2021
STANDARD POSTAGE
STAMP CATALOGUE

ONE HUNDRED AND SEVENTY-SEVENTH EDITION IN SIX VOLUMES

VOLUME 5B

PIT-SAM

EDITOR-IN-CHIEF	Jay Bigalke
EDITOR-AT-LARGE	Donna Houseman
MANAGING EDITOR	Timothy A. Hodge
CONTRIBUTING EDITOR	Charles Snee
EDITOR EMERITUS	James E. Kloetzel
SENIOR EDITOR /NEW ISSUES & VALUING	Martin J. Frankevicz
ADMINISTRATIVE ASSISTANT/CATALOGUE LAYOUT	Eric Wiessinger
PRINTING AND IMAGE COORDINATOR	Stacey Mahan
SENIOR GRAPHIC DESIGNER	Cinda McAlexander
SALES DIRECTOR	David Pistello
SALES DIRECTOR	Eric Roth

Released August 2020

Includes New Stamp Listings through the June 2020 *Linn's Stamp News Monthly* Catalogue Update

Copyright© 2020 by

AMOS MEDIA

911 S. Vandemark Road, Sidney, OH 45365-4129

Publishers of *Linn's Stamp News*, *Linn's Stamp News Monthly*, *Coin World* and *Coin World Monthly*.

Table of Contents

Acknowledgments 4A
Letter from the Editor 5A
Information on Philatelic Societies 6A
Expertizing Services 10A
Information on Catalogue Values, Grade and Condition.................. 12A
Grading Illustrations 13A
Gum Chart 15A
Understanding the Listings 16A
Catalogue Listing Policy 18A
Special Notices 19A
Abbreviations 19A
Basic Stamp Information 21A
Terminology 29A
Pronunciation Symbols 31A
Currency Conversion 32A
Common Design Types 34A
The British Commonwealth of Nations 55A
Colonies, Former Colonies, Offices, Territories Controlled by Parent States ...57A
Dies of British Colonial Stamps Referred to in the Catalogue 58A
British Colonial and Crown Agents Watermarks 59A

Countries of the World Pit-Sam 1

Illustrated Identifier 916
Glossary of Philatelic Terms 931
Index and Identifier **951**
2021 Volumes 5A-5B Catalogue Number Additions, Deletions & Changes 959
Index to Advertisers 960
Dealer Directory Yellow Pages 961

See the following volumes for other country listings:
Volume 1A: United States, United Nations, Abu Dhabi-Australia; Volume 1B: Austria-B
Volume 2A: C-Cur; Volume 2B: Cyp-F
Volume 3A: G; Volume 3B: H-I
Volume 4A: J-L; Volume 4B: M
Volume 5A: N-Phil
Volume 6A: San-Tete; Volume 6B: Thai-Z

Scott Catalogue Mission Statement

The Scott Catalogue Team exists to serve the recreational,
educational and commercial hobby needs of stamp collectors and dealers.

We strive to set the industry standard for philatelic information and products by developing and
providing goods that help collectors identify, value, organize and present their collections.

Quality customer service is, and will continue to be, our highest priority.
We aspire toward achieving total customer satisfaction.

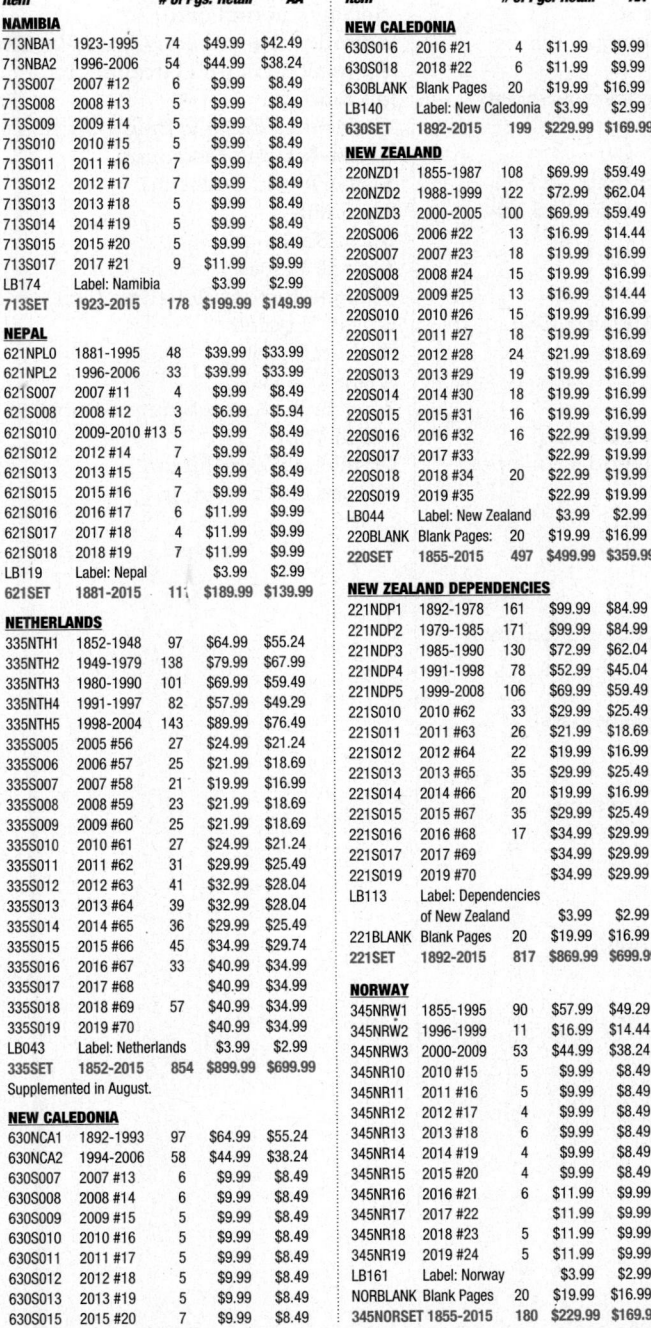

Acknowledgments

Our appreciation and gratitude go to the following individuals who have assisted us in preparing information included in this year's Scott Catalogues. Some helpers prefer anonymity. These individuals have generously shared their stamp knowledge with others through the medium of the Scott Catalogue.

Those who follow provided information that is in addition to the hundreds of dealer price lists and advertisements and scores of auction catalogues and realizations that were used in producing the catalogue values. It is from those noted here that we have been able to obtain information on items not normally seen in published lists and advertisements. Support from these people goes beyond data leading to catalogue values, for they also are key to editorial changes.

> A special acknowledgment to Liane and Sergio Sismondo of The Classic Collector for their assistance and knowledge sharing that have aided in the preparation of this year's Standard and Classic Specialized Catalogues.

Clifford J. Alexander
  (Carriers and Locals Society)
Roland Austin
Michael & Cecilia Ball (A to Z Stamps)
Jim Bardo (Bardo Stamps)
John Birkinbine II
James A. Booth
Les Bootman
Roger S. Brody
Keith & Margie Brown
Tina & John Carson (JET Stamps)
Carlson Chambliss
Bob Coale
Tony L. Crumble
  (Carolina Coin and Stamp, Inc.)
Christopher Dale
Markand Dave
Tony Davis
Bob and Rita Dumaine
  (Sam Houston Duck Co.)
Mark Eastzer
Paul G. Eckman
Steve Farago
Mike Farrell
Robert Finder (Korea Stamp Society)
Jeffrey M. Forster
Ernest E. Frick
  (France & Colonies Philatelic Society)
Bob Genisol (Sultan Stamp Center)
Henning Gmek
Stan Goldfarb
Marc E. Gonzes
Daniel Grau
Dan Harding
Sy Harvell
Bruce Hecht (Bruce L. Hecht Co.)
Armen Hovsan (ArmenStamp)

Robert Jack
Eric Jackson
Peter C. Jeannopoulos
William A. (Bill) Jones
Allan Katz (Ventura Stamp Co.)
Jon Kawaguchi
  (Ryukyu Philatelic Specialist Society)
Han Ki Klm
John R. Lewis
  (The William Henry Stamp Co.)
Ignacio Llach (Filatelia Llach, S.L.)
Nicolas Mallosetti
William K. McDaniel
Pat McElroy
Gary Morris (Pacific Midwest Co.)
Peter Mosiondz, Jr.
Phillip Moulay
Bruce M. Moyer
  (Moyer Stamps & Collectables)
Richard H. Muller (Richard's Stamps)
Scott Murphy
Leonard Nadybal
Dr. Tiong Tak Ngo
Nik & Lisa Oquist
Nicholas Pertwee
Don Peterson (International Philippine
  Philatelic Society)
Stanley M. Piller
  (Stanley M. Piller & Associates)
Dr. Charles Posner
Peter W. W. Powell
Siddique Mahmudur Rahman
  (Bangladesh Institute of Philatelic
  Studies)
Ghassan D. Riachi
Omar Rodriguez
Mehrdad Sadri (Persiphila)

Alex Schauss (Schauss Philatelics)
Joyce & Chuck Schmidt
Guy Shaw (Mexico-Elmhurst Philatelic
  Society International)
J. Randall Shoemaker (Philatelic Stamp
  Authenication and Grading, Inc.)
Jeff Siddiqui
  (Pakistan Philatelic Study Circle)
Sergio & Liane Sismondo
  (The Classic Collector)
Jay Smith
Telah Smith
Scott R. Trepel
  (Siegel Auction Galleries, Inc.)
Steven Unkrich
Herbert R. Volin
Philip T. Wall
Yong S. Yi (Korea Stamp Society)
Ralph Yorio
Dr. Michal Zika (Album)
Alfonso G. Zulueta, Jr.

SCOTT®

What's new for 2021 Scott Standard Volume 5?

Another catalog season is upon us as we continue the journey of the 152-year history of the Scott catalogs. The 2021 volumes are the 177th edition of the Scott *Standard Postage Stamp Catalogue*. Vol. 5A includes listings for countries of the world N through Philippines. Listings for countries of the world beginning with the Pitcairn Islands through Samoa can be found in Vol. 5B.

VOL. 5A

French New Hebrides was reviewed closely, and more than 300 changes were made with a mix of increases and decreases noted. One increase worth mentioning was for the 1977 Paris overprints set (Scott 236-248), which rose in unused condition from $65.25 to $79.35.

More than 1,200 value changes were made for Norfolk Island after a thorough review. Values increased for most of the issues before 1989. One of the key changes affected the 1960-62 definitive (regular-issue) set (Scott 29-41), which increased in unused condition from $53.85 to $65.25. In used condition, this set decreased from $41.95 to $35.10.

Nyassa was reviewed closely, with approximately 275 value changes made. Most of the changes were increases. Overprints remain of interest to collectors, and the 1910 Giraffe and Camel stamps overprinted "5 REIS PROVISORIO" (Scott 49-50) saw an increase from $1 each unused and 75¢ each used to $8 and $5.50, respectively.

A review of the Palestinian Authority listings netted approximately 90 changes. The 1999 Christmas stamp set of 14 (Scott 100-113A) increased from $35.35 in unused and used condition to $50.40 both ways in the 2021 catalog.

More than 600 value changes were made for Panama, with a mix of slight increases and decreases noted. For example the 1980 set of eight commemorating the 130th anniversary of the Transpanamanian Railroad and the 22nd Summer Olympic Games in Moscow (Scott 600-607) increased from $4.15 in unused condition to $5.10. Similar changes are noted throughout the listings for Panama.

A few changes were made to the stamps of Paraguay. One of the largest changes was noted for the 1930-39 set of six stamps marking the 60th anniversary of the first Paraguayan postage stamp (Scott 313-318), which increased from $5 in unused condition and $2.40 in used condition to $25 and $11, respectively. Both of these values are in italics because little market data is available for this set.

Approximately 350 changes were made for stamps of the Philippines. Notably the Scott editors moved post-1990 multiples, blocks and souvenir sheets up in value to a 1-1 ratio of unused to used. A handful of these items increased in used condition even more than that ratio. The largest increase for the Philippines was for a green

The 1960-62 set of Norfolk Islands definitive stamps (Scott 29-41) increased in unused condition from $53.85 to $65.25. Shown is one stamp from that set (29).

surcharged stamp of 1883 (Scott 95A), which jumped from $150 to $250 in unused condition.

VOL. 5B

A couple of dozen changes were made for Ponta Delgada stamps. Many of the changes were increases. The 1892-93 first set of 12 King Carlos stamps (Scott 1-12) increased from $192.50 unused and $122.05 used to $312.25 and $202.45, respectively.

A handful of changes were made for Portuguese Africa, with increases seen for the Vasco da Gama issue (Scott 1-8) and the war tax stamps (MR1-MR3).

Quality is key with Quelimane stamps. Of the changes made, the 1913 Vasco da Gama issue

This Russian World War II Ships sheet of eight (Scott 7446a) increased from $7.50 to $11 in mint condition.

(Scott 1-24) went from $142.50 in mint never-hinged condition to $195. The same set unused moved from $88 to $81.25.

Stamps of Russia issued from 1960 to date were looked at closely, and more than 1,800 value changes were made. Increases seemed to outweigh decreases, and values were added to the listings for a number of footnoted items. Many of the new minor listings added are for miniature sheets. Check the Number Additions, Deletions & Changes list in this volume for the specific number references. The 2013 World War II Ships sheet of eight (Scott 7446a) increased from $7.50 mint to $11.

The post-1920 stamps of St. Helena and St. Lucia were reviewed, with approximately 300 and 500 value changes made, respectively. There was a mix of increases and decreases throughout.

Some modern St. Helena issues from the past few decades are starting to increase in value. For example the 2009 souvenir sheet honoring the 500th anniversary of King Henry VIII's ascension (Scott 977) increased from $17.50 to $22.50.

St. Thomas and Prince Island was also reviewed, with approximately 700 value changes made for items issued prior to 1950. A number of increases were noted throughout.

And lastly, we encourage you to pay special attention to the Number Additions, Deletions & Changes in this volume. We also suggest reading the catalog introduction, which includes an abundance of useful information.

Best wishes in your stamp collecting pursuits!

Jay Bigalke, Scott catalog editor-in-chief

Addresses, Telephone Numbers, Web Sites, E-Mail Addresses of General & Specialized Philatelic Societies

Collectors can contact the following groups for information about the philately of the areas within the scope of these societies, or inquire about membership in these groups. Aside from the general societies, we limit this list to groups that specialize in particular fields of philately, particular areas covered by the Scott Standard Postage Stamp Catalogue, and topical groups. Many more specialized philatelic society exist than those listed below. These addresses are updated yearly, and they are, to the best of our knowledge, correct and current. Groups should inform the editors of address changes whenever they occur. The editors also want to hear from other such specialized groups not listed. Unless otherwise noted all website addresses begin with http://

General Societies

American Philatelic Society
100 Match Factory Place
Bellefonte, PA 16823-1367
(814) 933-3803
https://stamps.org
apsinfo@stamps.org

International Society of Worldwide Stamp Collectors
Joanne Murphy, M.D.
P.O. Box 19006
Sacramento, CA 95819
www.iswsc.org
executivedirector@iswsc.org

Royal Philatelic Society of Canada
P.O. Box 69080
St. Clair Post Office
Toronto, ON M4T 3A1
CANADA
(888) 285-4143
www.rpsc.org
info@rpsc.org

Royal Philatelic Society London
15 Abchurch Lane
London EX4N 7BW
UNITED KINGDOM
+44 (0) 20 7486 1044
www.rpsl.org.uk
secretary@rpsl.org.uk

Libraries, Museums, and Research Groups

American Philatelic Research Library
Scott Tiffney
100 Match Factory Place
Bellefonte, PA 16823
(814) 933-3803
www.stamplibrary.org
library@stamps.org

V. G. Greene Philatelic Research Foundation
P.O. Box 69100
St. Clair Post Office
Toronto, ON M4T 3A1
CANADA
(416) 921-2073
info@greenefoundation.ca

Aero/Astro Philately

American Air Mail Society
Stephen Reinhard
P.O. Box 110
Mineola, NY 11501
www.americanairmailsociety.org
sreinhard1@optonline.net

Postal History

Auxiliary Markings Club
Jerry Johnson
6621 W. Victoria Ave.
Kennewick, WA 99336
www.postal-markings.org
membership-2010@postal-markings.org

Postage Due Mail Study Group
Bob Medland
Camway Cottage
Nanny Hurn's Lane
Cameley, Bristol BS39 5AJ
UNITED KINGDOM
01761 45959
www.postageduemail.org.uk
secretary.pdmsg@gmail.com

Postal History Society
Yamil Kouri
405 Waltham St. #347
Lexington, MA 02421
www.postalhistorysociety.org
yhkouri@massmed.org

Post Mark Collectors Club
Bob Milligan
7014 Woodland Oaks Drive
Magnolia, TX 77354
(281) 259-2735
www.postmarks.org
bob.milligan@gmail.com

U.S. Cancellation Club
Roger Curran
18 Tressler Blvd.
Lewisburg, PA 17837
rdcnrc@ptd.net

Revenues & Cinderellas

American Revenue Association
Lyman Hensley
473 E. Elm St.
Sycamore, IL 60178-1934
www.revenuer.org
ilrno2@netzero.net

Christmas Seal & Charity Stamp Society
John Denune, Jr.
234 E. Broadway
Granville, OH 43023
(740) 814-6031
www.seal-society.org

National Duck Stamp Collectors Society
Anthony J. Monico
P.O. Box 43
Harleysville, PA 19438-0043
www.ndscs.org
ndscs@ndscs.org

State Revenue Society
Kent Gray
P.O. Box 67842
Albuquerque, NM 87193
www.staterevenue.org
srssecretary@comcast.net

Thematic Philately

Americana Unit
Dennis Dengel
17 Peckham Road
Poughkeepsie, NY 12603-2018
www.americanaunit.org
ddengel@americanaunit.org

American Topical Association
Jennifer Miller
P.O. Box 2143
Greer, SC 29652-2143
(618) 985-5100
www.americantopicalassn.org
americantopical@msn.com

Astronomy Study Unit
Leonard Zehr
1009 Treverton Crescent
Windsor, ON N8P 1K2
CANADA
(416) 833-9317
www.astronomystudyunit.net
lenzehr@gmail.com

Bicycle Stamps Club
Corey Hjalseth
1102 Broadway, Suite 200
Tacoma, WA 98402
(253) 318-6222
www.bicyclestampsclub.org
coreyh@evergreenhomeloans.com

Biology Unit
Chris Dahle
1401 Linmar Drive NE
Cedar Rapids, IA 52402-3724
www.biophilately.org
chris-dahle@biophilately.org

Bird Stamp Society
Mr. S. A. H. (Tony) Statham
Ashlyns Lodge
Chesham Road
Berkhamsted, Herts HP4 2ST
UNITED KINGDOM
www.bird-stamps.org/bss
tony.statham@sky.com

Captain Cook Society
Jerry Yucht
8427 Leale Ave.
Stockton, CA 95212
www.captaincooksociety.com
us@captaincooksociety.com

The CartoPhilatelic Society
Marybeth Sulkowski
2885 Sanford Ave., SW, #32361
Grandville, MI 49418-1342
www.mapsonstamps.org
secretary@mapsonstamps.org

Casey Jones Railroad Unit
Jeff Lough
2612 Redbud Land, Apt. C
Lawrence, KS 66046
www.uqp.de/cjr
jeffydplaugh@gmail.com

Cats on Stamps Study Unit
Robert D. Jarvis
2731 Teton Lane
Fairfield, CA 94533
www.catstamps.info
catmews1@yahoo.com

Chemistry & Physics on Stamps Study Unit
Dr. Roland Hirsch
13830 Metcalf Ave., Apt. 15218
Overland Park, KS 66223-8017
(301) 792-6296
www.cpossu.org
rfhirsch@cpossu.org

Chess on Stamps Study Unit
Barry Keith
511 1st St. N., Apt. 106
Charlottesville, VA 22902
www.chessonstamps.org
keithfam@embarqmail.com

Cricket Philatelic Society
A. Melville-Brown
11 Weppons, Ravens Road
Shorham-by-Sea
West Sussex BN43 5AW
UNITED KINGDOM
www.cricketstamp.net
mel.cricket.100@googlemail.com

Earth's Physical Features Study Group
Fred Klein
515 Magdalena Ave.
Los Altos, CA 94024
http://epfsu.jeffhayward.com
epfsu@jeffhayward.com

Ebony Society of Philatelic Events and Reflections (ESPER)
Don Neal
P.O. Box 5245
Somerset, NJ 08875-5245
www.esperstamps.org
esperdon@verizon.net

Europa Study Unit
Tonny E. Van Loij
3002 S. Xanthia St.
Denver, CO 80231-4237
(303) 752-0189
www.europastudyunit.org
tvanloij@gmail.com

Fire Service in Philately
John Zaranek
81 Hillpine Road
Cheektowaga, NY 14227-2259
(716) 668-3352
jczaranek@roadrunner.com

Gastronomy on Stamps Study Unit
David Wolfersburger
5062 NW 35th Lane Road
Ocala, FL 34482
(314) 494-3795
www.gastronomystamps.org

Gay & Lesbian History on Stamps Club
Joe Petronie
P.O. Box 190842
Dallas, TX 75219-0842
www.glhsonline.org
glhsc@aol.com

Gems, Minerals & Jewelry Study Unit
Fred Haynes
10 Country Club Drive
Rochester, NY 14618-3720
fredmhaynes55@gmail.com

Graphics Philately Association
Larry Rosenblum
1030 E. El Camino Real
PMB 107
Sunnyvale, CA 94087-3759
www.graphics-stamps.org
larry@graphics-stamps.org

Journalists, Authors and Poets on Stamps
Christopher D. Cook
7222 Hollywood Rd.
Berrien Springs, MI 49103
cdcook2@gmail.com

Lighthouse Stamp Society
Dalene Thomas
1805 S. Balsam St., #106
Lakewood, CO 80232
(303) 986-6620
www.lighthousestampsociety.org
dalene@lighthousestampsociety.org

Lions International Stamp Club
David McKirdy
s-Gravenwetering 248
3062 SJ Rotterdam
NETHERLANDS
31(0) 10 212 0313
www.lisc.nl
davidmckirdy@aol.com

Masonic Study Unit
Gene Fricks
25 Murray Way
Blackwood, NJ 08012-4400
genefricks@comcast.net

Medical Subjects Unit
Dr. Frederick C. Skvara
P.O. Box 6228
Bridgewater, NJ 08807
fcskvara@optonline.net

Napoleonic Age Philatelists
Ken Berry
4117 NW 146th St.
Oklahoma City, OK 73134-1746
(405) 748-8646
www.nap-stamps.org
krb4117@att.net

Old World Archaeological Study Unit
Caroline Scannell
14 Dawn Drive
Smithtown, NY 11787-1761
www.owasu.org
editor@owasu.org

Petroleum Philatelic Society International
Feitze Papa
922 Meander Drive
Walnut Creek, CA 94598-4239
www.ppsi.org.uk
oildad@astound.net

Rotary on Stamps Fellowship
Gerald L. Fitzsimmons
105 Calle Ricardo
Victoria, TX 77904
www.rotaryonstamps.org
glfitz@suddenlink.net

Scouts on Stamps Society International
Woodrow (Woody) Brooks
498 Baldwin Road
Akron, OH 44312
(330) 612-1294
www.sossi.org
secretary@sossi.org

Ships on Stamps Unit
Erik Th. Matzinger
Voorste Haververlden 30
4822 AL Breda
NETHERLANDS
www.shipsonstamps.org
erikships@gmail.com

Space Topic Study Unit
David Blog
P.O. Box 174
Bergenfield, NJ 07621
www.space-unit.com
davidblognj@gmail.com

Stamps on Stamps Collectors Club
Michael Merritt
73 Mountainside Road
Mendham, NJ 07945
www.stampsonstamps.org
stampsonstamps@yahoo.com

Windmill Study Unit
Walter J. Hallien
607 N. Porter St.
Watkins Glenn, NY 14891-1345
(607) 229-3541
www.windmillworld.com

Wine On Stamps Study Unit
David Wolfersburger
5062 NW 35th Lane Road
Ocala, FL 34482
(314) 494-3795
www.wine-on-stamps.org

United States

American Air Mail Society
Stephen Reinhard
P.O. Box 110
Mineola, NY 11501
www.americanairmailsociety.org
sreinhard1@optonline.net

American First Day Cover Society
Douglas Kelsey
P.O. Box 16277
Tucson, AZ 85732-6277
(520) 321-0880
www.afdcs.org
afdcs@afdcs.org

Auxiliary Markings Club
Jerry Johnson
6621 W. Victoria Ave.
Kennewick, WA 99336
www.postal-markings.org
membership-2010@postal-markings.org

American Plate Number Single Society
Rick Burdsall
APNSS Secretary
P.O. BOX 1023
Palatine, IL 60078-1023
www.apnss.org
apnss.sec@gmail.com

American Revenue Association
Lyman Hensley
473 E. Elm St.
Sycamore, IL 60178-1934
www.revenuer.org
ilrno2@netzero.net

American Society for Philatelic Pages and Panels
Ron Walenciak
P.O. Box 1042
Washington Township, NJ 07676
www.asppp.org
rwalenciak@aol.com

Canal Zone Study Group
Mike Drabik
P.O. Box 281
Bolton, MA 01740
www.canalzonestudygroup.com
czsgsecretary@gmail.com

Carriers and Locals Society
John Bowman
14409 Pentridge Drive
Corpus Christi, TX 78410
(361) 933-0757
www.pennypost.org
jbowman@stx.rr.com

Christmas Seal & Charity Stamp Society
John Denune, Jr.
234 E. Broadway
Granville, OH 43023
(740) 814-6031
www.seal-society.org
john@christmasseals.net

Confederate Stamp Alliance
Patricia A. Kaufmann
10194 N. Old State Road
Lincoln, DE 19960-3644
(302) 422-2656
www.csalliance.org
trishkauf@comcast.net

Error, Freaks, and Oddities Collectors Club
Scott Shaulis
P.O. Box 549
Murrysville, PA 15668-0549
(724) 733-4134
www.efocc.org
scott@shaulisstamps.com

National Duck Stamp Collectors Society
Anthony J. Monico
P.O. Box 43
Harleysville, PA 19438-0043
www.ndscs.org
ndscs@ndscs.org

Plate Number Coil Collectors Club (PNC3)
Gene Trinks
16415 W. Desert Wren Court
Surprise, AZ 85374
(623) 322-4619
www.pnc3.org
gctrinks@cox.net

Post Mark Collectors Club
Bob Milligan
7014 Woodland Oaks Drive
Magnolia, TX 77354
(281) 259-2735
www.postmarks.org
bob.milligan@gmail.com

Souvenir Card Collectors Society
William V. Kriebel
1923 Manning St.
Philadelphia, PA 19103-5728
www.souvenircards.org
kriebewv@drexel.edu

United Postal Stationery Society
Dave Kandziolka
404 Sundown Drive
Knoxville, TN 37934
www.upss.org
membership@upss.org

U.S. Cancellation Club
Roger Curran
18 Tressler Blvd.
Lewisburg, PA 17837
rdcnrc@ptd.net

U.S. Philatelic Classics Society
Rob Lund
2913 Fulton St.
Everett, WA 98201-3733
www.uspcs.org
membershipchairman@uspcs.org

US Possessions Philatelic Society
Daniel F. Ring
P.O. Box 113
Woodstock, IL 60098
http://uspps.tripod.com
danielfring@hotmail.com

United States Stamp Society
Rod Juell
P.O. Box 3508
Joliet, IL 60434-3508
www.usstamps.org
execsecretary@usstamps.org

Africa

Bechuanalands and Botswana Society
Otto Peetoom
Roos
East Yorkshire HU12 0LD
UNITED KINGDOM
44(0)1964 670239
www.bechuanalandphilately.com
info@bechuanalandphilately.com

Egypt Study Circle
Mike Murphy
11 Waterbank Road
Bellingham
London SE6 3DJ
UNITED KINGDOM
(44) 0203 6737051
www.egyptstudycircle.org.uk
secretary@egyptstudycircle.org.uk

Ethiopian Philatelic Society
Ulf Lindahl
21 Westview Place
Riverside, CT 06878
(203) 722-0769
https://ethiopianphilatelicsociety.weebly.com
ulindahl@optonline.net

Liberian Philatelic Society
P.O. Box 1570
Parker, CO 80134
www.liberiastamps.org
liberiastamps@comcast.net

Orange Free State Study Circle
J. R. Stroud, RDPSA
24 Hooper Close
Burnham-on-sea
Somerset TA8 1JQ
UNITED KINGDOM
44 1278 782235
www.orangefreestatephilately.org.uk
richard@richardstroud.plus.com

Philatelic Society for Greater Southern Africa
Alan Hanks
34 Seaton Drive
Aurora, ON L4G 2K1
CANADA
www.psgsa.org
alan.hanks@sympatico.ca

Rhodesian Study Circle
William R. Wallace
P.O. Box 16381
San Francisco, CA 94116
(415) 564-6069
www.rhodesianstudycircle.org.uk
bwall8rscr@earthlink.net

Society for Moroccan and Tunisian Philately
S.P.L.M.
206, Bld Pereire
75017 PARIS
FRANCE
http://splm-philatelie.org
splm206@aol.com

South Sudan Philatelic Society
William Barclay
1370 Spring Hill Road
South Londonderry, VT 05155
barclayphilatelics@gmail.com

Sudan Study Group
Andy Neal
Bank House, Coedway
Shrewsbury SY5 9AR
UNITED KINGDOM
www.sudanstamps.org
andywneal@gmail.com

Transvaal Study Circle
c/o 9 Meadow Road
Gravesend, Kent DA11 7LR
UNITED KINGDOM
www.transvaalstamps.org.uk
transvaalstudycircle@aol.co.uk

West Africa Study Circle
Martin Bratzel
1233 Virginia Ave.
Windsor, ON N8S 2Z1
CANADA
www.wasc.org.uk
marty_bratzel@yahoo.ca

Asia

Aden & Somaliland Study Group
Gary Brown
P.O. Box 106
Briar Hill, VIC 3088
AUSTRALIA
www.stampdomain.com/aden
garyjohn951@optushome.com.au

Burma (Myanmar) Philatelic Study Circle
Michael Whittaker
1, Ecton Leys, Hillside
Rugby
Warwickshire CV22 5SL
UNITED KINGDOM
https://burmamyanmarphilately.wordpress.com/burma-myanmar-philatelic-study-circle
manningham8@mypostoffice.co.uk

Ceylon Study Circle
Rodney W. P. Frost
42 Lonsdale Road
Cannington
Bridgwater, Somerset TA5 2JS
UNITED KINGDOM
01278 652592
www.ceylonsc.org
rodney.frost@tiscali.co.uk

China Stamp Society
H. James Maxwell
1050 W. Blue Ridge Blvd.
Kansas City, MO 64145-1216
www.chinastampsociety.org
president@chinastampsociety.org

Hong Kong Philatelic Society
John Tang
G.P.O. Box 446
HONG KONG
www.hkpsociety.com
hkpsociety@outlook.com

Hong Kong Study Circle
Robert Newton
www.hongkongstudycircle.com/index.html
newtons100@gmail.com

India Study Circle
John Warren
P.O. Box 7326
Washington, DC 20044
(202) 488-7443
https://indiastudycircle.org
jw-kbw@earthlink.net

International Philippine Philatelic Society
James R. Larot, Jr.
4990 Bayleaf Court
Martinez, CA 94553
(925) 260-5425
www.theipps.info
jlarot@ccwater.com

International Society for Japanese Philately
William Eisenhauer
P.O. Box 230462
Tigard, OR 97281
(503) 496-2634
www.isjp.org
secretary@isjp.org

Iran Philatelic Study Circle
Nigel Gooch
Marchwood, 56, Wickham Ave.
Bexhill-on-Sea
East Sussex TN39 3ER
UNITED KINGDOM
www.iranphilately.org
nigelmgooch@gmail.com

Korea Stamp Society
Peter Corson
1109 Gunnison Place
Raleigh, NC 27609
(919) 787-7611
https://koreastampsociety.org
pbcorson@aol.com

Nepal & Tibet Philatelic Study Circle
Colin Hepper
12 Charnwood Close
Peterborough, Cambs PE2 9BZ
UNITED KINGDOM
http://fuchs-online.com/ntpsc
ntpsc@fuchs-online.com

Pakistan Philatelic Study Circle
Jeff Siddiqui
P.O. Box 7002
Lynnwood, WA 98046
jeffsiddiqui@msn.com

Society of Indo-China Philatelists
Ron Bentley
2600 N. 24th St.
Arlington, VA 22207
(703) 524-1652
www.sicp-online.org
ron.bentley@verizon.net

Society of Israel Philatelists, Inc.
Sarah Berezenko
100 Match Factory Place
Bellefonte, PA 16823-1367
(814) 933-3803 ext. 212
www.israelstamps.com
israelstamps@gmail.com

Australasia and Oceana

Australian States Study Circle of the Royal Sydney Philatelic Club
Ben Palmer
G.P.O. 1751
Sydney, NSW 2001
AUSTRALIA
http://club.philas.org.au/states

Fellowship of Samoa Specialists
Trevor Shimell
18 Aspen Drive, Newton Abbot
Devon TQ12 4TN
UNITED KINGDOM
www.samoaexpress.org
trevor.shimell@gmail.com

Malaya Study Group
Michael Waugh
151 Roker Lane
Pudsey
Leeds LS28 9ND
UNITED KINGDOM
http://malayastudygroup.com
mawpud43@gmail.com

New Zealand Society of Great Britain
Michael Wilkinson
121 London Road
Sevenoaks
Kent TN13 1BH
UNITED KINGDOM
01732 456997
www.nzsgb.org.uk
mwilkin799@aol.com

Pacific Islands Study Circle
John Ray
24 Woodvale Ave.
London SE25 4AE
UNITED KINGDOM
www.pisc.org.uk
secretary@pisc.org.uk

Papuan Philatelic Society
Steven Zirinsky
P.O. Box 49, Ansonia Station
New York, NY 10023
(718) 706-0616
www.papuanphilatelicsociety.com
szirinsky@cs.com

Pitcairn Islands Study Group
Dr. Everett L. Parker
207 Corinth Road
Hudson, ME 04449-3057
(207) 573-1686
www.pisg.net
eparker@hughes.net

Ryukyu Philatelic Specialist Society
Laura Edmonds
P.O. Box 240177
Charlotte, NC 28224-0177
(336) 509-3739
www.ryukyustamps.org
secretary@ryukyustamps.org

Society of Australasian Specialists / Oceania
Steve Zirinsky
P.O. Box 230049
New York, NY 10023-0049
www.sasoceania.org
president@sosoceania.org

Sarawak Specialists' Society
Stephen Schumann
2417 Cabrallo Drive
Hayward, CA 94545
(510) 785-4794
www.britborneostamps.org.uk
vpnam@s-s-s.org.uk

Western Australia Study Group
Brian Pope
P.O. Box 423
Claremont, WA 6910
AUSTRALIA
(61) 419 843 943
www.wastudygroup.com
wastudygroup@hotmail.com

Europe

American Helvetia Philatelic Society
Richard T. Hall
P.O. Box 15053
Asheville, NC 28813-0053
www.swiss-stamps.org
secretary2@swiss-stamps.org

American Society for Netherlands Philately
Hans Kremer
50 Rockport Court
Danville, CA 94526
(925) 820-5841
www.asnp1975.com
hkremer@usa.net

Andorran Philatelic Study Circle
David Hope
17 Hawthorn Drive
Stalybridge
Cheshire SK15 1UE
UNITED KINGDOM
www.andorranpsc.org.uk
andorranpsc@btinternet.com

Austria Philatelic Society
Ralph Schneider
P.O. Box 978
Iowa Park, TX 76376
(940) 213-5004
www.austriaphilatelicsociety.com
rschneiderstamps@gmail.com

Channel Islands Specialists Society
Richard Flemming
Burbage, 64 Falconers Green
Hinckley
Leicestershire LE102SX
UNITED KINGDOM
www.ciss1950.org.uk
secretary@ciss1950.org.uk

Cyprus Study Circle
Rob Wheeler
47 Drayton Ave.
London W13 0LE
UNITED KINGDOM
www.cyprusstudycircle.org
robwheeler47@aol.com

Danish West Indies Study Unit of Scandinavian Collectors Club
Arnold Sorensen
7666 Edgedale Drive
Newburgh, IN 47630
(812) 480-6532
www.scc-online.org
valbydwi@hotmail.com

Eire Philatelic Association
John B. Sharkey
1559 Grouse Lane
Mountainside, NJ 07092-1340
www.eirephilatelicassoc.org
jsharkeyepa@me.com

Faroe Islands Study Circle
Norman Hudson
40 Queen's Road
Vicar's Cross
Chester CH3 5HB
UNITED KINGDOM
www.faroeislandssc.org
jntropics@hotmail.com

France & Colonies Philatelic Society
Edward Grabowski
111 Prospect St., 4C
Westfield, NJ 07090
(908) 233-9318
www.franceandcolsps.org
edjjg@alum.mit.edu

Germany Philatelic Society
P.O. Box 6547
Chesterfield, MO 63006-6547
www.germanyphilatelicusa.org
info@germanyphilatelicsocietyusa.org

Gibraltar Study Circle
Susan Dare
22, Byways Park, Strode Road
Clevedon
North Somerset BS21 6UR
UNITED KINGDOM
www.gibraltarstudycircle.wordpress.com
smldare@yahoo.co.uk

International Society for Portuguese Philately
Clyde Homen
1491 Bonnie View Road
Hollister, CA 95023-5117
www.portugalstamps.com
ispp1962@sbcglobal.net

Italy and Colonies Study Circle
Richard Harlow
7 Duncombe House
8 Manor Road
Teddington, Middlesex TW118BE
UNITED KINGDOM
44 208 977 8737
www.icsc-uk.com
richardharlow@outlook.com

Liechtenstudy USA
Paul Tremaine
410 SW Ninth St.
Dundee, OR 97115-9731
(503) 538-4500
www.liechtenstudy.org
tremaine@liechtenstudy.org

Lithuania Philatelic Society
Audrius Brazdeikis
9915 Murray Landing
Missouri City, TX 77459
(281) 450-6224
www.lithuanianphilately.com/lps
audrius@lithuanianphilately.com

Luxembourg Collectors Club
Gary B. Little
7319 Beau Road
Sechelt, BC V0N 3A8
CANADA
(604) 885-7241
http://lcc.luxcentral.com
gary@luxcentral.com

Plebiscite-Memel-Saar Study Group of the German Philatelic Society
Clayton Wallace
100 Lark Court
Alamo, CA 94507
claytonwallace@comcast.net

Polonus Polish Philatelic Society
Daniel Lubelski
P.O. Box 2212
Benicia, CA 94510
(419) 410-9115
www.polonus.org
info@polonus.org

Rossica Society of Russian Philately
Alexander Kolchinsky
1506 Country Lake Drive
Champaign, IL 61821-6428
www.rossica.org
alexander.kolchinsky@rossica.org

Scandinavian Collectors Club
Steve Lund
P.O. Box 16213
St. Paul, MN 55116
www.scc-online.org
steve88h@aol.com

Society for Czechoslovak Philately
Tom Cossaboom
P.O. Box 4124
Prescott, AZ 86302
(928) 771-9097
www.csphilately.org
klfck1@aol.com

Society for Hungarian Philately
Alan Bauer
P.O. Box 4028
Vineyard Haven, MA 02568
(617) 645-4045
www.hungarianphilately.org
alan@hungarianstamps.com

Spanish Study Circle
Edith Knight
www.spaincircle.wixsite.com/
spainstudycircle
spaincircle@gmail.com

Ukrainian Philatelic & Numismatic
 Society
Martin B. Tatuch
5117 8th Road N.
Arlington, VA 22205-1201
www.upns.org
treasurer@upns.org

Vatican Philatelic Society
Joseph Scholten
1436 Johnston St. SE
Grand Rapids, MI 49507-2829
www.vaticanphilately.org
jscholten@vaticanphilately.org

Yugoslavia Study Group
Michael Chant
1514 N. Third Ave.
Wausau, WI 54401
208-748-9919
www.yugosg.org
membership@yugosg.org

Interregional Societies

American Society of Polar Philatelists
Alan Warren
P.O. Box 39
Exton, PA 19341-0039
(610) 321-0740
www.polarphilatelists.org
alanwar@att.net

First Issues Collector's Club
Kurt Streepy
3128 E. Mattatha Drive
Bloomington, IN 47401
www.firstissues.org
secretary@firstissues.org

Former French Colonies Specialist Society
Col.fra
BP 628
75367 PARIS Cedex 08
FRANCE
www.colfra.org
postmaster@colfra.org

France & Colonies Philatelic Society
Edward Grabowski
111 Prospect St., 4C
Westfield, NJ 07090
(908) 233-9318
www.franceandcolsps.org
edjjg@alum.mit.edu

Joint Stamp Issues Society
Richard Zimmermann
29A, Rue Des Eviats
67220 LALAYE
FRANCE
www.philarz.net
richard.zimmermann@club-internet.fr

The King George VI Collectors Society
Brian Livingstone
21 York Mansions
Prince of Wales Drive
London SW11 4DL
UNITED KINGDOM
www.kg6.info
livingstone484@btinternet.com

International Society of Reply
 Coupon Collectors
Peter Robin
P.O. Box 353
Bala Cynwyd, PA 19004
peterrobin@verizon.net

Italy and Colonies Study Circle
Richard Harlow
7 Duncombe House
8 Manor Road
Teddington, Middlesex TW118BE
UNITED KINGDOM
44 208 977 8737
www.icsc-uk.com
richardharlow@outlook.com

St. Helena, Ascension & Tristan Da Cunha
 Philatelic Society
Dr. Everett L. Parker
207 Corinth Road
Hudson, ME 04449-3057
(207) 573-1686
www.shatps.org
eparker@hughes.net

United Nations Philatelists
Blanton Clement, Jr.
P.O. Box 146
Morrisville, PA 19067-0146
www.unpi.com
bclemjunior@gmail.com

Latin America

Asociación Filatélica de Panamá
Edward D. Vianna B
ASOFILPA
0819-03400
El Dorado, Panama
PANAMA
http://asociacionfilatelicadepanama.
blogspot.com
asofilpa@gmail.com

Asociacion Mexicana de Filatelia
 (AMEXFIL)
Alejandro Grossmann
Jose Maria Rico, 129
Col. Del Valle
3100 Mexico City, DF
MEXICO
www.amexfil.mx
amexfil@gmail.com

Associated Collectors of El Salvador
Joseph D. Hahn
301 Rolling Ridge Drive, Apt. 111
State College, PA 16801-6149
www.elsalvadorphilately.org
joehahn100@hotmail.com

Association Filatelic de Costa Rica
Giana Wayman (McCarty)
#SJO 4935
P.O. Box 025723
Miami, FL 33102-5723
011-506-2-228-1947
scotland@racsa.co.cr

Brazil Philatelic Association
William V. Kriebel
1923 Manning St.
Philadelphia, PA 19103-5728
www.brazilphilatelic.org
info@brazilphilatelic.org

Canal Zone Study Group
Mike Drabik
P.O. Box 281
Bolton, MA 01740
www.canalzonestudygroup.com
czsgsecretary@gmail.com

Colombia-Panama Philatelic Study Group
Thomas P. Myers
P.O. Box 522
Gordonsville, VA 22942
www.copaphil.org
tpmphil@hotmail.com

Falkland Islands Philatelic Study Groups
Morva White
42 Colton Road
Shrivenham
Swindon SN6 8AZ
UNITED KINGDOM
44(0) 1793 783245
www.fipsg.org.uk
morawhite@supanet.com

Federacion Filatelica de la Republica
 de Honduras
Mauricio Mejia
Apartado Postal 1465
Tegucigalpa, D.C.
HONDURAS
504 3399-7227
www.facebook.com/filateliadehonduras
ffrh@hotmail.com

International Cuban Philatelic Society
 (ICPS)
Ernesto Cuesta
P.O. Box 34434
Bethesda, MD 20827
(301) 564-3099
www.cubafil.org
ecuesta@philat.com

International Society of Guatemala
 Collectors
Jaime Marckwordt
449 St. Francis Blvd.
Daly City, CA 94015-2136
(415) 997-0295
www.guatemalastamps.com
president@guatamalastamps.com

Mexico-Elmhurst Philatelic Society
 International
Eric Stovner
P.O. Box 10097
Santa Ana, CA 92711-0097
www.mepsi.org
treasurer@mepsi.org

Nicaragua Study Group
Erick Rodriguez
11817 S. W. 11th St.
Miami, FL 33184-2501
nsgsec@yahoo.com

North America (excluding United States)

British Caribbean Philatelic Study Group
Bob Stewart
7 West Dune Lane
Long Beach Township, NJ 08008
(941) 379-4108
www.bcpsg.com
bcpsg@comcast.net

British North America Philatelic Society
Andy Ellwood
10 Doris Ave.
Gloucester, ON K1T 3W8
CANADA
www.bnaps.org
secretary@bnaps.org

British West Indies Study Circle
Steve Jarvis
5 Redbridge Drive
Andover
Hants SP10 2LF
UNITED KINGDOM
01264 358065
www.bwisc.org
info@bwisc.org

Bermuda Collectors Society
John Pare
405 Perimeter St.
Mount Horeb, WI 53572
(608) 852-7358
www.bermudacollectorssociety.com
pare16@mhtc.net
john@christmasseals.net

Haiti Philatelic Society
Ubaldo Del Toro
5709 Marble Archway
Alexandria, VA 22315
www.haitiphilately.org
u007ubi@aol.com

Hawaiian Philatelic Society
Gannon Sugimura
P.O. Box 10115
Honolulu, HI 96816-0115
www.stampshows.com/hps.html
hiphilsoc@gmail.com

Stamp Dealer Associations

American Stamp Dealers Association, Inc.
P.O. Box 692
Leesport, PA 19553
(800) 369-8209
www.americanstampdealer.com
asda@americanstampdealer.com

National Stamp Dealers Association
Sheldon Ruckens, President
3643 Private Road 18
Pinckneyville, IL 62274-3426
(618) 357-5497
www.nsdainc.org
nsda@nsdainc.org

Youth Philately

Young Stamp Collectors of America
100 Match Factory Place
Bellefonte, PA 16823
(814) 933-3803
https://stamps.org/stamps.org/Learn/
youth-in-philately
ysca@stamps.org

Expertizing Services

The following organizations will, for a fee, provide expert opinions about stamps submitted to them. Collectors should contact these organizations to find out about their fees and requirements before submiting philatelic material to them. The listing of these groups here is not intended as an endorsement by Amos Media Co.

General Expertizing Services

American Philatelic Expertizing Service (a service of the American Philatelic Society)
100 Match Factory Place
Bellefonte PA 16823-1367
(814) 237-3803
www.stamps.org/stamp-authentication
apex@stamps.org
Areas of Expertise: Worldwide

BPA Expertising, Ltd.
P.O. Box 1141
Guildford, Surrey, GU5 0WR
UNITED KINGDOM
www.bpaexpertising.com
sec@bpaexpertising.org
Areas of Expertise: British Commonwealth, Great Britain, Classics of Europe, South America and the Far East

Philatelic Foundation
22 E. 35th St., 4th Floor
New York NY 10016
(212) 221-6555
www.philatelicfoundation.org
philatelicfoundation@verizon.net
Areas of Expertise: U.S. & Worldwide

Philatelic Stamp Authentication and Grading, Inc.
P.O. Box 41-0880
Melbourne FL 32941-0880
(305) 345-9864
www.psaginc.com
info@psaginc.com
Areas of Expertise: U.S., Canal Zone, Hawaii, Philippines, Canada & Provinces

Professional Stamp Experts
P.O. Box 539309
Henderson NV 89053-9309
(702) 776-6522
www.gradingmatters.com
www.psestamp.com
info@gradingmatters.com
Areas of Expertise: Stamps and covers of U.S., U.S. Possessions, British Commonwealth

Royal Philatelic Society London Expert Committee
15 Abchurch Lane
London, EX4N 7BW
UNITED KINGDOM
www.rpsl.limited/experts.aspx
experts@rpsl.limited
Areas of Expertise: Worldwide

Expertizing Services Covering Specific Fields or Countries

China Stamp Society Expertizing Service
1050 W. Blue Ridge Blvd.
Kansas City MO 64145
(816) 942-6300
hjmesq@aol.com
Areas of Expertise: China

Confederate Stamp Alliance Authentication Service
C/O Stefan T. Jaronski
P.O. Box 232
Sidney, MT 59270-0232
www.csalliance.org/CSAAS.shtml
authentication@csalliance.org
Areas of Expertise: Confederate stamps and postal history

Errors, Freaks and Oddities Collectors Club Expertizing Service
138 East Lakemont Drive
Kingsland GA 31548
(912) 729-1573
Areas of Expertise: U.S. errors, freaks and oddities

Hawaiian Philatelic Society Expertizing Service
P.O. Box 10115
Honolulu HI 96816-0115
www.stampshows.com/hps.html
hiphilsoc@gmail.com
Areas of Expertise: Hawaii

Hong Kong Stamp Society Expertizing Service
P.O. Box 206
Glenside PA 19038
Areas of Expertise: Hong Kong

International Association of Philatelic Experts United States Associate members:

Paul Buchsbayew
119 W. 57th St.
New York NY 10019
(212) 977-7734
Areas of Expertise: Russia, Soviet Union

William T. Crowe
P.O. Box 2090
Danbury CT 06813-2090
wtcrowe@aol.com
Areas of Expertise: United States

John Lievsay
(see American Philatelic Expertizing Service and Philatelic Foundation)
Areas of Expertise: France

Robert W. Lyman
P.O. Box 348
Irvington on Hudson NY 10533
(914) 591-6937
Areas of Expertise: British North America, New Zealand

Robert Odenweller
P.O. Box 401
Bernardsville NJ 07924-0401
(908) 766-5460
Areas of Expertise: New Zealand, Samoa to 1900

Sergio Sismondo
The Regency Tower, Suite 1109
770 James St.
Syracuse NY 13203
(315) 422-2331
Areas of Expertise: British East Africa, Camerouns, Cape of Good Hope, Canada, British North America

International Society for Japanese Philately Expertizing Committee
132 North Pine Terrace
Staten Island NY 10312-4052
(718) 227-5229
Areas of Expertise: Japan and related areas, except WWII Japanese Occupation issues

International Society for Portuguese Philately Expertizing Service
P.O. Box 43146
Philadelphia PA 19129-3146
(215) 843-2106
s.s.washburne@worldnet.att.net
Areas of Expertise: Portugal and Colonies

Mexico-Elmhurst Philatelic Society International Expert Committee
Expert Committee Administrator
Marc E. Gonzales
P.O. Box 29040
Denver CO 80229-0040
www.mepsi.org/expert_committeee.htm
expertizations@mepsi.org
Areas of Expertise: Mexico

Ukrainian Philatelic & Numismatic Society Expertizing Service
30552 Dell Lane
Warren MI 48092-1862
Areas of Expertise: Ukraine, Western Ukraine

V. G. Greene Philatelic Research Foundation
P.O. Box 69100
St. Clair Post Office
Toronto, ON M4T 3A1
CANADA
(416) 921-2073
www.greenefoundation.ca
info@greenefoundation.ca
Areas of Expertise: British North America

Scott International Album

Prices have never been so low on selected album parts. It is a wonderful opportunity to collect internationally. The Ultimate Album for Worldwide Collectors! Pick a period in history and embark on a philatelic adventure. With the International Album, the whole world is divided chronologically into more than 40 parts. From the classic era of philately to present day, the International is one of the broadest and far reaching worldwide albums available. *Binders are sold separately.*

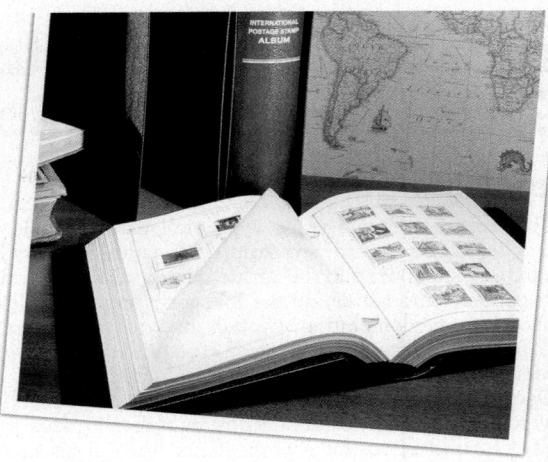

- More than 16,000 pages with spaces for over 220,000 stamps.
- Pages printed on 2 sides.

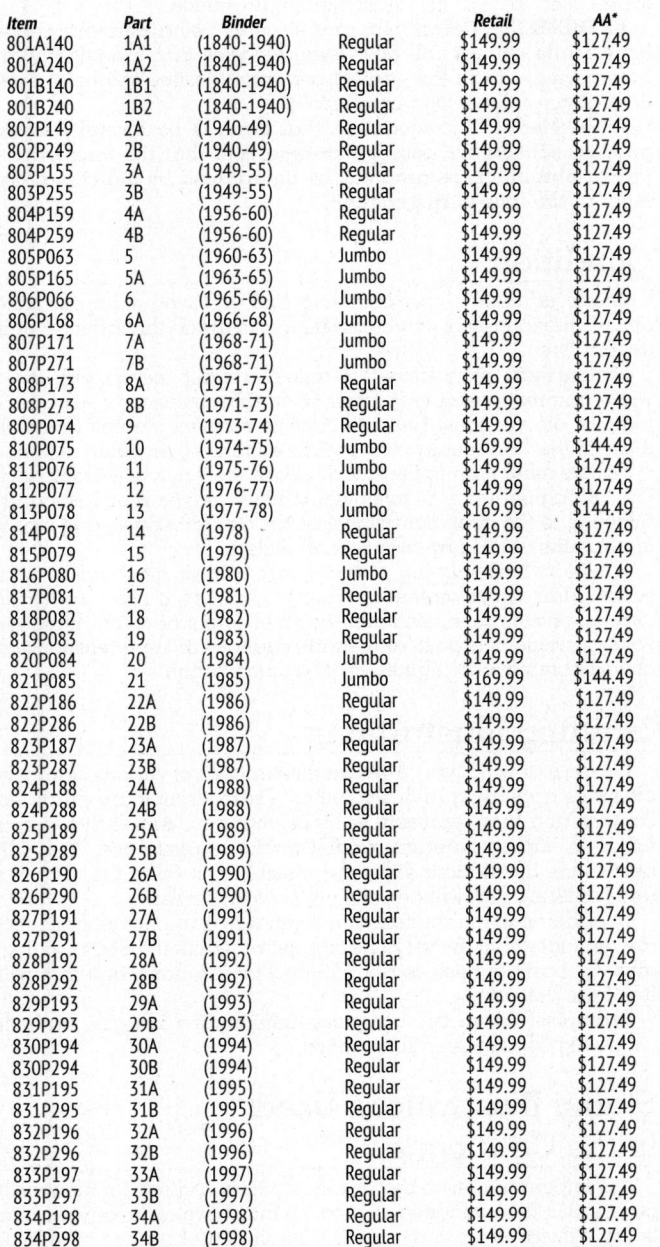

Item	Part	Binder		Retail	AA*
801A140	1A1	(1840-1940)	Regular	$149.99	$127.49
801A240	1A2	(1840-1940)	Regular	$149.99	$127.49
801B140	1B1	(1840-1940)	Regular	$149.99	$127.49
801B240	1B2	(1840-1940)	Regular	$149.99	$127.49
802P149	2A	(1940-49)	Regular	$149.99	$127.49
802P249	2B	(1940-49)	Regular	$149.99	$127.49
803P155	3A	(1949-55)	Regular	$149.99	$127.49
803P255	3B	(1949-55)	Regular	$149.99	$127.49
804P159	4A	(1956-60)	Regular	$149.99	$127.49
804P259	4B	(1956-60)	Regular	$149.99	$127.49
805P063	5	(1960-63)	Jumbo	$149.99	$127.49
805P165	5A	(1963-65)	Jumbo	$149.99	$127.49
806P066	6	(1965-66)	Jumbo	$149.99	$127.49
806P168	6A	(1966-68)	Jumbo	$149.99	$127.49
807P171	7A	(1968-71)	Jumbo	$149.99	$127.49
807P271	7B	(1968-71)	Jumbo	$149.99	$127.49
808P173	8A	(1971-73)	Regular	$149.99	$127.49
808P273	8B	(1971-73)	Regular	$149.99	$127.49
809P074	9	(1973-74)	Regular	$149.99	$127.49
810P075	10	(1974-75)	Jumbo	$169.99	$144.49
811P076	11	(1975-76)	Jumbo	$149.99	$127.49
812P077	12	(1976-77)	Jumbo	$149.99	$127.49
813P078	13	(1977-78)	Jumbo	$169.99	$144.49
814P078	14	(1978)	Regular	$149.99	$127.49
815P079	15	(1979)	Regular	$149.99	$127.49
816P080	16	(1980)	Jumbo	$149.99	$127.49
817P081	17	(1981)	Regular	$149.99	$127.49
818P082	18	(1982)	Regular	$149.99	$127.49
819P083	19	(1983)	Regular	$149.99	$127.49
820P084	20	(1984)	Jumbo	$149.99	$127.49
821P085	21	(1985)	Jumbo	$169.99	$144.49
822P186	22A	(1986)	Regular	$149.99	$127.49
822P286	22B	(1986)	Regular	$149.99	$127.49
823P187	23A	(1987)	Regular	$149.99	$127.49
823P287	23B	(1987)	Regular	$149.99	$127.49
824P188	24A	(1988)	Regular	$149.99	$127.49
824P288	24B	(1988)	Regular	$149.99	$127.49
825P189	25A	(1989)	Regular	$149.99	$127.49
825P289	25B	(1989)	Regular	$149.99	$127.49
826P190	26A	(1990)	Regular	$149.99	$127.49
826P290	26B	(1990)	Regular	$149.99	$127.49
827P191	27A	(1991)	Regular	$149.99	$127.49
827P291	27B	(1991)	Regular	$149.99	$127.49
828P192	28A	(1992)	Regular	$149.99	$127.49
828P292	28B	(1992)	Regular	$149.99	$127.49
829P193	29A	(1993)	Regular	$149.99	$127.49
829P293	29B	(1993)	Regular	$149.99	$127.49
830P194	30A	(1994)	Regular	$149.99	$127.49
830P294	30B	(1994)	Regular	$149.99	$127.49
831P195	31A	(1995)	Regular	$149.99	$127.49
831P295	31B	(1995)	Regular	$149.99	$127.49
832P196	32A	(1996)	Regular	$149.99	$127.49
832P296	32B	(1996)	Regular	$149.99	$127.49
833P197	33A	(1997)	Regular	$149.99	$127.49
833P297	33B	(1997)	Regular	$149.99	$127.49
834P198	34A	(1998)	Regular	$149.99	$127.49
834P298	34B	(1998)	Regular	$149.99	$127.49
835P199	35A	(1999)	Regular	$149.99	$127.49

Item	Part	Binder		Retail	AA*
835P299	35B	(1999)	Regular	$149.99	$127.49
836P100	36A	(2000)	Regular	$149.99	$127.49
836P200	36B	(2000)	Regular	$149.99	$127.49
837P101	37A	(2001)	Regular	$149.99	$127.49
837P201	37B	(2001)	Regular	$149.99	$127.49
838P102	38A	(2002)	Regular	$149.99	$127.49
838P202	38B	(2002)	Regular	$149.99	$127.49
839P103	39A	(2003)	Regular	$149.99	$127.49
839P203	39B	(2003)	Regular	$149.99	$127.49
840P104	40A	(2004)	Regular	$149.99	$127.49
840P204	40B	(2004)	Regular	$149.99	$127.49
841P105	41A	(2005)	Regular	$149.99	$127.49
841P205	41B	(2005)	Regular	$149.99	$127.49
842P106	42A	(2006)	Regular	$149.99	$127.49
842P206	42B	(2006)	Regular	$149.99	$127.49
843P107	43A	(2007)	Regular	$149.99	$127.49
843P207	43B	(2007)	Regular	$149.99	$127.49
844P108	44A	(2008)	Jumbo	$149.99	$127.49
844P208	44B	(2008)	Jumbo	$149.99	$127.49
845P109	45A	(2009)	Jumbo	$149.99	$127.49
845P209	45B	(2009)	Jumbo	$149.99	$127.49
846P110	46A	(2010)	Regular	$149.99	$127.49
846P210	46B	(2010)	Regular	$149.99	$127.49
847P111	47A	(2011)	Regular	$149.99	$127.49
847P211	47B	(2011)	Regular	$149.99	$127.49
848P112	48A	(2012)	Regular	$149.99	$127.49
848P212	48B	(2012)	Regular	$149.99	$127.49
849P113	49A	(2013)	Regular	$149.99	$127.49
849P213	49B	(2013)	Regular	$149.99	$127.49
850P114	50A	(2014)	Regular	$149.99	$127.49
850P214	50B	(2014)	Regular	$149.99	$127.49
851P115	51A	(2015)	Regular	$149.99	$127.49
851P215	51B	(2015)	Regular	$149.99	$127.49
852P116	52A	(2016)	Regular	$160.99	$140.00
852P216	52B	(2016)	Regular	$160.99	$140.00
853P117	53A	(2017)	Regular	$160.99	$140.00
853P217	53B	(2017)	Regular	$160.99	$140.00
854P118	54A	(2018)	Regular	$160.99	$140.00
854P218	54B	(2018)	Regular	$160.99	$140.00
855P119	55A	(2019)	Regular	$160.99	$140.00
855P219	55B	(2019)	Regular	$160.99	$140.00
800PC72		People's Republic of China		$49.99	$42.49
800BOH		Bosnia & Herzegovina 1879-2007		$49.99	$42.49

INTERNATIONAL SERIES BINDERS AND SLIPCASES

Attractive, blue two-post binder is available in two sizes. Features distinctive silver embossed spine. **Binder will hold International pages only.** Labels available for all parts. For a complete list see amosadvantage.com

Item		Retail	AA*
800B001	Regular Binder Holds 300 pages	$52.99	$40.99
800B002	Jumbo Binder Holds 400 pages.	$52.99	$40.99
800BC01	Regular Binder Slipcase	$32.99	$26.99
800BC02	Jumbo Binder Slipcase	$32.99	$26.99

www. AmosAdvantage.com

Call 800-572-6885 - Outside U.S. & Canada call: (937) 498-0800

Ordering Information: *AA prices apply to paid subscribers of Amos Media titles, or for orders placed online. Prices, terms and product availability subject to change. Shipping & Handling: U.S.: Orders total $0-$10.00 charged $3.99 shipping. U.S. Order total $10.01-$79.99 charged $7.99 shipping. U.S. Order total $80.00 or more charged 10% of order total for shipping. Canada: 20% of order total. Minimum charge $19.99 Maximum charge $200.00. Foreign orders are shipped via FedEx Intl. or USPS and billed actual freight. Taxes will apply in CA, OH, & IL.

Information on Catalogue Values, Grade and Condition

Catalogue Value

The Scott Catalogue value is a retail value; that is, an amount you could expect to pay for a stamp in the grade of Very Fine with no faults. Any exceptions to the grade valued will be noted in the text. The general introduction on the following pages and the individual section introductions further explain the type of material that is valued. The value listed for any given stamp is a reference that reflects recent actual dealer selling prices for that item.

Dealer retail price lists, public auction results, published prices in advertising and individual solicitation of retail prices from dealers, collectors and specialty organizations have been used in establishing the values found in this catalogue. Amos Media Co. values stamps, but Amos Media is not a company engaged in the business of buying and selling stamps as a dealer.

Use this catalogue as a guide for buying and selling. The actual price you pay for a stamp may be higher or lower than the catalogue value because of many different factors, including the amount of personal service a dealer offers, or increased or decreased interest in the country or topic represented by a stamp or set. An item may occasionally be offered at a lower price as a "loss leader," or as part of a special sale. You also may obtain an item inexpensively at public auction because of little interest at that time or as part of a large lot.

Stamps that are of a lesser grade than Very Fine, or those with condition problems, generally trade at lower prices than those given in this catalogue. Stamps of exceptional quality in both grade and condition often command higher prices than those listed.

Values for pre-1900 unused issues are for stamps with approximately half or more of their original gum. Stamps with most or all of their original gum may be expected to sell for more, and stamps with less than half of their original gum may be expected to sell for somewhat less than the values listed. On rarer stamps, it may be expected that the original gum will be somewhat more disturbed than it will be on more common issues. Post-1900 unused issues are assumed to have full original gum. From breakpoints in most countries' listings, stamps are valued as never hinged, due to the wide availability of stamps in that condition. These notations are prominently placed in the listings and in the country information preceding the listings. Some countries also feature listings with dual values for hinged and never-hinged stamps.

Grade

A stamp's grade and condition are crucial to its value. The accompanying illustrations show examples of Very Fine stamps from different time periods, along with examples of stamps in Fine to Very Fine and Extremely Fine grades as points of reference. When a stamp seller offers a stamp in any grade from fine to superb without further qualifying statements, that stamp should not only have the centering grade as defined, but it also should be free of faults or other condition problems.

FINE stamps (illustrations not shown) have designs that are quite off center, with the perforations on one or two sides very close to the design but not quite touching it. There is white space between the perforations and the design that is minimal but evident to the unaided eye. Imperforate stamps may have small margins, and earlier issues may show the design just touching one edge of the stamp design. Very early perforated issues normally will have the perforations slightly cutting into the design. Used stamps may have heavier than usual cancellations.

FINE-VERY FINE stamps will be somewhat off center on one side, or slightly off center on two sides. Imperforate stamps will have two margins of at least normal size, and the design will not touch any edge. For perforated stamps, the perfs are well clear of the design, but are still noticeably off center. *However, early issues of a country may be printed in such a way that the design naturally is very close to the edges. In these cases, the perforations may cut into the design very slightly.* Used stamps will not have a cancellation that detracts from the design.

VERY FINE stamps will be just slightly off center on one or two sides, but the design will be well clear of the edge. The stamp will present a nice, balanced appearance. Imperforate stamps will be well centered within normal-sized margins. *However, early issues of many countries may be printed in such a way that the perforations may touch the design on one or more sides. Where this is the case, a boxed note will be found defining the centering and margins of the stamps being valued.* Used stamps will have light or otherwise neat cancellations. This is the grade used to establish Scott Catalogue values.

EXTREMELY FINE stamps are close to being perfectly centered. Imperforate stamps will have even margins that are slightly larger than normal. Even the earliest perforated issues will have perforations clear of the design on all sides.

Amos Media Co. recognizes that there is no formally enforced grading scheme for postage stamps, and that the final price you pay or obtain for a stamp will be determined by individual agreement at the time of transaction.

Condition

Grade addresses only centering and (for used stamps) cancellation. *Condition* refers to factors other than grade that affect a stamp's desirability.

Factors that can increase the value of a stamp include exceptionally wide margins, particularly fresh color, the presence of selvage, and plate or die varieties. Unusual cancels on used stamps (particularly those of the 19th century) can greatly enhance their value as well.

Factors other than faults that decrease the value of a stamp include loss of original gum, regumming, a hinge remnant or foreign object adhering to the gum, natural inclusions, straight edges, and markings or notations applied by collectors or dealers.

Faults include missing pieces, tears, pin or other holes, surface scuffs, thin spots, creases, toning, short or pulled perforations, clipped perforations, oxidation or other forms of color changelings, soiling, stains, and such man-made changes as reperforations or the chemical removal or lightening of a cancellation.

Grading Illustrations

On the following two pages are illustrations of various stamps from countries appearing in this volume. These stamps are arranged by country, and they represent early or important issues that are often found in widely different grades in the marketplace. The editors believe the illustrations will prove useful in showing the margin size and centering that will be seen on the various issues.

In addition to the matters of margin size and centering, collectors are reminded that the very fine stamps valued in the Scott catalogues also will possess fresh color and intact perforations, and they will be free from defects.

Examples shown are computer-manipulated images made from single digitized master illustrations.

Stamp Illustrations Used in the Catalogue

It is important to note that the stamp images used for identification purposes in this catalogue may not be indicative of the grade of stamp being valued. Refer to the written discussion of grades on this page and to the grading illustrations on the following two pages for grading information.

Fine-Very Fine →

SCOTT CATALOGUES VALUE STAMPS IN THIS GRADE

Very Fine →

Extremely Fine →

Fine-Very Fine →

SCOTT CATALOGUES VALUE STAMPS IN THIS GRADE

Very Fine →

Extremely Fine →

Fine-Very Fine →

SCOTT CATALOGUES VALUE STAMPS IN THIS GRADE

Very Fine →

Extremely Fine →

Fine-Very Fine →

SCOTT CATALOGUES VALUE STAMPS IN THIS GRADE

Very Fine →

Extremely Fine →

For purposes of helping to determine the gum condition and value of an unused stamp, Scott presents the following chart which details different gum conditions and indicates how the conditions correlate with the Scott values for unused stamps. Used together, the Illustrated Grading Chart on the previous pages and this Illustrated Gum Chart should allow catalogue users to better understand the grade and gum condition of stamps valued in the Scott catalogues.

Gum Categories:	MINT N.H.	ORIGINAL GUM (O.G.)				NO GUM
	Mint Never Hinged *Free from any disturbance*	**Lightly Hinged** *Faint impression of a removed hinge over a small area*	**Hinge Mark or Remnant** *Prominent hinged spot with part or all of the hinge remaining*	**Large part o.g.** *Approximately half or more of the gum intact*	**Small part o.g.** *Approximately less than half of the gum intact*	**No gum** *Only if issued with gum*
Commonly Used Symbol:	★★	★	★	★	★	(★)
Pre-1900 Issues (Pre-1881 for U.S.)	*Very fine pre-1900 stamps in these categories trade at a premium over Scott value*			Scott Value for "Unused"		Scott "No Gum" listings for selected unused classic stamps
From 1900 to break-points for listings of never-hinged stamps	Scott "Never Hinged" listings for selected unused stamps	Scott Value for "Unused" (Actual value will be affected by the degree of hinging of the full o.g.)				
From breakpoints noted for many countries	Scott Value for "Unused"					

Never Hinged (NH; ★★): A never-hinged stamp will have full original gum that will have no hinge mark or disturbance. The presence of an expertizer's mark does not disqualify a stamp from this designation.

Original Gum (OG; ★): Pre-1900 stamps should have approximately half or more of their original gum. On rarer stamps, it may be expected that the original gum will be somewhat more disturbed than it will be on more common issues. Post-1900 stamps should have full original gum. Original gum will show some disturbance caused by a previous hinge(s) which may be present or entirely removed. The actual value of a post-1900 stamp will be affected by the degree of hinging of the full original gum.

Disturbed Original Gum: Gum showing noticeable effects of humidity, climate or hinging over more than half of the gum. The significance of gum disturbance in valuing a stamp in any of the Original Gum categories depends on the degree of disturbance, the rarity and normal gum condition of the issue and other variables affecting quality.

Regummed (RG; (★)): A regummed stamp is a stamp without gum that has had some type of gum privately applied at a time after it was issued. This normally is done to deceive collectors and/or dealers into thinking that the stamp has original gum and therefore has a higher value. A regummed stamp is considered the same as a stamp with none of its original gum for purposes of grading.

Understanding the Listings

On the opposite page is an enlarged "typical" listing from this catalogue. Below are detailed explanations of each of the highlighted parts of the listing.

❶ Scott number — Scott catalogue numbers are used to identify specific items when buying, selling or trading stamps. Each listed postage stamp from every country has a unique Scott catalogue number. Therefore, Germany Scott 99, for example, can only refer to a single stamp. Although the Scott catalogue usually lists stamps in chronological order by date of issue, there are exceptions. When a country has issued a set of stamps over a period of time, those stamps within the set are kept together without regard to date of issue. This follows the normal collecting approach of keeping stamps in their natural sets.

When a country issues a set of stamps over a period of time, a group of consecutive catalogue numbers is reserved for the stamps in that set, as issued. If that group of numbers proves to be too few, capital-letter suffixes, such as "A" or "B," may be added to existing numbers to create enough catalogue numbers to cover all items in the set. A capital-letter suffix indicates a major Scott catalogue number listing. Scott generally uses a suffix letter only once. Therefore, a catalogue number listing with a capital-letter suffix will seldom be found with the same letter (lower case) used as a minor-letter listing. If there is a Scott 16A in a set, for example, there will seldom be a Scott 16a. However, a minor-letter "a" listing may be added to a major number containing an "A" suffix (Scott 16Aa, for example).

Suffix letters are cumulative. A minor "b" variety of Scott 16A would be Scott 16Ab, not Scott 16b.

There are times when a reserved block of Scott catalogue numbers is too large for a set, leaving some numbers unused. Such gaps in the numbering sequence also occur when the catalogue editors move an item's listing elsewhere or have removed it entirely from the catalogue. Scott does not attempt to account for every possible number, but rather attempts to assure that each stamp is assigned its own number.

Scott numbers designating regular postage normally are only numerals. Scott numbers for other types of stamps, such as air post, semi-postal, postal tax, postage due, occupation and others have a prefix consisting of one or more capital letters or a combination of numerals and capital letters.

❷ Illustration number — Illustration or design-type numbers are used to identify each catalogue illustration. For most sets, the lowest face-value stamp is shown. It then serves as an example of the basic design approach for other stamps not illustrated. Where more than one stamp use the same illustration number, but have differences in design, the design paragraph or the description line clearly indicates the design on each stamp not illustrated. Where there are both vertical and horizontal designs in a set, a single illustration may be used, with the exceptions noted in the design paragraph or description line.

When an illustration is followed by a lower-case letter in parentheses, such as "A2(b)," the trailing letter indicates which overprint or surcharge illustration applies.

Illustrations normally are 70 percent of the original size of the stamp. Oversized stamps, blocks and souvenir sheets are reduced even more. Overprints and surcharges are shown at 100 percent of their original size if shown alone, but are 70 percent of original size if shown on stamps. In some cases, the illustration will be placed above the set, between listings or omitted completely. Overprint and surcharge illustrations are not placed in this catalogue for purposes of expertizing stamps.

❸ Paper color — The color of a stamp's paper is noted in italic type when the paper used is not white.

❹ Listing styles — There are two principal types of catalogue listings: major and minor.

Major listings are in a larger type style than minor listings. The catalogue number is a numeral that can be found with or without a capital-letter suffix, and with or without a prefix.

Minor listings are in a smaller type style and have a small-letter suffix or (if the listing immediately follows that of the major number) may show only the letter. These listings identify a variety of the major item. Examples include perforation and shade differences, multiples (some souvenir sheets, booklet panes and se-tenant combinations), and singles of multiples.

Examples of major number listings include 16, 28A, B97, C13A, 10N5, and 10N6A. Examples of minor numbers are 16a and C13Ab.

❺ Basic information about a stamp or set — Introducing each stamp issue is a small section (usually a line listing) of basic information about a stamp or set. This section normally includes the date of issue, method of printing, perforation, watermark and, sometimes, some additional information of note. *Printing method, perforation and watermark apply to the following sets until a change is noted.* Stamps created by overprinting or surcharging previous issues are assumed to have the same perforation, watermark, printing method and other production characteristics as the original. Dates of issue are as precise as Scott is able to confirm and often reflect the dates on first-day covers, rather than the actual date of release.

❻ Denomination — This normally refers to the face value of the stamp; that is, the cost of the unused stamp at the post office at the time of issue. When a denomination is shown in parentheses, it does not appear on the stamp. This includes the non-denominated stamps of the United States, Brazil and Great Britain, for example.

❼ Color or other description — This area provides information to solidify identification of a stamp. In many recent cases, a description of the stamp design appears in this space, rather than a listing of colors.

❽ Year of issue — In stamp sets that have been released in a period that spans more than a year, the number shown in parentheses is the year that stamp first appeared. Stamps without a date appeared during the first year of the issue. Dates are not always given for minor varieties.

❾ Value unused and Value used — The Scott catalogue values are based on stamps that are in a grade of Very Fine unless stated otherwise. Unused values refer to items that have not seen postal, revenue or any other duty for which they were intended. Pre-1900 unused stamps that were issued with gum must have at least most of their original gum. Later issues are assumed to have full original gum. From breakpoints specified in most countries' listings, stamps are valued as never hinged. Stamps issued without gum are noted. Modern issues with PVA or other synthetic adhesives may appear ungummed. Unused self-adhesive stamps are valued as appearing undisturbed on their original backing paper. Values for used self-adhesive stamps are for examples either on piece or off piece. For a more detailed explanation of these values, please see the "Catalogue Value," "Condition" and "Understanding Valuing Notations" sections elsewhere in this introduction.

In some cases, where used stamps are more valuable than unused stamps, the value is for an example with a contemporaneous cancel, rather than a modern cancel or a smudge or other unclear marking. For those stamps that were released for postal and fiscal purposes, the used value represents a postally used stamp. Stamps with revenue cancels generally sell for less.

Stamps separated from a complete se-tenant multiple usually will be worth less than a pro-rated portion of the se-tenant multiple, and stamps lacking the attached labels that are noted in the listings will be worth less than the values shown.

❿ Changes in basic set information — Bold type is used to show any changes in the basic data given for a set of stamps. These basic data categories include perforation gauge measurement, paper type, printing method and watermark.

⓫ Total value of a set — The total value of sets of three or more stamps issued after 1900 are shown. The set line also notes the range of Scott numbers and total number of stamps included in the grouping. The actual value of a set consisting predominantly of stamps having the minimum value of 25 cents may be less than the total value shown. Similarly, the actual value or catalogue value of se-tenant pairs or of blocks consisting of stamps having the minimum value of 25 cents may be less than the catalogue values of the component parts.

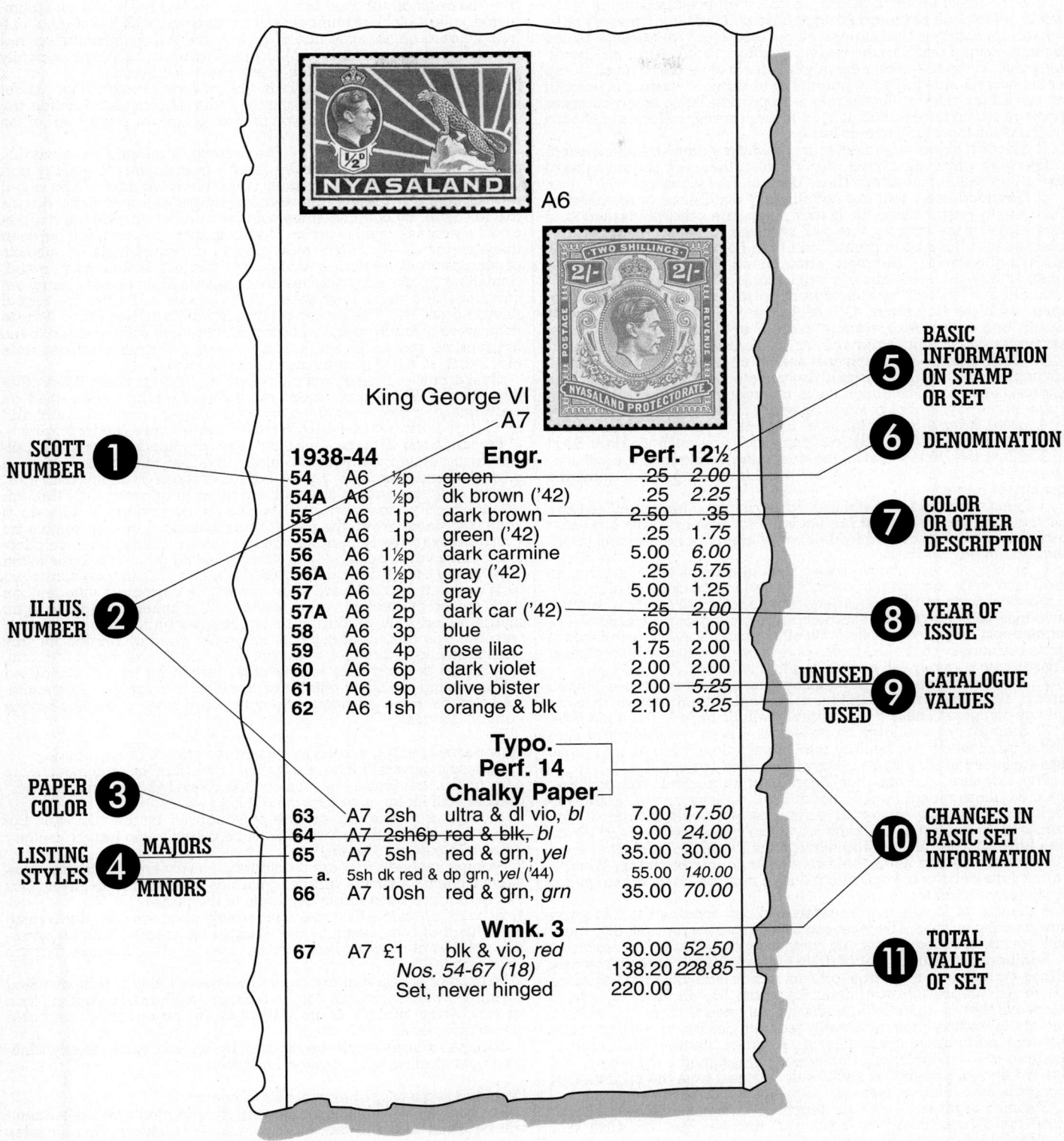

SCOTT NUMBER **1**

ILLUS. NUMBER **2**

PAPER COLOR **3**

LISTING STYLES **4**   MAJORS
                           MINORS

A6

King George VI
A7

5 BASIC INFORMATION ON STAMP OR SET

6 DENOMINATION

7 COLOR OR OTHER DESCRIPTION

8 YEAR OF ISSUE

9 CATALOGUE VALUES   UNUSED / USED

10 CHANGES IN BASIC SET INFORMATION

11 TOTAL VALUE OF SET

1938-44			**Engr.**	**Perf. 12½**	
54	A6	½p	green	.25	*2.00*
54A	A6	½p	dk brown ('42)	.25	*2.25*
55	A6	1p	dark brown	2.50	*.35*
55A	A6	1p	green ('42)	.25	*1.75*
56	A6	1½p	dark carmine	5.00	*6.00*
56A	A6	1½p	gray ('42)	.25	*5.75*
57	A6	2p	gray	5.00	*1.25*
57A	A6	2p	dark car ('42)	.25	*2.00*
58	A6	3p	blue	.60	*1.00*
59	A6	4p	rose lilac	1.75	*2.00*
60	A6	6p	dark violet	2.00	*2.00*
61	A6	9p	olive bister	2.00	*5.25*
62	A6	1sh	orange & blk	2.10	*3.25*

Typo.
Perf. 14
Chalky Paper

63	A7	2sh	ultra & dl vio, *bl*	7.00	*17.50*
64	A7	2sh6p	red & blk, *bl*	9.00	*24.00*
65	A7	5sh	red & grn, *yel*	35.00	*30.00*
a.		5sh dk red & dp grn, *yel* ('44)	55.00	*140.00*
66	A7	10sh	red & grn, *grn*	35.00	*70.00*

Wmk. 3

67	A7	£1	blk & vio, *red*	30.00	*52.50*
		Nos. 54-67 (18)		138.20	*228.85*
		Set, never hinged		220.00	

Catalogue Listing Policy

It is the intent of Amos Media Co. to list all postage stamps of the world in the *Scott Standard Postage Stamp Catalogue*. The only strict criteria for listing is that stamps be decreed legal for postage by the issuing country and that the issuing country actually have an operating postal system. Whether the primary intent of issuing a given stamp or set was for sale to postal patrons or to stamp collectors is not part of our listing criteria. Scott's role is to provide basic comprehensive postage stamp information. It is up to each stamp collector to choose which items to include in a collection.

It is Scott's objective to seek reasons why a stamp should be listed, rather than why it should not. Nevertheless, there are certain types of items that will not be listed. These include the following:

1. Unissued items that are not officially distributed or released by the issuing postal authority. If such items are officially issued at a later date by the country, they will be listed. Unissued items consist of those that have been printed and then held from sale for reasons such as change in government, errors found on stamps or something deemed objectionable about a stamp subject or design.

2. Stamps "issued" by non-existent postal entities or fantasy countries, such as Nagaland, Occusi-Ambeno, Staffa, Sedang, Torres Straits and others. Also, stamps "issued" in the names of legitimate, stamp-issuing countries that are not authorized by those countries.

3. Semi-official or unofficial items not required for postage. Examples include items issued by private agencies for their own express services. When such items are required for delivery, or are valid as prepayment of postage, they are listed.

4. Local stamps issued for local use only. Postage stamps issued by governments specifically for "domestic" use, such as Haiti Scott 219-228, or the United States non-denominated stamps, are not considered to be locals, since they are valid for postage throughout the country of origin.

5. Items not valid for postal use. For example, a few countries have issued souvenir sheets that are not valid for postage. This area also includes a number of worldwide charity labels (some denominated) that do not pay postage.

6. Egregiously exploitative issues such as stamps sold for far more than face value, stamps purposely issued in artificially small quantities or only against advance orders, stamps awarded only to a selected audience such as a philatelic bureau's standing order customers, or stamps sold only in conjunction with other products. All of these kinds of items are usually controlled issues and/or are intended for speculation. These items normally will be included in a footnote.

7. Items distributed by the issuing government only to a limited group, club, philatelic exhibition or a single stamp dealer or other private company. These items normally will be included in a footnote.

8. Stamps not available to collectors. These generally are rare items, all of which are held by public institutions such as museums. The existence of such items often will be cited in footnotes.

The fact that a stamp has been used successfully as postage, even on international mail, is not in itself sufficient proof that it was legitimately issued. Numerous examples of so-called stamps from non-existent countries are known to have been used to post letters that have successfully passed through the international mail system.

There are certain items that are subject to interpretation. When a stamp falls outside our specifications, it may be listed along with a cautionary footnote.

A number of factors are considered in our approach to analyzing how a stamp is listed. The following list of factors is presented to share with you, the catalogue user, the complexity of the listing process.

Additional printings — "Additional printings" of a previously issued stamp may range from an item that is totally different to cases where it is impossible to differentiate from the original. At least a minor number (a small-letter suffix) is assigned if there is a distinct change in stamp shade, noticeably redrawn design, or a significantly different perforation measurement. A major number (numeral or numeral and capital-letter combination) is assigned if the editors feel the "additional printing" is sufficiently different from the original that it constitutes a different issue.

Commemoratives — Where practical, commemoratives with the same theme are placed in a set. For example, the U.S. Civil War Centennial set of 1961-65 and the Constitution Bicentennial series of 1989-90 appear as sets. Countries such as Japan and Korea issue such material on a regular basis, with an announced, or at least predictable, number of stamps known in advance. Occasionally, however, stamp sets that were released over a period of years have been separated. Appropriately placed footnotes will guide you to each set's continuation.

Definitive sets — Blocks of numbers generally have been reserved for definitive sets, based on previous experience with any given country. If a few more stamps were issued in a set than originally expected, they often have been inserted into the original set with a capital-letter suffix, such as U.S. Scott 1059A. If it appears that many more stamps

than the originally allotted block will be released before the set is completed, a new block of numbers will be reserved, with the original one being closed off. In some cases, such as the U.S. Transportation and Great Americans series, several blocks of numbers exist. Appropriately placed footnotes will guide you to each set's continuation.

New country — Membership in the Universal Postal Union is not a consideration for listing status or order of placement within the catalogue. The index will tell you in what volume or page number the listings begin.

"No release date" items — The amount of information available for any given stamp issue varies greatly from country to country and even from time to time. Extremely comprehensive information about new stamps is available from some countries well before the stamps are released. By contrast some countries do not provide information about stamps or release dates. Most countries, however, fall between these extremes. A country may provide denominations or subjects of stamps from upcoming issues that are not issued as planned. Sometimes, philatelic agencies, those private firms hired to represent countries, add these later-issued items to sets well after the formal release date. This time period can range from weeks to years. If these items were officially released by the country, they will be added to the appropriate spot in the set. In many cases, the specific release date of a stamp or set of stamps may never be known.

Overprints — The color of an overprint is always noted if it is other than black. Where more than one color of ink has been used on overprints of a single set, the color used is noted. Early overprint and surcharge illustrations were altered to prevent their use by forgers.

Personalized Stamps — Since 1999, the special service of personalizing stamp vignettes, or labels attached to stamps, has been offered to customers by postal administrations of many countries. Sheets of these stamps are sold, singly or in quantity, only through special orders made by mail, in person, or through a sale on a computer website with the postal administrations or their agents for which an extra fee is charged, though some countries offer to collectors at face value personalized stamps having generic images in the vignettes or on the attached labels. It is impossible for any catalogue to know what images have been chosen by customers. Images can be 1) owned or created by the customer, 2) a generic image, or 3) an image pulled from a library of stock images on the stamp creation website. It is also impossible to know the quantity printed for any stamp having a particular image. So from a valuing standpoint, any image is equivalent to any other image for any personalized stamp having the same catalogue number. Illustrations of personalized stamps in the catalogue are not always those of stamps having generic images.

Personalized items are listed with some exceptions. These include:

1. Stamps or sheets that have attached labels that the customer cannot personalize, but which are nonetheless marketed as "personalized," and are sold for far more than the franking value.

2. Stamps or sheets that can be personalized by the customer, but where a portion of the print run must be ceded to the issuing country for sale to other customers.

3. Stamps or sheets that are created exclusively for a particular commercial client, or clients, including stamps that differ from any similar stamp that has been made available to the public.

4. Stamps or sheets that are deliberately conceived by the issuing authority that have been, or are likely to be, created with an excessive number of different face values, sizes, or other features that are changeable.

5. Stamps or sheets that are created by postal administrations using the same system of stamp personalization that has been put in place for use by the public that are printed in limited quantities and sold above face value.

6. Stamps or sheets that are created by licensees not directly affiliated or controlled by a postal administration.

Excluded items may or may not be footnoted.

Se-tenants — Connected stamps of differing features (se-tenants) will be listed in the format most commonly collected. This includes pairs, blocks or larger multiples. Se-tenant units are not always symmetrical. An example is Australia Scott 508, which is a block of seven stamps. If the stamps are primarily collected as a unit, the major number may be assigned to the multiple, with minors going to each component stamp. In cases where continuous-design or other unit se-tenants will receive significant postal use, each stamp is given a major Scott number listing. This includes issues from the United States, Canada, Germany and Great Britain, for example.

Special Notices

Classification of stamps

The *Scott Standard Postage Stamp Catalogue* lists stamps by country of issue. The next level of organization is a listing by section on the basis of the function of the stamps. The principal sections cover regular postage, semi-postal, air post, special delivery, registration, postage due and other categories. Except for regular postage, catalogue numbers for all sections include a prefix letter (or number-letter combination) denoting the class to which a given stamp belongs. When some countries issue sets containing stamps from more than one category, the catalogue will at times list all of the stamps in one category (such as air post stamps listed as part of a postage set).

The following is a listing of the most commonly used catalogue prefixes.

Prefix ....Category
- C.........Air Post
- M........Military
- P.........Newspaper
- N.........Occupation - Regular Issues
- O........Official
- Q........Parcel Post
- J.........Postage Due
- RA......Postal Tax
- B.........Semi-Postal
- E.........Special Delivery
- MR......War Tax

Other prefixes used by more than one country include the following:
- H.........Acknowledgment of Receipt
- I..........Late Fee
- CO......Air Post Official
- CQ......Air Post Parcel Post
- RAC....Air Post Postal Tax
- CF......Air Post Registration
- CB......Air Post Semi-Postal
- CBO ...Air Post Semi-Postal Official
- CE......Air Post Special Delivery
- EY.......Authorized Delivery
- S.........Franchise
- G ....Insured Letter
- GY......Marine Insurance
- MC .....Military Air Post
- MQ.....Military Parcel Post
- NC......Occupation - Air Post
- NO......Occupation - Official
- NJ........Occupation - Postage Due
- NRA....Occupation - Postal Tax
- NB ......Occupation - Semi-Postal
- NE ......Occupation - Special Delivery
- QY......Parcel Post Authorized Delivery
- AR......Postal-fiscal
- RAJ.....Postal Tax Due
- RAB ....Postal Tax Semi-Postal
- F ....Registration
- EB.......Semi-Postal Special Delivery
- EO......Special Delivery Official
- QE......Special Handling

New issue listings

Updates to this catalogue appear each month in the *Linn's Stamp News* monthly magazine. Included in this update are additions to the listings of countries found in the *Scott Standard Postage Stamp Catalogue* and the *Specialized Catalogue of United States Stamps and Covers*, as well as corrections and updates to current editions of this catalogue.

From time to time there will be changes in the final listings of stamps from the *Linn's Stamp News* magazine to the next edition of the catalogue. This occurs as more information about certain stamps or sets becomes available.

The catalogue update section of the *Linn's Stamp News* magazine is the most timely presentation of this material available. Annual subscriptions to *Linn's Stamp News* are available from Linn's Stamp News, Box 4129, Sidney, OH 45365-4129.

Number additions, deletions & changes

A listing of catalogue number additions, deletions and changes from the previous edition of the catalogue appears in each volume. See Catalogue Number Additions, Deletions & Changes in the table of contents for the location of this list.

Understanding valuing notations

The *minimum catalogue value* of an individual stamp or set is 25 cents. This represents a portion of the cost incurred by a dealer when he prepares an individual stamp for resale. As a point of philatelic-economic fact, the lower the value shown for an item in this catalogue, the greater the percentage of that value is attributed to dealer mark up and profit margin. In many cases, such as the 25-cent minimum value, that price does not cover the labor or other costs involved with stocking it as an individual stamp. The sum of minimum values in a set does not properly represent the value of a complete set primarily composed of a number of minimum-value stamps, nor does the sum represent the actual value of a packet made up of minimum-value stamps. Thus a packet of 1,000 different common stamps — each of which has a catalogue value of 25 cents — normally sells for considerably less than 250 dollars!

The *absence of a retail value* for a stamp does not necessarily suggest that a stamp is scarce or rare. A dash in the value column means that the stamp is known in a stated form or variety, but information is either lacking or insufficient for purposes of establishing a usable catalogue value.

Stamp values in *italics* generally refer to items that are difficult to value accurately. For expensive items, such as those priced at $1,000 or higher, a value in italics indicates that the affected item trades very seldom. For inexpensive items, a value in italics represents a warning. One example is a "blocked" issue where the issuing postal administration may have controlled one stamp in a set in an attempt to make the whole set more valuable. Another example is an item that sold at an extreme multiple of face value in the marketplace at the time of its issue.

One type of warning to collectors that appears in the catalogue is illustrated by a stamp that is valued considerably higher in used condition than it is as unused. In this case, collectors are cautioned to be certain the used version has a genuine and contemporaneous cancellation. The type of cancellation on a stamp can be an important factor in determining its sale price. Catalogue values do not apply to fiscal, telegraph or non-contemporaneous postal cancels, unless otherwise noted.

Some countries have released back issues of stamps in canceled-to-order form, sometimes covering as much as a 10-year period. The Scott Catalogue values for used stamps reflect canceled-to-order material when such stamps are found to predominate in the marketplace for the issue involved. Notes frequently appear in the stamp listings to specify which items are valued as canceled-to-order, or if there is a premium for postally used examples.

Many countries sell canceled-to-order stamps at a marked reduction of face value. Countries that sell or have sold canceled-to-order stamps at *full* face value include United Nations, Australia, Netherlands, France and Switzerland. It may be almost impossible to identify such stamps if the gum has been removed, because official government canceling devices are used. Postally used examples of these items on cover, however, are usually worth more than the canceled-to-order stamps with original gum.

Abbreviations

Scott uses a consistent set of abbreviations throughout this catalogue to conserve space, while still providing necessary information.

COLOR ABBREVIATIONS

amb. amber	crim. crimson	ol ..... olive
anil.. aniline	cr ..... cream	olvn . olivine
ap.... apple	dk .... dark	org... orange
aqua aquamarine	dl ..... dull	pck .. peacock
az .... azure	dp.... deep	pnksh pinkish
bis ... bister	db.... drab	Prus . Prussian
bl..... blue	emer emerald	pur... purple
bld... blood	gldn. golden	redsh reddish
blk... black	gryshgrayish	res ..... reseda
bril... brilliant	grn... green	ros ... rosine
brn... brown	grnsh greenish	ryl .... royal
brnsh brownish	hel ... heliotrope	sal ... salmon
brnz. bronze	hn.... henna	saph sapphire
brt.... bright	ind... indigo	scar . scarlet
brnt . burnt	int .... intense	sep .. sepia
car... carmine	lav ... lavender	sien . sienna
cer... cerise	lem .. lemon	sil..... silver
chlky chalky	lil ..... lilac	sl...... slate
chamchamois	lt ..... light	stl .... steel
chnt . chestnut	mag. magenta	turq.. turquoise
choc chocolate	man. manila	ultra ultramarine
chr... chrome	mar.. maroon	Ven.. Venetian
cit .... citron	mv ... mauve	ver ... vermilion
cl...... claret	multi multicolored	vio ... violet
cob .. cobalt	mlky milky	yel ... yellow
cop .. copper	myr.. myrtle	yelsh yellowish

When no color is given for an overprint or surcharge, black is the color used. Abbreviations for colors used for overprints and surcharges include: "(B)" or "(Blk)," black; "(Bl)," blue; "(R)," red; and "(G)," green.

Additional abbreviations in this catalogue are shown below:

Adm.	Administration
AFL.................	American Federation of Labor
Anniv............	Anniversary
APS	American Philatelic Society
Assoc.	Association
ASSR.	Autonomous Soviet Socialist Republic
b.	Born
BEP...............	Bureau of Engraving and Printing
Bicent...........	Bicentennial
Bklt.	Booklet
Brit.................	British
btwn.	Between
Bur.	Bureau
c. or ca..........	Circa
Cat.	Catalogue
Cent.	Centennial, century, centenary
CIO	Congress of Industrial Organizations
Conf.	Conference
Cong.	Congress
Cpl.	Corporal
CTO	Canceled to order
d.	Died
Dbl.	Double
EDU..............	Earliest documented use
Engr.	Engraved
Exhib.............	Exhibition
Expo.............	Exposition
Fed.	Federation
GB	Great Britain
Gen.	General
GPO	General post office
Horiz.	Horizontal
Imperf.	Imperforate
Impt.............	Imprint

Intl.	International
Invtd.............	Inverted
L	Left
Lieut., lt.........	Lieutenant
Litho.	Lithographed
LL	Lower left
LR	Lower right
mm	Millimeter
Ms.	Manuscript
Natl.	National
No.	Number
NY	New York
NYC	New York City
Ovpt.	Overprint
Ovptd............	Overprinted
P	Plate number
Perf.	Perforated, perforation
Phil.	Philatelic
Photo............	Photogravure
PO	Post office
Pr.	Pair
P.R.	Puerto Rico
Prec.	Precancel, precanceled
Pres.	President
PTT	Post, Telephone and Telegraph
R	Right
Rio.................	Rio de Janeiro
Sgt.................	Sergeant
Soc.	Society
Souv.	Souvenir
SSR	Soviet Socialist Republic, see ASSR
St.	Saint, street
Surch.	Surcharge
Typo.	Typographed
UL.................	Upper left
Unwmkd.	Unwatermarked
UPU	Universal Postal Union
UR	Upper Right
US	United States
USPOD	United States Post Office Department
USSR	Union of Soviet Socialist Republics
Vert................	Vertical
VP.................	Vice president
Wmk.............	Watermark
Wmkd.	Watermarked
WWI	World War I
WWII............	World War II

Examination

Amos Media Co. will not comment upon the genuineness, grade or condition of stamps, because of the time and responsibility involved. Rather, there are several expertizing groups that undertake this work for both collectors and dealers. Neither will Amos Media Co. appraise or identify philatelic material. The company cannot take responsibility for unsolicited stamps or covers sent by individuals.

All letters, E-mails, etc. are read attentively, but they are not always answered due to time considerations.

How to order from your dealer

When ordering stamps from a dealer, it is not necessary to write the full description of a stamp as listed in this catalogue. All you need is the name of the country, the Scott catalogue number and whether the desired item is unused or used. For example, "Japan Scott 422 unused" is sufficient to identify the unused stamp of Japan listed as "422 A206 5y brown."

Basic Stamp Information

A stamp collector's knowledge of the combined elements that make a given stamp issue unique determines his or her ability to identify stamps. These elements include paper, watermark, method of separation, printing, design and gum. On the following pages each of these important areas is briefly described.

Paper

Paper is an organic material composed of a compacted weave of cellulose fibers and generally formed into sheets. Paper used to print stamps may be manufactured in sheets, or it may have been part of a large roll (called a web) before being cut to size. The fibers most often used to create paper on which stamps are printed include bark, wood, straw and certain grasses. In many cases, linen or cotton rags have been added for greater strength and durability. Grinding, bleaching, cooking and rinsing these raw fibers reduces them to a slushy pulp, referred to by paper makers as "stuff." Sizing and, sometimes, coloring matter is added to the pulp to make different types of finished paper.

After the stuff is prepared, it is poured onto sieve-like frames that allow the water to run off, while retaining the matted pulp. As fibers fall onto the screen and are held by gravity, they form a natural weave that will later hold the paper together. If the screen has metal bits that are formed into letters or images attached, it leaves slightly thinned areas on the paper. These are called watermarks.

When the stuff is almost dry, it is passed under pressure through smooth or engraved rollers - dandy rolls - or placed between cloth in a press to be flattened and dried.

Wove — Laid — Granite

Quadrille — Oblong Quadrille — Laid Batonne

Stamp paper falls broadly into two types: wove and laid. The nature of the surface of the frame onto which the pulp is first deposited causes the differences in appearance between the two. If the surface is smooth and even, the paper will be of fairly uniform texture throughout. This is known as *wove paper*. Early papermaking machines poured the pulp onto a continuously circulating web of felt, but modern machines feed the pulp onto a cloth-like screen made of closely interwoven fine wires. This paper, when held to a light, will show little dots or points very close together. The proper name for this is "wire wove," but the type is still considered wove. Any U.S. or British stamp printed after 1880 will serve as an example of wire wove paper.

Closely spaced parallel wires, with cross wires at wider intervals, make up the frames used for what is known as *laid paper*. A greater thickness of the pulp will settle between the wires. The paper, when held to a light, will show alternate light and dark lines. The spacing and the thickness of the lines may vary, but on any one sheet of paper they are all alike. See Russia Scott 31-38 for examples of laid paper.

Batonne, from the French word meaning "a staff," is a term used if the lines in the paper are spaced quite far apart, like the printed ruling on a writing tablet. Batonne paper may be either wove or laid. If laid, fine laid lines can be seen between the batons.

Quadrille is the term used when the lines in the paper form little squares. *Oblong quadrille* is the term used when rectangles, rather than squares, are formed. Grid patterns vary from distinct to extremely faint. See Mexico-Guadalajara Scott 35-37 for examples of oblong quadrille paper.

Paper also is classified as thick or thin, hard or soft, and by color. Such colors may include yellowish, greenish, bluish and reddish.

Brief explanations of other types of paper used for printing stamps, as well as examples, follow.

Colored — Colored paper is created by the addition of dye in the paper-making process. Such colors may include shades of yellow, green, blue and red. *Surface-colored papers*, most commonly used for British colonial issues in 1913-14, are created when coloring is added only to the surface during the finishing process. Stamps printed on surface-colored paper have white or uncolored backs, while true colored papers are colored through. See Jamaica Scott 71-73.

Pelure — Pelure paper is a very thin, hard and often brittle paper that is sometimes bluish or grayish in appearance. See Serbia Scott 169-170.

Native — This is a term applied to handmade papers used to produce some of the early stamps of the Indian states. Stamps printed on native paper may be expected to display various natural inclusions that are normal and do not negatively affect value. Japanese paper, originally made of mulberry fibers and rice flour, is part of this group. See Japan Scott 1-18.

Manila — This type of paper is often used to make stamped envelopes and wrappers. It is a coarse-textured stock, usually smooth on one side and rough on the other. A variety of colors of manila paper exist, but the most common range is yellowish-brown.

Silk — Introduced by the British in 1847 as a safeguard against counterfeiting, silk paper contains bits of colored silk thread scattered throughout. The density of these fibers varies greatly and can include as few as one fiber per stamp or hundreds. U.S. revenue Scott R152 is a good example of an easy-to-identify silk paper stamp.

Silk-thread paper has uninterrupted threads of colored silk arranged so that one or more threads run through the stamp or postal stationery. See Great Britain Scott 5-6 and Switzerland Scott 14-19.

Granite — Filled with minute cloth or colored paper fibers of various colors and lengths, granite paper should not be confused with either type of silk paper. Austria Scott 172-175 and a number of Swiss stamps are examples of granite paper.

Chalky — A chalk-like substance coats the surface of chalky paper to discourage the cleaning and reuse of canceled stamps, as well as to provide a smoother, more acceptable printing surface. Because the designs of stamps printed on chalky paper are imprinted on what is often a water-soluble coating, any attempt to remove a cancellation will destroy the stamp. *Do not soak these stamps in any fluid.* To remove a stamp printed on chalky paper from an envelope, wet the paper from underneath the stamp until the gum dissolves enough to release the stamp from the paper. See St. Kitts-Nevis Scott 89-90 for examples of stamps printed on this type of chalky paper.

India — Another name for this paper, originally introduced from China about 1750, is "China Paper." It is a thin, opaque paper often used for plate and die proofs by many countries.

Double — In philately, the term double paper has two distinct meanings. The first is a two-ply paper, usually a combination of a thick and a thin sheet, joined during manufacture. This type was used experimentally as a means to discourage the reuse of stamps.

The design is printed on the thin paper. Any attempt to remove a cancellation would destroy the design. U.S. Scott 158 and other Banknote-era stamps exist on this form of double paper.

The second type of double paper occurs on a rotary press, when the end of one paper roll, or web, is affixed to the next roll to save time feeding the paper through the press. Stamp designs are printed over the joined paper and, if overlooked by inspectors, may get into post office stocks.

Goldbeater's Skin — This type of paper was used for the 1866 issue of Prussia, and was a tough, translucent paper. The design was printed in reverse on the back of the stamp, and the gum applied over the printing. It is impossible to remove stamps printed on this type of paper from the paper to which they are affixed without destroying the design.

Ribbed — Ribbed paper has an uneven, corrugated surface made by passing the paper through ridged rollers. This type exists on some copies of U.S. Scott 156-165.

Various other substances, or substrates, have been used for stamp manufacture, including wood, aluminum, copper, silver and gold foil, plastic, and silk and cotton fabrics.

Watermarks

Watermarks are an integral part of some papers. They are formed in the process of paper manufacture. Watermarks consist of small designs, formed of wire or cut from metal and soldered to the surface of the mold or, sometimes, on the dandy roll. The designs may be in the form of crowns, stars, anchors, letters or other characters or symbols. These pieces of metal - known in the paper-making industry as "bits" - impress a design into the paper. The design sometimes may be seen by holding the stamp to the light. Some are more easily seen with a watermark detector. This important tool is a small black tray into which a stamp is placed face down and dampened with a fast-evaporating watermark detection fluid that brings up the watermark image in the form of dark lines against a lighter background. These dark lines are the thinner areas of the paper known as the watermark. Some watermarks are extremely difficult to locate, due to either a faint impression, watermark location or the color of the stamp. There also are electric watermark detectors that come with plastic filter disks of various colors. The disks neutralize the color of the stamp, permitting the watermark to be seen more easily.

Multiple watermarks of Crown Agents and Burma

Watermarks of Uruguay, Vatican City and Jamaica

WARNING: Some inks used in the photogravure process dissolve in watermark fluids (Please see the section on Soluble Printing Inks). Also, see "chalky paper."

Watermarks may be found normal, reversed, inverted, reversed and inverted, sideways or diagonal, as seen from the back of the stamp. The relationship of watermark to stamp design depends on the position of the printing plates or how paper is fed through the press. On machine-made paper, watermarks normally are read from right to left. The design is repeated closely throughout the sheet in a "multiple-watermark design." In a "sheet watermark," the design appears only once on the sheet, but extends over many stamps. Individual stamps may carry only a small fraction or none of the watermark.

"Marginal watermarks" occur in the margins of sheets or panes of stamps. They occur on the outside border of paper (ostensibly outside the area where stamps are to be printed). A large row of letters may spell the name of the country or the manufacturer of the paper, or a border of lines may appear. Careless press feeding may cause parts of these letters and/or lines to show on stamps of the outer row of a pane.

Soluble Printing Inks

WARNING: Most stamp colors are permanent; that is, they are not seriously affected by short-term exposure to light or water. Many colors, especially of modern inks, fade from excessive exposure to light. There are stamps printed with inks that dissolve easily in water or in fluids used to detect watermarks. Use of these inks was intentional to prevent the removal of cancellations. Water affects all aniline inks, those on so-called safety paper and some photogravure printings - all such inks are known as fugitive colors. *Removal from paper of such stamps requires care and alternatives to traditional soaking.*

Separation

"Separation" is the general term used to describe methods used to separate stamps. The three standard forms currently in use are perforating, rouletting and die-cutting. These methods are done during the stamp production process, after printing. Sometimes these methods are done on-press or sometimes as a separate step. The earliest issues, such as the 1840 Penny Black of Great Britain (Scott 1), did not have any means provided for separation. It was expected the stamps would be cut apart with scissors or folded and torn. These are examples of imperforate stamps. Many stamps were first issued in imperforate formats and were later issued with perforations. Therefore, care must be observed in buying single imperforate stamps to be certain they were issued imperforate and are not perforated copies that have been altered by having the perforations trimmed away. Stamps issued imperforate usually are valued as singles. However, imperforate varieties of normally perforated stamps should be collected in pairs or larger pieces as indisputable evidence of their imperforate character.

PERFORATION

The chief style of separation of stamps, and the one that is in almost universal use today, is perforating. By this process, paper between the stamps is cut away in a line of holes, usually round, leaving little bridges of paper between the stamps to hold them together. Some types of perforation, such as hyphen-hole perfs, can be confused with roulettes, but a close visual inspection reveals that paper has been removed. The little perforation bridges, which project from the stamp when it is torn from the pane, are called the teeth of the perforation.

As the size of the perforation is sometimes the only way to differentiate between two otherwise identical stamps, it is necessary to be able to accurately measure and describe them. This is done with a perforation gauge, usually a ruler-like device that has dots or graduated lines to show how many perforations may be counted in the space of two centimeters. Two centimeters is the space universally adopted in which to measure perforations.

Perforation gauge

perce en arc

perce en lignes

perce en points

oblique roulette

perce en scie

perce serpentin

To measure a stamp, run it along the gauge until the dots on it fit exactly into the perforations of the stamp. If you are using a graduated-line perforation gauge, simply slide the stamp along the surface until the lines on the gauge perfectly project from the center of the bridges or holes. The number to the side of the line of dots or lines that fit the stamp's perforation is the measurement. For example, an "11" means that 11 perforations fit between two centimeters. The description of the stamp therefore is "perf. 11." If the gauge of the perforations on the top and bottom of a stamp differs from that on the sides, the result is what is known as *compound perforations.* In measuring compound perforations, the gauge at top and bottom is always given first, then the sides. Thus, a stamp that measures 11 at top and bottom and 10½ at the sides is "perf. 11 x 10½." See U.S. Scott 632-642 for examples of compound perforations.

Stamps also are known with perforations different on three or all four sides. Descriptions of such items are clockwise, beginning with the top of the stamp.

A perforation with small holes and teeth close together is a "fine perforation." One with large holes and teeth far apart is a "coarse perforation." Holes that are jagged, rather than clean-cut, are "rough perforations." *Blind perforations* are the slight impressions left by the perforating pins if they fail to puncture the paper. Multiples of stamps showing blind perforations may command a slight premium over normally perforated stamps.

The term *syncopated perfs* describes intentional irregularities in the perforations. The earliest form was used by the Netherlands from 1925-33, where holes were omitted to create distinctive patterns. Beginning in 1992, Great Britain has used an oval perforation to help prevent counterfeiting. Several other countries have started using the oval perfs or other syncopated perf patterns.

A new type of perforation, still primarily used for postal stationery, is known as microperfs. Microperfs are tiny perforations (in some cases hundreds of holes per two centimeters) that allows items to be intentionally separated very easily, while not accidentally breaking apart as easily as standard perforations. These are not currently measured or differentiated by size, as are standard perforations.

ROULETTING

In rouletting, the stamp paper is cut partly or wholly through, with no paper removed. In perforating, some paper is removed. Rouletting derives its name from the French roulette, a spur-like wheel. As the wheel is rolled over the paper, each point makes a small cut. The number of cuts made in a two-centimeter space determines the gauge of the roulette, just as the number of perforations in two centimeters determines the gauge of the perforation.

The shape and arrangement of the teeth on the wheels varies. Various roulette types generally carry French names:

Perce en lignes - rouletted in lines. The paper receives short, straight cuts in lines. This is the most common type of rouletting. See Mexico Scott 500.

Perce en points - pin-rouletted or pin-perfed. This differs from a small perforation because no paper is removed, although round, equidistant holes are pricked through the paper. See Mexico Scott 242-256.

Perce en arc and *perce en scie* - pierced in an arc or saw-toothed designs, forming half circles or small triangles. See Hanover (German States) Scott 25-29.

Perce en serpentin - serpentine roulettes. The cuts form a serpentine or wavy line. See Brunswick (German States) Scott 13-18.

Once again, no paper is removed by these processes, leaving the stamps easily separated, but closely attached.

DIE-CUTTING

The third major form of stamp separation is die-cutting. This is a method where a die in the pattern of separation is created that later cuts the stamp paper in a stroke motion. Although some standard stamps bear die-cut perforations, this process is primarily used for self-adhesive postage stamps. Die-cutting can appear in straight lines, such as U.S. Scott 2522, shapes, such as U.S. Scott 1551, or imitating the appearance of perforations, such as New Zealand Scott 935A and 935B.

Printing Processes

ENGRAVING (Intaglio, Line-engraving, Etching)

Master die — The initial operation in the process of line engraving is making the master die. The die is a small, flat block of softened steel upon which the stamp design is recess engraved in reverse.

Master die

Transfer roll

Photographic reduction of the original art is made to the appropriate size. It then serves as a tracing guide for the initial outline of the design. The engraver lightly traces the design on the steel with his graver, then slowly works the design until it is completed. At various points during the engraving process, the engraver hand-inks the die and makes an impression to check his progress. These are known as progressive die proofs. After completion of the engraving, the die is hardened to withstand the stress and pressures of later transfer operations.

Transfer roll — Next is production of the transfer roll that, as the name implies, is the medium used to transfer the subject from the master die to the printing plate. A blank roll of soft steel, mounted on a mandrel, is placed under the bearers of the transfer press to allow it to roll freely on its axis. The hardened die is placed on the bed of the press and the face of the transfer roll is applied to the die, under pressure. The bed or the roll is then rocked back and forth under increasing pressure, until the soft steel of the roll is forced into every engraved line of the die. The resulting impression on the roll is known as a "relief" or a "relief transfer." The engraved image is now positive in appearance and stands out from the steel. After the required number of reliefs are "rocked in," the soft steel transfer roll is hardened.

Different flaws may occur during the relief process. A defective relief may occur during the rocking in process because of a minute piece of foreign material lodging on the die, or some other cause. Imperfections in the steel of the transfer roll may result in a breaking away of parts of the design. This is known as a relief break, which will show up on finished stamps as small, unprinted areas. If a damaged relief remains in use, it will transfer a repeating defect to the plate. Deliberate alterations of reliefs sometimes occur. "Altered reliefs" designate these changed conditions.

Plate — The final step in pre-printing production is the making of the printing plate. A flat piece of soft steel replaces the die on the bed of the transfer press. One of the reliefs on the transfer roll is positioned over this soft steel. Position, or layout, dots determine the correct position on the plate. The dots have been lightly marked on the plate in advance. After the correct position of the relief is determined,

the design is rocked in by following the same method used in making the transfer roll. The difference is that this time the image is being transferred from the transfer roll, rather than to it. Once the design is entered on the plate, it appears in reverse and is recessed. There are as many transfers entered on the plate as there are subjects printed on the sheet of stamps. It is during this process that double and shifted transfers occur, as well as re-entries. These are the result of improperly entered images that have not been properly burnished out prior to rocking in a new image.

Modern siderography processes, such as those used by the U.S. Bureau of Engraving and Printing, involve an automated form of rocking designs in on preformed cylindrical printing sleeves. The same process also allows for easier removal and re-entry of worn images right on the sleeve.

Transferring the design to the plate

Following the entering of the required transfers on the plate, the position dots, layout dots and lines, scratches and other markings generally are burnished out. Added at this time by the siderographer are any required *guide lines*, *plate numbers* or other *marginal markings*. The plate is then hand-inked and a proof impression is taken. This is known as a plate proof. If the impression is approved, the plate is machined for fitting onto the press, is hardened and sent to the plate vault ready for use.

On press, the plate is inked and the surface is automatically wiped clean, leaving ink only in the recessed lines. Paper is then forced under pressure into the engraved recessed lines, thereby receiving the ink. Thus, the ink lines on engraved stamps are slightly raised, and slight depressions (debossing) occur on the back of the stamp. Prior to the advent of modern high-speed presses and more advanced ink formulations, paper had to be dampened before receiving the ink. This sometimes led to uneven shrinkage by the time the stamps were perforated, resulting in improperly perforated stamps, or misperfs. Newer presses use drier paper, thus both *wet* and *dry printings* exist on some stamps.

Rotary Press — Until 1914, only flat plates were used to print engraved stamps. Rotary press printing was introduced in 1914, and slowly spread. Some countries still use flat-plate printing.

After approval of the plate proof, older *rotary press plates* require additional machining. They are curved to fit the press cylinder. "Gripper slots" are cut into the back of each plate to receive the "grippers," which hold the plate securely on the press. The plate is then hardened. Stamps printed from these bent rotary press plates are longer or wider than the same stamps printed from flat-plate presses. The stretching of the plate during the curving process is what causes this distortion.

Re-entry — To execute a re-entry on a flat plate, the transfer roll is re-applied to the plate, often at some time after its first use on the press. Worn-out designs can be resharpened by carefully burnishing out the original image and re-entering it from the transfer roll. If the original impression has not been sufficiently removed and the transfer roll is not precisely in line with the remaining impression, the resulting double transfer will make the re-entry obvious. If the registration is true, a re-entry may be difficult or impossible to distinguish. Sometimes a stamp printed from a successful re-entry is identified by having a much sharper and clearer impression than its neighbors. With the advent of rotary presses, post-press re-entries were not possible. After a plate was curved for the rotary press, it was impossible to make a re-entry. This is because the plate had already been bent once (with the design distorted).

However, with the introduction of the previously mentioned modern-style siderography machines, entries are made to the preformed cylindrical printing sleeve. Such sleeves are dechromed and softened. This allows individual images to be burnished out and re-entered on the curved sleeve. The sleeve is then rechromed, resulting in longer press life.

Double Transfer — This is a description of the condition of a transfer on a plate that shows evidence of a duplication of all, or a portion of the design. It usually is the result of the changing of the registration between the transfer roll and the plate during the rocking in of the original entry. Double transfers also occur when only a portion of the design has been rocked in and improper positioning is noted. If the worker elected not to burnish out the partial or completed design, a strong double transfer will occur for part or all of the design.

It sometimes is necessary to remove the original transfer from a plate and repeat the process a second time. If the finished re-worked image shows traces of the original impression, attributable to incomplete burnishing, the result is a partial double transfer.

With the modern automatic machines mentioned previously, double transfers are all but impossible to create. Those partially doubled images on stamps printed from such sleeves are more than likely re-entries, rather than true double transfers.

Re-engraved — Alterations to a stamp design are sometimes necessary after some stamps have been printed. In some cases, either the original die or the actual printing plate may have its "temper" drawn (softened), and the design will be re-cut. The resulting impressions from such a re-engraved die or plate may differ slightly from the original issue, and are known as "re-engraved." If the alteration was made to the master die, all future printings will be consistently different from the original. If alterations were made to the printing plate, each altered stamp on the plate will be slightly different from each other, allowing specialists to reconstruct a complete printing plate.

Dropped Transfers — If an impression from the transfer roll has not been properly placed, a dropped transfer may occur. The final stamp image will appear obviously out of line with its neighbors.

Short Transfer — Sometimes a transfer roll is not rocked its entire length when entering a transfer onto a plate. As a result, the finished transfer on the plate fails to show the complete design, and the finished stamp will have an incomplete design printed. This is known as a "short transfer." U.S. Scott No. 8 is a good example of a short transfer.

TYPOGRAPHY (Letterpress, Surface Printing, Flexography, Dry Offset, High Etch)

Although the word "Typography" is obsolete as a term describing a printing method, it was the accepted term throughout the first century of postage stamps. Therefore, appropriate Scott listings in this catalogue refer to typographed stamps. The current term for this form of printing, however, is "letterpress."

As it relates to the production of postage stamps, letterpress printing is the reverse of engraving. Rather than having recessed areas trap the ink and deposit it on paper, only the raised areas of the design are inked. This is comparable to the type of printing seen by inking and using an ordinary rubber stamp. Letterpress includes all printing where the design is above the surface area, whether it is wood, metal or, in some instances, hardened rubber or polymer plastic.

For most letterpress-printed stamps, the engraved master is made in much the same manner as for engraved stamps. In this instance, however, an additional step is needed. The design is transferred to another surface before being transferred to the transfer roll. In this way, the transfer roll has a recessed stamp design, rather than one done in relief. This makes the printing areas on the final plate raised, or relief areas.

For less-detailed stamps of the 19th century, the area on the die not used as a printing surface was cut away, leaving the surface area raised. The original die was then reproduced by stereotyping or electrotyping. The resulting electrotypes were assembled in the required number and format of the desired sheet of stamps. The plate used in printing the stamps was an electroplate of these assembled electrotypes.

Once the final letterpress plates are created, ink is applied to the raised surface and the pressure of the press transfers the ink impression to the paper. In contrast to engraving, the fine lines of letterpress are impressed on the surface of the stamp, leaving a debossed surface. When viewed from the back (as on a typewritten page), the corresponding line work on the stamp will be raised slightly (embossed) above the surface.

PHOTOGRAVURE (Gravure, Rotogravure, Heliogravure)

In this process, the basic principles of photography are applied to a chemically sensitized metal plate, rather than photographic paper. The design is transferred photographically to the plate through a halftone, or dot-matrix screen, breaking the reproduction into tiny dots. The plate is treated chemically and the dots form depressions, called cells, of varying depths and diameters, depending on the degrees of shade in the design. Then, like engraving, ink is applied to the plate and the surface is wiped clean. This leaves ink in the tiny cells that is lifted out and deposited on the paper when it is pressed against the plate.

Gravure is most often used for multicolored stamps, generally using the three primary colors (red, yellow and blue) and black. By varying the dot matrix pattern and density of these colors, virtually any color can be reproduced. A typical full-color gravure stamp will be created from four printing cylinders (one for each color). The original multicolored image will have been photographically separated into its component colors.

Modern gravure printing may use computer-generated dot-matrix screens, and modern plates may be of various types including metal-coated plastic. The catalogue designation of Photogravure (or "Photo") covers any of these older and more modern gravure methods of printing.

For examples of the first photogravure stamps printed (1914), see Bavaria Scott 94-114.

LITHOGRAPHY (Offset Lithography, Stone Lithography, Dilitho, Planography, Collotype)

The principle that oil and water do not mix is the basis for lithography. The stamp design is drawn by hand or transferred from engraving to the surface of a lithographic stone or metal plate in a greasy (oily) substance. This oily substance holds the ink, which will later be transferred to the paper. The stone (or plate) is wet with an acid fluid, causing it to repel the printing ink in all areas not covered by the greasy substance.

Transfer paper is used to transfer the design from the original stone or plate. A series of duplicate transfers are grouped and, in turn, transferred to the final printing plate.

Photolithography — The application of photographic processes to lithography. This process allows greater flexibility of design, related to use of halftone screens combined with line work. Unlike photogravure or engraving, this process can allow large, solid areas to be printed.

Offset — A refinement of the lithographic process. A rubber-covered blanket cylinder takes the impression from the inked lithographic plate. From the "blanket" the impression is *offset* or transferred to the paper. Greater flexibility and speed are the principal reasons offset printing has largely displaced lithography. The term "lithography" covers both processes, and results are almost identical.

EMBOSSED (Relief) Printing

Embossing, not considered one of the four main printing types, is a method in which the design first is sunk into the metal of the die. Printing is done against a yielding platen, such as leather or linoleum. The platen is forced into the depression of the die, thus forming the design on the paper in relief. This process is often used for metallic inks.

Embossing may be done without color (see Sardinia Scott 4-6); with color printed around the embossed area (see Great Britain Scott 5 and most U.S. envelopes); and with color in exact registration with the embossed subject (see Canada Scott 656-657).

HOLOGRAMS

For objects to appear as holograms on stamps, a model exactly the same size as it is to appear on the hologram must be created. Rather than using photographic film to capture the image, holography records an image on a photoresist material. In processing, chemicals eat away at certain exposed areas, leaving a pattern of constructive and destructive interference. When the photoresist is developed, the result is a pattern of uneven ridges that acts as a mold. This mold is then coated with metal, and the resulting form is used to press copies in much the same way phonograph records are produced.

A typical reflective hologram used for stamps consists of a reproduction of the uneven patterns on a plastic film that is applied to a reflective background, usually a silver or gold foil. Light is reflected off the background through the film, making the pattern present on the film visible. Because of the uneven pattern of the film, the viewer will perceive the objects in their proper three-dimensional relationships with appropriate brightness.

The first hologram on a stamp was produced by Austria in 1988 (Scott 1441).

FOIL APPLICATION

A modern technique of applying color to stamps involves the application of metallic foil to the stamp paper. A pattern of foil is applied to the stamp paper by use of a stamping die. The foil usually is flat, but it may be textured. Canada Scott 1735 has three different foil applications in pearl, bronze and gold. The gold foil was textured using a chemical-etch copper embossing die. The printing of this stamp also involved two-color offset lithography plus embossing.

THERMOGRAPHY

In the 1990s stamps began to be enhanced with thermographic printing. In this process, a powdered polymer is applied over a sheet that has just been printed. The powder adheres to ink that lacks drying or hardening agents and does not adhere to areas where the ink has these agents. The excess powder is removed and the sheet is briefly heated to melt the powder. The melted powder solidifies after cooling, producing a raised, shiny effect on the stamps. See Scott New Caledonia C239-C240.

COMBINATION PRINTINGS

Sometimes two or even three printing methods are combined in producing stamps. In these cases, such as Austria Scott 933 or Canada 1735 (described in the preceding paragraph), the multiple-printing technique can be determined by studying the individual characteristics of each printing type. A few stamps, such as Singapore Scott 684-684A, combine as many as three of the four major printing types (lithography, engraving and typography). When this is done it often indicates the incorporation of security devices against counterfeiting.

INK COLORS

Inks or colored papers used in stamp printing often are of mineral origin, although there are numerous examples of organic-based pigments. As a general rule, organic-based pigments are far more subject to varieties and change than those of mineral-based origin.

The appearance of any given color on a stamp may be affected by many aspects, including printing variations, light, color of paper, aging and chemical alterations.

Numerous printing variations may be observed. Heavier pressure or inking will cause a more intense color, while slight interruptions in the ink feed or lighter impressions will cause a lighter appearance. Stamps printed in the same color by water-based and solvent-based inks can differ significantly in appearance. This affects several stamps in the U.S. Prominent Americans series. Hand-mixed ink formulas (primarily from the 19th century) produced under different conditions (humidity and temperature) account for notable color variations in early printings of the same stamp (see U.S. Scott 248-250, 279B, for example). Different sources of pigment can also result in significant differences in color.

Light exposure and aging are closely related in the way they affect stamp color. Both eventually break down the ink and fade colors, so that a carefully kept stamp may differ significantly in color from an identical copy that has been exposed to light. If stamps are exposed to light either intentionally or accidentally, their colors can be faded or completely changed in some cases.

Papers of different quality and consistency used for the same stamp printing may affect color appearance. Most pelure papers, for example, show a richer color when compared with wove or laid papers. See Russia Scott 181a, for an example of this effect.

The very nature of the printing processes can cause a variety of differences in shades or hues of the same stamp. Some of these shades are scarcer than others, and are of particular interest to the advanced collector.

Luminescence

All forms of tagged stamps fall under the general category of luminescence. Within this broad category is fluorescence, dealing with forms of tagging visible under longwave ultraviolet light, and phosphorescence, which deals with tagging visible only under shortwave light. Phosphorescence leaves an afterglow and fluorescence does not. These treated stamps show up in a range of different colors when exposed to UV light. The differing wavelengths of the light activates the tagging material, making it glow in various colors that usually serve different mail processing purposes.

Intentional tagging is a post-World War II phenomenon, brought about by the increased literacy rate and rapidly growing mail volume. It was one of several answers to the problem of the need for more automated mail processes. Early tagged stamps served the purpose of triggering machines to separate different types of mail. A natural outgrowth was to also use the signal to trigger machines that faced all envelopes the same way and canceled them.

Tagged stamps come in many different forms. Some tagged stamps have luminescent shapes or images imprinted on them as a form of security device. Others have blocks (United States), stripes, frames (South Africa and Canada), overall coatings (United States), bars (Great Britain and Canada) and many other types. Some types of tagging are even mixed in with the pigmented printing ink (Australia Scott 366, Netherlands Scott 478 and U.S. Scott 1359 and 2443).

The means of applying taggant to stamps differs as much as the intended purposes for the stamps. The most common form of tagging is a coating applied to the surface of the printed stamp. Since the taggant ink is frequently invisible except under UV light, it does not interfere with the appearance of the stamp. Another common application is the use of phosphored papers. In this case the paper itself either has a coating of taggant applied before the stamp is printed, has taggant applied during the papermaking process (incorporating it into the fibers), or has the taggant mixed into the coating of the paper. The latter method, among others, is currently in use in the United States.

Many countries now use tagging in various forms to either expedite mail handling or to serve as a printing security device against counterfeiting. Following the introduction of tagged stamps for public use in 1959 by Great Britain, other countries have steadily joined the parade. Among those are Germany (1961); Canada and Denmark (1962); United States, Australia, France and Switzerland (1963); Belgium and Japan (1966); Sweden and Norway (1967); Italy (1968); and Russia (1969). Since then, many other countries have begun using forms of tagging, including Brazil, China, Czechoslovakia, Hong Kong, Guatemala, Indonesia, Israel, Lithuania, Luxembourg, Netherlands, Penrhyn Islands, Portugal, St. Vincent, Singapore, South Africa, Spain and Sweden to name a few.

In some cases, including United States, Canada, Great Britain and Switzerland, stamps were released both with and without tagging. Many of these were released during each country's experimental period. Tagged and untagged versions are listed for the aforementioned countries and are noted in some other countries' listings. For at least a few stamps, the experimentally tagged version is worth far more than its untagged counterpart, such as the 1963 experimental tagged version of France Scott 1024.

In some cases, luminescent varieties of stamps were inadvertently created. Several Russian stamps, for example, sport highly fluorescent ink that was not intended as a form of tagging. Older stamps, such as early U.S. postage dues, can be positively identified by the use of UV light, since the organic ink used has become slightly fluorescent over time. Other stamps, such as Austria Scott 70a-82a (varnish bars) and Obock Scott 46-64 (printed quadrille lines), have become fluorescent over time.

Various fluorescent substances have been added to paper to make it appear brighter. These optical brightners, as they are known, greatly affect the appearance of the stamp under UV light. The brightest of these is known as Hi-Brite paper. These paper varieties are beyond the scope of the Scott Catalogue.

Shortwave UV light also is used extensively in expertizing, since each form of paper has its own fluorescent characteristics that are impossible to perfectly match. It is therefore a simple matter to detect filled thins, added perforation teeth and other alterations that involve the addition of paper. UV light also is used to examine stamps that have had cancels chemically removed and for other purposes as well.

Gum

The Illustrated Gum Chart in the first part of this introduction shows and defines various types of gum condition. Because gum condition has an important impact on the value of unused stamps, we recommend studying this chart and the accompanying text carefully.

The gum on the back of a stamp may be shiny, dull, smooth, rough, dark, white, colored or tinted. Most stamp gumming adhesives use gum arabic or dextrine as a base. Certain polymers such as polyvinyl alcohol (PVA) have been used extensively since World War II.

The *Scott Standard Postage Stamp Catalogue* does not list items by types of gum. The *Scott Specialized Catalogue of United States Stamps and Covers* does differentiate among some types of gum for certain issues.

Reprints of stamps may have gum differing from the original issues. In addition, some countries have used different gum formulas for different seasons. These adhesives have different properties that may become more apparent over time.

Many stamps have been issued without gum, and the catalogue

will note this fact. See, for example, United States Scott 40-47. Sometimes, gum may have been removed to preserve the stamp. Germany Scott B68, for example, has a highly acidic gum that eventually destroys the stamps. This item is valued in the catalogue with gum removed.

Reprints and Reissues

These are impressions of stamps (usually obsolete) made from the original plates or stones. If they are valid for postage and reproduce obsolete issues (such as U.S. Scott 102-111), the stamps are *reissues*. If they are from current issues, they are designated as *second, third,* etc., *printing*. If designated for a particular purpose, they are called *special printings.*

When special printings are not valid for postage, but are made from original dies and plates by authorized persons, they are *official reprints. Private reprints* are made from the original plates and dies by private hands. An example of a private reprint is that of the 1871-1932 reprints made from the original die of the 1845 New Haven, Conn., postmaster's provisional. *Official reproductions* or imitations are made from new dies and plates by government authorization. Scott will list those reissues that are valid for postage if they differ significantly from the original printing.

The U.S. government made special printings of its first postage stamps in 1875. Produced were official imitations of the first two stamps (listed as Scott 3-4), reprints of the demonetized pre-1861 issues (Scott 40-47) and reissues of the 1861 stamps, the 1869 stamps and the then-current 1875 denominations. Even though the official imitations and the reprints were not valid for postage, Scott lists all of these U.S. special printings.

Most reprints or reissues differ slightly from the original stamp in some characteristic, such as gum, paper, perforation, color or watermark. Sometimes the details are followed so meticulously that only a student of that specific stamp is able to distinguish the reprint or reissue from the original.

Remainders and Canceled to Order

Some countries sell their stock of old stamps when a new issue replaces them. To avoid postal use, the *remainders* usually are canceled with a punch hole, a heavy line or bar, or a more-or-less regular-looking cancellation. The most famous merchant of remainders was Nicholas F. Seebeck. In the 1880s and 1890s, he arranged printing contracts between the Hamilton Bank Note Co., of which he was a director, and several Central and South American countries. The contracts provided that the plates and all remainders of the yearly issues became the property of Hamilton. Seebeck saw to it that ample stock remained. The "Seebecks," both remainders and reprints, were standard packet fillers for decades.

Some countries also issue stamps *canceled-to-order (CTO),* either in sheets with original gum or stuck onto pieces of paper or envelopes and canceled. Such CTO items generally are worth less than postally used stamps. In cases where the CTO material is far more prevalent in the marketplace than postally used examples, the catalogue value relates to the CTO examples, with postally used examples noted as premium items. Most CTOs can be detected by the presence of gum. However, as the CTO practice goes back at least to 1885, the gum inevitably has been soaked off some stamps so they could pass as postally used. The normally applied postmarks usually differ slightly from standard postmarks, and specialists are able to tell the difference. When applied individually to envelopes by philatelically minded persons, CTO material is known as *favor canceled* and generally sells at large discounts.

Cinderellas and Facsimiles

Cinderella is a catch-all term used by stamp collectors to describe phantoms, fantasies, bogus items, municipal issues, exhibition seals, local revenues, transportation stamps, labels, poster stamps and many other types of items. Some cinderella collectors include in their collections local postage issues, telegraph stamps, essays and proofs, forgeries and counterfeits.

A *fantasy* is an adhesive created for a nonexistent stamp-issuing authority. Fantasy items range from imaginary countries (Occusi-Ambeno, Kingdom of Sedang, Principality of Trinidad or Torres Straits), to non-existent locals (Winans City Post), or nonexistent transportation lines (McRobish & Co.'s Acapulco-San Francisco Line).

On the other hand, if the entity exists and could have issued stamps (but did not) or was known to have issued other stamps, the items are considered *bogus* stamps. These would include the Mormon postage stamps of Utah, S. Allan Taylor's Guatemala and Paraguay inventions, the propaganda issues for the South Moluccas and the adhesives of the Page & Keyes local post of Boston.

Phantoms is another term for both fantasy and bogus issues.

Facsimiles are copies or imitations made to represent original stamps, but which do not pretend to be originals. A catalogue illustration is such a facsimile. Illustrations from the Moens catalogue of the last century were occasionally colored and passed off as stamps. Since the beginning of stamp collecting, facsimiles have been made for collectors as space fillers or for reference. They often carry the word "facsimile," "falsch" (German), "sanko" or "mozo" (Japanese), or "faux" (French) overprinted on the face or stamped on the back. Unfortunately, over the years a number of these items have had fake cancels applied over the facsimile notation and have been passed off as genuine.

Forgeries and Counterfeits

Forgeries and counterfeits have been with philately virtually from the beginning of stamp production. Over time, the terminology for the two has been used interchangeably. Although both forgeries and counterfeits are reproductions of stamps, the purposes behind their creation differ considerably.

Among specialists there is an increasing movement to more specifically define such items. Although there is no universally accepted terminology, we feel the following definitions most closely mirror the items and their purposes as they are currently defined.

Forgeries (also often referred to as *Counterfeits*) are reproductions of genuine stamps that have been created to defraud collectors. Such spurious items first appeared on the market around 1860, and most old-time collections contain one or more. Many are crude and easily spotted, but some can deceive experts.

An important supplier of these early philatelic forgeries was the Hamburg printer Gebruder Spiro. Many others with reputations in this craft included S. Allan Taylor, George Hussey, James Chute, George Forune, Benjamin & Sarpy, Julius Goldner, E. Oneglia and L.H. Mercier. Among the noted 20th-century forgers were Francois Fournier, Jean Sperati and the prolific Raoul DeThuin.

Forgeries may be complete replications, or they may be genuine stamps altered to resemble a scarcer (and more valuable) type. Most forgeries, particularly those of rare stamps, are worth only a small fraction of the value of a genuine example, but a few types, created by some of the most notable forgers, such as Sperati, can be worth as much or more than the genuine. Fraudulently produced copies are known of most classic rarities and many medium-priced stamps.

In addition to rare stamps, large numbers of common 19th- and early 20th-century stamps were forged to supply stamps to the early packet trade. Many can still be easily found. Few new philatelic forgeries have appeared in recent decades. Successful imitation of well-engraved work is virtually impossible. It has proven far easier to produce a fake by altering a genuine stamp than to duplicate a stamp completely.

Counterfeit (also often referred to as *Postal Counterfeit* or *Postal Forgery*) is the term generally applied to reproductions of stamps that have been created to defraud the government of revenue. Such items usually are created at the time a stamp is current and, in some cases, are hard to detect. Because most counterfeits are seized when the perpetrator is captured, postal counterfeits, particularly used on

cover, are usually worth much more than a genuine example to specialists. The first postal counterfeit was of Spain's 4-cuarto carmine of 1854 (the real one is Scott 25). Apparently, the counterfeiters were not satisfied with their first version, which is now very scarce, and they soon created an engraved counterfeit, which is common. Postal counterfeits quickly followed in Austria, Naples, Sardinia and the Roman States. They have since been created in many other countries as well, including the United States.

An infamous counterfeit to defraud the government is the 1-shilling Great Britain "Stock Exchange" forgery of 1872, used on telegraph forms at the exchange that year. The stamp escaped detection until a stamp dealer noticed it in 1898.

Fakes

Fakes are genuine stamps altered in some way to make them more desirable. One student of this part of stamp collecting has estimated that by the 1950s more than 30,000 varieties of fakes were known. That number has grown greatly since then. The widespread existence of fakes makes it important for stamp collectors to study their philatelic holdings and use relevant literature. Likewise, collectors should buy from reputable dealers who guarantee their stamps and make full and prompt refunds should a purchased item be declared faked or altered by some mutually agreed-upon authority. Because fakes always have some genuine characteristics, it is not always possible to obtain unanimous agreement among experts regarding specific items. These students may change their opinions as philatelic knowledge increases. More than 80 percent of all fakes on the philatelic market today are regummed, reperforated (or perforated for the first time), or bear forged overprints, surcharges or cancellations.

Stamps can be chemically treated to alter or eliminate colors. For example, a pale rose stamp can be re-colored to resemble a blue shade of high market value. In other cases, treated stamps can be made to resemble missing color varieties. Designs may be changed by painting, or a stroke or a dot added or bleached out to turn an ordinary variety into a seemingly scarcer stamp. Part of a stamp can be bleached and reprinted in a different version, achieving an inverted center or frame. Margins can be added or repairs done so deceptively that the stamps move from the "repaired" into the "fake" category.

Fakers have not left the backs of the stamps untouched either. They may create false watermarks, add fake grills or press out genuine grills. A thin India paper proof may be glued onto a thicker backing to create the appearance an issued stamp, or a proof printed on cardboard may be shaved down and perforated to resemble a stamp. Silk threads are impressed into paper and stamps have been split so that a rare paper variety is added to an otherwise inexpensive stamp. The most common treatment to the back of a stamp, however, is regumming.

Some in the business of faking stamps have openly advertised fool-proof application of "original gum" to stamps that lack it, although most publications now ban such ads from their pages. It is believed that very few early stamps have survived without being hinged. The large number of never-hinged examples of such earlier material offered for sale thus suggests the widespread extent of regumming activity. Regumming also may be used to hide repairs or thin spots. Dipping the stamp into watermark fluid, or examining it under longwave ultraviolet light often will reveal these flaws.

Fakers also tamper with separations. Ingenious ways to add margins are known. Perforated wide-margin stamps may be falsely represented as imperforate when trimmed. Reperforating is commonly done to create scarce coil or perforation varieties, and to eliminate the naturally occurring straight-edge stamps found in sheet margin positions of many earlier issues. Custom has made straight-edged stamps less desirable. Fakers have obliged by perforating straight-edged stamps so that many are now uncommon, if not rare.

Another fertile field for the faker is that of overprints, surcharges and cancellations. The forging of rare surcharges or overprints began in the 1880s or 1890s. These forgeries are sometimes difficult to detect, but experts have identified almost all. Occasionally, overprints or cancellations are removed to create non-overprinted stamps or seemingly unused items. This is most commonly done by removing a manuscript cancel to make a stamp resemble an unused example. "SPECIMEN" overprints may be removed by scraping and repainting to create non-overprinted varieties. Fakers use inexpensive revenues or pen-canceled stamps to generate unused stamps for further faking by adding other markings. The quartz lamp or UV lamp and a high-powered magnifying glass help to easily detect removed cancellations.

The bigger problem, however, is the addition of overprints, surcharges or cancellations - many with such precision that they are very difficult to ascertain. Plating of the stamps or the overprint can be an important method of detection.

Fake postmarks may range from many spurious fancy cancellations to a host of markings applied to transatlantic covers, to adding normally appearing postmarks to definitives of some countries with stamps that are valued far higher used than unused. With the increased popularity of cover collecting, and the widespread interest in postal history, a fertile new field for fakers has come about. Some have tried to create entire covers. Others specialize in adding stamps, tied by fake cancellations, to genuine stampless covers, or replacing less expensive or damaged stamps with more valuable ones. Detailed study of postal rates in effect at the time a cover in question was mailed, including the analysis of each handstamp used during the period, ink analysis and similar techniques, usually will unmask the fraud.

Restoration and Repairs

Scott bases its catalogue values on stamps that are free of defects and otherwise meet the standards set forth earlier in this introduction. Most stamp collectors desire to have the finest copy of an item possible. Even within given grading categories there are variances. This leads to a controversial practice that is not defined in any universal manner: stamp *restoration*.

There are broad differences of opinion about what is permissible when it comes to restoration. Carefully applying a soft eraser to a stamp or cover to remove light soiling is one form of restoration, as is washing a stamp in mild soap and water to clean it. These are fairly accepted forms of restoration. More severe forms of restoration include pressing out creases or removing stains caused by tape. To what degree each of these is acceptable is dependent upon the individual situation. Further along the spectrum is the freshening of a stamp's color by removing oxide build-up or the effects of wax paper left next to stamps shipped to the tropics.

At some point in this spectrum the concept of *repair* replaces that of restoration. Repairs include filling thin spots, mending tears by reweaving or adding a missing perforation tooth. Regumming stamps may have been acceptable as a restoration or repair technique many decades ago, but today it is considered a form of fakery.

Restored stamps may or may not sell at a discount, and it is possible that the value of individual restored items may be enhanced over that of their pre-restoration state. Specific situations dictate the resultant value of such an item. Repaired stamps sell at substantial discounts from the value of sound stamps.

Terminology

Booklets — Many countries have issued stamps in small booklets for the convenience of users. This idea continues to become increasingly popular in many countries. Booklets have been issued in many sizes and forms, often with advertising on the covers, the panes of stamps or on the interleaving.

The panes used in booklets may be printed from special plates or made from regular sheets. All panes from booklets issued by the United States and many from those of other countries contain stamps that are straight edged on the sides, but perforated between. Others are distinguished by orientation of watermark or other identifying features. Any stamp-like unit in the pane, either printed or blank, that is not a postage stamp, is considered to be a *label* in the catalogue listings.

Scott lists and values booklet panes. Modern complete booklets also are listed and valued. Individual booklet panes are listed only when they are not fashioned from existing sheet stamps and, therefore, are identifiable from their sheet stamp counterparts.

Panes usually do not have a used value assigned to them because there is little market activity for used booklet panes, even though many exist used and there is some demand for them.

Cancellations — The marks or obliterations put on stamps by postal authorities to show that they have performed service and to prevent their reuse are known as cancellations. If the marking is made with a pen, it is considered a "pen cancel." When the location of the post office appears in the marking, it is a "town cancellation." A "postmark" is technically any postal marking, but in practice the term generally is applied to a town cancellation with a date. When calling attention to a cause or celebration, the marking is known as a "slogan cancellation." Many other types and styles of cancellations exist, such as duplex, numerals, targets, fancy and others. See also "precancels," below.

Coil Stamps — These are stamps that are issued in rolls for use in dispensers, affixing and vending machines. Those coils of the United States, Canada, Sweden and some other countries are perforated horizontally or vertically only, with the outer edges imperforate. Coil stamps of some countries, such as Great Britain and Germany, are perforated on all four sides and may in some cases be distinguished from their sheet stamp counterparts by watermarks, counting numbers on the reverse or other means.

Covers — Entire envelopes, with or without adhesive postage stamps, that have passed through the mail and bear postal or other markings of philatelic interest are known as covers. Before the introduction of envelopes in about 1840, people folded letters and wrote the address on the outside. Some people covered their letters with an extra sheet of paper on the outside for the address, producing the term "cover." Used airletter sheets, stamped envelopes and other items of postal stationery also are considered covers.

Errors — Stamps that have some major, consistent, unintentional deviation from the normal are considered errors. Errors include, but are not limited to, missing or wrong colors, wrong paper, wrong watermarks, inverted centers or frames on multicolor printing, inverted or missing surcharges or overprints, double impressions, missing perforations, unintentionally omitted tagging and others. Factually wrong or misspelled information, if it appears on all examples of a stamp, are not considered errors in the true sense of the word. They are errors of design. Inconsistent or randomly appearing items, such as misperfs or color shifts, are classified as freaks.

Color-Omitted Errors — This term refers to stamps where a missing color is caused by the complete failure of the printing plate to deliver ink to the stamp paper or any other paper. Generally, this is caused by the printing plate not being engaged on the press or the ink station running dry of ink during printing.

Color-Missing Errors — This term refers to stamps where a color or colors were printed somewhere but do not appear on the finished stamp. There are four different classes of color-missing errors, and the catalog indicates with a two-letter code appended to each such listing what caused the color to be missing. These codes are used only for the United States' color-missing error listings.

FO = A *foldover* of the stamp sheet during printing may block ink from appearing on a stamp. Instead, the color will appear on the back of the foldover (where it might fall on the back of the selvage or perhaps on the back of the stamp or another stamp). FO also will be used in the case of foldunders, where the paper may fold underneath the other stamp paper and the color will print on the platen.

EP = When the extraneous paper is removed, an unprinted area of stamp paper remains and may show a color or colors to be totally missing on the finished stamp..

CM = A misregistration of the printing plates during printing will result in a *color misregistration*, and such a misregistraion may result in a color not appearing on the finished stamp.

PS = A *perforation shift* after printing may remove a color from the finished stamp. Normally, this will occur on a row of stamps at the edge of the stamp pane.

Measurements – When measurements are given in the Scott catalogues for stamp size, grill size or any other reason, the first measurement given is always for the top and bottom dimension, while the second measurement will be for the sides (just as perforation gauges are measured). Thus, a stamp size of 15mm x 21mm will indicate a vertically oriented stamp 15mm wide at top and bottom, and 21mm tall at the sides. The same principle holds for measuring or counting items such as U.S. grills. A grill count of 22x18 points (B grill) indicates that there are 22 grill points across by 18 grill points down.

Overprints and Surcharges — Overprinting involves applying wording or design elements over an already existing stamp. Overprints can be used to alter the place of use (such as "Canal Zone" on U.S. stamps), to adapt them for a special purpose ("Porto" on Denmark's 1913-20 regular issues for use as postage due stamps, Scott J1-J7) or to commemorate a special occasion (United States Scott 647-648).

A *surcharge* is a form of overprint that changes or restates the face value of a stamp or piece of postal stationery.

Surcharges and overprints may be handstamped, typeset or, occasionally, lithographed or engraved. A few hand-written overprints and surcharges are known.

Personalized Stamps — In 1999, Australia issued stamps with se-tenant labels that could be personalized with pictures of the customer's choice. Other countries quickly followed suit, with some offering to print the selected picture on the stamp itself within a frame that was used exclusively for personalized issues. As the picture used on these stamps or labels vary, listings for such stamps are for any picture within the common frame (or any picture on a se-tenant label), be it a "generic" image or one produced especially for a customer, almost invariably at a premium price.

Precancels — Stamps that are canceled before they are placed in the mail are known as precancels. Precanceling usually is done to expedite the handling of large mailings and generally allow the affected mail pieces to skip certain phases of mail handling.

In the United States, precancellations generally identified the point of origin; that is, the city and state. This information appeared across the face of the stamp, usually centered between parallel lines. More recently, bureau precancels retained the parallel lines, but the city and state designations were dropped. Recent coils have a service inscription that is present on the original printing plate. These show the mail service paid for by the stamp. Since these stamps are not intended to receive further cancellations when used as intended, they are considered precancels. Such items often do not have parallel lines as part of the precancellation.

In France, the abbreviation *Affranchts* in a semicircle together with the word *Postes* is the general form of precancel in use. Belgian precancellations usually appear in a box in which the name of the city appears. Netherlands precancels have the name of the city enclosed between concentric circles, sometimes called a "lifesaver." Precancellations of other countries usually follow these patterns, but may be any arrangement of bars, boxes and city names.

Precancels are listed in the Scott catalogues only if the precancel changes the denomination (Belgium Scott 477-478); if the precanceled stamp is different from the non-precanceled version (such as untagged U.S. precancels); or if the stamp exists only precanceled (France Scott 1096-1099, U.S. Scott 2265).

Proofs and Essays — Proofs are impressions taken from an approved die, plate or stone in which the design and color are the same as the stamp issued to the public. Trial color proofs are impressions taken from approved dies, plates or stones in colors that vary from the final version. An essay is the impression of a design that differs in some way from the issued stamp. "Progressive die proofs" generally are considered to be essays.

Provisionals — These are stamps that are issued on short notice and intended for temporary use pending the arrival of regular issues. They usually are issued to meet such contingencies as changes in government or currency, shortage of necessary postage values or military occupation.

During the 1840s, postmasters in certain American cities issued stamps that were valid only at specific post offices. In 1861, postmasters of the Confederate States also issued stamps with limited validity. Both of these examples are known as "postmaster's provisionals."

Se-tenant — This term refers to an unsevered pair, strip or block of stamps that differ in design, denomination or overprint.

Unless the se-tenant item has a continuous design (see U.S. Scott 1451a, 1694a) the stamps do not have to be in the same order as shown in the catalogue (see U.S. Scott 2158a).

Specimens — The Universal Postal Union required member nations to send samples of all stamps they released into service to the International Bureau in Switzerland. Member nations of the UPU received these specimens as samples of what stamps were valid for postage. Many are overprinted, handstamped or initial-perforated "Specimen," "Canceled" or "Muestra." Some are marked with bars across the denominations (China-Taiwan), punched holes (Czechoslovakia) or back inscriptions (Mongolia).

Stamps distributed to government officials or for publicity purposes, and stamps submitted by private security printers for official approval, also may receive such defacements.

The previously described defacement markings prevent postal use, and all such items generally are known as "specimens."

Tete Beche — This term describes a pair of stamps in which one is upside down in relation to the other. Some of these are the result of intentional sheet arrangements, such as Morocco Scott B10-B11. Others occurred when one or more electrotypes accidentally were placed upside down on the plate, such as Colombia Scott 57a. Separation of the tete-beche stamps, of course, destroys the tete beche variety.

Pronunciation Symbols

ə .... banana, collide, abut

ˈə, ˌə .... humdrum, abut

ə .... immediately preceding \l\, \n\, \m\, \ŋ\, as in battle, mitten, eaten, and sometimes open \ˈō-pᵊm\, lock and key \-ᵊŋ-\; immediately following \l\, \m\, \r\, as often in French table, prisme, titre

ər .... further, merger, bird

ˈər- } .... as in two different pronunciations
ˈə-r } .... of hurry \ˈhər-ē, ˈhə-rē\

a .... mat, map, mad, gag, snap, patch

ā .... day, fade, date, aorta, drape, cape

ä .... bother, cot, and, with most American speakers, father, cart

ȧ .... father as pronunced by speakers who do not rhyme it with bother; French patte

aú .... now, loud, out

b .... baby, rib

ch .... chin, nature \ˈnā-chər\

d .... did, adder

e .... bet, bed, peck

ˈē, ˌē .... beat, nosebleed, evenly, easy

ē .... easy, mealy

f .... fifty, cuff

g .... go, big, gift

h .... hat, ahead

hw .... whale as pronounced by those who do not have the same pronunciation for both whale and wail

i .... tip, banish, active

ī .... site, side, buy, tripe

j .... job, gem, edge, join, judge

k .... kin, cook, ache

k̲ .... German ich, Buch; one pronunciation of loch

l .... lily, pool

m .... murmur, dim, nymph

n .... no, own

ⁿ .... indicates that a preceding vowel or diphthong is pronounced with the nasal passages open, as in French un bon vin blanc \œⁿ -bōⁿ -vaⁿ -bläⁿ\

ŋ .... sing \ˈsiŋ\, singer \ˈsiŋ-ər\, finger \ˈfiŋ-gər\, ink \ˈiŋk\

ō .... bone, know, beau

ȯ .... saw, all, gnaw, caught

œ .... French boeuf, German Hölle

œ̄ .... French feu, German Höhle

ȯi .... coin, destroy

p .... pepper, lip

r .... red, car, rarity

s .... source, less

sh .... as in shy, mission, machine, special (actually, this is a single sound, not two); with a hyphen between, two sounds as in grasshopper \ˈgras-ˌhä-pər\

t .... tie, attack, late, later, latter

th .... as in thin, ether (actually, this is a single sound, not two); with a hyphen between, two sounds as in knighthood \ˈnīt-ˌhud\

t̲h̲ .... then, either, this (actually, this is a single sound, not two)

ü .... rule, youth, union \ˈyün-yən\, few \ˈfyü\

u̇ .... pull, wood, book, curable \ˈkyu̇r-ə-bəl\, fury \ˈfyu̇r-ē\

ue .... German füllen, hübsch

u̅e̅ .... French rue, German fühlen

v .... vivid, give

w .... we, away

y .... yard, young, cue \ˈkyü\, mute \ˈmyüt\, union \ˈyün-yən\

ʸ .... indicates that during the articulation of the sound represented by the preceding character the front of the tongue has substantially the position it has for the articulation of the first sound of yard, as in French digne \dēnʸ\

z .... zone, raise

zh .... as in vision, azure \ˈa-zhər\ (actually, this is a single sound, not two); with a hyphen between, two sounds as in hogshead \ˈhȯgz-ˌhed, ˈhägz-\

\ .... slant line used in pairs to mark the beginning and end of a transcription: \ˈpen\

ˈ .... mark preceding a syllable with primary (strongest) stress: \ˈpen-mən-ˌship\

ˌ .... mark preceding a syllable with secondary (medium) stress: \ˈpen-mən-ˌship\

- .... mark of syllable division

( ) .... indicate that what is symbolized between is present in some utterances but not in others: factory \ˈfak-t(ə-)rē\

÷ .... indicates that many regard as unacceptable the pronunciation variant immediately following: cupola \ˈkyü-pə-lə, ÷-ˌlō\

The system of pronunciation is used by permission from Merriam-Webster's Collegiate® Dictionary, Tenth Edition ©1993 by Merrian-Webster Inc., publisher of the Merriam-Webster® dictionaries.

Currency Conversion

Country	Dollar	Pound	S Franc	Yen	HK $	Euro	Cdn $	Aus $
Australia	1.6643	2.0383	1.7017	0.0153	0.2147	1.7956	1.1781	—
Canada	1.4127	1.7301	1.4445	0.0130	0.1822	1.5241	—	0.8488
European Union	0.9269	1.1352	0.9478	0.0085	0.1196	—	0.6561	0.5569
Hong Kong	7.7528	9.4950	7.9272	0.0714	—	8.3642	5.4879	4.6583
Japan	108.662	133.03	111.06	—	14.010	117.19	76.888	65.265
Switzerland	0.9780	1.1978	—	0.0090	0.1261	1.0551	0.6923	0.5876
United Kingdom	0.8165	—	0.8349	0.0075	0.1053	0.8809	0.5780	0.4906
United States	—	1.2247	1.0225	0.0092	0.1290	1.0789	0.7079	0.6009

Country	Currency	U.S. $ Equiv.
Pitcairn Islands	New Zealand dollar	.5857
Poland	zloty	.2361
Portugal	euro	1.0789
Azores	euro	1.0789
Maderia	euro	1.0789
Qatar	riyal	.2747
Romania	leu	.2235
Russia	ruble	.0130
Rwanda	franc	.0011
St. Helena	British pound	1.2247
St. Kitts.	East Caribbean dollar	.3704
St. Lucia	East Caribbean dollar	.3704
St. Martin	guilder	.5587
St. Pierre & Miquelon	euro	1.0789
St. Thomas & Prince	dobra	.0442
St. Vincent	East Caribbean dollar	.3704
St. Vincent Grenadines	East Caribbean dollar	.3704
El Salvador	U.S. dollar	1.0000
Samoa	tala (dollar)	.3573

*Source: **xe.com** Apr. 3, 2020. Figures reflect values as of Apr. 3, 2020.*

TOOLS OF THE EXPERTS!

6-IN-1 LED POCKET MAGNIFIER/MICROSCOPE (55X)

A powerful LED microscope (up to 55X magnification) teams up with two aspheric Perspex lenses (3X magnification large and 10X magnification small) to examine objects at various levels of detail. Built-in focus wheel ensures clarity. View objects even in low-light conditions with three lighting functions: three LED flashlight, simple UV light, one white LED. Black composite housing.

Item	Retail	AA*
MG61LED	$21.95	$19.95

3.2X LED ILLUMINATED MAGNIFIER

This 7" aluminum 3.2X magnifier is both beautiful and functional. Six LEDs surround the 1.375" lens to provide glare-free illumination. Zippered protective case and 2 AA batteries included.

Item	Retail	AA*
MG32XL	$35.95	$31.95

BLACK TRUE COLOR LIGHT

A versatile, compact light that provides superior image and color rendering while reducing glare and eye strain. Technologically advanced light produces a precise blend of light for contrast and brightness that makes colors vibrant and details incredibly clear. The lamp comes with an "E"(electronic) tube for a quicker starting time. This does plug into an outlet for long uses.

Item	Retail	AA*
ACC191BB	$79.99	$49.99

ZOOM 20X-40X MICROSCOPE WITH LED

This practical zoom microscope provides what collectors have been waiting for – outstanding clarity and resolution. Magnification is continuously adjustable between 20X and 40X. Powerful LED lighting illuminates the stage (3 #LR44 batteries included). Stand, examination slides, and slide covers also included.

Item	Retail	AA*
LHPM3	$29.95	$21.95

10X POCKET MAGNIFIER

This compact, portable and easy-to-use 10x pocket magnifier comes with its own illumination from a brilliant white LED. The glass lens is 18mm (3/4") in diameter.

Item	Retail	AA*
MG10XLED	$12.95	$11.95

PHONESCOPE DIGITAL MICROSCOPE

Clip this compact Lighthouse Phonescope lens on your smartphone or tablet to transform it into a powerful digital microscope. See the smallest details and instantly capture high-quality images and videos. The precision macro glass lens offers up to 60X magnification and requires no batteries. Field of view: 1/2" (13mm). Phonescope works with all popular smartphones without scratching display. Image resolution and zoom function dependent upon your device.

Item	Retail	AA*
LHSCOPE	$25.99	$21.99

DETECTAMARK SPECTRUM WATERMARK DETECTOR

Reveal every detail of your stamps whether it is watermarks or paper irregularities, quality defects, or repairs. Easy to use: Insert stamp, turn on the light, and you can already see the secrets of your stamps in every detail. The special feature of this watermark detector is the different light colors (white, red, green, and blue), which can be chosen to light up the stamp. The brightness can be infinitely adjusted.

Item	Retail	AA*
UK2570	$193.95	$184.95

13W DUOFLEX MAGNIFIER DESK LAMP

The OttLite DuoFlex has a two-pronged approach to enhance your vision. First, the large 3X-5X magnifier enlarges your subject. Then the energy-efficient 13w "E" bulb spotlights the field. Flexible arms allow nearly infinite positioning. Long-term bulb is rated to last up to 10,000 hours.

Item	Retail	AA*
ACC213W	$109.99	$59.99

PREMIUM MAGNIFIER VISOR

The Premium Binocular Headband Magnifier lets you free up your hands. This handy visor can be worn over eyeglasses.
- Receive 4 Lens set - 1.5x, 2x, 2.5x, 3.5x
- Receive 5x swivel eye loupe on the right eye
- Visor is adjustable +/- 60 degrees either way making it easy to flip up

Item	Retail	AA*
MG45H	$42.99	$39.99

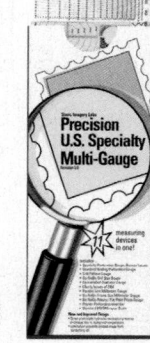

U.S. SPECIALIZED MULTI-GAUGE

The New and Improved U.S. Specialized Multi-Gauge is the essential tool for any collector interested in U.S. stamps from the Classics through the Liberty Issue of 1954. This multi gauge now contains 12 precision measuring devices!

Item	Retail	AA*
USSMG02	$15.99	$13.99

www.AmosAdvantage.com
Call: 1-800-572-6885
Outside U.S. & Canada Call: 1-937-498-0800

ORDERING INFORMATION: *AA prices apply to paid subscribers of Amos Media titles, or orders placed online. Prices, terms and product availability subject to change. Shipping and handling rates will apply. Taxes will apply in CA, OH, & IL.

COMMON DESIGN TYPES

Pictured in this section are issues where one illustration has been used for a number of countries in the Catalogue. Not included in this section are over-printed stamps or those issues which are illustrated in each country. Because the location of Never Hinged breakpoints varies from country to country, some of the values in the listings below will be for unused stamps that were previously hinged.

EUROPA
Europa, 1956

The design symbolizing the cooperation among the six countries comprising the Coal and Steel Community is illustrated in each country.

Belgium	496-497	
France	805-806	
Germany	748-749	
Italy	715-716	
Luxembourg	318-320	
Netherlands	368-369	
Nos. 496-497 (2)	9.00	.50
Nos. 805-806 (2)	5.25	1.00
Nos. 748-749 (2)	7.40	1.10
Nos. 715-716 (2)	9.25	1.25
Nos. 318-320 (3)	65.50	42.00
Nos. 368-369 (2)	25.75	1.50
Set total (13) Stamps	122.15	47.35

Europa, 1958

"E" and Dove — CD1

European Postal Union at the service of European integration.

1958, Sept. 13

Belgium	527-528	
France	889-890	
Germany	790-791	
Italy	750-751	
Luxembourg	341-343	
Netherlands	375-376	
Saar	317-318	
Nos. 527-528 (2)	3.75	.60
Nos. 889-890 (2)	1.65	.55
Nos. 790-791 (2)	2.95	.60
Nos. 750-751 (2)	1.05	.60
Nos. 341-343 (3)	1.35	.90
Nos. 375-376 (2)	1.25	.75
Nos. 317-318 (2)	1.05	2.30
Set total (15) Stamps	13.05	6.30

Europa, 1959

6-Link Enless Chain — CD2

1959, Sept. 19

Belgium	536-537	
France	929-930	
Germany	805-806	
Italy	791-792	
Luxembourg	354-355	
Netherlands	379-380	
Nos. 536-537 (2)	1.55	.60
Nos. 929-930 (2)	1.40	.80
Nos. 805-806 (2)	1.35	.60
Nos. 791-792 (2)	.80	.50
Nos. 354-355 (2)	2.65	1.00
Nos. 379-380 (2)	2.10	1.85
Set total (12) Stamps	9.85	5.35

Europa, 1960

19-Spoke Wheel CD3

First anniverary of the establishment of C.E.P.T. (Conference Europeenne des Admin-istrations des Postes et des Telecommunica-tions.) The spokes symbolize the 19 founding members of the Conference.

1960, Sept.

Belgium	553-554	
Denmark	379	
Finland	376-377	
France	970-971	
Germany	818-820	
Great Britain	377-378	
Greece	688	
Iceland	327-328	
Ireland	175-176	
Italy	809-810	
Luxembourg	374-375	
Netherlands	385-386	
Norway	387	
Portugal	866-867	
Spain	941-942	
Sweden	562-563	
Switzerland	400-401	
Turkey	1493-1494	
Nos. 553-554 (2)	1.25	.55
No. 379 (1)	.55	.50
Nos. 376-377 (2)	1.70	1.80
Nos. 970-971 (2)	.50	.50
Nos. 818-820 (3)	1.90	1.35
Nos. 377-378 (2)	8.00	5.00
No. 688 (1)	4.25	1.75
Nos. 327-328 (2)	1.30	1.85
Nos. 175-176 (2)	47.50	27.50
Nos. 809-810 (2)	.50	.50
Nos. 374-375 (2)	1.00	.80
Nos. 385-386 (2)	2.00	2.00
No. 387 (1)	1.00	.80
Nos. 866-867 (2)	3.00	1.75
Nos. 941-942 (2)	1.50	.75
Nos. 562-563 (2)	1.05	.55
Nos. 400-401 (2)	1.75	.75
Nos. 1493-1494 (2)	2.10	1.35
Set total (34) Stamps	80.85	50.05

Europa, 1961

19 Doves Flying as One — CD4

The 19 doves represent the 19 members of the Conference of European Postal and Tele-communications Administrations C.E.P.T.

1961-62

Belgium	572-573	
Cyprus	201-203	
France	1005-1006	
Germany	844-845	
Great Britain	382-384	
Greece	718-719	
Iceland	340-341	
Italy	845-846	
Luxembourg	382-383	
Netherlands	387-388	
Spain	1010-1011	
Switzerland	410-411	
Turkey	1518-1520	
Nos. 572-573 (2)	.75	.50
Nos. 201-203 (3)	2.10	1.20
Nos. 1005-1006 (2)	.50	.50
Nos. 844-845 (2)	.60	.75
Nos. 382-384 (3)	.75	.75
Nos. 718-719 (2)	.80	.50
Nos. 340-341 (2)	1.10	1.60
Nos. 845-846 (2)	.50	.50
Nos. 382-383 (2)	.55	.55
Nos. 387-388 (2)	.50	.50
Nos. 1010-1011 (2)	.70	.55
Nos. 410-411 (2)	1.90	.60
Nos. 1518-1520 (3)	1.55	.90
Set total (29) Stamps	12.30	9.40

Europa, 1962

Young Tree with 19 Leaves CD5

The 19 leaves represent the 19 original members of C.E.P.T.

1962-63

Belgium	582-583	
Cyprus	219-221	
France	1045-1046	
Germany	852-853	
Greece	739-740	
Iceland	348-349	
Ireland	184-185	
Italy	860-861	
Luxembourg	386-387	
Netherlands	394-395	
Norway	414-415	
Switzerland	416-417	
Turkey	1553-1555	
Nos. 582-583 (2)	.65	.65
Nos. 219-221 (3)	76.25	6.75
Nos. 1045-1046 (2)	.60	.50
Nos. 852-853 (2)	.65	.75
Nos. 739-740 (2)	2.00	1.15
Nos. 348-349 (2)	.85	.85
Nos. 184-185 (2)	2.00	.50
Nos. 860-861 (2)	1.00	.55
Nos. 386-387 (2)	.75	.55
Nos. 394-395 (2)	1.35	.90
Nos. 414-415 (2)	1.75	1.70
Nos. 416-417 (2)	1.65	1.00
Nos. 1553-1555 (3)	2.05	1.10
Set total (28) Stamps	91.55	16.95

Europa, 1963

Stylized Links, Symbolizing Unity — CD6

1963, Sept.

Belgium	598-599	
Cyprus	229-231	
Finland	419	
France	1074-1075	
Germany	867-868	
Greece	768-769	
Iceland	357-358	
Ireland	188-189	
Italy	880-881	
Luxembourg	403-404	
Netherlands	416-417	
Norway	441-442	
Switzerland	429	
Turkey	1602-1603	
Nos. 598-599 (2)	1.60	.55
Nos. 229-231 (3)	64.00	9.40
No. 419 (1)	1.25	.55
Nos. 1074-1075 (2)	.60	.50
Nos. 867-868 (2)	.50	.55
Nos. 768-769 (2)	4.65	1.65
Nos. 357-358 (2)	1.20	1.20
Nos. 188-189 (2)	4.75	3.25
Nos. 880-881 (2)	.50	.50
Nos. 403-404 (2)	.75	.55
Nos. 416-417 (2)	1.30	1.00
Nos. 441-442 (2)	2.60	2.40
No. 429 (1)	.90	.60
Nos. 1602-1603 (2)	1.20	.50
Set total (27) Stamps	85.80	23.20

Europa, 1964

Symbolic Daisy — CD7

5th anniverary of the establishment of C.E.P.T. The 22 petals of the flower symbolize the 22 members of the Conference.

1964, Sept.

Austria	738	
Belgium	614-615	
Cyprus	244-246	
France	1109-1110	
Germany	897-898	
Greece	801-802	
Iceland	367-368	
Ireland	196-197	
Italy	894-895	
Luxembourg	411-412	
Monaco	590-591	
Netherlands	428-429	
Norway	458	
Portugal	931-933	
Spain	1262-1263	
Switzerland	438-439	
Turkey	1628-1629	
No. 738 (1)	1.20	.80
Nos. 614-615 (2)	1.40	.60
Nos. 244-246 (3)	32.25	5.10
Nos. 1109-1110 (2)	.50	.50
Nos. 897-898 (2)	.50	.50
Nos. 801-802 (2)	4.15	1.55
Nos. 367-368 (2)	1.40	1.15
Nos. 196-197 (2)	17.00	4.25
Nos. 894-895 (2)	.50	.50
Nos. 411-412 (2)	.75	.55
Nos. 590-591 (2)	2.50	.70
Nos. 428-429 (2)	.75	.60
No. 458 (1)	3.50	3.50
Nos. 931-933 (3)	10.00	2.00
Nos. 1262-1263 (2)	1.30	.80
Nos. 438-439 (2)	1.65	.50
Nos. 1628-1629 (2)	2.00	.80
Set total (34) Stamps	81.35	24.40

Europa, 1965

Leaves and "Fruit" CD8

1965

Belgium	636-637	
Cyprus	262-264	
Finland	437	
France	1131-1132	
Germany	934-935	
Greece	833-834	
Iceland	375-376	
Ireland	204-205	
Italy	915-916	
Luxembourg	432-433	
Monaco	616-617	
Netherlands	438-439	
Norway	475-476	
Portugal	958-960	
Switzerland	469	
Turkey	1665-1666	
Nos. 636-637 (2)	.50	.50
Nos. 262-264 (3)	25.35	6.00
No. 437 (1)	1.25	.55
Nos. 1131-1132 (2)	.70	.55
Nos. 934-935 (2)	.50	.50
Nos. 833-834 (2)	2.25	1.15
Nos. 375-376 (2)	2.50	1.75
Nos. 204-205 (2)	16.00	3.35
Nos. 915-916 (2)	.50	.50
Nos. 432-433 (2)	.75	.55
Nos. 616-617 (2)	3.25	1.65
Nos. 438-439 (2)	.55	.50
Nos. 475-476 (2)	2.40	1.90
Nos. 958-960 (3)	10.00	2.75
No. 469 (1)	1.15	.50
Nos. 1665-1666 (2)	2.00	1.25
Set total (32) Stamps	69.65	23.95

Europa, 1966

Symbolic Sailboat — CD9

1966, Sept.

Andorra, French	172	
Belgium	675-676	
Cyprus	275-277	
France	1163-1164	
Germany	963-964	

Greece......862-863
Iceland......384-385
Ireland......216-217
Italy......942-943
Liechtenstein......415
Luxembourg......440-441
Monaco......639-640
Netherlands......441-442
Norway......496-497
Portugal......980-982
Switzerland......477-478
Turkey......1718-1719

No. 172 (1)	3.00	3.00
Nos. 675-676 (2)	.80	.50
Nos. 275-277 (3)	4.75	2.75
Nos. 1163-1164 (2)	.55	.50
Nos. 963-964 (2)	.50	.55
Nos. 862-863 (2)	2.10	1.05
Nos. 384-385 (2)	4.50	3.50
Nos. 216-217 (2)	6.75	2.00
Nos. 942-943 (2)	.50	.50
No. 415 (1)	.40	.35
Nos. 440-441 (2)	.70	.55
Nos. 639-640 (2)	2.00	.65
Nos. 441-442 (2)	.85	.50
Nos. 496-497 (2)	2.35	2.15
Nos. 980-982 (2)	9.75	2.25
Nos. 477-478 (2)	1.40	.60
Nos. 1718-1719 (2)	3.35	1.75
Set total (34) Stamps	44.25	23.15

Europa, 1967

Cogwheels
CD10

1967

Andorra, French......174-175
Belgium......688-689
Cyprus......297-299
France......1178-1179
Germany......969-970
Greece......891-892
Iceland......389-390
Ireland......232-233
Italy......951-952
Liechtenstein......420
Luxembourg......449-450
Monaco......669-670
Netherlands......444-447
Norway......504-505
Portugal......994-996
Spain......1465-1466
Switzerland......482
Turkey......B120-B121

Nos. 174-175 (2)	10.75	6.25
Nos. 688-689 (2)	1.05	.55
Nos. 297-299 (3)	4.25	2.50
Nos. 1178-1179 (2)	.55	.50
Nos. 969-970 (2)	.55	.55
Nos. 891-892 (2)	3.05	.85
Nos. 389-390 (2)	3.00	2.00
Nos. 232-233 (2)	5.90	2.30
Nos. 951-952 (2)	.60	.50
No. 420 (1)	.45	.40
Nos. 449-450 (2)	1.00	.70
Nos. 669-670 (2)	2.75	.70
Nos. 444-447 (4)	2.70	2.05
Nos. 504-505 (2)	2.00	1.80
Nos. 994-996 (3)	9.50	1.85
Nos. 1465-1466 (2)	.50	.50
No. 482 (1)	.60	.30
Nos. B120-B121 (2)	2.50	2.00
Set total (38) Stamps	51.70	26.30

Europa, 1968

Golden Key with C.E.P.T. Emblem
CD11

1968

Andorra, French......182-183
Belgium......705-706
Cyprus......314-316
France......1209-1210
Germany......983-984
Greece......916-917
Iceland......395-396
Ireland......242-243
Italy......979-980

Liechtenstein......442
Luxembourg......466-467
Monaco......689-691
Netherlands......452-453
Portugal......1019-1021
San Marino......687
Spain......1526
Switzerland......488
Turkey......1775-1776

Nos. 182-183 (2)	16.50	10.00
Nos. 705-706 (2)	1.25	.50
Nos. 314-316 (3)	2.90	2.50
Nos. 1209-1210 (2)	.85	.55
Nos. 983-984 (2)	.50	.55
Nos. 916-917 (2)	3.10	1.45
Nos. 395-396 (2)	3.00	2.20
Nos. 242-243 (2)	3.30	2.25
Nos. 979-980 (2)	.50	.50
No. 442 (1)	.45	.40
Nos. 466-467 (2)	.80	.70
Nos. 689-691 (3)	5.40	.95
Nos. 452-453 (2)	1.05	.70
Nos. 1019-1021 (3)	9.75	2.10
No. 687 (1)	.55	.35
No. 1526 (1)	.25	.25
No. 488 (1)	.40	.25
Nos. 1775-1776 (2)	2.50	1.25
Set total (35) Stamps	53.05	27.45

Europa, 1969

"EUROPA" and "CEPT"
CD12

Tenth anniversary of C.E.P.T.

1969

Andorra, French......188-189
Austria......837
Belgium......718-719
Cyprus......326-328
Denmark......458
Finland......483
France......1245-1246
Germany......996-997
Great Britain......585
Greece......947-948
Iceland......406-407
Ireland......270-271
Italy......1000-1001
Liechtenstein......453
Luxembourg......475-476
Monaco......722-724
Netherlands......475-476
Norway......533-534
Portugal......1038-1040
San Marino......701-702
Spain......1567
Sweden......814-816
Switzerland......500-501
Turkey......1799-1800
Vatican......470-472
Yugoslavia......1003-1004

Nos. 188-189 (2)	18.50	12.00
No. 837 (1)	.65	.30
Nos. 718-719 (2)	.75	.50
Nos. 326-328 (3)	3.00	2.25
No. 458 (1)	.75	.75
No. 483 (1)	3.50	.75
Nos. 1245-1246 (2)	.55	.50
Nos. 996-997 (2)	.70	.50
No. 585 (1)	.25	.25
Nos. 947-948 (2)	4.00	1.25
Nos. 406-407 (2)	4.20	2.40
Nos. 270-271 (2)	3.50	2.00
Nos. 1000-1001 (2)	.50	.50
No. 453 (1)	.45	.45
Nos. 475-476 (2)	.95	.50
Nos. 722-724 (3)	10.50	2.00
Nos. 475-476 (2)	1.35	1.00
Nos. 533-534 (2)	2.20	1.95
Nos. 1038-1040 (3)	17.75	2.40
Nos. 701-702 (2)	.90	.90
No. 1567 (1)	.25	.25
Nos. 814-816 (3)	4.00	2.85
Nos. 500-501 (2)	1.85	1.00
Nos. 1799-1800 (2)	2.50	1.65
Nos. 470-472 (3)	.75	.75
Nos. 1003-1004 (2)	4.00	4.00
Set total (51) Stamps	88.30	43.65

Europa, 1970

Interwoven Threads
CD13

1970

Andorra, French......196-197
Belgium......741-742
Cyprus......340-342
France......1271-1272
Germany......1018-1019
Greece......985, 987
Iceland......420-421
Ireland......279-281
Italy......1013-1014
Liechtenstein......470
Luxembourg......489-490
Monaco......768-770
Netherlands......483-484
Portugal......1060-1062
San Marino......729-730
Spain......1607
Switzerland......515-516
Turkey......1848-1849
Yugoslavia......1024-1025

Nos. 196-197 (2)	20.00	8.50
Nos. 741-742 (2)	1.10	.55
Nos. 340-342 (3)	2.70	2.75
Nos. 1271-1272 (2)	.65	.50
Nos. 1018-1019 (2)	.60	.50
Nos. 985,987 (2)	6.35	1.60
Nos. 420-421 (2)	6.00	4.00
Nos. 279-281 (3)	7.50	2.50
Nos. 1013-1014 (2)	.50	.50
No. 470 (1)	.45	.45
Nos. 489-490 (2)	.80	.55
Nos. 768-770 (3)	6.35	2.10
Nos. 483-484 (2)	1.30	1.15
Nos. 1060-1062 (3)	9.75	2.35
Nos. 729-730 (2)	.90	.55
No. 1607 (1)	.25	.25
Nos. 515-516 (2)	1.85	.70
Nos. 1848-1849 (2)	2.50	1.50
Nos. 1024-1025 (2)	.80	.80
Set total (40) Stamps	70.35	31.80

Europa, 1971

"Fraternity, Cooperation, Common Effort"
CD14

1971

Andorra, French......205-206
Belgium......803-804
Cyprus......365-367
Finland......504
France......1304
Germany......1064-1065
Greece......1029-1030
Iceland......429-430
Ireland......305-306
Italy......1038-1039
Liechtenstein......485
Luxembourg......500-501
Malta......425-427
Monaco......797-799
Netherlands......488-489
Portugal......1094-1096
San Marino......749-750
Spain......1675-1676
Switzerland......531-532
Turkey......1876-1877
Yugoslavia......1052-1053

Nos. 205-206 (2)	20.00	7.75
Nos. 803-804 (2)	1.30	.55
Nos. 365-367 (3)	2.60	3.25
No. 504 (1)	5.00	.75
No. 1304 (1)	.45	.40
Nos. 1064-1065 (2)	.60	.50
Nos. 1029-1030 (2)	4.00	1.80
Nos. 429-430 (2)	5.00	3.75
Nos. 305-306 (2)	4.50	1.50
Nos. 1038-1039 (2)	.65	.50
No. 485 (1)	.45	.45
Nos. 500-501 (2)	1.00	.65
Nos. 425-427 (3)	.80	.80
Nos. 797-799 (3)	15.00	2.80
Nos. 488-489 (2)	1.20	.95
Nos. 1094-1096 (3)	9.75	1.75
Nos. 749-750 (2)	.65	.55
Nos. 1675-1676 (2)	.75	.55
Nos. 531-532 (2)	1.85	.65
Nos. 1876-1877 (2)	2.50	1.25
Nos. 1052-1053 (2)	.50	.50
Set total (43) Stamps	78.55	31.65

Europa, 1972

Sparkles, Symbolic of Communications
CD15

1972

Andorra, French......210-211
Andorra, Spanish......62
Belgium......825-826
Cyprus......380-382
Finland......512-513
France......1341
Germany......1089-1090
Greece......1049-1050
Iceland......439-440
Ireland......316-317
Italy......1065-1066
Liechtenstein......504
Luxembourg......512-513
Malta......450-453
Monaco......831-832
Netherlands......494-495
Portugal......1141-1143
San Marino......771-772
Spain......1718
Switzerland......544-545
Turkey......1907-1908
Yugoslavia......1100-1101

Nos. 210-211 (2)	21.00	7.00
No. 62 (1)	60.00	60.00
Nos. 825-826 (2)	.95	.55
Nos. 380-382 (3)	5.95	4.25
Nos. 512-513 (2)	7.00	1.40
No. 1341 (1)	.50	.35
Nos. 1089-1090 (2)	1.10	.50
Nos. 1049-1050 (2)	2.00	1.55
Nos. 439-440 (2)	2.90	2.65
Nos. 316-317 (2)	13.00	4.50
Nos. 1065-1066 (2)	.55	.50
No. 504 (1)	.45	.45
Nos. 512-513 (2)	.95	.65
Nos. 450-453 (4)	1.05	1.40
Nos. 831-832 (2)	5.00	1.40
Nos. 494-495 (2)	1.20	.90
Nos. 1141-1143 (3)	9.75	1.50
Nos. 771-772 (2)	.70	.50
No. 1718 (1)	.50	.40
Nos. 544-545 (2)	1.65	.60
Nos. 1907-1908 (2)	4.00	2.00
Nos. 1100-1101 (2)	1.20	1.20
Set total (44) Stamps	141.40	94.25

Europa, 1973

Post Horn and Arrows
CD16

1973

Andorra, French......219-220
Andorra, Spanish......76
Belgium......839-840
Cyprus......396-398
Finland......526
France......1367
Germany......1114-1115
Greece......1090-1092
Iceland......447-448
Ireland......329-330
Italy......1108-1109
Liechtenstein......528-529
Luxembourg......523-524
Malta......469-471
Monaco......866-867
Netherlands......504-505
Norway......604-605
Portugal......1170-1172
San Marino......802-803
Spain......1753
Switzerland......580-581
Turkey......1935-1936
Yugoslavia......1138-1139

Nos. 219-220 (2)	20.00	11.00
No. 76 (1)	1.25	.85
Nos. 839-840 (2)	1.00	.65
Nos. 396-398 (3)	4.25	3.85
No. 526 (1)	1.25	.55
No. 1367 (1)	1.25	.75
Nos. 1114-1115 (2)	.85	.50
Nos. 1090-1092 (3)	2.10	1.85
Nos. 447-448 (2)	6.65	3.35

Nos. 329-330 (2)	5.25	2.00
Nos. 1108-1109 (2)	.50	.50
Nos. 528-529 (2)	.60	.60
Nos. 523-524 (2)	.90	.75
Nos. 469-471 (3)	.90	1.20
Nos. 866-867 (2)	15.00	2.40
Nos. 504-505 (2)	1.20	.95
Nos. 604-605 (2)	4.00	1.80
Nos. 1170-1172 (3)	13.00	2.15
Nos. 802-803 (2)	1.00	.60
No. 1753 (1)	.35	.25
Nos. 580-581 (2)	1.55	.60
Nos. 1935-1936 (2)	4.15	2.25
Nos. 1138-1139 (2)	1.15	1.10
Set total (46) Stamps	88.15	40.05

Europa, 2000

CD17

2000

Albania	2621-2622
Andorra, French	522
Andorra, Spanish	262
Armenia	610-611
Austria	1814
Azerbaijan	698-699
Belarus	350
Belgium	1818
Bosnia & Herzegovina (Moslem)	358
Bosnia & Herzegovina (Serb)	111-112
Croatia	428-429
Cyprus	959
Czech Republic	3120
Denmark	1189
Estonia	394
Faroe Islands	376
Finland	1129
Aland Islands	166
France	2771
Georgia	228-229
Germany	2086-2087
Gibraltar	837-840
Great Britain (Jersey)	935-936
Great Britain (Isle of Man)	883
Greece	1959
Greenland	363
Hungary	3699-3700
Iceland	910
Ireland	1230-1231
Italy	2349
Latvia	504
Liechtenstein	1178
Lithuania	668
Luxembourg	1035
Macedonia	187
Malta	1011-1012
Moldova	355
Monaco	2161-2162
Poland	3519
Portugal	2358
Portugal (Azores)	455
Portugal (Madeira)	208
Romania	4370
Russia	6589
San Marino	1480
Slovakia	355
Slovenia	424
Spain	3036
Sweden	2394
Switzerland	1074
Turkey	2762
Turkish Rep. of Northern Cyprus	500
Ukraine	379
Vatican City	1152

Nos. 2621-2622 (2)	11.00	11.00
No. 522 (1)	2.00	1.00
No. 262 (1)	1.75	.80
Nos. 610-611 (2)	4.75	4.75
No. 1814 (1)	1.40	1.40
Nos. 698-699 (2)	6.00	6.00
No. 350 (1)	1.75	1.75
No. 1818 (1)	1.40	.60
No. 358 (1)	4.75	4.75
Nos. 111-112 (2)	110.00	110.00
Nos. 428-429 (2)	6.25	6.25
No. 959 (1)	2.10	1.40
No. 3120 (1)	1.20	.40
No. 1189 (1)	3.50	2.25
No. 394 (1)	1.25	1.25
No. 376 (1)	2.40	2.40
No. 1129 (1)	2.00	.60
No. 166 (1)	2.00	1.10
No. 2771 (1)	1.25	.40
Nos. 228-229 (2)	9.00	9.00
Nos. 2086-2087 (2)	4.35	2.10
Nos. 837-840 (4)	5.50	5.30

Nos. 935-936 (2)	2.40	2.40
No. 883 (1)	1.75	1.75
No. 363 (1)	1.90	1.90
Nos. 3699-3700 (2)	6.50	2.50
No. 910 (1)	1.60	1.60
Nos. 1230-1231 (2)	4.35	4.35
No. 2349 (1)	1.50	.40
No. 504 (1)	5.00	2.40
No. 1178 (1)	2.25	1.75
No. 668 (1)	1.50	1.50
No. 1035 (1)	1.40	.85
No. 187 (1)	3.00	3.00
Nos. 1011-1012 (2)	4.35	4.35
No. 355 (1)	3.50	3.50
Nos. 2161-2162 (2)	2.80	1.40
No. 3519 (1)	1.25	.75
No. 2358 (1)	1.25	.65
No. 455 (1)	1.25	.50
No. 208 (1)	1.25	.50
No. 4370 (1)	2.50	1.25
No. 6589 (1)	4.00	.85
No. 1480 (1)	1.00	1.00
No. 355 (1)	1.60	.80
No. 424 (1)	3.25	3.25
No. 3036 (1)	.75	.40
No. 2394 (1)	3.00	2.25
No. 1074 (1)	2.10	1.05
No. 2762 (1)	2.75	2.00
No. 500 (1)	2.50	2.50
No. 379 (1)	4.50	3.00
No. 1152 (1)	1.25	1.25
Set total (68) Stamps	263.60	230.15

The Gibraltar stamps are similar to the stamp illustrated, but none have the design shown above. All other sets listed above include at least one stamp with the design shown, but some include stamps with entirely different designs. Bulgaria Nos. 4131-4132, Guernsey Nos. 802-803 and Yugoslavia Nos. 2485-2486 are Europa stamps with completely different designs.

PORTUGAL & COLONIES
Vasco da Gama

Fleet Departing
CD20

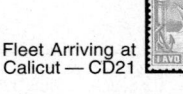

Fleet Arriving at Calicut — CD21

Embarking at Rastello
CD22

Muse of History
CD23

San Gabriel, da Gama and Camoens
CD24

Archangel Gabriel, the Patron Saint
CD25

Flagship San Gabriel — CD26

Vasco da Gama — CD27

Fourth centenary of Vasco da Gama's discovery of the route to India.

1898

Azores	93-100
Macao	67-74
Madeira	37-44
Portugal	147-154
Port. Africa	1-8
Port. Congo	75-98
Port. India	189-196
St. Thomas & Prince Islands	170-193
Timor	45-52

Nos. 93-100 (8)	113.50	73.50
Nos. 67-74 (8)	138.75	91.75
Nos. 37-44 (8)	60.55	37.25
Nos. 147-154 (8)	155.00	50.25
Nos. 1-8 (8)	35.00	23.50
Nos. 75-98 (24)	52.15	41.65
Nos. 189-196 (8)	25.25	15.50
Nos. 170-193 (24)	56.30	43.00
Nos. 45-52 (8)	39.75	27.25
Set total (104) Stamps	676.25	403.65

Pombal
POSTAL TAX
POSTAL TAX DUES

Marquis de Pombal — CD28

Planning Reconstruction of Lisbon, 1755 — CD29

Pombal Monument, Lisbon — CD30

Sebastiao Jose de Carvalho e Mello, Marquis de Pombal (1699-1782), statesman, rebuilt Lisbon after earthquake of 1755. Tax was for the erection of Pombal monument. Obligatory on all mail on certain days throughout the year. Postal Tax Dues are inscribed "Multa."

1925

Angola	RA1-RA3, RAJ1-RAJ3
Azores	RA9-RA11, RAJ2-RAJ4
Cape Verde	RA1-RA3, RAJ1-RAJ3
Macao	RA1-RA3, RAJ1-RAJ3
Madeira	RA1-RA3, RAJ1-RAJ3
Mozambique	RA1-RA3, RAJ1-RAJ3
Nyassa	RA1-RA3, RAJ1-RAJ3
Portugal	RA11-RA13, RAJ2-RAJ4
Port. Guinea	RA1-RA3, RAJ1-RAJ3
Port. India	RA1-RA3, RAJ1-RAJ3
St. Thomas & Prince Islands	RA1-RA3, RAJ1-RAJ3
Timor	RA1-RA3, RAJ1-RAJ3

Nos. RA1-RA3,RAJ1-RAJ3 (6)	6.60	6.60
Nos. RA9-RA11,RAJ2-RAJ4 (6)	6.60	6.60
Nos. RA1-RA3,RAJ1-RAJ3 (6)	4.50	3.90
Nos. RA1-RA3,RAJ1-RAJ3 (6)	21.25	13.20
Nos. RA1-RA3,RAJ1-RAJ3 (6)	7.95	14.70
Nos. RA1-RA3,RAJ1-RAJ3 (6)	2.40	2.55
Nos. RA1-RA3,RAJ1-RAJ3 (6)	63.00	63.00
Nos. RA11-RA13,RAJ2-RAJ4 (6)	5.95	5.20
Nos. RA1-RA3,RAJ1-RAJ3 (6)	5.10	4.65
Nos. RA1-RA3,RAJ1-RAJ3 (6)	3.45	3.45
Nos. RA1-RA3,RAJ1-RAJ3 (6)	4.50	4.50
Nos. RA1-RA3,RAJ1-RAJ3 (6)	2.10	3.90
Set total (72) Stamps	133.40	132.25

Vasco da Gama
CD34

Mousinho de Albuquerque
CD35

Dam
CD36

Prince Henry the Navigator
CD37

Affonso de Albuquerque
CD38

Plane over Globe
CD39

1938-39

Angola	274-291, C1-C9
Cape Verde	234-251, C1-C9
Macao	289-305, C7-C15
Mozambique	270-287, C1-C9
Port. Guinea	233-250, C1-C9
Port. India	439-453, C1-C8
St. Thomas & Prince Islands	302-319, 323-340, C1-C18
Timor	223-239, C1-C9

Nos. 274-291,C1-C9 (27)	129.40	22.85
Nos. 234-251,C1-C9 (27)	87.00	27.15
Nos. 289-305,C7-C15 (26)	495.70	149.20
Nos. 270-287,C1-C9 (27)	63.45	11.20
Nos. 233-250,C1-C9 (27)	130.20	49.15
Nos. 439-453,C1-C8 (23)	82.75	30.95
Nos. 302-319,323-340,C1-C18 (54)	467.70	244.80
Nos. 223-239,C1-C9 (26)	193.55	94.50
Set total (237) Stamps	1,650.	629.80

Lady of Fatima

Our Lady of the Rosary, Fatima, Portugal — CD40

1948-49

Angola	315-318
Cape Verde	266
Macao	336
Mozambique	325-328
Port. Guinea	271
Port. India	480
St. Thomas & Prince Islands	351
Timor	254

Nos. 315-318 (4)	68.00	17.25
No. 266 (1)	8.50	4.50
No. 336 (1)	42.50	12.00
Nos. 325-328 (4)	73.25	16.85
No. 271 (1)	6.50	3.50
No. 480 (1)	4.50	3.00
No. 351 (1)	8.50	7.00
No. 254 (1)	6.00	6.00
Set total (14) Stamps	217.75	70.10

A souvenir sheet of 9 stamps was issued in 1951 to mark the extension of the 1950 Holy Year. The sheet contains: Angola No. 316, Cape Verde No. 266, Macao No. 336, Mozambique No. 325, Portuguese Guinea No. 271, Portuguese India Nos. 480, 485, St. Thomas & Prince Islands No. 351, Timor No. 254. The sheet also contains a portrait of Pope Pius XII and is inscribed "Encerramento do

Ano Santo, Fatima 1951." It was sold for 11 escudos.

Holy Year

Church Bells and Dove CD41 — Angel Holding Candelabra CD42

Holy Year, 1950.

1950-51

Angola	331-332
Cape Verde	268-269
Macao	339-340
Mozambique	330-331
Port. Guinea	273-274
Port. India	490-491, 496-503
St. Thomas & Prince Islands	353-354
Timor	258-259

Nos. 331-332 (2)	7.60	1.35
Nos. 268-269 (2)	5.50	3.50
Nos. 339-340 (2)	60.00	14.00
Nos. 330-331 (2)	3.00	1.10
Nos. 273-274 (2)	11.25	3.50
Nos. 490-491,496-503 (10)	10.40	4.95
Nos. 353-354 (2)	7.75	4.90
Nos. 258-259 (2)	8.00	4.00
Set total (24) Stamps	113.50	37.30

A souvenir sheet of 8 stamps was issued in 1951 to mark the extension of the Holy Year. The sheet contains: Angola No. 331, Cape Verde No. 269, Macao No. 340, Mozambique No. 331, Portuguese Guinea No. 275, Portuguese India No. 490, St. Thomas & Prince Islands No. 354, Timor No. 258, some with colors changed. The sheet contains doves and is inscribed 'Encerramento do Ano Santo, Fatima 1951.' It was sold for 17 escudos.

Holy Year Conclusion

Our Lady of Fatima — CD43

Conclusion of Holy Year. Sheets contain alternate vertical rows of stamps and labels bearing quotation from Pope Pius XII, different for each colony.

1951

Angola	357
Cape Verde	270
Macao	352
Mozambique	356
Port. Guinea	275
Port. India	506
St. Thomas & Prince Islands	355
Timor	270

No. 357 (1)	5.25	1.50
No. 270 (1)	1.50	1.25
No. 352 (1)	45.00	10.00
No. 356 (1)	2.25	1.00
No. 275 (1)	1.75	.90
No. 506 (1)	2.50	1.00
No. 355 (1)	3.00	2.00
No. 270 (1)	5.75	2.40
Set total (8) Stamps	67.00	20.05

Medical Congress

CD44

First National Congress of Tropical Medicine, Lisbon, 1952. Each stamp has a different design.

1952

Angola	358
Cape Verde	287
Macao	364

Mozambique	359
Port. Guinea	276
Port. India	516
St. Thomas & Prince Islands	356
Timor	271

No. 358 (1)	1.50	.50
No. 287 (1)	.75	.60
No. 364 (1)	10.00	6.00
No. 359 (1)	1.25	.55
No. 276 (1)	1.00	.45
No. 516 (1)	5.50	2.00
No. 356 (1)	.35	.90
No. 271 (1)	2.50	1.30
Set total (8) Stamps	22.85	11.70

Postage Due Stamps

CD45

1952

Angola	J37-J42
Cape Verde	J31-J36
Macao	J53-J58
Mozambique	J51-J56
Port. Guinea	J40-J45
Port. India	J47-J52
St. Thomas & Prince Islands	J52-J57
Timor	J31-J36

Nos. J37-J42 (6)	4.30	2.55
Nos. J31-J36 (6)	2.80	2.30
Nos. J53-J58 (6)	17.45	6.85
Nos. J51-J56 (6)	1.80	1.55
Nos. J40-J45 (6)	2.55	2.55
Nos. J47-J52 (6)	6.10	6.10
Nos. J52-J57 (6)	3.85	3.85
Nos. J31-J36 (6)	6.20	3.50
Set total (48) Stamps	45.05	29.25

Sao Paulo

Father Manuel da Nobrega and View of Sao Paulo — CD46

Founding of Sao Paulo, Brazil, 400th anniv.

1954

Angola	385
Cape Verde	297
Macao	382
Mozambique	395
Port. Guinea	291
Port. India	530
St. Thomas & Prince Islands	369
Timor	279

No. 385 (1)	.80	.50
No. 297 (1)	.70	.60
No. 382 (1)	15.00	6.00
No. 395 (1)	.40	.30
No. 291 (1)	.35	.25
No. 530 (1)	.80	.40
No. 369 (1)	.70	.50
No. 279 (1)	3.00	1.25
Set total (8) Stamps	21.75	9.80

Tropical Medicine Congress

CD47

Sixth International Congress for Tropical Medicine and Malaria, Lisbon, Sept. 1958. Each stamp shows a different plant.

1958

Angola	409
Cape Verde	303
Macao	392
Mozambique	404
Port. Guinea	295
Port. India	569
St. Thomas & Prince Islands	371

Timor	289

No. 409 (1)	3.50	1.10
No. 303 (1)	5.50	2.10
No. 392 (1)	10.00	5.00
No. 404 (1)	2.50	.85
No. 295 (1)	3.00	1.10
No. 569 (1)	1.75	.75
No. 371 (1)	2.75	2.00
No. 289 (1)	3.50	2.75
Set total (8) Stamps	32.50	15.65

Sports

CD48

Each stamp shows a different sport.

1962

Angola	433-438
Cape Verde	320-325
Macao	394-399
Mozambique	424-429
Port. Guinea	299-304
St. Thomas & Prince Islands	374-379
Timor	313-318

Nos. 433-438 (6)	5.50	3.20
Nos. 320-325 (6)	15.25	5.20
Nos. 394-399 (6)	68.65	14.60
Nos. 424-429 (6)	5.70	2.45
Nos. 299-304 (6)	6.00	3.00
Nos. 374-379 (6)	6.75	3.20
Nos. 313-318 (6)	9.15	5.05
Set total (42) Stamps	117.00	36.70

Anti-Malaria

Anopheles Funestus and Malaria Eradication Symbol — CD49

World Health Organization drive to eradicate malaria.

1962

Angola	439
Cape Verde	326
Macao	400
Mozambique	430
Port. Guinea	305
St. Thomas & Prince Islands	380
Timor	319

No. 439 (1)	1.75	.90
No. 326 (1)	1.40	.90
No. 400 (1)	7.00	2.25
No. 430 (1)	1.40	.40
No. 305 (1)	1.25	.45
No. 380 (1)	2.25	1.25
No. 319 (1)	1.50	1.00
Set total (7) Stamps	16.55	7.15

Airline Anniversary

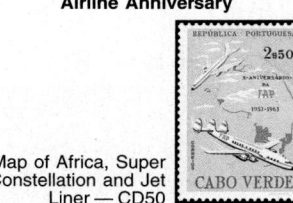

Map of Africa, Super Constellation and Jet Liner — CD50

Tenth anniversary of Transportes Aereos Portugueses (TAP).

1963

Angola	490
Cape Verde	327
Mozambique	434
Port. Guinea	318
St. Thomas & Prince Islands	381

No. 490 (1)	1.00	.35
No. 327 (1)	1.10	.70
No. 434 (1)	.40	.25

No. 318 (1)	.65	.35
No. 381 (1)	.80	.50
Set total (5) Stamps	3.95	2.15

National Overseas Bank

Antonio Teixeira de Sousa — CD51

Centenary of the National Overseas Bank of Portugal.

1964, May 16

Angola	509
Cape Verde	328
Port. Guinea	319
St. Thomas & Prince Islands	382
Timor	320

No. 509 (1)	.90	.30
No. 328 (1)	1.10	.75
No. 319 (1)	.65	.40
No. 382 (1)	.70	.50
No. 320 (1)	1.50	.85
Set total (5) Stamps	4.85	2.80

ITU

ITU Emblem and the Archangel Gabriel — CD52

International Communications Union, Cent.

1965, May 17

Angola	511
Cape Verde	329
Macao	402
Mozambique	464
Port. Guinea	320
St. Thomas & Prince Islands	383
Timor	321

No. 511 (1)	1.25	.65
No. 329 (1)	2.10	1.40
No. 402 (1)	6.00	2.25
No. 464 (1)	.45	.25
No. 320 (1)	1.90	.75
No. 383 (1)	2.00	1.00
No. 321 (1)	1.50	.90
Set total (7) Stamps	15.20	7.20

National Revolution

CD53

40th anniv. of the National Revolution. Different buildings on each stamp.

1966, May 28

Angola	525
Cape Verde	338
Macao	403
Mozambique	465
Port. Guinea	329
St. Thomas & Prince Islands	392
Timor	322

No. 525 (1)	.50	.25
No. 338 (1)	.60	.45
No. 403 (1)	9.00	2.25
No. 465 (1)	.50	.30
No. 329 (1)	.55	.35
No. 392 (1)	.80	.50
No. 322 (1)	1.75	.95
Set total (7) Stamps	13.70	5.05

Navy Club

CD54

Centenary of Portugal's Navy Club. Each stamp has a different design.

1967, Jan. 31

Angola		527-528
Cape Verde		339-340
Macao		412-413
Mozambique		478-479
Port. Guinea		330-331
St. Thomas & Prince Islands		393-394
Timor		323-324

Nos. 527-528 (2)	1.75	.75
Nos. 339-340 (2)	2.00	1.40
Nos. 412-413 (2)	11.25	4.00
Nos. 478-479 (2)	1.40	.65
Nos. 330-331 (2)	1.20	.90
Nos. 393-394 (2)	3.30	1.30
Nos. 323-324 (2)	4.65	1.90
Set total (14) Stamps	25.55	10.90

Admiral Coutinho

CD55

Centenary of the birth of Admiral Carlos Viegas Gago Coutinho (1869-1959), explorer and aviation pioneer. Each stamp has a different design.

1969, Feb. 17

Angola		547
Cape Verde		355
Macao		417
Mozambique		484
Port. Guinea		335
St. Thomas & Prince Islands		397
Timor		335

No. 547 (1)	.85	.35
No. 355 (1)	.50	.25
No. 417 (1)	5.00	1.75
No. 484 (1)	.25	.25
No. 335 (1)	.35	.25
No. 397 (1)	.60	.35
No. 335 (1)	2.50	1.05
Set total (7) Stamps	10.05	4.25

Administration Reform

Luiz Augusto Rebello da Silva — CD56

Centenary of the administration reforms of the overseas territories.

1969, Sept. 25

Angola		549
Cape Verde		357
Macao		419
Mozambique		491
Port. Guinea		337
St. Thomas & Prince Islands		399
Timor		338

No. 549 (1)	.35	.25
No. 357 (1)	.50	.25
No. 419 (1)	6.00	1.00
No. 491 (1)	.25	.25
No. 337 (1)	.25	.25
No. 399 (1)	.45	.45
No. 338 (1)	1.25	.50
Set total (7) Stamps	9.05	2.95

Marshal Carmona

CD57

Birth centenary of Marshal Antonio Oscar Carmona de Fragoso (1869-1951), President of Portugal. Each stamp has a different design.

1970, Nov. 15

Angola		563
Cape Verde		359
Macao		422
Mozambique		493
Port. Guinea		340
St. Thomas & Prince Islands		403
Timor		341

No. 563 (1)	.45	.25
No. 359 (1)	.55	.35
No. 422 (1)	2.00	1.00
No. 493 (1)	.40	.25
No. 340 (1)	.35	.25
No. 403 (1)	.75	.40
No. 341 (1)	1.00	.35
Set total (7) Stamps	5.50	2.85

Olympic Games

CD59

20th Olympic Games, Munich, Aug. 26-Sept. 11. Each stamp shows a different sport.

1972, June 20

Angola		569
Cape Verde		361
Macao		426
Mozambique		504
Port. Guinea		342
St. Thomas & Prince Islands		408
Timor		343

No. 569 (1)	.65	.25
No. 361 (1)	.85	.30
No. 426 (1)	4.25	1.00
No. 504 (1)	.30	.25
No. 342 (1)	.45	.25
No. 408 (1)	.45	.25
No. 343 (1)	1.60	.80
Set total (7) Stamps	8.55	3.10

Lisbon-Rio de Janeiro Flight

CD60

50th anniversary of the Lisbon to Rio de Janeiro flight by Arturo de Sacadura and Coutinho, March 30-June 5, 1922. Each stamp shows a different stage of the flight.

1972, Sept. 20

Angola		570
Cape Verde		362
Macao		427
Mozambique		505
Port. Guinea		343
St. Thomas & Prince Islands		409
Timor		344

No. 570 (1)	.35	.25
No. 362 (1)	1.50	.30
No. 427 (1)	22.50	8.50
No. 505 (1)	.25	.25
No. 343 (1)	.25	.25
No. 409 (1)	.50	.25
No. 344 (1)	1.40	.60
Set total (7) Stamps	26.75	10.40

WMO Centenary

WMO Emblem — CD61

Centenary of international meterological cooperation.

1973, Dec. 15

Angola		571
Cape Verde		363
Macao		429
Mozambique		509
Port. Guinea		344
St. Thomas & Prince Islands		410

Timor		345

No. 571 (1)	.45	.25
No. 363 (1)	.65	.30
No. 429 (1)	6.00	1.75
No. 509 (1)	.30	.25
No. 344 (1)	.45	.35
No. 410 (1)	.60	.50
No. 345 (1)	4.25	2.50
Set total (7) Stamps	12.70	5.90

FRENCH COMMUNITY

Upper Volta can be found under Burkina Faso in Vol. 1
Madagascar can be found under Malagasy in Vol. 3
Colonial Exposition

People of French Empire CD70

Women's Heads CD71

France Showing Way to Civilization CD72

"Colonial Commerce" CD73

International Colonial Exposition, Paris.

1931

Cameroun		213-216
Chad		60-63
Dahomey		97-100
Fr. Guiana		152-155
Fr. Guinea		116-119
Fr. India		100-103
Fr. Polynesia		76-79
Fr. Sudan		102-105
Gabon		120-123
Guadeloupe		138-141
Indo-China		140-142
Ivory Coast		92-95
Madagascar		169-172
Martinique		129-132
Mauritania		65-68
Middle Congo		61-64
New Caledonia		176-179
Niger		73-76
Reunion		122-125
St. Pierre & Miquelon		132-135
Senegal		138-141
Somali Coast		135-138
Togo		254-257
Ubangi-Shari		82-85
Upper Volta		66-69
Wallis & Futuna Isls.		85-88

Nos. 213-216 (4)	23.00	18.25
Nos. 60-63 (4)	22.00	22.00
Nos. 97-100 (4)	26.00	26.00
Nos. 152-155 (4)	22.00	22.00
Nos. 116-119 (4)	19.75	19.75
Nos. 100-103 (4)	18.00	18.00
Nos. 76-79 (4)	30.00	30.00
Nos. 102-105 (4)	19.00	19.00
Nos. 120-123 (4)	17.50	17.50
Nos. 138-141 (4)	19.00	19.00
Nos. 140-142 (3)	12.00	11.50
Nos. 92-95 (4)	22.50	22.50
Nos. 169-172 (4)	9.25	6.50
Nos. 129-132 (4)	21.00	21.00
Nos. 65-68 (4)	22.00	22.00
Nos. 61-64 (4)	20.00	18.50
Nos. 176-179 (4)	24.00	24.00
Nos. 73-76 (4)	20.50	20.50
Nos. 122-125 (4)	22.00	22.00
Nos. 132-135 (4)	24.00	24.00
Nos. 138-141 (4)	20.00	20.00
Nos. 135-138 (4)	22.00	22.00
Nos. 254-257 (4)	22.00	22.00

Nos. 82-85 (4)	21.00	21.00
Nos. 66-69 (4)	19.00	19.00
Nos. 85-88 (4)	31.00	35.00
Set total (103) Stamps	548.50	543.00

Paris International Exposition
Colonial Arts Exposition

"Colonial Resources"
CD74   CD77

Overseas Commerce CD75

Exposition Building and Women CD76

"France and the Empire" CD78

Cultural Treasures of the Colonies CD79

Souvenir sheets contain one imperf. stamp.

1937

Cameroun		217-222A
Dahomey		101-107
Fr. Equatorial Africa		27-32, 73
Fr. Guiana		162-168
Fr. Guinea		120-126
Fr. India		104-110
Fr. Polynesia		117-123
Fr. Sudan		106-112
Guadeloupe		148-154
Indo-China		193-199
Inini		41
Ivory Coast		152-158
Kwangchowan		132
Madagascar		191-197
Martinique		179-185
Mauritania		69-75
New Caledonia		208-214
Niger		77-83
Reunion		167-173
St. Pierre & Miquelon		165-171
Senegal		172-178
Somali Coast		139-145
Togo		258-264
Wallis & Futuna Isls.		89

Nos. 217-222A (7)	18.80	20.30
Nos. 101-107 (7)	23.60	27.60
Nos. 27-32, 73 (7)	28.10	32.10
Nos. 162-168 (7)	22.50	24.50
Nos. 120-126 (7)	24.00	28.00
Nos. 104-110 (7)	21.15	36.50
Nos. 117-123 (7)	58.50	75.00
Nos. 106-112 (7)	23.60	27.60
Nos. 148-154 (7)	19.55	21.05
Nos. 193-199 (7)	17.70	19.70
No. 41 (1)	21.00	27.50
Nos. 152-158 (7)	22.20	26.20
No. 132 (1)	9.25	11.00
Nos. 191-197 (7)	19.25	21.75
Nos. 179-185 (7)	19.95	21.95
Nos. 69-75 (7)	20.50	24.50
Nos. 208-214 (7)	39.00	50.50
Nos. 73-83 (11)	40.60	45.10
Nos. 167-173 (7)	21.70	23.20
Nos. 165-171 (7)	49.60	64.00
Nos. 172-178 (7)	21.00	23.80
Nos. 139-145 (7)	25.60	32.60
Nos. 258-264 (7)	20.40	20.40
No. 89 (1)	19.00	37.50
Set total (154) Stamps	606.55	742.10

Curie

Pierre and Marie Curie CD80

40th anniversary of the discovery of radium. The surtax was for the benefit of the Intl. Union for the Control of Cancer.

1938

Cameroun	B1
Cuba	B1-B2
Dahomey	B2
France	B76
Fr. Equatorial Africa	B1
Fr. Guiana	B3
Fr. Guinea	B2
Fr. India	B6
Fr. Polynesia	B5
Fr. Sudan	B1
Guadeloupe	B3
Indo-China	B14
Ivory Coast	B2
Madagascar	B2
Martinique	B2
Mauritania	B3
New Caledonia	B4
Niger	B1
Reunion	B4
St. Pierre & Miquelon	B3
Senegal	B3
Somali Coast	B2
Togo	B1

No. B1 (1)	10.00	10.00
Nos. B1-B2 (2)	12.00	3.35
No. B2 (1)	9.50	9.50
No. B76 (1)	21.00	12.50
No. B1 (1)	24.00	24.00
No. B3 (1)	13.50	13.50
No. B2 (1)	8.75	8.75
No. B6 (1)	10.00	10.00
No. B5 (1)	20.00	20.00
No. B1 (1)	12.50	12.50
No. B3 (1)	11.00	10.50
No. B14 (1)	12.00	12.00
No. B2 (1)	11.00	7.50
No. B2 (1)	11.00	11.00
No. B2 (1)	13.00	13.00
No. B3 (1)	7.75	7.75
No. B4 (1)	16.50	17.50
No. B1 (1)	16.50	16.50
No. B4 (1)	14.00	14.00
No. B3 (1)	21.00	22.50
No. B3 (1)	10.50	10.50
No. B2 (1)	7.75	7.75
No. B1 (1)	20.00	20.00
Set total (24) Stamps	313.25	294.60

Caillie

Rene Caillie and Map of Northwestern Africa — CD81

Death centenary of Rene Caillie (1799-1838), French explorer. All three denominations exist with colony name omitted.

1939

Dahomey	108-110
Fr. Guinea	161-163
Fr. Sudan	113-115
Ivory Coast	160-162
Mauritania	109-111
Niger	84-86
Senegal	188-190
Togo	265-267

Nos. 108-110 (3)	1.20	3.60
Nos. 161-163 (3)	1.20	3.20
Nos. 113-115 (3)	1.20	3.20
Nos. 160-162 (3)	1.05	2.55
Nos. 109-111 (3)	1.05	3.80
Nos. 84-86 (3)	2.35	2.35
Nos. 188-190 (3)	1.05	2.90
Nos. 265-267 (3)	1.05	3.30
Set total (24) Stamps	10.15	24.90

New York World's Fair

Natives and New York Skyline CD82

1939

Cameroun	223-224
Dahomey	111-112
Fr. Equatorial Africa	78-79
Fr. Guiana	169-170
Fr. Guinea	164-165
Fr. India	111-112
Fr. Polynesia	124-125
Fr. Sudan	116-117
Guadeloupe	155-156
Indo-China	203-204
Inini	42-43
Ivory Coast	163-164
Kwangchowan	133-134
Madagascar	209-210
Martinique	186-187
Mauritania	112-113
New Caledonia	215-216
Niger	87-88
Reunion	174-175
St. Pierre & Miquelon	205-206
Senegal	191-192
Somali Coast	179-180
Togo	268-269
Wallis & Futuna Isls.	90-91

Nos. 223-224 (2)	2.80	2.40
Nos. 111-112 (2)	1.60	3.20
Nos. 78-79 (2)	1.60	3.20
Nos. 169-170 (2)	2.60	2.60
Nos. 164-165 (2)	1.60	3.20
Nos. 111-112 (2)	3.00	8.00
Nos. 124-125 (2)	4.80	4.80
Nos. 116-117 (2)	1.60	3.20
Nos. 155-156 (2)	2.50	2.50
Nos. 203-204 (2)	2.05	2.05
Nos. 42-43 (2)	7.50	9.00
Nos. 163-164 (2)	1.50	3.00
Nos. 133-134 (2)	2.50	2.50
Nos. 209-210 (2)	1.50	2.50
Nos. 186-187 (2)	2.35	2.35
Nos. 112-113 (2)	1.40	2.80
Nos. 215-216 (2)	3.35	3.35
Nos. 87-88 (2)	1.60	2.80
Nos. 174-175 (2)	2.80	2.80
Nos. 205-206 (2)	4.80	6.00
Nos. 191-192 (2)	1.40	2.80
Nos. 179-180 (2)	1.40	2.80
Nos. 268-269 (2)	1.40	2.80
Nos. 90-91 (2)	5.00	6.00
Set total (48) Stamps	62.65	86.65

French Revolution

Storming of the Bastille CD83

French Revolution, 150th anniv. The surtax was for the defense of the colonies.

1939

Cameroun	B2-B6
Dahomey	B3-B7
Fr. Equatorial Africa	B4-B8, CB1
Fr. Guiana	B4-B8, CB1
Fr. Guinea	B3-B7
Fr. India	B7-B11
Fr. Polynesia	B6-B10, CB1
Fr. Sudan	B2-B6
Guadeloupe	B4-B8
Indo-China	B15-B19, CB1
Inini	B1-B5
Ivory Coast	B3-B7
Kwangchowan	B1-B5
Madagascar	B3-B7, CB1
Martinique	B3-B7
Mauritania	B4-B8
New Caledonia	B5-B9, CB1
Niger	B2-B6
Reunion	B5-B9, CB1
St. Pierre & Miquelon	B4-B8
Senegal	B4-B8, CB1
Somali Coast	B3-B7
Togo	B2-B6
Wallis & Futuna Isls.	B1-B5

Nos. B2-B6 (5)	60.00	60.00
Nos. B3-B7 (5)	47.50	47.50
Nos. B4-B8,CB1 (6)	120.00	120.00
Nos. B4-B8,CB1 (6)	79.50	79.50
Nos. B3-B7 (5)	47.50	47.50
Nos. B7-B11 (5)	28.75	32.50
Nos. B6-B10,CB1 (6)	122.50	122.50
Nos. B2-B6 (5)	50.00	50.00
Nos. B4-B8 (5)	50.00	50.00
Nos. B15-B19,CB1 (6)	85.00	85.00
Nos. B1-B5 (5)	80.00	100.00
Nos. B3-B7 (5)	43.75	43.75
Nos. B1-B5 (5)	46.25	46.25
Nos. B3-B7,CB1 (6)	65.50	65.50
Nos. B3-B7 (5)	52.50	52.50
Nos. B4-B8 (5)	42.50	42.50
Nos. B5-B9,CB1 (6)	101.50	101.50
Nos. B2-B6 (5)	60.00	60.00
Nos. B5-B9,CB1 (6)	87.50	87.50
Nos. B4-B8,CB1 (6)	67.50	72.50
Nos. B3-B7 (5)	45.00	45.00
Nos. B2-B6 (5)	42.50	42.50
Nos. B1-B5 (5)	80.00	110.00
Set total (128) Stamps	1,562.	1,621.

Plane over Coastal Area CD85

All five denominations exist with colony name omitted.

1940

Dahomey	C1-C5
Fr. Guinea	C1-C5
Fr. Sudan	C1-C5
Ivory Coast	C1-C5
Mauritania	C1-C5
Niger	C1-C5
Senegal	C12-C16
Togo	C1-C5

Nos. C1-C5 (5)	4.00	4.00
Nos. C1-C5 (5)	4.00	4.00
Nos. C1-C5 (5)	4.00	4.00
Nos. C1-C5 (5)	3.80	3.80
Nos. C1-C5 (5)	3.50	3.50
Nos. C1-C5 (5)	3.50	3.50
Nos. C12-C16 (5)	3.50	3.50
Nos. C1-C5 (5)	3.15	3.15
Set total (40) Stamps	29.45	29.45

Defense of the Empire

Colonial Infantryman — CD86

1941

Cameroun	B13B
Dahomey	B13
Fr. Equatorial Africa	B8B
Fr. Guiana	B10
Fr. Guinea	B13
Fr. India	B13
Fr. Polynesia	B12
Fr. Sudan	B12
Guadeloupe	B10
Indo-China	B19B
Inini	B7
Ivory Coast	B13
Kwangchowan	B7
Madagascar	B9
Martinique	B9
Mauritania	B14
New Caledonia	B11
Niger	B12
Reunion	B11
St. Pierre & Miquelon	B8B
Senegal	B14
Somali Coast	B9
Togo	B10B
Wallis & Futuna Isls.	B7

No. B13B (1)	1.60
No. B13 (1)	1.20
No. B8B (1)	3.50
No. B10 (1)	1.40
No. B13 (1)	1.40
No. B13 (1)	1.25
No. B12 (1)	3.50
No. B12 (1)	1.40
No. B10 (1)	1.00
No. B19B (1)	3.00
No. B7 (1)	1.75
No. B13 (1)	1.25
No. B7 (1)	.85

No. B9 (1)	1.50
No. B9 (1)	1.40
No. B14 (1)	.95
No. B12 (1)	1.40
No. B11 (1)	1.60
No. B8B (1)	4.50
No. B14 (1)	1.25
No. B9 (1)	1.60
No. B10B (1)	1.10
No. B7 (1)	1.75
Set total (23) Stamps	40.15

Each of the CD86 stamps listed above is part of a set of three stamps. The designs of the other two stamps in the set vary from country to country. Only the values of the Common Design stamps are listed here.

Colonial Education Fund

CD86a

1942

Cameroun	CB3
Dahomey	CB4
Fr. Equatorial Africa	CB5
Fr. Guiana	CB4
Fr. Guinea	CB4
Fr. India	CB3
Fr. Polynesia	CB4
Fr. Sudan	CB4
Guadeloupe	CB3
Indo-China	CB5
Inini	CB3
Ivory Coast	CB4
Kwangchowan	CB4
Malagasy	CB5
Martinique	CB3
Mauritania	CB4
New Caledonia	CB4
Niger	CB4
Reunion	CB4
St. Pierre & Miquelon	CB3
Senegal	CB5
Somali Coast	CB3
Togo	CB3
Wallis & Futuna	CB3

No. CB3 (1)	1.10	
No. CB4 (1)	.80	5.50
No. CB5 (1)	.80	
No. CB4 (1)	1.10	
No. CB4 (1)	.40	5.50
No. CB3 (1)	.90	
No. CB4 (1)	2.00	
No. CB4 (1)	.40	5.50
No. CB3 (1)	1.10	
No. CB5 (1)	2.00	
No. CB4 (1)	1.25	
No. CB4 (1)	1.00	5.50
No. CB4 (1)	1.00	
No. CB5 (1)	.65	
No. CB3 (1)	1.00	
No. CB4 (1)	.80	
No. CB4 (1)	2.25	
No. CB4 (1)	.35	
No. CB4 (1)	.90	
No. CB3 (1)	7.00	
No. CB5 (1)	.80	6.50
No. CB3 (1)	.70	
No. CB3 (1)	.35	
No. CB3 (1)	2.00	
Set total (24) Stamps	30.65	28.50

Cross of Lorraine & Four-motor Plane CD87

1941-5

Cameroun	C1-C7
Fr. Equatorial Africa	C17-C23
Fr. Guiana	C9-C10
Fr. India	C1-C6
Fr. Polynesia	C3-C9
Fr. West Africa	C1-C3
Guadeloupe	C1-C2
Madagascar	C37-C43

Martinique.................................. C1-C2
New Caledonia.......................... C7-C13
Reunion.................................... C18-C24
St. Pierre & Miquelon................ C1-C7
Somali Coast............................ C1-C7

Nos. C1-C7 (7)	6.30	6.30
Nos. C17-C23 (7)	10.40	6.35
Nos. C9-C10 (2)	3.80	3.10
Nos. C1-C6 (6)	9.30	15.00
Nos. C3-C9 (7)	13.75	10.00
Nos. C1-C3 (3)	9.50	3.90
Nos. C37-C43 (7)	5.60	3.80
Nos. C1-C2 (2)	3.00	1.60
Nos. C7-C13 (7)	8.85	7.30
Nos. C18-C24 (7)	7.05	5.00
Nos. C1-C7 (7)	11.60	9.40
Nos. C1-C7 (7)	13.95	11.10
Set total (71) Stamps	106.85	85.35

Somali Coast stamps are inscribed "Djibouti".

Transport Plane CD88

Caravan and Plane CD89

1942

Dahomey.................................. C6-C13
Fr. Guinea C6-C13
Fr. Sudan................................. C6-C13
Ivory Coast.............................. C6-C13
Mauritania................................ C6-C13
Niger....................................... C6-C13
Senegal................................... C17-C25
Togo....................................... C6-C13

Nos. C6-C13 (8)	7.15
Nos. C6-C13 (8)	5.75
Nos. C6-C13 (8)	8.00
Nos. C6-C13 (8)	11.15
Nos. C6-C13 (8)	9.75
Nos. C6-C13 (8)	6.20
Nos. C17-C25 (9)	9.45
Nos. C6-C13 (8)	6.75
Set total (65) Stamps	64.20

Red Cross

Marianne CD90

The surtax was for the French Red Cross and national relief.

1944

Cameroun.................................. B28
Fr. Equatorial Africa B38
Fr. Guiana B12
Fr. India B14
Fr. Polynesia B13
Fr. West Africa B1
Guadeloupe.............................. B12
Madagascar.............................. B15
Martinique................................ B11
New Caledonia B13
Reunion B15
St. Pierre & Miquelon B13
Somali Coast B13
Wallis & Futuna Isls. B9

No. B28 (1)	2.00	1.60
No. B38 (1)	1.60	1.20
No. B12 (1)	1.75	1.25
No. B14 (1)	1.50	1.25
No. B13 (1)	2.00	1.60
No. B1 (1)	6.50	4.75
No. B12 (1)	1.40	1.00
No. B15 (1)	.90	.90
No. B11 (1)	1.20	1.20
No. B13 (1)	1.50	1.50
No. B15 (1)	1.60	1.10
No. B13 (1)	2.60	2.60
No. B13 (1)	1.75	2.00
No. B9 (1)	3.00	3.00
Set total (14) Stamps	29.30	24.95

Eboue

CD91

Felix Eboue, first French colonial administrator to proclaim resistance to Germany after French surrender in World War II.

1945

Cameroun.................................296-297
Fr. Equatorial Africa 156-157
Fr. Guiana 171-172
Fr. India 210-211
Fr. Polynesia 150-151
Fr. West Africa 15-16
Guadeloupe..............................187-188
Madagascar..............................259-260
Martinique................................196-197
New Caledonia 274-275
Reunion 238-239
St. Pierre & Miquelon.................322-323
Somali Coast 238-239

Nos. 296-297 (2)	2.40	1.95
Nos. 156-157 (2)	2.55	2.00
Nos. 171-172 (2)	2.45	2.00
Nos. 210-211 (2)	2.20	1.95
Nos. 150-151 (2)	3.60	2.85
Nos. 15-16 (2)	2.40	2.40
Nos. 187-188 (2)	2.05	1.60
Nos. 259-260 (2)	2.00	1.45
Nos. 196-197 (2)	2.05	1.55
Nos. 274-275 (2)	3.40	3.00
Nos. 238-239 (2)	2.40	2.00
Nos. 322-323 (2)	4.40	3.45
Nos. 238-239 (2)	2.45	2.10
Set total (26) Stamps	34.35	28.30

Victory

Victory — CD92

European victory of the Allied Nations in World War II.

1946, May 8

Cameroun.....................................C8
Fr. Equatorial Africa C24
Fr. Guiana C11
Fr. India C7
Fr. Polynesia C10
Fr. West Africa C4
Guadeloupe..................................C3
Indo-China...................................C19
Madagascar..................................C44
Martinique...................................C3
New Caledonia C14
Reunion C25
St. Pierre & Miquelon.....................C8
Somali Coast C8
Wallis & Futuna Isls. C1

No. C8 (1)	1.60	1.20
No. C24 (1)	1.60	1.25
No. C11 (1)	1.75	1.25
No. C7 (1)	1.00	4.00
No. C10 (1)	2.75	2.00
No. C4 (1)	1.60	1.20
No. C3 (1)	1.25	1.00
No. C19 (1)	1.00	.55
No. C44 (1)	1.00	.35
No. C3 (1)	1.30	1.00
No. C14 (1)	1.50	1.25
No. C25 (1)	1.10	.90
No. C8 (1)	2.10	2.10
No. C8 (1)	1.75	1.40
No. C1 (1)	2.25	1.90
Set total (15) Stamps	23.55	21.35

Chad to Rhine

Leclerc's Departure from Chad — CD93

Battle at Cufra Oasis — CD94

Tanks in Action, Mareth — CD95

Normandy Invasion — CD96

Entering Paris — CD97

Liberation of Strasbourg — CD98

"Chad to the Rhine" march, 1942-44, by Gen. Jacques Leclerc's column, later French 2nd Armored Division.

1946, June 6

Cameroun.....................................C9-C14
Fr. Equatorial Africa C25-C30
Fr. Guiana C12-C17
Fr. India C8-C13
Fr. Polynesia C11-C16
Fr. West Africa C5-C10
Guadeloupe..................................C4-C9
Indo-China...................................C20-C25
Madagascar..................................C45-C50
Martinique...................................C4-C9
New Caledonia C15-C20
Reunion C26-C31
St. Pierre & Miquelon..............C9-C14
Somali Coast C9-C14
Wallis & Futuna Isls. C2-C7

Nos. C9-C14 (6)	12.05	9.70
Nos. C25-C30 (6)	14.70	10.80
Nos. C12-C17 (6)	12.65	10.35
Nos. C8-C13 (6)	12.80	15.00
Nos. C11-C16 (6)	17.55	13.40
Nos. C5-C10 (6)	16.05	11.95
Nos. C4-C9 (6)	12.00	9.60
Nos. C20-C25 (6)	6.40	6.40
Nos. C45-C50 (6)	10.30	8.40
Nos. C4-C9 (6)	8.85	7.30
Nos. C15-C20 (6)	13.40	11.90
Nos. C26-C31 (6)	10.25	6.55
Nos. C9-C14 (6)	17.30	14.35

Nos. C9-C14 (6)	18.10	12.65
Nos. C2-C7 (6)	13.75	10.45
Set total (90) Stamps	196.15	158.80

UPU

French Colonials, Globe and Plane — CD99

Universal Postal Union, 75th anniv.

1949, July 4

Cameroun.....................................C29
Fr. Equatorial Africa C34
Fr. India C17
Fr. Polynesia C20
Fr. West Africa C15
Indo-China...................................C26
Madagascar..................................C55
New Caledonia C24
St. Pierre & Miquelon.....................C18
Somali Coast C18
Togo..C18
Wallis & Futuna Isls. C10

No. C29 (1)	8.00	4.75
No. C34 (1)	16.00	12.00
No. C17 (1)	11.50	8.75
No. C20 (1)	20.00	15.00
No. C15 (1)	12.00	8.75
No. C26 (1)	4.75	4.00
No. C55 (1)	4.00	2.75
No. C24 (1)	7.50	5.00
No. C18 (1)	20.00	12.00
No. C18 (1)	14.00	10.50
No. C18 (1)	8.50	7.00
No. C10 (1)	11.00	8.25
Set total (12) Stamps	137.25	98.75

Tropical Medicine

Doctor Treating Infant CD100

The surtax was for charitable work.

1950

Cameroun.....................................B29
Fr. Equatorial Africa B39
Fr. India B15
Fr. Polynesia B14
Fr. West Africa B3
Madagascar..................................B17
New Caledonia B14
St. Pierre & Miquelon.....................B14
Somali Coast B14
Togo..B11

No. B29 (1)	7.25	5.50
No. B39 (1)	7.25	5.50
No. B15 (1)	6.00	4.00
No. B14 (1)	10.50	8.00
No. B3 (1)	9.50	7.25
No. B17 (1)	5.50	5.50
No. B14 (1)	6.75	5.25
No. B14 (1)	16.00	15.00
No. B14 (1)	7.75	6.25
No. B11 (1)	5.00	3.50
Set total (10) Stamps	81.50	65.75

Military Medal

Medal, Early Marine and Colonial Soldier — CD101

Centenary of the creation of the French Military Medal.

1952

Cameroun.....................................322
Comoro Isls. 39
Fr. Equatorial Africa 186

Fr. India		233
Fr. Polynesia		179
Fr. West Africa		57
Madagascar		286
New Caledonia		295
St. Pierre & Miquelon		345
Somali Coast		267
Togo		327
Wallis & Futuna Isls.		149

No. 322 (1)	7.25	3.25
No. 39 (1)	45.00	37.50
No. 186 (1)	8.00	5.50
No. 233 (1)	5.50	7.00
No. 179 (1)	13.50	10.00
No. 57 (1)	8.75	6.50
No. 286 (1)	3.75	2.50
No. 295 (1)	6.50	6.00
No. 345 (1)	16.00	15.00
No. 267 (1)	9.00	8.00
No. 327 (1)	5.50	4.75
No. 149 (1)	7.25	7.25
Set total (12) Stamps	136.00	113.25

Liberation

Allied Landing, Victory Sign and Cross of Lorraine — CD102

Liberation of France, 10th anniv.

1954, June 6

Cameroun		C32
Comoro Isls.		C4
Fr. Equatorial Africa		C38
Fr. India		C18
Fr. Polynesia		C22
Fr. West Africa		C17
Madagascar		C57
New Caledonia		C25
St. Pierre & Miquelon		C19
Somali Coast		C19
Togo		C19
Wallis & Futuna Isls.		C11

No. C32 (1)	7.25	4.75
No. C4 (1)	32.50	19.00
No. C38 (1)	12.00	8.00
No. C18 (1)	11.00	8.00
No. C22 (1)	10.00	8.00
No. C17 (1)	12.00	5.50
No. C57 (1)	3.25	2.00
No. C25 (1)	7.50	5.00
No. C19 (1)	19.00	12.00
No. C19 (1)	10.50	8.50
No. C19 (1)	7.00	5.50
No. C11 (1)	11.00	8.25
Set total (12) Stamps	143.00	94.50

FIDES

Plowmen CD103

Efforts of FIDES, the Economic and Social Development Fund for Overseas Possessions (Fonds d' Investissement pour le Developpement Economique et Social). Each stamp has a different design.

1956

Cameroun		326-329
Comoro Isls.		43
Fr. Equatorial Africa		189-192
Fr. Polynesia		181
Fr. West Africa		65-72
Madagascar		292-295
New Caledonia		303
St. Pierre & Miquelon		350
Somali Coast		268-269
Togo		331

Nos. 326-329 (4)	6.90	3.20
No. 43 (1)	2.25	1.60
Nos. 189-192 (4)	3.20	1.65
No. 181 (1)	4.00	2.00
Nos. 65-72 (8)	16.00	6.35
Nos. 292-295 (4)	2.25	1.20
No. 303 (1)	1.90	1.10
No. 350 (1)	6.00	4.00
Nos. 268-269 (2)	5.35	3.15
No. 331 (1)	4.25	2.10
Set total (27) Stamps	52.10	26.35

Flower

CD104

Each stamp shows a different flower.

1958-9

Cameroun		333
Comoro Isls.		45
Fr. Equatorial Africa		200-201
Fr. Polynesia		192
Fr. So. & Antarctic Terr.		11
Fr. West Africa		79-83
Madagascar		301-302
New Caledonia		304-305
St. Pierre & Miquelon		357
Somali Coast		270
Togo		348-349
Wallis & Futuna Isls.		152

No. 333 (1)	1.60	.80
No. 45 (1)	5.25	4.25
Nos. 200-201 (2)	3.60	1.60
No. 192 (1)	6.50	4.00
No. 11 (1)	8.75	7.50
Nos. 79-83 (5)	10.45	5.60
Nos. 301-302 (2)	1.60	.60
Nos. 304-305 (2)	8.00	3.00
No. 357 (1)	4.50	2.25
No. 270 (1)	4.25	1.40
Nos. 348-349 (2)	1.10	.50
No. 152 (1)	3.25	3.25
Set total (20) Stamps	58.85	34.75

Human Rights

Sun, Dove and U.N. Emblem CD105

10th anniversary of the signing of the Universal Declaration of Human Rights.

1958

Comoro Isls.		44
Fr. Equatorial Africa		202
Fr. Polynesia		191
Fr. West Africa		85
Madagascar		300
New Caledonia		306
St. Pierre & Miquelon		356
Somali Coast		274
Wallis & Futuna Isls.		153

No. 44 (1)	9.00	9.00
No. 202 (1)	2.40	1.25
No. 191 (1)	13.00	8.75
No. 85 (1)	2.40	2.00
No. 300 (1)	.80	.40
No. 306 (1)	2.00	1.50
No. 356 (1)	3.50	2.50
No. 274 (1)	3.50	2.10
No. 153 (1)	4.50	4.50
Set total (9) Stamps	41.10	32.00

C.C.T.A.

CD106

Commission for Technical Cooperation in Africa south of the Sahara, 10th anniv.

1960

Cameroun		339
Cent. Africa		3
Chad		66
Congo, P.R.		90
Dahomey		138
Gabon		150
Ivory Coast		180
Madagascar		317
Mali		9
Mauritania		117
Niger		104
Upper Volta		89

No. 339 (1)	1.60	.75
No. 3 (1)	1.60	.75
No. 66 (1)	1.75	.50
No. 90 (1)	1.00	1.00
No. 138 (1)	.50	.25
No. 150 (1)	1.25	1.10
No. 180 (1)	1.10	.50
No. 317 (1)	.60	.30
No. 9 (1)	1.20	.50
No. 117 (1)	.75	.40
No. 104 (1)	.85	.45
No. 89 (1)	.65	.40
Set total (12) Stamps	12.85	6.90

Air Afrique, 1961

Modern and Ancient Africa, Map and Planes — CD107

Founding of Air Afrique (African Airlines).

1961-62

Cameroun		C37
Cent. Africa		C5
Chad		C7
Congo, P.R.		C5
Dahomey		C17
Gabon		C5
Ivory Coast		C18
Mauritania		C17
Niger		C22
Senegal		C31
Upper Volta		C4

No. C37 (1)	1.00	.50
No. C5 (1)	1.00	.65
No. C7 (1)	1.00	.25
No. C5 (1)	1.75	.90
No. C17 (1)	.80	.40
No. C5 (1)	11.00	6.00
No. C18 (1)	2.00	1.25
No. C17 (1)	2.40	1.25
No. C22 (1)	1.75	.90
No. C31 (1)	.80	.30
No. C4 (1)	3.50	1.75
Set total (11) Stamps	27.00	14.15

Anti-Malaria

CD108

World Health Organization drive to eradicate malaria.

1962, Apr. 7

Cameroun		B36
Cent. Africa		B1
Chad		B1
Comoro Isls.		B1
Congo, P.R.		B3
Dahomey		B15
Gabon		B4
Ivory Coast		B15
Madagascar		B19
Mali		B1
Mauritania		B16
Niger		B14
Senegal		B16
Somali Coast		B15
Upper Volta		B1

No. B36 (1)	1.00	.45
No. B1 (1)	1.40	1.40
No. B1 (1)	1.00	.50
No. B1 (1)	3.50	3.50
No. B3 (1)	1.40	1.00
No. B15 (1)	.75	.75
No. B4 (1)	1.00	1.00
No. B15 (1)	1.25	1.25
No. B19 (1)	.75	.50
No. B1 (1)	1.25	.60
No. B16 (1)	.50	.50
No. B14 (1)	.75	.75
No. B16 (1)	1.10	.65
No. B15 (1)	7.00	7.00
No. B1 (1)	.75	.70
Set total (15) Stamps	23.40	20.55

Abidjan Games

CD109

Abidjan Games, Ivory Coast, Dec. 24-31, 1961. Each stamp shows a different sport.

1962

Cent. Africa		19-20, C6
Chad		83-84, C8
Congo, P.R.		103-104, C7
Gabon		163-164, C6
Niger		109-111
Upper Volta		103-105

Nos. 19-20,C6 (3)	4.15	2.85
Nos. 83-84,C8 (3)	5.80	1.55
Nos. 103-104,C7 (3)	3.85	1.80
Nos. 163-164,C6 (3)	5.00	3.00
Nos. 109-111 (3)	2.60	1.25
Nos. 103-105 (3)	2.80	1.75
Set total (18) Stamps	24.20	12.20

African and Malagasy Union

Flag of Union CD110

First anniversary of the Union.

1962, Sept. 8

Cameroun		373
Cent. Africa		21
Chad		85
Congo, P.R.		105
Dahomey		155
Gabon		165
Ivory Coast		198
Madagascar		332
Mauritania		170
Niger		112
Senegal		211
Upper Volta		106

No. 373 (1)	2.00	.75
No. 21 (1)	1.25	.75
No. 85 (1)	1.25	.25
No. 105 (1)	1.50	.50
No. 155 (1)	1.25	.90
No. 165 (1)	1.60	1.25
No. 198 (1)	2.10	.75
No. 332 (1)	.80	.80
No. 170 (1)	.75	.50
No. 112 (1)	.80	.50
No. 211 (1)	.80	.50
No. 106 (1)	1.10	.75
Set total (12) Stamps	15.20	8.20

Telstar

Telstar and Globe Showing Andover and Pleumeur-Bodou — CD111

First television connection of the United States and Europe through the Telstar satellite, July 11-12, 1962.

1962-63

Andorra, French		154
Comoro Isls.		C7
Fr. Polynesia		C29
Fr. So. & Antarctic Terr.		C5
New Caledonia		C33
St. Pierre & Miquelon		C26
Somali Coast		C31
Wallis & Futuna Isls.		C17

No. 154 (1)	2.00	1.60
No. C7 (1)	4.50	2.75
No. C29 (1)	11.50	8.00

No. C5 (1)	29.00	21.00
No. C33 (1)	25.00	18.50
No. C26 (1)	7.25	4.50
No. C31 (1)	1.00	1.00
No. C17 (1)	3.75	3.75
Set total (8) Stamps	84.00	61.10

Freedom From Hunger

World Map and Wheat Emblem CD112

U.N. Food and Agriculture Organization's "Freedom from Hunger" campaign.

1963, Mar. 21

Cameroun	B37-B38
Cent. Africa	B2
Chad	B2
Congo, P.R.	B4
Dahomey	B16
Gabon	B5
Ivory Coast	B16
Madagascar	B21
Mauritania	B17
Niger	B15
Senegal	B17
Upper Volta	B2

Nos. B37-B38 (2)	2.25	.75
No. B2 (1)	1.25	1.25
No. B2 (1)	1.10	.50
No. B4 (1)	1.40	1.00
No. B16 (1)	.80	.80
No. B5 (1)	1.00	1.00
No. B16 (1)	1.50	1.50
No. B21 (1)	.60	.45
No. B17 (1)	.60	.60
No. B15 (1)	.75	.75
No. B17 (1)	.80	.50
No. B2 (1)	.75	.70
Set total (13) Stamps	12.80	9.80

Red Cross Centenary

CD113

Centenary of the International Red Cross.

1963, Sept. 2

Comoro Isls.	55
Fr. Polynesia	205
New Caledonia	328
St. Pierre & Miquelon	367
Somali Coast	297
Wallis & Futuna Isls.	165

No. 55 (1)	7.50	6.00
No. 205 (1)	15.00	12.00
No. 328 (1)	8.00	6.75
No. 367 (1)	12.00	5.50
No. 297 (1)	6.25	6.25
No. 165 (1)	4.00	4.00
Set total (6) Stamps	52.75	40.50

African Postal Union, 1963

UAMPT Emblem, Radio Masts, Plane and Mail CD114

Establishment of the African and Malagasy Posts and Telecommunications Union.

1963, Sept. 8

Cameroun	C47
Cent. Africa	C10
Chad	C9
Congo, P.R.	C13

Dahomey	C19
Gabon	C13
Ivory Coast	C25
Madagascar	C75
Mauritania	C22
Niger	C27
Rwanda	36
Senegal	C32
Upper Volta	C9

No. C47 (1)	2.25	1.00
No. C10 (1)	1.90	.90
No. C9 (1)	1.80	.60
No. C13 (1)	1.40	.75
No. C19 (1)	.75	.25
No. C13 (1)	1.90	.80
No. C25 (1)	2.50	1.50
No. C75 (1)	1.25	.80
No. C22 (1)	1.50	.60
No. C27 (1)	1.25	.60
No. 36 (1)	1.00	.75
No. C32 (1)	1.75	.50
No. C9 (1)	1.50	.75
Set total (13) Stamps	20.75	9.80

Air Afrique, 1963

Symbols of Flight — CD115

First anniversary of Air Afrique and inauguration of DC-8 service.

1963, Nov. 19

Cameroun	C48
Chad	C10
Congo, P.R.	C14
Gabon	C18
Ivory Coast	C26
Mauritania	C26
Niger	C35
Senegal	C33

No. C48 (1)	1.25	.40
No. C10 (1)	1.80	.60
No. C14 (1)	1.60	.60
No. C18 (1)	1.25	.65
No. C26 (1)	1.00	.50
No. C26 (1)	.70	.25
No. C35 (1)	1.00	.55
No. C33 (1)	2.00	.65
Set total (8) Stamps	10.60	4.20

Europafrica

Europe and Africa Linked — CD116

Signing of an economic agreement between the European Economic Community and the African and Malagasy Union, Yaounde, Cameroun, July 20, 1963.

1963-64

Cameroun	402
Cent. Africa	C12
Chad	C11
Congo, P.R.	C16
Gabon	C19
Ivory Coast	217
Niger	C43
Upper Volta	C11

No. 402 (1)	2.25	.60
No. C12 (1)	2.50	1.75
No. C11 (1)	1.60	.90
No. C16 (1)	1.60	1.00
No. C19 (1)	1.25	.75
No. 217 (1)	1.10	.35
No. C43 (1)	.85	.50
No. C11 (1)	1.50	.80
Set total (8) Stamps	12.65	6.25

Human Rights

Scales of Justice and Globe CD117

15th anniversary of the Universal Declaration of Human Rights.

1963, Dec. 10

Comoro Isls.	56
Fr. Polynesia	206
New Caledonia	329
St. Pierre & Miquelon	368
Somali Coast	300
Wallis & Futuna Isls.	166

No. 56 (1)	7.50	6.00
No. 205 (1)	15.00	12.00
No. 329 (1)	7.00	6.00
No. 368 (1)	7.00	3.50
No. 300 (1)	8.50	8.50
No. 166 (1)	7.00	7.00
Set total (6) Stamps	52.00	43.00

PHILATEC

Stamp Album, Champs Elysees Palace and Horses of Marly CD118

Intl. Philatelic and Postal Techniques Exhibition, Paris, June 5-21, 1964.

1963-64

Comoro Isls.	60
France	1078
Fr. Polynesia	207
New Caledonia	341
St. Pierre & Miquelon	369
Somali Coast	301
Wallis & Futuna Isls.	167

No. 60 (1)	4.00	3.50
No. 1078 (1)	.25	.25
No. 206 (1)	15.00	10.00
No. 341 (1)	6.50	6.50
No. 369 (1)	11.00	8.00
No. 301 (1)	7.75	7.75
No. 167 (1)	3.00	3.00
Set total (7) Stamps	47.50	39.00

Cooperation

CD119

Cooperation between France and the French-speaking countries of Africa and Madagascar.

1964

Cameroun	409-410
Cent. Africa	39
Chad	103
Congo, P.R.	121
Dahomey	193
France	1111
Gabon	175
Ivory Coast	221
Madagascar	360
Mauritania	181
Niger	143
Senegal	236
Togo	495

Nos. 409-410 (2)	2.50	.50
No. 39 (1)	.90	.50
No. 103 (1)	1.00	.25
No. 121 (1)	.90	.35
No. 193 (1)	.80	.35
No. 1111 (1)	.25	.25
No. 175 (1)	.90	.60
No. 221 (1)	1.10	.35

No. 360 (1)	.60	.25
No. 181 (1)	.60	.35
No. 143 (1)	.80	.40
No. 236 (1)	1.60	.85
No. 495 (1)	.70	.25
Set total (14) Stamps	12.65	5.25

ITU

Telegraph, Syncom Satellite and ITU Emblem CD120

Intl. Telecommunication Union, Cent.

1965, May 17

Comoro Isls.	C14
Fr. Polynesia	C33
Fr. So. & Antarctic Terr.	C8
New Caledonia	C40
New Hebrides	124-125
St. Pierre & Miquelon	C29
Somali Coast	C36
Wallis & Futuna Isls.	C20

No. C14 (1)	18.00	9.00
No. C33 (1)	80.00	52.50
No. C8 (1)	200.00	160.00
No. C40 (1)	10.00	8.00
Nos. 124-125 (2)	32.25	27.25
No. C29 (1)	24.00	11.50
No. C36 (1)	15.00	9.00
No. C20 (1)	16.00	16.00
Set total (9) Stamps	395.25	293.25

French Satellite A-1

Diamant Rocket and Launching Installation — CD121

Launching of France's first satellite, Nov. 26, 1965.

1965-66

Comoro Isls.	C16a
France	1138a
Reunion	359a
Fr. Polynesia	C41a
Fr. So. & Antarctic Terr.	C10a
New Caledonia	C45a
St. Pierre & Miquelon	C31a
Somali Coast	C40a
Wallis & Futuna Isls.	C23a

No. C16a (1)	9.00	9.00
No. 1138a (1)	.65	.65
No. 359a (1)	3.50	3.50
No. C41a (1)	14.00	14.00
No. C10a (1)	29.00	24.00
No. C45a (1)	7.00	7.00
No. C31a (1)	14.50	14.50
No. C40a (1)	7.00	7.00
No. C23a (1)	8.50	8.50
Set total (9) Stamps	93.15	87.65

French Satellite D-1

D-1 Satellite in Orbit — CD122

Launching of the D-1 satellite at Hammaguir, Algeria, Feb. 17, 1966.

1966

Comoro Isls.	C17
France	1148

Fr. Polynesia...............................C42
Fr. So. & Antarctic Terr. C11
New Caledonia...........................C46
St. Pierre & Miquelon...................C32
Somali Coast.............................C49
Wallis & Futuna Isls. C24

No. C17 (1)	4.00	4.00
No. 1148 (1)	.25	.25
No. C42 (1)	7.00	4.75
No. C11 (1)	57.50	40.00
No. C46 (1)	2.25	2.00
No. C32 (1)	9.00	6.00
No. C49 (1)	4.25	2.75
No. C24 (1)	3.50	3.50
Set total (8) Stamps	87.75	63.25

Air Afrique, 1966

Planes and Air Afrique
Emblem — CD123

Introduction of DC-8F planes by Air Afrique.

1966

Cameroun..................................C79
Cent. Africa C35
Chad.......................................C26
Congo, P.R...............................C42
Dahomey..................................C42
Gabon.....................................C47
Ivory Coast..............................C32
Mauritania...............................C57
Niger......................................C63
Senegal...................................C47
Togo.......................................C54
Upper Volta..............................C31

No. C79 (1)	.80	.25
No. C35 (1)	1.00	.50
No. C26 (1)	.85	.25
No. C42 (1)	1.00	.25
No. C42 (1)	.75	.25
No. C47 (1)	.90	.35
No. C32 (1)	1.00	.60
No. C57 (1)	.60	.30
No. C63 (1)	.70	.35
No. C47 (1)	.80	.30
No. C54 (1)	.80	.25
No. C31 (1)	.75	.50
Set total (12) Stamps	9.95	4.15

African Postal Union, 1967

Telecommunications Symbols and Map
of Africa — CD124

Fifth anniversary of the establishment of the
African and Malagasy Union of Posts and
Telecommunications, UAMPT.

1967

Cameroun..................................C90
Cent. Africa C46
Chad.......................................C37
Congo, P.R...............................C57
Dahomey..................................C61
Gabon.....................................C58
Ivory Coast..............................C34
Madagascar..............................C85
Mauritania...............................C65
Niger......................................C75
Rwanda C1-C3
Senegal...................................C60
Togo.......................................C81
Upper Volta..............................C50

No. C90 (1)	2.40	.65
No. C46 (1)	2.25	.85
No. C37 (1)	2.00	.60
No. C57 (1)	1.60	.60
No. C61 (1)	1.75	.95
No. C58 (1)	2.00	.85
No. C34 (1)	3.50	1.50
No. C85 (1)	1.25	.60
No. C65 (1)	1.25	.60
No. C75 (1)	1.40	.60

Nos. C1-C3 (3)	2.30	1.25
No. C60 (1)	1.75	.50
No. C81 (1)	1.90	.30
No. C50 (1)	1.80	.70
Set total (16) Stamps	27.15	10.55

Monetary Union

Gold Token of the
Ashantis, 17-18th
Centuries — CD125

West African Monetary Union, 5th anniv.

1967, Nov. 4

Dahomey 244
Ivory Coast...............................259
Mauritania................................238
Niger.......................................204
Senegal 294
Togo..623
Upper Volta...............................181

No. 244 (1)	.65	.65
No. 259 (1)	.85	.40
No. 238 (1)	.45	.25
No. 204 (1)	.55	.25
No. 294 (1)	.60	.25
No. 623 (1)	.60	.25
No. 181 (1)	.65	.35
Set total (7) Stamps	4.35	2.40

WHO Anniversary

Sun,
Flowers
and WHO
Emblem
CD126

World Health Organization, 20th anniv.

1968, May 4

Afars & Issas 317
Comoro Isls. 73
Fr. Polynesia.......................241-242
Fr. So. & Antarctic Terr. 31
New Caledonia 367
St. Pierre & Miquelon...................377
Wallis & Futuna Isls. 169

No. 317 (1)	3.00	3.00
No. 73 (1)	2.40	1.75
Nos. 241-242 (2)	22.00	12.75
No. 31 (1)	62.50	47.50
No. 367 (1)	4.00	2.25
No. 377 (1)	12.00	9.00
No. 169 (1)	5.75	5.75
Set total (8) Stamps	111.65	82.00

Human Rights Year

Human Rights
Flame — CD127

1968, Aug. 10

Afars & Issas 322-323
Comoro Isls. 76
Fr. Polynesia.......................243-244
Fr. So. & Antarctic Terr. 32
New Caledonia 369
St. Pierre & Miquelon...................382
Wallis & Futuna Isls. 170

Nos. 322-323 (2)	6.75	4.00
No. 76 (1)	3.25	3.25
Nos. 243-244 (2)	24.00	14.00
No. 32 (1)	55.00	47.50
No. 369 (1)	2.75	1.50
No. 382 (1)	8.00	5.50
No. 170 (1)	3.25	3.25
Set total (9) Stamps	103.00	79.00

2nd PHILEXAFRIQUE

CD128

Opening of PHILEXAFRIQUE, Abidjan, Feb.
14. Each stamp shows a local scene and
stamp.

1969, Feb. 14

Cameroun..................................C118
Cent. Africa C65
Chad.......................................C48
Congo, P.R...............................C77
Dahomey..................................C94
Gabon.....................................C82
Ivory Coast.........................C38-C40
Madagascar..............................C92
Mali.......................................C65
Mauritania...............................C80
Niger......................................C104
Senegal...................................C68
Togo.......................................C104
Upper Volta..............................C62

No. C118 (1)	3.25	1.25
No. C65 (1)	1.75	1.75
No. C48 (1)	2.40	1.00
No. C77 (1)	2.00	1.75
No. C94 (1)	2.25	2.25
No. C82 (1)	2.00	2.00
Nos. C38-C40 (3)	14.50	14.50
No. C92 (1)	1.75	.85
No. C65 (1)	1.75	1.00
No. C80 (1)	1.90	.75
No. C104 (1)	3.00	1.90
No. C68 (1)	2.00	1.40
No. C104 (1)	2.25	.45
No. C62 (1)	4.00	3.25
Set total (16) Stamps	44.80	34.10

Concorde

Concorde in
Flight
CD129

First flight of the prototype Concorde supersonic plane at Toulouse, Mar. 1, 1969.

1969

Afars & Issas C56
Comoro Isls. C29
France.....................................C42
Fr. Polynesia.............................C50
Fr. So. & Antarctic Terr. C18
New Caledonia C63
St. Pierre & Miquelon...................C40
Wallis & Futuna Isls. C30

No. C56 (1)	26.00	16.00
No. C29 (1)	18.00	12.00
No. C42 (1)	.75	.35
No. C50 (1)	55.00	35.00
No. C18 (1)	55.00	37.50
No. C63 (1)	27.50	20.00
No. C40 (1)	32.50	11.00
No. C30 (1)	15.00	10.00
Set total (8) Stamps	229.75	141.85

Development Bank

Bank
Emblem — CD130

African Development Bank, fifth anniv.

1969

Cameroun...................................499
Chad..217
Congo, P.R..........................181-182

Ivory Coast................................281
Mali...................................127-128
Mauritania................................267
Niger.......................................220
Senegal 317-318
Upper Volta...............................201

No. 499 (1)	.80	.25
No. 217 (1)	.90	.25
Nos. 181-182 (2)	1.00	.50
No. 281 (1)	.70	.40
Nos. 127-128 (2)	1.00	.50
No. 267 (1)	.60	.25
No. 220 (1)	.70	.30
Nos. 317-318 (2)	1.55	.50
No. 201 (1)	.65	.30
Set total (12) Stamps	7.90	3.25

ILO

ILO Headquarters, Geneva, and
Emblem — CD131

Intl. Labor Organization, 50th anniv.

1969-70

Afars & Issas 337
Comoro Isls. 83
Fr. Polynesia.......................251-252
Fr. So. & Antarctic Terr. 35
New Caledonia 379
St. Pierre & Miquelon...................396
Wallis & Futuna Isls. 172

No. 337 (1)	2.75	2.00
No. 83 (1)	1.25	.75
Nos. 251-252 (2)	24.00	12.50
No. 35 (1)	15.00	10.00
No. 379 (1)	2.25	1.10
No. 396 (1)	10.00	5.50
No. 172 (1)	2.75	2.75
Set total (8) Stamps	58.00	34.60

ASECNA

Map of
Africa,
Plane and
Airport
CD132

10th anniversary of the Agency for the
Security of Aerial Navigation in Africa and
Madagascar (ASECNA, Agence pour la
Securite de la Navigation Aerienne en Afrique
et a Madagascar).

1969-70

Cameroun...................................500
Cent. Africa 119
Chad..222
Congo, P.R................................197
Dahomey...................................269
Gabon......................................260
Ivory Coast................................287
Mali..130
Niger.......................................221
Senegal 321
Upper Volta...............................204

No. 500 (1)	2.00	.60
No. 119 (1)	2.00	.80
No. 222 (1)	1.00	.25
No. 197 (1)	2.00	.40
No. 269 (1)	.90	.55
No. 260 (1)	1.75	.75
No. 287 (1)	.90	.40
No. 130 (1)	.90	.40
No. 221 (1)	1.40	.70
No. 321 (1)	1.60	.50
No. 204 (1)	1.75	1.00
Set total (11) Stamps	16.20	6.35

U.P.U. Headquarters

CD133

New Universal Postal Union headquarters,
Bern, Switzerland.

1970

Afars & Issas	342
Algeria	443
Cameroun	503-504
Cent. Africa	125
Chad	225
Comoro Isls.	84
Congo, P.R.	216
Fr. Polynesia	261-262
Fr. So. & Antarctic Terr.	36
Gabon	258
Ivory Coast	295
Madagascar	444
Mali	134-135
Mauritania	283
New Caledonia	382
Niger	231-232
St. Pierre & Miquelon	397-398
Senegal	328-329
Tunisia	535
Wallis & Futuna Isls.	173

No. 342 (1)	2.50	1.40
No. 443 (1)	1.10	.40
Nos. 503-504 (2)	2.60	.55
No. 125 (1)	1.75	.70
No. 225 (1)	1.20	.25
No. 84 (1)	5.50	2.00
No. 216 (1)	1.00	.25
Nos. 261-262 (2)	20.00	10.00
No. 36 (1)	40.00	27.50
No. 258 (1)	.90	.55
No. 295 (1)	1.10	.50
No. 444 (1)	.55	.25
Nos. 134-135 (2)	1.05	.50
No. 283 (1)	.60	.30
No. 382 (1)	3.00	1.50
Nos. 231-232 (2)	1.50	.60
Nos. 397-398 (2)	34.00	16.25
Nos. 328-329 (2)	1.55	.55
No. 535 (1)	.60	.25
No. 173 (1)	3.25	3.25
Set total (26) Stamps	123.75	67.55

De Gaulle

CD134

First anniversary of the death of Charles de Gaulle, (1890-1970), President of France.

1971-72

Afars & Issas	356-357
Comoro Isls.	104-105
France	1325a
Fr. Polynesia	270-271
Fr. So. & Antarctic Terr.	52-53
New Caledonia	393-394
Reunion	380a
St. Pierre & Miquelon	417-418
Wallis & Futuna Isls.	177-178

Nos. 356-357 (2)	12.50	7.50
Nos. 104-105 (2)	9.00	5.75
No. 1325a (1)	3.00	7.50
Nos. 270-271 (2)	51.50	29.50
Nos. 52-53 (2)	40.00	23.00
Nos. 393-394 (2)	23.00	11.75
No. 380a (1)	9.25	8.00
Nos. 417-418 (2)	56.50	31.00
Nos. 177-178 (2)	20.00	16.25
Set total (16) Stamps	224.75	141.75

African Postal Union, 1971

UAMPT Building, Brazzaville, Congo — CD135

10th anniversary of the establishment of the African and Malagasy Posts and Telecommunications Union, UAMPT. Each stamp has a different native design.

1971, Nov. 13

Cameroun	C177
Cent. Africa	C89
Chad	C94

Congo, P.R.	C136
Dahomey	C146
Gabon	C120
Ivory Coast	C47
Mauritania	C113
Niger	C164
Rwanda	C8
Senegal	C105
Togo	C166
Upper Volta	C97

No. C177 (1)	2.00	.50
No. C89 (1)	2.25	.85
No. C94 (1)	1.50	.50
No. C136 (1)	1.60	.75
No. C146 (1)	1.75	.80
No. C120 (1)	1.75	.70
No. C47 (1)	2.00	1.00
No. C113 (1)	1.10	.65
No. C164 (1)	1.25	.60
No. C8 (1)	2.75	2.50
No. C105 (1)	1.60	.50
No. C166 (1)	1.25	.40
No. C97 (1)	1.50	.70
Set total (13) Stamps	22.30	10.45

West African Monetary Union

African Couple, City, Village and Commemorative Coin — CD136

West African Monetary Union, 10th anniv.

1972, Nov. 2

Dahomey	300
Ivory Coast	331
Mauritania	299
Niger	258
Senegal	374
Togo	825
Upper Volta	280

No. 300 (1)	.65	.25
No. 331 (1)	1.00	.50
No. 299 (1)	.75	.25
No. 258 (1)	.65	.30
No. 374 (1)	.50	.30
No. 825 (1)	.60	.25
No. 280 (1)	.60	.25
Set total (7) Stamps	4.75	2.10

African Postal Union, 1973

Telecommunications Symbols and Map of Africa — CD137

11th anniversary of the African and Malagasy Posts and Telecommunications Union (UAMPT).

1973, Sept. 12

Cameroun	574
Cent. Africa	194
Chad	294
Congo, P.R.	289
Dahomey	311
Gabon	320
Ivory Coast	361
Madagascar	500
Mauritania	304
Niger	287
Rwanda	540
Senegal	393
Togo	849
Upper Volta	297

No. 574 (1)	1.75	.40
No. 194 (1)	1.25	.75
No. 294 (1)	1.75	.40
No. 289 (1)	1.60	.50
No. 311 (1)	1.25	.55
No. 320 (1)	1.40	.75
No. 361 (1)	2.50	1.00
No. 500 (1)	1.10	.35
No. 304 (1)	1.10	.40
No. 287 (1)	.90	.60
No. 540 (1)	4.00	2.00
No. 393 (1)	1.60	.50

No. 849 (1)	1.00	.35
No. 297 (1)	1.25	.70
Set total (14) Stamps	22.45	9.25

Philexafrique II — Essen

CD138

CD139

Designs: Indigenous fauna, local and German stamps. Types CD138-CD139 printed horizontally and vertically se-tenant in sheets of 10 (2x5). Label between horizontal pairs alternately commemorates Philexafrique II, Libreville, Gabon, June 1978, and 2nd International Stamp Fair, Essen, Germany, Nov. 1-5.

1978-1979

Benin	C286a
Central Africa	C201a
Chad	C239a
Congo Republic	C246a
Djibouti	C122a
Gabon	C216a
Ivory Coast	C65a
Mali	C357a
Mauritania	C186a
Niger	C292a
Rwanda	C13a
Senegal	C147a
Togo	C364a

No. C286a (1)	9.00	8.50
No. C201a (1)	7.50	7.50
No. C239a (1)	7.50	4.00
No. C246a (1)	7.00	7.00
No. C122a (1)	6.50	6.50
No. C216a (1)	6.50	4.00
No. C65a (1)	9.00	9.00
No. C357a (1)	5.00	5.00
No. C186a (1)	5.50	5.00
No. C292a (1)	6.00	6.00
No. C13a (1)	4.00	4.00
No. C147a (1)	10.00	4.00
No. C364a (1)	3.00	1.50
Set total (13) Stamps	86.50	70.00

BRITISH COMMONWEALTH OF NATIONS

The listings follow established trade practices when these issues are offered as units by dealers. The Peace issue, for example, includes only one stamp from the Indian state of Hyderabad. The U.P.U. issue includes the Egypt set. Pairs are included for those varieties issued with bilingual designs se-tenant.

Silver Jubilee

Windsor Castle and King George V CD301

Reign of King George V, 25th anniv.

1935

Antigua	77-80
Ascension	33-36
Bahamas	92-95
Barbados	186-189
Basutoland	11-14

Bechuanaland Protectorate	117-120
Bermuda	100-103
British Guiana	223-226
British Honduras	108-111
Cayman Islands	81-84
Ceylon	260-263
Cyprus	136-139
Dominica	90-93
Falkland Islands	77-80
Fiji	110-113
Gambia	125-128
Gibraltar	100-103
Gilbert & Ellice Islands	33-36
Gold Coast	108-111
Grenada	124-127
Hong Kong	147-150
Jamaica	109-112
Kenya, Uganda, Tanzania	42-45
Leeward Islands	96-99
Malta	184-187
Mauritius	204-207
Montserrat	85-88
Newfoundland	226-229
Nigeria	34-37
Northern Rhodesia	18-21
Nyasaland Protectorate	47-50
St. Helena	111-114
St. Kitts-Nevis	72-75
St. Lucia	91-94
St. Vincent	134-137
Seychelles	118-121
Sierra Leone	166-169
Solomon Islands	60-63
Somaliland Protectorate	77-80
Straits Settlements	213-216
Swaziland	20-23
Trinidad & Tobago	43-46
Turks & Caicos Islands	71-74
Virgin Islands	69-72

The following have different designs but are included in the omnibus set:

Great Britain	226-229
Offices in Morocco (Sp. Curr.)	67-70
Offices in Morocco (Br. Curr.)	226-229
Offices in Morocco (Fr. Curr.)	422-425
Offices in Morocco (Tangier)	508-510
Australia	152-154
Canada	211-216
Cook Islands	98-100
India	142-148
Nauru	31-34
New Guinea	46-47
New Zealand	199-201
Niue	67-69
Papua	114-117
Samoa	163-165
South Africa	68-71
Southern Rhodesia	33-36
South-West Africa	121-124

Nos. 77-80 (4)	20.25	23.25
Nos. 33-36 (4)	58.50	127.50
Nos. 92-95 (4)	25.00	46.00
Nos. 186-189 (4)	30.00	50.30
Nos. 11-14 (4)	11.60	21.25
Nos. 117-120 (4)	15.75	36.00
Nos. 100-103 (4)	16.80	58.50
Nos. 223-226 (4)	22.35	35.50
Nos. 108-111 (4)	15.25	16.35
Nos. 81-84 (4)	21.60	24.50
Nos. 260-263 (4)	10.40	21.60
Nos. 136-139 (4)	39.75	34.40
Nos. 90-93 (4)	18.85	19.85
Nos. 77-80 (4)	55.00	14.75
Nos. 110-113 (4)	20.25	34.00
Nos. 125-128 (4)	13.05	25.25
Nos. 100-103 (4)	28.75	62.75
Nos. 33-36 (4)	36.80	67.00
Nos. 108-111 (4)	25.75	78.10
Nos. 124-127 (4)	16.70	40.60
Nos. 147-150 (4)	59.00	18.75
Nos. 109-112 (4)	17.00	39.00
Nos. 42-45 (4)	8.75	11.00
Nos. 96-99 (4)	35.75	49.60
Nos. 184-187 (4)	22.00	33.70
Nos. 204-207 (4)	44.60	58.25
Nos. 85-88 (4)	10.25	30.25
Nos. 226-229 (4)	17.50	12.05
Nos. 34-37 (4)	17.50	70.00
Nos. 18-21 (4)	17.00	15.00
Nos. 47-50 (4)	39.75	80.25
Nos. 111-114 (4)	31.15	36.50
Nos. 72-75 (4)	10.80	18.65
Nos. 91-94 (4)	16.00	20.80
Nos. 134-137 (4)	9.45	21.25
Nos. 118-121 (4)	15.75	40.00
Nos. 166-169 (4)	23.60	50.35
Nos. 60-63 (4)	29.00	38.00
Nos. 77-80 (4)	17.00	48.25
Nos. 213-216 (4)	15.00	25.10
Nos. 20-23 (4)	6.80	18.25
Nos. 43-46 (4)	14.05	27.75
Nos. 71-74 (4)	8.40	14.50
Nos. 69-72 (4)	25.00	55.25
Nos. 226-229 (4)	5.15	4.40

Nos. 67-70 (4)	14.35	26.10
Nos. 226-229 (4)	8.20	28.90
Nos. 422-425 (4)	3.90	2.00
Nos. 508-510 (3)	18.80	23.85
Nos. 152-154 (3)	49.50	45.35
Nos. 211-216 (6)	23.85	13.35
Nos. 98-100 (3)	9.65	12.00
Nos. 142-148 (7)	28.85	14.00
Nos. 31-34 (4)	9.90	9.90
Nos. 46-47 (2)	4.35	1.70
Nos. 199-201 (3)	23.00	28.50
Nos. 67-69 (3)	11.80	26.50
Nos. 114-117 (4)	9.20	17.50
Nos. 163-165 (3)	4.40	6.50
Nos. 68-71 (4)	57.50	153.00
Nos. 33-36 (4)	27.75	45.25
Nos. 121-124 (4)	13.00	36.10
Set total (245) Stamps	1,337.	2,145.

Coronation

Queen Elizabeth and King George VI CD302

1937

Aden	13-15
Antigua	81-83
Ascension	37-39
Bahamas	97-99
Barbados	190-192
Basutoland	15-17
Bechuanaland Protectorate	121-123
Bermuda	115-117
British Guiana	227-229
British Honduras	112-114
Cayman Islands	97-99
Ceylon	275-277
Cyprus	140-142
Dominica	94-96
Falkland Islands	81-83
Fiji	114-116
Gambia	129-131
Gibraltar	104-106
Gilbert & Ellice Islands	37-39
Gold Coast	112-114
Grenada	128-130
Hong Kong	151-153
Jamaica	113-115
Kenya, Uganda, Tanzania	60-62
Leeward Islands	100-102
Malta	188-190
Mauritius	208-210
Montserrat	89-91
Newfoundland	230-232
Nigeria	50-52
Northern Rhodesia	22-24
Nyasaland Protectorate	51-53
St. Helena	115-117
St. Kitts-Nevis	76-78
St. Lucia	107-109
St. Vincent	138-140
Seychelles	122-124
Sierra Leone	170-172
Solomon Islands	64-66
Somaliland Protectorate	81-83
Straits Settlements	235-237
Swaziland	24-26
Trinidad & Tobago	47-49
Turks & Caicos Islands	75-77
Virgin Islands	73-75

The following have different designs but are included in the omnibus set:

Great Britain	234
Offices in Morocco (Sp. Curr.)	82
Offices in Morocco (Fr. Curr.)	439
Offices in Morocco (Tangier)	514
Canada	237
Cook Islands	109-111
Nauru	35-38
Newfoundland	233-243
New Guinea	48-51
New Zealand	223-225
Niue	70-72
Papua	118-121
South Africa	74-78
Southern Rhodesia	38-41
South-West Africa	125-132

Nos. 13-15 (3)	2.70	5.65
Nos. 81-83 (3)	1.85	8.00
Nos. 37-39 (3)	2.75	2.75
Nos. 97-99 (3)	1.05	3.05
Nos. 190-192 (3)	1.10	1.95
Nos. 15-17 (3)	1.15	3.00
Nos. 121-123 (3)	.95	3.35
Nos. 115-117 (3)	1.25	5.00
Nos. 227-229 (3)	1.45	3.05
Nos. 112-114 (3)	1.20	2.40
Nos. 97-99 (3)	1.10	2.70
Nos. 275-277 (3)	8.25	10.35

Nos. 140-142 (3)	3.75	6.50
Nos. 94-96 (3)	.85	2.40
Nos. 81-83 (3)	2.90	2.30
Nos. 114-116 (3)	1.35	5.75
Nos. 129-131 (3)	.85	3.95
Nos. 104-106 (3)	2.25	6.45
Nos. 37-39 (3)	.85	2.15
Nos. 112-114 (3)	3.10	10.00
Nos. 128-130 (3)	1.00	.85
Nos. 151-153 (3)	23.00	12.50
Nos. 113-115 (3)	1.25	1.25
Nos. 60-62 (3)	1.00	2.35
Nos. 100-102 (3)	1.55	4.00
Nos. 188-190 (3)	1.25	1.60
Nos. 208-210 (3)	1.75	3.50
Nos. 89-91 (3)	1.00	3.35
Nos. 230-232 (3)	7.00	2.80
Nos. 50-52 (3)	3.25	8.50
Nos. 22-24 (3)	.95	2.25
Nos. 51-53 (3)	1.05	1.30
Nos. 115-117 (3)	1.45	2.05
Nos. 76-78 (3)	.95	2.15
Nos. 107-109 (3)	1.05	2.05
Nos. 138-140 (3)	.80	4.75
Nos. 122-124 (3)	1.20	1.90
Nos. 170-172 (3)	1.95	5.65
Nos. 64-66 (3)	.90	2.00
Nos. 81-83 (3)	1.10	3.50
Nos. 235-237 (3)	3.25	1.60
Nos. 24-26 (3)	.75	2.70
Nos. 47-49 (3)	1.00	1.00
Nos. 75-77 (3)	1.30	1.15
Nos. 73-75 (3)	2.20	6.90

No. 234 (1)	.25	.25
No. 82 (1)	.80	.80
No. 439 (1)	.35	.25
No. 514 (1)	.55	.55
No. 237 (1)	.35	.25
Nos. 109-111 (3)	.85	.80
Nos. 35-38 (4)	1.10	5.50
Nos. 233-243 (11)	41.90	30.40
Nos. 48-51 (4)	1.40	7.90
Nos. 223-225 (3)	1.75	2.25
Nos. 70-72 (3)	.80	2.05
Nos. 118-121 (4)	1.60	5.25
Nos. 74-78 (5)	7.60	9.35
Nos. 38-41 (4)	3.55	15.50
Nos. 125-132 (8)	5.00	8.40
Set total (189) Stamps	170.50	261.90

Peace

King George VI and Parliament Buildings, London CD303

Return to peace at the close of World War II.

1945-46

Aden	28-29
Antigua	96-97
Ascension	50-51
Bahamas	130-131
Barbados	207-208
Bermuda	131-132
British Guiana	242-243
British Honduras	127-128
Cayman Islands	112-113
Ceylon	293-294
Cyprus	156-157
Dominica	112-113
Falkland Islands	97-98
Falkland Islands Dep	1L9-1L10
Fiji	137-138
Gambia	144-145
Gibraltar	119-120
Gilbert & Ellice Islands	52-53
Gold Coast	128-129
Grenada	143-144
Jamaica	136-137
Kenya, Uganda, Tanzania	90-91
Leeward Islands	116-117
Malta	206-207
Mauritius	223-224
Montserrat	104-105
Nigeria	71-72
Northern Rhodesia	46-47
Nyasaland Protectorate	82-83
Pitcairn Islands	9-10
St. Helena	128-129
St. Kitts-Nevis	91-92
St. Lucia	127-128
St. Vincent	152-153
Seychelles	149-150
Sierra Leone	186-187
Solomon Islands	80-81
Somaliland Protectorate	108-109
Trinidad & Tobago	62-63
Turks & Caicos Islands	90-91
Virgin Islands	88-89

The following have different designs but are included in the omnibus set:

Great Britain	264-265
Offices in Morocco (Tangier)	523-524

Aden	
Kathiri State of Seiyun	12-13
Qu'aiti State of Shihr and Mukalla	12-13
Australia	200-202
Basutoland	29-31
Bechuanaland Protectorate	137-139
Burma	66-69
Cook Islands	127-130
Hong Kong	174-175
India	195-198
Hyderabad	51-53
New Zealand	247-257
Niue	90-93
Pakistan-Bahawalpur	O16
Samoa	191-194
South Africa	100-102
Southern Rhodesia	67-70
South-West Africa	153-155
Swaziland	38-40
Zanzibar	222-223

Nos. 28-29 (2)	.95	2.50
Nos. 96-97 (2)	.50	.80
Nos. 50-51 (2)	.80	2.00
Nos. 130-131 (2)	.50	1.40
Nos. 207-208 (2)	.50	1.10
Nos. 131-132 (2)	.55	.55
Nos. 242-243 (2)	1.05	1.40
Nos. 127-128 (2)	.50	.50
Nos. 112-113 (2)	.80	.80
Nos. 293-294 (2)	.60	2.10
Nos. 156-157 (2)	.90	.70
Nos. 112-113 (2)	.50	.50
Nos. 97-98 (2)	.90	1.35
Nos. 1L9-1L10 (2)	1.30	1.00
Nos. 137-138 (2)	.75	1.75
Nos. 144-145 (2)	.50	.95
Nos. 119-120 (2)	.75	1.00
Nos. 52-53 (2)	.50	1.10
Nos. 128-129 (2)	1.85	3.75
Nos. 143-144 (2)	.50	.95
Nos. 136-137 (2)	.80	12.50
Nos. 90-91 (2)	.65	.65
Nos. 116-117 (2)	.50	1.50
Nos. 206-207 (2)	.65	2.00
Nos. 223-224 (2)	.50	1.05
Nos. 104-105 (2)	.50	.50
Nos. 71-72 (2)	.70	2.75
Nos. 46-47 (2)	1.25	2.00
Nos. 82-83 (2)	.50	.50
Nos. 9-10 (2)	1.40	1.40
Nos. 128-129 (2)	.65	.70
Nos. 91-92 (2)	.50	.50
Nos. 127-128 (2)	.50	.60
Nos. 152-153 (2)	.50	.50
Nos. 149-150 (2)	.55	.50
Nos. 186-187 (2)	.50	.50
Nos. 80-81 (2)	.50	1.50
Nos. 108-109 (2)	.70	.50
Nos. 62-63 (2)	.50	.50
Nos. 90-91 (2)	.50	.50
Nos. 88-89 (2)	.50	.50

Nos. 264-265 (2)	.50	.50
Nos. 523-524 (2)	1.50	3.00
Nos. 12-13 (2)	.50	.90
Nos. 12-13 (2)	.50	1.25
Nos. 200-202 (3)	1.60	1.25
Nos. 29-31 (3)	2.10	2.60
Nos. 137-139 (3)	2.05	4.75
Nos. 66-69 (4)	1.50	1.25
Nos. 127-130 (4)	2.00	1.85
Nos. 174-175 (2)	6.75	3.15
Nos. 195-198 (4)	5.60	5.50
Nos. 51-53 (3)	1.50	1.70
Nos. 247-257 (11)	3.35	3.65
Nos. 90-93 (4)	1.70	2.20
No. O16 (1)	5.50	7.00
Nos. 191-194 (4)	2.05	1.00
Nos. 100-102 (3)	1.00	3.25
Nos. 67-70 (4)	1.40	1.75
Nos. 153-155 (3)	1.85	3.25
Nos. 38-40 (3)	2.40	5.50
Nos. 222-223 (2)	.65	1.00
Set total (151) Stamps	74.55	114.15

Silver Wedding

King George VI and Queen Elizabeth

CD304   CD305

1948-49

Aden	30-31
Kathiri State of Seiyun	14-15
Qu'aiti State of Shihr and Mukalla	14-15
Antigua	98-99
Ascension	52-53
Bahamas	148-149
Barbados	210-211
Basutoland	39-40
Bechuanaland Protectorate	147-148
Bermuda	133-134
British Guiana	244-245
British Honduras	129-130
Cayman Islands	116-117
Cyprus	158-159
Dominica	114-115
Falkland Islands	99-100
Falkland Islands Dep	1L11-1L12
Fiji	139-140
Gambia	146-147
Gibraltar	121-122
Gilbert & Ellice Islands	54-55
Gold Coast	142-143
Grenada	145-146
Hong Kong	178-179
Jamaica	138-139
Kenya, Uganda, Tanzania	92-93
Leeward Islands	118-119
Malaya	
Johore	128-129
Kedah	55-56
Kelantan	44-45
Malacca	1-2
Negri Sembilan	36-37
Pahang	44-45
Penang	1-2
Perak	99-100
Perlis	1-2
Selangor	74-75
Trengganu	47-48
Malta	223-224
Mauritius	229-230
Montserrat	106-107
Nigeria	73-74
North Borneo	238-239
Northern Rhodesia	48-49
Nyasaland Protectorate	85-86
Pitcairn Islands	11-12
St. Helena	130-131
St. Kitts-Nevis	93-94
St. Lucia	129-130
St. Vincent	154-155
Sarawak	174-175
Seychelles	151-152
Sierra Leone	188-189
Singapore	21-22
Solomon Islands	82-83
Somaliland Protectorate	110-111
Swaziland	48-49
Trinidad & Tobago	64-65
Turks & Caicos Islands	92-93
Virgin Islands	90-91
Zanzibar	224-225

The following have different designs but are included in the omnibus set:

Great Britain	267-268
Offices in Morocco (Sp. Curr.)	93-94
Offices in Morocco (Tangier)	525-526
Bahrain	62-63
Kuwait	82-83
Oman	25-26
South Africa	106
South-West Africa	159

Nos. 30-31 (2)	40.40	56.50
Nos. 14-15 (2)	17.85	16.00
Nos. 14-15 (2)	18.55	12.50
Nos. 98-99 (2)	13.55	15.75
Nos. 52-53 (2)	55.55	50.45
Nos. 148-149 (2)	45.25	40.30
Nos. 210-211 (2)	18.35	13.55
Nos. 39-40 (2)	52.80	55.25
Nos. 147-148 (2)	42.85	47.75
Nos. 133-134 (2)	47.75	55.25
Nos. 244-245 (2)	24.25	28.45
Nos. 129-130 (2)	25.25	53.20
Nos. 116-117 (2)	25.25	33.50
Nos. 158-159 (2)	58.50	78.05
Nos. 114-115 (2)	25.25	32.75
Nos. 99-100 (2)	112.10	76.10
Nos. 1L11-1L12 (2)	4.25	6.00
Nos. 139-140 (2)	18.20	11.50
Nos. 146-147 (2)	21.25	21.25
Nos. 121-122 (2)	61.00	78.00
Nos. 54-55 (2)	14.25	26.25
Nos. 142-143 (2)	35.25	48.20
Nos. 145-146 (2)	21.75	21.75
Nos. 178-179 (2)	283.50	96.50
Nos. 138-139 (2)	27.85	60.25
Nos. 92-93 (2)	50.25	67.75
Nos. 118-119 (2)	7.00	8.25
Nos. 128-129 (2)	29.25	53.25
Nos. 55-56 (2)	35.25	50.25
Nos. 44-45 (2)	35.75	62.75
Nos. 1-2 (2)	35.40	49.75
Nos. 36-37 (2)	28.10	38.20
Nos. 44-45 (2)	28.00	38.05
Nos. 1-2 (2)	40.50	37.80

Nos. 99-100 (2)	27.80	37.75
Nos. 1-2 (2)	33.50	58.00
Nos. 74-75 (2)	30.25	25.30
Nos. 47-48 (2)	32.75	61.75
Nos. 223-224 (2)	40.55	45.25
Nos. 229-230 (2)	19.25	45.25
Nos. 106-107 (2)	8.75	17.25
Nos. 73-74 (2)	17.85	22.80
Nos. 238-239 (2)	35.30	45.75
Nos. 48-49 (2)	100.30	90.25
Nos. 85-86 (2)	18.25	30.25
Nos. 11-12 (2)	44.75	48.50
Nos. 130-131 (2)	32.80	42.80
Nos. 93-94 (2)	11.25	10.50
Nos. 129-130 (2)	22.25	40.25
Nos. 154-155 (2)	27.75	30.25
Nos. 174-175 (2)	50.40	52.90
Nos. 151-152 (2)	16.25	48.25
Nos. 188-189 (2)	25.25	29.75
Nos. 21-22 (2)	116.00	45.40
Nos. 82-83 (2)	13.40	13.40
Nos. 110-111 (2)	8.40	8.75
Nos. 48-49 (2)	40.30	47.75
Nos. 64-65 (2)	32.75	38.25
Nos. 92-93 (2)	11.25	16.25
Nos. 90-91 (2)	16.25	22.25
Nos. 224-225 (2)	29.60	38.00
Nos. 267-268 (2)	30.40	25.25
Nos. 93-94 (2)	20.10	25.35
Nos. 525-526 (2)	23.10	29.25
Nos. 62-63 (2)	38.50	57.75
Nos. 82-83 (2)	69.50	45.50
Nos. 25-26 (2)	41.00	42.50
No. 106 (1)	.80	1.00
No. 159 (1)	1.10	.35
Set total (136) Stamps	2,488.	2,681.

U.P.U.

Mercury and Symbols of Communications — CD306

Plane, Ship and Hemispheres — CD307

Mercury Scattering Letters over Globe CD308

U.P.U. Monument, Bern CD309

Universal Postal Union, 75th anniversary.

1949

Aden	32-35
Kathiri State of Seiyun	16-19
Qu'aiti State of Shihr and Mukalla	16-19
Antigua	100-103
Ascension	57-60
Bahamas	150-153
Barbados	212-215
Basutoland	41-44
Bechuanaland Protectorate	149-152
Bermuda	138-141
British Guiana	246-249
British Honduras	137-140
Brunei	79-82
Cayman Islands	118-121
Cyprus	160-163
Dominica	116-119
Falkland Islands	103-106
Falkland Islands Dep	1L14-1L17
Fiji	141-144
Gambia	148-151
Gibraltar	123-126

Gilbert & Ellice Islands	56-59
Gold Coast	144-147
Grenada	147-150
Hong Kong	180-183
Jamaica	142-145
Kenya, Uganda, Tanzania	94-97
Leeward Islands	126-129
Malaya	
Johore	151-154
Kedah	57-60
Kelantan	46-49
Malacca	18-21
Negri Sembilan	59-62
Pahang	46-49
Penang	23-26
Perak	101-104
Perlis	3-6
Selangor	76-79
Trengganu	49-52
Malta	225-228
Mauritius	231-234
Montserrat	108-111
New Hebrides, British	62-65
New Hebrides, French	79-82
Nigeria	75-78
North Borneo	240-243
Northern Rhodesia	50-53
Nyasaland Protectorate	87-90
Pitcairn Islands	13-16
St. Helena	132-135
St. Kitts-Nevis	95-98
St. Lucia	131-134
St. Vincent	170-173
Sarawak	176-179
Seychelles	153-156
Sierra Leone	190-193
Singapore	23-26
Solomon Islands	84-87
Somaliland Protectorate	112-115
Southern Rhodesia	71-72
Swaziland	50-53
Tonga	87-90
Trinidad & Tobago	66-69
Turks & Caicos Islands	101-104
Virgin Islands	92-95
Zanzibar	226-229

The following have different designs but are included in the omnibus set:

Great Britain	276-279
Offices in Morocco (Tangier)	546-549
Australia	223
Bahrain	68-71
Burma	116-121
Ceylon	304-306
Egypt	281-283
India	223-226
Kuwait	89-92
Oman	31-34
Pakistan-Bahawalpur	26-29, O25-O28
South Africa	109-111
South-West Africa	160-162

Nos. 32-35 (4)	5.85	8.45
Nos. 16-19 (4)	2.75	16.00
Nos. 16-19 (4)	2.60	8.00
Nos. 100-103 (4)	3.60	7.70
Nos. 57-60 (4)	11.10	9.00
Nos. 150-153 (4)	5.35	9.30
Nos. 212-215 (4)	4.40	14.85
Nos. 41-44 (4)	4.75	10.00
Nos. 149-152 (4)	3.35	7.25
Nos. 138-141 (4)	4.75	6.15
Nos. 246-249 (4)	2.75	4.20
Nos. 137-140 (4)	3.30	6.35
Nos. 79-82 (4)	9.50	8.45
Nos. 118-121 (4)	3.60	7.25
Nos. 160-163 (4)	4.60	10.70
Nos. 116-119 (4)	2.30	5.65
Nos. 103-106 (4)	14.00	17.10
Nos. 1L14-1L17 (4)	14.60	14.50
Nos. 141-144 (4)	3.35	15.75
Nos. 148-151 (4)	2.75	7.10
Nos. 123-126 (4)	5.90	8.75
Nos. 56-59 (4)	4.30	13.00
Nos. 144-147 (4)	2.55	10.35
Nos. 147-150 (4)	2.15	3.55
Nos. 180-183 (4)	57.25	18.25
Nos. 142-145 (4)	2.25	2.45
Nos. 94-97 (4)	2.90	3.40
Nos. 126-129 (4)	3.05	9.60
Nos. 151-154 (4)	4.70	8.90
Nos. 57-60 (4)	4.80	12.00
Nos. 46-49 (4)	4.25	12.65
Nos. 18-21 (4)	4.25	17.30
Nos. 59-62 (4)	3.50	10.75
Nos. 46-49 (4)	3.00	7.25
Nos. 23-26 (4)	5.10	11.75
Nos. 101-104 (4)	3.65	10.75
Nos. 3-6 (4)	3.95	14.25
Nos. 76-79 (4)	4.90	12.30
Nos. 49-52 (4)	5.55	12.25
Nos. 225-228 (4)	4.50	4.85
Nos. 231-234 (4)	3.70	7.05
Nos. 108-111 (4)	3.30	4.35
Nos. 62-65 (4)	1.60	4.25
Nos. 79-82 (4)	15.40	22.00

Nos. 75-78 (4)	2.80	9.25
Nos. 240-243 (4)	7.15	6.50
Nos. 50-53 (4)	5.00	6.50
Nos. 87-90 (4)	4.05	4.05
Nos. 13-16 (4)	18.50	16.50
Nos. 132-135 (4)	4.85	7.10
Nos. 95-98 (4)	3.35	5.55
Nos. 131-134 (4)	2.55	3.85
Nos. 170-173 (4)	2.20	5.05
Nos. 176-179 (4)	8.15	10.85
Nos. 153-156 (4)	3.00	5.15
Nos. 190-193 (4)	2.90	9.15
Nos. 23-26 (4)	19.00	13.70
Nos. 84-87 (4)	4.05	4.90
Nos. 112-115 (4)	3.95	8.70
Nos. 71-72 (2)	1.95	2.25
Nos. 50-53 (4)	2.80	4.65
Nos. 87-90 (4)	3.00	5.25
Nos. 66-69 (4)	3.15	3.15
Nos. 101-104 (4)	2.70	4.10
Nos. 92-95 (4)	2.60	5.90
Nos. 226-229 (4)	5.45	13.50
Nos. 276-279 (4)	1.35	1.00
Nos. 546-549 (4)	3.20	10.15
No. 223 (1)	.40	.40
Nos. 68-71 (4)	4.75	16.50
Nos. 116-121 (6)	7.30	5.35
Nos. 304-306 (3)	3.35	4.25
Nos. 281-283 (3)	5.75	2.70
Nos. 223-226 (4)	27.25	10.50
Nos. 89-92 (4)	6.10	10.25
Nos. 31-34 (4)	8.00	15.75
Nos. 26-29, O25-O28 (8)	2.00	42.00
Nos. 109-111 (3)	2.00	2.70
Nos. 160-162 (3)	3.00	5.50
Set total (313) Stamps	453.35	718.40

University

Arms of University College CD310

Alice, Princess of Athlone CD311

1948 opening of University College of the West Indies at Jamaica.

1951

Antigua	104-105
Barbados	228-229
British Guiana	250-251
British Honduras	141-142
Dominica	120-121
Grenada	164-165
Jamaica	146-147
Leeward Islands	130-131
Montserrat	112-113
St. Kitts-Nevis	105-106
St. Lucia	149-150
St. Vincent	174-175
Trinidad & Tobago	70-71
Virgin Islands	96-97

Nos. 104-105 (2)	1.35	3.75
Nos. 228-229 (2)	1.75	2.65
Nos. 250-251 (2)	1.10	1.25
Nos. 141-142 (2)	1.40	2.20
Nos. 120-121 (2)	1.40	1.75
Nos. 164-165 (2)	1.20	1.60
Nos. 146-147 (2)	.90	.70
Nos. 130-131 (2)	1.35	4.00
Nos. 112-113 (2)	.85	2.00
Nos. 105-106 (2)	.90	2.25
Nos. 149-150 (2)	1.40	1.50
Nos. 174-175 (2)	1.00	2.15
Nos. 70-71 (2)	.75	.75
Nos. 96-97 (2)	1.50	3.75
Set total (28) Stamps	16.85	30.30

Coronation

Queen Elizabeth II — CD312

1953

Aden	47
Kathiri State of Seiyun	28
Qu'aiti State of Shihr and Mukalla	28
Antigua	106
Ascension	61
Bahamas	157
Barbados	234
Basutoland	45
Bechuanaland Protectorate	153
Bermuda	142
British Guiana	252
British Honduras	143
Cayman Islands	150
Cyprus	167
Dominica	141
Falkland Islands	121
Falkland Islands Dependencies	1L18
Fiji	145
Gambia	152
Gibraltar	131
Gilbert & Ellice Islands	60
Gold Coast	160
Grenada	170
Hong Kong	184
Jamaica	153
Kenya, Uganda, Tanzania	101
Leeward Islands	132
Malaya	
Johore	155
Kedah	82
Kelantan	71
Malacca	27
Negri Sembilan	63
Pahang	71
Penang	27
Perak	126
Perlis	28
Selangor	101
Trengganu	74
Malta	241
Mauritius	250
Montserrat	127
New Hebrides, British	77
Nigeria	79
North Borneo	260
Northern Rhodesia	60
Nyasaland Protectorate	96
Pitcairn Islands	19
St. Helena	139
St. Kitts-Nevis	119
St. Lucia	156
St. Vincent	185
Sarawak	196
Seychelles	172
Sierra Leone	194
Singapore	27
Solomon Islands	88
Somaliland Protectorate	127
Swaziland	54
Trinidad & Tobago	84
Tristan da Cunha	13
Turks & Caicos Islands	118
Virgin Islands	114

The following have different designs but are included in the omnibus set:

Great Britain	313-316
Offices in Morocco (Tangier)	579-582
Australia	259-261
Bahrain	92-95
Canada	330
Ceylon	317
Cook Islands	145-146
Kuwait	113-116
New Zealand	280-284
Niue	104-105
Oman	52-55
Samoa	214-215
South Africa	192
Southern Rhodesia	80
South-West Africa	244-248
Tokelau Islands	4

No. 47 (1)	1.25	1.25
No. 28 (1)	.75	1.50
No. 28 (1)	1.10	.60
No. 106 (1)	.40	.75
No. 61 (1)	1.25	2.75
No. 157 (1)	1.40	.75
No. 234 (1)	1.00	.25
No. 45 (1)	.50	.60
No. 153 (1)	.75	.35
No. 142 (1)	.85	.50
No. 252 (1)	.45	.25
No. 143 (1)	.60	.40
No. 150 (1)	.40	1.75
No. 167 (1)	1.60	.75
No. 141 (1)	.40	.40
No. 121 (1)	.90	1.50
No. 1L18 (1)	1.80	1.40
No. 145 (1)	1.00	.60
No. 152 (1)	.50	.50
No. 131 (1)	.50	.50
No. 60 (1)	.65	2.25
No. 160 (1)	1.00	.25

No. 170 (1)	.30	.25
No. 184 (1)	6.00	.35
No. 153 (1)	.70	.25
No. 101 (1)	.40	.25
No. 132 (1)	1.00	2.25
No. 155 (1)	1.40	.30
No. 82 (1)	2.25	.60
No. 71 (1)	1.60	1.60
No. 27 (1)	1.10	1.50
No. 63 (1)	1.40	.65
No. 71 (1)	2.25	.25
No. 27 (1)	1.75	.30
No. 126 (1)	1.60	.25
No. 28 (1)	1.75	4.00
No. 101 (1)	1.75	.25
No. 74 (1)	1.50	1.00
No. 241 (1)	.50	.25
No. 250 (1)	1.10	.25
No. 127 (1)	.60	.45
No. 77 (1)	.75	.60
No. 79 (1)	.45	.25
No. 260 (1)	1.75	1.00
No. 60 (1)	.70	.25
No. 96 (1)	.75	.75
No. 19 (1)	2.25	2.25
No. 139 (1)	1.25	1.25
No. 119 (1)	.35	.25
No. 156 (1)	.70	.35
No. 185 (1)	.50	.30
No. 196 (1)	2.00	1.75
No. 172 (1)	.80	.80
No. 194 (1)	.40	.40
No. 27 (1)	2.50	.40
No. 88 (1)	1.00	1.00
No. 127 (1)	.40	.25
No. 54 (1)	.30	.25
No. 84 (1)	.25	.25
No. 13 (1)	1.00	1.75
No. 118 (1)	.40	1.10
No. 114 (1)	.40	1.00
Nos. 313-316 (4)	16.35	5.95
Nos. 579-582 (4)	7.40	5.20
Nos. 259-261 (3)	3.60	2.75
Nos. 92-95 (4)	15.20	12.75
No. 330 (1)	.25	.25
No. 317 (1)	1.40	.25
Nos. 145-146 (2)	2.65	2.65
Nos. 113-116 (4)	16.00	8.50
Nos. 280-284 (5)	3.30	4.55
Nos. 104-105 (2)	1.60	1.60
Nos. 52-55 (4)	14.25	6.50
Nos. 214-215 (2)	2.50	.80
No. 192 (1)	.45	.30
No. 80 (1)	7.25	7.25
Nos. 244-248 (5)	3.00	2.35
No. 4 (1)	2.75	2.75
Set total (106) Stamps	164.90	115.45

Separate designs for each country for the visit of Queen Elizabeth II and the Duke of Edinburgh.

Royal Visit 1953

1953

Aden		62
Australia		267-269
Bermuda		163
Ceylon		318
Fiji		146
Gibraltar		146
Jamaica		154
Kenya, Uganda, Tanzania		102
Malta		242
New Zealand		286-287

No. 62 (1)	.65	4.00
Nos. 267-269 (3)	2.75	2.05
No. 163 (1)	.50	.25
No. 318 (1)	1.00	.25
No. 146 (1)	.65	.35
No. 146 (1)	.50	.30
No. 154 (1)	.50	.25
No. 102 (1)	.50	.25
No. 242 (1)	.35	.25
Nos. 286-287 (2)	.50	.50
Set total (13) Stamps	7.90	8.45

West Indies Federation

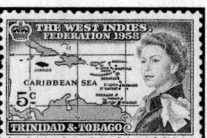

Map of the Caribbean
CD313

Federation of the West Indies, April 22, 1958.

1958

Antigua		122-124
Barbados		248-250
Dominica		161-163
Grenada		184-186
Jamaica		175-177
Montserrat		143-145
St. Kitts-Nevis		136-138
St. Lucia		170-172

St. Vincent		198-200
Trinidad & Tobago		86-88

Nos. 122-124 (3)	5.80	3.80
Nos. 248-250 (3)	1.60	2.90
Nos. 161-163 (3)	1.95	1.85
Nos. 184-186 (3)	1.50	1.20
Nos. 175-177 (3)	2.65	3.45
Nos. 143-145 (3)	2.35	1.35
Nos. 136-138 (3)	3.00	3.10
Nos. 170-172 (3)	2.05	2.80
Nos. 198-200 (3)	1.50	1.75
Nos. 86-88 (3)	.75	.90
Set total (30) Stamps	23.15	23.10

Freedom from Hunger

Protein Food
CD314

U.N. Food and Agricultural Organization's "Freedom from Hunger" campaign.

1963

Aden		65
Antigua		133
Ascension		89
Bahamas		180
Basutoland		83
Bechuanaland Protectorate		194
Bermuda		192
British Guiana		271
British Honduras		179
Brunei		100
Cayman Islands		168
Dominica		181
Falkland Islands		146
Fiji		198
Gambia		172
Gibraltar		161
Gilbert & Ellice Islands		76
Grenada		190
Hong Kong		218
Malta		291
Mauritius		270
Montserrat		150
New Hebrides, British		93
North Borneo		296
Pitcairn Islands		35
St. Helena		173
St. Lucia		179
St. Vincent		201
Sarawak		212
Seychelles		213
Solomon Islands		109
Swaziland		108
Tonga		127
Tristan da Cunha		68
Turks & Caicos Islands		138
Virgin Islands		140
Zanzibar		280

No. 65 (1)	1.50	1.75
No. 133 (1)	.35	.35
No. 89 (1)	1.00	.50
No. 180 (1)	.65	.65
No. 83 (1)	.50	.25
No. 194 (1)	.50	.50
No. 192 (1)	1.00	.50
No. 271 (1)	.45	.25
No. 179 (1)	.60	.25
No. 100 (1)	3.25	2.25
No. 168 (1)	.55	.30
No. 181 (1)	.30	.30
No. 146 (1)	10.50	2.50
No. 198 (1)	3.50	2.25
No. 172 (1)	.50	.25
No. 161 (1)	4.00	2.25
No. 76 (1)	1.40	.40
No. 190 (1)	.30	.25
No. 218 (1)	47.50	7.50
No. 291 (1)	2.00	2.00
No. 270 (1)	.45	.25
No. 150 (1)	.55	.35
No. 93 (1)	.60	.25
No. 296 (1)	1.90	.75
No. 35 (1)	10.00	4.50
No. 173 (1)	2.25	1.10
No. 179 (1)	.40	.40
No. 201 (1)	.90	.50
No. 212 (1)	1.60	1.75
No. 213 (1)	.85	.35
No. 109 (1)	3.00	.85
No. 108 (1)	.50	.50
No. 127 (1)	.60	.35
No. 68 (1)	.75	.35
No. 138 (1)	.50	.25
No. 140 (1)	.50	.50
No. 280 (1)	1.50	.80
Set total (37) Stamps	107.20	39.05

Red Cross Centenary

Red Cross and Elizabeth II
CD315

1963

Antigua		134-135
Ascension		90-91
Bahamas		183-184
Basutoland		84-85
Bechuanaland Protectorate		195-196
Bermuda		193-194
British Guiana		272-273
British Honduras		180-181
Cayman Islands		169-170
Dominica		182-183
Falkland Islands		147-148
Fiji		203-204
Gambia		173-174
Gibraltar		162-163
Gilbert & Ellice Islands		77-78
Grenada		191-192
Hong Kong		219-220
Jamaica		203-204
Malta		292-293
Mauritius		271-272
Montserrat		151-152
New Hebrides, British		94-95
Pitcairn Islands		36-37
St. Helena		174-175
St. Kitts-Nevis		143-144
St. Lucia		180-181
St. Vincent		202-203
Seychelles		214-215
Solomon Islands		110-111
South Arabia		1-2
Swaziland		109-110
Tonga		134-135
Tristan da Cunha		69-70
Turks & Caicos Islands		139-140
Virgin Islands		141-142

Nos. 134-135 (2)	1.00	2.00
Nos. 90-91 (2)	6.75	3.35
Nos. 183-184 (2)	2.30	2.80
Nos. 84-85 (2)	1.20	.90
Nos. 195-196 (2)	.95	.85
Nos. 193-194 (2)	3.00	2.80
Nos. 272-273 (2)	.85	.60
Nos. 180-181 (2)	1.00	2.50
Nos. 169-170 (2)	1.10	3.00
Nos. 182-183 (2)	.70	1.05
Nos. 147-148 (2)	18.00	5.50
Nos. 203-204 (2)	3.25	2.80
Nos. 173-174 (2)	.75	1.00
Nos. 162-163 (2)	6.25	5.40
Nos. 77-78 (2)	2.00	3.50
Nos. 191-192 (2)	.80	.50
Nos. 219-220 (2)	35.00	7.35
Nos. 203-204 (2)	.75	1.65
Nos. 292-293 (2)	2.50	4.75
Nos. 271-272 (2)	.85	.50
Nos. 151-152 (2)	1.00	.75
Nos. 94-95 (2)	1.00	1.00
Nos. 36-37 (2)	6.50	5.50
Nos. 174-175 (2)	1.70	2.30
Nos. 143-144 (2)	.90	.90
Nos. 180-181 (2)	1.25	1.25
Nos. 202-203 (2)	.90	.90
Nos. 214-215 (2)	1.00	1.50
Nos. 110-111 (2)	1.25	1.15
Nos. 1-2 (2)	1.25	1.25
Nos. 109-110 (2)	1.10	1.10
Nos. 134-135 (2)	1.00	1.25
Nos. 69-70 (2)	1.15	.80
Nos. 139-140 (2)	.85	.75
Nos. 141-142 (2)	.80	1.25
Set total (70) Stamps	110.65	73.95

Shakespeare

Shakespeare Memorial Theatre, Stratford-on-Avon — CD316

400th anniversary of the birth of William Shakespeare.

1964

Antigua		151
Bahamas		201
Bechuanaland Protectorate		197
Cayman Islands		171

Dominica		184
Falkland Islands		149
Gambia		192
Gibraltar		164
Montserrat		153
St. Lucia		196
Turks & Caicos Islands		141
Virgin Islands		143

No. 151 (1)	.35	.25
No. 201 (1)	.60	.35
No. 197 (1)	.35	.35
No. 171 (1)	.35	.30
No. 184 (1)	.35	.35
No. 149 (1)	1.60	.50
No. 192 (1)	.35	.25
No. 164 (1)	.65	.55
No. 153 (1)	.35	.25
No. 196 (1)	.45	.25
No. 141 (1)	.40	.25
No. 143 (1)	.45	.45
Set total (12) Stamps	6.25	4.10

ITU

ITU Emblem
CD317

Intl. Telecommunication Union, cent.

1965

Antigua		153-154
Ascension		92-93
Bahamas		219-220
Barbados		265-266
Basutoland		101-102
Bechuanaland Protectorate		202-203
Bermuda		196-197
British Guiana		293-294
British Honduras		187-188
Brunei		116-117
Cayman Islands		172-173
Dominica		185-186
Falkland Islands		154-155
Fiji		211-212
Gibraltar		167-168
Gilbert & Ellice Islands		87-88
Grenada		205-206
Hong Kong		221-222
Mauritius		291-292
Montserrat		157-158
New Hebrides, British		108-109
Pitcairn Islands		52-53
St. Helena		180-181
St. Kitts-Nevis		163-164
St. Lucia		197-198
St. Vincent		224-225
Seychelles		218-219
Solomon Islands		126-127
Swaziland		115-116
Tristan da Cunha		85-86
Turks & Caicos Islands		142-143
Virgin Islands		159-160

Nos. 153-154 (2)	1.45	1.35
Nos. 92-93 (2)	1.90	1.30
Nos. 219-220 (2)	1.35	1.50
Nos. 265-266 (2)	1.50	1.25
Nos. 101-102 (2)	.85	.65
Nos. 202-203 (2)	1.10	.75
Nos. 196-197 (2)	2.15	2.25
Nos. 293-294 (2)	.50	.50
Nos. 187-188 (2)	.75	.75
Nos. 116-117 (2)	1.75	1.75
Nos. 172-173 (2)	1.00	.85
Nos. 185-186 (2)	.55	.55
Nos. 154-155 (2)	6.75	3.15
Nos. 211-212 (2)	2.00	1.05
Nos. 167-168 (2)	9.00	5.95
Nos. 87-88 (2)	.85	.60
Nos. 205-206 (2)	.50	.50
Nos. 221-222 (2)	24.50	3.80
Nos. 291-292 (2)	1.10	.50
Nos. 157-158 (2)	1.05	1.15
Nos. 108-109 (2)	.65	.50
Nos. 52-53 (2)	6.25	4.30
Nos. 180-181 (2)	.80	.60
Nos. 163-164 (2)	.60	.60
Nos. 197-198 (2)	1.25	1.25
Nos. 224-225 (2)	.80	.50
Nos. 218-219 (2)	.75	.60
Nos. 126-127 (2)	.70	.55
Nos. 115-116 (2)	.70	.70
Nos. 85-86 (2)	1.00	.65
Nos. 142-143 (2)	.75	.50
Nos. 159-160 (2)	.85	.85
Set total (64) Stamps	75.70	42.15

Intl. Cooperation Year

ICY Emblem CD318

1965

Antigua	155-156
Ascension	94-95
Bahamas	222-223
Basutoland	103-104
Bechuanaland Protectorate	204-205
Bermuda	199-200
British Guiana	295-296
British Honduras	189-190
Brunei	118-119
Cayman Islands	174-175
Dominica	187-188
Falkland Islands	156-157
Fiji	213-214
Gibraltar	169-170
Gilbert & Ellice Islands	104-105
Grenada	207-208
Hong Kong	223-224
Mauritius	293-294
Montserrat	176-177
New Hebrides, British	110-111
New Hebrides, French	126-127
Pitcairn Islands	54-55
St. Helena	182-183
St. Kitts-Nevis	165-166
St. Lucia	199-200
Seychelles	220-221
Solomon Islands	143-144
South Arabia	17-18
Swaziland	117-118
Tristan da Cunha	87-88
Turks & Caicos Islands	144-145
Virgin Islands	161-162

Nos. 155-156 (2)	.55	.50
Nos. 94-95 (2)	1.30	1.40
Nos. 222-223 (2)	.65	1.90
Nos. 103-104 (2)	.75	.85
Nos. 204-205 (2)	.85	1.00
Nos. 199-200 (2)	2.05	1.25
Nos. 295-296 (2)	.55	.50
Nos. 189-190 (2)	.60	.55
Nos. 118-119 (2)	.85	.85
Nos. 174-175 (2)	1.00	.75
Nos. 187-188 (2)	.55	.55
Nos. 156-157 (2)	6.00	1.65
Nos. 213-214 (2)	1.95	1.25
Nos. 169-170 (2)	1.25	2.75
Nos. 104-105 (2)	.85	.60
Nos. 207-208 (2)	.50	.50
Nos. 223-224 (2)	22.00	3.10
Nos. 293-294 (2)	.65	.50
Nos. 176-177 (2)	.80	.65
Nos. 110-111 (2)	.50	.50
Nos. 126-127 (2)	12.00	12.00
Nos. 54-55 (2)	6.35	4.50
Nos. 182-183 (2)	.95	.50
Nos. 165-166 (2)	.80	.60
Nos. 199-200 (2)	.55	.55
Nos. 220-221 (2)	.80	.60
Nos. 143-144 (2)	.70	.60
Nos. 17-18 (2)	1.20	.50
Nos. 117-118 (2)	.75	.75
Nos. 87-88 (2)	1.05	.65
Nos. 144-145 (2)	.65	.50
Nos. 161-162 (2)	.65	.50
Set total (64) Stamps	70.65	43.85

Churchill Memorial

Winston Churchill and St. Paul's, London, During Air Attack CD319

1966

Antigua	157-160
Ascension	96-99
Bahamas	224-227
Barbados	281-284
Basutoland	105-108
Bechuanaland Protectorate	206-209
Bermuda	201-204
British Antarctic Territory	16-19
British Honduras	191-194
Brunei	120-123
Cayman Islands	176-179
Dominica	189-192
Falkland Islands	158-161
Fiji	215-218
Gibraltar	171-174
Gilbert & Ellice Islands	106-109
Grenada	209-212
Hong Kong	225-228
Mauritius	295-298
Montserrat	178-181
New Hebrides, British	112-115
New Hebrides, French	128-131
Pitcairn Islands	56-59
St. Helena	184-187
St. Kitts-Nevis	167-170
St. Lucia	201-204
St. Vincent	241-244
Seychelles	222-225
Solomon Islands	145-148
South Arabia	19-22
Swaziland	119-122
Tristan da Cunha	89-92
Turks & Caicos Islands	146-149
Virgin Islands	163-166

Nos. 157-160 (4)	3.05	3.05
Nos. 96-99 (4)	10.00	6.40
Nos. 224-227 (4)	2.30	3.20
Nos. 281-284 (4)	3.00	4.95
Nos. 105-108 (4)	2.80	3.25
Nos. 206-209 (4)	2.50	2.50
Nos. 201-204 (4)	4.00	4.75
Nos. 16-19 (4)	41.20	18.00
Nos. 191-194 (4)	2.45	1.30
Nos. 120-123 (4)	7.65	6.55
Nos. 176-179 (4)	3.10	3.65
Nos. 189-192 (4)	1.15	1.15
Nos. 158-161 (4)	12.75	9.55
Nos. 215-218 (4)	4.40	3.00
Nos. 171-174 (4)	3.05	5.30
Nos. 106-109 (4)	1.50	1.30
Nos. 209-212 (4)	1.10	1.10
Nos. 225-228 (4)	52.50	11.40
Nos. 295-298 (4)	3.70	3.75
Nos. 178-181 (4)	1.60	1.55
Nos. 112-115 (4)	2.30	1.00
Nos. 128-131 (4)	8.35	8.35
Nos. 56-59 (4)	11.00	6.75
Nos. 184-187 (4)	1.85	1.95
Nos. 167-170 (4)	1.50	1.70
Nos. 201-204 (4)	1.50	1.50
Nos. 241-244 (4)	1.50	1.75
Nos. 222-225 (4)	3.20	4.35
Nos. 145-148 (4)	1.50	1.60
Nos. 19-22 (4)	2.95	2.20
Nos. 119-122 (4)	1.70	2.55
Nos. 89-92 (4)	5.95	2.70
Nos. 146-149 (4)	1.60	1.75
Nos. 163-166 (4)	1.90	1.90
Set total (136) Stamps	210.60	135.75

Royal Visit, 1966

Queen Elizabeth II and Prince Philip CD320

Caribbean visit, Feb. 4 - Mar. 6, 1966.

1966

Antigua	161-162
Bahamas	228-229
Barbados	285-286
British Guiana	299-300
Cayman Islands	180-181
Dominica	193-194
Grenada	213-214
Montserrat	182-183
St. Kitts-Nevis	171-172
St. Lucia	205-206
St. Vincent	245-246
Turks & Caicos Islands	150-151
Virgin Islands	167-168

Nos. 161-162 (2)	3.50	2.60
Nos. 228-229 (2)	3.05	3.05
Nos. 285-286 (2)	3.00	2.00
Nos. 299-300 (2)	2.35	.85
Nos. 180-181 (2)	3.45	1.80
Nos. 193-194 (2)	3.00	.60
Nos. 213-214 (2)	.80	.50
Nos. 182-183 (2)	2.00	1.00
Nos. 171-172 (2)	.90	.75
Nos. 205-206 (2)	1.50	1.35
Nos. 245-246 (2)	2.75	1.35
Nos. 150-151 (2)	1.20	.55
Nos. 167-168 (2)	1.75	1.75
Set total (26) Stamps	29.25	18.15

World Cup Soccer

Soccer Player and Jules Rimet Cup CD321

World Cup Soccer Championship, Wembley, England, July 11-30.

1966

Antigua	163-164
Ascension	100-101
Bahamas	245-246
Bermuda	205-206
Brunei	124-125
Cayman Islands	182-183
Dominica	195-196
Fiji	219-220
Gibraltar	175-176
Gilbert & Ellice Islands	125-126
Grenada	230-231
New Hebrides, British	116-117
New Hebrides, French	132-133
Pitcairn Islands	60-61
St. Helena	188-189
St. Kitts-Nevis	173-174
St. Lucia	207-208
Seychelles	226-227
Solomon Islands	167-168
South Arabia	23-24
Tristan da Cunha	93-94

Nos. 163-164 (2)	.80	.85
Nos. 100-101 (2)	2.50	2.00
Nos. 245-246 (2)	.65	.65
Nos. 205-206 (2)	1.75	1.75
Nos. 124-125 (2)	1.30	1.25
Nos. 182-183 (2)	.75	.65
Nos. 195-196 (2)	1.20	.75
Nos. 219-220 (2)	1.70	.60
Nos. 175-176 (2)	1.85	1.75
Nos. 125-126 (2)	.70	.60
Nos. 230-231 (2)	.65	.95
Nos. 116-117 (2)	1.00	1.00
Nos. 132-133 (2)	7.00	7.00
Nos. 60-61 (2)	5.50	5.00
Nos. 188-189 (2)	1.25	.60
Nos. 173-174 (2)	.85	.80
Nos. 207-208 (2)	1.15	.90
Nos. 226-227 (2)	.85	.75
Nos. 167-168 (2)	1.10	1.10
Nos. 23-24 (2)	1.90	.55
Nos. 93-94 (2)	1.25	.80
Set total (42) Stamps	35.70	30.30

WHO Headquarters

World Health Organization Headquarters, Geneva — CD322

1966

Antigua	165-166
Ascension	102-103
Bahamas	247-248
Brunei	126-127
Cayman Islands	184-185
Dominica	197-198
Fiji	224-225
Gibraltar	180-181
Gilbert & Ellice Islands	127-128
Grenada	232-233
Hong Kong	229-230
Montserrat	184-185
New Hebrides, British	118-119
New Hebrides, French	134-135
Pitcairn Islands	62-63
St. Helena	190-191
St. Kitts-Nevis	177-178
St. Lucia	209-210
St. Vincent	247-248
Seychelles	228-229
Solomon Islands	169-170
South Arabia	25-26
Tristan da Cunha	99-100

Nos. 165-166 (2)	1.15	.55
Nos. 102-103 (2)	6.60	3.35
Nos. 247-248 (2)	.80	.80
Nos. 126-127 (2)	1.35	1.35
Nos. 184-185 (2)	2.25	1.20
Nos. 197-198 (2)	.75	.75
Nos. 224-225 (2)	4.70	3.30
Nos. 180-181 (2)	6.50	4.50
Nos. 127-128 (2)	.80	.70
Nos. 232-233 (2)	.80	.50
Nos. 229-230 (2)	11.25	2.30
Nos. 184-185 (2)	1.00	1.00
Nos. 118-119 (2)	.75	.50
Nos. 134-135 (2)	8.50	8.50
Nos. 62-63 (2)	7.25	6.50
Nos. 190-191 (2)	3.50	1.50
Nos. 177-178 (2)	.60	.60
Nos. 209-210 (2)	.80	.80
Nos. 247-248 (2)	1.15	1.05
Nos. 228-229 (2)	1.25	.65
Nos. 169-170 (2)	.95	.80
Nos. 25-26 (2)	2.10	.70
Nos. 99-100 (2)	1.90	1.25
Set total (46) Stamps	66.70	43.15

UNESCO Anniversary

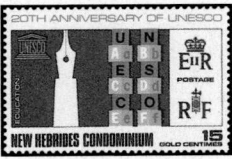

"Education" — CD323

"Science" (Wheat ears & flask enclosing globe). "Culture" (lyre & columns). 20th anniversary of the UNESCO.

1966-67

Antigua	183-185
Ascension	108-110
Bahamas	249-251
Barbados	287-289
Bermuda	207-209
Brunei	128-130
Cayman Islands	186-188
Dominica	199-201
Gibraltar	183-185
Gilbert & Ellice Islands	129-131
Grenada	234-236
Hong Kong	231-233
Mauritius	299-301
Montserrat	186-188
New Hebrides, British	120-122
New Hebrides, French	136-138
Pitcairn Islands	64-66
St. Helena	192-194
St. Kitts-Nevis	179-181
St. Lucia	211-213
St. Vincent	249-251
Seychelles	230-232
Solomon Islands	171-173
South Arabia	27-29
Swaziland	123-125
Tristan da Cunha	101-103
Turks & Caicos Islands	155-157
Virgin Islands	176-178

Nos. 183-185 (3)	1.90	2.50
Nos. 108-110 (3)	11.00	5.80
Nos. 249-251 (3)	2.35	2.35
Nos. 287-289 (3)	2.35	2.15
Nos. 207-209 (3)	3.80	3.90
Nos. 128-130 (3)	4.65	5.40
Nos. 186-188 (3)	2.50	1.50
Nos. 199-201 (3)	1.60	.75
Nos. 183-185 (3)	6.50	3.25
Nos. 129-131 (3)	2.50	2.45
Nos. 234-236 (3)	1.10	1.20
Nos. 231-233 (3)	69.50	17.50
Nos. 299-301 (3)	2.10	1.50
Nos. 186-188 (3)	2.40	2.40
Nos. 120-122 (3)	1.90	1.90
Nos. 136-138 (3)	7.75	7.75
Nos. 64-66 (3)	7.10	4.75
Nos. 192-194 (3)	5.25	3.65
Nos. 179-181 (3)	.90	.90
Nos. 211-213 (3)	1.15	1.15
Nos. 249-251 (3)	2.30	1.35
Nos. 230-232 (3)	2.40	2.40
Nos. 171-173 (3)	2.00	1.50
Nos. 27-29 (3)	5.50	5.50
Nos. 123-125 (3)	1.40	1.40
Nos. 101-103 (3)	2.00	1.40
Nos. 155-157 (3)	1.05	.90
Nos. 176-178 (3)	1.40	1.30
Set total (84) Stamps	156.35	88.50

Silver Wedding, 1972

Queen Elizabeth II and Prince Philip — CD324

Designs: borders differ for each country.

1972

Anguilla	161-162
Antigua	295-296
Ascension	164-165
Bahamas	344-345
Bermuda	296-297
British Antarctic Territory	43-44
British Honduras	306-307
British Indian Ocean Territory	48-49

Brunei 186-187
Cayman Islands.....................304-305
Dominica.........................352-353
Falkland Islands 223-224
Fiji 328-329
Gibraltar.............................292-293
Gilbert & Ellice Islands 206-207
Grenada.............................466-467
Hong Kong 271-272
Montserrat 286-287
New Hebrides, British 169-170
New Hebrides, French 188-189
Pitcairn Islands.....................127-128
St. Helena 271-272
St. Kitts-Nevis 257-258
St. Lucia 328-329
St.Vincent 344-345
Seychelles 309-310
Solomon Islands 248-249
South Georgia 35-36
Tristan da Cunha 178-179
Turks & Caicos Islands 257-258
Virgin Islands.....................241-242

Nos. 161-162 (2)	1.10	*1.50*
Nos. 295-296 (2)	.50	.50
Nos. 164-165 (2)	.70	.70
Nos. 344-345 (2)	.60	.60
Nos. 296-297 (2)	.50	*.65*
Nos. 43-44 (2)	6.50	5.65
Nos. 306-307 (2)	.80	.80
Nos. 48-49 (2)	2.00	1.00
Nos. 186-187 (2)	.70	.70
Nos. 304-305 (2)	.75	.75
Nos. 352-353 (2)	.65	.65
Nos. 223-224 (2)	1.00	1.15
Nos. 328-329 (2)	.70	.70
Nos. 292-293 (2)	.50	.50
Nos. 206-207 (2)	.50	.50
Nos. 466-467 (2)	.70	.70
Nos. 271-272 (2)	1.70	1.50
Nos. 286-287 (2)	.50	.50
Nos. 169-170 (2)	.50	.50
Nos. 188-189 (2)	1.25	1.25
Nos. 127-128 (2)	.90	.85
Nos. 271-272 (2)	.60	1.20
Nos. 257-258 (2)	.65	.50
Nos. 328-329 (2)	.75	.75
Nos. 344-345 (2)	.55	.55
Nos. 309-310 (2)	.90	.90
Nos. 248-249 (2)	.50	.50
Nos. 35-36 (2)	1.40	1.40
Nos. 178-179 (2)	.70	.70
Nos. 257-258 (2)	.50	.50
Nos. 241-242 (2)	.50	.50
Set total (62) Stamps	30.10	29.15

Princess Anne's Wedding

THE WEDDING OF H.R.H. THE PRINCESS ANNE
SEYCHELLES 95¢ — Princess Anne and Mark Phillips — CD325

Wedding of Princess Anne and Mark Phillips, Nov. 14, 1973.

1973

Anguilla.............................179-180
Ascension 177-178
Belize...............................325-326
Bermuda............................302-303
British Antarctic Territory..........60-61
Cayman Islands....................320-321
Falkland Islands 225-226
Gibraltar.............................305-306
Gilbert & Ellice Islands 216-217
Hong Kong 289-290
Montserrat 300-301
Pitcairn Islands.....................135-136
St. Helena 277-278
St. Kitts-Nevis 274-275
St. Lucia 349-350
St. Vincent 358-359
St. Vincent Grenadines 1-2
Seychelles 311-312
Solomon Islands 259-260
South Georgia 37-38
Tristan da Cunha 189-190
Turks & Caicos Islands 286-287
Virgin Islands.....................260-261

Nos. 179-180 (2)	.55	.55
Nos. 177-178 (2)	.60	.60
Nos. 325-326 (2)	.50	.50
Nos. 302-303 (2)	.50	.50
Nos. 60-61 (2)	1.10	1.10
Nos. 320-321 (2)	.50	.50

Nos. 225-226 (2)	.70	.60
Nos. 305-306 (2)	.55	.55
Nos. 216-217 (2)	.50	.50
Nos. 289-290 (2)	2.65	2.00
Nos. 300-301 (2)	.55	.55
Nos. 135-136 (2)	.70	.60
Nos. 277-278 (2)	.50	.50
Nos. 274-275 (2)	.50	.50
Nos. 349-350 (2)	.50	.50
Nos. 358-359 (2)	.50	.50
Nos. 1-2 (2)	.50	.50
Nos. 311-312 (2)	.65	.65
Nos. 259-260 (2)	.70	.70
Nos. 37-38 (2)	.75	.75
Nos. 189-190 (2)	.50	.50
Nos. 286-287 (2)	.50	.50
Nos. 260-261 (2)	.50	.50
Set total (46) Stamps	15.50	14.65

Elizabeth II Coronation Anniv.

CD326

CD327

CD328

Designs: Royal and local beasts in heraldic form and simulated stonework. Portrait of Elizabeth II by Peter Grugeon. 25th anniversary of coronation of Queen Elizabeth II.

1978

Ascension 229
Barbados 474
Belize...............................397
British Antarctic Territory........71
Cayman Islands....................404
Christmas Island 87
Falkland Islands 275
Fiji 384
Gambia 380
Gilbert Islands 312
Mauritius 464
New Hebrides, British 258
New Hebrides, French 278
St. Helena 317
St. Kitts-Nevis 354
Samoa 472
Solomon Islands 368
South Georgia 51
Swaziland 302
Tristan da Cunha 238
Virgin Islands.....................337

No. 229 (1)	2.00	2.00
No. 474 (1)	1.35	1.35
No. 397 (1)	1.40	1.75
No. 71 (1)	6.00	6.00
No. 404 (1)	2.00	2.00
No. 87 (1)	3.50	*4.00*
No. 275 (1)	4.00	5.50
No. 384 (1)	1.75	1.75
No. 380 (1)	1.50	1.50
No. 312 (1)	1.25	1.25
No. 464 (1)	2.10	2.10
No. 258 (1)	1.75	1.75
No. 278 (1)	3.50	3.50
No. 317 (1)	1.75	1.75
No. 354 (1)	1.00	1.00
No. 472 (1)	2.10	2.10
No. 368 (1)	2.50	2.50
No. 51 (1)	3.00	3.00
No. 302 (1)	1.60	1.60
No. 238 (1)	1.50	1.50
No. 337 (1)	1.80	1.80
Set total (21) Stamps	47.35	49.70

Queen Mother Elizabeth's 80th Birthday

CD330

Designs: Photographs of Queen Mother Elizabeth. Falkland Islands issued in sheets of 50; others in sheets of 9.

1980

Ascension...........................261
Bermuda.............................401
Cayman Islands....................443
Falkland Islands 305
Gambia 412
Gibraltar.............................393
Hong Kong 364
Pitcairn Islands......................193
St. Helena 341
Samoa 532
Solomon Islands 426
Tristan da Cunha 277

No. 261 (1)	.40	.40
No. 401 (1)	.45	.75
No. 443 (1)	.40	.40
No. 305 (1)	.40	.40
No. 412 (1)	.40	.50
No. 393 (1)	.35	.35
No. 364 (1)	1.10	1.25
No. 193 (1)	.60	.60
No. 341 (1)	.50	.50
No. 532 (1)	.55	.55
No. 426 (1)	.50	.50
No. 277 (1)	.45	.45
Set total (12) Stamps	6.10	6.65

Royal Wedding, 1981

Prince Charles and Lady Diana — CD331

CD331a

Wedding of Charles, Prince of Wales, and Lady Diana Spencer, St. Paul's Cathedral, London, July 29, 1981.

1981

Antigua 623-627
Ascension 294-296
Barbados 547-549
Barbuda 497-501
Bermuda 412-414
Brunei 268-270
Cayman Islands....................471-473
Dominica.............................701-705
Falkland Islands 324-326
Falkland Islands Dep............1L59-1L61
Fiji 442-444
Gambia 426-428
Ghana 759-764
Grenada.............................1051-1055
Grenada Grenadines 440-443
Hong Kong 373-375
Jamaica 500-503
Lesotho 335-337
Maldive Islands 906-909
Mauritius 520-522
Norfolk Island 280-282
Pitcairn Islands......................206-208
St. Helena 353-355
St. Lucia 543-549
Samoa 558-560
Sierra Leone 509-518
Solomon Islands 450-452
Swaziland 382-384
Tristan da Cunha 294-296
Turks & Caicos Islands 486-489
Caicos Island........................8-11
Uganda 314-317
Vanuatu 308-310
Virgin Islands.......................406-408

Nos. 623-627 (5)	6.55	2.55
Nos. 294-296 (3)	1.00	1.00

Nos. 547-549 (3)	.90	.90
Nos. 497-501 (5)	10.95	10.95
Nos. 412-414 (3)	2.00	2.00
Nos. 268-270 (3)	2.15	*4.50*
Nos. 471-473 (3)	1.20	1.30
Nos. 701-705 (5)	8.35	2.35
Nos. 324-326 (3)	1.65	1.70
Nos. 1L59-1L61 (3)	1.45	1.45
Nos. 442-444 (3)	1.35	1.35
Nos. 426-428 (3)	.80	.80
Nos. 759-764 (9)	6.20	6.20
Nos. 1051-1055 (5)	9.85	1.85
Nos. 440-443 (4)	2.35	2.35
Nos. 373-375 (3)	3.05	2.85
Nos. 500-503 (4)	1.45	1.35
Nos. 335-337 (3)	.90	.90
Nos. 906-909 (4)	1.55	1.55
Nos. 520-522 (3)	2.15	2.15
Nos. 280-282 (3)	1.75	1.75
Nos. 206-208 (3)	1.10	1.10
Nos. 353-355 (3)	.85	.85
Nos. 543-549 (3)	7.00	7.00
Nos. 558-560 (3)	.85	.85
Nos. 509-518 (10)	15.50	15.50
Nos. 450-452 (3)	1.25	1.25
Nos. 382-384 (3)	1.30	1.25
Nos. 294-296 (3)	.90	.90
Nos. 486-489 (4)	2.20	2.20
Nos. 8-11 (4)	5.00	5.00
Nos. 314-317 (4)	3.30	3.00
Nos. 308-310 (3)	1.15	1.15
Nos. 406-408 (3)	1.10	1.10
Set total (131) Stamps	109.10	92.95

Princess Diana

CD332

CD333

Designs: Photographs and portrait of Princess Diana, wedding or honeymoon photographs, royal residences, arms of issuing country. Portrait photograph by Clive Friend. Souvenir sheet margins show family tree, various people related to the princess. 21st birthday of Princess Diana of Wales, July 1.

1982

Antigua 663-666
Ascension 313-316
Bahamas 510-513
Barbados 585-588
Barbuda 544-547
British Antarctic Territory.............92-95
Cayman Islands....................486-489
Dominica.............................773-776
Falkland Islands 348-351
Falkland Islands Dep...........1L72-1L75
Fiji 470-473
Gambia 447-450
Grenada................................ 1101A-1105
Grenada Grenadines 485-491
Lesotho 372-375
Maldive Islands 952-955
Mauritius 548-551
Pitcairn Islands......................213-216
St. Helena 372-375
St. Lucia 591-594
Sierra Leone 531-534
Solomon Islands 471-474
Swaziland 406-409
Tristan da Cunha 310-313
Turks and Caicos Islands 531-534
Virgin Islands.......................430-433

Nos. 663-666 (4)	8.25	7.35
Nos. 313-316 (4)	3.50	3.50
Nos. 510-513 (4)	6.00	3.85
Nos. 585-588 (4)	3.40	3.25
Nos. 544-547 (4)	9.75	7.70
Nos. 92-95 (4)	4.25	3.45
Nos. 486-489 (4)	4.75	2.70
Nos. 773-776 (4)	7.05	7.05
Nos. 348-351 (4)	2.95	2.95
Nos. 1L72-1L75 (4)	2.50	2.60
Nos. 470-473 (4)	3.25	2.95
Nos. 447-450 (4)	2.85	2.85
Nos. 1101A-1105 (7)	16.05	15.55

Nos. 485-491 (7) ... 17.65 17.65
Nos. 372-375 (4) ... 4.00 4.00
Nos. 952-955 (4) ... 5.50 3.90
Nos. 548-551 (4) ... 5.00 5.00
Nos. 213-216 (4) ... 2.15 2.15
Nos. 372-375 (4) ... 2.00 2.00
Nos. 591-594 (4) ... 8.70 8.70
Nos. 531-534 (4) ... 7.20 7.20
Nos. 471-474 (4) ... 2.90 2.90
Nos. 406-409 (4) ... 3.85 2.25
Nos. 310-313 (4) ... 3.65 1.45
Nos. 486-489 (4) ... 2.20 2.20
Nos. 430-433 (4) ... 3.00 3.00
Set total (110) Stamps ... 142.35 128.15

250th anniv. of first edition of Lloyd's List (shipping news publication) & of Lloyd's marine insurance.

CD335

Designs: First page of early edition of the list; historical ships, modern transportation or harbor scenes.

1984
Ascension ... 351-354
Bahamas ... 555-558
Barbados ... 627-630
Cayes of Belize ... 10-13
Cayman Islands ... 522-526
Falkland Islands ... 404-407
Fiji ... 509-512
Gambia ... 519-522
Mauritius ... 587-590
Nauru ... 280-283
St. Helena ... 412-415
Samoa ... 624-627
Seychelles ... 538-541
Solomon Islands ... 521-524
Vanuatu ... 368-371
Virgin Islands ... 466-469

Nos. 351-354 (4) ... 2.90 2.55
Nos. 555-558 (4) ... 4.15 2.95
Nos. 627-630 (4) ... 6.10 5.15
Nos. 10-13 (4) ... 2.65 2.65
Nos. 522-526 (5) ... 9.30 8.45
Nos. 404-407 (4) ... 3.50 3.65
Nos. 509-512 (4) ... 5.30 4.90
Nos. 519-522 (4) ... 4.20 4.30
Nos. 587-590 (4) ... 9.40 9.40
Nos. 280-283 (4) ... 2.40 2.35
Nos. 412-415 (4) ... 2.40 2.40
Nos. 624-627 (4) ... 2.55 2.35
Nos. 538-541 (4) ... 5.00 5.00
Nos. 521-524 (4) ... 4.65 3.95
Nos. 368-371 (4) ... 2.40 2.40
Nos. 466-469 (4) ... 4.25 4.25
Set total (65) Stamps ... 71.15 66.70

Queen Mother 85th Birthday

CD336

Designs: Photographs tracing the life of the Queen Mother, Elizabeth. The high value in each set pictures the same photograph taken of the Queen Mother holding the infant Prince Henry.

1985
Ascension ... 372-376
Bahamas ... 580-584
Barbados ... 660-664
Bermuda ... 469-473
Falkland Islands ... 420-424
Falkland Islands Dep. ... 1L92-1L96
Fiji ... 531-535
Hong Kong ... 447-450
Jamaica ... 599-603
Mauritius ... 604-608
Norfolk Island ... 364-368
Pitcairn Islands ... 253-257
St. Helena ... 428-432
Samoa ... 649-653

Seychelles ... 567-571
Zil Elwannyen Sesel ... 101-105
Solomon Islands ... 543-547
Swaziland ... 476-480
Tristan da Cunha ... 372-376
Vanuatu ... 392-396

Nos. 372-376 (5) ... 4.65 4.65
Nos. 580-584 (5) ... 7.70 6.45
Nos. 660-664 (5) ... 8.00 6.70
Nos. 469-473 (5) ... 9.40 9.40
Nos. 420-424 (5) ... 7.35 6.65
Nos. 1L92-1L96 (5) ... 8.00 8.00
Nos. 531-535 (5) ... 6.15 6.15
Nos. 447-450 (4) ... 9.50 8.50
Nos. 599-603 (5) ... 6.15 7.00
Nos. 604-608 (5) ... 11.30 11.30
Nos. 364-368 (5) ... 5.00 5.00
Nos. 253-257 (5) ... 5.25 5.95
Nos. 428-432 (5) ... 5.25 5.25
Nos. 649-653 (5) ... 8.40 7.55
Nos. 567-571 (5) ... 8.70 8.70
Nos. 101-105 (5) ... 6.60 6.60
Nos. 543-547 (5) ... 3.95 3.95
Nos. 476-480 (5) ... 7.75 7.25
Nos. 372-376 (5) ... 5.40 5.40
Nos. 392-396 (5) ... 5.25 5.25
Set total (99) Stamps ... 139.75 135.70

Queen Elizabeth II, 60th Birthday

CD337

1986, April 21
Ascension ... 389-393
Bahamas ... 592-596
Barbados ... 675-679
Bermuda ... 499-503
Cayman Islands ... 555-559
Falkland Islands ... 441-445
Fiji ... 544-548
Hong Kong ... 465-469
Jamaica ... 620-624
Kiribati ... 470-474
Mauritius ... 629-633
Papua New Guinea ... 640-644
Pitcairn Islands ... 270-274
St. Helena ... 451-455
Samoa ... 670-674
Seychelles ... 592-596
Zil Elwannyen Sesel ... 114-118
Solomon Islands ... 562-566
South Georgia ... 101-105
Swaziland ... 490-494
Tristan da Cunha ... 388-392
Vanuatu ... 414-418
Zambia ... 343-347

Nos. 389-393 (5) ... 2.80 3.30
Nos. 592-596 (5) ... 2.75 3.70
Nos. 675-679 (5) ... 3.25 3.10
Nos. 499-503 (5) ... 4.65 5.15
Nos. 555-559 (5) ... 4.55 5.60
Nos. 441-445 (5) ... 3.95 4.95
Nos. 544-548 (5) ... 3.00 3.00
Nos. 465-469 (5) ... 8.75 6.75
Nos. 620-624 (5) ... 2.75 2.70
Nos. 470-474 (5) ... 2.10 2.10
Nos. 629-633 (5) ... 3.50 3.50
Nos. 640-644 (5) ... 4.10 4.10
Nos. 270-274 (5) ... 2.70 2.70
Nos. 451-455 (5) ... 2.50 3.05
Nos. 670-674 (5) ... 2.55 2.55
Nos. 592-596 (5) ... 2.70 2.70
Nos. 114-118 (5) ... 2.15 2.15
Nos. 562-566 (5) ... 2.90 2.90
Nos. 101-105 (5) ... 3.30 3.65
Nos. 490-494 (5) ... 2.15 2.15
Nos. 388-392 (5) ... 3.00 3.00
Nos. 414-418 (5) ... 3.10 3.10
Nos. 343-347 (5) ... 1.75 1.75
Set total (115) Stamps ... 74.95 77.65

Royal Wedding

Marriage of Prince Andrew and Sarah Ferguson
CD338

1986, July 23
Ascension ... 399-400
Bahamas ... 602-603
Barbados ... 687-688

Cayman Islands ... 560-561
Jamaica ... 629-630
Pitcairn Islands ... 275-276
St. Helena ... 460-461
St. Kitts ... 181-182
Seychelles ... 602-603
Zil Elwannyen Sesel ... 119-120
Solomon Islands ... 567-568
Tristan da Cunha ... 397-398
Zambia ... 348-349

Nos. 399-400 (2) ... 1.60 1.60
Nos. 602-603 (2) ... 2.75 2.75
Nos. 687-688 (2) ... 2.00 1.25
Nos. 560-561 (2) ... 1.70 2.35
Nos. 629-630 (2) ... 1.35 1.35
Nos. 275-276 (2) ... 2.40 2.40
Nos. 460-461 (2) ... 1.05 1.05
Nos. 181-182 (2) ... 1.50 2.25
Nos. 602-603 (2) ... 2.50 2.50
Nos. 119-120 (2) ... 2.30 2.30
Nos. 567-568 (2) ... 1.00 1.00
Nos. 397-398 (2) ... 1.40 1.40
Nos. 348-349 (2) ... 1.10 1.30
Set total (26) Stamps ... 22.65 23.50

Queen Elizabeth II, 60th Birthday

Queen Elizabeth II & Prince Philip, 1947 Wedding Portrait — CD339

Designs: Photographs tracing the life of Queen Elizabeth II.

1986
Anguilla ... 674-677
Antigua ... 925-928
Barbuda ... 783-786
Dominica ... 950-953
Gambia ... 611-614
Grenada ... 1371-1374
Grenada Grenadines ... 749-752
Lesotho ... 531-534
Maldive Islands ... 1172-1175
Sierra Leone ... 760-763
Uganda ... 495-498

Nos. 674-677 (4) ... 8.00 8.00
Nos. 925-928 (4) ... 5.50 6.20
Nos. 783-786 (4) ... 23.15 23.15
Nos. 950-953 (4) ... 7.25 7.25
Nos. 611-614 (4) ... 8.25 7.90
Nos. 1371-1374 (4) ... 6.80 6.80
Nos. 749-752 (4) ... 6.75 6.75
Nos. 531-534 (4) ... 5.25 5.25
Nos. 1172-1175 (4) ... 6.25 6.25
Nos. 760-763 (4) ... 5.25 5.25
Nos. 495-498 (4) ... 8.50 8.50
Set total (44) Stamps ... 90.95 91.30

Royal Wedding, 1986

CD340

Designs: Photographs of Prince Andrew and Sarah Ferguson during courtship, engagement and marriage.

1986
Antigua ... 939-942
Barbuda ... 809-812
Dominica ... 970-973
Gambia ... 635-638
Grenada ... 1385-1388
Grenada Grenadines ... 758-761
Lesotho ... 545-548
Maldive Islands ... 1181-1184
Sierra Leone ... 769-772
Uganda ... 510-513

Nos. 939-942 (4) ... 7.00 8.75
Nos. 809-812 (4) ... 14.55 14.55
Nos. 970-973 (4) ... 7.25 7.25
Nos. 635-638 (4) ... 7.80 7.80
Nos. 1385-1388 (4) ... 8.30 8.30
Nos. 758-761 (4) ... 9.00 9.00

Nos. 545-548 (4) ... 7.45 7.45
Nos. 1181-1184 (4) ... 8.45 8.45
Nos. 769-772 (4) ... 5.35 5.35
Nos. 510-513 (4) ... 9.25 10.00
Set total (40) Stamps ... 84.40 86.90

Lloyds of London, 300th Anniv.

CD341

Designs: 17th century aspects of Lloyds, representations of each country's individual connections with Lloyds and publicized disasters insured by the organization.

1986
Ascension ... 454-457
Bahamas ... 655-658
Barbados ... 731-734
Bermuda ... 541-544
Falkland Islands ... 481-484
Liberia ... 1101-1104
Malawi ... 534-537
Nevis ... 571-574
St. Helena ... 501-504
St. Lucia ... 923-926
Seychelles ... 649-652
Zil Elwannyen Sesel ... 146-149
Solomon Islands ... 627-630
South Georgia ... 131-134
Trinidad & Tobago ... 484-487
Tristan da Cunha ... 439-442
Vanuatu ... 485-488

Nos. 454-457 (4) ... 5.00 5.00
Nos. 655-658 (4) ... 8.90 4.95
Nos. 731-734 (4) ... 12.50 8.35
Nos. 541-544 (4) ... 8.00 6.60
Nos. 481-484 (4) ... 5.45 3.85
Nos. 1101-1104 (4) ... 4.25 4.25
Nos. 534-537 (4) ... 11.00 7.85
Nos. 571-574 (4) ... 8.35 8.35
Nos. 501-504 (4) ... 8.70 7.15
Nos. 923-926 (4) ... 8.80 8.80
Nos. 649-652 (4) ... 12.85 12.85
Nos. 146-149 (4) ... 11.25 11.25
Nos. 627-630 (4) ... 7.00 4.45
Nos. 131-134 (4) ... 6.30 3.70
Nos. 484-487 (4) ... 10.25 6.35
Nos. 439-442 (4) ... 7.60 7.60
Nos. 485-488 (4) ... 5.90 5.90
Set total (68) Stamps ... 142.10 117.25

Moon Landing, 20th Anniv.

CD342

Designs: Equipment, crew photographs, spacecraft, official emblems and report profiles created for the Apollo Missions. Two stamps in each set are square in format rather than like the stamp shown; see individual country listings for more information.

1989
Ascension ... 468-472
Bahamas ... 674-678
Belize ... 916-920
Kiribati ... 517-521
Liberia ... 1125-1129
Nevis ... 586-590
St. Kitts ... 248-252
Samoa ... 760-764
Seychelles ... 676-680
Zil Elwannyen Sesel ... 154-158
Solomon Islands ... 643-647
Vanuatu ... 507-511

Nos. 468-472 (5) ... 9.40 8.60
Nos. 674-678 (5) ... 23.00 19.70
Nos. 916-920 (5) ... 22.85 18.10
Nos. 517-521 (5) ... 12.50 12.50
Nos. 1125-1129 (5) ... 8.50 8.50
Nos. 586-590 (5) ... 7.50 7.50

Nos. 248-252 (5)	8.00	8.25
Nos. 760-764 (5)	9.85	9.30
Nos. 676-680 (5)	16.05	16.05
Nos. 154-158 (5)	26.85	26.85
Nos. 643-647 (5)	9.00	6.75
Nos. 507-511 (5)	9.90	9.90
Set total (60) Stamps	163.40	152.00

Queen Mother, 90th Birthday

CD343   CD344

Designs: Portraits of Queen Elizabeth, the Queen Mother. See individual country listings for more information.

1990

Ascension	491-492
Bahamas	698-699
Barbados	782-783
British Antarctic Territory	170-171
British Indian Ocean Territory	106-107
Cayman Islands	622-623
Falkland Islands	524-525
Kenya	527-528
Kiribati	555-556
Liberia	1145-1146
Pitcairn Islands	336-337
St. Helena	532-533
St. Lucia	969-970
Seychelles	710-711
Zil Elwannyen Sesel	171-172
Solomon Islands	671-672
South Georgia	143-144
Swaziland	565-566
Tristan da Cunha	480-481

Nos. 491-492 (2)	4.75	4.75
Nos. 698-699 (2)	5.25	5.25
Nos. 782-783 (2)	4.00	3.70
Nos. 170-171 (2)	6.00	6.00
Nos. 106-107 (2)	18.00	18.50
Nos. 622-623 (2)	4.00	5.50
Nos. 524-525 (2)	4.75	4.75
Nos. 527-528 (2)	7.00	7.00
Nos. 555-556 (2)	4.75	4.75
Nos. 1145-1146 (2)	3.25	3.25
Nos. 336-337 (2)	4.25	4.25
Nos. 532-533 (2)	5.25	5.25
Nos. 969-970 (2)	4.60	4.60
Nos. 710-711 (2)	6.60	6.60
Nos. 171-172 (2)	8.25	8.25
Nos. 671-672 (2)	5.00	5.30
Nos. 143-144 (2)	5.50	5.60
Nos. 565-566 (2)	4.10	4.10
Nos. 480-481 (2)	5.60	5.60
Set total (38) Stamps	110.90	113.90

Queen Elizabeth II, 65th Birthday, and Prince Philip, 70th Birthday

CD345

CD346

Designs: Portraits of Queen Elizabeth II and Prince Philip differ for each country. Printed in sheets of 10 + 5 labels (3 different) between. Stamps alternate, producing 5 different triptychs.

1991

Ascension	506a
Bahamas	731a

Belize	970a
Bermuda	618a
Kiribati	572a
Mauritius	734a
Pitcairn Islands	349a
St. Helena	555a
St. Kitts	319a
Samoa	791a
Seychelles	724a
Zil Elwannyen Sesel	178a
Solomon Islands	689a
South Georgia	150a
Swaziland	587a
Vanuatu	541a

No. 506a (1)	3.50	3.75
No. 731a (1)	4.00	4.00
No. 970a (1)	3.75	3.75
No. 618a (1)	3.50	4.00
No. 572a (1)	4.00	4.00
No. 734a (1)	4.00	4.00
No. 349a (1)	3.25	3.25
No. 555a (1)	2.75	2.75
No. 319a (1)	3.00	3.00
No. 791a (1)	3.75	3.75
No. 724a (1)	5.00	5.00
No. 178a (1)	6.25	6.25
No. 689a (1)	3.75	3.75
No. 150a (1)	4.75	7.00
No. 587a (1)	4.00	4.00
No. 541a (1)	2.50	2.50
Set total (16) Stamps	61.75	64.75

Royal Family Birthday, Anniversary

CD347

Queen Elizabeth II, 65th birthday, Charles and Diana, 10th wedding anniversary: Various photographs of Queen Elizabeth II, Prince Philip, Prince Charles, Princess Diana and their sons William and Henry.

1991

Antigua	1446-1455
Barbuda	1229-1238
Dominica	1328-1337
Gambia	1080-1089
Grenada	2006-2015
Grenada Grenadines	1331-1340
Guyana	2440-2451
Lesotho	871-875
Maldive Islands	1533-1542
Nevis	666-675
St. Vincent	1485-1494
St. Vincent Grenadines	769-778
Sierra Leone	1387-1396
Turks & Caicos Islands	913-922
Uganda	918-927

Nos. 1446-1455 (10)	21.70	20.05
Nos. 1229-1238 (10)	125.00	119.50
Nos. 1328-1337 (10)	30.20	30.20
Nos. 1080-1089 (10)	24.65	24.40
Nos. 2006-2015 (10)	25.45	22.10
Nos. 1331-1340 (10)	23.85	23.35
Nos. 2440-2451 (12)	21.40	21.15
Nos. 871-875 (5)	13.55	13.55
Nos. 1533-1542 (10)	28.10	28.10
Nos. 666-675 (10)	23.65	23.65
Nos. 1485-1494 (10)	26.75	25.90
Nos. 769-778 (10)	25.40	25.40
Nos. 1387-1396 (10)	26.35	26.35
Nos. 913-922 (10)	27.50	25.30
Nos. 918-927 (10)	26.60	26.60
Set total (147) Stamps	470.15	455.60

Queen Elizabeth II's Accession to the Throne, 40th Anniv.

CD348

Various photographs of Queen Elizabeth II with local Scenes.

1992

Antigua	1513-1518
Barbuda	1306-1311
Dominica	1414-1419
Gambia	1172-1177
Grenada	2047-2052
Grenada Grenadines	1368-1373
Lesotho	881-885

Maldive Islands	1637-1642
Nevis	702-707
St. Vincent	1582-1587
St. Vincent Grenadines	829-834
Sierra Leone	1482-1487
Turks and Caicos Islands	978-987
Uganda	990-995
Virgin Islands	742-746

Nos. 1513-1518 (6)	15.00	15.10
Nos. 1306-1311 (6)	125.25	83.65
Nos. 1414-1419 (6)	12.50	12.50
Nos. 1172-1177 (6)	14.95	14.85
Nos. 2047-2052 (6)	15.95	15.95
Nos. 1368-1373 (6)	17.00	15.35
Nos. 881-885 (5)	11.90	11.90
Nos. 1637-1642 (6)	17.55	17.55
Nos. 702-707 (6)	13.55	13.55
Nos. 1582-1587 (6)	14.40	14.40
Nos. 829-834 (6)	19.65	19.65
Nos. 1482-1487 (6)	22.50	22.50
Nos. 913-922 (10)	27.50	25.30
Nos. 990-995 (6)	19.50	19.50
Nos. 742-746 (5)	15.50	15.50
Set total (92) Stamps	362.70	317.25

CD349

1992

Ascension	531-535
Bahamas	744-748
Bermuda	623-627
British Indian Ocean Territory	119-123
Cayman Islands	648-652
Falkland Islands	549-553
Gibraltar	605-609
Hong Kong	619-623
Kenya	563-567
Kiribati	582-586
Pitcairn Islands	362-366
St. Helena	570-574
St. Kitts	332-336
Samoa	805-809
Seychelles	734-738
Zil Elwannyen Sesel	183-187
Solomon Islands	708-712
South Georgia	157-161
Tristan da Cunha	508-512
Vanuatu	555-559
Zambia	561-565

Nos. 531-535 (5)	6.10	6.10
Nos. 744-748 (5)	6.90	4.70
Nos. 623-627 (5)	7.40	7.55
Nos. 119-123 (5)	22.75	19.25
Nos. 648-652 (5)	7.60	6.60
Nos. 549-553 (5)	5.95	5.90
Nos. 605-609 (5)	5.15	5.50
Nos. 619-623 (5)	5.10	5.25
Nos. 563-567 (5)	9.10	9.10
Nos. 582-586 (5)	3.85	3.85
Nos. 362-366 (5)	5.35	5.35
Nos. 570-574 (5)	5.70	5.70
Nos. 332-336 (5)	6.60	5.50
Nos. 805-809 (5)	7.85	5.90
Nos. 734-738 (5)	10.55	10.55
Nos. 183-187 (5)	9.40	9.40
Nos. 708-712 (5)	5.00	5.30
Nos. 157-161 (5)	5.60	5.90
Nos. 508-512 (5)	8.75	8.30
Nos. 555-559 (5)	3.65	3.65
Nos. 561-565 (5)	5.60	5.60
Set total (105) Stamps	153.95	144.95

Royal Air Force, 75th Anniversary

CD350

1993

Ascension	557-561
Bahamas	771-775
Barbados	842-846
Belize	1003-1008
Bermuda	648-651
British Indian Ocean Territory	136-140
Falkland Is.	573-577
Fiji	687-691
Montserrat	830-834

St. Kitts	351-355

Nos. 557-561 (5)	15.60	14.60
Nos. 771-775 (5)	24.65	21.45
Nos. 842-846 (5)	14.15	12.85
Nos. 1003-1008 (6)	16.55	16.50
Nos. 648-651 (4)	9.65	10.45
Nos. 136-140 (5)	16.10	16.10
Nos. 573-577 (5)	10.85	10.85
Nos. 687-691 (5)	17.75	17.40
Nos. 830-834 (5)	14.10	14.10
Nos. 351-355 (5)	22.80	23.55
Set total (50) Stamps	162.20	157.85

Royal Air Force, 80th Anniv.

Design CD350 Re-inscribed

1998

Ascension	697-701
Bahamas	907-911
British Indian Ocean Terr	198-202
Cayman Islands	754-758
Fiji	814-818
Gibraltar	755-759
Samoa	957-961
Turks & Caicos Islands	1258-1265
Tuvalu	763-767
Virgin Islands	879-883

Nos. 697-701 (5)	16.10	16.10
Nos. 907-911 (5)	13.60	12.65
Nos. 136-140 (5)	16.10	16.10
Nos. 754-758 (5)	15.25	15.25
Nos. 814-818 (5)	14.00	12.75
Nos. 755-759 (5)	9.70	9.70
Nos. 957-961 (5)	15.70	14.90
Nos. 1258-1265 (2)	27.50	27.50
Nos. 763-767 (5)	9.75	9.75
Nos. 879-883 (5)	15.00	15.00
Set total (47) Stamps	152.70	149.70

End of World War II, 50th Anniv.

CD351

CD352

1995

Ascension	613-617
Bahamas	824-828
Barbados	891-895
Belize	1047-1050
British Indian Ocean Territory	163-167
Cayman Islands	704-708
Falkland Islands	634-638
Fiji	720-724
Kiribati	662-668
Liberia	1175-1179
Mauritius	803-805
St. Helena	646-654
St. Kitts	389-393
St. Lucia	1018-1022
Samoa	890-894
Solomon Islands	799-803
South Georgia	198-200
Tristan da Cunha	562-566

Nos. 613-617 (5)	21.50	21.50

Nos. 824-828 (5)	22.00	18.70
Nos. 891-895 (5)	14.20	11.90
Nos. 1047-1050 (4)	6.05	5.90
Nos. 163-167 (5)	16.25	16.25
Nos. 704-708 (5)	17.65	13.95
Nos. 634-638 (5)	18.65	17.15
Nos. 720-724 (5)	17.50	14.50
Nos. 662-668 (7)	16.30	16.30
Nos. 1175-1179 (5)	15.25	11.15
Nos. 803-805 (3)	7.50	7.50
Nos. 646-654 (9)	26.10	26.10
Nos. 389-393 (5)	16.40	16.40
Nos. 1018-1022 (5)	12.25	10.15
Nos. 890-894 (5)	15.25	14.50
Nos. 799-803 (5)	14.75	14.75
Nos. 198-200 (3)	14.50	15.50
Nos. 562-566 (5)	20.10	20.10
Set total (91) Stamps	292.20	272.30

UN, 50th Anniv.

CD353

1995

Bahamas	839-842
Barbados	901-904
Belize	1055-1058
Jamaica	847-851
Liberia	1187-1190
Mauritius	813-816
Pitcairn Islands	436-439
St. Kitts	398-401
St. Lucia	1023-1026
Samoa	900-903
Tristan da Cunha	568-571
Virgin Islands	807-810

Nos. 839-842 (4)	7.15	6.40
Nos. 901-904 (4)	7.00	5.75
Nos. 1055-1058 (4)	4.70	4.70
Nos. 847-851 (5)	5.40	5.45
Nos. 1187-1190 (4)	9.65	9.65
Nos. 813-816 (4)	4.55	4.55
Nos. 436-439 (4)	8.15	8.15
Nos. 398-401 (4)	6.15	7.15
Nos. 1023-1026 (4)	7.50	7.25
Nos. 900-903 (4)	9.35	8.20
Nos. 568-571 (4)	13.50	13.50
Nos. 807-810 (4)	7.45	7.45
Set total (49) Stamps	90.55	88.20

Queen Elizabeth, 70th Birthday

CD354

1996

Ascension	632-635
British Antarctic Territory	240-243
British Indian Ocean Territory	176-180
Falkland Islands	653-657
Pitcairn Islands	446-449
St. Helena	672-676
Samoa	912-916
Tokelau	223-227
Tristan da Cunha	576-579
Virgin Islands	824-828

Nos. 632-635 (4)	5.30	5.30
Nos. 240-243 (4)	9.45	8.15
Nos. 176-180 (5)	11.50	11.50
Nos. 653-657 (5)	13.55	11.20
Nos. 446-449 (4)	8.60	8.60
Nos. 672-676 (5)	12.45	12.70
Nos. 912-916 (5)	10.50	10.50
Nos. 223-227 (5)	10.50	10.50
Nos. 576-579 (4)	8.35	8.35
Nos. 824-828 (5)	11.30	11.30
Set total (46) Stamps	101.50	98.10

Diana, Princess of Wales (1961-97)

CD355

1998

Ascension	696
Bahamas	901A-902
Barbados	950
Belize	1091
Bermuda	753
Botswana	659-663
British Antarctic Territory	258
British Indian Ocean Terr.	197
Cayman Islands	752A-753
Falkland Islands	694
Fiji	819-820
Gibraltar	754
Kiribati	719A-720
Namibia	909
Niue	706
Norfolk Island	644-645
Papua New Guinea	937
Pitcairn Islands	487
St. Helena	711
St. Kitts	437A-438
Samoa	955A-956
Seychelles	802
Solomon Islands	866-867
South Georgia	220
Tokelau	252B-253
Tonga	980
Niuafo'ou	201
Tristan da Cunha	618
Tuvalu	762
Vanuatu	718A-719
Virgin Islands	878

No. 696 (1)	5.25	5.25
Nos. 901A-902 (2)	5.30	5.30
No. 950 (1)	6.25	6.25
No. 1091 (1)	5.00	5.00
No. 753 (1)	5.00	5.00
Nos. 659-663 (5)	8.25	8.80
No. 258 (1)	5.50	5.50
No. 197 (1)	5.50	5.50
Nos. 752A-753 (3)	7.40	7.40
No. 694 (1)	5.00	5.00
Nos. 819-820 (2)	5.25	5.25
No. 754 (1)	4.75	4.75
Nos. 719A-720 (2)	4.85	4.85
No. 909 (1)	1.75	1.75
No. 706 (1)	5.50	5.50
Nos. 644-645 (2)	5.60	5.60
No. 937 (1)	6.25	6.25
No. 487 (1)	4.75	4.75
No. 711 (1)	4.25	4.25
Nos. 437A-438 (2)	5.15	5.15
Nos. 955A-956 (2)	7.00	7.00
No. 802 (1)	6.25	6.25
Nos. 866-867 (2)	5.40	5.40
No. 220 (1)	4.50	5.00
Nos. 252B-253 (2)	6.00	6.00
No. 980 (1)	5.75	5.75
No. 201 (1)	6.50	6.50
No. 618 (1)	5.00	5.00
No. 762 (1)	4.00	4.00
Nos. 718A-719 (2)	8.00	8.00
No. 878 (1)	4.50	4.50
Set total (46) Stamps	169.45	170.50

Wedding of Prince Edward and Sophie Rhys-Jones

CD356

1999

Ascension	729-730
Cayman Islands	775-776
Falkland Islands	729-730
Pitcairn Islands	505-506
St. Helena	733-734
Samoa	971-972
Tristan da Cunha	636-637

Virgin Islands	908-909

Nos. 729-730 (2)	4.50	4.50
Nos. 775-776 (2)	4.95	4.95
Nos. 729-730 (2)	14.00	14.00
Nos. 505-506 (2)	7.00	7.00
Nos. 733-734 (2)	5.00	5.00
Nos. 971-972 (2)	5.00	5.00
Nos. 636-637 (2)	7.50	7.50
Nos. 908-909 (2)	7.50	7.50
Set total (16) Stamps	55.45	55.45

1st Manned Moon Landing, 30th Anniv.

CD357

1999

Ascension	731-735
Bahamas	942-946
Barbados	967-971
Bermuda	778
Cayman Islands	777-781
Fiji	853-857
Jamaica	889-893
Kiribati	746-750
Nauru	465-469
St. Kitts	460-464
Samoa	973-977
Solomon Islands	875-879
Tuvalu	800-804
Virgin Islands	910-914

Nos. 731-735 (5)	12.80	12.80
Nos. 942-946 (5)	14.10	14.10
Nos. 967-971 (5)	9.45	8.25
No. 778 (1)	9.00	9.00
Nos. 777-781 (5)	9.25	9.25
Nos. 853-857 (5)	9.25	8.45
Nos. 889-893 (5)	8.30	7.18
Nos. 746-750 (5)	8.85	8.85
Nos. 465-469 (5)	9.25	8.00
Nos. 460-464 (5)	11.35	11.65
Nos. 973-977 (5)	12.60	12.45
Nos. 875-879 (5)	7.50	7.50
Nos. 800-804 (5)	7.45	7.45
Nos. 910-914 (5)	11.75	11.75
Set total (66) Stamps	140.90	136.68

Queen Mother's Century

CD358

1999

Ascension	736-740
Bahamas	951-955
Cayman Islands	782-786
Falkland Islands	734-738
Fiji	858-862
Norfolk Island	688-692
St. Helena	740-744
Samoa	978-982
Solomon Islands	880-884
South Georgia	231-235
Tristan da Cunha	638-642
Tuvalu	805-809

Nos. 736-740 (5)	15.50	15.50
Nos. 951-955 (5)	13.75	12.65
Nos. 782-786 (5)	8.35	8.35
Nos. 734-738 (5)	30.00	28.25
Nos. 858-862 (5)	12.80	13.25
Nos. 688-692 (5)	9.50	9.50
Nos. 740-744 (5)	16.15	16.15
Nos. 978-982 (5)	12.50	12.10
Nos. 880-884 (5)	7.50	7.00
Nos. 231-235 (5)	29.75	30.00
Nos. 638-642 (5)	18.00	18.00
Nos. 805-809 (5)	8.65	8.65
Set total (60) Stamps	182.45	179.40

Prince William, 18th Birthday

CD359

2000

Ascension	755-759
Cayman Islands	797-801
Falkland Islands	762-766
Fiji	889-893
South Georgia	257-261
Tristan da Cunha	664-668
Virgin Islands	925-929

Nos. 755-759 (5)	15.50	15.50
Nos. 797-801 (5)	11.15	10.90
Nos. 762-766 (5)	24.60	22.50
Nos. 889-893 (5)	12.90	12.90
Nos. 257-261 (5)	29.00	28.75
Nos. 664-668 (5)	21.50	21.50
Nos. 925-929 (5)	14.50	14.50
Set total (35) Stamps	129.15	126.55

Reign of Queen Elizabeth II, 50th Anniv.

CD360

2002

Ascension	790-794
Bahamas	1033-1037
Barbados	1019-1023
Belize	1152-1156
Bermuda	822-826
British Antarctic Territory	307-311
British Indian Ocean Territory	239-243
Cayman Islands	844-848
Falkland Islands	804-808
Gibraltar	896-900
Jamaica	952-956
Nauru	491-495
Norfolk Island	758-762
Papua New Guinea	1019-1023
Pitcairn Islands	552
St. Helena	788-792
St. Lucia	1146-1150
Solomon Islands	931-935
South Georgia	274-278
Swaziland	706-710
Tokelau	302-306
Tonga	1059
Niuafo'ou	239
Tristan da Cunha	706-710
Virgin Islands	967-971

Nos. 790-794 (5)	14.10	14.10
Nos. 1033-1037 (5)	15.25	15.25
Nos. 1019-1023 (5)	12.90	12.90
Nos. 1152-1156 (5)	12.65	12.25
Nos. 822-826 (5)	18.00	18.00
Nos. 307-311 (5)	23.00	23.00
Nos. 239-243 (5)	19.40	19.40
Nos. 844-848 (5)	13.25	13.25
Nos. 804-808 (5)	23.00	22.00
Nos. 896-900 (5)	6.65	6.65
Nos. 952-956 (5)	16.65	16.65
Nos. 491-495 (5)	17.75	17.75
Nos. 758-762 (5)	15.90	15.90
Nos. 1019-1023 (5)	14.50	14.50
No. 552 (1)	9.25	9.25
Nos. 788-792 (5)	19.75	19.75
Nos. 1146-1150 (5)	12.25	12.25
Nos. 931-935 (5)	12.40	12.40
Nos. 274-278 (5)	28.00	28.50
Nos. 706-710 (5)	12.50	12.50
Nos. 302-306 (5)	14.50	14.50
No. 1059 (1)	8.50	8.50
No. 239 (1)	8.75	8.75
Nos. 706-710 (5)	18.50	18.50
Nos. 967-971 (5)	16.50	16.50
Set total (113) Stamps	383.90	383.00

Queen Mother Elizabeth (1900-2002)

CD361

2002

Ascension		799-801
Bahamas		1044-1046
Bermuda		834-836
British Antarctic Territory		312-314
British Indian Ocean Territory		245-247
Cayman Islands		857-861
Falkland Islands		812-816
Nauru		499-501
Pitcairn Islands		561-565
St. Helena		808-812
St. Lucia		1155-1159
Seychelles		830
Solomon Islands		945-947
South Georgia		281-285
Tokelau		312-314
Tristan da Cunha		715-717
Virgin Islands		979-983

Nos. 799-801 (3)	8.85	8.85
Nos. 1044-1046 (3)	9.10	9.10
Nos. 834-836 (3)	12.25	12.25
Nos. 312-314 (3)	18.75	18.75
Nos. 245-247 (3)	17.35	17.35
Nos. 857-861 (5)	15.00	15.00
Nos. 812-816 (5)	28.50	28.50
Nos. 499-501 (3)	14.00	14.00
Nos. 561-565 (5)	15.25	15.25
Nos. 808-812 (5)	12.00	12.00
Nos. 1155-1159 (5)	12.00	12.00
No. 830 (1)	6.50	6.50
Nos. 945-947 (3)	9.25	9.25
Nos. 281-285 (5)	19.50	19.50
Nos. 312-314 (3)	11.85	11.85
Nos. 715-717 (3)	16.25	16.25
Nos. 979-983 (5)	23.50	23.50
Set total (63) Stamps	249.90	249.90

Head of Queen Elizabeth II

CD362

2003

Ascension		822
Bermuda		865
British Antarctic Territory		322
British Indian Ocean Territory		261
Cayman Islands		878
Falkland Islands		828
St. Helena		820
South Georgia		294
Tristan da Cunha		731
Virgin Islands		1003

No. 822 (1)	12.50	12.50
No. 865 (1)	50.00	50.00
No. 322 (1)	9.50	9.50
No. 261 (1)	11.00	11.00
No. 878 (1)	14.00	14.00
No. 828 (1)	9.00	9.00
No. 820 (1)	9.00	9.00
No. 294 (1)	8.50	8.50
No. 731 (1)	10.00	10.00
No. 1003 (1)	10.00	10.00
Set total (10) Stamps	143.50	143.50

Coronation of Queen Elizabeth II, 50th Anniv.

CD363

2003

Ascension		823-825

Bahamas		1073-1075
Bermuda		866-868
British Antarctic Territory		323-325
British Indian Ocean Territory		262-264
Cayman Islands		879-881
Jamaica		970-972
Kiribati		825-827
Pitcairn Islands		577-581
St. Helena		821-823
St. Lucia		1171-1173
Tokelau		320-322
Tristan da Cunha		732-734
Virgin Islands		1004-1006

Nos. 823-825 (3)	12.50	12.50
Nos. 1073-1075 (3)	13.00	13.00
Nos. 866-868 (2)	14.25	14.25
Nos. 323-325 (3)	23.00	23.00
Nos. 262-264 (3)	28.00	28.00
Nos. 879-881 (3)	19.25	19.25
Nos. 970-972 (3)	10.00	10.00
Nos. 825-827 (3)	13.50	13.50
Nos. 577-581 (5)	14.40	14.40
Nos. 821-823 (3)	7.25	7.25
Nos. 1171-1173 (3)	8.75	8.75
Nos. 320-322 (3)	17.25	17.25
Nos. 732-734 (3)	16.75	16.75
Nos. 1004-1006 (3)	25.00	25.00
Set total (43) Stamps	222.90	222.90

Prince William, 21st Birthday

CD364

2003

Ascension		826
British Indian Ocean Territory		265
Cayman Islands		882-884
Falkland Islands		829
South Georgia		295
Tokelau		323
Tristan da Cunha		735
Virgin Islands		1007-1009

No. 826 (1)	7.25	7.25
No. 265 (1)	8.00	8.00
Nos. 882-884 (3)	6.95	6.95
No. 829 (1)	13.50	13.50
No. 295 (1)	8.50	8.50
No. 323 (1)	7.25	7.25
No. 735 (1)	6.00	6.00
Nos. 1007-1009 (3)	10.00	10.00
Set total (12) Stamps	67.45	67.45

STOCKBOOKS

Stockbooks are a classic and convenient storage alternative for many collectors.
These 9" x 12" Lighthouse stockbooks feature heavyweight archival quality paper with 9 pockets on each page and include double glassine interleaving between the pages for added protection.

COLOR: COVER/PAGES	PAGES	ITEM	RETAIL	AA*	COLOR: COVER/PAGES	PAGES	ITEM	RETAIL	AA*
BLACK/BLACK	16	LS48BK	$21.95	$18.66	BLACK/BLACK	32	LS416BK	$31.95	$27.16
BLACK/WHITE	16	LW48BK	$19.95	$16.96	BLUE/BLACK	32	LS416BL	$31.95	$27.16
BLUE/BLACK	16	LS48BL	$21.95	$18.66	GREEN/BLACK	32	LS416GR	$31.95	$27.16
BLUE/WHITE	16	LW48BL	$19.95	$16.96	RED/BLACK	32	LS416RD	$31.95	$27.16
GREEN/BLACK	16	LS48GR	$21.95	$18.66	BLACK/BLACK	64	LS432BK	$59.95	$50.96
GREEN/WHITE	16	LW48GR	$19.95	$16.96	BLUE/BLACK	64	LS432BL	$59.95	$50.96
RED/BLACK	16	LS48RD	$21.95	$18.66	GREEN/BLACK	64	LS432GR	$59.95	$50.96
RED/WHITE	16	LW48RD	$19.95	$16.96	RED/BLACK	64	LS432RD	$59.95	$50.96

Get yours today by visiting **AmosAdvantage.com**

Or call **1-800-572-6885** • Outside U.S. & Canada Call: **1-937-498-0800**

Mail to: P.O. Box 4129, Sidney, OH 45365

British Commonwealth of Nations

Dominions, Colonies, Territories, Offices and Independent Members

Comprising stamps of the British Commonwealth and associated nations.

A strict observance of technicalities would bar some or all of the stamps listed under Burma, Ireland, Kuwait, Nepal, New Republic, Orange Free State, Samoa, South Africa, South-West Africa, Stellaland, Sudan, Swaziland, the two Transvaal Republics and others but these are included for the convenience of collectors.

1. Great Britain

Great Britain: Including England, Scotland, Wales and Northern Ireland.

2. The Dominions, Present and Past

AUSTRALIA

The Commonwealth of Australia was proclaimed on January 1, 1901. It consists of six former colonies as follows:

New South Wales	Victoria
Queensland	Tasmania
South Australia	Western Australia

The following islands and territories are, or have been, administered by Australia: Australian Antarctic Territory, Christmas Island, Cocos (Keeling) Islands, Nauru, New Guinea, Norfolk Island, Papua.

CANADA

The Dominion of Canada was created by the British North America Act in 1867. The following provinces were former sepa- rate colonies and issued postage stamps:

British Columbia and Vancouver Island	Newfoundland
	Nova Scotia
New Brunswick	Prince Edward Island

FIJI

The colony of Fiji became an independent nation with dominion status on Oct. 10, 1970.

GHANA

This state came into existence Mar. 6, 1957, with dominion status. It consists of the former colony of the Gold Coast and the Trusteeship Territory of Togoland. Ghana became a republic July 1, 1960.

INDIA

The Republic of India was inaugurated on January 26, 1950. It succeeded the Dominion of India which was proclaimed August 15, 1947, when the former Empire of India was divided into Pakistan and the Union of India. The Republic is composed of about 40 predominantly Hindu states of three classes: governor's provinces, chief commissioner's provinces and princely states. India also has various territories, such as the Andaman and Nicobar Islands.

The old Empire of India was a federation of British India and the native states. The more important princely states were autonomous. Of the more than 700 Indian states, these 43 are familiar names to philatelists because of their postage stamps.

CONVENTION STATES

Chamba	Jhind
Faridkot	Nabha
Gwalior	Patiala

FEUDATORY STATES

Alwar	Jammu and Kashmir
Bahawalpur	Jasdan
Bamra	Jhalawar
Barwani	Jhind (1875-76)
Bhopal	Kashmir
Bhor	Kishangarh
Bijawar	Kotah
Bundi	Las Bela
Bussahir	Morvi
Charkhari	Nandgaon
Cochin	Nowanuggur
Dhar	Orchha
Dungarpur	Poonch
Duttia	Rajasthan
Faridkot (1879-85)	Rajpeepla
Hyderabad	Sirmur
Idar	Soruth
Indore	Tonk
Jaipur	Travancore
Jammu	Wadhwan

NEW ZEALAND

Became a dominion on September 26, 1907. The following islands and territories are, or have been, administered by New Zealand:

Aitutaki	Ross Dependency
Cook Islands (Rarotonga)	Samoa (Western Samoa)
Niue	Tokelau Islands
Penrhyn	

PAKISTAN

The Republic of Pakistan was proclaimed March 23, 1956. It succeeded the Dominion which was proclaimed August 15, 1947. It is made up of all or part of several Moslem provinces and various districts of the former Empire of India, including Bahawalpur and Las Bela. Pakistan withdrew from the Commonwealth in 1972.

SOUTH AFRICA

Under the terms of the South African Act (1909) the self-governing colonies of Cape of Good Hope, Natal, Orange River Colony and Transvaal united on May 31, 1910, to form the Union of South Africa. It became an independent republic May 3, 1961.

Under the terms of the Treaty of Versailles, South-West Africa, formerly German South-West Africa, was mandated to the Union of South Africa.

SRI LANKA (CEYLON)

The Dominion of Ceylon was proclaimed February 4, 1948. The island had been a Crown Colony from 1802 until then. On May 22, 1972, Ceylon became the Republic of Sri Lanka.

3. Colonies, Past and Present; Controlled Territory and Independent Members of the Commonwealth

Abu Dhabi	Barbados	British Central Africa
Aden	Barbuda	British Columbia and
Aitutaki	Basutoland	Vancouver Island
Alderney	Batum	British East Africa
Anguilla	Bechuanaland	British Guiana
Antigua	Bechuanaland Prot.	
Ascension	Belize	
Australia	Bermuda	
Bahamas	Botswana	
Bahrain	British Antarctic	
Bangladesh	Territory	

British Honduras
British Indian Ocean Territory
British New Guinea
British Solomon Islands
British Somaliland
Brunei
Burma
Bushire
Cameroons
Canada
Cape of Good Hope
Cayman Islands
Christmas Island
Cocos (Keeling) Islands
Cook Islands
Crete,
  British Administration
Cyprus
Dominica
East Africa & Uganda
  Protectorates
Egypt
Falkland Islands
Fiji
Gambia
German East Africa
Ghana
Gibraltar
Gilbert Islands
Gilbert & Ellice Islands
Gold Coast
Grenada
Griqualand West
Guernsey
Guyana
Heligoland
Hong Kong
Indian Native States
  (see India)
Ionian Islands
Jamaica
Jersey
Jordan
Kenya

Kenya, Uganda & Tanzania
Kiribati
Kuwait
Labuan
Lagos
Leeward Islands
Lesotho
Madagascar
Malawi
Malaya
  Federated Malay States
  Johore
  Kedah
  Kelantan
  Malacca
  Negri Sembilan
  Pahang
  Penang
  Perak
  Perlis
  Selangor
  Singapore
  Sungei Ujong
  Trengganu
Malaysia
Maldive Islands
Malta
Man, Isle of
Mauritius
Mesopotamia
Montserrat
Mozambique
Muscat
Namibia
Natal
Nauru
Nevis
New Britain
New Brunswick
Newfoundland
New Guinea
New Hebrides
New Republic
New South Wales

New Zealand
Niger Coast Protectorate
Nigeria
Niue
Norfolk Island
North Borneo
Northern Nigeria
Northern Rhodesia
North West Pacific Islands
Nova Scotia
Nyasaland Protectorate
Oman
Orange River Colony
Pakistan
Palestine
Papua New Guinea
Penrhyn Island
Pitcairn Islands
Prince Edward Island
Qatar
Queensland
Rhodesia
Rhodesia & Nyasaland
Ross Dependency
Rwanda
Sabah
St. Christopher
St. Helena
St. Kitts
St. Kitts-Nevis-Anguilla
St. Lucia
St. Vincent
Samoa
Sarawak
Seychelles
Sierra Leone
Singapore
Solomon Islands
Somaliland Protectorate
South Africa
South Arabia
South Australia
South Georgia
Southern Nigeria

Southern Rhodesia
South-West Africa
Sri Lanka
Stellaland
Straits Settlements
Sudan
Swaziland
Tanganyika
Tanzania
Tasmania
Tobago
Togo
Tokelau Islands
Tonga
Transvaal
Trinidad
Trinidad and Tobago
Tristan da Cunha
Trucial States
Turks and Caicos
Turks Islands
Tuvalu
Uganda
United Arab Emirates
Vanuatu
Victoria
Virgin Islands
Western Australia
Zambia
Zanzibar
Zimbabwe
Zululand

POST OFFICES IN FOREIGN COUNTRIES
  Africa
    East Africa Forces
    Middle East Forces
  Bangkok
  China
  Morocco
  Turkish Empire

Colonies, Former Colonies, Offices, Territories Controlled by Parent States

Belgium
Belgian Congo
Ruanda-Urundi

Denmark
Danish West Indies
Faroe Islands
Greenland
Iceland

Finland
Åland Islands

France
COLONIES PAST AND PRESENT, CONTROLLED TERRITORIES
Afars & Issas, Territory of
Alaouites
Alexandretta
Algeria
Alsace & Lorraine
Anjouan
Annam & Tonkin
Benin
Cambodia (Khmer)
Cameroun
Castellorizo
Chad
Cilicia
Cochin China
Comoro Islands
Dahomey
Diego Suarez
Djibouti (Somali Coast)
Fezzan
French Congo
French Equatorial Africa
French Guiana
French Guinea
French India
French Morocco
French Polynesia (Oceania)
French Southern & Antarctic Territories
French Sudan
French West Africa
Gabon
Germany
Ghadames
Grand Comoro
Guadeloupe
Indo-China
Inini
Ivory Coast
Laos
Latakia
Lebanon
Madagascar
Martinique
Mauritania
Mayotte
Memel
Middle Congo
Moheli
New Caledonia
New Hebrides
Niger Territory

Nossi-Be
Obock
Reunion
Rouad, Ile
Ste.-Marie de Madagascar
St. Pierre & Miquelon
Senegal
Senegambia & Niger
Somali Coast
Syria
Tahiti
Togo
Tunisia
Ubangi-Shari
Upper Senegal & Niger
Upper Volta
Viet Nam
Wallis & Futuna Islands

POST OFFICES IN FOREIGN COUNTRIES
China
Crete
Egypt
Turkish Empire
Zanzibar

Germany
EARLY STATES
Baden
Bavaria
Bergedorf
Bremen
Brunswick
Hamburg
Hanover
Lubeck
Mecklenburg-Schwerin
Mecklenburg-Strelitz
Oldenburg
Prussia
Saxony
Schleswig-Holstein
Wurttemberg

FORMER COLONIES
Cameroun (Kamerun)
Caroline Islands
German East Africa
German New Guinea
German South-West Africa
Kiauchau
Mariana Islands
Marshall Islands
Samoa
Togo

Italy
EARLY STATES
Modena
Parma
Romagna
Roman States
Sardinia
Tuscany
Two Sicilies
  Naples
  Neapolitan Provinces
  Sicily

FORMER COLONIES, CONTROLLED TERRITORIES, OCCUPATION AREAS
Aegean Islands
  Calimno (Calino)
  Caso
  Cos (Coo)
  Karki (Carchi)
  Leros (Lero)
  Lipso
  Nisiros (Nisiro)
  Patmos (Patmo)
  Piscopi
  Rodi (Rhodes)
  Scarpanto
  Simi
  Stampalia
Castellorizo
Corfu
Cyrenaica
Eritrea
Ethiopia (Abyssinia)
Fiume
Ionian Islands
  Cephalonia
  Ithaca
  Paxos
Italian East Africa
Libya
Oltre Giuba
Saseno
Somalia (Italian Somaliland)
Tripolitania

POST OFFICES IN FOREIGN COUNTRIES
"ESTERO"*
Austria
China
  Peking
  Tientsin
Crete
Tripoli
Turkish Empire
  Constantinople
  Durazzo
  Janina
Jerusalem
Salonika
Scutari
Smyrna
Valona
*Stamps overprinted "ESTERO" were used in various parts of the world.

Netherlands
Aruba
Caribbean Netherlands
Curacao
Netherlands Antilles (Curacao)
Netherlands Indies
Netherlands New Guinea
St. Martin
Surinam (Dutch Guiana)

Portugal
COLONIES PAST AND PRESENT, CONTROLLED TERRITORIES
Angola
Angra
Azores

Cape Verde
Funchal
Horta
Inhambane
Kionga
Lourenco Marques
Macao
Madeira
Mozambique
Mozambique Co.
Nyassa
Ponta Delgada
Portuguese Africa
Portuguese Congo
Portuguese Guinea
Portuguese India
Quelimane
St. Thomas & Prince Islands
Tete
Timor
Zambezia

Russia
ALLIED TERRITORIES AND REPUBLICS, OCCUPATION AREAS
Armenia
Aunus (Olonets)
Azerbaijan
Batum
Estonia
Far Eastern Republic
Georgia
Karelia
Latvia
Lithuania
North Ingermanland
Ostland
Russian Turkestan
Siberia
South Russia
Tannu Tuva
Transcaucasian Fed. Republics
Ukraine
Wenden (Livonia)
Western Ukraine

Spain
COLONIES PAST AND PRESENT, CONTROLLED TERRITORIES
Aguera, La
Cape Juby
Cuba
Elobey, Annobon & Corisco
Fernando Po
Ifni
Mariana Islands
Philippines
Puerto Rico
Rio de Oro
Rio Muni
Spanish Guinea
Spanish Morocco
Spanish Sahara
Spanish West Africa

POST OFFICES IN FOREIGN COUNTRIES
Morocco
Tangier
Tetuan

Dies of British Colonial Stamps

DIE A:

    1. The lines in the groundwork vary in thickness and are not uniformly straight.

    2. The seventh and eighth lines from the top, in the groundwork, converge where they meet the head.

    3. There is a small dash in the upper part of the second jewel in the band of the crown.

    4. The vertical color line in front of the throat stops at the sixth line of shading on the neck.

DIE B:

    1. The lines in the groundwork are all thin and straight.

    2. All the lines of the background are parallel.

    3. There is no dash in the upper part of the second jewel in the band of the crown.

    4. The vertical color line in front of the throat stops at the eighth line of shading on the neck.

DIE I:

    1. The base of the crown is well below the level of the inner white line around the vignette.

    2. The labels inscribed "POSTAGE" and "REVENUE" are cut square at the top.

    3. There is a white "bud" on the outer side of the main stem of the curved ornaments in each lower corner.

    4. The second (thick) line below the country name has the ends next to the crown cut diagonally.

DIE Ia.	DIE Ib.
1 as die II.	1 and 3 as die II.
2 and 3 as die I.	2 as die I.

DIE II:

    1. The base of the crown is aligned with the underside of the white line around the vignette.

    2. The labels curve inward at the top inner corners.

    3. The "bud" has been removed from the outer curve of the ornaments in each corner.

    4. The second line below the country name has the ends next to the crown cut vertically.

Wmk. 1
Crown and C C

Wmk. 2
Crown and C A

Wmk. 3
Multiple Crown
and C A

Wmk. 4
Multiple Crown
and Script C A

Wmk. 4a

Wmk. 46

Wmk. 314
St. Edward's Crown
and C A Multiple

Wmk. 373

Wmk. 384

Wmk. 406

British Colonial and Crown Agents Watermarks

Watermarks 1 to 4, 314, 373, 384 and 406, common to many British territories, are illustrated here to avoid duplication.

The letters "CC" of Wmk. 1 identify the paper as having been made for the use of the Crown Colonies, while the letters "CA" of the others stand for "Crown Agents." Both Wmks. 1 and 2 were used on stamps printed by De La Rue & Co.

Wmk. 3 was adopted in 1904; Wmk. 4 in 1921; Wmk. 46 in 1879; Wmk. 314 in 1957; Wmk. 373 in 1974; Wmk. 384 in 1985; Wmk 406 in 2008.

In Wmk. 4a, a non-matching crown of the general St. Edwards type (bulging on both sides at top) was substituted for one of the Wmk. 4 crowns which fell off the dandy roll. The non-matching crown occurs in 1950-52 printings in a horizontal row of crowns on certain regular stamps of Johore and Seychelles, and on various postage due stamps of Barbados, Basutoland, British Guiana, Gold Coast, Grenada, Northern Rhodesia, St. Lucia, Swaziland and Trinidad and Tobago. A variation of Wmk. 4a, with the non-matching crown in a horizontal row of crown-CA-crown, occurs on regular stamps of Bahamas, St. Kitts-Nevis and Singapore.

Wmk. 314 was intentionally used sideways, starting in 1966. When a stamp was issued with Wmk. 314 both upright and sideways, the sideways varieties usually are listed also – with minor numbers. In many of the later issues, Wmk. 314 is slightly visible.

Wmk. 373 is usually only faintly visible.

COVER SUPPLIES

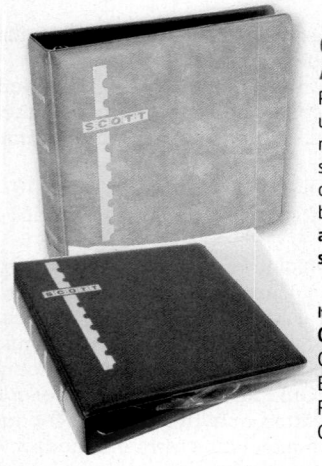

COVER BINDERS AND PAGES

Padded, durable, 3-ring binders will hold up to 100 covers. Features the "D" ring mechanism on the right hand side of album so you don't have to worry about creasing or wrinkling covers when opening or closing binder. Cover pages sold separately. **Binders and pages are also sold in a money saving sets. Call or go online for more details.**

Item		Retail	AA*
COVER BINDERS		$16.99	**$12.99**

Choose from four classic colors:
Black (CBBK); Blue (CBBL);
Red/Burgundy (CBRD);
Gray (CBGY)

COVER ALBUM PAGES WITH BLACK BACKGROUNDS

Item	Description	Retail	AA*
T2	Double-sided Page, 2 Pocket (25/pack)	$9.99	**$8.99**
SS2PG1B	Supersafe Page, 1 Pocket (10/pack)	$5.75	**$4.75**

COVER SLEEVES

Clear polyethylene sleeves protect your covers. **Sold in packages of 100.**

U.S. POSTAL CARD

3 11/16"
5 1/4"

Item	Retail	AA*
CVB05	$2.75	**$2.25**

U.S. FIRST DAY COVER #6

3 15/16"
6 7/8"

Item	Retail	AA*
CVB06	$3.25	**$2.75**

CONTINENTAL POSTCARD

4 3/8"
6"

Item	Retail	AA*
CVB07	$3.50	**$2.99**

EUROPEAN FIRST DAY COVER

5 1/8"
7 13/16"

Item	Retail	AA*
CVB09	$4.25	**$3.95**

#10 BUSINESS ENVELOPE

4 1/4"
9 5/8"

Item	Retail	AA*
CVB10	$5.75	$4.95

MINT SHEET BINDERS & PAGES

Keep those mint sheets intact in a handsome, 3-ring binder. Just like the cover album, the Mint Sheet album features the "D" ring mechanism on the right hand side of binder so you don't have to worry about damaging your stamps when turning the pages.

Binders and pages are also sold in a money saving sets. Call or go online for more details.

Item		Retail	AA*
MBRD	Red (Burgundy)	$21.99	**$17.99**
MBBL	Blue	$21.99	**$17.99**
MBGY	Gray	$21.99	**$17.99**
MBBK	Black	$21.99	**$17.99**
MS1	BLACK Mint Sheet Pages (25 per pack)	$16.99	**$14.99**
SSMP3C	CLEAR Mint Sheet Pages (12 per pack)	$9.95	**$8.95**

GLASSINE ENVELOPES

Perfect for organizing duplicates and sending approvals or mailing stamps. **Sold in packages of 100.**

Item	Size (Dimensions)	Retail-Inc	AA	AA-Disc 10+	Item	Size (Dimensions)	Retail-Inc	AA	AA-Disc 10+
GE01	#1 Glassine	5.49	4.99	**3.85**	GE06	#6 Glassine	10.50	9.50	**7.07**
GE02	#2 Glassine	5.99	5.49	**4.18**	GE07	#7 Glassine	11.00	10.00	**7.63**
GE03	#3 Glassine	6.99	5.99	**4.36**	GE08	#8 Glassine	11.50	10.50	**7.99**
GE04	#4 Glassine	7.99	6.99	**4.99**	GE10	#10 Glassine	17.99	16.99	**13.12**
GE4H	#4.5 Glassine	8.99	7.99	**5.45**	GE11	#11 Glassine	18.99	17.99	**13.65**
GE05	#5 Glassine	9.99	8.99	**6.05**					

GLASSINE BAGS

These larger glassine bags are ideal for storing panes, covers or prestige booklets. A handy accessory to keep around for all your collecting needs. Available in five different sizes. **Sold in packages of 100.**

Item	Size (Dimensions)	Retail	AA*
GB12	#12 (4 5/8" x 6 5/8")	$8.99	**$7.99**
GB13	#13 (5 3/4" x 7 3/4")	$9.99	**$8.99**
GB13A	#13A (6 3/4" x 9")	$10.99	**$9.99**
GB14	#14 (7 3/4" x 9 3/4")	$16.99	**$14.99**
GB15	#15 (8 1/2" x 11")	$18.99	**$15.99**

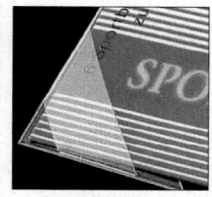

PRINZ CORNER MOUNTS

Clear, self-adhesive corner mounts are ideal for postal cards and covers. Mounts measure 7/8" each side and are made from transparent glass foil. There are 250 mounts in each pack.

Item	Retail	AA*
ACC176	$11.99	**$8.99**

AmosAdvantage.com • 1-800-572-6885

Outside U.S. and Canada, call (937) 498-0800
Mail to PO Box 4129, Sidney, OH 45365-4129

PITCAIRN ISLANDS

'pit-ˌkärn 'ī-lənds

LOCATION — South Pacific Ocean, nearly equidistant from Australia and South America
GOVT. — British colony under the British High Commissioner in New Zealand
AREA — 18 sq. mi. (includes all islands)
POP. — 43 (2007 est.)

The district of Pitcairn also includes the uninhabited islands of Ducie, Henderson and Oeno.

Postal affairs are administered by New Zealand.

12 Pence = 1 Shilling
100 Cents = 1 Dollar (1967)

> Catalogue values for all unused stamps in this country are for Never Hinged items.

Watermarks

Wmk. 387

Cluster of Oranges A1

Fletcher Christian with Crew and View of Pitcairn Island — A2

John Adams and His House A3

William Bligh and H. M. Armed Vessel "Bounty" A4

Map of Pitcairn and Pacific Ocean — A5

Bounty Bible — A6

H.M. Armed Vessel "Bounty" A7

Pitcairn School, 1949 — A8

Fletcher Christian and View of Pitcairn Island — A9

Fletcher Christian with Crew and Coast of Pitcairn A10

Perf. 12½, 11½x11

		1940-51	Engr.	Wmk. 4	
1	A1	½p blue grn & org		.95	1.00
2	A2	1p red lil & rose vio		1.15	.70
3	A3	1½p rose car & blk		1.15	.40
4	A4	2p dk brn & brt grn		2.00	1.25
5	A5	3p dk blue & yel grn		1.00	1.00
5A	A6	4p dk blue grn & blk		18.00	11.00
6	A7	6p sl grn & dp brn		5.50	1.25
6A	A8	8p lil rose & grn		18.50	7.50
7	A9	1sh slate & vio		5.00	2.00
8	A10	2sh6p dk brn & brt grn		13.50	3.50
		Nos. 1-8 (10)		66.75	29.60

Nos. 1-5, 6 and 7-8 exist in a booklet of eight panes of one. Value $2,750.
Issued: 4p, 8p, 9/1/51; others, 10/15/40.

Common Design Types pictured following the introduction.

Peace Issue
Common Design Type

		1946, Dec. 2		Perf. 13½x14	
9	CD303	2p brown		.65	.65
10	CD303	3p deep blue		.75	.75

Silver Wedding Issue
Common Design Types

		1949, Aug. 1	Photo.	Perf. 14x14½	
11	CD304	1½p scarlet		1.75	1.00

Perf. 11½x11
Engraved; Name Typographed

		1949			
12	CD305	10sh purple		43.00	47.50

UPU Issue
Common Design Types
Engr.; Name Typo. on 3p & 6p

		1949, Oct. 10		Perf. 13½, 11x11½	
13	CD306	2½p red brown		2.25	4.00
14	CD307	3p indigo		8.00	4.00
15	CD308	6p green		4.00	4.00
16	CD309	1sh rose violet		4.25	4.50
		Nos. 13-16 (4)		18.50	16.50

Coronation Issue
Common Design Type

		1953, June 2		Perf. 13½x13	
19	CD312	4p dk green & blk		2.25	2.25

Ti Plant — A11

Map — A12

Designs: 2p, John Adams and Bounty Bible. 2½p, Handicraft (Carving). 3p, Bounty Bay. 4p, School (actually Schoolteacher's House). 6p, Fiji-Pitcairn connection (Map). 8p, Inland scene. 1sh, Handicraft (Ship model). 2sh, Wheelbarrow. 2sh6p, Whaleboat.

Perf. 13x12½, 12½x13

		1957, July 2	Engr.	Wmk. 4	
20	A11	½p lilac & green		.75	1.00
21	A12	1p olive grn & blk		4.50	2.00
22	A12	2p blue & brown		2.25	.50
23	A11	2½p orange & brn		.65	.50
24	A11	3p ultra & emer		.90	.50
25	A11	4p ultra & rose red (Pitcairn School)		1.10	.65
26	A11	6p indigo & buff		3.25	.65
27	A11	8p magenta & grn		.65	.65
28	A11	1sh brown & blk		2.25	.90
29	A12	2sh dp org & grn		11.00	9.00
30	A11	2sh6p mag & ultra		25.00	10.00
		Nos. 20-30 (11)		52.30	26.35

See Nos. 31, 38.

Type of 1957 Corrected

		1958, Nov. 5		Perf. 13x12½	
31	A11	4p ultra & rose red (School-teacher's House)		5.00	2.50

Simon Young and Pitcairn A13

Designs: 6p, Maps of Norfolk and Pitcairn Islands. 1sh, Schooner Mary Ann.

Perf. 14½x13½

		1961, Nov. 15	Photo.	Wmk. 314	
32	A13	3p yellow & black		.50	.50
33	A13	6p blue & red brown		1.10	1.10
34	A13	1sh brt green & dp org		1.10	1.10
		Nos. 32-34 (3)		2.70	2.70

Pitcairn Islanders return from Norfolk Island.

Freedom from Hunger Issue
Common Design Type

		1963, June 4		Perf. 14x14½	
35	CD314	2sh6p ultra		10.00	4.50

Red Cross Centenary Issue
Common Design Type

		1963, Dec. 9	Litho.	Perf. 13	
36	CD315	2p black & red		1.00	1.00
37	CD315	2sh6p ultra & red		5.50	4.50

Type of 1957

		1963, Dec. 4	Engr.	Wmk. 314	
38	A11	½p lilac & green		1.25	2.25

Pitcairn Longboat A14

Queen Elizabeth II — A15

1p, H.M. Armed Vessel Bounty. 2p, Oarsmen rowing longboat. 3p, Great frigate bird. 4p, Fairy tern 6p, Pitcairn reed warbler. 8p, Red-footed booby. 10p, Red-tailed tropic birds. 1sh, Henderson Island flightless rail.

1sh6p, Henderson Island lory. 2sh6p, Murphy's petrel. 4sh, Henderson Island fruit pigeon.

		1964-65	Photo.	Perf. 14x14½	
39	A14	½p multicolored		.25	.30
a.		Blue omitted		750.00	
40	A14	1p multicolored		.30	.30
41	A14	2p multicolored		.30	.30
42	A14	3p multicolored		.75	.30
43	A14	4p multicolored		.75	.30
44	A14	6p multicolored		.80	.35
45	A14	8p multicolored		.85	.35
a.		Gray (beak) omitted		600.00	
46	A14	10p multicolored		.85	.40
47	A14	1sh multicolored		.85	.40
48	A14	1sh6p multicolored		2.50	1.25
49	A14	2sh6p multicolored		2.75	1.75
50	A14	4sh multicolored		4.00	2.25
51	A15	8sh multicolored		2.75	2.00
		Nos. 39-51 (13)		17.70	10.25

Issued: ½p-4sh, 8/5/64; 8sh, 4/5/65.
For surcharges see Nos. 72-84.

ITU Issue
Common Design Type

		1965, May 17	Litho.	Perf. 11x11½	
52	CD317	1p red lilac & org brn		1.00	.55
53	CD317	2sh6p grnsh blue & ultra		5.25	3.75

Intl. Cooperation Year Issue
Common Design Type

		1965, Oct. 25		Perf. 14½	
54	CD318	1p bl grn & cl		.35	.25
55	CD318	1sh6p lt vio & grn		6.00	4.25

Churchill Memorial Issue
Common Design Type

1966, Jan. 24 Photo. Perf. 14
Design in Black, Gold and Carmine Rose

56	CD319	2p brt blue		1.25	1.00
57	CD319	3p green		2.50	1.25
58	CD319	6p brown		3.00	1.50
59	CD319	1sh violet		4.25	3.00
		Nos. 56-59 (4)		11.00	6.75

World Cup Soccer Issue
Common Design Type

		1966, Aug. 1	Litho.	Perf. 14	
60	CD321	4p multi		1.00	1.00
61	CD321	2sh6p multi		4.50	4.00

WHO Headquarters Issue
Common Design Type

		1966, Sept. 20	Litho.	Perf. 14	
62	CD322	8p multi		3.00	3.00
63	CD322	1sh6p multi		4.25	3.50

UNESCO Anniversary Issue
Common Design Type

		1966, Dec. 1	Litho.	Perf. 14	
64	CD323	½p "Education"		.35	1.00
65	CD323	10p "Science"		2.25	1.00
66	CD323	2sh "Culture"		4.50	2.75
		Nos. 64-66 (3)		7.10	4.75

Mangarevan Canoe, c. 1325, and Pitcairn Island — A16

Designs: 1p, Pedro Fernandez de Quiros and galleon, 1606. 8p, "San Pedro," 17th century Spanish brigantine, 1606. 1sh, Capt. Philip Carteret and H.M.S. Swallow. 1sh6p, "Hercules," 1819.

Wmk. 314

		1967, Mar. 1	Photo.	Perf. 14½	
67	A16	½p multicolored		.25	.25
68	A16	1p multicolored		.25	.25
69	A16	8p multicolored		.25	.25
70	A16	1sh multicolored		.30	.30
71	A16	1sh6p multicolored		.40	.40
		Nos. 67-71 (5)		1.45	1.45

Bicentenary of the discovery of Pitcairn Islands by Capt. Philip Carteret.

Nos. 39-51
Surcharged
in Gold

1967, July 10   *Perf. 14x14½*
72	A14	½c on ½p	.25	.25
a.		Brown omitted	1,500.	
73	A14	1c on 1p	.35	.65
74	A14	2c on 2p	.30	.65
75	A14	2½c on 3p	.30	.65
76	A14	3c on 4p	.35	.25
77	A14	5c on 6p	.45	.75
78	A14	10c on 8p	.65	.40
a.		"10c" omitted	2,000.	
b.		Pale blue (beak) omitted	900.00	
79	A14	15c on 10p	1.60	.55
80	A14	20c on 1sh	1.75	.70
81	A14	25c on 1sh6p	2.00	1.00
82	A14	30c on 2sh6p	2.25	1.25
83	A14	40c on 4sh	2.50	1.50
84	A15	45c on 8sh	3.00	1.75
		Nos. 72-84 (13)	15.75	10.35

Size of gold rectangle and anchor varies.
The anchor symbol is designed after the
anchor of H.M.S. Bounty.

Admiral Bligh and Bounty's
Launch — A17

Designs: 8c, Bligh and his followers adrift in
a boat. 20c, Bligh's tomb, St. Mary's Cemetery, Lambeth, London.

            Unwmk.
1967, Dec. 7   **Litho.**   *Perf. 13*
85	A17	1c ultra, lt blue & blk	.25	.25
86	A17	8c brt rose, yel & blk	.35	.35
87	A17	20c brown, yel & blk	.55	.55
		Nos. 85-87 (3)	1.15	1.15

150th anniv. of the death of Admiral William
Bligh (1754-1817), capt. of the Bounty.

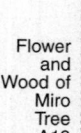

Human
Rights
Flame
A18

       Perf. 13½x13
1968, Mar. 4   **Litho.**   **Wmk. 314**
88	A18	1c rose & multi	.25	.25
89	A18	2c ocher & multi	.25	.25
90	A18	25c multicolored	.60	.45
		Nos. 88-90 (3)	1.10	.95

International Human Rights Year.

Flower
and
Wood of
Miro
Tree
A19

Pitcairn Handicraft: 10c, Carved flying fish.
15c, Two "hand" vases, vert. 20c, Old and new
woven baskets, vert.

     Perf. 14½x14, 14x14½
1968, Aug. 19   **Photo.**   **Wmk. 314**
91	A19	5c chocolate & multi	.30	.30
92	A19	10c dp green & multi	.30	.30
93	A19	15c brt violet & multi	.40	.40
94	A19	20c black & multi	.50	.50
		Nos. 91-94 (4)	1.50	1.50

       See Nos. 194-197.

Microscope, Cell, Germs and WHO
Emblem — A20

20c, Hypodermic and jars containing pills.

1968, Nov. 25   **Litho.**   *Perf. 14*
95	A20	2c vio blue, grnsh bl & blk	.25	.25
96	A20	20c black, magenta & org	.60	.60

       20th anniv. of WHO.

Capt. Bligh and his Larcum-Kendall
Chronometer — A21

1c, Pitcairn Island. 3c, Bounty's anchor,
vert. 4c, Plan of the Bounty, drawn 1787. 5c,
Breadfruit and method of transporting young
plants. 6c, Bounty Bay. 8c, Pitcairn longboat.
10c, Ship Landing Point and palms. 15c,
Fletcher Christian's Cave. 20c, Thursday
October Christian's house. 25c, "Flying Fox"
cable system (for hauling cargo), vert. 30c,
Radio Station at Taro Ground. 40c, Bounty
Bible.

    Perf. 13x12½, 12½x13
1969, Sept. 17   **Litho.**   **Wmk. 314**
97	A21	1c brn, yel & gold	1.25	*1.50*
98	A21	2c brn, blk & gold	.40	.25
99	A21	3c red, blk & gold	.40	.25
100	A21	4c buff, brn & gold	2.00	.25
101	A21	5c gold & multi	.80	.25
102	A21	6c gold & multi	.45	.30
103	A21	8c gold & multi	2.00	.30
104	A21	10c gold & multi	2.00	.80
105	A21	15c gold & multi	2.25	1.50
a.		Gold (Queen's head) omitted	1,100.	
106	A21	20c gold & multi	.70	.45
107	A21	25c gold & multi	.80	.45
108	A21	30c gold & multi	.65	.55
109	A21	40c red lil, blk & gold	1.00	.75
		Nos. 97-109 (13)	14.70	7.60

     For overprint see No. 118.

Lantana — A22

Pitcairn Flowers: 2c, Indian shot (canna
indica). 5c, Pulau (hibiscus tiliaceus). 25c,
Wild gladioli.

1970, Mar. 23   **Litho.**   *Perf. 14*
110	A22	1c black & multi	.25	.25
111	A22	2c black & multi	.35	.35
112	A22	5c black & multi	.55	.55
113	A22	25c black & multi	3.00	2.50
		Nos. 110-113 (4)	4.15	3.65

Rudderfish (Dream Fish) — A23

Fish: 5c, Groupers (Auntie and Ann). 15c,
Wrasse (Elwyn's trousers). 20c, Wrasse
(Whistling daughter).

       Perf. 14½x14
1970, Oct. 12   **Photo.**   **Wmk. 314**
114	A23	5c black & multi	1.50	.75
115	A23	10c grnsh bl & blk	1.75	1.25
116	A23	15c multicolored	2.00	1.75
117	A23	20c multicolored	2.75	2.50
		Nos. 114-117 (4)	8.00	6.25

**No. 104 Overprinted in Silver:
"ROYAL VISIT 1971"**
1971, Feb. 22   **Litho.**   *Perf. 13x12½*
118	A21	10c gold & multi	2.40	2.40

Polynesian Artifacts — A24

Polynesian Art on Pitcairn: 5c, Rock carvings, vert. 15c, Making of stone fishhook. 20c,
Seated deity, vert.

1971, May 3   **Litho.**   *Perf. 13½*
      Queen's Head in Gold
119	A24	5c dk brown & bis	1.00	1.00
120	A24	10c ol green & blk	1.10	1.10
121	A24	15c black & lt vio	1.25	1.25
122	A24	20c black & rose red	1.60	1.60
		Nos. 119-122 (4)	4.95	4.95

Health
Care
A25

4c, South Pacific Commission flag & Southern Cross, vert. 18c, Education (elementary
school). 20c, Economy (country store).

1972, Apr. 4   **Litho.**   *Perf. 14x14½*
123	A25	4c vio bl, yel & ultra	.65	.65
124	A25	8c brown & multi	.75	.75
125	A25	18c yellow grn & multi	.85	.85
126	A25	20c orange & multi	1.25	1.25
		Nos. 123-126 (4)	3.50	3.50

So. Pacific Commission, 25th anniv.

Silver Wedding Issue, 1972
    Common Design Type

Design: Queen Elizabeth II, Prince Philip,
skuas and longboat.

1972, Nov. 20   **Photo.**   **Wmk. 314**
127	CD324	4c slate grn & multi	.30	.25
128	CD324	20c ultra & multi	.60	.60

Pitcairn
Coat of
Arms
A26

1973, Jan. 2   **Litho.**   *Perf. 14½x14*
129	A26	50c multicolored	3.00	10.00

Rose Apple — A27

1973, June 25   *Perf. 14*
130	A27	4c shown	.85	.85
131	A27	8c Mountain apple	.95	.95
132	A27	15c Lata (myrtle)	1.25	1.25
133	A27	20c Cassia	1.40	1.40
134	A27	35c Guava	2.00	2.00
		Nos. 130-134 (5)	6.45	6.45

Princess Anne's Wedding Issue
    Common Design Type
1973, Nov. 14   **Litho.**   *Perf. 14*
135	CD325	10c lilac & multi	.30	.25
136	CD325	25c gray grn & multi	.40	.35

Miter
and
Horn
Shells
A28

1974, Apr. 15
137	A28	4c shown	.70	.70
138	A28	10c Dove shells	.95	.95
139	A28	18c Limpets and false limpet	1.10	1.10
140	A28	50c Lucine shells	2.00	2.00
a.		Souvenir sheet of 4, #137-140	5.50	5.50
		Nos. 137-140 (4)	4.75	4.75

Pitcairn
Post
Office,
UPU
Emblem
A29

UPU, cent.: 20c, Stampless cover, "Posted
at Pitcairn Island No Stamps Available." 35c,
Longboat leaving Bounty Bay for ship offshore.

1974, July 22   **Wmk. 314**   *Perf. 14½*
141	A29	4c multicolored	.40	.40
142	A29	20c multicolored	.55	.55
143	A29	35c multicolored	.65	.60
		Nos. 141-143 (3)	1.60	1.55

Churchill: "Lift up your
hearts . . ." — A30

Design: 35c, Churchill and "Give us the
tools and we will finish the job."

1974, Nov. 30   **Litho.**   **Wmk. 373**
144	A30	20c black & citron	.40	.40
145	A30	35c black & yellow	.75	.75

Sir Winston Churchill (1874-1965).

Queen
Elizabeth II — A31

1975, Apr. 21   **Wmk. 314**   *Perf. 14½*
146	A31	$1 multicolored	7.00	15.00

Mailboats — A32

1975, July 22   **Litho.**   *Perf. 14½*
147	A32	4c Seringapatam, 1830	.50	.50
148	A32	10c Pitcairn, 1890	.60	.60
149	A32	18c Athenic, 1901	.90	.90
150	A32	50c Gothic, 1948	1.25	1.25
a.		Souvenir sheet of 4, #147-150, perf. 14	12.00	12.00
		Nos. 147-150 (4)	3.25	3.25

Pitcairn Wasp A33

Insects: 6c, Grasshopper. 10c, Pitcairn moths. 15c, Dragonfly. 20c, Banana moth.

Wmk. 314

		1975, Nov. 9	**Litho.**	**Perf. 14½**	
151	A33	4c blue grn & multi	.45	.45
152	A33	6c carmine & multi	.55	.55
153	A33	10c purple & multi	.75	.75
154	A33	15c black & multi	.85	.85
155	A33	20c multicolored	1.00	1.00
		Nos. 151-155 (5)	3.60	3.60

Fletcher Christian — A34

H.M.S. Bounty — A35

American Bicentennial: 30c, George Washington. 50c, Mayflower.

		1976, July 4	**Wmk. 373**	**Perf. 13½**	
156	A34	5c multicolored	.30	.30
157	A35	10c multicolored	.55	.55
158	A34	30c multicolored	.70	.70
a.		Pair, #156, 158	1.40	1.40
159	A35	50c multicolored	.85	.85
a.		Pair, #157, 159	1.75	1.75
		Nos. 156-159 (4)	2.40	2.40

Prince Philip's Arrival, 1971 Visit — A36

20c, Chair of homage. 50c, The enthronement.

	1977, Feb. 6		**Perf. 13**	
160	A36	8c silver & multi	.25	.25
161	A36	20c silver & multi	.30	.30
162	A36	50c silver & multi	.55	.55
	Nos. 160-162 (3)		1.10	1.10

25th anniv. of the reign of Elizabeth II.

Building Longboat — A37

Designs: 1c, Man ringing Island Bell, vert. 5c, Landing cargo. 6c, Sorting supplies. 9c, Cleaning wahoo (fish), vert. 10c, Farming. 15c, Sugar mill. 20c, Women grating coconuts and bananas. 35c, Island church. 50c, Gathering miro logs, Henderson Island. 70c, Burning obsolete stamps, vert. $1, Prince Philip and "Britannia." $2, Elizabeth II, vert.

	1977-81		**Litho.**	**Perf. 14½**	
163	A37	1c multicolored	.30	.45
164	A37	2c multicolored	.30	.45
165	A37	5c multicolored	.30	.45
166	A37	6c multicolored	.30	.45
167	A37	9c multicolored	.30	.45
168	A37	10c multicolored	.30	.45
168A	A37	15c multicolored	1.10	2.25
169	A37	20c multicolored	.30	.50
170	A37	35c multicolored	.30	.65
171	A37	50c multicolored	.35	.75
171A	A37	70c multicolored	1.10	2.50

172	A37	$1 multicolored	.50	.90
173	A37	$2 multicolored	.70	1.00
		Nos. 163-173 (13)	6.15	11.25

Issued: #168A, 171A, 10/1/81; others, 9/12/77.

Building "Bounty" Model A38

Bounty Day: 20c, Bounty model afloat. 35c, Burning Bounty.

	1978, Jan. 9			**Perf. 14½**	
174	A38	6c yellow & multi	.40	.40
175	A38	20c yellow & multi	.55	.55
176	A38	35c yellow & multi	.70	.70
a.		Souvenir sheet of 3, #174-176	6.50	6.50
		Nos. 174-176 (3)	1.65	1.65

Souvenir Sheet

Elizabeth II in Coronation Regalia — A39

Wmk. 373

	1978, Sept.		**Litho.**	**Perf. 12**	
177	A39	$1.20 silver & multi	1.10	1.10

25th anniv. of coronation of Elizabeth II.

Unloading "Sir Geraint" A40

Designs: 15c, Harbor before development. 30c, Work on the jetty. 35c, Harbor after development.

Wmk. 373

	1978, Dec. 18		**Litho.**	**Perf. 13½**	
178	A40	15c multicolored	.30	.30
179	A40	20c multicolored	.40	.40
180	A40	30c multicolored	.55	.55
181	A40	35c multicolored	.70	.70
		Nos. 178-181 (4)	1.95	1.95

Development of new harbor on Pitcairn.

John Adams A41

Design: 70c, John Adams' grave.

	1979, Mar. 5		**Litho.**	**Perf. 14½**	
182	A41	35c multicolored	.45	.45
183	A41	70c multicolored	.75	.75

John Adams (1760-1829), founder of Pitcairn Colony, 150th death anniversary.

Pitcairn Island Seen from "Amphitrite" — A42

Engravings (c. 1850): 9c, Bounty Bay and Pitcairn Village, 20c, Lookout Ridge. 70c, Church and schoolhouse.

	1979, Sept. 12		**Litho.**	**Perf. 14**	
184	A42	6c multicolored	.25	.25
185	A42	9c multicolored	.25	.25
186	A42	20c multicolored	.25	.25
187	A42	70c multicolored	.40	.40
		Nos. 184-187 (4)	1.15	1.15

Taking Presents to the Square, IYC Emblem — A43

IYC Emblem and Children's Drawings: 9c, Decorating trees with presents. 20c, Distributing presents. 35c, Carrying the presents home.

Wmk. 373

	1979, Nov. 28		**Litho.**	**Perf. 13½**	
188	A43	6c multicolored	.25	.25
189	A43	9c multicolored	.25	.25
190	A43	20c multicolored	.25	.25
191	A43	35c multicolored	.35	.35
a.		Souvenir sheet of 4, #188-191	1.40	1.40
		Nos. 188-191 (4)	1.10	1.10

Christmas and IYC.

Souvenir Sheet

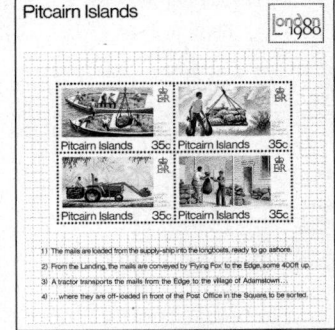

London 80 Intl. Phil. Exhibition — A44

Wmk. 373

	1980, May 6		**Litho.**	**Perf. 14½**	
192	A44	Sheet of 4	1.40	1.40
a.		35c Mail Transport by Longboat	.30	.30
b.		35c Mail crane lift	.30	.30
c.		35c Tractor transport	.30	.30
d.		35c Arrival at post office	.30	.30

London 80 Intl. Phil. Exhib., May 6-14.

Queen Mother Elizabeth Birthday Issue
Common Design Type
Wmk. 373

	1980, Aug. 4		**Litho.**	**Perf. 14**	
193	CD330	50c multicolored	.60	.60

Handicraft Type of 1968
Perf. 14½x14, 14x14½

	1980, Sept. 29		**Litho.**	**Wmk. 373**	
194	A19	9c Turtles	.25	.25
195	A19	20c Wheelbarrow	.25	.25
196	A19	35c Gannet, vert.	.25	.25
197	A19	40c Bonnet and fan, vert.	.30	.30
		Nos. 194-197 (4)	1.05	1.05

Big George — A45

Wmk. 373

	1981, Jan. 22		**Litho.**	**Perf. 14**	
198	A45	6c View of Adamstown	.25	.25
199	A45	9c shown	.25	.25
200	A45	20c Christian's Cave, Gannet's Ridge	.25	.25
201	A45	35c Pawala Valley Ridge	.25	.25
202	A45	70c Tatrimoa	.35	.35
		Nos. 198-202 (5)	1.35	1.35

Citizens Departing for Norfolk Island — A46

	1981, May 3		**Photo.**	**Perf. 13x14½**	
203	A46	9c shown	.25	.25
204	A46	35c Norfolk Isld. from Morayshire	.35	.35
205	A46	70c Morayshire	.65	.65
		Nos. 203-205 (3)	1.25	1.25

Migration to Norfolk Is., 125th anniv.

Royal Wedding Issue
Common Design Type
Wmk. 373

	1981, July 22		**Litho.**	**Perf. 14**	
206	CD331	20c Bouquet	.25	.25
207	CD331	35c Charles	.25	.25
208	CD331	$1.20 Couple	.60	.60
		Nos. 206-208 (3)	1.10	1.10

Lemon A47

	1982, Feb. 23		**Litho.**	**Perf. 14½**	
209	A47	9c shown	.25	.25
210	A47	20c Pomegranate	.30	.30
211	A47	35c Avocado	.35	.35
212	A47	70c Pawpaw	.50	.50
		Nos. 209-212 (4)	1.40	1.40

Princess Diana Issue
Common Design Type

	1982, July 1		**Litho.**	**Perf. 14½x14**	
213	CD333	6c Arms	.25	.25
214	CD333	9c Diana	.40	.40
215	CD333	70c Wedding	.55	.55
216	CD333	$1.20 Portrait	.95	.95
		Nos. 213-216 (4)	2.15	2.15

Christmas — A48

Designs: Various paintings of angels by Raphael. 50c, $1 vert.

	1982, Oct. 19		**Litho.**	**Perf. 14**	
217	A48	15c multicolored	.30	.30
218	A48	20c multicolored	.30	.30
219	A48	50c multicolored	.40	.40
220	A48	$1 multicolored	.60	.60
		Nos. 217-220 (4)	1.60	1.60

A48a

	1983, Mar. 14				
221	A48a	6c Radio operator	.25	.25
222	A48a	9c Postal clerk	.25	.25
223	A48a	70c Fisherman	.40	.40
224	A48a	$1.20 Artist	.75	.75
		Nos. 221-224 (4)	1.65	1.65

Commonwealth Day.

175th Anniv. of Capt. Folger's Discovery of the Settlers A49

6c, Topaz off Pitcairn Isld. 20c, Topaz, islanders. 70c, John Adams welcoming Folger. $1.20, Presentation of Chronometer.

Wmk. 373

1983, June 14		Litho.	*Perf. 14*	
225	A49	6c multicolored	.30	.30
226	A49	20c multicolored	.45	.45
227	A49	70c multicolored	.70	.70
228	A49	$1.20 multicolored	1.10	1.10
		Nos. 225-228 (4)	2.55	2.55

Local Trees A50

1983, Oct. 6		Litho.	*Perf. 13½*	
229		Pair	1.00	1.00
a.	A50	35c Hattie	.40	.40
b.	A50	35c Branch, wood painting	.40	.40
230		Pair	1.75	1.75
a.	A50	70c Pandanus	.70	.70
b.	A50	70c Branch, basket weaving	.70	.70

See Nos. 289-290.

Pseudojuloides Atavai — A51

4c, Halichoeres melasmapomus. 6c, Scarus longipinnis. 9c, Variola louti. 10c, Centropyge hotumatua. 15c, Stegastes emeryi. 20c, Chaetodon smithi. 35c, Xanthichthys mento. 50c, Chrysiptera galba. 70c, Genicanthus spinus. $1, Myripristis tiki. $1.20, Anthias ventralis. $2, Pseudocaranx dentex.

Wmk. 373

1984, Jan. 11		Litho.	*Perf. 14½*	
231	A51	1c multicolored	.25	.40
232	A51	4c multicolored	.40	.30
233	A51	6c multicolored	.40	.30
234	A51	9c multicolored	.40	.30
235	A51	10c multicolored	.40	.35
236	A51	15c multicolored	.40	.35
237	A51	20c multicolored	.50	.50
238	A51	35c multicolored	.70	.75
239	A51	50c multicolored	.70	1.00
240	A51	70c multicolored	1.00	1.25
241	A51	$1 multicolored	1.00	1.50
242	A51	$1.20 multicolored	1.20	1.75
243	A51	$2 multicolored	1.60	2.00
		Nos. 231-243 (13)	8.95	10.75

See Nos. 295-296.

Constellations — A52

1984, May 14			**Wmk. 373**	
244	A52	15c Crux Australis	.30	.30
245	A52	20c Piscis Australis	.40	.40
246	A52	70c Canis Minor	.70	.70
247	A52	$1 Virgo	1.20	1.20
		Nos. 244-247 (4)	2.60	2.60

Souvenir Sheet

AUSIPEX '84 — A53

Longboats.

1984, Sept. 21		Litho.	**Wmk. 373**	
248		Sheet of 2	2.50	2.50
a.	A53	50c multicolored	.50	.50
b.	A53	$2 multicolored	1.75	1.75

HMS Portland off Bounty Bay, by J. Linton Palmer, 1853 — A54

Paintings by J. Linton Palmer, 1853, and William Smyth, 1825: 9c, Christian's Look Out at Pitcairn Island. 35c, The Golden Age. $2, View of Village, by Smyth.

Wmk. 373

1985, Jan. 16		Litho.	*Perf. 14*	
249	A54	6c multicolored	.40	.40
250	A54	9c multicolored	.40	.40
251	A54	35c multicolored	.75	.75

Size: 48x32mm

252	A54	$2 multicolored	1.75	1.75
		Nos. 249-252 (4)	3.30	3.30

Examples of No. 252 with "1835" date were not issued. Value, $85.
See Nos. 291-294.

Queen Mother 85th Birthday
Common Design Type

6c, In Dundee, 1964. 35c, At 80th birthday celebration. 70c, Queen Mother. $1.20, Holding Prince Henry.
$2, In coach at the Races, Ascot.

Perf. 14½x14

1985, June 7		Litho.	**Wmk. 384**	
253	CD336	6c multi	.25	.30
254	CD336	35c multi	.35	.55
255	CD336	70c multi	.65	.85
256	CD336	$1.20 multi	1.25	1.50
		Nos. 253-256 (4)	2.50	3.20

Souvenir Sheet

257	CD336	$2 multi	2.75	2.75

Act 6 — A55

Essi Gina A56

1985, Aug. 28			*Perf. 14½x14*	
258	A55	50c shown	1.00	1.00
259	A55	50c Columbus Louisiana	1.00	1.00

Perf. 14

260	A56	50c shown	1.00	1.00
261	A56	50c Stolt Spirit	1.00	1.00
		Nos. 258-261 (4)	4.00	4.00

See Nos. 281-284.

Christmas A57

Madonna & child paintings: 6c, by Raphael. 9c, by Krause. 35c, by Andreas Mayer. $2, by an unknown Austrian master.

1985, Nov. 26			*Perf. 14*	
262	A57	6c multicolored	.65	.65
263	A57	9c multicolored	.65	.65
264	A57	35c multicolored	1.10	1.10
265	A57	$2 multicolored	3.50	3.50
		Nos. 262-265 (4)	5.90	5.90

Turtles A58

Designs: 9c, 20c, Chelonia mydas. 70c, $1.20, Eretmochelys imbricata.

Wmk. 384

1986, Feb. 12		Litho.	*Perf. 14½*	
266	A58	9c multicolored	1.00	1.00
267	A58	20c multi, diff.	1.50	1.50
268	A58	70c multicolored	2.40	2.40
269	A58	$1.20 multi, diff.	3.00	3.00
		Nos. 266-269 (4)	7.90	7.90

Queen Elizabeth II 60th Birthday
Common Design Type

Designs: 6c, In Royal Lodge garden, Windsor, 1946. 9c, Wedding of Princess Anne and Capt. Mark Philips, 1973. 20c, Wearing mantle and robes of Order of St. Paul's Cathedral, 1961. $1.20, Concert, Royal Festival Hall, London, 1971. $2, Visiting Crown Agents' offices, 1983.

1986, Apr. 21		Litho.	*Perf. 14½*	
270	CD337	6c multi	.25	.25
271	CD337	9c multi	.25	.25
272	CD337	20c multi	.35	.35
273	CD337	$1.20 multi	.75	.75
274	CD337	$2 multi	1.10	1.10
		Nos. 270-274 (5)	2.70	2.70

Royal Wedding Issue, 1986
Common Design Type

Designs: 20c, Informal portrait. $1.20, Andrew aboard royal navy vessel.

Wmk. 384

1986, July 23		Litho.	*Perf. 14*	
275	CD338	20c multi	.40	.40
276	CD338	$1.20 multi	2.00	2.00

7th Day Adventist Church, Cent. — A59

Designs: 6c, First church, 1886, and John I. Tay, missionary. 20c, Second church, 1907, and mission ship Pitcairn, 1890. 35c, Third church, 1945, baptism and Down Isaac. $2, Church, 1954, and sailing ship.

1986, Oct. 18				
277	A59	6c multicolored	.50	.50
278	A59	20c multicolored	1.25	1.25
279	A59	35c multicolored	1.50	1.50
280	A59	$2 multicolored	4.25	4.25
		Nos. 277-280 (4)	7.50	7.50

Ship Type of 1985

1987, Jan. 20			*Perf. 14x14½*	
281	A55	50c Brussel	1.40	1.40
282	A55	50c Samoan Reefer	1.40	1.40

Perf. 14

283	A56	50c Australian Exporter	1.40	1.40
284	A56	50c Taupo	1.40	1.40
		Nos. 281-284 (4)	5.60	5.60

Island Houses — A60

1987, May 21		**Wmk. 373**	*Perf. 14*	
285	A60	70c lt greenish blue, bluish grn & blk	.65	.65
286	A60	70c cream, yel bister & blk	.65	.65
287	A60	70c lt blue, brt blue & blk	.65	.65
288	A60	70c lt lil, brt vio & blk	.65	.65
		Nos. 285-288 (4)	2.60	2.60

Tree Type of 1983

1987, Aug. 10		**Wmk. 384**	*Perf. 14½*	
289		Pair	1.75	1.75
a.	A50	40c Leaves, blossoms	.80	.80
b.	A50	40c Monkey puzzle tree	.80	.80
290		Pair	6.00	6.00
a.	A50	$1.80 Leaves, blossoms, nuts	2.50	2.50
b.	A50	$1.80 Duduinut tree	2.50	2.50

Art Type of 1985

Paintings by Lt. Conway Shipley, 1848: 20c, House and Tomb of John Adams. 40c, Bounty Bay, with H.M.S. Calypso. 90c, School House and Chapel. $1.80, Pitcairn Island with H.M.S. Calypso.

1987, Dec. 7		Litho.	*Perf. 14*	
291	A54	20c multi	.65	.65
292	A54	40c multi	1.00	1.00
293	A54	90c multi	2.00	2.00

Size: 48x32mm

294	A54	$1.80 multi	3.00	3.00
		Nos. 291-294 (4)	6.65	6.65

Fish Type of 1984
Wmk. 384

1988, Jan. 14			*Perf. 14½*	
295	A51	90c Variola louti	3.50	3.50
296	A51	$3 Gymnothorax eurostus	5.00	5.00

Souvenir Sheet

Australia Bicentennial — A61

1988, May 9		**Wmk. 384**	*Perf. 14*	
297	A61	$3 HMS Bounty replica under sail	7.00	7.00

Visiting Ships A62

5c, HMS Swallow, 1767. 10c, HMS Pandora, 1791. 15c, HMS Briton and HMS Tagus, 1814. 20c, HMS Blossom, 1825. 30c, S.V. Lucy Anne, 1831. 35c, S.V. Charles Doggett, 1831. 40c, HMS Fly, 1840. 60c, LMS Camden, 1840. 90c, HMS Virago, 1853. $1.20, S.S. Rakaia, 1867. $1.80, HMS Sappho, 1882. $5, HMS Champion, 1893.

Wmk. 373

1988, Aug. 14		Litho.	*Perf. 13½*	
298	A62	5c multicolored	.50	.60
299	A62	10c multicolored	.50	.60
300	A62	15c multicolored	.50	.60
301	A62	20c multicolored	.60	.70
a.		Wmk. 384	1.75	2.00
b.		Booklet pane of 4, #301a	7.00	
302	A62	30c multicolored	.70	.80
303	A62	35c multicolored	.70	.80
304	A62	40c multicolored	.80	.80
305	A62	60c multicolored	1.00	1.25
306	A62	90c multicolored	1.10	4.00
a.		Wmk. 384	3.75	4.25
b.		Booklet pane of 4, #306a	15.00	
307	A62	$1.20 multicolored	1.10	1.50
308	A62	$1.80 multicolored	1.50	2.00
309	A62	$3.50 multicolored	3.50	5.00
		Nos. 298-309 (12)	12.50	18.65

Inscribed "1988" below design. Nos. 301a and 366a are inscribed "1990."
Issued: #301a-301b, 306a-306b, 5/3/90.

Constitution, 150th Anniv. — A63

Text and: 20c, Raising the Union Jack. 40c, Signing of the constitution aboard the H.M.S. "Fly," 1838. $1.05, Suffrage. $1.80, Equal education.

1988, Nov. 30		**Wmk. 373**	**Perf. 14**	
315	A63	20c multicolored	.40	.40
316	A63	40c multicolored	.60	.60
317	A63	$1.05 multicolored	.95	.95
318	A63	$1.80 multicolored	1.40	1.40
		Nos. 315-318 (4)	3.35	3.35

Christmas A64

a, Angel, animals in stable. b, Holy Family. c, Two Magi. d, Magus and shepherd boy.

1988, Nov. 30		**Wmk. 384**	**Perf. 14**	
319		Strip of 4	3.50	3.50
a.-d.	A64 90c any single		.80	.80

Miniature Sheets

Pitcairn Isls., Bicent. — A65

No. 320 (*Bounty* sets sail for the South Seas, Dec. 23, 1787): a, Fitting out the *Bounty* at Deptford. b, *Bounty* leaving Spithead. c, *Bounty* trying to round Cape Horn. d, Anchored in Adventure Bay, Tasmania. e, Ship's mates collecting breadfruit. f, Breadfruit in great cabin.

No. 321 (the mutiny, Apr. 28, 1789): a, *Bounty* leaving Matavai Bay. b, Mutineers waking Capt. Bligh. c, Confrontation between Fletcher Christian and Bligh. d, Bligh and crew members set adrift in an open boat. e, Castaways. f, Throwing breadfruit overboard.

No. 322: a, like No. 321e. b, Isle of Man #393. c, Norfolk Is. #453.

1989		**Litho.**	**Wmk. 373**	
320	A65	Sheet of 6	6.00	6.00
a.-f.	20c any single		.75	.75
321	A65	Sheet of 6	15.00	15.00
a.-f.	90c any single		2.00	2.25

Souvenir Sheet
Wmk. 384

322		Sheet of 3 + label	5.25	5.25
a.-c.	A65 90c any single		1.50	1.50

See #331, Isle of Man #389-394 and Norfolk Is. #452-456.

Issued: #320, Feb. 22; #321-322, Apr. 28. Difference between #. 321e and 322a is inscription at bottom of #322a: "C. Abbott 1989 BOT."

Aircraft A66

20c, RNZAF Orion. 80c, Beechcraft Queen Air. $1.05, Navy helicopter, USS *Breton*. $1.30, RNZAF Hercules.

		Wmk. 384		
1989, July 25		**Litho.**	**Perf. 14½**	
323	A66	20c multicolored	1.00	1.00
324	A66	80c multicolored	2.25	2.25
325	A66	$1.05 multicolored	2.50	2.50
326	A66	$1.30 multicolored	2.75	2.75
		Nos. 323-326 (4)	8.50	8.50

Second mail drop on Pitcairn, Mar. 21, 1985 (20c); photo mission from Tahiti, Jan. 14, 1983 (80c); diesel fuel delivery by the navy, Feb. 12, 1969 ($1.05); and parachute delivery of a bulldozer, May 31, 1983 ($1.30).

The Islands A67

		Wmk. 373		
1989, Oct. 23		**Litho.**	**Perf. 14**	
327	A67	15c Ducie Is.	.50	.50
328	A67	90c Henderson Is.	1.50	1.50
329	A67	$1.05 Oeno Is.	2.00	2.00
330	A67	$1.30 Pitcairn Is.	2.25	2.25
		Nos. 327-330 (4)	6.25	6.25

Bicentennial Type of 1989
Miniature Sheet

Designs: a, Mutineers aboard *Bounty* anticipating landing on Pitcairn. b, Landing. c, Exploration of the island. d, Carrying goods ashore. e, Burning the *Bounty*. f, Settlement.

1990, Jan. 15		**Wmk. 384**	**Perf. 14**	
331		Sheet of 6 + 3 labels	10.00	10.00
a.-f.	A65 40c any single		1.10	1.10

Stamp World London '90 — A68

Links with the UK: 80c, Peter Heywood and Ennerdale, Cumbria. 90c, John Adams and The Tower of St. Augustine, Hackney. $1.05, William Bligh and The Citadel Gateway, Plymouth. $1.30, Fletcher Christian and birthplace, Cockermouth.

1990, May 3		**Wmk. 373**	**Perf. 14**	
332	A68	80c multicolored	1.00	1.00
333	A68	90c multicolored	1.10	1.10
334	A68	$1.05 multicolored	1.25	1.25
335	A68	$1.30 multicolored	1.75	1.75
		Nos. 332-335 (4)	5.10	5.10

Queen Mother 90th Birthday
Common Design Types

1990, Aug. 4		**Wmk. 384**	**Perf. 14x15**	
336	CD343	40c Portrait, 1937	.75	.75
		Perf. 14½		
337	CD344	$3 King, Queen in carriage	3.50	3.50

First Pitcairn Island Postage Stamps, 50th Anniv — A69

Historical items and Pitcairn Islands stamps — 20c, Chronometer, #2. 80c, Bounty's Bible, #31. 90c, Bounty's Bell, #108. $1.05, Bounty, #172. $1.30, Penny Black, #300.

		Perf. 13½x14		
1990, Oct. 15			**Wmk. 373**	
338	A69	20c multicolored	.80	.80
339	A69	80c multicolored	1.60	1.60
340	A69	90c multicolored	1.75	1.75
341	A69	$1.05 multicolored	2.00	2.00
342	A69	$1.30 multicolored	2.25	2.25
		Nos. 338-342 (5)	8.40	8.40

Birds — A70

1990, Dec. 5		**Wmk. 373**	**Perf. 14**	
343	A70	20c Redbreast	1.00	1.00
344	A70	90c Wood pigeon	1.75	1.75
345	A70	$1.30 Sparrow	2.00	2.00
346	A70	$1.80 Flightless chicken	2.25	2.25
		Nos. 343-346 (4)	7.00	7.00

Birdpex '90, 20th Intl. Ornithological Congress, New Zealand.

Miniature Sheet

Pitcairn Islands, Bicent. — A71

Bicentennial celebrations: a, Re-enacting the landing. b, Commemorative plaque. c, Memorial church service. d, Cricket match. e, Bounty model burning. f, Fireworks.

		Wmk. 384		
1991, Mar. 24		**Litho.**	**Perf. 14½**	
347	A71	80c Sheet of 6, #a.-f.	12.00	12.00

Elizabeth & Philip, Birthdays
Common Design Types

		Wmk. 384		
1991, July 12		**Litho.**	**Perf. 14½**	
348	CD345	20c multicolored	.50	.50
349	CD345	$1.30 multicolored	2.00	2.00
a.	Pair, #348-349 + label		3.25	3.25

Cruise Ships A72

15c, Europa. 80c, Royal Viking Star. $1.30, World Discoverer. $1.80, Sagafjord.

1991, June 17				
350	A72	15c multicolored	1.25	1.25
351	A72	80c multicolored	2.25	2.25
352	A72	$1.30 multicolored	2.75	2.75
353	A72	$1.80 multicolored	3.25	3.25
		Nos. 350-353 (4)	9.50	9.50

Island Vehicles A73

1991, Sept. 25		**Wmk. 373**	**Perf. 14**	
354	A73	20c Bulldozer	.60	.60
355	A73	80c Motorcycle	1.50	1.50
356	A73	$1.30 Tractor	1.75	1.75
357	A73	$1.80 All-terrain vehicle	2.50	2.50
		Nos. 354-357 (4)	6.35	6.35

Christmas — A74

1991, Nov. 18			**Perf. 14x14½**	
358	A74	20c The Annunciation	.50	.50
359	A74	80c Shepherds	1.25	1.25
360	A74	$1.30 Nativity scene	1.50	1.50
361	A74	$1.80 Three wise men	2.10	2.10
		Nos. 358-361 (4)	5.35	5.35

Queen Elizabeth II's Accession to the Throne, 40th Anniv.
Common Design Type

		Wmk. 384		
1992, Feb. 6		**Litho.**	**Perf. 14**	
362	CD349	20c multicolored	.50	.50
363	CD349	60c multicolored	.85	.85
364	CD349	90c multicolored	1.10	1.10
365	CD349	$1 multicolored	1.15	1.15
		Wmk. 373		
366	CD349	$1.80 multicolored	1.75	1.75
		Nos. 362-366 (5)	5.35	5.35

Sharks — A75

Designs: 20c, Carcharhinus galapagensis. $1, Eugomphodus taurus. $1.50, Carcharhinus melanopterus. $1.80, Carcharhinus amblyrhynchos.

		Perf. 15x14½		
1992, June 30			**Wmk. 373**	
367	A75	20c multicolored	.75	.75
368	A75	$1 multicolored	2.25	2.25
369	A75	$1.50 multicolored	2.50	2.50
370	A75	$1.80 multicolored	3.00	3.00
		Nos. 367-370 (4)	8.50	8.50

Sir Peter Scott Commemorative Expedition to Pitcairn Islands, 1991-92 — A76

Designs: 20c, Montastrea, acropora coral sticks. $1, Henderson sandalwood. $1.50, Murphy's petrel. $1.80, Henderson hawkmoth.

		Perf. 14x15		
1992, Sept. 11		**Litho.**	**Wmk. 373**	
371	A76	20c multicolored	.80	.80
372	A76	$1 multicolored	1.75	1.75
373	A76	$1.50 multicolored	3.00	3.00
374	A76	$1.80 multicolored	3.50	3.50
		Nos. 371-374 (4)	9.05	9.05

Captain William Bligh, 175th Anniv. of Death A77

20c, Bligh's birthplace, St. Tudy, Cornwall, HMS Resolution. $1, On deck of HMAV Bounty, breadfruit plant. $1.50, Voyage in open boat, Bligh's answers at court martial. $1.80, Portrait by Rachel H. Combe, Battle of Camperdown, 1797.

Wmk. 373

1992, Dec. 7   **Litho.**   ***Perf. 14½***

375	A77	20c multicolored	.60	.60
376	A77	$1 multicolored	1.75	1.75
377	A77	$1.50 multicolored	2.25	2.25
378	A77	$1.80 multicolored	2.75	2.75
		Nos. 375-378 (4)	7.35	7.35

Royal Naval Vessels A78

Wmk. 384

1993, Mar. 10   **Litho.**   ***Perf. 14***

379	A78	15c HMS Chichester	.85	.85
380	A78	20c HMS Jaguar	1.00	1.00
381	A78	$1.80 HMS Andrew	4.25	4.25
382	A78	$3 HMS Warrior	6.75	6.75
		Nos. 379-382 (4)	12.85	12.85

Coronation of Queen Elizabeth II, 40th Anniv. A79

Wmk. 373

1993, June 17   **Litho.**   ***Perf. 13***

383	A79	$5 multicolored	7.00	7.00

Scenic Views A80

10c, Pawala Valley Ridge. 90c, St. Pauls. $1.20, Matt's Rocks from Water Valley. $1.50, Ridge Rope to St. Paul's Pool. $1.80, Ship Landing Point.

Wmk. 373

1993, Sept. 8   **Litho.**   ***Perf. 14***

384	A80	10c multicolored	.40	.40
385	A80	90c multicolored	1.10	1.10
386	A80	$1.20 multicolored	1.50	1.50
387	A80	$1.50 multicolored	1.60	1.60
388	A80	$1.80 multicolored	2.50	2.50
		Nos. 384-388 (5)	7.10	7.10

Lizards A81

Designs: 20c, Indopacific tree gecko. No. 390, Stump-toed gecko. No. 391, Mourning gecko. $1, Moth skink. No. 393, Snake-eyed skink. No. 394, White-bellied skink.

Perf. 13x13½

1993, Dec. 14   **Litho.**   **Wmk. 373**

389	A81	20c multicolored	.95	.95
390	A81	45c multicolored	1.00	1.00
391	A81	45c multicolored	1.00	1.00
a.		Pair, #390-391	2.50	2.50
392	A81	$1 multicolored	2.00	2.00
393	A81	$1.50 multicolored	2.50	2.50
394	A81	$1.50 multicolored	2.50	2.50
a.		Pair, #393-394	7.00	7.00
		Nos. 389-394 (6)	9.95	9.95

Nos. 390-391, 393-394 Ovptd. with Hong Kong '94 Emblem

Perf. 13x13½

1994, Feb. 18   **Litho.**   **Wmk. 373**

395	A81	45c on #390	.80	.80
396	A81	45c on #391	.80	.80
a.		Pair, #395-396	2.00	2.00

397	A81	$1.50 on #393	2.25	2.25
398	A81	$1.50 on #394	2.25	2.25
a.		Pair, #397-398	6.00	6.00
		Nos. 395-398 (4)	6.10	6.10

Early Pitcairners — A82

Designs: 5c, Friday October Christian. 20c, Moses Young. $1.80, James Russell McCoy. $3, Rosalind Amelia Young.

1994, Mar. 7   ***Perf. 14***

399	A82	5c multicolored	.30	.30
400	A82	20c multicolored	.60	.60
401	A82	$1.80 multicolored	2.50	2.50
402	A82	$3 multicolored	4.00	4.00
		Nos. 399-402 (4)	7.40	7.40

Shipwrecks A83

20c, Wildwave, Oeno Island, 1858. 90c, Cornwallis, Pitcairn Island, 1875. $1.80, Acadia, Ducie Island, 1881. $3, Oregon, Oeno Island, 1883.

Wmk. 373

1994, June 22   **Litho.**   ***Perf. 14***

403	A83	20c multicolored	.75	.75
404	A83	90c multicolored	2.00	2.00
405	A83	$1.80 multicolored	3.25	3.25
406	A83	$3 multicolored	4.75	4.75
		Nos. 403-406 (4)	10.75	10.75

Corals A84

Designs: 20c, Fire coral, vert. 90c, Cauliflower coral, arc-eye hawkfish. $1, Snubnose chub, lobe coral, vert. $3, Coral garden, butterflyfish, vert.

Wmk. 373

1994, Sept. 15   **Litho.**   ***Perf. 14***

407	A84	20c multicolored	.90	.90
408	A84	90c multicolored	2.00	2.00
409	A84	$1 multicolored	2.50	2.50
		Nos. 407-409 (3)	5.40	5.40

Souvenir Sheet

410	A84	$3 multicolored	5.50	5.50

Christmas A85

Flowers: 20c, Morning glory. 90c, Hibiscus, vert. $1, Frangipani. $3, Ginsey, vert.

Wmk. 373

1994, Nov. 24   **Litho.**   ***Perf. 14***

411	A85	20c multicolored	.45	.45
412	A85	90c multicolored	1.50	1.50
413	A85	$1 multicolored	1.75	1.75
414	A85	$3 multicolored	3.50	3.50
		Nos. 411-414 (4)	7.20	7.20

Birds A86

Designs: 5c, Fairy tern. 10c, Red-tailed tropicbird chick, vert. 15c, Henderson rail. 20c, Red-footed booby, vert. 45c, Blue-gray noddy. 50c, Henderson reed warbler. 90c, Common noddy. $1, Masked booby, chick, vert. $1.80, Henderson fruit dove. $2, Murphy's petrel. $3, Christmas shearwater. $5, Red-tailed tropicbird juvenile.

1995, Mar. 8   ***Perf. 13½***

415	A86	5c multicolored	.60	.60
416	A86	10c multicolored	.60	.60
417	A86	15c multicolored	.75	.75
418	A86	20c multicolored	.75	.75
419	A86	45c multicolored	1.00	1.00
420	A86	50c multicolored	1.25	1.25
421	A86	90c multicolored	1.50	1.50
422	A86	$1 multicolored	1.75	1.75
423	A86	$1.80 multicolored	2.50	2.50
424	A86	$2 multicolored	2.75	2.75
425	A86	$3 multicolored	3.00	3.00
426	A86	$5 multicolored	4.25	4.25
		Nos. 415-426 (12)	20.70	20.70

Oeno Island Vacation — A87

Designs: 20c, Boating. 90c, Volleyball on the beach. $1.80, Picnic. $3, Sing-a-long.

1995, June 26   ***Perf. 14x15***

427	A87	20c multicolored	.50	.50
428	A87	90c multicolored	1.25	1.25
429	A87	$1.80 multicolored	2.25	2.25
430	A87	$3 multicolored	3.75	3.75
		Nos. 427-430 (4)	7.75	7.75

Souvenir Sheet

Queen Mother, 95th Birthday — A88

1995, Aug. 4   ***Perf. 14½***

431	A88	$5 multicolored	7.50	7.50

Radio, Cent. — A89

Designs: 20c, Guglielmo Marconi, radio equipment, 1901. $1, Man, Pitcairn radio, 1938. $1.50, Woman, satellite earth station equipment, 1994. $3, Satellite in orbit, 1992.

1995, Sept. 5   ***Perf. 13***

432	A89	20c multicolored	.45	.45
433	A89	$1 multicolored	1.25	1.25
434	A89	$1.50 multicolored	2.00	2.00
435	A89	$3 multicolored	4.00	4.00
		Nos. 432-435 (4)	7.70	7.70

UN, 50th Anniv.
Common Design Type

Designs: 20c, Lord Mayor's Show. $1, RFA Brambleleaf. $1.50, UN ambulance. $3, Royal Air Force Tristar.

Wmk. 373

1995, Oct. 24   **Litho.**   ***Perf. 14***

436	CD353	20c multicolored	.40	.40
437	CD353	$1 multicolored	1.75	1.75
438	CD353	$1.50 multicolored	2.25	2.25
439	CD353	$3 multicolored	3.75	3.75
		Nos. 436-439 (4)	8.15	8.15

Supply Ship Day — A90

1996, Jan. 30   ***Perf. 14x14½***

440	A90	20c Early morning	.35	.35
441	A90	40c Meeting ship	.50	.50
442	A90	90c Unloading supplies	1.25	1.25
443	A90	$1 Landing work	1.40	1.40
444	A90	$1.50 Supply sorting	1.75	1.75
445	A90	$1.80 Last load	2.25	2.25
		Nos. 440-445 (6)	7.50	7.50

Queen Elizabeth II, 70th Birthday
Common Design Type

Various portraits of Queen, scenes from Pitcairn Islands: 20c, Bounty Bay. 90c, Jetty, Landing Point, Bounty Bay. $1.80, Matt's Rocks. $3, St. Paul's.

1996, Apr. 21   ***Perf. 13½x14***

446	CD354	20c multicolored	.60	.60
447	CD354	90c multicolored	1.75	1.75
448	CD354	$1.80 multicolored	2.50	2.50
449	CD354	$3 multicolored	3.75	3.75
		Nos. 446-449 (4)	8.60	8.60

CHINA '96, 9th Asian Intl. Philatelic Exhibition — A91

#450, Chinese junk. #451, HMAV Bounty. No. 452: a, Chinese rat. b, Polynesian rat.

1996, May 17   ***Perf. 14***

450	A91	$1.80 multicolored	2.75	2.75
451	A91	$1.80 multicolored	2.75	2.75

Souvenir Sheet

452	A91	90c Sheet of 2, #a.-b.	3.00	3.00

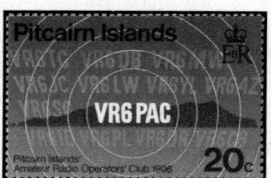

Amateur Radio — A92

Designs: 20c, Call signs of members in Amateur Radio Operator's Club, 1996. No. 454, VR6 1M calling for medical assistance. No. 455, Operator receiving transmission, physician standing by. $2.50, Andrew Young, Pitcairn's first operator, 1938.

1996, Sept. 4   **Wmk. 384**   ***Perf. 14***

453	A92	20c multicolored	.65	.65
454	A92	$1.50 multicolored	2.50	2.50
455	A92	$1.50 multicolored	2.50	2.50
a.		Pair, #454-455	6.00	6.00
456	A92	$2.50 multicolored	3.25	3.25
		Nos. 453-456 (4)	8.90	8.90

Birds A93 $2 PITCAIRN ISLANDS

World Wildlife Fund: 5c, Henderson Island reed-warbler, vert. 10c, Stephen's lorikeet, vert. 20c, Henderson Island rail, vert. 90c, Henderson Island fruit-dove, vert. No. 461, Masked booby. No. 462, Common fairy-tern.

1996, Nov. 20			Wmk. 373	
457	A93	5c multicolored	.65	.65
458	A93	10c multicolored	.65	.65
459	A93	20c multicolored	1.25	1.25
460	A93	90c multicolored	1.50	1.50
461	A93	$2 multicolored	2.00	2.00
462	A93	$2 multicolored	2.00	2.00
	Nos. 457-462 (6)		8.05	8.05

Nos. 461 and 462 do not include WWF emblem.

Souvenir Sheet

Coat of Arms — A94

1997, Feb. 12			*Perf. 14½x14*
463	A94	$5 multicolored	7.25 7.25

Hong Kong '97.

South Pacific Commission, 50th Anniv. — A95

a, MV David Baker. b, MV McLachlan.

Perf. 13½x14			
1997, May 26			Wmk. 373
464	A95	$2.50 Sheet of 2, #a.-	
		b.	7.00 7.00

Health Care A96

Designs: 20c, New Health Center. $1, Resident nurse treating patient. $1.70, Dental officer treating patient. $3, Patient being taken aboard ship.

	Wmk. 373			
1997, Sept. 12		Litho.	*Perf. 14*	
465	A96	20c multicolored	.50	.50
466	A96	$1 multicolored	1.25	1.25
467	A96	$1.70 multicolored	2.00	2.00
468	A96	$3 multicolored	4.50	4.50
	Nos. 465-468 (4)		8.25	8.25

Queen Elizabeth II and Prince Philip, 50th Wedding Anniv. — A97

Designs: No. 469, Prince driving team of horses. No. 470, Queen wearing wide-brimmed hat. No. 471, Prince in formal riding attire. No. 472, Queen, horse. No. 473, Queen and Prince standing behind flowers. No. 474, Prince Charles riding horse.

	Wmk. 373			
1997, Nov. 20		Litho.	*Perf. 13*	
469		20c multicolored	.40	.40
470		20c multicolored	.40	.40
a.	A97 Pair, #469-470		1.00	1.00
471		$1 multicolored	1.25	1.25
472		$1 multicolored	1.25	1.25
a.	A97 Pair, #471-472		3.00	3.00
473		$1.70 multicolored	1.75	1.75
474		$1.70 multicolored	1.75	1.75
a.	A97 Pair, #473-474		4.25	4.25
	Nos. 469-474 (6)		6.80	6.80

Christmas A98

Flower, picture: 20c, Gardenia taitensis, view of Island at night. 80c, Bauhinia variegata, ringing public bell. $1.20, Metrosideros collina, children's baskets hanging on line. $3, Hibiscus tiliaceus, Pitcairn Church, Square at Adamstown.

	Wmk. 373			
1997, Dec. 1		Litho.	*Perf. 13½*	
475	A98	20c multicolored	.50	.50
476	A98	80c multicolored	1.50	1.50
477	A98	$1.20 multicolored	1.75	1.75
478	A98	$3 multicolored	3.25	3.25
	Nos. 475-478 (4)		7.00	7.00

Views of Christian's Cave — A99

5c, Dorcas Apple, looking across Adamstown. 20c, Rocks near Betty's Edge looking past Tatinanny. 35c, Cave mouth. $5, Cave from road near where Fletcher Christian built home.

	Wmk. 384			
1998, Feb. 9		Litho.	*Perf. 13½*	
479	A99	5c multi	.35	.35
480	A99	20c multi	.65	.65
481	A99	35c multi, vert.	.85	.85
482	A99	$5 multi, vert.	5.00	5.00
	Nos. 479-482 (4)		6.85	6.85

Sailing Ships A100

Designs: 20c, HMS Bounty, 1790. 90c, HMS Swallow, 1767. $1.80, HMS Briton & HMS Tagus, 1814. $3, HMS Fly, 1838.

	Perf. 14½x14			
1998, May 28		Litho.	Wmk. 373	
483	A100	20c multicolored	.90	.90
484	A100	90c multicolored	1.50	1.50
485	A100	$1.80 multicolored	2.25	2.25
486	A100	$3 multicolored	3.25	3.25
	Nos. 483-486 (4)		7.90	7.90

Diana, Princess of Wales (1961-97)
Common Design Type

a, In evening dress. b, Wearing white hat, pearls. c, In houndstooth top. d, Wearing white hat, top.

1998, Aug. 31		Litho.	Wmk. 373	
487	CD355	90c Sheet of 4, #a.-d.	4.75	4.75

No. 487 sold for $3.60 + 40c with surtax being donated to the Princess Diana Memorial Fund.

Flowers A101

20c, Bidens mathewsii. 90c, Hibiscus. $1.80, Osteomeles anthyllidifolia. $3, Ipomoea littoralis.

	Wmk. 373			
1998, Oct. 20		Litho.	*Perf. 14*	
488	A101	20c multicolored	1.25	1.25
489	A101	90c multicolored	2.00	2.00
490	A101	$1.80 multicolored	3.50	3.50
491	A101	$3 multicolored	4.00	4.00
	Nos. 488-491 (4)		10.75	10.75

Flowers are below inscriptions on Nos. 489, 491.

Intl. Year of the Ocean A102

Designs: 20c, Fishing. 90c, Divers, vert. $1.80, Reef fish. $3, Murphy's petrel, vert.

	Unwmk.			
1998, Dec. 16		Litho.	*Perf. 14*	
492	A102	20c multicolored	1.40	1.40
493	A102	90c multicolored	2.50	2.50
494	A102	$1.80 multicolored	4.00	4.00
495	A102	$3 multicolored	5.75	5.75
a.	Souv. sheet of 4, #492-495 + label		16.00	16.00
	Nos. 492-495 (4)		13.65	13.65

Government Education on Pitcairn, 50th Anniv. — A103

Scenes on pages of books: 20c, Schoolmaster George Hunn Nobbs, students, 1828. 90c, Schoolmaster Simon Young, daughter Rosalind, teacher Hattie Andre, 1893. $1.80, Teacher Roy Clark, 1932. $3, Modern school at Palau, 1999.

	Unwmk.			
1999, Feb. 15		Litho.	*Perf. 14*	
496	A103	20c multicolored	1.00	1.00
497	A103	90c multicolored	1.50	1.50
498	A103	$1.80 multicolored	3.00	3.00
499	A103	$3 multicolored	5.00	5.00
	Nos. 496-499 (4)		10.50	10.50

PITCAIRN ISLANDS 50c

Archaeological Expedition to Survey Wreck of the Bounty — A104

Scenes of ship during last voyage and: a, 50c, Anchor. b, $1, Cannon. c, $1.50, Chronometer. d, $2, Copper caldron.

1999, Mar. 19				
500	A104	Sheet of 4, #a.-d.	13.00	13.00

19th Cent. Pitcairn Island A105

Designs: 20c, John Adams (d. 1829), Bounty Bay. 90c, Topaz, 1808. $1.80, George Hunn Nobbs, Norfolk Island. $3, HMS Champion, 1893.

	Perf. 14½x14			
1999, May 25		Litho.	Wmk. 373	
501	A105	20c multicolored	1.00	1.00
502	A105	90c multicolored	2.40	2.40
503	A105	$1.80 multicolored	3.00	3.00
504	A105	$3 multicolored	5.50	5.50
	Nos. 501-504 (4)		11.90	11.90

Wedding of Prince Edward and Sophie Rhys-Jones
Common Design Type

	Perf. 13¾x14			
1999, June 18			Wmk. 384	
505	CD356	$2.50 Separate portraits	3.50	3.50
506	CD356	$2.50 Couple	3.50	3.50

Honey Bees A106

Designs: 20c, Beekeepers, hives. $1, Bee, white and purple flower. $1.80, Bees, honeycomb. $3, Bee on flower, honey jar.

	Die Cut Perf. 9			
1999, Sept. 12			Litho.	
	Self-Adhesive			
507	A106	20c multicolored	1.00	1.00
508	A106	$1 multicolored	2.00	2.00
a.	Souvenir sheet of 1		6.00	6.00
509	A106	$1.80 multicolored	3.25	3.25
510	A106	$3 multicolored	4.50	4.50
	Nos. 507-510 (4)		10.75	10.75

China 1999 World Philatelic Exhibition, No. 508a. Issued 8/21.

Protection of Galapagos Tortoise "Mr. Turpen" A107

Designs: a, 5c, Arrival of the ship Yankee, 1937. b, 20c, Off-loading Mr. Turpen to a longboat. c, 35c, Mr. Turpen. d, $5, Close-up of tortoise's head.

Perf. 14¼

2000, Jan. 14		Litho.	Unwmk.
511 A107	Strip of 4 + label	9.50	9.50

Flowers
A108

Designs: 10c, Guettarda speciosa. 15c, Hibiscus tiliaceus. 20c, Selenicereus grandiflorus. 30c, Metrosideros collina. 50c, Alpinia zerumbet. $1, Syzygium jambos. $1.50, Commelina diffusa. $1.80, Canna indica. $2, Allamanda cathartica. $3, Calophyllum inophyllum. $5, Ipomea indica. $10, Bauhinia monandra (40x40mm).

Litho., Litho. with Foil Application ($10)
Perf. 13¾x13¼, 13¼x13¾ ($10)

2000, May 22			Unwmk.
512-523 A108	Set of 12	26.50	26.50
520a	Souvenir sheet, #518, 520	8.25	8.25

The Stamp Show 2000, London (No. 520a).

Millennium — A109

Old and modern pictures: 20c, Longboat at sea. 90c, Landing and longboat house. $1.80, Transportation of crops. $3, Communications.

Wmk. 373

2000, June 28	Litho.		Perf. 13¾
524-527 A109	Set of 4		12.00 12.00

Souvenir Sheets

Satellite Recovery Mission — A110

No. 528: a, Surveryor, helicopter. b, Military personnel, boat, ship, helicopter.

2000, July 7	Unwmk.		Perf. 14¼
528 A110	$2.50 Sheet of 2, #a-b		15.00 15.00

World Stamp Expo 2000, Anaheim. Illustration shows lower half of the entire sheet. The upper half, which has descriptive text, and is printed on the reverse, is the same size as the lower half. The entire sheet is folded where the halves meet.

Queen Mother, 100th Birthday — A111

No. 529: a, $2, Blue hat. b, $3, Maroon hat.

2000, Aug. 4			Perf. 14
529 A111	Sheet of 2, #a-b		7.00 7.00

Christmas
A112

Perf. 14½

2000, Nov. 22	Litho.		Unwmk.
530	Strip of 4	10.00	10.00
a.	A112 20c Woman	.75	.75
b.	A112 80c Man, boy	2.00	2.00
c.	A112 $1.50 Woman, child	3.00	3.00
d.	A112 $3 Three children	4.00	4.00

Cruise Ships
A113

Designs: No. 531, $1.50, Bremen. No. 532, $1.50, MV Europa. No. 533, $1.50, MS Rotterdam. No. 534, $1.50, Saga Rose.

Perf. 14¾

2001, Feb. 1	Litho.		Unwmk.
531-534 A113	Set of 4		12.00 12.00

Values are for stamps with surrounding selvage.

Tropical Fruit — A114

Designs: 20c, Cocos nucifera. 80c, Punica granatum. $1, Passiflora edulis. $3, Ananas comosus.

2001, Apr. 6	Litho.	Perf. 13½x13¼	
535-538 A114	Set of 4	7.50	7.50
538a	Souvenir sheet, #536, 538	5.25	5.25

Allocation of ".pn" Internet Domain Suffix — A115

CD and: 20c, Computer keyboard. 50c, Circuit board. $1, Integrated circuit. $5, Mouse.

2001, June 11		**Serpentine Die Cut**	
		Self-Adhesive	
539-542 A115	Set of 4	11.00	11.00

Tropical Fish — A116

Designs: 20c, Chaetodon ornatissimus. 80c, Chaetodon reticulatus. $1.50, Chaetodon lunula. $2, Henochus chrysostomus.

Perf. 13x13¼

2001, Sept. 4	Litho.		Unwmk.
543-546 A116	Set of 4	9.50	9.50
546a	Souvenir sheet, #543, 546	3.25	3.25

Wood Carving — A117

No. 547: a, 20c, Miro flower, man on beach carrying log. b, 50c, Toa flower, artisans carving fish. c, $1.50, Pulau flower, man using machine, woman looking at carved objects. d, $3, Ship, boat, carved objects.

2001, Oct. 11			
547 A117	Horiz. strip of 4, #a-d, + central label	8.50	8.50

Cowrie Shells
A118

Designs: 20c, Cypraea argus. 80c, Cypraea isabella. $1, Cypraea mappa. $3, Cypraea mauritana.

2001, Dec. 6		Perf. 13¼x13	
548-551 A118	Set of 4	7.75	7.75

Reign Of Queen Elizabeth II, 50th Anniv. Issue
Common Design Type
Souvenir Sheet

No. 552: a, 50c, With Queen Mother and Princess Margaret. b, $1, Wearing tiara. c, $1.20, Without hat. d, $1.50, Wearing hat. e, $2, 1955 portrait by Annigoni (38x50mm).

Perf. 14¼x14½, 13¾ (#552e)

2002, Feb. 6	Litho.	Wmk. 373	
552 CD360	Sheet of 5, #a-e	9.25	9.25

Famous Men — A119

Designs: No. 553, $1.50, Gerald DeLeo Bliss (1882-1957), Panamanian postmaster who expedited Pitcairn mail. No. 554, $1.50, Capt. Arthur C. Jones (1898-1987), shipper of trees to Pitcairn. No. 555, $1.50, James Russell McCoy (1845-1924), missionary. No. 556, $1.50, Adm. Sir Fairfax Moresby (1786-1877), philanthropist.

Perf. 14¼x14¾

2002, Apr. 5	Litho.		Unwmk.
553-556 A119	Set of 4		12.00 12.00

Cats — A120

Local cats: 20c, Simba Christian. $1, Miti Christian. $1.50, Nala Brown. $3, Alicat Pulau.

Perf. 13¼x13

2002, June 28	Litho.		Unwmk.
557-560 A120	Set of 4	8.25	8.25
a.	Souvenir sheet of 2, #557, 560	5.00	5.00

Queen Mother Elizabeth (1900-2002)
Common Design Type

Designs: 40c, As child, c. 1910 (black and white photograph). Nos. 562, 565a, $1, As young woman, without hat. $1.50, Wearing flowered hat. Nos. 564, 565b, $2, Wearing blue hat.

Wmk. 373

2002, Aug. 5	Litho.		Perf. 14¼
	With Purple Frames		
561 CD361	40c multicolored	1.25	1.25
562 CD361	$1 multicolored	2.00	2.00
563 CD361	$1.50 multicolored	2.50	2.50
564 CD361	$2 multicolored	3.00	3.00
Nos. 561-564 (4)		8.75	8.75
	Souvenir Sheet		
	Without Purple Frames		
	Perf. 14½x14¼		
565 CD361	Sheet of 2, #a-b	6.50	6.50

Weaving — A121

No. 566: a, 40c, Woman cutting thatch. b, 80c, Woman dyeing thatch. c, $1.50, Millie Christian weaving. d, $2.50, Thelma Brown with finished products.

Perf. 13¼x12¾

2002, Oct. 18	Litho.		Unwmk.
566 A121	Horiz. strip of 4, #a-d + central label		12.00 12.00

Trees
A122

Designs: 40c, Dudwi nut. $1, Toa. $1.50, Miro. $3, Hulianda.

Perf. 13¼

2002, Dec. 1	Litho.		Unwmk.
567-570 A122	Set of 4		9.50 9.50

Souvenir Sheet

Blue Star Line Ships — A123

2003, Jan. 8	Litho.	Perf. 14x13¼	
571 A123	$5 multi		11.00 11.00

Cone Shells
A124

Designs: 40c, Conus geographus. 80c, Conus textile. $1, Conus striatus. $1.20, Conus marmoreus. $3, Conus litoglyphus.

Perf. 13½x13¾

2003, Mar. 14	Litho.		Unwmk.
572-576 A124	Set of 5		10.00 10.00

Coronation of Queen Elizabeth II, 50th Anniv.
Common Design Type

Designs: Nos. 577, 581a, 40c, Queen wearing tiara. No. 578, 80c, Carriage in procession. No. 579, $1.50, Queen wearing tiara, diff. Nos. 580, 581b, $3, Queen in procession at coronation.

Perf. 14¼x14½
2003, June 2   Litho.   Wmk. 373
Vignettes Framed, Red Background
577	CD363	40c multicolored	.90	.90
578	CD363	80c multicolored	1.50	1.50
579	CD363	$1.50 multicolored	2.25	2.25
580	CD363	$3 multicolored	4.00	4.00

Nos. 577-580 (4)   8.65   8.65

Souvenir Sheet
Vignettes Without Frame, Purple Panel
581 CD363 Sheet of 2, #a-b   5.75   5.75

Painted Leaves — A125

No. 582: a, 40c, Women putting leaves in earthenware jar. b, 80c, Washing leaves. c, $1.50, Leaf painter. d, $3, Leaf painter, diff.

Perf. 13¼
2003, Aug. 18   Litho.   Unwmk.
582 A125 Horiz. strip of 4, #a-d, + central label   12.00   12.00

Squirrelfish
A126

Designs: 40c, Sargocentron diadema. 80c, Sargocentron spiniferum. $1.50, Sargocentron caudimaculatum. $3, Neoniphon sammara.

Perf. 13¼
2003, Oct. 8   Litho.   Unwmk.
583-586 A126 Set of 4   9.50   9.50
586a   Souvenir sheet of 1   8.00   8.00

Christmas
A127

Morning glory and: 40c, Holy Virgin in a Wreath of Flowers, by Peter Paul Rubens and Jan Brueghel. $1, Madonna della Rosa, by Raphael. $1.50, Stuppacher Madonna, by Matthias Grünewald. $3, Madonna with Cherries, by Titian.

Litho. with Foil Application
2003, Nov. 17   Perf. 13¾
587-590 A127 Set of 4   9.00   9.00

Shells
A128

Designs: 40c, Terebra maculata. 80c, Terebra subulata. $1.20, Terebra crenulata. $3, Terebra dimidata.

Perf. 14x14½
2004, Jan. 21   Litho.   Unwmk.
591-594 A128 Set of 4   9.00   9.00

Scenery
A129

Designs: 50c, Anchor, Bounty Bay and Hill of Difficulty, vert. $1, Flower, Christian's Cave on Rock Face. $1.50, Shells, St. Paul's Pool, vert. $2.50, Bird, Ridge Rope towards St. Paul's Point.

Perf. 13¼
2004, Apr. 28   Litho.   Unwmk.
595-598 A129 Set of 4   12.50   12.50

Souvenir Sheet

Commissioning of HMS Pitcairn, 60th Anniv. — A130

Perf. 13¼
2004, July 7   Litho.   Unwmk.
599 A130 $5.50 multi   12.00   12.00

HMAV Bounty Replica, Sydney
A131

Replica and: 60c, Sail and mast. 80c, Stern. $1, Figurehead. $3.50, Rigging.

2004, Sept. 8   Perf. 14¼x14
600-603 A131 Set of 4   12.00   12.00
603a   Souvenir sheet of 1   12.00   12.00

Murphy's Petrel
A132

Designs: 40c, Three in flight. 50c, Adult and chicks. $1, Adult nesting, flower, vert. $2, Head of adult, vert. $2.50, In flight.

2004, Nov. 17   Litho.   Perf. 14½
604-608 A132 Set of 5   9.50   9.50
608a   Souvenir sheet, #604-608   10.00   10.00

Views of Ducie and Oeno Islands
A133

Designs: 50c, Beach, Ducie Island, lizards. 60c, Rocks off Ducie Island, starfish. 80c, Sun on horizon, Ducie Island, birds. $1, Boat off Oeno Island, palm tree. $1.50, Beach and palm trees, Oeno Island, shells. $2.50, Boat with fishermen off Oeno Island, fish.

2005, Feb. 10   Litho.   Perf. 13¼
609-614 A133 Set of 6   12.50   12.50

Souvenir Sheet

Blue Moon Butterfly — A134

No. 615: a, $1.50, Male. b, $4, Female.

2005, Apr. 8   Litho.   Perf. 14½
615 A134 Sheet of 2, #a-b   16.00   16.00

Souvenir Sheet

Apr. 8, 2005 Solar Eclipse — A135

No. 616 — Eclipse and various solar prominences: a, $1. b, $2. c, $3.

2005, Apr. 8   Perf.
616 A135 Sheet of 3, #a-c   12.00   12.00

No. 616 contains three 38mm diameter stamps.

Wedding of Prince Charles and Camilla Parker Bowles
A136

Litho. With Foil Application
2005, Apr. 9   Perf. 14x14½
617 A136 $5 multi   18.00   18.00

HMS Bounty Replica, US
A137

Replica, map, emblem for Bounty Post and: 40c, Ship's wheel. $1, Lantern. $1.20, Bell. $3, Rigging.

2005, June 21   Litho.   Perf. 14¼x14
618-621 A137 Set of 4   15.00   15.00
621a   Souvenir sheet of 1   9.50   9.50

Bristle-thighed Curlew — A138

Designs: 60c, Curlews on rock. $1, Head of curlew. $1.50, Curlew with open beak, vert. $1.80, Head of curlew, two curlews in flight, vert. $2, Curlew on driftwood.

2005, Sept. 14   Litho.   Perf. 14½
622-626 A138 Set of 5   17.00   17.00
626a   Souvenir sheet, #622-626   17.00   17.00

Christmas
A139

Christmas ornament with: 40c, Hibiscus flower. 80c, Seabird. $1.80, Coat of arms. $2.50, HMS Bounty.

Litho. with Foil Application
2005, Nov. 23   Perf. 13¼
627-630 A139 Set of 4   14.00   14.00

Henderson Island — A140

Various scenes of Henderson Island and: 50c, Insects. 60c, Parrots. $1, Sea birds. $1.20, Lobsters. $1.50, Octopi. $2, Turtles.

2006, Feb. 15   Litho.   Perf. 13¼
631-636 A140 Set of 6   13.00   13.00

Souvenir Sheet

Washington 2006 World Philatelic Exhibition — A141

2006, Apr. 21   Litho.   Perf. 14½x14¾
637 A141 $5 multi   10.00   10.00

Queen Elizabeth II, 80th Birthday
A142

Queen: 40c, As young woman. 80c, Wearing tiara. No. 640, $1.80, Wearing yellow dress. No. 641, $3.50, Wearing red hat and jacket.
No. 642: a, $1.80, Wearing tiara. b, $3.50, Wearing yellow dress.

2006, Apr. 21   Perf. 14¼
Stamps With White Frames
638-641 A142 Set of 4   10.00   10.00

Souvenir Sheet
Stamps Without White Frames
642 A142 Sheet of 2, #a-b   9.00   9.00

Journey to Norfolk Island
A143

No. 643: a, Pitcairners preparing to leave Pitcairn Island. b, Ship, Morayshire, departing Pitcairn Island. c, Morayshire at anchor in Kingston Bay, Norfolk Island. d, Pitcairn settlers arrive in Kingston, Norfolk Island.

2006, June 7   Perf. 14½
643 Horiz. strip of 4 + central label   11.00   11.00
a.	A143 50c multi		1.25	1.25
b.	A143 $1 multi		1.75	1.75
c.	A143 $1.50 multi		2.75	2.75
d.	A143 $3 multi		5.00	5.00

See Norfolk Island Nos. 875-879.

Souvenir Sheet

Cave Dwellers of Henderson Island — A144

No. 644: a, 60c, Man carrying caught fish. b, $1.20, Child, bird, boat, horiz. c, $2, Man sitting on beach, horiz. d, $2.50, Two women.

2006, Aug. 30 — **Perf. 13¼**
644 A144   Sheet of 4, #a-d   10.50   10.50

Humpback Whales A145

Designs: $1.50, Whales underwater. $3.50, Tail of whale above water.

2006, Nov. 22 — **Perf. 14½**
645-646 A145   Set of 2   10.50   10.50
646a   Souvenir sheet, #645-646   10.50   10.50

Worldwide Fund for Nature (WWF) A146

2007, Feb. 28 — **Litho.** — **Perf. 14¼**
647   Horiz. strip of 4   9.00   9.00
a.   A146 50c Sooty tern   .70   .70
b.   A146 60c Blue-gray ternlet   .80   .80
c.   A146 $2 Brown noddies   2.75   2.75
d.   A146 $3 Black noddy   4.25   4.25
e.   Miniature sheet, 2 each #647a-647d   18.00   18.00

Raising of the Anchor of the Bounty, 50th Anniv. — A147

No. 648: a, Diver approaching anchor. b, Two divers at anchor. c, Pulling anchor onto ship. d, Anchor on shore.

2007, Apr. 20 — **Litho.** — **Perf. 13¼**
648   Horiz. strip of 4 + central label   12.00   12.00
a.   A147 60c multi   1.50   1.50
b.   A147 $1 multi   2.50   2.50
c.   A147 $1.20 multi   2.75   2.75
d.   A147 $2.50 multi   5.00   5.00

Souvenir Sheet

Rock Carvers of Pitcairn Island — A148

No. 649: a, 60c, Man carving on rock face. b, $1.20, Two men pounding rock, horiz. c, $2, Man near fire, horiz. d, $2.50, Man making stone ax.

2007, June 13
649 A148   Sheet of 4, #a-d   12.50   12.50

Utetheisa Pulchelloides A149

Design: $2, Moth on branch. $4, Moth in flight.

2007, Aug. 27 — **Litho.** — **Perf. 14½**
650-651 A149   Set of 2   12.00   12.00
651a   Souvenir sheet, #650-651   12.00   12.00

HMS Bounty Replica, United States A150

Designs: 10c, Crow's nest. 20c, Ropes and pulleys. 40c, Cannon. 50c, Compass. 80c, Captain's wheel. $1, Figurehead. $1.50, Mast. $2, Sails. $3.50, Sextant. $4, Lamp and transom. $5, Bell. $10, Chronometer.

2007, Oct. 17 — **Litho.** — **Perf. 14½**
652 A150   10c multi   .25   .25
653 A150   20c multi   .40   .40
654 A150   40c multi   .75   .75
655 A150   50c multi   .85   .85
656 A150   80c multi   1.00   1.00
657 A150 $1 multi   1.25   1.25
658 A150 $1.50 multi   1.75   1.75
659 A150 $2 multi   2.25   2.25
660 A150 $3.50 multi   4.00   4.00
a.   Souvenir sheet of 3, #656, 657, 660   9.50   9.50
661 A150 $4 multi   3.75   3.75
662 A150 $5 multi   4.25   4.25
663 A150 $10 multi   9.00   9.00
   Nos. 652-663 (12)   29.50   29.50

Issued: No. 660a, 5/8/10. London 2010 Festival of Stamps (No. 660a).

Fish — A151

No. 664: a, Dog tooth tuna. b, Wahoo. c, Dorado-Mahimahi. d, Yellowfin tuna. e, Giant trevally. f, Bonito.

2007, Dec. 12 — **Litho.** — **Perf. 14½**
664 A151 $1 Block of 6, #a-f   12.50   12.50

Pictures of Islands Taken By DigitalGlobe QuickBird Satellite A152

Islands: 60c, Oeno. $1, Pitcairn. $2, Henderson. $2.50, Ducie.

Serpentine Die Cut
2008, Feb. 27 — **Litho.**
Self-Adhesive
665-668 A152   Set of 4   12.00   12.00

Longboat History — A153

No. 669 — Inscriptions: a, From 1880 Timber framed longboat. b, 1983, Last wooden longboat launched. c, 1995, Diesel powered aluminum. d, Oeno sunsets brought within reach.

2008, Apr. 24 — **Litho.** — **Perf. 14x14¼**
669   Horiz. strip of 4 + central label   12.00   12.00
a.   A153 50c multi   1.25   1.25
b.   A153 $1 multi   1.75   1.75
c.   A153 $1.50 multi   2.75   2.75
d.   A153 $3.50 multi   5.00   5.00

Bees and Flowers A154

Apis mellifera ligustica and: $1, Yellow guava. $1.20, Portulaca. $1.50, Sunflower. $3, Mountain chestnut.

2008, June 25 — **Perf. 13¼**
670-673 A154   Set of 4   11.00   11.00
673a   Souvenir sheet, #672-673   9.00   9.00

Sunsets — A155

Sun and various photographs of sunsets: 50c, 60c, 80c, $1, $2, $2.50.

2008, Aug. 20 — **Litho.** — **Perf. 14¾**
674-679 A155   Set of 6   12.50   12.50

Souvenir Sheet

Discovery of Bounty Mutineer Community on Pitcairn by Capt. Mayhew Folger, Bicent. — A156

2008, Oct. 22 — **Litho.** — **Perf. 13¼**
680 A156 $5 multi   7.75   7.75

Miniature Sheet

Green Turtles of Henderson Island — A157

No. 681: a, 60c, Head of turtle, vert. b, $1, Turtle swimming. c, $2, Turtle coming ashore. d, $2.50, Hatchlings heading toward ocean, vert.

2008, Dec. 3 — **Litho.** — **Perf. 14**
681 A157   Sheet of 4, #a-d   9.00   9.00

Coconut Crab — A158

Crab: $2.80, Top view. $4, Side view.

2009, Feb. 17 — **Perf. 14½**
682-683 A158   Set of 2   11.00   11.00
683a   Souvenir sheet of 2, #682-683   11.00   11.00

Return of Pitcairn Islanders to Pitcairn Island, 150th Anniv. — A159

No. 684: a, Pitcairn islanders leave Kingston Jetty on Norfolk Island. b, Passengers approach the Mary Ann. c, Pitcairn Islanders on board the Mary Ann approach Pitcairn Island. d, Arrival of Pitcairn Islanders on Pitcairn Island.

2009, Apr. 22 — **Litho.** — **Perf. 14¾x13½**
684   Horiz. strip of 4 + central label   10.00   10.00
a.   A159 60c multi   1.00   1.00
b.   A159 $1 multi   1.75   1.75
c.   A159 $2 multi   2.50   2.50
d.   A159 $3.50 multi   3.75   3.75

Souvenir Sheet

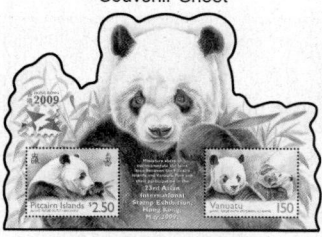

Hong Kong 2009 Intl. Stamp Exhibition — A160

2009, May 14 — **Perf. 13½**
685 A160   Sheet of 2, Pitcairn Islands #685a, Vanuatu #976a   8.50   8.50
a. $2.50 One panda   4.25   4.25

No. 685 sold for $5 and 310 Vanuatu vatus, and is identical to Vanuatu #976.

Charles Darwin (1809-82), Naturalist A161

Darwin and: 50c, Ship "Beagle" and fossil. $1.50, Tortoise and iguana. $2, Birds. $3.50, Darwin's book "On the Origin of Species by Means of Natural Selection" and ape.

2009, June 24 — **Perf. 14½**
686-689 A161   Set of 4   12.00   12.00

Wandering Glider Dragonfly A162

Dragonfly: $2.50, At flower's anthers. $4, On flower's petal.

2009, Aug. 26
690-691 A162   Set of 2   11.00   11.00
691a   Souvenir sheet, #690-691   11.00   11.00

Aircraft Flying Over Pitcairn Island A163

Designs: $1, Walrus amphibious biplane. $1.50, Alouette III helicopter. $1.80, Dassault VP-BMS Falcon 900. $2.50, Piper Comanche 260C.

2009, Oct. 21
692-695 A163   Set of 4   12.00   12.00

Miniature Sheet

Visiting Royal Navy Ships — A164

No. 696: a, 80c, HMS Actaeon, 1837. b, 80c, HMS Calypso, 1860. c, 80c, HMS Juno, 1855. d, $2, HMS Sutlej, 1864. e, $2, HMS Shah, 1878. f, $2, HMS Pelican, 1886.

2009, Dec. 9	Litho.	Perf. 14		
696	A164	Sheet of 6, #a-f	12.00	12.00

See No. 711.

Children's Art A165

Island sites and children's drawings of them: 50c, Flatland, by Bradley Christian. 60c, Tedside, by Torika Warren-Peu. $1, St. Pauls, by Jayden Warren-Peu. $1.80, Isaac's Valley, by Kimiora Warren-Peu. $2, Garnets Ridge, by Ralph Warren-Peu. $2.50, Ship Landing Point, by Ariel Brown.

2010, Feb. 24	Litho.	Perf. 14¼		
697-702	A165	Set of 6	12.00	12.00

ANZAC Day — A166

No. 703 — Poppy and: a, 50c, Tank. b, $1, Airplanes.
No. 704 — Poppy and: a, $1.80, Transport ship. b, $4, Gunboat.

2010, Apr. 23	Horiz. Pairs, #a-b	Perf. 14½x14		
703-704	A166	Set of 2	11.00	11.00

Worldwide Fund for Nature (WWF) A167

No. 705 — Fish: a, Centropyge flavissima. b, Chaetodon smithi. c, Centropyge loricula. d, Chaetodon lineolatus.

2010, June 23		Perf. 14¼		
705		Strip or block of 4	11.00	11.00
a.	A167 60c multi		1.10	1.10
b.	A167 $1 multi		1.50	1.50
c.	A167 $2 multi		2.25	2.25
d.	A167 $2.50 multi		2.75	2.50
e.	Sheet of 8, 2 each #705a-705d		20.00	20.00

Exploration of Volcanic Hotspots A168

No. 706: a, Research Vessel L'Atalante. b, Submersible Nautile. c, Photographing lava tube. d, Approaching Adams Volcano.

2010, Aug. 18		Perf. 14		
706		Horiz. strip of 4 + central label	11.50	11.50
a.	A168 80c multi		1.60	1.60
b.	A168 $1.20 multi		1.90	1.90
c.	A168 $1.50 multi		2.40	2.40
d.	A168 $3 multi		3.50	3.50

Snails A169

Designs: 80c, Orobophana solidula. $1, Philonesia filiceti. $1.80, Orobophana solidula, diff. $2.50, Philonesia filiceti, diff.

2010, Oct. 20	Serpentine Die Cut Self-Adhesive			
707-710	A169	Set of 4	10.00	10.00

Visiting Royal Navy Ships Type of 2009
Miniature Sheet

No. 711: a, $1, HMS Royalist, 1898. b, $1, HMS Cambrian, HMS Flora, 1906. c, $1, HMS Algerine, 1911. d, $1.80, HMS Leander, 1937. e, $1.80, HMS Monmouth, 1995. f, $1.80, HMS Sutherland, 2001.

2010, Dec. 9		Perf. 14		
711	A164	Sheet of 6, #a-f	15.00	15.00

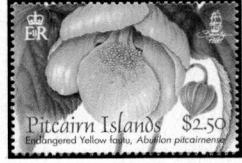

Yellow Fauta Flower A170

Designs: $2.50, Flower and bud. $3, Flower and three buds.

2011, Feb. 12		Litho.		
712	A170	$2.50 multi	4.50	4.50
713	A170	$3 multi	5.50	5.50
a.		Souvenir sheet of 1	5.75	5.75

Indipex 2011 World Philatelic Exhibition, New Delhi (No. 713a).

Peonies — A171

No. 714 — Peonies with denomination color of: a, White. b, Pink.

2011, Apr. 21				
714	A171	$1 Horiz. pair, #a-b	4.50	4.50

Printed in sheets containing 3 pairs.

Paper Wasp A172

Wasp on nest facing: $2.50, Right. $4, Left.

2011, Apr. 21				
715-716	A172	Set of 2	12.00	12.00
716a		Souvenr sheet of 2, #715-716	13.00	13.00

Wedding of Prince William and Catherine Middleton A173

Litho. With Foil Application

Supply Ships A174

2011, May 25		Perf. 14½x14¾		
717		Horiz. pair + central label	16.00	16.00
a.	A173 $2.80 Couple		6.00	6.00
b.	A173 $6 Couple at wedding		8.00	8.00

Designs: $1, Southern Salvor. $1.80, Claymore II. $2.10, Braveheart. $3, Taporo VIII.

2011, Aug. 31	Litho.	Perf. 14¼x14		
718-721	A174	Set of 4	14.50	14.50

Parkin Christian (1883-1971) A175

2011, Oct. 26		Perf. 14½		
722		Horiz. strip of 4 + central label	12.00	12.00
a.	A175 $1.50 Navigator		2.00	2.00
b.	A175 $1.80 Goodwill ambassador		2.25	2.25
c.	A175 $2.10 Magistrate		2.50	2.50
d.	A175 $2.40 Religious leader		2.75	2.75

Christmas — A176

Designs: $1, Magus and camel. $1.50, Magus and camel, diff. $2.10, Magus and camel, diff. $3, Holy Family.

2011, Dec. 7		Perf. 14¼		
723-726	A176	Set of 4	12.00	12.00

Henderson Island Birds — A177

Designs: 20c, Henderson crakes. 40c, Henderson fruit doves. $1.50, Henderson petrels. $2.10, Henderson reed warblers. $4.40, Henderson lorikeets.

2011, July 20		Perf. 14¼x14		
727-731	A177	Set of 5	17.00	17.00

Souvenir Sheet

Tapa Cloth Designs — A178

No. 732: a, $1.80, Lognboat. b, $2.20, Whale. c, $4.60, HMS Bounty.

2012, Feb. 21		Perf. 13¾x13½		
732	A178	Sheet of 3, #a-c	14.00	14.00

Dolphins A179

Designs: $1, Fraser's dolphin. $1.50, Spinner dolphin. $2.10, Spotted dolphin. $3, Bottlenose dolphin.

2012, Apr. 26		Perf. 14¼		
733-736	A179	Set of 4	12.00	12.00
736a		Souvenir sheet of 2, #734, 736	7.25	7.25

Reign of Queen Elizabeth II, 60th Anniv. A180

No. 737: a, Queen in uniform. b, Queen wearing blue green hat and dress.

2012, June 1		Perf. 14¼x14½		
737		Horiz. pair + central label	14.00	14.00
a.	A180 $2.80 multi		5.00	5.00
b.	A180 $4.40 multi		6.50	6.50

Photographs of Bounty Replicas — A181

Various photographs: 20c, $1, $2.10, $4.60.

2012, July 31				
738-741	A181	Set of 4	13.00	13.00
741a		Souvenir sheet of 1 #741	7.50	7.50

Roy P. Clark (1893-1980) A182

2012, Sept. 26		Perf. 14½		
742		Horiz. strip of 4 + central label	14.50	14.50
a.	A182 $1 Teacher		2.50	2.50
b.	A182 $1.50 Postmaster		3.25	3.25
c.	A182 $2.20 Writer		3.50	3.50
d.	A182 $2.80 Community and church elder		4.00	4.00

Worldwide Fund for Nature (WWF) A183

Various depictions of Fluted giant clam.

2012, Oct. 31		**Perf. 14¼x14½**	
743	Strip of 4	11.50	11.50
a.	A183 20c multi	.80	.80
b.	A183 $1 multi	2.00	2.00
c.	A183 $2.10 multi	2.75	2.75
d.	A183 $3 multi	3.25	3.25
e.	Souvenir sheet of 8, 2 each #743a-743d	20.00	20.00

Charles Dickens (1812-70), Writer A184

Various photographs of Dickens and characters from his novels: $1, $1.80, $2.10, $3.

2012, Dec. 5		**Perf. 14¾x14½**	
744-747	A184 Set of 4	13.00	13.00

Books in the Bounty Trilogy, by Charles Bernard Nordhoff and James Norman Hall — A185

Designs: $1, Mutiny on the Bounty. $2.10, Men Against the Sea. $3, Pitcairn's Island.

2013, Feb. 27		**Perf. 14½x14¾**	
748-750	A185 Set of 3	9.50	9.50
750a	Souvenir sheet of 3, #748-750, perf. 14¾	9.50	9.50

Cruise Ships — A186

Designs: No. 751, $2, MV Marina. No. 752, $2, Pacific Princess. No. 753, $2, Costa Neo Romantica. No. 754, $2, Arcadia.

2013, Apr. 24		**Perf. 14½x14**	
751-754	A186 Set of 4	13.50	13.50

Souvenir Sheet

Lobsters — A187

No. 755: a, $1, Easter Island spiny lobster. b, $2, Aesop slipper lobster. c, $3.40, Pronghorn spiny lobster.

2013, May 29		**Perf. 14**	
755	A187 Sheet of 3, #a-c	10.50	10.50

Coronation of Queen Elizabeth II, 60th Anniv. — A188

Litho. & Embossed

2013, July 11		**Perf. 14½x14**	
756	A188 $6 blue	9.50	9.50

No. 756 was printed in sheets of 2 stamps.

Souvenir Sheet

Birth of Prince George of Cambridge — A189

No. 757: a, $3.40, Duke, Duchess of Cambridge, Prince George. b, $4.40, Duke of Cambridge, Pricne George.

2013, Aug. 16	**Litho.**	**Perf. 14½**	
757	A189 Sheet of 2, #a-b	13.00	13.00

Lily Warren (1878-1969), Midwife A190

Varios photographs of Warren.

2013, Sept. 25			
758	Horiz. strip of 4 + central label	13.00	13.00
a.	A190 $1 multi	1.75	1.75
b.	A190 $1.50 multi	2.50	2.50
c.	A190 $2.20 multi	3.75	3.75
d.	A190 $2.80 multi	4.75	4.75

Pres. John F. Kennedy (1917-63) A191

Headlines for events in Kennedy's presidency: $1, Inaugural address, Jan. 20, 1961. $1.80, Announcement of plans to put a man on the Moon, May 25, 1961. $2.10, Announcement of naval blockade of Cuba, Oct. 22, 1962. $3, "Ich bin ein Berliner" speech, June 26, 1963.

2013, Nov. 22	**Litho.**	**Perf. 14½**	
759-762	A191 Set of 4	13.00	13.00

The April 18, 1962 date shown on the $2.10 stamp is incorrect for the headline. Kennedy announced plans for a nuclear disarmament treaty on April 18, 1962.

Ship Landing Point and Bounty Bay A192

Designs: 40c, Ship Landing Point as seen from Bounty Bay. No. 764, $1, Palm trees and Ship Landing Point. No. 765, $1, Bounty Bay framed by cliffs. No. 766, $2, Clouds above Ship Landing Point. No. 767, $2, Bounty Bay and rock promontory. $2.10, Aerial view of Bounty Bay.

2013, Dec. 18	**Litho.**	**Perf. 14**	
763-768	A192 Set of 6	14.00	14.00

Souvenir Sheet

Albatrosses — A193

No. 769: a, $1.80, Wandering albatrosses. b, $2.10, Black-browed albatrosses. c, $3, Butler's albatross.

2014, Feb. 27	**Litho.**	**Perf. 13½**	
769	A193 Sheet of 3, #a-c	11.50	11.50

Mutiny on the Bounty, 225th Anniv. A194

Designs: $1, Mutiny. $2, Captain Bligh and loyal crew set adrift in small boat. $2.10, Bounty leaving small boat with Captain Blight. $3, Bounty approaching Pitcairn Island.

2014, Apr. 28	**Litho.**	**Perf. 14½**	
770-773	A194 Set of 4	14.00	14.00

Flora — A195

Designs: 20c, Cerbera manghas. $1, Portulaca lutea. $1.80, Canna sp. $2, Chamaesyce sparrmannii. $2.10, Coprosma benefica. $3, Pandanus tectorius.

2014, June 12	**Litho.**	**Perf. 14x14¼**	
774-779	A195 Set of 6	18.00	18.00

Souvenir Sheet

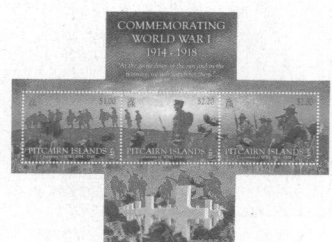

World War I, Cent. — A196

No. 780 — Poppies and: a, $1, Ten soldiers hiking. b, $2.20, Three soldiers. c, $2.80, Bugler and five soldiers at attention.

2014, July 28	**Litho.**	**Perf. 14**	
780	A196 Sheet of 3, #a-c	10.50	10.50

Actors Depicting Fletcher Christian in Movies — A197

Christian and actor portraying him: 20c, Wilton Power, 1916. $1, Errol Flynn, 1933. $2.10, Clark Gable, 1935. $2.80, Marlon Brando, 1962. $3, Mel Gibson, 1984.

2014, Sept. 25	**Litho.**	**Perf. 14**	
781-785	A197 Set of 5	14.50	14.50

Fletcher Christian (1764-93), mutiny leader.

Nelson Mandela (1918-2013), President of South Africa — A198

Various photographs of Mandela and quote beginning with: $1, "What counts in life. . ." $1.80, "A good head. . .", vert. $2.10, "For to be free. . . .", vert. $3, "Education is the most powerful weapon. . ."

	Perf. 14¼x14, 14x14¼		
2014, Nov. 3		**Litho.**	
786-789	A198 Set of 4	12.50	12.50

Visit to Pitcairn Islands of Richard E. Byrd Antarctic Expedition, 75th Anniv. A199

No. 790: a, Expedition members on Pitcairn, envelope cachet. b, USMS North Star, stamped cover to Philadelphia. c, USMS North Star, Snow Cruiser. d, Snow Cruiser, Admiral Byrd in parka.

Wmk. 387

2014, Dec. 11	**Litho.**	**Perf. 14½**	
790	Horiz. strip of 4 + central label	12.00	12.00
a.	A199 $1 multi	1.50	1.50
b.	A199 $1.80 multi	2.75	2.75
c.	A199 $2 multi	3.25	3.25
d.	A199 $2.80 multi	4.50	4.50

Souvenir Sheet

Red Lionfish — A200

No. 791: a, Denomination over fins. b, Fins above denomination. c, Fins touching "R" at UL.

Unwmk.

2015, Feb. 26	**Litho.**	**Perf. 14**	
791	A200 $2 Sheet of 3, #a-c	9.25	9.25

Paintings — A201

Designs: $1, Interior of Pitcairn, 1830, by F. W. Beechey. $2, Pitcairn Island, c. 1808, by E. Low. $2.10, Christian's House, Pitcairn Island, c. 1824, by Conway Shipley. $3, Landing in Bounty Bay, 1830, by Beechey.

2015, Apr. 29   Litho.   Perf. 14¾x14¼
792-795 A201   Set of 4   12.50 12.50

Ben Christian (1921-92), Island Secretary A202

No. 796 — Christian: a, On telephone. b, Carving wood. c, Holding caught fish. d, With medal.

2015, June 24   Litho.   Perf. 14½
796   Horiz. strip of 4 + central label   10.50 10.50
a.   A202 $1 multi   1.40 1.40
b.   A202 $1.50 multi   2.00 2.00
c.   A202 $2.10 multi   3.00 3.00
d.   A202 $2.80 multi   3.75 3.75

Souvenir Sheet

Breadfruit — A203

No. 797: a, $1, Flower. b, $2, Breadfruit half. c, $3, Mature breadfruit.

2015, Aug. 26   Litho.   Perf. 13½
797   A203   Sheet of 3, #a-c   7.75 7.75

First Pitcairn Islands Postage Stamps, 75th Anniv. A204

King George VI and: 10c, Cluster of oranges. 40c, Fletcher Christian with crew and view of Pitcairn Island. 60c, John Adams and his house. 80c, Map of Pitcairn and Pacific Ocean. $1, Bounty Bible. $2, H.M. Armed Vessel "Bounty." $4, William Bligh and H.M. Armed Vessel "Bounty." $5, Pitcairn School, 1949. $6, Fletcher Christian and view of Pitcairn Island. $10, Fletcher Christian with crew and coast of Pitcairn Island

2015, Oct. 15   Litho.   Perf. 14x14¼
798   A204 10c multi   .25 .25
799   A204 40c multi   .55 .55
800   A204 60c multi   .80 .80
801   A204 80c multi   1.10 1.10
802   A204 $1 multi   1.40 1.40
803   A204 $2 multi   2.75 2.75
804   A204 $4 multi   5.50 5.50
805   A204 $5 multi   6.75 6.75
806   A204 $6 multi   8.25 8.25
807   A204 $10 multi   13.50 13.50
    Nos. 798-807 (10)   40.85 40.85

Christmas A205

Carols: $1, Hark! The Herald Angels Sing. $2, Once in Royal David's City. $2.10, Away in a Manger. $3, Silent Night.

2015, Dec. 9   Litho.   Perf. 14¼
808-811 A205   Set of 4   11.00 11.00

Landscapes — A206

No. 812 — Inscriptions: a, Down the God from the sea. b, Rainbow over St. Paul's Pool. c, Sunset over Ship Landing Point. d, Cliff view towards Bounty Bay. e, Adamstown from inside Christian's cave. f, Tautama toward Aute Valley and Break Em Hip.

2016, Jan. 13   Litho.   Perf. 14¼x14
812   Block of 6   16.00 16.00
a.-f.   A206 $2 Any single   2.60 2.60
    Complete booklet, #812a-812f   16.00

Scenes from Plays by William Shakespeare (1564-1616) A207

No. 813: a, Macbeth. b, Hamlet. c, A Midsummer Night's Dream. d, Romeo and Juliet.

2016, Mar. 9   Litho.   Perf. 14¼x14½
813   Horiz. strip of 4 + central label   9.75 9.75
a.   A207 $1 multi   1.40 1.40
b.   A207 $1.80 multi   2.50 2.50
c.   A207 $2 multi   2.75 2.75
d.   A207 $2.20 multi   3.00 3.00

Queen Elizabeth II, 90th Birthday — A208

Queen Elizabeth II wearing: No. 814, $1.80, Gray lilac hat. No. 815, $1.80, Light blue hat. No. 816, $2.10, Gray brown and white hat with ribbon. No. 817, $2.10, Light yellow hat with black edge.

2016, Apr. 19   Litho.   Perf. 14x14¼
814-817 A208   Set of 4   11.00 11.00

Worldwide Fund for Nature (WWF) — A209

No. 818 — Phoenix petrel: a, Bird in nest. b, Two birds in nest. c, Two birds in flight. d, One bird in flight.

2016, July 6   Litho.   Perf. 14¼
818   Strip of 4   9.00 9.00
a.   A209 20c multi   .30 .30
b.   A209 $1 multi   1.40 1.40
c.   A209 $2.10 multi   3.00 3.00
d.   A209 $3 multi   4.25 4.25
e.   Souvenir sheet of 8, 2 each #818a-818d   18.00 18.00

Adamstown — A210

2016, Aug. 24   Litho.   Perf. 14½x14
819   Horiz. pair   1.75 1.75
a.   A210 20c multi   .30 .30
b.   A210 $1 Museum   1.40 1.40
820   Horiz. pair   9.75 9.75
a.   A210 $2 Church   3.00 3.00
b.   A210 $4.60 School   6.75 6.75

Ferns — A211

Designs: 20c, Dicranopteris linearis. $1, Loxoscaphe gibberosum. $3, Ctenitis cumingii. $3.40, Angiopteris chauliodonta.

2016, Oct. 19   Litho.   Perf. 14x14½
821-824 A211   Set of 4   11.00 11.00
824a   Souvenir sheet of 2, #823-824   9.25 9.25

Miniature Sheet

Pitcairn Language — A212

No. 825 — Pitcairn and English words for: a, 20c, Sea urchin. b, 20c, Goat. c, $1, Weaving strand. d, $1, Seedling. e, $1, Loader. f, $2, Melon. g, $2, Swimming. h, $2, Orange.

2016, Dec. 7   Litho.   Perf. 14x14¼
825   A212   Sheet of 8, #a-h   13.00 13.00

Rosalind Amelia Young (1853-1924), School Teacher A213

No. 826 — Young and: a, Blackboard. b, Her poetry, and husband, David. c, School children. d, Her book, Story of Pitcairn Island.

2017, Feb. 22   Litho.   Perf. 14½
826   Horiz. strip of 4 + central label   10.50 10.50
a.   A213 $1 multi   1.40 1.40
b.   A213 $1.50 multi   2.10 2.10
c.   A213 $2.10 multi   3.00 3.00
d.   A213 $2.80 multi   4.00 4.00

Souvenir Sheet

Women of the Bounty — A214

No. 827: a, $1.80, Polynesian women on board the Bounty. b, $2.20, Women watching the burning of the Bounty. c, $2.80, Women and men starting life on Pitcairn Island.

Perf. 13¼x13½
2017, Mar. 30   Litho.
827 A214   Sheet of 3, #a-c   9.50 9.50

See French Polynesia No. 1186.

Maps of Pitcairn Islands — A215

Map by: 20c, John Bayly, 1773. $1, Capt. Frederick Beechey, 1825. $2.10, Fred Christian, 1961. $4.40, David Evans, 2005.

2017, May 17   Litho.   Perf. 14½
828-831 A215   Set of 4   11.00 11.00

Miniature Sheet

Pitcairn Islands Marine Reserve — A216

No. 832: a, $1, Titan triggerfish. b, $1, Pitcairn angelfish. c, $1, Whitetip reef shark. d, $1, Multibar goatfish. e, $2, Whitemouth moray. f, $2, Lyretail hogfish. g, $2, Yellow-edged lyretail. h, $2, Peacock grouper.

2017, July 26   Litho.   Perf. 13x13¼
832   A216   Sheet of 8, #a-h   18.00 18.00

First Sighting of Pitcairn Islands, by Robert Pitcairn (1752-70?), 250th Anniv. — A217

No. 833 — Pitcairn: a, Pointing to island. b, Holding telescope.

2017, Sept. 13   Litho.   Perf. 14¼
833   A217 $3 Horiz. pair, #a-b, + central label   8.75 8.75

Transverse Ladybird A218

Ladybird on: $2.10, Green foliage. $3, Brown foliage.

No. 836: a, $1, Ladybird with elytra open and wings up. b, $4.60, Ladybird with elytra partially open.

2017, Oct. 25 Litho. Perf. 14¼x14
834-835 A218 Set of 2   7.00 7.00
Souvenir Sheet
836 A218 Sheet of 2, #a-b   7.75 7.75

William Bligh (1754-1817), Captain of HMAV Bounty — A219

Maps and paintings of Bligh and: $1, Capt. James Cook. $2.10, Mutiny on the Bounty. $2.80, Vice Admiral Horatio Nelson. $3, Statue of Bligh, Sydney, Australia.

2017, Dec. 7 Litho. Perf. 13¾x13¼
837-840 A219 Set of 4   13.00 13.00

Items Salvaged From the HMS Bounty A220

Designs: $1, Copper fragment. $1.80, Bronze bell strike. $2.10, Copper hull sheathing. $3, Large cannon ball.

Perf. 13½x13¼
2018, Feb. 27 Litho.
841-844 A220 Set of 4   11.50 11.50

Drafters of the Pitcairn Islands Constitution — A221

No. 845: a, Captain Russell Eliott (1802-81). b, George Hunn Nobbs (1799-1884).

2018, Apr. 5 Litho. Perf. 14¼
845 A221 $3 Horiz. pair, #a-b, +   central label   8.50 8.50

Wedding of Prince Harry and Meghan Markle — A222

No. 846: a, $3, Engagement photograph. b, $5, Wedding photograph.

Litho. With Foil Application
2018, May 30 Perf. 14¼
846 A222 Horiz. pair, #a-b, +   central label   11.50 11.50

Miniature Sheet

Flowers — A223

No. 847: a, $1, Hibiscus rosa-sinensis. b, $1, Strelitzia reginae. c, $1, Heliconia rostrata.

---

d, $2, Anthurium andraeanum. e, $2, Alpinia purpurata. f, $2, Allamanda blanchetii.

2018, July 18 Litho. Perf. 14¼
847 A223 Sheet of 6, #a-f   12.50 12.50

Souvenir Sheet

Big Blue Octopus — A224

No. 848 — Various depictions of Octopus cyanea: a, $1. b, $2.80. c, $3.

Perf. 13¼x13½
2018, Sept. 19 Litho.
848 A224 Sheet of 3, #a-c   9.00 9.00

Miniature Sheet

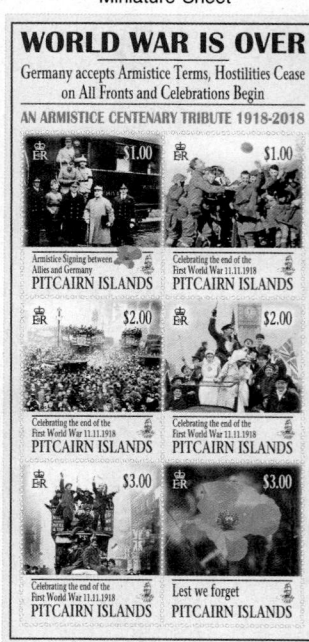

End of World War I, Cent. — A225

No. 849: a, $1, Armistice signing between Allies and Germany. b, $1, Soldiers celebrating end of World War I. c, $2, Crowd of people celebrating end of World War I, equestrian statue in background. d, $2, British people in automobile celebrating end of World War I, Big Ben in background. e, $3, People on double-decker bus celebrating end of World War I. f, $3, Poppy.

2018, Nov. 11 Litho. Perf. 14
849 A225 Sheet of 6, #a-f   17.00 17.00

Aerial Views of Pitcairn Island — A226

Various aerial photographs: 20c, $1, $3, $4.60.

2018, Dec. 12 Litho. Perf. 14½
850-853 A226 Set of 4   12.00 12.00

Paintings of the HMAV Bounty — A227

Painting by: $1, John Charles Alcott. $2.10, Roger Morris. $2.80, John Hagan. $3, Alfred Memelink.

2019, Feb. 27 Litho. Perf. 14½x14
854-857 A227 Set of 4   12.50 12.50

Miniature Sheet

Flowers — A228

No. 858: a, $1, Lilium longiflorum. b, $1.80, Brugmansia suaveolens. c, $2.80, Epiphyllum oxypetalum. d, $3, Cestrum nocturnum.

2019, Apr. 30 Litho. Perf. 14½
858 A228 Sheet of 4, #a-d   11.50 11.50

Pitcairn Reed Warbler A229

No. 859: a, Bird's head. b, Two birds. c, One bird.

2019, June 14 Litho. Perf. 14¼x14
859   Horiz. strip of 3   9.75 9.75
   a. A229 $1.80 multi   2.50 2.50
   b. A229 $2.10 multi   2.75 2.75
   c. A229 $3.40 multi   4.50 4.50

First Man on the Moon, 50th Anniv. A230

Designs: $1, Crew of Apollo 11. $2.20, Crew of Apollo 11 wearing space helmets. $3, Launch of Apollo 11. $3.40, Astronaut on ladder of Lunar Module.

2019, July 19 Litho. Perf. 14½
860-863 A230 Set of 4   12.50 12.50

Miniature Sheet

Mata ke Ti Randi Dark Sky Sanctuary — A231

No. 864 — Various views of Mata ki te Rangi at night: a, 20c. b, $2. c, $2.10. d, $3.

2019, Sept. 4 Litho. Perf. 14
864 A231 Sheet of 4, #a-d   9.25 9.25

Echinoderms — A232

Designs: 20c, Heterocentrotus mamillatus. $1, Brissus latecarinatus. $3, Neoferdina cumingi. $4.60, Macrophiothrix demessa.

2019, Oct. 23 Litho. Perf. 14½x14
865-868 A232 Set of 4   11.50 11.50

Christmas — A233

No. 869 — Angel over part of Pitcairn Island: a, $1.80. b, $2.20. c, $2.80.

2019, Dec. 4 Litho. Perf. 13¼x13½
869 A233 Horiz. strip o 3, #a-c   9.25 9.25

POLAND

'pō-lənd

LOCATION — Europe between Russia and Germany
GOVT. — Republic
AREA — 120,628 sq. mi.
POP. — 38,608,929 (1999 est.)
CAPITAL — Warsaw

100 Kopecks = 1 Ruble
100 Fenigi = 1 Marka (1918)
100 Halerzy = 1 Korona (1918)
100 Groszy = 1 Zloty (1924)

> Catalogue values for unused stamps in this country are for Never Hinged items, beginning with Scott 534 in the regular postage section, Scott B63 in the semipostal section, Scott C28 in the airpost section, Scott CB1 in the airpost semi-postal section, and Scott J146 in the postage due section.

Watermarks

Wmk. 145 — Wavy Lines

Wmk. 234 — Multiple Post Horns

Wmk. 326 — Multiple Post Horns

Issued under Russian Dominion

Coat of Arms — A1

Perf. 11½ to 12½

1860	Typo.		Unwmk.
1	A1	10k blue & rose	2,400.	300.
a.		10k blue & carmine	2,600.	375.
b.		10k dark blue & rose	3,000.	425.
c.		Added blue frame for inner oval	10,000.	1,400.
d.		Imperf.	—	7,500.

Used for letters within the Polish territory and to Russia. Postage on all foreign letters was paid in cash.
These stamps were superseded by those of Russia in 1865.
Counterfeits exist.

Issues of the Republic

Local issues were made in various Polish cities during the German occupation.

In the early months of the Republic many issues were made by overprinting the German occupation stamps with the words "Poczta Polska" and an eagle or bars often with the name of the city.
These issues were not authorized by the Government but were made by the local authorities and restricted to local use. In 1914 two stamps were issued for the Polish Legion and in 1918 the Polish Expeditionary Force used surcharged Russian stamps. The regularity of these issues is questioned.
Numerous counterfeits of these issues abound.

Warsaw Issues

Stamps of the Warsaw Local Post Surcharged

Statue of Sigismund III — A2

Coat of Arms of Warsaw — A3

Polish Eagle A4

Sobieski Monument A5

1918, Nov. 17   Wmk. 145   Perf. 11½

11	A2	5f on 2gr brn & buff	1.40	.90
a.		Inverted surcharge	200.00	200.00
12	A3	10f on 6gr grn & buff	.70	.65
a.		Inverted surcharge	15.00	15.00
13	A4	25f on 10gr rose & buff	7.00	3.25
a.		Inverted surcharge	27.50	27.50
14	A5	50f on 20gr bl & buff	8.50	6.25
a.		Inverted surcharge	350.00	350.00
		Nos. 11-14 (4)	17.60	11.05

Counterfeits exist.

Occupation Stamps Nos. N6-N16 Overprinted or Surcharged

a   b

1918-19   Wmk. 125   Perf. 14, 14½

15	A16	3pf brown ('19)	35.00	27.50
16	A22	5pf on 2½pf gray	1.40	.70
17	A16	5pf on 3pf brown	5.00	3.50
18	A16	5pf green	1.75	.70
19	A16	10pf carmine	1.40	.50
20	A22	15pf dark violet	1.00	.50
21	A16	20pf blue	1.40	.50
a.		20pf ultramarine	775.00	2,250.
23	A22	25pf on 7½pf org	1.00	.50
24	A16	30pf org & blk, buff	1.00	.50
25	A16	40pf lake & black	1.75	1.25
26	A16	60pf magenta	1.40	.50
		Nos. 15-26 (11)	52.10	36.65

There are two settings of this overprint. The first printing, issued Dec. 5, 1918, has space of 3½mm between the middle two bars. The second printing, issued Jan. 15, 1919, has space of 4mm. No. 15 comes only in the second setting; all others in both. The German overprint on No. 21a is very glossy.
Varieties of this overprint and surcharge are numerous: double; inverted; misspellings (Pocata, Poczat, Pelska); letters omitted, inverted or wrong font; 3 bars instead of 4, etc.
No. 21a requires competent expertization. A number of shades of the blue No. 21 exist. Counterfeits exist.

Lublin Issue

Austrian Military Semi-Postal Stamps of 1918 Overprinted

1918, Dec. 5   Unwmk.   Perf. 12½x13

27	MSP7	10h gray green	8.50	7.50
a.		Inverted overprint	80.00	80.00
b.		Double overprint	1,750.	700.00
c.		Double opt., one inverted	2,100.	850.00
28	MSP8	20h magenta	6.50	7.50
a.		Inverted overprint	50.00	50.00
b.		Double opt., one inverted	1,750.	500.00
29	MSP7	45h blue	6.50	7.50
a.		Inverted overprint	50.00	50.00
b.		Double opt., one inverted	1,750.	500.00
		Nos. 27-29 (3)	21.50	22.50

Austrian Military Stamps of 1917 Surcharged

1918-19   Perf. 12½

30	M3	3hal on 3h ol gray	27.50	20.00
a.		Inverted surcharge	3,900.	3,900.
b.		Perf. 11½	50.00	25.00
c.		Perf. 11½x12½	30.00	27.50
31	M3	3hal on 15h brt rose	7.00	7.00
a.		Inverted surcharge	25.00	30.00

Surcharged in Black

32	M3	10hal on 30h sl grn	7.00	7.00
a.		Inverted surcharge	25.00	30.00
b.		Brown surcharge (error)	75.00	65.00
34	M3	25hal on 40h ol bis	15.00	12.00
a.		Inverted surcharge	37.50	42.50
b.		Perf. 11½	52.50	27.50
c.		As "b," inverted surcharge	175.00	175.00
35	M3	45hal on 60h rose	7.00	7.00
a.		Inverted surcharge	30.00	27.50
36	M3	45hal on 80h dl blue	8.50	8.50
a.		Inverted surcharge	35.00	35.00
37	M3	50hal on 60h rose	18.00	14.00
a.		Inverted surcharge	52.50	35.00

Similar surcharge with bars instead of stars over original value

38	M3	45hal on 80h dl blue	20.00	10.00
a.		Inverted surcharge	40.00	35.00
b.		Double srch., one inverted	1,350.	

Overprinted

39	M3	50h deep green	27.50	27.50
a.		Inverted overprint	100.00	100.00
40	M3	90h dark violet	7.00	7.00
a.		Inverted overprint	140.00	100.00
		Nos. 30-40 (10)	136.50	120.00

Counterfeits

All Cracow issues, Nos. 41-60, J1-J12 and P1-P5 have been extensively counterfeited. Competent expertization is necessary. Prices apply only for authenticated stamps with identified plating position. Cost of certificate is not included in the catalogue value.

Cracow Issues

Austrian Stamps of 1916-18 Overprinted

1919, Jan. 17   Typo.

41	A37	3h brt violet	500.00	500.00
42	A37	5h lt green	550.00	550.00
43	A37	6h deep orange	70.00	65.00
a.		Inverted overprint	50,000.	
44	A37	10h magenta	500.00	500.00
45	A37	12h lt blue	75.00	75.00
46	A39	40h olive green	30.00	25.00
a.		Inverted overprint	550.00	—
b.		Double overprint	2,500.	
47	A39	50h blue green	15.00	15.00
a.		Inverted overprint		35,000.
48	A39	60h deep blue	10.00	10.00
a.		Inverted overprint	375.00	
49	A39	80h orange brown	14.00	14.00
a.		Inverted overprint	325.00	250.00
b.		Double overprint	1,750.	
50	A39	90h red violet	1,500.	1,400.
51	A39	1k carmine, yel	25.00	25.00

Engr.

52	A40	2k blue	12.00	14.00
53	A40	3k carmine rose	190.00	175.00
54	A40	4k yellow green	200.00	175.00
55	A40	10k deep violet	14,000.	13,000.

The 3k is on granite paper.
The overprint on Nos. 52-55 is litho. and slightly larger than illustration with different ornament between lines of type.

Same Overprint on Nos. 168-171

			1919		Typo.
56	A42	15h dull red		70.00	65.00
57	A42	20h dark green		300.00	160.00
58	A42	25h blue		2,000.	1,600.
59	A42	30h dull violet		600.00	400.00

Austria No. 157
Surcharged

1919, Jan. 24

60	A39	25h on 80h org brn	8.00	8.00
a.		Inverted surcharge	225.00	140.00

Excellent counterfeits of Nos. 27 to 60 exist.

Polish Eagle — A9

1919, Feb. 25   Litho.   Imperf.
Without gum
Yellowish Paper

61	A9	2h gray	1.75	1.40
62	A9	3h dull violet	1.00	1.00
63	A9	5h green	1.00	.70
64	A9	6h orange	17.50	20.00
65	A9	10h lake	1.00	.70
66	A9	15h brown	1.00	.70
67	A9	20h olive green	1.00	1.00

Bluish Paper

68	A9	25h carmine	.70	.70
69	A9	50h indigo	1.00	1.00
70	A9	70h deep blue	1.75	1.40
71	A9	1k ol gray & car	1.75	1.75
		Nos. 61-71 (11)	29.45	30.35

Nos. 61-71 exist with privately applied perforations.
Counterfeits exist.
For surcharges see Nos. J35-J39.

Posen (Poznan) Issue
Germany Nos. 84-85, 87, 96, 98
Overprinted in Black

Perf. 14, 14½

		1919, Aug. 5		Wmk. 125
72	A22	5pf on 2pf gray	30.00	18.00
73	A22	5pf on 7½pf org	2.00	1.40
a.		Double surcharge	1,550.	1,300.
74	A16	5pf on 20pf bl vio	2.00	1.25
75	A16	10pf on 25pf org & blk, yel	6.00	3.50
76	A16	10pf on 40pf lake & blk	3.50	1.40
		Nos. 72-76 (5)	43.50	25.55

Counterfeits exist.

Germany Nos. 96 and 98
Surcharged in Red or Green

a   b

1919, Sept. 15

77	A22	5pf on 2pf (R)	250.00	190.00
a.		Inverted surcharge	25,000.	
78	A22	10pf on 7½pf (G)	350.00	140.00

Nos. 77-78 are a provisional issue for use in Gniezno. Counterfeit surcharges abound.

Eagle and Fasces,
Symbolical of United Poland
A10   A11

"Agriculture"
A12

"Peace" — A13

Polish
Cavalryman
A14

For Northern Poland
Denominations as "F" or "M"

1919, Jan. 27   Imperf.
Wove or Ribbed Paper

81	A10	3f bister brn	.25	.35
82	A10	5f green	.25	.35
83	A10	10f red violet	.25	.35
84	A10	15f deep rose	.25	.50
85	A11	20f deep blue	.25	.50
86	A11	25f olive green	.25	.50
87	A11	50f blue green	.25	.50
88	A12	1m violet	2.50	3.75
89	A12	1.50m deep green	4.25	7.00
90	A12	2m dark brown	4.25	8.50
91	A13	2.50m orange brn	8.50	22.50
92	A14	5m red violet	17.50	40.00
		Nos. 81-92 (12)	38.75	84.55

Perf. 10, 11, 11½, 10x11½, 11½x10
1919-20

93	A10	3f bister brn	.25	.25
94	A10	5f green	.25	.25
95	A10	10f red violet	.25	.25
96	A10	10f brown ('20)	.25	.25
97	A10	15f deep rose	.25	.25
98	A10	15f vermilion ('20)	.25	.25
99	A11	20f deep blue	.25	.25
100	A11	25f olive green	.25	.25
101	A11	40f brt violet ('20)	.25	.25
102	A11	50f blue green	.25	.25
103	A12	1m violet	.70	.25
104	A12	1.50m deep green	.70	.35
105	A12	2m dark brown	1.75	.50
106	A13	2.50m orange brn	1.00	.70
107	A14	5m red violet	2.00	1.50
		Nos. 93-108 (15)	8.65	5.80

No. 108 exists in various shades of brown and violet.
Several denominations among Nos. 81-132 are found with double impression or in pairs imperf. between. See Nos. 109-132, 140-152C, 170-175. For surcharges & overprints, see Nos. 153, 199-200, B1-B14, 2K1-2K12, Eastern Silesia 41-50.

For Southern Poland
Denominations as "H" or "K"

1919, Jan. 27   Imperf.

109	A10	3h red brown	.35	.35
110	A10	5h emerald	.35	.25
111	A10	10h orange	.35	.25
112	A10	15h vermilion	.35	.25
113	A11	20h gray brown	.35	.25
114	A11	25h light blue	.35	.25
115	A11	50h orange brn	.35	.70
116	A12	1k dark green	.35	1.40
117	A12	1.50k red brown	4.75	4.00
118	A12	2k dark blue	2.00	3.50
119	A13	2.50k dark violet	12.50	8.00
120	A14	5k slate blue	15.00	12.00
		Nos. 109-120 (12)	37.05	31.20

Perf. 10, 11½, 10x11½, 11½x10

121	A10	3h red brown	.25	.25
122	A10	5h emerald	.25	.25
123	A10	10h orange	.25	.25
124	A10	15h vermilion	.25	.25
125	A11	20h gray brown	.25	.25
126	A11	25h light blue	.25	.25
127	A11	50h orange brn	.25	.25
128	A12	1k dark green	.25	.25

129	A12	1.50k red brown	.50	.25
130	A12	2k dark blue	.80	.25
131	A13	2.50k dark violet	2.00	.80
132	A14	5k slate blue	2.00	1.40
		Nos. 121-132 (12)	7.30	4.70

National Assembly Issue

A20

Ignacy Jan
Paderewski — A21

Adalbert
Trampczynski — A22

Eagle
Watching
Ship — A24

25f, Gen. Josef Pilsudski. 1m, Griffin.

1919-20   Perf. 11½
Wove or Ribbed Paper

133	A20	10f olive green	.40	.25
134	A21	15f brown red	.40	.25
a.		Imperf., pair	25.00	
135	A22	20f dp brown (21x25mm)		
136	A22	20f dp brown (17x20mm) ('20)	.40	.25
			1.75	2.25
137	A21	25f olive green	.40	.25
138	A24	50f Prus blue	.40	.25
139	A24	1m purple	1.25	.40
		Nos. 133-139 (7)	5.00	3.90

First National Assembly of Poland.

General Issue
1919   Perf. 9 to 14½ and Compound
Thin Laid Paper

140	A11	25f olive green	.25	.25
141	A11	50f blue green	.25	.25
142	A12	1m dark gray	.25	.25
143	A12	2m bister brn	.25	.25
144	A13	3m red brown	2.00	.35
a.		Pair, imperf. vert.	8.00	8.00
145	A14	5m red violet	1.25	.25
146	A14	6m deep rose	1.40	.25
a.		Pair, imperf. vert.	8.00	8.00
147	A14	10m brown red	.50	.20
a.		Horizontal pair, imperf.	8.00	8.00
148	A14	20m gray green	1.40	.50
		Nos. 140-148 (9)	7.55	2.65

Type of 1919 Redrawn
Perf. 9 to 14½ and Compound
1920-22   Thin Laid or Wove Paper

149	A10	1m red	.25	.25
150	A10	2m gray green	.25	.25
151	A10	3m light blue	.50	.35
152	A10	4m rose red	.25	.25
152A	A10	5m dark violet	.25	.25
b.		Horiz. pair, imperf. vert.	8.00	8.00
152C	A10	8m gray brown ('22)	.50	.50
		Nos. 149-152C (6)	2.00	1.85

The word "POCZTA" is in smaller letters and the numerals have been enlarged.
The color of No. 152A varies from dark violet to red brown.

No. 101 Surcharged

Perf. 10, 11½, 10x11½, 11½x10
1921, Jan. 25   Thick Wove Paper

153	A11	3m on 40f brt vio	.40	.25
a.		Double surcharge	25.00	25.00
b.		Inverted surcharge	—	—

Sower and
Rainbow of
Hope — A27

Thin Laid or Wove Paper
Perf. 9 to 14½ and Compound

	1921	Size: 28x22mm		Litho.
154	A27	10m grnsh blue	1.00	.30
155	A27	15m light brown	.65	.30
155A	A27	20m red	1.50	.30
		Nos. 154-155A (3)	3.15	.90

Signing of peace treaty with Russia.
Nos. 154-155A exist imperf. Value, unused, each $6.
See No. 191. For surcharges see Nos. 196-198.

Sun (Peace)
Breaking into
Darkness
(Despair) — A28

"Peace" and
"Agriculture"
A29

"Peace"
A30

Perf. 11, 11½, 12, 12½, 13 and Compound

1921, May 2

156	A28	2m green	.70	9.50
157	A28	3m blue	2.50	10.00
158	A28	4m red	.60	.70
a.		4m carmine rose (error)	600.00	
159	A29	6m carmine rose	.60	1.50
160	A29	10m slate blue	2.10	.80
161	A30	25m dk violet	3.50	.70
162	A30	50m slate bl & buff	2.10	.70
		Nos. 156-162 (7)	12.10	23.90

Issued to commemorate the Constitution.

Polish
Eagle — A31

Perf. 9 to 14½ and Compound
1921-23

163	A31	25m violet & buff	.80	.30
164	A31	50m carmine & buff	.80	.30
a.		Vert. pair, imperf. horiz.		
165	A31	100m blk brn & org	.80	.30
166	A31	200m black & rose ('23)		
			.80	.30
167	A31	300m olive grn ('23)	.40	.30
168	A31	400m brown ('23)	.55	.30
169	A31	500m brn vio ('23)	.70	.30
169A	A31	1000m orange ('23)	1.25	.30
169B	A31	2000m dull blue ('23)	.35	.30
		Nos. 163-169B (9)	6.45	2.70

For surcharge see No. 195.

Type of 1919 and

Miner — A32

Perf. 9 to 14½ and Compound
1922-23

170	A10	5f blue	.25	.75
171	A10	10f lt violet	.25	.75
172	A11	20f pale red	.25	1.50
173	A11	37f violet brn	.25	1.50
174	A11	50f orange	.25	1.50

175	A11	75f blue green	.25	2.25
176	A32	1m black	.25	1.50
177	A32	1.25m dark green	.25	3.25
178	A32	2m deep rose	.25	1.50
179	A32	3m emerald	.25	1.50
180	A32	4m deep ultra	.25	3.00
181	A32	5m yellow brn	.25	1.50
182	A32	6m red orange	.25	6.50
183	A32	10m lilac brn	.25	2.50
184	A32	20m deep violet	.25	3.00
185	A32	50m olive green	.25	2.50
187	A32	80m vermilion ('23)	1.00	20.00
188	A32	100m violet ('23)	.60	13.00
189	A32	200m orange ('23)	2.50	30.00
190	A32	300m pale blue ('23)	6.00	45.00
		Nos. 170-190 (20)	14.10	143.00

Union of Upper Silesia with Poland.
There were 2 printings of Nos. 176 to 190, the 1st being from flat plates, the 2nd from rotary press on thin paper, perf. 12½.
Nos. 173 and 175 are printed from new plates showing larger value numerals and a single "f."

Sower Type Redrawn
Size: 25x21mm

1922   Thick or Thin Wove Paper

191	A27	20m carmine	1.25	.50

In this stamp the design has been strengthened and made more distinct, especially the ground and the numerals in the upper corners.

Nicolaus Copernicus A33

Father Stanislaus Konarski — A34

1923   Perf. 10 to 12½

192	A33	1000m indigo	.60	.30
193	A34	3000m brown	.50	.60
a.		"Konarski"	18.00	17.00
194	A33	5000m rose	.90	.30
		Nos. 192-194 (3)	2.00	1.20

Nicolaus Copernicus (1473-1543), astronomer (Nos. 192, 194); Stanislaus Konarski (1700-1773), educator, and the creation by the Polish Parliament of the Commission of Public Instruction (No. 193).

No. 163 Surcharged

1923   Perf. 9 to 14½ and Compound

195	A31	10000m on 25m	5.00	.25
a.		Double surcharge	100.00	
b.		Inverted surcharge	75.00	

Stamps of 1921 Surcharged

196	A27	25000m on 20m red	3.50	1.75
a.		Double surcharge	100.00	
b.		Inverted surcharge	75.00	
197	A27	50000m on 10m grnsh bl	1.60	.25
a.		Double surcharge	100.00	
b.		Inverted surcharge	75.00	

No. 191 Surcharged

198	A27	25000m on 20m car	2.00	.25
a.		Double surcharge	100.00	
b.		Inverted surcharge	75.00	

No. 150 Surcharged with New Value
1924

199	A10	20000m on 2m gray grn	1.50	.25
a.		Inverted surcharge	75.00	—
b.		Double surcharge	100.00	—

Type of 1919 Issue Surcharged with New Value

200	A10	100000m on 5m red brn	1.60	.25
a.		Double surcharge	100.00	—
b.		Inverted surcharge	75.00	—
		Nos. 195-200 (6)	15.20	3.00

Arms of Poland — A35

Perf. 10 to 14½ and Compound

1924   Thin Paper   Litho.

205	A35	10,000m lilac brn	2.00	.40
206	A35	20,000m ol grn	1.20	.25
207	A35	30,000m scarlet	1.60	.25
208	A35	50,000m apple grn	4.75	.25
209	A35	100,000m brn org	1.60	.25
210	A35	200,000m lt blue	1.60	.25
211	A35	300,000m red vio	4.00	.65
212	A35	500,000m brn	4.00	.75
213	A35	1,000,000m ple rose	.40	26.00
214	A35	2,000,000m dk grn	.80	175.00
		Nos. 205-214 (10)	21.95	204.05
		Set, never hinged	65.00	

Arms of Poland A36

President Stanislaus Wojciechowski A37

Perf. 10 to 13½ and Compound

1924

215	A36	1g orange brown	.60	.50
216	A36	2g dark brown	.60	.25
217	A36	3g orange	.60	.25
218	A36	5g olive green	.60	.25
219	A36	10g blue green	1.75	.25
220	A36	15g red	2.50	.25
221	A36	20g blue	9.50	.25
222	A36	25g red brown	17.00	.25
a.		25g indigo	12,000.	6,000.
223	A36	30g deep violet	22.00	.25
a.		30g gray blue	250.00	125.00
224	A36	40g indigo	8.00	.70
225	A36	50g magenta	1.50	.25

Perf. 11½, 12

226	A37	1z scarlet	22.50	1.60
		Nos. 215-226 (12)	87.15	5.05
		Set, never hinged	300.00	

For overprints see Nos. 1K1-1K11.

Holy Gate of Wilno (Vilnius) — A38

Poznan Town Hall — A39

Sigismund Monument, Warsaw — A40

Wawel Castle at Cracow — A41

Sobieski Statue at Lwow — A42

Ship of State — A43

1925-27   Perf. 10 to 13

227	A38	1g bister brown	.55	.25
228	A42	2g brown olive	.65	.50
229	A40	3g blue	2.00	.25
230	A39	5g yellow green	2.75	.25
231	A40	10g violet	2.00	.25
232	A41	15g rose red	3.00	.25
233	A43	20g dull red	13.00	.25
234	A38	24g gray blue	5.50	.75
235	A42	30g dark blue	1.60	.25
236	A41	40g lt blue ('27)	1.60	.25
237	A43	45g dark violet	11.00	.25
		Nos. 227-237 (11)	43.65	3.50
		Set, never hinged	110.00	

For overprints see Nos. 1K11A-1K17.

1926-27   Redrawn

238	A40	3g blue	2.00	.25
239	A39	5g yellow green	2.50	.25
240	A40	10g violet	2.00	.25
241	A41	15g rose red	2.50	.25
		Nos. 238-241 (4)	9.00	1.00
		Set, never hinged	25.00	

On Nos. 229-232 the lines representing clouds touch the numerals. On the redrawn stamps the numerals have white outlines, separating them from the cloud lines.

Marshal Pilsudski — A44

Frederic Chopin — A45

1927   Typo.   Perf. 12½, 11½

242	A44	20g red brown	3.25	.50
243	A45	40g deep ultra	10.00	2.00
		Set, never hinged	35.00	

See No. 250. For overprint see No. 1K18.

President Ignacy Moscicki — A46

1927, May 4   Perf. 11½

245	A46	20g red	4.00	1.00
		Never hinged	10.50	

Dr. Karol Kaczkowski — A47

1927, May 27   Perf. 11½, 12½

246	A47	10g gray green	4.50	4.00
247	A47	25g carmine	6.50	4.00
248	A47	40g dark blue	9.00	2.00
		Nos. 246-248 (3)	20.00	10.00
		Set, never hinged	60.00	

4th Intl. Congress of Military Medicine and Pharmacy, Warsaw, May 30-June 4.

Juliusz Slowacki — A48

1927, June 28   Perf. 12½

249	A48	20g rose	4.00	1.10
		Never hinged	12.00	

Transfer from Paris to Cracow of the remains of Julius Slowacki, poet.

Pilsudski Type of 1927
Design Redrawn

1928   Perf. 11½, 12x11½, 12½x13

250	A44	25g yellow brown	3.00	.40
		Never hinged	10.00	

Souvenir Sheet

A49

1928, May 3   Engr.   Perf. 12½

251	A49	Sheet of 2	250.00	325.00
		Never hinged	475.00	
a.		50g black brown	25.00	85.00
b.		1z black brown	25.00	85.00

1st Natl. Phil. Exhib., Warsaw, May 3-13. Sold to each purchaser of a 1.50z ticket to the Warsaw Philatelic Exhibition. Counterfeits exist.

Marshal Pilsudski — A49a

Perf. 10½ to 14 and Compound

1928-31   Wove Paper

253	A49a	50g bluish slate	6.50	.25
254	A49a	50g blue grn ('31)	22.50	.40
		Set, never hinged	82.50	

See No. 315.

Pres. Moscicki — A50

Perf. 12x12½, 11½ to 13½ and Compound

1928   Laid Paper

255	A50	1z black, cream	15.00	.70
		Never hinged	50.00	
a.		Horizontally laid paper ('30)	40.00	2.25
		Never hinged	120.00	

See Nos. 305, 316. For surcharges and overprints see Nos. J92-J94, 1K19, 1K24.

General Josef Bem — A51

Wove Paper

1928, May　　Typo.　　Perf. 12½
256 A51 25g rose red　　3.75　.50
　　Never hinged　　8.50

Return from Syria to Poland of the ashes of General Josef Bern.

Henryk Sienkiewicz — A52

1928, Oct.
257 A52 15g ultra　　2.00　.40
　　Never hinged　　4.00

For overprint see No. 1K23.

Eagle Arms — A53

1928-29　　Perf. 12x12½
258 A53 5g dark violet　　.40　.25
259 A53 10g green　　.60　.25
260 A53 25g red brown　　.80　.30
　　Nos. 258-260 (3)　　1.80　.80
　　Set, never hinged　　4.25

See design A58. For overprints see Nos. 1K20-1K22.

"Swiatowid," Ancient Slav God — A54

1928, Dec. 15　　Perf. 12½x12
261 A54 25g brown　　2.00　.40
　　Never hinged　　5.00

Poznan Agricultural Exhibition.

King John III Sobieski — A55

1930, July　　Perf. 12x12½
262 A55 75g claret　　2.25　.40
　　Never hinged　　7.00

Stylized Soldiers — A56

1930, Nov. 1　　Perf. 12½
263 A56 5g violet brown　　.40　.25
264 A56 15g dark blue　　3.00　.45
265 A56 25g red brown　　.60　.25
266 A56 30g dull red　　6.50　4.00
　　Nos. 263-266 (4)　　10.50　4.95
　　Set, never hinged　　30.00

Centenary of insurrection of 1830.

Kosciuszko, Washington, Pulaski — A57

Laid Paper

1932, May 3　　Perf. 11½
267 A57 30g brown　　2.00　.45
　　Never hinged　　4.00

200th birth anniv. of George Washington.

A58

1932-33　　Typo.　　Wmk. 234

Perf. 12x12½
268 A58 5g dull vio ('33)　　.40　.25
269 A58 10g green　　.60　.25
270 A58 15g red brown ('33)　　.40　.25
271 A58 20g gray　　.65　.25
272 A58 25g buff　　.75　.25
273 A58 30g deep rose　　1.50　.25
274 A58 60g blue　　5.00　.50
　　Nos. 268-274 (7)　　9.30　2.00
　　Set, never hinged　　32.50

For overprints and surcharge see Nos. 280-281, 284, 292, 1K25-1K27.

Torun City Hall — A59

1933, Jan. 2　　Engr.　　Perf. 11½
275 A59 60g blue　　35.00　1.00
　　Never hinged　　92.50

700th anniversary of the founding of the City of Torun by the Grand Master of the Knights of the Teutonic Order.
See No. B28.

Altar Panel of St. Mary's Church, Cracow — A60

Perf. 11½-12½ & Compound
1933, July 10　　Laid Paper　　Unwmk.
277 A60 80g red brown　　14.00　1.25
　　Never hinged　　35.00

400th death anniv. of Veit Stoss, sculptor and woodcarver.
For surcharge see No. 285.

John III Sobieski and Allies before Vienna, painted by Jan Matejko — A61

1933, Sept. 12　　Laid Paper
278 A61 1.20z indigo　　24.00　6.50
　　Never hinged　　70.00

250th anniv. of the deliverance of Vienna by the Polish and allied forces under command of John III Sobieski, King of Poland, when besieged by the Turks in 1683.
For surcharge see No. 286.

Cross of Independence A62

Wmk. 234

1933, Nov. 11　　Typo.　　Perf. 12½
279 A62 30g scarlet　　3.00　.50
　　Never hinged　　8.00

15th anniversary of independence.

Type of 1932 Overprinted in Red or Black

1934, May 5　　Perf. 12
280 A58 20g gray (R)　　22.50　40.00
281 A58 30g deep rose　　32.50　45.00
　　Set, never hinged　　175.00

Katowice Philatelic Exhibition. Counterfeits exist.

Josef Pilsudski — A63

Perf. 11½ to 12½ and Compound
1934, Aug. 6　　Engr.　　Unwmk.
282 A63 25g gray blue　　3.00　.70
283 A63 30g black brown　　3.50　.70
　　Set, never hinged　　19.00

Polish Legion, 20th anniversary.
For overprint see No. 293.

Nos. 274, 277-278 Surcharged in Black or Red

1934　　Wmk. 234　　Perf. 12x12½
284 A58 55g on 60g blue　　3.75　.45

Perf. 11½-12½ & Compound
Unwmk.
285 A60 25g on 80g red brn　　5.00　.65
286 A61 1z on 1.20z ind (R)　　17.00　4.25
　a. Figure "1" in surcharge 5mm
　　high instead of 4½mm　　17.00　4.25
　　Never hinged　　50.00
　　Nos. 284-286 (3)　　25.75　5.35
　　Set, never hinged　　77.50

Surcharge of No. 286 includes bars.

Marshal Pilsudski — A64

1935　　Perf. 11 to 13 and Compound
287 A64 5g black　　.50　.25
288 A64 15g black　　.50　.35
289 A64 25g black　　.70　.25
290 A64 45g black　　3.25　.50
291 A64 1z black　　6.00　3.50
　　Nos. 287-291 (5)　　10.95　4.85
　　Set, never hinged　　32.50

Pilsudski mourning issue.
Nos. 287-288 are typo., Nos. 290-291 litho. No. 289 exists both typo. and litho.
See No. B35b.

Nos. 270, 282 Overprinted in Blue or Red

1935　　Wmk. 234　　Perf. 12x12½
292 A58 15g red brown　　.90　.25

Perf. 11½, 11½x12½

Unwmk.
293 A63 25g gray blue (R)　　2.75　.85
　　Set, never hinged　　12.00

Issued in connection with the proposed memorial to Marshal Pilsudski, the stamps were sold at Cracow exclusively.

"The Dog Cliff" — A65　　President Ignacy Moscicki — A75

Designs: 10g, "Eye of the Sea." 15g, M. S. "Pilsudski." 20g, View of Pieniny. 25g, Belvedere Palace. 30g, Castle in Mira. 45g, Castle at Podhorce. 50g, Cloth Hall, Cracow. 55g, Raczynski Library, Poznan. 1z, Cathedral, Wilno.

1935-36　　Typo.　　Perf. 12½x13
294 A65 5g violet blue　　.30　.25
295 A65 10g yellow green　　.50　.25
296 A65 15g Prus green　　3.00　.25
297 A65 20g violet black　　2.50　.25

Engr.
298 A65 25g myrtle green　　.30　.30
299 A65 30g rose red　　1.00　.25
300 A65 45g plum ('36)　　.30　.25
301 A65 50g black ('36)　　.25　.25
302 A65 55g blue ('36)　　1.50　.25
303 A65 1z brown ('36)　　5.00　3.00
304 A75 3z black brown　　1.25　4.00
　　Nos. 294-304 (11)　　15.90　9.30
　　Set, never hinged　　42.50

See Nos. 308-311. For overprints see Nos. 306-307, 1K28-1K32.

Type of 1928 inscribed "1926. 3. VI. 1936" on Bottom Margin

1936, June 3
305 A50 1z ultra　　3.00　5.00
　　Never hinged　　8.00

Presidency of Ignacy Moscicki, 10th anniv.

Nos. 299, 302 Overprinted in Blue or Red

1936, Aug. 15
306 A65 30g rose red　　4.00　3.50
307 A65 55g blue (R)　　7.00　2.25
　　Set, never hinged　　30.00

Gordon-Bennett Intl. Balloon Race. Counterfeits exist.

Scenic Type of 1935-36

Designs: 5g, Church at Czestochowa. 10g, Maritime Terminal, Gdynia. 15g, University, Lwow. 20g, Municipal Building, Katowice.

1937　　Engr.　　Perf. 12½
308 A65 5g violet blue　　.30　.25
309 A65 10g green　　.50　.25
310 A65 15g red brown　　.45　.25
311 A65 20g orange brown　　.45　.25
　　Nos. 308-311 (4)　　1.70　1.00
　　Set, never hinged　　5.00

For overprints see Nos. 1K31-1K32.

Marshal Smigly-Rydz — A80

1937　　Perf. 12½x13
312 A80 25g slate green　　.30　.25
313 A80 55g blue　　.30　.25
　　Set, never hinged　　2.25

For surcharges see Nos. N30, N32.

Types of 1928-37

1937	Souvenir Sheets		
314	Sheet of 4	14.00	20.00
a.	A80 25g, dark brown	1.75	2.75
315	Sheet of 4	14.00	20.00
a.	A49a 50g, deep blue	1.75	2.75
316	Sheet of 4	12.50	20.00
a.	A50 1z, gray black	1.75	2.75
	Set, never hinged	120.00	

Visit of King Carol of Romania to Poland, June 26-July 1. See No. B35c.

President Moscicki — A81

1938, Feb. 1		**Perf. 12½**	
317	A81 15g slate green	.70	.25
318	A81 30g rose violet	.35	.25
	Set, never hinged	3.00	

71st birthday of President Moscicki. For surcharge see No. N31.

Kosciuszko, Paine and Washington and View of New York City — A82

1938, Mar. 17		**Perf. 12x12½**	
319	A82 1z gray blue	1.40	1.00
	Never hinged	5.00	

150th anniv. of the US Constitution.

Boleslaus I and Emperor Otto III at Gnesen — A83

Marshal Pilsudski — A95

Designs: 10g, King Casimir III. 15g, King Ladislas II Jagello and Queen Hedwig. 20g, King Casimir IV. 25g, Treaty of Lublin. 30g, King Stephen Bathory commending Wielock, the peasant. 45g, Stanislas Zolkiewski and Jan Chodkiewicz. 50g, John III Sobieski entering Vienna. 55g, Union of nobles, commoners and peasants. 75g, Dabrowski, Kosciuszko and Poniatowski. 1z, Polish soldiers. 2z, Romuald Traugutt.

1938, Nov. 11		**Engr.**	**Perf. 12½**	
320	A83	5g red orange	.25	.25
321	A83	10g green	.25	.25
322	A83	15g fawn	.25	.25
323	A83	20g peacock blue	.25	.25
324	A83	25g dull violet	.40	.25
325	A83	30g rose red	.50	.25
326	A83	45g black	.40	.25
327	A83	50g brt red vio	.40	.25
328	A83	55g ultra	.40	.25
329	A83	75g dull green	2.60	1.00
330	A83	1z orange	3.25	1.75
331	A83	2z carmine rose	8.50	15.00
332	A95	3z gray black	5.00	10.00
	Nos. 320-332 (13)		22.45	30.00
	Set, never hinged		62.50	

20th anniv. of Poland's independence. See No. 339. For surcharges see Nos. N33-N47.

Souvenir Sheet

Marshal Pilsudski, Gabriel Narutowicz, President Moscicki, Marshal Smigly-Rydz — A96

1938, Nov. 11		**Perf. 12½**	
333	A96	Sheet of 4	13.00	20.00
	Never hinged		35.00	
a.	25g dull violet (Pilsudski)		1.40	1.90
b.	25g dull violet (Narutowicz)		1.40	1.90
c.	25g dull violet (Moscicki)		1.40	1.90
d.	25g dull violet (Smigly-Rydz)		1.40	1.90

20th anniv. of Poland's independence.

Poland Welcoming Teschen People — A97

1938, Nov. 11			
334	A97 25g dull violet	1.75	.60
	Never hinged	5.00	

Restoration of the Teschen territory ceded by Czechoslovakia.

Skier — A98

1939, Feb. 6			
335	A98 15g orange brown	.60	*.80*
336	A98 25g dull violet	.90	1.50
337	A98 30g rose red	2.00	1.50
338	A98 55g brt ultra	4.50	3.75
	Nos. 335-338 (4)	8.00	7.55
	Set, never hinged	23.00	

Intl. Ski Meet, Zakopane, Feb. 11-19.

Type of 1938

15g, King Ladislas II Jagello, Queen Hedwig.

Re-engraved

1939, Mar. 2		**Perf. 12½**	
339	A83 15g redsh brown	.45	.35
	Never hinged	.85	

No. 322 with crossed swords and helmet at lower left. No. 339, swords and helmet have been removed.

Marshal Pilsudski Reviewing Troops — A99

1939, Aug. 1		**Engr.**	
340	A99 25g dull rose violet	.40	*.50*
	Never hinged	1.10	

Polish Legion, 25th anniv. See No. B35a.

Polish Peoples Republic

Romuald Traugutt A100

Tadeusz Kosciuszko A101

Design: 1z, Jan Henryk Dabrowski.

Perf. 11½

1944, Sept. 7	**Litho.**	**Unwmk.**	
Without Gum			
341	A100 25g crimson rose	37.50	*55.00*
342	A101 50g deep green	35.00	*45.00*
343	A101 1z deep ultra	35.00	*50.00*
	Nos. 341-343 (3)	107.50	*150.00*

Counterfeits exist. For surcharges see Nos. 362-363.

Polish Eagle — A103

Grunwald Monument, Cracow — A104

1944, Sept. 13	**Photo.**	**Perf. 12½**	
344	A103 25g deep red	.60	.45
a.	25g dull red, typo.	1.00	
	Never hinged	2.75	
345	A104 50g dk slate green	.45	.30
	Set, never hinged	2.75	

No. 344a was not put on sale without surcharge. See Nos. 346, 349a. For surcharges see Nos. 345A-356, 364, B54, C19-C20.

No. 344 Surcharged in Black

a   b

c

1944-45			
345A	A103 1z on 25g	1.25	5.25
345B	A103 2z on 25g ('45)	1.25	6.50
345C	A103 3z on 25g ('45)	1.00	5.25
	Nos. 345A-345C (3)	3.50	17.00
	Set, never hinged	7.00	

Issued to honor Polish government agencies. K. R. N. — Krajowa Rada Narodowa (Polish National Council), P. K. W. N. — Polski Komitet Wyzwolenia Narodu (Polish National Liberation Committee) and R. T. R. P. — Rzad Tymczasowy Rzeczypospolitej Polskiej (Temporary Administration of the Polish Republic). Counterfeits exist.

No. 344a Surcharged in Brown

1945, Sept. 1			
346	A103 1.50z on 25g dull red	.45	.25
	Never hinged	1.50	
a.	1.50z on 25g deep red, #344	650.00	400.00

Counterfeits of No. 346a exist.

No. 344 Surcharged in Blue

1945, Feb. 12			
347	A103 3z on 25g	1.75	5.75
348	A103 3z on 25g *(Radom, 16. I. 1945)*	1.75	5.75
349	A103 3z on 25g *(Warszawa, 17. I. 1945)*	10.00	21.00
a.	3z on 25g dull red, #344a	125.00	150.00
350	A103 3z on 25g *(Czestochowa, 17. I. 1945)*	1.75	5.75
351	A103 3z on 25g *(Krakow, 19. I. 1945)*	1.75	5.75
352	A103 3z on 25g *(Lodz, 19. I. 1945)*	1.75	5.75
353	A103 3z on 25g *(Gniezno, 22. I. 1945)*	1.75	5.75
354	A103 3z on 25g *(Bydgoszcz, 23. I. 1945)*	2.00	5.75
355	A103 3z on 25g *(Kalisz, 24. I. 1945)*	1.75	5.75
356	A103 3z on 25g *(Zakopane, 29. I. 1945)*	2.50	5.75
	Nos. 347-356 (10)	26.75	72.75
	Set, never hinged	57.50	

Dates overprinted are those of liberation for each city. Counterfeits exist.

Grunwald Monument, Cracow — A105

Kosciuszko Statue, Cracow — A106

Cloth Hall, Cracow A107

Copernicus Memorial — A108

Wawel Castle — A109

1945, Apr. 10   Photo.   Perf. 10½, 11
357 A105 50g dk violet brn   .25   .25
  a.   50g dark brown   .50   .50
      Never hinged   1.00
358 A106 1z henna brown   .35   .25
359 A107 2z sapphire   .50   .35
360 A108 3z dp red violet   .85   .30
361 A109 5z blue green   2.00   7.25
      Nos. 357-361 (5)   3.95   8.40
  Set, never hinged   8.00

Liberation of Cracow Jan. 19, 1945.
Nos. 357-361 exist imperf. Value, set: unused $24; never hinged $55.
No. 357a is a coarser printing from a new plate showing designer's name (J. Wilczyk) in lower left margin. No. 357 does not show his name.

Nos. 341-342 Surcharged in Black or Red

d   e

1945   Perf. 11½
362 A100(d) 5z on 25g   30.00 60.00
363 A101(e) 5z on 50g (R)   5.00 40.00
      Never hinged   15.00

No. 362 was issued without gum.

No. 345 Surcharged in Brown

1945, Sept. 10   Perf. 12½
364 A104 1z on 50g dk sl grn   .40   .25
      Never hinged   1.40

Lodz Skyline   Kosciuszko
A110   Monument,
                      Lodz
                      A111

Flag Bearer Carrying Wounded Comrade — A112

1945, Mar. 9   Litho.   Perf. 11, 9 (3z)
365 A110 1z deep ultra   .55   .25
366 A111 3z dull red violet   1.25   .25
367 A112 5z deep carmine   1.50   1.90
      Nos. 365-367 (3)   3.30   2.40
  Set, never hinged   5.00

Nos. 365 and 367 commemorate the liberation of Lodz and Warsaw.

Grunwald Battle Scene — A113

1945, July 16
368 A113 5z deep blue   3.00 15.00
      Never hinged   8.00

Battle of Grunwald (Tannenberg), July 15, 1410.

Eagle Breaking Fetters and Manifesto of Freedom — A114

1945, July 22
369 A114 3z rose carmine   6.00 20.00
      Never hinged   12.00

1st anniv. of the liberation of Poland.

Crane Tower,   Stock Tower,
Gdansk — A115   Gdansk — A116

Ancient High Gate, Gdansk A117

1945, Sept. 15   Photo.   Unwmk.
370 A115 1z olive   .25   .25
371 A116 2z sapphire   .25   .25
372 A117 3z dark violet   .80   .50
      Nos. 370-372 (3)   1.30   1.00
  Set, never hinged   2.75

Recovery of Poland's access to the sea at Gdansk (Danzig).
Nos. 370-372 exist imperf. Value, set $25.

Civilian and Soldiers in Rebellion — A118

1945, Nov. 29
373 A118 10z black   4.25 20.00
      Never hinged   8.50

115th anniv. of the "November Uprising" against the Russians, Nov. 29, 1830.

Holy Cross Church — A119

Views of Warsaw, 1939 and 1945: 1.50z, Warsaw Castle, 1939 and 1945. 3z, Cathedral of St. John. 3.50z, City Hall. 6z, Post Office. 8z, Army General Staff Headquarters.

1945-46   Unwmk.   Imperf.
374 A119 1.50z crimson   .25   .25
375 A119 3z dark blue   .25   .25
376 A119 3.50z lt blue grn   .50   .50
377 A119 6z gray black   .50   .25
378 A119 8z brown ('46)   1.00   .50
379 A119 10z dark violet ('46)   .80   .25
      Nos. 374-379 (6)   3.30   2.00
  Set, never hinged   7.75

Nos. 374-379 exist with private produced rouletting.

Nos. 374-379 Overprinted in Black

1946, Jan. 17
383 A119 1.50z crimson   1.00   3.00
384 A119 3z dark blue   1.00   3.00
385 A119 3.50z lt blue grn   1.00   3.00
386 A119 6z gray black   1.00   3.00
387 A119 8z brown   1.00   3.00
388 A119 10z dark violet   .80   3.00
      Nos. 383-388 (6)   6.00 18.00
  Set, never hinged   14.00

Liberation of Warsaw, 1/17/45, 1st anniv.
Counterfeits exist.

Polish Revolutionist A125

1946, Jan. 22   Perf. 11
389 A125 6z slate blue   4.00 14.00
      Never hinged   8.00

Revolt of Jan. 22, 1863.

Infantry Advancing — A126

1946, May 9
390 A126 3z brown   .30   .25
      Never hinged   .60

Polish freedom, first anniversary.

Premier Edward Osubka-Morawski
Pres. Boleslaw Bierut and Marshal
Michael Rola-Zymierski — A127

Perf. 11x10½
1946, July 22   Unwmk.
391 A127 3z purple   .80 17.00
      Never hinged   2.10

For surcharge see No. B53.
No. 391 exists imperf. Value $55.

Bedzin Castle — A128

Duke Henry IV of Silesia, from Tomb at Wroclaw — A129

Lanckrona Castle A130

1946, Sept. 1   Photo.   Imperf.
392 A128 5z olive gray   .35   .25
393 A128 5z brown   .25   .25

Perf. 10½
394 A129 6z gray black   .35   .35

Imperf
395 A130 10z deep blue   1.00   .25
      Nos. 392-395 (4)   1.95   1.10
  Set, never hinged   3.50

Perforated examples of Nos. 392, 393 and 395 have been privately made. No. 394 exists imperf. Value, $175.
For surcharge see No. 404.

Jan Matejko, Jacek Malczewski, Josef Chelmonski — A131

Adam Chmielowski (Brother Albert) — A132

Designs: 3z, Chopin. 5z, Wojciech Bogus-lawski, Helena Modjeska and Stefan Jaracz. 6z, Alexander Swietochowski, Stephen Zer-omski and Boleslaw Prus. 10z, Marie Sklodowska Curie. 15z, Stanislaw Wyspianski, Juliusz Slowacki and Jan Kasprowicz. 20z, Adam Mickiewicz.

1947   Perf. 11
396 A131 1z blue   .35   .25
397 A132 2z brown   .35   .25
398 A132 3z Prus green   .35   .25
399 A131 5z olive green   .35   .25
400 A131 6z gray green   .75   .35
401 A132 10z gray brown   .50   .25
402 A132 15z sepia   1.40   .35
403 A132 20z gray black   1.00   .25
      Nos. 396-403 (8)   5.05   2.20
  Set, never hinged   13.00

Imperf
403A A131 1z blue   .30   .25
403B A132 2z brown   .40   .25
403C A132 3z Prus green   .40   .25
403D A131 5z olive green   .40   .25
403E A131 6z gray green   .60   .35
403F A132 10z gray brown   1.00   .25
403G A131 15z sepia   1.60   .35
403H A132 20z gray black   1.75   .25
      Nos. 403A-403H (8)   6.45   2.20

No. 394
Surcharged in
Red

1947, Feb. 25 *Perf. 10½*
104 A129 5z on 6z gray blk .50 .25
　Never hinged 1.00

　Exists imperf. Value $20.

Types of 1947

1947 **Photo.** *Perf. 11*
405 A131 1z slate gray .25 .25
406 A132 2z orange .25 .25
407 A132 3z olive green .25 .35
408 A131 5z olive brown .35 .25
409 A131 6z carmine rose .35 .25
410 A132 10z blue 1.25 .30
411 A131 15z chestnut brn .70 .35
412 A132 20z dark violet 1.40 .35
　a. Souv. sheet of 8, #405-
　　412 100.00 300.00
　　Never hinged 190.00
　Nos. 405-412 (8) 4.80 2.35
Set, never hinged 11.00

　No. 412a sold for 500z.

Imperf

412B A131 1z slate gray .75 .25
412C A132 2z orange .75 .25
412D A132 3z olive green 1.00 .25
412E A131 5z olive brown 2.40 .25
412F A131 6z carmine rose .75 .25
412G A132 10z blue 1.60 .25
412H A131 15z chestnut brn 3.00 .25
412I A132 20z dark violet 4.00 .25
　Nos. 412B-412I (8) 14.25 2.00

Laborer — A139　　Farmer — A140

Fisherman
A141

Miner
A142

1947, Aug. 20 **Engr.** *Perf. 13*
413 A139 5z rose brown .60 .25
414 A140 10z brt blue green .40 .25
415 A141 15z dark blue 1.75 .25
416 A142 20z brown black .40 .25
　Nos. 413-416 (4) 3.15 1.00
Set, never hinged 6.75

Allegory of the
Revolution — A143

1948, Mar. 15 **Photo.** *Perf. 11*
417 A143 15z brown .25 .25
　Never hinged .60

　Revolution of 1848. See Nos. 430-432.

Insurgents — A144

1948, Apr. 19
418 A144 15z gray black .65 5.75
　Never hinged 2.00

　Ghetto uprising, Warsaw, 5th anniv.
　Exists imperf., value $1,700.

Decorated
Bicycle
Wheel
A145

1948, May 1
419 A145 15z brt rose & blue 2.00 1.00
　Never hinged 2.75

　1st Intl. Bicycle Peace Race, Warsaw-
Prague-Warsaw.

Launching
Ship — A146

Loading
Freighter
A147

　35z, Racing yacht "Gen. Mariusz Zaruski."

1948, June 22
420 A146 6z violet .85 6.75
421 A147 15z brown car .85 2.75
422 A147 35z slate gray .85 4.50
　Nos. 420-422 (3) 2.55 14.00
Set, never hinged 6.00

　Polish Merchant Marine.

Cyclists
A148

1948, June 22
423 A148 3z gray 1.00 4.00
424 A148 6z brown 1.00 4.00
425 A148 15z green 1.00 5.50
　Nos. 423-425 (3) 3.00 13.50
Set, never hinged 7.00

　Poland Bicycle Race, 7th Circuit, 6/22-7/4.

A149

1948, July 15
426 A149 6z blue .50 .25
427 A149 15z red 1.00 .25
428 A149 18z rose brown .25 .25
429 A149 35z dark brown .50 .25
　Nos. 426-429 (4) 2.25 1.00
Set, never hinged 5.75

　Exhibition to commemorate the recovery of
Polish territories, Wroclaw, 1948.

Gen. Henryk
Dembinski
and Gen.
Josef
Bem — A150

　Designs: 35z, S. Worcell, P. Sciegienny and
E. Dembowski. 60z, Friedrich Engels and Karl
Marx.

1948, July 15
430 A150 30z dark brown .80 .40
431 A150 35z olive green 1.50 .55
432 A150 60z bright rose 1.25 .80
　Nos. 430-432 (3) 3.55 1.75
Set, never hinged 8.00

　Revolution of 1848, cent. See No. 417.

Symbolical of
United
Youth — A151

1948, Aug. 8
433 A151 15z blue .50 .35
　Never hinged 1.00

　Intl. Congress of Democratic Youth, Warsaw, Aug.

Stagecoach
Leaving
Torun
Gate — A152

1948, Sept. 4
434 A152 15z brown .70 .45
　Never hinged 1.40

　Philatelic Exhibition, Torun, Sept.

Clock Dial and
Locomotive
A153

1948, Oct. 6 *Perf. 11½*
435 A153 18z blue 2.75 16.00
　Never hinged 6.00

　European Railroad Schedule Conference,
Cracow.

Pres. Boleslaw
Bierut — A154

1948-49 **Unwmk.** *Perf. 11, 11½*
436 A154 2z orange ('49) .25 .25
437 A154 3z blue grn ('49) .25 .25
438 A154 5z brown .25 .25
439 A154 6z slate .90 .35
440 A154 10z violet ('49) .25 .25
441 A154 15z dp carmine .25 .25
442 A154 18z gray green 1.20 .25
443 A154 30z blue 1.20 .25
444 A154 35z violet brown 2.50 .35
　Nos. 436-444 (9) 7.05 2.45
Set, never hinged 15.00

Workers
Carrying
Flag
A155

　Designs: 15z, Marx, Engels, Lenin and Stalin. 25z, Ludwig Warynski.

　Inscribed: "Kongres Jednosci
Klasy Robotniczej 8. XII. 1948."

1948, Dec. 8 *Perf. 11*
445 A155 5z crimson .65 .25
446 A155 15z dull violet .50 .65
447 A155 25z brown 1.00 .60
　Nos. 445-447 (3) 2.15 1.50
Set, never hinged 5.75

Redrawn
Dated: "XII. 1948"

　Designs as before.

1948, Dec. 15 *Perf. 11½*
448 A155 5z brown carmine .50 .70
449 A155 15z bright blue 1.00 1.40
450 A155 25z dark green 1.90 4.00
　Nos. 448-450 (3) 3.40 6.10
Set, never hinged 8.25

　Congress of the Union of the Working
Class, Warsaw, Dec. 1948.

"Socialism"
A156

　Designs: 5z, "Labor." 15z, "Peace."

Perf. 11½
1949, May 31 **Unwmk.** **Photo.**
451 A156 3z carmine rose .60 .25
452 A156 5z deep blue .60 .25
453 A156 15z deep green .80 2.75
　Nos. 451-453 (3) 2.00 3.25
Set, never hinged 5.00

　8th Trade Union Congress, June 5, 1949.

Warsaw
Scene — A157

Pres. Boleslaw
Bierut — A158

Radio
Station — A159

Perf. 13x12½, 12½x13
1949, July 22 **Litho.**
454 A157 10z gray black 1.40 2.00
455 A158 15z lilac rose 1.20 2.00
456 A159 35z gray blue 1.40 2.00
　Nos. 454-456 (3) 4.00 6.00
Set, never hinged 9.25

　5th anniv. of "People's Poland."

A160

　UPU, 75th Anniv.: 6z, Stagecoach and
world map. 30z, Ship and map. 80z, Plane
and map.

1949, Oct. 10 **Engr.** *Perf. 13x12½*
457 A160 6z gray purple .30 .35
458 A160 30z blue .85 1.90
459 A160 80z dull green 2.10 5.75
　Nos. 457-459 (3) 3.25 8.00
Set, never hinged 7.25

A161

Symbolical of United Poland.

1949   *Perf. 13½x13*
460 A161 5z brown red   1.00 .25
461 A161 10z rose red   .25 .25
462 A161 15z green   .25 .25
463 A161 35z dark brown   2.00 1.00
   Nos. 460-463 (4)   3.50 1.75
   Set, never hinged   7.00

Congress of the People's Movement for Unity.

Adam Mickiewicz   Frederic Chopin
A162   A163

Design: 35z, Juliusz Slowacki.

1949, Dec. 5   *Perf. 12½*
464 A162 10z brown violet   .70 1.00
465 A163 15z brown rose   1.00 1.75
466 A162 35z deep blue   2.50 6.50
   Nos. 464-466 (3)   4.20 9.25
   Set, never hinged   9.50

Mail
Delivery — A164

1950, Jan. 21
467 A164 15z red violet   1.50 *4.25*
   Never hinged   3.25

3rd Congress of PTT Trade Unions, Jan. 21-23, 1950.

Adam Mickiewicz
and Pushkin — A165

1949, Dec. 15
468 A165 15z lilac   1.00 *4.75*
   Never hinged   3.25

Polish-Soviet friendship.

Pres. Boleslaw
Bierut — A166

1950, Feb. 25   **Engr.**   *Perf. 12x12½*
469 A166 15z red   .75 .25
   Never hinged   1.60

See Nos. 478-484, 490-496. For surcharge see No. 522.

Julian
Marchlewski — A167

1950, Mar. 23   **Photo.**   *Perf. 11x10½*
470 A167 15z gray black   .65 .40
       1.50

25th death anniv. of Julian Marchlewski, author and political leader.

Reconstruction,
Warsaw — A168

Perf. 11, 12 and Compounds of 13
1950, Apr. 15
471 A168 5z dark brown   .25 .25
   Never hinged   .45

See No. 497.

Worker Holding
Hammer, Flag
and Olive
Branch — A169

Workers of Three
Races with
Flag — A170

1950, Apr. 26   *Perf. 11½*
472 A169 10z deep lilac rose   .80 .70
473 A170 15z brown olive   1.00 .85
   Set, never hinged   4.75

60th anniversary of Labor Day.

Freedom Monument,
Poznan — A171

1950, Apr. 27
474 A171 15z chocolate   .35 .25
   Never hinged   .50

Poznan Fair, Apr. 29-May 14, 1950.

Dove on
Globe — A172

1950, May 15   **Unwmk.**
475 A172 10z dark green   .75 .30
476 A172 15z dark brown   .40 .25
   Set, never hinged   2.40

Day of Intl. Action for World Peace.

Polish
Workers — A173

1950, July 20   *Perf. 12½x13*
477 A173 15z violet blue   .25 .25
       .55

Poland's 6-year plan. See Nos. 507A-510, 539.

Bierut Type of 1950, No Frame
1950   **Engr.**   *Perf. 12x12½*
478 A166 5z dull green   .25 .25
479 A166 10z dull red   .25 .25
480 A166 15z deep blue   1.50 .25
481 A166 20z violet brown   .25 .25
482 A166 25z yellow brown   .25 .25
482A A166 30z rose brown   .75 .25
483 A166 40z brown   .40 .25
484 A166 50z olive   1.50 .35
   Nos. 478-484 (8)   5.15 2.10
   Set, never hinged   11.50

Hibner,
Kniewski and
Rutkowski
A174

1950, Aug. 18   **Photo.**   *Perf. 11*
485 A174 15z gray black   1.50 1.00
   Never hinged   3.50

25th anniv. of the execution of three Polish revolutionists, Wladyslaw Hibner, Wladyslaw Kniewski and Henryk Rutkowski.

Worker and
Dove — A175

1950, Aug. 31   **Engr.**   *Perf. 12½*
486 A175 15z gray green   .35 .25
   Never hinged   .70

Polish Peace Congress, Warsaw, 1950.

Dove by
Picasso — A176

"GROSZY"

To provide denominations needed as a result of the currency revaluation of Oct. 28, 1950, each post office was authorized to surcharge stamps of its current stock with the word "Groszy." Many types and sizes of this surcharge exist. The surcharge was applied to most of Poland's 1946-1950 issues. All stamps of that period could receive the surcharge upon request of anyone. Counterfeits exist.

1950, Nov. 13
487 A176 40g blue   1.00 .25
488 A176 45g brown red   .50 .45
   Set, never hinged   3.00

2nd World Peace Congress.
For Type A176 surcharged, see No. 500.

Josef Bem and Battle Scene — A177

1950, Dec. 10
489 A177 45g blue   .85 *1.75*
   Never hinged   2.40

Death centenary of Gen. Josef Bem.

Type of 1950 with Frame Omitted
Perf. 12x12½
1950, Dec. 16   **Engr.**   **Unwmk.**
490 A166 5g brown violet   .25 .25
491 A166 10g bluish green   .25 .25
492 A166 15g dp yellow grn   .25 .25
493 A166 25g dark red   .35 .25
493A A166 30g red   .35 .25
494 A166 40g vermilion   .60 .25
495 A166 45g deep blue   1.25 .50
496 A166 75g brown   1.00 .25
   Nos. 490-496 (8)   4.30 2.25
   Set, never hinged   10.00

Reconstruction Type of 1950
Perf. 11, 11x11½, 13x11
1950   **Photo.**
497 A168 15g green   .25 .25
       .40

Woman and
Doves — A178

1951, Mar. 2   **Engr.**   *Perf. 12½*
498 A178 45g dark red   .25 .25
   Never hinged   .50

Congress of Women, Mar. 3-4, 1951.

Gen. Jaroslaw Dabrowski — A179

1951, Mar. 24   *Perf. 12x12½*
499 A179 45g dark green   .35 .25
   Never hinged   .70

80th anniv. of the Insurrection of Paris and the death of Gen. Jaroslaw Dabrowski.

Dove Type of 1950 Surcharged
1951, Apr. 20   *Perf. 12½*
500 A176 45g on 15z brn red   .60 .35
   Never hinged   1.20

Worker and
Flag — A180

1951, Apr. 25   **Photo.**   *Perf. 14x11*
501 A180 45g scarlet   .50 .25
   Never hinged   1.00

Labor Day, May 1.

Steel Mill, Nowa Huta — A181

1951   **Engr.**   *Perf. 12½*
502	A181	40g dark blue	.25	.25
503	A181	45g black	.35	.25
504	A181	60g brown	.25	.25
505	A181	90g dark carmine	1.00	.25
		Nos. 502-505 (4)	1.85	1.00
		Set, never hinged	4.00	

Pioneer Saluting — A182   Boy and Girl Pioneers — A183

1951, Apr. 1   **Photo.**
506	A182	30g olive brown	1.00	.90
507	A183	45g brt grnish blue	2.25	1.50
		Set, never hinged	8.50	

Issued to publicize Children's Day, June 1, 1951.

Workers Type of 1950

1951   **Unwmk.**   **Engr.**   *Perf. 12½x13*
507A	A173	45g violet blue	.25	.25
508	A173	75g black brown	.25	.25
509	A173	1.15z dark green	.85	.25
510	A173	1.20z dark red	.35	.25
		Nos. 507A-510 (4)	1.70	1.00
		Set, never hinged	4.00	

Issued to publicize Poland's 6-year plan.

Stanislaw Staszik — A184   Congress Emblem — A186

Z. F. von Wroblewski and Karol S. Olszewski — A185

Portraits: 40g, Marie Sklodowska Curie. 60g, Marceli Nencki. 1.15z, Nicolaus Copernicus.

1951, Apr. 25   *Perf. 12½, 14x11*   **Photo.**
511	A184	25g carmine rose	1.75	3.00
512	A184	40g ultra	.35	.25
513	A184	45g purple	2.25	1.75
514	A184	60g green	.45	.25
515	A184	1.15z claret	.45	.25
516	A186	1.20z gray	.90	.70
		Nos. 511-516 (6)	6.15	6.20
		Set, never hinged	17.00	

1st Congress of Polish Science.

Feliks E. Dzerzhinski — A187

1951, July 5   **Engr.**   *Perf. 12x12½*
517	A187	45g chestnut brown	.25	.25
		Never hinged		.50

25th death anniv. of Feliks E. Dzerzhinski, Polish revolutionary, organizer of Russian secret police.

Pres. Boleslaw Bierut — A188

1951, July 22   *Perf. 12½*
518	A188	45g dark carmine	1.20	.35
519	A188	60g deep green	7.00	9.50
520	A188	90g deep blue	2.25	1.00
		Nos. 518-520 (3)	10.45	10.85
		Set, never hinged	26.00	

7th anniv. of the formation of the Polish People's Republic.

Flag and Sports Emblem — A189

1951, Sept. 8   **Photo.**   *Perf. 11x14*
521	A189	45g green	.80	.50
		Never hinged		1.75

National Sports Festival, 1951.
No. 521 exists perf. 12½. Values: unused, $1.75; never hinged, $4.

**Type of 1950 with Frame Omitted
Surcharged with New Value in Black**

1951, Sept. 1   **Engr.**   *Perf. 12½x11½*
522	A166	45g on 35z org red	.45	.35
		Never hinged		.90

Youths Encircling Globe — A190

1951, Aug. 5   **Photo.**   *Perf. 12½x11*
523	A190	40g deep ultra	.80	.35
		Never hinged		1.75

3rd World Youth Festival, Berlin, Aug. 5-19.

Joseph V. Stalin — A191

1951, Oct. 30   **Engr.**   *Perf. 12½*
524	A191	45g lake	.30	.25
525	A191	90g gray black	.50	.45
		Set, never hinged	1.75	

Month of Polish-Soviet friendship, Nov. 1951.

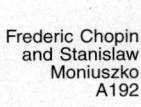

Frederic Chopin and Stanislaw Moniuszko — A192

1951, Nov. 15   **Unwmk.**
526	A192	45g gray	.25	.25
527	A192	90g brownish red	.80	.80
		Set, never hinged	1.90	

Festival of Polish Music, 1951.

Apartment House Construction A193   Coal Mining A194

Design: Nos. 529-530, Electrical installation.

1951-52   **Inscribed: "Plan 6," etc.**
528	A193	30g dull green	.25	.25
529	A193	30g gray black ('52)	.25	.25
530	A193	45g red ('52)	.25	.25
531	A194	90g chocolate	.25	.25
532	A193	1.15z violet brn ('52)	.25	.25
533	A194	1.20z deep blue ('52)	.25	.25
		Nos. 528-533,B68-B69A (9)	3.95	2.25
		Set, never hinged	4.50	

Poland's 6-year plan.

> **Catalogue values for unused stamps in this section, from this point to the end of the section, are for Never Hinged items.**

Pawel Finder — A195

Portrait: 1.15z, Malgorzata Fornalska.

1952, Jan. 18
534	A195	90g chocolate	.50	.25
535	A195	1.15z red orange	.30	.25
		Nos. 534-535,B63 (3)	1.05	.75

Polish Workers Party, 10th anniv.
See No. B63.

Flag, Two Women — A196

1952, Mar. 8   *Perf. 12½x12*
536	A196	1.20z deep carmine	.55	.25

Intl. Women's Day. See No. B64.

Gen. Karol Swierczewski-Walter A197

1952, Mar. 28   *Perf. 12½*
537	A197	90g blue gray	1.40	.25

Gen. Karol Swierczewski-Walter (1896-1947). See No. B65.

Pres. Boleslaw Bierut — A198

1952, Apr. 18
538	A198	90g dull green	1.60	.70
		Nos. 538,B66-B67 (3)	3.00	1.20

60th birth anniv. of Pres. Boleslaw Bierut.

Souvenir Sheet

A199

1951, Nov. 15
539	A199	Sheet of 4	40.00	15.00
a.		45g red brown (A173)	2.75	2.10
b.		75g red brown (A173)	2.75	2.10
c.		1.15z red brown (A173)	2.75	2.10
d.		1.20z red brown (A173)	2.75	2.10

Polish Philatelic Association Congress, Warsaw, 1951. Sold for 5 zloty.

Workers with Flag — A200

1952, May 1   **Unwmk.**   *Perf. 12½*
540	A200	75g deep green	.90	.25

Labor Day, May 1, 1952. See No. B70.

J. I. Kraszewski — A201

1z, Hugo Kollataj. 1.15z, Maria Konopnicka.

1952, May   **Various Frames**
541	A201	25g brown violet	1.00	.35
542	A201	1z yellow green	.70	.25
543	A201	1.15z red brown	.95	.25
		Nos. 541-543,B71-B72 (5)	3.50	1.85

Nikolai Gogol — A202

1952, June 5
544 A202 25g deep green   1.10   .70
    100th death anniv. of Nikolai V. Gogol, writer.

Gymnast — A203

1952, June 21   Photo.   Perf. 13
545 A203 1.15z Runners   4.50 3.50
546 A203 1.20z shown   .50   .25
    Nos. 545-546, B75-B76 (4)   10.00 5.00

Racing Cyclists — A204

1952, Apr. 25   Perf. 13½
547 A204 40g blue   1.75   .85
    5th Intl. Peace Bicycle Race, Warsaw-Berlin-Prague.

Shipyard Worker and Collier — A205

1952, June 28   Engr.   Perf. 12½
548 A205 90g violet brown   .90 1.75
    Nos. 548, B77-B78 (3)   7.40 3.50
    Shipbuilders' Day, 1952.

Concrete Works, Wierzbica — A206

1952, June 17
549 A206   3z gray   1.75   .30
550 A206 10z brown red   4.00 1.10

Bugler — A207

1952, July 17   Perf. 12½x12
551 A207 90g brown   1.00   .40
    Youth Festival, 1952. See Nos. B79-B80.

Celebrating New Constitution A208

1952, July 22   Photo.   Perf. 12½
552 A208 3z vio & dk brn   .90   .75
    Proclamation of a new constitution. See No. B81.

Power Plant, Jaworzno A209

1952, Aug. 7   Engr.
553 A209   1z black   3.00   .25
554 A209 1.50z deep green   .75   .25
    Nos. 553-554, B82 (3)   4.50   .75

Grywald — A210

1952, Aug. 18
555 A210 60g dark green   1.75 1.50
556 A210   1z red ("Niedzica")   4.75   .25
   a.   1z red ("Niedziga")   12.00   .75
    Nos. 555-556, B85 (3)   8.10 2.95

Parachute Descent — A211

1952, Aug. 23
557 A211 90g deep blue   1.50   .35
    Nos. 557, B86-B87 (3)   7.00 1.70
    Aviation Day, Aug. 23.

Avicenna — A212

Portrait: 90g, Victor Hugo.

1952, Sept. 1
558 A212 75g red brown   .60   .35
559 A212 90g sepia   .80   .35
    Anniversaries of the births of Avicenna (1000th) and Victor Hugo (150th).

Shipbuilding — A213

1952, Sept. 10
560 A213   5g deep green   .30   .25
561 A213 15g red brown   .60   .25
    Reconstruction of Gdansk shipyards.

Assault on the Winter Palace, 1917 A214

1952, Nov. 7   Perf. 12x12½
562 A214 60g dark brown   .90   .25
    Russian Revolution, 35th anniv. See No. B92.
    Nos. 562, B92 exist imperf. Values, set: never hinged $27.50; used $32.50.

Auto Assembly Plant, Zeran — A215

1952, Dec. 12   Perf. 12½
563 A215 1.15z brown   .75   .60
    See No. B99.

Dove — A216

1952, Dec. 12   Photo.
564 A216 30g green   .40   .30
565 A216 60g ultra   2.10   .80
    Congress of Nations for Peace, Vienna, Dec. 12-19, 1952.

Soldier with Flag — A217

1953, Feb. 2   Unwmk.   Perf. 11
Flag in Carmine
566 A217 60g olive gray   5.50 3.00
567 A217 80g blue gray   3.00   .70
    10th anniv. of the Battle of Stalingrad.

Karl Marx — A218

1953, Mar. 14   Perf. 12½
568 A218 60g dull blue   25.00 17.00
569 A218 80g dark brown   1.25   .25
    70th death anniv. of Karl Marx.

Cyclists and Arms of Warsaw — A219

Arms: No. 571, Berlin. No. 572, Prague.

1953, Apr. 30
570 A219 80g dark brown   .80   .25
571 A219 80g dark green   1.00   .25
572 A219 80g red   24.00 13.50
    Nos. 570-572 (3)   25.80 14.00
    6th Intl. Peace Bicycle Race, Warsaw-Berlin-Prague.

Flag and Globe — A220

1953, Apr. 28
573 A220 60g vermilion   15.00 3.75
574 A220 80g carmine   .40   .40
    Labor Day, May 1, 1953.

Boxer — A221

Design: 95g, Boxing match.

1953, May 17
575 A221 40g red brown   .85   .25
576 A221 80g orange   21.00 12.00
577 A221 95g violet brown   .85   .25
    Nos. 575-577 (3)   22.70 12.50
    European Championship Boxing Matches, Warsaw, May 17-24, 1953.

Copernicus Watching Heavens, by Jan Matejko — A222

Nicolaus Copernicus — A223

Perf. 12x12½, 12½x12
1953, May 22   Engr.
578 A222 20g brown   .80   .25
579 A223 80g deep blue   18.00 8.50
    480th birth anniv. of Nicolaus Copernicus, astronomer.

Fishing Boat — A224

Design: 1.35z, Freighter "Czech."

1953, July 15   Perf. 12½
580 A224   80g dark green   1.50   .25
581 A224 1.35z deep blue   3.50 1.50
    Issued for Merchant Marine Day.

Old Part of Warsaw — A225

1953, July 15   **Photo.**
582 A225   20g red brown   .25 .25
583 A225 2.35z blue   3.75 1.75
    36th anniv. of the proclamation of "People's Poland."

Students of Two Races — A226   Schoolgirl and Dove — A227

1.35z, Congress badge (similar to AP7).

1953, Aug. 24
584 A226   40g dark brown   .35 .25
585 A227 1.35z green   .50 .25
586 A227 1.50z blue   6.00 4.00
    Nos. 584-586,C32-C33 (5)   11.60 6.25
    3rd World Congress of Students, Warsaw, 1953.

Nurse Feeding Baby — A228

Design: 1.75z, Nurse instructing mother.

1953, Nov. 21
587 A228   80g rose carmine   8.25 7.25
588 A228 1.75z deep green   .25 .25
    Poland's Social Health Service.

Mieczylaw Kalinowski A229   Battle Scene, Polish and Soviet Flags A230

Portrait: 1.75z, Roman Pazinski.

1953, Oct. 10
589 A229   45g brown   4.75 2.25
590 A230   80g brown lake   .50 .25
591 A229 1.75z olive gray   .50 .25
    Nos. 589-591 (3)   5.75 2.75
    10th anniv. of Poland's People's Army.

Jan Kochanowski A231   Courtyard, Wawel Castle A232

Portrait: 1.35z, Mikolaj Rej.

1953, Nov. 10   **Engr.**
592 A231   20g red brown   .50 .25
593 A232   80g deep plum   .80 .25
594 A231 1.35z gray black   2.75 1.00
    Nos. 592-594 (3)   4.05 1.50
    Issued for the "Renaissance Year."

For surcharges see Nos. 733-736.

Palace of Culture, Warsaw A233

Designs: 1.75z, Constitution Square. 2z, Old Section, Warsaw.

1953, Nov. 30   **Perf. 12x12½**
595 A233   80g vermilion   11.00 .50
596 A233 1.75z deep blue   1.00 .25
597 A233   2z violet brown   8.00 4.25
    Nos. 595-597 (3)   20.00 5.00
    Issued for the reconstruction of Warsaw.

Ice Dancer — A236   Skier — A237

Design: 2.85z, Ice hockey player.

1953, Dec. 31   **Litho.**   **Perf. 12½**
602 A236   80g blue   1.60 .25
603 A237   95g blue green   1.60 .25
604 A236 2.85z dark red   4.75 2.25
    Nos. 602-604 (3)   7.95 2.75

Canceled to Order
    The government stamp agency began late in 1951 to sell canceled sets of new issues. Until 1990, at least, values in the second ("used") column are for these canceled-to-order stamps. Postally used stamps are worth more.

Children at Play — A238

Designs: 80g, Girls on the way to school. 1.50z, Two students in class.

1953, Dec. 31   **Photo.**
605 A238   10g violet   .25 .25
606 A238   80g red brown   .75 .25
607 A238 1.50z dark green   6.50 2.60
    Nos. 605-607 (3)   7.50 3.10

Krynica Spa A239   Dunajec Canyon, Pieniny Mountains A240

Designs: 80g, Morskie Oko, Tatra Mts. 2z, Windmill and framework, Ciechocinek.

1953, Dec. 16
608 A239   20g blue & rose brn   .40 .25
609 A240   80g bl grn & dk vio   5.50 2.50
610 A240 1.75z ol bis & dk grn   1.20 .25
611 A239   2z brick red & blk   1.20 .25
    Nos. 608-611 (4)   8.30 3.25

Electric Passenger Train — A241

Design: 80g, Electric locomotive and cars.

1954, Jan. 26   **Engr.**
612 A241   60g deep blue   6.00 3.00
613 A241   80g red brown   .55 .25

Spinning Mill, Worker — A242

Designs: 40g, Woman letter carrier. 80g, Woman tractor driver.

1954, Mar. 24   **Photo.**
614 A242   20g deep green   2.25 1.00
615 A242   40g deep blue   .50 .25
616 A242   80g dark brown   .55 .25
    Nos. 614-616 (3)   3.30 1.50

Flags and May Flowers — A243

1954, Apr. 28
617 A243   40g chocolate   .60 .25
618 A243   80g deep blue   1.00 .25
619 A243   80g carmine rose   .60 .25
    Nos. 617-619 (3)   2.20 .75
    Labor Day, May 1, 1954.

"Peace" Uniting Three Capitals — A244

No. 621, Dove, olive branch and wheel.

1954, Apr. 29   **Perf. 12½x12**
620 A244   80g red brown   .60 .25
621 A244   80g deep blue   .70 .45
    7th Intl. Bicycle Tour, May 2-17, 1954.

A245

1954, Apr. 30   **Engr.**   **Perf. 11½**
622 A245   25g gray   1.50 .50
623 A245   80g brown carmine   .35 .25
    3rd Trade Union Congress, Warsaw 1954.

Glider and Framed Clouds — A246

60g, Glider, flags. 1.35z, Glider, large cloud.

1954, May 31   **Photo.**   **Perf. 12½**
624 A246   45g dark green   .65 .25
625 A246   60g purple   3.75 2.50
626 A246   60g brown   1.25 .25
627 A246 1.35z blue   2.40 .25
    Nos. 624-627 (4)   8.05 3.25
    Intl. Glider Championships, Leszno.

Fencing — A247   Handstand on Horizontal Bars — A248

Design: 1z, Relay racers.

1954, July 17
628 A247   25g violet brown   2.10 .25
629 A248   60g Prus blue   1.60 .30
630 A247   1z violet blue   4.25 1.75
    Nos. 628-630 (3)   7.95 2.30

Javelin Throwers A249

1954, July 17   **Perf. 12**
631 A249   60g rose brn & dk red brn   1.00 .70
632 A249 1.55z gray & black   2.50 .70
    Nos. 628-632 were issued to publicize the second Summer Spartacist Games, 1954.

Studzianki Battle Scene — A250

Design: 1z, Soldier and flag bearer.

1954, Aug. 24   **Perf. 12½**
633 A250   60g dark green   2.00 .30
634 A250   1z violet blue   6.50 2.75
    10th anniversary, Battle of Studzianki.

Railway Signal — A251

Design: 60g, Modern train.

1954, Sept. 9
635 A251   40g dull blue   7.25 .25
636 A251   60g black   4.00 1.90
    Issued to publicize Railwaymen's Day.

Ivan Michurin, Horticulturalist A252

1954, Sept. 15
637 A252   40g violet   2.00 1.60
638 A252   60g black   .25 .25
    Month of Polish-Soviet friendship.

View of Elblag A253

Cities: 45g, Gdansk. 60g, Torun. 1.40z, Malbork. 1.55z, Olsztyn.

1954, Oct. 16   Engr.   Perf. 12x12½
639 A253 20g dk car, *bl*   5.20 1.50
640 A253 45g brown, *yel*   .40   .25
641 A253 60g dk green, *cit*   .40   .25
642 A253 1.40z dk blue, *pink*   .65   .25
643 A253 1.55z dk vio brn, *cr*   .65   .25
    Nos. 639-643 (5)   7.30 2.50

Pomerania's return to Poland, 500th anniv.
For overprint see No. 866.

Chopin and Piano — A254

1954, Nov. 8   Photo.   Perf. 12½
644 A254 45g dark brown   .30   .25
645 A254 60g dark green   .30   .25
646 A254 1z dark blue   3.25 1.60
    Nos. 644-646 (3)   3.85 2.10

5th Intl. Competition of Chopin's Music.

Coal Mine — A255

Designs: 20g, Soldier, flag and map. 25g, Steel mill. 40g, Relaxing worker in deck chair. 45g, Building construction. 60g, Tractor in field. 1.15z, Lublin Castle. 1.40z, Books and publications. 1.55z, Loading ship. 2.10z, Attacking tank.

Photo.; Center Engr.
1954-55   Perf. 12½x12
647 A255 10g red brn & choc   .80   .25
648 A255 20g rose & grnsh
            blk   .80   .25
649 A255 25g bister & blk   2.25   .25
650 A255 40g yel org & choc   .80   .25
651 A255 45g claret & vio brn   1.25   .25
652 A255 60g emerald & red
            brn   .55   .25
653 A255 1.15z brt bl grn & sep 2.00   .25
654 A255 1.40z orange & choc   17.00 3.50
655 A255 1.55z blue & indigo   7.00   .35
656 A255 2.10z ultra & indigo   6.50 1.75
    Nos. 647-656 (10)   38.95 7.35

10th anniversary of "People's Poland."
Issued: 25g, 60g, 1955; others, 12/23/54.

Photo.; Center Litho.
1954, Oct. 30
656A A255 25g bister & blk   12.00 1.75
656B A255 60g emer & red brn   3.00   .70

Insurgents Attacking Russians — A256

60g, Gen. Tadeusz Kosciuszko and insurgents. 1.40z, Kosciuszko leading attack in Cracow.

1954, Nov. 30   Engr.   Perf. 12½
657 A256 40g grnsh black   .60   .25
658 A256 60g violet brown   .80   .25
659 A256 1.40z dark gray   2.75 1.40
    Nos. 657-659 (3)   4.15 1.90

160th anniv. of the Insurrection of 1794.
No. 658 exists in a trial color proof in black blue.

Bison — A257

60g, European elk. 1.90z, Chamois. 3z, Beaver.

Engr.; Background Photo.
1954, Dec. 22
660 A257 45g yel grn & blk brn .30   .25
661 A257 60g emerald & dk
            brn   .30   .25
662 A257 1.90z blue & blk brn   .60   .25
663 A257 3z bl grn & dk brn   3.00 1.50
    Nos. 660-663 (4)   4.20 2.25

Exist imperf. Value, set: mint, $7, used $2.40.

Liberators Entering Warsaw — A258

60g, Allegory of freedom (Warsaw Mermaid).

1955, Jan. 17   Photo.
664 A258 40g red brown   1.75 1.40
665 A258 60g dull blue   1.75   .25

Liberation of Warsaw, 10th anniversary.

Frederic Chopin — A259

1955, Feb. 22   Engr.
666 A259 40g dark brown   .25   .25
667 A259 60g indigo   2.10 1.00

5th Intl. Competition of Chopin's Music, Feb. 22-Mar. 21.

Nicolaus Copernicus A260   Sigismund III A261

Warsaw monuments: 5g, Mermaid. 10g, Feliks E. Dzerzhinski. 20g, Brothers in Arms Monument. 45g, Marie Sklodowska Curie. 60g, Adam Mickiewicz. 1.55z, Jan Kilinski.

1955, May 3   Unwmk.   Perf. 12½
668 A260 5g dk grn, *grnsh*   .25   .25
669 A260 10g vio brn, *yel*   .25   .25
670 A261 15g blk brn, *bluish* .25   .25
671 A260 20g dk bl, *pink*   .25   .25
672 A260 40g vio, *vio*   .25   .25
673 A261 45g vio brn, *cr*   1.50   .25
674 A260 60g dk bl, *gray*   .35   .25
675 A261 1.55z sl bl, *grysh* 3.00 1.10
    Nos. 668-675 (8)   6.10 2.85

See Nos. 737-739.

Palace of Culture and Flags of Poland and USSR — A262

Design: 60g, Monument.

Perf. 12½x12, 11
1955, Apr. 21   Photo.
676 A262 40g rose red   .85   .30
677 A262 40g lt brown   .25   .25
678 A262 60g Prus blue   .25   .25
679 A262 60g dk olive brn   .25   .25
    Nos. 676-679 (4)   1.60 1.05

Polish-USSR treaty of friendship, 10th anniv.

Arms and Bicycle Wheels — A263

Design: 60g, Three doves above road.

1955, Apr. 25   Perf. 12
680 A263 40g chocolate   .80   .25
681 A263 60g ultra   .25   .25

8th Intl. Peace Bicycle Race, Prague-Berlin-Warsaw.

Poznan Town Hall and Fair Emblem — A264

1955, June 10   Photo.   Perf. 12½
682 A264 40g brt ultra   .45   .25
683 A264 60g dull red   .25   .25

24th Intl. Fair at Poznan, July 3-24, 1955.

"Laikonik" Carnival Costume A265

A265a

1955, June 16   Typo.   Perf. 12
Multicolored Centers
684 A265   20g emerald & henna 2.00   .70
685 A265a 40g brt org & lil   .25   .25
686 A265   60g blue & carmine   .30   .25
    Nos. 684-686 (3)   2.55 1.20

Cracow Celebration Days.

Pansies — A266

40g, 60g, (#690), Dove & Tower of Palace of Science & Culture. 45g, Pansies. 60g, (#691), 1z, "Peace" (POKOJ) & Warsaw Mermaid.

1955, July 13   Litho.   Perf. 12
687 A266 25g vio brn, org & car .25   .25
688 A266 40g gray bl & gray blk .25   .25
689 A266 45g brn lake, yel & car .85   .25
690 A266 60g sepia & orange   .30   .25
691 A266 60g ultra & lt blue   .30   .25
692 A266 1z purple & lt blue   1.00   .65
    Nos. 687-692 (6)   2.95 1.90

5th World Festival of Youth, Warsaw, July 31-Aug. 14, 1955.
Exist imperf. Value, set: mint, $5.50, used $3.50.

Motorcyclists A267

1955, July 20   Photo.   Perf. 12½
693 A267 40g chocolate   .80   .25
694 A267 60g dark green   .30   .25

13th Intl. Motorcycle Race in the Tatra Mountains, Aug. 7-9, 1955.

Stalin Palace of Culture and Science, Warsaw — A268

1955, July 21
695 A268 60g ultra   .25   .25
696 A268 60g gray   .25   .25
697 A268 75g blue green   .40   .30
698 A268 75g brown   .40   .30
    Nos. 695-698 (4)   1.30 1.10

Polish National Day, July 22, 1955. Sheets contain alternating stamps of the 60g values or the 75g values respectively.

Athletes — A269   Stadium — A270

Designs: 40g, Hammer throwing. 1z, Basketball. 1.35z, Sculling. 1.55z, Swimming.

1955, July 27   Unwmk.   Perf. 12½
699 A269 20g chocolate   .25   .25
700 A269 40g plum   .25   .25
701 A270 60g dull brown   .30   .25
702 A270 1z orange ver   .45   .25
703 A269 1.35z dull violet   .60   .25
704 A269 1.55z peacock green 1.75   .65
    Nos. 699-704 (6)   3.60 1.90

2nd International Youth Games, 1955. Exist imperf. Values, set: mint, $5; used, $4.

Town Hall, Szczecin (Stettin) — A271

Designs: 40g, Cathedral, Wroclaw (Breslau) 60g, Town Hall, Zielona Gora (Grunberg). 95g, Town Hall, Opole (Oppeln).

1955, Sept. 22   Engr.   Perf. 11½
705 A271 25g dull green   .25   .25
706 A271 40g red brown   .25   .25
707 A271 60g violet blue   .45   .25
708 A271 95g dark gray   1.40   .80
   Nos. 705-708 (4)   2.35 1.55

10th anniv. of the acquisition of Western Polish Territories.

Rebels with Flag — A272

1955, Sept. 30   Photo.   Perf. 12x12½
709 A272 40g dark brown   1.00   .30
710 A272 60g dk carmine rose   .25   .25

Revolution of 1905, 50th anniversary.

Adam Mickiewicz — A273

Mickiewicz Monument, Paris — A274

60g, Death mask. 95g, Statue, Warsaw.

1955, Oct. 10   Perf. 12x12½, 12½
711 A273 20g dark brown   .25   .25
712 A274 40g brn org & dk brn   .25   .25
713 A274 60g green & brown   .25   .25
714 A274 95g brn red & blk   1.75 1.20
   Nos. 711-714 (4)   2.50 1.95

Death cent. of Adam Mickiewicz, poet, and to publicize the celebration of Mickiewicz year.

Teacher and Child — A275

Design: 60g, Flame and open book.

Perf. 12½x13
1955, Oct. 21   Unwmk.
715 A275 40g brown   2.00   2.00
716 A275 60g ultra   2.00   .85

Polish Teachers' Trade Union, 50th anniv.

Rook and Hands — A276

Design: 60g, Chess knight and hands.

1956, Feb. 9   Perf. 12½
717 A276 40g dark red   2.50   .25
718 A276 60g blue   1.50 2.40

First World Chess Championship of the Deaf and Dumb, Feb. 9-23.

Captain and S. S. Kilinski A277

10g, Sailor and barges. 20g, Dock worker and S. S. Pokoj. 45g, Shipyard and worker. 60g, Fisherman, S. S. Chopin and trawlers.

1956, Mar. 16   Engr.   Perf. 12x12½
719 A277   5g green   .25   .25
720 A277 10g carmine lake   .25   .25
721 A277 20g deep ultra   .40   .25
722 A277 45g rose brown   2.10   .80
723 A277 60g violet blue   4.00   .25
   Nos. 719-723 (5)   7.00 1.80

Snowflake and Ice Skates — A278

Designs: 40g, Snowflake and Ice Hockey sticks. 60g, Snowflake and Skis.

1956, Mar. 7   Photo.   Perf. 12½
724 A278 20g brt ultra & blk   6.50 3.00
725 A278 40g brt grn & vio bl   .80   .25
726 A278 60g lilac & lake   .45   .25
   Nos. 724-726 (3)   7.75 3.50

XI World Students Winter Sport Championship, Mar. 7-13.

Cyclist — A279

1956, Apr. 25
727 A279 40g dark blue   1.25   .60
728 A279 60g dark green   .25   .25

9th Intl. Peace Bicycle Race, Warsaw-Berlin-Prague, May 1-15.

Zakopane Mountains and Shelter — A280

40g, Map, compass & knapsack. 60g, Map of Poland & canoe. 1.15z, Skis & mountains.

1956, May 25
729 A280 30g dark green   .40   .25
730 A280 40g lt red brown   .40   .25
731 A280 60g blue   2.60   .90
732 A280 1.15z dull purple   .40   .25
   Nos. 729-732 (4)   3.80 1.65

Polish Tourist industry.

No. 593 Surcharged

1956, July 6   Engr.   Perf. 12½
733 A232 10g on 80g dp plum   1.50   .45
734 A232 40g on 80g dp plum   .25   .25
735 A232 60g on 80g dp plum   .25   .25
736 A232 1.35z on 80g dp plum   2.25 1.10
   Nos. 733-736 (4)   4.25 2.05

The size and type of surcharge and obliteration of old value differ for each denomination.

Type of 1955

Warsaw Monuments: 30g, Ghetto Monument. 40g, John III Sobieski. 1.55z, Prince Joseph Poniatowski.

1956, July 10
737 A260 30g black   .25   .25
738 A260 40g red brn, grnsh   1.25   .25
739 A260 1.55z vio brn, pnksh   .25   .25
   Nos. 737-739 (3)   1.75   .75

No. 737 measures 22½x28mm, instead of 21x27mm.

A281

Polish-Soviet Friendship Month — A281a

Designs: 40g, Polish and Russian dancers. 60g, Open book and cogwheels.

1956, Sept. 14   Litho.   Perf. 12
740 A281   40g brn red & brn   1.00   .40
741 A281a 60g bister & red   .25   .25

Ludwika Wawrzynska and Children — A282

1956, Sept. 17   Photo.   Perf. 12½
742 A282 40g dull red brown   1.40   .40
743 A282 60g blue   .25   .25

Issued in honor of a heroic school teacher who saved three children from a burning house.

Bee on Clover and Beehive — A283

Design: 60g, Father Jan Dzierzon.

1956, Oct. 30   Litho.   Unwmk.
744 A283 40g org yel & brn   1.10   .45
745 A283 60g yel org & brn   .25   .25

50th death anniv. of Father Jan Dzierzon, the inventor of the modernized beehive.

"Lady with the Ermine" by Leonardo da Vinci A284

40g, Niobe. 60g, Madonna by Veit Stoss.

1956   Engr.   Perf. 11½x11
746 A284 40g dark green   3.00 1.40
747 A284 60g dark violet   .60   .25
748 A284 1.55z chocolate   1.75   .30
   Nos. 746-748 (3)   5.35 1.95

Intl. Museum Week (UNESCO), Oct. 8-14.

Fencer A285

Designs: 20g, Boxer. 25g, Sculling. 40g, Steeplechase racer. 60g, Javelin thrower. No. 755, Woman gymnast. No. 756, Woman broad jumper.

1956   Engr.   Perf. 11½
750 A285 10g slate & chnt   .25   .25
751 A285 20g lt brn & dl vio   .35   .25
   a.   Center inverted   17,500.
752 A285 25g lt blue & blk   1.20   .25
753 A285 40g brt bl grn &
              redsh brn   .25   .25
754 A285 60g rose car & ol
              brn   .25   .25
755 A285 1.55z lt vio & sepia   2.50   .65
756 A285 1.55z orange &
              chnt   1.25   .40
   Nos. 750-756 (7)   6.05 2.30

16th Olympic Games, Melbourne, 11/22-12/8.

15th Century Mailman — A286

Lithographed and Engraved
1956, Nov. 30   Unwmk.   Perf. 12½
757 A286 60g lt blue & blk   2.75 1.00

Reopening of the Postal Museum in Wroclaw.

Skier and Snowflake A287

Ski Jumper and Snowflake — A288

Design: 1z, Skier in right corner.

1957, Jan. 18   Photo.   Perf. 12½
758 A287 40g blue   .25   .25
759 A288 60g dark green   .25   .25
760 A287 1z purple   .70   .55
   Nos. 758-760 (3)   1.20 1.05

50 years of skiing in Poland.

Globe and Tree A289

UN Emblem — A290

UN Building, NY — A291

1957, Feb. 26   Photo.   Perf. 12
761 A289   5g mag & brt grnsh bl   .25   .25
762 A290 15g blue & gray   .55   .25
763 A291 40g brt bl grn & gray   .50   .45
        Nos. 761-763 (3)   1.30   .95

Issued in honor of the United Nations. Exist imperf. Value, set: mint $4, used $3.50.

An imperf. souvenir sheet exists, containing a 1.50z stamp in a redrawn design similar to A291. The stamp is blue and bright bluish green. Value, $25 unused, $14 canceled.

Skier — A292

1957, Mar. 22   Perf. 12½
764 A292 60g blue   1.25   .30
765 A292 60g brown   .25   .25

12th anniv. of the death of the skiers Bronislaw Czech and Hanna Marusarzowna.

Sword, Foil and Saber on World Map — A293

Designs: No. 767, Fencer facing right. No. 768, Fencer facing left.

1957, Apr. 20   Unwmk.   Perf. 12½
766 A293 40g deep plum   .55   .30
767 A293 60g carmine   .25   .25
768 A293 60g ultra   .25   .25
  a.   Pair, #767-768   .75   .50

World Youth Fencing Championships, Warsaw.
No. 768a has continuous design.

Dr. Sebastian Petrycy — A294

Doctors' Portraits: 20g Wojciech Oczko. 40g, Jedrzej Sniadecki. 60g, Tytus Chalubinski. 1z, Wladyslaw Bieganski. 1.35z, Jozef Dietl. 2.50z, Benedykt Dybowski. 3z, Henryk Jordan.

Portraits Engr., Inscriptions Typo.
1957   Perf. 11½
769 A294 10g sepia & ultra   .25   .25
770 A294 20g emerald & claret   .25   .25
771 A294 40g gray & org red   .25   .25
772 A294 60g blue & pale brn   1.10   .45
773 A294   1z org & dk blue   .25   .25
774 A294 1.35z gray brn & grn   .25   .25
775 A294 2.50z dull vio & lil rose .25 .25
776 A294   3z violet & ol brn   .25   .25
        Nos. 769-776 (8)   2.85 2.20

Bicycle Wheel and Carnation — A295

1957, May 4   Photo.   Perf. 12½
777 A295 60g shown   .50   .25
778 A295 1.50z Cyclist .40   .35

10th Intl. Peace Bicycle Race, Warsaw-Berlin-Prague.

Poznan Fair Emblem — A296

1957, June 8   Litho.   Unwmk.
779 A296 60g ultramarine   .25   .25
780 A296 2.50z lt blue green   .35   .25

Issued to publicize the 26th Fair at Poznan.

Turk's Cap — A297

Flowers: No. 782, Carline Thistle. No. 783, Sea Holly. No. 784, Edelweiss. No. 785, Lady's-slipper.

1957, Aug. 12   Photo.   Perf. 12
781 A297 60g bl grn & claret   .40   .25
782 A297 60g gray, grn & yel   .50   .25
783 A297 60g lt blue & grn   .50   .25
784 A297 60g gray & yel grn   1.60   .25
785 A297 60g lt grn, mar & yel   .70   .25
        Nos. 781-785 (5)   3.70 1.25

Fire Fighter — A298

60g, Child & flames. 2.50z, Grain & flames.

1957, Sept. 11   Perf. 12
786 A298 40g black & red   .25   .25
787 A298 60g dk grn & org red   .25   .25
788 A298 2.50z violet & red   .65   .30
        Nos. 786-788 (3)   1.15   .80

Intl. Fire Brigade Conf., Warsaw.

Town Hall, Leipzig and Congress Emblem — A299

1957, Sept. 25   Photo.   Perf. 12½
789 A299 60g violet   .25   .25

4th Intl. Trade Union Cong., Leipzig, Oct. 4-15.

"Girl Writing Letter" by Fragonard A300

1957, Oct. 9   Perf. 12
790 A300 2.50z dark blue green   .65   .25

Issued for Stamp Day, Oct. 9.

Karol Libelt — A301

1957, Nov. 15   Photo.   Perf. 12½
791 A301 60g carmine lake   .35   .25

Centenary of the Poznan Scientific Society and to honor Karol Libelt, politician and philosopher.

Broken Chain and Flag — A302

Design: 2.50z, Lenin Statue, Poronin.

1957, Nov. 7
792 A302 60g brt blue & red   .25   .25
793 A302 2.50z black & red brn .40   .25

40th anniv. of the Russian Revolution.

Jan A. Komensky (Comenius) A303

1957, Dec. 11   Perf. 12
794 A303 2.50z brt carmine   .40   .25

300th anniv. of the publication of "Didactica Opera Omnia."

Henri Wieniawski — A304

1957, Dec. 2   Perf. 12½
795 A304 2.50z blue   .55   .25

3rd Wieniawski Violin Competition in Poznan.

Andrzej Strug — A305

1957, Dec. 16   Unwmk.   Perf. 12½
796 A305 2.50z brown   .35   .25

20th death anniv. of Andrzej Strug, novelist.

Joseph Conrad and "Torrens" A306

1957, Dec. 30   Engr.   Perf. 12x12½
797 A306 60g brown, grnsh   .25   .25
798 A306 2.50z dk blue, pink .75   .40

Birth cent. of Joseph Conrad, Polish-born English writer.

Postilion and Stylized Plane — A307

Designs: 40g, Tomb of Prosper Prowana, globe with plane and satellite. 60g, St. Mary's Church, Cracow, mail coach and plane. 95g, Mail coach and postal bus. 2.10z, Medieval postman and train. 3.40z, Medieval galleon and modern ships.

1958   Litho.   Perf. 12½
799 A307 40g lt blue & vio brn .30   .25
800 A307 60g pale vio & blk   .25   .25
801 A307 95g lemon & violet   .25   .25
802 A307 2.10z gray & ultra   .40   .25
803 A307 2.50z brt blue & blk   .40   .25
804 A307 3.40z aqua & maroon   .50   .25
        Nos. 799-804 (6)   2.10 1.50

400th anniversary of the Polish posts. Imperfs. exist of all but No. 803.

Town Hall at Biecz — A308

Town Halls: 40g, Wroclaw. 60g, Tarnow, horiz. 2.10z, Danzig. 2.50z, Zamosc.

1958, Mar. 29   Engr.   Perf. 12½
805 A308 20g green   .25   .25
806 A308 40g brown   .25   .25
807 A308 60g dark blue   .35   .25
808 A308 2.10z rose lake   .50   .25
809 A308 2.50z violet   .65   .35
        Nos. 805-809 (5)   2.00 1.35

Giant Pike Perch A309

Fishes: 60g, Salmon, vert. 2.10z, Pike, vert. 2.50z, Trout, vert. 6.40z, Grayling.

1958, Apr. 22   Photo.   Perf. 12
810 A309 40g bl, blk, grn & yel   .75   .30
811 A309 60g yel grn, dk grn & bl .75 .25
812 A309 2.10z dk bl, grn & yel   .75   .25
813 A309 2.50z pur, blk & yel grn 2.40 .35
814 A309 6.40z bl grn, brn & red   .75   .35
        Nos. 810-814 (5)   5.40 1.50

Casimir Palace, Warsaw University — A310

1958, May 14   Unwmk.   Perf. 12½
815 A310 2.50z violet blue   .35   .25

140th anniv. of the University of Warsaw.

Stylized Glider and Cloud — A311

Design: 2.50z, Design reversed.

1958, June 14   Litho.
816 A311 60g gray blue & blk   .25   .25
817 A311 2.50z gray & blk   .40   .25

7th Intl. Glider Competitions.

Fair Emblem — A312

1958, June 9
818 A312 2.50z black & rose .40 .25
27th Fair at Poznan.

Armed Postman and Mail Box — A313

1958, Sept. 1 Engr. Perf. 11
819 A313 60g dark blue .35 .25
19th anniv. of the defense of the Polish post office at Danzig (Gdansk). Inscribed: "You were the first."

Letter, Quill and Postmark — A314

1958, Oct. 9 Litho.
820 A314 60g blk, bl grn & ver .60 .25
Issued for Stamp Day. Exists imperf., value $250.

Polar Bear — A315

Design: 2.50z, Rocket and Sputnik.

1958, Sept. 30 Photo. Perf. 12½x12
821 A315 60g gray & black .25 .25
822 A315 2.50z blue & dark blue .60 .25
Intl. Geophysical Year.

Partisan's Cross — A316

Designs: 60g, Virtuti Militari Cross. 2.50z, Grunwald Cross.

1958, Oct. 10 Perf. 11
823 A316 40g black, grn & ocher .25 .25
824 A316 60g black, blue & yel .25 .25
825 A316 2.50z multicolored 1.25 .30
 Nos. 823-825 (3) 1.75 .80
Polish People's Army, 15th anniv.

17th Century Ship — A317

Design: 2.50z, Polish immigrants.

1958, Oct. 29 Perf. 11
826 A317 60g dk slate grn .25 .25
827 A317 2.50z dk carmine rose .85 .25
350th anniversary of the arrival of the first Polish immigrants in America.

UNESCO Building, Paris — A318

1958, Nov. 3 Unwmk.
828 A318 2.50z yellow grn & blk .60 .25
UNESCO Headquarters in Paris, opening, Nov. 3.

Stagecoach — A319

Wmk. 326
1958, Oct. 26 Engr. Perf. 12½
829 A319 2.50z slate, buff 1.25 .35
 a. Souvenir sheet of 6 11.00 11.00
Philatelic exhibition in honor of the 400th anniv. of the Polish post, Warsaw, Oct. 25-Nov. 10.

Souvenir Sheet
1958, Dec. 12 Unwmk. Imperf.
Printed on Silk
830 A319 50z dark blue 135.00 52.50
400th anniversary of the Polish posts.

Stanislaw Wyspianski — A320

Portrait: 2.50z, Stanislaw Moniuszko.

1958, Nov. 25 Engr. Perf. 12½
831 A320 60g dark violet .25 .25
832 A320 2.50z dk slate grn .40 .25
Stanislaw Wyspianski, painter and poet, and Stanislaw Moniuszko, composer.

Kneeling Figure — A321

1958, Dec. 10 Litho.
833 A321 2.50z lt brn & red brn .50 .25
Signing of the Universal Declaration of Human Rights, 10th anniv.

Red Flag — A322

1958, Dec. 16 Photo.
834 A322 60g plum & red .30 .25
Communist Party of Poland, 40th anniv.

Sailing — A323

Sports: 60g, Girl archer. 95g, Soccer. 2z, Horsemanship.

1959, Jan. 3
835 A323 40g lt bl & vio bl .25 .25
836 A323 60g salmon & brn vio .25 .25
837 A323 95g green & brn vio .70 .25
838 A323 2z dp bl & lt grn .35 .25
 Nos. 835-838 (4) 1.55 1.00

Hand at Wheel — A324   Wheat, Hammer and Flag — A325

1959, Mar. 10 Wmk. 326 Perf. 12½
839 A324 40gr shown .25 .25
840 A325 60gr shown .25 .25
841 A324 1.55z Factory .40 .25
 Nos. 839-841 (3) .90 .75
3rd Workers Congress.

Amanita Phalloides — A326

Designs: Various mushrooms.

1959, May 8 Photo. Perf. 11½
842 A326 20g yel, grn & brn 4.00 2.10
843 A326 30g multicolored 1.40 .50
844 A326 40g multicolored .75 .25
845 A326 60g yel grn, brn & ocher .75 .25
846 A326 1z multicolored .75 .25
847 A326 2.50z blue, grn & brn 1.10 .35
848 A326 3.40z multicolored 2.00 .40
849 A326 5.60z dl yel, brn & grn 4.75 2.10
 Nos. 842-849 (8) 15.50 6.20

"Storks," by Jozef Chelmonski — A327

Paintings by Polish Artists: 60g, Mother and Child, Stanislaw Wyspianski, vert. 1z, Mme. de Romanet, Henryk Rodakowski, vert. 1.50z, Old Man and Death, Jacek Malczewski, vert. 6.40z, River Scene, Aleksander Gierymski.

1959 Engr. Perf. 12, 12½x12
850 A327 40g gray green .25 .25
851 A327 60g dull purple .25 .25
852 A327 1z intense black .35 .25

853 A327 1.50z brown .65 .25
854 A327 6.40z blue 3.00 .50
 Nos. 850-854 (5) 4.50 1.50
Nos. 850 and 854 measure 36x28mm; Nos. 851 and 853, 28x36mm; No. 852, 28x37mm.

Miner and Globe — A328

1959, July 1 Litho.
855 A328 2.50z multicolored 1.00 .25
3rd Miners' Conf., Katowice, July 1959.

Symbol of Industry — A329

Map of Poland and: 40g, Map of Poland and Symbol of Agriculture. 1.50z, Symbol of art and science.

Perf. 12x12½
1959, July 21 Wmk. 326
856 A329 40g black, bl & grn .25 .25
857 A329 60g black & ver .25 .25
858 A329 1.50z black & blue .30 .25
 Nos. 856-858 (3) .80 .75
15 years of the Peoples' Republic of Poland.

Lazarus Ludwig Zamenhof — A330

Design: 1.50z, Star, globe and flag.

1959, July 24 Perf. 12½
859 A330 60g blk & grn, ol .25 .25
860 A330 1.50z ultra, grn & red, gray 2.50 .40
Centenary of the birth of Lazarus Ludwig Zamenhof, author of Esperanto, and in conjunction with the Esperanto Congress in Warsaw.

Map of Austria and Flower — A331

1959, July 27 Litho.
861 A331 60g sep, red & grn, yel .25 .25
862 A331 2.50z bl, red, & grn, gray .75 .25
7th World Youth Festival, Vienna, July 26-Aug. 14.

Symbolic Plane — A332

1959, Aug. 24 Wmk. 326 Perf. 12½
863 A332 60g vio bl, grnsh bl & blk .30 .25
30th anniv. of LOT, the Polish airline.

Sejm (Parliament) Building — A333

1959, Aug. 27　Photo.　Perf. 12x12½
864　A333　60g lt grn, blk & red　.25　.25
865　A333　2.50z vio gray, blk &
　　　　　red　.75　.25
48th Interparliamentary Conf., Warsaw.

**No. 640 Overprinted in Blue:
"BALPEX I — GDANSK 1959"**
1959, Aug. 30　Engr.　Unwmk.
866　A253　45g brown, *yel*　.75　.50
Intl. Phil. Exhib. of Baltic States at Gdansk.

Stylized Dove
and
Globe — A334

Wmk. 326
1959, Sept. 1　Photo.　Perf. 12½
867　A334　60g blue & gray　.30　.25
World Peace Movement, 10th anniv.

Red Cross
Nurse — A335

Designs: 60g, Nurse. 2.50z, Henri Dunant.
Size: 21x26mm
1959, Sept. 21　Litho.　Perf. 12½
868　A335　40g red, lt grn & blk　.25　.25
869　A335　60g bis brn, brn &
　　　　　red　.25　.25
Perf. 11
Size: 23x23mm
870　A335　2.50z red, pink & blk　1.00　.35
　　Nos. 868-870 (3)　1.50　.85
Polish Red Cross, 40th anniv.; Red Cross, cent.

Polish-Chinese
Friendship Society
Emblem — A336

Wmk. 326
1959, Sept. 28　Litho.　Perf. 11
871　A336　60g multicolored　1.20　.60
872　A336　2.50z multicolored　.50　.25
Polish-Chinese friendship.

Flower Made of
Stamps — A337

1959, Oct. 9　Perf. 12½
873　A337　60g lt grnsh bl, grn &
　　　　　red　.25　.25
874　A337　2.50z red, grn & vio　.40　.25
Issued for Stamp Day, 1959.

Sputnik 3 — A338

60g, Luna I, sun. 2.50z, Earth, moon, Sputnik 2.

1959, Nov. 7　Photo.　Wmk. 326
875　A338　40g Prus blue & gray　.25　.25
876　A338　60g maroon & black　.30　.25
877　A338　2.50z green & dk blue　.90　.50
　　Nos. 875-877 (3)　1.45　1.00
42nd anniv. of the Russian Revolution and the landing of the Soviet moon rocket.
Exist imperf. Value, set: mint $2.75, used $2.

Child Doing
Homework — A339

Design: 60g, Three children leaving school.

Lithographed and Engraved
1959, Nov. 14　Perf. 11½
878　A339　40g green & dk brn　.25　.25
879　A339　60g blue & red　.25　.25
"1,000 Schools" campaign for the 1,000th anniversary of Poland.

Charles
Darwin — A340

Scientists: 40g, Dmitri I. Mendeleev. 60g, Albert Einstein. 1.50z, Louis Pasteur. 1.55z, Isaac Newton. 2.50z, Nicolaus Copernicus.

1959, Dec. 10　Engr.　Perf. 11
880　A340　20g dark blue　.25　.25
881　A340　40g olive gray　.25　.25
882　A340　60g claret　.35　.25
883　A340　1.50z dk violet brn　.35　.25
884　A340　1.55z dark green　.35　.25
885　A340　2.50z violet　1.25　.50
　　Nos. 880-885 (6)　2.80　1.75

Man from
Rzeszow
A341

Woman from
Rzeszow
A342

Regional Costumes: 40g, Cracow. 60g, Kurpiow. 1z, Silesia. 2z, Lowicz. 2.50z, Mountain people. 3.10z, Kujawy. 3.40z, Lublin. 5.60z, Szamotuli. 6.50z, Lubuski.

Engraved and Photogravure
1959-60　Wmk. 326　Perf. 12, Imperf.
886　A341　20g slate grn & blk　.25　.25
887　A342　20g slate grn & blk　.25　.25
　a.　Pair, #886-887　.25　.25

888　A341　40g lt bl & rose car
　　　　　('60)　.25　.25
889　A342　40g rose car & bl
　　　　　('60)　.25　.25
　a.　Pair, #888-889　.25　.25
890　A341　60g black & pink　.25　.25
891　A342　60g black & pink　.25　.25
　a.　Pair, #890-891　.25　.25
892　A341　1z grnsh red & dk
　　　　　red　.25　.25
893　A342　1z grnsh bl & dk
　　　　　red　.25　.25
　a.　Pair, #892-893　.25　.25
894　A341　2z yel & ultra ('60)　.25　.25
895　A342　2z yel & ultra ('60)　.25　.25
　a.　Pair, #894-895　.40　.25
896　A341　2.50z green & rose lil　.75　.25
897　A342　2.50z green & rose lil　.75　.25
　a.　Pair, #896-897　1.50　.50
898　A341　3.10z yel grn & sl grn
　　　　　('60)　.25　.25
899　A342　3.10z yel grn & sl grn
　　　　　('60)　.25　.25
　a.　Pair, #898-899　.50　.50
900　A341　3.40z gray grn & brn
　　　　　('60)　.25　.25
901　A342　3.40z gray grn & brn
　　　　　('60)　.25　.25
　a.　Pair, #900-901　.50　.50
902　A341　5.60z yel grn & gray
　　　　　bl　.75　.25
903　A342　5.60z yel grn & gray
　　　　　bl　.75　.25
　a.　Pair, #902-903　1.50　.50
904　A341　6.50z vio & gray grn
　　　　　('60)　1.50　.60
905　A342　6.50z vio & gray grn
　　　　　('60)　1.50　.60
　a.　Pair, #904-905　3.00　1.20
　　Nos. 886-905 (20)　9.50　5.70
Nos. 886-905 exist imperf. Value, same as perf.

Piano — A343　　Frederic
　　　　　　　　Chopin — A344

Design: 1.50z, Musical note and manuscript.

1960, Feb. 22　Litho.　Perf. 12
906　A343　60g brt violet & blk　.40　.25
907　A343　1.50z black, gray & red　.60　.25
Perf. 12½x12
Engr.
908　A344　2.50z black　2.50　1.00
　　Nos. 906-908 (3)　3.50　1.50
150th anniversary of the birth of Frederic Chopin and to publicize the Chopin music competition.

Stamp of
1860
A345

Designs: 60g, Ski meet stamp of 1939. 1.35z, Design from 1860 issue. 1.55z, 1945 liberation stamp. 2.50z, 1957 stamp day stamp.

Litho. (40g, 1.35z); Litho. and Photo.
Perf. 11½x11
1960, Mar. 21　Wmk. 326
909　A345　40g multicolored　.25　.25
910　A345　60g violet, ultra & blk　.25　.25
911　A345　1.35z gray, red & bl　.55　.25
912　A345　1.55z green, car & blk　.80　.25
913　A345　2.50z ap grn, dk grn &
　　　　　blk　1.40　.40
　　Nos. 909-913 (5)　3.25　1.40
Centenary of Polish stamps. Nos. 909-913 were also issued in sheets of 4. Values, set of 4 sheets: $625 mint, $675 used.
For overprint see No. 934.

Discus Thrower, Amsterdam
1928 — A346

Polish Olympic Victories: No. 915, Runner. No. 916, Bicyclist. No. 917, Steeplechase. No. 918, Trumpeters. No. 919, Boxers. No. 920, Olympic flame. No. 921 Woman jumper.

Lithographed and Embossed
Perf. 12x12½
1960, June 15　Unwmk.
914　A346　60g blue & blk　.25　.25
915　A346　60g car rose & blk　.25　.25
916　A346　60g violet & blk　.25　.25
917　A346　60g blue grn & blk　.25　.25
　a.　Block of 4, #914-917　1.50　.75
918　A346　2.50z ultra & blk　.55　.25
919　A346　2.50z chestnut & blk　.55　.25
920　A346　2.50z red & blk　.55　.25
921　A346　2.50z emerald & blk　.55　.25
　a.　Block of 4, #918-921　4.25　2.00
　　Nos. 914-921 (8)　3.20　2.00
17th Olympic Games, Rome, 8/25-9/11.
Nos. 917a and 921a have continuous design forming the stadium oval.
Nos. 914-921 exist imperf. Value, same as perf.

Tomb of King
Wladyslaw II
Jagiello — A347

Battle of Grunwald by Jan
Matejko — A348

90g, Detail from Grunwald monument.

Perf. 11x11½
1960　Wmk. 326　Engr.
922　A347　60g violet brown　.35　.25
923　A347　90g olive gray　.70　.35
Size: 78x37mm
924　A348　2.50z dark gray　2.50　1.00
　　Nos. 922-924 (3)　3.55　1.60
550th anniversary, Battle of Grunwald.

The Annunciation — A349

Carvings by Veit Stoss, St. Mary's Church, Cracow: 30g, Nativity. 40g, Adoration of the Kings. 60g, The Resurrection. 2.50z, The Ascension. 5.60z, Descent of the Holy Ghost. 10z, The Assumption of the Virgin, vert.

1960　Wmk. 326　Engr.　Perf. 12
925　A349　20g Prus blue　.25　.25
926　A349　30g lt red brown　.25　.25
927　A349　40g violet　.25　.25
928　A349　60g dull green　.25　.25
929　A349　2.50z rose lake　1.25　.25
930　A349　5.60z dark brown　8.00　3.25
　　Nos. 925-930 (6)　10.25　4.50

Miniature Sheet
Imperf

931 A349 10z black 8.00 5.50

No. 931 contains one vertical stamp which measures 72x95mm.

A350

1960, Sept. 26 *Perf. 12½*
932 A350 2.50z black .35 .25

Birth cent. of Ignacy Jan Paderewski, statesman and musician.

A351

Lukasiewicz and kerosene lamp.

Engr. & Photo.
1960, Sept. 14 *Perf. 11*
933 A351 60g citron & black .35 .25

5th Pharmaceutical Congress; Ignacy Lukasiewicz, chemist-pharmacist.

No. 909 Overprinted: "DZIEN ZNACZKA 1960"
1960 **Litho.** *Perf. 11½x11*
934 A345 40g multicolored 1.00 .45

Issued for Stamp Day, 1960.

Great Bustard A352

Birds: 20g, Raven. 30g, Great cormorant. 40g, Black stork. 50g, Eagle owl. 60g, White-tailed sea eagle. 75g, Golden eagle. 90g, Short-toed eagle. 2.50z, Rock thrush. 4z, European kingfisher. 5.60z, Wall creeper. 6.50z, European roller.

1960 Unwmk. Photo. *Perf. 11½*
Birds in Natural Colors

935	A352	10g gray & blk	.25	.25
936	A352	20g gray & blk	.25	.25
937	A352	30g gray & blk	.25	.25
938	A352	40g gray & blk	.25	.25
939	A352	50g pale grn & blk	.30	.25
940	A352	60g pale grn & blk	.40	.25
941	A352	75g pale grn & blk	.40	.25
942	A352	90g pale grn & blk	.65	.25
943	A352	2.50z pale ol gray & blk	6.75	3.00
944	A352	4z pale ol gray & blk	2.75	1.00
945	A352	5.60z pale ol gray & blk	4.50	1.00
946	A352	6.50z pale ol gray & blk	5.50	2.00
		Nos. 935-946 (12)	22.25	9.00

Gniezno — A353

Historic Towns: 10g, Cracow. 20g, Warsaw. 40g, Poznan. 50g, Plock. 60g, Kalisz. No. 952A, Tczew. 80g, Frombork. 90g, Torun. 95g, Puck (ships). 1.15z, Slupsk. 1.15z, Gdansk (Danzig). 1.35z, Wroclaw. 1.50z, Szczecin.

1.55z, Opole. 2z, Kolobrzeg. 2.10z, Legnica. 2.50z, Katowice. 3.10z, Lodz. 5.60z, Walbrzych.

1960-61 Engr. *Perf. 11½, 13x12½*

947	A353	5g red brown	.25	.25
948	A353	10g green	.25	.25
949	A353	20g dark brown	.25	.25
950	A353	40g vermilion	.25	.25
951	A353	50g violet	.25	.25
952	A353	60g rose claret	.25	.25
952A	A353	60g lt ultra ('61)	.50	.25
953	A353	80g blue	.25	.25
954	A353	90g brown ('61)	1.20	.25
955	A353	95g olive gray	.35	.25

Engraved and Lithographed

956	A353	1z orange & gray	.25	.25
957	A353	1.15z slate grn & sal	.25	.25
958	A353	1.35z lil rose & lt grn	.25	.25
959	A353	1.50z sep & pale grn	.35	.25
960	A353	1.55z car lake & buff	.25	.25
961	A353	2z dk blue & pink	.25	.25
962	A353	2.10z sepia & yel	.35	.25
963	A353	2.50z dl vio & pale grn	.25	.25
964	A353	3.10z ver & gray	1.50	.75
965	A353	5.60z sl grn & lt grn	5.00	1.75
		Nos. 947-965 (20)	12.60	7.00

Front Page of "Merkuriusz" A354

Newspapers: 60g, "Proletaryat," first issue, Sept. 15, 1883. 2.50z, "Rzeczpospolita," first issue, July 23, 1944.

Lithographed and Embossed
1961 **Wmk. 326** *Perf. 12*

966	A354	40g black, ultra & emer	.35	.25
967	A354	60g black, org brn & yel	.35	.25
968	A354	2.50z black, violet & bl	2.75	2.00
		Nos. 966-968 (3)	3.45	2.50

300th anniv. of the Polish newspaper Merkuriusz.

Ice Hockey — A355

60g, Ski jump. 1z, Soldiers on skis. 1.50z, Slalom.

1961, Feb. 1 Litho. Wmk. 326

969	A355	40g lt violet, blk & yel	.30	.25
970	A355	60g lt ultra, blk & car	.30	.25
971	A355	1z lt blue, ol & red	5.50	2.00
972	A355	1.50z grnsh bl, blk & yel	.30	.25
		Nos. 969-972 (4)	6.40	2.75

1st Winter Spartacist Games of Friendly Armies.

Part of Cogwheel — A356

1961, Feb. 11 *Perf. 12½*
973 A356 60g red & black .25 .25

Fourth Congress of Polish Engineers.

Maj. Yuri A. Gagarin A357

Design: 60g, Globe and path of rocket.

1961, Apr. 27 Photo. *Perf. 12*
974 A357 40g dark red & black .50 .25
975 A357 60g ultra, black & car .50 .25

1st man in space, Yuri A. Gagarin, Apr. 12, 1961.

Emblem of Poznan Fair — A358

1961, May 25 Litho. *Perf. 12½x12*
977 A358 40g brt bl, blk & red org .25 .25
978 A358 1.50z red org, blk & brt bl .35 .25
a. Souvenir sheet of 2 4.00 2.75

30th Intl. Fair at Poznan.

No. 978a contains two of No. 978 with simulated perforation and blue marginal inscriptions. Sold for 4.50z. Issued July 29, 1961.

Famous Poles A359

No. 979, Mieszko I. No. 980, Casimir Wielki. No. 981, Casimir Jagiello. No. 982, Nicolaus Copernicus. No. 983, Andrzej Frycz-Modrzewski. No. 984, Tadeusz Kosciuszko.

Photogravure and Engraved
1961, June 15 *Perf. 11x11½*
Black Inscriptions and Designs

979	A359	60g chalky blue	.25	.25
980	A359	60g deep rose	.25	.25
981	A359	60g slate	.25	.25
982	A359	60g dull violet	.35	.25
983	A359	60g lt brown	.25	.25
984	A359	60g olive gray	.60	.25
		Nos. 979-984 (6)	1.95	1.50

See Nos. 1059-1064, 1152-1155.

Trawler — A360

Designs: Various Polish Cargo Ships.

Unwmk.
1961, June 24 **Litho.** *Perf. 11*

985	A360	60g multicolored	.25	.25
986	A360	1.55z multicolored	.35	.25
987	A360	2.50z multicolored	.50	.25
988	A360	3.40z multicolored	.65	.30
989	A360	4z multicolored	1.25	.60
990	A360	5.60z multicolored	3.50	1.50
		Nos. 985-990 (6)	6.50	3.15

Polish ship industry. Sizes (width): 60g, 2.50z, 54mm; 1.55z, 3.40z, 4z, 80mm; 5.60z, 108mm.

Post Horn and Telephone Dial — A361

Post horn and: 60g, Radar screen. 2.50z, Conference emblem, globe.

1961, June 26

991	A361	40g sl, gray & red org	.25	.25
992	A361	60g gray, yel & vio	.25	.25
993	A361	2.50z ol bis, brt bl & vio bl	.35	.25
a.		Souvenir sheet of 3, #991-993	4.75	2.00
		Nos. 991-993 (3)	.85	.75

Conference of Communications Ministers of Communist Countries, Warsaw. No. 993a sold for 5z.

Seal of Opole, 13th Century — A362

Cement Works, Opole A363

Designs: No. 996, Tombstone of Henry IV and seal, Wroclaw. No. 997, Apartment houses, Wroclaw. No. 998, Seal of Conrad II and Silesian eagle. No. 999, Textile mill, Gorzow. No. 1000, Seal of Prince Barnim I. No. 1001, Seaport, Szczecin. No. 1002, Seal of Princess Elizabeth. No. 1003, Factory, Szczecinek. No. 1004, Seal of Unislaw. No. 1005, Shipyard, Gdansk. No. 1005A, Copernicus Tower, Frombork. No. 1005B, Agricultural College, Kortow.

1961-62 Wmk. 326 Engr. *Perf. 11*
Western Territories

994	A362	40g brown, *grysh*	.25	.25
995	A363	40g brown, *grysh*	.25	.25
a.		"Block," #994-995 + label	.25	.25
996	A362	60g violet, *pink*	.25	.25
997	A363	60g violet, *pink*	.25	.25
a.		"Block," #996-997 + label	.25	.25
998	A362	95g green, *bluish*	.50	.25
999	A363	95g green, *bluish*	.50	.25
a.		"Block," #998-999 + label	1.00	.25
1000	A362	2.50z ol grn, *grnsh*	.50	.25
1001	A363	2.50z ol grn, *grnsh*	.50	.25
a.		"Block," #1000-1001 + label	1.00	.40

Northern Territories

1002	A362	60g vio bl, *bluish*	.25	.25
1003	A363	60g vio bl, *bluish*	.25	.25
a.		"Block," #1002-1003 + label	.25	.25
1004	A362	1.55z brown, *buff*	.25	.25
1005	A363	1.55z brown, *buff*	.25	.25
c.		"Block," #1004-1005 + label	.50	.35
1005A	A362	2.50z slate bl, *grysh*	.75	.25
1005B	A363	2.50z slate bl, *grysh*	.75	.25
d.		"Block," #1005A-1005B + label	1.50	.40
		Nos. 994-1005B (14)	5.50	3.50

Issued: #994-997, 1000-1001, 7/21; 95g, 2/23/62; #1002-1005B, 7/21/62.

Kayak Race Start and "E" — A364

Designs: 60g, Four-man canoes and "E." 2.50z, Paddle, Polish flag and "E," vert.

Wmk. 326
1961, Aug. 18 **Litho.** *Perf. 12½*

1006	A364	40g bl grn, yel & red	.25	.25
1007	A364	60g multicolored	.25	.25
1008	A364	2.50z multicolored	.90	.25
		Nos. 1006-1008 (3)	1.40	.75

6th European Canoe Championships, Poznan, Aug. 18-20. Exist imperf. Value, set: mint $2.25, used $2.

Maj. Gherman Titov, Star, Globe, Orbit A365

Dove and Earth A366

Perf. 12x12½
1961, Aug. 24   Photo.   Unwmk.
1009 A365 40g pink, blk & red   .40   .25
1010 A366 60g blue & black   .40   .25
Manned space flight of Vostok 2, Aug. 6-7, in which Russian Maj. Gherman Titov orbited the earth 17 times.

Insurgents' Monument, St. Ann's Mountain A367

Design: 1.55z, Cross of Silesian Insurgents.

Wmk. 326
1961, Sept. 15   Litho.   Perf. 12
1011 A367 60g gray & emerald   .25   .25
1012 A367 1.55z gray & blue   .25   .25
40th anniv. of the third Silesian uprising.

"PKO," Initials of Polish Savings Bank A368

Initials and: #1014, Bee and clover. #1015, Ant. #1016, Squirrel. 2.50z, Savings bankbook.

1961, Oct. 2   Wmk. 326   Perf. 12
1013 A368 40g ver, blk & org   .25   .25
1014 A368 60g blue, blk & brt pink   .25   .25
1015 A368 60g bis brn, blk & ocher   .25   .25
1016 A368 60g brt grn, blk & dl red   .50   .25
1017 A368 2.50z car rose, gray & blk   1.50   .50
    Nos. 1013-1017 (5)   2.75   1.50
Issued to publicize Savings Month.

Mail Cart, by Jan Chelminski — A369

1961, Oct. 9   Engr.   Perf. 12x12½
1018 A369 60g deep green   .25   .25
1019 A369 60g violet brown   .25   .25
Polish Postal Museum, 40th anniv; Stamp Day.

Congress Emblem A370

1961, Nov. 20   Wmk. 326   Perf. 12
1020 A370 60g black   .25   .25
Issued to publicize the Fifth World Congress of Trade Unions, Moscow, Dec. 4-16.

Seal of Kopasyni Family, 1284 — A371

60g, Seal of Bytom, 14th century. 2.50z, Emblem of International Miners Congress, 1958.

1961, Dec. 4   Litho.   Perf. 11x11½
1021 A371 40g multicolored   .25   .25
1022 A371 60g bl, gray bl & vio bl   .25   .25
1023 A371 2.50z yel grn, grn & blk   .50   .25
    Nos. 1021-1023 (3)   1.00   .75
1,000 years of the Polish mining industry.

Child and Syringe — A372

Designs: 60g, Children of three races, horiz. 2.50z, Mother, child and milk bottle.

1961, Dec. 11   Perf. 12½x12, 12x12½
1024 A372 40g lt blue & blk   .25   .25
1025 A372 60g orange & blk   .25   .25
1026 A372 2.50z brt bl grn & blk   .50   .25
    Nos. 1024-1026 (3)   1.00   .75
15th anniversary of UNICEF.

Emblem A373

Design: 60g, Map with oil pipe line from Siberia to Central Europe.

1961, Dec. 12   Wmk. 326   Perf. 12
1027 A373 40g dk red, yel & vio bl   .25   .25
1028 A373 60g vio bl, bl & red   .25   .25
15th session of the Council of Mutual Economic Assistance of the Communist States.

Ground Beetle — A374

Black Apollo Butterfly A375

Insects: 30g, Violet runner. 40g, Alpine longicorn beetle. 50g, Great oak capricorn beetle. 60g, Gold runner. 80g, Stag-horned beetle. 1.35z, Death's-head moth. 1.50z, Tiger-striped swallowtail butterfly. 1.55z, Apollo butterfly. 2.50z, Red ant. 5.60z, Bumble bee.

Perf. 12½x12
1961, Dec. 30   Photo.   Unwmk.
Insects in Natural Colors
1029 A374 20g bister brown   .35   .25
1030 A374 30g pale gray grn   .35   .25
1031 A374 40g pale yellow grn   .35   .25
1032 A374 50g blue green   .35   .25
1033 A374 60g dull rose lilac   .35   .25
1034 A374 80g pale green   .70   .25

Perf. 11½
1035 A375 1.15z ultra   .70   .25
1036 A375 1.35z sapphire   .70   .25
1037 A375 1.50z bluish green   .70   .25
1038 A375 1.55z brt purple   1.00   .25
1039 A375 2.50z brt green   1.75   .85
1040 A375 5.60z orange brown   8.00   3.50
    Nos. 1029-1040 (12)   15.30   6.85

Worker with Gun — A376

#1042, Worker with trowel and gun. #1043, Worker with hammer. #1044, Worker at helm. #1045, Worker with dove and banner.

Perf. 12½x12
1962, Jan. 5   Litho.   Unwmk.
1041 A376 60g red, blk & green   .25   .25
1042 A376 60g red, blk & slate   .25   .25
1043 A376 60g blk & vio bl, red   .25   .25
1044 A376 60g blk & bis, red   .25   .25
1045 A376 60g blk & gray, red   .25   .25
    Nos. 1041-1045 (5)   1.25   1.25
Polish Workers' Party, 20th anniversary.

Women Skiers A377

Designs: 60g, Long distance skier. 1.50z, Ski jump, vert. 10z, FIS emblem, vert.

Lithographed and Embossed
1962, Feb. 14   Perf. 12
1046 A377 40g gray, red & gray bl   .25   .25
a.   40g sepia, red & dull blue   .35   .25
1047 A377 60g gray, red & gray bl   .25   .25
a.   60g sepia, red & dull blue   .45   .25
1048 A377 1.50z gray, red & gray bl   .35   .25
a.   1.50z gray, lilac & red   1.40   .70
    Nos. 1046-1048 (3)   .85   .75

Souvenir Sheet
Imperf
1049 A377 10z gray, red & gray bl   3.25   .85
World Ski Championships at Zakopane (FIS). No. 1049 contains one stamp with simulated perforation. The sheet sold for 15z.
Each of Nos. 1046-1048 exists in a souvenir sheet of four. Value, set of 3, $200.

Broken Flower and Prison Cloth (Auschwitz) — A378

Majdanek Concentration Camp — A379

Design: 1.50z, Proposed memorial, Treblinka concentration camp.

Wmk. 326
1962, Apr. 3   Engr.   Perf. 11½
1050 A378 40g slate blue   .25   .25
1051 A379 60g dark gray   .25   .25
1052 A378 1.50z dark violet   .40   .25
    Nos. 1050-1052 (3)   .90   .75
International Resistance Movement Month to commemorate the millions who died in concentration camps, 1940-45.

Bicyclist A380

2.50z, Cyclists in race. 3.40z, Wheel & arms of Berlin, Prague & Warsaw.

1962, Apr. 27   Unwmk.   Litho.   Perf. 12
1053 A380 60g blue & blk   .25   .25
1054 A380 2.50z yellow & blk   .35   .25
1055 A380 3.40z lilac & blk   .50   .25
    Nos. 1053-1055 (3)   1.10   .75
15th Intl. Peace Bicycle Race, Warsaw-Berlin-Prague.
Size of No. 1053, 1055: 36x22mm, No. 1054: 74x22mm.

Lenin in Bialy Dunajec — A381

Designs: 60g, Lenin. 2.50z, Lenin and Cloth Hall, Cathedral, Cracow.

Engraved and Photogravure
Perf. 11x11½
1962, May 25   Wmk. 326
1056 A381 40g pale grn & Prus grn   .25   .25
1057 A381 60g pink & dp claret   .25   .25
1058 A381 2.50z yellow & dk brn   .50   .25
    Nos. 1056-1058 (3)   1.00   .75
50th anniv. of Lenin's arrival in Poland.

Famous Poles Type of 1961
Famous Poles: No. 1059, Adam Mickiewicz. No. 1060, Juliusz Slowacki. No. 1061, Frederic Chopin. No. 1062, Romuald Traugutt. No. 1063, Jaroslaw Dabrowski. No. 1064, Maria Konopnicka.

1962, June 20   Engr. & Photo.
Black Inscriptions and Designs
1059 A359 60g dull green   .25   .25
1060 A359 60g brown orange   .25   .25

Perf. 12x12½
Litho.
1061 A359 60g dull blue   .25   .25
1062 A359 60g brown olive   .25   .25
1063 A359 60g rose lilac   .25   .25
1064 A359 60g blue green   .25   .25
    Nos. 1059-1064 (6)   1.50   1.50

Karol Swierczewski-Walter — A382

Perf. 11x11½

1962, July 14   Engr.   Unwmk.
1065 A382 60g black   .25 .25

15th death anniv. of General Karol Swierczewski-Walter, organizer of the new Polish army.

Crocus — A383

Flowers: No. 1067, Orchid. No. 1068, Monkshood. No. 1069, Gas plant. No. 1070, Water lily. No. 1071, Gentian. No. 1072, Daphne mezereum. No. 1073, Cowbell. No. 1074, Anemone. No. 1075, Globeflower. No. 1076, Snowdrop. No. 1077, Adonis vernalis.

Unwmk.
1962, Aug. 8   Photo.   Perf. 12
Flowers in Natural Colors
1066	A383	60g dull yel & red	.75	.25
1067	A383	60g redsh brn & vio	.25	.25
1068	A383	60g pink & lilac	.25	.25
1069	A383	90g olive & green	.25	.25
1070	A383	90g yel grn & red	.25	.25
1071	A383	90g lt ol grn & red	.25	.25
1072	A383	1.50z gray bl & bl	.35	.25
1073	A383	1.50z yel grn & dk grn	.35	.25
1074	A383	1.50z Prus grn & dk bl	.35	.25
1075	A383	2.50z gray grn & dk bl	.65	.35
1076	A383	2.50z dk bl grn & dk bl	.90	.35
1077	A383	2.50z gray bl & grn	1.75	1.25
		Nos. 1066-1077 (12)	6.35	4.20

The Poisoned Well by Jacek Malczewski — A384

1962, Aug. 15   Engr.   Wmk. 326
1078 A384 60g black, *buff*   .50 .25

Issued in sheets of 40 with alternating label for FIP Day (Federation Internationale de Philatelie), Sept. 1. Also issued in miniature sheet of 4. Value: mint $30, used $22.50.

Pole Vault — A385

Designs: 60g, Relay race. 90g, Javelin. 1z, Hurdles. 1.50z, High jump. 1.55z, Discus. 2.50z, 100m. dash. 3.40z, Hammer throw.

Unwmk.
1962, Sept. 12   Litho.   Perf. 11
1079	A385	40g multicolored	.25	.25
1080	A385	60g multicolored	.25	.25
1081	A385	90g multicolored	.25	.25
1082	A385	1z multicolored	.25	.25
1083	A385	1.50z multicolored	.25	.25
1084	A385	1.55z multicolored	.25	.25
1085	A385	2.50z multicolored	.45	.25
1086	A385	3.40z multicolored	.75	.25
		Nos. 1079-1086 (8)	2.70	2.00

7th European Athletic Championships, Belgrade, Sept. 12-16.
Exist imperf. Value, set: mint $3.50, used $2.25.

Anopheles Mosquito A386

Designs: 1.50z, Malaria blood cells. 2.50z, Cinchona flowers. 3z, Anopheles mosquito.

1962, Oct. 1   Wmk. 326   Perf. 13x12
1087	A386	60g ol blk, dk brn & bl grn	.25	.25
1088	A386	1.50z red, gray & brt vio	.25	.25
1089	A386	2.50z multicolored	.90	.30
		Nos. 1087-1089 (3)	1.40	.80

Miniature Sheet
Imperf
1090 A386   3z multicolored   1.25 .70

WHO drive to eradicate malaria.

Pavel R. Popovich and Andrian G. Nikolayev — A387

Design: 2.50z, Two stars in orbit around earth. 1z, Two stars in orbit.

1962, Oct. 6   Perf. 12½x12
1091	A387	60g violet, blk & citron	.30	.25
1092	A387	2.50z Prus bl, blk & red	.30	.25

Souvenir Sheet
Perf. 12x11
1093 A387   10z sl bl, blk & red   2.40 1.40

1st Russian group space flight, Vostoks III and IV, Aug. 11-15, 1962.

Woman Mailing Letter Warsaw — A388

1962, Oct. 9   Engr.   Perf. 12½x12
1094 A388 60g black   .25 .25
1095 A388 2.50z red brown   .45 .25

Stamp Day. The design is from the painting "A Moment of Decision," by Aleksander Kaminski.

Mazovian Princes' Mansion, A389

1962, Oct. 13   Litho.
1096 A389 60g red & black   .25 .25

25th anniversary of the founding of the Polish Democratic Party.

Cruiser "Aurora" — A390

Photo. & Engr.
1962, Nov. 3   Perf. 11
1097 A390 60g red & dk blue   .25 .25

Russian October revolution, 45th anniv.

Janusz Korczak by K. Dunikowski A391

King on Horseback A392

Illustrations from King Matthew books: 90g, King giving watch to Island girl. 1z, King handcuffed and soldier with sword. 2.50z, King with dead bird. 5.60z, King ice skating in moonlight.

Perf. 13x12
1962, Nov. 12   Unwmk.   Litho.
1098	A391	40g brn, bis & sep	.25	.25
1099	A392	60g multicolored	.25	.25
1100	A392	90g multicolored	.40	.25
1101	A392	1z multicolored	.40	.25
1102	A392	2.50z brn, yel & brt grn	.70	.45
1103	A392	5.60z brn, dk bl & grn	1.75	.75
		Nos. 1098-1103 (6)	3.75	2.20

20th anniversary of the death of Dr. Janusz Korczak (Henryk Goldszmit), physician, pedagogue and writer, in the Treblinka concentration camp, Aug. 5, 1942.

View of Old Warsaw — A393

1962, Nov. 26   Wmk. 326   Perf. 11
1104 A393 3.40z multicolored   .55 .30
　　a.　　Sheet of 4   5.00 3.00

5th Trade Union Cong., Warsaw, 11/26-12/1.

Orphan Mary and the Dwarf — A394

Various Scenes from "Orphan Mary and the Dwarfs" by Maria Konopnicka.

Perf. 13x12
1962, Dec. 31   Unwmk.   Litho.
1105	A394	40g multicolored	.35	.25
1106	A394	60g multicolored	2.00	.35
1107	A394	1.50z multicolored	.75	.25
1108	A394	1.55z multicolored	.75	.25
1109	A394	2.50z multicolored	.75	.30
1110	A394	3.40z multicolored	2.75	1.40
		Nos. 1105-1110 (6)	7.35	2.80

120th anniversary of the birth of Maria Konopnicka, poet and fairy tale writer.

Romuald Traugutt A395

Perf. 11½x11
1963, Jan. 31   Wmk. 326
1111 A395 60g aqua, blk & pale pink   .25 .25

Centenary of the 1863 insurrection and to honor its leader, Romuald Traugutt.

Tractor and Wheat A396

Designs: 60g, Man reaping and millet. 2.50z, Combine and rice.

Perf. 12x12½
1963, Feb. 25   Litho.   Wmk. 326
1112	A396	40g gray, bl, blk & ocher	.25	.25
1113	A396	60g brn red, blk, brn & grn	.50	.25
1114	A396	2.50z yel, buff, blk & grn	.70	.25
		Nos. 1112-1114 (3)	1.45	.75

FAO "Freedom from Hunger" campaign.

Cocker Spaniel — A397

30g, Polish sheep dog. 40g, Boxer. 50g, Airedale terrier, vert. 60g, French bulldog, vert. 1z, Poodle, vert. 2.50z, Hunting dog. 3.40z, Sheep dog, vert. 6.50z, Great Dane.

1963, Mar. 25   Unwmk.   Perf. 12½
1115	A397	20g lil, blk & org brn	.25	.25
1116	A397	30g rose car & blk	.25	.25
1117	A397	40g lil, blk & yel grn	.25	.25
1118	A397	50g multicolored	.25	.25
1119	A397	60g lt blue & blk	.30	.25
1120	A397	1z yel grn & blk	.50	.25
1121	A397	2.50z org, blk & brn	1.00	.35
1122	A397	3.40z red org & blk	2.75	1.00
1123	A397	6.50z brt yel & blk	6.50	2.40
		Nos. 1115-1123 (9)	12.05	5.25

Egyptian
Ship — A398

Ancient Ships: 10g, Phoenician merchant ship. 20g, Greek trireme. 30g, 3rd century merchantman. 40g, Scandinavian "Gokstad." 60g, Frisian "Kogge." 1z. 14th century "Holk." 1.15z, 15th century "Caraca."

Photo. (Background) & Engr.

1963, Apr. 19			Perf. 11½	
1124	A398	5g brown, *tan*	.25	.25
1125	A398	10g green, *gray grn*	.25	.25
1126	A398	20g ultra, *gray*	.25	.25
1127	A398	30g black, *gray ol*	.25	.25
1128	A398	40g lt bl, *bluish*	.25	.25
1129	A398	60g claret, *gray*	.25	.25
1130	A398	1z black, *bl*	.25	.25
1131	A398	1.15z grn, *pale rose*	.25	.25
		Nos. 1124-1131 (8)	2.00	2.00

See Nos. 1206-1213, 1299-1306.

Fighter and Ruins of Warsaw Ghetto — A399

Perf. 11½x11

1963, Apr. 5			Wmk. 326	
1132	A399	2.50z gray brn & gray	.50	.25

Warsaw Ghetto Uprising, 20th anniv.

Centenary
Emblem — A400

Perf. 12½x12

1963, May 8			Unwmk.	
1133	A400	2.50z blue, yel & red	.75	.25

Intl. Red Cross, cent. Every other stamp in sheet inverted.

Sand
Lizard
A401

40g, Smooth snake. 50g, European pond turtle. 60g, Grass snake. 90g, Slow worm. 1.15z, European tree frog. 1.35z, Alpine newt. 1.50z, Crested newt. 1.55z, Green toad. 2.50z, Firebellied toad. 3z, Fire salamander. 3.40z, Natterjack.

Perf. 11½

1963, June 1		Unwmk.	Photo.
Reptiles and Amphibians in Natural Colors			

1134	A401	30g grnsh gray & blk	.25	.25
1135	A401	40g gray ol & blk	.25	.25
1136	A401	50g bis brn & blk	.25	.25
1137	A401	60g tan & blk	.25	.25
1138	A401	90g gray grn & blk	.25	.25
1139	A401	1.15z gray & blk	.25	.25
1140	A401	1.35z gray bl & dk bl	.25	.25
1141	A401	1.50z bluish grn & blk	.50	.25
1142	A401	1.55z bluish gray & blk	.50	.25
1143	A401	2.50z gray vio & blk	.50	.25

1144	A401	3z gray grn & blk	.85	.35
1145	A401	3.40z gray & blk	2.40	1.25
		Nos. 1134-1145 (12)	6.60	4.10

Foil, Saber, Sword and Helmet A402

Designs: 40g, Fencers and knights in armor. 60g, Fencers and dragoons. 1.15z, Contemporary and 18th cent. fencers. 1.55z, Fencers and old houses, Gdansk. 6.50z, Arms of Gdansk, vert.

Perf. 12x12½, 12½x12

1963, June 29		Litho.	Unwmk.	
1146	A402	20g brown & orange	.25	.25
1147	A402	40g dk blue & blue	.25	.25
1148	A402	60g red & dp org	.25	.25
1149	A402	1.15z green & emer	.25	.25
1150	A402	1.55z violet & lilac	.35	.25
1151	A402	6.50z yel brn, mar & yel	1.10	.40
		Nos. 1146-1151 (6)	2.45	1.65

28th World Fencing Championships, Gdansk, July 15-28. A souvenir sheet exists containing one each of Nos. 1147-1150. Value: mint $40, used $32.50.

Famous Poles Type of 1961

No. 1152, Ludwik Warynski. No. 1153, Ludwik Krzywicki. No. 1154, Marie Sklodowska Curie. No. 1155, Karol Swierczewski-Walter.

Perf. 12x12½

1963, July 20			Wmk. 326	
Black Inscriptions and Designs				
1152	A359	60g red brown	.25	.25
1153	A359	60g gray brown	.25	.25
1154	A359	60g blue	.30	.25
1155	A359	60g green	.25	.25
		Nos. 1152-1155 (4)	1.05	1.00

Valeri Bykovski — A403

Designs: 60g, Valentina Tereshkova. 6.50z, Rockets "Falcon" and "Mew" and globe.

Unwmk.

1963, Aug. 26		Litho.	Perf. 11	
1156	A403	40g ultra, emer & blk	.25	.25
1157	A403	60g green, ultra & blk	.25	.25
1158	A403	6.50z multicolored	.85	.35
		Nos. 1156-1158 (3)	1.35	.85

Space flights of Valeri Bykovski June 14-19, and Valentina Tereshkova, first woman cosmonaut, June 16-19, 1963.
For overprints see Nos. 1175-1177.

Basketball
A404

Designs: Various positions of ball, hands and players. 10z, Town Hall, People's Hall and Arms of Wroclaw.

1963, Sept. 16		Unwmk.	Perf. 11½	
1159	A404	40g multicolored	.25	.25
1160	A404	50g fawn, grn & blk	.25	.25
1161	A404	60g red, lt grn & blk	.25	.25
1162	A404	90g multicolored	.25	.25
1163	A404	2.50z multicolored	.25	.25
1164	A404	5.60z multicolored	1.00	.25
		Nos. 1159-1164 (6)	2.25	1.50

Souvenir Sheet
Imperf

1965	A404	10z multicolored	2.00	1.10

13th European Men's Basketball Championship, Wroclaw, Oct. 4-13. No. 1165 contains one stamp; inscription on margin also commemorates the simultaneous European Sports Stamp Exhibition. Sheet sold for 15z.

Eagle and Ground-to-Air
Missile — A405

Eagle and: 40g, Destroyer. 60g, Jet fighter plane. 1.15z, Radar. 1.35z, Tank. 1.55z, Self-propelled rocket launcher. 2.50z, Amphibious troop carrier. 3z, Swords and medieval and modern soldiers.

1963, Oct. 1			Perf. 12x12½	
1166	A405	20g multicolored	.25	.25
1167	A405	40g violet, grn & red	.25	.25
1168	A405	60g multicolored	.25	.25
1169	A405	1.15z multicolored	.25	.25
1170	A405	1.35z multicolored	.25	.25
1171	A405	1.55z multicolored	.25	.25
1172	A405	2.50z multicolored	.35	.25
1173	A405	3z multicolored	.80	.35
		Nos. 1166-1173 (8)	2.65	2.10

Polish People's Army, 20th anniversary.

"Love Letter" by Wladyslaw
Czachórski — A406

Perf. 11½

1963, Oct. 9		Unwmk.	Engr.	
1174	A406	60g dark red brown	.40	.25

Issued for Stamp Day.

Nos. 1156-1158 Overprinted "23-28 X. 1963" and name of astronaut in Red or Black

1963		Litho.	Perf. 11	
1175	A403	40g multi (R)	.40	.25
1176	A403	60g multi (Blk)	.40	.25
1177	A403	6.50z multi (Blk)	2.00	.50
		Nos. 1175-1177 (3)	2.80	1.00

Visit of Valentina Tereshkova and Valeri Bykovski to Poland, Oct. 23-28. The overprints are: 40g, W. F. Bykowski / w Polsce; 60g, W. W. Tierieszkowa / w Polsce; 6.50z, W. F. BYKOWSKI I W. W. TIERIESZKOWA W POLSCE.

Konstantin E. Tsiolkovsky's Rocket and Rocket Speed Formula — A407

American and Russian Spacecrafts: 40g, Sputnik 1. 50g, Explorer 1. 60g, Lunik 2. 1z, Lunik 3. 1.50z, Vostok 1. 1.55z, Friendship 7. 2.50z, Vostoks 3 & 4. 5.60z, Mariner 2. 6.50z, Mars 1.

Perf. 12½x12

1963, Nov. 11		Litho.	Unwmk.	
Black Inscriptions				
1178	A407	30g dull bl grn & gray	.25	.25
1179	A407	40g lt ol grn & gray	.25	.25
1180	A407	50g violet bl & gray	.25	.25
1181	A407	60g brn org & gray	.25	.25
1182	A407	1z brt grn & gray	.25	.25
1183	A407	1.50z org red & gray	.25	.25

1184	A407	1.55z blue & gray	.25	.25
1185	A407	2.50z lilac & gray	.25	.25
1186	A407	5.60z brt yel grn & gray	.40	.25
1187	A407	6.50z grnsh bl & gray	.80	.25
		Nos. 1178-1187 (10)	3.20	2.50

Conquest of space. A souvenir sheet containing 2 each of Nos. 1186-1187 exists with top and bottom perfs, value: mint $60, used $40; and with bottom perfs only, value: mint $125, used $75.

Arab Stallion "Comet" — A408

Horses from
Mazury
Region — A409

Horses: 30g, Tarpans (wild horses). 40g, Horse from Sokolka. 50g, Arab mares and foals, horiz. 90g, Steeplechasers, horiz. 1.55z, Arab stallion "Witez II." 2.50z, Head of Arab horse, facing right. 4z, Mixed breeds, horiz. 6.50z, Head of Arab horse, facing left.

Perf. 11½x11 (A408); 12½x12, 12

1963, Dec. 30			Photo.	
1188	A408	20g black, yel & car	.25	.25
1189	A408	30g multicolored	.25	.25
1190	A408	40g multicolored	.25	.25

Sizes: 75x26mm (50g, 90g, 4z); 28x38mm (60g, 1.55z, 2.50z, 6.50z)

1191	A409	50g multicolored	.25	.25
1192	A409	60g multicolored	.25	.25
1193	A409	90g multicolored	.35	.25
1194	A409	1.55z multicolored	.45	.25
1195	A409	2.50z multicolored	.95	.30
1196	A409	4z multicolored	2.10	.75
1197	A409	6.50z yel, dl bl & blk	3.25	1.50
		Nos. 1188-1197 (10)	8.35	4.30

Issued to publicize Polish horse breeding.

Ice Hockey
A410

Sports: 30g, Slalom. 40g, Skiing. 60g, Speed skating. 1z, Ski jump. 2.50z, Tobogganing. 5.60z, Cross-country skiing. 6.50z, Figure skating pair.

1964, Jan. 25		Litho.	Perf. 12x12½	
1198	A410	20g multicolored	.25	.25
1199	A410	30g multicolored	.25	.25
1200	A410	40g multicolored	.25	.25
1201	A410	60g multicolored	.25	.25
1202	A410	1z multicolored	.35	.25
1203	A410	2.50z multicolored	.35	.25
1204	A410	5.60z multicolored	.65	.25
1205	A410	6.50z multicolored	1.25	.60
		Nos. 1198-1205 (8)	3.60	2.35

9th Winter Olympic Games, Innsbruck, Jan. 29-Feb. 9. A souvenir sheet contains 2 each of Nos. 1203, 1205. Value $35.

Ship Type of 1963

Sailing Ships: 1.35z, Caravel of Columbus, vert. 1.50z, Galleon. 1.55z, Polish warship, 1627, vert. 2z, Dutch merchant ship, vert. 2.10z, Line frigate. 2.50z, Frigate. 3z, 19th century merchantman. 3.40z, "Dar Pomorza," 20th century school ship, vert.

1964, Mar. 19		Engr.	Perf. 12½	
1206	A398	1.35z ultra	.25	.25
1207	A398	1.50z claret	.25	.25
1208	A398	1.55z black	.25	.25
1209	A398	2z violet	.25	.25
1210	A398	2.10z green	.25	.25
1211	A398	2.50z carmine rose	.25	.25

1212	A398	3z olive green	.40	.25
1213	A398	3.40z brown	.60	.25
		Nos. 1206-1213 (8)	2.50	2.00

European Cat — A411

40g, 60g, 1.55z, 2.50z, 6.50z, Various European cats. 50g, Siamese cat. 90g, 1.35z, 3.40z, Various Persian cats. 60g, 90g, 1.35z, 1.55z horiz.

1964, Apr. 30   Litho.   Perf. 12½
Cats in Natural Colors; Black
Inscriptions

1216	A411	30g yellow	.25	.25
1217	A411	40g orange	.25	.25
1218	A411	50g yellow	.25	.25
1219	A411	60g brt green	.25	.25
1220	A411	90g lt brown	.35	.25
1221	A411	1.35z emerald	.40	.25
1222	A411	1.55z violet blue	.40	.25
1223	A411	2.50z lilac	.50	.25
1224	A411	3.40z rose	2.25	.60
1225	A411	6.50z violet	3.50	1.75
		Nos. 1216-1225 (10)	8.40	4.35

King Casimir III, the Great — A412

Designs: No. 1227, Hugo Kollataj. No. 1228, Jan Dlugosz. No. 1229, Nicolaus Copernicus. 2.50z, King Wladyslaw II Jagiello and Queen Jadwiga.

1964, May 5   Engr.   Perf. 11x11½
Size: 22x35mm

1226	A412	40g dull claret	.25	.25
1227	A412	40g green	.25	.25
1228	A412	60g violet	.25	.25
1229	A412	60g dark blue	.50	.25

Size: 35½x37mm

1230	A412	2.50z gray brown	.50	.25
		Nos. 1226-1230 (5)	1.75	1.25

Jagiellonian University, Cracow, 600th anniv.

Lapwing A413

Waterfowl: 40g, White-spotted bluethroat. 50g, Black-tailed godwit. 60g, Osprey. 90g, Gray heron. 1.35z, Little gull. 1.55z, Shoveler. 5.60z, Arctic loon. 6.50z, Great crested grebe.

Perf. 11½
1964, June 5   Unwmk.   Photo.
Birds in Natural Colors; Black
Inscriptions
Size: 34x34mm

1231	A413	30g chalky blue	.25	.25
1232	A413	40g bister	.25	.25
1233	A413	50g brt yellow grn	.25	.25

Perf. 11½x11
Size: 34x48mm

1234	A413	60g blue	.25	.25
1235	A413	90g lemon	.25	.25
1236	A413	1.35z green	.35	.25

Perf. 11½
Size: 34x34mm

1237	A413	1.55z olive	.35	.25
1238	A413	5.60z blue green	.85	.25
1239	A413	6.50z brt green	1.40	.60
		Nos. 1231-1239 (9)	4.20	2.60

Hands Holding Red Flag — A414

Designs: No. 1241, Red and white ribbon around hammer. No. 1242, Hammer and rye. No. 1243, Brick wall under construction and red flag.

1964, June 15   Litho.   Perf. 11

1240	A414	60g ol bis, red, blk & pink	.25	.25
1241	A414	60g red, gray & black	.25	.25
1242	A414	60g magenta, blk & yel	.25	.25
1243	A414	60g gray, red, sal & blk	.25	.25
		Nos. 1240-1243 (4)	1.00	1.00

4th congress of the Polish United Workers Party.

Symbols of Peasant-Worker Alliance — A415

Atom Symbol and Book — A416

Shipyard, Gdansk — A417

Designs: No. 1245, Stylized oak. No. 1247, Factory and cogwheel. No. 1248, Tractor and grain. No. 1249, Pen, brush, mask and ornament. No. 1251, Lenin Metal Works, Nowa Huta. No. 1252, Cement factory, Chelm. No. 1253, Power Station, Turoszow. No. 1254, Oil refinery, Plock. No. 1255, Sulphur mine, Tarnobrzeg.

1964   Litho.   Perf. 12x12½

1244	A415	60g red, org & blk	.25	.25
1245	A415	60g grn, red, ocher, bl & blk	.25	.25

Photo.
Perf. 11

1246	A416	60g gray & dp vio bl	.25	.25
1247	A416	60g brt blue & blk	.25	.25
1248	A416	60g emerald & blk	.25	.25
1249	A416	60g orange & red	.25	.25

Photogravure and Engraved

1250	A417	60g dl bl grn & ultra	.25	.25
1251	A417	60g brt pink & pur	.25	.25
1252	A417	60g gray & gray brn	.25	.25
1253	A417	60g grn & slate grn	.25	.25
1254	A417	60g salmon & claret	.25	.25
1255	A417	60g citron & sepia	.25	.25
		Nos. 1244-1255 (12)	3.00	3.00

Polish People's Republic, 20 anniv.

Warsaw Fighters, 1944 — A418

1964, Aug. 1   Litho.   Perf. 12½x12

1256	A418	60g multicolored	.25	.25

20th anniv. of the Warsaw insurrection against German occupation.

Long Jump — A419

Women's High Jump — A420

Olympic Sports — A421

Sport: 40g, Rowing (single). 60g, Weight lifting. 90g, Relay race (square). 1z, Boxing (square). 2.50z, Soccer (square). 6.50z, Diving.

Unwmk.
1964, Aug. 17   Litho.   Perf. 11

1257	A419	20g multicolored	.25	.25
1258	A419	40g grnsh bl, bl & yel	.25	.25
1259	A419	60g vio bl, red & rose lil	.25	.25
1260	A419	90g dk brown, red & yel	.25	.25
1261	A419	1z dk violet, lil & gray	.25	.25
1262	A419	2.50z multicolored	.30	.25
1263	A420	5.60z multicolored	.75	.30
1264	A420	6.50z multicolored	1.50	.50
		Nos. 1257-1264 (8)	3.80	2.30

Souvenir Sheet
Imperf

1265	A421	Sheet of 4	3.00	1.60
a.		2.50z Sharpshooting	.40	.25
b.		2.50z Canoeing	.40	.25
c.		5z Fencing	.40	.25
d.		5z Basketball	.40	.25

18th Olympic Games, Tokyo, Oct. 10-25. Size of stamps in No. 1265: 24x24mm. A souvenir sheet containing 2 each of Nos. 1263-1264 with black marginal inscription exists. Value: mint $42.50, used $32.50.

Warsaw Mermaid and Stars — A422

1964, Sept. 7   Perf. 12½x12

1266	A422	2.50z violet & black	.55	.25

15th Astronautical Congress, Warsaw, Sept. 7-12.

Stefan Zeromski by Monika Zeromska — A423

1964, Sept. 21   Photo.   Perf. 12½

1267	A423	60g olive gray	.25	.25

Stefan Zeromski (1864-1925), writer.

Gun and Hand Holding Hammer — A424

1964, Sept. 21   Litho.   Perf. 11

1268	A424	60g brt grn, blk & red	.35	.25

Union of Fighters for Freedom and Democracy Congress, Warsaw, 9/24-26.

Globe and Red Flag — A425

1964, Sept. 28   Photo.   Perf. 12½

1269	A425	60g black & red org	.35	.25

First Socialist International, centenary.

Stagecoach by Jozef Brodowski — A426

1964, Oct. 9   Engr.   *Perf. 11½*
1270	A426	60g green	.25 .25
1271	A426	60g lt brown	.25 .25

Issued for Stamp Day.

Eleanor Roosevelt (1884-1962) — A427

1964, Oct. 10   *Perf. 12½*
1272	A427	2.50z black	.45 .25

Proposed Monument for Defenders of Westerplatte, 1939 — A428

Polish Soldiers Crossing Oder River, 1945 A429

Designs: No. 1274, Virtuti Military Cross. No. 1275, Nike, proposed monument for the martyrs of Bydgoszcz (woman with sword and torch). No. 1277, Battle of Studzianki, 1944.

Perf. 12x11, 11x12

1964, Nov. 16   Engr.   Unwmk.
1273	A428	40g gray violet	.25 .25
1274	A428	40g slate	.25 .25
1275	A428	60g dark blue	.25 .25
1276	A429	60g dark blue grn	.25 .25
1277	A429	60g grnsh black	.25 .25
		Nos. 1273-1277 (5)	1.25 1.25

Struggle and martyrdom of the Polish people, 1939-45. The vertical stamps are printed in sheets of 56 stamps (8x7) with 7 labels in each outside vertical row. The horizontal stamps are printed in sheets of 50 stamps (5x10) with 10 labels in each outside vertical row. See Nos. 1366-1368.

Souvenir Sheet

Col. Vladimir M. Komarov, Boris B. Yegorov and Dr. Konstantin Feoktistov — A430

1964, Nov. 21   Litho.   *Perf. 11½x11*
1278	A430	Sheet of 3	1.40 .85
a.		60g red & black (Komarov)	.25 .25
b.		60g brt grn & blk (Feoktistov)	.25 .25
c.		60g ultra & blk (Yegorov)	.25 .25

Russian three-manned space flight in space ship Voskhod, Oct. 12-13, 1964. Size of stamps: 27x36mm.

Cyclamen A431

Garden Flowers: 30g, Freesia. 40g, Monique rose. 50g, Peony. 60g, Royal lily.

90g, Oriental poppy. 1.35z, Tulip. 1.50z, Narcissus. 1.55z, Begonia. 2.50z, Carnation. 3.40z, Iris. 5.60z, Camellia.

1964, Nov. 30   Photo.   *Perf. 11*
Size: 35½x35½mm
Flowers in Natural Colors
1279	A431	20g violet	.25 .25
1280	A431	30g deep lilac	.25 .25
1281	A431	40g blue	.25 .25
1282	A431	50g violet blue	.25 .25
1283	A431	60g lilac	.25 .25
1284	A431	90g deep green	.25 .25

Size: 26x37½mm
1285	A431	1.35z dark blue	.25 .25
1286	A431	1.50z deep carmine	.50 .30
1287	A431	1.55z green	.25 .25
1288	A431	2.50z ultra	.45 .25
1289	A431	3.40z redsh brown	.85 .35
1290	A431	5.60z olive gray	2.00 .90
		Nos. 1279-1290 (12)	5.80 3.80

Future Interplanetary Spacecraft A432

Designs: 30g, Launching of Russian rocket. 40g, Dog Laika and launching tower. 60g, Lunik 3 photographing far side of the Moon. 1.55z, Satellite exploring the ionosphere. 2.50z, Satellite "Elektron 2" exploring radiation belt. 5.60z, "Mars 1" between Mars and Earth.

Perf. 12½x12

1964, Dec. 30   Litho.   Unwmk.
1291	A432	20g multicolored	.25 .25
1292	A432	30g multicolored	.25 .25
1293	A432	40g ol grn, blk & bl	.25 .25
1294	A432	60g dk bl, blk & dk red	.25 .25
1295	A432	1.55z gray & multi	.25 .25
1296	A432	2.50z multicolored	.35 .25
1297	A432	5.60z multicolored	.75 .35
		Nos. 1291-1297,B108 (8)	3.60 2.30

Issued to publicize space research.

Warsaw Mermaid, Ruins and New Buildings A433

1965, Jan. 15   Engr.   *Perf. 11x11½*
1298	A433	60g slate green	.25 .25

Liberation of Warsaw, 20th anniversary.

Ship Type of 1963
Designs as before.

1965, Jan. 25   Engr.   *Perf. 12½*
1299	A398	5g dark brown	.25 .25
1300	A398	10g slate green	.25 .25
1301	A398	20g slate blue	.25 .25
1302	A398	30g gray olive	.25 .25
1303	A398	40g dark blue	.25 .25
1304	A398	60g claret	.25 .25
1305	A398	1z red brown	.25 .25
1306	A398	1.15z dk red brown	.30 .25
		Nos. 1299-1306 (8)	2.05 2.00

Edaphosaurus — A434

Dinosaurs: 30g, Cryptocleidus, vert. 40g, Brontosaurus. 60g, Mesosaurus, vert. 90g, Stegosaurus. 1.15z, Brachiosaurus, vert. 1.35z, Styracosaurus. 3.40z, Corythosaurus, vert. 5.60z, Rhamphorhynchus, vert. 6.50z, Tyrannosaurus.

1965, Mar. 5   Litho.   *Perf. 12½*
1307	A434	20g multicolored	.25 .25
1308	A434	30g multicolored	.25 .25
1309	A434	40g multicolored	.25 .25
1310	A434	60g multicolored	.25 .25
1311	A434	90g multicolored	.25 .25
1312	A434	1.15z multicolored	.75 .25
1313	A434	1.35z multicolored	.75 .25
1314	A434	3.40z multicolored	.75 .25
1315	A434	5.60z multicolored	1.60 .70
1316	A434	6.50z multicolored	2.50 1.40
		Nos. 1307-1316 (10)	7.60 4.10

See Nos. 1395-1403.

Symbolic Wax Seal — A435

Russian and Polish Flags, Oil Refinery-Chemical Plant, Plock — A436

1965, Apr. 21   *Perf. 12½x12, 12½*
1317	A435	60g multicolored	.25 .25
1318	A436	60g multicolored	.25 .25

20th anniversary of the signing of the Polish-Soviet treaty of friendship, mutual assistance and postwar cooperation.

Polish Eagle and Town Coats of Arms A437

1965, May 8   Engr.   *Perf. 11½*
1319	A437	60g carmine rose	.35 .25

20th anniversary of regaining the Western and Northern Territories.

Dove A438

1965, May 8   Litho.   *Perf. 12x12½*
1320	A438	60g red & black	.35 .25

Victory over Fascism, 20th anniversary.

ITU Emblem — A439

Perf. 12½x12

1965, May 17   Litho.   Unwmk.
1321	A439	2.50z brt bl, lil, yel & blk	.65 .25

ITU, cent.

"The People's Friend" and Clover — A440

Factory and Rye A441

1965, June 5   *Perf. 11*
1322	A440	40g multicolored	.25 .25
1323	A441	60g multicolored	.25 .25

"Popular Movement" in Poland, 70th anniv.

Finn Class Yachts — A442

Yachts: 30g, Dragon class. 40g, 5.5-m. class. 50g, Group of Finn class. 60g, V-class. 1.35z, Group of Cadet class. 4z, Group of Star class. 5.60z, Two Flying Dutchmen. 6.50z, Two Amethyst class. 15z, Finn class race. (30g, 40g, 60g, 5.60z vertical.)

1965, June 14   Litho.   *Perf. 12½*
1324	A442	30g multicolored	.25 .25
1325	A442	40g multicolored	.25 .25
1326	A442	50g multicolored	.25 .25
1327	A442	60g multicolored	.25 .25
1328	A442	1.35z multicolored	.25 .25
1329	A442	4z multicolored	.45 .25
1330	A442	5.60z multicolored	.85 .35
1331	A442	6.50z multicolored	1.40 .30
		Nos. 1324-1331 (8)	3.95 2.15

Miniature Sheet
Perf. 11
1332	A442	15z multicolored	1.75 .85

World Championships of Finn Class Yachts, Gdynia, July 22-29. No. 1332 contains one stamp 48x22mm.

Marx and Lenin — A443

Photogravure and Engraved
1965, June 14   *Perf. 11½x11*
1333	A443	60g black, *ver*	.35 .25

6th Conference of Ministers of Post of Communist Countries, Peking, June 21-July 15.

Warsaw's Coat of Arms, 17th Cent. — A444

Old Town Hall, 18th Cent. — A445

Designs: 10g, Artifacts, 13th century. 20g, Tombstone of last Duke of Mazovia. 60g, Barbican, Gothic-Renaissance castle. 1.50z,

Arsenal, 19th century. 1.55z, National Theater. 2.50z, Staszic Palace. 3.40z, Woman with sword from Heroes' Memorial and Warsaw Mermaid seal.

Perf. 11x11½, 11½x11, 12x12½, 12½x12

1965, July 21		Engr.	Unwmk.	
1334	A444	5g carmine rose	.25	.25
1335	A444	10g green	.25	.25
1336	A445	20g violet blue	.25	.25
1337	A445	40g brown	.25	.25
1338	A445	60g orange	.25	.25
1339	A445	1.50z black	.25	.25
1340	A445	1.55z gray blue	.25	.25
1341	A445	2.50z lilac	.25	.25

Perf. 11½
Photogravure and Engraved

1342	A444	3.40z citron & blk	1.10	.50
		Nos. 1334-1342 (9)	3.10	2.50

700th anniversary of Warsaw.

No. 1342 is perforated all around, with lower right quarter perforated to form a 21x26mm stamp within a stamp. It was issued in sheets of 25 (5x5).

For surcharges see Nos. 1919-1926.

IQSY Emblem A446

Designs: 2.50z, Radio telescope dish, Torun. 3.40z, Solar system.

1965, Aug. 9				Litho.
1343	A446	60g vio, ver, brt grn & blk	.25	.25
a.		60g ultra, org, yel, bl & blk	.25	.25
1344	A446	2.50z red, yel, pur & blk	.40	.25
a.		2.50z red brn, yel, gray & blk	.40	.25
1345	A446	3.40z orange & multi	.65	.25
a.		3.40z ol gray & multi	.65	.25
		Nos. 1343-1345 (3)	1.30	.75
		Nos. 1343a-1345a (3)	1.30	.75

International Quiet Sun Year, 1964-65.

Odontoglossum Grande — A447

Orchids: 30g, Cypripedium hibridum. 40g, Lycaste skinneri. 50g, Cattleya. 60g, Vanda sanderiana. 1.35z, Cypripedium hibridum. 4z, Sobralia. 5.60z, Disa grandiflora. 6.50z, Cattleya labiata.

1965, Sept. 6		Photo.	Perf. 12½x12	
1346	A447	20g multicolored	.25	.25
1347	A447	30g multicolored	.25	.25
1348	A447	40g multicolored	.25	.25
1349	A447	50g multicolored	.25	.25
1350	A447	60g multicolored	.25	.25
1351	A447	1.35z multicolored	.25	.25
1352	A447	4z multicolored	.50	.25
1353	A447	5.60z multicolored	.95	.30
1354	A447	6.50z multicolored	1.60	.75
		Nos. 1346-1354 (9)	4.55	2.80

Weight Lifting — A448

Sport: 40g, Boxing. 50g, Relay race, men. 60g, Fencing. 90g, Women's 80-meter hurdles. 3.40z, Relay race, women. 6.50z, Hop, step and jump. 7.10z, Volleyball, women.

1965, Oct. 8		Photo.	Unwmk.	
1355	A448	30g gold & multi	.25	.25
1356	A448	40g gold & multi	.25	.25
1357	A448	50g silver & multi	.25	.25
1358	A448	60g gold & multi	.25	.25
1359	A448	90g silver & multi	.25	.25
1360	A448	3.40z gold & multi	.35	.25
1361	A448	6.50z gold & multi	.65	.25
1362	A448	7.10z bronze & multi	1.00	.35
		Nos. 1355-1362 (8)	3.25	2.10

Victories won by the Polish team in 1964 Olympic Games. Each denomination printed in sheets of eight stamps and two center labels showing medals.

Mail Coach, by Piotr Michalowski — A449

Design: 2.50z, Departure of Coach, by Piotr Michalowski.

1965, Oct. 9		Engr.	Perf. 11x11½	
1363	A449	60g brown	.25	.25
1364	A449	2.50z slate green	.40	.25

Issued for Stamp Day, 1965. Sheets of 50 with labels se-tenant inscribed "Dzien Znaczka 1965 R."

UN Emblem — A450

1965, Oct. 24		Litho.	Perf. 12½x12	
1365	A450	2.50z ultra	.40	.25

20th anniversary of United Nations.

Memorial, Plaszow — A451

No. 1367, Kielce Memorial. No. 1368, Chelm Memorial.

Perf. 12x11, 11x12

1965, Nov. 29			Engr.	
1366	A451	60g grnsh gray	.25	.25
1367	A451	60g chocolate	.25	.25
1368	A451	60g black, horiz.	.25	.25
		Nos. 1366-1368 (3)	.75	.75

Note after #1277 applies also to #1366-1368.

Wolf A452

1965, Nov. 30		Photo.	Perf. 11½	
1369	A452	20g shown	.25	.25
1370	A452	30g Lynx	.25	.25
1371	A452	40g Red fox	.25	.25
1372	A452	50g Badger	.25	.25
1373	A452	60g Brown bear	.25	.25
1374	A452	1.50z Wild Boar	.35	.25
1375	A452	2.50z Red deer	.35	.25
1376	A452	5.60z European bison	1.00	.45
1377	A452	7.10z Moose	1.25	.75
		Nos. 1369-1377 (9)	4.20	2.95

Gig — A453

Horse-drawn carriages, Lancut Museum: 40g, Coupé. 50g, Lady's basket. 60g, Vis-a-vis. 90g, Cab. 1.15z, Berlinka. 2.50z, Hunting break. 6.50z, Caleche à la Daumont. 7.10z, English break.

1965, Dec. 30		Litho.	Perf. 11	
		Size: 50x23mm		
1378	A453	20g multicolored	.25	.25
1379	A453	40g lilac & multi	.25	.25
1380	A453	50g orange & multi	.25	.25
1381	A453	60g fawn & multi	.25	.25
1382	A453	90g yellow & multi	.25	.25
		Size: 76x23mm		
1383	A453	1.15z multicolored	.25	.25
1384	A453	2.50z olive & multi	.35	.25
1385	A453	6.50z multicolored	1.00	.35
		Size: 103x23mm		
1386	A453	7.10z blue & multi	1.40	.60
		Nos. 1378-1386 (9)	4.25	2.70

Cargo Ship (No. 1389) — A454

No. 1387, Supervising Technical Organization (NOT) emblem, symbols of industry. No. 1388, Pit head & miners' badge, vert. No. 1390, Chemical plant, Plock. No. 1391, Combine. No. 1392, Railroad train. No. 1393, Building crane, vert. No. 1394, Pavilion & emblem of 35th Intl. Poznan Fair.

1966		Litho.	Perf. 11	
1387	A454	60g multicolored	.25	.25
1388	A454	60g multicolored	.25	.25
1389	A454	60g multicolored	.25	.25
1390	A454	60g multicolored	.25	.25
1391	A454	60g multicolored	.25	.25
1392	A454	60g multicolored	.25	.25
1393	A454	60g multicolored	.25	.25
1394	A454	60g multicolored	.25	.25
		Nos. 1387-1394 (8)	2.00	2.00

20th anniversary of the nationalization of Polish industry. No. 1394 also commemorates the 35th International Poznan Fair. Nos. 1387-1388 issued in connection with the 5th Congress of Polish Technicians, Katowice. Printed in sheets of 20 stamps and 20 labels with commemorative inscription within cogwheel on each label.

Issued: #1387-1388, 2/10; others, 5/21.

Dinosaur Type of 1965

Prehistoric Vertebrates: 20g, Dinichthys. 30g, Eusthenopteron. 40g, Ichthyostega. 50g, Mastodonsaurus. 60g, Cynognathus. 2.50z, Archaeopteryx, vert. 3.40z, Brontotherium. 6.50z, Machairodus. 7.10z, Mammoth.

1966, Mar. 5		Litho.	Perf. 12½	
1395	A434	20g multicolored	.25	.25
1396	A434	30g multicolored	.25	.25
1397	A434	40g multicolored	.25	.25
1398	A434	50g multicolored	.25	.25
1399	A434	60g multicolored	.25	.25
1400	A434	2.50z multicolored	.35	.25
1401	A434	3.40z multicolored	.50	.25
1402	A434	6.50z multicolored	1.25	.40
1403	A434	7.10z multicolored	2.00	1.75
		Nos. 1395-1403 (9)	5.35	3.90

Henryk Sienkiewicz A455

Photogravure and Engraved

1966, Mar. 30			Perf. 11½	
1404	A455	60g black, dl yel	.35	.25

Henryk Sienkiewicz (1846-1916), author and winner of 1905 Nobel Prize.

Soccer Game — A456

Designs: Various phases of soccer. Each stamp inscribed with the place and the result of final game in various preceding soccer championships.

1966, May 6			Perf. 13x12	
1405	A456	20g multicolored	.25	.25
1406	A456	40g multicolored	.25	.25
1407	A456	60g multicolored	.25	.25
1408	A456	90g multicolored	.25	.25
1409	A456	1.50z multicolored	.45	.25
1410	A456	3.40z multicolored	.65	.25
1411	A456	6.50z multicolored	1.25	.40
1412	A456	7.10z multicolored	1.75	.75
		Nos. 1405-1412 (8)	5.10	2.65

World Cup Soccer Championship, Wembley, England, July 11-30. Each denomination printed in sheets of 10 (5x2).

See No. B109.

Peace Dove and War Memorial — A457

Typo. & Engr.

1966, May 9			Perf. 11½	
1413	A457	60g silver & multi	.35	.25

21st anniversary of victory over Fascism.

Women's Relay Race A458

20g, Start of men's short distance race. 60g, Javelin. 90g, Women's 80-meter hurdles. 1.35z, Discus. 3.40z, Finish of men's medium distance race. 6.50z, Hammer throw. 7.10z, High jump.

5z, Long distance race.

Perf. 11½x11, 11x11½

1966, June 18			Litho.	
1414	A458	20g multi, vert.	.25	.25
1415	A458	40g multi	.25	.25
1416	A458	60g multi, vert.	.25	.25
1417	A458	90g multi	.25	.25
1418	A458	1.35z multi	.25	.25
1419	A458	3.40z multi	.40	.25
1420	A458	6.50z multi, vert.	.65	.25
1421	A458	7.10z multi	.65	.30
		Nos. 1414-1421 (8)	2.95	2.05

Souvenir Sheet
Imperf

1422	A458	5z multicolored	1.75	1.10

European Athletic Championships, Budapest, August, 1966. No. 1422 contains one 57x27mm stamp.

Polish Eagle — A459

Designs: Nos. 1424, 1426, Flag of Poland. No. 1425, Polish Eagle.

Photogravure and Embossed
Perf. 12½x12

			Unwmk.	
1966, July 21				
1423	A459	60g gold, red & blk	.25	.25
1424	A459	60g gold, red & blk	.25	.25
1425	A459	2.50z gold, red & blk	.25	.25
1426	A459	2.50z gold, red & blk	.25	.25
		Nos. 1423-1426 (4)	1.00	1.00

1000th anniversary of Poland. Nos. 1423-1424 and 1425-1426 printed in 2 sheets of 10 (5x2); top row in each sheet in eagle design, bottom row in flag design.

Flowers and Farm Produce — A460

Designs: 60g, Woman holding loaf of bread. 3.40z, Farm girls holding harvest wreath.

1966, Aug. 15		**Photo.**		**Perf. 11**
		Size: 22x50mm		
1427	A460	40g gold & multi	.40	.25
1428	A460	60g gold & multi	.40	.25
		Size: 48x50mm		
1429	A460	3.40z violet bl & multi	.65	.45
		Nos. 1427-1429 (3)	1.45	.95

Issued to publicize the harvest festival.

Chrysanthemum — A461

Flowers: 20g, Poinsettia. 30g, Centaury. 40g, Rose. 60g, Zinnias. 90g, Nasturtium. 5.60z, Dahlia. 6.50z, Sunflower. 7.10z, Magnolia.

1966, Sept. 1				**Perf. 11½**
Flowers in Natural Colors				
1430	A461	10g gold & black	.25	.25
1431	A461	20g gold & black	.25	.25
1432	A461	30g gold & black	.25	.25
1433	A461	40g gold & black	.25	.25
1434	A461	60g gold & black	.25	.25
1435	A461	90g gold & black	.25	.25
1436	A461	5.60z gold & black	.75	.25
1437	A461	6.50z gold & black	1.00	.30
1438	A461	7.10z gold & black	1.75	.50
		Nos. 1430-1438 (9)	5.00	2.55

Map Showing Tourist Attractions A462

Designs: 20g, Lighthouse, Hel. 40g, Amethyst yacht on Masurian Lake. No. 1442, Poniatowski Bridge, Warsaw, and sailboat. No. 1443, Mining Academy, Kielce. 1.15z, Dunajec Gorge. 1.35z, Old oaks, Rogalin. 1.55z, Planetarium, Katowice. 2z, M.S. Batory and globe.

Perf. 12½x12, 11½x12

1966, Sept. 15				**Engr.**
1439	A462	10g carmine rose	.25	.25
1440	A462	20g olive gray	.25	.25
1441	A462	40g grysh blue	.25	.25
1442	A462	60g redsh brown	.25	.25
1443	A462	60g black	.25	.25
1444	A462	1.15z green	.25	.25
1445	A462	1.35z vermilion	.25	.25

1446	A462	1.55z violet	.25	.25
1447	A462	2z dark gray	.25	.25
		Nos. 1439-1447 (9)	2.25	2.25

Stableman with Percherons, by Piotr Michalowski — A463

2.50z, "Horses and Dogs" by Michalowski.

1966, Sept. 8				**Perf. 11x11½**
1448	A463	60g gray brown	.25	.25
1449	A463	2.50z green	.40	.25

Issued for Stamp Day, 1966.

Capital of Romanesque Column from Tyniec and Polish Flag — A464

Engraved and Photogravure
1966, Oct. 7				**Perf. 11½**
1450	A464	60g dark brn & rose	.35	.25

Polish Cultural Congress.

Soldier A465

1966, Oct. 20		**Litho.**		**Perf. 11x11½**
1451	A465	60g blk, ol grn, & dl red	.40	.25

Participation of the Polish Jaroslaw Dabrowski Brigade in the Spanish Civil War.

Green Woodpecker — A466

Forest Birds: 10g, The eight birds of the set combined. 30g, Eurasian jay. 40g, European golden oriole. 60g, Hoopoe. 2.50z, European redstart. 4z, Siskin (finch). 6.50z, Chaffinch. 7.10z, Great tit.

1966, Nov. 17		**Photo.**		**Perf. 11½**
Birds in Natural Colors; Black Inscription				
1452	A466	10g lt green	.25	.25
1453	A466	20g dull violet bl	.25	.25
1454	A466	30g dull green	.35	.25
1455	A466	40g gray	.35	.25
1456	A466	60g gray green	.35	.25
1457	A466	2.50z lt olive grn	.50	.25
1458	A466	4z dull violet	1.25	.25
1459	A466	6.50z green	1.00	.35
1460	A466	7.10z gray blue	1.75	.75
		Nos. 1452-1460 (9)	6.05	2.85

Ceramic Ram, c. 4000 B.C. — A467

Designs: No. 1462, Bronze weapons and ornaments, c. 3500 B.C., horiz. No. 1463, Biskupin, settlement plan, 2500 B.C.

1966, Dec. 10		**Engr.**		**Perf. 11x11½**
1461	A467	60g dull violet blue	.25	.25
1462	A467	60g brown	.25	.25
1463	A467	60g green	.25	.25
		Nos. 1461-1463 (3)	.75	.75

Polish Eagle, Hammer and Grain — A468

Designs: 60g, Eagle and map of Poland.

1966, Dec. 20		**Litho.**		**Perf. 11**
1464	A468	40g brn, red & bluish lil	.25	.25
1465	A468	60g brn, red & ol grn	.25	.25

Millenium of Poland.

Vostok (USSR) — A469

Spacecraft: 40g, Gemini, American Spacecraft. 60g, Ariel 2 (Great Britain). 1.35z, Proton 1 (USSR). 1.50z, FR 1 (France). 3.40z, Alouette (Canada). 6.50z, San Marco 1 (Italy). 7.10z, Luna 9 (USSR).

1966, Dec. 20				**Perf. 11½x11**
1466	A469	20g tan & multi	.25	.25
1467	A469	40g brown & multi	.25	.25
1468	A469	60g gray & multi	.25	.25
1469	A469	1.35z multicolored	.25	.25
1470	A469	1.50z multicolored	.25	.25
1471	A469	3.40z multicolored	.25	.25
1472	A469	6.50z multicolored	.90	.25
1473	A469	7.10z multicolored	1.25	.35
		Nos. 1466-1473 (8)	3.65	2.10

Dressage — A470

Horses: 20g, Horse race. 40g, Jump. 60g, Steeplechase. 90g, Trotting. 5.90z, Polo. 6.60z, Stallion "Ofir." 7z, Stallion "Skowronek."

1967, Feb. 25		**Photo.**		**Perf. 12½**
1474	A470	10g ultra & multi	.25	.25
1475	A470	20g orange & multi	.25	.25
1476	A470	40g ver & multi	.25	.25
1477	A470	60g multicolored	.25	.25
1478	A470	90g green & multi	.25	.25
1479	A470	5.90z multicolored	.80	.25
1480	A470	6.60z multicolored	1.50	.50
1481	A470	7z violet & multi	2.10	.50
		Nos. 1474-1481 (8)	5.65	2.50

Janov Podlaski stud farm, 150th anniv.

Memorial at Auschwitz (Oswiecim) A471

Emblem of Memorials Administration A472

Memorials at: No. 1484, Oswiecim-Monowice. No. 1485, Westerplatte (Walcz). No. 1486, Lodz-Radugoszcz. No. 1487, Stutthof. No. 1488, Lambinowice-Jencom. No. 1489, Zagan.

1967		**Engr.**	**Perf. 11½x11, 11x11½**	
1482	A471	40g brown olive	.25	.25
1483	A472	40g dull violet	.25	.25
1484	A472	40g black	.25	.25
1485	A472	40g green	.25	.25
1486	A472	40g black	.25	.25
1487	A471	40g ultra	.25	.25
1488	A471	40g brown	.25	.25
1489	A472	40g deep plum	.25	.25
		Nos. 1482-1489 (8)	2.00	2.00

Issued to commemorate the martyrdom and fight of the Polish people, 1939-45.

Issue dates: Nos. 1482-1484, Apr. 10. Nos. 1485-1487, Oct. 9. Nos. 1488-1489, Dec. 28. See Nos. 1620-1624.

Striped Butterflyfish — A473

Tropical fish: 10g, Imperial angelfish. 40g, Barred butterflyfish. 60g, Spotted triggerfish. 90g, Undulate triggerfish. 1.50z, Striped triggerfish. 4.50z, Black-eye butterflyfish. 6.60z, Blue angelfish. 7z, Saddleback butterflyfish.

1967, Apr. 1		**Litho.**		**Perf. 11x11½**
1492	A473	5g multicolored	.25	.25
1493	A473	10g multicolored	.25	.25
1494	A473	40g multicolored	.25	.25
1495	A473	60g multicolored	.25	.25
1496	A473	90g multicolored	.25	.25
1497	A473	1.50z multicolored	.25	.25
1498	A473	4.50z multicolored	.65	.25
1499	A473	6.60z multicolored	1.00	.75
1500	A473	7z multicolored	1.25	.25
		Nos. 1492-1500 (9)	4.40	2.75

Bicyclists — A474

1967, May 5		**Litho.**		**Perf. 11**
1501	A474	60g multicolored	.25	.25

20th Warsaw-Berlin-Prague Bicycle Race.

Men's 100-meter Race — A475

Sports and Olympic Rings: 40g, Steeplechase. 60g, Women's relay race. 90g, Weight lifter. 1.35z, Hurdler. 3.40z, Gymnast on vaulting horse. 6.60z, High jump. 7z, Boxing.

1967, May 24   Litho.   *Perf. 11*

1502	A475	20g multicolored	.25	.25
1503	A475	40g multicolored	.25	.25
1504	A475	60g multicolored	.25	.25
1505	A475	90g multicolored	.25	.25
1506	A475	1.35z multicolored	.25	.25
1507	A475	3.40z multicolored	.25	.25
1508	A475	6.60z multicolored	.75	.25
1509	A475	7z multicolored	.75	.25
	Nos. 1502-1509 (8)		3.00	2.00

19th Olympic Games, Mexico City, 1968. Nos. 1502-1509 printed in sheets of 8, (2x4) with label showing emblem of Polish Olympic Committee between each two horizontal stamps. See No. B110.

Badge of Socialist Working Brigade A476

1967, June 2

1510	A476	60g multicolored	.25	.25

6th Congress of Polish Trade Unions. Printed in sheets of 20 stamps and 20 labels and in miniature sheets of 4 stamps and 4 labels.

Mountain Arnica — A477

Medicinal Plants: 60g, Columbine. 3.40z, Gentian. 4.50z, Ground pine. 5z, Iris sibirica. 10z, Azalea pontica.

1967, June 14   *Perf. 11½x11*
Flowers in Natural Colors

1511	A477	40g black & brn org	.25	.25
1512	A477	60g black & lt blue	.25	.25
1513	A477	3.40z black & dp org	.35	.25
1514	A477	4.50z black & lt vio	.25	.25
1515	A477	5z black & maroon	.45	.25
1516	A477	10z black & bister	.85	.25
	Nos. 1511-1516 (6)		2.40	1.50

Monument for Silesian Insurgents A478

1967, July 21   Litho.   *Perf. 11½*

1517	A478	60g multicolored	.25	.25

Unveiling of the monument for the Silesian Insurgents of 1919-21 at Katowice, July, 1967.

Marie Curie — A479

1967, Aug. 1   Engr.   *Perf. 11½x11*

1518	A479	60g dk carmine rose	.25	.25
1519	A479	60g violet	.25	.25
1520	A479	60g sepia	.25	.25
	Nos. 1518-1520 (3)		.75	.75

Marie Sklodowska Curie (1867-1934), discoverer of radium and polonium.

Designs: No. 1519, Curie statue, Warsaw. No. 1520, Nobel Prize diploma.

Sign Language and Emblem A480

1967, Aug. 1   Litho.   *Perf. 11x11½*

1521	A480	60g brt blue & blk	.25	.25

5th Congress of the World Federation of the Deaf, Warsaw, Aug. 10-17.

Flowers of the Meadows A481

Flowers: 40g, Poppy. 60g, Morning glory. 90g, Pansy. 1.15z, Common pansy. 2.50z, Corn cockle. 3.40z, Wild aster. 4.50z, Common pimpernel. 7.90z, Chicory.

1967, Sept. 5   Photo.   *Perf. 11½*

1522	A481	20g multicolored	.25	.25
1523	A481	40g multicolored	.25	.25
1524	A481	60g multicolored	.25	.25
1525	A481	90g multicolored	.25	.25
1526	A481	1.15z multicolored	.25	.25
1527	A481	2.50z multicolored	.30	.25
1528	A481	3.40z multicolored	.45	.25
1529	A481	4.50z multicolored	.80	.25
1530	A481	7.90z multicolored	1.70	.35
	Nos. 1522-1530 (9)		4.50	2.35

Wilanow Palace, by Wincenty Kasprzycki — A482

Engraved and Photogravure
1967, Oct. 9   *Perf. 11½*

1531	A482	60g olive blk & lt bl	.25	.25

Issued for Stamp Day, 1967.

Cruiser Aurora — A483

Designs: No. 1533, Lenin and library. No. 1534, Luna 10, earth and moon.

1967, Oct. 9   Litho.   *Perf. 11*

1532	A483	60g gray, red & blk	.25	.25
1533	A483	60g gray, dull red & blk	.25	.25
1534	A483	60g gray, red & blk	.25	.25
	Nos. 1532-1534 (3)		.75	.75

Russian Revolution, 50th anniv.

Tadeusz Kosciusko — A485

Engraved and Photogravure
1967, Oct. 14   *Perf. 12x11*

1540	A485	60g choc & ocher	.25	.25
1541	A485	2.50z sl grn & rose car	.25	.25

Tadeusz Kosciusko (1746-1817), Polish patriot and general in the American Revolution.

Vanessa Butterfly A486

Designs: Various Butterflies.

1967, Oct. 14   Litho.   *Perf. 11½*
Butterflies in Natural Colors

1542	A486	10g green	.25	.25
1543	A486	20g lt violet bl	.25	.25
1544	A486	40g yellow green	.25	.25
1545	A486	60g gray	.25	.25
1546	A486	2z lemon	.30	.25
1547	A486	2.50z Prus green	.35	.25
1548	A486	3.40z blue	.55	.35
1549	A486	4.50z rose lilac	1.25	.50
1550	A486	7.90z bister	1.75	.70
	Nos. 1542-1550 (9)		5.20	3.05

Polish Woman, by Antoine Watteau A487

Paintings from Polish Museums: 20g, Lady with the Ermine, by Leonardo da Vinci. 60g, Dog Fighting Heron, by Abraham Hondius. 2z, Guitarist after the Hunt, by J. Baptiste Greuze. 2.50z, Tax Collectors, by Marinus van Reymerswaele. 3.40z, Portrait of Daria Flodorowna, by Fyodor Rokotov. 4.50z, Still Life with Lobster, by Jean de Heem, horiz. 6.60z, Landscape (from the Good Samaritan), by Rembrandt, horiz.

Perf. 11½x11, 11x11½
1967, Nov. 15   Photo.

1551	A487	20g gold & multi	.25	.25
1552	A487	40g gold & multi	.25	.25
1553	A487	60g gold & multi	.25	.25
1554	A487	2z gold & multi	.25	.25
1555	A487	2.50z gold & multi	.25	.25
1556	A487	3.40z gold & multi	.25	.25
1557	A487	4.50z gold & multi	.70	.25
1558	A487	6.60z gold & multi	.95	.35
	Nos. 1551-1558 (8)		3.15	2.10

Printed in sheets of 5 + label. Pairs, stamp and label, set: mint $6, used $2.50.

Ossolinski Medal, Book and Flags — A488

1967, Dec. 12   Litho.   *Perf. 11*

1559	A488	60g lt bl, red & lt brn	.25	.25

150th anniversary of the founding of the Ossolineum, a center for scientific and cultural activities, by Count Josef Maximilian Ossolinski.

Wladyslaw S. Reymont (1867-1924), Writer, Nobel Prize Winner — A489

1967, Dec. 12

1560	A489	60g dk brn, ocher & red	.25	.25

Ice Hockey A490

Designs: 60g, Skiing. 90g, Slalom. 1.35z, Speed skating. 1.55z, Long-distance skiing. 2z, Sledding. 7z, Biathlon. 7.90z, Ski jump.

1968, Jan. 10

1561	A490	40g multicolored	.25	.25
1562	A490	60g multicolored	.25	.25
1563	A490	90g multicolored	.25	.25
1564	A490	1.35z multicolored	.25	.25
1565	A490	1.55z multicolored	.25	.25
1566	A490	2z multicolored	.25	.25
1567	A490	7z multicolored	.35	.25
1568	A490	7.90z multicolored	.70	.30
	Nos. 1561-1568 (8)		2.55	2.05

10th Winter Olympic Games, Grenoble, France, Feb. 6-18, 1968.

Puss in Boots — A491

Fairy Tales: 40g, The Fox and the Raven. 60g, Mr. Twardowski (man flying on a cock). 2z, The Fisherman and the Fish. 2.50z, Little Red Riding Hood. 3.40z, Cinderella. 5.50z, Thumbelina. 7z, Snow White.

1968, Mar. 15   Litho.   *Perf. 12½*

1569	A491	20g multicolored	.25	.25
1570	A491	40g lt violet & multi	.25	.25
1571	A491	60g multicolored	.25	.25
1572	A491	2z olive & multi	.25	.25
1573	A491	2.50z ver & multi	.30	.25
1574	A491	3.40z multicolored	.45	.25
1575	A491	5.50z multicolored	.75	.35
1576	A491	7z multicolored	1.10	.35
	Nos. 1569-1576 (8)		3.60	2.20

Bird-of-Paradise Flower — A492

Exotic Flowers: 10g, Clianthus dampieri. 20g, Passiflora quadrangularis. 40g, Coryphanta vivipara. 60g, Odontonia. 90g, Protea cynaroides.

1968, May 15   Litho.   *Perf. 11½*

1577	A492	10g sepia & multi	.25	.25
1578	A492	20g multicolored	.25	.25
1579	A492	30g brown & multi	.25	.25
1580	A492	40g ultra & multi	.25	.25
1581	A492	60g multicolored	.25	.25
1582	A492	90g multicolored	.25	.25
	Nos. 1577-1582,B111-B112 (8)		3.75	2.20

"Peace" by
Henryk
Tomaszewski
A493

2.50z, Poster for Gounod's Faust, by Jan Lenica.

1968, May 29   Litho.   Perf. 11½x11
1583 A493 60g gray & multi   .25 .25
1584 A493 2.50z gray & multi   .25 .25

2nd Intl. Poster Biennial Exhibition, Warsaw.

Zephyr Glider — A494

Polish Gliders: 90g, Storks. 1.50z, Swallow. 3.40z, Flies. 4z, Seal. 5.50z, Pirate.

1968, May 29   Perf. 12½
1585 A494 60g multicolored   .25 .25
1586 A494 90g multicolored   .25 .25
1587 A494 1.50z multicolored   .25 .25
1588 A494 3.40z multicolored   .45 .25
1589 A494 4z multicolored   .55 .25
1590 A494 5.50z multicolored   .80 .35
      Nos. 1585-1590 (6)   2.55 1.60

11th Intl. Glider Championships, Leszno.

Child Holding
Symbolic
Stamp — A495

No. 1592, Balloon over Poznan Town Hall.

1968, July 2   Litho.   Perf. 11½x11
1591 A495 60g multicolored   .25 .25
1592 A495 60g multicolored   .25 .25

75 years of Polish philately; "Tematica 1968" stamp exhibition in Poznan. Printed in sheets of 12 (4x3) se-tenant, arranged checkerwise.

Sosnowiec
Memorial — A496

Photogravure and Engraved
1968, July 20   Perf. 11x11½
1593 A496 60g brt rose lilac &
           blk   .25 .25

The monument by Helena and Roman Husarski and Witold Ceckiewicz was unveiled Sept. 16, 1967, to honor the revolutionary deeds of Silesian workers and miners.

Relay Race
and
Sculptured
Head
A497

Sports and Sculptures: 40g, Boxing. 60g. Basketball. 90g, Long jump. 2.50z, Women's javelin. 3.40z, Athlete on parallel bars. 4z, Bicycling. 7.90z, Fencing.

1968, Sept. 2   Litho.   Perf. 11x11½
Size: 35x26mm
1594 A497 30g sepia & multi   .25 .25
1595 A497 40g brn org, brn &
           blk   .25 .25
1596 A497 60g gray & multi   .25 .25
1597 A497 90g violet & multi   .25 .25
1598 A497 2.50z multicolored   .25 .25
1599 A497 3.40z brt grn, blk & lt
           ultra   .30 .35
1600 A497 4z multicolored   .30 .35
1601 A497 7.90z multicolored   .50 .30
      Nos. 1594-1601,B113 (9)   3.85 2.55

19th Olympic Games, Mexico City, 10/12-27.

Jewish
Woman
with
Lemons,
by
Aleksander
Gierymski
A498

Polish Paintings: 40g, Knight on Bay Horse, by Piotr Michalowski. 60g, Fisherman, by Leon Wyczolkowski. 1.35z, Eliza Parenska, by Stanislaw Wyspianski. 1.50z, "Manifest," by Wojciech Weiss. 4.50z, Stancyk (Jester), by Jan Matejko, horiz. 5z, Children's Band, by Tadeusz Makowski, horiz. 7z, Feast II, by Zygmunt Waliszewski, horiz.

Perf. 11½x11, 11x11½
1968, Oct. 10   Litho.
1602 A498 40g gray & multi   .25 .25
1603 A498 60g gray & multi   .25 .25
1604 A498 1.15z gray & multi   .25 .25
1605 A498 1.35z gray & multi   .25 .25
1606 A498 1.50z gray & multi   .35 .25
1607 A498 4.50z gray & multi   .40 .25
1608 A498 5z gray & multi   .65 .25
1609 A498 7z gray & multi   .85 .25
      Nos. 1602-1609 (8)   3.25 2.00

Issued in sheets of 4 stamps and 2 labels inscribed with painter's name. Pair with label, set: mint $3.50, used $2.25.

"September, 1939" by M.
Bylina — A499

Paintings: No. 1611, Partisans, by L. Maciag. No. 1612, Tank in Battle, by M. Bylina. No. 1613, Monte Cassino, by A. Boratynski. No. 1614, Tanks Approaching Warsaw, by S. Garwatowski. No. 1615, Battle on the Neisse, by M. Bylina. No. 1616, On the Oder, by K. Mackiewicz. No. 1617, "In Berlin," by M. Bylina. No. 1618, Warship "Blyskawica" by M. Mokwa. No. 1619, "Pursuit" (fighter planes), by T. Kulisiewicz.

Litho., Typo. & Engr.
1968, Oct. 12   Perf. 11½
1610 A499 40g pale yel, ol & vio   .25 .25
1611 A499 40g lil, red lil & ind   .25 .25
1612 A499 40g gray, dk bl & ol   .25 .25
1613 A499 40g pale sal, org brn
           & blk   .25 .25
1614 A499 40g pale grn, dk grn
           & plum   .25 .25
1615 A499 60g gray, vio bl & blk   .25 .25

1616 A499 60g pale grn, ol grn &
           vio brn   .25 .25
1617 A499 60g pink, car & grnsh
           blk   .25 .25
1618 A499 60g pink, brn & grn   .25 .25
1619 A499 60g lt bl, grnsh bl &
           blk   .25 .25
      Nos. 1610-1619 (10)   2.50 2.50

Polish People's Army, 25th anniversary.

Memorial Types of 1967

Designs: No. 1620, Tomb of the Unknown Soldier, Warsaw. No. 1621, Nazi War Crimes Memorial, Zamosc. No. 1622, Guerrilla Memorial, Plichno. No. 1623, Guerrilla Memorial, Kartuzy. No. 1624, Polish Insurgents' Memorial, Poznan.

Perf. 11½x11, 11x11½
1968, Nov. 15   Engr.
1620 A471 40g slate   .25 .25
1621 A472 40g dull red   .25 .25
1622 A471 40g dark blue   .25 .25
1623 A471 40g sepia   .25 .25
1624 A472 40g sepia   .25 .25
      Nos. 1620-1624 (5)   1.25 1.25

Martyrdom & fight of the Polish people, 1939-45.

Strikers, S.
Lentz
A500

No. 1626, "Manifesto," by Wojciech Weiss. No. 1627, Party members, by F. Kowarski, horiz.

Perf. 11½x11, 11x11½
1968, Nov. 11   Litho.
1625 A500 60g dark red & multi   .25 .25
1626 A500 60g dark red & multi   .25 .25
1627 A500 60g dark red & multi   .25 .25
      Nos. 1625-1627 (3)   .75 .75

5th Cong. of the Polish United Workers' Party.

Departure for the Hunt, by Wojciech
Kossak — A501

Hunt Paintings: 40g, Hunting with Falcon, by Juliusz Kossak. 60g, Wolves' Raid, by A. Wierusz-Kowalski. 1.50z, Bear Hunt, by Julian Falat. 2.50z, Fox Hunt, by T. Sutherland. 3.40z, Boar Hunt, by Frans Snyders. 4.50z, Hunters' Rest, by W. G. Perov. 8.50z, Lion Hunt in Morocco, by Delacroix.

1968, Nov. 20   Perf. 11
1628 A501 20g multicolored   .25 .25
1629 A501 40g multicolored   .25 .25
1630 A501 60g multicolored   .25 .25
1631 A501 1.50z multicolored   .25 .25
1632 A501 2.50z multicolored   .25 .25
1633 A501 3.40z multicolored   .30 .25
1634 A501 4.50z multicolored   .60 .25
1635 A501 8.50z multicolored   1.00 .45
      Nos. 1628-1635 (8)   3.15 2.20

Afghan
Greyhound
A502

Dogs: 20g, Maltese. 40g, Rough-haired fox terrier, vert. 1.50z, Schnauzer. 2.50z, English setter. 3.40z, Pekinese. 4.50z, German shepherd. 8.50z, Pointer.

1969, Feb. 2   Perf. 11x11½, 11½x11½
Dogs in Natural Colors
1636 A502 20g gray & brt grn   .25 .25
1637 A502 40g gray & orange   .40 .25
1638 A502 60g gray & lilac   .40 .25
1639 A502 1.50z gray & black   .40 .25
1640 A502 2.50z gray & brt pink   .50 .25
1641 A502 3.40z gray & dk grn   .60 .25
1642 A502 4.50z gray & ver   1.10 .40
1643 A502 8.50z gray & violet   2.25 .75
      Nos. 1636-1643 (8)   5.90 2.65

General Assembly of the Intl. Kennel Federation, Warsaw, May 1969.

Eagle-on-Shield
House Sign — A503

1969, Feb. 23   Litho.   Perf. 11½x11
1644 A503 60g gray, red & blk   .25 .25

9th Congress of Democratic Movement.

Sheaf of
Wheat
A504

1969, Mar. 29   Litho.   Perf. 11½x11
1645 A504 60g multicolored   .25 .25

5th Congress of the United Peasant Party, Warsaw, March 29-31.

Runner — A505

Olympic Rings and: 20g, Woman gymnast. 40g, Weight lifting. 60g, Women's javelin.

1969, Apr. 25   Litho.   Perf. 11½x11
1646 A505 10g orange & multi   .25 .25
1647 A505 20g ultra & multi   .25 .25
1648 A505 40g yellow & multi   .25 .25
1649 A505 60g red & multi   .25 .25
      Nos. 1646-1649,B114-B117 (8)   3.00 2.10

50th anniv. of the Polish Olympic Committee, and the 75th anniv. of the Intl. Olympic Committee.

Sailboat and Lighthouse, Kolobrzeg
Harbor — A506

40g, Tourist map of Swietokrzyski National Park. 60g, Ruins of 16th cent. castle, Niedzica, vert. 1.50z, Castle of the Dukes of Pomerania & ship, Szczecin. 2.50z, View of Torun & Vistula. 3.40z, View of Klodzko, vert. 4z, View of Sulejow. 4.50z, Market Place, Kazimierz Dolny, vert.

1969, May 20   Litho.   Perf. 11
1650 A506 40g multicolored   .25 .25
1651 A506 60g multicolored   .25 .25
1652 A506 1.35z multicolored   .25 .25
1653 A506 1.50z multicolored   .25 .25

1654	A506	2.50z multicolored	.25	.25
1655	A506	3.40z multicolored	.25	.25
1656	A506	4z multicolored	.40	.25
1657	A506	4.50z multicolored	.45	.25
		Nos. 1650-1657 (8)	2.35	2.00

Issued for tourist publicity. Printed in sheets of 15 stamps and 15 labels. Domestic plants on labels of 40g, 60g and 1.35z, coats of arms on others.

See Nos. 1731-1735.

World Map and Sailboat Opty A507

1969, June 21   Litho.   Perf. 11x11½

1658	A507	60g multicolored	.25	.25

Leonid Teliga's one-man voyage around the world, Casablanca, Jan. 21, 1967, to Las Palmas, Apr. 16, 1969.

Nicolaus Copernicus, Woodcut by Tobias Stimer — A508

Designs: 60g, Copernicus, by Jeremias Falck, 15th century globe and map of constellations. 2.50z, Copernicus, painting by Jan Matejko and map of heliocentric system.

Photo., Engr. & Litho.
1969, June 26   Perf. 11½

1659	A508	40g dl yel, sep & dp car	.25	.25
1660	A508	60g grnsh gray, blk & dp car	.25	.25
1661	A508	2.50z lt vio brn, ol & dp car	.30	.25
		Nos. 1659-1661 (3)	.80	.75

"Memory" Pathfinders' Cross and Protectors' Badge — A509

#1663, "Defense," military eagle and Pathfinders' cross. #1664, "Labor," map of Poland and Pathfinders' cross.

Photo., Engr. & Litho.
1969, July 19   Perf. 11x11½

1662	A509	60g ultra, blk & red	.25	.25
1663	A509	60g green, blk & red	.25	.25
1664	A509	60g carmine, blk & grn	.25	.25
		Nos. 1662-1664 (3)	.75	.75

5th Natl. Alert of Polish Pathfinders' Union.

Frontier Guard and Embossed Arms of Poland — A510

Coal Miner — A511

Designs: No. 1666, Oil refinery-chemical plant, Plock. No. 1667, Combine harvester. No. 1668, Rebuilt Grand Theater, Warsaw. No. 1669, Marie Sklodowska-Curie Monument and University, Lublin. No. 1671, Chemical industry (sulphur) worker. No. 1672, Steelworker. No. 1673, Ship builder and ship.

1969, July 21   Litho. & Embossed

1665	A510	60g red & multi	.25	.25
1666	A510	60g red & multi	.25	.25
1667	A510	60g red & multi	.25	.25
1668	A510	60g red & multi	.25	.25
1669	A510	60g red & multi	.25	.25
a.		Strip of 5, #1665-1669	.40	.40

Perf. 11½x11
Litho.

1670	A511	60g gray & multi	.25	.25
1671	A511	60g gray & multi	.25	.25
1672	A511	60g gray & multi	.25	.25
1673	A511	60g gray & multi	.25	.25
a.		Strip of 4, #1670-1673	.35	.35
		Nos. 1669a,1673a (2)	.75	.75

25th anniv. of the Polish People's Republic.

Landing Module on Moon, and Earth A512

1969, Aug. 21   Litho.   Perf. 12x12½

1674	A512	2.50z multicolored	.90	.35

Man's first landing on the moon, July 20, 1969. US astronauts Neil A. Armstrong and Col. Edwin E. Aldrin, Jr., with Lieut. Col. Michael Collins piloting Apollo 11. Issued in sheets of 8 stamps and 2 tabs, with decorative border. One tab shows Apollo 11 with lunar landing module, the other shows module's take-off from moon. Value, sheet: mint, $22.50, used $16.

"Hamlet," by Jacek Malczewski — A513

Polish Paintings: 20g, Motherhood, by Stanislaw Wyspianski. 60g, Indian Summer (sleeping woman), by Jozef Chelmonski. 2z, Two Girls, by Olga Boznanska, vert. 2.50z, "The Sun of May" (Breakfast on the Terrace), by Jozef Mehoffer, vert. 3.40z, Woman Combing her Hair, by Wladyslaw Slewinski. 5.50z, Still Life, by Jozef Pankiewicz. 7z, The Abduction of the King's Daughter, by Witold Wojtkiewicz.

Perf. 11x11½, 11½x11
1969, Sept. 4   Photo.

1675	A513	20g gold & multi	.25	.25
1676	A513	40g gold & multi	.25	.25
1677	A513	60g gold & multi	.25	.25
1678	A513	2z gold & multi	.25	.25
1679	A513	2.50z gold & multi	.25	.25
1680	A513	3.40z gold & multi	.25	.25
1681	A513	5.50z gold & multi	.55	.30
1682	A513	7z gold & multi	1.00	.35
		Nos. 1675-1682 (8)	3.05	2.15

Issued in sheets of 4 stamps and 2 labels inscribed with painter's name. Pairs, with label, set: mint $3.50, used $2.50.

Nike — A514

1969, Sept. 19   Litho.   Perf. 11½x11

1683	A514	60g gray, red & bister	.25	.25

4th Congress of the Union of Fighters for Freedom and Democracy.

Details from Memorial, Majdanek Concentration Camp — A515

1969, Sept. 20   Perf. 11

1684	A515	40g brt lil, gray & blk	.25	.25

Unveiling of a monument to the victims of the Majdanek concentration camp. The monument was designed by the sculptor Wiktor Tolkin.

Costumes from Krczonow, Lublin — A516

Regional Costumes: 60g, Lowicz, Lodz. 1.15z, Rozbark, Katowice. 1.35z, Lower Silesia, Wroclaw. 1.50z, Opoczno, Lodz. 4.50z, Sacz, Cracow. 5z, Highlanders, Cracow. 7z, Kurpiow, Warsaw.

1969, Sept. 30   Litho.   Perf. 11½x11

1685	A516	40g multicolored	.25	.25
1686	A516	60g multicolored	.25	.25
1687	A516	1.15z multicolored	.25	.25
1688	A516	1.35z multicolored	.25	.25
1689	A516	1.50z multicolored	.25	.25
1690	A516	4.50z multicolored	.40	.25
1691	A516	5z multicolored	.55	.25
1692	A516	7z multicolored	.55	.35
		Nos. 1685-1692 (8)	2.75	2.10

"Walk at Left" — A517

Traffic safety: 60g, "Drive Carefully" (horses on road). 2.50z, "Lower your Lights" (automobile on road).

1969, Oct. 4   Perf. 11

1693	A517	40g multicolored	.25	.25
1694	A517	60g multicolored	.25	.25
1695	A517	2.50z multicolored	.25	.25
		Nos. 1693-1695 (3)	.75	.75

ILO Emblem and Welder's Mask — A518

1969, Oct. 20   Perf. 11x11½

1696	A518	2.50z violet bl & ol	.25	.25

ILO, 50th anniversary.

Bell Foundry A519

Miniatures from Behem's Code, completed 1505: 60g, Painter's studio. 1.35z, Wood carvers. 1.55z, Shoemaker. 2.50z, Cooper. 3.40z, Bakery. 4.50z, Tailor. 7z, Bowyer's shop.

1969, Nov. 12   Perf. 12½

1697	A519	40g gray & multi	.25	.25
1698	A519	60g gray & multi	.25	.25
1699	A519	1.35z gray & multi	.25	.25
1700	A519	1.55z gray & multi	.25	.25
1701	A519	2.50z gray & multi	.25	.25
1702	A519	3.40z gray & multi	.35	.25
1703	A519	4.50z gray & multi	.35	.25
1704	A519	7z gray & multi	.65	.35
		Nos. 1697-1704 (8)	2.60	2.10

Angel — A520

Folk Art (Sculptures): 40g, Sorrowful Christ (head). 60g, Sorrowful Christ (seated figure). 2z, Crying woman. 2.50z, Adam and Eve. 3.40z, Woman with birds.

1969, Dec. 19   Litho.   Perf. 12½
Size: 21x36mm

1705	A520	20g lt blue & multi	.25	.25
1706	A520	40g lilac & multi	.25	.25
1707	A520	60g multicolored	.25	.25
1708	A520	2z multicolored	.25	.25
1709	A520	2.50z multicolored	.25	.25
1710	A520	3.40z multicolored	.25	.25
		Nos. 1705-1710,B118-B119 (8)	2.65	2.00

Leopold Staff (1878-1957) A521

Polish Writers: 60g, Wladyslaw Broniewski (1897-1962). 1.35z, Leon Kruczkowski (1900-1962). 1.50z, Julian Tuwim (1894-1953). 1.55z, Konstanty Ildefons Galczynski (1905-1953). 2.50z, Maria Dabrowska (1889-1965). 3.40z, Zofia Nalkowska (1885-1954).

Litho., Typo. & Engr.
1969, Dec. 30   Perf. 11x11½

1711	A521	40g ol grn & blk, grnsh	.25	.25
1712	A521	60g dp car & blk, pink	.25	.25
1713	A521	1.35z vio bl & blk, grysh	.25	.25
1714	A521	1.50z pur & blk, pink	.25	.25
1715	A521	1.55z dp grn & blk, grnsh	.25	.25

1716 A521 2.50z ultra & blk, *gray* .25 .25
1717 A521 3.40z red brn & blk,
pink .25 .25
Nos. 1711-1717 (7) 1.75 1.75

Statue of
Nike and
Polish
Colors
A522

1970, Jan. 17 Photo. Perf. 11½
1718 A522 60g sil, gold, red &
blk .25 .25

Warsaw liberation, 25th anniversary.

Medieval Print
Shop and
Modern Color
Proofs — A523

1970, Jan. 20 Litho. Perf. 11½x11
1719 A523 60g multicolored .25 .25

Centenary of Polish printers' trade union.

Ringnecked Pheasant — A524

Game Birds: 40g, Mallard drake. 1.15z,
Woodcock. 1.35z, Ruffs (males). 1.50z, Wood
pigeon. 3.40z, Black grouse. 7z, Gray par-
tridges (cock and hen). 8.50z, Capercaillie
cock giving mating call.

1970, Feb. 28 Litho. Perf. 11½
1720 A524 40g multicolored .25 .25
1721 A524 60g multicolored .30 .25
1722 A524 1.15z multicolored .45 .25
1723 A524 1.35z multicolored .45 .25
1724 A524 1.50z multicolored .45 .25
1725 A524 3.40z multicolored .95 .25
1726 A524 7z multicolored 1.25 .50
1727 A524 8.50z multicolored 2.50 .65
Nos. 1720-1727 (8) 6.60 2.65

Lenin in his Kremlin Study, Oct. 1918,
and Polish Lenin Steel Mill — A525

Designs: 60g, Lenin addressing 3rd International Congress in Leningrad, 1920, and Luna
13. 2.50z, Lenin with delegates to 10th Russian Communist Party Congress, Moscow,
1921, dove and globe.

Engr. & Typo.
1970, Apr. 22 Perf. 11
1728 A525 40g grnsh blk & dl
red .25 .25
1729 A525 60g sep & dp lil
rose .25 .25
a. Souvenir sheet of 4 2.50 1.10
1730 A525 2.50z bluish blk & ver .25 .25
Nos. 1728-1730 (3) .75 .75

Lenin (1870-1924), Russian communist
leader.
No. 1729a commemorates the Cracow Intl.
Phil. Exhib.

Tourist Type of 1969
No. 1731, Townhall, Wroclaw, vert. No.
1732, Cathedral, Piast Castle tower and
church towers, Opole. No. 1733, Castle,
Legnica. No. 1734, Castle Tower, Bolkow. No.
1735, Town Hall, Brzeg.

1970, May 9 Litho. Perf. 11
1731 A506 60g Wroclaw .25 .25
1732 A506 60g Opole .25 .25
1733 A506 60g Legnica .25 .25
1734 A506 60g Bolkow .25 .25
1735 A506 60g Brzeg .25 .25
Nos. 1731-1735 (5) 1.25 1.25

Issued for tourist publicity. Printed in sheets
of 15 stamps and 15 labels, showing coats of
arms.

Polish and Russian Soldiers before
Brandenburg Gate — A526

Flower, Eagle
and Arms of 7
Cities — A527

Lithographed and Engraved
1970, May 9 Perf. 11
1736 A526 60g tan & multi .25 .25
Perf. 11½
1737 A527 60g sil, red & sl grn .25 .25

25th anniv. of victory over Germany and of
Polish administration of the Oder-Neisse border area.

Peasant
Movement
Flag
A528

1970, May 15 Litho. Perf. 11½
1738 A528 60g olive & multi .25 .25

Polish peasant movement, 75th anniv.

A529

1970, May 20
1739 A529 2.50z blue & vio bl .25 .25

Inauguration of new UPU headquarters,
Bern.

A530

1970, May 30 Perf. 11½x11
1740 A530 60g multicolored .25 .25

European Soccer Cup Finals. Printed in
sheets of 15 stamps and 15 se-tenant labels
inscribed with the scores of the games.

Lamp of
Learning
A531

1970, June 3 Perf. 11½
1741 A531 60g black, bis & red .25 .25

Plock Scientific Society, 150th anniversary.

Cross-country Race — A532

No. 1743, Runners from ancient Greek
vase. No. 1744, Archer, drawing by W.
Skoczylas.

1970, June 16 Photo. Perf. 11x11½
1742 A532 60g yellow & multi .25 .25
1743 A532 60g black & multi .25 .25
1744 A532 60g dark blue & multi .25 .25
Nos. 1742-1744 (3) .75 .75

10th session of the Intl. Olympic Academy.
See No. B120.

Copernicus, by
Bacciarelli and
View of
Bologna — A533

Designs: 60g, Copernicus, by W. Lesseur
and view of Padua. 2.50z, Copernicus, by
Zinck Nora and view of Ferrara.

Photo., Engr. & Typo.
1970, June 26 Perf. 11½
1745 A533 40g orange & multi .25 .25
1746 A533 60g olive & multi .25 .25
1747 A533 2.50z multicolored .35 .25
Nos. 1745-1747 (3) .85 .75

Aleksander Orlowski (1777-1832),
Self-portrait — A534

Miniatures: 40g, Jan Matejko (1838-1893),
self-portrait. 60g, King Stefan Batory (1533-
1586), anonymous painter. 2z, Maria
Leszczynska (1703-1768), anonymous French
painter. 2.50z, Maria Walewska (1789-1817),
by Marie-Victoire Jaquotot. 3.40z, Tadeusz
Kosciuszko (1746-1817), by Jan Rustem.
5.50z, Samuel Bogumil Linde (1771-1847), by
G. Landolfi. 7z, Michal Oginski (1728-1800),
by Nanette Rosenzweig-Windisch.

Litho. & Photo.
1970, Aug. 27 Perf. 11½
1748 A534 20g gold & multi .25 .25
1749 A534 40g gold & multi .25 .25
1750 A534 60g gold & multi .25 .25
1751 A534 2z gold & multi .25 .25
1752 A534 2.50z gold & multi .25 .25
1753 A534 3.40z gold & multi .25 .25
1754 A534 5.50z gold & multi .45 .25
1755 A534 7z gold & multi .85 .25
Nos. 1748-1755 (8) 2.80 2.00

Nos. 1748-1755 printed in sheets of 4
stamps and 2 labels. Pairs, with label, set:
mint $3.50, used $2.50. The miniatures show
famous Poles and are from collections in the
National Museums in Warsaw and Cracow.

Poster for Chopin
Competition
A535

Photogravure and Engraved
1970, Sept. 8 Perf. 11x11½
1756 A535 2.50z black & vio .25 .25

8th Intl. Chopin Piano Competition, Warsaw,
Oct. 7-25.

UN
Emblem
A536

1970, Sept. 8 Photo. Perf. 11½
1757 A536 2.50z multicolored .25 .25

United Nations, 25th anniversary.

Poles — A537

Design: 60g, Family, home and Polish flag.

1970, Sept. 15 Litho. Perf. 11½x11
1758 A537 40g gray & multi .25 .25
1759 A537 60g multicolored .25 .25

National Census, Dec. 8, 1970.

Grunwald Cross and Warship Piorun
(Thunderbolt) — A538

Grunwald Cross and Warship: 60g, Orzel
(Eagle). 2.50z, Garland.

1970, Sept. 25 Engr. Perf. 11½x11
1760	A538	40g sepia	.25	.25
1761	A538	60g black	.25	.25
1762	A538	2.50z deep brown	.45	.25
		Nos. 1760-1762 (3)	.95	.75

Polish Navy during World War II.

Cellist, by Jerzy Nowosielski A539

Paintings: 40g, View of Lodz, by Benon Liberski. 60g, Studio Concert, by Waclaw Taranczewski. 1.50z, Still Life, by Zbigniew Pronaszko. 2z, Woman Hanging up Laundry, by Andrzej Wroblewski. 3.40z, "Expressions," by Maria Jarema, horiz. 4z, Canal in the Forest, by Piotr Potworowski, horiz. 8.50z, "The Sun," by Wladyslaw Strzeminski, horiz.

1970, Oct. 9 Photo. Perf. 11½
1763	A539	20g multicolored	.25	.25
1764	A539	40g multicolored	.25	.25
1765	A539	60g multicolored	.25	.25
1766	A539	1.50z multicolored	.25	.25
1767	A539	2z multicolored	.25	.25
1768	A539	3.40z multicolored	.25	.25
1769	A539	4z multicolored	.35	.25
1770	A539	8.50z multicolored	.85	.25
		Nos. 1763-1770 (8)	2.70	2.00

Issued for Stamp Day.

Luna 16 Landing on Moon — A540

1970, Nov. 20 Litho. Perf. 11½x11
1771	A540	2.50z multicolored	.35	.25

Luna 16 Russian unmanned, automatic moon mission, Sept. 12-24. Issued in sheets of 8 stamps and 2 tabs. One tab shows rocket launching; the other, parachute landing of capsule. Value, sheet: mint $8.50, used $4.75.

Stag — A541

16th Cent. Tapestries in Wawel Castle: 1.15z, Stork. 1.35z, Leopard fighting dragon. 2z, Man's head. 2.50z, Child holding bird. 4z, God, Adam & Eve. 4.50z, Panel with monogram of King Sigismund Augustus. 5.50z, Poland's coat of arms.

1970, Dec. 23 Photo. Perf. 11½x12
1772	A541	60g multicolored	.25	.25
1773	A541	1.15z purple & multi	.25	.25
1774	A541	1.35z multicolored	.25	.25
1775	A541	2z sepia & multi	.30	.25
1776	A541	2.50z dk blue & multi	.30	.25
1777	A541	4z green & multi	.50	.25
1778	A541	4.50z multicolored	.80	.35
		Nos. 1772-1778 (7)	2.65	1.85

Souvenir Sheet
Imperf
1779	A541	5.50z black & multi	1.25	1.00

No. 1779 contains one 48x57mm stamp. See No. B121.

School Sailing Ship Dar Pomorza — A542

Polish Ships: 60g, Transatlantic Liner Stefan Batory. 1.15z, Ice breaker Perkun. 1.35z, Rescue ship R-1. 1.50z, Freighter Ziemia Szczecinska. 2.50z, Tanker Beskidy. 5z, Express freighter Hel. 8.50z, Ferry Gryf.

1971, Jan. 30 Photo. Perf. 11
1780	A542	40g ver & multi	.25	.25
1781	A542	60g multicolored	.25	.25
1782	A542	1.15z blue & multi	.25	.25
1783	A542	1.35z yellow & multi	.25	.25
1784	A542	1.50z multicolored	.25	.25
1785	A542	2.50z violet & multi	.25	.25
1786	A542	5z multicolored	.40	.25
1787	A542	8.50z blue & multi	.65	.30
		Nos. 1780-1787 (8)	2.55	2.05

Checiny Castle A543

Polish Castles: 40g, Wisnicz. 60g, Bedzin. 2z, Ogrodzieniec. 2.50z, Niedzica. 3.40z, Kwidzyn. 4z, Pieskowa Skala. 8.50z, Lidzbark Warminski.

1971, Mar. 5 Litho. Perf. 11
1788	A543	20g multicolored	.25	.25
1789	A543	40g multicolored	.25	.25
1790	A543	60g multicolored	.25	.25
1791	A543	2z multicolored	.25	.25
1792	A543	2.50z multicolored	.25	.25
1793	A543	3.40z multicolored	.25	.25
1794	A543	4z multicolored	.30	.25
1795	A543	8.50z multicolored	.65	.35
		Nos. 1788-1795 (8)	2.45	2.10

Fighting in Pouilly Castle, Jaroslaw Dabrowski and Walery Wroblewski — A544

1971, Mar. 3 Perf. 12½x12½
1796	A544	60g vio bl, brn & red	.25	.25

Centenary of the Paris Commune.

Seedlings A545

1971, Mar. 30 Photo. Perf. 11½x11
Sizes: 26x34mm (40g, 1.50z);
26x47mm (60g)
1797	A545	40g shown	.25	.25
1798	A545	60g Forest	.25	.25
1799	A545	1.50z Clearing	.25	.25
		Nos. 1797-1799 (3)	.75	.75

Proper forest management.

Bishop Marianos A546

Frescoes from Faras Cathedral, Nubia, 8th-12th centuries: 60g, St. Anne. 1.15z, 1.50z, 7z, Archangel Michael (diff. frescoes). 1.35z, Hermit Anamon of Tuna el Gabel. 4.50z, Cross with symbols of four Evangelists. 5z, Christ protecting Nubian dignitary.

1971, Apr. 20
1800	A546	40g gold & multi	.25	.25
1801	A546	60g gold & multi	.25	.25
1802	A546	1.15z gold & multi	.25	.25
1803	A546	1.35z gold & multi	.25	.25
1804	A546	1.50z gold & multi	.25	.25
1805	A546	4.50z gold & multi	.35	.25
1806	A546	5z gold & multi	.35	.25
1807	A546	7z gold & multi	.50	.25
		Nos. 1800-1807 (8)	2.45	2.00

Polish archaeological excavations in Nubia.

Silesian Insurrectionists — A547

1971, May 3 Photo. Perf. 11
1808	A547	60g dk red brn & gold	.25	.25
a.		Souv. sheet of 3+3 labels	1.00	.50

50th anniversary of the 3rd Silesian uprising. Printed in sheets of 15 stamps and 15 labels showing Silesian Insurrectionists monument in Katowice.

Peacock on the Lawn, by Dorota, 4 years old — A548

Children's Drawings and UNICEF Emblem: 40g, Our Army, horiz. 60g, Spring. 2z, Cat with Ball, horiz. 2.50z, Flowers in Vase. 3.40z, Friendship, horiz. 5.50z, Clown. 7z, The Unknown Planet, horiz.

1971, May 20 Perf. 11½x11, 11x11½
1809	A548	20g multicolored	.25	.25
1810	A548	40g multicolored	.25	.25
1811	A548	60g multicolored	.25	.25
1812	A548	2z multicolored	.25	.25
1813	A548	2.50z multicolored	.25	.25
1814	A548	3.40z multicolored	.25	.25
1815	A548	5.50z multicolored	.35	.25
1816	A548	7z multicolored	.55	.25
		Nos. 1809-1816 (8)	2.40	2.00

25th anniversary of UNICEF.

Fair Emblem — A549

1971, June 1 Photo. Perf. 11½x11
1817	A549	60g ultra, blk & dk car	.25	.25

40th International Poznan Fair, June 13-22.

Collegium Maius, Cracow — A550

40g, Copernicus House, Torun, vert. 2.50z, Olsztyn Castle. 4z, Frombork Cathedral, vert.

1971, June Litho. Perf. 11
1818	A550	40g multicolored	.25	.25
1819	A550	60g blk, red brn & sep	.25	.25
1820	A550	2.50z multicolored	.35	.25
1821	A550	4z multicolored	.50	.25
		Nos. 1818-1821 (4)	1.35	1.00

Nicolaus Copernicus (1473-1543), astronomer. Printed in sheets of 15 with labels showing portrait of Copernicus, page from "Euclid's Geometry," astrolabe or drawing of heliocentric system, respectively.

Paper Cut-out — A551

Designs: Various paper cut-outs (folk art).

Photo., Engr. & Typo.
1971, July 12 Perf. 12x11½
1822	A551	20g blk & brt grn, bluish	.25	.25
1823	A551	40g sl grn & dk ol, lt gray	.25	.25
1824	A551	60g brn & bl, gray	.25	.25
1825	A551	1.15z plum & brn, buff	.25	.25
1826	A551	1.35z dk grn & ver, yel grn	.25	.25
		Nos. 1822-1826 (5)	1.25	1.25

Worker, by Xawery Dunikowski A552

Sculptures: No. 1828, Founder, by Xawery Dunikowski. No. 1829, Miners, by Magdalena Wiecek. No. 1830, Woman harvester, by Stanislaw Horno-Poplawski.

1971, July 21 Photo. Perf. 11½x12
1827	A552	40g silver & multi	.25	.25
1828	A552	40g silver & multi	.25	.25
1829	A552	60g silver & multi	.25	.25
1830	A552	60g silver & multi	.25	.25
a.		Souv. sheet of 4, #1827-1830	2.50	.85
		Nos. 1827-1830 (4)	1.00	1.00

Punched Tape and Cogwheel — A553

1971, Sept. 2 Litho. Perf. 11x11½
1831	A553	60g purple & red	.25	.25

6th Congress of Polish Technicians, held at Poznan, February, 1971.

Angel, by Jozef
Mehoffer,
1901 — A554

Water Lilies, by
Wyspianski
A555

Stained Glass Windows: 60g, Detail from
"The Elements" by Stanislaw Wyspianski.
1.35z, Apollo, by Wyspianski, 1904. 1.55z,
Two Kings, 14th century. 3.40z, Flight into
Egypt, 14th century. 5.50z, St. Jacob the
Elder, 14th century.

1971, Sept. 15   Photo.   Perf. 11½x11

1832	A554	20g gold & multi	.25	.25
1833	A555	40g gold & multi	.25	.25
1834	A555	60g gold & multi	.25	.25
1835	A555	1.35z gold & multi	.25	.25
1836	A554	1.55z gold & multi	.25	.25
1837	A554	3.40z gold & multi	.25	.25
1838	A554	5.50z gold & multi	.35	.25
	Nos. 1832-1838,B122 (8)		2.60	2.10

Mrs. Fedorowicz, by Witold
Pruszkowski (1846-1896) — A556

Paintings of Women: 50g, Woman with
Book, by Tytus Czyzewski (1885-1945). 60g,
Girl with Chrysanthemums, by Olga Boznan-
ska (1865-1940). 2.50z, Girl in Red Dress, by
Jozef Pankiewicz (1866-1940), horiz. 3.40z,
Nude, by Leon Chwistek (1884-1944), horiz.
4.50z, Strange Garden (woman), by Jozef
Mehoffer (1869-1946). 5z, Artist's Wife with
White Hat, by Zbigniew Pronaszko (1885-
1958).

Perf. 11½x11, 11x11½

1971, Oct. 9   Litho.

1839	A556	40g gray & multi	.25	.25
1840	A556	50g gray & multi	.25	.25
1841	A556	60g gray & multi	.25	.25
1842	A556	2.50z gray & multi	.25	.25
1843	A556	3.40z gray & multi	.25	.25
1844	A556	4.50z gray & multi	.35	.25
1845	A556	5z gray & multi	.75	.30
	Nos. 1839-1845,B123 (8)		3.20	2.40

Stamp Day, 1971. Printed in sheets of 4
stamps and 2 labels inscribed "Women in
Polish Paintings." Pairs, with label, set: mint
$5, used $2.75.

Royal
Castle,
Warsaw
A557

1971, Oct. 14   Photo.   Perf. 11x11½

1846	A557	60g gold, blk & brt red	.25	.25

P-11C Dive
Bombers
A558

Planes and Polish Air Force Emblem: 1.50z,
PZL 23-A Karas fighters. 3.40z, PZL Los
bomber.

1971, Oct. 14

1847	A558	90g multicolored	.25	.25
1848	A558	1.50z blue, red & blk	.25	.25
1849	A558	3.40z multicolored	.30	.25
	Nos. 1847-1849 (3)		.80	.75

Martyrs of the Polish Air Force, 1939.

Lunokhod 1 on
Moon — A559

No. 1850, Lunar Rover and Astronauts.

Perf. 11x11½, 11½x11

1971, Nov. 17

1850	A559	2.50z multicolored	.65	.25
1851	A559	2.50z multicolored	.65	.25

Apollo 15 US moon exploration mission,
July 26-Aug. 7 (No. 1850); Luna 17 unmanned
automated USSR moon mission, Nov. 10-17
(No. 1851). Printed in sheets of 6 stamps and
2 labels, with marginal inscriptions.

Worker at
Helm — A560

Shipbuilding
A561

No. 1853, Worker. No. 1855, Apartment
houses under construction. No. 1856, "Bison"
combine harvester. No. 1857, Polish Fiat 125.
No. 1858, Mining tower. No. 1859, Chemical
plant.

1971, Dec. 8   Perf. 11½x11

1852	A560	60g gray, ultra & red	.25	.25
1853	A560	60g red & gray	.25	.25
a.	Pair, #1852-1853 + label		.25	.25

Perf. 11x11½

1854	A561	60g red, gold & blk	.25	.25
1855	A561	60g red, gold & blk	.25	.25
1856	A561	60g red, gold & blk	.25	.25
1857	A561	60g red, gold & blk	.25	.25
1858	A561	60g red, gold & blk	.25	.25
1859	A561	60g red, gold & blk	.25	.25
a.	Souv. sheet of 6, #1854-1859		.90	.50
b.	Block of 6, #1854-1859		.60	.50
	Nos. 1853a,1859b (2)		.85	.75

6th Congress of the Polish United Worker's
Party. No. 1859b has outline of map of Poland
extending over the block.

Cherry Blossoms — A562

Blossoms: 20g, Niedzwiecki's apple. 40g,
Pear. 60g, Peach. 1.15z, Japanese magnolia.
1.35z, Red hawthorne. 2.50z, Apple. 3.40z,
Red chestnut. 5z, Acacia robinia. 8.50z,
Cherry.

1971, Dec. 28   Litho.   Perf. 12½
Blossoms in Natural Colors

1860	A562	10g dull blue & blk	.25	.25
1861	A562	20g grnsh blue & blk	.25	.25
1862	A562	40g lt violet & blk	.25	.25
1863	A562	60g green & blk	.25	.25
1864	A562	1.15z Prus bl & blk	.25	.25
1865	A562	1.35z ocher & blk	.25	.25
1866	A562	2.50z green & blk	.25	.25
1867	A562	3.40z ocher & blk	.35	.25
1868	A562	5z tan & blk	.85	.25
1869	A562	8.50z bister & blk	1.40	.65
	Nos. 1860-1869 (10)		4.35	2.90

Fighting Worker, by J.
Jarnuszkiewicz — A563

Photogravure and Engraved

1972, Jan. 5   Perf. 11½

1870	A563	60g red & black	.25	.25

Polish Workers' Party, 30th anniversary.

Luge and Sapporo '72
Emblem — A564

Sapporo '72 Emblem and: 60g, Women's
slalom, vert. 1.65z, Biathlon, vert. 2.50z, Ski
jump.

1972, Jan. 12   Photo.   Perf. 11

1871	A564	40g silver & multi	.25	.25
1872	A564	60g silver & multi	.25	.25
1873	A564	1.65z silver & multi	.25	.25
1874	A564	2.50z silver & multi	.40	.25
	Nos. 1871-1874 (4)		1.15	1.00

11th Winter Olympic Games, Sapporo,
Japan, Feb. 3-13. See No. B124.

Heart and Electro-cardiogram — A565

1972, Mar. 28   Photo.   Perf. 11½x11

1875	A565	2.50z blue, red & blk	.25	.25

"Your heart is your health," World Health
Day.

Bicyclists
Racing — A566

1972, May 2   Perf. 11

1876	A566	60g silver & multi	.25	.25

25th Warsaw-Berlin-Prague Bicycle Race.

Berlin Monument
A567

1972, May 9   Engr.   Perf. 11½x11

1877	A567	60g grnsh black	.25	.25

Unveiling of monument for Polish soldiers
and German anti-Fascists in Berlin, May 14.

Olympic
Runner — A568

Olympic Rings and "Motion" Symbol and:
30g, Archery. 40g, Boxing. 60g, Fencing.
2.50z, Wrestling. 3.40z, Weight lifting. 5z,
Bicycling. 8.50z, Sharpshooting.

1972, May 20   Perf. 11½x11

1878	A568	20g multicolored	.25	.25
1879	A568	30g multicolored	.25	.25
1880	A568	40g multicolored	.25	.25
1881	A568	60g gray & multi	.25	.25
1882	A568	2.50z multicolored	.25	.25
1883	A568	3.40z multicolored	.25	.25
1884	A568	5z blue & multi	.70	.25
1885	A568	8.50z multicolored	.70	.25
	Nos. 1878-1885 (8)		2.45	2.00

20th Olympic Games, Munich, Aug. 26-
Sept. 10. See No. B125.

Vistula and
Cracow — A569

1972, May 28   Photo.   Perf. 11½x11

1886	A569	60g red, grn & ocher	.25	.25

50th anniversary of Polish Immigrants Society in Germany (Rodlo).

Knight of King Mieszko I — A570

1972, June 12
1887 A570 60g gold, red brn, yel & blk .25 .25

Millennium of the Battle of Cedynia (Cidyny).

Zoo Animals — A571

1972, Aug. 20 Litho. Perf. 12½
1888	A571	20g Cheetah	.25	.25
1889	A571	40g Giraffe, vert	.25	.25
1890	A571	60g Toco toucan	.25	.25
1891	A571	1.35z Chimpanzee	.35	.25
1892	A571	1.65z Gibbon	.35	.25
1893	A571	3.40z Crocodile	.35	.25
1894	A571	4z Kangaroo	1.25	
1895	A571	4.50z Tiger, vert	1.75	.85
1896	A571	7z Zebra	4.00	1.50
		Nos. 1888-1896 (9)	8.80	4.10

Ludwik Warynski — A572

1972, Sept. 1 Photo. Perf. 11
1897 A572 60g multicolored .25 .25

90th anniversary of Proletariat Party, founded by Ludwik Warynski. Printed in sheets of 25 stamps each se-tenant with label showing masthead of party newspaper "Proletariat."

Feliks Dzerzhinski A573

1972, Sept. 11 Litho. Perf. 11x11½
1898 A573 60g red & black .25 .25

Feliks Dzerzhinski (1877-1926), Russian politician of Polish descent.

Congress Emblem — A574

1972, Sept. 15 Photo. Perf. 11½x11
1899 A574 60g multicolored .25 .25

25th Congress of the International Cooperative Union, Warsaw, Sept. 1972.

"In the Barracks," by Moniuszko A575

Scenes from Operas or Ballets by Moniuszko: 20g, The Countess. 40g, The Frightful Castle. 60g, Halka. 1.15z, A New Don Quixote. 1.35z, Verbum Nobile. 1.55z, Ideal. 2.50z, Paria.

Photogravure and Engraved
1972, Sept. 15 Perf. 11½
1900	A575	10g gold & violet	.25	.25
1901	A575	20g gold & dk brn	.25	.25
1902	A575	40g gold & slate grn	.25	.25
1903	A575	60g gold & indigo	.25	.25
1904	A575	1.15z gold & dk blue	.25	.25
1905	A575	1.35z gold & dk blue	.25	.25
1906	A575	1.55z gold & grnsh blk	.25	.25
1907	A575	2.50z gold & dk blue	.30	.25
		Nos. 1900-1907 (8)	2.05	2.00

Stanislaw Moniuszko (1819-72), composer.

"Amazon," by Piotr Michalowski — A576

Paintings: 40g, Ostafi Daszkiewicz, by Jan Matejko. 60g, "Summer Rain" (dancing woman), by Wojciech Gerson. 2z, Woman from Naples, by Aleksander Kotsis. 2.50z, Girl Taking Bath, by Pantaleon Szyndler. 3.40z, Count of Thun (child), by Artur Grottger. 4z, Rhapsodist (old man), by Stanislaw Wyspianski. 60g and 2.50z inscribed "DZIEN ZNACZKA 1972."

1972, Sept. 28 Photo. Perf. 10½x11
1908	A576	30g gold & multi	.25	.25
1909	A576	40g gold & multi	.25	.25
1910	A576	60g gold & multi	.25	.25
1911	A576	2z gold & multi	.25	.25
1912	A576	2.50z gold & multi	.25	.25
1913	A576	3.40z gold & multi	.35	.25
1914	A576	4z gold & multi	.85	.25
		Nos. 1908-1914,B126 (8)	3.85	2.30

Stamp Day.

Copernicus, by Jacob van Meurs, 1654, Heliocentric System — A577

Portraits of Copernicus: 60g, 16th century etching and Prussian coin, 1530. 2.50z, by Jeremiah Falck, 1645, and coat of arms of King of Prussia, 1520. 3.40z, Copernicus with lily of the valley, and page from Theophilactus Simocatta's "Letters on Customs."

1972, Sept. 28 Litho. Perf. 11x11½
1915	A577	40g brt blue & blk	.25	.25
1916	A577	60g ocher & blk	.25	.25
1917	A577	2.50z red & blk	.25	.25
1918	A577	3.40z yellow grn & blk	.40	.25
		Nos. 1915-1918 (4)	1.15	1.00

See No. B127.

Nos. 1337-1338 Surcharged in Red or Black

a   b

1972 Engr. Perf. 11½x11
1919	A445(a)	50g on 40g (R)	.25	.25
1920	A445(a)	90g on 40g (R)	.25	.25
1921	A445(a)	1z on 40g (R)	.25	.25
1922	A445(b)	1.50z on 60g	.25	.25
1923	A445(b)	2.70z on 60g (R)	.25	.25
1924	A445(b)	4z on 60g	.25	.25
1925	A445(b)	4.50z on 60g	.25	.25
1926	A445(b)	4.90z on 60g	.35	.25
		Nos. 1919-1926 (8)	2.10	2.00

Issued: #1919-1920, 11/17; others, 10/2.

The Little Soldier, by E. Piwowarski A578

1972, Oct. 16 Litho. Perf. 11½
1927 A578 60g rose & black .25 .25

Children's health center (Centrum Zdrowia Dzieck), to be built as memorial to children killed during Nazi regime.

Warsaw Royal Castle, 1656, by Erik J. Dahlbergh — A579

1972, Oct. 16 Photo. Perf. 11x11½
1928 A579 60g violet, bl & blk .25 .25

Rebuilding of Warsaw Castle, destroyed during World War II.

Ribbons with Symbols of Trade Union Activities — A580

1972, Nov. 13 Perf. 11½x11
1929 A580 60g multicolored .25 .25

7th and 13th Polish Trade Union congresses, Nov. 13-15.

Mountain Lodge, Chocholowska Valley — A581

Mountain Lodges in Tatra National Park: 60g, Hala Ornak, West Tatra, horiz. 1.55z, Hala Gasienicowa. 1.65z, Pieciu Stawow Valley, horiz. 2.50z, Morskie Oko, Rybiego Potoku Valley

1972, Nov. 13 Perf. 11
1930	A581	40g multicolored	.25	.25
1931	A581	60g multicolored	.25	.25
1932	A581	1.55z multicolored	.25	.25
1933	A581	1.65z multicolored	.25	.25
1934	A581	2.50z multicolored	.35	.25
		Nos. 1930-1934 (5)	1.35	1.25

Japanese Azalea — A582

Flowering Shrubs: 50g, Alpine rose. 60g, Pomeranian honeysuckle. 1.65z, Chinese quince. 2.50z, Viburnum. 3.40z, Rhododendron. 4z, Mock orange. 8.50z, Lilac.

1972, Dec. 15 Litho. Perf. 12½
1935	A582	40g gray & multi	.25	.25
1936	A582	50g blue & multi	.25	.25
1937	A582	60g multicolored	.25	.25
1938	A582	1.65z ultra & multi	.25	.25
1939	A582	2.50z ocher & multi	.35	.25
1940	A582	3.40z multicolored	.35	.25
1941	A582	4z multicolored	.70	.25
1942	A582	8.50z multicolored	1.00	.45
		Nos. 1935-1942 (8)	3.40	2.20

Emblem — A583

1972, Dec. 15 Photo. Perf. 11½
1943 A583 60g red & multi .25 .25

5th Congress of Socialist Youth Union.

Copernicus — A584

Coil Stamps

1972, Dec. 28 Photo. Perf. 14
1944	A584	1z deep claret	.25	.25
1945	A584	1.50z yellow brown	.25	.25

Nicolaus Copernicus (1473-1543), astronomer. Black control number on back of every 5th stamp.

Piast Knight, 10th Century A585

Polish Cavalry: 40g, Knight, 13th century. 60g, Knight of Ladislas Jagello, 15th century, horiz. 1.35z, Hussar, 17th century. 4z, National Guard Uhlan, 18th century. 4.50z, Congress Kingdom Period, 1831. 5z, Light cavalry, 1939, horiz. 7z, Light cavalry, People's Army, 1945.

1972, Dec. 28   **Perf. 11**
1946	A585	20g violet & multi	.25	.25
1947	A585	40g multicolored	.25	.25
1948	A585	60g orange & multi	.25	.25
1949	A585	1.35z orange & multi	.25	.25
1950	A585	4z orange & multi	.25	.25
1951	A585	4.50z orange & multi	.35	.25
1952	A585	5z brown & multi	.70	.25
1953	A585	7z multicolored	1.20	.75
	Nos. 1946-1953 (8)		3.50	2.50

Man and Woman, Sculpture by Wiera Muchina — A586

Design: 60g, Globe with Red Star.

1972, Dec. 30
1954	A586	40g gray & multi	.25	.25
1955	A586	60g blk, red & vio bl	.25	.25

50th anniversary of the Soviet Union.

Nicolaus Copernicus, by M. Bacciarelli A587

Portraits of Copernicus: 1.50z, painted in Torun, 16th century. 2.70z, by Zinck Nor. 4z, from Strasbourg clock. 4.90z, Copernicus in his Observatory, by Jan Matejko, horiz.

Perf. 11½x11, 11x11½
1973, Feb. 18   **Photo.**
1956	A587	1z brown & multi	.25	.25
1957	A587	1.50z multicolored	.25	.25
1958	A587	2.70z multicolored	.25	.25
1959	A587	4z multicolored	.35	.25
1960	A587	4.90z multicolored	.45	.25
	Nos. 1956-1960 (5)		1.55	1.25

Piast Coronation Sword, 12th Century — A588

Polish Art: No. 1962, Kruzlowa Madonna, c. 1410. No. 1963, Hussar's armor, 17th century. No. 1964, Wawel head, wood, 16th century. No. 1965, Cock, sign of Rifle Fraternity, 16th century. 2.70z, Cover of Queen Anna Jagiellonka's prayer book (eagle), 1582. 4.90z,

Skarbimierz Madonna, wood, c. 1340. 8.50z, The Nobleman Tenczynski, portrait by unknown artist, 17th century.

1973, Mar. 28   Photo.   Perf. 11½x11
1961	A588	50g violet & multi	.25	.25
1962	A588	1z lt blue & multi	.25	.25
1963	A588	1z ultra & multi	.25	.25
1964	A588	1.50z blue & multi	.25	.25
1965	A588	1.50z green & multi	.25	.25
1966	A588	2.70z multicolored	.25	.25
1967	A588	4.90z multicolored	.45	.25
1968	A588	8.50z black & multi	.75	.25
	Nos. 1961-1968 (8)		2.70	2.00

Lenin Monument, Nowa Huta — A589

1973, Apr. 28   Litho.   Perf. 11x11½
1969	A589	1z multicolored	.25	.25

Unveiling of Lenin Monument at Nowa Huta.

Envelope Showing Postal Code A590

1973, May 5   **Perf. 11x11½**
1970	A590	1.50z multicolored	.25	.25

Introduction of postal code system in Poland.

Wolf — A591

1973, May 21   Photo.   Perf. 11
1971	A591	50g shown	.25	.25
1972	A591	1z Mouflon	.25	.25
1973	A591	1.50z Moose	.25	.25
1974	A591	2.70z Capercaillie	.35	.25
1975	A591	3z Deer	.70	.25
1976	A591	4.50z Lynx	1.20	.25
1977	A591	4.90z European hart	2.00	.85
1978	A591	5z Wild boar	2.00	1.00
	Nos. 1971-1978 (8)		7.00	3.35

Intl. Hunting Committee Congress and 50th anniv. of Polish Hunting Assoc.

US Satellite "Copernicus" over Earth — A592

No. 1980, USSR satellite Salyut over earth.

1973, June 20
1979	A592	4.90z multicolored	.35	.25
1980	A592	4.90z multicolored	.35	.25

American and Russian astronomical observatories in space. No. 1979 and No. 1980 issued in sheets of 6 stamps and 2 labels. Value: mint $14, used $7.

Flame Rising from Book — A593

1973, June 26   **Litho.**
1981	A593	1.50z blue & multi	.25	.25

2nd Polish Science Cong., Warsaw, June 26-29.

Arms of Poznan on 14th Century Seal — A594

Polska '73 Emblem and: 1.50z, Tombstone of Nicolas Tomicki, 1524. 2.70z, Kalisz paten, 12th century. 4z, Lion knocker from bronze gate, Gniezno, 12th century, horiz.

Perf. 11½x11, 11x11½
1973, June 30
1982	A594	1z pink & multi	.25	.25
1983	A594	1.50z orange & multi	.25	.25
1984	A594	2.70z buff & multi	.25	.25
1985	A594	4z yellow & multi	.30	.25
	Nos. 1982-1985 (4)		1.05	1.00

POLSKA '73 Intl. Phil. Exhib., Poznan, Aug. 19-Sept. 2. See No. B128.

Marceli Nowotko — A595

1973, Aug. 8   Litho.   Perf. 11½x11
1986	A595	1.50z red & black	.25	.25

Marceli Nowotko (1893-1942), labor leader, member of Central Committee of Communist Party of Poland.

Emblem and Orchard — A596

Human Environment Emblem and: 90g, Grazing cows. 1z, Stork's nest. 1.50z, Pond with fish and water lilies. 2.70z, Flowers on meadow. 4.90z, Underwater fauna and flora. 5z, Forest scene. 6.50z, Still life.

1973, Aug. 30   Photo.   Perf. 11
1987	A596	50g black & multi	.25	.25
1988	A596	90g black & multi	.25	.25
1989	A596	1z black & multi	.25	.25
1990	A596	1.50z black & multi	.25	.25
1991	A596	2.70z black & multi	.25	.25
1992	A596	4.90z black & multi	.45	.25
1993	A596	5z black & multi	1.00	.40
1994	A596	6.50z black & multi	1.50	.70
	Nos. 1987-1994 (8)		4.20	2.60

Protection of the environment.

Motorcyclist — A597

1973, Sept. 2   **Perf. 11½**
1995	A597	1.50z silver & multi	.25	.25

Finals in individual world championship motorcycle race on cinder track, Chorzów, Sept. 2.

Tank — A598

1973, Oct. 12   Litho.   Perf. 12½
1996	A598	1z shown	.25	.25
1997	A598	1z Fighter plane	.25	.25
1998	A598	1.50z Missile	.50	.25
1999	A598	1.50z Warship	.35	.25
	Nos. 1996-1999 (4)		1.35	1.00

Polish People's Army, 30th anniversary.

Grzegorz Piramowicz — A599

Design: 1.50z, J. Sniadecki, Hugo Kollataj and Julian Ursyn Niemcewicz.

Photogravure and Engraved
1973, Oct. 13   **Perf. 11½x11**
2000	A599	1z buff & dk brn	.25	.25
2001	A599	1.50z gray & sl grn	.25	.25

Natl. Education Commission, bicent.

Henryk Arctowski, and Penguins A600

Polish Scientists: No. 2003, Pawel Edmund Strzelecki and Kangaroo. No. 2004, Benedykt Tadeusz Dybowski and Lake Baikal. No. 2005, Stefan Rogozinski, sailing ship "Lucja-Malgorzata." 2z, Bronislaw Malinowski, Trobriand Island drummers. 2.70z, Stefan Drzewiecki and submarine. 3z, Edward Adolf Strasburger and plants. 8z, Ignacy Domeyko, geological strata.

1973, Nov. 30   Photo.   Perf. 10½x11
2002	A600	1z gold & multi	.25	.25
2003	A600	1z gold & multi	.25	.25
2004	A600	1.50z gold & multi	.25	.25
2005	A600	1.50z gold & multi	.25	.25
2006	A600	2z gold & multi	.25	.25
2007	A600	2.70z gold & multi	.25	.25
2008	A600	3z gold & multi	.40	.30
2009	A600	8z gold & multi	.85	.50
	Nos. 2002-2009 (8)		2.75	2.30

Polish Flag — A601

1973, Dec. 15 Photo. Perf. 11½x11
2010 A601 1.50z dp ultra, red & gold   .25 .25

Polish United Workers' Party, 25th anniv.

Jelcz-Berliet Bus — A602

Designs: Polish automotives.

1973, Dec. 28 Photo. Perf. 11x11½
2011 A602 50g shown   .25 .25
2012 A602 90g Jelcz 316   .35 .25
2013 A602 1z Polski Fiat 126p .25 .25
2014 A602 1.50z Polski Fiat 125p .25 .25
2015 A602 4z Nysa M-521 bus   .35 .25
2016 A602 4.50z Star 660 truck .50 .25
      Nos. 2011-2016 (6)   1.95 1.50

Iris — A603

Flowers: 1z, Dandelion. 1.50z, Rose. 3z, Thistle. 4z, Cornflowers. 4.50z, Clover. (Paintings by Stanislaw Wyspianski.)

1974, Jan. 22 Engr. Perf. 12x11½
2017 A603 50g lilac   .25 .25
2018 A603 1z green   .25 .25
2019 A603 1.50z red orange   .25 .25
2020 A603 3z deep violet   .25 .25
2021 A603 4z violet blue   .30 .25
2022 A603 4.50z emerald   .35 .25
      Nos. 2017-2022 (6)   1.65 1.50

Cottage, Kurpie A604

Designs: 1.50z, Church, Sekowa. 4z, Town Hall, Sulmierzyce. 4.50z, Church, Lachowice. 4.90z, Windmill, Sobienie-Jeziory. 5z, Orthodox Church, Ulucz.

1974, Mar. 5 Photo. Perf. 11x11½
2023 A604 1z multicolored   .25 .25
2024 A604 1.50z yellow & multi .25 .25
2025 A604 4z pink & multi   .25 .25
2026 A604 4.50z lt blue & multi .25 .25
2027 A604 4.90z multicolored .35 .25
2028 A604 5z pink & multi   .70 .25
      Nos. 2023-2028 (6)   2.05 1.50

Mail Coach and UPU Emblem — A605

1974, Mar. 30   Perf. 11½x12
2029 A605 1.50z multicolored   .25 .25

Centenary of Universal Postal Union.

Embroidery from Cracow — A606

Embroideries from: 1.50z, Lowicz. 4z, Slask.

1974, May 7 Photo. Perf. 11½x11
2030 A606 50g multicolored   .25 .25
2031 A606 1.50z multicolored .25 .25
2032 A606 4z multicolored   .30 .25
  a. Souvenir sheet of 3 #2032, imperf.   1.25 1.00
  b. As "a," perf. 11½x11   5.00 5.00
      Nos. 2030-2032 (3)   .80 .75

SOCPHILEX IV International Philatelic Exhibition, Katowice, May 18-June 2.
No. 2032a sold for 17z.
No. 2032b sold for 17z plus 15z for 4 envelopes.

Association Emblem — A607

1974, May 8 Litho. Perf. 12x11½
2033 A607 1.50z gray & red   .25 .25

5th Congress of the Assoc. of Combatants for Liberty & Democracy, Warsaw, May 8-9.

Soldier and Dove — A608

1974, May 9   Perf. 11½x11
2034 A608 1.50z org, lt bl & blk .25 .25

29th anniversary of victory over Fascism.

Comecon Building, Moscow A609

1974, May 15   Perf. 11x11½
2035 A609 1.50z gray bl, bis & red   .25 .25

25th anniv. of the Council of Mutual Economic Assistance.

Soccer Ball and Games' Emblem A610

Design: No. 2037, Soccer players, Olympic rings and 1972 medal.

1974, June 15 Photo. Perf. 11x11½
2036 A610 4.90z olive & multi   .50 .25
  a. Souv. sheet of 4 + 2 labels 4.50 2.00
2037 A610 4.90z olive & multi   .50 .25
  a. Souv. sheet, 2 each #2036-2037   12.00 7.00

World Cup Soccer Championship, Munich, June 13-July 7.

No. 2036a issued to commemorate Poland's silver medal in 1974 Championship.

Sailing Ship, 16th Century — A611

Polish Sailing Ships: 1.50z, "Dal," 1934. 2.70z, "Opty," sailed around the world, 1969. 4z, "Dar Pomorza," winner "Operation Sail," 1972. 4.90z, "Polonez," sailed around the world, 1973.

1974, June 29 Litho. Perf. 11½x11
2038 A611 1z multicolored   .25 .25
2039 A611 1.50z multicolored .25 .25
2040 A611 2.70z multicolored .25 .25
2041 A611 4z green & multi   .35 .25
2042 A611 4.90z dp blue & multi .70 .25
      Nos. 2038-2042 (5)   1.80 1.25

Chess, by Jan Kochanowski A612

Design: 1.50z, "Education," etching by Daniel Chodowiecki.

1974, July 15 Litho. Perf. 11½x11
2043 A612 1z multicolored   .25 .25
2044 A612 1.50z multicolored .30 .25

10th International Chess Festival, Lublin.

Man and Map of Poland — A613

Polish Eagle — A614

1974, July 21 Photo. Perf. 11½x11
2045 A613 1.50z black, gold & red   .25 .25
2046 A614 1.50z silver & multi .25 .25
2047 A614 1.50z red & multi   .25 .25
      Nos. 2045-2047 (3)   .75 .75

People's Republic of Poland, 30th anniv.

Lazienkowska Bridge Road — A615

1974, July 21   Perf. 11x11½
2048 A615 1.50z multicolored   .25 .25

Opening of Lazienkowska Bridge over Vistula south of Warsaw.

Strawberries and Congress Emblem — A616

1974, Sept. 10 Photo. Perf. 11½
2049 A616 50g shown   .25 .25
2050 A616 90g Black currants .25 .25
2051 A616 1z Apples   .25 .25
2052 A616 1.50z Cucumbers   .35 .25
2053 A616 2.70z Tomatoes   .35 .25
2054 A616 4.50z Peas   .35 .25
2055 A616 4.90z Pansies   .70 .35
2056 A616 6.50z Nasturtiums   1.25 .75
      Nos. 2049-2056 (8)   3.75 2.60

19th Intl. Horticultural Cong., Warsaw, Sept.

Civic Militia and Security Service Badge — A617

1974, Oct. 3 Photo. Perf. 11½x11
2057 A617 1.50g multicolored   .25 .25

30th anniv. of the Civic Militia and the Security Service.

Polish Child, by Lukasz Orlowski — A618

Polish paintings of Children: 90g, Girl with Pigeon, Anonymous artist, 19th century. 1z, Girl, by Stanislaw Wyspianski. 1.50z, The Orphan from Poronin, by Wladyslaw Slewinski. 3z, Peasant Boy, by Kazimierz Sichulski. 4.50z, Florentine Page, by Aleksander Gierymski. 4.90z, The Artist's Son Tadeusz, by Piotr Michalowski. 6.50z, Boy with Doe, by Aleksander Kotsis.

1974, Oct. 9
2058 A618 50g multicolored   .25 .25
2059 A618 90g multicolored   .25 .25
2060 A618 1z multicolored   .25 .25
2061 A618 1.50z multicolored .25 .25
2062 A618 3z multicolored   .25 .25
2063 A618 4.50z multicolored .30 .25
2064 A618 4.90z multicolored .50 .25
2065 A618 6.50z multicolored .50 .30
      Nos. 2058-2065 (8)   2.55 2.05

Children's Day. The 1z and 1.50z are inscribed "Dzien Znaczka (Stamp Day) 1974."

Cracow
Manger — A619

King Sigismund
Vasa — A620

Masterpieces of Polish art: 1.50z, Flight into
Egypt, 1465. 4z, King Jan Olbracht.

1974, Dec. 2   Litho.   Perf. 11½x11
2066 A619   1z multicolored   .25 .25
2067 A620   1.50z multicolored   .25 .25
2068 A620   2z multicolored   .25 .25
2069 A619   4z multicolored   .45 .25
      Nos. 2066-2069 (4)   1.20 1.00

Angler — A621

Designs: 1.50z, Hunter with bow and arrow.
4z, Boy snaring geese. 4.50z, Beekeeper.
Designs from 16th century woodcuts.

1974-77   Engr.   Perf. 11½x11
2070   A621   1z black   .25 .25
2071   A621   1.50z indigo   .25 .25
2071A A621   4z slate green   .25 .25
2071B A621   4.50z dark brown   .25 .25
       Nos. 2070-2071B (4)   1.00 1.00

Issued: 1z-1.50z, 12/30; 4z-4.50z, 12/12/77.

Pablo Neruda,
by Osvaldo
Guayasamin
A622

1974, Dec. 31   Litho.   Perf. 11½x11
2072 A622   1.50z multicolored   .25 .25

Pablo Neruda (1904-1973), Chilean poet.

Nike Monument and Opera House,
Warsaw — A623

1975, Jan. 17   Photo.   Perf. 11
2073 A623   1.50z multicolored   .25 .25

30th anniversary of the liberation of Warsaw.

Hobby
Falcon — A624

No. 2074, Lesser kestrel, male. No. 2075,
Lesser kestrel, female. No. 2076, Red-footed
falcon, male. No. 2077, Red-footed falcon,
female. No. 2079, Kestrel. No. 2080, Merlin.
No. 2081, Peregrine.

1975, Jan. 23   Perf. 11½x12
2074 A624   1z multi   .25 .25
2075 A624   1z multi   .25 .25
   a.   Pair, #2074-2075   .35 .25
2076 A624   1.50z multi   .50 .25
2077 A624   1.50z multi   .50 .25
   a.   Pair, #2076-2077   1.00 .25
2078 A624   2z shown   .50 .25
2079 A624   3z multi   .65 .35
2080 A624   4z multi   2.00 1.20
2081 A624   8z multi   3.00 1.40
       Nos. 2074-2081 (8)   7.65 4.20

Falcons.

"Auschwitz"
A625

Photogravure and Engraved
1975, Jan. 27   Perf. 11½x11
2082 A625   1.50z red & black   .40 .25

30th anniversary of the liberation of
Auschwitz (Oswiecim) concentration camp.

Women's
Hurdle
Race
A626

Designs: 1.50z, Pole vault. 4z, Hop, step
and jump. 4.90z, Sprinting.

1975, Mar. 8   Litho.   Perf. 11x11½
2083 A626   1z multicolored   .25 .25
2084 A626   1.50z olive & multi   .25 .25
2085 A626   4z multicolored   .35 .25
2086 A626   4.90z green & multi   .45 .25
       Nos. 2083-2086 (4)   1.30 1.00

6th European Indoor Athletic Championships, Katowice, Mar. 1975.

St. Anne,
by Veit
Stoss,
Arphila
Emblem
A627

1975, Apr. 15   Photo.   Perf. 11x11½
2087 A627   1.50z multicolored   .25 .25

ARPHILA 75, International Philatelic Exhibition, Paris, June 6-10.

Amateur
Radio
Union
Emblem,
Globe
A628

1975, Apr. 15   Litho.   Perf. 11½
2088 A628   1.50z multicolored   .25 .25

International Amateur Radio Union Conference, Warsaw, Apr. 1975.

Mountain Guides' Badge and Sudetic
Mountains — A629

No. 2089, Pine, badge and Tatra Mountains,
vert. No. 2090, Gentian and Tatra Mountains,
vert. No. 2092, Yew branch with berries, and
Sudetic Mountains. No. 2093, River, Beskids
Mountains and badge, vert. No. 2094, Arnica
and Beskids Mountains, vert.

1975, Apr. 30   Photo.   Perf. 11
2089 A629   1z multicolored   .25 .25
2090 A629   1z multicolored   .25 .25
   a.   Pair, #2089-2090   .25 .25
2091 A629   1.50z multicolored   .25 .25
2092 A629   1.50z multicolored   .25 .25
   a.   Pair, #2091-2092   .30 .25
2093 A629   4z multicolored   .25 .25
2094 A629   4z multicolored   .25 .25
   a.   Pair, #2093-2094   .60 .25
       Nos. 2090a,2092a,2094a (3) 1.15 .75

Centenary of Polish Mountain Guides Organizations. Pairs have continuous design.

Hands Holding
Tulips and
Rifle — A630

1975, May 9   Perf. 11½x11
2095 A630   1.50z blue & multi   .25 .25

End of WWII, 30th anniv.; victory over
Fascism.

Warsaw Treaty
Members'
Flags — A631

1975, May 14
2096 A631   1.50z blue & multi   .25 .25

20th anniversary of the signing of the Warsaw Treaty (Bulgaria, Czechoslovakia, German Democratic Rep., Hungary, Poland,
Romania, USSR).

Cock and Hen, Congress
Emblem — A632

1975, June 23   Photo.   Perf. 12x11½
2097 A632   50g shown   .25 .25
2098 A632   1z Geese   .25 .25
2099 A632   1.50z Cattle   .25 .25
2100 A632   2z Cow   .25 .25
2101 A632   3z Arabian stallion .30 .25
2102 A632   4z Wielkopolska
             horses   .50 .25
2103 A632   4.50z Pigs   1.25 .50
2104 A632   5z Sheep   1.75 1.40
       Nos. 2097-2104 (8)   4.80 3.40

20th Congress of the European Zootechni-
cal Federation, Warsaw.

Apollo and
Soyuz
Linked in
Space
A633

1975, July 15   Perf. 11x11½
2105 A633   1.50z shown   .25 .25
2106 A633   4.90z Apollo   .35 .25
2107 A633   4.90z Soyuz   .35 .25
   a.   Souv. sheet, 2 each #2105-
        2107 + 2 labels   5.25 2.25
   b.   Pair, #2106-2107   .75 .35
       Nos. 2105-2107 (3)   .95 .75

Apollo Soyuz space test project (Russo-
American cooperation), launching July 15;
link-up, July 17.

Health Fund
Emblem — A634

1975, July 12   Perf. 11½x11
2108 A634   1.50z silver, blk & bl   .25 .25

National Fund for Health Protection.

"E" and
Polish Flag
A635

1975, July 30   Litho.   Perf. 11x11½
2109 A635   4z lt blue, red & blk   .40 .25

European Security and Cooperation Conference, Helsinki, July 30-Aug. 1.

UN Emblem
and
Sunburst
A636

1975, July 25
2110 A636   4z blue & multi   .45 .25

30th anniversary of the United Nations.

Bolek and Lolek A637

Cartoon Characters and Children's Health Center Emblem: 1z, Jacek and Agatka. 1.50z, Reksio, the dog. 4z, Telesfor, the dragon.

1975, Aug. 30   Photo.   Perf. 11x11½
2111	A637	50g violet bl & multi	.25	.25
2112	A637	1z multicolored	.25	.25
2113	A637	1.50z multicolored	.25	.25
2114	A637	4z multicolored	.35	.25
		Nos. 2111-2114 (4)	1.10	1.00

Children's television programs.

Circular Bar Graph and Institute's Emblem — A638

1975, Sept. 1   Litho.   Perf. 11½x11
2115	A638	1.50z multicolored	.25	.25

International Institute of Statistics, 40th session, Warsaw, Sept. 1975.

IWY Emblem, White, Yellow and Brown Women — A639

1975, Sept. 8   Photo.
2116	A639	1.50z multicolored	.25	.25

International Women's Year.

A640

George Washington A641

Designs: 1z, First Poles Arriving on "Mary and Margaret" 1608. 1.50z, Polish glass blower and glass works, Jamestown, 1608. 2.70z, Helena Modrzejewska (1840-1909), Polish actress, came to US in 1877. 4z, Casimir Pulaski (1747-1779), and 6.40z, Tadeusz Kosciusko (1748-1817), heroes of American War of Independence.

1975, Sept. 24   Litho.   Perf. 11x11½
2117	A640	1z black & multi	.25	.25
2118	A640	1.50z black & multi	.25	.25
2119	A640	2.70z black & multi	.25	.25
2120	A640	4z black & multi	.40	.25
2121	A640	6.40z black & multi	.60	.30
		Nos. 2117-2121 (5)	1.75	1.30

Souvenir Sheet
Perf. 12
2122		Sheet of 3+3 labels	1.75	.85
a.		A641 4.90z shown	.40	.25
b.		A641 4.90z Kosciusko	.40	.25
c.		A641 4.90z Pulaski	.40	.25

American Revolution, bicentenary.

Albatross Biplane, 1918-1925 A642

Design: 4.90z, IL 62 jet, 1975.

1975, Sept. 25   Perf. 11x11½
2123	A642	2.40z buff & multi	.25	.25
2124	A642	4.90z gray & multi	.30	.25

50th anniversary of Polish air post stamps.

Frederic Chopin — A643

1975, Oct. 7   Photo.
2125	A643	1.50z gold, lt vio & blk	.25	.25

9th International Chopin Piano Competition, Warsaw, Oct. 7-28.
Printed in sheets of 50 stamps with alternating labels with commemorative inscription.

Dunikowski, Self-portrait A644

Sculptures: 1z, "Breath." 1.50z, "Maternity."

1975, Oct. 9   Perf. 11½x11
2126	A644	50g silver & multi	.25	.25
2127	A644	1z silver & multi	.25	.25
2128	A644	1.50z silver & multi	.25	.25
		Nos. 2126-2128 (3)	.75	.75

Stamp Day. Xawery Dunikowski (1875-1964), sculptor. See No. B131.

Town Hall, Zamosc — A645

1z, Arcades, Kazimierz Dolny, horiz.

Coil Stamps

1975, Nov. 11   Photo.   Perf. 14
2129	A645	1z olive green	.25	.25
2130	A645	1.50z rose brown	.25	.25

European Architectural Heritage Year. Black control number on back of every fifth stamp of Nos. 2129-2130.

Lodz, by Wladyslaw Strzeminski A646

1975, Nov. 22   Litho.   Perf. 12½
2131	A646	4.50z multicolored	.35	.25
a.		Souvenir sheet	.80	.40

Lodz 75, 12th Polish Philatelic Exhibition, for 25th anniv. of Polish Philatelists Union.

Piast Family Eagle A647

1.50z, Seal of Prince Boleslaw of Legnica. 4z, Coin of Prince Jerzy Wilhelm (1660-1675).

1975, Nov. 29   Engr.   Perf. 11x11½
2132	A647	1z green	.25	.25
2133	A647	1.50z brown	.25	.25
2134	A647	4z dull violet	.25	.25
		Nos. 2132-2134 (3)	.75	.75

Piast dynasty's influence on the development of Silesia.

"7" Inscribed "ZJAZD" and "PZPR" — A648

"VII ZJAZD PZPR" — A649

1975, Dec. 8   Photo.   Perf. 11½x11
2135	A648	1z lt blue & multi	.25	.25
2136	A649	1.50z silver, red & ultra	.25	.25

7th Cong. of Polish United Workers' Party.

Ski Jump A650

Designs (Winter Olympic Games Emblem and): 1z, Ice hockey. 1.50z, Slalom. 2z, Speed skating. 4z, Luge. 6.40z, Biathlon.

1976, Jan. 10   Perf. 11x11½
2137	A650	50g silver & multi	.25	.25
2138	A650	1z silver & multi	.25	.25
2139	A650	1.50z silver & multi	.25	.25
2140	A650	2z silver & multi	.25	.25
2141	A650	4z silver & multi	.30	.25
2142	A650	6.40z silver & multi	.70	.35
		Nos. 2137-2142 (6)	2.00	1.60

12th Winter Olympic Games, Innsbruck, Austria, Feb. 4-15.

Engine by Richard Trevithick, 1803 — A651

Locomotives by: 1z, M. Murray and J. Blenkinsop, 1810. No. 2145, George Stephenson's Rocket, 1829. No. 2146, Polish electric locomotive, 1969. 2.70z, Stephenson, 1837. 3z, Joseph Harrison, 1840. 4.50z, Thomas Rogers, 1855. 4.90z, Chrzanow (Polish), 1922.

1976, Feb. 13   Photo.   Perf. 11½x12
2143	A651	50g multicolored	.25	.25
2144	A651	1z multicolored	.25	.25
2145	A651	1.50z multicolored	.25	.25
2146	A651	1.50z multicolored	.25	.25
2147	A651	2.70z multicolored	.25	.25
2148	A651	3z multicolored	.35	.25
2149	A651	4.50z multicolored	.55	.25
2150	A651	4.90z multicolored	.85	.35
		Nos. 2143-2150 (8)	3.00	2.10

History of the locomotive.

Telephone, Radar and Satellites, ITU Emblem — A652

1976, Mar. 10   Perf. 11
2151	A652	1.50z multicolored	.25	.25

Centenary of first telephone call by Alexander Graham Bell, Mar. 10, 1876.

Atom Symbol and Flags of Communist Countries A653

1976, Mar. 10   Litho.   Perf. 11½
2152	A653	1.50z multicolored	.25	.25

Joint Institute of Nuclear Research, Dubna, USSR, 20th anniversary.

Ice Hockey — A654

Design: 1.50z, like 1z, reversed.

1976, Apr. 8   Photo.   Perf. 11½x11
2153	A654	1z multicolored	.25	.25
2154	A654	1.50z multicolored	.25	.25

Ice Hockey World Championship 1976, Katowice.

Soldier and Map of Sinai A655

1976, Apr. 30   Photo.   Perf. 11x11½
2155	A655	1.50z multicolored	.25	.25

Polish specialist troops serving with UN Forces in Sinai Peninsula.
No. 2155 printed se-tenant with label with commemorative inscription.

Sappers' Monument, by Stanislaw Kulow, Warsaw — A656

Design: No. 2157, First Polish Army Monument, by Bronislaw Koniuszy, Warsaw.

1976, May 8   *Perf. 11½*
2156 A656 1z gold & multi   .25 .25
2157 A656 1z silver & multi   .25 .25
Memorials unveiled on 30th anniv. of WWII victory.

Interphil 76, Philadelphia
A657

1976, May 20 *Litho.* *Perf. 11½x11*
2158 A657 8.40z gray & multi   .45 .25
Interphil 76, Intl. Phil. Exhib., Philadelphia, May 29-June 6.

Wielkopolski Park and Owl — A658

National Parks: 1z, Wolinski Park and eagle. 1.50z, Slowinski Park and sea gull. 4.50z, Bieszczadzki Park and lynx. 5z, Ojcowski Park and bat. 6z, Kampinoski Park and elk.

1976, May 22 *Photo.* *Perf. 12x11½*
2159 A658 90g multicolored   .25 .25
2160 A658 1z multicolored   .25 .25
2161 A658 1.50z multicolored   .25 .25
2162 A658 4.50z multicolored   .30 .25
2163 A658 5z multicolored   .60 .25
2164 A658 6z multicolored   .75 .25
    Nos. 2159-2164 (6)   2.40 1.50

UN Headquarters, Dove-shaped Globe — A659

1976, June 29 *Litho.* *Perf. 11x11½*
2165 A659 8.40z multicolored   .45 .25
UN postage stamps, 25th anniversary.

Fencing and Olympic Rings
A660

1976, June 30   *Photo.*
2166 A660 50g shown   .25 .25
2167 A660 1z Bicycling   .25 .25
2168 A660 1.50z Soccer   .25 .25
2169 A660 4.20z Boxing   .30 .25
2170 A660 6.90z Weight lifting   .40 .25
2171 A660 8.40z Running   .55 .25
    Nos. 2166-2171 (6)   2.00 1.50

21st Olympic Games, Montreal, Canada, July 17-Aug. 1. See No. B132.

Polish Theater, Poznan — A662

1976, July 12 *Litho.* *Perf. 11x11½*
2173 A662 1.50z gray olive & org .25 .25
Polish Theater in Poznan, centenary.

Czekanowski, Lake Baikal — A663

1976, Sept. 3 *Photo.* *Perf. 11x11½*
2174 A663 1.50z silver & multi .25 .25
Aleksander Czekanowski (1833-1876), geologist, death centenary.

Siren
A664

Designs: 1z, Sphinx, vert. 2z, Lion. 4.20z, Bull. 4.50z, Goat. Designs from Corinthian vases, 7th century B.C.

    Perf. 11x11½, 11½x11
1976, Oct. 30   *Photo.*
2175 A664 1z gold & multi   .25 .25
2176 A664 1.50z gold & multi   .25 .25
2177 A664 2z gold & multi   .25 .25
2178 A664 4.20z gold & multi   .25 .25
2179 A664 4.50z gold & multi   .25 .25
    Nos. 2175-2179,B133 (6) 2.05 1.55
    Stamp Day.

Warszawa M20 — A665

Automobiles: 1.50z, Warszawa 223. 2z, Syrena 104. 4.90z, Polski Fiat 125.

1976, Nov. 6 *Photo.* *Perf. 11*
2180 A665 1z multicolored   .25 .25
2181 A665 1.50z multicolored   .25 .25
2182 A665 2z multicolored   .25 .25
2183 A665 4.90z multicolored   .30 .25
a.   Souvenir sheet of 4, #2180-
    2183 + 2 labels   1.50 1.00
    Nos. 2180-2183 (4)   1.05 1.00
Zeran Automobile Factory, Warsaw, 25th anniv.

Pouring Ladle — A666

1976, Nov. 26 *Litho.* *Perf. 11*
2184 A666 1.50z multicolored   .25 .25
First steel production at Katowice Foundry.

Virgin and Child, Epitaph, 1425 — A667

6z, The Beautiful Madonna, sculpture, c. 1410.

1976, Dec. 15
2185 A667 1z multicolored   .25 .25
2186 A667 6z multicolored   .30 .25

Polish Trade Union Emblem — A668

1976, Dec. 29
2187 A668 1.50z multicolored   .25 .25
8th Polish Trade Union Congress.

Tanker Zawrat Unloading, Gdansk — A669

Polish Ports: No. 2189, Ferry "Gryf" and cars at pier, Gdansk. No. 2190, Loading containers, Gdynia. No. 2191, "Stefan Batory" and "People of the Sea" monument, Gdynia. 2z, Barge and cargoship "Ziemia Szczecinska", Szczecin. 4.20z, Coal loading installations, Swinoujscie. 6.90z, Liner, hydrofoil and lighthouse, Kolobrzeg. 8.40z, Map of Polish Coast with ports, ships and emblem of Union of Polish Ports.

1976, Dec. 29 *Photo.* *Perf. 11*
2188 A669 1z multicolored   .25 .25
2189 A669 1z multicolored   .25 .25
2190 A669 1.50z multicolored   .25 .25
2191 A669 1.50z multicolored   .25 .25
2192 A669 2z multicolored   .25 .25
2193 A669 4.20z multicolored   .25 .25
2194 A669 6.90z multicolored   .45 .25
2195 A669 8.40z multicolored   .50 .30
    Nos. 2188-2195 (8)   2.45 2.05

Nurse Helping Old Woman — A670

1977, Jan. 24 *Litho.* *Perf. 11½x11*
2196 A670 1.50z multicolored   .25 .25
Polish Red Cross.

Civilian Defense Medal — A671

1977, Feb. 26 *Litho.* *Perf. 11*
2197 A671 1.50z multicolored   .25 .25
Civilian Defense.

Ball on the Road — A672

1977, Mar. 12   *Photo.*
2198 A672 1.50z olive & multi   .25 .25
Social Action Committee (founded 1966), "Stop, Child on the Road!"

Forest Fruits — A673

1977, Mar. 17   *Perf. 11½x11*
2199 A673 50g Dewberry   .25 .25
2200 A673 90g Cranberry   .25 .25
2201 A673 1z Wild strawberry .25 .25
2202 A673 1.50z Bilberry   .25 .25
2203 A673 2z Raspberry   .25 .25
2204 A673 4.50z Blueberry   .30 .25
2205 A673 6z Dog rose   .35 .25
2206 A673 6.90z Hazelnut   .75 .25
    Nos. 2199-2206 (8)   2.65 2.00

Flags of USSR and Poland as Computer Tape — A674

1977, Apr. 4 *Litho.* *Perf. 11½x11*
2207 A674 1.50z red & multi   .25 .25
Scientific and technical cooperation between Poland and USSR, 30th anniversary.

Emblem and Graph — A675

1977, Apr. 22
2208 A675 1.50z red & multi .25 .25
7th Congress of Polish Engineers.

Venus, by Rubens A676

Paintings by Flemish painter Peter Paul Rubens (1577-1640): 1.50z, Bathsheba. 5z, Helene Fourment. 6z, Self-portrait.

1977, Apr. 30 *Perf. 11½*
Frame in Gray Brown
2209 A676 1z multicolored .25 .25
2210 A676 1.50z multicolored .25 .25
2211 A676 5z multicolored .55 .25
2212 A676 6z multicolored .70 .25
Nos. 2209-2212 (4) 1.75 1.00
See No. B134.

Peace Dove A677

1977, May 6 *Perf. 11x11½*
2213 A677 1.50z black, ultra & yel .25 .25
Congress of World Council of Peace, Warsaw, May 6-11.

Bicyclist A678

1977, May 6 *Photo.*
2214 A678 1.50z gray & multi .25 .25
30th International Peace Bicycling Race, Warsaw-Berlin-Prague.

Wolf — A679

Wildlife Fund Emblem and: No. 2216, Great bustard. No. 2217, Kestrel. 6z, Otter.

1977, May 12 Photo. *Perf. 11½x11*
2215 A679 1z silver & multi .35 .25
2216 A679 1.50z silver & multi .40 .25
2217 A679 1.50z silver & multi .40 .25
2218 A679 6z silver & multi .90 .50
Nos. 2215-2218 (4) 2.05 1.25
Wildlife protection.

Violinist, by Jacob Toorenvliet A680

1977, May 16
2219 A680 6z gold & multi .45 .25
AMPHILEX '77 Intl. Phil. Exhib., Amsterdam, May 26-June 5. No. 2219 issued in sheets of 6.

Midsummer Bonfire — A681

Folk Customs: 1z, Easter cock. 1.50z, Dousing the women on Easter Monday. 3z, Harvest festival. 6z, Christmas procession with crèche. 8.40z, Wedding dance. 1z, 1.50z, 3z, 6z vertical.

Perf. 11x11½, 11½x11

1977, June 13 *Photo.*
2220 A681 90g multicolored .25 .25
2221 A681 1z multicolored .25 .25
2222 A681 1.50z multicolored .25 .25
2223 A681 3z multicolored .25 .25
2224 A681 6z multicolored .45 .25
2225 A681 8.40z multicolored .55 .25
Nos. 2220-2225 (6) 2.00 1.50

Henryk Wieniawski and Musical Symbol — A682

1977, June 30 Litho. *Perf. 11½x11*
2226 A682 1.50z gold, blk & red .30 .25
Wieniawski Music Festivals, Poznan: 5th Intl. Lute Competition, June 30-July 10, and 7th Intl. Violin Competition, Nov. 13-27.

Parnassius Apollo — A683

Butterflies: No. 2228, Nymphalis polychloros. No. 2229, Papilio machaon. No. 2230, Nymphalis antiopa. 5z, Fabriciana adippe. 6.90z, Argynnis paphia.

1977, Aug. 22 Photo. *Perf. 11*
2227 A683 1z multicolored .25 .25
2228 A683 1z multicolored .25 .25
2229 A683 1.50z multicolored .35 .25
2230 A683 1.50z multicolored .35 .25
2231 A683 5z multicolored .90 .35
2232 A683 6.90z multicolored 2.10 1.00
Nos. 2227-2232 (6) 4.20 2.35

Arms of Slupsk, Keyboard — A684

1977, Sept. 3 *Perf. 11½*
2233 A684 1.50z multicolored .25 .25
Slupsk Piano Festival.

Feliks Dzerzhinski A685

1977, Sept. 10 Litho. *Perf. 11½x11*
2234 A685 1.50z olive bis & sepia .25 .25
Feliks E. Dzerzhinski (1877-1926), organizer and head of Russian Secret Police (Cheka).

Earth and Sputnik A686

1977, Oct. 1 Litho. *Perf. 11x11½*
2235 A686 1.50z ultra & car .25 .25
a. Souvenir sheet of 3+3 labels .90 .35
60th anniv. of the Russian Revolution and 20th anniv. of Sputnik space flight. Printed in sheets of 15 stamps and 15 carmine labels showing Winter Palace, Leningrad.

Boleslaw Chrobry's Denarius, 11th Century — A687

Silver Coins: 1z, King Kazimierz Wielki's Cracow groszy, 14th century. 1.50z, Legniza-Brzeg-Wolow thaler, 17th century. 4.20z, King Augustus III guilder, Gdansk, 18th century. 4.50z, 5z (ship), 1936. 6z, 100z, Poland's millenium, 1966.

1977, Oct. 9 Photo. *Perf. 11½x11*
2236 A687 50g silver & multi .25 .25
2237 A687 1z silver & multi .25 .25
2238 A687 1.50z silver & multi .25 .25
2239 A687 4.20z silver & multi .25 .25
2240 A687 4.50z silver & multi .35 .25
2241 A687 6z silver & multi .50 .25
Nos. 2236-2241 (6) 1.85 1.50
Stamp Day.

Monastery, Przasnysz — A688

Architectural landmarks: No. 2242, Wolin Gate, vert. No. 2243, Church, Debno, vert. No. 2245, Cathedral, Plock. 6z, Castle, Kornik. 6.90z, Palace and Garden, Wilanow.

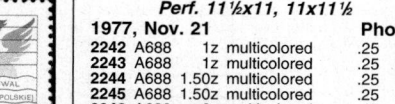

Perf. 11½x11, 11x11½
1977, Nov. 21 *Photo.*
2242 A688 1z multicolored .25 .25
2243 A688 1z multicolored .25 .25
2244 A688 1.50z multicolored .25 .25
2245 A688 1.50z multicolored .25 .25
2246 A688 6z multicolored .45 .25
2247 A688 6.90z multicolored .50 .30
Nos. 2242-2247 (6) 1.95 1.55

Vostok (USSR) and Mercury (USA) A689

1977, Dec. 28 Photo. *Perf. 11x11½*
2248 A689 6.90z ultra & multi .50 .30
a. Souvenir sheet of 6 4.75 2.40
20 years of space conquest. No. 2248a contains 6 No. 2248 (2 tete-beche pairs) and 2 labels, one showing Sputnik 1 and "4.X.1957," the other Explorer 1 and "31.1.1958."

DN Class Iceboats — A690

Design: No. 2250, One iceboat.

1978, Feb. 6 Litho. *Perf. 11*
2249 A690 1.50z lt ultra & blk .25 .25
2250 A690 1.50z lt ultra & blk .25 .25
a. Pair, #2249-2250 + label .50 .25
6th World Iceboating Championships, Feb. 6-11.

Electric Locomotive, Katowice Station, 1957 — A691

Locomotives in Poland: No. 2252, Narrow-gauge engine and Gothic Tower, Znin. No. 2253, Pm36 and Cegielski factory, Poznan, 1936. No. 2254, Electric train and Otwock Station, 1936. No. 2255, Marki Train and Warsaw Stalow Station, 1907. 4.50z, Ty51 coal train and Gdynia Station, 1933. 5z, Tr21 and Chrzanow factory, 1920. 6z, "Cockerill" and Vienna Station, 1848.

1978, Feb. 28 Photo. *Perf. 12x11½*
2251 A691 50g multicolored .25 .25
2252 A691 1z multicolored .25 .25
2253 A691 1z multicolored .25 .25
2254 A691 1.50z multicolored .25 .25
2255 A691 1.50z multicolored .25 .25
2256 A691 4.50z multicolored .35 .25
2257 A691 5z multicolored .40 .25
2258 A691 6z multicolored .85 .45
Nos. 2251-2258 (8) 2.85 2.20

Pierwsze Wzloty, 1896, and Czeslaw Tanski A692

Polish Aviation: 1z, Zwyciezcy-Challenge, 1932, F. Zwirko and S. Wigura, vert. 1.50z, RWD-5 bis over South Atlantic, 1933, and S. Skarzynski. 4.20z, MI-2 helicopter over mountains, Pezetel emblem, vert. 6.90z, PZL-104 Wilga 35, Pezetel emblem. 8.40z, Motoszybowiec SZD-45 Ogar.

1978, Apr. 15 *Perf. 11x11½, 11½x11*
2259 A692 50g multicolored .25 .25
2260 A692 1z multicolored .25 .25
2261 A692 1.50z multicolored .25 .25
2262 A692 4.20z multicolored .30 .25

2263	A692	6.90z multicolored	.65	.40
2264	A692	8.40z multicolored	.50	.40
		Nos. 2259-2264 (6)	2.20	1.80

Soccer — A693

Design: 6.90z, Soccer ball, horiz.

Perf. 11½x11, 11x11½

1978, May 12   Litho.

2265	A693	1.50z multicolored	.25	.25
2266	A693	6.90z multicolored	.50	.25

11th World Cup Soccer Championships, Argentina, June 1-25.

Poster — A694

1978, June 1   *Perf. 12x11½*

2267	A694	1.50z multicolored	.25	.25

7th International Poster Biennale, Warsaw.

Fair Emblem — A695

1978, June 10   *Perf. 11*

2268	A695	1.50z multicolored	.25	.25

50th International Poznan Fair.

Polonez Passenger Car — A696

1978, June 10   Photo.   *Perf. 11*

2269	A696	1.50z multicolored	.25	.25

Maj. Miroslaw Hermaszewski A697

6.90z, Hermaszewski, globe & trajectory.

Perf. 11½x11, 11x11½

1978, June 27   Photo.

2270	A697	1.50z multi	.25	.25
a.		Without date	.25	.25
2271	A697	6.90z multi, horiz.	.35	.25
a.		Without date	.65	.65

1st Polish cosmonaut on Russian space mission. Nos. 2270a, 2271a printed in sheets of 6 stamps and 2 labels.
Stamps and sheets showing Zenon Jankowski were prepared but not issued.

Youth Festival Emblem A698

1978, July 12   Litho.   *Perf. 11½*

2272	A698	1.50z multicolored	.25	.25

11th Youth Festival, Havana, July 28-Aug. 5.

Souvenir Sheet

Flowers — A699

1978, July 20   *Perf. 11½x11*

2273	A699	1.50z gold & multi	.45	.25

30th anniv. of Polish Youth Movement.

Anopheles Mosquito and Blood Cells — A700

Design: 6z, Tsetse fly and blood cells.

1978, Aug. 19   Litho.   *Perf. 11½x11*

2274	A700	1.50z multicolored	.25	.25
2275	A700	6z multicolored	.45	.25

4th International Parasitological Congress.

Norway Maple, Environment Emblem — A701

Emblem and: 1z, English oak. 1.50z, White poplar. 4.20z, Scotch pine. 4.50z, White willow. 6z, Birch.

1978, Sept. 6   Photo.   *Perf. 14*

2276	A701	50g gold & multi	.25	.25
2277	A701	1z gold & multi	.25	.25
2278	A701	1.50z gold & multi	.25	.25
2279	A701	4.20z gold & multi	.30	.25
2280	A701	4.50z gold & multi	.35	.25
2281	A701	6z gold & multi	.50	.30
		Nos. 2276-2281 (6)	1.90	1.55

Protection of the environment.

Souvenir Sheet

Jan Zizka, Battle of Grunwald, by Jan Matejko — A702

1978, Sept. 8   *Perf. 11½x11*

2282	A702	6z gold & multi	1.10	.60

PRAGA '78 Intl. Phil. Exhib., Prague, Sept. 8-17.

Letter, Telephone and Satellite — A703

1978, Sept. 20   Litho.   *Perf. 11*

2283	A703	1.50z multicolored	.25	.25

20th anniversary of the Organization of Ministers of Posts and Telecommunications of Warsaw Pact countries.

Peace, by Andre le Brun — A704

1978-79   Litho.   *Perf. 11½ (1z), 12½*

2284	A704	1z violet	.25	.25
2285	A704	1.50z steel blue ('79)	.25	.25
2286	A704	2z brown ('79)	.25	.25
2287	A704	2.50z ultra ('79)	.25	.25
		Nos. 2284-2287 (4)	1.00	1.00

Polish Unit, UN Middle East Emergency Force — A706

Designs: No. 2289, Color Guard, Kosziusko Division (4 soldiers). No. 2290, Color Guard, field training (3 soldiers).

1978, Oct. 6   Photo.   *Perf. 12x11½*

2289	A706	1.50z multicolored	.25	.25
2290	A706	1.50z multicolored	.25	.25
2291	A706	1.50z multicolored	.25	.25
		Nos. 2289-2291 (3)	.75	.75

35th anniversary of People's Army.

Young Man, by Raphael A707

1978, Oct. 9   *Perf. 11*

2292	A707	6z multicolored	.30	.25

Stamp Day.

Dr. Korczak and Children — A708

1978, Oct. 11   Litho.   *Perf. 11½x11*

2293	A708	1.50z multicolored	.25	.25

Dr. Janusz Korczak, physician, educator, writer, birth centenary.

Wojciech Boguslawski (1757-1829) — A709

Polish dramatists: 1z, Aleksander Fredro (1793-1878). 1.50z, Juliusz Slowacki (1809-1849). 2z, Adam Mickiewicz (1798-1855). 4.50z, Stanislaw Wyspianski (1869-1907). 6z, Gabriela Zapolska (1857-1921).

1978, Nov. 11   Litho.   *Perf. 11½*

2294	A709	50g multicolored	.25	.25
2295	A709	1z multicolored	.25	.25
2296	A709	1.50z multicolored	.25	.25
2297	A709	2z multicolored	.25	.25
2298	A709	4.50z multicolored	.30	.25
2299	A709	6z multicolored	.40	.25
		Nos. 2294-2299 (6)	1.70	1.50

Polish Combatants Monument, and Eiffel Tower, Paris — A710

1978, Nov. 2   Photo.   *Perf. 11x11½*

2300	A710	1.50z brown, red & bl	.25	.25

Przewalski Mare and Colt — A711

Animals: 1z, Polar bears. 1.50z, Indian elephants. 2z, Jaguars. 4.20z, Gray seals. 4.50z, Hartebeests. 6z, Mandrills.

1978, Nov. 10

2301	A711	50g multicolored	.25	.25
2302	A711	1z multicolored	.25	.25
2303	A711	1.50z multicolored	.25	.25
2304	A711	2z multicolored	.25	.25
2305	A711	4.20z multicolored	.40	.25
2306	A711	4.50z multicolored	.40	.25
2307	A711	6z multicolored	1.10	.40
		Nos. 2301-2307 (7)	2.90	1.90

Warsaw Zoological Gardens, 50th anniv.

Adolf Warski
(1868-1937)
A712

Party
Emblem
A713

#2309, Julian Lenski (1889-1937). #2310, Aleksander Zawadzki (1899-1964). #2311, Stanislaw Dubois (1901-1942).

Perf. 11½x11, 11x11½

1978, Dec. 15   Photo.

2308	A712	1.50z red & brown	.25	.25
2309	A712	1.50z red & black	.25	.25
2310	A712	1.50z red & dk vio	.25	.25
2311	A712	1.50z red & dk blue	.25	.25
2312	A713	1.50z black, red & gold	.25	.25
		Nos. 2308-2312 (5)	1.25	1.25

Polish United Workers' Party, 30th anniv.

LOT
Planes,
1929 and
1979
A714

1979, Jan. 2   Photo.   *Perf. 11x11½*

2313	A714	6.90z gold & multi	.35	.25

LOT, Polish airline, 50th anniversary.

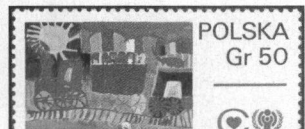

Train and IYC Emblem — A715

Children's Paintings: 1z, Children with toys. 1.50z, Children in meadow. 6z, Family.

1979, Jan. 13   *Perf. 11*

2314	A715	50g multicolored	.25	.25
2315	A715	1z multicolored	.25	.25
2316	A715	1.50z multicolored	.25	.25
2317	A715	6z multicolored	.35	.25
		Nos. 2314-2317 (4)	1.10	1.00

International Year of the Child.

Artist's Wife, by
Karol
Mondral — A716

Modern Polish Graphic Arts: 50g, "Lightning," by Edmund Bartlomiejczyk, horiz. 1.50z, Musicians, by Tadeusz Kulisiewicz. 4.50z, Portrait of a Brave Man, by Wladyslaw Skoczylas.

1979, Mar. 5   Engr.

2318	A716	50g brt violet	.25	.25
2319	A716	1z slate green	.25	.25
2320	A716	1.50z blue gray	.25	.25
2321	A716	4.50z violet brown	.30	.25
		Nos. 2318-2321 (4)	1.05	1.00

Andrzej Frycz-Modrzewski, Stefan Batory, Jan Zamoyski — A717

Photogravure and Engraved

1979, Mar. 12   *Perf. 12x11½*

2322	A717	1.50z cream & sepia	.25	.25

Royal Tribunal in Piotrkow Trybunalski, 400th anniversary.

Pole Vault and Olympic
Emblem — A718

Olympic Emblem and: 1.50z, High jump. 6z, Cross-country skiing. 8.40z, Equestrian.

1979, Mar. 26   Photo.   *Perf. 12x11½*

2323	A718	1z multicolored	.25	.25
2324	A718	1.50z multicolored	.25	.25
2325	A718	6z multicolored	.30	.25
2326	A718	8.40z multicolored	.45	.25
		Nos. 2323-2326 (4)	1.25	1.00

1980 Olympic Games.

Flounder — A720

Fish and Emblem: 90g, Perch. 1z, Grayling. 1.50z, Salmon. 2z, Trout. 4.50z, Pike. 5z, Carp. 6z, Catfish and frog.

1979, Apr. 26   Photo.   *Perf. 11½x11*

2327	A720	50g multicolored	.25	.25
2328	A720	90g multicolored	.25	.25
2329	A720	1z multicolored	.25	.25
2330	A720	1.50z multicolored	.25	.25
2331	A720	2z multicolored	.25	.25
2332	A720	4.50z multicolored	.25	.25
2333	A720	5z multicolored	.55	.25
2334	A720	6z multicolored	.85	.40
		Nos. 2327-2334 (8)	2.90	2.15

Polish angling, centenary, and protection of the environment.

A721

1979, Apr. 30   Litho.   *Perf. 11x11½*

2335	A721	1.50z multicolored	.25	.25

Council for Mutual Economic Aid of Socialist Countries, 30th anniversary.

Faces and
Emblem — A722

1979, May 7   *Perf. 11*

2336	A722	1.50z red & black	.25	.25

6th Congress of Association of Fighters for Liberty and Democracy, Warsaw, May 7-8.

St.
George's
Church,
Sofia
A722a

1979, May 15   Photo.   *Perf. 11x11½*

2337	A722a	1.50z multicolored	.25	.25

Philaserdica '79 Phil. Exhib., Sofia, Bulgaria, May 18-27.

Pope John
Paul II,
Cracow
Cathedral
A723

Designs: 8.40z, Pope John Paul II, Auschwitz-Birkenau Memorial. 50z, Pope John Paul II.

1979, June 2   Photo.   *Perf. 11x11½*

2338	A723	1.50z multicolored	.25	.25
2339	A723	8.40z multicolored	.60	.25

Souvenir Sheet

Perf. 11½x11

2340	A723	50z multicolored & gold	5.50	3.50

Visit of Pope John Paul II to Poland, June 2-11. No. 2340 contains one 26x35mm stamp. A variety of No. 2340 with silver margin exists. Values, unused $25, used $17.50.

Paddle Steamer Prince Ksawery and
Old Warsaw — A724

Designs: 1.50z, Steamer Gen. Swierczewski and Gdansk, 1914. 4.50z, Tug Aurochs and Plock, 1960. 6z, Motor ship Mermaid and modern Warsaw, 1959.

1979, June 15   Litho.   *Perf. 11*

2341	A724	1z multicolored	.25	.25
2342	A724	1.50z multicolored	.25	.25
2343	A724	4.50z multicolored	.25	.25
2344	A724	6z multicolored	.40	.25
		Nos. 2341-2344 (4)	1.15	1.00

Vistula River navigation, 150th anniversary.

Kosciuszko
Monument,
Philadelphia
A725

1979, July 1   Photo.   *Perf. 11½*

2345	A725	8.40z multicolored	.50	.30

Gen. Tadeusz Kosziuszko (1746-1807), Polish soldier and statesman who served in American Revolution.

Mining
Machinery — A726

Design: 1.50z, Salt crystals.

1979, July 14   Photo.   *Perf. 14*

2346	A726	1z lt brown & blk	.25	.25
2347	A726	1.50z blue grn & blk	.25	.25

Wieliczka ancient rock-salt mines.

Eagle and
People — A727

No. 2349, Man with raised hand and flag.

1979, July 21   *Perf. 11½x11*

2348	A727	1.50z red, blue & gray	.25	.25
2349	A727	1.50z silver, red & blk	.25	.25

35 years of Polish People's Republic.

Souvenir Sheet

1979, Sept. 2   Photo.   *Perf. 11½x11*

2350	A727	Sheet of 2, #2348-2349 + label	.55	.30

13th National Philatelic Exhibition.

Poland No. 1, Rowland Hill (1795-1879), Originator of Penny Postage — A728

1979, Aug. 16   Litho.   *Perf. 11½x11*

2351	A728	6z multicolored	.30	.25

Souvenir Sheet

The Rape of Europa, by Bernardo Strozzi — A729

1979, Aug. 20 Photo. Perf. 11x11½
2352 A729 10z multicolored .75 .35
Europhil '79, Intl. Phil. Exhib.

Wojciech Jastrzebowski A730

1979, Aug. 27 Perf. 11½x11
2353 A730 1.50z multicolored .25 .25
International Ergonomics Society Congress.

Postal Workers' Monument A731

1979, Sept. 1 Perf. 11x11½
2354 A731 1.50z multicolored .25 .25
40th anniversary of Polish postal workers' resistance to Nazi invaders. See No. B137.

ITU Emblem, Radio Antenna A732

1979, Sept. 24 Perf. 11x11½
2355 A732 1.50z multicolored .25 .25
Intl. Radio Consultative Committee (CCIR) of the ITU, 50th anniv.

Violin A733

1979, Sept. 25 Litho.
2356 A733 1.50z dk blue, org, grn .25 .25
Henryk Wieniawski Young Violinists' Competition, Lublin.

Pulaski Monument, Buffalo — A734

1979, Oct. 1 Photo. Perf. 11½x12
2357 A734 8.40z multicolored .35 .25
Gen. Casimir Pulaski (1748-1779), Polish nobleman who served in American Revolutionary War.

Gen. Franciszek Jozwiak — A735

1979, Oct. 3 Perf. 11½x11
2358 A735 1.50z gray blue, dk blue & gold .25 .25
35th anniv. of Civil and Military Security Service, founded by Gen. Franciszek Jozwiak (1895-1966).

Drive-in Post Office — A736

Designs: 1.50z, Parcel sorting. 4.50z, Loading mail train. 6z, Mobile post office.

1979, Oct. 9 Perf. 11½
2359 A736 1z multicolored .25 .25
2360 A736 1.50z multicolored .25 .25
2361 A736 4.50z multicolored .30 .25
2362 A736 6z multicolored .40 .25
   Nos. 2359-2362 (4) 1.20 1.00
Stamp Day.

Christmas A737

Designs: 2z, Holy Family. 6.90z, Nativity, horiz.

Perf. 11½x11, 11x11½
1979, Dec. 4 Photo.
2363 A737 2z multicolored .25 .25
2364 A737 6.90z multicolored .35 .25

A738

Space Achievements: 1z, Soyuz 30 and Salyut 6. 1.50z, Kopernik 500 and Copernicus satellite. 2z, Lunik 2 and Ranger 7. 4.50z, Yuri Gagarin and Vostok. 6.90z, Neil Armstrong and Apollo 11.

1979, Dec. 28 Photo. Perf. 11½x11
2365 A738 1z multi .25 .25
2366 A738 1.50z multi .25 .25
2367 A738 2z multi .25 .25
2368 A738 4.50z multi .30 .25
2369 A738 6.90z multi .30 .25
a. Souvenir sheet of 5 1.50 1.00
   Nos. 2365-2369 (5) 1.30 1.25
No. 2369a contains Nos. 2365-2369, tete beche plus label.

A739

Designs: Horse Paintings.

1980, Jan. 31 Photo. Perf. 11½x12
2370 A739 1z Stagecoach .25 .25
2371 A739 2z Horse, trainer .25 .25
2372 A739 2.50z Trotters .25 .25
2373 A739 3z Fox hunt .25 .25
2374 A739 4z Sled .25 .25
2375 A739 6z Hay cart .35 .25
2376 A739 6.50z Pairs .40 .25
2377 A739 6.90z Hurdles .60 .35
   Nos. 2370-2377 (8) 2.60 2.10
Sierakov horse stud farm, 150th anniv.

Party Slogan on Map of Poland — A740

Worker, by Janusz Stanny — A741

1980, Feb. 11 Photo. Perf. 11½x11
2378 A740 2.50z multi .25 .25
2379 A741 2.50z multi .25 .25
Polish United Workers' Party, 8th Congress.

Equestrian, Olympic Rings — A742

1980, Mar. 31 Perf. 12x11½
2380 A742 2z shown .25 .25
2381 A742 2.50z Archery .25 .25
2382 A742 6.50z Biathlon .35 .25
2383 A742 8.40z Volleyball .60 .25
   Nos. 2380-2383 (4) 1.45 1.00
13th Winter Olympic Games, Lake Placid, NY, Feb. 12-24 (6.50z); 22nd Summer Olympic Games, Moscow, July 19-Aug. 3. See No. B138.

Map and Old Town Hall, 1591, Zamosc A743

1980, Apr. 3 Litho. Perf. 11½
2384 A743 2.50z multi .25 .25
Zamosc, 400th anniversary.

Arms of Poland and Russia A744

1980, Apr. 21 Litho. Perf. 11½
2385 A744 2.50z multi .25 .25
Treaty of Friendship, Cooperation and Mutual Assistance between Poland and USSR, 35th anniversary.

Lenin, 110th Birth Anniversary — A745

1980, Apr. 22 Photo. Perf. 11
2386 A745 2.50z multi .25 .25

Workers Marching A746

1980, May 1 Perf. 11½x11
2387 A746 2.50z multi .25 .25
Revolution of 1905, 75th anniversary.

Dove Over Liberation Date — A747

1980, May 9 Perf. 11½x12
2388 A747 2.50z multi .25 .25
Victory over fascism, 35th anniversary.

Arms of Treaty-signing Countries A748

1980, May 14   Litho.   Perf. 11½x11
2389 A748 2z red & blk   .25 .25
Signing of Warsaw Pact (Bulgaria, Czechoslovakia, German Democratic Rep., Hungary, Poland, Romania, USSR), 25th anniversary.

A749

No. 2390, Caverns, (1961 Expedition) Map of Cuba. No. 2391, Seals, Antarctica, 1959. No. 2392, Ethnology, Mongolia, 1963. No. 2393, Archaeology, Syria, 1959. No. 2394, Mountain climbing, Nepal, 1978. No. 2395, Paleontology, Mongolia, 1963.

1980, May 22   Photo.   Perf. 14
2390 A749 2z multi   .25 .25
2391 A749 2z multi   .25 .25
2392 A749 2.50z multi   .25 .25
2393 A749 2.50z multi   .25 .25
2394 A749 6.50z multi   .35 .25
2395 A749 8.40z multi   .85 .35
      Nos. 2390-2395 (6)   2.20 1.60

Malachowski Lyceum Arms — A750

1980, June 7   Photo.   Perf. 11x12
2396 A750 2z blk & dl grn   .25 .25
Malachowski Lyceum (oldest school in Plock), 800th anniversary.

A751

No. 2397, Xerocomus Parasiticus. No. 2398, Clathrus ruber. No. 2399, Phallus hadriani. No. 2400, Strobilomyces floccopus. No. 2401, Sparassis crispa. No. 2402, Langermannia gigantea.

1980, June 30   Perf. 11½x11
2397 A751 2z multi   .25 .25
2398 A751 2z multi   .25 .25
2399 A751 2.50z multi   .25 .25
2400 A751 2.50z multi   .25 .25
2401 A751 8z multi   .60 .25
2402 A751 10.50z multi   .70 .30
      Nos. 2397-2402 (6)   2.30 1.55

Sandomierz Millennium — A752

1980, July 12   Photo.   Perf. 11x11½
2403 A752 2.50z dk brown   .25 .25

"Lwow," T. Ziolkowski — A753

Ships and Teachers: 2.50z, Antoni Garnuszewski, A. Garnuszewski. 6z, Zenit, A. Ledochowski. 6.50z, Jan Turlejski, K. Porebski. 6.90z, Horyzon, G. Kanski. 8.40z, Dar Pomorza, K. Maciejewicz.

1980, July 21   Litho.   Perf. 11
2404 A753 2z multi   .25 .25
2405 A753 2.50z multi   .25 .25
2406 A753 6z multi   .35 .25
2407 A753 6.50z multi   .45 .25
2408 A753 6.90z multi   .45 .25
2409 A753 8.40z multi   .55 .25
      Nos. 2404-2409 (6)   2.30 1.50
Training ships and teachers.

A754

Designs: Medicinal plants — No. 2410, Atropa belladonna. No. 2411, Datura innoxia. No. 2412, Valeriana. No. 2413, Mentha piperita. No. 2414, Calendula. No. 2415, Salvia officinalis.

1980, Aug. 15   Litho.   Perf. 11½x11
2410 A754 2z multicolored   .25 .25
2411 A754 2.50z multicolored .25 .25
2412 A754 3.40z multicolored .25 .25
2413 A754 5z multicolored   .35 .25
2414 A754 6.50z multicolored .45 .25
2415 A754 8z multicolored   .35 .30
      Nos. 2410-2415 (6)   1.90 1.55

A755

1980, Aug. 20   Perf. 11
2416 A755 2.50z multi   .25 .25
Jan Kochanowski (1530-1584), poet.

United Nations, 35th Anniversary — A756

1980, Sept. 19   Photo.   Perf. 11x11½
2417 A756 8.40z multi   .50 .25

Chopin Piano Competition — A757

1980, Oct. 2   Litho.   Perf. 11½
2418 A757 6.90z blk & tan   .45 .25

Mail Pick-up — A758

1980, Oct. 9   Photo.   Perf. 12x11½
2419 A758 2z shown   .25 .25
2420 A758 2.50z Letter sorting .25 .25
2421 A758 6z Loading mail
             plane   .40 .25
2422 A758 6.50z Mail boxes   .40 .25
  a.   Souvenir sheet of 4, #2419-
       2422   3.25 2.75
      Nos. 2419-2422 (4)   1.30 1.00
Stamp Day.

Girl Embracing Dove, UN Emblem A759

1980, Nov. 21   Litho.   Perf. 11x11½
2423 A759 8.40z multicolored .50 .25
UN Declaration on the Preparation of Societies for Life in Peace.

Battle of Olzynska Grochowska, by W. Kossak — A760

1980, Nov. 29   Photo.   Perf. 11
2424 A760 2.50z multicolored .25 .25
Battle of Olzynska Grochowska, 1830.

Horse-drawn Fire Engine — A761

Designs: Horse-drawn vehicles.

1980, Dec. 16
2425 A761 2z shown   .25 .25
2426 A761 2.50z Passenger
             coach   .25 .25
2427 A761 3z Beer wagon   .25 .25
2428 A761 5z Sled   .35 .25
2429 A761 6z Bus   .40 .25
2430 A761 6.50z Two-seater   .65 .30
      Nos. 2425-2430 (6)   2.15 1.55

Honor to the Silesian Rebels, by Jan Borowczak — A762

1981, Jan. 22   Engr.   Perf. 11½
2431 A762 2.50z gray grn   .25 .25
Silesian uprising, 60th anniversary.

Pablo Picasso — A763

1981, Mar. 10   Photo.   Perf. 11½x11
2432 A763 8.40z multi   .40 .25
  a.   Miniature sheet of 2 + 2 labels 1.90 1.00
Pablo Picasso (1881-1973), artist, birth centenary. No. 2432 se-tenant with label showing A Crying Woman. Sold for 20.80z.

Balloon Flown by Pilatre de Rozier, 1783 — A764

Gordon Bennett Cup (Balloons): No. 2434, J. Blanchard, J. Jeffries, 1875. 2.50z, F. Godard, 1850. 3z, F. Hynek, Z. Burzynski, 1933. 6z, Z. Burzynski, N. Wysocki, 1935. 6.50z, B. Abruzzo, M. Anderson, L. Newman, 1978. 10.50z, Winners' names, 1933-1935, 1938.

1981, Mar. 25   Photo.   Perf. 11½x12
2433 A764 2z multi   .25 .25
2434 A764 2z multi   .25 .25
2435 A764 2.50z multi   .25 .25
2436 A764 3z multi   .25 .25
2437 A764 6z multi   .45 .25
2438 A764 6.50z multi   .50 .25
      Nos. 2433-2438 (6)   1.95 1.50

Souvenir Sheet
Imperf
2439 A764 10.50z multi   .85 .60

Iphigenia, by Franz Anton Maulbertsch (1724-1796), WIPA '81 Emblem — A765

1981, May 11   Litho.   Perf. 11½
2440 A765 10.50z multi   .95 .25
WIPA '81 Intl. Phil. Exhib., Vienna, 5/22-31.

Wroclaw, 1493 — A766

1981, May 15   Photo.   Perf. 14
2441 A766 6.50z brown   .35 .25
See Nos. 2456-2459. For surcharge see No. 2526.

Gen. Wladyslaw Sikorski (1881-1943) A767

1981, May 20   Perf. 11½x11
2442 A767 6.50z multi   .30 .25

Kwan Vase, 18th Cent. — A768

2z, Cup, saucer, 1820. 2.50z, Jug, 1820. 5z, Portrait plate, 1880. 6.50z, Vase, 1900. 8.40z, Basket, 1840.

1981, June 15
2443 A768   1z shown   .25 .25
2444 A768   2z multi   .25 .25
2445 A768   2.50z multi   .25 .25
2446 A768   5z multi   .35 .25
2447 A768   6.50z multi   .45 .25
2448 A768   8.40z multi   .60 .25
    Nos. 2443-2448 (6)   2.15 1.50
See Nos. 2502-2507.

Intl. Architects Union, 14th Congress, Warsaw — A769

1981, July 15   Litho.
2449 A769 2.50z multi   .25 .25

Moose, Rifle and Pouch — A770

1981, July 30
2450 A770   2z shown   .25 .25
2451 A770   2z Boar   .25 .25
2452 A770   2.50z Fox   .30 .25
2453 A770   2.50z Elk   .30 .25
2454 A770   6.50z Greylag goose, horiz.   .80 .25
2455 A770   6.50z Fen duck   .85 1.50
    Nos. 2450-2455 (6)   2.75 1.50

City Type of 1981
4z, Gdansk, 1652, vert. 5z, Krakow, 1493, vert. 6z, Legnica, 1744. 8z, Warsaw, 1618.

Perf. 11x11½, 11½x13
1981, July 28   Photo.
2456 A766 4z multicolored   .35 .25
2457 A766 5z multicolored   .40 .25
2458 A766 6z multicolored   .50 .25
2459 A766 8z multicolored   .60 .30
    Nos. 2456-2459 (4)   1.85 1.05
For surcharge see #2939.

A770a

1982, Nov. 2   Photo.   Perf. 11½
2461 A770a 12z Vistula River   .25 .25
2463 A770a 17z Kasimierz Dolny   .25 .25
2466 A770a 25z Gdansk   .35 .25
    Nos. 2461-2466 (3)   .85 .75

Wild Bison — A771

No. 2471 — Bison bonasus: a, Adult looking forward in center, adult grazing at right, tree without leaves at UR. b. Adult grazing at left, adult at center, hindquarters of juvenile at right, tree with leaves at UL. c, Adults and juvenile, inscribed "Karat-2000" at bottom. d, Juvenile suckling female. e, Two adults facing right.

1981, Aug. 27   Perf. 11½x11
2471   Horiz. strip of 5   3.00 1.25
    a.-e. A771 6.50z Any single   .50 .25

60th Anniv. of Polish Tennis Federation — A772

1981, Sept. 17 Photo. Perf. 11x11½
2472 A772 6.50z multi   .75 .25

Model Airplane — A773

1981, Sept. 24   Perf. 14
2473 A773   1z shown   .25 .25
2474 A773   2z Boats   .25 .25
2475 A773   2.50z Racing cars   .25 .25
2476 A773   4.20z Gliders   .35 .25
2477 A773   6.50z Radio-controlled racing cars   .40 .25
2478 A773   8z Yachts   .60 .30
    Nos. 2473-2478 (6)   2.10 1.55

Intl. Year of the Disabled — A774

1981, Sept. 25 Litho. Perf. 11½x11
2479 A774 8.40z multi   .60 .25

Stamp Day — A775

2.50z, Pistol, 18th cent., horiz. 8.40z, Sword, 18th cent.

1981, Oct. 9   Photo.   Perf. 14
2480 A775 2.50z multi   .25 .25
2481 A775 8.40z multi   .50 .25

A776

1981, Oct. 10   Perf. 11½x12
2482 A776 2.50z multi   .25 .25
Henryk Wieniawski (1835-1880), violinist and composer.

A777

Working Movement Leaders: 50g, Bronislaw Wesolowski (1870-1919). 2z, Malgorzata Fornalska (1902-1944). 2.50z, Maria Koszutska (1876-1939). 6.50z, Marcin Kasprzak (1860-1905).

1981, Oct. 15   Litho.
2483 A777 50g grn & blk   .25 .25
2484 A777 2z bl & blk   .25 .25
2485 A777 2.50z brn & blk   .25 .25
2486 A777 6.50z lil rose & blk   .35 .25
    Nos. 2483-2486 (4)   1.10 1.00

World Food Day — A778

1981, Oct. 16   Perf. 11½x11
2487 A778 6.90z multi   .45 .25

Old Theater, Cracow, 200th Anniv. — A779

Theater Emblem and: 2z, Helena Modrzejewska (1840-1909), actress. 2.50z, Stanislaw Kozmian (1836-1922), theater director, 1865-1885, founder of Cracow School. 6.50z, Konrad Swinarski (1929-1975), stage manager.

Photo. & Engr.
1981, Oct. 17   Perf. 12x11½
2488 A779   2z multi   .25 .25
2489 A779   2.50z multi   .45 .25
2490 A779   6.50z multi   .45 .25
2491 A779   8z multi   .45 .25
    Nos. 2488-2491 (4)   1.60 1.00

Souvenir Sheet

Vistula River Project — A780

1981, Dec. 20 Litho. Perf. 11½x12
2492 A780 10.50z multi   1.25 .75

Flowering Succulent Plants A781

No. 2493, Epiphyllopsis gaertneri. No. 2494, Cereus tonduzii. No. 2495, Cylindropuntia leptocaulis. No. 2496, Cylindroppuntia fulgida. No. 2497, Caralluma lugardi. No. 2498, Nopalea cochenillifera. No. 2499, Lithopsps helmutii. No. 2500, Cylindropuntia spinosior.

1981, Dec. 22   Photo.   Perf. 13
2493 A781 90g multicolored   .25 .25
2494 A781 1z multicolored   .25 .25
2495 A781 2z multicolored   .25 .25
2496 A781 2.50z multicolored   .25 .25
2497 A781 2.50z multicolored   .25 .25
2498 A781 6.50z multicolored   .40 .25
2499 A781 6.50z multicolored   .40 .25
2500 A781 10.50z multicolored   1.00 .45
    Nos. 2493-2500 (8)   3.05 2.20

Polish Workers' Party, 40th Anniv. — A782

1982, Jan. 5   Photo.   Perf. 11½x11
2501 A782 2.50z multi   .25 .25

Stoneware Plate, 1890 — A783

Porcelain or Stoneware: 2z, Plate, mug, 1790. 2.50z, Soup tureen, gravy dish, 1830. 6z, Salt and pepper dish, 1844, 8z, Stoneware jug, 1840. 10.50z, Stoneware figurine, 1740.

1982, Jan. 20
2502	A783	1z multi	.25 .25
2503	A783	2z multi	.25 .25
2504	A783	2.50z multi	.25 .25
2505	A783	6z multi	.40 .25
2506	A783	8z multi	.50 .25
2507	A783	10.50z multi	.75 .30
		Nos. 2502-2507 (6)	2.40 1.55

Ignacy Lukasiewicz (1822-1882), Oil Lamp Inventor — A784

Designs: Various oil lamps.

1982, Mar. 22   Photo.   Perf. 11½x11
2508	A784	1z multi	.25 .25
2509	A784	2z multi	.25 .25
2510	A784	2.50z multi	.25 .25
2511	A784	3.50z multi	.25 .25
2512	A784	9z multi	.50 .25
2513	A784	10z multi	.55 .25
		Nos. 2508-2513 (6)	2.05 1.50

Karol Szymanowski (1882-1937), Composer A785

1982, Apr. 8
2514	A785 2.50z dk brn & gold	.25 .25

Victory in Challenge Trophy Flights A786

1982, May 5   Photo.   Perf. 11x11½
2515	A786	27z RWD-6 mono-plane	.75 .25
2516	A786	31z RWD-9	1.25 .25
a.		Souv. sheet of 2, #2515-2516	2.25 1.25

Henryk Sienkiewicz (1846-1916), Writer — A787

Polish Nobel Prize Winners: 15z, Wladyslaw Reymont (1867-1925), writer, 1924. 25z, Marie Curie (1867-1934), physicist 1903, 1911. 31z, Czeslaw Milosz (b. 1911), poet, 1980.

1982, May 10   Litho.   Perf. 11½x11
2517	A787	3z black & dk grn	.25 .25
2518	A787	15z black & brown	.40 .25
2519	A787	25z black	.50 .25
2520	A787	31z black & gray	.90 .25
		Nos. 2517-2520 (4)	2.05 1.00

1982 World Cup — A788

Perf. 11½x11, 11x11½
1982, May 28   Photo.
2521	A788	25z Ball	.75 .25
2522	A788	27z Bull, ball, horiz.	.75 .25

Souvenir Sheet

Maria Kaziera Sobieska — A789

1982, June 11   Photo.   Perf. 11½x11
2523	A789 65z multi	2.50 1.50

PHILEXFRANCE '82 Intl. Stamp Exhibition, Paris, June 11-21.

Assoc. Presidents Stanislaw Sierakowski and Boleslaw Domanski — A790

1982, July 20   Litho.
2524	A790 4.50z multi	.35 .25

Assoc. of Poles in Germany, 60th anniv.

2nd UN Conference on Peaceful Uses of Outer Space, Vienna, Aug. 9-21 — A791

1982, Aug. 9   Photo.
2525	A791 31z Globe	.75 .25

No. 2441 Surcharged

1982, Aug. 20
2526	A766 10z on 6.50z brn	.30 .25

Black Madonna of Jasna Gora, 600th Anniv. A792

2.50z, Father Augustin Kordecki (1603-1673). 25z, Siege of Jasna Gora by Swedes, 1655, horiz.

1982, Aug. 26   Perf. 11
2527	A792	2.50z multi	.25 .25
2528	A792	25z multi	.40 .25
2529	A792	65z multi	1.20 .35
		Nos. 2527-2529 (3)	1.85 .85

A souvenir sheet of 2 No. 2529 exists. Value: mint $10, used $9.

Workers' Movement A793

1982, Sept. 3   Perf. 11½x11
2530	A793 6z multicolored	.30 .25

Norbert Barlicki (1880-1941) — A794

Workers' Activists: 6z, Pawel Finder (1904-1944). 15z, Marian Buczek (1896-1939). 20z, Cezaryna Wojnarowska (1861-1911). 29z, Ignacy Daszynski (1866-1936).

1982, Sept. 10   Perf. 12x11½
2531	A794	5z multi	.25 .25
2532	A794	6z multi	.25 .25
2533	A794	15z multi	.25 .25
2534	A794	20z multi	.25 .25
2535	A794	29z multi	.25 .25
		Nos. 2531-2535 (5)	1.25 1.25

Carved Head, Wawel Castle — A795

1982, Sept. 25
2536	A795	60z Woman's head	.75 .25
2537	A795	100z Man's head	.75 .25

TB Bacillus Centenary A796

10z, Koch. 25z, Oko Bujwid (1857-1942), bacteriologist.

1982, Sept. 22   Perf. 11½x11
2538	A796	10z multicolored	.30 .25
2539	A796	25z multicolored	.50 .25

St. Maximilian Kolbe (1894-1941) A797

1982, Oct.
2540	A797 27z multi	.65 .25

50th Anniv. of Polar Research A798

1982, Oct. 25   Litho.   Perf. 11½
2541	A798 27z multi	.65 .25

Stanislaw Zaremba (1863-1942), Mathematician — A799

Mathematicians: 6z, Waclaw Sierpinski (1882-1969). 12z, Zygmunt Janiszewski (1888-1920). 15z, Stefan Banach (1892-1945).

1982, Nov. 23   Photo.   Perf. 11x11½
2542	A799	5z multicolored	.25 .25
2543	A799	6z multicolored	.25 .25
2544	A799	12z multicolored	.30 .25
2545	A799	15z multicolored	.40 .25
		Nos. 2542-2545 (4)	1.20 1.00

First Anniv. of Military Rule — A800

1982, Dec. 13   Perf. 12x11½
2546	A800	2.50z Medal obverse and reverse	.25 .25

Cracow Monuments Restoration A801

1982, Dec. 20   Litho.   Perf. 11½x11
2547	A801	15z Deanery portal	.35 .25
2548	A801	25z Law College portal	.50 .25

Souvenir Sheet
Lithographed and Engraved
Imperf
2549	A801 65z City map	1.00 .75

No. 2549 contains one stamp 22x27mm. See Nos. 2593-2594, 2656-2657, 2717-2718, 2809, 2847.

Map of Poland, by Bernard Wapowski, 1526
A802

Maps: 6z, Warsaw, Polish Kingdom Quartermaster, 1839. 8z, Poland, Romer's Atlas, 1908. 25z, Krakow, by A. Buchowiecki, 1703, astrolabe, 17th cent.

1982, Dec. 28   Litho.   Perf. 11½
2550 A802 5z multicolored .25 .25
2551 A802 6z multicolored .25 .25
2552 A802 8z multicolored .25 .25
2553 A802 25z multicolored .65 .25
    Nos. 2550-2553 (4) 1.40 1.00

120th Anniv. of 1863 Uprising — A803

1983, Jan. 22   Photo.   Perf. 12x11½
2554 A803 6z The Battle, by Arthur Grottger
    (1837-67) .25 .25

Warsaw Theater Sesquicentennial — A804

1983, Feb. 24   Photo.   Perf. 11
2555 A804 6z multicolored .25 .25

10th Anniv. of UN Conference on Human Environment, Stockholm — A805

1983, Mar. 24   Litho.   Perf. 11½
2556 A805 5z Wild flowers .25 .25
2557 A805 6z Swan, carp, eel .25 .25
2558 A805 17z Hoopoe .40 .25
2559 A805 30z Fish .50 .50
2560 A805 31z Deer, fawn, buffalo .50 .50
2561 A805 38z Fruit .75 .30
    Nos. 2556-2561 (6) 2.65 2.05

Karol Kurpinski (1785-1857), Composer
A806

Famous People: 6z, Maria Jasnorzewska Pawlikowska (1891-1945), poet. 17z, Stanislaw Szober (1879-1938), linguist. 25z,

Tadeusz Banachiewicz (1882-1954), astronomer. 27z, Jaroslaw Iwaszkiewicz (1894-1980), writer. 31z, Wladyslaw Tatarkiewicz (1886-1980), philosopher, art historian.

1983, Mar. 25   Photo.   Perf. 11½x11
2562 A806 5z tan & brn .25 .25
2563 A806 6z pink & vio .25 .25
2564 A806 17z dk grn & lt grn .35 .25
2565 A806 25z bister & brn .60 .25
2566 A806 27z lt bl & dk bl .60 .25
2567 A806 31z violet & pur .75 .25
    Nos. 2562-2567 (6) 2.80 1.50

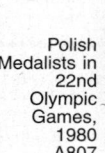

Polish Medalists in 22nd Olympic Games, 1980
A807

1983, Apr. 5   Perf. 11x11½
2568 A807 5z Steeplechase .25 .25
2569 A807 6z Equestrian .25 .25
2570 A807 15z Soccer, 1982
    World Cup .35 .25
2571 A807 27z + 5z Pole vault .70 .25
    Nos. 2568-2571 (4) 1.55 1.00

Warsaw Ghetto Uprising, 40th Anniv. — A808

Heroes' Monument, by Natan Rappaport.

1983, Apr. 19   Photo.   Perf. 11½x11
2572 A808 6z multicolored .25 .25
Se-tenant with label showing anniversary medal.

Customs Cooperation Council, 30th Anniv. — A809

1983, Apr. 28
2573 A809 5z multicolored .25 .25

Second Visit of Pope John Paul II — A810

Portraits of Pope. 31z vert.

1983, June 16   Photo.   Perf. 11
2574 A810 31z multicolored .80 .25
2575 A810 65z multicolored 1.50 .75
    a. Souvenir sheet 1.75 1.25

Army of King John III Sobieski — A811

No. 2576, Dragoons. No. 2577, Knight in armor. No. 2578, Non-commissioned infantry officers. No. 2579, Light cavalryman. No. 2580, Hussars.

1983, July 5   Perf. 11½x11
2576 A811 5z multi .25 .25
2577 A811 5z multi .25 .25
2578 A811 6z multi .25 .25
2579 A811 15z multi .35 .25
2580 A811 27z multi .70 .25
    Nos. 2576-2580 (5) 1.80 1.25

750th Anniv. of Torun Municipality — A812

1983, Aug. 25   Photo.   Perf. 11
2581 A812 6z multicolored .25 .25
    a. Souvenir sheet of 4 3.00 5.50
No. 2581a had limited distribution.

60th Anniv. of Polish Boxing Union
A813

1983, Nov. 4   Litho.   Perf. 11½x11
2582 A813 6z multicolored .25 .25

Enigma Decoding Machine, 50th Anniv. — A813a

1983, Aug. 16   Litho.   Perf. 11½x11
2582A A813a 5z multicolored .25 .25

Girl Near House — A813b

1983   Photo.   Perf. 11½x12
2582B A813b 6z multicolored .25 .25
Public courtesy campaign.

Portrait of King John III Sobieski
A814

King's Portraits by: #2584, Unknown court painter. #2585, Sobieski on Horseback, by Francesco Trevisani (1656-1746). 25z, Jerzy Eleuter Szymonowicz-Siemiginowski (1660-1711). 65z+10z, Sobieski at Vienna, by Jan Matejko (1838-1893).

1983, Sept. 12   Perf. 11
2583 A814 5z multicolored .25 .25
2584 A814 5z multicolored .25 .25
2585 A814 6z multicolored .25 .25
2586 A814 25z multicolored .60 .25
    Nos. 2583-2586 (4) 1.35 1.00

Souvenir Sheet
Imperf
2587 A814 65z + 10z multi 1.50 1.25
Victory over the Turks in Vienna, 300th anniv.

Polish Peoples' Army, 40th Anniv. — A815

#2588, General Zygmunt Berling (1896-1980). #2589, Wanda Wasilewska (1905-64). #2591, Troop formation.

1983, Oct. 12   Photo.   Perf. 11
2588 A815 5z multicolored .25 .25
2589 A815 5z multicolored .25 .25
2590 A815 6z multicolored .25 .25
2591 A815 6z multi, horiz. .25 .25
    Nos. 2588-2591 (4) 1.00 1.00

World Communications Year — A816

1983, Oct. 18   Photo.   Perf. 11
2592 A816 15z multicolored .35 .25

Cracow Restoration Type of 1982
1983, Nov. 25   Litho.   Perf. 11
2593 A801 5z Cloth Hall, horiz. .25 .25
2594 A801 6z Town Hall Tower .30 .25

Traditional Hats — A818

1983, Dec. 16   Photo.   Perf. 11½x11
2595 A818 5z Biskupianski .25 .25
2596 A818 5z Rozbarski .25 .25
2597 A818 6z Warminsko-
    Mazurski .25 .25
2598 A818 6z Cieszynski .25 .25

2599	A818	25z Kurpiowski	.45	.25
2600	A818	38z Lubuski	.75	.25
		Nos. 2595-2600 (6)	2.20	1.50

Natl. People's Council, 40th Anniv. — A819

Hand holding sword (poster).

1983, Dec. 31

2601	A819	6z multicolored	.25	.25

People's Army, 40th Anniv. — A820

1984, Jan. 1 Litho. Perf. 11½x11

2602	A820	5z Gen. Bem Brigade badge	.25	.25

Musical Instruments A821

1984, Feb. 10 Photo.

2603	A821	5z Dulcimer	.25	.25
2604	A821	6z Drum, tambourine	.25	.25
2605	A821	10z Accordion	.25	.25
2606	A821	15z Double bass	.30	.25
2607	A821	17z Bagpipes	.45	.25
2608	A821	29z Figurines by Tadeusz Zak	.60	.25
		Nos. 2603-2608 (6)	2.10	1.50

See Nos. 2682-2687.

Wincenty Witos (1874-1945), Prime Minister — A822

1984, Mar. 2 Litho. Perf. 11½x11

2609	A822	6z green & sepia	.25	.25

Local Flowers (Clematis Varieties) A823

1984, Mar. 26 Photo. Perf. 11x11½

2610	A823	5z Lanuginosa	.25	.25
2611	A823	6z Tangutica	.25	.25
2612	A823	10z Texensis	.25	.25
2613	A823	17z Alpina	.40	.25
2614	A823	25z Vitalba	.60	.35
2615	A823	27z Montana	.75	.50
		Nos. 2610-2615 (6)	2.50	1.85

The Ecstasy of St. Francis, by El Greco — A824

1984, Apr. 21 Perf. 11

2616	A824	27z multicolored	1.10	.50

1984 Olympics A825

1984, Apr. 25 Litho. Perf. 11x11½

2617	A825	5z Handball	.25	.25
2618	A825	6z Fencing	.25	.25
2619	A825	15z Bicycling	.35	.25
2620	A825	16z Running	.40	.25
2621	A825	17z Running, diff.	.45	.25
a.		Souv. sheet of 2, #2620-2621	1.25	1.00
2622	A825	31z Skiing	.75	.30
		Nos. 2617-2622 (6)	2.45	1.55

No. 2621a sold for 43z.

Battle of Monte Cassino, 40th Anniv. — A826

1984, May 18 Photo. Perf. 11½x11

2623	A826	15z Memorial Cross	.40	.25

View of Warsaw from the Praga Bank, by Bernardo Belotto Canaletto — A827

Paintings of Vistula River views: 6z, Trumpet Festivity, by Aleksander Gierymski. 25z, The Vistula near the Bielany District, by Jozef Rapacki. 27z, Steamship Harbor in the Powisle District, by Franciszek Kostrzewski.

1984, June 20 Photo. Perf. 11

2624	A827	5z multicolored	.25	.25
2625	A827	6z multicolored	.25	.25
2626	A827	25z multicolored	.60	.25
2627	A827	27z multicolored	.60	.25
		Nos. 2624-2627 (4)	1.70	1.00

Eastern Ruler — A828

Sculptures: 3.50z, Eastern ruler. No. 2628A, Woman wearing wreath. 10z, Man wearing hat. No. 2629, Warrior's Head, Wawel Castle.

1984-85 Photo. Perf. 11½x12

2628	A828	3.50z brown	.25	.25
2628A	A828	5z dark claret	.25	.25
2628B	A828	10z brt ultra	.25	.25
		Nos. 2628-2628B (3)	.75	.75

Coil Stamp Perf. 13½x14

2629	A828	5z dk blue grn	.25	.25

Issued: 3.50z, 1/24/85; No. 2628A, 10z, 7/8/85; No. 2629, 7/10/84.
No. 2629 has black control number on back of every fifth stamp.
See Nos. 2738-2744.

Order of Grunwald Cross — A829

Designs: 6z, Order of Revival of Poland. 10z, Order of the Banner of Labor, First Class. 16z, Order of Builders of People's Poland.

1984, July 21 Photo. Perf. 11½

2630	A829	5z multicolored	.25	.25
2631	A829	6z multicolored	.25	.25
2632	A829	10z multicolored	.25	.25
2633	A829	16z multicolored	.25	.25
a.		Sheet of 4, #2630-2633, perf. 11½x12	2.40	2.25
		Nos. 2630-2633 (4)	1.00	1.00

40th anniversary of July Manifesto (Origin of Polish People's Republic).

Warsaw Uprising, 40th Anniv. A830

1984, Aug. 1

2634	A830	4z multicolored	.25	.25
2635	A830	5z multicolored	.25	.25
2636	A830	6z multicolored	.25	.25
2637	A830	25z multicolored	.75	.25
		Nos. 2634-2637 (4)	1.50	1.00

Broken Heart Monument, Lodz — A831

1984, Aug. 31

2638	A831	16z multicolored	.40	.25

Defense of Oksywie Holm, Col. S. Dabek — A832

6z, Bzura River battle, Gen. T. Kutrzeba.

1984, Sept. 1

2639	A832	5z shown	.25	.25
2640	A832	6z multicolored	.25	.25

Invasion of Poland, 45th anniversary.
See Nos. 2692-2693, 2757, 2824-2826, 2864-2866, 2922-2925.

Polish Militia, 40th Anniv. A833

6z, Militiaman at Control Center.

1984, Sept. 29 Photo. Perf. 11½

2641	A833	5z shown	.25	.25
2642	A833	6z multicolored	.25	.25

Polish Aviation A834

No. 2643, Balloon ascent, 1784. No. 2644, Powered flight, 1911. No. 2645, Balloon Polonez, 1983. No. 2646 Modern gliders. No. 2647, Wilga, 1983. No. 2648, Farman, 1914. No. 2649, Los and PZL P-7.

1984, Nov. 6 Photo. Perf. 11x11½

2643	A834	5z multi	.25	.25
2644	A834	5z multi	.25	.25
2645	A834	6z multi	.25	.25
2646	A834	10z multi	.25	.25
2647	A834	16z multi	.35	.25
2648	A834	27z multi	.60	.25
2649	A834	31z multi	.65	.25
		Nos. 2643-2649 (7)	2.60	1.75

Protected Animals A835

1984, Dec. 4 Photo. Perf. 11x11½

2650	A835	4z Mustela nivalis	.25	.25
2651	A835	5z Martes foina	.25	.25
2652	A835	5z Mustela erminea	.25	.25

Perf. 11½x11

2653	A835	10z Castor fiber, vert.	.25	.25
2654	A835	10z Lutra lutra, vert.	.25	.25
2655	A835	65z Marmota marmota, vert.	1.50	.75
		Nos. 2650-2655 (6)	2.75	2.00

Cracow Restoration Type of 1982

5z, Royal Cathedral, Wawel. 15z, Royal Castle, Wawel, horiz.

Perf. 11½x11, 11x11½

1984, Dec. 10 Litho.

2656	A801	5z multi	.25	.25
2657	A801	15z multi	.30	.25

Religious Buildings A837

5z, Protestant Church, Warsaw. 10z, Saint Andrew Church, Cracow. 15z, Greek Orthodox Church, Rychwald. 20z, Orthodox Church, Warsaw. 25z, Tykocin Synagogue, horiz. 31z, Tartar Mosque, Kruszyniany, horiz.

Perf. 11½x12, 12x11½

1984, Dec. 28 Photo.

2658	A837	5z multicolored	.25	.25
2659	A837	10z multicolored	.25	.25
2660	A837	15z multicolored	.25	.25
2661	A837	20z multicolored	.25	.25
2662	A837	25z multicolored	.25	.25
2663	A837	31z multicolored	.45	.25
		Nos. 2658-2663 (6)	1.70	1.50

Classic and Contemporary Fire Engines — A838

Designs: 4z, Horse-drawn fire pump, 19th cent. 10z, Polski Fiat, c. 1930. 12z, Jelcz 315, 1970s. 15z, Horse-drawn hand pump, 1899. 20z, Jelcz engine, Magirus power ladder, 1970s. 30z, Hand pump, 18th cent.

1985, Feb. 25   Photo.   Perf. 11x11½
2664	A838	4z multicolored	.25	.25
2665	A838	10z multicolored	.25	.25
2666	A838	12z multicolored	.25	.25
2667	A838	15z multicolored	.25	.25
2668	A838	20z multicolored	.25	.25
2669	A838	30z multicolored	.85	.25
		Nos. 2664-2669 (6)	2.10	1.50

Battle of Raclawice, April, 1794, by Jan Styka, 1894 — A839

1985, Apr. 4   Perf. 11
| 2670 | A839 | 27z multicolored | .50 | .25 |

Kosciuszko Insurrection cent.

A840

1985, Apr. 11   Litho.   Perf. 11½
| 2671 | A840 | 10z sal rose & dk vio bl | .25 | .25 |

Wincenty Rzymowski (1883-1950), Democratic Party founder.

Blue Jeans, Badge — A841

1985, Apr. 25   Photo.   Perf. 11½x11
| 2672 | A841 | 15z multicolored | .25 | .25 |

Intl. Youth Year.

Prince Boleslaw Krzywousty (1085-1138) — A842

Regional maps and: 10z, Wladyslaw Gomulka (1905-82), sec.-gen. of the Polish Workers Party, prime minister 1945-49. 20z, Piotr Zaremba (b. 1910), president of Gdansk Province 1945-50.

1985, May 8   Litho.   Perf. 11½
2673	A842	5z multicolored	.25	.25
2674	A842	10z multicolored	.25	.25
2675	A842	20z multicolored	.35	.25
		Nos. 2673-2675 (3)	.85	.75

Restoration of the Western & Northern Territories to Polish control, 40th anniv.

Victory Berlin 1945, by Jozef Mlynarski (b. 1925) — A843

Painting: Polish and Soviet soldiers at Brandenburg Gate, May 9, 1945.

1985, May 9   Photo.   Perf. 12x11½
| 2676 | A843 | 5z multicolored | .25 | .25 |

Liberation from German occupation, 40th anniv.

Warsaw Treaty Org., 30th Anniv. — A844

1985, May 14   Litho.   Perf. 11½x11
| 2677 | A844 | 5z Emblem, member flags | .25 | .25 |

World Wildlife Fund A845

Endangered Wildlife: Canis lupus — No. 2678, Wolves, winter landscape. No. 2679, Female, cubs. No. 2680, Wolf. No. 2681, Wolves, summer landscape.

1985, May 25   Photo.   Perf. 11x11½
2678	A845	5z multicolored	.25	.25
2679	A845	10z multicolored	.35	.25
2680	A845	10z multicolored	.35	.25
2681	A845	20z multicolored	2.50	.75
		Nos. 2678-2681 (4)	3.45	1.50

A846

Folk instruments.

1985, June 25   Perf. 11½x11
2682	A846	5z Wooden rattle	.25	.25
2683	A846	10z Jingle	.25	.25
2684	A846	12z Clay whistles	.25	.25
2685	A846	20z Wooden fiddles	.30	.25
2686	A846	25z Tuned bells	.35	.25
2687	A846	31z Shepherd's flutes, ram's horn, ocarina	.45	.25
		Nos. 2682-2687 (6)	1.85	1.50

A847

Design: O.R.P. Iskra and emblem.

Photogravure and Engraved
1985, June 29
| 2688 | A847 | 5z bluish blk & yel | .25 | .25 |

Polish Navy, 40th anniv.

Tomasz Nocznicki (1862-1944) — A848

Polish Labor Movement founders: 20z, Maciej Rataj (1884-1940).

1985, July 26   Engr.   Perf. 11x11½
| 2689 | A848 | 10z grnsh black | .25 | .25 |
| 2690 | A848 | 20z brown black | .25 | .25 |

Natl. labor movement, 90th anniv.

Polish Field Hockey Assn., 50th Anniv. A849

1985, Aug. 22   Litho.   Perf. 11½x11
| 2691 | A849 | 5z multicolored | .25 | .25 |

World War II Battles Type of 1984
Designs: 5z, Defense of Wizny, Capt. Wladyslaw Raginis. 10z, Attack on Mlawa, Col. Wilhelm Andrzej Liszka-Lawicz.

1985, Sept. 1   Photo.   Perf. 12x11½
| 2692 | A832 | 5z multicolored | .25 | .25 |
| 2693 | A832 | 10z multicolored | .25 | .25 |

Pafawag Railway Rolling Stock Co. A850

1985, Sept. 18   Litho.   Perf. 11½
2694	A850	5z Box car	.25	.25
2695	A850	10z 201 E locomotive	.25	.25
2696	A850	17z Two-axle coal car	.25	.25
2697	A850	20z Passenger car	.50	.25
		Nos. 2694-2697 (4)	1.25	1.00

Wild Ducks A851

No. 2698, Anas crecca. No. 2699, Anas querquedula. No. 2700, Aythya fuligula. No. 2701, Bucephala clangula. No. 2702, Somateria mollissima. No. 2703, Netta rufina.

1985, Oct. 21   Photo.   Perf. 11x11½
2698	A851	5z multicolored	.25	.25
2699	A851	5z multicolored	.25	.25
2700	A851	10z multicolored	.30	.25
2701	A851	15z multicolored	.35	.25
2702	A851	25z multicolored	.50	.25
2703	A851	29z multicolored	.65	.35
		Nos. 2698-2703 (6)	2.30	1.60

UN, 40th Anniv. A852

1985, Oct. 24   Litho.   Perf. 11½x11
| 2704 | A852 | 27z multicolored | .50 | .25 |

Polish Ballet, 200th Anniv. — A853

1985, Dec. 4
| 2705 | A853 | 5z Prima ballerina | .25 | .25 |
| 2706 | A853 | 15z Male dancer | .25 | .25 |

Paintings by Stanislaw Ignacy Witkiewicz (1885-1939) — A854

5z, Marysia and Burek in Ceylon. No. 2708, Woman with a Fox. No. 2709, Self-portrait, 1931. 20z, Compositions, 1917. 25z, Portrait of Nena Stachurska, 1929. Nos. 2707, 2709-2711 vert.

Perf. 11½x11, 11x11½
1985, Dec. 6   Photo.
2707	A854	5z multicolored	.25	.25
2708	A854	10z multicolored	.25	.25
2709	A854	10z multicolored	.25	.25
2710	A854	20z multicolored	.25	.25
2711	A854	25z multicolored	.50	.25
		Nos. 2707-2711 (5)	1.50	1.25

Souvenir Sheet

Johann Sebastian Bach — A855

1985, Dec. 30   Perf. 11½x11
| 2712 | A855 | 65z multicolored | 1.25 | .45 |
| a. | | With inscription | 6.00 | 6.00 |

No. 2712a inscribed "300 Rocznica Urodzin Jana Sebastiana Bacha." Distribution was limited.

Profile, Emblem, Sigismond III Column, Royal Castle Tower — A856

1986, Jan. 16   *Perf. 11½x11*
2713 A856 10z lt ultra, brt ultra & ultra   .25 .25

Congress of Intellectuals for World Peace, Warsaw.

Halley's Comet
A857

Designs: No. 2714, Michal Kamienski (1879-1973), astronomer, orbit diagram. No. 2715, Comet, Vega, Giotto, Planet-A, ICE-3 space probes.

1986, Feb. 7   *Photo.*   *Perf. 11½*
2714 A857 25z multicolored   .40 .25
2715 A857 25z multicolored   .40 .25
    a.   Pair, #2714-2715   .90 .50

Intl. Peace Year — A858

1986, Mar. 20   *Photo.*   *Perf. 11½x11*
2716 A858 25z turq bl, yel & ultra   .35 .25

Cracow Restoration Type of 1982

Designs: 5z, Collegium Maius, Jagiellonian Museum. 10z, Town Hall, Kazimierz.

1986, Mar. 20   *Litho.*   *Perf. 11½*
2717 A801 5z multicolored   .25 .25
2718 A801 10z multicolored   .25 .25

Wildlife A859

No. 2719, Perdix perdix. No. 2720, Oryctolagus cuniculus. No. 2721, Dama dama. No. 2722, Phasianus colchicus. No. 2723, Lepus europaeus. No. 2724, Ovis ammon.

1986, Apr. 15   *Photo.*   *Perf. 11½x11*
2719 A859 5z multicolored   .25 .25
2720 A859 5z multicolored   .25 .25
2721 A859 10z multicolored   .25 .25
2722 A859 10z multicolored   .25 .25
2723 A859 20z multicolored   .35 .25
2724 A859 40z multicolored   .75 .50
    Nos. 2719-2724 (6)   2.10 1.75

Nos. 2719-2720, 2723-2724 vert.

Stanislaw Kulczynski (1895-1975), Scientist, Party Leader — A860

Photogravure and Engraved
1986, May 3   *Perf. 11½x11*
2725 A860 10z buff & choc   .25 .25

Warsaw Fire Brigade, 150th Anniv. — A861

Painting detail: The Fire Brigade on the Cracow Outskirts on Their Way to a Fire, 1871, by Josef Brodowski (1828-1900).

1986, May 16   *Perf. 11*
2726 A861 10z dl brn & dk brn   .25 .25

Paderewski A862

1986, May 22   *Perf. 11½x11*
2727 A862 65z multicolored   1.00 .25

AMERIPEX'86.

1986 World Cup Soccer Championships, Mexico — A863

1986, May 26   *Perf. 11½*
2728 A863 25z multicolored   .35 .25

Ferryboats – A864

1986, June 18   *Photo.*   *Perf. 11*
2729 A864 10z Wilanow   .25 .25
2730 A864 10z Wawel   .25 .25
    a.   Souv. sheet of 2, #2729-2730   1.25 .75
2731 A864 15z Pomerania   .30 .25
2732 A864 25z Rogalin   .35 .25
    a.   Souv. sheet of 2, #2731-2732   2.50 2.50
    Nos. 2729-2732 (4)   1.15 1.00

Nos. 2729-2732 printed se-tenant with labels picturing historic sites from the names of cities serviced. No. 2730a sold for 30z; No. 2732a for 55z. Surtax for the Natl. Assoc. of Philatelists.

Antarctic Agreement, 25th Anniv. — A865

Map of Antarctica and: 5z, A. B. Dobrowolski, Kopernik research ship. 40z, H. Arctowski, Professor Siedlecki research ship.

1986, June 23   *Litho.*   *Perf. 11½x11*
2733 A865 5z ver, pale grn & blk   .25 .25
2734 A865 40z org, pale vio & dk vio   .75 .40

Polish United Workers' Party, 10th Congress A866

1986, July 29   *Photo.*   *Perf. 11x11½*
2735 A866 10z red & dk gray bl   .25 .25

Wawel Heads Type of 1984-85

Designs: 15z, Woman wearing a wreath (like No. 2628A). No. 2739, Thinker. No. 2740, Eastern ruler. 40z, Youth wearing beret. 60z, Warrior. 200z, Man's head.

Perf. 11½x12, 14 (15z, No. 2740, 60z)
Engr., Photo. (15z, No. 2740, 60z)
1986-89
2738 A828 15z rose brown   .25 .25
2739 A828 20z green   .25 .25
2740 A828 20z peacock blue   .25 .25
2742 A828 40z gray   .25 .35
2743 A828 60z dark green   .25 .25
2744 A828 200z dark gray   .25 .25
    Nos. 2738-2744 (6)   1.50 1.60

Issued: 15z, 9/22/88; #2739, 2742, 7/30/86; #2740, 3/31/89; 60z, 12/15/89; #2744, 11/11/86.

No. 2740 and 60z are coil stamps, have black control number on back of every 5th stamp.

For surcharge see No. 2954.

Jasna Gora Monastery Collection A867

Designs: No. 2746, The Paulinite Church on Skalka in Cracow, oil painting detail, circa 1627. No. 2747, Jesse's Tree, oil on wood, 17th cent. No. 2748, Gilded chalice, 18th cent. No. 2749, Virgin Mary embroidery, 15th cent.

1986, Aug. 15   *Photo.*   *Perf. 11½x11*
2746 A867 5z multicolored   .25 .25
2747 A867 5z multicolored   .25 .25
2748 A867 20z multicolored   .35 .25
2749 A867 40z multicolored   .50 .25
    Nos. 2746-2749 (4)   1.35 1.00

Victories of Polish Athletes at 1985 World Championships — A868

Designs: No. 2750, Precision Flying, Kissimmee, Florida, won by Waclaw Nycz. No. 2751, Wind Sailing. Tallinn, USSR, won by Malgorzata Palasz-Piasecka. No. 2752, Glider Acrobatics, Vienna, won by Jerzy Makula. No. 2753, Greco-Roman Wrestling (82kg), Kolboten, Norway, won by Bogdan Daras. No. 2754, Road Cycling, Giavera del Montello, Italy, won by Lech Piasecki. No. 2755, Women's Modern Pentathlon, Montreal, won by Barbara Kotowska.

1986, Aug. 21   *Perf. 11½*
2750 A868 5z multicolored   .25 .25
2751 A868 10z multicolored   .25 .25
2752 A868 10z multicolored   .25 .25
2753 A868 15z multicolored   .25 .25
2754 A868 20z multicolored   .25 .25
2755 A868 30z multicolored   .50 .25
    Nos. 2750-2755 (6)   1.75 1.50

STOCKHOLMIA '86 — A869

1986, Aug. 28   *Perf. 11x11½*
2756 A869 65z multicolored   1.00 .35
    a.   Souvenir sheet   1.00 .50

World War II Battles Type of 1984

Design: Battle of Jordanow, Col. Stanislaw Maczek, motorized cavalry 10th brigade commander-in-chief.

1986, Sept. 1   *Perf. 12x11½*
2757 A832 10z multicolored   .25 .25

Albert Schweitzer — A870

Photogravure and Engraved
1986, Sept. 26   *Perf. 12x11½*
2758 A870 5z pale bl vio, sep & buff   .25 .25

World Post Day — A871

1986, Oct. 9   *Litho.*   *Perf. 11x11½*
2759 A871 40z org, ultra & sep   .50 .25
    a.   Souvenir sheet of 2   8.50 8.50

No. 2759a sold for 120z.

Folk and Fairy Tale Legends A872

Designs: No. 2760, Basilisk. No. 2761, Duke Popiel, vert. No. 2762, Golden Duck. No. 2763, Boruta, the Devil, vert. No. 2764, Janosik the Thief, vert. No. 2765, Lajkonik, conqueror of the Tartars, 13th cent., vert.

1986, Oct. 28   *Photo.*   *Perf. 11½x11*
2760 A872 5z multicolored   .25 .25
2761 A872 5z multicolored   .25 .25
2762 A872 10z multicolored   .25 .25
2763 A872 10z multicolored   .25 .25
2764 A872 20z multicolored   .30 .25
2765 A872 50z multicolored   .80 .35
    Nos. 2760-2765 (6)   2.10 1.60

Prof. Tadeusz Kotarbinski (1886-1981) — A873

1986, Nov. 19   *Litho.*   *Perf. 11½*
2766 A873 10z sepia, buff & brn blk   .25 .25

17th-20th Cent. Architecture — A874

Designs: No. 2767, Church, Baczal Dolny. No. 2768, Windmill, Zygmuntow. 10z, Oravian cottage, Zubrzyca Gorna. 15z, Kashubian Arcade cottage, Wazydze. 25z, Barn, Grzawa. 30z, Water mill, Molkowice Stare.

Perf. 11x11½, 11½x11

				Photo.
1986, Nov. 26				
2767	A874	5z multicolored	.25	.25
2768	A874	5z multi, vert.	.25	.25
2769	A874	10z multicolored	.25	.25
2770	A874	15z multicolored	.25	.25
2771	A874	25z multicolored	.35	.25
2772	A874	30z multicolored	.65	.40
		Nos. 2767-2772 (6)	2.00	1.65

Royalty A875

Photogravure and Engraved

1986, Dec. 4				Perf. 11
2773	A875	10z Mieszko I	.40	.25
2774	A875	25z Dobrava	.50	.40

See Nos. 2838-2839, 2884-2885, 2932-2933, 3033-3034, 3068-3069, 3141-3144, 3191-3192, 3222-3225, 3309-3312, 3366-3369, 3394-3397, 3479-3482, 3553-3556. For surcharges see Nos. 3016-3017.

New Year 1987 A876

1986, Dec. 12	Photo.	Perf. 11x11½
2775	A876	25z multicolored	.35	.25

Warsaw Cyclists Soc., Cent. A877

No. 2776, First trip to Bielany, uniformed escort, 1887. No. 2777, Jan Stanislaw Skrodzki (1867-1957), 1895 record-holder. No. 2778, Dynasy Society building, 1892-1937. No. 2779, Mieczyslaw Baranski, champion, 1896. No. 2780, Karolina Kociecka (b. 1875), female competitor. No. 2781, Henryk Weiss (d. 1912), Dynasy champion, 1904-1908.

Perf. 13x12½, 12½x13

1986, Dec. 19				Litho.
2776	A877	5z multi	.25	.25
2777	A877	5z multi, vert.	.25	.25
2778	A877	10z multi, vert.	.25	.25
2779	A877	10z multi, vert.	.25	.25
2780	A877	30z multi, vert.	.35	.25
2781	A877	50z multi, vert.	.65	.25
		Nos. 2776-2781 (6)	2.00	1.50

Henryk Arctowski Antarctic Station, King George Island, 10th Anniv. A878

Wildlife and ships: No. 2782, Euphausia superba, training freighter Antoni Garnuszewski. No. 2783, Notothenia rossi, Dissostichus mawsoni, Zulawy transoceanic ship. No. 2784, Fulmarus glacialoides, yacht Pogoria. No. 2785, Pigoscelis adeliae, yacht Gedania. 30z, Arctocephalus, research boat Dziunia. 40z, Hydrurga leptonyx, ship Kapitan Ledochowski.

1987, Feb. 13			Litho.	Perf. 11½
2782	A878	5z multicolored	.25	.25
2783	A878	5z multicolored	.25	.25
2784	A878	10z multicolored	.25	.25
2785	A878	10z multicolored	.25	.25
2786	A878	30z multicolored	.45	.30
2787	A878	40z multicolored	.65	.35
		Nos. 2782-2787 (6)	2.10	1.65

Paintings by Leon Wyczolkowski (1852-1936) — A879

No. 2788, Cineraria Flowers, 1924. No. 2789, Portrait of a Woman, 1883. No. 2790, Wood Church, 1910. No. 2791, Harvesting Beetroot, 1910. No. 2792, Wading Fishermen, 1891. No. 2793, Self-portrait, 1912.

1987, Mar. 20			Photo.	Perf. 11
2788	A879	5z multicolored	.25	.25
2789	A879	10z multicolored	.25	.25
2790	A879	10z multicolored	.25	.25
2791	A879	25z multicolored	.35	.25
2792	A879	30z multicolored	.45	.30
2793	A879	40z multicolored	.75	.40
		Nos. 2788-2793 (6)	2.30	1.70

Nos. 2789 and 2791 vert.

The Ravage, 1866, by Artur Grottger (1837-1867) — A880

1987, Mar. 26		Photo.	Perf. 11
2794	A880	15z dk brown & buff	.25	.25

Gen. Karol Swierczewski-Walter (1897-1947) — A881

1987, Mar. 27		Engr.	Perf. 11½x12
2795	A881	15z olive green	.25	.25

Pawel Edmund Strzelecki (1797-1873), Explorer — A882

1987, Apr. 23		Photo.	Perf. 11½x11
2796	A882	65z olive black	.80	.30

Colonization of Australia, bicentennial.

2nd PRON Congress A883

1987, May 8		Litho.	Perf. 11½
2797	A883	10z pale gray, brn, red & brt ultra	.25	.25

Patriotic Movement of the National Renaissance Congress.

Motor Vehicles — A884

No. 2798, 1936 Saurer-Zawrat. No. 2799, 1928 CWS T-1. No. 2800, 1928 Ursus-A. No. 2801, 1936 Lux-Sport. No. 2802, 1939 Podkowa 100. No. 2803, 1935 Sokol 600 RT.

1987, May 19			Photo.	Perf. 12x11½
2798	A884	10z multicolored	.25	.25
2799	A884	10z multicolored	.25	.25
2800	A884	15z multicolored	.25	.25
2801	A884	15z multicolored	.25	.25
2802	A884	25z multicolored	.35	.25
2803	A884	45z multicolored	.60	.35
		Nos. 2798-2803 (6)	1.95	1.60

Royal Castle, Warsaw — A885

1987, June 5			
2804	A885	50z multicolored	.60	.25

A souvenir sheet of 1 exists. Value $50.

A886

State Visit of Pope John Paul II — A887

1987, June 8			Perf. 11
2805	A886	15z shown	.25	.25
2806	A886	45z Portrait, diff.	.50	.30
a.	Pair, #2805-2806		.75	.50

Souvenir Sheet
Perf. 12x11½

2807	A887	50z shown	1.00	1.00

No. 2806a has continuous design.

Cracow Restoration Type of 1982

1987, July 6		Litho.	Perf. 11½
2809	A801	10z Barbican Gate, Wawel, horiz.	.25	.25

Esperanto Language, Cent. — A890

1987, July 25		Litho.	Perf. 11½
2811	A890	45z Ludwig L. Zamenhof	.40	.25

A891

Poznan and Town Hall, by Stanislaw Wyspianski.

1987, Aug. 3			
2812	A891	15z blk & pale salmon	.25	.25

POZNAN '87, Aug. 8-16.

A892

No. 2813, Queen. No. 2814, Worker. No. 2815, Drone. No. 2816, Box hive, orchard. No. 2817, Bee collecting pollen. No. 2818, Beekeeper collecting honey.

1987, Aug. 20			Photo.	Perf. 11½x11
2813	A892	10z multicolored	.25	.25
2814	A892	10z multicolored	.25	.25
2815	A892	15z multicolored	.25	.25
2816	A892	15z multicolored	.25	.25
2817	A892	40z multicolored	.25	.50
2818	A892	50z multicolored	.70	.25
		Nos. 2813-2818 (6)	1.95	1.75

31st World Apiculture Congress, Warsaw.

Success of Polish Athletes at World Championship Events — A894

10z, Acrobatics, France. 15z, Kayak, Canada. 20z, Marksmanship, E. Germany. 25z, Wrestling, Hungary.

1987, Sept. 24   Litho.   Perf. 14
2820 A894 10z multicolored   .25 .25
2821 A894 15z multicolored   .25 .25
2822 A894 20z multicolored   .25 .25
2823 A894 25z multicolored   .25 .25
    Nos. 2820-2823 (4)   1.00 1.00

World War II Battles Type of 1984
Designs: No. 2824, Battle of Mokra, Julian Filipowicz. No. 2825, Battle scene near Oleszycami, Brig.-Gen. Josef Rudolf Kustron. 15z, Air battles over Warsaw, pilot Stefan Pawlikowski.

1987, Sept. 1   Photo.   Perf. 12x11½
2824 A832 10z multicolored   .25 .25
2825 A832 20z multicolored   .25 .25
2826 A832 15z multicolored   .35 .25
    Nos. 2824-2826 (3)   .85 .75

Jan Hevelius (1611-1687), Astronomer, and Constellations — A895

1987, Sept. 15   Litho.   Perf. 11½
2827 A895 15z Hevelius, sextant, vert.   .25 .25
2828 A895 40z shown   .40 .30

Souvenir Sheet

1st Artificial Satellite, Sputnik, 30th Anniv. — A896

1987, Oct. 2   Photo.   Perf. 11½x11
2829 A896 40z Stacionar 4 satellite   .90 .75

World Post Day A897

Design: Ignacy Franciszek Przebendowski (1730-1791), postmaster general, and post office building, 19th cent., Krakowskie Przedmiescie, Warsaw.

1987, Oct. 9   Litho.
2830 A897 15z lt olive grn & rose claret   .25 .25

Col. Stanislaw Wieckowski — A898

Photo. & Engr.
1987, Oct. 16   Perf. 12x11½
2831 A898 15z deep blue & blk   .25 .25
Col. Wieckowski (1884-1942), physician and social reformer executed by the Nazis at Auschwitz.

HAFNIA '87 — A899

Fairy tales by Hans Christian Andersen (1805-1875): No. 2832, The Little Mermaid. No. 2833, The Nightingale. No. 2834, The Wild Swan. No. 2835, The Match Girl. 30z, The Snow Queen. 40z, The Brave Toy Soldier.

1987, Oct. 16   Photo.   Perf. 11x11½
2832 A899 10z multicolored   .25 .25
2833 A899 10z multicolored   .25 .25
2834 A899 20z multicolored   .35 .25
2835 A899 20z multicolored   .35 .25
2836 A899 30z multicolored   .35 .30
2837 A899 40z multicolored   .50 .30
    Nos. 2832-2837 (6)   2.05 1.60

Royalty Type of 1986
Photo. & Engr.
1987, Dec. 4   Perf. 11
2838 A875 10z Boleslaw I Chrobry   .35 .25
2839 A875 15z Mieszko II   .75 .25

No. 2838 exists with label. Value: mint $4, used $6.25.

New Year 1988 A900

1987, Dec. 14   Photo.   Perf. 11x11½
2840 A900 15z multicolored   .25 .25

Dragonflies — A901

No. 2841, Anax imperator. No. 2842, Libellula quadrimaculata, vert. No. 2843, Calopteryx splendens. No. 2844, Cordulegaster annulatus, vert. No. 2845, Sympetrum pedemontanum. No. 2846, Aeschna viridis, vert.

Perf. 11x11½, 11½x11
1988, Feb. 23   Photo.
2841 A901 10z multicolored   .25 .25
2842 A901 10z multicolored   .25 .25
2843 A901 15z multicolored   .25 .25
2844 A901 20z multicolored   .25 .25
2845 A901 30z multicolored   .35 .25
2846 A901 50z multicolored   .75 .40
    Nos. 2841-2846 (6)   2.10 1.65

Cracow Restoration Type of 1982
1988, Mar. 8   Litho.   Perf. 11½x11
2847 A801 15z Florianska Gate, 1300   .25 .25

Intl. Year of Graphic Design A903

1988, Apr. 28   Photo.   Perf. 11x11½
2848 A903 40z multicolored   .35 .25

Antique Clocks — A904

Clocks in the Museum of Artistic and Precision Handicrafts, Warsaw, and clockworks: No. 2849, Frisian wall clock, 17th cent., vert. No. 2850, Anniversary clock and rotary pendulum, 20th cent. No. 2851, Carriage clock, 18th cent., vert. No. 2852, Louis XV rococo bracket clock, 18th cent., vert. 20z, Pocket watch, 19th cent. 40z, Gdansk six-sided clock signed by Benjamin Zoll, 17th cent.

Perf. 11½x12, 12x11½
1988, May 19   Photo.
2849 A904 10z lt green & multi   .25 .25
2850 A904 10z purple & multi   .25 .25
2851 A904 15z dull org & multi   .25 .25
2852 A904 15z brown & multi   .25 .25
2853 A904 20z multicolored   .35 .25
2854 A904 40z multicolored   .50 .25
    Nos. 2849-2854 (6)   1.85 1.50

1988 Summer Olympics, Seoul A905

1988, June 27   Photo.   Perf. 11x11½
2855 A905 15z Triple jump   .25 .25
2856 A905 20z Wrestling   .25 .25
2857 A905 20z Two-man kayak   .25 .25
2858 A905 25z Judo   .25 .25
2859 A905 40z Shooting   .40 .25
2860 A905 55z Swimming   .50 .30
    Nos. 2855-2860 (6)   1.90 1.55

See No. B148.

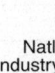

Natl. Industry A906

1988, Aug. 23   Photo.   Perf. 11x11½
Size: 35x27mm
2861 A906 45z Los "Elk" aircraft   .30 .25

State Aircraft Works, 60th anniv.
See Nos. 2867, 2871, 2881-2883.

16th European Regional FAO Conference, Cracow — A907

15z, Computers and agricultural growth. 40z, Balance between industry and nature.

1988, Aug. 22   Perf. 11½x11
2862 A907 15z multicolored   .25 .25
2863 A907 40z multicolored   .40 .25

World War II Battles Type of 1984
Battle scenes and commanders: 15z, Modlin, Brig.-Gen. Wiktor Thommee. No. 2865, Warsaw, Brig.-Gen. Walerian Czuma. No. 2866, Tomaszow Lubelski, Brig.-Gen. Antoni Szylling.

1988, Sept. 1   Photo.   Perf. 12x11½
2864 A832 15z multicolored   .25 .25
2865 A832 20z multicolored   .25 .25
2866 A832 20z multicolored   .25 .25
    Nos. 2864-2866 (3)   .75 .75

Natl. Industries Type of 1988
Design: Stalowa Wola Ironworks, 50th anniv.

1988, Sept. 5   Perf. 11x11½
Size: 35x27mm
2867 A906 15z multicolored   .25 .25

World Post Day A909

Design: Postmaster Tomasz Arciszewski (1877-1955), Post and Telegraph Administration emblem used from 1919 to 1927.

1988, Oct. 9   Litho.   Perf. 11½x11
2868 A909 20z multicolored   .25 .25

Also printed in sheet of 12 plus 12 labels.

World War II Combat Medals — A910

No. 2869, Battle of Lenino Cross. No. 2870, On the Field of Glory Medal.

1988, Oct. 12   Photo.
2869 A910 20z multicolored   .25 .25
2870 A910 20z multicolored   .25 .25

See Nos. 2930-2931.

Natl. Industries Type of 1988
Air Force Medical Institute, 60th anniv.

1988, Oct. 12   Perf. 11x11½
Size: 38x27mm
2871 A906 20z multicolored   .25 .25

Stanislaw Malachowski, Kazimierz Nestor Sapieha — A912

1988, Oct. 16   Perf. 11
2872 A912 20z multicolored   .25 .25

Four Years' Sejm (Parliament) (1788-1792), bicent.

National Leaders — A913

No. 2873, Wincenty Witos. No. 2874, Ignacy Daszynski. No. 2875, Wojciech Korfanty. No. 2876, Stanislaw Wojciechowski. No. 2877,

Julian Marchlewski. No. 2878, Ignacy Pade-rewski. No. 2879, Jozef Pilsudski. No. 2880, Gabriel Narutowicz.

1988, Nov. 11   *Perf. 12x11½*
2873	A913	15z multicolored	.25	.25
2874	A913	15z multicolored	.25	.25
2875	A913	20z multicolored	.25	.25
2876	A913	20z multicolored	.25	.25
2877	A913	20z multicolored	.25	.25
2878	A913	20z multicolored	.25	.25
2879	A913	200z multicolored	.25	.25
2880	A913	200z multicolored	.25	.25
a.		Souvenir sheet of 3, #2878-2880	25.00	25.00
		Nos. 2873-2880 (8)	2.00	2.00

Natl. independence, 70th anniv.

Natl. Industries Type of 1988

15z, Wharf, Gdynia. 20z, Industrialist Hipolit Cegielski, 1883 steam locomotive. 40z, Poznan fair grounds, Upper Silesia Tower.

1988   **Photo.**   *Perf. 11x11½*
Size: 39x27mm
2881	A906	15z multicolored	.25	.25
2882	A906	20z multicolored	.25	.25

Size: 35x27mm
2883	A906	40z multicolored	.25	.25
		Nos. 2881-2883 (3)	.75	.75

70th anniv. of Polish independence. Gdynia Port, 65th anniv (15z); Metal Works in Poznan, 142nd anniv. (20z); and Poznan Intl. Fair 60th anniv. (40z).
Issued: 15z, 12/12; 20z, 11/28; 40z, 12/21.

Royalty Type of 1986

10z, Rycheza. 15z, Kazimierz I Odnowiciel.

Photo. & Engr.
1988, Dec. 4   *Perf. 11*
2884	A875	10z multicolored	.35	.25
2885	A875	15z multicolored	.55	.25

New Year 1989
A914

1988, Dec. 9   **Photo.**   *Perf. 11x11½*
2886	A914	20z multicolored	.25	.25

Unification of Polish Workers' Unions, 40th Anniv. — A915

1988, Dec. 15   *Perf. 11½x12*
2887	A915	20z black & ver	.25	.25

Fire Boats — A916

1988, Dec. 29   **Litho.**   *Perf. 14*
2888	A916	10z Blysk	.25	.25
2889	A916	15z Zar	.25	.25
2890	A916	15z Plomien	.25	.25
2891	A916	20z Strazak 4	.25	.25
2892	A916	20z Strazak 11	.25	.25
2893	A916	45z Strazak 25	.45	.40
		Nos. 2888-2893 (6)	1.70	1.65

Horses — A917

1989, Mar. 6   **Photo.**   *Perf. 11*
2894	A917	15z Lippizaner	.25	.25
2895	A917	15z Arden, vert.	.25	.25
2896	A917	20z English	.25	.25
2897	A917	20z Arabian, vert.	.25	.25
2898	A917	30z Wielkopolski	.35	.25
2899	A917	70z Polish, vert.	.75	.25
		Nos. 2894-2899 (6)	2.10	1.50

Dogs — A918

No. 2900, Wire-haired dachshund. No. 2901, Cocker spaniel. No. 2902, Czech fousek pointer. No. 2903, Welsh terrier. No. 2904, English setter. No. 2905, Pointer.

1989, May 3   **Photo.**   *Perf. 11½x11*
2900	A918	15z multicolored	.25	.25
2901	A918	15z multicolored	.25	.25
2902	A918	20z multicolored	.25	.25
2903	A918	20z multicolored	.25	.25
2904	A918	25z multicolored	.35	.25
2905	A918	45z multicolored	.85	.60
		Nos. 2900-2905 (6)	2.20	1.85

Battle of Monte Cassino, 45th Anniv. — A919

Design: 80z, Gen. W. Anders. 165z, Battle of Falaise, General Stanislaw Maczek, horiz. 210z, Battle of Arnhem, Gen. Stanislaw Sosabowski, vert.

1989, May 18   *Perf. 11½x12*
2906	A919	80z multicolored	.25	.25
2907	A919	165z multicolored	.50	.25
2907A	A919	210z multicolored	.60	.25
		Nos. 2906-2907A (3)	1.35	.75

1st Armored Division at the Battle of Falaise, 45th anniv. Battle of Arnhem, 45th anniv.
See No. 2968.

A 50z stamp for Gen. Grzegorz Korczynski was prepared but not released. Value: mint $25, cto $35.

Woman Wearing a Phrygian Cap — A920

1989, July 3   **Litho.**   *Perf. 11½x11*
2908	A920	100z blk, dark red & dark ultra	.25	.25
a.		Souv. sheet of 2+2 labels	1.00	.75

French revolution bicent., PHILEXFRANCE '89. No. 2908 printed se-tenant with inscribed label picturing exhibition emblem. No. 2908a sold for 270z. Surcharge benefited the Polish Philatelic Union.

Polonia House, Pultusk — A921

1989, July 16   **Photo.**   *Perf. 11½*
2909	A921	100z multicolored	.35	.25

First Moon Landing, 20th Anniv. A922

1989, July 21   *Perf. 11x11½*
2910	A922	100z multicolored	.35	.25
a.		Souvenir sheet of 1	1.25	.50

No. 2910a exists imperf. Value $20.

Polish People's Republic, 45th Anniv. — A923

Winners of the Order of the Builders of People's Poland: No. 2911, Ksawery Dunikowski (1875-1964), artist. No. 2912, Stanislaw Mazur (1897-1964), agriculturist. No. 2913, Natalia Gasiorowska (1881-1964), historian. No. 2914, Wincenty Pstrowski (1904-1948), coal miner.

1989, July 21   *Perf. 11½x11*
2911	A923	35z multicolored	.25	.25
2912	A923	35z multicolored	.25	.25
2913	A923	35z multicolored	.25	.25
2914	A923	35z multicolored	.25	.25
		Nos. 2911-2914 (4)	1.00	1.00

Security Service and Militia, 45th Anniv. A924

1989, July 21   *Perf. 11x11½*
2915	A924	35z dull brn & slate blue	.25	.25

World Fire Fighting Congress, July 25-30, Warsaw — A925

1989, July 25   *Perf. 11½x11*
2916	A925	80z multicolored	.35	.25

Daisy — A926

Designs: 60z, Juniper. 150z, Daisy. 500z, Wild rose. 1000z, Blue corn flower.

1989   **Photo.**   *Perf. 11x12*
2917	A926	40z slate green	.25	.25
2918	A926	60z violet blue	.25	.25
2919	A926	150z rose lake	.25	.25
2920	A926	500z bright violet	.25	.25
2921	A926	1000z bright blue	.25	.25
		Nos. 2917-2921 (5)	1.25	1.25

Issue dates: 40z, 60z, Aug. 25. 150z, Dec. 4; 500z, 1000z, Dec. 19.
See Nos. 2978-2979, 3026. For surcharge see No. 2970.

World War II Battles Type of 1984

Battle scenes and commanders: No. 2922, Westerplatte, Capt. Franciszek Dabrowski. No. 2923, Hel, Artillery Capt. B. Przybyszewski. No. 2924, Kock, Brig.-Gen. Franciszek Kleeberg. No. 2925, Lwow, Brig.-Gen. Wladyslaw Langner.

1989, Sept. 1   *Perf. 12x11½*
2922	A832	25z multicolored	.25	.25
2923	A832	25z multicolored	.25	.25
2924	A832	35z multicolored	.25	.25
2925	A832	35z multicolored	.25	.25
		Nos. 2922-2925 (4)	1.00	1.00

Nazi invasion of Poland, 50th anniv.

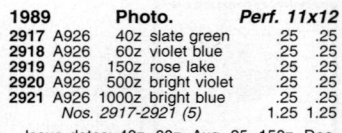

Caricature Museum — A927

1989, Sept. 15   **Photo.**   *Perf. 11½x11*
2926	A927	40z multicolored	.25	.25

Teaching Surgery at Polish Universities, Bicent., and Surgeon's Soc. Cent. — A928

Surgeons: 40z, Rafal Jozef Czerwiakowski (1743-1813), 1st professor of surgery and founder of the 1st surgical department, Jagellonian University, Cracow. 60z, Ludwik Rydygier (1850-1920), founder of the Polish Surgeons Society.

1989, Sept. 18   *Perf. 11½x12*
2927	A928	40z black & brt ultra	.25	.25
2928	A928	60z black & brt green	.25	.25

World Post Day — A929

Design: Emil Kalinski (1890-1973), minister of the Post and Telegraph from 1933-1939.

1989, Oct. 9   *Perf. 12x11½*
2929	A929	60z multicolored	.35	.25

Printed se-tenant with label picturing postal emblem of the second republic.

WWII Decorations Type of 1988

Medals: No. 2930, Participation in the Struggle for Control of the Nation. No. 2931, Defense of Warsaw, 1939-45.

1989, Oct. 12   **Photo.**   *Perf. 11½x11*
2930	A910	60z multicolored	.25	.25
2931	A910	60z multicolored	.25	.25

Royalty Type of 1986

20z, Boleslaw II Szczodry. 30z, Wladyslaw I Herman.

Photo. & Engr.
1989, Oct. 18   *Perf. 11*
2932	A875	20z multicolored	.50	.30
2933	A875	30z multicolored	.60	.50

World Stamp Expo '89, Washington, DC, Nov. 17-Dec.3 — A930

1989, Nov. 14 Photo. Perf. 11x11½
2934 A930 500z multicolored .90 .35
Exists imperf. Value: mint $1.50, used $1.40.

Polish Red Cross Soc., 70th Anniv. — A931

1989, Nov. 17 Perf. 11½x11
2935 A931 200z blk, brt yel grn & scar .35 .25

Treaty of Versailles, 70th Anniv. A932

Design: State arms and representatives of Poland who signed the treaty, including Ignacy Jan Paderewski (1860-1941), pianist, composer, statesman, and Roman Dmowski (1864-1939), statesman.

1989, Nov. 21 Perf. 11x11½
2936 A932 350z multicolored .65 .25

Camera Shutter as the Iris of the Eye — A933

Designs: 40z, Photographer in silhouette, Maksymilian Strasz (1804-1870), pioneer of photography in Poland.

Perf. 11½x12, 12x11½
1989, Nov. 27
2937 A933 40z multicolored .25 .25
2938 A933 60z shown .25 .25

Photography, 150th anniv.

No. 2456 Surcharged
1989, Nov. 30 Photo. Perf. 11x11½
2939 A766 500z on 4z dark violet .25 .25

Flowers, Still-life Paintings in the National Museum, Warsaw A934

25z, Jan Ciaglinski. 30z, Wojciech Weiss. 35z, Antoni Kolasinski. 50z, Stefan Nacht-Samborski. 60z, Jozef Pankiewicz. 85z, Henryka Beyer. 110z, Wladyslaw Slewinski. 190z, Czeslaw Wdowiszewski.

1989, Dec. 18 Perf. 13
2940 A934 25z multicolored .25 .25
2941 A934 30z multicolored .25 .25
2942 A934 35z multicolored .25 .25
2943 A934 50z multicolored .25 .25
2944 A934 60z multicolored .25 .25
2945 A934 85z multicolored .25 .25

2946 A934 110z multicolored .25 .25
2947 A934 190z multicolored .50 .30
Nos. 2940-2947 (8) 2.25 2.05

Religious Art — A935

50z, Jesus, shroud. 60z, Two saints. 90z, Three saints. 150z, Jesus, Mary, Joseph. 200z, Madonna and Child Enthroned. 350z, Holy Family with angels.

1989, Dec. 21 Perf. 11½x11
2948 A935 50z multicolored .25 .25
2949 A935 60z multicolored .25 .25
2950 A935 90z multicolored .25 .25

Perf. 11x11½
2951 A935 150z multicolored .25 .25
2952 A935 200z multicolored .30 .25
2953 A935 350z multicolored .50 .30
Nos. 2948-2953 (6) 1.80 1.55

Nos. 2951-2953 vert.

Republic of Poland
No. 2738 Surcharged
1990, Jan. 31 Photo. Perf. 11½x12
2954 A828 350z on 15z rose brn .25 .25

Opera Singers — A936

Portraits: 100z, Krystyna Jamroz (1923-1986). 150z, Wanda Werminska (1900-1988). 350z, Ada Sari (1882-1968). 500z, Jan Kiepura (1902-1966).

1990, Feb. 9 Perf. 12x11½
2955 A936 100z multicolored .25 .25
2956 A936 150z multicolored .25 .25
2957 A936 350z multicolored .25 .25
2958 A936 500z multicolored .35 .25
Nos. 2955-2958 (4) 1.10 1.00

Yachting A937

1990, Mar. 29 Perf. 11x11½
2959 A937 100z shown .25 .25
2960 A937 200z Rugby .25 .25
2961 A937 400z High jump .25 .25
2962 A937 500z Figure skating .25 .25
2963 A937 500z Diving .25 .25
2964 A937 1000z Rhythmic gymnastics .55 .25
Nos. 2959-2964 (6) 1.80 1.50

Roman Kozlowski (1889-1977), Paleontologist — A938

1990, Apr. 17 Photo. Perf. 11x11½
2965 A938 500z red & olive bis .30 .25

Pope John Paul II, 70th Birthday A939

1990, May 18 Perf. 11
2966 A939 1000z multicolored .55 .30

Souvenir Sheet

First Polish Postage Stamp, 130th Anniv. — A940

Design includes No. 1 separated by simulated perforations from 1000z commemorative version at right.

1990, May 25 Perf. 11½
2967 A940 1000z multicolored .90 .60

World War II Battle Type of 1989
Design: Battle of Narvik, 1940, General Z. Bohusz-Szyszko.

1990, May 28 Perf. 11½x12
2968 A919 1500z multicolored .45 .25

World Cup Soccer Championships, Italy — A941

1990, June 8 Perf. 11½x11
2969 A941 1000z multicolored .35 .30

No. 2918 Surcharged in Vermilion

1990, June 18 Photo. Perf. 11x12
2970 A926 700z on 60z vio bl .25 .25

Memorial to Victims of June 1956 Uprising, Poznan — A942

1990, June 28 Photo. Perf. 12x11½
2971 A942 1500z multicolored .30 .25

Social Insurance Institution, 70th Anniv. — A943

1990, July 5 Perf. 11x11½
2972 A943 1500z multicolored .30 .25

Shells — A944

#2973, Mussel. #2974, Fresh water snail.

1990, July 16 11½, 14 (#2974)
2973 A944 B (500z) dk pur .65 .25
2974 A944 A (700z) olive grn .65 .25

Katyn Forest Massacre, 50th Anniv. — A945

1990, July 20
2975 A945 1500z gray, red & blk .30 .25

Polish Meteorological Service — A946

1990, July 27 Perf. 11x11½
2976 A946 500z shown .25 .25
2977 A946 700z Water depth gauge .35 .25

Flower Type of 1989
2000z, Nuphar. 5000z, German iris.

1990, Aug. 13 Die Cut
Self Adhesive
2978 A926 2000z olive grn .35 .25
2979 A926 5000z violet .50 .25

World Kayaking Championships, Poznan — A947

Design: 1000z, One-man kayak.

1990, Aug. 22 Photo. Perf. 11x11½
2980 A947 700z multicolored .25 .25
2981 A947 1000z multicolored .30 .25
a. Souv. sheet of 1 + label 2.50 2.50

A948

1990, Aug. 31   **Perf. 11½x11**
2982 A948 1500z blk, red & gray   .50   .25
     Solidarity, 10th anniv.

A949

Flowers — No. 2983, Polemonium coeruleum. No. 2984, Nymphoides peltata. No. 2985, Dracocephalum ruyschiana. No. 2986, Helleborus purpurascens. No. 2987, Daphne cneorum. No. 2988, Dianthus superbus.

1990, Sept. 24   **Photo.**   **Perf. 11½x11**
2983 A949 200z multi   .25   .25
2984 A949 700z multi   .25   .25
2985 A949 700z multi   .25   .25
2986 A949 1000z multi   .25   .25
2987 A949 1500z multi   .50   .35
2988 A949 1700z multi   .65   .35
    Nos. 2983-2988 (6)   2.15 1.70

Cmielow Porcelain Works, Bicentennial — A950

Designs: 700z, Platter, 1870-1887. 800z, Plate, 1887-1890, vert. No. 2991, Figurine, 1941-1944, vert. No. 2992, Cup, saucer, c. 1887. 1500z, Candy box, 1930-1990. 2000z, Vase, 1979, vert.

1990, Oct. 31   **Photo.**   **Perf. 11**
2989 A950 700z multicolored   .25   .25
2990 A950 800z multicolored   .25   .25
2991 A950 1000z multicolored   .25   .25
2992 A950 1000z multicolored   .25   .25
2993 A950 1500z multicolored   .30   .25
2994 A950 2000z multicolored   .65   .25
    Nos. 2989-2994 (6)   1.95 1.50

Owls — A951

1990, Nov. 6   **Litho.**   **Perf. 14**
2995 A951 200z Athene noctua   .25   .25
2996 A951 500z shown   .35   .25
2997 A951 500z Strix aluco,
          winter   .25   .25
2998 A951 1000z Asio flammeus   .30   .25
2999 A951 1500z Asio otus   .40   .40
3000 A951 2000z Tyto alba   1.25   .75
    Nos. 2995-3000 (6)   2.80 2.15

Pres. Lech Walesa, 1983 Nobel Peace Prize Winner A952

1990, Dec. 12   **Litho.**   **Perf. 11x11½**
3001 A952 1700z multicolored   .60   .25

A953

1990, Dec. 21   **Photo.**   **Perf. 11½x11**
3002 A953 1500z multicolored   .40   .25
    Polish participation in Battle of Britain, 50th anniv.

A954

Architecture: 700z, Collegiate Church, 12th cent., Leczyca. 800z, Castle, 14th cent., Reszel. 1500z, Town Hall, 16th cent., Chelmno. 1700z, Church of the Nuns of the Visitation, 18th cent., Warsaw.

1990, Dec. 28   **Litho.**   **Perf. 11½**
3003 A954 700z multicolored   .25   .25
3004 A954 800z multicolored   .25   .25
3005 A954 1500z multicolored   .50   .25
3006 A954 1700z multicolored   .50   .25
    Nos. 3003-3006 (4)   1.50 1.00

No. 3006 printed with se-tenant label for World Philatelic Exhibition, Poland '93.

Art Treasures of the Natl. Gallery, Warsaw A955

Paintings: 500z, King Sigismund Augustus. 700z, The Adoration of the Magi, Pultusk Codex. 1000z, St. Matthew, Pultusk Codex. 1500z, Christ Removing the Moneychangers by Mikolaj Haberschrack. 1700z, The Annunciation. 2000z, The Three Marys by Haberschrack.

1991, Jan. 11   **Photo.**   **Perf. 11**
3007 A955 500z multicolored   .25   .25
3008 A955 700z multicolored   .25   .25
3009 A955 1000z multicolored   .25   .25
3010 A955 1500z multicolored   .30   .30
3011 A955 1700z multicolored   .40   .25
3012 A955 2000z multicolored   .60   .35
    Nos. 3007-3012 (6)   2.05 1.65

Pinecones — A956

1991, Feb. 22   **Perf. 12x11½**
3013 A956 700z Abies alba   .40   .25
3014 A956 1500z Pinus strobus   .40   .25
    See Nos. 3163-3164, 3231-3232.

Radziwill Palace A957

1991, Mar. 3   **Photo.**   **Perf. 11x12**
3015 A957 1500z multicolored   1.00   .50
    Admission to CEPT.

Royalty Type of 1986 Srchd. in Red

Designs: 1000z, Boleslaw III Krzywousty. 1500z, Wladyslaw II Wygnaniec.

Photo. & Engr.
1991, Mar. 25   **Perf. 11**
3016 A875 1000z on 40z, grn &
            blk   .60   .25
3017 A875 1500z on 50z, red vio
            & gray blk   .80   .40
    Not issued without surcharge.

Brother Albert (Adam Chmielowski, 1845-1916) — A958

1991, Mar. 29   **Photo.**   **Perf. 12x11½**
3018 A958 2000z multicolored   .55   .30

Battle of Legnica, 750th Anniv. A959

Photo. & Engr.
1991, Apr. 9   **Perf. 14½x14**
3019 A959 1500z multicolored   .65   .35
    See Germany No. 1635.

Polish Icons A960

Designs: 500z, 1000z, 1500z, Various paintings of Madonna and Child. 700z, 2000z, 2200z, Various paintings of Jesus.

1991, Apr. 22   **Photo.**   **Perf. 11**
3020 A960 500z multicolored   .25   .25
3021 A960 700z multicolored   .25   .25
3022 A960 1000z multicolored   .25   .25
3023 A960 1500z multicolored   .25   .25
3024 A960 2000z multicolored   .45   .25
3025 A960 2200z multicolored   .75   .40
    Nos. 3020-3025 (6)   2.20 1.65

Flower Type of 1989

Design: 700z, Lily of the Valley.

1991, Apr. 26   **Litho.**   **Perf. 14**
3026 A926 700z dk blue green   .25   .25

Royalty Type of 1986

Designs: 1000z, Boleslaw IV Kedzierzawy. 1500z, Mieszko III Stary.

Photo. & Engr.
1991, Apr. 30   **Perf. 11x11½**
3033 A875 1000z brn red & black .75   .25
3034 A875 1500z brt bl & bluish
            blk   1.00   .45

A961

2000z, Title page of act. 2500z, Debate in the Sejm. 3000z, Adoption of Constitution, May 3, 1791, by Jan Matejko (1838-1893).

1991, May 2   **Litho.**   **Perf. 11½**
3035 A961 2000z brown & ver   .35   .25
3036 A961 2500z brown & ver   .50   .35
        Souvenir Sheet
3037 A961 3000z multicolored   .85   .50
    May 3, 1791 Polish constitution, bicent.

A962

1991, May 6   **Litho.**   **Perf. 11½x11**
3038 A962 1000z multicolored   1.60   .75
    Europa.

European Conference for Protection of Cultural Heritage, Cracow — A963

1991, May 27   **Litho.**   **Perf. 11½**
3039 A963 2000z blue & lake   .55   .30

Sinking of the Bismarck, 50th Anniv. — A964

1991, May 27
3040 A964 2000z multicolored .60 .25

A965

Designs: 1000z, Pope John Paul II. 2000z, Pope wearing white.

1991, June 1   Litho.   Perf. 11½x11
3041 A965 1000z multicolored .40 .30
3042 A965 2000z multicolored .65 .40

A966

1991, June 21   Litho.   Perf. 11½
3043 A966 2000z multicolored .50 .25
Antarctic Treaty, 30th anniv.

Polish Paper Industry, 500th Anniv. A967

1991, July 8
3044 A967 2500z lake & gray .40 .25

Victims of Stalin — A968

1991, July 29   Litho.   Perf. 11½x12
3045 A968 2500z black & red .40 .25

Souvenir Sheet

Pope John Paul II — A969

1991, Aug. 15   Photo.   Perf. 11½x11
3046 A969 3500z multicolored .95 .50

Basketball, Cent. — A970

1991, Aug. 19   Litho.   Perf. 11x11½
3047 A970 2500z multicolored .45 .25

Leon Wyczolkowski (1852-1936), painter — A971

1991, Sept. 7   Photo.   Perf. 11½x12
3048 A971 3000z olive brown .40 .25
a.   Sheet of 4 2.25 3.00
16th Polish Philatelic Exhibition, Bydgoszcz '91.

Kazimierz Twardowski (1866-1938) — A972

1991, Oct. 10   Perf. 11x11½
3049 A972 2500z sepia & blk .50 .25

Butterflies — A973

No. 3050, Papilio machaon. No. 3051, Mormonia sponsa. No. 3052, Vanessa cardui. No. 3053, Iphiclides podalirius. No. 3054, Panaxia dominula. No. 3055, Nymphalis io. No. 3056, Aporia crataegi.

1991, Nov. 16   Litho.   Perf. 12½
3050 A973 1000z multi .25 .25
3051 A973 1000z multi .25 .25
3052 A973 1500z multi .25 .25
3053 A973 1500z multi .25 .25
3054 A973 2500z multi .50 .30
3055 A973 2500z multi .50 .30
a.   Block of 6, #3050-3055 2.25 1.60

Souvenir Sheet
3056 A973 15,000z multi 2.00 2.00

No. 3056 has a holographic image on the stamp and comes se-tenant with a Phila Nippon '91 label. The image may be affected by soaking in water. Varieties such as missing hologram, double and shifted images, and imperfs exist.

On Jan. 15, 1994, the Polish postal administration demonetized No. 3056.

Nativity Scene, by Francesco Solimena A974

1991, Nov. 25   Photo.   Perf. 11
3057 A974 1000z multicolored .50 .25

Polish Armed Forces at Tobruk, 50th Anniv. — A975

1991, Dec. 10   Photo.   Perf. 11½
3058 A975 2000z Gen. Stanislaw Kopanski .65 .25

A976

World War II Commanders: 2000z, Brig. Gen. Michal Tokarzewski-Karaszewicz (1893-1964). 2500z, Gen. Kazimierz Sosukowski (1885-1969). 3000z, Gen. Stefan Rowecki (1895-1944). 5000z, Gen. Tadeusz Komorowski (1895-1966). 6500z, Brig. Gen. Leopold Okulicki (1898-1946).

1991, Dec. 20   Litho.
3059 A976 2000z vermilion & blk .35 .25
3060 A976 2500z violet bl & lake .45 .25
3061 A976 3000z mag & dk bl .55 .25
3062 A976 5000z olive & brn 1.00 .30
3063 A976 6500z brn org & brn 1.25 .35
Nos. 3059-3063 (5) 3.60 1.40

A977

Boy Scouts in Poland, 80th anniv.: 1500z, Lord Robert Baden-Powell, founder of Boy Scouts. 2000z, Andrzej Malkowski (1889-1919), founder of Boy Scouts in Poland. 2500z, Scout standing guard, 1920. 3500z, Soldier scout, 1944.

1991, Dec. 30   Photo.   Perf. 12x11½
3064 A977 1500z multicolored .35 .25
3065 A977 2000z multicolored .35 .25
3066 A977 2500z multicolored .40 .25
3067 A977 3500z multicolored .85 .40
Nos. 3064-3067 (4) 1.95 1.15

Royalty Type of 1986
Designs: 1500z, Kazimierz II Sprawiedliwy. 2000z, Leszek Bialy.

Photo. & Engr.
1992, Jan. 15   Perf. 11
3068 A875 1500z olive green & brn .45 .25
3069 A875 2000z gray blue & blk 1.00 .35

Paintings A978

Paintings (self-portraits except for 2200z) by: 700z, Sebastien Bourdon. 1000z, Sir Joshua Reynolds. 1500z, Sir Gottfried Kneller. 2000z, Murillo. 2200z, Rubens. 3000z, Diego de Silva y Velazquez.

1992, Jan. 16   Photo.
3070 A978 700z multicolored .25 .25
3071 A978 1000z multicolored .25 .25
3072 A978 1500z multicolored .25 .25
3073 A978 2000z multicolored .25 .25
3074 A978 2200z multicolored .55 .25
3075 A978 3000z multicolored .60 .50
Nos. 3070-3075 (6) 2.15 1.75

1992 Winter Olympics, Albertville A979

1992, Feb. 8   Litho.   Perf. 11x11½
3076 A979 1500z Skiing .35 .25
3077 A979 2500z Hockey .60 .35
See Nos. 3095-3098.

Tadeusz Manteuffel (1902-1970), Historian A980

1992, Mar. 5   Photo.   Perf. 11½x11
3078 A980 2500z brown .45 .25

Famous Poles A981

Designs: 1500z, Nicolaus Copernicus, astronomer. 2000z, Frederic Chopin, composer. 2500z, Henryk Sienkiewicz, novelist. 3500z, Marie Sklodowska Curie, scientist. 5000z, Casimir Funk, biochemist.

1992, Mar. 5 Litho. Perf. 11x11½

3079	A981	1500z multicolored	.25	.25
3080	A981	2000z multicolored	.40	.25
3081	A981	2500z multicolored	.65	.25
3082	A981	3500z multicolored	1.00	.50
		Nos. 3079-3082 (4)	2.30	1.25

Souvenir Sheet

3083	A981	5000z multicolored	2.75	.75

Expo '92, Seville (No. 3083).

Discovery of America, 500th Anniv. — A982

No. 3084, Columbus, chart. No. 3085, Chart, Santa Maria.

1992, May 5

3084	A982	1500z multicolored	.30	.25
3085	A982	3000z multicolored	.45	.25
a.		Pair, #3084-3085	1.50	1.10

Europa.

Waterfalls A983

2000z, Pstrag (trout). 2500z, Zimorodek (kingfisher). 3000z, Jelec (whiting). 3500z, Pluszcz.

1992, June 1 Litho. Perf. 11½

3086	A983	2000z multicolored	.25	.25
3087	A983	2500z multicolored	.50	.25
3088	A983	3000z multicolored	.80	.35
3089	A983	3500z multicolored	.95	.35
		Nos. 3086-3089 (4)	2.50	1.20

Order of Virtuti Militari, Bicent. A984

Designs: 1500z, Prince Jozef Poniatowski (1763-1813), 3000z, Marshal Jozef Pilsudski (1867-1935). No. 3092, Black Madonna of Czestochowa.

1992, June 18 Perf. 11

3090	A984	1500z multi	.40	.25
3091	A984	3000z multi	.55	.25

Souvenir Sheet
Imperf

3092	A984	20,000z multi	3.50	2.50

No. 3092 contains one 39x60mm stamp.

Children's Drawings of Love — A985

1500z, Heart between woman and man. 3000z, Butterfly, animals with sun and rain.

1992, June 26 Litho. Perf. 11½x11

3093	A985	1500z multicolored	.25	.25
3094	A985	3000z multicolored	.40	.25
a.		Pair, #3093-3094	.55	.50

Olympics Type of 1992

1992, July 25 Litho. Perf. 11x11½

3095	A979	1500z Fencing	.50	.25
3096	A979	2000z Boxing	.25	.25
3097	A979	2500z Sprinting	.35	.30
3098	A979	3000z Cycling	.50	.35
		Nos. 3095-3098 (4)	1.60	1.15

1992 Summer Olympics, Barcelona.

Souvenir Sheet

OLYMPHILEX '92, Barcelona — A986

1992, July 29

3099	A986	20,000z Runners	3.00	3.00

Exists imperf. Value: mint $6, used $7.

Janusz Korczak (1879-1942), Physician, Concentration Camp Victim — A987

1992, Aug. 5 Photo. Perf. 11x11½

3100	A987	1500z multicolored	.35	.25

Polish Emigrants Assoc. World Meeting — A988

1992, Aug. 19 Perf. 12x11½

3101	A988	3000z multicolored	.65	.30

World War II Combatants World Meeting — A989

1992, Aug. 14 Perf. 11½x11

3102	A989	3000z multicolored	.50	.30

Stefan Cardinal Wyszynski (1901-1981) — A990

3000z, Pope John Paul II embracing person.

1992, Aug. 15 Litho.

3103	A990	1500z multicolored	.45	.25
3104	A990	3000z multicolored	.65	.50
a.		Block of 2, #3103-3104 + 2 labels	1.60	1.10

6th World Youth Cong., Czestochowa (#3104).

Adampol, Polish Village in Turkey, 150th Anniv. A991

1992, Sept. 15 Photo. Perf. 11x11½

3105	A991	3500z multicolored	.60	.35

World Post Day — A992

1992, Oct. 9 Perf. 11½x11

3106	A992	3500z multicolored	.65	.35

Bruno Schulz (1892-1942), Author — A993

1992, Oct. 26 Litho. Perf. 11x11½

3107	A993	3000z multicolored	.55	.30

Polish Sculptures, Natl. Museum, Warsaw A994

Designs: 2000z, Seated Girl, by Henryk Wicinski. 2500z, Portrait of Tytus Czyzewski, by Zbigniew Pronaszko. 3000z, Polish Nike, by Edward Wittig. 3500z, The Nude, by August Zamoyski.

1992, Oct. 29 Perf. 11½

3108	A994	2000z multicolored	.35	.25
3109	A994	2500z multicolored	.35	.25
3110	A994	3000z multicolored	.40	.25
3111	A994	3500z multicolored	.40	.25
a.		Souvenir sheet of 4, #3108-3111	1.50	.75
		Nos. 3108-3111 (4)	1.50	1.00

Polska '93 (No. 3111a).

Posters — A995

Designs: 1500z, 10th Theatrical Summer in Zamosc, by Jan Mlodozeniec, vert. 2000z, Red Magic, by Franciszek Starowieyski. 2500z, Circus, by Waldemar Swierzy, vert. 3500z, Mannequins, by Henryk Tomaszewski.

1992, Oct. 30 Perf. 13½

3112	A995	1500z multicolored	.25	.25
3113	A995	2000z multicolored	.40	.25
3114	A995	2500z multicolored	.50	.30
3115	A995	3500z multicolored	.65	.40
		Nos. 3112-3115 (4)	1.80	1.20

Illustrations by Edward Lutczyn A996

Designs: 1500z, Girl using snake as jump rope. 2000z, Boy on rocking horse with rockers reversed. 2500z, Boy using bird as arrow. 3500z, Girl with ladder, wind-up giraffe with keys on back.

1992, Nov. 16 Photo. Perf. 11

3116	A996	1500z multicolored	.25	.25
3117	A996	2000z multicolored	.40	.25
3118	A996	2500z multicolored	.55	.25
3119	A996	3500z multicolored	.85	.40
		Nos. 3116-3119 (4)	2.05	1.15

Polska '93.

Home Army A997

1992, Nov. 20 Litho. Perf. 13½

3120	A997	1500z shown	.30	.25
3121	A997	3500z Soldiers, diff.	.60	.25
a.		Pair, #3120-3121	1.00	.75

Souvenir Sheet

3122	A997	20,000z +500z "WP AK," vert.	2.50	2.00

Christmas A998

1992, Nov. 25 Photo. Perf. 11½

3123	A998	1000z multicolored	.25	.25

A999

1992, Dec. 5   Photo.   *Perf. 11½x11*
3124 A999 1500z Wheat stalks   .25 .25
3125 A999 3500z Food products   .40 .30
Intl. Conference on Nutrition, Rome.

A1000

1992, Dec. 10   Litho.
3126 A1000 3000z multicolored   .55 .30
Postal Agreement with the Sovereign Military Order of Malta, Aug. 1, 1991.

Natl. Arms — A1001

1992, Dec. 14   Photo.   *Perf. 12x11½*
3127 A1001 2000z 1295   .30 .25
3128 A1001 2500z 15th cent.   .30 .25
3129 A1001 3000z 18th cent.   .35 .25
3130 A1001 3500z 1919   .35 .25
3131 A1001 5000z 1990   .70 .25
    Nos. 3127-3131 (5)   2.00 1.25

Polish Philatelic Society, Cent. A1002

1993, Jan. 6   Photo.   *Perf. 11½*
3132 A1002 1500z multicolored   .35 .25

A1003

1993, Feb. 5   *Perf. 11½x11*
3133 A1003 3000z multicolored   .55 .30
1993 Winter University Games, Zakopane.

A1004

Design: I Love You.

1993, Feb. 14
3134 A1004 1500z shown   .30 .25
3135 A1004 3000z Heart on en-
                    velope   .45 .30

Amber — A1005

Various pieces of amber.
20,000z, Necklace, map, horiz.

1993, Jan. 29   Litho.   *Perf. 13½*
3136 A1005 1500z multicolored   .30 .25
3137 A1005 2000z multicolored   .40 .25
3138 A1005 2500z multicolored   .45 .30
3139 A1005 3000z multicolored   .85 .40
    Nos. 3136-3139 (4)   2.00 1.20
              Souvenir Sheet
3140 A1005 20,000z multi   2.25 1.40
Polska '93 (No. 3140).

Royalty Type of 1986

Designs: 1500z, Wladyslaw Laskonogi. 2000z, Henryk I Brodaty (1201-38). 2500z, Konrad I Mazowiecki. 3000z, Boleslaw V Wstydliwy.

Photo. & Engr.
1993, Mar. 25   *Perf. 11*
3141 A875 1500z yel grn & brn   .25 .25
3142 A875 2000z red vio & ind   .25 .25
3143 A875 2500z gray & black   .50 .25
3144 A875 3000z yel brn & brn   2.00 .50
    Nos. 3141-3144 (4)   3.00 1.25
No. 3144 printed with se-tenant label for Polska '93. Value, without label $1.25.

Battle of the Arsenal, 50th Anniv. — A1006

1993, Mar. 26   Photo.   *Perf. 11½*
3145 A1006 1500z multicolored   .40 .25

Intl. Medieval Knights' Tournament, Golub-Dobrzyn — A1007

Various knights on horseback.

1993, Mar. 29   *Perf. 11x11½*
3146 A1007 1500z multicolored   .25 .25
3147 A1007 2000z multicolored   .35 .25
3148 A1007 2500z multicolored   .40 .30
3149 A1007 3500z multicolored   .75 .25
    Nos. 3146-3149 (4)   1.75 1.05

City of Szczecin, 750th Anniv. A1008

1993, Apr. 3   Litho.   *Perf. 11½x11*
3150 A1008 1500z multicolored   .40 .25

Warsaw Ghetto Uprising, 50th Anniv. — A1009

1993, Apr. 19   Litho.   *Perf. 14*
3151 A1009 4000z gray, blk & yel .65 .30
See Israel No. 1163.

Europa — A1010

Contemporary art by: No. 3152, A. Szapocznikow and J. Lebenstein. No. 3153, S. Gierowski and B. Linke.

1993, Apr. 30   Photo.   *Perf. 11x11½*
3152 A1010 1500z multicolored   .40 .25
3153 A1010 4000z multicolored   .70 .35
  a.   Pair, #3152-3153   1.10 .50

Polish Parliament (Sejm), 500th Anniv. — A1011

1993, May 2   Photo.   *Perf. 11*
3154 A1011 2000z multicolored   .40 .25

Death of Francesco Nullo, 130th Anniv. — A1012

1993, May 5   Litho.   *Perf. 11x11½*
3155 A1012 2500z multicolored   .45 .30

Souvenir Sheet

Legend of the White Eagle — A1013

1993, May 7   Engr.   *Perf. 13½*
3156 A1013 50,000z dark brn   6.25 6.25
Polska '93.
No. 3156 exists imperf., value: mint $10.50, used $12.

Cadets of Second Polish Republic — A1014

1993, May 21   Litho.   *Perf. 11x11½*
3157 A1014 2000z multicolored   .35 .25

Nicolaus Copernicus (1473-1543) — A1015

1993, May 24
3158 A1015 2000z multicolored   .70 .35

Kornel Makuszymski, 40th Death Anniv. — A1016

Illustrations: 1500z, Lion, monkey. 2000z, Goat walking. 3000z, Monkey. 5000z, Goat riding bird.

1993, June 1
3159 A1016 1500z multicolored   .25 .25
3160 A1016 2000z multicolored   .40 .25
3161 A1016 3000z multicolored   .80 .30
3162 A1016 5000z multicolored   1.15 .70
    Nos. 3159-3162 (4)   2.60 1.50

Pine Cone Type of 1991

10,000z, Pinus cembra. 20,000z, Pinus sylvestris.

1993, June 30   Photo.   *Perf. 12x11½*
3163 A956 10,000z multi   1.50 .50
3164 A956 20,000z multi   2.75 .75

Birds — A1017

No. 3165, Passer montanus. No. 3166, Motacilla alba. No. 3167, Dendrocopos syriacus. No. 3168, Carduelis carduelis. No. 3169, Sturnus vulgaris. No. 3170, Pyrrhula pyrrhula.

1993, July 15   Litho.   Perf. 11½
3165	A1017	1500z multi	.25	.25
3166	A1017	2000z multi	.35	.25
3167	A1017	3000z multi	.40	.25
3168	A1017	4000z multi	.65	.30
3169	A1017	5000z multi	1.90	.80
3170	A1017	6000z multi	1.60	1.00
		Nos. 3165-3170 (6)	5.15	2.85

Polish Natl. Anthem, Bicent. A1018

1993, July 20   Photo.   Perf. 11x11½
3171 A1018 1500z multicolored   .35   .25
See No. 3206.

Madonna and Child A1019

Designs: 1500z, Stone carving from Basilica, Lesna Podlaska. 2000z, Statue, Swieta Lipska.

Perf. 11x11½ Syncopated Type A
1993, Aug. 15
3172	A1019	1500z multicolored	.50	.30
3173	A1019	2000z multicolored	.85	.30

World Post Day — A1020

Photo. & Engr.
1993, Oct. 9   Perf. 11½x11
3174 A1020 2500z multicolored   .55   .30

Polish Parachute Brigade A1021

Perf. 11x11½, Syncopated Type A
1993, Sept. 25   Photo.
3175 A1021 1500z multicolored   .45   .25

Death of St. Hedwig (Jadwiga), 750th Anniv. — A1022

1993, Oct. 14   Litho.   Perf. 14
3176 A1022 2500z multicolored   .75   .40
See Germany No. 1816.

35th Intl. Jazz Jamboree — A1023

Perf. 11½ Syncopated Type A
1993, Sept. 27   Litho.
3177 A1023 2000z multicolored   .50   .30

Souvenir Sheet

Election of Pope John Paul II, 15th Anniv. — A1024

1993, Oct. 16
3178 A1024 20,000z multicolored 2.60 2.00

A1025

1993, Nov. 11
3179 A1025 4000z Eagle, crown   1.00   .60
Souvenir Sheet
3180 A1025 20,000z Dove   2.50 1.75
Independence, 75th anniv. No. 3180 has a continuous design.

A1026

1993, Nov. 25
3181 A1026 1500z multicolored   .45   .25
Christmas.

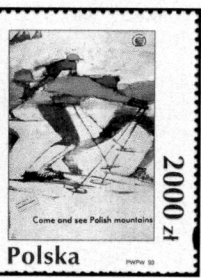

Posters A1027

Designs: 2000z, "Come and see Polish mountains." 5000z, Alban Berg Wozzeck.

1993, Dec. 10
3182	A1027	2000z multicolored	.50	.35
3183	A1027	5000z multicolored	.80	.50
See Nos. 3203-3204, 3259-3260.

"I Love You" — A1028

Perf. 11½x11 Syncopated Type A
1994, Jan. 14   Litho.
3184 A1028 1500z multicolored   .55   .35

A1029

2500z, Cross-country skiing. 5000z, Ski jumping. 10,000z, Downhill skiing.

1994, Feb. 12   Photo.   Perf. 11½x11
3185	A1029	2500z multi	.70	.35
3186	A1029	5000z multi	1.10	.70
Souvenir Sheet
| 3187 | A1029 | 10,000z multi | 1.90 | 1.40 |
1994 Winter Olympics, Lillehammer. Intl. Olympic Committee, cent. (No. 2187).

Kosciuszko Insurrection, Bicent. — A1030

Perf. 11½x11 Syncopated Type A
1994, Mar. 24   Photo.
3188 A1030 2000z multicolored   .55   .30

Zamosc Academy, 400th Anniv. — A1031

1994, Mar. 15
3189 A1031 5000z brn, blk & gray   .95   .50

Gen. Jozef Bem (1794-1850) — A1032

Perf. 11½ Syncopated Type A
1994, Mar. 14   Litho.
3190 A1032 5000z multicolored   .95   .50

Royalty Type of 1986 with Denomination at Bottom
Photo. & Engr.
1994, Apr. 15   Perf. 11
3191	A875	2500z Leszek Czarny	.75	.75
3192	A875	5000z Przemysl II	1.75	.75

Inventions A1033

Europa: 2500z, Petroleum lamp, invented by I. Lukasiewicz (1822-82). 6000z, Astronomical sighting device, with profile of Copernicus (1473-1543).

Perf. 11½x11 Syncopated Type A
1994, Apr. 30   Litho.
3193	A1033	2500z multicolored	.50	.35
3194	A1033	6000z multicolored	1.10	.70

St. Mary's Sanctuary A1034

4000z, Our Lady of Kalwaria Zebrzydowska.

Perf. 11½x11 Syncopated Type A
1994, May 16   Litho.
3195 A1034 4000z multicolored   1.00   .60

Battle of Monte Cassino, 50th Anniv. A1035

Perf. 11x11½ Syncopated Type A
1994, May 18
3196 A1035 6000z multicolored   .80   .40

Traditional Dances A1036

Perf. 11½ Syncopated Type A
1994, May 25
3197	A1036	3000z Mazurka	.50	.35
3198	A1036	4000z Goralski	.85	.50
3199	A1036	9000z Krakowiak	1.10	.50
		Nos. 3197-3199 (3)	2.45	1.35

ILO, 75th Anniv. A1037

Perf. 11½x11 Syncopated Type A
1994, June 7   Litho.
3200 A1037 6000z multicolored   .65   .35

Polish Electricians Assoc., 75th Anniv. A1038

Perf. 11x11½ Syncopated Type A
1994, June 10
3201 A1038 4000z multicolored .75 .35

1994 World Soccer Cup Championships, U.S. — A1039

Perf. 11½x11 Syncopated Type A
1994, June 17
3202 A1039 6000z multicolored .90 .50

Poster Art Type of 1993
4000z, Mr. Fabre, by Wiktor Gorka. 6000z, VIII OISTAT Congress, by Hubert Hilscher, horiz.

Perf. 11x11½, 11½x11 Syncopated Type A
1994, July 4 Litho.
3203 A1027 4000z multicolored .55 .35
3204 A1027 6000z multicolored .75 .50

Florian Znaniecki (1882-1958), Sociologist A1040

Perf. 11½ Syncopated Type A
1994, July 15 Litho.
3205 A1040 9000z multicolored .75 .45

Polish Natl. Anthem Type of 1993
Design: 2500z, Battle of Raclawice, 1794.

1994, July 20 Photo. Perf. 11x11½
3206 A1018 2500z multicolored .40 .25

A1042

Perf. 11½x11 Syncopated Type A
1994, Aug. 1 Litho.
3207 A1042 2500z Natl. arms .55 .25
Warsaw Uprising, 50th anniv.

PHILAKOREA '94 — A1043

1994, Aug. 16
3208 A1043 4000z multicolored .70 .35
Stamp Day.

Basilica of St. Brigida, Gdansk A1044

1994, Aug. 28
3209 A1044 4000z multicolored .85 .55

Modern Olympic Games, Cent. A1045

Perf. 11x11½ Syncopated Type A
1994, Sept. 5
3210 A1045 4000z multicolored .75 .60

Krzysztof Komeda (1931-69), Jazz Muscian — A1046

Perf. 11½ Syncopated Type A
1994, Sept. 22 Litho.
3211 A1046 6000z multicolored .85 .50

Aquarium Fish — A1047

Designs: No. 3212a, Ancistrus dolichopterus. b, Pterophyllum scalare. c, Xiphophorus helleri, paracheirodon innesi. d, Poecilia reticulata.

Perf. 11½x11 Syncopated Type A
1994, Sept. 28 Litho.
3212 Strip of 4 2.40 1.75
a.-d. A1047 4000z any single .50 .40

World Post Day — A1048

1994, Oct. 9
3213 A1048 4000z Postal Arms, 1858 .80 .50

St. Maximilian Kolbe (1894-1941), Concentration Camp Victim — A1049

1994, Oct. 24 Photo. Perf. 11x11½
3214 A1049 2500z multicolored .65 .35

Pigeons A1050

a, Mewka polska. b, Krymka biatostacka. c, Srebrniak polski. d, Sokot gdanski. 10,000z, Polski golab pocztowy.

Perf. 11x11½ Syncopated Type A
1994, Oct. 28 Litho.
3215 Block of 4 2.50 1.60
a.-b. A1050 4000z any single .50 .35
c.-d. A1050 6000z any single .50 .35
Souvenir Sheet
3216 A1050 10,000z multicolored 1.60 1.00

Christmas A1051

Perf. 11x11½ Syncopated Type A
1994, Nov. 25 Litho.
3217 A1051 2500z multicolored .80 .40

European Union A1052

1994, Dec. 15
3218 A1052 6000z multicolored 1.20 .70

Love Stamp — A1053

Perf. 11½x11 Syncopated Type A
1995, Jan. 31 Litho.
3219 A1053 35g dk bl & rose car .80 .40

Hydro-Meteorological Service, 75th Anniv. — A1054

Perf. 11x11½ Syncopated Type A
1995, Jan. 31
3220 A1054 60g multicolored .80 .40

Poland's Renewed Access to the Sea, 75th Anniv. A1055

1995, Feb. 10
3221 A1055 45g multicolored .50 .30

Royalty Type of 1986 with Denomination at Bottom
35g, Waclaw II. 45g, Wladyslaw I Lotiek. 60g, Kazimierz III, the Great. 80g, Ludwik Wegierski.

Photo. & Engr.
1995, Feb. 28 Perf. 11
3222 A875 35g multicolored .35 .25
3223 A875 45g multicolored .45 .25
3224 A875 60g multicolored .60 .35
3225 A875 80g multicolored 1.10 .50
Nos. 3222-3225 (4) 2.50 1.35

St. John of God (1495-1550), Initiator of Order — A1056

Perf. 12x11½ Syncopated Type A
1995, Mar. 8 Litho.
3226 A1056 60g multicolored .50 .30

Easter Eggs A1057

Each stamp showing various designs on 3 eggs.

Perf. 11½ Syncopated Type A
1995, Mar. 16 Background Color
3227 A1057 35g dull red .35 .25
3228 A1057 35g violet .35 .25
3229 A1057 45g bright blue .45 .35
3230 A1057 45g blue green .45 .35
Nos. 3227-3230 (4) 1.60 1.20

Pine Cone Type of 1991
1995, Mar. 27 Photo. Perf. 11½
3231 A956 45g Larix decidua .30 .25
3232 A956 80g Pinus mugo .45 .25

Katyn Forest Massacre, 55th Anniv. A1058

Perf. 11½ Syncopated Type A
1995, Apr. 13 Litho.
3233 A1058 80g multicolored .60 .40

Europa A1060

Perf. 11x11½ Syncopated Type A

1995, Apr. 28			**Litho.**
3234	A1060	35g shown	.40 .30
3235	A1060	80g Flowers in helmet	.70 .40

Ruturn of Western Polish Territories, 50th Anniv. — A1061

Perf. 11½ Syncopated Type A

1995, May 6			**Litho.**
3236	A1061	45g multicolored	.50 .25

Pope John Paul II, 75th Birthday A1062

Perf. 11½ Syncopated Type A

1995, May 18			**Litho.**
3237	A1062	80g multicolored	.90 .60

Groteska Theatre of Fairy Tales, 50th Anniv. — A1063

Designs: No. 3238, Two performing. No. 3239, Stage scene. No. 3240, Puppet leaning on barrel, vert. No. 3241, Character holding flower, vert.

1995, May 25			
3238	35g multicolored		.35 .30
3239	35g multicolored		.35 .30
a.	A1063 Pair, #3238-3239		1.10 .75
3240	45g multicolored		.45 .30
3241	45g multicolored		.45 .30
a.	A1063 Pair, #3240-3241		.90 .65
	Nos. 3238-3241 (4)		1.60 1.20

Polish Railways, 150th Anniv. A1064

Designs: 35g, Warsaw-Vienna steam train, 1945. 60g, Combustion fuel powered train, 1927. 80g, Electric train, 1936. 1z, Euro City Sobieski, Warsaw-Vienna, 1992.

1995, June 9			
3242	35g multicolored		.35 .25
3243	60g multicolored		.35 .25
a.	A1064 Pair, #3242-3243		.75 .50
3244	80g multicolored		.50 .35
3245	1z multicolored		.85 .55
a.	A1064 Pair, #3244-3245		1.50 1.00
	Nos. 3242-3245 (4)		2.05 1.40

UN, 50th Anniv. A1065

Perf. 11½ Syncopated Type A

1995, June 26			**Litho.**
3246	A1065	80g multicolored	.75 .35

Handlowy Bank, Warsaw, 125th Anniv. — A1066

1995, June 30			
3247	A1066	45g multicolored	.55 .25

Polish Peasants' Movement, Cent. A1067

Perf. 11½ Syncopated Type A

1995, July 13			**Litho.**
3248	A1067	45g multicolored	.45 .25

Polish Natl. Anthem, Bicent. A1068

1995, July 20	**Photo.**		**Perf. 11x11½**
3249	A1068	35g multicolored	.40 .25

Deciduous Trees — A1069

1995, July 31			**Perf. 12x11½**
3250	A1069	B Quercus petraea	.85 .25
3251	A1069	A Sorbus aucuparia	.85 .25

On day of issue, No. 3250 was valued at 35g; No. 3551 at 45g.

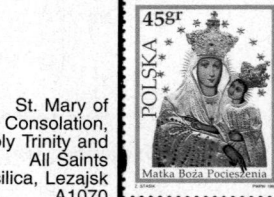

St. Mary of Consolation, Holy Trinity and All Saints Basilica, Lezajsk A1070

Perf. 11½ Syncopated Type A

1995, Aug. 2			**Litho.**
3252	A1070	45g multicolored	.35 .25

Battle of Warsaw, 75th Anniv. A1071

Design: 45g, Jósef Pilsudski (1867-1935).

1995, Aug. 14			
3253	A1071	45g multicolored	.45 .25

Horse-Equipage Driving World Championships, Poznan — A1072

Designs: 60g, Horses pulling carriage, men in formal attire. 80g, Marathon race through water, around pylons.

Perf. 11½ Syncopated Type A

1995, Aug. 23			**Litho.**
3254	A1072	60g multicolored	.70 .35
3255	A1072	80g multicolored	.70 .50
a.	Pair, #3254-3255		1.50 .95

18th All Polish Philatelic Exhibition, Warsaw A1073

Designs: 35g, Warsaw Technical University, School of Architecture. 1z, Warsaw Castle Place, Old Town, horiz.

Perf. 11½ Syncopated Type A

1995, Aug. 30			**Litho.**
3256	A1073	35g multicolored	.35 .25
Souvenir Sheet			
3257	A1073	1z multicolored	1.25 1.00

11th World Congress of Space Flight Participants, Warsaw A1074

Perf. 11½ Syncopated Type A

1995, Sept. 10			**Litho.**
3258	A1074	80g multicolored	.65 .45

Poster Art Type of 1993

35g, The Crazy Locomotive, by Jan Sawka. 45g, The Wedding, by Eugeniusz Get Stankiewicz.

Perf. 11½ Syncopated Type A

1995, Sept. 27			**Litho.**
3259	A1027	35g multicolored	.45 .25
3260	A1027	45g multicolored	.55 .30

13th Intl. Chopin Piano Festival A1076

Perf. 11½ Syncopated Type A

1995, Oct. 1			**Litho.**
3261	A1076	80g Polonaise score	.65 .45

A1077

World Post Day 45g, Postman in uniform, Polish Kingdom. 80g, Feather, wax seal of Stanislaw II Poniatowski.

1995, Oct. 9			
3262	A1077	45g multicolored	.35 .25
3263	A1077	80g multicolored	.50 .45

A1078

1995, Oct. 26			
3264	A1078	45g multicolored	.35 .25

Acrobatic Sports World Championships, Wroclaw.

Janusz Groszkowski (1898-1984), Physicist — A1079

Perf. 11½ Syncopated Type A

1995, Nov. 10			**Litho.**
3265	A1079	45g multicolored	.35 .25

Christmas — A1080

1995, Nov. 27			
3266	35g Nativity		.35 .25
3267	45g Magi, tree		.45 .25
a.	A1080 Pair, Nos. 3266-3267		.90 .50

No. 3267a is a continuous design.

Songbird Chicks — A1081

Designs: a, 35g, Parus caeruleus. b, 45g, Aegithalos caudatus. c, 60g, Lanius excubitor. d, 80g, Coccothraustes.

1995, Dec. 15			
3268	A1081	Block of 4, #a.-d.	2.00 1.10

See No. 3377.

.Krzysztof Kamil Baczynski (1921-44), Poet A1082

Perf. 11½ Syncopated Type A
1996, Jan. 22 **Litho.**
3269 A1082 35g multicolored .40 .25

Love — A1083

1996, Jan. 31
3270 A1083 40g Cherries .40 .25

Architecture A1084

40g, Romanesque style church, Inowlodz, 11-12th cent. 55g, Gothic syle, St. Virgin Mary's Church, Cracow, 14th cent. 70g, Renaissance period, St. Sigismundus Chapel of Cracow, Wawel Castle, 1519-33. 1z, Order of Holy Sacrament Nuns Baroque Church, Warsaw, 1688-92.

Perf. 11½ Syncopated Type A
1996, Feb. 27 **Litho.**
3271 A1084 40g multicolored .35 .25
3272 A1084 55g multicolored .50 .25
3273 A1084 70g multicolored .65 .30
3274 A1084 1z multicolored 1.00 .60
Nos. 3271-3274 (4) 2.50 1.40

Polish Sailing Ships — A1085

Designs: a, 40g, Topmast schooner, "Oceania," 1985. b, 55g, Staysail schooner, "Zawisza Czarny," 1961. c, 70g, Schooner, "General Zaruski," 1939. d, 75g, Brig, "Fryderyk Chopin," 1992.

1996, Mar. 11
3275 A1085 Strip of 4, #a.-d. 2.25 1.40

Warsaw, Capital of Poland, 400th Anniv. A1086

1996, Mar. 18
3276 A1086 55g multicolored .50 .25

Signs of the Zodiac — A1087

1996 **Photo.** **Perf. 12x11½**
3277 A1087 5g Aquarius .25 .25
3278 A1087 10g Pisces .25 .25
3279 A1087 20g Taurus .25 .25
3280 A1087 25g Gemini .25 .25
3281 A1087 30g Cancer .25 .25
3282 A1087 40g Virgo .25 .25
3283 A1087 50g Leo .35 .25
3284 A1087 55g Libra .40 .25
3285 A1087 70g Aries .50 .25
3286 A1087 1z Scorpio .70 .25
3287 A1087 2z Sagittarius 1.40 .25
3288 A1087 5z Capricorn 3.50 .30
Nos. 3277-3288 (12) 8.35 3.05

Design will dissolve when soaked on at least three denominations, 5g, 20g and 25g, from the second printing which is on fluorescent paper.
Issued: 70g, 3/21; 20g, 4/21; 25g, 5/10; 30g, 5/20; 40g, 50g, 5/31; 55g, 6/10; 1z, 6/20; 2z, 6/28; 5z, 7/10; 5g, 7/19; 10g, 7/31.

Famous Women A1088

Europa: 40g, Hanka Ordonówa (1902-50), singer. 1z, Pola Negri (1896-1987), actress.

Perf. 11½ Syncopated Type A
1996, Apr. 30 **Litho.**
3289 A1088 40g multicolored .35 .30
3290 A1088 1z multicolored .90 .60

3rd Silesian Uprising, 75th Anniv. A1089

Perf. 11 ½ Syncopated Type A
1996, May 2 **Litho.**
3291 A1089 55g multicolored .50 .25

UNICEF, 50th Anniv. — A1090

Illustrations from tales of Jan Brzechwa: No. 3292, Cat and mouse. No. 3293. Man at table, waiters. No. 3294, People with "onion heads." No. 3295, Chef, duck, vegetables at table. No. 3296, Man talking to bird with human head. No. 3297, Fox standing in front of bears.

1996, May 31
3292 A1090 40g multicolored .30 .25
3293 A1090 40g multicolored .30 .25
3294 A1090 55g multicolored .40 .25
3295 A1090 55g multicolored .40 .25
3296 A1090 70g multicolored .50 .35
3297 A1090 70g multicolored .50 .35
Nos. 3292-3297 (6) 2.40 1.70

Drawings by Stanislaw Noakowski (1867-1928) A1091

Designs: 40g, Renaissance building. 55g, Renaissance bedroom. 70g, Gothic village church. 1z, Stanislaw August Library, 18th cent.

1996, June 28
3298 A1091 40g multicolored .35 .25
3299 A1091 55g multicolored .35 .25
3300 A1091 70g multicolored .50 .25
3301 A1091 1z multicolored .90 .90
Nos. 3298-3301 (4) 2.10 1.65

1996 Summer Olympic Games, Atlanta A1092

40g, Discus as medallion, vert. 55g, Tennis ball. 70g, Polish flag, Olympic rings. 1z, Tire & wheel of mountain bicycle, vert.

1996, July 5
3302 A1092 40g multicolored .30 .25
3303 A1092 55g multicolored .35 .25
3304 A1092 70g multicolored .55 .35
3305 A1092 1z multicolored .90 .35
Nos. 3302-3305 (4) 2.10 1.20

OLYMPHILEX '96, Atlanta — A1093

1996, July 5
3306 A1093 1z multicolored .70 .40

National Anthem, Bicent. A1094

1996, July 20 **Photo.** **Perf. 11x11½**
3307 A1094 40g multicolored .35 .25

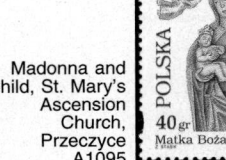

Madonna and Child, St. Mary's Ascension Church, Przeczyce A1095

Perf. 11½x11 Syncopated Type A
1996, Aug. 2 **Litho.**
3308 A1095 40g multicolored .45 .25

Royalty Type of 1986
Designs: 40g, Jadwiga. 55g, Wladyslaw II Jagiello. 70g, Wladyslaw II Warnenczyk. 1z, Kazimierz Jagiellonczyk.

1996, Aug. 29 **Engr.** **Perf. 11**
3309 A875 40g olive brown & brown .40 .25
3310 A875 55g red violet & violet .50 .25
3311 A875 70g gray & black .70 .35
3312 A875 1z yellow green & green 1.25 .60
Nos. 3309-3312 (4) 2.85 1.45

Mountain Scenes, Tatra Natl. Park A1096

Perf. 11½ Syncopated Type A
1996, Sept. 5 **Litho.**
3313 A1096 40g Giewont .30 .25
3314 A1096 40g Krzesanica .30 .25
3315 A1096 55g Swinica .40 .25
3316 A1096 55g Koscielec .40 .25
3317 A1096 70g Rysy .65 .35
3318 A1096 70g Miguszowieckie Szczyty .65 .35
Nos. 3313-3318 (6) 2.70 1.70

Zbigniew Seifert (1946-79), Jazz Musician A1097

Perf. 11½ Syncopated Type A
1996, Sept. 25 **Litho.**
3319 A1097 70g multicolored .65 .35

Post and Telecommunications Museum, Wroclaw, 75th Anniv. — A1098

Paintings: 40g, Horse Exchange and Post Station, by M. Watorski. 1z+20g, Stagecoach in Jagniatkowo, by Prof. Täger.

1996, Oct. 9 **Photo.** **Perf. 12x11½**
3320 A1098 40g multicolored .35 .25

Souvenir Sheet
Perf. 11x11½
3321 A1098 1z +20g multi 1.40 1.00
Nos. 3321 contains one 43x31mm stamp.

Christmas A1099

Perf. 11½ Syncopated Type A
1996, Nov. 27 **Litho.**
3322 A1099 40g Santa in sleigh .30 .25
3323 A1099 55g Carolers .40 .30

Bison Bonasus A1100

1996, Dec. 4
3324 A1100 55g shown .35 .25
3325 A1100 55g Facing .35 .25
3326 A1100 55g Two animals .35 .25
3327 A1100 55g Adult male .35 .25
a. Strip of 4, #3324-3327 2.00 1.40

Wislawa Szymborska, 1996 Nobel Laureate in Literature
A1101

1996, Dec. 10
3328 A1101 1z multicolored   .70   .45

Queen of Hearts
A1102

Perf. 11x11½ Syncopated Type A
1997, Jan. 14   **Litho.**
3329 A1102 B King of Hearts   .75   .25
3330 A1102 A Queen of Hearts   .75   .35
   a.   Pair, #3329-3330   1.60   .65
       Complete booklet, 4 #3330a   6.50

Nos. 3329-3330 sold for 40g and 55g, respectively, on day of issue.

Easter Traditions
A1103

50g, Man, woman in traditional costumes holding palms. 60g, Decorating eggs. 80g, Blessing the Easter meal. 1.10z, Man pouring water on woman.

Perf. 11x11½ Syncopated Type A
1997, Mar. 14   **Litho.**
3331 A1103 50g multicolored   .30   .25
3332 A1103 60g multicolored   .40   .25
3333 A1103 80g multicolored   .55   .30
3334 A1103 1.10z multicolored   .70   .35
     Nos. 3331-3334 (4)   1.95 1.15

A1104

St. Adalbert (956-97)
A1105

50g, St. Adalbert among heathen, horiz.

1997   **Engr.**   ***Perf. 11x11½x 11½x11***
3335 A1104 50g brown   .30   .25
3336 A1104 60g slate   .40   .25
3337 A1105 1.10z purple   .75   .50
     Nos. 3335-3337 (3)   1.45 1.00

See Czech Republic No. 3012, Germany No. 1964, Hungary No. 3569, Vatican City No. 1040.

Issued: Nos. 3335-3336, 4/19; No. 3337, 4/23.

Stories and Legends
A1106

Europa: 50g, shown. 1.10z, Mermaid.

Perf. 11½ Syncopated Type A
1997, May 5
3338 A1106 50g multicolored   .40   .25
3339 A1106 1.10z multicolored   .85   .50

46th Eucharistic Congress — A1107

1997, May 6
3340 A1107 50g multicolored   .50   .30

Souvenir Sheet

Pope John Paul II — A1108

Perf. 11x11½ Syncopated Type A
1997, May 28
3341 A1108 1.10z multicolored   1.75 1.25

City of Gdansk, 1000th Anniv. — A1109

Design: 1.10z, View of city, horiz.

Perf. 11½x11, 11x11½
1997, Apr. 18   **Engr.**
3342 A1109 50g multicolored   .35   .25
Souvenir Sheet
3343 A1109 1.10z multicolored   1.50 1.40
   No. 3343 exists imperf., value $12.

Polish Country Estates — A1110

1997   **Photo.**   **Perf. 11½x12**
3344 A1110 50g Lopusznej   .35   .25
3345 A1110 60g Zyrzyna   .45   .25
3346 A1110 1.10z Ozarowie   .80   .40
3347 A1110 1.70z Tulowicach   1.20   .50
3348 A1110 2.20z Kuznocinie   1.60   .60
3349 A1110 10z Koszutach   6.50 2.25
     Nos. 3344-3349 (6)   10.90 4.25

Issued: 50g, 60g, 4/26/97; 1.10z, 1.70z, 2.20z, 10z, 5/23/97.

See Nos. 3385-3390, 3463-3467, 3511-3514, 3571-3574

PACIFIC 97 — A1111

Design: San Francisco-Oakland Bay Bridge.

Perf. 11½ Syncopated Type A
1997, May 20   **Litho.**
3350 A1111 1.30z multicolored   .85   .45

Bats
A1113

50g, Plecotus auritus. 60g, Nyctalus noctula. 80g, Myotis myotis. 1.30z, Vespertilio murinus.

1997, May 30
3352 A1113 50g multicolored   .35   .25
3353 A1113 60g multicolored   .45   .25
3354 A1113 80g multicolored   .55   .30
3355 A1113 1.30z multicolored   .95   .65
     Nos. 3352-3355 (4)   2.30 1.45

Jagiellon University School of Theology, 600th Anniv.
A1114

Painting by Jan Matejko.

1997, June 6   **Perf. 11**
3356 A1114 80g multicolored   .60   .30

Polish Settlement in Argentina, Cent. — A1115

Perf. 11½ Syncopated Type A
1997, June 6
3357 A1115 1.40z multicolored   1.00   .45

Paintings, by Juliusz Kossak (1824-99) — A1116

Designs: 50g, Man on horse, woman, child. 60g, Men on galloping horses, carriage. 80g,

Feeding horses in stable. 1.10z, Man with horses.

1997, July 4   **Photo.**   **Perf. 11**
3358 A1116 50g multicolored   .35   .25
3359 A1116 60g multicolored   .45   .25
3360 A1116 80g multicolored   .65   .30
3361 A1116 1.10z multicolored   .80   .50
     Nos. 3358-3361 (4)   2.25 1.30

Polish Natl. Anthem, Bicent.
A1117

Designs: 50g, People in city waving hats at Gen. Jan Henryk Dabrowski. 1.10z, Words to Natl. Anthem, Dabrowski.

1997, July 18   ***Perf. 11x11½***
3362 A1117 50g multicolored   .35   .25
Souvenir Sheet
3363 A1117 1.10z multicolored   1.10   .80

Pawel Edmund Strzelecki (1797-1873), Geographer — A1118

Perf. 11½ Syncopated Type A
1997, July 20   **Litho.**
3364 A1118 1.50z multicolored   1.10   .50

Virgin of Consolation, Church of the Virgin of Consolation and St. Michael Archangel, Gorka Duchowna
A1119

Perf. 11½x11 Syncopated Type A
1997, Aug. 28
3365 A1119 50g multicolored   .50   .25

Royalty Type of 1986

Kings: 50g, Jan I Olbracht (1459-1501). 60g, Aleksander (1461-1506). 80g, Sigismundus I Stary (1467-48). 1.10z, Sigismundus II Augustus (1520-72).

1997, Sept. 22   **Engr.**   **Perf. 11**
3366 A875 50g brn & dk brn   .40   .25
3367 A875 60g blue & dp brn   .50   .25
3368 A875 80g grn & dk slate   .65   .30
3369 A875 1.10z mag & dk mag   .85   .55
     Nos. 3366-3369 (4)   2.40 1.35

Mieczyslaw Kosz (1944-73), Jazz Musician — A1120

Perf. 11½ Syncopated Type A
1997, Oct. 3   **Litho.**
3370 A1120 80g multicolored   .55   .40

World Post Day — A1121

1997, Oct. 9
3371 A1121 50g multicolored   .50   .25

Moscow '97 Intl. Philatelic Exhibition A1122

Perf. 11½ Syncopated Type B

1997, Oct. 13
3372 A1122 80g multicolored .70 .35

Theater Poster Art — A1123

#3373, "Sam Pierze Radion," black cat becoming white cat, by T. Gronowski, 1926. #3374, "Szewcy" (Bootmakers), by R. Cieslewicz, 1971. #3375, "Goya," by W. Sadowski, 1983. #3376, "Maz i zona," by A. Pagowski, 1977.

Perf. 11x11½, 11½x11 Syncopated Type A

1997, Nov. 14 Litho.
3373 A1123 50g multi .30 .25
3374 A1123 50g multi, vert. .30 .25
3375 A1123 60g multi, vert. .40 .25
3376 A1123 60g multi, vert. .40 .25
Nos. 3373-3376 (4) 1.40 1.00

Chick Type of 1995

Designs: a, Tadorna tadorna. b, Mergus merganser. c, Gallinago gallinago. d, Gallinula chloropus.

Perf. 11½ Syncopated Type A

1997, Dec. 5
3377 A1081 50g Block of 4, #a.-
d. 2.00 1.20

Christmas A1124

50g, Nativity. 60g, Food, candles. 80g, Outdoor winter scene, star, church. 1.10z, Carolers.

Perf. 11½x11, 11x11½ Syncopated Type A

1997, Nov. 27
3378 A1124 50g multi, vert. .35 .25
3379 A1124 60g multi .45 .25
3380 A1124 80g multi .55 .35
3381 A1124 1.10z multi, vert. .75 .40
Nos. 3378-3381 (4) 2.10 1.25

A1125

Perf. 11½ Syncopated Type A

1998, Jan. 5 Litho.
3382 A1125 1.40z multicolored .95 .50
1998 Winter Olympic Games, Nagano.

A1126

Love Stamps: B, Face of dog, cat on shirt. A, Face of cat, dog on shirt.

Perf. 12x11½ Syncopated Type A

1998, Jan. 14
3383 A1126 B multicolored .65 .35
3384 A1126 A multicolored .65 .35

Nos. 3383-3384 were valued at 55g and 65g, respectively, on day of issue.

Polish Country Estates Type of 1997

Designs: B, Gluchach. 55g, Oblegorku. A, Czarnolesie. 65g, Bronowicach. 90g, Oborach. 1.20z, Romanowie.

1998 **Photo.** **Perf. 11½x12**
3385 A1110 B multicolored .70 .35
3386 A1110 55g multicolored .40 .25
3387 A1110 A multicolored .70 .25
3388 A1110 65g multicolored .45 .25
3389 A1110 90g multicolored .65 .25
3390 A1110 1.20z multicolored .85 .30
Nos. 3385-3390 (6) 3.75 1.65

No. 3385 was valued at 55g, and No. 3387 was valued at 65g on day of issue.
Issued: B, A, 1/15; 55g, 65g, 90g, 1.20z, 3/3.

Easter — A1127

Perf. 11½ Syncopated Type A

1998, Mar. 12 Litho.
3391 A1127 55g shown .40 .25
3392 A1127 65g Image of Christ .45 .30

European Revolutionary Movements of 1848, 150th Anniv. — A1128

1998, Mar. 20 Engr. Perf. 11x11½
3393 A1128 55g gray violet .80 .25

Royalty Type of 1986

Designs: 55g, Henryk Walezy. 65g, Anna Jagiellonka. 80g, Stefan Batory. 90g, Zygmunt III.

1998, Mar. 31 **Perf. 11**
3394 A875 55g multicolored .40 .25
3395 A875 65g multicolored .45 .25
3396 A875 80g multicolored .55 .25
3397 A875 90g multicolored .65 .30
Nos. 3394-3397 (4) 2.05 1.05

Protection of the Baltic Sea — A1129

Marine life: #3398, Halichoerus grypus. #3399, Pomatoschistus microps. #3400, Alosa fallax, syngnathus typhle. #3401, Acipenser sturio. #3402, Salmo salar. #3403, Phocoena phocoena.

1.20z, Halichoerus grypus.

Perf. 11½ Syncopated Type B

1998, Apr. 28 Litho.
3398 A1129 65g multicolored .45 .25
3399 A1129 65g multicolored .45 .25
3400 A1129 65g multicolored .45 .25
3401 A1129 65g multicolored .45 .25
3402 A1129 65g multicolored .45 .25
3403 A1129 65g multicolored .45 .25
a. Strip of 6, #3398-3403 2.75 1.75

Souvenir Sheet

3404 A1129 1.20z multicolored 1.00 .75

Israel '98 World Philatelic Exhibition, Tel Aviv — A1130

Perf. 11½ Syncopated Type A

1998, Apr. 30
3405 A1130 90g Israel No. 8,
logo .70 .45

Natl. Holidays and Festivals A1131

Europa: 55g, Logo of Warwaw Autumn, Intl. Festival of Contemporary Music. 1.20z, First bars of song, "Welcome the May Dawn," 3rd of May Constitution Day.

1998, May 5
3406 A1131 55g multicolored .40 .25
3407 A1131 1.20z multicolored .85 .40
a. Pair, #3406-3407 1.40 .85

Coronation of Longing Holy Mother — A1132

Perf. 11½x12 Syncopated Type A

1998, June 28 Litho.
3408 A1132 55g multicolored .45 .30

Nikifor (Epifan Drowniak) (1895-1968), Artist — A1133

Paintings: 55g, "Triple Self-portrait." 65g, "Cracow Office." 1.20z, "Orthodox Church." 2.35z, "Ucrybów Station."

Perf. 11½ Syncopated Type A

1998, July 10 Litho.
3409 A1133 55g multicolored .40 .25
3410 A1133 65g multicolored .40 .25
3411 A1133 1.20z multicolored .85 .30
3412 A1133 2.35z multicolored 1.60 .55
Nos. 3409-3412 (4) 3.25 1.35

Main Board of Statistics, 80th Anniv. A1134

Perf. 11x11½ Syncopated Type A

1998, July 13
3413 A1134 55g multicolored .45 .30

15th Cent. Statue of Madonna and Child, Sejny Basilica A1135

Perf. 11½ Syncopated Type A

1998, Aug. 14
3414 A1135 55g multicolored .45 .30

Warsaw Diocese, Bicent. A1136

1998, Aug. 28
3415 A1136 65g multicolored .45 .30

Souvenir Sheet

17th Polish Philatelic Exhibition, Szczecin — A1137

View of city, 1624: a, People on raft, pier. b, Sailing ships, pier.

1998, Sept. 18 Engr. Perf. 11x11½
3416 A1137 65g Sheet of 2, #a.-
b. 1.15 1.00

No. 3416 exists imperf. Value, $14.

Discovery of Radium and Polonium, Cent. A1138

Perf. 11½ Syncopated Type A

1998, Sept. 18 Litho.
3417 A1138 1.20z Pierre, Marie
Curie .85 .50

Mazowsze Song and Dance Ensemble, 50th Anniv. — A1139

Couple dancing, denomination at: No. 3418, LL. No. 3419, LR.

1998, Sept. 22
3418	65g multicolored		.40	.25
3419	65g multicolored		.40	.25
a.	A1139 Pair, #3418-3419		.90	.60

Mniszech Palace (Belgian Embassy), Warsaw, Bicent. A1140

Photo. & Engr.
1998, Sept. 28   Perf. 11½
3420	A1140 1.20z multicolored	.85	.50

See Belgium No. 1706.

Sigismund III Vasa (1566-1632), King of Sweden and Poland — A1141

1998, Oct. 3   Engr.   Perf. 11½x11
3421	A1141 1.20z deep claret	.85	.55

See Sweden No. 2312.

World Stamp Day — A1142

Perf. 11½x11 Syncopated Type A
1998, Oct. 9   Litho.
3422	A1142 65g multicolored	.45	.30

Pontificate of John Paul II, 20th Anniv. — A1143

Perf. 11½x12 Syncopated Type A
1998, Oct. 16
3423	A1143 65g multicolored	.70	.40

Independence, 80th Anniv. — A1144

Perf. 12x11½ Syncopated Type A
1998, Nov. 11
3424	A1144 65g multicolored	.45	.30

Christmas A1145

Paintings: 55g, Nativity scene. 65g, Adoration of the Magi.

1998, Nov. 27 Photo.   Perf. 11½x11
3425	A1145 55g multicolored	.35	.25
3426	A1145 65g multicolored	.45	.25

Universal Declaration of Human Rights, 50th Anniv. A1146

Perf. 11x11½ Syncopated Type A
1998, Dec. 10   Litho.
3427	A1146 1.20z blue & dark blue	.90	.45

Adam Mickiewicz (1798-1855), Poet — A1147

Scenes, quotations from poems: 55g, Maryla Wereszczakówna, flower, night landscape. 65g, Cranes flying over tomb of Maria Potocka. 90g, Burning candles, cross. 1.20z, Nobleman's house, flowers, uhlan's cap. 2.45z, Bust of Mickiewicz, by Jean David d'Angers.

Perf. 12x11½ Syncopated Type A
1998, Dec. 24
3428	A1147 55g multicolored	.40	.25
3429	A1147 65g multicolored	.45	.25
3430	A1147 90g multicolored	.65	.25
3431	A1147 1.20z multicolored	.85	.40
	Nos. 3428-3431 (4)	2.35	1.15

Souvenir Sheet
3432	A1147 2.45z multicolored	1.75	1.25

No. 3432 contains one 27x35mm stamp.

Polish Navy, 80th Anniv. (in 1998) A1148

No. 3433, Destroyer ORP Piorun, 1942-46. No. 3434, Frigate ORP Piorun, 1994.

Perf. 11¼x11½ Syncopated Type A
1999, Jan. 4   Litho.
3433	A1148 55g multicolored	.40	.25
3434	A1148 55g multicolored	.40	.25
a.	Pair, #3433-3434	1.00	.50

Love Stamps A1149

Perf. 11½x11¼ Syncopated Type A
1999, Feb. 5
3435	A1149 B Dominoes	.75	.30
3436	A1149 A Dominoes, diff.	.75	.35

Nos. 3535-3436 were valued at 55g and 65g, respectively, on day of issue.

Famous Polish Men A1150

Designs: 1z, Ernest Malinowski (1818-99), constructor of Central Trans-Andean Railway, Peru. 1.60z, Rudolf Modrzejewski (Ralph Modjeski) (1861-1940), bridge builder.

Perf. 11½ Syncopated Type A
1999, Feb. 12
3437	A1150 1z multicolored	.55	.30
3438	A1150 1.60z multicolored	.90	.40

Easter — A1151

Scenes from Srudziadz Polyptych: 60g, Prayer in Ogrójec. 65g, Carrying cross. 1.40z, Resurrection. 1z, Tubadzin Pieta, 15th cent.

1999, Mar. 5   Perf. 11½x11¼
3439	A1151 60g multicolored	.35	.25
3440	A1151 65g multicolored	.35	.25
3441	A1151 1z multicolored	.60	.30
3442	A1151 1.40z multicolored	.85	.40
	Nos. 3439-3442 (4)	2.15	1.20

Souvenir Sheet

China 1999, World Philatelic Exhibition — A1152

Perf. 11½x11¼ Syncopated Type A
1999, Mar. 31
3443	A1152 1.70z Ideogram, dragon	1.60	1.00

Virgin Mary, Patron Saint of Soldiers A1153

Perf. 11½x11¾ Syncopated Type A
1999, Apr. 2   Litho.
3444	A1153 60g shown	.40	.25
3445	A1153 70g Katyn	.50	.25

Characters from Works by Henryk Sienkiewicz — A1154

No. 3446, Jan Skrzetuski. No. 3447, Onufry Zagloba. No. 3448, Longin Podbipieta. No. 3449, Bohun. No. 3450, Andrzej Kmicic. No. 3451, Michal Jerzy Wolodyjowski.

Perf. 11¾x11½ Syncopated Type B
1999, Apr. 6   Litho.
3446	A1154 70g multicolored	.50	.30
3447	A1154 70g multicolored	.50	.30
3448	A1154 70g multicolored	.50	.30
3449	A1154 70g multicolored	.50	.30
3450	A1154 70g multicolored	.50	.30
3451	A1154 70g multicolored	.50	.30
a.	Block of 6, # 3446-3451	3.50	2.10

Poland's Admission to NATO — A1155

Perf. 11½ Syncopated Type B
1999, Apr. 22   Litho.
3452	A1155 70g multicolored	.50	.30

Council of Europe, 50th Anniv. — A1156

Perf. 11½x11 Syncopated Type A
1999, May 5   Litho.
3453	A1156 1z multicolored	.70	.30

Europa A1157

Perf. 11½ Syncopated Type A
1999, May 5   Litho.
3454	A1157 1.40z multicolored	1.00	.70

Sports A1158

Perf. 11½ Syncopated Type B
1999, June 1   Litho.
3455	A1158 60g Cycling	.40	.25
3456	A1158 70g Snowboarding	.40	.25
3457	A1158 1z Skateboarding	.65	.30
3458	A1158 1.40z Roller blading	.90	.35
	Nos. 3455-3458 (4)	2.35	1.15

Visit of Pope John Paul II — A1159

Pope and: 60g, Church of the Virgin Mary, Cracow, crowd with Solidarity banners. 70g, Crowd with crosses. 1z, Crowd with flags. 1.40z, Eiffel Tower, Monument to Christ the Redeemer, Rio, Shrine of Our Lady of Fatima.

Perf. 11¾x11½ Syncopated Type A

1999, June 5			Litho.	
3459	A1159	60g multicolored	.40	.25
	Complete booklet, 10 #3459		4.00	
3460	A1159	70g multicolored	.50	.25
	Complete booklet, 10 #3460		5.00	
3461	A1159	1z multicolored	.70	.35
3462	A1159	1.40z multicolored	1.00	.45
	Nos. 3459-3462 (4)		2.60	1.30

Country Estates Type of 1997
Perf. 11½x11¾

1999, June 15			Photo.	
3463	A1110	70g Modlnicy	.50	.35
3464	A1110	1z Krzeslawicach	.70	.35
3465	A1110	1.40z Winnej Górze	1.00	.35
3466	A1110	1.60z Potoku Zlotym	1.10	.40
3467	A1110	1.85z Kasnej Dolnej	1.25	.45
	Nos. 3463-3467 (5)		4.55	1.85

Versailles Treaty, 80th Anniv. A1159a

Perf. 11¼x11½ Syncopated Type A

1999, June 29			Litho.	
3467A	A1159a	1.40z multi	1.00	.50

Depictions of the Virgin Mary — A1160

Designs: 60g, Painting from church in Rokitno. 70g, Crowned statue.

Perf. 11½x11¼ Syncopated Type A

1999, July 9			Litho.	
3468	A1160	60g multi	.40	.30
3469	A1160	70g multi	.50	.30

Insects — A1161

Designs: No. 3470, Corixa punctata. No. 3471, Dytiscus marginalis. No. 3472, Perla marginata. No. 3473, Limnophilus. No. 3474, Anax imperator. No. 3475, Ephemera vulgata.

Perf. 11½x11¾ Syncopated Type B

1999, July 16			Litho.	
3470	A1161	60g multi	.45	.30
3471	A1161	60g multi	.45	.30
3472	A1161	70g multi	.50	.30
3473	A1161	70g multi	.50	.30
3474	A1161	1.40z multi	.90	.50
3475	A1161	1.40z multi	.90	.50
	Nos. 3470-3475 (6)		3.70	2.20

Souvenir Sheet

Ksiaz Castle — A1162

Engr. (Margin Photo.)

1999, Aug. 14			Perf. 11¼x11	
3476	A1162	1z blue	1.10	.85

Natl. Philatelic Exhibition, Walbrzych, Czeslaw Slania's 1001st stamp design.
No. 3476 exists imperf., value $12.

Polish-Ukrainian Cooperation in Nature Conservation — A1163

Designs: No. 3477, Cervus elaphus. No. 3478, Felis silvestris.

Perf. 11x11½ Syncopated Type A

1999, Sept. 22			Litho.	
3477	A1163	1.40z multi	.90	.60
3478	A1163	1.40z multi	.90	.60
a.	Pair, #3477-3478		2.00	1.50

See Ukraine No. 354.

Royalty Type of 1986 with Denomination at Bottom

Designs: 60g, Wladyslaw IV. 70g, Jan II Kazimierz. 1z, Michal Korybut Wisniowiecki. 1.40z, Jan III Sobieski.

Photo. & Engr.

1999, Sept. 25			Perf. 10¾x11	
3479	A875	60g olive & black	.40	.25
3480	A875	70g brn & dk brn	.50	.25
3481	A875	1z blue & black	.70	.35
3482	A875	1.40z lilac & claret	.90	.40
	Nos. 3479-3482 (4)		2.50	1.25

UPU, 125th Anniv., World Post Day A1164

Perf. 11¾x11½ Syncopated Type A

1999, Oct. 9			Litho.	
3483	A1164	1.40z multi	1.00	.50

Frédéric Chopin (1810-49), Composer — A1165

1999, Oct. 17		Engr.	Perf. 11x11½	
3484	A1165	1.40z dark green	1.10	.55

See France No. 2744.

Jerzy Popieluszko (1947-84), Priest Murdered by Secret Police — A1166

Perf. 11½x11¼ Syncopated Type A

1999, Oct. 19			Litho.	
3485	A1166	70g multi	.55	.30

Souvenir Sheet

Memorial to Heroes of World War II — A1167

1999, Oct. 21				
3486	A1167	1z multi	1.10	.85

Christmas A1168

Various angels.

Perf. 11¼x11½ Syncopated Type A

1999, Nov. 26		Panel Color	Litho.	
3487	A1168	60g orange	.45	.25
3488	A1168	70g blue	.50	.25
3489	A1168	1z red	.70	.35
3490	A1168	1.40z olive green	1.00	.45
	Nos. 3487-3490 (4)		2.65	1.25

Polish Cultural Buildings in Foreign Countries A1169

Designs: 1z, Polish Museum, Rapperswil, Switzerland. 1.40z, Marian Fathers' Museum at Fawley Court Historic House, United Kingdom. 1.60z, Polish History and Literary Society Library, Paris. 1.80z, Polish Institute and Sikorski Museum, London.

Perf. 11½x11¾ Syncopated Type A

1999, Dec. 6			Litho.	
3491	A1169	1z multi	.70	.35
3492	A1169	1.40z multi	1.00	.45
3493	A1169	1.60z multi	1.10	.50
3494	A1169	1.80z multi	1.25	.60
	Nos. 3491-3494 (4)		4.05	1.90

New Year 2000 — A1170

Perf. 11½x11¾ Syncopated Type A

2000, Jan. 2			Litho.	
3495	A1170	A multi	1.00	.25

No. 3495 sold for 70g on day of issue.

Famous Poles A1171

Designs: 1.55z, Bronislaw Malinowski (1884-1942), ethnologist. 1.95z, Józef Zwierzycki (1888-1961), geologist.

Perf. 11¼x11½ Syncopated Type A

2000, Feb. 22				
3496	A1171	1.55z multi	1.10	.40
3497	A1171	1.95z multi	1.40	.55

Gniezno Summit, 1000th Anniv. — A1172

Designs: 70g, Holy Roman Emperor Otto III granting crown to Boleslaw Chrobry. 80g, Four bishops.
1.55z, Sclaunia, Germania, Gallia, Roma and Otto III, horiz.

Perf. 11½x11¼

2000, Mar. 12			Photo.	
3498	A1172	70g multi	.50	.25
3499	A1172	80g multi	.55	.25

Souvenir Sheet
Perf. 11¼x11½

3500	A1172	1.55z multi	1.40	.85

Organization of Roman Catholic Church in Poland, 1000th anniv.

Easter A1173

Designs: 70g, Christ in tomb. 80g, Resurrected Christ.

Perf. 11¼x11½ Syncopated Type B

2000, Mar. 24			Litho.	
3501	A1173	70g multi	.50	.25
3502	A1173	80g multi	.55	.25

Dinosaurs — A1174

No. 3503, Saurolophus. No. 3504, Gallimimus. No. 3505, Saichania. No. 3506, Protoceratops. No. 3507, Prenocephale. No. 3508, Velociraptor.

Perf. 11¾x11½ Syncopated Type A

2000, Mar. 24			Litho.	
3503	A1174	70g multi	.50	.25
3504	A1174	70g multi	.50	.25
3505	A1174	80g multi	.55	.25
3506	A1174	80g multi	.55	.25
3507	A1174	1.55z multi	.90	.40
3508	A1174	1.55z multi	.90	.40
a.	Souvenir sheet, #3503-3508		5.50	3.25
	Nos. 3503-3508 (6)		3.90	1.80

Awarding of Honorary Academy Award to Director Andrzej Wajda A1175

2000, Mar. 26				
3509	A1175	1.10z blk & gray	.75	.25
a.	Tete beche pair		1.75	.85

Holy Year 2000 — A1176

Perf. 11½x11¼ Syncopated Type B

2000, Apr. 7				
3510	A1176	80g multi	.50	.35

Country Estates Type of 1997

80g, Grabonóg. 1.55z, Zelazowa Wola. 1.65z, Sucha, Wegrów. 2.65z, Liwia, Wegrów.

Perf. 11½x11¾

2000, Apr. 14			Photo.	
3511	A1110	80g multicolored	.55	.25
3512	A1110	1.55z multicolored	1.10	.40
3513	A1110	1.65z multicolored	1.20	.45
3514	A1110	2.65z multicolored	1.75	.75
	Nos. 3511-3514 (4)		4.60	1.85

Cracow, 2000 European City of Culture — A1177

70g, Jan Matejko, Franciszek Joseph, Stanislaw Wyspianski, Konstanty Ildefons Galczynski, Stanislaw Lem, Slawomir Mrozek, Piotr Skrzynecki and Cloth Hall. 1.55z, Queen Jadwiga, Józef Dietl, Krzysztof Penderecki, Casimir the Great, Pope John Paul II, Jerzy Turowicz, Brother Albert, Copernicus, Collegium Maius and St. Mary's Church. 1.75z, Panorama of Cracow from 1493 wood engraving.

Perf. 11½x11¼ Syncopated Type A

2000, Apr. 26			Litho.	
3515	A1177	70g multi	.50	.30
3516	A1177	1.55z multi	1.10	.45

Souvenir Sheet
Engr.

Perf. 11¼x11½ Syncopated Type A

3517	A1177	1.75z blue	1.50	1.10

No. 3517 contains one 39x31mm stamp. No. 3517 exists imperf. Value $11.

Fight Against Drug Addiction A1178

Perf. 11¼x11½ Syncopated Type B

2000, Apr. 28			Litho.	
3518	A1178	70g multi	.50	.25

Europa, 2000
Common Design Type

Perf. 11½x11¾ Syncopated Type B

2000, May 9				
3519	CD17	1.55z multi	1.25	.75

Pope John Paul II, 80th Birthday A1179

Designs: 80g, Pope. 1.10z, Black Madonna of Jasna Gora. 1.55z, Pope's silver cross.

Engr., Litho. & Engr. (1.10z)

2000, May 9			Perf. 12¾	
3520	A1179	80g purple	.55	.25
3521	A1179	1.10z multi	.75	.35
3522	A1179	1.55z green	1.10	.50
	Nos. 3520-3522 (3)		2.40	1.10

See Vatican City Nos. 1153-1155.

España 2000 Intl. Philatelic Exhibition A1180

Perf. 11½x11¼ Syncopated Type A

2000, May 26			Litho.	
3523	A1180	1.55z multi	1.10	.50

Parenthood A1181

Perf. 11½x11¼ Syncopated Type B

2000, May 31				
3524	A1181	70g multi	.50	.25

Souvenir Sheet

Wroclaw, 1000th Anniv. — A1182

Perf. 11¼x11½ Syncopated Type A

2000, June 15				
3525	A1182	1.55z multi	1.25	.70

Social Activists A1183

70g, Karol Marcinkowski (1800-46), philantropist. 80g, Blessed Josemaría Escrivá de Balaguer, (1902-75), founder of Opus Dei.

Perf. 11¼x11½ Suncopated Type B

2000, June 23				
3526-3527	A1183	Set of 2	1.00	.50

Illustrations of Characters from Pan Tadeusz, by Adam Mickiewicz A1184

No. 3528, 70g, Gerwazy & Count. No. 3529, 70g, Telimena & Judge. No. 3530, 80g, Father Robak, Judge & Gerwazy. No. 3531, 80g, Wojski. No. 3532, 1.10z, Jankiel. No. 3533, 1.10z, Zofia & Tadeusz.

2000, June 30	Engr.		Perf. 11x11¼	
3528-3533	A1184	Set of 6	3.50	1.90

National Pilgrimage to Rome — A1185

Designs: 80g, Pope John Paul II, St. Peter's Basilica. 1.55z, Cross, Colosseum.

Perf. 11½x11¾ Syncopated Type B

2000, July 1			Litho.	
3534-3535	A1185	Set of 2	1.60	.70

Piotr Michalowski (1800-55), Artist — A1186

70g, Self-portrait, vert. 80g, Portrait of Boy in a Hat, vert. 1.10z, Stableboy Bridling Percherons. 1.55z, Horses & a Horse Cart.

Perf. 11½x11¼ (no syncopation), 11¾x11½ Syncopated Type A

2000, July 2				
3536-3539	A1186	Set of 4	2.75	1.00

Depictions of the Virgin Mary — A1187

Designs: 70g, Rózanostok. 1.55z, Lichen.

Perf. 11½x11¼ Syncopated Type A

2000, Aug. 14				
3540-3541	A1187	Set of 2	1.60	.65

St. John Bosco and Adolescents A1188

Perf. 11¼x11½ Syncopated Type B

2000, Aug. 25				
3542	A1188	80g multi	.55	.25

Educational work of Salesian order.

Souvenir Sheet

Solidarity Labor Union, 20th Anniv. — A1189

Perf. 11½x11¼ Syncopated Type B

2000, Aug. 31				
3543	A1189	1.65z multi	1.40	.75

2000 Summer Olympics, Sydney A1190

Designs: 70g, Runners. 80g, Diving, sailing, rowing. 1.10z, High jump, weight lifting, fencing. 1.55z, Basketball, judo, runner.

Perf. 11¾x11½ Syncopated Type A
2000, Sept. 1
3544-3547 A1190 Set of 4   2.75 1.25

World Post Day — A1191

Children's art by: 70g, Tomasz Wistuba, vert. 80g, Katarzyna Chrzanowska. 1.10z, Joanna Zbik. 1.55z, Katarzyna Lonak.

Perf. 11½x11¼, 11¼x11½ All Sync. Type B
2000, Oct. 9   Litho.
3548-3551 A1191   Set of 4   2.75 1.10

Souvenir Sheet

Polish Philatelic Union, 50th Anniv. — A1192

Perf. 11¼x11½ Sync. Type B
2000, Oct. 12
3552 A1192 1.55z multi   1.25 .75

Royalty Type of 1986 With Denominations at Bottom

Designs: 70g, August II. 80g, Stanislaw Leszczynski. 1.10z, August III. 1.55z, Stanislaw August Poniatowski.

2000, Oct. 23   Engr.   Perf. 10¾x11
3553-3556 A875 Set of 4   3.00 1.25

Katyn Massacre, 60th Anniv. — A1193

Designs: 70g, Priest and cross. 80g, Pope John Paul II at monument in Warsaw.

Perf. 11½x11¾ Sync. Type A
2000, Nov. 15   Litho.
3557-3558 A1193 Set of 2   1.10 .50

Christmas A1194

Scenes from the life of Jesus: 70g, Nativity. 80g, Wedding at Cana. 1.10g, Last Supper. 1.55z, Ascension.

Perf. 11½ Sync. Type A
2000, Nov. 27
3559-3562 A1194   Set of 4   2.75 1.25

Zacheta Art Museum, Warsaw, Cent. — A1195

Perf. 11½x11¼ Sync. Type B
2000, Dec. 4
3563 A1195 70g multi   .50 .25

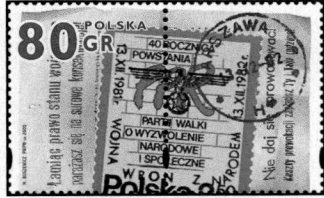

Underground Post During Martial Law — A1196

Perf. 11½x11¼ Sync. Type A
2000, Dec. 13
3564 A1196 80g multi + label   .85 .35
a.   Tete beche block of 2 stamps
     + 2 labels   2.25 1.10

End of Holy Year 2000 — A1197

Type C Syncopation (1st stamp #3565): Like Type A Syncopation but with oval hole on shorter sides rather than longer sides.

Perf. 11¾x11½ Sync. Type C
2001, Jan. 6   Litho.
3565 A1197 A multi   .85 .35

Sold for 1z on day of issue.

20th Winter Universiade, Zakopane — A1198

Perf. 11¼x11½ Sync. Type B
2001, Feb. 7
3566 A1198 1z multi   .65 .30

Internet A1199

Perf. 11¼x11½ Sync. Type A
2001, Feb. 22
3567 A1199 1z multi   .65 .30

World Ski Championships, Lahti, Finland — A1200

Perf. 11½ Sync. Type A
2001, Feb. 23
3568 A1200 1z shown   .70 .30
With Inscription "Adam Malysz" in Black
3569 A1200 1z multi   .70 .30
As #3569, With Inscription "Mistrzem Swiata" in Red
3570 A1200 1z multi   .70 .30
     Nos. 3568-3570 (3)   2.10 .90

Country Estates Type of 1997
Perf. 11½x11¾
2001, Feb. 28   Photo.
3571 A1110 10g Lipków   .25 .25
3572 A1110 1.50z Sulejówek   1.10 .35
3573 A1110 1.90z Petrykozy   1.40 .45
3574 A1110 3z Janowiec   2.10 .75
     Nos. 3571-3574 (4)   4.85 1.80

Issued: 1.90z, 3z, 2/28. 10g, 1.50z, 6/20.

Easter A1201

Designs: 1z, Women at empty tomb. 1.90z, Resurrected Christ with apostles.

Perf. 11½ Sync. Type A
2001, Mar. 16   Litho.
3575-3576 A1201 Set of 2   2.00 .70

12th Salesian Youth World Championships — A1202

Perf. 11¾x11½ Sync. Type C
2001, Apr. 28
3577 A1202 1z multi   .65 .30

Europa — A1203

Perf. 11½x11¼ Sync. Type A
2001, May 5
3578 A1203 1.90z multi   1.25 .75

Greetings A1204

Designs: No. 3579, 1z, All the best (couple in field of flowers). No. 3580, 1z, Vacation greetings (merman and mermaid at beach).

Perf. 11½x11¾ Syncopated Type B
2001, May 10   Litho.
3579-3580 A1204 Set of 2   1.40 .50

Wrzesnia Children's Strike Against German Language, Cent. — A1205

Perf. 11½x11¾ Syncopated Type A
2001, May 20
3581 A1205 1z multi   .70 .30

Polish Cultural Buildings in North America A1206

Designs: 1z, Poland Scientific Institute and Wanda Stachiewicz Polish Library, Montreal. 1.90z, Josef Pilsudski Institute, New York. 2.10z, Polonia Archives, Library and Museum, Orchard Lake, Mich. 2.20z, Polish Museum, Chicago.

Perf. 11½ Syncopated Type B
2001, June 29
3582 A1206   1z multi   .80 .30
a.   Tete beche pair   1.60 .70
3583 A1206 1.90z multi   1.50 .50
a.   Tete beche pair   3.00 1.40
3584 A1206 2.10z multi   1.60 .55
a.   Tete beche pair   3.25 1.60
3585 A1206 2.20z multi   1.60 .60
a.   Tete beche pair   3.25 1.75
     Nos. 3582-3585 (4)   5.50 1.95

Endangered Flora and Fauna — A1207

Convention on Intl. Trade in Endangered Species emblem and: No. 3586, 1z, Parnassius apollo, Orchis sambucina. No. 3587, 1z, Bubo bubo, Adonis vernalis. No. 3588, 1z, Galanthus nivalis, Lynx lynx. No. 3589, 1.90z, Orchis latifolia, Lutra lutra. No. 3590, 1.90z, Falco peregrinus, Orchis pallens. No. 3591, 1.90z, Cypripedium calceolus, Ursus arctos. 2z, World map.

Perf. 11½ Syncopated Type A
2001, July 10
3586-3591 A1207 Set of 6   6.00 2.25
Souvenir Sheet
Perf. 11¼x11½ Syncopated Type A
3592 A1207 2z multi   1.50 .95

No. 3592 contains one 39x30mm stamp.

Stefan Cardinal Wyszynski (1901-81) A1208

Perf. 11¾x11½ Syncopated Type A
2001, Aug. 3
3593 A1208 1z multi .70 .35

St. Maximilian Kolbe (1894-1941) — A1209

Perf. 11¾x11½ Syncopated Type B
2001, Aug. 14
3594 A1209 1z multi .70 .35

Depictions of the Virgin Mary — A1210

Designs: No. 3595, 1z, Piekniej Milosci, Bydgoszcz. No. 3596, 1z, Królowa Podhala, Ludzmierz. 1.90z, Mariampol, Wroclaw.

Perf. 11½x11¼ Syncopated Type A
2001, Aug. 14
3595-3597 A1210 Set of 3 2.75 1.10
See Nos. 3650-3652, 3694-3696.

Extension of God's Mercy Sanctuary, Cracow — A1211

2001, Aug. 31
3598 A1211 1z multi .70 .35

Euro Cuprum 2001 Philatelic Exhibition, Lubin — A1212

Designs: 1z, Copper smelter. 1.90z, Copper engravers at work. 2z, Copying with a copper engraving press.
3z, Engraver's burin, view of Lubin, 18th cent.

Perf. 11½x11¼ Syncopated Type A
2001, Sept. 1 **Litho. & Engr.**
3599-3601 A1212 Set of 3 3.50 1.40
Souvenir Sheet
Litho.
3602 A1212 3z multi 2.25 1.10
No. 3602 exists imperf. Value: mint $4, used $11.

Premiere of Movie "Quo Vadis," Directed by Jerzy Kawalerowicz — A1213

No. 3603: a, Ligia, Vinicius, Petrinius (red and light yellow inscriptions). b, Nero singing (blue and red inscriptions). c, Apostle Peter in catacombs, baptism of Chilon Chilonides (orange and yellow inscriptions). d, Chilon Chilonides, fire in Rome (white and yellow inscriptions). e, Ligia tied to back of aurochs, Ursus holding Ligia (red and white inscriptions). f, Apostle Peter blessing Vinicius and Ligia, close-up of Peter (purple and pink inscriptions).

Perf. 11¾x11½ Syncopated Type A
2001, Sept. 1 **Litho.**
3603 A1213 1z Sheet of 6, #a-f 4.25 2.75

A1214

Design: Exhibition on Christian Traditions in Military at Polish Army Museum.

Perf. 11¾x11½ Syncopated
2001, Sept. 10 **Litho.**
3604 A1214 1z multi .70 .35

Polish State Railways, 75th Anniv. — A1215

2001, Sept. 24
3605 A1215 1z multi .70 .35

Children's Stamp Design Contest Winners A1216

Art by: 1z, Marcin Kuron. 1.90z, Agata Grzyb, vert. 2z, Joanna Sadrakula.

Perf. 11½ Syncopated
2001, Sept. 28
3606-3608 A1216 Set of 3 3.25 1.40

Poland's Advancement to 2002 World Cup Soccer Championships A1217

Perf. 11½x11¾ Syncopated
2001, Oct. 6
3609 A1217 1z multi .70 .35

Year of Dialogue Among Civilizations A1218

2001, Oct. 9
3610 A1218 1.90z multi 3.00 .65
a. Tete beche pair 6.50 1.60

12th Intl. Henryk Wieniawski Violin Competition — A1219

Perf. 11¾x11½ Syncopated
2001, Oct. 13
3611 A1219 1z multi .70 .35

Papal Day — A1220

Perf. 11½x11¾ Syncopated
2001, Oct. 14
3612 A1220 1z multi .85 .40

Warsaw Philharmonic, Cent. — A1221

Perf. 11½x11¼ Syncopated
2001, Nov. 5
3613 A1221 1z multi .70 .35
a. Tete beche pair 1.75 .90

Millennium — A1222

No. 3614: a, Pope John Paul II, Gniezno Doors. b, Pres. Lech Walesa taking oath, cover of May 1791 Constitution. c, Covers of three magazines. d, Playwright Wojciech Boguslawski and Director Jerzy Grotowski, manuscript by Adam Mickiewicz. e, Marshal Józef Pilsudski, Solidarity posters. f, NATO emblem, Gen. Casimir Pulaski. g, Astronomers Nicolaus Copernicus and Aleksander Wolszczan, text from De Revolutionibus Orbium Coelestium, by Copernicus. h, Woodcut of mathematician Jan of Glogow, physicist Tadeusz Kotarbinski. i, Detail from 1920 poster and painting, Battle of Grunwald, by Jan Matejko. j, Four members of the Belvedere

Group, masthead of Warszawa Walczy newspaper, soldiers at Warsaw Uprising of 1944, seal of Marian Langiewicz. k, Head of John the Apostle, by Veit Stoss, and self-sculpture, by Magdalena Abakanowicz. l, Composers Krzysztof Penderecki and Frederic Chopin, Mazurka No. 10, Opus 50, by Karol Szymanowski. m, Engraving of Cracow and Royal Castle, Warsaw. n, Portrait of Jan III Sobieski, flag of European Union. o, Writers Wislawa Szymborska and Mikolaj Rej. p, Runners Janusz Kusocinski and Robert Korzeniowski.

Perf. 11¼x11½ Syncopated
2001, Nov. 11
3614 A1222 1z Sheet of 16, #a-p 12.00 6.00

Christmas A1223

Creches from Lower Silesia: 1z, 1.90z.

2001, Nov. 27
3615-3616 A1223 Set of 2 2.00 .85

Radio Maryja, 10th Anniv. A1224

Designs: No. 3617, 1z, Head of Virgin Mary statue, building.
No. 3618: a, 1z, Statue of Virgin Mary praying, crowd with flag. b, 1z, Statue of crowned Virgin Mary, crowd with flag.

2001, Dec. 7
3617 A1224 1z multi .70 .35
Souvenir Sheet
3618 A1224 1z Sheet, #a-b, 3617 2.10 1.10

Love A1225

Perf. 11¾x11½ Syncopated
2002, Feb. 4 **Litho.**
3619 A1225 1.10z multi .75 .35

2002 Winter Olympics, Salt Lake City — A1226

Perf. 11½x11¼ Syncopated
2002, Feb. 8
3620 A1226 1.10z multi .75 .35
a. Stamp + label .85 .50
No. 3620a was issued 2/22, and lists medals won by Adam Malysz.

Famous Poles A1227

Designs: No. 3621, 2z, Jan Czerski (1845-92), geologist. No. 3622, 2z, Bronislaw Pilsudski (1866-1918), linguist.

Perf. 11¾x11½ Syncopated
2002, Feb. 22
3621-3622 A1227 Set of 2 2.75 1.25

City Landmarks — A1228

Designs: 2z, Cathedral, St. Adalbert's coffin, Gniezno. 2.10z, Wawel Cathedral, St. Mary's Church, Lajkonik, Cracow. 3.20z, Mermaid monument, Royal Palace, Warsaw.

2002, Mar. 1 Photo. Perf. 11¾x11½
3623 A1228 2z multi 1.25 .50
3624 A1228 2.10z multi 1.35 .55
3625 A1228 3.20z multi 2.00 .90
   Nos. 3623-3625 (3) 4.60 1.95

See Nos. 3643-3644, 3665-3666, 3709-3712, 3763.

Easter — A1229

Designs: 1.10z, Flowers. 2z, Chicks.

Perf. 11½x11¾ Syncopated
2002, Mar. 8 Litho.
3626-3627 A1229 Set of 2 2.10 .85

Mammals and Their Young — A1230

No. 3628: a, Dog (purple denomination). b, Cat (brown denomination). c, Wolf (red denomination). d, Lynx (blue denomination).

Perf. 11¾x11½ Syncopated
2002, Mar. 25
3628 Horiz. strip of 4 3.00 1.75
a.-d. A1230 1.10z Any single .75 .35

Evacuation of Gen. Wladyslaw Anders' Army from USSR, 60th Anniv. A1231

Perf. 11½ Syncopated
2002, Mar. 26
3629 A1231 1.10z multi .75 .35

Paintings by Disabled Artists A1232

Unnamed works by: No. 3630, 1.10z, Henryk Paraszczuk, vert. No. 3631, 1.10z,

Amanda Zejmis, vert. 2z, Lucjan Matula. 3.20z, Józefa Laciak.

Perf. 11½x11¼ Sync., 11¼x11½ Sync.
2002, Apr. 17 Litho.
3630-3633 A1232 Set of 4 5.00 2.50

Census A1233

2002, Apr. 30 Perf. 11¼x11½ Sync.
3634 A1233 1.10z multi .75 .35

Radio Free Europe, 50th Anniv. — A1234

2002, May 2 Perf. 11¾x11½ Sync.
3635 A1234 2z multi 1.40 .60

State Fire Brigade, 10th Anniv. A1235

2002, May 4 Perf. 11¼x11½ Sync.
3636 A1235 1.10z multi .75 .50

Europa A1236

2002, May 5
3637 A1236 2z multi 1.20 .70

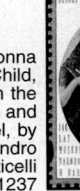

Madonna With Child, St. John the Baptist and Angel, by Sandro Botticelli A1237

2002, May 18 Perf. 11½ Sync.
3638 A1237 1.10z multi .75 .35

National Gallery, Warsaw, 140th anniv.

Maria Konopnicka (1842-1910), Poet — A1238

Photo. & Engr.
2002, May 23 Perf. 11½x11¼
3639 A1238 1.10z multi .75 .35

Children's Activities — A1239

No. 3640: a, Child playing badminton. b, Child flying kite. c, Child riding scooter.

Perf. 11½x11¼ Syncopated
2002, May 31 Litho.
3640 A1239 1.10z Horiz. strip of 3, #a-c 2.25 1.10

2002 World Cup Soccer Championships, Japan and Korea — A1240

Soccer ball and: 1.10z, Map. 2z, Players.

2002, June 1
3641-3642 A1240 Set of 2 2.00 1.00
3642a Souvenir sheet, 2 each #3641-3642 4.50 3.50

City Landmarks Type of 2002

Designs: 1.80z, Roman paten, St. Joseph's Sanctuary, Kalisz. 2.60z, Castle, reliquary of St. Sigismund, Plock, horiz.

Perf. 11¾x11½, 11½x11¾
2002, July 1 Photo.
3643 A1228 1.80z multi 1.25 .70
3644 A1228 2.60z multi 1.90 1.10

Ignacy Domeyko (1802-89), Mineralogist — A1241

Perf. 11¾x11½ Syncopated
2002, July 3 Litho.
3645 A1241 2.60z multi 1.75 .90

See Chile No. 1389.

Philakorea 2002 and Anphilex 2002 Stamp Exhibitions — A1242

2002, July 12
3646 A1242 2z multi 1.40 .60

Seventh Visit of Pope John Paul II A1243

Pope at: 1.10z, Kalwaria Zebrzydowska. 1.80z, Lagiewniki, Cracow. 3.20z, Wawel Castle, Cracow.

Perf. 11¾x11½ Syncopated
2002 Litho.
3647-3648 A1243 Set of 2 2.00 .80
Souvenir Sheet
Engr.
Perf. 11x11½
3649 A1243 3.20z blue 2.25 1.25
   Issued: 1.10z, 1.80z, 8/5; 3.20z, 8/16.

Depictions of the Virgin Mary Type of 2001

Designs: No. 3650, 1.10z, Holy Lady of Incessant Assistance (Matka Boza Nieustajacej Pomocy), Jaworzno. No. 3651, 1.10z, Holy Lady of Opole. 2z, Holy Lady of Trabki, Trabki Wielkie.

Perf. 11½x11¼ Syncopated
2002, Aug. 14 Litho.
3650-3652 A1210 Set of 3 3.00 1.00

Souvenir Sheet

23rd Polish Philatelic Association Convention, Ciechocinek — A1244

Engr. (Margin Photo. & Engr.)
2002, Sept. 1 Perf. 11x10¾
3653 A1244 3.20z brown 2.50 1.50
   Exists imperf. Value $7.50.

Premiere of Film "Zemsta," Directed by Andrzej Wajda — A1245

No. 3654: a, Czesnik and Dyndalski reading letter. b, Klara and Waclaw kissing. c, Papkin with mandolin. d, Rejent and Papkin, in chair. e, Rejent and Czesnik shaking hands. f, Attendant and Klara.

Perf. 11¾x11½ Syncopated
2002, Sept. 12 Litho.
3654 A1245 1.10z Sheet of 6, #a-f 8.50 4.75

Steam Locomotives — A1246

Designs: No. 3655, 1.10z, Ok1-359. No. 3656, 1.10z, Ol49-7. No. 3657, 2z, TKi3-87. No. 3658, 2z, Pm36-2.

Perf. 11¾x11½ Syncopated
2002, Sept. 21 Litho.
3655-3658 A1246 Set of 4 4.25 1.50
a. Horiz. strip of 4, #3655-3658 4.50 1.75

World Post
Day
A1247

Perf. 11¼x11½ Syncopated
2002, Oct. 9
3659 A1247 2z multi 1.40 .65

Fight
Against
Cancer
A1248

Perf. 11¾x11½ Syncopated
2002, Oct. 25
3660 A1248 1.10z multi .75 .35

Polish Television, 50th Anniv. — A1249

No. 3661 — Programs: a, Wiadomosci
(News, red background). b, Teatru Televizji
(Television theater, green background). c,
Pegaz (Cultural program). d, Teleranek (children's program).

Perf. 11¼x11½ Syncopated
2002, Oct. 25
3661 A1249 1.10z Sheet of 4,
#a-d 3.00 1.50

Saints — A1250

No. 3662: a, St. Stanislaw of Szczepanow
(1030-79). b, St. Kazimierz (1458-84). c, St.
Faustyna Kowalska (1905-38). d, St. Benedict
(480-547). e, Sts. Cyril (826-869) and
Methodius (815-85). f, St. Catherine of Siena
(1347-80).

Perf. 11½x11¼ Syncopated
2002, Nov. 8
3662 A1250 1.10z Sheet of 6,
#a-f 4.50 2.25

Christmas
A1251

Ornaments: 1.10z, 2z.

Perf. 11¼x11½ Syncopated
2002, Nov. 27
3663-3664 A1251 Set of 2 2.10 .80
Booklet, 10 #3663 7.50

City Landmarks Type of 2002
Designs: 1.20z, Towers of Old City Hall,
Statue of Nicolaus Copernicus, Torun, horiz.
3.40z, Church and well, Kazimierz Dolny,
horiz.

2003 Photo. **Perf. 11½x11¾**
3665 A1228 1.20z multi .70 .35
3666 A1228 3.40z multi 2.00 1.00

Issued: 1.20z, 1/31; 3.40z, 4/10.

1998-2002
Negotiations
to Join
European
Union
A1252

2003, Feb. 18 **Perf. 11x11½**
3667 A1252 1.20z multi .85 .45

A1253

**Pontificate of John
Paul II, 25th
Anniv. — A1254**

No. 3668: a, Election as Pope, 1978. b, In
Poland, 1979. c, In France, 1980. d, Assassination attempt, 1981. e, At Fatima, Portugal,
1982. f, Extraordinary Holy Year, 1983. g, At
Quirinale Palace, Rome, 1984. h, World Youth
Day, 1985. i, At synagogue, Rome, 1986. j,
Pentecost vigil, 1987. k, At European Parliament, Strasbourg, France, 1988. l, Meeting
with Mikhail Gorbachev, 1989. m, At Guinea-
Bissau leper colony, 1990. n, At European
Bishops' Synod, 1991. o, Publication of Catechism of the Catholic Church, 1992. p, Praying
for the Balkans in Assisi, 1993. q, At Sistine
Chapel, 1994. r, At UN Headquarters for 50th
anniv. celebrations, 1995. s, In Germany,
1996. t, In Sarajevo, Bosnia & Herzegovina,
1997. u, In Cuba, 1998. v, Opening Holy
Doors, 1999. w, World Youth Day, 2000. x,
Closing Holy Doors, 2001. y, Addressing Italian Parliament, 2002.

2003, Mar. 20 Litho. **Perf. 13x13¼**
3668 Sheet of 25 22.50 12.50
a.-y. A1253 1.20z Any single .85 .35

Etched on Silver Foil
Die Cut Perf. 12½x13
Self-Adhesive
3669 A1254 10z Pope John
Paul II 8.00 *12.00*

Cancels can be easily removed from No.
3669. See Vatican City Nos. 1236-1237.

Andrzej Frycz-Modrzewski (1503-72),
Writer — A1255

2003, Mar. 28 Engr. **Perf. 11½x11**
3670 A1255 1.20z brown .85 .35

Easter — A1256

Folk representations: 1.20z, Jesus seated.
2.10z, Jesus standing.

2003, Mar. 28 Photo. **Perf. 11½x11**
3671-3672 A1256 Set of 2 2.00 .90

Granting of Municipal Rights to
Poznan, 750th Anniv. — A1257

Designs: 1.20z, Old and modern skylines of
Poznan.
3.40z, View of Poznan, 1626.

Perf. 11¾x11½
2003, Apr. 15 Photo.
3673 A1257 1.20z multi .75 .35
Souvenir Sheet
Photo. & Engr.
Perf. 11¼x11½
3674 A1257 3.40z brown & lt
brown 2.10 .90
No. 3674 contains one 39x31mm stamp.

Signing of
European
Union
Accession
Treaty —
A1257a

2003, Apr. 16 Photo. **Perf. 11x11½**
3674A A1257a 1.20z multi .85 .45

Europa
A1258

2003, May 5 Photo. **Perf. 11**
3675 A1258 2.10z multi 1.25 .85

European Union Referendum —
A1258a

2003, May 26 Photo. **Perf. 11x11½**
3675A A1258a 1.20z multi .85 .45

**Lazienkowski Park Landmarks,
Warsaw — A1259**

Designs: 1.20z, Palac Na Wyspie. 1.80z,
Palac Na Wyspie, diff. 2.10z, Palac Myslewicki. 2.60z, Amphitheater.

2003, May 30 Photo.
3676-3679 A1259 Set of 4 5.25 2.25

Children's Dream Vacations — A1260

Children's art by: 1.20z, Anna Golebiewska.
1.80z, Marlena Krejpcio, vert. 2.10z, Michal
Korzen. 2.60z, Ewa Zajdler.

2003, June 20 **Perf. 11**
3680-3683 A1260 Set of 4 5.25 2.25

Fairy Tales
A1261

Designs: 1.20z, Krak, traditional tale. 1.80z,
Stupid Mateo, by Jozef Ignacy Kraszewski.
2.10z, The Princess Enchanted Into a Frog, by
Antoni Jozef Glinski. 2.60z, The Crock of Gold,
by Kraszewski.

2003, June 30
3684-3687 A1261 Set of 4 5.25 2.25

Souvenir Sheet

**19th National Philatelic Exhibition,
Katowice — A1262**

Photo. & Engr.
2003, Aug. 18 **Perf. 11½x11¼**
3688 A1262 3.40z multi 2.40 1.10

No. 3688 exists imperf. Value: mint $6, used
$9.

**Paintings of Julian Falat (1853-
1929) — A1263**

Designs: 1.20z, Self-portrait, vert. 1.80z, Spearsmen, vert. 2.10z, Winter Landscape with River and Bird. 2.60z, On the Ship — Merchants at Ceylon.

Perf. 11½x11¼, 11¼x11½

2003, Sept. 30		Photo.
3689-3692 A1263	Set of 4	5.25 2.10

World Post
Day — A1264

2003, Oct. 9		**Perf. 11½x11¼**
3693 A1264 2.10z multi		1.25 .60

Depictions of the Virgin Mary Type of 2001

Designs: 1.20z, Mother of the Redeemer. 1.80z, Holy Mother Benevolent, Krzeszowice. 2.10z, Holy Mother, Zieleniec.

2003, Oct. 14		
3694-3696 A1210	Set of 3	3.50 2.00

Motorcycle Racing in Poland,
Cent. — A1265

No. 3697 — Motorcycles of various eras with text in: a, Yellow. b, Green. c, Pink.

2003, Oct. 20	**Perf. 11¼x11½**
3697 Horiz. strip of 3	2.25 1.15
a.-c. A1265 1.20z Any single	.80 .35

Silesian Folk Ensemble — A1266

No. 3698: a, Denomination at left. b, Denomination at right.

2003, Oct. 29	**Perf. 11½x11¼**
3698 A1266 1.20z Horiz. pair, #a-b	1.75 .70

Cranes and Polish Government
Internet Address — A1267

2003, Oct. 31	**Perf. 11¼x11½**
3699 A1267 2.10z multi	1.50 .60

Worldwide Fund
for Nature
(WWF) — A1268

No. 3700 — Pandion haliaetus: a, On branch holding fish. b, Adult and young at nest. c, Adult hunting for prey. d, Adult flying with fish in talons.

2003, Oct. 31	**Perf. 11½x11¼**
3700 Horiz. strip of 4	3.25 1.75
a.-d. A1268 1.20z Any single	.80 .35

Christmas — A1269

Designs: 1.20z, Nativity. 1.80z, The Magi. 2.10z, The Annunciation, vert. 2.60z, Holy Family, vert.

Perf. 11½ Syncopated

2003, Nov. 27		Litho.
3701-3704 A1269	Set of 4	4.75 2.25

Foreign
Stamps
Depicting
Polish
Subjects
A1270

Designs: 1.20z, Sweden No. 2399a (Wislawa Szymborska), vert. 1.80z, France No. 1195 (Marie Curie). 2.10z, Sweden No. 1598 (Czeslaw Milosz), vert. 2.60z, Vatican City No. 437 (Black Madonna of Czestochowa).

2003, Dec. 12		
3705-3708 A1270	Set of 4	4.75 2.25

City Landmarks Type of 2002

Designs: 5g, Town Hall, church archway, Sandomierz, horiz. 1.25z, Town Hall, Neptune Fountain, Gdansk. 1.90z, Church of the Descent of the Holy Ghost, Israel Poznanski House, Lódz, horiz. 3.45z, Union Monument, Lublin Castle, Lublin, horiz.

Perf. 11½x11¾, 11¾x11½

2004			Photo.
3709 A1228	5g	multi	.25 .25
3710 A1228	1.25z	multi	.85 .35
3711 A1228	1.90z	multi	1.25 .60
3712 A1228	3.45z	multi	2.40 1.00
Nos. 3709-3712 (4)			4.75 2.20

Issued: 5g, 1/1; 1.25z, 1/9; 1.90z, 5/14; 3.45z, 2/23. Sheet margins of No. 3711 served as etiquettes.

12th Concert of the Great Holiday
Help Orchestra — A1271

2004, Jan. 5	**Perf. 11x11½**
3713 A1271 1.25z multi	.85 .35

LOT
(Polish
National
Airlines),
75th
Anniv.
A1272

2004, Jan. 21	
3714 A1272 1.25z multi	.85 .35

Love
A1273

2004, Feb. 2	
3715 A1273 1.25z multi	.85 .35

Famous
Poles
A1274

Designs: No. 3716, 2.10z, Helena Paderewska (1856-1934), chairwoman of Polish White Cross. No. 3717, 2.10z, Father Lucjan Bójnowski (1868-1960), Polish Army recruiter in US.

2004, Feb. 27		
3716-3717 A1274	Set of 2	3.00 1.00

Easter — A1275

Designs: 1.25z, Rabbit. 2.10z, Lamb.

2004, Mar. 12	**Perf. 11½x11¾**
3718-3719 A1275 Set of 2	2.25 .90

Flora and Fauna in
Reservoirs — A1276

No. 3720: a, Beaver, frog, flowers. b, Kingfisher holding fish, crawfish holding fish, snail, beetle and water lilies. c, Grayling, leech, mussel, snail. d, Pike chasing smaller fish, grebe, snail.

Perf. 11¾x11½ Syncopated

2004, Mar. 30	Litho.
3720 Horiz. strip of 4	3.50 1.50
a.-d. A1276 1.25z Any single	.85 .35

Admission to
European
Union — A1277

Perf. 11½x11¾ Syncopated

2004, May 1	
3721 A1277 2.10z multi + label	1.50 .80

Europa
A1278

2004, May 5		
3722 A1278 2.10z multi	1.50	.70

Tenth
Government
Postage Stamp
Printers'
Conference,
Krakow
A1279

Photo. & Engr.

2004, May 7	**Perf. 11½x11¾**
3723 A1279 3.45z multi + label	2.25 .90

A1280

WIZYTY DUSZPASTERSKIE OJCA ŚWIĘTEGO JANA PAWŁA II W POLSCE
WSPÓLNA EMISJA
POLSKI I WATYKANU

Visits to Poland by Pope John Paul II — A1281

No. 3724: a, Wearing red stole, hand on chin. b, Wearing red stole, praying. c, Holding crucifix with rays. d, Holding crucifix.

No. 3725: a, Wearing gold stole, holding crucifix. b, With arm raised. c, Wearing white vestments, seated. d, Wearing red stole, seated.

Litho. (Embossed Labels)
2004, June 2   **Perf. 13¼x13**
Country Name in Blue

3724 A1280 1.25z Sheet of 4,
#a-d, + 8 labels   3.50 2.00

Country Name in Red

3725 A1281 1.25z Sheet of 4,
#a-d, + 8 labels   3.50 2.00

See Vatican City Nos. 1264-1265.

Birds — A1282

No. 3726: a, Platycercus elegans, Platycercus eximius. b, Nymphicus hollandicus. c, Melopsittacus undulatus. d, Chloebia gouldiae, Poephila guttata, Padda oryzivora.

Perf. 11½x11¾ Syncopated
2004, June 30   **Litho.**
3726 A1282 1.25z Block of 4, #a-d   3.50 1.25

Paintings by Jacek Malczewski (1854-1929) — A1283

Designs: 1.20z, Self-portrait, vert. 1.90z, Ellenai, vert. 2.10z, Tobias and Harpy. 2.60z, The Unknown Note.

Perf. 11½x11¼, 11¼x11½
2004, July 15   **Photo.**
3727-3730 A1283   Set of 4   5.50 2.00

Souvenir Sheet

Singapore World Stamp Championship 2004 — A1284

Perf. 11¼x11½ Syncopated
2004, July 30   **Litho.**
3731 A1284 3.45z multi   2.50 1.00
   a.   Imperf.   9.50 11.00

Miniature Sheet

2004 Summer Olympics, Athens — A1285

No. 3732: a, Boxing. b, Women's track. c, Equestrian. d, Wrestling.

Perf. 11¾x11½ Syncopated
2004, Aug. 2
3732 A1285 1.25z Sheet of 4, #a-d   3.25 1.50

Witold Gombrowicz (1904-69), Writer — A1286

Perf. 11½x11¼ Syncopated
2004, Aug. 4
3733 A1286 1.25z blue   .85 .35

Depictions of the Virgin Mary — A1287

Inscriptions: No. 3734, 1.25z, Matka Boza Dzikowska. No. 3735, 1.25z, Matka Boza Fatimska. No. 3736, 1.25z, Matka Boza Jasnagórska. No. 3737, 1.25z, Matka Boza Laskawa. No. 3738, 1.25z, Matka Boza Lomzynska. No. 3739, 1.25z, Matka Boza Miedzenska. No. 3740, 1.25z, Matka Boza Nieustajacej Pomocy. No. 3741, 1.25z, Matka Boza Bolesna Oborska. No. 3742, 1.25z, Matka Boza Piekarska. No. 3743, 1.25z, Matka Boza Placzaca. No. 3744, 1.25z, Matka Boza Pokorna Rudzka. No. 3745, 1.25z, Matka Boza Rychwaldzka. No. 3746, 1.25z, Matka Boza Rywaldzka. No. 3747, 1.25z, Matka Boza Rzeszowska. No. 3748, 1.25z, Matka Boza Sianowska. No. 3749, 1.25z, Bolesna Matka Boza Skrzatuska. No. 3750, 1.25z, Matka Boza Swietorodzinna.

Perf. 11½x11¼ Syncopated
2004, Aug. 14   **Litho.**
3734-3750 A1287   Set of 17   14.00 6.25

Czeslaw Niemen (1939-2004), Musician — A1288

Perf. 11¾x11½ Syncopated
2004, Aug. 30   **Litho.**
3751 A1288 1.25z black & gray   .85 .35

Dunajec River Raftsmen — A1289

2004, Sept. 3
3752 A1289 2.10z multi   1.40 .75
See Slovakia No. 463.

Motor Sports A1290

No. 3753: a, Cinder track motorcycle racing (four motorcycles). b, Auto racing. c, Go-kart racing. d, Motorcycle racing (one motorcycle).

Perf. 11¼x11½ Syncopated
2004, Sept. 11
3753   Horiz. strip of 4   3.50 1.50
  a.-d. A1290 1.25z Any single   .85 .30

World Post Day A1291

Perf. 11¼x11½ Syncopated
2004, Oct. 9   **Litho.**
3754 A1291 2.10z multi   1.40 .60

UNESCO World Heritage Sites — A1292

Designs: No. 3755, 1.25z, Castle of the Teutonic Order, Malbork. No. 3756, 1.25z, Historic Center of Warsaw. No. 3757, 1.25z, Historic Center of Cracow, vert. No. 3758, 1.25z, Medieval Town of Torun, vert. No. 3759, 1.25z, Old City of Zamosc.

2004, Oct. 20   **Perf. 11½ Syncopated**
3755-3759 A1292   Set of 5   4.25 1.60

Christmas A1293

Designs: 1.25z, Worshippers at shrine. 2.10z, Window, ornaments, candle, poinsettia.

2004, Nov. 5   Photo.   Perf. 11½x11¾
3760-3761 A1293   Set of 2   2.25 .85

History of the Earth — A1294

No. 3762: a, Birth (narodziny). b, Infancy (dziecinstwo). c, Youth (mlodosc). d, Maturity (dojrzalosc).

Perf. 11½ Syncopated
2004, Dec. 3   1.25z Block of 4, #a-d   **Litho.**
3762 A1294   3.50 1.25

City Landmarks Type of 2002

Design: Monument of Hygea, Raczynski Library, Poznan.

2005, Jan. 3   Photo.   Perf. 11½x11¾
3763 A1228 1.30z multi   .80 .35

13th Concert of the Great Holiday Help Orchestra — A1295

2005, Jan. 6   **Perf. 11¼x11½**
3764 A1295 1.30z multi   .90 .40

Konstanty Ildefons Galczynski (1905-53), Poet — A1296

2005, Jan. 14   **Perf. 11½x11¼**
3765 A1296 1.30z multi   .90 .40

Mikolaj Rej (1505-69), Writer A1297

2005, Jan. 26   **Perf. 11¼x11½**
3766 A1297 1.30z black & red   .90 .40

Love
A1298

2005, Feb. 1 Photo. Perf. 11¼x11½
3767 A1298 1.30z multi   .90 .40

Easter — A1299

Flowers and: 1.30z, Rabbit. 2.20z, Chick.

2005, Mar. 1   Perf. 11¾x11½
3768-3769 A1299 Set of 2   2.10 1.00

Hans Christian Andersen (1805-75), Author — A1300

Designs: No. 3770, 1.30z, The Little Mermaid (Mala Syrenka), No. 3771, 1.30z, The Snow Queen (Królowa Sniegu).

Perf. 11½x11¾ Syncopated
2005, Mar. 15   Litho.
3770-3771 A1300 Set of 2   1.60 .70

Pope John Paul II (1920-2005)
A1301

Perf. 11½x11¾ Syncopated
2005, Apr. 8   Litho.
3772 A1301 1.30z multi   .90 .40

Extreme Sports — A1302

No. 3773: a, Parachuting. b, Bungee jumping. c, Rock climbing. d, White water rafting.

Perf. 11¾x11½ Syncopated
2005, Apr. 15   Litho.
3773 A1302 1.30z Block of 4, #a-d   3.50 1.50

Souvenir Sheet

Pacific Explorer 2005 World Stamp Expo, Sydney — A1303

Perf. 11¼x11½ Syncopated
2005, Apr. 21
3774 A1303 3.50z multi   2.40 1.00
No. 3774 exists imperf., value: mint $7.50, used $9.

Souvenir Sheet

JEZU UFAM TOBIE

Pope John Paul II (1920-2005) — A1304

Perf. 11½x11¼ Syncopated
2005, Apr. 22
3775 A1304 3.50z multi   2.25 1.10

All Saints Collegiate Church, Sieradz — A1305

Buildings, Katowice A1306

Baltic Shore, Sopot — A1307

Buildings, Szczecin A1308

St. John the Baptist Cathedral, Przemysl A1309

Perf. 11¾x11½, 11½x11¾
2005			Photo.	
3776	A1305	20g multi	.25	.25
3777	A1306	30g multi	.25	.25
3778	A1307	2.20z multi	1.25	.65
3779	A1308	2.80z multi	1.60	.80
3780	A1309	3.50z multi	2.00	.90
	Nos. 3776-3780 (5)		5.35	2.85

Issued: 20g, 7/29; 2.20z, 6/15; 2.80z, 5/30; 30g, 10/5; 3.50z, 4/30.

Europa
A1310

Perf. 11¼x11½ Syncopated
2005, May 5   Litho. & Embossed
3781 A1310 2.20z multi   1.50 .85

End of World War II, 60th Anniv. — A1311

Perf. 11¾x11½ Syncopated
2005, May 6   Litho.
3782 A1311 1.30z multi   .85 .40

Souvenir Sheet

Youth Literature — A1312

No. 3783: a, 1.30z, *Hour of the Crimson Rose*, by Maria Krüger. b, 2z, *The Little Prince*, by Antoine de Saint-Exupery. c, 2.20z, *20,000 Leagues Under the Sea*, by Jules Verne. d, 2.80z, *In Desert and Wilderness*, by Henryk Sienkiewicz.

Perf. 11½ Syncopated
2005, June 1   Litho.
3783 A1312 Sheet of 4, #a-d   5.75 2.75

Souvenir Sheet

Items in the Wilanow Museum — A1313

No. 3784: a, 1.30z, Portrait of Stanislaw Kostka Potocki, by Jacques Louis David, 1781. b, 2z, Nautilus wine cup, 17th cent. c, 2.20z, Porcelain figurine of flower girl, 18th cent. d, 2.80z, Decorative clock, 19th cent.

2005, June 21   Photo.
Perf. 11½x11¼
3784 A1313 Sheet of 4, #a-d   5.75 2.50

Embroidered Roses — A1314

Embroidered roses from: 1.30z, Podhale region. 2z, Lowicz region. 2.20z, Lowicz region, diff. 2.80z, Lowicz region, diff.

Perf. 11½x11¼ Syncopated
2005, July 15   Litho.
3785-3788 A1314 Set of 4   5.00 2.25

Souvenir Sheet

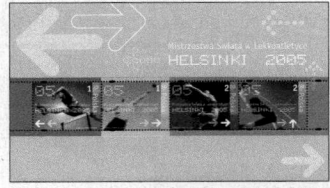

World Track and Field Championships, Helsinki — A1315

No. 3789: a, 1.30z, Hurdles. b, 1.30z, Shot put. c, 2z, Long jump. d, 2z, Pole vault.

Perf. 11¾x11½ Syncopated
2005, Aug. 8
3789 A1315 Sheet of 4, #a-d   4.50 1.75

Souvenir Sheet

Polish Eagle and Józef Pilsudski — A1316

Perf. 11¼x11½
2005, Aug. 12   Photo.
3790 A1316 3.50z multi   2.40 1.00
"Miracle on the Vistula," repulse of Red Army counter-offensive, 85th anniv.

Lech Walesa and Solidarity Emblem A1317

Perf. 11½x11¼ Syncopated
2005, Aug. 17 Litho.
3791 A1317 2.20z red & gray 1.50 .65
Solidarity Trade Union, 25th anniv.

Polish Radio, 80th Anniv. — A1318

Perf. 11½x11¾ Syncopated
2005, Sept. 1 Photo.
3792 A1318 1.30z multi .90 .40

15th Frederic Chopin Piano Competition A1319

Perf. 11¼x11½ Syncopated
2005, Sept. 16 Litho.
3793 A1319 2.20z multi 1.50 .65
a. Souvenir sheet of 4 7.50 7.50

Zoo Animals A1320

Designs: 1.30z, Lemuridae, Opole Zoo. 2z, Panthera tigris altaica, Wroclaw Zoo. 2.20z, Ceratotherium simum, Poznan Zoo. 2.80z, Myrmecophagidae, Warsaw Zoo.

Perf. 11½x11¾ Syncopated
2005, Sept. 30
3794-3797 A1320 Set of 4 5.00 2.50

Main Post Office, Cracow A1321

Perf. 11¾x11½ Syncopated
2005, Oct. 7
3798 A1321 1.30z multi .90 .40
World Post Day.

United Nations, 60th Anniv. A1322

Perf. 11¼x11½ Syncopated
2005, Oct. 14
3799 A1322 2.20z multi 1.40 .70

Landmarks in European Union Capitals A1323

Designs: No. 3800, 1.30z, Vilnius Cathedral, Vilnius, Lithuania. No. 3801, 1.30z, St. Matthias's Church, Statue of St. Stephen, Budapest, Hungary. No. 3802, 2.20z, Government building, Dublin, Ireland. No. 3803, 2.20z, Monument, Lisbon, Portugal. 2.80z, Arc de Triomphe, Paris, France.

Perf. 11¼x11½ Syncopated
2005, Oct. 24
3800-3804 A1323 Set of 5 6.25 2.75
See Nos. 3838-3842, 3875-3879, 3914-3918, 3957-3961, 4095.

Souvenir Sheet

Paintings by Polish Impressionists — A1324

No. 3805: a, 1.30z, Plowing in the Ukraine, by L. J. Wyczolkowski. b, 1.30z, Still Life, by J. Pankiewicz. c, 2z, Flower Sellers, by O. Boznanska. d, 2z, Gooseberry Bushes, by W. Podkowinski.

2005, Nov. 3 Photo.
3805 A1324 Sheet of 4, #a-d, + 2 labels 4.50 3.00

Polish Doctors' Association, Bicent. — A1325

Perf. 11½x11¼ Syncopated
2005, Nov. 24 Litho.
3806 A1325 1.30z multi .90 .40

Christmas — A1326

Christmas trees and angel in: 1.30z, Blue. 2.20z, Rose pink.

Perf. 11¾x11½
2005, Nov. 28 Photo.
3807-3808 A1326 Set of 2 2.25 .90

2006 Winter Olympics, Turin — A1327

Perf. 11¾x11½ Syncopated
2006, Feb. 7 Litho.
3809 A1327 2.40z multi + label 1.60 .75

Love — A1328

Perf. 11½x11¼
2006, Feb. 10 Photo.
3810 A1328 1.30z multi .90 .50

Wolfgang Amadeus Mozart (1756-91), Composer — A1329

Perf. 11¾x11½ Syncopated
2006, Feb. 15 Litho.
3811 A1329 2.40z multi 1.50 .75

Independent Students Association, 25th Anniv. — A1330

2006, Feb. 17
3812 A1330 1.30z multi .90 .50

Museum of Industry, Warsaw, and Zygmunt Gloger (1845-1910), First President of Polish Touring Society — A1331

2006, Feb. 20
3813 A1331 1.30z multi .90 .50
Polish Touring Society, cent.

Endangered Flora — A1332

Designs: 1.30z, Pedicularis sudetica. 2.40z, Trapa natans.

2006, Mar. 14
3814-3815 A1332 Set of 2 2.50 1.00

A1333

Sculptures by Igor Mitoraj — A1334

2006, Mar. 27
3816 A1333 1.30z Lips of Eros .90 .40
3817 A1334 1.30z Dream II .90 .40
a. Souvenir sheet, 2 each #3816-3817 3.50 4.00

Easter — A1335

Traditional customs: 1.30z, Women holding paper flower palms. 2.40z, Man dousing woman with water.

2006, Apr. 3 **Perf. 11½x11¾**
3818-3819 A1335 Set of 2 2.00 1.10

Convent of Jasna Gora, Czestochowa A1336

2006, Apr. 24 Photo.
3820 A1336 2.40z multi 1.30 .70

Europa — A1337

Perf. 11½x11¾ Syncopated
2006, May 5 Litho.
3821 A1337 2.40z multi 1.60 .70

Souvenir Sheet

Washington 2006 World Philatelic Exhibition — A1338

Perf. 11¼x11½
2006, May 19 Photo.
3822 A1338 2.40z multi + label 1.60 .70

Visit of Pope
Benedict
XVI — A1339

Perf. 11½x11¼ Syncopated
2006, May 25   Litho.
3823 A1339 1.30z multi   .80 .45

Souvenir Sheet

Lighthouses — A1340

No. 3824: a, Stilo. b, Krynica Morska. c,
Gaski. d, Niechorze.

Perf. 11½x11¼
2006, May 29   Photo.
3824 A1340 2.40z Sheet of 4,
              #a-d   6.25 2.75

Toys — A1341

Designs: No. 3825, 1.30z, Pinwheel. No.
3826, 1.30z, Top.

Perf. 11 Syncopated
2006, June 1   Litho.
3825-3826 A1341 Set of 2   1.75 .80
    See Nos. 3896-3897.

Souvenir Sheets

Worker Uprisings — A1342

Photo. & Engr.
2006   **Perf. 11¼x11½**
3827 A1342 3.50z Poznan, 1956 2.00 1.00
3828 A1342 3.50z Radom, 1976   2.00 1.00
    Issued: No. 3827, 6/25; No. 3828, 6/28.

Silver and Gold Objects — A1343

No. 3829: a, Tankard with Biblical designs,
by Peter Rohde, Poland. b, Jeweled Qing
Dynasty cup, China.

Perf. 11½x11¼
2006, June 20   Photo.
3829 A1343 1.30z Horiz. pair, #a-
        b   1.25 .75
See People's Republic of China Nos. 3506-
3507.

Jerzy Giedroyc
(1906-2000),
Literary
Magazine
Editor — A1344

2006, July 27   Engr.
3830 A1344 1.30z black   .80 .40

Polish Society of Internal Medicine,
Cent. — A1345

Doctors: No. 3831, 1.30z, Witold Eugeniusz
Orlowski (1874-1966). No. 3832, 1.30z,
Edward Szczeklik (1898-1985). 3z, Antoni
Wladyslaw Gluzinski (1856-1935).

Perf. 11¾x11½ Syncopated
2006, Sept. 8   Litho.
3831-3833 A1345 Set of 3   3.00 1.50

Souvenir Sheet

19th Polish Philatelic Congress,
Lubin — A1346

Photo. & Engr.
2006, Sept. 20   **Perf. 11¼x11½**
3834 A1346 3.50z multi   2.00 1.00
    No. 3834 exists imperf. Value, $6.50.

Miniature Sheets

Polish Alphabet — A1347

No. 3835 — Depictions of Polish words
starting with letters of the alphabet: a, 10gr,
Man shouting "E". b, 10gr, Indian. c, 30gr,
Angels. d, 30gr, House. e, 30gr, Ink-splattered
"K." f, 1z, Wave. g, 1z, Driver and "L." h, 1.30z,
Snowman. i, 1.30z, Lemon. j, 1.30z, Cake. k,
1.30z, Pear. l, 1.30z, Hammock. m, 1.30z, Liz-
ard's tongue.
No. 3836: a, 10gr, Musical notes. b, 10gr,
Child. c, 30gr, Carrots. d, 30gr, Eagle. e, 30gr,
Zebra. f, 1z, Peacock. g, 1z, Strawberry. h,
1.30z, Patch on "L." i, 1.30z, Lobster. j, 1.30z,
Elephant. k, 1.30z, Snail. l, 1.30z, Face with
large lips. m, 1.30z, Wolf.

2006 Litho. **Perf. 11½ Syncopated**
     Sheets of 13, #a-m
3835-3836 A1347 Set of 2   14.00 7.00
    Issued: No. 3835, 9/29; No. 3836, 11/7.
Nos. 3835c and 3836e are 41x19mm; other
stamps are 18x19mm.

World
Post Day
A1348

2006, Oct. 9 Photo. **Perf. 11¼x11½**
3837 A1348 2.40z multi   1.40 .60

**Landmarks in European Capitals
Type of 2005**
Designs: No. 3838, 2.40z, Brandenburg
Gate, Berlin, Germany. No. 3839, 2.40z, Col-
osseum, Rome, Italy. No. 3840, 2.40z, Royal
Dramatic Theater, Stockholm, Sweden. No.
3841, 2.40z, St. Alexander Nevski Cathedral,
Tallinn, Estonia. No. 3842, 2.40z, St. Paul's
Cathedral, Valletta, Malta.

Perf. 11¼x11½ Syncopated
2006, Oct. 24   Litho.
3838-3842 A1323 Set of 5   6.75 3.25

Dogs
A1349

No. 3843: a, Ogar polski (Polish bloodhound). b, Gonczy polski (Polish hound). c,
Polski owczarek nizinny (Polish Lowland
sheepdog). d, Chart polski (Polish greyhound).
e, Polski owczarek podhalanski (Polish
Podhale sheepdog).

2006, Nov. 6
3843   Horiz. strip of 5   4.50 3.00
a.-e. A1349 1.30z Any single   .80 .45

Christmas
A1350

Designs: 1.30z, Nativity. 2.40z, Angel,
"Christmas" in Polish, Italian, English, French
and German.

Perf. 11½x11¾
2006, Nov. 30   Photo.
3844-3845 A1350 Set of 2   2.10 .90

Wujek Coal Mine Massacre, 25th
Anniv. — A1351

Perf. 11¾ Syncopated
2006, Dec. 16   Litho.
3846 A1351 1.30z multi   .80 .40

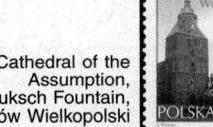

15th Concert of the Great Holiday
Help Orchestra — A1352

2007, Jan. 4 Photo. **Perf. 11¼x11½**
3847 A1352 1.35z multi   .85 .40

Cathedral of the
Assumption,
Pauksch Fountain,
Gorzów Wielkopolski
A1353

2007, Jan. 19   **Perf. 11¾x11½**
3848 A1353 1.35z multi   .85 .40

2007 European Figure Skating
Championships, Warsaw — A1354

Perf. 11¾x11½ Syncopated
2007, Jan. 22   Litho.
3849 A1354 2.40z multi   1.50 .70

Love — A1355

Perf. 11½x11¾ Syncopated
2007, Feb. 8   Litho.
3850 A1355 1.35z multi   .85 .40
    No. 3850 exists in a sheet of eight with eight
labels that could be personalized. Value, $50.

Easter
A1356

Folk art: 1.35z, Lamb made of straw. 2.40z, Chicken made from wooden eggs.

2007, Mar. 8 Photo. Perf. 11¼x11½
3851-3852 A1356 Set of 2 2.40 1.10

Treaty of Rome, 50th Anniv. — A1357

Perf. 11½x11¾ Syncopated
2007, Mar. 20 Litho.
3853 A1357 3.55z multi 2.25 1.00

Greetings for Special Days — A1358

Designs: No. 3854, 1.35z, Birthday cake and confetti. No. 3855, 1.35z, Grapes, chalice, bread, monogram of Jesus. No. 3856, 1.35z, Wedding rings, rose.

Perf. 11½ Syncopated
2007, Mar. 30 Litho.
3854-3856 A1358 Set of 3 2.50 1.25

Earth Day A1359

Perf. 11¾x11½ Syncopated
2007, Apr. 22 Litho.
3857 A1359 1.35z multi .95 .40

Railway Cars A1360

No. 3858: a, Type 5G postal car, 1956. b, Type Cd21b passenger car, 1924. c, Type C3Pr07 passenger car, 1909. d, Type Ci29 passenger car, 1929.

2007, Apr. 28
3858 Horiz. strip of 4 5.00 2.25
 a.-b. A1360 1.35z Either single .90 .40
 c.-d. A1360 2.40z Either single 1.60 .70

Europa A1361

2007, May 5
3859 A1361 3z multi 2.25 1.00
Scouting, cent.

Little Helen with a Vase of Flowers, by Stanislaw Wyspianski — A1362

2007, May 18
3860 A1362 1.35z multi .90 .40
Stanislaw Wyspianski Year.

Karol Szymanowski (1882-1937), Composer A1363

2007, May 26 Perf. 11½x11¼
3861 A1363 1.35z multi .90 .40
Karol Szymanowski Year.

Granting of Municipal Rights to Cracow, 750th Anniv. — A1364

Photo. & Engr.
2007, May 29 Perf. 11¾x11½
3862 A1364 2.40z multi 1.75 .80

Souvenir Sheet

St. Petersburg Intl. Philatelic Exhibition — A1365

2007, June 12 Perf. 11¼x11
3863 A1365 3z multi 2.25 .90

Nicolaus Copernicus Planetarium, Chorzów A1366

Perf. 11½x11¾
2007, June 15 Photo.
3864 A1366 3.55z multi 2.40 1.10

Souvenir Sheet

Lighthouses — A1367

No. 3865: a, 1.35z, Gdansk Lighthouse. b, 2.40z. Rozewie Lighthouse. c, 3z, Kolobrzeg Lighthouse. d, 3.55z, Hel Lighthouse.

2007, June 15 Perf. 11½x11¼
3865 A1367 Sheet of 4, #a-d 7.50 3.00

Holy Virgin of Lesniów A1368

Perf. 11½x11¼ Syncopated
2007, July 2 Litho.
3866 A1368 1.35z multi .90 .40
Lesniów Jubilee Year.

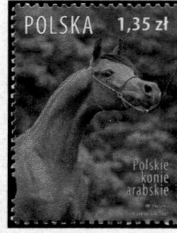

Arabian Horses — A1369

No. 3867 — Color of horse: a, Brown. b, White. c, Brown, diff. d, White, diff.

Perf. 11½x11¾ Syncopated
2007, Aug. 31
3867 Horiz. strip of 4 8.00 4.00
 a. A1369 1.35z multi .95 .40
 b. A1369 3z multi 2.10 1.00
 c.-d. A1369 3.55z Either single 2.40 1.25

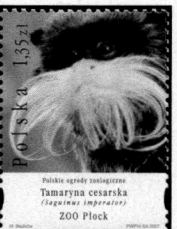

Animals in Polish Zoos — A1370

Designs: 1.35z, Saguinus imperator, Plock Zoo. 2.40z, Ciconia nigra, Lódz Zoo. 3z, Loxodonta africana, Gdansk Zoo. 3.55z, Uncia uncia, Cracow Zoo.

Perf. 11½x11¾ Syncopated
2007, Sept. 11 Litho.
3868-3871 A1370 Set of 4 7.75 3.50

50th Warsaw Autumn Intl. Contemporary Music Festival — A1371

Perf. 11¼x11½ Syncopated
2007, Sept. 21
3872 A1371 3z multi 2.10 .90

Theater in Katowice, Cent. A1372

Perf. 11x11½ Syncopated
2007, Oct. 5 Litho.
3873 A1372 1.35z multi 1.10 .55

World Post Day A1373

Perf. 11¾x11½ Syncopated
2007, Oct. 9 Litho.
3874 A1373 1.35z multi 1.10 .55

Landmarks in European Union Capitals Type of 2005

Designs: No. 3875, 1.35z, Statue of St. Roland and House of Blackheads, Riga, Latvia. No. 3876, 1.35z, Dragon's Bridge, Ljubljana, Slovenia. No. 3877, 3z, Plaza de Cibeles, Madrid. No. 3878, 3z, Luxembourg Philharmonic Building, Luxembourg. 3.55z, Tower Bridge, London.

Perf. 11¼x11½ Syncopated
2007, Oct. 24 Litho.
3875-3879 A1323 Set of 5 9.75 3.25

Pope John Paul II Foundation, 25th Anniv. A1374

2007, Oct. 30
3880 A1374 1.35z multi 1.10 .55

Self-portrait, by Jerzy Duda-Gracz (1941-2004) — A1375

2007, Nov. 5
3881 A1375 1.35z multi   1.10 .55

Teddy Bear and Christmas Tree — A1376

Adoration of the Magi, by Mikolaj Haberschrack A1377

Perf. 11½x11¼
2007, Nov. 27   Photo.
3882 A1376 1.35z multi   .95 .40
3883 A1377   3z multi   2.00 .75

Joseph Conrad (1857-1924), Writer — A1378

2007, Dec. 3 Engr.   Perf. 11¼x11½
3884 A1378 3z black   2.00 .90

Souvenir Sheet

PostEurop Plenary Assembly, Cracow — A1379

Perf. 11½x11¼ Syncopated
2008, Jan. 15   Litho.
3885 A1379 3z multi   2.00 .90

Love A1380

Perf. 11¾x11½ Syncopated
2008, Feb. 7   Litho.
3886 A1380 1.35z multi   .95 .40

Easter — A1381

Designs: 1.35z, Easter eggs. 2.40z, Easter eggs, diff.

Perf. 11½x11¼
2008, Feb. 29   Photo.
3887-3888 A1381 Set of 2   2.25 1.00

Photography by Karol Beyer (1818-77) A1382

No. 3889: a, Self-portrait, 1858. b, Peasants from Wilanów, 1866. c, Holy Cross Church, Warsaw, 1858, d, Russian Army in Castle Square, Warsaw, 1861.

Perf. 11½x11¾ Syncopated
2008, Feb. 29   Litho.
3889   Horiz. strip of 4   3.75 1.75
a.-d. A1382 1.35z Any single   .90 .35

Border Guards, 80th Anniv. — A1383

Perf. 11½x11¼ Syncopated
2008, Mar. 22   Litho.
3890 A1383 2.10z multi   1.50 .70

Military Aircraft — A1384

No. 3891: a, 3z, TS-11 Iskra (Spark). b, 3.55z, F-16 Jastrzab (Falcon).

Perf. 11½x11¾ Syncopated
2008, Mar. 31
3891 A1384   Horiz. pair, #a-b   4.50 2.25

Meteorological Phenomena — A1385

No. 3892: a, Sandstorm. b, Lightning. c, Rainbow. d, Tornado.

Perf. 11¾x11½ Syncopated
2008, Apr. 25
3892   Horiz. strip of 4   6.00 3.00
a.-b. A1385 1.35z Either single   1.10 .40
c.-d. A1385 2.40z Either single   1.90 1.00

Europa A1386

2008, May 5
3893 A1386 3z multi   2.00 .90

European Organization of Supreme Audit Institutions Congress, Cracow A1387

Perf. 11½x11¾ Syncopated
2008, May 30
3894 A1387 3.55z multi   2.40 1.00

UEFA Euro 2008 Soccer Championships, Austria and Switzerland A1388

Perf. 11½x11¼ Syncopated
2008, May 30   Photo.
3895 A1388 1.35z multi   .90 .40

Toys Type of 2006

Designs: 1.35z, Wooden train. 3z, Xylophone.

Perf. 11 Syncopated
2008, June 1   Litho.
3896-3897 A1341 Set of 2   3.00 1.00

Boy and Iranian Rug — A1389

Perf. 11½x11¼ Syncopated
2008, June 10
3898 A1389 2.40z multi   1.60 .65
Esfahan, Iran, city of Polish exiled orphan children.

Souvenir Sheet

EFIRO 2008 Philatelic Exhibition, Bucharest, Romania — A1390

Photo. & Engr.
2008, June 20   Perf. 11x11½
3899 A1390 3z multi   2.00 1.00

No. 3899 exists imperf. Value: mint $7, used $8.

Coronation of St. Mary of the Snow Icon, 25th Anniv. — A1391

Perf. 11½x11¼ Syncopated
2008, June 21   Litho.
3900 A1391 1.35z multi   .90 .40

Towns — A1392

Designs: 1.45z, Tower and column, Racibórz. 3.65z, Town Hall and Neptune Fountain, Jelenia Góra.

2008   Photo.   Perf. 11¾x11½
3901 A1392 1.45z multi   1.00 .40
3902 A1392 3.65z multi   2.50 .90
Issued: 1.45z, 7/1. 3.65z, 8/1.

2008 Summer Olympics, Beijing — A1393

No. 3903: a, Swimming. b, Women's volley-ball. c, Women's pole vault. d, Fencing.

Perf. 11½ Syncopated
2008, Aug. 8   Litho.
3903   Horiz. strip of 4   2.00 1.25
a.-b. A1393 10g Either single   .25 .25
c.-d. A1393 1.45z Either single   1.00 .60
e.   Souvenir sheet, #3903   3.00 3.00

Bridges A1394

No. 3904: a, Siekierkowski Bridge, Warsaw. b, Poniatowski Bridge, Warsaw. c, Welded bridge over Sludwia River, Maurzyce. d, Ernest Malinowski Bridge, Torun.

Perf. 11¾x11½ Syncopated
2008, Aug. 29   Litho. & Embossed
3904   Horiz. strip of 4   6.00 3.25
a.-b.   A1394 1.45z Either single   1.00 .55
c.-d.   A1394 3z Either single   2.00 1.00

Souvenir Sheet

Polish Post, 450th Anniv. — A1395

No. 3905: a, Prosper Provana, first supervisor of Krakow to Venice postal service. b, King Sigismund II August and grant to Provana (50x30mm). c, Sebastian Montelupi, administrator of royal postal service in 1564.

Photo. & Engr.
2008, Sept. 15   Perf. 11¾x11½
3905 A1395 1.45z Sheet of 3,
      #a-c   3.25 1.50
Sheet margin of No. 3905 is embossed.

Miniature Sheet

Presidents of the Republic of Poland
in Exile — A1396

No. 3906: a, Wladyslaw Raczkiewicz (1885-1947), 1939-47 President. b, August Zaleeski (1883-1972), 1947-72 President. c, Stanislaw Ostrowski (1892-1982), 1972-79 President. d, Edward Raczynski (1891-1993), 1979-86 President. e, Kazimierz Sabbat (1913-89), 1986-89 President. f, Ryszard Kaczorowski, 1989-90 President.

Perf. 11¾x11½ Syncopated
2008, Sept. 24   Litho.
3906 A1396 1.45z Sheet of 6,
      #a-f   6.50 2.75

Lódz
Sports
Club, Cent.
A1397

Perf. 11¼x11½
2008, Sept. 30   Photo.
3907 A1397 1.45z red & silver 1.25 .60

Arrival of
Poles in
America,
400th
Anniv.
A1398

Perf. 11¾x11½ Syncopated
2008, Sept. 30   Litho.
3908 A1398 3z multi   2.00 1.00

World
Post Day
A1399

Perf. 11¾x11½ Syncopated
2008, Oct. 9   Litho.
3909 A1399 2.10z multi   1.40 .60

Composers
A1400

Designs: No. 3910, 1.45z, Henryk Mikolaj Górecki. No. 3911, 1.45z, Mieczylaw Karlowicz (1876-1909). No. 3912, 1.45z, Wojciech Kilar. No. 3913, 1.45z, Witold Lutoslawski (1913-94).

Perf. 11½x11¾ Syncopated
2008, Oct. 18   Litho.
3910-3913 A1400   Set of 4   4.50 1.75

**Landmarks in European Union
Capitals Type of 2005**

Designs: No. 3914, 1.45z, Rijksmuseum, Amsterdam, Netherlands. No. 3915, 1.45z, Royal Library, Copenhagen, Denmark. No. 3916, 3z, Acropolis, Athens, Greece. No. 3917, 3z, Charles Bridge, Prague, Czech Republic. 3.65z, Parliament, Vienna, Austria.

Perf. 11¼x11½ Syncopated
2008, Oct. 24
3914-3918 A1323   Set of 5   8.00 3.50

Jeremi Przybora (1915-2004) and
Jerzy Wasowski (1913-84), Television
Performers — A1401

Perf. 11¾x11½ Syncopated
2008, Oct. 30
3919 A1401 1.45z multi   1.10 .45
Television show, Kabaret Starszych Panów (Senior Men's Cabaret), 50th anniv.

The Oath, Poem by Maria Konopnicka,
Cent. — A1402

2008, Nov. 7
3920 A1402 3.65z multi + label 2.40 1.00

Independence, 90th Anniv. — A1403

2008, Nov. 11 Engr. Perf. 11x11¼
3921 A1403 1.45z carmine lake 1.00 .40

Election of Karol
Woytyla as Pope
John Paul II,
30th
Anniv. — A1404

Perf. 11½x11¼
2008, Nov. 27   Photo.
3922 A1404 2.40z multi   1.75 .85

Christmas
A1405

Stars and snowflakes with background color of: 1.45z, Blue. 3z, Red violet.

Perf. 11½x11¼
2008, Nov. 27   Photo.
3923-3924 A1405   Set of 2   3.00 1.25

Zbigniew
Herbert (1924-
98),
Writer — A1406

Perf. 11½x11¼ Syncopated
2008, Dec. 1   Litho.
3925 A1406 2.10z multi   1.40 .60

United Nations
Conference on
Climate Change,
Poznan
A1407

2008, Dec. 1 Photo. Perf. 11½x11¼
3926 A1407 2.40z multi   1.60 .70

Souvenir Sheet

Polish Post, 450th Anniv. — A1408

**Printed On Silk
Self-Adhesive
Silk-screened**
2008, Dec. 19   Imperf.
3927 A1408 20z multi   14.00 11.00

Louis Braille (1809-52), Educator of
the Blind — A1409

Perf. 11¾x11½ Syncopated
2009, Jan. 4   Litho.
3928 A1409 1.45z multi + label 1.00 .45

Concentration
Camp Survivors
A1410

No. 3929: a, Witold Pilecki (1901-48), organizer of resistance movement at Auschwitz. b, Józef Wladyslaw Wolski (1910-2008), historian. c, Bishop Ignacy Ludwik Jez (1914-2007). d, Stanislawa Maria Sawicka (1895-1982), art and music historian.

Perf. 11½x11¼ Syncopated
2009, Jan. 30   Litho.
3929   Horiz. strip of 4   5.75 2.25
a.   A1410 1.45z multi   .95 .40
b.   A1410 2.10z multi   1.40 .40
c.   A1410 2.40z multi   1.40 .65
d.   A1410 3z multi   2.00 .80

No. 3929 was initially issued with the name "Jozef" missing on No. 3929b. It was quickly withdrawn from sale. Value, $30.

Love — A1411

Perf. 11½x11¾ Syncopated
2009, Feb. 6
3930 A1411 1.45z multi   1.00 .45

Sculpture and
Fabric Art by
Wladyslaw
Hasior (1928-99)
A1412

Designs: No. 3930A, 1.45z, Zwiastowanie (The Herald). No. 3930B, 1.45z, Mucha (The

Fly). No. 3930C, 2.10z, Sztandar Zielonej Poetki (Banner of the Green Poet). No. 3930D, 2.40z, Sztandar Rozbieranie do snu (The Night Undressing Banner).

Perf. 11½x11¾ Syncopated

2009, Mar. 6				**Litho.**
3930A-3930D	A1412	Set of 4	5.25	3.75
3930De		*Sheet of 4, #3930A-3930D*	5.25	3.50

Easter — A1413

Paintings by Szymon Czechowicz (1689-1775): 1.55z, Chrystus Zmartwychwstaly (Christ Resurrected). 3z, Zlozenie do Grobu (Entombment), vert.

Perf. 11½x11¾, 11¾x11½

2009, Apr. 1				**Photo.**
3932-3933	A1413	Set of 2	3.00	1.10

Souvenir Sheet

China 2009 World Philatelic Exhibition, Luoyang — A1414

Perf. 11½x11¼ Syncopated

2009, Apr. 16				**Litho.**
3934	A1414	3z multi		2.00 1.00

Souvenir Sheet

Berek Joselewicz, A Jewish Fighter for Polish Freedom's Last Battle, Kock, by Juliusz Kossak — A1415

Perf. 11¼x11½ Syncopated

2009, Apr. 22				
3935	A1415	3z multi		2.00 1.00

See Israel No. 1772.

Miniature Sheet

Photographs of African Animals by Tomasz Gudzowaty — A1416

No. 3936: a, 1.55z, First Lesson of Killing (cheetahs and antelope). b, 1.95z, Zebras at Waterhole. c, 2.40z, Paradise Crossing (crocodile and gnus in water). d, 3z, Elephants.

Perf. 11¾x11½ Syncopated

2009, Apr. 30				
3936	A1416	Sheet of 4, #a-d	6.50	3.00

Europa — A1417

No. 3937 — Star map drawings and overlapping text with: a, Syncopation near "O" in Polska. b, Syncopation near "Europa."

Perf. 11½x11¾ Syncopated

2009, May 5				
3937	A1417	3z Horiz. pair, #a-b	4.00	1.75

Intl. Year of Astronomy.

Grazyna Bacewicz (1909-69), Composer A1418

2009, May 28				
3938	A1418	1.55z multi	.95	.50

Tytus, Romek, and A'Tomek, Comic Book Characters by Papcio Chmiel — A1419

No. 3939: a, Tytus (ape). b, Romek (boy in boots). c, A'Tomek (man in suit).

2009, May 29				
3939	A1419	1.55z Horiz. strip of 3, #a-c	3.00	1.50

Souvenir Sheet

Lech Walesa — A1420

Perf. 11¼x11½ Syncopated

2009, May 30				
3940	A1420	3.75z multi	2.50	1.10

Victories of Solidarity candidates in June 4, 1989 parliamentary elections, 20th anniv.

St. Bruno of Querfurt (c. 974-1009) A1421

Perf. 11½x11¼

2009, June 19				**Photo.**
3941	A1421	3z multi	2.00	1.10

Souvenir Sheet

Ship "Dar Mlodzilzy" — A1422

Photo. & Engr.

2009, June 30		**Perf. 11¼x11**		
3942	A1422	3.75z multi	2.40	1.00

2009 Tall Ships Race, Gdynia.

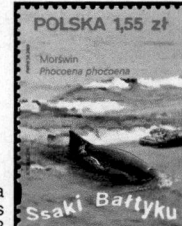

Baltic Sea Mammals A1423

No. 3943: a, Phocoena phocoena. b, Halichoerus grypus. c, Phoca vitulina. d, Phoca hispida.

Perf. 11½x11¾ Syncopated

2009, July 31				**Litho.**
3943		Horiz. strip of 4	4.50	2.00
a.-b.	A1423	1.55z Either single	.60	.40
c.-d.	A1423	1.95z Either single	.75	.60

Souvenir Sheet

Warsaw Uprising, 65th Anniv. — A1424

Photo. & Engr.

2009, Aug. 1		**Perf. 11½x11¼**		
3944	A1424	3.75z multi	2.60	1.00

Fruit and Flowers A1425

Designs: 1.95z, Cerasus avium. 3.75z, Calendula officinalis.

Perf. 11½x11¾

2009, Aug. 10				**Photo.**
3945-3946	A1425	Set of 2	3.50	1.00

See Nos. 3986, 4029, 4178-4180, 4205-4207, 4234-4236, 4255, 4331-4332.

Famous Polish Emigrés A1426

Designs: No. 3947, 1.55z, Jan Czochralski (1885-1953), metallurgist. No. 3948, 1.55z, Antoni Patek (1812-77), watchmaker. No. 3949, 1.95z, Ludwik Hirszfeld (1884-1954), serologist. No. 3950, 1.95z, Jerzy Rózycki (1909-42), Marian Rejewski (1905-80) and Henryk Zygalski (1907-78), cryptologists who broke the Enigma code.

Perf. 11½x11¾ Syncopated

2009, Aug. 28				**Litho.**
3947-3950	A1426	Set of 4	4.50	2.00

Juliusz Slowacki (1809-49), Writer — A1427

Perf. 11¼x11½

2009, Aug. 31				**Photo.**
3951	A1427	1.55z multi	1.10	.50

Start of World War II, 70th Anniv. A1428

Battles of: 1.55z, Wegierska Górka. 2.40z, Wielun.

2009, Sept. 1				
3952-3953	A1428	Set of 2	2.60	1.25

European Men's Basketball Championships, Poland — A1429

Perf. 11½x11¾ Syncopated

2009, Sept. 7				**Litho.**
3954	A1429	3z multi	2.25	.75

Selection of Tadeusz Mazowiecki as Prime Minister, 20th Anniv. — A1430

Perf. 11¾x11½ Syncopated Litho. & Embossed

2009, Sept. 11				
3955	A1430	1.55z multi	1.00	.40

European Women's Volleyball Championships, Poland — A1431

Perf. 11¾x11½ Syncopated

2009, Sept. 25				**Litho.**
3956	A1431	3z multi	2.25	.80

Landmarks in European Capitals Type of 2005

Designs: No. 3957, 1.55z, Castle, Bratislava, Slovakia. No. 3958, 1.55z, Famagusta Gate, Nicosia, Cyprus. No. 3959, 3z, Grand Place, Brussels, Belgium. No. 3960, 3z, Plac Zamkowy (Castle Square), Warsaw. 3.75z, National Museum, Helsinki, Finland.

Perf. 11¼x11½ Syncopated
2009, Oct. 6   Litho.
3957-3961 A1323 Set of 5   9.00 4.00

World Post Day — A1432

Photo. & Engr.
2009, Oct. 9   **Perf. 11½x11¼**
3962 A1432 3z multi   2.10 .80

Father Jerzy Popieluszko (1947-84), Murdered Supporter of Solidarity Movement — A1433

Perf. 11¾x11½ Syncopated
2009, Oct. 19   Litho.
3963 A1433 1.55z multi   1.00 .45

Tatra Mountain Volunteer Rescue Corps, Cent. — A1434

Perf. 11½x11¾ Syncopated
2009, Oct. 24   Litho.
3964 A1434 1.55z multi   1.10 .40

Pawel Jasienica (1909-70), Writer — A1435

Perf. 11½x11¼ Syncopated
2009, Nov. 10   Photo.
3965 A1435 1.55z blk & silver   1.10 .45

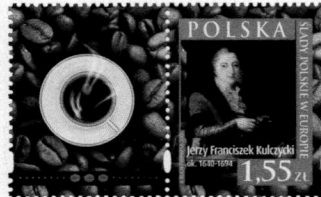

Jerzy Franciszek Kulczycki (1640-94), Hero of Battle of Vienna and Viennese Café Proprietor — A1436

2009, Nov. 16   Litho.
3966 A1436 1.55z multi + label 1.00 .50

Lost Artworks — A1437

No. 3967: a, Exlibris Willibald Pirckheimer, by Albrecht Dürer. b, Christ Falling Under the Cross, by Peter Paul Rubens. c, Joseph's Dream, by Rembrandt.

Perf. 11½x11¼
2009, Nov. 20   Photo.
3967 A1437 1.55z Horiz. strip of 3, #a-c   3.00 1.50

Christmas
A1438   A1439
2009, Nov. 27   **Perf. 11¾x11½**
3968 A1438 1.55z multi   1.00 .30
3969 A1439 2.40z multi   1.60 .60

Souvenir Sheet

First Polish Postage Stamp, 150th Anniv. — A1440

Perf. 11½x11¼ Syncopated
2010, Jan. 15   Litho.
3970 A1440 4.15z multi   2.75 1.40
No. 3970 exists with an overprint celebrating the 60th anniversary of the Polish Philatelic Union. Five hundred sheets were issued thus.

2010 Winter Olympics, Vancouver — A1441

Perf. 11¾x11½ Syncopated
2010, Jan. 27
3971 A1441 3z multi   1.90 .85

Miniature Sheet

Cats — A1442

No. 3972 — Breeds: a, 1.55z, Brytyjski krótkowlosy (British shorthair). b, 1.55z, Tajski (Siamese). c, 1.95z, Somalijski (Somali). d, 1.95z, Maine Coon. e, 3z, Pers (Persian). f, 3z, Egzotyk (Exotic).

Perf. 11½x11¾ Syncopated
2010, Feb. 17   Litho.
3972 A1442 Sheet of 6, #a-f   9.00 5.00

Souvenir Sheet

Frédéric Chopin (1810-49), Composer — A1443

Perf. 11¼x11½ Syncopated
2010, Feb. 22
3973 A1443 4.15z multi   3.00 1.50
No. 3973 exists imperf. Value, $20.

Easter — A1444

Designs: 1.55z, Lamb and banner. 2.40z, Eggs in basket.
2010, Mar. 5 Photo. **Perf. 11¾x11½**
3974-3975 A1444 Set of 2   2.75 1.10

Historical Photographs by Jan Bulhak (1876-1950) A1445

No. 3976: a, House of Stanislaw Stazic, Warsaw, 1920 (shown). b, 16 Poselska Street, Cracow, 1921. c, Vestibule of house in Old Town, Warsaw, 1920. d, Chapel of St. Casimir's Cathedral, Vilnius, 1912.

Perf. 11½x11¾ Syncopated
2010, Mar. 31   Litho.
3976   Horiz. strip of 4   5.75 2.50
a.-d.   A1445 1.95z Any single   1.40 .55

Special Services of the Republic of Poland, 20th Anniv. — A1446

2010, Apr. 6
3977 A1446 1.55z multi   1.10 .55

Souvenir Sheet

Katyn Massacre Remembrance Day — A1447

Perf. 11¾x11½ Syncopated
2010, Apr. 7
3978 A1447 3z multi   2.10 1.10

Souvenir Sheet

Portugal 2010 Intl. Philatelic Exhibition, Lisbon — A1448

Perf. 11½x11¾ Syncopated
2010, Apr. 30
3979 A1448 3z multi   2.10 1.10

Europa — A1449

2010, May 5
3980 A1449 3z multi   1.90 .95

Pope John Paul II (1920-2005) and St. Peter Apostle Church, Wadowice — A1450

Perf. 11¾x11½ Syncopated
2010, May 18   Litho. & Embossed
3981 A1450 1.95z multi + label   1.40 .70

Tczew Bridge — A1451

Perf. 11½x11¼
2010, May 27 Photo.
3982 A1451 1.55z multi 1.00 .45
Tczew, 750th anniv.

Beatification of Father Jerzy Popieluszko (1947-84) — A1452

Perf. 11¾x11½ Syncopated
2010, June 6 Litho.
3983 A1452 1.95z multi 1.40 .50

Dominican Convent of Ursuline Sisters, Sieradz, 750th Anniv. — A1453

Perf. 11¼x11½
2010, June 24 Photo.
3984 A1453 1.55z multi 1.00 .45

Souvenir Sheet

Battle of Grunwald, 600th Anniv. — A1454

2010, July 15 **Perf. 11x11¼**
3985 A1454 8.30z multi 5.50 2.75

Fruit and Flowers Type of 2009
Design: 4.15z, Myosotis arvensis.

Perf. 11½x11¾
2010, Aug. 10 Photo.
3986 A1425 4.15z multi 3.00 1.50

Scouting in Poland, Cent. — A1455

2010, Aug. 17 **Perf. 11½x11¼**
3987 A1455 1.95z multi 1.40 .70

Lech Walesa and Gdansk Shipyard A1456

Perf. 11¾x11½ Syncopated
2010, Aug. 31 **Litho. & Embossed**
3988 A1456 3.75z multi 2.75 1.00
Government cessions after settlement of Solidarity-led strikes, 30th anniv.

Minerals A1457

Perf. 11¾x11½ Syncopated
2010, Sept. 3 Litho.
3989 Vert. strip of 4 7.00 3.00
a. A1457 1.55z Sphalerite 1.15 .40
b. A1457 1.95z Gypsum 1.50 .55
c. A1457 2.40z Agate 1.90 .70
d. A1457 3z Chrysoprase 2.25 .80

World Post Day — A1458

2010, Oct. 9 Photo. **Perf. 11½x11¼**
3990 A1458 1.95z multi 1.40 .70
a. Tete-beche pair 2.80 1.40

Landmarks in European Capitals Type of 2005
Designs: 1.95z, Alexander Nevsky Cathedral, Sofia, Bulgaria. 3z, Romanian Athenaeum, Bucharest, Romania.

Perf. 11¼x11½ Syncopated
2010, Oct. 24 Litho.
3991-3992 A1323 Set of 2 3.75 1.90

Personalized Stamp — A1459

Perf. 11½x11¾ Syncopated
2010, Oct. 29 Litho.
3993 A1459 A multi + label 5.75 5.75
No. 3993 had a franking value of 1.55z on day of issue and was printed in sheets of 8 stamps + 8 labels that could be personalized for 56z.

Widzew Lódz Soccer Team, Cent. A1460

2010, Nov. 5 Photo. **Perf. 11¼x11½**
3994 A1460 1.55z multi 1.00 .50

Ignacy Jan Paderewski (1860-1941), Pianist, Prime Minister A1461

Perf. 11½x11¾ Syncopated
2010, Nov. 18 Litho.
3995 A1461 3z multi 2.10 1.10

Christmas A1462

Star of Bethlehem, text in Polish and: 1.55z, Christmas tree. 2.40z, Night sky.

Perf. 11½x11¾
2010, Nov. 27 Photo.
3996-3997 A1462 Set of 2 2.75 1.40

Love — A1463

Perf. 11½x11¾
2010, Dec. 30 Photo.
3998 A1463 A multi 1.10 .55
No. 3998 sold for 1.55z on day of issue.

Johannes Hevelius (1611-87), Astronomer — A1464

Perf. 11¾x11½ Syncopated
2011, Jan. 28 Litho.
3999 A1464 3z multi + label 2.10 1.10
No. 3999 was printed in sheets of 6 + 6 labels.

Field Hockey A1465

2011, Feb. 4
4000 A1465 2.40z multi 1.75 .85

Visegrád Group, 20th Anniv. — A1466

2011, Feb. 11 **Perf. 12**
4001 A1466 3z multi 3.00 1.50
See Czech Republic No. 3490, Hungary No. 4183, Slovakia No. 611.

Governmental Registration of Lódz Independent Student's Union, 30th Anniv. — A1467

Perf. 11¼x11½ Syncopated
2011, Feb. 17
4002 A1467 1.95z multi 1.40 .70

Cystic Fibrosis Week — A1468

Perf. 11½x11¼
2011, Feb. 28 Photo.
4003 A1468 1.55z multi 1.10 .55

Stefan Kisielewski (1911-91), Composer and Writer — A1469

Perf. 11¾x11½ Syncopated
2011, Mar. 7 Litho.
4004 A1469 1.95z multi 1.40 .70
a. Tete beche pair 2.80 1.40

Easter — A1470

Flowers and: 1.55z, Chick. 2.40z, Rabbit.

Perf. 11¾x11½
2011, Mar. 25 Photo.
4005-4006 A1470 Set of 2 3.00 1.50

Adam Cardinal Kozlowiecki (1911-2007) — A1471

2011, Mar. 31 Photo. **Perf. 11x11¼**
4007 A1471 1.95z multi 1.50 .75

Miniature Sheet

Photographs of People by Elzbieta
Dzikowska — A1472

No. 4008: a, 1.95z, Monk from Myanmar
(red panel). b, 1.95z, Hamer girl from Ethiopia
(purple panel). c. 2.40z, Girl from Myanmar
(yellow green panel). d, 2.40z, man from Palestine and camel (yellow orange panel). e, 3z,
Woman from Nepal (blue panel). f, 3z, Indian
woman from Peru (red violet panel).

Perf. 11½x11¾ Syncopated
2011, Apr. 18　　　　**Litho.**
4008　A1472　Sheet of 6, #a-f　11.00 5.50

Souvenir Sheet

Beatification of Pope John Paul
II — A1473

Perf. 11½x11¼ Syncopated
2011, Apr. 28
4009　A1473　8.30z multi　　6.00 3.00
See Vatican City No. 1471.

Europa
A1474

Perf. 11¾x11½ Syncopated
2011, May 5
4010　A1474　3z multi　　2.25 1.10
Intl. Year of Forests.

Cartoon
Characters by
Bohdan Butenko
A1475

No. 4011: a, Cezar (blue dog). b, Gucio
(brown hippopotamus). c, Kwapiszon (boy with
white hat). d, Gapiszon (boy with striped stocking hat).

2011, May 27　*Perf. 11½ Syncopated*
4011　　Horiz. strip of 4　5.75 3.00
a.-b.　A1475 1.55z Either single　1.10　.55
c.-d.　A1475 2.40z Either single　1.75　.85

Polish Presidency of European Union
Council — A1476

Perf. 11¾x11½ Syncopated
2011, June 30
4012　A1476　3z multi + label　2.25 1.10

Souvenir Sheet

Czeslaw Milosz (1911-2004), 1980
Nobel Laureate in Literature — A1477

Photo. & Engr.
2011, June 30　　*Perf. 11x11½*
4013　A1477　4.15z multi　　3.00 1.50

St. Maximilian
Kolbe (1894-
1941)
A1478

Perf. 11½x11¾ Syncopated
2011, Aug. 12　　　　**Litho.**
4014　A1478　1.95z multi　　1.40　.70

Famous
Poles
A1479

Designs: 1.55z, Michal Sedziwój (1566-
1636), chemist. 1.95z, Jan Szczepanik (1872-
1926), inventor. No. 4017, 3z, Jan Józef Bara-
nowski (1805-88), inventor. No. 4018, 3z,
Rudolf Stefan Weigl (1883-1957), biologist.

Perf. 11¾x11½ Syncopated
2011, Aug. 29
4015-4018 A1479　Set of 4　7.00 3.50

Father Jan
Dzierzon (1811-
1906), Apiarist
A1480

Perf. 11½x11¾ Syncopated
2011, Sept. 2
4019　A1480　1.55z multi　　1.00　.50

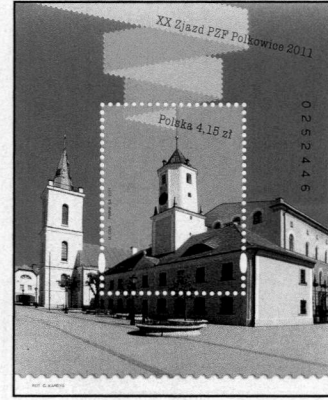

Church of the Assumption of the Virgin
Mary, Niegowic, First Pastoral
Assignment of Pope John Paul
II — A1481

Perf. 11¾x11½ Syncopated
2011, Sept. 22
4020　A1481　1.95z multi + label　1.50　.75

Souvenir Sheet

20th Congress of Polish Association of
Philatelists, Polkowice — A1482

Perf. 11½x11¾ Syncopated
2011, Sept. 30
4021　A1482　4.15z multi　　2.75 1.40

Lost
Works of
Art
A1483

No. 4022: a, Double Portrait of Eliza Parenska, by Stanislaw Wyspianski. b, Scene from
the Legends of Theophilus of Adana, by Veit
Stoss. c, Woman Looking Backwards, by
Jean-Antoine Watteau.

2011, Oct. 21　　*Perf. 11¼x11½*
4022　　Horiz. strip of 3　4.75 2.40
a.　A1483 1.95z multi　　1.25　.60
b.　A1483 2.40z multi　　1.60　.80
c.　A1483 3z multi　　1.90　.95

Souvenir Sheet

First Polish Scientific
Satellite — A1484

Perf. 11¾x11½ Syncopated
2011, Nov. 4
4023　A1484　4.15z multi　　2.60 1.40

Souvenir Sheet

Intl. Year of Chemistry — A1485

No. 4024: a, 3z, Nobel medal and radium
(36x28mm). b, Marie Curie (1867-1934), 1911
Nobel laureate for Chemistry (40x55mm).

Perf. 12¾ (#4024a), 13x12¾ (#4024b)
2011, Nov. 17　　**Litho. & Engr.**
4024　A1485　Sheet of 2, #a-b　7.75 3.75
See Sweden No. 2672.

Christmas
A1486

Designs: 1.55z, Santa Claus, reindeer and
sleigh. 2.40z, Nativity.

Perf. 11½x11¾
2011, Nov. 25　　　　**Photo.**
4025　A1486　1.55z multi　　.95　.45
Self-Adhesive
Litho.
Die Cut Perf. 11½x11¾
4026　A1486　2.40z multi　　1.50　.75

Souvenir Sheet

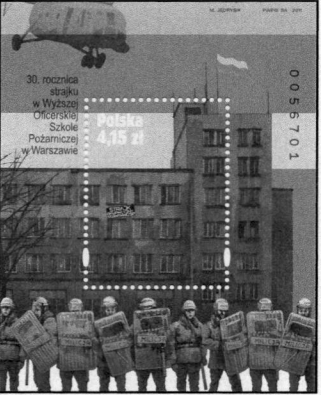

Military Suppression of Warsaw Fire
Academy Strike, 30th Anniv. — A1487

Perf. 11½x11¾ Syncopated
2011, Dec. 2
4027　A1487　4.15z multi　　2.60 1.30

Independence of Kazakhstan, 20th Anniv. — A1488

2011, Dec. 8 **Photo.** **Perf. 11¼x11½**
4028 A1488 2.40z multi 1.50 .75

Fruit and Flowers Type of 2009
Perf. 11½x11¾

2011, Dec. 16 **Photo.**
4029 A1425 1.55z Rubus idaeus 1.00 .50

Souvenir Sheet

20th Concert of the Great Holiday Help Orchestra — A1489

Litho. (With Foil Application in Sheet Margin)
Perf. 11¾x11½ Syncopated
2012, Jan. 8
4030 A1489 1.95z multi 1.25 .60

National Army, 70th Anniv. — A1490

Perf. 11½x11¼
2012, Feb. 14 **Photo.**
4031 A1490 1.55z multi 1.00 .50

Souvenir Sheet

Zygmunt Krasinski (1812-59), Poet — A1491

Perf. 11½x11¾ Syncopated
2012, Feb. 19 **Litho.**
4032 A1491 4.15z multi 2.75 1.40

Easter — A1492

Stylized flowers and: 1.55z, Lamb. 1.95z, Easter egg. 3z, Rabbit.

2012, Mar. 9 **Perf. 11¾x11½**
4033-4035 A1492 Set of 3 4.25 2.10

Leopold Kronenberg (1812-78), Banker and Leader of January 1863 Uprising A1493

2012, Mar. 20 **Photo.** **Perf. 11½x11**
4036 A1493 2.40z multi 1.50 .75

Photographs of Warsaw by Konrad Brandel (1838-1920) — A1494

No. 4037: a, Dworzec Wiedenski (Vienna Station), c. 1890. b, Krakowskie Przedmiescie, c. 1880. c, Plac Trzech Krzyzy (Three Crosses Square), c. 1875. d, Wiadukt Pancera (Pancera Viaduct), c. 1890.

Perf. 11¾x11½ Syncopated
2012, Mar. 28 **Litho.**
4037 Vert. strip of 4 5.50 2.75
a.-b. A1494 1.95z Either single 1.25 .60
c.-d. A1494 2.40z Either single 1.50 .75

Suwalki, 300th Anniv. A1495

2012, Mar. 30 **Photo.** **Perf. 11x11½**
4038 A1495 1.95z multi 1.25 .60

Miniature Sheet

First Polish Discoveries in Egypt, 150th Anniv. — A1496

No. 4039: a, 1.,55z, Porcelain statue. b, 1.95z, Porcelain statue, diff. c, 2.40z,

Nefertem amulet. d, 3z, Michal Tyszkiewicz (1828-97), Egyptologist.

2012, Apr. 30 **Perf. 11½x11**
4039 A1496 Sheet of 4, #a-d 5.75 3.00

Souvenir Sheet

Masquerade, by Tadeusz Makowski — A1497

2012, May 17 **Perf. 11¼x10¾**
4040 A1497 4.15z multi 2.40 1.25

National Museum, Warsaw, 150th anniv.

Europa A1498

Perf. 11½ Syncopated
2012, May 22 **Litho.**
4041 A1498 3z multi 1.75 .85

Heart, by Michal Batory — A1499

Piano, by Michal Batory A1500

2012, May 25
4042 A1499 1.95z multi 1.10 .55
4043 A1500 3z multi 1.75 .85

Souvenir Sheet

Animated Film *Parauszek the Rabbit* — A1501

2012, May 30
4044 A1501 4.15z multi 2.40 1.25

2012 European Soccer Championships, Poland and Ukraine — A1502

Tournament stadiums in Poland: 1.55z, Municipal Stadium, Poznan. 1.95z, National Stadium, Warsaw. 2.40z, PGE Arena, Gdansk. 3z, Municipal Stadium, Wroclaw.

2012, June 8
4045-4048 A1502 Set of 4 5.25 2.60
4048a Souvenir sheet of 4, 5.25 2.60
 #4045-4048

Nos. 4045-4048 each were printed in sheets of 8 + central label.

Soccer Ball, Flags of Ukraine and Poland A1503

2012, June 15
4049 A1503 3z multi 1.75 .85

2012 European Soccer Championships, Poland and Ukraine. No. 4049 was printed in sheets of 6. Selvage surrounding each stamp on the sheet differs. Values are for stamps with surrounding selvage.

Muzakowski Park UNESCO World Heritage Site, Poland and Germany — A1504

Perf. 11¾x11½ Syncopated
2012, July 12
4050 A1504 3z multi 1.90 .95

See Germany No. 2683.

Miniature Sheet

2012 Summer Olympics, London — A1505

No. 4051: a, 1.55z, Rowing. b, 1.95z, Volleyball. c, 2.40z, Weight lifting. d, 3z, Shot put.

2012, July 27
4051 A1505 Sheet of 4, #a-d 5.50 2.75

Józef Ignacy Kraszewski (1812-87), Writer — A1506

Perf. 11½x11¼
2012, July 28   **Photo.**
4052 A1506 4.15z multi + label   2.60 1.25

Miniature Sheet

Mushrooms — A1507

No. 4053: a, 1.55z, Russula virescens. b, 1.95z, Morchella esculenta. c, 3z, Macrolepiota procera. d, 4.15z, Armillaria ostoyae.

Perf. 11¾x11½ Syncopated
2012, Aug. 31   **Litho.**
4053 A1507   Sheet of 4, #a-d, +
         4 labels   6.75 3.50

2012 Polish-German Philatelic Exhibition, Kargowa — A1508

Perf. 11½x11¾ Syncopated
2012, Sept. 6
4054 A1508 2.40z multi   1.50 .75

Piotr Skarga (1536-1612), Counter-reformation Preacher — A1509

Perf. 11¼x11½
2012, July 27   **Photo.**
4055 A1509 1.55z multi   1.00 .55

Piotr Kwit (1929-2002), Painter — A1510

2012, Oct. 10   **Perf. 11½x11¼**
4056 A1510 1.55z multi   .95 .50

Pope John Paul II and Wawel Cathedral — A1511

Perf. 11¾x11½ Syncopated
2012, Oct. 13   **Litho.**
4057 A1511 1.95z multi + label   1.50 .75

Stage and Film Stars — A1512

Designs: 1.55z, Jadwiga Smosarska (1898-1971). 1.95z, Aleksander Zabczynski (1900-58). 3z, Eugeniusz Bodo (1899-1943).

Perf. 11½x11¾ Syncopated
2012, Oct. 31   **Litho.**
4058-4060 A1512   Set of 3   4.00 2.00
4060a   Souvenir sheet of 3,
        #4058-4060   4.00 2.00

See Nos. 4098-4100, 4149-4151, 4194-4196, 4258-4260, 4306-4308, 4371-4373, 4456-4458.

Souvenir Sheet

Turczynek Villa, Milanówek — A1513

Perf. 11¾x11½ Syncopated
2012, Oct. 31
4061 A1513 4.15z multi   2.60 1.25

Christmas — A1514

Designs: A, Angels. 2.40z, Children with gifts, horiz.

Perf. 11¾x11½, 11½x11¾
2012, Nov. 30   **Photo.**
4062-4063 A1514   Set of 2   2.50 1.25
No. 4062 sold for 1.55z on day of issue.

Jerzy Turowicz (1912-99), Journalist — A1515

Perf. 11½x11¾ Syncopated
2012, Dec. 10   **Litho.**
4064 A1515 1.55z multi   1.00 .50

21st Concert of the Great Holiday Help Orchestra — A1516

2013, Jan. 13   **Die Cut Perf.**
Self-Adhesive
4065 A1516 A multi   1.10 .55
No. 4065 sold for 1.60z on day of issue and was printed in sheets of 6. Unused values are for stamps with surrounding selvage.

A1517   A1518

A1519   A1520

2013, Mar. 8 Photo.   **Perf. 11¾x11½**
4066 A1517 (1.60z) multi   1.00 .50
4067 A1518 (2.35z) multi   1.50 .75
4068 A1519 (3.75z) multi   2.40 1.25
4069 A1520 (5.10z) multi   3.25 1.60
    Nos. 4066-4069 (4)   8.15 4.10

A1521   A1522

A1523   A1524

2013, Mar. 29
4070 A1521 (3.70z) multi   2.25 1.10
4071 A1522 (4.50z) multi   2.75 1.40
4072 A1523 (4.75z) multi   3.00 1.50
4073 A1524 (7.10z) multi   4.50 2.25
    Nos. 4070-4073 (4)   12.50 6.25

Souvenir Sheet

Alcedo Atthis — A1525

Perf. 11½ Syncopated
2013, Apr. 12   **Litho.**
4074 A1525 4.55z multi   3.00 1.50

Wieslaw Chrzanowski (1923-2012), Marshal of the Sejm — A1526

2013, Apr. 16
4075 A1526 3.80z multi   2.40 1.25

Warsaw Ghetto Uprising, 70th Anniv. — A1527

2013, Apr. 19 Photo.   **Perf. 11½x11**
4076 A1527 3.80z multi   2.40 1.25

Flag Day A1528

Perf. 11½ Syncopated
2013, May 2   **Litho.**
4077 A1528 1.60z multi   1.00 .50

Europa A1529

2013, May 6
4078 A1529 4.60z multi   3.00 1.50

Souvenir Sheet

Disney Cartoon Characters — A1530

2013, June 1
4079 A1530 4.60z multi   3.00 1.50

Miniature Sheet

Lighthouses — A1531

No. 4080: a, 1.60z, Darlowo Lighthouse. b, 2.35z, Jaroslawiec Lighthouse. c, 3.75z, Ustka Lighthouse. d, 3.80z, Czolpino Lighthouse.

2013, June 14   Photo.   Perf. 11½x11
4080 A1531 Sheet of 4, #a-d   7.25 3.75

A1532

A1534

A1533

A1535

Perf. 11¾x11½
2013, June 20   Photo.
4081 A1532 (6.30z) multi   4.00 2.00
4082 A1533 (7.30z) multi   4.50 2.25
4083 A1534 (8.80z) multi   5.50 2.75
4084 A1535 (10.90z) multi   6.75 3.50
   Nos. 4081-4084 (4)   20.75 10.50

Souvenir Sheet

Prince Boleslaw III the Wrymouthed
(1086-1138) — A1536

Photo. & Engr.
2013, June 28   Perf. 11½x11¼
4085 A1536 8.50z red & brn blk   5.25 2.60

Deeds of the Princes of the Poles, chronicle of Polish history by Gallus Anonymus, 900th anniv. of publication.

Strawberry — A1537

2013, July 18   Litho.   Perf. 11¼x11½
4086 A1537 4.60z multi   3.00 1.50

Tour de Pologne Bicycle
Race — A1538

No. 4087: a, One cyclist. b, Two cyclists.

Perf. 11½ Syncopated
2013, July 30   Litho.
4087 A1538 Horiz. pair   4.00 2.00
   a.   1.60z multi   1.00 .50
   b.   4.60z multi   3.00 1.50

Souvenir Sheet

Heweliusz Satellite — A1539

Perf. 11¾x11½ Syncopated
2013, July 31   Litho.
4088 A1539 4.55z multi   3.00 1.50

Woodstock
Festival
Poland,
Kostrzyn
nad Odra
A1540

Die Cut Perf. 11½
2013, Aug. 1   Litho.
Self-Adhesive
4089 A1540 2.35z multi   1.50 .75

Souvenir Sheet

Szczecin 2013 Tall Ships
Regatta — A1541

Photo. & Engr.
2013, Aug. 3   Perf. 11¼x11
4090 A1541 8.50z black & blue   5.50 2.75

Modernization of Polish Armed
Forces — A1542

No. 4091: a, General Dynamics F-16 Block 52+ jets. b, Rosomak armored vehicle. c, ORP Kontradmiral Xawery Czernicki support ship.

Perf. 11¾x11½ Syncopated
2013, Aug. 14   Litho.
4091 A1542 1.60z Vert. strip of 3,
     #a-c   3.00 1.50

Souvenir Sheet

Traditional Costumes of Poland and
Romania — A1543

Perf. 11½x11¾ Syncopated
2013, Sept. 11   Litho.
4092 A1543 4.60z multi   3.00 1.50
   See Romania No. 5483.

Minerals
A1544

No. 4093: a, Salt (gray violet panel). b, Malachite and azurite (blue panel). c, Marcasite (blue green panel). d, Gypsum (red panel).

Perf. 11¾x11½ Syncopated
Litho. & Silk-screened
2013, Sept. 20
4093   Vert. strip of 4   5.50 2.75
   a.-b. A1544 1.60z Either single   1.10 .55
   c.-d. A1544 2.35z Either single   1.60 .80

Pres. Lech
Walesa, 70th
Birthday
A1545

Perf. 11½x11¼ Syncopated
2013, Sept. 29   Litho.
4094 A1545 3.80z multi   2.50 1.25

Landmarks in European Capitals Type of 2005

Design: St. Mark's Church, Zagreb, Croatia.

Perf. 11¼x11½ Syncopated
2013, Oct. 11   Litho.
4095 A1323 4.60z multi   3.00 1.50

World Post
Day
A1546

Perf. 11¼x11½
2013, Oct. 18   Photo.
4096 A1546 4.60z multi   3.00 1.50

Polish postal services, 455th anniv.

Lost
Works of
Art
A1547

No. 4097 — Pastel drawings by Stanislaw Wyspianski of the actor Ludwik Solski in costume in plays: a, Treasure, by Leopold Staff. b, The Twelfth Night, by William Shakespeare. c, Varsovian Anthem, by Wyspianski.

Perf. 11¼x11½
2013, Oct. 21   Photo.
4097   Horiz. strip of 3   5.00 2.50
   a. A1547 1.60z multi   1.00 .50
   b. A1547 2.35z multi   1.50 .75
   c. A1547 3.80z multi   2.50 1.25

Stage and Film Stars Type of 2012

Designs: 1.60z, Helena Grossówna (1904-94). 2.35z, Adolf Dymsza (1900-75). 3.80z, Mieczyslawa Cwiklinska (1879-1972).

Perf. 11½x11¾ Syncopated
2013, Oct. 31   Litho.
4098 A1512 1.60z multi   1.00 .50
4099 A1512 2.35z multi   1.50 .75
4100 A1512 3.80z multi   2.50 1.25
   a.   Souvenir sheet of 3, #4098-
     4100   5.00 2.50

Krzystof
Penderecki,
Composer, 80th
Birthday
A1548

Perf. 11½x11¼
2013, Nov. 23   Photo.
4101 A1548 3.80z multi   2.50 1.25

Spiders
A1549

Designs: 1.60z, Argiope bruennichi. 2.35z, Atypus muralis. 3.80z, Eresus kollari. 4.55z, Philaeus chrysops.

Perf. 11¾x11½ Syncopated
Litho. & Silk-screened
2013, Nov. 29
4102-4105 A1549 Set of 4 8.25 4.25
Nos. 4102-4105 were each printed in sheets of 8 + label.

2014
Winter
Olympics,
Sochi,
Russia
A1550

No. 4106: a, Ski jumping. b, Cross-country skiing.

Perf. 11¾x11½ Syncopated
2014, Feb. 7   Litho. & Embossed
4106 A1550 Vert. pair 4.50 2.25
  a. 1.75z multi 1.25 .60
  b. 5z multi 3.25 1.60
No. 4106 was printed in sheets containing two pairs.

Oskar Kolberg
(1814-90),
Ethnologist and
Composer
A1551

2014, Feb. 22 Photo.   Perf. 11½x11
4107 A1551 4.20z multi 2.75 1.40

World Indoors Track and Field
Championships, Sopot — A1552

Perf. 11¼x11½ Syncopated
Litho. & Silk-Screened
2014, Mar. 7
4108 A1552 5z multi 3.00 1.75
No. 4108 was printed in sheets of 4.

Easter — A1553

Color of egg: 1.75z, Green. 5z, Purple.

Perf. 11¾x11½
2014, Mar. 26   Photo.
4109-4110 A1553 Set of 2 4.25 2.25
See Nos. 4162-4163.

Souvenir Sheet

Consecration of Wawel Cathedral,
650th Anniv. — A1554

No. 4111: a, 4.20z, Wawel Cathedral spires, 14th-15th cent.. b, 8.30z, Wawel Cathedral, Sigismund Bell.

Photo. & Engr.
2014, Mar. 28   Perf. 11
4111 A1554 Sheet of 2, #a-b 7.50 4.25

Souvenir Sheet

Canonization of Popes John Paul II
and John XXIII — A1555

No. 4112: a, Pope John Paul II. b, Pope John XXIII.

Perf. 11½x11¼ Syncopated
2014, Apr. 2   Litho.
4112 A1555 5z Sheet of 2, #a-b 6.25 3.25
See Vatican City No. 1558.

A1556

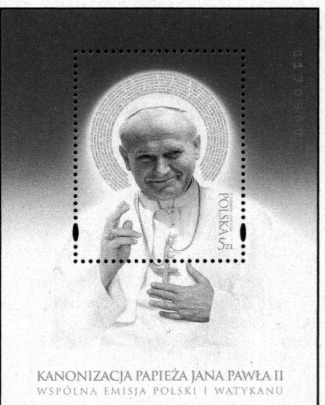

Canonization of Pope John Paul
II — A1557

Perf. 11½x11¾ Syncopated
2014, Apr. 2   Litho.
4113 A1556 2.35z multi 1.40 .80
Souvenir Sheets
Perf. 11¼x11½ Syncopated
4114 A1557 5z multi 3.25 1.75
Engr.
4115 A1557 8.50z brown 5.25 2.75
See Vatican City Nos. 1559-1561.

Souvenir Sheet

Polish Gold Medalists at 2014 Winter
Olympics — A1558

No. 4116: a, Kamil Stoch, ski jumping. b, Justyna Kowalczyk, cross-country skiing. c, Zbigniew Bródka, speed skating.

Perf. 11¾x11½ Syncopated
2014, Apr. 11   Litho.
4116 A1558 4.20z Sheet of 3, #a-c 7.50 4.25

Jan Karski
(1914-2000),
World War II
Resistance
Fighter — A1559

Perf. 11½x11¼
2014, Apr. 24   Photo.
4117 A1559 4.20z multi 2.50 1.40
  a. Tete-beche pair 5.50 3.00

Admission
to the
European
Union, 10th
Anniv.
A1560

Perf. 11¼x11½ Syncopated
2014, May 1   Litho.
4118 A1560 5.20z multi 3.00 1.75

Bagpipes
A1561

Perf. 11½x11¾ Syncopated
2014, May 5   Litho.
4119 A1561 5.20z multi 3.00 1.75
Europa.

International Year of the
Family — A1562

Perf. 11¼x11½
2014, May 15   Photo.
4120 A1562 2.35z multi 1.50 .80

Battle of Monte
Cassino, 70th
Anniv. — A1563

Perf. 11½x11¾ Syncopated
2014, May 18   Litho.
4121 A1563 1.75z multi 1.10 .60

Freedom
Festival — A1564

Perf. 11½x11¼
2014, May 28   Photo.
4122 A1564 2.35z multi 1.40 .80
Elections of June 4, 1989, 25th anniv.

Souvenir Sheet

Premiere of Animated Film *The Pirate
Fairy* — A1565

Perf. 11¾x11½ Syncopated
2014, June 1   Litho.
4123 A1565 5.20z multi 3.00 1.75

Miniature Sheet

Coaches — A1566

No. 4124: a, Kazimierz Górski (1921-2006), soccer coach. b, Hubert Wagner (1941-2002), volleyball coach. c, Feliks Stamm (1901-76), boxing coach. d, Henryk Lasak (1932-73), cycling coach.

Perf. 11¼x11½

2014, June 27   Photo.
4124 A1566 2.35z Sheet of 4,
#a-d   5.75 3.25

Historic Photographs by Henryk
Poddebski (1890-1945) — A1567

No. 4125: a, Zinc smelter, Szopienice. b,
Machinery at Kleofas colliery. c, Smokestacks
and buildings, Krolewska Huta. d, Coal transport at Gdynia Harbor.

Perf. 11¾x11½ Syncopated

2014, July 11   Litho.
4125   Vert. strip of 4   7.00 4.00
a. A1567 1.75z multi   1.00 .55
b. A1567 2.35z multi   1.25 .75
c. A1567 3.25z multi   2.25 1.25
d. A1567 4.20z multi   2.50 1.40

Apple
A1568

Perf. 11¼x11½

2014, July 18   Photo.
4126 A1568 5z multi   3.00 1.60

Souvenir Sheet

Merops Apiaster — A1569

Perf. 11½x11¾ Syncopated

2014, July 31   Litho.
4127 A1569 5.50z multi   3.25 1.75

Souvenir Sheet

Warsaw Uprising, 70th
Anniv. — A1570

Perf. 11½x11¾ Syncopated

2014, Aug. 1   Litho.
4128 A1570 5.20z multi   3.00 1.75

Souvenir Sheet

Józef Pilsudski (1867-1935), Prime
Minister, and Members of Polish
Legion — A1571

Photo. & Engr.   **Perf. 11¼**

2014, Aug. 6
4129 A1571 8.50z multi   5.00 2.60

Icons
A1572

Designs: 1.75z, Our Lady of Drohobycz.
4.20z. Our Lady of Kochawinskiej.

2014, Aug. 14   Photo.   Perf. 10¾x11
4130-4131 A1572   Set of 2   3.50 1.90

Miniature Sheet

Mushrooms — A1573

No. 4132: a, 1.75z, Cantharellus cibarius. b,
2.35z, Agaricus campestris. c, 3.75z, Russula
vesca. d, 4.20z, Boletus edulis.

Perf. 11¾x11½ Syncopated

2014, Aug. 29   Litho.
4132 A1573   Sheet of 4, #a-d, +
4 labels   7.25 3.75

Miniature Sheet

2014 Men's World Volleyball
Championships, Poland — A1574

No. 4133 — Color of player's shirt: a, 1.75z,
White. b, 1.75z, Dark blue. c, 2.35z, Green. d,
5z, Red. e, 5.10z, White. f, 5.50z, Yellow.

Perf. 11½x11¾ Syncopated

2014, Aug. 30   Litho.
4133 A1574   Sheet of 6, #a-f   15.00 7.50

Dr. Clown Charitable
Foundation — A1575

Perf. 11½x11¼

2014, Sept. 5   Photo.
4134 A1575 1.75z multi   1.10 .55

Souvenir Sheet

Mural by Natalia Rak — A1576

Perf. 11¾x11½ Syncopated

2014, Sept. 26   Litho.
4135 A1576 4.20z multi   2.50 1.25

Alternative Energy Sources — A1577

No. 4136: a, Hydroelectric dam. b, Geothermal energy. c, Wind generator. d, Solar panel.

Perf. 11½x11¼

2014, Sept. 29   Photo.
4136 A1577   Block of 4   7.00 3.75
a. 1.75z multi   1.00 .55
b. 2.35z multi   1.40 .75
c. 3.75z multi   2.10 1.10
d. 4.20z multi   2.40 1.25

Meteorological Phenomena — A1578

No. 4137: a, Aurora. b, Sun dog. c, Smoke.
d, Frost.

Perf. 11¾x11½ Syncopated

Litho. & Silk-Screened

2014, Sept. 30
4137   Horiz. strip of 4   8.00 4.50
a. A1578 1.75z multi   1.00 .55
b. A1578 2.35z multi   1.25 .75
c. A1578 4.20z multi   2.40 1.25
d. A1578 5.50z multi   3.25 1.75

Jan Nowak-Jezioranski (1914-2005),
Head of Polish Section for Radio Free
Europe — A1579

2014, Oct. 2   Photo.   Perf. 11½x11¼
4138 A1579 4.20z multi   2.40 1.25

Fish — A1580

Designs: 35g, Acanthurus sohal. 45g, Chaetodon capistratus. 55g, Rhinomuraena
quaesita. 65g, Hippocampus sp. 1.10z, Balistoides conspicillum. 1.20z, Pomacanthus
xanthometopon. 1.30z, Chelmon rostratus.
1.40z, Amphiprion ocellaris.

Perf. 11½x11¼

2014, Oct. 10   Photo.
4139-4146 A1580   Set of 8   4.50 2.25
4146a   Souvenir sheet of 8,
#4139-4146 + 4 labels   52.50 32.50

2014 National Philatelic Exhibition, Warsaw.
Nos. 4139-4146 each were printed in sheets
of 12 + 4 labels. Value, set of eight sheets $45.

Stefan Zeromski
(1864-1925),
Writer — A1581

Perf. 11½x11¼ Syncopated

2014, Oct. 14   Litho.
4147 A1581 4.20z multi   2.50 1.25

Miniature Sheet

Victory of Polish Men's Volleyball
Team and 2014 World
Championships — A1582

No. 4148: a, Stéphan Antiga. b, Piotr Nowa-
kowski. c, Michal Winiarski. d, Dawid Konarski.
e, Rafal Buszek. f, Pawel Zagumny. g, Karol
Klos. h, Andrzej Wrona. i, Mariusz Wlazly. j,
Fabian Drzyzga. k, Michal Kubiak. l, Krzysztof
Ignaczak. m, Pawel Zatorski. n, Marcin
Mozdzonek. o, Mateusz Mika. p, Philippe
Blain.

Perf. 11¾x11½ Syncopated
2014, Oct. 18   Litho.
4148 A1582 1z Sheet of 16, #a-
       p, + 4 labels   9.00 4.75

Stage and Film Stars Type of 2012
Designs: 1.75z, Tola Mankiewiczówna
(1900-85). 2.35z, Antoni Fertner (1874-1959).
4.20z, Loda Halama (1911-96).

Perf. 11½x11¾ Syncopated
2014, Oct. 31   Litho.
4149-4151 A1512   Set of 3   4.75 2.50
4151a   Souvenir sheet of 3,
            #4149-4151   4.75 2.50

Christmas — A1583

Stained-glass windows depicting: 2.35z,
Holy Family. 5.20z, Adoration of the Magi.

2014, Nov. 14   Photo.   Perf. 11¼
4152-4153 A1583   Set of 2   4.25 2.25

William
Shakespeare
(1564-1616),
Writer — A1584

Perf. 11½x11¾
2014, Nov. 21   Photo.
4154 A1584 4.20z multi   2.50 1.25

Souvenir Sheet

Diplomatic Relations Between Poland
and Turkey, 600th Anniv. — A1585

Perf. 11¼x11½ Syncopated
2014, Nov. 28   Litho.
4155 A1585 5z multi   2.75 1.50
       See Turkey No. 3416.

Ring of
Youths
A1586

Main
Square,
Cracow
A1587

Perf. 11¼ Syncopated
2014, Dec. 19   Litho.
4156 A1586 1.75z multi   1.00   .50

Perf. 11½ Syncopated
4157 A1587 5z multi   2.75 1.50
       Selection of Cracow as host city of 2016
World Youth Day.

23rd Concert of
the Great
Holiday Help
Orchestra
A1588

Perf. 11½x11¾ Syncopated
2015, Jan. 7   Litho.
4158 A1588 2.35z multi   1.25   .65

Love
A1589

Litho. & Silk-Screened
4159 A1589 2.35z multi   *Perf. 11½ Syncopated*   1.25   .65
       Values are for stamps with surrounding
selvage.

Kazimierz Przerwa-Tetmajer (1865-
1940), Poet — A1590

Perf. 11½x11¼ Syncopated
2015, Feb. 12   Litho.
4160 A1590 1.75z multi   .90   .45

Souvenir Sheet

Witkacy (1885-1939), Writer and
Painter — A1591

Perf. 11½x11¾ Syncopated
2015, Feb. 24   Litho.
4161 A1591 5.20z multi   2.75 1.40

Easter Type of 2014
Color of egg: 2.35z, Purplish black. 5.20z,
Red.

2015, Mar. 6   Photo.   *Perf. 11¾x11½*
4162-4163 A1553   Set of 2   4.00 2.10

Organ Transplantation — A1592

2015, Mar. 20   Photo.   *Perf. 11x11½*
4164 A1592 1.75z multi   .95   .45

Awarding of Best Foreign Film
Academy Award to Polish Movie "Ida"
A1593

Perf. 11½ Syncopated
2015, Mar. 31   Litho.
4165 A1593 2.35z multi   1.25   .65
       No. 4165 was printed in sheets of 8 + cen-
tral label.

Tadeusz Kantor
(1915-90),
Theater
Director — A1594

Perf. 11½x11¾ Syncopated
2015, Apr. 3   Photo.
4166 A1594 1.75z multi   .95   .45

Katyn Massacre,
75th
Anniv. — A1595

Perf. 11½x11¼ Syncopated
2015, Apr. 7   Litho.
4167 A1595 1.75z multi   1.00   .50

2016 World
Youth Day,
Cracow — A1596

Emblem and: 1.75z, St. John Paul II. 5z,
Map of Poland, signature of St. John Paul II.

Perf. 11½x11¼
2015, Apr. 27   Photo.
4168-4169 A1596   Set of 2   3.50 1.90

Toy Made
of Nuts
A1597

Perf. 11¾x11½ Syncopated
2015, May 5   Litho.
4170 A1597 5z multi   2.50 1.50
             Europa.

Souvenir Sheet

End of World War II, 70th
Anniv. — A1598

2015, May 8   Photo.   *Perf. 11½x11¼*
4171 A1598 2.35z multi   1.25   .65

Souvenir Sheet

Expo 2015, Milan — A1599

Perf. 11½x11¾ Syncopated
2015, May 28   Litho.
4172 A1599 5.20z multi   2.50 1.50

Father Jan Twardowski (1915-2006), Poet — A1600

Perf. 11½x11¾ Syncopated
2015, May 29   Litho.
4173 A1600 1.75z multi   .95 .45

Souvenir Sheet

Characters From Animated Film *Frozen* — A1601

No. 4174: a, Anna, denomination at UL. b, Elsa, denomination at UR.

Perf. 11½ Syncopated
2015, June 1   Litho.
4174 A1601 2.35z Sheet of 2,
          #a-b   2.60 1.25

World Blood Donor Day — A1602

Perf. 11½x11¼
2015, June 14   Photo.
4175 A1602 1.75z multi   .95 .45

Miniature Sheet

Lighthouses — A1603

No. 4176: a, Rozewie II Lighthouse. b, Kikut Lighthouse. c, Swinoujscie Lighthouse. d, Jastarnia Lighthouse. e, Gdansk North Port Lighthouse.

Perf. 11½x11¼
2015, June 19   Photo.
4176 A1603 2.35z Sheet of 5,
          #a-e, + label 5.75 3.25

Count Jan Potocki (1761-1815), Writer — A1604

Perf. 11½x11¼ Syncopated
2015, June 25   Litho.
4177 A1604 5z multi   2.50 1.40

Fruit and Flowers Type of 2009
2015   Photo.   **Perf. 11½x11¾**
4178 A1425 10g Nymphaea   .25 .25
4179 A1425 1z Helianthus   .50 .25
4180 A1425 5z Rose   2.40 1.40
     Nos. 4178-4180 (3)   3.15 1.90
     Issued: 1z, 6/26, 10g, 5z, 9/15.

Polish Presidency of Council of Baltic Sea States for 2015-16 A1605

Perf. 11½x11¼ Syncopated
2015, July 1   Litho.
4181 A1605 5z multi   2.50 1.40

Cows and Korycinski Cheese — A1606

Perf. 11¾x11½ Syncopated
2015, July 17   Litho. & Embossed
4182 A1606 5z multi   2.50 1.40

Souvenir Sheet

Pipe Organ, Cistercian Monastery Church, Jedrzejów — A1607

No. 4183: a, 4.20z, Organ pipes and balcony railing. b, 8.30z, Organ pipes and ceiling.

Perf. 11½x11¼ Syncopated
2015, July 30   Litho. & Engr.
4183 A1607   Sheet of 2, #a-b 6.00 3.50

Souvenir Sheet

St. John Bosco (1815-88) — A1608

Photo. & Engr.
2015, Aug. 16   **Perf. 11x11¼**
4184 A1608 5.20z multi   2.50 1.40

2015 Radom Air Show — A1609

No. 4185: a, Helicopter. b, Airplane.

Perf. 11¼x11½ Syncopated
2015, Aug. 22   Litho.
4185 A1609 2.35z Pair, #a-b   2.25 1.25

Optimist Class Sailboat World Championships — A1610

Perf. 11¾x11½ Syncopated
2015, Aug. 26   Litho.
4186 A1610 1.75z multi   .95 .45

Miniature Sheet

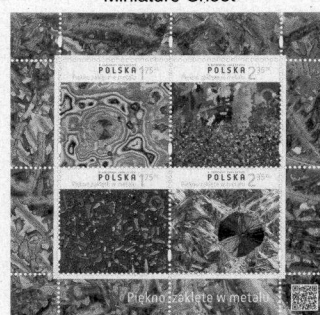

Metal Crystals — A1611

No. 4187: a, 1.75fr, Cast iron (green, yellow, pink & black). b, 1.75z, Bronze (blue violet, red and orange). c, 2.35z, Iron (large crystals at top, small crystals at bottom). d, 2.35z, Iron (large round crystal).

Litho. & Silk-Screened
Perf. 11½ Syncopated
2015, Sept. 11
4187 A1611   Sheet of 4, #a-d 4.00 2.25

Warsaw Post Office, Cent. — A1612

Perf. 11½x11¾ Syncopated
2015, Sept. 23   Litho.
4188 A1612 2.35z multi   1.25 .60

Depictions of Quotations from Polish Literature — A1613

Designs: No. 4189, 2.35z, Woman, man holding crocodile balloon (quotation from Revenge, by Aleksander Fredro). No. 4190, 2.35z, Dogs (quotation from Ashes, by Stefan Zeromski).

Perf. 11¾x11½ Syncopated
2015, Sept. 23   Litho.
4189-4190 A1613 Set of 2 2.50 1.25

17th Chopin Intl. Piano Competition A1614

Perf. 11½x11¼ Syncopated
2015, Oct. 1   Litho.
4191 A1614 1.75z multi   .95 .45

Letter of Reconciliation from Polish Bishops to German Bishops, 50th Anniv. — A1615

Perf. 11½x11¼
2015, Oct. 23   Photo.
4192 A1615 1.75z multi   .90 .45

Miniature Sheet

Owls — A1616

No. 4193: a, Bubo bubo. b, Aegolius funereus. c, Tyto alba. d, Strix nebulosa.

Perf. 11¾x11½ Syncopated
2015, Oct. 23   Litho. & Embossed
4193 A1616 2.35z Sheet of 4,
#a-d, + 4 la-
bels   5.00 2.50

Stage and Film Stars Type of 2012

Designs: 1.75z, Jerzy Pichelski (1903-63).
2.35z, Hanka Bielicka (1915-2006). 4.20z,
Aleksander Zelwerowicz (1877-1955).

Perf. 11½x11¾ Syncopated
2015, Oct. 30   Litho.
4194-4196 A1512 Set of 3   4.50 2.25
4196a   Souvenir sheet of 3,
#4194-4196   4.50 2.25

Christmas — A1617

Designs: 1.75z, Holy Family and animals.
2.35z, Annunciation. 5.20z, Adoration of the
Magi.

Perf. 11¾x11½
2015, Nov. 16   Photo.
4197-4199 A1617 Set of 3   4.75 2.40

Wojciech
Boguslawski
(1757-1829),
Director of
National Theater,
Warsaw
A1618

Perf. 11½x11¼
2015, Nov. 19   Photo.
4200 A1618 1.75z gold & multi   .90 .45
National Theater, 250th anniv.

National Day of
Rights of the
Child — A1619

Perf. 11½x11¼
2015, Nov. 20   Photo.
4201 A1619 1.75z multi   .90 .45

Wladyslaw Bartoszewski (1922-2015),
Minister of Foreign Affairs — A1620

Perf. 11¾x11½ Syncopated
2015, Nov. 25   Litho.
4202 A1620 1.75z gold & multi   .90 .45

City of Cracow and Jan Dlugosz
(1415-80), Diplomat and Chronicler of
Polish History
A1621

Perf. 11¼x11½
2015, Nov. 30   Photo.
4203 A1621 1.75z gold & multi   .90 .45

Beatification of Fathers
Michal Tomaszek
(1960-91), and
Zbigniew Strzalkowski
(1958-91), Murdered
Missionaries to
Peru — A1622

Perf. 11½x11¾ Syncopated
2015, Dec. 5   Litho.
4204 A1622 1.75z gold & multi   .90 .45

Fruit and Flowers Type of 2009
2015-16   Photo.   Perf. 11½x11¾
4205 A1425 5g Lilacs   .25 .25
4206 A1425 50g Coneflower   .25 .25
4207 A1425 10z Poppy   5.25 2.60
Nos. 4205-4207 (3)   5.75 3.10

Issued: 5g, 12/7; 50g, 1/20/16; 10z, 4/22/16.

St. Paraskevi Church, Kwiaton, Poland
and St. George's Church, Drohobych,
Ukraine — A1623

Photo. & Engr.
2015, Dec. 18   Perf. 11x10¾
4208 A1623 5z multi   2.60 1.25

Wooden Churches of the Carpathian
Region of Poland and Ukraine UNESCO
World Heritage Site. See Ukraine No. 1045.

24th Concert of the Great Orchestra of
Christmas Charity — A1624

Litho. & Silk-screened
2016, Jan. 5   Perf. 11½ Syncopated
4209 A1624 2.35z multi   1.25 .60

Values are for stamps with surrounding
selvage.

European Men's Handball
Championships, Poland — A1625

No. 4210 — Handball and: a, Player. b,
Hand.

Perf. 11½ Syncopated
2016, Jan. 15   Litho.
4210   Vert. pair   3.75 1.90
a.   A1625 2.35z multi   1.25 .60
b.   A1625 5z multi   2.50 1.25

Souvenir Sheet

Wroclaw, 2016 European Capital of
Culture — A1626

Perf. 11¾x11½ Syncopated
2016, Jan. 15   Litho.
4211 A1626 5z multi   2.50 1.25

Warsaw Mint,
250th
Anniv. — A1627

Perf. 11½x11¾ Syncopated
2016, Jan. 21   Litho.
4212 A1627 2.35z brnz & dark
brn   1.25 .60

First
Successful
Kidney
Transplant
in Poland,
50th Anniv.
A1628

Perf. 11¼x11½
2016, Jan. 22   Photo.
4213 A1628 1.75z multi   .90 .45

National Day of
Remembrance
A1629

Perf. 11½x11¾
2016, Feb. 28   Photo.
4214 A1629 A multi   1.00 .50

No. 4214 sold for 2z on day of issue.

Easter — A1630

Easter eggs: 2z, Pisanka huculska. 2.50z,
Pisanka lemkowska. 6z, Pisanka lubelska.

2016, Mar. 3 Photo. Perf. 11¾x11½
4215-4217 A1630 Set of 3   5.75 2.75

Historic Photographs — A1631

No. 4218: a, Summer in Warsaw, by Jan
Kosidowski, 1966. b, Construction of the
Turow Power Plant, by Wieslaw Prazuch,
1961. c, Aleja Jerozolimskie Near Kruczej,
Warsaw, by Kosidowski, 1963. d, May 1 Pro-
cession, Warsaw, by Prazuch, 1953.

Perf. 11¾x11½ Syncopated
2016, Mar. 23   Litho.
4218   Vert. strip of 4   5.00 2.50
a.-b. A1631 2z Either single   1.10 .55
c.-d. A1631 2.50z Either single 1.40 .70

Souvenir Sheet

Bringing Christianity, by Jan
Matejko — A1632

Photo. & Engr.
2016, Mar. 30   Perf. 11½x11¼
4219 A1632 6z multi   3.25 1.60

Adoption of Christianity in Poland, 1050th
anniv.

Extraordinary
Jubilee Year of
Mercy — A1633

2016, Apr. 2 Photo. Perf. 11½x11¾
4220 A1633 2.50z multi   1.40 .70

Souvenir Sheet

Legia Warszawa Soccer Team, Cent. — A1634

Perf. 11½x11¼ Syncopated

2016, Apr. 20		Litho.
4221 A1634 6z blk & gold	3.25	1.60

Europa A1635

2016, May 9 Litho.	Perf. 11¾x11½
4222 A1635 5z multi	2.60 1.40

Think Green Issue.

World Youth Day, Cracow A1636

Designs: 2.50z, Pope Francis and youths. 6z, Pope Francis.

Perf. 11¼x11½

2016, May 10		Photo.
4223 A1636 2.50z multi	1.25	.65

Souvenir Sheet
Photo. & Engr.
Perf. 11¼x11

4224 A1636 6z multi	3.00 1.50

No. 4224 contains one 54x41mm stamp. See Vatican City Nos. 1626-1627.

Souvenir Sheet

University of Warsaw, 200th Anniv. — A1637

Perf. 11½ Syncopated

2016, May 13		Litho.
4225 A1637 5z multi	2.60	1.40

Characters From "Reksio" Animated Films — A1638

No. 4226 — Chickens and: a, Reksio painting bird house. b, Reksio picking up eggs.

Perf. 11¼x10¾

2016, May 20		Photo.
4226 A1638 Pair	2.25	1.10
a. 2z multi	1.00	.50
b. 2.50z multi	1.25	.60

No. 4226 was printed in sheets containing two pairs.

Souvenir Sheet

World Stamp Show 2016, New York — A1639

Litho. & Silk-screened

2016, May 28 Perf. 11½ Syncopated
4227 A1639 6z multi 3.25 1.60

Family with Cat and Dog A1640

Perf. 11¾x11½ Syncopated

2016, June 1		Litho.
4228 A1640 3.70z multi	1.90	.95

Polish-German Youth Office, 25th Anniv. — A1641

Perf. 11¾x11½ Syncopated

2016, June 2		Litho.
4229 A1641 2.50z multi	1.25	.60

See Germany No. 2927.

Canonization of St. Stanislaus Papczynski (1631-1701) A1642

Perf. 11½x11¼ Syncopated

2016, June 5		Photo.
4230 A1642 3.70z multi	1.90	.95

Miniature Sheet

Clouds — A1643

No. 4231: a, Cumulonimbus capillatus praecipitatio arcus. b, Cirrus uncinus. c, Cumulonimbus mamma. d, Cumulonimbus capillatus.

Perf. 11½x11¼ Syncopated

2016, June 15		Litho.
4231 A1643 Sheet of 4	4.50	2.25
a.-b. 2z Either stamp	1.00	.50
c.-d. 2.50z Either stamp	1.25	.60

Jan Jessenius (1566-1621), Physician and Professor of Anatomy — A1644

Photo. & Engr.

2016, June 22		Perf. 11
4232 A1644 6z multi + label	3.00	1.50

See Czech Republic No. 3677, Hungary No. 4393, Slovakia No. 743.

NATO Summit, Warsaw A1645

Perf. 11¼x11½ Syncopated

2016, June 24		Litho.
4233 A1645 5z multi	2.50	1.25

Fruit and Flowers Type of 2009

Design: 20g, Saffron crocus. 2z, Iris. 6z, Lily.

2016	Photo.	Perf. 11½x11¾
4234 A1425 20g multi		.25 .25
4235 A1425 2z multi		1.10 .55
4236 A1425 6z multi		3.25 1.60

Issued: 20g, 7/6; 2z, 7/22; 6z, 7/15.

Miniature Sheet

2016 Summer Olympics, Rio de Janeiro — A1646

No. 4237: a, Sailboarding. b, Cycling. c, Discus. d, Women's tennis.

2016, July 8 Photo.	Perf. 11¼x11½
4237 A1646 2z Sheet of 4, #a-d	4.25 2.10

Postcrossing — A1647

Perf. 11½ Syncopated

2016, July 14		Photo.
4238 A1647 5z multi	2.60	1.40

Bees and Jar of Honey A1648

Perf. 11½ Syncopated

2016, July 18		Litho. & Embossed
4239 A1648 5z multi	2.60	1.40

Gen. Wladyslaw Anders (1892-1970), and Soldiers in Anders' Army — A1649

Perf. 11¼x11½ Syncopated

2016, July 21		Litho.
4240 A1649 2.50z multi	1.40	.70

Depictions of the Virgin Mary A1650

Designs: 2.50z, Our Lady of Fraga. 3.70z, Our Lady of Zólkiewska. No. 4243, 6z, Our Lady of Bialokamienska. No. 4244, 6z, Our Lady, Queen of the Polish Crown (with flags).

2016, Aug. 30 Photo.	Perf. 11x11¼
4241-4244 A1650 Set of 4	9.25 4.75

Endangered Fish — A1651

Designs: 2z, Rhodeus sericeus. 2.50z, Carassius carassius. 3.70z, Eupallasella percnurus. 6z, Acipenser oxyrinchus.

Perf. 11½x11¼ Syncopated
2016, Aug. 31   Litho.
4245-4248 A1651 Set of 4   7.25 3.75

Year of the Cichociemni (World War II Paratroopers) — A1652

2016, Sept. 1   Photo.   Perf. 11
4249 A1652 3.70z multi   1.90 .95

21st Assembly of Polish Philatelic Union, Ilawa A1653

Perf. 11¼x11½ Syncopated
2016, Sept. 8   Litho.
4250 A1653 2.50z multi   1.40 .70
No. 4250 was printed in sheets of 12 + 4 labels. Exists imperf.

Beatification of Father Wladyslaw Bukowinski (1904-74), Prisoner in Soviet Gulag — A1654

Perf. 11½x11¾ Syncopated
2016, Sept. 11   Litho.
4251 A1654 6z multi   3.25 1.60
No. 4251 was printed in sheets of 4.

Souvenir Sheet

Geralt of Rivia, Fictional Character From *The Witcher,* by Andrzej Sapkowski — A1655

Perf. 11½x11¼
2016, Sept. 16   Photo.
4252 A1655 6z multi   3.25 1.60

Polish Bible Society, 200th Anniv. — A1656

2016, Oct. 3 Photo. Perf. 11½x11¼
4253 A1656 2.50z multi   1.40 .70

Our Lady of Perpetual Help — A1657

2016, Oct. 5 Photo. Perf. 11½x11¼
4254 A1657 3.70z multi   1.90 .95

Fruit and Flowers Type of 2009
Perf. 11½x11¾
2016, Oct. 20   Photo.
4255 A1425 15g Vaccinium oxycoccus   .25 .25

Lost Works of Art — A1658

No. 4256: a, Shepherd with a Whip in a Meadow, by Józef Chelmonski, 1892. b, Self-portrait, by Aleksander Gierymski, 1899 or 1900. c, Portrait of Wife, Olga, by Leon Chwistek, before 1933.

Perf. 11½x11¼
2016, Oct. 24   Photo.
4256   Vert. strip of 3   3.00 1.50
  a.-c. A1658 2z Any single   1.00 .50

Miniature Sheet

Historians and Scientists — A1659

No. 4257: a, Aleksander Gieysztor (1916-99), medieval historian, and Royal Castle, Warsaw. b, Witold Kula (1916-88), historian, and balance. c, Gerard Labuda (1916-2010), medieval historian, and Ostrów Lednicki Church. d, Edmund Faustyn Biernacki (1866-1911), physician, and measuring tube, blood drop. e, Hilary Koprowski (1916-2013), virologist, and polio virus. f, Wladyslaw Kunicki-Goldfinger (1916-95), microbiologist, and bacteria.

2016, Oct. 29   Photo.   Perf. 11
4257 A1659 2.50z Sheet of 6,   7.75 4.00
          #a-f

Stage and Film Stars Type of 2012
Designs: 2z, Franciszek Brodniewicz (1892-1944). 2.50z, Elzbieta Barszczewska (1913-87). 6z, Tadeusz Fijewski (1911-78).

Perf. 11½x11¾ Syncopated
2016, Oct. 31   Litho.
4258-4260 A1512 Set of 3   5.50 2.75
4260a   Souvenir sheet of 3,   5.50 2.75
          #4258-4260

Christmas — A1660

Icons: 2z, Annunciation. 6z, Holy Family.

Perf. 11¾x11½
2016, Nov. 16   Photo.
4261-4262 A1660 Set of 2   4.00 2.00

Radio Maryja, 25th Anniv. A1661

Perf. 11¼x11½
2016, Nov. 25   Photo.
4263 A1661 A multi   .95 .50
No. 4263 sold for 2z on day of issue.

Polish Gold Medalists at 2016 Summer Olympics, Rio de Janeiro A1662

Designs: No. 4264, 2.50z, Anita Wlodarczyk, women's hammer throw. No. 4265, 2.50z, Natalia Madaj and Magdalena Fularczyk-Kozlowska, women's double sculls.

2016, Nov. 28 Photo. Perf. 10¾x11
4264-4265 A1662 Set of 2   2.40 1.25

Rafal Wilk, 2016 Paralympics Handcycling Gold Medalist — A1663

2016, Dec. 3 Photo. Perf. 11x10¾
4266 A1663 B multi   1.25 .60
No. 4266 sold for 2.50z on day of issue.

Vive Kielce, 2016 European Handball Federation Champions A1664

2016, Dec. 9 Photo. Perf. 10¾x11
4267 A1664 3.70z multi   1.75 .90

Souvenir Sheet

1960 Syrena Sport Prototype Automobile — A1665

Perf. 11¼x11½ Syncopated
2016, Dec. 30   Litho.
4268 A1665 6z multi   3.00 1.50

Erwin Axer (1917-2012), Theater Director — A1666

Perf. 11½x11 Syncopated
2017, Jan. 2   Litho.
4269 A1666 2.50z multi   1.25 .60

Adoration of the Magi, by Santi di Tito — A1667

2017, Jan. 6 Photo. Perf. 11½x11
4270 A1667 B multi   1.25 .60
Epiphany. No. 4270 sold for 2.50z on day of issue.

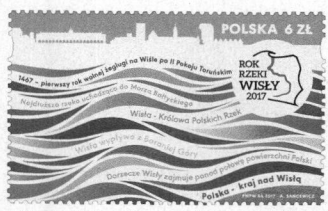

Year of the Vistula River — A1668

Perf. 11½x11¼ Syncopated
Photo. & Silk-Screened
2017, Jan. 30
4271 A1668 6z multi 3.00 1.50

General Mariusz Zaruski (1867-1941), Yachtsman A1669

Perf. 11½x11¾ Syncopated
2017, Jan. 31 Litho.
4272 A1669 B multi 1.25 .60
No. 4272 sold for 2.50z on day of issue.

Tadeusz Kosciuszko (1746-1817), General — A1670

Perf. 11¾x11½ Syncopated
2017, Feb. 4 Litho.
4273 A1670 3.20z multi 1.60 .80

World Day of the Sick A1671

2017, Feb. 11 Photo. **Perf. 11x11½**
4274 A1671 5z multi 2.50 1.25

Protestant Reformation, 500th Anniv. — A1672

2017, Feb. 28 Photo. **Perf. 11½x11**
4275 A1672 3.20z multi 1.60 .80

Souvenir Sheet

Soldier's Gorgets — A1673

No. 4276 — Gorget depicting: a, Black Madonna above eagle, belonging to Franciszek Majewski. b, Black Madonna on eagle with motto, belonging to Mieczyslaw Dziemieszkiewicz.

Perf. 11¼ Syncopated
2017, Mar. 1 Litho. & Embossed
4276 A1673 6z Sheet of 2, #a-b, + 2 labels 6.00 3.00

Souvenir Sheet

Apparition of the Virgin Mary at Fatima, Portugal, Cent. — A1674

Perf. 11½x12 Syncopated
2017, Mar. 12 Litho.
4277 A1674 6.80z multi 3.50 1.75
See Luxembourg No. 1461, Portugal No. 3888, Slovakia No. 759.

Easter — A1675

Background color of egg: A, White. 6z, Black.

Perf. 11¾x11½
2017, Mar. 15 Photo.
4278-4279 A1675 Set of 2 4.50 2.25
No. 4278 sold for 2.60z on day of issue.

Lublin, 700th Anniv. A1676

Perf. 11¼x11½
2017, Mar. 15 Photo.
4280 A1676 2.60z multi 1.40 .70

Souvenir Sheet

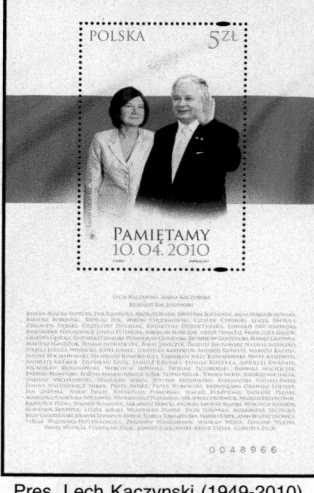

Pres. Lech Kaczynski (1949-2010), and Wife, Maria (1942-2010) — A1677

Perf. 11¼ Syncopated
2017, Apr. 10 Litho. & Embossed
4281 A1677 5z multi 2.60 1.40

Europa A1678

Perf. 11½x11¼ Syncopated
2017, May 5 Litho.
4282 A1678 5z multi 2.75 1.40

Wladyslaw Reymont (1867-1925), Writer — A1679

2017, May 7 Photo. **Perf. 11¼x11½**
4283 A1679 2.60z multi 1.40 .70

Souvenir Sheet

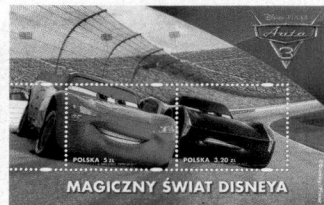

Characters from *Cars 3* Animated Film — A1680

No. 4284: a, 3.20z, Jackson Storm. b, 5z, Lightning McQueen.

Perf. 11x11½ Syncopated
Litho. & Silk-Screened
2017, May 30
4284 A1680 Sheet of 2 4.50 2.25
a. 3.20z multi 1.75 .85
b. 5z multi 2.75 1.40

Lieutenant General Józef Haller (1873-1960), Creator of Blue Army — A1681

Perf. 11½x11¾ Syncopated
2017, May 31 Litho.
4285 A1681 2.60z multi 1.40 .70
Blue Army, cent.

Franciszek Stefczyk (1861-1924), Founder of Savings and Loan Cooperatives A1682

2017, June 8 Photo. **Perf. 11½x11**
4286 A1682 2.60z multi 1.40 .70

10th World Games, Wroclaw A1683

Perf. 11x11½ Syncopated
2017, June 9 Litho.
4287 A1683 5z multi 2.75 1.40

Expo 2017, Astana, Kazakhstan A1684

Perf. 11½x11¼ Syncopated
2017, June 16 Litho.
4288 A1684 2.60z multi 1.40 .70
No. 4288 was printed in sheets of 12 + 4 central labels.

St. Albert Chmielowski (1845-1916), Founder of Servants of the Poor — A1685

Perf. 11½ Syncopated
2017, June 17 Litho.
4289 A1685 2.60z multi 1.40 .70
St. Albert Chmielowski Year. Values are for stamps with surrounding selvage.

Solidarity Fighters, 35th Anniv. A1686

Perf. 11x11½ Syncopated
2017, June 20   Litho.
4290 A1686 2.60z multi   1.40 .70

Souvenir Sheet

Rysy and Nearby Mountain Peaks — A1687

Perf. 11¾x11½
2017, June 30   Photo.
4291 A1687 6z multi   3.25 1.60

Arabian Horses Bred at Janów Podlaski Stud Farm — A1688

No. 4292: a, Algeria. b, Etruria. c, Pogrom. d, Pilarka. e, Pinga. f, Echao. g, Bandos. h, Pianissima. i, Bandola.

Perf. 11¾x11½ Syncopated
2017, July 31   Litho.
4292   Sheet of 9   13.50 6.75
  a.-i A1688 2.60z Any single   1.50 .75

Souvenir Sheet

2017 Tall Ships Race, Szczecin — A1689

2017, Aug. 5   Photo. **Perf. 11¼x11½**
4293 A1689 6z multi   3.50 1.75

A1690

A1691

A1692

2017 European Men's Volleyball Championships, Poland — A1693

Perf. 11½ Syncopated
2017, Aug. 10   Litho.
4294   Horiz. strip of 4   6.00 3.00
  a. A1690 2.60z multi   1.50 .75
  b. A1691 2.60z multi   1.50 .75
  c. A1692 2.60z multi   1.50 .75
  d. A1693 2.60z multi   1.50 .75
Printed in sheets containing two strips.

Coronation of Icon of Our Lady of Lichen, 50th Anniv. — A1694

Perf. 11½x11¾
2017, Aug. 12   Photo.
4295 A1694 2.60z multi   1.50 .75

Coronation of Icon of Our Lady of Czestochowa, 300th Anniv. — A1695

Perf. 11½x11¾
2017, Aug. 26   Photo.
4296 A1695 2.60z multi   1.50 .75

Miniature Sheet

Herbs — A1696

No. 4297: a, Centaurea cyanus. b, Matricaria chamomilla. c, Achillea millefolium. d, Thymus serpyllum.

Perf. 11¼ Syncopated
2017, Aug. 31   Litho.
4297 A1696 2.60z Sheet of 4,
            #a-d   5.75 3.00

Ecstascy of Saint Francis, by El Greco — A1697

Perf. 11½x11¼ Syncopated
2017, Sept. 2   Photo.
4298 A1697 2.60z multi   1.50 .75
No. 4298 was printed in sheets of 8 + central label.

Souvenir Sheet

Organ, Cathedral Basilica of the Assumption, Pelplin — A1698

Perf. 11½x11¼ Syncopated
2017, Sept. 16   Litho. & Engr.
4299 A1698 11z multi   6.00 3.00

Knotted Rope — A1699

Perf. 11¾x11½
2017, Sept. 29   Photo.
4300 A1699 A multi   1.50 .75
1937-38 purge and execution of Poles by Soviet NKVD. No. 4300 sold for 2.60z on day of issue.

Our Lady of Piekary — A1700

Perf. 11½x11¾
2017, Oct. 13   Photo.
4301 A1700 5z multi   2.75 1.40

Knights of the Immaculata, Cent. — A1701

Perf. 11½x11¼
2017, Oct. 14   Photo.
4302 A1701 5z multi + label   2.75 1.40

Feliks Selmanowicz (1904-46), Anti-Communist Soldier Executed by Communists A1702

Perf. 11½ Syncopated
2017, Oct. 18   Litho.
4303 A1702 3.20z multi   1.75 .90

Souvenir Sheet

Children's Art on Theme of Health — A1703

No. 4304: a, Girl and horse, by Ariadna Kruszy. b, Girl and bird, by Kamila Rylska. c, Clock and bicycle, by Sandra Marwitz.

Perf. 11½x11¼ Syncopated
2017, Oct. 25   Litho.
4304 A1703 2.60z Sheet of 3,
            #a-c   4.50 2.25

Miniature Sheet

Polish Avant-Garde Typography,
Cent. — A1704

No. 4305: a, Cover of *Kurier Blok* magazine, by Mieczyslaw Szczuka. b, Cover of sheet music for song *Szósta! Szósta!* by Wladyslaw Strzeminski. c, Cover of *Praesens* journal, by Henryk Stazewski. d, Cover of *Zdrój* magazine, by Wladyslaw Skotarek.

Perf. 11¼x11½ Syncopated

2017, Oct. 27		Litho.
4305	A1704 Sheet of 4	6.75 3.50
a.-b.	2.60z Either single	1.50 .75
c.	3.20z multi	1.75 .90
d.	3.70z multi	2.00 1.00

Stage and Film Stars Type of 2012

Designs: 2.60z, Mieczyslaw Cybulski (1903-84). 3.20z, Ina Benita (1912-44). 3.70z, Kazimierz Junosza-Stepowski (1880-1943).

Perf. 11½x11¾ Syncopated

2017, Oct. 30		Litho.
4306-4308	A1512 Set of 3	5.25 2.60
4308a	Souvenir sheet of 3, #4306-4308	5.25 2.60

Badge of 22nd Artillery Supply Company of the Second Polish Corps Depicting Wojtek the Bear — A1705

Perf. 11½x11¼

2017, Oct. 31		Photo.
4309	A1705 A multi	1.50 .75

No. 4309 sold for 2.60z on day of issue.

Croissant, Walnuts and Poppies — A1706

Perf. 11½ Syncopated

2017, Nov. 3		Litho. & Embossed
4310	A1706 5z multi	3.00 1.50

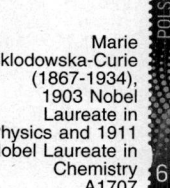

Marie Sklodowska-Curie (1867-1934), 1903 Nobel Laureate in Physics and 1911 Nobel Laureate in Chemistry A1707

Perf. 11½x11¾ Syncopated

2017, Nov. 7		Litho.
4311	A1707 6z multi	3.50 1.75

No. 4311 was printed in sheets of 8 + central label.

Statue of St. Margaret and Town Hall, Nowy Sacz — A1708

2017, Nov. 8	Photo.	**Perf. 11½x11¼**
4312	A1708 20g multi	.25 .25

Christmas — A1709

Illustrations from the Olbracht Missal: A, Madonna and Child. B, Adoration of the Magi. 6z, Annunciation.

Perf. 11¾x11½

2017, Nov. 16		Photo.
4313-4315	A1709 Set of 3	6.75 3.50

On day of issue, No. 4313 sold for 2.60z, and No. 4314 sold for 3.20z.

Snowflake A1710

Perf. 11½x11¾ Syncopated

2017, Nov. 18		Litho.
4316	A1710 2.60z multi	1.50 .75

Gold medal by ski jumping team of Maciej Kot, Dawid Kubacki, Kamil Stoch and Piotr Zyla at 2017 Nordic World Skiing Championships, Lahti, Finland.

Jarek Smietana (1951-2013), Jazz Guitarist and Composer — A1711

Perf. 11¾x11½ Syncopated

2017, Nov. 27		Litho.
4317	A1711 2.60z multi	1.50 .75

Miniature Sheet

Owls — A1712

No. 4318 — Face of: a, Bubo scandiacus. b, Athene noctua. c, Surnia ulula. d, Asio otus.

Perf. 11¾x11½ Syncopated

2017, Nov. 30		Litho. & Embossed
4318	A1712 5z Sheet of 4, #a-d, + 4 labels	11.50 5.75

Souvenir Sheet

1516 Bookplate — A1713

Perf. 11½x11¼ Syncopated

2017, Dec. 3		Litho.
4319	A1713 6z multi	3.50 1.75

Marshal Józef Pilsudski (1867-1935) — A1714

Photo. & Engr.

2017, Dec. 5		Perf. 10¾x11
4320	A1714 10z gold & multi	5.75 3.00

Gen. Wladyslaw Anders (1892-1970), and His Soldiers in Kazakhstan — A1715

Perf. 11¼x11½ Syncopated

2017, Dec. 6		Litho.
4321	A1715 5z multi	3.00 1.50

See Kazakhstan No. 839.

Nine Coal Miners Massacred in 1981 Wujek Mine Strike — A1716

Perf. 11¾x11½

2017, Dec. 16		Photo.
4322	A1716 2.60z multi	1.50 .75

Supreme Court, Cent. — A1717

Perf. 11½x11¼

2017, Dec. 29		Photo.
4323	A1717 3.70z multi	2.25 1.10

Poland's 2018-19 Term on United Nations Security Council A1718

Perf. 11¼x11½

2017, Dec. 29		Photo.
4324	A1718 3.70z multi	2.25 1.10

Sign at Entrance to Auschwitz Concentration Camp — A1719

Perf. 11¼x11½ Syncopated

2018, Jan. 27		Litho.
4325	A1719 2.60z black & red	1.60 .80

2018 Winter Olympics, PyeongChang, South Korea — A1720

Perf. 11½x11 Syncopated
2018, Feb. 1 Litho.
4326 A1720 5.20z multi 3.25 1.60
Perforate and imperforate souvenir sheets of 1 of No. 4326 with the denomination obliterated were given to members of the Polish Philatelic Union.

Virgin Mary, Teacher of Youth — A1721

Perf. 11½ Syncopated
2018, Feb. 24 Litho.
4327 A1721 2.60z multi 1.50 .75

2018 Winter Paralympics, PyeongChang, South Korea — A1722

2018, Mar. 1 Photo. **Perf. 11x10¾**
4328 A1722 5.20z multi 3.00 1.50

Souvenir Sheet

Soldier's Gorgets — A1723

No. 4329 — Gorget depicing: a, Black Madonna and eagle, belonging to Witold Pilecki. b, Black Madonna and eagle on banner with red cross, belonging to 5th Vilnius Brigade.

Perf. 11¼ Syncopated
2018, Mar. 1 Litho. & Embossed
4329 A1723 6z Sheet of 2, #a-b, + 2 labels 7.00 3.50

Easter — A1724

2018, Mar. 6 Photo. **Perf. 11¾x11½**
4330 A1724 B multi 1.90 .95
No. 4330 sold for 3.20z on day of issue.

Fruit and Flowers Type of 2009
Designs: 25g, Narcissus jonquilla. 6.80z, Lily of the valley.

2018 Photo. **Perf. 11½x11¾**
4331 A1425 25g multi .25 .25
4332 A1425 6.80z multi 3.75 1.90
Issued: 25g, 3/9. 6.80z, 5/11.

Irena Sendler (1910-2008), Resistance Leader in World War II — A1725

2018, Mar. 24 Photo. **Perf. 11x11½**
4333 A1725 2.60z multi 1.60 .80

Bar Confederation Soldier, Madonna and Child — A1726

Perf. 11¾x11½
2018, Mar. 31 Photo.
4334 A1726 1z multi .60 .30
Bar Confederation, 250th anniv.

Kamil Stoch, 2018 Winter Olympics Gold Medalist Ski Jumper — A1727

Perf. 11½x11¾
2018, Apr. 14 Photo.
4335 A1727 3.70z multi 2.10 1.10

Photographs by Ignacy Krieger (1817-89) A1728

No. 4336 — Photograph of: a, Krieger. b, Man from Szaflary holding boots. c, Boy carrying bagels. d, Chimney sweeps.

Perf. 11½ Syncopated
2018, Apr. 24 Litho.
4336 Block or horiz. strip of 4 6.00 3.00
a.-d. A1728 2.60z Any single 1.50 .75

Map of Poland in Ribbon — A1729

2018, May 2 Photo. **Perf. 11¾x11½**
4337 A1729 A multi 1.40 .70
No. 4337 sold for 2.60z on day of issue.

Tczew Bridge — A1730

Perf. 11½x11 Syncopated
2018, May 2 Litho.
4338 A1730 5z multi 2.75 1.40
Europa.

Coronation of Dabrowa Górnicza Icon of Madonna and Child, 50th Anniv. — A1731

Perf. 11¾x11½
2018, May 19 Photo.
4339 A1731 B multi 1.75 .85
No. 4339 sold for 3.20z on day of issue.

Souvenir Sheet

Prosze Slonia (Please, Elephant) Animated Film Series, 50th Anniv. — A1732

No. 4340: a, 2.60z, Boy on elephant. b, 3.20z, Boy, parents and sofa on elephant.

Perf. 11½ Syncopated
2018, May 30 Litho.
4340 A1732 Sheet of 2, #a-b 3.25 1.60

Souvenir Sheet

Pipe Organ, St. Mary's Church, Gdansk — A1733

Perf. 11½x11 Syncopated
2018, June 3 Litho. & Embossed
4341 A1733 6.80z multi 3.75 1.90

Robert Lewandowski, Captain of 2018 Polish National Soccer Team — A1734

Perf. 11¾x11½
2018, June 14 Photo.
4342 A1734 6z multi 3.25 1.60

St. Pio of Pietrelcina (1887-1968) A1735

2018, June 16 Photo. **Perf. 11½x11**
4343 A1735 2.60z multi 1.40 .70

Bishop Jordan, First Bishop of Poland, and Poznan Cathedral A1736

2018, June 22 Photo. **Perf. 10¾x11**
4344 A1736 A multi 1.40 .70
Poznan Bishopric, 1050th anniv. No. 4344 sold for 2.60z on day of issue.

Statue and Zywiec Castle, Zywiec — A1737

Perf. 11½x11¾
2018, June 22 Photo.
4345 A1737 10z multi 5.25 2.60

St. Dorothea of Montau (1347-94) A1738

2018, June 24 Photo. **Perf. 11½x11**
4346 A1738 2.60z multi 1.40 .70

Polish-Lithuanian Commonwealth, 550th Anniv. — A1739

Perf. 11½ Syncopated
2018, June 27 Litho.
4347 A1739 3.20z multi 1.75 .85

Tourist Attractions — A1740

No. 4348: a, 2.60z, Weimar Chamber, Wieliczka Salt Mines. b, 5.20z, Baltic Sea coast.

Perf. 11¼ Syncopated
2018, July 23 Litho.
4348 A1740 Pair, #a-b 4.25 2.10

Coronation of Our Lady of Trakai, 300th Anniv. — A1741

2018, July 27 Photo. Perf. 11x11¼
4349 A1741 3.20z multi + label 1.75 .85

No. 4349 was printed in sheets of 2 + 2 labels.

Gen. Wladyslaw Sikorski (1881-1943) A1742

Perf. 11¼x11¾ Syncopated
2018, July 28 Litho.
4350 A1742 2.60z multi 1.50 .75

Lisiecka Sausage A1743

Perf. 11¾x11½ Syncopated
2018, July 30 Litho. & Embossed
4351 A1743 6z multi 3.25 1.60

Coronation of Our Lady of Swieta Lipka, 50th Anniv. — A1744

Perf. 11½x11¼
2018, Aug. 11 Photo.
4352 A1744 2.60z gold & multi 1.40 .70

St. Stanislaw Kostka (1550-68) A1745

Perf. 11¼x11½
2018, Aug. 19 Photo.
4353 A1745 2.60z gold & multi 1.40 .70

Icons A1746

Designs: No. 4354, 2.60z, Our Lady of Zbaraski icon (black panels). No. 4355, 2.60z, Our Lady Queen of the Polish Crown from Kalusz (blue panels). No. 4356, 2.60z, Our Lady of Lutsk (gray panels). No. 4357, 2.60z, Our Lady, Queen of the Polish Crown from Porchowa, Ukraine (red panels).

2018, Aug. 23 Photo. Perf. 11
4354-4357 A1746 Set of 4 5.75 2.75

Roundhouse, Kedzierzyn-Kozle, Cent. — A1747

No. 4358: a, 2.60z, TKt48 locomotive. b, 3.20z, Ty42 locomotive.

Perf. 11¾x11½ Syncopated
2018, Aug. 31 Litho.
4358 A1747 Horiz. pair, #a-b 3.25 1.60

Botanical Garden of the University of Warsaw, 200th Anniv. — A1748

Perf. 11¼x11 Syncopated
2018, Sept. 10 Litho.
4359 A1748 3.20z multi 1.75 .85

No. 4359 was printed in sheets of 8 + central label.

World Congress of the Polish Diaspora and Poles Abroad, Warsaw A1749

Perf. 11¼x11½ Syncopated
2018, Sept. 20 Litho.
4360 A1749 2.60z multi 1.40 .70

Waclaw Sieroszewski (1858-1945), Writer Exiled to Siberia — A1750

2018, Sept. 24 Photo. Perf. 11x11½
4361 A1750 5.20z multi 3.00 1.50

Souvenir Sheet

Children's Art — A1751

No. 4362 — Winning designs in children's art contest on theme of saving the climate: a, Necessary Changes, by Oliwia Gola (green denomination). b, To Rescue our Planet, by Benjamin Czajkowski (red denomination). c, Fight Against Smog, by Natalia Gaska (blue denomination).

Perf. 11¼ Syncopated
2018, Sept. 26 Litho.
4362 A1751 2.60z Sheet of 3, #a-c 4.25 2.10

Beetles — A1752

Designs: No. 4363, 3.20z, Oryctes nasicornis. No. 4364, 3.20z, Cucujus cinnaberinus.

Perf. 11¼ Syncopated
2018, Sept. 28 Litho.
4363-4364 A1752 Set of 2 3.50 1.75

Nos. 4363-4364 were each printed in sheets of 8 + label.

Father Idzi Radziszewski (1871-1922), Founder of Catholic University of Lublin — A1753

2018, Oct. 1 Photo. Perf. 11½x11¼
4365 A1753 2.60z multi 1.40 .70

Catholic University of Lublin, cent.

Planned Via Carpathia Highway — A1754

2018, Oct. 3 Photo. Perf. 11¾x11½
4366 A1754 20g multi .25 .25

Town Hall Clock, Poznan — A1755

Perf. 11½ Syncopated
2018, Oct. 3 Litho.
4367 A1755 2.60z gold & multi 1.40 .70

National Philatelic Exhibition, Poznan. No. 4367 was printed in sheets of 12 + 4 labels.

Election of Cardinal Karol Wojtyla as Pope, 40th Anniv. — A1756

Perf. 11½x11¼ Syncopated
2018, Oct. 16 Litho.
4368 A1756 3.20z gold & multi 1.75 .85

Souvenir Sheet

Polish Postal Service, 460th Anniv. — A1757

Perf. 11½x11 Syncopated
2018, Oct. 18 Engr.
4369 A1757 10z gold & multi 5.25 2.60

Cardinal August Hlond (1881-1948) A1758

Perf. 11¾x11½
2018, Oct. 22 Photo.
4370 A1758 5z multi 2.75 1.40

Stage and Film Stars Type of 2012

Designs: No. 4371, 2.60z, Stefan Jaracz (1883-1945). No. 4372, 2.60z, Adam Brodzisz (1906-86). 3.20z, Maria Bogda (1909-81).

Perf. 11½x11¾ Syncopated
2018, Oct. 31 Photo.
4371-4373 A1512 Set of 3 4.50 2.25
4373a Souvenir sheet of 3, #4371-4373 4.50 2.25

Lost
Works of
Art
A1759

No. 4374: a, 2.60z, View of Zamosc, by Marcin Zaleski. b, 2.60z, Solec Harbor, by Aleksander Gierymski. c, 3.20z, View of Kraków, by Julian Falat.

Perf. 11¼x11½
2018, Oct. 31   Photo.
4374 A1759 Vert. strip of 3, #a-
c   4.50 2.25

Brühl
Palace,
Warsaw
A1760

Perf. 11¼x11½
2018, Oct. 31   Photo.
4375 A1760 2.60z multi   1.40 .70
Polish Foreign Service, cent.

Fireworks
and Flags
of Israel
and Poland
A1761

2018, Nov. 5   Litho.   **Perf. 13x13¼**
4376 A1761 2.60z multi   1.40 .70
Independence of Israel, 70th anniv.; and of Poland, cent. See Israel No. 2201.

End of
World War
I, Cent.
A1762

Perf. 11¼ Syncopated
2018, Nov. 11   Litho.
4377 A1762 2.60z multi   1.40 .70

Miniature Sheet

First Days of Polish
Independence — A1763

No. 4378: a, Nine Silesian insurgents. b, Marshal Edward Rydz-Smigly (1886-1941), vert. c, Major General Franciszek Ksawery Latinik (1864-1949), vert. d, Officers of the First Polish Guard Czeslaw Zajaczkowski, Wilhelm Stec and Jan Gawron in Kraków, vert. e, Seven soldiers guarding Lwów.

Die Cut Perf. 11½x11¾, 11¾x11½
2018, Nov. 11   Litho.
    Self-Adhesive
4378 A1763 2.60z Sheet of 5,
#a-e   7.00 3.50

Miniature Sheet

Independence, Cent. — A1764

No. 4379: a, Ignacy Jan Paderewski (1860-1941), prime minister and pianist. b, Marshal Józef Pilsudski (1867-1935), prime minister and military leader. c, Roman Dmowski (1864-1939), politician. d, Order of the Rebirth of Poland. e, Mother of God, Hetman of the Polish Soldier icon. f, Wincenty Witos (1874-1945), prime minister. g, Ignacy Daszynski (1866-1936), prime minister. h, Wojciech Korfanty (1873-1939), deputy prime minister.

**Litho., Litho. With Hologram Affixed
on Central Label
Perf. 11½ Syncopated**
2018, Nov. 11
4379 A1764 2.60z Sheet of 8,
#a-h, + cen-
tral label   11.00 5.50

Miniature Sheet

Armed Forces of Re-established
Republic of Poland, Cent. — A1765

No. 4380 — Members of: a, Army (54x27mm). b, Horse cavalry (54x27mm). c, Navy (54x27mm). d, Air Force (54x27mm). e, Modern armed forces (108x27mm).

2018, Nov. 11   Photo.   **Perf. 11x11¼**
4380 A1765 2.60z Sheet of 5,
#a-e   7.00 3.50

Miniature Sheet

Items Patented by Patent Office of
Republic of Poland — A1766

No. 4381: a, Triggo electric vehicle. b, Aeroscope compressed air camera. c, Bulletproof vest. d, Atlas of the human brain.

Perf. 11½x11 Syncopated
2018, Nov. 26   Litho.
4381 A1766 3.20z Sheet of 4,
#a-d   7.00 3.50
Patent Office of the Republic of Poland, cent.

Jedrzej Sniadecki (1768-1838),
Chemist and Writer — A1767

Perf. 11¼x11½
2018, Nov. 30   Photo.
4382 A1767 2.60z gold & multi   1.40 .70

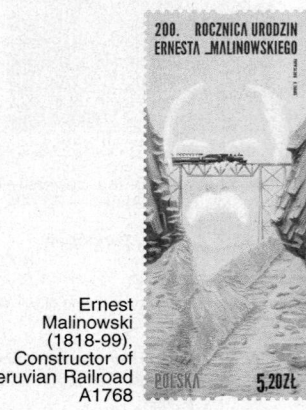

Ernest
Malinowski
(1818-99),
Constructor of
Peruvian Railroad
A1768

Perf. 11½x11¾ Syncopated
2018, Dec. 10   Litho.
4383 A1768 5.20z multi   2.75 1.40

Polish Industrial Design — A1769

No. 4384: a, Figurine of sitting girl, by Henryk Jedrasiak. b, RM58 chair, by Roman Modzelewski.

Perf. 11¼ Syncopated
2018, Dec. 21   Litho.
4384 A1769 2.60z Pair, #a-b   2.75 1.40
Printed in sheets of 4 containing two each of Nos. 4384a-4384b.

Greater Poland
Uprising,
Cent. — A1770

Perf. 11½x11¾ Syncopated
2018, Dec. 27   Litho.
4385 A1770 2.60z gold & multi   1.40 .70
Printed in sheets of 8 + central label.

Adult and
Juvenile Animals
A1771

Designs: No. 4386, 1.30z, Rhinocerso unicornis. No. 4387, 1.30z, Pan troglodytes. No. 4388, 3z, Choloepus didactylus. No. 4389, 3z, Giraffa camelopardalis.

**Perf. 11½x11¾ Syncopated
Litho. & Silk-Screened**
2018, Dec. 28
4386-4389 A1771   Set of 4   4.50 2.25
Nos. 4386-4389 were each printed in sheets of 12 + 4 labels.

Miniature Sheet

2018 World Champion Polish Men's
Volleyball Team — A1772

No. 4390: a, Piotr Nowakowski. b, Dawid Konarski. c, Bartosz Kurek. d, Artur Szalpuk. e, Damian Schulz. f, Damian Wojtaszek. g, Fabian Drzyzga. h, Grzegorz Lomacz. i, Michal Kubiak. j, Aleksander Sliwka. k, Jakub Kochanowski. l, Pawel Zatorski. m, Bartosz Kwolek. n, Mateusz Bieniek. o, Vital Heynen, trainer. p, Trophy and gold medal.

Perf. 11½x11¾ Syncopated
2018, Dec. 28   Litho.
4390 A1772 1z Sheet of 16, #a-
p, + 4 labels   8.50 4.25

Self-portrait of
Stanislaw
Wyspianski
(1869-1907),
Painter and
Poet — A1773

2019, Jan. 15   Photo.   **Perf. 11½x11**
4391 A1773 3.20z gold & multi   1.75 .85

Polish Red Cross, Cent. — A1774

Perf. 11½x11¼ Syncopated
2019, Jan. 18   **Litho.**
4392 A1774 3.20z multi   1.75 .85

Souvenir Sheet

Pres. Ignacy Jan Paderewski (1860-1941) — A1775

Perf. 11¼x11½ Syncopated
2019, Jan. 25   **Litho. & Engr.**
4393 A1775 14.50z multi   7.75 4.00
Polish Security Printing Works, cent.

LOT Polish Airlines, 90th Anniv. — A1776

Perf. 11½x11¾ Syncopated
2019, Jan. 31   **Litho.**
4394 A1776 5.20z multi   2.75 1.40

Archbishop Achille Ratti (Later Pope Pius XI, 1857-1939) and Archbishop Stanislaw Galla (1865-1942) — A1777

2019, Feb. 5   **Photo.**   **Perf. 11x11½**
4395 A1777 2.60z gold & multi   1.40 .70
Military Ordinariate of Poland, cent.

PKO Bank Polski, Cent. — A1778

2019, Feb. 7   **Photo.**   **Perf. 11½x11**
4396 A1778 3.20z sil & multi   1.75 .85

State Archives Network, Cent. — A1779

2019, Feb. 7   **Photo.**   **Perf. 11½x11**
4397 A1779 3.20z sil & multi   1.75 .85

Supreme Audit Office, Cent. A1780

Perf. 11½ Syncopated
2019, Feb. 7   **Litho.**
4398 A1780 5z sil & multi   2.60 1.40
No. 4398 was printed in sheets of 8 + central label.

Polish Prison Service, Cent. A1781

2019, Feb. 8   **Photo.**   **Perf. 11x11½**
4399 A1781 2.60z gold & multi   1.40 .70

Wojciech Trampczynski (1860-1953), First Marshal of Sejm — A1782

Perf. 11½x11 Syncopated
2019, Feb. 8   **Litho.**
4400 A1782 5z multi   2.60 1.40
Sejm, cent.

Branicki Palace and Sculpture Atop Palace Gate, Bialystok A1783

Perf. 11½x11¾
2019, Feb. 19   **Photo.**
4401 A1783 5z multi   2.60 1.40

Major Marian Bernaciak (1917-46), Leader of Polish Anti-Communist Forces, and People of Ryki — A1784

2019, Mar. 1   **Photo.**   **Perf. 11½x11¾**
4402 A1784 2.60z sil & multi   1.40 .70
Remembrance of the "Cursed Soldiers" (anti-Communist forces).

2019 Summer Special Olympics, Abu Dhabi A1785

Perf. 11½ Syncopated
2019, Mar. 7   **Litho.**
4403 A1785 2.60z multi   1.40 .70

Easter
A1786   A1787

Perf. 11¾x11½
2019, Mar. 18   **Photo.**
4404 A1786 A gold & multi   1.75 .85
4405 A1787 6z gold & multi   3.25 1.60
No. 4404 sold for 3.20z on day of issue.

Nazi Execution of Family of Józef (1900-44) and Wiktoria Ulma (1912-44) for Hiding Jews, 75th Anniv. A1788

Perf. 11x11½ Syncopated
2019, Mar. 24   **Litho.**
4406 A1788 3.30z multi   1.75 .85
No. 4406 was printed in sheets of 8 + central label.

End of Independence Cruise of the Dar Mlodziedzy — A1789

Perf. 11¼ Syncopated
2019, Mar. 28   **Litho.**
4407 A1789 3.30z multi   1.75 .85

Marshal Józef Pilsudski (1867-1935) and Pope Benedict XV (1854-1922) A1790

Perf. 11x11½ Syncopated
2019, Mar. 29   **Litho.**
4408 A1790 5z gold & multi   2.60 1.40
Diplomatic relations between Poland and Vatican City, cent. See Vatican City No. 1715.

Souvenir Sheet

Diplomatic Relations Between Poland and France, Cent. — A1791

No. 4409: a, Charles de Gaulle (1890-1970), French army captain, later president of France. b, Józef Haller (1873-1960), Polish lieutenant general.

Perf. 11½ Syncopated
2019, Apr. 2   **Litho.**
4409 A1791 5z Sheet of 2, #a-b   5.25 2.60
See France No. 5638.

Sokol Gymnastic Society, Cent. — A1792

2019, Apr. 17   **Photo.**   **Perf. 11½x11**
4410 A1792 3.30z gold & multi   1.75 .85

Fringilla Coelebs A1793

Perf. 11¼x11½ Syncopated
2019, Apr. 24   **Litho.**
4411 A1793 5z multi   2.60 1.40
Europa.

St. Adalbert of Prague (956-97), Patron Saint of Poland A1794

2019, Apr. 27   **Photo.**   **Perf. 11x11½**
4412 A1794 3.30z multi   1.75 .85

Diplomatic Relations Between Poland and Greece, Cent. A1795

Perf. 11x11½ Syncopated
2019, Apr. 30   **Litho.**
4413 A1795 3.30z multi   1.75 .85
See Greece No.

Miniature Sheet

Polish Landscapes — A1796

No. 4414: a, Fields and forests, Central Poland. b, Islands in Warta River Delta. c, Meadow near Tatra Mountains. d, Snow-covered forest in Bieszczady Mountains.

Perf. 11x11½ Syncopated
2019, Apr. 30   Litho.
4414 A1796 3.30zl Sheet of 4,
      #a-d   7.00 3.50

Poland's Admission to the European Union, 15th Anniv. — A1797

Perf. 11½x11 Syncopated
2019, May 1   Litho.
4415 A1797 3.30z multi   1.75 .85

Stanislaw Moniuszko (1819-72), Composer A1798

2019, May 5 Photo.   Perf. 11½x11
4416 A1798 3.30z multi   1.75 .85

Sluzewiec Racetrack, Warsaw, 80th Anniv. A1799

Perf. 11½ Syncopated
2019, May 5   Litho.
4417 A1799 3.30z multi   1.75 .85

Heliodor Swiecicki (1854-1923), First Rector of Poznan University — A1800

2019, May 7   Photo.   Perf. 11½x11
4418 A1800 8.40z multi   4.50 2.25
Poznan University, cent.

Polish Olympic Committee, Cent. A1801

Perf. 11x11½ Syncopated
2019, May 16   Litho.
4419 A1801 4.10z multi   2.25 1.10

Royal Castle, Warsaw, 400th Anniv. — A1802

Perf. 11¾x11½ Syncopated
2019, May 29   Litho.
4420 A1802 3.30z multi   1.75 .85

Miniature Sheet

Buildings in Baku, Azerbaijan Designed by Polish Architects — A1803

No. 4421: a, Junior High School for Boys, by Konstanty Borysoglebski. b, City Council Building (with spire), by Józef Goslawski. c, Taghiyev School for Girls (with balcony), by Goslawski. d, House of Tigran Melikov (on street corner), by Goslawski. e, Haji Sultan Ali Mosque, by Józef Ploszko. f, Mukhtarov Palace, by Ploszko. g, House of Agabala Guliyev, by Eugeniusz Skibinski. h, Rothschild Office Building, by Kazimierz Skorewicz.

Perf. 11¼x11½ Syncopated
2019, May 31   Litho.
4421 A1803 3.30z Sheet of 8,
      #a-h   14.00 7.00
See Azerbaijan No. 1226.

Souvenir Sheet

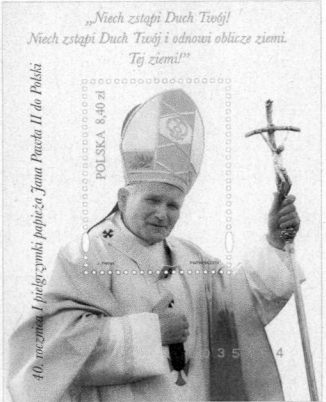

First Pilgrimage to Poland by Pope John Paul II, 40th Anniv. — A1804

Perf. 11½ Syncopated
2019, June 2   Litho.
4422 A1804 8.40z multi   4.50 2.25

Marshal's Staff of Polish Senate — A1805

Perf. 11½x11¾ Syncopated
2019, June 4   Litho.
4423 A1805 5z multi   2.60 1.40
Re-establishment of the Polish Senate, and free elections, 30th anniv.

Beatification of 108 Polish Martyrs of World War II, 20th Anniv. — A1806

2019, June 15 Photo.   Perf. 10¾x11
4424 A1806 3.30z multi   1.75 .90

Painted Wooden Bird — A1807

Perf. 11¾x11½
2019, June 19   Photo.
4425 A1807 4.10z multi   2.25 1.10
Beskid Culture Week.

Souvenir Sheet

Organ From St. John the Baptist and St. John the Evangelist Cathedral, Torun — A1808

Perf. 11½x11 Syncopated
2019, June 21   Litho.
4426 A1808 6.60z multi   3.50 1.75

Anna Walentynowicz (1929-2010), Co-Founder of Solidarity Labor Union — A1809

Perf. 11¾x11½
2019, June 24   Photo.
4427 A1809 8.70z multi   4.75 2.40

Miniature Sheet

Clematis Varieties — A1810

No. 4428 — Clematis variety: a, General Sikorski (purple flowers). b, Cardinal Wyszynski (two magenta flowers). c, Solidarity (three red flowers). d, Marie Sklodowska-Curie (white flowers).

Perf. 11½x11¾ Syncopated
2019, June 25   Litho.
4428 A1810 3.30z Sheet of 4,
      #a-d   7.00 3.50

1877 Apparitions of the Virgin Mary in Gietrzwald A1811

2019, June 27 Photo. Perf. 11½x11
4429 A1811 3.30z multi   1.75   .90

Teczynski Family Arms — A1812

2019, June 28 Photo. Perf. 11½x11
4430 A1812 3.30z multi   1.75   .90

Garlic A1813

Perf. 11½ Syncopated
2019, June 28 Litho. & Embossed
4431 A1813 6z multi   3.25 1.60

Souvenir Sheet

Union of Lublin, by Jan Matejko (1838-93) — A1814

2019, July 1 Photo. Perf. 11½x11
4432 A1814 8.40z multi   4.50 2.25
Union of Lublin, 450th anniv.

Souvenir Sheet

First Man on the Moon, 50th Anniv. — A1815

Perf. 11½ Syncopated
2019, July 20   Litho.
4433 A1815 8.40z multi   4.50 2.25

Polish State Police, Cent. — A1816

2019, July 24 Photo. Perf. 11½x11
4434 A1816 3.30z multi   1.75   .85

Henryk Slawik (1894-1944), Diplomat Who Saved Jews In World War II — A1817

Perf. 11¾x11½
2019, July 26   Photo.
4435 A1817 4z multi   2.10 1.10

Polish Soccer Association, Cent. — A1818

Perf. 11½ Syncopated
2019, July 30   Litho.
4436 A1818 4z multi   2.10 1.10

Souvenir Sheet

Zbigniew Scibor-Rylski (1917-2018), Brigadier General, and Warsaw Uprising Memorial Wall — A1819

Perf. 11½ Syncopated
2019, Aug. 1   Litho.
4437 A1819 7.30z multi   3.75 1.90
Warsaw Uprising, 75th anniv.

Racers in Solidarity Street Run, Kolobrzeg Lighthouse — A1820

2019, Aug. 2 Photo. Perf. 11¾x11½
4438 A1820 30g multi   .25   .25

Blessed Stefan Wincenty Frelichowski (1913-45), Priest Who Died at Dachau Concentration Camp — A1821

2019, Aug. 8 Photo. Perf. 11¾x11½
4439 A1821 6.30z multi   3.25 1.60

Kazimierz Deyna (1947-89), Soccer Player — A1822

Perf. 11¾x11½
2019, Aug. 12   Photo.
4440 A1822 5.90z multi   3.00 1.50

Striking Coal Miners, Map of Silesia, and Alfons Zgrzebniok (1891-1937), Leader of Polish Forces in Silesian Uprisings A1823

Perf. 11½ Syncopated
2019, Aug. 16   Litho.
4441 A1823 3.30z multi   1.75   .85

Central Road Administration, 200th Anniv. — A1824

Perf. 11¼x11½
2019, Aug. 28   Photo.
4442 A1824 3.30z multi   1.75   .85

Jerzy Milian (1935-2018), Jazz Musician and Composer A1825

Perf. 11½x11 Syncopated
2019, Aug. 30   Litho.
4443 A1825 3.30z multi   1.75   .85

Start of World War II, 80th Anniv. — A1826

2019, Sept. 1 Photo. Perf. 11x10¾
4444 A1826 3.30z multi   1.75   .85

Defense of the Gdansk Post Office, 80th Anniv. — A1827

Perf. 11½ Syncopated
2019, Sept. 1   Litho.
4445 A1827 3.30z multi   1.75   .85

Confederation of Independent Poland Political Party, 40th Anniv. — A1828

Perf. 11¼x11½
2019, Sept. 1   Photo.
4446 A1828 3.30z multi   1.75   .85

Zegrze Military Communications Training Center, Cent. — A1829

Perf. 11½x11¾
2019, Sept. 12   Photo.
4447 A1829 3.30z multi   1.75   .85

Souvenir Sheet

Finance of Poland Anniversaries — A1830

No. 4448: a, Public financing, cent. ("100" from banknote). b, Budget, 250th anniv. (arms of King Stanislaw II Augustus). c, National Treasury Administration, cent. (emblem).

Perf. 11x11½ Syncopated
2019, Sept. 20   Litho.
4448 A1830 3.30z Sheet of 3,
              #a-c   5.25 2.60

Polish Underground State, 80th Anniv. — A1831

Perf. 11¼x11½
2019, Sept. 27   Photo.
4449 A1831 3.30z multi   1.75   .85

Souvenir Sheet

Children's Art — A1832

No. 4450: a, Ruddy Orchard, by Paulina Malarz. b, Beauty of the Orchard, by Karolina Rupik. c, Bee's Paradise, by Patryk Zielanski.

Perf. 11½x11 Syncopated
2019, Sept. 27   Litho.
4450 A1832 3.30z Sheet of 3,
    #a-c   5.25   2.60

Origami Stork on Japan Flag — A1833

Perf. 11½x11 Syncopated
2019, Sept. 30   Litho.
4451 A1833 3.30z multi   1.75   .85

Assistance for Polish orphans from Eastern Siberia by Fukudenkai Orphanage in Japan, cent.

Mohandas K. Gandhi (1869-1948), Indian Nationalist Leader — A1834

Perf. 11½x11¼
2019, Sept. 30   Photo.
4452 A1834 3.30z multi   1.75   .85

Memorial to Victims of Piasnica Massacre — A1835

2019, Oct. 3   Photo.   **Perf. 11¾x11½**
4453 A1835 2.60z multi   1.40   .70

Mass murder committed by Nazis in Piasnica, 80th anniv.

Souvenir Sheet

Organ, Basilica of St. Andrew the Apostle, Olkusz. — A1836

Perf. 11½x11 Syncopated
2019, Oct. 5   Litho.
4454 A1836 6.60z multi   3.50   1.75

Settlement of Poznan by Bambergs, 300th Anniv. — A1837

Perf. 11½ Syncopated
2019, Oct. 19   Litho.
4455 A1837 3.30z multi   1.75   .85

Stage and Film Stars Type of 2012
Designs: No. 4456, 3.30z, Michal Znicz (1888-1943). No. 4457, 3.30z, Jadwiga Andrzejewska (1915-77). No. 4458, 3.30z, Józef Wegrzyn (1884-1952).

Perf. 11½ Syncopated
2019, Oct. 25   Litho.
4456-4458 A1512   Set of 3   5.25   2.60
4458a   Souvenir sheet of 3,
    #4456-4458   5.25   2.60

Liberation of Breda, Netherlands by Polish Troops of Gen. Stanislaw Maczek, 75th Anniv. — A1838

2019, Oct. 26   Photo.   **Perf. 11½x11**
4459 A1838 3.30z multi   1.75   .85

Sermon of St. John the Baptist, by Pieter Brueghel the Younger (1564-1638) — A1839

Perf. 11½x11 Syncopated
2019, Oct. 28   Litho.
4460 A1839 6z multi   3.25   1.60

No. 4460 was printed in sheets of 5 + label.

Souvenir Sheet

Birds of Singapore and Poland — A1840

No. 4461: a, Anthracoceros albirostris. b, Falco peregrinus.

Perf. 11½x11 Syncopated
2019, Oct. 30   Litho.
4461 A1840 3.30z Sheet of 2,
    #a-b   3.50   1.75

See Singapore No.

Miniature Sheet

First Days of Polish Independence — A1841

No. 4462: a, Lieutenant General Józef Haller (1873-1960). b, Parade of Polish cavalry, Sejny, horiz. c, Seizure of Vilnius, horiz. d, Lieutenant General Józef Dowbor-Musnicki (1867-1937). e, Government ministers of Prime Minister Jedrzej Moraczewski (1870-1944), horiz. f, Soldiers parading in Bialystok, horiz.

Die Cut Perf. 11¾x11½ (vert. stamps), 11½x11¾ (horiz. stamps)
2019, Nov. 11   Litho.
    Self-Adhesive
4462 A1841 3.30z Sheet of 6,
    #a-f   10.50   5.25

Gabriela Balicka (1871-1962), Botanist and Politician A1842

Perf. 11½x11 Syncopated
2019, Nov. 28   Litho.
4463 A1842 3.30z multi   1.75   .85

Woman suffrage in Poland, 101st anniv.

Polish President Ignacy Jan Paderewski (1860-1941) and U.S. President Woodrow Wilson (1856-1924) A1843

Perf. 11½ Syncopated
2019, Dec. 20   Litho.
4464 A1843 3.30z multi   1.75   .85

Diplomatic relations between Poland and the United States, cent.

Monument to Insurgents and Town Hall, Leszno — A1844

Perf. 11¾x11½
2020, Jan. 17   Photo.
4465 A1844 3.30z multi   1.75   .85

New Year 2020 (Year of the Rat) A1845

Perf. 11½ Syncopated
2020, Jan. 27   Litho.
4466 A1845 3.30z multi   1.75   .85

Values are for stamps with surrounding selvage.

Liberation of Auschwitz Concentration Camp, 75th Anniv. — A1846

Perf. 11½x11¾
2020, Jan. 27   Photo.
4467 A1846 3.30z multi   1.75   .85

First Polish Postage Stamp, 160th Anniv. — A1847

Perf. 11½x11 Syncopated
2020, Jan. 31   Litho.
4468 A1847 3.30z multi   1.75   .85

No. 4468 was printed in sheets of 8 + label.

The Marriage of Poland and the Baltic Sea, by Wojciech Kossak (1856-1942) A1848

Perf. 11x11½ Syncopated
2020, Feb. 10   Litho.
4469 A1848 3.30z multi   1.75   .85

Recovery of Pomerania by troops of Gen. Józef Haller, cent.

SEMI-POSTAL STAMPS

Regular Issue of 1919 Surcharged in Violet

    a   b

1919, May 3		**Unwmk.**	*Imperf.*	
B1	A10(a)	5f + 5f grn	.40	.40
B2	A10(a)	10f + 5f red vio	.40	.55
B3	A10(a)	15f + 5f dp red	.40	.55
B4	A11(b)	25f + 5f ol grn	.40	.40
B5	A11(b)	50f + 5f bl grn	.40	.75

Perf. 11½

B6	A10(a)	5f + 5f grn	.30	.30
B7	A10(a)	10f + 5f red vio	.55	.30
B8	A10(a)	15f + 5f dp red	.30	.30
B9	A11(b)	25f + 5f ol grn	.30	.30
B10	A11(b)	50f + 5f bl grn	.40	.40
		Nos. B1-B10 (10)	3.85	4.50
		Set, never hinged	18.00	

First Polish Philatelic Exhibition. The surtax benefited the Polish White Cross Society.

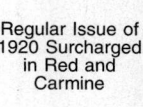

Regular Issue of 1920 Surcharged in Red and Carmine

1921, Mar. 5   *Perf. 9*

Thin Laid Paper

B11	A14	5m + 30m red vio	1.50	*8.50*
B12	A14	6m + 30m dp rose	1.50	*8.50*
B13	A14	10m + 30m lt red	3.00	*8.50*
B14	A14	20m + 30m gray grn	65.00	*120.00*
		Nos. B11-B14 (4)	71.00	145.50
		Set, never hinged	150.00	

Counterfeits, differently perforated, exist of Nos. B11-B14.

SP1

1925, Jan. 1   **Typo.**   *Perf. 12½*

B15	SP1	1g orange brn	4.50	26.00
B16	SP1	2g dk brown	4.50	26.00
B17	SP1	3g orange	4.50	26.00
B18	SP1	5g olive grn	4.50	26.00
B19	SP1	10g blue grn	4.50	26.00
B20	SP1	15g red	4.50	26.00
B21	SP1	20g blue	4.50	26.00
B22	SP1	25g red brown	4.50	26.00
B23	SP1	30g dp violet	4.50	26.00
B24	SP1	40g indigo	110.00	26.00
B25	SP1	50g magenta	4.50	26.00
		Nos. B15-B25 (11)	155.00	286.00
		Set, never hinged	325.00	

"Na Skarb" means "National Funds." These stamps were sold at a premium of 50 groszy each, for charity.

Light of Knowledge — SP2

1927, May 3   *Perf. 11½*

B26	SP2	10g + 5g choc & grn	6.25	7.00
B27	SP2	20g + 5g dk bl & buff	7.50	12.00
		Set, never hinged	40.00	

"NA OSWIATE" means "For Public Instruction." The surtax aided an Association of Educational Societies.

Torun Type of 1933

1933, May 21   **Engr.**

B28	A59	60g (+40g) red brn, buff	11.00	21.00
		Never hinged	30.00	

Philatelic Exhibition at Torun, May 21-28, 1933, and sold at a premium of 40g to aid the exhibition funds.

Souvenir Sheet

Stagecoach and Wayside Inn — SP3

1938, May 3   **Engr.**   *Imperf.*

B29	SP3	Sheet of 4	52.50	125.00
		Never hinged	125.00	
a.		45g green	5.25	8.75
b.		55g blue	5.25	8.75

Perf. 12

B29C	SP3	Sheet of 4	67.50	145.00
		Never hinged	150.00	
d.		45g green	6.50	10.00
e.		55g blue	6.50	10.00

5th Phil. Exhib., Warsaw, May 3-8. The sheets each contain two 45g and two 55g stamps. Sold for 3z.

Souvenir Sheet

Stratosphere Balloon over Mountains — SP4

1938, Sept. 15   *Perf. 12½*

B31	SP4	75g dp vio, sheet	40.00	65.00
		Never hinged	120.00	

Issued in advance of a proposed Polish stratosphere flight. Sold for 2z.

Winterhelp Issue

SP5

1938-39

B32	SP5	5g + 5g red org	.45	*.25*
B33	SP5	25g + 10g dk vio ('39)	.90	*.25*
B34	SP5	55g + 15g brt ultra ('39)	1.10	*3.75*
		Nos. B32-B34 (3)	2.45	4.25
		Set, never hinged	9.50	

For surcharges see Nos. N48-N50.

Souvenir Sheet

SP6

1939, Aug. 1

B35	SP6	Sheet of 3, dark blue gray	15.00	26.00
		Never hinged	40.00	
a.		25g Marshal Pilsudski Reviewing Troops	3.50	3.00
b.		25g Marshal Pilsudski	3.50	3.00
c.		25g Marshal Smigly-Rydz	3.50	3.00

25th anniv. of the founding of the Polish Legion. The sheets sold for 1.75z, the surtax going to the National Defense fund.

See types A64, A80, A99.

Polish People's Republic

Polish Warship SP7

Sailing Vessel — SP8   Polish Naval Ensign and Merchant Flag — SP9

Crane and Crane Tower, Gdansk SP10

1945, Apr. 24   **Typo.**   *Perf. 11*

B36	SP7	50g + 2z red	2.50	19.00
B37	SP8	1z + 3z dp bl	1.75	10.00
B38	SP9	2z + 4z dk car	1.50	10.00
B39	SP10	3z + 5z ol grn	1.50	13.00
		Nos. B36-B39 (4)	7.25	52.00
		Set, never hinged	20.00	

Polish Maritime League, 25th anniv.

City Hall, Poznan — SP11

1945, June 16   **Photo.**

B40	SP11	1z + 5z green	8.50	30.00
		Never hinged	20.00	

Postal Workers' Convention, Poznan, June 16, 1945. Exists imperf. Value, never hinged *$90.*

Last Stand at Westerplatte — SP12

1945, Sept. 1

B41	SP12	1z + 9z steel blue	7.00	27.50
		Never hinged	29.00	

Polish army's last stand at Westerplatte, Sept. 1, 1939. Exists imperf. Value, never hinged *$100.*

"United Industry" — SP13

1945, Nov. 18   **Unwmk.**   *Perf. 11*

B42	SP13	1.50z + 8.50z sl blk	2.00	10.00
		Never hinged	7.25	

Trade Unions Congress, Warsaw, Nov. 18. No. B42 exists imperf. Value, never hinged *$2,500.*

Polish Volunteers in Spain — SP14

1946, Mar. 10

B43	SP14	3z + 5z red	1.50	15.00
		Never hinged	3.50	

Participation of the Jaroslaw Dabrowski Brigade in the Spanish Civil War.

14th Century Piast Eagle and Soldiers — SP15

1946, May 2

B44	SP15	3z + 7z brn	.40	3.50
		Never hinged	1.10	

Silesian uprisings of 1919-21, 1939-45.

"Death" Spreading Poison Gas over Majdanek Prison Camp — SP16

1946, Apr. 29

B45	SP16	3z + 5z Prus grn	4.25	*16.00*
		Never hinged	9.25	

Issued to recall Majdanek, a concentration camp of World War II near Lublin.

Bydgoszcz
(Bromberg)
Canal — SP17

1946, Apr. 19   Unwmk.   Perf. 11
B46 SP17 3z + 2z ol blk   1.50 13.00
      Never hinged   3.25
600th anniv. of Bydgoszcz (Bromberg).

Map of Polish
Coast and
Baltic
Sea — SP18

1946, July 21
B47 SP18 5z + 7z dp bl   .70 11.00
      Never hinged   2.00
Maritime Holiday of 1946. The surtax was
for the Polish Maritime League.

Salute to P.T.T. Casualty and Views of
Gdansk — SP19

1946, Sept. 14
B48 SP19 3z + 12z slate   1.00 14.00
      Never hinged   2.25
Polish postal employees killed in the Ger-
man attack on Danzig (Gdansk), Sept. 1939.
No. B48 exists imperf. Value, never hinged
$160.

School
Children — SP20

Designs: 6z+24z, Courtyard of Jagiellon
University, Cracow. 11z+19z, Gregor
Piramowicz (1735-1801), founder of Education
Commission.

1946, Oct. 10   Unwmk.   Perf. 11½
B49   SP20 3z + 22z dk
                      red   16.50 65.00
B49A SP20 6z + 24z dk blk   16.50 65.00
B49B SP20 11z + 19z dk
                      grn   16.50 65.00
    c.   Souv. sheet of 3, #B49-
           B49B   210.00 575.00
           Never hinged   425.00
      Nos. B49-B49B (3)   49.50 195.00
      Never hinged   95.00
Polish educational work. Surtax was for
International Bureau of Education.
No. B49Bc sold for 100z.

Stanislaw Stojalowski, Jakob Bojko,
Jan Stapinski and Wincenty
Witos — SP21

1946, Dec. 1
B50 SP21 5z + 10z bl grn   .45 12.00
B51 SP21 5z + 10z dull blue   .50 12.00
B52 SP21 5z + 10z dk olive   .45 12.00
      Nos. B50-B52 (3)   1.40 36.00
      Set, never hinged   3.25
50th anniv. of the Peasant Movement. The
surtax was for education and cultural improvement among the Polish peasantry.

No. 391 Surcharged in Red

1947, Feb. 4   Perf. 11x10½
B53 A127 3z + 7z purple   3.50 22.50
      Never hinged   7.00
Opening of the Polish Parliament, 1/19/47.

**No. 344 Surcharged
in Blue**

1947, Feb. 21   Perf. 12½
B54 A103 5z + 15z on 25g   1.50   8.50
      Never hinged   3.25
Ski Championship Meet, Zakopane. Coun-
terfeits exist.

Emil Zegadlowicz — SP22

1947, Mar. 1   Photo.   Perf. 11
B55 SP22 5z + 15z dl gray grn 1.00 12.00
      Never hinged   2.25

Nurse and War
Victims — SP23

1947, June 1   Perf. 10½
B56 SP23 5z + 5z ol blk & red 1.75 10.00
      Never hinged   4.00
The surtax was for the Red Cross.

Adam Chmielowski
SP24

1947, Dec. 21   Perf. 11
B57 SP24 2z + 18z dk vio   .45   9.50
      Never hinged   1.10

Zamkowy
Square and
Proposed
Highway
SP25

1948, Nov. 1
B58 SP25 15z + 5z green   .40   1.10
The surtax was to aid in the reconstruction
of Warsaw.

Infant and TB
Crosses — SP26

Various Portraits of Children

1948, Dec. 16   Perf. 11½
B59 SP26 3z + 2z dl grn   1.75   5.00
B60 SP26 5z + 5z brn   1.40   3.50
B61 SP26 6z + 4z vio   .85   2.40
B62 SP26 15z + 10z car lake   .35   1.00
      Nos. B59-B62 (4)   4.35 11.90
      Set, never hinged   8.50
Alternate vertical rows of stamps ten
different labels. The surtax was for anti-tuber-
culosis work among children.

┌─────────────────────────────────┐
│ Catalogue values for unused   │
│ stamps in this section, from this │
│ point to the end of the section, are │
│ for Never Hinged items.   │
└─────────────────────────────────┘

Workers Party Type of 1952
Perf. 12½
1952, Jan. 18   Engr.   Unwmk.
B63 A195 45g + 15g Marceli
                      Nowotko   .25   .25

Women's Day Type of 1952
1952, Mar. 8   Perf. 12½x12
B64 A196 45g + 15g chocolate   .35   .35

Swierczewski-Walter Type of 1952
1952, Mar. 28   Perf. 12½
B65 A197 45g + 15g chocolate   .65   .30

Bierut Type of 1952
1952, Apr. 18
B66 A198 45g + 15g red   .70   .25
B67 A198 1.20z + 15g ultra   .70   .25

**Type of Regular Issue of 1951-52
Inscribed "Plan 6," etc.**
Design: 45g+15g, Electrical installation.

1952
B68   A193 30g + 15g brn red   .75   .25
B69   A193 45g + 15g choco-
                      late   1.15   .25
B69A A194 1.20z + 15g red org .55   .25
      Nos. B68-B69A (3)   2.45   .75

**Labor Day Type of Regular Issue of
1952**
1952, May 1
B70 A200 45g + 15g car rose   .50   .25

Similar to Regular Issue of 1952
No. B71, Maria Konopnicka. No. B72, Hugo
Kollataj.

1952, May   Different Frames
B71 A201 30g + 15g blue green .50   .60
B72 A201 45g + 15g brown   .35   .40
Issued: No. B71, May 10. No. B72, May 20.

Leonardo da
Vinci — SP28

1952, June 1
B73 SP28 30g + 15g ultra   1.10   .65
500th birth anniv. of Leonardo da Vinci.

Pres. Bierut and Children — SP29

1952, June 1   Photo.   Perf. 13½x14
B74 SP29 45g + 15g blue   2.50 1.20
Intl. Children's Day, June 1.

Sports Type
1952, June 21   Perf. 13
45g+15g, Soccer players and trophy.
B75 A203 30g + 15g blue   3.75 1.00
B76 A203 45g + 15g purple   1.25   .25

Yachts   "Dar Pomorza"
SP31   SP32

1952, June 28   Engr.   Perf. 12½
B77 SP31 30g + 15g dp bl grn   4.25 1.40
B78 SP32 45g + 15g dp ultra   2.25   .35
Shipbuilders' Day, 1952.

Workers on
Holiday — SP33

Students
SP34

1952, July 17   Perf. 12½x12, 12x12½
B79 SP33 30g + 15g dp grn   .50   .25
B80 SP34 45g + 15g red   .50   .25
Issued to publicize the Youth Festival, 1952.

Constitution Type of Regular Issue
1952, July 22   Photo.   Perf. 11
B81 A208 45g + 15g lt bl grn &
                      dk brn   2.75   .25

Power Plant Type of Regular Issue
1952, Aug. 7   Engr.   Perf. 12½
B82 A209 45g + 15g red   .75   .25

Ludwik Warynski
SP36

1952, July 31
B83 SP36 30g + 15g dk red .45 .25
B84 SP36 45g + 15g blk brn 1.15 .40
70th birth anniv. of Ludwik Warynski, political organizer.

Church of Frydman — SP37

1952, Aug. 18
B85 SP37 45g + 15g vio brn 1.60 1.20

Aviator Watching Glider — SP38

Design: 45g+15g, Pilot entering plane.

1952, Aug. 23
B86 SP38 30g + 15g grn 1.75 .85
B87 SP38 45g + 15g brn red 3.75 .50
Aviation Day, Aug. 23.

Henryk Sienkiewicz — SP39

1952, Oct. 25
B88 SP39 45g + 15g vio brn 1.00 .40
Henryk Sienkiewicz (1846-1916), author of "Quo Vadis" and other novels, Nobel prizewinner (literature, 1905).

Revolution Type of Regular Issue
1952, Nov. 7   Perf. 12x12½
B92 A214 45g + 15g red brn 1.50 .25
Exists imperforate. See No. 562.

Lenin — SP42

1952, Nov. 7   Perf. 12½
B93 SP42 30g + 15g vio brn .70 .60
B94 SP42 45g + 15g brn 1.10 .25
a. "LENIN" omitted 32.50
Month of Polish-Soviet friendship, Nov. 1952.

Miner — SP43

1952, Dec. 4
B95 SP43 45g + 15g blk brn .80 .25
B96 SP43 1.20z + 15g brn 1.20 .60
Miners' Day, Dec. 4.

Henryk Wieniawski and Violin — SP44

1952, Dec. 5   Photo.
B97 SP44 30g + 15g dk grn 1.50 .85
B98 SP44 45g + 15g purple 1.50 .40
Henryk Wieniawski; 2nd Intl. Violin Competition.

Type of Regular Issue of 1952
1952, Dec. 12   Engr.
B99 A215 45g + 15g dp grn .35 .25

Truck Factory, Lublin — SP45

1953, Feb. 20
B100 SP45 30g + 15g dp bl 1.40 .60
B101 SP45 60g + 20g vio brn .35 .25

Souvenir Sheet

Town Hall in Poznan — SP46

Photo. & Litho.
1955, July 7   Imperf.
B102 SP46 2z pck grn & ol grn 1.75 1.40
B103 SP46 3z car rose & ol blk 24.00 14.00
6th Polish Philatelic Exhibition in Poznan. Sheets sold for 3z and 4.50z respectively.

Souvenir Sheet

"Peace" (POKOJ) and Warsaw Mermaid — SP47

Design: 1z, Pansies (A266) and inscription on map of Europe, Africa and Asia.

1955, Aug. 3
B104 SP47 1z bis, rose vio & yel 1.75 .75
B105 SP47 2z ol gray, ultra & lt bl 20.00 9.50
Intl. Phil. Exhib., Warsaw, Aug. 1-14, 1955. Sheets sold for 2z and 3z respectively.

Souvenir Sheet

Chopin and Liszt — SP48

1956, Oct. 25   Photo.   Imperf.
B106 SP48 4z dk blue grn 27.50 16.00
Day of the Stamp; Polish-Hungarian friendship. The sheet sold for 6z.

Souvenir Sheet

Stamp of 1860 — SP49

Wmk. 326
1960, Sept. 4   Litho.   Perf. 11
B107 SP49 Sheet of 4 50.00 42.50
a. 10z + 10z blue, red & black 9.00 9.00
Intl. Phil. Exhib. "POLSKA 60," Warsaw, 9/3-11.
Sold only with 5z ticket to exhibition.

Type of Space Issue, 1964
Design: Yuri A. Gagarin in space capsule.

Perf. 12½x12
1964, Dec. 30   Unwmk.
B108 A432 6.50z + 2z Prus grn & multi 1.25 .45

Souvenir Sheet

Jules Rimet Cup and Flags of Participating Countries — SP50

1966, May 9   Litho.   Imperf.
B109 SP50 13.50z + 1.50z multi 2.00 1.00
World Cup Soccer Championship, Wembley, England, July 11-30.

Souvenir Sheet

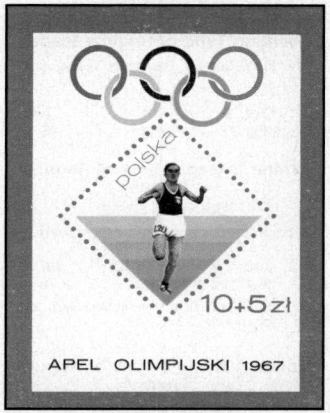

J. Kusocinski, Olympic Winner 10,000-Meter Race, 1932 — SP51

1967, May 24   Litho.   Imperf.
B110 SP51 10z + 5z multi 1.50 .80
19th Olympic Games, Mexico City, 1968. Simulated perforations.

Flower Type of Regular Issue
Flowers: 4z+2z, Abutilon. 8z+4z, Rosa polyantha hybr.

1968, May 15   Litho.   Perf. 11½
B111 A492 4z + 2z vio & multi .85 .30
B112 A492 8z + 4z lt vio & multi 1.40 .40

Olympic Type of Regular Issue, 1968
Design: 10z+5z, Runner with Olympic torch and Chin cultic carved stone disc showing Mayan ball player and game's scoreboard.

1968, Sept. 2   Litho.   Perf. 11½
Size: 56x45mm
B113 A497 10z + 5z multi 1.50 .40
19th Olympic Games, Mexico City, Oct. 12-27. The surtax was for the Polish Olympic Committee.

Olympic Type of Regular Issue, 1969
Olympic Rings and: 2.50z+50g, Women's discus. 3.40z+1z, Running. 4z+1.50z, Boxing. 7z+2z, Fencing.

1969, Apr. 25   Litho.   Perf. 11½x11
B114 A505 2.50z + 50g multi .25 .25
B115 A505 3.40z + 1z multi .25 .25
B116 A505 4z + 1.50z multi .50 .25
B117 A505 7z + 2z multi 1.00 .35
Nos. B114-B117 (4) 2.00 1.10

Folk Art Type of Regular Issue

5.50z+1.50z, Choir. 7z+1.50z, Organ grinder.

1969, Dec. 19   Litho.   Perf. 11½x11
Size: 24x36mm
B118 A520 5.50z + 1.50z multi   .50 .25
B119 A520 7z + 1.50z multi   .65 .25

Sports Type of Regular Issue
Souvenir Sheet

Design: "Horse of Glory," by Z. Kaminski.

1970, June 16   Photo.   Imperf.
B120 A532 10z + 5z multi   1.50 .75
The surtax was for the Polish Olympic Committee. No. B120 contains one imperf. stamp with simulated perforations.

Tapestry Type of Regular Issue
Souvenir Sheet

Design: 7z+3z, Satyrs holding monogram of King Sigismund Augustus.

1970, Dec. 23   Photo.   Imperf.
B121 A541 7z + 3z multi   1.40 .75

Type of Regular Issue

Design: 8.50z+4z, Virgin Mary, 15th century stained glass window.

1971, Sept. 15   Perf. 11½x11
B122 A555 8.50z + 4z multi   .75 .35

Painting Type of Regular Issue

7z+1z, Nude, by Wojciech Weiss (1875-1950).

1971, Oct. 9   Litho.
B123 A556 7z + 1z multi   .85 .60

Winter Olympic Type of Regular Issue
Souvenir Sheet

Slalom and Sapporo '72 emblem, vert.

1972, Jan. 12   Photo.   Imperf.
B124 A564 10z + 5z multi   2.25 1.00
No. B124 contains one stamp with simulated perforations, 27x52mm.

Summer Olympic Type of Regular Issue
Souvenir Sheet

Design: 10z+5z, Archery (like 30g).

1972, May 20   Photo.   Perf. 11½x11
B125 A568 10z + 5z multi   1.50 .75

Painting Type of Regular Issue, 1972

Design: 8.50z+4z, Portrait of a Young Lady, by Jacek Malczewski, horiz.

1972, Sept. 28   Photo.   Perf. 11x10½
B126 A576 8.50z + 4z multi   1.40 .55

Souvenir Sheet

Copernicus — SP52

Engraved and Photogravure
1972, Sept. 28   Perf. 11½
B127 SP52 10z + 5z vio bl, gray
& car   1.75 .80
Nicolaus Copernicus (1473-1543), astronomer. No. B127 shows the Ptolemaic and Copernican concepts of solar system from L'Harmonica Microcosmica, by Cellarius, 1660.

Souvenir Sheet

Poznan, 1740, by F. B. Werner — SP53

1973, Aug. 19   Imperf.
B128 SP53 10z + 5z ol & dk brn   1.00 .60
a.   10z + 5z pale lilac & dk brn   5.00 5.25
POLSKA 73 Intl. Phil. Exhib., Poznan, Aug. 19-Sept. 2. No. B128 contains one stamp with simulated perforations.
No. B128a was sold only in combination with an entrance ticket.

Copernicus, by Marcello Bacciarelli — SP54

1973, Sept. 27   Photo.   Perf. 11x11½
B129 SP54 4z + 2z multi   .40 .25
Stamp Day. The surtax was for the reconstruction of the Royal Castle in Warsaw.

Souvenir Sheet

Montreal Olympic Games Emblem — SP55

Photo. & Engr.
1975, Mar. 8   Perf. 12
B130 SP55 10z + 5z sil & grn   1.75 .65
21st Olympic Games, Montreal, July 17-Aug. 8, 1976.
Outer edge of souvenir sheet is perforated.

Dunikowski Type of 1975

Design: 8z+4z, Mother and Child, from Silesian Insurrectionist Monument, by Dunikowski.

1975, Oct. 9   Photo.   Perf. 11½x11
B131 A644 8z + 4z multi   .50 .25

Souvenir Sheet

Volleyball — SP56

Engraved and Photogravure
1976, June 30   Perf. 11½
B132 SP56 10z + 5z blk & car   1.50 .75
21st Olympic Games, Montreal, Canada, July 17-Aug. 1. No. B132 contains one perf. 11½ stamp and is perf. 11½ all around.

Corinthian Art Type 1976

Design: 8z+4z, Winged Sphinx, vert.

1976, Oct. 30   Photo.   Perf. 11½x11
B133 A664 8z + 4z multi   .80 .30

Souvenir Sheet

Stoning of St. Stephen, by Rubens — SP57

1977, Apr. 30   Engr.   Perf. 12x11½
B134 SP57 8z + 4z sepia   1.00 .40
Peter Paul Rubens (1577-1640), Flemish painter.
Outer edge of souvenir sheet is perforated.

Souvenir Sheet

Kazimierz Gzowski — SP58

1978, June 6   Photo.   Perf. 11½x11
B135 SP58 8.40z + 4z multi   1.10 .60
CAPEX, '78 Canadian Intl. Phil. Exhib., Toronto, June 9-18.
K. S. Gzowski (1813-1898), Polish engineer and lawyer living in Canada, built International Bridge over Niagara River.

Souvenir Sheet

Olympic Rings — SP59

1979, May 19   Engr.   Imperf.
B136 SP59 10z + 5z black   .90 .65
1980 Olympic Games.

Monument Type of 1979
Souvenir Sheet

1979, Sept. 1   Photo.   Imperf.
B137 A731 10z + 5z multi   1.00 .60
Surtax was for monument.

Summer Olympic Type of 1980
Souvenir Sheet

1980, Mar. 31   Photo.   Perf. 11x11½
B138 A742 10.50z + 5z Kayak   1.00 .60
No. B138 contains one stamp 42x30mm.

Souvenir Sheet

Intercosmos Cooperative Space Program — SP60

1980, Apr. 12   Perf. 11½x11
B139 SP60 6.90z + 3z multi   .80 .60

SP61

1970 Uprising Memorial: 2.50z + 1z, Triple Crucifix, Gdansk (27x46mm). 6.50z + 1z, Monument, Gdynia.

1981, Dec. 16   Photo.   Perf. 11½x12
B140 SP61 2.50 + 1z blk & red   .35 .25
B141 SP61 6.50 + 1z blk & lil   .40 .25

SP62

Portrait of a German Princess, by Lucas Cranach.

1984, May 15 Photo. Perf. 11½x12
B142 SP62 27z + 10z multi   1.25 1.00

1984 UPU Congress, Hamburg. No. B142 issued se-tenant with multicolored label showing UPU emblem and text.

Souvenir Sheet

Madonna with Child, St. John and the Angel, by Sandro Botticelli (1445-1510), Natl. Museum, Warsaw — SP63

1985, Sept. 25 Photo. Perf. 11
B143 SP63 65z + 15z multi   2.25 1.25
 a. Inscribed: 35 LAT POL-
      SKIEGO . . .   5.00 5.00

ITALIA '85. Surtax for Polish Association of Philatelists.
No. B143a was for the 35th anniv. of the Polish Philatelic Union. Distribution was limited.

Joachim Lelewel (1786-1861), Historian — SP64

1986, Dec. 22 Photo. Perf. 11½x12
B144 SP64 10z + 5z multi   .40 .25

Surtax for the Natl. Committee for School Aid.

Polish Immigrant Settling in Kasubia, Ontario — SP65

1987, June 13 Photo. Perf. 12x11½
B145 SP65 50z + 20z multi   .75 .30

CAPEX '87, Toronto, Canada. Surtaxed for the Polish Philatelists' Union.

Souvenir Sheet

OLYMPHILEX '87, Rome — SP66

1987, Aug. 28 Litho. Perf. 14
B146 SP66 45z + 10z like #2617 1.10 1.10

FINLANDIA '88 — SP67

1988, June 1 Photo. Perf. 12x11½
B147 SP67 45z +20z Salmon,
         reindeer   .75 .30

Souvenir Sheet

Jerzy Kukuczka, Mountain Climber Awarded Medal by the Intl. Olympic Committee for Climbing the Himalayas — SP68

1988, Aug. 17 Photo. Perf. 11x11½
B148 SP68 70z +10z multi   1.00 .65

Surtax for the Polish Olympic Fund.

Aid for Victims of 1997 Oder River Flood — SP69

1997, Aug. 18 Photo. Perf. 11½x12
B149 SP69 60g +30g multi   .65 .40

Souvenir Sheet

Museum of Posts and Telecommunications, 80th Anniv. — SP70

2001, Oct. 9 Photo. Perf. 11¼x11½
B150 SP70 3z +75g multi   2.40 1.25

AIR POST STAMPS

Biplane — AP1

Perf. 12½

1925, Sept. 10 Typo. Unwmk.
C1 AP1 1g lt blue   .65 9.00
C2 AP1 2g orange   .65 9.00
C3 AP1 3g yellow brn   .65 9.00
C4 AP1 5g dk brown   .65 .80
C5 AP1 10g dk green   .65 .80
C6 AP1 15g red violet 3.25 .80
C7 AP1 20g olive grn   7.50 4.00

C8 AP1 30g dull rose   7.50 2.25
C9 AP1 45g dk violet   8.50 3.75
  Nos. C1-C9 (9)   30.00 39.40
  Set, never hinged   95.00

Counterfeits exist.
Nos. C1-C9 exist imperf. Value, set $125.
For overprint see No. C11.

Capt. Franciszek Zwirko and Stanislaus Wigura — AP2

Perf. 11½ to 12½ and Compound
1933, Apr. 15 Engr. Wmk. 234
C10 AP2 30g gray green   16.50 1.40
     Never hinged   47.50

Winning of the circuit of Europe flight by two Polish aviators in 1932. The stamp was available for both air mail and ordinary postage.
For overprint see No. C12.

Nos. C7 and C10 Ovptd. in Red

1934, Aug. 28 Unwmk. Perf. 12½
C11 AP1 20g olive green   7.75 7.00

Wmk. 234
Perf. 11½
C12 AP2 30g gray green   8.75 2.00
  Set, never hinged   45.00

Polish People's Republic

Douglas Plane over Ruins of Warsaw — AP3

Unwmk.
1946, Mar. 5 Photo. Perf. 11
C13 AP3 5z grnsh blk   .35 .25
 a. Without control number 5.75 1.20
      Never hinged   11.00
C14 AP3 10z dk violet   .35 .25
C15 AP3 15z blue   1.15 .25
C16 AP3 20z rose brn   .70 .25
C17 AP3 25z dk bl grn   1.50 .40
C18 AP3 30z red   2.25 .55
     Nos. C13-C18 (6)   6.30 1.95
  Set, never hinged   13.50

The 10z, 20z and 30z were issued only with control number in lower right stamp margin. The 15z and 25z exist only without number. The 5z comes both ways.
Nos. C13-C18 exist imperforate. Value, set $125.

Nos. 345, 344 and 344a Surcharged in Red or Black

a   b

1947, Sept. 10 Perf. 12½
C19 A104(a) 40z on 50g (R)   1.75 1.50
C20 A103(b) 50z on 25g dl red 2.25 2.50
 a. 50z on 25g deep red   3.00 2.75
      Never hinged, #C20a   4.50 2.25
  Set, never hinged   9.00

Counterfeits exist.

Centaur AP4

1948 Perf. 11
C21 AP4 15z dk violet   1.50 .25
C22 AP4 25z deep blue   .80 .25
C23 AP4 30z brown   .65 .25
C24 AP4 50z dk green   1.25 .25
C25 AP4 75z gray black   1.50 .25
C26 AP4 100z red orange   1.50 .25
     Nos. C21-C26 (6)   7.20 1.50
  Set, never hinged   15.00

Nos. C21-C26 exist imperf.

Pres. F. D. Roosevelt AP5

100z, Casimir Pulaski. 120z, Tadeusz Kosciusko.

1948, Dec. 30 Photo. Perf. 11½
Granite Paper
C26A AP5 80z blue blk   13.00 27.00
C26B AP5 100z purple   14.00 27.00
C26C AP5 120z deep blue   14.00 27.00
  d.   Souvenir sheet of 3 210.00 300.00
        Never hinged   325.00
     Nos. C26A-C26C (3)   41.00 81.00
  Set, never hinged   67.50

Nos. C26A-C26C were issued in panes containing 16 stamps and 4 labels. Value, never hinged set of three with labels $140.
No. C26Cd contains stamps similar to Nos. C26A-C26C with colors changed: 80z ultramarine, 100z carmine rose, 120z dark green. Sold for 500z.

Airplane Mechanic and Propeller — AP5a

1950, Feb. 6 Engr. Perf. 12½
C27 AP5a 500z rose lake   3.75 6.50
     Never hinged   6.00

> **Catalogue values for unused stamps in this section, from this point to the end of the section, are for Never Hinged items.**

Seaport AP6

Designs: 90g, Mechanized farm. 1.40z, Warsaw. 5z, Steel mill.

1952, Apr. 10 Perf. 12x12½
C28 AP6 55g intense blue   1.00 .25
C29 AP6 90g dull green   1.25 .35
C30 AP6 1.40z violet brn   1.10 .25
C31 AP6 5z gray black   1.25 .35
     Nos. C28-C31 (4)   4.60 1.20

Nos. C28-C31 exist imperf. Value $29.

Congress Badge — AP7

1953, Aug. 24   Photo.   *Imperf.*

C32	AP7	55g brown lilac	1.75	.35
C33	AP7	75g brown org	3.00	1.40

3rd World Congress of Students, Warsaw 1953.

Souvenir Sheet

AP8

1954, May 23   Engr.   *Perf. 12x12½*

C34	AP8	5z gray green	40.00 25.00

3rd congress of the Polish Phil. Assoc., Warsaw, 1954. Sold for 7.50 zlotys. A similar sheet, imperf. and in dark blue, was issued but had no postal validity. Value: mint $275; cto $275.

Paczkow Castle, Luban — AP9

80g, Kazimierz Dolny. 1.15z, Wawel castle, Cracow. 1.50z, City Hall, Wroclaw. 1.55z, Lazienki Park, Warsaw. 1.95z, Cracow gate, Lublin.

1954, July 13   *Perf. 12½*

C35	AP9	60g dk gray grn	.60	.25
C36	AP9	80g red	.60	.25
C37	AP9	1.15z black	3.75	1.25
C38	AP9	1.50z rose lake	.60	.25
C39	AP9	1.55z dp gray bl	.60	.25
C40	AP9	1.95z chocolate	1.75	.85
		Nos. C35-C40 (6)	7.90	3.10

Plane over "Peace" Steelworks — AP10

Plane over: 1.50z, Castle Square, Warsaw. 3.40z, Old Market, Cracow. 3.90z, King Boleslaw Chrobry Wall, Szczecin. 4z, Karkonosze mountains. 5z, Gdansk. 10z, Ruins of Liwa Castle. 15z, Old City, Lublin. 20z, Kasprowy Wierch Peak and cable car. 30z, Porabka dam. 50z, M. S. Batory and Gdynia harbor.

Wmk. 326 ('58 Values); Unwmkd.

1957-58   Engr. & Photo.   *Perf. 12½*

C41	AP10	90g black & pink	.35	.25
C42	AP10	1.50z brn & salmon	.35	.25
C43	AP10	3.40z sep & buff	.35	.25
C44	AP10	3.90z dk brn & cit	.35	.25
C45	AP10	4z ind & lt grn	.35	.25
C46	AP10	5z maroon & gray	.75	.25
C47	AP10	10z sepia & grn	1.40	.25
C48	AP10	15z vio bl & pale bl	1.40	.70
C49	AP10	20z vio blk & lem	1.50	.70

C50	AP10	30z ol gray & bis	4.25	3.25
C51	AP10	50z dk bl & gray	10.00	4.50
		Nos. C41-C51 (11)	21.05	10.90

Issue dates: 5z, 10z, 20z, 30z, 50z, Dec. 15, 1958. Others, Dec. 6, 1957.

1959, May 23   Litho.   Wmk. 326

C52	AP10	10z sepia	2.00	1.75
a.		With 5z label	3.50	3.50

65th anniv. of the Polish Philatelic Society. Sheet of 6 stamps and 2 each of 3 different labels. Each label carries an added charge of 5z for a fund to build a Society clubhouse in Warsaw.

Jantar Glider — AP11

Contemporary aviation: 10z, Mi6 transport helicopter. 20z, PZL-106 Kruk, crop spraying plane. 50z, Plane over Warsaw Castle.

1976-78   Unwmk.   Engr.   *Perf. 11½*

C53	AP11	5z dk blue grn	.45	.30
C54	AP11	10z dk brown	.95	.60
C55	AP11	20z grnsh black	1.60	.30
C56	AP11	50z claret	2.75	.65
		Nos. C53-C56 (4)	5.75	1.85

Issued: 5z, 10z, 3/27/76; 20z, 2/15/77; 50z, 2/2/78.

AIR POST SEMI-POSTAL STAMP

> **Catalogue values for unused stamps in this section are for Never Hinged items.**

Polish People's Republic

Wing of Jet Plane and Letter — SPAP1

Perf. 11½

1957, Mar. 28   Unwmk.   Photo.

CB1	SPAP1	4z + 2z blue	2.75	2.75
a.		Souv. sheet of 1, ultra, imperf.	10.00	5.00

7th Polish National Philatelic Exhibition, Warsaw. Sheet of 12 with 4 diagonally arranged gray labels.

REGISTRATION STAMPS

Insects — R1

Designs: (3.80z), Polyommatus semiargus. (5.90z), Rosalia alpina. (6.70z), Gerris paludum. (9.30z), Sympetrum flaveolum.

Perf. 11¾x11½

2013, Aug. 16   Photo.

F1	R1	(3.80z) multi	2.40	2.40
F2	R1	(5.90z) multi	3.75	3.75
F3	R1	(6.70z) multi	4.25	4.25
F4	R1	(9.30z) multi	6.00	6.00
		Nos. F1-F4 (4)	16.40	16.40

Insects — R2

Designs: (5.90z), Coccinella septempunctata. (6.70z), Chorthippus parallelus. (6.95z), Inachis io. (9.30z), Formica rufa.

Perf. 11¾x11½

2013, Sept. 30   Photo.

F5	R2	(5.90z) multi	4.00	4.00
F6	R2	(6.70z) multi	4.50	4.50
F7	R2	(6.95z) multi	4.50	4.50
F8	R2	(9.30z) multi	6.00	6.00
		Nos. F5-F8 (4)	19.00	19.00

Insects — R3

Designs: (8.50z), Arctia caja. (9.50z), Papilio machaon caterpillar. (11z), Apis mellifera. (13.10z), Lucanus cervus.

Perf. 11¾x11½

2013, Oct. 18   Photo.

F9	R3	(8.50z) multi	5.50	5.50
F10	R3	(9.50z) multi	6.00	6.00
F11	R3	(11z) multi	7.00	7.00
F12	R3	(13.10z) multi	8.50	8.50
		Nos. F9-F12 (4)	27.00	27.00

POSTAGE DUE STAMPS

Cracow Issues

Postage Due Stamps of Austria, 1916, Overprinted in Black or Red

1919, Jan. 10   Unwmk.   *Perf. 12½*

J1	D4	5h rose red	15.50	15.50
J2	D4	10h rose red	4,000.	6,500.
J3	D4	15h rose red	10.50	9.00
a.		Inverted overprint	7,750.	2,250.
J4	D4	20h rose red	650.00	525.00
J5	D4	25h rose red	32.50	35.00
J6	D4	30h rose red	1,600.	1,200.
J7	D4	40h rose red	300.00	300.00
J8	D5	1k ultra (R)	4,250.	4,750.
J9	D5	5k ultra (R)	4,250.	4,750.
J10	D5	10k ultra (R)	17,000.	20,000.
a.		Black overprint	65,000.	77,500.

Overprint on Nos. J1-J7, J10a is type. Overprint on Nos. J8-J10 is slightly larger than illustration, has a different ornament between lines of type and is litho.

Austria Nos. J61 and J63 Surcharged in Black

1919, Jan. 10

J11	A38	15h on 36h vio	525.00	325.00
J12	A38	50h on 42h choc	65.00	37.50
a.		Double surcharge	2,750.	4,250.

> **See note above No. 41. Counterfeits exist of Nos. J1-J12.**

Regular Issues

Numerals of Value — D7

1919   Typo.   *Perf. 11½*

For Northern Poland

J13	D7	2f red orange	.25	.25
J14	D7	4f red orange	.25	.25
J15	D7	5f red orange	.25	.25
J16	D7	10f red orange	.25	.25
J17	D7	20f red orange	.25	.25
J18	D7	30f red orange	.25	.25
J19	D7	50f red orange	.25	.25
J20	D7	100f red orange	.50	.35
J21	D7	500f red orange	2.50	2.40

For Southern Poland

J22	D7	2h dark blue	.25	.25
J23	D7	4h dark blue	.25	.25
J24	D7	5h dark blue	.25	.25
J25	D7	10h dark blue	.25	.25
J26	D7	20h dark blue	.25	.25
J27	D7	30h dark blue	.25	.25
J28	D7	50h dark blue	.35	.25
J29	D7	100h dark blue	.45	.80
J30	D7	500h dark blue	1.40	1.60
		Nos. J13-J30 (18)	8.45	8.65
		Set, never hinged	33.00	

Counterfeits exist.

1920   *Perf. 9, 10, 11½*

Thin Laid Paper

J31	D7	20f dark blue	.25	.25
J32	D7	100f dark blue	.25	.25
J33	D7	200f dark blue	.35	.25
J34	D7	500f dark blue	.35	.25
		Nos. J31-J34 (4)	1.20	1.00
		Set, never hinged	4.25	

Regular Issue of 1919 Surcharged

1921, Jan. 25   *Imperf.*

Wove Paper

J35	A9	6m on 15h brown	.75	.75
J36	A9	6m on 25h car	.75	.75
J37	A9	20m on 10h lake	5.00	7.00
J38	A9	20m on 50h indigo	4.00	5.25
J39	A9	35m on 70h dp bl	7.00	9.25
		Nos. J35-J39 (5)	17.50	23.00
		Set, never hinged	21.00	

Counterfeits exist.

Numerals of Value — D8

Thin Laid or Wove Paper
Size: 17x22mm

Perf. 9 to 14½ and Compound

1921-22   Typo.

J40	D8	1m indigo	.25	.25
J41	D8	2m indigo	.25	.25
J42	D8	4m indigo	.25	.25
J43	D8	6m indigo	.45	.25
J44	D8	8m indigo	.45	.25
J45	D8	20m indigo	.45	.25
J46	D8	50m indigo	.45	.25
J47	D8	100m indigo	.70	.35
		Nos. J40-J47 (8)	3.25	2.10
		Set, never hinged	13.00	

Nos. J44-J45, J41 Surcharged
Perf. 9 to 14½ and Compound

1923, Nov.

J48	D8	10,000(m) on 8m indigo	.35	.25
J49	D8	20,000(m) on 20m indigo	.35	.25
J50	D8	50,000(m) on 2m indigo	.45	.45
		Nos. J48-J50 (3)	1.15	.95
		Set, never hinged	5.75	

Type of 1921-22 Issue
Size: 19x24mm

1923   Typo.   *Perf. 12½*

J51	D8	50m indigo	.25	.25
J52	D8	100m indigo	.25	.25
J53	D8	200m indigo	.25	.25
J54	D8	500m indigo	.60	.25
J55	D8	1000m indigo	.35	.25
J56	D8	2000m indigo	.40	.30
J57	D8	10,000m indigo	.25	.25
J58	D8	20,000m indigo	.35	.25
J59	D8	30,000m indigo	.35	.25
J60	D8	50,000m indigo	.35	.25

J61	D8	100,000m indigo	.40	.25
J62	D8	200,000m indigo	.40	.25
J63	D8	300,000m indigo	5.00	.35
J64	D8	500,000m indigo	1.75	.35
J65	D8	1,000,000m indigo	1.00	.30
J66	D8	2,000,000m indigo	1.75	.35
J67	D8	3,000,000m indigo	3.00	1.40
		Nos. J51-J67 (17)	16.70	5.70
		Set, never hinged	67.50	

D9

Perf. 10 to 13½ and Compound
1924 Size: 20x25½mm

J68	D9	1g brown	.25	.25
J69	D9	2g brown	.25	.25
J70	D9	4g brown	.30	.25
J71	D9	6g brown	.30	.25
J72	D9	10g brown	1.25	.25
J73	D9	15g brown	4.50	.25
J74	D9	20g brown	3.25	.25
J75	D9	25g brown	6.25	.25
J76	D9	30g brown	.75	.25
J77	D9	40g brown	1.00	.25
J78	D9	50g brown	1.00	.25
J79	D9	1z brown	.45	.25
J80	D9	2z brown	.45	.25
J81	D9	3z brown	.75	1.50
J82	D9	5z brown	.40	.60
		Nos. J68-J82 (15)	21.15	5.35
		Set, never hinged	92.50	

Nos. J68-J69 and J72-J75 exist measuring 19½x24½mm.
For surcharges see Nos. J84-J91.

D10

1930, July *Perf. 12½*

J83	D10	5g olive brown	.70	.25
		Never hinged	1.00	

Postage Due
Stamps of 1924
Surcharged

Perf. 10 to 13½ and Compound
1934-38

J84	D9	10g on 2z brown ('38)	.25	.25
J85	D9	15g on 2z brown	.25	.25
J86	D9	20g on 1z brown	.40	.25
J87	D9	20g on 5z brown	6.00	.25
J88	D9	25g on 40g brown	.85	.25
J89	D9	30g on 40g brown	1.40	.25
J90	D9	50g on 40g brown	1.40	.50
J91	D9	50g on 3z brown ('35)	.85	.35
		Nos. J84-J91 (8)	11.40	2.35
		Set, never hinged	52.50	

No. 255a
Surcharged in Red
or Indigo

1934-36 Laid Paper

J92	A50	10g on 1z (R) ('36)	.80	.25
a.		Vertically laid paper (No. 255)	25.00	18.00
J93	A50	20g on 1z (R) ('36)	2.50	.80
J94	A50	25g on 1z (I)	.80	.30
a.		Vertically laid paper (No. 255)	30.00	18.00
		Nos. J92-J94 (3)	4.10	1.35
		Set, never hinged	13.00	

D11

1938-39 Typo. *Perf. 12½x12*

J95	D11	5g dark blue green	.25	.25
J96	D11	10g dark blue green	.25	.25
J97	D11	15g dark blue green	.25	.25
J98	D11	20g dark blue green	.35	.25
J99	D11	25g dark blue green	.35	.25
J100	D11	30g dark blue green	.60	.25
J101	D11	50g dark blue green	.95	.25
J102	D11	1z dark blue green	5.00	1.65
		Nos. J95-J102 (8)	8.00	3.40
		Set, never hinged	14.00	

For surcharges see Nos. N51-N55.

Polish People's Republic

Post Horn with
Thunderbolts
D12

Size: 26½x19½mm

Perf. 11x10½
1945, May 20 Litho. Unwmk.

J103	D12	1z orange brown	.25	.25
J104	D12	2z orange brown	.25	.25
J105	D12	3z orange brown	.25	.25
J106	D12	5z orange brown	.35	.30
		Nos. J103-J106 (4)	1.10	1.05
		Set, never hinged	3.25	

Nos. J103-J106 exist imperf. Value, set $40.

Type of 1945
Perf. 11, 11½ (P) or Imperf. (I)
1946-49 Size: 29x21½mm Photo.

J106A	D12	1z org brn (P) ('49)	.25	.25
J107	D12	2z org brn (P,I)	.25	.25
J108	D12	3z org brn (P,I)	.25	.25
J109	D12	5z org brn (I)	.25	.25
J110	D12	6z org brn (I)	.25	.25
J111	D12	10z org brn (I)	.25	.25
J112	D12	15z org brn (P,I)	.55	.30
J113	D12	25z org brn (P,I)	.75	.60
J114	D12	100z brn (P) ('49)	1.50	.90
J115	D12	150z brn (P) ('49)	2.00	1.00
		Nos. J106A-J115 (10)	6.30	4.30
		Set, never hinged	8.00	

Polish Eagle — D13

1950 Engr. *Perf. 12x12½*

J116	D13	5z red brown	.25	.25
J117	D13	10z red brown	.25	.25
J118	D13	15z red brown	.25	.25
J119	D13	20z red brown	.25	.25
J120	D13	25z red brown	.25	.25
J121	D13	50z red brown	.50	.30
J122	D13	100z red brown	.50	.35
		Nos. J116-J122 (7)	2.25	1.90
		Set, never hinged	3.00	

1951-52

J123	D13	5g red brown	.25	.25
J124	D13	10g red brown	.25	.25
J125	D13	15g red brown	.25	.25
J126	D13	20g red brown	.25	.25
J127	D13	25g red brown	.25	.25
J128	D13	30g red brown	.25	.25
J129	D13	50g red brown	.25	.25
J130	D13	60g red brown	.25	.25
J131	D13	90g red brown	.50	.45
J132	D13	1z red brown	.25	.25
J133	D13	2z red brown	.25	.25
J134	D13	5z brown violet	.60	.60
		Nos. J123-J134 (12)	3.60	3.55
		Set, never hinged	4.00	

Without imprint

1953, Apr. Photo.

J135	D13	5g red brown	.25	.25
J136	D13	10g red brown	.25	.25
J137	D13	15g red brown	.25	.25
J138	D13	20g red brown	.25	.25
J139	D13	25g red brown	.25	.25
J140	D13	30g red brown	.25	.25
J141	D13	50g red brown	.25	.25
J142	D13	60g red brown	.25	.25
J143	D13	90g red brown	.30	.25

J144	D13	1z red brown	.25	.25
J145	D13	2z red brown	.55	.55
		Nos. J135-J145 (11)	3.20	3.05
		Set, never hinged	3.50	

> Catalogue values for unused stamps in this section, from this point to the end of the section, are for Never Hinged items.

1980, Sept. 2 Litho. *Perf. 12½*

J146	D13	1z lt red brown	.25	.25
J147	D13	2z gray olive	.25	.25
J148	D13	3z dull violet	.25	.25
J149	D13	5z brown	.40	.25
		Nos. J146-J149 (4)	1.15	1.00

D14

1998, June 18 Litho. *Perf. 14*

J150	D14	5g lilac, blk & yel	.25	.25
J151	D14	10g green blue, blk & yel	.25	.25
J152	D14	20g green, blk & yel	.25	.25
J153	D14	50g yellow & black	.30	.30
J154	D14	80g orange, blk & yel	.40	.45
J155	D14	1z red, blk & yel	.60	.70
		Nos. J150-J155 (6)	2.05	2.20

OFFICIAL STAMPS

O1

Perf. 10, 11½, 10x11½, 11½x10
1920, Feb. 1 Litho. Unwmk.

O1	O1	3f vermilion	.25	.25
O2	O1	5f vermilion	.25	.25
O3	O1	10f vermilion	.25	.25
O4	O1	15f vermilion	.25	.25
O5	O1	25f vermilion	.25	.25
O6	O1	50f vermilion	.25	.25
O7	O1	100f vermilion	.25	.25
O8	O1	150f vermilion	.25	.25
O9	O1	200f vermilion	.65	.45
O10	O1	300f vermilion	.75	.50
O11	O1	600f vermilion	1.40	1.75
		Nos. O1-O11 (11)	4.80	4.70
		Set, never hinged	14.00	

The stars on either side of the denomination do not appear on Nos. O7-O11. Nos. O7-O11 exist imperf. Value, set $27.50.

Numerals Larger
Stars inclined outward
1920, Nov. 20 *Perf. 11½*
Thin Laid Paper

O12	O1	5f red	.25	.25
O13	O1	10f red	.25	.25
O14	O1	15f red	.25	.25
O15	O1	25f red	.60	.25
O16	O1	50f red	.35	.25
		Nos. O12-O16 (5)	1.70	1.25
		Set, never hinged	6.50	

Polish Eagle — O3

Perf. 12x12½
1933, Aug. 1 Typo. Wmk. 234

O17	O3	(30g) vio (Zwyczajna)	.35	.25
O18	O3	(80g) red (Polecona)	.35	.25
		Set, never hinged	3.00	

Polish Eagle — O4

1935, Apr. 1

O19	O4	(25g) bl vio (Zwyczajna)	.25	.25
O20	O4	(55g) car (Polecona)	.25	.25
		Set, never hinged	1.40	

Stamps inscribed "Zwyczajna" or "Zwykla" were for ordinary official mail. Those with "Polecona" were for registered official mail.

Polish People's Republic

Polish Eagle — O5

Perf. 11, 14
1945, July 1 Photo. Unwmk.

O21	O5	(5z) bl vio (Zwykla)	.25	.25
a.		Imperf.	3.50	3.50
O22	O5	(10z) red (Polecona)	.25	.25
a.		Imperf.	7.00	7.00
		Set, never hinged, #O21, O22	1.40	
		Set, never hinged, #O21a, O22a	10.00	

Control number at bottom right: M-01705 on No. O21; M-01706 on No. O22.

Type of 1945 Redrawn
1946, July 31

O23	O5	(5z) dl bl vio (Zwykla)	.25	.25
O24	O5	(10z) dl rose red (Polecona)	.25	.25
		Set, never hinged	1.50	

The redrawn stamps appear blurred and the eagle contains fewer lines of shading. Control number at bottom right: M-01709 on Nos. O23-O26.

Redrawn Type of 1946
1946, July 31 *Imperf.*

O25	O5	(60g) dl bl vio (Zwykla)	.25	.25
O26	O5	(1.55z) dl rose red (Polecona)	.25	.25
		Set, never hinged	1.50	

Type of 1945, 2nd Redrawing
No Control Number at Lower Right
Perf. 11, 11½, 11x12½
1950-53 Unwmk.

O27	O5	(60g) blue (Zwykla)	.25	.25
O28	O5	(1.55z) red (Polecona) ('53)	.25	.25
		Set, never hinged	1.50	

Redrawn Type of 1952
1954 *Perf. 13x11, 11½, 14*

O29	O5	(60g) slate gray (Zwykla)	3.00	1.00
		Never hinged	5.00	

O6

Perf. 11x11½, 12x12½
1954, Aug. 15 Engr.

O30	O6	(60g) dark blue (Zwykla)	.25	.25
O31	O6	(1.55z) red (Polecona)	.30	.25
		Set, never hinged	2.00	

Polish People's Republic, 10th anniversary.

NEWSPAPER STAMPS

Austrian Newspaper
Stamps of 1916
Overprinted

1919, Jan. 10 Unwmk. *Imperf.*

P1	N9	2h brown	19.00	19.00
P2	N9	4h green	18.00	15.00
P3	N9	6h dark blue	15.00	14.00
P4	N9	10h orange	240.00	175.00
P5	N9	30h claret	19.00	17.00
		Nos. P1-P5 (5)	311.00	240.00

See note above No. 41.
Counterfeits exist of Nos. P1-P5.

OCCUPATION STAMPS

Issued under German Occupation

German Stamps of
1905 Overprinted

Perf. 14, 14½

1915, May 12			Wmk. 125	
N1	A16	3pf brown	.65	.85
N2	A16	5pf green	1.40	.85
N3	A16	10pf carmine	1.40	.85
N4	A16	20pf ultra	2.75	1.25
N5	A16	40pf lake & blk	8.25	6.25
		Nos. N1-N5 (5)	14.45	10.05
		Set, never hinged	45.00	

German Stamps of
1905-17 Overprinted

1916-17				
N6	A22	2½pf gray	1.50	2.50
N7	A16	3pf brown	1.50	2.50
N8	A16	5pf green	1.50	2.50
N9	A22	7½pf orange	1.50	2.50
N10	A16	10pf carmine	1.50	2.50
N11	A22	15pf yel brn	4.25	3.50
N12	A22	15pf dk vio ('17)	1.50	2.50
N13	A16	20pf ultra	2.10	2.50
N14	A16	30pf org & blk, *buff*	8.50	15.00
N15	A16	40pf lake & blk	3.00	2.50
N16	A16	60pf magenta	3.50	3.50
		Nos. N6-N16 (11)	30.35	42.00
		Set, never hinged	95.00	

For overprints and surcharges see #15-26.

German Stamps of
1934 Surcharged in
Black

1939, Dec. 1			Wmk. 237	Perf. 14
N17	A64	6g on 3pf bister	.25	.40
N18	A64	8g on 4pf dl bl	.25	.40
N19	A64	12g on 6pf dk grn	.25	.40
N20	A64	16g on 8pf vermilion	.50	1.25
N21	A64	20g on 10pf choc	.25	.40
N22	A64	24g on 12pf dp car	.25	.25
N23	A64	30g on 15pf maroon	.50	1.25
N24	A64	40g on 20pf brt bl	.50	.40
N25	A64	50g on 25pf ultra	.50	.80
N26	A64	60g on 30pf ol grn	.50	.40
N27	A64	80g on 40pf red vio	.55	.80
N28	A64	1z on 50pf dk grn & blk	1.10	1.60
N29	A64	2z on 100(pf) org & blk	2.25	3.00
		Nos. N17-N29 (13)	7.65	11.35
		Set, never hinged	27.50	

Stamps of Poland
1937, Surcharged in
Black or Brown

1940			Unwmk.	Perf. 12½, 12½x13
N30	A80	24g on 25g sl grn	1.25	3.25
N31	A81	40g on 30g rose vio	.40	1.25
N32	A80	50g on 55g blue	.30	.80

Similar Surcharge on Stamps of 1938-39

N33	A83	2g on 5g red org	.25	.40
N34	A83	4(g) on 5g red org	.25	.40
N35	A83	6(g) on 10g grn		

N36	A83	8(g) on 10g grn (Br)	.25	.40
N37	A83	10(g) on 10g grn	.25	.40
N38	A83	12(g) on 15g redsh brn (#339)	.25	.40
N39	A83	16(g) on 15g redsh brn (#339)	.25	.40
N40	A83	24g on 25g dl vio	.25	.40
N41	A83	30(g) on 30g rose red	.25	.40
N42	A83	50(g) on 50g brt red vio	.25	.65
N43	A83	60(g) on 55g ultra	6.00	17.00
N44	A83	80(g) on 75g dl grn	6.00	17.00
N45	A83	1z on 1z org	6.25	17.00
N46	A83	2z on 2z car rose	3.00	7.50
N47	A95	3z on 3z gray blk	4.00	10.00

Similar Surcharge on Nos. B32-B34

N48	SP5	30g on 5g+5g	.25	.65
N49	SP5	40g on 25g+10g	.25	.65
N50	SP5	1z on 55g+15g	4.00	10.00

Similar Surcharge on Nos. J98-J102

Perf. 12½x12

N51	D11	50(g) on 20g	1.25	3.25
N52	D11	50(g) on 25g	6.00	17.50
N53	D11	50(g) on 30g	14.00	37.50
N54	D11	50(g) on 50g	.75	2.40
N55	D11	50(g) on 1z	1.75	4.75
		Nos. N30-N55 (26)	57.95	154.75
		Set, never hinged	160.00	

The surcharge on Nos. N30 to N55 is arranged to fit the shape of the stamp and obliterate the original denomination. On some values, "General Gouvernement" appears at the bottom. Counterfeits exist.

St. Florian's Gate, Cracow — OS1   Palace, Warsaw — OS13

Designs: 8g, Watch Tower, Cracow. 10g, Cracow Gate, Lublin. 12g, Courtyard and statue of Copernicus. 20g, Dominican Church, Cracow. 24g, Wawel Castle, Cracow. 30g, Church, Lublin. 40g, Arcade, Cloth Hall, Cracow. 48g, City Hall, Sandomierz. 50g, Court House, Cracow. 60g, Courtyard, Cracow. 80g, St. Mary's Church, Cracow.

1940-41			Unwmk. Photo.	Perf. 14
N56	OS1	6g brown	.25	.75
N57	OS1	8g brn org	.25	.75
N58	OS1	8g bl blk ('41)	.45	.50
N59	OS1	10g emerald	.25	.25
N60	OS1	12g dk grn	2.00	.70
N61	OS1	12g dp vio ('41)	.30	.25
N62	OS1	20g dk ol brn	.25	.25
N63	OS1	24g henna brn	.25	.25
N64	OS1	30g purple	.25	.25
N65	OS1	30g vio brn ('41)	.30	.25
N66	OS1	40g slate blk	.25	.25
N67	OS1	48g chnt brn ('41)	.60	1.50
N68	OS1	50g brt bl	.25	.25
N69	OS1	60g slate grn	.25	.25
N70	OS1	80g dull pur	.25	.50
N71	OS13	1z rose lake	2.00	1.25
N72	OS13	1z Prus grn ('41)	.55	1.00
		Nos. N56-N72 (17)	8.70	9.20
		Set, never hinged	22.50	

For surcharges see Nos. NB1-NB4.

Cracow Castle and City, 15th Century OS14

1941, Apr. 20			Engr.	Perf. 14½
N73	OS14	10z red & ol blk	1.10	2.75
		Never hinged	2.50	

Printed in sheets of 8.

Rondel and Florian's Gate, Cracow OS15

Design: 4z, Tyniec Monastery, Vistula River.

1941				Perf. 13½x14
N74	OS15	2z dk ultra	.90	1.00
N75	OS15	4z slate grn	.90	1.75
		Set, never hinged	3.50	

Adolf Hitler — OS17

1941-43			Unwmk. Photo.	Perf. 14
N76	OS17	2g gray blk	.25	.25
N77	OS17	6g golden brn	.25	.25
N78	OS17	8g slate blue	.25	.25
N79	OS17	10g green	.25	.25
N80	OS17	12g purple	.25	.25
N81	OS17	16g org red	1.60	2.00
N82	OS17	20g blk brn	.25	.25
N83	OS17	24g henna	.25	.25
N84	OS17	30g rose vio	.25	.25
N85	OS17	32g dk bl grn	.50	.50
N86	OS17	40g brt blue	.25	.25
N87	OS17	48g chestnut	1.40	.80
N88	OS17	50g vio bl ('43)	.30	.50
N89	OS17	60g dk olive ('43)	.30	.50
N90	OS17	80g dk vio ('43)	.30	.50
		Nos. N76-N90 (15)	6.65	7.05
		Set, never hinged	12.00	

A 20g black brown exists with head of Hans Frank substituted for that of Hitler. It was printed and used by Resistance movements. Nos. N76-N90 exist imperf. Value, set unused $300.

1942-44			Engr.	Perf. 12½
N91	OS17	50g vio bl	.50	1.00
N92	OS17	60g dk ol	.50	1.00
N93	OS17	80g dk red vio	.50	1.00
N94	OS17	1z slate grn	.50	1.00
a.		Perf. 14 ('44)	1.00	12.00
N95	OS17	1.20z dk brn	.80	1.60
a.		Perf. 14 ('44)	2.00	16.00
N96	OS17	1.60z bl vio	.80	1.60
a.		Perf. 14 ('44)	2.00	20.00
		Nos. N91-N96 (6)	3.60	7.20
		Set, never hinged	7.25	
		Set, #N94a, N95a, N96a, never hinged	9.50	

Nos. N91-N96 exist imperf. Value, set unused $1,250.

Rondel and Florian's Gate, Cracow OS18

Designs: 4z, Tyniec Monastery, Vistula River. 6z, View of Lwow. 10z, Cracow Castle and City, 15th Century.

1943-44				Perf. 13½x14
N100	OS18	2z slate grn	.40	.80
N101	OS18	4z dk gray vio	1.20	2.40
N102	OS18	6z sepia ('44)	.60	1.20
N103	OS18	10z org brn & gray blk	.60	1.60
		Nos. N100-N103 (4)	2.80	6.00
		Set, never hinged	5.50	

OCCUPATION SEMI-POSTAL STAMPS

Issued under German Occupation

Types of 1940 Occupation Postage Stamps Surcharged in Red

1940, Aug. 17			Photo.	Perf. 14	Unwmk.
NB1	OS1	12g + 8g olive gray		2.00	3.50
NB2	OS1	24g + 16g olive gray		2.00	3.50
NB3	OS1	50g + 50g olive gray		2.00	4.50
NB4	OS1	80g + 80g olive gray		2.00	6.00
		Nos. NB1-NB4 (4)		8.00	17.50
		Set, never hinged		16.00	

German Peasant Girl in Poland OSP1

Designs: 24g+26g, Woman wearing scarf. 30g+20g, Similar to type OSP4.

1940, Oct. 26			Engr.	Perf. 14½	Thick Paper
NB5	OSP1	12g + 38g dk sl grn		1.20	2.75
NB6	OSP1	24g + 26g cop red		1.20	2.75
NB7	OSP1	30g + 20g vio pur		2.00	5.00
		Nos. NB5-NB7 (3)		4.40	10.50
		Set, never hinged		8.75	

1st anniversary of the General Government.

German Peasant OSP4

1940, Dec. 1				Perf. 12
NB8	OSP4	12g + 8g blk grn	.80	1.60
NB9	OSP4	24g + 16g rose red	.80	2.00
NB10	OSP4	30g + 30g vio brn	1.40	2.50
NB11	OSP4	50g + 50g ultra	1.40	3.00
		Nos. NB8-NB11 (4)	4.40	9.10
		Set, never hinged	8.75	

The surtax was for war relief.

Adolf Hitler — OSP5

1942, Apr. 20			Engr.	Perf. 11	Thick Cream Paper
NB12	OSP5	30g + 1z brn car		.60	1.60
NB13	OSP5	50g + 1z dk ultra		.60	1.60
NB14	OSP5	1.20z + 1z brown		.60	1.60
		Nos. NB12-NB14 (3)		1.80	4.80
		Set, never hinged		3.50	

To commemorate Hitler's 53rd birthday. Printed in sheets of 25.

Ancient Lublin — OSP6

Designs: 24g+6g, 1z+1z, Modern Lublin.

1942, Aug. 15   Photo.   *Perf. 12½*

NB15	OSP6	12g + 8g rose vio	.30	.65
NB16	OSP6	24g + 6g henna	.30	.65
NB17	OSP6	50g + 50g dp bl	.30	1.20
NB18	OSP6	1z + 1z dp grn	.65	1.60
	Nos. NB15-NB18 (4)		1.55	4.10
	Set, never hinged		3.25	

600th anniversary of Lublin.

Veit Stoss — OSP8

Designs: 24g+26g, Hans Durer. 30g+30g, Johann Schuch. 50g+50g, Joseph Elsner. 1z+1z, Nicolaus Copernicus.

1942, Nov. 20   Engr.   *Perf. 13½x14*

NB19	OSP8	12g + 18g dl pur	.25	.40
NB20	OSP8	24g + 26g dl henna	.25	.40
NB21	OSP8	30g + 30g dl rose vio	.25	.40
NB22	OSP8	50g + 50g dl bl vio	.25	.65
NB23	OSP8	1z + 1z dl myr grn	.25	.80
	Nos. NB19-NB23 (5)		1.25	2.65
	Set, never hinged		1.60	

For overprint see No. NB27.

Adolf Hitler — OSP13

1943, Apr. 20

NB24	OSP13	12g + 1z purple	.60	1.35
NB25	OSP13	24g + 1z rose car	.60	1.35
NB26	OSP13	84g + 1z myrtle grn	.60	1.35
	Nos. NB24-NB26 (3)		1.80	4.05
	Set, never hinged		3.50	

To commemorate Hitler's 54th birthday.

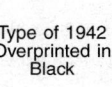

Type of 1942 Overprinted in Black

1943, May 24

NB27	OSP8	1z + 1z rose lake	.55	1.60
	Never hinged		.90	

Nicolaus Copernicus. Printed in sheets of 10, with marginal inscription.

Cracow Gate, Lublin — OSP14

Designs: 24g+76g, Cloth Hall, Cracow. 30g+70g, New Government Building, Radom. 50g+1z, Bruhl Palace, Warsaw. 1z+2z, Town Hall, Lwow.
The center of the designs is embossed with the emblem of the National Socialist Party.

1943   Photogravure, Embossed

NB28	OSP14	12g + 38g dk grn	.30	.95
NB29	OSP14	24g + 76g red	.30	.95
NB30	OSP14	30g + 70g rose vio	.30	.95
NB31	OSP14	50g + 1z brt bl	.30	.95
NB32	OSP14	1z + 2z bl blk	.30	.95
	Nos. NB28-NB32 (5)		1.50	4.75
	Set, never hinged		3.25	

3rd anniversary of the National Socialist Party in Poland.

Adolf Hitler — OSP19

1944, Apr. 20   Photo.   *Perf. 14x13½*

NB33	OSP19	12g + 1z green	.25	.95
NB34	OSP19	24g + 1z brn red	.25	.95
NB35	OSP19	84g + 1z dk vio	.25	.95
	Nos. NB33-NB35 (3)		.75	2.85
	Set, never hinged		1.25	

To commemorate Hitler's 55th birthday. Printed in sheets of 25.

Conrad Celtis — OSP20

Designs: 24g+26g, Andreas Schluter. 30g+30g, Hans Boner. 50g+50g, Augustus II. 1z+1z, Georg Gottlieb Pusch.

1944, July 15   Engr.   *Perf. 13½x14*

NB36	OSP20	12g + 18g dk grn	.25	1.20
NB37	OSP20	24g + 26g dk red	.25	1.20
NB38	OSP20	30g + 30g rose vio	.25	1.60
NB39	OSP20	50g + 50g ultra	.25	2.00
NB40	OSP20	1z + 1z dl red brn	.25	2.00
	Nos. NB36-NB40 (5)		1.25	8.00
	Set, never hinged		1.60	

Cracow Castle OSP25

1944, Oct. 26   *Perf. 14½*

NB41	OSP25	10z + 10z red & blk	7.50	40.00
	Never hinged		15.00	
a.	Imperf.		12.00	
	Never hinged		24.00	
b.	10z + 10z car & greenish blk		12.50	25.00
	Never hinged		25.00	
c.	Horiz. pair, imperf. btwn.		65.00	
	Never hinged		90.00	

5th anniv. of the General Government, Oct. 26, 1944. Printed in sheets of 8.

OCCUPATION RURAL DELIVERY STAMPS

Issued under German Occupation

OSD1

1940, Dec. 1   Photo.   Unwmk.
Perf. 13½

NL1	OSD1	10g red orange	.60	1.20
NL2	OSD1	20g red orange	.60	1.25
NL3	OSD1	30g red orange	.60	1.25
NL4	OSD1	50g red orange	1.40	3.00
	Nos. NL1-NL4 (4)		3.20	6.70
	Set, never hinged		6.50	

OCCUPATION OFFICIAL STAMPS

Issued under German Occupation

Eagle and Swastika OOS1

Perf. 12, 13½x14

1940, Apr.   Photo.   Unwmk.
Size: 31x23mm

NO1	OOS1	6g lt brown	.80	2.40
NO2	OOS1	8g gray	.80	2.40
NO3	OOS1	10g green	.80	2.40
NO4	OOS1	12g dk green	.80	1.75
NO5	OOS1	20g dk brown	.80	2.75
NO6	OOS1	24g henna brn	10.00	1.75
NO7	OOS1	30g rose lake	.80	2.60
NO8	OOS1	40g dl violet	.80	5.00
NO9	OOS1	48g dl olive	3.25	5.00
NO10	OOS1	50g royal bl	.80	2.60
NO11	OOS1	60g dk ol grn	.60	2.40
NO12	OOS1	80g rose vio	.60	2.40

Size: 35x26mm

NO13	OOS1	1z gray blk & brn vio	1.50	4.75
NO14	OOS1	3z gray blk & chnt	1.50	4.75
NO15	OOS1	5z gray blk & org brn	2.50	6.50
	Nos. NO1-NO15 (15)		26.35	49.45
	Set, never hinged		75.00	

1940   Size: 21¼x16¼mm   *Perf. 12*

NO16	OOS1	6g brown	.65	1.20
NO17	OOS1	8g slate	.65	1.40
NO18	OOS1	10g dp grn	1.00	2.00
NO19	OOS1	12g slate grn	.65	1.40
NO20	OOS1	20g blk brn	.65	1.20
NO21	OOS1	24g cop brn	1.00	1.20
NO22	OOS1	30g rose lake	.80	1.60
NO23	OOS1	40g dl pur	.80	2.00
NO24	OOS1	50g royal blue	.80	2.00
	Nos. NO16-NO24 (9)		7.00	14.00
	Set, never hinged		25.00	

Nazi Emblem and Cracow Castle — OOS2

1943   Photo.   *Perf. 14*

NO25	OOS2	6g brown	.30	.80
NO26	OOS2	8g slate blue	.30	.80
NO27	OOS2	10g green	.30	.80
NO28	OOS2	12g dk vio	.30	.80
NO29	OOS2	16g red org	.40	.80
NO30	OOS2	20g dk brn	.30	.80
NO31	OOS2	24g dk red	.30	.80
NO32	OOS2	30g rose vio	.30	.80
NO33	OOS2	40g blue	.30	.80
NO34	OOS2	60g olive grn	.30	.80
NO35	OOS2	80g dull claret	.30	.80
NO36	OOS2	100g slate blk	.60	1.60
	Nos. NO25-NO36 (12)		4.00	10.40
	Set, never hinged		18.00	

POLISH OFFICES ABROAD

OFFICES IN DANZIG

Poland Nos. 215-225 Overprinted

1925, Jan. 5   Unwmk.   *Perf. 11½x12*

1K1	A36	1g orange brn	.55	2.50
1K2	A36	2g dk brown	.55	5.25
1K3	A36	3g orange	.55	1.60
1K4	A36	5g olive grn	18.00	7.50
1K5	A36	10g blue grn	5.50	3.00
1K6	A36	15g red	30.00	7.50
1K7	A36	20g blue	1.60	1.50
1K8	A36	25g red brown	2.10	1.50
1K9	A36	30g dp violet	2.10	1.50
1K10	A36	40g indigo	2.10	1.50
1K11	A36	50g magenta	2.60	2.25
	Nos. 1K1-1K11 (11)		65.65	35.60
	Set, never hinged		375.00	

Same Ovpt. on Poland Nos. 230-231

1926   *Perf. 11½, 12*

1K11A	A39	5g yellow grn	60.00	40.00
1K12	A40	10g violet	16.00	16.00
	Set, never hinged		160.00	

Counterfeit overprints are known on Nos. 1K1-1K32.

No. 232 Overprinted

1926-27

1K13	A41	15g rose red	50.00	55.00

Same Overprint on Redrawn Stamps of 1926-27
Perf. 13

1K14	A39	5g yellow grn	1.60	2.00
1K15	A40	10g violet	2.75	2.25
1K16	A41	15g rose red	5.00	4.00
1K17	A43	20g dull red	3.25	2.25
	Nos. 1K14-1K17 (4)		12.60	10.50
	Set, never hinged		40.00	

Same Ovpt. on Poland Nos. 250, 255a

1928-30   *Perf. 12½*

1K18	A44	25g yellow brn	5.00	3.25
	Never hinged		20.00	

Laid Paper
Perf. 11½x12, 12½x11½

1K19	A50	1z blk, *cr* ('30)	20.00	32.50
	Never hinged		55.00	

Poland Nos. 258-260 Overprinted

1929-30   *Perf. 12x12½*

1K20	A53	5g dk violet	4.00	2.00
1K21	A53	10g green ('30)	4.00	2.00
1K22	A53	25g red brown	8.00	6.00
	Nos. 1K20-1K22 (3)		16.00	6.00
	Set, never hinged		32.50	

Same Overprint on Poland No. 257

1931, Jan. 5   *Perf. 12½*

1K23	A52	15g ultra	8.50	6.00
	Never hinged		20.00	

Poland No. 255 Overprinted in Dark Blue

1933, July 1   Laid Paper   *Perf. 11½*

1K24	A50	1z black, *cream*	70.00	140.00
	Never hinged		140.00	

Poland Nos. 268-270 Overprinted in Black

1934-36   Wmk. 234   *Perf. 12x12½*

1K25	A58	5g dl violet	3.75	6.50
1K26	A58	10g green ('36)	32.50	100.00
1K27	A58	15g red brown	3.75	6.50
	Nos. 1K25-1K27 (3)		40.00	113.00
	Set, never hinged		110.00	

Poland Nos. 294, 296, 298 Overprinted in Black in one or two lines

1935-36   Unwmk.   Perf. 12½x13

1K28	A65	5g violet blue	3.00	12.00
1K29	A65	15g Prus green	3.00	18.00
1K30	A65	25g myrtle green	4.00	9.00
		Nos. 1K28-1K30 (3)	10.00	39.00
		Set, never hinged	35.00	

Same Overprint in Black on Poland Nos. 308, 310

1937, June 5

1K31	A65	5g violet blue	1.75	6.00
1K32	A65	15g red brown	1.75	6.00
		Set, never hinged	11.00	

Polish Merchants Selling Wheat in Danzig, 16th Century — A2

1938, Nov. 11   Engr.   Perf. 12½

1K33	A2	5g red orange	.40	12.00
1K34	A2	15g red brown	.40	12.00
1K35	A2	25g dull violet	1.00	12.00
1K36	A2	55g brt ultra	1.50	12.00
		Nos. 1K33-1K36 (4)	3.30	48.00
		Set, never hinged	14.00	

OFFICES IN THE TURKISH EMPIRE

Stamps of Poland 1919, Overprinted in Carmine

1919, May   Unwmk.   Perf. 11½
Wove Paper

2K1	A10	3f bister brn	60.00	110.00
2K2	A10	5f green	60.00	110.00
2K3	A10	10f red vio	60.00	110.00
2K4	A10	15f red	60.00	110.00
2K5	A11	20f dp blue	60.00	110.00
2K6	A11	25f olive grn	60.00	110.00
2K7	A11	50f blue grn	60.00	110.00

Overprinted

2K8	A12	1m violet	150.00	130.00
2K9	A12	1.50m dp green	150.00	130.00
2K10	A12	2m dk brown	150.00	150.00
2K11	A13	2.50m orange brn	150.00	130.00
2K12	A14	5m red violet	150.00	150.00
		Nos. 2K1-2K12 (12)	1,170.	1,460.

Counterfeit cancellations are plentiful. Counterfeits exist of Nos. 2K1-2K12.
Reissues are lighter, shiny red. Value, set $25.

Polish stamps with "P.P.C." overprint (Poste Polonaise Constantinople) were used on consular mail for a time.

Seven stamps with these overprints were not issued. Value, set: unused $15, never hinged $35.

EXILE GOVERNMENT IN GREAT BRITAIN

These stamps were issued by the Polish government in exile for letters posted from Polish merchant ships and warships.

United States Embassy Ruins, Warsaw — A1

Polish Ministry of Finance Ruins, Warsaw — A2

Destruction of Mickiewicz Monument, Cracow — A3

Ruins of Warsaw A4

Polish Submarine "Orzel" — A8

Polish Machine Gunners A5

Armored Tank A6

Polish Planes in Great Britain A7

Perf. 12½, 11½x12
1941, Dec. 15   Engr.   Unwmk.

3K1	A1	5g rose violet	.60	1.25
3K2	A2	10g dk bl grn	.80	1.60
3K3	A3	25g black	1.25	2.00
3K4	A4	55g dark blue	1.60	2.75
3K5	A5	75g olive grn	3.50	7.25
3K6	A6	80g dk car rose	3.50	7.25
3K7	A7	1z slate blue	3.50	7.25
3K8	A8	1.50z copper brn	3.50	7.25
		Nos. 3K1-3K8 (8)	18.25	36.60
		Set, never hinged	35.00	

These stamps were used for correspondence carried on Polish ships and, on certain days, in Polish Military camps in Great Britain. For surcharges see Nos. 3K17-3K20.

Polish Air Force in Battle of the Atlantic — A9   Polish Army in France, 1939-40 — A11

Polish Merchant Navy A10

Polish Army in Narvik, Norway, 1940 — A12

The Homeland Fights On — A15

Polish Army in Libya, 1941-42 A13

General Sikorsky and Polish Soldiers in the Middle East, 1943 A14

The Secret Press in Poland A16

1943, Nov. 1

3K9	A9	5g rose lake	.50	1.20
3K10	A10	10g dk bl grn	.75	1.50
3K11	A11	25g dk vio	.75	1.50
3K12	A12	55g sapphire	1.25	2.00
3K13	A13	75g brn car	2.00	3.50
3K14	A14	80g rose car	2.50	5.25
3K15	A15	1z olive blk	2.50	5.00
3K16	A16	1.50z black	3.25	7.50
		Nos. 3K9-3K16 (8)	13.50	27.45
		Set, never hinged	22.50	

Nos. 3K5 to 3K8 Surcharged in Blue

Perf. 12½, 11½x12
1944, June 27   Unwmk.

3K17	A5	45g on 75g	7.50	22.50
3K18	A6	55g on 80g	7.50	22.50
3K19	A7	80g on 1z	7.50	22.50
3K20	A8	1.20z on 1.50z	7.50	22.50
		Nos. 3K17-3K20 (4)	30.00	90.00
		Set, never hinged	80.00	

Capture of Monte Cassino by the Poles, May 18, 1944.

EXILE GOVERNMENT IN GREAT BRITAIN SEMI-POSTAL STAMP

Heroic Defenders of Warsaw — SP1

Perf. 11½
1945, Feb. 3   Unwmk.   Engr.

3KB1	SP1	1z + 2z slate green	4.75	12.00
		Never hinged	9.50	

Warsaw uprising, Aug. 1-Oct. 3, 1944.

PONTA DELGADA

ˌpän-tə del-ˈgä-də

LOCATION — Administrative district of the Azores comprising the islands of Sao Miguel and Santa Maria
GOVT. — A district of Portugal
AREA — 342 sq. mi.
POP. — 124,000 (approx.)
CAPITAL — Ponta Delgada

1000 Reis = 1 Milreis

King Carlos — A1

1892-93   Typo.   Unwmk.
Perf. 12½, 11½ (25r), 13½ (75r, 150r)

1	A1	5r yellow	3.75	1.40
c.		Diagonal half used as 2½r on piece		18.00
2	A1	10r reddish vio	4.25	2.40
3	A1	15r chocolate	5.50	3.00
4	A1	20r lavender	5.50	3.00
a.		Perf. 13½	9.25	3.00
5d	A1	25r green	10.25	1.75
6	A1	50r ultra	11.00	4.25
7	A1	75r carmine	10.50	7.25
8	A1	80r yellow grn	16.00	12.00
9	A1	100r brn, *yel*	16.00	7.25
10	A1	150r car, *rose*	75.00	52.50
11	A1	200r dk bl, *bl*	75.00	52.50
12	A1	300r dk bl, *salmon*	80.00	55.00
		Nos. 1-12 (12)	312.75	202.30

Nos. 1, 4 and 9-12 were reprinted in 1900 (perf. 11½). Value, each $50. All values were reprinted in 1905 (perf. 13½). Value, each $25. The reprints are on paper slightly thinner than that of the originals, and unsurfaced. They have white gum and clean-cut perfs.
See the Scott Classic Specialized Catalogue for listings by perforation.

King Carlos — A2

Name and Value in Black except Nos. 25 and 34

1897-1905   Perf. 11½

13	A2	2½r gray	.60	.35
14	A2	5r orange	.60	.35
15	A2	10r lt green	.60	.35
16	A2	15r brown	9.00	7.25
17	A2	15r gray grn ('99)	2.40	1.75
18	A2	20r dull violet	2.40	1.40
19	A2	25r sea green	3.75	1.40
20	A2	25r rose red ('99)	2.40	.60
21	A2	50r blue	3.75	1.40
22	A2	50r ultra ('05)	22.50	13.00
23	A2	65r slate blue ('98)	1.40	.60
24	A2	75r rose	8.00	1.40
25	A2	75r brn & car, *yel* ('05)	17.00	8.50
26	A2	80r violet	2.40	1.40
27	A2	100r dk bl, *bl*	5.00	1.00
28	A2	115r org brn, *rose* ('98)	4.25	1.75
29	A2	130r gray brn, *buff* ('98)	3.00	1.75
30	A2	150r lt brn, *buff*	3.00	2.10
31	A2	180r sl, *pnksh* ('98)	3.00	2.10
32	A2	200r red vio, *pnksh*	8.50	6.00
33	A2	300r blue, *rose*	10.00	5.50
a.		Perf. 12½	57.50	35.00
34	A2	500r blk & red, *bl*	21.00	13.00
a.		Perf. 12½	32.00	18.00
		Nos. 13-34 (21)	133.95	72.60

Imperfs are proofs.
The stamps of Ponta Delgada were superseded by those of the Azores, which in 1931 were replaced by those of Portugal.

PORTUGAL

'pōr-chi-gəl

LOCATION — Southern Europe, on the western coast of the Iberian Peninsula
GOVT. — Republic
AREA — 35,516 sq. mi.
POP. — 9,918,040 (1999 est.)
CAPITAL — Lisbon

Figures for area and population include the Azores and Madeira, which are integral parts of the republic. The republic was established in 1910. See Azores, Funchal, Madeira.

1000 Reis = 1 Milreis
10 Reis = 1 Centimo
100 Centavos = 1 Escudo (1912)
100 Cents = 1 Euro (2002)

Catalogue values for unused stamps in this country are for Never Hinged items, beginning with Scott 662 in the regular postage section, Scott C11 in the airpost section, Scott J65 in the postage due section, and Scott O2 in the officials section.

Queen Maria II
A1   A2

A3   A4

Typo. & Embossed

1853		Unwmk.		Imperf.
1	A1	5r reddish brown	2,850.	850.00
b.		Double impression		4,250.
2	A2	25r blue	925.	19.00
b.		Double impression	4,750.	1,500.
3	A3	50r dp yellow grn	3,400.	875.00
a.		50r blue green	6,750.	1,650.
c.		Double impression	14,000.	6,000.
4	A4	100r lilac	31,000.	1,900.

The stamps of the 1853 issue were reprinted in 1864, 1885, 1905 and 1953. Many stamps of subsequent issues were reprinted in 1885 and 1905. The reprints of 1864 are on thin white paper with white gum. The originals have brownish gum which often stains the paper. The reprints of 1885 are on a stout, very white paper. They are usually ungummed, but occasionally have a white gum with yellowish spots. The reprints of 1905 are on creamy white paper of ordinary quality with shiny white gum.

When perforated the reprints of 1885 have a rather rough perforation 13½ with small holes; those of 1905 have a clean-cut perforation 13½ with large holes making sharp pointed teeth.

The colors of the reprints usually differ from those of the originals, but actual comparison is necessary.

The reprints are often from new dies which differ slightly from those used for the originals.

5 reis: There is a defect in the neck which makes the Adam's apple appear very large in the first reprint. The later ones can be distinguished by the paper and the shades and by the absence of the pendant curl.

25 reis: The burelage of the ground work in the original is sharp and clear, while in the 1864 reprints it is blurred in several places; the upper and lower right hand corners are very thick and blurred. The central oval is less than ½mm from the frame at the sides in the originals and fully ¾mm in the 1885 and 1905 reprints.

50 reis: In the reprints of 1864 and 1885 there is a small break in the upper right hand diagonal line of the frame, and the initials of the engraver (F. B. F.), which in the originals

are plainly discernible in the lower part of the bust, do not show. The reprints of 1905 have not the break in the frame and the initials are distinct.

100 reis: The small vertical lines at top and bottom at each side of the frame are heavier in the reprints of 1864 than in the originals. The reprints of 1885 and 1905 can be distinguished only by the paper, gum and shades.

Reprints of 1953 have thick paper, no gum and dates "1853/1953" on back. Value $55 each.

Values of lowest-cost earlier reprints (1905) of Nos. 1, $100; No. 2, $120; Nos. 3, 4, $150.

King Pedro V
A5   A6

A7   A8

1855   With Straight Hair

TWENTY-FIVE REIS:
Type I — Pearls mostly touch each other and oval outer line.
Type II — Pearls are separate from each other and oval outer line.

5	A5	5r red brown	8,250.	900.00
6	A6	25r blue, type II	950.00	25.00
a.		25r blue, type I	1,150.	30.00
7	A7	50r green	600.00	70.00
b.		Double impression	1,900.	725.00
8	A8	100r lilac	800.00	90.00

1856   With Curled Hair

TWENTY-FIVE REIS:
Type I — The network is fine (single lines).
Type II — The network is coarse (double lines).

9	A5	5r brown	500.00	70.00
g.		Double impression	1,400.	375.00
10	A6	25r blue, type II	400.00	13.50
a.		25r blue, type I	9,500.	55.00

1858

11	A6	25r rose, type II	275.00	6.50
a.		Double impression	525.00	275.00

The 5r dark brown, formerly listed and sold at about $1, is now believed by the best authorities to be a reprint made before 1866. It is printed on thin yellowish white paper with yellowish white gum and is known only unused. The same remarks will apply to a 25r blue which is common unused but not known used. It is printed from a die which was not used for the issued stamps but the differences are slight and can only be told by expert comparison.

Nos. 9 and 10, also 10a in rose, were reprinted in 1885 and Nos. 9, 10, 10a and 11 in 1905. Value of lowest-cost reprints, $40 each.

See note after No. 4.

King Luiz
A9   A10

A11   A12

A13

FIVE REIS:
Type I — The distance between "5" and "reis" is 3mm.
Type II — The distance between "5" and "reis" is 2mm.

1862-64

12	A9	5r brown, type I	125.00	10.00
a.		5r brown, type II	160.00	25.00
b.		Double impression, type II	650.00	350.00
d.		Double embossing, type I	—	275.00
13	A10	10r orange	125.00	40.00
14	A11	25r rose	100.00	4.75
a.		Double impression	1,350.	375.00
15	A12	50r yellow green	725.00	77.50
16	A13	100r lilac ('64)	900.00	90.00
		Nos. 12-16 (5)	1,975.	222.25

All values were reprinted in 1885 and all except the 25r in 1905. Value of lowest-cost reprints, $10 each.
See note after No. 4.

King Luiz — A14

1866-67   Imperf.

17	A14	5r black	100.00	10.00
a.		Double impression	275.00	190.00
18	A14	10r yellow	225.00	140.00
19	A14	20r bister	175.00	67.50
20	A14	25r rose ('67)	200.00	6.00
a.		Double impression		225.00
21	A14	50r green	250.00	50.00
22	A14	80r orange	250.00	50.00
23	A14	100r dk lilac ('67)	300.00	75.00
24	A14	120r blue	325.00	70.00
a.		Double impression	725.00	450.00
		Nos. 17-24 (8)	1,825.	468.50

All values were reprinted in 1885 and all except the 25r in 1905. Value of lowest-cost reprints, $10 each. Some values with unofficial percé en croix (diamond) perforation were used in Madeira.

All values were reprinted in 1885 and 1905. Value: Nos. 17-23, each $30-$40; No. 24, $100.
See note after No. 4.

Typographed & Embossed

1867-70   Perf. 12½

25	A14	5r black	125.00	42.50
a.		Double impression	225.00	110.00
26	A14	10r yellow	250.00	110.00
27	A14	20r bister ('69)	300.00	110.00
28	A14	25r rose	65.00	5.00
a.		Double impression	550.00	200.00
29	A14	50r green ('68)	250.00	100.00
30	A14	80r orange ('69)	350.00	100.00
31	A14	100r lilac ('69)	250.00	100.00
32	A14	120r blue	300.00	67.50
a.		Double impression	625.00	160.00
33	A14	240r pale violet ('70)	1,000.	475.00
		Nos. 25-33 (9)	2,890.	1,110.

Nos. 25-33 frequently were separated with scissors. Slightly blunted perfs on one or two sides are to be expected for stamps of this issue.

Two types each of 5r and 100r differ in the position of the "5" at upper right and the "100" at lower right in relation to the end of the label.

Nos. 25-33 were reprinted in 1885 and 1905. Some of the 1885 reprints were perforated 12½ as well as 13½. Value of the lowest-cost reprints, $40 each.
See note after No. 4.

King Luiz — A15

Typographed & Embossed

1870-84   Perf. 12½, 13½

34	A15	5r black	55.00	5.00
a.		Imperf	550.00	
f.		Double impression	275.00	67.50
35	A15	10r yellow ('71)	77.50	27.50
a.		Imperf	550.00	
f.		Double impression	300.00	125.00
36	A15	10r blue grn ('79)	375.00	175.00
37b	A15	10r yellow grn ('80)	110.00	24.00
		On post card		160.00
d.		Double impression	250.00	130.00
38	A15	15r lilac brn ('75)	100.00	29.00
d.		Double impression	500.00	260.00
39	A15	20r bister	72.50	25.00
a.		Imperf	550.00	
g.		Double impression		175.00
40	A15	20r rose ('84)	325.00	55.00
b.		Double impression	—	1,050.
41	A15	25r rose	30.00	3.75
a.		Imperf	550.00	
f.		Double impression	240.00	30.00
42	A15	50r pale green	140.00	40.00
43	A15	50r blue ('79)	350.00	50.00
44e	A15	80r orange	125.00	19.00
45e	A15	100r pale lilac ('71)	65.00	12.00
46	A15	120r blue ('71)	300.00	62.50
47	A15	150r pale bl ('76)	375.00	110.00
d.		Double impression	1,050.	390.00
48b	A15	150r yellow ('80)	125.00	13.50
49	A15	240r pale violet ('73)	1,700.	1,050.
50a	A15	300r dull violet ('76)	110.00	27.50
51a	A15	1000r black ('84)	400.00	77.50

Nos. 34-51 were printed on three types of paper, plain, ribbed and enamel surfaced, and with perfs gauging 11, 12½, 13½, or 14¼. Values are for the least expensive varieties. For detailed listings, see the Scott Classic Specialized Catalogue.

Two types each of 15r, 20r and 80r differ in the distance between the figures of value.

Imperfs probably are proofs.

For overprints and surcharges see Nos. 86-87, 94-96.

All values of the issues of 1870-84 were reprinted in 1885 and 1905. Value of the lowest-cost reprints, $10 each.
See note after No. 4.

King Luiz
A16   A17

A18   A19

1880-81   Typo.   Perf. 12½, 13½

52	A16	5r black	40.00	4.00
53	A17	25r bluish gray	300.00	29.00
54	A18	25r gray	45.00	3.50
55	A18	25r brown vio ('81)	45.00	3.50
56	A19	50r blue ('81)	300.00	15.00
		Nos. 52-56 (5)	730.00	55.00

All values were reprinted in 1885 and 1905. Value of the lowest-cost reprints, $15 each.
See note after No. 4.

A20   A21

King Luiz
A22   A23

A24   A24a

1882-87   **Perf. 11½, 12½, 13½**

57	A20	2r black ('84)	20.00	15.00
58	A21	5r black ('84)	32.50	3.50
59	A22	10r green ('84)	35.00	4.00
60c	A23	25r brown	32.50	2.60
61	A24	50r blue	45.00	3.00
62	A24a	500r black ('84)	600.00	300.00
63	A24a	500r violet ('87)	300.00	52.50
		Nos. 57-63 (7)	1,065.	380.60

Nos. 57-63 were printed on both plain and enamel surfaced papers, with one or more perf varieties for each value. Values are for the least expensive varieties. For a detailed listing, see the *Scott Classic Specialized Catalogue*.

For overprints see Nos. 79-82, 85, 88-89, 93.

The stamps of the 1882-87 issues were reprinted in 1885, 1893 and 1905. Value of the lowest-cost reprints, $5 each.
See note after No. 4.

A25   A26

1887   **Perf. 11½**

64	A25	20r rose	50.00	17.00
65	A26	25r violet	40.00	3.00
66	A26	25r lilac rose	30.00	3.00
		Nos. 64-66 (3)	120.00	23.00

For overprints see Nos. 83-84, 90-92.
Nos. 64-66 were reprinted in 1905. Value $22.50 each. See note after No. 4.

King Carlos — A27

1892-93   **Perf. 11½, 12½, 13½**

67	A27	5r orange	11.00	2.00
68	A27	10r redsh violet	30.00	4.00
69b	A27	15r chocolate	27.50	5.00
70	A27	20r lavender	35.00	9.25
71a	A27	25r dark green	27.50	2.00
72	A27	50r blue	35.00	9.25
73	A27	75r carmine ('93)	67.50	8.00
74a	A27	80r yellow green	85.00	42.50
75	A27	100r brn, *buff* ('93)	65.00	6.25
76	A27	75r car, *rose* ('93)	160.00	42.50
77	A27	200r dk bl, *bl* ('93)	160.00	35.00
78	A27	300r dk bl, *sal* ('93)	150.00	57.50
		Nos. 67-78 (12)	878.50	223.25

Nos. 67-78 were issued on two types of paper: enamel surfaced, which is white, with a uniform low gloss; and chalky, which bears a low-gloss application in a pattern of tiny lozenges, producing a somewhat duller appearance.

Nos. 76-78 were reprinted in 1900 (perf. 11½). Value, each $100. All values were reprinted in 1905 (perf. 13½). Value, each $50. See note after No. 4.

Stamps and Types of Previous Issues Overprinted in Black or Red

a   b

c

1892

79	A21 (a)	5r gray blk	16.00	8.75
a.		Double overprint	650.00	450.00
80	A22 (b)	10r green	16.00	8.75
a.		Inverted overprint	—	—
b.		Double overprint	650.00	450.00

1892-93

81	A21 (c)	5r gray blk (R)	13.50	6.75
82	A22 (c)	10r green (R)	16.00	9.25
a.		Inverted overprint	160.00	160.00
83	A25 (c)	20r rose	42.50	22.50
a.		Inverted overprint	225.00	225.00
84	A26 (c)	25r rose lilac, perf. 11½	14.50	5.25
a.		Perf. 12½	475.00	70.00
85	A24 (c)	50r blue (R) ('93)	77.50	62.50
		Nos. 81-85 (5)	164.00	106.25

1893

86	A15 (c)	15r bister brn (R)	20.00	12.00
87	A15 (c)	80r yellow	110.00	87.50

Nos. 86-87 are found in two types each. See note below No. 51.
Some of Nos. 79-87 were reprinted in 1900 and all values in 1905. Value of lowest-cost reprint, $10.
See note after No. 4.

Stamps and Types of Previous Issues Overprinted or Surcharged in Black or Red

d   e

1893   **Perf. 11½, 12½**

88	A21 (d)	5r gray blk (R)	30.00	22.50
89	A22 (d)	10r grn, perf. 11½ (R)	24.00	20.00
a.		"1938"	300.00	300.00
b.		"1863"	300.00	300.00
c.		"1838"	300.00	300.00
d.		Perf. 12½	1,650.	1,100.
90	A25 (d)	20r rose	45.00	32.50
a.		Inverted overprint	125.00	100.00
b.		"1938"	300.00	300.00
91	A26 (e)	20r on 25r lil rose	60.00	47.50
92	A26 (e)	25r lilac rose	110.00	100.00
a.		Inverted overprint	275.00	275.00
93	A24 (d)	50r blue (R)	125.00	110.00

Perf. 12½

94	A15 (d)	50r on 80r yel	150.00	100.00
95	A15 (d)	75r on 80r yel	100.00	72.50
a.		"1893" and "50rs" double	350.00	200.00
96	A15 (d)	80r yellow	150.00	95.00
a.		"1893" double	450.00	450.00
		Nos. 88-96 (9)	794.00	600.00

Nos. 94-96 are found in two types each. See note below No. 51.
Some of Nos. 88-96 were reprinted in 1900 and all values in 1905. Value of lowest-cost reprint, $45 each.
See note after No. 4.

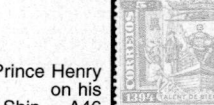

Prince Henry on his Ship — A46

Prince Henry Directing Fleet Maneuvers — A47

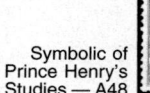

Symbolic of Prince Henry's Studies — A48

1894   **Litho.**   **Perf. 14**

97	A46	5r orange	3.25	.50
98	A46	10r magenta	3.25	.50
99	A46	15r red brown	10.00	3.00
100	A46	20r dull violet	10.00	3.50
101	A47	25r gray green	9.50	1.00
102	A47	50r blue	25.00	5.50
103	A47	75r car rose	47.50	10.50
104	A47	80r yellow grn	47.50	12.50
105	A47	100r lt brn, *pale buff*	37.50	9.50

Engr.

106	A48	150r lt car, *pale rose*	125.00	32.50
107	A48	300r dk bl, *sal buff*	140.00	37.50
108	A48	500r dp vio, *pale lil*	300.00	75.00
109	A48	1000r gray blk, *grysh*	550.00	110.00
		Nos. 97-109 (13)	1,309.	301.50

5th centenary of the birth of Prince Henry the Navigator.

King Carlos — A49

1895-1905   **Typo.**   **Perf. 11½**
Value in Black or Red (#122, 500r)

110	A49	2½r gray	.25	.25
111	A49	5r orange	.25	.25
112	A49	10r lt green	.50	.25
113	A49	15r brown	80.00	3.25
114	A49	15r gray grn ('99)	42.50	2.25
115	A49	20r gray violet	1.00	.30
116	A49	25r sea green	55.00	.25
117	A49	25r car rose ('99)	.50	.25
118	A49	50r blue	75.00	.35
119	A49	50r ultra ('05)	.50	.25
120	A49	65r slate bl ('98)	.50	.25
121	A49	75r rose	110.00	4.00
122	A49	75r brn, *yel* ('05)	2.00	.75
123	A49	80r violet	2.00	1.00
124	A49	100r dk bl, *bl*	1.00	.35
125	A49	115r org brn, *pink* ('98)	4.50	3.25
126	A49	130r gray brn, *straw* ('98)	3.50	1.40
127	A49	150r lt brn, *straw*	130.00	21.00
128	A49	180r sl, *pnksh* ('98)	16.00	9.50
129	A49	200r red lil, *pnksh*	4.00	1.00
130	A49	300r blue, *rose*	3.50	1.75
131	A49	500r blk, *bl* ('96)	10.00	4.00
a.		Perf. 12½	110.00	25.00
		Nos. 110-131 (22)	542.50	55.90

Several values of the above type exist without figures of value, also with figures inverted or otherwise misplaced but they were not regularly issued.

St. Anthony and his Vision — A50   St. Anthony Preaching to Fishes — A51

St. Anthony Ascends to Heaven — A52   St. Anthony, from Portrait — A53

Perf. 11½, 12½ and Compound
1895   **Typo.**

132	A50	2½r black	4.00	1.00

Litho.

133	A51	5r brown org	4.00	1.00
134	A51	10r red lilac	12.50	7.50
135	A51	15r chocolate	13.50	7.50
136	A51	20r gray violet	13.50	8.00
137	A51	25r grn & vio	12.50	1.00

138	A52	50r blue & brn	30.00	20.00
139	A52	75r rose & brn	45.00	35.00
140	A52	80r lt grn & brn	60.00	55.00
141	A52	100r choc & blk	50.00	27.50
142	A53	150r car & bis	150.00	90.00
143	A53	200r blue & bis	150.00	110.00
144	A53	300r slate & bis	210.00	140.00
145	A53	500r vio brn & grn	375.00	275.00
146	A53	1000r vio & grn	600.00	375.00
		Nos. 132-146 (15)	1,730.	1,154.

7th centenary of the birth of Saint Anthony of Padua. Stamps have eulogy in Latin printed on the back.

Common Design Types
pictured following the introduction.

Vasco da Gama Issue
Common Design Types

1898   **Perf. 12½ to 16**

147	CD20	2½r blue green	1.50	.25
148	CD21	5r red	1.50	.25
149	CD22	10r red violet	7.50	1.50
150	CD23	25r yel grn	4.50	.50
151	CD24	50r dark blue	10.00	2.75
152	CD25	75r violet brown	40.00	9.50
153	CD26	100r bister brown	27.50	9.50
154	CD27	150r bister	62.50	26.00
		Nos. 147-154 (8)	155.00	50.25

For overprints and surcharges see Nos. 185-192, 199-206.

King Manuel II
A62   A63

1910   **Typo.**   **Perf. 14½x15**

156	A62	2½r violet	.25	.25
157	A62	5r black	.25	.25
158	A62	10r gray green	.25	.25
159	A62	15r lilac brown	2.50	2.50
160	A62	20r carmine	.75	.60
161	A62	25r violet brn	.55	.25
162	A62	50r dark brn	1.40	.60
163	A62	75r bister brn	8.50	4.50
164	A62	80r slate	2.40	2.00
165	A62	100r brn, *lt grn*	9.00	2.75
166	A62	200r dk grn, *sal*	5.50	3.75
167	A62	300r blk, *azure*	6.00	4.50
168	A63	500r ol grn & vio brn	13.00	11.50
169	A63	1000r dk bl & blk	30.00	23.00
		Nos. 156-169 (14)	80.35	56.70

For overprint see No. RA1.

Preceding Issue Overprinted in Carmine or Green

1910

170	A62	2½r violet	.25	.25
171	A62	5r black	.25	.25
172	A62	10r gray green	3.25	1.10
173	A62	15r lilac brn	1.00	.80
174	A62	20r carmine (G)	4.00	1.50
175	A62	25r violet brn	.70	.25
176	A62	50r dk blue	5.50	2.00
177	A62	75r bister brn	8.50	4.00
178	A62	80r slate	3.00	2.25
179	A62	100r brn, *lt grn*	2.00	.75
180	A62	200r dk grn, *sal*	2.50	1.60
181	A62	300r blk, *azure*	3.50	3.00
182	A63	500r ol grn & vio brn	9.00	8.00
183	A63	1000r dk bl & blk	22.50	20.00
		Nos. 170-183 (14)	65.95	45.75

The numerous inverted and double overprints on this issue were unofficially and fraudulently made.
The 50r with blue overprint is a fraud.

Vasco da Gama Issue Overprinted or Surcharged

a

b

c

1911   Perf. 12½ to 16

185	CD20(a)	2½r blue grn	.50	.25
a.		Inverted overprint	15.00	13.00
186	CD21(b)	15r on 5r red	1.00	.50
a.		Inverted surcharge	10.00	9.50
187	CD23(a)	25r yel grn	.50	.25
a.		Inverted overprint	12.50	11.00
b.		Double overprint	17.50	16.00
188	CD24(a)	50r dk blue	3.00	2.10
a.		Inverted overprint	27.50	22.50
189	CD25(a)	75r vio brn	37.50	32.50
190	CD27(b)	80r on 150r bis	6.00	5.00
191	CD26(a)	100r bis brn	6.00	4.50
a.		Inverted overprint	30.00	21.00
192	CD22(c)	1000r on 10r red vio	55.00	40.00
a.		Inverted overprint	150.00	140.00
		Nos. 185-192 (8)	109.50	85.10

Postage Due Stamps of 1898 Overprinted or Surcharged for Regular Postage

d

e

1911   Perf. 12

193	D1(d)	5r black	1.00	.50
a.		Inverted overprint	15.00	11.00
b.		Double overprint	15.00	11.00
c.		Double ovpt., one inverted	15.00	11.00
194	D1(d)	10r magenta	1.50	.75
a.		Double ovpt., one inverted	15.00	11.00
195	D1(d)	20r orange	5.00	3.00
a.		Inverted overprint	22.50	17.50
b.		Double overprint	22.50	17.50
196	D1(d)	200r brn, buff	110.00	62.50
197	D1(e)	300r on 50r slate	80.00	40.00
198	D1(e)	500r on 100r car, pink	45.00	24.00
a.		Inverted surcharge	110.00	87.50
b.		Double surcharge	110.00	87.50
		Nos. 193-198 (6)	242.50	130.75

Vasco da Gama Issue of Madeira Ovptd. or Srchd. Types "a," "b" and "c"

1911   Perf. 12½ to 16

199	CD20(a)	2½r blue grn	11.00	8.00
200	CD21(b)	15r on 5r red	3.00	2.50
a.		Inverted surcharge	12.00	11.00
201	CD23(a)	25r yellow grn	5.00	4.50
202	CD24(a)	50r dk blue	10.00	7.50
203	CD25(a)	75r violet brn	10.00	5.00
a.		Inverted overprint	35.00	30.00
b.		Double overprint	45.00	35.00
204	CD27(b)	80r on 150r bis	11.00	10.50
a.		Inverted surcharge	45.00	42.50
205	CD26(a)	100r bister brn	35.00	8.00
a.		Inverted overprint	120.00	100.00
b.		Double overprint	120.00	100.00
206	CD22(c)	1000r on 10r red vio	35.00	25.00
		Nos. 199-206 (8)	120.00	71.00

Ceres — A64

Chalky Paper With Imprint

1912-20   Typo.   Perf. 15x14

207	A64	¼c dark olive	8.00	
208	A64	½c black	8.00	5.00
209	A64	1c deep green	6.50	2.50
210	A64	1½c chocolate	20.00	9.00
211	A64	2c carmine	20.00	9.00
212	A64	2½c violet	9.50	9.50
213	A64	5c dp blue	5.50	.55
214	A64	7½c yellow brn	65.00	13.50
215	A64	8c slate	3.00	3.00
216	A64	10c org brn	45.00	25.00
217	A64	15c plum	300.00	75.00
218	A64	20c vio brn, grn	13.00	1.50
219	A64	20c brn, buff ('20)	15.00	3.50
220	A64	30c brn, pink	100.00	9.50
221	A64	30c lt brn, yel ('17)	8.75	1.60
222	A64	50c org, sal ('18)	12.00	1.10
223	A64	1e dp grn, bl	19.00	1.40
		Nos. 207-223 (17)	658.25	175.65

1920   Typo.   Perf. 12x11½

224	A64	14c dk bl, yel	3.25	1.25
225	A64	20c choc, buff	800.00	200.00
226	A64	50c org, salmon	225.00	30.00
		Nos. 224-226 (3)	1,028.	231.25

1917-26   Typo.   Perf. 15x14
Ordinary Paper

227	A64	¼c dk ol ('18)	.65	.25
228	A64	½c black ('18)	.40	.25
229	A64	1c deep green	.65	.25
230	A64	1c chocolate	.25	.25
231	A64	1½c chocolate	5.50	2.50
232	A64	1½c dp grn ('18)	.30	.25
233	A64	2c carmine	5.50	2.50
234	A64	2c orange ('18)	.25	.25
235	A64	2½c violet	.25	.25
236	A64	3c car rose	.25	.25
237	A64	3c ultra ('21)	200.00	80.00
238	A64	3½c lt grn ('18)	.25	.25
239	A64	4c lt grn ('19)	.40	.30
240	A64	5c yel brn	.50	.30
240A	A64	5c deep blue	2.40	.25
241	A64	6c pale rose ('20)	.25	.25
242	A64	7½c dp blue	.50	.45
243	A64	7½c yellow brn	12.00	2.50
244	A64	8c slate	5.50	.75
245	A64	10c org brn	25.00	1.50
246	A64	12c bl gray ('20)	1.25	.65
247	A64	15c plum	3.25	.85
248	A64	20c choc ('20)	60.00	5.00
249	A64	30c gray brown	120.00	21.00
250	A64	36c red ('21)	4.50	1.25
251	A64	60c blue ('21)	4.00	1.90
252	A64	80c brn rose ('21)	1.40	1.10
253	A64	90c blue ('21)	5.50	4.75
254	A64	1e violet ('21)	185.00	65.00
		Nos. 227-254 (29)	645.70	195.05

1920-26   Perf. 12x11½
Ordinary Paper

255	A64	¼c dark olive	.40	.25
256	A64	½c black	.40	.25
257	A64	1c chocolate	.25	.25
258	A64	1½c dp grn	.25	.25
259	A64	2c orange	.70	.40
260	A64	2c yellow	.55	.25
261	A64	2c choc ('26)	1.40	8.00
262	A64	2½c violet	4.00	2.25
263	A64	3c car rose	.30	.30
264	A64	3c ultra ('21)	.50	.25
265	A64	4c lt grn ('19)	.25	.25
266	A64	4c org ('26)	1.40	1.60
267	A64	5c yel brn	1.00	.40
268	A64	5c ol brn ('23)	.25	.25
269	A64	6c pale rose	.40	.40
270	A64	6c brown ('24)	.55	.25
271	A64	7½c dp blue	.25	.25
272	A64	8c slate	.25	.25
273	A64	8c bl grn ('22)	.45	.25
274	A64	8c org ('24)	.45	.45
275	A64	10c org brn	.45	.25
276	A64	12c dp grn ('21)	.45	.40
277	A64	13½c chlky bl	1.40	.45
278	A64	14c brt vio ('21)	1.10	.45
279	A64	15c black ('23)	.40	.25
280	A64	16c brt ultra ('24)	.90	.65
281	A64	20c dk brn	.50	.25
282	A64	20c dp grn ('23)	.45	.25
283	A64	20c gray ('24)	.25	.25
284	A64	24c grnsh bl ('21)	.45	.25
285	A64	25c sal pink ('23)	.45	.25
286	A64	25c lt gray ('26)	.45	.25
287	A64	30c gray brn ('21)	.50	.25
288	A64	30c dk brn ('24)	20.00	4.00
289	A64	32c dp grn ('24)	1.10	.40
290	A64	36c red ('21)	1.75	.45
291	A64	40c dk bl ('23)	.90	.55
292	A64	40c choc ('24)	.45	.45
293	A64	40c green ('26)	.25	.25
294	A64	48c rose ('24)	7.50	4.00
295	A64	50c yellow ('21)	1.90	.70
296	A64	60c blue ('21)	1.40	.60
297	A64	64c pale ultra ('24)	9.50	5.50

298	A64	75c dull rose ('23)	15.00	7.50
298A	A64	80c brn rose ('21)	32.50	9.50
298B	A64	80c violet ('24)	1.00	.55
298C	A64	90c chalky bl ('21)	1.60	.85
298D	A64	96c dp rose ('26)	42.50	35.00
298E	A64	1e violet ('21)	4.50	1.90
298F	A64	1.10e yel brn ('21)	4.50	1.60
298G	A64	1.20e yel grn ('21)	2.50	1.40
298H	A64	2e sl grn ('21)	45.00	5.50
		Nos. 255-298H (52)	215.60	101.80

1923-26   Perf. 12x11½
Glazed Paper

298I	A64	1e dk blue	5.00	2.25
298J	A64	1e gray vio ('24)	1.50	1.10
298K	A64	1.20e buff ('24)	50.00	32.50
298L	A64	1.50e blk vio ('24)	17.50	3.25
298M	A64	1.50e lilac ('24)	30.00	5.00
298N	A64	1.60e dp bl ('24)	19.00	5.00
298O	A64	2e sl grn ('24)	37.50	5.50
298P	A64	2.40e ap grn ('26)	160.00	110.00
298Q	A64	3e pink ('26)	160.00	100.00
298R	A64	3.20e gray grn ('24)	32.50	12.00
298S	A64	5e emer ('24)	35.00	9.00
298T	A64	10e red ('24)	175.00	50.00
298U	A64	20e pale turq ('24)	300.00	160.00
		Nos. 298I-298U (13)	1,023.	495.60

See design A85. For surcharges & overprints see Nos. 453-495, RA2.
See 496A-496R.

Presidents of Portugal and Brazil and Aviators Cabral and Coutinho A65

1923   Litho.   Perf. 14

299	A65	1c brown	.25	.75
300	A65	2c orange	.25	.75
301	A65	3c ultra	.25	.75
302	A65	4c yellow grn	.25	.75
303	A65	5c bister brn	.25	.75
304	A65	10c brown org	.25	.75
305	A65	15c black	.25	.75
306	A65	20c blue grn	.25	.75
307	A65	25c rose	.25	.75
308	A65	30c olive brn	.60	2.00
309	A65	40c chocolate	.25	.75
310	A65	50c yellow	.30	.90
311	A65	75c violet	.30	1.10
312	A65	1e dp blue	.30	2.00
313	A65	1.50e olive grn	.65	2.50
314	A65	2e myrtle grn	.65	6.50
		Nos. 299-314 (16)	5.30	22.50

Flight of Sacadura Cabral and Gago Coutinho from Portugal to Brazil.

Camoens at Ceuta A66

Camoens Saving the Lusiads — A67

Luis de Camoens — A68

First Edition of the Lusiads — A69

Camoens Dying — A70

Tomb of Camoens A71

Monument to Camoens — A72

Engr.; Values Typo. in Black
1924, Nov. 11   Perf. 14, 14½

315	A66	2c lt blue	.25	.25
316	A66	3c orange	.25	.25
317	A66	4c dk gray	.25	.25
318	A66	5c yellow grn	.25	.25
319	A66	6c lake	.25	.25
320	A67	8c orange brn	.25	.25
321	A67	10c gray vio	.25	.25
322	A67	15c olive grn	.25	.25
323	A67	16c violet brn	.25	.25
324	A67	20c dp orange	.30	.40
325	A68	25c lilac	.30	.40
326	A68	30c dk brown	.30	.40
327	A68	32c dk green	.90	1.25
328	A68	40c ultra	.25	.35
329	A68	48c red brown	1.10	1.50
330	A69	60c red orange	1.25	1.60
331	A69	64c green	1.25	1.60
332	A69	75c dk violet	1.40	.90
333	A69	80c bister	1.00	1.25
334	A69	96c lake	1.00	1.25
335	A70	1e slate	1.00	1.25
336	A70	1.20e lt brown	6.00	4.75
337	A70	1.50e red	1.10	1.75
338	A70	1.60e dk blue	1.10	1.75
339	A70	2e apple grn	5.00	6.00
340	A71	2.40e green, grn	3.25	4.00
341	A71	3e dk bl, bl	1.40	2.00
a.		Value double	125.00	125.00
342	A71	3.20e blk, green	1.40	2.00
343	A71	4.50e blk, orange	3.75	5.00
344	A71	10e dk brn, pnksh	8.50	11.00
345	A72	20e dk vio, lil	8.50	11.00
		Nos. 315-345 (31)	52.30	63.65

Birth of Luis de Camoens, poet, 400th anniv.
For overprints see Nos. 1S6-1S71.

Castello-Branco's House at Sao Miguel de Seide — A73

Castello-Branco's Study — A74

Camillo Castello-Branco A75

Teresa de Albuquerque A76

Mariana and Joao de Cruz — A77   Simao de Botelho — A78

1925, Mar. 26   *Perf. 12½*

346	A73	2c orange	.25	.25
347	A73	3c green	.25	.25
348	A73	4c ultra	.25	.25
349	A73	5c scarlet	.25	.25
350	A73	6c brown vio	.25	.25
a.		"6" and "C" omitted		
351	A73	8c black brn	.25	.25
352	A75	10c pale blue	.25	.25
353	A75	15c olive grn	.25	.25
354	A74	16c red orange	.30	.30
355	A74	20c dk violet	.30	.30
356	A75	25c car rose	.30	.30
357	A74	30c bister brn	.30	.30
358	A74	32c green	1.75	1.75
359	A74	40c green & blk	.65	.65
360	A74	48c red brn	3.50	3.50
361	A76	50c blue green	.65	.65
362	A76	64c orange brn	3.50	3.50
363	A75	75c gray blk	.60	.60
364	A75	80c brown	.60	.60
365	A76	96c car rose	2.00	2.00
366	A76	1e gray vio	1.50	1.50
367	A76	1.20e yellow grn	1.50	1.50
368	A77	1.50e dk bl, *bl*	25.00	15.00
369	A75	1.60e indigo	4.75	3.75
370	A77	2e dk grn, *grn*	6.25	4.75
371	A77	2.40e red, *org*	52.50	32.50
372	A77	3e lake, *bl*	65.00	42.50
373	A77	3.20e *green*	30.00	30.00
374	A77	4.50e red & blk	11.00	4.00
375	A77	10e brn, *yel*	11.50	4.00
376	A78	20e *orange*	12.50	5.00
		Nos. 346-376 (31)	237.95	160.95
		Set, never hinged	400.00	

Centenary of the birth of Camillo Castello-Branco, novelist.

First Independence Issue

Alfonso the Conqueror, First King of Portugal — A79

Batalha Monastery and King John I — A80

Battle of Aljubarrota A81

Filipa de Vilhena Arming her Sons A82   King John IV (The Duke of Braganza) A83

Independence Monument, Lisbon — A84

Center in Black

1926, Aug. 13   *Perf. 14, 14½*

377	A79	2c orange	.25	.25
378	A79	3c ultra	.25	.25
379	A79	4c yellow grn	.25	.25
380	A80	5c black brn	.25	.25
381	A79	6c ocher	.25	.25
382	A80	15c dk green	.25	.25
383	A79	16c dp blue	.65	1.20
384	A81	20c dull violet	.65	1.20
385	A82	25c scarlet	.65	1.20
386	A81	32c dp green	.80	2.00
387	A82	40c yellow brn	.80	2.00
388	A80	46c carmine	3.00	4.00
389	A82	50c olive bis	3.00	4.00
390	A83	64c blue green	4.50	6.00
391	A82	75c brown red	4.50	6.00
392	A84	96c dull red	6.75	7.50
393	A83	1e black vio	6.75	8.50
394	A81	1.60e myrtle grn	8.50	11.00
395	A84	3e plum	25.00	29.00
396	A84	4.50e olive grn	32.50	35.00
397	A81	10e carmine	50.00	55.00
		Nos. 377-397 (21)	149.55	175.10
		Set, never hinged	250.00	

The use of these stamps instead of the regular issue was obligatory on Aug. 13th and 14th, Nov. 30th and Dec. 1st, 1926.

Stamps of 1926 Surcharged in Black

No. 397A

No. 397D

No. 397K

1926   **Center in Black**   *Perf. 13½x14*

397A	A80	2c on 5c blk brn	1.10	1.40
397B	A80	2c on 46c car	1.10	1.40
397C	A83	2c on 64c bl grn	1.50	2.00
397D	A82	3c on 75c brn red	1.50	2.00
397E	A84	3c on 96c dull red	2.00	2.50
397F	A83	3c on 1e blk vio	1.75	2.25
397G	A81	4c on 1.60e myr grn	11.00	12.00
397H	A84	4c on 3e plum	3.75	4.25
397J	A84	6c on 4.50e ol grn	3.75	4.25
397K	A81	6c on 10e carmine	4.25	5.00
		Nos. 397A-397K (10)	31.70	37.55
		Set, never hinged	60.00	

There are two styles of the ornaments in these surcharges.

Ceres — A85

Without Imprint

1926, Dec. 2   **Typo.**   *Perf. 13½x14*

398	A85	2c chocolate	.25	.25
399	A85	3c brt blue	.25	.25
400	A85	4c dp orange	.25	.25
401	A85	5c dp brown	.25	.25
402	A85	6c orange brn	.25	.25
403	A85	10c orange red	.25	.25
404	A85	15c black	.25	.25
405	A85	16c ultra	.25	.25
406	A85	25c gray	.25	.25
407	A85	32c dp green	.55	.35
408	A85	40c blue green	.35	.25
409	A85	48c rose	1.10	.90
410	A85	50c ocher	1.75	1.60
411	A85	64c deep blue	1.75	1.60
412	A85	80c violet	3.50	.55
413	A85	96c car rose	2.00	1.00
414	A85	1e red brown	9.00	1.00
415	A85	1.20e yellow brn	9.00	1.00
416	A85	1.60e dark blue	2.25	.55
417	A85	2e green	13.00	1.00
418	A85	3.20e olive grn	5.00	1.00
419	A85	4.50e yellow	5.00	1.00
420	A85	5e brown olive	65.00	3.75
421	A85	10e red	8.00	2.00
		Nos. 398-421 (24)	129.50	19.80
		Set, never hinged	290.00	

See design A64.

Second Independence Issue

Goncalo Mendes da Maia — A86   Dr. Joao das Regras — A88

Guimaraes Castle — A87

Battle of Montijo — A89

Brites de Almeida — A90   Joao Pinto Ribeiro — A91

Center in Black

1927, Nov. 29   **Engr.**   *Perf. 14*

422	A86	2c brown	.25	.25
423	A87	3c ultra	.25	.25
424	A86	4c orange	.25	.25
425	A88	5c olive brn	.25	.25
426	A89	6c orange brn	.25	.25
427	A87	15c black brn	.45	1.00
428	A88	16c deep blue	1.00	1.75
429	A86	25c gray	1.25	1.75
430	A89	32c blue grn	2.25	3.00
431	A90	40c yellow grn	.60	1.00
432	A86	48c brown red	10.00	12.50
433	A87	80c dk violet	7.50	9.00
434	A90	96c dull red	13.00	15.00
435	A88	1.60e myrtle grn	14.00	15.00
436	A91	4.50e bister	20.00	22.50
		Nos. 422-436 (15)	71.30	83.75
		Set, never hinged	125.00	

The use of these stamps instead of the regular issue was compulsory on Nov. 29-30, Dec. 1-2, 1927. The money derived from their sale was used for the purchase of a palace for a war museum, the organization of an international exposition in Lisbon, in 1940, and for fêtes to be held in that year in commemoration of the 8th cent. of the founding of Portugal and the 3rd cent. of its restoration.

Third Independence Issue

Gualdim Paes — A93   The Siege of Santarem — A94

Battle of Rolica — A95

Battle of Atoleiros A96

Joana de Gouveia A97   Matias de Albuquerque A98

1928, Nov. 28   **Center in Black**

437	A93	2c lt blue	.25	.25
438	A94	3c lt green	.25	.25
439	A95	4c lake	.25	.25
440	A96	5c olive grn	.25	.25
441	A97	6c orange brn	.25	.25
442	A94	15c slate	.65	.85
443	A95	16c dk violet	.65	.85
444	A93	25c ultra	.65	1.00
445	A97	32c dk green	3.50	4.00
446	A96	40c olive brn	.65	1.00
447	A95	50c red orange	8.50	10.00
448	A94	80c lt gray	9.00	10.00
449	A97	96c carmine	15.00	18.00
450	A96	1e claret	25.00	29.00
451	A93	1.60e dk blue	11.50	13.50
452	A98	4.50e yellow	12.50	15.00
		Nos. 437-452 (16)	88.85	104.45
		Set, never hinged	150.00	

Obligatory Nov. 27-30. See note after No. 436.

Type and Stamps of 1912-28 Surcharged in Black

1928-29   *Perf. 12x11½, 15x14*

453	A64	4c on 8c orange	.35	.30
454	A64	4c on 30c dk brn	.35	.30
455	A64	10c on ¼c dk ol	.35	.30
a.		Inverted surcharge	100.00	90.00
456	A64	10c on ½c blk (R)	.50	.40
a.		Perf. 15x14	17.50	14.00
457	A64	10c on 1c choc	.50	.40
a.		Perf. 15x14	65.00	50.00
458	A64	10c on 4c grn	.40	.35
a.		Perf. 15x14	75.00	60.00
459	A64	10c on 4c orange	.40	.35
460	A64	10c on 5c ol brn	.40	.35
461	A64	15c on 16c blue	1.00	.75
462	A64	15c on 16c ultra	1.00	.75
463	A64	15c on 20c brown	32.50	30.00
464	A64	15c on 20c gray	.35	.30
465	A64	15c on 24c grnsh bl	2.10	1.60
466	A64	15c on 25c gray	.35	.30
467	A64	15c on 25c sal pink	.35	.30
468	A64	16c on 32c dp grn	.75	.70
469	A64	40c on 2c orange	.35	.30
470	A64	40c on 2c yellow	4.00	3.00
471	A64	40c on 2c choc	.35	.30
472	A64	40c on 3c ultra	.40	.35
473	A64	40c on 50c yellow	.35	.30
474	A64	40c on 60c blue	.75	.65
a.		Perf. 15x14	9.00	7.50

475	A64	40c on 64c pale ultra	.75	.70
476	A64	40c on 75c dl rose	.85	.80
477	A64	40c on 80c violet	.60	.50
478	A64	40c on 90c chlky bl	4.00	3.00
a.		Perf. 15x14	10.00	8.50
479	A64	40c on 1e gray vio	.75	.70
480	A64	40c on 1.10e yel brn	.75	.70
481	A64	80c on 6c pale rose	.75	.70
482	A64	80c on 6c choc	.75	.70
483	A64	80c on 48c rose	1.10	1.00
484	A64	80c on 1.50e lilac	1.75	1.25
485	A64	96c on 1.20e yel grn	3.50	2.50
486	A64	96c on 1.20e buff	4.50	3.50
487	A64	1.60e on 2e slate grn	40.00	27.50
487A	A64	1.60e on 2e sl grn, *glazed paper*	32.50	27.50
488	A64	1.60e on 3.20e gray grn	9.00	7.00
489	A64	1.60e on 20e pale turq	12.00	10.00
		Nos. 453-489 (37)	128.90	102.90
		Set, never hinged	275.00	.30

Stamps of 1912-26
Overprinted in Black or Red

1929   **Perf. 12x11½**

490	A64	10c orange brn	.40	
a.		Perf. 15x14	275.00	275.00
491	A64	15c black (R)	.40	.30
492	A64	40c lt green	.60	.50
493	A64	40c chocolate	.60	.40
494	A64	96c dp rose	5.00	4.50
495	A64	1.60e brt blue	22.50	16.00
a.		Double overprint	110.00	100.00
		Nos. 490-495 (6)	29.50	21.70
		Set, never hinged	45.00	

Liberty — A100

1929, May   **Perf. 12x11½**
496	A100	1.60e on 5c red brn	13.00	10.00

Types of 1912-20 Issues
With Imprint

1930-31   **Typo.**   **Perf. 12x11½**

496A	A64	4c orange	.30	.25
496B	A64	5c blk brn ('31)	.30	.25
496C	A64	6c red brn	.30	.25
496D	A64	10c red ('31)	.30	.25
496E	A64	15c black	1.75	.30
496F	A64	25c lt gray	.45	.25
496G	A64	25c blue grn	.45	.25
496H	A85	32c dp green	.45	.25
496I	A64	40c green	3.50	.55
496J	A64	50c bister	1.75	.80
496K	A64	50c red brn ('30)	1.75	.80
496L	A64	75c car rose	1.75	.85
496M	A64	80c dk grn	1.75	.85
496N	A64	1e brn lake	3.50	.85
496O	A64	1.20e pur brn ('31)	3.00	1.00
496P	A64	1.25e dk bl ('31)	2.50	1.00
496Q	A64	2e red vio ('31)	17.50	6.50
496R	A64	4.50e org ('31)	45.00	40.00
		Nos. 496A-496R (18)	86.30	55.25
		Set, never hinged	160.00	

Nos. 496A-496R were printed at the Lisbon Mint from new plates produced from the original dies. The paper is whiter than the paper used for earlier Ceres stamps. The gum is white.

"Portugal" Holding Volume of "Lusiads" — A101

1931-38   **Typo.**   **Perf. 14**
497	A101	4c bister brn	.25	.25
498	A101	5c olive gray	.25	.25
499	A101	6c lt gray	.25	.25
500	A101	10c dk violet	.25	.25
501	A101	15c gray blk	.25	.25

502	A101	16c brt blue	1.10	.75
503	A101	25c deep green	3.00	.35
504	A101	25c brt bl ('33)	3.25	.40
505	A101	30c dk grn ('33)	1.75	.40
506	A101	40c orange red	5.50	.25
507	A101	48c fawn	1.10	.95
508	A101	50c lt brown	.30	.25
509	A101	75c car rose	4.50	1.10
510	A101	80c emerald	.35	.25
511	A101	95c car rose ('33)	15.00	6.50
512	A101	1e claret	27.50	.25
513	A101	1.20e olive grn	2.00	1.10
514	A101	1.25e dk blue	1.75	.25
515	A101	1.60e dk blue ('33)	30.00	4.00
516	A101	1.75e dk blue ('38)	.65	.25
517	A101	2e dull violet	.65	.25
518	A101	4.50e orange	1.50	.30
519	A101	5e yellow grn	1.50	.30
		Nos. 497-519 (23)	102.65	19.15
		Set, never hinged	200.00	

Birthplace of St. Anthony A102

Font where St. Anthony was Baptized A103

Lisbon Cathedral A104

St. Anthony with Infant Jesus A105

Santa Cruz Cathedral A106

St. Anthony's Tomb at Padua A107

1931, June   **Typo.**   **Perf. 12**
528	A102	15c plum	.65	.25

Litho.
529	A103	25c gray & pale grn	1.00	.25
530	A104	40c gray brn & buff	.65	.25
531	A105	75c dl rose & pale rose	21.00	14.00
532	A106	1.25e gray & pale bl	47.50	27.50
533	A107	4.50e gray vio & lil	23.00	3.50
		Nos. 528-533 (6)	93.80	45.75
		Set, never hinged	210.00	

7th centenary of the death of St. Anthony of Padua and Lisbon.
For surcharges see Nos. 543-548.

Nuno Alvares Pereira (1360-1431), Portuguese Warrior and Statesman — A108

1931, Nov. 1   **Typo.**   **Perf. 12x11½**
534	A108	15c black	1.10	1.10
535	A108	25c gray grn & blk	1.75	1.10
536	A108	40c orange	2.75	.50
a.		Value omitted	150.00	150.00
537	A108	75c car rose	32.50	27.50
538	A108	1.25e dk bl & pale bl	26.00	21.00

539	A108	4.50e choc & lt grn	120.00	52.50
a.		Value omitted	350.00	350.00
		Nos. 534-539 (6)	184.10	103.70
		Set, never hinged	350.00	

For surcharges see Nos. 549-554.

Nos. 528-533 Surcharged

1933   **Perf. 12**
543	A104	15c on 40c	.75	.35
544	A102	40c on 15c	2.50	1.25
545	A103	40c on 25c	2.00	.35
546	A105	40c on 75c	8.00	5.25
547	A106	40c on 1.25e	8.00	5.25
548	A107	40c on 4.50e	8.00	5.25
		Nos. 543-548 (6)	29.25	17.70
		Set, never hinged	52.50	

Nos. 534-539 Surcharged

1933   **Perf. 12x11½**
549	A108	15c on 40c	.90	.35
550	A108	40c on 15c	3.75	2.75
551	A108	40c on 25c	1.10	.90
552	A108	40c on 75c	8.00	6.50
553	A108	40c on 1.25e	8.00	4.00
554	A108	40c on 4.50e	8.00	4.00
		Nos. 549-554 (6)	29.75	18.50
		Set, never hinged	55.00	

President Carmona — A109

1934, May 28   **Typo.**   **Perf. 11½**
556	A109	40c brt violet	17.50	.35
		Never hinged	32.50	

Head of a Colonial — A110

1934, July   **Perf. 11½x12**
558	A110	25c dk brown	3.00	1.75
559	A110	40c scarlet	19.00	.40
560	A110	1.60e dk blue	29.00	13.00
		Nos. 558-560 (3)	51.00	15.15
		Set, never hinged	125.00	

Colonial Exposition.

Roman Temple, Evora A111

Prince Henry the Navigator A112

"All for the Nation" A113

Coimbra Cathedral A114

1935-41   **Perf. 11½x12**
561	A111	4c black	.40	.25
562	A111	5c blue	.45	.25
563	A111	6c choc ('36)	.75	.30

Perf. 11½, 12x11½ (1.75e)
564	A112	10c turq grn	.65	.25
565	A112	15c red brown	.25	.25
a.		Booklet pane of 4		
566	A113	25c dp blue	5.25	.40
a.		Booklet pane of 4		
567	A113	40c brown	1.75	.25
a.		Booklet pane of 4		
568	A113	1e rose red	8.50	.45
568A	A114	1.75e blue	70.00	1.25
568B	A113	10e gray blk ('41)	20.00	3.00
569	A113	20e turq grn ('41)	26.00	2.00
		Nos. 561-569 (11)	134.00	8.65
		Set, never hinged	240.00	

For overprint see No. O1.

Queen Maria — A115

Typographed, Head Embossed

1935, June 1   **Perf. 11½**
570	A115	40c scarlet	1.25	.25
		Never hinged	2.00	

First Portuguese Philatelic Exhibition.

Rod and Bowl of Aesculapius — A116

1937, July 24   **Typo.**   **Perf. 11½x12**
571	A116	25c blue	9.50	.90
		Never hinged	15.00	

Centenary of the establishment of the School of Medicine in Lisbon and Oporto.

Gil Vicente — A117

1937
572	A117	40c dark brown	17.00	.25
573	A117	1e rose red	2.00	.25
		Set, never hinged	32.50	

400th anniversary of the death of Gil Vicente (1465-1536), Portuguese playwright. Design shows him in cowherd role in his play, "Auto do Vaqueiro."

Grapes — A118

1938   *Perf. 11½*
575	A118	15c brt purple	1.25	.50
576	A118	25c brown	3.00	1.60
577	A118	40c dp red lilac	9.00	.30
578	A118	1.75e dp blue	26.00	24.00
		Nos. 575-578 (4)	39.25	26.40
		Set, never hinged	65.00	

International Vineyard and Wine Congress.

Emblem of Portuguese Legion — A119

1940, Jan. 27   **Unwmk.**   *Perf. 11½*
579	A119	5c dull yellow	.30	.25
580	A119	10c violet	.30	.25
581	A119	15c brt blue	.30	.25
582	A119	25c brown	20.00	1.10
583	A119	40c dk green	32.50	.40
584	A119	80c yellow grn	2.10	.60
585	A119	1e brt red	50.00	3.50
586	A119	1.75e dark blue	7.00	2.60
a.		Souv. sheet of 8, #579- 586	290.00	290.00
		Never hinged	600.00	
		Nos. 579-586 (8)	112.50	8.95
		Set, never hinged	190.00	

Issued in honor of the Portuguese Legion. No. 586a sold for 5.50e, the proceeds going to various charities.

Portuguese World Exhibition A120

King John IV — A121

Discoveries Monument, Belém — A122

King Alfonso I — A123

1940   **Engr.**   *Perf. 12x11½, 11½x12*
587	A120	10c brown violet	.25	.25
588	A121	15c dk grnsh bl	.25	.25
589	A122	25c dk slate grn	1.20	.25
590	A121	35c yellow green	1.10	.35
591	A123	40c olive bister	2.50	.25
592	A120	80c dk violet	5.00	.35
593	A122	1e dark red	11.00	1.60
594	A123	1.75e ultra	6.50	2.60
a.		Souv. sheet of 8, #587-594 ('41)	150.00	110.00
		Never hinged	300.00	
		Nos. 587-594 (8)	27.80	5.90
		Set, never hinged	47.50	

Portuguese Intl. Exhibition, Lisbon (10c, 80c); restoration of the monarchy, 300th anniv (15c, 35c); Portuguese independence, 800th anniv (40c, 1.75e). No. 594a sold for 10e.

Sir Rowland Hill — A124

1940, Aug. 12   **Typo.**   *Perf. 11½x12*
595	A124	15c dk violet brn	.25	.25
596	A124	25c dp org brn	.25	.25
597	A124	35c green	.30	.25
598	A124	40c brown violet	.45	.25
599	A124	50c turq green	17.00	3.25
600	A124	80c lt blue	2.00	1.10
601	A124	1e crimson	20.00	3.50
602	A124	1.75e dk blue	6.00	3.50
a.		Souv. sheet of 8, #595-602 ('41)	75.00	75.00
		Never hinged	120.00	
		Nos. 595-602 (8)	46.25	12.35
		Set, never hinged	75.00	

Postage stamp centenary. No. 602a sold for 10e.

Fisherwoman of Nazare A126

Native of Coimbra A127

Native of Saloio — A128

Fisherwoman of Lisbon — A129

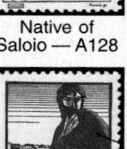

Native of Olhao — A130

Native of Aveiro — A131

Native of Madeira A132

Native of Viana do Castelo A133

Rancher of Ribatejo A134

Peasant of Alentejo A135

Ancient Sailing Vessel — A136

1943   *Perf. 14*
615	A136	5c black	.25	.25
616	A136	10c fawn	.25	.25
617	A136	15c lilac gray	.25	.25
618	A136	20c dull violet	.25	.25
619	A136	30c brown violet	.25	.25
620	A136	35c dk blue grn	.25	.25
621	A136	50c plum	.25	.25
622	A136	1e deep rose	6.75	.25
623	A136	1.75e indigo	21.00	.25
624	A136	2e dull claret	1.60	.25
625	A136	2.50e crim rose	2.40	.25
626	A136	3.50e grnsh blue	11.00	.50
627	A136	5e dp orange	1.25	.25
628	A136	10e blue gray	2.75	.25
629	A136	15e blue green	26.00	1.00
630	A136	20e olive gray	80.00	.70
631	A136	50e salmon	240.00	1.00
		Nos. 615-631 (17)	394.50	6.45
		Set, never hinged	850.00	

See Nos. 702-710.

Farmer — A137

1943, Oct.   *Perf. 11½*
632	A137	10c dull blue	.75	.25
633	A137	50c red	1.25	.35
		Set, never hinged	3.00	

Congress of Agricultural Science.

Postrider — A138

1944, May   **Unwmk.**
634	A138	10c dk violet brn	.25	.25
635	A138	50c purple	.25	.25
636	A138	1e cerise	3.25	.65
637	A138	1.75e brt blue	3.25	1.75
a.		Sheet of 4, #634-637	32.50	35.00
		Never hinged	52.50	
		Nos. 634-637 (4)	7.00	2.90
		Set, never hinged	10.50	

3rd Philatelic Exhibition, Lisbon. No. 637a sold for 7.50e.

Portrait of Avellar Brotero — A139

1941, Apr. 4   **Typo.**   *Perf. 11½*
605	A126	4c sage green	.25	.25
606	A127	5c orange brn	.25	.25
607	A128	10c red violet	3.25	1.25
608	A129	15c lt yel grn	.25	.25
609	A130	25c rose violet	2.25	.70
610	A131	40c yellow grn	.25	.25
611	A132	80c lt blue	3.25	2.10
612	A133	1e rose red	9.50	1.60
613	A134	1.75e dull blue	10.50	4.75
614	A135	2e red orange	40.00	22.50
a.		Sheet of 10, #605-614	125.00	125.00
		Never hinged	225.00	
		Nos. 605-614 (10)	69.75	33.90
		Set, never hinged	120.00	

No. 614a sold for 10e.

Statue of Brotero — A140

1944, Nov. 23   **Typo.**   *Perf. 11½x12*
638	A139	10c chocolate	.25	.25
639	A140	50c dull green	1.20	.25
640	A140	1e carmine	7.00	1.60
641	A139	1.75e dark blue	6.25	2.60
a.		Sheet of 4,#638-641 ('45)	32.50	32.50
		Never hinged	62.50	
		Nos. 638-641 (4)	14.70	4.70
		Set, never hinged	21.00	

Avellar Brotero, botanist, 200th birth anniv. No. 641a sold for 7.50e.

Gil Eannes — A141

Designs: 30c, Joao Goncalves Zarco. 35c, Bartolomeu Dias. 50c, Vasco da Gama. 1e, Pedro Alvares Cabral. 1.75e, Fernando Magellan. 2e, Goncalo Velho. 3.50e, Diogo Cao.

1945, July 29   **Engr.**   *Perf. 13½*
642	A141	10c violet brn	.25	.25
643	A141	30c yellow brn	.25	.25
644	A141	35c blue green	.35	.25
645	A141	50c dk olive grn	1.25	.25
646	A141	1e vermilion	3.00	.65
647	A141	1.75e slate blue	3.50	2.10
648	A141	2e black	4.50	2.40
649	A141	3.50e carmine rose	8.00	4.25
a.		Sheet of 8, #642-649	32.50	40.00
		Never hinged	50.00	
		Nos. 642-649 (8)	21.10	10.40
		Set, never hinged	32.50	

Portuguese navigators of 15th and 16th centuries. No. 649a sold for 15e.

Pres. Antonio Oscar de Fragoso Carmona — A149

     Perf. 11½
1945, Nov. 12   **Photo.**   **Unwmk.**
650	A149	10c bright violet	.25	.25
651	A149	30c copper brn	.25	.25
652	A149	35c dark green	.25	.25
653	A149	50c dark olive	.35	.25
654	A149	1e dark red	9.50	1.25
655	A149	1.75e dark blue	7.50	3.75
656	A149	2e deep claret	42.50	5.00
657	A149	3.50e slate black	30.00	7.50
a.		Sheet of 8, #650-657	110.00	110.00
		Never hinged	210.00	
		Nos. 650-657 (8)	90.60	18.50
		Set, never hinged	150.00	

No. 657a sold for 15e.

Astrolabe — A150

1945, Dec. 27   **Litho.**
658	A150	10c light brown	.25	.25
659	A150	50c gray green	.25	.25
660	A150	1e brown red	3.00	.75
661	A150	1.75e dull chalky bl	3.25	2.60
a.		Sheet of 4, #658-661 ('46)	26.00	27.50
		Never hinged	42.50	
		Nos. 658-661 (4)	6.75	3.85
		Set, never hinged	10.50	

Centenary of the Portuguese Naval School.

No. 661a, issued Apr. 29, sold for 7.50e.

Catalogue values for unused stamps in this section, from this point to the end of the section, are for Never Hinged items.

Silves Castle A151

Almourol Castle A152

Castles: 30c, Leiria. 35c, Feira. 50c, Guimaraes. 1.75e, Lisbon. 2e, Braganca. 3.50e, Ourem.

1946, June 1   **Engr.**
662	A151	10c brown vio	.25	.25
663	A151	30c brown red	.25	.25
664	A151	35c olive grn	.25	.25
665	A151	50c gray blk	.75	.25
666	A152	1e brt carmine	30.00	1.00
667	A152	1.75e dk blue	16.50	2.40
a.		Sheet of 4	175.00	100.00
		Hinged	95.00	
668	A152	2e dk gray grn	60.00	4.50
669	A152	3.50e orange brn	26.00	5.50
		Nos. 662-669 (8)	134.00	14.40

No. 667a printed on buff granite paper, size 135x102mm, sold for 12.50e.

Figure with Tablet and Arms — A153

1946, Nov. 19   **Perf. 12x11½**
670	A153	50c dark blue	1.00	.25
a.		Sheet of 4	155.00	120.00
		Hinged	80.00	

Establishment of the Bank of Portugal, cent. No. 670a measures 155x143½mm and sold for 7.50e.

Madonna and Child — A154

1946, Dec. 8   **Unwmk.**   **Perf. 13½**
671	A154	30c gray black	.30	.25
672	A154	50c deep green	.30	.25
673	A154	1e rose car	3.25	1.10
674	A154	1.75e brt blue	5.25	2.25
a.		Sheet of 4, #671-674 ('47)	67.50	52.50
		Hinged	37.50	
		Nos. 671-674 (4)	9.10	3.85

300th anniv. of the proclamation making the Virgin Mary patroness of Portugal. No. 674a sold for 7.50e.

Shepherdess, Caramullo — A155

30c, Timbrel player, Malpique. 35c, Flute player, Monsanto. 50c, Woman of Avintes. 1e, Field laborer, Maia. 1.75e, Woman of Algarve. 2e, Bastonet player, Miranda. 3.50e, Woman of the Azores.

1947, Mar. 1   **Photo.**   **Perf. 11½**
675	A155	10c rose violet	.25	.25
676	A155	30c dark red	.25	.25
677	A155	35c dk olive grn	.35	.25
678	A155	50c dark brown	.60	.25
679	A155	1e red	19.00	.55
680	A155	1.75e slate blue	4.00	4.00
681	A155	2e peacock bl	65.00	4.50
682	A155	3.50e slate blk	50.00	7.50
a.		Sheet of 8, #675-682	260.00	260.00
		Hinged	145.00	
		Nos. 675-682 (8)	155.45	17.55

No. 682a sold for 15e.

Surrender of the Moors, 1147 — A163

1947, Oct. 13   **Engr.**   **Perf. 12½**
683	A163	5c blue green	.25	.25
684	A163	20c dk carmine	.25	.25
685	A163	50c violet	.30	.25
686	A163	1.75e dark blue	7.25	5.00
687	A163	2.50e chocolate	11.00	6.50
688	A163	3.50e slate black	19.00	10.50
		Nos. 683-688 (6)	38.05	22.75

Conquest of Lisbon from the Moors, 800th anniv.

St. John de Britto A164 A165

1948, May 28   **Perf. 11½x12**
689	A164	30c green	.25	.25
690	A165	50c dark brown	.25	.25
691	A164	1e rose carmine	10.50	1.60
692	A165	1.75e blue	13.00	2.75
		Nos. 689-692 (4)	24.00	4.85

Birth of St. John de Britto, 300th anniv.

Architecture and Engineering A166

1948, May 28   **Perf. 13x12½**
693	A166	50c violet brn	.65	.25

Exposition of public Works and Natl. Congress of Engineering and Architecture, 1948.

King John I — A167

Designs: 30c, Philippa of Lancaster. 35c, Prince Ferdinand. 50c, Prince Henry the Navigator. 1e, Nuno Alvarez Pereira. 1.75e, John das Regras. 2e, Fernao Lopes. 3.50e, Affonso Domingues.

       Perf. 11½
1949, May 6   **Unwmk.**   **Photo.**
694	A167	10c brn vio & cr	.25	.25
695	A167	30c dk bl grn & cr	.25	.25
696	A167	35c dk ol grn & cr	.50	.25
697	A167	50c dp blue & cr	1.50	.25
698	A167	1e dk red & cr	1.50	.25
699	A167	1.75e dk gray & cr	27.00	15.00
700	A167	2e dk gray bl & cr	16.00	2.00

701	A167	3.50e dk brn & gray	55.00	17.00
a.		Sheet of 8, #694-701	80.00	80.00
		Nos. 694-701 (8)	102.00	35.25

No. 701a sold for 15e. Stamps from No. 701a differ from Nos. 694-701 in that they do not have "P. GUEDES" and "COURVOISIER S.A." below the design. Each stamp from the sheet of 8 has the same retail value.

Ship Type of 1942

1948-49   **Typo.**   **Perf. 14**
702	A136	80c dp green	4.75	.45
703	A136	1e dp claret ('48)	3.25	.25
704	A136	1.20e dp carmine	5.00	.25
705	A136	1.50e olive	55.00	.40
706	A136	1.80e yellow org	50.00	3.00
707	A136	2e deep blue	7.50	.50
708	A136	4e orange	75.00	2.75
709	A136	6e yellow grn	145.00	4.00
710	A136	7.50e grnsh gray	45.00	3.50
		Nos. 702-710 (9)	390.50	15.10
		Set, hinged	230.00	

Angel, Coimbra Museum — A168

1949, Dec. 20   **Engr.**   **Perf. 13x14**
711	A168	1e red brown	11.50	.25
712	A168	5e olive brown	3.00	.25

16th Intl. Congress of History and Art.

Symbols of the UPU — A169

1949, Dec. 29
713	A169	1e brown violet	.35	.25
714	A169	2e deep blue	1.10	.25
715	A169	2.50e deep green	5.75	1.25
716	A169	4e brown red	16.00	3.50
		Nos. 713-716 (4)	23.20	5.25

75th anniv. of the UPU.

Madonna of Fatima — A170

1950, May 13   **Perf. 11½x12**
717	A170	50c dark green	.65	.25
718	A170	1e dark brown	3.25	.25
719	A170	2e blue	8.50	1.60
720	A170	5e lilac	100.00	29.00
		Nos. 717-720 (4)	112.40	31.10

Holy Year, 1950, and to honor "Our Lady of the Rosary" at Fatima.

St. John of God Helping Ill Man — A171

1950, Oct. 30   **Engr.**   **Unwmk.**
721	A171	20c gray violet	.35	.25
722	A171	50c cerise	.50	.25
723	A171	1e olive grn	2.00	.45
724	A171	1.50e deep orange	17.00	3.00
725	A171	2e blue	14.50	2.25
726	A171	4e chocolate	60.00	8.50
		Nos. 721-726 (6)	94.35	14.70

400th anniv. of the death of St. John of God.

Guerra Junqueiro A172

1951, Mar. 2   **Litho.**   **Perf. 13½**
727	A172	50c dark brown	8.50	.35
728	A172	1e dk slate gray	2.00	.30

Birth centenary of Guerra Junqueiro, poet.

Fisherman and Catch — A173

1951, Mar. 9
729	A173	50c gray grn, *buff*	5.00	.50
730	A173	1e rose lake, *buff*	1.00	.25

3rd National Congress of Fisheries.

Dove — A174

Pope Pius XII — A175

1951, Oct. 11
731	A174	20c dk brn & buff	.40	.25
732	A174	90c dk ol grn & cr	9.00	1.75
733	A175	1e dp cl & pink	9.00	.25
734	A175	2.30e dk bl grn & bl	12.00	2.10
		Nos. 731-734 (4)	30.40	4.35

End of the Holy Year.

15th Century Colonists, Terceira A176

1951, Oct. 24   **Perf. 13x13½**
735	A176	50c dk bl, *salmon*	3.75	.45
736	A176	1e dk brn, *cream*	1.25	.35

500th anniversary (in 1950) of the colonizing of the island of Terceira.

Student, Soldiers and Workers A177

1951, Nov. 22   **Perf. 13½x13**
737	A177	1e violet brown	10.00	.25
738	A177	2.30e dark blue	7.50	1.40

25th anniversary of the national revolution.

16th Century Coach A178

Designs: Various coaches.

Perf. 13x13½

1952, Jan. 8		Engr.	Unwmk.	
739	A178	10c purple	.25	.25
740	A178	20c olive gray	.25	.25
741	A178	50c steel blue	1.00	.25
742	A178	90c green	3.50	1.50
743	A178	1e red orange	1.50	.25
744	A178	1.40e rose pink	8.00	4.50
745	A178	1.50e rose brown	7.50	2.25
746	A178	2.30e deep ultra	5.50	2.00
		Nos. 739-746 (8)	27.50	11.25

National Museum of Coaches.

Symbolical of NATO — A179

1952, Apr. 4		Litho.	Perf. 12½	
747	A179	1e green & blk	7.50	
748	A179	3.50e gray & vio bl	290.00	15.00
		Set, hinged	140.00	

North Atlantic Treaty signing, 3rd anniv.

Hockey Players on Roller Skates A180

1952, June 28		Perf. 13x13½		
749	A180	1e dk blue & gray	5.00	.25
750	A180	3.50e dk red brown	7.50	2.25

Issued to publicize the 8th World Championship Hockey-on-Skates matches.

Francisco Gomes Teixeira — A181

1952, Nov. 25		Perf. 14x14½		
751	A181	1e cerise	1.25	.25
752	A181	2.30e deep blue	8.00	4.25

Centenary of the birth of Francisco Gomes Teixeira (1851-1932), mathematician.

St. Francis and Two Boys — A182

1952, Dec. 23		Perf. 13½		
753	A182	1e dark green	1.25	.25
754	A182	2e dp claret	2.50	.35
755	A182	3.50e chalky blue	26.00	11.00
756	A182	5e dark purple	50.00	3.75
		Nos. 753-756 (4)	79.75	15.35

400th anniv. of the death of St. Francis Xavier.

Marshal Carmona Bridge A183

Designs: 1.40e, "28th of May" Stadium. 2e, University City, Coimbra. 3.50e, Salazar Dam.

1952, Dec. 10		Unwmk.	Perf. 12½	
		Buff Paper		
757	A183	1e red brown	1.00	.25
758	A183	1.40e dull purple	14.00	5.00
759	A183	2e dark green	7.50	2.50
760	A183	3.50e dark blue	11.50	4.00
		Nos. 757-760 (4)	34.00	11.75

Centenary of the foundation of the Ministry of Public Works.

Equestrian Seal of King Diniz — A184

1953-56			Litho.	
761	A184	5c green, citron	.25	.25
762	A184	10c ind, salmon	.25	.25
763	A184	20c org red, citron	.25	.25
763A	A184	30c rose lil, cr ('56)	.25	.25
764	A184	50c gray	.25	.25
765	A184	90c dk grn, cit	17.50	1.00
766	A184	1e vio brn, rose	.45	.25
767	A184	1.40e rose red	18.00	1.10
768	A184	1.50e red, cream	.65	.25
769	A184	2e gray	1.25	.25
770	A184	2.30e blue	24.00	.85
771	A184	2.50e gray blk, sal	1.60	.25
772	A184	5e rose vio, cr	1.60	.25
773	A184	10e blue, citron	10.00	.25
774	A184	20e bis brn, cit	20.00	.30
775	A184	50e rose violet	6.00	.45
		Nos. 761-775 (16)	102.30	6.45

St. Martin of Braga — A185

Perf. 13x13½

1953, Feb. 26			Unwmk.	
776	A185	1e gray blk & gray	1.60	.25
777	A185	3.50e dk brn & yel	14.00	4.00

14th centenary of the arrival of St. Martin of Dume on the Iberian peninsula.

Guilherme Gomes Fernandes — A186

1953, Mar. 28		Perf. 13		
778	A186	1e red violet	1.10	.25
779	A186	2.30e deep blue	11.00	5.50

Birth of Guilherme Gomes Fernandes, General Inspector of the Firemen of Porto.

Emblems of Automobile Club — A187

1953, Apr. 15		Perf. 12½		
780	A187	1e dk grn & yel grn	.80	.25
781	A187	3.50e dk brn & buff	13.50	5.00

Portuguese Automobile Club, 50th anniv.

Princess St. Joanna — A188

		Perf. 14½x14		
1953, May 14		Litho.	Unwmk.	
782	A188	1e blk & gray grn	2.00	.25
783	A188	3.50e dk blue & blue	13.50	6.00

Birth of Princess St. Joanna, 500th anniv.

Queen Maria II — A189

1953, Oct. 3		Photo.	Perf. 13½	
		Background of Lower Panel in Gold		
784	A189	50c red brown	.25	.25
785	A189	1e claret brn	.25	.25
786	A189	1.40e dk violet	2.10	.65
787	A189	2.30e dp blue	5.00	2.00
788	A189	3.50e violet blue	5.00	2.10
789	A189	4.50e dk blue grn	3.50	1.50
790	A189	5e dk ol grn	8.00	1.50
791	A189	20e red violet	72.50	8.00
		Nos. 784-791 (8)	96.60	16.25

Centenary of Portugal's first postage stamp.

Allegory A190

1954, Sept. 22			Perf. 13	
792	A190	1e bl & dk grnsh bl	.60	.25
793	A190	1.50e buff & dk brn	3.50	.65

150th anniversary of the founding of the State Secretariat for Financial Affairs.

Open Textbook A191

1954, Oct. 15			Litho.	
794	A191	50c blue	.40	.25
795	A191	1e red	.40	.25
796	A191	2e dk green	35.00	1.40
797	A191	2.50e orange brn	29.00	1.25
		Nos. 794-797 (4)	64.80	3.15

National literacy campaign.

Cadet and College Arms — A192

1954, Nov. 17				
798	A192	1e choc & lt grn	1.60	.25
799	A192	3.50e dk bl & gray grn	6.50	2.50

150th anniversary of the Military College.

Manuel da Nobrega and Crucifix — A193

1954, Dec. 17		Engr.	Perf. 14x13	
800	A193	1e brown	.80	.25
801	A193	2.30e deep blue	60.00	22.50
802	A193	3.50e gray green	17.00	3.25
803	A193	5e green	50.00	4.75
		Nos. 800-803 (4)	127.80	30.75

Founding of Sao Paulo, Brazil, 400th anniv.

King Alfonso I — A194

Kings: 20c, Sancho I. 50c, Alfonso II. 90c, Sancho II. 1e, Alfonso III. 1.40e, Diniz. 1.50e, Alfonso IV. 2e, Pedro I. 2.30e, Ferdinand I.

1955, Mar. 17		Perf. 13½x13		
804	A194	10c rose violet	.25	.25
805	A194	20c dk olive grn	.25	.25
806	A194	50c dk blue grn	.35	.25
807	A194	90c green	3.25	1.40
808	A194	1e red brown	1.40	.25
809	A194	1.40e carmine rose	9.00	3.00
810	A194	1.50e olive brn	4.00	1.10
811	A194	2e deep orange	11.00	3.00
812	A194	2.30e violet blue	10.00	2.50
		Nos. 804-812 (9)	39.50	12.00

Telegraph Pole — A195

1955, Sept. 16		Litho.	Perf. 13½	
813	A195	1e ocher & hn brn	.75	.25
814	A195	2.30e gray grn & Prus bl	27.50	3.50
815	A195	3.50e lemon & dp grn	3.25	
		Nos. 813-815 (3)	53.25	7.00

Centenary of the telegraph system in Portugal.

A. J. Ferreira da Silva — A196

1956, May 8		Photo.	Unwmk.	
816	A196	1e blue & dk blue	.50	.25
817	A196	2.30e grn & dk grn	16.00	5.00

Centenary of the birth of Prof. Antonio Joaquim Ferreira da Silva, chemist.

Steam Locomotive, 1856 — A197

Design: 1.50e, 2e, Electric train, 1956.

1956, Oct. 28		Litho.	Perf. 13	
818	A197	1e lt & dk ol grn	1.00	.25
819	A197	1.50e Prus bl & lt grnsh bl	4.75	.35
820	A197	2e dk org brn & bis	35.00	1.40
821	A197	2.50e choc & brn	47.50	2.25
		Nos. 818-821 (4)	88.25	4.25

Centenary of the Portuguese railways.

Madonna, 15th Century — A198

1956, Dec. 8   **Photo.**
822 A198   1e dp grn & lt ol grn   1.25   .25
823 A198   1.50e dk red brn & ol
       bis   2.50   .30
      Mothers' Day, Dec. 8.

J. B. Almeida Garrett — A199

1957, Mar. 7   **Engr.**   **Perf. 13½x14**
824 A199   1e sepia   .75   .25
825 A199   2.30e lt purple   45.00   11.00
826 A199   3.50e dull green   10.00   1.10
827 A199   5e rose carmine   85.00   10.50
    Nos. 824-827 (4)   140.75   22.85
   Issued in honor of Joao Baptista da Silva Leitao de Almeida Garrett, poet.

Cesarío Verde — A200

1957, Dec. 12   **Litho.**   **Perf. 13½**
828 A200   1e citron & brown   .40   .25
829 A200   3.30e gray grn, yel grn
       & dk ol   1.90   1.10
   Jose Joaquim de Cesario Verde (1855-86), poet.

Exhibition Emblems — A201

1958, Apr. 7
830 A201   1e multicolored   .35   .25
831 A201   3.30e multicolored   1.60   1.40
   Universal & Intl. Exposition at Brussels.

Queen St. Isabel — A202

Design: 2e, 5e, St. Teotonio.

       Perf. 14½x14
1958, July 10   **Photo.**   **Unwmk.**
832 A202   1e rose brn & buff   .25   .25
833 A202   2e dk green & buff   .65   .35
834 A202   2.50e purple & buff   5.50   .85
835 A202   5e brown & buff   7.00   1.00
    Nos. 832-835 (4)   13.40   2.45

Institute for Tropical Medicine — A203

1958, Sept. 4   **Litho.**   **Perf. 13**
836 A203   1e dk grn & lt gray   2.50   .25
837 A203   2.50e bl & pale bl   7.75   1.50
   6th Intl. Cong. for Tropical Medicine and Malaria, Lisbon, Sept. 1958, and opening of the new Tropical Medicine Institute.

Cargo Ship and Loading Crane — A204

1958, Nov. 27   **Unwmk.**   **Perf. 13**
838 A204   1e brn & dk brn   6.50   .25
839 A204   4.50e vio bl & dk bl   5.00   2.25
   2nd Natl. Cong. of the Merchant Marine, Porto.

Queen Leonor — A205

1958, Dec. 17
840 A205   1e multi   .25   .25
841 A205   1.50e bis, blk, bl & dk
       bis brn   4.00   .70
   a.   Dark bister brown omitted
842 A205   2.30e multi   3.75   1.10
843 A205   4.10e multi   3.75   1.60
    Nos. 840-843 (4)   11.75   3.65
   500th anniv. of the birth of Queen Leonor.

Arms of Aveiro — A206

1959, Aug. 30   **Litho.**   **Perf. 13**
844 A206   1e ol bis, brn, gold &
       sil   1.75   .25
845 A206   5e grnsh gray, gold &
       sil   13.00   1.90
      Millennium of Aveiro.

Symbols of Hope and Peace — A207

1960, Mar. 2   **Perf. 12½**
846 A207   1e lt violet & blk   .35   .25
847 A207   3.50e gray & dk grn   3.25   1.75
   10th anniversary (in 1959) of NATO.

Open Door to "Peace" and WRY Emblem — A208

1960, Apr. 7   **Unwmk.**   **Perf. 13**
848 A208   20c multi   .25   .25
849 A208   1e multi   .50   .25
850 A208   1.80e yel grn, org & blk   1.10   .95
    Nos. 848-850 (3)   1.85   1.45
   World Refugee Year, 7/1/59-6/30/60.

Glider — A209

Designs: 1.50e, Plane. 2e, Plane and parachutes. 2.50e, Model plane.

1960, May 2
851 A209   1e yel, gray & bl   .25   .25
852 A209   1.50e multicolored   .65   .25
853 A209   2e bl grn, yel & blk   1.25   .60
854 A209   2.50e grnsh bl, ocher &
       red   2.50   1.10
    Nos. 851-854 (4)   4.65   2.20
   Aero Club of Portugal, 50th anniv. (in 1959).

Father Cruz — A210

1960, July 18   **Unwmk.**   **Perf. 13**
855 A210   1e deep brown   .25   .25
856 A210   4.30e Prus blue & blk   8.75   6.25
     Father Cruz, "father of the poor."

University of Evora Seal — A211

1960, July 18   **Litho.**
857 A211   50c violet blue   .25   .25
858 A211   1e red brn & yel   .40   .25
859 A211   1.40e rose cl & rose   2.75   1.50
    Nos. 857-859 (3)   3.40   2.00
   Founding of the University of Evora, 400th anniv.

Arms of Prince Henry — A212

Designs: 2.50e, Caravel. 3.50e, Prince Henry. 5e, Prince Henry's motto. 8e, Prince Henry's sloop. 10e, Old chart of Sagres region of Portugal.

1960, Aug. 4   **Photo.**   **Perf. 12x12½**
860 A212   1e gold & multi   .35   .25
861 A212   2.50e gold & multi   3.50   .35
862 A212   3.50e gold & multi   5.00   1.40
863 A212   5e gold & multi   8.00   .80
864 A212   8e gold & multi   2.00   .75
865 A212   10e gold & multi   14.00   2.00
    Nos. 860-865 (6)   32.85   5.55
   500th anniversary of the death of Prince Henry the Navigator.

Europa Issue, 1960
Common Design Type

1960, Sept. 16   **Litho.**   **Perf. 13**
       Size: 31x21mm
866 CD3   1e ultra & gray blue   .25   .25
867 CD3   3.50e brn red & rose
       red   2.75   1.50
    Nos. 866-867 (2)   3.00   1.75

Arms of Lisbon and Symbolic Ship — A213

1960, Nov. 17   **Perf. 13**
868 A213   1e gray ol, blk & vio
       bl   .40   .25
869 A213   3.30e bl, blk & ultra   5.25   3.25
   5th Natl. Philatelic Exhibition, Lisbon, part of the Prince Henry the Navigator festivities. (The ship in the design is in honor of Prince Henry).

Flag and Laurel — A214

1960, Dec. 20   **Litho.**   **Perf. 13**
870 A214   1e multicolored   .30   .25
     50th anniversary of the Republic.

King Pedro V — A215

1961, Aug. 3   **Engr.**   **Perf. 13**
871 A215   1e gray brn & dk
       grn   .30   .25
872 A215   6.50e dk blue & blk   3.50   .65
   Centenary of the founding of the Faculty of Letters, Lisbon University.

Setubal Sea Gate and Ships — A216

1961, Aug. 24   **Litho.**   **Perf. 12x11½**
873 A216   1e gold & multi   .35   .25
874 A216   4.30e gold & multi   16.00   5.00
     Centenary of the city of Setubal.

Europa Issue

Clasped Hands and CEPT Emblem — A217

1961, Sept. 18   **Perf. 13½x13**
875 A217   1e blue & lt blue   .25   .25
876 A217   1.50e green & brt
       green   1.25   .75
877 A217   3.50e brown, pink &
       red   1.50   1.00
    Nos. 875-877 (3)   3.00   2.00

Tomar Castle and River Nabao — A218

1962, Jan. 26   **Perf. 11½x12**
878 A218   1e gold & multi   .25   .25
879 A218   3.50e gold & multi   1.40   .85
     800th anniversary of the city of Tomar.

National Guardsman — A219

1962, Feb. 20   Unwmk.   Perf. 13½
880 A219 1e multi   .25   .25
881 A219 2e multi   2.00   .60
882 A219 2.50e multi   2.00   .50
   Nos. 880-882 (3)   4.25 1.35
Republican National Guard, 50th anniv.

Archangel
Gabriel — A220

1962, Mar. 24   Litho.   Perf. 13
883 A220 1e ol, pink & red brn   .70   .25
884 A220 3.50e ol, pink & dk grn   .50   .40
Issued for St. Gabriel's Day. St. Gabriel is patron of telecommunications.

Tents and
Scout Emblem
A221

1962, June 11   Unwmk.   Perf. 13
885 A221 20c gray, bis, yel & blk   .25   .25
  a. Double impression of gray frame lettering
886 A221 50c multi   .25   .25
887 A221 1e multi   .60   .25
888 A221 2.50e multi   4.00   .50
889 A221 3.50e multi   .90   .50
890 A221 6.50e multi   1.25   .65
   Nos. 885-890 (6)   7.25 2.40
50th anniv. of the Portuguese Boy Scouts and the 18th Boy Scout World Conf., Sept. 19-24, 1961.

Children
Reading
A222

Designs: 1e, Vaccination. 2.80e, Children playing ball. 3.50e, Guarding sleeping infant.

1962, Sept. 10   Litho.   Perf. 13½
891 A222 50c bluish grn, yel & blk   .25   .25
892 A222 1e pale bl, yel & blk   .90   .25
893 A222 2.80e dp org yel & blk   2.50   .90
894 A222 3.50e dl rose, yel & blk   5.00 1.40
   Nos. 891-894 (4)   8.65 2.80
10th Intl. Cong. of Pediatrics, Lisbon, Sept. 9-15.

19-Cell
Honeycomb
A223

1962, Sept. 17
895 A223 1e bl, dk bl & gold   .25   .25
896 A223 1.50e lt & dk grn & gold   1.00   .55
897 A223 3.50e dp rose, mar & gold   1.40 1.00
   Nos. 895-897 (3)   2.65 1.80
Europa. The 19 cells represent the 19 original members of the Conference of European Postal and Telecommunications Administrations, C.E.P.T.

St. Zenon, the
Courier — A224

1962, Dec. 1   Unwmk.   Perf. 13½
898 A224 1e multi   .25   .25
899 A224 2e multi   .95   .70
900 A224 2.80e multi   1.90 1.50
   Nos. 898-900 (3)   3.10 2.45
Issued for Stamp Day.

European Soccer
Cup and
Emblem — A225

1963, Feb. 5   Perf. 13½
901 A225 1e multi   .80   .25
902 A225 4.30e multi   1.10   .90
Victories of the Benfica Club of Lisbon in the 1961 and 1962 European Soccer Championships.

Wheat
Emblem
A226

1963, Mar. 21   Litho.
903 A226 1e multi   .25   .25
904 A226 3.30e multi   1.40   .80
905 A226 3.50e multi   1.25   .75
   Nos. 903-905 (3)   2.90 1.80
FAO "Freedom from Hunger" campaign.

Stagecoach — A227

1963, May 7   Perf. 12x11½
906 A227 1e gray, lt & dk bl   .25   .25
907 A227 1.50e bis, dk brn & lil rose   1.75   .40
908 A227 5e org brn, dk brn & rose lil   .60   .30
   Nos. 906-908 (3)   2.60   .95
1st Intl. Postal Conference, Paris, 1863.

St. Vincent de Paul
by
Monsaraz — A228

**1963, July 10   Photo.   Perf. 13½x14
Gold Inscription**
909 A228 20c lt blue & ultra   .25   .25
  a. Gold inscription omitted   60.00
910 A228 1e gray & slate   .35   .25
911 A228 2.80e green & slate   3.50 1.40
  a. Gold inscription omitted   70.00
912 A228 5e dp rose car & sl   2.50 1.00
   Nos. 909-912 (4)   6.60 2.90
Tercentenary of the death of St. Vincent de Paul.

Emblem of
Order and
Knight
A229

1963, Aug. 13   Litho.   Perf. 11½
913 A229 1e multi   .25   .25
914 A229 1.50e multi   .55   .25
915 A229 2.50e multi   1.40   .70
   Nos. 913-915 (3)   2.20 1.20
800th anniv. of the Military Order of Avis.

Europa Issue

Stylized
Bird — A230

1963, Sept. 16   Perf. 13½
916 A230 1e lt bl, gray & blk   .25   .25
917 A230 1.50e grn, gray & blk   2.00   .60
918 A230 3.50e red, gray & blk   3.50   .90
   Nos. 916-918 (3)   5.75 1.75

Jet
Plane — A231

1963, Dec. 1   Unwmk.   Perf. 13½
919 A231 1e dk bl & lt bl   .25   .25
920 A231 2.50e dk grn & yel grn   1.25   .50
921 A231 3.50e org brn & org   1.60   .85
   Nos. 919-921 (3)   3.10 1.60
Transportes Aéreos Portugueses, TAP, 10th anniv.

Apothecary
Jar — A232

1964, Apr. 9   Litho.
922 A232 50c brn ol, dk brn & blk   .30   .25
923 A232 1e rose brn, dp cl & blk   .30   .25
924 A232 4.30e dk gray, sl & blk   3.75 2.75
   Nos. 922-924 (3)   4.35 3.25
4th centenary of the publication (in Goa, Apr. 10, 1563) of "Coloquios Dos Simples e Drogas" (Herbs and Drugs in India) by Garcia D'Orta.

Emblem of National
Overseas
Bank — A233

1964, May 19   Unwmk.   Perf. 13½
925 A233 1e bister, yel & dk bl   .25   .25
926 A233 2.50e ocher, yel & grn   2.50   .75
927 A233 3.50e bister, yel & brn   2.00   .90
   Nos. 925-927 (3)   4.75 1.90
Centenary of National Overseas Bank.

Mt. Sameiro
Church — A234

1964, June 5   Litho.
928 A234 1e red brn, bis & dl brn   .25   .25
929 A234 2e brn, bis & dl brn   1.75   .60
930 A234 5e dk vio bl, bis & gray   2.25   .80
   Nos. 928-930 (3)   4.25 1.65
Centenary of the Shrine of Our Lady of Mt. Sameiro, Braga.

Europa Issue
Common Design Type
**1964, Sept. 14   Unwmk.   Perf. 13½
Size: 19x32mm.**
931 CD7 1e bl, lt bl & dk bl   1.00   .25
932 CD7 3.50e rose brn, buff & dk brn   4.00   .50
933 CD7 4.30e grn, yel grn & dk grn   5.00 1.25
   Nos. 931-933 (3)   10.00 2.00

Partial Eclipse of
Sun — A235

1964
934 A235 1e multicolored   .25   .25
935 A235 8e multicolored   1.50 1.00
International Quiet Sun Year, 1964-65.

Olympic Rings,
Emblems of
Portugal and
Japan — A236

**Black Inscriptions; Olympic Rings
in Pale Yellow**

1964, Dec. 1   Unwmk.   Perf. 13½
936 A236 20c tan, red & vio bl   .25   .25
937 A236 1e ultra, red & vio bl   .25   .25
938 A236 1.50e yel grn, red & vio bl   1.75 1.00
939 A236 6.50e rose lil, red & vio bl   2.90 1.90
   Nos. 936-939 (4)   5.15 3.30
18th Olympic Games, Tokyo, Oct. 10-25.

Eduardo
Coelho — A237

1964, Dec. 28   Litho.   Perf. 13½
940 A237 1e multicolored   .45   .25
941 A237 5e multicolored   6.50 1.00
Centenary of the founding of Portugal's first newspaper, "Diario de Noticias," and to honor the founder, Eduardo Coelho, journalist.

Traffic Signs
and Signals
A238

1965, Feb. 15   Litho.
942 A238 1e yellow, red & emer   .25   .25
943 A238 3.30e multicolored   5.75 3.00
944 A238 3.50e red, yellow & emer   3.50 1.10
   Nos. 942-944 (3)   9.50 4.35
1st National Traffic Cong., Lisbon, 2/15-19.

Ferdinand I, Duke
of
Braganza — A239

1965, Mar. 16 Unwmk. Perf. 13½
945 A239 1e rose brown & blk .25 .25
946 A239 10e Prus green & blk 2.40 .65
500th anniv. of the city of Braganza (in 1964).

Coimbra Gate, Angel with Censer and Sword — A240

1965, Apr. 27 Perf. 11½x12
947 A240 1e blue & multi .25 .25
948 A240 2.50e multi 2.10 1.10
949 A240 5e multi 2.10 1.40
Nos. 947-949 (3) 4.45 2.75
9th centenary (in 1964) of the capture of the city of Coimbra from the Moors.

ITU Emblem — A241

1965, May 17 Perf. 13½
950 A241 1e bis brn, ol grn & ol .25 .25
951 A241 3.50e ol, rose cl & dp cl 1.60 1.00
952 A241 6.50e yel grn, dl bl & sl bl 1.40 .90
Nos. 950-952 (3) 3.25 2.15
International Telecommunication Union, cent.

Calouste Gulbenkian A242

1965, July 20 Litho. Perf. 13½
953 A242 1e multicolored .60 .25
954 A242 8e multicolored .55 .40
Gulbenkian (1869-1955), oil industry pioneer and sponsor of the Gulbenkian Foundation.

Red Cross — A243

1965, Aug. 17 Unwmk. Perf. 13½
955 A243 1e grn, red & blk .50 .25
956 A243 4e ol, red & blk 2.25 .90
957 A243 4.30e lt rose brn, red & blk 10.00 5.00
Nos. 955-957 (3) 12.75 6.15
Centenary of the Portuguese Red Cross.

Europa Issue
Common Design Type
1965, Sept. 27 Litho. Perf. 13
Size: 31x24mm
958 CD8 1e saph, grnsh bl & dk bl 2.00 .25
959 CD8 3.50e rose brn, sal & brn 3.00 .50
960 CD8 4.30e grn, yel grn & dk grn 5.00 2.00
Nos. 958-960 (3) 10.00 2.75

Military Plane — A244

1965, Oct. 20 Perf. 13½
961 A244 1e ol grn, red & dk grn .25 .25
962 A244 2e sepia, red & dk grn 1.25 .55
963 A244 5e chlky bl, red & dk grn 2.25 1.10
Nos. 961-963 (3) 3.75 1.90
Portuguese Air Force founding, 50th anniv.

Woman — A245

Designs: Characters from Gil Vicente Plays.

1965, Dec. 1 Litho. Perf. 13½
964 A245 20c ol, pale yel & blk .25 .25
965 A245 1e brn, pale yel & blk .30 .25
966 A245 2.50e dk red, buff & blk 2.90 .45
967 A245 6.50e blue, gray & blk 1.00 .55
Nos. 964-967 (4) 4.45 1.50
Gil Vicente (1465?-1536?).

Chrismon with Alpha and Omega A246

1966, Mar. 28 Litho. Perf. 13½
968 A246 1e ol bis, gold & blk .25 .25
969 A246 3.30e gray, gold & blk 5.00 2.75
970 A246 5e rose cl, gold & blk 4.00 .90
Nos. 968-970 (3) 9.25 3.90
Congress of the International Committee for the Defense of Christian Civilization, Lisbon.

Symbols of Peace and Labor — A247

1966, May 28 Litho. Perf. 13½
971 A247 1e dk bl, sl bl & lt sl bl .25 .25
972 A247 3.50e ol, ol brn, & lt ol 2.40 1.10
973 A247 4e dk brn, brn car & dl rose 2.50 .85
Nos. 971-973 (3) 5.15 2.20
40th anniversary of National Revolution.

Knight Giraldo on Horseback A248

1966, June 8
974 A248 1e multicolored .30 .25
975 A248 8e multicolored 1.10 .55
Conquest of Evora from the Moors, 800th anniv.

Salazar Bridge — A249

Designs: 2.80e, 4.30e, View of bridge, vert.

1966, Aug. 6 Litho. Perf. 13½
976 A249 1e gold & red .25 .25
977 A249 2.50e gold & ultra 1.25 .50
978 A249 2.80e silver & dp ultra 2.00 1.10
979 A249 4.30e silver & dk grn 2.25 1.25
Nos. 976-979 (4) 5.75 3.10
Issued to commemorate the opening of the Salazar Bridge over the Tejo River, Lisbon.

Europa Issue
Common Design Type
1966, Sept. 26 Litho. Perf. 11½x12
Size: 26x32mm
980 CD9 1e blue & blk 1.00 .25
981 CD9 3.50e red brn & blk 3.75 .75
982 CD9 4.30e yel grn & blk 5.00 1.25
Nos. 980-982 (3) 9.75 2.25

Pestana — A250

Portraits: 20c, Camara Pestana (1863-1899), bacteriologist. 50c, Egas Moniz (1874-1955), neurologist. 1e, Antonio Pereira Coutinho (1851-1939), botanist. 1.50e, José Corrèa da Serra (1750-1823), botanist. 2e, Ricardo Jórge (1858-1938), hygienist and anthropologist. 2.50e, J. Liete de Vasconcelos (1858-1941), ethnologist. 2.80e, Maximiano Lemos (1860-1923), medical historian. 4.30e, José Antonio Serrano, anatomist.

Portrait and Inscription in Dark Brown and Bister
1966, Dec. 1 Litho. Perf. 13½
983 A250 20c gray green .25 .25
984 A250 50c orange .25 .25
985 A250 1e lemon .25 .25
986 A250 1.50e bister brn .30 .25
987 A250 2e brown org 1.50 .25
988 A250 2.50e pale green 1.60 .40
989 A250 2.80e salmon 1.90 1.25
990 A250 4.30e Prus blue 3.25 2.10
Nos. 983-990 (8) 9.30 5.00
Issued to honor Portuguese scientists.

Bocage — A251

1966, Dec. 28 Litho. Perf. 11½x12
991 A251 1e bis, grnsh gray & blk .25 .25
992 A251 2e brn org, grnsh gray & blk .75 .35
993 A251 6e gray, grnsh gray & blk 1.20 .65
Nos. 991-993 (3) 2.20 1.25
200th anniversary of the birth of Manuel Maria Barbosa du Bocage (1765-1805), poet.

Europa Issue
Common Design Type
1967, May 2 Litho. Perf. 13
Size: 21½x31mm
994 CD10 1e lt bl, Prus bl & blk 1.00 .25
995 CD10 3.50e sal, brn red & blk 3.50 .60
996 CD10 4.30e yel grn, ol grn & blk 5.00 1.00
Nos. 994-996 (3) 9.50 1.85

Apparition of Our Lady of Fatima — A252

Designs: 2.80e, Church and Golden Rose. 3.50e, Statue of the Pilgrim Virgin, with lilies and doves. 4e, Doves holding crown over Chapel of the Apparition.

1967, May 13 Perf. 11½x12
997 A252 1e multicolored .25 .25
998 A252 2.80e multicolored .55 .40
999 A252 3.50e multicolored .35 .25
1000 A252 4e multicolored .50 .25
Nos. 997-1000 (4) 1.65 1.15
50th anniversary of the apparition of the Virgin Mary to 3 shepherd children at Fatima.

Statues of Roman Senators — A253

1967, June 1 Litho. Perf. 13
1001 A253 1e gold & rose claret .25 .25
1002 A253 2.50e gold & dull blue 1.90 1.00
1003 A253 4.30e gold & gray green 1.40 1.00
Nos. 1001-1003 (3) 3.55 2.25
Introduction of a new civil law code.

Shipyard, Margueira, Lisbon — A254

Design: 2.80e, 4.30e, Ship's hull and map showing location of harbor.

1967, June 23
1004 A254 1e aqua & multi .25 .25
1005 A254 2.80e multicolored 2.10 1.00
1006 A254 3.50e multicolored 1.40 .85
1007 A254 4.30e multicolored 2.10 .95
Nos. 1004-1007 (4) 5.85 3.05
Issued to commemorate the inauguration of the Lisnave Shipyard at Margueira, Lisbon.

Symbols of Healing — A255

1967, Oct. 8 Litho. Perf. 13½
1008 A255 1e multicolored .25 .25
1009 A255 2e multicolored 1.00 .50
1010 A255 5e multicolored 1.50 .95
Nos. 1008-1010 (3) 2.75 1.70
Issued to publicize the 6th European Congress of Rheumatology, Lisbon, Oct. 8-13.

Flags of EFTA Nations — A256

1967, Oct. 24   **Litho.**   **Perf. 13½**
1011	A256	1e bister & multi	.25 .25
1012	A256	3.50e buff & multi	1.10 1.00
1013	A256	4.30e gray & multi	3.00 2.50
		Nos. 1011-1013 (3)	4.35 3.75

Issued to publicize the European Free Trade Association. See note after Norway No. 501.

Tables of the Law — A257

1967, Dec. 27   **Litho.**   **Perf. 13½**
1014	A257	1e olive	.25 .25
1015	A257	2e red brown	1.25 .65
1016	A257	5e green	2.10 1.25
		Nos. 1014-1016 (3)	3.60 2.15

Centenary of abolition of death penalty.

Bento de Goes — A258

Perf. 13½ (#1017), 12x11½ (#1018)
1968, Feb. 14   **Engr.**
1017	A258	1e olive, indigo & dk brn	.75 .25
1018	A258	8e org brn, dl pur & ol grn	1.25 .50

360th anniversary (in 1967) of the death of Bento de Goes (1562-1607), Jesuit explorer of the route to China.

Europa Issue
Common Design Type
1968, Apr. 29   **Litho.**   **Perf. 13**
Size: 31x21mm
1019	CD11	1e multicolored	1.00 .25
1020	CD11	3.50e multicolored	3.75 .60
1021	CD11	4.30e multicolored	5.00 1.25
		Nos. 1019-1021 (3)	9.75 2.10

Mother's and Child's Hands — A259

1968, May 26   **Litho.**   **Perf. 13½**
1022	A259	1e lt gray, blk & red	.25 .25
1023	A259	2e salmon, blk & red	1.50 .60
1024	A259	5e lt bl, blk & red	3.00 1.40
		Nos. 1022-1024 (3)	4.75 2.25

Mothers' Organization for Natl. Education. 30th anniv.

"Victory over Disease" and WHO Emblem A260

1968, July 10   **Litho.**   **Perf. 12½**
1025	A260	1e multicolored	.60 .25
1026	A260	3.50e multicolored	1.40 .50
1027	A260	4.30e tan & multi	5.00 3.00
		Nos. 1025-1027 (3)	7.00 3.75

20th anniv. of WHO.

Madeira Grapes and Wine A261

Joao Fernandes Vieira — A262

Designs: 1e, Fireworks on New Year's Eve. 1.50e, Mountains and valley. 3.50e, Woman doing Madeira embroidery. 4.30e, Joao Gonçalves Zarco. 20e, Muschia aurea (flower.)

Perf. 12x11½, 11½x12
1968, Aug. 17   **Litho.**
1028	A261	50c multi	.25 .25
1029	A261	1e multi	.25 .25
1030	A261	1.50e multi	.30 .25
1031	A262	2.80e multi	2.25 1.50
1032	A262	3.50e multi	1.50 1.00
1033	A262	4.30e multi	8.00 6.00
1034	A262	20e multi	4.00 1.00
		Nos. 1028-1034 (7)	16.55 10.25

Issued to publicize Madeira and the Lubrapex 1968 stamp exhibition.
Design descriptions in Portuguese, French and English printed on back of stamps.

Pedro Alvares Cabral A263

Cabral's Fleet A264

Design: 3.50e, Cabral's coat of arms, vert.

Perf. 12x12½, 12½x12
1969, Jan. 30   **Engr.**
1035	A263	1e vio bl, bl & gray bl	.25 .25
1036	A263	3.50e deep claret	4.25 2.00

Litho.
1037	A264	6.50e green & multi	2.50 1.75
		Nos. 1035-1037 (3)	7.00 4.00

5th cent. of the birth of Pedro Alvarez Cabral (1468-1520), navigator, discoverer of Brazil. Nos. 1035-1037 have description of the designs printed on the back in Portuguese, French and English.

Europa Issue
Common Design Type
1969, Apr. 28   **Litho.**   **Perf. 13**
Size: 31x22½mm
1038	CD12	1e dp blue & multi	1.00 .25
1039	CD12	3.50e multicolored	6.75 .65
1040	CD12	4.30e grn & multi	10.00 1.50
		Nos. 1038-1040 (3)	17.75 2.40

King José I and Arms of National Press — A265

1969, May 14   **Litho.**   **Perf. 11½x12**
1041	A265	1e multicolored	.25 .25
1042	A265	2e multicolored	1.10 .45
1043	A265	8e multicolored	1.00 .60
		Nos. 1041-1043 (3)	2.35 1.30

Bicentenary of the National Press.

ILO Emblem A266

1969, May 28   **Perf. 13**
1044	A266	1e bluish grn, blk & sil	.25 .25
1045	A266	3.50e red, blk & sil	1.40 .65
1046	A266	4.30e brt bl, blk & sil	2.25 1.50
		Nos. 1044-1046 (3)	3.90 2.40

50th anniversary of the ILO.

Juan Cabrillo Rodriguez A267

1969, July 16   **Litho.**   **Perf. 11½x12**
1047	A267	1e multi	.25 .25
1048	A267	2.50e multi	1.60 .45
1049	A267	6.50e multi	1.75 .90
		Nos. 1047-1049 (3)	3.60 1.60

Bicent. of San Diego, Calif., & honoring Juan Cabrillo Rodriguez, explorer of California coast.
Backs inscribed. See note below No. 1034.

Vianna da Motta, by Columbano Bordalo Pinheiro — A268

1969, Sept. 24   **Litho.**   **Perf. 12**
1050	A268	1e multicolored	.90 .25
1051	A268	9e gray & multi	.90 .60

Centenary of the birth of Vianna da Motta (1868-1948), pianist and composer.

Gago Coutinho and 1922 Seaplane A269

Design: 2.80e, 4.30e, Adm. Coutinho and Coutinho sextant.

1969, Oct. 22
1052	A269	1e grnsh gray, dk & lt brn	.25 .25
1053	A269	2.80e yel bis, dk & lt brn	2.25 1.00
1054	A269	3.30e gray bl, dk & lt brn	2.10 1.40
1055	A269	4.30e lt rose brn, dk brn	2.10 1.50
		Nos. 1052-1055 (4)	6.70 4.15

Admiral Carlos Viegas Gago Coutinho (1869-1959), explorer and aviation pioneer.

Vasco da Gama A270

Designs: 2.80e, Da Gama's coat of arms. 3.50e, Map showing route to India and compass rose, horiz. 4e, Da Gama's fleet, horiz.

Perf. 12x11½, 11½x12
1969, Dec. 30   **Litho.**
1056	A270	1e multi	.50 .25
1057	A270	2.80e multi	3.00 1.75
1058	A270	3.50e multi	2.25 .75
1059	A270	4e multi	2.10 .60
		Nos. 1056-1059 (4)	7.85 3.35

Vasco da Gama (1469-1525), navigator who found sea route to India.
Design descriptions in Portuguese, French and English printed on back of stamps.

Europa Issue
Common Design Type
1970, May 4   **Litho.**   **Perf. 13½**
Size: 31x22mm
1060	CD13	1e multicolored	1.00 .25
1061	CD13	3.50e multicolored	3.75 .60
1062	CD13	4.30e multicolored	5.00 1.50
		Nos. 1060-1062 (3)	9.75 2.35

Distillation Plant — A271

Design: 2.80e, 6e, Catalytic cracking tower.

1970, June 5   **Litho.**   **Perf. 13**
1063	A271	1e dk bl & dl bl	.25 .25
1064	A271	2.80e sl grn & pale grn	2.25 1.40
1065	A271	3.30e dk ol grn & ol	1.40 1.00
1066	A271	6e dk brn & dl ocher	1.40 .85
		Nos. 1063-1066 (4)	5.30 3.50

Opening of the Oporto Oil Refinery.

Marshal Carmona and Oak Leaves A272

Designs: 2.50e, Carmona, Portuguese coat of arms and laurel. 7e, Carmona and ferns.

Litho. & Engr.
1970, July 1   **Perf. 12x12½**
1067	A272	1e ol grn & blk	.25 .25
1068	A272	2.50e red, ultra & blk	1.60 .60
1069	A272	7e slate bl & blk	1.50 .90
		Nos. 1067-1069 (3)	3.35 1.75

Centenary of the birth of Marshal Antonio Oscar de Fragoso Carmona (1869-1951), President of Portugal, 1926-1951.

Emblem of Plant Research Station A273

1970, July 29   **Litho.**
1070	A273	1e multi	.25	.25
1071	A273	2.50e multi	1.10	.40
1072	A273	5e multi	1.60	.60
		Nos. 1070-1072 (3)	2.95	1.25

25th anniv. of the Plant Research Station at Elvas.

Compass Rose and EXPO Emblem — A274

Designs: 5e, Monogram of Christ (IHS) and EXPO emblem. 6.50e, "Portugal and Japan" as written in old manuscripts, and EXPO emblem.

1970, Sept. 16   **Litho.**   **Perf. 13**
1073	A274	1e gold & multi	.25	.25
1074	A274	5e silver & multi	1.40	.90
1075	A274	6.50e multicolored	3.00	2.25
		Nos. 1073-1075,C11 (4)	5.35	3.80

EXPO '70 International Exhibition, Osaka, Japan, Mar. 15-Sept. 13.

Castle (from Arms of Santarem) A275

#1077, Star & wheel, from Covilha coat of arms. 2.80e, Ram & Covilha coat of arms. 4e, Knights on horseback & Santarem coat of arms.

1970, Oct. 7   **Litho.**   **Perf. 12x11½**
1076	A275	1e multicolored	.25	.25
1077	A275	1e ultra & multi	.25	.25
1078	A275	2.80e red & multi	2.50	1.25
1079	A275	4e gray & multi	1.50	.70
		Nos. 1076-1079 (4)	4.50	2.45

City of Santarem, cent. (#1076, 1079); City of Covilha, cent. (#1077-1078).

Paddlesteamer Great Eastern Laying Cable — A276

Designs: 2.80e, 4e, Cross section of cable.

1970, Nov. 21   **Litho.**   **Perf. 14**
1080	A276	1e multi	.25	.25
1081	A276	2.50e multi	1.60	.40
1082	A276	2.80e multi	3.00	2.25
1083	A276	4e multi	1.40	.70
		Nos. 1080-1083 (4)	6.25	3.60

Centenary of the Portugal-Great Britain submarine telegraph cable.

Grapes and Woman Filling Baskets A277

Designs: 1e, Worker carrying basket of grapes, and jug. 3.50e, Glass of wine, and barge with barrels on River Douro. 7e, Wine bottle and barrels.

1970, Dec. 20   **Litho.**   **Perf. 12x11½**
1084	A277	50c multi	.25	.25
1085	A277	1e multi	.25	.25
1086	A277	3.50e multi	1.00	.25
1087	A277	7e multi	1.00	.50
		Nos. 1084-1087 (4)	2.50	1.25

Publicity for port wine export.

Mountain Windmill, Bussaco Hills — A278

Windmills: 50c, Beira Litoral Province. 1e, Estremadura Province. 2e, St. Miguel, Azores. 3.30e, Porto Santo, Madeira. 5e, Pico, Azores.

1971, Feb. 24   **Litho.**   **Perf. 13**
1088	A278	20c multicolored	.25	.25
1089	A278	50c lt blue & multi	.25	.25
1090	A278	1e gray & multi	.25	.25
1091	A278	2e multicolored	.90	.25
1092	A278	3.30e ocher & multi	2.00	1.00
1093	A278	5e multicolored	1.75	.55
		Nos. 1088-1093 (6)	5.40	2.55

Backs inscribed. See note below No. 1034.

Europa Issue
Common Design Type

1971, May 3   **Photo.**   **Perf. 14**
Size: 32x22mm
1094	CD14	1e dk bl, lt grn & blk	1.00	.25
1095	CD14	3.50e red brn, yel & blk	3.75	.50
1096	CD14	7.50e olive, yel & blk	5.00	1.00
		Nos. 1094-1096 (3)	9.75	1.75

Francisco Franco (1885-1955) A279

Portuguese Sculptors: 1e, Antonio Teixeira Lopes (1866-1942). 1.50e, Antonio Augusto da Costa Mota (1862-1930). 2.50e, Rui Roque Gameiro (1906-1935). 3.50e, José Simoes de Almeida (nephew; 1880-1950). 4e, Francisco dos Santos (1878-1930).

Perf. 11½x12½; 13½ (2.50e, 4e)

1971, July 7   **Engr.**
1097	A279	20c black	.25	.25
a.		Perf. 13½	2.50	.30
1098	A279	1e claret	.30	.25
1099	A279	1.50e sepia	.50	.40
1100	A279	2.50e dark blue	.90	.30
1101	A279	3.50e carmine rose	1.40	.45
1102	A279	4e gray green	2.40	1.50
		Nos. 1097-1102 (6)	5.75	3.15

Pres. Antonio Salazar — A280

1971, July 27   **Engr.**   **Perf. 13½**
1103	A280	1e multicolored	.25	.25
a.		Perf. 12½x12	100.00	2.75
1104	A280	5e multicolored	1.50	.35
1105	A280	10e multicolored	2.50	.95
a.		Perf. 12½x12	25.00	1.75
		Nos. 1103-1105 (3)	4.25	1.55

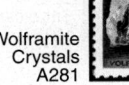

Wolframite Crystals A281

Minerals: 2.50e, Arsenopyrite (gold). 3.50e, Beryllium. 6.50e, Chalcopyrite (copper).

1971, Sept. 24   **Litho.**   **Perf. 12**
1106	A281	1e multicolored	.25	.25
1107	A281	2.50e carmine & multi	1.90	.40
1108	A281	3.50e green & multi	.65	.30
1109	A281	6.50e blue & multi	1.10	.45
		Nos. 1106-1109 (4)	3.90	1.40

Spanish-Portuguese-American Economic Geology Congress.

Town Gate, Castelo Branco — A282

Designs: 3e, Memorial column. 12.50e, Arms of Castelo Branco, horiz.

1971, Oct. 7   **Perf. 14**
1110	A282	1e multi	.25	.25
1111	A282	3e multi	1.25	.50
1112	A282	12.50e multi	1.00	.50
		Nos. 1110-1112 (3)	2.50	1.25

Bicentenary of Castelo Branco as a town.

Weather Recording Station and Barograph Charts — A283

Designs: 4e, Stratospheric weather balloon and weather map of southwest Europe and North Africa. 6.50e, Satellite and aerial map of Atlantic Ocean off Portugal.

1971, Oct. 29   **Perf. 13½**
1113	A283	1e buff & multi	.25	.25
1114	A283	4e multicolored	2.10	.85
1115	A283	6.50e blk, dl red brn & org	1.50	.45
		Nos. 1113-1115 (3)	3.85	1.55

25 years of Portuguese meteorological service.

Missionaries and Ship — A284

1971, Nov. 24
1116	A284	1e gray, ultra & blk	.25	.25
1117	A284	3.30e dp bis, lil & blk	1.75	1.00
1118	A284	4.80e olive, grn & blk	1.90	1.10
		Nos. 1116-1118 (3)	3.90	2.35

400th anniv. of the martyrdom of a group of Portuguese missionaries on the way to Brazil.

"Man" A285

Nature Conservation: 3.30e, "Earth" (animal, vegetable, mineral). 3.50e, "Air" (birds). 4.50e, "Water" (fish).

1971, Dec. 22   **Litho.**   **Perf. 12**
1119	A285	1e brown & multi	.25	.25
1120	A285	3.30e lt bl, yel & grn	.55	.30
1121	A285	3.50e lt bl, rose & vio	.65	.25
1122	A285	4.50e lt bl, grn & ultra	2.25	1.25
		Nos. 1119-1122 (4)	3.70	2.05

City Hall, Sintra — A286

Designs: 5c, Aqueduct, Lisbon. 50c, University, Coimbra. 1e, Torre dos Clerigos, Porto. 1.50e, Belem Tower, Lisbon. 2.50e, Castle, Vila da Feira. 3e, Misericordia House, Viana do Castelo. 3.50e, Window, Tomar Convent. 8e, Ducal Palace, Guimaraes. 10e, Cape Girao, Madeira. 20e, Episcopal Garden, Castelo Branco. 100e, Lakes of Seven Cities, Azores.

1972-73   **Litho.**   **Perf. 12½**
Size: 22x17½mm
1123	A286	5c gray, grn & blk, "1973"	.25	.25
1124	A286	50c gray bl, blk & org, "1972"	.25	.25
a.		"1973"	.65	.25
b.		"1974"	.45	.25
c.		"1975"	.25	.25
d.		"1976"	.25	.25
1125	A286	1e green, blk & brn, "1972"	.45	.25
a.		"1973"	.90	.25
b.		"1976"	.45	.25
c.		"1977"	.45	.25
d.		Unlettered paper, "1978"	.25	.25
1126	A286	1.50e blue, bis & blk, "1972"	.40	.25
a.		"1973"	.90	.25
b.		"1974"	.25	.25
c.		Unlettered paper, "1981"	.25	.25
1127	A286	2.50e brn, dk brn & gray, "1973"	.80	.25
a.		"1975"	2.75	.25
b.		Unlettered paper, "1978"	.25	.25
1128	A286	3e yellow, blk & brn, "1972"	.25	.25
a.		"1974"	.50	.25
b.		"1976"	.25	.25
1129	A286	3.50e dp org, sl & brn, "1973"	1.40	.25
a.		"1975"	1.40	.25
b.		Unlettered paper, "1978"	.25	.25
1130	A286	8e blk, ol & grn, "1973"	1.40	.25
a.		"1975"	1.40	.25
b.		Unlettered paper, "1978"	1.10	.25

Perf. 13½
Size: 31x22mm
1131	A286	10e gray & multi, "1972"	.55	.25
a.		"1974"	1.00	.25
b.		"1977"	1.40	.25
c.		Unlettered paper, "1978"	.45	.25
1132	A286	20e green & multi, "1972"	5.50	.25
a.		"1974"	3.50	.25
b.		"1975"	3.50	.25
c.		"1977"	7.25	.25
1133	A286	50e gray bl, ocher & blk, "1972"	4.50	.25
a.		"1973"	6.75	.25
b.		"1977"	3.50	.25
c.		Unlettered paper, "1978"	1.75	.25
1134	A286	100e green & multi, "1972"	7.25	.55
a.		Unlettered paper, "1978"	9.00	.60
		Nos. 1123-1134 (12)	23.00	3.30

"CTT" and year date printed in minute gray multiple rows on back of stamps. Values are for most common dates.
Issue dates: 1e, 1.50e, 50e, 100e, Mar. 1; 50c, 3e, 10e, 20e, Dec. 6, 1972; 5c, 2.50e, 3.50e, 8e, Sept. 5, 1973.
See Nos. 1207-1214.

Tagging
Starting in 1975, phosphor (bar or L-shape) was applied to the face of most definitives and commemoratives.
Stamps issued both with and without tagging include Nos. 1124-1125, 1128, 1130-1131, 1209, 1213-1214, 1250, 1253, 1257, 1260, 1263.

Window, Pinhel Church — A287

1e, Arms of Pinhel, horiz. 7.50e, Stone lantern.

1972, Mar. 29   **Perf. 13½**
1135	A287	1e blue & multi	.25	.25
a.		Perf. 11½x12½	70.00	3.00
1136	A287	2.50e multicolored	1.50	.30
1137	A287	7.50e blue & multi	1.40	.50
		Nos. 1135-1137 (3)	3.15	1.05

Bicentenary of Pinhel as a town.

Heart and Pendulum A288

Designs: 4e, Heart and spiral pattern. 9e, Heart and continuing coil pattern.

1972, Apr. 24

1138	A288	1e violet & red	.25	.25
1139	A288	4e green & red	2.40	.90
1140	A288	9e brown & red	1.20	.60
		Nos. 1138-1140 (3)	3.85	1.75

"Your heart is your health," World Health Day.

Europa Issue
Common Design Type

1972, May 1   *Perf. 13½*

Size: 21x31mm

1141	CD15	1e gray & multi	1.00	.25
1142	CD15	3.50e salmon & multi	2.75	.35
1143	CD15	6e grn & multi	6.00	.90
		Nos. 1141-1143 (3)	9.75	1.50

Trucks — A289

1972, May 17   Litho.   *Perf. 13½*

1144	A289	1e shown	.25	.25
1145	A289	4.50e Taxi	1.90	.90
1146	A289	8e Autobus	1.50	.70
		Nos. 1144-1146 (3)	3.65	1.85

13th Congress of International Union of Road Transport (I.R.U.), Estoril, May 15-18.

Soccer, Olympic Rings A290

1e, Running. 1.50e, Equestrian. 3.50e, Swimming, women's. 4.50e, Yachting. 5e, Gymnastics, women's.

1972, July 26   Litho.   *Perf. 14*

1147	A290	50c shown	.25	.25
1148	A290	1e multicolored	.25	.25
1149	A290	1.50e multicolored	.40	.25
1150	A290	3.50e multicolored	.95	.30
1151	A290	4.50e multicolored	1.20	.85
1152	A290	5e multicolored	2.50	.80
		Nos. 1147-1152 (6)	5.55	2.70

20th Olympic Games, Munich, 8/26-9/11.

Marquis of Pombal — A291

2.50e, Scientific apparatus. 8e, Seal of Univ. of Coimbra.

1972, Aug. 28   *Perf. 13½*

1153	A291	1e shown	.25	.25
1154	A291	2.50e multicolored	1.50	.60
1155	A291	8e multicolored	1.60	.95
		Nos. 1153-1155 (3)	3.35	1.80

Bicentenary of the Pombaline reforms of University of Coimbra.

Tomé de Sousa — A292

Designs: 2.50e, José Bonifacio. 3.50e, Dom Pedro IV. 6e, Allegory of Portuguese-Brazilian Community.

1972, Oct. 5   Litho.   *Perf. 13½*

1156	A292	1e gray & multi	.25	.25
1157	A292	2.50e green & multi	.65	.25
1158	A292	3.50e multicolored	.65	.30
1159	A292	6e blue & multi	1.40	.65
		Nos. 1156-1159 (4)	2.95	1.45

150th anniv. of Brazilian independence.

Sacadura Cabral, Gago Coutinho and Plane — A293

2.50e, 3.80e, Map of flight from Lisbon to Rio.

1972, Nov. 15   *Perf. 11½x12½*

1160	A293	1e blue & multi	.25	.25
a.		Perf. 13½	40.00	.95
1161	A293	2.50e multi	.80	.30
1162	A293	2.80e multi	1.00	.60
1163	A293	3.80e multi	1.60	1.00
a.		Perf. 13½	125.00	37.50
		Nos. 1160-1163 (4)	3.65	2.15

50th anniv. of the Lisbon to Rio flight by Commander Arturo de Sacadura Cabral and Adm. Carlos Viegas Gago Coutinho, Mar. 30-June 5, 1922.

Luiz Camoens A294

Designs: 3e, Hand saving manuscript from sea. 10e, Symbolic of man's questioning and discovering the unknown.

1972, Dec. 27   Litho.   *Perf. 13*

1164	A294	1e org brn, buff & blk	.25	.25
1165	A294	3e dull bl, lt grn & blk	1.20	.50
1166	A294	10e red brn, buff & yel	1.50	.65
		Nos. 1164-1166 (3)	2.95	1.40

4th centenary of the publication of The Lusiads by Luiz Camoens (1524-1580).

Graphs and Sequence Count — A295

1973, Apr. 11   Litho.   *Perf. 14½*

1167	A295	1e shown	.25	.25
1168	A295	4e Odometer	1.10	.50
1169	A295	9e Graphs	1.00	.45
		Nos. 1167-1169 (3)	2.35	1.20

Productivity Conference '72, 1/17-22/72.

Europa Issue
Common Design Type

1973, Apr. 30   *Perf. 13*

Size: 31x29mm

1170	CD16	1e multicolored	1.00	.25
1171	CD16	4e brn red & multi	5.00	.65
1172	CD16	6e green & multi	7.00	1.25
		Nos. 1170-1172 (3)	13.00	2.15

Gen. Medici, Arms of Brazil and Portugal A296

2.80e, 4.80e, Gen. Medici and world map.

Lithographed and Engraved

1973, May 16   *Perf. 12x11½*

1173	A296	1e dk grn, blk & sep	.25	.25
1174	A296	2.80e olive & multi	.70	.50
1175	A296	3.50e dk bl, blk & buff	.80	.45
1176	A296	4.80e multicolored	.90	.50
		Nos. 1173-1176 (4)	2.65	1.70

Visit of Gen. Emilio Garrastazu Medici, President of Brazil, to Portugal.

Child and Birds — A297

4e, Child and flowers. 7.50e, Child.

1973, May 28   Litho.   *Perf. 13*

1177	A297	1e ultra & multi	.25	.25
1178	A297	4e multicolored	1.25	.50
1179	A297	7.50e bister & multi	1.40	.80
		Nos. 1177-1179 (3)	2.90	1.55

To pay renewed attention to children.

Transportation, Weather Map — A298

3.80e, Communications: telegraph, telephone, radio, satellite. 6e, Postal service: mailbox, truck, mail distribution diagram.

1973, June 25

1180	A298	1e multi	.25	.25
1181	A298	3.80e multi	.40	.30
1182	A298	6e multi	1.00	.50
		Nos. 1180-1182 (3)	1.65	1.05

Ministry of Communications, 25th anniv.

Pupil and Writing Exercise — A299

Designs: 4.50e, Illustrations from 18th century primer. 5.30e, School and children, by 9-year-old Marie de Luz, horiz. 8e, Symbolic chart of teacher-pupil link, horiz.

1973, Oct. 24   Litho.   *Perf. 13*

1183	A299	1e blue & multi	.25	.25
1184	A299	4.50e brown & multi	1.40	.40
1185	A299	5.30e lt blue & multi	1.10	.50
1186	A299	8e green & multi	3.00	1.10
		Nos. 1183-1186 (4)	5.75	2.25

Primary state school education, bicent.

Oporto Streetcar, 1910 A300

Designs: 1e, Horse-drawn streetcar, 1872. 3.50e, Double-decker Leyland bus, 1972.

1973, Nov. 7   *Size: 31½x34mm*

1187	A300	1e brn, yel & blk	.25	.25
1188	A300	3.50e choc & multi	1.75	1.00

Size: 37½x27mm

Perf. 12½

1189	A300	7.50e buff & multi	2.00	.90
		Nos. 1187-1189 (3)	4.00	2.15

Cent. of public transportation in Oporto.

Servicemen's League Emblem — A301

Designs: 2.50e, Sailor, soldier and aviator. 11e, Military medals.

1973, Nov. 28   Litho.   *Perf. 13*

1190	A301	1e multi	.25	.25
1191	A301	2.50e multi	1.90	.55
1192	A301	11e dk blue & multi	1.50	.45
		Nos. 1190-1192 (3)	3.65	1.25

50th anniv. of the Servicemen's League.

Death of Nuño Gonzalves — A302

1973, Dec. 19

1193	A302	1e slate blue & org	.30	.25
1194	A302	10e violet brn & org	1.50	.85

600th anniv. of the heroism of Nuno Gonzalves, alcaide of Faria Castle.

Damiao de Gois, by Dürer (?) A303

Designs: 4.50e, Title page of Cronica de Principe D. Joao. 7.50e, Lute and score of Dodecachordon.

1974, Apr. 5   Litho.   *Perf. 12*

1195	A303	1e multi	.25	.25
1196	A303	4.50e multi	2.10	.45
1197	A303	7.50e multi	1.10	.40
		Nos. 1195-1197 (3)	3.45	1.10

400th anniversary of the death of Damiao de Gois (1502-1574), humanist, writer, composer.

Europa Issue

"The Exile," by Soares dos Reis — A304

1974, Apr. 29   Litho.   *Perf. 13*

1198	A304	1e multicolored	2.00	.25
1199	A304	4e dk red & multi	5.00	.50
1200	A304	6e dk grn & multi	10.00	1.00
		Nos. 1198-1200 (3)	17.00	1.75

Pattern of Light Emission A305

Designs: 4.50e, Spiral wave radiation pattern. 5.30e, Satellite and earth.

1974, June 26   Litho.   *Perf. 14*
1201	A305	1.50e gray olive	.25	.25
1202	A305	4.50e dark blue	1.25	.50
1203	A305	5.30e brt rose lilac	2.00	.75
		Nos. 1201-1203 (3)	3.50	1.50

Establishment of satellite communications network via Intelsat among Portugal, Angola and Mozambique.

Diffusion of Hertzian Waves A306

1974, Sept. 4   Litho.   *Perf. 12*
1204	A306	1.50e multi	.50	.25
1205	A306	3.30e multi	2.00	.60
1206	A306	10e multi	1.25	.40
		Nos. 1204-1206 (3)	3.75	1.25

Guglielmo Marconi (1874-1937), Italian electrical engineer and inventor.

Buildings Type of 1972-73

Designs: 10c, Ponte do Lima (Roman bridge). 30c, Alcobaça Monastery, interior. 2e, City Hall, Bragança. 4e, New Gate, Braga. 4.50e, Dolmen of Carrazeda. 5e, Roman Temple, Evora. 6e, Leca do Balio Monastery. 7.50e, Almourol Castle.

1974, Sept. 18   Litho.   *Perf. 12½*
Size: 22x17½mm
1207	A286	10c multi, "1974"	.25	.25
1208	A286	30c multi, "1974"	.25	.25
1209	A286	2e multi, "1974"	2.00	.25
a.		"1975"	2.00	.25
b.		"1977"	.50	.25
c.		Unlettered paper "1978"	.25	.25
1210	A286	4e multi, "1974"	.55	.25
1211	A286	4.50e multi, "1974"	.90	.25
1212	A286	5e multi, "1974"	7.50	.25
a.		"1975"	15.00	.25
b.		"1976"	7.50	.25
1213	A286	6e multi, "1974"	2.50	.25
a.		"1975"	25.00	.50
1214	A286	7.50e multi, "1974"	1.00	.25
a.		"1977"	2.50	.25
		Nos. 1207-1214 (8)	14.95	2.00

"CTT" and year date printed in minute gray multiple rows on back of stamps. Values are for most common dates.

Postillion, Truck and Letter A307

Designs: 2e, Hand holding letter. 3.30e, Packet and steamship. 4.50e, Pigeon and letters. 5.30e, Hand holding sealed letter. 20e, Old and new locomotives.

1974, Oct. 9   Litho.   *Perf. 13*
1220	A307	1.50e brown & multi	.25	.25
1221	A307	2e multicolored	.65	.25
1222	A307	3.30e olive & multi	.35	.25
1223	A307	4.50e multicolored	1.10	.45
1224	A307	5.30e multicolored	.45	.30
1225	A307	20e multicolored	2.10	.95
a.		Souvenir sheet of 6	6.50	6.50
		Nos. 1220-1225 (6)	4.90	2.45

Centenary of UPU. No. 1225a contains one each of Nos. 1220-1225, arranged to show a continuous design with a globe in center. Sold for 50e.

Luisa Todi, Singer (1753-1833) A308

Marcos Portugal, Composer (1762-1838) A309

Portuguese Musicians: 2e, Joao Domingos Bomtempo (1775-1842). 2.50e, Carlos Seixas (1704-1742). 3e, Duarte Lobo (1565-1646). 5.30e, Joao de Sousa Carvalho (1745-1798).

1974, Oct. 30   Litho.   *Perf. 12*
1226	A308	1.50e brt pink	.25	.25
1227	A308	2e vermilion	1.10	.25
1228	A308	2.50e brown	.65	.25
1229	A308	3e bluish black	1.10	.30
1230	A308	5.30e slate green	.65	.40
1231	A309	11e rose lake	.80	.45
		Nos. 1226-1231 (6)	4.55	1.90

Coat of Arms of Beja A310

2,000th Anniv. of Beja: 3.50e, Men of Beja in costumes from Roman times to date. 7e, Moorish Arches and view across plains.

1974, Nov. 13
1232	A310	1.50e multi	.25	.25
1233	A310	3.50e multi	2.00	.80
1234	A310	7e multi	2.25	.95
		Nos. 1232-1234 (3)	4.50	2.00

Annunciation A311

Christmas: 4.50e, Adoration of the Shepherds. 10e, Flight into Egypt. Designs show Portuguese costumes from Nazare township.

1974, Dec. 4   Litho.   *Perf. 13*
1235	A311	1.50e red & multi	.25	.25
1236	A311	4.50e multicolored	3.00	.45
1237	A311	10e blue & multi	2.25	.60
		Nos. 1235-1237 (3)	5.50	1.30

Rainbow and Dove — A312

1974, Dec. 18   *Perf. 12*
1238	A312	1.50e multi	.25	.25
1239	A312	3.50e multi	2.90	1.40
1240	A312	5e multi	1.60	.50
		Nos. 1238-1240 (3)	4.75	2.15

Armed Forces Movement of Apr. 25, 1974.

Egas Moniz — A313

3.30e, Lobotomy probe and Nobel Prize medal, 1949. 10e, Cerebral angiography, 1927.

1974, Dec. 27   Engr.   *Perf. 11½x12*
1241	A313	1.50e yellow & multi	.25	.25
1242	A313	3.30e brown & ocher	1.10	.35
1243	A313	10e gray & ultra	4.25	.60
		Nos. 1241-1243 (3)	5.60	1.20

Egas Moniz (1874-1955), brain surgeon, birth centenary.

Soldier as Farmer, Farmer as Soldier — A314

1975, Mar. 21   Litho.   *Perf. 12*
1244	A314	1.50e green & multi	.25	.25
1245	A314	3e gray & multi	1.90	.50
1246	A314	4.50e multicolored	2.25	.75
		Nos. 1244-1246 (3)	4.40	1.50

Cultural progress and citizens' guidance campaign.

Hands and Dove — A315

4.50e, Brown hands reaching for dove. 10e, Dove with olive branch and arms of Portugal.

1975, Apr. 23   Litho.   *Perf. 13½*
1247	A315	1.50e red & multi	.25	.25
1248	A315	4.50e brown & multi	2.00	.55
1249	A315	10e green & multi	2.60	.80
		Nos. 1247-1249 (3)	4.85	1.60

Movement of April 25th, first anniversary. Slogans in Portuguese, French and English printed on back of stamps.

God's Hand Reaching Down — A316

Designs: 4.50e, Jesus' hand holding up cross. 10e, Dove (Holy Spirit) descending.

1975, May 13   Litho.   *Perf. 13½*
1250	A316	1.50e multicolored	.25	.25
1251	A316	4.50e plum & multi	2.75	.45
1252	A316	10e blue & multi	3.25	.80
		Nos. 1250-1252 (3)	6.25	1.80

Holy Year 1975.

Horseman of the Apocalypse, 12th Century A317

Europa: 10e, The Poet Fernando Pessoa, by Almada Negreiros (1893-1970).

1975, May 26
1253	A317	1.50e multi	2.00	.25
1254	A317	10e multi	14.00	1.25

Assembly Building A318

1975, June 2   Litho.   *Perf. 13½*
1255	A318	2e red, blk & yel	.30	.25
1256	A318	20e emer, blk & yel	4.25	.75

Opening of Constituent Assembly.

Hikers — A319

Designs: 4.50e, Campsite on lake. 5.30e, Mobile homes on the road.

1975, Aug. 4   Litho.   *Perf. 13½*
1257	A319	2e multicolored	.75	.25
1258	A319	4.50e multicolored	2.25	.80
1259	A319	5.30e multicolored	1.40	.75
		Nos. 1257-1259 (3)	4.40	1.80

36th Rally of the International Federation of Camping and Caravanning, Santo Andre Lake.

People and Sapling A320

Designs (UN Emblem and): 4.50e, People and dove. 20e, People and grain.

1975, Sept. 17   Litho.   *Perf. 13½*
1260	A320	2e green & multi	.25	.25
1261	A320	4.50e vio & multi	1.40	.40
1262	A320	20e multicolored	3.00	1.00
		Nos. 1260-1262 (3)	4.65	1.65

United Nations, 30th anniversary.

Icarus and Rocket — A321

Designs: 4.50e, Apollo and Soyuz in space. 5.30e, Robert H. Goddard, Robert Esnault-Pelterie, Hermann Oberth and Konstantin Tsiolkovski. 10e, Sputnik, man in space, moon landing module.

1975, Sept. 26   Litho.   *Perf. 13½*
Size: 30½x26½mm
1263	A321	2e green & multi	.40	.25
1264	A321	4.50e brown & multi	2.00	.60
1265	A321	5.30e lilac & multi	.95	.60

Size: 65x28mm
1266	A321	10e blue & multi	3.50	1.00
		Nos. 1263-1266 (4)	6.85	2.45

26th Congress of International Astronautical Federation, Lisbon, Sept. 1975.

Land Survey A322

Designs: 8e, Ocean survey. 10e, People of many races and globe.

1975, Nov. 19   Litho.   *Perf. 12x12½*
1267	A322	2e ocher & multi	.25	.25
1268	A322	8e blue & multi	1.40	.55
1269	A322	10e dk vio & multi	3.00	.85
		Nos. 1267-1269 (3)	4.65	1.65

Centenary of Lisbon Geographical Society.

Arch and Trees — A323

Designs: 8e, Plan, pencil and ruler. 10e, Hand, old building and brick tower.

1975, Nov. 28   **Perf. 13½**
1270	A323	2e dk bl & gray	.25	.25
1271	A323	8e dk car & gray	2.50	.65
1272	A323	10e ocher & multi	3.00	.90
		Nos. 1270-1272 (3)	5.75	1.80

European Architectural Heritage Year 1975.

Nurse and Hospital Ward — A324

Designs (IWY Emblem and): 2e, Farm workers. 3.50e, Secretary. 8e, Factory worker.

1975, Dec. 30   **Litho.**   **Perf. 13½**
1273	A324	50c multicolored	.25	.25
1274	A324	2e multicolored	.75	.25
1275	A324	3.50e multicolored	.85	.45
1276	A324	8e multicolored	1.40	.90
	a.	Souvenir sheet of 4	6.00	4.00
		Nos. 1273-1276 (4)	3.25	1.85

International Women's Year 1975. No. 1276a contains 4 stamps similar to Nos. 1273-1276 in slightly changed colors. Sold for 25e.

Pen Nib as Plowshare A325

1976, Feb. 6   **Litho.**   **Perf. 12**
1277	A325	3e dk bl & red org	.35	.25
1278	A325	20e org, ultra & red	3.25	.90

Portuguese Soc. of Writers, 50th anniv.

Telephones, 1876, 1976 — A326

10.50e, Alexander Graham Bell & telephone.

1976, Mar. 10   **Litho.**   **Perf. 12x12½**
1279	A326	3e yel grn, grn & blk	.65	.25
1280	A326	10.50e rose, red & blk	2.50	.65

Centenary of first telephone call by Alexander Graham Bell, March 10, 1876.

Industry and Shipping — A327

1e, Garment, food and wine industries.

1976, Apr. 7   **Litho.**   **Perf. 12½**
1281	A327	50c red brown	.25	.25
1282	A327	1e slate	.45	.25

Support of national production.

Carved Spoons, Olive Wood A328

Europa: 20e, Gold filigree pendant, silver box and CEPT emblem.

1976, May 3   **Litho.**   **Perf. 12x12½**
1283	A328	3e olive & multi	2.00	.25
1284	A328	20e tan & multi	15.00	1.75

Stamp Collectors A329

Designs: 7.50e, Stamp exhibition and hand canceler. 10e, Printing and designing stamps.

1976, May 29   **Litho.**   **Perf. 14½**
1285	A329	3e multicolored	.25	.25
1286	A329	7.50e multicolored	1.00	.45
1287	A329	10e multicolored	1.40	.50
		Nos. 1285-1287 (3)	2.65	1.20

Interphil 76, International Philatelic Exhibition, Philadelphia, Pa., May 29-June 6.

King Ferdinand I — A330

Designs: 5e, Plowshare, farmers chasing off hunters. 10e, Harvest.

1976, July 2   **Litho.**   **Perf. 12**
1288	A330	3e lt bl & multi	.25	.25
1289	A330	5e yel grn & multi	1.50	.30
1290	A330	10e multicolored	1.60	.60
	a.	Souv. sheet of 3, #1288-1290	4.25	4.25
		Nos. 1288-1290 (3)	3.35	1.15

Agricultural reform law (compulsory cultivation of uncultivated lands), 600th anniversary. No. 1290a sold for 30e.

Torch Bearer A331

7e, Women's relay race. 10.50e, Olympic flame.

1976, July 16   **Perf. 13½**
1291	A331	3e red & multi	.25	.25
1292	A331	7e red & multi	1.50	.90
1293	A331	10.50e red & multi	2.00	.80
		Nos. 1291-1293 (3)	3.75	1.95

21st Olympic Games, Montreal, Canada, July 17-Aug. 1.

Farm A332

1976, Sept. 15   **Litho.**   **Perf. 12**
1294	A332	3e shown	.55	.25
1295	A332	3e Ship	.55	.25
1296	A332	3e City	.55	.25
1297	A332	3e Factory	.55	.25
	b.	Souv. sheet of 4, #1294-1297	12.50	12.50
		Nos. 1294-1297 (4)	2.75	1.00

Fight against illiteracy. #1297b sold for 25e.

        Perf. 13½
1294a	A332	3e	24.00	.50
1295a	A332	3e	.80	.25
1296a	A332	3e	24.00	.50
1297a	A332	3e	.80	.25
		Nos. 1294a-1297a (4)	49.60	1.50

Azure-winged Magpie A333

Designs: 5e, Lynx. 7e, Portuguese laurel cherry. 10.50e, Little wild carnations.

1976, Sept. 30   **Perf. 12**
1298	A333	3e multi	.50	.25
1299	A333	5e multi	1.10	.25
1300	A333	7e multi	1.25	.65
1301	A333	10.50e multi	1.25	.85
		Nos. 1298-1301 (4)	4.10	2.00

Portucale 77, 2nd International Thematic Exhibition, Oporto, Oct. 29-Nov. 6, 1977.

Exhibition Hall — A334

Design: 20e, Symbolic stamp and emblem.

1976, Oct. 9   **Litho.**   **Perf. 13½**
1302	A334	3e bl & multi	.35	.25
1303	A334	20e ocher & multi	2.00	1.10
	a.	Souv. sheet of 2, #1302-1303	3.75	3.75

6th Luso-Brazilian Phil. Exhib., LUBRAPEX 76, Oporto, Oct. 9. #1303a sold for 30e.

Bank Emblem and Family A335

7e, Grain. 15e, Cog wheels.

1976, Oct. 29   **Perf. 12**
1304	A335	3e org & multi	.25	.25
1305	A335	7e grn & multi	1.75	.60
1306	A335	15e bl & multi	2.25	.85
		Nos. 1304-1306 (3)	4.25	1.70

Trust Fund Bank centenary.

Sheep Grazing on Marsh A336

Designs: 3e, Drainage ditches. 5e, Fish in water. 10e, Ducks flying over marsh.

1976, Nov. 24   **Litho.**   **Perf. 14**
1307	A336	1e multicolored	.25	.25
1308	A336	3e multicolored	.90	.25
1309	A336	5e multicolored	1.50	.30
1310	A336	10e multicolored	2.75	.75
		Nos. 1307-1310 (4)	5.40	1.55

Protection of wetlands.

"Liberty" — A337

1976, Nov. 30   **Litho.**   **Perf. 13½**
1311	A337	3e gray, grn & ver	.65	.25

Constitution of 1976.

Mother Examining Child's Eyes A338

Designs: 5e, Welder with goggles. 10.50e, Blind woman reading Braille.

1976, Dec. 13
1312	A338	3e multicolored	.25	.25
1313	A338	5e multicolored	1.75	.25
1314	A338	10.50e multicolored	1.40	.80
		Nos. 1312-1314 (3)	3.40	1.30

World Health Day and campaign against blindness.

Hydroelectric Energy — A339

Abstract Designs: 4e, Fossil fuels. 5e, Geothermal energy. 10e, Wind power. 15e, Solar energy.

1976, Dec. 30
1315	A339	1e multicolored	.25	.25
1316	A339	4e multicolored	.50	.25
1317	A339	5e multicolored	.65	.25
1318	A339	10e multicolored	1.25	.60
1319	A339	15e multicolored	2.40	1.10
		Nos. 1315-1319 (5)	5.05	2.45

Sources of energy.

Map of Council of Europe Members A340

1977, Jan. 28   **Litho.**   **Perf. 12**
1320	A340	8.50e multicolored	1.25	.95
1321	A340	10e multicolored	1.25	.85

Portugal's joining Council of Europe.

Alcoholic and Bottle — A341

Designs (Bottle and): 5e, Symbolic figure of broken life. 15e, Bars blotting out the sun.

1977, Feb. 4   **Perf. 13**
1322	A341	3e multicolored	.25	.25
1323	A341	5e ocher & multi	.85	.30
1324	A341	15e org & multi	2.00	.95
		Nos. 1322-1324 (3)	3.10	1.50

Anti-alcoholism Day and 10th anniversary of Portuguese Anti-alcoholism Society.

Trees Tapped for Resin — A342

Designs: 4e, Trees stripped for cork. 7e, Trees and logs. 15e, Trees at seashore as windbreakers.

1977, Mar. 21   **Litho.**   **Perf. 13½**
1325	A342	1e multicolored	.25	.25
1326	A342	4e multicolored	.65	.25
1327	A342	7e multicolored	1.40	.95
1328	A342	15e multicolored	1.50	.95
		Nos. 1325-1328 (4)	3.80	2.40

Forests, a natural resource.

"Suffering"
A343

6e, Man exercising. 10e, Group exercising. All designs include emblems of WHO & Portuguese Institute for Rheumatology.

1977, Apr. 13   Litho.   Perf. 12x12½

1329	A343	4e blk, brn & ocher	.25	.25
1330	A343	6e blk, bl & vio	1.10	.75
1331	A343	10e blk, pur & red	1.00	.50
		Nos. 1329-1331 (3)	2.35	1.50

International Rheumatism Year.

Southern Plains Landscape A344

Europa: 8.50e, Northern mountain valley.

1977, May 2

1332	A344	4e multi	1.00	.25
1333	A344	8.50e multi	3.00	.60
a.		Min. sheet, 3 each #1332-1333	15.00	14.00

Pope John XXI Enthroned A345

Petrus Hispanus, the Physician A346

1977, May 20   Litho.   Perf. 13½

1334	A345	4e multicolored	.25	.25
1335	A346	15e multicolored	.60	.35

Pope John XXI (Petrus Hispanus), only Pope of Portuguese descent, 7th death centenary.

Compass Rose, Camoens Quotation A347

1977, June 8   Perf. 12

1336	A347	4e multi	.25	.25
1337	A347	8.50e multi	1.10	.80

Camoens Day and to honor Portuguese overseas communities.

Student, Computer and Book — A348

Designs (Book and): No. 1339, Folk dancers, flutist and boat. No. 1340, Tractor drivers. No. 1341, Atom and people.

1977, July 20   Litho.   Perf. 12x12½

1338	A348	4e multicolored	.40	.25
1339	A348	4e multicolored	.40	.25
1340	A348	4e multicolored	.40	.25
1341	A348	4e multicolored	.40	.25
a.		Souv. sheet of 4, #1338-1341	4.50	4.50
		Nos. 1338-1341 (4)	1.60	1.00

Continual education. #1341a sold for 20e.

Pyrites, Copper, Chemical Industry A349

Designs: 5e, Marble, statue, public buildings. 10e, Iron ore, girders, crane. 20e, Uranium ore, atomic diagram.

1977, Oct. 4   Litho.   Perf. 12x11½

1342	A349	4e multicolored	.25	.25
1343	A349	5e multicolored	.75	.25
1344	A349	10e multicolored	1.20	.35
1345	A349	20e multicolored	1.90	.90
		Nos. 1342-1345 (4)	4.10	1.75

Natural resources from the subsoil.

Alexandre Herculano — A350

1977, Oct. 19   Engr.   Perf. 12x11½

1346	A350	4e multicolored	.25	.25
1347	A350	15e multicolored	1.60	.50

Alexandre Herculano de Carvalho Araujo (1810-1877), historian, novelist, death centenary.

Maria Pia Bridge A351

4e, Arrival of first train, ceramic panel by Jorge Colaco, St. Bento railroad station.

1977, Nov. 4   Litho.   Perf. 12x11½

1348	A351	4e multicolored	.25	.25
1349	A351	10e multicolored	1.25	1.25

Centenary of extension of railroad across Douro River.

Poveiro Bark A352

Coastal Fishing Boats: 3e, Do Mar bark. 4e, Nazaré bark. 7e, Algarve skiff. 10e, Xavega bark. 15e, Bateira de Buarcos.

1977, Nov. 19   Perf. 12

1350	A352	2e multicolored	.40	.25
1351	A352	3e multicolored	.25	.25
1352	A352	4e multicolored	.25	.25
1353	A352	7e multicolored	.50	.25
1354	A352	10e multicolored	.80	.40
1355	A352	15e multicolored	1.25	.65
a.		Souv. sheet of 6, #1350-1355	4.00	4.00
		Nos. 1350-1355 (6)	3.45	2.05

PORTUCALE 77, 2nd International Topical Exhibition. Oporto, Nov. 19-20. No. 1355a sold for 60e.

Nativity A353

Children's Drawings: 7e, Nativity. 10e, Holy Family, vert. 20e, Star and Christ Child, vert.

Perf. 12x11½, 11½x12

1977, Dec. 12   Litho.

1356	A353	4e multicolored	.25	.25
1357	A353	7e multicolored	.90	.30
1358	A353	10e multicolored	1.00	.45
1359	A353	20e multicolored	2.25	.80
		Nos. 1356-1359 (4)	4.40	1.80

Christmas 1977.

Old Desk and Computer — A354

Designs: Work tools, old and new — 50c, Medical. 1e, Household. 2e, Communications. 3e, Garment making. 4e, Office. 5e, Fishing craft. 5.50e, Weaving. 6e, Plows. 6.50e, Aviation. 7e, Printing. 8e, Carpentry. 8.50e, Potter's wheel. 9e, Photography. 10e, Saws. 12.50e, Compasses ('83). 16e, Mail processing ('83). 20e, Construction. 30e, Steel industry. 40e, Transportation. 50e, Chemistry. 100e, Shipbuilding. 250e, Telescopes.

1978-83   Litho.   Perf. 12½
Size: 22x17mm

1360	A354	50c multi	.25	.25
1361	A354	1e multi	.25	.25
1362	A354	2e multi	.25	.25
1363	A354	3e multi	.25	.25
1364	A354	4e multi	.25	.25
1365	A354	5e multi	.25	.25
1366	A354	5.50e multi	.25	.25
1367	A354	6e multi	.25	.25
1368	A354	6.50e multi	.25	.25
1369	A354	7e multi	.25	.25
1370	A354	8e multi	.25	.25
1371	A354	8.50e multi	.25	.25
1372	A354	9e multi	.25	.25
1373	A354	10e multi	.25	.25
1373A	A354	12.50e multi	.30	.25
1373B	A354	16e multi	.30	.25

Perf. 13½
Size: 31x22mm

1374	A354	20e multi	.50	.25
1375	A354	30e multi	.60	.30
a.		Incomplete arch	1.00	.30
1376	A354	40e multi	.60	.25
1377	A354	50e multi	1.00	.25
1378	A354	100e multi	1.60	.30
1379	A354	250e multi	4.25	.60
		Nos. 1360-1379 (22)	12.65	5.95

Red Mediterranean Soil — A355

Designs: 5e, Stone formation. 10e, Alluvial soil. 20e, Black soil.

1978, Mar. 6   Litho.   Perf. 12

1380	A355	4e multicolored	.25	.25
1381	A355	5e multicolored	.40	.25
1382	A355	10e multicolored	.80	.45
1383	A355	20e multicolored	2.25	.60
		Nos. 1380-1383 (4)	3.70	1.55

Soil, a natural resource.

Street Crossing A356

Designs: 2e, Motorcyclist. 2.50e, Children in back seat of car. 5e, Hands holding steering wheel. 9e, Driving on country road. 12.50e, "Avoid drinking and driving."

1978, Apr. 19   Litho.   Perf. 12

1384	A356	1e multi	.25	.25
1385	A356	2e multi	.25	.25
1386	A356	2.50e multi	.55	.25
1387	A356	5e multi	1.00	.25
1388	A356	9e multi	1.90	.50
1389	A356	12.50e multi	2.90	1.25
		Nos. 1384-1389 (6)	6.85	2.75

Road safety campaign.

Roman Tower, Belmonte A357

Europa: 40e, Belém Monastery of Hieronymite monks (inside).

1978, May 2

1390	A357	10e multicolored	1.75	.25
1391	A357	40e multicolored	3.75	.75
a.		Souv. sheet, 2 each #1390-1391	15.00	12.00

No. 1391a sold for 120e.

Trajan's Bridge — A358

Roman Tablet from Bridge — A359

1978, June 14   Litho.   Perf. 13½

1392	A358	5e multicolored	.40	.25
1393	A359	20e multicolored	2.50	.80

1900th anniv. of Chaves (Aquae Flaviae).

Running A360

1978, July 24   Litho.   Perf. 12

1394	A360	5e shown	.25	.25
1395	A360	10e Bicycling	.40	.25
1396	A360	12.50e Watersport	.85	.50
1397	A360	15e Soccer	.85	.65
		Nos. 1394-1397 (4)	2.35	1.65

Sport for all the people.

Pedro Nunes A361

Design: 20e, "Nonio" navigational instrument and diagram from "Tratado da Rumaçao do Globo."

1978, Aug. 9   Litho.   Perf. 12x11½

1398	A361	5e multicolored	.25	.25
1399	A361	20e multicolored	1.40	.35

Nunes (1502-78), navigator and cosmographer.

Trawler, Frozen Fish Processing, Can of Sardines — A362

Fishing Industry: 9e, Deep-sea trawler, loading and unloading at dock. 12.50e, Trawler with radar and instruction in use of radar. 15e, Trawler with echo-sounding equipment, microscope and test tubes.

1978, Sept. 16   Litho.   *Perf. 12x11½*
1400	A362	5e multi	.25	.25
1401	A362	9e multi	.65	.25
1402	A362	12.50e multi	1.20	.70
1403	A362	15e multi	1.75	.90
	Nos. 1400-1403 (4)		3.85	2.10

Natural resources.

Postrider
A363

Designs: No. 1405, Carrier pigeon. No. 1406, Envelopes. No. 1407, Pen.

1978, Oct. 30   Litho.   *Perf. 12*
1404	A363	5e yel & multi	.35	.25
1405	A363	5e bl gray & multi	.35	.25
1406	A363	5e grn & multi	.35	.25
1407	A363	5e red & multi	.35	.25
	Nos. 1404-1407 (4)		1.40	1.00

Introduction of Postal Code.

Human Figure, Flame Emblem
A364

Design: 40e, Human figure pointing the way and flame emblem.

1978, Dec. 7   Litho.   *Perf. 12*
1408	A364	14e multicolored	.50	.30
1409	A364	40e multicolored	1.40	.90
a.	Souv. sheet, 2 ea #1408-1409		5.50	6.25

Universal Declaration of Human Rights, 30th anniv. and 25th anniv. of European Declaration.

Sebastiao Magalhaes Lima — A365

1978, Dec. 7
1410	A365	5e multicolored	.30	.25

Sebastiao Magalhaes Lima (1850-1928), lawyer, journalist, statesman.

Mail Boxes and Scale
A366

Designs: 5e, Telegraph and condenser lens. 10e, Portugal Nos. 2-3 and postal card printing press, 1879. 14e, Book and bookcases, 1879, 1979.

1978, Dec. 20
1411	A366	4e multicolored	.25	.25
1412	A366	5e multicolored	.25	.25
1413	A366	10e multicolored	.90	.25
1414	A366	14e multicolored	2.25	1.25
a.	Souv. sheet of 4, #1411-1414		5.00	5.00
	Nos. 1411-1414 (4)		3.65	2.00

Centenary of Postal Museum and Postal Library; 125th anniversary of Portuguese stamps (10e). No. 1414a sold for 40e.

Emigrant at Railroad Station
A367

Designs: 14e, Farewell at airport. 17e, Emigrant greeting child at railroad station.

1979, Feb. 21   Litho.   *Perf. 12*
1415	A367	5e multicolored	.25	.25
1416	A367	14e multicolored	.70	.35
1417	A367	17e multicolored	1.10	.80
	Nos. 1415-1417 (3)		2.05	1.40

Portuguese emigration.

Automobile Traffic — A368

Combat noise pollution: 5e, Pneumatic drill. 14e, Man with bull horn.

1979, Mar. 14   *Perf. 13½*
1418	A368	4e multicolored	.25	.25
1419	A368	5e multicolored	.55	.25
1420	A368	14e multicolored	1.40	.50
	Nos. 1418-1420 (3)		2.20	1.00

NATO Emblem
A369

1979, Apr. 4   Litho.   *Perf. 12*
1421	A369	5e multicolored	.30	.25
1422	A369	50e multicolored	2.50	1.60
a.	Souv. sheet, 2 ea #1421-1422		6.00	6.00

NATO, 30th anniv.

Mail Delivery, 16th Century
A370

Europa: 40e, Mail delivery, 19th century.

1979, Apr. 30   Litho.   *Perf. 12*
1423	A370	14e multicolored	1.00	.30
1424	A370	40e multicolored	1.75	1.60
a.	Souv. sheet, 2 ea #1423-1424		8.00	6.00

Mother, Infant, Dove
A371

Designs (IYC Emblem and): 5.50e, Children playing ball. 10e, Child in nursery school. 14e, Black and white boys.

1979, June 1   Litho.   *Perf. 12x12½*
1425	A371	5.50e multi	.25	.25
1426	A371	6.50e multi	.30	.25
1427	A371	10e multi	.45	.25
1428	A371	14e multi	.90	.65
a.	Souv. sheet of 4, #1425-1428		3.50	3.50
	Nos. 1425-1428 (4)		1.90	1.40

Intl. Year of the Child. No. 1428a sold for 40e.

Salute to the Flag — A372

1979, June 8
1429	A372	6.50e multicolored	.35	.25
a.	Souvenir sheet of 9		4.50	4.50

Portuguese Day.

Pregnant Woman
A373

Designs: 17e, Boy sitting in a cage. 20e, Face, and hands using hammer.

1979, June 6   Litho.   *Perf. 12x12½*
1430	A373	6.50e multi	.25	.25
1431	A373	17e multi	.65	.50
1432	A373	20e multi	.90	.60
	Nos. 1430-1432 (3)		1.80	1.35

Help for the mentally retarded.

Children Reading Book, UNESCO Emblem
A374

17e, Teaching deaf child, and UNESCO emblem.

1979, June 25
1433	A374	6.50e multi	.30	.25
1434	A374	17e multi	1.60	.70

Intl. Bureau of Education, 50th anniv.

Water Cart, Brasiliana '79 Emblem
A375

Brasiliana '79 Philatelic Exhibition: 5.50e, Wine sledge. 6.50e, Wine cart. 16e, Covered cart. 19e, Mogadouro cart. 20e, Sand cart.

1979, Sept. 15   Litho.   *Perf. 12*
1435	A375	2.50e multi	.25	.25
1436	A375	5.50e multi	.25	.25
1437	A375	6.50e multi	.35	.25
1438	A375	16e multi	.80	.55
1439	A375	19e multi	1.10	.75
1440	A375	20e multi	1.20	.30
	Nos. 1435-1440 (6)		3.95	2.35

Antonio Jose de Almeida (1866-1929)
A376

Republican Leaders: 6.50e, Afonso Costa (1871-1937). 10e, Teofilo Braga (1843-1924). 16e, Bernardino Machado (1851-1944). 19.50e, Joao Chagas (1863-1925). 20e, Elias Garcia (1830-1891).

1979, Oct. 4   *Perf. 12½x12*
1441	A376	5.50e multi	.25	.25
1442	A376	6.50e multi	.25	.25
1443	A376	10e multi	.45	.25
1444	A376	16e multi	.75	.45

1445	A376	19.50e multi	1.25	.80
1446	A376	20e multi	1.00	.35
	Nos. 1441-1446 (6)		3.95	2.35

See Nos. 1454-1459.

Red Cross and Family
A377

20e, Doctor examining elderly man.

1979, Oct. 26   *Perf. 12x12½*
1447	A377	6.50e multi	.30	.25
1448	A377	20e multi	1.25	.40

National Health Service Campaign.

Holy Family, 17th Century Mosaic
A378

Mosaics, Lisbon Tile Museum: 6.50e, Nativity, 16th century. 16e, Flight into Egypt, 18th century.

1979, Dec. 5   Litho.   *Perf. 12x12½*
1449	A378	5.50e multi	.35	.25
1450	A378	6.50e multi	.35	.25
1451	A378	16e multi	.90	.70
	Nos. 1449-1451 (3)		1.60	1.20

Christmas 1979.

Rotary International, 75th Anniversary — A379

1980, Feb. 22   *Perf. 12x11½*
1452	A379	16e shown	1.00	.45
1453	A379	50e Emblem, torch	2.75	1.25

Portrait Type of 1979

Leaders of the Republican Movement: 3.50e, Alvaro de Castro (1878-1928). 5.50e, Antonio Sergio (1883-1969). 6.50e, Norton de Matos (1867-1955). 11e, Jaime Cortesao (1884-1960). 16e, Teixeira Gomes (1860-1941). 20e, Jose Domingues dos Santos (1885-1958). Nos. 1454-1459 horizontal.

1980, Mar. 19
1454	A376	3.50e multi	.25	.25
1455	A376	5.50e multi	.25	.25
1456	A376	6.50e multi	.25	.25
1457	A376	11e multi	1.40	.75
1458	A376	16e multi	.85	.50
1459	A376	20e multi	.90	.30
	Nos. 1454-1459 (6)		3.90	2.30

Europa Issue

Serpa Pinto (1864-1900), Explorer of Africa
A380

60e, Vasco da Gama.

1980, Apr. 14
1460	A380	16e shown	.70	.30
1461	A380	60e multicolored	2.00	1.00
a.	Souv. sheet, 2 each #1460-1461		5.00	3.00

Barn Owl
A381

1980, May 6   Litho.   Perf. 12x11½
1462 A381   6.50e shown   .25   .25
1463 A381   16e Red fox   .70   .30
1464 A381   19.50e Timber wolf 1.00 .40
1465 A381   20e Golden eagle   1.10 .35
   a.   Souv. sheet of 4, #1462-1465 3.75 3.25
      Nos. 1462-1465 (4)   3.05 1.30

European Campaign for the Protection of Species and their Habitat (Lisbon Zoo animals); London 1980 International Stamp Exhibition, May 6-14.

Luiz Camoens
(1524-80)
A382

Lithographed & Engraved
1980, June 9   Perf. 11½x12
1466 A382   6.50e multi + label .40   .25
1467 A382   20e multi + label   .90   .75

Mendes Pinto and Chinese Men
A383

1980, June 30   Litho.   Perf. 12x11½
1468 A383   6.50e shown   .30   .25
1469 A383   10e Battle at sea .90 .40

A Peregrinacao (The Peregrination,) by Fernao Mendes Pinto (1509-1583), written in 1580, published in 1614.

St. Vincent and Old Lisbon
A384

Designs: 8e, Lantern Tower, Evora Cathedral. 11e, Jesus with top hat, Miranda do Douro Cathedral, and mountain. 16e, Our Lady of the Milk, Braga Cathedral, and Canicada Dam. 19.50e, Pulpit, Santa Cruz Monastery, Coimbra, and Aveiro River. 20e, Algarve chimney, and Rocha Beach.

1980, Sept. 17   Litho.   Perf. 12x12½
1470 A384   6.50e multi   .30   .25
1471 A384   8e multi   .35   .25
1472 A384   11e multi   .80   .35
1473 A384   16e multi   1.10 .55
1474 A384   19.50e multi 1.50 .65
1475 A384   20e multi   1.25 .40
      Nos. 1470-1475 (6)   5.30 2.45

World Tourism Conf., Manila, Sept. 27.

Caravel, Lubrapex '80 Emblem
A385

8e, Three-master Nau. 16e, Galleon. 19.50e, Paddle steam.

1980, Oct. 18   Litho.   Perf. 12x11½
1476 A385   6.50e shown   .30   .25
1477 A385   8e multicolored   .60   .30
1478 A385   16e multicolored   1.20 .45
1479 A385   19.50e multicolored 1.75 .50
   a.   Souv. sheet of 4, #1476-1479 6.00 6.00
      Nos. 1476-1479 (4)   3.85 1.50

Lubrapex '80 Stamp Exhib., Lisbon, Oct. 18-26.

Car Emitting Gas Fumes
A386

1980, Oct. 31
1480 A386   6.50e Light bulbs .25   .25
1481 A386   16e shown   1.60 .55

Energy conservation.

Student, School and Sextant
A387

1980, Dec. 19   Litho.   Perf. 12x11½
1482 A387   6.50e Founder, book, emblem .30 .25
1483 A387   19.50e shown   1.40 .50

Lisbon Academy of Science bicentennial.

Man with Diseased Heart and Lungs, Hand Holding Cigarette
A388

19.50e, Healthy man rejecting cigarette.

1980, Dec. 19   Perf. 13½
1484 A388   6.50e shown   .30   .25
1485 A388   19.50e multicolored 1.75 .80

Anti-smoking campaign.

Census Form and Houses
A389

1981, Jan. 28   Litho.   Perf. 13½
1486 A389   6.50e Form, head   .30   .25
1487 A389   16e shown   1.40 .95

Fragata on Tejo River
A390

8.50e, Rabelo, Douro River. 10e, Moliceiro, Aveiro River. 16e, Barco, Lima River. 19.50e, Carocho, Minho River. 20e, Varino, Tejo River.

1981, Feb. 23   Litho.   Perf. 12x12½
1488 A390   8e multicolored   .25   .25
1489 A390   8.50e multicolored .25   .25
1490 A390   10e multicolored   .45   .25
1491 A390   16e multicolored   .65   .45
1492 A390   19.50e multicolored .75   .45
1493 A390   20e multicolored   .75   .35
      Nos. 1488-1493 (6)   3.10 2.00

Rajola Tile, Valencia, 15th Century
A391

Designs: No. 1495, Moresque tile, Coimbra 16th cent. No. 1496, Arms of Duke of Braganza, 1510. No. 1497, Pisanos design, 1595.

1981   Litho.   Perf. 11½x12
1494 A391   8.50e multi   .75   .25
   a.   Miniature sheet of 6   4.50 5.00
1495 A391   8.50e multi   .75   .25
   a.   Miniature sheet of 6   4.50 4.50
1496 A391   8.50e multi   .75   .25
   a.   Miniature sheet of 6   4.50 4.50
1497 A391   8.50e multi   .75   .25
   a.   Miniature sheet of 6   4.50 4.50
   b.   Souv. sheet of 4, #1494-1497 5.00 5.00
      Nos. 1494-1497 (4)   3.00 1.00

Issued: #1494, 3/16; #1495, 6/13; #1496, 8/28; #1497, 12/16. See #1528-1531, 1563-1566, 1593-1596, 1617-1620.

Perdigueiro
A392

7e, Cao de agua. 8.50e, Serra de aires. 22e, Podengo. 22.50e, Castro laboreiro. 33.50e, Serra da estrela.

1981, Mar. 16   Perf. 12
1498 A392   7e multi   .40   .25
1499 A392   8.50e multi   .40   .25
1500 A392   15e shown   1.00 .25
1501 A392   22e multi   1.10 .65
1502 A392   25.50e multi 1.75 1.00
1503 A392   33.50e multi 2.25 .65
      Nos. 1498-1503 (6)   6.90 3.05

Portuguese Kennel Club, 50th anniversary.

Workers and Rainbow
A393

25.50e, Rainbow, demonstration.

1981, Apr. 30   Litho.   Perf. 12x12½
1504 A393   8.50e shown   .25   .25
1505 A393   25.50e multi 1.25 .85

International Workers' Day.

Europa Issue

Dancer in National Costume — A394

48e, Painted boat, horiz.

1981, May 11   Perf. 13½
1506 A394   22e shown   .80   .50
1507 A394   48e multi   1.60 1.25
   a.   Souv. sheet, 2 ea #1506-1507 6.00 4.00

St. Anthony Writing
A395

St. Anthony of Lisbon, 750th Anniversary of Death: 70e, Blessing people.

1981, June 13   Perf. 12x11½
1508 A395   8.50e multi   .50   .25
1509 A395   70e multi   3.00 1.75

500th Anniv. of King Joao II
A396

27e, Joao II leading army.

1981, Aug. 28   Perf. 12x11½
1510 A396   8.50e shown   .45   .25
1511 A396   27e multi   2.00 .95

125th Anniv. of Portuguese Railroads — A397

Designs: Locomotives — 8.50e, Dom Luis, 1862. 19e, Pacific 500, 1925. 27e, ALCO 1500, 1948. 33.50e, BB 2600 ALSTHOM, '74.

1981, Oct. 28   Litho.   Perf. 12x11½
1512 A397   8.50e multi   .65   .25
1513 A397   19e multi   1.90 .90
1514 A397   27e multi   1.90 1.00
1515 A397   33.50e multi 2.75 .85
      Nos. 1512-1515 (4)   7.20 3.00

Pearier Pump Fire Engine, 1856 — A398

8.50e, Ford, 1927. 27e, Renault, 1914. 33.50e, Snorkel, Ford 1978.

1981, Nov. 18   Litho.   Perf. 12x12½
1516 A398   7e shown   .45   .25
1517 A398   8.50e multi   .65   .25
1518 A398   27e multi   2.25 .95
1519 A398   33.50e multi 2.90 .90
      Nos. 1516-1519 (4)   6.25 2.35

A399

Christmas: Clay creches.

1981, Dec. 16   Perf. 12½x12
1520 A399   7e multi   .45   .30
1521 A399   8.50e multi   .65   .25
1522 A399   27e multi   2.10 1.40
      Nos. 1520-1522 (3)   3.20 1.95

A400

8.50e, With animals. 27e, Building church.

1982, Jan. 20 Litho.   Perf. 12½x12
| 1523 | A400 | 8.50e multi | .35 | .25 |
| 1524 | A400 | 27e multi | 1.90 | 1.40 |

800th birth anniv. of St. Francis of Assisi.

Centenary of Figueira da Foz
A401

10e, St. Catherine Fort. 19e, Tagus Bridge, ships.

1982, Feb. 24 Litho.   Perf. 13½
| 1525 | A401 | 10e multi | .45 | .25 |
| 1526 | A401 | 19e multi | 1.40 | .85 |

25th Anniv. of European Economic Community A402

1982, Feb. 24   Perf. 12x11½
| 1527 | A402 | 27e multi | 1.25 | .65 |
| a. | | Souvenir sheet of 4 | 4.50 | 2.50 |

Tile Type of 1981

Designs: No. 1528, Italo-Flemish pattern, 17th cent. No. 1529, Oriental fabric pattern altar frontal, 17th cent. No. 1530, Greek cross, 1630-1640. No. 1531, Blue and white design, Mother of God Convent, Lisbon, 1670.

1982   Litho.   Perf. 12x11½
1528	A391	10e multi	.75	.25
a.		Miniature sheet of 6	5.00	5.00
1529	A391	10e multi	.75	.25
a.		Miniature sheet of 6	5.00	4.50
1530	A391	10e multi	.75	.25
a.		Miniature sheet of 6	5.00	4.50
1531	A391	10e red & blue	.75	.25
a.		Miniature sheet of 6	5.00	4.50
b.		Souv. sheet of 4, #1528-1531	5.00	4.50
		Nos. 1528-1531 (4)	3.00	1.00

Issued: No. 1528, Mar. 24; No. 1529, June 11; No. 1530, Sept. 22; No. 1531, Dec. 15.

A403

Major Sporting Events of 1982: 27e, Lisbon Sail. 33.50e, 25th Roller-hockey Championships, Lisbon and Barcelos, May 1-16. 50e, Intl. 470 Class World Championships, Cascais Bay. 75e, Espana '82 World Cup Soccer.

1982, Mar. 24   Perf. 12x12½
1532	A403	27e multi	1.25	.80
1533	A403	33.50e multi	1.60	1.10
1534	A403	50e multi	2.40	1.25
1535	A403	75e multi	4.00	1.50
		Nos. 1532-1535 (4)	9.25	4.65

A404

1982, Apr. 14 Litho.   Perf. 11½x12
| 1536 | A404 | 10e Phone, 1882 | .35 | .25 |
| 1537 | A404 | 27e 1887 | 1.25 | 1.00 |

Telephone centenary.

Europa 1982 A405

Embassy of King Manuel to Pope Leo X, 1514.

1982, May 3   Perf. 12x11½
| 1538 | A405 | 33.50e multi | 1.50 | .75 |
| a. | | Miniature sheet of 4 | 6.00 | 4.00 |

Visit of Pope John Paul II — A406

Designs: Pope John Paul and cathedrals.

1982, May 13   Perf. 14
1539	A406	10e Fatima	.35	.25
1540	A406	27e Sameiro	1.75	1.10
1541	A406	33.50e Lisbon	1.90	1.00
a.		Min. sheet, 2 each #1539-1541	7.50	7.50
		Nos. 1539-1541 (3)	4.00	2.35

Tejo Estuary Nature Reserve Birds — A407

10e, Dunlin. 19e, Red-crested pochard. 27e, Greater flamingo. 33.50e, Black-winged stilt.

1982, June 11   Perf. 11½x12
1542	A407	10e multi	.40	.25
1543	A407	19e multi	1.25	.55
1544	A407	27e multi	1.60	.80
1545	A407	33.50e multi	1.75	.90
		Nos. 1542-1545 (4)	5.00	2.50

PHILEXFRANCE '82 Stamp Exhibition, Paris, June 11-21.

TB Bacillus Centenary — A408

1982, July 27   Perf. 12x11½
| 1546 | A408 | 27e Koch | 1.25 | 1.00 |
| 1547 | A408 | 33.50e Virus, lungs | 1.50 | 1.10 |

Don't Drink and Drive! — A409

1982, Sept. 22   Perf. 12
| 1548 | A409 | 10e multicolored | .50 | .25 |

Boeing 747 A410

Lubrapex '82 Stamp Exhibition (Historic Flights): 10e, South Atlantic crossing, 1922.

19e, South Atlantic night crossing, 1927. 33.50e, Lisbon-Rio de Janeiro discount fare flights, 1960-1967. 50e, Portugal-Brazil service, 10th anniv.

1982, Oct. 15   Perf. 12x11½
1549	A410	10e Fairey III D MK2	.25	.25
1550	A410	19e Dornier DO	1.00	.70
1551	A410	33.50e DC-7C	1.50	.70
1552	A410	50e shown	1.75	1.00
a.		Souv. sheet of 4, #1549-1552	4.50	4.50
		Nos. 1549-1552 (4)	4.50	2.65

Marques de Pombal, Statesman, 200th Anniv. of Death — A411

1982, Nov. 24 Litho.   Perf. 12x11½
| 1553 | A411 | 10e multicolored | .50 | .25 |

75th Anniv. of Port Authority of Lisbon — A412

1983, Jan. 5   Perf. 12½
| 1554 | A412 | 10e Ships | .50 | .25 |

French Alliance Centenary A413

1983, Jan. 5   Perf. 12x11½
| 1555 | A413 | 27e multicolored | 1.25 | .70 |

Export Effort A414

1983, Jan. 28
| 1556 | A414 | 10e multicolored | .50 | .25 |

World Communications Year — A415

1983, Feb. 23 Litho.   Perf. 11½x12
| 1557 | A415 | 10e blue & multi | .50 | .25 |
| 1558 | A415 | 33.50e lt brown & multi | 1.60 | 1.00 |

Naval Uniforms and Ships — A416

12.50e, Midshipman, 1782, Vasco da Gama. 25e, Sailor, 1845, Estefania. 30e, Sergeant, 1900, Adamastor. 37.50e, Midshipman, 1892, Comandante Joao Belo.

1983, Feb. 23   Perf. 13½
1559	A416	12.50e multi	.55	.25
1560	A416	25e multi	1.40	.35
1561	A416	30e multi	1.60	.50
1562	A416	37.50e multi	2.00	.70
a.		Bklt. pane of 4, #1559-1562	5.75	
		Nos. 1559-1562 (4)	5.55	1.80

See Nos. 1589-1592.

Tile Type of 1981

No. 1563, Hunting scene, 1680. No. 1564, Birds, 18th cent. No. 1565, Flowers and Birds, 18th cent. No. 1566, Figurative tile, 18th cent.

1983   Perf. 12x11½
1563	A391	12.50e multi	.85	.25
a.		Miniature sheet of 6	5.25	5.25
1564	A391	12.50e multi	.85	.25
a.		Miniature sheet of 6	5.00	5.00
1565	A391	12.50e multi	.85	.25
a.		Miniature sheet of 6	5.00	5.00
1566	A391	12.50e multi	.85	.25
a.		Miniature sheet of 6	5.00	5.00
b.		Souv. sheet of 4, #1563-1566	4.50	4.50
		Nos. 1563-1566 (4)	3.40	1.00

Issued: No. 1563, Mar. 16; No. 1564, June 16; No. 1565, Oct. 19; No. 1566, Nov. 23.

17th European Arts and Sciences Exhibition, Lisbon — A417

Portuguese Discoveries and Renaissance Europe: 11e, Helmet, 16th cent. 12.50e, Astrolabe. 25e, Ships, Flemish tapestry. 30e, Column capital, 12th cent. 37.50e, Hour glass. 40e, Chinese panel painting.

1983, Apr. 6
1567	A417	11e multi	.40	.25
1568	A417	12.50e multi	.55	.25
1569	A417	25e multi	1.25	.55
1570	A417	30e multi	1.50	.55
1571	A417	37.50e multi	1.60	.85
1572	A417	40e multi	1.75	.80
a.		Souv. sheet of 6, #1567-1572	9.00	9.00
		Nos. 1567-1572 (6)	7.05	3.25

Europa Issue

Antonio Egas Moniz (1874-1955), Cerebral Angiography and Pre-frontal Leucotomy Pioneer — A418

1983, May 5 Litho.   Perf. 12½
| 1573 | A418 | 37.50e multi | 1.50 | .60 |
| a. | | Souvenir sheet of 4 | 6.00 | 4.00 |

European Conference of Ministers of Transport — A419

1983, May 16
| 1574 | A419 | 30e multi | 2.00 | .65 |

Endangered Sea Mammals — A420

1983, July 29 Litho. Perf. 12x11½

1575	A420	12.50e	Sea wolf	.75	.25
1576	A420	30e	Dolphin	1.75	.45
1577	A420	37.50e	Killer whale	2.40	1.10
1578	A420	80e	Humpback whale	4.00	1.00
a.			Souv. sheet of 4, #1575-1578	11.00	11.00
			Nos. 1575-1578 (4)	8.90	2.80

BRASILIANA '83 Intl. Stamp Exhibition, Rio de Janeiro, July 29-Aug. 7.

600th Anniv. of Revolution of 1383 — A421

12.50e, Death of Joao Fernandes Andeiro. 30e, Rebellion.

1983, Sept. 14 Perf. 13½

1579	A421	12.50e multi	.70	.25
1580	A421	30e multi	2.25	1.10

First Manned Balloon Flight A422

Designs: 16e, Bartolomeu Lourenco de Gusmao, Passarola flying machine. 51e, Montgolfier Balloon, first flight.

1983, Nov. 9 Litho. Perf. 12x11½

1581	A422	16e multicolored	.65	.25
1582	A422	51e multicolored	1.60	.85

Christmas 1983 — A423

Stained Glass Windows, Monastery at Batalha: 12.50e, Adoration of the Magi. 30e, Flight to Egypt.

1983, Nov. 23 Perf. 12½

1583	A423	12.50e multi	.65	.25
1584	A423	30e multi	2.00	.85

Lisbon Zoo Centenary — A424

1984, Jan. 18 Litho. Perf. 12x11½

1585	A424	16e	Siberian tigers	1.40	.25
1586	A424	16e	White rhinoceros	1.40	.25
1587	A424	16e	Damalisco Albifronte	1.40	.25
1588	A424	16e	Cheetahs	1.40	.25
a.			Strip of 4, #1585-1588	6.00	2.50

Military Type of 1983

Air Force Dress Uniforms and Planes: 16e, 1954; Hawker Hurricane II, 1943. 35e, 1960; Republic F-84G Thunderjet. 40e, Paratrooper, 1966; 2502 Nord Noratlas, 1960. 51e, 1966; Corsair II, 1982.

1984, Feb. 5 Litho. Perf. 13½

1589	A416	16e multi	.40	.25
1590	A416	35e multi	1.60	.55
1591	A416	40e multi	1.60	.60
1592	A416	51e multi	2.10	.85
a.		Bklt. pane of 4, #1589-1592	11.00	
		Nos. 1589-1592 (4)	5.70	2.25

Tile Type of 1981

Design: No. 1593, Royal arms, 19th cent. No. 1594, Pombal Palace wall tile, 19th cent. No. 1595, Facade covering, 19th cent. No. 1596, Grasshoppers, by Rafael Bordallo Pinhiero, 19th cent.

1984, Mar. 8 Litho. Perf. 12x11½

1593	A391	16e multi	.85	.25
a.		Miniature sheet of 6	5.00	4.00
1594	A391	16e multi	.85	.25
a.		Miniature sheet of 6	5.00	4.00
1595	A391	16e multi	.85	.25
a.		Miniature sheet of 6	5.00	4.00
1596	A391	16e multi	.85	.25
a.		Miniature sheet of 6	5.00	4.00
b.		Souv. sheet of 4, #1593-1596	6.00	4.50
		Nos. 1593-1596 (4)	3.40	1.00

Issued: No. 1593, Mar. 8; No. 1594, July 18; No. 1595, Aug. 3; No. 1596, Oct. 17 .

25th Lisbon Intl. Fair, May 9-13 A425

Events: 40e, World Food Day. 51e, 15th Rehabilitation Intl. World Congress, Lisbon, June 4-8, vert.

1984, Apr. 3

1597	A425	35e multicolored	1.50	.50
1598	A425	40e multicolored	1.60	.65
1599	A425	51e multicolored	2.00	.85
		Nos. 1597-1599 (3)	5.10	2.00

April 25th Revolution, 10th Anniv. — A426

1984, Apr. 25 Perf. 13½

1600	A426	16e multicolored	1.10	.25

Europa (1959-84) A427

1984, May 2 Perf. 13½

1601	A427	51e multicolored	1.50	.80
a.		Souvenir sheet of 4	6.00	4.00

LUBRAPEX '84 and Natl. Early Art Museum Centenary — A428

Paintings: 16e, Nun, 15th cent. 40e, St. John, by Master of the Retable of Santiago, 16th cent. 51e, View of Lisbon, 17th cent. 66e, Cabeca de Jovem, by Domingos Sequeira, 19th cent.

1984, May 9 Litho. Perf. 12x11½

1602	A428	16e multicolored	.55	.25
1603	A428	40e multicolored	1.75	.55
1604	A428	51e multicolored	2.50	.90
1605	A428	66e multicolored	2.75	1.10
a.		Souv. sheet of 4, #1602-1605	8.00	8.00
		Nos. 1602-1605 (4)	7.55	2.80

1984 Summer Olympics A429

1984, June 5

1606	A429	35e	Fencing	1.25	.30
1607	A429	40e	Gymnastics	1.75	.55
1608	A429	51e	Running	2.40	.95
1609	A429	80e	Pole vault	2.60	1.00
			Nos. 1606-1609 (4)	8.00	2.80

Souvenir Sheet

1610	A429	100e Hurdles	7.00	7.00

Historical Events — A430

Designs: 16e, Gil Eanes, explorer who reached west coast of Africa, 1434. 51e, King Peter I of Brazil and IV of Portugal.

1984, Sept. 24 Perf. 12x11½

1611	A430	16e multicolored	.45	.25
1612	A430	51e multicolored	2.00	.90

See Brazil No. 1954.

Infantry Grenadier, 1740 — A431

46e, 5th Cavalry Regiment Officer, 1810. 60e, Artillery Corporal, 1892. 100e, Engineering Soldier, 1985.

1985, Jan. 23 Litho. Perf. 13½

1613	A431	20e multi	.45	.25
1614	A431	46e multi	2.10	.55
1615	A431	60e multi	2.25	.70
1616	A431	100e multi	2.60	1.10
a.		Bklt. pane of 4, #1613-1616	8.50	
		Nos. 1613-1616 (4)	7.40	2.60

Tile Type of 1981

Designs: No. 1617, Tile from entrance hall of Lisbon's Faculdade de Letras, by Jorge Barradas, 20th cent.; No. 1618, Explorer and sailing ship, detail from tile panel by Maria Keil, Avenida Infante Santo, Lisbon; No. 1619, Profile and key, detail from a 20th century tile mural by Querubim Lapa; No. 1620, Geometric designs and flowers, by Manuel Cargaleiro.

1985 Litho. Perf. 12x11½

1617	A391	20e multicolored	.85	.25
a.		Miniature sheet of 6	5.00	5.00
1618	A391	20e multicolored	.85	.25
a.		Miniature sheet of 6	5.00	5.00
1619	A391	20e multicolored	.85	.25
a.		Miniature sheet of 6	5.00	5.00
1620	A391	20e multicolored	.85	.25
a.		Miniature sheet of 6	5.00	5.00
b.		Souv. sheet of 4, #1617-1620	5.00	5.00
		Nos. 1617-1620 (4)	3.40	1.00

Issued: No. 1617, Feb. 13; No. 1618, June 11; No. 1619, Aug. 20; No. 1620, Nov. 15.

Kiosks — A432

1985, Mar. 19 Litho. Perf. 11½x12

1621	A432	20e Green kiosk	1.00	.25
1622	A432	20e Red kiosk	1.00	.25
1623	A432	20e Gray kiosk	1.00	.25
1624	A432	20e Blue kiosk	1.00	.25
a.		Strip of 4, #1621-1624	5.00	

25th Anniv., European Free Trade Association — A433

1985, Apr. 10 Litho. Perf. 12x11½

1625	A433	46e Flags of members	1.40	.55

Intl. Youth Year A434

60e, Heads of boy and girl.

1985, Apr. 10 Litho.

1626	A434	60e multicolored	1.25	.80

Europa 1985-Music A435

60e, Woman playing tambourine.

1985, May 6 Litho. Perf. 11½x12

1627	A435	60e multicolored	1.75	1.00
a.		Souvenir sheet of 4	7.50	4.00

Historic Anniversaries — A436

20e, King John I at the Battle of Aljubarrota, 1385. 46e, Queen Leonor (1458-1525) founding the Caldas da Rainha Hospital. 60e, Cartographer Pedro Reinel, earliest Portuguese map, c. 1483.

1985, July 5 Litho. Perf. 12x11½

1628	A436	20e multicolored	.60	.25
1629	A436	46e multicolored	1.90	.70
1630	A436	60e multicolored	2.00	.95
		Nos. 1628-1630 (3)	4.50	1.90

See Nos. 1678-1680.

Traditional Architecture A437

50c, Saloia, Estremadura. 1e, Beira interior. 1.50e, Ribatejo. 2.50e, Transmontanas. 10e, Minho and Douro Litoral. 20e, Farm house, Minho. 22.50e, Alentejo. 25e, African Sitio, Algarve. 27e, Beira Interior. 29e, Hill country. 30e, Algarve. 40e, Beira Interior. 50e, Private home, Beira Litoral. 55e, Tras-os-Montes. 60e, Beira Litoral. 70e, Estremadura Sul and Alentejo. 80e, Estremadura. 90e, Minho. 100e, Adobe Monte, Alentejo. 500e, Algarve.

1985-89 Litho. Perf. 12

1631	A437	50c multi	.25	.25
1632	A437	1e multi	.25	.25
1633	A437	1.50e multi	.25	.25
1634	A437	2.50e multi	.25	.25
1635	A437	10e multi	.25	.25
1636	A437	20e multi	.25	.25
1637	A437	22.50e multi	.25	.25
1638	A437	25e multi	.30	.25
1639	A437	27e multi	.45	.25
1640	A437	29e multi	.45	.25
1641	A437	30e multi	.45	.25
1642	A437	40e multi	.55	.25
1643	A437	50e multi	.65	.25

1644 A437	55e multi	.65	.25
1645 A437	60e multi	.85	.25
1646 A437	70e multi	.90	.25
1647 A437	80e multi	.95	.35
1648 A437	90e multi	1.10	.35
1649 A437	100e multi	1.40	.35
1650 A437	500e multi	5.50	.75
	Nos. 1631-1650 (20)	15.95	5.80

Issued: 20e, 25e, 50e, 100e, 8/20; 2.50e, 22.50e, 80e, 90e, 3/10/86; 10e, 40e, 60e, 70e, 3/6/87; 1.50e, 27e, 30e, 55e, 3/15/88; 50c, 1e, 29e, 500e, 3/8/89.

Aquilino Ribeiro
(1885-1963),
Author — A438

46e, Fernando Pessoa (1888-1935), poet.

1985, Oct. 2   Litho.   Perf. 12
1651 A438	20e multicolored	.65	.25
1652 A438	46e multicolored	1.25	.60

Natl. Parks
and
Reserves
A439

20e, Berlenga Island. 40e, Estrela Mountain Chain. 46e, Boquilobo Marsh. 80e, Formosa Lagoon. 100e, St. Jacinto Dunes.

1985, Oct. 25
1653 A439	20e multi	.45	.25
1654 A439	40e multi	1.40	.55
1655 A439	46e multi	2.10	.80
1656 A439	80e multi	2.40	.85
	Nos. 1653-1656 (4)	6.35	2.45

Souvenir Sheet
1657 A439	100e multi	7.00	5.00

ITALIA '85.

Christmas
1985 — A440

Illuminated codices from The Prayer Times Book, Book of King Manuel, 1517-1538.

1985, Nov. 15   Perf. 11½x12
1658 A440	20e The Nativity	.50	.25
1659 A440	46e Adoration of the Magi	1.75	.65

Postrider
A441

1985, Dec. 13   Litho.   Perf. 13½
1660 A441	A(22.50e) lt yel grn & dp yel grn	.80	.25

See No. 1938 for another stamp with postrider inscribed "Serie A."

Flags of
EEC
Member
Nations
A442

Design: 57.50e, Map of EEC, flags.

1986, Jan. 7   Litho.   Perf. 12
1661 A442	20e multi	.50	.25
1662 A442	57.50e multi	2.00	.80
a.	Souv. sheet, 2 ea #1661-1662	6.00	2.50

Admission of Portugal and Spain to the European Economic Community, Jan. 1. See Spain Nos. 2463-2466.
No. 1662a contains 2 alternating pairs of Nos. 1661-1662.

Castles
A443

1986, Feb. 18   Litho.   Perf. 12
1663 A443	22.50e Beja	.75	.25
a.	Booklet pane of 4	3.50	
1664 A443	22.50e Feira	.75	.25
a.	Booklet pane of 4	3.50	

1986, Apr. 10
1665 A443	22.50e Guimaraes	.75	.25
a.	Booklet pane of 4	3.50	
1666 A443	22.50e Braganca	.75	.25
a.	Booklet pane of 4	3.50	

1986, Sept. 18
1667 A443	22.50e Montemor-o-Velho	.75	.25
a.	Booklet pane of 4	3.50	
1668 A443	22.50e Belmonte	.75	.25
a.	Booklet pane of 4	3.50	
	Nos. 1663-1668 (6)	4.50	1.50

See Nos. 1688-1695, 1723-1726.

Intl. Peace
Year
A445

1986, Feb. 18   Litho.   Perf. 12
1669 A445	75e multicolored	2.00	1.00

Automobile Centenary — A446

1986, Apr. 10   Litho.   Perf. 12
1670	22.50e 1886 Benz	.90	.25
1671	22.50e 1886 Daimler	.90	.25
a.	A446 Pair, #1670-1671	2.25	2.25

Europa
1986
A447

1986, May 5   Litho.
1672 A447	68.50e Shad	3.00	1.00
a.	Souvenir sheet of 4	15.00	6.00

Horse
Breeds
A448

1986, May 22   Litho.   Perf. 12
1673 A448	22.50e Alter	.55	.25
1674 A448	47.50e Lusitano	1.75	.70
1675 A448	52.50e Garrano	2.25	.90
1676 A448	68.50e Sorraia	2.60	.95
	Nos. 1673-1676 (4)	7.15	2.80

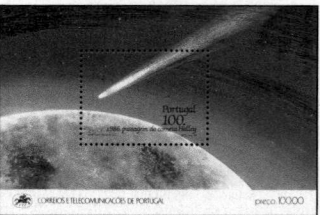

Souvenir Sheet

Halley's Comet — A449

1986, June 24
1677 A449 100e multi	11.00	7.50

Anniversaries Type of 1985

Designs: 22.50e, Diogo Cao, explorer, heraldic pillar erected at Cape Lobo, 1484, 1st expedition. No. 1679, Manuel Passos, Corinthian column. No. 1680, Joao Baptista Ribeiro, painter, Oporto Academy director, c. 1836, and musicians.

1986, Aug. 28   Litho.
1678 A436	22.50e multi	.50	.25
1679 A436	52.50e multi	1.40	.70
1680 A436	52.50e multi	1.40	.70
	Nos. 1678-1680 (3)	3.30	1.65

Diogo Cao's voyages, 500th anniv. Academies of Fine Art, 150th anniv.

Stamp
Day — A450

Natl. Guard, 75th
Anniv. — A451

Order of
Engineers, 50th
Anniv. — A452

No. 1681, Postal card, 100th anniv.

1986, Oct. 24   Litho.
1681 A450	22.50e multi	.85	.25
1682 A451	47.50e multi	1.50	.65
1683 A452	52.50e multi	1.50	.70
	Nos. 1681-1683 (3)	3.85	1.60

Watermills
A453

1986, Nov. 7
1684 A453	22.50e Duoro	.50	.25
1685 A453	47.50e Coimbra	1.25	.85
1686 A453	52.50e Gerez	1.75	.90
1687 A453	90e Braga	2.75	.80
a.	Souv. sheet of 4, #1684-1687	10.00	7.50
	Nos. 1684-1687 (4)	6.25	2.80

LUBRAPEX '86. #1687a issued Nov. 21.

Castle Type of 1986
1987-88   Litho.
1688 A443	25e Silves	.75	.25
a.	Booklet pane of 4	3.50	
1689 A443	25e Evora Monte	.75	.25
a.	Booklet pane of 4	3.50	
1690 A443	25e Leiria	.75	.25
a.	Booklet pane of 4	3.50	
1691 A443	25e Trancoso	.75	.25
a.	Booklet pane of 4	3.50	
1692 A443	25e St. George	.75	.25
a.	Booklet pane of 4	3.50	
1693 A443	25e Marvao	.75	.25
a.	Booklet pane of 4	3.50	
1694 A443	27e Fernando's Walls of Oporto	.75	.25
a.	Booklet pane of 4	3.50	
1695 A443	27e Almourol	.75	.25
a.	Booklet pane of 4	3.50	
	Nos. 1688-1695 (8)	6.00	2.00

Issued: #1688-1689, 1/16; #1690-1691, 4/10; #1692-1693, 9/15; #1694-1695, 1/19/88.

Natl. Tourism Organization, 75th
Anniv. — A454

25e, Beach houses, Tocha. 57e, Boats, Espinho. 98e, Chafariz Fountain, Arraioles.

1987, Feb. 10   Litho.   Perf. 12
1696 A454	25e multicolored	.50	.25
1697 A454	57e multicolored	2.10	.90
1698 A454	98e multicolored	2.75	.85
	Nos. 1696-1698 (3)	5.35	2.00

European Nature
Conservation
Year — A455

57e, Hands, flower, map. 74.50e, Hands, star, rainbow.

1987, Mar. 20   Perf. 12x12½
1699 A455	25e shown	.50	.25
1700 A455	57e multicolored	1.50	.75
1701 A455	74.50e multicolored	2.00	.85
	Nos. 1699-1701 (3)	4.00	1.85

Europa
1987
A456

Modern architecture: Bank Borges and Irmao Agency, 1986, Vila do Conde.

1987, May 5   Litho.   Perf. 12
1702 A456	74.50e multi	1.75	1.00
a.	Souvenir sheet of 4	7.00	6.00

A457

Lighthouses

1987, June 12   Perf. 11½x12
1703 A457	25e Aveiro	1.00	.25
1704 A457	25e Berlenga	1.00	.25
1705 A457	25e Cape Mondego	1.00	.25
1706 A457	25e Cape St. Vincente	1.00	.25
a.	Strip of 4, #1703-1706	5.00	5.00

A458

1987, Aug. 27   Litho.   Perf. 12
1707 A458   74.50e multi   2.00   .75

Amadeo de Souza-Cardoso (1887-1919), painter.

Portuguese Royal Library, Rio de Janeiro, 150th anniv. A459

1987, Aug. 27   Perf. 12x11½
1708 A459   125e multicolored   2.25 1.00

Paper Currency of Portugal, 300th Anniv. A460

1987, Aug. 27   Perf. 12x11½
1709 A460   100e multicolored   2.00   .75

Voyages of Bartolomeu Dias (d. 1499), 500th Anniv. — A461

No. 1710, Departing from Lisbon, 1487. No. 1711, Discovering the African Coast, 1488.

1987, Aug. 27   Perf. 12x11½
1710 A461   25e multicolored   1.00   .25
1711 A461   25e multicolored   1.00   .25
   a. A461 Pair, #1710-1711   3.00 2.00

No. 1711a has continuous design.
See Nos. 1721-1722.

Souvenir Sheet

Phonograph Record, 100th Anniv. — A462

1987, Oct. 9   Litho.   Perf. 12
1712 A462   Sheet of 2   9.00 7.00
   a. 75e Compact-disc player   3.25 2.90
   b. 125e Gramophone   5.00 4.50

Christmas A463

Various children's drawings, Intl. Year of the Child emblem — 25e, Angels, magi, tree. 57e, Friendship circle. 74.50e, Santa riding dove.

1987, Nov. 6
1713 A463   25e multi   .60   .25
1714 A463   57e multi   1.60   .70
1715 A463   74.50e multi   2.00 1.00
   a. Souv. sheet of 3, #1713-1715 5.00 5.00
   Nos. 1713-1715 (3)   4.20 1.95

World Wildlife Fund A464

Lynx, Lynx pardina.

1988, Feb. 3   Litho.   Perf. 12
1716 A464   27e Stalking   1.25   .50
1717 A464   27e Carrying prey   1.25   .50
1718 A464   27e Two adults   1.25   .50
1719 A464   27e Adult, young   1.25   .50
   a. Strip of 4, Nos. 1716-1719   7.50 5.00

Printed in a continuous design.

Journey of Pero da Covilha to the East, 500th Anniv. A465

1988, Feb. 3
1720 A465   105e multi   2.50   .95

Bartolomeu Dias Type of 1987

Discovery of the link between the Atlantic and Indian Oceans by Dias, 500th Anniv.: No. 1721, Tidal wave, ship. No. 1722, Henricus Martelus Germanus's map (1489), picturing the African coast and linking the two oceans.

1988, Feb. 3
1721 A461   27e multi   .85   .25
1722 A461   27e multi   .85   .25
   a. Bklt. pane of 4, Nos. 1710-
        1711, 1721-1722   6.00
   b. Pair, #1721-1722   1.75 1.75

No. 1722b has continuous design.

Castle Type of 1986

No. 1723, Vila Nova de Cerveira. No. 1724, Palmela.

1988, Mar. 15   Litho.   Perf. 12
1723 A443   27e multicolored   .75   .25
   a. Bklt. pane of 4   3.50
1724 A443   27e multicolored   .75   .25
   a. Bklt. pane of 4   3.50
1988, July 1
1725 A443   27e Chaves   .75   .25
   a. Bklt. pane of 4   3.50
1726 A443   27e Penedono   .75   .25
   a. Bklt. pane of 4   3.50
   Nos. 1723-1726 (4)   3.00 1.00

Europa 1988 A466

Transportation: Mail coach, Lisbon-Oporto route, 1855-1864.

1988, Apr. 21   Litho.   Perf. 12
1735 A466   80e multi   2.50 1.00
   a. Souv. sheet of 4   10.00 4.00

Jean Monnet (1888-1979), Economist — A467

1988, May 9   Litho.
1736 A467   60e multi   1.25   .55

Souvenir Sheet

National Heritage (Patrimony) — A468

Design: 150e, Belvedere of Cordovil House and Fountain of Porta de Moura reflected in the Garcia de Resende balcony window, Evora, 16th cent.

1988, May 13   Perf. 13½x12½
1737 A468   150e multi   7.00 7.00

No. 1737 has inscribed margin picturing LUBRAPEX '88 and UNESCO emblems.

20th Cent. Paintings by Portuguese Artists — A469

Designs: 27e, Viola, c. 1916, by Amadeo de Souza-Cardoso (1887-1918). 60e, Jugglers and Tumblers Do Not Fall, 1949, by Jose de Almada Negreiros (1893-1970). 80e, Still-life with Guitar, c. 1940, by Eduardo Viana (1881-1967).

1988, Aug. 23   Litho.   Perf. 11½x12
1738 A469   27e multi   .50   .25
1739 A469   60e multi   1.50   .70
1740 A469   80e multi   1.75   .85
   a. Min. sheet of 3, #1738-1740 5.00 5.00
   Nos. 1738-1740 (3)   3.75 1.80

See Nos. 1748-1750, 1754-1765.

1988 Summer Olympics, Seoul A470

1988, Sept. 16   Litho.   Perf. 12x11½
1741 A470   27e Archery   .45   .25
1742 A470   55e Weight lifting 1.25   .75
1743 A470   60e Judo   1.40   .80
1744 A470   80e Tennis   2.10   .80
   Nos. 1741-1744 (4)   5.20 2.60

Souvenir Sheet

1745 A470   200e Yachting   9.00 7.00

Remains of the Roman Civilization in Portugal A471

Mozaics: 27e, "Winter Image," detail of Mosaic of the Four Seasons, limestone and glass, 3rd cent., House of the Waterworks, Coimbra. 80e, Fish in Marine Water, limestone, 3rd-4th cent., cover of a tank wall, public baths, Faro.

1988, Oct. 18   Litho.   Perf. 12
1746 A471   27e multi   .50   .25
1747 A471   80e multi   1.50   .75

20th Cent. Art Type of 1988

Paintings by Portuguese artists: 27e, Burial, 1938, by Mario Eloy. 60e, Lisbon Roofs, c. 1936, by Carlos Botelho. 80e, Avejao Lirico, 1939, by Antonio Pedro.

1988, Nov. 18   Litho.   Perf. 11½x12
1748 A469   27e multi   .45   .25
1749 A469   60e multi   1.40   .65
1750 A469   80e multi   1.75   .75
   a. Souv. sheet of 3, #1748-
        1750   5.00 5.00
   b. Souv. sheet of 6, #1738-
        1740, 1748-1750   9.00 9.00
   Nos. 1748-1750 (3)   3.60 1.65

Braga Cathedral, 900th Anniv. A472

1989, Jan. 20   Perf. 12
1751 A472   30e multi   .80   .25

INDIA '89 — A473

55e, Caravel, Sao Jorge da Mina Fort, 1482. 60e, Navigator using astrolabe, 16th cent.

1989, Jan. 20
1752 A473   55e multi   1.25   .65
1753 A473   60e multi   1.75   .80

20th Cent. Art Type of 1988

Paintings by Portuguese artists: 29e, Antithesis of Calm, 1940, by Antonio Dacosta. 60c, Lunch of the Unskilled Mason, c. 1926, by Julio Pomar. 87e, Simums, 1949, by Vespeira.

1989, Feb. 15   Litho.   Perf. 11½x12
1754 A469   29e multi   .45   .25
1755 A469   60e multi   1.20   .60
1756 A469   87e multi   1.50   .90
   a. Souv. sheet of 3, #1754-1756 6.00 6.00
   Nos. 1754-1756 (3)   3.15 1.75

1989, July 7

Paintings by Portuguese artists: 29e, 046-72, 1972, by Fernando Lanhas. 60e, Les Spirales, 1954, by Nadir Afonso. 87e, Sim, 1987, by Carlos Calvet.

1757 A469   29e multi   .45   .25
1758 A469   60e multi   1.20   .55
1759 A469   87e multi   1.50   .90
   a. Souv. sheet of 3, #1757-
        1759   6.00 6.00
   b. Souv. sheet of 6, #1754-
        1759   11.00 11.00
   Nos. 1757-1759 (3)   3.15 1.70

1990, Feb. 14

Paintings by Portuguese artists: 32e, Aluenda-Tordesillas by Joaquim Rodrigo. 60e, Pintura by Noronha da Costa. 95e, Pintura by Vasco Costa (1917-1985).

1760 A469   32e multicolored   .45   .25
1761 A469   60e multicolored   1.20   .50
1762 A469   95e multicolored   1.50   .85
   a. Souv. sheet of 3, #1760-1762 6.00 6.00
   Nos. 1760-1762 (3)   3.15 1.60

1990, Sept. 21

Paintings by Portuguese artists: 32e, Costa Pinheiro. 60e, Paula Rego. 95e, Jose De Guimaraes.

1763	A469	32e multicolored	.45	.25
1764	A469	60e multicolored	1.20	.55
1765	A469	95e multicolored	1.50	.85
a.		Min. sheet of 3, #1763-1765	6.00	6.00
b.		Min. sheet of 6, #1760-1765	11.00	11.00
		Nos. 1763-1765 (3)	3.15	1.65

A474

1989, Feb. 15　Litho.　Perf. 12

1772	A474	29e multi	.50	.25
a.		Bklt. pane of 8	4.00	
1773	A474	60e With love	1.00	.50
a.		Bklt. pane of 8	8.00	

Special occasions.

A475

1989, Mar. 8　Litho.　Perf. 11½x12

1774	A475	60e multi	1.25	.60

European Parliament elections.

Europa 1989 A476

Children's toys.

1989, Apr. 26　Litho.　Perf. 12

1775	A476	80e Top	1.75	1.00

Souvenir Sheet

1776		Sheet of 4, 2 each #1775, 1776a	12.50	5.00
a.	A476	80e Tops	2.00	1.25

Surface Transportation, Lisbon — A477

29e, Carris Co. elevated railway, Bica Street. 65e, Carris electric tram. 87e, Carmo Elevator, Santa Justa Street. 100e, Carris doubledecker bus. 250e, Transtejo Co. riverboat *Cacilheiro*, horiz.

1989, May 22　　　　　　Litho.

1777	A477	29e multi	.45	.25
1778	A477	65e multi	1.40	.75
1779	A477	87e multi	1.60	1.00
1780	A477	100e multi	2.00	.75
		Nos. 1777-1780 (4)	5.45	2.75

Souvenir Sheet

1781	A477	250e multi	7.50	6.50

Windmills A478

29e, Ansiao. 60e, Santiago do Cacem. 87e, Afife. 100e, Caldas da Rainha.

1989, June 14　　　　　　Litho.

1782	A478	29e multicolored	.50	.25
1783	A478	60e multicolored	1.60	.75
1784	A478	87e multicolored	1.75	.90
1785	A478	100e multicolored	2.00	.85
a.		Bklt. pane of 4, #1782-1785	7.00	
		Nos. 1782-1785 (4)	5.85	2.75

Souvenir Sheet

French Revolution, 200th Anniv. — A479

1989, July 7　Litho.　Perf. 11½x12

1786	A479	250e Drummer	8.50	8.50

No. 1786 has multicolored inscribed margin picturing the PHILEXFRANCE '89 emblem and the storming of the Bastille.

Natl. Palaces A480

1989, Oct. 18　Litho.　Perf. 12

1787	A480	29e Ajuda, Lisbon, and King Luiz I	.30	.25
1788	A480	60e Queluz	1.20	.80

Death cent. of King Luiz.

Exhibition Emblem and Wildflowers A481

29e, Armeria pseudarmeria. 60e, Santolina impressa. 87e, Linaria lamarckii. 100e, Limonium multiforum.

1989, Nov. 17　　　　　　Litho.

1789	A481	29e multicolored	.40	.25
1790	A481	60e multicolored	1.10	.60
1791	A481	87e multicolored	1.60	.95
1792	A481	100e multicolored	2.25	1.10
a.		Bklt. pane of 4, #1789-1792	7.00	
		Nos. 1789-1792 (4)	5.35	2.80

World Stamp Expo '89, Washington, DC.

Portuguese Faience, 17th Cent. A482

No. 1794, Nobleman (plate). No. 1795, Urn. No. 1796, Fish (pitcher). No. 1797, Crown, shield (plate). No. 1798, Lidded bowl. No. 1799, Plate.

1990, Jan. 24　Litho.　Perf. 12x11½

1793	A482	33e shown	.50	.25
1794	A482	33e multicolored	.50	.25
1795	A482	35e multicolored	.70	.25
1796	A482	60e multicolored	1.25	.70
1797	A482	60e multicolored	1.25	.70
1798	A482	60e multicolored	1.25	.70
		Nos. 1793-1798 (6)	5.45	2.85

Souvenir Sheet
Perf. 12

1799	A482	250e multicolored	6.00	5.00

No. 1799 contains one 52x45mm stamp. See Nos. 1829-1835, 1890-1896.

Score, Alfred Keil and Henrique Lopes de Mondonca A483

1990, Mar. 6　　　　Perf. 12x11½

1804	A483	32e multicolored	.45	.25

A Portuguesa, the Natl. Anthem, cent. (32e).

University Education in Portugal, 700th Anniv. — A484

1990, Mar. 6　　　　Perf. 11½x12

1805	A484	70e multicolored	1.60	.70

Europa 1990 A485

1990, Apr. 11　　　　Perf. 12x11½

1806	A485	80e Santo Tirso P.O.	1.25	1.00

Souvenir Sheet

1807		Sheet of 4, 2 each #1806, 1807a	9.00	4.50
a.	A485	80e Mala Posta P.O.	1.50	1.25

Souvenir Sheet

Gentleman Using Postage Stamp, 1840 — A486

1990, May 3

1808	A486	250e multicolored	9.00	5.00

Stamp World London '90 and 150th anniv. of the Penny Black.

Greetings Issue A487

"FELICITACOES" and street scenes. No. 1809, Stairway. No. 1810, Automobile. No. 1811, Man in street. No. 1812, Street scene, girl with bouquet behind mail box.

1990, June 5　Litho.　Perf. 12

1809	A487	60e multi	1.00	.45
1810	A487	60e multi	1.00	.45
1811	A487	60e multi	1.00	.45
1812	A487	60e multi	1.00	.45
		Nos. 1809-1812 (4)	4.00	1.80

Perf. 13 Vert.

1809a	A487	60e	1.25	1.25
1810a	A487	60e	1.25	1.25
1811a	A487	60e	1.25	1.25
1812a	A487	60e	1.25	1.25
b.		Bklt. pane of 4, #1809a-1812a	5.00	

Camilo Castelo Branco (1825-1890), Writer — A488

Designs: 70e, Friar Bartolomeu dos Martires (1514-1590), theologian.

1990, July 11　Litho.　Perf. 12x11½

1813	A488	65e multicolored	1.00	.65
1814	A488	70e multicolored	1.25	.70

Ships A489

1990, Sept. 21　Litho.　Perf. 12

1815	A489	32e Barca	.40	.25
1816	A489	60e Caravela Pescareza	.95	.50
1817	A489	70e Barinel	1.10	.75
1818	A489	95e Caravela	1.75	1.00
		Nos. 1815-1818 (4)	4.20	2.50

Perf. 13½ Vert.

1815a	A489	32e	1.25	1.25
1816a	A489	60e	1.25	1.25
1817a	A489	70e	1.25	1.25
1818a	A489	95e	1.25	1.25
b.		Bklt. pane of 4, #1815a-1818a	5.00	

National Palaces — A490

1990, Oct. 11　　　　Perf. 12

1819	A490	32e Pena	.45	.25
1820	A490	60e Vila	1.00	.50
1821	A490	70e Mafra	1.20	.75
1822	A490	120e Guimaraes	1.60	1.00
		Nos. 1819-1822 (4)	4.25	2.50

Francisco Sa Carneiro (1934-1980),
Politician — A491

1990, Nov. 7
1823 A491 32e ol brn & blk .55 .25

Rossio
Railway
Station,
Cent.
A492

Various locomotives.

1990, Nov. 7
1824	A492	32e Steam, 1887	.65	.25
1825	A492	60e Steam, 1891	1.10	.50
1826	A492	70e Steam, 1916	1.25	.75
1827	A492	95e Electric, 1956	1.75	1.00

Nos. 1824-1827 (4) 4.75 2.50

Souvenir Sheet
1828 A492 200e Railway station 5.00 4.00

Ceramics Type of 1990
1991, Feb. 7 Litho. Perf. 12
1829	A482	35e Lavabo	.50	.25
1830	A482	35e Tureen and plate	.50	.25
1831	A482	35e Flower vase	.50	.25
1832	A482	60e Finger bowl	1.00	.50
1833	A482	60e Coffee pot	1.00	.50
1834	A482	60e Mug	1.00	.50

Nos. 1829-1834 (6) 4.50 2.25

Souvenir Sheet
1835 A482 250e Plate 5.00 4.00

No. 1835 contains one 52x44mm stamp.

European
Tourism
Year
A494

1991, Mar. 6 Litho. Perf. 12
1836	A494	60e Flamingos	1.00	.50
1837	A494	110e Chameleon	1.70	.85

Souvenir Sheet
1838 A494 250e Deer 5.00 4.00

Portuguese
Navigators
A495

2e, Joao Goncalves Zarco. 3e, Pedro Lopes
de Sousa. 4e, Duarte Pacheco Pereira. 5e,
Tristao Vaz Teixeira. 6e, Pedro Alvares Cabral.
10e, Joao de Castro. 32e, Bartolomeu Per-
estrelo. 35e, Gil Eanes. 38e, Vasco da Gama.
42e, Joao de Lisboa. 45e, Joao Rodriques
Cabrillo. 60e, Nuno Tristao. 65e, Joao da
Nova. 70e, Ferdinand Magellan. 75e, Pedro
Fernandes de Queiros. 80e, Diogo Gomes.
100e, Diogo de Silves. 200e, Estevao Gomes.
250e, Diogo Cao. 350e, Bartolomeu Dias.

1990-94 Litho. Perf. 12x11½
1839	A495	2e multi	.25	.25
1840	A495	3e multi	.25	.25
1841	A495	4e multi	.25	.25
1842	A495	5e multi	.25	.25
1843	A495	6e multi	.25	.25
1844	A495	10e multi	.25	.25
1845	A495	32e multi	.40	.25
1846	A495	35e multi	.35	.25
1847	A495	38e multi	.30	.25
1848	A495	42e multi	.40	.25
1849	A495	45e multi	.35	.25
1850	A495	60e multi	.40	.30
1851	A495	65e multi	.80	.25
1852	A495	70e multi	.80	.25

1853	A495	75e multi	.70	.45
1854	A495	80e multi	1.10	.50
1855	A495	100e multi	1.50	.65
1856	A495	200e multi	2.25	.60
1857	A495	250e multi	3.50	1.25
1858	A495	350e multi	4.25	1.50

Nos. 1839-1858 (20) 18.60 8.50

Issued: 2e, 5e, 32e, 100e, 3/6; 6e, 38e, 65e,
350e, 3/6/91; 35e, 60e, 80e, 250e, 3/6/92; 4e,
42e, 70e, 200e, 4/6/93; 3e, 10e, 45e, 75e,
4/29/94.

Europa
A496

1991, Apr. 11 Litho. Perf. 12
1859 A496 80e Eutelsat II 1.50 1.00

Souvenir Sheet
1860 Sheet, 2 ea #1859,
1860a 10.00 5.00
a. A496 80e Olympus I 2.00 1.50

Souvenir Sheet

Princess Isabel & Philip le
Bon — A497

1991, May 27 Litho. Perf. 12½
1861 A497 300e multicolored 7.50 4.00

Europalia '91. See Belgium No. 1402.

Discovery
Ships
A498

1991, May 27 Litho. Perf. 12
1862	A498	35e Caravel	.40	.25
1863	A498	75e Nau	1.10	.55
1864	A498	80e Nau, stern	1.20	.60
1865	A498	110e Galleon	1.50	.75

Nos. 1862-1865 (4) 4.20 2.15

Perf. 13½ Vert.
1862a	A498	35e	1.25	1.25
1863a	A498	75e	1.25	1.25
1864a	A498	80e	1.25	1.25
1865a	A498	110e	1.25	1.25
b.		Bklt. pane of 4, #1862a-1865a	5.00	

Portuguese
Crown
Jewels — A499

Designs: 35e, Running knot, diamonds &
emeralds, 18th cent. 60e, Royal scepter, 19th
cent. 70e, Sash of the Grand Cross, ruby &
diamonds, 18th cent. 80e, Court saber, gold &
diamonds in hilt, 19th cent. 140e, Royal crown,
19th cent.

1991, July 8 Litho. Perf. 12
1866	A499	35e multicolored	.35	.25
1867	A499	60e multicolored	.85	.50
1868	A499	80e multicolored	.90	.60
1869	A499	140e multicolored	1.40	.85

Nos. 1866-1869 (4) 3.50 2.20

Perf. 13½ Vert.
1870 A499 70e multicolored 1.00 .55
a. Booklet pane of 5 5.00

See Nos. 1898-1902.

Antero de Quental (1842-1891),
Poet — A500

First Missionaries to Congo, 500th
Anniv. — A501

1991, Aug. 2 Perf. 12
1871 A500 35e multicolored .45 .25
1872 A501 110e multicolored 1.70 .85

Architectural Heritage — A502

Designs: 35e, School of Architecture,
Oporto University, by Siza Vieira. 60e, Torre
do Tombo, by Ateliers Associates of Arsenio
Cordeiro. 80e, Railway Bridge over Douro
River, by Edgar Cardoso. 110e, Setubal-Braga
highway bridge.

1991, Sept. 4 Litho. Perf. 12
1873	A502	35e multicolored	.50	.25
1874	A502	60e multicolored	.80	.45
1875	A502	80e multicolored	1.25	.60
1876	A502	110e multicolored	1.70	.75

Nos. 1873-1876 (4) 4.25 2.05

1992
Summer
Olympics,
Barcelona
A503

1991, Oct. 9 Litho. Perf. 12
1877	A503	35e Equestrian	.45	.25
1878	A503	60e Fencing	.85	.40
1879	A503	80e Shooting	1.25	.60
1880	A503	110e Sailing	1.70	.75

Nos. 1877-1880 (4) 4.25 2.00

History of Portuguese
Communications — A504

Designs: 35e, King Manuel I appointing first
Postmaster, 1520. 60e, Mailbox, telegraph,
1881. 80e, Automobile, telephone, 1911.
110e, Airplane, mail truck, 1991.

1991, Oct. 9
1881	A504	35e multicolored	.45	.25
1882	A504	60e multicolored	.90	.45
1883	A504	80e multicolored	1.25	.60

Nos. 1881-1883 (3) 2.60 1.30

Souvenir Sheet
1884 A504 110e multicolored 1.90 1.40

Automobile
Museum,
Caramulo
A505

35e, Peugeot, 1899. 60e, Rolls Royce,
1911. 80e, Bugatti 35B, 1930. 110e, Ferrari
195 Inter, 1950.
No. 1889a, Mercedes 380K, 1934. b, His-
pano-Suiza, 1924.

1991, Nov. 15
1885	A505	35e multi	.50	.25
1886	A505	60e multi	1.10	.45
1887	A505	80e multi	1.60	.65
1888	A505	110e multi	2.00	.70

Nos. 1885-1888 (4) 5.20 2.05

Souvenir Sheet
1889 Sheet, 2 each #1889a-
1889b 4.50 4.50
a.-b. A505 70e any single 1.10 .55

Phila Nippon '91 (#1889). See #1903-1906A.

Ceramics Type of 1990
No. 1890, Tureen with lid. No. 1891, Plate.
No. 1892, Pitcher with lid. No. 1893, Violin.
No. 1894, Bottle in form of woman. No. 1895,
Man seated on barrel.
No. 1896, Political caricature.

1992, Jan. 24 Litho. Perf. 12
1890	A482	40e multicolored	.60	.30
1891	A482	40e multicolored	.60	.30
1892	A482	40e multicolored	.60	.30
1893	A482	65e multicolored	.95	.50
1894	A482	65e multicolored	.95	.50
1895	A482	65e multicolored	.95	.50

Nos. 1890-1895 (6) 4.65 2.40

Souvenir Sheet
1896 A482 260e multicolored 4.75 3.00

No. 1896 contains one 51x44mm stamp.

Portuguese
Presidency
of the
European
Community
Council of
Ministers
A506

1992, Jan. 24
1897 A506 65e multicolored 1.10 .45

Crown Jewels Type of 1991
Designs: 38e, Coral flowers, 19th cent. 65e,
Clock of gold, enamel, ivory and diamonds,
20th cent. 70e, Tobacco box encrusted with
diamonds and emeralds, 1755. 85e, Royal
scepter, 1828. 125e, Eighteen star necklace
with diamonds, 1863.

1992, Feb. 7 Litho. Perf. 11½x12
1898	A499	38e multicolored	.45	.25
1899	A499	70e multicolored	.85	.40
1900	A499	85e multicolored	1.10	.65
1901	A499	125e multicolored	1.50	.80

Perf. 13½ Vert.
1902 A499 65e multicolored 1.10 .50
a. Booklet pane of 5 5.00

Nos. 1898-1902 (5) 5.00 2.60

Automobile Museum Type of 1991
Designs: 38e, Citroen Torpedo, 1922. 65e,
Rochet Schneider, 1914. 85e, Austin Seven,
1933. 120e, Mercedes Benz 770, 1938. No.
1906b, Renault, 1911. c, Ford Model T, 1927.

1992, Mar. 6 Litho. Perf. 12
1903	A505	38e multicolored	.50	.25
1904	A505	65e multicolored	1.25	.50
1905	A505	85e multicolored	1.50	.65
1906	A505	120e multicolored	1.90	.75

Nos. 1903-1906 (4) 5.15 2.15

Souvenir Sheet
1906A Sheet of 2 each, #b.-c. 4.75 4.50
b.-c. A505 70e any single 1.10 .55

Automobile Museum, Oeiras.

Portuguese Arrival in Japan, 450th Anniv. A508

Granada '92: 120e, Three men with gifts, Japanese.

1992, Apr. 24   Litho.   Perf. 12
1907 A508 38e shown   .45 .25
1908 A508 120e multicolored   1.75 .75

Portuguese Pavilion, Expo '92, Seville — A509

1992, Apr. 24   Litho.   Perf. 11½x12
1909 A509 65e multicolored   .90 .40

Instruments of Navigation — A510

1992, May 9   Litho.   Perf. 12x11½
1910 A510 60e Cross staff   .90 .25
1911 A510 70e Quadrant   1.10 .50
1912 A510 100e Astrolabe   1.50 .55
1913 A510 120e Compass   1.90 .70
    a.   Souv. sheet of 4, #1910-
          1913   6.00 6.00
    Nos. 1910-1913 (4)   5.40 2.00

Lubrapex '92 (#1913a).

Royal Hospital of All Saints, 500th Anniv. A511

1992, May 11
1914 A511 38e multicolored   .60 .30

Apparitions of Fatima, 75th Anniv. A512

1992, May 11
1915 A512 70e multicolored   1.00 .40

Port of Leixoes, Cent. A513

1992, May 11
1916 A513 120e multicolored   1.75 .65

A514

Voyages of Columbus — A515

Designs: 85e, King John II with Columbus. No. 1918, Columbus in sight of land. No. 1919, Landing of Columbus. No. 1920, Columbus soliciting aid from Queen Isabella. No. 1921, Columbus welcomed at Barcelona. No. 1922, Columbus presenting natives. No. 1923, Columbus.
    Nos. 1918-1923 are similar in design to US Nos. 230-231, 234-235, 237, 245.

1992, May 22   Litho.   Perf. 12x11½
1917 A514 85e gold & multi   2.50 .60
Souvenir Sheets
Perf. 12
1918 A515 260e blue   4.50 4.50
1919 A515 260e brown violet   4.50 4.50
1920 A515 260e brown   4.50 4.50
1921 A515 260e violet black   4.50 4.50
1922 A515 260e black   4.50 4.50
1923 A515 260e black   4.50 4.50
    Nos. 1918-1923 (6)   27.00 27.00
                Europa.
    See US Nos. 2624-2629, Italy Nos. 1883-1888, and Spain Nos. 2677-2682.

UN Conference on Environmental Development — A516

70e, Bird flying over polluted water system. 120e, Clean water system, butterfly, bird, flowers.

1992, June 12   Litho.   Perf. 12x11½
1924 A516 70e multicolored   2.00 .55
1925 A516 120e multicolored   3.00 1.00
    a.   A516 Pair, #1924-1925   6.00 4.50

1992 Summer Olympics, Barcelona A517

1992, July 29   Litho.   Perf. 11½x12
1926 A517 38e Women's run-
            ning   .55 .30
1927 A517 70e Soccer   1.15 .60
1928 A517 85e Hurdles   1.40 .70
1929 A517 120e Roller hockey   1.75 1.00
    Nos. 1926-1929 (4)   4.85 2.60
Souvenir Sheet
Perf. 12
1930 A517 250e Basketball   9.00 6.00

Olymphilex '92 (#1930).

Campo Pequeno Bull Ring, Lisbon, Cent. A518

Various scenes of picadors.

1992, Aug. 18   Perf. 12x11½
1931 A518 38e multicolored   .55 .30
1932 A518 65e multicolored   1.00 .55
1933 A518 70e multicolored   1.25 .60
1934 A518 155e multicolored   2.10 1.25
    Nos. 1931-1934 (4)   4.90 2.70
Souvenir Sheet
Perf. 13½x12½
1935 A518 250e Bull ring, vert.   4.50 3.00

No. 1935 contains one 35x50mm stamp.

Single European Market A519

1992, Nov. 4   Litho.   Perf. 12x11½
1936 A519 65e multicolored   1.10 .50

European Year for Security, Hygiene and Health at Work A520

1992, Nov. 4   Perf. 12x11½
1937 A520 120e multicolored   1.60 .90

Postrider A521

1993, Mar. 9   Litho.   Perf. 12x12½
1938 A521 (A) henna brown, gray
            & black   .80 .30

No. 1938 sold for 42e on date of issue. See No. 2276A.

Almada Negreiros (1893-1970), Artist — A522

1993, Mar. 9   Litho.   Perf. 11½x12
1939 A522 40e Portrait   .60 .30
1940 A522 65e Ships   .95 .50

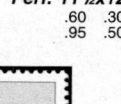

Instruments of Navigation — A523

1993, Apr. 6   Perf. 12x11½
1941 A523 42e Hourglass   .60 .30
1942 A523 70e Nocturlabe   1.00 .50
1943 A523 90e Kamal   1.30 .65
1944 A523 130e Backstaff   1.90 .95
    Nos. 1941-1944 (4)   4.80 2.40

Contemporary Paintings by Jose Escada (1934-1980) — A524

Europa: No. 1945, Cathedral, 1979. No. 1946a, Abstract shapes, 1966.

1993, May 5   Litho.   Perf. 12x11½
1945 A524 90e multicolored   1.25 .60
Souvenir Sheet
1946   Sheet, 2 each #1945,
        1946a   6.00 4.00
    a.   A524 90e multicolored   1.50 1.00

Assoc. of Volunteer Firemen of Lisbon, 125th Anniv. A525

1993, June 21   Litho.   Perf. 12x11½
1947 A525 70e multicolored   1.10 .45

Sao Carlos Natl. Theatre, Bicent. A526

1993, June 21
1948 A526 42e Rossini   .55 .25
1949 A526 70e Verdi   1.25 .45
1950 A526 90e Wagner   1.40 .55
1951 A526 130e Mozart   2.10 .80
    Nos. 1948-1951 (4)   5.30 2.05
Souvenir Sheet
1952 A526 300e Theatre   5.00 4.00

Union of Portuguese Speaking Capitals — A527

1993, July 30   Litho.   Perf. 11½x12
1953 A527 130e multicolored   1.75 .80
    a.   Miniature sheet of 4 + 2 labels 7.50 5.00

Brasiliana '93 (#1953a).

Sculpture — A528

Designs: 42e, Annunciation Angel, 12th cent. 70e, St. Mark, 16th cent., horiz. No. 1956, Virgin and Child, 17th cent. 90e, Archangel St. Michael, 18th cent. 130e, Conde de Ferreira, 19th cent. 170e, Modern sculpture, 20th cent.
    No. 1960a, Head of Agrippina, the Elder, 1st cent. No. 1960b, Virgin of the Annunciation, 16th cent. No. 1960c, The Widow, 19th cent. No. 1960d, Love Ode, 20th cent.

Perf. 11½x12, 12x11½
1993, Aug. 18
1954 A528 42e multicolored   .55 .30
1955 A528 70e multicolored   .90 .45
1956 A528 75e multicolored   .95 .50

1957	A528	90e multicolored	1.10	.60
1958	A528	130e multicolored	1.60	.80
1959	A528	170e multicolored	2.25	1.10
		Nos. 1954-1959 (6)	7.35	3.75

Souvenir Sheet

1960		Sheet of 4	4.50	3.50
a.-d.	A528 75e any single		.95	.95

See Nos. 2001-2007, 2067-2073.

Railway World Congress A529

90e, Cars on railway overpass, train. 130e, Traffic jam, train. 300e, Train, track skirting tree.

1993, Sept. 6   **Perf. 12x11½**

1961	A529	90e multicolored	.90	.55
1962	A529	130e multicolored	2.10	.80

Souvenir Sheet

1963	A529	300e multicolored	4.50	3.50

Portuguese Arrival in Japan, 450th Anniv. A530

Designs: 42e, Japanese using musket. 130e, Catholic priests. 350e, Exchanging items of trade.

1993, Sept. 22   **Litho.**   **Perf. 12**

1964	A530	42e multicolored	.55	.30
1965	A530	130e multicolored	1.60	.85
1966	A530	350e multicolored	4.50	2.25
		Nos. 1964-1966 (3)	6.65	3.40

See Macao Nos. 704-706.

Trawlers A531

1993, Oct. 1   **Litho.**   **Perf. 12x11½**

1967	A531	42e Twin-mast	.55	.30
1968	A531	70e Single-mast	.90	.45
1969	A531	90e SS Germano 3	1.10	.55
1970	A531	130e Steam-powered	1.75	.85
		Nos. 1967-1970 (4)	4.30	2.15

Perf. 11½

1967a	A531	42e	.55	.30
1968a	A531	70e	.90	.45
1969a	A531	90e	1.10	.55
1970a	A531	130e	1.75	.85
b.		Booklet pane of 4, #1967a-1970a	5.00	

A532

Mailboxes: 42e, Rural mail bag, 1880. 70e, Railroad wall-mounted mailbox, 19th cent. 90e, Free-standing mailbox, 19th cent. 130e, Modern mailbox, 1992. 300e, Mailbox from horse-drawn postal vehicle, 19th cent.

1993, Oct. 9   **Litho.**   **Perf. 12**

1971	A532	42e multicolored	.55	.25
1972	A532	70e multicolored	.85	.40
1973	A532	90e multicolored	1.20	.50
1974	A532	130e multicolored	1.60	.75
		Nos. 1971-1974 (4)	4.20	1.90

Souvenir Sheet

1975	A532	300e multicolored	4.50	3.50

No. 1975 has continuous design.

A533

Endangered birds of prey.

1993, Oct. 9

1976	A533	42e Imperial eagle	.50	.25
1977	A533	70e Royal eagle owl	1.10	.40
1978	A533	130e Peregrine falcon	1.75	.75
1979	A533	350e Hen harrier	4.00	2.00
		Nos. 1976-1979 (4)	7.35	3.40

Brazil-Portugal Treaty of Consultation and Friendship, 40th Anniv. — A534

1993, Nov. 3

1980	A534	130e multicolored	1.60	.75

See Brazil No. 2430.

Souvenir Sheet

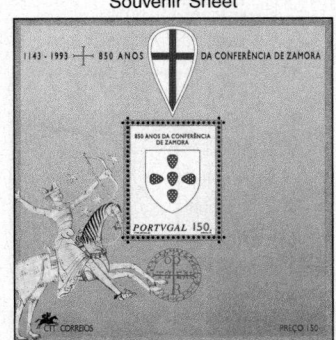

Conference of Zamora, 850th Anniv. — A535

1993, Dec. 9

1981	A535	150e multicolored	3.00	2.00

West European Union, 40th Anniv. A536

1994, Jan. 27   **Litho.**   **Perf. 12**

1982	A536	85e multicolored	1.20	.55

Intl. Olympic Committee, Cent. A537

Design: No. 1984, Olympic torch, rings.

1994, Jan. 27

1983	A537	100e multicolored	1.50	.65
1984	A537	100e multicolored	1.50	.65

Issued in sheets of 8, 4 each + label.

Oliveira Martins (1845-94), Historian A538

100e, Florbela Espanca (1894-1930), poet.

1994, Feb. 21

1985	A538	45e multicolored	.65	.30
1986	A538	100e multicolored	1.50	.65

Prince Henry the Navigator (1394-1460) — A539

1994, Mar. 4

1987	A539	140e multicolored	2.40	.85

See Brazil No. 2463, Cape Verde No. 664, Macao No. 719.

Transfer of Power, 20th Anniv. A540

1994, Apr. 22   **Litho.**   **Perf. 12x11½**

1988	A540	75e multicolored	1.10	.45

Europa A541

1994, May 5   **Litho.**   **Perf. 12x11½**

1989	A541	100e People of Ormuz	1.25	.65

Souvenir Sheet

1990		Sheet of 4, 2 each #1989, 1990a	4.50	3.50
a.	A541 100e Ears of corn		1.00	.50

Intl. Year of the Family A542

1994, May 15   **Litho.**   **Perf. 12x11½**

1991	A542	45e blk, red & brn	.55	.30
1992	A542	140e blk, red & grn	1.75	.85

Treaty of Tordesillas, 500th Anniv. — A543

1994, June 7   **Litho.**   **Perf. 12x11½**

1993	A543	140e multicolored	1.75	.90

1994 World Cup Soccer Championships, US — A544

1994, June 7

1994	A544	100e shown	1.25	.60
1995	A544	140e Ball, 4 shoes	1.90	.95

Lisbon '94, European Capital of Culture A545

Birds and: 45e, Music. 75e, Photography. 100e, Theater and ballet. 145e, Art.

1994, July 1

1996	A545	45e multicolored	.55	.30
1997	A545	75e multicolored	1.00	.50
1998	A545	100e multicolored	1.25	.60
1999	A545	140e multicolored	2.00	.95
a.		Souvenir sheet of 4, #1996-1999	6.00	5.00
		Nos. 1996-1999 (4)	4.80	2.35

Year of Road Safety — A545a

1994, Aug. 16   **Litho.**   **Perf. 11½x12**

2000	A545a	45e blk, red & grn	.60	.30

Sculpture Type of 1993

Designs: 45e, Pedra Formosa, Castreja culture. No. 2002, Carved pilaster, 7th cent., vert. 80e, Capital carved with figures, 12th cent. 100e, Laying Christ in the Tomb, 16th cent. 140e, Reliquary chapel, 17th cent. 180e, Bas relief, 20th cent.

No. 2007: a, Sarcophagus of Queen Urraca, 13th cent. b, Sarcophagus of Dom Afonso. c, Tomb of Dom Joao de Noronha and Dona Isabel de Sousa, 16th cent. d, Mausoleum of Adm. Machado Santos, 20th cent.

Perf. 12x11½, 11½x12

1994, Aug. 16

2001	A528	45e multicolored	.55	.30
2002	A528	75e multicolored	.75	.50
2003	A528	80e multicolored	1.10	.50
2004	A528	100e multicolored	1.40	.60
2005	A528	140e multicolored	1.75	.85
2006	A528	180e multicolored	2.50	1.10
		Nos. 2001-2006 (6)	8.05	3.85

Souvenir Sheet

Perf. 12x11½

2007		Sheet of 4	5.00	4.00
a.-d.	A528 75e any single		.95	.95

Falconry A546

Designs: 45e, Falconer, hooded bird, dog. 75e, Falcon flying after prey. 100e, Falcon, prey on ground. 140e, Three falcons on perches. 250e, Hooded falcon.

1994, Sept. 16   **Litho.**   **Perf. 12**

2008	A546	45e multicolored	.55	.30
2009	A546	75e multicolored	1.10	.50
2010	A546	100e multicolored	1.25	.60
2011	A546	140e multicolored	1.90	.85
		Nos. 2008-2011 (4)	4.80	2.25

Souvenir Sheet

2012	A546	250e multicolored	5.00	4.00

Trawlers
A547

1994, Sept. 16   **Perf. 12x11½**
2013 A547 45e Maria Arminda   .55   .30
2014 A547 75e Bom Pastor   1.10 .50
2015 A547 100e With triplex
                   haulers   1.25 .60
2016 A547 140e Sueste   2.00 .85
          Nos. 2013-2016 (4)   4.90 2.25
          Perf. 11½ Vert.
2013a A547 45e   .50   .30
2014a A547 75e   .95   .50
2015a A547 100e   1.25 .60
2016a A547 140e   1.75 .85
  b.   Booklet pane of 4, #2013a-
            2016a   6.00

Modern Railway Transport — A548

45e, Sintra Railway, electric multiple car unit. 75e, 5600 series locomotives. 140e, Lisbon subway cars.

1994, Oct. 10   Litho.   **Perf. 12**
2017 A548 45e multicolored   .75   .30
2018 A548 75e multicolored   1.00 .45
2019 A548 140e multicolored   1.75 .90
          Nos. 2017-2019 (3)   3.50 1.65

Vehicles of Postal
Transportation — A549

45e, Horse-drawn mail coach, 19th cent. 75e, Railway postal ambulance, 1910. 100e, Mercedes station wagon, No. 222, 1950. 140e, Volkswagen van, 1952. 250e, DAF 2500 truck, 1983.

1994, Oct. 10
2020 A549 45e multicolored   .55   .30
2021 A549 75e multicolored   1.00 .45
2022 A549 100e multicolored   1.25 .65
2023 A549 140e multicolored   1.90 .90
          Nos. 2020-2023 (4)   4.70 2.30
          Souvenir Sheet
2024 A549 250e multicolored   5.00 4.00

First
Savings
Bank in
Portugal,
150th
Anniv.
A550

45e, Pelican medallion. 100e, Modern coins.

1994, Oct. 31
2025 A550 45e multicolored   .60   .30
2026 A550 100e multicolored   1.40 .65
          World Wide Savings Day (#2026).

American
Society of
Travel
Agents,
64th
Congress,
Lisbon
A551

1994, Nov. 7
2027 A551 140e multicolored   1.75 .90

Historical
Inns
A552

45e, S. Filipe Fort, Setubal. 75e, Obidos Castle. 100e, Dos Loios Convent, Evora. 140e, St. Marinha Guimaraes Monastery.

1994, Nov. 7
2028 A552 45e multicolored   .55   .30
2029 A552 75e multicolored   1.00 .45
2030 A552 100e multicolored   1.25 .60
2031 A552 140e multicolored   1.90 .90
          Nos. 2028-2031 (4)   4.70 2.25

Evangelization and Meeting of
Cultures — A553

45e, Carving of missionary, Mozambique, 19th cent., vert. 75e, Sculpture, young Jesus ministering to the people, India, 17th cent., vert. 100e, Chalice, Macao, 17th cent., vert. 140e, Carving of native, Angola, 19th cent.

1994, Nov. 17   Litho.   **Perf. 12**
2032 A553 45e multicolored   .55   .30
2033 A553 75e multicolored   1.00 .45
2034 A553 100e multicolored   1.25 .60
2035 A553 140e multicolored   1.90 .90
          Nos. 2032-2035 (4)   4.70 2.25

Arrival of
Portuguese
in Senegal,
550th
Anniv.
A554

1994, Nov. 17
2036 A554 140e multicolored   1.75 .90
          See Senegal No. 1083.

Souvenir Sheet

Battle of Montijo, 350th Anniv. — A555

1994, Dec. 1
2037 A555 150e multicolored   2.50 2.00

Christmas — A556

1994, Dec. 8
2038 A556 150e Magi   2.50 1.25

Nature Conservation in
Europe — A557

Designs: 42e, Otis tarda. 90e, Pandion haliaetus. 130e, Lacerta schreiberi.

1995, Feb. 22   Litho.   **Perf. 12**
2039 A557 42e multicolored   .60   .30
2040 A557 90e multicolored   1.40 .60
2041 A557 130e multicolored   2.00 .85
  a.   Souvenir sheet of 3, #2039-
            2041   5.00 4.00
          Nos. 2039-2041 (3)   4.00 1.75

St. Joao de Deus
(1495-1550),
Founder of Order
of Hospitalers
A558

1995, Mar. 8   Litho.   **Perf. 12**
2042 A558 45e multicolored   .70   .30

Trams & Automobiles in Portugal,
Cent. — A559

Designs: 90e, 1895 Electric tram, 1895. 130e, 1895 Panhard & Levassor automobile.

1995, Mar. 8
2043 A559 90e multicolored   1.50 .60
2044 A559 130e multicolored   2.00 .95

19th Century
Professions
A560

Designs: 1e, Baker woman. 20e, Spinning wheel and spoon vendor. 45e, Junk dealer. 50e, Fruit vendor. 75e, Whitewasher.

1995, Apr. 20   Litho.   **Perf. 12**
2045 A560 1e multicolored   .25   .25
2046 A560 20e multicolored   .25   .25
2047 A560 45e multicolored   .45   .30
          Complete booklet, 10 #2047   4.50

2048 A560 50e multicolored   .65   .35
2049 A560 75e multicolored   1.00 .50
          Complete booklet, 10 #2049   10.00
          Nos. 2045-2049 (5)   2.60 1.65
          See Nos. 2088-2092, 2147-2151, 2210-
          2214, 2277-2281B.

Peace & Freedom — A561

Europa: No. 2050, People awaiting ships for America, Aristides de Sousa Mendes signing entrance visas, 1940. No. 2051, Transportation of refugees from Gibraltar to Madeira, 1940.

1995, May 5   Litho.   **Perf. 12**
2050 A561 95e multicolored   1.25 .50
2051 A561 95e multicolored   1.25 .50

UN, 50th
Anniv.
A562

135e, like #2052, clouds in background.

1995, May 5
2052 A562 75e multicolored   1.00 .50
2053 A562 135e multicolored   1.75 .90
  a.   Souv. sheet, 2 ea #2052-2053 6.00 5.00

A563

St. Antony of
Padua (1195-
1231)
A564

45e, *St. Anthony Holding Child Jesus.* 75e, St. Anthony with flowers. 135e, Statue of St. Antony holding child Jesus. 250e, Statue of St. Antony holding child Jesus, diff.

1995, June 13   Litho.   **Perf. 12**
2054 A563 45e multicolored   2.00 .30
2055 A564 75e multicolored   3.50 .50
2056 A564 135e multicolored   6.00 .95
          Nos. 2054-2056 (3)   11.50 1.75
          Souvenir Sheet
2057 A563 250e multicolored   5.00 4.00
          See Italy Nos. 2040-2041, Brazil No. 2539.

Firemen in
Portugal,
600th
Anniv.
A565

Designs: No. 2058, Carpenters with axes, women with pitchers, 1395. No. 2059, Dutch firemen, water pumper, 1701. 75e, Fireman of Lisbon, water wagon, 1780, firemen, 1782. 80e, Firemen pulling pumper, carrying water kegs, 1834. 95e, Fire chief directing firemen on Merryweather steam pumper, 1867. 135e, Firemen, hydrant, early fire truck, 1908.

1995, July 4   Litho.   **Perf. 12**
2058 A565 45e multicolored   .45   .30
2059 A565 45e multicolored   .65   .30
  a.   Miniature sheet of 4   3.00 1.25

2060	A565 75e multicolored	1.00	.50
a.	Miniature sheet of 4	5.00	2.00
2061	A565 80e multicolored	1.10	.55
2062	A565 95e multicolored	1.10	.65
2063	A565 135e multicolored	1.50	.90
	Nos. 2058-2063 (6)	5.80	3.20

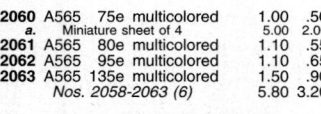

Dom Manuel I, 500th Anniv. of Acclamation — A566

1995, Aug. 4 Litho. Perf. 12
2064	A566 45e buff, brown & red	.60	.30
a.	Miniature sheet of 4	3.00	2.50

New Electric Railway Tram — A567

1995, Sept. 1
2066	A567 80e multicolored	1.10	.55
a.	Booklet pane of 4	4.50	
	Complete booklet, No. 2066a	5.00	

Sculpture Type of 1993

Designs: 45e, Warrior, Castreja culture. 75e, Two-headed fountain. 80e, Statue, "The Truth," by Texeira Lopes. 95e, Monument to the war dead. 135e, Statue of Fernão Lopes, by Martins Correia. 190e, Monument to Fernando Pessoa, by Lagoa Henriques.

Equestrian statues: No. 2073: a, Medieval cavalryman. b, D. José I. c, D. João IV. d, Vímara Peres.

1995, Sept. 27 Litho. Perf. 11½x12
2067	A528 45e multicolored	.55	.30
2068	A528 75e multicolored	1.00	.50
2069	A528 80e multicolored	1.00	.55
2070	A528 95e multicolored	1.10	.65
2071	A528 135e multicolored	1.60	.90
2072	A528 190e multicolored	2.50	1.25
	Nos. 2067-2072 (6)	7.75	4.15

Souvenir Sheet
2073	Sheet of 4	4.50	3.50
a.-d.	A528 75e any single	1.00	1.00

Portuguese Expansion Period Art — A568

45e, Statue of the Guardian Angel of Portugal. 75e, Reliquary of Queen D. Leonor. 80e, Statue of Dom Manuel. 95e, Painting, St. Anthony, by Nuno Goncalves. 135e, Painting, Adoration of the Magi, by Vasco Fernandez. 190e, Painting, Christ on the Way to Mount Calvary, by Jorge Afonso.

200e, Altarpiece for Convent of St. Vincent, by Nuno Goncalves.

1995, Oct. 9 Litho. Perf. 12
2074	A568 45e multicolored	.60	.25
2075	A568 75e multicolored	1.00	.50
2076	A568 80e multicolored	1.00	.50
2077	A568 95e multicolored	1.25	.60
2078	A568 135e multicolored	1.75	.90
2079	A568 190e multicolored	2.50	1.25
	Nos. 2074-2079 (6)	8.10	4.00

Souvenir Sheet
2080	A568 200e multicolored	3.00	2.50

No. 2080 contains one 76x27mm stamp.

José Maria Eca de Queiroz (1845-1900), Writer — A569

1995, Oct. 27 Litho. Perf. 12
2081	A569 135e multicolored	1.75	.90

Christmas A570

1995, Nov. 14
2082	A570 80e Annunciation angel	1.20	.50
a.	"PORTUGAL" omitted	1.40	
b.	Miniature sheet, 4 #2082	5.00	4.00
c.	Miniature sheet, 4 #2082a	7.50	4.00

TAP Air Portugal, 50th Anniv. A571

1995, Nov. 14
2083	A571 135e Airbus A340/300	1.75	.90

Oceanographic Voyages of King Charles I of Portugal and Prince Albert I of Monaco, Cent. — A572

95e, Ship, King Charles I holding sextant, microscope, sea life. 135e, Fish in sea, net, Prince Albert I holding binoculars, ship.

1996, Feb. 1
2084	A572 95e multicolored	1.25	.60
2085	A572 135e multicolored	2.00	.90

See Monaco Nos. 1992-1993.

Natl. Library, Bicent. A573

1996, Feb. 29
2086	A573 80e multicolored	1.20	.50

Use of Portuguese as Official Language, 700th Anniv. — A574

1996, Feb. 29
2087	A574 200e multicolored	2.50	1.25

19th Cent. Professions Type

Designs: 3e, Exchange broker. 47e, Woman selling chestnuts. 78e, Cloth seller. 100e, Black woman selling mussels. 250e, Water seller.

1996, Mar. 20 Litho. Perf. 11½x12
2088	A560 3e multicolored	.25	.25
2089	A560 47e multicolored	.50	.30
a.	Booklet pane, 10 #2089	5.00	
	Complete booklet, #2089a	5.00	
2090	A560 78e multicolored	.90	.50
a.	Booklet pane, 10 #2090	9.00	
	Complete booklet, #2090a	9.00	
2091	A560 100e multicolored	1.10	.65
2092	A560 250e multicolored	2.75	1.60
	Nos. 2088-2092 (5)	5.50	3.30

Joao de Deus (1830-96), Founder of New Method to Teach Reading A576

1996, Apr. 12 Perf. 12
2093	A576 78e multicolored	1.10	.50

UNICEF, 50th Anniv. — A577

1996, Apr. 12
2094	A577 78e shown	1.00	.50
2095	A577 140e Children	1.75	.90
a.	Bklt. pane, 2 ea #2094-2095	5.50	
	Complete booklet, #2095a	5.50	

Joao de Barros (1496-1570), Writer — A578

1996, Apr. 12
2096	A578 140e multicolored	1.75	.90

Helena Vieira da Silva (1908-92), Painter — A579

1996, May 3
2097	A579 98e multicolored	1.25	.60
a.	Souvenir sheet of 3	3.75	3.75

Europa.

Euro '96, European Soccer Championships, Great Britain — A580

1996, June 7 Litho. Perf. 12
2098	A580 78e Soccer players	1.00	.50
2099	A580 140e Soccer players, diff.	1.75	.90
a.	Souvenir sheet, #2098-2099	3.00	2.75

Joao Vaz Corte-Real, Explorer, 500th Death Anniv. — A581

1996, June 7
2100	A581 140e multicolored	1.75	.90

Souvenir Sheet
2101	A581 315e like #2100	4.25	4.00

No. 2101 contains one 40x31 stamp with a continuous design.

1996 Summer Olympics, Atlanta A582

1996, June 24
2102	A582 47e Wrestling	.60	.30
2103	A582 78e Equestrian	1.00	.50
2104	A582 98e Boxing	1.25	.65
2105	A582 140e Running	1.75	.90
	Nos. 2102-2105 (4)	4.60	2.35

Souvenir Sheet
2106	A582 300e Early track event	4.00	3.00

Olymphilex '96 (#2106).

Augusto Hilário (1864-96), Singer A583

1996, July 1 Litho. Perf. 12x11½
2107	A583 80e multicolored	1.20	.50

Alphonsine Condification of Statutes, 550th Anniv. — A584

1996, Aug. 7
2108	A584 350e multicolored	4.25	2.25

Motion Pictures, Cent. A585

Directors, stars of motion pictures: 47e, António Silva. 78e, Vasco Santana. 80e, Laura Alves. 98e, Aurélio Pais dos Reis. 100e, Leitao de Barros. 140e, António Lopes Ribeiro.

1996, Aug. 7
2109	A585 47e multicolored	.60	.30
2110	A585 78e multicolored	1.00	.50
2111	A585 80e multicolored	1.00	.50
a.	Souvenir sheet, #2109-2111	2.75	2.75
2112	A585 98e multicolored	1.25	.65
2113	A585 100e multicolored	1.25	.65
2114	A585 140e multicolored	1.75	.90
a.	Souvenir sheet, #2112-2114	5.00	5.00
b.	Souvenir sheet, #2109-2114	7.50	7.50
	Nos. 2109-2114 (6)	6.85	3.50

Azeredo Perdigao (1896-1993), Lawyer, Chairman of Calouste Gulbenkian Foundation — A586

1996, Sept. 19	**Litho.**		**Perf. 12**
2115 A586 47e multicolored		.75	.30

Arms of the Districts of Portugal A587

1996, Sept. 27

2116	A587	47e Aveiro	.60	.30
2117	A587	78e Beja	1.00	.50
2118	A587	80e Braga	1.00	.50
a.		Souvenir sheet, #2116-2118	2.75	2.75
2119	A587	98e Branganca	1.25	.65
2120	A587	100e Castelo Branco	1.25	.65
2121	A587	140e Coimbra	1.75	.90
a.		Souvenir sheet, #2119-2121	4.50	4.50
		Nos. 2116-2121 (6)	6.85	3.50

County of Portucale, 900th Anniv. A588

1996, Oct. 9

2122 A588 47e multicolored	.75	.30

Home Mail Delivery, 175th Anniv. — A589

Designs: 47e, Mail carrier, 1821. 78e, Postman, 1854. 98e, Rural mail distrubutor, 1893. 100e, Postman, 1939. 140e, Postman, 1992.

1996, Oct. 9

2123	A589	47e multicolored	.60	.30
2124	A589	78e multicolored	1.00	.50
2125	A589	98e multicolored	1.25	.65
2126	A589	100e multicolored	1.25	.65
2127	A589	140e multicolored	1.90	.90
		Nos. 2123-2127 (5)	6.00	3.00

Traditional Food A590

47e, Minho-style pork. 78e, Trout, Boticas. 80e, Tripe, Oporto. 98e, Baked codfish, potatoes. 100e, Eel chowder, Aveiro. 140e, Lobster, Peniche.

1996, Oct. 9

2128	A590	47e multicolored	.60	.30
2129	A590	78e multicolored	1.00	.50
2130	A590	80e multicolored	1.00	.50
2131	A590	98e multicolored	1.25	.65
2132	A590	100e multicolored	1.25	.65
2133	A590	140e multicolored	2.00	.90
		Nos. 2128-2133 (6)	7.10	3.50

See Nos. 2170-2175.

Bank of Portugal, 150th Anniv. A591

1996, Nov. 12	**Litho.**	**Perf. 12**
2134 A591 78e multicolored	1.00	.50

Rights of the People of East Timor A592

1996, Nov. 12

2135 A592 140e black & red	1.75	.90

Discovery of Maritime Route to India, 500th Anniv. — A593

Voyage of Vasco da Gama: 47e, Visit of D. Manuel I to shipyards. 78e, Departure from Lisbon, July 8, 1497. 98e, Trip over Atlantic Ocean. 140e, Passing Cape of Good Hope. 315e, Dream of Manuel.

1996, Nov. 12		**Perf. 13½**
2136 A593 47e multicolored	.60	.30
2137 A593 78e multicolored	1.00	.50
2138 A593 98e multicolored	1.25	.60
2139 A593 140e multicolored	1.75	.85
Nos. 2136-2139 (4)	4.60	2.25
Souvenir Sheet		
2140 A593 315e multicolored	4.00	4.00

See Nos. 2191-2195, 2265-2270.

Souvenir Sheet

1996 Organization for Security and Cooperation in Europe Summit, Lisbon — A594

1996, Dec. 2	**Perf. 12**
2141 A594 200e multicolored	2.50 2.50

Ships of the Indian Shipping Line A595

Designs: 49e, Portuguese galleon, 16th cent. 80e, "Principe da Beira," 1780. 100e, Bow of Frigate "D. Fernando II e Gloria," 1843. 140e, Stern of "D. Fernando II e Gloria."

1997, Feb. 12		**Litho.**	**Perf. 12**
2142	A595	49e multicolored	.60	.30
2143	A595	80e multicolored	1.00	.50
2144	A595	100e multicolored	1.25	.65
2145	A595	140e multicolored	1.75	.90
		Nos. 2142-2145 (4)	4.60	2.35

Project Life — A596

1997, Feb. 20

2146 A596 80e multicolored	1.20	.50
a. Booklet pane of 5	6.00	
Complete booklet, #2146a	6.00	

19th Cent. Professions Type

Designs: 2e, Laundry woman. 5e, Broom seller. 30e, Olive oil seller. 49e, Woman with cape. 80e, Errand boy.

1997, Mar. 12		**Litho.**	**Perf. 11½x12**
2147	A560	2e multicolored	.25	.25
2148	A560	5e multicolored	.25	.25
2149	A560	30e multicolored	.35	.25
2150	A560	49e multicolored	.60	.30
a.		Booklet pane of 10	6.00	
		Complete booklet, #2150a	6.00	
2151	A560	80e multicolored	1.00	.50
a.		Booklet pane of 10	10.00	
		Complete booklet, #2151a	10.00	
		Nos. 2147-2151 (5)	2.45	1.55

Managing Institute of Public Credit, Bicent. A597

1997, Mar. 12	**Litho.**	**Perf. 12**
2152 A597 49e multicolored	.65	.30

World Wildlife Fund — A598

Galemys pyreanicus: No. 2153, Looking upward. No. 2154, Paws around nose. No. 2155, Eating earthworm. No. 2156, Heading downward.

1997, Mar. 12		**Perf. 12**
2153	49e multicolored	.65	.45
2154	49e multicolored	.65	.45
2155	49e multicolored	.65	.45
2156	49e multicolored	.65	.45
a.	A598 Strip of 4, #2153-2156	3.50	3.50

Stories and Legends — A599

Europa: Moorish girl watching over treasures.

1997, May 5	**Litho.**	**Perf. 12**
2157 A599 100e multicolored	1.25	.65
a. Souvenir sheet of 3	4.50	3.25

Sports A600

#2162: a, BMX bike riding. b, Hang gliding.

1997, May 29		**Perf. 12**
2158	A600	49e Surfing	.60	.30
2159	A600	80e Skate boarding	1.00	.50
2160	A600	100e Roller blading	1.25	.65
2161	A600	140e Parasailing	1.75	.90
		Nos. 2158-2161 (4)	4.60	2.35
		Souvenir Sheet		
2162		Sheet of 2	4.00	3.00
a.-b.		A600 150e any single	1.60	1.60

Capture of Lisbon and Santarém from the Moors, 850th Anniv. — A601

Designs: No. 2163, Soldier on horse, front of fortress of Lisbon. No. 2164, Soldiers climbing ladders into Santareém at night.

1997, June 9		**Perf. 12**
2163	80e multicolored	1.00	.50
2164	80e multicolored	1.00	.50
a.	A601 Pair, #2163-2164	2.00	2.00
b.	Souvenir sheet, 2 #2164a	4.25	4.25

Fr. Luís Fróis (1532-97), Missionary, Historian — A602

80e, Fróis on mission in Orient. #2166, Fróis holding hands across chest. #2167, Fróis, church.

1997, June 9

2165	A602	80e multi, horiz.	1.00	.50
2166	A602	140e multi	1.90	.90
2167	A602	140e multi	1.90	.90
		Nos. 2165-2167 (3)	4.80	2.30

See Macao 878-879.

Fr. José de Anchieta (1534-97), Missionary in Brazil — A603

Design: No. 2169, Fr. António Vieira (1608-97), missionary in Brazil, diplomat.

1997, June 9

2168	A603	140e multicolored	1.75	.90
2169	A603	350e multicolored	4.75	2.25

See Brazil Nos. 2639-2640.

Traditional Food Type of 1996

10e, Roasted kid, Beira Baixa. 49e, Fried shad. 80e, Lamb stew. 100e, Fish chowder. 140e, Swordfish fillets with corn. 200e, Stewed octopus, Azores.

1997, July 5		**Litho.**	**Perf. 12**
2170	A590	10e multicolored	.25	.25
2171	A590	49e multicolored	.60	.30
2172	A590	80e multicolored	1.00	.50
2173	A590	100e multicolored	1.25	.65
2174	A590	140e multicolored	1.75	.85
2175	A590	200e multicolored	2.50	1.25
		Nos. 2170-2175 (6)	7.35	3.80

Souvenir Sheet

City of Oporto, UNESCO World
Heritage Site — A605

1997, July 5   **Litho.**   *Perf. 12*
2176 A605 350e multicolored   4.50 4.50

A606

1997, July 19   **Litho.**   *Perf. 12*
2177 A606 100e multicolored   1.25 .65

Brotherhood of the Yeoman of Beja, 700th anniv.

A607

1997, Aug. 29   **Litho.**   *Perf. 12*
2178 A607 50e multicolored   1.00 .30

Natl. Laboratory of Civil Engineering, 50th anniv.

Treaty of
Alcanices,
700th
Anniv.
A608

1997, Sept. 12
2179 A608 80e multicolored   1.00 .50

Arms of the
Districts of
Portugal
A609

1997, Sept. 17
2180	A609	10e Evora	.25	.25
2181	A609	49e Faro	.55	.30
2182	A609	80e Guarda	.85	.50
2183	A609	100e Leiria	1.40	.65
2184	A609	140e Lisboa	1.60	.90
a.		Souv. sheet, #2180, 2182, 2184	3.50	3.00
2185	A609	200e Portalegre	2.25	1.25
a.		Souv. sheet, #2181, 2183, 2185	4.50	4.00
		Nos. 2180-2185 (6)	6.90	3.85

See Nos. 2249-2254.

Incorporation of Postal Service in
State Administration, Bicent. — A610

1997, Oct. 9
2186 A610 80e multicolored   1.00 .50

Portuguese Cartography — A611

Designs: 49e, Map from atlas of Lopo Homen-Reineis, 1519. 80e, Map from atlas of Joao Freire, 1546. 100e, Chart by Diogo Ribeiro, 1529. 140e, Anonymous map, 1630.

1997, Oct. 9
2187	A611	49e multicolored	.60	.30
2188	A611	80e multicolored	1.00	.50
2189	A611	100e multicolored	1.25	.60
2190	A611	140e multicolored	1.75	.90
a.		Souvenir sheet, #2187-2190	4.75	4.75
		Nos. 2187-2190 (4)	4.60	2.30

Discovery of Maritime Route to India Type of 1996

Voyage of Vasco da Gama: 49e, St. Gabriel's cross, Quelimane. 80e, Stop at island off Mozambique. 100e, Arrival in Mombasa. 140e, Reception for king of Melinde. 315e, Trading with natives, Natal.

1997, Nov. 5   *Perf. 13½*
2191	A593	49e multicolored	.60	.30
2192	A593	80e multicolored	1.00	.50
2193	A593	100e multicolored	1.25	.60
2194	A593	140e multicolored	1.75	.90
		Nos. 2191-2194 (4)	4.60	2.30

Souvenir Sheet
2195 A593 315e multicolored   4.25 4.25

Expo
'98 — A612

Plankton: 49e, Loligo vulgaris. 80e, Scyllarus arctus. 100e, Pontellina plumata. 140e, Solea senegalensis.
No. 2200: a, Calcidiscus leptoporus. b, Tabellaria.

1997, Nov. 5   *Perf. 12*
2196	A612	49e multicolored	.60	.30
2197	A612	80e multicolored	1.00	.50
2198	A612	100e multicolored	1.25	.65
2199	A612	140e multicolored	1.75	.90
		Nos. 2196-2199 (4)	4.60	2.35

Souvenir Sheet
Perf. 12½
2200		Sheet of 2	3.00	3.00
a.-b.		A612 100e any single	1.50	1.50

See Nos. 2215-2219, 2226-2244.

Souvenir Sheet

Sintra, UNESCO World Heritage
Site — A613

1997, Dec. 5   *Perf. 12*
2201 A613 350e multicolored   4.50 4.50

Portuguese Military Engineering, 350th
Anniv. — A614

Engineering officer, map of fortress: 50e, Almeida. 80e, Miranda do Douro. 100e, Moncao. 140e, Elvas.

1998, Jan. 28   **Litho.**   *Perf. 12*
2202	A614	50e multicolored	.60	.30
2203	A614	80e multicolored	1.00	.50
2204	A614	100e multicolored	1.25	.65
2205	A614	140e multicolored	1.75	.90
a.		Booklet pane, #2202-2205, perf. 12 vert.	6.00	
		Complete booklet, #2205a	6.00	
		Nos. 2202-2205 (4)	4.60	2.35

Roberto
Ivens
(1850-98),
Naturalist
A615

1998, Jan. 28
2206 A615 140e multicolored   1.75 .90

Misericórdias (Philanthropic
Organizations), 500th Anniv. — A616

Sculptures: 80e, Madonna wearing crown surrounded by angels, people kneeling in praise, vert. 100e, People of antiquity gathered around another's bedside.

1998, Feb. 20
2207	A616	80e multicolored	1.00	.50
2208	A616	100e multicolored	1.25	.65

Souvenir Sheet

Aqueduct of the Free Waters, 250th
Anniv. — A617

1998, Feb. 20
2209 A617 350e multicolored   4.50 2.25

19th Cent. Professions Type

10e, Fish seller. 40e, Collector of alms. 50e, Ceramics seller. 85e, Duck and eggs vendor. 250e, Queijadas (small cakes made of cheese) seller.

1998, Mar. 20   *Perf. 11½x12*
2210	A560	10e multicolored	.25	.25
2211	A560	40e multicolored	.40	.25
2212	A560	50e multicolored	.50	.30
a.		Booklet pane of 10	5.00	
		Complete booklet, #2212a	5.00	
2213	A560	85e multicolored	1.00	.55
a.		Booklet pane of 10	10.00	
		Complete booklet, #2213a	10.00	
2214	A560	250e multicolored	3.00	1.60
		Nos. 2210-2214 (5)	5.15	2.95

Expo '98 Type of 1997

Plankton: 50e, Pilumnus hirtellus. 85e, Lophius piscatorius. 100e, Sparus aurata. 140e, Cladonema radiatum.
No. 2219: a, Noctiluca miliaris. b, Dinophysis acuta.

1998, Mar. 20   *Perf. 12*
2215	A612	50e multicolored	.55	.30
2216	A612	85e multicolored	.90	.50
2217	A612	100e multicolored	1.20	.65
2218	A612	140e multicolored	1.60	.90
		Nos. 2215-2218 (4)	4.25	2.35

Souvenir Sheet
2219	A612	100e Sheet of 2, #a.-b.	2.50	2.50
c.		Sheet of 12, #2196-2199, 2200a-2200b, 2215-2218, 2219a-2219b	15.00	15.00

Opening of
the Vasco
Da Gama
Bridge
A618

1998, Mar. 29   **Litho.**   *Perf. 12*
2220 A618 200e multicolored   2.50 1.25

Souvenir Sheet
2221 A618 200e like #2220   2.50 2.50

Stamp in No. 2221 is a continuous design and shows bridge cables overlapping at far left.

Oporto
Industrial
Assoc.,
150th
Anniv.
A619

1998, Apr. 30
2222 A619 80e multicolored   1.00 .50

Vasco da
Gama
Aquarium,
Cent.
A620

1998, May 13
2223	A620	50e Seahorse	.60	.30
2224	A620	80e Fish	1.00	

National Festivals A621

1998, May 21
2225 A621 100e People's Saints 1.25 .65
a. Souvenir sheet of 3 3.75 3.75
Europa.

Expo '98 Type of 1997

Designs: No. 2226, Portuguese sailing ship, face on stone cliff. No. 2227, Diver, astrolabe. No. 2228, Various fish. No. 2229, Research submersible, fish. No. 2230, Mermaid swimming. No. 2231, Children under water holding globe.

No. 2232: a, Portuguese Pavilion. b, Pavilion of the Future. c, Oceans Pavilion. d, Knowledge of the Seas Pavilion. e, Pavilion of Utopia. f, Mascot putting letter into mailbox.

No. 2233, Like #2216, inscribed "Larva de Tamboril" only. No. 2234, Like #2219a, inscribed "Protozário Broluminiscente" only. No. 2235, Like #2215, inscribed "Larvas de Carangueijos" only. No. 2236, Like #2217, inscribed "Larvas de Dourada" only. No. 2237, Like #2219b, inscribed "Dinoflagelados" only. No. 2238, Like #2218, inscribed "Medusa" only.

No. 2239, like #2227. No. 2240, like #2229. No. 2241, like #2231. No. 2242, like #2226. No. 2243, like #2228. No. 2244, like #2230.

1998, May 21
2226 A612 50e multicolored .60 .30
2227 A612 50e multicolored .60 .30
2228 A612 85e multicolored 1.00 .50
2229 A612 85e multicolored 1.00 .50
2230 A612 140e multicolored 1.75 .90
2231 A612 140e multicolored 1.75 .90
a. Sheet of 6, #2226-2231 6.75 6.75
2232 Sheet of 6, #a.-f. 6.75 6.75
a. A612 50e multicolored .60 .30
b.-c. A612 85e any single 1.00 .50
d.-e. A612 140e any single 1.75 .90
f. A612 80e multicolored 1.00 .50
g. Souvenir sheet, #2232a-2232e 6.25 6.25

Die Cut 11½
Self-Adhesive Coil Stamps
Size: 29x24mm

2233 A612 50e multicolored .60 .30
2234 A612 50e multicolored .60 .30
2235 A612 50e multicolored .60 .30
2236 A612 50e multicolored .60 .30
2237 A612 50e multicolored .60 .30
2238 A612 50e multicolored .60 .30
a. Strip of 6, #2233-2238 3.75
2239 A612 85e multicolored 1.00 .45
2240 A612 85e multicolored 1.00 .45
2241 A612 85e multicolored 1.00 .45
2242 A612 85e multicolored 1.00 .45
2243 A612 85e multicolored 1.00 .45
2244 A612 85e multicolored 1.00 .45
a. Strip of 6, #2239-2244 6.00

Nos. 2233-2238 are not inscribed with Latin names.

Discovery of Radium, Cent. — A622

1998, June 1   **Perf. 12**
2245 A622 140e Marie Curie 1.75 .90

Ferreira de Castro (1898-1974), Writer — A623

1998, June 10
2246 A623 50e multicolored .70 .30

Bernardo Marques, Artist, Birth Cent. — A624

1998, June 10
2247 A624 85e multicolored 1.10 .50

Souvenir Sheet

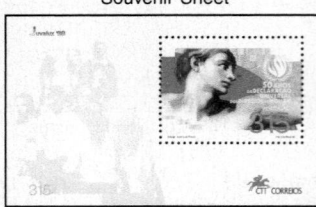

Universal Declaration of Human Rights, 50th Anniv. — A625

1998, June 18
2248 A625 315e multicolored 4.00 2.00

District Arms Type of 1997

1998, June 23
2249 A609 50e Vila Real .65 .30
2250 A609 85e Setubal .95 .50
2251 A609 85e Viana do Castelo .95 .50
2252 A609 100e Santarem 1.20 .65
2253 A609 100e Viseu 1.20 .65
a. Souvenir sheet of 3, #2250, 2252-2253 4.00 4.00
2254 A609 200e Porto 2.25 1.25
a. Souvenir sheet of 3, #2249, 2251, 2254 3.25 3.25
Nos. 2249-2254 (6) 7.20 3.85

Marinha Grande Glass Industry, 250th Anniv. A626

Designs: 50e, Blowing glass, furnace. 80e, Early worker heating glass, ornament. 100e, Factory, bottles. 140e, Modern worker heating glass, vases.

1998, July 7
2255 A626 50e multicolored .55 .30
2256 A626 80e multicolored .90 .50
2257 A626 100e multicolored 1.10 .65
2258 A626 140e multicolored 1.75 .90
Nos. 2255-2258 (4) 4.30 2.35

1998 Vasco da Gama Regatta A627

Sailing ship, country represented: 50e, Sagres, Portugal. No. 2260, Asgard II, Ireland. No. 2261, Rose, US. No. 2262, Kruzenshtern, Russia. No. 2263, Amerigo Vespucci, Italy. 140e, Creoula, Portugal.

1998, July 31
2259 A627 50e multicolored .60 .30
2260 A627 85e multicolored 1.00 .50
2261 A627 85e multicolored 1.00 .50
2262 A627 100e multicolored 1.25 .65
2263 A627 100e multicolored 1.25 .65
2264 A627 140e multicolored 1.75 .90
Nos. 2259-2264 (6) 6.85 3.50

Discovery of Maritime Route to India Type of 1996

Voyage of Vasco da Gama: No. 2265, Meeting with pilot, Ibn Madjid. 80e, Storm in the Indian Ocean. 100e, Arrival in Calicut. 140e, Meeting with the Samorin of Calicut.

No. 2269: a, like #2136. b, like #2137. c, like #2138. d, like #2139. e, like #2191. f, like #2192. g, like #2193. h, like #2194. i, like #2266. j, like #2267. k, like #2268.

315e, King of Melinde listening to narration of the history of Portugal.

1998, Sept. 4   **Perf. 13½**
2265 A593 50e multicolored .60 .30
2266 A593 80e multicolored .85 .50
2267 A593 100e multicolored 1.25 .65
2268 A593 140e multicolored 1.60 .90
Nos. 2265-2268 (4) 4.30 2.35

Sheet of 12
2269 A593 50e #a.-k. + #2265 7.50 7.50

Souvenir Sheet
2270 A593 315e multicolored 4.00 4.00

Lisbon-Coimbra Mail Coach, Decree to Reorganize Maritime Mail to Brazil, Bicent. — A628

50e, Modern van delivering mail, postal emblm. 140e, Sailing ship, Postilhao da America, mail coach.

1998, Oct. 9   **Perf. 12x11½**
2271 A628 50e multicolored 1.00 .30
2272 A628 140e multicolored 2.00 .90

See Brazil No. 2691.

Souvenir Sheet

8th Iberian-American Summit, Oporto — A629

1998, Oct. 18   **Perf. 12½**
2273 A629 140e multicolored 1.75 1.75

Souvenir Sheet

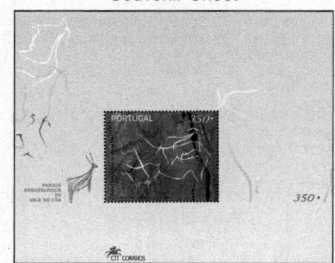

Coa Valley Archaeological Park — A630

1998, Oct. 23   **Perf. 13½**
2274 A630 350e multicolored 4.25 2.25

Health in Portugal — A631

1998, Nov. 5   **Perf. 12**
2275 A631 100e multicolored 1.25 .65

Souvenir Sheet

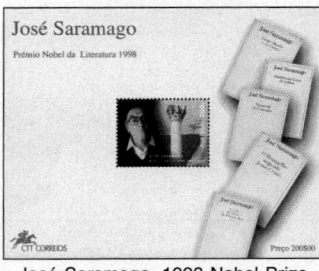

José Saramago, 1998 Nobel Prize Winner for Literature — A632

1998, Dec. 15   **Litho.**   **Perf. 12**
2276 A632 200e multicolored 2.50 1.25

Postrider Type of 1993

1999, Jan. 11   **Litho.**   **Perf. 13¼**
2276A A521 A brown, gray & black 1.00 .50

No. 2276A sold for 51e on date of issue. Inscription at LR reads "Imp: Lito Maia 99."

19th Cent. Professions Type

Designs: 51e, Knife grinder. 86e, Female bread seller. 95e, Coachman. 100e, Milkmaid. 210e, Basket seller.

1999, Feb. 26   **Litho.**   **Perf. 11½x12**
2277 A560 51e multicolored .45 .35
2278 A560 86e multicolored .90 .55
2279 A560 95e multicolored 1.00 .65
2280 A560 100e multicolored 1.10 .65
2281 A560 210e multicolored 2.50 1.40
Nos. 2277-2281 (5) 5.95 3.60

Booklet Stamps
Self-Adhesive
Serpentine Die Cut 11¼

2281A A560 51e like #2277 .65 .35
c. Booklet pane of 10 6.50
2281B A560 95e like #2279 1.25 .65
d. Booklet pane of 10 12.50

Nos. 2281A and 2281B were issued as coil rolls of 100 (No. 2281A) or 50 (No. 2281B) as well as in booklet form. Values the same. Used examples of each denomination are identical. Nos. 2281Ac, 2281Bd are complete booklets. The peelable backing serves as a booklet cover.

Beginning with No. 2282 denominations are on the stamps in both escudos and euros. Listings show the value in escudos.

Introduction of the Euro — A633

1999, Mar. 15   **Perf. 12**
2282 A633 95e multicolored 1.25 1.00

Australia '99, World Stamp Expo — A634

Portuguese in Australia: No. 2283, Sailing ship offshore, kangaroos. No. 2284, Sailing ship, natives watching. 350e, like #2283-2284.

1999, Mar. 19
2283 140e multicolored 1.75 .90
2284 140e multicolored 1.75 .90
a. A634 Pair, #2283-2284 3.50 3.50

Souvenir Sheet
2285 A634 350e multicolored 4.25 4.25

No. 2285 contains one 80x30mm stamp and is a continuous design.

Presidential Campaign of José Norton de Matos, 50th Anniv. — A635

1999, Mar. 24
2286 A635 80e multicolored   1.10   .50

Joao Almeida Garrett (1799-1854), Writer — A636

1999, Mar. 24
2287 A636 95e multicolored   1.25   .65

Souvenir Sheet
2288 A636 210e like #2287   2.50 1.40

Flight Between Portugal and Macao, 75th Anniv. A637

Airplanes: No. 2289, Breguet 16 Bn2, "Patria." No. 2290, DH9.

1999, Apr. 19
2289 A637 140e multicolored   1.75   .90
2290 A637 140e multicolored   1.75   .90
  a.   Souvenir sheet, #2289-2290 3.50 3.50
         See Macao 979-980.

Carnation A638

Assembly building — A639

1999, Apr. 25
2291 A638 51e multicolored   .55   .30
2292 A639 80e multicolored   .95   .50
  a.   Souvenir sheet, #2291-2292 1.50 1.50
         Revolution, 25th Anniv.

Council of Europe, 50th Anniv. A640

1999, May 5   Litho.   Perf. 12x11¾
2293 A640 100e multicolored   1.25   .65

Europa A641

100e, Wolf, iris, Peneda-Gerês Natl. Park.

1999, May 5
2294 A641 100e multicolored   1.25   .65
  a.   Souvenir sheet of 3   3.75 3.75

Marquis de Pombal (1699-1782), Statesman — A642

No. 2295: 80e, Portrait.
No. 2296: a, 80e, Portrait and portion of statue. b, 210e, Hand, quill pen.

1999, May 13
2295 A642 80e multicolored   1.10 1.00

Souvenir Sheet
2296 A642   Sheet of 2, #a.-b. 3.50 3.50

Meeting of Portuguese and Chinese Cultures in Macao — A643

Designs: 51e, Ship, junk, bridge. 80e, Macao dancers in Portuguese outfits. 95e, Virgin Mary statue, dragon heads. 100e, Church, temple. 140e, Statues in park, horiz.

Perf. 11¾x12, 12x11¾
1999, June 24   Litho.
2297 A643 51e multicolored   .50   .30
2298 A643 80e multicolored   .90   .50
2299 A643 95e multicolored   1.00   .60
2300 A643 100e multicolored   1.10   .65
2301 A643 140e multicolored   1.50   .90
        Nos. 2297-2301 (5)   5.00 2.95

Portuguese Air Force, 75th Anniv. A644

Designs: No. 2302, De Havilland DH 82A Tiger Moth. No. 2303, Supermarine Spitfire Vb. No. 2304, Breguet Bre XIV A2. No. 2305, Spad S. VII-C1. No. 2306, Caudron G.III. No. 2307, Junkers Ju-52/3m g3e.

1999, July 1   Perf. 12x11¾
2302 A644 51e multicolored   .55   .30
2303 A644 51e multicolored   .55   .30
2304 A644 85e multicolored   .90   .55
2305 A644 85e multicolored   .90   .55
2306 A644 95e multicolored   1.10   .65
2307 A644 95e multicolored   1.10   .65
  a.   Souv. sheet of 6, #2302-2307 5.00 5.00
        Nos. 2302-2307 (6)   5.10 3.00

Surrealist Group of Lisbon, 50th Anniv. A645

Sections of Painting "Cadavre Exquis" by: 51e, António Pedro (1909-66). 80e, Marcellino Vespeira (b. 1926). 95e, Joao Moniz Pereira (1920-89). 100e, Fernando de Azevedo (b. 1923). 140e, António Domingues (b. 1921).

1999, July 2   Litho.   Perf. 13¼
2308 A645 51e multicolored   .50   .30
2309 A645 80e multicolored   .85   .50
2310 A645 95e multicolored   1.00   .60
2311 A645 100e multicolored   1.10   .65
2312 A645 140e multicolored   1.60   .90
  a.   Souv. sheet of 5, #2308-2312 5.25 5.25
        Nos. 2308-2312 (5)   5.05 2.95
        PhilexFrance 99, No. 2312a.

Inauguration of Rail Link Over 25th of April Bridge — A646

51e, No. 2315, Train, tunnel entrance. 95e, No. 2316, Train, viaduct, Tagus River.

1999, July 29   Litho.   Perf. 12x11¾
2313 A646 51e multicolored   .60   .30
2314 A646 95e multicolored   1.25   .60

Souvenir Sheets
2315 A646 350e multicolored   4.25 4.25
2316 A646 350e multicolored   4.25 4.25
Nos. 2315-2316 each contain one 80x30mm stamp.

UPU, 125th Anniv. A647

Designs: 95e, Heinrich von Stephan, earth, letter. 140e, Computer, earth, letter. 315e, Von Stephan, computer, earth, letters.

1999, Aug. 21
2317 A647 95e multicolored   1.10   .65
2318 A647 140e multicolored   1.60   .90

Souvenir Sheet
2319 A647 315e multicolored   3.75 3.75
No. 2319 contains one 80x30mm stamp.

Desserts Originating in Convents A648

Designs: 51e, Trouxas de ovos. 80e, Pudim de ovos (egg pudding). 95e, Papos de anjo. 100e, Palha de Abrantes. 140e, Castanhas de Viseu. 210e, Bolo de mel (honey cake).

1999, Aug. 30
2320 A648 51e multicolored   .60   .30
2321 A648 80e multicolored   .95   .50
2322 A648 95e multicolored   1.10   .60
2323 A648 100e multicolored   1.20   .65
2324 A648 140e multicolored   1.60   .90
2325 A648 210e multicolored   2.25 1.40
        Nos. 2320-2325 (6)   7.70 4.35
        See Nos. 2366-2371.

Conquest of Algarve, 750th Anniv. A649

1999, Sept. 3   Litho.   Perf. 12x11¾
2326 A649 100e multicolored   1.25   .65

Medical Pioneers A650

#2327, Ricardo Jorge (1858-1939), Natl. Health Inst. #2328, Camara Pestana (1863-99), microscope, Pestana Bacteriological Inst. #2329, Francisco Gentil (1878-1964), Portuguese Inst. of Oncology. #2330, Egas Moniz (1874-1955), cerebral angiogram. #2331, Reynaldo dos Santos (1880-1970), arteriogram. #2332, Joao Cid dos Santos (1907-76), performer of 1st endarterectomy.

1999, Sept. 20
2327 A650 51e multicolored   .60   .30
2328 A650 51e multicolored   .60   .30
2329 A650 80e multicolored   .90   .50
2330 A650 80e multicolored   .90   .50
2331 A650 95e multicolored   1.10   .60
2332 A650 95e multicolored   1.10   .60
        Nos. 2327-2332 (6)   5.20 2.80

José Diogo de Mascarenhas Neto, First Superintendent of Posts — A651

1999, Oct. 9
2333 A651 80e multicolored   1.10   .50
Postal reorganization and provisional mail regulations, bicent.

Jaime Martins Barata (1899-1970), Painter, Philatelic Art Consultant — A652

1999, Oct. 9
2334 A652 80e multicolored   1.10   .50

Christmas A653

Art by handicapped persons: 51e, Maria F. Gonçalves (Magi). 95e, Marta Silva. 140e, Luis F. Farinha. 210e, Gonçalves (Nativity).

1999, Nov. 19
2335 A653 51e multicolored   .55   .30
2336 A653 95e multicolored   1.10   .60
2337 A653 140e multicolored   1.50   .90
2338 A653 210e multicolored   2.40 1.40
        Nos. 2335-2338 (4)   5.55 3.20

Souvenir Sheet

Meeting of Portuguese and Chinese Cultures — A654

1999, Nov. 19   Perf. 11¾x12
2339 A654 140e multicolored   2.00 1.25
See Macao No. 1009.

Souvenir Sheet

Retrospective of Macao's Portuguese History — A655

1999, Dec. 19   Litho.   Perf. 12x11¾
2340 A655 350e multicolored   4.50 4.50
See Macao No. 1011.

Birth of Jesus Christ, 2000th Anniv. — A656

2000, Feb. 15   Litho.   Perf. 11¾x12
2341 A656 52e multicolored   .60   .30

The 20th Century A657

Designs: 86e, Astronaut and spacecraft.
No. 2343: a, Human rights. b, Fashions (60x30mm). c, Ecology (60x30mm). d, Transportation (old). e, Transportation (modern). f, Like No. 2342. g, Space shuttle.
No. 2344: a, Authors Marcel Proust, Thomas Mann, James Joyce, Franz Kafka, Fernando Pessoa, Jorge Luis Borges, Samuel Beckett (50x30mm). b, Musicians and composers Claude Debussy, Igor Stravinsky, Arnold Schoenberg, Béla Bartók, George Gershwin, Charlie Parker, Bill Evans (50x30mm). c, Stage. d, Stage, diff. (60x30mm). e, Art (50x30mm). f, Art (30x30mm). g, Cinema (50x30mm). h, Cinema and television (30x30mm). i, Architecture (denomination at LL). j, Architecture (denomination at LR). k, Architecture (denomination at center).
No. 2345: a, Philosophers Edmund Husserl, Ludwig Wittgenstein, Martin Heidegger. b, Mathematicians Jules-Henri Poincaré, Kurt Gödel, Andrei Kolmogorov. c, Physicists Max Planck, Albert Einstein, Niels Bohr (50x30mm). d, Anthropologists Franz Boas, Claude Lévi-Strauss, Margaret Mead. e, Psychoanalyst Sigmund Freud and medical researcher Sir Alexander Fleming (30x30mm). f, Transplant pioneer Dr. Christiaan Barnard. g, Economists Joseph Schumpeter, John Maynard Keynes. h, Technology. i, Technology (30x30mm). j, Computer pioneers Alan Turing, John von Neumann. k, Radio pioneer Guglielmo Marconi. l, Information and communications (30x30mm).

2000, Feb. 18   Perf. 12x11¾
2342 A657 86e multicolored   1.20 .55

Souvenir Sheets of 7, 11, 12
2343 A657 52e #a.-g.   4.50 4.50
2344 A657 52e #a.-k.   7.00 7.00
2345 A657 52e #a.-l.   7.75 7.75

Birds — A658

Designs: 52e, Golden eagle. 85e, Great crested grebe. 90e, Flamingo. 100e, Gannet. 215e, Teal.

2000, Mar. 2   Litho.   Perf. 11¾x11½
2346 A658 52e multi   .60   .30
2347 A658 85e multi   1.10 .55
2348 A658 90e multi   1.10 .55
2349 A658 100e multi   1.25 .65
2350 A658 215e multi   2.75 1.40
          Nos. 2346-2350 (5)   6.80 3.45

Booklet Stamps
Serpentine Die Cut 11¼
Self-Adhesive
2351 A658 52e Like #2346   .60   .30
   a.   Booklet, 10 #2351   6.00
2352 A658 100e Like #2349   1.25 .65
   a.   Booklet, 10 #2352   12.50
   See Nos. 2401-2407, 2465-2471, 2472, 2473, 2530-2535, 2537-2537A, 2621-2626, 2628.

Portuguese Presidency of Council of Europe A659

2000, Mar. 23   Perf. 12x11¾
2353 A659 100e multi   1.40 .65

Discovery of Brazil, 500th Anniv. A660

Designs: 52e, Two sailors, three natives, parrot. 85e, sailor, ships, four natives. 100e, Sailors, natives, sails. 140e, Sailor and natives inspecting tree.

2000, Apr. 11   Litho.   Perf. 12x11¾
2354 A660 52e multi   .60   .30
2355 A660 85e multi   1.10 .55
2356 A660 100e multi   1.25 .65
2357 A660 140e multi   1.75 .90
   a.   Souvenir sheet, #2354-2357   4.50 2.40
          Nos. 2354-2357 (4)   4.70 2.40
   Lubrapex 2000 (#2357a). See Brazil No. 2738.

Europa, 2000
Common Design Type
2000, May 9   Perf. 11¾x12
2358 CD17 100e multi   1.25 .65
   a.   Souvenir sheet of 3   3.75 3.75

Visit of Pope John Paul II A661

2000, May 12   Perf. 12x11¾
2359 A661 52e multi   1.00 .40

Intl. Cycling Union, Cent. and The Stamp Show 2000, London A662

Bicycles: 52e, Draisenne, 1817. 85e, Michaux, 1868. 100e, Ariel, 1871. 140e, Rover, 1888. 215e, BTX, 2000. 350e, GT, 2000.

2000, May 22
2360 A662 52e multi   .60   .30
2361 A662 85e multi   1.10 .55
2362 A662 100e multi   1.25 .65
2363 A662 140e multi   1.75 .90
2364 A662 215e multi   2.75 1.40
2365 A662 350e multi   4.50 2.25
   a.   Souvenir sheet, #2360-2365   12.00 12.00
          Nos. 2360-2365 (6)   11.95 6.05

Desserts Type of 1999
Designs: 52e, Fatias de Tomar. 85e, Dom rodrigos. 100e, Sericaia. 140e, Pao-de-ló. 215e, Pao de rala. 350e, Bolo real paraíso.
2000, May 30
2366 A648 52e multi   .60   .30
2367 A648 85e multi   1.10 .55
2368 A648 100e multi   1.25 .65
2369 A648 140e multi   1.75 .90
2370 A648 215e multi   2.75 1.40
2371 A648 350e multi   4.50 2.25
          Nos. 2366-2371 (6)   11.95 6.05

Fishermen's Day — A663

2000, May 31
2372 A663 52e multi   .70   .35

Expo 2000, Hanover — A664

Designs: 100e, Portuguese landscapes. 350e, Portuguese pavilion.
2000, June 1
2373 A664 100e multi   1.25 .65
Souvenir Sheet
2374 A664 350e multi   4.25 4.25
No. 2374 contains one 40x31mm stamp.

Constituent Assembly, 25th Anniv. A665

2000, June 2
2375 A665 85e multi   1.10 .55

Cod Fishing A666

Cod, various fishermen and boats.

2000, June 24   Perf. 12x11¾
Color of Denominations
2376 A666 52e rose   .55   .30
2377 A666 85e claret   .90   .45
2378 A666 100e green   1.10 .55
2379 A666 100e red   1.10 .55

2380 A666 140e yellow   1.50 .75
2381 A666 215e brown   2.50 1.25
   a.   Souvenir sheet, #2376-2381   8.00 8.00
          Nos. 2376-2381 (6)   7.65 3.85

Eça de Queiroz (1845-1900), Writer — A667

2000, Aug. 16   Litho.   Perf. 12x11¾
2382 A667 85e multi   1.10 .55

2000 Summer Olympics, Sydney A668

Designs: 52e, Runner. 85e, Show jumping. 100e, Yachting. 140e, Diving.
No. 2387: a, 85e, Fencing. b, 215e, Beach volleyball.
2000, Sept. 15
2383-2386 A668 Set of 4   4.25 2.10
Souvenir Sheet
2387 A668 Sheet of 2, #a-b   3.75 3.75
Olymphilex 2000, Sydney (No. 2387).

Snoopy A669

Snoopy: No. 2388, 52e, At computer on dog house. No. 2389, 52e, Mailing letter. 85e, Driving mail truck. 100e, At letter sorting machine. 140e, Delivering mail. 215e, Reading letter.
2000, Oct. 6
2388-2393 A669 Set of 6   7.75 3.75
2393a   Souvenir sheet, #2288-2393   7.75 7.75

Lisbon Geographic Society, 125th Anniv. — A670

No. 2394: a, 85e, African native, geographer, theodolite, sextant. b, 100e, Sextant, society emblem, map, zebras.
2000, Nov. 10
2394 A670 Horiz. pair, #a-b   2.25 1.10

Famous People — A671

No. 2395: a, Carolina Michaelis de Vasconcellos (1851-1925), teacher. b, Miguel Bombarda (1851-1910), doctor, politician. c, Bernardino Machado (1851-1944), politician. d, Tomás Alcaide (1901-67), singer. e, José Régio (1901-69), writer. f, José Rodrigues Miguéis (1901-80), writer. g, Vitorino Nemésio

(1901-78), writer. h, Bento de Jesus Caraça (1901-48), mathematician.

2001, Feb. 20   **Litho.**   ***Perf. 12x11¾***
2395 A671   Sheet of 8 + 4 labels   8.00   8.00
a.-h.   85e Any single   1.00   .55

World Indoor Track and Field
Championships — A672

Designs: 85e, Runners. 90e, Pole vault. 105e, Shot put. 250e, High jump.

2001, Mar. 1
2396-2399 A672   Set of 4   6.00   3.00
Souvenir Sheet
2400 A672 350e Hurdles   4.25   2.10

Bird Type of 2000 and

A672a

Designs: 53e, Sisao. No. 2402, Caimao. 105e, Perdiz-do-mar. 140e, Peneireiro cinzento. 225e, Abutre do Egipto.

2001, Mar. 6   **Litho.**   ***Perf. 11¾x11½***
2401   A658   53e multi   .65   .35
2402   A658   85e multi   1.10   .55
2403   A658   105e multi   1.25   .65
2404   A658   140e multi   1.75   .90
2405   A658   225e multi   2.75   1.40
   Nos. 2401-2405 (5)   7.50   3.85
Serpentine Die Cut 11½x12
Self-Adhesive
2406   A658   53e multi   .65   .35
a.   Booklet of 10   6.50
2406B A672a   85e shown   1.10   .55
2407   A658   105e multi   1.25   .65
a.   Booklet of 10   12.50

Arab Heritage in Portugal
A673

Designs: 53e, Plate with ship design, 15th cent. 90e, Tiles, 16th cent. 105e, Tombstone, 14th cent. 140e, Gold dinar, 12th cent. 225e, container, 11th cent. 350e, Ceramic jug, 12th-13th cent.

2001, Mar. 28   **Litho.**   ***Perf. 12x11¾***
2408-2413 A673   Set of 6   12.00   6.00

Stampin' the Future Children's Stamp Design Contest Winners
A674

Art by: 85e, Angela M. Lopes. 90e, Maria G. Silva, vert. 105e, Joao A. Ferreira.

Perf. 12x11¾, 11¾x12
2001, Apr. 10   **Litho.**
2414-2416 A674   Set of 3   3.50   1.75

Natl. Fine Arts Society, Cent.
A675

Designs: 85e, Sculpture, building, stained glass window. 105e, Artist, painting. 350p, Hen and Chicks, by Girao.

2001, Apr. 19   ***Perf. 12x11¾***
2417-2418 A675   Set of 2   2.40   1.25
Souvenir Sheet
2419 A675 350e multi   4.25   4.25

Constitution, 25th Anniv. — A676

2001, Apr. 25
2420 A676 85e multi   1.10   .55

Europa
A677

2001, May 9
2421 A677 105e multi   1.25   .65
a.   Souvenir sheet of 3   3.75   3.75

Congratulations
A678

Designs: No. 2422, 85e, Couple, hearts. No. 2423, 85e, Birthday cake. No. 2424, 85e, Drinks. No. 2425, 85e, Flowers.

2001, May 16   ***Perf. 11¾x12***
2422-2425 A678   Set of 4   4.00   2.00
2425a   Souvenir sheet, #2422-2425   4.00   4.00

Porto, European City of Culture
A679

Bridge and: 53e, Open book. 85e, Globe, binary code. 105e, Piano. 140e, Stage curtain. 225e, Picture frame. 350e, Fireworks.

2001, May 23   ***Perf. 12x11¾***
2426-2431 A679   Set of 6   11.00   5.50
2431a   Souvenir sheet, #2426-2431   11.00   11.00

Military Museum, 150th Anniv.
A680

Designs: 85e, Shell, 1773. 105e, Suit of armor, 16th cent.
No. 2434: a, 53e, Pistol of King Joseph I, 1757. b, 53e, Cannon, 1797. c, 140e, Cannon, 1533. d, 140e, Helmet, 14th-15th cent.

2001, June 7
2432-2433 A680   Set of 2   2.50   1.25
Souvenir Sheet
2434 A680   Sheet of 4, #a-d   5.00   5.00

Animals at Lisbon Zoo
A681

Designs: 53e, Bear. 85e, Monkey. 90e, Iguana. 105e, Penguin. 225e, Toucan. 350e, Giraffe.
No. 2441, vert.: a, 85e, Elephant. b, 85e, Zebra. c, 225e, Lion. d, 225e, Rhinoceros.

2001, June 11   ***Perf. 12x11¾***
2435-2440 A681   Set of 6   11.00   5.50
Souvenir Sheet
2441 A681   Sheet of 4, #a-d   7.50   7.50
Belgica 2001 Intl. Stamp Exhibition, Brussels (#2441).

2001 Lions Intl. European Forum
A682

2001, Sept. 6   **Litho.**   ***Perf. 12x11¾***
2442 A682 85e multi   1.10   .55

Pillars
A683

No. 2443: a, Azinhoso. b, Soajo. c, Bragança. d, Linhares. e, Arcos de Valdevez. f, Vila de Rua. g, Sernancelhe. h, Frechas.

2001, Sept. 19
2443   Block of 8   4.50   2.25
a.-h.   A683 53e Any single   .65   .35

Year of Dialogue Among Civilizations
A684

2001, Oct. 9
2444 A684 140e multi   1.60   .80

Walt Disney (1901-66)
A685

Designs: No. 2445, Disney and sketches.
No. 2446 — Various tiles and: a, Huey, Dewey and Louie. b, Mickey Mouse. c, Minnie Mouse. d, Goofy. e, Pluto. f, Donald Duck. g, Scrooge McDuck. h, Daisy Duck.

2001, Oct. 18   **Litho.**   ***Perf. 12x11¾***
2445 A685 53e multi   .70   .35
Souvenir Sheet
2446   Sheet of 9, #a-h, 2445   6.25   6.25
a.-h.   A685 53e Any single   .65   .35

Security Services, 200th Anniv.
A686

Designs: 53e, Royal police guards, Lisbon, 1801. 85e, Municipal guard, Lisbon, 1834.

90e, National infantry guard, 1911. 105e, National cavalry guard, 1911. 140e, Transit brigade guard, 1970. 350e, Fiscal brigade guard, 1993.
225e, National cavalry guard, 1911, diff.

2001, Oct. 22
2447-2452 A686   Set of 6   10.00   5.00
Souvenir sheet
2453 A686 225e multi   2.50   2.50

Sailing Ships — A687

No. 2454: a, Chinese junk, 13th cent. b, Portuguese caravel, 15th cent.

2001, Nov. 8
2454 A687 53e Horiz. pair, #a-b   1.25   1.25
See People's Republic of China No. 3146.

100 Cents = 1 Euro (€)

Introduction of the Euro
A688

2002, Jan. 2   **Litho.**   ***Perf. 12x11¾***
2455 A688   1c   1c coin   .25   .25
2456 A688   2c   2c coin   .25   .25
2457 A688   5c   5c coin   .25   .25
2458 A688   10c   10c coin   .25   .25
2459 A688   20c   20c coin   .50   .25
2460 A688   50c   50c coin   1.00   .50
2461 A688   €1   €1 coin   2.25   1.25
2462 A688   €2   €2 coin   4.50   2.25
   Nos. 2455-2462 (8)   9.25   5.25

Postrider
A689

2002, Jan. 2   ***Perf. 13¼***
2463 A689 A multi   .85   .40
No. 2463 sold for 28c on day of issue.

Damiao de Góis (1502-74), Diplomat and Historian — A690

2002, Feb. 26   ***Perf. 12x11¾***
2464 A690 45c multi   1.10   .55

Bird Type of 2000 with Euro Denominations Only and

A690a

Designs: 2c, Abelharuco. No. 2466, 28c, Andorinha do mar ana. No. 2467, 43c, Bufo real. No. 2468, 54c, Cortiçol de barriga branca. 60c, Noitibó de nuca vermelha. 70c, Cuco rabilongo. Nos. 2472A, 28c, Cuco-rabilongo. No. 2471A, 43c, Andorinha do mar ana. Nos. 2472, 2473, 54c, Bufo real.

2002, Feb. 26   ***Perf. 11¾x11½***
2465 A658   2c multi   .25   .25
2466 A658   28c multi   .60   .30
2467 A658   43c multi   .90   .45
2468 A658   54c multi   1.20   .60
2469 A658   60c multi   1.40   .70
2470 A658   70c multi   1.60   .80

Serpentine Die Cut 11½x12, 11x11½ (#2471A)

2471	A658	28c multi	.75	.35
2471A	A690a	43c multi	1.00	.50
2472	A658	54c multi	1.40	.70

Booklet Stamps
Serpentine Die Cut 11¼x11

2472A	A658	28c multi	.75	.35
b.		Booklet pane of 10	7.50	
2473	A658	54c multi	1.20	.60
a.		Booklet pane of 10	12.00	
	Nos. 2465-2473 (11)		11.05	5.60

No. 2472A has thicker numerals than No. 2471. No. 2473 lacks dot between "bufo" and "real" found on No. 2472. No. 2472A lacks dot between "cuco" and "rebilongo" found on No. 2471.

Pedro Nunes (1502-78), Mathematician and Geographer — A691

Designs: No. 2474, 28c, Ship. Earth. No. 2475, 28c, Ship, sextant. €1.15, Nunes.

2002, Mar. 6   **Perf. 12x11¾**

2474-2476	A691	Set of 3	3.50	1.75
2476a		Souvenir sheet, #2474-2476	4.50	4.50

America Issue — Youth, Education and Literacy A692

Children and: No. 2477, 70c, Flower. No. 2478, 70c, Pencil. No. 2479, 70c, Book.

2002, Mar. 12

2477-2479	A692	Set of 3	5.00	2.50

Astronomy A693

Designs: No. 2480, 28c, Nobres College, 16th cent. astrolabe, solar eclipse. No. 2481, Polytechnic Observatory, Lisbon, telescope, Jupiter. 43c, Coimbra Observatory, quadrant, stars. No. 2483, 45c, King Pedro V, telescope, sun. No. 2484, 45c, King Luis, Cassegrain telescope, comet. 54c, Ajuda Observatory, telescope, Moon. €1.15, Porto Observatory Cassegrain telescope, Saturn. €1.75 Projector of C. Gulbenkian Planetarium, planets.
No. 2488: a, 18th cent. armillary sphere. b, 19th cent. theodolite.

2002, Apr. 23   **Litho.**   **Perf. 12x11¾**

2480-2487	A693	Set of 8	12.00	6.00

Souvenir Sheet

2488	A693	70c Sheet of 2, #a-b	3.50	3.00

Grande Oriente Lusitano Masonic Organization, Bicent. — A694

2002, May 9

2489	A694	43c multi	1.10	.55

Europa A695

2002, May 9

2490	A695	54c multi	1.20	.70
a.		Souvenir sheet of 3, perf. 12½	3.75	3.75

Portuguese Air Force, 50th Anniv. A696

Designs: 28c, F-16. 43c, SA-300 Puma helicopter. 54c, A-Jet. 70c, C-130. €1.25, P-3P.
No. 2496, €1.75, Fiat G91.
No. 2497: a, €1.15, Asas de Portugal. b, €1.75, Epsilon.

2002, July 1   **Litho.**   **Perf. 12x11¾**

2491-2496	A696	Set of 6	12.00	6.00

Souvenir Sheet

2497	A696	Sheet of 2, #a-b	7.00	7.00

Sports A697

Designs: No. 2498, 28c, Race walking. No. 2499, 28c, Gymnastics. No. 2500, 45c, Basketball. No. 2501, 45c, Handball. No. 2502, 54c, Fencing. No. 2503, 54c, Women's roller hockey. No. 2504, €1.75, Golf. No. 2505, €1.75, Soccer.
No. 2506: a, €1, Soccer players. b, €2, Soccer players, diff.

2002, Aug. 2

2498-2505	A697	Set of 8	14.00	7.00

Souvenir Sheet

2506	A697	Sheet of 2, #a-b	7.00	7.00

Portuguese Gymnastics Federation, 50th anniv. (#2499), World Fencing Championships (#2502), 6th Women's Roller Hockey Championships (#2503), 2002 World Cup Soccer Championships, Japan and Korea (#2505-2506), PhilaKorea 2002 World Stamp Exhibition (#2506).

13th World Economics Congress A698

2002, Sept. 9

2507	A698	70c multi	1.60	.80

Ministry of Public Works, 150th Anniv. — A699

Designs: No. 2508, Anniversary emblem. No. 2509: a, Port administration. b, Rail transportation. c, Air transportation. d, Infrastructure. e, Public buildings. f, Housing.

2002, Sept. 30   **Litho.**   **Perf. 12x12½**

2508	A699	43c shown	1.00	.50

Miniature Sheet

2509		Sheet of 6	6.50	6.50
a.-f.		A699 43c Any single	1.00	.85

Technical Education in Portugal, 150th Anniv. A700

2002, Oct. 9   **Perf. 12x11¾**

2510	A700	43c multi	1.10	.55

UNESCO World Heritage Sites — A701

Various views of: No. 2511, 28c, No. 2518, 70c, No. 2519, €1.25, Alcobaça Monastery. No. 2512, 28c, No. 2517, 70c, No. 2520, €1.25, Monastery of the Hieronymites. No. 2513, 43c, No. 2516, 54c, No. 2521, €1.25, Historic Center of Guimaraes. No. 2514, 43c, No. 2515, 54c, No. 2522, €1.25, Alto Douro Wine Region.

2002, Nov. 7   **Perf. 11¾x12, 12x11¾**

2511-2518	A701	Set of 8	10.00	5.00

Souvenir Sheets

2519-2522	A701	Set of 4	12.00	12.00

Size of Nos. 2515-2518: 80x30mm.

Portuguese Military College, Bicent. — A702

Military uniforms from: 20c, 1870. 30c, 1806. 43c, 1837. 55c, 1861. 70c, 1866. €2, 1912.
No. 2529: a, 1802. b, 1948.

2003, Feb. 22   **Litho.**   **Perf. 11¾x12**

2523-2528	A702	Set of 6	10.00	4.50

Souvenir Sheet

2529	A702	€1 Sheet of 2, #a-b	4.50	4.50

Bird Type of 2000 With Euro Denominations Only and

A703

Designs: 1c, Peto verde. 30c, Pombo das rochas. 43c, Melro azul. 55c, Toutinegra carrasqueira. 70c, Chasco ruivo.

2003, Mar. 7   **Perf. 11¾x11½**

2530	A658	1c multi	.25	.25
2531	A658	30c multi	.60	.30
2532	A658	43c multi	.85	.45
2533	A658	55c multi	1.10	.60
2534	A658	70c multi	1.50	.75

Self-Adhesive
Serpentine Die Cut 11¾
With Dots Between Words

2535	A658	30c multi	.60	.30
2536	A703	43c multi	.85	.45
2537	A658	55c multi	1.10	.60
	Nos. 2530-2537 (8)		6.85	3.70

Coil Stamp
Self-Adhesive
Without Dots Between Words

2537A	A658	30c multi	1.60	.60

Position of country name is at UL on No. 2531 but at LR on No. 2535; UR on No. 2533 but LL on No. 2537.
Nos. 2535-2537 have dots between the words in the bird's name. Two other stamps exist in this set. The editors would like to examine any examples.

European Year of Disabled People — A704

Crowd of people in design of: 30c, Person in wheelchair. 55c, Head with blue brain. 70c, Head with pink ear, eye and mouth.

2003, Mar. 12   **Perf. 13¼**

2538-2540	A704	Set of 3	3.50	1.75

Portuguese Postage Stamps, 150th Anniv. A705

Designs: 30c, #1. 43c, #2. 55c, #3. 70c, #4.

2003, Mar. 13   **Perf. 12x11¾**

2541-2544	A705	Set of 4	4.25	2.10

See No. 2578.

Orchids — A706

Designs: No. 2545, 46c, Aceras anthropophorum. No. 2546, 46c, Dactylorhiza maculata.
No. 2547, 30c: a, Orchis champagneuxii. b, Orchis morio. c, Serapias cordigera. d, Orchis coriophora. e, Ophrys bombyliflora. f, Ophrys vernixia. g, Ophrys speculum. h, Ophrys scolopax. i, Anacamptis pyramidalis.
No. 2548, 30c: a, Orchis italica. b, Ophrys tenthredinifera. c, Ophrys fusca fusca. d, Orchis papilionacea. e, Barlia robertiana. f, Ophrys lutea. g, Ophrys fusca. h, Ophrys apifera. i, Dactylorhiza ericetorum.

2003, Apr. 29   **Litho.**   **Perf. 11¾x12**

2545-2546	A706	Set of 2	2.40	1.10

Sheets of 9, #a-i

2547-2548	A706	Set of 2	12.00	12.00

Europa A707

Poster art by: No. 2549, 55c, Fred Kradolfer, 1931. No. 2550, 55c, Joao Machado, 1997.

2003, May 5   **Perf. 12x12½**

2549-2550	A707	Set of 2	2.50	1.25
2550a		Souvenir sheet, #2549-2550	2.50	2.00

History of Law A708

Designs: 30c, Lawyer in black robe, lawyer in red robe, order of Portuguese lawyers. 43c, Two lawyers in black robes, national arms. 55c, Lawyer, bishop, manuscript. 70c, Lawyer in black robe, order of Portuguese lawyers, diff.

No. 2555: a, €1, Lawyer in red robe, left half of order of Portuguese lawyers. b, €2, Right half of order of Portuguese lawyers, bishop.

2003, May 13　　　**Perf. 12x11¾**
2551-2554　A708　Set of 4　　4.50 2.40
Souvenir Sheet
2555　A708　Sheet of 2, #a-b　6.50 6.50

Traveling Exhibition on the 150th Anniv. of the First Portuguese Stamp A709

Exhibition stops: No. 2556, Viseu. No. 2557, Faro. No. 2558, Porto.

2003　　　**Perf. 14x13½**
Background Color
2556　A709　30c yellow　　.75　.35
2557　A709　30c white　　.75　.35
2558　A709　30c blue　　.75　.35
　Nos. 2556-2558 (3)　2.25 1.05
Issued: No. 2556, 5/23; No. 2557, 7/21.

2004 European Soccer Championships, Portugal — A710

Emblem with background color of: 30c, White. 43c, Dark blue. 47c, Brown carmine. 55c, Green. 70c, Brown orange.
No. 2564 — Emblem and quadrant of emblem with denomination at: a, LL. b, LR. c, UL. d, UR.

2003, May 28　　**Litho.**　**Perf. 14x13½**
2559-2563　A710　Set of 5　　6.00 2.75
Souvenir Sheet
2564　A710　Sheet of 4　　5.50 5.50
　a.-d.　55c Any single　1.25 1.25
　e.　Souvenir sheet, #2559-2563, 2564a-2564d　12.00 12.00

Portuguese Automobile Club, Cent. A711

Emblems and: 30c, Driver in old automobile. 43c, Motorcyclist. €2, Driver in old automobile, blurred race car.

2003, June 24　　　**Perf. 12x11¾**
2565-2567　A711　Set of 3　　6.00 3.50

Ricardo do Espírito Santo Silva Foundation, 50th Anniv. — A712

Designs: No. 2568, 30c, Portrait of Ricardo do Espírito Santo Silva, by Eduardo Malta. No. 2569, 30c, Chess table, 18th cent. No. 2570, 43c, Cutlery in decorated case, c. 1720-1750. No. 2571, 43c, Salver, 15th cent. No. 2572, 55c, Chinese cutlery case, c, 1700-1722. No. 2573, 55c, Wooden tub, 18th cent.
No. 2574: a, €1, Chest with drawers, 17th cent. b, €2, Carpet, 18th cent.

2003, July 9　　　**Perf. 11¾x12**
2568-2573　A712　Set of 6　　5.50 3.00
Souvenir Sheet
2574　A712　Sheet of 2, #a-b　7.00 7.00

Experimental Design — A713

No. 2575: a, 2 lobes, black "EXD," white denomination circle to right. b, 3 lobes, black "EXD," white denomination circle below and to left. c, 3 lobes, black "EXD," white denomination circle above. d, 2 lobes, black "EXD," white denomination circle to left. e, 2 lobes, red "EXD," black denomination circle to right. f, 3 lobes, red "EXD," black denomination circle above. g, 3 lobes, red "EXD," black denomination circle below and to right. h, 2 lobes, red "EXD," black denomination circle to left. i, 2 lobes, red "EXD," white denomination circle to right. j, 3 lobes, red "EXD," white denomination circle below and to left. k, 3 lobes, red "EXD," white denomination circle above. l, 2 lobes, red "EXD," white denomination circle to left.

Serpentine Die Cut
2003, Sept. 17　　　**Litho.**
Self-Adhesive
2575　A713　Sheet of 12　12.00 12.00
　a.-d.　30c Any single　.65　.35
　e.-h.　43c Any single　1.00　.50
　i.-l.　55c Any single　1.20　.60

Souvenir Sheet

Portuguese Stamps, 150th Anniv. — A714

Litho. & Embossed
2003, Sept. 19　　　**Perf. 12x11¾**
2576　A714　€3 Queen Maria II, Type A2　　7.00 7.00

Souvenir Sheet

Francisco de Borja Freire (1790-1869), Designer and Engraver of First Portuguese Stamp — A715

Litho. With Hologram Applied
2003, Sept. 23　　　**Perf. 12x12½**
2577　A715　€2.50 multi　　6.00 6.00

Souvenir Sheet

Lubrapex 2003 Philatelic Exhibition, Lisbon — A716

2003, Sept. 25　Litho.　Perf. 12x11¾
2578　A716　Sheet, #2578a, 4　
　　#2541　　4.00 4.00
　a.　30c Queen Maria II　1.00 1.00
　Size of No. 2578a: 40x60mm.

Fountains A717

Designs: 30c, Sao Joao Fountain, Moucós. 43c, Fountain of Virtues, Porto. 55c, Giraldo Square Fountain, Evora. 70c, Blessed Woman Fountain, Sao Marcos de Tavira. €1, Town Fountain, Castelo de Vide. €2, Santo André Fountain, Guarda.

2003, Oct. 1　　　**Perf. 12x11¾**
2579-2584　A717　Set of 6　11.00 6.00

Glass — A718

Designs: 30c, Glass of King José I, 18th cent. 55c, Glass of Queen Maria II, 19th cent. 70c, Glass by Carmo Valente, 20th cent. €2, Glass by M. Helena Matos, 20th cent.
€1.50, Stained glass by Fernando Santos, 19th cent.

2003, Oct. 9　　　**Perf. 11¾x12**
2585-2588　A718　Set of 4　　8.00 4.25
Souvenir Sheet
2589　A718　€1.50 multi　　3.50 3.50

Apothecary Items A719

Designs: 30c, Persian jar, 12th-13th cent., Roman Empire medicine dropper, 1st-2nd cent. 43c, Bottle and bowl, 17th cent. 55c, Mortars and pestle, 16th and 17th cent. 70c, Alembic, 1910, and flask, 1890-1930.

2003, Oct. 23　　　**Perf. 12x11¾**
2590-2593　A719　Set of 4　　4.50 2.40

Portuguese Design A720

Designs: No. 2594, 43c, Secretary, by Daciano da Costa, 1962. No. 2595, 43c, Chair, by António Garcia, 1970, vert. No. 2596, 43c, Drawing table, by José Espinho, 1970. No. 2597, 43c, Chairs by Leonor and

António Sena da Silva, 1973. No. 2598, 43c, Telephone booth, by Pedro Silva Dias, 1998, vert. No. 2599, 43c, Cutlery, by Eduardo Afonsa Dias, 1976. No. 2600, 43c, Faucet, by Carlos Aguiar, 1998. No. 2601, 43c, Thermos bottle, by Carlos Rocha, 1982, vert. No. 2602, 43c, Tea cart, by Cruz de Carvalho, 1957.

2003, Oct. 31　Perf. 12x11¾, 11¾x12
2594-2602　A720　Set of 9　11.00 4.50

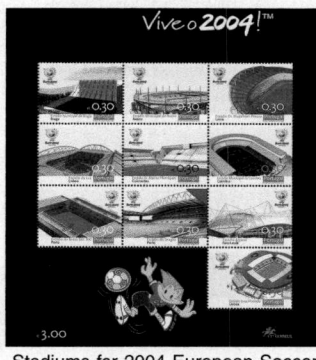

Stadiums for 2004 European Soccer Championships — A721

No. 2603: a, Braga Municipal Stadium, Braga. b, Aveiro Municpal Stadium, Aveiro. c, Dr. Magalhaes Pessoa Stadium, Leiria. d, Luz Stadium, Lisbon. e, D. Afonso Henriques Stadium, Guimaraes. f, Coimbra Municipal Stadium, Coimbra. g, Bessa 21st Century Stadium, Porto. h, Dragao Stadium, Porto. i, Algarve Stadium, Faro-Loulé. j, José Alvalade Stadium, Lisbon.

2003, Nov. 28　Litho.　Perf. 14x13½
2603　A721　Sheet of 10　　7.00 7.00
　a.-j.　30c Any single　　.65　.55

Souvenir Sheet

Coin Commemorating 150th Anniv. of First Portuguese Stamps, Bust and Portrait of Queen Maria II — A722

2003, Dec. 12　　　**Perf. 12**
2604　A722　€1 multi　　2.40 2.40

Mascot of 2004 European Soccer Championships — A723

Mascot and: 45c, CorreioAzul emblem. €1.75, Priority air mail emblem.

Serpentine Die Cut 11½
2004, Mar. 16　　　**Litho.**
Self-Adhesive
2605　A723　45c multi　　1.00　.55
2606　A723　€1.75 multi　　4.00 2.10
　No. 2606 is airmail.

King John IV (1604-56) — A724

No. 2607 — Vila Viçosa, birthplace and: a, 45c, Head of King. b, €1, King with sword.

2004, Mar. 19   *Perf. 14x13½*
2607 A724   Horiz. pair, #a-b   3.00 1.75

Lisbon Oceanarium — A725

Designs: 30c, Phyllopteryx taeniolatus. 45c, Spheniscus magellanicus. 56c, Hypsypops rubicundus. 72c, Enhydra lutris. €1, Charcarias taurus. €2, Fratercula arctica.
€1.50, Eudyptes chysolophus, people at Oceanarium.

2004, Mar. 22
2608-2613 A725   Set of 6   11.00 6.25
Souvenir Sheet
2614 A725   €1.50 multi   3.50 3.50
No. 2614 contains one 80x30mm stamp.

2004 European Soccer Championships A726

Designs: Nos. 2615a, 2616, 10c, Foot kicking soccer ball. Nos. 2615b, 2617, 20c, Soccer ball in air. Nos. 2615c, 2618, 30c, Soccer ball on chalk line. Nos. 2615d, 2619, 50c, Soccer ball, corner of goal.

2004, Mar. 30   *Perf.*
Souvenir Sheet
2615 A726   Sheet of 4, #a-d   3.25 3.25
Self-Adhesive
Serpentine Die Cut
2616-2619 A726   Set of 4   2.40 1.40
No. 2615 contains four 24mm diameter stamps.

Flags of Countries in 2004 European Soccer Championships and Mascot — A727

No. 2620: a, Portugal. b, France. c, Sweden. d, Czech Republic. e, Greece. f, England. g, Bulgaria. h, Latvia. i, Spain. j, Switzerland. k, Denmark. l, Germany. m, Russia. n, Croatia. o, Italy. p, Netherlands.

2004, Apr. 6   *Perf. 13x13¼*
2620 A727   Sheet of 16   12.00 12.00
a.-p.   30c Any single   .75 .40

Bird Type of 2000 With Euro Denominations Only and

Andorinha Daurica — A728

Designs: 30c, Cruza bico comun. No. 2622, Andorinha daurica, diff. 56c, Papa figos. 58c, Cotovia montesina. 72c, Chapim de poupa.

2004, Apr. 15   *Perf. 11¾x11½*
2621 A658 30c multi   .65 .35
2622 A658 45c multi   .95 .55
2623 A658 56c multi   1.20 .65
2624 A658 58c multi   1.25 .70
2625 A658 72c multi   1.60 .85
Self-Adhesive
Size: 26x21mm (#2626, 2628)
Serpentine Die Cut 11½, 11½x11¾
(#2627)
2626 A658 30c multi   .65 .35
2627 A728 45c multi   .95 .55
2628 A658 56c multi   1.20 .65
  Nos. 2621-2628 (8)   8.45 4.65

Landmarks in Host Cities of 2004 European Soccer Championships and Players — A729

Host city: No. 2629, 30c, Aveiro. No. 2630, 30c, Braga. No. 2631, 30c, Coimbra. No. 2632, 30c, Faro-Loulé. No. 2633, 30c, Guimaraes. No. 2634, 30c, Leiria. No. 2635, 30c, Lisbon. No. 2636, 30c, Porto.

2004, Apr. 20   *Perf. 14x13¼*
2629-2636 A729   Set of 8   5.50 3.00

Coup of Apr. 25, 1974, 30th Anniv. — A730

2004, Apr. 25   *Perf. 13¼x13*
2637 A730 45c multi   1.10 .55

Stadiums for 2004 European Soccer Championships — A731

Designs: No. 2638, 30c, Aveiro Municipal Stadium, Aveiro. No. 2639, 30c, Braga Municipal Stadium, Braga. No. 2640, 30c, Coimbra Municipal Stadium, Coimbra. No. 2641, 30c, D. Afonso Henriques Stadium, Guimaraes. No. 2642, 30c, Algarve Stadium, Faro-Loulé. No. 2643, 30c, Dr. Magalhaes Pessoa Stadium, Leiria. No. 2644, 30c, José Alvalade Stadium, Lisbon. No. 2645, 30c, Luz Stadium, Lisbon. No. 2646, 30c, Bessa 21st Century Stadium, Porto. No. 2647, 30c, Dragao Stadium, Porto.

2004, Apr. 28   *Perf. 14x13¼*
2638-2647 A731   Set of 10   7.00 3.50

2004 European Parliament Elections A732

2004, May 3
2648 A732 30c multi   .85 .35

Expansion of the European Union — A733

Designs: 56c, Flags of newly-added nations, stars. €2, Flags of newly-added nations, flags of previous members.

2004, May 3   *Litho.*
2649 A733 56c multi   1.40 .65
Souvenir Sheet
2650 A733 €2 multi   4.50 4.50

Europa — A734

Designs: No. 2651, 56c, Woman looking at painting. No. 2652, 56c, Vacationer with gear on beach.

2004, May 10   *Perf. 13¼x14*
2651-2652 A734   Set of 2   2.50 1.40
2652a   Souvenir sheet, #2651-2652   2.50 2.50

First Telephone Line Between Lisbon and Porto, Cent. — A735

Designs: 30c, Old telephone. 45c, Telephone pole. 56c, Fiber-optic cables. 72c, Picture phone.
No. 2657: a, Old telephone, diff. b, Like 72c.

2004, May 17
2653-2656 A735   Set of 4   4.50 2.50
Souvenir Sheet
2657 A735   €1 Sheet of 2, #a-b   4.50 4.50

Jewish Heritage of Portugal — A736

Designs: 30c, Mishnah Torah of Maimonides, British Library. 45c, Star of David with lion, Cervera Bible, National Library. 56c, Menorah, Cervera Bible, National Library. 72c, Menorah carved on rock, Mértola Museum. €1, Abravanel Bible, Coimbra University Library. €2, Statue of prophet, Christ Convent, Tomar.
€1.50, Interior of Shaare Tikva Synagogue.

2004, May 20
2658-2663 A736   Set of 6   11.00 6.00
Souvenir Sheet
2664 A736   €1.50 multi   3.50 3.50
  Shaare Tikva Synagogue, Cent.

Souvenir Sheet

Final Match of 2004 European Soccer Championships — A737

2004, May 27   *Perf. 13¼x13*
2665 A737 €1 multi   2.25 2.25

Portuguese Philatelic Federation, 50th Anniv. — A738

Designs: 30c, Anniversary emblem, #761, 2652. €1.50, Handstamp and letter.

2004, June 18   *Perf. 14x13¼*
2666 A738 30c multi   .85 .35
Souvenir Sheet
2667 A738 €1.50 multi   3.50 3.50

Souvenir Sheet

UEFA (European Football Union), 50th Anniv. — A739

2004, July 29   *Litho.*   *Perf. 13x13¼*
2668 A739 €1 multi   2.40 2.40

2004 Summer Olympics, Athens A740

Designs: 30c, Hurdles. 45c, High jump.

2004, Aug. 13   *Perf. 14x13¼*
2669-2670 A740   Set of 2   1.75 .95

2004 Paralympics, Athens — A741

Designs: 30c, Swimming. 45c, Wheelchair racing. 56c, Cycling. 72c, Running.

2004, Sept. 2   *Perf. 13¼x14*
2671-2674 A741   Set of 4   4.50 2.50

Souvenir Sheet

Pedro Homem de Mello (1904-84), Poet — A742

2004, Sept. 6   **Perf. 14x13¼**
2675 A742 €2 multi   4.50 4.50

Opening of Presidential Museum — A743

Designs: 45c, Museum exterior. €1, Museum interior.

2004, Oct. 5
2676 A743 45c multi   1.10 .55
Souvenir Sheet
2677 A743 €1 multi   2.50 2.50

Comic Strips A744

Designs: 30c, Quim e Manecas, by Stuart de Carvalhais. 45c, Guarda Abília, by Júlio Pinto and Nuno Saraiva. 56c, Simao Infante, by Raul Correia and Eduardo Teixeira Coelho. 72c, A Pior Bando do Mundo, by José Carlos Fernandes.
No. 2682: a, O Espiao Acácio, by Relvas. b, Jim del Monaco, by Louro and Simoes. c, Tomahawk Tom, by Vitor Péon. d, Pitanga, by Arlindo Fagundes.

2004, Oct. 8
2678-2681 A744 Set of 4   5.00 2.50
Souvenir Sheet
2682 A744 50c Sheet of 4, #a-d   5.00 5.00

Viticulture A745

Designs: 30c, Sarcophagus depicting seasonal scenes, detail of mosaic of Autumn, 3rd cent. 45c, Detail of mosaic of Autumn, Apocalypse of Lorvao, 12th cent. 56c, Lorvao Missal illustration, 14th cent., detail of illustration from Book of Hours, by D. Fernando, 15th-16th cent. 72c, Detail of illustration from Book of Hours, detail of Group of the Lion, Columbano, 19th cent. €1, Detail of Group of the Lion, stained glass window, by Lino António, 20th cent.
No. 2688: a, Grapes, harvester. b, Harvester, wine jugs. c, Winery. d, Wine barrels, bottles and glasses.

2004, Oct. 15
2683-2687 A745 Set of 5   7.50 3.75
Souvenir Sheet
2688 A745 50c Sheet of 4, #a-d   5.00 5.00

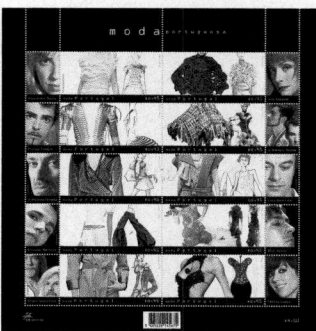

Women's Fashion — A746

No. 2689 — Clothing designed by: a, Alexandra Moura. b, Ana Salazar. c, Filipe Faisca. d, J. Branco and L. Sanchez. e, J. António Tenente. f, Luís Buchinho. g, Osvaldo Martins. h, Dino Alves. i, Alves and Gonçalves. j, Fátima Lopes. Designers names and pictures are on labels adjacent to stamps showing their clothing.

2004, Nov. 10   **Perf. 13¾x14¼**
2689 A746 45c Sheet of 10 +   11.00 11.00
10 labels

Christmas A747

Paintings: 30c, Adoration of the Magi, attributed to Jorge Afonso. 45c, Adoration of the Magi, by Flemish School. 56c, Flight into Egypt, by Francisco Vieira. 72c, Nativity, by Portuguese School.
€3, Nativity, by Josefa de Obidos.

2004, Nov. 19   **Perf. 13x13¼**
2690-2693 A747 Set of 4   4.50 2.75
Souvenir Sheet
Perf. 13½x13¼
2694 A747 €3 multi   7.00 7.00
No. 2694 contains one 50x35mm stamp.

Masks — A748

A748a

Designs: 10c, Entrudo, Lazarim. 30c Festa dos Rapazes, Salsas. 45c, Festa dos Rapazes, Salsa, different. 57c, Cardador, Vale de Ilhavo. 74c, Festa dos Rapazes, Aveleda.

Perf. 11¾x11½
2005, Feb. 17   **Litho.**
2695 A748 10c multi   .25 .25
2696 A748 30c brn red &
    multi   .65 .25
2697 A748 45c dk blue &
    multi   1.00 .60
2698 A748 57c multi   1.25 .75
2699 A748 74c multi   1.75 1.00
Nos. 2695-2699 (5)   4.90 2.85
Self-Adhesive
Serpentine Die Cut 11½, 11 (45c)
2699A A748 30c multi   .65 .40
2699B A748 45c multi   1.00 .60
2699C A748 57c multi   1.25 .75
Nos. 2699A-2699C (3)   2.90 1.75
See Nos. 2797-2799, 2827-2832. No. 2696 has denomination at left; No. 2829 has denomination at right.

Public Transportation — A749

Lines of people and: 30c, Train, front of trolley. 50c, Trolley, rear of train. 57c, Ferry, rear of trolley. €1, Rear of articulated bus, front of train. €2, Front of articulated bus, rear of train.

2005, Mar. 17   **Perf. 12x11¾**
2700-2704 A749 Set of 5   11.50 11.50

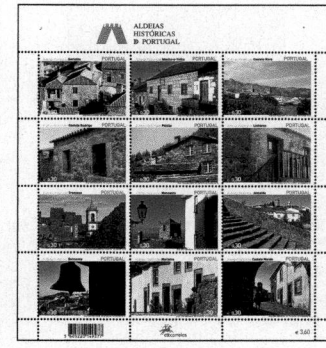

Historic Villages — A750

No. 2705: a, Sortelha. b, Idanha-a-Velha. c, Castelo Novo. d, Castelo Rodrigo. e, Piódao. f, Linhares. g, Trancoso. h, Monsanto. i, Almeida. j, Belmonte. k, Marialva. l, Castelo Mendo.

2005, Apr. 28   **Litho.**   **Perf. 14x13¼**
2705 A750 Sheet of 12   9.25 9.25
a.-l.   30c Any single   .75 .40

Paintings by José Malhoa (1855-1933) — A751

Designs: 30c, A Beira-Mar. 45c, The Pious Offerings.
€1.77, Conversation with a Neighbor.

2005, Apr. 28   **Perf. 12x11¾**
2706-2707 A751 Set of 2   1.75 1.40
Souvenir Sheet
2708 A751 €1.77 multi   4.00 4.00

Europa A752

Designs: No. 2709, Cozido à Portuguesa. No. 2710a, Bacalhau Assado com Batatas a Murro (dried cod and baked potatoes).

2005, May 5   **Perf. 14x13¼**
2709 A752 57c multi   1.50 .75
Souvenir Sheet
2710 Sheet of 2 #2710a   2.50 2.50
a. A752 57c multi   1.25 1.25

Rotary International, Cent. — A753

2005, May 20   **Perf. 12x11¾**
2711 A753 74c Paul Harris   1.75 .95
Souvenir Sheet
2712 A753 €1.75 Harris, diff.   3.75 3.75

National Coach Museum, Cent. A754

Designs: No. 2713, 30c, Porto Covo carriage, 19th cent. No. 2714, 30c, Carriage, 19th cent. No. 2715, 45c, Coach of Francisca Sabóia, 17th cent. No. 2716, 45c, Sege "Das Plumas," 18th cent. 57c, Palanquin, 18th cent. 74c, Coche Dos Oceanos, 18th cent.
€1.75, Coaches and Queen Amelia.

2005, May 23   **Perf. 14x13¼**
2713-2718 A754 Set of 6   6.00 3.00
Souvenir Sheet
2719 A754 €1.75 multi   3.75 3.75

Era of Kings Philip I to Philip III — A755

Arms and: 5c, Pegoes Aqueduct, Tomar. 30c, Chalice from Elvas Cathedral. 45c, Tile panel of cross from Christ Convent, Tomar. 57c, Fort St. John the Baptist, Angra. €1, Armada. €2, St. Vincent of Fora Church, Lisbon.
€1.20, Cross and reliquary from Lisbon Cathedral.

2005, June 7   **Perf. 11¾x12**
2720-2725 A755 Set of 6   10.00 5.00
Souvenir Sheet
2726 A755 €1.20 multi   2.50 2.50

Miniature Sheet

Caricatures — A756

No. 2727 — Caricatures by: a, Raphael Bordallo Pinheiro. b, Sebastiao Sanhudo. c, Celso Herminio. d, Leal da Camara. e, Francisco Valença. f, Stuart Carvalhais. g, Sam. h, Joao Abel Manta. i, Augusto Cid. j, António Antunes. k, Pinheiro (Zé Povinho).

2005, June 12   **Perf. 13¼x14**
2727 A756 Sheet of 11 + label 7.00 7.00
a.-k.   30c Any single   .65 .35

Souvenir Sheets

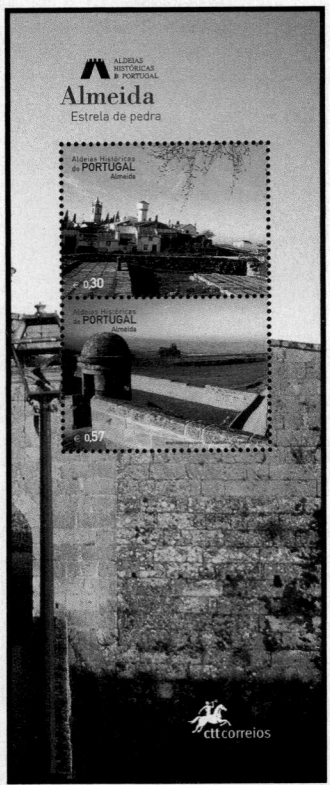

Historic Villages — A757

Various views of named villages.

2005, June 8 Litho. Perf. 14x13¼
Sheets of 2, #a-b

2728	A757	Almeida	2.25	2.25
a.		30c multi	.75	.35
b.		57c multi	1.40	.70
2729	A757	Belmonte	2.25	2.25
a.		30c multi	.75	.35
b.		57c multi	1.40	.70
2730	A757	Castelo Mendo	2.25	2.25
a.		30c multi	.75	.35
b.		57c multi	1.40	.70
2731	A757	Castelo Novo	2.25	2.25
a.		30c multi	.75	.35
b.		57c multi	1.40	.70
2732	A757	Castelo Rodrigo	2.25	2.25
a.		30c multi	.75	.35
b.		57c multi	1.40	.70
2733	A757	Idanha-a-Velha	2.25	2.25
a.		30c multi	.75	.35
b.		57c multi	1.40	.70
2734	A757	Linhares da Beira	2.25	2.25
a.		30c multi	.75	.35
b.		57c multi	1.40	.70
2735	A757	Marialva	2.25	2.25
a.		30c multi	.75	.35
b.		57c multi	1.40	.70
2736	A757	Monsanto	2.25	2.25
a.		30c multi	.75	.35
b.		57c multi	1.40	.70
2737	A757	Piodao	2.25	2.25
a.		30c multi	.75	.35
b.		57c multi	1.40	.70
2738	A757	Sortelha	2.25	2.25
a.		30c multi	.75	.35
b.		57c multi	1.40	.70
2739	A757	Trancoso	2.25	2.25
a.		30c multi	.75	.35
b.		57c multi	1.40	.70
		Nos. 2728-2739 (12)	27.00	27.00

Faro, 2005 National Cultural Capital A758

Designs: 30c, Conductor's hands and baton. 45c, Broken pot. 57c, Shell. 74c, Hands applauding.

2005, June 15
2740-2743 A758 Set of 4 4.50 2.25

Tourism A759

Various scenes from: No. 2744, 45c, Lisbon. No. 2745, 45c, Porto e Norte. No. 2746, 48c, Lisbon, diff. No. 2747, 48c, Porto e Norte, diff. No. 2748, 57c, Lisbon, diff. No. 2749, 57c, Porto e Norte, diff.

2005, July 8 Perf. 12x11¾
2744-2749 A759 Set of 6 6.50 3.25

Nature Conservation — A760

Designs: 30c, Man with hatchet inspecting tree. 45c, Forest fire prevention squad. 57c, Bird on branch, building in forest. €2, Bird on fence, large trees.

2005, Aug. 19 Perf. 12x11¾
2750-2752 A760 Set of 3 3.00 1.50
Souvenir Sheet
Perf. 12x12½
2753 A760 €2 multi 4.75 4.75

United Nations, 60th Anniv. A761

Intl. Day of Peace A762

Children at Risk A763

Intl. Year of Physics A764

2005, Sept. 21 Perf. 12x11¾

2754	A761	30c multi	.70	.35
2755	A762	45c multi	1.00	.50
2756	A763	57c multi	1.40	.70
2757	A764	74c multi	1.75	.90
		Nos. 2754-2757 (4)	4.85	2.45

Sundials — A765

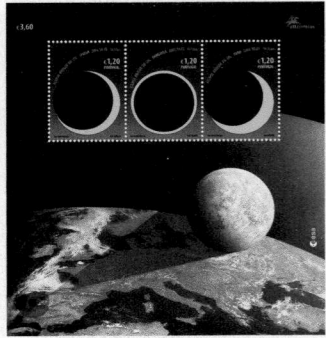

Annular Solar Eclipse, Oct. 3, 2005 — A766

Sundial from: 45c, St. John the Baptist Church, Sintra. €1, Maritime Museum, Lisbon. No. 2760 — view of eclipsed Sun from: a, Lisbon at 9:53. b, Bragança at 9:55. c, Faro at 9:55.

2005, Oct. 3 Perf. 12½x12
2758-2759 A765 Set of 2 3.25 1.60
Souvenir Sheet
Perf. 12

2760	A766	Sheet of 3	8.00	8.00
a.-c.		€1.20 multi	2.50	1.40

A767

Communications Media — A768

Designs: 30c, Press (fountain pen). 45c, Radio (microphone). 57c, Television (portable camera). 74c, Internet (globe and "@."
No. 2765: a, Press (newspaper). b, Radio (studio).
No. 2766: a, Television (studio). b, Internet (beginning of website address).

2005, Oct. 13 Perf. 12x12½
2761-2764 A767 Set of 4 4.50 1.25
Souvenir Sheets

2765	A768	Sheet of 2	6.00	6.00
a.		€1.10 multi	2.50	1.40
b.		€1.55 multi	3.50	1.90
2766	A768	Sheet of 2	6.00	6.00
a.		€1.10 multi	2.50	1.40
b.		€1.55 multi	3.50	1.90

Fishing Villages — A769

No. 2767, 30c — Aldeia da Carrasquiera, Portugal: a, Denomination at R. b, Denomination at L.
No. 2768, 30c — Tai O, Hong Kong: a, Denomination at R. b, Denomination at L.

2005, Oct. 18 Perf. 13¼x13¾
Horiz. Pairs, #a-b
2767-2768 A769 Set of 2 2.75 1.40
See Hong Kong Nos. 1160-1163.

Alvaro Cunhal (1913-2005), Communist Politician — A770

Designs: 30c, Cunhal in crowd. €1, Cunhal with young girl.

2005, Nov. 10 Perf. 12x12½
2769 A770 30c multi .75 .35
Souvenir Sheet
2770 A770 €1 multi 2.25 2.25

Serralves Foundation A771

Designs: No. 2771, 30c, White building. No. 2772, 45c, Silhouette of seated person. 48c, Red brown building entrance, diff. 57c, Sculpture of garden shovel. 74c, Person painting. No. 2776, €1, Walkway and hedges.
No. 2777: a, 30c, Red brown building entrance, horiz. b, 45c, Walkway and trees. c, 45c, Columns in building. d, 45c, Tower. e, 45c, Walkway and hedges, diff.
No. 2778: a, €1, White building, horiz. (80x30mm). b, €1, Art in gallery, horiz. (80x30mm). c, €1, Trees and lawn.

2005, Nov. 15 Perf. 13¼x14
2771-2776 A771 Set of 6 7.50 3.75
Souvenir Sheets

2777		Sheet of 5	4.50	4.50
a.	A771	30c multi	.65	.35
b.-e.	A771	45c Any single	.95	.50
		Perf. 14x13¼		
2778		Sheet of 3	6.50	6.50
a.-c.	A771	€1 Any single	2.10	1.10

Lisbon Earthquake, 250th Anniv. — A772

Designs: 45c, Fire after earthquake. €2, Victims, braced buildings. €2.65, Victims and damaged buildings.

2005, Nov. 25 Perf. 14x13¼
2779-2780 A772 Set of 2 5.25 2.75
Souvenir Sheet
2781 A772 €2.65 multi 6.25 6.25
No. 2781 contains one 40x30mm stamp.

Modernization of the Navy — A773

Designs: 45c, Navpol ship. 57c, Hydrographic ship. 74c, Ocean patrol boat and helicopter. €2, Submarine.

2005, Nov. 25 Perf. 12x12½
2782-2785 A773 Set of 4 9.00 4.50

Soccer Teams A774

Players and team emblems: No. 2786, N, Sporting Clube de Portugal. No. 2787, N, Sport Lisboa e Benfica. No. 2788, N, Futebol Clube do Porto.

No. 2789, €1, Sporting Clube de Portugal, diff. No. 2790, €1, Sport Lisboa e Benfica, diff. No. 2791, €1, Player lifting trophy, Futebol Clube do Porto.

2005, Nov. 25   *Perf. 12x12¼*
2786-2788 A774   Set of 3   2.10 1.10
Souvenir Sheets
Perf. 12x11¾
2789-2791 A774   Set of 3   6.50 6.50

Nos. 2786-2788 each sold for 30c on day of issue.

Greetings
A775

Designs: No. 2792, Parabens (birthday party). No. 2793, Amote (men and women dancing and exchanging gifts, child). No. 2794, Parabens (man, woman and two children, stork with baby). No. 2795, Parabens (conductor, cocktail party). No. 2796, Parabens (man, woman, fairy, Cupid).

2006, Feb. 7   *Perf. 12x12½*
2792 A775 N multi   .75 .35
   a.   Perf. 12 vert. (from booklet pane)   .75 .35
2793 A775 N multi   .75 .35
   a.   Perf. 12 vert. (from booklet pane)   .75 .35
2794 A775 N multi   .75 .35
   a.   Perf. 12 vert. (from booklet pane)   .75 .35
2795 A775 N multi   .75 .35
   a.   Perf. 12 vert. (from booklet pane)   .75 .35
2796 A775 N multi   .75 .35
   a.   Perf. 12 vert. (from booklet pane)   .75 .35
   b.   Booklet pane, #2792a-2796a   3.75 —
    Complete booklet, #2796b   3.75
    Nos. 2792-2796 (5)   3.75 1.75

Nos. 2792-2796 each sold for 30c on day of issue.

Masks Type of 2005
Designs: N, Like No. 2696. A, "Carnaval" Lazarim, Bragança. E, "Dia de Ano Novo" Mogadouro, Bragança.

Serpentine Die Cut 11½
2006, Mar. 1   Self-Adhesive
2797 A748 N multi   .75 .35
2798 A748 A multi   1.10 .55
2799 A748 E multi   1.40 .70
    Nos. 2797-2799 (3)   3.25 1.60

No. 2797 sold for 30c, No. 2798 sold for 45c, and No. 2799 sold for 57c on day of issue.

Water
A776

Designs: No. 2800, N, Glass of water. No. 2801, N, Water cycle. No. 2802, A, Spigot. No. 2803, A, Turbines. No. 2804, E, Sailboat. No. 2805, E, Flower.

2006, Mar. 22   **Litho.**   *Perf. 12x11¾*
2800-2805 A776   Set of 6   6.00 3.00

On the day of issue Nos. 2800-2801 each sold for 30c; Nos. 2802-2803 each sold for 45c, and Nos. 2804-2805 each sold for 57c.

St. Francis Xavier (1506-52), Missionary A777

St. Francis Xavier: 45c, Baptizing man. €1, Holding cross. €2.75, Wearing black robe.

2006, Apr. 5
2806-2807 A777   Set of 2   3.00 1.50
Souvenir Sheet
2808 A777   €2.75 multi   6.00 6.00

Europa
A778

No. 2810 — Children's drawings: a, Child in stroller. b, Four children.

2006, May 9   *Perf. 12x12½*
2809 A778 60c shown   1.60 .80
Souvenir Sheet
Perf. 12x11¾
2810 A778 60c Sheet of 2, #a-b   2.50 2.25

UEFA Under 21 Soccer Championships, Portugal — A780

2006, May 23   *Perf. 12x12½*
2816 A780 €2.75 multi   6.00 6.00

2006 World Cup Soccer Championships, Germany — A781

Silhouettes of soccer players in action: 45c, €1. €2.40, World Cup.

2006, June 7   *Perf. 12x11¾*
2817-2818 A781   Set of 2   3.75 1.90
Souvenir Sheet
2819 A781   €2.40 multi   5.25 5.25

Intl. Year of Deserts and Desertification — A782

Designs: 30c, Sand dune. 60c, Dead and living trees.

2006, June 17
2820-2821 A782   Set of 2   2.25 1.10

Roman Heritage A783

Designs: 30c, Mosaic of Oceanus. 40c, Roman temple, Evora. 50c, Patera. 60c, Two-headed sculpture. €2.40, Mosaic of seahorse.

2006, June 21
2822-2825 A783   Set of 4   4.00 2.00
Souvenir Sheet
2826 A783   €2.40 multi   5.25 5.25

Masks Type of 2005
Designs: 3c, "Carnaval" Lazarim, Viseu. 5c, "Festa dos Rapazes," Baçal, Bragança. 30c, Like #2797. 45c, Like #2798. 60c, Like #2799. 75c, "Dia dos Diablos" Vinhais, Bragança.

2006, June 29   *Perf. 11¾x11½*
2827 A748 3c multi   .25 .25
2828 A748 5c multi   .25 .25
2829 A748 30c dk red & multi   .75 .35
2830 A748 45c blue & multi   1.25 .60
2831 A748 60c multi   1.50 .75
2832 A748 75c multi   1.90 .95
    Nos. 2827-2832 (6)   5.90 3.15

No. 2829 has denomination at right. No. 2696 has denomination at left.

Wolfgang Amadeus Mozart (1756-91), Composer. A784

Mozart and: 60c, Musical score. €2.75, Handwritten text.

2006, July 7   *Perf. 12x11¾*
2833 A784 60c multi   1.25 .60
Souvenir Sheet
2834 A784 €2.75 multi   6.00 6.00

Souvenir Sheet

Community of Portuguese-speaking Countries, 10th Anniv. — A785

2006, July 12   *Perf. 12½x13*
2835 A785 €2.85 multi   6.00 6.00

Calouste Gulbenkian Foundation, 50th Anniv. — A786

Designs: 30c, Portrait of a Young Woman by Domenico Ghirlandaio. 45c, Peacock, jewelry by René Lalique. 60c, Ceramic tile from Turkey. 75c, Flora, sculpture by Jean-Baptise Carpeaux, Roman medal. €1, Jade jar from Samarkand. €2, Portrait of Calouste Gulbenkian, by C. J. Watelet.

No. 2842, vert.: a, Sculpture and "arte." b, Bookshelf and "educaçao." c, Microscope and "ciencia." d, Painting of mother and child and "caridade."

2006, July 18   **Litho.**   *Perf. 12½x13*
2836-2841 A786   Set of 6   11.00 5.50
Souvenir Sheet
Perf. 13x12½
2842 A786 30c Sheet of 4, #a-d   2.50 2.50

Modern Architecture — A787

Designs: No. 2843, 30c, Building, Bouça neighborhood of Porto, by Alvaro Siza. No. 2844, 30c, Apartments, Lisbon, by Teotónio Pereira, Nuno Portas, Pedro Botelho, and Joao Paciencia. No. 2845, 30c, José Gomes Ferreira School, Lisbon, by Raul Hestnes Ferreira. No. 2846, 30c, Matosinhos Town Hall, by Alcino Soutinho. No. 2847, 30c, Borges & Irmao Bank, Vila do Conde, by Siza. No. 2848, 30c, Art House, Porto, by Eduardo Souto Moura. No. 2849, 30c, University of Santiago Campus, Aveiro, by Portas. No. 2850, 30c, Social Communications School, Lisbon, by Carrilho da Graça. No. 2851, 30c, Architect's Building, Lisbon, by Manuel Graça Diaz and Egas José Vieira. No. 2852, 30c, Santa Maria Church, Marco de Canaveses, by Siza.

2006, Aug. 21   *Perf. 12½x13*
2843-2852 A787   Set of 10   6.50 3.25

Television Broadcasting in Portugal, 50th Anniv. — A788

Men and: 30c, Camera at right. 60c, Camera at left.

2006, Sept. 4   *Perf. 12x11¾*
2853-2854 A788   Set of 2   2.00 1.00

Bridges Between Portugal and Spain — A789

Designs: 30c, Alcantara Bridge. 52c, Vila Real de Santo António (Ayamonte International) Bridge.

2006, Sept. 14   **Litho.**
2855-2856 A789   Set of 2   1.75 .90

See Spain No. 3441.

Famous Men — A779

Designs, No. 2811, €1, Humberto Delgado (1906-65), founder of TAP Airlines. No. 2812, €1, Thomaz de Mello (Tom) (1906-90), artist. No. 2313, €1, Agostinho da Silva (1906-94), philosopher. No. 2814, €1, Fernando Lopes-Graça (1906-94), composer. No. 2815, €1, Rómulo de Carvalho (1906-97), poet.

2006, May 15   *Perf. 11¾x12*
2811-2815 A779   Set of 5   11.00 5.50

Souvenir Sheet

Douro Demarcated Region, 250th Anniv. — A790

2006, Sept. 14
2857 A790 €2.40 multi   5.25 5.25

Fish
A791

Designs: 30c, Capros aper. 45c, Anthias anthias. 60c, Lepadogaster lepadogaster. 75c, Gobiusculus flavescens. €1, Coris julis. €2, Callionymus lyra.
No. 2864, 80c: a, Macroramphosus scolopax. b, Echiichthys vipera.
No. 2865, 80c: a, Thalassoma pavo. b, Blennius ocellaris.

2006, Oct. 7   Perf. 12¼x11¾
2858-2863 A791 Set of 6   11.00 5.50
Souvenir Sheets of 2, #a-b
2864-2865 A791 Set of 2   7.00 7.00
España 06 Intl. Philatelic Exhibition, Malaga, Spain.

School Correspondence — A792

Various letters with denomination at: No. 2866, N, Upper left. No. 2867, N, Upper right.

2006, Oct. 9   Perf. 12½x13
2866-2867 A792 Set of 2   1.40 .70

Portuguese Railroads, 150th Anniv. — A793

Designs: 30c, Flecha de Prata. 45c, Sud-Express. 60c, Foguete. €2, Alfa Pendular. €1.60, Inaugural ceremonies, 1856.

2006, Oct. 28   Perf. 12x11¾
2868-2871 A793 Set of 4   7.50 3.75
Souvenir Sheet
2872 A793 €1.60 multi   3.50 3.50
No. 2872 contains one 80x30mm stamp.

Portuguese Arrival in Ceylon, 500th Anniv. — A794

Designs: 30c, Map. 75c, Carvings. €2.40, Map, horiz.

2006, Oct. 30   Perf. 13x13¼
2873-2874 A794 Set of 2   2.50 1.25
Souvenir Sheet
Perf. 12½x13
2875 A794 €2.40 multi   5.25 5.25
Lubrapex Intl. Philatelic Exhibition, Rio.

Islamic Influences in Lisbon A795

Designs: 30c, Ceramic tile, 16th cent. 45c, Frieze, 9th-10th cent. 52c, Sousa Leal Palace. 61c, Film Museum. 75c, Casa do Alentejo. €1, Ribeiro da Cunha Palace. €2.95, Pitcher.

2007, Feb. 15   Litho.   Perf. 12½x13
2876-2881 A795 Set of 6   7.50 7.50
Souvenir Sheet
2882 A795 €2.95 multi   6.50 6.50

Miniature Sheets

Regional Garments — A796

No. 2883: a, Capote and capelo, Azores. b, Campones, Beira Litoral. c, Viloa, Madeira. d, Camponesa, Ribatejo.
No. 2884: a, Lavradeira, Minho. b, Noiva, Minho. c, Capa de honras, Trás-os-Montes. d, Pauliteiro, Trás-os-Montes. e, Camisola de pescador, Douro Litoral. f, Coroça, Beiras and Trás-os-Montes. g, Saias da Nazaré, Estremadura. h, Campino, Ribatejo. i, Camponesa, Algarve. j, Capote, Alentejo.

2007, Feb. 28
2883   A796   Sheet of 4   2.75 2.75
a.-d.   30c Any single   .65 .40
2884   A796   Sheet of 10   6.50 6.50
a.-j.   30c Any single   .65 .40

Art by Manuel Cargaleiro A797

Designs: 30c, Carreaux Diamants. 45c, Composizione Floreale. 61c, Decoraçao Mural.

2007, Mar. 16
2885-2887 A797 Set of 3   3.00 1.50

Audit Offices in Europe, Bicent. A798

Designs: 30c, King John I Reinforces the Audit Office, by Jaime Martins Barata. 61c, Creation of Audit Tribunal, by Almada Negreiros. €2, Audit Tribunal Building. €2.95, The Accountant, tapestry by Negreiros.

2007, Mar. 17
2888-2890 A798 Set of 3   6.50 4.50
Souvenir Sheet
2891 A798 €2.95 multi   7.00 7.00

Treaty of Rome, 50th Anniv. — A799

2007, Mar. 23   Perf. 13x12½
2892 A799 61c multi   1.25 .65

Historical Urban Public Transport A800

Designs: 30c, Ox-drawn carriage, 1840. 45c, Horse-drawn streetcar, 1872. 50c, Horse-drawn streetcar, 1873. 61c, Electric trolley, 1895. 75c, Electric trolley, 1901.

2007, Mar. 30   Perf. 11¾x11½
2893 A800 30c multi   .60 .30
2894 A800 45c multi   .95 .50
2895 A800 50c multi   1.00 .50
2896 A800 61c multi   1.25 .60
2897 A800 75c multi   1.75 .90
   Nos. 2893-2897 (5)   5.55 2.80

A801

Dams — A802

Designs: No. 2898, Castelo do Bode Dam. No. 2899, Aguieira Dam and Reservoir. 61c, Valeira Dam and Reservoir. 75c, Alto Lindoso Dam and Reservoir. €1, Castelo do Bode Dam and Reservoir.

2007, Apr. 19   Litho.   Perf. 12½x13
2898 A801 30c multi   .60 .30
2899 A802 30c multi   .60 .30
2900 A802 61c multi   1.40 .70
2901 A802 75c multi   1.50 .55
2902 A802 €1 multi   2.40 1.20
   Nos. 2898-2902 (5)   6.50 3.05

Europa A803

Designs: No. 2903, Lord Robert Baden-Powell.
No. 2904: a, Compass. b, Boy Scouts looking at map.

2007, May 9
2903 A803 61c multi   1.50 .75
Souvenir Sheet
2904   Sheet of 2   3.00 3.00
a.-b.   A803 61c Either single   1.50 .85
    Scouting, cent.

Historical Urban Public Transport Type of 2007
Designs: N, Horse-drawn streetcar, 1872. A, Electric trolley, 1895. E, Electric trolley, 1901.

Serpentine Die Cut 11½
2007, May 30   Self-Adhesive
2905 A800 N red & black   .60 .30
2906 A800 A blue & black   1.00 .50
2907 A800 E brown & black   1.40 .70
   Nos. 2905-2907 (3)   3.00 1.50
Nos. 2905-2907 sold for 30c, 45c and 61c, respectively, on day of issue.

Modern Architecture — A804

Designs: No. 2908, 30c, Casa dos 24, Porto, by Fernando Távora. No. 2909, 30c, Documentation and Information Center of the President of the Republic, Lisbon, by Carrilho da Graça. No. 2910, 30c, Portugal Pavilion, Lisbon, by Alvaro Siza. No. 2911, 30c, Ilhavo Maritime Museum, Ilhavo, by ARX Portugal. No. 2912, 30c, Visual Arts Center, Coimbra, by Joao Mendes Ribeiro. No. 2913, 30c, Superior School of Art and Design, Caldas da Rainha, by Vitor Figueiredo. No. 2914, 30c, VTS Tower, Lisbon, by Gonçalo Byrne. No. 2915, 30c, Braga Municipal Stadium, Braga, by Eduardo Souto Moura. No. 2916, 30c, José Saramago Library, Loures, by Fernando Martins. No. 2917, 30c, Sines Art Center, Sines, by Aires Mateus.
€1.85, Portugal Pavilion, by Siza, diff.

2007, May 31   Perf. 12½x13
2908-2917 A804 Set of 10   6.50 3.25
Souvenir Sheet
2918 A804 €1.85 multi   4.00 4.00

World Sailing Championships — A805

Designs: No. 2919, 61c, Catamarans. No. 2920, 61c, Sailboats 23 and 105. No. 2921, 75c, Sailboat 75 and other sailboat. No. 2922, 75c, Sailboats CHI 34 and POR 16. €2.95, Like #2921.

2007, June 12   Perf. 12x11¾
2919-2922 A805 Set of 4   6.00 3.00
Souvenir Sheet
2923 A805 €2.95 multi   7.00 7.00

Miniature Sheets

Seven Wonders of Portugal — A806

No. 2924: a, Vila Vicosa Ducal Palace. b, Roman temple, Evora. c, Pena National Palace, Sintra. d, Queluz National Palace, Sintra. e, Jéronimos Monastery, Lisbon. f, Belem Tower, Lisbon. g, Sagres Fort, Vila do Bispo.
No. 2925: a, Christ Convent, Tomar. b, Almourol Castle, Vila Nova da Barquinha. c, Alcobaça Monastery. d, Obidos Castle. e, Mafra Convent and Basilica. f, Marvao Castle. g, Monsaraz Fortifications.

No. 2926: a, Guimaraes Castle. b, Mateus Palace, Vila Real. c, Sao Francisco Church, Porto. d, Clergymen Church and Tower, Porto. e, Coimbra University Palace. f, Conimbriga Ruins, Condeixa-a-Nova. g, Batalha Monastery.

2007, June 14			**Perf. 12x11¾**		
2924	A806	Sheet of 7 + label		6.00	6.00
a.-g.		30c Any single		.85	.40
2925	A806	Sheet of 7 + label		6.00	6.00
a.-g.		30c Any single		.85	.40
2926	A806	Sheet of 7 + label		6.00	6.00
a.-g.		30c Any single		.85	.40
		Nos. 2924-2926 (3)		18.00	18.00

Art From Berardo Museum — A807

Designs: 45c, Bridge, by Amadeo de Souza Cardoso. No. 2928, 61c, Les Baigneuses, by Niki de Saint Phalle, vert. €1, Interior with Restful Paintings, by Roy Lichtenstein, vert. €2, Femme Dans un Fauteuil, by Pablo Picasso, vert.

No. 2931, 61c, vert.: a, Le Couple, by Oscar Dominguez. b, Café Man Ray, by Man Ray. c, Néctar, by Joana Vasconcelos. d, Head, by Jackson Pollock.

2007, June 25			**Perf. 12**		
2927-2930	A807	Set of 4		9.00	4.50
		Souvenir Sheet			
2931		Sheet of 4		7.00	7.00
a.-d.	A807	61c Any single		1.75	.85

Portuguese Presidency of European Union Council of Ministers — A808

Designs: 61c, Building, stars running from UL to LR. €2.45, Building, stars running from LL to UR.

		Perf. 12x11¾ Syncopated			
2007, July 1					
2932	A808	61c multi		1.40	.70
		Souvenir Sheet			
2933	A808	€2.45 multi		6.75	6.75

Motorcycles — A809

Designs: 30c, 1935 SMC-Nacional 500cc. 52c, 1959 FAMEL Foguete. No. 2936, 61c, 1954 Vilar Cucciolo. €1, 1969, Casal Carina. No. 2938, 61c: a, 1952 Quimera Alma. b, 1958 CINAL Pachancho. c, 1965 SIS Sachs VS. d, 1985 Casal K287.

2007, July 4					
2934-2937	A809	Set of 4		5.50	2.75
		Souvenir Sheet			
2938		Sheet of 4		6.00	6.00
a.-d.	A809	61c Any single		1.50	1.50

Souvenir Sheet

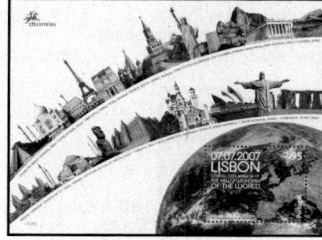

New Seven Wonders of the World — A810

2007, July 7			**Perf. 12½x13¼**		
2939	A810	€2.95 multi		7.00	7.00

Raul Maria Pereira, Architect, and Postal Headquarters, Lima, Peru — A811

2007, Aug. 10			**Perf. 12x11¾**		
2940	A811	75c multi		1.75	.90
		See Peru No. 1574.			

Famous Men — A812

Designs: No. 2941, 45c, Miguel Torga (1907-95), writer. No. 2942, 45c, Fialho de Almeida (1857-1911), writer. No. 2943, 45c, Columbano (1857-1929); painter.

2007, Aug. 12			**Perf. 11¾x12**		
2941-2943	A812	Set of 3		3.00	1.50

Souvenir Sheet

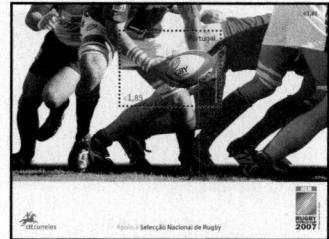

Portuguese Rugby Team — A813

2007, Aug. 22			**Perf. 12½x13¼**		
2944	A813	€1.85 multi		4.50	4.50

Art by Nadir Afonso — A814

Designs: 30c, Horus. 45c, Veneza. 61c, Processao em Veneza.

2007, Sept. 5		**Litho.**	**Perf. 12½x13**		
2945-2947	A814	Set of 3		3.00	1.50

Flora and Fauna of the Americas A815

Designs: No. 2948, 30c, Potatoes. No. 2949, 30c, Corn. No. 2950, 30c, Jacaranda. 45c, Cacao pods. 61c, Turkeys. 75c, Passion fruits. €1.85, Hummingbird at passion fruit blossom, horiz.

2007, Sept. 25			**Perf. 11¾x12**		
2948-2953	A815	Set of 6		6.00	3.00
		Souvenir Sheet			
		Perf. 12x11¾			
2954	A815	€1.85 multi		4.50	4.50

Buildings — A816

Designs: 30c, Tower, Arzila, Morocco. 75c, Silves Castle, Portugal.

2007, Sept. 26			**Perf. 13x12½**		
2955-2956	A816	Set of 2		2.40	1.20
		See No. 3623, Morocco Nos. 1043-1044.			

Flags A817

Flag of: Nos. 2957, 2958a, Portugal. No. 2958 — Flag of: b, Portuguese President. c, Portuguese Assembly. d, Azores. e, Madeira.

		Perf. 12x11¾ Syncopated			
2007, Oct. 5					
2957	A817	30c multi		.65	.30
		Perf. 13¼x13			
2958		Sheet of 5		3.50	3.50
a.-e.	A817	30c Any single		.65	.30
		No. 2958 contains five 36x28mm stamps.			

Children's Art A818

Designs: No. 2959, (30c), Children and flowers, by Ines Filipa Navrat. No. 2960, (30c), Children and globe, by Sofia Fiteiro Passeira. No. 2961, (30c), Hands and globe, by Maria Correia Borges.

		Perf. 12x11¾ Syncopated			
2007, Oct. 9					
2959-2961	A818	Set of 3		2.10	1.00

Mafra National Reserve A819

Fauna: 30c, Cervus dama. 45c, Sus scrofa. 61c, Vulpes vulpes. 75c, Cervus elaphus. €1, Bubo bubo. €2, Hieraaetus fasciatus. €1.25, Cervus elaphus, diff.

2007, Oct. 16			**Perf. 12x11¾**		
2962-2967	A819	Set of 6		12.00	6.00
		Souvenir Sheet			
2968	A819	€1.25 multi		3.25	3.25

Islamic Center, Lisbon A820

2007, Nov. 7			**Perf. 13¼**		
2969	A820	N Ground-level view		.60	.30
2970	A820	I Aerial view		1.75	.90

Reign of Aga Khan IV, 50th anniv. On day of issue, No. 2969 sold for 30c, and No. 2970 sold for 75c.

Cork Industry A821

		Serpentine Die Cut 12½			
2007, Nov. 28			**Litho.**		
		Self-Adhesive			
		Printed on Cork Veneer			
2971	A821	€1 multi		8.00	7.00

Souvenir Sheet

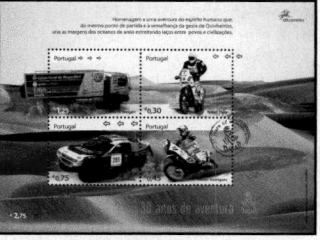

Lisbon to Dakar Rally — A822

No. 2972: a, Ruben Faria on motorcycle. b, Hélder Rodrigues on motorcycle. c, Automobile of Carlos Sousa. d, Truck of Rainer Weigart.

2008, Jan. 5		**Litho.**	**Perf. 13¼x13**		
2972	A822	Sheet of 4		6.00	6.00
a.		30c multi		.70	.35
b.		45c multi		1.10	.55
c.		75c multi		1.75	.90
d.		€1.25 multi		3.00	1.50

Arrival of Portuguese Royal Family in Brazil, 200th Anniv. — A823

No. 2973: a, N, Royal family and ship. b, I, King John VI and ships.

2008, Jan. 22			**Perf. 12 Syncopated**		
2973	A823	Horiz. pair, #a-b		2.50	2.50

On day of issue, Nos. 2973a and 2973b sold for 30c and 75c, respectively.
See Brazil No. 3032.

Infertility — A824

Perf. 11¾x12 Syncopated
2008, Mar. 12 Litho.
2974 A824 30c multi .65 .30

Intl. Year
of Planet
Earth
A825

Designs: 30c, Forest. 45c, Clouds. 61c, Volcano. 75c, Coral reef.

Perf. 12x11¾ Syncopated
2008, Mar. 25
2975-2978 A825 Set of 4 4.50 4.50

2008 European Judo Championships,
Lisbon — A826

Various action photos of judo opponents.

2008, Apr. 7
2979 A826 30c multi .65 .35
2980 A826 61c multi 1.40 .70
Souvenir Sheet
2981 Sheet of 2 6.00 6.00
a. A826 45c multi 1.00 .75
b. A826 €2 multi 4.50 3.25

Famous
People — A827

Designs: No. 2982, 30c, Maria Helena Vieira da Silva (1908-92), painter. No. 2983, 30c, Father António Vieira (1608-97), Inquisition reformer. No. 2984, 30c, Aureliano Mira Fernandes (1884-1958), mathematician. No. 2985, 30c, José Relvas (1858-1929), Prime Minister of Portugal. No. 2986, 30c, Manoel de Oliveira (b. 1908), film director. No. 2987, 30c, Ricardo Jorge (1858-1939), physician.

Perf. 11¾x12 Syncopated
2008, Apr. 18
2982-2987 A827 Set of 6 4.00 2.00

2008
Summer
Olympics,
Beijing
A828

Emblem of 2008 Summer Olympics and: No. 2988, 30c, Runners. No. 2989, 30c, Cyclists. 75c, Triple jump.

Perf. 12x11¾ Syncopated
2008, Apr. 30
2988-2990 A828 Set of 3 3.00 1.50

Miniature Sheet

Olympex 2008, Beijing — A829

No. 2991 — Olympic athletes: a, Equestrian. b, Canoeing. c, Shooting. d, Rhythmic gymnastics.

Perf. 12x11¾ Syncopated
2008, Apr. 30
2991 A829 Sheet of 4 7.00 7.00
a.-d. 75c Any single 1.75 1.10

European Triathlon
Championships — A830

Perf. 12x11¾ Syncopated
2008, May 9 Litho.
2992 A830 €2 multi 4.50 2.25

Europa
A831

Designs: No. 2993, Man sitting on envelope, mail truck. No. 2994a, Mail truck, bull.

2008, May 9
2993 A831 61c multi 1.25 .75
Souvenir Sheet
2994 Sheet of 2, #2993, 2994a 3.00 2.00
a. A831 61c multi 1.75 .95

Historic Public
Transportation
A832

Designs: N, Oldsmobile taxicab, Lisbon, 1928. A, Electric trolley, Cascais, 1926. E, Bus, Lisbon, 1944.

Serpentine Die Cut 11½
2008, May 13 Self-Adhesive
2995 A832 N multi .65 .35
2996 A832 A multi 1.00 .50
2997 A832 E multi 1.40 .70
Nos. 2995-2997 (3) 3.05 1.55

On day of issue, Nos. 2995-2997 sold for 30c, 45c, and 61c, respectively.
See Nos. 3026-3030.

Children's Right
to Education
A833

Designs: 30c, Child arriving at school. 45c, Children in classroom. 61c, Children reading and painting. 75c, Child reading with parents. €2.95, Man hugging "4," paint brushes.

Perf. 11¾x12 Suncopated
2008, June 2
2998-3001 A833 Set of 4 4.50 2.25
Souvenir Sheet
3002 A833 €2.95 multi 7.00 4.75

UEFA Euro 2008
Soccer
Championships,
Austria and
Switzerland.
A834

Silhouettes of soccer players in: 30c, Orange and red. 61c, Blue green and lilac.
No. 3005: a, Red and lilac. b, Orange and brown.

2008, June 5
3003-3004 A834 Set of 2 2.00 1.00
Souvenir Sheet
3005 Sheet of 2 7.00 4.50
a. A834 €1.20 multi 2.75 1.90
b. A834 €1.66 multi 4.25 2.60

Lighthouses — A835

Designs: No. 3006, 30c, Bugio. No. 3007, 30c, Cabo de Sao Vicente. No. 3008, 30c, Cabo da Roca. No. 3009, 30c, Cabo Sardao. No. 3010, 30c, Esposende, vert. No. 3011, 30c, Santa Marta, vert. No. 3012, 30c, Cabo Espichel, vert. No. 3013, 30c, Penedo da Saudade, vert. No. 3014, 30c, Montedor, vert. No. 3015, 30c, Leça, vert.

Perf. 12x11¾, 11¾x12 Syncopated
2008, June 19
3006-3015 A835 Set of 10 9.00 4.50

International Polar Year — A836

Designs: 30c, Calidris alba. 52c, Alca torda. 61c, Oceanites oceanicus. €1, Sterna paradisea.
€2.95, Phoca hispida, Ursus maritimus.

Perf. 12x11¾ Syncopated
2008, June 23
3016-3019 A836 Set of 4 5.25 2.75
Souvenir Sheet
3020 A836 €2.95 multi 6.50 4.75

EFIRO 2008 World Philatelic Exhibition, Bucharest, Romania (#3020). No. 3020 contains one 80x30mm stamp.

Formula 1
Racing in
Portugal,
50th Anniv.
A837

Race cars driven by: 31c, Stirling Moss. 67c, Jack Brabham. 80c, Mark Haywood. €2, Bobby Vernon-Roe.
€2.45, 1960 Grand Prix race at Boavista Racetrack.

Perf. 12x11¾ Syncopated
2008, Sept. 11 Litho.
3021-3024 A837 Set of 4 8.00 4.00
Souvenir Sheet
3025 A837 €2.45 multi 6.00 3.50
No. 3025 contains one 80x30mm stamp.

Historic Public Transportation Type of 2008

Designs: 6c, Electric trolley, Porto, 1927. 31c, Oldsmobile taxicab, Lisbon, 1928. 47c, Electric trolley, Cascais, 1926. 67c, Bus, Lisbon, 1944. 80c, Electric trolley, Coimbra, 1911.

2008, Sept. 12 Perf. 11¾x11½
3026 A832 6c multi .25 .25
3027 A832 31c multi .65 .35
3028 A832 47c multi 1.10 .55
3029 A832 67c multi 1.50 .75
3030 A832 80c multi 1.75 .90
Nos. 3026-3030 (5) 5.25 2.80

Souvenir Sheet

Escola School Computer
Program — A838

Perf. 12x11¾ Syncopated
2008, Sept. 15
3031 A838 €3 multi 6.50 4.25

Companhia Uniao Fabril,
Cent. — A839

Designs: 31c, Metalworking industry. 67c, Textile industry. €1, Naval construction industry. €2, Chemical industry.
€2.45, Alfredo da Silva, company founder, vert.

Perf. 12x11¾ Syncopated
2008, Sept. 19
3032-3035 A839 Set of 4 9.00 4.50
Perf. 11¾x12 Syncopated
3036 A839 €2.45 multi 6.00 3.50

Ceramic
Pharmacy
Jars
A840

Designs: 31c, Two jars, 17th cent. 47c, Jar, 18th cent. 67c, Three jars, 17th-18th cent. 80c, Two jars with lids, 19th cent.
€2.48, Pharmacy, 17th-18th cent.

Perf. 12x11¾ Syncopated
2008, Sept. 26
3037-3040 A840 Set of 4 5.00 2.50
Souvenir Sheet
3041 A840 €2.48 multi 6.00 3.50

Demarcated Wine Regions,
Cent. — A841

No. 3042, 31c: a, Colares vineyard and grapes. b, Carcavelos barrels and grapes.
No. 3043, 31c: a, Setúbal Muscatel bottles and grapes. b, Setúbal Muscatel vineyards and grapes.
No. 3044, 31c: a, Bucelas vineyard and grapes. b, Bucelas barrels and grapes.
No. 3045, 31c: a, Dao vineyard and grapes. b, Dao barrels and grapes.
No. 3046, 31c: a, Green Wine vineyard and grapes. b, Green Wine terraced vineyard.

Perf. 12x11¾ Syncopated
2008, Oct. 2 — Litho.
Horiz. Pairs, #a-b
3042-3046 A841 Set of 5 6.00 3.00

Republican Ideas A842

Bust and: No. 3047, 31c, First Executive Republican Chamber. No. 3048, 31c, School and children. No. 3049, 47c, Row houses and family. No. 3050, 47c, Factory. 57c, Postal workers. No. 3052, 67c, Civil registry. No. 3053, 67c, Public health. 80c, Civic participation.
€2.95, Tagus River Railroad Bridge.

2008, Oct. 5
3047-3054 A842 Set of 8 10.00 5.00
Souvenir Sheet
3055 A842 €2.95 multi 7.00 4.00
No. 3055 contains one 80x30mm stamp.

Olive Oil Production A843

Designs: 31c, Olive grove. 47c, Olive pickers. 57c, Olive sorters. 67c, Olive mill. 80c, Oil vats. €2, Containers of herbed olive oil.
€1.85, Hands holding olives.

2008, Oct. 7
3056-3061 A843 Set of 6 11.00 5.50
Souvenir Sheet
3062 A843 €1.85 multi 4.50 2.50

School Correspondence — A844

Children's drawings by: 31c, Erica Bluemel Portocarrero. 47c, Eloísa O. Pereira. 67c, Joao Maria Martins Branco.

2008, Oct. 9
3063-3065 A844 Set of 3 3.25 1.75

Bridges A845

Designs: 31c, April 25th Bridge, Lisbon. 47c, Arrábida Bridge, Oporto. 57c, Arade River Bridge, Portimao. 67c, Mosteiro Bridge, Cinfães. 80c, Amizade Bridge, Vila Nova de Cerveira. €1, Santa Clara Bridge, Coimbra.
No. 3072, €1.85, April 25th Bridge, Lisbon, diff. No. 3073, €1.85, Arrábida Bridge, Oporto, diff.

2008, Oct. 16
3066-3071 A845 Set of 6 8.50 4.25
Souvenir Sheets
3072-3073 A845 Set of 2 9.00 4.75
Nos. 3072-3073 each contain one 80x30mm stamp. See Nos. 3837, 3889.

European Year of Intercultural Dialogue — A846

Designs: 31c, Sculpture, tile design. 47c, Mask, bust. 67c, Window, feather headdress. 80c, African and Chinese masks.

2008, Oct. 23
3074-3077 A846 Set of 4 5.00 2.50

Waiting for Success, Painting by Henrique Pousao (1859-84) A847

Joaquim Soeiro Pereira Gomes (1909-49), Writer A848

Perf. 11¾x12 Syncopated
2009, Jan. 27 — Litho.
3078 A847 32c multi .70 .35
Perf. 12x11¾ Syncopated
3079 A848 32c multi .70 .35

Creation of the Euro, 10th Anniv. A849

Euro symbols, stars and: 47c, Three stylized euro coins. €1, Two stylized euro coins.

Perf. 12x11¾ Syncopated
2009, Jan. 28
3080-3081 A849 Set of 2 3.25 1.60

Historic Public Transportation A850

Designs: 20c, Bus, 1957. Nos. 3083, 3087, Electric train, 1957. Nos. 3084, 3088, ML7 train car, 1959. Nos. 3085, 3089, Double-decker bus, 1960. 80c, Electric trolley bus, 1961.

2009 — Litho. — **Perf. 11¾x11½**
3082 A850 20c multi .45 .25
3083 A850 32c multi .70 .35
3084 A850 47c multi 1.10 .60
3085 A850 68c multi 1.50 .75
3086 A850 80c multi 1.75 .90
Nos. 3082-3086 (5) 5.50 2.85

Booklet Stamps
Self-Adhesive
Serpentine Die Cut 11½
3087 A850 N multi .70 .35
 a. Booklet pane of 10 7.00
 Complete booklet, 10 #3087a 70.00
3088 A850 A multi 1.10 .60
 a. Booklet pane of 10 11.00
 Complete booklet, 5 #3088a 55.00
3089 A850 E multi 1.50 .75
 a. Booklet pane of 10 15.00
 Complete booklet, 5 #3089a 75.00
Nos. 3087-3089 (3) 3.30 1.70
Issued: Nos. 3082-3086, 2/9; Nos. 3087-3089, 4/30. On day of issue, Nos. 3087-3089 sold for 32c, 47c and 68c respectively.

Charles Darwin (1809-82), Naturalist A851

Darwin and: No. 3090, 32c, Finches. No. 3091, 32c, Iguana. No. 3092, 68c, Diana monkey. No. 3093, 68c, Orchids. No. 3094, 80c, Shells and fossil skull. No. 3095, 80c, Platypus.
€2.50, Darwin and finches, vert.

Perf. 12x11¾ Syncopated
2009, Feb. 12
3090-3095 A851 Set of 6 7.50 3.75
Souvenir Sheet
Perf. 11¾x12 Syncopated
3096 A851 €2.50 multi 6.00 3.25

African Heritage in Portugal A852

Africans as depicted in: 32c, Ceramic figurine, 19th cent. 47c, Santa Auta retable, 1522. 57c, Painting by José Conrado Roza, 1788. 68c, Ceramic tile, 19th cent. 80c, Portuguese faience, 18th cent. €2, Painted wood, 19th cent.
€2.50, Painting by Joaquim Marques, 1789.

Perf. 12x11¾ Syncopated
2009, Feb. 26
3097-3102 A852 Set of 6 11.00 5.50
Souvenir Sheet
3103 A852 €2.50 multi 6.00 3.25

Molecular Models A853

Multiplication Equations — A854

2009, Mar. 4
3104 A853 32c multi .70 .35
3105 A854 32c multi .70 .35

Franciscan Order, 800th Anniv. A855

Designs: 32c, St. Francis of Assisi with dog.

No. 3107, vert.: a, 50c, St. Francis receiving tonsure. b, €2, Pope Innocent III.

Perf. 12x11¾ Syncopated
2009, Mar. 11
3106 A855 32c multi .70 .35
Souvenir Sheet
Perf. 11¾x12 Syncopated
3107 A855 Sheet of 2, #a-b 7.50 3.25

Canonization of St. Nuno de Santa Maria — A856

Perf. 12x11¾ Syncopated
2009, Aug. 26
3108 A856 32c multi .70 .35

Europa A857

Designs: No. 3109, Three images from Mar. 3, 2007 lunar eclipse. No. 3110a, European Southern Observatory.

2009, May 8
3109 A857 68c multi 1.60 .80
Souvenir Sheet
3110 Sheet of 2, #3109, 3110a 4.00 2.00
 a. A857 68c multi 1.90 .95
Intl. Year of Astronomy.

Ceramics A858

Designs: 32c, Faience mosque lamp, Turkey. 68c, Ceramic pot, Portugal.

2009, May 12 — **Perf. 12½x13**
3111-3112 A858 Set of 2 2.25 1.10
See Turkey Nos. 3160-3161.

Cristo Rei Sanctuary, Lisbon, 50th Anniv. — A859

Designs: 32c, Statue of Christ and base. 68c, Statue of Christ.
€2.48, Head of statue and 25 de Abril Bridge.

Perf. 11¾x12 Syncopated
2009, May 17
3113-3114 A859 Set of 2 2.25 1.20
Souvenir Sheet
Perf. 12x11¾ Syncopated
3115 A859 €2.48 multi 6.00 3.50
No. 3115 contains one 80x30mm stamp. See No. 3838.

Foods of Portuguese-speaking
Areas — A860

Designs; No. 3116, 32c, Leitoa num ar de
sarapatel, Brazil. No. 3117, 32c, Bebinca das
sete colinas, India. No. 3118, 68c, Caldeirada
de cabrito, Angola. No. 3119, 68c, Bacalhau,
pao, vinho e aziete, Portugal. No. 3120, 80c,
No caldeiro a tempura, Asia. No. 3121, 80c,
Do cozido à cachupa, Cape Verde.
€1.85, Bacalhau, pao, vinho e aziete, diff.,
vert.

Perf. 12x11¾ Syncopated
2009, June 5
3116-3121 A860   Set of 6   8.00 4.00
Souvenir Sheet
Perf. 11¾x12 Syncopated
3122   A860   €1.85 multi   4.50 2.60

Lusitano
Horses — A861

Designs: No. 3123, 32c, White horse with
rider. No. 3124, 32c, Black horse with rider.
57c, Brown horse with rider. 68c, Brown horse
rearing. 80c, Horses in team.
€2.50, Horse walking.

Perf. 11¾x12 Syncopated
2009, June 11
3123-3127 A861   Set of 5   6.00 3.00
Souvenir Sheet
3128   A861   €2.50 multi   6.00 3.50
See No. 3624.

King
Afonso I
(1109-85),
First King
of Portugal
A862

Designs: 32c, Sculpture of King Afonso I.
€3.07, Drawing of King Afonso I on horse.

Perf. 12x11¾ Syncopated
2009, June 24
3129   A862   32c multi   .70 .35
Souvenir Sheet
3130   A862   €3.07 multi   7.00 4.50

Jazz in
Portugal — A863

Inscriptions: 32c, Cascais Jazz. 47c, Jazz
num Dia de Verao. 57c, Fundaçao Calouste
Gulbenkian Jazz em Agosto. 68c, Jazz
Europeu no Porto. 80c, Guimaraes Jazz. €1,
Seixal Jazz.
€3.16, Quarteto Hot Club, horiz.

Perf. 11¾x12 Syncopated
2009, June 26
3131-3136 A863   Set of 6   9.00 4.50
Souvenir Sheet
Perf. 12x11¾ Syncopated
3137   A863   €3.16 black   7.50 4.50

Traditional
Breads
A864

Designs: No. 3138, 32c, Pao de Centeio
(rye bread). No. 3139, 32c, Pao de Quartos.
47c, Regueifa. No. 3141, 68c, Pao de Testa.
No. 3142, 68c, Pao com Chouriço (bread with
sausage). 80c, Pao de Mealhada.
No. 3144, €2, Bolo de Caco. No. 3145, €2,
Pao de Milho (corn bread).

Perf. 12x11¾ Syncopated
2009, July 28   Litho.
3138-3143 A864   Set of 6   7.50 3.75
Souvenir Sheets
3144-3145 A864   Set of 2   9.50 5.75
3144a   Booklet pane of 1   4.50
3145a   Booklet pane of 1   4.50 —
See No. 3667.

António
Pedro
(1909-66),
Theater
Founder
A865

Designs: 32c, Pedro and stage art. €3.16,
Pedro.

2009, Sept. 1
3146   A865   32c multi   .70 .35
Souvenir Sheet
3147   A865   €3.16 multi   7.50 4.50

Belém Palace (Presidential
Residence), Lisbon — A866

Designs: 32c, Palace exterior, 1841-42. 47c,
Decorative painting. 57c, Writing desk. 68c,
Bas-relief depicting satyrs. 80c, Decorative
head from Gold Room. €1, Painting from
Fountain Room.
€2.50, Fountain Room.

2009, Sept. 17
3148-3153 A866   Set of 6   8.50 4.25
Souvenir Sheet
3154   A866   €2.50 multi   6.00 3.75

Birds — A867

Designs: 32c, Pandion haliaetus. 80c,
Haliaeetus albicilla.

2009, Sept. 21   Perf. 13x12½
3155-3156 A867   Set of 2   2.50 1.25
See Iran No. 3002.

The
Senses — A868

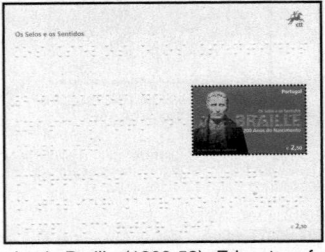

Louis Braille (1809-52), Educator of
the Blind — A869

Senses: 32c, Smell (cup of coffee). 68c,
Taste (ice cream bar). 80c, Sight (eyeglasses).
€1, Touch (tube of paint). €2, Hearing (file).

Perf. 11¾x12 Syncopated
2009, Oct. 2   Litho.
3157   A868   32c multi   .70 .40
3158   A868   68c multi   1.50 .75
Litho. with Hologram Affixed
3159   A868   80c multi   1.75 1.00
Litho. & Embossed
3160   A868   €1 multi   2.50 1.25
Litho.
3161   A868   €2 multi   5.00 2.50
   Nos. 3157-3161 (5)   11.45 5.90
Souvenir Sheet
Litho. & Embossed
Perf. 13¼x13½
3162   A869   €2.50 multi   6.00 3.75
No. 3157 is impregnated with a coffee
scent. Parts of the design of No. 3161 are
covered with a gritty substance.

Famous
Women — A870

Designs: No. 3163, 32c, Maria Veleda
(1871-1955), teacher and writer of children's
books. No. 3164, 32c, Adelaide Cabete (1867-
1935), doctor and feminist leader. 57c, Ana de
Castro Osório (1872-1935), writer and feminist
leader. 68c, Angelina Vidal (1853-1917),
teacher. 80c, Carolina Beatriz Angelo (1877-
1911), surgeon and feminist leader. €1, Carolina Michaelis de Vasconcelos (1851-1925),
novelist.
No. 3169: a, Virginia Quaresma (1882-
1973), journalist. b, Emília de Sousa Costa
(1877-1959), writer and educator.

Perf. 11¾x12 Syncopated
2009, Oct. 5   Litho.
3163-3168 A870   Set of 6   8.00 4.00
Souvenir Sheet
3169   A870   €1.15 Sheet of 2,
           #a-b   5.50 3.50

School Correspondence — A871

Children's art by: 32c, Martina Marques Teixeira Santos. 47c, Joel Filipe Silva Carmo.
68c, Manuel Pedro A. B. Paiva Martins.

Perf. 12x11¾ Syncopated
2009, Oct. 9
3170-3172 A871   Set of 3   3.50 1.75

Christmas
A872

Santa Claus and: 32c, Star and hearts. 47c,
Door and sack of letters. 68c, Christmas tree
and gift. 80c, Reindeer and gift.
No. 3177: a, 50c, Toy reindeer, "0" and "9."
b, €1, Christmas stocking

Perf. 11¾x12 Syncopated
2009, Oct. 21
3173-3176 A872   Set of 4   5.00 2.50
Souvenir Sheet
3177   A872   Sheet of 2, #a-b   4.00 2.25

Abandoned
Dog — A873

Viriathus (d. 138
B.C.), Lusitanian
Rebel Against
Roman
Empire — A874

Perf. 11¾x12 Syncopated
2010, Feb. 22   Litho.
3178   A873   32c multi   .70 .35
3179   A874   32c multi   .70 .35

Composers — A875

Designs: No. 3180, 68c, Frédéric Chopin
(1810-49). No. 3181, 68c, Robert Schumann
(1810-56).
No. 3182, €2, Chopin, diff. No. 3183, €2,
Schumann, diff.

Perf. 12x11¾ Syncopated
2010, Mar. 1
3180-3181 A875   Set of 2   3.00 1.50
Souvenir Sheets
3182-3183 A875   Set of 2   9.50 5.50

Urban
Transportation of
the 1970s to
1990s — A876

Designs: 1c, Volvo articulated bus, Porto.
Nos. 3185, 3189, Carris articulated tram, Lis-
bon. Nos. 3186, 3190, ML 79 subway train,
Lisbon. Nos. 3187, 3191, Ferry boat
Madragoa, Lisbon. 80c, CP electric train.

2010, Mar. 8   Litho.   **Perf. 11¾x11½**
3184   A876   1c multi   .25 .25
3185   A876   32c multi   .70 .35
3186   A876   47c multi   1.10 .55

3187	A876	68c multi	1.50	.75
3188	A876	80c multi	1.90	.95
	Nos. 3184-3188 (5)		5.45	2.85

Self-Adhesive
Serpentine Die Cut 11½

3189	A876	N multi	.70	.35
3190	A876	A multi	1.10	.55
3191	A876	E multi	1.60	.80
	Nos. 3189-3191 (3)		3.40	1.70

On day of isse Nos. 3189-3191 sold for 32c, 47c, and 68c, respectively.

Intl. Year of Biodiversity A877

Designs: 32c, Thunnus thynnus. 47c, Centrophorus granulosus. 68c, Ailuropoda melanoleuca. 80c, Hummingbird. €2.50, Lion tamarin.

Perf. 12x11¾ Syncopated
2010, Mar. 8

| 3192-3195 | A877 | Set of 4 | 5.00 | 2.50 |

Souvenir Sheet

| 3196 | A877 | €2.50 multi | 6.00 | 3.50 |

Precious Stones in Sacred Art — A878

Designs: 32c, Archdiocese of Evora bouquet pin. 68c, Bodice ornament of Virgin of Carmo. €1, Processional cross of King Sancho I. €2.50, Crown of Our Lady of Fatima sculpture.

Perf. 12x11¾ Syncopated
2010, Mar. 22

| 3197-3199 | A878 | Set of 3 | 4.50 | 2.25 |

Souvenir Sheet

| 3200 | A878 | €2.50 multi | 5.50 | 3.50 |

Breads A879

Designs: 32c, Broa. 47c, Padas. 68c, Broa de Avintes. 80c, Alentejano bread. No. 3205: a, 80c, Carcaça. b, €1, Mafra bread.

Perf. 12x11¾ Syncopated
2010, Apr. 6

| 3201-3204 | A879 | Set of 4 | 5.00 | 2.50 |

Souvenir Sheet

| 3205 | A879 | Sheet of 2, #a-b | 4.00 | 2.50 |

Famous Men A880

Designs: No. 3206, 32c, Gomes Eanes de Azurara (1410-74), royal chronicler and archive keeper. No. 3207, 32c, Fernao Mendes Pinto (1510-83), travel writer. No. 3208, 32c, Alexandre Herculano (1810-77), historian. No. 3209, 32c, Francisco Keil do Amaral (1910-75), architect.

2010, Apr. 22

| 3206-3209 | A880 | Set of 4 | 3.00 | 1.50 |

Europa — A881

Characters from children's story: No. 3210, Monkey. No. 3211a, Barber with razor.

Perf. 11¾x12 Syncopated
2010, May 7

| 3210 | A881 | 68c multi | 1.50 | .75 |

Souvenir Sheet

| 3211 | | Sheet of 2, #3210, 3211a | 3.00 | 1.75 |
| a. | A881 | 68c multi | 1.50 | .85 |

Popes A882

Designs: 68c, Pope Benedict XVI. No. 3213, vert. — Popes who visited Portugal: a, Pope Paul VI. b, Pope John Paul II. c, Pope Benedict XVI, diff.

Perf. 12x11¾ Syncopated
2010, May 10

| 3212 | A882 | 68c multi | 1.60 | .80 |

Souvenir Sheet
Perf. 11¾x12 Syncopated

| 3213 | A882 | 80c Sheet of 3, #a-c | 5.50 | 3.00 |

Visit of Pope Benedict XVI to Portugal.

Public Elevators and Funicular Railroads A883

Designs: 32c, Santa Justa Elevator, Lisbon. 47c, Glória Funicular, Lisbon. 57c Guindais Funicular, Porto. 68c, Bom Jesus Funicular, Braga. 80c, Santa Luiza Funicular, Viana do Castelo. €1, Nazaré Funicular, Nazaré. No. 3220: a, Bica Funicular, Lisbon. b, Lavra Funicular, Lisbon.

Perf. 11¾x12 Syncopated
2010, May 17

| 3214-3219 | A883 | Set of 6 | 8.50 | 4.25 |

Souvenir Sheet

| 3220 | A883 | €1.25 Sheet of 2, #a-b | 5.50 | 3.00 |

A884

2010 World Cup Soccer Championships, South Africa — A885

Perf. 12x11¾ Syncopated
2010, May 31 — Souvenir Sheet

| 3221 | A884 | €2.50 multi | 5.50 | 2.75 |

Self-Adhesive
Serpentine Die Cut

| 3222 | A885 | 80c multi | 1.75 | .95 |

Theater in Portugal A886

Designs: No. 3223, 32c, Estrangeiros and Vilhalpandos, by Francisco de Sá de Miranda. No. 3224, 32c, Auto da Barca do Inferno, by Gil Vicente. 57c, A Castro, by António Ferreira. No. 3226, 68c, O Fidalgo Aprendiz, by Dom Francisco Manuel de Mello. No. 3227, 68c, El-Rei Seleuco, by Luis de Camoens. 80c, Guerras de Alecrim e Manjerona, by António José da Silva.

Perf. 12x11¾ Syncopated
2010, June 7

| 3223-3228 | A886 | Set of 6 | 7.50 | 3.75 |

Cheeses A887

Designs: No. 3229, 32c, Serra de Estrela. No. 3230, 32c, Rabaçal. 47c, Azeitao. 68c, Cabra Transmontano. 80c, Sao Jorge. €2.50, Serra de Estrela, diff.

Perf. 12x11¾ Syncopated
2010, June 21

| 3229-3233 | A887 | Set of 5 | 6.00 | 3.00 |

Souvenir Sheet

| 3234 | A887 | €2.50 multi | 5.50 | 3.25 |

Miniature Sheet

Heads of "The Republic" by Various Artists — A888

No. 3235 — Depictions by: a, 32c, Júlio Pomar. b, 32c, Francisco dos Santos. c, 32c, Costa Pinheiro. d, 32c, Bento Condado. e, 32c, Luís Maceira. f, 68c, Joao Abel Manta. g, 68c, Joao Machado. h, 80c, André Carrilho.

Perf. 11¾x12 Syncopated
2010, June 24

| 3235 | A888 | Sheet of 8, #a-h, + central label | 9.50 | 4.75 |

Portugal 2010 World Philatelic Exhibition, Lisbon.

Tiles — A889

No. 3236 — Tile from: a, 68c, Portugal, 18th cent. b, 80c, Romania, 19th cent.

2010, June 30 — Litho.

| 3236 | A889 | Pair, #a-b | 3.50 | 1.75 |

See Romania Nos. 5188-5189.

Jewish Culture A890

Designs: 32c, Synagogue, Tomar. 57c, Arched doorway, Rua Nova, Lamego. 68c, Jewish neighborhood, Castelo de Vide. €2.50, Illuminated manuscript depicting Jews building structure.

Perf. 12x11¾ Syncopated
2010, July 5

| 3237-3239 | A890 | Set of 3 | 3.75 | 2.00 |

Souvenir Sheet

| 3240 | A890 | €2.50 multi | 6.00 | 3.25 |

Rock Music Album Covers A891

Designs: 32c, Ar de Rock, by Rui Veloso. 47c, Heróis do Mar, by Heróis do Mar. 57c, Psicopátria, by GNR. 68c, A Flor da Pele, by UHF. 80c, Compacto, by Xutos & Pontapes. €1, Wolfheart, by Moonspell. €2.50, A Lenda de El-Rei D. Sebastiao, by Quarteto 1111.

Perf. 12x11¾ Syncopated
2010, July 10
3241-3246 A891 Set of 6   9.00 4.50
Souvenir Sheet
3247 A891 €2.50 multi   6.00 3.25

Portuguese Assembly Building (St. Benedict's Palace), Lisbon — A892

Designs: 32c, Sala dos Sessoes. 68c, Senate Chambers. 80c, Sala dos Passos Perdidos.
€2, Building exterior.

Perf. 12x11¾ Syncopated
2010, Sept. 15
3247A A892 32c multi   .75 .35
3248 A892 68c multi   1.60 .80
3249 A892 80c multi   2.00 1.00
Souvenir Sheet
3250 A892 €2 multi   4.50 2.75
Portugal 2010 World Philatelic Exhibition, Lisbon (#3250).

Peninsular War, Bicent. — A893

No. 3251: a, 32c, Battle of Vimeiro. b, 68c, Battle of Buçaco.
€2.50, Battle of Pombal.

2010, Sept. 15
3251 A893 Horiz. pair, #a-b   2.50 1.25
Souvenir Sheet
3252 A893 €2.50 multi   6.00 3.50
No. 3252 contains one 80x30mm stamp.

Hydrographic Institute, 50th Anniv. — A894

No. 3253: a, 32c, Lighthouse, ship's bow. b, 68c, Ship's stern, man inspecting equipment.

2010, Sept. 22
3253 A894 Horiz. pair, #a-b   2.40 1.20

Circus Performers A895

Designs: 32c, Clown with broom. 47c, Clown on unicycle. 68c, Acrobat with hoops. 80c, Juggler with bowling pins.
€2.50, Trapeze artists.

Perf. 11¾x12 Syncopated
2010, Sept. 29
3254-3257 A895 Set of 4   5.25 2.75
Souvenir Sheet
3258 A895 €2.50 multi   6.00 3.50
No. 3258 contains one 30x80mm stamp.

Ceres — A896

Litho. & Engr.
2010, Oct. 1   Perf. 14x13¼
3259 A896 80c multi   2.00 1.00
Republic of Portugal, cent.

History of Freedom A897

Designs: No. 3260, 32c, Liberty with Portuguese flag. No. 3261, 32c, Man with Portuguese flag, man with rifle. 47c, Soldier with cannon, man with rifle. 68c, Liberty with French flag, French man with rifle. 80c, Uncle Sam pointing at British soldiers. €1, Bishop, king and peasant.

Perf. 12x11¾ Syncopated
2010, Oct. 2   Litho.
3260-3265 A897 Set of 6   8.00 4.00
Portugal 2010 World Philatelic Exhibition, Lisbon

School Correspondence — A898

Children's art by: 32c, Guilherme Pereira. 47c, Diogo Gouveia. 68c, Ana Marques.

2010, Oct. 9
3266-3268 A898 Set of 3   3.50 1.75

UN High Commissioner for Refugees, 60th Anniv. — A899

Designs: 80c, Refugees walking on road. €2.50, Refugee in framework for hut, vert.

Perf. 12x11¾ Syncopated
2010, Oct. 18
3269 A899 80c multi   1.75 .90
Souvenir Sheet
Perf. 11¾x12 Syncopated
3270 A899 €2.50 multi   5.50 3.50

Friendship Between Portugal and Japan, 150th Anniv. — A900

No. 3271 — Detail of Japanese screen painting depicting Portuguese ship's: a, 32c, Bow. b, 80c, Stern.

2010, Oct. 22   Perf. 13¼x12½
3271 A900 Horiz. pair, #a-b   2.50 1.25
See Japan No. 3267.

Assoc. of Postal and Telecommunications Operators of Portuguese-Speaking Countries and Territories, 20th Anniv. — A901

Perf. 12x11¾ Syncopated
2010, Oct. 25
3272 A901 80c multi   1.75 .90

Messenger on Horseback, Sculpture by Jorge Pé-Curto — A902

Designs: €1, Entire sculpture. €2.50, Head of sculpture, horiz.

Perf. 11¾x12 Syncopated
2010, Nov. 2
3273 A902 €1 multi   2.50 1.25
Souvenir Sheet
Perf. 12x11¾ Syncopated
3274 A902 €2.50 multi   6.00 3.50
No. 3274 contains one 80x30mm stamp.

In 2010, Portugal began issuing self-adhesive personalizable stamps as shown in the example above. These stamps, each of which were sold only in full sheets, have the inscription "Portugal CTT" at lower left, and are inscribed at the lower right with perhaps as many as 33 different denominations initially, with many more new denominations possible as postage rates change. Vignettes could be personalized or chosen from a library of stock designs.

Wind Turbines, Bridge, Buildings A903

Animals on Floating Island A904

2011, Feb. 17   Perf. 13 Syncopated
3275 A903 32c multi   .70 .35
3276 A904 47c multi   1.10 .70

Traditional Portuguese Festivals — A905

Designs: 10c, People watching fireworks. 32c, Festa dos Tabulieros, Tomar. 47c, Festa do Sao Joao, Porto. 68c, Carneval, Loulé. 80c, Flower Festival, Madeira.

Perf. 11¾x11½
2011, Feb. 21   Litho.
3277 A905 10c multi   .25 .25
3278 A905 32c multi   .70 .45
3279 A905 47c multi   1.10 .70
3280 A905 68c multi   1.50 .95
3281 A905 80c multi   1.90 1.10
  Nos. 3277-3281 (5)   5.45 3.45

Cheeses — A906

Designs: 32c, Serpa. 47c, Castelo Branco. 68c, Pico. 80c, Nisa. €1, Terrincho. €2.50, Castelo Branco, diff.

2011, Mar. 1   Perf. 13 Syncopated
3282-3286 A906 Set of 5   7.50 3.75
Souvenir Sheet
3287 A906 €2.50 multi   6.00 3.50

Famous People A907

Designs: 32c, Alves Redol (1911-69), writer. 47c, Manuel da Fonseca (1911-93), writer. 57c, Trindade Coelho (1861-1908), writer. 68c, Antónia Ferreira (1811-96), businesswoman. 80c, Eugénio dos Santos (1711-60), architect.

2011, Mar. 14
3288-3292 A907 Set of 5   7.00 3.50

Centenaries of Institutes of Higher Education — A908

Designs: No. 3293, 32c, University of Lisbon. No. 3294, 32c, University of Porto. No. 3295, 80c, Higher Institute of Economics and Management. No. 3296, 80c, Higher Institute of Technology.

2011, Mar. 22
3293-3296 A908 Set of 4   5.00 2.50

Crédito Agrícola, Cent. A909

Hills, plants and: No. 3297, N, Tall buildings. No. 3298, E, Small buildings.

2011, Mar. 25
3297-3298 A909   Set of 2   2.50 1.25

On day of issue, No. 3297 sold for 32c and No. 3298 sold for 68c.

Fish
A910

Designs: 32c, Lampetra fluviatilis. 47c, Alosa alosa. 68c, Platichthys flesus. 80c, Liza ramada.

No. 3303, €1.80, Salmo salar. No. 3304, €1.80, Anguilla anguilla.

2011, Apr. 7
3299-3302 A910   Set of 4   5.50 2.75
Souvenir Sheets
3303-3304 A910   Set of 2   8.00 5.25

Diplomatic Relations Between Portugal and the Republic of Korea, 50th Anniv.
A911

Designs: No. 3305, N, Korean turtle ship. No. 3306, I, Portuguese nau.

2011, Apr. 15   *Perf. 12½x13*
3305-3306 A911   Set of 2   2.50 1.25

On day of issue, No. 3305 sold for 32c and No. 3306 sold for 80c. See South Korea No. 2355.

Republican National Guard, Cent. — A912

Designs: N, Hats. €3.60, Gloves, sword and uniform, horiz.

2011, Apr. 21   *Perf. 13 Syncopated*
3307 A912   N multi   .75   .40
Souvenir Sheet
3308 A912   €3.60 multi   8.00 5.25

No. 3307 sold for 32c on day of issue.

Europa
A913

Designs: No. 3309, Man cutting bark from cork oak, pigs. No. 3310a, Deer at edge of forest.

Perf. 12x11¾ Syncopated
2011, May 9
3309 A913   68c multi   1.60   .80
Souvenir Sheet
3310   Sheet of 2, #3309,
            3310a   3.50 2.00
  a. A913 68c multi   1.60 1.00

Intl. Year of Forests.

Postal Union of the Americas, Spain and Portugal ((UPAEP), Cent. — A914

2011, May 16   *Perf. 13 Syncopated*
3311 A914   80c multi   1.75 1.00

Portuguese Military Academy, Cent. — A915

Designs: 32c, Shako. €1, Cadets in electronics laboratory.

€2.50, Cadet holding flag, cadet wearing shako, horiz.

2011, May 25
3312-3313 A915   Set of 2   3.00 1.50
Souvenir Sheet
3314 A915   €2.50 multi   5.50 3.75

Souvenir Sheet

Emblems of Portuguese Soccer Teams in 2010-11 UEFA Europa League Championship Match — A916

No. 3315 — Emblem of: a, Porto. b, Braga.

Perf. 11¾x12 Syncopated
2011, May 25
3315 A916   €1 Sheet of 2, #a-b 5.25 3.00

Museum of Contemporary Art, Lisbon, Cent. — A917

Designs: No. 3316, 32c, A Luva Cinzenta, by Columbano. No. 3317, 32c, Tristezas, Cabeça, by Amadeo de Souza-Cardoso. 47c, A Sesta, by Almada Negreiros. No. 3319, 68c, Cais 44, by Fernando Lanhas. No. 3320, 68c, Sombra Projectada de René Bertholo, by Lourdes Castro. 80c, A Esquiva, by Joao Maria Gusmao and Pedro Paiva.

No. 3322: a, Landscape, by Juliao Sarmento. b, Estrada da Vida, by Fernando Taborda.

2011, May 26   *Perf. 13 Syncopated*
3316-3321 A917   Set of 6   8.00 4.00
Souvenir Sheet
3322 A917   €1.50 Sheet of 2,
              #a-b   6.50 4.50

Marine Training School, 50th Anniv.
A918

Designs: 32c, Marine coming ashore. 80c, Marines in boat.

€2.50, Monument.

2011, June 3   Litho.
3323-3324 A918   Set of 2   2.50 1.25
Souvenir Sheet
3325 A918   €2.50 multi   6.50 3.75

Embroidery
A919

Embroidery designs from: 32c, Vila Verde. 47c, Arraiolos. 57c, Castelo Branco. 68c, Viana. 80c, Madeira. €1, Azores.

No. 3332, €1.75, Guimaraes. No. 3333, €1.75, Ribatejo.

Perf. 11¾x12 Syncopated
2011, June 28
3326-3331 A919   Set of 6   9.00 4.50
  3330a   Booklet pane of 1   2.00
  3331a   Booklet pane of 1   2.50   —
Souvenir Sheets
3332-3333 A919   Set of 2   8.00 5.00

Nos. 3330a and 3331a are found in booklets listed under Azores and Madeira. See Nos. 3625, 3668.

A920

Diplomatic Relations Between Thailand and Portugal, 500th Anniv. — A921

No. 3334: a, 32c, Portuguese caravel, rowboats, Thai buildings and temples. b, 80c, Elephants and riders at dockside.

No. 3335: a, 32c, Portuguese caravel, Thai buildings. b, 80c, Thai boats and buildings.

2011, July 20   *Perf. 13x13¼*
3334 A920 Horiz. pair, #a-b   1.50   .80
3335 A921 Horiz. pair, #a-b   3.50 2.00

See Thailand Nos. 2617-2618.

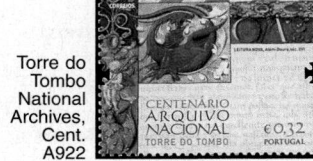

Torre do Tombo National Archives, Cent.
A922

Various historical documents and illuminations: 32c, 68c, €2.

€2.30, Torre de Tombo National Archive, document.

2011, July 27   *Perf. 13 Syncopated*
3336-3338 A922   Set of 3   6.50 3.50
Souvenir Sheet
3339 A922   €2.30 multi   6.50 3.50

Intl. Year of Veterinary Medicine
A923

Designs: 32c, Pigs in farm trailer. 68c, Horse, DNA strands. 80c, Cat, medicines. €1, Cow, milk bottles.

€2.50, Owl in tree.

2011, Sept. 7   Litho.
3340-3343 A923   Set of 4   6.50 3.00
Souvenir Sheet
3344 A923   €2.50 multi   6.00 3.50

Theater in Portugal
A924

Actors and actresses: No. 3345, 32c, Laura Alves (1927-86). No. 3346, 32c, Amélia Rey Colaço (1898-1990). 47c, Raul Solnado (1929-2009). 68c, Armando Cortez (1928-2002). 80c, Eunice Muñoz. €1, Ruy de Carvalho.

No. 3351, €1: a, Scene from "Frei Luis de Sousa," by Almeida Garrett. b, Scene from "Os Velhos," by D. Joao da Câmara.

No. 3352, €1: a, Scene from "A Promessa," by Bernardo Santareno. b, Scene from "Bernilde ou a Virgem-Mâe," by José Régio.

2011, Sept. 14
3345-3350 A924   Set of 6   8.00 4.00
Souvenir Sheets of 2, #a-b
3351-3352 A924   Set of 2   8.50 5.50

Archaeology in Portugal — A925

Artifacts from archaeological sites in: 32c, Citânia de Briteiros. 47c, Foz Côa. 68c, Conímbriga. 80c, Milreu. €1, Alcalar.

€2.50, José Leite de Vasconcelos (1858-1941), first director of National Museum of Archaeology.

2011, Sept. 21   *Perf. 13 Syncopated*
3353-3357 A925   Set of 5   7.50 3.50
Souvenir Sheet
3358 A925   €2.50 multi   5.50 3.50

See Nos. 3626-3627.

Protection of Water Resources and the Environment — A926

Designs: 32c, Hand holding glass under running faucet. 47c, Bandage on hose. 68c, Water bucket, filter and flowers. 80c, Recycling bins.

2011, Sept. 30
3359-3362 A926   Set of 4   5.50 3.00

Fado Musicians A927

Designs: 32c, Alfredo Marceneiro (1891-1982). 47c, Carlos Ramos (1907-69). 57c, Hermínia Silva (1907-93). 68c, Maria Teresa de Noronha (1918-93). 80c, Amália Rodrigues (1920-99). €1, Carlos do Carmo. €2.50, O Fado, painting by José Malhoa.

2011, Oct. 3
3363-3368 A927 Set of 6   9.00 4.50
Souvenir Sheet
3369 A927 €2.50 multi   5.50 3.50

Festival of the Trays, Tomar — A928

Festival of St. John the Baptist, Porto — A929

Loulé Carnival — A930

Serpentine Die Cut 11½
2011, Oct. 3   Self-Adhesive
3370 A928 N multi   .75   .25
3371 A929 A multi   1.10   .40
3372 A930 E multi   1.50   .45
    Nos. 3370-3372 (3)   3.35 1.10
On day of issue, No. 3370 sold for 32c; No. 3371, 47c; No. 3372, 68c.

School Correspondence — A931

Children's art: 32c, Bird and fish. 68c, Earth and sun as wheels on boy's bicycle. 80c, Three girls, duck.

2011, Oct. 11   *Perf. 13 Syncopated*
3373-3375 A931 Set of 3   4.00 2.00

Portuguese Military Academy, 175th Anniv. — A932

Designs: 32c, Academy building, Marquis de Sá da Bandeira (1795-1876). 68p, Academy crest and regalia. €2.50, Sword and regalia, vert.

2012, Jan. 12   *Perf. 12 Syncopated*
3376-3377 A932 Set of 2   2.25 1.10
Souvenir Sheet
3378 A932 €2.50 multi   5.50 3.25

Famous Men — A933

Designs: 32c, Marcos Portugal (1762-1830), composer. 68c, Brito Camacho (1862-1934), journalist and politician. 80c, António Vilar (1912-95), actor.

Perf. 13¼x13 Syncopated
2012, Feb. 13
3379-3381 A933 Set of 3   4.25 2.00

Art Depicting Biblical Scenes — A934

Designs: 47c, Creation of Eve (Criação de Eva). 68c, Moses in the Desert (Moisés no Deserto). 80c, Adoration of the Magi (Adoração dos Reis Magos). €1, The Last Supper (Ultima Ceia).
    No. 3386, €1.50, Crucifixion (Paixao de Cristo). No. 3387, €1.50, Pentecost (Pentecostes).

2012, Feb. 23
3382-3385 A934 Set of 4   6.50 3.25
Souvenir Sheets
3386-3387 A934 Set of 2   7.00 4.00

Colors and Associated Color-Blindness Shapes For Them — A935

Designs: 32c, Red (Vermelho). 47c, Blue (Azul). 68c, Yellow (Amarelo). 80c, Black (Preto). €1, White (Branco).

Perf. 13x13¼ Syncopated
2012, Mar. 20
3388-3392 A935 Set of 5   7.50 3.75

Guimares, 2012 European Capital of Culture A936

Designs: 32c, Largo da Oliveira. 47c, Vila Flor Cultural Center. 68c, Nicolinas Festival. 80c, Santa Marinha da Costa Inn. €3, Guimaraes Castle, sculpture by Joao Cutiliero.

Perf. 12x11¾ Syncopated
2012, Apr. 10
3393-3396 A936 Set of 4   5.25 2.50
Souvenir Sheet
3397 A936 €3 multi   6.75 4.00
No. 3397 contains one 80x30mm stamp.

Erasmus Foreign Exchange Program, 25th Anniv. A937

European landmarks and: 68c, Female student on bicycle. €3, Student on motor scooter, female student.

2012, Apr. 17
3398 A937 68c multi   1.50   .75
Souvenir Sheet
3399 A937 €3 multi   6.75 4.00
No. 3399 contains one 80x30mm stamp.

Europa A938

Designs: No. 3400, Steamer Principe Perfeito. No. 3401a, Lisbon waterfront.

2012, May 9
3400 A938 68c multi   1.50   .75
Souvenir Sheet
3401   Sheet of 2, #3400,
            3401a   3.50 1.75
    a. A938 68c multi   1.50   .75

Cathedrals A939

Cathedrals at: No. 3402, N, Braga. No. 3403, N, Faro. No. 3404, N, Guarda. No. 3405, N, Lamego. No. 3406, N, Porto. No. 3407, N, Santarém. No. 3408, N, Silves. No. 3409, N, Viana do Castelo. No. 3410, N, Vila Real. No. 3411, N, Viseu.

2012, May 18   *Perf. 13 Syncopated*
3402-3411 A939 Set of 10   8.00 4.00
Nos. 3402-3411 each sold for 32c on day of issue. See No. 3890.

University of Lisbon Institute of Social Sciences, 50th Anniv. A940

Designs: N, Adérito Sedas Nunes and *Análise Social* Magazine. E, Institute of Social Sciences Building.

Perf. 12x11¾ Syncopated
2012, May 31
3412 A940 N multi   .75   .35
3413 A940 E multi   1.60   .80
On day of issue, No. 3412 sold for 32c and No. 3413 sold for 68c.

2012 European Soccer Championships, Poland and Ukraine — A941

Design: 68c, Foosball figure and soccer ball. €2.50, Foosball figures and soccer ball, horiz.

Perf. 11¾x12 Syncopated
2012, June 4
3414 A941 68c multi   1.50   .75
Souvenir Sheet
Perf. 12x11¾ Syncopated
3415 A941 €2.50 multi   5.50 3.25

2012 Summer Olympics and Paralympics, London — A942

Designs: No. 3416, N, Stylized Olympic athlete. No. 3417, N, Two stylized Paralympic athletes. No. 3418, I, Stylized Olympic fencer. No. 3419, I, Stylized athlete in wheelchair.

Perf. 11¾x12 Syncopated
2012, June 19
3416-3419 A942 Set of 4   5.00 2.50
On day of issue, Nos. 3416-3417 each sold for 32c, and Nos. 3418-3419 each sold for 80c.

Transit of Venus A943

Designs: €2, Teodoro de Almeida (1722-1804), observer of 1761 transit, Venus and Sun. €3, Diagram showing Earth, Venus and Sun.

2012, June 27   *Perf. 13 Syncopated*
3420 A943 €2 multi   4.50 2.25
Souvenir Sheet
3421 A943 €3 multi   6.50 3.75

Souvenir Sheet

Victory of Portuguese Team at 2012 European Soccer Championships — A944

Perf. 11¾x12 Syncopated
2012, July 4
3422 A944 €1.50 multi   3.50 1.90

Traditional Portuguese Festivals A945

Designs: 5c, People watching fireworks. 32c, Festa de Santo António, Lisbon. 47c, Festas do Espirito Santo, Azores. 68c, Carnaval, Ilhavo. 90c, Golega Fair.

2012, July 20   *Perf. 11¾x11½*
3423 A945 5c multi   .25   .25
3424 A945 32c multi   .80   .40
3425 A945 47c multi   1.10   .50
3426 A945 68c multi   1.50   .75
3427 A945 80c multi   1.90   .80
    Nos. 3423-3427 (5)   5.55 2.70
Compare with Types A956-A958.

Douro River A946

Designs: 32c, Riverside cliffs. 57c, Boat on river. 68c, Terraced fields and road near river. 80c, Buildings near river. €3, Porto buildings, bridge and boats.

2012, July 30   Perf. 13 Syncopated
3428-3431 A946   Set of 4   5.50 2.75
Souvenir Sheet
3432 A946 €3 multi   6.50 3.75
No. 3432 contains one 80x30mm stamp. See No. 3891.

Training Ships — A947

Designs: 32c, NRP Sagres. 80c, NTM Creoula.
No. 3435, €1.75, Bell, silhouette of NRP Sagres. No. 3436, €1.75, Lifeboats, silhouette of NTM Creoula.

Perf. 11¾x12 Syncopated, 12x11¾ Syncopated (#3436)
2012, Aug. 3
3433-3434 A947   Set of 2   2.75 1.40
Souvenir Sheets
3435-3436 A947   Set of 2   8.50 4.25
See No. 3839.

Fernando Pessoa (1888-1935), Poet — A948

Joao da Cruz e Sousa (1861-98), Poet — A949

Perf. 11¾x12 Syncopated
2012, Sept. 7
3437 A948 80c multi + label   1.90 .95
3438 A949 80c multi + label   1.90 .95
See Brazil Nos. 3225-3226.

Sausages and Hams A950

Sausages: No. 3439, 32c, Guarda chouriço. No. 3440, 32c, Vinhais chouriça. No. 3441, 47c, Ponte de Lima onion chouriça. No. 3442, 47c, Barroso-Montalegre chouriça. 57c, Vinhais salpicao. No. 3444, 68c, Guarda

morcela. No. 3445, 68c, Vila Real moura. No. 3446, 80c, Mirandela alheira.
No. 3447, 80c, vert. — Hams from: a, Melgaço. b, Vinhais. c, Barroso.

Perf. 12x11¾ Syncopated
2012, Sept. 25
3439-3446 A950   Set of 8   10.00 5.00
Souvenir Sheet
Perf. 11¾x12 Syncopated
3447 A950 80c Sheet of 3, #a-c   6.25 3.25
See Nos. 3483-3491.

Palaces — A951

Rooms and exterior views of: No. 3448, 32c, Pena National Palace, Sao Pedro de Penaferrim. No. 3449, 32c, Ajuda National Palace, Lisbon, Queen Consort Maria Pia of Savoy (1847-1911). No. 3450, 68c, Mafra National Palace, Mafra. No. 3451, 68c, Sintra National Palace, Sintra. No. 3452, 80c, Monserrate Palace, Sintra. No. 3453, 80c, Queluz National Palace, Queluz.

Perf. 11¾x12 Syncopated
2012, Oct. 3
3448-3453 A951   Set of 6   8.50 4.25

School Correspondence A952

Children's art by: 32c, Martim dos Santos Onofre. 68c, Matilde Amaro Nunes. 80c, Ana Carolina Marques.

Perf. 13¼x13 Syncopated
2012, Oct. 9
3454-3456 A952   Set of 3   4.25 2.10

Fado Musicians A953

Designs: No. 3457, 32c, Vicente da Câmara. No. 3458, 32c, Argentina Santos. 57c, Maria da Fé. 68c, Rodrigo. 80c, Camané. No. 3462, €1, Mariza. No. 3463, Caricature of Fado guitarist, neck of Fado guitar.

2012, Oct. 11   Litho.
3457-3463 A953   Set of 7   11.00 5.50

First Humorists Exhibition, Cent. — A954

Caricutures and cartoon art by: No. 3464, 32c, Rafael Bordalo Pinheiro. No. 3465, 47c, Stuart Carvalhais. No. 3466, 68c, Emmerico Nunes. No. 3467, 80c, Almada Negreiros.
No. 3468: a, 32c, Francisco Valenca. b, 32c, Manuel Gustavo Bordalo Pinheiro. c, 47c, Jorge Barradas. d, 47c, Américo Amarelhe. e, 68c, Celso Herminio. f, 68c, Canto da Maya. g, 80c, Cristiano Cruz. h, 80c, Menezes Ferreira.

Perf. 13¼x13 Syncopated
2012, Oct. 16
3464-3467 A954   Set of 4   5.00 2.50
Souvenir Sheet
3468 A954   Sheet of 8, #a-h   11.50 5.75

Order of Engineers — A955

Designs: 32c, Civil, geological and mining engineering. 47c, Electrical and informational engineering. 57c, Naval and mechanical engineering. 68c, Material, chemical and biological engineering. 80c, Forestry and agronomic engineering. €1, Geographical and environmental engineering. €3, Arch and angels.

Perf. 13x13¼ Syncopated
2012, Oct. 19
3469-3474 A955   Set of 6   9.00 4.50
Souvenir Sheet
3475 A955 €3 multi   6.50 4.00

Festa do Santo António, Lisbon — A956

Festas do Espirito Santo, Azores — A957

Carnaval, Ilhavo — A958

Serpentine Die Cut11½
2012, Nov. 13   Self-Adhesive
3476 A956 N multi   .75 .30
3477 A957 (47c) multi   1.10 .50
3478 A958 E multi   1.60 .70
    Nos. 3476-3478 (3)   3.85 1.90
Compare with type A945. On day of issue, No. 3476 sold for 32c and No. 3478 sold for 68c.

Composers A959

Designs: No. 3479, E, Giuseppe Verdi (1813-1901). No. 3480, E, Richard Wagner (1813-83).

No. 3481, €1.50, Falstaff. No. 3482, €1.50, Valkyrie.

Perf. 11¾x12 Syncopated
2013, Jan. 31
3479-3480 A959   Set of 2   3.25 1.60
Souvenir Sheets
3481-3482 A959   Set of 2   7.00 4.25
On day of issue, Nos. 3479-3480 each sold for 68c.

Sausages and Hams Type of 2012

Designs: No. 3483, N, Portalegre chouriço mouro. No. 3484, N, Estremoz and Borba farinheira. No. 3485, A, Estremoz and Borba chouriço. No. 3486, A, Monchique farinheira. No. 3487, E, Portalegre paio enguitado. No. 3488, E, Sao Miguel morcela. No. 3489, I, Serta maranhos. No. 3490, I, Portalegre paio ou lombo branco.
No. 3491, vert. — Hams from: a, Barrancos. b, Santana da Serra.

Perf. 12x11¾ Syncopated
2013, Mar. 15
3483-3490 A950   Set of 8   10.00 5.00
Souvenir Sheet
Perf. 11¾x12 Syncopated
3491 A950 €1 Sheet of 2, #a-b   4.50 2.60
On day of issue, Nos. 3483-3484 each sold for 32c, Nos. 3485-3486 each sold for 47c, Nos. 3487-3488 each sold for 68c and Nos. 3489-3490 each sold for 80c.

Falconry — A960

Designs: N, Falco peregrinus, falcon hood. A, Accipiter gentilis, pouch. E, Accipiter nisus, lure. I, Aquila chrysaetos, gauntlet.
€1.50, Royal Falconry Building, Salvaterra do Magos.

Perf. 11¾x12 Syncopated
2013, Mar. 23
3492 A960 N multi   .75 .30
3493 A960 A multi   1.10 .55
3494 A960 E multi   1.60 .70
3495 A960 I multi   1.90 .95
    Nos. 3492-3495 (4)   5.35 2.50
Souvenir Sheet
3496 A960 €1.50 multi   3.50 2.00
On day of issue Nos. 3492-3495 each sold for 32c, 47c, 68c and 80c, respectively.

Famous People A961

Designs: 36c, Joao Villaret (1913-61), actor. 60c, Ilse Losa (1913-2006), writer. 70c, Joao Dos Santos (1913-87), psychiatrist. 80c, Edgar Cardoso (1913-2000), civil engineer. €1, Raúl Rego (193-2002), journalist.

Perf. 12x11¾ Syncopated
2013, Apr. 15
3497-3501 A961   Set of 5   7.50 3.75

Traditional Portuguese Festivals — A962

Designs: 3c, Icon, men in red vestments. 4c, Icon, men in blue vestments. 36c, Woman and girl, Sao Mateus Fair, Viseu. 50c, Woman, icon on boat, Feast of Our Lady of Agony, Viana do Castelo. 70c, People in costumes, Feast of Santo Estevao, Ousilhao. 80c, Men wearing hats, Feast of Our Lady of Guadalupe, Serpa. €1, Three participants,

People's Festival, Campo Maior. €1.70, Man, woman and icon, Pilgrimage of Our Lady of Almortao, Idanha-a-Nova.

2013, Apr. 30   *Perf. 11¾x11½*

3502	A962	3c multi	.25	.25
3503	A962	4c multi	.25	.25
3504	A962	36c multi	.80	.30
3505	A962	50c multi	1.10	.55
3506	A962	70c multi	1.50	.75
3507	A962	80c multi	1.90	.90
3508	A962	€1 multi	2.40	1.20
3509	A962	€1.70 multi	4.00	2.00
		Nos. 3502-3509 (8)	12.20	6.20

Arrival of Explorer Jorge Alvares in China, 500th Anniv. — A963

Old map of Chinese coast and: 36c, Chinese compass. 80c, Compass rose. €3, Chinese vase, old map of Chinese coast.

Perf. 11¾x12 Syncopated

2013, May 8   Litho.

3510-3511 A963 Set of 2   2.75 1.40

Souvenir Sheet

3512 A963 €3 multi   7.00 4.00

No. 3512 contains one 30x80mm stamp.

Europa A964

Designs: No. 3513, Portuguese postal van facing left. No. 3514a, Postal worker and Portuguese postal van.

Perf. 12x11¾ Syncopated

2013, May 9   Litho.

3513 A964 70c multi   1.50 .75

Souvenir Sheet

3514		Sheet of 2, #3513, 3514a	3.50	1.90
a.	A964	70c multi	1.75	.80

Lay Missions in Africa, Cent. — A965

Designs: 36c, Eight missionaries to Angola. 80c, Seven missionaries to Mozambique. €2.60, Colonial Missions Institute, Cernache do Bonjardim.

Perf. 11¾x12 Syncopated

2013, May 13   Litho.

3515-3516 A965 Set of 2   2.50 1.25

Souvenir Sheet

3517 A965 €2.60 multi   6.25 3.50

Intl. Year of Statistics A966

Graph and: 36c, Gears. €1, People carrying streamers. €2, Graph, trees and rain clouds.

Perf. 12x11¾ Syncopated

2013, May 24   Litho.

3518-3519 A966 Set of 2   3.00 1.50

Souvenir Sheet

3520 A966 €2 multi   4.50 2.75

No. 3520 contains one 80x30mm stamp.

Cathedrals A967

Designs: No. 3521, 36c, Old Coimbra Cathedral (Velha). No. 3522, 36c, New Coimbra Cathedral (Nova). No. 3523, 36c, Portalegre Cathedral. No. 3524, 36c, Castelo Branco Cathedral. No. 3525, 36c, Leiria Cathedral. No. 3526, 36c, Aveiro Cathedral. No. 3527, 80c, Funchal Cathedral. No. 3528, 80c, Angra Cathedral.

Perf. 11¾x12 Syncopated

2013, June 6   Litho.

3521-3528 A967 Set of 8   9.00 4.50

See Madeira No. 363.

Antique Works of Jewelers A968

Designs: 36c, Bronze Age bracelet. 70c, Iron Age earring. 80c, Roman Era phiale. €1.70, Visigoth Era fibula. €3, Iron Age necklace, vert.

Perf. 12x11¾ Syncopated

2013, June 21   Litho.

3529-3532 A968 Set of 4   8.00 4.00

Souvenir Sheet

Perf. 11¾x12 Syncopated

3533 A968 €3 multi   6.50 4.00

Woman and Girl, Sao Mateus Fair, Viseu — A969

Woman, Icon on Boat, Feast of Our Lady of Agony, Viana do Castelo — A970

People in Costumes, Feast of Santo Estevao, Ousilhao — A971

Die Cut Perf. 11½

2013, July 22   Litho.

Self-Adhesive

3534	A969	N multi	.85	.30
3535	A970	A multi	1.20	.60
3536	A971	E multi	1.60	.80
		Nos. 3534-3536 (3)	3.65	1.70

On day of issue, No. 3534 sold for 36c; No. 3535, 50c; No. 3536, 70c.

Catholic Missions in Africa A972

Designs: 36c, Child at blackboard (education). 50c, Nurses and patient (health care). 70c, Children at sink (building of infrastructure). 80c, Man watering plants (agricultural development). €1, Adult education. €1.70, Priest and children (evangelization).

Perf. 12x11¾ Syncopated

2013, Aug. 19   Litho.

3537-3542 A972 Set of 6   11.00 5.50

Compilation of the Canon of Medicine, by Avicenna, 1000th Anniv. — A973

Designs: €1.70, Avicenna taking notes. €3.30, Avicenna examining patient, horiz.

2013, Aug. 23   Litho.   *Perf. 11¾x12*

3543 A973 €1.70 multi   4.00 2.00

Souvenir Sheet

3544 A973 €3.30 multi   7.00 4.50

No. 3544 contains one 61x40mm stamp.

Presentation of 12th Aga Khan Awards for Architecture — A974

Designs: 80c, Tiles. €1, Embroidery design €3, Sao Jorge Castle, Lisbon, site of awards ceremony, vert.

2013, Sept. 6   Litho.   *Perf. 12x12½*

3545-3546 A974 Set of 2   4.00 2.00

Souvenir Sheet
Silk-faced Paper
Perf. 12½x12

3547 A974 €3 multi   7.00 4.00

No. 3547 contains one 30x80mm stamp.

Sculptures of Joana Vasconcelos A975

Designs: 50c, Red Independent Heart. 80c, Cinderella.

Perf. 11¾x12 Syncopated

2013, Sept. 16   Litho.

3548-3549 A975 Set of 2   3.00 1.50

Apiculture — A976

Designs: 36c, Bees, honeycomb, beekeeper tending hive. 50c, Bees at hive entrance and in flight. 70c, Bees in flight over field. 80c, Bees and flowers.

€1.70, Bee on flower. €1.90, Bee, beekeeper removing honey from honeycomb.

Perf. 12x11¾ Syncopated

2013, Sept. 23   Litho.

3550-3553 A976 Set of 4   5.00 2.50

Souvenir Sheets

3554-3555 A976 Set of 2   8.00 5.00

Papal Recognition of Sovereign Military Order of Malta, 900th Anniv. — A977

Grand Masters: 36c, Afonso of Portugal (1137-1207). 70c, Luís Mendes de Vasconcelos (c. 1542-1623). 80c, António Manoel de Vilhena (1663-1736). €1, Manuel Pinto da Fonseca (1681-1773). €1.95, Ship of Grand Master Pinto da Fonseca.

Perf. 11¾x12 Syncopated

2013, Sept. 27   Litho.

3556-3559 A977 Set of 4   6.50 3.25

Souvenir Sheet

3560 A977 €1.95 multi   4.50 2.60

No. 3560 contains one 30x80mm stamp.

School Correspondence — A978

Children's art by: N, Martim Ferreira Simao. E, David Serafim Reis. I, Francisco Maria Rasquilha.

Perf. 12x11¾ Syncopated

2013, Oct. 9   Litho.

3561-3563 A978 Set of 3   4.00 2.00

On day of issue, No. 3561 sold for 36c; No. 3562, 70c; No. 3563, 80c.

Christmas A979

Various creche figures: N, 50c, 60c, 70c, 80c, €1.70,

Perf. 12x11¾ Syncopated

2013, Oct. 9   Litho.

3564-3569 A979 Set of 6   11.00 5.50

No. 3564 sold for 36c on day of issue.

Souvenir Sheet

Public Trading of Shares of CTT Portugal — A980

Perf. 12x11¾ Syncopated

2014, Jan. 27   Litho.

3570 A980 €1.70 multi   4.00 2.40

Extreme Sports — A981

Designs: 40c, Surfing. 50c, Mountain biking. 70c, Skateboarding. 80c, Kayaking. €1.70, Paragliding.

Perf. 11¾x11½

2014, Feb. 10			Litho.	
3571	A981	40c multi	.95	.30
3572	A981	50c multi	1.20	.60
3573	A981	70c multi	1.60	.80
3574	A981	80c multi	1.90	.90
3575	A981	€1.70 multi	4.00	2.00
	Nos. 3571-3575 (5)		9.65	4.60

See Nos. 3602-3604, 3669-3671, 3685-3689, 3765-3767, 3778-3782.

Publication of Peregrinaço (Pilgrimage), Travel Writings of Fernao Mendes Pinto, 400th Anniv. — A982

Designs: €1, Front page of Peregrinaço, ships, Buddhist deity on peacock, horseman. €3, Old map.

Perf. 12x11¾ Syncopated

2014, Feb. 24			Litho.	
3576	A982	€1 multi	2.40	1.20

Souvenir Sheet

| 3577 | A982 | €3 multi | 7.00 | 4.25 |

Portuguese Notary Publics, 800th Anniv. A983

Designs: 80c, Documents. €3, Notary public writing in book.

Perf. 12x11¾ Syncopated

2014, Mar. 6			Litho.	
3578	A983	80c multi	1.90	.95

Souvenir Sheet

| 3579 | A983 | €3 multi | 7.00 | 4.25 |

No. 3579 contains one 80x30mm stamp.

Famous People — A984

Designs: 40c, Florbela Espanca (1894-1930), poet. 50c, Maria Keil (1914-2012), painter. 60c, Joaquim Namorado (1914-86), poet. 70c, Joao Hogan (1914-88), painter. 80c, António Dacosta (1914-90), painter. €1, José Sebastiao e Silva (1914-72), mathematician.

Perf. 11¾x12 Syncopated

2014, Mar. 24			Litho.	
3580-3585	A984	Set of 6	9.00	4.50

Architects and Their Buildings — A985

Designs: No. 3586, I, Paula Rego Museum, by Eduardo Souto de Moura. No. 3587, I, Júlio

Pomar Museum, by Alvaro Siza Vieira. No. 3588, I, Green Corridor of Lisbon, by Gonçalo Ribeiro Telles.

Perf. 12x11¾ Syncopated

2014, Apr. 7			Litho.	
3586-3588	A985	Set of 3	5.50	2.75

On day of issue, Nos. 3586-3588 each sold for 80c.

Military Coup of April 25, 1974, 40th Anniv. A986

Designs: No. 3589, N, Soldiers and vehicles in Palace Square, Lisbon. No. 3590. I, Crowd surrounding soldiers in transport vehicle. €3, Flags of Portugal, Greece and Spain.

Perf. 12x11¾ Syncopated

2014, Apr. 14			Litho.	
3589-3590	A986	Set of 2	2.75	1.40

Souvenir Sheet

| 3591 | A986 | €3 multi | 7.00 | 4.25 |

On day of issue, No. 3589 sold for 42c; No. 3590, for 80c. No. 3591 contains one 80x30mm stamp.

Miniature Sheet

Anatomical Drawings by Andreas Vesalius (1514-64) — A987

No. 3592: a, 40c, Nude man. b, 60c, Skeleton. c, 70c, Nervous system. d, 80c, Muscular system. e, €1, Circulatory system.

Photo. & Engr.

2014, Apr. 21			Perf. 11½	
3592	A987	Sheet of 5, #a-e	8.50	5.00

See Belgium No. 2689.

Archbishop Bartholomew of Braga (1514-90) — A988

Designs: 70c, Archbishop standing. €3, Archbishop seated.

Perf. 11¾x12 Syncopated

2014, Apr. 28			Litho.	
3593	A988	70c multi	1.60	.80

Souvenir Sheet

| 3594 | A988 | €3 multi | 7.00 | 4.25 |

No. 3594 contains one 30x80mm stamp.

Eusébio (1942-2014), Soccer Player — A989

Designs: No. 3595, N, Eusébio chasing soccer ball. No. 3596, E, Eusébio dribbling ball. €2.50, Eusébio kicking ball.

Perf. 11¾x12 Syncopated

2014, May 2			Litho.	
3595-3596	A989	Set of 2	2.75	1.40

Souvenir Sheet

| 3597 | A989 | €2.50 multi | 6.00 | 3.50 |

On day of issue, No. 3595 sold for 42c; No. 3596, for 72c.

Portuguese Language, 800th Anniv. A990

Designs: 80c, Arms of Portugal, flags of Portuguese-speaking countries, hand with pen.
€2.50, Pen nib, green and red lines, vert.

Perf. 12x11¾ Syncopated

2014, May 5			Litho.	
3598	A990	80c multi	1.90	.95

Souvenir Sheet

Perf. 11¾x12 Syncopated

| 3599 | A990 | €2.50 multi | 6.00 | 3.50 |

Europa — A991

Designs: No. 3600, Bagpiper. No. 3601a, Bagpipes.

Perf. 11¾x12 Syncopated

2014, May 9			Litho.	
3600	A991	E multi	1.60	.80

Souvenir Sheet

| 3601 | | Sheet of 2, #3600, 3601a | 3.50 | 2.00 |
| a. | A991 | E multi | 1.75 | 1.00 |

On day of issue Nos. 3600 and 3601a each sold for 72c. See No. 3892.

Extreme Sports Type of 2014

Designs: N, Surfing. A, Mountain biking. E, Skateboarding.

Die Cut Perf. 11½

2014, May 27			Litho.	
		Self-Adhesive		
3602	A981	N multi	1.00	.35
3603	A981	A multi	1.20	.50
3604	A981	E multi	1.75	.90
	Nos. 3602-3604 (3)		3.95	1.75

On day of issue, No. 3602 sold for 42c; No. 3603, 50c; No. 3604, 72c.

Diplomatic Relations Between Portugal and Mexico, 150th Anniv. A992

Portuguese and Mexican flags with denomination color of: 42c, Gray. 80c, White.

Perf. 12x11¾ Syncopated

2014, June 6			Litho.	
3605-3606	A992	Set of 2	2.75	1.40

See Mexico Nos. 2876-2877.

2014 World Cup Soccer Championships, Brazil — A993

Designs: 42c, 2014 World Cup emblem and flag of Portugal. 72c, 2014 World Cup mascot and flag of Brazil.
€1, Silhouettes of soccer players, World Cup trophy, flag of Portugal.

Perf. 12x11¾ Syncopated

2014, June 16			Litho.	
3607-3608	A993	Set of 2	2.75	1.40

Souvenir Sheet

| 3609 | A993 | €1 multi | 2.50 | 1.40 |

No. 3609 contains one 80x30mm stamp.

Gardens A994

Designs: No. 3610, 42c, Chalet da Condessa D'Edla, Sintra. No. 3611, 42c, Palácio Fronteira, Lisbon. 50c, Palácio Nacional de Queluz, Sintra. 62c, Parque de Serralves, Porto. No. 3614, 72c, Mosteiro de Tibaes, Braga. No. 3615, 72c, Jardim Botânico da Universidade, Coimbra. No. 3616, 80c, Quinta do Palheiro Ferreira, Madeira. No. 3617, 80c, Parque Terra Nostra, Sao Miguel, Azores.

Perf. 12x11¾ Syncopated

2014, June 26			Litho.	
3610-3617	A994	Set of 8	12.00	6.00

See Nos. 3759, 4117, Madeira No. 364.

Garrison Border Town of Elvas and Its Fortifications UNESCO World Heritage Site — A995

Designs: 42c, Graça Fort. 50c, Amoreira Aqueduct. 72c, Santa Luzia Fort. 80c, Pelourinho.
€1.70, Olivença Gate.

Perf. 12x11¾ Syncopated

2014, June 30			Litho.	
3618-3621	A995	Set of 4	5.50	2.75

Souvenir Sheet

| 3622 | A995 | €1.70 multi | 4.00 | 2.40 |

See Nos. 3840, 4126.

Types of 2007-11

Die Cut Perf. 10½

2014, July 21			Litho.	
		Self-Adhesive		
3623	A816	E Like #2956	1.60	.80
3624	A861	E Like #3126	1.60	.80
3625	A919	E Like #3327	1.60	.80
3626	A925	E Like #3356	1.60	.80
3627	A925	E Like #3357	1.60	.80
	Nos. 3623-3627 (5)		8.00	4.00

Nos. 3623-3627 each sold for 72c on day of issue.

Intl. Year of Crystallography — A996

Designs: 42c, Chalcopyrite. 50c, Sodium chloride. 72c, Patterson function and crystal lattice. 80c, Caffeine molecular model, coffee beans. €1, Hemoglobin.
€1.70, Snowflake, vert.

Perf. 12x11¾ Syncopated
2014, July 21 Litho.
3628-3632 A996 Set of 5 7.50 3.75
Souvenir Sheet
Perf. 11¾x12 Syncopated
3633 A996 €1.70 multi 4.00 2.40

King Manuel I's Diplomatic Mission to Pope Leo X, 500th Anniv. — A997

Designs: 42c, Display of Portuguese wealth before Pope Leo X. €2, Hanno, elephant gift from King Manuel I, and crowd.

Perf. 12x11¾ Syncopated
2014, July 29 Litho.
3634-3635 A997 Set of 2 5.50 2.75

Cathedrals A998

Designs: No. 3636, 42c, Old Bragança Cathedral (antiga). No. 3637, 42c, New Bragança Cathedral (nova). No. 3638, 42c, Beja Cathedral. No. 3639, 42c, Elvas Cathedral. No. 3640, 42c, Evora Cathedral. No. 3641, 42c, Lisbon Cathedral. No. 3642, 42c, Miranda do Douro Cathedral. No. 3643, 42c, Setúbal Cathedral.

Perf. 12x11¾ Syncopated
2014, Aug. 18 Litho.
3636-3643 A998 Set of 8 8.00 4.00
See Nos. 4118, 4127.

University of Coimbra UNESCO World Heritage Site — A999

Designs: 42c, College of Nuestra Senhora da Graça. 50c, Joanine Library. 72c, Chemistry Laboratory. 80c, Humanities Faculties Building.
€1.70, Main courtyard.

Perf. 11¾x12 Syncopated
2014, Sept. 24 Litho.
3644-3647 A999 Set of 4 5.50 2.75
Souvenir Sheet
3648 A999 €1.70 multi 4.00 2.25
See No. 3893.

Coffee — A1000

Coffee bushes and plantation workers from: 42c, Timor. 62c, Angola. 72c, Brazil. 80c, St. Thomas and Prince Islands.
€3.50, Hand holding coffee bush seedling.

Perf. 11¾x12 Syncopated
2014, Sept. 29 Litho.
3649-3652 A1000 Set of 4 6.00 3.00
Souvenir Sheet
3653 A1000 €3.50 multi 8.00 4.50

University of Coimbra Geophysical Institute, 150th Anniv. A1001

Fields of study: 42c, Seismology. 62c, Geomagnetism. 72c, Meteorology. 80c, Planetary science.
€2.80, Geophysical Institute, vert.

Perf. 12x11¾ Syncopated
2014, Oct. 3 Litho.
3654-3657 A1001 Set of 4 6.50 3.25
Souvenir Sheet
Perf. 11¾x12 Syncopated
3658 A1001 €2.80 multi 7.00 3.50
No. 3658 contains one 30x80mm stamp.

Modern Portuguese Tapestries A1002

Designs: No. 3659, 42c, Ambiguous Structure, by Eduardo Nery. No. 3660, 42c, Endless Purpose, by Cruzeiro Seixas. 50c, Egypte, by Vieira da Silva. 62c, Arruto, by Júlio Pomar. 72c, Racial Integration, by Almada Negreiros. 80c, Magenta, by Joana Vasconcelos.
€1.70, Weaver at loom.

Perf. 11¾x12 Syncopated
2014, Oct. 9 Litho.
3659-3664 A1002 Set of 6 8.75 4.50
Souvenir Sheet
3665 A1002 €1.70 multi 4.25 2.10

Sustainable Transportation — A1003

No. 3666: a, 42c, Train, bus, man on Segway. b, 80c, Bicycle riders, electric automobile.

Perf. 12x11¾ Syncopated
2015, Jan. 27 Litho.
3666 A1003 Horiz. pair, #a-b 2.75 1.40

Types of 2009-11
Die Cut Perf. 10½
2015, Jan. 19 Litho.
Self-Adhesive
3667 A864 E Like #3144 1.75 .85
3668 A919 E Like #3330 1.75 .85
Nos. 3667-3668 each sold for 72c on day of issue.

Extreme Sports Type of 2014
Designs: N, Kitesurfing. A, Rock climbing. E, Rafting.

Die Cut Perf. 10x9½
2015, Feb. 12 Litho.
Self-Adhesive
3669 A981 N multi .95 .45
3670 A981 A multi 1.10 .55
3671 A981 E multi 1.60 .80
Nos. 3669-3671 (3) 3.65 1.80
On day of issue, No. 3669 sold for 42c; No. 3670, 50c; No. 3671, 72c.

Orpheu Magazine, Cent. — A1004

Cover from: 42c, First edition. 72c, Second edition.
€2.50, Painting of person reading second edition.

Perf. 11¾x12 Syncopated
2015, Feb. 20 Litho.
3672-3673 A1004 Set of 2 2.60 1.40
Souvenir Sheet
3674 A1004 €2.50 multi 5.50 2.75

Music Personalities A1005

Designs: 72c, Jean Sibelius (1865-1957), composer. 80c, Elisabeth Schwarzkopf (1915-2006), opera singer.
No. 3677, €1.50, Sibelius, horiz. No. 3678, €1.50, Schwarzkopf, horiz.

Perf. 11¾x12 Syncopated
2015, Mar. 26 Litho.
3675-3676 A1005 Set of 2 3.50 1.75
Souvenir Sheets
Perf. 12x11¾ Syncopated
3677-3678 A1005 Set of 2 6.75 3.50

Famous People A1006

Designs: N, Francisco Vieira (1765-1805), painter. A, Manuel Maria Barbosa du Bocage (1765-1805), poet. 62c, Ramalho Ortigao (1836-1915), writer. 72c, Ruy Cinatti (1915-86), poet. 80c, Agostinho Ricca (1913-2010),

architect. €1, Frederico George (1915-94), architect.

Perf. 12x11¾ Syncopated
2015, Mar. 31 Litho.
3679-3684 A1006 Set of 6 9.25 4.75
On day of issue, No. 3679 sold for 45c; No. 3680, 55c.

Extreme Sports Type of 2014
Designs: 2c, Wingsuit flying. 45c, Kitesurfing. 55c, Rock climbing. 72c, Rafting. 80c, BMX cycling.
2015, Apr. 17 Litho. Perf. 11¾x11½
3685 A981 2c multi .25 .25
3686 A981 45c multi 1.00 .55
3687 A981 55c multi 1.25 .60
3688 A981 72c multi 1.75 .85
3689 A981 80c multi 1.90 .95
Nos. 3685-3689 (5) 6.15 3.15

Clay Figurines A1007

Figurines from: No. 3690, 45c, Barcelos. No. 3691, 45c, Vila Nova de Gaia. No. 3692, 55c, Estremoz. No. 3693, 55c, Ribolhos.

Perf. 12x11¾ Syncopated
2015, Apr. 21 Litho.
3690-3693 A1007 Set of 4 4.50 2.25
See No. 4128, Azores No. 568, Madeira No. 338.

Intl. Association of Portuguese-Speaking Countries, 25th Anniv. — A1008

Perf. 11¾x12 Syncopated
2015, Apr. 27 Litho.
3694 A1008 80c multi 1.75 .90
Souvenir Sheet
Perf. 12x11¾ Syncopated
3695 A1008 €2 Emblem, horiz. 4.50 2.25
See Angola No. , Brazil No. 3300, Cape Verde No. 1004, Guinea-Bissau No. , Macao No. 1440. Mozambique No. , St. Thomas and Prince Islands No. 2954, Timor No.

Reintroduction of the Iberian Lynx to Portugal — A1009

Designs: 45c, Head of lynx. 55c, Lynx, flower. 72c, Lynx and rabbits. 80c, Lynx facing left.
€2, Pride of lynx.

Perf. 12x11¾ Syncopated
2015, Apr. 30 Litho.
3696-3699 A1009 Set of 4 5.75 3.00
Souvenir Sheet
3700 A1009 €2 multi 4.50 2.25
No. 3700 contains one 80x30mm stamp.

Europa
A1010

Old toys: No. 3701, Helicopter. No. 3702a, Cabinet.

Perf. 12x11¾ Syncopated
2015, May 8 **Litho.**
3701 A1010 72c multi 1.60 .80
Souvenir Sheet
3702 Sheet of 2, #3701, 3.25 1.60
3702a
a. A1010 72c multi 1.60 .80

Way of St. James — A1011

Inscriptions: 45c, Sao Tiago Maior. 55c, Lisboa, Santarém. 72c, Porto, San Pedro de Rates. 80c, Viseu, Chaves.
€2, Catedral de Santiago de Compostela.

Perf. 12x11¾ Syncopated
2015, May 8 **Litho.**
3703-3706 A1011 Set of 4 5.75 3.00
Souvenir Sheet
3707 A1011 €2 multi 4.50 2.25

International Telecommunication
Union, 150th Anniv. — A1012

Designs: 80c, 150th anniv. emblem. €1, 150th anniv. emblem, world map.

2015, May 18 Litho. Perf. 12x11¾
3708-3709 A1012 Set of 2 4.00 2.00

Belém
Tower,
Lisbon,
500th
Anniv.
A1013

Designs: 45c, Drawing of tower, king. 72c, Tower, flag and boats, rhinoceros. 80c, Photograph of tower, seaplane.
€2, Photograph of tower, diff.

Perf. 12x11¾ Syncopated
2015, July 1 **Litho.**
3710-3712 A1013 Set of 3 4.50 2.25
Souvenir Sheet
3713 A1013 €2 sil & multi 4.50 2.25
No. 3713 contains one 80x30mm stamp. See No. 3841.

Boats of the Mediterranean — A1014

Designs: 45c, Canoa do alto. 72c, Calao. 80c, Canoa da picada.
€1.80, Caique and Galeao.

Office of the
Ombudsman,
40th
Anniv. — A1015

Designs: 45c, Man, woman, child, building. €2, Building, birds.

Perf. 11¾x12 Syncopated
2015, July 15 **Litho.**
3718 A1015 45c multi 1.00 .50
Souvenir Sheet
3719 A1015 €2 multi 4.50 2.25
No. 3719 contains one 30x80mm stamp.

Mediterranean Diet — A1016

Dishes: No. 3720, 45c, Sopa de beldroegas (purslane soup). No. 3721, 45c, Carapaus de escabeche (fish in vinegar sauce). 72c, Cozido do grao com peras (bean stew with pears). 80c, Broas de batata doce (sweet potato scones).
€1.80, Caldeirada de polvo (octopus stew).

Perf. 12x11¾ Syncopated
2015, July 20 **Litho.**
3720-3723 A1016 Set of 4 5.50 2.75
Souvenir Sheet
3724 A1016 €1.80 multi 4.00 2.00

Rules of
Heredity, 150th
Anniv. — A1017

Pea plant and: 45c, Gregor Mendel (1822-84), scientist. €1, Peas on chart.

Perf. 11¾x12 Syncopated
2015, Aug. 4 **Litho.**
3725-3726 A1017 Set of 2 3.25 1.60

Coimbra
Question, 150th
Anniv. — A1018

Designs: 45c, Antonio Feliciano de Castilho (1800-75), writer. 55c, Antero de Quental (1842-91), writer.
€2, Writers José Maria Eça de Queirós, Joaquim Pedro de Oliveira Martins, Antero de Quental, Ramalho Ortigao and Abilio Manuel Guerra Junqueiro, horiz.

Perf. 12x11¾ Syncopated
2015, July 9 **Litho.**
3714-3716 A1014 Set of 3 4.50 2.25
Souvenir Sheet
3717 A1014 €1.80 multi 4.00 2.00
No. 3717 contains one 80x30mm stamp.

Perf. 11¾x12 Syncopated
2015, Aug. 12 **Litho.**
3727-3728 A1018 Set of 2 2.25 1.10
Souvenir Sheet
Perf. 12x11¾ Syncopated
3729 A1018 €2 multi 4.50 2.25
No. 3729 contains one 80x30mm stamp.

Fruits and
Nuts — A1019

Designs: No. 3730, 45c, Castanea sativa (chestnuts). No. 3731, 45c, Prunus avium (cherries). No. 3732, 55c, Pyrus communis (pears). No. 3733, 55c, Citrus spp. (oranges). 72c, Musa acuminata (bananas). 80c, Ananas comosus (pineapples).

Perf. 11¾x12 Syncopated
2015, Sept. 1 **Litho.**
3730-3735 A1019 Set of 6 8.00 4.00
3735a Souvenir sheet of 6, 8.00 4.00
#3730-3735
See No. 4129, Madeira No. 365.

St. John Bosco
(1815-88)
A1020

Designs: 45c, Bosco and children.
€2.50, Bosco, horiz.

Perf. 11¾x12 Syncopated
2015, Sept. 3 **Litho.**
3736 A1020 45c multi 1.00 .50
Souvenir Sheet
Perf. 12x11¾ Syncopated
3737 A1020 €2.50 gold & multi 5.75 3.00

St. Teresa of
Avila (1515-82)
A1021

Designs: 45c, Painting of St. Teresa. €2.50, St. Teresa, manuscript, horiz.

Perf. 11¾x12 Syncopated
2015, Sept. 11 **Litho.**
3738 A1021 45c gold & multi 1.00 .50
Souvenir Sheet
Perf. 12x11¾ Syncopated
3739 A1021 €2.50 gold & multi 5.75 3.00
No. 3739 contains one 80x30mm stamp.

Portugal's
Use of the
Sea
A1022

Designs: 45c, Tourism. 62c, Fishing. 72c, Transportation. 80c, Energy.
€2, Science.

Perf. 12x11¾ Syncopated
2015, Sept. 17 **Litho.**
3740-3743 A1022 Set of 4 6.00 3.00
Souvenir Sheet
3744 A1022 €2 multi 4.50 2.25

Portuguese
Capture of
Ceuta, 600th
Anniv. — A1023

Designs: 55c, Map, Church of Our Lady of Africa. €1, Map, Manzanna del Revellín Cultural Center.
€2.50, Royal Walls of Ceuta, 1572 depiction of Ceuta.

Perf. 11¾x12 Syncopated
2015, Sept. 28 **Litho.**
3745-3746 A1023 Set of 2 3.50 1.75
Souvenir Sheet
3747 A1023 €2.50 multi 5.75 3.00

Montepio Mutual Benefit Association,
175th Anniv. — A1024

Designs: 45c, Pelican emblem. 80c, Family and money box.
€2.50, Montepio headquarters, Lisbon, vert.

Perf. 12x11¾ Syncopated
2015, Oct. 1 **Litho.**
3748-3749 A1024 Set of 2 3.00 1.50
Souvenir Sheet
Perf. 11¾x12 Syncopated
3750 A1024 €2.50 multi 5.75 3.00
No. 3750 contains one 30x80mm stamp.

Dancers and
Choreographers
A1025

Designs: 45c, Francis Graça (1902-80), dancer. 55c, Margarida de Abreu (1915-2006), choreographer. 62c, Fernando Lima (1928-2005), choreographer. 72c, Agueda Sena, dancer. 80c, Isabel Santa Rosa (1931-2001), dancer. €1, Carlos Trincheiras (1937-93), dancer.

Perf. 11¾x12 Syncopated
2015, Oct. 9 **Litho.**
3751-3756 A1025 Set of 6 9.25 4.50

Intl. Year of
Light — A1026

No. 3757: a, Sun, galaxy, Earth, Moon, satellite. b, Lighthouse, solar panels.

Perf. 11¾x12 Syncopated
2015, Oct. 14   **Litho.**
3757 A1026 45c Vert. pair, #a-b   2.00 1.00

Intl. Year of
Soils — A1027

No. 3758: a, Earth, plant, roots, top of hourglass. b, Apple tree, apples, flowers, bottom of hourglass.

Perf. 11¾x12 Syncopated
2015, Oct. 14   **Litho.**
3758 A1027 45c Vert. pair, #a-b   2.00 1.00

Gardens Type of 2014
Die Cut Perf. 10½
2015, Oct. 23   **Litho.**
Self-Adhesive
3759 A994 E Like #3617   1.60 .80
No. 3759 sold for 72c on day of issue.

Arrival of Portuguese in Timor, 500th
Anniv. — A1028

Designs: 80c, Settlement near hills, flower, woman. €1, Timorese house, Dom Aleixo Corte-Real (1886-1943), leader of revolt against Japanese occupation, Timorese sash. €2.50, Model of Timorese house, scuplture.

Perf. 12x11¾ Syncopated
2015, Oct. 28   **Litho.**
3760-3761 A1028   Set of 2   4.00 2.00
Souvenir Sheet
3762 A1028 €2.50 multi   5.50 2.25

Abade de Baçal Museum, Bragança,
Cent. — A1029

Designs: 80c, Museum displays. €2.05, Sculpture, cabinet and painting.

Perf. 12x11¾ Syncopated
2016, Feb. 16   **Litho.**
3763 A1029   80c multi   1.75 .85
Souvenir Sheet
3764 A1029 €2.05 multi   4.50 2.25

Extreme Sports Type of 2014
Designs: N, Paddleboarding. A, Skydiving. E, Skiing.

Die Cut Perf. 11½
2016, Feb. 25   **Litho.**
Self-Adhesive
3765 A981   N multi   1.00 .50
3766 A981   A multi   1.25 .65
3767 A981   E multi   1.60 .80
    Nos. 3765-3767 (3)   3.85 1.95
On day of issue, No. 3765 sold for 47c; No. 3766, 58c; No. 3767, 75c.

Famous
Men
A1030

Designs: No. 3768, N, Vergílio Ferreira (1916-96), writer. No. 3769, A, President António José de Almeida (1866-1929). No. 3770, E, Mário Dionísio (1916-93), writer and painter.

Perf. 12x11¾ Syncopated
2016, Mar. 14   **Litho.**
3768-3770 A1030   Set of 3   4.25 2.10
On day of issue, No. 3768 sold for 47c; No. 37696, 58c; No. 3770, 75c.

Grao Vasco National Museum, Viseu,
Cent. — A1031

Designs: 80c, Painting and museum displays. €2.05, Pitcher and painting.

Perf. 12x11¾ Syncopated
2016, Mar. 16   **Litho.**
3771 A1031   80c multi   1.90 .95
Souvenir Sheet
3772 A1031 €2.05 multi   4.75 2.40

Jesuits
A1032

Designs: 47c, St. Francis Xavier (1506-52). 58c, St. John de Britto (1647-93). 75c, Father Manuel Antunes (1918-85), educator and writer. 80c, Father Luís Archer (1926-2011), geneticist. €2, Father António Vieira (1608-97), philosopher.

Perf. 12x11¾ Syncopated
2016, Mar. 18   **Litho.**
3773-3776 A1032   Set of 4   6.00 3.00
Souvenir Sheet
3777 A1032 €2 gold & multi   4.75 2.40
No. 3777 contains one 80x30mm stamp.

Extreme Sports Type of 2014
Designs: 3c, Snowboarding. 47c, Paddleboarding. 58c, Skydiving. 75c, Skiing. 80c, Windsurfing.

Perf. 11¾x11½
2016, Mar. 31   **Litho.**
3778 A981   3c multi   .25 .25
3779 A981   47c multi   1.10 .55
3780 A981   58c multi   1.40 .70
3781 A981   75c multi   1.75 .85
3782 A981   80c multi   1.90 .95
    Nos. 3778-3782 (5)   6.40 3.30

Lubrapex
Philatelic
Exhibitions,
50th Anniv.
A1033

Designs: No. 3783, 80c, Filigree heart, Portugal. No. 3784, 80c, Headdress, Brazil.
No. 3785: a, Beaded necklace, Angola. b, Beaded necklace, Cape Verde. c, Sculpture, Guinea-Bissau. d, Fan, Macao. e, Necklace, Mozambique. f, Mask, St. Thomas and Prince Islands. g, Necklace, Timor.

Perf. 12x11¾ Syncopated
2016, Apr. 26   **Litho.**
3783-3784 A1033   Set of 2   3.75 1.90
Miniature Sheet
3785 A1033 47c Sheet of 7, #a-g, + label   7.75 4.00
    See Brazil No. 3325.

Cante Alentejano
Choral
Singing — A1034

Various costumes of singers: 47c, 80c.
No. 3788: a, Singers with flowers on hats. b, Singers with miner's helmets and jackets with gray stripes.

Perf. 11¾x12 Syncopated
2016, Apr. 27   **Litho.**
3786-3787 A1034   Set of 2   3.00 1.50
Souvenir Sheet
3788 A1034 €1 Sheet of 2, #a-b   4.75 2.40

Statue of
Virgin Mary
and
Basilica,
Fatima
A1035

Statue and Basilica: 80c, At night. €2, In daylight.

Perf. 12x11¾ Syncopated
2016, May 2   **Litho.**
3789 A1035 80c multi   1.90 .95
Souvenir Sheet
3790 A1035 €2 multi   4.75 2.40
No. 3790 contains one 80x30mm stamp. See No. 4119.

Europa
A1036

Designs: No. 3791, Bicyclist, buildings, wind generators.
No. 3792a, Mountain climbers, castle.

Perf. 12x11¾ Syncopated
2016, May 9   **Litho.**
3791 A1036 75c multi   1.75 .85
Souvenir Sheet
3792   Sheet of 2, #3791, 3792a   3.50 1.75
  a. A1036 75c multi   1.75 .85
    Think Green Issue.

Art Treasures From Portuguese
Museums — A1037

Details from: No. 3793, 80c, Middle left panel of St. Vincent, by Nuno Gonçalves. No. 3794, 80c, Middle rightside panel The Temptation of St. Anthony, by Hieronymus Bosch.
Details from: No. 3795, €1.80, Middle right panel of St. Vincent, by Nuno Gonçalves, diff. No. 3796, €1.80, Middle center panel The Temptation of St. Anthony, by Hieronymus Bosch, diff.

Perf. 12x11¾ Syncopated
2016, May 30   **Litho.**
3793-3794 A1037   Set of 2   3.75 1.90
Souvenir Sheets
3795-3796 A1037   Set of 2   8.00 4.00

Predatory
Mammals
A1038

Designs: No. 3797, 47c, Canis lupus. No. 3798, 47c, Vulpes vulpes. 58c, Felis silvestris. 65c, Genetta genetta. 75c, Lutra lutra. 80c, Meles meles.

Perf. 11¾x12 Syncopated
2016, June 7   **Litho.**
3797-3802 A1038   Set of 6   8.25 4.25

Bilateral
Trade
Between
Portugal
and Viet
Nam, 500th
Anniv.
A1039

Flags of Viet Nam and Portugal and: 47c, Plate, map of Lisbon. 80c, Vase, map of Hoi An, Viet Nam.

2016, July 1   **Litho.**   **Perf. 12x11¾**
3803-3804 A1039   Set of 2   3.00 1.50
    See Viet Nam Nos. 3549-3550.

Fish of the Mediterranean
Sea — A1040

Designs: No. 3805, 47c, Thunnus thynnus. 58c, Katsuwonus pelamis. 75c, Sarda sarda. 80c, Scomber scombrus.
No. 3809, 47c: a, Serranus atricauda. b, Serranus scriba. c, Epinephilus marginatus. d, Serranus cabrilla.

Perf. 12x11¾ Syncopated
2016, July 9   **Litho.**
3805-3808 A1040   Set of 4   5.75 3.00
Miniature Sheet
3809 A1040 47c Sheet of 4, #a-d   4.25 2.10

Souvenir Sheet

Portuguese Soccer Team, 2016
European Champions — A1041

Perf. 12x11¾ Syncopated
2016, July 11   **Litho.**
3810   A1041   €2 multi   4.50   2.25

First Portuguese Military Flight, Cent. A1042

Designs: 47c, Two airplanes. 80c, Airplane and pilot.
€1.50, Airplane, people around airplane near hangar.

Perf. 12x11¾ Syncopated
2016, July 15   **Litho.**
3811-3812   A1042   Set of 2   3.00   1.50
Souvenir Sheet
3813   A1042   €1.50 multi   3.50   1.75
No. 3813 contains one 80x30mm stamp.

Vineyards A1043

Designs: 47c, Vineyard workers and horses, grape buds. 58c, Aerial view of vineyard, white grapes. 75c, Grape harvesting, wine testing. 80c, Grape arbor, wine barrels.
€1.80, Ripe grapes on vine.

Perf. 11¾x12 Syncopated
2016, July 22   **Litho.**
3814-3817   A1043   Set of 4   5.75   3.00
Souvenir Sheet
3818   A1043   €1.80 multi   4.00   2.00
No. 3818 contains one 30x80mm stamp.

Decorative Walkways A1044

Location of walkway: No. 3819, 47c, Lisbon. 58c, Porto. 75c, Madeira. 80c, Azores.
No. 3823, 47c — Location of walkway: a, Macao. b, United States (E.U.A.). c, Spain. d, Brazil.

Perf. 12x11¾ Syncopated
2016, July 28   **Litho.**
3819-3822   A1044   Set of 4   5.75   3.00
Miniature Sheet
3823   A1044   47c Sheet of 4, #a-d   4.25   2.10
See No. 4120.

Sites in Lisbon A1045

Designs: 47c, Waterside pillars. 65c, Buildings on hillside near water. 75c, Ribiera das Naus walkway. 80c, Topiary, Edward VIII Park.

Perf. 12x11¾ Syncopated
2016, Aug. 26   **Litho.**
3824-3827   A1045   Set of 4   6.00   3.00
See No. 4121.

Radio Personalities — A1046

Designs: No. 3828, 47c, Artur Agostinho (1920-2011), reporter. No. 3829, 47c, António Sala, radio show host. No. 3830, 47c, Fernando Pessa (1902-2002), reporter. 58c, Francisco Sena Santos, reporter. 75c, Herman José, comedian. 80c, Ana Galvao, radio show host.

Perf. 12x11¾ Syncopated
2016, Aug. 30   **Litho.**
3828-3833   A1046   Set of 6   8.00   4.00

Publication of *Petri Nonii Salaciensis Opera (The Works of Pedro Nunes From Alcácer do Sal),* 450th Anniv. — A1047

Nunes and: 47c, Title page. €1, Loxodrome illustration.

Perf. 11¾x12 Syncopated
2016, Aug. 31   **Litho.**
3834-3835   A1047   Set of 2   3.25   1.60

Souvenir Sheet

Opening of Banco CTT — A1048

Perf. 12x11¾ Syncopated
2016, Sept. 21   **Litho.**
3836   A1048   €2 multi   4.50   2.25

Types of 2008-15
Die Cut Perf. 10½
2016, Sept. 23   **Litho.**
Self-Adhesive
3837   A845   E Like #3066   1.75   .85
3838   A859   E Like #3113   1.75   .85
3839   A947   E Like #3433   1.75   .85

3840   A995   E Like #3621   1.75   .85
3841   A1013   E Like #3712   1.75   .85
    Nos. 3837-3841 (5)   8.75   4.25

Nos. 3837-3841 each sold for 75c on day of issue.

Portuguese Postal System, 500th Anniv. A1049

Designs: 47c, Messenger with large pot. 58c, Messenger delivering message. 75c, Messenger with boat. 80c, Messenger on horse.
€1.80, Messenger delivering message, diff.

Perf. 12x11¾ Syncopated
2016, Oct. 10   **Litho.**
3842-3845   A1049   Set of 4   5.75   3.00
Souvenir Sheet
3846   A1049   €1.80 multi   4.00   2.00
No. 3846 contains one 80x30mm stamp.

Architecture of Paris and Lisbon — A1050

Designs: 47c, Rua Augusta Arch, Lisbon. 75c, Buildings along Rue Royale, Paris.

2016, Oct. 21   **Engr.**   **Perf. 13x13¼**
3847-3848   A1050   Set of 2   2.75   1.40
See France Nos. 5111-5112.

Army Heraldry A1051

Inscriptions at lower left: No. 3849, 47c, Exército (Army). No. 3850, 47c, Direçao de História e Cultura Militar (Military History and Culture Directorate). No. 3851, 47c, Comando do Instruçao e Doutrina (Training and Doctrine Command). No. 3852, 47c, Comando da Logistica (Logistics Command). No. 3853, 47c, Comando dos Forças Terrestres (Land Forces Command). No. 3854, 47c, Comando do Pessoal (Personnel Command).

Perf. 11¾x12 Syncopated
2016, Oct. 21   **Litho.**
3849-3854   A1051   Set of 6   6.25   3.25

Diplomatic Relations Between Philippines and Portugal, 70th Anniv. A1052

Flags of Philippines and Portugal and: 47c, Lavandula pedunculata, national flower of Portugal. 80c, Jasminum sambac, national flower of Philippines.

2016, Oct. 24   **Litho.**   **Perf. 12x11¾**
3855-3856   A1052   Set of 2   3.00   1.50
See Philippines No. 3691.

Historic Cafes A1053

Designs: No. 3857, 47c, Apolo Cafe, Funchal. No. 3858, 47c, Athanásio Cafe, Angra do Heroísmo. No. 3859, 47c, Arcada Cafe, Evora. No. 3860, 47c, Paraíso Cafe, Tomar. No. 3861, 47c, A Brasileira Cafe, Lisbon. No. 3862, 47c, Santa Cruz Cafe, Coimbra.
€1.50, Majestic Cafe, Porto, vert.

Perf. 12x11¾ Syncopated
2016, Oct. 27   **Litho.**
3857-3862   A1053   Set of 6   6.25   3.25
Souvenir Sheet
Perf. 11¾x12 Syncopated
3863   A1053   €1.50 multi   3.50   1.75
No. 3863 contains one 30x80mm stamp.

Fish Canning Industry — A1054

Designs: 47c, Fishing boat, illustration of fishermen, catch and cans, two anchovies. 58c, Fishermen hauling in catch, illustration of women preparing fish, two sardines. 65c, Dock for unloading fish, illustration of boat, woman and fish in net, two mackerels. 75c, Women packing fish in cans, illustration of open cans of fish, two tunas. 80c, People working in canning factory, illustration of woman holding basket, two squids. €1, Workers at canning factory, illustration of woman holding canned fish, two eels.

Perf. 12x11¾ Syncopated
2016, Oct. 31   **Litho.**
3864   A1054   47c multi   1.10   .55
3865   A1054   58c multi   1.25   .65
  a.   Horiz. pair, #3864-3865   2.40   —
    Complete booklet, #3865a   2.40
3866   A1054   65c multi   1.50   .75
3867   A1054   75c multi   1.75   .85
  a.   Horiz. pair, #3866-3867   3.25   —
    Complete booklet, #3867a   3.25
3868   A1054   80c multi   1.75   .90
3869   A1054   €1 multi   2.25   1.10
  a.   Horiz. pair, #3868-3869   4.00   —
    Complete booklet, #3869a   4.00
    Nos. 3864-3869 (6)   9.60   4.80

The three complete booklets were sold packed in a metal can similar to those in which fish are packed.

Election of António Guterres as United Nations Secretary-General — A1055

Guterres: 80c, Meeting African people. €2, Speaking at United Nations General Assembly, vert.

Perf. 12x11¾ Syncopated
2017, Jan. 4   **Litho.**
3870   A1055   80c multi   1.75   .85
Souvenir Sheet
Perf. 11¾x12 Syncopated
3871   A1055   €2 multi   4.50   2.25
No. 3871 contains one 30x80mm stamp.

Dancers A1056

Designs: 47c, Pauliteiros dancers, Portugal. 80c, Dandiya dancers, India.

2017, Jan. 7 Litho. Perf. 12x11¾
3872-3873 A1056 Set of 2 2.75 1.40
3873a Souvenir sheet of 2,
#3872-3873 2.75 1.40
See India Nos. 2896-2897.

Lisbon, 2017 Ibero-American Capital of Culture — A1057

Designs: 47c, Machu Picchu, Peru, ceramic pot. 65c, Sao Francisco Church, Salvador da Bahia, Brazil, berimbau. No. 3876, 80c, Palace of the Argentine National Congress, Buenos Aires, Argentina, emigrants (blue panel). No. 3877, 80c, Sport City, Oaxaca, Mexico (red panel). €2, Praça de Município, Lisbon, horiz.

Perf. 11¾x12 Syncopated
2017, Jan. 7 Litho.
3874-3877 A1057 Set of 4 6.00 3.00
Souvenir Sheet
Perf. 12x11¾ Syncopated
3878 A1057 €2 multi 4.50 2.25
No. 3878 contains one 80x30mm stamp.

Dominican Order, 800th Anniv. — A1058

Designs: €1, St. Dominic (1170-1221), founder of order. €2, Pope Honorius III Accepting the Rule of St. Dominic in 1216, painting by Leandro Bassano, horiz.

Perf. 11¾x12 Syncopated
2017, Jan. 9 Litho.
3879 A1058 €1 multi 2.25 1.10
Souvenir Sheet
Perf. 12x11¾ Syncopated
3880 A1058 €2 multi 4.50 2.25
No. 3880 contains one 80x30mm stamp.

Fruits — A1059

Designs: No. 3881, 47c, Ficus carica. No. 3882, 47c, Vitis vinifera. No. 3883, 58c, Prunus amygdalus. No. 3884, 58c, Malus domestica. 75c, Passiflora edulis. 80c, Annona cherimola.

Perf. 11¾x12 Syncopated
2017, Feb. 22
3881-3886 A1059 Set of 6 7.75 4.00
3886a Souvenir sheet of 6,
#3881-3886 7.75 4.00

Miniature Sheet

Visit of Pope Francis to Fatima — A1060

No. 3887 — Portion of Our Lady of Fatima statue and: a, 47c, Pope Francis at base of statue, 2015. b, 58c, Lúcia Santos, Jacinta and Francisco Marto, witnesses of apparition. c, 75c, Shrine of Fatima at night. d, 80c, Pilgrims in daylight.

Perf. 12x11¾ Syncopated
2017, Mar. 13 Litho.
3887 A1060 Sheet of 4, #a-d 5.50 2.75

Souvenir Sheet

Apparition of the Virgin Mary at Fatima, Cent. — A1061

Perf. 11¾x12 Syncopated
2017, Mar. 13 Litho.
3888 A1061 €2 multi 4.25 2.10
See Luxembourg No. 1461, Poland No. 4277, Slovakia No. 759.

Types of 2008-14
Serpentine Die Cut 11
2017, Mar. 24 Litho.
Self-Adhesive
3889 A845 E Like #3067 1.75 .85
3890 A939 E Like #3402 1.75 .85
3891 A946 E Like #3430 1.75 .85
3892 A991 E Like #3600 1.75 .85
3893 A999 E Like #3646 1.75 .85
Nos. 3889-3893 (5) 8.75 4.25
On day of issue, Nos. 3889-3893 each sold for 80c.

Dolphin Reserarch A1062

2017, Apr. 4 Litho. Perf. 12x12¼
3894 A1062 80c multi 1.75 .85
Joint issue between Portugal and Israel. See Israel No. 2139.

Famous Men — A1063

Designs: No. 3895, N, Pedro Manuel de Nóbrega (1517-70), missionary in Brazil. No. 3896, N, Raul Brandao (1867-1930), writer. No. 3897, N, Francisco da Holanda (1517-85), painter. No. 3898, A, Luís de Albuquerque (1917-92), historian and mathematician. No. 3899, A, Oscar Lopes (1917-2013), linguist. No. 3900, E, Júlio Resende (1917-2011), painter. No. 3901, I, António José Saraiva (1917-93), historian.

Perf. 11¾x12 Syncopated
2017, Apr. 27 Litho.
3895-3901 A1063 Set of 7 8.25 4.25
On day of issue, Nos. 3895-3897 each sold for 50c; Nos. 3898-3899, for 63c; No. 3900, for 80c; No. 3901, for 85c.

Mário Soares (1924-2017), Prime Minister — A1064

Designs: N, Photograph of Soares. €2, Drawing of Soares, vert.

Perf. 12x11¾ Syncopated
2017, Apr. 28 Litho.
3902 A1064 N multi 1.10 .55
Souvenir Sheet
Perf. 11¾x12 Syncopated
3903 A1064 €2 multi 4.50 2.25
No. 3902 sold for 50c on day of issue. No. 3903 contains on 30x80mm stamp.

Lions Clubs International, Cent. — A1065

Lions Club International emblem and: 80c, Secretary-treasurer Melvin Jones (1879-1961). €2, Lions from 2017 U.S. $1 Lions Clubs International coin.

Perf. 12x11¾ Syncopated
2017, Apr. 29 Litho.
3904 A1065 80c multi 1.75 .85
Souvenir Sheet
3905 A1065 €2 multi 4.50 2.25
No. 3905 contains on 80x30mm stamp.

Europa A1066

Designs: No. 3906, Almourol Castle. No. 3907a, Castle of Marvao.

Perf. 12x11¾ Syncopated
2017, May 9 Litho.
3906 A1066 80c multi 1.75 .90
Souvenir Sheet
3907 Sheet of 2, #3906, 3907a 3.50 1.80
a. A1066 80c multi 1.75 .90

Desserts A1067

Designs: N, Pastel de Belém. A, Ovos moles de Aveiro. E, Pastel de Tentúgal. I, Queijadas de Vila Franca do Campo.

Serpentine Die Cut 11
2017, May 12 Litho.
Self-Adhesive
3908 A1067 N multi 1.10 .55
3909 A1067 A multi 1.40 .70
3910 A1067 E multi 1.75 .90
3911 A1067 I multi 1.90 .95
On day of issue, No. 3908 sold for 50c; No. 3909, for 63c; No. 3910, for 80c; No. 3911, for 85c. See Nos. 3917-3922.

Rally de Portugal, 50th Anniv. A1068

Race cars: 50c, 1967 Renault 8 Gordini. 63c, 1981 Fiat 131 Abarth. 70c, 1982 Audi Quattro S1. 80c, 1992 Lancia Delta Integrale. 85c, 2015 Volkswagen Polo WRC.

Perf. 12x11¾ Syncopated
2017, May 17 Litho.
3912-3916 A1068 Set of 5 7.75 4.00

Desserts Type of 2017
Designs: 50c, Pastel de Belém. 63c, Ovos moles de Aveiro. 70c, Rebuçados de ovo de Portalegre. 80c, Pastel de Tentúgal. 85c, Queijadas de Vila Franca do Campo. €1, Tigeladas de Abrantes.

2017, May 31 Litho. Perf. 11¾x11½
3917 A1067 50c multi 1.10 .55
3918 A1067 63c multi 1.40 .70
3919 A1067 70c multi 1.60 .80
3920 A1067 80c multi 1.75 .90
3921 A1067 85c multi 1.90 .95
3922 A1067 €1 multi 2.25 1.10
Nos. 3917-3922 (6) 10.00 5.00

Portuguese Textile Industry — A1069

Designs: 50c, Skein of yarn, fabric, woman at loom, painting of shepherd. 63c, Flower, embroidery, looms, painting of woman at loom. 80c, Silk moth on silk, fabric, women in textile factory, painting of woman, man and spinning wheel. 85c, Spools of thread, fabric, machinery at textile factory. €2, Cotton plant, fabric, woman in textile factory, painting of woman and gear wheel.

Perf. 12x11¾ Syncopated
2017, June 17 Litho.
3923-3926 A1069 Set of 4 6.50 3.25
Souvenir Sheet
Flocked Paper
Perf. 12x12½
3927 A1069 €2 multi 4.75 2.40

World War I, Cent. — A1070

Designs: 50c, Alberto Lello Portela (1893-1949), pilot, and airplanes. 63c, Admiral Afonso Cerqueira (1872-1957), NRP Adamastor, batallion in Angola. 85c, Aníbal Milhais (1895-1970), most highly-decorated Portuguese soldier in World War I, and soldiers in France.

Perf. 12x11¾ Syncopated
2017, June 30   **Litho.**
3928-3930 A1070   Set of 3   4.50 2.25

Abolition of Death Penalty in Portugal, 150th Anniv. A1071

Designs: 50c, Augusto César Barjona de Freitas (1834-1900), Minister of Justice. €1, King Luiz (1838-89).

Perf. 12x11¾ Syncopated
2017, July 1   **Litho.**
3931-3932 A1071   Set of 2   3.50 1.75

Archbishops of Braga — A1072

Designs: No. 3933, 50c, St. Martin of Braga (c. 520-80). No. 3934, 50c, St. Fructuosus of Braga (?-665). No. 3935, 50c, St. Gerald of Braga (?-1109). No. 3936, 50c, Blessed Bartholomew of Braga (1514-90), and his coat of arms. No. 3937, 50c, Rodrigo de Moura Teles (1644-1728), and his coat of arms. No. 3938, 50c, Jorge Ferreira da Costa Ortiga, current archbishop, and his coat of arms. €1.40, Bom Jesus do Monte Sanctuary, Braga.

Perf. 11¾x12 Syncopated
2017, July 7   **Litho.**
3933-3938 A1072   Set of 6   7.25 3.75
Souvenir Sheet
3939 A1072 €1.40 multi   3.50 1.75

No. 3939 contains one 30x80mm stamp.

Trees of the Mediterranean Region — A1073

Euromed emblem and: 50c, Quercus suber. 63c, Pyrus bourgaeana. 80c, Arbutus unedo. 85c, Olea europaea.

Perf. 12x11¾ Syncopated
2017, July 10   **Litho.**
3940-3943 A1073   Set of 4   6.75 3.25
See No. 4130.

Portuguese Public Security Police, 150th Anniv. A1074

Designs: 50c, Emblem and shoulder patch. No. 3945: a, Policeman and policewoman, motorcycle policeman near statue. b, Policemen on motorcycle, policewomen walking.

Perf. 12x11¾ Syncopated
2017, July 13   **Litho.**
3944 A1074 50c multi   1.25 .60
Souvenir Sheet
3945 A1074 70c Sheet of 2, #a-b   3.50 1.75

Star Wars Movie Series, 40th Anniv. A1075

Characters: No. 3946, 50c, No. 3953a, N, Luke Skywalker. No. 3947, 50c, No. 3953b, N, Princess Leia. No. 3948, 85c, No. 3953c, E, Han Solo. No. 3949, 80c, No. 3953d, E, Chewbacca. No. 3950, 85c, No. 3953e, I, Darth Vader. No. 3951, 85c, No. 3953f, I, Yoda.
No. 3952 — Movie posters for: a, *Star Wars: A New Hope.* b, *Star Wars: The Empire Strikes Back.* c, *Star Wars: The Return of the Jedi.*

Perf. 12x11¾ Syncopated
2017, Aug. 25   **Litho.**
3946-3951   Set of 6   10.50 5.25
Souvenir Sheet
3952   Sheet of 3   3.75 1.80
a.-c.   A1075 50c Any single   1.25 .60
Self-Adhesive
Die Cut Perf. 10½
3953   Booklet pane of 6   10.50
a.-b. A1075 N Either single   1.25 .60
c.-d. A1075 E Either single   1.90 .95
e.-f. A1075 I Either single   2.00 1.00

On day of issue, Nos. 3953a-3953b each sold for 50c; Nos. 3953c-3953d, for 80c; Nos. 3953e-3953f, for 85c.

Historic Cafes A1076

Designs: No. 3954, 50c, Manuel Natário Cafe, Viana do Castelo. No. 3955, 50c, Aliança Cafe, Faro. No. 3956, 50c, A Brasileira Cafe, Braga. No. 3957, 50c, Milenário Cafe, Guimaraes. No. 3958, 50c, Piolho (Ancora d'Ouro) Cafe, Porto. €1.40, Versailles Cafe, Lisbon, vert.

Perf. 12x11¾ Syncopated
2017, Aug. 31   **Litho.**
3954-3958 A1076   Set of 5   6.00 3.00
Souvenir Sheet
Perf. 11¾x12 Syncopated
3959 A1076 €1.40 multi   3.50 1.75

No. 3959 contains one 30x80mm stamp.

Cascais, 2018 European Youth Capital A1077

Designs: 50c, Cascaes, Mural by Frederico Draw. 63c, Avarina, Mural by Add Fuel. 80c, Mermaid statue with added necklace. 85c, Terra Mar, by Alexandre Farto. €1.40, Santa Marta Lighthouse and Casa Santa Maria.

Perf. 12x11¾ Syncopated
2017, Sept. 8   **Litho.**
3960-3963 A1077   Set of 4   6.50 3.25
Souvenir Sheet
3964 A1077 €1.40 multi   3.50 1.75

No. 3964 contains one 80x30mm stamp.

National Palace of Mafra — A1078

Designs: 50c, Library, statue of King John V, by Alessandro Giusti. €1, Palace exterior, statue of St. Sebastian, by Carlo Monaldi.

Perf. 12x11¾ Syncopated
2017, July 18   **Litho.**
3965-3966 A1078   Set of 2   3.50 1.75

Porto A1079

Designs: 50c, Porto Music Hall. 70c, Dom Luis I Bridge. 80c, Boat on Douro River. 85c, City skyline.

Perf. 12x11¾ Syncopated
2017, Sept. 20   **Litho.**
3967-3970 A1079   Set of 4   6.75 3.50

University of Coimbra Joanina Library, 300th Anniv. — A1080

Various library holdings: 50c, €1.

Perf. 12x11¾ Syncopated
2017, Sept. 28   **Litho.**
3971-3972 A1080   Set of 2   3.50 1.75

Portuguese Postal System, 500th Anniv. A1081

Designs: No. 3973, 50c, Luís Gomes de Mata Coronel (?-1607), 5th High Courier. No. 3974, 50c, José Diogo Mascarenhas Neto (1752-c.1824), General Superintendent of the Mail and Post of the Kingdom. 63c, Guilhermino Augusto de Barros (1828-1900), 2nd Director General of the Posts. 80c, António Maria da Silva (1872-1950), 1st General Administrator of Posts and Telegraphs. 85c, Luís de Albuquerque Couto dos Santos (1896-?), General Administrator of Posts. €1.40, Queen Maria II (1819-53), vert.

Perf. 12x11¾ Syncopated
2017, Oct. 9   **Litho.**
3973-3977 A1081   Set of 5   7.75 3.75
Souvenir Sheet
Perf. 11¾x12 Syncopated
3978 A1081 €1.40 multi   3.25 1.60

No. 3978 contains one 30x80mm stamp.

Portuguese Catholic University, 50th Anniv. — A1082

No. 3979 — Half of university emblem and: a, 50c, Denomination at LL. b, 85c, Denomination at UR.

Perf. 12x11¾ Syncopated
2017, Oct. 13   **Litho.**
3979 A1082   Horiz. pair, #a-b   3.25 1.60

UNESCO Creative Cities in Portugal A1083

Designs: No. 3980, 85c, Idanha-a-Nova. No. 3981, 85c, Obidos.

Perf. 12x11¾ Syncopated
2017, Oct. 16   **Litho.**
3980-3981 A1083   Set of 2   4.00 2.00

Desserts A1084

Designs: N, Pastel de Feijao de Torres Vedras. A, Crista de Galo de Vila Real. E, Travesseiro de Sintra. I, Queijada de Evora.

Die Cut Perf. 11½x11¾
2018, Jan. 31   **Litho.**
Self-Adhesive
3982 A1084 N multi   1.25 .60
3983 A1084 A multi   1.60 .80
3984 A1084 E multi   2.00 1.00
3985 A1084 I multi   2.10 1.10
Nos. 3982-3985 (4)   6.95 3.50

On day of issue, No. 3982 sold for 50c; No. 3983, for 63c; No. 3984, for 80c; No. 3985, for 85c.

Portuguese Breeds of Farm Animals A1085

Designs: No. 3986, 50c, Mertolenga bull. No. 3987, 50c, Barrosa cow. No. 3988, 65c, Galega Mirandesa sheep. No. 3989, 65c, Merina Preta sheep. No. 3990, 85c, Algarvia goat. No. 3991, 85c, Serrana goat.

Perf. 12x11¾ Syncopated
2018, Feb. 8   **Litho.**
3986-3991 A1085   Set of 6   9.75 5.00
3991a   Souvenir sheet of 6, #3986-3991   9.75 5.00

Tagus River — A1086

Various views of river and: 50c, Rock carving. 70c, Horse and rider. 80c, Bird. 85c, Sailboat. €2, Monument and Square overlooking Tagus River and drawing of ships in river.

Perf. 11¾x12 Syncopated
2018, Feb. 26   **Litho.**
3992-3995 A1086   Set of 4   7.00 3.50
Souvenir Sheet
3996 A1086 €2 multi   5.00 2.50

Islamic Community of Lisbon, 50th Anniv. A1087

Designs: N, Muslim woman at mosque entrance. A, Men performing ablutions. E, Congregation listening to lecture. I, Interior of mosque. €2, Koran in book holder, mosque floor, vert.

2018, Mar. 16   **Litho.**   *Perf. 12x12¼*
3997-4000 A1087   Set of 4   7.25 3.75
Souvenir Sheet
Perf. 12¼x12
4001 A1087 €2 multi   5.00 2.50

On day of issue, No. 3997 sold for 53c; No. 3998, 65c; No. 3999, 86c; No. 4000, 91c.

Electricity in Portugal
A1088

Lightbulb and: N, Wind generators. A, Hydroelectric dam. E, Solar panels. I, Geothermal station.
€2, Lightbulb, exterior and interior of power station.

Perf. 12x11¾ Syncopated
2018, Mar. 19   Litho.
4002-4005 A1088 Set of 4   7.25 3.75
Souvenir Sheet
4006 A1088 €2 multi   5.00 2.50

On day of issue, No. 4002 sold for 53c; No. 4003, 65c; No. 4004, 86c; No. 4005, 91c. No. 4006 contains one 80x30mm stamp.

Lisbon Water Supply Company (EPAL), 150th Anniv. — A1089

No. 4007: a, Boy in brown drinking water, rural area. b, Girl in light blue green drinking water, city skyline.
€2.50, Water towers, city gate, bicyclist, vert.

Perf. 12x11¾ Syncopated
2018, Apr. 2   Litho.
4007 A1089   Horiz. pair, #a-b 3.75 1.90
a.   N multi   1.40   .70
b.   I multi   2.25 1.10
Souvenir Sheet
Perf. 11¾x12 Syncopated
4008 A1089 €2.50 multi   6.25 3.25

On day of issue, No. 4007a sold for 53c; No. 4007b, 91c. No. 4008 contains one 30x80mm stamp.

Battle of the Lys, Cent. A1090

Designs: E, Soldiers and their gear.
€2, Soldiers, vert.

Perf. 12x11¾ Syncopated
2018, Apr. 9   Litho.
4009 A1090 E multi   2.10 1.10
Souvenir Sheet
Perf. 11¾x12 Syncopated
4010 A1090 €2 multi   4.75 2.40

No. 4009 sold for 86c on day of issue. No. 4010 contains one 30x80mm stamp.

Fernando Peyroteo (1918-78), Soccer Player
A1091

Perf. 12x11¾ Syncopated
2018, Apr. 30   Litho.
4011 A1091 N multi   1.25   .65

No. 4011 sold for 53c on day of issue.

Ajuda Botanical Gardens, 250th Anniv.
A1092

Designs: N, Fountain and gardens. A, Trees. E, Path, wall and trees. I, Stairway.
€2, Fountain and King Joseph, vert.

Perf. 12x11¾ Syncopated
2018, May 7   Litho.
4012-4015 A1092 Set of 4   7.00 3.50
Souvenir Sheet
Perf. 11¾x12 Syncopated
4016 A1092 €2 multi   4.75 2.40

On day of issue, No. 4012 sold for 53c; No. 4013, 65c; No. 4014, 86c; No. 4015, 91c. No. 4016 contains one 30x80mm stamp.

Orient Foundation, 30th Anniv. and Orient Museum, Lisbon, 10th Anniv.
A1093

Designs: 65c, Robe. No. 4018, €1, Statue of Buddha.
No. 4019, €1: a, Pair of stirrups. b, Dragon.

Perf. 12x11¾ Syncopated
2018, May 8   Litho.
4017-4018 A1093 Set of 2   4.00 2.00
Souvenir Sheet
4019 A1093 €1 Sheet of 2, #a-b 4.75 2.40

Europa
A1094

Designs: No. 4020, Vasco da Gama Bridge, Lisbon. No. 4021a, Roman Bridge, Chaves.

Perf. 12x11¾ Syncopated
2018, May 9   Litho.
4020 A1094 E multi   2.00 1.00
Souvenir Sheet
4021   Sheet of 2, #4020,
       4021a   4.00 2.00
a.   A1094 E multi   2.00 1.00

On day of issue, Nos. 4020 and 4021a each sold for 86c.

European Cultural Heritage Year
A1095

Designs: N, Ceramic figurine of devil, plate, Alcobaça Monastery. A, Pena Palace, container with ducks and duckling, pendant. E, St. Vincent with the Portuguese Royal Family, by Nuno Gonçalves, sculpture of Adam and Eve, by Ernesto Canto da Maia, chest. I, Sculpture of St. Lucia, tile, untitled painting by Joao Vieira.
No. 4026, €1: a, Praia de Maças, by José Malhoa, drinking glass, The Banished, sculpture by António Soares dos Reis, door, African mask. b, Tram and building, Portuguese guitar, sculpture of soldier, drawing of man, carriage of Pope Clement XI.

Perf. 12x11¾ Syncopated
2018, May 9   Litho.
4022-4025 A1095 Set of 4   7.00 3.50
Souvenir Sheet
4026 A1095 €1 Sheet of 2,
              #a-b   4.75 2.40

On day of issue, No. 4022 sold for 53c; No. 4023, 65c; No. 4024, 86c; No. 4025, 91c. No. 4026 contains two 80x30mm stamps.

Famous Men
A1096

Designs: No. 4027, 53c, Domingos Sequeira (1768-1837), painter. No. 4028, 53c, Bernardino António Gomes (1768-1823), botanist. No. 4029, 53c, Tomás da Annunciaçao (1818-79), painter. No. 4030, 53c, José Vianna da Motta (1868-1948), composer. No. 4031, 53c, Padre Himalaya (1868-1933), priest and inventor. No. 4032, 53c, António Champalimaud (1918-2004), industrialist. No. 4033, 53c, Vitorino Magalhaes Godinho (1918-2011), historian.

Perf. 12x11¾ Syncopated
2018, June 20   Litho.
4027-4033 A1096 Set of 7   8.75 4.50

Desserts
A1097

Designs: 1c, Bolo de Ança. 20c, Marmelada Branca de Odivelas. 53c, Pastel de Feijao de Torres Vedras. 65c, Crista de Galo de Vila Real. 86c, Travesseiro de Sintra. 91c, Queijada de Evora. €1, Bonecas de Massa do Caniço.

2018, July 6 Litho. *Perf. 11¾x11½*
4034 A1097 1c multi   .25   .25
4035 A1097 20c multi   .45   .25
4036 A1097 53c multi   1.25   .60
4037 A1097 65c multi   1.50   .75
4038 A1097 86c multi   2.00 1.00
4039 A1097 91c multi   2.10 1.10
4040 A1097 €1 multi   2.40 1.25
       Nos. 4034-4040 (7)   9.95 5.20

Houses
A1098

House from: 53c, Alentejo region. 86c, Algarve region.

Perf. 12x11¾ Syncopated
2018, July 9   Litho.
4041-4042 A1098 Set of 2   3.25 1.60

Henrique Mendonça Palace, Lisbon — A1099

Reign of Aga Khan IV, 60th Anniv. — A1100

2018, July 9 Litho. *Perf. 12½x12*
4043 A1099 91c sil & multi   2.10 1.10
Souvenir Sheet
Perf. 13
4044 A1100 €2 blue green   4.75 2.40

Chocolate
A1101

Designs: 53c, Opened and unopened cacao pod, cocoa beans. 65c, Colima Culture vessel for chocolate. 70c, Lady Pouring Chocolate, by Jean-Etienne Liotard, European cocoa pot. 86c, Chocolate truffle and chocolate factory.
€1.50, Chocolate bar, sculpture of Aztec carrying cacao pod, map, King John V of Portugal Being Served Chocolate by His Uncle, the Duke of Lafoes, by Alessandro Castrioto.

Perf. 12x11¾ Syncopated
2018, July 13   Litho.
4045-4048 A1101 Set of 4   6.50 3.25
Souvenir Sheet
4049 A1101 €1.50 multi   3.50 1.75

No. 4049 contains one 80x30mm stamp.

49th International Physics Olympiad, Lisbon — A1102

Flag bearer, marchers, physics concepts, with background color of: 53c, Yellow orange. €1, Light blue lavender.

Perf. 12x11¾ Syncopated
2018, July 21   Litho.
4050-4051 A1102 Set of 2   3.75 1.90

Publication of *Os Maias,* by José Maria de Eça de Queiroz, 130th Anniv. — A1103

Characters: No. 4052, 53c, Carlos da Maia. No. 4053, 53c, Condessa de Gouvarinho. No. 4054, 53c, Joao da Ega. No. 4055, 53c, Dâmaso Salcede. No. 4056, 53c, Maria Eduarda. No. 4057, 53c, Afonso da Maia.
€1, José Maria de Eça de Queiroz (1845-1900), writer.

Perf. 11¾x12 Syncopated
2018, July 25   Litho.
4052-4057 A1103 Set of 6   7.50 3.75
Souvenir Sheet
4058 A1103 €1 multi   2.40 1.25

No. 4058 contains one 30x80mm stamp.

End of World War I, Cent. — A1104

Designs: 91c, Soldier. €1.50, Soldiers and young girl, horiz.

Perf. 11¾x12 Syncopated
2018, Aug. 9   Litho.
4059 A1104 91c multi   2.10 1.10
Souvenir Sheet
Perf. 12x11¾ Syncopated
4060 A1104 €1.50 multi   3.50 1.75

No. 4060 contains one 80x30mm stamp.

Manufacture of Cowbells — A1105

Manufacture of Estremoz Clay
Figurines — A1106

Manufacture of Bisalhaes Black
Pottery — A1107

Perf. 12x11¾ Syncopated

2018, Aug. 31			Litho.	
4061	A1105	86c multi	2.00	1.00
4062	A1106	86c multi	2.00	1.00
4063	A1107	86c multi	2.00	1.00
	Nos. 4061-4063 (3)		6.00	3.00

UNESCO Intangible Cultural Heritage.

A1108

A1109

A1110

A1111

A1112

A1113

A1114

A1115

A1116

A1117

A1118

Mickey Mouse,
90th
Anniv. — A1119

Perf. 11¾x12 Syncopated

2018, Sept. 14			Litho.	
4064	A1108	53c multi	1.25	.60
4065	A1109	91c multi	2.10	1.10

Miniature Sheet

4066	Sheet of 8, #4064-4065, 4066a-4066f		12.00	5.25
a.	A1110	53c multi	1.25	.60
b.	A1111	53c multi	1.25	.60
c.	A1112	53c multi	1.25	.60
d.	A1113	53c multi	1.25	.60
e.	A1114	53c multi	1.25	.60
f.	A1115	53c multi	1.25	.60

Booklet Stamps
Self-Adhesive
Die Cut Perf. 10½

4067	Booklet pane of 4		5.00	
a.	A1116 N multi		1.25	.60
b.	A1117 N multi		1.25	.60
c.	A1118 N multi		1.25	.60
d.	A1119 N multi		1.25	.60

On day of issue, Nos. 4067a-4067d each
sold for 53c.

Ships — A1120

Various ships: 53c, 70c, 86c.
€1.50, Ships, vert.

Perf. 12x11¾ Syncopated

2018, Sept. 20			Litho.	
4068-4070	A1120	Set of 3	5.00	2.50

Souvenir Sheet
Perf. 11¾x12 Syncopated

4071	A1120	€1.50 multi	3.50	1.75

Archaeology — A1121

Designs: 53c, Paleolithic Age carved stone,
Côa River Valley. 70c, Neolithic Age container,
banks of Tagus River. 75c, Megalithic Age
carved schist plaque, Praia das Maças. 86c,
Chalcolithic Age ivory idol, Guadiana River
Valley.

Perf. 12x11¾ Syncopated

2018, Oct. 2			Litho.	
4072-4075	A1121	Set of 4	6.50	3.25

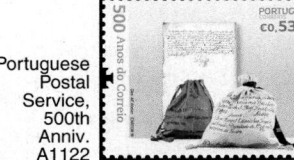

Portuguese
Postal
Service,
500th
Anniv.
A1122

Designs: 53c, 18th century silk mail bags
and royal charter of 1756. 65c, 19th century
letter scale, Alentejo Mail Coach box. 86c,
1850s stagecoach, 1850s Postal Directorate
plaque. 91c, Electric tricycle for mail delivery,
21st cent.
€2, Estoril Post Office, 20th cent.

Perf. 12x11¾ Syncopated

2018, Oct. 9			Litho.	
4076-4079	A1122	Set of 4	6.75	3.50

Souvenir Sheet
Perf. 12½x13 Syncopated

4080	A1122	€2 multi	4.75	2.40

No. 4080 contains one 54x49mm stamp.

Archbishops of
Braga — A1123

Designs: No. 4081, 53c, St. Martin of Braga
(c. 520-80). No. 4082, 53c, St. Fructosus of
Braga (d.665). No. 4083, 53c, St. Gerald of
Braga (d. 1109).

Perf. 11¾x12 Syncopated

2018, Oct. 22			Litho.	
4081-4083	A1123	Set of 3	3.75	1.90

Portuguese Mint and Printing Office,
250th Anniv. — A1124

No. 4084: a, Printing Office Library. b, Commemorative text.

Perf. 12x11¾ Syncopated

2018, Oct. 24			Litho.	
4084	A1124	Horiz. pair	3.25	1.60
a.		53c sil & multi	1.25	.60
b.		86c gold, silver & blk	2.00	1.00

Portuguese
Breeds of
Farm
Animals
A1125

Designs: No. 4085, 53c, Serra da Estrela
sheep. No. 4086, 53c, Pedrês chicken. No.
4087, 70c, Bísaro pig. No. 4088, 70c,
Alentajano pig. No. 4089, 91c, Alentajana bull.
No. 4090, 91c, Mirandês burro.

Perf. 12x11¾ Syncopated

2019, Jan. 28			Litho.	
4085-4090	A1125	Set of 6	10.00	5.00
4090a		Souvenir sheet of 6, #4085-4090	10.00	5.00

Diplomatic Relations Between Portugal
and People's Republic of China, 40th
Anniv.
A1126

Designs: 53c, Silver tea pot. 91c, Earthenware tea pot and cup.

Perf. 12x11¾ Syncopated

2019, Feb. 8			Litho.	
4091-4092	A1126	Set of 2	3.25	1.60

See People's Republic of China Nos. 4601-
4602.

Famous
People
A1127

Designs: No. 4093, 53c, Joel Serrao (1919-
2008), historian. No. 4094, 53c, Jorge de
Sena (1919-78), poet. No. 4095, 53c, Gago
Coutinho (1869-1959), geographer and aviation pioneer. No. 4096, 53c, Fernando Namora
(1919-89), writer. No. 4097, 53c, Sophia de
Mello Breyner Andresen (1919-2004), writer.
No. 4098, 53c, Francisco de Lacerda (1869-
1934), composer. No. 4099, 53c, Fontes Pereira de Melo (1819-87), Prime Minister.

Perf. 12x11¾ Syncopated

2019, Feb. 19			Litho.	
4093-4099	A1127	Set of 7	8.50	4.25

Queen
Maria II
(1819-53)
A1128

Various artistic depictions of Queen Maria II:
53c, 65c, 86c, 91c.
€2, Queen Maria II and street scene, vert.

Perf. 12x11¾ Syncopated
2019, Feb. 25　　　　　Litho.
4100-4103 A1128 Set of 4 　6.75 3.50
Souvenir Sheet
Perf. 11¾x12 Syncopated
4104 A1128 €2 multi 　　　4.50 2.25
No. 4104 contains one 30x80mm stamp.

Abolition of Slavery in Portugal, 150th Anniv. — A1129

No. 4105 — Shackle and: a, Two slaves. b, One slave.

Perf. 12x11¾ Syncopated
2019, Feb. 25　　　　　Litho.
4105 A1129 Horiz. pair 　　3.00 1.50
　a.　53c multi 　　　　　　1.25 　.60
　b.　75c multi 　　　　　　1.75 　.85

Order of Christ, 700th Anniv. A1130

Designs: 53c, King Denis (1261-1325) and 1319 bull from Pope John XXII. €1, Prince Henry the Navigator (1394-1460) and caravel. €2, Cross of the Order of Christ and angel.

Perf. 12x11¾ Syncopated
2019, Mar. 14　　　　　Litho.
4106-4107 A1130 Set of 2 　3.50 1.75
Souvenir Sheet
Perf. 11¾x12 Syncopated
4108 A1130 €2 multi 　　　4.50 2.25
No. 4108 contains one 30x80mm stamp.

Calouste Sarkis Gulbenkian (1869-1955), Businessman and Philanthropist — A1131

Gulbenkian and: 53c, Jeweled peacock. 91c, Ceramic bowl, 18th cent.

Perf. 12x11¾ Syncopated
2019, Mar. 23　　　　　Litho.
4109-4110 A1131 Set of 2 　3.25 1.60
See Armenia No. 1183.

Desserts A1132

Designs: N, Queijadas de Sintra. A, Fatias do Freixo. E, Cavacas das Caldas da Rainha. I, Morgados do Algarve.

Die Cut Perf. 12½x12¼
2019, Mar. 29　　　　　Litho.
Self-Adhesive
4111 A1132 N multi 　　　1.25 　.65
4112 A1132 A multi 　　　1.50 　.75
4113 A1132 E multi 　　　1.60 　.80
4114 A1132 I multi 　　　2.00 1.00
　Nos. 4111-4114 (4) 　　　6.35 3.20
On day of issue, No. 4111 sold for 53c; No. 4112, 65c; No. 4113, 70c; No. 4114, 86c. See Nos. 4156-4160.

Souvenir Sheet

Aga Khan Music Awards — A1133

2019, Mar. 29　Litho.　Perf. 13¼
4115 A1133 €2.50 multi 　　5.75 5.75

Museums A1134

No. 4116: a, University of Coimbra Museum of Science, 1772. b, Soares dos Reis National Museum, Porto, 1833. c, Military Museum, Lisbon, 1851. d, University of Lisbon National Museum of Natural History and Science, 1858. e, Geological Museum, Lisbon, c. 1860. f, Carmo Archaeological Museum, Lisbon, 1864. g, Carlos Machado Museum, Ponta Delgada, Azores, 1880. h, Lisbon Geographic Society Historical and Ethnographic Museum, 1884. i, Museum of Fine Arts, Lisbon, 1884. j, Martins Sarmento Archaeological Museum, Guimaraes, 1885. k, National Archaeological Museum, Lisbon, 1893. l, Santos Rocha Municipal Museum, Figueira da Foz, 1894. m, Faro Municipal Museum, 1894.

Perf. 12x11¾ Syncopated
2019, Apr. 5
4116　Vert. strip of 13 　　　6.50 8.00
　a.-m.　A1134 N Any single 　1.25 　.60
On day of issue, Nos. 4116a-4116m each sold for 53c.

Types of 2014-16
Die Cut Perf. 10½
2019, Apr. 29　　　　　Litho.
Self-Adhesive
4117 A994　 I Like #3612 　2.10 1.10
4118 A998　 I Like #3643 　2.10 1.10
4119 A1035 I Like #3789 　2.10 1.10
4120 A1044 I Like #3819 　2.10 1.10
4121 A1045 I Like #3827 　2.10 1.10
　Nos. 4117-4121 (5) 　　　10.50 5.50
Nos. 4117-4121 each sold for 91c on day of issue.

International Labor Organization, Cent. — A1135

Albert Thomas (1878-1932), first Director General of International Labor Organization, and: 53c, Delegates to early assembly. 91c, Delegates to modern assembly.

Perf. 12x11¾ Syncopated
2019, May 3　　　　　Litho.
4122-4123 A1135 Set of 2 　3.25 1.60

Europa A1136

Birds: No. 4124, Erithacus rubecula. No. 4125a, Luscinia svecica.

Perf. 12x11¾ Syncopated
2019, May 9　　　　　Litho.
4124 A1136 86c multi 　　　2.00 1.00
Souvenir Sheet
4125　Sheet of 2, #4124, 4125a 　　　　　　4.00 4.00
　a.　A1136 86c multi 　　　2.00 1.00

Types of 2014-17
Die Cut Perf. 10½
2019, May 13　　　　　Litho.
Self-Adhesive
4126 A995 　I Like #3619 　2.10 1.10
4127 A998 　I Like #3638 　2.10 1.10
4128 A1007 I Like #3692 　2.10 1.10
4129 A1019 I Like #3733 　2.10 1.10
4130 A1073 I Like #3942 　2.10 1.10
　Nos. 4126-4139 (5) 　　　10.50 5.50
Nos. 4126-4130 each sold for 91c on day of issue.

Observation of Eclipse Proving Light Waves Are Bent by Gravity, Cent. — A1137

Designs: 53c, Albert Einstein (1879-1955), physicist who theorized light waves are bent by gravity in general theory of relativity. 91c, Total solar eclipse of May 29, 1919. €2.50, Diagram of gravity of sun bending light waves from distant star.

Perf. 11¾x12 Syncopated
2019, May 16　　　　　Litho.
4131-4132 A1137 Set of 2 　3.25 1.60
Souvenir Sheet
4133 A1137 €2.50 multi 　　5.75 5.75
No. 4133 contains one 30x80mm stamp.

Traditional Costumes — A1138

Costumes of men and women from: 53c, Alentejo region. 86c, Algarve region.

Perf. 12x11¾ Syncopated
2019, July 8　　　　　Litho.
4134-4135 A1138 Set of 2 　3.25 1.60

Famous People — A1139

Designs: No. 4136, 86c, Clara Schumann (1819-96), composer. No. 4137, 86c, Jacques Offenbach (1819-80), composer. No. 4138, 86c, Margot Fonteyn (1919-91), ballerina.

Perf. 11¾x12 Syncopated
2019, July 12　　　　　Litho.
4136-4138 A1139 Set of 3 　5.75 3.00

International Year of the Periodic Table — A1140

Designs: N, Periodic table information for hydrogen, sun, clouds, water, plant. I, Periodic table information for mendelevium, Dmitri Mendeleev (1834-1907), formulator of periodic table of elements. €2, Periodic table information for carbon.

Perf. 12x11¾ Syncopated
2019, July 24　　　　　Litho.
4139-4140 A1140 Set of 2 　3.25 1.60
Souvenir Sheet
4141 A1140 €2 multi 　　　4.50 4.50
On day of issue, No. 4139 sold for 53c; No. 4140, 91c.

Artur "Pinga" de Sousa (1909-63), Soccer Player and Coach A1141

Perf. 12x11¾ Syncopated
2019, Aug. 22　　　　　Litho.
4142 A1141 N multi 　　　1.25 　.60
No. 4142 sold for 53c on day of issue.

Characters from *Harry Potter* Movies — A1142

Designs: 70c, Harry Potter and his owl, Hedwig. 75c, Hermione Granger and her cat, Crookshanks. 86c, Ron Weasley and his rat, Scabbers. 91c, Lord Voldemort and his snake, Nagini.
No. 4147: a, Albus Dumbledore and his phoenix, Fawkes. b, Minerva McGonagall and books. c, Severus Snape and potions. d, Rubeus Hagrid, his dragon, Norbert, and spider, Aragog.

Perf. 11¾x12 Syncopated
2019, Aug. 27　　　　　Litho.
4143-4146 A1142 Set of 4 　7.00 3.50
Souvenir Sheet
4147 A1142 50c Sheet of 4, #a-d 4.50 4.50

Souvenir Sheet

Ferdinand Magellan (c. 1480-1521), Explorer — A1143

Perf. 11¾x12 Syncopated
2019, Sept. 12　　　　　Litho.
4148 A1143 €3.50 multi 　　7.75 7.75
Magellan-Elcano Expedition around the world, 500th anniv. See Spain No. 4378.

National Health Service, 40th Anniv. — A1144

Designs: N, Child with balloons. E, Woman with hearts. I, Man sitting on blocks.

Perf. 11¾x12 Syncopated

2019, Sept. 17   **Litho.**

4149-4151 A1144   Set of 3   5.00 2.50

On day of issue, No. 4149 sold for 53c; No. 4150, 86c; No. 4151, 91c.

Directorate General for Livestock Services, Cent. — A1145

Designs: 53c, Animal identification tags, ranchers attaching tag to animal. 65c, Instrument for disease detection, animal being milked. 86c, Inspection mark on finished cheese, cheese maker.
€1.50, Flock of sheep and bells.

Perf. 11¾x12 Syncopated

2019, Sept. 27   **Litho.**

4152-4154 A1145   Set of 3   4.50 2.25

Souvenir Sheet

4155 A1145 €1.50 multi   3.75 3.75

Desserts Type of 2019

Designs: 10c, Cavacas de Resende. 53c, Queijadas de Sintra. 65c, Fatias de Freixo. 86c, Cavacas das Caldas da Rainha. 91c, Morgados do Algarve.

2019, Oct. 1   **Litho.**   **Perf. 11¾x11½**

4156	A1132	10c multi	.25 .25
4157	A1132	53c multi	1.25 .60
4158	A1132	65c multi	1.40 .70
4159	A1132	86c multi	1.90 .95
4160	A1132	91c multi	2.00 1.00
		Nos. 4156-4160 (5)	6.80 3.50

Mohandas K. Gandhi (1869-1948), Indian Nationalist Leader — A1146

Gandhi facing: 91c, Right. €3, Left.

2019, Oct. 2   **Litho.**   **Perf. 12¼x12**

4161 A1146 91c multi   2.00 1.00

Souvenir Sheet

4162 A1146 €3 multi   6.75 6.75

No. 4162 contains one 30x80mm stamp.

Portuguese Postal System, 500th Anniv. — A1147

Designs: 53c, 1880 Postal emblem, postmen, cover of official report on postal service. 70c, 1936 Postal emblem, post office. 86c, 1953 Postal emblem, postal workers and van. 91c, 1964 Postal emblem, postman holding letter showing postal codes.
No. 4167: a, 1991 Postal emblem, CorreioAzul mail box. b, 2015 Postal emblem, BancoCTT building.

Perf. 12½x13¼ Syncopated

2019, Oct. 9   **Litho.**

4163-4166 A1147   Set of 4   6.75 3.50

Souvenir Sheet

Litho., Sheet Margin Litho. & Engr.

4167 A1147 €1 Sheet of 2, #a-b   4.50 4.50

A1148

National Communications Authority, 30th Anniv. — A1149

Perf. 12x11½ Syncopated

2019, Oct. 17   **Litho.**

4168	A1148	53c multi	1.25 .60
4169	A1149	53c multi	1.25 .60

Archbishops of Braga — A1150

Sanctuary of Our Lady of the Immaculate Conception of Monte Sameiro — A1151

Portrait and coat of arms of: No. 4170, 53c, Archbishop Diogo de Sousa (c. 1461-1532). No. 4171, 53c, Archbishop Gaspar de Bragança (1716-89). No. 4172, 53c, Archbishop Manuel Vieira de Matos (1861-1932).

Perf. 11¾x12 Syncopated

2019, Oct. 18   **Litho.**

4170-4172 A1150   Set of 3   3.50 1.75

Souvenir Sheet

4173 A1151 €1.50 gold & multi   3.50 3.50

Liberal Revolution of 1820 — A1152

Various illustrations of the Revolution: 53c, 86c.
€2, Allegrory with figures holding banners promoting constitution, vert.

Perf. 12x11¾ Syncopated

2019, Oct. 21   **Litho.**

4174-4175 A1152   Set of 2   3.25 1.60

Souvenir Sheet

Perf. 11¾x12 Syncopated

4176 A1152 €2 multi   4.50 4.50

Christmas A1153

Designs: 53c, Magus holding chest and camel. 86c, Magus holding bottle on camel. 91c, Magus on camel.
€3.50, Nativity scene, vert.

Perf. 12x11¾ Syncopated

2019, Oct. 22   **Litho.**

4177-4179 A1153   Set of 3   5.25 2.60

Souvenir Sheet

Perf. 11¾x12 Syncopated

4180 A1153 €3.50 multi   7.75 7.75

No. 4180 contains one 30x80mm stamp, which has an oval hole into which a small stone in a metal mount is glued to a piece of paper that is affixed to the back of the stamp.

Chronicle of 1419 — A1154

Designs: 53c, Lines and "Cronica." 91c, Lines and names of Portuguese kings.

Perf. 12x11¾ Syncopated

2019, Oct. 28   **Litho.**

4181-4182 A1154   Set of 2   3.25 1.60

Unabridged Almeida Bible, 200th Anniv. A1155

Designs: 53c, Bible, map of Europe and Africa. €1, Map of Africa and Asia.

Perf. 12x11¾ Syncopated

2019, Oct. 31   **Litho.**

4183-4184 A1155   Set of 2   3.50 1.75

AIR POST STAMPS

Symbol of Aviation AP1

Perf. 12x11½

1936-41		Unwmk.	Typo.
C1	AP1	1.50e dark blue	.50 .30
C2	AP1	1.75e red orange	.75 .35
C3	AP1	2.50e rose red	.75 .35
C4	AP1	3e brt blue ('41)	12.50 12.00
C5	AP1	4e dp yel grn ('41)	18.00 18.00
C6	AP1	5e car lake	1.50 1.25
C7	AP1	10e brown lake	3.00 1.25
C8	AP1	15e orange ('41)	11.50 7.00
C9	AP1	20e black brn	8.00 2.75
C10	AP1	50e brn vio ('41)	145.00 75.00
		Nos. C1-C10 (10)	201.50 118.25
		Set, never hinged	390.00

Stamps issued in 1941 have decimals "00" in the denomination.
Nos. C1-C10 exist imperf.

Catalogue values for unused stamps in this section, from this point to the end of the section, are for Never Hinged items.

EXPO Type of Regular Issue

1970, Sept. 16   **Litho.**   **Perf. 13**

C11 A274 3.50e silver & multi   .70 .40

TAP-Airline of Portugal 35th Anniversary AP2

Design: 19e, Jet flying past sun.

1979, Sept. 21   **Litho.**   **Perf. 12x11½**

C12	AP2	16e multicolored	1.10 .55
C13	AP2	19e multicolored	1.25 .80

POSTAGE DUE STAMPS

Vasco da Gama Issue

The Zamorin of Calicut Receiving Vasco da Gama — D1

Unwmk.

1898, May 1   **Typo.**   **Perf. 12**

Denomination in Black

J1	D1	5r black	2.00 1.25
a.		Value and "Continente" omitted	50.00 5.00
J2	D1	10r lilac & blk	3.50 1.75
J3	D1	20r orange & blk	6.00 2.50
J4	D1	50r slate & blk	45.00 11.00
J5	D1	100r car & blk, pink	75.00 40.00
J6	D1	200r brn & blk, buff	85.00 60.00

For overprints and surcharges see Nos. 193-198.

D2

1904			**Perf. 11½x12**
J7	D2	5r brown	.40 .35
J8	D2	10r orange	2.50 .90
a.		Imperf.	
J9	D2	20r lilac	8.00 3.75
J10	D2	30r gray green	5.00 2.75
J11	D2	40r gray violet	10.00 2.75
J12	D2	50r carmine	50.00 4.50
a.		Imperf.	
J13	D2	100r dull blue	8.75 6.50
a.		Imperf.	
		Nos. J7-J13 (7)	84.65 21.50

Preceding Issue Overprinted in Carmine or Green

1910			
J14	D2	5r brown	.50 .25
a.		Inverted overprint	17.50 14.00
J15	D2	10r orange	.50 .25
a.		Inverted overprint	17.50 14.00
J16	D2	20r lilac	1.50 1.00
J17	D2	30r gray green	1.50 .25
a.		Inverted overprint	17.50 14.00
J18	D2	40r gray violet	1.50 .25
a.		Inverted overprint	20.00 15.00
J19	D2	50r carmine (G)	6.00 4.50
a.		Inverted overprint	20.00 15.00
J20	D2	100r dull blue	7.50 5.25
		Nos. J14-J20 (7)	19.00 11.75

See note after No. 183.

D3

1915, Mar. 18   Typo.

J21	D3	½c brown	.75	.60
J22	D3	1c orange	.75	.60
J23	D3	2c claret	.75	.60
J24	D3	3c green	.75	.60
J25	D3	4c gray violet	.75	.60
J26	D3	5c carmine	.75	.60
J27	D3	10c dark blue	.75	.60
		Nos. J21-J27 (7)	5.25	4.20

1921-27

J28	D3	½c gray green ('22)	.50	.35
J29	D3	4c gray green ('27)	.50	.35
J30	D3	8c gray green ('23)	.50	.35
J31	D3	10c gray green ('22)	.50	.35
J32	D3	12c gray green	.60	.50
J33	D3	16c gray green ('23)	.60	.50
J34	D3	20c gray green	.60	.50
J35	D3	24c gray green	.60	.50
J36	D3	32c gray green ('23)	.85	.50
J37	D3	36c gray green	1.50	.75
J38	D3	40c gray green ('23)	1.50	.75
J39	D3	48c gray green ('23)	.75	.65
J40	D3	50c gray green	.75	.65
J41	D3	60c gray green	.75	.65
J42	D3	72c gray green	.75	.65
J43	D3	80c gray green ('23)	8.50	7.50
J44	D3	1.20e gray green	3.00	3.00
		Nos. J28-J44 (17)	22.75	18.50

D4

1932-33

J45	D4	5c buff	.50	.45
J46	D4	10c lt blue	.50	.45
J47	D4	20c pink	1.25	1.00
J48	D4	30c blue green	1.50	1.00
J49	D4	40c lt green	1.50	1.00
a.		Figure of value inverted		
J50	D4	50c gray	1.60	1.00
J51	D4	60c rose	4.25	2.00
J52	D4	80c violet brn	10.00	4.00
J53	D4	1.20e gray ol ('33)	13.00	12.00
		Nos. J45-J53 (9)	34.10	22.90

D5

1940, Feb. 1   Unwmk.   Perf. 12½

J54	D5	5c bister, perf. 14	.50	.35
J55	D5	10c rose lilac	.30	.25
J56	D5	20c dk car rose	.30	.25
J57	D5	30c purple	.30	.25
J58	D5	40c cerise	.30	.25
J59	D5	50c brt blue	.30	.25
J60	D5	60c yellow grn	.30	.25
J61	D5	80c scarlet	.30	.25
J62	D5	1e brown	.30	.25
J63	D5	2e dk rose vio	.55	.45
J64	D5	5e org yel, perf. 14	11.00	9.00
a.		Perf. 12½	175.00	125.00
		Nos. J54-J64 (11)	14.45	11.80

Nos. J54-J64 were first issued perf. 14. In 1955 all but the 5c were reissued in perf. 12½.

> **Catalogue values for unused stamps in this section, from this point to the end of the section, are for Never Hinged items.**

D6

1967-84   Litho.   Perf. 11½

J65	D6	10c dp org, red brn & yel	.25	.25
J66	D6	20c bis, dk brn & yel	.25	.25
J67	D6	30c org, red brn & yel	.25	.25
J68	D6	40c ol bis, dk brn & yel	.25	.25
J69	D6	50c ultra, dk bl & bl	.25	.25
J70	D6	60c grnsh bl, dk grn & lt bl	.25	.25
J71	D6	80c bl, dk bl & lt bl	.25	.25
J72	D6	1e vio bl, dk bl & lt bl	.25	.25
J73	D6	2e grn, dk grn & lt grn	.25	.25
J74	D6	3e lt grn, grn & yel ('75)	.25	.25
J75	D6	4e bl grn, dk grn & yel ('75)	.25	.25
J76	D6	5c cl, dp cl & pink	.25	.25

J77	D6	9e vio, dk vio & pink ('75)	.25	.25
J78	D6	10e lil, pur & pale vio ('75)	.25	.25
J79	D6	20e red, brn & pale vio ('75)	.70	.25
J80	D6	40e dp red lil, rose vio & bluish lil ('84)	3.00	1.25
J81	D6	50e lil, brn & pale gray ('84)	4.50	1.50
		Nos. J65-J81 (17)	11.70	6.50

D7

1992-93   Litho.   Perf. 12x11½

J82	D7	1e multicolored	.25	.25
J83	D7	2e multicolored	.25	.25
J84	D7	5e multicolored	.25	.25
J85	D7	10e multicolored	.30	.25
J86	D7	20e multicolored	.50	.25
J87	D7	50e multicolored	1.00	.25
J88	D7	100e multicolored	2.00	.55
J89	D7	200e multicolored	3.00	1.25
		Nos. J82-J89 (8)	7.55	3.30

Issued: 1e, 2e, 5e, 200e, 10/7/92; 10e, 20e, 50e, 100e, 3/9/93.

Type D7 Inscribed "CTT CORREIOS"

1995-96

J90	D7	3e multicolored	.25	.25
J91	D7	4e multicolored	.25	.25
J92	D7	5e multicolored	.25	.25
J93	D7	9e multicolored	.50	.25
J94	D7	10e multicolored	.25	.25
J95	D7	20e multicolored	.25	.25
J96	D7	40e multicolored	.85	.75
J97	D7	50e multicolored	.75	.60
J98	D7	100e multicolored	1.10	.95
		Nos. J90-J98 (9)	4.45	3.80

Issued: 3e, 4e, 9e, 40e, 4/20/95; 50e, 5/22/95; 5e, 10e, 20e, 100e, 5/24/96.

Numerals — D8

2002, Jan. 2   Litho.   Perf. 11¾x11½

J99	D8	1c multi	.25	.25
J100	D8	2c multi	.25	.25
J101	D8	5c multi	.25	.25
J102	D8	10c multi	.25	.25
J103	D8	25c multi	.55	.25
J104	D8	50c multi	1.10	.35
J105	D8	€1 multi	2.00	.70
		Nos. J99-J105 (7)	4.65	2.30

OFFICIAL STAMPS

No. 567 Overprinted in Black

1938   Unwmk.   Perf. 11½

O1	A113	40c brown	.45	.25

> **Catalogue values for unused stamps in this section, from this point to the end of the section, are for Never Hinged items.**

O1

1952, Sept.   Litho.   Perf. 12½

O2	O1	black & cream	.45	.25

O2

1975, June

O3	O2	black & yellow	1.00	.25

NEWSPAPER STAMPS

N1

Perf. 11½, 12½, 13½

1876   Typo.   Unwmk.

P1	N1	2½r bister	9.50	1.40
a.		2½r olive green	9.50	1.40

Various shades.

PARCEL POST STAMPS

Mercury and Commerce
PP1

1920-22   Unwmk.   Typo.   Perf. 12

Q1	PP1	1c lilac brown	.25	.25
Q2	PP1	2c orange	.25	.25
Q3	PP1	5c lt brown	.25	.25
Q4	PP1	10c red brown	.25	.25
Q5	PP1	20c gray blue	.30	.25
Q6	PP1	40c carmine rose	.35	.25
Q7	PP1	50c black	.50	.45
Q8	PP1	60c dk blue ('21)	.50	.45
Q9	PP1	70c gray brn ('21)	3.00	2.00
Q10	PP1	80c ultra ('21)	3.50	3.25
Q11	PP1	90c lt vio ('21)	3.50	2.25
Q12	PP1	1e lt green	4.00	2.25
Q13	PP1	2e pale lilac ('22)	11.00	3.50
Q14	PP1	3e olive ('22)	21.00	4.00
Q15	PP1	4e ultra ('22)	42.50	7.00
Q16	PP1	5e gray ('22)	55.00	4.75
Q17	PP1	10e chocolate ('22)	82.50	9.25
		Nos. Q1-Q17 (17)	228.65	40.65

Parcel Post Package
PP2

1936   Perf. 11½

Q18	PP2	50c olive brown	.65	.50
Q19	PP2	1e bister brown	.65	.50
Q20	PP2	1.50e purple	.65	.50
Q21	PP2	2e carmine lake	2.75	.60
Q22	PP2	2.50e olive green	2.75	.60
Q23	PP2	4.50e brown lake	5.75	.65
Q24	PP2	5e violet	9.00	.75
Q25	PP2	10e orange	12.00	1.75
		Nos. Q18-Q25 (8)	34.20	5.85

POSTAL TAX STAMPS

These stamps represent a special fee for the delivery of postal matter on certain days in each year. The money derived from their sale is applied to works of public charity.

Regular Issues Overprinted in Carmine

1911, Oct. 4   Unwmk.   Perf. 14½x15

RA1	A62	10r gray green	8.50	2.25

The 20r carmine of this type was for use on telegrams. Value, $8.50.

1912, Oct. 4   Perf. 15x14½

RA2	A64	1c deep green	6.00	1.75

The 2c carmine of this type was for use on telegrams. Value, $10.

"Lisbon" — PT1

1913, June 8   Litho.   Perf. 12x11½

RA3	PT1	1c dark green	.95	.70

The 2c dark brown of this type was for use on telegrams. Value, $5.

"Charity" — PT2

1915, Oct. 4   Typo.

RA4	PT2	1c carmine	.35	.30

The 2c plum of this type was for use on telegrams. Value, $5.
See No. RA6.

No. RA4 Surcharged

1924, Oct. 4

RA5	PT2	15c on 1c dull red	1.25	.70

The 30c on 2c claret of this type was for use on telegrams. Value, $5.

Charity Type of 1915 Issue

1925, Oct. 4   Perf. 12½

RA6	PT2	15c carmine	.55	.50

The 30c brown violet of this type was for use on telegrams. Value, $6.50.

Comrades of the Great War Issue

Muse of History with Tablet — PT3

1925, Apr. 8   Litho.   Perf. 11

RA7	PT3	10c brown	1.10	1.10
RA8	PT3	10c green	1.10	1.10
RA9	PT3	10c rose	1.10	1.10
RA10	PT3	10c ultra	1.10	1.10
		Nos. RA7-RA10 (4)	4.40	4.40

The use of these stamps, in addition to the regular postage, was obligatory on certain days of the year. If the tax represented by these stamps was not prepaid, it was collected by means of Postal Tax Due Stamp No. RAJ1.

Pombal Issue
Common Design Types
Engraved; Value and "Continente" Typographed in Black

		1925, May 8		Perf. 12½
RA11	CD28	15c ultra	.65	.40
RA12	CD29	15c ultra	1.00	.75
RA13	CD30	15c ultra	1.00	.75
		Nos. RA11-RA13 (3)	2.65	1.90

Olympic Games Issue

Hurdler — PT7

		1928	Litho.	Perf. 12
RA14	PT7	15c dull red & blk	3.50	2.50

The use of this stamp, in addition to the regular postage, was obligatory on May 22-24, 1928. 10% of the money thus obtained was retained by the Postal Administration; the balance was given to a Committee in charge of Portuguese participation in the Olympic games at Amsterdam.

POSTAL TAX DUE STAMPS

Comrades of the Great War Issue

PTD1

		1925	Unwmk. Typo.	Perf. 11x11½
RAJ1	PTD1	20c brown orange	.55	.45

See Note after No. RA10.

Pombal Issue
Common Design Types

		1925		Perf. 12½
RAJ2	CD28	30c ultra	1.10	1.10
RAJ3	CD29	30c ultra	1.10	1.10
RAJ4	CD30	30c ultra	1.10	1.10
		Nos. RAJ2-RAJ4 (3)	3.30	3.30

When the compulsory tax was not paid by the use of stamps #RA11-RA13, double the amount was collected by means of #RAJ2-RAJ4.

Olympic Games Issue

PTD2

		1928	Litho.	Perf. 11½
RAJ5	PTD2	30c lt red & blk	2.50	1.75

FRANCHISE STAMPS

These stamps are supplied by the Government to various charitable, scientific and military organizations for franking their correspondence. This franking privilege was withdrawn in 1938.

FOR THE RED CROSS SOCIETY

F1

		Perf. 11½		
		1889-1915	Unwmk.	Typo.
1S1	F1	rose & blk ('15)	.50	.40
a.		Vermilion & black ('08)	5.75	1.25
b.		Red & black, perf. 12½	65.00	6.25

No. 1S1 Overprinted in Green

		1917		
1S3	F1	rose & black	80.00	72.50
a.		Inverted overprint	150.00	150.00

"Charity" Extending Hope to Invalid — F1a

		1926	Litho.	Perf. 14
		Inscribed "LISBOA"		
1S4	F1a	black & red	8.00	8.00
		Inscribed "DELEGACOES"		
1S5	F1a	black & red	8.00	8.00

No. 1S4 was for use in Lisbon. No. 1S5 was for the Red Cross chapters outside Lisbon. For overprints see Nos. 1S72-1S73.

Camoens Issue of 1924 Overprinted in Black or Red

		1927		
1S6	A68	40c ultra	1.10	1.00
1S7	A68	48c red brown	1.10	1.00
1S8	A69	64c green	1.10	1.00
1S9	A69	75c dk violet	1.10	1.00
1S10	A71	4.50e blk, org (R)	1.10	1.00
1S11	A71	10e dk brn, pnksh	1.10	1.00
		Nos. 1S6-1S11 (6)	6.60	6.00

Camoens Issue of 1924 Overprinted in Red

		1928		
1S12	A67	15c olive grn	1.10	1.00
1S13	A67	16c violet brn	1.10	1.00
1S14	A68	25c lilac	1.10	1.00
1S15	A68	40c ultra	1.10	1.00
1S16	A70	1.20e lt brown	1.10	1.00
1S17	A70	2e apple green	1.10	1.00
		Nos. 1S12-1S17 (6)	6.60	6.00

Camoens Issue of 1924 Overprinted in Red

		1929		
1S18	A68	30c dk brown	1.10	1.00
1S19	A68	40c ultra	1.10	1.00
1S20	A69	80c bister	1.10	1.00
1S21	A70	1.50e red	1.10	1.00
1S22	A70	1.60e dark blue	1.10	1.00
1S23	A71	2.40e green, grn	1.10	1.00
		Nos. 1S18-1S23 (6)	6.60	6.00

Same Overprint Dated "1930"

		1930		
1S24	A68	40c ultra	1.10	1.00
1S25	A69	50c red orange	1.10	1.00
1S26	A69	96c lake	1.10	1.00
1S27	A70	1.60e dk blue	1.10	1.00
1S28	A71	3e dk blue, bl	1.10	1.00
1S29	A72	20e dk violet, lil	1.10	1.00
		Nos. 1S24-1S29 (6)	6.60	6.00

Camoens Issue of 1924 Overprinted in Red

		1931		
1S30	A68	25c lilac	1.25	1.10
1S31	A68	32c dk green	1.25	1.10
1S32	A68	40c ultra	1.25	1.10
1S33	A69	96c lake	1.25	1.10
1S34	A70	1.60e dark blue	1.25	1.10
1S35	A71	3.20e black, green	1.25	1.10
		Nos. 1S30-1S35 (6)	7.50	6.60

Same Overprint Dated "1932"

		1931		
1S36	A67	20c dp orange	1.75	1.75
1S37	A68	40c ultra	1.75	1.75
1S38	A68	48c red brown	1.75	1.75
1S39	A69	64c green	1.75	1.75
1S40	A70	1.60e dark blue	1.75	1.75
1S41	A71	10e dk brown, pnksh	1.75	1.75
		Nos. 1S36-1S41 (6)	10.50	10.50

Nos. 1S6-1S11 Overprinted in Red

		1932		
1S42	A68	40c ultra	1.75	1.75
1S43	A68	48c red brown	1.75	1.75
1S44	A69	64c green	1.75	1.75
1S45	A69	75c dk violet	1.75	1.75
1S46	A71	4.50e blk, orange	1.75	1.75
1S47	A71	10e dk brn, pnksh	1.75	1.75
		Nos. 1S42-1S47 (6)	10.50	10.50

		1933		Dated "1934"
1S48	A68	40c ultra	2.25	2.25
1S49	A68	48c red brown	2.25	2.25
1S50	A69	64c green	2.25	2.25
1S51	A69	75c dark violet	2.25	2.25
1S52	A71	4.50e blk, orange	2.25	2.25
1S53	A71	10e dk brown, pnksh	2.25	2.25
		Nos. 1S48-1S53 (6)	13.50	13.50

		1935		Dated "1935"
1S54	A68	40c ultra	2.60	2.60
1S55	A68	48c red brown	2.60	2.60
1S56	A69	64c green	2.60	2.60
1S57	A69	75c dk violet	2.60	2.60
1S58	A71	4.50e black, orange	2.60	2.60
1S59	A71	10e dk brn, pnksh	2.60	2.60
		Nos. 1S54-1S59 (6)	15.60	15.60

Camoens Issue of 1924 Overprinted in Black or Red

		1935		
1S60	A68	25c lilac	1.10	1.00
1S61	A68	40c ultra (R)	1.10	1.00
1S62	A69	50c red orange	1.10	1.00
1S63	A70	1e slate	1.10	1.00
1S64	A70	2e apple green	1.10	1.00
1S65	A72	20e dk violet, lilac	1.10	1.00
		Nos. 1S60-1S65 (6)	6.60	6.00

Camoens Issue of 1924 Overprinted in Red

		1936		
1S66	A68	30c dk brown	1.10	1.10
1S67	A68	32c dk green	1.10	1.10
1S68	A69	80c bister	1.10	1.10
1S69	A70	1.20e lt brown	1.10	1.10
1S70	A71	3e dk blue, bl	1.10	1.10
1S71	A71	4.50e black, yel	1.10	1.10
		Nos. 1S66-1S71 (6)	6.60	6.60

No. 1S4 Overprinted "1935"

		1936	Unwmk.	Perf. 14
1S72	F1a	black & red	10.00	10.00

Same Stamp with Additional Overprint "Delegacoes"

1S73	F1a	black & red	10.00	10.00

After the government withdrew the franking privilege in 1938, the Portuguese Red Cross Society distributed charity labels which lacked postal validity.

FOR CIVILIAN RIFLE CLUBS

Rifle Club Emblem — F2

		Perf. 11½x12		
		1899-1910	Typo.	Unwmk.
2S1	F2	bl grn & car ('99)	10.00	10.00
2S2	F2	brn & yel grn ('00)	10.00	10.00
2S3	F2	car & buff ('01)	1.00	1.00
2S4	F2	bl & org ('02)	1.00	1.00
2S5	F2	grn & org ('03)	1.00	1.00
2S6	F2	lt brn & car ('04)	1.60	1.60
2S7	F2	mar & ultra ('05)	4.25	4.25
2S8	F2	ultra & buff ('06)	1.00	1.00
2S9	F2	choc & yel ('07)	1.00	1.00
2S10	F2	car & ultra ('08)	1.60	1.60
2S11	F2	bl & yel grn ('09)	1.00	1.00
2S12	F2	bl grn & brn, pink ('10)	4.00	4.00
		Nos. 2S1-2S12 (12)	37.45	37.45

FOR THE GEOGRAPHICAL SOCIETY OF LISBON

Coat of Arms
F3   F4

1903-34		Unwmk. Litho.	Perf. 11½	
3S1	F3	blk, rose, bl & red	9.00	5.00
3S2	F3	bl, yel, red & grn ('09)	12.00	5.00
3S3	F4	blk, org, bl & red ('11)	5.50	4.00
3S4	F4	blk & brn org ('22)	6.75	4.75
3S5	F4	blk & bl ('24)	15.00	8.50
3S6	F4	blk & rose ('26)	6.75	4.75
3S7	F4	blk & grn ('27)	6.75	4.75
3S8	F4	blk, yel & red ('29)	4.75	3.50
3S9	F4	bl, red & vio ('30)	4.75	3.50
3S10	F4	dp bl, lil & red ('31)	4.75	3.50
3S11	F4	bis brn & red ('32)	4.75	3.50
3S12	F4	lt grn & red ('33)	4.75	3.50
3S13	F4	blue & red ('34)	4.75	3.50
		Nos. 3S1-3S13 (13)	90.25	57.75

No. 3S12 with three-line overprint, "C.I.C.I. Portugal 1933," was not valid for postage and was sold only to collectors.

No. 3S2 was reprinted in 1933. Green vertical lines behind "Porte Franco" omitted. Value $7.50.

F5

1934		Litho.	Perf. 11½	
3S15	F5	blue & red	6.00	3.50

1935-38			Perf. 11	
3S16	F5	blue	18.00	5.25
3S17	F5	dk bl & red ('36)	4.75	4.25
3S18	F5	lil & red ('37)	3.50	2.75
3S19	F5	blk, grn & car ('38)	3.50	2.75
		Nos. 3S16-3S19 (4)	29.75	15.00

The inscription in the inner circle is omitted on No. 3S16.

FOR THE NATIONAL AID SOCIETY FOR CONSUMPTIVES

F10

		Perf. 11½x12		
1904, July		Typo.	Unwmk.	
4S1	F10	brown & green	5.00	5.00
4S2	F10	carmine & yellow	5.00	5.00

AZORES

Starting in 1980, stamps inscribed Azores and Madeira were valid and sold in Portugal. See Vols. 1 and 4 for prior issues.

Azores No. 2 — A33

Design: 19.50e, Azores No. 6.

1980, Jan. 2		Litho.	Perf. 12	
314	A33	6.50e multi	.25	.25
315	A33	19.50e multi	.85	.50
a.		Souvenir sheet of 2, #314-315	3.75	3.75

No. 315a exists overprinted for Capex 87.

Map of Azores A34

1980, Sept. 17		Litho.	Perf. 12x11½	
316	A34	50c shown	.25	.25
317	A34	1e Cathedral	.25	.25
318	A34	5e Windmill	.40	.25
319	A34	6.50e Local women	.50	.25
320	A34	8e Coastline	.70	.25
321	A34	30e Ponta Delgada	1.60	.45
		Nos. 316-321 (6)	3.70	1.70

World Tourism Conf., Manila, Sept. 27.

Europa Issue

St. Peter's Cavalcade, St. Miguel Island A35

1981, May 11		Litho.	Perf. 12	
322	A35	22e multicolored	1.00	.60
a.		Souvenir sheet of 2	4.50	1.50

Bulls Attacking Spanish Soldiers A36

Battle of Salga Valley, 400th Anniv.: 33.50e, Friar Don Pedro leading citizens.

1981, July 24		Litho.	Perf. 12x11½	
323	A36	8.50e multi	.55	.25
324	A36	33.50e multi	2.00	.75

Tolpis Azorica — A37

Designs: Local flora — 8.50e, Ranunculus azoricus. 20e, Platanthera micranta. 50e, Laurus azorica.

1981, Sept. 21		Litho.	Perf. 12½x12	
325	A37	7e multicolored	.25	.25
326	A37	8.50e multicolored	.35	.25
327	A37	20e multicolored	.65	.35
328	A37	50e multicolored	1.40	.75
a.		Booklet pane of 4, #325-328	5.00	
		Nos. 325-328 (4)	2.65	1.60

1982, Jan. 29				
329	A37	4e Myosotis azorica	.25	.25
330	A37	10e Lactuca watsoniana	.50	.25
331	A37	27e Vicia dennesiana	1.10	.60
332	A37	33.50e Azorina vidalii	1.10	.75
a.		Booklet pane of 4	5.00	
		Nos. 329-332 (4)	2.95	1.85

See Nos. 338-341.

Europa Type of Portugal

Heroes of Mindelo embarkation, 1832.

1982, May 3		Litho.	Perf. 12x11½	
333	A405	33.50e multi	1.50	.65
a.		Souvenir sheet of 3	5.00	3.00

Chapel of the Holy Ghost — A39

Various Chapels of the Holy Ghost.

1982, Nov. 24		Litho.	Perf. 12½x12	
334	A39	27e multi	1.25	.75
335	A39	33.50e multi	1.75	.90

Europa 1983 A40

1983, May 5		Litho.	Perf. 12½	
336	A40	37.50e Geothermal energy	1.50	.55
a.		Souvenir sheet of 3	6.00	3.50

Flag of the Autonomous Region — A41

1983, May 23		Litho.	Perf. 12x11½	
337	A41	12.50e multi	1.00	.25

Flower Type of 1981

1983, June 16			Perf. 12½x12	
338	A37	12.50e St. John's wort	.25	.25
339	A37	30e Prickless bramble	.80	.30
340	A37	37.50e Romania bush	1.10	.55
341	A37	100e Common juniper	2.25	1.00
a.		Booklet pane of 4, #338-341	6.00	
		Nos. 338-341 (4)	4.40	2.10

Woman Wearing Terceira Cloaks — A42

1984, Mar. 8		Litho.	Perf. 13½	
342	A42	16e Jesters costumes, 18th cent.	.60	.25
343	A42	51e shown	2.00	1.00

Europa Type of Portugal

1984, May 2			Perf. 12x11½	
344	A427	51e multicolored	1.50	.95
a.		Souvenir sheet of 3	7.00	4.00

Megabombus Ruderatus — A44

35e, Pieris brassicae azorensis. 40e, Chrysomela banksi. 51e, Phlogophora interrupta.

1984, Sept. 3		Litho.	Perf. 12x11½	
345	A44	16e multicolored	.30	.25
346	A44	35e multicolored	1.00	.50
347	A44	40e multicolored	1.40	.50
348	A44	51e multicolored	1.60	.80
		Nos. 345-348 (4)	4.30	2.05
		Perf. 12 Vert.		
345a	A44	16e	1.50	1.50
346a	A44	35e	1.50	1.50
347a	A44	40e	1.50	1.50
348a	A44	51e	1.50	1.50
b.		Bklt. pane of 4, #345a-348a	7.50	

1985, Feb. 13			Perf. 12x11½	

20e, Polyspilla polyspilla. 40e, Sphaerophoria nigra. 46e, Colias croceus. 60e, Hipparchia azorina.

349	A44	20e multicolored	.35	.25
350	A44	40e multicolored	1.00	.40
351	A44	46e multicolored	1.50	.60
352	A44	60e multicolored	1.60	.65
		Nos. 349-352 (4)	4.45	1.90
		Perf. 12 Vert.		
349a	A44	20e	2.50	2.50
350a	A44	40e	2.50	2.50
351a	A44	46e	2.50	2.50
352a	A44	60e	2.50	2.50
b.		Bklt. pane of 4, #349a-352a	10.00	

Europa Type of Portugal

1985, May 6		Litho.	Perf. 11½x12	
353	A435	60e Man playing folia drum	1.75	.80
a.		Souvenir sheet of 3	5.50	3.50

Native Boats — A46

1985, June 19		Litho.	Perf. 12x12½	
354	A46	40e Jeque	1.40	.70
355	A46	60e Bote	2.00	1.00

Europa Type of Portugal

1986, May			Litho.	
356	A447	68.50e Pyrrhula murina	2.25	.90
a.		Souvenir sheet of 3	7.00	4.00

Regional Architecture A48

19th Century fountains: 22.50e, Alto das Covas, Angra do Heroismo. 52.50e, Faja de Baixo, San Miguel. 68.50e, Gates of St. Peter, Terceira. 100e, Agua d'Alto, San Miguel.

1986, Sept. 18		Litho.	Perf. 12	
357	A48	22.50e multi	.50	.25
358	A48	52.50e multi	1.50	.70
359	A48	68.50e multi	2.25	.90
360	A48	100e multi	3.00	.75
a.		Booklet pane of 4, #357-360	6.00	
		Nos. 357-360 (4)	7.25	2.60

Traditional Modes of Transportation — A49

1986, Nov. 7			Litho.	
361	A49	25e Isle of Santa Maria ox cart	.65	.25
362	A49	75e Ram cart	3.00	1.40

Europa Type of Portugal

Modern architecutre: Regional Assembly, Horta, designed by Manuel Correia Fernandes and Luis Miranda.

1987, May 5		Litho.	Perf. 12	
363	A456	74.50e multicolored	1.50	.90
a.		Souvenir sheet of 4	6.00	4.00

Windows and Balconies A51

51e, Santa Cruz, Graciosa. 74.50e, Ribiera Grande, San Miguel.

1987, July 1 *Perf. 12*
364 A51 51e multicolored 1.75 1.00
365 A51 74.50e multicolored 2.25 .85

Aviation History
A52

Seaplanes — 25e, NC-4 Curtiss Flyer, 1919. 57e, Dornier DO-X, 1932. 74.50e, Savoia-Marchetti S 55-X, 1933. 125e, Lockheed Sirius, 1933.

1987, Oct. 9 *Perf. 12x11½*
366 A52 25e multi .45 .25
367 A52 57e multi 1.75 .90
368 A52 74.50e multi 2.60 1.25
369 A52 125e multi 3.00 1.50
    Nos. 366-369 (4) 7.80 3.90
    Perf. 12 Vert.
366a A52 25e 2.25 2.25
367a A52 57e 2.25 2.25
368a A52 74.50e 2.25 2.25
369a A52 125e 2.25 2.25
  b. Bklt. pane of 4, #366a-369a 9.00

Europa Type of Portugal

1988, Apr. 21 Litho. *Perf. 12*
370 A466 80e multicolored 6.00 1.20
  a. Souvenir sheet of 4 7.00 4.00

Birds — A54

1988, Oct. 18 Litho.
371 A54 27e Columba
        palumbus azorica .60 .25
372 A54 60e Scolopax rusticola 1.90 1.50
373 A54 80e Sterna dougallii 2.00 1.00
374 A54 100e Buteo buteo 2.50 .90
  a. Booklet pane of 4, #371-374 7.00
    Nos. 371-374 (4) 7.00 3.65

Coats of Arms
A55

1988, Nov. 18 Litho.
375 A55 55e Dominion of Azores 1.25 .60
376 A55 80e Bettencourt family 1.75 .80

Wildlife Conservation
A56

Various kinglets, Regulus regulus.

1989, Jan. 20 Litho.
377 A56 30e Adult on branch .75 .25
378 A56 30e Two adults .75 .25
379 A56 30e Adult, nest .75 .25
380 A56 30e Bird in flight .75 .25
  a. Strip of 4, Nos. 377-380 3.25 3.25
    See Nos. 385-388.

Europa Type of Portugal

Children's toys.

1989, Apr. 26 Litho.
381 A476 80e Tin boat 2.50 .80

Souvenir Sheet
382 Sheet, 2 each #381, 382a 10.00 4.00
  a. A476 80e Tin boat, diff. 2.50 1.20

Settlement of the Azores, 550th Anniv.
A58

1989, Sept. 20 Litho.
383 A58 29e Friar Goncalvo
        Velho .65 .25
384 A58 87e Settlers farming 2.40 1.00

Bird Type of 1989 With World Wildlife Fund Emblem

Various Pyrrhula murina.

1990, Feb. 14 Litho. *Perf. 12*
385 A56 32e Adult on branch 1.00 .50
386 A56 32e Two adults 1.00 .50
387 A56 32e Brooding 1.00 .50
388 A56 32e Bird in flight 1.00 .50
  a. Strip of 4, #385-388 4.50 4.50

No. 388a has continuous design.

Europa Type of Portugal

1990, Apr. 11 Litho. *Perf. 12x11½*
389 A486 80e Vasco da Gama
        P.O. 1.50 .55

Souvenir Sheet
390 Sheet of 4, 2 each #389,
        390a 7.50 4.50
  a. A486 80e Maia P.O. 1.50 1.75

Professions
A61

1990, July 11 Litho. *Perf. 12*
391 A61 5e Cart maker .25 .25
392 A61 32e Potter .55 .30
393 A61 60e Metal worker 1.50 1.00
394 A61 100e Cooper 2.10 1.10
    Nos. 391-394 (4) 4.40 2.65
    Perf. 13½ Vert.
391a A61 5e 1.25 1.25
392a A61 32e 1.25 1.25
393a A61 60e 1.25 1.25
394a A61 100e 1.25 1.25
  b. Bklt. pane of 4, #391a-394a 5.25
    See Nos. 397-400, 406-409.

Europa
A62

1991, Apr. 11 Litho. *Perf. 12*
395 A62 80e Hermes space
        shuttle 2.00 .75

Souvenir Sheet
396 Sheet, 2 each
        #395, 396a 10.00 4.00
  a. A62 80e Sanger 2.00 1.75

Professions Type of 1990

1991, Aug. 2 Litho. *Perf. 12x11½*
397 A61 35e Tile makers .45 .25
398 A61 65e Mosaic artists 1.20 .65
399 A61 70e Quarrymen 1.25 .75
400 A61 110e Stonemasons 2.00 1.50
    Nos. 397-400 (4) 4.90 3.15
    Perf. 13½ Vert.
397a A61 35e 1.25 1.25
398a A61 65e 1.25 1.25
399a A61 70e 1.25 1.25
400a A61 110e 1.25 1.25
  b. Bklt. pane of 4, #397a-400a 5.00

Transportation in the Azores — A63

Ships and Planes: 35e, Schooner Helena, 1918. 60e, Beechcraft CS, 1947. 80e, Yacht, Cruzeiro do Canal, 1987. 110e, British Aerospace ATP, 1991.

1991, Nov. 15 Litho. *Perf. 12x11½*
401 A63 35e multicolored .45 .25
402 A63 60e multicolored .90 .45
403 A63 80e multicolored 1.25 .60
404 A63 110e multicolored 1.60 .80
    Nos. 401-404 (4) 4.20 2.10
    See Nos. 410-413.

Europa Type of Portugal

85e, Columbus aboard Santa Maria.

1992, May 22 Litho. *Perf. 12x11½*
405 A514 85e gold & multi 4.00 .70

Professions Type of 1990

1992, June 12 Litho. *Perf. 12x11½*
406 A61 10e Guitar maker .25 .25
407 A61 38e Carpenter .45 .25
408 A61 85e Basket maker 1.10 .50
409 A61 120e Boat builders 1.40 .75
    Nos. 406-409 (4) 3.20 1.75
    Perf. 13½ Vert.
406a A61 10e 1.25 1.25
407a A61 38e 1.25 1.25
408a A61 85e 1.25 1.25
409a A61 120e 1.25 1.25
  b. Bklt. pane of 4, #406a-409a 5.25

Transportation Type of 1991

Ships.

1992, Oct. 7 Litho. *Perf. 12x11½*
410 A63 38e Insulano .45 .25
411 A63 65e Carvalho Araujo 1.00 .60
412 A63 85e Funchal 1.20 .65
413 A63 120e Terceirense 1.60 .80
    Nos. 410-413 (4) 4.25 2.30

Contemporary Paintings by Antonio Dacosta (1914-90) — A64

Europa: No. 414, Two Mermaids at the Entrance to a Cave, 1980. No. 415a, Acoriana, 1986.

1993, May 5 Litho. *Perf. 12x11½*
414 A64 90e multicolored 1.25 .60

Souvenir Sheet
415 Sheet, 2 each #414, 415a 7.00 5.00
  a. A64 90e multicolored 1.25 .60

Grinding Stones
A64a

Designs: 42e, Animal-powered mill. 130e, Woman using hand-driven mill.

1993, May 5 Litho. *Perf. 12x11*
416 A64a 42e multicolored .50 .25
417 A64a 130e multicolored 2.25 1.00

Architecture
A65

Church of Praia da Vitoria: 42e, Main entry. 70e, South entry.
Church of Ponta Delgada: 90e, Main entry. 130e, South entry.

1993, Nov. 3 Litho. *Perf. 12*
418 A65 42e multicolored .45 .25
419 A65 70e multicolored 1.00 .50
420 A65 90e multicolored 1.20 .60
421 A65 130e multicolored 1.60 .80
    Nos. 418-421 (4) 4.25 2.15

Tile Used in Religious Architecture
A66

Designs: 40e, Blue and white pattern, Caloura church, Sao Miguel. 70e, Blue, white and yellow pattern, Caloura church, Sao Miguel. 100e, Drawing of Adoration of the Wise Men, by Bartolomeu Antunes, Esperanca monastery, Ponta Delgada. 150e, Drawing, frontal altar, Nossa Senhora dos Anjos chapel.

1994, Mar. 28 Litho. *Perf. 12*
422 A66 40e multicolored .40 .25
423 A66 70e multicolored .90 .70
424 A66 100e multicolored 1.20 .60
425 A66 150e multicolored 1.75 .90
    Nos. 422-425 (4) 4.25 2.45
    Perf. 11½ Vert.
422a A66 40e .45 .25
423a A66 70e .90 .60
424a A66 100e 1.20 .90
425a A66 150e 1.50 1.00
  b. Bklt. pane of 4, #422a-425a 4.50

Europa Type of Portugal

Wildlife, country: No. 426, Monkey, Brazil. No. 427a, Armadillo, Africa.

1994, May 5 Litho. *Perf. 12*
426 A541 100e multicolored 1.25 .60
Souvenir Sheet
427 Sheet, 2 each #426, 427a 6.00 5.00
  a. A541 100e multicolored 1.25 .60

Architecture Type of 1993

45e, Church of Santa Barbara, Manueline Entry, Cedros. 140e, Railed window, Ribeira Grande.

1994, Sept. 16 Litho. *Perf. 12*
428 A65 45e multicolored .45 .30
429 A65 140e multicolored 1.75 .85

Advocates of Local Autonomy
A67

42e, Aristides Moreira da Motta (1855-1942). 130e, Gil Mont'Alverne de Sequeira (1859-1931).

1995, Mar. 2 Litho. *Perf. 12*
430 A67 42e multicolored .50 .30
431 A67 130e multicolored 1.50 .95

19th Century Architecture
A68

Designs: 45e, Santana Palace, Ponta Delgada. 80e, Our Lady of Victories Chapel, Furnas Lake. 95e, Hospital of the Santa Casa da Misericórdia, Ponta Delgada. 135e, Residence of Ernesto do Canto, Myrthes Park, Furnas Lake

1995, Sept. 1   Litho.   Perf. 12

432	A68	45e multicolored	.50	.30
433	A68	80e multicolored	.95	.50
434	A68	95e multicolored	1.10	.60
435	A68	135e multicolored	1.50	.90
	Nos. 432-435 (4)		4.05	2.30

Perf. 11½ Vert.

432a	A68	45e	.60	.60
433a	A68	80e	1.00	1.00
434a	A68	95e	1.25	.60
435a	A68	135e	1.75	.90
b.	Bklt. pane, #432a-435a		4.75	
	Complete booklet, No. 435b		6.00	

Natália Correia (1923-93), Writer A69

1996, May 3   Litho.   Perf. 12

436	A69	98e multicolored	1.50	.60
a.	Souvenir sheet of 3		6.00	5.00

Europa.

Lighthouses — A70

Designs: 47e, Contendas, Terceira Island. 78e, Molhe, Port of Ponte Delgada, San Miguel Island. 98e, Arnel, San Miguel. 140e, Santa Clara, San Miguel. 200e, Ponta da Barca, Graciosa Island.

1996, May 3

437	A70	47e multicolored	.55	.30
438	A70	78e multicolored	1.10	.55
439	A70	98e multicolored	1.25	.60
440	A70	140e multicolored	1.90	1.00
	Nos. 437-440 (4)		4.80	2.45

Souvenir Sheet

441	A70	200e multicolored	3.00	3.00

Carved Work from Church Altar Pieces A71

49e, Leaves, berries, bird, St. Peter Church, Ponta Delgada, Sao Miguel. 80e, Cherub, Church of the Convent of St. Peter de Alcântara, Sao Roque, Pico. 100e, Cherub, All Saints Church, former Jesuits' College, Ponta Delgada. 140e, Figure holding scroll above head, St. Joseph Church, Ponta Delgada.

1997, Apr. 16   Litho.   Perf. 12

442	A71	49e multicolored	.55	.30
443	A71	80e multicolored	.90	.45
444	A71	100e multicolored	1.10	.60
445	A71	140e multicolored	1.60	.80
	Nos. 442-445 (4)		4.15	2.15

Perf. 11½ Vert.

442a	A71	49e	.55	.30
443a	A71	80e	.90	.45
444a	A71	100e	1.10	.60
445a	A71	140e	1.60	.80
b.	Bklt. pane, #442a-445a		5.00	
	Complete booklet, #445b		5.25	

Stories and Legends Type of Portugal

Europa: Man on ship from "Legend of the Island of Seven Cities," horiz.

1997, May 5   Litho.   Perf. 12

446	A599	100e multicolored	1.25	.50
a.	Souvenir sheet of 3		4.50	3.00

Natl. Festivals Type of Portugal

1998, May 21   Litho.   Perf. 12

447	A621	100e Holy Spirit	1.25	.55
a.			5.00	1.75

Europa.

Ocean Creatures A72

Designs: 50e, Stenella frontalis. 140e, Physeter macrocephalus.

1998, Aug. 4   Litho.   Perf. 12

448	A72	50e multicolored	.60	.30

Size: 80x30mm

449	A72	140e multicolored	1.75	.80

Perf. 11½ Vert.

448a	A72	50e	.70	.30
449a	A72	140e	2.00	.80
b.	Booklet pane, #448a-449a + label		3.50	
	Complete booklet, #449b		3.50	

Europa Type of Portugal

100e, Flowers, Pico Mountain Natural Reserve.

1999, May 5   Litho.   Perf. 12x11¾

450	A641	100e multi	1.25	.50
a.	Souvenir sheet of 3		3.75	3.75

Paintings of the Azores A73

51e, Emigrants, by Domingos Rebelo (1891-1975). 95e, Portrait of Vitorino Nemésio, by Antonio Dacosta (1914-90), vert. 100e, Espera de Gado no Alto das Covas (1939-98), by José Van der Hagen (1940e, The Vila Franca Islands, by Duarte Maia (1867-1922).

Perf. 12x11¾, 11¾x12

1999, Sept. 3   Litho.

451	A73	51e multi	.60	.25
452	A73	95e multi	1.10	.45
453	A73	100e multi	1.25	.50
454	A73	140e multi	1.75	.70

Perf. 11¾ Vert., 11¾ Horiz. (#452a)

451a	A73	51e multi	.60	.25
452a	A73	95e multi	1.10	.45
453a	A73	100e multi	1.25	.50
454a	A73	140e multi	1.75	.70
b.	Bklt. pane of 4, #451a-454a		4.00	
	Complete booklet, #454b		4.75	

Europa Issue
Common Design Type

2000, May 9   Perf. 11¾x12

455	CD17	100e multi	1.25	.50
a.	Souvenir sheet of 3		3.75	1.50

Mail Delivery Systems of the Past — A74

Designs: 85e, Buoy mail. 140e, Zeppelin mail, vert.

Perf. 12x11¾, 11¾x12

2000, Oct. 9   Litho.

456-457	A74	Set of 2	2.75	1.10

Europa Type of Portugal

2001, May 9   Litho.   Perf. 12x11¾

458	A677	105e Marine life	1.25	.45
a.	Souvenir sheet of 3		3.75	3.75

Angra do Heroismo World Heritage Site — A75

View of town, sea and: 53e, Archway. 85e, Monument. 140e, Window.

2001, June 4

459-461	A75	Set of 3	3.25	1.25

Souvenir Sheet

462	A75	350e Map	4.00	4.00

Europa Type of Portugal

2002, May 9   Litho.   Perf. 12x11¾

463	A695	54c Clown, diff.	1.25	.50
a.	Souvenir sheet of 3, perf. 12½	3.75	3.75

Flowers A76

Designs: 28c, Scabiosa nitens. 45c, Viburnum tinus. 54c, Euphorbia azorica. 70c, Lysimachia nemorum. No. 468, €1.15, Bellis azorica. No. 469, €1.75, Spergularia azorica. No. 470: a, €1.15, Azorina vidalli. b, €1.75, Senecio malvifolius.

2002, May 20   Perf. 12x11¾

464-469	A76	Set of 6	11.50	4.50

Souvenir Sheet

470	A76	Sheet of 2, #a-b	6.50	6.50

Windmills — A77

Designs: 43c, Ilha do Faial windmill, Azores. 54c, Onze-Lieve-Vrouw-Lombeek windmill, Belgium.

2002, July 12   Litho.   Perf. 11¾x12

471-472	A77	Set of 2	2.10	1.20

See Belgium Nos. 1925-1926.

Europa Type of Portugal

Design: Poster art by Sebastiao Rodrigues, 1983.

2003, May 5   Litho.   Perf. 12x12½

473	A707	55c multi	1.25	.65
a.	Souvenir sheet of 2		2.50	2.50

Heritage of the Azores A78

Designs: 30c, Pineapple and plants. 43c, Grapes, vines. 55c, Tea leaves and plants. 70c, Tobacco leaf and plants.
No. 478: a, €1, Carnival dancers, Terceira Island. b, €2, Festival of the Holy Spirit.

2003, June 6   Litho.   Perf. 12x11¾

474-477	A78	Set of 4	4.50	2.25

Souvenir Sheet

478	A78	Sheet of 2, #a-b	6.25	6.25

Europa Type of Portugal

Design: People in flower garden.

2004, May 10   Litho.   Perf. 13¼x14

479	A734	56c multi	1.20	.70
a.	Souvenir sheet of 2		2.40	2.40

Worldwide Fund for Nature (WWF) A79

No. 480: a, Front of Makaira nigricans. b, Rear of Makira nigricans, fish in background. c, Front of Tetrapturus albidus. d, Rear of Tetrapturus albidus, fish in background.

2004, June 28   Perf. 13x13¼

480		Horiz. strip of 4	3.00	1.50
a.-d.	A79 30c Any single		.75	.40

Europa Type of Portugal

Designs: No. 481, Torresmos. No. 482a, Polvo Guisado (stewed octopus).

2005, May 5   Perf. 14x13¼

481	A752	57c multi	1.50	.75

Souvenir Sheet

482		Sheet of 2 #482a	3.00	3.00
a.	A752 57c multi		1.50	1.50

Tourism A80

Designs: No. 483, 30c, Cow. No. 484, 30c, Arch. No. 485, 45c, Building. No. 486, 45c, Windmill. 57c, Arm of windmill, whale, pineapple. 74c, Pineapple, volcanic lake.
No. 489: a, 30c, Statue of Jesus. b, €1.55, Embroidered dove.

2005, May 13

483-488	A80	Set of 6	6.00	3.00

Souvenir Sheet

489	A80	Sheet of 2, #a-b	4.50	4.50

Europa A81

No. 491 — Children's drawings: a, Child with one leg. b, People of many colors.

2006, May 9   Litho.   Perf. 12x12½

490	A81	60c shown	1.40	.70
a.	Booklet pane of 1, perf. 12x11¾	1.40	—

Souvenir Sheet
Perf. 12x11¾

491	A81	60c Sheet of 2, #a-b	2.75	2.75
c.	Booklet pane of 2, #491a-491b	2.75	—

Booklet panes are separated from binding stub at left by row of rouletting.

Hydrothermal Vents — A82

Designs: 20c, Crabs and mussels. 30c, Fish and mussels. 75c, Active vent. €2, Shrimp.

2006, July 22   Perf. 12½x13

492-495	A82	Set of 4	7.00	3.50
493a		Booklet pane of 2, #492-493	1.10	
495a		Souvenir sheet of 1	4.50	4.50
495b		Booklet pane of 2, #494-495	6.50	
495c		Booklet pane of 1, #495	4.75	—

Lubrapex Intl. Philatelic Exhibition, Rio (#495a). Booklet panes are separated from binding stub at left by row of rouletting.

Wines of Pico Island A83

Designs: 30c, Wine barrels, vineyard, grapes. No. 497, 60c, Grapes and vineyard. No. 498, 75c, Grape harvesters, wine barrels. No. 499, €1, Wine press, workers moving wine barrel.

No. 500: a, 45c, Vineyard, small grape vines, grapes. b, 60c, Grapes, grape harvester. c, 75c, Grapes, vats, and barrels. d, €1, Barrels, men inspecting barrels.

2006, Sept. 14

496-499	A83	Set of 4	5.50	2.75
497a		Booklet pane of 2, #496-497	2.00	—
499a		Booklet pane of 2, #498-499	3.50	—

Souvenir Sheet

500	A83	Sheet of 4, #a-d	6.00	6.00
500e		Booklet pane of 5, #500a-500d	6.00	—
		Complete booklet, #490a, 491c, 493a, 495b, 495c, 497a, 499a, 500e	29.00	

Booklet panes are separated from binding stub at left by a row of rouletting. Complete booklet also contains a pane of four progressive proofs of No. 490. These were not valid for postage.

Europa
A84

Designs: No. 501, Scout neckerchief. No. 502: a, Knot. b, Scouts and leader at tent.

2007, May 9   Litho.   Perf. 12½x13

501	A84	61c multi	1.50	.75
a.		Booklet pane of 1	1.50	—

Souvenir Sheet

502		Sheet of 2	3.00	3.00
a.-b.		A84 61c Either single	1.50	.75
c.		Booklet pane of 2, #502a-502b	3.00	—

Scouting, cent.
Booklet panes are separated from binding stub at left by a row of rouletting.

Windmills
A85

Designs: 30c, Windmill with red domed roof. No. 504, 45c, Windmill with red conical roof. 61c, White windmill with metal roof. 75c, Blue windmill.
No. 507: a, 45c, Windmill with black conical roof. b, €2, Red striped windmill.

2007, May 28

503-506	A85	Set of 4	4.50	2.50
506a		Booklet pane of 4, #503-506	4.50	—

Souvenir Sheet

507		Sheet of 2	5.50	5.50
a.		A85 45c multi	1.00	.50
b.		A85 €2 multi	4.50	2.25
c.		Booklet pane of 2, #507a-507b	5.50	—

Booklet panes are separated from binding stub at left by a row of rouletting.

Sept. 27, 1957 Eruption of Capelinhos Volcano, 50th Anniv.
A86

Designs: 30c, Erupting volcano, as seen from ocean. 75c, Erupting volcano and lighthouse.
€2.45, Cliff and lighthouse.

2007, Sept. 27   Litho.   Perf. 12½x13

508-509	A86	Set of 2	2.50	1.25
509a		Booklet pane of 2, #508-509	2.50	—

Souvenir Sheet

510	A86	€2.45 multi	6.00	6.00
a.		Booklet pane of 1	6.00	—
		Complete booklet, #501a, 502c, 506a, 507c, 509a, 510a	23.00	

No. 510 contains one 80x30mm stamp. Booklet panes are separated from binding stub at left by a row of rouletting. Complete booklet also contains a pane of four progressive proofs of No. 501. These were not valid for postage.

Europa
A87

Designs: No. 511, Man in rowboat, envelope, whale. No. 512a, Windmill, envelopes.

Perf. 12x11¾ Syncopated

2008, May 9   Litho.

511	A87	61c multi	1.25	.60
a.		Booklet pane of 1	1.25	—

Souvenir Sheet

512		Sheet of 2, #511, 512a	3.00	1.50
a.		A87 61c multi	1.25	.60
b.		Booklet pane of 2, #511, 512b	2.50	—

Booklet panes are separated from binding stub at left by a row of rouletting.

Pyrrhula Murina
A88

Various depictions of Pyrrhula murina: 30c, 61c, 75c, €1.
€2.45, Pyrrhula murina feeding. €2.95, Pyrrhula murina with beak open.

2008, May 28

513-516	A88	Set of 4	5.50	2.75
514a		Booklet pane of 2, #513-514	2.00	—
516a		Booklet pane of 2, #515-516	3.50	—

Souvenir Sheets

517-518	A88	Set of 2	12.00	7.50
517a		Booklet pane of 1	5.00	—
518a		Booklet pane of 1	7.00	—

Booklet panes are separated from binding stub at left by a row of rouletting.

Lighthouse Type of Portugal of 2008

2008, June 19

519	A835	61c Arnel Lighthouse	1.40	.70
a.		Booklet pane of 1	1.40	—
		Complete booklet, #511a, 512b, 514a, 516a, 517a, 518a, 519a	23.00	

Booklet panes are separated from binding stub at left by a row of rouletting. Complete booklet also contains a pane of four progressive proofs of No. 511. These were not valid for postage.

Biodiversity of Lakes and Lagoons — A89

Designs: 32c, Galinhola (bird). 68c, Sátiro dos Açores (butterflies). 80c, Libélula (dragonflies). €2, Cedro-das-ilhas (tree).
No. 524, €2.50, Améijoa-boa, polvo-comun, moreia-pintada (clams, octopus, moray eel). No. 525, €2.50, Zarro, marrequinha, garçareal (ducks and kingfisher).

Perf. 12x11¾ Syncopated

2009, Apr. 22   Litho.

520-523	A89	Set of 4	7.50	3.75
521a		Booklet pane of 2, #520-521	2.00	—
523a		Booklet pane of 2, #522-523	5.50	—

Souvenir Sheets

524-525	A89	Set of 2	10.50	6.00
524a		Booklet pane of 1	5.25	—
525a		Booklet pane of 1	5.25	—

Nos. 524-525 each contain one 80x30mm stamp.
Booklet panes are separated from binding stub at left by a row of rouletting.

Europa
A90

Designs: No. 526, Dish antenna of European Space Agency Satellite Tracking Center, Santa Maria Island. No. 527a, Ribeira Grande Astronomical Observatory, Sao Miguel Island.

2009, May 8

526	A90	68c multi	1.50	.75
a.		Booklet pane of 1	1.50	—

Souvenir Sheet

527		Sheet of 2, #526, 527a	3.00	2.00
a.		A90 68c multi	1.50	.75
b.		Booklet pane of 2, #526, 527a	3.00	—
		Complete booklet, #521a, 523a, 524a, 525a, 526a, 527b, Portugal #3145a	27.00	

Intl. Year of Astronomy.
Booklet panes are separated from binding stub at left by a row of rouletting. Complete booklet also contains a pane of 4 progressive proofs of No. 526. These were not valid for postage.

Europa — A91

Characters from children's story: No. 528, Woman in green. No. 529a, King on horseback in blue.

Perf. 11¾x12 Syncopated

2010, May 7   Litho.

528	A91	68c multi	1.50	.75
a.		Booklet pane of 1	1.50	—

Souvenir Sheet

529		Sheet of 2, #528, 529a	3.00	1.50
a.		A91 68c multi	1.50	.75
b.		Booklet pane of 2, #528, 529a	3.00	—

Issued: Nos. 528a, 529b, Nov.
Booklet panes are separated from binding stub at left by a row of rouletting.

Marine Invertebrates — A92

Designs: 32c, Dardanus callidus. 68c, Alicia mirabilis. 80c, Ophidiaster ophidianus. No. 533, €2, Sabella spallanzanii.
No. 534, €2, Grapsus adscencionis. No. 535, €2, Sphaerechinus granularis.

Perf. 12x11¾ Syncopated

2010, July 1

530-533	A92	Set of 4	8.25	4.00
531a		Booklet pane of 2, #530-531	2.25	—
533a		Booklet pane of 2, #532-533	6.00	—

Souvenir Sheets

534-535	A92	Set of 2	8.50	5.00
534a		Booklet pane of 1	4.25	—
535a		Booklet pane of 1	4.25	—
		Complete booklet, #528a, 529b, 531a, 533a, 534a, 535a	22.00	

Issued: Nos. 531a, 533a, 534a, 535a, Nov.
Booklet panes are separated from binding stub at left by a row of rouletting.

Europa
A93

Designs: No. 536, Cows in pasture, bird in tree. No. 537a, Cows in pasture.

2011, May 9

536	A93	68c multi	1.50	.75
a.		Booklet pane of 1	1.50	—

Souvenir Sheet

537		Sheet of 2, #536, 537a	3.00	2.00
a.		A93 68c multi	1.50	.75
b.		Booklet pane of 2, #536, 537a	3.00	—

Intl. Year of Forests. See No. 577.

Azores Whaling Heritage
A94

Designs: 32c, Whaling boats from Azores and America. 68c, Harpooned whale, whalers. 80c, Whale hunt, whalers, whale boats. €2, Whale caught near lighthouse, whale on shore, religious statue.
No. 542, €1.75, Children, whalers and boats. No. 543, €2.30, Whalers capturing whale, whaler and boat, partially-constructed whale boat.

2011, Aug. 26

538-541	A94	Set of 4	8.00	4.00
539a		Booklet pane of 2, #538-539	2.00	—
541a		Booklet pane of 2, #540-541	6.00	—

Souvenir Sheets

542-543	A94	Set of 2	9.00	3.50
542a		Booklet pane of 1	3.50	—
543a		Booklet pane of 1	5.50	—
		Complete booklet, #536a, 537b, 539a, 541a, 542a, 543a, Portugal #3331a	23.00	

Europa
A95

Designs: No. 544, Steamer Funchal. No. 545a, Pico waterfront.

2012, May 9

544	A95	68c multi	1.50	.75
a.		Booklet pane of 1	1.50	—

Souvenir Sheet

545		Sheet of 2, #544, 545a	3.00	1.75
a.		A95 68c multi	1.50	.75
b.		Booklet pane of 2, #544, 545a	3.00	—

Issued: Nos. 544a, 545b, Nov.
Booklet panes are separated from binding stub at left by a row of rouletting. See No. 578.

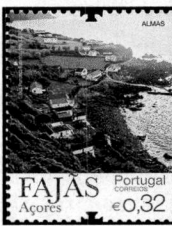

Aerial Views of Towns — A96

Designs: 32c, Almas. 68c, D'Além Norte. 80c, Grande. €2, Sao Joao.
No. 550, €1.75, Caldeira de Santo Cristo. No. 551, €2.30, Cubres.

Perf. 11¾x12 Syncopated

2012, June 5

546-549	A96	Set of 4	8.50	4.25
547a		Booklet pane of 2, #546-547	2.25	—
549a		Booklet pane of 2, #548-549	6.25	—

Souvenir Sheets

550-551	A96	Set of 2	9.00	5.25
550a		Booklet pane of 1	4.00	—
551a		Booklet pane of 1	5.00	—
		Complete booklet, #544a, 545b, 547a, 549a, 550a, 551a	22.50	

Issued: Nos. 547a, 549a, 550a, 551a, Nov.
Booklet panes are separated from binding stub at left by a row of rouletting. Complete booklet contains a pane of four imperforate progressive proofs of No. 544. These were not valid for postage. See No. 579.

Europa
A97

Designs: No. 552, Portuguese postal motorcycle. No. 553a, Rider on Portuguese postal motorcycle.

Perf. 12x11¾ Syncopated
2013, May 9   **Litho.**
552	A97	70c multi	1.50	.75
a.		Booklet pane of 1	1.50	—

Souvenir Sheet
553		Sheet of 2, #552, 553a	3.00	2.00
a.		A97 70c multi	1.50	.75
b.		Booklet pane of 2, #552, 553a	3.00	—

Booklet panes are separated from binding stub at left by a row of rouletting.

Apiculture
A98

Designs: 36c, Beekeepers tending hives, Sao Jorge. 70c, Beekeeper using smoker near hives, Pico. 80c, Beekeepers, bees and hives, Santa María. No. 557, €1.70, Beekeeper near hives near fruit trees, Flores.
No. 558, €1.70, Beehives on farm, Sao Miguel. €1.90, Beekeepers, hives, cattle, Terceira.

Perf. 12x11¾ Syncopated
2013, Oct. 9   **Litho.**
554-557	A98	Set of 4	8.00	4.00
555a		Booklet pane of 2, #554-555	2.25	—
557a		Booklet pane of 2, #556-557	5.75	—

Souvenir Sheets
558-559	A98	Set of 2	8.00	5.00
558a		Booklet pane of 1	3.75	—
559a		Booklet pane of 1	4.25	—
		Complete booklet, #552a, 553b, 555a, 557a, 558a, 559a	21.00	

Nos. 558-559 each contain one 80x30mm stamp. See No. 580.
Booklet panes are separated from binding stub at left by a row of rouletting. Complete booklet also contains a pane of 4 progressive proofs of No. 552. These were not valid for postage.

Europa — A99

Designs: No. 560, Viola da terra player. No. 561a, Viola da terra.

Perf. 11¾x12 Syncopated
2014, May 9   **Litho.**
560	A99	E multi	1.60	.80
a.		Booklet pane of 1	1.60	—

Souvenir Sheet
561		Sheet of 2, #560, 561a	3.00	2.00
a.		A99 E multi	1.60	.80
b.		Booklet pane of 2, #560, 561a	3.00	—

On day of issue Nos. 560 and 561a each sold for 72c.
Booklet panes are separated from binding stub at left by a row of rouletting.

Airplanes
A100

Designs: 42c, Boeing 314 Clipper. 50c, Douglas C-47. 72c, Lockheed Constellation. 80c, Hawker-Siddeley HS-748 Avro. €1, Boeing 314 Clipper, diff. €1.70, Lockheed Super Constellation.

Perf. 12x11¾ Syncopated
2014, Sept. 4   **Litho.**
562-565	A100	Set of 4	5.25	2.75
563a		Booklet pane of 2, #562-563	2.00	—
565a		Booklet pane of 2, #564-565	3.25	—

Souvenir Sheets
566-567	A100	Set of 2	6.00	3.50
566a		Booklet pane of 1	2.00	—
567a		Booklet pane of 1	4.00	—
		Complete booklet, #560a, 561b, 563a, 565a, 566a, 567a	16.00	

Nos. 566-567 each contain one 80x30mm stamp.
Booklet panes are separated from binding stub at left by a row of rouletting. Complete booklet also contains a pane of 4 progressive proofs of No. 560. These were not valid for postage.

Figurines Type of Portugal of 2015
Perf. 12x11¾ Syncopated
2015, Apr. 21   **Litho.**
568	A1007	80c Azores figurines	1.60	.80
a.		Booklet pane of 1	1.60	—

Issued: No. 568a, 10/19.

Europa
A101

Old toys: No. 569, Horse-drawn cart. No. 570a, Stove.

Perf. 12x11¾ Syncopated
2015, May 8   **Litho.**
569	A101	72c multi	1.60	.80
a.		Booklet pane of 1	1.60	—

Souvenir Sheet
570		Sheet of 2, #569, 570a	3.25	1.60
a.		A101 72c multi	1.60	.80
b.		Booklet pane of 2, #569, 570a	3.25	—

Issued: No. 569a, 570b, 10/19. Booklet panes are separated from binding stub at left by a row of rouletting.

Handicrafts
A102

Designs: 45c, Ceramics. 72c, Weaving. 80c, Woodworking. €1, Lace. €1.80, Plant fiber items. €2, Embroidery.

Perf. 11¾x12 Syncopated
2015, May 8   **Litho.**
571-574	A102	Set of 4	6.50	3.25
572a		Booklet pane of 2, #571-572	2.50	—
574a		Booklet pane of 2, #573, 574	4.00	—

Souvenir Sheets
575-576	A102	Set of 2	8.50	4.25
575a		Booklet pane of 1	4.00	—
576a		Booklet pane of 1	4.50	—
		Complete booklet, #568a, 569a, 570b, 572a, 574a, 575a, 576a	22.00	

Issued: No. 572a, 574a, 575a, 576a, 10/19. Booklet panes are separated from binding stub at left by a row of rouletting. Complete booklet contains a pane of four imperforate progressive proofs of No. 569. These were not valid for postage.

Types of 2011-13
Die Cut Perf. 10½
2015, Oct. 23   **Litho.**
Self-Adhesive
577	A93	E Like #536	1.60	.80
578	A95	E Like #544	1.60	.80
579	A96	E Like #547	1.60	.80
580	A98	E Like #555	1.60	.80
		Nos. 577-580 (4)	6.40	3.20

Nos. 577-580 each sold for 72c on day of issue.

Europa
A103

Designs: No. 581, Bicyclist, buildings, wind generators.
No. 582a, Hikers, whale, sailboats.

Perf. 12x11¾ Syncopated
2016, May 9   **Litho.**
581	A103	75c multi	1.75	.85

Souvenir Sheet
582		Sheet of 2, #581, 582a	3.50	1.75
a.		A103 75c multi	1.75	.85

Think Green Issue.

Activities in Natural Settings
A104

Designs: 47c, Bird watching. 75c, Whale watching. 80c, Canyoning. €1, Surfing. No. 587, €1.80, Walking tours. No. 588, €1.80, Diving.

Perf. 12x11¾ Syncopated
2016, May 16   **Litho.**
583-586	A104	Set of 4	6.75	3.50

Souvenir Sheets
587-588	A104	Set of 2	8.00	4.00

Europa
A105

Designs: No. 589, St. John the Baptist Fortress, Pico. No. 590a, Sao Brás Fort, Ponta Delgada.

Perf. 12x11¾ Syncopated
2017, May 9   **Litho.**
589	A105	80c multi	1.75	.90

Souvenir Sheet
590		Sheet of 2, #589, 590a	3.50	1.80
a.		A105 80c multi	1.75	.90

Azores Geopark — A106

Natural feature and map of: 50c, Furnas Caldera, Sao Miguel Island. 80c, Capelinhos Volcano, Faial Island. No. 593, 85c, Mount Pico, Pico Island. No. 594, €1, Faja Grande and Fajazinha, Flores Island.
No. 595: a, 85c, Algar do Carvao, Terceira Island. b, €1, Caldera and Furna do Enxofre, Graciosa Island

Perf. 11¾x12 Syncopated
2017, Sept. 7   **Litho.**
591-594	A106	Set of 4	7.50	3.75

Souvenir Sheet
595		Sheet of 2	4.50	2.25
a.		A106 85c multi	2.00	1.00
b.		A106 €1 multi	2.40	1.25

Europa
A107

Designs: No. 596, Despe-te-que-suas Bridge, Nordeste. No. 597a, 8 Arches Bridge, Ribeira Grande.

Perf. 12x11¾ Syncopated
2018, May 9   **Litho.**
596	A107	E multi	2.00	1.00

Souvenir Sheet
597		Sheet of 2, #596, 597a	4.00	2.00
a.		A107 E multi	2.00	1.00

On day of issue, Nos. 596 and 597a each sold for 86c.

Peter Café Sport, Horta, Cent. — A108

Designs: No. 598, 53c, Café entrance. No. 599, 53c, Café interior. 86c, Host behind counter. 91c, Café's scrimshaw museum. €1.50, Café exterior.

Perf. 11¾x12 Syncopated
2018, June 18   **Litho.**
598-601	A108	Set of 4	6.75	3.50

Souvenir Sheet
602	A108	€1.50 multi	3.50	1.75

No. 602 contains one 30x80mm stamp. Nos. 598-602 are not inscribed "Açores."

Tea Cultivation
A110

Designs: 53c, Tea picker and blossom. 86c, Basket for tea leaves, machinery. 91c, Tea sorter and tea pot. €2, Tea pickers, woman drinking tea, tea plantation.

Perf. 12x11¾ Syncopated
2019, June 27   **Litho.**
605-607	A110	Set of 3	5.25	2.60

Souvenir Sheet
608	A110	€2 multi	4.50	4.50

No. 608 contains one 80x30mm stamp.

MADEIRA

Type of Azores, 1980
6.50e, Madeira #2. 19.50e, Madeira #5.

1980, Jan. 2   **Litho.**   *Perf. 12*
66	A33	6.50e multi	.25	.25
67	A33	19.50e multi	.85	.55
a.		Souvenir sheet of 2, #66-67	3.25	3.25

No. 67a exists overprinted for Capex 87.

Grapes and Wine — A7

1980, Sept. 17   **Litho.**   *Perf. 12x11½*
68	A7	50c Bullock cart	.25	.25
69	A7	1e shown	.25	.25
70	A7	5e Produce map of Madeira	.40	.25
71	A7	6.50e Basket and lace	.50	.25
72	A7	8e Orchid	.80	.25
73	A7	30e Madeira boat	1.60	.45
		Nos. 68-73 (6)	3.80	1.70

World Tourism Conf., Manila, Sept. 27.

Europa Issue

O Bailinho
Folk Dance
A8

1981, May 11   Litho.   Perf. 12
74   A8   22e multi   1.25   .65
a.   Souvenir sheet of 2   3.75 1.50

Explorer
Ship — A9

1981, July 1   Litho.   Perf. 12x11½
75   A9   8.50e shown   .45   .25
76   A9   33.50e Map   1.60   .55
Discovery of Madeira anniv.

A10

Designs: Local flora.

1981, Oct. 6   Litho.   Perf. 12½x12
77   A10   7e Dactylorhiza foliosa   .30   .25
78   A10   8.50e Echium candicans   .35   .25
79   A10   20e Geranium mader-
            ense   .65   .35
80   A10   50e Isoplexis sceptrum   1.40   .75
a.   Booklet pane of 4, #77-80   6.00
        Nos. 77-80 (4)   2.70 1.60

See Nos. 82-85, 90-93.

Europa Type of Portugal

1982, May 3   Litho.   Perf. 12x11½
81   A405   33.50e Sugar mills,
            15th cent.   1.50   .65
a.   Souvenir sheet of 3   18.00 3.00

Type of 1981

9e, Goodyera macrophylla. 10e, Armeria
maderensis. 27e, Viola paradoxa. 33.50e,
Scilla maderensis.

1982, Aug. 31   Litho.   Perf. 12½x12
82   A10   9e multicolored   .40   .25
83   A10   10e multicolored   .45   .25
84   A10   27e multicolored   1.10   .50
85   A10   33.50e multicolored   1.10   .70
a.   Booklet pane of 4, #82-85   6.00
        Nos. 82-85 (4)   3.05 1.70

A12

1982, Dec. 15   Litho.   Perf. 13½
86   A12   27e Brinco dancing
            dolls   1.25   .60
87   A12   33.50e Dancers   1.75   .80

Europa
1983
A13

1983, May 5   Litho.   Perf. 12½
88   A13   37.50e Levadas irriga-
            tion system   1.50   .50
a.   Souvenir sheet of 3   5.00 3.00

Flag of the Autonomous
Region — A14

1983, July 1   Litho.   Perf. 12x11½
89   A14   12.50e multi   .95   .25

Flower Type of 1981

1983, Oct. 19   Litho.   Perf. 12½x12
90   A10   12.50e Matthiola mader-
            ensis   .25   .25
91   A10   30e Erica maderensis   .75   .35
92   A10   37.50e Cirsium latifolium   1.00   .60
93   A10   100e Clethra arborea   2.10   .90
a.   Booklet pane of 4, #90-93   6.00
        Nos. 90-93 (4)   4.10 2.10

Europa Type of Portugal

1984, May 2   Litho.   Perf. 12x11½
94   A427   51e multi   1.50   .75
a.   Souvenir sheet of 3   5.00 3.00

Madeira Rally (Auto
Race), 25th
Anniv. — A16

Various cars.

1984, Aug. 3   Litho.   Perf. 11½x12
95   A16   16e multicolored   .60   .25
96   A16   51e multicolored   2.00 1.25

Traditional Means of
Transportation — A17

1984, Nov. 22   Perf. 12
97   A17   16e Mountain sledge   .35   .25
98   A17   35e Hammock   .90   .50
99   A17   40e Winebag carriers'
            procession   1.25   .50
100 A17   51e Carreira Boat   1.60   .65
a.   Booklet pane of 4, Nos. 97-100   9.00
        Nos. 97-100 (4)   4.10 1.90

See Nos. 104-107.

Europa Type of Portugal

1985, May 6   Litho.   Perf. 11½x12
101 A435   60e Man playing gui-
            tar   1.90   .80
a.   Souvenir sheet of 3   6.00 3.50

Marine
Life — A19

1985, July 5   Litho.   Perf. 12
102 A19   40e Aphanopus carbo   1.25   .60
103 A19   60e Lampris guttatus   1.75   .90

See Nos. 108-109.

Transportation type of 1984

1985, Sept. 11   Litho.   Perf. 12x11½
104 A17   20e Ox-drawn sledge   .35   .25
105 A17   40e Mountain train   1.00   .50
106 A17   46e Fish vendors   1.40   .80

107 A17   60e Coastal steamer   1.60   .80
a.   Booklet pane of 4, Nos. 104-107   5.00
        Nos. 104-107 (4)   4.35 2.35

Marine Life Type of 1985

1986, Jan. 7   Litho.
108 A19   20e Thunnus obesus   .65   .25
109 A19   75e Beryx decadactylus   3.00   .90

Europa Type of Portugal

1986, May 5   Litho.
110 A447   68.50e Great Shear-
            water   2.75   .90
a.   Souvenir sheet of 3   9.00 3.50

Forts in
Funchal
and
Machico
A21

22.50e, Sao Lourenco, 1583. 52.50e, Sao
Joao do Pico, 1611. 68.50e, Sao Tiago, 1614.
100e, Sao do Amparo, 1706.

1986, July 1   Perf. 12
111 A21   22.50e multi   .50   .25
112 A21   52.50e multi   1.50   .70
113 A21   68.50e multi   2.25   .90
114 A21   100e multi   3.00   .75
a.   Booklet pane of 4, #111-114   7.50
        Nos. 111-114 (4)   7.25 2.60

A22

Indigenous birds: 25e, Regulus ignicapillus
madeirensis. 57e, Columba trocaz. 74.50e,
Tyto alba schmitzi. 125e, Pterodroma madeira.

1987, Mar. 6   Litho.
115 A22   25e multi   .55   .25
116 A22   57e multi   1.60   .80
117 A22   74.50e multi   2.40 1.20
118 A22   125e multi   3.00 1.25
a.   Booklet pane of 4, #115-118   11.00
        Nos. 115-118 (4)   7.55 3.50

See Nos. 123-126.

Europa Type of Portugal

Modern Architecture: Social Services
Center, Funchal, designed by Raul Chorao
Ramalho.

1987, May 5   Perf. 12
119 A456   74.50e multicolored   1.50   .75
a.   Souvenir sheet of 4   6.00 4.00

A24

Natl. Monuments — 51e, Funchal Castle,
15th cent. 74.50e, Old Town Hall, Santa Cruz,
16th cent.

1987, July 1   Perf. 12x12½
120 A24   51e multi   1.40   .70
121 A24   74.50e multi   1.75   .70

Europa Type of Portugal

Transportation Modern mail boat PS 13 TL.

1988, Apr. 21   Litho.   Perf. 12
122 A466   80e multicolored   4.00 1.20
a.   Souvenir sheet of 4   10.00 4.00

Bird Type of 1987

1988, June 15   Litho.
123 A22   27e Erithacus rubecula   .45   .25
124 A22   60e Petronia   1.40   .75
125 A22   80e Fringilla coelebs   2.00   .80

126 A22   100e Accipiter nisus   2.25   .80
a.   Booklet pane of 4, #123-126   6.00
        Nos. 123-126 (4)   6.10 2.60

Portraits of
Christopher
Columbus
and
Purported
Residences
on Madeira
A27

55e, Funchal, 1480-1481, vert. 80e, Porto
Santo.

1988, July 1   Litho.
127 A27   55e multicolored   1.60   .80
128 A27   80e multicolored   2.00 1.00

Europa Type of Portugal

Children's toys.

1989, Apr. 26   Litho.
129 A476   80e Kite   2.50   .80

Souvenir Sheet
130   Sheet, 2 each #129,
            130a   10.00 4.50
a.   A476 80e Kite, diff.   2.50 1.25

Monuments
A29

Churches: 29e, Church of the Colegio (St.
John the Evangelist Church). 87e, Santa Clara
Church and convent.

1989, July 28   Litho.
131 A29   29e multi   .45   .25
132 A29   87e multi   1.90   .90

Fish — A30

29e, Argyropelecus aculeatus. 60e,
Pseudolepidaplois scrofa. 87e, Coris julis.
100e, Scorpaena maderensis.

1989, Sept. 20   Litho.
133 A30   29e multi   .45   .25
134 A30   60e multi   1.25   .65
135 A30   87e multi   2.00   .85
136 A30   100e multi   2.00 1.25
a.   Booklet pane of 4, #133-136   6.00
        Nos. 133-136 (4)   5.70 3.00

Europa Type of Portugal

1990, Apr. 11   Litho.   Perf. 12x11½
137 A486   80e Zarco P.O.   1.50   .55

Souvenir Sheet
138   Sheet, 2 ea #137, 138a   7.50 4.00
a.   A486 80e Porto da Cruz P.O.   1.50 1.40

Subtropical Fruits
and
Plants — A32

1990, June 5   Litho.   Perf. 12
139 A32   5e Banana   .25   .25
140 A32   32e Avocado   .45   .25
141 A32   60e Sugar apple   1.25   .85
142 A32   100e Passion fruit   1.90   .85
        Nos. 139-142 (4)   3.85 1.90

Perf. 13½ Vert.

139a	A32	5e	1.50	1.50
140a	A32	32e	1.50	1.50
141a	A32	60e	1.50	1.50
142a	A32	100e	1.50	1.50
b.		Bklt. pane of 4, #139a-142a	6.00	

See Nos. 153-160.

Boats of Madeira
A33

1990, Aug. 24　　Perf. 12

143	A33	32e Tuna	.45	.25
144	A33	60e Desert islands	1.10	.60
145	A33	70e Maneiro	1.40	.65
146	A33	95e Chavelha	2.00	1.20
		Nos. 143-146 (4)	4.95	2.70

See Nos. 162-165.

Columba Trocaz Heineken — A34

1991, Jan. 23　Litho.　Perf. 12

147		35e shown	.90	.40
148		35e On branch	.90	.40
149		35e In flight	.90	.40
150		35e On nest	.90	.40
a.	A34	Strip of 4, #147-150	4.00	4.00

Europa
A35

1991, Apr. 11　Litho.　Perf. 12

151	A35	80e ERS-1	1.25	.75

Souvenir Sheet

152		Sheet, 2 each #151, 152a	10.00	5.00
a.	A35	80e SPOT	2.25	1.75

Subtropical Fruits Type of 1990

1991, June 7　Litho.　Perf. 12

153	A32	35e Mango	.50	.25
154	A32	65e Surinam cherry	1.10	.55
155	A32	70e Brazilian guava	1.25	.60
156	A32	110e Papaya	1.90	.95
		Nos. 153-156 (4)	4.75	2.35

Perf. 13½ Vert.

153a	A32	35e	1.10	1.10
154a	A32	65e	1.10	1.10
155a	A32	70e	1.10	1.10
156a	A32	110e	1.10	1.10
b.		Bklt. pane of 4, #153a-156a	5.00	

1992, Feb. 21　Litho.　Perf. 11½x12

157	A32	10e Prickly pear	.25	.25
158	A32	38e Tree tomato	.55	.30
159	A32	85e Ceriman	1.50	.75
160	A32	125e Guava	2.00	1.00
		Nos. 157-160 (4)	4.30	2.30

Perf. 13½ Vert.

157a	A32	10e	.25	.25
158a	A32	38e	.45	.25
159a	A32	85e	1.30	.65
160a	A32	125e	1.90	.95
b.		Bklt. pane of 4, #157a-160a	5.00	

Europa Type of Portugal

Europa: 85e, Columbus at Funchal.

1992, May 22　Litho.　Perf. 12x11½

161	A514	85e gold & multi	2.50	.70

Ships Type of 1990

1992, Sept. 18　Litho.　Perf. 12x11½

162	A33	38e Gaviao	.50	.25
163	A33	65e Independencia	1.00	.50
164	A33	85e Madeirense	1.25	.70
165	A33	120e Funchalense	1.75	1.00
		Nos. 162-165 (4)	4.50	2.45

Contemporary Paintings by Lourdes Castro — A36

Europa: No. 166, Shadow Projection of Christa Maar, 1968. No. 167a, Shadow Projection of a Dahlia, c. 1970.

1993, May 5　Litho.　Perf. 11½x12

166	A36	90e multicolored	1.25	.60

Souvenir Sheet

167		Sheet, 2 each #166, 167a	6.00	4.00
a.	A36	90e multicolored	1.25	.60

Nature Preservation — A37

Monachus monachus: No. 168, Adult on rock. No. 169, Swimming. No. 170, Mother nursing pup. No. 171, Two on rocks.

1993, June 30　Litho.　Perf. 12x11½

168		42e multicolored	.75	.50
169		42e multicolored	.75	.50
170		42e multicolored	.75	.50
171		42e multicolored	.75	.50
a.	A37	Strip of 4, #168-171	4.00	3.00

Architecture
A38

Designs: 42e, Window from Sao Francisco Convent, Funchal. 130e, Window of Mercy (Old Hospital), Funchal.

1993, July 30　　Perf. 11½x12

172	A38	42e multicolored	.60	.25
173	A38	130e multicolored	1.90	.80

Europa Type of Portugal

Discoveries: No. 174, Native with bow and arrows. No. 175a, Palm tree.

1994, May 5　Litho.　Perf. 12

174	A541	100e multicolored	1.25	.60

Souvenir Sheet

175		Sheet, 2 each, #174-175a	6.00	4.00
a.	A541	100e multicolored	1.25	.60

Native Handicrafts
A39

1994, May 5　　Perf. 12x11½

176	A39	45e Embroidery	.55	.30
177	A39	75e Tapestry	.90	.45
178	A39	100e Shoes	1.25	.60
179	A39	140e Wicker work	1.60	.85
		Nos. 176-179 (4)	4.30	2.20

Perf. 11½ Vert.

176a	A39	45e	.55	.30
177a	A39	75e	.90	.45
178a	A39	100e	1.25	.60
179a	A39	140e	1.60	.85
b.		Bklt. pane of 4, #176a-179a	6.00	

Arms of Madeira Districts — A40

1994, July 1　Litho.　Perf. 11½x12

180	A40	45e Funchal	.55	.30
181	A40	140e Porto Santo	1.90	.95

Traditional Arts & Crafts — A41

Designs: 45e, Chicken puppets made of flour paste. 80e, Inlaid wood furniture piece. 95e, Wicker bird cage. 135e, Knitted wool bonnet.

1995, June 30　Litho.　Perf. 11½x12

182	A41	45e multicolored	.55	.30
183	A41	80e multicolored	1.00	.50
184	A41	95e multicolored	1.10	.65
185	A41	135e multicolored	1.50	.95
		Nos. 182-185 (4)	4.15	2.40

Perf. 11½ Vert.

182a	A41	45e	.55	.30
183a	A41	80e	1.00	.50
184a	A41	95e	1.10	.65
185a	A41	135e	1.50	.95
b.		Booklet pane, #182a-185a	5.00	
		Complete booklet, #185b	5.00	

Famous Woman Type of Azores, 1996

Europa: Guiomar Vilhena (1705-89), entrepeneur.

1996, May 3　Litho.　Perf. 12

186	A69	98e multicolored	1.25	.60
a.		Souvenir sheet of 3	3.75	1.90

Paintings from Flemish Group, Museum of Sacred Paintings of Funchal (Madeira)
A42

Designs: 47e, The Adoration of the Magi, vert. 78e, St. Mary Magdalene, vert. 98e, Annunciation. 140e, St. Peter, St. Paul and St. Andrew.

Perf. 11½x12, 12x11½

1996, July 1　　　　Litho.

187	A42	47e multicolored	.50	.30
188	A42	78e multicolored	.90	.50
189	A42	98e multicolored	1.10	.65
190	A42	140e multicolored	1.40	.90
		Nos. 187-190 (4)	3.90	2.35

Perf. 11½ on 2 Sides

187a	A42	47e	.50	.30
188a	A42	78e	.90	.50
189a	A42	98e	1.00	.65
190a	A42	140e	1.40	.90
b.		Booklet pane, #187a-190a	4.50	
		Complete booklet, #190b	5.00	

Moths & Butterflies
A43

Designs: 49e, Eumichtis albostigmata. 80e, Menophra maderae. 100e, Vanessa indica vulcania. 140e, Pieris brassicae wollastoni.

1997, Feb. 12　Litho.　Perf. 12

191	A43	49e multicolored	.55	.30
192	A43	80e multicolored	1.00	.45
193	A43	100e multicolored	1.10	.60
194	A43	140e multicolored	2.40	1.25
		Nos. 191-194 (4)	5.05	2.60

Perf. 11½ Vert.

191a	A43	49e multicolored	.55	.30
192a	A43	80e multicolored	1.00	.45
193a	A43	100e multicolored	1.10	.60
194a	A43	140e multicolored	2.40	.80
b.		Booklet pane, #191a-194a	6.00	
		Complete booklet, #194b	6.50	

See Nos. 197-200.

Stories and Legends Type of Portugal

Europa: Man holding woman from "Legend of Machico," horiz.

1997, May 5　Litho.　Perf. 12

195	A599	100e multicolored	1.25	.55
a.		Souvenir sheet of 3	5.00	3.00

Natl. Festivals Type of Portugal

1998, May 21　Litho.　Perf. 12

196	A621	100e New Year's Eve	1.25	.55
a.		Souvenir sheet of 3	5.00	3.00

Europa.

Moths and Butterflies Type of 1997

Designs: 50e, Gonepteryx cleopatra. 85e, Xanthorhoe rupicola. 100e, Noctua teixeirai. 140e, Xenochlorodes nubigena.

1998, Sept. 6　Litho.　Perf. 12

197	A43	50e multicolored	.60	.30
198	A43	85e multicolored	1.00	.45
199	A43	100e multicolored	1.25	.55
200	A43	140e multicolored	1.60	.90
a.		Booklet pane, #197-200, perf. 12 vert.	6.00	
		Complete booklet, #200a	6.00	
		Nos. 197-200 (4)	4.45	2.10

Europa Type of Portugal

100e, Flowers, Madeira Island Natural Park.

1999, May 5　Litho.　Perf. 12x11¾

201	A641	100e multi	1.25	.50
a.		Souvenir sheet of 3	3.75	3.75

Glazed Tiles From Frederico de Freitas Museum, Funchal
A44

Designs: 51e, Griffin, from Middle East, 13th-14th cent. 80e, Flower, from England, 19th-20th cent. 95e, Bird, from Persia, 14th cent. 100e, Geometric, from Moorish Spain, 13th cent. 140e, Ship, from Holland, 18th cent. 210e, Flowers from Syria, 13th-14th cent.

1999, July 1

202	A44	51e multicolored	.55	.25
203	A44	80e multicolored	.85	.40
204	A44	95e multicolored	1.10	.50
205	A44	100e multicolored	1.10	.50
206	A44	140e multicolored	1.50	.75
207	A44	210e multicolored	2.10	1.10
a.		Souvenir sheet of 6, #202-207	8.00	8.00
		Nos. 202-207 (6)	7.20	3.50

Europa Issue
Common Design Type

2000, May 9　　Perf. 11¾x12

208	CD17	100e multi	1.25	.50
a.		Souvenir sheet of 3	3.75	3.75

Plants from Laurissilva Forest
A45

52e, Purple orchid. 85e, White orchid. No. 211, 100e, Folhado. No. 212, 100e, Laurel tree. 140e, Barbusano. 350e, Visco.

2000, July 4　Litho.　Perf. 12x11¾

209-214	A45	Set of 6	9.00	4.00
214a		Souvenir sheet, #209-214	9.00	9.00

Expansion of Madeira Airport
A46

2000, Sept. 15
215 A46 140e multi 2.00 1.00
a. Souvenir sheet of 1 2.50 1.50

Europa Type of Portugal
2001, May 9 Litho. Perf. 12x11¾
216 A677 105e Signals *1.25 .45*
a. Souvenir sheet of 3 5.00 3.75

Scenes of Traditional Life — A47

Designs: 53e, People retruning home. 85e, On the road to the marketplace. 105e, Traditional clothes.
350e, Leisure time.

2001, July 19 Litho. Perf. 12x11¾
217-219 A47 Set of 3 3.00 1.10
Souvenir Sheet
220 A47 350e multi 3.75 3.75

Europa Type of Portugal
2002, May 9 Litho. Perf. 12x11¾
221 A695 54c Clown, diff. *1.25 .50*
a. Souvenir sheet of 3, perf. 12½ 5.00 3.00

Worldwide Fund for Nature (WWF) — A48

Streptopelia turtur: a, On nest with chicks. b, On branch, with wings extended. c, Pair on branch. d, One on branch.

2002, Aug. 30 Litho. Perf. 11¾x12
222 A48 28c Horiz. strip or block
of 4, #a.-d. 4.50 2.50

Europa Type of Portugal
Design: Poster art by José Brandao, 1992.

2003, May 5 Litho. Perf. 12x12½
223 A707 55c multi *1.25 .65*
a. Souvenir sheet of 2 2.50 2.50

Items in Madeira Museums
A49

Designs: 30c, Funchal Bay, by W. G. James. 43c, Creche, by Manuel Orlando Noronha Gois. 55c, O Largo da Fonte, by Andrew Picken. 70c, Le Depart, by Martha Teles.
No. 228: a, €1, Photograph of Vicente Gomes da Silva. b, €2, Photograph of Jorge Bettencourt.

2003, Aug. 30 Litho. Perf. 12x11¾
224-227 A49 Set of 4 4.50 2.25
Souvenir Sheet
228 A49 Sheet of 2, #a-b 6.75 6.75

Europa Type of Portugal
Design: Hiker in flower garden.

2004, May 10 Litho. Perf. 13¼x14
229 A734 56c multi *1.40 .70*
a. Souvenir sheet of 2 2.80 2.80

Flora and Fauna of the Selvagens Islands
A50

Designs: 30c, Pelagodroma marina hypoleuca. 45c, Monanthes lowei. 72c, Tarentola bischoffi.

2004, May 24 Perf. 13x13¼
230-232 A50 Set of 3 3.50 1.75
232a Souvenir sheet, #230-232 3.50 3.50

Europa Type of Portugal
Designs: No. 233, Espetada em pau de louro. No. 234a, Filete de espada (Scabbard fish filet).

2005, May 5 Perf. 14x13¼
233 A752 57c multi *1.50 .75*
Souvenir Sheet
234 Sheet of 2 #234a 3.00 3.00
a. A752 57c multi 1.50 1.50

Tourism
A51

Designs: No. 235, 30c, Coastal village, offshore rocks, flowers. No. 236, 30c, Flowers, bird, waterfall. No. 237, 45c, Man and woman on footpath, golf course. No. 238, 45c, Windmill on beach. 57c, Horses and riders, scuba diver. 74c, Flowers, fireworks.
No. 241: a, 30c, Wicker chair, girls with flower baskets, lace. b, €1.55, Lace, clock tower.

2005, July 1 Litho. Perf. 14x13¼
235-240 A51 Set of 6 6.75 3.50
Souvenir Sheet
241 A51 Sheet of 2, #a-b 4.50 4.50

Flowers
A52

Designs: 30c, Euphorbia pulcherrima. No. 243, 45c, Aloe arborescens. 57c, Senna didymobotrya. 74c, Anthurium andraeanum. €1, Strelitzia reginae. €2, Hydrangea macrophylla.
No. 248, 45c: a, Rosa cultivar. b, Leucospermum nutans. c, Paphiopedilum insigne. d, Hippeastrum vittatum.
No. 249, 45c: a, Bougainvillea cultivar. b, Cymbidium cultivar. c, Hibiscus rosa-sinensis. d, Erythrina crista-galli.

2006, Mar. 7 Litho. Perf. 12x11¾
242-247 A52 Set of 6 11.00 5.00
243a Booklet pane of 2, #242-243 1.50 —
245a Booklet pane of 2, #244-245 2.50 —
247a Booklet pane of 2, #246-247 7.00 —
Souvenir Sheets
248 Sheet of 4 4.00 4.50
a.-d. A52 45c Any single 1.00 .55
e. Booklet pane of 4, #248a-248d 4.00 —
249 Sheet of 4 4.00 4.50
a.-d. A52 45c Any single 1.00 .55
e. Booklet pane of 4, #249a-249d 4.00 —

Booklet panes are separated from binding stub at left by row of rouletting.

Europa
A53

No. 251 — Children's drawings: a, Children in swimming pool. b, Boy walking dog.

2006, May 9 Litho. Perf. 12x12½
250 A53 60c shown 1.50 .75
a. Booklet pane of 1, perf. 12x11¾ 1.50 —
Souvenir Sheet
Perf. 12x11¾
251 A53 60c Sheet of 2, #a-b 3.25 3.25
c. Booklet pane of 2, #251a-251b 3.25 —

Booklet panes are separated from binding stub at left by row of rouletting.

Wines of Madeira
A54

Designs: 30c, Wine bottles, terraces. 52c, Bottles, grape harvesters. No. 254, 60c, Bottles, barrels in cellar. No. 255, 75c, Bottles, barrels, wine glass.
No. 256: a, 45c, Vineyards. b, 60c, Grape harvester, grape masher. c, 75c, Bottles. d, €1, Bottles, barrels, grapes.

2006, July 1 Perf. 12½x13
252-255 A54 Set of 4 5.00 2.50
253a Booklet pane of 2, #252-253 1.75 —
255a Booklet pane of 2, #254-255 3.25 —
Souvenir Sheet
256 A54 Sheet of 4, #a-d 6.00 6.00
e. Booklet pane of 4, #256a-256d 6.00 —
Complete booklet, #243a, 245a, 247a, 248e, 249e, 250a, 251c, 253a, 255a, 256e 35.00

Booklet panes are separated from binding stub at left by row of rouletting. Complete booklet also contains a pane of four progressive proofs of No. 250. These were not valid for postage.

Marine Creatures
A55

Designs: 30c Monachus monachus. 45c, Caretta caretta. No. 259, 61c, Calonectris diomedea borealis. 75c, Aphanopus carbo.
No. 261, 61c: a, Telmatactis cricoides. b, Charonia lampas. c, Patella aspera. d, Sparisoma cretense.

2007, Apr. 17 Litho. Perf. 12½x13
257-260 A55 Set of 4 4.75 2.50
260a Booklet pane of 4, #257-260 4.75 —
Souvenir Sheet
261 Sheet of 4 5.50 5.50
a.-d. A55 61c Any single 1.40 .70
e. Booklet pane of 4, #261a-261d 5.50 —

Booklet panes are separated from binding stub at left by row of rouletting.

Europa
A56

Designs: No. 262, Scout emblem.
No. 263: a, Lord Robert Baden-Powell. b, Scout hat.

2007, May 9
262 A56 61c multi 1.50 .75
a. Booklet pane of 1 1.50 —
Souvenir Sheet
263 Sheet of 2 3.50 3.50
a.-b. A56 61c Either single 1.75 .85
c. Booklet pane of 2, #263a-263b 3.50 —

Scouting, cent.
Booklet panes are separated from binding stub at left by row of rouletting.

Sugar Mills
A57

Designs: 30c, Man stirring syrup, man grinding cane. 75c, Oxen, man grinding cane. €2.45, Man leading oxen, man grinding cane, man carrying cane.

2007, July 1 Perf. 12½x13
264-265 A57 Set of 2 2.50 1.25
265a Booklet pane of 2, #264-265 2.50 —
Souvenir Sheet
Perf. 13¼x13
266 A57 €2.45 multi 6.00 6.00
a. Booklet pane of 1 6.00 —
Complete booklet, #260a, 261e, 262a, 263c, 265a, 266a 24.00

No. 266 contains one 60x40mm stamp.
Booklet panes are separated from binding stub at left by a row of rouletting. Complete booklet also contains a pane of four progressive proofs of No. 262. These were not valid for postage.

Funchal, 500th Anniv.
A58

Designs: 30c, Funchal Harbor. 61c, Map. 75c, Coat of arms. €1, Boat in harbor.
No. 271, €2.45, Boat in harbor, diff. No. 272, €2.45, Man, harbor, town.

Perf. 12x11¾ Syncopated
2008, Apr. 15 Litho.
267-270 A58 Set of 4 6.00 3.00
268a Booklet pane of 2, #267-268 2.00 —
270a Booklet pane of 2, #269-270 4.00 —
Souvenir Sheets
271-272 A58 Set of 2 11.00 11.00
271a Booklet pane of 1 5.50 —
272a Booklet pane of 1 5.50 —

Booklet panes are separated from binding stub at left by a row of rouletting.

Europa
A59

Designs: No. 273, Man, envelopes. No. 274a, Houses, envelopes.

Perf. 12x11¾ Syncopated
2008, May 9 Litho.
273 A59 61c multi 1.40 .70
a. Booklet pane of 1 1.40 —
Souvenir Sheet
274 Sheet of 2, #273, 274a 3.00 2.00
a. A59 61c multi 1.40 .70
b. Booklet pane of 2, #273, 274a 2.75 —

Booklet panes are separated from binding stub at left by a row of rouletting.

Lighthouse Type of Portugal of 2008
2008, June 19
275 A835 61c Ponta do Pargo
Lighthouse 1.40 .70
a. Booklet pane of 1 1.40 —
Complete booklet, #268a, 270a, 271a, 272a, 273a, 274b, 275a 23.00

Booklet panes are separated from binding stub at left by a row of rouletting. Complete booklet also contains a pane of four progressive proofs of No. 273. These were not valid for postage.

Fruits
A60

Designs: 32c, Annona cherimola. 68c, Eugenia uniflora. 80c, Persea americana. €2, Psidium guajava.
No. 280, €2.50, Dwarf Cavendish bananas. No. 281, €2.50, Passiflora edulis.

Perf. 12x11¾ Syncopated
2009, Apr. 27   Litho.

276-279	A60	Set of 4	9.00	4.50
277a	Booklet pane of 2, #276-277		2.25	—
279a	Booklet pane of 2, #278-279		6.75	—

Souvenir Sheets

280-281	A60	Set of 2	11.00	7.50
280a	Booklet pane of 1		5.50	—
281a	Booklet pane of 1		5.50	—

Nos. 280-281 each contain one 80x30mm stamp. See No. 316.
Booklet panes are separated from binding stub at left by a row of rouletting.

Europa
A61

Designs: No. 282, M51 galaxy. No. 283a, Telescope built by astronomy student from University of Madeira.

2009, May 8

282	A61	68c multi	1.60	.80
a.	Booklet pane of 1		1.60	—

Souvenir Sheet

283	Sheet of 2, #282, 283a		3.50	2.00
a.	A61 68c multi		1.75	.85
b.	Booklet pane of 2, #282, 283a		3.50	—
	Complete booklet, #277a, 279a, 280a, 281a, 282a, 283b, Portugal #3144a		30.00	

Intl. Year of Astronomy.
Booklet panes are separated from binding stub at left by a row of rouletting. Complete booklet also contains a pane of 4 progressive proofs of No. 282. These were not valid for postage.

Botanical Gardens, 50th Anniv.
A62

Designs: 32c, Musschia aurea, topiary garden. 68c, Geranium maderense, path. 80c, Ranunculus cortusifolius, path and roads. No. 287, €2, Convolvulus massonii, people in gardens.
No. 288, €2, Patterned flower gardens. No. 289, €2, Building, scientist, botanist inspecting plant, seeds.

Perf. 12x11¾ Syncopated
2010, Apr. 30   Litho.

284-287	A62	Set of 4	8.50	4.00
285a	Booklet pane of 2, #284-285		2.25	—
287a	Booklet pane of 2, #286-287		6.25	—

Souvenir Sheets

288-289	A62	Set of 2	9.00	5.50
288a	Booklet pane of 1		4.50	—
289a	Booklet pane of 1		4.50	—

Issued: Nos. 285a, 287a, 288a, 289a, Nov.
Booklet panes are separated from binding stub at left by a row of rouletting.
See Nos. 317, 349.

Europa — A63

Characters from children's story: No. 290, Woman. No. 291a, Man.

Perf. 11¾x12 Syncopated
2010, May 7   Litho.

290	A63	68c multi	1.60	.80
a.	Booklet pane of 1		1.60	—

Souvenir Sheet

291	Sheet of 2, #290, 291a		3.50	1.75
a.	A63 68c multi		1.75	.85
b.	Booklet pane of 2, #290, 291a		3.50	—
	Complete booklet, #285a, 287a, 288a, 289a, 290a, 291b		23.00	

Issued: Nos. 290a, 291b, Nov.
Booklet panes are separated from binding stub at left by a row of rouletting.

Europa
A64

Designs: No. 292, People walking on forest path, bird in tree. No. 293a, Birds in flight and on branch..

Perf. 12x11¾ Syncopated
2011, May 9

292	A64	68c multi	1.50	.75
a.	Booklet pane of 1		1.50	—

Souvenir Sheet

293	Sheet of 2, #292, 293a		3.00	2.00
a.	A64 68c multi		1.50	.75
b.	Booklet pane of 2, #292, 293a		3.00	—

Intl. Year of Forests.

Country Houses
A65

Designs: 32c, Quinta dos Cruzes. 68c, Quinta Jardins do Lago. 80c, Quinta Monte Palace. €2, Quinta Serra Golf.
No. 298, €1.75, Quinta do Palheiro - Casa Velha. No. 299, €2.30, Quinta Vigia.

2011, Sept. 23

294-297	A65	Set of 4	8.50	4.25
295a	Booklet pane of 2, #294-295		2.60	—
297a	Booklet pane of 2, #296-297		6.50	—

Souvenir Sheets

298-299	A65	Set of 2	8.50	5.50
298a	Booklet pane of 1		3.50	—
299a	Booklet pane of 1		5.00	—
	Complete booklet, #292a, 293b, 295a, 297a, 298a, 299a, Portugal #3330a		24.00	

Europa
A66

Designs: No. 300, Steamer Santa Maria. No. 301a, Funchal waterfront.

2012, May 9

300	A66	68c multi	1.50	.75
a.	Booklet pane of 1		1.50	—

Souvenir Sheet

301	Sheet of 2, #300, 301a		3.00	1.75
a.	A66 68c multi		1.50	.75
b.	Booklet pane of 2, #300, 301a		3.00	—

Issued: Nos. 300a, 301b, Nov.
Booklet panes are separated from binding stub at left by a row of rouletting.

Levadas
A67

Irrigation canals at: 32c, Rei. 68c, Caldeirao Verde. 80c, Faja do Rodrigues. €2, 25 Fontes. €1.75. Cedros, vert. €2.30, Furado, vert.

2012   Perf. 12x11¾ Syncopated

302-305	A67	Set of 4	8.50	4.25
303a	Booklet pane of 2, #302-303		2.25	—
305a	Booklet pane of 2, #304-305		6.25	—

Souvenir Sheets
Perf. 11¾x12 Syncopated

306-307	A67	Set of 2	9.00	5.25
306a	Booklet pane of 1		4.00	—
307a	Booklet pane of 1		5.00	—
	Complete booklet, #300a, 301b, 303a, 305a, 306a, 307a		24.00	

Issued: Nos. 302-307, 9/21; Nos. 303a, 305a, 306a, 307a, Nov. Nos. 306-307 each contain one 30x80mm stamp.
Booklet panes are separated from binding stub at left by a row of rouletting. Complete booklet contains a pane of four imperforate progressive proofs of No. 300. These were not valid for postage.
See Nos. 318, 350, 361.

Europa
A68

Designs: No. 308, Portuguese postal all-terrain vehicle. No. 309a, Rider on Portuguese all-terrain vehicle.

Perf. 12x11¾ Syncopated
2013, May 9   Litho.

308	A68	70c multi	1.60	.80
a.	Booklet pane of 1		1.60	—

Souvenir Sheet

309	Sheet of 2, #308, 309a		3.25	2.00
a.	A68 70c multi		1.60	.85
b.	Booklet pane of 2, #308, 309a		3.25	—

See No. 319.
Booklet panes are separated from binding stub at left by a row of rouletting.

Apiculture
A69

Designs: 36c, Bee near water. 70c, Bee at flower. 80c, Bee at flower, diff. No. 313, €1.70, Beekeeper and bees near hives.
No. 314, €1.70, Bee approaching flower. €1.90, Hives, bee on leaf near flower.

Perf. 12x11¾ Syncopated
2013, May 17   Litho.

310-313	A69	Set of 4	8.00	4.00
311a	Booklet pane of 2, #310-311		2.50	—
313a	Booklet pane of 2, #312-313		5.50	—

Souvenir Sheets

314-315	A69	Set of 2	9.00	5.00
314a	Booklet pane of 1		4.00	—
315a	Booklet pane of 1		5.00	—
	Complete booklet, #308a, 309b, 311a, 313a, 314a, 315a		22.00	

Nos. 314-315 each contain one 80x30mm stamp. See No. 320.
Booklet panes are separated from binding stub at left by a row of rouletting. Complete booklet also contains a pane of 4 progressive proofs of No. 308. These were not valid for postage.

Types of 2009-13
Die Cut Perf. 10½
2014, Jan. 27   Litho.
Self-Adhesive

316	A60	E Like #277	1.60	.95
317	A62	E Like #285	1.60	.95
318	A67	E Like #303	1.60	.95
319	A68	E Like #308	1.60	.95
320	A69	E Like #311	1.60	.95
	Nos. 316-320 (5)		8.00	4.75

On day of issue, Nos. 316-320 each sold for 70c.

Europa — A70

Designs: No. 321, Brinquinho player. No. 322a, Brinquinho.

Perf. 11¾x12 Syncopated
2014, May 9   Litho.

321	A70	E multi	1.60	.80
a.	Booklet pane of 1		1.60	—

Souvenir Sheet

322	Sheet of 2, #321, 322a		3.50	2.00
a.	A70 E multi		1.60	.80
b.	Booklet pane of 2, #321, 322a		3.50	—

On day of issue Nos. 321 and 322a each sold for 72c.
Booklet panes are separated from binding stub at left by a row of rouletting.
See No. 351.

Diocese of Funchal, 500th Anniv. — A71

Designs: 42c, Processional cross. 50c, St. James, the Lesser. 72c, Our Lady of the Mount. 80c, Pope John Paul II.
€1, Papal bull creating Diocese of Funchal. €1.70, Funchal Cathedral.

Perf. 11¾x12 Syncopated
2014, June 12   Litho.

323-326	A71	Set of 4	5.50	3.00
324a	Booklet pane of 2, #323-324		2.00	—
326a	Booklet pane of 2, #325-326		3.50	—

Souvenir Sheets

327-328	A71	Set of 2	6.00	3.75
327a	Booklet pane of 1		2.25	—
328a	Booklet pane of 1		3.75	—
	Complete booklet, #321a, 322b, 324a, 326a, 327a, 328a		18.00	

Booklet panes are separated from binding stub at left by a row of rouletting. Complete booklet also contains a pane of 4 progressive proofs of No. 321. These were not valid for postage.

Types of 2011-12
Die Cut Perf. 10½
2015, Jan. 19   Litho.
Self-Adhesive

329	A64	E Like #292	1.50	.75
330	A65	E Like #296	1.50	.75
331	A66	E Like #300	1.50	.75
	Nos. 329-331 (3)		4.50	2.25

Nos. 329-331 each sold for 72c on day of issue.

Flower Festival
A72

Designs: 45c, Flower market. 72c, Street decorations. 80c, Children in costumes carrying flowers. €1, Street garden.
€1.80, Anthurium andraeanum. €2, Heliconia rostrata.

Perf. 12x11¾ Syncopated
2015, Apr. 16   Litho.

332-335	A72	Set of 4	6.75	3.50
333a	Booklet pane of 2, #332-333		2.75	—
335a	Booklet pane of 2, #334-335		4.25	—

Souvenir Sheets

336-337	A72	Set of 2	8.75	4.25
336a	Booklet pane of 1		4.25	—
337a	Booklet pane of 1		4.50	—

Issued: No. 333a, 335a, 336a, 337a, 10/19.
Booklet panes are separated from binding stub at left by a row of rouletting.

See Nos. 352, 362.

Figurines Type of Portugal of 2015
Perf. 12x11¾ Syncopated

2015, Apr. 21			Litho.
338	A1007 72c Madeira figurines	1.60	.80
a.	Booklet pane of 1	1.60	—

Issued: No. 338a, 10/19.

Europa
A73

Old toys: No. 339, Sink, bucket and watering can. No. 340a, Taxi.

Perf. 12x11¾ Syncopated

2015, May 8			Litho.
339	A73 72c multi	1.60	.80
a.	Booklet pane of 1	1.60	—

Souvenir Sheet

340	Sheet of 2, #339, 340a	3.25	1.60
a.	A73 72c multi	1.60	.80
b.	Booklet pane of 2, #339, 340a	3.25	
	Complete booklet, #333a, 335a, 336a, 337a, 338a, 339a, 340b	22.50	

Issued: Nos. 339a, 340b, 10/19. Booklet panes are separated from binding stub at left by a row of rouletting. Complete booklet contains a pane of four imperforate progressive proofs of No. 339. These were not valid for postage.

Christmas and New Year's Day — A74

Designs: 47c, Outdoor creche. 75c, Fruit market. 80c, Christmas decoration. €1, New Year's fireworks display.
No. 345a, Infant Jesus creche figurine. No. 346a, Fireworks display near ship.

Perf. 12x11¾ Syncopated

2016, Apr. 7			Litho.
341-344	A74 Set of 4	6.50	3.25

Souvenir Sheets

345	Sheet of 2, #343, 345a	4.25	2.10
a.	A74 €1 multi	2.40	1.25
346	Sheet of 2, #344, 346a	4.25	2.10
a.	A74 80c multi	1.90	.95

See No. 353.

Europa
A75

Designs: No. 347, Bicyclist, buildings, wind generators. No. 348a, Skydiver, boats.

Perf. 12x11¾ Syncopated

2016, May 9			Litho.
347	A75 75c multi	1.75	.85

Souvenir Sheet

348	Sheet of 2, #347, 348a	3.50	1.75
a.	A75 75c multi	1.75	.85

Think Green Issue.

Types of 2010-16
Die Cut Perf. 10½

2016, Aug. 8			Litho.
	Self-Adhesive		
349	A62 E Like #286	1.60	.80
350	A67 E Like #305	1.60	.80
351	A70 E Like #321	1.60	.80
352	A72 E Like #334	1.60	.80
353	A74 E Like #344	1.60	.80
	Nos. 349-353 (5)	8.00	4.00

On day of issue, Nos. 349-353 each sold for 75c.

Europa
A76

Designs: No. 354, St. John the Baptist Fortress, Angra do Heroísmo. No. 355a, Sao Tiago Fortress, Funchal.

Perf. 12x11¾ Syncopated

2017, May 9			Litho.
354	A76 80c multi	1.75	.90

Souvenir Sheet

355	Sheet of 2, #354, 355a	3.50	1.80
a.	A76 80c multi	1.75	.90

Mountain Peaks — A77

Designs: 50c, Pico Ruivo. 80c, Pico do Castelo. No. 358, 85c, Pico do Veado. No. 359, €1, Pico Branco.
No. 360: a, 85c, Pico Ana Ferreira. b, €1, Pico do Arieiro.

Perf. 11¾x12 Syncopated

2017, Nov. 17			Litho.
356-359	A77 Set of 4	7.50	3.75

Souvenir Sheet

360	Sheet of 2	4.50	2.40
a.	A77 85c multi	2.10	1.10
b.	A77 €1 multi	2.40	1.25

Types of Madeira 2012-15
Die Cut Perf. 10½

2018, Jan. 15			Litho.
	Self-Adhesive		
361	A67 E Like #304	2.25	1.10
362	A72 E Like #332	2.25	1.10

On day of issue, Nos. 361-362 each sold for 86c.

Types of Portugal 2013-15
Die Cut Perf. 10½

2018, Jan. 15			Litho.
	Self-Adhesive		
363	A967 E Like #3527	2.25	1.10
364	A994 E Like #3616	2.25	1.10
365	A1019 E Like #3734	2.25	1.10
	Nos. 363-365 (3)	6.75	3.30

On day of issue, Nos. 363-365 each sold for 86c.

Europa
A78

Designs: No. 366, Socorridos Bridge, Câmara de Lobos. No. 367a, Ribeira de Metade Bridge, Faial.

Perf. 12x11¾ Syncopated

2018, May 9			Litho.
366	A78 E multi	2.00	1.00

Souvenir Sheet

367	Sheet of 2, #366, 367a	4.00	2.00
a.	A78 E multi	2.00	1.00

On day of issue, Nos. 366 and 367a each sold for 86c.

Discovery of Madeira, 600th Anniv. — A79

Porto Santo buildings and: No. 368, 53c, Cowherd and cows. No. 369, 53c, Cows, corn. 86c, Man, woman and dragon tree. 91c, Cows, sugar cane.
€1.50, Man, dragon tree, ship, horiz.

Perf. 11¾x12 Syncopated

2018, June 22			Litho.
368-371	A79 Set of 4	6.75	3.50

Souvenir Sheet
Perf. 12x11¾ Syncopated

372	A79 €1.50 multi	3.50	1.75

No. 372 contains one 80x30mm stamp.

Discovery of Madeira, 600th Anniv. A81

Designs: 53c, Woman and cat. 86c, Two men. 91c, Guitarist and ships. €2, Statues, vert.

Perf. 12x11¾ Syncopated

2019, June 7			Litho.
375-377	A81 Set of 3	5.25	2.60

Souvenir Sheet
Perf. 11¾x12 Syncopated

378	A81 €2 multi	4.50	4.50

No. 378 contains one 30x80mm stamp.

PORTUGUESE AFRICA

ˈpōr-chə-ˌgēz ˈa-fri-kə

For use in any of the Portuguese possessions in Africa.

1000 Reis = 1 Milreis
100 Centavos = 1 Escudo

Common Design Types pictured following the introduction.

Vasco da Gama Issue
Common Design Types
Inscribed "Africa - Correios"
Perf. 13½ to 15½

1898, Apr. 1			Engr.	Unwmk.
1	CD20	2½r blue green	1.20	.85
2	CD21	5r red	1.20	.85
3	CD22	10r red violet	1.20	.85
4	CD23	25r yellow green	1.20	.85
5	CD24	50r dark blue	1.20	.85
6	CD25	75r violet brown	8.50	7.25
7	CD26	100r bister brown	8.50	6.00
8	CD27	150r bister	12.00	6.00
	Nos. 1-8 (8)		35.00	23.50
Set, never hinged			120.00	

Vasco da Gama's voyage to India.

POSTAGE DUE STAMPS

D1

1945	Unwmk.	Typo.	*Perf. 11½x12*	
	Denomination in Black			
J1	D1	10c claret	.75	.50
J2	D1	20c purple	.75	.50
J3	D1	30c deep blue	.75	.50
J4	D1	40c chocolate	.75	.50
J5	D1	50c red violet	.75	.75
J6	D1	1e orange brown	3.00	3.00
J7	D1	2e yellow green	6.00	6.00
J8	D1	3e bright carmine	9.00	9.00
J9	D1	5e orange yellow	17.50	17.50
	Nos. J1-J9 (9)		39.25	38.25
Set, never hinged			52.50	

WAR TAX STAMPS

Liberty
WT1

Overprinted in Black, Orange or Carmine
Perf. 12x11½, 15x14

1919		Typo.	Unwmk.	
MR1	WT1 1c green (Bk)		1.50	1.50
a.	Figures of value omitted		15.00	7.50
MR2	WT1 4c green (O)		3.00	
MR3	WT1 5c green (C)		1.50	1.50
	Nos. MR1-MR3 (3)		6.00	3.00

Values the same for either perf.
No. MR2 used is known only with fiscal cancelation. Some authorities consider No. MR2 a revenue stamp.

PORTUGUESE CONGO

'pōr-chi-gēz 'kän₋₌gō

LOCATION — The northernmost district of the Portuguese Angola Colony on the southwest coast of Africa
CAPITAL — Cabinda

Stamps of Angola replaced those of Portuguese Congo.

1000 Reis = 1 Milreis
100 Centavos = 1 Escudo (1913)

King Carlos — A1

Perf. 12½

1894, Aug. 5		Typo.	Unwmk.	
1	A1	5r yellow	1.60	1.40
2	A1	10r redsh violet	2.40	1.45
a.		Perf. 13½	27.50	14.50
3	A1	15r chocolate	4.00	3.00
a.		Perf. 11½	8.00	4.50
4	A1	20r lav, ordinary paper	4.25	3.00
b.		Perf. 11½	8.00	4.50
5	A1	25r green	2.40	1.00
b.		Perf. 11½	5.50	1.20

Perf. 13½

6	A1	50r light blue	4.50	2.75
a.		Perf. 11½	22.00	9.75

Perf. 11½

7	A1	75r rose	8.00	4.50
a.		Perf. 12½	33.00	19.00
8	A1	80r yellow green	11.00	7.25
a.		Perf. 12½	97.50	57.50
9	A1	100r brown, yel	9.00	6.00
a.		Perf. 13½	55.00	29.00

Perf. 12½

10	A1	150r carmine, rose	18.00	13.50
11	A1	200r dk blue, bl	18.00	13.50
12	A1	300r dk blue, salmon	22.00	18.00
		Nos. 1-12 (12)	105.15	75.35

For surcharges and overprints see Nos. 36-47, 127-131.

King Carlos — A2

Name & Value in Black except 500r

1898-1903			Perf. 11½	
13	A2	2½r gray	.50	.30
14	A2	5r orange	.50	.30
15	A2	10r lt green	.85	.30
16	A2	15r brown	1.75	1.75
17	A2	15r gray grn ('03)	1.50	.35
18	A2	20r gray violet	1.50	1.00
19	A2	25r sea green	1.75	1.00
20	A2	25r car rose ('03)	1.50	.35
21	A2	50r deep blue	2.60	1.60
22	A2	50r brown ('03)	3.50	1.90
23	A2	65r dull blue ('03)	12.00	8.25
24	A2	75r rose	4.50	3.00
25	A2	75r red lilac ('03)	4.50	3.75
26	A2	80r violet	4.50	3.00
27	A2	100r dk bl, bl	3.75	2.50
28	A2	115r org brn, pink ('03)	10.25	7.00
29	A2	130r brn, straw ('03)	20.00	11.00
30	A2	150r brown, buff	5.25	3.75
31	A2	200r red lilac, pnksh	7.25	4.25
32	A2	300r dk blue, rose	6.50	4.00
33	A2	400r dl bl, straw ('03)	14.00	11.00
34	A2	500r blk & red, bl ('01)	25.00	11.50
35	A2	700r vio, yelsh ('01)	40.00	22.00
		Nos. 13-35 (23)	173.45	103.85

For overprints and surcharges see Nos. 49-53, 60-74, 117-126, 136-138.

Surcharged in Black

Perf. 12½, 11½ (#41, 43), 13½ (#44)

1902		On Issue of 1894		
36	A1	65r on 15r choc	6.00	4.00
a.		Perf. 11½	27.50	14.50
37	A1	65r on 20r lav (#4)	6.00	4.00
38	A1	65r on 25r green (#5)	6.00	4.00
a.		Perf. 11½	27.50	17.00
39	A1	65r on 300r bl, sal	8.00	7.25
40	A1	115r on 10r red vio	6.00	4.00
41	A1	115r on 50r lt bl	6.00	4.00
			6.00	4.00
42	A1	130r on 5r yellow	6.00	4.00
a.		Inverted surcharge	55.00	50.00
b.		Perf. 13½	6.00	4.50
43	A1	130r on 75r rose	6.00	4.25
a.		Perf. 12½	10.50	9.00
44	A1	130r on 100r brn, yel	6.00	4.50
a.		Inverted surcharge	50.00	45.00
b.		Perf. 11½	33.00	19.50
45	A1	400r on 80r yel grn	3.00	1.75
a.		Perf. 12½	6.00	4.50
46	A1	400r on 150r car, rose	4.25	3.00
47	A1	400r on 200r bl, bl	4.25	3.00

On Newspaper Stamps of 1894

48	N1	115r on 2½r brn	6.00	3.75
a.		Inverted surcharge	45.00	40.00
b.		Perf. 13½	6.00	3.75
		Nos. 36-48 (13)	73.50	51.50

Nos. 16, 19, 21 and 24 Overprinted in Black

1902			Perf. 11½	
49	A2	15r brown	3.25	1.75
50	A2	25r sea green	3.25	1.75
51	A2	50r blue	3.25	1.75
a.		Double overprint	67.50	55.00
52	A2	75r rose	6.75	4.25
a.		Double ovpt, one albino	30.00	24.00
		Nos. 49-52 (4)	16.50	9.50

No. 23 Surcharged

1905				
53	A2	50r on 65r dull blue	7.00	3.75

Angola Stamps of 1898-1903 (Port. Congo type A2) Overprinted or Surcharged

a	b

1911				
54	(a)	2½r gray	2.75	1.75
55	(a)	5r orange	3.00	2.10
a.		"REPUBLICA" inverted	15.00	12.50
56	(a)	10r lt green	3.00	2.10
a.		"REPUBLICA" inverted	15.00	11.00
57	(a)	15r gray green	3.00	2.10
a.		"REPUBLICA" inverted	15.00	11.00
58	(b)	25r on 200r red vio, pnksh	3.50	2.40
a.		"REPUBLICA" inverted	15.00	11.00
b.		"CONGO" double	15.00	11.00

Thin Bar and "CONGO" as Type "b"

59	(a)	2½r gray	3.75	2.75
		Nos. 54-59 (6)	19.00	13.20

Issue of 1898-1903 Overprinted in Carmine or Green — c

1911				
60	A2	2½r gray	.35	.25
61	A2	5r orange	.35	.35
62	A2	10r lt green	.35	.35
63	A2	15r gray grn	.35	.35
64	A2	20r gray vio	.35	.35
65	A2	25r car rose (G)	.60	.50
66	A2	50r brown	.70	.45
67	A2	75r red lilac	1.20	.75
68	A2	100r dk bl, bl	1.30	.75
69	A2	115r org brn, pink	2.25	1.50
70	A2	130r brown, straw	2.25	1.50
71	A2	200r red vio, pnksh	3.75	2.40
72	A2	400r dull bl, straw	7.00	4.25
73	A2	500r blk & red, bl	7.00	4.50
74	A2	700r violet, yelsh	9.50	5.50
		Nos. 60-74 (15)	37.30	23.75

Numerous inverts and doubles exist. These are printer's waste or made to order.

Common Design Types pictured following the introduction.

Vasco da Gama Issue of Various Portuguese Colonies Surcharged

1913		On Stamps of Macao		
75	CD20	¼c on ½a bl grn	1.75	1.60
76	CD21	½c on 1a red	1.75	1.60
77	CD22	1c on 2a red vio	1.90	1.60
78	CD23	2½c on 4a yel grn	1.90	1.60
79	CD24	5c on 8a dk blue	1.90	1.60
80	CD25	7½c on 12a vio brn	4.00	2.60
81	CD26	10c on 16a bis brn	2.50	1.75
a.		Inverted surcharge	50.00	50.00
82	CD27	15c on 24a bister	2.50	1.75
		Nos. 75-82 (8)	18.20	14.10

On Stamps of Portuguese Africa

83	CD20	¼c on 2½r bl grn	1.50	1.60
84	CD21	½c on 5r red	1.50	1.60
85	CD22	1c on 10r red vio	1.50	1.60
86	CD23	2½c on 25r yel grn	1.50	1.60
87	CD24	5c on 50r dk bl	1.75	1.60
88	CD25	7½c on 75r vio brn	3.50	2.25
89	CD26	10c on 100r bis brn	2.40	1.60
a.		Inverted surcharge	42.50	42.50
90	CD27	15c on 150r bister	2.10	1.60
		Nos. 83-90 (8)	15.75	13.45

On Stamps of Timor

91	CD20	¼c on ½a bl grn	1.75	1.60
92	CD21	½c on 1a red	1.75	1.60
93	CD22	1c on 2a red vio	1.90	1.60
94	CD23	2½c on 4a yel grn	1.90	1.60
95	CD24	5c on 8a dk blue	1.90	1.60
a.		Double surcharge	42.50	42.50
96	CD25	7½c on 12a vio brn	4.00	2.60
97	CD26	10c on 16a bis brn	2.50	1.75
98	CD27	15c on 24a bister	2.50	1.75
		Nos. 91-98 (8)	18.20	14.10
		Nos. 75-98 (24)	52.15	41.65

Ceres — A3

Name and Value in Black
Chalky Paper

1914		Typo.	Perf. 15x14	
99	A3	¼c olive brn	1.10	.50
a.		Inscriptions inverted	20.00	
100	A3	½c black	1.15	.50
101	A3	1c blue grn	3.25	2.10
102	A3	1½c lilac brn	2.25	1.35
103	A3	2c carmine	2.50	2.10
104	A3	2½c lt violet	.80	.65
105	A3	5c dp blue	1.15	1.20
106	A3	7½c yellow brn	1.90	1.50
107	A3	8c slate	1.90	1.75
108	A3	10c orange brn	1.90	1.75
109	A3	15c plum	2.50	2.10
110	A3	20c yellow grn	2.50	2.10
111	A3	30c brown, grn	5.25	3.50
112	A3	40c brown, pink	5.25	3.50
113	A3	50c orange, salmon	6.75	4.00
114	A3	1e green, blue	8.50	5.25
		Nos. 99-114 (16)	48.65	33.85

1920		Ordinary Paper		
115	A3	¼c olive brn	.90	.80
116	A3	2c carmine	1.25	.90

Issue of 1898-1903 Overprinted Locally in Green or Red

1914-18			Perf. 11½	
117	A2	50r brown (G)	2.10	1.50
118	A2	75r rose (G)	500.00	
119	A2	75r red lilac (R)	17.50	10.25
120	A2	100r blue, bl (R)	2.10	1.50
121	A2	200r red vio, pink (G)	7.50	6.75
122	A2	400r dl bl, straw (R) ('18)	110.00	110.00
123	A2	500r blk & red, bl	90.00	90.00

Same on Nos. 51-52

124	A2	50r blue (R)	2.10	1.50
125	A2	75r rose (G)	2.75	2.10

Same on No. 53

126	A2	50r on 65r dl bl (R)	2.10	1.75
		Nos. 117,119-126 (9)	236.15	225.35

No. 118 was not regularly issued.

Provisional Issue of 1902
Overprinted Type "c" in Red

Perf. 11½ (#130-131), 12½ (#127), 13½ (#128-129)

1915				
127	A1	115r on 10r red vio	1.20	.75
a.		Perf. 13½	27.00	23.00
128	A1	115r on 50r lt bl	2.50	1.35
a.		Perf. 11½	2.50	1.35
129	A1	130r on 5r yellow	1.75	1.25
a.		Perf. 12½	2.50	1.35
130	A1	130r on 75r rose	2.50	1.35
a.		Perf. 12½	3.50	2.10
131	A1	130r on 100r brn, buff	1.35	.85
a.		Perf. 13½	1.35	.85
135	N1	115r on 2½r brn	1.75	1.25

Nos. 49, 51 Overprinted Type "c"

136	A2	15r brown	1.75	1.25
a.		Perf. 12½	2.10	1.40
137	A2	50r blue	1.75	1.25

No. 53 Overprinted Type "c"

138	A2	50r on 65r dull blue	1.75	1.25
		Nos. 127-138 (9)	16.30	10.95

NEWSPAPER STAMP

N1

Perf. 12½

1894, Aug. 5		Typo.	Unwmk.	
P1	N1	2½r brown	1.75	1.40
a.		Perf. 13½	1.75	1.40

For surcharge and overprint see Nos. 48, 135.

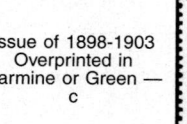

PORTUGUESE GUINEA

'pōr-chi-gēz 'gi-nē

LOCATION — On the west coast of Africa between Senegal and Guinea
GOVT. — Portuguese Overseas Territory
AREA — 13,944 sq. mi.
POP. — 560,000 (est. 1970)
CAPITAL — Bissau

The territory, including the Bissagos Islands, became an independent republic on Sept. 10, 1974. See Guinea-Bissau in Vol. 3.

1000 Reis = 1 Milreis
100 Centavos = 1 Escudo (1913)

Catalogue values for unused stamps in this country are for Never Hinged items, beginning with Scott 273 in the regular postage section, Scott J40 in the postage due section, and Scott RA17 in the postal tax section.

Nos. 1-7 are valued with small faults such as short perfs or small thins. Completely fault-free examples of any of these stamps are very scarce and are worth more than the values given.

Stamps of Cape Verde, 1877-85 Overprinted in Black

1881		Unwmk.	Perf. 12½
Without Gum (Nos. 1-7)			
1	A1	5r black	1,100.	900.
1A	A1	10r yellow	2,000.	975.
2	A1	20r bister	600.	350.
3	A1	25r rose	1,600.	975.
4	A1	40r blue	1,400.	975.
a.	Cliché of Mozambique in Cape Verde plate		18,000.	17,000.
4B	A1	50r green	2,000.	975.
5	A1	100r lilac	350.	240.
6	A1	200r orange	725.	600.
7	A1	300r brown	725.	600.

Excellent forgeries exist of Nos. 1-7.

Overprinted in Red or Black

1881-85			Perf. 12½, 13½
8	A1	5r black (R)	6.50	4.25
9	A1	10r yellow	190.00	190.00
10	A1	10r green ('85)	9.75	8.00
11	A1	20r bister	4.50	3.75
12	A1	20r rose ('85)	11.00	8.00
a.	Double overprint			
13	A1	25r carmine	3.75	3.00
a.	Perf. 13½		97.50	45.00
14	A1	25r violet ('85)	4.50	3.00
a.	Double overprint			
15	A1	40r blue	240.00	150.00
a.	Cliché of Mozambique in Cape Verde plate		1,500.	1,100.
16	A1	40r yellow ('85)	3.00	2.40
a.	Cliché of Mozambique in Cape Verde plate		67.50	50.00
b.	Imperf.			
g.	As "a," imperf.			
	Double overprint			
17	A1	50r green	240.00	150.00
18	A1	50r blue ('85)	9.00	4.25
a.	Imperf.			
b.	Double overprint			
19	A1	100r lilac	13.00	10.00
a.	Inverted overprint			
20	A1	200r orange	18.00	13.00
21	A1	300r yellow brn	22.00	16.50
a.	300r lake brown		22.00	16.50

Varieties of this overprint may be found without accent on "E" of "GUINE," or with grave instead of acute accent.

Stamps of the 1881-85 issues were reprinted on a smooth white chalky paper,

ungummed, and on thin white paper with shiny white gum and clean-cut perforation 13½.
See Scott Classic Catalogue for listings by perforation.

King Luiz — A3

1886		Typo.	Perf. 12½, 13½
22	A3	5r gray black	9.75	8.50
a.	Imperf.			
23	A3	10r green	11.50	6.00
a.	Perf. 13½		13.00	10.00
b.	Imperf.			
24	A3	20r carmine	17.00	6.00
25	A3	25r red lilac	17.00	7.00
a.	Imperf.			
26	A3	40r chocolate	14.00	9.75
a.	Perf. 12½		120.00	90.00
27	A3	50r blue	26.00	9.75
a.	Imperf.			
28	A3	80r gray	24.00	16.50
a.	Perf. 12½		120.00	90.00
29	A3	100r brown	24.00	16.50
a.	Perf. 12½		60.00	33.00
30	A3	200r gray lilac	60.00	33.00
31	A3	300r orange	72.50	50.00
a.	Perf. 13½		270.00	270.00
	Nos. 22-31 (10)		275.75	163.00

Varieties of this overprint may be found without accent on "E" of "GUINE," or with grave instead of acute accent. For surcharges and overprints see Nos. 67-76, 180-183.
Reprinted in 1905 on thin white paper with shiny white gum and clean-cut perforation 13½.

King Carlos — A4

1893-94			Perf. 11½
32	A4	5r yellow	3.00	1.75
a.	Perf. 11½		4.25	2.40
33	A4	10r red violet	3.00	1.75
34	A4	15r chocolate	3.75	2.40
35	A4	20r lavender	3.75	2.40
36	A4	25r blue green	3.75	2.40
37	A4	50r lt blue	6.75	4.00
a.	Perf. 12½		25.00	18.00
38	A4	75r rose	18.00	11.00
39	A4	80r lt green	18.00	11.00
40	A4	100r brn, buff	18.00	11.00
41	A4	150r car, rose	19.00	11.00
42	A4	200r dk bl, bl	27.50	21.00
43	A4	300r dk bl, sal	30.00	21.00
	Nos. 32-43 (12)		154.50	100.70

Almost all of Nos. 32-43 were issued without gum.
For surcharges and overprints see #77-88, 184-188, 203-205.

King Carlos — A5

1898-1903			Perf. 11½
Name & Value in Black except 500r			
44	A5	2½r gray	.50	.35
45	A5	5r orange	.50	.35
46	A5	10r lt green	.50	.35
47	A5	15r brown	4.50	3.50
48	A5	15r gray grn ('03)	2.75	1.45
49	A5	20r gray violet	2.40	1.35
50	A5	25r sea green	2.75	1.35
51	A5	25r carmine ('03)	1.50	1.00
52	A5	50r dark blue	3.75	1.75
53	A5	50r brown ('03)	3.75	2.75
54	A5	65r dl blue ('03)	14.00	9.00
55	A5	75r rose	22.50	13.00
56	A5	75r lilac ('03)	5.50	4.50
57	A5	80r brt violet	4.50	2.75
58	A5	100r dk bl, bl	4.50	2.75
a.	Perf. 12½		300.00	150.00
59	A5	115r org brn, pink ('03)	13.00	9.00
a.	115r orange brown, yellowish		15.00	9.00
60	A5	130r brn, straw ('03)	13.50	9.00
61	A5	150r lt brn, buff	14.00	5.75
62	A5	200r red lilac, pnksh	14.00	5.75
63	A5	300r blue, rose	13.00	7.25
64	A5	400r dl bl, straw ('03)	17.50	10.00

65	A5	500r blk & red, bl	19.50	11.00
66	A5	700r vio, yelsh ('01)	26.00	19.50
	Nos. 44-66 (23)		204.40	123.45

Stamps issued in 1903 were without gum.
For overprints and surcharges see Nos. 90-115, 190-194, 197.

Issue of 1886 Surcharged in Black or Red

1902, Oct. 20			Perf. 12½
67	A3	65r on 10r green	10.00	5.75
a.	Inverted surcharge		60.00	55.00
b.	Perf. 13½		67.50	55.00
68	A3	65r on 20r car	10.00	5.75
69	A3	65r on 25r red lilac	10.00	5.75
70	A3	115r on 40r choc	9.00	5.50
a.	Perf. 13½		21.00	9.75
71	A3	115r on 50r blue	9.00	5.50
a.	Inverted surcharge		60.00	55.00
72	A3	115r on 300r orange	12.00	10.25
73	A3	130r on 80r gray	8.00	8.50
a.	Perf. 13½		21.00	9.75
74	A3	130r on 100r brown	13.00	8.50
a.	Perf. 13½		31.00	22.00
75	A3	400r on 200r gray lil	67.50	60.00
76	A3	400r on 5r gray blk (R)	23.00	13.50
	Nos. 67-76 (10)		175.50	129.00

Reprints of No. 76 are in black and have clean-cut perforation 13½.

Same Surcharge on Issue of 1893-94

		Perf. 11½, 12½ (#80)	
77	A4	65r on 10r red vio	8.50	4.25
a.	Perf. 11½		5.75	3.50
78	A4	65r on 15r choc	8.50	4.25
79	A4	65r on 20r lav	8.50	4.25
80	A4	65r on 50r lt bl	5.00	3.75
a.	Perf. 12½		21.00	18.00
81	A4	115r on 5r yel	8.50	4.25
a.	Inverted surcharge		60.00	55.00
b.	Perf. 12½		80.00	72.50
82	A4	115r on 25r bl grn	9.00	4.50
83	A4	130r on 150r car, rose	9.00	4.50
84	A4	130r on 200r dk bl, bl	9.75	5.25
85	A4	130r on 300r dk bl, sal	9.75	5.50
86	A4	400r on 75r rose	6.75	5.50
87	A4	400r on 80r lt grn	4.25	2.40
a.	Inverted surcharge		60.00	55.00
88	A4	400r on 100r brn, buff	5.50	2.40

Same Surcharge on No. P1

		Perf. 13½	
89	N1	115r on 2½r brn	6.00	4.00
a.	Inverted surcharge		60.00	55.00
b.	Perf. 12½		8.50	4.25
c.	As "b," inverted surcharge		60.00	55.00
	Nos. 77-89 (13)		99.00	54.80

Issue of 1898 Overprinted in Black

1902, Oct. 20			Perf. 11½
90	A5	15r brown	3.75	2.25
91	A5	25r sea green	3.75	2.25
92	A5	50r dark blue	5.00	2.60
93	A5	75r rose	9.00	7.25
	Nos. 90-93 (4)		21.50	14.35

No. 54 Surcharged in Black

1905			
94	A5	50r on 65r dull blue	7.25	4.25

Issue of 1898-1903 Overprinted in Carmine or Green

1911			Perf. 11½
95	A5	2½r gray	.70	.50
a.	Inverted overprint		24.00	24.00
96	A5	5r orange	.70	.50
97	A5	10r lt green	.90	.60
98	A5	15r gray green	.90	.75
99	A5	20r gray violet	.90	.75
100	A5	25r carmine (G)	.90	.75
a.	Double overprint		21.00	18.00
101	A5	50r brown	.85	.75
102	A5	75c lilac	.85	.75
103	A5	100r dk bl, bl	2.40	.85
104	A5	115r org brn, pink	2.40	1.00
105	A5	130r brn, straw	2.40	1.00
106	A5	200r red lil, pink	10.25	4.50
107	A5	400r dl bl, straw	3.50	2.75
108	A5	500r blk & red, bl	3.50	2.75
109	A5	700r vio, yelsh	5.50	4.50
	Nos. 95-109 (15)		36.65	22.70

Issued without gum: #101-102, 104-105, 107.

Issue of 1898-1903 Overprinted in Red

1913			Perf. 11½
Without Gum (Nos. 110-115)			
110	A5	15r gray grn	21.00	14.00
111	A5	75r lilac	21.00	14.00
a.	Inverted overprint		72.50	55.00
112	A5	100r bl, bl	11.00	8.50
a.	Inverted overprint		72.50	55.00
113	A5	200r red lil, pnksh	52.50	40.00
a.	Inverted overprint		90.00	92.50

Same Overprint on Nos. 90, 93 in Red

114	A5	15r brown	21.00	14.00
a.	"REPUBLICA" double, one inverted		90.00	80.00
b.	"REPUBLICA" inverted		72.50	55.00
115	A5	75r rose	21.00	14.00
a.	"REPUBLICA" inverted		72.50	55.00
	Nos. 110-115 (6)		147.50	104.50

Vasco da Gama Issue of Various Portuguese Colonies Surcharged

1913		On Stamps of Macao	
116	CD20	¼c on ½a bl grn	2.40	2.00
117	CD21	½c on 1a red	2.40	2.00
118	CD22	1c on 2a red vio	2.40	2.00
119	CD23	2½c on 4a yel grn	2.40	2.00
120	CD24	5c on 8a dk bl	2.40	2.00
121	CD25	7½c on 12a vio brn	5.00	3.75
122	CD26	10c on 16a bis brn	4.25	3.75
a.	Inverted surcharge		42.50	42.50
123	CD27	15c on 24a bis	6.00	4.00
	Nos. 116-123 (8)		27.25	21.50

		On Stamps of Portuguese Africa	
124	CD20	¼c on 2½c bl grn	2.10	1.75
125	CD21	½c on 5r red	2.10	1.75
126	CD22	1c on 10r red vio	2.10	1.75
127	CD23	2½c on 25r yel grn	2.10	1.75
128	CD24	5c on 50r dk bl	2.10	1.75
129	CD25	7½c on 75r vio brn	5.00	3.75
130	CD26	10c on 100r bis brn	2.75	1.75
131	CD27	15c on 150r bis	6.00	5.00
	Nos. 124-131 (8)		24.25	19.25

		On Stamps of Timor	
132	CD20	¼c on ½a bl grn	2.40	2.00
133	CD21	½c on 1a red	2.40	2.00
134	CD22	1c on 2a red vio	2.40	2.00
135	CD23	2½c on 4a yel grn	2.40	2.00
136	CD24	5c on 8a dk blue	2.40	2.00
137	CD25	7½c on 12a vio brn	5.00	3.75
138	CD26	10c on 16a bis brn	4.25	3.75
139	CD27	15c on 24a bister	6.00	4.00
	Nos. 132-139 (8)		27.25	21.50
	Nos. 116-139 (24)		78.75	62.25

Ceres — A6

Name and Value in Black

1914		Chalky Paper	Perf. 15x14
140	A6	¼c olive brown	.55	.40
141	A6	½c black	.55	.40
142	A6	1c blue green	1.60	.95
143	A6	1½c lilac brn	1.00	.65
144	A6	2c carmine	1.05	.70

145	A6	2½c lt violet	1.60	.50
146	A6	5c deep blue	1.05	.65
147	A6	7½c yellow brn	1.75	1.10
148	A6	8c slate	1.20	.90
149	A6	10c orange brn	1.50	1.10
150	A6	15c plum	12.00	8.50
151	A6	20c yellow grn	3.00	1.50
152	A6	30c brown, *grn*	8.00	6.00
153	A6	40c brown, *pink*	5.25	1.40
154	A6	50c orange, *salmon*	5.25	1.40
155	A6	1e green, *blue*	7.25	4.50
		Nos. 140-155 (16)	52.60	30.65

1919-20   **Ordinary Paper**

156	A6	¼c olive brown	1.20	1.00
157	A6	½c black ('20)	.25	.25
158	A6	1c blue green	3.75	3.00
159	A6	2c carmine	1.50	1.10
		Nos. 156-159 (4)	6.70	5.35

1921-26   **Perf. 12x11½**

160	A6	¼c olive brown	.50	.45
161	A6	½c black	.25	.25
162	A6	1c yellow green		
		('22)	.25	.25
163	A6	1½c lilac brn	.25	.25
164	A6	2c carmine	.25	.25
165	A6	2c gray ('25)	.25	.60
166	A6	2½c lt violet	.25	.25
167	A6	3c orange ('22)	.25	.50
168	A6	4c deep red		
		('22)	.25	.50
169	A6	4½c gray ('22)	.25	.50
170	A6	5c brt blue ('22)	.25	.25
171	A6	6c lilac ('22)	.25	.50
172	A6	7c ultra ('22)	.75	.50
173	A6	7½c yellow brn	.25	.25
174	A6	8c slate	.25	.25
175	A6	10c orange brn	.25	.25
176	A6	12c blue grn		
		('22)	1.50	.60
177	A6	15c brn rose		
		('22)	.50	.35
178	A6	20c yellow grn	.25	.25
179	A6	24c ultra ('25)	2.75	2.10
179A	A6	25c brown ('25)	2.00	.65
179B	A6	30c gray grn		
		('22)	1.50	.60
179C	A6	40c turq bl ('22)	1.50	.70
179D	A6	50c violet ('25)	2.00	1.35
179E	A6	60c dk blue ('22)	2.40	1.75
179F	A6	60c dp rose ('26)	3.00	1.75
179G	A6	80c brt rose		
		('22)	3.75	2.40
179H	A6	1e indigo ('26)	5.00	3.25
		Nos. 160-179H (28)	30.90	21.55

1922-25   **Glazed Paper**

179I	A6	1e pale rose	5.00	2.00
179J	A6	2e dk violet	5.00	3.00
179K	A6	5e buff ('25)	23.00	12.50
179L	A6	10e pink ('25)	42.50	16.50
179M	A6	20e pale turq		
		('25)	87.50	47.50
		Nos. 179I-179M (5)	163.00	81.50

For surcharges see Nos. 195-196, 211-213.

Provisional Issue of
1902 Overprinted in
Carmine

1915   **Perf. 11½, 12½, 13½**

180	A3	115r on 40r choc	1.50	1.40
a.		Perf. 13½	10.50	8.50
181	A3	115r on 50r blue	1.50	1.40
182	A3	130r on 80r gray	5.00	3.00
a.		Perf. 12½	60.00	35.00
183	A3	130r on 100r brn	4.00	3.50
a.		Perf. 13½	15.00	11.50
184	A4	115r on 5r yellow	1.75	1.20
a.		Perf. 11½	7.25	5.75
185	A4	115r on 25r bl grn	1.75	1.50
186	A4	130r on 150r car, *rose*	1.75	1.50
187	A4	130r on 200r bl, *bl*	1.75	1.50
188	A4	130r on 300r dk bl, *sal*	1.75	1.50
189	N1	115r on 2½r brn	5.00	3.00
a.		Perf. 13½		
b.		Inverted overprint	67.50	60.00

Nos. 90, 92, 94
Overprinted

Perf. 11½

190	A5	15r brown	1.75	1.50
191	A5	50r dark blue	1.75	1.50
192	A5	50r on 65r dl bl	1.75	1.50
		Nos. 180-192 (13)	31.00	24.00

Nos. 64, 66
Overprinted

1919   **Without Gum**   **Perf. 11½**

193	A5	400r dl bl, *straw*	80.00	45.00
194	A5	700r vio, *yelsh*	26.00	18.00

Nos. 140, 141 and 59 Surcharged

      a   b

1920, Sept.   **Perf. 15x14, 11½**

Without Gum

195	A6(a)	4c on ¼c	6.00	4.50
196	A6(a)	6c on ½c	6.00	4.50
197	A5(b)	12c on 115r	15.00	11.00
		Nos. 195-197 (3)	27.00	20.00

Nos. 86-88
Surcharged

1925   **Perf. 11½**

203	A4	40c on 400r on 75r	1.75	1.50
204	A4	40c on 400r on 80r	1.75	1.50
205	A4	40c on 400r on 100r	1.75	1.50
		Nos. 203-205 (3)	5.25	4.50

Nos. 179F-179G, 179J
Surcharged

1931   **Perf. 12x11½**

211	A6	50c on 60c dp rose	3.50	2.40
212	A6	70c on 80c pink	3.50	3.00
213	A6	1.40e on 2e dk vio	8.50	6.00
		Nos. 211-213 (3)	15.50	11.40

Ceres — A7

1933   **Wmk. 232**

214	A7	1c bister	.25	.25
215	A7	5c olive brn	.25	.25
216	A7	10c violet	.25	.25
217	A7	15c black	.25	.25
218	A7	20c gray	.25	.25
219	A7	30c dk green	.25	.25
220	A7	40c red orange	1.20	.50
221	A7	45c lt blue	1.20	.60
222	A7	50c lt brown	1.20	.60
223	A7	60c olive grn	1.40	.60
224	A7	70c orange brn	1.40	.70
225	A7	80c emerald	2.00	.95
226	A7	85c deep rose	4.00	1.75
227	A7	1e red brown	1.75	1.20
228	A7	1.40e dk blue	6.75	4.25
229	A7	2e red violet	3.50	2.10
230	A7	5e apple green	11.50	8.00
231	A7	10e olive bister	23.00	9.75
232	A7	20e orange	60.00	34.00
		Nos. 214-232 (19)	120.40	66.50

Common Design Types
pictured following the introduction.

Common Design Types
Engr.; Name & Value Typo. in Black

1938   **Unwmk.**   **Perf. 13½x13**

233	CD34	1c gray grn	.25	.25
234	CD34	5c orange brn	.25	.25
235	CD34	10c dk carmine	.30	.30
236	CD34	15c dk vio brn	.30	.30
237	CD34	20c slate	.60	.30
238	CD35	30c rose violet	.70	.45
239	CD35	35c brt green	.70	.45
240	CD35	40c brown	.70	.45
241	CD35	50c brt red vio	.70	.45
242	CD36	60c gray black	.70	.45
243	CD36	70c brown vio	.70	.45
244	CD36	80c orange	1.40	.60
245	CD36	1e red	1.60	.60
246	CD37	1.75e blue	2.10	1.20
247	CD37	2e brown car	5.75	2.00
248	CD37	5e olive grn	8.00	4.25
249	CD38	10e blue vio	10.25	5.00
250	CD38	20e red brown	34.00	8.00
		Nos. 233-250 (18)	69.00	25.75

Fort of
Cacheu
A8

   Nuno   Ulysses S.
Tristam — A9   Grant — A10

Designs: 3.50e, Teixeira Pinto. 5e, Honorio Barreto. 20e, Bissau Church.

Unwmk.

1946, Jan. 12   **Litho.**   **Perf. 11**

251	A8	30c gray & lt gray	.95	.50
252	A9	50c black & pink	.70	.40
253	A9	50c gray grn & lt grn	.70	.40
254	A10	1.75e blue & lt blue	2.75	1.40
255	A10	3.50e red & pink	5.00	1.75
256	A10	5e lt brn & buff	12.50	5.75
257	A8	20e vio & lt vio	21.00	9.00
a.		Sheet of 7, #251-257 ('47)	110.00	95.00
		Nos. 251-257 (7)	43.60	19.20

Discovery of Guinea, 500th anniversary.
No. 257a sold for 40 escudos.

Guinea
Village — A11

Designs: 10c, Crowned crane. 20c, 3.50e, Tribesman. 35c, 5e, Woman in ceremonial dress. 50c, Musician. 70c, Man. 80c, 20e, Girl. 1e, 2e, Drummer. 1.75e, Antelope.

1948, Apr.   **Photo.**   **Perf. 11½**

258	A11	5c chocolate	.25	.25
259	A11	10c lt violet	2.75	1.25
260	A11	20c dull rose	.70	.45
261	A11	35c green	.90	.45
262	A11	50c dp orange	.45	.25
263	A11	70c dp gray bl	.70	.40
264	A11	80c dk ol grn	1.00	.40
265	A11	1e rose red	1.00	.40
266	A11	1.75e ultra	13.00	5.00
267	A11	2e blue	15.00	1.50
268	A11	3.50e orange brn	3.25	1.25
269	A11	5e slate	5.75	2.50
270	A11	20e violet	24.00	6.50
a.		Sheet of 13, #258-270 + 2 labels	130.00	120.00
		Nos. 258-270 (13)	68.75	20.60

No. 270a sold for 40 escudos.

Lady of Fatima Issue
Common Design Type

1948, Oct.   **Litho.**   **Perf. 14½**

271	CD40	50c deep green	6.50	3.50

UPU
Symbols — A12

1949, Oct.   **Perf. 14**

272	A12	2e dp org & cream	4.50	2.50

Universal Postal Union, 75th anniversary.

> **Catalogue values for unused stamps in this section, from this point to the end of the section, are for Never Hinged items.**

Holy Year Issue
Common Design Types

1950, May   **Perf. 13x13½**

273	CD41	1e brown lake	4.75	1.50
274	CD42	3e blue green	6.50	2.00

Holy Year Extension Issue
Common Design Type

1951, Oct.   **Perf. 14**

275	CD43	1e choc & pale brn + label	1.75	.90

Stamps without label attached sell for less.

Medical Congress Issue
Common Design Type

Design: Physical examination.

1952   **Perf. 13½**

276	CD44	50c purple & choc	1.00	.45

Exhibition
Entrance — A13

1953, Jan.   **Litho.**   **Perf. 13**

277	A13	10c brn lake & ol	.25	.25
278	A13	50c dk blue & bister	1.60	.25
279	A13	3e blk, dk brn & sal	3.50	1.00
		Nos. 277-279 (3)	5.35	1.50

Exhibition of Sacred Missionary Art held at Lisbon in 1951.

Stamp of Portugal
and Arms of
Colonies — A14

1953   **Photo.**   **Unwmk.**

280	A14	50c multicolored	1.75	.90

Centenary of Portugal's first postage stamps.

Analeptes
Trifasciata — A15

1953   **Perf. 11½**
Various Beetles in Natural Colors

281	A15	5c yellow	.40	.25
282	A15	10c blue	.40	.25
283	A15	30c org vermilion	.40	.25
284	A15	50c yellow grn	.40	.25
285	A15	70c gray brn	.60	.25
286	A15	1e orange	.60	.25
287	A15	2e pale ol grn	1.50	.25
288	A15	3e lilac rose	2.25	.70

289 A15 5e lt blue grn 3.75 1.10
290 A15 10e lilac 6.00 3.00
Nos. 281-290 (10) 16.30 6.55

Sao Paulo Issue
Common Design Type
1954 Litho. Perf. 13½
291 CD46 1e lil rose, bl gray & blk .35 .25

Belem Tower, Lisbon, and Colonial Arms — A16

1955, Apr. 14
292 A16 1e blue & multi .25 .25
293 A16 2.50e gray & multi .50 .25

Visit of Pres. Francisco H. C. Lopes.

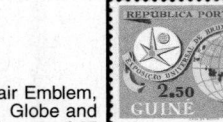

Fair Emblem, Globe and Arms — A17

1958 Unwmk. Perf. 12x11½
294 A17 2.50e multicolored .65 .55

World's Fair at Brussels.

Tropical Medicine Congress Issue
Common Design Type
Design: Maytenus senegalensis.

1958 Perf. 13½
295 CD47 5e multicolored 3.00 1.10

Honorio Barreto — A18

1959, Apr. 29 Litho. Perf. 13½
296 A18 2.50e multicolored .40 .25

Centenary of the death of Honorio Barreto, governor of Portuguese Guinea.

Nautical Astrolabe — A19

1960, June 25 Perf. 13½
297 A19 2.50e multicolored .40 .25

500th anniversary of the death of Prince Henry the Navigator.

Traveling Medical Unit — A20

1960 Unwmk. Perf. 14½
298 A20 1.50e multicolored .40 .25

10th anniv. of the Commission for Technical Cooperation in Africa South of the Sahara (C.C.T.A.).

Sports Issue
Common Design Type
1962, Jan. 18 Litho. Perf. 13½
299 CD48 50c Automobile race .50 .25
300 CD48 1e Tennis .80 .40
301 CD48 1.50e Shot put .50 .25
302 CD48 2.50e Wrestling .90 .45
303 CD48 3.50e Trapshooting .90 .45
304 CD48 15e Volleyball 2.40 1.20
Nos. 299-304 (6) 6.00 3.00

Anti-Malaria Issue
Common Design Type
Design: Anopheles gambiae.

1962 Unwmk. Perf. 13½
305 CD49 2.50e multicolored 1.25 .45

African Spitting Cobra — A21

Snakes: 35c, African rock python. 70c, Boomslang. 80c, West African mamba. 1.50e, Smythe's water snake. 2e, Common night adder, horiz. 2.50e, Green swamp snake. 3.50e, Brown house snake. 4e, Spotted wolf snake. 5e, Common puff adder. 15e, Striped beauty snake. 20e, African egg-eating snake, horiz.

1963, Jan. 17 Litho. Perf. 13½
306 A21 20c multicolored .25 .25
307 A21 35c multicolored .25 .25
308 A21 70c multicolored .75 .30
309 A21 80c multicolored .75 .25
310 A21 1.50e multicolored .75 .25
311 A21 2e multicolored .35 .25
312 A21 2.50e multicolored 3.25 .35
313 A21 3.50e multicolored .50 .25
314 A21 4e multicolored .65 .25
315 A21 5e multicolored 1.20 .35
316 A21 15e multicolored 2.40 1.25
317 A21 20e multicolored 4.00 2.00
Nos. 306-317 (12) 15.10 6.00

For overprints see Guinea-Bissau Nos. 696-703.

Airline Anniversary Issue
Common Design Type
1963 Litho. Perf. 14½
318 CD50 2.50e lt brown & multi .65 .35

National Overseas Bank Issue
Common Design Type
Design: 2.50e, Joao de Andrade Córvo.

1964, May 16 Perf. 13½
319 CD51 2.50e multicolored .65 .40

ITU Issue
Common Design Type
1965, May 17 Unwmk. Perf. 14½
320 CD52 2.50e lt blue & multi 1.90 .75

Soldier, 1548 — A22

40c, Rifleman, 1578. 60c, Rifleman, 1640. 1e, Grenadier, 1721. 2.50e, Fusiliers captain, 1740. 4.50e, Infantryman, 1740. 7.50e, Sergeant major, 1762. 10e, Engineers' officer, 1806.

1966, Jan. 8 Litho. Perf. 13½
321 A22 25c multicolored .25 .25
322 A22 40c multicolored .25 .25
323 A22 60c multicolored .35 .25
324 A22 1e multicolored .40 .25
325 A22 2.50e multicolored .90 .25

---

326 A22 4.50e multicolored 2.25 .60
327 A22 7.50e multicolored 3.75 1.75
328 A22 10e multicolored 4.00 1.90
Nos. 321-328 (8) 12.15 5.50

National Revolution Issue
Common Design Type
2.50e, Berta Craveiro Lopes School and Central Pavilion of Bissau Hospital.

1966, May 28 Litho. Perf. 11½
329 CD53 2.50e multicolored .55 .35

Navy Club Issue
Common Design Type
Designs: 50c, Capt. Oliveira Muzanty and cruiser Republica. 1e, Capt. Afonso de Cerqueira and torpedo boat Guadiana.

1967, Jan. 31 Litho. Perf. 13
330 CD54 50c multicolored .40 .25
331 CD54 1e multicolored .80 .65

Sacred Heart of Jesus Monument and Chapel of the Apparition — A23

1967, May 13 Perf. 12½x13
332 A23 50c multicolored .35 .35

50th anniv. of the appearance of the Virgin Mary to three shepherd children at Fatima.

Pres. Rodrigues Thomaz — A24

1968, Feb. 2 Litho. Perf. 13½
333 A24 1e multicolored .25 .25

Issued to commemorate the 1968 visit of Pres. Americo de Deus Rodrigues Thomaz.

Cabral's Coat of Arms — A25

1968, Apr. 22 Litho. Perf. 14
334 A25 2.50e multicolored .55 .25

Pedro Alvares Cabral, navigator who took possession of Brazil for Portugal, 500th birth anniv.

Admiral Coutinho Issue
Common Design Type
Design: 1e, Adm. Coutinho and astrolabe.

1969, Feb. 17 Litho. Perf. 14
335 CD55 1e multicolored .35 .25

Vasco da Gama Issue

Da Gama Coat of Arms — A26

1969, Aug. 29 Litho. Perf. 14
336 A26 2.50e multicolored .35 .25

Vasco da Gama (1469-1524), navigator.

Administration Reform Issue
Common Design Type
1969, Sept. 25 Litho. Perf. 14
337 CD56 50c multicolored .25 .25

King Manuel I Issue

Arms of King Manuel I — A27

1969, Dec. 1 Litho. Perf. 14
338 A27 2e multicolored .35 .25

Pres. Ulysses S. Grant and View of Bolama — A28

1970, Oct. 25 Litho. Perf. 13½
339 A28 2.50e multicolored .45 .25

Centenary of Pres. Grant's arbitration in 1868 of Portuguese-English dispute concerning Bolama.

Marshal Carmona Issue
Common Design Type
Design: 1.50e, Antonio Oscar Carmona in general's uniform.

1970, Nov. 15 Litho. Perf. 14
340 CD57 1.50e multicolored .35 .25

Luiz Camoens — A29

1972, May 25 Litho. Perf. 13
341 A29 50c brn org & multi .25 .25

4th centenary of publication of The Lusiads by Luiz Camoens (1524-1580).

Olympic Games Issue
Common Design Type
Design: 2.50e, Weight lifting, hammer throw and Olympic emblem.

1972, June 20 Perf. 14x13½
342 CD59 2.50e multicolored .45 .25

Lisbon-Rio de Janeiro Flight Issue
Common Design Type
1e, "Lusitania" taking off from Lisbon.

1972, Sept. 20 Litho. Perf. 13½
343 CD60 1e multicolored .25 .25

WMO Centenary Issue
Common Design Type
1973, Dec. 15 Litho. Perf. 13
344 CD61 2e lt brown & multi .45 .35

AIR POST STAMPS

Common Design Type
Perf. 13½x13
1938, Sept. 19 Engr. Unwmk.
Name and Value in Black
C1 CD39 10c red orange 1.40 .75
C2 CD39 20c purple 1.40 .75
C3 CD39 50c orange 1.40 .75
C4 CD39 1e ultra 1.50 .75
C5 CD39 2e lilac brown 11.50 5.25
C6 CD39 3e dark green 5.00 1.60
C7 CD39 5e red brown 6.50 1.05

C8	CD39	9e rose carmine	12.00	5.75
C9	CD39	10e magenta	20.50	6.75
		Nos. C1-C9 (9)	61.20	23.40

No. C7 exists with overprint "Exposicao Internacional de Nova York, 1939-1940" and Trylon and Perisphere. Value $300.

POSTAGE DUE STAMPS

D1

Without Gum

1904		Unwmk. Typo.	*Perf. 12*	
J1	D1	5r yellow green	1.40	.60
J2	D1	10r slate	1.40	.60
J3	D1	20r yellow brown	1.40	.60
J4	D1	30r red orange	2.50	1.75
J5	D1	50r gray brown	2.50	1.75
J6	D1	60r red brown	6.50	3.75
J7	D1	100r lilac	6.50	3.75
J8	D1	130r dull blue	6.50	3.75
J9	D1	200r carmine	10.00	8.00
J10	D1	500r violet	22.50	9.00
		Nos. J1-J10 (10)	61.20	33.55

Same Overprinted in Carmine or Green

1911			**Without Gum**	
J11	D1	5r yellow green	.25	.25
J12	D1	10r slate	.35	.25
J13	D1	20r yellow brown	.60	.35
J14	D1	30r red orange	.60	.35
J15	D1	50r gray brown	.70	.40
J16	D1	60r red brown	1.75	1.35
J17	D1	100r lilac	4.00	2.40
J18	D1	130r dull blue	4.00	2.40
J19	D1	200r carmine (G)	4.00	2.40
J20	D1	500r violet	3.25	2.10
		Nos. J11-J20 (10)	19.50	12.25

Nos. J2-J10 Overprinted

1919			**Without Gum**	
J21	D1	10r slate	7.75	7.00
J22	D1	20r yellow brown	9.25	7.75
J23	D1	30r red orange	7.00	4.25
J24	D1	50r gray brown	3.50	2.40
J25	D1	60r red brown	325.00	
J26	D1	100r lilac	3.50	3.00
J27	D1	130r dull blue	45.00	29.00
J28	D1	200r carmine	6.50	3.75
J29	D1	500r violet	35.00	24.00
		Nos. J21-J24,J26-J29 (8)	117.50	81.15

No. J25 was not regularly issued but exists on genuine covers.

D2

1921				
J30	D2	½c yellow green	.25	.25
J31	D2	1c slate	.25	.25
J32	D2	2c orange brown	.25	.25
J33	D2	3c orange	.25	.25
J34	D2	5c gray brown	.25	.25
J35	D2	6c light brown	1.25	1.00
J36	D2	10c red violet	1.25	1.00
J37	D2	13c dull blue	1.25	1.00
a.		Double impression	140.00	95.00

J38	D2	20c carmine	1.25	1.00
J39	D2	50c gray	1.25	1.00
		Nos. J30-J39 (10)	7.50	6.25

> Catalogue values for unused stamps in this section, from this point to the end of the section, are for Never Hinged items.

Common Design Type
Photogravure and Typographed

1952		**Unwmk.**	*Perf. 14*	
Numeral in Red, Frame Multicolored				
J40	CD45	10c olive green	.25	.25
J41	CD45	30c purple	.25	.25
J42	CD45	50c dark green	.25	.25
J43	CD45	1e violet blue	.30	.30
J44	CD45	2e olive black	.50	.50
J45	CD45	5e brown red	1.00	1.00
		Nos. J40-J45 (6)	2.55	2.55

WAR TAX STAMPS

WT1

		Perf. 11½x12		
1919, May 20		**Typo.**	**Unwmk.**	
MR1	WT1	10r brn, buff & blk	120.00	100.00
MR2	WT1	40r brn, buff & blk	120.00	100.00
MR3	WT1	50r brn, buff & blk	120.00	100.00
		Nos. MR1-MR3 (3)	360.00	300.00

The 40r is not overprinted "REPUBLICA." Some authorities consider Nos. MR2-MR3 to be revenue stamps.

NEWSPAPER STAMP

N1

1893		**Typo.**	**Unwmk.**	*Perf. 12½*	
P1	N1	2½r brown		2.50	1.50
a.		Perf. 13½		2.50	1.50

For surcharge and overprint see Nos. 89, 189.

POSTAL TAX STAMPS

Pombal Issue
Common Design Types

1925		**Unwmk.**	**Engr.**	*Perf. 12½*	
RA1	CD28	15c red & black		.95	.80
RA2	CD29	15c red & black		.95	.80
RA3	CD30	15c red & black		.95	.80
		Nos. RA1-RA3 (3)		2.85	2.40

Coat of Arms — PT7

Without Gum

1934, Apr. 1		**Typo.**	*Perf. 11½*	
RA4	PT7	50c red brn & grn	17.00	8.50
a.		Tête beche pair		200.00

Coat of Arms — PT8

1938-40		**Without Gum**		
RA5	PT8	50c ol bis & citron	15.50	8.50
RA6	PT8	50c lt grn & ol brn ('40)	15.50	8.50

Coat of Arms — PT9

1942		**Without Gum**	*Perf. 11*	
RA7	PT9	50c black & yellow	4.25	3.00

1959, July		**Unwmk.**	**Without Gum**	
RA8	PT9	30c dark ocher & blk	.50	.25

See Nos. RA24-RA26.

Lusignian Cross — PT10

1967		**Typo.**	*Perf. 11x11½*	
Without Gum				
RA9	PT10	50c pink, red & blk	1.00	1.00
RA10	PT10	1e grn, red & blk	1.40	.90
RA11	PT10	5e gray, red & blk	3.00	1.75
RA12	PT10	10e lt bl, red & blk	4.75	3.75
		Nos. RA9-RA12 (4)	10.15	7.40

The tax was for national defense. A 50e was used for revenue only.

Lusignian Cross — PT11

1967, Aug.		**Typo.**	*Perf. 11*	
Without Gum				
RA13	PT11	50c pink, blk & red	.25	.25
RA14	PT11	1e pale grn, blk & red	.50	.50
RA15	PT11	5e gray, blk & red	1.00	1.00
RA16	PT11	10e lt bl, blk & red	3.25	2.75
		Nos. RA13-RA16 (4)	5.00	4.50

The tax was for national defense.

> Catalogue values for unused stamps in this section, from this point to the end of the section, are for Never Hinged items.

Carved Figurine — PT12

Art from Bissau Museum: 1e, Tree of Life, with 2 birds, horiz. No. RA19, Man wearing horned headgear ("Vaca Bruto"). 2.50e, The Magistrate. 5e, Man bearing burden on head. 10e, Stylized pelican.

1968		**Litho.**	*Perf. 13½*	
RA17	PT12	50c gray & multi	.25	.25
a.		Yellow paper	4.25	4.25
RA18	PT12	1e multi	.25	.25
RA19	PT12	2e multi	.25	.25
RA21	PT12	2.50e multi	.70	.45
RA22	PT12	5e multi	1.00	.60
RA23	PT12	10e multi	1.75	1.10
		Nos. RA17-RA19,RA21-RA23 (6)	4.20	2.90

Obligatory on all inland mail Mar. 15-Apr. 15 and Dec. 15-Jan. 15, and all year on parcels.
A souvenir sheet containing Nos. RA17-RA23 exists. The stamps have simulated perforations. Value $30.
A 2e stamp with the design of RA19, inscribed "Tocador de Bombolon" was printed but not issued. The stamp was used for RA27-RA28. Value, unsurcharged example, $22.50.
For surcharges see Nos. RA27-RA28.

Arms Type of 1942

1968		**Typo.**	*Perf. 11*	
Without Gum				
RA24	PT9	2.50e lt blue & blk	3.00	1.50
RA25	PT9	5e green & blk	4.25	3.50
RA26	PT9	10e dp blue & blk	7.00	5.50
		Nos. RA24-RA26 (3)	14.25	10.50

PT12a

1968		**Litho.**	*Perf. 13½*	
RA27	PT12a	50c on 2e multi	1.00	.50

RA27 does not exist without surcharge.

RA28	PT12a	1e on 2e multi	1.00	.50

Black and White Hands Holding Sword — PT13

1968		**Litho.**	*Perf. 13½*	
RA29	PT13	50c pink & multi	.25	.25
RA30	PT13	1e multicolored	.25	.25
RA31	PT13	2e yellow & multi	.45	.25
RA32	PT13	2.50e buff & multi	.80	.45
RA33	PT13	3e multicolored	.95	.60
RA34	PT13	4e gray & multi	1.20	.75
RA35	PT13	5e multicolored	1.55	.90
RA36	PT13	10e multicolored	5.75	3.75
		Nos. RA29-RA36 (8)	11.20	7.20

The surtax was for national defense. Other denominations exist: 8e, 9e, 15e. Value, $4 each.

Mother and Children — PT14

1971, June		**Litho.**	*Perf. 13½*	
RA37	PT14	50c multicolored	.25	.25
RA38	PT14	1e multicolored	.25	.25
RA39	PT14	2e multicolored	.45	.40
RA40	PT14	3e multicolored	1.25	1.00
RA41	PT14	4e multicolored	1.50	1.15
RA42	PT14	5e multicolored	2.50	1.75
RA43	PT14	10e multicolored	4.25	3.25
		Nos. RA37-RA43 (7)	10.45	8.05

A 20e exists. Value $4.

D2

Coat of Arms — PT7

POSTAL TAX DUE STAMPS

Pombal Issue
Common Design Types

1925		Unwmk.	Perf. 12½	
RAJ1	CD28	30c red & black	.75	.75
RAJ2	CD29	30c red & black	.75	.75
RAJ3	CD30	30c red & black	.75	.75
	Nos. RAJ1-RAJ3 (3)		2.25	2.25

PORTUGUESE INDIA

'pōr-chi-gēz 'in-dē-ə

LOCATION — West coast of the Indian peninsula
GOVT. — Portuguese colony
AREA — 1,537 sq. mi.
POP. — 649,000 (1958)
CAPITAL — Panjim (Nova-Goa)

The colony was seized by India on Dec. 18, 1961, and annexed by that republic.

1000 Reis = 1 Milreis
12 Reis = 1 Tanga (1881-82)
(Real = singular of Reis)
16 Tangas = 1 Rupia
100 Centavos = 1 Escudo (1959)

> **Catalogue values for unused stamps in this country are for Never Hinged items, beginning with Scott 490 in the regular postage section, Scott J43 in the postage due section, and Scott RA6 in the postal tax section.**

Expect Nos. 1-55, 70-112 to have rough perforations. Stamps frequently were cut apart because of the irregular and missing perforations. Scissor separations that do not remove perfs do not negatively affect value.

Numeral of Value — A1

A1: Large figures of value.
"REIS" in Roman capitals. "S" and "R" of "SERVICO" smaller and "E" larger than the other letters. 33 lines in background. Side ornaments of four dashes.
A2: Large figures of value.
"REIS" in block capitals. "S," "E" and "R" same size as other letters of "SERVICO." 44 lines in background. Side ornaments of five dots.

Handstamped from a Single Die
Perf. 13 to 18 & Compound

1871, Oct. 1			Unwmk.	
Thin Transparent Brittle Paper				
1	A1	10r black	650.00	325.00
2	A1	20r dk carmine	1,550.	350.00
a.		20r orange vermilion	1,550.	425.00
3	A1	40r Prus blue	525.00	400.00
4	A1	100r yellow grn	650.00	425.00
5	A1	200r ocher yel	1,025.	550.00

1872		**Thick Soft Wove Paper**		
5A	A1	10r black	1,600.	425.00
6	A1	20r dk carmine	1,700.	500.00
7	A1	20r orange ver	2,000.	500.00
7A	A1	100r yellow grn	2,400.	1,550.
8	A1	200r ocher yel	2,400.	1,350.
9	A1	300r dp red violet		3,000.

The 600r and 900r of type A1 are bogus.
See Nos. 24-28. For surcharges see Nos. 70-71, 73, 83, 94, 99, 104, 108.

Numeral of Value — A2

Perf. 12½ to 14½ & Compound

1872				
10	A2	10r black	330.00	130.00
11	A2	20r vermilion	260.00	115.00
a.		"20" omitted		1,500.
12	A2	40r blue	100.00	75.00
a.		Tête bêche pair	7,000.	7,000.
		40r dark blue	115.00	75.00
13	A2	100r deep green	80.00	57.50
14	A2	200r yellow	325.00	275.00
15	A2	300r red violet	325.00	275.00
a.		Imperf.		
16	A2	600r red violet	220.00	175.00
a.		"600" double	900.00	
17	A2	900r red violet	260.00	175.00
		Nos. 10-17 (8)	1,900.	1,278.

An unused 100r blue green exists with watermark of lozenges and gray burelage on back. Experts believe it to be a proof.

White Laid Paper

18	A2	10r black	52.50	42.50
a.		Tête bêche pair	17,000.	10,000.
b.		10r brownish black	52.50	40.00
19	A2	20r vermilion	45.00	40.00
20	A2	40r blue	97.50	75.00
a.		"40" double	1,750.	—
b.		Tête bêche pair	—	—
21	A2	100r green	87.50	60.00
a.		"100" double	1,500.	
22	A2	200r yellow	225.00	200.00
		Nos. 18-22 (5)	507.50	417.50

See No. 23. For surcharges see Nos. 72, 82, 95-96, 100-101, 105-106, 109-110.

Re-issues

1873		**Thin Bluish Toned Paper**		
23	A2	20r vermilion	250.00	175.00
24	A1	10r black	15.00	10.00
a.		"1" inverted	125.00	100.00
b.		"10" double	500.00	240.00
25	A1	20r vermilion	21.00	14.00
a.		"20" double	500.00	
b.		"20" inverted		
26	A1	300r dp violet	140.00	110.00
a.		"300" double	600.00	
27	A1	600r dp violet	175.00	135.00
a.		"600" double	725.00	
b.		"600" inverted	725.00	
28	A1	900r dp violet	175.00	135.00
a.		"900" double	850.00	
b.		"900" triple	1,000.	
		Nos. 23-28 (6)	776.00	579.00

Nos. 23 to 26 are re-issues of Nos. 11, 5A, 7, and 9. The paper is thinner and harder than that of the 1871-72 stamps and slightly transparent. It was originally bluish white but is frequently stained yellow by the gum.

A3

A3: Same as A1 with small figures.

1874		**Thin Bluish Toned Paper**		
29	A3	10r black	45.00	35.00
a.		"10" and "20" superimposed	600.00	550.00
30	A3	20r vermilion	600.00	425.00
a.		"20" double		900.00

For surcharge see No. 84.

A4

A4: Same as A2 with small figures.

1875				
31	A4	10r black	52.50	30.00
a.		Value sideways		800.00
32	A4	15r rose	16.00	12.00
a.		"15" inverted	600.00	
b.		"15" double		
c.		Value omitted	1,400.	
33	A4	20r vermilion	97.50	57.50
a.		"0" missing	1,000.	
b.		"20" sideways	1,000.	725.00
c.		"20" double		
		Nos. 31-33 (3)	166.00	99.50

For surcharges see Nos. 74, 78, 85.

A5   A6

A5: Re-cutting of A1.
Small figures. "REIS" in Roman capitals. Letters larger. "V" of "SERVICO" barred. 33 lines in background. Side ornaments of five dots.
A6: First re-cutting of A2.
Small figures. "REIS" in block capitals. Letters re-cut. "V" of "SERVICO" barred. 41 lines above and 43 below "REIS." Side ornaments of five dots.

Perf. 12½ to 13½ & Compound

1876				
34	A5	10r black	29.00	19.50
35	A5	20r vermilion	23.00	15.00
a.		"20" double	—	350.00
36	A5	10r black	8.00	6.00
a.		Double impression	600.00	
b.		"10" double	600.00	
37	A5	15r rose	550.00	400.00
a.		"15" omitted	2,100.	
38	A6	20r vermilion	33.00	24.00
39	A6	40r blue	135.00	110.00
40	A6	100r green	210.00	190.00
a.		Imperf.		
41	A6	200r yellow	1,000.	825.00
42	A6	300r violet	600.00	500.00
a.		"300" omitted		
43	A6	600r violet	850.00	700.00
44	A6	900r violet	1,200.	800.00
a.		"900" omitted		

For surcharges see Nos. 75-76, 78C-80, 86-87, 91-92, 98, 102, 107, 111.

A7   A8

A9

A7: Same as A5 with addition of a star above and a bar below the value.
A8: Second re-cutting of A2. Same as A6 but 41 lines both above and below "REIS." Star above and bar below value.
A9: Third re-cutting of A2. 41 lines above and 38 below "REIS." Star above and bar below value. White line around central oval.

1877				
45	A7	10r black	40.00	30.00
46	A8	10r black	60.00	50.00
47	A9	10r black	40.00	30.00
a.		"10" omitted		
48	A9	15r rose	42.50	34.00
49	A9	20r vermilion	12.00	11.00
50	A9	40r blue	24.00	21.00
a.		"40" omitted	240.00	175.00
51	A9	100r green	115.00	72.50
a.		"100" omitted		
52	A9	200r yellow	100.00	90.00
53	A9	300r violet	160.00	100.00
54	A9	600r violet	160.00	100.00
55	A9	900r violet	160.00	100.00
		Nos. 45-55 (11)	913.50	638.50

For surcharges see Nos. 77, 81, 88-90, 93, 112.
No. 47, 20r, 40r and 200r exist imperf.

Portuguese Crown — A10

1877, July 15	Typo.	Perf. 12½, 13½		
56	A10	5r black	8.00	3.50
57	A10	10r yellow	13.50	11.00
a.		Imperf.		
58	A10	20r bister	13.00	11.00
59	A10	25r rose	14.50	11.50
60	A10	50r blue	19.50	13.50
a.		Perf. 12½	220.00	175.00
61	A10	50r yellow grn	35.00	25.00
62	A10	100r lilac	18.50	14.50
63	A10	200r orange	32.00	24.00
64	A10	300r yel brn	34.00	32.00
		Nos. 56-64 (9)	188.00	146.00

1880-81				
65a	A10	10r green	14.50	13.50
66	A10	25r slate	60.00	42.50
67a	A10	25r violet	42.50	30.00

68a	A10	40r yellow	52.50	40.00
69a	A10	50r dk blue	52.50	35.00
		Nos. 65a-69a (5)	222.00	161.00

For surcharges see Nos. 113-161. The 1880-81 issue exists perf 12½ and 13½ on thin paper, and 13½ on medium paper. Nos. 65a-69a above are the most common varieties. For detailed listings, see the *Scott Classic Specialized Catalogue*.

The stamps of the 1877-81 issues were reprinted in 1885, on stout very white paper, ungummed and with rough perforation 13½. They were again reprinted in 1905 on thin white paper with shiny white gum and clean-cut perforation 13½ with large holes. Value of the lowest-cost reprint, $3 each.

Stamps of 1871-77
Surcharged with New Values

1881			**Black Surcharge**	
70	A1	1½r on 20r (#2)	450.00	500.00
71	A1	1½r on 20r (#7)		400.00
72	A2	1½r on 20r (#11)		260.00
73	A1	1½r on 20r (#25)	250.00	225.00
74	A4	1½r on 20r (#33)	160.00	140.00
a.		Inverted surcharge		250.00
75	A5	1½r on 20r (#35)	105.00	90.00
76	A6	1½r on 20r (#38)	140.00	120.00
77	A9	1½r on 20r (#49)	210.00	160.00
78	A4	5r on 15r (#32)	14.00	14.00
a.		Double surcharge		
b.		Inverted surcharge	—	
78C	A6	5r on 15r (#37)	190.00	180.00
79	A5	5r on 20r (#35)	5.00	5.00
a.		Double surcharge		
b.		Inverted surcharge	—	
80	A6	5r on 20r (#38)	5.00	5.00
a.		Double surcharge		
b.		Inverted surcharge	—	
81	A9	5r on 20r (#49)	5.75	5.00
a.		Double surcharge		
b.		Invtd. surcharge	—	

			Red Surcharge	
82	A2	5r on 10r (#18)	400.00	400.00
83	A1	5r on 10r (#24)	400.00	400.00
84	A3	5r on 10r (#29)		1,750.
85	A4	5r on 10r (#31)	180.00	180.00
86	A5	5r on 10r (#34)	13.00	13.00
a.		Double surcharge		
87	A6	5r on 10r (#36)	10.00	10.00
a.		Inverted surcharge		
88	A7	5r on 10r (#45)	100.00	42.50
a.		Inverted surcharge		
89	A8	5r on 10r (#46)	85.00	70.00
90	A9	5r on 10r (#47)	60.00	50.00
a.		Inverted surcharge		
b.		Double surcharge	—	

Similar Surcharge, Handstamped Black Surcharge

1883				
91	A5	1½r on 10r (#34)	1,650.	600.00
92	A6	1½r on 10r (#36)	1,100.	600.00
93	A9	1½r on 10r (#47)	825.00	400.00
94	A1	4½r on 40r (#3)	2,000.	775.00
95	A2	4½r on 40r (#12)	45.00	45.00
96	A2	4½r on 40r (#20)	45.00	45.00
98	A6	4½r on 40r (#39)	45.00	45.00
99	A1	4½r on 100r (#4)	2,000.	775.00
100	A2	4½r on 100r (#13)	52.50	45.00
101	A2	4½r on 100r (#21)	52.50	45.00
102	A6	4½r on 100r (#40)	42.50	32.00
104	A1	6r on 100r (#4)	2,200.	900.00
105	A2	6r on 100r (#13)	425.00	290.00
106	A2	6r on 100r (#21)	275.00	225.00
107	A6	6r on 100r (#40)	280.00	250.00
108	A1	6r on 200r (#5)	825.00	700.00
109	A2	6r on 200r (#14)		600.00
110	A2	6r on 200r (#22)	275.00	210.00
111	A6	6r on 200r (#40)	500.00	525.00
112	A9	6r on 200r (#52)	575.00	525.00

Stamps of 1877-81
Surcharged in Black

1881-82				
113	A10	1½r on 5r blk	2.75	1.75
a.		With additional surcharge "4 ½" in blue	175.00	125.00
114	A10	1½r on 10r grn	2.75	2.10
a.		With additional surch. "6"	200.00	175.00
115	A10	1½r on 20r bis	26.00	19.50
a.		Inverted surcharge	27.50	
b.		Double surcharge	27.50	
c.		Pair, one without surcharge		
116	A10	1½r on 25r slate	90.00	70.00
117	A10	1½r on 100r lil	115.00	87.50
118	A10	4½r on 40r yel	240.00	240.00
119	A10	4½r on 20r bis	6.00	5.00
a.		Inverted surcharge	82.50	65.00

120	A10	4½r on 25r vio	24.00	19.50
121	A10	4½r on 100r lil	200.00	175.00
122	A10	6r on 10r yel	97.50	90.00
123	A10	6r on 20r grn	21.00	16.50
124	A10	6r on 20r bis	27.50	19.50
125	A10	6r on 25r slate	85.00	57.50
126	A10	6r on 25r vio	7.25	5.00
127	A10	6r on 40r blue	220.00	190.00
128	A10	6r on 40r yel	90.00	75.00
129	A10	6r on 50r grn	115.00	90.00
130	A10	6r on 50r blue	120.00	100.00
	Nos. 113-130 (18)		1,490.	1,264.

Surcharged in Black

131	A10	1t on 10r grn	325.00	275.00
a.	With additional surch. "6"		600.00	525.00
132	A10	1t on 20r bis	85.00	67.50
133	A10	1t on 25r slate	90.00	72.50
134	A10	1t on 25r vio	24.00	18.00
135	A10	1t on 40r blue	31.00	24.00
136	A10	1t on 50r grn	100.00	80.00
137	A10	1t on 50r blue	45.00	31.00
138	A10	1t on 100r lil	40.00	23.00
139	A10	1t on 200r org	67.50	57.50
140	A10	2t on 25r slate	72.50	57.50
a.	Small "T"		55.00	40.00
141	A10	2t on 25r vio	24.00	17.00
142	A10	2t on 40r blue	115.00	75.00
143	A10	2t on 40r yel	57.50	45.00
144	A10	2t on 50r grn	45.00	35.00
a.	Inverted surcharge		110.00	100.00
145	A10	2t on 50r blue	145.00	120.00
146	A10	2t on 100r lil	21.00	17.00
147	A10	2t on 200r org	75.00	57.50
148	A10	2t on 300r brn	65.00	57.50
149	A10	4t on 10r grn	35.00	27.50
a.	Inverted surcharge		45.00	45.00
150	A10	4t on 50r grn	35.00	24.00
a.	With additional surch. "2"		200.00	110.00
151	A10	4t on 200r org	80.00	57.50
152	A10	4t on 20r bis	87.50	65.00
153	A10	8t on 25r rose	350.00	300.00
154	A10	8t on 40r blue	75.00	65.00
155	A10	8t on 100r lil	67.50	57.50
156	A10	8t on 200r org	67.50	57.50
157	A10	8t on 300r brn	67.50	52.50
	Nos. 131-157 (27)		2,293.	1,837.

1882 Blue Surcharge

158	A10	4½r on 5r black	13.00	13.00

Similar Surcharge, Handstamped

1883

159	A10	1½r on 5r black	35.00	30.00
160	A10	1½r on 10r grn	30.00	25.00
161	A10	4½r on 100r lil	*400.00*	*325.00*

The "2" in "½" is 3mm high, instead of 2mm as on Nos. 113, 114 and 121.

The handstamp is known double on #159-161.

A12

There were three printings of the 1882-83 issue.

The first had "REIS" in thick letters with acute accent on the "E."

The second had "REIS" in thin letters with accent on the "E."

The third had the "E" without accent. In the first printing the "E" sometimes had a grave or circumflex accent.

The third printing may be divided into two sets, with or without a small circle in the cross of the crown.

With or Without Accent on "E" of "REIS"

1882-83				**Typo.**
162	A12	1½r black	1.00	.85
a.	"½" for "1 ½"			
163	A12	4½r olive bister	1.10	.60
164	A12	6r green	1.25	1.00
165	A12	1t rose	1.25	1.00
166	A12	2t blue	1.25	1.00
167	A12	4t lilac	6.00	3.50
168	A12	8t orange	6.00	5.00
	Nos. 162-168 (7)		17.85	12.95

Stamps doubly printed or with value omitted, double, inverted or misplaced are printer's waste.

Nos. 162-168 were reprinted on thin white paper, with shiny white gum and clean-cut perforation 13½. Value of lowest-cost reprint, $1 each.

"REIS" no serifs — A13   "REIS" with serifs — A14

1883		**Litho.**		**Imperf.**
169	A13	1½r black	2.40	1.75
a.	Tête bêche pair		*3,500.*	
b.	"1 ½" double		675.00	525.00
170	A13	4½r olive grn	24.00	17.00
a.	"4 ½" omitted		525.00	450.00
171	A13	6r green	21.00	14.50
a.	Tête bêche pair		*1,800.*	
b.	"6" omitted		675.00	600.00
172	A14	1½r black	240.00	67.50
a.	"1 ½" omitted		600.00	500.00
173	A14	6r green	90.00	55.00
a.	"6" omitted		600.00	500.00
	Nos. 169-173 (5)		377.40	155.75

Nos. 169-171 exist with unofficial perf. 12.

King Luiz — A15

1886, Apr. 29				**Embossed**
174	A15	1½r black	3.75	1.75
a.	Perf. 13 ½		150.00	87.50
175	A15	4½r bister	4.25	2.10
a.	Perf. 13 ½		30.00	14.00
176	A15	6r dp green	5.75	2.75
a.	Perf. 13 ½		35.00	15.00
177	A15	1t brt rose	7.25	4.25
178	A15	2t deep blue	14.00	6.75
179	A15	4t gray vio	14.00	6.75
180	A15	8t orange	14.00	6.75
	Nos. 174-180 (7)		63.00	31.10

For surcharges and overprints see Nos. 224-230, 277-278, 282, 317-323, 354, 397.

Nos. 178-179 were reprinted. Originals have yellow gum. Reprints have white gum and clean-cut perforation 13½. Value, $4 each.

King Carlos — A16

1895-96 Typo.		**Perf. 11½, 12½, 13½**		
181	A16	1½r black	2.60	.85
182	A16	4½r pale orange	2.10	.85
a.	Perf. 13 ½		11.00	2.00
183	A16	6r green	2.10	.85
a.	Perf. 12 ½		5.50	2.00
184	A16	9r gray lilac	7.50	4.50
185	A16	1t lt blue	3.00	1.75
a.	Perf. 13 ½		8.00	3.75
186	A16	2t rose	2.40	1.00
a.	Perf. 12 ½		24.00	13.50
187	A16	4t dk blue	3.50	1.50
a.	Perf. 12 ½		6.75	4.00
188	A16	8t brt violet	5.50	3.75
	Nos. 181-188 (8)		28.70	15.05

For surcharges and overprints see Nos. 231-238, 275-276, 279-281, 324-331, 352.

No. 184 was reprinted. Reprints have white gum, and clean-cut perforation 13½. Value $10.

Common Design Types pictured following the introduction.

Vasco da Gama Issue Common Design Types

1898, May 1		**Engr.**	**Perf. 14 to 15**	
189	CD20	1½r blue green	1.25	.70
190	CD21	4½r red	1.25	.70
191	CD22	6r red violet	1.25	.90
192	CD23	9r yellow green	2.00	1.00
193	CD24	1t dk blue	3.50	2.10
194	CD25	2t violet brn	4.25	2.10
195	CD26	4t bister brn	4.25	3.00
196	CD27	8t bister	7.50	5.00
	Nos. 189-196 (8)		25.25	15.50

For overprints and surcharges see Nos. 290-297, 384-389.

King Carlos — A17

Name and Value in Black except No. 219

1898-1903		**Typo.**	**Perf. 11½**	
197	A17	1r gray ('02)	.35	.25
198	A17	1½r orange	.35	.25
199	A17	1½r slate ('02)	.45	.25
200	A17	2r orange ('02)	.35	.25
201	A17	2½r yel brn ('02)	.45	.25
202	A17	3r dp blue ('02)	.45	.25
203	A17	4½r lt green	1.25	.55
204	A17	6r brown	1.25	.55
205	A17	6r gray grn ('02)	.45	.25
206	A17	9r dull vio	1.25	.55
a.	9r gray lilac		1.75	1.00
208	A17	1t sea green	1.50	.60
209	A17	1t car rose ('02)	.75	.25
210	A17	2t blue	1.75	.60
a.	Perf. 13 ½		55.00	21.00
211	A17	2t brown ('02)	3.50	1.60
212	A17	2½t dull bl ('02)	13.50	6.50
213	A17	4t blue, *blue*	3.75	2.50
214	A17	5t brn, *straw*	4.25	2.50
215	A17	8t red lil, *pnksh*	4.25	2.10
216	A17	8t red vio, *pink* ('02)	7.25	3.50
217	A17	12t blue, *pink*	6.50	3.50
218	A17	12t grn, *pink* ('02)	8.50	3.50
219	A17	1rp blk & red, *bl*	13.00	5.25
220	A17	1rp dl bl, *straw* ('02)	17.00	14.50
221	A17	2rp vio, *yelsh*	17.00	8.50
222	A17	2rp gray blk, *straw* ('03)	29.00	27.50
	Nos. 197-222 (25)		138.10	86.30

Several stamps of this issue exist without value or with value inverted but they are not known to have been issued in this condition. The 1r and 6r in carmine rose are believed to be color trials.

For surcharges and overprints see Nos. 223, 239-259, 260C-274, 283-289, 300-316, 334-350, 376-383, 390-396, 398-399.

No. 210 Surcharged in Black

1900

223	A17	1½r on 2t blue	4.25	2.40
a.	Inverted surcharge		240.00	240.00
b.	Perf. 13 ½		180.00	150.00

Stamps of 1885-96 Surcharged in Black or Red

On Stamps of 1886

1902			**Perf. 12½, 13½**	
224	A15	1r on 2t blue	1.20	.50
225	A15	2r on 4½r bis	.65	.50
a.	Inverted surcharge		22.50	22.50
b.	Double surcharge			
226	A15	2½r on 6r green	.55	.25
227	A15	3r on 1t rose	.55	.25
228	A15	2½t on 1½r blk (R)	3.00	2.10
229	A15	2½t on 4t gray vio	3.00	2.10
230	A15	5t on 8t orange	1.75	1.00
a.	Perf. 12 ½		35.00	21.00

On Stamps of 1895-96

			Perf. 11½, 12½, 13½	
231	A16	1r on 6r green	.50	.25
232	A16	2r on 8t brt vio	.35	.25
233	A16	2½r on 9r gray vio	.35	.35
234	A16	3r on 4½r yel	2.25	1.40
a.	Inverted surcharge		28.00	28.00
235	A16	3r on 1t lt bl	2.10	1.50
236	A16	2½t on 1½r blk (R)	2.60	1.50
237	A16	5t on 2t rose	2.60	1.50
a.	Perf. 12 ½		210.00	160.00
238	A16	5t on 4t dk bl	2.60	1.50
	Nos. 224-238 (15)		24.05	14.95

Nos. 224, 229, 231, 233, 234, 235 and 238 were reprinted in 1905. They have whiter gum than the originals and very clean-cut perf. 13½. Value $2.50 each.

Nos. 204, 208, 210 Overprinted

1902			**Perf. 11½**	
239	A17	6r brown	3.25	1.50
a.	Inverted overprint			
240	A17	1t sea green	3.25	1.50
241	A17	2t blue	3.25	1.50
a.	Perf. 13 ½		725.00	500.00
	Nos. 239-241 (3)		9.75	4.50

No. 212 Surcharged in Black

1905

243	A17	2t on 2½t dull blue	3.50	2.75

Stamps of 1898-1903 Overprinted in Lisbon in Carmine or Green

1911

244	A17	1r gray	.25	.25
a.	Inverted overprint		11.00	11.00
245	A17	1½r slate	.25	.25
a.	Double overprint		11.00	11.00
246	A17	2r orange	.25	.25
a.	Double overprint		15.00	15.00
b.	Inverted overprint		11.00	11.00
247	A17	2½r yellow brn	.40	.25
248	A17	3r deep blue	.40	.25
249	A17	4½r light green	.40	.25
250	A17	6r gray green	.35	.25
251	A17	9r gray lilac	.40	.25
252	A17	1t car rose (G)	.60	.25
253	A17	2t brown	.60	.25
254	A17	4t blue, *blue*	1.50	1.25
255	A17	5t brn, *straw*	2.40	1.25
256	A17	8t vio, *pink*	6.75	3.75
257	A17	12t grn, *pink*	7.25	4.00
258	A17	1rp dl bl, *straw*	11.50	9.50
259	A17	2rp gray blk, *straw*	14.50	10.00
	Nos. 244-259 (16)		47.80	32.25

A18

Values are for pairs, both halves.

1911 Perforated Diagonally

260	A18	1r on 2r orange	1.00	.85
a.	Without diagonal perf.		42.50	34.00
b.	Cut diagonally instead of perf.		21.00	17.00

Stamps of Preceding Issues Perforated Vertically through the Middle and Each Half Surcharged

a   b

Values are for pairs, both halves of the stamp.

1912-13		**On Issue of 1898-1903**		
260C	A17(a)	1r on 2r org	1.00	.75
261	A17(a)	1r on 1t car	1.00	.75
262	A17(a)	1r on 5t brn, *straw*	140.00	85.00
263	A17(b)	1r on 5t brn, *straw*	6.50	5.00
264	A17(a)	1½r on 2½r yel brn	2.40	1.75
264C	A17(a)	1½r on 4½r lt grn	21.00	12.00
265	A17(a)	1½r on 9r gray lil	1.50	1.25

266	A17(a)	1½r on 4t bl, *bl*	3.25	2.00
267	A17(a)	2r on 2½r yel		
		brn	1.50	1.25
268	A17(a)	2r on 4t bl, *bl*	2.25	1.75
269	A17(a)	3r on 2½r yel		
		brn	1.50	1.25
270	A17(a)	3r on 2t brown	2.00	1.50
271	A17(a)	6r on 4½r lt grn	1.75	1.50
272	A17(a)	6r on 9r gray lil	1.75	1.50
273	A17(a)	6r on 9r dull vio	2.50	2.10
274	A17(b)	6r on 8t red vio,		
		pink	3.00	2.50

On Nos. 237-238, 230, 226, 233

275	A16(b)	1r on 5t on 2t	24.00	17.00
276	A16(b)	1r on 5t on 4t	14.00	10.00
277	A15(b)	1r on 5t on 8t	5.00	3.25
278	A15(b)	2r on 2½r on 6r	5.00	3.25
279	A16(a)	2r on 2½r on 9r	45.00	37.50
280	A16(b)	2r on 5t on 2t	22.50	17.50
281	A16(b)	3r on 5t on 4t	14.00	10.00
282	A15(b)	3r on 5t on 8t	2.75	2.00

On Issue of 1911

283	A17(a)	1r on 1r gray	.50	.45
283B	A17(a)	1r on 2r org	.50	.45
284	A17(a)	1r on 1t car	.50	.45
285	A17(a)	1r on 5t brn,		
		straw	.50	.45
285A	A17(b)	1r on 5t brn,		
		straw	1,150.	975.00
285B	A17(a)	1½r on 4½r lt		
		grn	1.25	1.00
286	A17(a)	3r on 2t brn	21.00	16.50
289	A17(a)	6r on 9r gray		
		lil	1.25	1.00

There are several settings of these surcharges and many minor varieties of the letters and figures, notably a small "6." Nos. 260-289 were issued mostly without gum.

More than half of Nos. 260C-289 exist with inverted or double surcharge, or with bisecting perforation omitted. The legitimacy of these varieties is questioned. Price of inverted surcharges, $3-$15; double surcharges, $1-$4; perf. omitted, $1.50-$15.

Similar surcharges made without official authorization on stamps of type A17 are: 2r on 2½r, 3r on 2½r, 3r on 5t, and 6r on 4½r.

Vasco da Gama Issue Overprinted

1913

290	CD20	1½r blue green	.35	.25
291	CD21	4½r red	.35	.25
a.		Double overprint	22.50	
292	CD22	6r red violet	.45	.40
a.		Double overprint	22.50	
293	CD23	9r yellow grn	.50	.45
294	CD24	1t dark blue	1.40	.60
295	CD25	2t violet brown	2.40	2.10
296	CD26	4t orange brn	1.75	.60
297	CD27	8t bister	3.00	1.50
		Nos. 290-297 (8)	10.20	6.15

Issues of 1898-1913 Overprinted Locally in Red

1913-15   On Issues of 1898-1903

300	A17	2r orange	30.00	24.00
301	A17	2½r yellow brn	7.50	6.00
302	A17	3r dp blue	19.00	
303	A17	4½r lt green	12.00	8.50
304	A17	6r gray grn	25.00	
305	A17	9r gray lilac	18.00	15.00
306	A17	1t sea green	45.00	
307	A17	2t blue	50.00	
309	A17	4t blue, *blue*	60.00	55.00
310	A17	5t brn, *straw*	55.00	
311	A17	8t red vio, *pink*	65.00	
312	A17	12t grn, *pink*	24.00	18.00
313	A17	1rp blk & red, *bl*	100.00	
314	A17	1rp dl bl, *straw*	57.50	50.00
315	A17	2rp gray blk, *straw*	85.00	72.50
316	A17	2rp vio, *yelsh*	85.00	72.50
		Nos. 300-316 (16)	738.00	321.50

Inverted or double overprints exist on 2½r, 4½r, 9r, 1rp and 2rp.

Nos. 300-316 were issued without gum except 4½r and 9r.

Nos. 302, 304, 306, 307, 310, 311 and 313 were not regularly issued. Value the 1½r, 2t brown and 12t blue on pink with preceding overprint.

Same Overprint in Red or Green on Provisional Issue of 1902

317	A15	1r on 2t blue	45.00	
a.		"REPUBLICA" inverted	140.00	

318	A15	2r on 4½r bis	45.00	
a.		"REPUBLICA" inverted	140.00	
319	A15	2r on 6r grn	9.00	7.25
a.		"REPUBLICA" inverted	19.00	
320	A15	3r on 1t rose (R)	11.00	
321	A15	2½t on 4t gray vio	110.00	
323	A15	5t on 8t org (G)	17.50	12.00
a.		Red overprint	50.00	40.00
324	A16	1r on 6r grn	35.00	22.50
325	A16	2r on 8t vio	50.00	42.50
a.		Inverted surcharge	110.00	
327	A16	3r on 4½r yel	82.50	
328	A16	3r on 1t lt bl	82.50	
329	A16	5t on 2t rose (G)	24.00	18.00
330	A16	5t on 4t bl (G)	15.00	11.00
331	A16	5t on 4t bl (R)	33.00	27.00
a.		"REPUBLICA" inverted	55.00	
b.		"REPUBLICA" double	55.00	
		Nos. 317-331 (13)	559.50	140.25

The 2½r on 1½r of types A15 and A16, the 3r on 1t (A15) and 2½r on 9r (A16) were clandestinely printed.

Some authorities question the status of No. 317-318, 320-321, 324, 327-328.

Same Overprint on Nos. 240-241
1913-15

334	A17	1t sea green	72.50	60.00
335	A17	2t blue	72.50	60.00

This overprint was applied to No. 239 without official authorization. Value $35.

On Issue of 1912-13 Perforated through the Middle

Values are for pairs, both halves of the stamp.

336	A17(a)	1r on 2r org	135.00	12.00
340	A17(a)	1½r on 4½r lt grn	17.50	13.50
341	A17(a)	1½r on 9r gray lil	20.00	
342	A17(a)	1½r on 4t bl, *bl*	27.50	
343	A17(a)	2r on 2½r yel		
		brn	20.00	
344	A17(a)	2r on 4t bl, *bl*	27.50	
345	A17(a)	3r on 2½r yel		
		brn	22.50	
346	A17(a)	3r on 2t brn	13.00	7.25
347	A17(a)	6r on 4½r lt grn	6.75	5.25
348	A17(a)	6r on 9r gray lil	9.75	7.25
350	A17(b)	6r on 8t red vio,		
		pink	9.75	8.50
352	A16(b)	1r on 5t on 4t bl	110.00	
354	A15(a)	2r on 2½r on 6r		
		grn	13.00	
		Nos. 334-354 (15)	577.25	

The 1r on 5t (A15), 1r on 1t (A17), 1½r on 2½r (A17), 3r on 5t on 8t (A15), and 6r on 9r (A17) were clandestinely printed.

Nos. 336, 347 exist with inverted surcharge. Some authorities question the status of Nos. 341-345, 352 and 354.

Ceres — A21

Name and Value in Black
Chalky Paper

1914		Typo.	Perf. 15x14	
357	A21	1r olive brn	.75	.70
358	A21	1½r yellow grn	.75	.70
359	A21	2r black	1.10	.70
360	A21	2½r olive grn	1.10	.70
361	A21	3r lilac	1.20	.70
362	A21	4½r orange brn	1.20	.70
363	A21	5r blue green	1.20	.70
364	A21	6r lilac brown	.90	.70
365	A21	9r ultra	1.20	.70
366	A21	10r carmine	1.50	.85
367	A21	1t lt violet	2.40	.85
368	A21	2t deep blue	3.00	1.20
369	A21	3t yellow brown	3.75	1.50
370	A21	4t slate	2.40	1.75
371	A21	8t plum	7.25	6.00
372	A21	12t brown, *green*	6.75	5.50
373	A21	1rp brown, *pink*	35.00	21.00
374	A21	2rp org, *salmon*	21.00	17.00
375	A21	3rp green, *blue*	28.00	42.50
		Nos. 357-375 (19)	120.45	104.45

The 1r, 2r, 2½r, 3r, 4½r, 5r, 6r and 10r, 1t and 3t exist on glazed paper.

1916-20   Ordinary Paper

375A	A21	1r olive brn	2.75	2.50
375B	A21	1½r yellow grn	2.75	2.50
b.		Imperf.		
375C	A21	2r black ('19)	5.25	5.00
375D	A21	2½r olive grn ('19)	2.75	2.50
375E	A21	3r lilac ('16)	2.75	2.50
375F	A21	4½r orange brn ('19)	2.75	2.50
375G	A21	6r lilac brown ('16)	2.75	2.50
375H	A21	1t lt violet ('16)	2.75	2.50
375I	A21	2t deep blue ('16)	5.25	3.00
		Nos. 375A-375I (9)	29.75	25.50

1921-23			Perf. 12x11½	
375J	A21	1r olive brn	2.75	2.40
375K	A21	1½r yellow grn	2.75	2.40
375L	A21	2r black	3.75	3.00
375M	A21	3r lilac ('22)	2.75	2.40
375N	A21	4r blue ('22)	2.10	1.75
375O	A21	4½r orange brn	11.00	9.00
375P	A21	5r blue green	14.50	12.00
375Q	A21	6r lilac brown	2.10	1.75
375R	A21	9r ultra	6.75	5.00
375S	A21	10r carmine	30.00	21.00
375T	A21	1t lt violet	9.75	6.00
375U	A21	1½t gray green		
		('22)	2.10	1.20
375V	A21	2t deep blue	9.75	7.25
375W	A21	2½t turquoise blue		
		('22)	2.40	1.75
375X	A21	3t4r yellow brown		
		('23)	6.75	4.25
375Y	A21	4t slate	9.75	7.25
375Z	A21	8t plum	16.00	13.00
		Nos. 375J-375Z (17)	134.95	101.40

The 1, 2, 2½, 3, 4½, 1, 2, and 4t exist with the black inscriptions inverted and the 2½r with them double, one inverted, but it is not known that any of these were regularly issued.

For surcharges see Nos. 400, 400A, 420, 421, 423.

Nos. 249, 251-253, 256-259 Surcharged in Black

1914

376	A17	1½r on 4½r grn	1.35	1.00
377	A17	1½r on 9r gray lil	1.35	1.00
378	A17	1½r on 12t grn, *pink*	2.10	1.75
379	A17	3r on 1t car rose	1.50	1.25
380	A17	3r on 2t brn	8.00	6.75
381	A17	3r on 8t red vio,		
		pink	10.00	8.00
382	A17	3r on 1rp dl bl,		
		straw	2.10	1.35
383	A17	3r on 2rp gray blk,		
		straw	2.75	1.75

There are 3 varieties of the "2" in "1½."
Nos. 376-377 exist with inverted surcharge.

Vasco da Gama Issue Surcharged in Black

384	CD21	1½r on 4½r red	1.00	.60
385	CD23	1½r on 9r yel grn	1.00	.60
386	CD24	3r on 1t dk bl	1.10	.60
387	CD25	3r on 2t vio brn	4.25	3.50
388	CD26	3r on 4t org brn	1.10	.60
389	CD27	3r on 8t bister	3.75	2.75
		Nos. 376-389 (14)	41.35	31.50

Double, inverted and other surcharge varieties exist on Nos. 384-386, 389.

Nos. 303, 305, 312 and 315 Surcharged in Black

1915

390	A17	1½r on 4½r grn	45.00	22.50
a.		"REPUBLICA" omitted	77.50	47.50
b.		"REPUBLICA" inverted	82.50	
391	A17	1½r on 9r gray lil	14.00	8.25
a.		"REPUBLICA" omitted	35.00	
392	A17	1½r on 12t grn, *pink*	6.00	4.25
396	A17	3r on 2rp gray blk,		
		straw	15.50	13.00
		Nos. 390-396 (4)	80.50	48.00

Nos. 390, 390a, 390b, 391, and 391a were not regularly issued. The 3r on 2½r (A17) was surcharged without official authorization.

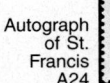

Preceding Issues Overprinted in Carmine

1915   On No. 230

397	A15	5t on 8t org	3.25	1.75

On Nos. 241, 243

398	A17	2t blue	2.50	1.75
399	A17	2t on 2½t dl bl	3.00	1.75
		Nos. 397-399 (3)	8.75	5.25

Nos. 375C, 359 Surcharged in Carmine

1922

400	A21	1½r on 2r black (ordinary paper)	2.10	1.20
400A	A21	1½r on 2r black (chalky paper)	1.20	.75

No. 400 also exists on glazed paper.

Ceres Type of 1913-23
Name and Value in Black

1922		Typo.	Perf. 12x11½	
		Glazed Paper		
407	A21	1rp gray brn	24.00	20.00
408	A21	2rp yellow	28.00	28.00
409	A21	3rp bluish grn	42.50	42.50
410	A21	5rp carmine rose	50.00	50.00
		Nos. 407-410 (4)	144.50	140.50

Vasco da Gama and Flagship A22

1925, Jan. 30   Litho.
Without Gum

411	A22	6r brown	6.75	6.00
412	A22	1t red violet	9.00	7.25

400th anniv. of the death of Vasco da Gama (1469?-1524), Portuguese navigator.

Monument to St. Francis — A23

Image of St. Francis — A25

Autograph of St. Francis A24

Image of St. Francis — A26

Tomb of St. Francis — A28

Church of Bom Jesus at Goa — A27

1931, Dec. 3 *Perf. 14*

414	A23	1r gray green	1.00	.80
415	A24	2r brown	1.00	.80
416	A25	6r red violet	2.00	1.00
417	A26	1½t yellow brn	7.75	5.00
418	A27	2t deep blue	11.50	7.25
419	A28	2½t light red	16.50	8.00
		Nos. 414-419 (6)	39.75	22.85

Exposition of St. Francis Xavier at Goa, in December, 1931.

Nos. 371 and 375X
Surcharged

1931-32 *Perf. 15x14*
Chalky Paper

420	A21	1½r on 8t plum ('32)	5.50	3.00

Ordinary Paper
Perf. 12x11½

421	A21	1½r on 8t plum ('32)	3.75	2.40
423	A21	2½r on 3t4r yel brn	77.50	57.50

"Portugal" and Vasco da Gama's Flagship "San Gabriel" — A29

1933 Typo. *Perf. 11½x12* Wmk. 232

424	A29	1r bister	.25	.25
425	A29	2r olive brn	.25	.25
426	A29	4r violet	.25	.25
427	A29	6r dk green	.25	.25
428	A29	8r black	.30	.25
429	A29	1t gray	.30	.25
430	A29	1½t dp rose	.30	.25
431	A29	2t brown	.30	.25
432	A29	2½t dk blue	1.60	.50
433	A29	3t brt blue	1.75	.50
434	A29	5t red orange	1.75	.50
435	A29	1rp olive grn	7.75	3.25
436	A29	2rp maroon	19.50	7.50
437	A29	3rp orange	28.00	8.75
438	A29	5rp apple grn	40.00	25.00
		Nos. 424-438 (15)	102.55	48.00

For surcharges see Nos. 454-463, 472-474, J34-J36.

Common Design Types
Perf. 13½x13

1938, Sept. 1 Engr. Unwmk.
Name and Value in Black

439	CD34	1r gray brn	.25	.25
440	CD34	2r orange brn	.25	.25
441	CD34	3r dk vio brn	.25	.25
442	CD34	6r brt green	.25	.25
443	CD35	10r dk carmine	.40	.25
444	CD35	1t brt red vio	.40	.25
445	CD35	1½t red	.40	.25
446	CD37	2t orange	.40	.25
447	CD37	2½t blue	.40	.25
448	CD37	3t slate	1.00	.35
449	CD36	5t rose vio	1.75	.40
450	CD36	1rp brown car	4.50	1.00
451	CD36	2rp olive grn	7.00	2.75
452	CD38	3rp blue vio	13.00	6.00
453	CD38	5rp red brown	27.00	8.50
		Nos. 439-453 (15)	57.25	21.25

For surcharges see Nos. 492-495, 504-505.

Stamps of 1933
Surcharged in Black

1941, June Wmk. 232 Perf. 11½x12

454	A29	1t on 1½t dp rose	2.50	2.00
455	A29	1t on 1rp olive grn	2.50	2.00
456	A29	1t on 2rp maroon	2.50	2.00
457	A29	1t on 5rp apple grn	2.50	2.00
		Nos. 454-457 (4)	10.00	8.00

Nos. 430-431
Surcharged

1943

458	A29	3r on 1½t dp rose	1.25	.80
459	A29	1t on 2t brown	2.75	2.25

Nos. 434, 428, 437 and 432
Surcharged in Dark Blue or Carmine

a   b

1945-46 Wmk. 232 Perf. 11½x12

460	A29(a)	1r on 5t red org (DB)	.90	.80
461	A29(b)	2r on 8r blk (C)	.90	.80
462	A29(b)	3r on 3rp org (DB) ('46)	2.25	1.75
463	A29(b)	6r on 2½t dk bl (C)	2.25	1.75
		Nos. 460-463 (4)	6.30	5.10

St. Francis Xavier A30   Luis de Camoens A31

Garcia de Orta — A32   St. John de Britto — A33

Arch of the Viceroy A34   Affonso de Albuquerque A35

Vasco da Gama — A36   Francisco de Almeida — A37

Perf. 11½

1946, May 28 Litho. Unwmk.

464	A30	1r black & gray blk	.50	.25
465	A31	2r rose brn & pale rose brn	.50	.25
466	A32	6r ocher & dl yel	.50	.25
467	A33	7r vio & pale vio	3.00	3.00
468	A34	9r sepia & buff	3.00	1.40
469	A35	1t dk sl grn & sl grn	2.25	1.40

470	A36	3½t ultra & pale ultra	2.25	2.10
471	A37	1rp choc & bis brn	6.25	2.75
a.		Miniature sheet of 8, (#464-471)	35.00	30.00
		Nos. 464-471 (8)	18.25	11.40

No. 471a sold for 1½ rupias.
See #476. For surcharges see #595, J43-J46.

No. 428, 431 and 433
Surcharged in
Carmine or Black

1946 Wmk. 232 Perf. 11½x12

472	A29 (c)	1r on 8r blk (C)	.80	.80
473	A29 (b)	3r on 2t brn	.80	.80
474	A29 (b)	6r on 3t brt bl	2.25	1.90
		Nos. 472-474 (3)	3.85	3.50

Type of 1946 and

Joao de Castro — A38   José Vaz — A39

Luis de Ataide — A40   Duarte Pacheco Pereira — A41

1948 Unwmk. Litho. Perf. 11½

475	A38	3r brt ultra & lt bl	1.10	.55
476	A30	1t dk grn & yel grn	1.10	.65
477	A39	1½t dk pur & dl vio	2.25	1.25
478	A40	2½t brt ver	3.00	1.60
479	A41	7½t dk brn & org brn	4.75	2.60
a.		Miniature sheet of 5	35.00	27.50
		Nos. 475-479 (5)	12.20	6.65

No. 476 measures 21x31mm.
No. 479a measures 106x146mm. and contains one each of Nos. 475-479. Marginal inscriptions in gray. The sheet sold for 16 tangas (1 rupia).
For surcharge see No. 591.

Lady of Fatima Issue
Common Design Type

1948 *Perf. 14½*

480	CD40	1t dk blue green	4.50	3.00

A souvenir sheet of nine, including Nos. 480 and 485 and stamps from seven Portuguese colonies, exists. Value, $100. For additional information, see note following Common Design No. 40 listings in the Common Design Types section of the catalog.

Our Lady of Fatima — A42

1949 Litho. Perf. 14

481	A42	1r blue	1.00	.75
482	A42	3r orange yel	1.00	.75
483	A42	9r dk car rose	1.50	1.00
484	A42	2t green	5.00	1.90
485	A42	9t orange red	4.50	2.50
486	A42	2rp dk vio brn	8.25	3.00
487	A42	5rp olive grn	16.50	7.25
488	A42	8rp violet blue	34.00	13.50
		Nos. 481-488 (8)	71.75	30.65

Our Lady of the Rosary at Fatima, Portugal.

UPU Symbols — A42a

1949, Oct.

489	A42a	2½t scarlet & pink	4.25	2.25

UPU, 75th anniversary.

> **Catalogue values for unused stamps in this section, from this point to the end of the section, are for Never Hinged items.**

Holy Year Issue
Common Design Types

1950, May *Perf. 13x13½*

490	CD41	1r olive bister	1.25	.45
491	CD42	2t dk gray green	1.75	.60

See Nos. 496-503.
A souvenir sheet of eight, including No. 490 and stamps from seven Portuguese colonies, exists. Value, $100. For additional information, see note following Common Designs No. 41 and 42 listings in the Common Design Types section of the catalog.

No. 443
Surcharged in Black

1950 *Perf. 13½x13*

492	CD35	1r on 10r dk car	.75	.40
493	CD35	2r on 10r dk car	.75	.40

Similar Surcharge on No. 447
in Black or Red

494	CD37	1r on 2½t blue	.75	.40
495	CD37	3r on 2½t blue (R)	.75	.40
		Nos. 492-495 (4)	3.00	1.60

Letters with serifs, small (lower case) "r" in "real" and "réis."

Holy Year Issue
Common Design Types

1951 Litho. *Perf. 13½*

496	CD41	1r dp car rose	.60	.30
497	CD41	2r emerald	.60	.30
498	CD42	3r red brown	.60	.30
499	CD41	6r gray	.60	.40
500	CD42	9r brt pink	1.25	.60
501	CD41	1t blue violet	1.25	.60
502	CD42	2t yellow	1.25	.70
503	CD41	4t violet brown	1.25	.70
		Nos. 496-503 (8)	7.40	3.90

No. 447 with Surcharge Similar to
Nos. 492-493 in Red

1951 *Perf. 13½x13*

504	CD37	6r on 2½t blue	.75	.40
505	CD37	1t on 2½t blue	.75	.40

Letters with serifs, small (lower case) "r" in "réis."

Holy Year Extension Issue
Common Design Type

1951 Litho. *Perf. 14*

506	CD43	1rp bl vio & pale vio + label	2.50	1.00

Stamp without label sells for less.

José Vaz — A43   Ruins of Sancoale Church — A44

Design: 12t, Altar.

Dated: "1651-1951"

1951		Litho.	Perf. 14½
507	A43	1r Prus bl & pale bl	.25 .25
508	A44	2r ver & red brn	.25 .25
509	A43	3r gray blk & gray	.70 .25
510	A44	1t vio bl & ind	.40 .25
511	A43	2t dp cl & cl	.40 .25
512	A44	3t ol grn & blk	.60 .25
513	A43	9t indigo & ultra	.60 .45
514	A44	10t lilac & vio	1.40 .65
515	A44	12t blk brn & brn	2.00 .95
		Nos. 507-515 (9)	6.60 3.55

300th anniversary of the birth of José Vaz.

Medical Congress Issue
Common Design Type

Design: Medical School, Goa.

1952	Unwmk.	Perf. 13½
516 CD44	4½t blk & lt blue	5.50 2.00

St. Francis Xavier Issue

Statue of Saint Francis Xavier — A44a

A45

St. Francis Xavier and his Tomb, Goa — A46

Designs: 2t, Miraculous Arm of St. Francis. 4t, 5t, Tomb of St. Francis.

1952, Oct. 25	Litho.	Perf. 14
517 A44a	6r aqua & multi	.45 .25
518 A44a	2t cream & multi	2.25 .60
519 A44a	5t pink & silver	4.25 1.40
	Nos. 517-519 (3)	6.95 2.25

Souvenir Sheets
Perf. 13

520	A45	9t brn & dk brn	14.50 11.00
521	A46	12t Sheet of 2	14.50 11.00
a.		4t orange buff & black	3.25 3.25
b.		8t slate & black	3.25 3.25

400th anniv. of the death of St. Francis Xavier.

Numeral A47

St. Francis Xavier A48

1952, Dec. 4	Litho.	Perf. 13½
522 A47	3t black	9.50 8.50
523 A48	5t dk violet & blk	9.50 8.50
a.	Strip of 2 + label	25.00 21.00

Issued to publicize Portuguese India's first stamp exhibition, Goa, 1952.
No. 523a consists of a tête bêche pair of Nos. 522-523 separated by a label publicizing the exhibition.

Statue of Virgin Mary — A49

1953, Jan.

524	A49	6r dk & lt blue	.25 .25
525	A49	1t brown & buff	1.25 .70
526	A49	3t dk pur & pale ol	2.75 1.25
		Nos. 524-526 (3)	4.25 2.20

Exhibition of Sacred Missionary Art held at Lisbon in 1951.
For surcharge see No. 594.

Stamp Centenary Issue

Stamp of Portugal and Arms of Colonies — A49a

1953		Typo.
527 A49a	1t multicolored	2.00 .95

Centenary of Portugal's first postage stamps.

Claudio da Gama Pinto, Ophthalmologist and Author, Birth Cent. — A50

1954, Apr. 10	Litho.	Perf. 11½
528 A50	3r gray & ol grn	.40 .25
529 A50	2t black & gray blk	.80 .30

Sao Paulo Issue
Common Design Type

1954, Oct. 2	Unwmk.	Perf. 13½
530 CD46	2t dk Prus bl, bl & blk	.80 .40

For surcharge see No. 593.

Affonso de Albuquerque School — A51

1955, Feb. 26

| 531 A51 | 9t multicolored | 1.75 .55 |

Centenary (in 1954) of the founding of the Affonso de Albuquerque National School.

Msgr. Sebastiao Rodolfo Dalgado — A52

1955, Nov. 15	Unwmk.	Perf. 13½
532 A52	1r multicolored	.25 .25
533 A52	1t multicolored	.75 .25

Birth cent. of Msgr. Sebastiao Rodolfo Dalgado.

Francisco de Almeida — A53

Manuel Antonio de Sousa — A54

Map of Bassein by Pedro Barreto de Resendo, 1635 — A55

Portraits: 9r, Affonso de Albuquerque. 1t, Vasco da Gama. 1½t, Filipe Nery Xavier. 3t, Nuno da Cunha. 4t, Agostinho Vicente Lourenco. 8t, Jose Vaz. 9t, Manuel Godinho de Heredia. 10t, Joao de Castro. 2rp, Antonio Caetano Pacheco. 3rp, Constantino de Braganca.
Maps of ancient forts, drawn in 1635: 2½t, Mombaim (Bombay). 3½t, Damao (Daman). 5t, Diu. 12t, Cochin. 1rp, Goa.

Inscribed: "450 Aniversario da Fundacao do Estado da India 1505-1955."

Perf. 11½x12 (A53), 14½ (A54), 12½ (A55)

1956, Mar. 24		Unwmk.
534	A53	3r multicolored	.25 .25
535	A54	6r multicolored	.25 .25
536	A53	9r multicolored	.25 .25
537	A53	1t multicolored	.35 .25
538	A54	1½t multicolored	.25 .25
539	A55	2t multicolored	3.50 1.90
540	A55	2½t multicolored	1.50 1.00
541	A53	3t multicolored	.65 .30
542	A55	3½t multicolored	1.50 1.00
543	A54	4t multicolored	.30 .25
544	A54	5t multicolored	.80 .40
545	A54	8t multicolored	.85 .35
546	A54	9t multicolored	.85 .35
547	A53	10t multicolored	1.00 .35
548	A55	12t multicolored	1.25 .75
549	A55	1rp multicolored	3.00 1.50
550	A54	2rp multicolored	3.50 1.75
551	A53	3rp multicolored	4.50 1.90
		Nos. 534-551 (18)	24.55 13.10

Portuguese settlements in India, 450th anniv.
For surcharges see Nos. 575-577, 579-581, 592.

Map of Damao and Nagar Aveli — A56

Map and Inscriptions in Black, Red, Ocher and Blue

1957		Litho.	Perf. 11½
552	A56	3r gray & buff	.25 .25
553	A56	6r bl grn & pale lem	.30 .25
554	A56	3t pink & lt gray	.35 .25
555	A56	6t blue	.35 .25
556	A56	11t ol bis & lt vio gray	1.00 .45
557	A56	2rp lt vio & pale gray	2.00 .90
558	A56	3rp citron & pink	2.75 1.75
559	A56	5rp magenta & pink	4.50 2.40
		Nos. 552-559 (8)	11.50 6.50

For surcharges see Nos. 571, 578, 584-585, 588-590.

Arms of Vasco da Gama — A57

Arms of: 6r, Lopo Soares de Albergaria. 9r, Francisco de Almeida. 1t, Garcia de Noronha. 4t, Alfonso de Albuquerque. 5t, Joao de Castro. 11t, Luis de Ataide. 1rp, Nuno da Cunha.

Arms in Original Colors Inscriptions in Black and Red

1958, Apr. 3		Unwmk.	Perf. 13x13½
560	A57	2r buff & ocher	.30 .25
561	A57	6r gray & ocher	.30 .25
562	A57	9r pale blue & emer	.30 .25
563	A57	1t pale citron & brn	.40 .25
564	A57	4t pale bl grn & lil	.45 .25
565	A57	5t buff & blue	.55 .35
566	A57	11t pink & lt brn	1.00 .75
567	A57	1rp pale grn & maroon	1.40 .90
		Nos. 560-567 (8)	4.70 3.25

For surcharges see Nos. 570, 572-574, 582-583, 586-587.

Exhibition Emblem and View — A58

1958, Dec. 15	Litho.	Perf. 14½
568 A58	1rp multicolored	.95 .50

World's Fair, Brussels, Apr. 17-Oct. 19.
For surcharge see No. 597.

Tropical Medicine Congress Issue
Common Design Type

Design: Holarrhena antidysenterica.

1958, Dec. 15		Perf. 13½
569 CD47	5t gray, brn, grn & red	1.75 .75

For surcharge see No. 596.

Stamps of 1955-58 Surcharged with New Values and Bars

1959, Jan. 1		Litho.	Unwmk.
570	A57	5c on 2r (#560)	.30 .25
571	A56	10c on 3r (#552)	.30 .25
572	A57	15c on 6r (#561)	.30 .25
573	A57	20c on 9r (#562)	.30 .25
574	A57	30c on 1t (#563)	.30 .25
575	A55	40c on 2t (#539)	.65 .30
576	A55	40c on 2½t (#540)	.80 .35
577	A55	40c on 3½t (#542)	.40 .25
578	A56	50c on 3t (#554)	.40 .25
579	A53	80c on 3t (#541)	.40 .25
580	A53	80c on 10t (#547)	1.10 .80
581	A53	80c on 3rp (#551)	1.60 .95
582	A57	1e on 4t (#564)	.40 .25
583	A57	1.50e on 5t (#565)	.40 .25
584	A56	2e on 6t (#555)	.65 .35
585	A56	2.50e on 11t (#556)	.95 .25
586	A57	4e on 11t (#566)	1.10 .55
587	A57	4.50e on 1rp (#567)	1.10 .55
588	A56	5e on 2rp (#557)	1.20 .55
589	A56	10e on 3rp (#558)	2.25 1.60
590	A56	30e on 5rp (#559)	5.00 2.25
		Nos. 570-590 (21)	19.90 11.00

Types of 1946-1958 Surcharged with New Values, Old Values Obliterated

1959		Litho.	Unwmk.
591	A39	40c on 1½t dl pur	.65 .25
592	A44	40c on 1½t multi	.65 .25
593	CD46	40c on 2t bl & gray	1.10 .80
594	A49	80c on 3t blk & pale cit	.65 .25
595	A36	80c on 3½t dk bl	.80 .25
596	CD47	80c on 5t gray, brn, grn & red	.80 .45
597	A58	80c on 1rp multi	2.25 .65
		Nos. 591-597 (7)	6.90 2.90

Coin, Manuel I — A59

Various Coins from the Reign of Manuel I (1495-1521) to the Republic.

Inscriptions in Black and Red

Perf. 13½x13

1959, Dec. 1		Litho.	Unwmk.
598	A59	5c lt bl & gold	.30 .25
599	A59	10c pale brn & gold	.30 .25
600	A59	15c pale grn & gray	.30 .25

601	A59	30c salmon & gray	.30	.25
602	A59	40c pale yel & gray	.30	.25
603	A59	50c lilac & gray	.30	.25
604	A59	60c pale yel grn & gray	.30	.25
605	A59	80c lt bl & gray	.30	.25
606	A59	1e ocher & gray	.30	.25
607	A59	1.50e blue & gray	.30	.25
608	A59	2e pale bl & gold	.30	.25
609	A59	2.50e pale gray & gold	.35	.25
610	A59	3e citron & gray	.35	.25
611	A59	4e pink & gray	.75	.25
612	A59	4.40e pale bis & vio brn	.90	.35
613	A59	5e pale dl vio & gray	1.00	.45
614	A59	10e brt yel & gray	2.00	.80
615	A59	20e beige & gray	4.00	2.25
616	A59	30e brt yel grn & lt cop brn	5.00	3.00
617	A59	50e lt gray & gray	10.00	5.00
		Nos. 598-617 (20)	27.65	15.35

Arms of Prince
Henry — A60

1960, June 25   **Perf. 13½**
618 A60 3e multicolored   2.75   .60

500th anniversary of the death of Prince Henry the Navigator.

Portugal continued to print special-issue stamps for its lost colony after its annexation by India Dec. 18, 1961: Sports, six stamps issued Dec. 1961, value (set) $3; Anti-Malaria, one stamp issued April, 1962, value 75c.

Stamps of India were first used on Dec. 29. Stamps of Portuguese India remained valid until Jan. 5, 1962.

AIR POST STAMPS

Common Design Type
Perf. 13½x13

1938, Sept. 1   **Engr.**   **Unwmk.**
Name and Value in Black

C1	CD39	1t red orange	1.50	.75
C2	CD39	2½t purple	1.50	.75
C3	CD39	3½t orange	1.50	.75
C4	CD39	4½t ultra	1.50	.75
C5	CD39	7t lilac brown	2.25	.85
C6	CD39	7½t dark green	2.25	.85
C7	CD39	9t red brown	7.00	2.50
C8	CD39	11t magenta	8.00	2.50
		Nos. C1-C8 (8)	25.50	9.70

No. C4 exists with overprint "Exposicao Internacional de Nova York, 1939-1940" and Trylon and Perisphere. Value, unused $90, never hinged $125.
Counterfeits exist.

POSTAGE DUE STAMPS

D1

1904   **Unwmk.**   **Typo.**   **Perf. 11½**
Name and Value in Black

J1	D1	2r gray green	.60	.45
J2	D1	3r yellow grn	.60	.45
J3	D1	4r orange	.60	.50
J4	D1	5r slate	.60	.50
J5	D1	6r gray	.60	.50
J6	D1	9r yellow brn	1.00	1.00
J7	D1	1t red orange	1.25	1.10
J8	D1	2t gray brown	2.10	1.40
J9	D1	5t dull blue	4.75	3.50
J10	D1	10t carmine	5.00	4.00
J11	D1	1rp dull vio	19.00	8.50
		Nos. J1-J11 (11)	36.10	21.90

Nos. J1-J11
Overprinted in
Carmine or Green

1911

J12	D1	2r gray grn	.25	.25
J13	D1	3r yellow grn	.25	.25
J14	D1	4r orange	.25	.25
J15	D1	5r slate	.25	.25
J16	D1	6r gray	.50	.25
J17	D1	9r yellow brn	.60	.45
J18	D1	1t red org	.70	.45
J19	D1	2t gray brn	1.10	.70
J20	D1	5t dull blue	2.50	1.75
J21	D1	10t carmine (G)	6.00	4.00
J22	D1	1rp dull violet	7.00	4.00
		Nos. J12-J22 (11)	19.40	12.60

Nos. J1-J11
Overprinted

1914

J23	D1	2r gray grn	1.00	.90
J24	D1	3r yellow grn	1.00	.90
J25	D1	4r orange	1.00	.90
J26	D1	5r slate	1.00	.90
J27	D1	6r gray	1.00	.90
J28	D1	9r yellow brn	1.00	.90
J29	D1	1t red org	1.00	.90
J30	D1	2t gray brn	7.75	1.00
J31	D1	5t dull blue	8.25	5.25
J32	D1	10t carmine	13.00	6.50
J33	D1	1rp dull violet	21.00	11.00
		Nos. J23-J33 (11)	57.00	30.05

Nos. 432, 433 and
434 Surcharged In
Red or Black

1943   **Wmk. 232**   **Perf. 11½x12**

J34	A29	3r on 2½t dk bl (R)	.60	.50
J35	A29	6r on 3t brt bl (R)	1.20	.75
J36	A29	1t on 5t red org (Bk)	2.10	2.10
		Nos. J34-J36 (3)	3.90	3.35

D2

1945   **Typo.**   **Unwmk.**
Country Name and Denomination in Black

J37	D2	2r brt carmine	1.00	.85
J38	D2	3r blue	1.00	.85
J39	D2	4r orange yel	1.00	.85
J40	D2	6r yellow grn	1.00	.85
J41	D2	1t bister brn	1.25	1.10
J42	D2	2t chocolate	1.40	1.25
		Nos. J37-J42 (6)	6.65	5.75

> **Catalogue values for unused stamps in this section, from this point to the end of the section, are for Never Hinged items.**

Nos. 467 and 471
Surcharged in
Carmine or Black

1951, Jan. 1   **Perf. 11½**

J43	A33	2r on 7r vio & pale vio (C)	1.25	.60
J44	A33	3r on 7r vio & pale vio (C)	1.25	.60

J45	A37	1t on 1rp choc & bis brn	1.25	.60
J46	A37	2t on 1rp choc & bis brn	1.25	.60
		Nos. J43-J46 (4)	5.00	2.40

Common Design Type
Photogravure and Typographed
1952   **Perf. 14**
Numeral in Red; Frame Multicolored

J47	CD45	2r olive	.25	.25
J48	CD45	3r black	.40	.40
J49	CD45	6r dark blue	.55	.55
J50	CD45	1t dk carmine	.80	.80
J51	CD45	2t orange	1.10	1.10
J52	CD45	10t violet blue	3.00	3.00
		Nos. J47-J52 (6)	6.10	6.10

Nos. J47-J49 and J51-J52
Surcharged with New Value and
Bars

1959, Jan.
Numeral in Red; Frame Multicolored

J53	CD45	5c on 2r olive	.25	.25
J54	CD45	10c on 3r black	.35	.45
J55	CD45	15c on 6r dk blue	.65	.80
J56	CD45	60c on 2t orange	1.00	1.40
J57	CD45	60c on 10t vio blue	2.25	2.25
		Nos. J53-J57 (5)	4.50	5.15

WAR TAX STAMPS

Overprinted in Black or Carmine

WT1

Denomination in Black
Perf. 15x14

1919, Apr. 15   **Typo.**   **Unwmk.**

MR1	WT1	0:00:05,48rp grn	3.50	2.75
MR2	WT1	0:01:09,94rp grn	6.75	4.50
MR3	WT1	0:02:03,43rp grn (C)	6.75	4.50
		Nos. MR1-MR3 (3)	17.00	11.75

Some authorities consider No. MR2 a revenue stamp.

POSTAL TAX STAMPS

Pombal Issue
Common Design Types

1925   **Unwmk.**   **Perf. 12½**

RA1	CD28	6r rose & black	.50	.50
RA2	CD29	6r rose & black	.50	.50
RA3	CD30	6r rose & black	.50	.50
		Nos. RA1-RA3 (3)	1.50	1.50

Mother and
Child — PT1

1948   **Litho.**   **Perf. 11**

RA4	PT1	6r yellow green	4.00	3.00
RA5	PT1	1t carmine	4.00	3.00

See Nos. RA7-RA7A, RA9, RA12. For surcharge and overprint see Nos. RA6, RA8.

> **Catalogue values for unused stamps in this section, from this point to the end of the section, are for Never Hinged items.**

Type of 1948 Surcharged with New
Value and Bar in Black

1951
RA6 PT1 1t on 6r carmine   4.00   2.25

Type of 1948

1952-53

RA7	PT1	1t gray	5.00	2.50
RA7A	PT1	1t red orange ('53)	4.00	2.10

No. RA5 Overprinted
in Black

1953
RA8 PT1 1t carmine   11.00   6.50

Type of 1948

1954   **Typo.**
RA9 PT1 6r pale bister   4.50   3.25

Mother and
Child — PT2

Surcharged in Black

1956   **Typo.**   **Perf. 11**
RA10 PT2 1t on 4t lt blue   13.50   11.00

Mother and
Child — PT3

1956   **Litho.**   **Perf. 13**
RA11 PT3 1t blk, pale grn & red   1.40   1.00

See No. RA14. For surcharges see Nos. RA13, RA15-RA16.

Type of 1948 Redrawn
1956   **Perf. 11**

Without Gum
RA12 PT1 1t bluish green   6.50   3.25

Denomination in white oval at left.

No. RA11 Surcharged with New
Value and Bars in Red

1957   **Perf. 13½**
RA13 PT3 6r on 1t   1.50   1.10

Type of 1956
1958   **Unwmk.**   **Perf. 13**
RA14 PT3 1t dk bl, sal & grn   1.00   .75

No. RA14 Surcharged with New
Values and Four Bars

1959, Jan.   **Litho.**   **Perf. 13**

RA15	PT3	20c on 1t	.75	.60
RA16	PT3	40c on 1t	.75	.60

Arms and People
Seeking Help — PT4

1960   **Perf. 13½**
RA17 PT4 20c brown & red   .75   .50

POSTAL TAX DUE STAMPS

Pombal Issue
Common Design Types

1925	**Unwmk.**	**Perf. 12½**
RAJ1 CD28 1t rose & black	.65	.65
RAJ2 CD29 1t rose & black	.65	.65
RAJ3 CD30 1t rose & black	.65	.65
Nos. RAJ1-RAJ3 (3)	1.95	1.95

See note after Portugal No. RAJ4.

PUERTO RICO

ˌpwer-tə-'rē-ˌkō

(Porto Rico)

LOCATION — A large island in the West Indies, east of Hispaniola
GOVT. — Former Spanish Colony
AREA — 3,435 sq. mi.
POP. — 953,243 (1899)
CAPITAL — San Juan

The island was ceded to the United States by the Treaty of 1898.

100 Centimes = 1 Peseta
1000 Milesimas = 100 Centavos = 1 Peso (1881)
100 Cents = 1 Dollar (1898)

Puerto Rican stamps of 1855-73, a part of the Spanish colonial period, were also used in Cuba. They are listed as Cuba Nos. 1-4, 9-14, 18-21, 31-34, 39-41, 47-49, 51-53, 55-57.

Issued under Spanish Dominion

Values for unused stamps are for examples with original gum as defined in the catalogue introduction. Very fine examples of Nos. 1-170, MR1-MR13 will have perforations clear of the design but will be noticeably poorly centered. Extremely fine examples will be well centered; these are scarce and command substantial premiums.

Stamps of Cuba Overprinted in Black

a   b

c   d

1873	**Unwmk.**	**Perf. 14**
1 A10 (a) 25c gray	62.50	2.10
2 A10 (a) 50c brown	140.00	6.25
3 A10 (a) 1p red brown	600.00	21.00
Nos. 1-3 (3)	802.50	29.35

1874		
4 A11 (b) 25c ultra	47.50	10.00
a. Double overprint	275.00	
b. Inverted overprint	275.00	

1875		
5 A12 (b) 25c ultra	37.50	3.25
a. Inverted overprint	95.00	55.00
6 A12 (b) 50c green	45.00	3.50
a. Inverted overprint	210.00	105.00
7 A12 (b) 1p brown	160.00	17.50
Nos. 5-7 (3)	242.50	24.25

1876		
8 A13 (c) 25c pale violet	4.25	1.90
a. 25c bluish gray	5.00	2.75
9 A13 (c) 50c blue	10.50	3.25
10 A13 (c) 1p black	75.00	12.00

11 A13 (d) 25c pale violet	35.00	1.40
12 A13 (d) 1p black	75.00	11.00
Nos. 8-12 (5)	199.75	29.55

Varieties of overprint on Nos. 8-11 include: inverted, double, partly omitted and sideways. Counterfeit overprints exist.

King Alfonso XII — A5

1877		**Typo.**
13 A5 5c yellow brown	13.00	2.75
a. 5c carmine (error)	300.00	
14 A5 10c carmine	45.00	7.50
a. 10c brown (error)	300.00	
15 A5 15c deep green	65.00	15.50
16 A5 25c ultra	25.00	2.60
17 A5 50c bister	45.00	6.50
Nos. 13-17 (5)	193.00	34.85

Imperf. examples of Nos. 13-17 are from proof or trial sheets. Value, set $400.

1878		**Dated "1878"**
18 A5 5c ol bister	22.00	22.00
19 A5 10c red brown	350.00	120.00
20 A5 25c deep green	2.75	1.75
21 A5 50c ultra	9.00	3.50
22 A5 1p bister	18.00	8.50
Nos. 18-22 (5)	401.75	155.75

Imperf. examples of Nos. 18-22 are from proof or trial sheets. Value, set $600.

1879		**Dated "1879"**
23 A5 5c lake	20.00	6.50
24 A5 10c dark brown	20.00	6.50
25 A5 15c dk olive grn	20.00	6.50
26 A5 25c blue	5.00	2.25
27 A5 50c dark green	20.00	6.50
28 A5 1p gray	110.00	30.00
Nos. 23-28 (6)	195.00	58.25

Imperf. examples of Nos. 23-28 are from proof or trial sheets.

King Alfonso XII — A6

1880		
29 A6 ¼c deep green	37.50	25.00
30 A6 ½c brt rose	9.00	3.25
31 A6 1c brown lilac	16.50	13.00
32 A6 2c gray lilac	8.50	5.50
33 A6 3c buff	9.50	6.00
34 A6 4c black	9.50	6.00
35 A6 5c gray green	4.75	2.50
36 A6 10c rose	5.25	3.00
37 A6 15c yellow brn	9.50	4.50
38 A6 25c gray blue	4.75	2.10
39 A6 40c gray	18.00	22.00
40 A6 50c dark brown	40.00	20.00
41 A6 1p olive bister	150.00	26.50
Nos. 29-41 (13)	322.75	139.35

1881		**Dated "1881"**
42 A6 ½m lake	.55	.50
43 A6 1m violet	.55	.30
44 A6 2m pale rose	.75	.50
45 A6 4m brt yellowish green	1.30	.30
46 A6 6m brown lilac	1.30	.70
47 A6 8m ultra	3.25	1.75
48 A6 1c gray green	4.25	1.50
49 A6 2c lake	5.75	4.75
50 A6 3c dark brown	12.50	7.75
51 A6 5c grayish ultra	4.75	.55
52 A6 8c brown	4.75	2.25
53 A6 10c slate	75.00	11.50
54 A6 20c olive bister	90.00	21.00
Nos. 42-54 (13)	204.70	53.35

Alfonso XII — A7

1882-86		
55 A7 ½m rose	.30	.25
a. ½m salmon rose	.55	.35
56 A7 ½m lake ('84)	.90	.40
57 A7 1m pale lake	.90	1.10
58 A7 1m brt rose ('84)	.30	.25
59 A7 2m violet	.30	.25

60 A7 4m brown lilac	.30	.25
61 A7 6m brown	.45	.25
62 A7 8m yellow green	.45	.25
63 A7 1c gray green	.30	.25
64 A7 2c rose	1.15	.25
65 A7 3c yellow	4.25	2.25
a. Cliché of 8c in plate of 3c	120.00	
66 A7 3c yellow brn ('84)	4.25	.90
a. Cliché of 8c in plate of 3c	25.00	
67 A7 5c gray blue	15.00	1.25
68 A7 5c gray bl, 1st retouch ('84)	15.00	3.00
69 A7 5c gray bl, 2nd retouch ('86)	115.00	5.75
70 A7 8c gray brown	3.75	.25
71 A7 10c dark green	3.75	.30
72 A7 20c gray lilac	5.50	.30
a. 20c olive brown (error)	120.00	
73 A7 40c blue	65.00	15.00
74 A7 80c olive bister	70.00	21.00
Nos. 55-74 (20)	306.85	53.50

For differences between the original and the retouched stamps see note on the 1883-86 issue of Cuba.

Alfonso XIII — A8

1890-97		
75 A8 ½m black	.30	.25
76 A8 ½m olive gray ('92)	.25	.25
77 A8 ½m red brn ('94)	.25	.25
78 A8 ½m dull vio ('96)	.25	.25
79 A8 1m emerald	.25	.25
80 A8 1m dk violet ('92)	.25	.25
81 A8 1m ultra ('94)	.25	.25
82 A8 1m dp brown ('96)	.25	.25
83 A8 2m lilac rose	.25	.25
84 A8 2m violet brn ('92)	.25	.25
85 A8 2m red orange ('94)	.25	.25
86 A8 2m yellow grn ('96)	.25	.25
87 A8 4m dk olive grn	11.50	5.75
88 A8 4m ultra ('92)	.25	.25
89 A8 4m yellow brn ('94)	.25	.25
90 A8 4m blue grn ('96)	1.00	.35
91 A8 6m dk brown	50.00	15.00
92 A8 6m pale rose ('92)	.25	.25
93 A8 8m olive bister	35.00	22.00
94 A8 8m yellow grn ('92)	.25	.25
95 A8 1c yellow brown	.30	.25
96 A8 1c blue grn ('91)	.55	.25
97 A8 1c violet brn ('94)	6.00	.45
98 A8 1c claret ('96)	.65	.25
99 A8 2c brownish violet	1.00	.85
100 A8 2c red brown ('92)	.95	.25
101 A8 2c lilac ('94)	2.25	.45
102 A8 2c orange brn ('96)	.65	.25
103 A8 3c slate blue	7.50	1.00
104 A8 3c orange ('92)	.90	.25
105 A8 3c ol gray ('94)	6.00	.45
106 A8 3c blue ('96)	22.00	.35
107 A8 3c claret brn ('97)	.30	.25
108 A8 4c slate bl ('94)	1.50	.45
109 A8 4c gray brn ('96)	.70	.25
110 A8 5c brown violet	13.00	.45
111 A8 5c yellow grn ('94)	5.75	1.10
112 A8 5c blue green ('92)	.90	.25
113 A8 5c blue ('96)	.30	.25
114 A8 6c orange ('94)	.45	.25
115 A8 6c violet ('96)	.35	.25
116 A8 8c ultra	16.00	1.75
117 A8 8c gray brown ('92)	.25	.25
118 A8 8c dull vio ('94)	13.00	5.00
119 A8 8c car rose ('96)	3.00	1.50
120 A8 10c rose	4.75	1.10
a. 10c salmon rose	11.50	2.75
121 A8 10c lilac rose ('92)	1.50	.35
122 A8 20c red orange	5.25	4.75
123 A8 20c lilac ('92)	2.50	.55
124 A8 20c car rose ('94)	1.50	.45
125 A8 20c olive gray ('96)	6.75	1.50
126 A8 40c orange	200.00	57.50
127 A8 40c slate brown ('92)	5.75	4.00
128 A8 40c claret ('94)	7.50	13.50
129 A8 40c salmon ('96)	7.00	1.60
130 A8 80c yellow green	700.00	240.00
131 A8 80c orange ('92)	14.50	11.50
132 A8 80c black ('97)	27.50	23.50

Imperforates of type A8 were not issued and are variously considered to be proofs or printer's waste.

Shades of No. 129 are often mistaken for No. 126. Value for No. 126 is for expertized examples.
For overprints see Nos. 154A-170, MR1-MR13.

Landing of Columbus on Puerto Rico — A9

1893	**Litho.**	**Perf. 12**
133 A9 3c dark green	350.00	100.00

400th anniversary, landing of Columbus on Puerto Rico.
This stamp was valid for postage for only one day and for internal use only.
Counterfeits exist.

Alfonso XIII — A10

1898		**Typo.**
135 A10 1m orange brown	.25	.25
136 A10 2m orange brown	.25	.25
137 A10 3m orange brown	.25	.25
138 A10 4m orange brown	2.40	.75
139 A10 5m orange brown	.25	.25
140 A10 1c black violet	.25	.25
a. Tête bêche pair	1,700.	
141 A10 2c dk blue green	.25	.25
142 A10 3c dk brown	.25	.25
143 A10 4c orange	2.40	1.60
144 A10 5c brt rose	.30	.25
145 A10 6c dark blue	.85	.25
146 A10 8c gray brown	.30	.25
147 A10 10c vermilion	.30	.25
148 A10 15c dull olive grn	.30	.25
149 A10 20c maroon	3.00	.75
150 A10 40c violet	2.25	2.00
151 A10 60c black	2.25	2.00
152 A10 80c red brown	8.50	7.25
153 A10 1p yellow green	18.00	14.50
154 A10 2p slate blue	50.00	22.00
Nos. 135-154 (20)	92.60	53.85

Nos. 135-154 exist imperf. Value, set $1,300.

Stamps of 1890-97 Handstamped in Rose or Violet

1898		
154A A8 ½m dull violet	27.50	11.00
155 A8 1m deep brown	2.00	1.75
156 A8 2m yellow green	.50	.50
157 A8 4m blue green	.50	.50
158 A8 1c claret	6.00	5.00
159 A8 2c orange brown	.75	1.00
160 A8 3c blue	55.00	18.00
161 A8 3c claret brn	4.00	3.25
162 A8 4c gray brn	.80	.80
163 A8 4c slate blue	29.00	16.50
164 A8 5c yellow grn	13.00	8.50
165 A8 5c blue	1.00	.80
166 A8 6c violet	1.00	.55
167 A8 8c car rose (V)	2.00	1.00
a. Rose overprint	26.00	21.00
168 A8 20c olive gray	2.50	1.40
169 A8 40c salmon	4.50	3.25
170 A8 80c black	60.00	27.50
Nos. 154A-170 (17)	210.05	101.30

As usual with handstamps there are many inverted, double and similar varieties. Counterfeits of Nos. 154A-170 abound.

Issued under U.S. Administration
LOCAL ISSUES
Ponce Issue

A11

Handstamped
1898   Unwmk.   *Imperf.*
200 A11 5c violet

No. 200 is a violet handstamp and control mark used on envelopes. Some examples have no control mark. There are three types of circular markings known, and two control marks. Uses on 2c U.S. stamps on cover were strictly as a cancellation, not as local postage. Because genuine usage is extremely difficult to authenticate with certainty, certification by competent authorities is essential.

Coamo Issue

A12

Typeset, setting of 10
1898, Aug.
201 A12 5c black   700.   *1,250.*

See the Scott U.S. Specialized Catalogue for more detailed listings.

The stamps bear the control mark "F. Santiago" in violet. About 500 were issued.

Dangerous forgeries exist.

Regular Issue

United States Nos. 279, 279Bf, 281, 272 and 282C Overprinted in Black at 36 degree angle

1899	**Wmk. 191**		**Perf. 12**	
210 A87	1c yellow green		6.00	1.40
	Never hinged		13.00	
a.	Overprint at 25 degree angle		8.00	2.25
	Never hinged		17.50	
211 A88	2c redsh car, type IV		5.00	1.25
	Never hinged		11.00	
a.	Overprint at 25 degree angle, *Mar. 15*		6.50	2.25
	Never hinged		14.00	
212 A91	5c blue		12.50	2.50
	Never hinged		27.50	
213 A93	8c violet brown		40.00	17.50
	Never hinged		90.00	
a.	Overprint at 25 degree angle		45.00	19.00
	Never hinged		100.00	
c.	"PORTO RIC"		150.00	110.00
214 A94	10c brown, type I		22.50	6.00
	Never hinged		50.00	
	Nos. 210-214 (5)		86.00	28.65

Misspellings of the overprint on Nos. 210-214 (PORTO RICU, PORTU RICO, FORTO RICO) are actually broken letters.

United States Nos. 279 and 279B Overprinted Diagonally in Black

1900				
215 A87	1c yellow green		7.50	1.40
	Never hinged		17.50	
216 A88	2c red, type IV		5.50	2.00
	Never hinged		12.50	
b.	Inverted overprint			*12,500.*

POSTAGE DUE STAMPS

United States Nos. J38, J39 and J42 Overprinted in Black at 36 degree angle

1899	**Wmk. 191**		**Perf. 12**	
J1 D2	1c deep claret		22.50	5.50
	Never hinged		50.00	
a.	Overprint at 25 degree angle		22.50	7.50
	Never hinged		50.00	

J2 D2	2c deep claret		20.00	6.00
	Never hinged		45.00	
a.	Overprint at 25 degree angle		20.00	7.00
	Never hinged		45.00	
J3 D2	10c deep claret		180.00	55.00
	Never hinged		375.00	
a.	Overprint at 25 degree angle		160.00	75.00
	Never hinged		330.00	
	Nos. J1-J3 (3)		222.50	66.50

Stamps of Puerto Rico were replaced by those of the United States.

WAR TAX STAMPS

Stamps of 1890-94 Overprinted or Surcharged by Handstamp

1898	**Unwmk.**		**Perf. 14**	
Purple Overprint or Surcharge				
MR1	A8	1c yellow brn	8.00	5.75
MR2	A8	2c on 2m orange	3.75	3.00
MR3	A8	2c on 5c blue grn	5.00	3.50
MR4	A8	2c dark violet	.95	.95
MR5	A8	2c lilac	.90	.90
MR6	A8	2c red brown	.50	.30
MR7	A8	5c blue green	1.90	1.90
MR8	A8	5c on 5c bl grn	8.75	6.00
Rose Surcharge				
MR9	A8	2c on 2m orange	1.90	1.90
MR10	A8	5c on 1m dk vio	.30	.30
MR11	A8	5c on 1m dl bl	.85	.85
Magenta Surcharge				
MR12	A8	5c on 1m dk vio	.50	.30
MR13	A8	5c on 1m dl bl	3.00	3.00
		Nos. MR1-MR13 (13)	36.30	28.65

Nos. MR2-MR13 were issued as War Tax Stamps (2c on letters or sealed mail; 5c on telegrams) but, during the early days of the American occupation, they were accepted for ordinary postage.

Double, inverted and similar varieties of overprints are numerous in this issue.

Counterfeit overprints exist.

QATAR
'kät-ər

LOCATION — A peninsula in eastern Arabia
GOVT. — Independent state
AREA — 4,575 sq. mi.
POP. — 580,000 (1998 est.)
CAPITAL — Doha

Qatar was a British protected sheikdom until Sept. 1, 1971, when it declared its independence. Stamps of Muscat were used until 1957.

100 Naye Paise = 1 Rupee
100 Dirhams = 1 Riyal (1967)

Catalogue values for all unused stamps in this country are for Never Hinged items.

Watermarks

Wmk. 368 — JEZ Multiple

The market for Qatar stamps is extremely volatile, and dealer stocks are quite limited. All values for this country are tentative.

Great Britain Nos. 317-325, 328, 332-333 and 309-311 Surcharged "QATAR" and New Value in Black

Perf. 14½x14

		1957, Apr. 1	Photo.	Wmk. 308	
1	A129	1np on 5p lt brn		.45	.25
2	A126	3np on ½p red org		.45	.25
3	A126	6np on 1p ultra		.45	.25
4	A126	9np on 1½p grn		.45	.25
5	A126	12np on 2p red brn		.55	2.50
6	A127	15np on 2½p scarlet		.50	.65
7	A127	20np on 3p dk pur		.50	.25
8	A128	25np on 4p ultra		.70	2.00
9	A129	40np on 6p lil rose		.50	.30
10	A130	50np on 9p dp ol grn		.80	2.00
11	A132	75np on 1sh3p dk grn		1.00	4.00
12	A131	1ru on 1sh6p dk bl		14.50	.65

Engr. *Perf. 11x12*

13	A133	2ru on 2sh6p dk brn		5.00	4.00
14	A133	5ru on 5sh crimson		6.75	6.50
15	A133	10ru on 10sh brt ultra		8.50	15.00
		Nos. 1-15 (15)		41.10	38.85

Both typeset and stereotyped overprints were used on Nos. 13-15. The typeset have bars close together and thick, bold letters. The stereotyped have bars wider apart and thinner letters. Value, 13-15 with stereotyped overprints $95.

Great Britain Nos. 334-336 Surcharged "QATAR," New Value and Square of Dots in Black

Perf. 14½x14

		1957, Aug. 1	Photo.	Wmk. 308	
16	A138	15np on 2½p scarlet		.50	.40
17	A138	25np on 4p ultra		.90	.75
18	A138	75np on 1sh3p dk grn		1.75	1.50
		Nos. 16-18 (3)		3.15	2.65

50th anniv. of the Boy Scout movement and the World Scout Jubilee Jamboree, Aug. 1-12.

Great Britain Nos. 353-358, 362 Surcharged "QATAR" and New Value

		1960	Wmk. 322	Perf. 14½x14	
19	A126	3np on ½p red org		.75	1.75
20	A126	6np on 1p ultra		3.00	3.00
21	A126	9np on 1½p grn		.80	1.50
22	A126	12np on 2p red brn		5.00	6.50
23	A127	15np on 2½p scar		2.75	.25

24	A127	20np on 3p dk pur		.60	.25
25	A129	40np on 6p lil rose		3.00	2.00
		Nos. 19-25 (7)		15.90	15.25

Sheik Ahmad bin Ali al Thani — A1

Dhow — A2

Oil Derrick — A3

Designs: 40np, 50np, Peregrine Falcon. 5r, 10r, Mosque.

Perf. 14½

		1961, Sept. 2	Unwmk.	Photo.	
26	A1	5np rose carmine		.40	.35
27	A1	15np brown black		.50	.35
28	A1	20np claret		.50	.35
29	A1	30np deep green		.50	.45
30	A2	40np red		2.75	.45
31	A2	50np sepia		3.50	.60
32	A2	75np ultra		1.75	3.00

Engr. *Perf. 13*

33	A3	1ru rose red		3.75	.50
34	A3	2ru blue		4.00	2.00
35	A3	5ru green		35.00	7.00
36	A3	10ru black		70.00	12.00
		Nos. 26-36 (11)		122.65	27.05

For surcharges see Nos. 108-108J.

Nos. 31-32, 34-36 Overprinted or Surcharged

		1964, Oct. 25	Photo.	Perf. 14½	
37	A2	50np sepia		3.00	2.50
38	A2	75np ultra		4.50	3.75

Engr. *Perf. 13*

39	A3	1ru on 10r black		6.00	2.00
40	A3	2ru blue		14.00	3.75
41	A3	5ru green		30.00	10.00
		Nos. 37-41 (5)		57.50	22.00

18th Olympic Games, Tokyo, Oct. 10-25.
For surcharges see Nos. 110-110D.

Nos. 31-32, 34-36 with Typographed Overprint or Surcharge

		1964, Nov. 22	Photo.	Perf. 14½	
42	A2	50np sepia		3.00	1.25
43	A2	75np ultra		4.50	1.75

Engr. *Perf. 13*

44	A3	1ru on 10ru blk		6.25	3.00
45	A3	2ru blue		13.00	8.00
46	A3	5ru green		32.50	13.00
		Nos. 42-46 (5)		59.25	27.00

Pres. John F. Kennedy (1917-63).
For surcharges see Nos. 111-111D.

Column — A4

Designs: 2np, 1.50r, Isis Temple and Colonnade, Philae. 3np, 1r, Trajan's kiosk, Philae.

Perf. 14½x14

		1965, Jan. 17	Photo.	Unwmk.	
47	A4	1np multicolored		2.25	.60
48	A4	2np multicolored		2.75	.60
49	A4	3np multicolored		2.75	.60
50	A4	1ru multicolored		4.00	1.50
51	A4	1.50ru multicolored		8.50	2.50
52	A4	2ru multicolored		2.75	2.00
		Nos. 47-52 (6)		23.00	7.80

UNESCO world campaign to save historic monuments in Nubia. Nos. 47-52 exist imperf. Value, set $32.50.

Qatar Scout Emblem, Tents and Sheik Ahmad — A5

Scouts Saluting and Sheik Ahmad — A6

Designs: 1np, 4np, Qatar scout emblem.

Perf. 14 (A5), 14½x14 (A6)

		1965, May 22	Photo.	Unwmk.	
53	A5	1np ol grn & dk red brn		.90	.45
54	A5	2np sal & dk vio bl		.90	.45
55	A5	3np dk vio bl & grn		.90	.45
56	A5	4np bl & dk red brn		.90	.45
57	A5	5np dk vio bl & grnsh bl		.90	.45
58	A6	30np multi		8.25	3.50
59	A6	40np multi		12.50	5.00
60	A6	1ru multi		24.00	10.00
		Nos. 53-60 (8)		49.25	20.75

Issued to honor the Qatar Boy Scouts. Nos. 53-60 exist imperf. Value, set $45. Perf. and imperf. souvenir sheets contain one each of Nos. 58-60 with red brown marginal inscription. Size: 108x76mm. Value, perf. $40, imperf. $60.
For surcharges see Nos. 113-113G.

Eiffel Tower, Telstar, ITU Emblem and "Qatar" in Morse Code — A7

Designs: 2np, 1ru, Tokyo Olympic Games emblem and Syncom III. 3np, 40np, Radar tracking station and Relay satellite. 4np, 50np, Post Office Tower, London, and Echo II, Syncom III, Telstar and Relay satellites around globe.

Perf. 13½x14

		1965, Oct. 16	Photo.	Unwmk.	
61	A7	1np dk bl & red brn		1.25	.55
62	A7	2np bl & dk red brn		1.25	.55
63	A7	3np dp yel grn & brt pur		1.25	.55
64	A7	4np org brn & brt bl		1.25	.55
65	A7	5np dl vio & dk ol bis		1.25	.55
66	A7	40np dk car rose & blk		6.50	1.50
67	A7	50np sl grn & bis		10.00	1.75
68	A7	1ru emer & car		13.00	2.75
a.		Souvenir sheet of 2, #67-68		40.00	40.00
		Nos. 61-68 (8)		35.75	8.75

Cent. of the ITU. Nos. 61-68 exist imperf. Value, set $42.50. No. 68a exists imperf. Value $60.
For overprints and surcharges see Nos. 91-98, 114-114G, 117-117G.

Triggerfish — A8

Various Fish, including: 2np, 50np, Clown grunt. 3np, 10ru, Saddleback butterflyfish. 4np, 5ru, Butterflyfish. 15np, 3ru, Paradisefish. 20np, 1ru, Río Grande perch. 75np, Triggerfish.

		1965, Oct. 18		Perf. 14x14½	
69	A8	1np multi & black		.50	.40
70	A8	2np multi & black		.50	.40
71	A8	3np multi & black		.50	.40
72	A8	4np multi & black		.50	.40
73	A8	5np multi & black		.50	.40
74	A8	15np multi & black		1.50	.40
75	A8	20np multi & black		1.75	.40
76	A8	30np multi & black		2.50	.60
77	A8	40np multi & black		3.00	.75
78	A8	50np multi & gold		3.75	1.25
79	A8	75np multi & gold		5.00	1.75
80	A8	1ru multi & gold		6.00	
81	A8	2ru multi & gold		16.00	4.00
82	A8	3ru multi & gold		22.50	6.50
83	A8	4ru multi & gold		32.50	8.00
84	A8	5ru multi & gold		42.50	10.00
85	A8	10ru multi & gold		95.00	14.00
		Nos. 69-85 (17)		234.50	49.65

Nos. 69-85 exist imperf. Values about 25-50 percent higher.
For surcharges see Nos. 115-115P.

Basketball — A9

No. 87, Horse jumping. No. 88, Running. No. 89, Soccer. No. 90, Weight lifting.

| | | 1966, Jan. 10 | Photo. | Perf. 11½ | |
		Granite Paper			
86	A9	1ru gray, blk & dk red		4.25	2.00
87	A9	1ru brn & dk red		4.25	2.00
88	A9	1ru dull rose & blue		4.25	2.00
89	A9	1ru grn & blk		4.25	2.00
90	A9	1ru bl & brn		4.25	2.00
a.		Strip of 5, #86-90		35.00	
		Nos. 86-90 (5)		21.25	10.00

4th Pan Arab Games, Cairo, Sept. 2-11. Nos. 86-90 were printed in sheets of 25 in se-tenant horizontal rows of five. Nos. 86-90 exist imperf. Value, set $25.

Nos. 61-68 Overprinted in Black

		1966, Feb. 9	Photo.	Perf. 13½x14	
91	A7	1np dk bl & red brn		1.50	.40
92	A7	2np bl & dk red brn		1.50	.40
93	A7	3np dp yel grn & brt pur		1.50	.40
94	A7	4np org brn & brt bl		1.50	.40
95	A7	5np dl vio & dk ol bis		1.50	.40

96	A7	40np dk car rose & blk	7.00	.45
97	A7	50np slate grn & bis	7.50	.55
98	A7	1ru emer & car	17.50	1.10
a.		Souvenir sheet of 2, #97-98	55.00	32.50
		Nos. 91-98 (8)	39.50	4.10

Issued to commemorate the rendezvous in space of Gemini 6 and 7, Dec. 15, 1965. Nos. 91-98 exist overprinted in red. Value, set $200. Nos. 96-98 also exist overprinted in blue. Value, set $150. No. 98a exists imperf. Value, $800 each.

For surcharges see Nos. 117-117G.

Sheik Ahmad — A9a

Designs: 3np, 5np, 40np, 80np, 2ru, 10ru, Reverse of coin with Arabic inscription.

Litho. & Embossed Gold or Silver Foil

			1966, Feb. 24	**Imperf.**
99	A9a	1np ol & lil (S)	.75	.40
99A	A9a	3np blk & org (S)	.75	.40
99B	A9a	4np pur & red	.75	.40
99C	A9a	5np brt grn & red brn	.75	.40

Diameter: 55mm

99D	A9a	10np brn & brt vio (S)	2.25	.40
99E	A9a	40np org red & bl (S)	3.50	.75
99F	A9a	70np Prus bl & bl vio	7.25	1.60
99G	A9a	80np car & grn	7.25	1.60

Diameter: 65mm

99H	A9a	1ru red vio & blk (S)	10.50	2.10
99J	A9a	2ru bl grn & cl (S)	18.50	4.00
99K	A9a	5ru red lil & ver	40.00	9.00
99L	A9a	10ru bl vio & brn car	80.00	21.00
		Nos. 99-99L (12)	172.25	42.05

John F. Kennedy, UN Headquarters, NY, and ICY Emblem — A10

Designs (ICY emblem and): #100, UN emblem. #100B, Dag Hammarskjold and UN General Assembly. #100C, Jawaharlal Nehru and dove.

1966, Mar. 8   Perf. 11½
Granite Paper

100	A10	40np brt bl, vio bl & red brn	5.00	2.50
100A	A10	40np brt grn, vio & brn	5.00	2.50
100B	A10	40np red brn, brt bl & blk	5.00	2.50
100C	A10	40np dk vio & brt grn	5.00	2.50
d.		Block of 4, #100-100C	27.50	25.00
		Nos. 100-100C (4)	20.00	10.00

UN Intl. Cooperation Year, 1965. Printed in sheets of 16 + 9 labels in shape of a cross. Nos. 100-100C exist imperf. Value, set $30. No. 100Cd exists imperf.

An imperf. souvenir sheet of 4 contains one each of Nos. 100-100C. Value $55.

For overprints see Nos. 101E-101H. For surcharges see Nos. 117H-117K.

Telstar, Rocket — A10a

Nos. 100-100C Overprinted in Blue, Black or Red

Designs: No. 101, John F. Kennedy, "In Memoriam / John F. Kennedy / 1917-1963." No. 101A, Olive branches, Churchill quote and "In Memoriam / 1874-1965." No. 101B, like #101 portrait facing left, no overprint. No. 101C, Eternal flame, Arabic inscription. No. 101D, Telstar, Rocket.

1966, Mar. 8   Granite Paper

101	A10a	5np bl grn, car & blk (BL)	15.00	8.00
j.		5np Like #101, bl grn, blk & car (BL)	—	—
101A	A10a	5np bl grn, rose & blk	15.00	8.00
k.		5np Like #101A (R)	—	—
101B	A10a	5np bl grn, car & blk	15.00	8.00
l.		5np Like #101B, bl grn, blk & car	—	—
101C	A10a	5np bl grn, rose & blk	15.00	8.00
m.		5np Like #101C, bl grn, blk & car (R)	—	—
101D	A10a	5np bl grn, car & blk	15.00	8.00
n.		5np Like #101D, bl grn, blk & car (R)	—	—
101E	A10	40np on No. 100	5.00	3.00
o.		40np Like #101E (R)	—	—
101F	A10	40np on No. 100A	5.00	3.00
p.		40np Like #101F (R)	—	—
101G	A10	40np on No. 100B	5.00	3.00
q.		40np Like #101G (R)	—	—
101H	A10	40np on No. 100C	5.00	3.00
i.		Sheet of 21, #101-101D, 4 ea #101E-101H+4 labels	—	—
r.		40np Like #101H (R)	—	—
s.		Sheet of 21, #101j-101n, 4 ea #101o-101r+4 labels	—	—
		Nos. 101-101H (9)	95.00	52.00

Nos. 101-101H were made from the sheets of Nos. 100-100C. The 4 outer labels and the center label were surcharged to create Nos. 101-101D. The other 4 labels were overprinted but have no denomination. Kennedy's portrait is in carmine on Nos. 101, 101B and in black on Nos. 101j and 101Bl.

The imperf. souvenir sheet exists with overprint in margin: "IN VICTORY, / MAGNANIMITY. / IN PEACE / GOODWILL / WINSTON CHURCHILL." The margin overprint overlaps onto No. 101A on an upper left quarter of stamp. Nos. 101-101H exist imperf.

For surcharges see Nos. 118-118H.

John F. Kennedy (1917-1963) — A10b

Kennedy and: No. 102c, 10np, No. 102Af, 70np, NYC. No. 102d, 30np, No. 102Ag, 80np, Rocket lifting off at Cape Kennedy. No. 102e, 60np, No. 102Ah, 1ru, Statue of Liberty. No. 102B, Statue of Liberty.

1966, July 18   Perf. 13½

102	A10b	Strip of 3, #c.-e.	4.00	4.00
102A	A10b	Strip of 3, #f.-h.	7.00	7.00

Souvenir Sheet
Imperf

102B	A10b	50np multicolored	42.50	—

Nos. 102-102A exist imperf. Value, set of 2 strips $17.50.

For surcharges see Nos. 119-119B.

1968 Summer Olympics, Mexico City — A10c

Designs: #103c, 1np, #103Af, 70np, #103B, Equestrian. #103d, 4np, #103Ag, 80np, Running. #103e, 5np, #103Ah, 90np, Javelin.

1966, July 20   Perf. 13½

103	A10c	Strip of 3, #c.-e.	4.00	4.00
103A	A10c	Strip of 3, #f.-h.	10.00	15.00

Souvenir Sheet
Imperf

103B	A10c	50np multicolored	42.50	—

Nos. 103-103A exist imperf. Value, set $30. For surcharges see Nos. 120-120B.

A10d

American Astronauts — A10e

Astronaut and space vehicle: No. 104c, 5np, James A. Lovell. d, 10np, Thomas P. Stafford. e, 15np, Alan B. Shepard.

No. 104Af, 20np, John H. Glenn. No. 104Ag, 30np, M. Scott Carpenter. No. 104Ah, 40np, Walter M. Schirra. No. 104Ai, 50np, Virgil I. Grissom. No. 104Aj, 60np, L. Gordon Cooper, Jr.

No. 104B, Stafford, Schirra, Frank Borman, Lovell and diagram of space rendezvous.

1966, Aug. 20   Perf. 12

104	A10d	Strip of 3, #c.-e.	4.00	4.00
104A	A10e	Strip of 5, #f.-j.	12.50	12.50

Souvenir Sheet
Imperf
Size: 115x75mm

104B	A10e	50np multicolored	52.50	—

The name of James A. Lovell is spelled "Lovel" on No. 104c. Nos. 104-104A exist imperf. For surcharges see Nos. 121-121B.

A10h   A10i

1966 World Cup Soccer Championships, London

Designs: 1np-4np, Jules Rimet Cup. 60np, #107H, Hands holding Cup, soccer ball. 70np, #107J, Cup, soccer ball. 80np, #107K, Soccer players, ball. 90np, #107L, Wembley Stadium.

1966, Nov. 27   Photo.   Perf. 13½

107	A10h	1np blue	5.00	—
107A	A10h	2np blue	5.00	—
107B	A10h	3np blue	5.00	—
107C	A10h	4np blue	5.00	—
m.		Block of 4, #107-107C	20.00	
107D	A10i	60np multi	15.00	—
107E	A10i	70np multi	15.00	—
107F	A10i	80np multi	15.00	—
107G	A10i	90np multi	15.00	—
n.		Block of 4, #107D-107G	60.00	

Souvenir Sheets
Imperf

107H	A10i	25np multi	50.00	50.00
107J	A10i	25np multi	50.00	50.00
107K	A10i	25np multi	50.00	50.00
107L	A10i	25np multi	50.00	50.00
		Nos. 107-107L (12)	280.00	200.00

Nos. 107-107C are airmail. Issued in sheets of 36 containing 5 #107m and 4 #107n. Nos. 107-107G exist imperf.

Nos. 26-36 Surcharged with New Currency

			1966, Oct.	**Perf.**
108	A1	5d on 5np rose car	11.00	7.50
108A	A1	15d on 15np brn blk	11.00	7.50
108B	A1	20d on 20np clar	11.00	7.50
108C	A1	30d on 30np dp grn	40.00	15.00
108D	A2	40d on 40np red	75.00	27.50
108E	A2	50d on 50np sepia	85.00	32.50
108F	A2	75d on 75np ultra	125.00	40.00
108G	A3	1r on 1ru rose red	150.00	50.00
108H	A3	2r on 2ru blue	160.00	110.00
108I	A3	5r on 5ru green	200.00	150.00
108J	A3	10r on 10ru black	300.00	225.00
		Nos. 108-108J (11)	1,168.	672.50

Nos. 37-41 Surcharged with New Currency in Gray or Red

			1966 Photo.	**Perf. 14½**
110	A2	50d on 50np #37 (G)	25.00	—
110A	A2	75d on 75np #38	35.00	—

Engr.
Perf. 13

110B	A3	1r on 1ru on 10ru #39	50.00	—
110C	A3	2r on 2ru #40	75.00	—
110D	A3	5r on 5ru #41	50.00	—
		Nos. 110-110D (5)	285.00	

Nos. 42-46 Surcharged with New Currency in Gray or Red

			1966 Photo.	**Perf. 14½**
111	A2	50d on 50np #42 (G)	40.00	—
111A	A2	75d on 75np #43	50.00	—

Engr.
Perf. 13

111B	A3	1r on 1ru on 10ru #44	75.00	—
111C	A3	2r on 2ru #45	100.00	—
111D	A3	5r on 5ru #46	125.00	—
		Nos. 111-111D (5)	390.00	

Nos. 53-60 Surcharged with New Currency

			Perf. 14 (A5), 14½x14 (A6)	
			1966	**Photo.**
113	A5	1d on 1np #53	2.00	—
113A	A5	2d on 2np #54	3.00	—
113B	A5	3d on 3np #55	5.00	—
113C	A5	4d on 4np #56	8.00	—
113D	A5	5d on 4np #57	10.00	—
113E	A6	30d on 30np #58	20.00	—
113F	A6	40d on 40np #59	30.00	—
113G	A6	1r on 1ru #60	45.00	—
		Nos. 113-113G (8)	123.00	

Exist imperf. Perf and imperf souvenir sheets contain one each of #113E-113G surcharged with new currency.

Nos. 61-68 Surcharged with New Currency in Black or Red

			1966	**Perf. 13½x14**
114	A7	1d on 1np #61	2.00	—
114A	A7	2d on 2np #62	3.00	—
114B	A7	3d on 3np #63	4.00	—
114C	A7	4d on 4np #64	6.00	—
114D	A7	5d on 5np #65	8.00	—
114E	A7	40d on 40np #66	20.00	—
114F	A7	50d on 50np #67	30.00	—
114G	A7	1r on 1ru #68	40.00	—
		Nos. 114-114G (8)	113.00	

Exist imperf.

Nos. 69-85 Surcharged with New Currency

1966, Oct.

115	A8	1d on 1np multi & black	3.00	1.75
115A	A8	2d on 2np multi & black	3.00	1.75
115B	A8	3d on 3np multi & black	3.00	1.75
115C	A8	4d on 4np multi & black	3.00	1.75
115D	A8	5d on 5np multi & black	3.00	1.75

115E	A8	15d on 15np multi & black	3.50	1.75
115F	A8	20d on 20np multi & black	4.00	1.75
115G	A8	30d on 30np multi & black	4.00	1.75
115H	A8	40d on 40np multi & black	5.00	4.50
115I	A8	50d on 50np multi & gold	6.50	6.50
115J	A8	75d on 75np multi & gold	7.50	20.00
115K	A8	1r on 1 ru multi & gold	75.00	35.00
115L	A8	2r on 2ru multi & gold	110.00	45.00
115M	A8	3r on 3ru multi & gold	125.00	55.00
115N	A8	4r on 4ru multi & gold	200.00	75.00
115O	A8	5r on 5 ru multi & gold	225.00	100.00
115P	A8	10r on 10ru multi & gold	275.00	150.00
		Nos. 115-115P (17)	1,056.	505.00

Nos. 69-85 exist imperf. Value, set $1,600.

Nos. 91-98 Surcharged with New Currency

1966 Photo. Perf. 13½x14

117	A7	1d on 1np #91	—	—
117A	A7	2d on 2np #92	—	—
117B	A7	3d on 3np #93	—	—
117C	A7	4d on 4np #94	—	—
117D	A7	5d on 5np #95	—	—
117E	A7	40d on 40np #96	—	—
117F	A7	50d on 50np #97	—	—
117G	A7	1r on 1ru #98	—	—
		Set, #117-117G	75.00	—

A sheet similar to No. 98a surcharged in new currency exists. Value, $800.

Nos. 100-100C Surcharged in Black

1966 Perf. 11½

Granite Paper

117H	A10	40d on 40np #100	—	—
117I	A10	40d on 40np #100A	—	—
117J	A10	40d on 40np #100B	—	—
117K	A10	40d on 40np #100C	—	—
l.		Block of 4, #117H-117K	—	—

Printed in sheets of 16 + 9 labels in shape of a cross. Nos. 117H-117K exist imperf.

Nos. 101-101H Surcharged in Black with New Currency Like Nos. 117H-117K

1966 Photo. Perf. 11½

Granite Paper

118	A10a	5d on 5np #101	—	—
j.		5d on 5np #101j	—	—
118A	A10a	5d on 5np #101A	—	—
k.		5d on 5np #101k	—	—
118B	A10a	5d on 5np #101B	—	—
l.		5d on 5np #101l	—	—
118C	A10a	5d on 5np #101C	—	—
m.		5d on 5np #101m	—	—
118D	A10a	5d on 5np #101D	—	—
n.		5d on 5np #101n	—	—
118E	A10	40d on 40np #101E	—	—
o.		40d on 40np #101o	—	—
118F	A10	40d on 40np #101F	5.00	3.00
p.		40d on 40np #101p	—	—
118G	A10	40d on 40np #101G	—	—
q.		40d on 40np #101q	—	—
118H	A10	40d on 40np #101H	—	—
i.		Sheet of 21, #118-118D, 4 ea #118E-118H+4 labels	—	—
r.		40d on 40np #101r	—	—
s.		Sheet of 21, #118j-118n, 4 ea #118o-118r+4 labels	—	—

Exist imperf. Imperf. souvenir sheets mentioned after Nos. 100C, 101H exist surcharged with new currency.

Nos. 102-102B Surcharged with New Currency

1966 Perf. 13½

119		Strip of 3	30.00	—
c.		A10b 10d on 10np #102c	5.00	—
d.		A10b 30d on 30np #102d	7.50	—
e.		A10b 60d on 60np #102e	10.00	—
119A		Strip of 3	50.00	—
f.		A10b 70d on 70np #102f	12.50	—
g.		A10b 80d on 80np #102g	15.00	—
h.		A10b 1r on 1ru #102h	17.50	—

Souvenir Sheet

Imperf

119B		A10b 50d on 50np #102B	80.00	50.00
		Nos. 119-119B (3)	160.00	50.00

Nos. 119-119A exist imperf.

Nos. 103-103B Surcharged with New Currency

1966 Perf. 13½

120		Strip of 3	65.00	—
c.		A10c 1d on 1np #103c	10.00	—
d.		A10c 4d on 4np #103d	15.00	—
e.		A10c 5d on 5np #103e	22.50	—
120A		Strip of 3	100.00	—
f.		A10c 70d on 70np #103f	25.00	—
g.		A10c 80d on 80np #103g	27.50	—
h.		A10c 90d on 90np #103h	32.50	—

Souvenir Sheet

Imperf

120B		A10c 50d on 50np #103	100.00	—
		Nos. 120-120B (3)	265.00	

Nos. 120-120B exist imperf.

Nos. 104-104B Surcharged with New Currency

1966 Perf. 12

121		Strip of 3	30.00	—
c.		A10d 5d on 5np #104c	5.00	—
d.		A10d 10d on 10np #104d	7.00	—
e.		A10d 15d on 15np #104e	8.00	—
121A		Strip of 5	75.00	—
f.		A10e 20d on 20np #104f	9.00	—
g.		A10e 30d on 30np #104g	10.00	—
h.		A10e 40d on 40np #104h	12.00	—
i.		A10e 50d on 50np #104i	15.00	—
j.		A10e 60d on 60np #104j	17.00	—

Souvenir Sheet

Imperf

121B		A10e 50d on 50np #104B	115.00	—
		Nos. 121-121B (3)	220.00	

Nos. 121-121A printed se-tenant with five labels showing Arabic inscription.

Arab Postal Union Emblem — A11

1967, Apr. 15 Photo. Perf. 11x11½

122	A11	70d magenta & sepia	4.50	2.00
122A	A11	80d dull blue & sepia	6.50	2.00

Qatar's joining the Arab Postal Union.

Apollo Project A11a

Designs: 5d, 70d, Two astronauts on Moon. 10d, 80d, Command and lunar modules in lunar orbit. 20d, 1r, Lunar module on Moon. 30d, 1.20r, Lunar module ascending from Moon. 40d, 2r, Saturn 5 rocket.

1967, May 1 Perf. 12½

123	A11a	5d multicolored	.75	.35
123A	A11a	10d multicolored	.75	.35
123B	A11a	20d multicolored	.75	.35
123C	A11a	30d multicolored	1.00	.45
123D	A11a	40d multicolored	1.50	.65
123E	A11a	70d multicolored	3.00	1.50
123F	A11a	80d multicolored	3.25	2.25
123G	A11a	1r multicolored	3.50	2.75
123H	A11a	1.20r multicolored	4.25	3.00
123J	A11a	2r multicolored	6.00	4.00
		Nos. 123-123J (10)	24.75	15.70

#123J exists in an imperf. souv. sheet of one. Value $30.

Traffic Light and Intersection — A12

1967, May 24 Litho. Perf. 13½

124	A12	20d vio & multi	1.00	.40
124A	A12	30d multi	2.00	.65
124B	A12	50d multi	3.00	.80
124C	A12	1r ultra & multi	5.00	2.50
		Nos. 124-124C (4)	11.00	4.35

Issued for Traffic Day.

Boy Scouts and Sheik Ahmad A13

Designs: 1d, First Boy Scout camp, Brownsea Island, 1907, and tents, Idaho, US, 1967. 2d, Lord Baden-Powell. 5d, Boy Scout canoeing. 15d, Swimming. 75d, Mountain climbing. 2r, Boy Scout saluting flag and emblem of 12th World Jamboree. 1d and 2d lack head of Sheik Ahmad.

1967, Sept. 15 Litho. Perf. 11½x11

125	A13	1d multicolored	1.00	.45
125A	A13	2d buff & multi	1.00	.45

Litho. and Engr.

125B	A13	3d rose & multi	1.00	.45
125C	A13	5d lilac & multi	1.25	.45
125D	A13	15d multicolored	2.50	.55
125E	A13	75d green & multi	5.00	1.75
125F	A13	2r sepia & multi	14.00	6.00
		Nos. 125-125F (7)	25.75	10.10

Nos. 125-125A for 60th anniv. of the Boy Scouts, Nos. 125B-125F for 12th Boy Scout World Jamboree, Farragut State Park, Idaho, Aug. 1-9.

Viking Ship (from Bayeux Tapestry) — A14

Famous Ships: 2d, Santa Maria (Columbus). 3d, San Gabriel (Vasco da Gama). 75d, Victoria (Ferdinand Magellan). 1r, Golden Hind (Sir Francis Drake). 2r, Gipsy Moth IV (Sir Francis Chichester).

1967, Nov. 27 Litho. Perf. 13½

126	A14	1d org & multi	.80	.35
126A	A14	2d lt bl, tan & blk	.90	.35
126B	A14	3d lt bl & multi	1.25	.35
126C	A14	75d fawn & multi	5.75	1.75
126D	A14	1r gray, yel grn & red	7.50	2.75
126E	A14	2r multi	14.50	3.75
		Nos. 126-126E (6)	30.70	9.30

Professional Letter Writer — A15

Designs: 2d, Carrier pigeon and man releasing pigeon, vert. 3d, Postrider. 60d, Mail transport by rowboat, vert. 1.25r, Mailman riding camel, jet plane and modern buildings. 2r,

Qatar No. 1, hand holding pen, paper, envelopes and inkwell.

1968, Feb. 14

127	A15	1d multicolored	.75	.40
127A	A15	2d multicolored	.75	.40
127B	A15	3d multicolored	.75	.40
127C	A15	60d multicolored	4.00	1.25
127D	A15	1.25r multicolored	8.00	2.50
127E	A15	2r multicolored	14.00	4.25
		Nos. 127-127E (6)	28.25	9.20

Ten years of Qatar postal service.

Human Rights Flame and Barbed Wire A16

2d, Arab refugee family leaving concentration camp. 3d, Scales of Justice. 60d, Hands opening gates to the sun. 1.25r, Family and sun, vert. 2r, Stylized family groups.

1968, Apr. 10

128	A16	1d gray & multi	.60	.30
129	A16	2d multicolored	.60	.30
130	A16	3d brt grn, org & blk	.75	.30
131	A16	60d org, brn & blk	4.00	2.25
132	A16	1.25r brt grn, blk & yel	5.50	4.75
133	A16	2r multicolored	11.00	6.50
		Nos. 128-133 (6)	22.45	14.40

International Human Rights Year.

Nurse Attending Premature Baby — A17

Designs (WHO Emblem and): 2d, Operating room. 3d, Dentist. 60d, X-ray examination. 1.25r, Medical laboratory. 2r, State Hospital.

1968, June 20

134	A17	1d multi	.75	.40
135	A17	2d multi	.75	.40
136	A17	3d multi	.85	.40
137	A17	60d multi	3.75	.70
138	A17	1.25r multi	8.50	2.25
139	A17	2r multi	14.00	3.25
		Nos. 134-139 (6)	28.60	7.40

20th anniv. of the World Health Organization.

Olympic Rings and Gymnast A18

Designs (Olympic Rings and): 1d, Discobolus and view of Mexico City. 2d, Runner and flaming torch. 60d, Weight lifting and torch. 1.25r, Olympic flame as a mosaic, vert. 2r, Mythological bird.

1968, Aug. 24

140	A18	1d multicolored	.55	.50
141	A18	2d multicolored	.65	.50
142	A18	3d multicolored	1.00	.50
143	A18	60d multicolored	4.50	1.75
144	A18	1.25r multicolored	8.00	2.75
145	A18	2r multicolored	14.00	4.25
		Nos. 140-145 (6)	28.70	10.25

19th Olympic Games, Mexico City, 10/12-27.

A19

Sheik Ahmad bin
Ali al Thani — A21

Dhow
A20

Designs: 40d, Desalination plant. 60d, Loading platform and oil tanker. 70d, Qatar Mosque. 1r, Clock Tower, Market Place, Doha. 1.25r, Doha Fort. 1.50r, Falcon.

1968   Litho.   **Perf. 13½**

146	A19	5d blue & green	.50	.50
147	A19	10d brt bl & red brn	.65	.50
148	A19	20d blk & vermilion	1.00	.50
149	A19	25d brt mag & brt grn	2.25	.50

Lithographed and Engraved
Perf. 13

150	A20	35d grn & brt pink	4.00	.50
151	A20	40d pur, lt bl & org	5.00	.50
152	A20	60d lt bl, brn & lil	6.50	.85
153	A20	70d blk, lt bl & brt grn	7.00	1.10
154	A20	1r vio bl, yel & brt grn	9.00	1.40
155	A20	1.25r ind, brt bl & ocher	10.00	1.75
156	A20	1.50r lt bl, dk grn & rose lil	12.50	2.10

Perf. 11½

157	A21	2r brn, ocher & bl gray	17.50	3.00
158	A21	5r grn, lt grn & pur	30.00	7.25
159	A21	10r ultra, lt bl & sep	60.00	13.50
		Nos. 146-159 (14)	165.90	33.95

UN Headquarters, NY, and
Flags — A22

1d, Flags. 4d, World map and dove. 60d, Classroom. 1.50r, Farmers, wheat and tractor. 2r, Sec. Gen. U Thant and General Assembly Hall.

1968, Oct. 24   Litho.   **Perf. 13½x13**

160	A22	1d multi	.50	.50
161	A22	4d multi	.65	.50
162	A22	5d multi	.75	.50
163	A22	60d multi	4.75	1.50
164	A22	1.50r multi	7.50	2.40
165	A22	2r multi	8.50	4.00
		Nos. 160-165 (6)	22.65	9.40

United Nations Day, Oct. 24, 1968.

Fishing
Vessel
Ross
Rayyan
A23

Progress in Qatar: 4d, Elementary School and children playing. 5d, Doha Intl. Airport. 60d, Cement factory and road building. 1.50r, Power station. 2r, Housing development.

1969, Jan. 13

166	A23	1d brt bl & multi	.40	.40
167	A23	4d green & multi	.40	.40
168	A23	5d dl org & multi	.75	.40
169	A23	60d lt brn & multi	4.00	1.50
170	A23	1.50r brt lil & multi	9.00	2.00
171	A23	2r buff & multi	13.00	3.00
		Nos. 166-171 (6)	27.55	7.70

Armored
Cars
A24

Designs: 2d, Traffic police. 3d, Military helicopter. 60d, Military band. 1.25r, Field gun. 2r, Mounted police.

1969, May 6   Litho.   **Perf. 13½**

172	A24	1d multicolored	.75	.45
173	A24	2d lt blue & multi	.75	.45
174	A24	3d gray & multi	.90	.50
175	A24	60d multicolored	5.00	1.50
176	A24	1.25r multi	8.50	2.25
177	A24	2r blue & multi	15.00	4.00
		Nos. 172-177 (6)	30.90	9.15

Issued to honor the public security forces.

Oil
Tanker
A25

2d, Research laboratory. 3d, Off-shore oil rig, helicopter. 60d, Oil rig, storage tanks. 1.50r, Oil refinery. 2r, Oil tankers, 1890-1968.

1969, July 4

178	A25	1d gray & multi	.65	.40
179	A25	2d olive & multi	.65	.40
180	A25	3d ultra & multi	1.00	.40
181	A25	60d lilac & multi	4.00	1.75
182	A25	1.50r red brn & multi	11.00	3.25
183	A25	2r brown & multi	16.50	4.25
		Nos. 178-183 (6)	33.80	10.45

Qatar oil industry.

Boy
Scouts
Building
Boats
A26

Designs: 2d, Scouts at work and 10 symbolic candles. 3d, Parade. 60d, Gate to camp interior. 1.25r, Main camp gate. 2r, Hoisting Qatar flag, and Sheik Ahmad.

1969, Sept. 18   Litho.   **Perf. 13½x13**

184	A26	1d multicolored	.35	.30
185	A26	2d multicolored	.35	.30
186	A26	3d multicolored	.75	.30
187	A26	60d multicolored	6.00	1.10
a.		Souvenir sheet of 4, #184-187	40.00	20.00
188	A26	1.25r multicolored	9.50	2.25
189	A26	2r multicolored	13.00	3.50
		Nos. 184-189 (6)	29.95	7.75

10th Qatar Boy Scout Jamboree. No. 187a sold for 1r.

Neil A.
Armstrong
A27

Designs: 2d, Col. Edwin E. Aldrin, Jr. 3d, Lt. Col. Michael Collins. 60d, Astronaut walking on moon. 1.25r, Blast-off from moon. 2r, Capsule and raft in Pacific, horiz.

1969, Dec. 6   **Perf. 13x13½, 13½x13**

190	A27	1d blue & multi	.50	.50
191	A27	2d multicolored	.50	.50
192	A27	3d grn & multi	.85	.50
193	A27	60d multicolored	3.50	1.25
194	A27	1.25r pur & multi	7.00	3.00
195	A27	2r multicolored	12.50	4.75
		Nos. 190-195 (6)	24.85	10.50

See note after US No. C76.

UPU
Emblem,
Boeing
Jet
Loading
in Qatar
A28

2d, Transatlantic ocean liner. 3d, Mail truck and mail bags. 60d, Qatar Post Office. 1.25r, UPU Headquarters, Bern. 2r, UPU emblem.

1970, Jan. 31   Litho.   **Perf. 13½x13**

196	A28	1d multi	.50	.50
197	A28	2d multi	.50	.50
198	A28	3d multi	.90	.50
199	A28	60d multi	3.50	1.50
200	A28	1.25r multi	6.50	2.75
201	A28	2r brt yel grn, blk & lt brn	11.00	3.50
		Nos. 196-201 (6)	22.90	9.25

Qatar's admission to the UPU.

Map of Arab League Countries, Flag
and Emblem — A28a

1970, Mar.   **Perf. 13x13½**

202	A28a	35d yellow & multi	2.25	.80
203	A28a	60d blue & multi	3.75	1.25
204	A28a	1.25r multi	7.00	2.25
205	A28a	1.50r vio & multi	9.50	4.00
		Nos. 202-205 (4)	22.50	8.30

25th anniversary of the Arab League.

VC10
Touching
down for
Landing
A29

Designs: 2d, Hawk, and VC10 in flight. 3d, VC10 and airport. 60d, Map showing route Doha to London. 1.25r, VC10 over Gulftown. 2r, Tail of VC10 with emblem of Gulf Aviation.

1970, Apr. 5   **Perf. 13½x13**

206	A29	1d multi	.45	.45
207	A29	2d multi	.75	.45
208	A29	3d multi	.85	.45
209	A29	60d multi	5.50	1.50
210	A29	1.25r multi	10.00	3.00
211	A29	2r multi	17.50	4.50
		Nos. 206-211 (6)	35.05	10.35

Issued to publicize the first flight to London from Doha by Gulf Aviation Company.

Education Year Emblem, Spaceship
Trajectory, Koran Quotation — A30

1970, May 24   **Perf. 13x12½**

212	A30	35d blue & multi	4.00	1.60
213	A30	60d blue & multi	8.00	2.50

Intl. Education Year. Translation of Koran quotation: "And say, O God, give me more knowledge."

Flowers — A31

1970, July 2   **Perf. 13x13½**

214	A31	1d Freesia	.90	.45
215	A31	2d Azalea	.90	.45
216	A31	3d Ixia	1.25	.45
217	A31	60d Amaryllis	5.50	1.60
218	A31	1.25r Cineraria	9.50	3.50
219	A31	2r Rose	12.50	4.50
		Nos. 214-219 (6)	30.55	10.95

For surcharges see Nos. 287-289.

EXPO Emblem
and Fisherman
on Shikoku
Beach — A32

1d, Toyahama fishermen honoring ocean gods. 2d, Map of Japan. 60d, Mt. Fuji. 1.50r, Camphorwood torii. 2r, Tower of Motherhood, EXPO Tower and Mt. Fuji.

Perf. 13½x13, 13x13½
1970, Sept. 29

220	A32	1d multi, horiz.	.45	.45
221	A32	2d multi, horiz.	.60	.45
222	A32	3d multi	.90	.45
223	A32	60d multi	4.25	1.10
a.		Souvenir sheet of 4	55.00	27.50
224	A32	1.50r multi, horiz.	12.00	3.50
225	A32	2r multi	17.50	6.00
		Nos. 220-225 (6)	35.70	11.95

EXPO '70 Intl. Exhib., Osaka, Japan, Mar. 15-Sept. 13. No. 223a contains 4 imperf. stamps similar to Nos. 220-223 with simulated perforations. Sold for 1r.

Globe and UN
Emblem — A33

UN, 25th anniv.: 2d, Cannon used as flower vase. 3d, Birthday cake and dove. 35d, Emblems of UN agencies forming wall. 1.50r, Trumpet and emblems of UN agencies. 2r, Two men, black and white, embracing, and globe.

1970, Dec. 7   Litho.   **Perf. 14x13½**

226	A33	1d blue & multi	.70	.35
227	A33	2d multicolored	.70	.35
228	A33	3d brt pur & multi	1.00	.40
229	A33	35d green & multi	3.25	1.00
230	A33	1.50r multi	9.50	2.25
231	A33	2r brn red & multi	11.50	3.75
		Nos. 226-231 (6)	26.65	8.10

Al
Jahiz
and
Old
World
Map
A34

Designs: 2d, Sultan Saladin and palace. 3d, Al Farabi, sailboat and musical instruments. 35d, Iben al Haithum and palace. 1.50r, Al Motanabbi and camels. 2r, Avicenna and old world map.

1971, Feb. 20   *Perf. 13½x14*
232	A34	1d brt pink & multi	.90	.40
233	A34	2d pale bl & multi	.90	.40
234	A34	3d dl yel & multi	1.50	.40
235	A34	35d lt bl & multi	5.00	.95
236	A34	1.50r yel grn & multi	20.00	3.75
237	A34	2r pale grn & multi	25.00	5.00
		Nos. 232-237 (6)	53.30	10.90

Famous men of Islam.

Cormorant — A35

Designs: 2d, Lizard and prickly pear. 3d, Flamingos and palms. 60d, Oryx and yucca. 1.25r, Gazelle and desert dandelion. 2r, Camel, palm and bronzed chenopod.

1971, Apr. 14   **Litho.**   *Perf. 11x12*
238	A35	1d multi	2.50	.45
239	A35	2d multi	2.50	.45
240	A35	3d multi	2.50	.50
241	A35	60d multi	11.00	2.00
242	A35	1.25r multi	22.50	5.00
243	A35	2r multi	30.00	7.50
		Nos. 238-243 (6)	71.00	15.90

Goonhilly Satellite Tracking Station A36

Designs: 2d, Cable ship, and section of submarine cable. 3d, 35d, London Post Office Tower, and television control room. 4d, Various telephones. 5d, 75d, Video telephone. 3r, Telex machine and telephone.

1971, May 17   *Perf. 13½x13*
244	A36	1d vio bl & multi	.40	.35
245	A36	2d multicolored	.40	.35
246	A36	3d rose red & multi	.40	.35
247	A36	4d magenta & multi	.40	.35
248	A36	5d rose red & multi	.40	.35
249	A36	35d multicolored	3.25	1.00
250	A36	75d magenta & multi	4.75	1.25
251	A36	3r ocher & multi	17.50	3.50
		Nos. 244-251 (8)	27.50	7.50

3rd World Telecommunications Day.

State of Qatar

Arab Postal Union Emblem — A37

1971, Sept. 4   *Perf. 13*
252	A37	35d red & multi	1.25	.40
253	A37	55d blue & multi	2.25	.80
254	A37	75d brown & multi	3.25	1.25
255	A37	1.25r violet & multi	5.25	1.90
		Nos. 252-255 (4)	12.00	4.35

25th anniv. of the Conf. of Sofar, Lebanon, establishing the Arab Postal Union.

Boy Reading — A38

1971, Aug. 10   *Perf. 13x13½*
256	A38	35d brown & multi	2.00	.40
257	A38	55d ultra & multi	4.25	.75
258	A38	75d green & multi	5.75	1.10
		Nos. 256-258 (3)	12.00	2.25

International Literacy Day, Sept. 8.

Men Splitting Racism A39

2d, 3r, People fighting racism. 3d, Soldier helping war victim. 4d, Men of 4 races rebuilding. 5d, Children on swing. 35d, Wave of racism engulfing people. 75d, like 1d.

Perf. 13½x13, 13x13½
1971, Oct. 12   **Litho.**
259	A39	1d multi	.60	.40
260	A39	2d multi	.60	.40
261	A39	3d multi	.60	.40
262	A39	4d multi, vert.	.60	.40
263	A39	5d multi, vert.	.60	.40
264	A39	35d multi	3.50	.90
265	A39	75d multi	7.50	1.75
266	A39	3r multi	17.50	3.75
		Nos. 259-266 (8)	31.50	8.40

Intl. Year Against Racial Discrimination.

UNICEF Emblem, Mother and Child — A40

UNICEF, 25th anniv.: 2d, Child's head, horiz. 3d, 75d, Child with book. 4d, Nurse and child, horiz. 5d, Mother and child, horiz. 35d, Woman and daffodil. 3r, like 1d.

1971, Dec. 6   *Perf. 14x13½, 13½x14*
267	A40	1d blue & multi	.60	.50
268	A40	2d lil rose & multi	.60	.50
269	A40	3d blue & multi	.60	.50
270	A40	4d yellow & multi	.60	.50
271	A40	5d blue & multi	.60	.50
272	A40	35d lil rose & multi	2.50	.65
273	A40	75d yellow & multi	6.75	1.50
274	A40	3r multicolored	16.00	3.50
		Nos. 267-274 (8)	28.25	8.15

Sheik Ahmad, Flags of Arab League and Qatar A41

"International Cooperation" A42

75d, Sheik Ahmad, flags of UN and Qatar. 1.25r, Sheik Ahmad bin Ali al Thani.

1972, Jan. 17   *Perf. 13½x13, 13x13½*
275	A41	35d black & multi	2.00	.50
276	A41	75d black & multi	3.75	1.25
277	A42	1.25r lt brn & blk	5.50	1.50
278	A42	3r multicolored	13.00	3.50
a.		Souvenir sheet	50.00	25.00
		Nos. 275-278 (4)	24.25	6.75

Independence 1971. No. 278a contains one stamp with simulated perforations.

European Roller — A43

Birds: 2d, European kingfisher. 3d, Rock thrush. 4d, Caspian tern. 5d, Hoopoe. 35d, European bee-eater. 75d, European golden oriole. 3r, Peregrine falcon.

1972, Mar. 1   **Litho.**   *Perf. 12x11*
279	A43	1d sepia & multi	2.00	.85
280	A43	2d emerald & multi	2.25	.85
281	A43	3d bister & multi	2.25	.85
282	A43	4d lt blue & multi	2.50	.85
283	A43	5d yellow & multi	2.50	.85
284	A43	35d vio bl & multi	8.00	1.00
285	A43	75d pink & multi	18.00	2.75
286	A43	3r blue & multi	47.50	11.00
		Nos. 279-286 (8)	85.00	19.00

Nos. 217-219 Surcharged

1972, Mar. 7   *Perf. 13x13½*
287	A31	10d on 60d multi	5.00	.80
288	A31	1r on 1.25r multi	20.00	4.00
289	A31	5r on 2r multi	70.00	13.00
		Nos. 287-289 (3)	95.00	17.80

Sheik Khalifa bin Hamad al Thani
A44   A44a

1972   **Size: 23x27mm**   *Perf. 14*
290	A44	5d pur & ultra	.75	.30
291	A44	10d brn & rose red	.75	.60
291A	A44a	10d lt brn & lt red	240.00	100.00
291B	A44a	25d vio & emer	240.00	100.00
292	A44	35d org & dl grn	2.50	.75
293	A44	55d brt grn & lil	4.25	1.75
294	A44	75d vio & lil rose	5.50	2.00

     Size: 26½x32mm
295	A44	1r bister & blk	9.50	2.50
296	A44	5r olive & blk	11.00	3.50
297	A44	5r blue & blk	40.00	10.00
298	A44	10r red & blk	70.00	24.00
		Nos. 290-298 (11)	624.25	
		Nos. 290-291,292-298 (9)	144.25	45.40

Issued: Type A44, Mar. 7.

Book Year Emblem A45

1972, Apr. 23   *Perf. 13½x13*
299	A45	35d lt ultra & blk	2.50	.45
300	A45	55d lt brown & blk	3.75	.75
301	A45	75d green & blk	5.00	1.10
302	A45	1.25r violet & blk	8.25	1.75
		Nos. 299-302 (4)	19.50	4.05

International Book Year 1972.

Olympic Rings, Soccer A46

2d, 3r, Running. 3d, Bicycling. 4d, Gymnastics. 5d, Basketball. 35d, Discus. 75d, Like 1d.

1972, June 12   *Perf. 13½x13*
303	A46	1d green & multi	.80	.40
304	A46	2d yel grn & multi	.80	.40
305	A46	3d blue & multi	.80	.40
306	A46	4d lilac & multi	.80	.40
307	A46	5d blue & multi	.90	.40
308	A46	35d gray & multi	2.25	.60
a.		Souvenir sheet of 6	40.00	25.00
309	A46	75d green & multi	4.00	1.00
310	A46	3r multicolored	15.00	4.00
		Nos. 303-310 (8)	25.35	7.60

20th Olympic Games, Munich, Aug. 26-Sept. 10. No. 308a contains stamps with simulated perforations similar to Nos. 303-308.

Installation of Underwater Pipe Line — A47

1d, Drilling for oil, vert. 5d, Drilling platform. 35d, Ship searching for oil.

1972, Aug. 8   **Litho.**   *Perf. 13x13½*
311	A47	1d multicolored	.65	.40
312	A47	4d shown	.65	.40
313	A47	5d multicolored	.65	.40
314	A47	35d multicolored	2.75	.55
315	A47	75d like 1d, vert.	5.75	1.25
316	A47	3r like 5d	27.50	6.00
		Nos. 311-316 (6)	37.95	9.00

Oil from the sea.

Government Palace — A48

Designs: 35d, Clasped hands, Qatar flag. 75d, Clasped hands, UN flag. 1.25r, Sheik Khalifa bin Hamad al-Thani, vert.

1972, Sept. 3   *Perf. 13½x13, 13x13½*
317	A48	10d yel & multi	1.50	.50
318	A48	35d blk & multi	4.00	.65
319	A48	75d blk & multi	7.50	1.25
320	A48	1.25r gold & multi	14.00	2.00
a.		Souvenir sheet of 1	42.50	22.50
		Nos. 317-320 (4)	27.00	4.40

Independence Day, 1st anniv. of independence.
No. 320a contains one stamp with simulated perforations similar to No. 320.

Qatar Flag, Council Emblem and Flag A49

1972, Dec. 4   **Litho.**   *Perf. 14x13½*
321	A49	25d blue & multi	4.00	1.00
322	A49	30d vio bl & multi	6.00	1.50

Civil Aviation Council of Arab States, 10th session.

Tracking Station, Satellite, Telephone, ITU and UN Emblems A50

Designs (Agency and UN Emblems): 2d, Surveyor, artist; UNESCO. 3d, Tractor, helicopter, fish, grain and fruit; FAO. 4d, Reading children, teacher; UNICEF. 5d, Weather satellite and map; WMO. 25d, Workers and crane; ILO. 55d, Health clinic; WHO. 1r, Mail plane and post office; UPU.

1972, Oct. 24   Perf. 13½x14

323	A50	1d multicolored	.60	.35
324	A50	2d multicolored	.60	.35
325	A50	3d multicolored	.60	.35
326	A50	4d multicolored	.60	.35
327	A50	5d multicolored	.75	.50
328	A50	25d multicolored	5.75	1.00
329	A50	55d multicolored	10.00	3.00
330	A50	1r multicolored	20.00	6.00
		Nos. 323-330 (8)	38.90	11.90

United Nations Day, Oct. 24, 1972. Each stamp dedicated to a different UN agency.

Road Building — A51

3d, Housing development. 4d, Operating room. 5d, Telephone operators. 15d, School, classroom. 20d, Television studio. 35d, Sheik Khalifa. 55d, New Gulf Hotel. 1r, Fertilizer plant. 1.35r, Flour mill.

1973, Feb. 22   Litho.   Perf. 13x13½

331	A51	2d multicolored	.80	.40
332	A51	3d multicolored	.80	.40
333	A51	4d multicolored	.80	.40
334	A51	5d multicolored	.80	.40
335	A51	15d multicolored	1.75	.40
336	A51	20d multicolored	2.00	.40
337	A51	35d multicolored	3.00	.50
338	A51	55d multicolored	3.75	.80
339	A51	1r multicolored	5.25	1.60
340	A51	1.35r multicolored	8.25	2.25
		Nos. 331-340 (10)	27.20	7.55

1st anniv. of the accession of Sheik Khalifa bin Hamad al Thani as Emir of Qatar.

Aerial Pest Control — A52

WHO, 25th anniv.: 3d, Medicines. 4d, Poliomyelitis prevention. 5d, Malaria control. 55d, Mental health. 1r, Pollution control.

1973, May 14   Litho.   Perf. 14

341	A52	2d blue & multi	.85	.50
342	A52	3d blue & multi	.85	.50
343	A52	4d blue & multi	.85	.50
344	A52	5d blue & multi	1.75	.65
345	A52	55d blue & multi	11.00	2.00
346	A52	1r blue & multi	25.00	3.75
		Nos. 341-346 (6)	40.30	7.90

Weather Ship A53

Designs (WMO Emblem and): 3d, Launching of radiosonde balloon. 4d, Plane and meteorological data checking. 5d, Cup anemometers and meteorological station. 10d, Weather plane in flight. 1r, Nimbus I weather satellite. 1.55r, Launching of rocket carrying weather satellite.

1973, July   Litho.   Perf. 14x13

347	A53	2d multicolored	.60	.40
348	A53	3d multicolored	.60	.40
349	A53	4d multicolored	.60	.40
350	A53	5d multicolored	.60	.40
351	A53	10d multicolored	2.00	.60
352	A53	1r multicolored	13.50	1.75
353	A53	1.55r multicolored	20.00	3.00
		Nos. 347-353 (7)	37.90	6.95

Cent. of intl. meteorological cooperation.

Sheik Khalifa — A54

Clock Tower, Doha — A55

1973-74   Litho.   Perf. 14
Size: 18x27mm

354	A54	5d green & multi	1.25	.40
355	A54	10d lt bl & multi	1.75	.40
356	A54	20d ver & multi	2.25	.40
357	A54	25d org & multi	3.00	.40
358	A54	35d purple & multi	4.00	.75
359	A54	55d dk gray & multi	6.00	1.00

Engr.
Perf. 13½

360	A55	75d lil, bl & yel grn	9.00	2.00

Photo.
Perf. 13
Size: 27x32mm

360A	A54	1r multicolored	22.50	5.00
360B	A54	5r multicolored	75.00	24.00
360C	A54	10r multicolored	160.00	55.00
		Nos. 354-360C (10)	284.75	89.35

Issue dates: 20d, 75d, July 3, 1973; 1r-10r, July 1974; others, Jan. 27, 1973.

Flag of Qatar, Handclasp, Sheik Khalifa — A56

Flag, Sheik and: 35d, Harvest. 55d, Government Building. 1.35r, Market and Clock Tower, Doha. 1.55r, Illuminated fountain.

1973, Oct. 4   Litho.   Perf. 13

361	A56	15d red & multi	.45	.30
362	A56	35d buff & multi	.80	.30
363	A56	55d multi	2.00	.50
364	A56	1.35r vio & multi	4.50	1.25
365	A56	1.55r multi	5.00	1.60
		Nos. 361-365 (5)	12.75	3.95

2nd anniversary of independence.

Planting Tree, Qatar and UN Flags, UNESCO Emblem — A57

Qatar and UN Flags and: 4d, UN Headquarters and flags. 5d, Pipe laying, cement mixer, helicopter and ILO emblem. 35d, Nurse, patient and UNICEF emblem. 1.35r, Telecommunications and ITU emblem. 3r, Cattle, wheat disease analysis and FAO emblem.

1973, Oct. 24

366	A57	2d multi	.50	.50
367	A57	4d multi	.50	.50
368	A57	5d multi	.60	.50
369	A57	35d multi	1.60	.50
370	A57	1.35r multi	6.50	1.75
371	A57	3r multi	15.00	5.50
		Nos. 366-371 (6)	24.70	9.25

United Nations Day.

Prison Gates Opening — A58

4d, Marchers with flags. 5d, Scales of Justice. 35d, Teacher and pupils. 1.35r, UN General Assembly. 3r, Human Rights flame, vert.

1973, Dec.   Litho.   Perf. 13x13½

372	A58	2d yellow & multi	.45	.40
373	A58	4d pale lil & multi	.45	.40
374	A58	5d rose & multi	.70	.40
375	A58	35d ocher & multi	2.00	.75
376	A58	1.35r lt bl & multi	7.00	3.00
377	A58	3r citron & multi	13.00	4.25
		Nos. 372-377 (6)	23.60	9.20

25th anniversary of the Universal Declaration of Human Rights.

Highway Overpass — A59

1974, Feb. 22   Perf. 14x13½

378	A59	2d shown	.70	.35
379	A59	3d Symbol of learning	.70	.35
380	A59	5d Oil field	.70	.35
381	A59	35d Gulf Hotel, Doha	2.25	.50
382	A59	1.55r Radar station	10.00	3.25
383	A59	2.25r Sheik Khalifa	13.00	4.00
		Nos. 378-383 (6)	27.35	8.80

Accession of Sheik Khalifa as Emir, 2nd, anniv.

Mail Truck, Camel Caravan and UPU Emblem — A60

UPU cent.: 3d, Old and new trains, Arab Postal Union emblem. 10d, Old and new ships and Qatar coat of arms. 35d, Old and new planes. 75d, Mail sorting by hand and computer, and Arab Postal Union emblem. 1.25r, Old and new post offices, and Qatar coat of arms.

1974, May 22   Litho.   Perf. 13½

384	A60	2d brt yel & multi	.85	.45
385	A60	3d lt bl & multi	.85	.45
386	A60	10d dp org & multi	.85	.45
387	A60	35d slate & multi	3.25	.65
388	A60	75d yellow & multi	7.75	1.00
389	A60	1.25r lt bl & multi	11.00	2.25
		Nos. 384-389 (6)	24.55	5.50

Doha Hospital — A61

1974, July 13   Litho.   Perf. 13½

390	A61	5d shown	.55	.40
391	A61	10d WPY emblem and people	.55	.40
392	A61	15d WPY emblem	.75	.40
393	A61	35d World map	1.75	.75
394	A61	1.75r Clock and infants	6.75	3.00
395	A61	2.25r Family	9.75	4.00
		Nos. 390-395 (6)	20.10	8.95

World Population Year 1974.

Television Station — A62

1974, Sept. 2   Perf. 13½x13

399	A62	5d shown	.45	.45
400	A62	10d Palace of Doha	.45	.45
401	A62	15d Teachers' College	.45	.45
402	A62	75d Clock Tower and Mosque	5.25	1.10
403	A62	1.55r Traffic circle, Doha	8.50	1.75
404	A62	2.25r Sheik Khalifa	13.50	2.75
		Nos. 399-404 (6)	28.60	6.95

3rd anniversary of independence.

Operating Room and WHO Emblem — A63

UN Day: 10d, Satellite earth station and ITU emblem. 20d, Tractor, UN and FAO emblems. 25d, School children, UN and UNESCO emblems. 1.75r, Open air court, UN Headquarters, emblems. 2r, UPU and UN emblems.

1974, Oct. 24   Litho.   Perf. 13x13½

405	A63	5d multi	.60	.45
406	A63	10d multi	1.10	.45
407	A63	20d multi	2.25	.45
408	A63	25d multi	3.50	.55
409	A63	1.75r multi	13.50	2.00
410	A63	2r multi	16.00	2.75
		Nos. 405-410 (6)	36.95	6.65

VC-10, Gulf Aviation Airliner — A64

Arab League and Qatar Flags, Civil Aviation Emblem — A65

Design: 25d, Doha Airport.

1974, Dec. 1   Litho.   Perf. 13½

411	A64	20d multi	3.00	.55
412	A64	25d yel & dk bl	4.50	.70
413	A65	30d multi	5.75	.85
414	A65	50d multi	8.50	1.00
		Nos. 411-414 (4)	21.75	3.10

Arab Civil Aviation Day.

Caspian Terns, Hoopoes and Shara'o Island — A66

Dhow by Moonlight — A67

5d, Clock Tower, Doha, vert. 15d, Zubara Fort. 35d, Gulf Hotel & sailboats. 75d, Arabian oryx. 1.25r, Khor Al-Udein. 1.75r, Ruins, Wakrah.

1974, Dec. 21		Litho.	Perf. 13½	
415	A66	5d multi	1.25	.40
416	A66	10d multi	1.60	.40
417	A66	15d multi	2.00	.40
418	A66	35d multi	3.25	.40
419	A67	55d multi	3.75	.70
420	A67	75d multi	5.75	1.00
421	A67	1.25r multi	9.50	1.60
422	A66	1.75r multi	12.50	3.50
	Nos. 415-422 (8)		39.60	6.90

Traffic Circle, Doha A68

Sheik Khalifa — A69

35d, Pipe line from offshore platform. 55d, Laying underwater pipe line. 1r, Refinery.

1975, Feb. 22		Litho.	Perf. 13½	
423	A68	10d multi	.40	.40
424	A68	35d multi	2.10	.85
425	A68	55d multi	3.25	1.10
426	A68	1r multi	6.25	1.75
427	A69	1.35r sil & multi	7.25	2.50
428	A69	1.55r gold & multi	9.50	3.50
	Nos. 423-428 (6)		28.75	10.10

Accession of Sheik Khalifa, 3rd anniv.

Qatar Flag and Arab Labor Charter Emblem — A70

1975, May 28		Litho.	Perf. 13	
429	A70	10d bl, red brn & blk	.55	.55
430	A70	35d multicolored	4.25	1.00
431	A70	1r green & multi	11.00	2.75
	Nos. 429-431 (3)		15.80	4.30

Arab Labor Charter and Constitution, 10th anniversary.

Flintlock Pistol with Ornamental Grip — A71

Designs: 3d, Ornamental mosaic. 35d, View of museum. 75d, Arch and museum, vert. 1.25r, Flint arrowheads and tool. 3r, Gold necklace, vert.

1975, June 23			Perf. 13	
432	A71	2d multi	.50	.40
433	A71	3d ver blk & gold	1.00	.40
434	A71	35d bis & multi	2.50	.60
435	A71	75d ver & multi	5.75	1.00
436	A71	1.25r vio & multi	9.00	1.75
437	A71	3r fawn & multi	20.00	3.25
	Nos. 432-437 (6)		38.75	7.30

Opening of Qatar National Museum.

Traffic Signs, Policeman, Doha — A72

Designs: 15d, 55d, Cars, arrows, traffic lights, Doha Clock Tower. 35d, like 5d.

1975, June 24				
438	A72	5d lt green & multi	.50	.50
439	A72	15d lt blue & multi	3.25	.50
440	A72	35d lemon & multi	7.75	1.10
441	A72	55d lt violet & multi	13.00	1.90
	Nos. 438-441 (4)		24.50	4.00

Traffic Week.

Constitution, Arabic Text — A73

5d, Government buildings, horiz. 15d, Museum & Clock Tower, horiz. 55d, 1.25r, Sheik Khalifa & Qatar flag. 75d, Constitution, English text.

1975, Sept. 2				
442	A73	5d multi	.40	.40
443	A73	15d multi	2.10	.95
444	A73	35d multi	2.50	.65
445	A73	55d multi	4.25	.95
446	A73	75d multi	5.75	1.25
447	A73	1.25r multi	9.00	2.10
	Nos. 442-447 (6)		24.00	6.30

4th anniversary of independence.

Satellite over Globe, ITU Emblem — A74

UN, 30th anniv.: 15d, UN Headquarters, NY and UN emblem. 35d, UPU emblem over Eastern Arabia, UN emblem. 55d, Nurses and infant, WHO emblem. 1.25r, Road building equipment, ILO emblem. 2r, Students, UNESCO emblem.

1975, Oct. 25		Litho.	Perf. 13x13½	
448	A74	5d multi	.55	.55
449	A74	15d multi	1.40	.50
450	A74	35d multi	2.10	.50
451	A74	1r multi	6.25	1.40
452	A74	1.25r multi	7.00	1.60
453	A74	2r multi	12.50	2.75
	Nos. 448-453 (6)		29.80	7.35

Fertilizer Plant — A75

Designs: 10d, Flour mill, vert. 35d, Natural gas plant. 75d, Oil refinery. 1.25r, Cement works. 1.55r, Steel mill.

1975, Dec. 6				
454	A75	5d salmon & multi	.50	.50
455	A75	10d yellow & multi	1.25	.50
456	A75	35d multi	2.50	.60
457	A75	75d multi	5.00	1.50
458	A75	1.25r mag & multi	10.00	2.50
459	A75	1.55r multi	15.00	3.50
	Nos. 454-459 (6)		34.25	9.10

Modern Building, Doha — A76

10d, 35d, 1.55r, Various modern buildings. 55d, 75d, Sheik Khalifa & Qatar flag, diff.

1976, Feb. 22		Litho.	Perf. 13	
460	A76	5d multi	.55	.55
461	A76	10d multi	.55	.55
462	A76	35d multi	2.25	.55
463	A76	55d multi	4.25	.85
464	A76	75d multi	5.50	1.25
465	A76	1.55r multi	11.00	2.50
	Nos. 460-465 (6)		24.10	6.25

Accession of Sheik Khalifa, 4th anniv.

Satellite Earth Station — A77

Designs: 55d, 1r, Satellite. 75d, Like 35d.

1976, Mar. 1				
466	A77	35d multicolored	2.50	.40
467	A77	55d dp bis & multi	3.25	.50
468	A77	75d vermilion & multi	4.75	.70
469	A77	1r violet & multi	7.25	.95
	Nos. 466-469 (4)		17.75	2.55

Inauguration of satellite earth station in Qatar.

Telephones, 1876 and 1976 — A78

1976, Mar. 10				
470	A78	1r rose & multi	4.75	2.00
471	A78	1.35r lt bl & multi	6.50	2.75

Centenary of first telephone call by Alexander Graham Bell, Mar. 10, 1876.

Arabian Soccer League Emblem — A79

Designs: 10d, 1.25r, Stadium, Doha. 35d, Like 5d. 55d, Players. 75d, One player.

1976, Mar. 25		Litho.	Perf. 13½x13	
472	A79	5d lil & multi	.45	.45
473	A79	10d pink & multi	1.25	.45
474	A79	35d bl grn & multi	2.00	.60
475	A79	55d multi	4.00	.95
476	A79	75d multi	6.75	1.40
477	A79	1.25r multi	8.75	2.40
	Nos. 472-477 (6)		23.20	6.25

4th Arabian Gulf Soccer Cup Tournament, Doha, Mar. 22-Apr.

Dhow A80

Designs: Various dhows.

1976, Apr. 19			Perf. 13½x14	
478	A80	10d blue & multi	2.50	.35
479	A80	35d blue & multi	3.00	.40
480	A80	80d blue & multi	9.00	1.25
481	A80	1.25r blue & multi	13.00	2.00
482	A80	1.50r blue & multi	15.00	2.50
483	A80	2r blue & multi	22.50	4.00
	Nos. 478-483 (6)		65.00	10.50

Soccer — A81

10d, Yachting. 35d, Steeplechase. 80d, Boxing. 1.25r, Weight lifting. 1.50r, Basketball.

1976, May 15		Litho.	Perf. 14x13½	
484	A81	5d multicolored	.85	.40
485	A81	10d blue & multi	.85	.40
486	A81	35d orange & multi	.85	.40
487	A81	80d bister & multi	5.50	.85
488	A81	1.25r lilac & multi	9.50	1.60
489	A81	1.50r rose & multi	12.50	2.10
	Nos. 484-489 (6)		30.05	5.75

21st Olympic Games, Montreal, Canada, July 17-Aug. 1.

Village and Emblems — A82

35d, Emblems. 80d, Village. 1.25r, Sheik Khalifa.

1976, May 31			Perf. 13½x14	
490	A82	10d orange & multi	.65	.30
491	A82	35d yellow & multi	1.75	.30
492	A82	80d citron & multi	4.25	.70
493	A82	1.25r dp blue & multi	7.25	2.00
	Nos. 490-493 (4)		13.90	3.30

Habitat, UN Conf. on Human Settlements, Vancouver, Canada, May 31-June 11.

Snowy Plover A83

Birds: 10d, Great cormorant. 35d, Osprey. 80d, Flamingo. 1.25r, Rock thrush. 2r, Saker falcon. 35d, 80d, 1.25r, 2r, vertical.

Perf. 13½x14, 14x13½

1976, July 19 Litho.
494	A83	5d multi	1.25	.40
495	A83	10d multi	3.00	.55
496	A83	35d multi	8.25	.90
497	A83	80d multi	17.50	2.00
498	A83	1.25r multi	27.50	3.00
499	A83	2r multi	30.00	4.00
		Nos. 494-499 (6)	87.50	10.85

Sheik Khalifa and Qatar Flag — A84

Government Building — A85

Designs: 10d, like 5d. 80d, Government building. 1.25r, Offshore oil platform. 1.50r, UN emblem and Qatar coat of arms.

1976, Sept. 2 Perf. 14x13½, 13½x14
500	A84	5d gold & multi	.50	.50
501	A84	10d silver & multi	.50	.50
502	A85	40d multicolored	1.90	.60
503	A85	80d multicolored	3.50	1.25
504	A85	1.25r multicolored	5.50	1.25
505	A85	1.50r multicolored	7.50	1.75
		Nos. 500-505 (6)	19.40	6.10

5th anniversary of independence.

Qatar Flag and UN Emblem — A86

1976, Oct. 24 Litho. Perf. 13½x14
506	A86	2r multi	7.00	1.75
507	A86	3r multi	9.50	2.50

United Nations Day 1976.

Sheik Khalifa — A87

1977, Feb. 22 Litho. Perf. 14x13½
508	A87	20d silver & multi	1.50	.50
509	A87	1.80r gold & multi	11.00	2.50

Accession of Sheik Khalifa, 5th anniv.

Sheik Khalifa — A88

1977, Mar. 1 Litho. Perf. 14x14½
Size: 22x27mm
510	A88	5d multicolored	.50	.30
511	A88	10d aqua & multi	.75	.30
512	A88	35d orange & multi	1.25	.35
513	A88	80d multicolored	2.50	.50

Perf. 13½
Size: 25x30mm
514	A88	1r vio bl & multi	5.00	.75
515	A88	5r yellow & multi	16.00	3.25
516	A88	10r multicolored	37.50	6.75
		Nos. 510-516 (7)	63.50	12.20

Letter, APU Emblem, Flag — A89

1977, Apr. 12 Perf. 14x13½
517	A89	35d blue & multi	1.75	.50
518	A89	1.35r blue & multi	5.25	2.00

Arab Postal Union, 25th anniversary.

Waves and Sheik Khalifa A90

1977, May 17 Litho. Perf. 13½x14
519	A90	35d multi	1.00	.45
520	A90	1.80r multi	6.25	2.50

World Telecommunications Day.

Sheik Khalifa — A90a

Perf. 13½x13
1977, June 29 Litho. Wmk. 368
520A	A90a	5d multi	1.00	1.00
520B	A90a	10d multi	2.00	2.00
520C	A90a	35d multi	3.00	3.00
520D	A90a	80d multi	10.00	10.00
e.		Bklt. pane, 4 5d, 3 10d, 2 35d, 80d	50.00	25.00
		Nos. 520A-520D (4)	16.00	16.00

Issued in booklets only.

Parliament, Clock Tower, Minaret — A91

Designs: No. 522, Main business district, Doha. No. 523, Highway crossings, Doha.

1977, Sept. 1 Litho. Perf. 13½x13½
521	A91	80d multicolored	4.25	1.50
522	A91	80d multicolored	4.25	1.50
523	A91	80d multicolored	4.25	1.50
		Nos. 521-523 (3)	12.75	4.50

6th anniversary of independence.

UN Emblem, Flag — A92

1977, Oct. 24 Litho. Perf. 13½x14
524	A92	20d green & multi	1.50	.55
525	A92	1r blue & multi	6.00	2.25

United Nations Day.

Surgery — A93

20d, Steel mill. 1r, Classroom. 5r, Sheik Khalifa.

1978, Feb. 22 Litho. Perf. 13½x14
526	A93	20d multicolored	1.40	.40
527	A93	80d multicolored	3.00	.65
528	A93	1r multicolored	5.00	1.00
529	A93	5r multicolored	16.00	3.00
		Nos. 526-529 (4)	25.40	5.05

Accession of Sheik Khalifa, 6th anniv.

Oil Refinery — A94

80d, Office buildings, Doha. 1.35r, Traffic Circle, Doha. 1.80r, Sheik Khalifa and flag.

1978, Aug. 31 Litho. Perf. 13½x14
530	A94	35d multi	1.00	.40
531	A94	80d multi	2.50	.95
532	A94	1.35r multi	4.00	1.40
533	A94	1.80r multi	5.25	1.90
		Nos. 530-533 (4)	12.75	4.65

7th anniversary of independence.

Man Learning to Read — A95

1978, Sept. 8 Litho. Perf. 13½x14
534	A95	35d multicolored	1.75	.50
535	A95	80d multicolored	5.00	1.60

International Literacy Day.

Flag and UN Emblem — A96

1978, Oct. 14 Perf. 13x13½
536	A96	35d multi	1.50	.50
537	A96	80d multi	4.50	1.25

United Nations Day.

Human Rights Emblem — A97

Designs: 80d, like 35d. 1.25r, 1.80r, Scales and Human Rights emblem.

1978, Dec. 10 Litho. Perf. 14x13½
538	A97	35d multi	1.00	.35
539	A97	80d multi	2.50	1.00
540	A97	1.25r multi	3.75	1.50
541	A97	1.80r multi	5.25	2.25
		Nos. 538-541 (4)	12.50	5.10

30th anniversary of Universal Declaration of Human Rights.

IYC Emblem — A98

Wmk. JEZ Multiple (368)
1979, Jan. 1 Litho. Perf. 13½x13
542	A98	35d multi	1.25	1.00
543	A98	1.80r multi	4.25	4.00

International Year of the Child.

A99

1979, Jan. 15 Unwmk. Perf. 14
544	A99	5d multi	.30	.30
545	A99	10d multi	.35	.30
546	A99	20d multi	.65	.30
547	A99	25d multi	1.00	.30
548	A99	35d multi	1.50	.55
549	A99	60d multi	1.90	.65
550	A99	80d multi	2.50	.70

Size: 27x32mm
551	A99	1r multi	2.75	1.00
552	A99	1.25r multi	3.00	1.10
553	A99	1.35r multi	3.25	1.50
554	A99	1.80r multi	5.00	1.75
555	A99	5r multi	12.00	3.25
556	A99	10r multi	22.50	7.00
		Nos. 544-556 (13)	56.70	18.70

Sheik Khalifa — A100

1979, Feb. 22 Wmk. 368
557	A100	35d multi	.80	.50
558	A100	80d multi	1.75	1.10
559	A100	1r multi	2.75	1.50
560	A100	1.25r multi	3.25	1.90
		Nos. 557-560 (4)	8.55	5.00

7th anniv. of accession of Sheik Khalifa.

Cables and People — A101

1979, May 17   Litho.   Perf. 14x13½
561 A101   2r multi   4.75 2.00
562 A101   2.80r multi   5.75 3.00

World Telecommunications Day.

Children Holding Globe, UNESCO Emblem — A102

Perf. 13x13½
1979, July 15   Litho.   Unwmk.
563 A102   35d multicolored   1.00 .45
564 A102   80d multicolored   4.25 1.10

International Bureau of Education, Geneva, 50th anniversary.

Rolling Mill — A103

Wmk. 368
1979, Sept. 2   Litho.   Perf. 13½
565 A103   5d shown   .75 .40
566 A103   10d Doha, aerial view   1.10 .40
567 A103   1.25r Qatar flag   4.50 1.25
568 A103   2r Sheik Khalifa   6.25 1.75
    Nos. 565-568 (4)   12.60 3.80

Independence, 8th anniversary.

UN Day — A104

1979, Oct. 24   Litho.   Perf. 13½x13
569 A104   1.25r multi   4.25 1.25
570 A104   2r multi   7.50 1.75

Conference Emblem — A105

1979, Nov. 24   Perf. 13x13½
571 A105   35d multi   3.25 1.00
572 A105   1.80r multi   10.00 2.25

Hegira (Pilgrimage Year); 3rd World Conference on Prophets.

Sheik Khalifa, 8th Anniversary of Accession — A106

1980, Feb. 22   Litho.   Perf. 13x13½
573 A106   20d multi   1.25 .30
574 A106   60d multi   3.25 .65
575 A106   1.25r multi   5.00 1.25
576 A106   2r multi   11.00 2.10
    Nos. 573-576 (4)   20.50 4.30

Map of Arab Countries — A107

1980, Mar. 1   Litho.   Perf. 13½x14
577 A107   2.35r multi   8.25 1.75
578 A107   2.80r multi   12.00 2.10

6th Congress of Arab Town Organization, Doha, Mar. 1-4.

Oil Refinery — A108

1980, Sept. 2   Litho.   Perf. 14½
579 A108   10d shown   .75 .40
580 A108   35d View of Doha   3.00 .50
581 A108   2r Telecommunications tower   11.00 2.50
582 A108   2.35r Hospital   13.00 3.75
    Nos. 579-582 (4)   27.75 7.15

9th anniversary of independence.

Men Holding OPEC Emblem — A109

1980, Sept. 15   Perf. 14x13½
583 A109   1.35r multi   4.75 1.40
584 A109   2r multi   7.00 2.10

OPEC, 20th anniversary.

United Nations Day 1980 — A110

1980, Oct. 24
585 A110   1.35r multi   3.25 1.25
586 A110   1.80r multi   4.75 1.60

Hegira (Pilgrimage Year) — A111

1980, Nov. 8   Litho.   Perf. 14½
587 A111   10d multi   .50 .50
588 A111   35d multi   1.00 .65
589 A111   1.25r multi   2.25 1.50
590 A111   2.80r multi   5.50 3.75
    Nos. 587-590 (4)   9.25 6.40

International Year of the Disabled — A112

1981, Jan. 5   Photo.   Perf. 11½
Granite Paper
591 A112   2r multi   4.75 2.75
592 A112   3r multi   7.25 3.25

Education Day — A113

Perf. 14x13½
1981, Feb. 22   Litho.   Wmk. 368
593 A113   2r multi   5.50 2.00
594 A113   3r multi   6.75 2.75

Sheik Khalifa, 9th Anniversary of Accession A114

1981, Feb. 22
595 A114   10d multi   .50 .40
596 A114   35d multi   1.50 .40
597 A114   80d multi   3.00 .70
598 A114   5r multi   15.00 3.75
    Nos. 595-598 (4)   20.00 5.25

A115

1981, May 17   Litho.   Perf. 13½x13
599 A115   2r multi   5.00 1.25
600 A115   2.80r multi   7.25 2.40

13th World Telecommunications Day.

A116

Championship emblem.

1981, June 11   Litho.   Perf. 14x13½
601 A116   1.25r multi   6.00 1.60
602 A116   2.80r multi   10.00 3.00

30th Intl. Military Soccer Championship, Doha.

10th Anniv. of Independence — A117

Perf. 13½x14
1981, Sept. 2   Litho.   Wmk. 368
603 A117   5d multicolored   .75 .40
604 A117   60d multicolored   2.25 .60
605 A117   80d multicolored   3.00 .75
606 A117   5r multicolored   17.50 5.00
    Nos. 603-606 (4)   23.50 7.00

World Food Day A118

1981, Oct. 16   Litho.   Perf. 13
607 A118   2r multi   6.50 3.25
608 A118   2.80r multi   8.50 4.00

Red Crescent Society — A119

1982, Jan. 16   Litho.   Perf. 14x13½
609 A119   20d multi   1.25 .30
610 A119   2.80r multi   7.75 3.25

10th Anniv. of Sheik Khalifa's Accession — A120

Perf. 13½x14
1982, Feb. 22   Litho.   Wmk. 368
611 A120   10d multi   1.00 .45
612 A120   20d multi   2.00 .45
613 A120   1.25r multi   7.00 1.40
614 A120   2.80r multi   15.00 3.00
    Nos. 611-614 (4)   25.00 5.30

Sheik
Khalifa — A121

Oil
Refinery — A122

Designs: 5r, 10r, 15r, Hoda Clock Tower.

1982, Mar. 1　Photo.　Perf. 11½x12
Granite Paper
615	A121	5d multi	.30	.30
616	A121	10d multi	.35	.30
617	A121	15d multi	.40	.30
618	A121	20d multi	.45	.30
619	A121	25d multi	.60	.30
620	A121	35d multi	.85	.30
621	A121	60d multi	1.25	.35
622	A121	80d multi	2.00	.50
623	A122	1r multi	2.25	.65
624	A122	1.25r multi	3.00	1.00
625	A122	2r multi	4.75	1.90
626	A122	5r multi	12.50	4.50
627	A122	10r multi	22.50	9.25
628	A122	15r multi	32.50	13.50
	Nos. 615-628 (14)		83.70	33.45

Hamad General Hospital — A123

1982, Mar.　Litho.　Perf. 13x13½
629	A123	10d multi	.75	.35
630	A123	2.35r multi	6.75	3.00

6th Anniv. of United Arab Shipping
Co. — A124

1982, Mar. 6　Litho.　Perf. 13x13½
631	A124	20d multi	1.25	.35
632	A124	2.35r multi	11.00	3.00

A125

1982, Apr. 12　Litho.　Perf. 13½x13
633	A125	35d yellow & multi	1.50	.35
634	A125	2.80r blue & multi	10.50	2.25

30th anniv. of Arab Postal Union.

A126

1982, Sept. 2　Litho.　Perf. 13½x13
635	A126	10d multi	1.00	.30
636	A126	80d multi	2.25	.60
637	A126	1.25r multi	4.00	1.50
638	A126	2.80r multi	7.75	2.25
	Nos. 635-638 (4)		15.00	4.65

11th anniv. of Independence.

World
Communications
Year — A127

1983, Jan. 10　Litho.　Perf. 13½x13
639	A127	35d multi	1.75	.50
640	A127	2.80r multi	8.75	2.50

Gulf Postal Org., 2nd Conference,
Doha, Apr. — A128

1983, Apr. 9　Litho.　Perf. 13½x14
641	A128	1r multi	4.00	1.25
642	A128	1.35r multi	5.75	2.00

A129

1983, Sept. 2　Litho.　Perf. 14
643	A129	10d multi	.45	.45
644	A129	35d multi	.90	.45
645	A129	80d multi	2.00	.75
646	A129	2.80r multi	6.75	2.50
	Nos. 643-646 (4)		10.10	4.15

12th anniv. of Independence.

A130

1983, Nov. 7　Litho.　Perf. 13½x14
647	A130	35d multi	3.00	.50
648	A130	2.80r multi	10.00	3.00

GCC Supreme Council, 4th regular session.

35th Anniv. of UN Declaration of
Human Rights — A131

1983, Dec. 10　Litho.　Perf. 13½x14
649	A131	1.25r Globe, emblem	4.00	1.50
650	A131	2.80r Scale	7.75	2.50

A132　　　　A133

1984, Mar. 1　Litho.　Perf. 13x13½
651	A132	15d multi	.50	.25
652	A132	40d multi	1.25	.45
653	A132	50d multi	1.25	.55

Perf. 14½x13½
654	A133	1r multi	3.00	1.50
655	A133	1.50r multi	3.50	1.75
656	A133	2.50r multi	6.00	2.75
657	A133	3r multi	8.00	3.00
658	A133	5r multi	14.00	5.75
659	A133	10r multi	24.00	11.00
	Nos. 651-659 (9)		61.50	27.00

See Nos. 707-709, 792-801.

13th Anniv. of Independence — A134

1984, Sept. 2　Photo.　Perf. 12
660	A134	15d multi	1.00	.45
661	A134	1r multi	3.00	1.00
662	A134	2.50r multi	6.00	2.25
663	A134	3.50r multi	8.75	3.25
	Nos. 660-663 (4)		18.75	6.95

Literacy Day,
1984 — A135

1984, Sept. 8　Litho.　Perf. 14x13½
664	A135	1r lilac & multi	5.25	1.10
665	A135	1r orange & multi	5.25	1.10

40th Anniv.,
ICAO — A136

1984, Dec. 7　Litho.　Perf. 13½x13
666	A136	20d multi	.50	.40
667	A136	3.50r multi	8.50	3.00

League of
Arab
States,
40th Anniv.
A137

1985, Mar. 22　Photo.　Perf. 11½
668	A137	50d multi	1.50	.40
669	A137	4r multi	7.75	3.00

Intl. Youth
Year — A138

1985, Mar. 4　　　Perf. 11½x12
Granite Paper
670	A138	50d multi	2.25	.65
671	A138	1r multi	4.75	1.25

Traffic
Crossing — A139

1985, Mar. 9　　　Perf. 14x13½
672	A139	1r lt bl & multi	4.00	1.25
673	A139	1r pink & multi	4.00	1.25

Gulf Cooperation Council Traffic Safety
Week, Mar. 16-22.

Natl. Independence, 14th
Anniv. — A140

1985, Sept. 2　　　Perf. 11½x12
Granite Paper
674	A140	40d Doha	1.25	.35
675	A140	50d Earth satellite station	2.00	.55
676	A140	1.50r Oil refinery	5.50	1.25
677	A140	4r Storage facility	12.50	4.00
	Nos. 674-677 (4)		21.25	6.15

Org. of Petroleum Exporting Countries,
25th Anniv. — A141

1985, Sept. 14　　　Perf. 13½x14
678	A141	1r brt yel grn & multi	5.00	1.25
679	A141	1r salmon rose & multi	5.00	1.25

UN,
40th
Anniv.
A142

1985, Oct. 24　Litho.　Perf. 13½x14
680	A142	1r multi	1.75	1.25
681	A142	3r multi	5.00	3.50

Population and Housing
Census — A143

1986, Mar. 1   Photo.   Perf. 11½x12
682 A143 1r multi — 3.25 1.25
683 A143 3r multi — 7.25 4.00

United Arab Shipping Co., 10th Anniv. — A144

1986, May 30   Litho.   Perf. 13½x14
684 A144 1.50r Qatari ibn al Fuja'a — 3.00 2.75
685 A144 4r Al Wajba — 9.25 6.00

Natl. Independence, 15th Anniv. — A145

Perf. 13x13½
1986, Sept. 2   Litho.   Unwmk.
686 A145 40d multi — .75 .55
687 A145 50d multi — 1.10 .65
688 A145 1r multi — 2.25 1.25
689 A145 4r multi — 7.00 4.75
Nos. 686-689 (4) — 11.10 7.20

Sheik Khalifa — A146

1987, Jan. 1   Photo.   Perf. 11½x12
Granite Paper
690 A146 15r multi — 19.00 12.00
691 A146 20r multi — 24.00 16.00
692 A146 30r multi — 42.50 25.00
Nos. 690-692 (3) — 85.50 53.00

15th Anniv. of Sheik Khalifa's Accession A147

1987, Feb. 22   Perf. 12x11½
Granite Paper
693 A147 50d multi — .95 .50
694 A147 1r multi — 2.00 1.00
695 A147 1.50r multi — 2.75 1.40
696 A147 4r multi — 6.50 4.50
Nos. 693-696 (4) — 12.20 7.40

Arab Postal Union, 35th Anniv. — A148

Perf. 14x13½
1987, Apr. 12   Litho.   Unwmk.
697 A148 1r multi — 3.00 1.25
698 A148 1.50r multi — 3.50 2.00

Natl. Independence, 16th Anniv. — A149

1987, Sept. 2   Litho.   Perf. 13x13½
699 A149 25d Housing complex — 1.00 .35
700 A149 75d Water tower, city — 3.25 .90
701 A149 2r Modern office building — 5.00 2.25
702 A149 4r Oil refinery — 11.00 4.75
Nos. 699-702 (4) — 20.25 8.25

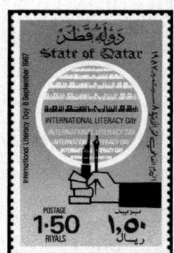

A150

Perf. 13½x13
1987, Sept. 8   Litho.   Unwmk.
703 A150 1.50r multicolored — 2.75 1.25
704 A150 4r multicolored — 4.75 2.00
Intl. Literacy Day.

A151

Perf. 14x13½
1987, Apr. 24   Litho.   Wmk. 368
705 A151 1r multicolored — 2.25 1.25
706 A151 4r multicolored — 5.75 4.00
Gulf Environment Day.

Sheik Type of 1984
1988, Jan. 1   Perf. 13x13½
Size of 25d, 75d: 22x27mm
707 A133 25d multicolored — 2.00 .75
708 A133 75d multicolored — 4.50 2.00
Perf. 14½x13
709 A133 2r multicolored — 15.00 4.75

WHO, 40th Anniv. — A152

1988, Apr. 7   Perf. 14x13½
714 A152 1.50r multicolored — 3.25 2.25
715 A152 2r multicolored — 7.00 3.50

Independence, 17th Anniv. — A153

Perf. 11½x12
1988, Sept. 2   Litho.   Unwmk.
Granite Paper
716 A153 50d multicolored — 1.00 .55
717 A153 75d multicolored — 1.75 .80
718 A153 1.50r multicolored — 3.00 2.00
719 A153 2r multicolored — 3.75 2.40
Nos. 716-719 (4) — 9.50 5.75

Opening of the Doha General P.O. — A154

1988, Sept. 3   Perf. 13x13½
720 A154 1.50r multicolored — 2.25 2.00
721 A154 4r multicolored — 5.00 4.75

Arab Housing Day — A155

1988, Oct. 3   Perf. 11½x12
Granite Paper
722 A155 1.50r multicolored — 3.00 1.75
723 A155 4r multicolored — 7.75 3.75

A156

Perf. 14x13½
1988, Dec. 10   Wmk. 368
724 A156 1.50r multicolored — 3.25 2.50
725 A156 2r multicolored — 4.25 3.75
Declaration of Human Rights, 40th anniv.

A157

Perf. 12x11½
1989, May 17   Unwmk.
Granite Paper
726 A157 2r multicolored — 3.00 2.25
727 A157 4r multicolored — 6.00 4.00
World Telecommunications Day.

Qatar Red Crescent Soc., 10th Anniv. — A158

Perf. 13½x14
1989, Aug. 8   Wmk. 368
728 A158 4r multicolored — 11.00 4.75

Natl. Independence, 18th Anniv. — A159

Perf. 13x13½
1989, Sept. 2   Unwmk.
729 A159 75d multicolored — 1.25 .85
730 A159 1r multicolored — 2.25 1.50
731 A159 1.50r multicolored — 2.75 2.00
732 A159 2r multicolored — 4.00 2.40
Nos. 729-732 (4) — 10.25 6.75

Gulf Air, 40th Anniv. A160

1990, Mar. 24   Litho.   Perf. 13x13½
733 A160 50d multicolored — 1.25 .50
734 A160 75d multicolored — 2.00 1.00
735 A160 4r multicolored — 8.50 4.00
Nos. 733-735 (3) — 11.75 5.50

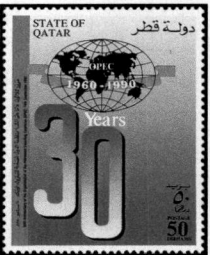

Independence, 19th Anniv. — A161

Designs: 75d, Map, sunburst. 1.50r, 2r, Swordsman, musicians.

1990, Sept. 2   Perf. 14x13½
736 A161 50d multicolored — 1.25 .50
737 A161 75d multicolored — 1.75 .90
738 A161 1.50r multicolored — 3.50 1.60
739 A161 2r multicolored — 5.50 2.75
Nos. 736-739 (4) — 12.00 5.75

Organization of Petroleum Exporting Countries (OPEC), 30th Anniv. A162

1990, Sept. 14
740 A162 50d shown — 2.00 .55
741 A162 1.50r Flags — 5.00 1.60

A163

GCC Supreme Council, 11th Regular Session: 1r, Leaders of member nations. 1.50r, Flag, council emblem. 2r, State seal, emblem.

Perf. 14x13½

1990, Dec. 22		Litho.	Wmk. 368	
742	A163	50d multicolored	1.50	.50
743	A163	1r multicolored	2.50	1.10
744	A163	1.50r multicolored	4.00	1.75
745	A163	2r multicolored	4.75	2.10
		Nos. 742-745 (4)	12.75	5.45

A164

Plants — 10d, Glossonema edule. 25d, Lycium shawii. 50d, Acacia tortilis. 75d, Acacia ehrenbergiana. 1r, Capparis spinosa. 4r, Cymhopogon parkeri.

Perf. 12½x13½

1991, June 20		Litho.	Wmk. 368	
747	A164	10d multi	1.00	.35
748	A164	25d multi	1.10	.40
749	A164	50d multi	1.25	1.00
750	A164	75d multi	2.25	1.25
751	A164	1r multi	3.25	2.50
752	A164	4r multi	13.00	8.50
		Nos. 747-752 (6)	21.85	14.00

Independence, 20th Anniv. — A165

1991, Aug. 15		Litho.	Perf. 14x14½	
		Granite Paper		
762	A165	25d shown	.85	.30
763	A165	75d red vio & multi	1.75	.65

Perf. 14½x14

764	A165	1r Doha skyline, horiz.	2.50	1.00
765	A165	1.50r Palace, horiz.	3.75	1.75
		Nos. 762-765 (4)	8.85	3.70

Fish A166

Various species of fish.

1991, Dec. 1			Perf. 14x13½	
767	A166	10d multicolored	1.00	.50
768	A166	15d multicolored	1.25	.55
769	A166	25d multicolored	2.00	.90
770	A166	50d multicolored	4.50	1.75
771	A166	75d multicolored	6.50	2.75
772	A166	1r multicolored	8.00	4.50
773	A166	1.50r multicolored	12.00	7.00
774	A166	2r multicolored	14.50	8.50
		Nos. 767-774 (8)	49.75	26.45

A167

Sheik Khalifa, 20th Anniv. of Accession A168

Perf. 14x13½

1992, Feb. 22		Litho.	Wmk. 368	
781	A167	25d multicolored	.75	.35
782	A167	50d multicolored	1.25	.50
783	A168	75d multicolored	2.00	.75
784	A168	1.50r multicolored	3.75	1.75
		Nos. 781-784 (4)	7.75	3.35

World Health Day A169

1992, Apr. 7		Perf. 14x13½, 13½x14		
785	A169	50d Heart with face, vert.	1.10	.60
786	A169	1.50r shown	3.00	2.00

Children's Paintings A170

25d, Girls dancing. 50d, Children playing. 75d, Ships. 1.50r, Fishing from boats.

1992, June 15		Unwmk.	Perf. 11½	
787	A170	25d multi	.75	.40
788	A170	50d multi	1.75	.50
789	A170	75d multi	3.25	.65
790	A170	1.50r multi	5.00	1.25
a.		Souvenir sheet of 4, #787-790	375.00	375.00
		Nos. 787-790 (4)	10.75	2.80

Type of 1984 with Smaller Arabic Inscription and

A171   A172

Designs: 25d, 1.50r, Offshore oil field. 50d, 2r, 5r, Map. 75d, 3r, Storage tanks, horiz. 1r, 4r, 10r, Oil refinery, horiz.

1992		Litho.	Perf. 13x13½	
791	A171	10d multicolored	.35	.25
792	A132	25d multicolored	.35	.25
793	A132	50d multicolored	.55	.50

Perf. 13½x13

794	A132	75d multicolored	.95	.55
795	A132	1r multicolored	1.25	.75

Size: 25x32mm
Perf. 14½x13, 13x14½

796	A132	1.50r multicolored	1.60	1.10
797	A132	2r multicolored	2.10	1.25
798	A132	3r multicolored	4.25	2.50
799	A132	4r multicolored	4.75	3.00
800	A132	5r multicolored	5.50	3.75
801	A132	10r multicolored	12.00	7.00
802	A172	15r multicolored	16.00	12.00
803	A172	20r multicolored	27.50	14.00
804	A172	30r multicolored	32.50	24.00
		Nos. 791-804 (14)	109.65	70.90

Issued: 10-50d, 1.50, 2, 5, 15, 30r, 2/15; others, 5/14.

1992 Summer Olympics, Barcelona A174

1992, July 25		Litho.	Perf. 15	
805	A174	50d Running	1.50	.40
806	A174	1.50r Soccer	3.75	1.25

11th Persian Gulf Soccer Cup A175

1992, Nov. 27		Litho.	Perf. 14½	
807	A175	50d shown	1.75	.60
808	A175	1r Ball, net, vert.	3.50	1.25

A176

Independence, 21st Anniv. — A177

Sheik Khalifa and: No. 810, "21" in English and Arabic. No. 811, Tree, dhow in harbor. No. 812, Natural gas well, pen, dhow.

Unwmk.

1992, Sept. 2		Litho.	Perf. 12	
		Granite Paper		
809	A176	50d shown	1.25	.55
810	A176	50d multicolored	1.25	.55
811	A177	1r multicolored	2.00	1.25
812	A177	1r multicolored	2.00	1.25
a.		Strip of 8, 2 each #809-812	14.00	9.00
		Nos. 809-812 (4)	6.50	3.60

Intl. Conference on Nutrition, Rome — A178

50d, Globe, emblems, vert. 1r, Cornucopia.

1992, Dec. 12			Perf. 14½	
813	A178	50d multicolored	2.00	.40
814	A178	1r multicolored	3.25	.70

Qatar Broadcasting, Silver Jubilee — A179

Designs: 25d, Man at microphone, satellite dish. 50d, Rocket lift-off, satellite. 75d, Communications building. 1r, Technicians working on books.

1993, June 25		Photo.	Perf. 12x11½	
		Granite Paper		
819	A179	25d multicolored	1.00	.40
820	A179	50d multicolored	2.50	.75
821	A179	75d multicolored	3.25	1.00
822	A179	1r multicolored	4.75	1.25
a.		Souvenir sheet of 4, #819-822	225.00	225.00
		Nos. 819-822 (4)	11.50	3.40

Ruins A180

Mosque with: a, Minaret (at left, shown). b, Minaret with side projections (at right). c, Minaret with catwalk, inside wall. d, Minaret at right, outside wall.

1993, May 10		Litho.	Perf. 12	
		Granite Paper		
823	A180	1r Strip of 4, #a.-d.	9.00	3.75

Independence, 22nd Anniv. — A181

Designs: 25c, Oil pumping station. 50d, Flag, clock tower. 75d, Coat of arms, "22." 1.50r, Flag, fortress tower.

1993, Sept. 2		Litho.	Perf. 11½	
		Granite Paper		
824	A181	25d multicolored	.50	.30
825	A181	50d multicolored	1.00	.60
826	A181	75d multicolored	1.50	1.00
827	A181	1.50r multicolored	3.50	2.25
		Nos. 824-827 (4)	6.50	4.15

Intl. Literacy Day — A182

Designs: 25d, Quill, paper. 50d, Papers with English letters, pen. 75d, Papers with Arabic letters, pen. 1.50r, Scroll, Arabic letters, pen.

Perf. 14x13½

1993, Sept. 2		Litho.	Wmk. 368	
828	A182	25d multicolored	.50	.30
829	A182	50d multicolored	1.00	.60
830	A182	75d multicolored	1.50	.90
831	A182	1.50r multicolored	3.50	2.25
		Nos. 828-831 (4)	6.50	4.05

Children's Games
A183

Designs: 25d, Girls with thread and spinners. 50d, Boys with stick and disk, vert. 75r, Children guiding wheels with sticks, vert. 1.50r, Girls with jump rope.

1993, Dec. 5   Litho.   Perf. 11½
Granite Paper
832	A183	25d multicolored	.85	.35
833	A183	50d multicolored	1.75	.50
834	A183	75d multicolored	2.75	.75
a.		Souvenir sheet, 2 each #833, #834	90.00	90.00
835	A183	1.50r multicolored	5.25	2.00
a.		Souvenir sheet, 2 each #832, #835	90.00	90.00
		Nos. 832-835 (4)	10.60	3.60

Falcons — A184

1993, Dec. 22   Granite Paper
836	A184	25d Lanner	.75	.40
837	A184	50d Saker	1.25	.50
838	A184	75d Barbary	2.25	.75
839	A184	1.50r Peregrine	4.75	2.00
a.		Souvenir sheet, #836-839	175.00	
		Nos. 836-839 (4)	9.00	3.65

A185

Society for Handicapped Welfare and Rehabilition: 75d, Hands above and below handicapped symbol.

1994, May 6   Litho.   Perf. 14
840	A185	25d shown	1.10	.50
841	A185	75d multi	2.75	1.10

A186

Qatar Insurance Co., 30th Anniv.: 50d, Building. 1.50r, Co. arms, global tourist attractions.

Perf. 14½
1994, Mar. 11   Litho.   Unwmk.
842	A186	50d gold & multi	1.50	.40
843	A186	1.50r gold & multi	4.50	1.60

A187

World Day for Water: 1r, UN emblem, hands catching water drop, tower, grain.

1994, Mar. 22   Litho.   Perf. 11½
844	A187	25d shown	1.50	.40
845	A187	1r multicolored	2.75	1.50

A188

1994, Mar. 22   Litho.   Perf. 11½
846	A188	75d shown	1.25	.75
847	A188	2r Scales, gavel	2.75	2.50

Intl. Law Conference.

A189

1r, Family, UN emblem.

Perf. 12x11½
1994, July 16   Litho.   Unwmk.
848	A189	25d shown	1.00	.65
849	A189	1r multicolored	3.00	1.25

Intl. Year of the Family.

Independence, 23rd Anniv. — A190

25d, 2r, Text. 75d, Island. 1r, Oil drilling plant.

1994, Sept. 2   Photo.   Perf. 12
Granite Paper
850	A190	25d green & multi	.60	.35
851	A190	75d multicolored	1.25	.75
852	A190	1r multicolored	2.00	1.10
853	A190	2r pink & multi	4.50	2.25
		Nos. 850-853 (4)	8.35	4.45

ILO, 75th
Anniv. — A191

1994, May 28   Perf. 14
854	A191	25d salmon & multi	.75	.40
855	A191	2r green & multi, diff.	4.75	1.60

ICAO, 50th Anniv. A192

1994, Dec. 7   Perf. 13½x14
856	A192	25d shown	1.00	.40
857	A192	75d Emblem, airplane	4.75	1.00

A193

A194

A195

A196

Rock Carvings at Jabal
Jusasiyah — A197

1995, Mar. 18   Litho.   Perf. 14½x15
858	A193	1r multicolored	1.40	.80
859	A194	1r multicolored	1.40	.80
860	A195	1r multicolored	1.40	.80
861	A196	1r multicolored	1.40	.80
862	A197	1r multicolored	1.40	.80
863	A197	1r multi, diff.	1.40	.80
a.		Vert. strip of 6, #858-863	11.00	8.50
		Nos. 858-863 (6)	8.40	4.80

Gulf Environment Day — A198

Shells: No. 864a, Conus pennaceus. b, Cerithidea cingulata. c, Hexaplex kuesterianus. d, Epitonium scalare.
No. 865a, Murex scolopax. b, Thais mutabilis. c, Fusinus arabicus. d, Lambis truncata sebae.

1995, Apr. 24
864	A198	75d Strip of 4, #a.-d.	5.50	4.50
865	A198	1r Strip of 4, #a.-d.	6.50	5.50

Intl. Nursing
Day — A199

Designs: 1r, Nurse adjusting IV for patient. 1.50r, Injecting shot into arm of infant.

1995, May 12
866	A199	1r multicolored	2.50	1.10
867	A199	1.50r multicolored	4.25	1.60

Independence, 24th Anniv. — A200

Designs: a, 1.50r, Shipping dock, city. b, 1r, Children in classroom. c, 1.50r, Aerial view of city. d, 1r, Palm trees.

1995, Sept. 2   Litho.   Perf. 13½x14
868	A200	Block of 4, #a.-d.	7.00	4.75

UN, 50th
Anniv. — A201

1995, Oct. 24   Perf. 13½
869	A201	1.50r multicolored	2.50	1.25

Gazelles
A202

No. 870; a, 75c, Gazella dorcas pelzelni. b, 50d, Dorcatragus megalotis. c, 25d, Gazella dama. d, 1.50r, Gazella spekei. e, 2r, Gazella soemmeringi. f, 1r, Gazella dorcas.
3r, Gazella spekei, gazella dorcas pelzelni, gazella soemmeringi.

1996, Jan.   Litho.   Perf. 11½
870	A202	Strip of 6, #a.-f.	10.00	10.00

Size: 121x81mm
Imperf
871	A202	3r multicolored	67.50	50.00

Fight Against
Drug
Abuse — A203

1996, June 26 Litho. Perf. 14x13
872	A203	50d shown	1.40	.55
873	A203	1r "NO," needles, hand	2.50	1.00

1996 Summer
Olympic Games,
Atlanta — A204

a, 10d, Olympic emblem, map of Qatar. b, 15d, Shooting. c, 25d, Bowling. d, 50d, Table tennis. e, 1r, Athletics. f, 1.50r, Yachting.

1996, July 19 Litho. Perf. 14x13½
874	A204	Strip of 6, #a.-f.	9.00	8.00

Independence, 25th Anniv. — A204a

Litho. & Typo.
1996, Sept. 2 Perf. 12
Granite Paper
875	A204a	1.50r silver & multi	2.50	1.25
876	A204a	2r gold & multi	4.75	1.75

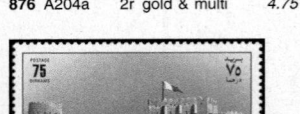

Forts
A204b

25d, Al-Wajbah, vert. 75d, Al-Zubarah. 1r, Al-Kout. 3r, Umm Salal Mohammed.

1997, Jan. 15 Litho. Perf. 14½
877	A204b	25d multicolored	.60	.35
878	A204b	75d multicolored	1.50	1.00
879	A204b	1r multicolored	2.00	1.25
880	A204b	3r multicolored	5.50	4.25
		Nos. 877-880 (4)	9.60	6.85

A205   A206

Sheik Hamad —
A206a

1996-2012 (?) Photo. Perf. 11½x12
Granite Paper
881	A205	25d pink & multi	.40	.25
881A	A205	25d green & multi	—	
882	A205	50d green & multi	.65	.40
882A	A205	50d org brn & multi	—	
883	A205	75d bl grn & multi	1.00	.50
884	A205	1r gray & multi	1.25	.60

Perf. 11½
885	A206	1.50r grn bl & multi	2.25	.90
886	A206	2r green & multi	2.50	1.00
886A	A206	2r pur brn & multi	—	
887	A206	4r ver & multi	4.75	2.50
888	A206	5r purple & multi	5.75	5.00
888A	A206	5r red vio & multi	—	
888B	A206a	5r purple & multi	—	
889	A206	10r brown & multi	14.50	7.00
889A	A206	10r red & multi	—	
889B	A206a	10r brown & multi	—	
890	A206	20r blue & multi	25.00	14.00
890A	A206a	20r blue & multi	—	
890B	A206	20r gray grn & multi	—	
891	A206	30r orange & multi	37.50	21.00
891A	A206a	30r org & multi	—	

Issued: Nos. 881-888, 889, 890, 891, 11/16/96; No. 890B, 2012 ? Others, 2009?

A207

UNICEF, 50th Anniv.: No. 893, Children, open book emblem.

1996, Dec. 11 Litho. Perf. 14½
892	A207	75d blue & multi	1.25	.85
893	A207	75d violet & multi	1.25	.85

A208

17th Session of GCC Supreme Council: 1.50r, Emblem, dove with olive branch, Sheik Khalifa.

1996, Dec. 7
894	A208	1r multicolored	2.00	.75
895	A208	1.50r multicolored	3.50	1.50

Opening of Port of Ras Laffan — A209

1997, Feb. 24 Litho. Perf. 13½
896	A209	3r multicolored	8.00	3.00

Arabian
Horses
A210

25d, Red horse with tan mane. 75d, Black horse. 1r, White horse. 1.50r, Red brown horse. 3r, Mares, foals.

1997, Mar. 19 Photo. Perf. 12x11½
897	A210	25d multi	1.00	.45
898	A210	75d multi	1.75	.90
899	A210	1r multi	2.25	1.25
900	A210	1.50r multi	3.50	2.00
		Nos. 897-900 (4)	8.50	4.60

Size: 115x75mm
Imperf
901	A210	3r multi	125.00	65.00

Independence, 26th Anniv. — A211

1997, Sept. 2 Photo. Perf. 11½x12
Granite Paper
902	A211	1r shown	1.75	.85
903	A211	1.50r Oil refinery	2.75	1.25

Doha '97, Doha-Mena Economic
Conference — A212

1997, Nov. 16 Litho. Perf. 11
904	A212	2r multicolored	2.50	1.25

Insects — A213

a, Nubian flower bee. b, Domino beetle. c, Seven-spot ladybird. d, Desert giant ant. e, Eastern death's-head hawkmoth. f, Arabian darkling beetle. g, Yellow digger. h, Mole cricket. i, Migratory locust. j, Elegant rhinoceros beetle. k, Oleander hawkmoth. l, American cockroach. m, Girdled skimmer. n, Sabre-toothed beetle. o, Arabian cicada. p, Pinstriped ground weevil. q, Praying mantis. r, Rufous bombardier beetle. s, Diadem. t, Shore earwing.

1998, July 20 Litho. Perf. 11½x12
Granite Paper
905	A213	2r Sheet of 20, #a.-t.	40.00	32.50
u.		Souvenir sheet, #905i	22.50	17.50
v.		Souvenir sheet, #905s	22.50	17.50

Early Diving Equipment — A214

Perf. 11½x12, 12x11½
1998, Aug. 15 Photo.
Granite Paper
906	A214	25d Meflaja	.70	.25
907	A214	75d Mahar	1.40	.75
908	A214	1r Dasta	2.00	1.10
909	A214	1.50r Deyen, vert.	3.00	2.00
		Nos. 906-909 (4)	7.10	4.10

Souvenir Sheet
910	A214	2r Man seated in boat	16.00	12.00

Qatar University,
25th
Anniv. — A215

1998, Sept. 2 Litho. Perf. 13½x13
911	A215	1r blue & multi	1.40	.85
912	A215	1.50r gray & muti	2.25	1.25

Independence, 27th Anniv. — A216

1998, Sept. 2 Perf. 14
913	A216	1r Sheik Khalifa, vert.	1.40	.85
914	A216	1.50r Sheik Khalifa	2.25	1.25

Camels — A217

1999, Jan. 25 Litho. Perf. 11½
Granite Paper
915	A217	25d shown	.25	.25
916	A217	75d One standing	1.50	1.25
917	A217	1r Three standing	2.10	1.50
918	A217	1.50r Four standing, group	3.00	2.50
		Nos. 915-918 (4)	6.85	5.50

Souvenir Sheet
919	A217	2r Adult, juvenile	24.50	20.00

1999 FEI General
Assembly
Meeting,
Doha — A218

1999 Litho. Perf. 13¼x13
920	A218	1.50r multicolored	3.50	2.00

Ancient Coins — A219

Obverse, reverse of dirhams — #921: a, Umayyad (shown). b, Umayyad, diff. c, Abbasid (3 lines of text on obv.). d, Abbasid (6 lines of text obv.). e, Umayyad, diff. (small circles near edge at top of obv. & rev.).

Obv., rev. of dinars — #922: a, Abbasid (3 lines of text obv.). b, Umayyad. c, Abbasid (5 lines of text obv.). d, Marabitid. e, Fatimid.

Obverse and reverse of: No. 923, Arab Sasanian dirham. 3r, Umayyad dinar, diff.

1999 Litho. Perf. 11½
Granite Paper
921	A219	1r Strip of 5, #a.-e.	6.00	4.50
922	A219	2r Strip of 5, #a.-e.	11.00	7.00

QATAR

227

Souvenir Sheets

923	A219	2r multicolored	16.00	12.00
924	A219	3r multicolored	18.00	14.00

Independence, 28th Anniv. — A220

Perf. 12¾x13¾

1999, Sept. 2 Litho. Wmk. 368

925	A220	1r violet & multi	1.40	1.25
926	A220	1.50r yellow & multi	2.00	1.75

A221

UPU, 125th anniv.: 1r, Tree with letters. 1.50r, Building, horiz.

Perf. 11½

1999, Oct. 9 Litho. Unwmk.
Granite Paper

927	A221	1r multicolored	1.40	1.25
928	A221	1.50r multicolored	2.00	1.75

A222

Fifth Stamp Exhibition for the Arab Gulf Countries: 1r, Emblem, stamps. 1.50r, Emblem, horiz.

1999, Oct. 30 Granite Paper

929	A222	1r multicolored	1.25	.75
930	A222	1.50r multicolored	1.75	1.25

National Committee for Children with Special Needs — A223

Perf. 12¾x13¼

1999, Nov. 2 Litho. Wmk. 368

931	A223	1.50r multi	2.40	2.00

Millennium
A224

Photo. & Embossed
2000, Jan. 1 Unwmk. Perf. 11¾
Granite Paper

932	A224	1.50r red & gold	2.25	2.00
933	A224	2r blue & gold	3.00	2.50

Qatar Tennis Open — A225

Trophy and: 1r, Stadium. 1.50r, Racquet.

2000, Jan. 3 Litho. Perf. 13¼x13½

934	A225	1r multi	2.00	1.60
935	A225	1.50r multi	2.75	2.40

GCC Water Week — A226

2000, Mar. 1 Perf. 13¾

936	A226	1r Map, water drop	1.60	1.25
937	A226	1.50r Hands, water drop	2.40	1.75

15th Asian Table Tennis Championships, Doha — A227

2000, May 1 Photo. Perf. 11¾
Granite Paper

938	A227	1.50r multi	2.50	2.00

Independence, 29th Anniv. — A228

Sheik Hamad and: 1r, Fort. 1.50r, Oil derrick, city skyline.

Perf. 11½x11¾

2000, Sept. 2 Photo.
Granite Paper

939-940	A228	Set of 2	4.50	4.50

Post Office, 50th Anniv. A229

Monument, building and: 1.50r, Bird. 2r, Magnifying glass.

Photo. & Embossed
2000, Oct. 9 Perf. 11¾
Granite Paper

941-942	A229	Set of 2	5.25	5.25

9th Islamic Summit Conference — A230

No. 943: a, 1r, Emblem (size: 21x28mm). b, 1.50r, Emblem, olive branch (size: 45x28mm).

2000, Nov. 12 Photo.
Granite Paper

943	A230	Pair, #a-b	4.25	4.25

Clean Environment Day — A231

Designs: 1r, Qatar Gas emblem, tanker ship, coral reef. 1.50r, RasGas emblem, refinery, antelopes. 2r, Ras Laffan Industrial City emblem, flamingos near industrial complex. 3r, Qatar Petroleum emblem, view of Earth from space.

2001, Feb. 26 Photo. Perf. 11½
Granite Paper

944-947	A231	Set of 4	9.25	9.25

Independence, 30th Anniv. — A232

Background colors: 1r, Olive. 1.50r, Blue.

2001, Sept. 2 Litho. Perf. 14x14½

948-949	A232	Set of 2	3.75	3.75

Year of Dialogue Among Civilizations A233

Designs: 1.50r, Shown. 2r, Branch with leaves of many colors.

2001, Oct. 9 Perf. 13¼

950-951	A233	Set of 2	6.00	6.00

4th World Trade Organization Ministerial Conference — A234

Background colors: 1r, Yellow brown. 1.50r, Blue.

2001, Nov. 9

952-953	A234	Set of 2	5.25	5.25

Old Doors — A235

Various doors: 25d, 75d, 1.50r, 2r.

2001, Dec. 30 Perf. 14½

954-957	A235	Set of 4	6.00	6.00

Souvenir Sheet

958	A235	3r multi	20.00 20.00

2002 World Cup Soccer Championships, Japan and Korea — A236

No. 959 — World Cup Posters (except for #959r) from: a, 1930. b, 1934 (Italian). c, 1938. d, 1950. e, 1954. f, 1958. g, 1962. h, 1966. i, 1970. j, 1974. k, 1978. l, 1982. m, 1986. n, 1990. o, 1994. p, 1998. q, 2002. r, World Cup Trophy.

2002 Litho. Perf. 14

959		Sheet of 18	52.50	52.50
a.-r.		A236 2r Any single	2.00	1.75
s.		Souvenir sheet, #959q-959r	8.00	8.00

Asian Games Emblems — A237

No. 960: a, 1r, 2002 Asian Games emblem, Busan, South Korea. b, 3r, 2006 Asian Games Emblem, Doha, Qatar.

2002, Sept. 29 Photo. Perf. 14¼
Granite Paper

960	A237	Sheet of 2, #a-b	7.00	7.00

Qatar General Postal Corporation, 1st Anniv. — A238

Background colors: 1r, White. 3r, Light blue.

2002, Oct. 25 Litho. Perf. 12½

961-962	A238	Set of 2	5.25	5.25

World No Tobacco Day — A239

2003, May 31 Perf. 13¼x14

963	A239	1.50r red	2.00	2.00

Qatar Red Crescent, 25th Anniv. — A240

No. 964: a, Red crescent, boy (30mm diameter). b, Headquarters building.

Litho. With Foil Application
2003, July 1 Perf. 13¼

964	A240	75d Horiz. pair, #a-b	4.25	4.25

Jewelry — A241

Designs: No. 965, 25d, Al-mashmoom. No. 966, 25d, Al-mertash. No. 967, 50d, Khatim. No. 968, 50d, Ishqab. No. 969, 1.50r, Tassa. No. 970, 1.50r, Shmailat.

Photo. & Embossed
2003, Oct. 1   **Perf. 14½x14¼**
965-970 A241 Set of 6   8.25 8.25

Souvenir Sheet

Powered Flight, Cent. — A242

No. 971: a, Wright Flyer. b, Man with winged glider. c, Qatar Airways jet. d, Plane with propellers.

2003, Dec. 17   Litho.   Perf. 13½
971 A242 50d Sheet of 4, #a-d   5.00 5.00

Intl. Year of the Family, 10th Anniv. A243

2004, Apr. 15   **Perf. 14½**
972 A243 2.50r multi   4.00 4.00

FIFA (Fédération Internationale de Football Association), Cent. — A244

2004, May 21   **Perf. 13**
973 A244 50d multi   2.00 2.00
Values are for stamps with selvage adjacent to diagonal sides.

Permanent Constitution — A245

2004, June 8   Litho.   Perf. 13½x13¾
974 A245 75d multi   2.25 2.25

Souvenir Sheet

2004 Summer Olympics, Athens — A246

No. 975: a, Denomination at left. b, Denomination at right.

2004, Aug. 13   Litho.   Perf. 13
975 A246 3r Sheet of 2, #a-d   5.00 5.00

Souvenir Sheet

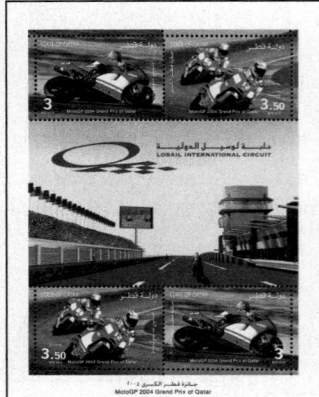

MotoGP 2004 Grand Prix Motorcycle Race — A247

No. 976: a, 3r, Motorcycle, denomination at left. b, 3.50r, Two motorcycles, denomination at right. c, 3.50r, Two motorcycles, denomination at left. d, 3r, Motorcycle, denomination at right.

Perf. 13x14x14x14, 14x14x13x14
2004, Sept. 30
976 A247 Sheet of 4, #a-d   8.50 8.50

Numeral — A248

2004, Nov. 1   Litho.   Perf. 13½x12½
Stamp + Label
977 A248 50d blue   .50   .50
978 A248 50d red   .50   .50
979 A248 50d orange   .50   .50
980 A248 50d blue green   .50   .50
981 A248 50d olive green   .50   .50
  a.   Vert. strip, #977-981, + 5 labels 3.50 3.50
      Nos. 977-981 (5)   2.50 2.50

National Human Rights Committee — A249

2004, Nov. 11   Litho.   Perf. 13¼x13
982 A249 50d multi   .45   .45

Souvenir Sheet

17th Arabian Gulf Cup — A250

No. 983: a, Mascot, emblem, stadium (35x25mm). b, Mascot, emblem, player kicking ball (25x35mm). c, Mascot, emblem (35x35mm). d, Mascot, emblem, goalie catching ball (25x35mm). e, Emblem, two mascots (35x25mm).

2004, Dec. 10   **Perf. 12¾x13¼**
983 A250 1.50r Sheet of 5, #a-e,
      + 4 labels   7.50 7.50

2006 Asian Games, Doha — A251

Mascot Orry: Nos. 984, 990a, 50d, Pointing to Doha. Nos. 985, 990b, 1r, On dhow in Doha harbor, horiz. Nos. 986, 990c, 1.50r, Counting down days on calendar, horiz. Nos. 987, 990d, 2r, Carrying torch. Nos. 988, 990e, 3r, Lighting flame. Nos. 989, 990f, Carrying Qatari flag.

Perf. 13¼x13, 13x13¼
2004, Dec. 31   **Litho.**
984-989 A251 Set of 6   8.00 8.00
Self-Adhesive
Serpentine Die Cut 12½
990 A251 Booklet pane of 6,
      #a-f   8.00 8.00

Miniature Sheet

Cars and Trucks — A252

No. 991: a, 1949 DeSoto (green car). b, 1958 Cadillac Sedan de Ville (white car facing left). c, 1938 Buick (white car facing right). d, 1953 Chrysler Windsor (black car). e, 1962 Dodge Powerwagon (red truck facing right). f, 1958 Chevrolet Pickup (orange red truck facing left). g, 1948 Chevrolet Pickup (green truck). h, 1957 Dodge Sweptside (white and red truck).

2005, Feb. 1   **Perf. 13½x13¾**
991 A252 50d Sheet of 8, #a-h   2.75 2.75

Oryx Quest 2005 Catamaran Race — A253

Designs: No. 992, 50d, Qatar 2006. No. 993, 50d, Daedalus. No. 994, 50d, Cheyenne, vert. No. 995, 50d, Geronimo, vert.

2005, Feb. 1   **Perf. 14½**
992-995 A253 Set of 4   1.25 1.25

Expo 2005, Aichi, Japan — A254

Designs: No. 996, 50d, Mascots. No. 997, 50d, Flag of Qatar.

2005, Mar. 25   Litho.   Perf. 13
996-997 A254 Set of 2   2.00 2.00

Souvenir Sheet

Doha Development Forum — A255

No. 998: a, Denomination in white. b, Denomination in maroon.

2005, Apr. 9   Litho.   Perf. 12¼x13¼
998 A255 6r Sheet of 2, #a-b   7.00 7.00

Souvenir Sheet

Accession of Emir Sheikh Hamad bin Khalifa Al Thani, 10th Anniv. — A256

Litho. & Embossed with Foil Application
2005, June 27   **Perf. 13¼x13¾**
999 A256 2.50r multi   2.25 2.25

Friendship Between Doha, Qatar and Sarajevo, Bosnia and Herzegovina — A257

2005, July 13   Litho.   Perf. 13
1000 A257 2.50r multi   3.00 3.00
See Bosnia & Herzegovina No. 504.

National Flag — A258

Serpentine Die Cut 12¾

2005, Aug. 1   **Self-Adhesive**
1001	Booklet pane of 6	8.50	
a.	A258 50d maroon	.30	.30
b.	A258 1r maroon	.65	.65
c.	A258 1.50r maroon	.95	.95
d.	A258 2.50r maroon	1.60	1.60
e.	A258 3r maroon	1.90	1.90
f.	A258 3.50r maroon	2.25	2.25

Souvenir Sheet

Al Jazeera Children's Channel — A259

No. 1002: a, Children playing. b, Children and balloon. c, Children running. d, Family.

2005, Sept. 9   **Litho.**   **Perf.**
1002 A259 50d Sheet of 4, #a-d   1.25   1.25

Souvenir Sheet

Qatar Philatelic and Numismatics Club — A260

No. 1003: a, Denomination in maroon. b, Denomination in blue.

Litho. & Embossed with Foil Application

2005, Dec. 16   **Perf. 12¾**
1003 A260 1r Sheet of 2, #a-b   1.25   1.25

11th Gulf Cooperation Council Stamp Exhibition — A261

No. 1004: a, Mascots. b, Emblems of exhibition and Qatar General Postal Corporation.

2005, Dec. 21   **Litho.**   **Perf. 13¾**
1004 A261 1r Pair, #a-b   1.25   1.25

Intl. Civil Defense Day — A262

Fire trucks and firefighters on: 50d, Metal ladder. 2.50r, Rope ladder.

2006, Mar. 5   **Litho.**   **Perf. 13x12¾**
1005-1006 A262   Set of 2   2.10   2.10

A263

Gulf Cooperation Council, 25th Anniv. — A264

Litho. with Foil Application

2006, May 25   **Perf. 14**
1007 A263 50d multi   .40   .40

Imperf
Size: 165x105mm

1008 A264 5r multi   3.25   3.25

See Bahrain Nos. 628-629, Kuwait Nos. 1646-1647, Oman Nos. 477-478, Saudi Arabia No. 1378, and United Arab Emirates Nos. 831-832.

2006 World Cup Soccer Championships, Germany — A265

2006, June 9   **Litho.**   **Perf. 13¼**
1009 A265 2r multi + label   1.25   1.25

Printed in sheets of 8 + 8 labels.

2006 Asian Games, Doha — A266

Designs: 50d, Torch bearers. 75d, Volunteers.

2006, Oct. 8   **Litho.**   **Perf. 13¼x13½**
1010-1011 A266   Set of 2   .80   .80

2006 Asian Games, Doha A267

Designs: No. 1012, 1.50r, Athlete's village. No. 1013, 1.50r, Khalifa Stadium. No. 1014, 1.50r, Aspire Dome. No. 1015, 1.50r, Al-Dana Club.
5r, Vignettes of Nos. 1012-1015, Khalifa Stadium, vert.

2006, Nov. 15   **Litho.**   **Perf. 12¾**
1012-1015 A267   Set of 4   3.50   3.50

Imperf
Size: 126x179mm

1016 A267 5r multi   2.75   2.75

Sports of the 2006 Asian Games, Doha — A268

No. 1017: a, Runner breaking tape at finish line. b, Karate. c, Tennis. d, Swimming. e, Cycling.

2006, Nov. 26   **Litho.**   **Perf. 12¾**
1017 A268 50d Vert. strip of 5, a-
     e, + 5 labels   5.50   5.50

Labels on Nos. 1017a-1017e could be personalized.

2006 Asian Games, Doha — A269

Designs: No. 1018, 50d, Mascot Orry playing soccer. No. 1019, 50d, Mascot Orry cycling. No. 1020, 50d, Soccer. No. 1021, 50d, Women's volleyball. No. 1022, 50d, Table tennis.

2006, Dec. 1   **Perf. 13¼**
1018-1022 A269   Set of 5   5.50   5.50

Pan-Arab Equestrian Federation General Assembly Meeting, Doha — A270

2007, Sept. 1   **Litho.**   **Perf. 13¾x14**
1027 A270 2.50r multi   1.60   1.60

Souvenir Sheet

Doha's Bid For 2016 Summer Olympics and Paralympics — A271

No. 1029: a, Runner in starting position, denomination in red violet. b, Runner in starting position, violet denomination. c, Children with raised arms, orange denomination. d, Children with raised arms, red denomination.

2007, Oct. 25   **Litho.**   **Perf. 14x14½**
1029 A271 50d Sheet of 4, #a-d   1.25   1.25

28th Session of Supreme Council of Gulf Cooperation Council — A272

2007, Dec. 3   **Litho.**   **Perf. 12¾**
1030 A272 50d multi   .30   .30

Miniature Sheet

Qatar Rulers and National Emblem — A273

No. 1031: a, National emblem (light blue panel, 38x28mm). b, Sheikh Hamad bin Khalifa Al Thani (38x55mm). c, National emblem (maroon panel, 38x28mm). d, Sheikh Ali bin Abdullah Al Thani (1895-1974, blue green panel, 38x28mm). e, Sheikh Abdullah bin Jassim Al Thani (1876-1957, pale green panel, 38x28mm). f, Sheikh Khalifa bin Hamad Al Thani (buff panel, 38x28mm). g, Sheikh Ahmad bin Ali Al Thani (1917-77, gray brown panel, 38x28mm).

Litho. With Foil Application

2007, Dec. 18   **Perf. 12¼**
1031 A273 2.50r Sheet of 7, #a-
     g, + label   9.75   9.75

Islamic Holy Sites — A274

No. 1032: a, Green Dome of the Holy Prophet, Medina (olive green frame). b, Holy Ka'aba, Mecca (yellow brown frame). c, Dome of the Rock, Jerusalem (blue frame).

Litho. & Embossed

2007, Dec. 19   **Perf. 14x13½**
1032 A274   Horiz. strip of 3   4.25   4.25
a.-c.   2.50r Any single   1.40   1.40

Souvenir Sheet

Holy Ka'aba, Green Dome of the Holy Prophet, and Dome of the Rock — A274a

Litho. & Embossed

2007, Dec. 19   **Perf. 14x13½**
1033 A274a 5r multi   6.50   6.50

First Arab Stamp Exhibition, Doha A275

2008, Jan. 30 Litho. *Perf. 13x12¾*
1034 A275 50d multi .30 .30

Miniature Sheet

Traditional Perfumes — A276

No. 1035: a, Al Marash. b, Oud perfume oil. c, Agar wood. d, Al Mogbass.

2008, Mar. 31 *Perf. 13¾*
1035 A276 1.50r Sheet of 4, #a-d 3.50 3.50

No. 1035 is impregnated with a sandalwood scent.

Miniature Sheet

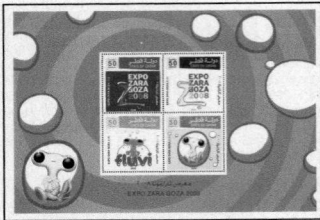

Expo Zaragoza 2008, Zaragoza, Spain — A277

No. 1036: a, Emblem, denomination in Prussian blue. b, Emblem, denomination in dark blue. c, Mascot, denomination in yellow brown. d, Mascot, denomination in gray.

2008, June 14 *Perf. 14x14¼*
1036 A277 50d Sheet of 4, #a-d 1.10 1.10

Souvenir Sheet

Arab Post Day — A278

No. 1037 — Emblem and: a, World map, pigeon. b, Camel caravan.

Litho. & Silk-screened With Foil Application
2008, Aug. 3 *Perf. 13½x13¼*
1037 A278 5r Sheet of 2, #a-b 5.50 5.50

Miniature Sheet

2008 Summer Olympics, Beijing — A279

No. 1038 — Beijing Olympics emblem and: a, 50d, Blue background (34x36mm). b, 50d, Green background (34x36mm). c, 3r, Stylized people (69x36mm).

2008, Aug. 8 Litho. *Perf. 14½*
1038 A279 Sheet of 3, #a-c 2.25 2.25

14th Gulf Cooperation Council Stamp Exhibition, Doha — A280

2008, Oct. 14 *Perf. 14x14½*
1039 A280 50d multi .30 .30

Arab Police Sporting Federation — A281

No. 1040 — Color of denomination. a, White, b, Olive green.

2008, Oct. 14 *Perf. 13¾x13¼*
1040 A281 50d Horiz. pair, #a-b .55 .55

Museum of Islamic Art, Doha A282

2008, Nov. 22 Litho. *Perf. 13x13¼*
1041 A282 50d multi .30 .30

Souvenir Sheet
1042 A282 5r multi 2.75 2.75

A283

Souq Waqif A283a

2008, Dec. 18 *Perf. 13¾*
1043 A283 1.50r multi — —
1044 A283a 1.50r multi — —
1045 A283b 1.50r multi — —
1046 A283c 1.50r multi — —

Campaign for Responsible Media — A284

2009, Jan. 13 Litho. *Perf. 13¼*
1047 A284 50d multi .30 .30

Tears for Gaza — A285

2009, Jan. 21 Litho. *Perf. 12¾*
1048 A285 1r multi .55 .55

First Democratic City Council Elections, 10th Anniv. — A286

2009, Mar. 15 Litho. *Perf. 13¾*
1050 A286 50d multi .30 .30

Jerusalem, 2009 Capital of Arab Culture A287

2009, Aug. 3 *Perf. 13*
1051 A287 1r multi .55 .55

Souvenir Sheet

RasGas Liquified Natural Gas Sales, 10th Anniv., and Train 6 Inauguration — A288

No. 1052 — RasGas emblem and: a, Drop. b, Large globe. c, Small glove, numbers 1 to 10.

2009, Oct. 27 *Perf.*
1052 A288 1r Sheet of 3, #a-c 1.75 1.75

Birds A289

Designs: No. 1053, Orphean warbler. No. 1054, Woodchat shrike. No. 1055, Isabelline shrike. No. 1056, Lesser gray shrike. No. 1057, Chiffchaf. No. 1058, Yellow wagtail. No. 1059: a, Head of Orphean warbler. b, Head of Woodchat shrike. c, Head of Isabelline shrike. d, Head of Lesser gray shrike. e, Head of Chiffchaf. f, Head of Yellow wagtail. 5r, Cream-colored courser.

2009, Dec. 18 Litho. *Perf. 13*
1053 A289 50d multi .30 .30
1054 A289 50d multi .30 .30
1055 A289 50d multi .30 .30
1056 A289 50d multi .30 .30
1057 A289 50d multi .30 .30
1058 A289 50d multi .30 .30
Nos. 1053-1058 (6) 1.80 1.80

Booklet Stamps
1059 Booklet pane of 6 1.80 —
a-.f. A289 50d Any single .30 .30

Souvenir Sheet
1060 A289 5r multi 2.75 2.75

Organization of Petroleum Exporting Countries, 50th Anniv. — A290

2010, Jan. 28 Litho. *Perf. 13x13¼*
1061 A290 1r multi .55 .55

Distribution of Mus-haf Qatar (Koran With Calligraphic Writing) A291

2010, Mar. 9 *Perf. 12¾x13*
1062 A291 3r multi 1.75 1.75

2010 Population and Housing Census A292

2010, Apr. 20 *Perf. 13¾*
1063 A292 1r multi .55 .55

25th Universal Postal Union Congress, Doha — A293

2010, Sept. 24 *Perf. 13¼x13¾*
1064 A293 50d multi .30 .30

See Nos. 1076, 1084.

A294

Doha, 2010 Capital of Arab
Culture — A295

No. 1065: a, Horsemen with flags. b, Masks.
c, Open book. d, Stringed instrument and
musical notes.
5r, Stylized peacock.

2010, Oct. 10   *Perf. 14½*
1065 A294 1.50r Sheet of 4, #a-d 3.50 3.50

Size:60x100mm
Imperf
1066 A295   5r multi   2.75 2.75

Souvenir Sheet

2010 Aga Khan Award for
Architecture — A296

2010, Nov. 24   *Perf. 13¼x12¾*
1067 A296 1.50r multi   .85 .85

Souvenir Sheets

A297

A298

A299

Qatar's Annual Production of 77
Million Tonnes of Liquified Natural
Gas — A300

2010, Dec. 13   *Perf. 14x13½*
1068 A297 1r multi   .55 .55
1069 A298 1r multi   .55 .55
1070 A299 1r multi   .55 .55
1071 A300 1r multi   .55 .55
    Nos. 1068-1071 (4)   2.20 2.20

Souvenir Sheet

Qatar News Agency, 35th
Anniv. — A301

2010, Dec. 18   *Perf. 13¼*
1072 A301 1r blue & red   .55 .55

Qatar Amateur Radio Society — A302

2010, Dec. 26   *Perf. 13¾*
1073 A302 50d multi   .30 .30

Arab Deaf
Week — A303

2011, Apr. 20   *Perf. 12¾x13*
1074 A303 1r multi   .55 .55

First Postal Agency, 50th
Anniv. — A304

Litho. With Foil Application
2011, May 17   *Perf. 14x13¼*
1075 A304 50d multi   .30 .30

25th UPU Congress Type of 2010
2011, Sept. 24 Litho.   *Perf. 14x14½*
1076 A293 1r multi   .55 .55

Miniature Sheet

11th Qatar Classic Squash
Championship — A305

No. 1077 — Color of top panel: a, Light
green. b, Tan. c, Light blue. d, Rose lilac.

2011, Oct. 16   *Perf. 14½x14¾*
1077 A305 1r Sheet of 4, #a-d 2.25 2.25

2011 Arab Games,
Doha — A306

No. 1078 — Text with denomination color in:
a, Orange. b, Gray. c, Yellow green.

2011, Dec. 9   *Perf. 12½*
1078 A306 50d Vert. strip of 3,
    #a-c   .85 .85

Qatari Endowment Deed, 90th
Anniv. — A307

Designs: No. 1079, 50d, Emblem. No. 1080,
50d, Building.
3r, Scroll, vert.

2012, Mar. 4   *Perf. 13½x13¼*
1079-1080 A307   Set of 2   .55 .55
Souvenir Sheet
Perf. 13¼x13½
1081 A307 3r multi   1.75 1.75

Arab
Postal
Day
A308

2012, Aug. 3   *Perf. 13¼*
1082 A308 1r multi   .55 .55

25th UPU Congress Type of 2010
2012, Sept. 24 Litho.   *Perf. 14x14½*
1084 A293 2r multi   1.10 1.10

Falcon,
Flags of
Qatar and
Morocco
A310

2012, Oct. 9   *Perf. 12¾*
1085 A310 2.50r multi   1.40 1.40

See Morocco No. 1155.

2012 United Nations Climate Change
Conference, Doha — A311

2012, Nov. 1
1086 A311 2.50r blue & lt blue   1.40 1.40

First Compressed Natural Gas Bus in
Qatar — A312

2013, Mar. 25 Litho.   *Perf. 12¾*
1087 A312 50d multi   .30 .30

Miniature Sheet

Jeemtv.net — A313

No. 1088: a, Girl, horse made of ribbons, orange panel. b, Boy, automobiles, purple panel. c, Boy in soccer uniform, red panel. d, Girl, stylized butterflies, turquoise green panel.

2013, June 23   Litho.   Perf. 13¾
1088 A313 2.50r Sheet of 4, #a-d 5.50 5.50

World Social Security Forum, Doha — A314

2013, Nov. 10   Litho.   Perf. 14¼x14
1089 A314 3r multi   1.75 1.75

Sheikh Tamim — A315

2013, Dec. 17   Litho.   Perf. 13¼x13
Panel Color at Bottom
1090 A315 50d pale green   .30   .30
1091 A315 1r rose lilac   .55   .55
1092 A315 2r brt yel grn   1.10   1.10
1093 A315 3r pale yel grn   1.75   1.75
1094 A315 4r pale yellow   2.25   2.25
1095 A315 5r light blue   2.75   2.75
Size: 25x30mm
Perf. 13½x13¼
1096 A315 10r turq grn   5.50   5.50
1097 A315 20r pale gray   11.00 11.00
1098 A315 30r tan   16.50 16.50
      Nos. 1090-1098 (9)   41.70 41.70

See Nos. 1113-1115, 1123.

Qatar Insurance Company, 50th Anniv. A316

Litho. & Embossed With Foil Application
2014, Feb. 16   Perf. 13½
1099 A316 1r gold & carmine   .55   .55

Souvenir Sheet

Media Training, 10th Anniv. — A317

Litho. & Embossed With Foil Application
2014, Feb. 24   Perf. 13¾x13½
1100 A317 4r multi   2.25   2.25

No. 1100 was printed with three different sheet margins.

Oryx Leucoryx, Vultur Gryphus, Flags of Ecuador and Qatar — A318

Litho. With Foil Application
2014, Oct. 22   Perf. 12¾x13¼
1101 A318 3r silver & gold   1.75   1.75

See Ecuador No. 2133.

Souvenir Sheet

2014 World Arabian Horse Conference, Doha — A319

2014, Nov. 2   Litho.   Perf. 12¼
1102 A319 5r multi   3.25   3.25

Souvenir Sheet

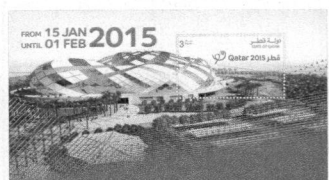

2015 Men's World Handball Championships, Qatar — A321

2015, Jan. 15   Litho.   Perf. 13x12¾
1108 A321 3r copper & blk   1.75   1.75

International Al-Bawasil Diabetic Camp — A322

2015, Jan. 16   Litho.   Perf. 13½
1109 A322 3r multi   1.75   1.75

Souvenir Sheet

Katara Prize for Arabic Novels — A323

Litho. & Embossed
2015, Jan. 18   Perf. 12¾x13¼
1110 A323 5r multi   2.75   2.75

Miniature Sheet

Jeem Cup Children's Soccer Tournament — A324

No. 1111 — Mascot, with panel color of: a, Brown orange. b, Purple. c, Brown red. d, Yellow orange.

2015, Mar. 16   Litho.   Perf. 13¾
1111 A324 2.50r Sheet of 4, #a-d 5.50 5.50

Miniature Sheet

13th United Nations Congress on Crime Prevention and Criminal Justice, Doha — A325

No. 1112 — Emblems and text: a, With red arch at top. b, Without red arch at top.

2015, Apr. 12   Litho.   Perf. 14½x14¼
1112 A325 1r Sheet of 4, 2 each
              #a-b   2.25   2.25

Sheikh Tamim Type of 2013
Perf. 13½x13¼
2015, Aug. 10   Litho.
Size: 25x30mm
Panel Color at Bottom
1113 A315 10r light orange   5.50   5.50
1114 A315 20r red   11.00 11.00
1115 A315 30r dark blue   16.50 16.50
      Nos. 1113-1115 (3)   33.00 33.00

Souvenir Sheet

National Day — A326

Perf. 13¾x13½
2015, Dec. 17   Litho.
1116 A326 5r gold & multi   2.75   2.75

20th Gulf Cooperation Council Stamp Exhibition, Doha — A327

Designs: 3r, Gulf Cooperation Council and Exhibition emblems. 5r, Gulf Cooperation Council and Exhibition emblems, triangles.

2015, Sept. 29   Litho.   Perf. 13¼
1117 A327 3r multi   1.75   1.75
Size: 90x57mm
Imperf
1118 A327 5r multi   2.75   2.75

National Sports Day — A328

2016, Feb. 8   Litho.   Perf. 13¼
1119 A328 5r multi   2.75   2.75

Miniature Sheet

"With Education, We Build Qatar" — A329

No. 1120: a, Arabic characters. b, Beakers, molecular models and formulas. c, Dhows and buildings. d, Computer keyboard and open book.

Perf. 13¾ Syncopated
2016, Sept. 18   Litho.
1120 A329 3.50r Sheet of 4, #a-d 7.75 7.75

Arab Postal Day — A330

No. 1121 — Globe, envelopes and emblem with denomination at: a, LR. b, LL.

2016, Sept. 25   Litho.   Perf. 12¾
1121 A330 4.50r Horiz. pair, #a-b 4.50 4.50

Souvenir Sheet

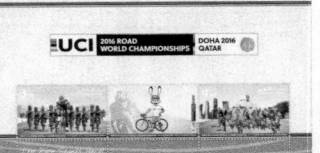

2016 Road Cycling World Championships, Qatar — A331

No. 1122: a, 3.50r, Cyclists wearing same jerseys. b, 4r, Cyclist and mascot. c, 4.50r, Cyclists wearing different jerseys.

Perf. 13¼x13½
2016, Sept. 26   Litho.
1122 A331 Sheet of 3, #a-c   6.75   6.75

Sheikh Tamim Type of 2013

2016, Oct. 10 Litho. Perf. 13¼x13
Panel Color at Bottom
1123 A315 5r dull mauve   2.75 2.75

Miniature Sheet

QatarDebate Initiative — A332

No. 1124: a, 3.50r, Man and woman debating, magenta frame. b, 4.50r, Man and woman debating, dull blue frame. c, 5r, Woman and two men, magenta background.´d, 5r, Woman and two men, greenish blue background.

2016, Oct. 16 Litho. Perf. 13¼x13
1124 A332 Sheet of 4, 3a-d   10.00 10.00

National Day A333

Denomination in: 50r, Red. 100r, Gold.

2016, Dec. 17 Litho. Perf. 14
1125-1126 A333 Set of 2   — —

Souvenir Sheet

National Day — A334

No. 1127: a, People pulling on ropes. b, Falcon.

Litho. With Foil Application
2016, Dec. 17 Perf. 13½x13¼
1127 A334 5r Sheet of 2, #a-b   5.50 5.50

Souvenir Sheet

Opening of Port Hamad — A335

No. 1128 — Ship, crane and dock: a, 4.50r. b, 8.50r.

2017, Jan. 4 Litho. Perf. 14¼
1128 A335 Sheet of 2, #a-b   7.25 7.25

Marine Life — A336

Designs: No. 1129, 50d, Hermit crab. No. 1130, 50d, Cnidaria. No. 1131, 3r, Sea slug. No. 1132, 3r, Crustacean. No. 1133, 4r, Sea anemone. No. 1134, 4r, Coral polyps. No. 1135, 5r, Sea anemone, diff. No. 1136, 5r, Phylum Annelida.

2017, Feb. 26 Litho. Perf. 13¼
1129-1134 A336 Set of 6   8.25 8.25
Size: 100x60mm
Imperf
1135-1136 A336 Set of 2   5.50 5.50

Education Excellence Day — A337

2017, Mar. 1 Litho. Perf. 13¼x14
1137 A337 3.50r multi   2.00 2.00

Souvenir Sheet

Qatar Stars Professional Soccer League — A338

No. 1138: a, Soccer ball with red flower designs. b, Stylized soccer player. c, Ring of five colored flower designs.

2017, Sept. 12 Litho. Perf. 14
1138 A338 4r Sheet of 3, #a-c   6.75 6.75

Miniature Sheet

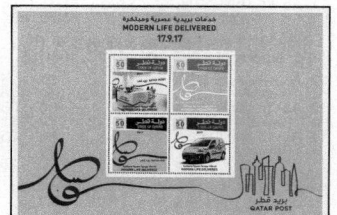

Qatar Post — A339

No. 1139: a, Post office counter. b, Arabic calligraphy and English slogan in white. c, Arabic calligraphy and English slogan in dark blue and blackish purple. d, Mail van.

2017, Sept. 17 Litho. Perf. 14x14½
1139 A339 50d Sheet of 4, #a-d 1.10 1.10

Souvenir Sheet

Teacher's Day — A340

Litho. With Foil Application
2017, Oct. 5 Perf. 13
1140 A340 5r silver & multi   2.60 2.60

Miniature Sheet

Qatar Airways, 20th Anniv. — A341

No. 1140: a, Jet on runway. b, Front view of jet in flight. c, Side view of jet in flight. d, Doha skyline, 20th anniversary emblem, 2017 Airline of the Year award.

Litho. & Embossed With Foil Application
2017, Nov. 30 Perf. 13x12¾
1141 A341 5r Sheet of 4, #a-d   11.00 11.00

Souvenir Sheet

National Day — A342

No. 1142 — Arabic text and: a, Clouds. b, Doha skyline.

Litho. With Foil Application
2017, Dec. 17 Perf. 13¾x13¼
1142 A342 10r Sheet of 2, #a-b, + central label   11.00 11.00

Souvenir Sheet

Diplomatic Relations Between Qatar and Turkey, 45th Anniv. — A343

No. 1143: a, Rumeli Fortress, Istanbul, and Al Zubara Castle, Qatar. b, Barzan Castle, Qatar, and Ankara Castle, Ankara.

Litho., Sheet Margin Litho. With Foil Application
2018, Feb. 21 Perf. 13½x13¼
1143 A343 8.50r Sheet of 2, #a-b 9.50 9.50

See Turkey No. 3588.

A344

Qatar National Library, Doha — A345

2018, Apr. 16 Litho. Perf. 13¼x13¾
1144 A344 1r multi   — —
1145 A345 1r multi   — —

A346

A347

A348

Al Wadha Arches at 5/6 Interchange, Doha — A349

Serpentine Die Cut 11 Syncopated
Litho. With Foil Application
2018, June 5 Self-Adhesive
1146   Sheet of 4   — —
  a. A346 3.50r silver & multi   — —
  b. A347 3.50r silver & multi   — —
  c. A348 3.50r silver & multi   — —
  d. A349 3.50r silver & multi   — —

Souvenir Sheet

Reign of Sheikh Tamim, 5th Anniv. — A350

No. 1147 — Sheikh Tamim and: a, Flags. b, Building, horiz. c, Emblem of Qatar, horiz.

Litho. With Foil Application
2018, July 2 Perf. 13
1147 A350 25r Sheet of 3, #a-c   — —

QUELIMANE

ˌkel-ə-'män-ə

LOCATION — A district of the Mozambique Province in Portuguese East Africa
GOVT. — Part of the Portuguese East Africa Colony
AREA — 39,800 sq. mi.
POP. — 877,000 (approx.)
CAPITAL — Quelimane

This district was formerly a part of Zambezia. Quelimane stamps were replaced by those of Mozambique.

100 Centavos = 1 Escudo

Vasco da Gama Issue

Various Portuguese Colonies Surcharged

1913   Unwmk.   *Perf. 12½ to 16*
On Stamps of Macao

1	CD20	¼c on ½a bl grn	3.50	3.50
2	CD21	½c on 1a red	3.00	2.60
3	CD22	1c on 2a red vio	3.00	2.60
4	CD23	2½c on 4a yel grn	3.00	2.60
5	CD24	5c on 8a dk bl	3.00	2.60
6	CD25	7½c on 12a vio brn	5.75	4.25
7	CD26	10c on 16a bis brn	3.50	2.60
8	CD27	15c on 24a bister	3.50	2.60
		Nos. 1-8 (8)	28.25	23.35
		Set, never hinged	67.50	

On Stamps of Portuguese Africa

9	CD20	¼c on 2½r bl grn	2.60	2.60
10	CD21	½c on 5r red	2.60	2.60
11	CD22	1c on 10r red vio	2.60	2.60
12	CD23	2½c on 25r yel grn	2.60	2.60
13	CD24	5c on 50r dk bl	2.60	2.60
14	CD25	7½c on 75r vio brn	5.75	4.00
15	CD26	10c on 100r bister	3.25	2.60
16	CD27	15c on 150r bister	3.25	2.60
		Nos. 9-16 (8)	25.25	22.20
		Set, never hinged	60.00	

On Stamps of Timor

17	CD20	¼c on ½a bl grn	3.00	3.00
18	CD21	½c on 1a red	3.00	3.00
19	CD22	1c on 2a red vio	3.00	3.00
20	CD23	2½c on 4a yel grn	3.00	3.00
21	CD24	5c on 8a dk bl	3.00	3.00
22	CD25	7½c on 12a vio brn	5.75	4.00
23	CD26	10c on 16a bis brn	3.50	3.00
24	CD27	15c on 24a bister	3.50	3.00
		Nos. 17-24 (8)	27.75	25.00
		Set, never hinged	67.50	
		Nos. 1-24 (24)	81.25	70.55
		Set, never hinged	195.00	

Ceres — A1

1914   Typo.   *Perf. 15x14*
Name and Value in Black
Chalky Paper

25	A1	¼c olive brown	1.60	2.25
26	A1	½c black	2.25	2.25
27	A1	1c blue green	2.60	2.25
a.		Imperf.		
28	A1	1½c lilac brown	3.25	2.40
29	A1	2c carmine	3.25	2.40
30	A1	2½c light violet	1.60	1.20
31	A1	5c deep blue	2.40	2.40
32	A1	7½c yellow brown	4.00	2.40
33	A1	8c slate	4.00	2.40
34	A1	10c orange brown	4.00	2.40
35	A1	15c plum	4.00	3.75
36	A1	20c yellow green	6.50	2.75
37	A1	30c brown, *green*	7.25	6.50
38	A1	40c brown, *pink*	7.25	7.25
39	A1	50c orange, *salmon*	8.00	8.00
40	A1	1e green, *blue*	10.00	9.00
		Nos. 25-40 (16)	71.95	59.80

Ordinary Paper

25B	A1	¼c olive brown	2.10	2.25
27B	A1	1c blue green	2.50	2.25
32B	A1	7½c yellow brown	3.25	2.40
34B	A1	10c orange brown	2.50	2.40
36B	A1	20c yellow green	4.00	2.10
		Nos. 25B-36B (5)	14.35	11.40

RAS AL KHAIMA

ˌräs al 'kī-mə

LOCATION — Oman Peninsula, Arabia, on Persian Gulf
GOVT. — Sheikdom under British protection

Ras al Khaima was the 7th Persian Gulf sheikdom to join the United Arab Emirates, doing so in Feb. 1972.
See United Arab Emirates.

100 Naye Paise = 1 Rupee
100 Fils = 1 Rupee (1966)
100 Dirhams = 1 Riyal (1966)

> **Catalogue values for all unused stamps in this country are for Never Hinged items.**

> **Used values are for canceled to order stamps, except for Nos. 66-141, and where otherwise stated.**

> **Imperforate stamps and deluxe sheets are footnoted where they are known to exist. All are believed to have been valid for postage and sold at the post office in Ras Al Khaima, but were produced in limited quanities. Orders were often limited to one set per order or to one set for every 10 regularly perforated sets ordered.**

Sheik Saqr bin Mohammed al Qasimi — A1

Seven Palm Trees — A2

Dhow A3

Perf. 14½x14
1964, Dec. 21   Photo.   Unwmk.

1	A1	5np brown & black	.25	.25
2	A1	15np deep blue & blk	.25	.25
3	A2	30np ocher & black	.25	.35
4	A2	40np blue & black	.30	.45
5	A2	75np brn red & blk	1.25	.90
6	A3	1r lt grn & sepia	3.75	1.25
7	A3	2r brt vio & sepia	10.00	2.75
8	A3	5r blue gray & sepia	25.00	8.25
		Nos. 1-8 (8)	41.05	14.45

Used values are for postally used examples.
For overprints and surcharges see Nos. 21-29, 66-73, 86-93, 140-141.

Pres. John Kennedy (1917-63), Lyndon Johnson (1908-73), and Astronaut John Glenn (1921-2016) — A4

Pres. John Kennedy (1917-63) A5

Design: Nos. 10 and 13, President John F. Kennedy and Jackie Kennedy shaking hands.

1965, July 21   Photo.   *Perf. 14½*

9	A4	2r sepia & bl	.75	.40
10	A4	3r sepia, bl & blk	1.20	.60
11	A5	4r sepia & bl	1.75	.85
		Nos. 9-11 (3)	3.70	1.85

Nos. 9-11 were printed in sheets of six.
For surcharges see Nos. 74-76, 160-162.

12	A4	1r sepia & bl	.60	.25
a.		Pane of 4	2.50	1.20
13	A4	1r sepia, bl & blk	.60	.25
a.		Pane of 4	2.50	1.20
14	A5	1r sepia & bl	.60	.25
a.		Pane of 4	2.50	1.20
		Nos. 12-14 (3)	1.80	.75

Nos. 12-14 were printed in sheets of four.
For surcharges see Nos. 77-79, 163-165.

Winston Churchill (1874-1965) — A6

Funeral Procession, Winston Churchill (1874-1965) — A7

Design: Nos. 16 and 19, Winston Churchill with Franklin Roosevelt, horiz.

1965, Nov. 30   Photo.   *Perf. 14½*

15	A6	2r sepia, bl & blk	.75	.40
16	A6	3r sepia & bl	1.20	.60
17	A7	4r sepia, bl & blk	1.75	.85
		Nos. 15-17 (3)	3.70	1.85

Nos. 15-17 were printed in sheets of six.
For overprints and surcharges see Nos. 80-82.

Souvenir Sheets

18	A6	1r sepia, bl & blk	.60	.25
a.		Pane of 4	2.50	1.20
19	A6	1r sepia & sepia	.60	.25
a.		Pane of 4	2.50	1.20

20	A7	1r sepia, bl & blk	.60	.25
a.		Pane of 4	2.50	1.20
			1.80	.75
		Nos. 18-20 (3)		

Nos. 18-20 were printed in sheets of four.
For surcharges see Nos. 83-85.

Nos. 6-8 Overprinted

1965, Oct. 10   *Perf. 14½x14*

21	A3	1r lt grn & sepia	.60	.60
22	A3	2r brt vio & sepia	1.20	1.20
23	A3	5r blue gray & sepia	3.25	3.25
		Nos. 21-23 (3)	5.05	5.05

Overprinted for the 1964 Tokyo Olympic Games.
Nos. 21-23 exist with inverted or double overprints.

Nos. 6-8 Overprinted

1965, Nov. 1

24	A3	1r lt grn & sepia	.60	.60
25	A3	2r brt vio & sepia	1.20	1.20
26	A3	5r blue gray & sepia	3.25	3.25
		Nos. 24-26 (3)	5.05	5.05

Overprinted for the 100th anniversary of the death Abraham Lincoln (1809-65).
Nos. 24-26 exist with inverted or double overprints.

Nos. 6-8 Overprinted

1965, Nov. 30

27	A3	1r lt grn & sepia	.60	.60
28	A3	2r brt vio & sepia	1.20	1.20
29	A3	5r blue gray & sepia	3.25	3.25
		Nos. 27-29 (3)	5.05	5.05

Overprinted for the 20th anniversary of the death of Franklin Roosevelt (1882-1945).
Nos. 27-29 exist with inverted or double overprints.

Satellite and Dish — A8

Designs: 15np, 1r, Satellite and satellite dish with radio waves. 50np, 2r, Satellite and tower. 85np, 3r, Satellite and rocket on launch pad.
5r, Two satellites orbiting globe.

1966, May 10   Litho.   *Perf. 13¼x13½*

30	A8	15np multi	.25	.25
31	A8	50np multi	.45	.25
32	A8	85np multi	.95	.30
33	A8	1r multi	1.10	.40
34	A8	2r multi	1.90	.45
35	A8	3r multi	2.25	.50
		Nos. 30-35 (6)	6.90	2.15

Souvenir Sheet
Imperf

36	A8	5r multi		5.00

100th anniversary of the ITU.
Nos. 30-35 exist imperf. Value, set $9.
For surcharges see Nos. 94-100.

Running — A9

Designs: 1np, 5np, Running. 2np, 25np, Boxing. 3np, 50np, Soccer. 4np, 75np, 5r, Fencing. 10np, 1r, Swimming.

1966, June 9   Photo.   Perf. 12

37	A9	1np shown	.25	.25
38	A9	2np multi	.25	.25
39	A9	3np multi	.25	.25
40	A9	4np multi	.25	.25
41	A9	5np multi	.25	.25
42	A9	10np multi	.25	.25
43	A9	25np multi	.40	.25
44	A9	50np multi	.75	.25
45	A9	75np multi	1.00	.25
46	A9	1r multi	1.60	.25
		Nos. 37-46 (10)	5.25	2.50

Souvenir Sheet
Imperf

| 47 | A9 | 5r multi | 5.00 | — |

Pan-Arab Games.
Nos. 37-46 exist imperf. Value, set $6.75.
For surcharges see Nos. 100-111.

Scott Carpenter (1925-2013), Astronaut — A10

Designs: 25np, Scott Carpenter (1925-2013). 50np, John Glenn (1921-2016). 75np, Alan Shepard (1923-98). 1r, Leroy Gordon Cooper (1927-2004). 2r, Virgil Ivan Grissom (1926-67). 3r, Walter Marty Schirra (1923-2007). 4r, Thomas P. Stafford (b. 1930). 5r, James A. Lovell (b. 1928).

1966, June 30   Photo.   Perf. 12

48	A10	25np gold & multi	.25	.25
49	A10	50np silver & multi	.25	.25
50	A10	75np silver & multi	.25	.25
51	A10	1r silver & multi	.35	.25
52	A10	2r silver & multi	.70	.30
53	A10	3r gold & multi	1.00	.30
54	A10	4r gold & multi	1.25	.40
55	A10	5r gold & multi	1.50	.50
		Nos. 48-55 (8)	5.55	2.50

Souvenir Sheet
Size: 155x105mm
Simulated Perfs

| 56 | A10 | 4r multi | 5.00 | 5.00 |
| 57 | A10 | 4r multi | 5.00 | 5.00 |

Nos. 48-55 exist imperf. Value, set $9.
No. 56 is a single 4r stamp containing the designs of Nos. 49-52. No. 57 is a single 4r stamp containing the designs of Nos. 48 and 53-55.
For surcharges and overprints see Nos. 122-131, 173-182.

Sheikh Saqr bin Mohammed al Qasimi (1918-2010) and Sheikh Ahmad — A11

Designs: Sheikh Saqr bin Mohammed al Qasimi (1918-2010) with other world leaders. No. 58, Sheikh Ahmad. No. 59, Sheikh Ahmed Bin Ali Al Thani (1922-77), Qatar. No. 60, Pres. Gamal Abdel Nasser (1918-70), Egypt and the United Arab Republic. No. 61, King Hussein bin Talal (1935-99), Jordan. No. 62, Pres. Lyndon B. Johnson (1908-73), United

States. No. 63, Pres. Charles de Gaulle (1890-1970), France. No. 64, Pope Paul VI (1897-1978). No. 65, Prime Minister Harold Wilson (1916-95), Great Britain.

1966, July 28   Litho.   Perf. 13½x14½

58	A11	1r peach & blk	.65	.25
59	A11	1r purple & blk	.65	.25
60	A11	1r pink & blk	.65	.25
61	A11	1r steel grn & blk	.65	.25
a.		Sheet of 4, #58-61, simulated perfs.	5.00	
62	A11	1r yelsh grn & blk	.65	.25
63	A11	1r yellow & blk	.65	.25
64	A11	1r org & blk	.65	.25
65	A11	1r steel blue & blk	.65	.25
a.		Sheet of 4, #62-65, simulated perfs.	5.00	
		Nos. 58-65 (8)	5.20	2.00

Issued for the 20th anniversary of the United Nations.
Nos. 58-65 exist imperf. Value, set $10.
For surcharges see Nos. 132-139.

Nos. 66-85 were surcharged for the currency change from Rupee to Fils, which occurred on Aug. 1, 1966.
Nos. 30-35 and 58-65 surcharged with Fils are likely bogus. The editors would like more information on these.

Nos. 1-8 Surcharged New Currency in Fils With Three Bar Obliterators

1966, Aug. 1   Photo.   Perf. 14½x14

66	A1	5f on 5np	—	—
67	A1	15f on 15np	—	—
68	A2	30f on 30np	—	—
69	A2	40f on 40np	—	—
70	A2	75f on 75np	—	—
71	A3	100f on 1r	—	—
72	A3	200f on 2r	—	—
73	A3	500f on 5r	—	—

See Nos. 86-93. For surcharge see No. 141.

Nos. 9-11 Surcharged in English and Arabic

1966, Aug. 1

74	A4	200f on 2r	.75	.75
75	A4	300f on 3r	1.00	1.00
76	A5	400f on 4r	1.25	1.25
		Nos. 74-76 (3)	3.00	3.00

Same Surcharge on Nos. 12-14
Souvenir Sheets

77	A4	100f on 1r (#12)	.50	.50
a.		Pane of 4	2.00	2.00
78	A4	100f on 1r (#13)	.50	.50
a.		Pane of 4	2.00	2.00
79	A5	100f on 1r (#14)	.50	.50
a.		Pane of 4	2.00	2.00
		Nos. 77-79 (3)	1.50	1.50

Nos. 15-17 Surcharged in English and Arabic

1966, Aug. 1   Perf. 14½

80	A6	200f on 2r	.75	.75
81	A6	300f on 3r	1.00	1.00
82	A7	400f on 4r	1.25	1.25
		Nos. 80-82 (3)	3.00	3.00

Same Surcharge on Nos. 18-20
Souvenir Sheets

83	A6	100f on 1r (#18)	.50	.50
a.		Pane of 4	2.00	2.00
84	A6	100f on 1r (#19)	.50	.50
a.		Pane of 4	2.00	2.00

85	A7	100f on 1r (#20)	.50	.50
a.		Pane of 4	2.00	2.00
		Nos. 83-85 (3)	1.50	1.50

For Nos. 74-79, used values are for postally used examples.

Nos. 86-141 were surcharged for the currency change from Fils to Dirhams, which occurred on Nov. 20, 1966.

Nos. 1-8 Surcharged

1966   Perf. 14½x14

86	A1	5d on 5np	—	5.50
87	A1	15d on 15np	—	5.50
88	A2	30d on 30np	—	5.50
89	A2	40d on 40np	—	5.50
90	A2	75d on 75np	—	35.00
91	A3	1rl on 1r	—	10.00
92	A3	2rl on 2r	—	10.00
93	A3	5rl on 5r	—	10.00
		Nos. 86-93 (8)		87.00

Nos. 30-36 Surcharged

1966, Nov. 20   Perf. 13¼x13½

94	A8	15d on 15np	.35	.35
95	A8	50d on 50np	1.20	1.20
96	A8	85d on 85np	2.25	2.25
97	A8	1rl on 1r	2.40	2.40
98	A8	2rl on 2r	3.75	3.75
99	A8	3rl on 3r	5.00	5.00
		Nos. 94-99 (6)	14.95	14.95

Souvenir Sheet
Imperf

| 100 | A8 | 5rl on 5r | 20.00 | — |

Nos. 94-99 exist imperf. Value, set $25.

Nos. 37-47 Surcharged

1966, Nov. 20   Perf. 12

101	A9	1d on 1np	.30	.30
102	A9	2d on 2np	.30	.30
103	A9	3d on 3np	.30	.30
104	A9	4d on 4np	.30	.30
105	A9	5d on 5np	.30	.30
106	A9	10d on 10np	.45	.45
107	A9	25d on 25np	.75	.75
108	A9	50d on 50np	1.60	1.60
109	A9	75d on 75np	2.40	2.40
110	A9	1rl on 1r	3.50	3.50
		Nos. 101-110 (10)	10.20	10.20

Souvenir Sheet
Simulated Perfs

| 111 | A9 | 5rl on 5r | 50.00 | — |

Nos. 101-110 exist imperf.
For overprints see Nos. 112-121.

Overprinted "PRO OLYMPIC GAMES MEXICO" Diagonally in English and Arabic on Nos. 101-110

1966

112	A9	1d on 1np	1.00	—
113	A9	2d on 2np	1.00	—
114	A9	3d on 3np	1.00	—
115	A9	4d on 4np	1.00	—
116	A9	5d on 5np	1.00	—
117	A9	10d on 10np	1.00	—
118	A9	25d on 25np	1.00	—
119	A9	50d on 50np	1.60	—
120	A9	75d on 75np	2.40	—
121	A9	1rl on 1r	3.50	—
		Nos. 112-121 (10)	14.50	

Nos. 112-121 exist imperf.

Nos. 48-57 Surcharged

1966, Nov. 20

122	A10	25d on 25np	.50	—
123	A10	50d on 50np	.90	—
124	A10	75d on 75np	1.25	—
125	A10	1rl on 1r	1.60	—
126	A10	2rl on 2r	2.50	—
127	A10	3rl on 3r	3.25	—
128	A10	4rl on 4r	3.75	—
129	A10	5rl on 5r	4.50	—
		Nos. 122-129 (8)	18.25	

Souvenir Sheet
Size: 155x105mm
Simulated Perfs

| 130 | A10 | 4rl on 4r (#56) | 30.00 | — |
| 131 | A10 | 4rl on 4r (#57) | 30.00 | — |

Nos. 122-129 exist imperf. Value, set $27.50.
For similar surcharges see Nos. 173-182.

Nos. 58-65 Surcharged

1966, Nov. 20

132	A11	1rl on 1r (#58)	.90	.90
133	A11	1rl on 1r (#59)	.90	.90
134	A11	1rl on 1r (#60)	.90	.90
135	A11	1rl on 1r (#61)	.90	.90
a.		On #61a	5.00	
136	A11	1rl on 1r (#62)	.90	.90
137	A11	1rl on 1r (#63)	.90	.90
138	A11	1rl on 1r (#64)	.90	.90
139	A11	1rl on 1r (#65)	.90	.90
a.		On #65a	5.00	
		Nos. 132-139 (8)	7.20	7.20

Nos. 132-139 exist imperf. Value, set $8.

No. 5 Surcharged in Black

1966

| 140 | A2 | 5d on 75np | | 150.00 |

No. 70 Surcharged in Black

1966

| 141 | A2 | 5d on 75f on 75np | — | 1,200. |

W.H.O. Headquarters — A12

1966, Dec. 1   Litho.   Perf. 12

142	A12	15d shown	.25	.25
143	A12	35d multi	.50	.25
144	A12	50d multi	.60	.25
145	A12	3rl multi	1.60	.25
a.		Sheet of 1, imperf.	5.00	5.00
		Nos. 142-145 (4)	2.95	1.00

Nos. 144-145 are airmail.
Nos. 142-145 exist imperf. Value, set $5.

1 dh. **RAS AL KHAIMA**

Domestic Cat A13

1967, Mar. 30   Photo.   Perf. 11¼

146	A13	1d shown	.25 .25
147	A13	2d blue & multi	.25 .25
148	A13	3d pink & multi	.25 .25
149	A13	4d green & multi	.25 .25
150	A13	5d brown & multi	.25 .25
151	A13	3rl lilac & multi	3.00 1.25
		Nos. 146-151 (6)	4.25 2.50

No. 151 is airmail.

Solon and His Students — A14

Designs: 2d, Monarch and Attendants, vert. 3d and 1rl, Al Hairth to Abu Zayd. 4d, Monarch on His Throne, vert. 10d, Herons. 20d, Archangel Israfil, vert. 30d, Two Horsemen.

1967, May 10   Litho.   Perf. 12

152	A14	1d shown	.25 .25
153	A14	2d multi	.25 .25
154	A14	3d multi	.25 .25
155	A14	4d multi	.25 .25
156	A14	10d multi	.60 .25
157	A14	20d multi	1.40 .50
158	A14	30d multi	1.60 .80
		Nos. 152-158 (7)	4.60 2.55

Souvenir Sheet
Imperf

159	A14	1rl multi	3.50 3.50

Nos. 152-158 were issued in sheets of 10.
Nos. 152-158 exist imperf. Value, set $8.
For similar designs see Nos. C10-C16.

Nos. 9-11 Overprinted in English and Arabic in a Circle and Surcharged

1967, June 30

160	A4	2rl on 2r	1.60 —
161	A4	3rl on 3r	2.10 —
162	A5	4rl on 4r	3.25 —
		Nos. 160-162 (3)	6.95

Same Overprinted on Nos. 12-14

163	A4	1rl on 1r (#12)	1.00 1.00
a.		Pane of 4	4.00 4.00
164	A4	1rl on 1r (#13)	1.00 1.00
a.		Pane of 4	4.00 4.00
165	A5	1rl on 1r (#14)	1.00 1.00
a.		Pane of 4	4.00 4.00
		Nos. 163-165 (3)	3.00 6.00

Nos. 160-162 may exist imperf. The editors would like to examine any examples.

12th Boy Scout Jamboree, Idaho — A15

Designs: 1d, Bugler. 2d and 75d, Sir Baden-Powell (1857-1941). 3d, Campfire and four scouts, horiz. 4d, Three scouts hiking, horiz. 35d, Scout emblem. 1rl, Gemini capsule and boy scout.

1967, July 20   Litho.   Perf. 12

166	A15	1d shown	.45 .25
167	A15	2d multi	.45 .25
168	A15	3d multi	.45 .25
169	A15	4d multi	.45 .25
170	A15	35d multi	.90 .75
171	A15	75d multi	1.75 .75
a.		Imperf. sheet of 2, #170-171	4.75 4.75
172	A15	1rl multi	2.10 .75
a.		Imperf. sheet of 1	4.75 4.75
		Nos. 166-172 (7)	6.55 3.25

Nos. 170-172 are airmail.
Nos. 166-172 exist imperf. Value, set $9.

Nos. 48-57 Surcharged and Overprinted in English and Arabic

Nos. 173-174, 179

Nos. 175-176, 178, 180

No. 177

1967, Aug. 20

173	A10	25d on 25np	.25 —
174	A10	50d on 50np	.30 —
175	A10	75d on 75np	.50 —
176	A10	1rl on 1r	.75 —
177	A10	2rl on 2r	1.50 —
178	A10	3rl on 3r	2.25 —
179	A10	4rl on 4r	3.25 —
180	A10	5rl on 5r	4.00 —
		Nos. 173-180 (8)	12.80

Souvenir Sheet
Size: 155x105mm
Simulated Perfs

181	A10	4rl on 4r (#56)	7.00 —
182	A10	4rl on 4r (#57)	7.00 —

Nos. 173-180 have additional images commemorating the three astronauts killed aboard Apollo 1 were printed in the gutter.
On No. 181 the simulated stamps have Arabic inscription. On No. 182 the simulated stamps have Arabic inscription, whereas #177 has English.
Nos. 173-182 exist imperf. Value, set $35.

Discus thrower and Atlantes of Tula — A16

Designs: Olympic rings, athlete and Mexico tourist attraction. 20d, Weightlifter and Palacio de Bellas Artes. 30d, Soccer player and University of Mexico Library. 40d, Fencer and fishing boats. 1rl, Runner and Guadalajara Cathedral. 2rl, Boxer and Paseo de la Reforma.

1967, Oct. 20   Photo.   Perf. 12½

183	A16	10d shown	.25 .25
184	A16	20d multi	.25 .25
185	A16	30d multi	.25 .25
186	A16	40d multi	.25 .25
187	A16	1rl multi	.75 .30
188	A16	2rl multi	1.40 .50
a.		Imperf. sheet of 1	4.00 2.00
		Nos. 183-188 (6)	3.15 1.80

Nos. 187-188 are airmail.
Nos. 183-188 exist imperf. Value, set $8.

Grenoble Olympics, Ice Hockey — A17

Grenoble Olympics A18

Designs: 2d, Ski jumping. 3d, Speed skating. 4d, 2rl, Bobsled. 5d, No. 196, Figure skating pair.
No. 197, Aerial map of Grenoble.

1967, Dec. 24   Litho.   Perf. 12½

189	A17	1d shown	.25 .25
190	A17	2d multi	.25 .25
191	A17	3d multi	.25 .25
192	A17	4d multi	.25 .25
193	A17	5d multi	.25 .25
194	A18	85d shown	.60 .25
195	A17	2rl multi	1.20 .25
196	A17	3rl multi	1.75 .25
		Nos. 189-196 (8)	4.80 2.00

Souvenir Sheet
Imperf

197	A17	3rl multi	6.50 6.50

Nos. 194-197 are airmail.
Nos. 189-196 exist imperf. Value, set $8.

Beatrice d'Este, by Leonardo da Vinci — A19

Designs: 30d, The Goldfinch Madonna, by Raphael. 40d, La Donna Velata, by Raphael. 50d, Fabiola, by Jean-Jacques Henner. 1rl, Portrait of Anne Henriette, by Jean-Marc Nattier the Younger, horiz. 2rl, Study, by Jean Honore Fragonard. 3rl, Portrait of Mary Adelaide, by Jean-Marc Nattier the Younger, horiz. 4rl, Virgin with Green Cushion, by Andrea Solari.
5rl, Mona Lisa, by Leonardo da Vinci.

1968, Mar. 21   Litho.   Perf. 11¼

198	A19	20d shown	.25 .25
199	A19	30d multi	.25 .25
200	A19	40d multi	.25 .25
201	A19	50d multi	.25 .25
202	A19	1rl multi	.25 .25
203	A19	2rl multi	.40 .25
204	A19	3rl multi	.60 .25
205	A19	4rl multi	.90 .25
		Nos. 198-205 (8)	3.15 2.00

Souvenir Sheet
Imperf

206	A19	5rl multi	8.00 1.00

Issued in panes of six and 10.
Nos. 202-205 are airmail.
Nos. 198-205 exist imperf. Value, set $8.50. And in imperf. deluxe sheets of one.
No. 206 exists perforated around the design. Without the selvage this becomes simply a label. Value unused, $8, CTO, $1.

Abraham Lincoln (1809-65) — A20

Designs: No. 208, John Kennedy (1917-63). No. 209, Martin Luther King, Jr. (1929-68).

1968, May 25   Litho.   Perf. 11¼

207	A20	2rl shown	1.90 .50
208	A20	2rl multi	1.90 .50
209	A20	2rl multi	1.90 .50
a.		Imperf. sheet of 3, #207-209	7.00 1.50
		Nos. 207-209 (3)	5.70 1.50

Issued for the International Human Rights Year, in panes of six.
Nos. 207-209 exist imperf. Value, set $7.50. No. 209a exists perforated.
For overprint see No. 312.

Young Child, by Gerard Terborch A21

Designs: Paintings. No. 211, Lady on Horseback, by Edouard Manet, horiz. 20d, A Little Girl, by Jan Gossaert. 25d, The Hay Wain, by

John Constable, horiz. 35d, Helene, by Peter Paul Rubens. 40d, Young Beggars Playing Dice, by Bortolome Esteban Murillo. 45d, A Horse Frightened by Lightning, by Thoedore Gericault, horiz. 60d, Plaster Torso, by Henri Matisse. 70d, Portrait of M. Fourcade, by Henri de Toulouse-Lautrec. 80d, Madonna and Child, by Leonardo da Vinci. 90d, Balerina with Bouquet, by Edgar Degas. 1rl, Concert, by Gerrit van Honthorst. 1.25rl, The Milkmaid, by Jean-Baptiste Greuze. 1.50rl, The Poor Fisherman, by Paul Gauguin. 2.50rl, Sunflowers, by Vincent Van Gogh. 2.75rl, The Land of Cockaigne, by Peter Brueghel.

No. 226a, Pleasure Boat, by Claude Monet. No. 226b, The Bridge at Mantes, by Jean-Baptiste Corot. No. 227a, Girl Reading Letter, by Jan Vermeer. No. 227b, Self-portrait with Saskia, by Rembrandt. No. 228a, The Painter's Daughters, by Thomas Gainsborough. No. 228b, A Child with an Apple, by Jean-Baptiste Greuze. No. 229a, Coeur in the Forest, by Pierre Auguste Renoir. No. 229b, The Negro Scipio, by Paul Cezanne.

1968, May 25   Litho.   Perf. 11¼

210	A21	15d shown	.25 .25
211	A21	15d multi	.25 .25
212	A21	20d multi	.25 .25
213	A21	25d multi	.25 .25
214	A21	35d multi	.25 .25
215	A21	40d multi	.25 .25
216	A21	45d multi	.25 .25
217	A21	60d multi	.30 .25
218	A21	70d multi	.35 .25
219	A21	80d multi	.35 .25
220	A21	90d multi	.45 .25
221	A21	1rl multi	.45 .25
222	A21	1.25rl multi	.55 .25
223	A21	1.50rl multi	.70 .25
224	A21	2.50rl multi	1.10 .25
225	A21	2.75rl multi	1.25 .25
		Nos. 210-225 (16)	7.25 4.00

Souvenir Sheets

226		Sheet of 2, #a.-b.	5.00 5.00
a.	A21	2rl multi	1.50 1.50
b.	A21	3rl multi	1.50 1.50
227		Sheet of 2, #a.-b.	5.00 5.00
a.	A21	2rl multi	1.50 1.50
b.	A21	3rl multi	1.50 1.50
228		Sheet of 2, #a.-b.	5.00 5.00
a.	A21	2rl multi	1.50 1.50
b.	A21	3rl multi	1.50 1.50
229		Sheet of 2, #a.-b.	5.00 5.00
a.	A21	2rl multi	1.50 1.50
b.	A21	3rl multi	1.50 1.50
		Nos. 226-229 (4)	20.00 20.00

Nos. 210-225 exist imperf. Value, set $24. Nos. 226-229 exist imperf. Value unused, $5 each, CTO, $1.75 each.

Winter Olympics Champions, Marielle Goitschel — A22

Designs: 1rl, Franco Nones. 1.50rl, Jean-Claude Killy and Guy Perillat. 2rl, Olga Pall. 2.50rl, Nancy Greene. 3rl, Peggy Fleming.
No. 236 Marielle Goitschel, same design as No. 230.

1968, Aug 31   Litho.   Perf. 11¼

230	A22	50d shown	.25 .25
231	A22	1rl multi	.40 .25
232	A22	1.50rl multi	.60 .25
233	A22	2rl multi	.75 .25
234	A22	2.50rl multi	.90 .25
235	A22	3rl multi	1.00 .25
		Nos. 230-235 (6)	3.90 1.50

Embossed on Foil Coated Paper

Perf. 8

236	A22	50d gold	15.00 —

Printed in panes of 6.
Nos. 230-235 exist imperf. Value, set $7. No. 236 exists imperf. Value, $15. Nos. 230-235 exist in deluxe sheets of one. Value, $13 each. No. 236 exists in an imperf. sheet of one. Value, $23.
See Nos. C22-C23.

Christmas Paintings - The Virgin and Child with John the Baptist, by Sandro Botticelli — A23

Rest during the Flight into Egypt, by Gentile da Fabriano — A24

Adoration of the Child, by Gerrit van Honthorst — A25

Designs: 30d, The Adoration of the Child, by Antonio Correggio. 40d, Nativity, by Carle van Loo. 50d, Adoration, by Susan Tu Luca Ch'en. 60d, Madonna and Child, by Bartolome Estiban Murillo. 1rl, Adoration of the Shepherds, by Gerrit van Honthorst. 3rl, Nativity, by Neri di Bicci. 4rl, Nativity, by unknown Florentine master.

1968, Dec.   Litho.   Perf. 11¼

237	A23	20d shown	.25 .25
238	A23	30d multi	.25 .25
239	A23	40d multi	.30 .25
240	A23	50d multi	.30 .25
241	A23	60d multi	.40 .25
242	A23	1rl multi	.60 .25

Perf. 11

243	A24	2rl shown	1.00 .25
244	A24	3rl multi	1.40 .25
245	A24	4rl multi	2.00 .25
		Nos. 237-245 (9)	6.50 2.25

Souvenir Sheet

Size: 120x94mm

Simulated Perfs

246	A25	5rl shown	3.00 .75
a.		Size: 132x134mm	50.00 —

Issue dates: Nos. 237-242 and 246, Dec. 10; Nos. 243-245, Dec. 7.
Nos. 237-245 were printed in sheets of five plus one label. The top right and the top left stamps in the pane show parts of the marginal design.
Nos. 243-246 are airmail.
Nos. 237-245 exist imperf. Value, set $15.
Nos. 237-245 exist in deluxe sheets of one. Value, $4.75 each.
Nos. 243-245 exist in sheetlets of five overprinted "APOLLO 8 - XMAS TRIP AROUND THE MOON 25.12.68." This overprint spans the entire miniature sheet. Values for miniature sheets of No. 243 perf. overprinted, $15, imperf., $25; No. 244 perf. overprinted, $20, imperf., $35; No. 245 perf. overprinted, $25, imperf., $40. No. 246 was similarly overprinted. Value, $22.50.

Paintings of Composers, Frederic Chopin, by Eugene Delacroix — A26

Designs: 50d, Hector Berlioz, by Gustave Courbet. 75d, Richard Strauss, by Max Liebermann. 1.50rl, Wolfgang Mozart, by Raoul Dufy. 2.50rl, Giuseppe Verdi, by Giovanni Boldini.

1969, Jan. 5   Litho.   Perf. 11¼

247	A26	25d shown	.25 .25
248	A26	50d multi	.45 .25
249	A26	75d multi	.65 .25
250	A26	1.50rl multi	1.30 .25
251	A26	2.50rl multi	2.40 .25
		Nos. 247-251 (5)	5.05 1.25

Nos. 247-251 were issued in panes of six.
Nos. 247-251 exist imperf. Value, set $6. And as deluxe sheets of one. Value, set $25.

Scenes from Operas, Othello, by Giuseppe Verdi — A27

Designs: 40d, Faust, by Charles Gounod. 60d, Aida, by Giuseppe Verdi. 80d, Madame Butterfly, by Giacomo Puccini. 1rl, Lohengrin, by Richard Wagner. 2rl and 10rl, Abduction of the Seraglio, by Wolfgang Mozart.

1969, Feb. 5   Litho.   Perf. 11¼

252	A27	20d shown	.25 .25
253	A27	40d multi	.50 .30
254	A27	60d multi	.75 .45
255	A27	80d multi	1.00 .50
256	A27	1rl multi	1.25 .60
257	A27	2rl multi	2.25 .75
		Nos. 252-257 (6)	6.00 2.90

Souvenir Sheet

258	A27	10rl multi	12.00 —

Nos. 252-257 were issued in panes of six.
Nos. 252-257 exist imperf. Value, set $7.50. Also issued as deluxe sheets of one, Value, set $17.50.
No. 258 exists imperf. Value, $13.
A miniature sheet of 4, depicting "The Four Seasons" by Abel Grimmer (1573-1619) exists both perforated and imperforate. The sheet has a face value of 10rl, printed in the selvage of the sheet. It is uncertain whether this sheet was legitimately issued and valid for postage. The editors are seeking additional information. Value perf., $9, imperf., $17.50.

Famous People and Scenes, Sheikh Ahmed Bin Majid and Ship — A28

Designs: 30d and No. 268, Charles de Gaulle and Europa emblem. 50d, Napoleon Bonaparte and Napoleon on a horse. 1.50rl, Vincent van Gogh with brushes and palette. Nos. 264 and 270, Lord Baden Powell and scout tents. Nos. 265 and 271, Pierre de Coubertin and columns. Nos. 266 and 272,

Wernher von Braun with satellite and rocket. Nos. 267, 269 and 273, John Kennedy and United States Capitol building.

1969, Feb. 5   Litho.   Perf. 12

260	A28	20d shown	.25 .25
261	A28	30d multi	.25 .25
262	A28	50d multi	.40 .25
263	A28	1.50rl multi	.90 .25
264	A28	2rl multi	1.50 .25
265	A28	3rl multi	1.75 .25
266	A28	4rl multi	2.50 .25
267	A28	5rl multi	3.00 .25
		Nos. 260-267 (8)	10.55 2.00

Souvenir Sheets

268	A28	10rl multi	7.50 —
269	A28	10rl multi	7.50 —

Embossed on Foil Coated Paper

Perf. 8

270	A28	2rl gold	10.00 —
271	A28	3rl gold	10.00 —
272	A28	4rl gold	10.00 —
273	A28	5rl gold	10.00 —
		Nos. 270-273 (4)	40.00 —

Nos 263-273 are airmail.
Nos. 260-267 exist imperf. Value, set $50. Also exists in deluxe sheets of one. Value, set $125.
Nos. 268-269 exist imperf. Value, set $50.
Nos. 270-273 exist imperf. Value, $10 each.
Also exists in imperf. sheets of one. Value, $20 each.
For overprint see No. C38.

United States No. 1332b — A29

Designs: 25d, Japan No. B28. 35d, Germany No. 988. 40d, Greece No. 670. 50d, United Nations No. 29. 60d, Mali No. C31. 70d, Belgium No. 706. 1rl, France No. 1150. 2rl, Monaco No. 596. 3rl, San Marino No. 653. Nos. 284 and 289, Vatican No. 397. Nos. 285 and 290, Mexico No. 966.
No. 286 as No. 274 in gold.

1969, Feb. 20   Litho.   Perf. 11

274	A29	Pair, #a.-b.	.25 .25
a.-b.		10d either single	.25 .25
275	A29	25d multi	.25 .25
276	A29	35d multi	.25 .25
277	A29	40d multi	.25 .25
278	A29	50d multi	.25 .25
279	A29	60d multi	.25 .25
280	A29	70d multi	.25 .25

Perf. 11¼

281	A29	1rl multi	.35 .25
282	A29	2rl multi	.65 .30
283	A29	3rl multi	.95 .35
284	A29	5rl multi	1.60 .50
285	A29	5rl multi	1.60 .50
a.		Souvenir sheet of 2, #284-285	2.50 1.00
		Nos. 274-285 (12)	6.90 3.65

Embossed on Foil Coated Paper

Perf. 7½

286	A29	Pair, #a.-b.	14.00 —
c.		Sheet of 2, imperf.	20.00 —
d.		With ovpt. "...APOLLO 13" on tab	50.00 —
e.		As "c," with margin ovpt. "...APOLLO 13"	50.00 —
287	A29	2rl gold	14.00 —
a.		Sheet of 1, imperf.	20.00 —
b.		As "a," with margin ovpt. "...APOLLO 13..."	50.00 —
288	A29	3rl gold	14.00 —
a.		Sheet of 1, imperf.	20.00 —
b.		With ovpt. "...U.P.U."	50.00 50.00
c.		As "a," with margin ovpt. "CHRISTMAS 1970"	60.00 —
d.		As "a," with margin ovpt. "...U.P.U."	60.00 —
289	A29	5rl gold	14.00 —
a.		Sheet of 1, imperf.	20.00 —
b.		As "a," with margin ovpt. "CHRISTMAS 1970"	60.00 —
290	A29	5rl gold	14.00 —
a.		Sheet of 1, imperf.	20.00 —
b.		With ovpt. "MUNICH 1972"	50.00 —
c.		As "a," with margin ovpt. "SUPPORT..."	60.00 —
d.		As "a," with margin ovpt. "Transmission..."	60.00 —
		Nos. 286-290 (5)	70.00

Nos. 281-285 and 287-290 are airmail and are in a larger format than the rest of the set.
Nos. 274-285 exist imperf. Value, set $14.
Nos. 286-290 exist imperf. Value, $14 each.
Nos. 275-285 exist in deluxe sheets of one, No. 274 exists as a deluxe sheet of two. Value, set $120.
No. 285a exists imperf. Value, $2.50.
Nos. 288b and 290b exist imperf. Value, $50 each.

Soccer — A30

Designs: 2rl, Skiing. 3rl, Ice hockey. 4rl,
Running.
10rl, Three gold medalists.

1969, June 10	**Litho.**	**Perf. 11**	
291 A30	1rl shown	.50	.25
292 A30	2rl multi	.75	.25
293 A30	3rl multi	1.25	.25
294 A30	4rl multi	1.75	.25
Nos. 291-294 (4)		4.25	1.00

Souvenir Sheet

| 295 A30 | 10rl multi | 4.00 | — |

Issued in panes of 10.
Nos. 291-294 exist imperf. Value, set $4.50.
Also issued in imperf. deluxe sheets of one.
Value, set $10.
No. 295 exists imperf. Value, $12.

Napoleon I
Bonaparte,
Bicentennial
of
Birth — A31

Designs: 1.75rl, Bonaparte, Premier Con-
sul, on Horseback, by Antoine-Jean Gros.
2.75rl, Bonaparte, Franchissant les Alpes au
Grand Saint-Bernard, by Jacques-Louis
David. 3.75rl, Napoleon with the Coronation
Dress, by Simon Gerard.

1969, Aug. 15	**Litho.**	**Perf. 11**	
296 A31	75d shown	.35	.25
297 A31	1.75rl multi	.80	.25
298 A31	2.75rl multi	1.25	.25
299 A31	3.75rl multi	1.60	.25
Nos. 296-299 (4)		4.00	1.00

Issued in panes of 16, composed of four
strips of four.
No. 296 is airmail.
Nos. 296-299 exist imperf. Value, set $7. An
imperf. deluxe sheet of four of Nos. 296-299
exists. Value, $20.
See No. C31.

Nos. 230-232 Surcharged

Method and Perfs as Before
1969, Nov.

299A A22	5d on 50d	—	950.
299B A22	5d on 1rl	—	1,250.
299C A22	5d on 1.50rl	—	800.

Paintings of Philippe de Champaigne
(1602-74) — A32

Designs: Paintings: No. 300, Various paint-
ings of Philippe de Champaigne (1602-74).
No. 301, Various paintings of Andrea del Sarto
(1486-1531). No. 302, Various paintings of
Jean-Battista Tiepolo (1693-1770). No. 303,
Various paintings of Barolome Esteban Murillo
(1617-82). No. 304, Various paintings of Paul
Gauguin (1848-1903). No. 305, Various paint-
ings of Titian (1488-1576).
No. 306, Le Reve D'Elie, by Philippe de
Champaigne. No. 307, La Madone des Har-
pies, by Andrea del Sarto. No. 308, La
Crocifissione, by Jean-Battista Tiepolo. No.
309, Rebecca et Elieze, by Barolome Esteban
Murillo. No. 310, Nafea Foa Ipoipo, by Paul
Gauguin. No. 311, La Vierge Au Lapin, by
Titian.

1970, Jan. 2	**Litho.**	**Perf. 14½**	
300 A32	Horiz. strip of 3, #a.-	2.00	.75
a.	50d multi	.50	.25
b.	3rl multi	.50	.25
c.	3.50rl multi	.50	.25
301 A32	Horiz. strip of 3, #a.-	2.00	.75
a.	50d multi	.50	.25
b.	3rl multi	.50	.25
c.	3.50rl multi	.50	.25
302 A32	Horiz. strip of 3, #a.-	2.00	.75
a.	50d multi	.50	.25
b.	3rl multi	.50	.25
c.	3.50rl multi	.50	.25
303 A32	Horiz. strip of 3, #a.-	2.00	.75
a.	50d multi	.50	.25
b.	3rl multi	.50	.25
c.	3.50rl multi	.50	.25
304 A32	Horiz. strip of 3, #a.-	2.00	.75
a.	50d multi	.50	.25
b.	3rl multi	.50	.25
c.	3.50rl multi	.50	.25
305 A32	Horiz. strip of 3, #a.-	2.00	.75
a.	50d multi	.50	.25
b.	3rl multi	.50	.25
c.	3.50rl multi	.50	.25
Nos. 300-305 (6)		12.00	4.50

Souvenir Sheets

306 A32	10rl multi	3.50	2.25
307 A32	10rl multi	3.50	2.25
308 A32	10rl multi	3.50	2.25
309 A32	10rl multi	3.50	2.25
310 A32	10rl multi	3.50	2.25
311 A32	10rl multi	3.50	2.25
Nos. 306-311 (6)		21.00	13.50

Nos. 300-305 we printed in sheets of 12.
The central stamp of Nos. 303 and 311 is
inscribed "CHRISTMAS 1969." The central
stamp of Nos. 300 and 308 is inscribed
"EASTER 1970."
Nos. 300-305 exist imperf. Value, $3 each.
Nos. 306-311 exist imperf. Value, $4 each.
Nos. 301-305 exist in imperf. deluxe sheets
of 3. Value, $12 each. It is likely that No. 300
also exists in that format. The editors would
like to examine any examples.

No. 208 Overprinted

1970, May?		**Perf. 11¼**	
312 A20	2rl multi	4.50	4.50
a.	Imperf. sheet of 3, #207, 209, 312	8.00	—

Printed in panes of six.
No. 312 exists imperf. Value, $8. No. 312a
exists perforated.
No. 312 and 312a exist with the overprint
inverted, "29th may" on right. Value, $15 and
$20, respectively. This was an intentionally
created variety, presumably with a limited print
run.

Great Britain Pavilion — A33

Tower of the Sun, Globe and Emblem,
Japan No. B34 — A34

Designs: 50d,   Japan-Midori-Kan
"Astrorama." 55d, Cherry Blossoms, Japan
No. B35. 60d, Japan Tower of the Sun and
Saudi Arabia pavilion. 65d, Globe and cherry
blossoms, Japan Nos. 1024, and 1023. 70d,
Federal Republic of Germany pavilion. 75d,
The Irises, Japan No. 1025. 80d, France pavil-
ion. 85d, Winter landscape, Japan No. 984,
vert. 90d, Japan Gas Association. 95d, Bud-
dah Fugen, Japan No. 953, vert. 1.60rl, United
States of America pavilion. 1.65rl, Ichikawa
Ebizo, Japan No. 630, vert. 1.85rl, Girl with
flute, Japan No. 619, vert. 2rl, Fiji Group,
Japan Pavilion.
5rl, Japan Pavilion. 10rl, Japan No. 931.

1970, June 18	**Litho.**	**Perf. 11¼**	
313 A33	40d shown	.25	.25
314 A34	45d shown	.25	.25
315 A34	50d multi	.25	.25
316 A34	55d multi	.40	.25
317 A34	60d multi	.40	.25
318 A34	65d multi	.40	.25
319 A34	70d multi	.50	.25
320 A34	75d multi	.50	.25
321 A34	80d multi	.50	.25
322 A34	85d multi	.55	.25
323 A34	90d multi	.60	.25
324 A34	95d multi	.60	.25
325 A34	1.60rl multi	1.10	.25
326 A34	1.65rl multi	1.10	.25
327 A34	1.85rl multi	1.20	.25
328 A33	2rl multi	1.25	.25
Nos. 313-328 (16)		9.85	4.00

Souvenir Sheets

| 329 A33 | 5rl multi | 7.00 | 1.50 |
| 330 A34 | 10rl multi | 7.00 | 1.50 |

Issued in panes of six for the World Exhibi-
tion EXPO '70 Osaka, Japan.
Nos. 321-330 are airmail.
Nos. 313-328 exist imperf. Value, set $16.
Nos. 329-330 exist imperf. Value, $9 each.

Iris and Birds, by
Harunobu Sazuki
(1724-70) — A35

Designs: Various Japanese paintings. 55d,
Snow, Moon, and Blossoms, by Katsukawa
Shunsho (1726-92). 65d, Spring, by Sakai
Hoitsu (1761-1828). 75d, Flowering Grasses,
by Tatebayashi Kagei. 85d, Ivy-bound Lane,
by Fukae Roshu (1699-1755). 95d, Two Beau-
ties, by Katsushika Hokusai (1760-1849).

1.50rl, Spring, by Sakai Hoitsu. 1.75rl, Cock
and Hen, by Ito Jakuchu (1713-1800).
5rl, Palm and Children, by Maruyama Ohkyo
(1733-95).

1970, June 18	**Litho.**	**Perf. 14**	
331 A35	25d shown	.25	.25
332 A35	55d multi	.40	.25
333 A35	65d multi	.55	.25
334 A35	75d multi	.65	.25
335 A35	85d multi	.75	.25
336 A35	95d multi	1.00	.25
337 A35	1.50rl multi	1.40	.25
338 A35	1.75rl multi	2.00	.25
Nos. 331-338 (8)		7.00	2.00

Souvenir Sheet
Simulated Perfs

| 339 A35 | 5rl multi | 4.00 | 1.25 |

Issued in panes of 10 for the World Exhibi-
tion EXPO '70 Osaka, Japan.
Nos. 331, 335-339 are airmail.
Nos. 331-338 exist imperf. Value, set $9.
No. 339 exists imperf. Value, $5.50.
Nos. 331-338 exist as imperf. deluxe sheets
of one, with a white background. Value, $5
each. Also exists with a yellow background.
Value, $8 each.

Sapporo Olympics 1972, Ice
Hockey — A36

Embossed on Foil Coated Paper
1970, June 30		**Perf. 8**
340 A36	3rl gold	10.00

No. 340 exists imperf. and in an imperf
sheet of one. Values, $10 and $12,
respectively.

Stations of the Cross, Jesus
Condemned — A37

Designs: a, 10d, Station 1, Jesus condemned b, 20d, Station 2, Jesus carries the
cross. c, 30d, Station 3, Jesus falls carrying
the cross. d, 40d, Station 4, Jesus carrying the
cross, meets Mary. e, 50d, Station 5, Simon of
Cyrene helps Jesus carry the cross. f, 60d,
Station 6, Veronica wipes the face of Jesus. g,
70d, Station 7, Jesus falls carrying the cross.
h, 80d, Station 8, Jesus carrying the cross
meets the women of Jerusalem. i, 1rl, Station
9, Jesus falls carrying the cross. j, 1.50rl, Station 10, Jesus' clothes are removed. k, 2rl,
Station 11, Jesus is nailed to the cross. l,
2.50rl, Station 12, Jesus dies on the cross. m,
3rl, Station 13, Jesus' body is taken down. n,
3.50rl, Station 14, Jesus is laid in the tomb.

1970, Aug. 5	**Photo.**	**Perf. 13½**	
341	Sheet of 14 + label	40.00	5.00
a.-n.	A37 any single	1.40	.25

Easter.
No. 341 exists imperf. Value, $75.

The Life of Jesus Christ — A38

Designs: Paintings of the life of Jesus —5d, Jesus in the Temple, by Duccio di Buoninsegna. 10d, Calling of Peter and Andrew, by Duccio di Buoninsegna. 25d, Sinite Parvulos, by Ludwig Vogel. 50d, Christ at the Sea of Galilee, Jacopo Tintoretto. 1rl, Entry into Jerusalem, by Giotto di Bondone. 2rl, The Kiss of Judas, by Giotto di Bondone. 5rl, The Ascent to Calvary, by Jacopo Tintoretto.

10rl, Adoration of the Magi, by Gentile da Fabriano.

1970, Nov. 6   Litho.   Perf. 13
342	A38	5d shown	.25	.25
343	A38	10d multi	.25	.25
344	A38	25d multi	.25	.25
345	A38	50d multi	.30	.25
346	A38	1rl multi	.70	.25
347	A38	2rl multi	1.25	.25
348	A38	5rl multi	3.00	.25
		Nos. 342-348 (7)	6.00	1.75

Souvenir Sheet

349	A38	10rl multi	6.00	2.50

Nos. 342-348 exist imperf. Value, set $9.
No. 349 exists imperf. Value, $12.

The Marriage of the Virgin, by the Master of Mary's Life (ca. 1463-90) A39

Designs: Paintings of the Life of the Virgin Mary. 15d, The Annunciation, by Fra Angelico. 30d, The Visitation, by the Master of Mary's Life. 60d, The Nativity, by Sandro Botticelli. 75d, Presentation at the Temple, by Hans Memling. 3rl, Madonna and Child Adored by Angels, by the Master of Moulins. 4rl, The Canigiani Madonna, by Raphael.

10rl, Madonna and Child.

1970, Dec. 5   Litho.   Perf. 13½
350	A39	10d shown	.25	.25
351	A39	15d multi	.25	.25
352	A39	30d multi	.25	.25
353	A39	60d multi	.60	.25
354	A39	75d multi	.75	.25
355	A39	3rl multi	3.00	.25
356	A39	4rl multi	4.00	.25
		Nos. 350-356 (7)	9.10	1.75

Souvenir Sheet

357	A39	10rl multi	5.50	1.90

No. 357 exists imperf. Value, $8.

AIR POST STAMPS

Wembley Stadium — AP1

Designs: 2r, Goalie diving for ball and another player. 3r, Two players, one dribbling ball. 4r, Presentaion of the Jules Rimet Cup to Bobby Moore by Queen Elizabeth II.

Perf. 12¼x11¼

1966, Dec. 30   Unwmk.   Photo.
C1	AP1	1rl shown	.60	.25
C2	AP1	2rl multi	1.00	.25
C3	AP1	3rl multi	1.50	.25
C4	AP1	4rl multi	2.00	.25
		Nos. C1-C4 (4)	5.10	1.00

Nos. C1-C4 exist imperf. Value, set $7.50.
Nos. C1 and C4 exist as imperf. sheets of one. Value, $3.50 each.

The Magic Garden — AP2

Designs: 70d, Aladdin and the Genie, vert. 1rl, Girl riding a flying black horse. 2rl, Sinbad carried by an eagle, vert. 3rl, Ali Baba surrounded by treasure.

1967, Feb 1   Litho.   Perf. 12
C5	AP2	30d shown	.25	.25
C6	AP2	70d multi	.25	.25
C7	AP2	1rl multi	.45	.25
C8	AP2	2rl multi	.90	.25
C9	AP2	3rl multi	1.20	.25
		Nos. C5-C9 (5)	3.05	1.25

Nos. C5-C9 exist imperf. Value, set $5.50.
No. C9 exists as an imperf. sheet of one. Value, $4.

Arab Saddling His Horse, by Eugene Delacroix AP3

Designs: 70d, Pierrot and Harlequin, by Paul Cezanne. 1rl, The Fifer, by Edouard Manet. 2rl, Fishing Boats on the Beach at Saites-Maries, by Vincent van Gogh, horiz. 3rl, A Young Man with a Glove, by Frans Hals. 5rl, Vase of Flowers, by Jean Baptiste Simeon Chardin. Hendrickje Stoffels in the Window, by Rembrandt.

1967   Litho.   Perf. 12
C10	AP3	60d shown	.30	.25
C11	AP3	70d multi	.30	.25
a.		Sheet of 2, #C10-C11, imperf.	9.50	—
C12	AP3	1rl multi	.50	.25
C13	AP3	2rl multi	.75	.25
C14	AP3	3rl multi	1.25	.25
C15	AP3	5rl multi	2.25	.50
C16	AP3	10rl multi	4.25	1.00
		Nos. C10-C16 (7)	9.60	2.75

Issue Dates: Nos. C10-C13, 5/30; Nos C14-C16, 9/10.
Nos. C10-C16 exist imperf. Value, set $12.

Weightlifting — AP4

Designs: Mexican artifacts and athlete. 2rl, Discus throw. 3rl, Shot put. Nos. C20-C21, Running.

1968, Aug. 31   Litho.   Perf. 11¼
C17	AP4	1rl shown	.70	.25
C18	AP4	2rl multi	1.40	.25
C19	AP4	3rl multi	2.00	.25
C20	AP4	4rl multi	2.90	.25
		Nos. C17-C20 (4)	7.00	1.00

Embossed on Foil Coated Paper

C21	AP4	4rl gold	12.50	

Nos. C17-C20 exist imperf. Value, set $8.
No. C21 exists imperf. Value, $12.50.
Nos. C17-C20 exist in deluxe sheets of one. Value, $6.50 each.
No. C21 exists in an imperf. sheet of one. Value, $19. Additionally the imperf. sheet of one exists with green overprint "F.I.S./1970/VALGARDENA" in the lower selvage. Value, $35.

Grenoble Olympic Champions, Peggy Flemming with President Lyndon B. Johnson — AP5

Design: 5rl, Jean-Claude Killy (France)

1968, Aug 31   Litho.   Perf. 11¼
C22	AP5	2rl shown	.75	.25
C23	AP5	5rl multi	1.15	.25
a.		Souvenir sheet of 2, #C22-C23	3.00	1.25

Issued in panes of six.
Nos. C22-C23 exist imperf. Value, set $2.50. No. C23a exists imperf. Value, $3.
Imperf. deluxe sheets of one, and of the pair exist. Values, $10 and $6 respectively.

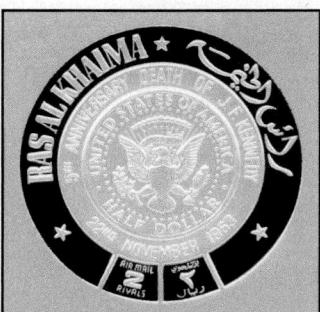

Reverse of United States 1964 50-Cent Coin — AP6

Designs: No. C24-C25, shown. Nos. C26-C27, Obverse of United States 1964 50-cent coin showing John Kennedy.

Embossed on Foil Coated Paper

1968, Nov. 22   Imperf.
C24	AP6	2rl black & silver	6.00	6.00
C25	AP6	2rl gold	6.00	6.00
C26	AP6	3rl black & silver	9.00	9.00
C27	AP6	3rl gold	9.00	9.00
		Nos. C24-C27 (4)	30.00	30.00

Nos. C24-C27 exist in miniature sheets of one. Value, set $65.
Nos. C25 and C27 were not available on the day of issue, but were made available later. Miniature sheets and singles exist in nine different colored frames in all four designs, totaling 36 singles and 36 miniature sheets. Only 500 sets were issued and came in a vinyl faux leather wallet with 18 stamps. Value for either set of 18 singles, $110. Value for either set of 18 miniature sheets, $200.

Soviet Space Program — AP7

Designs: 2.50rl, Apollo Program. 3.50rl, French Program. 4.50rl, Moonlanding. 10rl, Apollo 11.

1969, June 19   Litho.   Perf. 11
C28	AP7	1.50rl shown	.50	.25
C29	AP7	2.50rl multi	.75	.25
C30	AP7	3.50rl multi	1.00	.25
C31	AP7	4.50rl multi	1.25	.25
		Nos. C28-C31 (4)	3.50	1.00

Souvenir Sheet

C32	AP7	10rl multi	6.50	—

Issued in panes of 10.
Nos. C28-C31 exist imperf. Value, set $7.75. Also exists in imperf. deluxe sheets of one. Value, set $20.
No. C32 exists imperf. Value, $10.
See no. C50.

Coronation of Napoleon — AP8

Napoleon Bonaparte, Bicentennial of Birth — AP9

1969, Aug. 15   Litho.   Perf. 11
C33	AP8	10rl multi	7.00	3.00

Embossed on Foil Coated Paper

Perf. 7½
C34	AP8	10rl gold	10.00	—

Perf. 11
C35	AP9	10rl gold	10.00	—

No. C33 exists imperf. Value, $9. Nos. C34-C35 exist imperf. and in imperf sheets of one. Value, $7.50 each and $15 each, respectively.
See Nos. 296-299.

Apollo 10 — AP10

Design: C37, Apollo 11.

1969, Aug. 15	Litho.	Perf. 11	
C36	Strip of 4, #a.-d.	6.00	1.00
a.	AP10 2rl multi	1.00	.25
b.	AP10 3rl multi	1.00	.25
c.	AP10 4rl multi	1.00	.25
d.	AP10 5rl multi	1.00	.25
C37	Strip of 4, #a.-d.	6.00	1.00
a.	AP10 2.50rl multi	1.00	.25
b.	AP10 3.50rl multi	1.00	.25
c.	AP10 4.50rl multi	1.00	.25
d.	AP10 5.50rl multi	1.00	.25

Overprint on No. 269
Souvenir Sheet
Perf. 12

| C38 | A28 10rl multi | 7.00 | — |

Issued in sheets of 16 and 20.
Nos. C36-C37 exist imperf. Value, set $15.
No. C38 exists imperf. Value, $35.
Nos. C36 and C37 were each produced in imperf. deluxe sheets of four. Value, set $32.
No. C38 exists with intentionally created inverted overprints. Value, $60.

Apollo 10 — AP11

Designs: No. C40, Apollo 11. No. C41 and C43, Apollo 11, lunar research. No. C42 and C44, Apollo 12, inspection of Surveyor, vert.

Souvenir Sheets

1969, Aug. 15	Litho.	Perf. 11	
C39	AP11 10rl shown	6.00	2.00
C40	AP11 10rl multi	6.00	2.00
C41	AP11 10rl multi	6.00	2.00
C42	AP11 10rl multi	6.00	2.00

Embossed on Foil Coated Paper
Perf. 11

| C43 | AP11 10rl gold | 12.00 | — |

Perf. 14½

| C44 | AP11 10rl gold | 12.00 | — |

Nos. C39-C41 exist imperf. Value, set $7.50. Nos. C43-C44 exist imperf. Value, set $12. They also exist as miniature sheets of 1. Value, set $20.

Designs: No. C45, As No. C39, with President Kennedy's mouth open. No. C46, As No. C39, with President Kennedy's mouth closed. No. C47, As No. C40.

Embossed on Foil Coated Paper

1969, Aug. 30		Perf. 8	
C45	AP11 10rl gold	30.00	—
C46	AP11 10rl gold	10.00	—
C47	AP11 10rl gold	10.00	—

No. C45 was withdrawn from sale due to design flaws.
No. C45 exists imperf. Value, $35. No. C45 exists as a deluxe sheet of one with red inscriptions. Value, $55.
Nos. C46-C47 exist imperf. Value, $12 each. Nos. C46-C47 exist as deluxe sheets of one with red or black inscriptions. Value, $22.50 and $85 each, respectively.

Michael Collins, Apollo 11 — AP12

Designs: 3.25rl, Neil Armstrong. 4.25rl, Edward Aldrin. 5.25rl, Nixon and three Apollo 11 astronauts.

1969, Aug. 15	Litho.	Perf. 11	
C48	Strip of 4, #a.-d.	5.00	1.50
a.	AP12 2.25rl multi	1.00	.25
b.	AP12 3.25rl multi	1.00	.25
c.	AP12 4.25rl multi	1.00	.25
d.	AP12 5.25rl multi	1.00	.25

Issued in sheets of 16 and 20.
No. C48 exists imperf. Value, $8. No. C48 exists in imperf. deluxe sheets of four, and as imperf deluxe sheets of one of each value with a white background, and with a pink background.
On No. C48c Edwin Aldrin is misspelled Edward Aldrin.

Apollo 12 — AP13

Designs: 60d, Command center. 2.60rl, Richard F. Gordon Jr. 3.60rl, Charles Conrad, Jr. 4.60rl, Alan L. Bean. 5.60rl, John F. Kennedy, Wernher von Braun, and rocket.

1969, Aug.	Litho.	Perf. 11	
C49	AP13 Sheet of 5, #a.-e., + 4 labels	9.50	4.25
a.	60d multi	1.50	.50
b.	2.60rl multi	1.50	.50
c.	3.60rl multi	1.50	.50
d.	4.60rl multi	1.50	.50
e.	5.60rl multi	1.50	.50

No. C49 exists imperf. Value, $15.
Nos. C49b-C49e exist in deluxe sheets of one, both perf and imperf. Value, $65. No. C49a exists in a deluxe sheet of one plus two labels, both perf. and imperf. Value, $65.
See No. C56.

Type of Soviet Space Program
Embossed on Foil Coated Paper
Perf. 8

1969, Sept.			
C50	AP7 4.50rl gold	15.00	—

No. C50 exists imperf. Value, $15. Also exists as an imperf. sheet of one. Value, $20.

1968 Mexico Olympics, Mask — AP14

Design: 3rl, Mask with red background.

1969, Dec.	Litho.	Perf. 11¼	
C51	AP14 2rl shown	.75	.25
C52	AP14 3rl multi	2.00	.25
a.	Souvenir sheet of 2, #C51-C52	3.50	1.50

Issued in panes of six.
Nos. C51-C52 exist imperf. Value, set $3.
No. C52a exists imperf. Value, $3.50.
Imperf. deluxe sheets of one, and of the pair exist. Values, $10 and $6, respectively.

Type of 1969

Designs: Apollo 11. No. C53, Apollo 11, eagle and moon. No. C54, Michael Collins, Niel Armstrong and Edwin "Buzz" Aldrin. No. C55, Lunar module and moon.

Embossed on Foil Coated Paper

1970, Jan. 20		Perf. 7½	
C53	AP9 10rl gold	12.00	—
C54	AP9 10rl gold	12.00	—
C55	AP9 10rl gold	12.00	—

Nos. C53-C55 exist imperf. Value, $17 each.
Nos. C53-C55 exist as imperf. sheets of one. Value, $25 each.

Type of Apollo XII
Embossed on Foil Coated Paper

1970, Feb. 24		Perf. 14½	
C56	AP13 5.60rl gold	12.00	—

No. C56 exists imperf, and as an imperf sheet of one. Values, $12 and $15, respectively.

AP15

1970 World Cup, Mexico — AP16

Designs: Various soccer scenes and artifacts. 1rl, red background. 2rl, olive background. 3rl, yellow background. 4rl, green background. 5rl, blue background. 6rl, pink background.

1970, Mar. 10	Litho.	Perf. 11	
C57	Block of 6, #a.-f.	8.00	2.25
a.	AP15 1rl shown	1.00	.25
b.	AP15 2rl multi	1.00	.25
c.	AP15 3rl multi	1.00	.25
d.	AP15 4rl multi	1.00	.25
e.	AP15 5rl multi	1.00	.25
f.	AP15 6rl multi	1.00	.25

Souvenir Sheet

| C58 | AP16 10rl multi | 5.75 | 1.50 |

Printed in panes of 12 plus three labels.
No. C57 exists imperf. Value, $11. No. C58 exists imperf. Value, $7.
Nos. C57a-C57f exist in imperf deluxe sheets of one, with an image of a mask and a soccer ball in the margins. Value, $5 each.
For gold foil version see No. C63. For overprints see Nos. C65-C66.

1972 Sapporo Olympics, Downhill Skiing — AP17

Designs: 2rl, Ski jumping. 3rl. Speed skating. 4rl, Slalom skiing. 5rl, Figure skating. 6rl, Ice hockey.
10rl, Downhill skiing.

1970, Mar. 10	Litho.	Perf. 11	
C59	Block of 6, #a.-f.	6.00	2.00
a.	AP17 1rl shown	.80	.25
b.	AP17 2rl multi	.80	.25
c.	AP17 3rl multi	.80	.25
d.	AP17 4rl multi	.80	.25
e.	AP17 5rl multi	.80	.25
f.	AP17 6rl multi	.80	.25

Souvenir Sheet

| C60 | AP17 10rl multi | 5.00 | 1.50 |

Printed in panes of 12 plus three labels.
No. C59 exists imperf. Value, $9. No. C60 exists imperf. Value, $5.50.
Nos. C59a-C59f exist in imperf deluxe sheets of one. Value, $5 each.
No. C60 was also overprinted, both perf. and imperf. However the overprint is entirely in the selvage. Value, perf. $6, imperf. $7.
No. C60 contains one 38x50½.
See No. C64. For overprints see No. C67.

1972 Munich Olympics, Hurdling — AP18

Designs: 2rl, Diving. 3rl, Running. 4rl, High jump. 5rl, Riding. 6rl, Gymnastics.
10rl, Stadium.

1970, Mar. 10	Litho.	Perf. 11	
C61	Block of 6, #a.-f.	7.00	3.00
a.	AP18 1rl shown	.90	.35
b.	AP18 2rl multi	.90	.35
c.	AP18 3rl multi	.90	.35
d.	AP18 4rl multi	.90	.35
e.	AP18 5rl multi	.90	.35
f.	AP18 6rl multi	.90	.35

Souvenir Sheet

| C62 | AP18 10rl multi | 5.00 | 1.50 |

Printed in panes of 12 plus three labels.
No. C61 exists imperf. Value, $9. No. C62 exists imperf. Value, $6.
Nos. C61a-C61f exist in imperf deluxe sheets of one. Value, $5 each.
No. C62 contains one 38x50½.
See No. C64. For overprints see Nos. C68-C69.

Types of 1969-70

Designs: No. C63, as No. C58. No. C64, as No. C61d.

Embossed on Foil Coated Paper

1970, June 6		Perf. 13	
C63	AP16 20rl gold	7.00	—

1970, July			
C64	AP16 4rl gold		8.00 —

Nos. C63-C64 exist imperf. Value, $8 each.
Nos. C63-C64 exist in imperf. sheets of one. Value, $10 and $12, respectively.

A 25rl and 30rl set of two was issued June 20, 1970, embossed in gold foil and rouletted, bearing the images of the Queen of Saba and a camel, and Winston Churchill and Sheikh Saqr Bin Mohammed Al Qasimi, respectively. The editors question the validity of this issue and would like more information.

No. C57 Overprinted in Gold

1970, July   Litho.   Perf. 11

C65		Block of 6, #a.-f.	9.50	—
a.	AP15	1rl shown	1.25	—
b.	AP15	2rl multi	1.25	—
c.	AP15	3rl multi	1.25	—
d.	AP15	4rl multi	1.25	—
e.	AP15	5rl multi	1.25	—
f.	AP15	6rl multi	1.25	—

No. C58 Overprinted In Blue

C66	AP16	10rl multi	6.50	—

Printed in panes of 12 plus three labels.
No. C65 exists imperf. Value, *$13.* No. C66 exists imperf. Value, *$8.50.*
Nos. C65a-C65f exist in imperf. deluxe sheets of one. Value, *$6* each.

No. C59 Overprinted in Gold

1970, July   Litho.   Perf. 11

C67		Block of 6, #a.-f.	7.00	—
a.	AP17	1rl shown	.90	—
b.	AP17	2rl multi	.90	—
c.	AP17	3rl multi	.90	—
d.	AP17	4rl multi	.90	—
e.	AP17	5rl multi	.90	—
f.	AP17	6rl multi	.90	—

Printed in panes of 12 plus 3 labels.
No. C67 exists imperf. Value, *$12.*
Nos. C67a-C67f exist in imperf. deluxe sheets of one. Value, *$6* each.
See footnote after No. C60.

Nos. C61-C62 Overprinted in Gold

1970, July   Litho.   Perf. 11

C68		Block of 6, #a.-f.	8.25	—
a.	AP18	1rl multi	1.10	—
b.	AP18	2rl multi	1.10	—
c.	AP18	3rl multi	1.10	—
d.	AP18	4rl multi	1.10	—
e.	AP18	5rl multi	1.10	—
f.	AP18	6rl multi	1.10	—

Souvenir Sheet

C69	AP18	10rl multi	6.00	—

Printed in panes of 12 plus three labels.
No. C68 exists imperf. Value, *$12.* No. C69 exists imperf. Value, *$7.*
Nos. C68a-C68f exist in imperf. deluxe sheets of one. Value, *$6.*

Apollo 12 — AP19

Designs: No. C71, Apollo 13: a, Apollo 13 struck by space debris. b, Nos. C82-C83, command module releasing lunar module. c, command module reentering atmosphere.

No. C72, Symphonie satellites: a, Diamant B, assembly. b, Nos. C84-C85, WIKA satellite. c, Diamant B rocket.
No. C73, Apollo 13: a, Apollo 13 orbiting the moon. b, Apollo 13 astronauts c, Apollo 13 water landing.
No. C74, a, Zond satellite orbitting moon. b, Mars probe and Mars. c, Mariner VII and Mars.
No. C75, a, Vladimir Komarov. b, Soyuz 1. c, Yuri Gagarin.
No. C76, Exploring Surveyor 3. No. C77, Command and lunar modules. No. C78, Intelsat IV. No. C79, Apollo 13 splashdown. No. C80, Mariner VII passes Mars. No. C81, Soyuz 4 and Soyuz 5 join.

1970, July 22   Litho.   Perf. 14½

C70	AP19	Strip of 3, #a.-c.	6.00	.75
a.		1rl multi	1.00	.25
b.		2rl multi	1.00	.25
c.		4rl multi	1.00	.25
C71	AP19	Strip of 3, #a.-c.	6.00	.75
a.		1rl multi	1.00	.25
b.		2rl multi	1.00	.25
c.		4rl multi	1.00	.25
C72	AP19	Strip of 3, #a.-c.	6.00	.75
a.		1rl multi	1.00	.25
b.		2rl multi	1.00	.25
c.		4rl multi	1.00	.25
C73	AP19	Strip of 3, #a.-c.	6.00	.75
a.		1rl multi	1.00	.25
b.		2rl multi	1.00	.25
c.		4rl multi	1.00	.25
C74	AP19	Strip of 3, #a.-c.	6.00	.75
a.		1rl multi	1.00	.25
b.		2rl multi	1.00	.25
c.		4rl multi	1.00	.25
C75	AP19	Strip of 3, #a.-c.	6.00	.75
a.		1rl multi	1.00	.25
b.		2rl multi	1.00	.25
c.		4rl multi	1.00	.25
		Nos. C70-C75 (6)	36.00	4.50

Souvenir Sheets

C76	AP19	10rl multi	16.50	5.00
C77	AP19	10rl multi	16.50	5.00
C78	AP19	10rl multi	16.50	5.00
C79	AP19	10rl multi	16.50	5.00
C80	AP19	10rl multi	16.50	5.00
C81	AP19	10rl multi	16.50	5.00
		Nos. C76-C81 (6)	99.00	30.00

Embossed on Foil Coated Paper
Perf. 13

C82	AP19	2rl silver	15.00	—
C83	AP19	2rl gold	15.00	—
C84	AP19	2rl silver	15.00	—
C85	AP19	2rl gold	15.00	—
		Nos. C82-C85 (4)	60.00	

Issued in panes of 12, in 4 strips of 3.
Nos. C70-C75 exist imperf. Value, set *$40.*
Nos. C76-C81 exist imperf. Value, *$25* each.
Nos. C70a-C75c exist as imperf. deluxe sheets of one. Value, *$150* for set of 18.
Nos. C82-C85 exist imperf. Value, *$15* each. Also exists in imperf. deluxe sheets of one. Value, *$25* each.

Napoleon Bonaparte — AP20

Designs: No. C86: a, Napoleon Bonaparte, portrait. b, Napoleon in Tilsit. c, Napoleon in Alexandria.
No. C87: a, Surrender of Madrid. b, Napoleon at the hospice of St. Bernard Pass. c, Napoleon visits the Louvre.
No. C88: a, Napoleon establishes the constitution of the Duchy of Warsaw. b, Napoleon after the Battle of Aspern. c, Napoleon receives the Ambassador of Persia.
No. C89: Louis XIV. a, Portrait as a boy. b, Framed portrait and musical instruments. c, Portrait by Henri Testelin.
No. C90: a, Queen Marie-Louise, portrait. b, Queen Marie-Louise in Compiegne. c, Josephine Bonaparte, portrait.
No. C91: Charles De Gaulle. a, Charles De Gaulle meeting Sir Winston Churchill. b, Charles De Gaulle, Heinrich Lubke and Konrad Adenauer. c, Charles De Gaulle and Dwight D. Eisenhower.
No. C92, Napoleon Meeting the King of Prussia at Tilsit, by Nicolas-Henri Tardieu. No. C93, Napoleon Proclaimed Emperor by Georges Rouget. No. C94, Napoleon Meets the Baron Vincent at Erfurt, by Sylvia Gosse. No. C95, Family of Divinites by Jean Nocret. No. C96, Arrival of Napoleon and Marie-Louise in Tuileries, by Etienne Barthelemy Garnier. No. C97, John F. Kennedy, Charles De Gaulle and Jackie Kennedy.
Nos. C98-C99, design as No. C86a. Nos. C100-C101, design as No. C91b.

1970, July 22   Litho.   Perf. 14½

C86	AP20	Strip of 3, #a.-c.	6.00	1.75
a.		1rl multi	1.00	.50
b.		2rl multi	1.00	.50
c.		4rl multi	1.00	.50

C87	AP20	Strip of 3, #a.-c.	6.00	1.75
a.		1rl multi	1.00	.50
b.		2rl multi	1.00	.50
c.		4rl multi	1.00	.50
C88	AP20	Strip of 3, #a.-c.	6.00	1.75
a.		1rl multi	1.00	.50
b.		2rl multi	1.00	.50
c.		4rl multi	1.00	.50
C89	AP20	Strip of 3, #a.-c.	6.00	1.75
a.		1rl multi	1.00	.50
b.		2rl multi	1.00	.50
c.		4rl multi	1.00	.50
C90	AP20	Strip of 3, #a.-c.	6.00	1.75
a.		1rl multi	1.00	.50
b.		2rl multi	1.00	.50
c.		4rl multi	1.00	.50
C91	AP20	Strip of 3, #a.-c.	6.00	1.75
a.		1rl multi	1.00	.50
b.		2rl multi	1.00	.50
c.		4rl multi	1.00	.50
		Nos. C86-C91 (6)	36.00	10.50

Souvenir Sheets

C92	AP20	10rl multi	16.50	5.00
C93	AP20	10rl multi	16.50	5.00
C94	AP20	10rl multi	16.50	5.00
C95	AP20	10rl multi	16.50	5.00
C96	AP20	10rl multi	16.50	5.00
C97	AP20	10rl multi	16.50	5.00
		Nos. C92-C97 (6)	99.00	30.00

Embossed on Foil Coated Paper
Perf. 13

C98	AP20	2rl silver	15.00	—
C99	AP20	2rl gold	15.00	—
C100	AP20	2rl silver	15.00	—
C101	AP20	2rl gold	15.00	—
		Nos. C98-C101 (4)	60.00	

Issued in panes of 12, in four strips of three.
Nos. C86-C91 exist imperf. Nos. C92-C97 exist imperf. Value, *$20* each.
Nos. C86a-C91c exist as imperf. deluxe sheets of one.
Nos. C98-C101 exist imperf. Value, *$15* each. Also exists in imperf. deluxe sheets of one. Value, *$25* each. Nos. C100-C101 deluxe sheets exist with marginal inscription "AUSTERLITZ 1805." Value, *$50* each.

PHILYMPIA '70 London, Belgium No. 726 — AP21

Designs: No. C102: a, Belgium No. 726. b, Nicaragua No. C713. c, Panama No. C363. d, Romania No. 2160. e, United States No. C76. f, El Salvador No. C282. g, Ecuador No. 764E. h, Singapore No. 1240. i, Paraguay No. 1240. j, Togo No. 733. k, Monaco No. 772. l, Vatican City No. 481. m, Monaco No. 757. n, Bulgaria No. 1842. o, Rwanda No. 130. p, Chile No. C294. q, Romania No. 2137. r, Romania No. 2177. s, Aden, Kathiri State of Hadhramaut unlisted stamp. t, Monaco No. 757.
No. C103, Musketeer and Cupid, by Pablo Picasso. No. C104, El Salvador No. C276. No. C105, Germany No. 901. No. C106, Togo No. 674.
Nos. C107-C108, design as No. C102e. Nos. C109-C110, design as No. C102o.

1970, Sept. 30   Litho.   Perf. 11

C102		Sheet of 20, #a.-t.	30.00	15.00
a.-d.	AP21	1rl any single	1.25	.60
e.-h.	AP21	1.50rl any single	1.25	.60
i.-l.	AP21	2.50rl any single	1.25	.60
m.-p.	AP21	3rl any single	1.25	.60
q.-t.	AP21	3rl any single	1.25	.60

Souvenir Sheets

C103	AP21	10rl multi	27.50	7.00
C104	AP21	10rl multi	9.00	4.00
C105	AP21	10rl multi	—	4.00
C106	AP21	10rl multi	12.00	4.00
		Nos. C103-C106 (4)	48.50	19.00

Embossed on Foil Coated Paper
Perf. 13

C107	AP21	1.50rl silver	15.00	—
C108	AP21	1.50rl gold	15.00	—
C109	AP21	3rl silver	17.50	—
C110	AP21	3rl gold	17.50	—
		Nos. C107-C110 (4)	65.00	

No. C102 exists imperf. Nos. C103-C106 exist imperf. Nos. C107-C110 exist imperf.
Nos. C102a-C102t exist in deluxe sheets of one. Value CTO, perf. $2.50 each. Value CTO, imperf. $2.50 each.
Nos. C107-C110 exist in imperf sheets of one.

RHODESIA
rō-'dē-zh͞ē-ə

(British South Africa)

LOCATION — Southeastern Africa
GOVT. — Administered by the British South Africa Company
AREA — 440,653 sq. mi.
POP. — 1,738,000 (estimated 1921)
CAPITAL — Salisbury

In 1923 the area was divided and the portion south of the Zambezi River became the British Crown Colony of Southern Rhodesia. In the following year the remaining territory was formed into the Protectorate of Northern Rhodesia. The Federation of Rhodesia and Nyasaland (comprising Southern Rhodesia, Northern Rhodesia and Nyasaland) was established Sept. 3, 1953.

12 Pence = 1 Shilling
20 Shillings = 1 Pound

A1   A2

Coat of Arms — A3

Thin Paper
Engr. (A1, A3); Engr., Typo. (A2)

1890-94		Unwmk.	Perf. 14, 14½	
1	A2	½p blue & ver ('91)	4.75	5.25
2	A1	1p black	19.00	4.50
3	A2	2p gray grn & ver ('91)	28.00	8.00
4	A2	3p gray & grn ('91)	25.00	5.00
5	A2	4p red brn & blk ('91)	47.50	6.50
6	A1	6p ultra	80.00	28.00
7	A1	6p deep blue	50.00	4.25
8	A2	8p rose & bl ('91)	22.50	24.00
9	A1	1sh gray brown	55.00	16.00
10	A1	2sh vermilion	77.50	42.50
11	A1	2sh6p dull lilac	47.50	55.00
		Revenue cancellation		1.00
12	A2	3sh brn & grn ('94)	195.00	100.00
		Revenue cancellation		2.50
13	A2	4sh gray & ver ('93)	48.00	60.00
		Revenue cancellation		1.00
14	A1	5sh yellow	92.50	65.00
		Revenue cancellation		1.50
15	A1	10sh deep green	130.00	110.00
		Revenue cancellation		1.25
16	A3	£1 dark blue	325.00	175.00
		Revenue cancellation		6.75
17	A3	£2 rose	550.00	200.00
		Revenue cancellation		22.50
18	A3	£5 yellow grn	1,775.	500.00
		Revenue cancellation		50.00
19	A3	£10 orange brn	3,000.	800.00
		Revenue cancellation		75.00
		Nos. 1-16 (16)	1,247.	709.00

The paper of the 1891 issue has the trademark and initials of the makers in a monogram watermarked in each sheet. Some of the lower values were also printed on a slightly thicker paper without watermark.
Examples of Nos. 16-19 with cancellations removed are frequently offered as unused specimens.
See Nos. 24-25, 58.
For surcharges see Nos. 20-23, 40-42. For overprints see British Central Africa Nos. 1-20.

Nos. 6 and 9
Surcharged in Black

1891, Mar.

No.	Type	Description		
20	A1	½p on 6p ultra	150.00	525.00
21	A1	2p on 6p ultra	195.00	700.00
22	A1	4p on 6p ultra	210.00	825.00
23	A1	8p on 1sh brown	225.00	925.00
		Nos. 20-23 (4)	780.00	2,975.

Beware of forged surcharges.

1895 Thick Soft Paper Perf. 12½

No.	Type	Description		
24	A2	2p green & red	32.50	20.00
25	A2	4p ocher & black	32.50	21.00
a.		Imperf., pair	2,250.	

A4

1896 Engraved, Typo. Perf. 14

No.	Type	Description		
26	A4	½p slate & vio	5.00	3.75
27	A4	1p scar & emer	14.00	5.50
28	A4	2p brn & rose lil	30.00	4.00
29	A4	3p red brn & ultra	11.00	2.50
30	A4	4p blue & red lil	24.00	.60
d.		Horiz. pair, imperf. btwn.		
31	A4	6p vio & pale rose	19.00	1.10
32	A4	8p dp grn & vio, buff	20.00	.70
a.		Imperf. pair	4,500.	
b.		Horiz. pair, imperf. btwn.		
33	A4	1sh brt grn & ultra	27.50	4.00
34	A4	2sh dk bl & grn, buff	55.00	14.00
35	A4	2sh6p brn & vio, yel	92.50	65.00
36	A4	3sh grn & red vio, bl	90.00	47.50
a.		Imperf. pair	13,000.	
37	A4	4sh red & bl, grn	75.00	4.00
38	A4	5sh org red & grn	65.00	14.00
39	A4	10sh sl & car, rose	150.00	75.00
		Nos. 26-39 (14)	678.00	241.65

The plates for this issue were made from two dies. Stamps of die I have a small dot at the right of the tail of the supporter at the right of the shield, and the body of the lion is not fully shaded. Stamps of die II have not the dot and the lion is heavily shaded.
See type A7.

Nos. 4, 13-14 Surcharged in Black

1896, Apr. Perf. 14

No.	Type	Description		
40	A2	1p on 3p	650.00	850.00
a.		"P" of "Penny" inverted	50,000.	
b.		"y" of "Penny" inverted	—	
c.		Double surcharge	—	

No.	Type	Description		
41	A2	1p on 4sh	325.00	350.00
a.		"P" of "Penny" inverted	37,500.	
b.		Single bar in surch.	1,250.	1,400.
c.		"y" of "Penny" inverted	37,500.	
42	A1	3p on 5sh yellow	225.00	275.00
a.		"T" of "THREE" inverted	50,000.	
b.		"R" of "THREE" inverted	37,500.	
		Nos. 40-42 (3)	1,200.	1,475.

Cape of Good Hope Stamps Overprinted in Black

1896, May 22 Wmk. 16

No.	Type	Description		
43	A6	½p slate	20.00	25.00
44	A15	1p carmine	22.50	29.00
45	A6	2p bister brown	27.50	15.00
46	A6	4p deep blue	34.00	27.50
a.		"COMPANY" omitted	11,000.	
47	A3	6p violet	77.50	90.00
48	A6	1sh yellow buff	175.00	165.00

Wmk. 2

No.	Type	Description		
49	A6	3p claret	60.00	85.00
		Nos. 43-49 (7)	416.50	436.50

Nos. 42-49 were used at Bulawayo during the Matabele Rebellion.
Forgeries are known.

Remainders

Rhodesian authorities made available remainders in large quantities of all stamps in 1897, 1898-1908, 1905, 1909 and 1910 issues, CTO. Some varieties exist only as remainders. See notes following Nos. 100 and 118.

A7

Type A7 differs from type A4 in having the ends of the scroll which is below the shield curved between the hind legs of the supporters instead of passing behind one leg of each. There are other minor differences.

Perf. 13½ to 16

No.	Type	1897 Unwmk.		Engr.
50	A7	½p slate & violet	7.75	9.50
51	A7	1p ver & gray grn	13.00	11.50
52	A7	2p brn & lil rose	27.50	4.50
53	A7	3p red brn & gray bl	11.00	.55
a.		Vert. pair, imperf. btwn.	5,000.	
54	A7	4p ultra & red lil	32.50	4.50
a.		Horiz. pair, imperf. btwn.	18,000.	17,500.
55	A7	6p vio & sal	22.50	4.00
56	A7	8p dk grn & vio, buff	32.50	.55
			—	4,000.
a.		Vert. pair, imperf. btwn.		
57	A7	£1 blk & red, grn	450.00	250.00
		Revenue cancellation		12.00
		Nos. 50-56 (7)	146.75	35.10

Thick Paper Perf. 15

No.	Type	Description		
58	A3	£2 bright red	1,900.	500.00
		Revenue cancellation		65.00

See note on remainders following No. 49.

A8 A9

A10

1898-1908 Perf. 13½ to 16

No.	Type	Description		
59	A8	½p yel grn ('04)	7.50	4.00
a.		Imperf. pair	1,000.	
b.		Horiz. pair, imperf. vert.	975.00	
c.		Vert. pair, imperf between	1,675.	
60	A8	1p rose (shades)	17.50	1.10
a.		Horiz. pair, imperf. btwn.		1,150.
b.		Vert. pair, imperf between	825.00	
c.		Imperf. pair	1,000.	900.00
d.		1p red (shades) ('05)	13.00	.80
61	A8	2p brown	14.50	3.00
62	A8	2½p dull blue (shades)	26.00	2.00
a.		Horiz. pair, imperf vert.	1,100.	1,300.
63	A8	3p clar ('08)	22.50	1.00
a.		Vert. pair, imperf between	800.00	
64	A8	4p ol grn	21.00	.75
a.		Vert. pair, imperf. between	800.00	
65	A8	6p lilac	27.50	3.75
66	A9	1sh bister	42.50	6.00
a.		Vert. pair, imperf. btwn.	3,500.	3,500.
b.		Horiz. pair, imperf between	4,000.	4,000.
67	A9	2sh6p bluish gray ('06)	75.00	2.25
a.		Vert. pair, imperf. between	1,300.	575.00
68	A9	3sh pur ('02)	42.50	4.50
69	A9	5sh org ('01)	70.00	29.00
70	A9	7sh6p blk ('01)	110.00	32.50
71	A9	10sh bluish grn ('08)	65.00	3.00
72	A10	£1 gray vio, perf 15½ ('01)	425.00	170.00
		Revenue cancellation		17.50
73	A10	£2 red brn ('08)	130.00	7.50
74	A10	£5 dk blue ('01)	3,750.	3,000.
		Revenue cancellation		125.00
75	A10	£10 blue lil ('01)	3,750.	3,000.
		Revenue cancellation		125.00
75A	A10	£20 bister ('01?)	22,500.	
		Revenue cancellation		175.00
75B	A10	£100 cherry red ('01)	185,000.	
		Revenue cancellation		900.00
		Nos. 59-73 (15)	1,097.	270.35

For overprints and surcharges see #82-100.
See note on remainders following #49.

Victoria Falls — A11

Perf. 14, 14½x15 (#78)

1905, July 13

No.	Type	Description		
76	A11	1p rose red	9.50	11.50
77	A11	2½p ultra	45.00	12.00
78	A11	5p magenta	47.50	60.00
79	A11	1sh blue green	42.50	57.50
a.		Imperf., pair	35,000.	
b.		Horiz. pair, imperf. vert.	37,500.	
c.		Horiz. pair, imperf. btwn.	45,000.	
d.		Vert. pair, imperf. btn.	45,000.	
e.		Perf 14 ½x15		425.00

No.	Type	Description		
80	A11	2sh6p black	145.00	180.00
81	A11	5sh violet	145.00	50.00
		Nos. 76-81 (6)	434.50	371.00

Opening of the Victoria Falls bridge across the Zambezi River.
See note on remainders following No. 49.

Stamps of 1898-1908 Overprinted or Surcharged

1909 Perf. 14, 15

No.	Type	Description		
82	A8	½p green (shades)	6.50	3.50
83	A8	1p car rose	11.00	1.75
a.		Horiz. pair, imperf between	525.00	
84	A8	2p brown	7.50	9.00
85	A8	2½p cobalt blue	5.00	.90
86	A8	3p claret	5.00	3.00
a.		Double overprint	1,600.	1,600.
b.		Inverted overprint	—	20.00
87	A8	4p ol grn	17.50	4.25
a.		Inverted overprint		16.50
88	A8	5p on 6p lilac	16.00	22.50
a.		Violet surcharge	100.00	
89	A8	6p lilac	12.00	12.00
b.		6p dull purple	27.50	12.00
90	A9	7½p on 2sh6p	7.00	4.25
a.		Violet surcharge	27.50	11.00
b.		Double surcharge	10,000.	
91	A9	10p on 3sh pur, vio srch.	9.00	5.00
a.		Black surcharge	18.50	11.00
92	A9	1sh dp brnsh bister	18.00	9.00
93	A9	2sh on 5sh org	17.00	8.50
94	A9	2sh6p bluish gray	42.50	14.00
b.		Inverted overprint		25.00
95	A9	3sh purple	30.00	13.50
96	A9	5sh orange	57.50	87.50
97	A9	7sh6p black	110.00	40.00
98	A9	10sh bluish grn	77.50	24.00
99	A10	£1 gray vio	220.00	110.00
a.		Vert. pair, lower stamp without overprint	47,500.	
b.		Violet overprint	425.00	220.00
100	A10	£2 red brn, bluish, perf 14½x15 ('12)	4,500.	330.00
100B	A10	£5 dp blue, bluish	9,000.	5,000.
		Nos. 82-99 (18)	669.00	372.65

See note on remainders following No. 49.
Nos. 86b, 87a and 94b are from the remainders.
Nos. 82-87, 89, 92, 94, 96 and 98 exist without period after "Rhodesia." See the Scott Classic Specialized Catalogue of Stamps & Covers for listings.

Queen Mary and King George V — A12

1910 Engr. Perf. 14, 15x14, 14x15

No.	Type	Description		
101	A12	½p green	15.00	2.50
a.		½p olive green	45.00	5.50
b.		Perf. 15	350.00	14.50
c.		Imperf., pair	16,000.	8,000.
d.		Perf. 13½	350.00	55.00
102	A12	1p rose car	37.50	4.50
a.		Vertical pair, imperf. btwn.	22,500.	14,500.
b.		Perf. 15	350.00	10.00
c.		Perf. 13½	2,250.	55.00
103	A12	2p gray & blk	60.00	12.50
b.		Perf. 15	1,000.	47.50
104	A12	2½p ultra	27.50	12.00
a.		2½p light blue	29.00	24.00
b.		Perf. 15	82.50	45.00
c.		Perf. 13½	45.00	77.50
105	A12	3p ol yel & vio	50.00	52.00
a.		Perf. 15	3,650.	82.50
b.		Perf. 14x15	7,750.	325.00
106	A12	4p org & blk	55.00	27.50
a.		4p orange & violet black	95.00	72.50
b.		Perf. 15x14	550.00	
c.		Perf. 15	65.00	82.50
107	A12	5p ol grn & brn	60.00	60.00
a.		5p olive yel & brn (error)	725.00	165.00
b.		Perf. 15	875.00	115.00

108	A12	6p claret & brn	72.50	25.00
a.		Perf. 15	1,000.	67.50
109	A12	8p brn vio & gray blk	190.00	110.00
a.		Perf. 13½	67.50	275.00
110	A12	10p plum & rose red	55.00	55.00
111	A12	1sh turq grn & black	72.50	24.00
a.		Perf. 14x15	32,500.	3,250.
b.		Perf. 15	1,325.	62.50
112	A12	2sh gray bl & black	125.00	82.50
a.		Perf. 15	2,500.	400.00
113	A12	2sh6p car rose & blk	400.00	450.00
114	A12	3sh vio & bl grn	250.00	210.00
115	A12	5sh yel grn & brn red	325.00	225.00
116	A12	7sh6p brt bl & car	725.00	500.00
117	A12	10sh red org & bl grn	475.00	550.00
a.		10sh red org & myrtle grn	725.00	325.00
118	A12	£1 bluish sl & car	1,650.	775.00
a.		£1 black & red	1,550.	425.00
c.		Perf. 15	19,000.	4,750.
d.		As "a," carmine and reddish mauve (error)	14,500.	
		Nos. 101-118 (18)	4,645.	3,178.

See note on remainders following No. 49. The £1 in plum and red is from the remainders.

King George V — A13

Three dies were used for Nos. 122, 124-138: I, Outline at top of cap absent or very faint and broken. Left ear not shaded or outlined and appears white; II, Outline at top of cap faint and broken. Ear shaded all over, with no outline; III, Outline at top of cap continuous. Ear shaded all over, with continuous outline. Die types are noted in parentheses.

1913-23 **Perf. 14**

119	A13	½p dp grn	9.25	2.50
a.		Vert. pair, imperf horiz.	925.00	
b.		Vert. strip of 5, imperf between	4,250.	
d.		½p blue green, perf 15	9.50	30.00
120	A13	1p brn rose	4.50	4.00
a.		Perf. 15	7.50	10.00
b.		1p bright rose	7.25	2.50
c.		As "b," horiz. pair, imperf btwn.	1,100.	950.00
121	A13	1½p bis brn ('17)	6.00	2.50
a.		Horiz. pair, imperf between	900.00	900.00
b.		Perf. 15 ('19)	50.00	8.00
c.		As "b," horiz. pair, imperf between	26,500.	
122	A13	2p vio blk & blk (III) '22	13.50	9.00
a.		2p gray & black (III)	11.50	4.00
b.		Perf. 15 (II)	13.50	25.00
c.		Horiz. pair, imperf. btwn. (III)	6,750.	
d.		2p gray & brnish blk (III), perf 15	6,500.	
123	A13	2½p ultra	8.25	40.00
a.		Perf. 15	17.50	65.00
124	A13	3p org yel & blk (III)	20.00	4.75
a.		3p yellow & black (III)	17.50	4.25
b.		Perf. 15 (I)	9.00	27.50
125	A13	4p org red & blk (I)	12.00	42.50
a.		Perf. 15 (I)	175.00	32.50
126	A13	5p yel grn & blk (I)	7.25	22.50
127	A13	6p lilac & blk (III)	16.50	8.75
a.		Perf. 15 (I)	10.50	12.00
128	A13	8p gray grn & vio (II)	19.00	82.50
a.		Perf. 15 (III)	77.50	
b.		8p green & violet (II)	225.00	190.00
129	A13	10p car rose & bl, perf. 15	16.50	50.00
a.		Perf. 14 (III) '22	18.50	75.00
130	A13	1sh turq bl & blk (III) '22	15.00	22.50
a.		1sh lt grn & blk (III) ('19)	95.00	60.00
b.		Perf. 15 (II)	77.50	22.50
132	A13	2sh brn & blk, perf. 14 (III)('19)	22.50	20.00
a.		Perf. 15 (I)	17.50	55.00

133	A13	2sh6p ol gray & vio bl (III) '22	65.00	110.00
a.		2sh6p gray & blue (II)	82.50	60.00
b.		Perf. 15 (II)	55.00	105.00
134	A13	3sh brt blue & red brn (II)	130.00	165.00
a.		Perf. 15 (II)	195.00	
135	A13	5sh grn & bl (II)	95.00	100.00
a.		Perf. 15 (II)	210.00	225.00
136	A13	7sh6p blk & vio, perf. 15	175.00	300.00
a.		Perf. 14 (III) '22	250.00	425.00
137	A13	10sh yel grn & car (III) '23	275.00	360.00
a.		Perf. 15 (II)	250.00	425.00
138	A13	£1 vio & blk (II)	450.00	675.00
a.		£1 magenta & black (III) '23	950.00	1,250.
b.		Perf. 15 (III) '23	1,100.	
c.		Perf. 15, black & purple (II)	1,750.	1,750.
		Nos. 119-138 (19)	1,360.	2,022.

No. 120 Surcharged in Dark Violet

No. 139

No. 140

1917

139	A13	½p on 1p	2.75	10.50
a.		Inverted surcharge	1,600.	1,650.
140	A13	½p on 1p	2.00	10.00

Nos. 141-190 are accorded to Rhodesia and Nyasaland.

RHODESIA & NYASALAND

rō-'dē-zhē-ə ənd͵ nī-'a-sə-͵land

LOCATION — Southern Africa
GOVT. — Federal State in British Commonwealth
AREA — 486,972 sq. mi.
POP. — 8,510,000 (est. 1961)
CAPITAL — Salisbury, Southern Rhodesia

The Federation of Southern Rhodesia, Northern Rhodesia and Nyasaland was created in 1953, dissolved at end of 1963.

12 Pence = 1 Shilling
20 Shillings = 1 Pound

Catalogue values for all unused stamps in this country are for Never Hinged items.

A14

A15

Queen Elizabeth II
A16

Perf. 13½x14 (A14), 13½x13 (A15), 14x13 (A16)

1954-56 **Engr.** **Unwmk.**

141	A14	½p vermilion	.25	.25
a.		Booklet pane of 6	1.25	
b.		Perf. 12½x14	.75	.50
142	A14	1p ultra	.25	.25
a.		Booklet pane of 6	1.25	
b.		Perf. 12½x14	1.50	15.00
143	A14	2p emerald	.25	.25
a.		Booklet pane of 6	1.60	
143B	A14	2½p ocher ('56)	5.00	.25
144	A14	3p carmine	.25	.25

145	A14	4p red brown	.60	.25
146	A14	4½p blue green	.40	1.50
147	A14	6p red lilac	2.00	.25
148	A14	9p purple	2.25	.90
149	A14	1sh gray	2.00	.25
150	A15	1sh3p ultra & ver	6.50	.40
151	A15	2sh brn & dp bl	7.50	5.00
152	A15	2sh6p car & blk	7.50	2.00
153	A15	5sh ol & pur	21.00	6.50
154	A16	10sh red org & aqua	21.00	9.50
155	A16	£1 brn car & ol	37.50	27.50
		Nos. 141-155 (16)	114.25	55.30

Issue dates: 2½p, Feb. 15, others, July 1.
Nos. 141b and 142b are coils.

A17

A18

Victoria Falls

1955, June 15 **Perf. 13½**

156	A17	3p Plane	.80	.35
157	A18	1sh David Livingstone	.90	.75

Centenary of discovery of Victoria Falls.

Tea Picking — A19

Rhodes' Grave, Matopos — A20

Designs: 1p, V. H. F. Mast. 2p, Copper mining. 2½p, Kingsley Fairbridge Memorial. 4p, Boat on Lake Bangweulu. 6p, Victoria Falls. 9p, Railroad trains. 1sh, Tobacco. 1sh3p, Ship on Lake Nyasa. 2sh, Chirundu Bridge, Zambezi River. 2sh6p, Salisbury Airport. 5sh, Cecil Rhodes statue, Salisbury. 10sh, Mlanje mountain. £1, Coat of arms.

Perf. 13½x14, 14x13½

1959-63 **Engr.** **Unwmk.**

Size: 18½x22½mm, 22½x18½mm

158	A19	½p emer & blk	1.25	2.00
a.		Perf. 12½x13½	3.50	5.50
159	A19	1p blk & rose red	.30	.25
a.		Perf. 12½x13½	3.50	11.00
b.		Rose red (center) omitted	325.00	
160	A19	2p ocher & vio	2.00	.50
161	A19	2½p slate & lil, perf. 14½	1.75	2.00
162	A20	3p blue & blk	1.00	.25
a.		Booklet pane of 4 ('63)	4.00	
b.		Black omitted	30,000.	

Perf. 14½

Size: 24x27mm, 27x24mm

163	A19	4p ol & mag	1.50	.25
164	A19	6p grn & ul-tra	2.50	.25
164A	A20	9p pur & ocher ('62)	7.50	3.25
165	A20	1sh ultra & yel grn	1.25	.25
166	A20	1sh3p sep & brt grn, perf. 14	4.75	.25
167	A20	2sh lake & grn	4.00	.60
168	A20	2sh6p ocher & bl	9.50	1.00

Perf. 11½

Size: 32x27mm

169	A20	5sh yel grn & choc	13.00	2.50
170	A20	10sh brt rose & ol	22.50	19.00
171	A20	£1 vio & blk	40.00	45.00
		Nos. 158-171 (15)	112.80	77.35

Nos. 158a and 159a are coils.
Issue dates: 9p, May 15, others, Aug. 12.

Kariba Gorge, 1955
A21

Designs: 6p, Power lines. 1sh, View of dam. 1sh3p, View of dam and lake. 2sh6p, Power station. 5sh, Dam and Queen Mother Elizabeth.

1960, May 17 Photo. Perf. 14½x14

172	A21	3p org & sl grn	.80	.25
a.		Orange omitted	6,000.	
173	A21	6p yel brn & brn	1.00	.25
174	A21	1sh dull bl & em-er	2.25	4.25
175	A21	1sh3p grnsh bl & ocher	2.50	3.50
176	A21	2sh6p org ver & blk	3.75	8.50
177	A21	5sh grnsh bl & li-lac	10.00	12.00
		Nos. 172-177 (6)	20.30	28.75

Miner with Drill — A22

Design: 1sh3p, Mining surface installations.

1961, May 8 **Unwmk.**

178	A22	6p chnt brn & ol grn	.75	.25
179	A22	1sh3p lt blue & blk	.75	.90

7th Commonwealth Mining and Metallurgical Cong., Apr. 10-May 20.

DH Hercules Biplane A23

Designs: 1sh3p, Flying boat over Zambezi River. 2sh6p, DH Comet, Salisbury Airport.

1962, Feb. 6

180	A23	6p ver & ol grn	2.50	.75
181	A23	1sh3p bl, blk, grn & yel	1.90	.50
182	A23	2sh6p dk pur & car rose	4.25	6.50
		Nos. 180-182 (3)	8.65	7.75

30th anniv. of the inauguration of the Rhodesia-London airmail service.

Tobacco Plant — A24

Designs: 6p, Tobacco field. 1sh3p, Auction floor. 2sh6p, Cured tobacco.

1963, Feb. 18 Photo. Perf. 14x14½

184	A24	3p gray brown & grn	.30	.25
185	A24	6p blue, grn & brn	.40	.30
186	A24	1sh3p slate & red brn	1.40	.40
187	A24	2sh6p brown & org yel	1.60	3.00
		Nos. 184-187 (4)	3.70	3.95

3rd World Tobacco Scientific Cong., Salisbury, Feb. 18-26 and the 1st Intl. Tobacco Trade Cong., Salisbury, March 6-16.

Red Cross A25

1963, Aug. 6 *Perf. 14½x14*
188 A25 3p red 1.10 .25
Centenary of the International Red Cross.

"Round Table" Emblem A26

1963, Sept. 11 **Unwmk.**
189 A26 6p multicolored .65 *1.25*
190 A26 1sh3p multicolored .90 *.95*

World Council of Young Men's Service Clubs at University College of Rhodesia and Nyasaland, Sept. 8-15.

POSTAGE DUE STAMPS

D1

Perf. 12½
1961, Apr. 19 Unwmk. **Typo.**
J1 D1 1p vermilion 4.25 *5.75*
 a. Horiz. pair, imperf. btwn. 750.00 850.00
J2 D1 2p dark blue 3.50 *3.50*
J3 D1 4p emerald 3.75 10.00
J4 D1 6p dark purple 5.25 8.00
 a. Horiz. pair, imperf. btwn. 1,900.
  Nos. J1-J4 (4) 16.75 27.25

Nos. 142-143 exist with provisional "Poastage Due" handstamp.

RHODESIA

rō-'dē-zhę̄ȩ̄-ə

Self-Governing State (formerly Southern Rhodesia)

LOCATION — Southeastern Africa, bordered by Zambia, Mozambique, South Africa and Botswana
GOVT. — Self-governing member of British Commonwealth
AREA — 150,333 sq. mi.
POP. — 4,670,000 (est. 1968)
CAPITAL — Salisbury

In Oct. 1964, Southern Rhodesia assumed the name Rhodesia. On Nov. 11, 1965, the white minority government declared Rhodesia independent. Rhodesia became Zimbabwe on Apr. 18, 1980. For earlier issues, see Southern Rhodesia and Rhodesia and Nyasaland.

12 Pence = 1 Shilling
20 Shillings = 1 Pound
100 Cents = 1 Dollar (1967)

> **Catalogue values for all unused stamps in this country are for Never Hinged items.**

ITU Emblem, Old and New Communication Equipment — A27

Unwmk.
1965, May 17 Photo. *Perf. 14*
200 A27 6p apple grn & brt vio 1.50 .45
201 A27 1sh3p brt vio & dk vio 1.50 .45
202 A27 2sh6p org brn & dk vio 4.50 *4.50*
  Nos. 200-202 (3) 7.50 5.40

Cent. of the ITU.

Bangala Dam — A28

Designs: 4p, Irrigation canal through sugar plantation. 2sh6p, Worker cutting sugar cane.

1965, July 19 Photo. *Perf. 14*
203 A28 3p dull bl, grn & ocher .40 .25
204 A28 4p blue, grn & brn 1.25 1.25
205 A28 2sh6p multicolored 2.25 *3.50*
  Nos. 203-205 (3) 3.90 5.00

Issued to publicize Conservation Week of the Natural Resources Board.

Churchill, Parliament, Quill and Sword — A29

1965, Aug. 16
206 A29 1sh3p ultra & black .70 .45

Sir Winston Spencer Churchill (1874-1965), statesman and WWII leader.
For surcharge see No. 222.

Issues of Smith Government

Arms of Rhodesia A30

1965, Dec. 8 Photo. *Perf. 11*
207 A30 2sh6p violet & multi .35 .25
 a. Imperf., pair 900.00

Declaration of independence by the government of Prime Minister Ian Smith.

Southern Rhodesia Nos. 95-108 Overprinted

Perf. 14½
1966, Jan. 17 Unwmk. **Photo.**
Size: 23x19mm
208 A30 ½p lt bl, yel & grn .25 .25
 a. Pair, one without overprint 7,500.
209 A30 1p ocher & pur .25 .25
210 A30 2p vio & org yel .25 .25
211 A30 3p lt blue & choc .25 .25
212 A30 4p sl grn & org .25 .25

Perf. 13½x13
Size: 27x23mm
213 A30 6p dull grn, red & yel .40 .25
 a. Pair, one without overprint
214 A30 9p ol grn, yel & brn .45 .25
 a. Double overprint 800.00
 b. Pair, one without overprint
215 A30 1sh ocher & brt grn .50 .25
 a. Double overprint 800.00
 b. Pair, one without overprint
216 A30 1sh3p grn, vio & dk red .60 .40
217 A30 2sh dull bl & yel .75 *2.75*
218 A30 2sh6p ultra & yel .85 .90
 a. Red omitted

Perf. 14½x14
Size: 32x27mm
Overprint 26mm Wide
219 A30 5sh bl, grn, ocher & lt brn 2.25 *5.50*
 a. Double overprint 850.00
220 A30 10sh ocher, blk, red & bl 4.00 2.50
221 A30 £1 rose, sep, ocher & grn 1.50 *2.50*
  Nos. 208-221 (14) 12.55 16.55

No. 206 Surcharged in Red

Perf. 14
222 A29 5sh on 1sh3p 6.25 14.00
 a. "5/-" omitted

Ansellia Orchid — A31

Designs: 1p, Cape Buffalo. 2p, Oranges. 3p, Kudu. 4p, Emeralds. 6p, Flame lily. 9p, Tobacco. 1sh, Corn. 1sh3p, Lake Kyle. 2sh, Aloe. 2sh6p, Tigerfish. 5sh, Cattle. 10sh, Gray-breasted helmet guinea fowl. £1, Arms of Rhodesia.

Printed by Harrison & Sons, London
1966, Feb. 9 Photo. *Perf. 14½*
Size: 23x19mm
223 A31 1p ocher & pur .25 .25
224 A31 2p slate grn & org .25 .25
 b. Orange omitted 3,250.
225 A31 3p lt blue & choc .25 .25
 b. Queen's head omitted 6,500.
 c. Booklet pane of 4 1.00
 d. Lt blue omitted 4,750.
226 A31 4p gray & brt grn 1.75 .25

Perf. 13½x13
Size: 27x23mm
227 A31 6p dull grn, red & yel .25 .25
228 A31 9p purple & ocher .75 .25
229 A31 1sh lt bl, yel & grn .25 .25
230 A31 1sh3p dull blue & yel .35 .25
 b. Yellow omitted 4,000.
231 A31 1sh6p ol grn, yel & brn 2.25 .35
232 A31 2sh lt ol grn, vio & dk red .75 *.95*
233 A31 2sh6p brt grnsh bl, ultra & ver 1.50 .25

Perf. 14½x14
Size: 32x27mm
234 A31 5sh bl, grn, ocher & lt brn 1.25 1.00
235 A31 10sh dl yel, blk, red & bl 4.25 3.75
236 A31 £1 sal pink, sep, ocher & grn 3.50 *7.50*
  Nos. 223-236 (14) 17.60 15.80

Printed by Mardon Printers, Salisbury
1966-68 Litho. *Perf. 14½*
223a A31 1p ocher & pur .25 .25
224a A31 2p sl grn & org ('68) 1.00 .50
225a A31 3p lt bl & choc ('68) 2.00 .25
226a A31 4p sep & brt grn 1.00 .55
227a A31 6p gray grn, red & yel 1.00 .50
228a A31 9p pur & ocher ('68) .80 .25
230a A31 1sh3p dl bl & yel 2.00 .40
232a A31 2sh lt ol grn, vio & dk red 2.25 3.50

Perf. 14
234a A31 5sh brt bl, grn, ocher & brn 3.00 5.00
235a A31 10sh ocher, blk, red & bl 8.50 15.00
236a A31 £1 sal pink, sep, ocher & grn 12.50 22.50
  Nos. 223a-236a (11) 34.30 48.70

See Nos. 245-248A.

Zeederberg Coach — A32

Designs: 9p, Sir Rowland Hill. 1sh6p, Penny Black. 2sh6p, Rhodesia No. 18, £5.

Perf. 14½
1966, May 2 Litho. **Unwmk.**
237 A32 3p blue, org & blk .30 .25
238 A32 9p beige & brown .30 .25
239 A32 1sh6p blue & black .45 .50
240 A32 2sh6p rose, yel grn & blk .55 *.90*
 a. Souvenir sheet of 4, #237-240 10.00 14.00
  Nos. 237-240 (4) 1.60 1.90

28th Cong. of the Southern Africa Phil. Fed. and the RHOPEX Exhib., Bulawayo, May 2-7. No. 240a was printed in sheets of 12 and comes with perforations extending through the margins in four different versions. Many stamps have holes in the top margin made when the sheet was cut into individual panes. Sizes of panes vary. Nos. 237, 240-240a exist imperf.

De Havilland Dragon Rapide A33

Planes: 1sh3p, Douglas DC-3. 2sh6p, Vickers Viscount. 5sh, Jet.

1966, June 1
241 A33 6p multicolored 1.00 .50
242 A33 1sh3p multicolored 1.25 .60
243 A33 2sh6p multicolored 2.25 1.50
244 A33 5sh blue & black 3.25 *4.50*
  Nos. 241-244 (4) 7.75 7.10

20th anniv. of Central African Airways.

Dual Currency Issue
Type of 1966 with Denominations in Cents and Pence-Shillings
1967-68 Litho. *Perf. 14½*
245 A31 3p/2½c lt blue & choc .75 .25
246 A31 1sh/10c multi 1.00 .45
247 A31 1sh6p/15c multi 5.00 1.00
248 A31 2sh/20c multi 4.75 *6.00*
248A A31 2sh6p/25c multi 20.00 27.50
  Nos. 245-248A (5) 31.50 35.20

These locally printed stamps were issued to acquaint Rhodesians with the decimal currency to be introduced in 1969-1970.
Issued: 3p, 3/15; 1sh, 11/1/67; 1sh6p, 2sh, 3/11/68; 2sh6p, 12/9/68.

Leander Starr Jameson, by Frank Moss Bennett — A34

1967, May 17
249 A34 1sh6p emerald & multi .50 .50
Dr. Leander Starr Jameson (1853-1917), pioneer with Cecil Rhodes and Prime Minister of Cape Colony. See No. 262.

Soapstone Sculpture, by Joram Mariga A35

9p, Head of Burgher of Calais, by Auguste Rodin. 1sh3p, "Totem," by Roberto Crippa. 2sh6p, St. John the Baptist, by Michele Tosini.

1967, July 12   Litho.   Perf. 14
250 A35 3p brn, blk & ol grn .25 .25
251 A35 9p brt bl, blk & ol grn .30 .25
a. Perf. 13½ 8.25 17.50
252 A35 1sh3p multicolored .30 .30
253 A35 2sh6p multicolored .40 .50
Nos. 250-253 (4) 1.25 1.30
10th anniv. of the Rhodes Natl. Gallery, Salisbury.

White Rhinoceros — A36

#255, Parrot's beak gladioli, vert. #256, Baobab tree. #257, Elephants.

1967, Sept. 6   Unwmk.   Perf. 14½
254 A36 4p olive & black .25 .25
255 A36 4p dp orange & blk .35 .25
256 A36 4p brown & blk .35 .25
257 A36 4p gray & blk .25 .25
Nos. 254-257 (4) 1.20 1.00
Issued to publicize nature conservation.

Wooden Hand Plow, c. 1820 A37

Designs: 9p, Ox-drawn plow, c. 1860. 1sh6p, Steam tractor and plows, c. 1905. 2sh6p, Tractor and moldboard plow, 1968.

1968, Apr. 26   Litho.   Perf. 14½
258 A37 3p multicolored .25 .25
259 A37 9p multicolored .25 .25
260 A37 1sh6p multicolored .30 .30
261 A37 2sh6p multicolored .30 .75
Nos. 258-261 (4) 1.10 1.55
15th world plowing contest, Kent Estate, Norton.

Portrait Type of 1967
Design: 1sh6p, Alfred Beit (portrait at left).

1968, July 15   Unwmk.   Perf. 14½
262 A34 1sh6p orange, blk & red .50 .50
Alfred Beit (1853-1906), philanthropist and friend of Cecil Rhodes.

Allan Wilson, Matopos Hills — A38

Matabeleland, 75th Anniversary: 3p, Flag raising, Bulawayo, 1893. 9p, Bulawayo arms, view of Bulawayo.

1968, Nov. 4   Litho.   Perf. 14½
263 A38 3p multicolored .25 .25
264 A38 9p multicolored .25 .25
265 A38 1sh6p multicolored .40 .40
Nos. 263-265 (3) .90 .90

William Henry Milton (1854-1930), Adminstrator — A39

1969, Jan. 15
266 A39 1sh6p multicolored .50 .50
See Nos. 298-303.

Locomotive, 1890's — A40

Beira-Salisbury Railroad, 70th Anniversary: 9p, Steam locomotive, 1901. 1sh6p, Garratt articulated locomotive, 1950. 2sh6p, Diesel, 1955.

1969, May 22
267 A40 3p multicolored .75 .25
268 A40 9p multicolored 1.25 .60
269 A40 1sh6p multicolored 2.25 .80
270 A40 2sh6p multicolored 3.00 4.00
Nos. 267-270 (4) 7.25 5.65

Low Level Bridge A41

Bridges: 9p, Mpudzi River. 1sh6p, Umniati River. 2sh6p, Birchenough over Sabi River.

1969, Sept. 18
271 A41 3p multicolored .60 .25
272 A41 9p multicolored 1.00 .50
273 A41 1sh6p multicolored 1.75 1.25
274 A41 2sh6p multicolored 2.50 2.75
Nos. 272-274 (3) 5.25 4.50

Blast Furnace — A42   Devil's Cataract, Victoria Falls — A43

1c, Wheat harvest. 2½c, Ruins, Zimbabwe. 3c, Trailer truck. 3½c, 4c, Cecil Rhodes statue. 5c, Mining. 6c, Hydrofoil, "Seaflight." 7½c, like 8c. 10c, Yachting, Lake McIlwaine. 12½c, Hippopotamus. 14c, 15c, Kariba Dam. 20c, Irrigation canal. 25c, Bateleur eagles. 50c, Radar antenna and Viscount plane. $1, "Air Rescue." $2, Rhodesian flag.

1970-73   Litho.   Perf. 14½
Size: 22x18mm
275 A42 1c multicolored .25 .25
a. Booklet pane of 4 .25
b. Min. sheet of 4, Rhophil 3.75 *
276 A42 2c multicolored .25 .25
277 A42 2½c multicolored .25 .25
a. Booklet pane of 4 1.00
b. Min. sheet of 4, Rhophil 3.75
278 A42 3c multi ('73) 1.25 .25
a. Booklet pane of 4 5.00
279 A42 3½c multicolored .25 .25
a. Booklet pane of 4 1.00
b. Min. sheet of 4, Rhophil 3.75
280 A42 4c multi ('73) 2.00 1.00
a. Booklet pane of 4 8.00
281 A42 5c multicolored .25 .25

Size: 27x23mm
282 A43 6c multi ('73) 4.50 4.50
283 A43 7½c multi ('73) 7.50 .80
284 A43 8c multicolored .90 .50
285 A43 10c multicolored .75 .25
286 A43 12½c multicolored 1.75 .25
287 A43 14c multi ('73) 12.50 1.00
288 A43 15c multi 1.50 .25
289 A43 20c multicolored 1.25 .25

Size: 30x25mm
290 A43 25c multi ('73) 4.25 .70
291 A43 50c multicolored 1.40 .75
292 A43 $1 multicolored 5.50 3.00
293 A43 $2 multicolored 9.00 16.00
Nos. 275-293 (19) 55.30 30.75

Booklet panes and miniature sheets were made by altering the plates used to print the stamps, eliminating every third horizontal and vertical row of stamps. The perforations extend through the margins in four different versions. In 1972 sheets of 4 overprinted in the margins were issued for Rhophil '72 Philatelic Exhibition.
Issue dates: Feb. 17, 1970, Jan. 1, 1973.

Despatch Rider, c. 1890 A44

Posts and Telecommunications Corporation, Inauguration: 3½c, Loading mail, Salisbury Airport. 15c, Telegraph line construction, c.1890. 25c, Telephone and telecommunications equipment.

1970, July 1
294 A44 2½c multicolored .45 .25
295 A44 3½c multicolored .55 .55
296 A44 15c multicolored .75 1.25
297 A44 25c multicolored 1.25 2.00
Nos. 294-297 (4) 3.00 4.05

Famous Rhodesians Type of 1969
13c Dr. Robert Moffat (1795-1883), missionary. #299, Dr. David Livingstone (1813-73), explorer. #300, George Pauling (1854-1919), engineer. #301, Thomas Baines (1820-75), self-portrait. #302, Mother Patrick (1863-1900), Dominican nurse and teacher. #303, Frederick Courteney Selous (1851-1917), explorer, big game hunter.

1970-75   Litho.   Perf. 14½
298 A39 13c multi ('72) .90 .90
299 A39 14c multi ('73) .90 .90
300 A39 14c multi ('74) .90 .90
301 A39 14c multi ('75) .90 .90
302 A39 15c multi .90 .90
303 A39 15c multi ('71) .90 .90
Nos. 298-303 (6) 5.40 5.40
Issued: 2/14/72; 4/2/73; 5/15/74; 2/12/75; 11/16/70; 3/1/71.

African Hoopoe — A45

Birds: 2½c, Half-collared kingfisher, horiz. 5c, Golden-breasted bunting. 7½c, Carmine bee-eater. 8c, Red-eyed bulbul. 25c, Wattled plover, horiz.

1971, June 1
304 A45 2c multicolored 1.25 .30
305 A45 2½c multicolored 1.50 .25
306 A45 5c multicolored 1.75 .50
307 A45 7½c multicolored 2.00 .55
308 A45 8c multicolored 2.75 1.25
309 A45 25c multicolored 3.25 3.25
Nos. 304-309 (6) 12.50 6.10

Porphyritic Granite — A46

Granite '71, Geological Symposium, 8/30-9/19: 7½c, Muscovite mica, seen through microscope. 15c, Granite, seen through microscope. 25c, Geological map of Rhodesia.

1971, Aug. 30
310 A46 2½c multicolored .75 .50
311 A46 7½c multicolored 1.25 .50
312 A46 15c multicolored 1.50 .50
313 A46 25c multicolored 2.00 3.50
Nos. 310-313 (4) 5.50 5.00

"Be Airwise" A47

Prevent Pollution: 3½c, Antelope (Be Country-wise). 7c, Fish (Be Waterwise). 13c, City (Be Citywise).

1972, July 17
314 A47 2½c multicolored .25 .25
315 A47 3½c multicolored .25 .25
316 A47 7c multicolored .30 .25
317 A47 13c multicolored .35 .30
Nos. 314-317 (4) 1.15 1.05

The Three Kings — A48

1972, Oct. 18
318 A48 2c multicolored .25 .25
319 A48 5c multicolored .25 .25
320 A48 13c multicolored .40 .40
Nos. 318-320 (3) .90 .90
Christmas.

W.M.O. Emblem — A49

1973, July 2
321 A49 3c multicolored .25 .25
322 A49 14c multicolored .40 .30
323 A49 25c multicolored .75 .75
Nos. 321-323 (3) 1.40 1.30
Intl. Meteorological Cooperation, cent.

Arms of Rhodesia A50

1973, Oct. 10

324	A50	2½c multicolored	.25	.25
325	A50	4c multicolored	.25	.25
326	A50	7½c multicolored	.30	.25
327	A50	14c multicolored	.45	1.00
		Nos. 324-327 (4)	1.25	1.75

Responsible Government, 50th Anniversary.

Kudu
A51

Thunbergia
A52

Pearl
Charaxes — A53

1974-76   Litho.   Perf. 14½

328	A51	1c shown	.25	.25
329	A51	2½c Eland	.75	.25
330	A51	3c Roan antelope	.25	.25
331	A51	4c Reedbuck	.25	.25
332	A51	5c Bushbuck	.30	.50
333	A52	6c shown	.50	.25
334	A52	7½c Flame lily	1.00	.45
335	A52	8c like 7½c ('76)	.35	.25
336	A52	10c Devil thorn	.30	.25
337	A52	12c Hibiscus ('76)	1.00	2.00
338	A52	12½c Pink sabi star	1.25	.45
339	A52	14c Wild pimpernel	1.50	.45
340	A52	15c like 12½c ('76)	.70	1.00
341	A52	16c like 14c ('76)	.70	.40
342	A53	20c shown	1.25	.50
343	A53	24c Yellow pansy ('76)	.85	.50
344	A53	25c like 24c	3.00	2.00
345	A53	50c Queen purple tip	1.00	.80
346	A53	$1 Striped swordtail	1.50	1.00
347	A53	$2 Guinea fowl butterfly	1.50	1.00
		Nos. 328-347 (20)	18.20	12.80

Issue dates: Aug. 14, 1974, July 1, 1976.
For surcharges see Nos. 364-366.

Mail Collection
and UPU
Emblem
A54

1974, Nov. 20   Perf. 14½

348	A54	3c shown	.25	.25
349	A54	4c Mail sorting	.25	.25
350	A54	7½c Mail delivery	.35	.30
351	A54	14c Parcel post	.60	.90
		Nos. 348-351 (4)	1.45	1.70

Universal Postal Union Centenary.

Euphorbia
Confinalis — A55

1975, July 16

352	A55	2½c shown	.30	.30
353	A55	3c Aloe excelsa	.30	.30
354	A55	4c Hoodia lugardii	.35	.30
355	A55	7½c Aloe ortholopha	.40	.25
356	A55	14c Aloe musapana	.45	.30
357	A55	25c Aloe saponaria	.90	2.00
		Nos. 352-357 (6)	2.70	3.50

Intl. Succulent Cong., Salisbury, July 1975.

Head Injury
and Safety
Helmet — A56

Occupational Safety: 4c, Bandaged hand
and safety glove. 7½c, Injured eye and safety
eyeglass. 14c, Blind man and protective
shield.

1975, Oct. 15

358	A56	2½c multicolored	.25	.25
359	A56	4c multicolored	.25	.25
360	A56	7½c multicolored	.30	.25
361	A56	14c multicolored	.40	.30
		Nos. 358-361 (4)	1.20	1.05

Telephones, 1876
and 1976 — A57

Alexander
Graham
Bell — A58

1976, Mar. 10

362	A57	3c light blue & blk	.25	.25
363	A58	14c buff & black	.25	.25

Centenary of first telephone call, by Alexander Graham Bell, Mar. 10, 1876.

**Nos. 334, 339 and 344 Surcharged
with New Value and Two Bars**

1976, July 1

364	A52	8c on 7½c multi	.30	.25
365	A52	16c on 14c multi	.35	.30
366	A53	24c on 25c multi	.45	.80
		Nos. 364-366 (3)	1.10	1.35

Wildlife
Protection
A59

1976, July 21

367	A59	4c Roan Antelope	.30	.25
368	A59	6c Brown hyena	.40	.60
369	A59	8c Wild dog	.40	.30
370	A59	16c Cheetah	.50	.50
		Nos. 367-370 (4)	1.60	1.65

Brachystegia
Spiciformis — A60

1976, Nov. 17

371	A60	4c shown	.25	.25
372	A60	6c Red mahogany	.25	.25
373	A60	8c Pterocarpus angolensis	.25	.25
374	A60	16c Rhodesian teak	.30	.50
		Nos. 371-374 (4)	1.05	1.25

Flowering trees.

Black-eyed
Bulbul — A61

Birds: 4c, Yellow-mantled whydah. 6c,
Orange-throated longclaw. 8c, Long-tailed
shrike. 16c, Lesser blue-eared starling. 24c,
Red-billed wood hoopoe.

1977, Mar. 16

375	A61	3c multicolored	.25	.25
376	A61	4c multicolored	.30	.25
377	A61	6c multicolored	.35	.30
378	A61	8c multicolored	.40	.35
379	A61	16c multicolored	.55	.35
380	A61	24c multicolored	1.00	1.00
		Nos. 375-380 (6)	2.85	2.50

Lake Kyle,
by Joan
Evans
A62

Landscape Paintings: 4c, Chimanimani
Mountains, by Evans. 6c, Rocks near Bonsor
Reef, by Alice Balfour. 8c, Dwala (rock) near
Devil's Pass, by Balfour. 16c, Zimbabwe, by
Balfour. 24c, Victoria Falls, by Thomas Baines.

1977, July 20   Litho.   Perf. 14½

381	A62	3c multicolored	.25	.25
382	A62	4c multicolored	.25	.25
383	A62	6c multicolored	.25	.25
384	A62	8c multicolored	.25	.25
385	A62	16c multicolored	.35	.35
386	A62	24c multicolored	.40	.65
		Nos. 381-386 (6)	1.75	1.95

Virgin and
Child — A63

1977, Nov. 16

387	A63	3c multicolored	.25	.25
388	A63	6c multicolored	.25	.25
389	A63	8c multicolored	.25	.25
390	A63	16c multicolored	.30	.25
		Nos. 387-390 (4)	1.05	1.00

Christmas.

Fair Spire and
Fairgrounds — A64

19th Rhodesian Trade Fair, Bulawayo: 8c,
Fair spire.

1978, Mar. 15

391	A64	4c multicolored	.25	.25
392	A64	8c multicolored	.30	.25

Morganite
A65

Black Rhinoceros
A66

Odzani
Falls — A67

1978, Aug. 16   Litho.   Perf. 14½

393	A65	1c shown	.25	.25
394	A65	3c Amethyst	.25	.25
395	A65	4c Garnet	.25	.25
396	A65	5c Citrine	.25	.25
397	A65	7c Blue topaz	.25	.25
398	A66	9c shown	.25	.25
399	A66	11c Lion	.35	.35
400	A66	13c Warthog	.35	1.25
401	A66	15c Giraffe	.35	.35
402	A66	17c Zebra	.35	.25
403	A67	21c shown	.35	.40
404	A67	25c Goba Falls	.50	.25
405	A67	30c Inyangombe Falls	.60	.25
406	A67	$1 Bridal Veil Falls	1.25	.45
407	A67	$2 Victoria Falls	1.50	.65
		Nos. 393-407 (15)	7.10	5.70

Wright's
Flyer A
A68

1978, Oct. 18

408	A68	4c shown	.25	.25
409	A68	5c Bleriot XI	.25	.25
410	A68	7c Vickers Vimy	.25	.25
411	A68	9c A.W. 15 Atalanta	.25	.25
412	A68	17c Vickers Viking 1B	.35	.25
413	A68	25c Boeing 720	.45	.50
		Nos. 408-413 (6)	1.80	1.75

75th anniversary of powered flight.

POSTAGE DUE STAMPS

**Type of Rhodesia and Nyasaland,
1961, Inscribed "RHODESIA"**

Hyphen Hole Perf. 5

1965, June 17   Typo.   Unwmk.

J5	D1	1p vermilion	.60	14.00
a.		Rouletted 9½	5.50	14.00

Rouletted 9½

J6	D1	2p dark blue	.45	9.00
J7	D1	4p emerald	.60	9.00
J8	D1	6p purple	.65	6.50
		Nos. J5-J8 (4)	2.30	38.50

Soapstone
Zimbabwe
Bird — D2

1966, Dec. 15   Litho.   Perf. 14½

J9	D2	1p crimson	1.50	4.50
J10	D2	2p violet blue	1.75	3.00
J11	D2	4p emerald	1.75	4.00
J12	D2	6p lilac	1.75	2.75
J13	D2	1sh dull red brown	1.75	2.75
J14	D2	2sh black	2.00	6.00
		Nos. J9-J14 (6)	10.50	23.00

1970-73   Litho.   Perf. 14½
Size: 26x22½mm

J15	D2	1c bright green	.90	1.50
J16	D2	2c ultramarine	.90	.75
J17	D2	5c red violet	1.75	2.75
J18	D2	6c lemon	7.00	5.00
J19	D2	10c rose red	1.75	5.00
		Nos. J15-J19 (5)	12.30	15.00

Issued: 6c, 5/7/73; others, 2/1/70.

RIO DE ORO

ˌrē-ō dē ˈȯr-ˌō

LOCATION — On the northwest coast
of Africa, bordering on the Atlantic
Ocean
GOVT. — Spanish Colony
AREA — 71,600 sq. mi.
POP. — 24,000
CAPITAL — Villa Cisneros

Prior to the issuance of Rio de Oro
stamps, Spanish stamps were used
1901-1904, canceled "Rio de Oro."
Rio de Oro became part of Spanish
Sahara in 1924.

100 Centimos = 1 Peseta

King Alfonso XIII — A1

Control Numbers on Back in Blue

1905		Unwmk.	Typo.	Perf. 14	
1	A1	1c blue green		4.00	3.00
2	A1	2c claret		5.00	3.00
3	A1	3c bronze green		5.00	3.00
4	A1	4c dark brown		5.00	3.00
5	A1	5c orange red		5.00	3.00
6	A1	10c dk gray brown		5.00	3.00
7	A1	15c red brown		5.00	3.00
8	A1	25c dark blue		95.00	32.50
9	A1	50c dark green		45.00	13.50
10	A1	75c dark violet		45.00	19.00
11	A1	1p orange brown		32.50	8.00
12	A1	2p buff		100.00	57.50
13	A1	3p dull violet		70.00	20.00
14	A1	4p blue green		70.00	20.00
15	A1	5p dull blue		100.00	45.00
16	A1	10p pale red		250.00	150.00
		Nos. 1-16 (16)		841.50	386.50
		Set, never hinged		1,700.	

For surcharges see Nos. 17, 34-36, 60-66.

No. 8 Handstamp
Surcharged in Rose —
a

1907

17	A1	15c on 25c dk blue	250.00	60.00
		Never hinged	400.00	

The surcharge exists inverted, double and in
violet, normally positioned. Value for each,
$450.

King Alfonso XIII — A2

Control Numbers on Back in Blue

1907				Typo.
18	A2	1c claret	3.00	2.75
19	A2	2c black	3.50	2.75
20	A2	3c dark brown	3.50	2.75
21	A2	4c red	3.50	2.75
22	A2	5c black brown	3.50	2.75
23	A2	10c chocolate	3.50	2.75
24	A2	15c dark blue	3.50	2.75
25	A2	25c deep green	9.50	2.75
26	A2	50c black violet	9.50	2.75
27	A2	75c orange brown	9.50	2.75
28	A2	1p orange	16.00	2.75
29	A2	2p dull violet	5.50	2.75
30	A2	3p blue green	5.50	2.75
a.		Cliché of 4p in plate of 3p	400.00	260.00
31	A2	4p dark blue	9.00	5.00
32	A2	5p red	9.00	5.25
33	A2	10p deep green	9.00	12.00
		Nos. 18-33 (16)	106.50	58.00
		Set, never hinged	250.00	

For surcharges see Nos. 38-43, 67-70.

Nos. 9-10 Handstamp
Surcharged in Red

1907

34	A1	10c on 50c dk green	100.00	30.00
		Never hinged	175.00	
a.		"10" omitted	175.00	100.00
		Never hinged	250.00	
35	A1	10c on 75c dk violet	100.00	32.00
		Never hinged	175.00	

No. 12 Handstamp
Surcharged in Violet

1908

36	A1	2c on 2p buff	52.50	24.00
		Never hinged	100.00	

No. 36 is found with "1908" measuring
11mm and 12mm.

Same Surcharge in Red on No. 26

38	A2	10c on 50c blk vio	22.50	3.75
		Never hinged	37.50	

A 5c on 10c (No. 23) was not officially
issued.

Nos. 25, 27-28 Handstamp Surcharged Type "a" in Red, Violet or Green

1908				
39	A2	15c on 25c dp grn (R)	25.00	3.75
40	A2	15c on 75c org brn (V)	32.50	17.50
a.		Green surcharge	50.00	6.75
		Never hinged	72.50	
41	A2	15c on 1p org (V)	37.50	15.00
42	A2	15c on 1p org (R)	35.00	15.00
43	A2	15c on 1p org (G)	25.00	12.00
		Nos. 39-43 (5)	155.00	63.25
		Set, never hinged	325.00	

As this surcharge is handstamped, it exists
in several varieties: double, inverted, in pairs
with one surcharge omitted, etc.

A3

Revenue stamps overprinted and surcharged

1908				Imperf.
44	A3	5c on 50c green (C)	90.00	30.00
		Never hinged	160.00	
45	A3	5c on 50c green (V)	130.00	52.50
		Never hinged	225.00	

The surcharge, which is handstamped,
exists in many variations.
Nos. 44-45 are found with and without control numbers on back. Stamps with control
numbers sell at about double the above values. Counterfeits exist.
See Spanish Guinea Nos. 98-101C for additional revenue stamps surcharged for postal
use.

King Alfonso XIII — A4

Control Numbers on Back in Blue

1909			Typo.	Perf. 14½
46	A4	1c red	.85	.50
47	A4	2c orange	.85	.50
48	A4	5c dark green	.85	.50
49	A4	10c orange red	.85	.50
50	A4	15c blue green	.85	.50
51	A4	20c dark violet	2.10	.70
52	A4	25c deep blue	2.10	.70
53	A4	30c claret	2.10	.70
54	A4	40c chocolate	2.10	.70
55	A4	50c red violet	4.00	.70
56	A4	1p dark brown	5.25	3.25
57	A4	4p carmine rose	6.25	4.75
58	A4	10p claret	14.00	7.75
		Nos. 46-58 (13)	42.15	21.75
		Set, never hinged	80.00	

Stamps of 1905
Handstamped in Black

1910

60	A1	10c on 5p dull bl	21.00	8.50
a.		Red surcharge	90.00	55.00
		Never hinged	145.00	
62	A1	10c on 10p pale red	21.00	8.50
a.		Violet surcharge	145.00	62.50
		Never hinged	210.00	
b.		Green surcharge	145.00	62.50
		Never hinged	210.00	
65	A1	15c on 3p dull vio	21.00	8.50
a.		Imperf.	110.00	
		Never hinged	190.00	
66	A1	15c on 4p blue grn	21.00	8.50
a.		10c on 4p bl grn	925.00	275.00
		Never hinged	1,300.	
		Nos. 60-66 (4)	84.00	34.00
		Set, never hinged	160.00	

See note after No. 43.

Nos. 31 and 33
Surcharged in Red or
Violet

1911-13

67	A2	2c on 4p dk blue (R)	12.50	9.00
68	A2	5c on 10p dp grn (V)	37.50	9.00

Nos. 29-30 Surcharged
in Black

69	A2	10c on 2p dull vio	19.00	8.25
69A	A2	10c on 3p bl grn ('13)	225.00	50.00

Nos. 30, 32 Handstamped Type "a"

69B	A2	15c on 3p bl grn ('13)	200.00	24.00
70	A2	15c on 5p red	13.50	9.00
		Nos. 67-70 (6)	507.50	109.25
		Set, never hinged	650.00	

King Alfonso XIII — A5

Control Numbers on Back in Blue

1912			Typo.	Perf. 13½
71	A5	1c carmine rose	.40	.35
72	A5	2c lilac	.40	.35
73	A5	5c deep green	.40	.35
74	A5	10c red	.40	.35
75	A5	15c brown orange	.40	.35
76	A5	20c brown	.40	.35
77	A5	25c dull blue	.40	.35
78	A5	30c dark violet	.40	.35
79	A5	40c blue green	.40	.35
80	A5	50c lake	.40	.35
81	A5	1p red	4.00	.80
82	A5	4p claret	7.50	4.00
83	A5	10p dark brown	11.00	6.00
		Nos. 71-83 (13)	26.50	14.30
		Set, never hinged	60.00	

For overprints see Nos. 97-109.

King Alfonso XIII — A6

Control Numbers on Back in Blue

1914

84	A6	1c olive black	.40	.35	Perf. 13
85	A6	2c maroon	.40	.35	
86	A6	5c deep green	.40	.35	
87	A6	10c orange red	.40	.35	
88	A6	15c orange red	.40	.35	
89	A6	20c deep claret	.40	.35	
90	A6	25c dark blue	.40	.35	
91	A6	30c blue green	.40	.35	
92	A6	40c brown orange	.40	.35	
93	A6	50c dark brown	.40	.35	
94	A6	1p dull lilac	3.00	2.40	
95	A6	4p carmine rose	7.25	6.25	
96	A6	10p dull violet	7.50	6.25	
		Nos. 84-96 (13)	21.75	18.40	
		Set, never hinged	50.00		

Nos. 71-83 Overprinted
in Black

1917

97	A5	1c carmine rose	17.50	1.40	Perf. 13½
98	A5	2c lilac	17.50	1.40	
99	A5	5c deep green	3.50	1.40	
100	A5	10c red	3.50	1.40	
101	A5	15c orange brn	3.50	1.40	
102	A5	20c brown	3.50	1.40	
103	A5	25c dull blue	3.50	1.40	
104	A5	30c dark violet	3.50	1.40	
105	A5	40c blue green	3.50	1.40	
106	A5	50c lake	3.50	1.40	
107	A5	1p red	19.00	4.75	
108	A5	4p claret	22.50	6.25	
109	A5	10p dark brown	42.50	7.75	
		Nos. 97-109 (13)	147.00	34.25	
		Set, never hinged	300.00		

Nos. 97-109 exist with overprint inverted or
double (value 50 percent over normal) and in
dark blue (value twice normal). Forgeries
exist.

King Alfonso XIII — A7

Control Numbers on Back in Blue

1919

114	A7	1c brown	1.25	.55	Typo. Perf. 13
115	A7	2c claret	1.25	.55	
116	A7	5c light green	1.25	.55	
117	A7	10c carmine	1.25	.55	
118	A7	15c orange	4.00	2.00	
119	A7	20c orange	1.25	.55	
120	A7	25c blue	1.25	.55	
121	A7	30c green	1.25	.55	
122	A7	40c vermilion	1.25	.55	
123	A7	50c brown	1.25	.55	
124	A7	1p lilac	8.00	4.50	
125	A7	4p rose	14.50	7.50	
126	A7	10p violet	25.00	10.00	
		Nos. 114-126 (13)	62.75	28.95	
		Set, never hinged	100.00		

A8

Control Numbers on Back in Blue

1920

127	A8	1c gray lilac	1.10	.55	Perf. 13
128	A8	2c rose	1.10	.55	
129	A8	5c light red	1.10	.55	
130	A8	10c lilac	1.10	.55	
131	A8	15c light brown	1.10	.55	
132	A8	20c greenish blue	1.10	.55	
133	A8	25c yellow	1.10	.55	
134	A8	30c dull blue	6.25	4.50	
135	A8	40c orange	3.75	2.10	
136	A8	50c dull rose	3.75	2.10	
137	A8	1p gray green	5.25	2.10	
138	A8	4p lilac rose	7.00	4.25	
139	A8	10p brown	25.00	10.00	
		Nos. 127-139 (13)	58.70	28.90	
		Set, never hinged	100.00		

A9

King Alfonso XIII — A6

King Alfonso XIII — A5

Control Numbers on Back in Blue

1922

140	A9	1c yellow	1.00	.60
141	A9	2c red brown	1.00	.60
142	A9	5c blue green	1.00	.60
143	A9	10c pale red	1.00	.60
144	A9	15c myrtle green	1.00	.60
145	A9	20c turq blue	1.00	.65
146	A9	25c deep blue	1.00	.65
147	A9	30c deep rose	1.75	1.25
148	A9	40c violet	1.75	1.25
149	A9	50c orange	1.75	1.25
150	A9	1p lilac	5.50	1.75
151	A9	4p claret	12.00	4.00
152	A9	10p dark brown	20.00	8.25
		Nos. 140-152 (13)	49.75	22.05
		Set, never hinged	100.00	

For subsequent issues see Spanish Sahara.

RIO MUNI

ˌrē-ō ˈmü-nē

LOCATION — West Africa, bordering on Cameroun and Gabon Republics
GOVT. — Province of Spain
AREA — 9,500 sq. mi.
POP. — 183,377 (1960)
CAPITAL — Bata

Rio Muni and the island of Fernando Po are the two provinces that constitute Spanish Guinea. Separate stamp issues for the two provinces were decreed in 1960.
Spanish Guinea Nos. 1-84 were used only in the territory now called Rio Muni.
Rio Muni united with Fernando Po on Oct. 12, 1968, to form the Republic of Equatorial Guinea.

100 Centimos = 1 Peseta

Catalogue values for all unused stamps in this country are for Never Hinged items.

Boy Reading and Missionary — A1

1960　Unwmk.　Photo.　Perf. 13x12½

1	A1	25c dull vio bl	.25	.25
2	A1	50c olive brown	.25	.25
3	A1	75c dull grysh pur	.25	.25
4	A1	1p orange ver	.25	.25
5	A1	1.50p brt blue grn	.25	.25
6	A1	2p red lilac	.25	.25
7	A1	3p sapphire	.30	.25
8	A1	5p red brown	1.00	.25
9	A1	10p lt olive grn	1.75	.25
		Nos. 1-9 (9)	4.55	2.25

Quina Plant — A2

1960　　　　　　　Perf. 13x12½

10	A2	35c shown	.25	.25
11	A2	80c Croton plant	.25	.25

See Nos. B1-B2.

Map of Rio Muni — A3

Designs: 50c, 1p, Gen. Franco. 70c, Government Palace.

1961, Oct. 1　　　　　Perf. 12½x13

12	A3	25c gray violet	.25	.25
13	A3	50c olive brown	.25	.25
14	A3	70c brt green	.25	.25
15	A3	1p red orange	.25	.25
		Nos. 12-15 (4)	1.00	1.00

25th anniversary of the nomination of Gen. Francisco Franco as Chief of State.

Rio Muni Headdress — A4

Design: 50c, Rio Muni idol.

1962, July 10　　　　Perf. 13x12½

16	A4	25c violet	.25	.25
17	A4	50c green	.25	.25
18	A4	1p orange brown	.25	.25
		Nos. 16-18 (3)	.75	.75

Issued for child welfare.

Cape Buffalo A5

Design: 35c, Gorilla, vert.

Perf. 13x12½, 12½x13

1962, Nov. 23　Photo.　Unwmk.

19	A5	15c dark olive grn	.25	.25
20	A5	35c magenta	.25	.25
21	A5	1p brown orange	.25	.25
		Nos. 19-21 (3)	.75	.75

Issued for Stamp Day.

Mother and Child — A6

1963, Jan. 29　　　　Perf. 13x12½

22	A6	50c green	.25	.25
23	A6	1p brown orange	.25	.25

Issued to help the victims of the Seville flood.

Father Joaquin Juanola — A7

50c, Blessing hand, cross and palms.

1963, July 6　　　　　Perf. 13x12½

24	A7	25c dull violet	.25	.25
25	A7	50c brown olive	.25	.25
26	A7	1p orange red	.25	.25
		Nos. 24-26 (3)	.75	.75

Issued for child welfare.

Praying Child and Arms — A8

1963, July 12

27	A8	50c dull green	.25	.25
28	A8	1p redsh brown	.25	.25

Issued for Barcelona flood relief.

Branch of Copal Tree — A9

50c, Flowering quina, horiz.

Perf. 13x12½, 12½x13

1964, Mar. 6　　　　　　Photo.

29	A9	25c brt violet	.25	.25
30	A9	50c blue green	.25	.25
31	A9	1p dk carmine rose	.25	.25
		Nos. 29-31 (3)	.75	.75

Issued for Stamp Day 1963.

Tree Pangolin A10

Design: 50c, Chameleon.

1964, June 1　　　　　Perf. 13x12½

32	A10	25c violet blk	.25	.25
33	A10	50c olive gray	.25	.25
34	A10	1p fawn	.25	.25
		Nos. 32-34 (3)	.75	.75

Issued for child welfare.

Dwarf Crocodile A11

15c, 70c, 3p, Dwarf crocodile. 25c, 1p, 5p, Leopard. 50c, 1.50p, 10p, Black rhinoceros.

1964, July 1

35	A11	15c lt brown	.25	.25
36	A11	25c violet	.25	.25
37	A11	50c olive	.25	.25
38	A11	70c green	.25	.25
39	A11	1p brown car	.85	.25
40	A11	1.50p blue green	.90	.25
41	A11	3p dark blue	1.75	.25
42	A11	5p brown	4.50	.50
43	A11	10p green	8.50	1.10
		Nos. 35-43 (9)	17.50	3.35

Greshoff's Tree Frog A12

Stamp Day: 1p, Helmet guinea fowl, vert.

Perf. 13x12½, 12½x13

1964, Nov. 23　Photo.　Unwmk.

44	A12	50c green	.25	.25
45	A12	1p deep claret	.25	.25
46	A12	1.50p blue green	.25	.25
		Nos. 44-46 (3)	.75	.75

Issued for Stamp Day, 1964.

Woman's Head — A13　　Woman Chemist — A14

1964　　　Photo.　　Perf. 13x12½

47	A13	50c shown	.25	.25
48	A14	1p shown	.25	.25
49	A14	1.50p Logger	.25	.25
		Nos. 47-49 (3)	.75	.75

Issued to commemorate 25 years of peace.

Goliath Beetle A15

Beetle: 1p, Acridoxena hewaniana.

1965, June 1　Photo.　Perf. 12½x13

50	A15	50c Prus green	.25	.25
51	A15	1p sepia	.25	.25
52	A15	1.50p black	.25	.25
		Nos. 50-52 (3)	.75	.75

Issued for child welfare.

Ring-necked Pheasant — A16

Leopard and Arms of Rio Muni A17

Perf. 13x12½, 12½x13

1965, Nov. 23　　　　　　Photo.

53	A16	50c grnsh gray	.35	.25
54	A17	1p sepia	.65	.25
55	A16	2.50p lilac	3.00	.90
		Nos. 53-55 (3)	4.00	1.40

Issued for Stamp Day, 1965.

Elephant and Parrot A18

Design: 1.50p, Lion and boy.

Perf. 12½x13

1966, June 1　　Photo.　　Unwmk.

56	A18	50c olive	.25	.25
57	A18	1p dk purple	.25	.25
58	A18	1.50p brt Prus blue	.25	.25
		Nos. 56-58 (3)	.75	.75

Issued for child welfare.

Water Chevrotain A19

Designs: 40c, 4p, Tree pangolin, vert.

1966, Nov. 23   Photo.   Perf. 13

59	A19	10c brown & yel brn	.25	.25
60	A19	40c brown & yellow	.25	.25
61	A19	1.50p blue & rose lilac	.25	.25
62	A19	4p dk bl & emerald	.25	.25
		Nos. 59-62 (4)	1.00	1.00

Issued for Stamp Day, 1966.

A20

Designs: 40c, 4p, Vine creeper.

1967, June 1   Photo.   Perf. 13

63	A20	10c green & yellow	.25	.25
64	A20	40c blk, rose car & grn	.25	.25
65	A20	1.50p blue & orange	.25	.25
66	A20	4p black & green	.25	.25
		Nos. 63-66 (4)	1.00	1.00

Issued for child welfare.

Potto — A21

Designs: 1p, River hog, horiz. 3.50p, African golden cat, horiz.

1967, Nov. 23   Photo.   Perf. 13

67	A21	1p black & red brn	.30	.30
68	A21	1.50p brown & grn	.30	.30
69	A21	3.50p org brn & grn	.45	.45
		Nos. 67-69 (3)	1.05	1.05

Issued for Stamp Day 1967.

Zodiac Issue

Cancer — A22

1.50p, Taurus. 2.50p, Gemini.

1968, Apr. 25   Photo.   Perf. 13

70	A22	1p brt mag, *lt yel*	.30	.30
71	A22	1.50p brown, *pink*	.30	.30
72	A22	2.50p dk vio, *yel*	.75	.75
		Nos. 70-72 (3)	1.35	1.35

Issued for child welfare.

SEMI-POSTAL STAMPS

Type of Regular Issue, 1960

Designs: 10c+5c, Croton plant. 15c+5c, Flower and leaves of croton.

1960 Unwmk. Photo.   Perf. 13x12½

B1	A2	10c + 5c maroon	.25	.25
B2	A2	15c + 5c bister brown	.25	.25

The surtax was for child welfare.

Bishop Juan de Ribera — SP1

20c+5c, The clown Pablo de Valladolid by Velazquez. 30c+10c, Juan de Ribera statue.

1961   Perf. 13x12½

B3	SP1	10c + 5c rose brown	.25	.25
B4	SP1	20c + 5c dk slate grn	.25	.25
B5	SP1	30c + 10c olive brown	.25	.25
B6	SP1	50c + 20c brown	.25	.25
		Nos. B3-B6 (4)	1.00	1.00

Issued for Stamp Day, 1960.

Mandrill SP2

Design: 25c+10c, Elephant, vert.

Perf. 12½x13, 13x12½
1961, June 21   Unwmk.

B7	SP2	10c + 5c rose brown	.25	.25
B8	SP2	25c + 10c gray violet	.25	.25
B9	SP2	80c + 20c dark green	.25	.25
		Nos. B7-B9 (3)	.75	.75

The surtax was for child welfare.

Statuette — SP3

Design: 25c+10c, 1p+10c, Male figure.

1961, Nov. 23   Perf. 13x12½

B10	SP3	10c + 5c rose brown	.25	.25
B11	SP3	25c + 10c dark purple	.25	.25
B12	SP3	30c + 10c olive black	.25	.25
B13	SP3	1p + 10c red orange	.25	.25
		Nos. B10-B13 (4)	1.00	1.00

Issued for Stamp Day 1961.

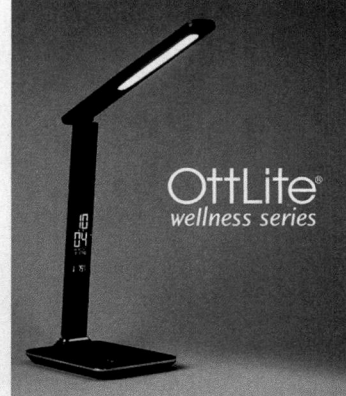

ROMANIA

rō-'mā-nēə

(Rumania, Roumania)

LOCATION — Southeastern Europe, bordering on the Black Sea
GOVT. — Republic
AREA — 91,699 sq. mi.
POP. — 22,600,000 (est. 1984)
CAPITAL — Bucharest

Romania was formed in 1861 from the union of the principalities of Moldavia and Walachia in 1859. It became a kingdom in 1881. Following World War I, the original territory was considerably enlarged by the addition of Bessarabia, Bukovina, Transylvania, Crisana, Maramures and Banat. The republic was established in 1948.

40 Parale = 1 Piaster
100 Bani = 1 Leu (plural "Lei") (1868)

Catalogue values for unused stamps in this country are for Never Hinged items, beginning with Scott 475 in the regular postage section, Scott B82 in the semi-postal section, Scott C24 in the airpost section, Scott CB1 in the airpost semi-postal section, Scott J82 in the postage due section, Scott O1 in the official section, Scott RA16 in the postal tax section, and Scott RAJ1 in the postal tax postage due section.

Watermarks

Wmk. 95 — Wavy Lines

Wmk. 163 — Coat of Arms

Wmk. 164 — PR

Wmk. 165 — PR Interlaced

Wmk. 167 — Coat of Arms Covering 25 Stamps

Wmk. 200 — PR

Wmk. 225 — Crown over PTT, Multiple

Wmk. 230 — Crowns and Monograms

Wmk. 276 — Cross and Crown Multiple

Wmk. 289 — RPR Multiple

Wmk. 358 — RPR Multiple in Endless Rows

Wmk. 398 — Fr Multiple

Values for unused stamps are for examples with original gum as defined in the catalogue introduction except for Nos. 1-4 which are valued without gum.

Moldavia

Coat of Arms — A1

Laid Paper
Handstamped

1858, July		**Unwmk.**		*Imperf.*	
1	A1	27pa blk, *rose*		60,000.	25,000.
a.	Tête bêche pair				
2	A1	54pa blue, *grn*		15,500.	10,000.
3	A1	108pa blue, *rose*		35,000.	16,000.

Wove Paper

4	A1	81pa blue, *bl*		50,000.	55,000.

Cut to shape or octagonally, Nos. 1-4 sell for one-fourth to one-third of these values.

Coat of Arms — A2

1858			**Bluish Wove Paper**	
5	A2	5pa black	15,000.	15,000.
a.	Tête bêche pair			
6	A2	40pa blue	275.	225.
a.	Tête bêche pair		1,300.	2,650.
7	A2	80pa red	7,750.	875.
a.	Tête bêche pair			

1859			**White Wove Paper**	
8	A2	5pa black	15,000.	10,000.
a.	Tête bêche pair			
b.	Frame broken at bottom		175.	
c.	As "b," tête bêche pair		600.	
9	A2	40pa blue	175.	190.
b.	Tête bêche pair		650.	1,500.
10	A2	80pa red	475.	300.
b.	Tête bêche pair		1,750.	3,250.

Nos. 6-7, 9-10 are inscribed "Posta Scrisorei." No. 8b has a break in the frame at bottom below "A." It was never placed in use.

Moldavia-Walachia

Coat of Arms — A3

Printed by Hand from Single Dies

1862			**White Laid Paper**	
11	A3	3pa orange	300.00	2,250.
a.	3pa yellow		300.00	2,250.
12	A3	6pa carmine	300.00	475.00
13	A3	6pa red	300.00	475.00
14	A3	30pa blue	87.50	115.00
	Nos. 11-14 (4)		987.50	3,315.

White Wove Paper

15	A3	3pa orange yel	85.00	275.00
a.	3pa lemon		85.00	275.00
16	A3	6pa carmine	95.00	275.00
17	A3	6pa vermilion	77.50	225.00
18	A3	30pa blue	60.00	65.00
	Nos. 15-18 (4)		317.50	840.00

Greenish-Blue Paper

15C	A3	3pa orange yel	—	2,500.

Tête bêche pairs

11b	A3	3pa orange	1,550.	
12a	A3	6pa carmine	1,000.	1,250.
14a	A3	30pa blue	190.00	1,550.
15b	A3	3pa orange yellow	210.00	1,600.
16a	A3	6pa carmine	275.00	1,750.
17a	A3	6pa vermilion	190.00	1,600.
18a	A3	30pa blue	175.00	1,600.

Nos. 11-18 were printed with a hand press, one at a time, from single dies. The impressions were very irregularly placed and occasionally overlapped. Sheets of 32 (4x8). The 3rd and 4th rows were printed inverted, making the second and third rows tête bêche. All values come in distinct shades, frequently even on the same sheet. The paper of this and the following issues through No. 52 often shows a bluish, grayish or yellowish tint.

White Wove Paper

1864		**Typographed from Plates**		
19	A3	3pa yellow	60.00	1,500.
a.	Tête bêche pair		350.00	
b.	Pair, one sideways		150.00	
20	A3	6pa deep rose	22.50	
a.	Tête bêche pair		52.50	
b.	Pair, one sideways		52.50	
21	A3	30pa deep blue	17.50	100.00
a.	Tête bêche pair		57.50	
b.	Pair, one sideways		57.50	2,650.
c.	Bluish wove paper		150.00	
	Nos. 19-21 (3)		100.00	

Stamps of 1862 issue range from very clear to blurred impressions but rarely have broken or deformed characteristics. The 1864 issue, though rarely blurred, usually have various imperfections in the letters and numbers. These include breaks, malformations, occasional dots at left of the crown or above the "R" of "PAR," a dot on the middle stroke of the "F," and many other bulges, breaks and spots of color.

The 1864 issue were printed in sheets of 40 (5x8). The first and second rows were inverted. Clichés in the third row were placed sideways, 4 with head to right and 4 with head to left, making one tête bêche pair. The fourth and fifth rows were normally placed.

No. 20 was never placed in use.

All values exist in shades, light to dark.

Counterfeit cancellations exist on #11-21.

Three stamps in this design- 2pa, 5pa, 20pa- were printed on white wove paper in 1864, but never placed in use. Value, set $12.

Romania

Prince Alexandru Ioan Cuza — A4

TWENTY PARALES:
Type I — The central oval does not touch the inner frame. The "I" of "DECI" extends above and below the other letters.
Type II — The central oval touches the frame at the bottom. The "I" of the "DECI" is the same height as the other letters.

1865, Jan.	**Unwmk.**	**Litho.**	*Imperf.*	
22	A4	2pa orange	70.00	250.00
a.	2pa yellow		77.50	325.00
b.	2pa ocher		325.00	325.00
23	A4	5pa blue	45.00	275.00
24	A4	20pa red, type I	35.00	47.50
a.	Bluish paper		350.00	
25	A4	20pa red, type II	35.00	40.00
a.	Bluish paper		350.00	
	Nos. 22-25 (4)		185.00	612.50

The 20pa types are found se-tenant.

White Laid Paper

26	A4	2pa orange	60.00	275.00
a.	2pa ocher		125.00	
27	A4	5pa blue	95.00	450.00

Prince Carol — A5

Type I — A6

Type II — A7

TWENTY PARALES:
Type I — A6. The Greek border at the upper right goes from right to left.
Type II — A7. The Greek border at the upper right goes from left to right.

1866-67		**Thin Wove Paper**		
29	A5	2pa blk, *yellow*	35.00	95.00
a.	Thick paper		65.00	400.00
30	A5	5pa blk, *dk bl*	60.00	575.00
a.	5pa black, *indigo*		100.00	—
b.	Thick paper		70.00	525.00
31	A6	20pa blk, *rose*, (I)	30.00	26.50
a.	Dot in Greek border, thin paper		400.00	150.00
b.	Thick paper		175.00	87.50
c.	Dot in Greek border, thick paper		125.00	72.50
32	A7	20pa blk, *rose*, (II)	30.00	26.50
a.	Thick paper		175.00	87.50
	Nos. 29-32 (4)		155.00	723.00

The 20pa types are found se-tenant.
Faked cancellations are known on Nos. 22-27, 29-32.
The white dot of Nos. 31a and 31c occurs in extreme upper right border.
Thick paper was used in 1866, thin in 1867.

Prince Carol — A8

1868-70

33	A8	2b orange	42.50	40.00
a.		2b yellow	45.00	40.00
34	A8	3b violet ('70)	42.50	40.00
35	A8	4b dk blue	55.00	47.50
36	A8	18b scarlet	225.00	30.00
a.		18b rose	225.00	30.00
		Nos. 33-36 (4)	365.00	157.50

Prince Carol — A9

1869

37	A9	5b orange yel	72.50	42.50
a.		5b deep orange	75.00	42.50
38	A9	10b blue	40.00	35.00
a.		10b ultramarine	77.50	52.50
b.		10b indigo	85.00	40.00
40	A9	15b vermilion	40.00	35.00
41	A9	25b orange & blue	40.00	26.50
42	A9	50b blue & red	150.00	52.50
a.		50b indigo & red	175.00	55.00
		Nos. 37-42 (5)	342.50	191.50

No. 40 on vertically laid paper was not issued. Value $1,250.

Prince Carol — A10

1871-72 *Imperf.*

43	A10	5b rose	42.50	35.00
a.		5b vermilion	45.00	45.00
44	A10	10b orange yel	55.00	35.00
a.		Vertically laid paper	450.00	450.00
45	A10	10b blue	125.00	70.00
46	A10	15b red	210.00	210.00
47	A10	25b olive brown	47.50	47.50
		Nos. 43-47 (5)	480.00	397.50

1872

48	A10	10b ultra	42.50	52.50
a.		Vertically laid paper	175.00	300.00
b.		10b greenish blue	150.00	175.00
49	A10	50b blue & red	225.00	240.00

No. 48 is a provisional issue printed from a new plate in which the head is placed further right.

Faked cancellations are found on No. 49.

1872 **Wove Paper** *Perf. 12½*

50	A10	5b rose	65.00	52.50
a.		5b vermilion	1,300.	700.00
51	A10	10b blue	57.50	52.50
a.		10b ultramarine	60.00	25.00
52	A10	25b dark brown	47.50	47.50
		Nos. 50-52 (3)	170.00	152.50

No. 43a with faked perforation is frequently offered as No. 50a.

Prince Carol — A11

Paris Print, Fine Impression Tinted Paper

1872 *Typo.* *Perf. 14x13½*

53	A11	1½b brnz grn, *bluish*	25.00	5.00
54	A11	3b green, *bluish*	32.50	5.00
55	A11	5b bis, *pale buff*	21.00	4.50
56	A11	10b blue	21.00	5.00
57	A11	15b red brn, *pale buff*	140.00	15.00
58	A11	25b org, *pale buff*	145.00	18.50
59	A11	50b rose, *pale rose*	150.00	42.50
		Nos. 53-59 (7)	534.50	95.50

Nos. 53-59 exist imperf.

Bucharest Print, Rough Impression
Perf. 11, 11½, 13½, and Compound
1876-79

60	A11	1½b brnz grn, *bluish*	6.50	4.25
61	A11	5b bis, *yelsh*	17.00	3.25
b.		Printed on both sides		75.00
62	A11	10b bl, *yelsh* ('77)	27.50	5.00
a.		10b pale bl, *yelsh*	25.00	5.00
b.		10b dark blue, *yelsh*	42.50	5.00
d.		Cliché of 5b in plate of 10b ('79)	425.00	425.00
63	A11	10b ultra, *yelsh* ('77)	47.50	5.00
64	A11	15b red brn, *yelsh*	72.50	9.25
a.		Printed on both sides		100.00
65	A11	30b org red, *yelsh* ('78)	190.00	50.00
a.		Printed on both sides		210.00
		Nos. 60-65 (6)	361.00	76.75

#60-65 are valued in the grade of fine.
#62d has been reprinted in dark blue. The originals are in dull blue. Value of reprint, $175.

Perf. 11, 11½, 13½ and Compound
1879

66	A11	1½b blk, *yelsh*	6.25	4.25
b.		Imperf.		12.00
67	A11	3b ol grn, *bluish*	17.50	12.50
a.		Diagonal half used as 1½b on cover		
68	A11	5b green, *bluish*	6.75	4.25
69	A11	10b rose, *yelsh*	13.50	2.50
b.		Cliché of 5b in plate of 10b	3.75.00	475.00
70	A11	15b rose red, *yelsh*	50.00	12.50
71	A11	25b blue, *yelsh*	140.00	25.00
72	A11	50b bister, *yelsh*	120.00	35.00
		Nos. 66-72 (7)	354.00	96.00

#66-72 are valued in the grade of fine.
There are two varieties of the numerals on the 15b and 50b.
No. 69b has been reprinted in dark rose. Originals are in pale rose. Value of reprint, $40.

King Carol I — A12

1880 **White Paper**

73	A12	15b brown	12.50	2.50
74	A12	25b blue	23.50	3.25

#73-74 are valued in the grade of fine.
No. 74 exists imperf.

King Carol I — A13

Perf. 13½, 11½ & Compound
1885-89

75	A13	1½b black	3.50	1.75
a.		Printed on both sides		
76	A13	3b violet	5.00	1.75
a.		Half used as 1½b on cover		21.00
77	A13	5b green	75.00	1.75
78	A13	15b red brown	14.50	2.50
79	A13	25b blue	17.00	6.00
		Nos. 75-79 (5)	115.00	13.75

Tinted Paper

80	A13	1½b blk, *bluish*	5.00	1.75
81	A13	3b vio, *bluish*	5.00	1.75
82	A13	3b ol grn, *bluish*	5.00	1.75
83	A13	5b bl grn, *bluish*	5.00	1.75
84	A13	10b rose, *pale buff*	5.00	2.50
85	A13	15b red brn, *pale buff*	18.50	2.75
86	A13	25b bl, *pale buff*	18.50	6.00
87	A13	50b bis, *pale buff*	75.00	21.00
		Nos. 80-87 (8)	137.00	39.25

Thin Pale Yellowish Paper

1889 **Wmk. 163**

88	A13	1½b black	30.00	6.00
89	A13	3b violet	21.00	6.00
90	A13	5b green	21.00	6.00
91	A13	10b rose	21.00	6.00
92	A13	15b red brown	72.50	13.00
93	A13	25b dark blue	47.50	10.00
		Nos. 88-93 (6)	213.00	47.00

King Carol I — A14

1890 *Perf. 13½, 11½ & Compound*

94	A14	1½b maroon	5.00	3.50
95	A14	3b violet	25.00	3.50
96	A14	5b emerald	12.00	3.50
97	A14	10b red	13.00	5.00
a.		10b rose		17.00	6.75
98	A14	15b dk brown	30.00	3.50
99	A14	25b gray blue	25.00	3.50
100	A14	50b orange	65.00	32.50
		Nos. 94-100 (7)	175.00	55.00

1891 **Unwmk.**

101	A14	1½b lilac rose	1.75	1.25
b.		Printed on both sides		65.00
102	A14	3b lilac	2.00	1.75
a.		3b violet	2.25	2.25
b.		Printed on both sides		
c.		Impressions of 5b on back	100.00	75.00
103	A14	5b emerald	3.50	1.75
104	A14	10b pale red	21.00	1.75
a.		Printed on both sides	140.00	110.00
105	A14	15b gray brown	13.00	1.25
106	A14	25b gray blue	13.00	1.75
107	A14	50b orange	85.00	13.00
		Nos. 101-107 (7)	139.25	22.50

Nos. 101-107 exist imperf.

King Carol I — A15

1891

108	A15	1½b claret	6.00	7.00
109	A15	3b lilac	6.00	7.00
110	A15	5b emerald	7.50	8.50
111	A15	10b red	7.50	8.50
112	A15	15b gray brown	7.50	8.50
		Nos. 108-112 (5)	34.50	39.50

25th year of the reign of King Carol I.

1894 **Wmk. 164**

113	A14	3b lilac	9.25	5.00
114	A14	5b pale green	9.25	5.00
115	A14	25b gray blue	13.50	6.25
116	A14	50b orange	27.50	12.50
		Nos. 113-116 (4)	59.50	28.75

King Carol I
A17   A18

A19

A20

A21   A23

1893-98 **Wmk. 164 & 200**

117	A17	1b pale brown	1.25	1.25
118	A17	1½b black	.85	1.25
119	A18	3b chocolate	1.25	.85
120	A19	5b blue	1.75	.85
a.		Cliché of the 25b in the plate of 5b	185.00	200.00
121	A19	5b yel grn ('98)	5.00	3.00
a.		5b emerald	5.00	3.00
122	A20	10b emerald	2.50	1.75
123	A20	10b rose ('98)	6.00	2.50
124	A21	15b rose	2.50	.85
125	A21	15b black ('98)	6.00	2.00
126	A19	25b violet	3.75	1.25
127	A19	25b indigo ('98)	9.25	3.25
128	A19	40b gray grn	21.00	3.50
129	A19	50b orange	12.50	2.00
130	A23	1 l bis & rose	30.00	2.00
131	A23	2 l orange & brn	35.00	5.00
		Nos. 117-131 (15)	138.60	29.55

This watermark may be found in four versions (Wmks. 164, 200 and variations). The paper also varies in thickness.

A 3b orange of type A18; 10b brown, type A20; 15b rose, type A21, and 25b bright green with similar but different border, all watermarked "P R," were prepared but never issued. Value, each $15.

See Nos. 132-157, 224-229. For overprints and surcharges see Romanian Post Offices in the Turkish Empire Nos. 1-6, 10-11.

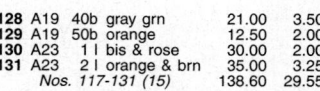

King Carol I — A24

Thin Paper, Tinted Rose on Back

Perf. 11½, 13½ and Compound
1900-03 **Unwmk.**

132	A17	1b pale brown	1.75	1.75
133	A24	1b brown ('01)	1.75	1.25
134	A24	1b black ('03)	1.75	1.25
135	A18	3b red brown	1.75	.85
136	A19	5b emerald	2.50	.85
137	A20	10b rose	3.00	1.25
138	A21	15b black	2.50	.85
139	A21	15b lil gray ('01)	2.50	.85
140	A21	15b dk vio ('03)	2.50	1.25
141	A19	25b blue	4.25	1.75
142	A19	40b gray grn	8.50	1.75
143	A19	50b orange	17.00	1.75
144	A23	1 l bis & rose ('01)	34.00	3.00
145	A23	1 l grn & blk ('03)	30.00	3.50
146	A23	2 l org & brn ('01)	30.00	3.50
147	A23	2 l red brn & blk ('03)	25.00	4.25
		Nos. 132-147 (16)	168.75	29.65

#132 inscribed BANI; #133-134 BAN.

1900, July **Wmk. 167**

148	A17	1b pale brown	12.00	5.00
149	A18	3b red brown	12.00	5.50
150	A19	5b emerald	10.00	5.00
151	A20	10b rose	15.00	6.00
152	A21	15b black	17.00	7.25
153	A19	25b blue	19.00	12.50
154	A19	40b gray grn	30.00	12.50
155	A19	50b orange	30.00	12.50
156	A23	1 l bis & rose	34.00	17.00
157	A23	2 l orange & brn	42.50	21.00
		Nos. 148-157 (10)	221.50	104.25

Mail Coach Leaving PO — A25

Thin Paper, Tinted Rose on Face

1903 **Unwmk.** *Perf. 14x13½*

158	A25	1b gray brown	2.25	1.60
159	A25	3b brown violet	3.75	1.60
160	A25	5b pale green	7.50	2.50
161	A25	10b rose	4.50	2.50
162	A25	15b black	4.50	3.25
163	A25	25b blue	22.50	9.50
164	A25	40b dull green	32.50	12.50
165	A25	50b orange	37.50	16.00
		Nos. 158-165 (8)	115.00	49.45

Counterfeits are plentiful. See note after No. 172. See No. 428.

King Carol I and Façade of New Post Office — A26

Thick Toned Paper

1903 **Engr.** *Perf. 13½x14*

166	A26	15b black	5.00	3.75
167	A26	25b blue	11.00	6.50
168	A26	40b gray grn	19.00	9.00
169	A26	50b orange	21.00	11.00
170	A26	1 l dk brown	16.00	9.00

171	A26	2 l dull red	130.00	65.00
a.		2 l orange (error)	180.00	150.00
172	A26	5 l dull violet	160.00	110.00
a.		5 l red violet	80.00	32.50
		Nos. 166-172 (7)	362.00	214.25

Opening of the new PO in Bucharest (Nos. 158-172).
Counterfeits exist.

Prince Carol Taking Oath of Allegiance, 1866 — A27

Prince in Royal Carriage A28

Prince Carol at Calafat in 1877 — A29

Prince Carol Shaking Hands with His Captive, Osman Pasha — A30

Carol I as Prince in 1866 and King in 1906 — A31

Romanian Army Crossing Danube A32

Romanian Troops Return to Bucharest in 1878 — A33

Prince Carol at Head of His Command in 1877 — A34

King Carol I at the Cathedral in 1896 — A35

King Carol I at Shrine of St. Nicholas, 1904 — A36

1906   **Engr.**   **Perf. 12**

176	A27	1b bister & blk	.65	.45
177	A28	3b red brn & blk	1.40	.45
178	A29	5b dp grn & blk	1.75	.45
179	A30	10b carmine & blk	1.10	.45
180	A31	15b dull vio & blk	1.10	.45
181	A32	25b ultra & blk	7.00	5.25
a.		25b olive green & black	9.00	5.25

182	A33	40b dk brn & blk	1.90	1.60
183	A34	50b bis brn & blk	2.00	1.60
184	A35	1 l vermilion & blk	2.25	1.90
185	A36	2 l orange & blk	2.50	2.40
		Nos. 176-185 (10)	21.65	15.00

40 years' rule of Carol I as Prince & King. No. 181a was never placed in use. Cancellations were by favor.

King Carol I — A37

1906

186	A37	1b bister & blk	.90	.45
187	A37	3b red brn & blk	2.25	.85
188	A37	5b dp grn & blk	1.50	.75
189	A37	10b carmine & blk	1.50	.75
190	A37	15b dl vio & blk	1.50	.75
191	A37	25b ultra & blk	13.50	7.00
192	A37	40b dk brn & blk	6.00	1.50
193	A37	50b bis brn & blk	6.00	1.50
194	A37	1 l red & blk	6.00	1.50
195	A37	2 l orange & blk	6.00	1.50
		Nos. 186-195 (10)	45.15	16.55

25th anniversary of the Kingdom.

Plowman and Angel — A38

Exposition Building — A39

Exposition Buildings
A40   A41

King Carol I — A42   Queen Elizabeth (Carmen Sylva) — A43

1906   **Typo.**   **Perf. 11½, 13½**

196	A38	5b yel grn & blk	4.50	1.40
197	A38	10b car & blk	4.50	1.40
198	A39	15b violet & blk	6.50	2.25
199	A39	25b blue & blk	6.50	2.25
200	A40	30b red & blk brn	8.75	2.25
201	A40	40b grn & blk brn	9.50	2.75
202	A41	50b orange & blk	8.75	3.25
203	A41	75b lt brn & dk brn	7.75	3.25
204	A42	1.50 l red lil & brn	97.50	45.00
a.		Center inverted		450.00

205	A42	2.50 l yellow & brn	37.50	26.00
a.		Center inverted		
206	A43	3 l brn org & brn	28.00	26.00
		Nos. 196-206 (11)	219.75	115.80

General Exposition. They were sold at post offices July 29-31, 1906, and were valid only for those three days. Those sold at the exposition are overprinted "S E" in black. Remainders were sold privately, both unused and canceled to order, by the Exposition promoters. Value, set: unused or used, $450.

A44   A45

Perf. 11½, 13½ & Compound
1908-18   **Engr.**

207	A44	5b pale yel grn	2.50	.25
208	A44	10b carmine	.70	.25
209	A45	15b purple	11.50	2.25
210	A44	25b deep blue	1.75	.25
211	A44	40b brt green	.85	.25
212	A44	40b dk brn ('18)	5.25	2.25
213	A44	50b orange	.65	.25
214	A44	50b lt red ('18)	2.00	.70
215	A44	1 l brown	2.00	.40
216	A44	2 l red	10.00	2.50
		Nos. 207-216 (10)	37.20	9.35

King Carol I — A46

Perf. 13½x14, 11½, 13½ & Compound
1909-18   **Typo.**

217	A46	1b black	.60	.25
218	A46	3b red brown	1.25	.25
219	A46	5b yellow grn	.60	.25
220	A46	10b rose	1.25	.25
221	A46	15b dull violet	21.00	12.50
222	A46	15b olive green	1.25	.25
223	A46	15b red brn ('18)	1.10	.65
		Nos. 217-223 (7)	27.05	14.40

Nos. 217-219, 222 exist imperf.
No. 219 in black is a chemical changeling. For surcharge and overprints see Nos. 240-242, 245-247, J50-J51, RA1-RA2, RA11-RA12, Romanian Post Offices in the Turkish Empire 7-9.

Types of 1893-99
1911-19   White Paper   Unwmk.

224	A17	1½b straw	1.75	.45
225	A19	25b deep blue ('18)	1.00	.85
226	A19	40b gray brn ('19)	1.25	.85
227	A19	50b dull red ('19)	1.75	.85
228	A23	1 l gray grn ('18)	2.25	.50
229	A23	2 l orange ('18)	2.25	.85
		Nos. 224-229 (6)	10.25	4.35

For overprints see Romanian Post Offices in the Turkish Empire Nos. 10-11.

Romania Holding Flag — A47   Romanian Crown and Old Fort on Danube — A48

Troops Crossing Danube — A49

View of Turtucaia — A50

Mircea the Great and Carol I — A51

View of Silistra — A52

Perf. 11½x13½, 13½x11½
1913, Dec. 25

230	A47	1b black	.85	.40
231	A48	3b ol gray & choc	2.25	.85
232	A49	5b yel grn & blk brn	1.75	.40
233	A50	10b org & gray	.85	.40
234	A51	15b bister & vio	2.25	.85
235	A52	25b blue & choc	3.00	1.25
236	A49	40b bis & red vio	6.00	4.75
237	A48	50b yellow & bl	16.00	6.50
238	A48	1 l bl & ol bis	25.00	14.50
239	A48	2 l org red & rose	40.00	20.00
		Nos. 230-239 (10)	97.95	49.90

Romania's annexation of Silistra.

No. 217 Handstamped in Red

Perf. 13½x14, 11½, 13½ & Compound
1918, May 1

240	A46	25b on 1b black	2.25	2.25

This handstamp is found inverted.

No. 219 and 220 Overprinted in Black

1918

241	A46	5b yellow green	.60	.55
a.		Inverted overprint	3.25	3.25
b.		Double overprint	3.25	3.25
242	A46	10b rose	.60	.55
a.		Inverted overprint	3.25	3.25
b.		Double overprint	3.25	3.25

Nos. 217, 219 and 220 Overprinted in Red or Black

1919, Nov. 8

245	A46	1b black (R)	.40	.25
a.		Inverted overprint	6.75	
b.		Double overprint	10.00	2.25
246	A46	5b yel grn (Bk)	.40	.25
a.		Double overprint	10.00	3.25
b.		Inverted overprint	6.75	2.00
247	A46	10b rose (Bk)	.40	.25
a.		Inverted overprint	6.75	2.00
b.		Double overprint	10.00	3.00
		Nos. 245-247 (3)	1.20	.75

Recovery of Transylvania and the return of the King to Bucharest.

King Ferdinand — A53

1920-22   Typo.

248	A53	1b black	.25	.25
249	A53	5b yellow grn	.25	.25
250	A53	10b rose	.25	.25
251	A53	15b red brown	.75	.25
252	A53	25b deep blue	1.50	.40
253	A53	25b brown	.75	.25
254	A53	40b gray brown	1.25	.35
255	A53	50b salmon	.35	.25
256	A53	1 l gray grn	1.25	.25
257	A53	1 l rose	.75	.25
258	A53	2 l orange	1.25	.25
259	A53	2 l dp blue	1.25	.25
260	A53	2 l rose ('22)	3.00	1.75
		Nos. 248-260 (13)	12.85	5.00

Nos. 248-260 are printed on two papers: coarse, grayish paper with bits of colored fiber, and thinner white paper of better quality.
Nos. 248-251, 253 exist imperf.

King Ferdinand — A54

Type I   Type II   Type III

Type I   Type II   Type I   Type II

TWO LEI:
Type I — The "2" is thin, with tail 2½mm wide. Top of "2" forms a hook.
Type II — The "2" is thick, with tail 3mm wide. Top of "2" forms a ball.
Type III — The "2" is similar to type II. The "E" of "LEI" is larger and about 2mm wide.

THREE LEI:
Type I — Top of "3" begins in a point. Top and middle bars of "E" of "LEI" are without serifs.
Type II — Top of "3" begins in a ball. Top and middle bars of "E" of "LEI" have serifs.

FIVE LEI:
Type I — The "5" is 2½mm wide. The end of the final stroke of the "L" of "LEI" almost touches the vertical stroke.
Type II — The "5" is 3mm wide and the lines are broader than in type I. The end of the final stroke of the "L" of "LEI" is separated from the vertical by a narrow space.

Perf. 13½x14, 11½, 13½ & Compound

1920-26

261	A54	3b black	.25	.25
262	A54	5b black	.25	.25
263	A54	10b yel grn ('25)	.25	.25
a.		10b olive green ('25)	.40	
264	A54	25b bister brn	.25	.25
265	A54	25b salmon	.25	.25
266	A54	30b violet	.25	.25
267	A54	50b orange	.25	.25
268	A54	60b gray brn	1.00	.55
269	A54	1 l violet	.25	.25
270	A54	2 l rose (I)	1.25	.25
a.		2 l claret (I)	47.50	
271	A54	2 l lt green (II)	.70	.25
a.		2 l light green (I)	.95	.40
b.		2 l light green (III)	.80	.25
272	A54	3 l blue (I)	2.60	.80
273	A54	3 l buff (II)	2.60	.80
		3 l buff (I)	12.50	2.25
274	A54	3 l salmon (II)	.25	.25
a.		3 l salmon (I)	1.60	1.25
275	A54	5 l car rose (II)	.65	.25
276	A54	5 l emer (I)	2.10	.50
277	A54	5 l lt brn (II)	.45	.25
a.		5 l light brown (I)	1.60	.80
278	A54	6 l blue	2.60	1.25
279	A54	6 l carmine	5.75	3.25
280	A54	6 l ol grn ('26)	2.50	.80
281	A54	7½ l pale bl	2.10	.45
282	A54	10 l deep blue	2.10	.45
		Nos. 261-282 (22)	28.65	12.10

#273 and 273a, 274 and 274a, exist se-tenant. The 50b exists in three types.
For surcharge see No. Q7.

Alba Iulia Cathedral A55   King Ferdinand A56

Coat of Arms — A57   Queen Marie as Nurse — A58

Michael the Brave and King Ferdinand A59   King Ferdinand A60

Queen Marie — A61

Perf. 13½x14, 13½, 11½ & Compound

1922, Oct. 15   Photo.   Wmk. 95

283	A55	5b black	.40	.30
284	A56	25b chocolate	1.25	.40
285	A57	50b dp green	1.25	.60
286	A58	1 l olive grn	1.50	.85
287	A59	2 l carmine	1.50	.85
288	A60	3 l blue	4.00	1.25
289	A61	6 l violet	11.50	8.00
		Nos. 283-289 (7)	21.40	12.25

Coronation of King Ferdinand I and Queen Marie on Oct. 15, 1922, at Alba Iulia. All values exist imperforate. Value, set $150, unused or used.

King Ferdinand A62   A63

1926, July 1   Unwmk.   Perf. 11

291	A62	10b yellow grn	.35	.25
292	A62	25b orange	.35	.25
293	A62	50b orange brn	.25	.25
294	A63	1 l dk violet	.50	.25
295	A63	2 l dk green	.50	.25
296	A63	3 l brown car	.50	.50
297	A63	5 l black brn	.50	.50
298	A63	6 l dk olive	.50	.50
a.		6 l bright blue (error)	150.00	175.00
300	A63	9 l slate	.75	.50
301	A63	10 l brt blue	.75	.50
b.		10 l brown carmine (error)	150.00	175.00
		Nos. 291-301 (10)	5.05	3.75

60th birthday of King Ferdinand.
Exist imperf. Value, set unused $150; used $175. Imperf. examples with watermark 95 are proofs.

King Carol I and King Ferdinand A69

King Ferdinand A70

A71

1927, Aug. 1   Perf. 13½

308	A69	25b brown vio	.50	.35
309	A70	30b gray blk	.50	.35
310	A71	50b dk green	.50	.35
311	A71	1 l bluish slate	.50	.35
312	A70	2 l dp green	.50	.45
313	A70	3 l violet	.50	.55
314	A71	4 l dk brown	.50	.65
315	A71	4.50 l henna brn	3.00	2.25
316	A71	5 l red brown	.50	.55
317	A71	6 l carmine	2.00	1.25
318	A69	7.50 l grnsh bl	.50	.55
319	A69	10 l brt blue	3.00	1.10
		Nos. 308-319 (12)	12.50	8.75

50th anniversary of Romania's independence from Turkish suzerainty.
Some values exist imperf. All exist imperf. and with value numerals omitted.

King Michael A72   A73

Perf. 13½x14 (25b, 50b); 13½

1928-29   Typo.   Unwmk.

Size: 19x25mm

320	A72	25b black	.25	.25
321	A72	30b fawn ('29)	.40	.25
322	A72	50b olive grn	.25	.25

Photo.
Size: 18½x24½mm

323	A73	1 l violet	.45	.25
324	A73	2 l dp green	.45	.25
325	A73	3 l brt rose	.90	.25
326	A73	5 l red brown	1.40	.25
327	A73	7.50 l ultra	6.25	.90
328	A73	10 l blue	5.25	.35
		Nos. 320-328 (9)	15.60	3.00

See Nos. 343-345, 353-357. For overprints see Nos. 359-368A.

Parliament House, Bessarabia — A74

Designs: 1 l, 2 l, Parliament House, Bessarabia. 3 l, 5 l, 20 l, Hotin Fortress. 7.50 l, 10 l, Fortress Cetatea Alba.

1928, Apr. 29   Wmk. 95   Perf. 13½

329	A74	1 l deep green	1.75	.65
330	A74	2 l deep brown	1.75	.65
331	A74	3 l black brown	1.75	.65
332	A74	5 l carmine lake	2.25	.80
333	A74	7.50 l ultra	2.25	.80
334	A74	10 l Prus blue	5.00	2.00
335	A74	20 l black vio	8.00	2.75
		Nos. 329-335 (7)	22.75	8.30

Reunion of Bessarabia with Romania, 10th anniv.

King Carol I and King Michael A77

View of Constanta Harbor A78

Trajan's Monument at Adam Clisi A79

Cernavoda Bridge — A80

1928, Oct. 25

336	A77	1 l blue green	1.10	.45
337	A78	2 l red brown	1.10	.45
338	A79	3 l gray black	1.40	.50
339	A79	5 l dull lilac	1.75	.60
340	A79	7.50 l ultra	2.10	.80
341	A80	10 l blue	3.25	1.90
342	A80	20 l carmine rose	5.50	3.25
		Nos. 336-342 (7)	16.20	7.95

Union of Dobruja with Romania, 50th anniv.

Michael Types of 1928-29

Perf. 13½x14

1928, Sept. 1   Typo.   Wmk. 95

343	A72	25b black	.60	.25

Photo.

344	A73	7.50 l ultra	2.00	.75
345	A73	10 l blue	4.00	.60
		Nos. 343-345 (3)	6.60	1.60

Ferdinand I; Stephen the Great; Michael the Brave; Corvin and Constantine Brancoveanu — A81

Union with Transylvania A82

Avram Jancu — A83   Prince Michael the Brave — A84

Castle Bran — A85

King Ferdinand I — A86

1929, May 10   Photo.   Wmk. 95

347	A81	1 l dark violet	2.25	1.75
348	A82	2 l olive green	2.25	1.75
349	A83	3 l violet brown	2.50	1.75
350	A84	4 l cerise	2.75	2.25
351	A85	5 l orange	4.50	2.25
352	A86	10 l brt blue	7.50	4.25
	Nos. 347-352 (6)		21.75	14.00

Union of Transylvania and Romania.

Michael Type of 1928

1930   Unwmk.   Perf. 14½x14
Size: 18x23mm

353	A73	1 l deep violet	.80	.25
354	A73	2 l deep green	1.25	.25
355	A73	3 l carmine rose	2.40	.25
356	A73	7.50 l ultra	5.00	1.10
357	A73	10 l deep blue	16.00	7.00
	Nos. 353-357 (5)		25.45	8.85

Stamps of 1928-30 Overprinted

On Nos. 320-322, 326, 328
Perf. 13½x14, 13½

1930, June 8   Typo.

359	A72	25b black	.40	.25
360	A72	30b fawn	.80	.25
361	A72	50b olive green	.80	.25

Photo.
Size: 18½x24½mm

362	A73	5 l red brown	1.60	.25
362A	A73	10 l brt blue	8.25	1.50

On Nos. 353-357
Perf. 14½x14
Size: 18x23mm

363	A73	1 l deep violet	.80	.25
364	A73	2 l deep green	.80	.25
365	A73	3 l carmine rose	1.60	.25
366	A73	7.50 l ultra	4.00	.75
367	A73	10 l deep blue	3.25	.75

On Nos. 343-344
Perf. 13½x14, 13½

		Typo.	**Wmk. 95**
368	A72	25b black	1.25	.35

Photo.
Size: 18½x24½mm

368A	A73	7.50 l ultra	5.00	1.50
	Nos. 359-368A (12)		28.55	6.60

Accession to the throne by King Carol II. This overprint exists on Nos. 323, 345.

A87

A88

King Carol II — A89

1930   Wmk. 225
Perf. 13½, 14, 14x13½

369	A87	25b black	1.10	.25
370	A87	50b chocolate	3.25	.45
371	A87	1 l dk violet	2.25	.25
372	A87	2 l gray green	2.75	.25
373	A88	3 l carmine rose	2.25	.25
374	A88	4 l orange red	3.25	.25
375	A88	6 l carmine brn	4.25	.25
376	A88	7.50 l ultra	4.25	.30
377	A89	10 l deep blue	2.25	.25
378	A89	16 l peacock grn	4.75	.25
379	A89	20 l orange	1.40	.60
	Nos. 369-379 (11)		31.75	3.35

Exist imperf. Value, unused or used, $250.
See Nos. 405-414.

A90

A91

1930, Dec. 24   Unwmk.   Perf. 13½

380	A90	1 l dull violet	1.25	.45
381	A91	2 l green	2.25	.50
382	A91	4 l vermilion	2.50	.35
383	A91	6 l brown carmine	6.50	.45
	Nos. 380-383 (4)		12.50	1.75

First census in Romania.

King Carol II — A92

King Carol I — A93   King Ferdinand — A96

King Carol II — A94

King Carol II, King Ferdinand and King Carol I — A95

1931, May 10   Photo.   Wmk. 225

384	A92	1 l gray violet	2.50	1.75
385	A93	2 l green	4.25	2.00
386	A94	6 l red brown	11.00	3.25
387	A95	10 l blue	16.00	6.00
388	A96	20 l orange	22.50	8.50
	Nos. 384-388 (5)		56.25	21.50

50th anniversary of Romanian Kingdom.

Using Bayonet — A97

Romanian Infantryman 1870 — A98

Romanian Infantry 1830 — A99

King Carol I A100

Infantry Advance A101

King Ferdinand A102

King Carol II A103

1931, May 10

389	A97	25b gray black	1.40	.75
390	A98	50b dk red brn	2.10	1.10
391	A99	1 l gray violet	2.75	1.10
392	A100	2 l deep green	4.25	1.50
393	A101	3 l carmine rose	10.00	3.50
394	A102	7.50 l ultra	13.00	9.00
395	A103	16 l blue green	16.00	4.00
	Nos. 389-395 (7)		49.50	20.95

Centenary of the Romanian Army.

Naval Cadet Ship "Mircea" A104

10 l, Ironclad. 16 l, Light cruiser. 20 l, Destroyer.

1931, May 10

396	A104	6 l red brown	7.00	4.00
397	A104	10 l blue	9.50	4.50
398	A104	16 l blue green	40.00	6.00
399	A104	20 l orange	17.50	10.00
	Nos. 396-399 (4)		74.00	24.50

50th anniversary of the Romanian Navy.

King Carol II — A108

1931   Unwmk.   Engr.   Perf. 12

400	A108	30 l ol bis & dk bl	1.75	1.00
401	A108	50 l red & dk bl	4.50	1.50
402	A108	100 l dk grn & dk bl	7.25	3.50
	Nos. 400-402 (3)		13.50	6.00

Exist imperf. Value, unused or used, $150.

Carol II, Ferdinand, Carol I — A109

Wmk. 230
1931, Nov. 1   Photo.   Perf. 13½

403	A109	16 l Prus green	12.00	.90

Exists imperf. Value, unused or used, $300.

Carol II Types of 1930
Perf. 13½, 14, 14½ and Compound
1932   Wmk. 230

405	A87	25b black	.50	.25
406	A87	50b dark brown	1.00	.25
407	A87	1 l dark violet	1.40	.25
408	A87	2 l gray green	1.75	.25
409	A88	3 l carmine rose	2.25	.25
410	A88	4 l orange red	5.25	.25
411	A88	6 l carmine brn	12.50	.25
412	A88	7.50 l ultra	21.50	.75
413	A89	10 l deep blue	125.00	.90
414	A89	20 l orange	110.00	9.00
	Nos. 405-414 (10)		281.15	12.40

Alexander the Good — A110

1932, May   Perf. 13½

415	A110	6 l carmine brown	12.00	6.00

500th death anniv. of Alexander the Good, Prince of Moldavia, 1400-1432.

King Carol II — A111

1932, June

416	A111	10 l brt blue	12.00	.45

Exists imperf. Value, unused or used, $200.

Cantacuzino and Gregory Ghika, Founders of Coltea and Pantelimon Hospitals — A112

Session of the Congress A113

Aesculapius and Hygeia — A114

1932, Sept.   Perf. 13½

417	A112	1 l carmine rose	7.50	7.50
418	A113	6 l deep orange	20.00	11.00
419	A114	10 l brt blue	34.00	18.50
	Nos. 417-419 (3)		61.50	37.00

9th Intl. History of Medicine Congress, Bucharest.

Bull's Head and Post Horn A116

Lion Rampant and Bridge A117

Dolphins
A118

Eagle and
Castles
A119

Coat of
Arms — A120

Eagle and
Post
Horn — A121

Bull's Head and Post
Horn — A122

1932, Nov. 20   Typo.   Imperf.

421	A116	25b black	.85	.40
422	A117	1 l violet	2.00	.70
423	A118	2 l green	2.50	.90
424	A119	3 l car rose	2.80	1.10
425	A120	6 l red brown	3.50	1.25
426	A121	7.50 l lt blue	4.25	1.75
427	A122	10 l dk blue	8.00	3.00
		Nos. 421-427 (7)	23.90	9.10

75th anniv. of the first Moldavian stamps.

Mail Coach Type of 1903

1932, Nov. 20   Perf. 13½

428	A25	16 l blue green	11.00	5.50

30th anniv. of the opening of the new post
office, Bucharest, in 1903.

Arms of City of Turnu-Severin, Ruins
of Tower of Emperor Severus — A123

Inauguration of Trajan's
Bridge — A124

Prince Carol Landing at Turnu-
Severin — A125

Bridge
over the
Danube
A126

1933, June 2   Photo.   Perf. 14½x14

429	A123	25b gray green	.75	.30
430	A124	50b dull blue	1.10	.45
431	A125	1 l black brn	1.75	.75
432	A126	2 l olive blk	3.25	1.10
		Nos. 429-432 (4)	6.85	2.60

Centenary of the incorporation in Walachia
of the old Roman City of Turnu-Severin.
Exist imperf. Value, unused or used, $150.

Queen
Elizabeth
and King
Carol
I — A127

Profiles of
Kings
Carol I,
Ferdinand
and Carol
II — A128

Castle
Peles,
Sinaia
A129

1933, Aug.

433	A127	1 l dark violet	2.50	2.00
434	A128	3 l olive brown	3.00	2.75
435	A129	6 l vermilion	4.25	3.25
		Nos. 433-435 (3)	9.75	8.00

50th anniversary of the erection of Castle
Peles, the royal summer residence at Sinaia.
Exist imperf. Value, unused or used, $125.

A130

A131

King Carol
II — A132

1934, Aug.   Perf. 13½

436	A130	50b brown	1.00	.40
437	A131	2 l gray green	2.00	.40
438	A131	4 l red	3.50	.55
439	A132	6 l deep claret	8.00	.40
		Nos. 436-439 (4)	14.50	1.75

See Nos. 446-460 for stamps inscribed
"Posta." Nos. 436, 439 exist imperf. Value for
both, unused or used, $100.

Child and
Grapes — A133

Woman and
Fruit — A134

1934, Sept. 14

440	A133	1 l dull green	5.00	2.25
441	A134	2 l violet brown	5.00	2.25

Natl. Fruit Week, Sept. 14-21. Exist imperf.
Value, unused or used, $125.

Crisan,
Horia and
Closca
A135

1935, Feb. 28

442	A135	1 l shown	.65	.50
443	A135	2 l Crisan	.90	.60
444	A135	6 l Closca	2.25	1.00
445	A135	10 l Horia	5.00	2.25
			8.80	4.35

150th anniversary of the death of three
Romanian martyrs. Exist imperf. Value,
unused or used, $110.

A139

A140

A141

A142

King Carol
II — A143

Wmk. 230

1935-40   Photo.   Perf. 13½

446	A139	25b black brn	.25	.25
447	A142	50b brown	.25	.25
448	A140	1 l purple	.25	.25
449	A141	2 l green	.45	.25
449A	A141	2 l dk bl grn ('40)	.65	.25
450	A142	3 l deep rose	.70	.25
450A	A142	3 l grnsh bl ('40)	.85	.30
451	A141	4 l vermilion	1.25	.25
452	A140	5 l rose car ('40)	1.25	.80
453	A143	6 l maroon	1.60	.25
454	A140	7.50 l ultra	1.90	.30
454A	A142	8 l magenta ('40)	1.90	.25
455	A141	9 l brt ultra ('40)	2.50	.80
456	A142	10 l brt blue	1.00	.25
456A	A143	12 l slate bl ('40)	1.60	1.25
457	A139	15 l dk brn ('40)	1.60	.95
458	A143	16 l Prus blue	2.10	.25
459	A143	20 l orange	1.25	.35
460	A143	24 l dk car ('40)	2.10	.95
		Nos. 446-460 (19)	23.45	8.90

Exist imperf. Value, unused or used, $240.

Nos. 454, 456
Overprinted in Red

1936, Dec. 5

461	A140	7.50 l ultra	9.25	6.50
462	A142	10 l brt blue	9.25	6.50

16th anniversary of the Little Entente.
Overprints in silver or gold are fraudulent.

Birthplace
of Ion
Creanga
A144

Ion
Creanga
A145

1937, May 15

463	A144	2 l green	1.25	.80
464	A145	3 l carmine rose	1.75	.90
465	A144	4 l dp violet	2.00	1.10
466	A145	6 l red brown	5.00	2.50
		Nos. 463-466 (4)	10.00	5.30

Creanga (1837-89), writer. Exist imperf.
Value, unused or used, $125.

Cathedral at
Curtea de
Arges — A146

1937, July 1

467	A146	7.50 l ultra	2.50	1.10
468	A146	10 l blue	3.25	.80

The Little Entente (Romania, Czechoslovakia, Yugoslavia). Exist imperf. Value, unused
or used, $125.

Souvenir Sheet

A146a

**Surcharged in Black with New
Values**

1937, Oct. 25   Unwmk.   Perf. 13½

469	A146a	Sheet of 4	9.00	9.00
a.		2 l on 20 l orange	.35	.35
b.		6 l on 10 l bright blue	.35	.35
c.		10 l on 6 l maroon	.45	.45
d.		20 l on 2 l orange	1.00	1.00

Promotion of the Crown Prince Michael to
the rank of Lieutenant on his 17th birthday.

Arms of
Romania,
Greece, Turkey
and Yugoslavia
A147

Perf. 13x13½

1938, Feb. 10   Wmk. 230

470	A147	7.50 l ultra	1.50	.90
471	A147	10 l blue	2.00	.80

The Balkan Entente.
Exist imperf. Value, unused or used, $100.

A148

King Carol II

A149   A150

1938, May 10 — **Perf. 13½**

472	A148	3 l dk carmine	.75	.50
473	A149	6 l violet brn	1.25	.50
474	A150	10 l blue	2.00	.90

Nos. 472-474 (3) — 4.00 1.90

New Constitution of Feb. 27, 1938.
Exist imperf. Value, unused or used, $100.

> **Catalogue values for unused stamps in this section, from this point to the end of the section, are for Never Hinged items.**

Prince Carol's Calatorie, 1866 — A151

Examining Plans for a Monastery — A153

Prince Carol and Carmen Sylva (Queen Elizabeth) — A155

Sigmaringen and Peles Castles — A154

Prince Carol, Age 6 — A156

Equestrian Statue — A159

Battle of Plevna — A160

On Horseback A161

Cathedral of Curtea de Arges A164

King Carol I and Queen Elizabeth A163

Designs: 50b, At Calafat. 4 l, In 1866. 5 l, In 1877. 12 l, in 1914.

Perf. 14, 13½

1939, Apr. 10 — **Wmk. 230**

475	A151	25b olive blk	.25	.25
476	A151	50b violet brn	.25	.25
477	A153	1 l dk purple	.25	.25
478	A154	1.50 l green	.25	.25
479	A155	2 l myrtle grn	.25	.25
480	A156	3 l red orange	.25	.25
481	A156	4 l rose lake	.25	.25
482	A156	5 l black	.25	.25
483	A159	7 l olive blk	.25	.25
484	A160	8 l dark blue	.25	.25
485	A161	10 l deep mag	.80	.25
486	A161	12 l dull blue	1.20	.25
487	A163	15 l ultra	1.20	.25
488	A164	16 l Prus green	1.20	.60

Nos. 475-488 (14) — 6.90 3.85

Centenary of the birth of King Carol I.
Nos 475-488 exist imperf. Value, unused or used, $150.

Souvenir Sheets

1939 — **Perf. 14x13½**

488A	Sheet of 3, #475-476, 478	3.50	3.50
d.	Imperf. ('40)	7.00	7.00

Perf. 14x15½

488B	Sheet of 4, #480-482, 486	3.50	3.50
e.	Imperf. ('40)	7.00	7.00
488C	Sheet of 4, #479, 483-485	3.50	3.50
f.	Imperf. ('40)	7.00	7.00

No. 488A sold for 20 l, Nos. 488B-488C for 50 l, the surtax for national defense.

Nos. 488A-488C and 488Ad-488Cf were overprinted "PRO-PATRIA 1940" to aid the armament fund. Value, set of 6, $100.

Nos. 488A-488C exist with overprint of "ROMA BERLIN 1940" and bars, but these are not recognized as having been officially issued.

Romanian Pavilion A165

Romanian Pavilion A166

1939, May 8 — **Perf. 14x13½, 13½**

489	A165	6 l brown carmine	1.25	.60
490	A166	12 l brt blue	1.25	.60

New York World's Fair.
Nos 489-490 exist imperf. Value, unused or used, $250.

Mihail Eminescu
A167　　　　　A168

1939, May 22 — **Perf. 13½**

491	A167	5 l olive gray	3.00	1.75
492	A168	7 l brown carmine	3.00	1.75

Mihail Eminescu, poet, 50th death anniv.
Nos 491-492 exist imperf. Value, unused or used, $300.

Three Types of Locomotives — A169

Modern Train A170

Wood-burning Locomotive A171

Streamlined Locomotive A172

Railroad Terminal A173

1939, June 10 — **Typo.** — **Perf. 14**

493	A169	1 l red violet	1.75	.60
494	A170	4 l deep rose	1.75	.60
495	A171	5 l gray lilac	1.75	.60
496	A171	7 l claret	1.75	.60
497	A172	12 l blue	3.50	1.75
498	A173	15 l green	3.50	2.40

Nos. 493-498 (6) — 14.00 6.55

Romanian Railways, 70th anniversary.
Nos 493-498 exist imperf. Value, unused or used, $200.

Arms of Romania, Greece, Turkey and Yugoslavia — A174

Wmk. 230

1940, May 27 — **Photo.** — **Perf. 13½**

504	A174	12 l lt ultra	1.25	.75
505	A174	16 l dull blue	1.25	.75

The Balkan Entente.
Nos 504-505 exist imperf. Value, unused or used, $125.

King Michael — A175

1940-42 — **Wmk. 230** — **Perf. 14**

506	A175	25b Prus green	.25	.25
506A	A175	50b dk grn ('42)	.25	.25
507	A175	1 l purple	.25	.25
508	A175	2 l red orange	.25	.25
508A	A175	4 l slate ('42)	.25	.25
509	A175	5 l rose pink	.25	.25
509A	A175	7 l dp blue ('42)	.25	.25
510	A175	10 l dp magenta	.40	.25
511	A175	12 l dull blue	.25	.25
511A	A175	13 l dk vio ('42)	.25	.25
512	A175	16 l Prus blue	.55	.25
513	A175	20 l brown	1.75	.25
514	A175	30 l yellow grn	.25	.25
515	A175	50 l olive brn	.25	.25
516	A175	100 l rose brown	.25	.25

Nos. 506-516 (15) — 6.20 3.75

See Nos. 535A-553.

Prince Duca — A176

1941, Oct. 6 — **Perf. 13½**

517	A176	6 l lt brown	.40	.40
518	A176	12 l dk violet	.80	.80
519	A176	24 l brt blue	1.10	1.10

Nos. 517-519 (3) — 2.30 2.30

Crossing of the Dniester River by Romanian forces invading Russia.

Nos. 517-519 each exist in an imperf., ungummed souvenir sheet of 4. These were prepared by the civil government of Trans-Dniestria to be sold for 300 lei apiece to aid the Red Cross, but were not recognized by the national government at Bucharest. The sheets reached philatelic channels in 1946. Value, set of 3 sheets $40.
See Nos. 554-557.

Hotin Chapel, Bessarabia A177

Sucevita Monastery, Bucovina A179

Designs: 50b, 9.50 l, Hotin Fortress, Bessarabia. 1.50 l, Soroca Fortress, Bessarabia. 2 l, 5.50 l, Tighina Fortress, Bessarabia. 3 l, Dragomirna Monastery, Bucovina. 6.50 l, Cetatea Alba Fortress, Bessarabia. 10 l, 130 l, Putna Monastery, Bucovina. 13 l, Milisauti Monastery, Bucovina. 26 l, St. Nicholas Monastery, Suceava, Bucovina. 39 l, Rughi Monastery, Bessarabia.

Inscribed "Basarabia" or "Bucovina" at bottom

1941, Dec. 1 — **Perf. 13½**

520	A177	25b rose car	.25	.25
521	A179	50b red brn	.25	.25
522	A179	1 l dp vio	.25	.25
523	A179	1.50 l green	.25	.25
524	A179	2 l brn org	.30	.25
525	A177	3 l dk ol grn	.30	.25
526	A177	5 l olive blk	.30	.25
527	A179	5.50 l brown	.30	.25
528	A179	6.50 l magenta	.40	.25
529	A179	9.50 l gray blk	.40	.25
530	A179	10 l dk vio brn	.35	.25
531	A177	13 l slate blue	.70	.25
532	A179	17 l brn car	1.00	.25
533	A179	26 l gray grn	1.25	.40
534	A179	39 l bl grn	1.75	.60
535	A179	130 l yel org	5.00	2.75

Nos. 520-535,B179-B187 (25) — 19.50 11.75

Type of 1940-42

1943-45 — **Wmk. 276** — **Perf. 14**

535A	A175	25b Prus grn ('44)	.25	.25
536	A175	50b dk grn ('44)	.25	.25
537	A175	1 l dk vio ('43)	.25	.25
538	A175	2 l red org ('43)	.25	.25
539	A175	3 l red brn ('44)	.25	.25
540	A175	3.50 l brn ('43)	.25	.25
541	A175	4 l slate	.25	.25
542	A175	4.50 l dk brn ('43)	.25	.25
543	A175	5 l rose car	.25	.25
544	A175	6.50 l dl vio	.25	.25
545	A175	7 l dp bl	.25	.25
546	A175	10 l dp mag	.25	.25
547	A175	11 l brt ultra	.25	.25
548	A175	12 l dark blue	.25	.25
549	A175	15 l royal blue	.25	.25
550	A175	16 l dp blue	.25	.25
551	A175	20 l brn ('43)	.25	.25
551A	A175	29 l ultra ('45)	.55	.35
552	A175	30 l yel org	.25	.25
553	A175	50 l olive blk	.25	.25

Nos. 535A-553 (20) — 5.30 5.10

Prince Duca Type of 1941

1943   **Perf. 13½**
554	A176	3 l red org	.40	.75
555	A176	6 l dl brn	.40	.75
556	A176	12 l dl vio	.80	1.10
557	A176	24 l brt bl	1.10	1.50
		Nos. 554-557 (4)	2.70	4.10

Andrei
Saguna — A188

Andrei
Muresanu
A189

Transylvanians: 4.50 l, Samuel Micu. 11 l, Gheorghe Sincai. 15 l, Michael the Brave. 31 l, Gheorghe Lazar. 35 l, Avram Jancu. 41 l, Simeon Barnutiu. 55 l, Three Heroes. 61 l, Petru Maior.

1945   Inscribed "1944"   Perf. 14
558	A188	25b rose red	.60	.70
559	A189	50b orange	.40	.70
560	A189	4.50 l brown	.40	.70
561	A188	11 l lt ultra	.40	.70
562	A188	15 l Prus grn	.40	.70
563	A189	31 l dl vio	.40	.70
564	A189	35 l bl blk	.40	.70
565	A188	41 l olive gray	1.10	.70
566	A189	55 l red brown	.40	.70
567	A189	61 l deep magenta	.40	.70
		Nos. 558-567,B251 (11)	5.40	7.75

Romania's liberation.

A198   A199

King Michael
A200   A201

1945   **Photo.**
568	A198	50b gray blue	.25	.25
569	A199	1 l dl brn	.25	.25
570	A199	2 l violet	.25	.25
571	A198	2 l sepia	.25	.25
572	A199	4 l yel grn	.25	.25
573	A200	5 l dp mag	.25	.25
574	A198	10 l blue	.25	.25
575	A198	15 l magenta	.25	.25
576	A199	20 l dl blue	.25	.25
577	A200	25 l red org	.25	.25
578	A200	35 l brown	.25	.25
579	A200	40 l car rose	.25	.25
580	A199	50 l pale ultra	.25	.25
581	A200	55 l red	.25	.25
582	A200	75 l Prus grn	.25	.25
583	A201	80 l orange	.25	.25
584	A201	100 l dp red brn	.25	.25
585	A201	160 l yel grn	.25	.25
586	A201	200 l dk ol grn	.25	.25
587	A201	400 l dl vio	.25	.25
		Nos. 568-587 (20)	5.00	5.00

Nos. 571, 573, 580, 581, 585 and 587 are printed on toned paper, Nos. 576, 577, 583, 584 and 586 on both toned and white papers, others on white paper only.
See Nos. 610-624, 651-660.

Mail
Carrier
A202

Telegraph
Operator
A203

Lineman
A204

Post
Office,
Bucharest
A205

1945, July 20   Wmk. 276   Perf. 13
588	A202	100 l dk brn	1.00	1.00
589	A202	100 l gray olive	1.00	1.00
590	A203	150 l brown	1.65	1.65
591	A203	150 l brt rose	1.65	1.65
592	A204	250 l lt gray ol	2.00	2.00
593	A204	250 l blue	2.00	2.00
594	A205	500 l dp mag	14.00	14.00
		Nos. 588-594 (7)	23.30	23.30

Issued in sheets of 4. Value, set of 7 sheets $150.

I. Ionescu, G. Titeica, A. O.
Idachimescu and V. Cristescu — A207

Allegory
of
Learning
A208

1945, Sept. 5   Perf. 13½
596	A207	2 l sepia	.25	.25
597	A208	80 l bl blk	.55	.55

50th anniversary of "Gazeta Matematica," mathematics journal.

Cernavoda Bridge, 50th
Anniv. — A209

1945, Sept. 26   Perf. 14
598	A209	80 l bl blk	.40	.25

Blacksmith and
Plowman — A210

1946, Mar. 6
599	A210	80 l blue	.50	.25
		Nos. 599,B326-B329 (5)	2.10	3.25

Agrarian reform law of Mar. 23, 1945.
See No. CB4.

Atheneum,   Numeral in
Bucharest   Wreath
A211   A212

Georges
Enescu — A213

Wmk. 276

1946, Apr. 26   Photo.   Perf. 13½
600	A211	10 l dk bl	.25	.25
601	A212	20 l red brn	.25	.25
602	A212	55 l peacock bl	.25	.25
603	A213	80 l purple	.40	.25
a.		Tête bêche pair	.80	.80
604	A212	160 l red org	.25	.25
		Nos. 600-604,B330-B331 (7)	3.10	4.50

Philharmonic Society, 25th anniv.

Mechanic — A214

Labor Day: No. 606, Laborer. No. 607, Sower. No. 608, Reaper. 200 l, Students.

1946, May 1   Perf. 13½x13
605	A214	10 l Prus grn	.75	.75
606	A214	10 l dk car rose	.25	.25
607	A214	20 l dl bl	.75	.75
608	A214	20 l dk red brn	.25	.25
609	A214	200 l brt red	.40	.40
		Nos. 605-609 (5)	2.40	2.40

Michael Types of 1945

1946   Wmk. 276   Photo.   Perf. 14
Toned Paper
610	A198	10 l brt red brn	.25	.25
611	A198	20 l vio brn	.25	.25
612	A201	80 l blue	.25	.25
613	A198	137 l yel grn	.25	.25
614	A201	160 l chalky bl	.25	.25
615	A201	200 l red org	.25	.25
616	A201	300 l sapphire	.25	.25
617	A201	360 l sepia	.25	.25
618	A199	400 l red org	.25	.25
619	A201	480 l brn red	.25	.25
620	A201	600 l dk ol grn	.25	.25
621	A201	1000 l Prus grn	.25	.25
622	A198	1500 l Prus grn	.25	.25
623	A201	2400 l magenta	.25	.25
624	A201	3700 l dull bl	.25	.25
		Nos. 610-624 (15)	3.75	3.75

Demetrius
Cantemir — A219

Designs: 100 l, "Cultural Ties." 300 l, "Economic Ties."

1946, Oct. 20   Perf. 13½
625	A219	80 l dk brn	.40	.40
626	A219	100 l dp bl	.40	.40
627	A219	300 l bl blk	.40	.40
		Nos. 625-627,B338 (4)	1.90	2.45

Romania-Soviet friendship. See No. B339.

Soccer — A222

Designs: 20 l, Diving. 50 l, Running. 80 l, Mountain climbing.

1946, Sept. 1   Perf. 11½, Imperf.
628	A222	10 l dp blue	.40	.40
629	A222	20 l brt red	.40	.40
630	A222	50 l dp violet	.40	.40
631	A222	80 l chocolate	.40	.40
		Nos. 628-631,B340,C26,CB6 (7)	4.10	4.60

Issued in sheets of 16.

Weaving — A226

Wmk. 276

1946, Nov. 20   Photo.   Perf. 14
636	A226	80 l dk ol brn	.30	.30
		Nos. 636,B342-B345 (5)	1.70	3.30

Democratic Women's Org. of Romania. See No. CB7.

Child Receiving
Bread — A227

Transporting Relief Supplies — A228

1947, Jan. 15   Perf. 13½x14, 14x13½
637	A227	300 l dk ol brn	.40	.40
638	A228	600 l magenta	.40	.40
		Nos. 637-638,B346-B347 (4)	1.40	2.00

Social relief fund. See #B348.

CGM Congress
Emblem — A229

1947, Feb. 10   Perf. 13½
639	A229	200 l blue	.55	.55
640	A229	300 l orange	.55	.55
a.		Pair, #639-640	1.10	1.10
b.		Pair, #640-641	1.25	1.25
641	A229	600 l crimson	.70	.70
		Nos. 639-641 (3)	1.80	1.80

Congress of the United Labor Unions ("CGM").
Printed in sheets of 18 comprising 3 pairs of each denomination. Sheet yields 3 each of Nos. 640a and 640b.

Peace in
Chariot
A230

Peace — A231

Flags of US,
Russia, GB &
Romania — A232

Dove of
Peace — A233

1947, Feb. 25　Perf. 14x13½, 13½x14
642 A230　　300 l dl vio　　　.50　.50
643 A231　　600 l dk org brn　.50　.50
644 A232　3000 l blue　　　　.50　.50
645 A233　7200 l sage grn　　.50　.50
　　Nos. 642-645 (4)　　　2.00 2.00
Signing of the peace treaty of Feb. 10, 1947.

King
Michael — A234

1947　Size: 25x30mm　Perf. 13½
646 A234　3000 l blue　　　　.25　.25
647 A234　7200 l dl vio　　　　.25　.25
648 A234　15,000 l brt bl　　　.40　.25
649 A234　21,000 l magenta　.40　.25
650 A234　36,000 l violet　　　.75　.60
　　Nos. 646-650 (5)　　　2.05 1.60
　　See Nos. 661-664.

Michael Types of 1945
1947　Wmk. 276　Photo.　Perf. 14
651 A199　　10 l red brn　　　.25　.25
652 A200　　20 l magenta　　.25　.25
653 A198　　80 l blue　　　　.25　.25
654 A199　　200 l brt red　　　.25　.25
655 A200　　500 l magenta　　.25　.25
656 A200　　860 l vio brn　　　.25　.25
657 A199　2500 l ultra　　　　.25　.25
658 A198　5000 l sl gray　　　.25　.25
659 A198　8000 l Prus grn　　.75　.25
660 A201　10,000 l dk brn　　1.00　.25

Type of 1947
Size: 18x21½mm
661 A234　1000 l gray bl　　　.25　.25
662 A234　5500 l yel grn　　　.25　.25
663 A234　20,000 l ol brn　　　.55　.30
664 A234　50,000 l red org　　1.00　.45
　　Nos. 651-664 (14)　　　5.80 3.75
　　For surcharge see No. B368.

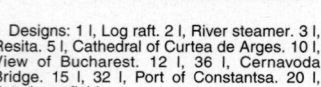

Harvesting
Wheat
A235

Designs: 1 l, Log raft. 2 l, River steamer. 3 l,
Resita. 5 l, Cathedral of Curtea de Arges. 10 l,
View of Bucharest. 12 l, 36 l, Cernavoda
Bridge. 15 l, 32 l, Port of Constantsa. 20 l,
Petroleum field.

1947, Aug. 15　　　Perf. 14½x14
666 A235　50b red org　　　.25　.25
667 A235　　1 l red brn　　.25　.25
668 A235　　2 l bl gray　　.25　.25
669 A235　　3 l rose crim　.50　.25
670 A235　　5 l brt ultra　　.50　.25
671 A235　10 l brt blue　　.65　.30
672 A235　12 l violet　　　.85　.35
673 A235　15 l dp ultra　1.50　.35
674 A235　20 l dk brown　2.50　.50
675 A235　32 l violet brn　5.75 2.50
676 A235　36 l dk car rose　6.00 2.50
　　Nos. 666-676 (11)　19.00 7.75
　For overprints & surcharge see #684-694,
B369.

Beehive, Savings
Emblem — A236

1947, Oct. 31　　　Perf. 13½
677 A236 12 l dk car rose　　.55　.35
World Savings Day, Oct. 31, 1947.

People's Republic

Map,
Workers
and
Children
A237

1948, Jan. 25　　　Perf. 14½x14
678 A237 12 l brt ultra　　1.00　.30
1948 census. For surcharge see #819A.

Government Printing Plant and
Press — A238

1948　　　　　　　Perf. 14½x14
679 A238　　6 l magenta　　2.00 1.10
680 A238　7.50 l dk Prus grn　1.10　.25
　b.　Tête bêche pair　　3.25 3.25
75th anniversary of Stamp Division of
Romanian State Printing Works.
　Issued: No. 680, Feb. 12; No. 679, May 20.

Romanian
and
Bulgarian
Peasants
Shaking
Hands
A239

1948, Mar. 25　　　Wmk. 276
680A A239 32 l red brown　　1.50　.75
Romanian-Bulgarian friendship.
For surcharge see No. 696.

Allegory of the
People's
Republic — A240

1948, Apr. 8　Photo.　Perf. 14x14½
681 A240　　1 l car rose　　.55　.40
682 A240　　2 l dl org　　　.80　.55
683 A240　12 l deep blue　2.40　.90
　　Nos. 681-683 (3)　　3.75 1.85
New constitution.
For surcharge see No. 820.

**Nos. 666 to 676 Overprinted in
Black**

1948, Mar.　　　　Perf. 14½x14
684 A235　50b red org　　　.30　.25
685 A235　　1 l red brn　　.30　.25
686 A235　　2 l bl gray　　.60　.25
687 A235　　3 l rose crim　.60　.25
688 A235　　5 l brt ultra　1.25　.30
689 A235　10 l brt bl　　　1.50　.30
690 A235　12 l violet　　　1.75　.35
691 A235　15 l dp ultra　1.75　.40
692 A235　20 l dk brn　　2.50　.55
693 A235　32 l vio brn　　7.50 2.50
694 A235　36 l dk car rose　7.50 2.50
　　Nos. 684-694 (11)　25.55 7.90

Romanian Newspapers — A241

1948, Sept. 12
695 A241 10 l red brn　　　.40　.25
　　Nos. 695,B396-B398 (4)　3.70 3.55
Week of the Democratic Press, Sept. 12-19.

**No. 680A Surcharged with New
Value in Black**
1948, Aug. 17
696 A239 31 l on 32 l red brn　1.00　.35

Monument to Soviet
Soldier — A242

1948, Oct. 29　Photo.　Perf. 14x14½
697 A242 10 l dk red　　　.80　.80
　　Nos. 697,B399-B400 (3)　6.30 8.30
Sheets of 50 stamps and 50 labels.

Proclamation of
Islaz — A243

1948, June 1　　　Perf. 14½x14
698 A243 11 l car rose　　.85　.25
　　Nos. 698,B409-B412 (5)　4.30 5.05
Centenary of Revolution of 1848.
For surcharge see No. 820A.

Arms of Romanian
People's
Republic — A243a

1948, July 8　　　Wmk. 276
698A A243a 50b red ("Lei 0.50")　.30　.25
698B A243a　1 l red brn　　.30　.25
698C A243a　2 l dk grn　　.30　.25
698D A243a　3 l grnsh blk　.55　.25
698E A243a　4 l chocolate　.55　.25
698F A243a　5 l ultra　　　.70　.25
698G A243a 10 l dp bl　　　.85　.25

"Bani" instead of "Lei"
698H A243a 50b red ("Bani
　　　　　0.50")　　　.55　.55
　　Nos. 698A-698H (8)　4.10 2.30
　　See Nos. 712-717.

Nicolae Balcescu (1819-1852),
Writer — A244

1948, Dec. 20　　　Wmk. 289
699 A244 20 l scarlet　　1.00　.35

Release from
Bondage — A245

1948, Dec. 30　　　Perf. 13½
700 A245 5 l brt rose　　.55　.25
First anniversary of the Republic.

Lenin, 25th Death
Anniv. — A246

1949, Jan. 21
701 A246 20 l black　　　.70　.25
Exists imperf. Value, unused or used, $1.25.

Folk
Dance — A247

1949, Jan. 24　　　Perf. 13½
702 A247 10 l dp bl　　　.55　.30
90th anniv. of the union of the Danubian
Principalities.

Ion C. Frimu and Revolutionary
Scene — A248

1949, Mar. 22　　　Perf. 14½x14
703 A248 20 l red　　　　.55　.25
Exists imperf. Value, unused or used, $1.25.

Aleksander S.
Pushkin, 150th Birth
Anniv. — A249

1949, May 20   *Perf. 14x14½*
704 A249 11 l car rose   1.25 .75
705 A249 30 l Prus grn   1.60 .75
   For surcharges see Nos. 821-822.

Globe and Post
Horn — A250

Evolution of Mail
Transportation — A251

    Perf. 13½, 14½x14
1949, June 30   **Photo.**   **Wmk. 289**
706 A250 20 l org brn   2.25 2.25
707 A251 30 l brt bl   4.75 1.25
   UPU, 75th anniv.
   For surcharges see Nos. C43-C44.

Russian Army Entering Bucharest,
August, 1944 — A252

1949, Aug. 23   *Perf. 14½x14*
708 A252 50 l choc, bl grn   .95 .60
   5th anniv. of the liberation of Romania by
the Soviet army, Aug. 1944.
   Exists imperf. Value, unused or used, $2.

"Long Live Romanian-Soviet
Amity" — A253

1949, Nov. 1   *Perf. 13½x14½*
709 A253 20 l dp red   .65 .35
   Natl. week of Romanian-Soviet friendship
celebration, 11/1-7/49. Exists imperf. Value,
unused or used, $1.50.

Symbols of
Transportation
A254

1949, Dec. 10   *Perf. 13½*
710 A254 11 l blue   1.50 1.50
711 A254 20 l crimson   1.50 1.50
   Intl. Conference of Transportation Unions,
Dec. 10, 1949.
   Alternate vertical rows of stamps and labels
in sheet. Exist imperf. Value for set, unused or
used, $3.75.

Arms Type of 1948

1949-50   **Wmk. 289**   *Perf. 14x13½*
712 A243a 50b red ("Lei 0.50")   .40 .25
713 A243a 1 l red brn   .40 .25
714 A243a 2 l dk grn   .40 .25
714A A243a 3 l grnsh blk   .65 .25
715 A243a 5 l ultra   .50 .25

716 A243a 5 l rose vio ('50)   .80 .25
717 A243a 10 l dp blue   1.00 .25
   Nos. 712-717 (7)   4.15 1.75

Joseph V.
Stalin — A256

1949, Dec. 21   *Perf. 13½*
718 A256 31 l olive black   .65 .25
   Stalin's 70th birthday. Exists imperf. Value,
unused or used, $1.60.

Mihail
Eminescu — A257

Poem:
"Life" — A258

   No. 721, "Third Letter." No. 722, "Angel and
Demon." No. 723, "Emperor and Proletariat."

1950, Jan. 15   **Photo.**   **Wmk. 289**
719 A257 11 l blue   1.00 .30
720 A258 11 l purple   1.75 .65
721 A258 11 l dk grn   1.00 .30
722 A258 11 l red brn   1.00 .30
723 A258 11 l rose pink   1.00 .30
   Nos. 719-723 (5)   5.75 1.85
   Birth cent. of Mihail Eminescu, poet.
   For surcharges see Nos. 823-827.

Fair at
Dragaica
A259

Ion Andreescu (Self-
portrait)
A260

Village
Well
A261

1950, Mar. 25   *Perf. 14½x14, 14x14½*
724 A259 5 l dk gray grn   1.00 .60
725 A260 11 l ultra   1.60 .60
726 A261 20 l brown   1.75 1.00
   Nos. 724-726 (3)   4.35 2.20
   Birth cent. of Ion Andreescu, painter. No.
725 also exists imperf. Value, unused or used,
$3.50.
   For surcharges see Nos. 827A-827B.

Graph and
Factories
A262

   Design: 31 l, Tractor and Oil Derricks.

   Inscribed: "Planul de Stat 1950."

    Perf. 14½x14
1950, Apr. 23   **Wmk. 289**
727 A262 11 l red   .60 .25
728 A262 31 l violet   1.10 .50
   1950 plan for increased industrial production. No. 727 exists imperf. Value, unused or
used, $2.
   For surcharges see Nos. 827C-827D.

Young Man Holding
Flag — A263

1950, May 1   *Perf. 14x14½*
729 A263 31 l orange red   .65 .25
   Labor Day, May 1.
   Exists imperf. Value, unused or used, $1.25.
   For surcharge see No. 827E.

    Canceled to Order
   Canceled sets of new issues have
long been sold by the government.
Values in the second ("used") column
are for these canceled-to-order
stamps. Postally used stamps are
worth more.

Arms of
Republic — A264

1950   **Photo.**   *Perf. 12½*
730 A264 50b black   .25 .25
731 A264 1 l red orange   .25 .25
732 A264 2 l ol gray   .25 .25
733 A264 3 l violet   .25 .25
734 A264 4 l rose lilac   .25 .25
735 A264 5 l red brn   .25 .25
736 A264 6 l dp grn   .25 .25
737 A264 7 l vio brn   .25 .25
738 A264 7.50 l blue   .40 .25
739 A264 10 l dk brn   .80 .25
740 A264 11 l rose car   .80 .25
741 A264 15 l dp bl   .40 .25
742 A264 20 l Prus grn   .40 .25
743 A264 31 l dl grn   .80 .25
744 A264 36 l dk org brn   1.25 .30
   Nos. 730-744 (15)   6.85 3.80
   See Nos. 947-961 which have similar
design with white denomination figures.
   For overprint & surcharges see Nos. 758,
828-841.

Bugler
and
Drummer
A265

   Designs: 11 l, Three school children. 31 l,
Drummer, flag-bearer and bugler.

1950, May 25   *Perf. 14½x14*
745 A265 8 l blue   1.40 .60
746 A265 11 l rose vio   1.75 1.00
747 A265 31 l org ver   3.00 2.00
   Nos. 745-747 (3)   6.15 3.60
   Young Pioneers, 1st anniv.
   For surcharges see Nos. 841A-841C.

Factory
Worker — A266

1950, July 20   **Photo.**   *Perf. 14x14½*
748 A266 11 l red brn   .50 .35
749 A266 11 l red   .85 .35
750 A266 11 l blue   .50 .35
751 A266 11 l blk brn   .85 .35
   Nos. 748-751 (4)   2.70 1.40
   Nationalization of industry, 2nd anniv.

Aurel Vlaicu and
his First
Plane — A267

1950, July 22   **Wmk. 289**   *Perf. 12½*
752 A267 3 l dk grn   .40 .25
753 A267 6 l dk bl   .60 .25
754 A267 8 l ultra   .75 .35
   Nos. 752-754 (3)   1.75 .85
   Aurel Vlaicu (1882-1913), pioneer of
Romanian aviation.
   For surcharges see Nos. 842-844.

Mother and
Child — A268   Lathe and
       Operator — A269

1950, Sept. 9   *Perf. 13½*
755 A268 11 l rose red   .40 .25
756 A269 20 l dk ol brn   .45 .25
   Congress of the Committees for the Struggle for Peace.
   For surcharge see No. 844A.

Statue of Soviet
Soldier — A270

1950, Oct. 6   *Perf. 14x14½*
757 A270 30 l red brn   .85 .35
   Celebration of Romanian-Soviet friendship,
Oct. 7-Nov. 7, 1950.

No. 741 Overprinted
in Carmine

1950, Oct. 6   *Perf. 12½*
758 A264 15 l deep blue   1.10 .35
   Romanian-Hungarian friendship.

"Agriculture," "Manufacturing" and
Sports Badge — A271

5 l, Student workers & badge. 11 l, Track
team & badge. 31 l, Calisthenics & badge.

1950, Oct. 30 *Perf. 14½x14*
759	A271	3 l rose car	1.40	1.40
760	A271	5 l red brn	1.00	1.00
761	A271	5 l brt bl	1.00	1.00
762	A271	11 l green	1.00	1.00
763	A271	31 l brn ol	2.50	2.50
	Nos. 759-763 (5)		6.90	6.90

For surcharge see No. 845.

A272

1950, Nov. 2 *Perf. 13½*
764	A272	11 l blue	.50	.35
765	A272	11 l red org	.50	.35

3rd Soviet-Romanian Friendship Congress.

"Industry" — A273

"Agriculture" — A274

Perf. 14x14½, 14½x14
1951, Feb. 9 **Photo.** **Wmk. 289**
766	A273	11 l red brn	.40	.25
767	A274	31 l deep bl	.75	.35

Industry and Agriculture Exposition. Exist
imperf. Value for set, unused or used, $2.
For surcharge see No. 846.

Ski
Jump — A275

Ski Descent
A276

5 l, Skating. 20 l, Hockey. 31 l, Bobsledding.

1951, Jan. 28 *Perf. 13½*
768	A275	4 l blk brn	1.50	1.50
769	A275	5 l vermilion	1.25	1.25
770	A276	11 l dp bl	1.25	1.25
771	A275	20 l org brn	1.25	1.25
772	A275	31 l dk gray grn	3.50	3.25
	Nos. 768-772 (5)		8.75	8.50

9th World University Winter Games.
For surcharges see Nos. 847-848.

Medal for
Work — A277

Orders: 4 l, Star of the Republic, Classes III,
IV & V. 11 l, Work. 35 l, As 4 l, Classes I & II.

1951, May 1 *Perf. 13½*
773	A277	2 l ol gray	.25	.25
774	A277	4 l blue	.35	.25
775	A277	11 l crimson	.50	.25
776	A277	35 l org brn	.75	.40
	Nos. 773-776 (4)		1.85	1.15

Labor Day. Exist imperf. Value for set,
unused or used, $2.50.
For surcharges see Nos. 849-852.

Camp of
Young
Pioneers
A278

Pioneers Greeting
Stalin — A279

Admitting
New
Pioneers
A280

1951, May 8 *Perf. 14x14½, 14½x14*
777	A278	1 l gray grn	1.00	.45
778	A279	11 l blue	1.00	.45
779	A280	35 l red	1.50	.70
	Nos. 777-779 (3)		3.50	1.60

Romanian Young Pioneers Organization.
For surcharge see No. 853.

Woman Orator and
Flags — A281

1951, Mar. 8 *Perf. 14x14½*
780	A281	11 l org brn	.50	.25

Woman's Day, March 8. Exists imperf.
Value, unused or used, 80c.

Ion Negulici — A282

1951, June 20 *Perf. 14x14½*
781	A282	35 l rose red	3.50	2.10

Death cent. of Ion Negulici, painter.

Bicyclists
A283

1951, July 9 *Perf. 14½x14*
782	A283	11 l chnt brn	2.10	.80
a.	Tête bêche pair		7.00	7.00

The 1951 Bicycle Tour of Romania.

Festival
Badge — A284

Boy and Girl with
Flag — A285

Youths Encircling
Globe — A286

1951, Aug. 1 *Perf. 13½*
783	A284	1 l scarlet	.80	.40
784	A285	5 l deep blue	1.50	.40
785	A286	11 l deep plum	2.25	.80
	Nos. 783-785 (3)		4.55	1.60

3rd World Youth Festival, Berlin.

Filimon
Sarbu — A287

1951, July 23 *Perf. 14x14½*
786	A287	11 l dk brn	.70	.25

10th death anniv. of Filimon Sarbu, patriot.

"Romania Raising
the Masses" — A288

"Revolutionary Romania" — A289

1951, July 23 *Perf. 14x14½, 14½x14*
787	A288	11 l yel brn	2.00	.75
788	A288	11 l rose vio	2.00	.75
789	A289	11 l dk grn	2.00	.75
790	A289	11 l org red	2.00	.75
	Nos. 787-790 (4)		8.00	3.00

Death cent. of C. D. Rosenthal, painter.

Scanteia
Building
A290

1951, Aug. 16 *Perf. 14½x14*
791	A290	11 l blue	.75	.35

20th anniv. of the newspaper Scanteia.

Miner in Dress
Uniform — A291

Design: 11 l, Miner in work clothes.

1951, Aug. 12 *Perf. 14x14½*
792	A291	5 l blue	.60	.35
793	A291	11 l plum	.70	.25

Miner's Day. For surcharge see No. 854.

Order for National
Defense — A293

1951, Aug. 12 *Perf. 14x14½*
794	A293	10 l crimson	.55	.25

For surcharge see No. 855.

Choir — A294

Music Week
Emblem — A295

Design: No. 796, Orchestra and dancers.

Wmk. 358
1951, Sept. 22 **Photo.** *Perf. 13½*
795	A294	11 l blue	.50	.35
796	A294	11 l red brown	.75	.40
797	A295	11 l purple	.50	.35
	Nos. 795-797 (3)		1.75	1.10

Music Week, Sept. 22-30, 1951.

Soldier — A296

1951, Oct. 2
798	A296	11 l blue	.55	.25

Army Day, Oct. 2, 1951.

Oil Field — A297

Designs: 2 l, Coal mining. 3 l, Romanian soldier. 4 l, Smelting ore. 5 l, Agricultural machinery. 6 l, Canal construction. 7 l, Agriculture. 8 l, Self-education. 11 l, Hydroelectric production. 35 l, Manufacturing.

1951-52

799	A297	1 l	black brn	.70 .25
800	A297	2 l	chocolate	.40 .25
801	A297	3 l	scarlet	.75 .45
802	A297	4 l	yel brn ('52)	.50 .25
803	A297	5 l	green	.50 .25
804	A297	6 l	brt bl ('52)	2.00 1.10
805	A297	7 l	emerald	1.10 .50
806	A297	8 l	brown ('52)	.90 .50
807	A297	11 l	blue	.90 .25
808	A297	35 l	purple	1.25 .75
		Nos. 799-808,C35-C36 (12)		15.75 10.05

1951-55 Five Year Plan.
2 l and 11 l exist with wmk. 289. Values same.
For surcharges see Nos. 860-869.

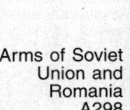

Arms of Soviet Union and Romania A298

1951, Oct. 7   Wmk. 358

809	A298	4 l	chestnut brn, cr	.40 .25
810	A298	35 l	orange red	.85 .45

Month of Romanian-Soviet friendship, Oct. 7-Nov. 7.
For surcharges see Nos. 870-871.

Pavel Tcacenco — A299

1951, Dec. 15   Perf. 14x14½

811	A299	10 l	ol brn & dk brn	.75 .40

Revolutionary, 26th death anniv.
For surcharge see No. 872.

Railroad Conductor — A300

1952, Mar. 24   Perf. 13½

812	A300	55b	dark brown	3.00 .40

Railroad Workers' Day, Feb. 16.

Ion L. Caragiale — A301

Announcing Caragiale Celebration — A302

Designs: No. 814, Book and painting "1907." No. 815, Bust and wreath.

Inscribed: ". . . . I. L. Caragiale."

1952, Apr. 1   Perf. 13½, 14½x14

813	A301	55b	chalky blue	1.50 .55
814	A302	55b	scarlet	1.50 .55
815	A302	55b	deep green	1.50 .55
816	A302	1 l	brown	4.00 .70
		Nos. 813-816 (4)		8.50 2.35

Birth cent. of Ion L. Caragiale, dramatist.
For surcharges see Nos. 817-819.

Types of 1952 Surcharged with New Value in Black or Carmine

1952-53

817	A302	20b on 11 l scar (as #814)		1.25 .65
818	A302	55b on 11 l dp grn (as #815) (C)		1.75 .80
819	A301	75b on 11 l chlky bl (C)		3.00 1.10

Various Issues Surcharged with New Values in Carmine or Black

On No. 678, Census

Perf. 14x13½

819A	A237	50b on 12 l ultra		3.25 2.00

On No. 683, New Constitution

Perf. 14

820	A240	50b on 12 l dp bl		4.00 1.25

On No. 698, Revolution

820A	A243	1.75 l on 11 l car rose (Bk)		18.00 5.00

On Nos. 704-705, Pushkin

1952   Wmk. 358

821	A249	10b on 11 l (Bk)		4.00 1.75
822	A249	10b on 30 l		4.00 1.75

On Nos. 719-723, Eminescu

Perf. 13½x13, 13x13½

823	A257	10b on 11 l blue		3.00 1.90
824	A258	10b on 11 l pur		3.00 1.90
825	A258	10b on 11 l dk grn		3.00 1.90
826	A258	10b on 11 l red brn (Bk)		3.00 1.90
827	A258	10b on 11 l rose pink (Bk)		3.00 1.90

On Nos. 724-725, Andreescu

Perf. 14

827A	A259	55b on 5 l dk gray grn		10.00 3.25
827B	A260	55b on 11 l ultra		10.00 3.25

On Nos. 727-728, Production Plan

Perf. 14½x14

827C	A262	20b on 11 l red (Bk)		4.00 1.25
827D	A262	20b on 31 l vio		4.00 1.25

On No. 729, Labor Day

Perf. 14

827E	A263	55b on 31 l (Bk)		5.00 3.25

On Nos. 730-739 and 741-744, National Arms

Perf. 12½

828	A264	3b on 1 l red (Bk)		2.50 1.10
829	A264	3b on 2 l ol gray (Bk)		2.50 1.10
830	A264	3b on 4 l rose lil (Bk)		2.50 1.10
831	A264	3b on 5 l red brn (Bk)		2.50 1.10
832	A264	3b on 7.50 l bl (Bk)		2.50 1.10
833	A264	3b on 10 l dk brn (Bk)		2.50 1.10
834	A264	55b on 50b blk brn		7.00 1.90
835	A264	55b on 3 l vio		7.00 1.90
836	A264	55b on 6 l dp grn		7.00 1.90
837	A264	55b on 7 l vio brn		7.00 1.90
838	A264	55b on 15 l dp bl		9.00 1.90
839	A264	55b on 20 l Prus grn		7.00 1.90
840	A264	55b on 31 l dl grn		7.00 1.90
841	A264	55b on 36 l dk org brn		9.00 1.90

On Nos. 745-747, Young Pioneers

Perf. 14

841A	A265	55b on 8 l		10.00 5.75
841B	A265	55b on 11 l		10.00 5.75
841C	A265	55b on 31 l (Bk)		10.00 5.75

On Nos. 752-754, Vlaicu

Perf. 12½

842	A267	10b on 3 l dk grn		3.00 1.10
843	A267	10b on 6 l dk bl		3.00 1.10
844	A267	10b on 8 l ultra		3.00 1.10

Original denomination canceled with an "X."

On No. 756, Peace Congress

Perf. 13½

844A	A269	20b on 20 l		4.00 1.90

On No. 759, Sports

Perf. 14½x14

845	A271	55b on 3 l (Bk)		24.00 15.00

On No. 767, Exposition

846	A274	55b on 31 l dp bl		6.00 3.75

On Nos. 771-772, Winter Games

Perf. 13½

847	A275	55b on 20 l (Bk)		35.00 15.00
848	A275	55b on 31 l		35.00 15.00

On Nos. 773-776, Labor Medals

849	A277	20b on 2 l		5.00 2.40
850	A277	20b on 5 l		5.00 2.40
851	A277	20b on 11 l (Bk)		5.00 2.40
852	A277	20b on 35 l (Bk)		5.00 2.40

On Nov. 779, Young Pioneers

Perf. 14x14½

853	A280	55b on 35 l (Bk)		10.00 4.75

On No. 792, Miners' Day

854	A291	55b on 5 l bl		10.00 2.75

On No. 794, Defense Order

855	A293	55b on 10 l (Bk)		10.00 2.75

On Nos. B409-B412, 1848 Revolution

1952   Wmk. 276   Perf. 13x13½

856	SP280	1.75 l on 2 l + 2 l (Bk)		18.00 4.75
857	SP281	1.75 l on 5 l + 5 l		18.00 4.75
858	SP282	1.75 l on 10 l + 10 l		18.00 4.75
859	SP280	1.75 l on 36 l + 18 l		18.00 4.75

On Nos. 799-808, 5-Year Plan

Wmk. 358   Perf. 13½

860	A297	35b on 1 l blk brn		2.10 .95
861	A297	35b on 2 l choc		2.50 .95
862	A297	35b on 3 l scar (Bk)		4.50 2.00
863	A297	35b on 4 l yel brn (Bk)		5.25 2.25
a.		Red surcharge		25.00 15.00
864	A297	35b on 5 l grn		4.25 4.00
865	A297	1 l on 6 l brt bl		6.25 5.00
866	A297	1 l on 7 l emer		6.25 2.25
867	A297	1 l on 8 l brn		6.25 5.00
868	A297	1 l on 11 l bl		6.25 2.75
869	A297	1 l on 35 l pur		8.00 2.25

Nos. 861, 868 exist with wmk. 289.

On Nos. 809-810, Romanian-Soviet Friendship

870	A298	10b on 4 l (Bk)		2.25 1.25
871	A298	10b on 35 l (Bk)		2.25 1.25

On No. 811, Tcacenco

Perf. 13½x14

872	A299	10b on 10 l		2.25 1.00

A302a

Perf. 13½x13

1952, Apr. 14   Photo.   Wmk. 358

873	A302a	1 l	Ivan P. Pavlov	.75 .40

Meeting of Romanian-Soviet doctors in Bucharest.

Labor Day — A303

1952, May 1

874	A303	55b	Hammer & sickle medal	2.75 .25

Medal for Motherhood A304

Medals: 55b, Maternal glory. 1.75 l, Mother-Heroine.

1952, Apr. 7   Perf. 13x13½

875	A304	20b	plum & sl gray	.90 .25
876	A304	55b	henna brn	2.00 .45
877	A304	1.75 l	rose red & brn buff	4.25 .55
		Nos. 875-877 (3)		7.15 1.25

International Women's Day.

Leonardo da Vinci — A305

1952, July 3

878	A305	55b	purple	5.00 .55

500th birth anniv. of Leonardo da Vinci.

Gogol and Scene from Taras Bulba A306

Nikolai V. Gogol — A307

1952, Apr. 1   Perf. 13½x14, 14x13½

879	A306	55b	deep blue	2.25 .35
880	A307	1.75 l	olive gray	2.75 .55

Gogol, Russian writer, death cent.

Pioneers Saluting — A308

Labor Day Paraders Returning A309

Design: 55b, Pioneers studying nature.

1952, May 21   *Perf. 14*
881 A308 20b brown   1.50 .25
882 A308 55b dp green   4.00 .25
883 A309 1.75 l blue   7.00 .55
   Nos. 881-883 (3)   12.50 1.05
Third anniversary of Romanian Pioneers.

Infantry Attack, Painting by Grigorescu A310

1.10 l, Romanian and Russian soldiers.

1952, June 7   *Perf. 13x13½*
884 A310 50b rose brown   1.10 .25
885 A310 1.10 l blue   1.75 .50
Independence Proclamation of 1877, 75th anniv.

Miner — A311

1952, Aug. 11   Wmk. 358
902 A311 20b rose red   2.00 .45
903 A311 55b purple   2.00 .40
Day of the Miner.

Book and Globe — A312

Chemistry Student A313

Students in Native Dress — A314

Design: 55b, Students playing soccer.

Perf. 13½x13, 13½x14, 13x13½
1952, Sept. 5
904 A312 10b deep blue   .50 .25
905 A313 20b orange   2.75 .35
906 A312 55b deep green   2.75 .45
907 A314 1.75 l rose red   5.50 1.10
   Nos. 904-907 (4)   11.50 2.15
Intl. Student Union Congr., Bucharest, Sept.

Soldier, Sailor and Aviator — A316

1952, Oct. 2   *Perf. 14*
909 A316 55b blue   1.75 .25
Armed Forces Day, Oct. 2, 1952.

"Russia" Leading Peace Crusade — A317

Allegory: Romanian-Soviet Friendship — A318

1952, Oct. 7   *Perf. 13½x13, 13x13½*
910 A317 55b vermilion   1.10 .25
911 A318 1.75 l black brown   3.00 .60
Month of Romanian-Soviet friendship, Oct.

Rowing on Lake Snagov — A319

1.75 l, Athletes marching with flags.

1952, Oct. 20
912 A319 20b deep blue   5.00 .50
913 A319 1.75 l rose red   8.00 1.10
Values are for stamps with poor perforations.

Nicolae Balcescu — A320

1952, Nov. 29
914 A320 55b gray   4.00 .50
915 A320 1.75 l lemon bister   8.00 1.25
Death cent. of Nicolae Balcescu, poet.

Arms of Republic — A321

1952, Dec. 6   Wmk. 358
916 A321 55b dull green   1.75 .35
5th anniversary of socialist constitution.

Arms and Industrial Symbols A322

1953, Jan. 8   *Perf. 12½x13½*
917 A322 55b blue, yellow & red   3.50 .50
5th anniv. of the proclamation of the People's Republic.

Matei Millo, Costache Caragiale and Aristita Romanescu A323

1953, Feb.   Photo.   *Perf. 13x13½*
918 A323 55b brt ultra   3.50 .35
National Theater of I. L. Caragiale, cent.

Iron Foundry Worker — A324

Worker — A325

Design: No. 921, Driving Tractor.

1953, Feb.   *Perf. 13½x13, 13x13½*
919 A324 55b slate green   1.25 .25
920 A325 55b black brown   1.25 .25
921 A325 55b orange   1.50 .55
   Nos. 919-921 (3)   4.00 1.05
3rd Congress of the Syndicate of the Romanian People's Republic.

"Strike at Grivita," Painted by G. Miclossy A326

1953, Feb. 16   *Perf. 13x13½*
922 A326 55b chestnut   2.75 .25
Oil industry strike, Feb. 16, 1933, 20th anniv.

Arms of Romanian People's Republic — A327

1953   *Perf. 12½*
923 A327 5b crimson   .80 .25
924 A327 55b purple   1.40 .25

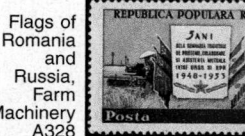

Flags of Romania and Russia, Farm Machinery A328

1953, Mar. 24   *Perf. 14*
925 A328 55b dk brn, *bl*   4.00 .50
5th anniv. of the signing of a treaty of friendship and mutual assistance between Russia and Romania.

Map and Medal — A329

1953, Mar. 24
926 A329 55b dk gray green   10.00 1.75
927 A329 55b chestnut   10.00 1.75
20th World Championship Table Tennis Matches, Budapest, 1953.

Ceramics — A330

Costume of Campulung (Muscel) — A330a

Folk Dance — A330b

Designs: 55b, Apuseni Mts. costume. 1 l, Rug.

Inscribed: "Arta Populara Romaneasca"

1953
928 A330 10b deep green   1.00 .25
929 A330a 20b red brown   1.75 .25
929A A330b 35b purple   3.00 .25
930 A330a 55b violet blue   4.00 .25
931 A330 1 l brt red violet   6.00 .35
   Nos. 928-931 (5)   15.75 1.35
Romanian Folk Arts.

Karl Marx — A331

1953, May 21   *Perf. 13½x13*
932 A331 1.55 l olive brown   3.50 .45
70th death anniv. of Karl Marx.

Children Planting Tree — A332

Physics Class A333

Design: 55b, Flying model planes.

1953, May 21   *Perf. 14*
933 A332 35b deep green   1.75 .25
934 A332 55b dull blue   2.10 .30
935 A333 1.75 l brown   4.00 .65
   Nos. 933-935 (3)   7.85 1.20

Women and Flags — A334

1953, June 18   *Perf. 13½x13*
936 A334 55b red brown   2.10 .30
3rd World Congress of Women, Copenhagen, 1953.

Discus Thrower — A335

Students Offering Teacher Flowers A336

Designs: 55b, Students reaching toward dove. 1.75 l, Dance in local costumes.

1953, Aug. 2   **Wmk. 358**   *Perf. 14*
937 A335   20b orange   1.00 .35
938 A335   55b deep blue   1.75 .75
939 A335   65b scarlet   2.25 1.10
940 A336 1.75 l red violet   6.50 1.75
    Nos. 937-940 (4)   11.50 3.95
4th World Youth Festival, Bucharest, 8/2-16.

Waterfall — A337

Wheat Field — A338

Design: 55b, Forester holding seedling.

1953, July 29   **Photo.**
941 A337 20b violet blue   1.25 .25
942 A338 38b dull green   3.00 1.00
943 A337 55b lt brown   3.50 .35
    Nos. 941-943 (3)   7.75 1.60
Month of the Forest.

Vladimir V. Mayakovsky, 60th Birth Anniv. — A339

1953, Aug. 22
944 A339 55b brown   2.50 .50

Miner Using Drill A340

1953, Sept. 19
945 A340 1.55 l slate black   4.00 .50
Miners' Day.

Arms of Republic — A342

Size: 20x24mm

1952-53   *Perf. 12½*
947 A342   3b deep orange   .60 .25
948 A342   5b crimson   .80 .25
949 A342   7b dk blue grn   .80 .25
950 A342   10b chocolate   1.00 .25
951 A342   20b deep blue   1.25 .25
952 A342   35b black brn   2.75 .25
953 A342   50b dk gray grn   3.25 .25
954 A342   55b purple   7.25 .25

Size: 24x29mm

955 A342 1.10 l dk brown   6.50 .30
956 A342 1.75 l violet   26.00 .50
957 A342   2 l olive black   6.75 .60
958 A342 2.35 l orange brn   8.00 .40
959 A342 2.55 l dp orange   10.00 .50
960 A342   3 l dk gray grn   10.00 .40
961 A342   5 l deep crimson   13.00 .75
   Nos. 947-961 (15)   97.95 5.45

Stamps of similar design with value figures in color are Nos. 730-744.

Postal Administration Building and Telephone Employees — A343

Designs: 55b, Postal Adm. Bldg. and Letter carrier. 1 l, Map and communications symbols. 1.55 l, Postal Adm. Bldg. and Telegraph employees.

1953, Oct. 20   **Wmk. 358**   *Perf. 14*
964 A343   20b dk red brn   .40 .25
965 A343   55b olive green   .75 .25
966 A343   1 l brt blue   1.75 .25
967 A343 1.55 l rose brown   3.25 .50
    Nos. 964-967 (4)   6.15 1.25
50th anniv. of the construction of the Postal Administration Building.

Liberation Medal — A344

1953, Oct. 20   *Perf. 14x13½*
968 A344 55b dark brown   1.75 .25
9th anniv. of the liberation of Romania.

Soldier and Flag — A345

1953, Oct. 2   *Perf. 13½*
969 A345 55b olive green   1.75 .25
Army Day, Oct. 2.

Girl with Model Plane A346

Civil Aviation: 20b, Parachute landing. 55b, Glider and pilot. 1.75 l, Plane in flight.

1953, Oct. 20   *Perf. 14*
970 A346   10b org & dk gray
           grn   3.00 .40
971 A346   20b org brn & dk ol
           grn   5.75 .25
972 A346   55b dk scar & rose
           lil   9.50 .60
973 A346 1.75 l dk rose vio &
           brn   12.50 .90
    Nos. 970-973 (4)   30.75 2.15

Workers and Flags — A347

1.55 l, Spasski Tower, lock on Volga-Don Canal.

1953, Nov. 25   *Perf. 13x13½*
974 A347   55b brown   1.10 .25
975 A347 1.55 l rose brown   1.60 .35
Month of Romanian-Soviet friendship, Oct. 7-Nov. 7.

Hemispheres and Clasped Hands — A348

Workers, Flags and Globe — A349

1953, Nov. 25   *Perf. 14*
976 A348   55b dark olive   .90 .25
977 A349 1.25 l crimson   1.75 .45
World Congress of Trade Unions.

Ciprian Porumbescu A350

1953, Dec. 16
978 A350 55b purple   8.50 .45
Ciprian Porumbescu (1853-1883), composer.

Harvesting Machine A351

Designs: 35b, Tractor in field. 2.55 l, Cattle.

Perf. 13x13½
1953, Dec. 16   **Wmk. 358**
979 A351   10b sepia   .30 .25
980 A351   35b dark green   .50 .25
981 A351 2.55 l orange brown   3.75 .80
    Nos. 979-981 (3)   4.55 1.30

Aurel Vlaicu — A352

1953, Dec. 26   *Perf. 14*
982 A352 50b violet blue   1.75 .25
Vlaicu, aviation pioneer, 40th death anniv.

Lenin — A353

1954, Jan. 21   *Perf. 13½*
983 A353 55b dk red brn, *buff*   2.00 .25
30th death anniv. of Lenin.

Red Deer — A354

Designs: 55b, Children planting trees. 1.75 l, Mountain scene.

Yellow Surface-colored Paper

1954, Apr. 1
984 A354   20b dark brown   4.00 .45
985 A354   55b violet   3.25 .45
986 A354 1.75 l dark blue   5.75 1.00
    Nos. 984-986 (3)   13.00 1.90
Month of the Forest.

Calimanesti Rest Home — A355

Workers' Rest Homes: 1.55 l, Sinaia. 2 l, Predeal. 2.35 l, Tusnad. 2.55 l, Govora.

1954, Apr. 15   *Perf. 14*
987 A355   5b blk brn, *cream*   .40 .25
988 A355 1.55 l dk vio brn, *bl*   2.00 .25
989 A355   2 l dk grn, *pink*   3.00 .30
990 A355 2.35 l ol blk, *grnsh*   3.00 .60
991 A355 2.55 l dk red brn, *cit*   4.00 .80
    Nos. 987-991 (5)   12.40 2.20

Octav Bancila — A356

1954, May 26   *Perf. 13½*
992 A356 55b red brn & dk grn   6.50 2.75
10th death anniv. of Octav Bancila, painter.

Globe, Child, Dove and Flowers A357

1954, June 1   **Perf. 13x13½**
993 A357 55b brown   1.75 .25
    Children's Day, June 1.

Girl Feeding Calf A358

Designs: 55b, Girl holding sheaf of grain. 1.75 l, Young students.

1954, July 5   **Perf. 14**
994 A358   20b grnsh blk   .45   .25
995 A358   55b blue   .80   .30
996 A358   1.75 l car rose   2.50   .50
    Nos. 994-996 (3)   3.75 1.05

Stephen the Great — A359

1954, July 10
997 A359 55b violet brown   2.75 .45
    Stephen of Moldavia (1433?-1504).

Loading Coal on Conveyor Belt — A360

1954, Aug. 8   **Perf. 13x13½**
998 A360 1.75 l black   3.00 .50
    Miners' Day.

Victor Babes — A361

1954, Aug. 15   **Perf. 14**
999 A361 55b rose red   2.25 .40
    Birth cent. of Victor Babes, serologist.

Applicant Requesting Loan — A362

Design: 55b, Mutual aid declaration.

1954, Aug. 20
1000 A362 20b deep violet   .40   .25
1001 A362 55b dk redsh brn   .80   .25
    5th anniv. of the Mutual Aid Organization.

Sailor and Naval Scene — A363

1954, Aug. 19   **Perf. 13x13½**
1002 A363 55b deep blue   1.75 .35
    Navy Day.

Monument to Soviet Soldier — A364

1954, Aug. 23   **Perf. 13½x13**
1003 A364 55b scarlet & purple   1.50 .30
    10th anniv. of Romania's liberation.

House of Culture A365

Academy of Music, Bucharest — A366

55b, Scanteia building. 1.55 l, Radio station.

1954, Sept. 6   **Perf. 14, 13½x13**
1004 A365   20b violet blue   .50   .25
1005 A366   38b violet   1.00   .30
1006 A365   55b violet brown   1.00   .30
1007 A366   1.55 l red brown   2.00   .30
    Nos. 1004-1007 (4)   4.50 1.15
    Publicizing Romania's cultural progress during the decade following liberation.

Aviator — A367

       Perf. 13½x13
1954, Sept. 13   **Wmk. 358**
1008 A367 55b blue   2.75 .40
    Aviation Day.

Chemical Plant and Oil Derricks A368

1954, Sept. 21   **Perf. 13x13½**
1009 A368 55b gray   2.50 .40
    Intl. Conference of chemical and petroleum workers, Bucharest, Sept. 1954.

Dragon Pillar, Peking — A369

1954, Oct. 7   **Perf. 14**
1010 A369 55b dk ol grn, cream   2.50 .40
    Week of Chinese Culture.

Dumitri T. Neculuta — A370

1954, Oct. 17   **Perf. 13½x13**
1011 A370 55b purple   2.00 .30
    Neculuta, poet, 50th death anniv.

ARLUS Emblem — A371

65b, Romanian & Russian women embracing.

1954, Oct. 22   **Perf. 14**
1012 A371 55b rose carmine   .70   .25
1013 A371 65b dark purple   1.00   .25
    Month of Romanian-Soviet Friendship.

Gheorghe Tattarescu — A372

1954, Oct. 24   **Perf. 13½x13**
1014 A372 55b cerise   2.50 .40
    Gheorghe Tattarescu (1820-1894), painter.

Barbu Iscovescu — A373

1954, Nov. 3   **Perf. 14**
1015 A373 1.75 l red brown   3.25 .60
    Death cent. of Barbu Iscovescu, painter.

Wild Boar — A374

Month of the Forest: 65b, Couple planting tree. 1.20 l, Logging.

      Perf. 13½x13
1955, Mar. 15   **Wmk. 358**
1016 A374   35b brown   1.40   .25
1017 A374   65b turq blue   1.60   .30
1018 A374   1.20 l dark red   3.50   .65
    Nos. 1016-1018 (3)   6.50 1.20

Globe and Clasped Hands — A375

1955, Apr. 5   **Photo.**
1019 A375 25b carmine rose   .70 .25
    Intl. Conference of Universal Trade Unions (Federation Syndicale Mondiale), Vienna, Apr. 1955.

Teletype — A376

1954, Dec. 31   **Perf. 13½x13**
1020 A376 50b lilac   1.75 .30
    Romanian telegraph system, cent.

Lenin — A377

Various Portraits of Lenin.

1955, Apr. 22   **Perf. 13½x14**
1021 A377   20b ol bis & brn   .65   .25
1022 A377   55b copper brown   1.25   .30
1023 A377   1 l vermilion   2.00   .35
    Nos. 1021-1023 (3)   3.90 .90
    85th anniversary of the birth of Lenin.

Chemist — A378

Designs: 5b, Steelworker. 10b, Aviator. 20b, Miner. 30b, Tractor driver. 35b, Pioneer. 40b, Girl student. 55b, Mason. 1 l, Sailor. 1.55 l, Spinner. 2.35 l, Soldier. 2.55 l, Electrician.

1955-56   **Wmk. 358**   **Perf. 14**
1024   A378   3b blue   .40   .25
1025   A378   5b violet   .25   .25
1026   A378   10b chocolate   .40   .25
1027   A378   20b lilac rose   .50   .25
1027A A378   30b vio bl ('56)   1.00   .25
1028   A378   35b grnsh blue   .75   .25
1028A A378   40b slate   1.60   .25
1029   A378   55b ol gray   1.50   .25
1030   A378   1 l purple   2.00   .25
1031   A378   1.55 l brown lake   3.00   .25
1032   A378   2.35 l bister brn   4.00   .75
1033   A378   2.55 l slate   6.25   .55
    Nos. 1024-1033 (12)   21.65 3.80

Volleyball — A379

Design: 1.75 l, Woman volleyball player.

1955, June 17
1034 A379 55b red vio, *pink*   5.00 .80
1035 A379 1.75 l lil rose, *cr*   11.00 .80
European Volleyball Championships, Bucharest.

Globe, Flag and Dove — A379a

1955, May 7 Photo. Perf. 13½
1035A A379a 55b ultra   1.75 .25
Peace Congress, Helsinki.

Girls with Dove and Flag — A380

1955, June 1 Perf. 13½x14
1036 A380 55b dark red brown 1.60 .25
International Children's Day, June 1.

Russian War Memorial, Berlin — A381

1955, May 9
1037 A381 55b deep blue 1.40 .25
Victory over Germany, 10th anniversary.

Theodor Aman Museum A382

Bucharest Museums: 55b, Lenin and Stalin Museum. 1.20 l, Popular Arts Museum. 1.75 l, Arts Museum. 2.55 l, Simu Museum.

1955, June 28 Perf. 13½, 14
1038 A382 20b rose lilac .45 .25
1039 A382 55b brown .70 .25
1040 A382 1.20 l gray black 1.60 .45
1041 A382 1.75 l slate green 2.50 .45
1042 A382 2.55 l rose violet 4.75 .60
   Nos. 1038-1042 (5) 10.00 2.00

#1038, 1040, 1042 measure 29x24½mm, #1039, 1041 32½x23mm.

Sharpshooter A383

1955, Sept. 11 Perf. 13½
1043 A383 1 l pale brn & sepia 6.00 .60
European Sharpshooting Championship meeting, Bucharest, Sept. 11-18.

Fire Truck, Farm and Factory — A384

1955, Sept. 13 Wmk. 358
1044 A384 55b carmine 2.50 .35
Firemen's Day, Sept. 13.

Bishop Dosoftei A385

Romanian writers: No. 1046, Stolnicul Constantin Cantacuzino. No. 1047, Dimitrie Cantemir. No. 1048, Enachita Vacarescu. No. 1049, Anton Pann.

1955, Sept. 9 Photo.
1045 A385 55b bluish gray 1.25 .30
1046 A385 55b dp vio 1.25 .30
1047 A385 55b ultra 1.25 .30
1048 A385 55b rose vio 1.25 .30
1049 A385 55b ol gray 1.25 .30
   Nos. 1045-1049 (5) 6.25 1.50

Mother and Child — A386

1955, July 7 Perf. 13½x14
1050 A386 55b ultra 1.75 .30
World Congress of Mothers, Lausanne.

Pioneers and Train Set — A387

Designs: 20b, Pioneers studying nature. 55b, Home of the Pioneers.

1955 Perf. 12½
1051 A387 10b brt ultra .70 .25
1052 A387 20b grnsh bl 1.40 .25
1053 A387 55b dp plum 3.00 .30
   Nos. 1051-1053 (3) 5.10 .80

Fifth anniversary of the Pioneer headquarters, Bucharest.

Rowing — A388

1955, Aug. 22 Perf. 13x13½
1054 A388 55b shown 8.00 .60
1055 A388 1 l Sculling 14.00 1.00
European Women's Rowing Championship on Lake Snagov, Aug. 4-7.

Insect Pest Control A389

20b, Orchard. 55b, Vineyard. 1 l, Truck garden.

1955, Oct. 15 Perf. 14x13½
1056 A389 10b brt grn 1.00 .25
1057 A389 20b lil rose 1.00 .25
1058 A389 55b vio bl 2.50 .30
1059 A389 1 l dp claret 3.50 .40
   Nos. 1056-1059 (4) 8.00 1.20

Quality products of Romanian agriculture. See Nos. 1068-1071.

I. V. Michurin — A390

1955, Oct. 25 Perf. 13½x14
1060 A390 55b Prus bl 1.75 .30
Birth cent. of I. V. Michurin, Russian agricultural scientist.

Congress Emblem A391

1955, Oct. 20 Perf. 13x13½
1061 A391 20b cream & ultra 1.00 .25
4th Soviet-Romanian Cong., Bucharest, Oct.

Globes and Olive Branches — A392

1 l, Three workers holding FSM banner.

1955, Oct. 1 Perf. 13½x13
1062 A392 55b dk ol grn .50 .25
1063 A392 1 l ultra .80 .25
Intl. Trade Union Org. (Federation Syndicale Mondiale), 10th anniv.

Sugar Beets — A393

20b, Cotton. 55b, Flax. 1.55l, Sunflower.

1955, Nov. 10 Perf. 13½
1064 A393 10b plum .75 .25
1065 A393 20b sl grn 1.00 .30
1066 A393 55b brt ultra 2.25 .70
1067 A393 1.55 l dk red brn 4.75 1.00
   Nos. 1064-1067 (4) 8.75 2.25

Sheep and Shepherd A394

Stock Farming: 10b, Pigs. 35b, Cattle. 55b, Horses.

1955, Dec. 10 Perf. 14x13½
1068 A394 5b yel grn & brn 1.00 .25
1069 A394 10b ol bis & dk vio 1.00 .25
1070 A394 35b brick red & brn 2.75 .50
1071 A394 55b dk ol bis & brn 3.25 .70
   Nos. 1068-1071 (4) 8.00 1.70

Animal husbandry.

Hans Christian Andersen — A395

Portraits: 55b, Adam Mickiewicz. 1 l, Friedrich von Schiller. 1.55 l, Baron de Montesquieu. 1.75 l, Walt Whitman. 2 l, Miguel de Cervantes.

1955, Dec. 17 Engr. Unwmk.
1072 A395 20b sl bl .50 .25
1073 A395 55b dp ultra 1.25 .25
1074 A395 1 l grnsh blk 2.25 .30
1075 A395 1.55 l vio brn 4.00 .55
1076 A395 1.75 l dl vio 4.25 .90
1077 A395 2 l rose lake 5.25 1.00
   Nos. 1072-1077 (6) 17.50 3.25

Anniversaries of famous writers.

Bank Book and Savings Bank A396

1955, Dec. 29 Photo. Wmk. 358
1078 A396 55b dp vio 2.75 .50
1079 A396 55b blue 8.25 4.50

Advantages of systematic saving in a bank.

Census Date — A397

Family Group — A397a

Inscribed: "Recensamintul Populatiei"

1956, Feb. 3 Perf. 13½
1080 A397 55b dp org .45 .25
1081 A397a 1.75 l emer & red brn 1.90 .35
 a. Center inverted 550.00 500.00
National Census, Feb. 21, 1956.

Ring-necked Pheasant A398

Great Bustard — A399

Animals: No. 1082, Hare. No. 1083, Bustard. 35b, Trout. 50b, Boar. No. 1087, Brown bear. 1 l, Lynx. 1.55 l, Red squirrel. 2 l, Chamois. 3.25 l, Pintail (duck). 4.25 l, Fallow deer.

1956		**Wmk. 358**		**Perf. 14**
1082	A398	20b grn & blk	2.50	.40
1083	A399	20b cit & gray blk	2.50	.40
1084	A398	35b brt bl & blk	2.50	.40
1085	A398	50b dp ultra & brn blk	2.50	.40
1086	A398	55b ol bis & ind	2.50	.40
1087	A398	55b dk bl grn & dk red brn	2.50	.40
1088	A398	1 l dk grn & red brn	4.75	.75
1089	A399	1.55 l lt ultra & red brn	4.75	.75
1090	A399	1.75 l sl grn & dk brn	4.75	.75
1091	A398	2 l ultra & brn blk	17.50	15.00
1092	A398	3.25 l lt grn & blk brn	17.50	15.00
1093	A399	4.25 l brn org & dk brn	17.50	15.00
		Nos. 1082-1093 (12)	81.75	49.65

Exist imperf. in changed colors. Value, set $50.

Street Fighting, Paris, 1871 — A400

1956, May 29   **Perf. 13½**
1094 A400 55b vermilion   1.75   .35
85th anniversary of Commune of Paris.

Globe and Child — A400a

1956, June 1   **Photo.**   **Perf. 13½x14**
1095 A400a 55b dp vio   2.50   .30
Intl. Children's Day. The sheet of 100 contains 10 labels, each with "Peace" printed on it in one of 10 languages. Value for stamp with label, unused or used, $20.

Oak Tree — A401

Design: 55b, Logging train in timberland.

1956, June 11   **Litho.**   **Wmk. 358**
1096 A401 20b dk bl grn, *pale grn*   1.40   .25
1097 A401 55b brn blk, *pale grn*   4.00   .50
Month of the Forest.

Romanian Academy A402

1956, June 19   **Photo.**   **Perf. 14**
1098 A402 55b dk grn & dl yel   1.75   .30
90th anniversary of Romanian Academy.

Red Cross Worker — A403

1956, June 7
1099 A403 55b olive & red   2.75   .40
Romanian Red Cross Congress, June 7-9.

Woman Speaker and Globe — A404

1956, June 14
1100 A404 55b dk bl grn   1.75   .30
Intl. Conference of Working Women, Budapest, June 14-17.

Traian Vuia and Planes — A405

1956, June 21   **Perf. 13x13½**
1101 A405 55b grnsh blk & brn   2.25   .30
1st flight by Vuia, near Paris, 50th anniv.

Ion Georgescu A406

1956, June 25   **Perf. 14x13½**
1102 A406 55b dk red brn & dk grn   2.75   .30
Ion Georgescu (1856-1898), sculptor.

White Cabbage Butterfly A407

June Bug — A408

Design: 55b, Colorado potato beetle.

1956, July 30   **Perf. 14x13½, 13½x14**
1103	A407	10b dp vio, pale yel & blk	3.75	.45
1104	A407	55b ol blk & yel	5.50	.50
1105	A408	1.75 l lt ol & dp plum	15.00	10.00
1106	A408	1.75 l gray ol & dk brn	12.00	1.25
		Nos. 1103-1106 (4)	36.25	12.20

Campaign against insect pests.

Girl Holding Sheaf of Wheat — A409

1956   **Perf. 13½x14**
1107 A409 55b "1949-1956"   2.75   .30
   a.   "1951-1956" (error)   12.00   12.00
7th anniversary of collective farming.

Dock Workers on Strike — A410

1956, Aug. 6
1108 A410 55b dk red brn   1.75   .30
Dock workers' strike at Galati, 50th anniv.

Title Page and Printer — A411

1956, Aug. 13   **Perf. 13½**
1109 A411 55b ultra   1.50   .25
25th anniv. of the publication of "Scanteia" (The Spark).

Maxim Gorki — A412

1956, Aug. 29   **Perf. 13½x14**
1110 A412 55b brown   1.75   .30
Maxim Gorki (1868-1936), Russian writer.

Theodor Aman — A413

1956, Sept. 24   **Engr.**
1111 A413 55b gray blk   2.75   .30
Aman, painter, 125th birth anniv.

Primrose and Snowdrops — A414

55b, Daffodil and violets. 1.75 l, Snapdragon and bellflowers. 3 l, Poppies and lilies of the valley.

Flowers in Natural Colors

1956, Sept. 26   **Photo.**   **Perf. 14x14½**
1112	A414	5b bl, yel & red	1.00	.40
1113	A414	55b blk, yel & red	3.00	.80
1114	A414	1.75 l ind, pink & yel	7.00	1.00
1115	A414	3 l bl grn, dk bl grn & yel	12.00	1.75
		Nos. 1112-1115 (4)	23.00	3.95

Olympic Rings and Torch — A415

Designs: 55b, Water polo. 1 l, Gymnastics. 1.55 l, Canoeing. 1.75 l, High jump.

1956, Oct. 25   **Perf. 13½x14**
1116	A415	20b vermilion	.55	.25
1117	A415	55b ultra	.80	.25
1118	A415	1 l lil rose	1.60	.30
1119	A415	1.55 l lt bl grn	2.10	.30
1120	A415	1.75 l dp pur	3.00	.40
		Nos. 1116-1120 (5)	8.05	1.50

16th Olympic Games, Melbourne, 11/22-12/8.

Janos Hunyadi — A416

1956, Oct.   **Wmk. 358**
1121 A416 55b dp vio   1.40   .30
Janos Hunyadi (1387-1456), national hero of Hungary. No. 1121 is found se-tenant with label showing Hunyadi Castle. Value for stamp with label, unused or used, $20.

Benjamin Franklin — A417

Portraits: 35b, Sesshu (Toyo Oda). 40b, G. B. Shaw. 50b, Ivan Franco. 55b, Pierre Curie. 1 l, Henrik Ibsen. 1.55 l, Fedor Dostoevski. 1.75 l, Heinrich Heine. 2.55 l, Mozart. 3.25 l, Rembrandt.

1956   **Unwmk.**
1122	A417	20b vio bl	.50	.25
1123	A417	35b rose lake	.60	.25
1124	A417	40b chocolate	.70	.25
1125	A417	50b brn blk	.90	.25
1126	A417	55b dk ol	.90	.25
1127	A417	1 l dk bl grn	1.75	.25
1128	A417	1.55 l dp pur	2.50	.25
1129	A417	1.75 l brt bl	3.25	.25
1130	A417	2.55 l rose vio	4.50	.40
1131	A417	3.25 l dk bl	4.75	.90
		Nos. 1122-1131 (10)	20.35	3.30

Great personalities of the world.

George Enescu as
a Boy — A418

Portrait: 1.75 l, George Enescu as an adult.

1956, Dec. 29   **Engr.**
1132 A418   55b ultramarine   1.25   .30
1133 A418   1.75 l deep claret   2.25   .40
   75th birth anniv. of George Enescu, musician and composer.

A419

Fighting Peasants, by Octav Bancila.

1957, Feb. 28   **Photo.**   **Wmk. 358**
1134 A419 55b dk bl gray   1.50   .30
   50th anniversary of Peasant Uprising.

A420

1957, Apr. 24   **Perf. 13½x14**
1147 A420 55b brown   1.25   .25
1148 A420 55b olive black   .75   .40
   Enthronement of Stephen the Great, Prince
of Moldavia, 500th anniv.

Dr. George Marinescu, Marinescu
Institute and Congress
Emblem — A421

Dr. N. Kretzulescu, Medical School,
Dr. C. Davila — A422

   35b, Dr. I. Cantacuzino & Cantacuzino Hospital. 55b, Dr. V. Babes & Babes Institute.

1957, May 5   **Perf. 14x13½**
1149 A421   20b dp grn   .45   .25
1150 A421   35b dp red brn   .60   .25
1151 A421   55b red lil   1.00   .30
1152 A422   1.75 l brt ultra & dk
         red   3.75   .70
    Nos. 1149-1152 (4)   5.80 1.50
   National Congress of Medical Science,
Bucharest, May 5-6.
   No. 1152 also for centenary of medical and
pharmaceutical teaching in Bucharest. It measures 66x23mm.

Dove and
Handle
Bars — A423

1957, May 29   **Perf. 13½x14**
1153 A423 20b shown   .40   .25
1154 A423 55b Cyclist   1.25   .30
   10th International Bicycle Peace Race.

Woman Watching
Gymnast — A424

Woman
Gymnast on
Bar — A425

1957, May 21   **Perf. 13½**
1155 A424   20b shown   .60   .25
1156 A425   35b shown   .90   .25
1157 A425   55b Vaulting horse   1.75   .30
1158 A424   1.75 l Acrobat   5.00   .75
    Nos. 1155-1158 (4)   8.25 1.55
   European Women's Gymnastic meet,
Bucharest.

Slide Rule, Caliper
& Atomic
Symbol — A426

            Wmk. 358
1957, May 29   **Photo.**   **Perf. 14**
1159 A426 55b blue   1.40   .25
1160 A426 55b brn red   1.60   .30
   2nd Congress of the Society of Engineers
and Technicians, Bucharest, May 29-31.

Rhododendron
Hirsutum — A427

   Carpathian Mountain Flowers: 10b, Daphne
Blagayana. 20b, Lilium Bulbiferum L. 35b,
Leontopodium Alpinum. 55b, Gentiana Acaulis
L. 1 l, Dianthus Callizonus. 1.55 l, Primula
Carpatica Griseb. 1.75 l, Anemone Montana
Hoppe.

Light Gray Background

1957, June 22   **Litho.**   **Unwmk.**
1161 A427   5b brt rose   .35   .25
1162 A427   10b dk grn   .45   .25
1163 A427   20b red org   .50   .25
1164 A427   35b olive   .90   .25
1165 A427   55b ultra   1.25   .25
1166 A427   1 l red   2.50   .25
1167 A427   1.55 l yellow   2.50   .30
1168 A427   1.75 l dk pur   4.25   .45
    Nos. 1161-1168 (8)   12.70 2.25
   Nos. 1161-1168 also come se-tenant with a
decorative label. Value, set $50.

"Oxcart" by
Grigorescu
A428

Nicolae
Grigorescu — A429

   Painting: 1.75 l, Battle scene.

1957, June 29   **Photo.**   **Wmk. 358**
1169 A428   20b dk bl grn   .60   .25
1170 A429   55b deep brown   1.50   .25
1171 A428   1.75 l chalky blue   5.50   .70
    Nos. 1169-1171 (3)   7.60 1.20
   Grigorescu, painter, 50th death anniv.

Warship
A430

1957, Aug. 3   **Perf. 13x13½**
1172 A430 1.75 l Prus bl   2.00   .30
   Navy Day.

Young
Couple — A431

Festival Emblem — A432

Folk Dance — A433

Design: 55b, Girl with flags on hoop.

**Perf. 14x14½, 14x14x12½ (A432),
13½x12½ (A433)**
1957, July 28
1173 A431   20b red lilac   .25   .25
1174 A431   55b emerald   .45   .25
1175 A432   1 l red orange   1.10   .30
1176 A433   1.75 l ultra   1.75   .25
    Nos. 1173-1176 (4)   3.55 1.05
   Moscow 1957 Youth Festival. No. 1173
measures 23x34mm, No. 1174 22x38mm.
   No. 1175 was printed in sheets of 50, alternating with 40 labels inscribed "Peace and
Friendship" in 20 languages. Value for stamp
with label, unused or used, $10.

Bugler — A434

1957, Aug. 30   **Wmk. 358**   **Perf. 14**
1177 A434 20b brt pur   2.50   .50
   80th anniv. of the Russo-Turkish war.

Girl Holding
Dove — A435

1957, Sept. 3   **Perf. 13½**
1178 A435 55b Prus grn & red   2.75   .50
   Honoring the Red Cross.

Battle Scene
A436

1957, Aug. 31
1179 A436 1.75 l brown   1.75   .30
   Battle of Marasesti, 40th anniv.

Jumper and
Dove — A437

   55b, Javelin thrower, bison. 1.75 l, Runner,
stag.

1957, Sept. 14   **Photo.**   **Perf. 13½**
1180 A437   20b brt bl & blk   .40   .25
1181 A437   55b yel & blk   1.25   .25
1182 A437   1.75 l brick red & blk   3.50   .50
    Nos. 1180-1182 (3)   5.15 1.00
   International Athletic Meet, Bucharest.

Statue of Ovid,
Constanta
A438

1957, Sept. 20   **Photo.**   **Wmk. 358**
1183 A438 1.75 l vio bl   2.75   .60
   2000th anniv. of the birth of the Roman poet
Publius Ovidius Naso.

Oil
Field — A439

Design: 55b, Horse pulling drill, 1857.

1957, Oct. 5
1184	A439	20b dl red brn	.45 .25
1185	A439	20b indigo	.45 .25
1186	A439	20b vio blk	1.10 .30
	Nos. 1184-1186 (3)		2.00 .80

Centenary of Romanian oil industry.

Congress Emblem A440

1957, Sept. 28
1187	A440	55b ultra	1.00 .25

4th Intl. Trade Union Cong., Leipzig, 10/4-15.

Young Couple, Lenin Banner — A441

35b, Lenin & Flags. 55b, Lenin statue.

1957, Nov. 6   Perf. 14x14½, 14½x14
1188	A441	10b crimson	.30 .25
1189	A441	35b plum, horiz.	.60 .25
1190	A441	55b brown	.90 .25
	Nos. 1188-1190 (3)		1.80 .75

Russian Revolution, 40th anniversary.

Endre Ady — A442

1957, Dec. 5   Perf. 14
1191	A442	55b ol brn	1.25 .25

Ady, Hungarian poet, 80th birth anniv.

Oath of Bobilna A443

Bobilna Monument — A444

1957, Nov. 30
1192	A443	50b deep plum	.35 .25
1193	A444	55b slate blue	.50 .25

520th anniversary of the insurrection of the peasants of Bobilna in 1437.

Black-winged Stilt — A445

Animals: 10b, Great white egret. 20b, White spoonbill. 50b, Sturgeon. 55b, Ermine, horiz. 1.30 l, White pelican, horiz.

Perf. 13½x14, 14x13½

1957, Dec. 27   Photo.   Wmk. 358
1194	A445	5b red brn & gray	.25 .25
1195	A445	10b emer & ocher	.25 .25
1196	A445	20b brt red & ocher	.35 .25
1197	A445	50b bl grn & ocher	.65 .25
1198	A445	55b dp cl & gray	1.00 .25
1199	A445	1.30 l pur & org	1.75 .30
	Nos. 1194-1199,C53-C54 (8)		14.00 3.80

Sputnik 2 and Laika A446

1957, Dec. 20   Perf. 14x13½
1200	A446	1.20 l bl & dk brn	5.00 .60
1201	A446	1.20 l grnsh bl & choc	5.00 .60

Dog Laika, "first space traveler."

Romanian Arms, Flags — A447

Designs: 55b, Arms, "Industry and Agriculture." 1.20 l, Arms, "Art, Science and Sport (soccer)."

1957, Dec. 30   Perf. 13½
1202	A447	25b ultra, red & ocher	.35 .25
1203	A447	55b dull yellow	.60 .25
1204	A447	1.20 l crimson rose	1.25 .30
	Nos. 1202-1204 (3)		2.20 .80

Proclamation of the Peoples' Republic, 10th anniv.

Flag and Wreath — A448

1958, Feb. 15   Unwmk.   Perf. 13½
1205	A448	1 l dk bl & red, *buff*	.90 .25
1206	A448	1 l brn & red, *buff*	.90 .25

Grivita Strike, 25th anniversary.

Television, Radio Antennas A449

Design: 1.75 l, Telegraph pole and wires.

1958, Mar. 21   Perf. 14x13½
1207	A449	55b brt vio	.50 .25
1208	A449	1.75 l dp mag	1.00 .30

Telecommunications Conference, Moscow, Dec. 3-17, 1957.

Nicolae Balcescu — A450

Romanian Writers: 10b, Ion Creanga. 35b, Alexandru Vlahuta. 55b, Mihail Eminescu.

1.75 l, Vasile Alecsandri. 2 l, Barbu S. Delavrancea.

1958   Wmk. 358   Perf. 14x14½
1209	A450	5b bluish blk	.35 .25
1210	A450	10b int blk	.35 .25
1211	A450	35b dk bl	.35 .25
1212	A450	55b dk red brn	.60 .25
1213	A450	1.75 l blk brn	1.25 .30
1214	A450	2 l dk sl grn	2.10 .35
	Nos. 1209-1214 (6)		5.00 1.65

See Nos. 1309-1314.

Fencer in Global Mask A451

1958, Apr. 5   Perf. 14½x14
1215	A451	1.75 l brt pink	1.75 .30

Youth Fencing World Championships, Bucharest.

Stadium and Health Symbol — A452

1958, Apr. 16   Perf. 14x14½
1216	A452	1.20 l lt grn & red	1.75 .30

25 years of sports medicine.

Globe and Dove — A453

1958, May 15   Photo.
1217	A453	55b brt bl	1.10 .25

4th Congress of the Intl. Democratic Women's Federation, June 1958.

Carl von Linné — A454

Portraits: 20b, Auguste Comte. 40b, William Blake. 55b, Mikhail I. Glinka. 1 l, Henry W. Longfellow. 1.75 l, Carlo Goldoni. 2 l, Jan A. Komensky.

Perf. 14x14½

1958, May 31   Unwmk.
1218	A454	10b Prus grn	.25 .25
1219	A454	20b brown	.35 .25
1220	A454	40b dp lil	.60 .25
1221	A454	55b dp bl	.90 .25
1222	A454	1 l dp mag	1.25 .25
1223	A454	1.75 l dp vio bl	1.50 .30
1224	A454	2 l olive	2.75 .35
	Nos. 1218-1224 (7)		7.60 1.90

Great personalities of the world.

Clavaria Aurea — A456

Mushrooms: 5b, Lepiota Procera. 20b, Amanita caesarea. 30b, Lactarius deliciosus. 35b, Armillaria mellea. 55b, Coprinus comatus. 1 l, Morchella conica. 1.55 l, Psalliota campestris. 1.75 l, Boletus edulis. 2 l, Cantharellus cibarius.

1958, July   Litho.   Unwmk.
1225	A456	5b gray bl & brn	.25 .25
1226	A456	10b ol, ocher & brn	.25 .25
1227	A456	20b gray, red & yel	.45 .25
1228	A456	30b grn & dp org	.60 .25
1229	A456	35b lt bl & yel brn	.65 .25
1230	A456	55b pale grn, fawn & brn	.90 .25
1231	A456	1 l bl grn, ocher & brn	1.25 .25
1232	A456	1.55 l gray, lt gray & pink	2.10 .30
1233	A456	1.75 l emer, brn & buff	2.40 .35
1234	A456	2 l dl bl & org yel	3.50 .40
	Nos. 1225-1234 (10)		12.35 2.80

Antarctic Map and Emil Racovita A457

Design: 1.20 l, Cave and Racovita.

1958, July 30   Photo.   Perf. 14½x14
1235	A457	55b indigo & lt bl	1.10 .30
1236	A457	1.20 l ol bis & dk vio	2.50 .30

90th birth anniv. of Emil Racovita, explorer and naturalist.

Armed Forces Monument — A458

Designs: 75b, Soldier guarding industry. 1.75 l, Sailor raising flag and ship.

1958, Oct. 2   Perf. 13½x13
1237	A458	55b orange brown	.30 .25
1238	A458	75b deep magenta	.45 .25
1239	A458	1.75 l bright blue	1.00 .25
	Nos. 1237-1239,C55 (4)		3.35 1.25

Armed Forces Day.

Woman & Man from Oltenia — A459

Regional Costumes: 40b, Tara Oasului. 50b, Transylvania. 55b, Muntenia. 1 l, Banat. 1.75 l, Moldavia. Pairs: "a" woman, "b" man.

1958   Unwmk.   Perf. 13½x14
1240	A459	35b Pair, #a.-b. + label	.75 .25
1241	A459	40b Pair, #a.-b. + label	.75 .25
1242	A459	50b Pair, #a.-b. + label	.95 .25
1243	A459	55b Pair, #a.-b. + label	1.50 .25
1244	A459	1 l Pair, #a.-b. + label	3.25 .45

1245 A459 1.75 l Pair, #a.-b. + label 3.75 .55
Nos. 1240-1245 (6) 10.95 2.00
Nos. 1240-1245 exist imperf. Value, set $20, unused or used.

Printer and Hand Press A461

Moldavia Stamp of 1858 A462

55b, Scissors cutting strips of 1858 stamps. 1.20 l, Postillion, mail coach. 1.30 l, Postillion blowing horn, courier on horseback. 1.75 l, 2 l, 3.30 l, Various denominations of 1858 issue.

1958, Nov. 15 **Engr.** **Perf. 14½x14**
1252 A461 35b vio bl .30 .25
1253 A461 55b dk red brn .50 .25
1254 A461 1.20 l dull bl .90 .25
1255 A461 1.30 l brown vio 1.20 .25
1256 A462 1.55 l gray brn 1.50 .25
1257 A462 1.75 l rose claret 1.50 .25
1258 A462 2 l dull vio 1.90 .50
1259 A462 3.30 l dull red brn 2.50 .60
Nos. 1252-1259 (8) 10.30 2.60
Cent. of Romanian stamps. See No. C57. Exist imperf. Value, set $25.

Bugler — A463

1958, Dec. 10 **Photo.** **Perf. 13½x13**
1260 A463 55b crimson rose .75 .30
Decade of teaching reforms.

Runner — A464

Perf. 13½x14
1958, Dec. 9 **Wmk. 358**
1261 A464 1 l deep brown 1.25 .30
Third Youth Spartacist Sports Meet. For overprint, see No. 1287.

Building and Flag — A465

1958, Dec. 16
1262 A465 55b dk car rose .80 .25
Workers' Revolution, 40th anniversary.

Prince Alexandru Ioan Cuza A466

Perf. 14x13½
1959, Jan. 27 **Unwmk.**
1263 A466 1.75 l dk blue 1.50 .30
Centenary of the Romanian Union.

Friedrich Handel — A467

Portraits: No. 1265, Robert Burns. No. 1266, Charles Darwin. No. 1267, Alexander Popov. No. 1268, Shalom Aleichem.

1959, Apr. 25 **Photo.** **Perf. 13½x14**
1264 A467 55b brown .60 .25
1265 A467 55b indigo .60 .25
1266 A467 55b slate .60 .25
1267 A467 55b carmine .60 .25
1268 A467 55b purple .60 .25
Nos. 1264-1268,C59 (6) 7.00 1.85
Various cultural anniversaries in 1959.

Corn — A468

Sheep A469

No. 1270, Sunflower and bee. No. 1271, Sugar beet and refinery. No. 1273, Cattle. No. 1274, Rooster and hens. No. 1275, Tractor and grain. No. 1276, Loaded farm wagon. No. 1277, Farm couple and "10."

Perf. 13½x14, 14x13½
1959, June 1 **Photo.** **Wmk. 358**
1269 A468 55b brt green .40 .25
1270 A468 55b red org .40 .25
1271 A468 55b red lilac .40 .25
1272 A469 55b olive grn .40 .25
1273 A469 55b red brown .40 .25
1274 A469 55b yellow brn .40 .25
1275 A469 55b blue .40 .25
1276 A469 55b brown .40 .25

Unwmk.
1277 A469 5 l dp red lilac 3.00 .60
Nos. 1269-1277 (9) 6.20 2.60
10th anniv. of collective farming. Sizes: #1272-1276 33x23mm; #1277 38x27mm.

Young Couple — A470

Design: 1.60 l, Dancer in folk costume.

Perf. 13½x14
1959, July 15 **Unwmk.**
1278 A470 1 l brt blue .75 .25
1279 A470 1.60 l car rose 1.00 .25
7th World Youth Festival, Vienna, 7/26-8/14.

Steel Worker and Farm Woman — A471

1959, Aug. 23 **Litho.** **Perf. 13½x14**
1280 A471 55b multicolored .60 .25
a. Souvenir sheet of 1 1.75 .65
15th anniv. of Romania's liberation from the Germans.
No. 1280a is ungummed and imperf. The blue, yellow and red vignette shows large "XV" and Romanian flag. Brown 1.20 l denomination and inscription in margin.

Prince Vlad Tepes and Document — A472

Designs: 40b, Nicolae Balcescu Street. No. 1283, Atheneum. No. 1284, Printing Combine. 1.55 l, Opera House. 1.75 l, Stadium.

1959, Sept. 20 **Photo.**
Centers in Gray
1281 A472 20b blue .95 .25
1282 A472 40b brown 1.40 .25
1283 A472 55b bister brn 1.60 .25
1284 A472 55b rose lilac 2.00 .35
1285 A472 1.55 l pale violet 4.25 .60
1286 A472 1.75 l bluish grn 4.75 .85
Nos. 1281-1286 (6) 14.95 2.55
500th anniversary of the founding of Bucharest. See No. C71.

No. 1261 Overprinted with Shield in Silver, inscribed: "Jocurile Bucaresti Balcanice 1959"
1959, Sept. 12 **Wmk. 358**
1287 A464 1 l deep brown 10.00 3.50
Balkan Games.

Soccer — A473

Motorcycle Race — A474

Perf. 13½
1959, Oct. 5 **Unwmk.** **Litho.**
1288 A473 20b shown .25 .25
1289 A474 35b shown .30 .25
1290 A474 40b Ice hockey .40 .25
1291 A473 55b Handball .45 .25
1292 A473 1 l Horse race .80 .25
1293 A473 1.50 l Boxing 1.40 .25
1294 A474 1.55 l Rugby 1.60 .25
1295 A474 1.60 l Tennis 2.00 .30
Nos. 1288-1295,C72 (9) 9.70 2.55

Russian Icebreaker "Lenin" A475

Perf. 14½x13½
1959, Oct. 25 **Photo.**
1296 A475 1.75 l blue vio 2.50 .40
First atomic ice-breaker.

Stamp Album and Magnifying Glass — A476

1959, Nov. 15 **Wmk. 358** **Perf. 14**
1297 A476 1.60 l + 40b label 1.25 .40
Issued for Stamp Day.
Stamp and label were printed alternately in sheet. The 40b went to the Romanian Association of Philatelists.

Purple Foxglove — A477

1959, Dec. 15 **Typo.** **Unwmk.**
Medicinal Flowers in Natural Colors
1298 A477 20b shown .25 .25
1299 A477 40b Peppermint .30 .25
1300 A477 55b Cornflower .50 .25
1301 A477 55b Daisies .65 .25
1302 A477 1 l Autumn crocus .90 .25
1303 A477 1.20 l Monkshood 1.00 .25
1304 A477 1.55 l Poppies 1.50 .25
1305 A477 1.60 l Linden 1.50 .30
1306 A477 1.75 l Dog rose 1.50 .30
1307 A477 3.20 l Buttercup 2.50 .50
Nos. 1298-1307 (10) 10.60 2.85

Cuza University, Jassy, Centenary A478

1959, Nov. 26 **Photo.** **Wmk. 358**
1308 A478 55b brown .70 .25

Romanian Writers Type of 1958
20b, Gheorghe Cosbuc. 40b, Ion Luca Caragiale. 50b, Grigore Alexandrescu. 55b, Alexandru Donici. 1 l, Costache Negruzzi. 1.55 l, Dimitrie Bolintineanu.

1960, Jan. 20 **Perf. 14**
1309 A450 20b bluish blk .25 .25
1310 A450 40b dp lilac .55 .25
1311 A450 50b brown .65 .25
1312 A450 55b violet brn .65 .25
1313 A450 1 l violet 1.10 .25
1314 A450 1.55 l dk blue 1.50 .35
Nos. 1309-1314 (6) 4.70 1.60

Huchen (Salmon) — A480

55b, Greek tortoise. 1.20 l, Shelduck.

1960, Feb. 1 **Engr.** **Unwmk.**
1315 A480 20b blue .30 .25
1316 A480 55b brown .50 .25
1317 A480 1.20 l dk purple 1.25 .30
Nos. 1315-1317,C76-C78 (6) 7.30 2.10

Woman, Dove and
Globe — A481

1960, Mar. 1   Photo.   Perf. 14
1318 A481 55b violet blue   .50   .25
50 years of Intl. Women's Day, Mar. 8.

A482

40b, Lenin. 55b, Lenin statue, Bucharest.
1.55 l, Head of Lenin.

1960, Apr. 22   Wmk. 358   Perf. 13½
1319 A482 40b magenta   .35   .25
1320 A482 55b violet blue   .50   .25

Souvenir Sheet
1321 A482 1.55 l carmine   3.00 2.00
90th birth anniv. of Lenin.

A483

40b, Heroes Monument. 55b, Soviet war
memorial.

1960, May 9   Wmk. 358   Perf. 14
1322 A483 40b multicolored   .35   .25
1323 A483 55b multicolored   .45   .25
  a.   Strip of 2, #1322-1323 + label   1.50 .75
15th anniversary of the liberation.
Nos. 1322-1323 exist imperf., printed in
deep magenta. Value, set $3.25; label strip,
$4.50.

Swimming
A484

Sports: 55b, Women's gymnastics. 1.20 l,
High jump. 1.60 l, Boxing. 2.45 l, Canoeing.

1960, June   Unwmk. Typo.   Perf. 14
Gray Background
1326 A484 40b blue & yel   3.00 3.00
1327 A484 55b blk, yel &
              emer   3.00 3.00
1328 A484 1.20 l emer & brick
              red   3.00 3.00
  a.   Strip of 3, #1326-1328   10.00 10.00
1329 A484 1.60 l blue, yel &
              blk   3.00 3.00
1330 A484 2.45 l blk, emer &
              brick red   3.00 3.00
  a.   Pair, #1329-1330 + 2 labels   10.00 10.00
      Nos. 1326-1330 (5)   15.00 15.00
17th Olympic Games, Rome, 8/25-9/11.
Nos. 1326-1330 were printed in one sheet,
the top half containing No. 1328a, the bottom
half No. 1330a, with gutter between. When the
two strips are placed together, the Olympic
rings join in a continuous design.
  Exist imperf. (3.70 l replaced 2.45 l). Value,
set, two strips $35.

R.P. ROMINA

Swimming — A485

Olympic Flame, Stadium — A486

40b, Women's gymnastics. 55b, High jump.
1 l, Boxing. 1.60 l, Canoeing. 2 l, Soccer.

1960   Photo.   Wmk. 358
1331 A485 20b chalky blue   .25   .25
1332 A485 40b dk brn red   .35   .25
1333 A485 55b blue   .55   .25
1334 A485 1 l rose red   .75   .25
1335 A485 1.60 l rose lilac   1.00   .25
1336 A485 2 l dull violet   1.50   .35
      Nos. 1331-1336 (6)   4.40 1.60

Souvenir Sheets
Perf. 11½
1337 A486 5 l ultra   12.50 7.00
Imperf
1338 A486 6 l dull red   20.00 10.00
17th Olympic Games.

A487

Perf. 13½
1960, June 20   Unwmk.   Litho.
1339 A487 55b red org & dk car   .50   .25
Romanian Workers' Party, 3rd congress.

A488

Portraits: 10b, Leo Tolstoy. 20b, Mark
Twain. 35b, Hokusai. 40b, Alfred de Musset.
55b, Daniel Defoe. 1 l, Janos Bolyai. 1.20 l,
Anton Chekov. 1.55 l, Robert Koch. 1.75 l,
Frederick Chopin.

1960   Wmk. 358   Photo.   Perf. 14
1340 A488 10b dull pur   .25   .25
1341 A488 20b olive   .30   .25
1342 A488 35b blue   .40   .25
1343 A488 40b slate green   .50   .25
1344 A488 55b dull brn vio   .75   .25
1345 A488 1 l Prus grn   1.25   .45
1346 A488 1.20 l dk car rose   1.40   .25
1347 A488 1.55 l gray blue   1.60   .25
1348 A488 1.75 l brown   2.25   .50
      Nos. 1340-1348 (9)   8.70 2.70
Various cultural anniversaries.

Students
A489

Piano and Books
A490

Designs: 5b, Diesel locomotive. 10b, Dam.
20b, Miner with drill. 30b, Ambulance and doctor. 35b, Textile worker. 50b, Nursery. 55b,
Timber industry. 60b, Harvester. 75b, Feeding
cattle. 1 l, Atomic reactor. 1.20 l, Oil derricks.
1.50 l, Coal mine. 1.55 l, Loading ship. 1.60 l,
Athlete. 1.75 l, Bricklayer. 2 l, Steam roller.
2.40 l, Chemist. 3 l, Radio and television.

1960   Wmk. 358   Photo.   Perf. 14
1349 A489 3b brt lil rose   .25   .25
1350 A489 5b olive bis   .25   .25
1351 A489 10b violet gray   .25   .25
1352 A489 20b blue vio   .25   .25
1353 A489 30b vermilion   .25   .25
1354 A489 35b crimson   .25   .25
1355 A490 40b ocher   .25   .25
1356 A489 50b bluish vio   .25   .25
1357 A489 55b blue   .25   .25
1358 A490 60b green   .25   .25
1359 A490 75b gray ol   .30   .25
1360 A489 1 l car rose   .50   .25
1361 A489 1.20 l black   .40   .25
1362 A489 1.50 l plum   .50   .25
1363 A490 1.55 l Prus grn   .50   .25
1364 A490 1.60 l dp blue   .55   .25
1365 A489 1.75 l red brown   .75   .25
1366 A489 2 l dk ol gray   1.00   .25
1367 A489 2.40 l brt lilac   1.25   .25
1368 A489 3 l grysh blue   1.75   .25
      Nos. 1349-1368,C86 (21)   11.50 5.25

Ovid Statue
at Constanta
A491

Black Sea Resorts: 35b, Constanta harbor.
40b, Vasile Rosita beach and vase. 55b,
Ionian column and Mangalia beach. 1 l, Eforie
at night. 1.60 l, Eforie and sailboat.

1960, Aug. 2   Litho.   Unwmk.
1369 A491 20b multicolored   .25   .25
1370 A491 35b multicolored   .25   .25
1371 A491 40b multicolored   .25   .25
1372 A491 55b multicolored   .30   .25
1373 A491 1 l multicolored   .75   .25
1374 A491 1.60 l multicolored   1.10   .25
      Nos. 1369-1374,C87 (7)   4.40 2.00

Emblem — A492

Petrushka,
Russian
Puppet — A493

Designs: Various Puppets.

1960, Aug. 20   Typo.
1375 A492 20b multi   .25   .25
1376 A493 40b multi   .25   .25
1377 A493 55b multi   .25   .25
1378 A493 1 l multi   .50   .25
1379 A493 1.20 l multi   .50   .25
1380 A493 1.75 l multi   .75   .25
      Nos. 1375-1380 (6)   2.50 1.50
International Puppet Theater Festival.

Children on
Sled — A494

Children's Sports: 35b, Boys playing ball,
horiz. 55b, Ice skating, horiz. 1 l, Running.
1.75 l, Swimming, horiz.

Unwmk.
1960, Oct. 1   Litho.   Perf. 14
1381 A494 20b multi   .25   .25
1382 A494 35b multi   .25   .25
1383 A494 55b multi   .30   .25
1384 A494 1 l multi   .45   .25
1385 A494 1.75 l multi   .90   .25
      Nos. 1381-1385 (5)   2.15 1.25

Globe and Peace
Banner — A495

Perf. 13½x14
1960, Nov. 26   Photo.   Wmk. 358
1386 A495 55b brt bl & yel   .40   .25
Intl. Youth Federation, 15th anniv.

Worker
and Flags
A496

Perf. 14x13
1960, Nov. 26   Litho.   Unwmk.
1387 A496 55b dk car & red org   .40   .25
40th anniversary of the general strike.

Carp
A497

Fish: 20b, Pikeperch. 40b, Black Sea tur-
bot. 55b, Allis shad. 1 l, Wels (catfish). 1.20 l,
Sterlet. 1.60 l, Huchen (salmon).

1960, Dec. 5   Typo.
1388 A497 10b multi   .25   .25
1389 A497 20b multi   .30   .25
1390 A497 40b multi   .35   .25
1391 A497 55b multi   .40   .25
1392 A497 1 l multi   1.00   .25
1393 A497 1.20 l multi   1.10   .25
1394 A497 1.60 l multi   1.75   .35
      Nos. 1388-1394 (7)   5.15 1.85

Kneeling Woman
and
Grapes — A498

Designs: 30b, Farmers drinking, horiz. 40b,
Loading grapes into basket, horiz. 55b,
Woman cutting grapes. 75b, Vintner with basket. 1 l, Woman filling basket with grapes. 1.20
l, Vintner with jug. 5 l, Antique wine jug.

1960, Dec. 20   Litho.   Perf. 14
1395 A498 20b brn & gray   .25   .25
1396 A498 30b red org & pale
              grn   .30   .25
1397 A498 40b dp ultra & gray
              ol   .40   .25
1398 A498 55b emer & buff   .50   .25
1399 A498 75b dk car rose &
              pale grn   .50   .25
1400 A498 1 l Prus grn & gray
              ol   .65   .25
1401 A498 1.20 l org brn & pale
              bl   1.00   .30
      Nos. 1395-1401 (7)   3.60 1.80

Souvenir Sheet
Imperf

1402	A498	5 l	dk car rose & bis	4.00 1.90

Each stamp represents a different wine-growing region: Dragasani, Dealul Mare, Odobesti, Cotnari, Tirnave, Minis, Murfatlar and Pietroasa.

Steelworker by I. Irimescu — A499

Modern Sculptures: 10b, G. Doja, I. Vlad. 20b, Meeting, B. Caragea. 40b, George Enescu, A. Anghel. 50b, Mihail Eminescu, C. Baraschi. 55b, Peasant Revolt, 1907, M. Constantinescu, horiz. 1 l, "Peace," I. Jalea. 1.55 l, Building Socialism, C. Medrea. 1.75 l, Birth of an Idea, A. Szobotka.

Perf. 13½x14, 14x13½

1961, Feb. 16		Photo.	Unwmk.	
1403	A499	5b car rose	.25	.25
1404	A499	10b violet	.25	.25
1405	A499	20b ol blk	.25	.25
1406	A499	40b ol bis	.35	.25
1407	A499	50b blk brn	.40	.25
1408	A499	55b org ver	.60	.25
1409	A499	1 l dp plum	.80	.25
1410	A499	1.55 l brt ultra	1.00	.25
1411	A499	1.75 l green	1.40	.25
		Nos. 1403-1411 (9)	5.30	2.25

Peter Poni, and Chemical Apparatus — A500

Romanian Scientists: 20b, A. Saligny and Danube bridge, Cernavoda. 55b, C. Budeanu and electrical formula. 1.55 l, Gh. Titeica and geometrical symbol.

1961, Apr. 11	Litho.	**Perf. 13½x13**	
Portraits in Brown Black			
1412	A500	10b pink & vio bl	.25 .25
1413	A500	20b citron & mar	.25 .25
1414	A500	55b blue & red	.30 .25
1415	A500	1.55 l ocher & lilac	1.00 .25
		Nos. 1412-1415 (4)	1.80 1.00

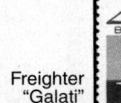

Freighter "Galati" A501

Ships: 40b, Passenger ship "Oltenita." 55b, Motorboat "Tomis." 1 l, Freighter "Arad." 1.55 l, Tugboat. 1.75 l, Freighter "Dobrogea."

1961, Apr. 25	Typo.	**Perf. 14x13**	
1416	A501	20b multi	.25 .25
1417	A501	40b multi	.25 .25
1418	A501	55b multi	.40 .25
1419	A501	1 l multi	.50 .25
1420	A501	1.55 l multi	.75 .25
1421	A501	1.75 l multi	1.10 .25
		Nos. 1416-1421 (6)	3.25 1.50

Marx, Lenin and Engels on Red Flag — A502

Designs: 55b, Workers. 1 l, "Industry and Agriculture" and Workers Party Emblem.

1961, Apr. 29		Litho.	
1422	A502	35b red, bl & ocher	.40 .25
1423	A502	55b mar, red & gray	.60 .25

Souvenir Sheet
Imperf

1424	A502	1 l multi		1.75 .70

40th anniv. of the Romanian Communist Party. #1424 contains one 55x33mm stamp.

Roe Deer and Bronze Age Hunting Scene — A503

Lynx and Prehistoric Hunter A504

35b, Boar, Roman hunter. 40b, Brown bear, Roman tombstone. 55b, Red deer, 16th cent. hunter. 75b, Red fox, feudal hunter. 1 l, Black goat, modern hunter. 1.55 l, Rabbit, hunter with dog. 1.75 l, Badger, hunter. 2 l, Roebuck, hunter.

1961, July		**Perf. 13x14, 14x13**		
1425	A503	10b multi	.25	.25
1426	A504	20b multi	.25	.25
1427	A504	35b multi	.35	.25
1428	A504	40b multi	.60	.25
1429	A504	55b multi	.75	.25
1430	A504	75b multi	.90	.25
1431	A503	1 l multi	1.00	.25
1432	A503	1.55 l multi	1.25	.25
1433	A503	1.75 l multi	1.50	.30
1434	A503	2 l multi	1.75	.45
		Nos. 1425-1434 (10)	8.60	2.75

Georges Enescu A505

1961, Sept. 7	Litho.	**Perf. 14x13**	
1435	A505	3 l pale vio & vio brn	1.40 .30

2nd Intl. George Enescu Festival, Bucharest.

Peasant Playing Panpipe — A506

Peasants playing musical instruments: 20b, Alpenhorn, horiz. 40b, Flute. 55b, Guitar. 60b, Bagpipe. 1 l, Zither.

Perf. 13x14, 14x13

1961		Unwmk.	Typo.	
Tinted Paper				
1436	A506	10b multi	.25	.25
1437	A506	20b multi	.25	.25
1438	A506	40b multi	.25	.25
1439	A506	55b multi	.45	.25
1440	A506	60b multi	.45	.25
1441	A506	1 l multi	.70	.25
		Nos. 1436-1441 (6)	2.35	1.50

Heraclitus — A507

Portraits: 20b, Francis Bacon. 40b, Rabindranath Tagore. 55b, Domingo F. Sarmiento. 1.35 l, Heinrich von Kleist. 1.75 l, Mikhail V. Lomonosov.

Perf. 13½x13

1961, Oct. 25		Photo.	Wmk. 358	
1442	A507	10b maroon	.25	.25
1443	A507	20b brown	.25	.25
1444	A507	40b Prus grn	.25	.25
1445	A507	55b cerise	.25	.25
1446	A507	1.35 l brt bl	.75	.25
1447	A507	1.75 l purple	1.00	.25
		Nos. 1442-1447 (6)	2.75	1.50

Swimming — A508

Gold Medal, Boxing A509

#1449, Olympic torch. #1450, Water polo, Melbourne. #1451, Women's high jump, Rome.

Perf. 14x14½

1961, Oct. 30		Photo.	Unwmk.	
1448	A508	20b bl gray	.25	.25
1449	A508	20b vermilion	.25	.25
1450	A508	55b ultra	.60	.25
1451	A508	55b blue	.60	.25
		Nos. 1448-1451 (4)	1.70	1.00

Perf. 10½
Size: 33x33mm

Gold Medals: 35b, Pistol shooting, Melbourne. 40b, Sharpshooting, Rome. 55b, Wrestling. 1.35 l, Woman's high jump. 1.75 l, Three medals for canoeing.

Medals in Ocher

1452	A509	10b Prus grn	.25	.25
1453	A509	35b brown	.40	.25
1454	A509	40b plum	.45	.25
1455	A509	55b org red	.60	.25
1456	A509	1.35 l dp ultra	.90	.25

Size: 46x32mm

1457	A509	1.75 l dp car rose	1.75	.35
		Nos. 1452-1457 (6)	4.35	1.60
		Nos. 1448-1457 (10)	6.05	2.60

Romania's gold medals in 1956, 1960 Olympics.
#1452-1457 exist imperf. Value, set: unused $5; used $3.50.
A souvenir sheet of one 4 l dark red & ocher was issued. Value, unused $5.50, canceled $4.50.

Congress Emblem — A510

1961, Dec.	Litho.	**Perf. 13½x14**	
1458	A510	55b dk car rose	.50 .25

5th World Congress of Trade Unions, Moscow, Dec. 4-16.

Primrose A511

Designs: 20b, Sweet William. 25b, Peony. 35b, Prickly pear. 40b, Iris. 55b, Buttercup.

1 l, Hepatica. 1.20 l, Poppy. 1.55 l, Gentian. 1.75 l, Carol Davilla and Dimitrie Brindza. 20b, 25b, 40b, 55b, 1.20 l, 1.55 l, are vertical.

Perf. 14x13½, 13½x14

1961, Sept. 15				
1459	A511	10b multi	.25	.25
1460	A511	20b multi	.25	.25
1461	A511	25b multi	.25	.25
1462	A511	35b multi	.30	.25
1463	A511	40b multi	.30	.25
1464	A511	55b multi	.35	.25
1465	A511	1 l multi	.50	.25
1466	A511	1.20 l multi	.65	.25
1467	A511	1.55 l multi	1.10	.25
		Nos. 1459-1467 (9)	3.95	2.25

Souvenir Sheet
Imperf

1468	A511	1.75 l car, blk & grn	4.50 3.00

Bucharest Botanical Garden, cent. No. 1459-1467 exist imperf. Value, set $12.

United Nations Emblem — A512

Designs: 20b, Map of Balkan peninsula and dove. 40b, Men of three races.

1961, Nov. 27			**Perf. 13½x14**	
1469	A512	20b bl, yel & pink	.25	.25
1470	A512	40b multi	.55	.25
1471	A512	55b org, lil & yel	.80	.25
		Nos. 1469-1471 (3)	1.60	.75

UN, 15th anniv. Nos. 1469-1470 are each printed with alternating yellow labels.
Exist imperf. Value, set: unused $2.75; used $2.

Cock and Savings Book — A513

Savings Day: 55b, Honeycomb, bee and savings book.

1962, Feb. 15	Typo.	**Perf. 13½**	
1472	A513	40b multi	.30 .25
1473	A513	55b multi	.30 .25

Soccer Player and Map of Europe — A514

1962, Apr. 20	Litho.	**Perf. 13x14**	
1474	A514	55b emer & red brn	2.00 .75

European Junior Soccer Championships, Bucharest. For surcharge see No. 1510.

Wheat, Map and Tractor — A515

Designs: 55b, Medal honoring agriculture. 1.55Nl, Sheaf of wheat, hammer & sickle.

1962, Apr. 27   **Perf. 13½x14**
1475 A515   40b org & dk car   .25   .25
1476 A515   55b yel, car & brn   .25   .25
1477 A515   1.55 l multi   .25   .25
     Nos. 1475-1477 (3)   1.35   .75
     Collectivization of agriculture.

Canoe Race A516

20b, Kayak. 40b, 8-man shell. 55b, 2-man skiff. 1 l, Yachts. 1.20 l, Motorboats. 1.55 l, Sailboat. 3 l, Water slalom.

1962, May 15   Photo.   Perf. 14x13
Vignette in Bright Blue
1478 A516   10b lil rose   .25   .25
1479 A516   20b ol gray   .25   .25
1480 A516   40b red brn   .25   .25
1481 A516   55b ultra   .25   .25
1482 A516   1 l red   .30   .25
1483 A516   1.20 l dp plum   .70   .25
1484 A516   1.55 l orange   1.00   .25
1485 A516   3 l violet   1.75   .25
     Nos. 1478-1485 (8)   4.75   2.00
These stamps were also issued imperf. with color of denomination and inscription changed. Value, set unused $6, canceled $2.75.

Ion Luca Caragiale — A517

40b, Jean Jacques Rousseau. 1.75 l, Aleksander I. Herzen. 3.30 l, Ion Luca Caragiale (as a young man).

1962, June 9   **Perf. 13½x14**
1486 A517   40b dk sl grn   .25   .25
1487 A517   55b magenta   .25   .25
1488 A517   1.75 l dp bl   .75   .25
     Nos. 1486-1488 (3)   1.25   .75
Souvenir Sheet
Perf. 11½
1489 A517   3.30 l brown   4.25   4.25
Rousseau, French philosopher, 250th birth anniv.; Caragiale, Romanian author, 50th death anniv.; Herzen, Russian writer, 150th birth anniv. No. 1489 contains one 32x55mm stamp.

Globes Surrounded with Flags — A518

1962, July 6   Typo.   Perf. 11
1490 A518   55b multi   .60   .25
8th Youth Festival for Peace and Friendship, Helsinki, July 28-Aug. 6.

Traian Vuia — A519

Portraits: 20b, Al. Davila. 35b, Vasile Pirvan. 40b, Ion Negulici. 55b, Grigore Cobilcescu. 1 l, Dr. Gheorghe Marinescu. 1.20 l, Ion Cantacuzino. 1.35 l, Victor Babes. 1.55 l, C. Levaditi.

1962, July 20   Photo.   Wmk. 358
1491 A519   15b brown   .25   .25
1492 A519   20b dl red brn   .25   .25
1493 A519   35b brn mag   .25   .25
1494 A519   40b bl vio   .25   .25
1495 A519   55b brt bl   .25   .25
1496 A519   1 l dp ultra   .30   .25
1497 A519   1.20 l crimson   .45   .25
1498 A519   1.35 l Prus grn   .60   .25
1499 A519   1.55 l purple   1.10   .25
     Nos. 1491-1499 (9)   3.70   2.25

Fieldball Player and Globe — A520

Perf. 13x14
1962, May 12   Litho.   Unwmk.
1500 A520   55b yel & vio   2.50   .50
2nd Intl. Women's Fieldball Championships, Bucharest.

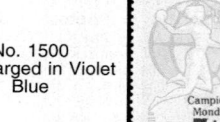

No. 1500 Surcharged in Violet Blue

1962, July 31
1501 A520   5 l on 55b yel & vio   7.50   5.00
   a.   Pair, one without surcharge   500.00
Romanian victory in the 2nd Intl. Women's Fieldball Championships.

Rod Fishing A521

Various Fishing Scenes.

1962, July 25   **Perf. 14x13**
1502 A521   10b multi   .25   .25
1503 A521   25b multi   .25   .25
1504 A521   40b bl & brick red   .25   .25
1505 A521   55b multi   .25   .25
1506 A521   75b sl, gray & bl   .40   .25
1507 A521   1 l multi   .55   .25
1508 A521   1.75 l multi   .90   .25
1509 A521   3.25 l multi   1.50   .25
     Nos. 1502-1509 (8)   4.35   2.00

No. 1474 Surcharged "1962 Campioana Europeana 2 lei" in Dark Blue

1962, July 31
1510 A514   2 l on 55b   3.75   3.75
Romania's victory in the European Junior Soccer Championships, Bucharest.

Child and Butterfly — A522

Designs: 30b, Girl feeding bird. 40b, Boy and model sailboat. 55b, Children writing,

---

horiz. 1.20 l, Girl at piano, and boy playing violin. 1.55 l, Pioneers camping, horiz.

Perf. 13x14, 14x13
1962, Aug. 25   **Litho.**
1511 A522   20b lt bl, red & brn   .35   .25
1512 A522   30b org, bl & red
          brn   .35   .25
1513 A522   40b chalky bl, dp
          org & Prus bl   .35   .25
1514 A522   55b citron, bl & red   .45   .25
1515 A522   1.20 l car, brn & dk
          vio   .65   .25
1516 A522   1.55 l bis, red & vio   1.25   .25
     Nos. 1511-1516 (6)   3.40   1.50

Handicraft — A523

Designs: 10b, Food and drink. 20b, Chemical industry. 40b, Chinaware. 55b, Leather industry. 75b, Textiles. 1 l, Furniture. 1.20 l, Electrical appliances. 1.55 l, Household goods (sewing machine and pots).

1962, Oct. 12   **Perf. 13x14**
1517 A523   5b multi   .25   .25
1518 A523   10b multi   .25   .25
1519 A523   20b multi   .25   .25
1520 A523   40b multi   .25   .25
1521 A523   55b multi   .25   .25
1522 A523   75b multi   .25   .25
1523 A523   1 l multi   .40   .25
1524 A523   1.20 l multi   .75   .25
1525 A523   1.55 l multi   1.10   .25
     Nos. 1517-1525,C126 (10)   5.25   2.50
     4th Sample Fair, Bucharest.

Lenin — A524

1962, Nov. 7   **Perf. 10½**
1526 A524   55b vio bl, red & bis   .50   .25
Russian October Revolution, 45th anniv.

Bull — A525

Designs: 20b, Sheep, horiz. 40b, Merino ram, horiz. 1 l, York pig. 1.35 l, Cow. 1.55 l, Heifer, horiz. 1.75 l, Pigs, horiz.

1962, Nov. 20   Perf. 14x13, 13x14
1527 A525   20b ultra & blk   .25   .25
1528 A525   40b bl, yel & sep   .30   .25
1529 A525   55b ocher, buff & sl
          grn   .50   .25
1530 A525   1 l gray, yel & brn   .75   .25
1531 A525   1.35 l dl grn, choc &
          blk   1.25   .25
1532 A525   1.55 l org red, dk brn
          & blk   1.25   .25
1533 A525   1.75 l dk vio bl, yel &
          org   2.00   .30
     Nos. 1527-1533 (7)   6.30   1.80

Arms, Factory and Harvester A526

Perf. 14½x13½
1962, Dec. 30   **Litho.**
1534 A526   1.55 l multi   .85   .25
Romanian People's Republic, 15th anniv.

Strikers at Grivita, 1933 A527

1963, Feb. 16   **Perf. 14x13½**
1535 A527   1.75 l red, vio & yel   .80   .25
30th anniv. of the strike of railroad and oil industry workers at Grivita.

Tractor Driver and "FAO" Emblem A528

55b, Farm woman, cornfield & combine. 1.55 l, Child drinking milk & milking machine. 1.75 l, Woman with basket of grapes & vineyard.

1963, Mar. 21   Photo.   Perf. 14½x13½
1536 A528   40b vio bl   .25   .25
1537 A528   55b bis brn   .25   .25
1538 A528   1.55 l rose red   .50   .25
1539 A528   1.75 l green   .85   .25
     Nos. 1536-1539 (4)   1.85   1.00
FAO "Freedom from Hunger" campaign.

Tomatoes — A529

40b, Hot peppers. 55b, Radishes. 75b, Eggplant. 1.20 l, Mild peppers. 3.25 l, Cucumbers, horiz.

Perf. 13½x14, 14x13½
1963, Apr. 25   Litho.   Unwmk.
1540 A529   35b multi   .25   .25
1541 A529   40b multi   .25   .25
1542 A529   55b multi   .25   .25
1543 A529   75b multi   .25   .25
1544 A529   1.20 l multi   .70   .25
1545 A529   3.25 l multi   1.50   .30
     Nos. 1540-1545 (6)   3.20   1.55

Woman Swimmer at Start — A530

Designs: 30b, Crawl, horiz. 55b, Butterfly stroke, horiz. 1 l, Backstroke, horiz. 1.35 l, Breaststroke, horiz. 1.55 l, Woman diver. 2 l, Water polo.

1963, June 15   Perf. 13x14, 14x13

1546	A530	25b yel brn, emer & gray	.25	.25
1547	A530	30b ol grn, gray & yel	.25	.25
1548	A530	55b bl, gray & red	.25	.25
1549	A530	1 l grn, gray & red	.25	.25
1550	A530	1.35 l ultra, car & gray	.40	.25
1551	A530	1.55 l pur, gray & org	.85	.25
1552	A530	2 l car rose, gray & org	.90	.35

Nos. 1546-1552 (7)   3.15   1.85

Chicks — A531

Domestic poultry: 30b, Hen. 40b, Goose. 55b, White cock. 70b, Duck. 1 l, Hen. 1.35 l, Tom turkey. 3.20 l, Hen.

Fowl in Natural Colors; Inscription in Dark Blue

1963, May 23   Perf. 10½

1553	A531	20b ultra	.25	.25
1554	A531	30b tan	.25	.25
1555	A531	40b org brn	.25	.25
1556	A531	55b brt yel	.25	.25
1557	A531	70b lilac	.25	.25
1558	A531	1 l blue	.35	.25
1559	A531	1.35 l ocher	.50	.25
1560	A531	3.20 l yel grn	1.10	.35

Nos. 1553-1560 (8)   3.20   2.10

Women and Globe A532

1963, June 15   Photo.   Perf. 14x13

1561   A532   55b dark blue   .40   .25

Intl. Women's Cong., Moscow, June 24-29.

William M. Thackeray, Writer A533

Portraits: 50b, Eugene Delacroix, painter. 55b, Gheorghe Marinescu, physician. 1.55 l, Giuseppe Verdi, composer. 1.75 l, Stanislavski, actor and producer.

1963, July   Unwmk.   Perf. 14x13
Portrait in Black

1562	A533	40b pale vio	.25	.25
1563	A533	50b bister brn	.25	.25
1564	A533	55b olive	.25	.25
1565	A533	1.55 l rose brn	.50	.25
1566	A533	1.75 l pale vio bl	.85	.25

Nos. 1562-1566 (5)   2.10   1.25

Walnuts A534

Designs: 20b, Plums. 40b, Peaches. 55b, Strawberries. 1 l, Grapes. 1.55 l, Apples. 1.60 l, Cherries. 1.75 l, Pears.

1963, Sept. 15   Litho.   Perf. 14x13½
Fruits in Natural Colors

1567	A534	10b pale yel & brn ol	.25	.25
1568	A534	20b pale pink & red org	.25	.25
1569	A534	40b lt bl & bl	.25	.25
1570	A534	55b dl yel & rose car	.25	.25
1571	A534	1 l rose vio & vio	.25	.25
1572	A534	1.55 l yel grn & ultra	.45	.25

1573	A534	1.60 l yel & bis	.75	.25
1574	A534	1.75 l lt bl & grn	.75	.25

Nos. 1567-1574 (8)   3.20   2.00

Women Playing Volleyball and Map of Europe — A535

40b, 3 men players. 55b, 3 women players. 1.75 l, 2 men players. 3.20 l, Europa Cup.

1963, Oct. 22   Perf. 13½x14

1575	A535	5b gray & lil rose	.25	.25
1576	A535	40b gray & vio bl	.25	.25
1577	A535	55b gray & grnsh bl	.30	.25
1578	A535	1.75 l gray & org brn	.55	.25
1579	A535	3.20 l gray & vio	1.25	.35

Nos. 1575-1579 (5)   2.60   1.35

European Volleyball Championships, Oct. 22-Nov. 4.

Pine Tree, Branch and Cone A536

Design: 1.75 l, Beech forest and branch.

Perf. 13½

1963, Dec. 5   Unwmk.   Photo.

1580	A536	55b dk grn	.25	.25
1581	A536	1.75 l dk bl	.60	.25

Reforestation program.

Silkworm Moth — A537

Designs: 20b, Chrysalis, moth and worm. 40b, Silkworm on leaf. 55b, Bee over mountains, horiz. 60b, 1.20 l, 1.35 l, 1.60 l, Bees pollinating various flowers, horiz.

1963, Dec. 12   Litho.   Perf. 13x14

1582	A537	10b multi	.30	.25
1583	A537	20b multi	.30	.25
1584	A537	40b multi	.30	.25
1585	A537	55b multi	.40	.25
1586	A537	60b multi	.50	.25
1587	A537	1.20 l multi	.80	.25
1588	A537	1.35 l multi	1.00	.25
1589	A537	1.60 l multi	1.40	.25

Nos. 1582-1589 (8)   5.00   2.00

18th Century House, Ploesti — A538

Peasant Houses from Village Museum, Bucharest: 40b, Oltenia, 1875, horiz. 55b, Hunedoara, 19th Cent., horiz. 75b, Oltenia, 19th Cent. 1 l, Brasov, 1847. 1.20 l, Bacau, 19th Cent. 1.75 l, Arges, 19th Cent.

1963, Dec. 25   Engr.   Perf. 13

1590	A538	20b claret	.35	.25
1591	A538	40b blue	.35	.25
1592	A538	55b dl vio	.35	.25
1593	A538	75b green	.35	.25
1594	A538	1 l brn & mar	.65	.25
1595	A538	1.20 l gray ol	.80	.25
1596	A538	1.75 l dk brn & ultra	1.60	.25

Nos. 1590-1596 (7)   4.45   1.75

Ski Jump A539

20b, Speed skating. 40b, Ice hockey. 55b, Women's figure skating. 60b, Slalom. 75b, Biathlon. 1 l, Bobsledding. 1.20 l, Cross-country skiing.

1963, Nov. 25   Litho.   Perf. 14

1597	A539	10b red & dk bl	.30	.25
1598	A539	20b ultra & red brn	.30	.25
1599	A539	40b emer & red brn	.30	.25
1600	A539	55b vio & red brn	.40	.25
1601	A539	60b org & vio bl	.65	.25
1602	A539	75b lil rose & dk bl	.80	.25
1603	A539	1 l bis & vio bl	1.50	.30
1604	A539	1.20 l grnsh bl & vio	1.60	.40

Nos. 1597-1604 (8)   5.85   2.20

9th Winter Olympic Games, Innsbruck, Jan. 29-Feb. 9, 1964.
Exist imperf. in changed colors. Value, set $6.50.
A souvenir sheet contains one imperf. 1.50 l ultramarine and red stamp showing the Olympic Ice Stadium at Innsbruck and the Winter Games emblem. Value $6.50.

Elena Teodorini as Carmen — A540

Designs: 10b, George Stephanescu, founder of Romanian opera. 35b, Ion Bajenaru as Petru Rares. 40b, D. Popovici as Alberich. 55b, Hariclea Darclée as Tosca. 75b, George Folescu as Boris Godunov. 1 l, Jean Athanasiu as Rigoletto. 1.35 l, Traian Grosavescu as Duke in Rigoletto. 1.55 l, N. Leonard as Hoffmann.

1964, Jan. 20   Photo.   Perf. 13
Portrait in Dark Brown

1605	A540	10b olive	.25	.25
1606	A540	20b ultra	.25	.25
1607	A540	35b green	.25	.25
1608	A540	40b grnsh bl	.25	.25
1609	A540	55b car rose	.30	.25
1610	A540	75b lilac	.30	.25
1611	A540	1 l blue	.65	.25
1612	A540	1.35 l brt vio	.90	.25
1613	A540	1.55 l red brn	1.00	.25

Nos. 1605-1613 (9)   4.15   2.25

Munteanu Murgoci and Congress Emblem — A541

1964, Feb. 5   Unwmk.   Perf. 13

1614   A541   1.60 l brt bl, ind & bis   .80   .25

8th Intl. Soil Congress, Bucharest.

Asculaphid A542

Insects: 10b, Thread-waisted wasp. 35b, Wasp. 40b, Rhyparioides metelkana moth. 55b, Tussock moth. 1.20 l, Kanetisa circe butterfly. 1.55 l, Beetle. 1.75 l, Horned beetle.

1964, Feb. 20   Litho.   Perf. 14x13
Insects in Natural Colors

1615	A542	5b pale lilac	.25	.25
1616	A542	10b lt bl & red	.25	.25
1617	A542	35b pale grn	.25	.25
1618	A542	40b olive green	.25	.25
1619	A542	55b ultra	.30	.25
1620	A542	1.20 l pale grn & red	.50	.25
1621	A542	1.55 l yel & brn	.70	.25
1622	A542	1.75 l orange & red	.75	.25

Nos. 1615-1622 (8)   3.25   2.00

Tobacco Plant — A543

Garden flowers: 20b, Geranium. 40b, Fuchsia. 55b, Chrysanthemum. 75b, Dahlia. 1 l, Lily. 1.25 l, Day lily. 1.55 l, Marigold.

1964, Mar. 25   Perf. 13x14

1623	A543	10b dk bl, grn & bis	.25	.25
1624	A543	20b gray, grn & red	.25	.25
1625	A543	40b pale grn, grn & red	.25	.25
1626	A543	55b grn, lt grn & lil	.30	.25
1627	A543	75b cit, red & grn	.35	.25
1628	A543	1 l dp cl, rose cl, grn & org	.50	.25
1629	A543	1.25 l sal, vio bl & grn	.60	.25
1630	A543	1.55 l red brn, yel & grn	.70	.25

Nos. 1623-1630 (8)   3.20   2.00

Jumping — A544

Horse Show Events: 40b, Dressage, horiz. 1.35 l, Jumping. 1.55 l, Galloping, horiz.

Unwmk.

1964, Apr. 25   Photo.   Perf. 13

1631	A544	40b lt bl, rose brn & blk	.25	.25
1632	A544	55b lil, red & brn	.25	.25
1633	A544	1.35 l brt grn, red & dk brn	.65	.25
1634	A544	1.55 l pale yel, bl & dp claret	.90	.25

Nos. 1631-1634 (4)   2.05   1.00

Hogfish A545

Fish (Constanta Aquarium): 10b, Peacock blenny. 20b, Mediterranean scad. 40b, Sturgeon. 50b, Sea horses. 55b, Yellow gurnard. 1 l, Beluga. 3.20 l, Stingray.

1964, May 10   Litho.   Perf. 14

1635	A545	5b multi	.40	.25
1636	A545	10b multi	.40	.25
1637	A545	20b multi	.40	.25
1638	A545	40b multi	.40	.25
1639	A545	50b multi	.40	.25
1640	A545	55b multi	.40	.25
1641	A545	1 l multi	1.10	.25
1642	A545	3.20 l multi	2.50	.25

Nos. 1635-1642 (8)   6.00   2.00

Mihail
Eminescu — A546

Portraits: 20b, Ion Creanga. 35b, Emil
Girleanu. 55b, Michelangelo. 1.20 l, Galileo
Galilei. 1.75 l, William Shakespeare.

1964, June 20   Photo.   Perf. 13
Portraits in Dark Brown

1643	A546	5b green	.25	.25
1644	A546	20b magenta	.25	.25
1645	A546	35b vermilion	.35	.25
1646	A546	55b bister	.35	.25
1647	A546	1.20 l ultra	.60	.25
1648	A546	1.75 l violet	1.00	.25
		Nos. 1643-1648 (6)	2.70	1.50

50th death anniv. of Emil Girleanu, writer;
the 75th death anniversaries of Ion Creanga
and Mihail Eminescu, writers; the 400th anniv.
of the death of Michelangelo and the births of
Galileo and Shakespeare.

Road through
Gorge — A547

Tourist Publicity: 55b, Lake Bilea and cot-
tage. 1 l, Ski lift, Polana Brasov. 1.35 l,
Ceahlaul peak and Lake Bicaz, horiz. 1.75 l,
Hotel Alpin.

1964, June 29   Engr.

1649	A547	40b rose brn	.25	.25
1650	A547	55b dk bl	.25	.25
1651	A547	1 l dl pur	.40	.25
1652	A547	1.35 l pale brn	.55	.25
1653	A547	1.75 l green	.65	.25
		Nos. 1649-1653 (5)	2.10	1.25

High Jump — A548

1964 Balkan Games: 40b, Javelin throw.
55b, Running. 1 l, Discus throw. 1.20 l, Hurdling. 1.55 l, Map and flags of Balkan
countries.

Size: 23x37½mm

1964, July 28   Photo.

1654	A548	30b ver, yel & yel grn	.25	.25
1655	A548	40b grn, yel, brn & vio	.25	.25
1656	A548	55b gldn brn, yel & bl grn	.25	.25
1657	A548	1 l brt bl, yel, brn & red	.50	.25
1658	A548	1.20 l pur, yel, brn & grn	.65	.25

Litho.
Size: 23x45mm

1659	A548	1.55 l multi	1.00	.25
		Nos. 1654-1659 (6)	2.90	1.50

Factory — A549

55b, Flag, Coat of Arms, vert. 75b, Combine. 1.20 l, Apartment buildings. 2 l, Flag,
coat of arms, industrial & agricultural scenes.
55b, 2 l, Inscribed "A XX A aniversare a eliber-
arii patriei!"

1964, Aug. 23   Photo.   Perf. 13

1660	A549	55b multi	.25	.25
1661	A549	60b multi	.25	.25
1662	A549	75b multi	.25	.25
1663	A549	1.20 l multi	.60	.25
		Nos. 1660-1663 (4)	1.35	1.00

Souvenir Sheet
Imperf

1664	A549	2 l multi	1.50	.50

20th anniv. of Romania's liberation. No.
1664 contains one stamp 110x70mm.

High Jump — A550

Sport: 30b, Wrestling. 35b, Volleyball. 40b,
Canoeing. 55b, Fencing. 1.20 l, Women's
gymnastics. 1.35 l, Soccer. 1.55 l,
Sharpshooting.

Olympic Rings in Blue, Yellow,
Black, Green and Red

1964, Sept. 1   Litho.

1665	A550	20b yel & blk	.25	.25
1666	A550	30b lilac & blk	.25	.25
1667	A550	35b grnsh bl & blk	.25	.25
1668	A550	40b pink & blk	.25	.25
1669	A550	55b lt yel grn & blk	.45	.25
1670	A550	1.20 l org & blk	.75	.25
1671	A550	1.35 l ocher & blk	1.00	.25
1672	A550	1.55 l bl & blk	1.10	.35
		Nos. 1665-1672 (8)	4.30	2.10

18th Olympic Games, Tokyo, Oct. 10-25.
Nos. 1665-1669 exist imperf., in changed
colors. Three other denominations exist,
1.60 l, 2 l and 2.40 l, imperf. Value, set of 8,
unused $7, canceled $6.
An imperf. souvenir sheet contains a 3.25 l
stamp showing a runner. Value unused $7
canceled $6.

George Enescu,
Piano Keys and
Neck of
Violin — A551

Designs: 55b, Enescu at piano. 1.60 l,
Enescu Festival medal. 1.75 l, Enescu bust by
G. Anghel.

1964, Sept. 5   Engr.

1673	A551	10b bl grn	.30	.25
1674	A551	55b vio blk	.50	.25
1675	A551	1.60 l dk red brn	1.50	.65
1676	A551	1.75 l dk bl	2.00	.40
		Nos. 1673-1676 (4)	4.30	1.55

3rd Intl. George Enescu Festival, Bucharest,
Sept., 1964.

Black
Swans
A552

5b, Indian python. 35b, Ostriches. 40b,
Crowned cranes. 55b, Tigers. 1 l, Lions. 1.55 l,
Grevy's zebras. 2 l, Bactrian camels.

Perf. 14x13

1964, Sept. 28   Litho.   Unwmk.

1677	A552	5b multi	.25	.25
1678	A552	10b multi	.25	.25
1679	A552	35b multi	.25	.25
1680	A552	40b multi	.25	.25
1681	A552	55b multi	.25	.25
1682	A552	1 l multi	.45	.25

1683	A552	1.55 l multi	.90	.25
1684	A552	2 l multi	1.25	.25
		Nos. 1677-1684 (8)	3.85	2.00

Issued to publicize the Bucharest Zoo.
No. 1683 inscribed "BANI."

C. Brincoveanu, Stolnicul Cantacuzino,
Gheorghe Lazar and
Academy — A553

Designs: 40b, Alexandru Ioan Cuza, medal
and University. 55b, Masks, curtain, harp,
keyboard and palette, vert. 75b, Women students in laboratory and auditorium. 1 l, Savings Bank building.

Perf. 13x13½, 13½x13

1964, Oct. 14   Photo.

1685	A553	20b multi	.25	.25
1686	A553	40b multi	.25	.25
1687	A553	55b multi	.25	.25
1688	A553	75b multi	.25	.25
1689	A553	1 l dk brn, yel & org	.50	.25
		Nos. 1685-1689 (5)	1.50	1.25

No. 1685 for 250th anniv. of the Royal Academy; Nos. 1686, 1688 cent. of the University
of Bucharest; No. 1687 cent. of the Academy
of Art and No. 1689 cent. of the Savings Bank.

Soldier's Head and
Laurel — A554

1964, Oct. 25   Litho.   Perf. 12x12½

1690	A554	55b ultra & lt bl	.40	.25

Army Day.

Canadian
Kayak
Singles
Gold Medal,
Melbourne,
1956
A555

Romanian Olympic Gold Medals: 30b, Boxing, Melbourne, 1956. 35b, Rapid Silhouette
Pistol, Melbourne, 1956. 40b, Women's High
Jump, Rome, 1960. 55b, Wrestling, Rome,
1960. 1.20 l, Clay Pigeon Shooting, Rome,
1960. 1.35 l, Women's High Jump, Tokyo,
1964. 1.55 l, Javelin, Tokyo, 1964.

1964, Nov. 30   Photo.   Perf. 13½
Medals in Gold and Brown

1691	A555	20b pink & ultra	.25	.25
1692	A555	30b yel grn & ultra	.25	.25
1693	A555	35b bluish grn & ul-tra	.25	.25
1694	A555	40b lil & ultra	.50	.25
1695	A555	55b org & ultra	.60	.25
1696	A555	1.20 l ol grn & ultra	.90	.25
1697	A555	1.35 l gldn brn & ultra	1.00	.25
1698	A555	1.55 l rose lil & ultra	1.50	.35
		Nos. 1691-1698 (8)	5.25	2.10

Romanian athletes who won gold medals in
three Olympic Games.
Nos. 1691-1695 exist imperf., in changed
colors. Three other denominations exist,
1.60 l, 2 l and 2.40 l, imperf. Value, set of 8,
unused $7, canceled $5.
A 10 l souvenir sheet shows the 1964
Olympic gold medal and world map. Value
unused $7, canceled $5.

Strawberries
A556

Designs: 35b, Blackberries. 40b, Raspberries. 55b, Rose hips. 1.20 l, Blueberries.
1.35 l, Cornelian cherries. 1.55 l, Hazelnuts.
2.55 l, Cherries.

1964, Dec. 20   Litho.   Perf. 13½x14

1703	A556	5b gray, red & grn	.25	.25
1704	A556	35b ocher, grn & dk vio bl	.25	.25
1705	A556	40b pale vio, car & grn	.30	.25
1706	A556	55b yel grn, grn & red	.30	.25
1707	A556	1.20 l sal pink, grn, brn & ind	.50	.25
1708	A556	1.35 l lt bl, grn & red	.60	.25
1709	A556	1.55 l gldn brn, grn & ocher	1.00	.25
1710	A556	2.55 l ultra, grn & red	1.25	.25
		Nos. 1703-1710 (8)	4.45	2.00

Syncom 3 — A557

Space Satellites: 40b, Syncom 3 over TV
antennas. 55b, Ranger 7 reaching moon,
horiz. 1 l, Ranger 7 and moon close-up, horiz.
1.20 l, Voskhod. 5 l, Konstantin Feoktistov,
Vladimir M. Komarov, Boris B. Yegorov and
Voskhod.

Perf. 13x14, 14x13
1965, Jan. 5   Litho.   Unwmk.
Size: 22x38mm, 38x22mm

1711	A557	30b multi	.30	.25
1712	A557	40b multi	.30	.25
1713	A557	55b multi	.50	.25
1714	A557	1 l multi	.60	.25
1715	A557	1.20 l multi, horiz.	.90	.25

Perf. 13½x13
Size: 52x30mm

1716	A557	5 l multi	2.10	.75
		Nos. 1711-1716 (6)	4.70	2.00

For surcharge see No. 1737.

UN Headquarters,
NY — A558

1.60 l, Arms, flag of Romania, UN emblem.

1965, Jan. 25   Perf. 12x12½

1717	A558	55b ultra, red & gold	.45	.25
1718	A558	1.60 l ultra, red, gold & yel	.80	.25

20th anniv. of the UN and 10th anniv. of
Romania's membership in the UN.

Greek Tortoise — A559

Reptiles: 10b, Bull lizard. 20b, Three-lined lizard. 40b, Sand lizard. 55b, Slow worm. 60b, Sand viper. 1 l, Desert lizard. 1.20 l, Orsini's viper. 1.35 l, Caspian whipsnake. 3.25 l, Four-lined snake.

1965, Feb. 25   Photo.   Perf. 13½

1719	A559	5b multi	.25	.25
1720	A559	10b multi	.25	.25
1721	A559	20b multi	.25	.25
1722	A559	40b multi	.40	.25
1723	A559	55b multi	.40	.25
1724	A559	60b multi	.45	.25
1725	A559	1 l multi	.60	.25
1726	A559	1.20 l multi	.70	.25
1727	A559	1.35 l multi	.90	.25
1728	A559	3.25 l multi	1.75	.25
		Nos. 1719-1728 (10)	5.95	2.50

White Persian Cats — A560

Designs: 1.35 l, Siamese cat. Others; Various European cats. (5b, 10b, 3.25 l, horiz.)

1965, Mar. 20   Litho.
Size: 41x29mm, 29x41mm
Cats in Natural Colors

1729	A560	5b brn org & blk	.25	.25
1730	A560	10b brt bl & blk	.25	.25
1731	A560	40b yel grn, yel & blk	.40	.25
1732	A560	55b rose red & blk	.55	.25
1733	A560	60b yel & blk	.90	.25
1734	A560	75b lt vio & blk	1.10	.25
1735	A560	1.35 l red org & blk	1.40	.25

Perf. 13x13½
Size: 62x29mm

1736	A560	3.25 l blue	2.50	.75
		Nos. 1729-1736 (8)	7.35	2.50

No. 1714 Surcharged in Violet

1737	A557	5 l on 1 l multi	14.00 14.00

1965, Apr. 25   Perf. 14x13

Flight of the US rocket Ranger 9 to the moon, Mar. 24, 1965.

Dante Alighieri — A561

40b, Ion Bianu, philologist and historian. 55b, Anton Bacalbasa, writer. 60b, Vasile

---

Conta, philosopher. 1 l, Jean Sibelius, Finnish composer. 1.35 l, Horace, Roman poet.

1965, May 10   Photo.   Perf. 13½
Portrait in Black

1738	A561	40b chalky blue	.25	.25
1739	A561	55b bister	.25	.25
1740	A561	60b light lilac	.25	.25
1741	A561	1 l dl red brn	.45	.25
1742	A561	1.35 l olive	.60	.25
1743	A561	1.75 l orange red	1.10	.25
		Nos. 1738-1743 (6)	2.90	1.50

ITU Emblem, Old and New Communication Equipment — A562

1965, May 15   Engr.

1744	A562	1.75 l ultra	.90 .40

ITU, centenary.

Iron Gate, Danube — A562a

Arms of Yugoslavia and Romania and Djerdap Dam — A562b

55b (50d), Iron Gate hydroelectric plant & dam.

Perf. 12½x12

1965, Apr. 30   Litho.   Unwmk.

1745	A562a	30b (25d) lt bl & grn	.25	.25
1746	A562a	55b (50d) lt bl & dk red	.45	.25

Miniature Sheet
Perf. 13½x13

1747	A562b	Sheet of 4	3.00	2.25
a.		80b multi	.35	.35
b.		1.20 l multi	.70	.70

Issued simultaneously by Romania and Yugoslavia for the start of construction of the Iron Gate hydroelectric plant and dam. Valid for postage in both countries.
No. 1747 contains one each of Nos. 1747a, 1747b and Yugoslavia Nos. 771a and 771b. Only Nos. 1747a and 1747b were valid in Romania. Sold for 4 l. See Yugoslavia Nos. 769-771.

Small-bore Rifle Shooting, Kneeling — A563

Designs: 40b, Rifle shooting, prone. 55b, Rapid-fire pistol and map of Europe. 1 l, Free pistol and map of Europe. 1.60 l, Small-bore rifle, standing, and map of Europe. 2 l, 5 l, Marksmen in various shooting positions (all horizontal).

Perf. 12x12½, 12½x12

1965, May 30   Litho.   Unwmk.
Size: 23x43mm, 43x23mm

1748	A563	20b multi	.25	.25
1749	A563	40b dl grn, pink & blk	.25	.25
1750	A563	55b multi	.25	.25
1751	A563	1 l pale grn, blk & ocher	.35	.25
1752	A563	1.60 l multi	.60	.25

Perf. 13½
Size: 51x28mm

1753	A563	2 l multi	.70	.25
		Nos. 1748-1753 (6)	2.40	1.50

European Shooting Championships, Bucharest.
Nos. 1749-1752 were issued imperf. in changed colors. Two other denominations exist, 3.25 l and 5 l, imperf. Value, set of 6, unused $5, canceled $2.

Fat-Frumos and the Giant — A564

Fairy Tales: 40b, Fat-Frumos on horseback and Ileana Cosinzeana. 55b, Harap Alb and the Bear. 1 l, "The Moralist Wolf." 1.35 l, "The Ox and the Calif." 2 l, Wolf and bear pulling sled.

1965, June 25   Photo.   Perf. 13

1756	A564	20b multi	.25	.25
1757	A564	40b multi	.25	.25
1758	A564	55b multi	.30	.25
1759	A564	1 l multi	.45	.25
1760	A564	1.35 l multi	.70	.25
1761	A564	2 l multi	1.00	.25
		Nos. 1756-1761 (6)	2.95	1.50

Bee and Blossoms — A565

Design: 1.60 l, Exhibition Hall, horiz.

Perf. 12x12½, 12½x12

1965, July 28   Litho.   Unwmk.

1762	A565	55b org, bl & pink	.35	.25
1763	A565	1.60 l multi	.60	.25

20th Congress of the Intl Federation of Bee-keeping Assocs. (Apimondia), Bucharest, Aug. 26-31.

Space Achievements A566

Designs: 1.75 l, Col. Pavel Belyayev, Lt. Col. Alexei Leonov and Voskhod 2. 2.40 l, Early Bird over globe. 3.20 l, Lt. Col. Gordon Cooper and Lt. Com. Charles Conrad, Gemini 3 and globe.

1965, Aug. 25   Litho.   Perf. 12x12½

1764	A566	1.75 l dk bl, bl & ver	.80	.25
1765	A566	2.40 l multi	1.10	.25
1766	A566	3.20 l dk bl, lt bl & ver	2.25	.35
		Nos. 1764-1766 (3)	4.15	.85

European Quail — A567

Birds: 10b, Eurasian woodcock. 20b, Eurasian snipe. 40b, Turtle dove. 55b, Mallard. 60b, White-fronted goose. 1 l, Eurasian crane. 1.20 l, Glossy ibis. 1.35 l, Mute swan. 3.25 l, White pelican.

1965, Sept. 10   Photo.   Perf. 13½
Size: 34x34mm
Birds in Natural Colors

1767	A567	5b red brn & rose lil	.25	.25
1768	A567	10b red brn & yel grn	.25	.25
1769	A567	20b brn & bl grn	.25	.25
1770	A567	40b lil & org brn	.25	.25
1771	A567	55b brt grn & lt brn	.25	.25
1772	A567	60b dl org & bl	.30	.25
1773	A567	1 l red & lil	.40	.25
1774	A567	1.20 l dk brn & grn	.60	.25
1775	A567	1.35 l org & ultra	.80	.25

Size: 32x73mm

1776	A567	3.25 l ultra & sep	2.10	.30
		Nos. 1767-1776 (10)	5.45	2.55

Marx and Lenin — A568

1965, Sept. 6   Photo.

1777	A568	55b red, blk & yel	.50 .25

6th Conference of Postal Ministers of Communist Countries, Peking, June 21-July 15.

Vasile Alecsandri — A569

1965, Oct. 9   Unwmk.   Perf. 13½

1778	A569	55b red brn, dk brn & gold	.50 .25

Alecsandri (1821-1890), statesman and poet.

Bird-of-Paradise Flower — A570

Flowers from Cluj Botanical Gardens: 10b, Stanhope orchid. 20b, Paphiopedilum insigne. 30b, Zanzibar water lily, horiz. 40b, Ferocactus, horiz. 55b, Cotton blossom, horiz. 1 l, Hibiscus, horiz. 1.35 l, Gloxinia. 1.75 l, Victoria water lily, horiz. 2.30 l, Hibiscus, bird-of-paradise flower and greenhouse.

Perf. 12x12½, 12½x12

1965, Oct. 25   **Litho.**
Size: 23x43mm, 43x23mm
Flowers in Natural Colors

1779	A570	5b brown	.25	.25
1780	A570	10b green	.25	.25
1781	A570	20b dk bl	.30	.25
1782	A570	30b vio bl	.30	.25
1783	A570	40b red brn	.30	.25
1784	A570	55b dk red	.30	.25
1785	A570	1 l ol grn	.45	.25
1786	A570	1.35 l violet	.60	.25
1787	A570	1.75 l dk grn	1.00	.25

Perf. 13½
Size: 52x30mm

1788	A570	2.30 l green	1.50	.35
		Nos. 1779-1788 (10)	5.25	2.60

The orchid on No. 1780 is attached to the bottom of the limb.

Running — A571

1965, Nov. 10   **Photo.**   *Perf. 13½*

1789	A571	55b shown	.25	.25
1790	A571	1.55 l Soccer	.50	.25
1791	A571	1.75 l Woman diver	.65	.25
1792	A571	2 l Mountaineering	.70	.25
1793	A571	5 l Canoeing, horiz.	1.60	.40
		Nos. 1789-1793 (5)	3.70	1.40

Spartacist Games. No. 1793 commemorates the Romanian victory in the European Kayak Championships.

Pigeon and Post Horn — A572

Designs: 1 l, Pigeon on television antenna and post horn, horiz. 1.75 l, Flying pigeon and post horn, horiz.

1965, Nov. 15   **Engr.**

1794	A572	55b + 45b label	.50	.25
1795	A572	1 l green & brown	.50	.25
1796	A572	1.75 l ol grn & sepia	1.00	.25
		Nos. 1794-1796 (3)	2.00	.75

Issued for Stamp Day. No. 1794 is printed with alternating label showing post rider and emblem of Romanian Philatelists' Association and 45b additional charge. Stamp and label are imperf. between.

Chamois and Hunting Trophy A573

Hunting Trophy and: 1 l, Brown bear. 1.60 l, Red deer. 1.75 l, Wild boar. 3.20 l, Antlers of red deer.

1965, Dec. 10   **Photo.**   *Perf. 13½*
Size: 37x22mm

1797	A573	55b rose lil, yel & brn	.35	.25
1798	A573	1 l brt grn, red & brn	.45	.25
1799	A573	1.60 l lt vio bl, org & brn	1.25	.25
1800	A573	1.75 l rose, grn & blk	1.60	.25

Size: 48x36½mm

1801	A573	3.20 l gray, gold, blk & org	2.50	.40
		Nos. 1797-1801 (5)	6.15	1.40

Probe III Photographing Moon — A574

Designs: 5b, Proton I space station, vert. 15b, Molniya I telecommunication satellite, vert. 3.25 l, Mariner IV and Mars picture, vert. 5 l, Gemini 5.

Perf. 12x12½, 12½x12

1965, Dec. 25   **Litho.**

1802	A574	5b multi	.25	.25
1803	A574	10b vio bl, red & gray	.25	.25
1804	A574	15b pur, gray & org	.25	.25
1805	A574	3.25 l vio bl, blk & red	2.25	.25
1806	A574	5 l dk bl, gray & red org	3.50	.45
		Nos. 1802-1806 (5)	6.50	1.45

Achievements in space research.

Cocker Spaniel — A575

Hunting Dogs: 5b, Dachshund (triangle). 40b, Retriever. 55b, Terrier. 60b, Red setter. 75b, White setter. 1.55 l, Pointers (rectangle). 3.25 l, Duck hunter with retriever (rectangle).

1965, Dec. 28   **Photo.**   *Perf. 13½*
Size: 30x42mm

1807	A575	5b multi	.25	.25

Size: 33½x33½mm

1808	A575	10b multi	.25	.25
1809	A575	40b multi	.30	.25
1810	A575	55b multi	.45	.25
1811	A575	60b multi	.65	.25
1812	A575	75b multi	.90	.25

Size: 43x28mm

1813	A575	1.55 l multi	1.75	.25
1814	A575	3.25 l multi	3.50	.75
		Nos. 1807-1814 (8)	8.05	2.50

Chessboard, Queen and Jester — A576

Chessboard and: 20b, 1.60 l, Pawn and emblem. 55b, 1 l, Rook and knight on horseback.

1966, Feb. 25   **Litho.**   *Perf. 13*

1815	A576	20b multi	.25	.25
1816	A576	40b multi	.30	.25
1817	A576	55b multi	.45	.25
1818	A576	1 l multi	.75	.25
1819	A576	1.60 l multi	1.25	.25
1820	A576	3.25 l multi	2.00	1.60
		Nos. 1815-1820 (6)	5.00	2.85

Chess Olympics in Cuba.

Tractor, Grain and Sun — A577

1966, Mar. 5

1821	A577	55b lt grn & ocher	.40	.25

Founding congress of the National Union of Cooperative Farms.

Gheorghe Gheorghiu-Dej A578

1966, Mar.   **Photo.**   *Perf. 13½*

1822	A578	55b gold & blk	.60	.40
a.		5 l souvenir sheet	4.50	3.75

1st death anniv. of Pres. Gheorghe Gheorghiu-Dej (1901-65). No. 1822a contains design similar to No. 1822 with signature of Gheorghiu-Dej.

Congress Emblem — A579

1966, Mar. 21   *Perf. 13x14½*

1823	A579	55b yel & red	.40	.25

1966 Congress of Communist Youth.

Folk Dancers of Moldavia — A580

Folk Dances: 40b, Oltenia. 55b, Maramaros. 1 l, Muntenia. 1.60 l, Banat. 2 l, Transylvania.

1966, Apr. 4   **Engr.**   *Perf. 13½*
Center in Black

1824	A580	30b lilac	.25	.25
1825	A580	40b brick red	.25	.25
1826	A580	55b brt bl grn	.30	.25
1827	A580	1 l maroon	.50	.25
1828	A580	1.60 l dk bl	1.00	.25
1829	A580	2 l yel grn	1.75	.30
		Nos. 1824-1829 (6)	4.05	1.55

Soccer Game — A581

Designs: 10b, 15b, 55b, 1.75 l, Scenes of soccer play. 4 l, Jules Rimet Cup.

1966, Apr. 25   **Litho.**   **Unwmk.**

1830	A581	5b multi	.25	.25
1831	A581	10b multi	.25	.25
1832	A581	15b multi	.25	.25
1833	A581	55b multi	.45	.25
1834	A581	1.75 l multi	1.10	.25
1835	A581	4 l gold & multi	2.50	.60
a.		10 l souv. sheet	6.00	5.50
		Nos. 1830-1835 (6)	4.80	1.85

World Cup Soccer Championship, Wembley, England, July 11-30.
No. 1835a contains imperf. 10 l multicolored stamp in design of 4 l, but larger (32x46mm). No gum. Issued June 20.

Symbols of Industry A582

1966, May 14   **Photo.**

1836	A582	55b multi	.40	.25

Romanian Trade Union Congress.

Red-breasted Flycatcher A583

Song Birds: 10b, Red crossbill. 15b, Great reed warbler. 20b, European redstart. 55b, European robin. 1.20 l, White-spotted bluethroat. 1.55 l, Yellow wagtail. 3.20 l, Common penduline tit.

1966, May 25   **Photo.**   *Perf. 13½*

1837	A583	5b gold & multi	.40	.25
1838	A583	10b sil & multi	.40	.25
1839	A583	15b gold & multi	.40	.25
1840	A583	20b sil & multi	.40	.25
1841	A583	55b sil & multi	.50	.25
1842	A583	1.20 l gold & multi	.75	.25
1843	A583	1.55 l sil & multi	2.25	.30
1844	A583	3.20 l gold & multi	3.50	.50
		Nos. 1837-1844 (8)	8.60	2.85

Venera 3 (USSR) — A584

Designs: 20b, FR-1 (France). 1.60 l, Luna 9 (USSR). 5 l, Gemini 6 and 7 (US).

1966, June 25

1845	A584	10b dp vio, gray & red	.30	.25
1846	A584	20b ultra, blk & red	.30	.25
1847	A584	1.60 l dk bl, blk & red	.85	.25
1848	A584	5 l bl, blk, brn & red	2.25	.40
		Nos. 1845-1848 (4)	3.70	1.15

International achievements in space.

Urechia
Nestor — A585

Portraits: 5b, George Cosbuc. 10b, Gheorghe Sincai. 40b, Aron Pumnul. 55b, Stefan Luchian. 1 l, Sun Yat-sen. 1.35 l, Gottfried Wilhelm Leibnitz. 1.60 l, Romain Rolland. 1.75 l, Ion Ghica. 3.25 l, Constantin Cantacuzino.

1966, June 28

1849	A585	5b grn, blk & dk bl	.25	.25
1850	A585	10b rose car, grn & blk	.25	.25
1851	A585	20b grn, plum & blk	.25	.25
1852	A585	40b vio bl, brn & blk	.25	.25
1853	A585	55b brn org, bl grn & blk	.25	.25
1854	A585	1 l ocher, vio & blk	.35	.25
1855	A585	1.35 l bl & blk	.35	.25
1856	A585	1.60 l brt grn, dl vio & blk	.55	.25
1857	A585	1.75 l org, dl vio & blk	.55	.25
1858	A585	3.25 l bl, dk car & blk	1.00	.25
		Nos. 1849-1858 (10)	3.95	2.50

Cultural anniversaries.

Country House, by Gheorghe
Petrascu — A586

Paintings: 10b, Peasant Woman, by Nicolae Grigorescu, vert. 20b, Reapers at Rest, by Camil Ressu. 55b, Man with the Blue Cap, by Van Eyck, vert. 1.55 l, Train Compartment, by Daumier. 3.25 l, Betrothal of the Virgin, by El Greco, vert.

1966, July 25   **Unwmk.**

Gold Frame

1859	A586	5b Prus grn & brn org	.25	.25
1860	A586	10b red brn & crim	.25	.25
1861	A586	20b brn & brt grn	.30	.25
1862	A586	55b vio bl & lil	.40	.25
1863	A586	1.55 l dk sl grn & org	1.90	.40
1864	A586	3.25 l vio & ultra	4.00	1.25
		Nos. 1859-1864 (6)	7.10	2.65

See Nos. 1907-1912.

Hottonia
Palustris
A587

Marine Flora: 10b, Ceratophyllum submersum. 20b, Aldrovanda vesiculosa. 40b, Callitriche verna. 55b, Vallisneria spiralis. 1 l, Elodea Canadensis rich. 1.55 l, Hippuris vulgaris. 3.25 l, Myriophyllum spicatum.

1966, Aug. 25   **Litho.**   **Perf. 13½**

Size: 28x40mm

1865	A587	5b multi	.25	.25
1866	A587	10b multi	.25	.25
1867	A587	20b multi	.25	.25
1868	A587	40b multi	.25	.25
1869	A587	55b multi	.25	.25
1870	A587	1 l multi	.45	.25
1871	A587	1.55 l multi	.70	.25

Size: 28x50mm

1872	A587	3.25 l multi	1.40	.35
		Nos. 1865-1872 (8)	3.80	2.10

Derivation of
the
Meter — A588

Design: 1 l, Metric system symbols.

1966, Sept. 10   **Photo.**   **Perf. 13½**

1873	A588	55b salmon & ultra	.30	.25
1874	A588	1 l lt grn & vio	.40	.25

Introduction of metric system in Romania, centenary.

Statue of Ovid
and Medical
School
Emblem — A589

Line Integral
Denoting
Work — A590

I. H. Radulescu, M. Kogalniceanu and
T. Savulescu — A591

Design: 1 l, Academy centenary medal.

1966, Sept. 30   **Size: 22x27mm**

1875	A589	40b lil gray, ultra, sep & gold	.25	.25
1876	A590	55b gray, brn, red & gold	.25	.25

Size: 22x34mm

1877	A589	1 l ultra, brn & gold	.45	.25

Size: 66x28mm

1878	A591	3 l org, dk brn & gold	1.10	.30
		Nos. 1875-1878 (4)	2.05	1.05

Centenary of the Romanian Academy.

Stone
Crab
A592

Molluscs and Crustaceans:5b, Crawfish. 10b, Nassa reticulata, vert. 40b, Campylaea trizona. 55b, Helix lucorum. 1.35 l, Mytilus galloprovincialis. 1.75 l, Lymnaea stagnalis. 3.25 l, Anodonta cygnaea. (10b, 40b, 55b, 1.75 l, are snails; 1.35 l, 3.25 l, are bivalves).

1966, Oct. 15

Animals in Natural Colors

1879	A592	5b dp org	.25	.25
1880	A592	10b lt bl	.25	.25
1881	A592	20b pale lil	.25	.25
1882	A592	40b yel grn	.25	.25
1883	A592	55b car rose	.25	.25
1884	A592	1.35 l brt grn	.55	.25
1885	A592	1.75 l ultra	.65	.25
1886	A592	3.25 l brt org	1.60	.35
		Nos. 1879-1886 (8)	4.05	2.10

Cave Bear
A593

Prehistoric Animals: 10b, Mammoth. 15b, Bison. 55b, Cave elephant. 1.55 l, Stags. 4 l, Dinotherium.

1966, Nov. 25   **Size: 36x22mm**

1887	A593	5b ultra, bl grn & red brn	.25	.25
1888	A593	10b vio, emer & brn	.25	.25
1889	A593	15b ol, grn & dk brn	.25	.25
1890	A593	55b lil, emer & brn	.30	.25
1891	A593	1.55 l ultra, grn & brn	.95	.25

Size: 43x27mm

1892	A593	4 l rose car, grn & brn	1.50	.50
		Nos. 1887-1892 (6)	3.50	1.75

Putna
Monastery,
500th Anniv.
A594

1966   **Photo.**   **Perf. 13½**

1893	A594	2 l multi	.70	.25

Yuri A. Gagarin and
Vostok 1 — A595

Russian Achievements in Space: 10b, Trajectory of Sputnik 1 around globe, horiz. 25b, Valentina Tereshkova and globe with trajectory of Vostok 6. 40b, Andrian G. Nikolayev, Pavel R. Popovich and globe with trajectory of Vostok 3 and 4. 55b, Alexei Leonov walking in space.

1967, Feb. 15   **Photo.**   **Perf. 13½**

1894	A595	10b silver & multi	.25	.25
1895	A595	20b silver & multi	.25	.25
1896	A595	25b silver & multi	.25	.25
1897	A595	40b silver & multi	.35	.25
1898	A595	55b silver & multi	.45	.25
		Nos. 1894-1898,C163-C166 (9)	5.40	2.85

Ten years of space exploration.

Barn Owl
A596

Birds of Prey: 20b, Eagle owl. 40b, Saker falcon. 55b, Egyptian vulture. 75b, Osprey. 1 l, Griffon vulture. 1.20 l, Lammergeier. 1.75 l, Cinereous vulture.

1967, Mar. 20   **Photo.**   **Unwmk.**

Birds in Natural Colors

1899	A596	10b vio & olive	.30	.25
1900	A596	20b bl & grn	.35	.25
1901	A596	40b emer & org	.30	.25
1902	A596	55b yel grn & ocher	.35	.25
1903	A596	75b rose lil & grn	.35	.25
1904	A596	1 l yel org & blk	.70	.25
1905	A596	1.20 l claret & yel	1.25	.25
1906	A596	1.75 l sal pink & gray	1.75	.50
		Nos. 1899-1906 (8)	5.35	2.25

Painting Type of 1966

10b, Woman in Fancy Dress, by Ion Andreescu. 20b, Washwomen, by J. Al. Steriadi. 40b, Women weavers, by St. Dimitrescu, vert. 1.55 l, Venus and Amor, by Lucas Cranach, vert. 3.20 l, Hercules & the Lion of Nemea, by Rubens, vert. 5 l, Haman Asking Esther's Forgiveness, by Rembrandt, vert.

1967, Mar. 30   **Perf. 13½**

Gold Frame

1907	A586	10b dp bl & rose red	.25	.25
1908	A586	20b dp grn & bis	.25	.25
1909	A586	40b carmine & bl	.25	.25
1910	A586	1.55 l dp plum & lt ultra	.50	.25
1911	A586	3.20 l brown & grn	.90	.25
1912	A586	5 l ol grn & org	2.00	.45
		Nos. 1907-1912 (6)	4.15	1.70

Mlle.
Pogany, by
Brancusi
A597

Sculptures: 5b, Girl's head. 10b, The Sleeping Muse, horiz. 20b, The Infinite Column. 40b, The Kiss, horiz. 55b, Earth Wisdom (seated woman). 3.25 l, Gate of the Kiss.

1967, Apr. 27   **Photo.**   **Perf. 13½**

1913	A597	5b dl yel, blk brn & ver	.25	.25
1914	A597	10b bl grn, blk & lil	.25	.25
1915	A597	20b lt bl, blk & rose red	.25	.25
1916	A597	40b pink, sep & brt grn	.25	.30
1917	A597	55b yel grn, blk & ultra	.35	.25
1918	A597	1.20 l bluish lil, ol blk & org	.85	.25
1919	A597	3.25 l emer, blk & cer	1.50	.75
		Nos. 1913-1919 (7)	3.70	2.30

Constantin Brancusi (1876-1957), sculptor.

Coins
of
1867
A598

Design: 1.20 l, Coins of 1966.

1967, May 4

1920	A598	55b multicolored	.25	.25
1921	A598	1.20 l multicolored	1.00	.25

Centenary of Romanian monetary system.

Infantry Soldier,
by Nicolae
Grigorescu
A599

1967, May 9

1922	A599	55b multicolored	.70	.25

90th anniv. of Romanian independence.

Peasants Marching, by Stefan
Luchian — A600

Painting: 40b, Fighting Peasants, by Octav Bancila, vert.

1967, May 20   **Unwmk.**   **Perf. 13½**

1923	A600	40b multicolored	.25	.25
1924	A600	1.55 l multicolored	1.10	.70

60th anniversary of Peasant Uprising.

Centaury — A601

Carpathian Flora: 40b, Hedge mustard. 55b, Columbine. 1.20 l, Alpine violet. 1.75 l, Bell flower. 4 l, Dryas, horiz.

1967, June 10   **Photo.**
Flowers in Natural Colors

1925	A601	20b ocher	.30	.25
1926	A601	40b violet	.30	.25
1927	A601	55b bis & brn red	.30	.25
1928	A601	1.20 l yel & red brn	.50	.25
1929	A601	1.75 l bluish grn & car	.70	.25
1930	A601	4 l lt ultra	2.00	.25
		Nos. 1925-1930 (6)	4.10	1.50

Fortifications, Sibiu — A602

Designs: 40b, Cris Castle. 55b, Wooden Church, Plopis. 1.60 l, Ruins of Nuamtulua Fortress. 1.75 l, Mogosoaia Palace. 2.25 l, Voronet Church.

1967, June 29   **Photo.**   *Perf. 13½*
Size: 33x33mm

1931	A602	20b ultra & multi	.40	.25
1932	A602	40b vio & multi	.60	.25
1933	A602	55b multi	.85	.25
1934	A602	1.60 l multi	1.50	.25
1935	A602	1.75 l multi	1.75	.35

Size: 48x36mm

1936	A602	2.25 l bl & multi	2.75	1.50
		Nos. 1931-1936 (6)	7.85	2.85

Souvenir Sheet
Imperf

1937	A603	5 l lt bl, ultra & blk	4.50	4.50

International Tourist Year.

Map of Romania and ITY Emblem — A603

The Attack at Marasesti, by E. Stoica — A604

1967, July 24   **Unwmk.**   *Perf. 13½*
1938	A604	55b gray, Prus bl & brn	.45	.25

Battle of Marasesti & Oituz, 50th anniv.

Dinu Lipatti, Pianist — A605

Designs: 20b, Al. Orascu, architect. 40b, Gr. Antipa, zoologist. 55b, M. Kogalniceanu, statesman. 1.20 l, Jonathan Swift, writer. 1.75 l, Marie Curie, scientist.

1967, July 29   **Photo.**   *Perf. 13½*
1939	A605	10b ultra, blk & pur	.25	.25
1940	A605	20b org brn, blk & ultra		.25	.25
1941	A605	40b bl grn, blk & org brn		.25	.25
1942	A605	55b dp rose, blk & dk ol grn		.25	.25
1943	A605	1.20 l ol, blk & brn	.40	.25
1944	A605	1.75 l dl bl, blk & bl grn	.80	.25
		Nos. 1939-1944 (6)	2.20	1.50

Cultural anniversaries.

Wrestlers — A606

Designs: 20b, 55b, 1.20 l, 2 l, Various fight scenes and world map (20b, 2 l horizontal); on 2 l maps are large and wrestlers small.

1967, Aug. 28
1945	A606	10b olive & multi	.25	.25
1946	A606	20b citron & multi	.25	.25
1947	A606	55b bister & multi	.25	.25
1948	A606	1.20 l multi	.25	.25
1949	A606	2 l ultra, gold & dp car	1.00	.30
		Nos. 1945-1949 (5)	2.00	1.30

World Greco-Roman Wrestling Championships, Bucharest.

Congress Emblem — A607

1967, Aug. 28
1950	A607	1.60 l lt bl, ultra & dp car	.70	.40

Intl. Linguists' Cong., Bucharest, 8/28-9/2.

Ice Skating — A608

Designs: 40b, Biathlon. 55b, 5 l, Bobsledding. 1 l, Skiing. 1.55 l, Ice Hockey. 2 l, Emblem of 10th Winter Olympic Games. 2.30 l, Ski jump.

1967, Sept. 28   **Photo.**   *Perf. 13½x13*
1951	A608	20b lt bl & multi	.25	.25
1952	A608	40b multi	.25	.25
1953	A608	55b bl & multi	.25	.25
1954	A608	1 l lil & multi	.25	.25
1955	A608	1.55 l multi	.30	.25
1956	A608	2 l gray & multi	.50	.25
1957	A608	2.30 l multi	.85	.35
		Nos. 1951-1957 (7)	2.65	1.85

Souvenir Sheet
Imperf

1958	A608	5 l lt bl & multi	3.25	2.75

10th Winter Olympic Games, Grenoble, France, Feb. 6-18, 1968.
Nos. 1951-1957 issued in sheets of 10 (5x2) and 5 labels.

Curtea de Arges Monastery, 450th Anniv. — A609

1967, Nov. 1   **Unwmk.**   *Perf. 13½*
1959	A609	55b multicolored	.40	.25

Romanian Academy Library, Bucharest, Cent. — A610

1967, Sept. 25   **Litho.**
1960	A610	55b ocher, gray & dk bl	.40	.25

Karl Marx and Title Page — A611

1967, Nov. 4   **Photo.**
1961	A611	40b rose claret, blk & yel	.40	.25

Centenary of the publication of "Das Kapital" by Karl Marx.

Lenin — A612

1967, Nov. 3
1962	A612	1.20 l red, blk & gold	.40	.25

Russian October Revolution, 50th anniv.

Monorail Leaving US EXPO Pavilion A613

Designs: 1 l, EXPO emblem and atom symbol. 1.60 l, Cup, world map and EXPO emblem. 2 l, EXPO emblem.

1967, Nov. 28   **Photo.**
1963	A613	55b grnsh bl, vio & blk	.25	.25
1964	A613	1 l red, blk & gray	.25	.25
1965	A613	1.60 l multicolored	.40	
1966	A613	2 l multicolored	.60	.25
		Nos. 1963-1966 (4)	1.50	1.00

EXPO '67 Intl. Exhib., Montreal, Apr. 28-Oct. 27. No. 1965 also for Romania's victory in the World Fencing Championships in Montreal. Issued in sheets of four.

Truck — A614   Arms of the Republic — A615

Diesel Locomotive — A616

Map Showing Telephone Network A617

Designs: 10b, Communications emblem, vert. 20b, Train. 35b, Plane. 50b, Telephone, vert. 60b, Small loading truck. 1.20 l, Autobus. 1.35 l, Helicopter. 1.50 l, Trolley bus. 1.55 l, Radio station and tower. 1.75 l, Highway. 2 l, Mail truck. 2.40 l, Television tower. 3.20 l, Jet plane. 3.25 l, Steamship. 4 l, Electric train. 5 l, World map and teletype.

Photo.; Engr. (type A615)
1967-68   *Perf. 13½*
1967	A614	5b lt ol grn ('68)	.25	.25
1968	A614	10b henna brn ('68)	.25	.25
1969	A614	20b gray ('68)	.25	.25
1970	A614	35b bl blk ('68)	.25	.25
1971	A615	40b violet blue	.25	.25
1972	A614	50b orange ('68)	.25	.25
1973	A615	55b dull orange	.25	.25
1974	A614	60b orange brn ('68)	.25	.25

Size: 22½x28mm, 28x22½mm
1975	A616	1 l emerald ('68)	.25	.25
1976	A617	1 l red lil ('68)	.25	.25
1977	A617	1.35 l brt blue ('68)	.30	.25
1978	A616	1.50 l rose red ('68)	.35	.25
1979	A616	1.55 l dk brown ('68)	.35	.25
1980	A615	1.60 l rose red	.40	.25
1981	A617	1.75 l dp green ('68)	.40	.25
1982	A617	2 l citron ('68)	.60	.25
1983	A616	2.40 l dk blue ('68)	.75	.25
1984	A617	3 l grnsh blue	.75	.25
1985	A617	3.20 l ocher ('68)	1.00	.25
1986	A616	3.25 l ultra ('68)	1.00	.25
1987	A617	4 l lil rose ('68)	1.25	.25
1988	A617	5 l violet ('68)	1.40	.25
		Nos. 1967-1988 (22)	11.05	5.50

Issue dates: 1967, Nov. 6, Nos. 1971, 1973, 1980; 1967, Dec. 20, No. 1984; 1968, Jan. 20, Nos. 1975, 1976, 1978, 1979, 1981; 1968, Feb. 6, all others.
40th anniv. of the first automatic telephone exchange; introduction of automatic telephone service (No. 1984).
See Nos. 2078-2079, 2269-2284 and design A792.

Coat of Arms, Symbols of Agriculture and Industry A618

55b, Coat of arms. 1.60 l, Romanian flag. 1.75 l, Coat of arms, symbols of arts and education.

1967, Dec. 26   Photo.   Perf. 13½
Size: 27x48mm

1989	A618	40b multicolored	.25	.25
1990	A618	55b multicolored	.25	.25

Size: 33½x48mm

1991	A618	1.60 l multicolored	.50	.25

Size: 27x48mm

1992	A618	1.75 l multicolored	1.00	.55
	Nos. 1989-1992 (4)		2.00	1.30

20th anniversary of the republic.

Souvenir Sheet

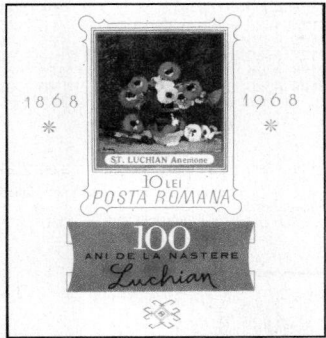

Anemones, by Stefan Luchian — A619

1968, Mar. 30   Litho.   Imperf.

1993	A619	10 l multi	6.00	6.00

Stefan Luchian, Romanian painter, birth cent.

Portrait of a Lady, by Misu Popp A620

Paintings: 10b, The Reveille of Romania, by Gheorghe Tattarescu. 20b, Composition, by Teodorescu Sionion, horiz. 35b, The Judgment of Paris, by Hendrick van Balen, horiz. 55b, Little Girl with Red Kerchief, by Nicolae Grigorescu. 60b, The Mystical Betrothal of St. Catherine, by Lamberto Sustris, horiz. 1 l, Old Nicolas, the Zither Player, by Stefan Luchian. 1.60 l, Man with a Skull, by Dierick Bouts (?). 1.75 l, Madonna and Child with Fruit Basket, by Jan van Bylert. 2.40 l, Medor and Angelica, by Sebastiano Ricci, horiz. 3 l, Summer, by Jacob Jordaens, horiz. 3.20 l, 5 l, Ecce Homo, by Titian.

Gold Frame
Size: 28x49mm

1968   Photo.   Perf. 13½

1994	A620	10b multi	.25	.25

Size: 48½x36½mm, 36x48½mm

1995	A620	20b multi	.25	.25
1996	A620	35b multi	.25	.25
1997	A620	40b multi	.25	.25
1998	A620	55b multi	.25	.25
1999	A620	60b multi	.25	.25
2000	A620	1 l multi	.65	.25

2001	A620	1.60 l multi	.80	.25
2002	A620	1.75 l multi	1.10	.25
2003	A620	2.40 l multi	1.25	.30
2004	A620	3 l multi	2.50	.50
2005	A620	3.20 l multi	2.25	.70
	Nos. 1994-2005 (12)		10.05	3.75

Miniature Sheet
Imperf

2006	A620	5 l multi	5.00	5.00

Issued: 40, 55b, 1, 1.60, 2.40, 3.20, 5 l, 3/28; others, 9/9.
See Nos. 2088-2094, 2124-2130.

Human Rights Flame — A621

1968, May 9   Unwmk.   Perf. 13½

2007	A621	1 l multicolored	.45	.25

Intl. Human Rights Year.

WHO Emblem — A622

1968, May 14   Photo.

2008	A622	1.60 l multi	.50	.25

WHO, 20th anniversary.

"Prince Dragos Hunting Bison," by Nicolae Grigorescu — A623

1968, May 17

2009	A623	1.60 l multi	.70	.25

15th Hunting Cong., Mamaia, May 23-29.

Pioneers and Liberation Monument — A624

Pioneers: 40b, receiving scarfs. 55b, building model planes and boat. 1 l, as radio amateurs. 1.60 l, folk dancing. 2.40 l, Girl Pioneers in camp.

1968, June 9   Photo.   Perf. 13½

2010	A624	5b multi	.25	.25
2011	A624	40b multi	.25	.25
2012	A624	55b multi	.25	.25
2013	A624	1 l multi	.30	.25
2014	A624	1.60 l multi	.50	.25
2015	A624	2.40 l multi	.70	.25
	Nos. 2010-2015 (6)		2.25	1.50

Ion Ionescu de la Brad — A625

Designs: 55b, Emil Racovita. 1.60 l, Prince Mircea of Walachia.

1968   Size: 28x43mm

2016	A625	40b multicolored	.25	.25
2017	A625	55b green & multi	.25	.25

Size: 28x48mm

2018	A625	1.60 l gold & multi	.55	.25
	Nos. 2016-2018 (3)		1.05	.75

Ion Ionescu de la Brad (1818-91); Emil Racovita (1868-1947), explorer and naturalist; 1.60 l, Prince Mircea (1386-1418). Issue dates: 40b, 55b, June 24; 1.60 l, June 22.

Geranium A626

Designs: Various geraniums.

1968, July 20   Photo.   Perf. 13½

2019	A626	10b multicolored	.25	.25
2020	A626	20b multicolored	.25	.25
2021	A626	40b multicolored	.25	.25
2022	A626	55b multicolored	.25	.25
2023	A626	60b multicolored	.25	.25
2024	A626	1.20 l multicolored	.25	.25
2025	A626	1.35 l multicolored	.35	.25
2026	A626	1.60 l multicolored	.75	.25
	Nos. 2019-2026 (8)		2.60	2.00

Avram Iancu, by B. Iscovescu and Demonstrating Students — A627

Demonstrating Students and: 55b, Nicolae Balcescu, by Gheorghe Tattarescu. 1.60 l, Vasile Alecsandri, by N. Livaditti.

1968, July 25

2027	A627	55b gold & multi	.25	.25
2028	A627	1.20 l gold & multi	.45	.25
2029	A627	1.60 l gold & multi	.70	.25
	Nos. 2027-2029 (3)		1.40	.75

120th anniversary of 1848 revolution.

Boxing — A628

Aztec Calendar Stone and: 10b, Javelin, Women's. 20b, Woman diver. 40b, Volleyball.

60b, Wrestling. 1.20 l, Fencing. 1.35 l, Canoeing. 1.60 l, Soccer. 5 l, Running.

1968, Aug. 28

2030	A628	10b multi	.25	.25
2031	A628	20b multi	.25	.25
2032	A628	40b multi	.25	.25
2033	A628	55b multi	.25	.25
2034	A628	60b multi	.25	.25
2035	A628	1.20 l multi	.35	.25
2036	A628	1.35 l multi	.40	.25
2037	A628	1.60 l multi	.65	.25
	Nos. 2030-2037 (8)		2.65	2.00

Souvenir Sheet
Imperf

2038	A628	5 l multi	3.00	2.00

19th Olympic Games, Mexico City, 10/12-17.

Atheneum and Harp — A629

1968, Aug. 20   Litho.   Perf. 12x12½

2039	A629	55b multicolored	.40	.25

Centenary of the Philharmonic Orchestra.

Globe and Emblem — A630

1968, Oct. 4   Litho.   Perf. 13½

2040	A630	1.60 l ultra & gold	.60	.25

Intl. Fed. of Photograpic Art, 20th anniv.

Moldovita Monastery Church — A631

Historic Monuments: 10b, "The Triumph of Trajan," Roman metope, vert. 55b, Cozia monastery church. 1.20 l, Court of Tirgoviste Palace. 1.55 l, Palace of Culture, Jassy. 1.75 l, Corvinus Castle, Hunedoara.

1968, Nov. 25   Engr.   Perf. 13½

2041	A631	10b dk bl, ol & brn	.25	.25
2042	A631	40b rose car, bl & brn	.25	.25
2043	A631	55b ol, brn & vio	.25	.25
2044	A631	1.20 l yel, mar & gray	.30	.25
2045	A631	1.55 l vio brn, dk bl & lt grn	.50	.25
2046	A631	1.75 l org, blk & ol	1.00	.25
	Nos. 2041-2046 (6)		2.55	1.50

Mute Swan — A632

Protected Birds and Animals: 20b, European stilts. 40b, Sheldrakes. 55b, Egret feeding young. 60b, Golden eagle. 1.20 l, Great bustards. 1.35 l, Chamois. 1.60 l, Bison.

1968, Dec. 20   Photo.   Perf. 13½

2047	A632	10b pink & multi	.30	.25
2048	A632	20b multicolored	.30	.25
2049	A632	40b lilac & multi	.30	.25
2050	A632	55b olive & multi	.30	.25
2051	A632	60b multicolored	.30	.25
2052	A632	1.20 l multicolored	.65	.25

2053	A632	1.35 l blue & multi	.75 .25
2054	A632	1.60 l multicolored	.90 .25
		Nos. 2047-2054 (8)	3.80 2.00

Michael the Brave's Entry into Alba Iulia, by D. Stoica — A633

Designs: 1 l, "The Round Dance of Union," by Theodor Aman. 1.75 l, Assembly of Alba Iulia.

1968, Dec. 1   Litho.   Perf. 13½

2055	A633	55b gold & multi	.25 .25
2056	A633	1 l gold & multi	.40 .25
2057	A633	1.75 l gold & multi	.60 .35
a.		Souv. sheet of 3, #2055-2057, imperf.	1.75 1.50
		Nos. 2055-2057 (3)	1.25 .85

50th anniv. of the union of Transylvania and Romania. No. 2057a sold for 4 l.

Woman from Neamt — A634

Regional Costumes: 40b, Man from Neamt. 55b, Woman from Hunedoara. 1 l, Man from Hunedoara. 1.60 l, Woman from Brasov. 2.40 l, Man from Brasov.

1968, Dec. 28   Perf. 12x12½

2058	A634	5b orange & multi	.25 .25
2059	A634	40b blue & multi	.25 .25
2060	A634	55b multi	.25 .25
2061	A634	1 l brown & multi	.25 .25
2062	A634	1.60 l brown & multi	.50 .25
2063	A634	2.40 l multi	.95 .35
		Nos. 2058-2063 (6)	2.45 1.60

1969, Feb. 15

Regional Costumes: 5b, Woman from Dolj. 40b, Man from Dolj. 55b, Woman from Arges. 1 l, Man from Arges. 1.60 l, Woman from Timisoara. 2.40 l, Man from Timisoara.

2064	A634	5b multi	.25 .25
2065	A634	40b multi	.25 .25
2066	A634	55b lil & multi	.25 .25
2067	A634	1 l rose & multi	.25 .25
2068	A634	1.60 l multi	.55 .25
2069	A634	2.40 l brn & multi	1.00 .35
		Nos. 2064-2069 (6)	2.55 1.50

Fencing — A635

Sports: 20b, Women's javelin. 40b, Canoeing. 55b, Boxing. 1 l, Volleyball. 1.20 l, Swimming. 1.60 l, Wrestling. 2.40 l, Soccer.

1969, Mar. 10   Photo.   Perf. 13½
Denominations Black, Athletes in Gray

2070	A635	10b pale brown	.25 .25
2071	A635	20b violet	.25 .25
2072	A635	40b blue	.25 .25
2073	A635	55b red	.25 .25
2074	A635	1 l green	.25 .25
2075	A635	1.20 l brt blue	.25 .25
2076	A635	1.60 l cerise	.45 .25
2077	A635	2.40 l dp green	.85 .25
		Nos. 2070-2077 (8)	2.80 2.00

Type of Regular Issue

1969, Jan. 10   Photo.   Perf. 13½

2078	A614	40b Power lines, vert.	.25 .25
2079	A614	55b Dam, vert.	.25 .25

Painting Type of 1968

Paintings (Nudes): 10b, Woman Carrying Jug, by Gheorghe Tattarescu. 20b, Reclining Woman, by Theodor Pallady, horiz. 35b, Seated Woman, by Nicolae Tonitza. 60b, Venus and Amor, 17th century Flemish School. 1.75 l, 5 l, Diana and Endimion, by Marco Liberi. 3 l, The Three Graces, by Hans von Aachen.

1969, Mar. 27   Photo.   Perf. 13½
Gold Frame
Size: 37x49mm, 49x37mm

2088	A620	10b multi	.25 .25
2089	A620	20b multi	.25 .25
2090	A620	35b multi	.25 .25
2091	A620	60b multi	.30 .25
2092	A620	1.75 l multi	.80 .25

Size: 27½x48½mm

2093	A620	3 l multi	1.75 .45
		Nos. 2088-2093 (6)	3.60 1.70

Miniature Sheet
Imperf

2094	A620	5 l multi	4.50 4.50

No. 2094 contains one stamp 36½x48½mm. with simulated perforations.
No. 2093 is incorrectly inscribed Hans von Achen.

ILO, 50th Anniv. — A636

1969, Apr. 9   Photo.   Perf. 13½

2095	A636	55b multicolored	.50 .25

Symbolic Head — A637

1969, Apr. 28

2096	A637	55b ultra & multi	.35 .25
2097	A637	1.50 l red & multi	1.00 .35

Romania's cultural and economic cooperation with European countries.

Communications Symbol — A638

1969, May 12   Photo.   Perf. 13½

2098	A638	55b vio bl & bluish gray	.40 .25

7th Session of the Conference of Postal and Telecommunications Ministers, Bucharest.

Boxers, Referee and Map of Europe A639

Map of Europe and: 40b, Two boxers. 55b, Sparring. 1.75 l, Referee declaring winner.

1969, May 24

2099	A639	35b multicolored	.25 .25
2100	A639	40b multicolored	.25 .25
2101	A639	55b multicolored	.25 .25
2102	A639	1.75 l blue & multi	.25 .25
		Nos. 2099-2102 (4)	1.35 1.00

European Boxing Championships, Bucharest, May 31-June 8.

Apatura Ilia — A640

Designs: Various butterflies and moths.

1969, June 25   Photo.   Perf. 13½
Insects in Natural Colors

2103	A640	5b yellow grn	.30 .25
2104	A640	10b rose mag	.30 .25
2105	A640	20b violet	.30 .25
2106	A640	40b blue grn	.30 .25
2107	A640	55b brt blue	.30 .25
2108	A640	1 l blue	.45 .25
2109	A640	1.20 l violet bl	.60 .25
2110	A640	2.40 l yellow bis	1.25 .25
		Nos. 2103-2110 (8)	3.80 2.00

Communist Party Flag — A641

1969, Aug. 6   Photo.   Perf. 13½

2111	A641	55b multicolored	.40 .25

10th Romanian Communist Party Congress.

Torch, Atom Diagram and Book — A642

Designs: 40b, Symbols of agriculture, science and industry. 1.75 l, Pylon, smokestack and cogwheel.

1969, Aug. 10

2112	A642	35b multicolored	.25 .25
2113	A642	40b green & multi	.25 .25
2114	A642	1.75 l multicolored	.50 .25
		Nos. 2112-2114 (3)	1.00 .75

Exhibition showing the achievements of Romanian economy during the last 25 years.

Broken Chain — A643

55b, Construction work. 60b, Flags.

1969, Aug. 23

2115	A643	10b multicolored	.25 .25
2116	A643	55b yellow & multi	.25 .25
2117	A643	60b multicolored	.25 .25
		Nos. 2115-2117 (3)	.75 .75

25th anniversary of Romania's liberation from fascist rule.

Juggler on Unicycle — A644

Circus Performers: 20b, Clown. 35b, Trapeze artists. 60b, Dressage and woman trainer. 1.75 l, Woman in high wire act. 3 l, Performing tiger and trainer.

1969, Sept. 29   Photo.   Perf. 13½

2118	A644	10b lt blue & multi	.25 .25
2119	A644	20b lemon & multi	.25 .25
2120	A644	35b lilac & multi	.25 .25
2121	A644	60b multicolored	.25 .25
2122	A644	1.75 l multicolored	.55 .25
2123	A644	3 l ultra & multi	.90 .35
		Nos. 2118-2123 (6)	2.45 1.60

Painting Type of 1968

10b, Venetian Senator, Tintoretto School. 20b, Sofia Kretzulescu, by Gheorghe Tattarescu. 35b, Phillip IV, by Velazquez. 60b, Man Reading and Child, by Hans Memling. 1.75 l, Doamnei d'Aguesseau, by Madame Vigée-Lebrun. 3 l, Portrait of a Woman, by Rembrandt. 5 l, The Return of the Prodigal Son, by Bernardino Licinio, horiz.

Gold Frame

1969		**Size: 36½x49mm**	
2124	A620	10b multi	.25 .25
2125	A620	20b multi	.25 .25
2126	A620	35b multi	.25 .25
2127	A620	60b multi	.40 .25
2128	A620	1.75 l multi	.80 .25
2129	A620	3 l multi	1.40 .40
		Nos. 2124-2129 (6)	3.35 1.65

Miniature Sheet
Imperf

2130	A620	5 l gold & multi	3.00 2.25

No. 2130 contains one stamp with simulated perforations.
Issue dates: 5 l, July 31. Others, Oct. 1.

Masks — A645

1969, Nov. 24   Photo.   Perf. 13½

2131	A645	40b Branesti	.25 .25
2132	A645	55b Tudora	.25 .25
2133	A645	1.55 l Birsesti	.50 .25
2134	A645	1.75 l Rudaria	.60 .25
		Nos. 2131-2134 (4)	1.60 1.00

Armed Forces Memorial A646

1969, Oct. 25

2135	A646	55b red, blk & gold	.40 .25

25th anniversary of the People's Army.

Locomotives of 1869 and 1969 — A647

1969, Oct. 31

2136	A647	55b silver & multi	.40 .25

Bucharest-Filaret-Giurgevo railroad, cent.

Apollo 12 landing module.

1969, Nov. 24

2137	A648	1.50 l multi	.50	.40

2nd landing on the moon, Nov. 19, 1969, astronauts Captains Alan Bean, Charles Conrad, Jr. and Richard Gordon.

Printed in sheets of 4 with 4 labels (one label with names of astronauts, one with Apollo 12 emblem and 2 silver labels with picture of landing module, Intrepid). Value, unused $2.50; used $2.25.

A649

New Year: 40b, Mother Goose in Goat Disguise. 55b, Children singing and decorated tree, Sorcova. 1.50 l, Drummer, and singer, Buhaiul. 2.40 l, Singer and bell ringer, Plugusurol.

1969, Dec. 25   Photo.   Perf. 13½

2138	A649	40b bister & multi	.25	.25
2139	A649	55b lilac & multi	.25	.25
2140	A649	1.50 l blue & multi	.60	.25
2141	A649	2.40 l multicolored	1.10	.25
		Nos. 2138-2141 (4)	2.20	1.00

The Last Judgment (detail), Voronet Monastery — A650

North Moldavian Monastery Frescoes: 10b, Stephen the Great and family, Voronet. 20b, Three prophets, Sucevita. 60b, St. Nicholas (scene from his life), Sucevita, vert. 1.75 l, Siege of Constantinople, 7th century, Moldovita. 3 l, Plowman, Voronet, vert.

1969, Dec. 15

2142	A650	10b gold & multi	.25	.25
2143	A650	20b gold & multi	.25	.25
2144	A650	35b gold & multi	.25	.25
2145	A650	60b gold & multi	.30	.25
2146	A650	1.75 l gold & multi	.50	.25
2147	A650	3 l gold & multi	1.40	.25
		Nos. 2142-2147 (6)	2.95	1.50

Ice Hockey A651

Designs: 55b, Goalkeeper. 1.20 l, Two players with puck. 2.40 l, Player and goalkeeper.

1970, Jan. 20   Perf. 13½

2148	A651	20b yellow & multi	.25	.25
2149	A651	55b multicolored	.25	.25
2150	A651	1.20 l pink & multi	.50	.25
2151	A651	2.40 l lt blue & multi	1.10	.30
		Nos. 2148-2151 (4)	2.10	1.05

World Ice Hockey Championships, Bucharest and Galati, Feb. 24-Mar. 5.

Pasqueflower A652

Flowers: 10b, Adonis vernalis. 20b, Thistle. 40b, Almond tree blossoms. 55b, Iris. 1 l, Flax. 1.20 l, Sage. 2.40 l, Peony.

1970, Feb. 25   Photo.   Perf. 13½

2152	A652	5b yellow & multi	.25	.25
2153	A652	10b green & multi	.25	.25
2154	A652	20b lt bl & multi	.25	.25
2155	A652	40b violet & multi	.25	.25
2156	A652	55b ultra & multi	.25	.25
2157	A652	1 l multicolored	.25	.25
2158	A652	1.20 l red & multi	.45	.25
2159	A652	2.40 l multicolored	.95	.25
		Nos. 2152-2159 (8)	2.90	2.00

Japanese Print and EXPO '70 Emblem A653

Design: 1 l, Pagoda, EXPO '70 emblem.

1970, Mar. 23

2160	A653	20b gold & multi	.25	.25

Size: 29x92mm

2161	A653	1 l gold & multi	.50	.25

EXPO '70 Intl. Exhib., Osaka, Japan, Mar. 15-Sept. 13.

A souvenir sheet exists with perforated label in pagoda design of 1 l. Issued Nov. 28, 1970. Value $3.

Camille, by Claude Monet (Maximum Card) — A654

1970, Apr. 19   Photo.   Perf. 13½

2162	A654	1.50 l gold & multi	.55	.25

Franco-Romanian Maximafil Phil. Exhib.

Cuza, by C. Popp de Szathmary — A655

1970, Apr. 20   Perf. 13½

2163	A655	55b gold & multi	.35	.25

Alexandru Ioan Cuza (1820-1866), prince of Romania.

Lenin (1870-1924) A656

1970, Apr. 21   Photo.   Perf. 13½

2164	A656	40b dk red & multi	.35	.25

Map of Europe with Capital Cities A657

1970, Apr. 28

2165	A657	40b grn, brn org & blk	.50	.35
2166	A657	1.50 l ultra, yel brn & blk	1.00	.70

Inter-European cultural and economic cooperation.

Victory Monument, Romanian and Russian Flags — A658

1970, May 9

2167	A658	55b red & multi	.35	.25

25th anniv. of victory over the Germans.

Greek Silver Drachm, 5th Century B.C. — A659

Coins: 20b, Getic-Dacian silver didrachm, 2nd-1st centuries B.C. 35b, Emperor Trajan's copper sestertius, 106 A.D. 60b, Mircea ducat, 1400. 1.75 l, Stephen the Great's silver groschen, 1460. 3 l, Brasov klippe-taler, 1601, vert.

1970, May 15

2168	A659	10b ultra, blk & sil	.25	.25
2169	A659	20b hn brn, blk & sil	.25	.25
2170	A659	35b grn, dk brn & gold	.25	.25
2171	A659	60b brn, blk & sil	.25	.25
2172	A659	1.75 l brt bl, blk & sil	.25	.25
2173	A659	3 l dk car, blk & sil	1.00	.25
		Nos. 2168-2173 (6)	2.50	1.50

Soccer Players and Ball — A660

Soccer ball & various scenes from soccer game.

1970, May 26   Perf. 13½

2174	A660	40b multi	.25	.25
2175	A660	55b multi	.25	.25
2176	A660	1.75 l blue & multi	.60	.25
2177	A660	3.30 l multi	1.00	.30
		Nos. 2174-2177 (4)	2.10	1.05

Souvenir Sheet

2178		Sheet of 4	3.00	2.00
a.		A660 1.20 l multi	.35	.25
b.		A660 1.50 l multi	.50	.25
c.		A660 1.55 l multi	.60	.25
d.		A660 1.75 l multi	.60	.25

9th World Soccer Championships for the Jules Rimet Cup, Mexico City, May 30-June 21. No. 2178 contains 4 stamps similar to Nos. 2174-2177, but with only one quarter of the soccer ball on each stamp, forming one large ball in the center of the block.

Moldovita Monastery — A661

Frescoes from North Moldavian Monasteries.

1970, June 29   Perf. 13½

Size: 36½x49mm

2179	A661	10b gold & multi	.25	.25

Size: 27½x49mm

2180	A661	20b gold & multi	.25	.25

Size: 36½x49mm, 48x37mm

2181	A661	40b gold & multi	.25	.25
2182	A661	55b gold & multi	.25	.25
2183	A661	1.75 l gold & multi	.35	.25
2184	A661	3 l gold & multi	1.00	.35
		Nos. 2179-2184 (6)	2.35	1.60

Miniature Sheet

2185	A661	5 l gold & multi	2.50	2.25

Friedrich Engels (1820-1895), German Socialist — A662

1970, July 10   Photo.   Perf. 13½

2186	A662	1.50 l multi	.45	.25

Aerial View of Iron Gate Power Station A663

1970, July 13

2187	A663	35b blue & multi	.30	.25

Hydroelectric plant at the Iron Gate of the Danube.

Cargo Ship A664

1970, July 17

2188	A664	55b blue & multi	.30	.25

Romanian merchant marine, 75th anniv.

Exhibition Hall and Oil Derrick A665

1970, July 20
2189 A665 1.50 l multi .45 .25
International Bucharest Fair, Oct. 13-24.

Opening of UPU Headquarters, Bern — A666

1970, Aug. 17   Photo.   Perf. 13½
2190 A666 1.50 l ultra & slate green .45 .25

Education Year Emblem — A667

1970, Aug. 17
2191 A667 55b black, pur & red .40 .25
International Education Year.

Iceberg Rose — A668

Roses: 35b, Wiener charme. 55b, Pink luster. 1 l, Piccadilly. 1.50 l, Orange Delbard. 2.40 l, Sibelius.

1970, Aug. 21
2192 A668 20b dk red, grn & yel .25 .25
2193 A668 35b vio, yel & grn .25 .25
2194 A668 55b blue, rose & grn .25 .25
2195 A668 1 l grn, car rose & yel .40 .25
2196 A668 1.50 l dk bl, red & grn .55 .25
2197 A668 2.40 l brt bl, dp red & grn 1.00 .25
Nos. 2192-2197 (6) 2.70 1.50

Spaniel and Pheasant, by Jean B. Oudry A669

Paintings: 10b, The Hunt, by Domenico Brandi. 35b, The Hunt, by Jan Fyt. 60b, After the Chase, by Jacob Jordaens. 1.75 l, 5 l, Game Merchant, by Frans Snyders (horiz.). 3 l, The Hunt, by Adriaen de Gryeff. Sizes: 37x49mm (10b, 35b); 35x33mm (20b, 60b, 3 l); 49x37mm (1.75 l, 3 l).

1970, Sept. 20   Photo.   Perf. 13½
2198 A669 10b gold & multi .25 .25
2199 A669 20b gold & multi .25 .25
2200 A669 35b gold & multi .25 .25
2201 A669 60b gold & multi .40 .25

2202 A669 1.75 l gold & multi .90 .30
2203 A669 3 l gold & multi 1.75 .60
Nos. 2198-2203 (6) 3.80 1.90
Miniature Sheet
2204 A669 5 l gold & multi 3.75 3.25

UN Emblem — A670

1970, Sept. 29
2205 A670 1.50 l lt bl, ultra & blk .60 .25
25th anniversary of the United Nations.

Mother and Child — A671

Designs: 1.50 l, Red Cross relief trucks and tents. 1.75 l, Rebuilding houses.

1970, Sept. 25
2206 A671 55b bl gray, blk & ol .25 .25
2207 A671 1.50 l ol, blk & car .45 .25
a. Strip of 3, #2206-2207, C179 1.40 .55
2208 A671 1.75 l blue & multi .70 .25
Nos. 2206-2208, C179 (4) 1.65 1.00
Plight of the Danube flood victims.

Arabian Thoroughbred — A672

Horses: 35b, American trotter. 55b, Ghidran (Anglo-American). 1 l, Northern Moravian. 1.50 l, Trotter thoroughbred. 2.40 l, Lippizaner.

1970, Oct. 10   Photo.   Perf. 13½
2209 A672 20b blk & multi .25 .25
2210 A672 35b blk & multi .25 .25
2211 A672 55b blk & multi .25 .25
2212 A672 1 l blk & multi .30 .25
2213 A672 1.50 l blk & multi .50 .25
2214 A672 2.40 l blk & multi 1.10 .25
Nos. 2209-2214 (6) 2.65 1.50

Ludwig van Beethoven (1770-1827), Composer — A673

1970, Nov. 2
2215 A673 55b multicolored 1.25 .25

Abstract, by Joan Miró — A674

1970, Dec. 10   Photo.   Perf. 13½
2216 A674 3 l ultra & multi 2.75 2.75
Souvenir Sheet
Imperf
2217 A674 5 l ultra & multi 5.00 5.00
Plight of the Danube flood victims. No. 2216 issued in sheets of 5 stamps and label with signature of Miró and date of flood. No. 2217 contains one stamp with simulated perforation.

The Sense of Sight, by Gonzales Coques A675

"The Senses," paintings by Gonzales Coques (1614-1684): 20b, Hearing. 35b, Smell. 60b, Taste. 1.75 l, Touch. 3 l, Bruckenthal Museum, Sibiu. 5 l, View of Sibiu, 1808, horiz.

1970, Dec. 15   Photo.   Perf. 13½
2218 A675 10b gold & multi .25 .25
2219 A675 20b gold & multi .25 .25
2220 A675 35b gold & multi .25 .25
2221 A675 60b gold & multi .25 .25
2222 A675 1.75 l gold & multi .60 .25
2223 A675 3 l gold & multi 1.00 .45
Nos. 2218-2223 (6) 2.60 1.70
Miniature Sheet
Imperf
2224 A675 5 l gold & multi 2.75 2.50

Men of Three Races A676

1971, Feb. 23   Photo.   Perf. 13½
2225 A676 1.50 l multi .60 .25
Intl. year against racial discrimination.

Tudor Vladimirescu, by Theodor Aman — A677

1971, Feb. 20
2226 A677 1.50 l gold & multi .60 .25
Vladimirescu, patriot, 150th death anniv.

German Shepherd A677a

Dogs: 35b, Bulldog. 55b, Fox terrier. 1 l, Setter. 1.50 l, Cocker spaniel. 2.40 l, Poodle.

1971, Feb. 22
2227 A677a 20b blk & multi .25 .25
2228 A677a 35b blk & multi .25 .25
2229 A677a 55b blk & multi .25 .25
2230 A677a 1 l blk & multi .40 .25
2231 A677a 1.50 l blk & multi .65 .25
2232 A677a 2.40 l blk & multi 1.25 .40
Nos. 2227-2232 (6) 3.05 1.65

Paris Commune — A678

1971, Mar. 15   Photo.   Perf. 13½
2233 A678 40b multicolored .40 .25
Centenary of the Paris Commune.

Congress Emblem — A679

1971, Mar. 23
2234 A679 55b multicolored .40 .25
Romanian Trade Unions Congress.

Rock Formation A680

Designs: 10b, Bicazului Gorge, vert. 55b, Winter resort. 1 l, Danube Delta view. 1.50 l, Lakeside resort. 2.40 l, Venus, Jupiter, Neptune Hotels on Black Sea.

Size: 23x38mm, 38x23mm
1971, Apr. 15
2235 A680 10b multi .25 .25
2236 A680 40b multi .25 .25
2237 A680 55b multi .25 .25
2238 A680 1 l multi .30 .25
2239 A680 1.50 l multi .50 .25
Size: 76½x28mm
2240 A680 2.40 l multi 1.00 .35
Nos. 2235-2240 (6) 2.55 1.60
Tourist publicity.

Arrow Pattern A681

Design: 1.75 l, Wave pattern.

1971, Apr. 28   Photo.   Perf. 13½
2241 A681 55b multi   .75   .60
2242 A681 1.75 l multi   1.50 1.00
Inter-European Cultural and Economic Collaboration. Sheets of 10.

Historical
Museum — A682

1971, May 7   Photo.   Perf. 13½
2243 A682 55b blue & multi   .40   .25
For Romania's Historical Museum.

Communist Party Emblem — A683

Demonstration, by
A.
Anastasiu — A684

35b, Reading Proclamation, by Stefan Szonyi.

1971, May 8
2244 A684 35b multicolored   .25   .25
2245 A683 40b multicolored   .25   .25
2246 A684 55b multicolored   .25   .25
      Nos. 2244-2246 (3)   .75   .75
Romanian Communist Party, 50th anniv.

Souvenir Sheets

Motra
Tone, by
Kole
Idromeno
A685

Dancing the Hora, by Theodor
Aman — A686

Designs: b, Girl from Kalotina, by V. Dimitrov-Maystora. c, Rosa Botzaris, by Joseph Stieler. d, Woman in Costume, by Katarina Ivanovic. e, Argeseanca, by Carol Popp de Szathmary. f, Woman in Modern Dress, by Ibrahim Calli.

1971, May 25   Photo.   Perf. 13½
2247 A685 Sheet of 6   4.00 3.50
  a.-f. 1.20 l any single   .55   .40
2248 A686 5 l multicolored   3.00 3.00
Balkanphila III Stamp Exhibition, Bucharest, June 27-July 2.
No. 2247 contains 6 stamps in 3 rows and 6 labels showing exhibition emblem and "60b."

Pomegranate
Flower — A687

Flowers: 35b, Slipperwort. 55b, Lily. 1 l, Mimulus. 1.50 l, Morning-glory. 2.40 l, Leaf cactus, horiz.

1971, June 20
2249 A687 20b ultra & multi   .25   .25
2250 A687 35b red & multi   .25   .25
2251 A687 55b ultra & multi   .25   .25
2252 A687 1 l car & multi   .45   .25
2253 A687 1.50 l car & multi   .75   .25
2254 A687 2.40 l ultra & multi   1.10   .30
      Nos. 2249-2254 (6)   3.05 1.55

Nude, by
Iosif Iser
A688

Paintings of Nudes: 20b, by Camil Ressu. 35b, by Nicolae Grigorescu. 60b, by Eugene Delacroix (odalisque). 1.75 l, by Auguste Renoir. 3 l, by Palma il Vecchio (Venus and Amor). 5 l, by Il Bronzino (Venus and Amor). 60b, 3 l, 5 l, horiz.

1971, July 25   Photo.   Perf. 13½
**Size: 38x50mm, 49x39mm,
29x50mm (20b)**
2255 A688 10b gold & multi   .25   .25
2256 A688 20b gold & multi   .25   .25
2257 A688 35b gold & multi   .25   .25
2258 A688 60b gold & multi   .25   .25
2259 A688 1.75 l gold & multi   .35   .25
2260 A688 3 l gold & multi   1.40   .35
      Nos. 2255-2260 (6)   2.75 1.60

Miniature Sheet
Imperf
2261 A688 5 l gold & multi   3.25 3.25

Ships in Storm, by B. Peters — A689

Paintings of Ships by: 20b, Ludolf Backhuysen. 35b, Andries van Eertvelt. 60b, M. W. Arnold. 1.75 l, Ivan Konstantinovich Aivazovski. 3 l, Jean Steriadi. 5 l, N. Darascu, vert.

1971, Sept. 15   Photo.   Perf. 13½
2262 A689 10b gold & multi   .25   .25
2263 A689 20b gold & multi   .25   .25
2264 A689 35b gold & multi   .25   .25
2265 A689 60b gold & multi   .25   .25
2266 A689 1.75 l gold & multi   .45   .25
2267 A689 3 l gold & multi   1.00   .35
      Nos. 2262-2267 (6)   2.45 1.60

Miniature Sheet
2268 A689 5 l gold & multi   2.50 2.50

Type of Regular Issue
Designs as Before and: 3.60 l, Mail collector. 4.80 l, Mailman. 6 l, Ministry of Posts.

1971   Photo.   Perf. 13½
Size: 16½x23mm, 23x16½mm
2269 A616 1 l emerald   .25   .25
2270 A617 1.20 l red lilac   .25   .25
2271 A617 1.35 l brt blue   .30   .25
2272 A616 1.50 l orange red   .35   .25
2273 A616 1.55 l sepia   .35   .25
2274 A617 1.75 l deep green   .40   .25
2275 A617 2 l citron   .45   .25
2276 A616 2.40 l dark blue   .55   .25
2277 A617 3 l greenish bl   .75   .25
2278 A617 3.20 l ocher   .75   .25
2279 A616 3.25 l ultra   .85   .25
2280 A616 3.60 l blue   .90   .25
2281 A617 4 l lilac rose   1.10   .25
2282 A616 4.80 l grnsh blue   1.20   .25
2283 A617 5 l violet   1.25   .25
2284 A616 6 l dp magenta   1.60   .25
      Nos. 2269-2284 (16)   11.30 4.00

Prince Neagoe
Basarab
A690

1971, Sept. 20   Perf. 13½
2288 A690 60b gold & multi   .40   .25
450th anniversary of the death of Prince Neagoe Basarab of Walachia.

Theodor Pallady
(Painter) — A691

Portraits of: 55b, Benvenuto Cellini (1500-1571), sculptor. 1.50 l, Antoine Watteau (1684-1721), painter. 2.40 l, Albrecht Dürer (1471-1528), painter.

1971, Oct. 12   Photo.   Perf. 13½
2289 A691 40b gold & multi   .25   .25
2290 A691 55b gold & multi   .25   .25
2291 A691 1.50 l gold & multi   .50   .25
2292 A691 2.40 l gold & multi   1.00   .25
      Nos. 2289-2292 (4)   2.00 1.00

Anniversaries of famous artists.

Proclamation of
Cyrus the
Great — A692

1971, Oct. 12
2293 A692 55b multicolored   .50   .25
2500th anniversary of the founding of the Persian empire by Cyrus the Great.

Figure
Skating — A693

Designs: 20b, Ice hockey. 40b, Biathlon (skier). 55b, Bobsledding. 1.75 l, Skiing. 3 l, Sapporo '72 emblem. 5 l, Olympic flame and emblem.

1971, Oct. 25
2294 A693 10b lt bl, blk & red   .25   .25
2295 A693 20b multicolored   .25   .25
2296 A693 40b multicolored   .25   .25
2297 A693 55b lt bl, blk & red   .25   .25
2298 A693 1.75 l lt bl, blk & red   .50   .25
2299 A693 3 l lt bl, blk & red   .80   .25
      Nos. 2294-2299 (6)   2.30 1.50

Miniature Sheet
Imperf
2300 A693 5 l multicolored   2.75 2.75

11th Winter Olympic Games, Sapporo, Japan, Feb. 3-13, 1972. Nos. 2294-2296 printed se-tenant in sheets of 15 (5x3); Nos. 2297-2298 printed se-tenant in sheets of 10 (5x2). No. 2300 contains one stamp 37x50mm.

St.
George
and the
Dragon
A694

Frescoes from North Moldavian Monasteries: 10b, 20b, 40b, Moldovita. 55b, 1.75 l, 5 l, Voronet. 3 l, Arborea, horiz.

1971, Nov. 30   Photo.   Perf. 13½
2301 A694 10b gold & multi   .25   .25
2302 A694 20b gold & multi   .25   .25
2303 A694 40b gold & multi   .25   .25
2304 A694 55b gold & multi   .25   .25
2305 A694 1.75 l gold & multi   .70   .25
2306 A694 3 l gold & multi   1.00   .40
      Nos. 2301-2306 (6)   2.70 1.65

Miniature Sheet
Imperf
2307 A694 5 l gold & multi   2.50 2.50
No. 2307 contains one stamp 44x56mm.

Ferdinand
Magellan
A695

Designs: 55b, Johannes Kepler and observation tower. 1 l, Yuri Gagarin and rocket orbiting earth. 1.50 l, Baron Ernest R. Rutherford, atom, nucleus and chemical apparatus.

1971, Dec. 20
2308 A695 40b grn, brt rose &
              dk bl   .25   .25
2309 A695 55b lil, bl & gray grn   .25   .25
2310 A695 1 l violet & multi   .35   .25
2311 A695 1.50 l red brn, grn &
              bl   .60   .25
      Nos. 2308-2311 (4)   1.45 1.00

Magellan (1480?-1521), navigator; Kepler (1571-1630), astronomer; Gagarin, 1st man in space, 10th anniv.; Ernest R. Rutherford (1871-1937), British physicist.

Matei Millo — A696

Design: 1 l, Nicolae Iorga.

1971, Dec.
2312	A696	55b blue & multi	.25	.25
2313	A696	1 l purple & multi	.30	.25

Millo (1814-1896), playwright; Iorga (1871-1940), historian and politician.

Young Communists Union Emblem — A697

1972, Feb.
2314	A697	55b dk bl, red & gold	.40	.25

Young Communists Union, 50th anniv.

Young Animals — A698

1972, Mar. 10   Photo.   Perf. 13½
2315	A698	20b Lynx	.25	.25
2316	A698	35b Foxes	.25	.25
2317	A698	55b Roe fawns	.25	.25
2318	A698	1 l Wild pigs	.25	.25
2319	A698	1.50 l Wolves	.50	.25
2320	A698	2.40 l Bears	1.00	.25
	Nos. 2315-2320 (6)		2.50	1.50

Wrestling — A699

Olympic Rings and: 20b, Canoeing. 55b, Soccer. 1.55 l, Women's high jump. 2.90 l, Boxing. 6.70 l, Field ball.

1972, Apr. 25   Photo.   Perf. 13½
2321	A699	10b yel & multi	.25	.25
2322	A699	20b multicolored	.25	.25
2323	A699	55b gray & multi	.25	.25
2324	A699	1.55 l grn & multi	.35	.25
2325	A699	2.90 l multicolored	.80	.25
2326	A699	6.70 l lil & multi	1.25	.50
	Nos. 2321-2326 (6)		3.15	1.75

20th Olympic Games, Munich, Aug. 26-Sept. 10. See Nos. C186-C187.

Stylized Map of Europe and Links A700

Design: 2.90 l, Entwined arrows and links.

1972, Apr. 28
2327	A700	1.75 l dp car, gold & blk	1.10	.75
2328	A700	2.90 l grn, gold & blk	1.50	1.00
a.	Pair, #2327-2328		2.60	2.00

Inter-European Cultural and Economic Collaboration.

UIC Emblem and Trains A701

1972, May 20   Photo.   Perf. 13½
2329	A701	55b dp car rose, blk & gold	.35	.25

50th anniv., Intl. Railroad Union (UIC).

Souvenir Sheet

"Summer," by Peter Brueghel, the Younger — A702

1972, May 20   Perf. 13x13½
2330	A702	6 l gold & multi	3.00	3.00

Belgica 72, Intl. Phil. Exhib., Brussels, June 24-July 9.

Peony — A703

Protected Flowers: 40b, Pink. 55b, Edelweiss. 60b, Nigritella rubra. 1.35 l, Narcissus. 2.90 l, Lady's slipper.

1972, June 5   Photo.   Perf. 13
Flowers in Natural Colors
2331	A703	20b dk vio bl	.25	.25
2332	A703	40b chocolate	.25	.25
2333	A703	.55b dp blue	.25	.25
2334	A703	60b dk green	.30	.25
2335	A703	1.35 l violet	.65	.25
2336	A703	2.90 l dk Prus bl	1.25	.40
	Nos. 2331-2336 (6)		2.95	1.65

Saligny Bridge, Cernavoda — A704

Danube Bridges: 1.75 l, Giurgeni Bridge, Vadul. 2.75 l, Friendship Bridge, Giurgiu-Ruse.

1972, June 25   Photo.   Perf. 13½
2337	A704	1.35 l multi	.35	.25
2338	A704	1.75 l multi	.50	.25
2339	A704	2.75 l multi	.85	.25
	Nos. 2337-2339 (3)		1.70	.75

North Railroad Station, Bucharest, Cent. A705

1972, July 4
2340	A705	55b ultra & multi	.35	.25

Water Polo and Olympic Rings A706

Olympic Rings and: 20b, Pistol shoot. 55b, Discus. 1.55 l, Gymnastics, women's. 2.75 l, Canoeing. 6.40 l, Fencing.

1972, July 5   Photo.   Perf. 13½
2341	A706	10b ol, gold & lil	.25	.25
2342	A706	20b red, gold & grn	.25	.25
2343	A706	55b grn, gold & brn	.25	.25
2344	A706	1.55 l vio, gold & ol	.40	.25
2345	A706	2.75 l bl, gold & gray	.70	.25
2346	A706	6.40 l pur, gold & gray	1.50	.45
	Nos. 2341-2346 (6)		3.35	1.70

20th Olympic Games, Munich, Aug. 26-Sept. 11. See No. C187.

Stamp Printing Press — A707

1972, July 25
2347	A707	55b multicolored	.35	.25

Centenary of the stamp printing office.

Stefan Popescu, Self-portrait — A708

1972, Aug. 10
2348	A708	55b shown	.25	.25
2349	A708	1.75 l Octav Bancila	.25	.25
2350	A708	2.90 l Gheorghe Petrascu	.50	.25
2351	A708	6.50 l Ion Andreescu	1.25	.30
	Nos. 2348-2351 (4)		2.25	1.05

Self-portraits by Romanian painters.

Runner with Torch, Olympic Rings — A709

1972, Aug. 13
2352	A709	55b sil, bl & claret	.75	.25

Olympic torch relay from Olympia, Greece, to Munich, Germany, passing through Romania.

City Hall Tower, Sibiu — A710

Designs: 1.85 l, St. Michael's Cathedral, Cluj. 2.75 l, Sphinx Rock, Mt. Bucegi, horiz. 3.35 l, Heroes' Monument, Bucharest. 3.45 l, Sinaia Castle, horiz. 5.15 l, Hydroelectric Works, Arges, horiz. 5.60 l, Church of the Epiphany, Iasi. 6.20 l, Bran Castle. 6.40 l, Hunedoara Castle, horiz. 6.80 l, Polytechnic Institute, Bucharest, horiz. 7.05 l, Black Church, Brasov. 8.45 l, Atheneum, Bucharest. 9.05 l, Excavated Coliseum, Sarmizegetusa, horiz. 9.10 l, Hydroelectric Station, Iron Gate, horiz. 9.85 l, Monument, Cetatea. 11.90 l, Republic Palace, horiz. 12.75 l, Television Station. 13.30 l, Arch, Alba Iulia, horiz. 16.20 l, Clock Tower, Sighisoara.

1972   Photo.   Perf. 13
Size: 23x18mm, 17x24mm
2353	A710	1.85 l brt purple	.25	.25
2354	A710	2.75 l gray	.40	.25
2355	A710	3.35 l magenta	.55	.25
2356	A710	3.45 l green	.55	.25
2357	A710	5.15 l brt blue	.80	.25
2358	A710	5.60 l blue	1.00	.25
2359	A710	6.20 l cerise	1.00	.25
2360	A710	6.40 l sepia	1.00	.25
2361	A710	6.80 l rose red	1.25	.25
2362	A710	7.05 l black	1.25	.25
2363	A710	8.45 l rose red	1.50	.25
2364	A710	9.05 l dull green	1.40	.25
2365	A710	9.10 l ultra	1.40	.25
2366	A710	9.85 l green	1.60	.25

Size: 19½x29mm, 29x21mm
2367	A710	10 l dp brown	1.60	.25
2368	A710	11.90 l bluish blk	1.75	.25
2369	A710	12.75 l dk violet	1.75	.25
2370	A710	13.30 l dull red	2.10	.25
2371	A710	16.20 l olive grn	2.75	.25
	Nos. 2353-2371,C193 (20)		25.40	5.15

View of Satu-Mare — A711

1972, Oct. 5
2372	A711	55b multicolored	.50	.25

Millennium of Satu-Mare.

Tennis Racket and Davis Cup A712

1972, Oct. 10   **Perf. 13½**
2373 A712 2.75 l multi   1.40 .25
Davis Cup finals between Romania and US, Bucharest, Oct. 13-15.

Venice, by Gheorge Petrascu — A713

Paintings of Venice by: 20b, N. Darascu. 55b, Petrascu. 1.55 l, Marius Bunescu. 2.75 l, N. Darascu, vert. 6 l, Petrascu. 6.40 l, Marius Bunescu.

1972, Oct. 20
2374 A713   10b gray & multi   .25 .25
2375 A713   20b gray & multi   .25 .25
2376 A713   55b gray & multi   .25 .25
2377 A713   1.55 l gray & multi   .25 .25
2378 A713   2.75 l gray & multi   .55 .25
2379 A713   6.40 l gray & multi   1.40 .35
    Nos. 2374-2379 (6)   2.95 1.60
Souvenir Sheet
2380 A713   6 l gray & multi   2.00 2.00

Fencing, Bronze Medal — A714

20b, Team handball, bronze medal. 35b, Boxing, silver medal. 1.45 l, Hurdles, women's, silver medal. 2.75 l, Pistol shoot, silver medal. 6.20 l, Wrestling, gold medal.

1972, Oct. 28
2381 A714   10b red org & multi   .25 .25
2382 A714   20b lt grn & multi   .25 .25
2383 A714   35b multicolored   .25 .25
2384 A714   1.45 l multi   .25 .25
2385 A714   2.75 l ocher & multi   .85 .25
2386 A714   6.20 l blk & multi   2.00 .45
    Nos. 2381-2386 (6)   3.85 1.70
Romanian medalists at 20th Olympic Games. See No. C191. For surcharge see No. 2493.

Charity Labels
Stamp day issues frequently have an attached, fully perforated label with a face value. These are Romanian Philatelic Association charity labels. They are inscribed "AFR." The stamps are valued with label attached. When the "label" is part of the stamp, the stamp is listed in the semi-postal section. See Nos. B426-B430.

Stamp Day Semi-Postal Type of 1968
Design: Traveling Gypsies, by Emil Volkers.
1972, Nov. 15   **Photo.**   **Perf. 13½**
2386A SP288 1.10 l + 90b label   1.00 .40
    Stamp Day.

Apollo 1, 2 and 3 — A715

1972, Dec. 27   **Photo.**   **Perf. 13½**
2387 A715   10b shown   .25 .25
2388 A715   35b Grissom, Chaffee and White, 1967   .25 .25
2389 A715   40b Apollo 4, 5, 6   .25 .25
2390 A715   55b Apollo 7, 8   .25 .25
2391 A715   1 l Apollo 9, 10   .25 .25
2392 A715   1.20 l Apollo 11, 12   .25 .25
2393 A715   1.85 l Apollo 13, 14   .35 .25
2394 A715   2.75 l Apollo 15, 16   .60 .25
2395 A715   3.60 l Apollo 17   1.10 .30
    Nos. 2387-2395 (9)   3.55 2.30
Highlights of US Apollo space program. See No. C192.

"25" and Flags — A716

Designs: 1.20 l, "25" and national emblem. 1.75 l, "25" and factory.

1972, Dec. 25
2396 A716   55b blue & multi   .25 .25
2397 A716   1.20 l yel & multi   .35 .25
2398 A716   1.75 l ver & multi   .60 .25
    Nos. 2396-2398 (3)   1.20 .75
25th anniversary of the Republic.

European Bee-eater A717

Globeflowers A718

Nature Protection: No. 2400, Red-breasted goose. No. 2401, Penduline tit. No. 2403, Garden Turk's-cap. No. 2404, Gentian.

1973, Feb. 5   **Photo.**   **Perf. 13**
2399 A717   1.40 l gray & multi   .25 .25
2400 A717   1.85 l multi   .35 .25
2401 A717   2.75 l blue & multi   .70 .25
   a.   Strip of 3, #2399-2401   1.40 .60
2402 A718   1.40 l multi   .25 .25
2403 A718   1.85 l yellow & multi   .35 .25
2404 A718   2.75 l multi   .70 .25
   a.   Strip of 3, #2402-2404   1.40 .60

Nicolaus Copernicus — A719

1973, Feb. 19   **Photo.**   **Perf. 13x13½**
2405 A719   2.75 l multi   1.00 .35
Nicolaus Copernicus (1473-1543), Polish astronomer. Printed with alternating label publicizing Intl. Phil. Exhib., Poznan, 8/19-9/2.

Suceava Woman A720

Regional Costumes: 40b, Suceava man. 55b, Harghita woman. 1.75 l, Harghita man. 2.75 l, Gorj woman. 6.40 l, Gorj man.

1973, Mar. 15
2406 A720   10b lt bl & multi   .25 .25
2407 A720   40b multicolored   .25 .25
2408 A720   55b bis & multi   .25 .25
2409 A720   1.75 l lil & multi   .30 .25
2410 A720   2.75 l multi   .45 .25
2411 A720   6.40 l multi   1.25 .35
    Nos. 2406-2411 (6)   2.75 1.60

D. Paciurea (Sculptor) — A721

Portraits: 40b, I. Slavici (1848-1925), writer. 55b, G. Lazar (1779-1823), writer. 6.40 l, A. Flechtenmacher (1823-1898), composer.

1973, Mar. 26
2412 A721   10b multi   .25 .25
2413 A721   40b multi   .25 .25
2414 A721   55b multi   .25 .25
2415 A721   6.40 l multi   1.25 .40
    Nos. 2412-2415 (4)   2.00 1.15
Anniversaries of famous artists.

Map of Europe A722

Design: 3.60 l, Symbol of collaboration.

1973, Apr. 28   **Photo.**   **Perf. 13½**
2416 A722   3.35 l dp bl & gold   1.10 .70
2417 A722   3.60 l brt mag & gold   1.25 1.00
   a.   Pair, #2416-2417   2.40 2.00
Inter-European cultural and economic cooperation. Printed in sheets of 10 with blue marginal inscription.

Souvenir Sheet

The Rape of Proserpina, by Hans von Aachen — A723

1973, May 5
2418 A723   12 l gold & multi   3.50 3.25
IBRA Munchen 1973, Intl. Stamp Exhib., Munich, May 11-20.

Prince Alexander I. Cuza — A724

1973, May 5   **Photo.**   **Perf. 13½**
2419 A724   1.75 l multi   .50 .25
Alexander Ioan Cuza (1820-1873), prince of Romania, Moldavia and Walachia.

Hand with Hammer and Sickle — A725

1973, May 5
2420 A725   40b gold & multi   .40 .25
Workers and Peasants Party, 25th anniv.

Romanian Flag, Bayonets Stabbing Swastika — A726

1973, May 5
2421 A726   55b multicolored   .40 .25
Anti-fascist Front, 40th anniversary.

WMO Emblem, Weather Satellite — A727

1973, June 15
2422 A727   2 l ultra & multi   .60 .25
Intl. meteorological cooperation, cent.

Dimitrie Ralet Holding Letter — A728

Portraits with letters. 60b, Enachita Vacarescu, by A. Chladek. 1.55 l, Serdarul Dimitrie Aman, by C. Lecca.

1973, June 20
2423 A728   40b multi   .25 .25
2424 A728   60b multi   .25 .25
2425 A728   1.55 l multi   .50 .25
    Nos. 2423-2425,B432 (4)   2.50 1.35
"The Letter on Romanian Portraits." Socfilex III Philatelic Exhibition, Bucharest, July 20-29. See No. B433.

Dimitrie Cantemir — A729

6 l, Portrait of Cantemir in oval frame.

1973, June 25
2426 A729 1.75 l multi .50 .25

Souvenir Sheet
2427 A729 6 l multi 2.50 1.75

Dimitrie Cantemir (1673-1723), Prince of Moldavia, writer. No. 2427 contains one 38x50mm stamp.

Plate — A730

Designs: 10b, Fibulae, vert. 55b, Jug, vert. 1.55 l, Necklaces and fibula. 2.75 l, Plate, vert. 6.80 l, Octagonal bowl with animal handles. 12 l, Breastplate, vert.

1973, July 25 Photo. Perf. 13½
2428 A730 10b vio bl & multi .25 .25
2429 A730 20b green & multi .25 .25
2430 A730 55b red & multi .25 .25
2431 A730 1.55 l multi .35 .25
2432 A730 2.75 l plum & multi .55 .25
2433 A730 6.80 l multi 1.50 .35
 Nos. 2428-2433 (6) 3.15 1.60

Souvenir Sheet
2434 A730 12 l multi 3.00 2.75

Roman gold treasure of Pietroasa, 4th century.

Symbolic Flower, Map of Europe A731

Design: 5 l, Map of Europe, symbolic tree.

1973, Oct. 2 Photo. Perf. 13½
2435 A731 2.75 l multi 1.10 .70
2436 A731 5 l multi 1.75 1.00
 a. Sheet 2 each + 2 labels 5.25 5.25

Conference for European Security and Cooperation, Helsinki, Finland, July 1973.

Jug and Cloth, Oboga — A732

Designs: 20b, Plate and Pitcher, Vama. 55b, Bowl, Marginea. 1.55 l, Pitcher and plate, Sibiu-Saschiz. 2.75 l, Bowl and jug, Pisc. 6.80 l, Figurine (fowl), Oboga.

1973, Oct. 15 Perf. 13
2437 A732 10b multi .25 .25
2438 A732 20b multi .25 .25
2439 A732 55b multi .25 .25
2440 A732 1.55 l multi .35 .25
2441 A732 2.75 l multi .55 .25
2442 A732 6.80 l multi 1.25 .35
 Nos. 2437-2442 (6) 2.90 1.60

Pottery and cloths from various regions of Romania.

Postilion, by A. Verona A732a

1973, Nov. 15 Photo. Perf. 13½
2442A A732a 1.10 l + 90b label .50 .25
 Stamp Day.

Women Workers, by G. Saru A733

Paintings of Workers: 20b, Construction Site, by M. Bunescu, horiz. 55b, Shipyard Workers, by H. Catargi, horiz. 1.55 l, Worker, by Catargi. 2.75 l, Miners, by A. Phoebus. 6.80 l, Spinner, by Nicolae Grigorescu. 12 l, Farmers at Rest, by Stefan Popescu, horiz.

1973, Nov. 26 Photo. Perf. 13½
2443 A733 10b gold & multi .25 .25
2444 A733 20b gold & multi .25 .25
2445 A733 55b gold & multi .25 .25
2446 A733 1.55 l gold & multi .25 .25
2447 A733 2.75 l gold & multi .50 .25
2448 A733 6.80 l gold & multi 1.25 .35
 Nos. 2443-2448 (6) 2.75 1.60

Miniature Sheet
2449 A733 12 l gold & multi 3.00 2.75

City Hall, Craiova — A734   Tugboat under Bridge — A735

Designs: 10b, Infinite Column, by Constantin Brancusi, vert. 20b, Heroes' Mausoleum, Marasesti. 35b, Risnov Citadel. 40b, Densus Church, vert. 50b, Dej Church, vert. 55b, Maldaresti Fortress. 60b, National Theater, Iasi. 1 l, Curtea-de-Arges Monastery, vert. 1.20 l, Tirgu-Mures Citadel. 1.45 l, Cargoship Dimbovita. 1.50 l, Muntenia passenger ship. 1.55 l, Three-master Mircea. 1.75 l, Motorship Transilvania. 2.20 l, Ore carrier Oltul. 3.65 l, Trawler Mures. 4.70 l, Tanker Arges.

1973-74 Photo. Perf. 13
2450 A734 5b lake .25 .25
2451 A734 10b brt blue .25 .25
2452 A734 20b orange .25 .25
2453 A734 35b green .25 .25
2454 A734 40b dk violet .25 .25
2455 A734 50b ultra .25 .25
2456 A734 55b orange brn .25 .25
2457 A734 60b carmine .25 .25
2458 A734 1 l dp ultra .25 .25
2459 A734 1.20 l olive grn .30 .25
2460 A735 1.35 l gray .35 .25
2461 A735 1.45 l dull blue .35 .25
2462 A735 1.50 l car rose .35 .25
2463 A735 1.55 l violet bl .35 .25
2464 A735 1.75 l slate grn .45 .25
2465 A735 2.20 l brt blue .60 .25
2466 A735 3.65 l dull lilac 1.00 .25
2467 A735 4.70 l violet brn 1.40 .25
 Nos. 2450-2467 (18) 7.40 4.50

Issued: #2450-2459, 12/15/73; #2460-2467, 1/28/74.

Boats at Montfleur, by Claude Monet — A736

Impressionistic paintings: 40b, Church of Moret, by Alfred Sisley, vert. 55b, Orchard in Bloom, by Camille Pissarro. 1.75 l, Portrait of Jeanne, by Pissarro, vert. 2.75 l, Landscape, by Auguste Renoir. 3.60 l, Portrait of a Girl, by Paul Cezanne, vert. 10 l, Women Taking Bath, by Renoir, vert.

1974, Mar. 15 Photo. Perf. 13½
2468 A736 20b blue & multi .25 .25
2469 A736 40b blue & multi .25 .25
2470 A736 55b blue & multi .25 .25
2471 A736 1.75 l blue & multi .40 .25
2472 A736 2.75 l blue & multi .60 .25
2473 A736 3.60 l blue & multi .80 .25
 Nos. 2468-2473 (6) 2.55 1.50

Souvenir Sheet
2474 A736 10 l blue & multi 2.25 2.00

Harness Racing A737

Designs: Various horse races.

1974, Apr. 5 Photo. Perf. 13½
2475 A737 40b ver & multi .25 .25
2476 A737 55b bis & multi .25 .25
2477 A737 60b multi .25 .25
2478 A737 1.55 l multi .35 .25
2479 A737 2.75 l multi .60 .25
2480 A737 3.45 l multi .80 .30
 Nos. 2475-2480 (6) 2.50 1.55

Centenary of horse racing in Romania.

Nicolae Titulescu (1883-1941) A738

1974, Apr. 16
2481 A738 1.75 l multi .50 .25

Interparliamentary Session, Bucharest, Apr. 1974. Titulescu was the first Romanian delegate to the League of Nations.

Roman Memorial with First Reference to Napoca (Cluj) — A739

1974, Apr. 18 Photo. Perf. 13
2482 A739 10 l multi 2.50 2.50

1850th anniv. of the elevation of the Roman settlement of Napoca (Cluj) to a municipality.

Stylized Map of Europe A740

Design: 3.45 l, Satellite over earth.

1974, Apr. 25 Photo. Perf. 13½x13
2483 A740 2.20 l multi 1.00 .70
2484 A740 3.45 l multi 1.50 1.00
 a. Pair, #2483-2484 2.50 2.00

Inter-European Cultural Economic Cooperation.

Young Pioneers with Banners, by Pepene Cornelia — A741

1974, Apr. 25 Photo. Perf. 13½
2485 A741 55b multicolored .50 .25

25th anniv. of the Romanian Pioneers Org.

Mail Motorboat, UPU Emblem A742

UPU Emblem and: 40b, Mail train. 55b, Mailplane and truck. 1.75 l, Mail delivery by motorcycle. 2.75 l, Mailman delivering letter to little girl. 3.60 l, Young stamp collectors. 4 l, Mail collection. 6 l, Modern post office.

1974, May 15
2486 A742 20b gray & multi .25 .25
2487 A742 40b multicolored .25 .25
2488 A742 55b ultra & multi .25 .25
2489 A742 1.75 l multi .50 .25
2490 A742 2.75 l brn & multi .70 .25
2491 A742 3.60 l org & multi 1.00 .30
 Nos. 2486-2491 (6) 2.95 1.55

Souvenir Sheet
2492 Sheet of 2 3.00 2.75
 a. A742 4 l multi .90
 b. A742 6 l multi 1.60

Centenary of Universal Postal Union. Size of stamps of No. 2492, 28x24mm. An imperf airmail UPU souvenir sheet of one (10 l) exists. The multicolored stamp is 49x38mm. This sheet is not known to have been sold to the public at post offices. Value, unused $30, used $27.50.

No. 2382 Surcharged with New Value and Overprinted: "ROMÂNIA / CAMPIOANA / MONDIALA / 1974"

1974, May 13
2493 A714 1.75 l on 20b multi   2.50 1.75

Romania's victory in World Handball Championship, 1974.

Soccer and Games Emblem A743

Designs: Games emblem and various scenes from soccer game.

1974, June 25   **Perf. 13½**
2494	A743	20b purple & multi	.25	.25
2495	A743	40b multi	.25	.25
2496	A743	55b ultra & multi	.25	.25
2497	A743	1.75 l brn & multi	.25	.25
2498	A743	2.75 l multi	.50	.25
2499	A743	3.60 l vio & multi	.75	.30
		Nos. 2494-2499 (6)	2.25	1.55

Souvenir Sheet
2500 A743 10 l multi   2.50 2.00

World Cup Soccer Championship, Munich, June 13-July 7. No. 2500 contains one horizontal stamp 50x38mm.

An imperf. 10 l airmail souvenir sheet exists showing a globe as soccer ball and satellite. Gray blue margin showing Soccer Cup, radio tower and stadium; black control number. Value, unused or used, $65.

"25" — A744

1974, June 10
2501 A744 55b blue & multi   .40 .25

25th anniv. of the Council for Mutual Economic Assistance (COMECON).

UN Emblem and People — A745

1974, June 25   Photo.   Perf. 13½
2502 A745 2 l multicolored   .60 .25
World Population Year.

Hand Drawing Peace Dove — A746

1974, June 28
2503 A746 2 l ultra & multi   .60 .25

25 years of the National and Intl. Movement to Uphold the Cause of Peace.

Ioan, Prince of Wallachia — A747

Soldier, Industry and Agriculture A748

Hunedoara Iron and Steel Works — A749

Designs: 1.10 l, Avram Iancu (1824-1872). 1.30 l, Dr. C. I. Parhon (1874-1969). 1.40 l, Bishop Dosoftei (1624-1693).

1974   Photo.   Perf. 13
2504	A747	20b blue	.25	.25
2505	A748	55b carmine rose	.25	.25
2506	A749	1 l slate green	.25	.25
2507	A747	1.10 l dk gray olive	.25	.25
2508	A747	1.30 l deep magenta	.30	.25
2509	A747	1.40 l dark violet	.35	.25
		Nos. 2504-2509 (6)	1.65	1.50

No. 2505 for Army Day, No. 2506 for 220th anniv. of Hunedoara Iron and Steel works; others for anniversaries of famous Romanians.

Issue dates: 1l, June 17; others June 25.

Romanians and Flags — A750

Design: 40b, Romanian and Communist flags forming "XXX," vert.

1974, Aug. 20
2510 A750 40b gold, ultra & car   .25 .25
2511 A750 55b yellow & multi   .25 .25

Romania's liberation from Fascist rule, 30th anniv.

Souvenir Sheet

View, Stockholm — A751

1974, Sept. 10   Photo.   Perf. 13
2512 A751 10 l multicolored   2.50 2.50

Stockholmia 74 International Philatelic Exhibition, Stockholm, Sept. 21-29.

Thistle — A752

Nature Protection: 40b, Checkered lily. 55b, Yew. 1.75 l, Azalea. 2.75 l, Forget-me-not. 3.60 l, Pinks.

1974, Sept. 15
2513	A752	20b plum & multi	.25	.25
2514	A752	40b multi	.25	.25
2515	A752	55b multi	.25	.25
2516	A752	1.75 l multi	.50	.25
2517	A752	2.75 l brn & multi	.70	.25
2518	A752	3.60 l multi	1.00	.30
		Nos. 2513-2518 (6)	2.95	1.55

Isis, First Century A.D. A753

Archaeological art works excavated in Romania: 40b, Serpent, by Glycon. 75b, Emperor Trajan, bronze bust. 1.75 l, Roman woman, statue, 3rd century. 2.75 l, Mithraic bas-relief. 3.60 l, Roman man, statue, 3rd century.

1974, Oct. 20   Photo.   Perf. 13
2519	A753	20b multi	.25	.25
2520	A753	40b ultra & multi	.25	.25
2521	A753	55b multi	.25	.25
2522	A753	1.75 l multi	.40	.25
2523	A753	2.75 l brn & multi	.60	.25
2524	A753	3.60 l multi	.85	.30
		Nos. 2519-2524 (6)	2.60	1.55

Romanian Communist Party Emblem — A754

Design: 1 l, similar to 55b.

1974, Nov. 20
2525 A754 55b blk, red & gold   .25 .25
2526 A754 1 l blk, red & gold   .30 .25

9th Romanian Communist Party Congress.

Discobolus and Olympic Rings — A755

1974, Nov. 11
2527 A755 2 l ultra & multi   .75 .25

Romanian Olympic Committee, 60th anniv.

Skylab A756

1974, Dec. 14   Photo.   Perf. 13
2528 A756 2.50 l multi   .70 .35

Skylab, manned US space laboratory. No. 2528 printed in sheets of 4 stamps and 4 labels. A 10 l imperf. souvenir sheet exists showing Skylab. Value, unused or used, $65.

Field Ball and Games' Emblem A757

Designs: 1.75 l, 2.20 l, Various scenes from field ball; 1.75 l, vert.

1975, Jan. 3
2529	A757	55b ultra & multi	.25	.25
2530	A757	1.75 l yellow & multi	.30	.25
2531	A757	2.20 l multi	.45	.25
		Nos. 2529-2531 (3)	1.00	.75

World University Field Ball Championship.

Rocks and Birches, by Andreescu A758

Paintings by Ion Andreescu (1850-1882): 40b, Farm Woman with Green Kerchief. 55b, Winter in the Woods. 1.75 l, Winter in Barbizon, horiz. 2.75 l, Self-portrait. 3.60 l, Main Road, horiz.

1975, Jan. 24
2532	A758	20b multi	.25	.25
2533	A758	40b multi	.25	.25
2534	A758	55b multi	.25	.25
2535	A758	1.75 l multi	.40	.25
2536	A758	2.75 l multi	.60	.25
2537	A758	3.60 l multi	.85	.30
		Nos. 2532-2537 (6)	2.60	1.55

Torch with Flame in Flag Colors and Coat of Arms — A759

1975, Feb. 1
2538 A759 40b multicolored   .40   .25
Romanian Socialist Republic, 10th anniv.

Vaslui Battle, by O. Obedeanu A760

1975, Feb. 25   Photo.   Perf. 13½
2539 A760 55b gold & multi   .40   .25
Battle at the High Bridge, Stephan the Great's victory over the Turks, 500th anniv.

Woman Spinning, by Nicolae Grigorescu — A761

1975, Mar. 1
2540 A761 55b gold & multi   .40   .25
International Women's Year.

Michelangelo, Self-portrait A762

1975, Mar. 10
2541 A762 5 l multicolored   1.40   .30
Michelangelo Buonarroti (1475-1564), Italian sculptor, painter and architect.
For overprint see No. 2581.

Souvenir Sheet

Escorial Palace and España 75 Emblem — A763

1975, Mar. 15   Photo.   Perf. 13
2542 A763 10 l multi   2.50   2.25
Espana 75 Intl. Phil. Exhib., Madrid, 4/4-13.

Letter with Postal Code, Pigeon A764

1975, Mar. 26   Photo.   Perf. 13½
2543 A764 55b blue & multi   .40   .25
Introduction of postal code system.

Children's Science Pavilion — A765

1975, Apr. 10   Photo.   Perf. 13
2544 A765 4 l multicolored   1.20   .25
Oceanexpo 75, International Exhibition, Okinawa, July 20, 1975-Jan. 1976.

Peonies, by N. Tonitza A766

3.45 l, Chrysanthemums, by St. Luchian.

1975, Apr. 28
2545 A766 2.20 l gold & multi   .85   .50
2546 A766 3.45 l gold & multi   1.25   .95
  a. Pair, #2545-2546   2.25   1.75
Inter-European Cultural and Economic Cooperation. Printed checkerwise in sheets of 10 (2x5).

1875 Meter Convention Emblem — A767

1975, May 10   Photo.   Perf. 13
2547 A767 1.85 l bl, blk & gold   .65   .25
Cent. of Intl. Meter Convention, Paris, 1875.

Mihail Eminescu and his Home — A768

1975, June 5
2548 A768 55b multicolored   .40   .25
Milhail Eminescu (1850-1889), poet.

Marble Plaque and Dacian Coins 1st-2nd Centuries — A769

1975, May 26
2549 A769 55b multicolored   .40   .25
2000th anniv. of the founding of Alba Iulia (Apulum).

Souvenir Sheet

"On the Bank of the Seine," by Th. Pallady — A770

1975, May 26
2550 A770 10 l multicolored   2.25   1.75
ARPHILA 75, Paris, June 6-16.

Dr. Albert Schweitzer (1875-1965), Medical Missionary — A771

1974, Dec. 20   Photo.   Perf. 13½
2551 A771 40b black brown   .40   .25

Ana Ipatescu — A772

1975, June 2   Photo.   Perf. 13½
2552 A772 55b lilac rose   .40   .25
Ana Ipatescu, fighter in 1848 revolution.

Policeman with Walkie-talkie — A773

1975, Sept. 1
2553 A773 55b brt blue   .40   .25
Publicity for traffic rules.

Monument and Projected Reconstruction, Adam Clissi — A777

Roman Monuments: 55b, Emperor Trajan, bas-relief, vert. 1.20 l, Trajan's column, Rome, vert. 1.55 l, Governor Decibalus, bas-relief, vert. 2 l, Excavated Roman city, Turnu-Severin. 2.25 l, Trajan's Bridge, ruin and projected reconstruction. No. 2569, Roman fortifications, vert.

1975, June 26   Photo.   Perf. 13½
2563 A777   55b red brn & blk   .25   .25
2564 A777 1.20 l vio bl & blk   .25   .25
2565 A777 1.55 l green & blk   .35   .25
2566 A777 1.75 l dl rose & multi   .50   .25
2567 A777   2 l dl yel & blk   .60   .25
2568 A777 2.25 l brt bl & blk   1.10   .25
  Nos. 2563-2568 (6)   3.05   1.50

Souvenir Sheet

2569 A777 10 l multicolored   4.50   3.75
European Architectural Heritage Year.
An imperf. 10 l gold and dark brown souvenir sheet exists showing the Roman wolf suckling Romulus and Remus. Value $70, unused or used.
A similar souvenir sheet was issued in 1978 to honor the Essen International Stamp Fair. It contains a 10 l stamp, depicting the design of the stamp described above, within a blue frame. Value $10, unused or used.

Michael the Brave, by Sadeler A778

Michael the Brave Statue — A779

Designs: 1.20 l, Ottoman Messengers Offering Gifts to Michael the Brave, by Theodor Aman, horiz. 2.75 l, Michael the Brave in Battle of Calugareni, by Aman.

1975, July 7
2571 A778   55b gold & blk   .25   .25
2572 A778 1.20 l gold & multi   .25   .25
2573 A778 2.75 l gold & multi   .65   .25
  Nos. 2571-2573 (3)   1.15   .75

Souvenir Sheet
Imperf

2574 A779 10 l gold & multi 20.00 20.00

First political union of Romanian states under Michael the Brave, 375th anniv. No. 2574 issued Sept. 20.

Larkspur — A780

1975, Aug. 15 Photo. Perf. 13½
2575	A780	20b shown	.25	.25
2576	A780	40b Field poppies	.25	.25
2577	A780	55b Xeranthemum annuum	.25	.25
2578	A780	1.75 l Rockrose	.30	.25
2579	A780	2.75 l Meadow sage	.60	.25
2580	A780	3.60 l Wild chicory	.75	.25
		Nos. 2575-2580 (6)	2.40	1.50

No. 2541 Overprinted in Red

1975, Aug. 23
2581 A762 5 l multicolored 4.50 4.50

Intl. Phil. Exhib., Riccione, Italy, Aug. 23-25.

Map Showing Location of Craiova, 1750 — A781

1975, Sept. 15 Photo. Perf. 13½
2582	A781	Strip of 3	.65	.30
a.		20b ocher, yellow, red & black	.25	.25
b.		55b ocher, yellow, red & black	.25	.25
c.		1 l ocher, yellow, red & black	.25	.25

1750th anniv. of first documentation of Daco-Getian settlement of Pelendava and 500th anniversary of documentation of Craiova.

Size of Nos. 2582a, 2582c: 25x32mm; of No. 2582b: 80x32mm.

Muntenian Rug — A782

Romanian Peasant Rugs: 40b, Banat. 55b, Oltenia. 1.75 l, Moldavia. 2.75 l, Oltenia. 3.60 l, Maramures.

1975, Oct. 5 Photo. Perf. 13½
2583	A782	20b dk bl & multi	.25	.25
2584	A782	40b black & multi	.25	.25
2585	A782	55b multicolored	.25	.25
2586	A782	1.75 l black & multi	.30	.25
2587	A782	2.75 l multicolored	.55	.25
2588	A782	3.60 l black & multi	.70	.25
		Nos. 2583-2588 (6)	2.30	1.50

Minibus A783

1975, Nov. 5 Photo. Perf. 13½
2589	A783	20b shown	.25	.25
2590	A783	40b Gasoline truck	.25	.25
2591	A783	55b Jeep	.25	.25
2592	A783	1.75 l Flat-bed truck	.40	.25
2593	A783	2.75 l Dacia automobile	.55	.25
2594	A783	3.60 l Dump truck	.70	.25
		Nos. 2589-2594 (6)	2.40	1.50

Souvenir Sheet

Winter, by Peter Brueghel, the Younger — A784

1975, Nov. 25 Photo. Perf. 13½
2595 A784 10 l multicolored 3.25 3.00

THEMABELGA Intl. Topical Phil. Exhib., Brussels, Dec. 13-21.

Luge and Olympic Games' Emblem — A785

Innsbruck Olympic Games' Emblem and: 40b, Biathlon, vert. 55b, Woman skier. 1.75 l, Ski jump. 2.75 l, Woman figure skater. 3.60 l, Ice hockey. 10 l, Two-man bobsled.

1976, Jan. 12 Photo. Perf. 13½
2596	A785	20b blue & multi	.25	.25
2597	A785	40b multicolored	.25	.25
2598	A785	55b multicolored	.25	.25
2599	A785	1.75 l ol & multi	.40	.25
2600	A785	2.75 l multi	.60	.25
2601	A785	3.60 l multi	.80	.35
		Nos. 2596-2601 (6)	2.55	1.60

Souvenir Sheet

2602 A785 10 l multi 4.50 4.25

12th Winter Olympic Games, Innsbruck, Austria, Feb. 4-15. An imperf. 10 l souvenir sheet exists showing slalom; Romanian flag, Games' emblem. Values: unused $50; used, $30.

Washington at Valley Forge, by W. T. Trego — A786

Paintings: 40b, Washington at Trenton, by John Trumbull, vert. 55b, Washington Crossing the Delaware, by Emanuel Leutze. 1.75 l, The Capture of the Hessians, by Trumbull. 2.75 l, Jefferson, by Thomas Sully, vert. 3.60 l,

Surrender of Cornwallis at Yorktown, by Trumbull. 10 l, Signing of the Declaration of Independence, by Trumbull.

1976, Jan. 25 Photo. Perf. 13½
2603	A786	20b gold & multi	.25	.25
2604	A786	40b gold & multi	.25	.25
2605	A786	55b gold & multi	.30	.25
2606	A786	1.75 l gold & multi	.40	.25
2607	A786	2.75 l gold & multi	.80	.30
2608	A786	3.60 l gold & multi	1.00	.35
		Nos. 2603-2608 (6)	3.00	1.65

Souvenir Sheet

2609 A786 10 l gold & multi 3.00 2.50

American Bicentennial. No. 2609 also for Interphil 76 Intl. Phil. Exhib., Philadelphia, Pa., May 20-June 6. Printed in horizontal rows of 4 stamps with centered label showing Bicentennial emblem.

Prayer, by Brancusi A787

Designs: 1.75 l, Architectural Assembly, by Brancusi. 3.60 l, Constantin Brancusi.

1976, Feb. 15 Photo. Perf. 13½
2610	A787	55b purple & multi	.25	.25
2611	A787	1.75 l blue & multi	.30	.25
2612	A787	3.60 l multicolored	.85	.35
		Nos. 2610-2612 (3)	1.40	.85

Constantin Brancusi (1876-1957), sculptor. For surcharge see No. B440.

Anton Davidoglu A788   Archives Museum A789

55b, Vlad Tepes. 1.20 l, Costache Negri.

1976, Feb. 25
2613	A788	40b green & multi	.25	.25
2614	A788	55b green & multi	.25	.25
2615	A788	1.20 l green & multi	.25	.25
2616	A789	1.75 l green & multi	.25	.25
		Nos. 2613-2616 (4)	1.00	1.00

Anniversaries: Anton Davidoglu (1876-1958), mathematician; Prince Vlad Tepes, commander in war against the Turks (d. 1476); Costache Negri (1812-1876), Moldavian freedom fighter; Romanian National Archives Museum, founded 1926.

Dr. Carol Davila — A790

1.75 l, Nurse with patient. 2.20 l, First aid.

1976, Apr. 20
2617	A790	55b multi	.25	.25
2618	A790	1.75 l multi	.40	.25
2619	A790	2.20 l yellow & multi	.50	.25
		Nos. 2617-2619, C199 (4)	1.85	1.00

Romanian Red Cross cent.

Vase with King Decebalus Portrait — A791

Design: 3.45 l, Vase with portrait of King Michael the Bold.

1976, May 13
2620	A791	2.20 l bl & multi	.35	.35
2621	A791	3.45 l multi	.35	.35

Inter-European Cultural Economic Cooperation. Nos. 2620-2621 each printed in sheets of 4 with marginal inscriptions.

Coat of Arms — A792

1976, June 12
2622 A792 1.75 l multi .75 .25

See design A615.

Spiru Haret — A793

1976, June 25
2628 A793 20b multicolored .40 .25

Spiru Haret (1851-1912), mathematician.

Woman Athlete — A794

Romanian Olympic Emblem and: 40b, Boxing. 55b, Team handball. 1.75 l, 2-man scull. 2.75 l, Gymnast on rings, horiz. 3.60 l, 2-man canoe, horiz. 10 l, Woman gymnast, horiz.

1976, June 25 Photo. Perf. 13½
2629	A794	20b org & multi	.25	.25
2630	A794	40b multi	.25	.25
2631	A794	55b multi	.25	.25
2632	A794	1.75 l multi	.35	.25
2633	A794	2.75 l vio & multi	.50	.25
2634	A794	3.60 l bl & multi	.75	.45
		Nos. 2629-2634 (6)	2.35	1.70

Souvenir Sheet

2635 A794 10 l rose & multi 3.25 2.25

21st Olympic Games, Montreal, Canada, July 17-Aug. 1. No. 2635 contains one stamp 49x37mm.

An imperf. airmail 10 l souvenir sheet exists showing Olympic Stadium, Montreal. Values: unused $40; used $25.

Inscribed Stone Tablets,
Banat — A795

Designs: 40b, Hekate, Bacchus, bas-relief.
55b, Ceramic fragment, bowl, coins. 1.75 l,
Bowl, urn and cup. 2.75 l, Sword, lance and
tombstone. 3.60 l, Lances, urn. 10 l, Clay vessel and silver coins.

1976, July 25

2636	A795	20b multi	.25	.25
2637	A795	40b multi	.25	.25
2638	A795	55b org & multi	.25	.25
2639	A795	1.75 l multi	.40	.25
2640	A795	2.75 l fawn & multi	.60	.25
2641	A795	3.60 l multi	.85	.35
		Nos. 2636-2641 (6)	2.60	1.60

Souvenir Sheet

2642	A795	10 l yel & multi	3.25	2.25

Daco-Roman archaeological treasures. No.
2642 issued Mar. 25. An imperf. 10 l souvenir
sheet exists showing a silver and gold vase
and silver coins. Values: unused $10; used
$6.

Wolf
Statue,
4th
Century
Map
A796

1976, Aug. 25

2643	A796	55b multi	.40	.25

Founding of Buzau, 1600th anniv.

Game
A797

1976, Sept. 20

2644	A797	20b Red deer	.25	.25
2645	A797	40b Brown bear	.25	.25
2646	A797	55b Chamois	.25	.25
2647	A797	1.75 l Boar	.40	.25
2648	A797	2.75 l Red fox	.60	.25
2649	A797	3.60 l Lynx	.85	.25
		Nos. 2644-2649 (6)	2.60	1.50

Dan Grecu, Bronze Medal — A798

Nadia
Comaneci — A799

40b, Fencing, bronze medal. 55b Gheorge
Megelea (Javelin), bronze medal. 1.75 l,
Handball, silver medal. 2.75 l, Boxing, 1
bronze, 2 silver medals. 3.60 l, Wrestling, silver and bronze medals. 10 l, Vasile Daba
(kayak), gold and silver medals, vert.

1976, Oct. 20　　Photo.　　Perf. 13½

2650	A798	20b multi	.25	.25
2651	A798	40b car & multi	.25	.25
2652	A798	55b grn & multi	.25	.25
2653	A798	1.75 l red & multi	.25	.25
2654	A798	2.75 l bl & multi	.40	.25
2655	A798	3.60 l multi	.60	.30
2656	A798	5.70 l multi	1.50	.45
		Nos. 2650-2656 (7)	3.50	2.00

Souvenir Sheet

2657	A798	10 l multi	3.25	2.25

Romanian Olympic medalists. No. 2657
contains one 37x50mm stamp.
An imperf airmail 10 l souvenir sheet exists
picturing gymnast, Nadia Comaneci. Values:
unused $45; used $25.

Milan Cathedral — A800

1976, Oct. 20　　Photo.　　Perf. 13½

2658	A800	4.75 l multi	1.00	.40

ITALIA 76 Intl. Phil. Exhib., Milan, 10/14-24.

Oranges and Carnations, by
Luchian — A801

Paintings by Stefan Luchian (1868-1916):
40b, Flower arrangement. 55b, Vase with flowers. 1.75 l, Roses. 2.75 l, Cornflowers. 3.60 l,
Carnations in vase.

1976, Nov. 5

2659	A801	20b multi	.25	.25
2660	A801	40b multi	.25	.25
2661	A801	55b multi	.25	.25
2662	A801	1.75 l multi	.25	.25
2663	A801	2.75 l multi	.35	.25
2664	A801	3.60 l multi	.65	.35
		Nos. 2659-2664 (6)	2.00	1.60

Arms of
Alba — A802

Designs: Arms of Romanian counties.

1976-77　　　Photo.　　Perf. 13½

2665	A802	55b shown	.25	.25
2666	A802	55b Arad	.25	.25
2667	A802	55b Arges	.25	.25
2668	A802	55b Bacau	.25	.25
2669	A802	55b Bihor	.25	.25
2670	A802	55b Bistrita-Nasaud	.25	.25
2671	A802	55b Botosani	.25	.25
2672	A802	55b Brasov	.25	.25
2673	A802	55b Braila	.25	.25
2674	A802	55b Buzau	.25	.25
2675	A802	55b Caras-Severin	.25	.25
2676	A802	55b Cluj	.25	.25
2677	A802	55b Constanta	.25	.25
2678	A802	55b Covasna	.25	.25
2679	A802	55b Dimbovita	.25	.25
2680	A802	55b Dolj	.25	.25
2681	A802	55b Galati	.25	.25
2682	A802	55b Gorj	.25	.25
2683	A802	55b Harghita	.25	.25
2684	A802	55b Hunedoara	.25	.25
2685	A802	55b Ialomita	.25	.25
2686	A802	55b Iasi	.25	.25
2687	A802	55b Ilfov	.25	.25
2688	A802	55b Maramures	.25	.25
2689	A802	55b Mehedinti	.25	.25
2690	A802	55b Mures	.25	.25
2691	A802	55b Neamt	.25	.25
2692	A802	55b Olt	.25	.25
2693	A802	55b Prahova	.25	.25
2694	A802	55b Salaj	.25	.25
2695	A802	55b Satu-Mare	.25	.25
2696	A802	55b Sibiu	.25	.25
2697	A802	55b Suceava	.25	.25
2698	A802	55b Teleorman	.25	.25
2699	A802	55b Timis	.25	.25
2700	A802	55b Tulcea	.25	.25
2701	A802	55b Vaslui	.25	.25
2702	A802	55b Vilcea	.25	.25
2703	A802	55b Vrancea	.25	.25
2704	A802	55b Postal emblem	.25	.25
		Nos. 2665-2704 (40)	10.00	10.00

Sheets of 50 (10x5) contain 5 designs: Nos.
2665-2669; 2670-2674; 2675-2679; 2680-
2684; 2685-2689; 2690-2694; 2695-2699;
2700-2704. Each row of 10 contains 5 pairs of
each design.
Issued: #2665-2679, 12/20; #2680-2704,
9/5/77.

Oxcart, by Grigorescu — A803

Paintings by Nicolae Grigorescu (1838-
1907): 1 l, Self-portrait, vert. 1.50 l, Shepherdess. 2.15 l, Woman Spinning with Distaff.
3.40 l, Shepherd, vert. 4.80 l, Rest at Well.

1977, Jan. 20　　Photo.　　Perf. 13½

2705	A803	55b gray & multi	.25	.25
2706	A803	1 l gray & multi	.25	.25
2707	A803	1.50 l gray & multi	.25	.25
2708	A803	2.15 l gray & multi	.40	.25
2709	A803	3.40 l gray & multi	.55	.30
2710	A803	4.80 l gray & multi	.85	.35
		Nos. 2705-2710 (6)	2.55	1.65

Cheia Telecommunications
Station — A804

1977, Feb. 1

2711	A804	55b multi	.25	.25

Red Deer
A805

Protected Birds and Animals: 1 l, Mute
swan. 1.50 l, Egyptian vulture. 2.15 l, Bison.
3.40 l, White-headed ruddy duck. 4.80 l,
Kingfisher.

1977, Mar. 20　　Photo.　　Perf. 13½

2712	A805	55b multi	.25	.25
2713	A805	1 l multi	.25	.25
2714	A805	1.50 l multi	.25	.25
2715	A805	2.15 l multi	.40	.25
2716	A805	3.40 l multi	.60	.25
2717	A805	4.80 l multi	.85	.25
		Nos. 2712-2717 (6)	2.60	1.50

Calafat Artillery Unit, by Sava
Hentia — A806

Paintings: 55b, Attacking Infantryman, by
Oscar Obedeanu, vert. 1.50 l, Infantry Attack
in Winter, by Stefan Luchian, vert. 2.15 l, Battle of Plevna (after etching). 3.40 l, Artillery, by
Nicolae Ion Grigorescu. 10 l, Battle of Grivita,
1877.

1977

2718	A806	55b gold & multi	.25	.25
2719	A806	1 l gold & multi	.25	.25
2720	A806	1.50 l gold & multi	.25	.25
2721	A806	2.15 l gold & multi	.60	.25
2722	A806	3.40 l gold & multi	.75	.25
		Nos. 2718-2722,B442 (6)	3.60	1.65

Souvenir Sheet

2723	A806	10 l gold & multi	3.00	2.25

Centenary of Romania's independence. A
10 l imperf. souvenir sheet exists showing victorious return of army, Dobruja, 1878. Values:
unused $10; used, $6.
Issued: #2718-2722, May 9; #2723, Apr. 25.

Sinaia, Carpathian Mountains — A807

Design: 2.40 l, Hotels, Aurora, Black Sea.

1977, May 17

2724	A807	2 l gold & multi	1.00	.85
2725	A807	2.40 l gold & multi	1.40	1.25

Inter-European Cultural and Economic
Cooperation. Nos. 2724-2725 printed in
sheets of 4 with marginal inscriptions.

Petru
Rares — A808

1977, June 10   Photo.   Perf. 13½
2726 A808 40b multi   .35 .25
  450th anniversary of the elevation of Petru
Rares to Duke of Moldavia.

Ion Luca
Caragiale — A809

1977, June 10
2727 A809 55b multi   .35 .25
  Ion Luca Caragiale (1852-1912), writer.

Red
Cross
Nurse,
Children,
Emblems
A810

1977, June 10
2728 A810 1.50 l multi   .40 .25
  23rd Intl. Red Cross Conf., Bucharest.

Arch of
Triumph,
Bucharest
A811

1977, June 10
2729 A811 2.15 l multi   .75 .25
  Battles of Marasesti and Oituz, 60th anniv.

Peaks of San Marino, Exhibition
Emblem — A812

1977, Aug. 28   Photo.   Perf. 13½
2730 A812 4 l brt bl & multi   1.20 .25
  Centenary of San Marino stamps, and San
Marino '77 Phil. Exhib., San Marino, 8/28-9/4.

Man on
Pommel
Horse — A813

  Gymnasts: 40b, Woman dancer. 55b, Man
on parallel bars. 1 l, Woman on balance beam.
2.15 l, Man on rings. 4.80 l, Woman on double
bars.

1977, Sept. 25   Photo.   Perf. 13½
2731 A813 20b multi   .25 .25
2732 A813 40b multi   .25 .25
2733 A813 55b multi   .25 .25
2734 A813 1 l multi   .25 .25
2735 A813 2.15 l multi   .35 .25
2736 A813 4.80 l multi   1.25 .25
      Nos. 2731-2736 (6)   2.60 1.50

"Carpati" near Cazane, Iron
Gate — A814

  Designs: 1 l, "Mircesti" at Orsova. 1.50 l,
"Oltenita" at Calafat. 2.15 l, Water bus at
Giurgiu. 3 l, "Herculane" at Tulcea. 3.40 l,
"Muntenia" in Nature preserve, Sulina. 4.80 l,
Map of Danube Delta with Sulina Canal. 10 l,
Danubius, god of Danube, from Trajan's Col-
umn, Rome, vert.

1977, Dec. 28
2737 A814 55b multi   .25 .25
2738 A814 1 l multi   .25 .25
2739 A814 1.50 l multi   .25 .25
2740 A814 2.15 l multi   .40 .25
2741 A814 3 l multi   .60 .25
2742 A814 3.40 l multi   .65 .25
2743 A814 4.80 l multi   1.25 .30
      Nos. 2737-2743 (7)   3.65 1.80

Souvenir Sheet

2744 A814 10 l multi   2.75 2.00
  European Danube Commission.
  A 10 l imperf. souvenir sheet exists showing
map of Danube from Regensburg to the Black
Sea. Value, unused or used, $50.

Flag and
Arms of
Romania
A815

  Designs: 1.20 l, Computer production in
Romania. 1.75 l, National Theater, Craiova.

1977, Dec. 30
2745 A815 55b multi   .25 .25
2746 A815 1.20 l multi   .25 .25
2747 A815 1.75 l multi   .40 .25
      Nos. 2745-2747 (3)   .90 .75
  Proclamation of Republic, 30th anniversary.

Dancers
A816

  Designs: Romanian male folk dancers.

1977, Nov. 28   Photo.   Perf. 13½
2748 A816 20b multi   .25 .25
2749 A816 40b multi   .25 .25
2750 A816 55b multi   .25 .25
2751 A816 1 l multi   .25 .25
2752 A816 2.15 l multi   .35 .25
2753 A816 4.80 l multi   1.25 .25
      Nos. 2748-2753 (6)   2.60 1.50

Souvenir Sheet

2754 A816 10 l multi   2.50 2.25

Firiza
Dam
A817

  Hydroelectric Stations and Dams: 40b,
Negovanu. 55b, Piatra Neamt. 1 l, Izvorul
Muntelui-Bicaz. 2.15 l, Vidraru. 4.80 l, Iron
Gate.

1978, Mar. 10   Photo.   Perf. 13½
2755 A817 20b multi   .25 .25
2756 A817 40b multi   .25 .25
2757 A817 55b multi   .25 .25
2758 A817 1 l multi   .25 .25
2759 A817 2.15 l multi   .35 .25
2760 A817 4.80 l multi   1.00 .25
      Nos. 2755-2760 (6)   2.35 1.50

Soccer and
Argentina '78
Emblem
A818

  Various soccer scenes & Argentina '78
emblem.

1978, Apr. 15
2761 A818 55b bl & multi   .25 .25
2762 A818 1 l org & multi   .25 .25
2763 A818 1.50 l yel grn & multi   .25 .25
2764 A818 2.15 l ver & multi   .30 .25
2765 A818 3.40 l bl grn & multi   .60 .25
2766 A818 4.80 l lil rose & multi   1.00 .25
      Nos. 2761-2766 (6)   2.55 1.50
  11th World Cup Soccer Championship,
Argentina '78, June 1-25. See No. C222.

King
Decebalus
of Dacia
Statue,
Deva
A819

  Design: 3.40 l, King Mircea the Elder of Wallachia statue, Tulcea, and ship.

1978, May 22   Photo.   Perf. 13½
2767 A819 1.30 l gold & multi   .90 .70
2768 A819 3.40 l gold & multi   1.60 1.25
  Inter-European Cultural and Economic
Cooperation. Each printed in sheet of 4.

Worker, Factory,
Flag — A821

1978, June 11   Photo.   Perf. 13½
2770 A821 55b multi   .35 .25
  Nationalization of industry, 30th anniv.

Spindle and
Handle,
Transylvania
A822

  Wood Carvings: 40b, Cheese molds,
Muntenia. 55b, Spoons, Oltenia. 1 l, Barrel,
Moldavia. 2.15 l, Ladle and mug, Transylvania.
4.80 l, Water bucket, Oltenia.

1978, June 20
2771 A822 20b multi   .25 .25
2772 A822 40b multi   .25 .25
2773 A822 55b multi   .25 .25
2774 A822 1 l multi   .25 .25
2775 A822 2.15 l multi   .30 .25
2776 A822 4.80 l multi   1.00 .25
      Nos. 2771-2776 (6)   2.30 1.50

Danube Delta — A823

  Tourist Publicity: 1 l, Bran Castle, vert.
1.50 l, Monastery, Suceava, Moldavia. 2.15 l,
Caves, Oltenia. 3.40 l, Ski lift, Brasov. 4.80 l,
Mangalia, Black Sea. 10 l, Strehaia Fortress,
vert.

1978, July 20   Photo.   Perf. 13½
2777 A823 55b multi   .25 .25
2778 A823 1 l multi   .25 .25
2779 A823 1.50 l multi   .25 .25
2780 A823 2.15 l multi   .30 .25
2781 A823 3.40 l multi   .50 .25
2782 A823 4.80 l multi   1.00 .35
      Nos. 2777-2782 (6)   2.55 1.60

Miniature Sheet

2783 A823 10 l multi   3.00 2.50
  No. 2783 contains one 37x51mm stamp.
Issued July 30.

Electronic
Microscope
A824

  Designs: 40b, Hydraulic excavator. 55b,
Computer center. 1.50 l, Oil derricks. 3 l, Harvester combine. 3.40 l, Petrochemical plant.

1978, Aug. 15   Photo.   Perf. 13½
2784 A824 20b multi   .25 .25
2785 A824 40b multi   .25 .25
2786 A824 55b multi   .25 .25
2787 A824 1.50 l multi   .25 .25

2788	A824	3 l multi, horiz.	.55	.25
2789	A824	3.40 l multi	.70	.25

Nos. 2784-2789 (6) 2.25 1.50

Industrial development.

Polovraci Cave, Carpathians A825

Caves: 1 l, Topolnita. 1.50 l, Ponoare. 2.15 l, Ratei, Mt. Bucegi. 3.40 l, Closani, Mt. Motrului. 4.80 l, Epuran. 1 l, 1.50 l, 4.80 l, Mt. Mehedinti.

1978, Aug. 25   Photo.   Perf. 13½

2790	A825	55b multi	.25	.25
2791	A825	1 l multi	.25	.25
2792	A825	1.50 l multi	.25	.25
2793	A825	2.15 l multi	.30	.25
2794	A825	3.40 l multi	.50	.25
2795	A825	4.80 l multi	1.00	.25

Nos. 2790-2795 (6) 2.55 1.50

"Racial Equality" — A826

1978, Sept. 28

2796	A826	3.40 l multi	.70	.25

Anti-Apartheid Year.

Gold Bas-relief — A827

Designs: 40b, Gold armband. 55b, Gold cameo ring. 1 l, Silver bowl. 2.15 l, Eagle from Roman standard, vert. 4.80 l, Silver armband.

1978, Sept. 25

2797	A827	20b multi	.25	.25
2798	A827	40b multi	.25	.25
2799	A827	55b multi	.25	.25
2800	A827	1 l multi	.25	.25
2801	A827	2.15 l multi	.30	.25
2802	A827	4.80 l multi	1.00	.35

Nos. 2797-2802 (6) 2.30 1.60

Daco-Roman archaeological treasures. An imperf. 10 l souvenir sheet exists showing gold helmet, vert. Values: unused $10; used $6.

Woman Gymnast, Games' Emblem A828

1 l, Running. 1.50 l, Skiing. 2.15 l, Equestrian. 3.40 l, Soccer. 4.80 l, Handball.

1978, Sept. 15

2803	A828	55b multi	.25	.25
2804	A828	1 l multi	.25	.25
2805	A828	1.50 l multi	.25	.25
2806	A828	2.15 l multi	.30	.25

2807	A828	3.40 l multi	.50	.25
2808	A828	4.80 l multi	1.00	.25

Nos. 2803-2808 (6) 2.55 1.50

Ptolemaic Map of Dacia A829

Designs: 55b, Meeting House of Romanian National Council, Arad. 1.75 l, Pottery vases, 8th-9th centuries, found near Arad.

1978, Oct. 21   Photo.   Perf. 13½

2809	A829	40b multi	.25	.25
2810	A829	55b multi	.25	.25
2811	A829	1.75 l multi	.35	.25
b.		Strip of 3, #2809-2811	.50	.30

2,000th anniversary of founding of Arad.

Dacian Warrior, from Trajan's Column, Rome — A829a

1978, Nov. 5   Photo.   Perf. 13x13½

2811A	A829a	6 l + 3 l label	1.60	.85

NATIONALA '78 Phil. Exhib., Bucharest. Stamp Day.

Assembly at Alba Iulia, 1919 — A830

Design: 1 l, Open book and Romanian flag.

1978, Dec. 1

2812	A830	55b gold & multi	.25	.25
2813	A830	1 l gold & multi	.25	.25

60th anniversary of national unity.

Warrior, Bas-relief — A831

1.50 l, Warrior on horseback, bas-relief.

1979   Photo.   Perf. 13½

2814	A831	55b multi	.25	.25
2815	A831	1.50 l multi	.25	.25

2,050 years since establishment of first centralized and independent Dacian state.

"Heroes of Vaslui" — A832

Children's Drawings: 1 l, Building houses. 1.50 l, Folk music of Tica. 2.15 l, Industrial landscape, horiz. 3.40 l, winter customs, horiz. 4.80 l, Pioneer festival, horiz.

1979, Mar. 1

2816	A832	55b multi	.25	.25
2817	A832	1 l multi	.25	.25
2818	A832	1.50 l multi	.25	.25
2819	A832	2.15 l multi	.30	.25
2820	A832	3.40 l multi	.50	.25
2821	A832	4.80 l multi	.75	.25

Nos. 2816-2821 (6) 2.30 1.50

International Year of the Child.

A833

1.30 l, Ice Hockey, Globe, Emblem. 3.40 l, Ice hockey players, globe & emblem.

1979, Mar. 16   Photo.   Perf. 13½

2822		1.30 l multi	.30	.25
2823		3.40 l multi	.55	.25
a.	A833	Pair, #2822-2823	.85	.50

European Youth Ice Hockey Championship, Miercurea-Ciuc (1.30 l) and World Ice Hockey Championship, Galati (3.40 l).

Dog's-tooth Violet — A834

Protected Flowers: 1 l, Alpine violet. 1.50 l, Linum borzaeanum. 2.15 l, Persian bindweed. 3.40 l, Primula auricula. 4.80 l, Transylvanian columbine.

1979, Apr. 25   Photo.   Perf. 13½

2824	A834	55b multi	.25	.25
2825	A834	1 l multi	.25	.25
2826	A834	1.50 l multi	.25	.25
2827	A834	2.15 l multi	.35	.25
2828	A834	3.40 l multi	.50	.25
2829	A834	4.80 l multi	.75	.25

Nos. 2824-2829 (6) 2.35 1.50

Mail Coach and Post Rider, 19th Century A835

1979, May 3   Photo.   Perf. 13

2830	A835	1.30 l multi	.40	.25

Inter-European Cultural and Economic Cooperation. Printed in sheets of 4. See No. C231.

Oil Rig and Refinery — A836

1979, May 24   Photo.   Perf. 13

2832	A836	3.40 l multi	.60	.25

10th World Petroleum Congress, Bucharest.

Girl Pioneer — A837

1979, June 20

2833	A837	55b multi	.35	.25

30th anniversary of Romanian Pioneers.

Children with Flowers, IYC Emblem A838

IYC Emblem and: 1 l, Kindergarten. 2 l, Pioneers with rabbit. 4.60 l, Drummer, trumpeters, flags.

1979, July 18   Photo.   Perf. 13½

2834	A838	40b multi	.25	.25
2835	A838	1 l multi	.25	.25
2836	A838	2 l multi	.30	.25
2837	A838	4.60 l multi	.70	.25

Nos. 2834-2837 (4) 1.50 1.00

International Year of the Child.

Lady in a Garden, by Tattarescu A839

Paintings by Gheorghe Tattarescu: 40b, Mountain woman. 55b, Mountain man. 1 l, Portrait of Gh. Magheru. 2.15 l, The artist's daughter. 4.80 l, Self-portrait.

1979, June 16

2838	A839	20b multi	.25	.25
2839	A839	40b multi	.25	.25
2840	A839	55b multi	.25	.25
2841	A839	1 l multi	.25	.25
2842	A839	2.15 l multi	.30	.25
2843	A839	4.80 l multi	.90	.25

Nos. 2838-2843 (6) 2.20 1.50

Stefan Gheorghiu — A840

Designs: 55b, Gheorghe Lazar monument. 2.15 l, Lupeni monument. 4.60 l, Women in front of Memorial Arch.

1979, Aug.
2844	A840	40b multi	.25	.25
2845	A840	55b multi	.25	.25
2846	A840	2.15 l multi	.40	.25
2847	A840	4.60 l multi	1.10	.25
	Nos. 2844-2847 (4)		2.00	1.00

State Theater, Tirgu-Mures — A841

Modern Architecture: 40b, University, Brasov. 55b, Political Administration Buildings, Baia Mare. 1 l, Stefan Gheorghiu Academy, Bucharest. 2.15 l, Political Administration Building, Botosani. 4.80 l, House of Culture, Tirgoviste.

1979, June 25
2848	A841	20b multi	.25	.25
2849	A841	40b multi	.25	.25
2850	A841	55b multi	.25	.25
2851	A841	1 l multi	.25	.25
2852	A841	2.15 l multi	.25	.25
2853	A841	4.80 l multi	.70	.25
	Nos. 2848-2853 (6)		1.95	1.50

Flags of Russia and Romania — A842

1 l, Workers' Militia, by L. Suhar, horiz.

1979, Aug. 20   Photo.   Perf. 13½
2854	A842	55b multi	.25	.25
2855	A842	1 l multi	.25	.25

Liberation from Fascism, 35th anniversary.

Cargo Ship Galati A843

Romanian Ships: 1 l, Cargo ship Bucuresti. 1.50 l, Ore carrier Resita. 2.15 l, Ore carrier Tomis. 3.40 l, Tanker Dacia. 4.80 l, Tanker Independenta.

1979, Aug. 27   Photo.   Perf. 13½
2856	A843	55b multi	.25	.25
2857	A843	1 l multi	.25	.25
2858	A843	1.50 l multi	.25	.25
2859	A843	2.15 l multi	.25	.25
2860	A843	3.40 l multi	.45	.25
2861	A843	4.80 l multi	.90	.25
	Nos. 2856-2861 (6)		2.35	1.50

Olympic Stadium, Melbourne, 1956, Moscow '80 Emblem — A844

Moscow '80 Emblem and Olympic Stadiums: 1 l, Rome, 1960. 1.50 l, Tokyo, 1964. 2.15 l, Mexico City, 1968. 3.40 l, Munich, 1972. 4.80 l, Montreal, 1976. 10 l, Moscow, 1980.

1979, Oct. 23   Photo.   Perf. 13½
2862	A844	55b multi	.25	.25
2863	A844	1 l multi	.25	.25
2864	A844	1.50 l multi	.25	.25
2865	A844	2.15 l multi	.30	.25
2866	A844	3.40 l multi	.45	.25
2867	A844	4.80 l multi	.65	.25
	Nos. 2862-2867 (6)		2.15	1.50

Souvenir Sheet
2868	A844	10 l multi	3.00	2.50

22nd Summer Olympic Games, Moscow, July 19-Aug. 3, 1980. No. 2868 contains one 50x38mm stamp.
No. 2868 airmail.
Imperf 10 l souvenir sheets exist for the European Sports Conference and 1980 Olympics. Value for former, unused or used, $15. Value for latter, unused or used, $20.

Arms of Alba Iulia — A845

Designs: Arms of Romanian cities.

1979, Oct. 25
2869	A845	1.20 l shown	.30	.25
2870	A845	1.20 l Arad	.30	.25
2871	A845	1.20 l Bacau	.30	.25
2872	A845	1.20 l Baia-Mare	.30	.25
2873	A845	1.20 l Birlad	.30	.25
2874	A845	1.20 l Botosani	.30	.25
2875	A845	1.20 l Braila	.30	.25
2876	A845	1.20 l Brasov	.30	.25
2877	A845	1.20 l Buzau	.30	.25
2878	A845	1.20 l Calarasi	.30	.25
2879	A845	1.20 l Cluj	.30	.25
2880	A845	1.20 l Constanta	.30	.25
2881	A845	1.20 l Craiova	.30	.25
2882	A845	1.20 l Dej	.30	.25
2883	A845	1.20 l Deva	.30	.25
2884	A845	1.20 l Turnu-Severin	.30	.25
2885	A845	1.20 l Focsani	.30	.25
2886	A845	1.20 l Galati	.30	.25
2887	A845	1.20 l Gheorghe Gheorghiu-Dej	.30	.25
2888	A845	1.20 l Giurgiu	.30	.25
2889	A845	1.20 l Hunedoara	.30	.25
2890	A845	1.20 l Iasi	.30	.25
2891	A845	1.20 l Lugoj	.30	.25
2892	A845	1.20 l Medias	.30	.25
2893	A845	1.20 l Odorheiu Seguiesc	.30	.25

1980, Jan. 5
2894	A845	1.20 l Oradea	.30	.25
2895	A845	1.20 l Petrosani	.30	.25
2896	A845	1.20 l Piatra-Neamt	.30	.25
2897	A845	1.20 l Pitesti	.30	.25
2898	A845	1.20 l Ploiesti	.30	.25
2899	A845	1.20 l Resita	.30	.25
2900	A845	1.20 l Rimnicu-Vilcea	.30	.25
2901	A845	1.20 l Roman	.30	.25
2902	A845	1.20 l Satu-Mare	.30	.25
2903	A845	1.20 l Sibiu	.30	.25
2904	A845	1.20 l Siget-Marma-tiei	.30	.25
2905	A845	1.20 l Sighisoara	.30	.25
2906	A845	1.20 l Suceava	.30	.25
2907	A845	1.20 l Tecuci	.30	.25
2908	A845	1.20 l Timisoara	.30	.25
2909	A845	1.20 l Tirgoviste	.30	.25
2910	A845	1.20 l Tirgu-Jiu	.30	.25
2911	A845	1.20 l Tirgu-Mures	.30	.25
2912	A845	1.20 l Tulcea	.30	.25
2913	A845	1.20 l Turda	.30	.25
2914	A845	1.20 l Turnu Magurele	.30	.25
2915	A845	1.20 l Bucharest	.30	.25
	Nos. 2869-2915 (47)		14.10	11.75

A846

Regional Costumes: 20b, Maramures Woman. 40b, Maramures man. 55b, Vrancea woman. 1.50 l, Vrancea man. 3 l, Padureni woman. 3.40 l, Padureni man.

1979, Oct. 27
2916	A846	20b multi	.25	.25
2917	A846	40b multi	.25	.25
2918	A846	55b multi	.25	.25
2919	A846	1.50 l multi	.25	.25
2920	A846	3 l multi	.40	.25
2921	A846	3.40 l multi	.45	.25
	Nos. 2916-2921 (6)		1.85	1.50

A847

Flower Paintings by Stefan Luchian: 40b, Snapdragons. 60b, Triple chrysanthemums. 1.55 l, Potted flowers on stairs.

1979, July 27
2922	A847	40b multi	.25	.25
2923	A847	60b multi	.25	.25
2924	A847	1.55 l multi	.25	.25
	Nos. 2922-2924,B445 (4)		1.85	1.85

Socfilex, International Philatelic Exhibition, Bucharest. See No. B446.

Souvenir Sheet

Romanian Communist Party, 12th Congress — A848

1979, Oct.
2925	A848	5 l multi	1.75	.70

Figure Skating, Lake Placid '80 Emblem, Olympic Rings — A849

1979, Dec. 27   Photo.   Perf. 13½
2926	A849	55b shown	.25	.25
2927	A849	1 l Downhill skiing	.25	.25
2928	A849	1.50 l Biathlon	.25	.25
2929	A849	2.15 l Two-man bob-sledding	.25	.25
2930	A849	3.40 l Speed skating	.50	.25
2931	A849	4.80 l Ice hockey	1.00	.25
	Nos. 2926-2931 (6)		2.50	1.50

Souvenir Sheet
2932	A849	10 l Ice hockey, diff.	3.25	2.50

13th Winter Olympic Games, Lake Placid, NY, Feb. 12-24, 1980. No. 2932 contains one 38x50mm stamp. An imperf. 10 l air post souvenir sheet exists showing four-man bobsledding. Value, unused or used, $30.

"Calugareni", Expo Emblem — A850

No. 2934, "Orleans". No. 2935, #1059, type fawn. No. 2936, #15021, type 1E. No. 2937, "Pacific". No. 2938, Electric engine 060-EA. 10 l, Diesel electric.

1979, Dec. 29
2933	A850	55b multicolored	.25	.25
2934	A850	1 l multicolored	.25	.25
2935	A850	1.50 l multicolored	.25	.25
2936	A850	2.15 l multicolored	.35	.25
2937	A850	3.40 l multicolored	.60	.25
2938	A850	4.80 l multicolored	.80	.25
	Nos. 2933-2938 (6)		2.50	1.50

Souvenir Sheet
2939	A850	10 l multicolored	3.00	2.50

Intl. Transport Expo., Hamburg, June 8-July 1. #2939 contains one 50x40mm stamp.

Dacian Warrior, Trajan's Column, Rome — A851

Design: 1.50 l, Two warriors.

1980, Feb. 9   Photo.   Perf. 13½
2940	A851	55b multi	.25	.25
2941	A851	1.50 l multi	.30	.25

2,050 years since establishment of first centralized and independent Dacian state.

Kingfisher — A852

1 l, Great white heron, vert. 1.50 l, Red-breasted goose. 2.15 l, Red deer, vert. 3.40 l, Roe deer. 4.80 l, European bison, vert.

1980, Mar. 25   Photo.   Perf. 13½
2942	A852	55b multicolored	.25	.25
2943	A852	1 l multicolored	.25	.25
2944	A852	1.50 l multicolored	.25	.25
2945	A852	2.15 l multicolored	.25	.25
2946	A852	3.40 l multicolored	.45	.25
2947	A852	4.80 l multicolored	.90	.25
	Nos. 2942-2947 (6)		2.35	1.50

European Nature Protection Year. A 10 l imperf. souvenir sheet exists showing bears; red control number. Value, unused or used, $30.
See No. C232.

Souvenir Sheets

George Enescu — A853

1980, May 6
2948	A853	Sheet of 4	3.50	3.00
a.		1.30 l Playing violin	.70	.25
b.		1.30 l Conducting	.70	.25
c.		1.30 l Playing piano	.70	.25
d.		1.30 l Composing	.70	.25

2949	A853	Sheet of 4	3.50	3.00
a.		3.40 l Beethoven in library	.70	.25
b.		3.40 l Portrait	.70	.25
c.		3.40 l At piano	.70	.25
d.		3.40 l Composing	.70	.25

Inter-European Cultural and Economic Cooperation.

Vallota Purpurea — A854

1 l, Eichhornia crasipes. 1.50 l, Sprekelia formosissima. 2.15 l, Hypericum calycinum. 3.40 l, Camellia japonica. 4.80 l, Nelumbo nucifera.

1980, Apr. 10　　Photo.　　Perf. 13½

2950	A854	55b multicolored	.25	.25
2951	A854	1 l multicolored	.25	.25
2952	A854	1.50 l multicolored	.25	.25
2953	A854	2.15 l multicolored	.40	.25
2954	A854	3.40 l multicolored	.60	.25
2955	A854	4.80 l multicolored	1.00	.25
		Nos. 2950-2955 (6)	2.75	1.50

Tudor Vladimirescu A855

55b, Mihail Sadoveanu. 1.50 l, Battle against Hungarians. 2.15 l, Tudor Arghezi. 3 l, Horea.

1980, Apr. 24

2956	A855	40b multicolored	.25	.25
2957	A855	55b multicolored	.25	.25
2958	A855	1.50 l multicolored	.25	.25
2959	A855	2.15 l multicolored	.40	.25
2960	A855	3 l multicolored	.50	.25
		Nos. 2956-2960 (5)	1.65	1.25

Anniversaries: 40b, Tudor Vladimirescu (1780-1821), leader of 1821 revolution; 55b, Mihail Sadoveanu (1880-1961), author; 1.50 l, Victory of Posada; 2.15 l, Tudor Arghezi (1880-1967), poet; 3 l, Horea (1730-1785), leader of 1784 uprising.

A856

Dacian fruit bowl and cup.

1980, May 8

2961	A856	1 l multicolored	.35	.25

Petrodava City, 2000th anniversary.

A857

1980, June 20　　Photo.　　Perf. 13½

2962	A857	55b Javelin	.25	.25
2963	A857	1 l Fencing	.25	.25
2964	A857	1.50 l Shooting	.30	.25
2965	A857	2.15 l Kayak	.35	.25
2966	A857	3.40 l Wrestling	.55	.25
2967	A857	4.80 l Rowing	.80	.25
		Nos. 2962-2967 (6)	2.50	1.50

Souvenir Sheet

2968	A857	10 l Handball	2.75	2.25

22nd Summer Olympic Games, Moscow, July 19-Aug. 3. No. 2968 contains one 38x50mm stamp. An imperf. 10 l air post souvenir sheet exists showing gymnast. Value, unused or used, $27.50.

Congress Emblem — A858

1980, Aug. 10　　Photo.　　Perf. 13½

2969	A858	55b multicolored	.50	.50

15th Intl. Historical Sciences Congress, Bucharest.

Fireman Rescuing Child — A859

1980, Aug. 25

2970	A859	55b multicolored	.35	.25

Firemen's Day, Sept. 13.

Chinese and Romanian Young Pioneers at Stamp Show — A860

1980, Sept. 18

2971	A860	1 l multicolored	.35	.25

Romanian-Chinese Phil. Exhib., Bucharest.

Souvenir Sheet

Parliament Building, Bucharest — A861

1980, Sept. 30

2972	A861	10 l multicolored	2.00	1.65

European Security Conference, Madrid. An imperf. 10 l air post souvenir sheet exists showing Plaza Mayor, Madrid. Value, unused or used, $20.

Knights and Chessboard — A862

1980, Oct. 1　　Photo.　　Perf. 13½

2973	A862	55b shown	.25	.25
2974	A862	1 l Rooks	.25	.25
2975	A862	2.15 l Man	.30	.25
2976	A862	4.80 l Woman	1.00	1.00
		Nos. 2973-2976 (4)	1.80	1.00

Chess Olympiad, Valletta, Malta, Nov. 20-Dec. 8.

Dacian Warrior — A863

40b, Moldavian soldier, 15th cent. 55b, Walachian horseman, 17th cent. 1 l, Flag bearer, 19th cent. 1.50 l, Infantryman, 19th cent. 2.15 l, Lancer, 19th cent. 4.80 l, Mounted Elite Corps Guard, 19th cent.

1980, Oct. 15

2977	A863	20b multi	.25	.25
2978	A863	40b multi	.25	.25
2979	A863	55b multi	.25	.25
2980	A863	1 l multi	.25	.25
2981	A863	1.50 l multi	.25	.25
2982	A863	2.15 l multi	.35	.25
2983	A863	4.80 l multi	.75	.35
		Nos. 2977-2983 (7)	2.35	1.85

Burebista Sculpture — A864

1980, Nov. 5　　Photo.　　Perf. 13½

2984	A864	2 l multicolored	.35	.25

2050 years since establishment of first centralized and independent Dacian state.

George Oprescu (1881-1969), Art Critic — A865

Famous Men: 2.15 l, Marius Bunescu (1881-1971), painter. 3.40 l, Ion Georgescu (1856-1898), sculptor.

1981, Feb. 20　　Photo.　　Perf. 13½

2985	A865	1.50 l multicolored	.25	.25
2986	A865	2.15 l multicolored	.40	.25
2987	A865	3.40 l multicolored	.70	.25
		Nos. 2985-2987 (3)	1.35	.75

National Dog Show — A866

Designs: Dogs — 40b, Mountain sheepdog, horiz. 55b, Saint Bernard. 1 l, Fox terrier, horiz. 1.50 l, German shepherd, horiz. 2.15 l, Boxer. 3.40 l, Dalmatian, horiz. 4.80 l, Poodle.

1981, Mar. 15

2988	A866	40b multicolored	.25	.25
2989	A866	55b multicolored	.25	.25
2990	A866	1 l multicolored	.25	.25
2991	A866	1.50 l multicolored	.25	.25
2992	A866	2.15 l multicolored	.45	.25
2993	A866	3.40 l multicolored	.70	.25
2994	A866	4.80 l multicolored	1.00	.25
		Nos. 2988-2994 (7)	3.15	1.75

River Steamer Stefan cel Mare — A867

1 l, Vas de Supraveghere. 1.50 l, Tudor Vladimirescu. 2.15 l, Dredger Sulina. 3.40 l, Republica Populara Romana. 4.80 l, Sulina Canal. 10 l, Galati.

1981, Mar. 25

2995	A867	55b multi	.25	.25
2996	A867	1 l multi	.25	.25
2997	A867	1.50 l multi	.25	.25
2998	A867	2.15 l multi	.25	.25
2999	A867	3.40 l multi	.40	.25
3000	A867	4.80 l multi	.80	.35
		Nos. 2995-3000 (6)	2.20	1.60

Souvenir Sheet

3001	A867	10 l multi	2.00	2.00

European Danube Commission, 125th anniv. An imperf. 10 l souvenir sheet exists showing map of Danube. Value, unused or used, $22.50.

Carrier Pigeon A868

Various carrier pigeons and doves.

1981, Apr. 15　　Photo.　　Perf. 13½

3002	A868	40b multi	.25	.25
3003	A868	55b multi	.25	.25
3004	A868	1 l multi	.25	.25
3005	A868	1.50 l multi	.25	.25
3006	A868	2.15 l multi	.30	.25
3007	A868	3.40 l multi	.60	.25
		Nos. 3002-3007 (6)	1.90	1.50

Romanian
Communist Party,
60th Anniv. — A869

1981, Apr. 22   Photo.   Perf. 13½
3008 A869 1 l multicolored   .35 .25

Folkdance, Moldavia — A870

Designs: Regional folkdances.

1981, May 4   Photo.   Perf. 13½
3009   Sheet of 4   2.50 2.50
 a.   A870 2.50 l shown   .45   .45
 b.   A870 2.50 l Transylvania   .45   .45
 c.   A870 2.50 l Banat   .45   .45
 d.   A870 2.50 l Muntenia   .45   .45
3010   Sheet of 4   2.50 2.50
 a.   A870 2.50 l Maramures   .45   .45
 b.   A870 2.50 l Dobruja   .45   .45
 c.   A870 2.50 l Oltenia   .45   .45
 d.   A870 2.50 l Crisana   .45   .45

Inter-European Cultural and Economic
Cooperation.

Singing
Romania
Festival — A871

1981, July 15
3011 A871   55b Industry   .25 .25
3012 A871 1.50 l Electronics   .25 .25
3013 A871 2.15 l Agriculture   .35 .25
3014 A871 3.40 l Culture   .50 .30
      Nos. 3011-3014 (4)   1.35 1.05

University '81
Games,
Bucharest — A872

1981, July 17
3015 A872   1 l Book, flag   .25 .25
3016 A872 2.15 l Emblem   .35 .25
3017 A872 4.80 l Stadium, horiz.   .75 .35
      Nos. 3015-3017 (3)   1.35 .85

Theodor Aman, Artist, Birth
Sesquicentennial — A873

Aman Paintings: 40b, Self-portrait. 55b, Battle of Giurgiu. 1 l, The Family Picnic. 1.50 l,
The Painter's Studio. 2.15 l, Woman in Interior.
3.40 l, Aman Museum, Bucharest. 55b, 1 l,
1.50 l, 3.40 l horiz.

1981, July 28
3018 A873   40b multi   .25 .25
3019 A873   55b multi   .25 .25
3020 A873   1 l multi   .25 .25
3021 A873 1.50 l multi   .25 .25
3022 A873 2.15 l multi   .30 .25
3023 A873 3.40 l multi   .50 .25
      Nos. 3018-3023 (6)   1.80 1.50

Thinker of
Cernavoda, 3rd
Cent. BC — A874

1981, July 30
3024 A874 3.40 l multi   .65 .30
      16th Science History Congress.

Blood Donation
Campaign — A875

1981, Aug. 15   Photo.   Perf. 13½
3025 A875 55b multicolored   .35 .25

Bucharest Central Military Hospital
Sesquicentennial — A876

1981, Sept. 1
3026 A876 55b multicolored   .35 .25

Romanian
Musicians — A877

Designs: 40b, George Enescu (1881-1955).
55b, Paul Constantinescu (1909-1963). 1 l,
Dinu Lipatti (1917-1950). 1.50 l, Ionel Periea
(1900-1970). 2.15 l, Ciprian Porumbescu
(1853-1883). 3.40 l, Mihail Jora (1891-1971).

1981, Sept. 20
3027 A877   40b multi   .25 .25
3028 A877   55b multi   .25 .25
3029 A877   1 l multi   .25 .25
3030 A877 1.50 l multi   .25 .25
3031 A877 2.15 l multi   .35 .25
3032 A877 3.40 l multi   .50 .25
      Nos. 3027-3032 (6)   1.85 1.50

Stamp
Day
A879

1981, Nov. 5   Photo.   Perf. 13½
3034 A879 2 l multicolored   .35 .25

Children's
Games — A880

Illustrations by Eugen Palade (40b, 55b, 1 l)
and Norman Rockwell (1.50 l, 2.15 l, 3 l, 4 l).
40b, Hopscotch. 55b, Soccer. 1 l, Riding
stick horse. 1.50 l, Snagging the Big One. 2.15
l, A Patient Friend. 3 l, Doggone It. 4 l, Puppy
Love.

1981, Nov. 25
3035 A880   40b multicolored   .25 .25
3036 A880   55b multicolored   .25 .25
3037 A880   1 l multicolored   .25 .25
3038 A880 1.50 l multicolored   .25 .25
3039 A880 2.15 l multicolored   .30 .25
3040 A880   3 l multicolored   .40 .25
3041 A880   4 l multicolored   .45 .35
      Nos. 3035-3041,C243 (8)   2.85 2.55

A881

1981, Dec. 28
3042 A881   55b multi   .25 .25
3043 A881   1 l multi   .25 .25
3044 A881 1.50 l multi   .25 .25
3045 A881 2.15 l multi   .35 .25
3046 A881 3.40 l multi   .40 .25
3047 A881 4.80 l multi   .65 .35
      Nos. 3042-3047 (6)   2.15 1.60

Souvenir Sheet
3048 A881   10 l multi   2.00 2.00

Espana '82 World Cup Soccer.
No. 3048 contains one 38x50mm stamp. An
imperf. 10 l air post souvenir sheet exists
showing game. Value, unused or used,
$27.50.

A882

Designs: 1 l, Prince Alexander the Good of
Moldavia (ruled 1400-1432). 1.50 l, Bogdan
Petriceicu Hasdeu (1838-1907), scholar. 2.15
l, Nicolae Titulescu (1882-1941), diplomat.

1982, Jan. 30   Photo.   Perf. 13½
3049 A882   1 l multi   .25 .25
3050 A882 1.50 l multi   .25 .25
3051 A882 2.15 l multi   .40 .25
      Nos. 3049-3051 (3)   .90 .75

Bucharest
Subway
System
A883

60b, Union Square station entrance. 2.40 l,
Heroes' Station platform.

1982, Feb. 25
3052 A883   60b multi   .25 .25
3053 A883 2.40 l multi   .45 .25

60th Anniv. of
Communist Youth
Union — A884

1.20 l, Construction worker. 1.50 l, Farm
workers. 2 l, Research. 2.50 l, Workers. 3 l,
Musicians, dancers.

1982
3054 A884   1 l shown   .25 .25
3055 A884 1.20 l multicolored   .25 .25
3056 A884 1.50 l multicolored   .25 .25
3057 A884   2 l multicolored   .30 .25
3058 A884 2.50 l multicolored   .35 .25
3059 A884   3 l multicolored   .40 .25
      Nos. 3054-3059 (6)   1.80 1.50

Dog
Sled
A885

55b, Dog rescuing child. 1 l, Shepherd, dog,
vert. 3 l, Hunting dog, vert. 4 l, Spitz, woman,
vert. 4.80 l, Guide dog, woman, vert. 5 l, Dalmatian, girl, vert. 6 l, Saint Bernard.

1982, Mar. 28   Photo.   Perf. 13½
3060 A885   55b multicolored   .25 .25
3061 A885   1 l multicolored   .25 .25
3062 A885   3 l multicolored   .45 .25
3063 A885 3.40 l shown   .55 .25
3064 A885   4 l multicolored   .60 .25
3065 A885 4.80 l multicolored   .70 .25
3066 A885   5 l multicolored   .75 .25
3067 A885   6 l multicolored   .90 .25
      Nos. 3060-3067 (8)   4.45 2.00

Bran
Castle,
Brasov,
1377
A886

1982, May 6
3068   Sheet of 4   1.75 1.75
 a.   A886 2.50 l shown   .35   .35
 b.   A886 2.50 l Hunedoara, Corvinilor,
             1409   .35   .35
 c.   A886 2.50 l Sinaia, 1873   .35   .35
 d.   A886 2.50 l Iasi, 1905   .35   .35
3069   Sheet of 4   1.75 1.75
 a.   A886 2.50 l Neuschwanstein   .35   .35
 b.   A886 2.50 l Stolzenfels   .35   .35
 c.   A886 2.50 l Katz-Loreley   .35   .35
 d.   A886 2.50 l Linderhof   .35   .35

Inter-European Cultural and Economic
Cooperation.

Souvenir Sheet

Constantin Brancusi in Paris
Studio — A887

1982, June 5
3070 A887 10 l multicolored   2.50 2.00
PHILEXFRANCE '82 Intl. Stamp Exhibition,
Paris, June 11-21.
For surcharge see No. 6067.

Gloria C-16 Combine
Harvester — A888

1982, June 29
3071 A888   50b shown   .25 .25
3072 A888   1 l Dairy farm   .25 .25
3073 A888 1.50 l Apple orchard   .25 .25
3074 A888 2.50 l Vineyard   .30 .25
3075 A888   3 l Irrigation   .50 .25
    Nos. 3071-3075,C250 (6)   2.15 1.50

Souvenir Sheet
3076 A888   10 l Village   2.50 2.00
Agricultural modernization. No. 3076 contains one 50x38mm stamp.

A890

Resort Hotels and Beaches. 1 l, 2.50 l, 3 l, 5
l horiz.

1982, Aug. 30   Photo.   Perf. 13½
3078 A890   50b Baile Felix   .25 .25
3079 A890   1 l Predeal   .25 .25
3080 A890 1.50 l Baile Herculane   .25 .25
3081 A890 2.50 l Eforie Nord   .40 .25
3082 A890   3 l Olimp   .50 .25
3083 A890   5 l Neptun   .85 .30
    Nos. 3078-3083 (6)   2.50 1.55

A891

Designs: 1 l, Legend, horiz. 1.50 l, Contrasts, horiz. 3.50 l, Relay Runner, horiz. 4 l,
Genesis of Romanian People, by Sabin
Balasa.

1982, Sept. 6
3084 A891   1 l multicolored   .25 .25
3085 A891 1.50 l multicolored   .25 .25
3086 A891 3.50 l multicolored   .65 .25
3087 A891   4 l multicolored   .80 .35
    Nos. 3084-3087 (4)   1.95 1.10

An imperf. 10 l souvenir sheet showing a rainbow over a map of Europe was
issued 1982, Sept. 25, with limited distribtuion. Value, $12.

Souvenir Sheet

Merry Peasant Girl, by Nicolae
Grigorescu (d. 1907) — A892

1982, Sept. 30   Photo.   Perf. 13½
3088 A892   10 l multicolored   2.50 2.50

Bucharest
Intl. Fair
A893

1982, Oct. 2
3089 A893   2 l Exhibition Hall,
                flag   .40 .25

Savings Week, Oct.
25-31 — A894

1982, Oct. 25
3090 A894   1 l Girl holding bank
                book   .25 .25
3091 A894   2 l Poster   .35 .25

Stamp Day — A895

1982, Nov. 10
3092 A895   1 l Woman letter carrier .25 .25
3093 A895   2 l Mailman   .35 .25

Scene from
Ileana Sinziana,
by Petre
Ispirescu
A896

Fairytales: 50b, The Youngest Child and the
Golden Apples, by Petre Ispirescu. 1 l, The
Bear Hoaxed by the Fox, by Ion Creanga. 1.50
l, The Prince of Tear, by Mihai Eminescu. 2.50
l, The Little Bag with Two Coins Inside, by Ion
Creanga. 3 l, Ileana Simziana, by Petre
Ispirescu. 5 l, Danila Prepeleac, by Ion
Creanga.

1982, Nov. 30
3094 A896   50b multicolored   .25 .25
3095 A896   1 l multicolored   .25 .25
3096 A896 1.50 l multicolored   .25 .25
3097 A896 2.50 l multicolored   .40 .25
3098 A896   3 l multicolored   .40 .25
3099 A896   5 l multicolored   .80 .30
    Nos. 3094-3099 (6)   2.35 1.55

Arms, Colors,
Book — A897

1982, Dec. 16
3100 A897   1 l Closed book   .25 .25
3101 A897   2 l Open book   .35 .25
Natl. Communist Party Conference,
Bucharest, Dec. 16-18.

A898

50b, Wooden flask, Suceava. 1 l, Ceramic
plate, Radauti. 1.50 l, Wooden scoop, Valea
Mare, horiz. 2 l, Plate, jug, Vama. 3 l, Butter
churn, wooden bucket, Moldavia. 3.50 l,
Ceramic plates, Leheceni, horiz. 4 l, Wooden
spoon, platter, Cluj. 5 l, Bowl, pitcher,
Marginea. 6 l, Jug, flask, Bihor. 7 l, Spindle,
shuttle, Transylvania. 7.50 l, Water buckets,
Suceava. 8 l, Jug, Oboga; plate, Horezu. 10 l,
Water buckets, Hunedoara, Suceava, horiz.
20 l, Wooden flask, beakers, Horezu. 30 l,
Wooden spoons, Alba, horiz. 50 l, Ceramic
dishes, Horezu.

1982, Dec. 22   Photo.   Perf. 13½
3102 A898   50b red orange   .25 .25
3103 A898   1 l dark blue   .25 .25
3104 A898 1.50 l orange brn   .25 .25
3105 A898   2 l brt blue   .30 .25
3106 A898   3 l olive green   .40 .25
3107 A898 3.50 l dk green   .55 .25
3108 A898   4 l lt brown   .60 .25
3109 A898   5 l gray blue   .75 .25
    Size: 23x29mm, 29x23mm
3110 A898   6 l blue   .90 .25
3111 A898   7 l lake   1.10 .25
3112 A898 7.50 l red violet   1.25 .25
3113 A898   8 l brt green   1.25 .25
3114 A898   10 l red   1.50 .25
3115 A898   20 l purple   3.25 .25
3116 A898   30 l Prus blue   4.50 .35
3117 A898   50 l dark brown   8.00 .65
    Nos. 3102-3117 (16)   25.10 4.50

35th Anniv. of
Republic — A899

1982, Dec. 27
3118 A899   1 l Symbols of development   .25 .25
3119 A899   2 l Flag   .35 .25

Grigore
Manolescu
(1857-92), as
Hamlet — A900

Actors or Actresses in Famous Roles: 50b,
Matei Millo (1814-1896) in The Discontented.
1 l, Mihail Pascaly (1829-1882) in Director
Milo. 1.50 l, Aristizza Romanescu (1854-
1918), in The Dogs. 2 l, C. I. Nottara (1859-
1935) in Snowstorm. 3 l, Agatha Birsescu
(1857-1939) in Medea. 4 l, Ion Brezeanu
(1869-1940) in The Lost Letter. 5 l, Aristide
Demetriad (1872-1930) in The Despotic
Prince.

1983, Feb. 28
3120 A900   50b multi   .25 .25
3121 A900   1 l multi   .25 .25
3122 A900 1.50 l multi   .30 .25
3123 A900   2 l multi   .35 .25
3124 A900 2.50 l multi   .45 .25
3125 A900   3 l multi   .60 .25
3126 A900   4 l multi   .70 .25
3127 A900   5 l multi   .90 .25
    Nos. 3120-3127 (8)   3.80 2.00

Hugo Grotius
(1583-1645), Dutch
Jurist — A901

1983, Apr. 30
3128 A901   2 l brown   .45 .25

Romanian-Made Vehicles — A902

50b, ARO-10. 1 l, Dacia, 1300 station
wagon. 1.50 l, ARO-242 jeep. 2.50 l, ARO-
244. 4 l, Dacia 1310. 5 l, OLTCIT club passenger car.

1983, May 3
3129 A902   50b multi   .25 .25
3130 A902   1 l multi   .25 .25
3131 A902 1.50 l multi   .35 .25
3132 A902 2.50 l multi   .60 .25
3133 A902   4 l multi   .95 .35
3134 A902   5 l multi   1.20 .40
    Nos. 3129-3134 (6)   3.60 1.75

Johannes Kepler (1571-1630) — A903

Famous Men: No. 3135: b, Alexander von Humboldt (1769-1859), explorer. c, Goethe (1749-1832). d, Richard Wagner (1813-1883), composer.

No. 3136: a, Ioan Andreescu (1850-1882), painter. b, George Constantinescu (1881-1965), engineer. c, Tudor Arghezi (1880-1967), poet. d, C.I. Parhon (1874-1969), endocrinologist.

1983, May 16

3135		Sheet of 4	2.50	2.50
a.-d.	A903	3 l Any single	.55	.55
3136		Sheet of 4	2.50	2.50
a.-d.	A903	3 l Any single	.55	.55

Inter-European Cultural and Economic Cooperation.

Workers' Struggle, 50th Anniv. — A904

1983, July 22   Photo.   Perf. 13½

3137	A904	2 l silver & multi	.35	.25

Birds — A905

50b, Luscinia svecica. 1 l, Sturnus roseus. 1.50 l, Coracias garrulus. 2.50 l, Merops apiaster. 4 l, Emberiza schoeniclus. 5 l, Lanius minor.

1983, Oct. 28   Photo.   Perf. 13½

3138	A905	50b multi	.25	.25
3139	A905	1 l multi	.25	.25
3140	A905	1.50 l multi	.35	.25
3141	A905	2.50 l multi	.50	.25
3142	A905	4 l multi	.80	.35
3143	A905	5 l multi	1.00	.40
		Nos. 3138-3143 (6)	3.15	1.75

Water Sports A906

1983, Sept. 16   Photo.   Perf. 13½

3144	A906	50b Kayak	.25	.25
3145	A906	1 l Water polo	.25	.25
3146	A906	1.50 l Canadian one-man canoes	.35	.25
3147	A906	2.50 l Diving	.60	.25
3148	A906	4 l Singles rowing	.95	.25
3149	A906	5 l Swimming	1.20	.25
		Nos. 3144-3149 (6)	3.60	1.50

Stamp Day A907

1 l, Mailman on bicycle. 3.50 l, with 3 l label, flag.
10 l, Unloading mail plane.

1983, Oct. 24

3150	A907	1 l multicolored	.25	.25
3151	A907	3.50 l multicolored	1.00	.55

Souvenir Sheet

3152	A907	10 l multicolored	3.00	3.00

#3152 is airmail, contains one 38x51mm stamp.

Geum Reptans A908

Flora (No. 3154): b, Papaver dubium. c, Carlina acaulis. d, Paeonia peregrina. e, Gentiana excisa. Fauna (No. 3155): a, Sciurus vulgaria. b, Grammia quenselii. c, Dendrocopos medius. d, Lynx. e, Tichodroma muraria.

1983, Oct. 28   Photo.   Perf. 13½

3154		Strip of 5	2.25	2.25
a.-e.	A908	1 l Any single	.45	.45
3155		Strip of 5	2.25	2.25
a.-e.	A908	1 l Any single	.45	.45

Issued in sheets of 15.

Lady with Feather, by Cornelius Baba — A909

1983, Nov. 3

3156	A909	1 l shown	.25	.25
3157	A909	2 l Citizens	.40	.25
3158	A909	3 l Farmers, horiz.	.60	.25
3159	A909	4 l Resting in the Field, horiz.	.80	.25
		Nos. 3156-3159 (4)	2.05	1.00

A910

1983, Nov. 30

3160	A910	1 l Banner, emblem	.25	.25
3161	A910	2 l Congress building, flags	.40	.25

Pact with Romania, 65th anniv.

A911

Designs: 1 l, Flags of participating countries, post office, mailman. 2 l, Congress building, woman letter carrier. 10 l, Flags, Congress building.

1983, Dec. 17

3162	A911	1 l multicolored	.25	.25
3163	A911	2 l multicolored	.45	.25

Souvenir Sheet

3164	A911	10 l multicolored	2.25	2.25

BALKANFILA '83 Stamp Exhibition, Bucharest. #3164 contains one 38x50mm stamp.

Souvenir Sheet

Orient Express Centenary (Paris-Istanbul) — A912

Leaving Gara de Nord, Bucharest, 1883

1983, Dec. 30

3165	A912	10 l multi	3.25	3.25

1984 Winter Olympics A913

1984, Jan. 14

3166	A913	50b Cross-country skiing	.25	.25
3167	A913	1 l Biathlon	.25	.25
3168	A913	1.50 l Figure skating	.25	.25
3169	A913	2 l Speed skating	.30	.25
3170	A913	3 l Hockey	.40	.25
3171	A913	3.50 l Bobsledding	.50	.25
3172	A913	4 l Luge	.60	.25
3173	A913	5 l Skiing	.75	.30
		Nos. 3166-3173 (8)	3.30	2.05

A 10 l imperf souvenir sheet exists showing ski jumping. Value, unused or used, $27.50.

Souvenir Sheet

Prince Alexandru Ioan Cuza, Arms — A914

1984, Jan. 24   Photo.   Perf. 13½

3174	A914	10 l multi	2.25	2.25

Union of Moldavia and Walachia Provinces, 125th anniv.

Palace of Udriste Nasturel (1596-1658), Chancery Official — A915

Miron Costin (1633-91), Poet — A916

Famous Men: 1.50 l, Crisan (Marcu Giurgiu), (1733-85), peasant revolt leader. 2 l, Simion Barnutiu (1808-64), scientist. 3.50 l, Duiliu Zamfirescu (1858-1922), poet. 4 l, Nicolas Milescu (1636-1708), Court official.

1984, Feb. 8

3175	A915	50b multi	.25	.25
3176	A916	1 l multi	.25	.25
3177	A916	1.50 l multi	.35	.25
3178	A916	2 l multi	.35	.25
3179	A916	3.50 l multi	.50	.25
3180	A916	4 l multi	.75	.25
		Nos. 3175-3180 (6)	2.45	1.50

See Nos. 3210-3213.

Souvenir Sheet

15th Balkan Chess Match, Herculane A917

4 successive moves culminating in checkmate.

1984, Feb. 20   Photo.   Perf. 13½

3181		Sheet of 4	4.50	4.50
a.-d.	A917	3 l, any single	1.00	1.00

Bridges A918

No. 3182 — Romanian bridges: a, Orsova Bridge. b, Arges Bridge. c, Basarabi Bridge. d, Ohaba Bridge.

No. 3183 — Foreign bridges: a, Kohlbrand Bridge, Germany. b, Bosfor (Bosporus) Bridge, Turkey. c, Europa Bridge, Austria. d, Turnului (Tower Bridge), England.

1984, Apr. 24

3182		Sheet of 4	2.50	2.50
a.-d.	A918	3 l Any single	.55	.55
3183		Sheet of 4	2.50	2.50
a.-d.	A918	3 l Any single	.55	.55

Inter-European Cultural and Economic Cooperation.

Summer Olympics — A919

1984, May 25   Photo.   Perf. 13½

3184	A919	50b High jump	.25	.25
3185	A919	1 l Swimming	.25	.25
3186	A919	1.50 l Running	.25	.25
3187	A919	3 l Handball	.50	.30
3188	A919	4 l Rowing	.70	.40
3189	A919	5 l 2-man canoe	.85	.50
		Nos. 3184-3189 (6)	2.80	1.95

A 10 l imperf. airmail souvenir sheet containing a vert. stamp picturing a gymnast exists. Value, unused or used, $27.50.

Environmental Protection — A920

1984, Apr. 26   Photo.   Perf. 13½

3190	A920	1 l Sunflower	.25	.25
3191	A920	2 l Stag	.45	.25
3192	A920	3 l Fish	.70	.25
3193	A920	4 l Bird	.90	.30
		Nos. 3190-3193 (4)	2.30	1.05

Danube
Flowers — A921

50b, Sagittaria sagittifolia. 1 l, Iris
pseudacorus. 1.50 l, Butomus umbellatus. 3 l,
Nymphaea alba, horiz. 4 l, Nymphoides
peltata, horiz. 5 l, Nuphar luteum, horiz.

1984, Apr. 30　　Photo.　　Perf. 13½

3194	A921	50b multi	.25	.25
3195	A921	1 l multi	.25	.25
3196	A921	1.50 l multi	.40	.25
3197	A921	3 l multi	.70	.25
3198	A921	4 l multi	1.00	.30
3199	A921	5 l multi	1.10	.45
		Nos. 3194-3199 (6)	3.70	1.75

45th Anniv.,
Youth Anti-
Fascist
Committee
A922

1984, Apr. 30　　Photo.　　Perf. 13½

3200	A922	2 l multicolored	.65	.25

25th Congress,
Ear, Nose and
Throat
Medicine — A923

1984, May 30　　Photo.　　Perf. 13½

3201	A923	2 l Congress seal	.40	.25

Souvenir Sheets

European Soccer Cup Championships
A923a

Soccer players and flags of: c, Romania. d,
West Germany. e, Portugal. f, Spain. g,
France. h, Belgium. i, Yugoslavia. j, Denmark.

1984, June 7　　Photo.　　Perf. 13½

3201A		Sheet of 4	2.50	2.50
c.-f.	A923a	3 l, any single	.60	.60
3201B		Sheet of 4	2.50	2.50
g.-i.	A923a	3 l, any single	.60	.60

Summer Olympics — A924

1984, July 2　　Photo.　　Perf. 13½

3202	A924	50b Boxing	.25	.25
3203	A924	1 l Rowing	.25	.25
3204	A924	1.50 l Team handball	.25	.25
3205	A924	2 l Judo	.25	.25
3206	A924	3 l Wrestling	.40	.25
3207	A924	3.50 l Fencing	.50	.25
3208	A924	4 l Kayak	.65	.25
3209	A924	5 l Swimming	.75	.30
		Nos. 3202-3209 (8)	3.30	2.05

Two imperf. 10 l airmail souvenir sheets,
showing long jumping and gymnastics exist.
Value for each sheet, unused or used, $15.

Famous Romanians Type

1984, July 28　　Photo.　　Perf. 13½

3210	A916	1 l Mihai Ciuca	.25	.25
3211	A916	2 l Petre Aurelian	.35	.25
3212	A916	3 l Alexandru Vlahuta	.50	.25
3213	A916	4 l Dimitrie Leonida	.70	.30
		Nos. 3210-3213 (4)	1.80	1.05

40th Anniv.,
Romanian
Revolution
A925

1984, Aug. 17　　Photo.　　Perf. 13½

3214	A925	2 l multicolored	.40	.25

Romanian Horses — A926

1984, Aug. 30　　Photo.　　Perf. 13½

3215	A926	50b Lippizaner	.25	.25
3216	A926	1 l Hutul	.25	.25
3217	A926	1.50 l Bucovina	.30	.25
3218	A926	2.50 l Nonius	.50	.25
3219	A926	4 l Arabian	1.00	.30
3220	A926	5 l Romanian Mixed-breed	.80	.40
		Nos. 3215-3220 (6)	3.10	1.70

1784 Uprisings,
200th
Anniv. — A927

1984, Nov. 1　　Photo.　　Perf. 13½

3221	A927	2 l Monument	.40	.25

Children
A928

Paintings: 50b, Portrait of Child, by T.
Aman. 1 l, Shepherd, by N. Grigorescu. 2 l,
Girl with Orange, by S. Luchian. 3 l, Portrait of
Child, by N. Tonitza. 4 l, Portrait of Boy, by S.
Popp. 5 l, Portrait of Girl, by I. Tuculescu.

1984, Nov. 10　　Photo.　　Perf. 13½

3222	A928	50b multicolored	.25	.25
3223	A928	1 l multicolored	.25	.25
3224	A928	2 l multicolored	.35	.25
3225	A928	3 l multicolored	.50	.25
3226	A928	4 l multicolored	.70	.30
3227	A928	5 l multicolored	.85	.35
		Nos. 3222-3227 (6)	2.90	1.65

Stamp
Day
A929

1984, Nov. 15　　Photo.　　Perf. 13½

3228	A929	2 l + 1 l label	.50	.30

Souvenir Sheet

13th Party Congress — A930

1984, Nov. 17　　Photo.　　Perf. 13½

3229	A930	10 l Party symbols	4.00	4.00

Souvenir Sheets

Romanian Medalists, 1984 Summer
Olympic Games — A931

No. 3230: a, Ecaterina Szabo, gymnastic
floor exercise. b, 500-meter four-women
kayak. c, Anisoara Stanciu, long jump. d,
Greco-Roman wrestling. e, Mircea Fratica, half
middleweight judo. f, Corneliu Ion, rapid fire
pistol.
No. 3231: a, 1000-meter two-man scull. b,
Weight lifting. c, Women's relays. d, Canoeing,
pair oars without coxswain. e, Fencing, team
foil. f, Ecaterina Szabo, all-around gymnastics.

1984, Oct. 29　　Photo.　　Perf. 13½

3230		Sheet of 6	3.25	3.25
a.-f.	A931	3 l, any single	.50	.50
3231		Sheet of 6	3.25	3.25
a.-f.	A931	3 l, any single	.50	.50

Pelicans of the Danube Delta.

A932

1984, Dec. 15

3232	A932	50b Flying	.25	.25
3233	A932	1 l On ground	.55	.25
3234	A932	1 l In water	.65	.25
3235	A932	2 l Nesting	.95	.45
		Nos. 3232-3235 (4)	2.40	1.20

A933

Famous Men: 50b, Dr. Petru Groza (1884-
1958). 1 l, Alexandru Odobescu (1834-1895).
2 l, Dr. Carol Davila (1828-1884). 3 l, Dr. Nicolae G. Lupu (1884-1966). 4 l, Dr. Daniel
Danielopolu (1884-1955). 5 l, Panait Istrati
(1884-1935).

1984, Dec. 26

3236	A933	50b multi	.25	.25
3237	A933	1 l multi	.25	.25
3238	A933	2 l multi	.35	.25
3239	A933	3 l multi	.50	.25
3240	A933	4 l multi	.70	.30
3241	A933	5 l multi	.85	.35
		Nos. 3236-3241 (6)	2.90	1.65

Timisoara
Power
Station,
Electric
Street
Lights,
Cent.
A934

1984, Dec. 29

3242	A934	1 l Generator, 1884	.25	.25
3243	A934	2 l Street arc lamp, Timisoara, 1884, vert.	.35	.25

Souvenir Sheets

European Music Year — A935

Composers and opera houses, No. 3244a,
Moscow Theater, Tchaichovsky (1840-1893).
b, Bucharest Theater, George Enescu (1881-
1955). c, Dresden Opera, Wagner (1813-
1883). d, Warsaw Opera, Stanislaw Moniuszko (1819-1872).
No. 3245a, Paris Opera, Gounod (1818-
1893). b, Munich Opera, Strauss (1864-1949).
c, Vienna Opera, Mozart (1756-1791). d, La
Scala, Milan, Verdi (1813-1901).

1985, Mar. 28

3244	A935	Sheet of 4	2.50	2.50
a.-d.		3 l, any single	.60	.60
3245	A935	Sheet of 4	2.50	2.50
a.-d.		3 l, any single	.60	.60

August T. Laurian
(1810-1881),
Linguist and
Historian — A936

Famous men: 1 l, Grigore Alexandrescu
(1810-1885), author. 1.50 l, Gheorghe Pop de
Basesti (1835-1919), politician. 2 l, Mateiu
Caragiale (1885-1936), author. 3 l, Gheorghe
Ionescu-Sisesti (1885-1967), scientist. 4 l,
Liviu Rebreanu (1885-1944), author.

1985, Mar. 29

3246	A936	50b multi	.25	.25
3247	A936	1 l multi	.25	.25
3248	A936	1.50 l multi	.25	.25
3249	A936	2 l multi	.35	.25
3250	A936	3 l multi	.50	.30
3251	A936	4 l multi	.70	.40
	Nos. 3246-3251 (6)		2.30	1.70

Intl. Youth Year — A937

1985, Apr. 15

3252	A937	1 l Scientific research	.25	.25
3253	A937	2 l Construction	.35	.25

Souvenir Sheet

3254	A937	10 l Intl. solidarity	2.50	2.25

No. 3254 contains one 54x42mm stamp.

Wildlife Conservation A938

1985, May 6

3255	A938	50b Nyctereutes procyonoides	.25	.25
3256	A938	1 l Perdix perdix	.25	.25
3257	A938	1.50 l Nyctea scandiaca	.30	.25
3258	A938	2 l Martes martes	.40	.25
3259	A938	3 l Meles meles	.65	.25
3260	A938	3.50 l Lutra lutra	.80	.25
3261	A938	4 l Tetrao urogallus	.90	.30
3262	A938	5 l Otis tarda	1.10	.35
	Nos. 3255-3262 (8)		4.65	2.15

End of World War II, 40th Anniv. — A939

War monument, natl. and party flags.

1985, May 9

3263	A939	2 l multicolored	.50	.25

Union of Communist Youth, 12th Congress A940

1985, May 14

3264	A940	2 l Emblem	.35	.25

An imperf. 10 l EUROPA souvenir sheet showing a man, a woman and a baby with arms raised was issued 1985, June 3, with limited distribution. Value, $16.

Danube-Black Sea Canal Opening, May 26, 1984 — A942

1 l, Canal, map. 2 l, Bridge over lock, Cernavoda. 3 l, Bridge over canal, Medgidea. 4 l, Agigea lock, bridge.
10 l, Opening ceremony, Cernavoda, Ceaucescu.

1985, June 7 — *Perf. 13½*

3266	A942	1 l multi	.25	.25
3267	A942	2 l multi	.50	.25
3268	A942	3 l multi	.70	.25
3269	A942	4 l multi	1.00	.35
	Nos. 3266-3269 (4)		2.45	1.10

Souvenir Sheet

3270	A942	10 l multi	4.50	4.00

No. 3270 contains one 54x42mm stamp.

Audubon Birth Bicentenary — A943

American bird species — 50b, Turdus migratorius. 1 l, Pelecanus occidentalis. 1.50 l, Nyctanassa violarea. 2 l, Icterus galbula. 3 l, Podiceps grisegena. 4 l, Anas platyrhynchos. Nos. 3272-3275 vert.

1985, June 26

3271	A943	50b multi	.25	.25
3272	A943	1 l multi	.25	.25
3273	A943	1.50 l multi	.30	.25
3274	A943	2 l multi	.35	.25
3275	A943	3 l multi	.70	.25
3276	A943	4 l multi	.95	.35
	Nos. 3271-3276 (6)		2.80	1.60

20th Century Paintings by Ion Tuculescu — A944

1985, July 13

3277	A944	1 l Fire, vert.	.25	.25
3278	A944	2 l Circuit, vert.	.35	.25
3279	A944	3 l Interior	.50	.25
3280	A944	4 l Sunset	.65	.35
	Nos. 3277-3280 (4)		1.75	1.10

Butterflies A945

1985, July 15

3281	A945	50b Inachis io	.25	.25
3282	A945	1 l Papilio machaon	.25	.25
3283	A945	2 l Vanessa atalanta	.40	.25
3284	A945	3 l Saturnia pavonia	.60	.30
3285	A945	4 l Ammobiota festiva	.80	.40
3286	A945	5 l Smerinthus ocellatus	1.00	.50
	Nos. 3281-3286 (6)		3.30	1.95

Natl. Communist Party Achievements — A946

Natl. and party flags, and: 1 l, Transfagarasan Mountain Road. 2 l, Danube-Black Sea Canal. 3 l, Bucharest Underground Railway. 4 l, Irrigation.

1985, July 29

3287	A946	1 l multicolored	.25	.25
3288	A946	2 l multicolored	.50	.25
3289	A946	3 l multicolored	.75	.25
3290	A946	4 l multicolored	1.00	.35
	Nos. 3287-3290 (4)		2.50	1.10

20th annivs.: Election of Gen.-Sec. Nicolae Ceausescu; Natl. Communist Congress.

Romanian Socialist Constitution, 20th Anniv. — A947

1985, Aug. 5

3291	A947	1 l Arms, wheat, dove	.25	.25
3292	A947	2 l Arms, torch	.60	.25

1986 World Cup Soccer Preliminaries — A948

Flags of participants; Great Britain, Northern Ireland, Romania, Finland, Turkey and: 50b, Sliding tackle. 1 l, Trapping the ball. 1.50 l, Heading the ball. 2 l, Dribble. 3 l, Tackle. 4 l, Scissor kick. 10 l, Dribble, diff.

1985, Oct. 15

3293	A948	50b multi	.25	.25
3294	A948	1 l multi	.25	.25
3295	A948	1.50 l multi	.30	.25
3296	A948	2 l multi	.35	.25
3297	A948	3 l multi	.55	.30
3298	A948	4 l multi	.70	.35
	Nos. 3293-3298 (6)		2.40	1.65

An imperf airmail 10 l souvenir sheet exists, showing flags, stadium and soccer players. Value, unused or used, $13.

Souvenir Sheet

Motorcycle Centenary — A949

1985, Aug. 22 — **Photo.** — *Perf. 13½*

3300	A949	10 l 1885 Daimler Einspur	2.25 2.25

Retezat Natl. Park, 50th Anniv. — A950

50b, Senecio glaberrimus. 1 l, Rupicapra rupicapra. 2 l, Centaurea retezatensis. 3 l, Viola dacica. 4 l, Marmota marmota. 5 l, Aquila chrysaetos.
10 l, Lynx lynx.

1985, Aug. 29

3301	A950	50b multi	.25	.25
3302	A950	1 l multi	.25	.25
3303	A950	2 l multi	.35	.25
3304	A950	3 l multi	.55	.25
3305	A950	4 l multi	.80	.35
3306	A950	5 l multi	1.00	.45
	Nos. 3301-3306 (6)		3.20	1.80

Souvenir Sheet

3307	A950	10 l multi	3.00	2.75

No. 3307 contains one 42x54mm stamp.

Tractors Manufactured by Universal — A951

1985, Sept. 10

3308	A951	50b 530 DTC	.25	.25
3309	A951	1 l 550 M HC	.25	.25
3310	A951	1.50 l 650 Super	.25	.25
3311	A951	2 l 850	.30	.25
3312	A951	3 l S 1801 IF	.60	.25
3313	A951	4 l A 3602 IF	.75	.30
	Nos. 3308-3313 (6)		2.40	1.55

Folk Costumes — A952

Women's and men's costumes from same region printed in continuous design.

1985, Sept. 28

3314		50b Muscel woman	.25	.25
3315		50b Muscel man	.25	.25
a.		A952 Pair, #3314-3315	.25	.25
3316		1.50 l Bistrita-Nasaud woman	.25	.25
3317		1.50 l Bistrita-Nasaud man	.25	.25
a.		A952 Pair, #3316-3317	.50	.30
3318		2 l Vrancea woman	.35	.25
3319		2 l Vrancea man	.35	.25
a.		A952 Pair, #3318-3319	.70	.30
3320		3 l Vilcea woman	.50	.25
3321		3 l Vilcea man	.50	.25
a.		A952 Pair, #3320-3321	1.00	.50
	Nos. 3314-3321 (8)		2.70	2.00

Admission to UN, 30th Anniv. — A953

1985, Oct. 21
3322 A953 2 l multicolored .40 .25

UN, 40th
Anniv. — A954

1985, Oct. 21
3323 A954 2 l multicolored .35 .25

Mineral
Flowers — A955

50b, Quartz and calcite, Herja. 1 l, Copper, Altin Tepe. 2 l, Gypsum, Cavnic. 3 l, Quartz, Ocna de Fier. 4 l, Stibium, Baiut. 5 l, Tetrahedrite, Cavnic.

1985, Oct. 28
3324	A955	50b multi	.25	.25
3325	A955	1 l multi	.25	.25
3326	A955	2 l multi	.30	.25
3327	A955	3 l multi	.60	.30
3328	A955	4 l multi	.75	.40
3329	A955	5 l multi	.90	.50
	Nos. 3324-3329 (6)		3.05	1.95

Stamp Day — A956

1985, Oct. 29
3330 A956 2 l + 1 l label .40 .25

A Connecticut Yankee in King Arthur's
Court, by Mark Twain — A957

The Three Brothers, by Jacob and
Wilhelm Grimm — A958

Disney characters in classic fairy tales — No. 3331, Hank Morgan awakes in Camelot. No. 3332, Predicts eclipse of sun. No. 3333, Mounting horse. No. 3334, Sir Sagramor. No. 3335, Fencing with shadow. No. 3336, Fencing, father. No. 3337, Shoeing a horse. No. 3338, Barber, rabbit. No. 3339, Father, three sons.
No. 3340, Tournament of knights. No. 3341, Cottage.

1985, Nov. 28
3331	A957	50b multi	2.00	2.00
3332	A957	50b multi	2.00	2.00
3333	A957	50b multi	2.00	2.00
3334	A957	50b multi	2.00	2.00
3335	A958	1 l multi	4.50	4.50
3336	A958	1 l multi	4.50	4.50
3337	A958	1 l multi	4.50	4.50
3338	A958	1 l multi	4.50	4.50
3339	A958	1 l multi	4.50	4.50
	Nos. 3331-3339 (9)		30.50	30.50

Souvenir Sheets
3340	A957	5 l multi	15.00	15.00
3341	A958	5 l multi	15.00	15.00

Miniature Sheets

Intereuropa 1986 — A959

Fauna & flora: #3343: a, Felis silvestris. b, Mustela erminea. c, Tetrao urogallus. d, Urso arctos.
#3344: a, Dianthus callizonus. b, Pinus cembra. c, Salix sp. d, Rose pendulina.

1986, Mar. 25   Photo.   Perf. 13½
3343	A959	Sheet of 4	2.50	2.50
a.-d.		3 l, any single	.60	.60
3344	A959	Sheet of 4	2.50	2.50
a.-d.		3 l, any single	.60	.60

Inventors and Adventurers — A960

Designs: 1 l, Orville and Wilbur Wright, Wright Flyer. 1.50 l, Jacques Cousteau, research vessel Calypso. 2 l, Amelia Earhart, Lockheed Electra. 3 l, Charles Lindbergh, Spirit of St. Louis. 3.50 l, Sir Edmund Hillary (1919-), first man to reach Mt. Everest summit. 4 l, Robert Edwin Peary, Arctic explorer. 5 l, Adm. Richard Byrd, explorer. 6 l, Neil Armstrong, first man on moon.

1985, Dec. 25   Photo.   Perf. 13½
3345	A960	1 l multi	.25	.25
3346	A960	1.50 l multi	.30	.25
3347	A960	2 l multi	.40	.30
3348	A960	3 l multi	.60	.40
3349	A960	3.50 l multi	.65	.50
3350	A960	4 l multi	.75	.60
3351	A960	5 l multi	1.00	.70
3352	A960	6 l multi	1.25	.85
	Nos. 3345-3352 (8)		5.20	3.85

Paintings by
Nicolae
Tonitza — A961

1986, Mar. 12   Photo.   Perf. 13½
3353	A961	1 l Nina in Green	.25	.25
3354	A961	2 l Irina	.40	.25
3355	A961	3 l Woodman's Daughter	.55	.25
3356	A961	4 l Woman on the Verandah	.75	.30
	Nos. 3353-3356 (4)		1.95	1.05

Color Animated Films, 50th
Anniv. — A962

Walt Disney characters in the Band Concert, 1935 — No. 3357, Clarabelle. No. 3358, Mickey Mouse. No. 3359, Paddy and Peter. No. 3360, Goofy. No. 3361, Donald Duck. No. 3362, Mickey Mouse, diff. No. 3363, Mickey and Donald. No. 3364, Horace. No. 3365, Donald and trombonist.
No. 3366, Finale.

1986, Apr. 10   Photo.   Perf. 13½
3357	A962	50b multi	2.00	2.00
3358	A962	50b multi	2.00	2.00
3359	A962	50b multi	2.00	2.00
3360	A962	50b multi	2.00	2.00
3361	A962	1 l multi	4.50	4.50
3362	A962	1 l multi	4.50	4.50
3363	A962	1 l multi	4.50	4.50
3364	A962	1 l multi	4.50	4.50
3365	A962	1 l multi	4.50	4.50
	Nos. 3357-3365 (9)		30.50	30.50

Souvenir Sheet
3366	A962	5 l multi	15.00	15.00

1986 World Cup Soccer
Championships, Mexico — A963

Various soccer plays and flags: 50b, Italy vs. Bulgaria. 1 l, Mexico vs. Belgium. 2 l, Canada vs. France. 3 l, Brazil vs. Spain. 4 l, Uruguay vs. Germany. 5 l, Morocco vs. Poland.

1986, May 9
3367	A963	50b multi	.25	.25
3368	A963	1 l multi	.25	.25
3369	A963	2 l multi	.30	.25
3370	A963	3 l multi	.45	.25
3371	A963	4 l multi	.90	.25
3372	A963	5 l multi	1.00	.35
	Nos. 3367-3372 (6)		3.15	1.60

An imperf. 10 l airmail souvenir sheet exists picturing stadium, flags of previous winners, satellite and map. Value, unused or used, $22.50.

Hotels — A964

50b, Diana, Herculane. 1 l, Termal, Felix. 2 l, Delfin, Meduza and Steaua de Mare, Eforie Nord. 3 l, Caciulata, Calimanesti Caciulata. 4 l, Palas, Slanic Moldova. 5 l, Bradet, Sovata.

1986, Apr. 23   Photo.   Perf. 13½
3373	A964	50b multi	.25	.25
3374	A964	1 l multi	.25	.25
3375	A964	2 l multi	.35	.25
3376	A964	3 l multi	.50	.25
3377	A964	4 l multi	.70	.25
3378	A964	5 l multi	1.00	.35
	Nos. 3373-3378 (6)		3.05	1.60

Nicolae Ceausescu, Party
Flag — A965

1986, May 8   Photo.   Perf. 13½
3379 A965 2 l multicolored 1.00 .75

Natl. Communist Party, 65th anniv.

Flowers — A966

1986, June 25   Photo.   Perf. 13½
3380	A966	50b Tulipa gesneriana	.25	.25
3381	A966	1 l Iris hispanica	.25	.25
3382	A966	2 l Rosa hybrida	.35	.25
3383	A966	3 l Anemone coronaria	.55	.25
3384	A966	4 l Freesia refracta	.80	.25
3385	A966	5 l Chrysanthemum indicum	1.00	.35
	Nos. 3380-3385 (6)		3.20	1.60

Mircea the Great, Ruler of Wallachia,
1386-1418 — A967

1986, July 17   Photo.   Perf. 13½
3386 A967 2 l multicolored .60 .30

Ascent to the throne, 600th anniv.

Open Air Museum of Historic Dwellings, Bucharest, 50th Anniv. — A968

1986, July 21
3387	A968	50b Alba	.25	.25
3388	A968	1 l Arges	.25	.25
3389	A968	2 l Constantia	.35	.25
3390	A968	3 l Timis	.55	.25
3391	A968	4 l Neamt	.80	.25
3392	A968	5 l Gorj	1.00	.35
	Nos. 3387-3392 (6)		3.20	1.60

Polar Research — A969

Exploration: 50b, Julius Popper, exploration of Tierra del Fuego (1886-93). 1 l, Bazil G. Assan, exploration of Spitzbergen (1896). 2 l, Emil Racovita, Antarctic expedition (1897-99). 3 l, Constantin Dumbrava, exploration of Greenland (1927-8). 4 l, Romanians with the 17th Soviet Antarctic expedition (1971-72). 5 l, Research on krill fishing (1977-80).

1986, July 23   Photo.   Perf. 13½
3393	A969	50b multi	.25	.25
3394	A969	1 l multi	.25	.25
3395	A969	2 l multi	.35	.25
3396	A969	3 l multi	.55	.25
3397	A969	4 l multi	.80	.25
3398	A969	5 l multi	1.00	.35
	Nos. 3393-3398 (6)		3.20	1.60

Natl. Cycling Championships A970

Various athletes.

1986, Aug. 29
3399	A970	1 l multicolored	.25	.25
3400	A970	2 l multicolored	.35	.25
3401	A970	3 l multicolored	.55	.25
3402	A970	4 l multicolored	.75	.30
	Nos. 3399-3402 (4)		1.90	1.05

Souvenir Sheet
3403	A970	10 l multicolored	2.50	1.25

No. 3403 contains one 42x54mm stamp.

Souvenir Sheet

Intl. Peace Year — A971

1986, July 25
3404	A971	5 l multicolored	1.25	.60

Fungi — A972

50b, Amanita rubescens. 1 l, Boletus luridus. 2 l, Lactarius piperatus. 3 l, Lepiota clypeolaria. 4 l, Russula cyanoxantha. 5 l, Tremiscus helvelloides.

1986, Aug. 15
3405	A972	50b multi	.25	.25
3406	A972	1 l multi	.25	.25
3407	A972	2 l multi	.35	.25
3408	A972	3 l multi	.55	.25
3409	A972	4 l multi	.80	.25
3410	A972	5 l multi	1.00	.35
	Nos. 3405-3410 (6)		3.20	1.60

An imperf. 10 l EUROPA souvenir sheet with an oval stamp inscribed "CSCE" was issued, 1986, Oct. 28, with limited distribtion. Value, $20.

A973

Famous Men: 50b, Petru Maior (c. 1761-1821), historian. 1 l, George Topirceanu (1886-1937), doctor. 2 l, Henri Coanda (1886-1972), engineer. 3 l, Constantin Budeanu (1886-1959), engineer.

1986, Nov. 10   Photo.   Perf. 13½
3411	A973	50b dl cl, gold & dk bl grn	.25	.25
3412	A973	1 l sl grn, gold & dk lil rose	.25	.25
3413	A973	2 l rose cl, gold & brt bl	.45	.25
3414	A973	3 l chlky bl, gold & choc	.70	.25
	Nos. 3411-3414 (4)		1.65	1.00

UNESCO, 40th Anniv. A974

1986, Nov. 10
3415	A974	4 l multicolored	.75	.35

Stamp Day — A975

1986, Nov. 15
3416	A975	2 l + 1 l label	1.20	.25

Industry A976

50b, F-300 oil rigs, vert. 1 l, Promex excavator. 2 l, Pitesti refinery, vert. 3 l, 110-ton dump truck. 4 l, Coral computer, vert. 5 l, 350-megawatt turbine.

1986, Nov. 28
3417	A976	50b multi	.25	.25
3418	A976	1 l multi	.25	.25
3419	A976	2 l multi	.40	.25
3420	A976	3 l multi	.55	.25
3421	A976	4 l multi	.80	.25
3422	A976	5 l multi	1.00	.35
	Nos. 3417-3422 (6)		3.25	1.60

Folk Costumes — A977

1986, Dec. 26
3423	A977	50b Capra	.25	.25
3424	A977	1 l Sorcova	.25	.25
3425	A977	2 l Plugusorul	.35	.25
3426	A977	3 l Buhaiul	.55	.25
3427	A977	4 l Caiutii	.80	.25
3428	A977	5 l Uratorii	1.00	.35
	Nos. 3423-3428 (6)		3.20	1.60

Recycling Campaign — A978

1986, Dec. 30
3429	A978	1 l Metal	.25	.25
3430	A978	1 l Trees	.50	.25

Young Communists' League, 65th Anniv. — A979

1987, Mar. 18   Photo.   Perf. 13½
3431	A979	1 l Flags, youth	.25	.25
3432	A979	2 l Emblem	.45	.25
3433	A979	3 l Flags, youth, diff.	.65	.40
	Nos. 3431-3433 (3)		1.35	.90

Miniature Sheets

Intereuropa — A980

Modern architecture: No. 3434a, Exposition Pavilion, Bucharest. b, Intercontinental Hotel, Bucharest. c, Europa Hotel, Black Sea coast. d, Polytechnic Institute, Bucharest.

No. 3435a, Administration Building, Satu Mare. b, House of Young Pioneers, Bucharest. c, Valahia Hotel, Tirgoviste. d, Caciulata Hotel, Caciulata.

1987, May 18   Photo.   Perf. 13½
3434	A980	Sheet of 4	2.50	2.50
a.-d.		3 l any single	.60	.60
3435	A980	Sheet of 4	2.50	2.50
a.-d.		3 l any single	.60	.60

Collective Farming, 25th Anniv. — A981

1987, Apr. 25   Photo.   Perf. 13½
3436	A981	2 l multicolored	.50	.25

Birch Trees by the Lakeside, by I. Andreescu — A982

Paintings in Romanian museums: 1 l, Young Peasant Girls Spinning, by N. Grigorescu. 2 l, Washerwoman, by S. Luchian. 3 l, Inside the Peasant's Cottage, by S. Dimitrescu. 4 l, Winter Landscape, by A. Ciucurencu. 5 l, Winter in Bucharest, by N. Tonitza, vert.

1987, Apr. 28
3437	A982	50b multicolored	.25	.25
3438	A982	1 l multicolored	.25	.25
3439	A982	2 l multicolored	.35	.25
3440	A982	3 l multicolored	.50	.25
3441	A982	4 l multicolored	.75	.35
3442	A982	5 l multicolored	1.00	.50
	Nos. 3437-3442 (6)		3.10	1.85

Peasant Uprising of 1907, 80th Anniv. — A983

1987, May 30
3443	A983	2 l multicolored	.50	.25

Men's World Handball Championships — A984

Various plays.

1987, July 15
3444	A984	50b multi, vert.	.25	.25
3445	A984	1 l multi	.25	.25
3446	A984	2 l multi, vert.	.35	.25
3447	A984	3 l multi	.50	.25
3448	A984	4 l multi, vert.	.75	.35
3449	A984	5 l multi	1.00	.50
	Nos. 3444-3449 (6)		3.10	1.85

A985

Natl. Currency — A986

1987, July 15
3450	A985	1 l multicolored	.25	.25

Souvenir Sheet
3451	A986	10 l multicolored	2.50	2.50

Landscapes — A987

50b, Pelicans over the Danube Delta. 1 l, Transfagarasan Highway. 2 l, Hairpin curve, Bicazului. 3 l, Limestone peaks, Mt. Ceahlau. 4 l, Lake Capra, Mt. Fagaras. 5 l, Orchard, Borsa.

1987, July 31   Photo.   Perf. 13½
3452	A987	50b multi	.25	.25
3453	A987	1 l multi	.25	.25
3454	A987	2 l multi	.35	.25
3455	A987	3 l multi	.50	.25
3456	A987	4 l multi	.70	.35
3457	A987	5 l multi	.90	.50
		Nos. 3452-3457 (6)	2.95	1.85

A988

Scenes from Fairy Tale by Peter Ispirescu (b. 1887) — A988a

1987, Sept. 25   Photo.   Perf. 13½
3458	A988	50b shown	.25	.25
3459	A988	1 l multi, diff.	.25	.25
3460	A988	2 l multi, diff.	.35	.25
3461	A988	3 l multi, diff.	.50	.25
3462	A988	4 l multi, diff.	.70	.35
3463	A988	5 l multi, diff.	.85	.40
		Nos. 3458-3463 (6)	2.90	1.75

Souvenir Sheet
3464	A988a	10 l shown	2.50	2.50

Miniature Sheets

Flora and Fauna A989

Flora: No. 3465a, Aquilegia alpina. b, Pulsatilla vernalis. c, Aster alpinus. d, Soldanella pusilla baumg. e, Lilium bulbiferum. f, Arctostaphylos uva-ursi. g, Crocus vernus. h, Crepis aurea. i, Cypripedium calceolus. j, Centaurea nervosa. k, Dryas octopetala. l, Gentiana excisa.
Fauna: No. 3466a, Martes martes. b, Felis lynx. c, Ursus maritimus. d, Lutra lutra. e, Bison bonasus. f, Branta ruficollis. g, Phoenicopterus ruber. h, Otis tarda. i, Lyrurus tetrix. j, Gypaetus barbatus. k, Vormela peregusna. l, Oxyura leucocephala.

1987, Oct. 16   Sheets of 12
3465	A989	1 l #a.-l.	4.50	4.50
3466	A989	1 l #a.-l.	4.50	4.50

Souvenir Sheet

PHILATELIA '87, Cologne — A990

1987, Oct. 19
3467	A990	Sheet of 2 + 2 labels	2.50	2.50
a.		3 l Bucharest city seal	1.00	1.00
b.		3 l Cologne city arms	1.00	1.00

Locomotives — A991

1987, Oct. 15
3468	A991	50b L 45 H	.25	.25
3469	A991	1 l LDE 125	.25	.25
3470	A991	2 l LDH 70	.40	.25
3471	A991	3 l LDE 2100	.65	.30
3472	A991	4 l LDE 3000	.90	.40
3473	A991	5 l LE 5100	1.00	.50
		Nos. 3468-3473 (6)	3.45	1.95

Folk Costumes — A992

1987, Nov. 7
3474	A992	1 l Tirnave (woman)	.25	.25
3475	A992	1 l Tirnave (man)	.25	.25
a.	A992	Pair, #3474-3475	.40	.25
3476	A992	2 l Buzau (woman)	.40	.25
3477	A992	2 l Buzau (man)	.40	.25
a.	A992	Pair, #3476-3477	.80	.30
3478	A992	3 l Dobrogea (woman)	.60	.30
3479	A992	3 l Dobrogea (man)	.60	.30
a.	A992	Pair, #3478-3479	1.25	.60
3480	A992	4 l Ilfov (woman)	.80	.40
3481	A992	4 l Ilfov (man)	.80	.40
a.	A992	Pair, #3480-3481	1.60	.80
		Nos. 3474-3481 (8)	4.10	2.40

Postwoman Delivering Mail -- A993

1987, Nov. 15   Photo.   Perf. 13½
3482	A993	2 l + 1 l label	.75	.35

Stamp Day.

Apiculture — A994

1 l, Apis mellifica carpatica. 2 l, Bee pollinating sunflower. 3 l, Hives, Danube Delta. 4 l, Apiculture complex, Bucharest.

1987, Nov. 16   Photo.   Perf. 13½
3483	A994	1 l multi	.25	.25
3484	A994	2 l multi	.50	.25
3485	A994	3 l multi	.75	.35
3486	A994	4 l multi	1.00	.50
		Nos. 3483-3486 (4)	2.50	1.35

1988 Winter Olympics, Calgary A995

1987, Dec. 28   Photo.   Perf. 13½
3487	A995	50b Biathlon	.25	.25
3488	A995	1 l Slalom	.25	.25
3489	A995	1.50 l Ice hockey	.25	.25
3490	A995	2 l Luge	.25	.25
3491	A995	3 l Speed skating	.45	.25
3492	A995	3.50 l Women's figure skating	.45	.25
3493	A995	4 l Downhill skiing	.60	.25
3494	A995	5 l Two-man bobsled	.75	.35
		Nos. 3487-3494 (8)	3.25	2.10

An imperf. 10 l souvenir sheet picturing ski jumping also exists. Value, unused or used, $20.

Traffic Safety A996

Designs: 50b, Be aware of children riding bicycles in the road. 1 l, Young Pioneer girl as crossing guard. 2 l, Do not open car doors in path of moving traffic. 3 l, Be aware of pedestrian crossings. 4 l, Observe the speed limit; do not attempt curves at high speed. 5 l, Protect small children.

1987, Dec. 10   Photo.   Perf. 13½
3495	A996	50b multicolored	.25	.25
3496	A996	1 l multicolored	.25	.25
3497	A996	2 l multicolored	.40	.25
3498	A996	3 l multicolored	.65	.30
3499	A996	4 l multicolored	.85	.40
3500	A996	5 l multicolored	1.00	.45
		Nos. 3495-3500 (6)	3.40	1.90

October Revolution, Russia, 70th Anniv. — A997

1987, Dec. 26
3501	A997	2 l multicolored	.60	.25

40th Anniv. of the Romanian Republic — A998

1987, Dec. 30
3502	A998	2 l multicolored	.50	.25

70th Birthday of President Nicolae Ceausescu — A999

1988, Jan. 26
3503	A999	2 l multicolored	.90	.45

Pottery A1000

1988, Feb. 26   Photo.   Perf. 13½
3504	A1000	50b Marginea	.25	.25
3505	A1000	1 l Oboga	.25	.25
3506	A1000	2 l Horezu	.35	.25
3507	A1000	3 l Curtea De Arges	.55	.25
3508	A1000	4 l Birsa	.75	.25
3509	A1000	5 l Vama	1.00	.35
		Nos. 3504-3509 (6)	3.15	1.60

Miniature Sheets

Intereuropa — A1001

Transportation and communication: No. 3510a, Mail coach. b, ECS telecommunications satellite. c, Oltcit automobile. d, ICE high-speed electric train.

No. 3511a, Santa Maria, 15th cent. b, Cheia Ground Station satellite dish receivers. c, Bucharest subway. d, Airbus-A320.

1988, Apr. 27	Photo.		Perf. 13½
3510 A1001	Sheet of 4	2.50	2.50
a.-d.	3 l any single	.60	.60
3511 A1001	Sheet of 4	2.50	2.50
a.-d.	3 l any single	.60	.60

1988 Summer Olympics, Seoul — A1002

1988, Jun. 28			
3512 A1002	50b Gymnastics	.25	.25
3513 A1002	1.50 l Boxing	.30	.25
3514 A1002	2 l Tennis	.35	.25
3515 A1002	3 l Judo	.50	.25
3516 A1002	4 l Running	.80	.25
3517 A1002	5 l Rowing	1.00	.40
	Nos. 3512-3517 (6)	3.20	1.65

An imperf. 10 l souvenir sheet exists. Value, unused or used, $12.

19th-20th Cent. Clocks in the Ceasului Museum, Ploesti A1003

50b, Arad Region porcelain. 1.50 l, French bronze. 2 l, French bronze, diff. 3 l, Gothic bronze. 4 l, Saxony porcelain. 5 l, Bohemian porcelain.

1988, May 20	Photo.		Perf. 13½
3518 A1003	50b multicolored	.25	.25
3519 A1003	1.50 l multicolored	.25	.25
3520 A1003	2 l multicolored	.40	.25
3521 A1003	3 l multicolored	.55	.25
3522 A1003	4 l multicolored	.85	.25
3523 A1003	5 l multicolored	1.00	.35
	Nos. 3518-3523 (6)	3.30	1.60

20th cent. timepiece (50b); others 19th cent.

Miniature Sheets

European Soccer Championships, Germany — A1003a

Soccer players and flags of: c, Federal Republic of Germany. d, Spain. e, Italy. f, Denmark. g, England. h, Netherlands. i, Ireland. j, Soviet Union.

1988, June 9	Litho.		Perf. 13½
3523A A1003a	Sheet of 4	3.25	3.25
c.-f.	3 l any single	.80	.80
3523B A1003a	Sheet of 4	3.25	3.25
g.-j.	3 l any single	.80	.80

Accession of Constanin Brincoveanu as Prince Regent of Wallachia, 1688-1714, 300th Anniv. — A1004

1988, June 20
3524 A1004	2 l multicolored	.50	.25

1988 Summer Olympics, Seoul — A1005

50b, Women's running. 1 l, Canoeing. 1.50 l, Women's gymnastics. 2 l, Kayaking. 3 l, Weight lifting. 3.50 l, Women's swimming. 4 l, Fencing. 5 l, Women's rowing (double).

1988, Sept. 1	Photo.		Perf. 13½
3525 A1005	50b multicolored	.25	.25
3526 A1005	1 l multicolored	.25	.25
3527 A1005	1.50 l multicolored	.25	.25
3528 A1005	2 l multicolored	.25	.25
3529 A1005	3 l multicolored	.40	.25
3530 A1005	3.50 l multicolored	.50	.25
3531 A1005	4 l multicolored	.60	.25
3532 A1005	5 l multicolored	.75	.30
	Nos. 3525-3532 (8)	3.25	2.05

An imperf. 10 l souvenir sheet exists picturing women's gymnastics. Value, unused or used, $20.

Romania-China Philatelic Exhibition — A1006

1988, Aug. 5	Photo.		Perf. 13½
3533 A1006	2 l multicolored	.50	.25

Souvenir Sheet

PRAGA '88 — A1007

1988, Aug. 26
3534 A1007	5 l Carnations, by Stefan Luchian	2.00	2.00

Miniature Sheets

Orchids — A1008

#3535: a, Oncidium lanceanum. b, Cattleya trianae. c, Sophronitis cernua. d, Bulbophyllum lobbii. e, Lycaste cruenta. f, Mormolyce ringens. g, Phragmipedium schlimii. h, Angraecum sesquipedale. i, Laelia crispa. j, Encyclia atropurpurea. k, Dendrobium nobile. l, Oncidium splendidum.

#3536: a, Brassavola perrinii. b, Paphiopedilum maudiae. c, Sophronitis coccinea. d, Vandopsis lissochiloides. e, Phalaenopsis lueddemanniana. f, Chysis bractescens. g, Cochleanthes discolor. h, Phalaenopsis amabilis. i, Pleione pricei. j, Sobralia macrantha. k, Aspasia lunata. l, Cattleya citrina.

1988, Oct. 24			
3535 A1008	Sheet of 12	4.00	4.00
a.-l.	1 l any single	.30	.30
3536 A1008	Sheet of 12	4.00	4.00
a.-l.	1 l any single	.30	.30

Miniature Sheets

Events Won by Romanian Athletes at the 1988 Seoul Olympic Games A1009

Sporting event and medal: No. 3537a, Women's gymnastics. b, Free pistol shooting. c, Weight lifting (220 pounds). d, Featherweight boxing.

No. 3538a, Women's 1500 and 3000-meter relays. b, Women's 200 and 400-meter individual swimming medley. c, Wrestling (220 pounds). d, Rowing, coxless pairs and coxed fours.

1988, Dec. 7	Photo.		Perf. 13½
3537	Sheet of 4	3.00	3.00
a.-d. A1009	3 l any single	.75	.75
3538	Sheet of 4	3.00	3.00
a.-d. A1009	3 l any single	.75	.75

Stamp Day — A1010

1988, Nov. 13	Photo.		Perf. 13½
3539 A1010	2 l + 1 l label	.75	.35

Unitary Natl. Romanian State, 70th Anniv. A1011

1988, Dec. 29
3540 A1011	2 l multicolored	.50	.40

Anniversaries — A1012

Designs: 50b, Athenaeum, Bucharest. 1.50 l, Trajan's Bridge, Drobeta, on a Roman bronze sestertius used in Romania from 103 to 105 A.D. 2 l, Ruins, Suceava. 3 l, Pitesti municipal coat of arms, scroll, architecture. 4 l, Trajan's Column (detail), 113 A.D. 5 l, Gold helmet discovered in Prahova County.

1988, Dec. 30			
3541 A1012	50b shown	.25	.25
3542 A1012	1.50 l multi	.25	.25
3543 A1012	2 l multi	.35	.25
3544 A1012	3 l multi	.50	.25
3545 A1012	4 l multi	.80	.25
3546 A1012	5 l multi	1.00	.35
	Nos. 3541-3546 (6)	3.15	1.60

Athenaeum, Bucharest, cent. (50b), Suceava, capital of Moldavia from 1401-1565, 600th anniv. (2 l), & Pitesti municipal charter, 600th anniv. (3 l).

Miniature Sheets

Grand Slam Tennis Championships — A1013

No. 3547: a, Men's singles, stadium in Melbourne. b, Men's singles, scoreboard. c, Mixed doubles, spectators. d, Mixed doubles, Roland Garros stadium.

No. 3548: a, Women's singles, stadium in Wimbledon. b, Women's singles, spectators. c, Men's doubles, spectators. d, Men's doubles, stadium in Flushing Meadows.

1988, Aug. 22	Photo.		Perf. 13½
3547 A1013	Sheet of 4	3.00	3.00
a.-d.	3 l any single	.75	.75
3548 A1013	Sheet of 4	3.00	3.00
a.-d.	3 l any single	.75	.75

Australian Open (Nos. 3547a-3547b), French Open (Nos. 3547c-3547d), Wimbledon (Nos. 3548a-3548b) and US Open (Nos. 3548c-3548d).

Architecture — A1014

Designs: 50b, Zapodeni, Vaslui, 17th cent. 1.50 l, Berbesti, Maramures, 18th cent. 2 l, Voitinel, Suceava, 18th cent. 3 l, Chiojdu mic, Buzau, 18th cent. 4 l, Cimpanii de sus, Bihor, 19th cent. 5 l, Naruja, Vrancea, 19th cent.

1989, Feb. 8	Photo.		Perf. 13½
3549 A1014	50b multi	.25	.25
3550 A1014	1.50 l multi	.25	.25
3551 A1014	2 l multi	.35	.25
3552 A1014	3 l multi	.50	.25
3553 A1014	4 l multi	.80	.25
3554 A1014	5 l multi	1.00	.35
	Nos. 3549-3554 (6)	3.15	1.60

Rescue and Relief Services — A1015

50b, Relief worker. 1.50 l, Fireman, child. 2 l, Fireman's carry. 3 l, Rescue team on skis. 3.50 l, Mountain rescue. 4 l, Water rescue. 5 l, Water safety.

1989, Feb. 25
3555	A1015	50b multicolored	.25	.25
3556	A1015	1 l multicolored	.25	.25
3557	A1015	1.50 l multicolored	.25	.25
3558	A1015	2 l multicolored	.30	.25
3559	A1015	3 l multicolored	.50	.25
3560	A1015	3.50 l multicolored	.60	.25
3561	A1015	4 l multicolored	.70	.30
3562	A1015	5 l multicolored	.85	.35
		Nos. 3555-3562 (8)	3.70	2.15

Nos. 3555, 3557-3558, 3560-3561 vert.

Industries — A1016

Designs: 50b, Fasca Bicaz cement factory. 1.50 l, Bridge on the Danube near Cernavoda. 2 l, MS-2-2400/450-20 synchronous motor. 3 l, Bucharest subway. 4 l, Mangalia-Constanta ferry. 5 l, Gloria marine platform.

1989, Apr. 10   Photo.   Perf. 13½
3563	A1016	50b multi	.25	.25
3564	A1016	1.50 l multi	.25	.25
3565	A1016	2 l multi	.40	.25
3566	A1016	3 l multi	.55	.25
3567	A1016	4 l multi	.75	.25
3568	A1016	5 l multi	.85	.35
		Nos. 3563-3568 (6)	3.05	1.60

Anti-fascist March, 50th Anniv. — A1017

1989, May 1   Photo.   Perf. 13½
3569	A1017	2 l shown	.50	.25
		Souvenir Sheet		
3570	A1017	10 l Patriots, flag	4.00	4.00

Souvenir Sheet

BULGARIA '89, Sofia, May 22-31 — A1018

1989, May 20
3571	A1018	10 l Roses	2.50	2.50

Miniature Sheets

Intereuropa 1989 — A1019

Children's activities and games: No. 3572a, Swimming. No. 3572b, Water slide. No. 3572c, Seesaw. No. 3572d, Flying kites. No. 3573a, Playing with dolls. No. 3573b, Playing ball. No. 3573c, Playing in the sand. No. 3573d, Playing with toy cars.

1989, June 15
3572	A1019	Sheet of 4	2.25	2.25
a.-d.		3 l any single	.55	.55
3573	A1019	Sheet of 4	2.25	2.25
a.-d.		3 l any single	.55	.55

Socialist Revolution in Romania, 45th Anniv. A1020

1989, Aug. 21   Photo.   Perf. 13½
3574	A1020	2 l multicolored	.50	.25

Cartoons — A1021

50b, Pin-pin. 1 l, Maria. 1.50 l, Gore and Grigore. 2 l, Pisoiul, Balanel, Manole and Monk. 3 l, Gruia Lui Novac. 3.50 l, Mihaela. 4 l, Harap alb. 5 l, Homo sapiens.

1989, Sept. 25
3575	A1021	50b multi	.25	.25
3576	A1021	1 l multi	.25	.25
3577	A1021	1.50 l multi	.30	.25
3578	A1021	2 l multi	.35	.25
3579	A1021	3 l multi	.55	.25
3580	A1021	3.50 l multi	.60	.25
3581	A1021	4 l multi	.65	.25
3582	A1021	5 l multi	.75	.30
		Nos. 3575-3582 (8)	3.70	2.05

Famous Romanians A1022

Portraits: 1 l, Ion Creanga (1837-1889). 2 l, Mihail Eminescu (1850-1889), poet. 3 l, Nicolae Teclu (1839-1916), chemist and inventor.

1989, Aug. 18   Photo.   Perf. 13½
3583	A1022	1 l multicolored	.25	.25
3584	A1022	2 l multicolored	.45	.25
3585	A1022	3 l multicolored	.65	.35
		Nos. 3583-3585 (3)	1.35	.85

Stamp Day — A1023

1989, Oct. 7
3586	A1023	2 l + 1 l label	.75	.30

No. 3586 has a second label picturing posthorn.

Storming of the Bastille, 1789 A1024

1989, Oct. 14
3587	A1024	50b shown	.25	.25
3588	A1024	1.50 l multicolored	.30	.25
3589	A1024	2 l multicolored	.40	.25
3590	A1024	3 l multicolored	.60	.25
3591	A1024	4 l multicolored	.80	.30
3592	A1024	5 l multicolored	1.00	.40
		Nos. 3587-3592 (6)	3.35	1.70

Souvenir Sheet
3593	A1025	10 l shown	2.50	2.50

French revolution, bicent.

Emblems of PHILEXFRANCE '89 and the Revolution — A1025

Designs: 1.50 l, Gavroche. 2 l, Robespierre. 3 l, La Marseillaise, by Rouget de Lisle. 4 l, Diderot. 5 l, 1848 Uprising, Romania.

14th Romanian Communist Party Congress — A1025a

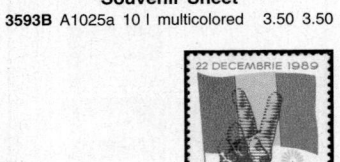

1989, Nov. 20   Photo.   Perf. 13½
3593A	A1025a	2 l multicolored	.60	.25
		Souvenir Sheet		
3593B	A1025a	10 l multicolored	3.50	3.50

Revolution of Dec. 22, 1989 — A1026

1990, Jan. 8   Photo.   Perf. 13½
3594	A1026	2 l multicolored	.45	.25

For surcharge, see No. 3633.

World Cup Soccer Preliminaries, Italy — A1027

Various soccer players in action.

1990, Mar. 19   Photo.   Perf. 13½
3595	A1027	50b multicolored	.25	.25
3596	A1027	1.50 l multicolored	.30	.25
3597	A1027	2 l multicolored	.40	.25
3598	A1027	3 l multicolored	.60	.25
3599	A1027	4 l multicolored	.80	.30
3600	A1027	5 l multicolored	1.00	.35
		Nos. 3595-3600 (6)	3.35	1.65

An imperf. 10 l airmail souvenir sheet exists. Value, $10.

Souvenir Sheet

First Postage Stamp, 150th Anniv. — A1028

1990, May 2   Litho.   Perf. 13½
3601	A1028	10 l multicolored	3.00	3.00

Stamp World London '90. For surcharge, see No. 5681.

World Cup Soccer Championships, Italy — A1029

Various soccer players in action.

1990, May 7   Photo.   Perf. 13½
3602	A1029	50b multicolored	.25	.25
3603	A1029	1 l multicolored	.25	.25
3604	A1029	1.50 l multicolored	.25	.25
3605	A1029	2 l multicolored	.30	.25
3606	A1029	3 l multicolored	.45	.25
3607	A1029	3.50 l multicolored	.50	.25

3608	A1029	4 l multicolored	.55	.25
3609	A1029	5 l multicolored	.65	.25

Nos. 3602-3609 (8) 3.20 2.00

An imperf. 10 l airmail souvenir sheet showing Olympic Stadium, Rome exists. Value, $10.

Intl. Dog Show, Brno, Czechoslovakia — A1030

50b, German shepherd. 1 l, English setter. 1.50 l, Boxer. 2 l, Beagle. 3 l, Doberman pinscher. 3.50 l, Great Dane. 4 l, Afghan hound. 5 l, Yorkshire terrier.

1990, June 6

3610	A1030	50b multicolored	.25	.25
3611	A1030	1 l multicolored	.25	.25
3612	A1030	1.50 l multicolored	.30	.25
3613	A1030	2 l multicolored	.35	.25
3614	A1030	3 l multicolored	.60	.25
3615	A1030	3.50 l multicolored	.75	.25
3616	A1030	4 l multicolored	.80	.25
3617	A1030	5 l multicolored	1.00	.25

Nos. 3610-3617 (8) 4.30 2.00

Riccione '90, Intl. Philatelic Exhibition A1031

1990, Aug. 24

3618	A1031	2 l multicolored	.50	.25

See No. 3856.

Romanian-Chinese Philatelic Exhibition, Bucharest — A1032

1990, Sept. 8   Photo.   Perf. 13½

3619	A1032	2 l multicolored	.40	.25

For surcharge see No. 4186.

Paintings Damaged in 1989 Revolution — A1033

Designs: 50b, Old Nicolas, the Zither Player, by Stefan Luchian. 1.50 l, Woman in Blue by Ion Andreescu. 2 l, The Gardener by Luchian. 3 l, Vase of Flowers by Jan Brueghel, the Elder. 4 l, Springtime by Peter Brueghel, the Elder, horiz. 5 l, Madonna and Child by G. B. Paggi.

1990, Oct. 25   Photo.   Perf. 13½

3620	A1033	50b multicolored	.25	.25
3621	A1033	1.50 l multicolored	.25	.25
3622	A1033	2 l multicolored	.25	.25
3623	A1033	3 l multicolored	.40	.25
3624	A1033	4 l multicolored	.55	.25
3625	A1033	5 l multicolored	.70	.30

Nos. 3620-3625 (6) 2.40 1.55

For surcharges see #4365-4369.

Stamp Day — A1033a

1990, Nov. 10   Photo.   Perf. 13½

3625A	A1033a	2 l + 1 l label	1.00	.70

Famous Romanians A1034

Designs: 50b, Prince Constantin Cantacuzino (1640-1716). 1.50 l, Ienachita Vacarescu (c. 1740-1797), historian. 2 l, Titu Maiorescu (1840-1917), writer. 3 l, Nicolae Iorga (1871-1940), historian. 4 l, Martha Bibescu (1890-1973). 5 l, Stefan Procopiu (1890-1972), scientist.

1990, Nov. 27   Photo.   Perf. 13½

3626	A1034	50b sepia & dk bl	.25	.25
3627	A1034	1.50 l grn & brt pur	.25	.25
3628	A1034	2 l claret & dk bl	.30	.25
3629	A1034	3 l dk bl & brn	.40	.25
3630	A1034	4 l brn & dk bl	.50	.25
3631	A1034	5 l brt pur & grn	.65	.25

Nos. 3626-3631 (6) 2.35 1.50

For surcharges see #4356-4360.

National Day — A1035

1990, Dec. 1   Photo.   Perf. 13½

3632	A1035	2 l multicolored	.40	.25

No. 3594 Surcharged in Brown

1990, Dec. 22   Photo.   Perf. 13½

3633	A1026	4 l on 2 l	.65	.25

Vincent Van Gogh, Death Cent. — A1036

Paintings: 50b, Field of Irises. 2 l, Artist's Room. 3 l, Night on the Coffee Terrace, vert. 3.50 l, Blossoming Fruit Trees. 5 l, Vase with Fourteen Sunflowers, vert.

1991, Mar. 29   Photo.   Perf. 13½

3634	A1036	50b multicolored	.25	.25
3635	A1036	2 l multicolored	.25	.25
3636	A1036	3 l multicolored	.35	.25
3637	A1036	3.50 l multicolored	.40	.25
3638	A1036	5 l multicolored	.60	.25

Nos. 3634-3638 (5) 1.85 1.25

For surcharges see #4371-4372.

A1037

Birds: 50b, Larus marinus. 1 l, Sterna hirundo. 1.50 l, Recurvirostra avosetta. 2 l, Stercorarius pomarinus. 3 l, Vanellus vanellus. 3.50 l, Mergus serrator. 4 l, Egretta garzetta. 5 l, Calidris alpina. 6 l, Limosa limosa. 7 l, Childonias hybrida.

1991, Apr. 3   Photo.   Perf. 13½

3639	A1037	50b ultra	.25	.25
3640	A1037	1 l blue green	.25	.25
3641	A1037	1.50 l bister	.25	.25
3642	A1037	2 l dark blue	.25	.25
3643	A1037	3 l light green	.25	.25
3644	A1037	3.50 l dark green	.30	.25
3645	A1037	4 l purple	.30	.25
3646	A1037	5 l brown	.35	.25
3647	A1037	6 l yel brown	.70	.25
3648	A1037	7 l light blue	.65	.25

Nos. 3639-3648 (10) 3.55 2.50

A1038

1991, Apr. 5   Photo.   Perf. 13½

3649	A1038	4 l multicolored	.35	.25

Easter.

Europa — A1039

1991, May 10   Photo.   Perf. 13½

3650	A1039	4.50 l Eutelsat I	2.00	.80

For surcharge see No. 4185.

Posthorn — A1040

1991, May 24   Photo.   Perf. 13½

3651	A1040	4.50 l blue	.40	.25

Gymnastics A1041

1991, June 14

3652	A1041	1 l Rings	.25	.25
3653	A1041	1 l Parallel bars	.25	.25
3654	A1041	4.50 l Vault	.25	.25
3655	A1041	4.50 l Uneven parallel bars	.25	.25
3656	A1041	8 l Floor exercise	.45	.25
3657	A1041	9 l Balance beam	.60	.25

Nos. 3652-3657 (6) 2.05 1.50

For surcharge on 5 l see No. 3735. For other surcharges see Nos. 3944, 3946, 4237-4238.

Monasteries — A1042

1991, July 4   Photo.   Perf. 13½

3658	A1042	1 l Curtea de Arges, vert.	.25	.25
3659	A1042	1 l Putna, vert.	.25	.25
3660	A1042	4.50 l Varatec, vert.	.25	.25
3661	A1042	4.50 l Agapia	.25	.25
3662	A1042	8 l Golia	.45	.25
3663	A1042	9 l Sucevita	.60	.25

Nos. 3658-3663 (6) 2.05 1.50

For surcharges see #4354-4355.

Hotels, Lodges, and Resorts A1043   A1044

Designs: 1 l, Hotel Continental, Timisoara, vert. 2 l, Valea Caprei Lodge, Fagaras. 4 l, Hotel Intercontinental, Bucharest, vert. 5 l, Lebada Hotel, Crisan. 6 l, Muntele Rosu Lodge, Ciucas. 8 l, Transylvania Hotel, Cluj-Napoca. 9 l, Hotel Orizont, Predeal. 10 l, Hotel Roman, Herculane, vert. 18 l, Rarau Lodge, Rarau, vert. 20 l, Alpine Hotel, Poiana Brasov. 25 l, Constanta Casino. 30 l, Miorija Lodge, Bucegi. 45 l, Sura Dacilor Lodge, Poiana Brasov. 60 l, Valea Draganului, Tourist Complex. 80 l, Hotel Florica, Venus Health Resort. 120 l, International Hotel, Baile Felix, vert. 160 l, Hotel Egreta, Tulcea, vert. 250 l, Motel Valea de Pesti, Valea Jiului. 400 l, Tourist Complex, Baisoara. 500 l, Hotel Bradul, Covasna. 800 l, Hotel Gorj, Tirgu Jiu.

1991   Photo.   Perf. 13½

3664	A1043	1 l blue	.25	.25
3665	A1043	2 l dark green	.25	.25
3666	A1043	4 l carmine	.25	.25
3667	A1043	5 l violet	.25	.25
3668	A1043	6 l olive brown	.25	.25
3669	A1043	8 l brown	.25	.25
3670	A1043	9 l red brown	.60	.25
3671	A1043	10 l olive green	.65	.25
3672	A1043	18 l bright red	.40	.25
3673	A1043	20 l brown org	.30	.25
3674	A1043	25 l bright blue	.65	.25
3675	A1043	30 l magenta	.85	.25
3676	A1043	45 l dark blue	.75	.30
3677	A1044	60 l brown olive	1.00	.40
3678	A1044	80 l purple	1.25	.55

Size: 27x41mm, 41x27mm

3679	A1044	120 l	gray bl & dk bl vio	1.50	.25
3680	A1044	160 l	lt ver & dk ver	2.00	.25
3681	A1044	250 l	lt bl & dk bl	2.50	.25
3682	A1044	400 l	tan & dk brn	3.25	.30
3683	A1044	500 l	lt bl grn & dk bl grn	3.75	.35
3684	A1044	800 l	pink & dk lil rose	4.50	.40
	Nos. 3664-3684 (21)			25.45	6.05

Issued: 1 l, 5 l, 9 l, 10 l, 8/27; 2 l, 4 l, 18 l, 25 l, 30 l, 10/8; 6 l, 8 l, 20 l, 45 l, 60 l, 80 l, 11/14; 120 l, 160 l, 250 l, 400 l, 500 l, 800 l, 12/5.

For surcharges see Nos. 4167-4174, 4204-4219, 4384.

Riccone '91, Intl. Philatelic Exhibition — A1045

1991, Aug. 27

3685	A1045	4 l	multicolored	.40	.25

A1046

Vases: a, Decorated with birds. b, Decorated with flowers.

1991, Sept. 12

3686	A1046	5 l	Pair, #a.-b.	.80	.35

Romanian-Chinese Philatelic Exhibition.

A1047

1991, Sept. 17

3687	A1047	1 l	blue	.35	.25

Romanian Academy, 125th anniv.
For surcharges, see Nos. 4266-4267.

A1048

Balkanfila '91 Philatelic Exhibition: 4 l, Flowers, by Nicu Enea. 5 l, Peasant Girl of Vlasca, by Gheorghe Tattarescu. 20 l, Sports Center, Bacau.

1991, Sept. 20

3688	A1048	4 l	multicolored	.35	.25
3689	A1048	5 l	multicolored	.35	.25

Souvenir Sheet

3690	A1048	20 l	multicolored	1.50	1.50

No. 3689 printed se-tenant with 2 l Romanian Philatelic Assoc. label. No. 3690 contains one 54x42mm stamp.

For surcharge see No. 4463.

Miniature Sheets

A1049

Birds: No. 3691a, Cissa erythrorhyncha. b, Malaconotus blanchoti. c, Sialia sialis. d, Sturnella neglecta. e, Harpactes fasciatus. f, Upupa epops. g, Malurus cyaneus. h, Brachypteracias squamigera. i, Leptopterus madagascariensis. j, Phoeniculus bollei. k, Melanerpes erythrocephalus. l, Pericrocotus flammeus.

No. 3692a, Melithreptus laetior. b, Rhynochetos jubatus. c, Turdus migratorius. d, Copsychus saularis. e, Monticola saxatilis. f, Xanthocephalus xanthocephalus. g, Scotopelia peli. h, Ptilogonys caudatus. i, Todus mexicanus. j, Copsychus malabaricus. k, Myzomela erythrocephala. l, Gymnostinops montezuma.

1991, Oct. 7   **Sheets of 12**

3691	A1049	2 l	#a.-l.	2.50	2.50
3692	A1049	2 l	#a.-l.	2.50	2.50

Natl. Census — A1050

1991, Oct. 15

3693	A1050	5 l	multicolored	.35	.25

Phila Nippon '91 — A1051

1991, Nov. 13   **Photo.**   *Perf. 13½*

3694	A1051	10 l	Sailing ship	.65	.25
3695	A1051	10 l	Bridge building	.65	.25

Miniature Sheets

Butterflies and Moths — A1052

Designs: No. 3696a, Ornithoptera paradisea. b, Bhutanitis lidderdalii. c, Morpho helena. d, Ornithoptera croesus. e, Phoebis avellaneda. f, Ornithoptera victoriae. g, Teinopalpus imperialis. h, Hypolimnas dexithea. i, Dabasa payeni. j, Morpho achilleana. k, Heliconius melpomene. l, Agrias claudina sardanapalus.

No. 3697a, Graellsia isabellae. b, Antocharis cardamines. c, Ammobiota festiva. d, Polygonia c-album. e, Catocala promissa. f, Rhyparia purpurata. g, Arctia villica. h, Polyommatus daphnis. i, Zerynthia polyxena. j, Daphnis nerii. k, Licaena dispar rutila. l, Pararge roxelana.

1991, Nov. 30   **Photo.**   *Perf. 13½*
Sheets of 12

3696	A1052	3 l	#a.-l.	3.00	3.00
3697	A1052	3 l	#a.-l.	3.00	3.00

A1053

1991, Nov. 21   **Photo.**   *Perf. 13½*

3698	A1053	1 l	Running	.25	.25
3699	A1053	4 l	Long jump	.25	.25
3700	A1053	5 l	High jump	.25	.25
3701	A1053	5 l	Runner in blocks	.25	.25
3702	A1053	9 l	Hurdles	.45	.25
3703	A1053	10 l	Javelin	.50	.25
	Nos. 3698-3703 (6)			1.95	1.50

World Track and Field Championships, Tokyo.

A1054

Famous People: 1 l, Mihail Kogalniceanu (1817-1891), politician. 4 l, Nicolae Titulescu (1882-1941), politician. No. 3706, Andrei Mureseanu (1816-1863), author. No. 3707, Aron Pumnul (1818-1866), author. 9 l, George Bacovia (1881-1957), author. 10 l, Perpessicius (1891-1971), writer.

1991, Dec. 10   **Photo.**   *Perf. 13½*

3704	A1054	1 l	multi	.25	.25
3705	A1054	4 l	multi	.25	.25
3706	A1054	5 l	multi	.25	.25
3707	A1054	5 l	multi	.25	.25
3708	A1054	9 l	multi	.60	.25
3709	A1054	10 l	multi	.70	.25
	Nos. 3704-3709 (6)			2.30	1.50

See Nos. 3759-3761, 3776-3781.
For surcharges see Nos. 4238A-4248.

Stamp Day — A1055

1991, Dec. 20

3710	A1055	8 l	+ 2 l label	.50	.25

Central University Library, Bucharest, Cent. A1056

1991, Dec. 23

3711	A1056	8 l	red brown	.50	.25

Christmas A1057

1991, Dec. 25   **Photo.**   *Perf. 13½*

3712	A1057	8 l	multicolored	.50	.25

See No. 3874.

1992 Winter Olympics, Albertville A1058

1992, Feb. 1   **Photo.**   *Perf. 13½*

3713	A1058	4 l	Biathlon	.25	.25
3714	A1058	5 l	Alpine skiing	.25	.25
3715	A1058	8 l	Cross-country skiing	.25	.25
3716	A1058	10 l	Two-man luge	.25	.25
3717	A1058	20 l	Speed skating	.35	.25
3718	A1058	25 l	Ski jumping	.40	.25
3719	A1058	30 l	Ice hockey	.50	.25
3720	A1058	45 l	Men's figure skating	.65	.25
	Nos. 3713-3720 (8)			2.90	2.00

Souvenir Sheets

3721	A1058	75 l	Women's figure skating	2.50	2.50

Imperf

3722	A1058	125 l	4-Man bobsled	7.00	7.00

No. 3721 is airmail and contains one 42x54mm stamp.
For surcharge see No. 4464.

Porcelain — A1059

Designs: 4 l, Sugar and cream service. 5 l, Tea service. 8 l, Goblet and pitcher, vert. 30 l, Tea service, diff. 45 l, Vase, vert.

1992, Feb. 20   **Photo.**   *Perf. 13½*

3723	A1059	4 l	multicolored	.25	.25
3724	A1059	5 l	multicolored	.25	.25
3725	A1059	8 l	multicolored	.25	.25
3726	A1059	30 l	multicolored	.45	.25
3727	A1059	45 l	multicolored	.65	.35
	Nos. 3723-3727 (5)			1.85	1.35

Fish A1060

Designs: 4 l, Scomber scombrus. 5 l, Tinca tinca. 8 l, Salvelinus fontinalis. 10 l, Romanichthys valsanicola. 30 l, Chondrostoma nasus. 45 l, Mullus barbatus ponticus.

1992, Feb. 28   **Photo.**   *Perf. 13½*

3728	A1060	4 l	multicolored	.25	.25
3729	A1060	5 l	multicolored	.25	.25
3730	A1060	8 l	multicolored	.25	.25
3731	A1060	10 l	multicolored	.25	.25
3732	A1060	30 l	multicolored	.35	.25
3733	A1060	45 l	multicolored	.60	.25
	Nos. 3728-3733 (6)			1.95	1.50

A1060a

1992, Mar. 11   Photo.   Perf. 13½
3734 A1060a 90 l on 5 l multi   1.50   .35
No. 3734 not issued without surcharge.

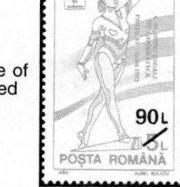

Gymnastics Type of
1991 Surcharged

1992, Mar. 11   Photo.   Perf. 13½
3735 A1041 90 l on 5 l like
#3657   1.50   .35
No. 3735 not issued without surcharge.

Horses
A1061

Various stylized drawings of horses walking, running, or jumping.

1992, Mar. 17   Photo.   Perf. 13½
3736 A1061   6 l multi, vert.   .25   .25
3737 A1061   7 l multi   .25   .25
3738 A1061 10 l multi, vert.   .25   .25
3739 A1061 25 l multi, vert.   .35   .25
3740 A1061 30 l multi   .45   .25
3741 A1061 50 l multi, vert.   .65   .25
Nos. 3736-3741 (6)   2.20   1.50

Miniature Sheet

Discovery of America, 500th
Anniv. — A1062

Columbus and ships: a, Green background. b, Violet background. c, Blue background. d, Ship approaching island.

1992, Apr. 22   Photo.   Perf. 13½
3742 A1062 35 l Sheet of 4,
#a.-d.   17.50   17.50
Europa.

Granada '92, Philatelic
Exhibition — A1063

a, 25 l, Spain No. 1 and Romania No. 1. b, 10 l, Expo emblem. c, 30 l, Building and courtyard, Granada

1992, Apr. 24   Photo.   Perf. 13½
3743 A1063 Sheet of 3, #a.-c.   1.60   1.60

Icon of Christ's
Descent into
Hell,
1680 — A1064

1992, Apr. 24   Photo.   Perf. 13½
3744 A1064 10 l multicolored   .35   .25
Easter.

Fire Station,
Bucharest,
Cent. — A1065

1992, May 2
3745 A1065 10 l multicolored   .50   .25

Chess Olympiad, Manila — A1066

No. 3747, Building, chess board.
75 l, Shore, chess board.

1992, June 7   Perf. 13½
3746 A1066 10 l shown   .30   .25
3747 A1066 10 l multicolored   .30   .25

Souvenir Sheet
3748 A1066 75 l multicolored   1.75   1.75
No. 3748 contains one 42x54mm stamp.

1992 Summer Olympics,
Barcelona — A1067

1992, July 17   Photo.   Perf. 13½
3749 A1067   6 l Shooting, vert.   .25   .25
3750 A1067   7 l Weight lifting,
vert.   .25   .25
3751 A1067   9 l Two-man cano-
ing   .25   .25
3752 A1067 10 l Handball, vert.   .25   .25
3753 A1067 25 l Wrestling   .25   .25
3754 A1067 30 l Fencing   .35   .25
3755 A1067 50 l Running, vert.   .40   .25
3756 A1067 55 l Boxing   .50   .25
Nos. 3749-3756 (8)   2.50   2.00

Souvenir Sheets
3757 A1067 100 l Rowing   1.00   1.00

Imperf
3758 A1067 200 l Gymnastics   5.00   5.00
Nos. 3757-3758 are airmail. No. 3757 contains one 54x42mm stamp, No. 3758 one 40x53mm stamp.

Famous People Type of 1991
Designs: 10 l, Ion I. C. Bratianu (1864-1927), prime minister. 25 l, Ion Gh. Duca (1879-1933). 30 l, Grigore Gafencu (1892-1957), journalist and politician.

1992, July 27   Photo.   Perf. 13½
3759 A1054 10 l green & violet   .25   .25
3760 A1054 25 l blue & lake   .25   .25
3761 A1054 30 l lake & blue   .25   .25
Nos. 3759-3761 (3)   .75   .75

Expo
'92,
Seville
A1068

Designs: 6 l, The Thinker, Cernavoda. 7 l, Trajan's bridge, Drobeta. 10 l, Mill. 25 l, Railroad bridge, Cernavoda. 30 l, Trajan Vuia's flying machine. 55 l, Herman Oberth's rocket. 100 l, Prayer sculpture, by C. Brancusi.

1992, Sept. 1
3762 A1068   6 l multicolored   .25   .25
3763 A1068   7 l multicolored   .25   .25
3764 A1068   10 l multicolored   .25   .25
3765 A1068   25 l multicolored   .25   .25
3766 A1068   30 l multicolored   .25   .25
3767 A1068   55 l multicolored   .50   .25
Nos. 3762-3767 (6)   1.75   1.50

Souvenir Sheet
3768 A1068 100 l multicolored   .75   .75
No. 3768 contains one 42x54mm stamp.

World Post Day — A1069

1992, Oct. 9
3769 A1069 10 l multicolored   .35   .25
For surcharge see No. 3945.

Discovery of America, 500th
Anniv. — A1070

Columbus and: 6 l, Santa Maria. 10 l, Nina. 25 l, Pinta. 55 l, Arrival in New World. 100 l, Sailing ship, vert.

1992, Oct. 30   Photo.   Perf. 13½
3770 A1070   6 l multicolored   .25   .25
3771 A1070   10 l multicolored   .25   .25
3772 A1070   25 l multicolored   .30   .25
3773 A1070   55 l multicolored   .50   .25
Nos. 3770-3773 (4)   1.30   1.00

Souvenir Sheet
3774 A1070 100 l multicolored   1.00   1.00
No. 3774 contains one 42x54mm stamp.

Romanian Postal Reorganization, 1st
Anniv. — A1071

1992, Nov. 5   Photo.   Perf. 13½
3775 A1071 10 l multicolored   .35   .25
For surcharge see No. 4113.

Famous People Type of 1991
Designs: 6 l, Iacob Negruzzi (1842-1932), author. 7 l, Grigore Antipa (1867-1944), naturalist. 9 l, Alexe Mateevici (1888-1917), poet. 10 l, Cezar Petrescu (1892-1961), author. 25 l, Octav Onicescu (1892-1983), mathematician. 30 l, Ecaterina Teodoroiu (1894-1917), World War I soldier.

1992, Nov. 9   Photo.   Perf. 13½
3776 A1054   6 l green & violet   .25   .25
3777 A1054   7 l lilac & green   .25   .25
3778 A1054   9 l gray blue & pur   .25   .25
3779 A1054 10 l brown & blue   .25   .25
3780 A1054 25 l blue & brown   .25   .25
3781 A1054 30 l slate & blue   .30   .25
Nos. 3776-3781 (6)   1.55   1.50

Wild Animals — A1072

Designs: 6 l, Haliaeetus leucocephalus, vert. 7 l, Strix occidentalis, vert. 9 l, Ursus arctos, vert. 10 l, Haematopus bachmani. 25 l, Canis lupus. 30 l, Odocoileus virginianus. 55 l, Alces alces.

1992, Nov. 16   Litho.   Perf. 13½
3782 A1072   6 l multicolored   .25   .25
3783 A1072   7 l multicolored   .25   .25
3784 A1072   9 l multicolored   .25   .25
3785 A1072   10 l multicolored   .25   .25
3786 A1072   25 l multicolored   .25   .25
3787 A1072   30 l multicolored   .30   .25
3788 A1072   55 l multicolored   .60   .25
Nos. 3782-3788 (7)   2.15   1.75

Souvenir Sheet
3789 A1072 100 l Orcinus orca   .90   .90

Romanian Anniversaries and
Events — A1073

7 l, Building, Galea Victoria St., 300th anniv. 9 l, Statue, School of Commerce, 600th anniv. 10 l, Curtea de Arges Monastery, 475th anniv. 25 l, School of Architecture, Bucharest, 80th anniv.

1992, Dec. 3   Photo.   Perf. 13½
3790 A1073   7 l multicolored   .25   .25
3791 A1073   9 l multicolored   .25   .25
3792 A1073 10 l multicolored   .25   .25
3793 A1073 25 l multicolored   .25   .25
Nos. 3790-3793 (4)   1.00   1.00
For surcharges see No. 4465-4466.

Natl.
Arms — A1074

1992, Dec. 7
3794 A1074 15 l multicolored   .25   .25

Christmas
A1075

1992, Dec. 15
3795 A1075 15 l multicolored   .35   .25
For surcharge see No. 4249.

New Telephone
Numbering
System
A1076

1992, Dec. 28   Photo.   Perf. 13½
3796 A1076 15 l blue, blk & red   .35   .25
For surcharges see #4268-4272.

Souvenir Sheets

1992
Summer
Olympics,
Barcelona
A1077

No. 3797: a, Shooting. b, Wrestling. c,
Weight lifting. d, Boxing.
No. 3798: a, Women's gymnastics. b, Four-
man sculls. c, Fencing. d, High jump.

1992, Dec. 30   Photo.   Perf. 13½
3797 A1077 35 l Sheet of 4, #a.-
              d.   1.00 1.00
3798 A1077 35 l Sheet of 4, #a.-
              d.   1.00 1.00

Historic Sites, Bucharest — A1078

Designs: 10 l, Mihai Voda Monastery. 15 l,
Vacaresti Monastery. 25 l, Multi-purpose hall.
30 l, Mina Minovici Medical Institute.

1993, Feb. 11   Photo.   Perf. 13½
3799 A1078 10 l multicolored   .25   .25
3800 A1078 15 l multicolored   .25   .25
3801 A1078 25 l multicolored   .25   .25
3802 A1078 30 l multicolored   .25   .25
      Nos. 3799-3802 (4)   1.00 1.00

Easter — A1079

1993, Mar. 25
3803 A1079 15 l multicolored   .25   .25

Medicinal
Plants — A1080

10 l, Crataegus monogyna. 15 l, Gentiana
phlogifolia. 25 l, Hippophae rhamnoides. 30 l,
Vaccinium myrtillus. 50 l, Arnica montana. 90
l, Rosa canina.

1993, Mar. 30
3804 A1080 10 l multi   .25   .25
3805 A1080 15 l multi   .25   .25
3806 A1080 25 l multi   .25   .25
3807 A1080 30 l multi   .25   .25
3808 A1080 50 l multi   .35   .25
3809 A1080 90 l multi   .65   .25
      Nos. 3804-3809 (6)   2.00 1.50

Nichita
Stanescu
(1933-1983),
Poet — A1081

1993, Mar. 31
3810 A1081 15 l brown and blue   .25   .25

Souvenir Sheet

Polska '93 — A1082

1993, Apr. 28   Photo.   Perf. 13½
3811 A1082 200 l multicolored   1.10 1.10

Birds
A1083

5 l, Pica pica. 10 l, Aquila chrysaetos. 15 l,
Pyrrhula pyrrhula. 20 l, Upupa epops. 25 l,
Dendrocopos major. 50 l, Oriolus oriolus. 65 l,
Loxia leucoptera. 90 l, Hirundo rustica. 160 l,
Parus cyanus. 250 l, Sturnus roseus.

1993, Apr. 30
3812 A1083 5 l multi   .25   .25
3813 A1083 10 l multi   .25   .25
3814 A1083 15 l multi   .25   .25
3815 A1083 20 l multi   .25   .25
3816 A1083 25 l multi   .25   .25
3817 A1083 50 l multi   .25   .25
3818 A1083 65 l multi   .25   .25
3819 A1083 90 l multi   .30   .25
3820 A1083 160 l multi   .50   .25
3821 A1083 250 l multi   .65   .25
      Nos. 3812-3821 (10)   3.20 2.50

Nos. 3812-3813 are horiz.

Cats — A1084

Various cats.

1993, May 24   Photo.   Perf. 13½
3822 A1084 10 l multicolored   .25   .25
3823 A1084 15 l multicolored   .25   .25
3824 A1084 30 l multicolored   .25   .25
3825 A1084 90 l multicolored   .35   .25
3826 A1084 135 l multicolored   .45   .25
3827 A1084 160 l multicolored   .60   .25
      Nos. 3822-3827 (6)   2.15 1.50

Souvenir Sheet

Europa — A1085

Paintings and sculpture by: a, Pablo
Picasso. b, Constantin Brancusi. c, Ion
Irimescu. d, Alexandru Ciucurencu.

1993, May 31   Photo.   Perf. 13½
3828 A1085 280 l Sheet of 4,
              #a.-d.   4.00 4.00

A1086

1993, June 30   Photo.   Perf. 13½
3829 A1086 10 l Vipera berus   .25   .25
3830 A1086 15 l Lynx lynx   .25   .25
3831 A1086 25 l Tadorna
              tadorna   .25   .25
3832 A1086 75 l Hucho hucho   .40   .25
3833 A1086 105 l Limenitis popu-
              li   .50   .25
3834 A1086 280 l Rosalia alpina   .75   .25
      Nos. 3829-3834 (6)   2.40 1.50

Nos. 3829, 3831-3834 are horiz.

A1087

10 l, Martes martes. 15 l, Oryctolagus cuniculus. 20 l, Sciurus vulgaris. 25 l, Rupicapra
rupicapra. 30 l, Vulpes vulpes. 40 l, Ovis
ammon. 75 l, Genetta genetta. 105 l, Eliomys
quercinus. 150 l, Mustela erminea. 280 l,
Herpestes ichneumon.

1993, June 30
3835 A1087 10 l multi   .25   .25
3836 A1087 15 l multi   .25   .25
3837 A1087 20 l multi   .25   .25
3838 A1087 25 l multi   .25   .25
3839 A1087 30 l multi   .25   .25
3840 A1087 40 l multi   .25   .25
3841 A1087 75 l multi   .25   .25
3842 A1087 105 l multi   .40   .25
3843 A1087 150 l multi   .45   .25
3844 A1087 280 l multi   1.00   .25
      Nos. 3835-3844 (10)   3.60 2.50

Nos. 3836, 3839, 3843-3844 are horiz.
For surcharges see Nos. 4427-4428.

Dinosaurs — A1088

1993, July 30   Photo.   Perf. 13½
3845 A1088 29 l Brontosaurus   .25   .25
3846 A1088 46 l Plesiosaurus   .25   .25
3847 A1088 85 l Triceratops   .30   .25
3848 A1088 171 l Stegosaurus   .65   .25
3849 A1088 216 l Tyrannosaurus   .75   .25
3850 A1088 319 l Archaeopteryx   1.00   .25
      Nos. 3845-3850 (6)   3.20 1.50

Souvenir Sheet

Telafila '93, Israel-Romanian Philatelic
Exhibition — A1089

Woman with Eggs, by Marcel Iancu.

1993, Aug. 21
3851 A1089 535 l multicolored   1.75 1.75

Icons — A1090

Designs: 75 l, St. Stephen. 171 l, Martyrs
from Brancoveanu and Vacarescu families.
216 l, St. Anthony.

1993, Aug. 31
3852 A1090 75 l multicolored   .25   .25
3853 A1090 171 l multicolored   .30   .25
3854 A1090 216 l multicolored   .70   .35
      Nos. 3852-3854 (3)   1.25   .85

Rural Mounted
Police,
Cent. — A1091

1993, Sept. 1
3855 A1091 29 l multicolored .25 .25

No. 3618 Surcharged in Red

1993, Sept. 3
3856 A1031 171 l on 2 l multi .60 .25

Souvenir Sheet

Bangkok '93 — A1092

1993, Sept. 20
3857 A1092 535 l multicolored 1.75 1.75

Famous
Men — A1093

Designs: 29 l, George Baritiu (1812-93), politician. 46 l, Horia Creanga (1892-1943), architect. 85 l, Armand Calinescu (1893-1939), politician. 171 l, Dumitru Bagdasar (1893-1946), physician. 216 l, Constantin Brailoiu (1893-1958), musician. 319 l, Iuliu Maniu (1873-1953), politician.

1993, Oct. 8
3858 A1093 29 l multicolored .25 .25
3859 A1093 46 l multicolored .25 .25
3860 A1093 85 l multicolored .25 .25
3861 A1093 171 l multicolored .30 .25
3862 A1093 216 l multicolored .35 .25
3863 A1093 319 l multicolored .60 .25
Nos. 3858-3863 (6) 2.00 1.50
For surcharge see No. 4407.

Souvenir Sheet

Romanian Entry into Council of
Europe — A1094

1993, Nov. 26 Photo. Perf. 13½
3864 A1094 1590 l multi 3.50 3.50

Expansion of Natl. Borders, 75th
Anniv. — A1095

Government leaders: 115 l, Iancu Flondor (1865-1924). 245 l, Ion I. C. Bratianu (1864-1927). 255 l, Iuliu Maniu (1873-1953). 325 l, Pantelimon Halippa (1883-1979). 1060 l, King Ferdinand I (1865-1927).

1993-94
3865 A1095 115 l multi .25 .25
3866 A1095 245 l multi .50 .25
3867 A1095 255 l multi .50 .25
3868 A1095 325 l multi .75 .35
Nos. 3865-3868 (4) 2.00 1.10

Souvenir Sheet
3869 A1095 1060 l Romania in
one color 2.50 2.50
a. Romania in four colors 8.00 8.00
No. 3869a was redrawn because of an error in the map.
Issued: No. 3869, Feb. 1994; Nos. 3865-3868, 3869a, Dec. 1, 1993.
For surcharge see No. 4472.

Anniversaries
and Events
A1096

Designs: 115 l, Emblem of the Diplomatic Alliance. 245 l, Statue of Johannes Honterus, founder of first Humanitarian School. 255 l, Arms, seal of Slatina, Olt River Bridge. 325 l, Map, arms of Braila.

1993, Dec. 15
3870 A1096 115 l multicolored .25 .25
3871 A1096 245 l multicolored .55 .25
3872 A1096 255 l multicolored .55 .25
3873 A1096 325 l multicolored .55 .30
Nos. 3870-3873 (4) 1.90 1.05
Diplomatic Alliance, 75th anniv. (#3870). Birth of Johannes Honterus, 450th anniv. (#3871). City of Slatina, 625th anniv. (#3872). County of Braila, 625th anniv. (#3873).
For surcharge see No. 4473.

Christmas Type of 1991
1993, Dec. 20
3874 A1057 45 l like #3712 .25 .25

Insects, Wildlife from Movile
Cavern — A1097

Designs: 29 l, Clivina subterranea. 46 l, Nepa anophthalma. 85 l, Haemopis caeca. 171 l, Lascona cristiani. 216 l, Semisalsa dobrogica. 319 l, Armadilidium tabacarui. 535 l, Exploring cavern, vert.

1993, Dec. 27
3875 A1097 29 l multicolored .25 .25
3876 A1097 46 l multicolored .25 .25
3877 A1097 85 l multicolored .25 .25
3878 A1097 171 l multicolored .40 .25
3879 A1097 216 l multicolored .55 .25
3880 A1097 319 l multicolored .80 .25
Nos. 3875-3880 (6) 2.50 1.50

Souvenir Sheet
3881 A1097 535 l multicolored 1.50 1.50

Alexandru Ioan
Cuza — A1098

1994, Jan. 24 Photo. Perf. 13
3882 A1098 45 l multicolored .25 .25

Historic Buildings, Bucharest — A1099

115 l, Opera House. 245 l, Vacaresti Monastery. 255 l, Church of St. Vineri. 325 l, Dominican House, Vacaresti Monastery.

1994, Feb. 7
3883 A1099 115 l multicolored .25 .25
3884 A1099 245 l multicolored .45 .25
3885 A1099 255 l multicolored .60 .25
3886 A1099 325 l multicolored .60 .25
Nos. 3883-3886 (4) 1.90 1.00

For surcharge see No. 4482.

1994 Winter
Olympics,
Lillehammer
A1100

1994, Feb. 12 Perf. 13½
3887 A1100 70 l Speed skating .25 .25
3888 A1100 115 l Slalom skiing .25 .25
3889 A1100 125 l Bobsled .30 .25
3890 A1100 245 l Biathlon .40 .25
3891 A1100 255 l Ski jumping .40 .25
3892 A1100 325 l Figure skating .60 .25
Nos. 3887-3892 (6) 2.20 1.50

Souvenir Sheet
3893 A1100 1590 l Luge 3.00 3.00
No. 3893 contains one 43x54mm stamp.

Mills — A1101

1994, Mar. 31 Perf. 13
3894 A1101 70 l Sarichioi .25 .25
3895 A1101 115 l Valea Nucarilor .25 .25
3896 A1101 125 l Caraorman .30 .25
3897 A1101 245 l Romanii de
Jos .40 .25
3898 A1101 255 l Enisala, horiz. .45 .25
3899 A1101 325 l Nistoresti .60 .30
Nos. 3894-3899 (6) 2.25 1.55
For surcharges see Nos. 4431-4434.

Dinosaurs — A1102

90 l, Struthiosaurs. 130 l, Megalosaurs. 150 l, Parasaurolophus. 280 l, Stenonychosaurus. 500 l, Camarasaurus. 635 l, Gallimimus.

1994, Apr. 30 Photo. Perf. 13½
3900 A1102 90 l multi .25 .25
3901 A1102 130 l multi .25 .25
3902 A1102 150 l multi .30 .25
3903 A1102 280 l multi .40 .25
3904 A1102 500 l multi .50 .25
3905 A1102 635 l multi .60 .30
Nos. 3900-3905 (6) 2.30 1.55
For surcharge see No. 4467.

Romanian
Legends
A1103

Designs: 70 l, Calin the Madman. 115 l, Ileana Cosanzeana. 125 l, Ileana Cosanzeana, diff. 245 l, Ileana Cosanzeana, diff. 255 l, Agheran the Brave. 325 l, Wolf as Prince Charming, Ileana Cosanzeana.

1994, Apr. 8 Photo. Perf. 13½
3906 A1103 70 l multicolored .25 .25
3907 A1103 115 l multicolored .25 .25
3908 A1103 125 l multicolored .30 .25
3909 A1103 245 l multicolored .45 .25
3910 A1103 255 l multicolored .45 .25
3911 A1103 325 l multicolored .65 .30
Nos. 3906-3911 (6) 2.35 1.55
For surcharge see No. 4474.

Easter
A1104

1994, Apr. 21
3912 A1104 60 l multicolored .25 .25

Trees — A1105

No. 3913, Abies alba. No. 3914, Pinus sylvestris. No. 3915, Populus alba. No. 3916, Quercus robur. No. 3917, Larix decidua. No. 3918, Fagus sylvatica. No. 3919, Acer pseudoplatanus. No. 3920, Fraxinus excelsior. No. 3921, Picea abies. No. 3922, Tilia platyphyllos.

Wmk. 398

1994, May 27		Photo.	Perf. 13¼	
3913	A1105	15 l multi	.25	.25
3914	A1105	35 l multi	.25	.25
3915	A1105	45 l multi	.25	.25
3916	A1105	60 l multi	.25	.25
3917	A1105	70 l multi	.25	.25
3918	A1105	125 l multi	.25	.25
3919	A1105	350 l multi	.40	.25
3920	A1105	940 l multi	1.25	.25
3921	A1105	1440 l multi	1.75	.25
3922	A1105	3095 l multi	3.50	.25
		Nos. 3913-3922 (10)	8.40	2.50

For surcharges see Nos. 4221-4224, 4422-4424.

1994 World Cup Soccer Championships, US — A1106

1994, June 17			Unwmk.	
3923	A1106	90 l Group A	.25	.25
3924	A1106	130 l Group B	.25	.25
3925	A1106	150 l Group C	.30	.25
3926	A1106	280 l Group D	.50	.25
3927	A1106	500 l Group E	.55	.25
3928	A1106	635 l Group F	.70	.25
		Nos. 3923-3928 (6)	2.55	1.50

Souvenir Sheet

3929	A1106	2075 l Action scene	3.00	3.00

No. 3929 is airmail and contains one 54x42mm stamp.

Intl. Olympic Committee, Cent. — A1107

Ancient Olympians: 150 l, Torchbearer. 280 l, Discus thrower. 500 l, Wrestlers. 635 l, Arbitrator.
2075 l, Runners, emblem of Romanian Olympic Committee.

1994, June 23				
3930	A1107	150 l multicolored	.25	.25
3931	A1107	280 l multicolored	.45	.25
3932	A1107	500 l multicolored	.60	.25
3933	A1107	635 l multicolored	1.20	.25
		Nos. 3930-3933 (4)	2.50	1.00

Souvenir Sheet

3934	A1107	2075 l multicolored	3.00	3.00

No. 3934 contains one 54x42mm stamp. Romanian Olympic Committee, 80th anniv. (#3934).

Miniature Sheets

Mushrooms — A1108

Edible: No. 3935a, 30 l, Craterellus cornucopiodes. b, 60 l, Lepista nuda. c, 150 l, Boletus edulis. d, 940 l, Lycoperdon perlatum.
Poisonous: No. 3936a, 90 l, Boletus satanas. b, 280 l, Amanita phalloides. c, 350 l, Inocybe patonillardi. d, 500 l, Amanita muscaria.

1994, Aug. 8		Photo.	Perf. 13½	
3935	A1108	Sheet of 4, #a.-d.	2.00	2.00
3936	A1108	Sheet of 4, #a.-d.	2.00	2.00
		Complete booklet, #3935-3936	4.50	

PHILAKOREA '94 — A1109

1994, Aug. 16			Perf. 13½	
3937	A1109	60 l Tuning fork	.30	.25

Souvenir Sheet

3938	A1109	2075 l Korean drummer	2.75	2.75

No. 3938 contains one 42x54mm stamp.

Environmental Protection in Danube River Delta — A1110

Designs: 150 l, Huso huso. 280 l, Vipera ursini. 500 l, Haliaeetus albicilla. 635 l, Mustela lutreola.
2075 l, Periploca graeca.

1994, Aug. 31				
3939	A1110	150 l multicolored	.25	.25
3940	A1110	280 l multicolored	.50	.25
3941	A1110	500 l multicolored	.95	.30
3942	A1110	635 l multicolored	1.10	.35
		Nos. 3939-3942 (4)	2.80	1.15

Souvenir Sheet

3943	A1110	2075 l multi	3.00	3.00

No. 3943 contains one 54x42mm stamp.

Nos. 3654-3655 Surcharged

No. 3769 Surcharged

1994		Perfs., Etc. as Before		
3944	A1041	150 l on 4.50 l		
		#3654	.25	.25
3945	A1069	150 l on 10 l #3769	.30	.25
3946	A1041	525 l on 4.50 l		
		#3655	.90	.30
		Nos. 3944-3946 (3)	1.45	.80

Issued: #3944, 3946 9/9/94; #3945, 10/7/94.

Circus Animal Acts — A1111

Designs: 90 l, Elephant. 130 l, Bear, vert. 150 l, Monkeys. 280 l, Tiger. 500 l, Tightrope walker, dogs. 635 l, Horse.

1994, Sept. 15		Photo.	Perf. 13	
3947	A1111	90 l multicolored	.25	.25
3948	A1111	130 l multicolored	.25	.25
3949	A1111	150 l multicolored	.30	.25
3950	A1111	280 l multicolored	.50	.25
3951	A1111	500 l multicolored	.65	.25
3952	A1111	635 l multicolored	.90	.25
		Nos. 3947-3952 (6)	2.85	1.50

20th Intl. Fair, Bucharest — A1112

1994, Oct. 10				
3953	A1112	525 l multicolored	.90	.30

Fish A1113

World Wildlife Fund: 150 l, Acipenser ruthenus. 280 l, Acipenser guldenstaedti. 500 l, Acipenser stellatus. 635 l, Acipenser sturio.

1994, Oct. 29		Photo.	Perf. 13½	
3954	A1113	150 l multicolored	.30	.25
3955	A1113	280 l multicolored	.50	.25
3956	A1113	500 l multicolored	.75	.25
3957	A1113	635 l multicolored	1.00	.25
		Nos. 3954-3957 (4)	2.55	1.00

Issued in sheets of 10.

Chinese-Romanian Philatelic Exhibition — A1114

1994, Oct. 29		Photo.	Perf. 13½	
3958	A1114	150 l Serpent	.30	.25
3959	A1114	1135 l Dragon	1.60	.30
a.		Pair, #3958-3959 + label	2.00	.60

Romanian State Railway, 125th Anniv. A1115

1994, Oct. 31				
3960	A1115	90 l multicolored	.25	.25

Famous People A1116

Designs: 30 l, Alexandru Orascu (1817-94). 60 l, Gh. Polizu (1819-86). 90 l, Gheorghe Tattarescu (1820-94), politician, prime minister. 150 l, Iulia Hasdeu (1869-88). 280 l, S. Mehedinti (1869-1962). 350 l, Camil Petrescu (1894-1957). 500 l, N. Paulescu (1869-1931). 940 l, L. Grigorescu (1894-1965).

1994		Photo.	Perf. 13½	
3961	A1116	30 l multicolored	.25	.25
3962	A1116	60 l multicolored	.25	.25
3962A	A1116	90 l multicolored	.25	.25
3963	A1116	150 l multicolored	.30	.25
3964	A1116	280 l multicolored	.30	.25
3965	A1116	350 l multicolored	.45	.25
3966	A1116	500 l multicolored	.50	.25
3967	A1116	940 l multicolored	1.25	.25
		Nos. 3961-3967 (8)	3.55	2.00

Issued; 90 l, 12/28/94; others, 11/30/94.

Christmas — A1117

1994, Dec. 14			Perf. 13½	
3968	A1117	60 l multicolored	.30	.25

For surcharge see No. 4250.

St. Mary's Romanian Orthodox Church, Cleveland, Ohio, 90th Anniv. — A1118

1994, Dec. 21		Photo.	Perf. 13½	
3969	A1118	610 l multicolored	.85	.30

World Tourism Organization, 20th Anniv. — A1119

1994, Dec. 22				
3970	A1119	525 l multicolored	1.00	.30

Miniature Sheet

Romanian Military
Decorations — A1120

Year of medal — No. 3971: a, 30 l, Distinguished Flying Cross, 1938. b, 60 l, Military Cross, 3rd class, 1916. c, 150 l, Distinguished Serivce Medal, 1st Class, 1880. d, 940 l, Order of the Romanian Star, 1877.

1994, Dec. 23
3971 A1120 Sheet of 4, #a.-d. 2.00 2.00

Baby Animals
A1121

1994, Dec. 27 **Photo.** **Perf. 13x½**
3972 A1121 90 l Kittens .25 .25
3973 A1121 130 l Puppies .25 .25
3974 A1121 150 l Kid goat .25 .25
3975 A1121 280 l Foal .30 .25
3976 A1121 500 l Bunnies .60 .25
3977 A1121 635 l Lambs .75 .25
 Nos. 3972-3977 (6) 2.40 1.50

For surcharge see No. 4468.

A1122

1995, Jan. 31 **Photo.** **Perf. 13½**
3978 A1122 60 l dark blue .35 .25

Save the Children organization.

A1123

The Young Men of Brasov: 40 l, Tanar. 60 l, Batran. 150 l, Curcan. 280 l, Dorobant. 350 l, Brasovechean. 500 l, Rosior. 635 l, Albior.

1995, Feb. 25 **Photo.** **Perf. 13½**
3979 A1123 40 l multicolored .25 .25
3980 A1123 60 l multicolored .25 .25
3981 A1123 150 l multicolored .25 .25
3982 A1123 280 l multicolored .30 .25
3983 A1123 350 l multicolored .50 .25
3984 A1123 500 l multicolored .60 .25
3985 A1123 635 l multicolored .75 .25
 Nos. 3979-3985 (7) 2.90 1.75

Liberation of Concentration Camps,
50th Anniv. — A1124

1995, Mar. 24 **Perf. 13½**
3986 A1124 960 l black & red .85 .30

FAO
& UN,
50th
Anniv.
A1125

Designs: 675 l, FAO emblem, grain. 960 l, "50," UN emblem. 1615 l, Hand holding pen with flags of UN Charter countries.

1995, Apr. 12 **Perf. 13½**
3987 A1125 675 l multicolored .50 .25
3988 A1125 960 l multicolored .75 .25
3989 A1125 1615 l multicolored 1.50 .25
 Nos. 3987-3989 (3) 2.75 .75

Easter
A1126

1995, Apr. 14
3990 A1126 60 l multicolored .25 .25

Romanian Fairy Tales — A1127

Designs: 90 l, King riding horse across town. 130 l, Woman feeding animals, vert. 150 l, Man riding on winged horse. 280 l, Old man, young man. 500 l, Archer aiming at apple tree, vert. 635 l, Two people riding log pulled by galloping horses.

1995, Apr. 20 **Perf. 13½**
3991 A1127 90 l multicolored .25 .25
3992 A1127 130 l multicolored .25 .25
3993 A1127 150 l multicolored .25 .25
3994 A1127 280 l multicolored .35 .25
3995 A1127 500 l multicolored .60 .25
3996 A1127 635 l multicolored .75 .25
 Nos. 3991-3996 (6) 2.45 1.50

For surcharge see No. 4405.

Georges Enescu (1881-1955),
Composer — A1128

1995, May 5 **Perf. 13½**
3997 A1128 960 l blk & dp yel .75 .30

Peace &
Freedom
A1129

Europa: 150 l, Dove carryng piece of rainbow. 4370 l, Dove under rainbow with wings forming "Europa."

1995, May 8
3998 A1129 150 l multicolored .25 .25
3999 A1129 4370 l multicolored 6.00 6.00

Lucian Blaga
(1895-1961),
Poet — A1130

1995, May 9
4000 A1130 150 l multicolored .35 .25
 See Nos. 4017-4021.

Methods of Transportation — A1131

Designs: 470 l, Bucharest Metro subway train, 1979. 675 l, Brasov aerial cable car, vert. 965 l, Sud Aviation SA 330 Puma helicopter. 2300 l, 1904 Trolleybus. 2550 l, Steam locomotive, 1869. 3410 l, Boeing 737-300.

1995, May 30 **Photo.** **Perf. 13½**
4001 A1131 470 l blk, gray & yel .40 .25
4002 A1131 675 l blk, gray & red .55 .25
4003 A1131 965 l bl, blk & gray .80 .25
4004 A1131 2300 l blk, gray & grn 2.00 .25
4005 A1131 2550 l blk, gray & red 2.00 .25
4006 A1131 3410 l bl, blk & gray 2.90 .25
 Nos. 4001-4006 (6) 8.65 1.50

Nos. 4003, 4006 are airmail. No. 4006, 75th anniversary of Romanian air transportation. See Nos. 4055-4060.

Romanian Maritime Service,
Cent. — A1132

Ships: 90 l, Dacia, liner, vert. 130 l, Imparatul Traian, steamer. 150 l, Romania, steamer. 280 l, Costinesti, tanker. 960 l, Caransebes, container ship. 3410 l, Tutova, car ferry.

1995, May 31 **Photo.** **Perf. 13½**
4007 A1132 90 l multicolored .25 .25
4008 A1132 130 l multicolored .25 .25
4009 A1132 150 l multicolored .25 .25
4010 A1132 280 l multicolored .25 .25
4011 A1132 960 l multicolored .60 .25
4012 A1132 3410 l multicolored 2.25 .50
 Nos. 4007-4012 (6) 3.85 1.75

For surcharge see No. 4469.

A1133

European Nature Conservation Year: 150 l, Dama dama. 280 l, Otis tarda. 960 l, Cypripedium caiceolus. 1615 l, Ghetarul scarisoara (stalagmites).

1995, June 5
4013 A1133 150 l multicolored .25 .25
4014 A1133 280 l multicolored .25 .25
4015 A1133 960 l multicolored .35 .50
4016 A1133 1615 l multicolored 1.25 .50
 Nos. 4013-4016 (4) 2.10 1.50

Famous Romanians Type of 1995

Designs: 90 l, D.D. Rosca (1895-1980). 130 l, Vasile Conta (1845-1882). 280 l, Ion Barbu (1895-1961). 960 l, Iuliu Hatieganu (1885-1959). 1650 l, Dimitrie Brandza (1846-95).

1995, June 26 **Photo.** **Perf. 13½**
4017 A1130 90 l multicolored .25 .25
4018 A1130 130 l multicolored .25 .25
4019 A1130 280 l multicolored .25 .25
4020 A1130 960 l multicolored .70 .25
4021 A1130 1650 l multicolored 1.00 .25
 Nos. 4017-4021 (5) 2.45 1.25

For surcharge see No. 4470.

A1134

1995, July 10 **Photo.** **Perf. 13½**
4022 A1134 1650 l multicolored 1.25 .40

European Youth Olympic days.

Stamp Day — A1135

1995, July 15
4023 A1135 960 l +715 l label 2.00 .50

Cernavoda Bridge, Cent. — A1136

1995, July 27 Photo. Perf. 13½
4024 A1136 675 l multicolored .75 .40

A1137

Fowl: 90 l, Anas platyrhynchos. 130 l, Gallus gallus (hen). 150 l, Numida meleagris. 280 l, Meleagris gallopavo. 960 l, Anser anser. 1650 l, Gallus gallus (rooster).

1995, July 31 Photo. Perf. 13½
4025 A1137 90 l multicolored .25 .25
4026 A1137 130 l multicolored .25 .25
4027 A1137 150 l multicolored .25 .25
4028 A1137 280 l multicolored .30 .25
4029 A1137 960 l multicolored .85 .25
4030 A1137 1650 l multicolored 1.25 .25
    Nos. 4025-4030 (6) 3.15 1.50

For surcharge see No. 4471.

A1138

Institute of Air Medicine, 75th Anniv.: Gen. Dr. Victor Anastasiu (1886-1972).

1995, Aug. 5 Photo. Perf. 13½
4031 A1138 960 l multicolored .80 .35

Battle of Calugareni, 400th Anniv. — A1139

1995, Aug. 13
4032 A1139 100 l multicolored .35 .25

Romanian Buildings — A1140

Structure, year completed: 250 l, Giurgiu Castle, 1395. 500 l, Neamtului Castle, 1395, vert. 960 l, Sebes-Alba Mill, 1245. 1615 l, Dorohoi Church, 1495, vert. 1650 l, Military Observatory, Bucharest, 1895, vert.

1995, Aug. 28
4033 A1140 250 l multicolored .25 .25
4034 A1140 500 l multicolored .30 .25
4035 A1140 960 l multicolored .50 .25

4036 A1140 1615 l multicolored .75 .25
4037 A1140 1650 l multicolored .90 .25
    Nos. 4033-4037 (5) 2.70 1.25

A1141

Buildings in Manastirea: 675 l, Moldovita Monastery. 960 l, Hurez Monastery. 1615 l, Biertan Castle, horiz.

1995, Aug. 31
4038 A1141 675 l multicolored .30 .25
4039 A1141 960 l multicolored .60 .25
4040 A1141 1615 l multicolored .90 .30
    Nos. 4038-4040 (3) 1.80 .80

A1142

1995, Sept. 8
4041 A1142 1020 l multicolored .85 .50
Romania Open Tennis Tournament, Bucharest.

Magazine "Mathematics," Cent. — A1143

Design: Ion N. Ionescu, founder.

1995, Sept. 15
4042 A1143 100 l multicolored .35 .25

Plants from Bucharest Botanical Garden — A1144

Designs: 50 l, Albizia julibrissin. 100 l, Taxus baccata. 150 l, Paulownia tomentosa. 500 l, Strelitzia reginae. 960 l, Victoria amazonica. 2300 l, Rhododendron indicum.

1995, Sept. 29 Photo. Perf. 13½
4043 A1144 *50 l multicolored .25 .25
4044 A1144 100 l multicolored .25 .25
4045 A1144 150 l multicolored .25 .25
4046 A1144 500 l multicolored .30 .25
4047 A1144 960 l multicolored .60 .25
4048 A1144 2300 l multicolored 1.20 .30
    Nos. 4043-4048 (6) 2.85 1.55

Church of St. John — A1145

1995, Oct. 1 Photo. Perf. 13½
4049 A1145 250 l multi .75 .50
City of Piatra Neamt, 600th anniv.

A1146

Emigres: 150 l, George Apostu (1934-86), sculptor. 250 l, Emil Cioran (1911-95), philosopher. 500 l, Eugen Ionescu (1909-94), writer. 960 l, Elena Vacarescu (1866-1947), writer. 1650 l, Mircea Eliade (1907-86), philosopher.

1995, Nov. 9
4050 A1146 150 l grn, gray & blk .25 .25
4051 A1146 250 l bl, gray & blk .25 .25
4052 A1146 500 l tan, brn & blk .40 .25
4053 A1146 960 l lake, mag & blk .80 .25
4054 A1146 1650 l tan, brn & blk 1.20 .25
    Nos. 4050-4054 (5) 2.90 1.25

Transportation Type of 1995

285 l, IAR 80 fighter planes. 630 l, Training ship, Mesagerul. 715 l, IAR-316 Red Cross helicopter. 755 l, Cargo ship, Razboieni. 1575 l, IAR-818H seaplane. 1615 l, First electric tram, Bucharest, 1896, vert.

1995, Nov. 16
4055 A1131 285 l blk, gray & grn .25 .25
4056 A1131 630 l bl & red .35 .25
4057 A1131 715 l gray bl & red .35 .25
4058 A1131 755 l blk, bl & gray .40 .25
4059 A1131 1575 l blk, grn & gray .90 .25
4060 A1131 1615 l blk, grn & gray .75 .25
    Nos. 4055-4060 (6) 3.00 1.50

Nos. 4055, 4057, 4059 are air mail.
For surcharges see Nos. 4475-4477.

1996 Summer Olympics, Atlanta — A1147

1995, Dec. 8
4061 A1147 50 l Track .25 .25
4062 A1147 100 l Gymnastics .25 .25
4063 A1147 150 l Two-man canoe .25 .25
4064 A1147 500 l Fencing .50 .25
4065 A1147 960 l Rowing-eights .85 .25
4066 A1147 2300 l Boxing 2.00 .35
    Nos. 4061-4066 (6) 4.10 1.60

Souvenir Sheet

4067 A1147 2610 l Gymnastics 2.50 2.50
No. 4067 contains one 42x54mm stamp.

Christmas A1148

100 l, The Holy Family.

1995, Dec. 15 Photo. Perf. 13½
4068 A1148 100 l multicolored .35 .25

Folk Masks & Costumes — A1149

1996, Jan. 31
4069 A1149 250 l Maramures .30 .25
4070 A1149 500 l Moldova .50 .25
4071 A1149 960 l Moldova, vert. .80 .25
4072 A1149 1650 l Moldova, diff., vert. 1.20 .25
    Nos. 4069-4072 (4) 2.80 1.00

Tristan Tzara (1896-1963), Writer — A1151

1500 l, Anton Pann (1796-1854), writer.

1996, Mar. 27 Photo. Perf. 13½
4078 A1151 150 l multicolored .25 .25
4079 A1151 1500 l multicolored 1.25 .25

Easter A1152

1996, Mar. 29
4080 A1152 150 l multicolored .35 .25

Romfilex '96, Romanian-Israeli Philatelic Exhibition — A1153

Paintings: a, 370 l, On the Terrace at Sinaia, by Theodor Aman. b, 150 l, The Post Office, by

M. Stoican. c, 1500 l, Old Jerusalem, by Reuven Rubin.

1996, Apr. 5
4081 A1153 Sheet of 3, #a.-c. 5.50 5.00
For surcharges see No. 4202.

Insects — A1154

Designs: 70 l, Chrysomela vigintipunctata. 220 l, Cerambyx cerdo. 370 l, Entomoscelis adonidis. 650 l, Coccinella bipunctata. 700 l, Calosoma sycophanta. 740 l, Hedobia imperialis. 960 l, Oryctes nasicornis. 1000 l, Trichius fasciatus. 1500 l, Purpuricenus kaehleri. 2500 l, Anthaxia salicis.

1996
4082	A1154	70 l	multicolored	.25 .25
4083	A1154	220 l	multicolored	.25 .25
4084	A1154	370 l	multicolored	.25 .25
4085	A1154	650 l	multicolored	.30 .25
4086	A1154	700 l	multicolored	.30 .25
4087	A1154	740 l	multicolored	.45 .25
4088	A1154	960 l	multicolored	.60 .25
4089	A1154	1000 l	multicolored	.60 .25
4090	A1154	1500 l	multicolored	.90 .25
4091	A1154	2500 l	multicolored	1.20 .30
	Nos. 4082-4091 (10)			5.10 2.55

Issued: 220, 740, 960, 1000, 1500, 4/16/96; 70, 370, 650, 700, 2500 l, 6/10/96.
For surcharges see Nos. 4283-4289, 4375-4377.

Souvenir Sheet

Dumitru Prunariu, First Romanian Cosmonaut — A1155

1996, Apr. 22
4092 A1155 2720 l multicolored 1.50 1.50
ESPAMER '96, Aviation and Space Philatelic Exhibition, Seville, Spain.
For surcharges see Nos. 4829-4830.

1996 Summer Olympic Games, Atlanta — A1158

1996, July 12 Photo. Perf. 13½
4093	A1158	220 l	Boxing	.25 .25
4094	A1158	370 l	Athletics	.25 .25
4095	A1158	740 l	Rowing	.40 .25
4096	A1158	1000 l	Judo	.80 .25
4097	A1158	2550 l	Gymnastics	1.75 .30
	Nos. 4093-4097 (5)			3.45 1.30

Souvenir Sheet
4098 A1158 4050 l Gymnastics, diff. 2.75 2.00
No. 4098 is airmail and contains one 54x42mm stamp. Olymphilex '96 (#4098).
For surcharge see No. 4877.

UNESCO World Heritage Sites — A1159

Designs: 150 l, Arbore Church. 1500 l, Voronet Monastery. 2550 l, Humor Monastery.

1996, Apr. 24 Photo. Perf. 13½
4099	A1159	150 l	multicolored	.25 .25
4100	A1159	1500 l	multicolored	.80 .25
4101	A1159	2550 l	multicolored	1.50 .35
	Nos. 4099-4101 (3)			2.55 .85

Famous Women — A1160

Europa: 370 l, Ana Aslan (1897-1988), physician. 4140 l, Lucia Bulandra (1873-1961), actress.

1996, May 6
4102	A1160	370 l	multicolored	.25 .25
4103	A1160	4140 l	multicolored	3.75 2.25
a.	Pair, #4102-4103 + 2 labels			4.00 2.50

UNICEF, 50th Anniv. — A1161

Children's paintings: 370 l, Mother and children. 740 l, Winter Scene. 1500 l, Children and Sun over House. 2550 l, House on Stilts.

1996, May 25
4104	A1161	370 l	multi	.25 .25
4105	A1161	740 l	multi	.45 .25
4106	A1161	1500 l	multi	.80 .25
4107	A1161	2550 l	multi, vert.	1.20 .25
	Nos. 4104-4107 (4)			2.70 1.00

Habitat II (#4107).

Euro '96, European Soccer Championships, Great Britain — A1162

Designs: a, 220 l, Goal keeper, ball. b, 370 l, Player with ball. c, Two players, ball. d, 1500 l, Three players, ball. e, 2550 l, Player dribbling ball.

4050 l, Two players, four balls.

1996, May 27
4108 A1162 Strip of 5, #a.-e. 3.75 1.25
Souvenir Sheet
4109 A1162 4050 l multicolored 2.75 2.10
No. 4109 contains one 42x54mm stamp.

CAPEX '96 — A1163

Designs: 150 l, Toronto Convention Center. 4050 l, CN Tower, Skydome, Toronto skyline.

1996, May 29
4110 A1163 150 l multicolored .25 .25
Souvenir Sheet
4111 A1163 4050 l multicolored 2.75 2.10
No. 4111 contains 42x54mm stamp.

Resita Factory, 225th Anniv. A1164

1996, June 20 Photo. Perf. 13½
4112 A1164 150 l dark red brown .35 .25

No. 3775 Surcharged

1996, June 22
4113 A1071 150 l on 10 l multi .35 .25

Stamp Day — A1165

1996, July 15
4114 A1165 1500 l + 650 l label 1.25 .25

Conifers — A1166

70 l, Picea glauca. 150 l, Picea omorica. 220 l, Picea pungens. 740 l, Picea sitchensis. 1500 l, Pinus sylvestris. 3500 l, Pinus pinaster.

1996, Aug. 1
4115	A1166	70 l	multi	.25 .25
4116	A1166	150 l	multi	.25 .25
4117	A1166	220 l	multi	.25 .25
4118	A1166	740 l	multi	.45 .25
4119	A1166	1500 l	multi	.85 .25
4120	A1166	3500 l	multi	2.00 .30
	Nos. 4115-4120 (6)			4.05 1.55

For surcharge see No. 4403.

Wildlife — A1167

Designs: 70 l, Natrix natrix, vert. 150 l, Testudo hermanni, vert. 220 l, Alauda arvensis. 740 l, Vulpes vulpes. 1500 l, Phocaena phocaena, vert. 3500 l, Aquila chrysaetos, vert.

1996, Sept. 12 Photo. Perf. 13½
4121	A1167	70 l	multicolored	.25 .25
4122	A1167	150 l	multicolored	.25 .25
4123	A1167	220 l	multicolored	.25 .25
4124	A1167	740 l	multicolored	.45 .25
4125	A1167	1500 l	multicolored	.85 .25
4126	A1167	3500 l	multicolored	2.00 .30
	Nos. 4121-4126 (6)			4.05 1.55

For surcharge see No. 4348.

Famous Men — A1168

100 l, Stan Golestan (1875-1956). 150 l, Corneliu Coposu (1914-95). 370 l, Vintila Horia (1915-92). 1500 l, Alexandru Papana (1906-46).

1996, Nov. 29
4127	A1168	100 l	black & rose red	.25 .25
4128	A1168	150 l	black & lake	.25 .25
4129	A1168	370 l	blk & yel brn	.35 .25
4130	A1168	1500 l	black & ver	1.00 .40
	Nos. 4127-4130 (4)			1.85 1.15

Madonna and Child — A1169

1996, Nov. 27
4131 A1169 150 l multicolored .35 .25

Antique Autombiles — A1170

No. 4132: a, 280 l, 1933 Mercedes Benz. b, 70 l, 1930 Ford Spider. c, 150 l, 1932 Citroen. d, 220 l, 1936 Rolls Royce.
No. 4133: a, 2550 l, 1936 Mercedes Benz 500k Roadster. b, 2500 l, 1934 Bugatti "Type 59." c. 2550 l, 1931 Alfa Romeo 8C. d, 120 l, 1937 Jaguar SS 100.

1996, Dec. 19 Photo. Perf. 13½
4132 A1170 Sheet of 4, #a.-d. .80 .40
4133 A1170 Sheet of 4, #a.-d. 7.00 3.50

Souvenir Sheet

Deng Xiaoping, China, and Margaret Thatcher, Great Britain — A1171

1997, Jan. 20　　Photo.　　Perf. 13½
4134　A1171　1500 l multicolored　.75　.75
Hong Kong '97.

Fur-Bearing Animals — A1172

Designs: 70 l, Mustela erminea. 150 l, Alopex lagopus. 220 l, Nyctereutes procyonoides. 740 l, Lutra lutra. 1500 l, Ondatra zibethica. 3500 l, Martes martes.

1997, Feb. 14
4135　A1172　70 l multicolored　.25　.25
4136　A1172　150 l multicolored　.25　.25
4137　A1172　220 l multicolored　.25　.25
4138　A1172　740 l multicolored　.25　.25
4139　A1172　1500 l multicolored　.40　.25
4140　A1172　3500 l multicolored　1.00　.25
　Nos. 4135-4140 (6)　2.40　1.50

For surcharge see No. 4349.

Greenpeace, 25th Anniv. — A1173

Various views of MV Greenpeace.

1997, Mar. 6
4141　A1173　150 l multicolored　.25　.25
4142　A1173　370 l multicolored　.25　.25
4143　A1173　1940 l multicolored　.50　.25
4144　A1173　2500 l multicolored　.75　.25
　Nos. 4141-4144 (4)　1.75　1.00
Souvenir Sheet
4145　A1173　4050 l multicolored　1.50　.85
No. 4145 contains one 49x38mm stamp.

Famous People — A1174

Designs: 200 l, Thomas A. Edison. 400 l, Franz Schubert. 3600 l, Miguel de Cervantes Saavedra (1547-1616), Spanish writer.

1997, Mar. 27　　Photo.　　Perf. 13½
4146　A1174　200 l multicolored　.25　.25
4147　A1174　400 l multicolored　.25　.25
4148　A1174　3600 l multicolored　1.75　.50
　Nos. 4146-4148 (3)　2.25　.75

Inauguration of Mobile Telephone Network in Romania — A1175

1997, Apr. 7　　Photo.　　Perf. 13½
4149　A1175　400 l multicolored　.35　.25

Churches — A1176

1997, Apr. 21　　Photo.　　Perf. 13½
4150　A1176　200 l Surdesti　.25　.25
4151　A1176　400 l Plopis　.25　.25
4152　A1176　450 l Bogdan Voda　.25　.25
4153　A1176　850 l Rogoz　.25　.25
4154　A1176　3600 l Calinesti　.80　.25
4155　A1176　6000 l Birsana　1.50　.30
　Nos. 4150-4155 (6)　3.30　1.55

A1177

Shakespeare Festival, Craiova: a, 400 l, Constantin Serghe (1819-87) as Othello, 1855. b, 200 l, Al. Demetrescu Dan (1870-1948) as Hamlet, 1916. c, 3600 l, Ion Manolescu (1881-1959) as Hamlet, 1924. d, 2400 l, Gheorghe Cozorici (1933-93) as Hamlet, 1957.

1997, Apr. 23　　Photo.　　Perf. 13½
4156　A1177　Sheet of 4, #a.-d. + 4 labels　2.25　1.50

A1178

Europa (Stories and Legends): 400 l, Vlad Tepes (Vlad the Impaler), prince upon whom legend of Dracula said to be based. 4250 l, Dracula.

1997, May 5
4157　A1178　400 l multicolored　.25　.25
4158　A1178　4250 l multicolored　1.90　1.90
　a.　Pair, #4157-4158 + label　2.00　2.00

A1179

Natl. Theater, Cathedral, Statue of Mihai Viteazul.

1997, June 27　　Photo.　　Perf. 13½
4159　A1179　450 l multicolored　.35　.25
Balcanmax '97, Maximum Cards Exhibition, Cluj-Napoca.

Cacti A1180

Designs: 100 l, Dolichothele uberiformis. 250 l, Rebutia. 450 l, Echinofossulocactus lamellosus. 500 l, Ferocactus glaucescens. 650 l, Thelocactus. 6150 l, Echinofossulocactus albatus.

1997, June 27
4160　A1180　100 l multicolored　.25　.25
4161　A1180　250 l multicolored　.25　.25
4162　A1180　450 l multicolored　.25　.25
4163　A1180　500 l multicolored　.25　.25
4164　A1180　650 l multicolored　.25　.25
4165　A1180　6150 l multicolored　2.40　.25
　Nos. 4160-4165 (6)　3.65　1.50

Stamp Day — A1181

1997, July 15　　Photo.　　Perf. 13½
4166　A1181　3600 l + 1500 l label　1.75　.40
Ten different labels exist.

Nos. 3664-3670, 3672 Srchd. in Brnish Purple (#4167-4171, 4174) or Black (#4172-4173)

1997, July 17
4167　A1043　250 l on 1 l #3664　.25　.25
4168　A1043　250 l on 2 l #3665　.25　.25
4169　A1043　250 l on 4 l #3666　.25　.25
4170　A1043　450 l on 5 l #3667　.25　.25
4171　A1043　450 l on 6 l #3668　.25　.25
4172　A1043　450 l on 18 l #3672　.25　.25
4173　A1043　950 l on 9 l #3670　.25　.25
4174　A1043　3600 l on 8 l #3669　.75　.25
　Nos. 4167-4174 (8)　2.50　2.00

Castle Dracula, Sighisoara — A1181a

Designs: 650 l, Clocktower on Town Hall. 3700 l, Steps leading to castle and clocktower.

1997, July 31
4175　A1181a　250 l shown　.25　.25
4175A　A1181a　650 l multi　.25　.25
4175B　A1181a　3700 l multi　1.20　.25
　Nos. 4175-4175B (3)　1.70　.75

A1181b

Tourism Monument, Banat.

1997, Aug. 3
4175C　A1181b　950 l multi　.35　.25

A1181c

1997, Aug. 13
4175D　A1181c　450 l multi　.35　.25
Stamp Printing Works, 125th anniv.

Belgian Antarctic Expedition, Cent. — A1181d

"Belgica" sailing ship and: 450 l, Emil Racovita, biologist. 650 l, Frederick A. Cook, anthropologist, photographer. 1600 l, Roald Amundsen. 3700 l, Adrien de Gerlache, expedition commander.

1997, Aug. 18
4175E　A1181d　450 l multi　.25　.25
4175F　A1181d　650 l multi　.25　.25
4175G　A1181d　1600 l multi　.40　.25
4175H　A1181d　3700 l multi　1.50　.25
　Nos. 4175E-4175H (4)　2.40　1.00

Sports A1182

500 l, Rugby. 700 l, American football, vert. 1750 l, Baseball. 3700 l, Mountain climbing, vert.

1997, Nov. 21　　Photo.　　Perf. 13½
4176　A1182　500 l multi　.25　.25
4177　A1182　700 l multi　.25　.25
4178　A1182　1750 l multi　.45　.25
4179　A1182　3700 l multi　1.40　.30
　Nos. 4176-4179 (4)　2.35　1.05

Romanian Scouts A1183

300 l, Tents at campsite. 700 l, Scouting emblem. 1050 l, Hands reaching toward each other. 1750 l, Carvings. 3700 l, Scouts seated around campfire.

1997, Oct. 25 Photo. Perf. 13½
4180	A1183	300 l multicolored	.25	.25
4181	A1183	700 l multicolored	.25	.25
4182	A1183	1050 l multicolored	.30	.25
4183	A1183	1750 l multicolored	.45	.25
4184	A1183	3700 l multicolored	1.10	.25
a.		Strip of 5, #4180-4184	2.50	1.00

No. 3650 Surcharged in Red

1997, Sept. 27
4185	A1039	1050 l on 4.50 l	.60	.25

No. 3619 Surcharged in Red

1997, Oct. 28 Photo. Perf. 13½
4186	A1032	500 l on 2 l multi	.25	.25

Ion Mihalache (1882-1963), Politician — A1184

Design: 1050 l, King Carol I (1866-1914).

1997, Nov. 8
4187	A1184	500 l multi	.25	.25
4188	A1184	1050 l pink & multi	.35	.30

King Carol I Type of 1997
Designs: Nos. 4188A-4188C, King Carol I.

1997, Nov. 8 Litho. Perf. 13½
4188A	A1184	1050 l blue & multi	.35	.35
4188B	A1184	1050 l clar & multi	.35	.35
4188C	A1184	1050 l blk & multi	.35	.35

No. 4188 is pink & multi.

Chamber of Commerce and Industry, Bucharest, 130th Anniv. — A1185

1998, Jan. 29 Photo. Perf. 13½
4189	A1185	700 l multicolored	.35	.25

No. 4189 is printed se-tenant with label.

1998 Winter Olympic Games, Nagano A1186

1998, Feb. 5
4190	A1186	900 l Skiing	.30	.25
4191	A1186	3900 l Figure skating	1.25	.65

Souvenir Sheet

Flag Day — A1187

„Emotion de tous es drapeaux Chaque nation dans sa verité et dans sa justice" (J. Michelet).

1998, Feb. 24 Photo. Perf. 13½
4192	A1187	900 l multicolored	.60	.25

National Festivals and Holidays — A1188

1998, Feb. 26 Photo. Perf. 13x13½
4193	A1188	900 l 4-Leaf clover	.80	1.00
4194	A1188	3900 l Heart	17.50	22.50

Europa.

Famous People and Events of the 20th Century A1189

Designs: 700 l, Alfred Nobel, creation of Nobel Foundation, 1901. 900 l, Guglielmo Marconi, first radio transmission across Atlantic, 1901. 1500 l, Albert Einstein, theory of relativity, 1905. 3900 l, Trajan Vuia, flying machine, 1906.

1998, Mar. 31 Photo. Perf. 13½
4195	A1189	700 l multicolored	.40	.25
4196	A1189	900 l multicolored	.40	.25
4197	A1189	1500 l multicolored	.50	.25
4198	A1189	3900 l multicolored	1.40	.40
		Nos. 4195-4198 (4)	2.70	1.15

See Nos. 4261-4265, 4312-4319, 4380-4383.

Roadside Shrines — A1190

1998, Apr. 17
4199	A1190	700 l Cluj	.25	.25
4200	A1190	900 l Prahova	.25	.25
4201	A1190	1500 l Arges	.50	.25
		Nos. 4199-4201 (3)	1.00	.75

No. 4081 Surcharged in Red

Designs: a, 900 l on 370 l. b, 700 l on 150 l, c, 3900 l on 1500 l.

1998, May 12
4202	A1153	Sheet of 3, #a.-c.	2.50	1.25

Surcharge on #4202a, 4202c does not include '98 show emblem. This appears in the selvage to the right and left of the stamps.

Romanian Surgical Society, Cent. — A1191

Thoma Ionescu (1860-1926), founder.

1998, May 18
4203	A1191	1050 l multicolored	.50	.25

Nos. 3665-3669, 3672, 3676 Surcharged in Black, Red, Bright Green, Violet, Red Violet, Orange Brown, Dark Green, Violet Brown or Deep Blue

1998 Photo. Perf. 13½
4204	A1043	50 l on 2 l #3665 (R)	.25	.25
4205	A1043	100 l on 8 l #3669 (BG)	.25	.25
4206	A1043	200 l on 4 l #3666	.25	.25
4207	A1043	250 l on 45 l #3676 (Bl)	.25	.25
4208	A1043	350 l on 45 l #3676	.25	.25
4209	A1043	400 l on 6 l #3668 (V)	.25	.25
4210	A1043	400 l on 45 l #3676 (BG)	.25	.25
4211	A1043	450 l on 45l #3676 (RV)	.25	.25
4212	A1043	500 l on 18 l #3672 (Bl)	.25	.25
4213	A1043	850 l on 45 l #3676 (OB)	.75	.35
4214	A1043	900 l on 45 l #3676 (V)	.75	.35
4215	A1043	1000 l on 45 l #3676 (DkG)	.75	.35
4216	A1043	1000 l on 9 l #3670	.40	.40
4217	A1043	1500 l on 5 l #3667 (R)	.40	.40
4218	A1043	1600 l on 45 l #3676 (VB)	1.75	.40
4219	A1043	2500 l on 45 l #3676 (R)	3.00	.75
		Nos. 4204-4219 (16)	10.05	5.25

Obliterator varies on Nos. 4204-4219.
Issued: Nos. 4204-4206, 4209, 4212, 5/21; Nos. 4216-4217, 7/6; others, 1998.

1998 World Cup Soccer Championships, France — A1192

Various soccer plays, stadium: a, 800 l. b, 1050 l. c, 1850 l. d, 4150 l.

1998, June 10 Photo. Perf. 13½
4220	A1192	Sheet of 4, #a.-d.	2.25	1.10

Nos. 3913-3915, 3918 Surcharged in Red Violet, Blue, Black, or Red

Wmk. 398
1998, June 30 Photo. Perf. 13
Design A1105
4221	700 l on 125 l #3918 (RV)	.25	.25
4222	800 l on 35 l #3914 (Bl)	.25	.25
4223	1050 l on 45 l #3915 (Blk)	.35	.25
4224	4150 l on 15 l #3913 (R)	1.25	.65
	Nos. 4221-4224 (4)	2.10	1.40

Night Birds A1193

Designs: 700 l, Apteryx australis, vert. 1500 l, Tyto alba, vert. 1850 l, Rallus aquaticus. 2450 l, Caprimulgus europaeus.

1998, Aug. 12 Unwmk.
4225	A1193	700 l multicolored	.30	.30
4226	A1193	1500 l multicolored	.30	.30
a.		Complete booklet, 4 each, #4225-4226	3.00	
4227	A1193	1850 l multicolored	.30	.30
4228	A1193	2450 l multicolored	1.10	1.10
a.		Complete booklet, 4 each, #4227-4228	5.75	
		Nos. 4225-4228 (4)	2.00	2.00

Stamp Day A1194

1998, July Litho. Perf. 13½
4229	A1194	700 l Romania #4	.25	.25
4230	A1194	1050 l multicolored Romania #1	.35	.25
a.		Complete booklet, #4225, 4 #4226	3.50	

Souvenir Sheet
4231	A1194	4150 l +850 l Romania #2-3	1.60	.80

No. 4231 contains one 54x42mm stamp.

Natl. Uprising, 150th Anniv. — A1195

1998, Sept. 28 Photo. Perf. 13½
4232	A1195	1050 l multicolored	.35	.25

A1196

German Personalities in Banat: 800 l, Niko-
laus Lenau (1802-50). 1850 l, Stefan Jäger
(1877-1962). 4150 l, Adam Müller-Gutten-
brunn (1852-1923).

1998, Oct. 16
4233	A1196	800 l multicolored	.25	.25
4234	A1196	1850 l multicolored	.50	.25
4235	A1196	4150 l multicolored	1.00	.50
	Nos. 4233-4235 (3)		1.75	1.00

A1197

1998, Nov. 4   Photo.   Perf. 13½
4236	A1197	1100 l multicolored	.40	.25

Intl. Year of the Ocean.

Nos. 3652-3653,
3704-3709, 3776-
3779, 3781, 3795,
3968 Srchd. in
Green, Black, Red,
Red Violet or Deep
Blue

1998   Photo.   Perf. 13½
4237	A1041	50 l on #3652 (G)	.25	.25
4238	A1041	50 l on #3653 (Blk)	.25	.25
4238A	A1054	50 l on 1 l #3704 (Blk)	.25	.25
4239	A1054	50 l on #3705 (R)	.90	.25
4240	A1054	50 l on #3706 (R)	.25	.25
4241	A1054	50 l on #3707 (Blk)	.25	.25
4242	A1054	50 l on #3708 (Blk)	.25	.25
4243	A1054	50 l on #3709 (R)	.25	.25
4244	A1054	50 l on #3776 (RV)	.25	.25
4245	A1054	50 l on #3777 (DB)	.25	.25
4246	A1054	50 l on #3778 (Blk)	.25	.25
4247	A1054	50 l on #3779 (G)	.25	.25
4248	A1054	50 l on #3781 (R)	.25	.25
4249	A1075	2000 l on #3795 (G)	.80	.50
4250	A1117	2600 l on #3968 (R)	.80	.50
	Nos. 4237-4250 (15)		5.50	4.25

Obliterator varies on Nos. 4237-4250.
Issued: 4237-4238, 11/10; 4238A, 11/27;
4249-4250, 12/22.

A1198

Lighthouses.

1998, Dec. 28
4251	A1198	900 l Genovez	.25	.25
4252	A1198	1000 l Constanta	.30	.25
4253	A1198	1100 l Sfantu Ghe-orghe	.35	.25
4254	A1198	2600 l Sulina	1.00	.40
	Nos. 4251-4254 (4)		1.90	1.15

A1199

Flowers: 350 l, Tulipa gesneriana. 850 l,
Dahlia variabilis. 1100 l, Lillium martagon.
4450 l, Rosa centifolia.

1998, Nov. 25
4255	A1199	350 l multicolored	.25	.25
4256	A1199	850 l multicolored	.30	.25
4257	A1199	1100 l multicolored	.30	.25
4258	A1199	4450 l multicolored	1.00	.65
	Nos. 4255-4258 (4)		1.85	1.40

Universal
Declaration of
Human Rights,
50th
Anniv. — A1200

1998, Dec. 10
4259	A1200	700 l multicolored	.35	.25

Dimitrie Paciurea (1873-1932),
Sculptor — A1200a

1998, Dec. 11   Photo.   Perf. 13¼
4259A	A1200a	850 l ocher & blk	.40	.25

Total Eclipse of the Sun, Aug. 11,
1999 — A1201

1998, Dec. 17
4260	A1201	1100 l multi + label	.35	.25

Events of the 20th Cent. Type

Designs: 350 l, Sinking of the Titanic, 1912.
1100 l, "Coanda 1910" aircraft with air-reactive
(jet) engine, 1919, by Henri Coanda (1886-
1972). 1600 l, Louis Blériot's (1872-1936) Cal-
ais-Dover flight, 1909. 2000 l, Opening of the
Panama Canal, 1914. 2600 l, Russian Revolution, 1917.

1998, Dec. 22   Photo.   Perf. 13½
4261	A1189	350 l multicolored	.25	.25
4262	A1189	1100 l multicolored	.30	.25
4263	A1189	1600 l multicolored	.30	.25
4264	A1189	2000 l multicolored	.30	.30
4265	A1189	2600 l multicolored	.75	.40
	Nos. 4261-4265 (5)		1.90	1.45

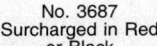

No. 3687
Surcharged in Red
or Black

1999, Feb. 10   Photo.   Perf. 13½
4266	A1047	100 l on 1 l (R)	.30	.25
4267	A1047	250 l on 1 l (Blk)	.30	.25

Obliterator is a guitar on #4266 and a saxophone on #4267.

No. 3796
Surcharged in
Black, Red,
Green, or
Brown

1999, Jan. 22
4268	A1076	50 l on 15 l (Blk)	.25	.25
4269	A1076	50 l on 15 l (R)	.25	.25
4270	A1076	400 l on 15 l (Grn)	.25	.25
4271	A1076	2300 l on 15 l (Brn)	.50	.35
4272	A1076	3200 l on 15 l (Blk)	1.00	.50
	Nos. 4268-4272 (5)		2.25	1.60

Obliterator varies on Nos. 4268-4272.

Monasteries — A1203

1999, Jan. 17
4273	A1203	500 l Arnota	.25	.25
4274	A1203	700 l Bistrita	.25	.25
4275	A1203	1100 l Dintr'un Lemn	.25	.25
4276	A1203	2100 l Govora	.50	.30
4277	A1203	4850 l Tismana	1.40	.70
	Nos. 4273-4277 (5)		2.65	1.75

Shrub
Flowers
A1204

350 l, Magnolia x soulangiana. 1000 l,
Stewartia malacodendron. 1100 l, Hibiscus
rosa-sinensis. 5350 l, Clematis patens.

1999, Feb. 15
4278	A1204	350 l multicolored	.25	.25
4279	A1204	1000 l multicolored	.25	.25
4280	A1204	1100 l multicolored	.25	.25
4281	A1204	5350 l multicolored	1.50	.75
	Nos. 4278-4281 (4)		2.25	1.50

Easter
A1205

1999, Mar. 15   Photo.   Perf. 13¼
4282	A1205	1100 l multi	.35	.25

**No. 4082 Surcharged in Bright Pink,
Red, Violet, Black, Green or Blue**

1999, Mar. 22   Litho.   Perf. 13½
4283	A1154	100 l on 70 l (BP)	.25	.25
4284	A1154	100 l on 70 l (R)	.25	.25
4285	A1154	200 l on 70 l (V)	.25	.25
4286	A1154	1500 l on 70 l	.50	.25
4287	A1154	1600 l on 70 l (G)	.50	.25
4288	A1154	3200 l on 70 l (Bl)	1.10	.45
4289	A1154	6000 l on 70 l (G)	1.90	.90
	Nos. 4283-4289 (7)		4.75	2.60

Obliterators on Nos. 4283-4289 are various
dinosaurs.

Jewelry — A1206

Designs: 1200 l, Keys on chain. 2100 l, Key
holder. 2600 l, Necklace. 3200 l, Necklace,
horiz.

1999, Mar. 29   Photo.   Perf. 13¼
4290-4293	A1206	Set of 4	1.75	.90

Birds — A1207

Perf. 13½x13¼
1999, Apr. 26   Photo.
4294	A1207	1100 l Ara macao	.30	.25
4295	A1207	2700 l Pavo albus	.60	.35
4296	A1207	3700 l Pavo cristatus	.80	.45
4297	A1207	5700 l Cacatua galerita	1.25	.65
	Nos. 4294-4297 (4)		2.95	1.70

Council of Europe, 50th
Anniv. — A1208

1999, May 5   Photo.   Perf. 13¼
4298	A1208	2300 l multi + label	.60	.35

A1209

Visit of Pope John Paul II to Romania: a,
6300 l, Pope John Paul II. b, 1300 l, St. Peter's
Basilica. c, 1600 l, Patriarchal Cathedral,
Bucharest. d, 2300 l, Patriarch Teoctist.

1999, May 7
4299	A1209	Sheet of 6, #a.-d.	2.50	1.90

Issued in sheets containing one strip of
#4299a-4299d, 1 ea #4299a, 4299d + 2
labels.

A1210

Europa: 1100 l, Anas clypeata. 5700 l, Ciconia nigra.

1999, May 17
4300	A1210	1100 l multicolored	.25	.25
4301	A1210	5700 l multicolored	1.50	1.25

Nos. 4300-4301 printed with se-tenant label.

Famous Personalities — A1211

Designs: 600 l, Gheorghe Cartan (1849-1911). 1100 l, George Calinescu (1899-1965), writer. 2600 l, Johann Wolfgang von Goethe (1749-1832), poet. 7300 l, Honoré de Balzac (1799-1850), novelist.

1999, May 31
4302	A1211	600 l multicolored	.25	.25
4303	A1211	1100 l multicolored	.25	.25
4304	A1211	2600 l multicolored	.40	.25
4305	A1211	7300 l multicolored	1.50	.75
		Nos. 4302-4305 (4)	2.40	1.50

Total Solar Eclipse, Aug. 11 — A1212

1999, June 21   Photo.   Perf. 13¼
4306	A1212	1100 l multicolored	.50	.25

No. 4306 printed se-tenant with label.

Health Dangers A1213

1999, July 29   Photo.   Perf. 13¼
4307	A1213	400 l Smoking	.25	.25
4308	A1213	800 l Alcohol	.25	.25
4309	A1213	1300 l Drugs	.25	.25
4310	A1213	2500 l AIDS	.50	.25
		Nos. 4307-4310 (4)	1.25	1.00

Luciano Pavarotti Concert in Bucharest on Day of Solar Eclipse — A1214

1999, Aug. 9
4311	A1214	8100 l multi	1.60	.80

Events of the 20th Century Type

Designs: 800 l, Alexander Fleming discovers penicillin, 1928. 3000 l, League of Nations, 1920. 7300 l, Harold C. Urey discovers heavy water, 1931. 17,000 l, First marine oil drilling platform, off Beaumont, Texas, 1934.

1999, Aug. 30
4312	A1189	800 l multi	.25	.25
4313	A1189	3000 l multi	.50	.40
4314	A1189	7300 l multi	1.25	.85
4315	A1189	17,000 l multi	3.50	1.90
		Nos. 4312-4315 (4)	5.50	3.40

1999, Sept. 24   Photo.   Perf. 13¼

1500 l, Karl Landsteiner (1868-1943), discoverer of blood groups. 3000 l, Nicolae C. Paulescu (1869-1931), diabetes researcher. 7300 l, Otto Hahn (1879-1968), discoverer of nuclear fission. 17,000 l, Ernst Ruska (1906-88), inventor of electron microscope.

4316	A1189	1500 l multi	.30	.25
4317	A1189	3000 l multi	.55	.30
4318	A1189	7300 l multi	1.40	.70
4319	A1189	17,000 l multi	3.25	1.60
		Nos. 4316-4319 (4)	5.50	2.85

UPU, 125th Anniv. — A1215

1999, Oct. 9
4320	A1215	3100 l multi	.70	.35

Comic Actors — A1216

Designs: 900 l, Grigore Vasiliu Birlic. 1500 l, Toma Caragiu. 3100 l, Constantin Tanase. 7950 l, Charlie Chaplin. 8850 l, Oliver Hardy and Stan Laurel, horiz.

1999, Oct. 21
4321	A1216	900 l blk & brn red	.25	.25
4322	A1216	1500 l blk & brn red	.25	.25
4323	A1216	3100 l blk & brn red	.40	.35
4324	A1216	7950 l blk & brn red	1.20	.95
4325	A1216	8850 l blk & brn red	1.60	1.00
		Nos. 4321-4325 (5)	3.70	2.80

Stavropoleos Church, 275th Anniv. — A1217

1999, Oct. 29
4326	A1217	2100 l multi	.50	.25

New Olympic Sports A1218

1999, Nov. 10
4327	A1218	1600 l Snowboarding	.25	.25
4328	A1218	1700 l Softball	.35	.25
4329	A1218	7950 l Taekwondo	1.40	.70
		Nos. 4327-4329 (3)	2.00	1.20

Christmas — A1219

Designs: 1500 l, Christmas tree, bell. 3100 l, Santa Claus.

1999, Nov. 29   Photo.   Perf. 13¼
4330-4331	A1219	Set of 2	.80	.40

UN Rights of the Child Convention, 10th Anniv. — A1220

Children's art by: 900 l, A. Vieriu. 3400 l, A. M. Bulete, vert. 8850 l, M. L. Rogojeanu.

1999, Nov. 30   Photo.   Perf. 13¼
4332	A1220	900 l multi	.25	.25
4333	A1220	3400 l multi	.60	.30
4334	A1220	8850 l multi	1.50	.75
		Nos. 4332-4334 (3)	2.35	1.30

Princess Diana — A1221

1999, Dec. 2
4335	A1221	6000 l multi	1.00	.60

Issued in sheets of 4. For surcharge, see No. 5992.

Ferrari Automobiles — A1222

Designs: 1500 l, 1968 365 GTB/4. 1600 l, 1970 Dino 246 GT. 1700 l, 1973 365 GT/4 BB. 7950 l, Mondial 3.2. 8850 l, 1994 F 355. 14,500 l, 1998 456M GT.

1999, Dec. 17
4336	A1222	1500 l multi	.25	.25
4337	A1222	1600 l multi	.30	.25
4338	A1222	1700 l multi	.30	.25
4339	A1222	7950 l multi	1.40	.70
4340	A1222	8850 l multi	1.50	.75
4341	A1222	14,500 l multi	2.50	1.25
		Nos. 4336-4341 (6)	6.25	3.45

Romanian Revolution, 10th Anniv. — A1223

1999, Dec. 21   Perf. 13¼
4342	A1223	2100 l multi	.50	.25

Start of Accession Negotiations With European Union — A1224

2000, Jan. 13   Photo.   Perf. 13¼
4343	A1224	6100 l multi	1.00	.50

Souvenir Sheet

Mihail Eminescu (1850-89), Poet — A1225

Scenes from poems and Eminescu: a, At R, clean-shaven. b, At R, with mustache. c, At L, with trimmed mustache. d, At L, with handlebar mustache.

2000, Jan. 15
4344	A1225	Sheet of 4	4.75	1.10
a.-d.		3400 l Any single	.55	.25

Valentine's Day — A1226

2000, Feb. 1   Photo.   Perf. 13¼
4345	A1226	1500 l Cupid	.25	.25
4346	A1226	7950 l Couple kissing	1.25	.65

Easter — A1227

2000, Feb. 29
4347	A1227	1700 l multi	.35	.25

Nos. 4121, 4135 Surcharged in Red

Methods and Perfs. as Before

2000
4348	A1167	1700 l on 70 l multi	.35	.25
4349	A1172	1700 l on 70 l multi	.35	.25

Issued: No. 4348, 3/14; No. 4349, 3/13. Obliterator on No. 4349 is a crown.

Birds
A1228

Designs: 1700 l, Paradisaea apoda. 2400 l,
Diphyllodes magnificus. 9050 l, Lophorina
superba. 10,050 l, Cicinnurus regius.

2000, Mar. 20　Photo.　Perf. 13¼

4350	A1228	1700 l	multi	.25	.25
4351	A1228	2400 l	multi	.35	.25
4352	A1228	9050 l	multi	1.40	.70
4353	A1228	10,050 l	multi	1.50	.75
	Nos. 4350-4353 (4)			3.50	1.95

Nos. 3658-
3659
Surcharged in
Red

Methods & Perfs. as Before
2000, Mar. 31

4354	A1042	1900 l on 1 l		.30	.25
		(#3658)			
4355	A1042	2000 l on 1 l		.30	.25
		(#3659)			

Nos. 3626-
3630
Surcharged

Methods & Perfs. as Before
2000, Apr. 12

4356	A1034	1700 l on 50b	.30	.30
4357	A1034	1700 l on 1.50 l	.30	.30
4358	A1034	1700 l on 2 l	.30	.30
4359	A1034	1700 l on 3 l	.30	.30
4360	A1034	1700 l on 4 l	.30	.30
	Nos. 4356-4360 (5)		1.50	1.50

Appearance of obliterator varies.

Flowers — A1229

Designs: 1700 l, Senecio cruentus. 3100 l,
Clivia miniata. 5800 l, Plumeria rubra.
10,050 l, Fuchsia hybrida.

2000, Apr. 20　Photo.　Perf. 13¼

4361	A1229	1700 l	multi	.25	.25
4362	A1229	3100 l	multi	.40	.25
4363	A1229	5800 l	multi	.80	.40
4364	A1229	10,050 l	multi	1.40	.70
	Nos. 4361-4364 (4)			2.85	1.60

Nos. 3620-3624 Surcharged

Methods & Perfs. as Before
2000, Apr. 24

4365	A1033	1700 l on 50b	.30	.30
4366	A1033	1700 l on 1.50 l	.30	.30
4367	A1033	1700 l on 2 l	.30	.30
4368	A1033	1700 l on 3 l	.30	.30
4369	A1033	1700 l on 4 l	.30	.30
	Nos. 4365-4369 (5)		1.50	1.50

Europa Issue
Common Design Type

2000, May 9　Photo.　Perf. 13¼

4370	CD17	10,150 l	multi	2.50	1.25

Nos. 3634, 3637 Surcharged in Red

Methods and Perfs as Before
2000, May 17

4371	A1036	1700 l on 50b	.40	.25
4372	A1036	1700 l on 3.50 l	.40	.25

Unification of Walachia, Transylvania
and Moldavia by Michael the Brave,
400th Anniv. — A1230

2000, May 19　Photo.　Perf. 13¼

4373	A1230	3800 l	multi	.50	.25

Printing of Bible in Latin by Johann
Gutenberg, 550th Anniv. — A1231

2000, May 19

4374	A1231	9050 l	multi	1.25	.60

No. 4084 Surcharged in Red

2000, May 31　Photo.　Perf. 13¼

4375	A1154	10,000 l on 370 l	1.40	.70
4376	A1154	19,000 l on 370 l	2.50	1.25
4377	A1154	34,000 l on 370 l	4.75	2.40
	Nos. 4375-4377 (3)		8.65	4.35

Souvenir Sheet

2000 European Soccer
Championships — A1232

No. 4378: a, 3800 l, Romania vs. Portugal
(red and green flag). b, 3800 l, England (red
and white flag) vs. Romania. c, 10,150 l,
Romania vs. Germany. d, 10,150 l, Goalie.

2000, June 20

4378	A1232	Sheet of 4, #a-d	3.75	1.90

First
Zeppelin
Flight,
Cent.
A1233

2000, July 12

4379	A1233	2100 l	multi	.35	.25
		Stamp Day.			

20th Century Type of 1998

2100 l, Enrico Fermi, formula, 1st nuclear
reactor, 1942. 2200 l, Signing of UN Charter,
1945. 2400 l, Edith Piaf sings "La Vie en
Rose," 1947. 6000 l, 1st ascent of Mt. Everest,
by Sir Edmund Hillary and Tenzing Norgay,
1953.

2000, July 12

4380-4383	A1189	Set of 4	1.60	.80

No. 3680
Surcharged
in Green

Methods and Perfs as Before
2000, July 31

4384	A1044	1700 l on 160 l	.30	.25

20th Century Type of 1998

Designs: 1700 l, First artificial satellite,
1957. 3900 l, Yuri Gagarin, first man in space,
1961. 6400 l, First heart transplant perfromed
by Christiaan Barnard, 1967. 11,300 l, Neil
Armstrong, first man on the moon, 1969.

2000, Aug. 28　Photo.　Perf. 13¼

4385-4388	A1189	Set of 4	3.50	1.75

2000
Summer
Olympics,
Sydney
A1234

Designs: 1700 l, Boxing. 2200 l, High jump.
3900 l, Weight lifting. 6200 l, Gymnastics.

2000, Sept. 7

4389-4392	A1234	Set of 4	2.25	1.00

Souvenir Sheet

4393	A1234	11,300 l	Runner	1.40	.70

No. 4393 contains one 42x54mm stamp.

Souvenir Sheet

Olymphilex 2000, Sydney — A1235

2000, Sept. 7　　Imperf.

4394	A1235	14,100 l	Gabriela Szabo	2.40	.85

Bucharest
Palaces
A1236

Designs: 1700 l, Agricultural Ministry Palace. 2200 l, Cantacuzino Palace. 2400 l,
Grigore Ghica Palace. 3900 l, Stirbei Palace.

2000, Sept. 29　　Perf. 13¼

4395-4398	A1236	Set of 4	1.60	.80

No. 4115 Surcharged in Brown

2000, Oct. 11　Photo.　Perf. 13½

4403	A1166	300 l on 70 l	multi	.25	.25

No. 3664 Surcharged in Blue

2000, Oct. 26　　Perf. 13½

4404	A1043	300 l on 1 l	blue	.35	.25

No. 3991 Surcharged in Red Violet

2000, Nov. 3　　Perf. 13½

4405	A1127	2000 l on 90 l	multi	.35	.25

European Human
Rights Convention,
50th
Anniv. — A1237

2000, Nov. 3   *Perf. 13¼*
4406 A1237 11,300 l multi   2.25 2.25

No. 3858
Surcharged

2000, Nov. 28   *Perf. 13½*
4407 A1093 2000 l on 29 l multi   .60 .25

Endangered Wild Cats — A1238

Designs: 1200 l, Panthera pardus. 2000 l,
Panthera uncia. 2200 l, Panthera leo. 2300 l,
Lynx rufus. 4200 l, Puma concolor. 6500 l,
Panthera tigris.
14,100 l, Panthera leo.

2000, Nov. 29   **Photo.**   *Perf. 13½*
4408 A1238   1200 l multi   .25 .25
4409 A1238   2000 l multi   .25 .25
4410 A1238   2200 l multi   .25 .25
4411 A1238   2300 l multi   .25 .25
4412 A1238   4200 l multi   .40 .25
4413 A1238   6500 l multi   1.20 .25
   Nos. 4408-4413 (6)   2.60 1.50

Souvenir Sheet
4414 A1238 14,100 l multi   2.00 .60
No. 4414 contains one 54x42mm stamp.

Self-portraits
A1239

Designs: 2000 l, Camil Ressu (1880-1962),
2400 l, Jean A. Steriadi (1880-1956). 4400 l,
Nicolae Tonitza (1886-1940). 15,000 l, Nicolae Grigorescu (1838-1907).

2000   **Photo.**   *Perf. 13½*
4415 A1239   2000 l multi   .25 .25
4416 A1239   2400 l multi   .25 .25
4417 A1239   4400 l multi   .40 .25
4418 A1239 15,000 l multi   2.00 .75
   Nos. 4415-4418 (4)   2.90 1.50

Issued: 2000 l, 12/8; others, 12/13.

Christmas — A1240

2000, Dec. 15   **Photo.**   *Perf. 13½*
4419 A1240 4400 l multi   .35 .25

Christianity,
2000th
Anniv. — A1241

Stained glass windows: 2000 l, Resurrection
of Jesus. 7000 l, Holy Trinity (22x38mm).

2000, Dec. 22   **Photo.**   *Perf. 13¼*
4420-4421 A1241   Set of 2   1.10 .40

No. 3922
Surcharged in Red
Brown

Wmk. 398
2000, Dec. 28   **Photo.**   *Perf. 13¼*
4422 A1105   7000 l on 3095 l
     multi   1.10 .30
4423 A1105 10,000 l on 3095 l
     multi   .75 .45
4424 A1105 11,500 l on 3095 l
     multi   1.10 .55
   Nos. 4422-4424 (3)   2.95 1.30
Obliterator on No. 4423 is a bear and on No.
4424 a bison.

Advent of the Third
Millennium — A1242

Perf. 13½
2001, Jan. 19   **Photo.**   **Unwmk.**
4425 A1242 11,500 l multi   1.90 .60

Sculptures by Constantin Brancusi
(1876-1957) — A1243

No. 4426: a, 4600 l, b, 7200 l.

2001, Feb. 2
4426 A1243   Horiz. pair, #a-b   1.50 .55

Methods and Perfs as Before
2001, Feb. 9
4427 A1087   7400 l on 280 l
     multi   .75 .35
4428 A1087 13,000 l on 280 l
     multi (R)   1.25 .60
Obliterator on No. 4428 is snake on branch.

Valentine's Day — A1244

Designs: 2200 l, Heart of rope. 11,500 l,
Rope running through heart.

2001, Feb. 15   **Photo.**   *Perf. 13½*
4429-4430 A1244   Set of 2   1.50 .75

Nos. 3894,
3895, 3897
Surcharged in
Brown or Green

Methods and Perfs as Before
2001, Feb. 21
4431 A1101   1300 l on 245 l   .25 .25
4432 A1101   2200 l on 115 l   .25 .25
4433 A1101   5000 l on 115 l (G)   .50 .25
4434 A1101 16,500 l on 70 l   2.00 .75
   Nos. 4431-4434 (4)   3.00 1.50
Appearance of obliterators differ. Obliterators on Nos 4432-4433 are ears of corn.

Famous
People
A1245

Designs: 1300 l, Hortensia Papadat-
Bengescu (1876-1955), writer. 2200 l, Eugen
Lovinescu (1881-1943), writer. 2400 l, Ion
Minulescu (1881-1944), writer. 4600 l, André
Malraux (1901-76), writer. 7200 l, George H.
Gallup (1901-84), pollster. 35,000 l, Walt Dis-
ney (1901-66), film producer.

2001   **Photo.**   *Perf. 13¼*
4435-4440 A1245   Set of 6   8.00 3.00
Issued: 2200 l, 4600 l, 7200 l, 3/9; others
3/15.

Easter — A1246

2001, Mar. 23
4441 A1246 2200 l multi   .35 .25

Fruit — A1247

Designs: 2200 l, Prunus spinosa. 4600 l,
Ribes rubrum. 7400 l, Ribes uva-crispa.
11,500 l, Vaccinium vitis-idaea.

2001, Apr. 12
4442-4445 A1247   Set of 4   3.00 1.25

Gheorge Hagi,
Soccer
Player — A1248

Designs: 2200 l, Wearing uniform. 35,000 l,
Wearing team jacket.

2001, Apr. 23   *Perf. 13¼*
4446 A1248   2200 l multi   .50 .25
Souvenir Sheet
Imperf
Without Gum
4447 A1248 35,000 l multi   4.75 1.40
No. 4447 is airmail and contains one
43x28mm stamp.

Europa — A1249

2001, May 4   *Perf. 13¼*
4448 A1249 13,000 l multi   1.75 .85

Dogs
A1250

Designs: 1300 l, Collie. 5000 l, Basset
hound. 8000 l, Siberian husky. 13,500 l,
Sheepdog.

2001, June 16
4449-4452 A1250   Set of 4   2.75 1.40

Romanian
Presidency of
Organization for
Security and
Cooperation in
Europe — A1251

2001, July 6
4453 A1251 11,500 l multi   1.25 .45

Millennium — A1252

Events of the 20th Century: 1300 l, Mariner 9, 1971. 1500 l, Telephone pioneer Augustin Maior and circuit diagram, 1906. 2400 l, Discovery of cave drawings in Ardeche, France, 1994. 5000 l, First Olympic perfect score of gymnast Nadia Comaneci, 1976. 5300 l, Pioneer 10, 1972. 8000 l, Fall of the Iron Curtain, 1989. 13,500 l, First microprocessor, 1971. 15,500 l, Hubble Space Telescope, 1990.

2001
4454-4461 A1252 Set of 8 5.50 2.75
Issued: 1300 l, 2400 l, 5000 l, 8000 l, 7/13; others, 9/25.

UN High Commissioner for Refugees, 50th Anniv. — A1253

2001, July 26
4462 A1253 13,500 l multi 1.50 .60

Nos. 3688, 3713, 3790, 3791, 3865, 3870, 3900, 3907, 3972, 4007, 4017, 4025, 4057, 4058, and 4060 Surcharged in Black, Red, Green or Blue

2001 Photo. Perf. 13½
4463 A1048 300 l on 4 l #3688	.40	.25
4464 A1058 300 l on 4 l #3713 (R)	.40	.25
4465 A1073 300 l on 7 l #3790 (R)	.40	.25
4466 A1073 300 l on 9 l #3791 (R)	.40	.25
4467 A1102 300 l on 90 l #3900	.40	.25
4468 A1121 300 l on 90 l #3972 (G)	.40	.25
4469 A1132 300 l on 90 l #4007	.40	.25
4470 A1130 300 l on 90 l #4017	.40	.25
4471 A1137 300 l on 90 l #4025 (G)	.40	.25
4472 A1095 300 l on 115 l #3865 (R)	.40	.25
4473 A1096 300 l on 115 l #3870 (R)	.40	.25
4474 A1103 300 l on 115 l #3907 (R)	.40	.25
4475 A1131 2500 l on 715 l #4057 (R)	.40	.25
4476 A1131 2500 l on 755 l #4058 (Bl)	.40	.25
4477 A1131 2500 l on 1615 l #4060	.40	.25
Nos. 4463-4477 (15)	6.00	3.75

Numbers have been reserved for additional surcharges. Design and location of obliterators and new value varies.
Issued: No. 4472, 8/20; No. 4473, 8/24; Nos. 4467, 4469, 8/28; No. 4470, 8/29; Nos. 4463, 4464, 4465, 4466, Nos. 4468, 4471, 4474-4477, 8/31.

Equestrian Sports A1254

Designs: 1500 l, Harness racing. 2500 l, Dressage. 5300 l, Steeplechase. 8300 l, Racing.

2001, Aug. 21 Photo. Perf. 13¼
4478-4481 A1254 Set of 4 2.00 1.00

No. 3883 Surcharged

2001, Aug. 29 Photo. Perf. 13½
4482 A1099 300 l on 115 l multi .25 .25

Souvenir Sheets

Corals and Anemones — A1255

No. 4483: a, 2500 l, Porites porites. b, 8300 l, Condylactis gigantea. c, 13,500 l, Anemonia telia. 37,500 l, Gorgonia ventalina.
No. 4484: a, 9000 l, Corallium rubrum. b, 9000 l, Acropora palmata. c, 16,500 l, Actinia equina. d, 16,500 l, Metridium senile.

2001-02 Sheets of 4, #a-d
4483-4484 A1255 Set of 2 10.50 5.25
Issued: No. 4483, 9/27/01; No. 4484, 1/30/02.

Year of Dialogue Among Civilizations A1256

2001, Oct. 9
4485 A1256 8300 l multi .80 .40

Comic Strip A1257

No. 4486: a, Cat, bear, king. b, Fox with drum, cat. c, Fox plays drum for king. d, Cat gives drum to fox. e, Fox, exploding drum.

2001, Oct. 31
4486 Horiz. strip of 5 7.00 3.50
a.-e. A1257 13,500 l Any single 1.40 .70

Christmas A1258

No. 4487: a, Ribbon extending from wreath. b, No ribbon extending from wreath.

2001, Nov. 5
4487 A1258 2500 l Pair, #a-b .35 .25
Booklet, 5 #4487 2.00

Zodiac Signs A1259

Designs: No. 4488, 1500 l, Scorpio. No. 4489, 1500 l, Aries. No. 4490, 2500 l, Libra. No. 4491, 2500 l, Taurus. No. 4492, 5500 l, Capricorn. No. 4493, 5500 l, Gemini. 8700 l, Cancer. No. 4495, 9000 l, Pisces. No. 4496, 9000 l, Leo. 13,500 l, Aquarius. 16,500 l, Sagittarius. 23,500 l, Virgo.

2001-02
4488-4499 A1259 Set of 12 10.00 5.00
Issued: Nos. 4488, 4490, 4492, 4495, 4497, 4498, 11/23/01; others 1/4/02.

Bucharest Post Office, Cent. — A1260

No. 4500: a, Building. b, Medal.

2001, Dec. 18 Photo. Perf. 13¼
4500 A1260 5500 l Horiz. pair, #a-b 1.20 .55

Emanuil Gojdu (1802-70), Promoter of Romanian Orthodox Church in Hungary A1261

2002, Feb. 6
4501 A1261 2500 l multi .35 .25

Valentine's Day A1262

Designs: 5500 l, Mice. 43,500 l, Elephants.

2002, Feb. 8
4502-4503 A1262 Set of 2 4.25 2.00

Famous Men A1263

Designs: 1500 l, Ion Mincu (1852-1912), architect. 2500 l, Costin D. Nenitescu (1902-70), chemist. 5500 l, Alexandre Dumas père (1802-70), writer. 9000 l, Serban Cioculescu (1902-88), writer. 16,500 l, Leonardo da Vinci (1452-1519), artist. 34,000 l, Victor Hugo (1802-85), writer.

2002, Mar. 1
4504-4509 A1263 Set of 6 6.50 3.25

United We Stand — A1264

No. 4510: a, Statue of Liberty, US flag. b, Romanian flag.

2002, Mar. 22
4510 A1264 25,500 l Horiz. pair, #a-b 5.00 3.25

German Fortresses in Romania — A1265

Designs: 1500 l, Saschiz, vert. 2500 l, Darjiu, vert. 6500 l, Viscri. 10,500 l, Vorumloc. 13,500 l, Calnic, vert. 17,500 l, Prejmer, vert.

2002, Apr. 2
4511-4516 A1265 Set of 6 4.50 2.75

Easter — A1266

Designs: 2500 l, Crucifixion. 10,500 l, Resurrection.

2002, Apr. 12 Photo. Perf. 13¼
4517-4518 A1266 Set of 2 1.25 .55

Souvenir Sheet

Proclamation of Independence, 125th Anniv. — A1267

2002, May 9
4519 A1267 25,500 l multi 2.50 1.75

Europa — A1268

Clown with: 17,500 l, Yellow hair. 25,500 l, Brown hair.

2002, May 9
4520-4521 A1268 Set of 2 4.50 2.00

Souvenir Sheet

Intl. Federation of Stamp Dealers' Associations, 50th Anniv. — A1269

No. 4522: a, 10,000 l, Romanian flags, #1, 2 and 4. b, 10,000 l, IFSDA emblem. c, 27,500 l, World Trade Center, Bucharest. d, 27,500 l, Romanian philatelic store.

2002, June 10
4522 A1269   Sheet of 4, #a-d   6.00 3.50

Intl. Year of Mountains A1270

2002, June 14
4523 A1270 2000 l multi   .30 .25

Intl. Year of Ecotourism A1271

2002, June 14
4524 A1271 3000 l multi   .40 .25

Sports A1272

Designs: 7000 l, Cricket. 11,000 l, Polo. 15,500 l, Golf. 19,500 l, Baseball.

2002, July 11
4525-4528 A1272   Set of 4   4.50 2.25

Stamp Day — A1273

No. 4529: a, Ion Luca Caragiale (1852-1912), writer. b, National Theater, Bucharest, 150th anniv.

2002, July 15
4529 A1273 10,000 l Horiz. pair, #a-b   1.75 .85

A1274

A1275

A1276

A1277

Postal Services A1278

2002, Aug. 9
4530 A1274   2000 l multi   .25 .25
4531 A1275   3000 l multi   .35 .25
4532 A1276   10,000 l multi   .85 .40
4533 A1277   15,500 l multi   1.50 .75
4534 A1278   27,500 l multi   2.25 1.10
   Nos. 4530-4534 (5)   5.20 2.75
See Nos. 4543-4545.

Souvenir Sheet

Butterflies — A1279

No. 4535: a, Boloria pales carpathomeridionalis. b, Erebia pharte romaniae. c, Peridea korbi herculana. d, Tomares nogelli dobrogensis.

2002, Sept. 2   Photo.   Perf. 13¼
4535 A1279 44,500 l Sheet of 4, #a-d   13.00 13.00

Locomotives — A1280

Designs: 4500 l, Series 50115, 1930. 6500 l, Series 50025, 1921. 7000 l, Series 230128, 1933. 11,000 l, Series 764493, 1956. 19,500 l, Series 142072, 1939. 44,500 l, Series 704209, 1909.
72,500 l, Locomotive #1, 1872, vert.

2002, Sept. 22   Photo.   Perf. 13¼
4536-4541 A1280   Set of 6   6.75 3.75
Souvenir Sheet
4542 A1280 72,500 l multi   5.25 3.25
No. 4542 contains one 54x41mm stamp.

A1281

A1282

Postal Services A1283

2002, Oct. 1
4543 A1281   8000 l multi   .60 .35
4544 A1282   13,000 l multi   .90 .55
4545 A1283   20,500 l multi   1.50 1.00
   Nos. 4543-4545 (3)   3.00 1.90

Souvenir Sheet

35th Chess Olympiad, Bled, Slovenia — A1284

No. 4546: a, Knight and bishop. b, Queen and knight. c, King and rook.

2002, Oct. 23
4546 A1284 20,500 l Sheet of 3, #a-c   4.50 2.50

Fruit — A1285

Designs: 15,500 l, Cydonia oblonga. 20,500 l, Armeniaca vulgaris. 44,500 l, Cerasus vulgaris. 73,500 l, Morus nigra.

2002, Nov. 11
4547-4550 A1285   Set of 4   12.00 6.00

Christmas A1286

Santa Claus and helper: 3000 l, With gifts. 15,500 l, At computers.

2002, Nov. 19
4551-4552 A1286   Set of 2   1.40 .80

Invitation to Join NATO A1287

Litho. With Hologram Applied
2002, Nov. 22   Perf. 12¾
4553 A1287 131,000 l multi   10.00 10.00
Printed in sheets of 2 + central label. Value, $20.

Paintings — A1288

Designs: 4500 l, Portul Braila, by J.A. Steriadi. 6500 l, Balcic, by N. Darascu. 30,500 l, Conversatie, by N. Vermont. 34,000 l, Dalmatia, by N. Darascu. 46,500 l, Barci Pescaresti, by Steriadi. 53,000 l, Nude, by B. Pietris.
83,500 l, Femeie pe Malul Marii, by N. Grigorescu, vert.

2003, Jan. 22   Photo.   Perf. 13¼
4554-4559 A1288   Set of 6   12.00 7.00
Souvenir Sheet
4560 A1288 83,500 l multi   6.00 3.25
No. 4560 contains one 41x54mm stamp.

Natl. Military Palace, 80th Anniv. A1289

2003, Jan. 28
4561 A1289 5000 l multi   .60 .30

St. Valentine's Day A1290

Designs: 3000 l, Ladybug with heart-shaped spots. 5000 l, Man with ladder, vert.

2003, Feb. 14
4562-4563 A1290   Set of 2   .80 .40

Admission to European Union, 10th Anniv. A1291

2003, Feb. 20
4564 A1291 142,000 l multi   10.00 5.00

Famous Men — A1292

Designs: 6000 l, Ion Irimescu, sculptor, cent. of birth. 18,000 l, Hector Berlioz (1803-69), composer. 20,000 l, Vincent Van Gogh (1853-90), painter. 36,000 l, Dr. Georges de Bellio (1828-94), art collector.

2003, Feb. 27
4565-4568 A1292   Set of 4   5.00 3.00
See also Nos. 4587-4590.

Buildings in
Bucharest
A1293

Designs: 4500 l, Postal Palace. 5500 l, Economics House. 10,000 l, National Bank of Romania, horiz. 15,500 l, Stock Exchange. 20,500 l, Carol I University. 46,500 l, Atheneum. 73,500 l, Palace of Justice.

2003, Mar. 27   **Photo.**   **Perf. 13¼**
4569-4574 A1293   Set of 6   7.00 4.00

Souvenir Sheet
4575 A1293 73,500 l multi   5.50 2.75

No. 4575 contains one 42x53mm stamp.

Natl. Map and Book Museum,
Bucharest — A1294

No. 4576 — Map of Dacia by Petrus Kaerius: a, Northwestern Dacia. b, Northeastern Dacia. c, Southwestern Dacia. d, Southeastern Dacia.
46,500 l, Museum, vert.

2003, Apr. 4   **Photo.**   **Perf. 13¼**
4576 A1294 30,500 l Sheet of 4,
     #a-d   9.00 4.50

Souvenir Sheet
4577 A1294 46,500 l multi   4.00 2.00

No. 4577 contains one 42x54mm stamp.

Easter — A1295

2003, Apr. 10
4578 A1295 3000 l multi   .35 .25

Owls — A1296

Designs: 5000 l, Otus scops. 8000 l, Strix uralensis. 10,000 l, Glaucidium passerinum. 13,000 l, Asio flammeus. 15,500 l, Asio otus. 20,500 l, Aegolius funereus.

2003, Apr. 25
4579-4584 A1296   Set of 6   4.75 2.75

Europa
A1297

Poster art: 20,500 l, Butterfly emerging from chrysalis. 73,500 l, Man holding framed picture.

2003, May 9
4585-4586 A1297   Set of 2   5.75 5.75

Famous Men Type of 2003
Designs: 4500 l, Dumitru Staniloae (1903-93), theologian. 8000 l, Alexandru Ciucurecu (1903-77), painter. 30,500 l, Ilarie Voronca (1903-46), writer. 46,500 l, Victor Brauner (1903-66), painter.

2003, June 6   **Photo.**   **Perf. 13¼**
4587-4590 A1292   Set of 4   5.75 3.25

Paintings by Victor Brauner — A1298

No. 4591 — Unidentified paintings: a, Two dragons in foreground. b, White and black arcs (20x30mm). c, Spheres at left. d, Landscape with house with red roof in center. e, Abstract with fish head (20x30mm). f, Landscape with white clouds at left and right. g, Mountain with rings. h, Line drawing of man (20x30mm). i, Fire-breathing dragon. j, Man standing (20x30mm).

2003, June 24
4591 A1298 10,000 l Sheet, #a-
     i, 3 #j   10.00 5.00

Nostradamus (1503-66),
Astrologer — A1299

No. 4592: a, Nostradamus, denomination at left. b, Astrological chart, denomination at bottom.

2003, July 2
4592 A1299 73,500 l Horiz. pair,
     #a-b   9.00 5.00

Stamp
Day
A1300

2003, July 15
4593 A1300 5000 l multi   .40 .25

Souvenir Sheets

Mushrooms — A1301

No. 4594, 15,500 l: a, Agaricus xanthodermus. b, Clathrus ruber. c, Amanita pantherina.
No. 4595, 20,500 l: a, Leccinum aurantiacum. b, Laetiporus sulphureus. c, Russula xerampelina.

2003, Sept. 19   **Sheets of 3, #a-c**
4594-4595 A1301   Set of 2   7.50 3.75

Extreme
Sports
A1302

Designs: 5000 l, Skydiving, vert. 8000 l, Windsurfing. 10,000 l, Motorcycle racing. 30,500 l, Skiing, vert.

2003, Sept. 30
4596-4599 A1302   Set of 4   3.50 1.75

Reptiles and Amphibians — A1303

No. 4600: a, Lacerta viridis. b, Hyla arborea. c, Ablepharus kitaibelii stepanekii. d, Rana temporaria.

2003, Oct. 28
4600 A1303 18,000 l Sheet of 4,
     #a-d   6.50 3.25

Musical Instruments — A1304

Designs: 1000 l, Lute (cobza). 4000 l, Horn (bucium). 6000 l, Fiddle with horn (vioara cu goarna).

2003, Oct. 31
4601-4603 A1304   Set of 3   .80 .40

Granting of Dobruja Region to
Romania, 125th Anniv. — A1305

2003, Nov. 11
4604 A1305 16,000 l multi   1.10 .55

Pope John Paul II and Patriarch
Teoctist — A1306

No. 4605: a, Holding crosses. b, Embracing.

2003, Nov. 29
4605   Horiz. pair with 2 central labels   2.00 1.25
   a.-b.   A1306 16,000 l Either single   1.00 .60

Pontificate of Pope John Paul II, 25th anniv.

Christmas — A1307

No. 4606: a, Santa Claus. b, Snowman.

2003, Dec. 5
4606 A1307 4000 l Horiz. pair,
     #a-b   .50 .25

Women's Fashions in the 20th
Century — A1308

No. 4607, 4000 l: a, 1921-30. b, 1931-40.
No. 4608, 21,000 l: a, 1901-10. b, 1911-20.

2003, Dec. 13
   Horiz. Pairs, #a-b, + Label
4607-4608 A1308   Set of 2   5.50 2.75

FIFA (Fédération Internationale de
Football Association), Cent. (in
2004) — A1309

Designs: 3000 l, Women soccer players. 4000 l, Soccer players, television camera. 6000 l, Men, FIFA charter. 10,000 l, Players, equipment. 34,000 l, Rule book, field diagram.

2003, Dec. 22   **Photo.**   **Perf. 13¼**
4609-4613 A1309   Set of 5   3.50 1.75

Miniature Sheet

Birds — A1310

No. 4614 — UPU emblem and: a, Ardea cinerea. b, Anas platyrhynchos. c, Podiceps cristatus. d, Pelecanus onocrotalus.

2004, Jan. 23 Photo. Perf. 13¼
4614 A1310 16,000 l Sheet of 4,
  #a-d 4.75 2.10

Miniature Sheet

Information Technology — A1311

No. 4615 — UPU emblem and: a, Earth, satellite, compact disc. b, Computer screen showing computer user. c, Earth, satellite dish. d, Computer keyboard, diskette.

2004, Jan. 26
4615 A1311 20,000 l Sheet of 4,
  #a-d 5.00 2.50

Amerigo Vespucci (1454-1512), Explorer — A1312

Designs: 16,000 l, Vespucci. 31,000 l, Ship.

2004, Jan. 31
4616-4617 A1312 Set of 2 3.00 1.50

St. Valentine's Day — A1313

2004, Feb. 10
4618 A1313 21,000 l multi 1.40 .70

23rd UPU Congress, Bucharest — A1314

No. 4619: a, UPU emblem. b, Congress emblem.

2004, Feb. 20
4619 A1314 31,000 l Horiz. pair,
  #a-b 4.00 2.00

Easter — A1315

2004, Mar.5
4620 A1315 4000 l multi .35 .25

High Speed Trains A1316

UPU Congress emblem and: 4000 l, Bullet Train, Japan. 6000 l, TGV, France. 10,000 l, KTX, South Korea. 16,000 l, AVE, Spain. 47,000 l, ICE, Germany. 56,000 l, Eurostar, Europe. 77,000 l, Sageata Albastra, Romania.

2004, Mar. 11
4621-4626 A1316 Set of 6 9.00 4.50
Souvenir Sheet
4627 A1316 77,000 l multi 5.00 2.50
No. 4627 contains one 54x42mm stamp.

Admission to NATO — A1317

2004, Mar. 24
4628 A1317 4000 l multi *2.00 1.00*

Women's Fashions Type of 2003
No. 4629, 5000 l: a, 1941-50. b, 1951-60.
No. 4630, 21,000 l: a, 1981-90. b, 1991-2000.
No. 4631, 31,000 l: a, 1961-70. b, 1971-80.

2004, Mar. 31
Horiz. Pairs, #a-b + Label
4629-4631 A1308 Set of 3 8.00 4.00

Intl. Council for Game and Wildlife Conservation, 51st General Assembly A1318

No. 4632 — Emblem and: a, Hunter. b, Dog and pheasant. c, Buck. d, Mountain goat. e, Bear.
No. 4633, Buck, horiz.

2004, Apr. 24
4632 Horiz. strip of 5 5.75 2.75
a.-e. A1318 16,000 l Any single 1.10 .55
Souvenir Sheet
4633 A1318 16,000 l multi 1.10 .55
No. 4633 contains one 54x42mm stamp.

Europa A1319

Stylized sun and: 21,000 l, Beach. 77,000 l, Mountains.

2004, May 7 Photo. Perf. 13¼
4634-4635 A1319 Set of 2 6.50 3.25

Michael the Brave (1558-1601), Prince of Walachia — A1320

2004, May 14
4636 A1320 3000 l multi .25 .25

National Philatelic and Romanian History Museum — A1321

2004, May 21
4637 A1321 4000 l multi .30 .25

Souvenir Sheet

Dracula — A1322

No. 4638: a, Bram Stoker, author of Dracula. b, Dracula and cross. c, Dracula and woman. d, Dracula in coffin.

2004, May 21
4638 A1322 31,000 l Sheet of 4,
  #a-d 8.50 4.25
23rd UPU Congress, Bucharest. Exists imperf.

Famous People A1323

Designs: 4000 l, Anghel Saligny (1854-1925), civil engineer. 16,000 l, Gheorge D. Anghel (1904-66), sculptor. 21,000 l, George Sand (1804-76), author. 31,000 l, Oscar Wilde (1854-1900), writer.

2004, May 27
4639-4642 A1323 Set of 4 5.00 2.25

Romanian Athenaeum — A1324

2004, May 28
4643 A1324 10,000 l multi .60 .30

Johnny Weissmuller (1904-84), Olympic Swimming Gold Medalist, Actor — A1325

2004, June 2 Photo. Perf. 13¼
4644 A1325 21,000 l multi 1.40 .70

TAROM Airlines, 50th Anniv. A1326

2004, June 7
4645 A1326 16,000 l multi 1.10 .55

FIFA (Fédération Internationale de Football Association), Cent. — A1327

2004, June 15
4646 A1327 31,000 l multi 2.10 1.00

Miniature Sheets

Stephen the Great (1437-1504), Prince of Moldavia — A1328

No. 4647, 10,000 l: a, Portrait of Stephen the Great, Dobrovat-Iasi Monastery Church. b, Sucevei Fortress. c, Portrait of Stephen the Great, Putna Monastery.
No. 4648, 16,000 l: a, Putna Monastery. b, Stephen the Great. c, Neamtului Fortress.

2004, June 16
Sheets of 3, #a-c
4647-4648 A1328 Set of 2 5.00 2.50

Famous Men A1329

Designs: 2000 l, Alexandru Macedonski (1854-1920), writer. 3000 l, Victor Babes (1854-1926), bacteriologist. 6000 l, Arthur Rimbaud (1854-91), writer. 56,000 l, Salvador Dali (1904-89), painter.

2004, June 30
4649-4652 A1329 Set of 4 5.00 2.25

Flight of Zeppelin LZ-127 Over Brasov, 75th Anniv. A1330

2004, July 29
4653   A1330   31,000 l multi   2.10   1.00

Savings Banks, 140th Anniv. A1331

2004, July 30
4654   A1331   5000 l multi   .35   .25

Fire Fighters — A1332

No. 4655: a, Fire fighters leaving truck. b, Fire fighters in protective suits.

Horiz. pair, #a-b, + flanking label
2004, Aug. 12
4655   A1332   12,000 l multi   1.50   .75

2004 Summer Olympics, Athens — A1333

Designs: 7000 l, Rowing. 12,000 l, Fencing. 21,000 l, Swimming. 31,000 l+9000 l, Gymnastics.

2004, Aug. 20   Litho.   Perf. 13¼
4656-4659   A1333   Set of 4   5.50   2.75
Olymphilex Philatelic Exhibition (#4659).

23rd UPU Congress, Bucharest A1334

Stamps commemorating UPU Congresses: 8000 l, Romania #4619b. 10,000 l, Switzerland #590. 19,000 l, South Korea #1794, horiz. 31,000 l, People's Republic of China #2868. 47,000 l, United States #2434, horiz. 77,000 l, Brazil #1629.

2004, Sept. 10
4660-4665   A1334   Set of 6   12.50   6.25

Sculptures by Idel Ianchelevici (1909-94) A1335

Designs: 21,000 l, L'appel. 31,000 l, Perennis Perdurat Poeta.

2004, Sept. 20
4666-4667   A1335   Set of 2   3.00   1.50
Each stamp printed in sheets of 8 + 2 labels. See Belgium Nos. 2036-2037.

Chinese and Romanian Handicrafts — A1336

No. 4668: a, Drum with tigers and birds, China. b, Cucuteni pottery jar, Romania.

2004, Sept. 24
4668   A1336   5000 l Pair, #a-b   .70   .35
See People's Republic of China Nos. 3390-3391.

Souvenir Sheet

23rd UPU Congress, Bucharest — A1337

No. 4669: a, Gerardus Mercator and Jodocus Hondius, cartographers. b, UPU emblem. c, Amerigo Vespucci (1454-1512), explorer.

2004, Oct. 5   Perf. 13½
4669   A1337   118,000 l Sheet of
                  3, #a-c   24.00   12.00
For surcharge see No. 4755.

Details From Trajan's Column, Rome A1338

Various details: 7000 l, 12,000 l, 19,000 l, 21,000 l, 31,000 l, 56,000 l, 145,000 l.

2004   Perf. 13¼
4670-4676   A1338   Set of 7   20.00   10.00
Issued: 7000 l, 12,000 l, 19,000 l, 56,000 l, 10/15; others, 12/4.

Roses — A1339

Designs: 8000 l, Simfonia. 15,000 l, Foc de Tabara. 25,000 l, Golden Elegance. 36,000 l, Doamna in Mov.

2004, Oct. 25
4677-4680   A1339   Set of 4   6.00   3.00
4680a   Souvenir sheet, #4677-
                  4680   6.00   3.00

Ilie Nastase, Tennis Player — A1340

2004, Nov. 16   Perf. 13¼
4681   A1340   10,000 l multi   .75   .35
Souvenir Sheets
Perf. 13¼x13¾
4682   A1340   72,000 l Nastase,
                  diff.   5.25   2.60
Imperf
4683   A1340   72,000 l Like No.
                  4682   5.25   2.60
No. 4682 contains one 42x51mm stamp. No. 4683 contains one 37x48mm stamp.

Christmas — A1341

2004, Nov. 27   Perf. 13¼
4684   A1341   5000 l multi   .40   .25

Organizations A1342

Prince Dimitrie Cantemir (1673-1723), Writer — A1343

Designs: 12,000 l, Romanian Boy Scouts. 16,000 l, Lions International. 19,000 l, Red Cross and Red Crescent.

2004, Dec. 8   Perf. 13¼
4685-4687   A1342   Set of 3   3.25   1.60
Souvenir Sheet
Perf. 13¼x13¾
4688   A1343   87,000 l multi   6.00   3.00

Olympic Gold Medalists A1344

Designs: 5000 l, Iolanda Balas, high jump. 33,000 l, Elisabeta Lipa, rowing. 77,000 l, Ivan Pazaichin, canoeing.

2004, Dec. 15   Perf. 13¼
4689-4691   A1344   Set of 3   7.00   4.50
Values are for stamps with surrounding selvage.

Souvenir Sheets

Modern Paintings — A1345

No. 4692, 7000 l: a, Tristan Tzara, by M. H. Maxy. b, Baroness, by Merica Ramniceanu. c, Portrait of a Woman, by Jean David.
No. 4693, 12,000 l: a, Composition, by Marcel Iancu. b, Femele Care Viseaza, by Victor Brauner. c, Composition, by Hans Mattis-Teutsch.

2004, Dec. 16   Litho.
Sheets of 3, #a-c
4692-4693   A1345   Set of 2   4.25   2.10

Famous People — A1346

Designs: 15,000 l, Gen. Gheorghe Magheru (1804-80), politician. 25,000 l, Christian Dior (1905-57), fashion designer. 35,000 l, Henry Fonda (1905-82), actor. 72,000 l, Greta Garbo (1905-90), actress. 77,000 l, George Valentin Bibescu (1880-1941), first president of Romanian Auto Club.

2005, Jan. 20   Litho.   Perf. 13¼
4694-4698   A1346   Set of 5   15.50   7.75
See Nos. 4722-4726.

Rotary International, Cent. A1347

2005, Feb. 23
4699   A1347   21,000 l multi   1.60   .80
Printed in sheets of 4.

Pottery — A1348

Pottery from: 3000 l, Oboga, Olt. 5000 l, Sacel, Maramures. 7000 l, Romana, Olt. 8000 l, Vadul Crisului, Bihor. 10,000 l, Tara Barsei, Brasov. 12,000 l, Horezu, Valcea. 16,000 l, Corund, Harghita.

2005   Litho.   Perf. 13¼
Pottery Actual Color; Background Color:
4700   A1348   3000 l lilac   .25   .25
4701   A1348   5000 l lt blue   .45   .25
4702   A1348   7000 l lt green   .55   .25
4703   A1348   8000 l rose brn   .70   .35
4704   A1348   10,000 l orange   .80   .40

4705 A1348 12,000 l green 1.00 .50
4706 A1348 16,000 l lt brown 1.40 .70
Nos. 4700-4706 (7) 5.15 2.70
Issued: 3000 l, 5000 l, 12,000 l, 16,000 l,
2/24. 7000 l, 8000 l, 10,000 l, 3/24.
See Nos. 4767-4775, 4804-4811, 4844-
4847.

Dinosaurs — A1349

Designs: 21,000 l, Elopteryx nopcsai.
31,000 l, Telmatosaurus transsylvanicus.
35,000 l, Struthiosaurus transilvanicus.
47,000 l, Hatzegopteryx thambema.

2005, Feb. 25   Litho.   Perf. 13¼
4707-4710 A1349 Set of 4 10.00 5.00
4710a Souvenir sheet, #4707-
4710, + 2 labels 10.00 5.00

Fish — A1350

Designs: 21,000 l, Carassius auratus.
31,000 l, Symphysodon discus. 36,000 l,
Labidochromis. 47,000 l, Betta splendens.

2005, Mar. 1   Stamp + Label
4711-4714 A1350 Set of 4 10.00 5.00
4714a Souvenir sheet, #4711-
4714, + 4 labels 10.00 5.00

Jules Verne
(1828-1905),
Writer — A1351

Scenes from stories: 19,000 l, The Castle in
the Carpathians. 21,000 l, The Danube Pilot.
47,000 l, Claudius Bombarnac. 56,000 l, Ker-
aban, the Inflexible.

2005, Mar. 29   Litho.   Perf. 13¼
4715-4718 A1351 Set of 4 10.50 5.25
4718a Souvenir sheet, #4715-
4718, + 2 labels 10.50 5.25

Easter — A1352

No. 4719: a, Last Supper. b, Crucifixion
(30mm diameter). c, Resurrection.

2005, Apr. 1
4719 A1352 Horiz. strip of 3 1.50 .55
a.-c. 5000 l Any single .40 .25

Pope John Paul II (1920-
2005) — A1353

Pope John Paul II and: 5000 l, Dove, map of
Romania. 21,000 l, St. Peter's Basilica.

2005, Apr. 8   Litho.   Perf. 13¼
4720-4721 A1353 Set of 2 2.10 1.00
4721a Souvenir sheet, 2 each
#4720-4721 4.50 2.25

Famous People Type of 2005

Designs: 3000 l, Hans Christian Andersen
(1805-75), author. 5000 l, Jules Verne (1828-
1905), writer. 12,000 l, Albert Einstein (1879-
1955), physicist. 21,000 l, Dimitrie Gusti
(1880-1955), sociologist. 22,000 l, George
Enescu (1881-1955), composer.

2005, Apr. 18
4722-4726 A1346 Set of 5 4.75 2.40

Romanian Accession to European
Union — A1354

No. 4727: a, Map in gold. b, Map in silver.

2005, Apr. 25
4727 A1354 Pair .80 .40
a.-b. 5000 l Either single .40 .25
c. Souvenir sheet, 2 each
#4727a-4727b 1.75 .85

**Pair of No. 3921 Surcharged in Red
and Silver**

No. 4728 — "Sprijin Pentru Semeni": a, In
box. b, Reading up at left.

Wmk. 398
2005, May 9   Photo.   Perf. 13¼
4728 A1105 Horiz. pair .80 .40
a.-b. 5000 l on 1440 Either single .40 .25
Nos. 4728a-4728b also have face values
expressed in revalued leu currency that was
used as of July 1.

Europa — A1355

Designs: 21,000 l, Map of Dacia, archer on
horseback, duck and stew pot. 77,000 l, Map,
hunting dog, roasted game bird, vegetables,
glass of wine.

Perf. 13¼
2005, May 9   Litho.   Unwmk.
4729-4730 A1355 Set of 2 6.75 3.25
4730a Souvenir sheet, 2 each
#4729-4730, #4729 at UL 13.50 6.75
4730b As "a," #4730 at UL 13.50 6.75

Miniature Sheet

Viticulture — A1356

No. 4731: a, Feteasca alba. b, Grasa de
Cotnari. c, Fetesaca neagra. d, Victoria.

2005, May 27
4731 A1356 21,000 l Sheet of 4,
#a-d, + 2
labels 6.50 3.25
Nos. 4731a-4731d also have face values
expressed in revalued leu currency that was
used as of July 1.

Scouting
A1357

Designs: No. 4732, 22,000 l, Scout climbing
rocks. No. 4733, 22,000 l, Scout following
marked trail. No. 4734, 22,000 l, Scouts building campfire. No. 4735, 22,000 l, Scouts reading map.

2005, June 15
4732-4735 A1357 Set of 4 6.00 3.00
4735a Horiz. strip of 4, #4732-
4735 6.00 3.00
4735b Souvenir sheet of 4,
#4732-4735 6.00 3.00
Nos. 4732-4735 also have face values
expressed in revalued leu currency that was
used as of July 1.

July 1 Currency Devaluation — A1358

National Bank of Romania, new and old
coins or banknotes depicting revaluation of:
30b, 100 old lei to 1 new ban. 50b, 10,000 old
lei to 1 new leu. 70b, 500 old lei to 5 new bani.
80b, 50,000 old lei to 5 new lei. 1 l, 100,000
old lei to 10 new lei. 1.20 l, 500,000 old lei to
50 new lei. 1.60 l, 1,000,000 old lei to 100 new
lei. 2.10 l, 1000 old lei to 10 new bani. 2.20 l,
5,000,000 old lei to 500 new lei. 3.10 l, 5000
old lei to 50 new bani.
In the pairs, the "a" stamp has the colored
denomination panel on the left and shows the
obverse of coins at left and reverse of coins at
right, or the obverse side of banknotes. The
"b" stamp has the panel on the right, shows
the reverse of coins at left and obverse of
coins at right, or the reverse side of
banknotes.

2005, July 1   Litho.
Horiz. or Vert. Pairs, #a-b
Panel Color
4736 A1358 30b gray .40 .25
4737 A1358 50b emerald .70 .35
4738 A1358 70b blue .95 .45
4739 A1358 80b red brown 1.10 .55
4740 A1358 1 l red violet 1.40 .70
4741 A1358 1.20 l dull brown 1.60 .80
4742 A1358 1.60 l olive green 2.25 1.10
4743 A1358 2.10 l blue green 2.75 1.40
4744 A1358 2.20 l bister 3.00 1.50
4745 A1358 3.10 l purple 4.25 2.10
c. Miniature sheet of 10 horiz.
pairs, #4736-4745 18.50 9.25

Military Ships — A1359

No. 4746: a, Training ship Constanta. b,
Corvette Contraadmiral Horia Macellariu. c,
Monitor ship Mihail Kogalniceanu. d, Frigate
Marasesti.

2005, July 15   Perf. 13¼
4746 Vert. strip of 4 6.00 3.00
a.-d. A1359 2.20 l Any single 1.50 .75
e. Souvenir sheet of 4, #4746a-
4746d 6.00 3.00

Stamp Day.

Rainbow and Genesis 1:9 — A1360

2005, Aug. 2
4747 A1360 50b multi + label .45 .25
July 2005 floods in Romania.

Election of Joseph
Cardinal Ratzinger
as Pope Benedict
XVI — A1361

Ratzinger in vestments of: 1.20 l, Cardinal.
2.10 l, Pope.

2005, Aug. 18
4748-4749 A1361 Set of 2 2.75 1.40
4749a Souvenir sheet, #4748-4749 2.75 1.40

European Philatelic Cooperation, 50th
Anniv. (in 2006) — A1362

No. 4750 — Christopher Columbus and: a,
Denomination to right of face. b, Ship, denomination at lower right. c, Ship, denomination at
lower left. d, Denomination to left of face.

2005, Aug. 22   Perf. 13¼
4750 A1362 Horiz. strip of 4 13.50 6.75
a.-d. 4.70 l Any single 3.25 1.60
e. Souvenir sheet, #4750a-
4750d +2 labels 13.50 6.75
Europa stamps, 50th anniv. (in 2006). The
vignettes of Nos. 4750a and 4750d are inside
a 31x27mm perf. 13 hexagon. Values for singles of these stamps are for examples with
surrounding selvage.
No. 4750 exists imperf.

Children's
Art — A1363

Designs: 30b, Forest Mailman, by Bianca
Paul. 40b, The Road to You, by Daniel Ciornei.
60b, A Messenger of Peace, by Stefan
Ghiliman, horiz. 1 l, Good News for Every-
body, by Adina Elena Mocanu, horiz.

2005, Aug. 31   Litho.   Perf. 13¼
4751-4754 A1363 Set of 4 1.75 .85

No. 4669 Surcharged in Black and Blue

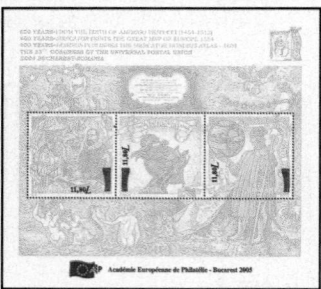

No. 4755: a, Gerardus Mercator and Jodocus Hondius, cartographers. b, UPU emblem. c, Amerigo Vespucci, explorer.

2005, Sept. 26   **Perf. 13½**
4755 A1337 11.80 l on
       118,000   25.00   25.00

Visit of members of European Philatelic Academy to Bucharest.

Dogs — A1364

No. 4756: a, Jagd terrier. b, Rhodesian ridgeback. c, Munsterlander. d, Bloodhound. e, Transylvanian hound (Copoi ardelenesc). f, Pointer.

2005, Sept. 28   **Perf. 13¼**
4756 A1364   Block of 6   10.50   5.25
  a.-f.   2.20 l Any single   1.75   .85
  g.   Sheet, #4756a-4756f   10.50   5.25

Natl. Philatelic Museum, 1st Anniv. — A1365

2005, Sept. 30
4757 A1365 40b multi   .40   .25

World Summit on the Information Society, Tunis — A1366

2005, Oct. 10
4758 A1366 5.60 l multi   4.75   2.25

United Nations — A1367

Dove, UN emblem, Romanian flag and: 40b, Flags. 1.50 l, Security Council. 2.20 l, General Assembly building.

2005, Oct. 24
4759-4761 A1367   Set of 3   3.50   1.75
4761a   Souvenir sheet, #4759-
         4761   3.50   1.75

Romania's admission to UN, 50th anniv. (#4759); Romania's presidency of Security Council, 2004-05 (#4760); UN, 60th anniv. (#4761).

Birthplace of Dimitrie Butculescu, Romanian Philatelic Federation Emblem — A1368

Dimitrie Butculescu, Founder of Romanian Philatelic Society — A1369

Design: No. 4762b, Butculescu, September 1892 edition of Romanian Philatelic Society Monitor.

2005, Nov. 4   **Perf. 13¼**
4762   Horiz. pair with flanking
     labels   .85   .40
  a.-b.   A1368 50b Either single + label   .40   .25

Souvenir Sheet
Imperf
4763 A1369 9 l multi   7.50   3.75

Central University Library, 110th Anniv. — A1370

No. 4764: a, Library building (47x32mm). b, Statue (23x32mm).

2005, Nov. 10   **Perf. 13¼**
4764 A1370 60b Horiz. pair, #a-b   1.00   .50
  c.   Souvenir sheet, #4764a-4764b   1.00   .50

Souvenir Sheet

Pigeon Breeds — A1371

No. 4765: a, English Pouter (green frame). b, Parlor rollers (lilac frame). c, Standard carrier (green frame). d, Andalusian (yellow orange frame).

2005, Nov. 18   **Litho.**
4765 A1371 2.50 l Sheet of 4,
       #a-d   8.25   4.00

UNESCO, 60th Anniv. — A1372

2005, Nov. 21
4766 A1372 60b multi + label   1.25   .60

Pottery Type of 2005

Pottery from: 30b, Leheceni, Bihor. 50b, Vladesti, Valcea. 1 l, Curtea de Arges, Arges. 1.20 l, Vamu, Satu Mare. 2.20 l, Barsa, Arad. 2.50 l, Corund, Harghita. 4.70 l, Targu Neamt, Neamt. 5.60 l, Polana Deleni, Iasi. 14.50 l, Valea Izei, Maramures.

2005   **Perf. 13¼**
Pottery Actual Color; Background Color:
4767 A1348   30b greenish
           yel   .25   .25
4768 A1348   50b blue green   .40   .25
4769 A1348   1 l red orange   .85   .40
4770 A1348   1.20 l pale salm-
           on   1.00   .50
4771 A1348   2.20 l gray   1.75   .85
4772 A1348   2.50 l pink   2.10   1.00
4773 A1348   4.70 l blue violet   4.00   2.00
4774 A1348   5.60 l red   4.75   2.25
4775 A1348 14.50 l lt bl grn   12.00   6.00
   Nos. 4767-4775 (9)   27.10   13.50

Issued: 4.70 l, 5.60 l, 12/19; others, 11/24.

Christmas — A1373

No. 4776: a, The Annunciation (23x32mm). b, Nativity (47x32mm). c, Madonna and Child with Angels (23x32mm).

2005, Dec. 2
4776 A1373 50b Horiz. strip of 3,
       #a-c   1.00   .50

Modern Art — A1374

No. 4777: a, Inscriptions, by Virgil Preda. b, The Suspended Garden, by Alin Gheorghiu. c, Still Life with Bottle, by Constantin Ceraceanu. d, Monster 1, by Cristian Paleologu.

2005, Dec. 12
4777 A1374 1.50 l Block of 4, #a-
         d   5.00   2.50

Cats
A1375

Designs: 30b, Norwegian Forest. 50b, Turkish Van. 70b, Siamese. 80b, Ragdoll. 1.20 l, Persian. 1.60 l, Birman.

2006, Jan. 20   **Perf. 13¼**
4778-4783 A1375   Set of 6   4.25   2.10
4783a   Souvenir sheet, #4778-
         4783, imperf.   4.25   2.10

Famous People — A1376

Designs: 50b, Wolfgang Amadeus Mozart (1756-91), composer. 1.20 l, Ion C. Bratianu (1821-91), Prime Minister. 2.10 l, Grigore Moisil (1906-73), mathematician.

2006, Jan. 27   **Perf. 13¼**
4784-4786 A1376   Set of 3   3.25   1.60

See Nos. 4825-4827.

Souvenir Sheet

2006 Winter Olympics, Turin — A1377

No. 4787: a, Figure skating. b, Downhill skiing. c, Bobsled. d, Biathlon.

2006, Feb. 1
4787 A1377 1.60 l Sheet of 4,
       #a-d   5.50   2.75

Gold Coins — A1378

Coin obverse and reverse: 30b, 1868 20 lei. 50b, 1906 50 lei. 70b, 1906 100 lei. 1 l, 1922 50 lei. 1.20 l, 1939 100 lei. 2.20 l, 1940 100 lei.

2006, Feb. 22
4788-4793 A1378   Set of 6   5.00   2.50
4788a   Sheet of 7 + 2 labels   1.75   .85
4789a   Sheet of 7 + 2 labels   3.00   1.50
4790a   Sheet of 7 + 2 labels   4.00   2.00
4791a   Sheet of 7 + 2 labels   6.00   3.00
4792a   Sheet of 7 + 2 labels   7.00   3.50
4793a   Sheet of 7 + 2 labels   13.00   6.50

A1379

A1380

A1381

A1382

Easter
A1383

2006, Mar. 15   Litho.   Perf. 13¼

4794	A1379 50b multi	.40	.25
4795	A1380 50b multi	.40	.25
4796	A1381 50b multi	.40	.25
4797	A1382 50b multi	.40	.25
4798	A1383 50b multi	.40	.25
a.	Souvenir sheet, #4794-4798, + 4 labels, with red labels at UL and LR	2.00	1.00
b.	As "a," with red labels at UR and LL	2.00	1.00
	Complete booklet, 4 each #4794-4798	8.00	
	Nos. 4794-4798 (5)	2.00	1.25

First Flight of Traian Vuia,
Cent. — A1384

Outline drawings of aircraft and: 70b, Traian Vuia. 80b, Vuia I aircraft. 1.60 l, Vuia II aircraft. 4.70 l, Vuia in airplane, vert.

2006, Mar. 18   Perf. 13¼

4799-4801	A1384 Set of 3	2.50	1.25
4799a	Sheet of 8 + label	4.75	2.40
4800a	Sheet of 8 + label	5.50	2.75
4801a	Souvenir sheet, #4799-4801 + label	1.25	.60
4801b	Sheet of 8 + label	11.00	5.50

Souvenir Sheet
Perf. 13¼x14

4802	A1384 4.70 l multi	4.00	2.00

No. 4802 contains one 42x52mm stamp.

Léopold Sédar Senghor (1906-2001), First President of Senegal — A1385

2006, Mar. 20   Perf. 13¼

4803	A1385 2.10 l multi	1.75	.85
a.	Souvenir sheet of 4	7.00	3.50

Pottery Type of 2005

Pottery from: 30b, Oboga, Olt. 40b, Radauti, Suceava. 60b, Poienita, Arges. 70b, Oboga, Olt. diff. 80b, Oboga, Olt. diff. 1.60 l, Romana, Olt. 2.50 l, Vladesti, Valcea. 3.10 l, Jupanesti, Timis.

2006   Perf. 13¼
Pottery Actual Color; Background Color:

4804	A1348 30b lilac	.25	.25
a.	Sheet of 9	2.25	1.10
4805	A1348 40b yellow	.35	.25
a.	Sheet of 9	3.25	1.60
4806	A1348 60b pale salmon	.50	.25
a.	Sheet of 9	4.50	2.25
4807	A1348 70b bister	.60	.30
a.	Sheet of 9	5.50	2.75
4808	A1348 80b gray blue	.70	.35
a.	Sheet of 9	6.25	3.00
4809	A1348 1.60 l gray	1.25	.60
a.	Sheet of 9	11.50	5.75

4810	A1348 2.50 l light green	2.10	1.00
a.	Sheet of 9	19.00	9.50
4811	A1348 3.10 l light blue	2.50	1.25
a.	Sheet of 9	22.50	11.00
	Nos. 4804-4811 (8)	8.25	4.25

Issued: 60b, 70b, 80b, 1.60 l, 3/30; others 4/20.

Tulip
Varieties — A1386

Designs: 30b, Turkestanica. 50b, Ice Follies. 1 l, Cardinal. 1.50 l, Yellow Empress, horiz. (47x32mm). 2.10 l, Donna Bella. 3.60 l, Don Quixote, horiz. (47x32mm).

2006, Apr. 14   Litho.   Perf. 13¼

4812-4817	A1386 Set of 6	7.50	3.75
a.	Block of 6, #4812-4817	7.50	3.75
b.	Souvenir sheet of 6, #4812-4817	7.50	3.75
c.	Miniature sheet, 2 each #4812-4817	15.00	7.50

Europa — A1387

Children's drawings: 2.10 l, Children, house, sun. 3.10 l, People, house, fence.

2006, May 4

4818-4819	A1387 Set of 2	4.50	2.25
4819a	Souvenir sheet, 2 each #4818-4819, #4818 at UL	9.00	4.50
4819b	Souvenir sheet, 2 each #4818-4819, #4819 at UL	9.00	4.50

Romanian Stamps Depicting Royalty A1388

Crown and: 30b, Prince Carol I (#29). 1 l, King Ferdinand I (#248). 2.10 l, King Carol II (#376). 2.50 l, King Michael (#513). 4.70 l, Carol I as Prince and King (#180), horiz.

2006, May 8

4820-4823	A1388 Set of 4	5.00	2.50
4823a	Miniature sheet, #4820-4823	5.00	2.50

Souvenir Sheet
Perf. 14x13¼

4824	A1388 4.70 l multi	4.00	2.00

Foundation of Romanian royal dynasty, 140th anniv., Proclamation of Romanian kingdom, 125th anniv. No. 4824 contains one 51x41mm stamp.

Famous People Type of 2006

Designs: 50b, Christopher Columbus (1451-1506), explorer. 1 l, Paul Cézanne (1839-1906), painter. 1.20 l, Henrik Ibsen (1828-1906), writer.

2006, May 17   Perf. 13¼

4825-4827	A1376 Set of 3	2.25	1.10

Dimitrie Gusti National Village Museum, 70th Anniv.
A1389

2006, May 17

4828	A1389 2.20 l multi	1.90	.95
a.	Sheet of 8 + central label	13.00	6.50

No. 4092 Surcharged in Gold or Silver

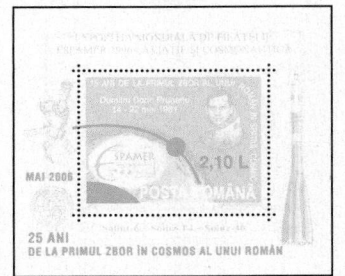

2006, May 19   Perf. 13½

4829	A1155 2.10 l on 2720 l #4092 (G)	1.75	.85
4830	A1155 2.10 l on 2720 l #4092 (S)	1.75	.85

First Romanian in space, 25th anniv.

1906 General Exhibition and Carol I Park, Bucharest, Cent. — A1390

Designs: 30b, Main entrance to Carol I Park. 50b, Tepes Castle. 1 l, Post Office Pavilion. 1.20 l, European Danube Commission Pavilion. 1.60 l, Industry Palace. No. 4836, 2.20 l, Roman arenas.
No. 4837, Arts Palace.

2006, June 6   Perf. 13¼

4831-4836	A1390 Set of 6	5.75	2.75
4836a	Miniature sheet, #4831-4836	5.75	2.75

Souvenir Sheet
Perf. 14x13¼

4837	A1390 2.20 l multi	1.90	.95

No. 4837 contains one 51x41mm stamp.

Composers — A1391

No. 4838: a, Béla Bartók (1881-1945) and Hungarian flag. b, George Enescu (1881-1955) and Romanian flag.

2006, June 8   Perf. 13¼

4838	A1391 1.20 l Horiz. pair, #a-b	2.00	1.00
c.	Souvenir sheet, #4838	2.00	1.00
d.	Sheet of 6 pairs	10.50	5.25

The stamps on No. 4838d are arranged so that the stamps in the middle of the sheet are tete-beche pairs of the same stamp. No. 4838d exists with two arrangements of the stamps, one with No. 4838a as the stamps in the middle of the sheet, the other with No. 4838b as the stamps in the middle of the sheet.

2006 World Cup Soccer Championships, Germany — A1392

Designs: 30b, World Cup. 50b, Ball in goal. 1 l, Player dribbling ball. 1.20 l, Player lifting World Cup.

2006, June 9

4839-4842	A1392 Set of 4	2.50	1.25
4842a	Souvenir sheet, #4839-4842	2.50	1.25

Intl. Day Against Drug Abuse and Illegal Trafficking — A1393

2006, June 26

4843	A1393 2.20 l multi	1.90	.95

Pottery Type of 2005

Pottery from: 30b, Golesti, Arges. 70b, Romana, Olt. 1 l, Oboga, Olt. 2.20 l, Vama, Satu Mare.

2006, July 10   Perf. 13¼
Pottery Actual Color; Background Color:

4844	A1348 30b tan	.25	.25
a.	Sheet of 9	2.25	1.10
4845	A1348 70b yel orange	.60	.30
a.	Sheet of 9	5.50	2.75
4846	A1348 1 l green	.85	.40
a.	Sheet of 9	7.75	3.75
4847	A1348 2.20 l blue green	1.90	.95
a.	Sheet of 9	17.00	8.50
	Nos. 4844-4847 (4)	3.60	1.90

Decebalus (d. 106), Dacian King — A1394

Map and: 30b, Coins and Decebalus. 50b, Head of Decebalus. 1.20 l, Dacian helmet. 3.10 l, Decebalus, diff.

2006, July 15

4848-4851	A1394 Set of 4	4.25	2.10
4851a	Souvenir sheet, #4848-4851	4.25	2.10

Stamp Day.

Minerals — A1395

Designs: 30b, Fluorite. 50b, Quartz. 1 l, Agate. 1.20 l, Blende. 1.50 l, Amethyst. 2.20 l, Stibnite.

2006, Aug. 7

4852-4857	A1395 Set of 6	5.50	2.75
4857a	Souvenir sheet, #4852-4857	5.50	2.75

Nos. 4852-4857 were each printed in sheets of 18 + 3 labels.

Bats — A1396

Designs: 30b, Myotis myotis. 50b, Rhinolophus hipposideros. 1 l, Plecotus auritus. 1.20 l, Pipistrellus pipistrellus. 1.60 l, Nyctalus lasiopterus. 2.20 l, Barbastella barbastellus.

2006, Aug. 15
4858-4863	A1396	Set of 6	5.50	2.75
4863a		Souvenir sheet, #4858-4863	5.50	2.75

Railroads in Romania, 150th Anniv. — A1397

Locomotives: 30b, StEG111 Wartberg, 1854. 50b, D. B. S. R. 1 Ovidiu, 1860. 1 l, L. C. J. E. 56 Curierulu, 1869. 1.20 l, C. F. R. 1 Berlad, 1869. 1.50 l, B. M. 1 Unirea, 1877. 1.60 l, Fulger and King Carol I Pullman Express, 1933. 2.20 l, StEG 500 Steyerdorf.

2006, Aug. 23
4864-4869	A1397	Set of 6	5.00	2.50

Souvenir Sheet
4870	A1397	2.20 l multi	1.90	.95

No. 4870 contains one 71x32mm stamp.

EFIRO 2008 World Philatelic Exhibition, Bucharest — A1398

Exhibition emblem and: 30b, Romania #1. 50b, Romania #2. 1.20 l, Romania #4. 1.60 l, Romania #3. 2.20 l, Bull and vignette of Romania #1.

2006, Aug. 30
4871-4874	A1398	Set of 4	4.00	2.00

Souvenir Sheet
Perf. 13¼x14
4875	A1398	2.20 l multi	1.90	.95

No. 4875 contains one 41x51mm stamp. Nos. 4871-4874 were each printed in sheets of 16 + 8 labels.

National Lottery, Cent. — A1399

2006, Sept. 14　　**Perf. 13¼**
4876	A1399	1 l multi	.85	.40

Printed in sheets of 27 + 1 label.

No. 4098 Surcharged in Gold

2006, Sept. 16　Litho.　Perf. 13½
4877	A1159	5.60 l on 4050 l #4098	4.75	2.25

Sculptures by Constantin Brancusi (1876-1957) — A1400

Designs: 2.10 l, Sleeping Muse. 3.10 l, Sleep.

2006, Sept. 25　　**Perf. 13¼**
4878-4879	A1400	Set of 2	4.50	2.25
4878a		Sheet of 12	18.00	9.00
4879a		Souvenir sheet, #4878-4879	4.50	2.25
4879b		Sheet of 12	27.00	13.50

The third stamp down in the middle column of Nos. 4878a and 4879b is inverted in relation to the other stamps in the sheet.
See France Nos. 3245-3246.

11th Francophone Summit, Bucharest A1401

2006, Sept. 28　　**Perf. 13¼**
4880	A1401	1.20 l multi	1.00	.50

Souvenir Sheet
Perf. 13¼x14
4881	A1401	5.60 l multi	4.75	2.25

No. 4881 contains one 41x51mm stamp.

Romanian Peasant Museum, Cent. — A1402

Designs: 40b, Headdress, 20th cent. 70b, Turkish belt, 19th cent. 1.60 l, Coin necklace, 19th cent. 3.10 l, Musuem founder Alexandru Tzgara-Samurcas.

2006, Oct. 5　　**Perf. 13¼**
4882-4885	A1402	Set of 4	5.00	2.50

Souvenir Sheet

Romanian Division of Intl. Police Association, 10th Anniv. — A1403

2006, Oct. 7
4886	A1403	8.70 l multi	7.25	3.50

Worldwide Fund for Nature (WWF) — A1404

Platalea leucorodia: No. 4887, 80b, Adult and chicks at nest. No. 4888, 80b, Birds in flight. No. 4889, 80b, Birds at water. No. 4890, 80b, Two birds.

2006, Oct. 20
4887-4890	A1404	Set of 4	3.25	2.25
4890a		Souvenir sheet, #4887-4890	3.25	3.25

Nos. 4887-4890 each were printed in sheets of 10 + 2 labels.

Romanian Orders — A1405

Designs: 30b, Order of Loyal Service. 80b, Order of Romanian Star. 2.20 l, Order of Merit. 2.50 l, First Class Order of Merit in Sports.

2006, Oct. 30　　**Perf. 13¼x14**
4891-4894	A1405	Set of 4	5.00	2.50

A small star-shaped hole was punched into Nos. 4891-4894.

Actors and Actresses A1406

Designs: 40b, Radu Beligan. 1 l, Carmen Stanescu. 1.50 l, Dina Cocea. 2.20 l, Colea Rautu.

2006, Nov. 15　　**Perf. 13¼**
4895-4898	A1406	Set of 4	4.25	2.10

Christmas A1407

Designs: No. 4899, 50b, Madonna and Child (shown). No. 4900, 50b, Adoration of the Magi. No. 4901, 50b, Madonna and Child enthroned with angels.

2006, Nov. 17
4899-4901	A1407	Set of 3	1.25	.60
4901a		Sheet of 9, 3 each #4899-4901	3.75	1.90

Art by Ciprian Paleologu — A1408

Designs: 30b, Ad Perpetuam Rei Memoriam. 1.50 l, Cui Bono? 3.60 l, Usqve Ad Finem.

2006, Nov. 30
4902-4904	A1408	Set of 3	4.50	2.25

2007 Admission of Romania and Bulgaria into European Union — A1409

Designs: 50b, "EU" in colors of Bulgarian and Romanian flags. 2.10 l, Flags of Bulgaria and Romania, map of Europe, European Union ballot box.

2006, Nov. 26　Litho.　Perf. 13¼
4905-4906	A1409	Set of 2	2.00	1.00
4906a		Sheet of 8, 4 each #4905-4906, + label	8.00	4.00

See Bulgaria Nos. 4412-4413.

Currency Devaluation Type of 2005

1,000,000 old lei bank notes and 200 lei note: 50b, Obverses of notes. 1.20 l, Reverses of notes.

2006, Dec. 1　Litho.　Perf. 13¼
4907-4908	A1358	Set of 2	1.40	.70
4908a		Sheet of 16, 8 each #4907-4908	11.50	5.75

UNICEF, 60th Anniv. — A1410

2006, Dec. 11
4909	A1410	3.10 l multi	2.50	1.25

Admission into European Union — A1411

2007, Jan. 3　Litho.　Perf. 13¼
4910	A1411	2.20 l multi + label	1.75	.85
a.		Sheet of 8 + 8 labels	14.00	7.00

Biospeleology, Cent. — A1412

Designs: 40b, Altar Rock Cave. 1.60 l, Emil Racovita (1868-1947), founder of Biospeleology Institute. 7.20 l, Ursus spelaeus. 8.70 l, Typhlocirolana moraguesi.

2007, Jan. 19
4911-4914 A1412 Set of 4 14.00 7.00
4914a Souvenir sheet, #4911-4914 14.00 7.00

Intl. Holocaust Remembrance Day — A1413

2007, Jan. 27
4915 A1413 3.30 l multi 2.60 1.40

Printed in sheets of 32 + 4 labels.

Black Sea Fauna A1414

Designs: 70b, Hypocampus hypocampus. 1.50 l, Delphinus delphis. 3.10 l, Caretta caretta. 7.70 l, Trigla lucerna.

2007, Feb. 9
4916-4919 A1414 Set of 4 10.50 5.25
4919a Souvenir sheet, #4916-4919 10.50 5.25

Famous People — A1415

Designs: 60b, Gustave Eiffel (1832-1923), engineer. 80b, Maria Cutarida (1857-1919), physician. 2.10 l, Virginia Woolf (1882-1941), writer. 3.50 l, Nicolae Titulescu (1882-1941), politician.

2007, Feb. 23
4920-4923 A1415 Set of 4 5.50 2.75

Easter — A1416

No. 4924: a, Decorated Easter egg, Olt (30mm diameter). b, Detail from painted glass icon. c, Decorated Easter egg, Bucovina (30mm diameter).

2007, Mar. 9
4924 A1416 50b Horiz. strip of 3,
#a-c 1.25 .60
d. Miniature sheet, 3 each
#4924a-4924c 3.75 1.90

Orchids A1417

Designs: 30b, Cephalanthera rubra. 1.20 l, Epipactis palustris. 1.60 l, Dactylorhiza maculata. 2.50 l, Anacamptis pyramidalis. 2.70 l, Limodorum abortivum. 6 l, Ophrys scolopax.

2007, Mar. 23
4925-4930 A1417 Set of 6 11.50 5.75
a. Souvenir sheet #4925-4930 11.50 5.75

Nos. 4925-4930 each were printed in sheets of 21. The right column of stamps in each sheet have 3 perforation holes separating the stamp from the right selvage, which promotes the 2008 Efiro Intl. Philatelic Exhibition, Bucharest.

Peasant Plates — A1418

Plates from: 70b, Oboga, Olt. 1 l, Varna, Satu Mare. 2.10 l, Valea Izei, Maramures. 2.20 l, Fagaras, Brasov.

2007, Apr. 13
4931 A1418 70b blue & multi .60 .30
a. Miniature sheet of 6 3.75 1.90
4932 A1418 1 l fawn & multi .85 .40
a. Miniature sheet of 6 5.25 2.60
4933 A1418 2.10 l lt grn & multi 1.75 .85
a. Miniature sheet of 6 10.50 5.25
4934 A1418 2.20 l yel & multi 1.90 .95
a. Miniature sheet of 6 11.50 5.75
Nos. 4931-4934 (4) 5.10 2.50

See Nos. 4950-4957.

Birds of Prey — A1419

Designs: 50b, Accipiter nisus. 80b, Circus aeruginosus. 1.60 l, Aquila pomarina. 2.50 l, Buteo buteo. 3.10 l, Athene noctua. 4.70 l, Falco subbuteo.

2007, Apr. 19 Litho. Perf. 13¼
4935-4939 A1419 Set of 5 7.00 3.50
Souvenir Sheet
Perf. 13¼x14
4940 A1419 4.70 l multi 4.00 2.00

No. 4940 contains one 42x52mm stamp.

Europa A1420

Designs: 2.10 l, Scouts. 7.70 l, Lord Robert Baden-Powell.

2007, May 3 Litho. Perf. 13¼
4941-4942 A1420 Set of 2 8.00 4.00
4942a Souvenir sheet, 2 each
#4941-4942, #4941 at UL 16.00 8.00
4942b As "a," #4942 at UL 16.00 8.00

Scouting, cent. Nos. 4941-4942 each printed in sheets of 6.

Old Bucharest — A1421

Designs: 30b, Vlad Tepes, Old Court, document mentioning Bucharest for first time. 50b, Sturdza Palace and arms. 70b, National Military Circle building and arms. 1.60 l, National Theater, Prince Alexandru Ioan Cuza. 3.10 l, I. C. Bratianu Square, King Carol I. 4.70 l, Senate Square and arms. 5.60 l, Romanian Athenaeum.

2007, May 15 Perf. 13¼
4943-4948 A1421 Set of 6 9.00 4.50
4948a Miniature sheet, #4943-4948, + 3 labels 9.00 4.50
Souvenir Sheet
Perf. 14x13¼
4949 A1421 5.60 l multi 4.75 2.40

No. 4949 contains one 42x42mm stamp

Peasant Plates Type of 2007

Plates from: 60b, Tirgu Lapus, Maramures. 70b, Vladesti, Valcea. No. 4952, 80b, Vistea, Brasov. No. 4953, 80b, Luncavita, Tulcea. 1.10 l, Horezu, Valcea. No. 4955, 1.60 l, Tansa, Iasi. No. 4956, 1.60 l, Radauti, Suceava. 3.10 l, Romana, Olt.

2007 Perf. 13¼
4950 A1418 60b gray & multi .50 .25
Miniature sheet of 6 3.00 1.50
4951 A1418 70b bl grn & multi .60 .30
Miniature sheet of 6 3.75 1.90
4952 A1418 80b org & multi .65 .35
Miniature sheet of 6 4.00 2.00
4953 A1418 80b pink & multi .70 .35
Miniature sheet of 6 4.25 2.10
4954 A1418 1.10 l gray & multi .95 .45
Miniature sheet of 6 5.75 2.75
4955 A1418 1.60 l grn & multi 1.40 .70
Miniature sheet of 6 8.50 4.25
4956 A1418 1.60 l yel org & multi 1.40 .70
Miniature sheet of 6 8.50 4.25
4957 A1418 3.10 l pink & multi 2.60 1.25
Miniature sheet of 6 16.00 8.00
Nos. 4950-4957 (8) 8.80 4.35

Issued: Nos. 4950, 4953, 4954, 4956, 8/3; Nos. 4951, 4952, 4955, 4957, 6/5.

Steaua Sports Club, 60th Anniv. — A1422

2007, June 7
4958 A1422 7.70 l multi 6.50 3.25

Printed in sheets of 8 + label.

Romanian Savings Bank Building, 110th Anniv. — A1423

Various views of building with frame color of: 4.70 l, Brown. 5.60 l, Olive green.

2007, June 8
4959 A1423 4.70 l multi 4.00 2.00
Souvenir Sheet
4960 A1423 5.60 l multi + label 4.75 2.40

No. 4959 printed in sheets of 12 with one stamp tete-beche in relation to others.

Sibiu, 2007 European Cultural Capital — A1424

Designs: 30b, Altemberger House, knights from church altar, Dupus. 50b, Liars' Bridge and Council Tower, 18th cent. Transylvanian Saxons. 60b, Parochial Evangelical Church, painting of the Crucifixion. 70b, Grand Square, 1780, 18th cent. peasants. 2.10 l, Brukenthal Palace, statue of St. Nepomuk, portrait of Samuel von Brukenthal. 5.60 l, Sibiu, 1790, Cisnadie Gate Tower. 4.70 l, Sibiu Fortress.

2007, June 11 Perf. 13¼
4961-4966 A1424 Set of 6 8.50 4.25
4966a Miniature sheet, #4961-4966, + 3 labels 8.50 4.25
Souvenir Sheet
Perf. 14x13¼
4967 A1424 4.70 l multi 4.25 2.10

No. 4967 contains one 52x42mm stamp.

Ducks and Geese — A1425

Designs: 40b, Anser erythropus. 60b, Branta ruficollis. 1.60 l, Anas acuta. 2.10 l, Anser albifrons. 3.60 l, Netta rufina. 4.70 l, Anas querquedula. 5.60 l, Anas clypeata.

2007, July 12 Perf. 13¼
4968-4973 A1425 Set of 6 11.50 5.75
4973a Miniature sheet, #4968-4973 11.50 5.75
Souvenir Sheet
Imperf
4974 A1425 5.60 l multi 5.00 2.50

Nos. 4968-4973 each printed in sheets of 10 + 5 labels. No. 4974 contains one 52x42mm stamp.

Bistra Resort Local Postage Stamps, Cent. — A1426

Designs: 50b, Carriage, Upper Colony cabins, 6 heller stamp. 2.10 l, Lower Colony cabins, postman, 2 heller stamp.

2007, July 18 Perf. 13¼
4975-4976 A1426 Set of 2 2.25 1.10

Teoctist (1915-2007), Patriarch of Romanian Orthodox Church A1427

2007, Aug. 3 Litho.
4977 A1427 80b multi .70 .35

Printed in sheets of 4 + 2 labels.

Pottery Baskets, Cups and Pitchers — A1428

Designs: 1.40 l, Basket, Horezu, Valcea. 1.80 l, Cup, Baia Mare, Maramures. 2.10 l, Pitcher, Transylvania. 2.90 l, Cup, Oboga, Olt. 3.10 l, Pitcher, Horezu, Valcea. 7.20 l, Cup, Obarsa, Hunedoara. 7.10 l, Cup, Baia Mare, Maramures, diff. 8.70 l, Cup, Baia Mare, Maramures, diff.

2007 **Perf. 13¼**
4978	A1428	1.40 l gray & multi	1.25	.60
a.		Miniature sheet of 4	5.00	2.50
4979	A1428	1.80 l pink & multi	1.60	.80
a.		Miniature sheet of 4	6.50	3.25
4980	A1428	2.10 l blue & multi	1.75	.90
a.		Miniature sheet of 4	7.00	3.75
4981	A1428	2.90 l bis & multi	2.50	1.25
a.		Miniature sheet of 4	10.00	5.00
4982	A1428	3.10 l lilac & multi	2.60	1.25
a.		Miniature sheet of 4	10.50	5.00
4983	A1428	7.20 l yel & multi	6.00	3.00
a.		Miniature sheet of 4	24.00	12.00
4984	A1428	7.70 l gray grn & multi	6.75	3.50
a.		Miniature sheet of 4	27.00	14.00
4985	A1428	8.70 l lt grn & multi	7.50	3.75
a.		Miniature sheet of 4	30.00	15.00
		Nos. 4978-4985 (8)	29.95	15.05

Issued: Nos. 4978, 4979, 4981, 4984, 8/10. Nos. 4980, 4982, 4983, 4985, 11/7.
See Nos. 5027-5030.

EFIRO 2008 World Philatelic Exhibition, Bucharest — A1429

EFIRO emblem and: 1.10 l, Romania #8. 2.10 l, Romania #9. 3.30 l, Romania #10. 5.60 l, Star, bull's head and post horn.

2007, Aug. 17 **Litho.** **Perf. 13¼**
Stamp + Label
4986-4988	A1429	Set of 3	5.50	2.75

Souvenir Sheet
Perf. 13¼x13¾
4989	A1429	5.60 l multi	4.75	2.40

No. 4989 contains one 42x52mm stamp.

Famous Germans Born in Romania A1430

Designs: 1.90 l, Johannes Honterus (1498-1549), author, cartographer. 2.10 l, Hermann Oberth (1894-1989), rocket scientist. 3.90 l, Stephan Ludwig Roth (1796-1849), educator.

2007, Aug. 24 **Litho.** **Perf. 13¼**
4990-4992	A1430	Set of 3	6.75	3.25

Nos. 4990-4992 each printed in sheets of 8 + label.

Casa Luxemburg, Sibiu — A1431

Various views of building.

2007, Sept. 3 **Perf. 13¼**
4993	A1431	3.60 l multi	3.00	1.50

Souvenir Sheet
Perf. 14x13¼
4994	A1431	4.30 l multi	3.75	1.90

No. 4994 contains one 52x42mm stamp. See Luxembourg No. 1222.

Modern Romanian Monetary System, 140th Anniv. — A1432

Coins: 3.90 l, Reverse of 1867 1-ban coin. 5.60 l, Reverse of 1870 1-leu coin.

2007, Sept. 12 **Litho.** **Perf. 13¼**
4995	A1432	3.90 l multi	3.25	1.60

Souvenir Sheet
Perf.
4996	A1432	5.60 l multi	4.75	2.40

Values for No. 4995 are for stamps with surrounding selvage.

2007 Rugby World Cup, France — A1433

Various players: 1.80 l, 3.10 l.

2007, Sept. 25 **Perf. 13¼**
4997-4998	A1433	Set of 2	4.25	2.10

Nos. 4997-4998 each printed in sheets of 8 + label.

Launch of Sputnik 1, 50th Anniv. — A1434

Sputnik 1 and: 3.10 l, Earth and Moon. 5.60 l, Earth.

2007, Oct. 4 **Perf. 13¼**
4999	A1434	3.10 l multi	2.60	1.25

Souvenir Sheet
Perf. 14x13¼
5000	A1434	5.60 l multi	4.75	2.40

No. 4999 printed in sheets of 8 + label.

Christmas — A1435

2007, Nov. 3 **Perf. 13¼**
5001	A1435	80b multi	.70	.35

Printed in sheets of 8 + label.

Support for the Blind — A1436

2007, Nov. 13 **Litho.** **Perf. 13¼**
5002	A1436	5.60 l multi	4.75	2.40

Printed in sheets of 10 + 2 labels.

Danube River Harbors and Ships — A1437

Ships and: 1 l, Orsova, Romania. 1.10 l, Novi Sad, Serbia.
No. 5005 — Ships: a, Orsova. b, Sirona.

2007, Nov. 14
5003-5004	A1437	Set of 2	1.75	.90

Souvenir Sheet
5005	A1437	2.10 l Sheet of 2, #a-b, + 2 labels	3.50	1.75

Nos. 5003 and 5004 each were printed in sheets of 10 + 5 labels. See Serbia Nos. 412-414.

Arctic Animals — A1438

Designs: 30b, Ursus maritimus. 50b, Pagophilus groenlandicus, vert. 1.90 l, Alopex lagopus, vert. 3.30 l, Aptenodytes forsteri. 3.60 l, Balaenoptera musculus. 4.30 l, Odobenus rosmarus, vert.

2007, Dec. 12 **Litho.** **Perf. 13¼**
5006-5011	A1438	Set of 6	11.50	5.75

Edible and Poisonous Mushrooms A1439

Designs: 1.20 l, Lepiota rhacodes. 1.40 l, Lactarius deliciosus. 2 l, Morchella esculenta. 2.40 l, Paxillus involutus. 3 l, Gyromitra exculenta. 4.50 l, Russula emetica.

2008, Jan. 18 **Litho.** **Perf. 13¼**
5012-5017	A1439	Set of 6	11.50	5.75
5017a		Miniature sheet of 6, #5012-5017	11.50	5.75

Henri Farman (1874-1958) and Voisin-Farman I Bis Airplane — A1440

2008, Jan. 25
5018	A1440	5 l multi	4.00	2.00

Printed in sheets of 8 + label. First flight of one kilometer over a circular course, cent.

Firearms in Natl. Military Museum A1441

Designs: 50b, Four-barreled flint pistol, 18th cent. 1 l, Flint pistol, 18th cent. 2.40 l, Mannlicher carbine pistol, 1903. 5 l, 8mm revolver, 1915.

2008, Feb. 8 **Litho.** **Perf. 13¼**
5019-5022	A1441	Set of 4	7.25	3.75
5022a		Souvenir sheet of 4, #5019-5022, + 2 labels	7.25	3.75

No. 5022a exists with top gun in top label pointing either left or right.

1958 Space Exploration Missions, 50th Anniv. — A1442

Designs: 1 l, Explorer 1. 2.40 l, Sputnik 3. 3.10 l, Jupiter AM-13.

2008, Feb. 22 **Set of 3** 5.00 5.00
5023-5025	A1442	Set of 3	5.00	5.00

Nos. 5023-5025 each were printed in sheets of 8 + central label.

Easter — A1443

2008, Mar. 12
5026	A1443	1 l multi	.85	.40

Printed in sheets of 8 + central label.

Pottery Cups and Pitchers Type of 2007

Designs: 2 l, Cup, Cosesti, Arges. 2.40 l, Pitcher, Radauti, Suceava. 6 l, Pitcher, Baia Mare, Maramures. 7.60 l, Lidded pot, Vladesti, Valcea.

2008, Mar. 21 **Perf. 13¼**
5027	A1428	2 l multi	1.75	.85
a.		Miniature sheet of 4	7.00	3.50
5028	A1428	2.40 l multi	2.10	1.10
a.		Miniature sheet of 4	8.50	4.50
5029	A1428	6 l multi	5.25	2.60
a.		Miniature sheet of 4	21.00	10.50
5030	A1428	7.60 l multi	6.50	3.25
a.		Miniature sheet of 4	26.00	13.00
		Nos. 5027-5030 (4)	15.60	7.80

NATO Summit, Bucharest A1444

2008, Apr. 2   **Litho.**
Color of NATO Emblem
5031 A1444 6 l blue   5.25 2.60
Litho. With Foil Application
5032 A1444 6 l gold   5.25 2.60
5033 A1444 6 l silver   5.25 2.60
   Nos. 5031-5033 (3)   15.75 7.80

Nos. 5032-5033 each were printed in sheets of 8 + central label.

Bears — A1445

Designs: 60b, Helarctos malayanus. 1.20 l, Ursus americanus, horiz. 1.60 l, Ailuropoda melanoleuca, horiz. 3 l, Melursus ursinus, horiz. 5 l, Tremarctos ornatus. 9.10 l, Ursus arctos.

2008, Apr. 21   **Litho.**   *Perf. 13¼*
5034-5038 A1445 Set of 5   9.75 4.50
Souvenir Sheet
Perf. 13¼x13¾
5039 A1445 9.10 l multi   7.75 3.75

Nos. 5034-5038 each were printed in sheets of 8 + label. No. 5039 contains one 42x52mm stamp.

Miniature Sheet

2008 Summer Olympics, Beijing — A1446

No. 5040: a, Track. b, Gymnastics. c, Swimming. d, Canoeing.

2008, May 1   *Perf. 13¼*
5040 A1446 1 l Sheet of 4, #a-d   3.50 1.75

Europa — A1447

Designs: 1.60 l, Envelope, map of Europe. 8.10 l, Stamped cover, European Union flag.

2008, May 8
5041-5042 A1447 Set of 2   8.25 4.00
5042a   Souvenir sheet of 4, 2 each
   #5041-5042, with #5041 at
   UL   16.50 8.25
5042b   As "a," with #5042 at UL   16.50 8.25

Grigore Antipa Natl. Natural History Museum, Cent. — A1448

Designs: 2.40 l, Flora and fauna. 3 l, Grigore Antipa (1867-1944), biologist.

2008, May 20
5043-5044 A1448 Set of 2   4.75 2.40

Nos. 5043-5044 each were printed in sheets of 8 + label.

European Central Bank, 10th Anniv. — A1449

2008, May 26
5045 A1449 3.10 l multi   2.00 2.00
   a.   Sheet of 6 + 6 labels   14.00 14.00

No. 5045 was printed in sheets of 40 stamps + 20 labels.

A1450

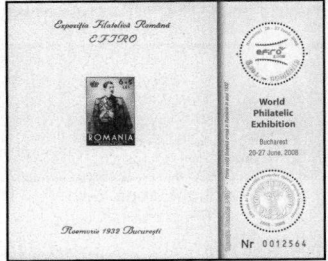

EFIRO 2008 World Philatelic Exhibition, Bucharest — A1451

Romanian stamps: 50b, #5. 1 l, #12. 2.40 l, #22. 3.10 l, #108. 4.50 l, #158. 6 l, #415.

2008, June 20   *Perf. 13¼*
5046 A1450 50b multi + label   .45 .25
   a.   Tete-beche pair   .90 .40
5047 A1450 1 l multi + label   .90 .45
   a.   Tete-beche pair   1.80 .90
5048 A1450 2.40 l multi + label   2.10 1.10
   a.   Tete-beche pair   4.20 2.20

5049 A1450 3.10 l multi + label   2.75 1.40
   a.   Tete-beche pair   5.50 2.80
5050 A1450 4.50 l multi + label   4.00 2.00
   a.   Tete-beche pair   8.00 4.00
5051 A1450 6 l multi + label   5.25 2.60
   a.   Tete-beche pair   10.50 5.20
   b.   Miniature sheet, #5046-5051,
    + 6 labels   15.50 7.75
   Nos. 5046-5051 (6)   15.45 7.80
Souvenir Sheet
Perf.
5052 A1451 8.10 l multi   7.00 3.00

Labels of Nos. 5046-5051 are separated from stamps by two sets of three perforation holes.

Diplomatic Relations Between Romania and Kuwait, 45th Anniv. — A1452

No. 5053: a, Romanian woman weaving. b, Kuwaiti man building ship model. 3.30 l, Romanian oil well fire vehicle.

2008, June 21
5053   Horiz. pair + 2 labels   3.50 1.75
  a.-b.   A1452 2 l Either single   1.75 .85
  c.   Miniature sheet, 2 #5053   7.00 3.50
Souvenir Sheet
5054 A1452 3.30 l multi   3.00 1.50

Labels of Nos. 5053a and 5053b are separated from stamps by a partial row of perforations. The labels show the flags on top and also at the bottom. On No. 5053c, both labels are shown adjacent to the two similar stamps. See Kuwait Nos. 1678-1679.

Selection of "7 Arts" as Best Animated Film at Tours Film Festival, 50th Anniv. — A1453

Designs: 1.40 l, Characters from film. 4.70 l, Character, award, and Ion Popescu-Gopo, director.

2008, June 22   *Perf. 13¼*
5055-5056 A1453 Set of 2   5.25 2.60
5056a   Souvenir sheet, #5055-5056   5.25 2.60

Cathedrals A1454

UNESCO World Heritage Sites: 3 l, St. George's Cathedral, Voronets Monastery, Romania, and chrismon. 4.30 l, St. Demetrius's Cathedral, Vladimir, Russia, and winged beast.

2008, June 23
5057-5058 A1454 Set of 2   6.50 3.25
5058a   Souvenir sheet, #5057-
   5058, + 2 labels   6.50 3.25

Nos. 5057-5058 each were printed in sheets of 10 stamps + 2 labels. See Russia No. 7074.

Castles — A1455

Designs: 1 l, Fagaras Castle, Fagaras. 2.10 l, Peles Castle, Sinaia. 3 l, Huniad Castle, Hunedoara. 5 l, Bethlen Castle, Cris.

2008, June 24
5059-5062 A1455 Set of 4   9.75 4.75
5062a   Miniature sheet of 4,
   #5059-5062   9.75 4.75

Nos. 5059-5062 each were printed in sheets of 9 stamps + 3 labels.

Printing of First Book in Romania, 500th Anniv. A1456

Designs: 4.30 l, Page from Macarie's Missal. 9.10 l, Two pages from Macarie's Missal.

2008, June 25   *Perf. 13¼*
5063 A1456 4.30 l multi   3.75 1.90
Souvenir Sheet
Perf. 13¾x13¼
5064 A1456 9.10 l multi   8.00 4.00

No. 5063 was printed in sheets of 9 stamps + 3 labels. No. 5064 contains one 52x42mm stamp.

Iasi, 600th Anniv. of Mention in Documents — A1457

Buildings in Iasi: 1 l, Church of the Three Holy Hierarchs. 1.60 l, Metropolitan Cathedral. 2.10 l, Vasile Alecsandri National Theater. 3.10 l, Museum of Unification. 7.60 l, Palace of Culture, vert.

2008, June 26   *Perf. 13¼*
Stamps + Label
5065-5068 A1457 Set of 4   6.75 3.25
5068a   Miniature sheet of 4,
   #5065-5068, + 4 labels   6.75 3.25
Souvenir Sheet
Perf. 13¼x13¾
5069 A1457 7.60 l multi   6.75 3.25

Nos. 5065-5068 have labels to both the right and left of the stamp. No. 5069 contains one 42x52mm stamp.

Queen Marie (1875-1938) A1458

2008, July 15   *Perf. 13¼*
Color of Queen
5070 A1458 1 l maroon   .90 .45
   a.   Sheet of 8 + central label   7.25 3.75
5071 A1458 3 l gray green   2.75 1.40
   a.   Sheet of 8 + central label   22.00 11.50
   b.   Souvenir sheet of 2, #5070-
    5071   3.75 1.90

Nos. 5070-5071 each were printed in sheets of 16 stamps + 4 labels.

Regional Coats of Arms
A1459

Arms of: 60b, Moldavia (Moldova). 1 l, Wallachia (Tara Romaneasca). 3 l, Transylvania. 3.10 l, Bucharest.
6 l, Seal of Bucharest, vert.

2008, Sept. 4   **Perf. 13¼**
5072 A1459   60b multi   .50   .25
  a.   Sheet of 8 + central label   4.00   2.00
5073 A1459   1 l multi   .80   .40
  a.   Sheet of 8 + central label   6.50   3.25
5074 A1459   3 l multi   2.40   1.25
  a.   Sheet of 8 + central label 19.50 10.00
5075 A1459   3.10 l multi   2.50   1.25
  a.   Sheet of 8 + central label 20.00 10.00
  b.   Miniature sheet of 4,
          #5072-5075   6.25   3.25
  Nos. 5072-5075 (4)   6.20   3.15

Souvenir Sheet
Perf. 13¼x13¾
5076 A1459   6 l multi   4.75   2.40

Nos. 5072-5075 each were printed in sheets of 16 stamps + 4 labels. No. 5076 contains one 42x52mm stamp.

Nuclearelectrica Power Company, 10th Anniv. — A1460

2008, Oct. 21   **Perf. 13¼**
5077 A1460 2.10 l multi + label 1.50   .75

Radio Romania, 80th Anniv.
A1461

2008, Oct. 28   Litho.   Perf. 13½
5078 A1461 2.40 l multi   1.75   .85
  a.   Souvenir sheet of 2   3.50   1.75

No. 5078 was printed in sheets of 16 having adjacent stamps rotated 90 degrees from each other.

Christmas
A1462

2008, Nov. 5   Litho.   Perf. 13¼
5079 A1462   1 l multi   .70   .35

Flora and Fauna of Paraul Petea Nature Reserve
A1463

Designs: 1.40 l, Nymphaea lotus thermalis. 1.60 l, Scardinius racovitzai. 3.10 l, Melanopsis parreyssi.

2008, Dec. 8   Litho.   Perf. 13½
5081-5083 A1463   Set of 3   4.25   2.10
  5083a Souvenir sheet, #5081-5083 4.25 2.10

Unification of the Romanian Principalities, 150th Anniv.
A1464

Various arms of the United Romanian Principalities.

2009, Jan. 24   **Perf. 13½**
5084 A1464 2.40 l multi   1.50   .75

Souvenir Sheet
Perf.
5085 A1464 9.10 l multi   5.50   2.75

Value for No. 5084 is for stamp with surrounding selvage.

Introduction of the Euro, 10th Anniv. — A1465

2009, Jan. 30   Litho.   Perf. 13¼
5086 A1465   3 l multi   1.90   .95
Litho. With Foil Application
5087 A1465   3 l multi   1.90   .95

Easter — A1466

No. 5088: a, Crucifixion. b, Resurrection. c, Ascension.

2009, Feb. 26   Litho.   Perf. 13½
5088 A1466   1 l Horiz. strip of 3,
              #a-c   1.90   .95

Birds of the Danube Delta — A1467

Designs: 50b, Alcedo atthis atthis. 1.60 l, Himantopus himantopus, horiz. (48x33mm). 2.10 l, Egretta alba, horiz. (48x33mm). 3.10 l, Falco cherrug.
8.10 l, Haliaeetus albicilla.

2009, Feb. 28   **Perf. 13¼**
5089-5092 A1467   Set of 4   4.50   2.25
  5092a Sheet of 4, #5089-5092 4.50 2.25

Souvenir Sheet
Perf. 13½
5093 A1467 8.10 l multi   4.75   2.40

No. 5093 contains one 50x50mm diamond-shaped stamp.

Preservation of Polar Regions and Glaciers
A1468

Designs: 1.60 l, Penguin, eye and teardrop. 8.10 l, Map of Antarctica, iceberg.

2009, Mar. 21   **Perf. 13¼**
5094 A1468 1.60 l multi   1.10   .55
  a.   Tete-beche pair   2.20   1.10
5095 A1468 8.10 l multi   5.25   2.60
  a.   Tete-beche pair   10.50   5.25
  b.   Souvenir sheet, #5094-5095 6.50 3.75

Flowers of the Rodna Mountains
A1469

Designs: 30b, Leontopodium alpinum. 60b, Aster alpinus. 1 l, Dianthus superbus. 1.20 l, Silene nivalis. 2.40 l, Campanula persicifolia. 3.10 l, Lilium martagon.

2009, Mar. 28   **Perf. 13½**
5096 A1469   30b multi   .25   .25
  a.   Sheet of 8 + central label 1.60   .80
5097 A1469   60b multi   .40   .25
  a.   Sheet of 8 + central label 3.25 1.60
5098 A1469   1 l multi   .65   .30
  a.   Sheet of 8 + central label 5.25 2.60
5099 A1469 1.20 l multi   .80   .40
  a.   Sheet of 8 + central label 6.50 3.25
5100 A1469 2.40 l multi   1.60   .80
  a.   Sheet of 8 + central label 13.00 6.50
5101 A1469 3.10 l multi   2.00 1.00
  a.   Sheet of 8 + central label 16.00 8.00
  Nos. 5096-5101 (6)   5.70   3.00

Romgaz, Cent. — A1470

2009, Apr. 24   **Perf. 13¼**
5102 A1470 2.40 l multi   1.50   .75
  a.   Sheet of 6 + 3 central labels 9.00 4.50

Europa — A1471

Designs: 2.40 l, Galileo and his telescope, Leaning Tower of Pisa. 9.10 l, Map of constellations.

2009, May 6   **Litho.**
5103 A1471 2.40 l multi   1.60   .80
5104 A1471 9.10 l multi   6.00   3.00
  a.   Sheet of 4, 2 each #5103-
          5104, #5103 at UL   15.50   7.75
  b.   As "a," with #5104 at UL 15.50 7.75

Intl. Year of Astronomy. Nos. 5103-5104 were each printed in sheets of 6 with and without an illustrated margin.

Council of Europe, 60th Anniv. — A1472

2009, May 11   **Perf. 13¼**
5105 A1472   6 l multi   4.00   2.00

31st Conference of Police Agencies of European Capitals, Bucharest — A1473

Conference emblem, map of Bucharest and: 1 l, Bucharest coat of arms. 1.60 l, Emblem of Romanian Police.

2009, May 25
5106 A1473   1 l multi   .70   .35
  a.   Tete-beche pair   1.40   .70
5107 A1473 1.60 l multi   1.10   .55
  a.   Tete-beche pair   2.20   1.10
  b.   Horiz. pair, #5106-5107 1.80 .90

Romania as Source of European Energy — A1474

Designs: 80b, Electric street light, electric tram and Timisoara Cathedral. 2.10 l, Gas street lamp and Orthodox Cathedral, Turda. 3 l, Iron Gates I Hydroelectric Station, power lines.

2009, June 2
5108-5110 A1474   Set of 3   4.00   2.00
  5110a Sheet of 3, #5108-5110 4.00 2.00

First Man on the Moon, 40th Anniv.
A1475

Designs: 3 l, Astronaut stepping onto Moon. 14.50 l, Bootprint on Moon.

2009, July 20   **Perf. 13¼**
5111 A1475   3 l multi   2.00   1.00
Souvenir Sheet
Perf.
5112 A1475 14.50 l multi   9.75   5.00

No. 5111 was printed in sheets of 8 + label. Values of No. 5111 are for stamps with surrounding selvage.

Historic Center of Sigisoara, UNESCO World Heritage Site — A1476

Arms of Sigisoara and: 1 l, Church on the Hill. 1.60 l, Historic city center. 6 l, Clock Tower, vert.
7.60 l, Aerial view of Sigisoara.

2009, July 24   **Perf. 13¼**
5113-5115 A1476   Set of 3   6.00   3.00
  5115a Sheet of 3 #5113-5115 6.00 3.00
Souvenir Sheet
Perf. 14x13¼
5116 A1476 7.60 l multi   5.25   2.60

Nos. 5113-5115 were each printed in sheets of 8 + central label. No. 5116 contains one 51x41mm stamp.

Stamp Day — A1477

Anghel I. Saligny (1854-1925), engineer and: 2.10 l, Cernavoda Railroad Bridge. 2.40 l, Cernavoda Railroad Bridge and statue.

2009, July 30   *Perf. 13¼*
5117-5118   A1477   Set of 2   3.00   1.50

Electric Trams of European Cities A1478

Arms and trams from: 80b, Frankfurt-am-Main, Germany. 1.20 l, Bucharest. 1.60 l, Vienna. 2.10 l, Brailia, Romania. 2.40 l, London. 8.10 l, Berlin.

2009, Aug. 14
5119-5123   A1478   Set of 5   5.50   2.75
     Souvenir Sheet
5124   A1478   8.10 l multi   5.50   2.75
No. 5124 contains one 48x33mm stamp.

Protected Animals — A1479

Designs: 30b, Aquila chrysaetos. 50b, Lynx lynx, vert. 60b, Cervus elaphus. 1.40 l, Huso huso, vert. 3 l, Testudo graeca ibera. 6 l, Otis tarda, vert.

2009, Aug. 28   *Perf. 13¼*
5125-5130   A1479   Set of 6   8.00   4.00
Nos. 5125-5130 were each printed in sheets of 8 + label.

     Miniature Sheet

Treasures of Romania — A1480

No. 5131: a, Dimitrie Cantemir (1673-1723), prince of Moldavia and writer. b, George Enescu (1881-1955), composer. c, Church of the Three Hierarchs, Iasi. d, Black Church, Brasov. e, Pelican and water lily, Danube Delta. f, Retezat National Park. g, Viticulture. h, Maramures pottery and wood carving.

2009, Sept. 16
5131   A1480   3 l Sheet of 8, #a-
     h, stamps adja-
     cent   17.00   8.50
   i.   As No. 5131, stamps sepa-
     rated   17.00   8.50

Bucharest, 550th Anniv. — A1481

Designs: 30b, Buna Vestire Church. 80b, Coltea Hospital. 3 l, Sutu Palace. 4.70 l, School of Architecture. 8.10 l, Bucharest Patriarchal Cathedral.

2009, Sept. 18   *Perf. 13¼*
5132-5135   A1481   Set of 4   6.25   3.25
5135a   Sheet of 4, #5132-5135   6.25   3.25
     Souvenir Sheet
     Perf. 14x13¼
5136   A1481   8.10 l multi   5.75   3.00
No. 5136 contains one 51x41mm stamp.

Intl. Day of Non-violence — A1482

2009, Oct. 6   *Perf. 13¼*
5137   A1482   3 l multi   2.10   1.10
   a.   Tete-beche pair   4.20   2.20
   b.   Sheet of 6   13.00   6.75

Transgaz, 35th Anniv. — A1483

2009, Oct. 14   *Litho.*
5138   A1483   5 l multi   3.50   1.75
   a.   Souvenir sheet of 3   10.50   5.25

General Staff of the Romanian Armed Forces, 150th Anniv. A1484

2009, Nov. 12
5139   A1484   7.60 l multi   5.25   2.60
   a.   Sheet of 6   32.00   16.00
No. 5139 was printed in sheets of 8 + central label.

Christmas A1485

2009, Nov. 20   *Litho.*   *Perf. 13¼*
5140   A1485   1 l multi   .70   .35
   a.   Sheet of 4, perf. 13¼ on 3
     sides   2.80   1.40
No. 5140 was printed in sheets of 8 + central label.

University of Bucharest Law Faculty, 150th Anniv. — A1486

2009, Nov. 25
5141   A1486   9.10 l multi   6.50   3.25
   a.   Souvenir sheet of 2   13.00   6.50
No. 5141 was printed in sheets of 8 + central label.

First Yiddish Theater, Iasi — A1487

2009, Nov. 26
5142   A1487   3.10 l multi   2.25   1.10
   a.   Souvenir sheet of 2   4.50   2.25
No. 5142a contains two stamps, one with its label to the left of the stamp. The labels on No. 5142a have a complete column of perforations separating them from the adjacent stamps. See Israel No. 1797.

Constanta Harbor, Cent. — A1488

Designs: 1 l, Ship "Mircea." 5 l, King Carol I Lighthouse.

2009, Dec. 23
5143-5144   A1488   Set of 2   4.25   2.10
5144a   Sheet of 2, #5143-5144   4.25   2.10

Honeybees A1489

Designs: 50b, Apis mellifera mellifera. 2.10 l, Apis mellifera ligustica. 3.10 l, Apis mellifera carnica. 4.30 l, Apis mellifera caucasica.

2010, Jan. 22   *Perf. 13¼*
5145   A1489   50b multi   .35   .25
   a.   Sheet of 4, perf. 13¼ on 2 or
     3 sides   1.40   .70
5146   A1489   2.10 l multi   1.50   .75
   a.   Sheet of 4, perf. 13¼ on 2 or
     3 sides   6.00   3.00
5147   A1489   3.10 l multi   2.10   1.10
   a.   Sheet of 4, perf. 13¼ on 2 or
     3 sides   8.50   4.50
5148   A1489   4.30 l multi   3.00   1.50
   a.   Sheet of 4, perf. 13¼ on 2 or
     3 sides   12.00   6.00
     Nos. 5145-5148 (4)   6.95   3.60

2010 Winter Olympics, Vancouver A1490

Designs: 60b, Cross-country skiing. 80b, Speed skating. 1 l, Skeleton, horiz. 7.60 l, Bobsled, horiz.

2010, Feb. 12   *Perf. 13¼*
5149-5152   A1490   Set of 4   6.75   3.50
Nos. 5149-5152 each were printed in sheets of 4.

Tarantulas A1491

Designs: 50b, Brachypelma albopilosum. 80b, Haplopelma lividum. 1.20 l, Brachypelma smithi. 9.10 l, Grammostola rosea.

2010, Feb. 19
5153-5156   A1491   Set of 4   7.75   4.00
Nos. 5153-5156 each were printed in sheets of 8 + central label.

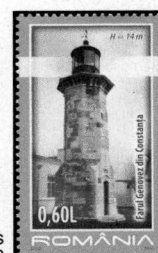

Lighthouses A1492

Designs: 60b, Genoese Lighthouse, Constanta. 80b, Old Lighthouse, Sulina. 1.20 l, Mangalia Lighthouse. 1.60 l, Landing Lighthouse, Tuzla. 8.10 l, White Lighthouse, Constanta North Harbor.

2010, Mar. 5   *Perf. 13¼*
5157-5161   A1492   Set of 5   8.25   4.25
Nos. 5157-5161 each were printed in sheets of 8 + label.

Easter A1493

2010, Mar. 12
5162   A1493   1 l multi   .65   .35
Printed in sheets of 8 + central label.

Intl. Civil Aviation Organization, 65th Anniv. — A1494

2010, Mar. 29   *Perf. 13¼x14*
5163 A1494 8.10 l multi   5.50 2.75
   a.   Souvenir sheet of 2   11.00 5.50
   No. 5163 was printed in sheets of 8 + 2 labels

Romanian Gendarmerie, 160th Anniv. — A1495

2010, Apr. 7   *Perf. 13¼*
5164 A1495 9.10 l multi   6.00 3.00
   a.   Souvenir sheet of 2   12.00 6.00
   No. 5164 was printed in sheets of 8 + central label.

Souvenir Sheet

Eugeniu Carada (1836-1910), Founder of National Bank of Romania — A1496

2010, Apr. 29
5165 A1496 9.10 l multi   6.00 3.00

Europa
A1497

   Designs: 4.30 l, Little Red Riding Hood and Wolf. 7.60 l, Boy and Dragon.

2010, May 6
5166-5167 A1497   Set of 2   7.25 3.75
5167a   Sheet of 4, 2 each #
    5166-5167, #5166 at
    UL   14.50 7.25
5167b   As "a," #5167 at UL   14.50 7.25

Coats of Arms and Landmarks of Countries Along the Danube River — A1498

Mother Baar with Her Daughter, the Young Danube, Sculpture by Adolf Heer, Donaueschingen, Germany — A1499

   Design on stamps and attached labels: 1.40 l, Melk Abbey, arms of Austria. 2.40 l, Bratislava Castle, arms of Slovakia. 3.10 l, Ilok Fortress, arms of Croatia. 4.30 l, Parliament Building, arms of Hungary.

2010, May 8
5168-5171 A1498   Set of 4   6.50 3.25
5171a   Souvenir sheet of 4,
    #5168-5171   6.50 3.25

Souvenir Sheet
5172 A1499 14.50 l multi   8.25 4.25

Minerals
A1500

   Designs: 50b, Quartz and calcite. 1.40 l, Quartz and gold. 1.60 l, Quartz and rhodochrosite. 2.40 l, Calcite. 7.60 l, Red barite.

2010, May 21   *Litho.*
5173-5177 A1500   Set of 5   7.75 4.00
   Nos. 5173-5177 each were printed in sheets of 4.

Horse Breeds — A1501

   Designs: 60b, Huçul. 1 l, Arabian thoroughbred. 2 l, Lippizaner, vert. 2.10 l, Furioso North Star. 5 l, Shagya Arab.

2010, May 29   *Perf. 13¼*
5178-5182 A1501   Set of 5   6.25 3.25
   Nos. 5178-5182 each were printed in sheets of 8 + label.

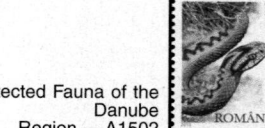

Protected Fauna of the Danube Region — A1502

   Designs: 1.40 l, Vipera ursinii. 1.60 l, Phalacrocorax pygmaeus. 2 l, Huso huso. 7.60 l, Pelecanus crispus.

2010, June 9
5183-5186 A1502   Set of 4   7.25 3.75
5186a   Souvenir sheet of 4,
    #5183-5186   7.25 3.25
   Nos. 5183-5186 each were printed in sheets of 8 + central label.

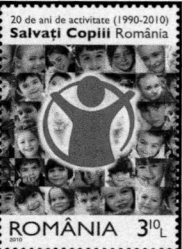

Save the Children Romania, 20th Anniv. A1503

2010, June 9
5187 A1503 3.10 l multi   1.75 .90
   Printed in sheets of 8 + central label.

Ceramic Tiles — A1504

   Tile from: 2.10 l, Portugal, 18th cent. 3.10 l, Romania, 19th cent.

2010, June 30
5188-5189 A1504   Set of 2   3.25 1.60
   Nos. 5188-5189 each were printed in sheets of 8 + central label, with or without an illustrated margin. Stamps from sheets with illustrated margins are perforated on 2 or 3 sides. See Portugal No. 3236.

Recognition of Romanian Orthodox Church Autocephaly, 125th Anniv. A1505

2010, July 15
5190 A1505 6 l multi   3.75 1.90
   Stamp Day. Printed in sheets of 8 + central label.

Botanical Garden of Bucharest, 150th Anniv. — A1506

Dr. Dimitrie Brandza (1846-95), Founder of Botanical Garden — A1507

   Designs: 1.60 l, Clivia miniata. 2.10 l, Magnolia kobus. 2.40 l, Strelitzia juncea. 3 l, Hepatica transsilvanica. 3.10 l, Dicentra spectabilis.

2010, July 23
5191-5195 A1506   Set of 5   7.50 3.75

Souvenir Sheet
5196 A1507 7.60 l multi   4.75 2.40

A1508

Carpathian Garden — A1509

   Designs: 1 l, Tourist looking at Carpathian Sphinx. 1.60 l, Tourist looking at valley. 9.10 l, Valley.

Perf. 13¼x14 on 3 Sides
2010, July 29
Stamp + Label
5197-5198 A1508   Set of 2   1.60 .80
5198a   Sheet, #5197-5198, perf.
    13¼x14, + 2 labels   1.60 .80

Souvenir Sheet
Perf. 13¼x14
5199 A1509 9.10 l multi + label   5.75 2.75

Souvenir Sheet

2010 Youth Olympics, Singapore — A1510

2010, Aug. 12   *Perf. 13¼*
5200 A1510 8.10 l multi   5.00 2.50

Mountain Lakes A1511

   Designs: 2.10 l, Lake Nahuel Huapi, Argentina. 3.10 l, Lake Balea, Romania.

2010, Aug. 14   *Perf. 13¼x14*
5201-5202 A1511   Set of 2   3.25 1.60
   Nos. 5201-5202 were each printed in sheets of 4. See Argentina Nos. 2588-2589.

National Bank of Romania, 130th Anniv. — A1512

   100-lei banknote of 1896: 2.40 l, Obverse. 4.30 l, Reverse.

2010, Sept. 5   *Perf. 14x13¼*
5203 A1512 2.40 l multi   1.50 .75
   a.   Tete-beche pair   3.00 1.50

5204 A1512 4.30 l multi   2.60 1.25
  a. Tete-beche pair   5.20 2.50
  b. Souvenir sheet of 2, #5203-5204   4.25 2.10

Nos. 5203-5204 each have a star punched into the paper next to denomination.

Orient Express — A1513

Locomotive and view of: 2.40 l, Salzburg, Austria. 4.70 l, Sinaia, Romania.

2010, Sept. 6   **Perf. 13¼**
5205-5206 A1513   Set of 2   4.25 2.10
5206a Souvenir sheet of 2, #5205-5206   4.25 2.10

See Austria No. 2275.

Ratification of UN Convention on the Rights of the Child, 20th Anniv. — A1514

2010, Sept. 27
5207 A1514 6 l multi   4.00 2.00

Printed in sheets of 8 + central label.

Danube River Countries Types of 2010

Designs of stamps and attached labels: 1.40 l, Ram Fortress, Serbia, arms of Serbia. 2.40 l, Sava Ognyanov Drama Theater, Ruse, Bulgaria, arms of Bulgaria. 3.10 l, Bogdan Petriceicu Hasdeu State University, Cahul, Moldova, arms of Moldova. 4.30 l, Assumption of the Virgin Church, Izmail, Ukraine, arms of Ukraine.
14.50 l, Navigation Palace, Galati, Romania.

2010, Oct. 1 **Litho.** **Perf. 13¼**
5208-5211 A1498   Set of 4   7.25 3.75
5211a Souvenir sheet of 4, #5208-5211   7.25 3.25
Souvenir Sheet
5212 A1499 14.50 l multi   9.50 4.75

Nos. 5208-5211 each were printed in sheets of 8 + central label. No. 5212 contains one 48x33mm stamp.

Souvenir Sheet

Henri Coanda (1886-1972), Aviation Pioneer and His 1910 Jet Airplane — A1515

2010, Oct. 15
5213 A1515 14.50 l multi + 2 labels   9.50 4.75

National Grand Masonic Lodge, 130th Anniv. — A1516

Designs: 3 l, Arms. 5 l, Compass and square.

2010, Nov. 4
5214-5215 A1516   Set of 2   5.25 2.60

Nos. 5214-5215 each were printed in sheets of 8 + central label.

Viticulture A1517

Designs: 2.10 l, Wine barrels, wine glass. 3.10 l, Grapes, pitcher.

2010, Nov. 10
5216-5217 A1517   Set of 2   3.50 1.75
5217a Souvenir sheet of 2, #5216-5217, perf. 13¼ on 3 sides   3.50 1.75

Nos. 5216-5217 each were printed in sheets of 8 + label. See Cyprus No. 1139.

Christmas A1518

Paintings: 1 l, The Birth of Jesus, by Gheorghe Tattarescu. 3.10 l, The Nativity and Adoration of the Shepherds, by the School of Murillo.

2010, Nov. 15   **Perf. 13¼**
5218-5219 A1518   Set of 2   2.60 1.25

Nos. 5218-5219 each were printed in sheets of 8 + central label. See Vatican City Nos. 1458-1461.

Romanian Innovations — A1519

Designs: 3 l, Brad-Barza gold mine ore car on track with switch, 16th cent. 4.30 l, Horizontal water wheel, 13th-14th cent. 5 l, Petrarche Poenaru and his fountain pen, 1827. 8.10 l, 1923 aerodynamic automobile designed by Aurel Persu.

2010, Dec. 17
5220-5223 A1519   Set of 4   13.00 6.50

Nos. 5220-5223 each were printed in sheets of 8 + central label.

Reptiles A1520

Designs: 60b, Zamenis longissimus. 2.40 l, Podarcis taurica. 3 l, Vipera ammodytes ammodytes. 9.10 l, Vipera ursinii moldavica.

2011, Jan. 19
5224 A1520 60b multi   .40 .25
  a. Souvenir sheet of 4   1.60 .80
5225 A1520 2.40 l multi   1.60 .80
  a. Souvenir sheet of 4   6.50 3.25
5226 A1520 3 l multi   1.90 .95
  a. Souvenir sheet of 4   7.75 4.00
5227 A1520 9.10 l multi   6.00 3.00
  a. Souvenir sheet of 4   24.00 12.00
    Nos. 5224-5227 (4)   9.90 5.00

Nos. 5224-5227 each were printed in sheets of 8 + central label.

Paintings in the National Bank of Romania Collection A1521

Designs: 1.40 l, Mercury, by George Demetrescu Mirea. 2.10 l, Marine, by Eugeniu Voinescu. 3 l, Rodica, by Nicolae Grigorescu. 7.60 l, Prometheus, by Mirea.

2011, Jan. 28   **Perf. 13¼x13¾**
5228 A1521 1.40 l multi   .90 .45
  a. Souvenir sheet of 4   3.75 1.90
  b. Tete-beche pair   1.80 .90
5229 A1521 2.10 l multi   1.40 .70
  a. Souvenir sheet of 4   5.75 3.00
  b. Tete-beche pair   2.80 1.40
5230 A1521 3 l multi   1.90 .95
  a. Souvenir sheet of 4   7.75 4.00
  b. Tete-beche pair   3.80 1.90
5231 A1521 7.60 l multi   5.00 2.50
  a. Souvenir sheet of 4   20.00 10.00
  b. Tete-beche pair   10.00 5.00
    Nos. 5228-5231 (4)   9.20 4.60

Nos. 5228-5231 each were printed in sheets of 8.

Caves A1522

Designs: 30b, Ursilor Cave. 50b, Closani Cave. 60b, Muierii Cave. 3 l, Meziad Cave, horiz. 3.10 l, Vantului Cave, horiz. 8.70 l, Sura Mare Cave, horiz.

2011, Feb. 17   **Perf. 13¼**
5232 A1522 30b multi   .25 .25
  a. Sheet of 8 + central label   1.60 .80
5233 A1522 50b multi   .35 .25
  a. Sheet of 8 + central label   3.00 1.50
5234 A1522 60b multi   .40 .25
  a. Sheet of 8 + central label   3.25 1.60
5235 A1522 3 l multi   2.00 1.00
  a. Sheet of 8 + central label   16.00 8.00
5236 A1522 3.10 l multi   2.10 1.10
  a. Sheet of 8 + central label   17.00 8.50
5237 A1522 8.70 l multi   5.75 3.00
  a. Sheet of 8 + central label   47.50 24.00
    Nos. 5232-5237 (6)   10.85 5.85

Parrots A1523

Designs: 1.60 l, Ara illiger. 2.10 l, Ara macao. 2.40 l, Primolius auricollis. 4.70 l, Platycercus eximius. 5 l, Melopsittacus undulatus.
9.10 l, Nymphicus hollandicus.

2011, Feb. 24
5238 A1523 1.60 l multi   1.10 .55
  a. Sheet of 8 + label   9.00 4.50
5239 A1523 2.10 l multi   1.40 .70
  a. Sheet of 8 + label   11.50 5.75
5240 A1523 2.40 l multi   1.60 .80
  a. Sheet of 8 + label   13.00 6.50
5241 A1523 4.70 l multi   3.25 1.60
  a. Sheet of 8 + label   26.00 13.00
5242 A1523 5 l multi   3.50 1.75
  a. Sheet of 8 + label   28.00 14.00
    Nos. 5238-5242 (5)   10.85 5.40
Souvenir Sheet
5243 A1523 9.10 l multi   6.00 3.00

World Down Syndrome Day — A1524

2011, Mar. 14
5244 A1524 3 l multi   2.10 1.10

Easter — A1525

2011, Mar. 24   **Litho.**
5245 A1525 1 l multi   .70 .35

Printed in sheets of 8 + central label.

Peonies A1526

Designs: 1 l, Paeonia peregrina. 2.10 l, Paeonia tenuifolia.

2011, Mar. 30   **Perf. 13¼**
5246 A1526 1 l multi   .70 .35
Souvenir Sheet
5247 A1526 2.10 l multi   1.50 .75

No. 5246 was printed in sheets of 4.

Butterflies and Moths — A1527

Designs: 50b, Parnassius apollo. 60b, Greta oto, vert. 2.40 l, Morpho nestira. 3 l, Papilio macahon. 4.50 l, Attacus atlas. 5 l, Inachis io. 8.10 l, Iphiclides podalirius.

2011, Apr. 12
5248 A1527 50b multi   .35 .25
  a. Sheet of 8 + central label   3.00 1.50
5249 A1527 60b multi   .45 .25
  a. Sheet of 8 + central label   3.75 1.90
5250 A1527 2.40 l multi   1.75 .85
  a. Sheet of 8 + central label   14.00 7.00
5251 A1527 3 l multi   2.10 1.10
  a. Sheet of 8 + central label   17.00 8.50
5252 A1527 4.50 l multi   3.25 1.60
  a. Sheet of 8 + central label   26.00 13.00
5253 A1527 5 l multi   3.50 1.75
  a. Sheet of 8 + central label   28.00 14.00
    Nos. 5248-5253 (6)   11.40 5.80
Souvenir Sheet
5254 A1527 8.10 l multi   5.75 3.00

Palace of the Parliament, Bucharest — A1528

Designs: 30b, Exterior. 50b, Senate entrance. 60b, Senate chamber. 3 l, Human

Rights Room. 4.30 l, Chamber of Deputies. 7.60 l, Exterior, diff.

2011, Apr. 26

5255	A1528	30b multi	.25	.25
a.		Sheet of 8 + central label	1.60	.80
5256	A1528	50b multi	.35	.25
a.		Sheet of 8 + central label	3.00	1.50
5257	A1528	60b multi	.45	.25
a.		Sheet of 8 + central label	3.75	1.90
5258	A1528	3 l multi	2.10	1.10
a.		Sheet of 8 + central label	17.00	8.50
5259	A1528	4.30 l multi	3.00	1.50
a.		Sheet of 8 + central label	24.00	12.00
5260	A1528	7.60 l multi	5.50	2.75
a.		Sheet of 8 + central label	45.00	22.50
b.		Souvenir sheet of 6, #5255-5260, + label	12.00	6.00
		Nos. 5255-5260 (6)	11.65	6.10

Europa
A1529

Forest and: 2.40 l, Buck. 9.10 l, Squirrel.

2011, Apr. 27

5261	A1529	2.40 l multi	1.75	.85
a.		Sheet of 6	10.50	5.25
5262	A1529	9.10 l multi	6.50	3.25
a.		Sheet of 6	39.00	19.50
b.		Souvenir sheet of 4, 2 each #5261-5262, #5261 at upper left	16.50	8.25
c.		As "b," with #5262 at upper left	16.50	8.25

Intl. Year of Forests.

Signs of the Zodiac
A1530

2011, May 5

5263	A1530	30b Aries	.25	.25
a.		Sheet of 8 + central label	1.60	.80
5264	A1530	50b Taurus	.35	.25
a.		Sheet of 8 + central label	3.00	1.50
5265	A1530	60b Gemini	.45	.25
a.		Sheet of 8 + central label	3.75	1.90
5266	A1530	80b Cancer	.55	.25
a.		Sheet of 8 + central label	4.50	2.25
5267	A1530	1.40 l Leo	1.00	.50
a.		Sheet of 8 + central label	8.00	4.00
5268	A1530	14.50 l Virgo	10.00	5.00
a.		Sheet of 8 + central label	80.00	40.00
b.		Souvenir sheet of 6, #5263-5268	13.00	6.50
		Nos. 5263-5268 (6)	12.60	6.50

See Nos. 5303-5308.

First Man in Space, 50th
Anniv. — A1531

Designs: 3 l, Dumitru Dorin Prunariu, first Romanian in space, Soyuz 40 rocket on launch pad. 4.70 l, Yuri Gagarin, first man in space, Vostok 1 on launch pad. 8.70, Earth as seen from space.

2011, May 9   *Perf. 13¼*

5269	A1531	3 l multi	2.10	1.10
a.		Sheet of 8 + central label	17.00	8.50
5270	A1531	4.70 l multi	3.25	1.60
a.		Sheet of 8 + central label	26.00	13.00

Souvenir Sheet
Perf.

5271	A1531	8.70 l multi	6.00	3.00

Circus
A1532

Designs: 50b, Circus tent, clown's face. 8.10 l, Clown with top hat.

2011, June 1   *Perf. 13¼*

5272	A1532	50b multi	.35	.25
a.		Sheet of 8 + central label	3.00	1.50
5273	A1532	8.10 l multi	5.75	3.00
a.		Sheet of 8 + central label	46.00	23.00
b.		Souvenir sheet of 2, #5272-5273	6.25	3.25

Campaign Against AIDS and HIV, 30th
Anniv. — A1533

2011, June 8   *Litho.*

5274	A1533	3 l multi	2.10	1.10

Opening of Basarab Overpass,
Bucharest — A1534

2011, June 21

5275	A1534	5 l multi	3.50	1.75
a.		Souvenir sheet of 2	7.00	3.50
b.		Sheet of 8	28.00	14.00

Peach Blossoms
A1535

Blossoms of Prunus persica with denomination at: No. 5276, 50b, UL. No. 5277, 50b, UR.

2011, June 30

5276-5277	A1535	Set of 2	.70	.35

Nos. 5276-5277 were printed in sheets of 6, containing 3 of each stamp.

Romanian Red Cross, 135th
Anniv. — A1536

2011, July 3

5278	A1536	3.10 l multi	2.10	1.10
a.		Sheet of 8 + central label	17.00	8.50

Transylvanian Association for Romanian Literature and Culture of the Romanian People, 150th
Anniv. — A1537

Anniversary emblem and: 3 l, Metropolitan Andrei Saguna (1808-73), first president of association. 9.10 l, Association library, Sibiu.

2011, July 15   *Perf. 13¼*

5279	A1537	3 l multi	2.10	1.10
a.		Sheet of 8 + central label	17.00	9.00
5280	A1537	9.10 l multi	6.25	3.25
a.		Sheet of 8 + central label	50.00	26.00

Stamp Day.

Animals and Birds in Nature
Preserves — A1538

Designs: 30b, Canis lupus. 4.50 l, Ardea purpurea. 5 l, Tetrao urogallus. 8.10 l, Nyctereutes procyonoides.

2011, July 25

5281	A1538	30b multi	.25	.25
a.		Sheet of 8 + label	2.00	2.00
5282	A1538	4.50 l multi	3.00	1.50
a.		Sheet of 8 + label	24.00	12.00
5283	A1538	5 l multi	3.50	1.75
a.		Sheet of 8 + label	28.00	14.00
5284	A1538	8.10 l multi	5.50	2.75
a.		Sheet of 8 + label	44.00	22.00
b.		Souvenir sheet of 4, #5281-5284	12.50	6.25
		Nos. 5281-5284 (4)	12.25	6.25

Stained Glass Windows
A1539

Windows in Dumitru Furnica-Minovici Western Old Art Museum of the Romanian Academy, Bucharest: 3.60 l, The Artist, 18th cent. Austrian window. 4.30 l, St. Catherine, 19th cent. Austrian window. 4.50 l, Hunter, 19th cent. Austrian window. 4.70 l, Lady in Green, 17th cent. German window.
St. Hieronymus and Resurrection of Lazarus, 15th cent. Tyrolean windows.

2011, Aug. 18

5285	A1539	3.60 l multi	2.40	1.25
a.		Sheet of 8 + central label	19.50	9.75
5286	A1539	4.30 l multi	2.75	1.40
a.		Sheet of 8 + central label	22.00	11.00
5287	A1539	4.50 l multi	3.00	1.50
a.		Sheet of 8 + central label	24.00	12.00
5288	A1539	4.70 l multi	3.00	1.50
a.		Sheet of 8 + central label	24.00	12.00
		Nos. 5285-5288 (4)	11.15	5.65

Souvenir Sheet

5289	A1539	8.10 l multi	5.25	2.60

Locomotives — A1540

Designs: 2 l, CFR 103 Romania, 1869. 3 l, CFR 28 Codaesti, 1887. 3.30 l, CFR 185 Domnita Maria, 1875. 9.10 l, CFR 001 Lespezi, 1884.
8.10 l, CFR 8008, 1901.

2011, Aug. 26

5290	A1540	2 l multi	1.25	.60
a.		Sheet of 8 + label	10.00	5.00
5291	A1540	3 l multi	1.90	.95
a.		Sheet of 8 + label	15.50	7.75
5292	A1540	3.30 l multi	2.10	1.10
a.		Sheet of 8 + label	17.00	9.00
5293	A1540	9.10 l multi	5.75	3.00
a.		Sheet of 8 + label	46.00	24.00
		Nos. 5290-5293 (4)	11.00	5.65

Souvenir Sheet
Perf. 14x13¼

5294	A1540	8.10 l multi	5.25	2.60

No. 5294 contains one 52x42mm stamp.

20th George Enescu Intl. Music
Festival and Competition — A1541

Designs: 1.40 l, Conductor, concert hall. 3 l, Musical score, Enescu's signature, opera libretto. 7.60 l, Romanian Athenaeum.

2011, Sept. 1   *Perf. 13¼*

5295	A1541	1.40 l multi	.90	.45
a.		Sheet of 8	7.25	3.75
5296	A1541	3 l multi	1.90	.95
a.		Sheet of 8	15.50	7.75
5297	A1541	7.60 l multi	5.00	2.50
a.		Sheet of 8	40.00	20.00
b.		Souvenir sheet of 3, #5295-5297	8.00	4.00
		Nos. 5295-5297 (3)	7.80	3.90

New National Arena,
Bucharest — A1542

2011, Sept. 6   *Perf. 14x13¼*

5298	A1542	5 l multi	3.25	1.60
a.		Souvenir sheet of 2	6.50	3.25
b.		Sheet of 10	32.50	16.00

Biertan Church Castle UNESCO World Heritage
Site — A1543

2011, Sept. 15   *Perf. 13¼*
Granite Paper

5299	A1543	2.10 l multi	1.40	.70
a.		Sheet of 2 + label	2.80	1.40

See Germany No. 2638.

Franz-Joseph Müller von Reichenstein (c. 1740-1825), Discoverer of Tellurium, Diagram of Tellurium Atom — A1544

2011, Sept. 26 — Litho.
| 5300 | A1544 | 5 l multi | 3.25 | 1.60 |
| | a. | Sheet of 8 + central label | 26.00 | 13.00 |

Intl. Year of Chemistry.

Diplomatic Relations Between Romania and Moldova, 20th Anniv. A1545

Designs: 1 l, Holy Gates, Chisinau, Moldova. 3.10 l, Arch of Triumph, Bucharest.

2011, Oct. 11 — Perf. 13¼
5301	A1545	1 l multi	.65	.30
	a.	Sheet of 8 + central label	5.25	2.60
5302	A1545	3.10 l multi	2.00	1.00
	a.	Sheet of 8 + central label	16.00	8.00
	b.	Souvenir sheet of 2, #5301-5302	2.75	1.40

See Moldova Nos. 728-729.

Signs of the Zodiac Type of 2011

2011, Oct. 14
5303	A1530	50b Libra	.35	.25
	a.	Sheet of 8 + central label	3.00	2.00
5304	A1530	60b Scorpio	.40	.25
	a.	Sheet of 8 + central label	3.25	2.00
5305	A1530	80b Sagittarius	.50	.25
	a.	Sheet of 8 + central label	4.00	2.00
5306	A1530	3 l Capricorn	1.90	.95
	a.	Sheet of 8 + central label	15.50	7.75
5307	A1530	6 l Aquarius	3.75	1.90
	a.	Sheet of 8 + central label	30.00	15.50
5308	A1530	8.10 l Pisces	5.25	2.60
	b.	Souvenir sheet of 6, #5303-5308	12.50	6.25
		Nos. 5303-5308 (6)	12.15	6.20

European Day of Civil Justice — A1546

2011, Oct. 25
| 5309 | A1546 | 5 l multi | 3.25 | 1.60 |
| | a. | Sheet of 8 + central label | 26.00 | 13.00 |

Christmas A1547

2011, Nov. 18
| 5310 | A1547 | 1 l multi | .65 | .30 |
| | a. | Sheet of 8 + central label | 5.25 | 2.60 |

Handicrafts A1548

Designs: No. 5311, Painted Easter eggs, Romania. No. 5312, Dough figurines, Hong Kong.

2011, Nov. 24
5311	A1548	2 l multi	1.25	.60
	a.	Sheet of 8	10.00	5.00
5312	A1548	2 l multi	1.25	.60
	a.	Sheet of 8	10.00	5.00
	b.	Souvenir sheet of 2, #5311-5312	2.50	1.25

Romanians and Their Innovations — A1549

Designs: 1.40 l, Stefan Odobleja (1902-78), neurologist, and computer chip. 1.60 l, Ioan Cantacuzino (1863-1934), discoverer of anticholera vaccine, bacillae and microscope. 2.10 l, Anastase Dragomir (1896-1966), inventor of airplane ejector seat. 7.60 l, Grigore Antipa (1867-1944), creator of biological dioramas for museums, and animals.

2011, Dec. 15
5313	A1549	1.40 l multi	.85	.40
	a.	Sheet of 8 + central label	7.00	3.50
5314	A1549	1.60 l multi	1.00	.50
	a.	Sheet of 8 + central label	8.00	4.00
5315	A1549	2.10 l multi	1.25	.60
	a.	Sheet of 8 + central label	10.00	5.00
5316	A1549	7.60 l multi	4.75	2.40
	a.	Sheet of 8 + central label	38.00	19.50
		Nos. 5313-5316 (4)	7.85	3.90

Cotroceni Palace A1550

Stained-glass windows in Union Hall: 50b, Tara Romaneasca window. 60b, Prince Basarab I window, pillar. 80b, Moldova window. 1 l, Prince Bogdan I window, pillar. 2.40 l, Transilvania window. 3.10 l, Prince Michael the Brave (Mihai Viteazul) window, pillar. 14.50 l, Cotroceni Palace.

2011, Dec. 21 — Perf. 13¼
5317	A1550	50b multi	.30	.25
	a.	Sheet of 8 + central label	2.40	2.00
5318	A1550	60b multi	.40	.25
	a.	Sheet of 8 + central label	3.25	2.00
5319	A1550	80b multi	.50	.25
	a.	Sheet of 8 + central label	4.00	2.00
5320	A1550	1 l multi	.60	.30
	a.	Sheet of 8 + central label	5.00	2.40
5321	A1550	2.40 l multi	1.50	.75
	a.	Sheet of 8 + central label	12.00	6.00
5322	A1550	3.10 l multi	1.90	.95
	a.	Sheet of 8 + central label	15.50	7.75
		Nos. 5317-5322 (6)	5.20	2.75

Souvenir Sheet
Imperf
| 5323 | A1550 | 14.50 l multi | 8.75 | 4.50 |

Flowers A1551

Designs: 50b, Eritrichium nanum and snake. 60b, Amaranthus caudatus and turkey. 1 l, Pulmonaria officinalis and bear. 1.20 l, Ranunculus repens and chicken. 1.60 l, Borago officinalis and lamb. 2 l, Potentilla anserina and lobster. 3.30 l, Antirrhinum majus and lion. 3.60 l, Oxalis acetosella and rabbit. 4.70 l, Callistephus chinensis and cow. 7.60 l, Convolvulus arvensis and bird.

2012 — Litho. — Perf. 13¼
5324	A1551	50b multi	.30	.25
	a.	Sheet of 8 + central label	2.40	1.25
5325	A1551	60b multi	.40	.25
	a.	Sheet of 8 + central label	3.25	1.60
5326	A1551	1 l multi	.60	.30
	a.	Sheet of 8 + central label	5.00	2.50
5327	A1551	1.20 l multi	.75	.35
	a.	Sheet of 8 + central label	6.00	3.00
5328	A1551	1.60 l multi	1.00	.50
	a.	Sheet of 8 + central label	8.00	4.00
5329	A1551	2 l multi	1.25	.60
	a.	Sheet of 8 + central label	10.00	5.00
5330	A1551	3.30 l multi	2.00	1.00
	a.	Sheet of 8 + central label	16.00	8.00
5331	A1551	3.60 l multi	2.25	1.10
	a.	Sheet of 8 + central label	18.00	9.00
5332	A1551	4.70 l multi	3.00	1.50
	a.	Sheet of 8 + central label	24.00	12.00
5333	A1551	7.60 l multi	4.75	2.40
	a.	Sheet of 8 + central label	38.00	19.50
		Nos. 5324-5333 (10)	16.30	8.25

Issued: 50b, 60b, 1.60 l, 2 l, 1/19; 1 l, 1.20 l, 3.30 l, 3.60 l, 4.70 l, 7.60 l, 1/17.

Ion Luca Caragiale (1852-1912), Writer — A1552

Designs: 5 l, Caragiale. 9.10 l, Sculpture of Caragiale by Ioan Bolborea, horiz.

2012, Jan. 30 — Perf. 13¼
| 5334 | A1552 | 5 l multi | 3.00 | 1.50 |
| | a. | Sheet of 8 + central label | 24.00 | 12.00 |

Souvenir Sheet
Perf. 14x13¼
| 5335 | A1552 | 9.10 l multi | 5.50 | 2.75 |

No. 5335 contains one 53x42mm stamp.

Selection of Bucharest as Capital of Romania, 150th Anniv. — A1553

Designs: 14.50 l, Sutu Palace, Bucharest coat of arms. 8.10 l, Prince Alexandru Ioan Cuza.

2012, Feb. 3 — Perf. 13¼
| 5336 | A1553 | 14.50 l multi | 9.00 | 4.50 |
| | a. | Sheet of 8 + central label | 72.00 | 36.00 |

Souvenir Sheet
Perf. 14x13¼
| 5337 | A1553 | 8.10 l multi | 5.00 | 2.50 |

No. 5337 contains one 53x42mm stamp.

Portraits on Romanian Banknotes — A1554

Portrait of: 80b, Nicolae Iorga (1871-1940), writer. 1.40 l, George Enescu (1881-1955), composer. 2.10 l, Nicolae Grigorescu (1838-1907), painter. 2.40 l, Aurel Vlaicu (1882-1913), aviation pioneer. 3 l, Ion Luca Caragiale (1852-1912), writer. 3.10 l, Lucian Blaga (1895-1961), writer. 6 l, Mihai Eminescu (1850-89), poet.

2012, Feb. 10 — Perf. 13¼
5338	A1554	80b multi	.50	.25
	a.	Sheet of 4	2.00	1.00
5339	A1554	1.40 l multi	.85	.40
	a.	Sheet of 4	3.50	1.60
5340	A1554	2.10 l multi	1.25	.65
	a.	Sheet of 4	5.00	2.60
5341	A1554	2.40 l multi	1.50	.75
	a.	Sheet of 4	6.00	3.00
5342	A1554	3 l multi	1.90	.95
	a.	Sheet of 4	7.75	4.00
5343	A1554	3.10 l multi	1.90	.95
	a.	Sheet of 4	7.75	4.00
5344	A1554	6 l multi	3.75	1.90
	a.	Souvenir sheet of 4	15.00	7.75
		Nos. 5338-5344 (7)	11.65	5.85

Irons A1555

Iron from: 50b, France, 18th cent. 80b, Germany, 18th cent. 1.40 l, United States, 19th cent. 4.70 l, Scotland, 19th cent. 5 l, Romania, 19th cent. 14.50 l, Romania, 20th cent.

2012, Feb. 17 — Perf. 13¼
5345	A1555	50b multi	.30	.25
	a.	Sheet of 8 + central label	2.40	1.25
5346	A1555	80b multi	.50	.25
	a.	Sheet of 8 + central label	4.00	2.00
5347	A1555	1.40 l multi	.85	.40
	a.	Sheet of 8 + central label	7.00	3.50
5348	A1555	4.70 l multi	3.00	1.50
	a.	Sheet of 8 + central label	24.00	12.00
5349	A1555	5 l multi	3.00	1.50
	a.	Sheet of 8 + central label	24.00	12.00
		Nos. 5345-5349 (5)	7.65	3.90

Souvenir Sheet
Perf. 13¼x14
| 5350 | A1555 | 14.50 l multi | 9.00 | 4.50 |

No. 5350 contains one 42x52mm stamp. See Nos. 5384-5389.

Easter — A1556

2012, Mar. 16 — Perf. 13¼
| 5351 | A1556 | 1 l multi | .60 | .30 |
| | a. | Sheet of 8 + central label | 5.00 | 2.50 |

First Mention of Timisoara in Documents, 800th Anniv. A1557

Designs: 2.10 l, Roman Catholic Cathedral. 5 l, Timisoara Fortress, horiz. 7.60 l, Hunyadi Castle, horiz. 14.50 l, Orthodox Metropolitan Cathedral.

2012, Mar. 26 — Litho.
5352	A1557	2.10 l multi	1.25	.60
	a.	Sheet of 8 + central label	10.00	5.00
5353	A1557	5 l multi	3.00	1.50
	a.	Sheet of 8 + central label	24.00	12.00
5354	A1557	7.60 l multi	4.75	2.40
	a.	Sheet of 8 + central label	38.00	19.50
5355	A1557	14.50 l multi	8.75	4.25
	a.	Sheet of 8 + central label	70.00	35.00
	b.	Souvenir sheet of 1	8.75	4.25
		Nos. 5352-5355 (4)	17.75	8.75

Europa
A1558

Map of Romania and: 1.40 l, Crane in Danube Delta. 8.10 l, Castle and mountains.

2012, Apr. 6

5356	A1558	1.40 l multi	.85	.40
a.		Sheet of 6	5.25	2.40
5357	A1558	8.10 l multi	5.00	2.50
a.		Sheet of 6	30.00	15.00
b.		Souvenir sheet of 4, 2 each #5356-5357, #5356 at UL	12.00	6.00
c.		As "b," with #5357 at UL	12.00	6.00

Romanian
Athletic
Federation,
Cent. — A1559

2012, Apr. 20　　　Perf. 13¼

5358	A1559	1.40 l multi	.85	.40
a.		Sheet of 8 + central label	7.00	3.50

Ministry of
Foreign Affairs,
150th Anniv.
A1560

2012, Apr. 25

5359	A1560	2.10 l multi	1.25	.60
a.		Sheet of 8 + central label	10.00	5.00
b.		Souvenir sheet of 1 + label	1.25	.60

Fruits and
Vegetables
A1561

Designs: 50b, Grapes, peach, tomatoes, garlic. 1.60 l, Apples. 2.10 l, Peppers.

2012, May 3

5360	A1561	50b multi	.30	.25
a.		Sheet of 8 + central label	2.40	1.25
5361	A1561	1.60 l multi	.95	.50
a.		Sheet of 8 + central label	7.75	4.00
5362	A1561	2.10 l multi	1.25	.60
a.		Sheet of 8 + central label	10.00	5.00
		Nos. 5360-5362 (3)	2.50	1.35

The upper right stamp in Nos. 5360a-5362a is tete-beche in relation to the other stamps in the sheet.

Intl.
Children's
Day — A1562

2012, June 1

5363	A1562	2.40 l multi	1.40	.70
a.		Sheet of 8 + central label	11.50	5.75

Fish
A1563

Designs: 1.40 l, Poecilia sphenops. 3 l, Eupomotis gibbosus. 3.10 l, Macropodus opercularis. 14.50 l, Thorichthys meeki.

2012, June 15

5364	A1563	1.40 l multi	.80	.40
a.		Sheet of 8 + central label	6.50	3.25
5365	A1563	3 l multi	1.60	.80
a.		Sheet of 8 + central label	13.00	6.50
5366	A1563	3.10 l multi	1.75	.85
a.		Sheet of 8 + central label	14.00	7.00
5367	A1563	14.50 l multi	8.00	4.00
a.		Sheet of 8 + central label	65.00	32.50
		Nos. 5364-5367 (4)	12.15	6.05

Birds — A1564

Designs: 1 l, Merops apiaster. 1.20 l, Egretta garzetta. 2.10 l, Ardeola ralloides. 8.10 l, Branta ruficollis. 9.10 l, Pelecanus onocrotalus.

2012, July 6　　　Perf. 14x13¼

5368	A1564	1 l multi	.55	.25
a.		Sheet of 9 + label	5.00	2.50
5369	A1564	1.20 l multi	.65	.30
a.		Sheet of 9 + label	6.00	3.00
5370	A1564	2.10 l multi	1.25	.60
a.		Sheet of 9 + label	11.50	5.50
5371	A1564	8.10 l multi	4.50	2.25
a.		Sheet of 9 + label	41.00	21.00
5372	A1564	9.10 l multi	5.00	2.50
a.		Sheet of 9 + label	45.00	22.50
b.		Souvenir sheet of 1	5.00	2.50
		Nos. 5368-5372 (5)	11.95	5.90

Eleventh meeting of the Conference of the Parties to the Convention on Wetlands of International Importance, Bucharest.

Victor Babes National Institute, 125th
Anniv. — A1565

Designs: 3.10 l, Building, Bucharest. 7.60 l, Babes (1854-1926), physician, and flasks.

2012, July 16　　　Perf. 13¼

5373	A1565	3.10 l multi	1.75	.85
a.		Sheet of 8 + central label	14.00	7.00
5374	A1565	7.60 l multi	4.25	2.10
a.		Sheet of 8 + central label	34.00	17.00
b.		Souvenir sheet of 2, #5373-5374	6.00	3.00

2012 Summer Olympics,
London — A1566

Designs: 1.20 l, Gymnastics. 1.40 l, Canoeing. 2.10 l, Fencing. 6 l, Javelin.

2012, July 27　　　Litho.

5375-5378	A1566	Set of 4	5.75	3.00

Nos. 5374-5378 each were printed in sheets of 4.

Dogs — A1567

Designs: 4.50 l, Short-haired dachshund. 5 l, Golden retriever. 8.10 l, Romanian Mioritic shepherd. 9.10 l, Romanian Carpathian shepherd.

2012, Aug. 10

5379	A1567	4.50 l multi	2.60	1.40
a.		Sheet of 8 + central label	21.00	11.50
5380	A1567	5 l multi	3.00	1.50
a.		Sheet of 8 + central label	24.00	12.00
5381	A1567	8.10 l multi	4.75	2.40
a.		Sheet of 8 + central label	38.00	19.50
5382	A1567	9.10 l multi	5.25	2.60
a.		Sheet of 8 + central label	42.00	21.00
b.		Souvenir sheet of 4, #5379-5382	16.00	8.00
		Nos. 5379-5382 (4)	15.60	7.90

Hagigadar Monastery, Moara, 500th
Anniv. — A1568

2012, Aug. 11

5383	A1568	4.70 l multi	2.75	1.40
a.		Sheet of 8 + central label	22.00	11.50
b.		Souvenir sheet of 2 + 2 labels	5.50	2.75

Examples of No. 5383b with gold foil applied were printed in limited quantities and sold for 135 l. See Armenia No. 911.

Irons Type of 2012

Irons from: 80b, Burma, 19th cent. 1 l, Sweden, 18th cent. 1.20 l, Belgium, 18th cent. 1.60 l, Italy, 18th cent. 5 l, Switzerland, 19th cent. 14.50 l, United States, 19th cent.

2012, Sept. 1

5384	A1555	80b multi	.45	.25
a.		Sheet of 8 + central label	3.75	2.00
5385	A1555	1 l multi	.60	.30
a.		Sheet of 8 + central label	5.00	2.40
5386	A1555	1.20 l multi	.70	.35
a.		Sheet of 8 + central label	5.75	3.00
5387	A1555	1.60 l multi	.95	.45
a.		Sheet of 8 + central label	7.75	3.75
5388	A1555	5 l multi	3.00	1.50
a.		Sheet of 8 + central label	24.00	12.00
5389	A1555	14.50 l multi	8.50	4.25
a.		Sheet of 8 + central label	68.00	34.00
b.		Souvenir sheet of 1, imperf.	8.50	4.25
		Nos. 5384-5389 (6)	14.20	7.10

Romanian Post, 150th Anniv. — A1569

Designs: 1 l, Romania #11, 12, 14. 8.10 l, Posthorn, Postal headquarters, Bucharest.

2012, Sept. 24

5390	A1569	1 l multi	.60	.30
a.		Sheet of 8 + central label	5.00	2.40
5391	A1569	8.10 l multi	4.75	2.40
a.		Sheet of 8 + central label	38.00	19.50
b.		Souvenir sheet of 1, imperf.	4.75	2.40

A sheet containing Nos. 5390-5391 was printed in limited quantities.

Treaty Between
Romania and
Germany, 20th
Anniv. — A1570

2012, Oct. 4

5392	A1570	2.10 l multi	1.25	.60
a.		Sheet of 8 + central label	10.00	5.00

Curtea de Arges Monastery Church,
500th Anniv. — A1571

Designs: 4.50 l, Church and icons. 14.50 l, Church.

2012, Oct. 12

5393	A1571	4.50 l multi	2.60	1.40
a.		Sheet of 8 + central label	21.00	11.50
5394	A1571	14.50 l multi	8.25	4.25
a.		Sheet of 8 + central label	66.00	34.00
b.		Souvenir sheet of 4, 2 each #5393-5394, + 2 labels	22.00	11.50

Mammals
A1572

Designs: No. 5395, Capra pyrenaica. No. 5396, Cervus elaphus.

2012, Oct. 19

5395	A1572	3.10 l multi	1.75	.90
a.		Sheet of 8 + central label	14.00	7.25
5396	A1572	3.10 l multi	1.75	.90
a.		Sheet of 8 + central label	14.00	7.25

A sheet containing Nos. 5395-5396 was printed in limited quantities. See Spain No. 3878.

ROMÂNIA 1³⁰L
Christmas
A1573

2012, Nov. 15

5397	A1573	1 l multi	.60	.30
a.		Sheet of 8 + central label	5.00	2.40

A souvenir sheet of 2 No. 5397 was printed in limited quantities.

Stone
Churches
A1574

Designs: 3 l, St. Nicholas Church, Densus. 5 l, Strei Church, Hunedoara. 7.60 l, Mintia Church, Vetel. 14.50 l, Colt Church, Suseni.

2012, Nov. 16

5398	A1574	3 l multi	1.75	.85
a.		Sheet of 8 + central label	14.00	7.00
5399	A1574	5 l multi	3.00	1.50
a.		Sheet of 8 + central label	24.00	12.00
5400	A1574	7.60 l multi	4.50	2.25
a.		Sheet of 8 + central label	36.00	18.00
5401	A1574	14.50 l multi	8.25	4.25
a.		Sheet of 8 + central label	66.00	34.00
		Nos. 5398-5401 (4)	17.50	8.85

Young
Animals
A1575

Designs: 4.30 l, Bear cub. 5 l, Fawn. 9.10 l, Fox pup. 14.50 l, Wolf pup.

2012, Dec. 7

5402	A1575	4.30 l multi	2.50	1.25
a.		Sheet of 8 + central label	20.00	10.00
5403	A1575	5 l multi	3.00	1.50
a.		Sheet of 8 + central label	24.00	12.00
5404	A1575	9.10 l multi	5.25	2.60
a.		Sheet of 8 + central label	42.00	21.00
5405	A1575	14.50 l multi	8.25	4.25
a.		Sheet of 8 + central label	66.00	34.00
b.		Sheet of 4, #5402-5405	19.00	9.75
		Nos. 5402-5405 (4)	19.00	9.60

Seal of Mircea cel Batran and Arms of Sovereign Military Order of Malta — A1576

2012, Dec. 14

5406	A1576	8.10 l multi	5.00	2.50
a.		Sheet of 8 + central label	40.00	20.00

Romanian relations with Sovereign Military Order of Malta, 80th anniv. A souvenir sheet of two No. 5406 exists from a limited printing.

Anti-terrorist Fighter's Day — A1577

Crest of Romanian Anti-terrorist Brigade and: 1 l, Soldier. 8.10 l, Five soldiers.

2012, Dec. 21

5407	A1577	1 l multi	.60	.30
a.		Sheet of 8 + 4 labels	5.00	2.40
5408	A1577	8.10 l multi	5.00	2.50
a.		Sheet of 8 + 4 labels	40.00	20.00
b.		Souvenir sheet of 1	5.00	2.50

Self-portraits
A1578

Self-portrait of: 4.50 l, Stefan Luchian (1868-1916). 9.10 l, Nicolae Grigorescu (1838-1907).

2013, Jan. 18

5409	A1578	4.50 l multi	2.75	1.40
a.		Sheet of 8 + central label	22.00	11.50
5410	A1578	9.10 l multi	5.75	2.75
a.		Sheet of 8 + central label	46.00	22.00
b.		Souvenir sheet of 1	5.75	2.75

Flowers and
Clocks — A1579

Designs: 60b, Papaver rhoeas, French mantel clock, 19th cent. 80b, Cichorium intybus, Austrian carriage clock, 19th cent. 1 l, Scorzonera rosea, French table clock, 19th cent. 1.60 l, Caltha palustris, German table clock, 20th cent. 2.40 l, Helianthus annuus, French portico clock, 19th cent. 5 l, Veronica chamaedrys, French table clock, 19th cent.

2013, Jan. 25

5411	A1579	60b multi	.40	.25
a.		Sheet of 8 + central label	3.25	2.00
5412	A1579	80b multi	.50	.25
a.		Sheet of 8 + central label	4.00	2.00
5413	A1579	1 l multi	.65	.30
a.		Sheet of 8 + central label	5.25	2.40
5414	A1579	1.60 l multi	1.00	.50
a.		Sheet of 8 + central label	8.00	4.00
5415	A1579	2.40 l multi	1.50	.75
a.		Sheet of 8 + central label	12.00	6.00
5416	A1579	5 l multi	3.25	1.60
a.		Sheet of 8 + central label	26.00	13.00
		Nos. 5411-5416 (6)	7.30	3.65

A sheet of six containing Nos. 5412-5417 exists in a limited printing. See Nos. 5454-5459.

Radauti Synagogue, 130th
Anniv. — A1580

Synagogue and: 8.10 l, Star of David. 14.50 l, Menorah.

2013, Feb. 8 Litho. Perf. 13¼

5417	A1580	8.10 l multi	5.00	2.50
a.		Sheet of 8 + central label	40.00	20.00
5418	A1580	14.50 l multi	8.75	4.50
a.		Sheet of 8 + central label	70.00	36.00

A sheet of two containing Nos. 5417-5418 exists in a limited printing.

Romanian Athenaeum. 125th
Anniv. — A1581

Designs: 5 l, Stage. 9.10 l, Exterior.

Perf. 13¾x13¼

2013, Feb. 22 Litho.

5419	A1581	5 l multi	3.00	1.50
a.		Sheet of 10	30.00	15.00
5420	A1581	9.10 l multi	5.50	2.75
a.		Sheet of 10	55.00	27.50
b.		Souvenir sheet of 1	5.50	2.75

Crowns
A1582

Crown of: 3.30 l, King Carol I. 4.30 l, Queen Elizabeth. 14.50 l, Queen Marie.

2013, Feb. 28 Litho. Perf. 13¼

5421	A1582	3.30 l multi	2.00	1.00
a.		Sheet of 6	12.00	6.00
5422	A1582	4.30 l multi	2.60	1.40
a.		Sheet of 6	16.00	8.50
5423	A1582	14.50 l multi	8.75	4.50
a.		Sheet of 6	52.50	27.00
		Nos. 5421-5423 (3)	13.35	6.90

Values are for stamps with surrounding selvage. A souvenir sheet of three containing Nos. 5421-5423 exists in a limited printing.

Tourist Attractions in
Transylvania — A1583

Arms of Transylvania and: 3.30 l, Fortified Church, Viscri. 3.60 l, House, Valea Zalanului, vert. 4.30 l, Hosman, vert. 5 l, St. Michael's Church, Cluj.

2013, Mar. 15 Litho. Perf. 13¼

5424	A1583	3.30 l multi	1.90	.95
a.		Sheet of 8 + central label	15.50	7.75
5425	A1583	3.60 l multi	2.10	1.10
a.		Sheet of 8 + central label	17.00	9.00
5426	A1583	4.30 l multi	2.50	1.25
a.		Sheet of 8 + central label	20.00	10.00
5427	A1583	5 l multi	3.00	1.50
a.		Sheet of 8 + central label	24.00	12.00
		Nos. 5424-5427 (4)	9.50	4.80

A sheet of four containing Nos. 5424-5427 exists in a limited printing.

Cameras
A1584

Designs: 50b, Goldmann camera, Austria. 80b, Suter camera, Switzerland. 1.40 l, Plaubel Makina camera, Germany. 2 l, Ernemann Tropen-Klapp camera, Germany. 2.10 l, Balda Pontina camera, Germany. 14.50 l, Welta camera, Germany.

2013, Mar. 29 Litho. Perf. 13¼

5428	A1584	50b multi	.30	.25
a.		Sheet of 8 + central label	2.40	1.25

5429	A1584	80b multi	.50	.25
a.		Sheet of 8 + central label	4.00	2.00
5430	A1584	1.40 l multi	.80	.40
a.		Sheet of 8 + central label	6.50	3.25
5431	A1584	2 l multi	1.25	.60
a.		Sheet of 8 + central label	10.00	5.00
5432	A1584	2.10 l multi	1.25	.60
a.		Sheet of 8 + central label	10.00	5.00
5433	A1584	14.50 l multi	8.50	4.25
a.		Sheet of 8 + central label	68.00	34.00
		Nos. 5428-5433 (6)	12.60	6.35

Easter — A1585

2013, Apr. 5 Litho. Perf. 13¼

5434	A1585	1 l multi	.60	.30
a.		Sheet of 8 + central label	4.80	2.40

King Carol I and Bucharest University of Economic Studies — A1586

2013, Apr. 6 Litho. Perf. 13¼

5435	A1586	8.10 l multi	5.00	2.50
a.		Sheet of 8 + central label	40.00	20.00

Bucharest University of Economic Studies, cent.

National Bank of Romania,
Bucharest — A1587

Designs: 3.10 l, Exterior. 3.60 l, Marble Hall. 4.50 l, Main hallway. 4.70 l, Staircase.

2013, Apr. 17 Litho. Perf. 13¼

5436	A1587	3.10 l multi	1.90	.95
a.		Sheet of 6	11.50	5.75
5437	A1587	3.60 l multi	2.25	1.10
a.		Sheet of 6	13.50	6.75
5438	A1587	4.50 l multi	2.75	1.40
a.		Sheet of 6	16.50	8.50
5439	A1587	4.70 l multi	3.00	1.50
a.		Sheet of 6	18.00	9.00
b.		Souvenir sheet of 4, #5436-5439	10.00	5.00
		Nos. 5436-5439 (4)	9.90	4.95

Earth
Day — A1588

2013, Apr. 22 Litho. Perf. 13¼

5440	A1588	5 l multi	3.00	1.50
a.		Sheet of 8 + central label	24.00	12.00

Famous Women — A1589

Designs: 1 l, Stefania Maracineanu (1882-1944), physicist. 3.30 l, Josephine Cochrane (1839-1913), inventor of dishwasher. 9.10 l, Rear Admiral Grace Murray Hopper (1906-92), computer scientist.

2013, Apr. 26		**Litho.**	**Perf. 13¼**	
5441	A1589	1 l multi	.60	.30
a.		Sheet of 6	3.60	1.80
5442	A1589	3.30 l multi	2.00	1.00
a.		Sheet of 6	12.00	6.00
5443	A1589	9.10 l multi	5.50	2.75
a.		Sheet of 6	33.00	16.50
		Nos. 5441-5443 (3)	8.10	4.05

Europa — A1590

Designs: 2.10 l, Biplane with airmail envelopes as wings. 14.50 l, Postman on bicycle delivering letter to driver of automobile.

2013, Apr. 30		**Litho.**	**Perf. 13¼**	
5444	A1590	2.10 l multi	1.25	.60
a.		Sheet of 6	7.50	3.75
5445	A1590	14.50 l multi	9.00	4.50
a.		Sheet of 6	54.00	27.00
b.		Souvenir sheet of 4, 2 each #5444-5445, #5444 at UL	20.50	10.50
c.		As "b," #5445 at UL	20.50	10.50

Edict of Milan, 1700th Anniv. — A1591

Emperor Constantine the Great and Empress Helen on: 4.70 l, Byzantine era icon. 9.10 l, Icon by Otilia Michail Otetelesanu from 1960s.

2013, May 21		**Litho.**	**Perf. 13¼**	
5446	A1591	4.70 l multi	3.00	1.50
a.		Sheet of 6	18.00	9.00
5447	A1591	9.10 l multi	5.50	2.75
a.		Sheet of 6	33.00	16.50

First Mention of Suceava in Documents, 625th Anniv. — A1592

Anniversary emblem and: 4.30 l, St. George's Church (Mirauti Church). 14.50 l, Suceava Fortress.

2013, May 30		**Litho.**	**Perf. 13¼**	
5448	A1592	4.30 l multi	2.60	1.40
a.		Sheet of 8 + label	21.00	11.50
5449	A1592	14.50 l multi	8.75	4.50
a.		Sheet of 8 + label	70.00	36.00

A souvenir sheet of two containing Nos. 5448-5449 was printed in limited quantities.

Healthy Foods A1593

Jar of honey and: 1 l, Walnuts, cinnamon sticks. 1.40 l, Hazelnuts. 6 l, Raspberries and blackberries. 8.10 l, Walnuts, cinnamon sticks, hazelnuts, raspberries and blackberries.

2013, June 7		**Litho.**	**Perf. 13¼**	
5450	A1593	1 l multi	.60	.30
a.		Sheet of 8 + label	5.00	2.40
5451	A1593	1.40 l multi	.85	.40
a.		Sheet of 8 + label	7.00	3.25
5452	A1593	6 l multi	3.75	1.90
a.		Sheet of 8 + label	30.00	15.50
5453	A1593	8.10 l multi	5.00	2.50
a.		Sheet of 8 + label	40.00	20.00
		Nos. 5450-5453 (4)	10.20	5.10

A souvenir sheet of four containing Nos. 5450-5453 was printed in limited quantities.

Flowers and Clocks Type of 2013

Designs: 50b, Anthericum ramosum, French table clock, 19th cent. 1.20 l, Mirabilis jalapa, German table clock, 19th cent. 1.40 l, Datura stramonium, Swiss pocket watch, 18th cent. 3 l, Silene latifolia, Austrian traveler's clock, 19th cent. 3.10 l, Nicotiana alata, French chimney clock, 19th cent. 4.70 l, Oenothera biennis, French miniature table clock, 19th cent.

2013, June 21		**Litho.**	**Perf. 13¼**	
5454	A1579	50b multi	.30	.25
a.		Sheet of 8 + central label	2.40	1.25
5455	A1579	1.20 l multi	.70	.35
a.		Sheet of 8 + central label	5.75	3.00
5456	A1579	1.40 l mulkti	.85	.40
a.		Sheet of 8 + central label	7.00	3.25
5457	A1579	3 l multi	1.75	.85
a.		Sheet of 8 + central label	14.00	7.00
5458	A1579	3.10 l multi	1.90	.95
a.		Sheet of 8 + central label	15.50	7.75
5459	A1579	4.70 l multi	2.75	1.40
a.		Sheet of 8 + central label	22.00	11.50
		Nos. 5454-5459 (6)	8.25	4.20

A sheet of six containing Nos. 5454-5459 exists in a limited printing.

Owls — A1594

Designs: 2 l, Athene noctua. 3.30 l, Asio otus. 4.50 l, Strix uralensis. 9.10 l, Strix nebulosa, horiz.

2013, June 28		**Litho.**	**Perf. 13¼**	
5460	A1594	2 l multi	1.25	.60
a.		Sheet of 6	7.50	3.75
5461	A1594	3.30 l multi	2.00	1.00
a.		Sheet of 6	12.00	6.00
5462	A1594	4.50 l multi	2.75	1.40
a.		Sheet of 6	16.50	8.50
5463	A1594	9.10 l multi	5.50	2.75
a.		Sheet of 6	33.00	16.50
		Nos. 5460-5463 (4)	11.50	5.75

Treaty of Friendly Relations and Cooperation Between Romania and Russia, 10th Anniv. — A1595

2013, July 9	**Litho.**	**Perf. 13¾x13¼**		
5464	A1595	8.10 l multi	4.75	2.40
a.		Sheet of 6 + 2 labels	28.50	14.50
b.		Souvenir sheet of 1	4.75	2.40

Sport Hunting and Fishing A1596

Designs: 2 l, Mouflon. 2.10 l, European hare. 6 l, Chamois. 7.60 l, Trout.

2013, July 9		**Litho.**	**Perf. 13¼**	
5465	A1596	2 l multi	1.25	.60
a.		Sheet of 8 + label	10.00	5.00
5466	A1596	2.10 l multi	1.25	.60
a.		Sheet of 8 + label	10.00	5.00
5467	A1596	6 l multi	3.50	1.75
a.		Sheet of 8 + label	28.00	14.00
5468	A1596	7.60 l multi	4.50	2.25
a.		Sheet of 8 + label	36.00	18.00
		Nos. 5465-5468 (4)	10.50	5.20

Antim Monastery, 300th Anniv. — A1597

Designs: 3.60 l, Monastery. 14.50 l, Bishop Antim Ivireanu (1650-1716).

2013, July 15		**Litho.**	**Perf. 13¼**	
5469	A1597	3.60 l multi	2.10	1.10
a.		Sheet of 4	8.50	4.50
5470	A1597	14.50 l multi	8.75	4.50
a.		Sheet of 4	35.00	18.00

A sheet of two containing Nos. 5469-5470 exists in a limited printing.

Romanian Gold Coins A1598

20-lei coins from: 3.30 l, 1870. 4.30 l, 1906. 4.50 l, 1922. 8.10 l, 1939.

2013, July 26		**Litho.**	**Perf. 13¼**	
5471	A1598	3.30 l multi	2.00	1.00
a.		Sheet of 6	12.00	6.00
5472	A1598	4.30 l multi	2.60	1.40
a.		Sheet of 6	16.00	8.50
5473	A1598	4.50 l multi	2.75	1.40
a.		Sheet of 6	16.50	8.50
5474	A1598	8.10 l multi	5.00	2.50
a.		Sheet of 6	30.00	15.00
		Nos. 5471-5474 (4)	12.35	6.30

Religion and Law — A1599

Designs: 1.20 l, Statue of Moses, by Michelangelo. 1.40 l, Ten Commandments. 3 l, Torahs, Great Synagogue of Bucharest. 14.50 l, St. Catherine's Monastery, Mount Sinai, Egypt.

2013, Aug. 14		**Litho.**	**Perf. 13¼**	
5475	A1599	1.20 l multi	.75	.35
a.		Sheet of 8 + central label	6.00	3.00
5476	A1599	1.40 l multi	.85	.40
a.		Sheet of 8 + central label	7.00	3.25
5477	A1599	3 l multi	1.75	.90
a.		Sheet of 8 + central label	14.00	7.25
5478	A1599	14.50 l multi	8.75	4.50
a.		Sheet of 8 + central label	70.00	36.00
		Nos. 5475-5478 (4)	12.10	6.15

A sheet of 4 containing Nos. 5475-5478 exists in a limited printing.

Mention of Oradea in Documents, 900th Anniv. — A1600

Designs: 2.10 l, Assumption of the Virgin Orthodox Cathedral. 4.30 l, Roman Catholic Cathedral. 4.70 l, Queen Marie Theater, horiz. 9.10 l, Oradea City Hall, horiz.

2013, Aug. 30		**Litho.**	**Perf. 13¼**	
5479	A1600	2.10 l multi	1.25	.60
a.		Sheet of 8 + central label	10.00	5.00
5480	A1600	4.30 l multi	2.60	1.40
a.		Sheet of 8 + central label	21.00	11.50
5481	A1600	4.70 l multi	3.00	1.50
a.		Sheet of 8 + central label	24.00	12.00
5482	A1600	9.10 l multi	5.50	2.75
a.		Sheet of 8 + central label	44.00	22.00
b.		Souvenir sheet of 1	5.50	2.75
		Nos. 5479-5482 (4)	12.35	6.25

A sheet of four containing Nos. 5479-5482 exists in a limited printing.

Traditional Costumes of Romania and Poland — A1601

		Perf. 13¾x13¼		
2013, Sept. 11			**Litho.**	
5483	A1601	8.10 l multi	5.00	2.50
a.		Sheet of 10	50.00	25.00
b.		Souvenir sheet of 1	5.00	2.50

See Poland No. 4092.

Statues of the National Bank of Romania A1602

Designs: 2 l, Justice. 3.30 l, Commerce. 3.60 l, Industry. 4.50 l, Agriculture. 8.10 l, Bust of bank founder Eugeniu Carada (1836-1910), by Ioan Bolborea.

2013, Sept. 20		**Litho.**	**Perf. 13¼**	
5484	A1602	2 l multi	1.25	.60
a.		Sheet of 6	7.50	3.75
5485	A1602	3.30 l multi	2.00	1.00
a.		Sheet of 6	12.00	6.00
5486	A1602	3.60 l multi	2.25	1.10
a.			2.25	1.10
5487	A1602	4.50 l multi	2.75	1.40
a.		Sheet of 6	16.50	8.50
		Nos. 5484-5487 (4)	8.25	4.10

Souvenir Sheet
Perf. 13¼x13¾

5488	A1602	8.10 l multi	5.00	2.50

No. 5488 contains one 42x52mm stamp. A sheet of four containing Nos. 5484-5487 exists in a limited printing, as does and example of No. 5488 with gold foil.

Maria Tanase (1913-63),
Singer — A1603

2013, Sept. 25   Litho.   Perf. 13¼
5489 A1603 9.10 l multi   5.50   2.75
  a. Sheet of 8   44.00 22.00
  b. Souvenir sheet of 1   5.50   2.75
No. 5489a exists with two different marginal
illustrations. Values are for either illustration.

Rogoz Wooden
Church From
Wooden
Churches of
Maramures
UNESCO
World Heritage
Site — A1604

2013, Sept. 27   Litho.   Perf. 13¼
5490 A1604 8.10 l multi   5.00   2.50
  a. Sheet of 6   30.00 15.00
Rogoz Wooden Church, 350th anniv.

Transylvanian Association for
Romanian Literature and Culture
Museum of Traditional Folk Civilization,
50th Anniv. — A1605

2013, Oct. 4   Litho.   Perf. 13¼
5491 A1605 14.50 l multi   9.00   4.50
  a. Sheet of 4 + 2 labels 36.00 18.00

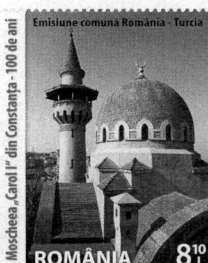

King Carol
I Mosque,
Constanta,
Cent.
A1606

2013, Oct. 10   Litho.   Perf. 13¼x13¾
5492 A1606 8.10 l multi   5.00   2.50
  a. Sheet of 6   30.00 15.00
  b. Souvenir sheet of 1   5.00   2.50
No. 5492b exists with a different sheet margin on a first day cover in a limited printing.
See Turkey No. 3365.

Fauna
A1607

Designs: 3.30 l, Marmota marmota. 4.30 l,
Picoides tridactylus. 4.50 l, Lynx lynx. 9.10 l,
Bison bonasus.

2013, Oct. 25   Litho.   Perf. 13¼
5493 A1607 3.30 l multi   2.00   1.00
  a. Sheet of 5 + label   10.00   5.00
5494 A1607 4.30 l multi   2.60   1.40
  a. Sheet of 5 + label   13.00   7.00
5495 A1607 4.50 l multi   2.75   1.40
  a. Sheet of 5 + label   14.00   7.00
5496 A1607 9.10 l multi   5.50   2.75
  a. Sheet of 5 + label   27.50 14.00
    Nos. 5493-5496 (4)   12.85   6.55

Radio
Romania,
85th Anniv.
A1608

Designs: 1 l, Nicolae Iorga (1871-1940),
writer and prime minister. 14.50 l, Elena
Vacarescu (1866-1947), writer.

2013, Nov. 4   Litho.   Perf. 13¼
5497 A1608 1 l multi   .60   .30
  a. Sheet of 4   2.40   1.25
5498 A1608 14.50 l multi   8.75   4.50
  a. Sheet of 4   35.00 18.00
  b. Sheet of 2, #5497-5498, +
    14 labels   9.50   4.75

Christmas — A1609

2013, Nov. 22   Litho.   Perf. 13¼
5499 A1609 1 l multi   .60   .30
  a. Sheet of 8 + central label 5.00 2.40
    Complete booklet, 8 #5499   5.00
A sheet containing four No. 5499 exists in a
limited printing.

Chess Pieces and Emblem of
Integrated Intelligence Office — A1610

2013, Nov. 29   Litho.   Perf. 13¼
5500 A1610 8.10 l multi   5.00   2.50
  a. Sheet of 6 + 3 labels 30.00 15.00

Paintings of
Roses — A1611

Designs: 1 l, Roses, by Nicolae Grigorescu.
3.60 l, Roses, by Theodor Aman. 4.50 l,
Roses, by Stefan Luchian, horiz. 14.50 l,
Roses, by Ion Andreescu, horiz.

2013, Dec. 12   Litho.   Perf. 13¼
5501 A1611 1 l multi   .60   .30
  a. Sheet of 6 + 2 labels   3.75   1.90
5502 A1611 3.60 l multi   2.25   1.10
  a. Sheet of 6 + 2 labels 13.50   6.75
5503 A1611 4.50 l multi   2.75   1.40
  a. Sheet of 6 + 2 labels 16.50   8.50
5504 A1611 14.50 l multi   9.00   4.50
  a. Sheet of 6 + 2 labels 54.00 27.00
    Nos. 5501-5504 (4)   14.60   7.30
A sheet of four containing Nos. 5501-5504
exists in a limited printing.

Corund
Ceramics
A1612

Designs: 3.30 l, Plate. 3.60 l, Cup. 5 l, Bowl.
8.10 l, Vase.

2013, Dec. 20   Litho.   Perf. 13¼
5505 A1612 3.30 l multi   2.00   1.00
  a. Sheet of 6   12.00   6.00
5506 A1612 3.60 l multi   2.25   1.10
  a. Sheet of 6   13.50   6.75
5507 A1612 5 l multi   3.00   1.50
  a. Sheet of 6   18.00   9.00
5508 A1612 8.10 l multi   5.00   2.50
  a. Sheet of 6   30.00 15.00
    Nos. 5505-5508 (4)   12.25   6.10

Churches
A1613

Designs: 1 l, Church of the Savior, Ber-
estovo, Ukraine. 9.10 l, Church of the Sucevita
Monastery, Romania.

2013, Dec. 21   Litho.   Perf. 13¼
5509 A1613 1 l multi   .60   .30
  a. Sheet of 8 + central label 4.80 2.40
5510 A1613 9.10 l multi   5.50   2.75
  a. Sheet of 8 + central label 44.00 22.00
See Ukraine No. 952.

Mihai Eminescu
(1850-89),
Poet — A1614

2014, Jan. 15   Litho.   Perf. 13¼
5511 A1614 9.10 l multi   5.50   2.75
  a. Souvenir sheet of 1   5.50   2.75
  b. Miniature sheet of 6   33.00 16.50
National Culture Day.

Buildings in Arad — A1615

Arms of Arad and: 2 l, City Hall. 2.10 l, Old
Orthodox Cathedral, vert. 3.60 l, Evangelical
Lutheran Church, vert. 14.50 l, Ioan Slavici
Classical Theater.

2014, Jan. 23   Litho.   Perf. 13¼
5512 A1615 2 l multi   1.25   .60
  a. Sheet of 5 + label   6.25   3.00
5513 A1615 2.10 l multi   1.25   .65
  a. Sheet of 5 + label   6.25   3.25
5514 A1615 3.60 l multi   2.25   1.10
  a. Sheet of 5 + label   11.50   5.50
5515 A1615 14.50 l multi   8.75   4.50
  a. Sheet of 5 + label   44.00 22.50
    Nos. 5512-5515 (4)   13.50   6.85

Desert
Flowers
A1616

Designs: 1 l, Echinocereus triglochidiatus.
1.40 l, Baileya multiradiata. 8.10 l, Solanum
elaeagnifolium. 14.50 l, Hibiscus denudatus.

2014, Jan. 29   Litho.   Perf. 13¼
5516 A1616 1 l multi   .60   .30
  a. Sheet of 4   2.40   1.20
5517 A1616 1.40 l multi   .85   .40
  a. Sheet of 4   3.50   1.60
5518 A1616 8.10 l multi   5.00   2.50
  a. Sheet of 4   20.00 10.00
5519 A1616 14.50 l multi   8.75   4.50
  a. Sheet of 4   35.00 18.00
    Nos. 5516-5519 (4)   15.20   7.70

Favorable Judgement in Black Sea
Boundary Dispute With Ukraine, 5th
Anniv. — A1617

2014, Feb. 3   Litho.   Perf. 13¼
5520 A1617 9.10 l multi   5.50   2.75
  a. Souvenir sheet of 1   5.50   2.75
  b. Sheet of 10 + 2 labels 55.00 27.50

2014 Winter Olympics, Sochi,
Russia — A1618

No. 5521: a, Biathlon. b, Bobsledding. c,
Figure skating. d, Skiing.

2014, Feb. 7   Litho.   Perf. 13¼
5521 A1618 2.10 l Block of 4, #a-
    d   5.25   2.60
No. 5521 was printed in sheets containing
two tete-beche blocks.

Miniature Sheet

Paintings of Roma People — A1619

No. 5522 — Painting of various Roma people by: a, 3.50 l, Iosif Iser (1881-1958). b,
4.30 l, Nicolae Grigorescu (1838-1907). c,
4.50 l, Pierre Bellet (1865-1924). d, 8.10 l,
Nicolae Vermont (1836-1932).

2014, Feb. 20   Litho.   Perf. 13¼x14
5522 A1619 Sheet of 4, #a-d 12.50 6.25

Actors and Actresses A1620

Designs: No. 5523, Draga Olteanu Matei. No. 5524, Florin Piersic. No. 5525, Olga Tudorache. No. 5526, Marin Moraru. No. 5527, Mircea Albulescu. No. 5528, Ileana Stana Ionescu. No. 5529, Tamara Buciuceanu-Botez. No. 5530, Mitica Popescu. No. 5531, Sebastian Papaiani. No. 5532, Valeria Gagealov. No. 5533, George Motoi. No. 5534, Sanda Toma.

2014, Mar. 1	Litho.	Perf. 13¼	
5523 A1620 1.60 l multi		1.00	.50
a.	Sheet of 4	4.00	2.00
5524 A1620 1.60 l multi		1.00	.50
a.	Sheet of 4	4.00	2.00
5525 A1620 1.60 l multi		1.00	.50
a.	Sheet of 4	4.00	2.00
5526 A1620 1.60 l multi		1.00	.50
a.	Sheet of 4	4.00	2.00
5527 A1620 1.60 l multi		1.00	.50
a.	Sheet of 4	4.00	2.00
5528 A1620 1.60 l multi		1.00	.50
a.	Sheet of 4	4.00	2.00
5529 A1620 1.60 l multi		1.00	.50
a.	Sheet of 4	4.00	2.00
5530 A1620 1.60 l multi		1.00	.50
a.	Sheet of 4	4.00	2.00
5531 A1620 1.60 l multi		1.00	.50
a.	Sheet of 4	4.00	2.00
5532 A1620 1.60 l multi		1.00	.50
a.	Sheet of 4	4.00	2.00
5533 A1620 1.60 l multi		1.00	.50
a.	Sheet of 4	4.00	2.00
5534 A1620 1.60 l multi		1.00	.50
a.	Sheet of 4	4.00	2.00
b.	Sheet of 12, #5523-5534, + 4 central labels	12.00	6.00
Nos. 5523-5534 (12)		12.00	6.00

See Nos. 5882-5887.

Easter — A1621

2014, Mar. 20	Litho.	Perf. 13¼	
5535 A1621 1 l multi		.65	.30
a.	Sheet of 8 + central label	5.25	2.60

Ducks A1622

Designs: 1.20 l, Anas platyrhynchos. 1.40 l, Aythya fuligula. 8.10 l, Anas clypeata. 14.50 l, Anas crecca.

2014, Mar. 24	Litho.	Perf. 13¼	
5536 A1622 1.20 l multi		.75	.35
a.	Sheet of 5 + label	3.75	1.75
5537 A1622 1.40 l multi		.85	.45
a.	Sheet of 5 + label	4.25	2.25
5538 A1622 8.10 l multi		5.00	2.50
a.	Sheet of 5 + label	25.00	12.50
5539 A1622 14.50 l multi		9.00	4.50
a.	Sheet of 5 + label	45.00	22.50
Nos. 5536-5539 (4)		15.60	7.80

Admission to North Atlantic Treaty Organization, 10th Anniv. — A1623

2014, Apr. 2	Litho.	Perf. 13¼	
5540 A1623 9.10 l multi		5.75	3.00
a.	Sheet of 6	35.00	18.00
b.	Souvenir sheet of 1	5.75	3.00

No. 5540 has 13 perforation holes within stamp; No. 5540b, has 5.

Traditional Foods A1624

Designs: 1 l, Red eggs and cozonac. 3.60 l, Fish on fir tree branches. 4.50 l, Roast lamb and vegetables. 8.10 l, Cheeses and vegetables.

2014, Apr. 18	Litho.	Perf. 13¼	
5541 A1624 1 l multi		.65	.30
a.	Sheet of 5 + 3 labels	3.25	1.50
5542 A1624 3.60 l multi		2.25	1.10
a.	Sheet of 5 + 3 labels	11.50	5.50
5543 A1624 4.50 l multi		3.00	1.50
a.	Sheet of 5 + 3 labels	15.00	7.50
5544 A1624 8.10 l multi		5.00	2.50
a.	Sheet of 5 + 3 labels	25.00	12.50
Nos. 5541-5544 (4)		10.90	5.40

Europa — A1625

Musicians playing: 2.10 l, Tulnics. 14.50 l, Lutes.

2014, May 5	Litho.	Perf. 13¼	
5545 A1625 2.10 l multi		1.40	.70
a.	Sheet of 6	8.50	4.25
5546 A1625 14.50 l multi		9.00	4.50
a.	Sheet of 6	54.00	27.00
b.	Souvenir sheet of 4, 2 each #5545-5546, #5545 at UL	21.00	10.50
c.	As "b," #5546 at UL	21.00	10.50

World Conference of Masonic Regular Grand Lodges, Romania A1626

Emblem and: 3.30 l, Olive branch. 9.10 l, Sever Frentiu (1931-97), painter.

2014, May 14	Litho.	Perf. 13¼	
5547 A1626 3.30 l multi		2.10	1.10
a.	Sheet of 4	8.50	4.50
5548 A1626 9.10 l multi		5.75	3.00
a.	Sheet of 4	23.00	12.00

Training Ship Mircea, 75th Anniv. — A1627

Designs: 1 l, Mircea with sails up. No. 5550, Mircea and military order, vert. No. 5551, Mircea with sails down.

2014, May 24	Litho.	Perf. 13¼	
5549 A1627 1 l multi		.65	.30
a.	Sheet of 6	4.00	2.00
5550 A1627 14.50 l multi		9.00	4.50
a.	Sheet of 6	54.00	27.00

Souvenir Sheet

5551 A1627 14.50 l multi + label		9.00	4.50

Theodor Aman (1831-91), Founder of National University of Arts, Bucharest A1628

2014, May 28	Litho.	Perf. 13¼	
5552 A1628 8.10 l multi		5.00	2.50
a.	Sheet of 6	30.00	15.00
b.	Souvenir sheet of 1	5.00	2.50

National University of Arts, 150th anniv.

UNICEF Campaign To End Violence Against Children A1629

2014, June 2	Litho.	Perf. 13¼	
5553 A1629 4.30 l aqua blue		2.75	1.40
a.	Sheet of 8 + central label	22.00	11.50

Emblem of Court of Accounts A1630

Emblem of Court of Accounts, Prince Alexandru Ioan Cuza (1820-73) — A1631

2014, June 6	Litho.	Perf. 13¾	
5554 A1630 2.40 l multi		1.50	.75
a.	Sheet of 8 + central label	12.00	6.00
5555 A1631 4.50 l gray grn & multi		3.00	1.50
a.	Sheet of 8 + central label	24.00	12.00

Souvenir Sheet

5556 A1631 14.50 l beige & multi		9.00	4.50

Court of Accounts, 150th anniv.

2014 World Cup Soccer Championships, Brazil — A1632

No. 5557: a, Two players, denomination at UR. b, Goaltender, denomination at UL. c, Two players, diff., denomination at LL. d, Two players, diff. denomination at LR.

2014, June 12	Litho.	Perf. 13¼	
5557 A1632 2.40 l Block of 4, #a-d		6.00	3.00
e.	Souvenir sheet of 4, #5557a-5557d	6.00	3.00

Romanian Senate, 150th Anniv. — A1633

Designs: 1 l, Senate Building and emblem. 14.50 l, Emblem.

2014, June 17	Litho.	Perf. 13¼	
5558 A1633 1 l multi		.65	.30
a.	Sheet of 8 + 2 labels	5.25	2.40

Souvenir Sheet

5559 A1633 14.50 l multi		9.00	4.50

No. 5559 contains one 36x36mm stamp.

Gymnastics Personalities A1634

Designs: 2.10 l, Octavian Bellu, head coach of national team. 9.10 l, Mariana Bitang, coach and trainer.

2014, June 20	Litho.	Perf. 13¼	
5560 A1634 2.10 l multi		1.40	.70
a.	Sheet of 6	8.50	4.25
5561 A1634 9.10 l multi		5.75	3.00
a.	Sheet of 6	35.00	18.00
b.	Souvenir sheet of 2, #5560-5561	7.25	3.75

Maramures Tourist Attractions A1635

Designs: 2 l, Stephen's Tower. 3.30 l, Berbesti roadside cross. 8.10 l, Wooden church, Sugatag. 14.50 l, Cemetery with decorations, Sapanta.

2014, July 4	Litho.	Perf. 13¼	
5562 A1635 2 l multi		1.25	.60
a.	Sheet of 5 + label	6.25	3.00
5563 A1635 3.30 l multi		2.00	1.00
a.	Sheet of 5 + label	10.00	5.00
5564 A1635 8.10 l multi		5.00	2.50
a.	Sheet of 5 + label	25.00	12.50
5565 A1635 14.50 l multi		8.75	4.50
a.	Sheet of 5 + label	44.00	22.50
Nos. 5562-5565 (4)		17.00	8.60

A1636

Church of the Three Holy Hierarchs Monastery, Iasi — A1637

2014, July 15   Litho.   *Perf. 13¼*
5566 A1636 14.50 l multi   8.75   4.50
     a.   Sheet of 8 + central label   70.00   36.00

Souvenir Sheet
5567 A1637   8.10 l multi   5.00   2.50

Stamp Day.

University of Bucharest, 150th Anniv. — A1638

Designs: 8.10 l. University building and statue.14.50 l, Watercolor depicting University Buildings by Alexandru Orascu.

2014, July 16   Litho.   *Perf. 13¼*
5568 A1638   8.10 l multi   5.00   2.50
     a.   Sheet of 8   40.00   20.00

Souvenir Sheet
5569 A1638 14.50 l multi + label   8.75   4.50

Remembrance of National Heroes — A1639

Designs: 1 l, Order of Michael the Brave first class, King Ferdinand I, Gen. Alexandru Averescu. 3.60 l, Heroes' Cross Monument, vert. 14.50 l, Mausoleum of Marasesti.

2014, July 25   Litho.   *Perf. 13¼*
5570 A1639   1 l multi   .60   .30
     a.   Sheet of 6   3.75   1.90
5571 A1639   3.60 l multi   2.25   1.10
     a.   Sheet of 6   13.50   6.75
5572 A1639 14.50 l multi   8.75   4.50
     a.   Sheet of 6   52.50   27.00
       Nos. 5570-5572 (3)   11.60   5.90

UNESCO Intangible Cultural Heritage in Romania — A1640

Designs: 3.10 l, Doina musician, sheep in pasture. 6 l, Calus dancers. No. 5575, Colindat Christmas ritual. No. 5576, Horezu plate and potter.

2014, Aug. 7   Litho.   *Perf. 13¼*
5573 A1640   3.10 l multi   1.75   .90
     a.   Sheet of 6   10.50   5.40
5574 A1640   6 l multi   3.75   1.90
     a.   Sheet of 6   22.50   11.50
5575 A1640   9.10 l multi   5.50   2.75
     a.   Sheet of 6   33.00   16.50
       Nos. 5573-5575 (3)   11.00   5.55

Souvenir Sheet
5576 A1640   9.10 l multi   5.50   2.75

Martyrdom of the Brancoveanu Saints, 300th Anniv. — A1641

Designs: 2.40 l, Constantin Brancoveanu (1654-1714), Prince of Wallachia. 5 l, Icon depicting martyrs and Ianache Vacarescu, vert. 14.50 l, St. George's New Church, Bucharest.

2014, Aug. 16   Litho.   *Perf. 13¼*
5577 A1641   2.40 l multi   1.50   .75
     a.   Sheet of 6   9.00   4.50
5578 A1641   5 l multi   3.00   1.50
     a.   Sheet of 6   18.00   9.00
5579 A1641 14.50 l multi   8.75   4.50
     a.   Sheet of 6   52.50   27.00
       Nos. 5577-5579 (3)   13.25   6.75

An imperforate sheet of Nos. 5577-5579 was printed in a limited edition.

Paintings — A1642

Designs: 4.70 l, Spring, by Pieter Breughel the Younger. 5 l, Summer, by Breughel the Younger. 7.60 l, The Marriage of the Virgin, by El Greco, vert. 8.10 l, The Martyrdom of St. Maurice and the 10,000 Thebans, by El Greco, vert.

2014, Aug. 22   Litho.   *Perf. 13¼*
5580 A1642 4.70 l multi   2.75   1.40
     a.   Sheet of 4   11.00   5.75
5581 A1642   5 l multi   3.00   1.50
     a.   Sheet of 4   12.00   6.00
5582 A1642 7.60 l multi   4.50   2.25
     a.   Sheet of 4   18.00   9.00
5583 A1642 8.10 l multi   5.00   2.50
     a.   Sheet of 4   20.00   10.00
       Nos. 5580-5583 (4)   15.25   7.65

Oltenia Tourism — A1643

Arms of Oltenia and: 2.40 l, Cula Greceanu, Maldaresti Museum complex, Valcea. 3 l, Art Museum of Craiova. 3.30 l, Tismana Monastery. 4.30 l, Biserica Monastery, Hurezi. 4.50 l, Horezu ceramics. 14.50 l, Grapes and vineyard.

2014, Aug. 29   Litho.   *Perf. 13¼*
5584 A1643   2.40 l multi   1.50   .75
     a.   Sheet of 5 + label   7.50   3.75
5585 A1643   3 l multi   1.75   .90
     a.   Sheet of 5 + label   8.75   4.50
5586 A1643   3.30 l multi   2.00   1.00
     a.   Sheet of 5 + label   10.00   5.00
5587 A1643   4.30 l multi   2.60   1.25
     a.   Sheet of 5 + label   13.00   6.25
5588 A1643   4.50 l multi   2.75   1.40
     a.   Sheet of 5 + label   14.00   7.00
5589 A1643 14.50 l multi   8.75   4.50
     a.   Sheet of 5 + label   44.00   22.50
       Nos. 5584-5589 (6)   19.35   9.80

Animals and Their Food — A1644

Designs: 1.40 l, Squirrel and hazel nuts. 2 l, Boar and acorns, vert. 8.10 l , Bear and berries, vert. 14.50 l, Starling and grapes.

2014, Sept. 5   Litho.   *Perf. 13¼*
5590 A1644   1.40 l multi   .80   .40
     a.   Sheet of 5 + label   4.00   2.00
5591 A1644   2 l multi   1.25   .60
     a.   Sheet of 5 + label   6.25   3.00
5592 A1644   8.10 l multi   4.75   2.40
     a.   Sheet of 5 + label   24.00   12.00
5593 A1644 14.50 l multi   8.50   4.25
     a.   Sheet of 5 + label   42.50   21.50
       Nos. 5590-5593 (4)   15.30   7.65

Romanian Olympic Committee, Cent. — A1645

"100" and: 1 l, Romanian Olympic Committee emblem. 14.50 l, Torch.

2014, Sept. 12   Litho.   *Perf. 13¼*
5594 A1645   1 l multi   .60   .30
     a.   Sheet of 8 + central label   4.80   2.40

Souvenir Sheet
5595 A1645 14.50 l multi   8.50   4.25

Bucharest, 555th Anniv. — A1646

Designs: 3.30 l, National Bank of Romania. 4.30 l, Palace of the Patriarchate. 4.50 l, Toma Stelian House. 5 l, Kretulescu Palace. 6 l, Carol Davila University of Medicine and Pharmacy. No. 5601, National Geology Museum. No. 5602, Zodiac Fountain.

2014, Sept. 20   Litho.   *Perf. 13¼*
5596 A1646   3.30 l multi   1.90   .95
     a.   Sheet of 5 + 5 labels   9.50   4.75
5597 A1646   4.30 l multi   2.50   1.25
     a.   Sheet of 5 + 5 labels   12.50   6.25
5598 A1646   4.50 l multi   2.60   1.25
     a.   Sheet of 5 + 5 labels   13.00   6.25
5599 A1646   5 l multi   3.00   1.50
     a.   Sheet of 5 + 5 labels   15.00   7.50
5600 A1646   6 l multi   3.50   1.75
     a.   Sheet of 5 + 5 labels   17.50   8.75
5601 A1646   9.10 l multi   5.25   2.60
     a.   Sheet of 5 + 5 labels   26.50   13.00
       Nos. 5596-5601 (6)   18.75   9.30

Souvenir Sheet
5602 A1646   9.10 l multi   5.25   2.60

Clock Towers — A1647

Designs: 3 l, Oradea City Hall. 3.10 l, Trumpeters' Tower, Medias. 3.30 l, Palace of Culture Tower, Iasi. 3.60 l, Communal Palace Tower, Buzau. 4.70 l, City Council Tower, Brasov. 14.50 l, Peles Castle Central Tower, Sinaia.

2014, Oct. 3   Litho.   *Perf. 13¼*
5603 A1647   3 l multi   1.75   .85
     a.   Sheet of 4   7.00   3.50
5604 A1647   3.10 l multi   1.75   .85
     a.   Sheet of 4   7.00   3.50
5605 A1647   3.30 l multi   1.90   .95
     a.   Sheet of 4   7.75   4.00
5606 A1647   3.60 l multi   2.00   1.00
     a.   Sheet of 4   8.00   4.00
5607 A1647   4.70 l multi   2.75   1.40
     a.   Sheet of 4   11.00   5.75
5608 A1647 14.50 l multi   8.25   4.25
     a.   Sheet of 4   33.00   17.00
       Nos. 5603-5608 (6)   18.40   9.30

Wild Cats — A1648

Designs: 3.30 l, Felis silvestris ocreata. 3.60 l, Felis silvestris ornata. 7.60 l, Felis silvestris. 8.10 l, Felis silvestris cafra.

2014, Oct. 10   Litho.   *Perf. 13¼*
5609 A1648   3.30 l multi   1.90   .95
     a.   Sheet of 5 + label   9.50   4.75
5610 A1648   3.60 l multi   2.00   1.00
     a.   Sheet of 5 + label   10.00   5.00
5611 A1648   7.60 l multi   4.25   2.10
     a.   Sheet of 5 + label   21.50   10.50
5612 A1648   8.10 l multi   4.75   2.40
     a.   Sheet of 5 + label   24.00   12.00
       Nos. 5609-5612 (4)   12.90   6.45

Coins From National Bank of Romania Numismatic Collection — A1649

Obverse and reverse of: 2 l, Dacian gold koson. 2.40 l, Istrian drachm. 8.10 l, Thaler. 14.50 l, Venetian gold ducat.

2014, Oct. 24   Litho.   *Perf. 13¼*
5613 A1649   2 l multi   1.10   .55
     a.   Sheet of 6   6.75   3.50
5614 A1649   2.40 l multi   1.40   .70
     a.   Sheet of 6   8.50   4.25
5615 A1649   8.10 l multi   4.75   2.40
     a.   Sheet of 6   28.50   14.50
5616 A1649 14.50 l multi   8.25   4.25
     a.   Sheet of 6   49.50   25.50
       Nos. 5613-5616 (4)   15.50   7.90

A souvenir sheet of 4 containing Nos. 5613-5616 was printed in limited quantities.

King Michael, 93rd Birthday A1650

Designs: 4.70 l, King Michael and monogram. 14.50 l, King Michael and Queen Anne.

2014, Oct. 25   Litho.   *Perf. 13¼*
5617 A1650   4.70 l multi   2.75   1.40
     a.   Sheet of 8 + central label   22.00   11.50

Souvenir Sheet
Perf. 13¼x14
5618 A1650 14.50 l multi   8.25   4.25

No. 5618 contains one 42x52mm stamp and exists imperforate.

Tourist Attractions in Tulcea — A1651

Designs: 3 l, Independence Monument. 3.30 l, Spiru Haret College in Dobrogea, horiz. 4.30 l, Aziziye Mosque, horiz. 14.50 l, St. Nicholas Episcopal Cathedral.

2014, Oct. 31	Litho.	Perf. 13¼	
5619 A1651	3 l multi	1.75	.85
a.	Sheet of 5 + label	8.75	4.25
5620 A1651	3.30 l multi	1.90	.95
a.	Sheet of 5 + label	9.50	4.75
5621 A1651	4.30 l multi	2.40	1.25
a.	Sheet of 5 + label	12.00	6.25
5622 A1651	8.25 l multi	4.25	
a.	Sheet of 5 + label	41.50	21.50
	Nos. 5619-5622 (4)	14.30	7.30

Carol I University Foundation, Cent. — A1652

Designs: 9.10 l, University Library, statue of King Carol I. 14.50 l, University Foundation Palace, horiz.

2014, Nov. 7	Litho.	Perf. 13¼	
5623 A1652	9.10 l multi	5.25	2.60
a.	Sheet of 4	21.00	10.50

Souvenir Sheet
Perf. 14x13¼

5624 A1652	14.50 l multi	8.25	4.25

No. 5624 contains one 52x42mm stamp. No. 5623a was printed with two different sheet margins.

Fortified Churches A1653

Designs: 1 l, St. Nicholas Church, Komiza, Croatia. 9.10 l, Evangelical Church, Cristian.

2014, Nov. 14	Litho.	Perf. 13¼	
5625 A1653	1 l multi	.55	.30
a.	Sheet of 8 + central label	4.50	2.40
5626 A1653	9.10 l multi	5.25	2.60
a.	Sheet of 8 + central label	42.00	21.00

See Croatia No. 930.

Hammer and Sickle, "XXV" — A1654

Wings Monument, by Mihai Buculei — A1655

2014, Nov. 20	Litho.	Perf. 13¼	
5627 A1654	14.50 l multi	8.25	4.25
a.	Sheet of 5 + label	41.50	21.50

Souvenir Sheet

5628 A1655	8.10 l multi	4.50	2.25

Fall of Communism, 25th anniv.

Christmas A1656

2014, Nov. 21	Litho.	Perf. 13¼	
5629 A1656	1 l multi	.55	.30
a.	Sheet of 8 + central label	4.50	2.40

No. 5629 exists imperforate in a limited printing. A souvenir sheet of 2 was printed in limited quantities.

Romanian Savings Bank, 150th Anniv. — A1657

Designs: 8.10 l, Building. 14.50 l, Decorative frieze on Savings Bank.

2014, Nov. 28	Litho.	Perf. 13¼	
5630 A1657	8.10 l multi	4.50	2.25
a.	Sheet of 6	36.00	18.00

Souvenir Sheet

5631 A1657	14.50 l gold & multi	8.25	4.25

No. 5631 contains one 36x36mm stamp.

Writers — A1658

Writers: 3.30 l, Ion Creanga (1837-89). 4.50 l, Vasile Alecsandri (1821-90). 7.60 l, George Cosbuc (1866-1918). 8.10 l, George Bacovia (1881-1957).

2014, Dec. 5	Litho.	Perf. 14x13¼	
5632 A1658	3.30 l multi	1.75	.90
a.	Sheet of 5 + label	8.75	4.50

5633 A1658	4.50 l multi	2.40	1.25
a.	Sheet of 5 + label	12.00	6.25
5634 A1658	7.60 l multi	4.25	2.10
a.	Sheet of 5 + label	21.50	10.50
5635 A1658	8.10 l multi	4.50	2.25
a.	Sheet of 5 + label	22.50	11.50
	Nos. 5632-5635 (4)	12.90	6.50

Inventors and Scientists — A1659

Designs: 3.30 l, Nikola Tesla (1856-1943), electrical engineer, induction motor. 3.60 l, Thomas Alva Edison (1847-1931), inventor, incandescent light bulb. 4.30 l, Albert Einstein (1879-1955), physicist, mass-energy equivalence equation. 14.50 l, Leonardo da Vinci (1452-1519), inventor and painter, irrigation machine.

2014, Dec. 17	Litho.	Perf. 13¼	
5636 A1659	3.30 l multi	1.75	.90
a.	Sheet of 5 + label	8.75	4.50
5637 A1659	3.60 l multi	2.00	1.00
a.	Sheet of 5 + label	10.00	5.00
5638 A1659	4.30 l multi	2.40	1.25
a.	Sheet of 5 + label	12.00	6.25
5639 A1659	14.50 l multi	7.75	4.00
a.	Sheet of 5 + label	39.00	20.00
	Nos. 5636-5639 (4)	13.90	7.15

Handicrafts A1660

Rugs and: 1 l, Copper vessel from Lahich, Azerbaijan. 9.10 l, Pottery jug from Horezu, Romania.

2014, Dec. 19	Litho.	Perf. 13¼	
5640 A1660	1 l multi	.55	.25
a.	Sheet of 6	3.50	1.50
5641 A1660	9.10 l multi	5.00	2.50
a.	Sheet of 6	30.00	15.00

See Azerbaijan No. 1075.

Wildlife A1661

Designs: 3.60 l, Antidorcas marsupialis. 4.30 l, Puma concolor. 8.10 l, Orcinus orca. 9.10 l, Acinonyx jubatus.

2015, Jan. 16	Litho.	Perf. 13¼	
5642-5645 A1661	Set of 4	13.00	6.50
5645a	Souvenir sheet of 4, #5642-5645	13.00	6.50

Paintings and Sculptures — A1662

Designs: 3.10 l, Hagar in the Desert, by Gheorghe Tattarescu (1820-94). 3.30 l, Girl with Tambourine, by Tattarescu, vert. 4.50 l, The Kiss, sculpture, by Auguste Rodin (1840-1917), vert. 14.50 l, The Spring, sculpture by Rodin.

Perf. 14x13¼, 13¼x14

2015, Jan. 23		Litho.	
5646 A1662	3.10 l gold & multi	1.60	.80
a.	Sheet of 4 + 2 labels	6.50	3.25
5647 A1662	3.30 l gold & multi	1.75	.85
a.	Sheet of 4 + 2 labels	7.00	3.50
5648 A1662	4.50 l sil & multi	2.40	1.25
a.	Sheet of 4 + 2 labels	9.75	5.00
5649 A1662	14.50 l sil & multi	7.50	3.75
a.	Sheet of 4 + 2 labels	30.00	15.00
	Nos. 5646-5649 (4)	13.25	6.65

Romanian Royalty A1663

Royalty and their monograms: 3.10 l, King Carol I (1839-1914), Queen Elisabeth (1843-1916). 3.30 l, King Ferdinand (1865-1927), Queen Marie (1875-1938). 6 l, King Carol II (1893-1953), Queen Helen (1896-1982). 14.50 l, King Michael, Queen Anne.

2015, Jan. 30	Litho.	Perf. 13¼x14	
5650 A1663	3.10 l multi	1.60	.80
a.	Sheet of 4 + 2 labels	6.50	3.25
5651 A1663	3.30 l multi	1.75	.85
a.	Sheet of 4 + 2 labels	7.00	3.50
5652 A1663	6 l multi	3.25	1.60
a.	Sheet of 4 + 2 labels	13.00	6.50
5653 A1663	14.50 l multi	7.50	3.75
a.	Sheet of 4 + 2 labels	30.00	15.00
	Nos. 5650-5653 (4)	14.10	7.00

The royal monograms on Nos. 5650-5653 are surrounded by perforations within the stamp. A souvenir sheet of 4 containing Nos. 5650-5653 was printed in limited quantities.

Songbirds A1664

Designs: 4.50 l, Coccothraustes cocothraustes. 5 l, Emberiza citrinella. 8.10 l, Bombycilla garrulus. 9.10 l, Pyrrhula pyrrhula.

2015, Feb. 6	Litho.	Perf. 13¼	
5654 A1664	4.50 l multi	2.25	1.10
a.	Sheet of 5 + label	11.50	5.50
5655 A1664	5 l multi	2.50	1.25
a.	Sheet of 5 + label	12.50	6.25
5656 A1664	8.10 l multi	4.00	2.00
a.	Sheet of 5 + label	20.00	10.00
5657 A1664	9.10 l multi	4.50	2.25
a.	Sheet of 5 + label	22.50	11.50
	Nos. 5654-5657 (4)	13.25	6.60

A souvenir sheet of 4 containing Nos. 5654-5657 was printed in a limited quantity.

Letters and Flowers A1665

Designs: 3 l, "T," roses. 3.10 l, "I," irises. 3.30 l, "M," poppies. 4.30 l, "B," begonias. 4.70 l, "R," flowering tobacco. 14.50 l, "E," purple coneflowers.

2015, Feb. 20	Litho.	Perf. 13¼	
5658 A1665	3 l multi	1.50	.75
a.	Sheet of 5 + label	7.50	3.75
5659 A1665	3.10 l multi	1.60	.80
a.	Sheet of 5 + label	8.00	4.00
5660 A1665	3.30 l multi	1.75	.85
a.	Sheet of 5 + label	8.75	4.25

5661	A1665	4.30 l	multi	2.25	1.10
a.		Sheet of 5 + label		11.50	5.50
5662	A1665	4.70 l	multi	2.40	1.25
a.		Sheet of 5 + label		12.00	6.25
5663	A1665	14.50 l	multi	7.25	3.75
a.		Sheet of 5 + label		36.50	19.00
b.		Souvenir sheet of 6, #5658-5663		17.00	8.50
		Nos. 5658-5663 (6)		16.75	8.50

Easter
A1666

Designs: 1 l, Icon depicting crucifixion from Nicula Monastery.
9.10 l, Icon depicting resurrection from Transylvanian Museum of Ethnography.

2015, Mar. 12   Litho.   Perf. 13¼

5664	A1666	1 l	multi	.50	.25
a.		Sheet of 4		2.00	1.00
b.		Sheet of 8 + central label		4.00	2.00

Souvenir Sheet

5665	A1666	9.10 l	multi	4.50	2.25

No. 5664a was printed with two different sheet margins. Two souvenir sheets of 2, one containing Nos. 5664-5665, and the other containing 2 No. 5664, were printed in limited quantities.

Archaeological Artifacts of
Dinogetia — A1667

Designs: 3 l, Rings, bracelet, loop of gold wire. 4.50 l, Gold coins, chain. 9.10 l, Ring, bracelet, loop of gold wire. 14.50 l, Reliquary cross.

2015, Mar. 20   Litho.   Perf. 14x13¼

5666	A1667	3 l	multi	1.50	.75
a.		Sheet of 4		6.00	3.00
5667	A1667	4.50 l	multi	2.25	1.10
a.		Sheet of 4		9.00	4.50
5668	A1667	9.10 l	multi	4.50	2.25
a.		Sheet of 4		18.00	9.00
5669	A1667	14.50 l	multi	7.25	3.75
a.		Sheet of 4		29.00	15.00
b.		Souvenir sheet of 4, #5666-5669, + 2 labels		15.50	8.00
		Nos. 5666-5669 (4)		15.50	7.85

Romanian Intelligence Service, 25th
Anniv. — A1668

Designs: 8.10 l, Emblem, map of Romania. 14.50 l, Emblem.

2015, Mar. 23   Litho.   Perf. 13¼

5670	A1668	8.10 l	multi	4.00	2.00
a.		Sheet of 6		24.00	12.00

Souvenir Sheet
Perf.

5671	A1668	14.50 l	multi	7.25	3.75

No. 5671 contains one 30mm diameter stamp.

Pelicans — A1669

Designs: 3.60 l, Six Pelecanus onocrotalus. 5 l, Two Pelecanus crispus. 8.10 l, Two Pelecanus onocrotalus. No. 5675, 9.10 l, Two Pelecanus crispus, close up of face.
No. 5676, 9.10 l, Head of Pelecanus crispus.

2015, Apr. 10   Litho.   Perf. 13¼

5672	A1669	3.60 l	multi	1.90	.95
a.		Sheet of 5 + label		9.50	4.75
5673	A1669	5 l	multi	2.60	1.40
a.		Sheet of 5 + label		13.00	7.00
5674	A1669	8.10 l	multi	4.25	2.10
a.		Sheet of 5 + label		21.50	10.50
5675	A1669	9.10 l	multi	4.75	2.40
a.		Sheet of 5 + label		24.00	12.00
		Nos. 5672-5675 (4)		13.50	6.85

Souvenir Sheet
Perf. 14x13¼

5676	A1669	9.10 l	multi	4.75	2.40

No. 5676 contains one 52x42mm stamp. A souvenir sheet of 4 containing Nos. 5672-5675 was printed in limited quantities.

Europa
A1670

Designs: 2.10 l, Wooden toys. 14.50 l, Rocking horse, tricycle.

2015, Apr. 17   Litho.   Perf. 13¼

5677	A1670	2.10 l	multi	1.10	.55
a.		Sheet of 6		6.75	3.50
5678	A1670	14.50 l	multi	7.50	3.75
a.		Sheet of 6		45.00	22.50
b.		Sheet of 4, 2 each #5677-5678, #5677 at UL		17.50	8.75
c.		As "b," #5678 at UL		17.50	8.75

Quill Pen, Book, Hand Touching Tablet
Screen — A1671

2015, Apr. 30   Litho.   Perf. 13¼

5679	A1671	4.70 l	multi	2.40	1.25
a.		Sheet of 5 + label		12.00	6.25

The Group, 10th anniv.

Victory in World
War II, 70th
Anniv. — A1672

2015, May 9   Litho.   Perf. 13¼

5680	A1672	4.30 l	multi	2.25	1.10
a.		Sheet of 8 + central label		18.00	9.00

No. 5680a was printed with two different central labels.

No. 3601 Surcharged in Gold

Methods and Perfs. As Before
2015, May 13

5681	A1028	9.10 l	on 10 l #3601	4.50	2.25

Europhilex 2015 Intl. Stamp Exhibition, London.

University of Medicine and Pharmacy,
Tirgu Mures, 70th Anniv. — A1673

Designs: 3.30 l, University building, emblem with 1945 date. 8.10 l, University building, emblem, without oval.
9.10 l, University building, emblem without oval, vert.

2015, May 15   Litho.   Perf. 13¼

5682	A1673	3.30 l	gold & multi	1.75	.85
a.		Sheet of 5 + label		8.75	4.25
5683	A1673	8.10 l	gold & multi	4.00	2.00
a.		Sheet of 5 + label		20.00	10.00

Souvenir Sheet
Perf. 13¼x14

5684	A1673	9.10 l	gold & multi	4.50	2.25

No. 5684 contains one 42x52mm stamp.

Romanian Mint, 145th Anniv. — A1674

Designs: 8.10 l, Mint building, horse and carriage, 1870 1-leu coin.
14.50 l, 1870 gold 20-lei coin.

2015, May 19   Litho.   Perf. 13¼

5685	A1674	8.10 l	multi	4.00	2.00
a.		Imperf.		4.00	2.00
b.		Sheet of 4 #5685 + 8 labels		16.00	8.00
c.		Sheet of 5, #5685a, 4 #5685		20.00	10.00

Souvenir Sheet

5686	A1674	14.50 l	multi	7.25	3.75

No. 5686 contains one 36x36mm stamp. A ring of perforations surrounds the image of the coin on No. 5685. The ring of perforations is not on No. 5685a. A souvenir sheet of 2 containing Nos. 5685-5686 was produced in limited quantities.

National Institute for Research and
Development in Informatics, 45th
Anniv. — A1675

2015, June 5   Litho.   Perf. 14x13¼

5687	A1675	7.60 l	multi	3.75	1.90
a.		Sheet of 5 + label		19.00	9.50

National Grand
Masonic Lodge
of Romania,
135th
Anniv. — A1676

Designs: 2.10 l, Masonic and astrological symbols. 14.50 l, Lodge, horiz.

2015, June 16   Litho.   Perf. 13¼

5688	A1676	2.10 l	multi	1.10	.55
a.		Sheet of 4		4.50	2.25
5689	A1676	14.50 l	multi	7.25	3.75
a.		Sheet of 4		29.00	15.00
b.		Sheet of 2, #5688-5689, imperf.		8.50	4.25

A souvenir sheet of 2 containing perforated examples of No. 5688-5689 was produced in limited quantities.

Flowers in
Botanical
Gardens
A1677

Designs: 1 l, Astragalus peterfii. 3.30 l, Iris brandzae. 8.10 l, Paeonia peregrina. 9.10 l, Hepatica transsilvanica.

2015, July 3   Litho.   Perf. 13¼

5690	A1677	1 l	multi	.50	.25
a.		Sheet of 5 + label		2.50	1.25
5691	A1677	3.30 l	multi	1.60	.80
a.		Sheet of 5 + label		8.00	4.00
5692	A1677	8.10 l	multi	4.00	2.00
a.		Sheet of 5 + label		20.00	10.00
5693	A1677	9.10 l	multi	4.50	2.25
a.		Sheet of 5 + label		22.50	11.50
		Nos. 5690-5693 (4)		10.60	5.30

Autocephaly of Romanian Orthodox
Church, 130th Anniv. — A1678

Designs: 5 l, Drawing for under-construction Romanian People's Salvation Cathedral. 8.10 l, Cathedral, arms of Patriarchate.

2015, July 15   Litho.   Perf. 13¼

5694	A1678	5 l	multi	2.50	1.25
a.		Sheet of 8 + central label		20.00	10.00

Souvenir Sheet
Perf. 14x13¼

5695	A1678	8.10 l	multi	4.00	2.00

No. 5695 contains one 52x42mm stamp. An souvenir sheet containing two imperforate examples of No. 5694 was printed in limited quantities.

Paintings Depicting Horses — A1679

Details of paintings: 3.60 l, The Plowing, by Ioan Andreescu (1850-82). 8.10 l, Mounted

Ranger Officer, by Nicolae Grigorescu (1838-1907), vert. 9.10 l, Peasant with a Carriage, by Rudolf Schweitzer-Cumpana (1886-1975).

Perf. 14x13¼, 13¼x14

2015, July 24			**Litho.**		
5696	A1679	3.60 l	gold & multi	1.90	.95
a.		Sheet of 4		7.75	4.00
5697	A1679	8.10 l	gold & multi	4.00	2.00
a.		Sheet of 4		16.00	8.00
5698	A1679	9.10 l	gold & multi	4.50	2.25
a.		Sheet of 4		18.00	9.00
		Nos. 5696-5698 (3)		10.40	5.20

Medicinal Plants — A1680

Designs: 1.20 l, Hypericum perforatum. 2 l, Lavandula angustifolia. 2.40 l, Calendula officinalis. 14.50 l, Matricaria chamomilla.

2015, Aug. 7			**Litho.**	**Perf. 13¼**	
5699	A1680	1.20 l	multi	.60	.30
a.		Sheet of 5 + 4 labels		3.00	1.50
5700	A1680	2 l	multi	1.00	.50
a.		Sheet of 5 + 4 labels		5.00	2.50
5701	A1680	2.40 l	multi	1.25	.60
a.		Sheet of 5 + 4 labels		6.25	3.00
5702	A1680	14.50 l	multi	7.50	3.75
a.		Sheet of 5 + 4 labels		37.50	19.00
b.		Souvenir sheet of 4, #5699-5702		10.50	5.25
		Nos. 5699-5702 (4)		10.35	5.15

Nicula Monastery A1681

Designs: 1 l, Icon of Virgin Mary and Child. 4.50 l, Wooden church.

2015, Aug. 15			**Litho.**	**Perf. 13¼**	
5703	A1681	1 l	multi	.50	.25
a.		Sheet of 8 + central label		4.00	2.00
5704	A1681	4.50 l	multi	2.40	1.25
a.		Sheet of 8 + central label		19.50	10.00

A souvenir sheet of 2 containing Nos. 5703-5704 was printed in limited quantities.

Birds A1682

Designs: 3.30 l, Sterna hirundo. 4.30 l, Larus michahellis. 4.70 l, Recurvirostra avosetta. 8.10 l, Tadorna ferruginea. 9.10 l, Cygnus olor.

2015, Aug. 21			**Litho.**	**Perf. 13¼**	
5705	A1682	3.30 l	multi	1.75	.85
a.		Sheet of 5 + label		8.75	4.25
5706	A1682	4.30 l	multi	2.25	1.10
a.		Sheet of 5 + label		11.50	5.50
5707	A1682	4.70 l	multi	2.40	1.25
a.		Sheet of 5 + label		12.00	6.25
5708	A1682	8.10 l	multi	4.25	2.10
a.		Sheet of 5 + label		21.50	10.50
		Nos. 5705-5708 (4)		10.65	5.30

Souvenir Sheet

5709	A1682	9.10 l	multi	4.75	2.40

A souvenir sheet of 5 containing Nos. 5705-5709 was printed in limited quantities.

Moldavian Tourist Attractions — A1683

Arms and: 3.30 l, Cucuteni Eneolithic Art Museum, Piatra Neamt, Cucuteni ceramic piece. 3.60 l, Neamt Fortress, sculpture of Stephen the Great. 6 l, St. Nicholas Church, Iasi, sculpture of Metropolitan Dosoftei. 9.10 l, Alexandru Ioan Cuza Palace, Ruginoasa, Prince Alexandru Ioan I

2015, Sept. 8			**Litho.**	**Perf. 13¼**	
5710	A1683	3.30 l	multi	1.75	.85
a.		Sheet of 5 + label		8.75	4.25
5711	A1683	3.60 l	multi	1.90	.95
a.		Sheet of 5 + label		9.50	4.75
5712	A1683	6 l	multi	3.00	1.50
a.		Sheet of 5 + label		15.00	7.50
5713	A1683	9.10 l	multi	4.75	2.40
a.		Sheet of 5 + label		24.00	12.00
		Nos. 5710-5713 (4)		11.40	5.70

A souvenir sheet of 4 containing Nos. 5710-5713 was printed in limited quantities.

Dobrudja Tourist Attractions — A1684

Map and: 2 l, Tropaeum Traiani, Adamclisi. 4.70 l, Enisala Fortress ruins and coins. 7.60 l, Church of St. Andrew, St. Andrew's Cave pilgrimage site. 8.10 l, Boats and pelican in Danube Delta.

2015, Sept. 18			**Litho.**	**Perf. 13¼**	
5714	A1684	2 l	multi	1.00	.50
a.		Sheet of 5 + label		5.00	2.50
5715	A1684	4.70 l	multi	2.40	1.25
a.		Sheet of 5 + label		12.00	6.25
5716	A1684	7.60 l	multi	4.00	2.00
a.		Sheet of 5 + label		20.00	10.00
5717	A1684	8.10 l	multi	4.25	2.10
a.		Sheet of 5 + label		21.50	10.50
		Nos. 5714-5717 (4)		11.65	5.85

A souvenir sheet of 4 containing Nos. 5714-5717 was printed in limited quantities.

National Bank of Romania, 135th Anniv. — A1685

Designs: 3.30 l, Obverse of 1881 20-lei banknote, Ion I. Campineanu, first governor of bank. 9.10 l, Reverse of 1881 20-lei banknote, Emil Costinescu, first director of Banknote Manufacturing and Accounting Service.

2015, Sept. 29			**Litho.**	**Perf. 13¼**	
5718	A1685	3.30 l	multi	1.75	.85
a.		Sheet of 4		7.00	3.50
5719	A1685	9.10 l	multi	4.75	2.40
a.		Sheet of 4		19.00	9.75
b.		Souvenir sheet of 2, #5718-5719		6.50	3.25

A numbered souvenir sheet of 2 containing Nos. 5718-5719 with gold foil was printed in limited quantities.

Peles Castle Stained-Glass Windows — A1686

Windows depicting hunters hunting: 2 l, Boar. 3.30 l, Stags. 4.30 l, Hares. 14.50 l, Bear.

2015, Oct. 9			**Litho.**	**Perf. 14x13¼**	
5720	A1686	2 l	multi	1.00	.50
a.		Sheet of 4 + 2 labels		4.00	2.00
5721	A1686	3.30 l	multi	1.75	.85
a.		Sheet of 4 + 2 labels		7.00	3.50
5722	A1686	4.30 l	multi	2.25	1.10
a.		Sheet of 4 + 2 labels		9.00	4.50
5723	A1686	14.50 l	multi	7.25	3.75
a.		Sheet of 4 + 2 labels		29.00	15.00
		Nos. 5720-5723 (4)		12.25	6.20

A souvenir sheet of 4 containing Nos. 5720-5723 was printed in limited quantities.

Ion Tiriac, Tennis Player — A1687

Designs: 2.10 l, Tiriac, tennis ball. 9.10 l, Tiriac.

2015, Oct. 16			**Litho.**	**Perf. 13¼**	
5724	A1687	2.10 l	multi	1.10	.55
a.		Sheet of 8 + central label		9.00	4.50

Souvenir Sheet

5725	A1687	9.10 l	multi	4.50	2.25

No. 5724a was printed with two different central labels.

Christmas A1688

2015, Nov. 6			**Litho.**	**Perf. 13¼**	
5726	A1688	1 l	multi	.50	.25
a.		Sheet of 8		4.00	2.00
b.		Sheet of 8 + central label		4.00	2.00

Values are for stamps with surrounding selvage.

Flags of Romania and United States, King Carol I and Pres. Rutherford B. Hayes — A1689

2015, Nov. 18			**Litho.**	**Perf. 13¼**	
5727	A1689	3.60 l	multi	1.75	.85
a.		Sheet of 7 + 2 labels		12.50	6.00

Diplomatic relations between Romania and the United States, 135th anniv.

Oct. 30, 2015 Bucharest Night Club Fire — A1690

2015, Nov. 20			**Litho.**	**Perf. 13¼**	
5728	A1690	1 l	multi	.50	.25
a.		Sheet of 9		4.50	2.25

Dogs A1691

Designs: 2.40 l, German shepherd. 5 l, Malinois. 8.10 l, Labrador retriever. 9.10 l, Rottweiler.

2015, Nov. 20			**Litho.**	**Perf. 13¼**	
5729	A1691	2.40 l	multi	1.25	.60
a.		Sheet of 5 + label		6.25	3.00
5730	A1691	5 l	multi	2.40	1.25
a.		Sheet of 5 + label		12.00	6.25
5731	A1691	8.10 l	multi	4.00	2.00
a.		Sheet of 5 + label		20.00	10.00
5732	A1691	9.10 l	multi	4.50	2.25
a.		Sheet of 5 + label		22.50	11.50
		Nos. 5729-5732 (4)		12.15	6.10

Alba Iulia A1692

Designs: 3 l, Roman 13th Twin Legion Fortress. 3.30 l, Third Gate. 8.10 l, St. Michael's Cathedral. 9.10 l, Coronation Cathedral, King Ferdinand.

2015, Nov. 27			**Litho.**	**Perf. 13¼**	
5733	A1692	3 l	multi	1.50	.75
a.		Sheet of 5 + label		7.50	3.75
5734	A1692	3.30 l	multi	1.60	.80
a.		Sheet of 5 + label		8.00	4.00
5735	A1692	8.10 l	multi	4.00	2.00
a.		Sheet of 5 + label		20.00	10.00
5736	A1692	9.10 l	multi	4.50	2.25
a.		Sheet of 5 + label		22.50	11.50
		Nos. 5733-5736 (4)		11.60	5.80

A souvenir sheet of 4 containing Nos. 5733-5736 was printed in limited quantities.

Coins in Numismatic Collection of National Bank of Romania — A1693

Designs: 2 l, Dacian silver coins. 2.40 l, Imperial Roman gold coins. 8.10 l, Dutch ducats. 14.50 l, Polish silver coins.

2015, Dec. 4			**Litho.**	**Perf. 13¼**	
5737	A1693	2 l	multi	1.00	.50
a.		Sheet of 6		6.00	3.00
5738	A1693	2.40 l	multi	1.25	.60
a.		Sheet of 6		7.50	3.75
5739	A1693	8.10 l	multi	4.00	2.00
a.		Sheet of 6		24.00	12.00
5740	A1693	14.50 l	multi	7.00	3.50
a.		Sheet of 6		42.00	21.00
		Nos. 5737-5740 (4)		13.25	6.60

A souvenir sheet of 4 containing Nos. 5737-5740 was printed in limited quantities.

Romania in United Nations, 60th
Anniv. — A1694

2015, Dec. 15   Litho.   Perf. 13¼
5741 A1694 4.50 l shown   2.25 1.10
 a. Sheet of 7 + 2 labels   16.00 7.75

Souvenir Sheet
Perf.

5742 A1694 8.10 l Globe   4.00 2.00

No. 5742 contains one 30mm diameter
stamp.

Sculptures
Depicting
Eve — A1695

Sculpture by: 1 l, Gheorghe Leonida. 9.10 l,
Victor Brecheret, horiz.

2015, Dec. 21   Litho.   Perf. 13¼
5743 A1695   1 l multi   .50   .25
 a. Sheet of 6   3.00 1.50
5744 A1695 9.10 l multi   4.50 2.25
 a. Sheet of 6   27.00 13.50

See Brazil No. 3321.

Flemish Paintings in Brukenthal
National Museum — A1696

Designs: 4.70 l, St. Jerome in Scriptorium,
by Marinus Claeszoon van Reymerswaele. 5 l,
Ceres, Bacchus and Venus, by Abraham Jan-
ssens van Nuyssen. 7.60 l, Lion in Front of the
Cave, by Roelant Savery. 9.10 l, Still Life with
Fruits and Parrot, by Jan Fyt.

2016, Jan. 6   Litho.   Perf. 13¼
5745 A1696 4.70 l multi   2.25 1.10
 a. Sheet of 5 + label   11.50 5.50
5746 A1696   5 l multi   2.50 1.25
 a. Sheet of 5 + label   12.50 6.25
5747 A1696 7.60 l multi   3.75 1.90
 a. Sheet of 5 + label   19.00 9.50
5748 A1696 9.10 l multi   4.50 2.25
 a. Sheet of 5 + label   22.50 11.50
     Nos. 5745-5748 (4)   13.00 6.50

Flowers
A1697

Designs: 4.70 l, Dipsacus fullonum. 5 l, Centaurea solstitialis. 6 l, Echinops ruthenicus.
8.10 l, Ononis spinosa.

2016, Jan. 14   Litho.   Perf. 13¼
5749 A1697 4.70 l multi   2.25 1.10
 a. Sheet of 4   9.00 4.50
5750 A1697   5 l multi   2.50 1.25
 a. Sheet of 4   10.00 5.00
5751 A1697   6 l multi   3.00 1.50
 a. Sheet of 4   12.00 6.00
5752 A1697 8.10 l multi   4.00 2.00
 a. Sheet of 4   16.00 8.00
     Nos. 5749-5752 (4)   11.75 5.85

Prehistoric Animals — A1698

Designs: 2 l, Balaur bondoc. 3 l, Theri-
osuchus sympiestodon. 3.30 l, Magy-
arosaurus dacus. 14.50 l, Kogaionon
ungureanui.

2016, Jan. 22   Litho.   Perf. 13¼
5753 A1698   2 l multi   1.00   .50
 a. Sheet of 5 + label   5.00 2.50
5754 A1698   3 l multi   1.50   .75
 a. Sheet of 5 + label   7.50 3.75
5755 A1698 3.30 l multi   1.60   .80
 a. Sheet of 5 + label   8.00 4.00
5756 A1698 14.50 l multi   7.00 3.50
 a. Sheet of 5 + label   35.00 17.50
     Nos. 5753-5756 (4)   11.10 5.55

Woodpeckers
A1699

Designs: 2 l, Picoides tridactylus. 4.50 l,
Picus viridis. 5 l, Dryocopus martius. 14.50 l,
Jynx torquilla.

2016, Feb. 9   Litho.   Perf. 13¼
5757 A1699   2 l multi   1.00   .50
 a. Sheet of 5 + label   5.00 2.50
5758 A1699 4.50 l multi   2.25 1.10
 a. Sheet of 5 + label   11.50 5.50
5759 A1699   5 l multi   2.50 1.25
 a. Sheet of 5 + label   12.50 6.25
5760 A1699 14.50 l multi   7.00 3.50
 a. Sheet of 5 + label   35.00 17.50
     Nos. 5757-5760 (4)   12.75 6.35

Brasov Tourist Attractions — A1700

Arms of Brasov and: 3 l, Black Church.
3.30 l, Catherine's Gate. 5 l, First Romanian
school. 14.50 l, Council Hall.

2016, Feb. 17   Litho.   Perf. 13¼
5761 A1700   3 l multi   1.50   .75
 a. Sheet of 5 + label   7.50 3.75
5762 A1700 3.30 l multi   1.60   .80
 a. Sheet of 5 + label   8.00 4.00
5763 A1700   5 l multi   2.50 1.25
 a. Sheet of 5 + label   12.50 6.25
5764 A1700 14.50 l multi   7.00 3.50
 a. Sheet of 5 + label   35.00 17.50
     Nos. 5761-5764 (4)   12.60 6.30

A souvenir sheet containing Nos. 5761-
5764 was printed in limited quantities.

Romanian Superlatives and
Curiosities — A1701

Designs: 3 l, World's smallest and lowest-
valued banknotes. 3.30 l, Gold from Gold
Museum, Brad. 5 l, Buchholz Organ, Black
Church, Brasov, largest mechanical organ in
Romania, vert. 14.50 l, Sculpture of King
Decebalus, largest stone sculpture in Europe,
vert.

2016, Feb. 24   Litho.   Perf. 13¼
5765 A1701   3 l multi   1.50   .75
 a. Sheet of 5 + label   7.50 3.75
5766 A1701 3.30 l multi   1.60   .80
 a. Sheet of 5 + label   8.00 4.00
5767 A1701   5 l multi   2.50 1.25
 a. Sheet of 5 + label   12.50 6.25
5768 A1701 14.50 l multi   7.00 3.50
 a. Sheet of 5 + label   35.00 17.50
     Nos. 5765-5768 (4)   12.60 6.30

Letters and
Flowers
A1702

Designs: 1.20 l, "C," chrysanthemums.
1.40 l, "U," houseleeks. 1.60 l, "D," dahlias.
4.50 l, "R," yellow pheasant's eye. 8 l, "A,"
azaleas. 16 l, "G," gladiolas.

2016, Mar. 8   Litho.   Perf. 13¼
5769 A1702 1.20 l multi   .65   .30
 a. Sheet of 5 + label   3.25 1.50
5770 A1702 1.40 l multi   .75   .35
 a. Sheet of 5 + label   3.75 1.75
5771 A1702 1.60 l multi   .85   .40
 a. Sheet of 5 + label   4.25 2.00
5772 A1702 4.50 l multi   2.40 1.25
 a. Sheet of 5 + label   12.00 6.25
5773 A1702   8 l multi   4.00 2.00
 a. Sheet of 5 + label   20.00 10.00
5774 A1702   16 l multi   8.25 4.25
 a. Sheet of 5 + label   41.50 21.50
 b. Sheet of 6, #5769-5774 17.00 8.75
     Nos. 5769-5774 (6)   16.90 8.55

Famous
Romanians
A1703

Designs: 1 l, Constantin Brâncusi (1876-
1957), sculptor. 2 l, George Enescu (1881-
1955), composer. 3.50 l, George Emil Palade
(1912-2008), 1974 Nobel laureate for Physiology or Medicine. 4 l, George Constantinescu
(1881-1965), inventor. 12 l, Ana Aslan (1897-
1988), gerontologist. 31 l, Dumitru Staniloae
(1903-93), theologian.

2016, Mar. 18   Litho.   Perf. 13¼
5775 A1703   1 l multi   .50   .25
 a. Sheet of 3 + label   1.50   .75
5776 A1703   2 l multi   1.00   .50
 a. Sheet of 3 + label   3.00 1.50
5777 A1703 3.50 l multi   1.75   .90
 a. Sheet of 3 + label   5.25 2.75
5778 A1703   4 l multi   2.10 1.10
 a. Sheet of 3 + label   6.50 3.50
5779 A1703   12 l multi   6.25 3.25
 a. Sheet of 3 + label   19.00 9.75
5780 A1703   31 l multi   16.00 8.00
 a. Sheet of 3 + label   48.00 24.00
     Nos. 5775-5780 (6)   27.60 14.00

Easter
A1704

Designs: No. 5781, Icon depicting crucifixion. No. 5782, Easter flowers.
8 l, Crucifixion, diff.

2016, Mar. 23   Litho.   Perf. 13¼
5781 A1704   1 l multi   .50   .25
 a. Sheet of 8   4.00 2.00
 b. Sheet of 8 + central label 4.00 2.00
5782 A1704   1 l multi   .50   .25
 a. Sheet of 8   4.00 2.00
 b. Sheet of 8 + central label 4.00 2.00

Souvenir Sheet
Perf.

5783 A1704   8 l multi   4.00 2.00

Values are for stamps with surrounding
selvage. A souvenir sheet of 2 containing Nos.
5781-5782 and a souvenir sheet of 3 containing No. 5781 and two No. 5782 were printed in
limited quantities.

Romanian Academy, 150th
Anniv. — A1705

Designs: 5 l, Romanian Academy building.
8 l, Building façade and goddess Minerva,
vert.

2016, Apr. 4   Litho.   Perf. 13¼
5784 A1705   5 l multi   2.60 1.25
 a. Sheet of 6 + 3 labels   16.00 7.50

Souvenir Sheet
Perf. 13¼x14

5785 A1705   8 l multi   4.25 2.10

No. 5785 contains one 42x53mm stamp.

Butterflies — A1706

Designs: 3 l, Lycaena dispar. 3.50 l, Scoli-
tantides orion. 5 l, Argynnis paphia. 15 l,
Plebejus argus.

2016, Apr. 15   Litho.   Perf. 14x13¼
5786 A1706   3 l multi   1.60   .80
 a. Sheet of 5 + label   8.00 4.00
5787 A1706 3.50 l multi   1.75   .90
 a. Sheet of 5 + label   8.75 4.50
5788 A1706   5 l multi   2.60 1.40
 a. Sheet of 5 + label   13.00 7.00
5789 A1706   15 l multi   7.75 4.00
 a. Sheet of 5 + label   39.00 20.00
     Nos. 5786-5789 (4)   13.70 7.10

A souvenir sheet containing Nos. 5786-
5789 was printed in limited quantities.

Romania in Interparliamentary Union,
125th Anniv. — A1707

Designs: 3 l, Vasile A. Urechia, member of
Romanian delegation to 1891 conference.
12 l, Interparliamentary Union emblem.

2016, Apr. 18   Litho.   Perf. 13¼
5790 A1707   3 l multi   1.60   .80
 a. Sheet of 8 + central label 13.00 6.50

Souvenir Sheet
Perf.

5791 A1707   12 l multi   6.25 3.25

No. 5791 contains one 30mm diameter
stamp.

A1708

Europa — A1709

2016, May 4   Litho.   Perf. 13¼
5792 A1708 5 l multi   2.50   1.25
   a.   Sheet of 6   15.00   7.50
5793 A1709 12 l multi   2.50   1.25
   a.   Sheet of 6   36.00 18.00
   b.   Sheet of 4, 2 each #5792-
          5793, #5792 at UL   17.00   8.50
   c.   As "b," #5793 at UL   17.00   8.50
Think Green Issue.

Romanian Dynasty, 150th Anniv. A1710

Designs: 4.50 l, Collar of the Order of Carol I. 16 l, Scepter of King Ferdinand I. 8 l, King Carol I and royal family, horiz.

2016, May 10   Litho.   Perf. 13¼x14
5794 A1710 4.50 l multi   2.25   1.10
   a.   Sheet of 5 + label   11.50   5.50
5795 A1710 16 l multi   8.00   4.00
   a.   Sheet of 5 + label   40.00 20.00

Souvenir Sheet
Perf. 14x13¼
5796 A1710 8 l multi   4.00   2.00
A souvenir sheet of 2 containing Nos. 5794-5795 was printed in limited quantities.

The Four Seasons at the Village Museum, Bucharest — A1711

Designs: 2 l, Sfintii Voievozi Church, flower. 2.40 l, Chiojdu-Mic Homestead, sunflower. 8 l, Jurilovca Homestead, autumn leaves. 15 l, Surdesti Homestead in winter.

2016, May 20   Litho.   Perf. 13¼
5797 A1711 2 l multi   1.00   .50
   a.   Sheet of 6   6.00   3.00
5798 A1711 2.40 l multi   1.25   .60
   a.   Sheet of 6   7.50   3.75
5799 A1711 8 l multi   4.00   2.00
   a.   Sheet of 6   24.00 12.00
5800 A1711 15 l multi   7.50   3.75
   a.   Sheet of 6   45.00 22.50
   b.   Souvenir sheet of 4, #5797-
          5800 + 2 labels   14.00   7.00
   Nos. 5797-5800 (4)   13.75   6.85
Village Museum, 80th anniv.

Souvenir Sheet

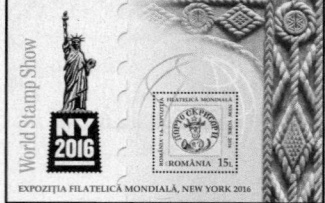

2016 World Stamp Show, New York — A1712

2016, May 28   Litho.   Perf. 13¼
5801 A1712 15 l Romania #1   7.50   3.75

Children's Stories — A1713

Characters from: 2 l, Two Penny Bag, by Ion Creanga. 2.40 l, Neghinita, by Barbu Stefanescu Delavrancea. 8 l, Prince Charming and Ileana Cosanzeanna, by Petre Ispirecu, vert. 15 l, Mr. Goe, by I. L. Caragiale, vert.

2016, June 1   Litho.   Perf. 13¼
5802 A1713 2 l multi   1.00   .50
   a.   Sheet of 5 + label   5.00   2.50
5803 A1713 2.40 l multi   1.25   .60
   a.   Sheet of 5 + label   6.25   3.00
5804 A1713 8 l multi   4.00   2.00
   a.   Sheet of 5 + label   20.00 10.00
5805 A1713 15 l multi   7.50   3.75
   a.   Sheet of 5 + label   37.50 19.00
   Nos. 5802-5805 (4)   13.75   6.85

Sibiu International Theater Festival — A1714

Masked character from festival poster and Sibiu towers: 5 l, Council Tower. 8 l, Potter's Tower.

2016, June 10   Litho.   Perf. 13¼
5806 A1714 5 l multi   2.50   1.25
   a.   Sheet of 5 + label   12.50   6.25
5807 A1714 8 l multi   4.00   2.00
   a.   Sheet of 5 + label   20.00 10.00

2016 European Soccer Championships, France — A1715

Various soccer players, flags of Romania and group opponents: 3 l, France. 3.50 l, Switzerland. 4.50 l, Albania. 16 l, France, Switzerland and Albania.

2016, June 10   Litho.   Perf. 13¼
5808 A1715 3 l multi   1.50   .75
   a.   Sheet of 5 + label   7.50   3.75
5809 A1715 3.50 l multi   1.75   .85
   a.   Sheet of 5 + label   8.75   4.25
5810 A1715 4.50 l multi   2.25   1.10
   a.   Sheet of 5 + label   11.50   5.50
5811 A1715 16 l multi   8.00   4.00
   a.   Sheet of 5 + label   40.00 20.00
   Nos. 5808-5811 (4)   13.50   6.70

Famous Romanian Women Wearing Traditional Blouses — A1716

Designs: 3.50 l, Queen Elisabeth (1843-1916), blouse from Olt County. 4 l, Queen Marie (1875-1938), blouse from Dolj County. 4.50 l, Smaranda Braescu (1897-1948), parachutist, blouse from Muscel. 16 l, Maria Tanase (1913-63), singer, blouse from Padureni.

2016, June 22   Litho.   Perf. 14x13¼
5812 A1716 3.50 l multi   1.75   .85
   a.   Sheet of 4   7.00   3.50

5813 A1716 4 l multi   2.00   1.00
   a.   Sheet of 4   8.00   4.00
5814 A1716 4.50 l multi   2.25   1.10
   a.   Sheet of 4   9.00   4.50
5815 A1716 16 l multi   8.00   4.00
   a.   Sheet of 4   32.00 16.00
   Nos. 5812-5815 (4)   14.00   6.95

Putna Monastery, 550th Anniv. — A1717

Designs: 3 l, Prince Stephen the Great, Putna Monastery. 15 l, Putna Monastery. 12 l, Tomb of Stephen the Great.

2016, July 5   Litho.   Perf. 13¼
5816 A1717 3 l multi   1.50   .75
   a.   Sheet of 5 + label   7.50   3.75
5817 A1717 15 l multi   7.50   3.75
   a.   Sheet of 5 + label   37.50 19.00

Souvenir Sheet
5818 A1717 12 l multi   6.00   3.00
No. 5818 contains one 36x36mm stamp.

First Documented Reference to Town of Sibiu, 825th Anniv. — A1718

Details from *General View of Sibiuy in 1808*, by Franz Neuhauser the Younger, with arms of Sibiu at: 3 l, Left. 15 l, Right.

2016, July 15   Litho.   Perf. 13¼
5819 A1718 3 l multi   1.50   .75
   a.   Sheet of 5 + label   7.50   3.75
5820 A1718 15 l multi   7.50   3.75
   a.   Sheet of 5 + label   37.50 19.00
Stamp Day. A souvenir sheet of 2 containing Nos. 5819-5820 was printed in limited quantities.

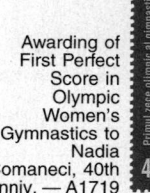

Awarding of First Perfect Score in Olympic Women's Gymnastics to Nadia Comaneci, 40th Anniv. — A1719

Designs: 4.50 l, Comaneci and "10." No. 5822, Comaneci with leg extended, denomination in black. No. 5823, Comaneci with leg raised, denomination in white.

2016, July 18   Litho.   Perf. 13¼
5821 A1719 4.50 l multi   2.25   1.10
   a.   Sheet of 5 + label   11.50   5.50

Souvenir Sheets
5822 A1719 31 l multi   15.50   7.75
Imperf
5823 A1719 31 l multi   15.50   7.75
Nos. 5822 and 5823 each contain one 36x36mm stamp.

2016 Summer Olympics, Rio de Janeiro A1720

Designs: 3 l, Judo. 4 l. Fencing. 8 l, Long jump. 16 l, Shooting.

2016, Aug. 5   Litho.   Perf. 13¼
5824 A1720 3 l multi   1.50   .75
   a.   Sheet of 5 + label   7.50   3.75
5825 A1720 4 l multi   2.00   1.00
   a.   Sheet of 5 + label   10.00   5.00
5826 A1720 8 l multi   4.00   2.00
   a.   Sheet of 5 + label   20.00 10.00
5827 A1720 16 l multi   8.00   4.00
   a.   Sheet of 5 + label   40.00 20.00
   b.   Souvenir sheet of 4, #5824-
          5827 + 2 labels   15.50   7.75
   Nos. 5824-5827 (4)   15.50   7.75

Transalpina, Highest Road in Romania A1721

Designs: 8 l, Hairpin turn. 15 l, Road and village, horiz.

2016, Aug. 12   Litho.   Perf. 13¼
5828 A1721 8 l multi   4.00   2.00
   a.   Sheet of 8 + central label   32.00 16.00

Souvenir Sheet
5829 A1721 15 l multi   7.50   3.75
No. 5829 contains one 48x35mm stamp.

Cluj-Napoca Tourist Attractions A1722

Arms of Cluj-Napoca and: 3.50 l, Dormition of the Virgin Mary Orthodox Metropolitan Cathedral. 4 l, Tailor's Bastion. 4.50 l, Lucian Blaga National Theater, horiz. 15 l, Babes-Bolyai University, horiz.

2016, Aug. 19   Litho.   Perf. 13¼
5830 A1722 3.50 l multi   1.75   .90
   a.   Sheet of 5 + label   8.75   4.50
5831 A1722 4 l multi   2.00   1.00
   a.   Sheet of 5 + label   10.00   5.00
5832 A1722 4.50 l multi   2.25   1.10
   a.   Sheet of 5 + label   11.50   5.50
5833 A1722 15 l multi   7.50   3.75
   a.   Sheet of 5 + label   37.50 19.00
   Nos. 5830-5833 (4)   13.50   6.75
A souvenir sheet of 4 containing Nos. 5830-5833 was printed in limited quantities.

Romanian Chapter of International Police Association, 20th Anniv. — A1723

Designs: 8 l, Emblem, map and flag of Romania. 15 l, Emblem and flag of Romania.

2016, Aug. 24   Litho.   Perf. 13¼
5834 A1723 8 l multi   4.00   2.00
   a.   Sheet of 8 + central label   32.00 16.00

Souvenir Sheet
Perf.
5835 A1723 15 l multi   7.50   3.75
No. 5835 contains one 30mm diameter stamp.

Flora and Fauna of Ceahlau National Park — A1724

Park emblem and: 80b, Edelweiss. 90b, Red crossbill, vert. 1.10 l, Liverwort. 1.20 l, Chamois, vert. 1.30 l, Arnica. 1.40 l, Brown bear, vert. 1.50 l, European robin. 1.60 l, Great yellow gentian, vert. 1.70 l, Water pipit. 1.80 l, Lady's slipper orchid, vert. 2.70 l, Common kingfisher. 16 l, Martagon lily, vert.

2016, Sept. 1 Litho. Perf. 13¼

5836 A1724	80b multi	.40	.25
a.	Sheet of 4	1.60	.80
5837 A1724	90b multi	.45	.25
a.	Sheet of 4	1.90	1.00
5838 A1724	1.10 l multi	.55	.25
a.	Sheet of 4	2.25	1.00
5839 A1724	1.20 l multi	.60	.30
a.	Sheet of 4	2.40	1.25
5840 A1724	1.30 l multi	.65	.30
a.	Sheet of 4	2.60	1.25
5841 A1724	1.40 l multi	.70	.35
a.	Sheet of 4	3.00	1.40
5842 A1724	1.50 l multi	.75	.40
a.	Sheet of 4	3.00	1.60
5843 A1724	1.60 l multi	.80	.40
a.	Sheet of 4	3.25	1.60
5844 A1724	1.70 l multi	.85	.40
a.	Sheet of 4	3.50	1.60
5845 A1724	1.80 l multi	.90	.45
a.	Sheet of 4	3.75	1.90
5846 A1724	2.70 l multi	1.40	.70
a.	Sheet of 4	5.75	3.00
5847 A1724	16 l multi	8.00	4.00
a.	Sheet of 4	32.00	16.00
Nos. 5836-5847 (12)		16.05	8.05

Designs: 2.50 l, Plecotus auritus. 4.50 l, Pipistrellus pipistrellus. 8 l, Miniopterus schreibersii. 15 l, Nyctalus noctula, vert.

Bats A1725

2016, Sept. 9 Litho. Perf. 13¼

5848 A1725	2.50 l multi	1.25	.60
a.	Sheet of 5 + label	6.25	3.00
5849 A1725	4.50 l multi	2.25	1.10
a.	Sheet of 5 + label	11.50	5.50
5850 A1725	8 l multi	4.00	2.00
a.	Sheet of 5 + label	20.00	10.00
5851 A1725	15 l multi	7.50	3.75
a.	Sheet of 5 + label	37.50	19.00
Nos. 5848-5851 (4)		15.00	7.45

A souvenir sheet of 4 containing Nos. 5848-5851 was printed in limited quantities.

Anti-Aircraft Artillery, Cent. — A1726

2016, Sept. 19 Litho. Perf. 13¼

5852 A1726	8 l multi	4.00	2.00
a.	Sheet of 6	24.00	12.00

Military Aircraft, Cent. — A1727

Designs: 4.50 l, IAR-93. 15 l, IAR-99. 16 l, F-16.

2016, Oct. 7 Litho. Perf. 13¼

5853 A1727	4.50 l multi	2.25	1.10
a.	Sheet of 4	9.00	4.50
5854 A1727	15 l multi	7.50	3.75
a.	Sheet of 4	30.00	15.00

Souvenir Sheet
Perf. 14x13¼

5855 A1727	16 l multi	8.00	4.00

No. 5855 contains one 52x42mm stamp.

Laser Valley Land of Lights Research Laboratory, Magurele — A1728

Designs: 4.50 l, Horia Hulubei (1896-1972), physicist. 8 l, Ion L. Agârbiceanu (1907-71), physicist. 15 l, Laser Valley Laboratory.

2016, Oct. 11 Litho. Perf. 13¼

5856 A1728	4.50 l multi	2.25	1.10
a.	Sheet of 5 + label	11.50	5.50
5857 A1728	8 l multi	4.00	2.00
a.	Sheet of 5 + label	20.00	10.00

Souvenir Sheet
Perf. 14x13¼

5858 A1728	15 l multi	7.50	3.75

No. 5858 contains one 52x42mm stamp.

Muntenia Tourist Attractions A1729

Arms of Muntenia and: 2.50 l, Curtea de Arges Monastery, founder Neagoe Basarab. 3.50 l, Constantin Brancoveanu (1654-1714), Prince of Wallachia, and building details. 8 l, Woman wearing traditional costume, carpets & decorative motifs, stone decorations. 15 l, Buildings, sculpture of Prime Minister Ion C. Bratianu.

2016, Oct. 14 Litho. Perf. 13¼

5859 A1729	2.50 l multi	1.25	.60
a.	Sheet of 5 + label	6.25	3.00
5860 A1729	3.50 l multi	1.75	.85
a.	Sheet of 5 + label	8.75	4.25
5861 A1729	8 l multi	4.00	2.00
a.	Sheet of 5 + label	20.00	10.00
5862 A1729	15 l multi	7.50	3.75
a.	Sheet of 5 + label	37.50	19.00
Nos. 5859-5862 (4)		14.50	7.20

A souvenir sheet of 4 containing Nos. 5859-5862 was printed in limited quantities.

Corkscrews A1730

Corkscrew from: 1.80 l, Italy, 19th cent. 2.20 l, France, 18th cent. 2.70 l, Great Britain, 19th cent. 3.50 l, Germany, 19th cent. 4.50 l, United States, 20th cent. 8 l, Netherlands, 19th cent. 16 l, Romanian corkscrew, 20th cent., horiz,

2016, Oct. 27 Litho. Perf. 13¼

5863 A1730	1.80 l multi	.90	.45
a.	Sheet of 8 + central label	7.25	3.75
b.	Sheet of 13 + 2 labels	12.00	6.00
5864 A1730	2.20 l multi	1.10	.55
a.	Sheet of 8 + central label	9.00	4.50
b.	Sheet of 13 + 2 labels	14.50	7.25
5865 A1730	2.70 l multi	1.40	.70
a.	Sheet of 8 + central label	11.50	5.75
b.	Sheet of 13 + 2 labels	18.50	9.25
5866 A1730	3.50 l multi	1.75	.85
a.	Sheet of 8 + central label	14.00	7.00
b.	Sheet of 13 + 2 labels	23.00	11.50
5867 A1730	4.50 l multi	2.25	1.10
a.	Sheet of 8 + central label	18.00	9.00
b.	Sheet of 13 + 2 labels	29.50	14.50
5868 A1730	8 l multi	4.00	2.00
a.	Sheet of 8 + central label	32.00	16.00
b.	Sheet of 13 + 2 labels	52.00	26.00

Souvenir Sheet
Imperf

5869 A1730	16 l multi	8.00	4.00

No. 5869 contains one 52x42mm stamp.
See Nos. 5921-5927.

Transportation of King Michael — A1731

King Michael and: 4 l, Aero 30 Roadster. 4.50 l, Motorcycle, vert. 8 l, Automobile, with Queen Anne, vert. 15 l, Airplane.

2016, Oct. 27 Litho. Perf. 14x13¼

5870 A1731	4 l multi	2.00	1.00
a.	Sheet of 5 + label	10.00	5.00
5871 A1731	4.50 l multi	2.25	1.10
a.	Sheet of 5 + label	11.50	5.50
5872 A1731	8 l multi	4.00	2.00
a.	Sheet of 5 + label	20.00	10.00
5873 A1731	15 l multi	7.50	3.75
a.	Sheet of 5 + label	37.50	19.00
Nos. 5870-5873 (4)		15.75	7.85

A souvenir sheet of 4 containing Nos. 5870-5873 was printed in limited quantities.

World Bank in Romania, 25th Anniv. A1732

2016, Nov. 1 Litho. Perf. 13¼x14

5874 A1732	12 l multi	6.00	3.00
a.	Sheet of 5 + label	30.00	15.00

Christmas A1733

Designs: No. 5875, Nativity icon from Putna Monastery. No. 5876, Poinsettia. 12 l, Madonna and Child icon from Putna Monastery.

2016, Nov. 11 Litho. Perf. 13¼

5875 A1733	1.30 l multi	.65	.30
a.	Sheet of 8 + central label	5.25	2.40
5876 A1733	1.30 l multi	.65	.30
a.	Sheet of 8 + central label	5.25	2.40

Souvenir Sheet

5877 A1733	12 l multi	5.75	3.00

Souvenir sheets of 2 containing one each of Nos. 5875-5876 and souvenir sheets of 3 containing No. 5875 and 2 examples of No. 5876 were printed in limited quantities.

Foods of the Bible A1734

Designs: 1.60 l, Wheat and bread. 4.50 l, Figs and pomegranates. 8 l, Grapes. 15 l, Olives and olive oil.

2016, Nov. 24 Litho. Perf. 13¼

5878 A1734	1.60 l multi	.75	.40
a.	Sheet of 5 + label	3.75	2.00
5879 A1734	4.50 l multi	2.25	1.10
a.	Sheet of 5 + label	11.50	5.50
5880 A1734	8 l multi	3.75	1.90
a.	Sheet of 5 + label	19.00	9.50
5881 A1734	15 l multi	7.25	3.75
a.	Sheet of 5 + label	36.50	19.00
Nos. 5878-5881 (4)		14.00	7.15

Actors and Actresses Type of 2014

Designs: No. 5882, Adela Marculescu. No. 5883, Florina Cercel. No. 5884, Ilinca Tomoroveanu. No. 5885, Ion Caramitru. No. 5886, Costel Constantin. No. 5887, Alexandru Arsinel.

2016, Dec. 19 Litho. Perf. 13¼

5882 A1620	4.50 l multi	2.10	1.10
a.	Sheet of 4	8.50	4.50
5883 A1620	4.50 l multi	2.10	1.10
a.	Sheet of 4	8.50	4.50
5884 A1620	4.50 l multi	2.10	1.10
a.	Sheet of 4	8.50	4.50
5885 A1620	4.50 l multi	2.10	1.10
a.	Sheet of 4	8.50	4.50
5886 A1620	4.50 l multi	2.10	1.10
a.	Sheet of 4	8.50	4.50
5887 A1620	4.50 l multi	2.10	1.10
a.	Sheet of 4	8.50	4.50
b.	Souvenir sheet of 6, #5882-5887 + 3 labels	13.00	6.75
Nos. 5882-5887 (6)		12.60	6.60

New Year's Customs — A1735

Designs: 2.20 l, Plugusorul (man pushing plow decorated with Christmas tree). 2.50 l, Buhaiul (carolers and drummer). 8 l, Ursul (dancers with bear costumes). 15 l, Capra (goat dance).

2016, Dec. 21 Litho. Perf. 13¼

5888 A1735	2.20 l multi	1.00	.50
a.	Sheet of 5 + label	5.00	2.50
5889 A1735	2.50 l multi	1.25	.60
a.	Sheet of 5 + label	6.25	3.00
5890 A1735	8 l multi	3.75	1.90
a.	Sheet of 5 + label	19.00	9.50
5891 A1735	15 l multi	7.00	3.50
a.	Sheet of 5 + label	35.00	17.50
Nos. 5888-5891 (4)		13.00	6.50

Palace of Culture, Iasi — A1736

Designs: 2.20 l, Palace at night. 2.50 l, Voivode Hall. 8 l, Henri Coanda Room. 15 l, Palace in daytime.

2017, Jan. 10 Litho. Perf. 13¼

5892 A1736	2.20 l multi	1.10	.55
a.	Sheet of 4	5.50	2.75
5893 A1736	2.50 l multi	1.25	.60
a.	Sheet of 4	6.25	3.00
5894 A1736	8 l multi	3.75	1.90
a.	Sheet of 4	19.00	9.50
5895 A1736	15 l multi	7.25	3.50
a.	Sheet of 4	36.50	17.50
Nos. 5892-5895 (4)		13.35	6.55

Orchids A1737

Designs: 2.20 l, Epipactis atrorubens. 4.50 l, Cephalanthera damasonium. 8 l, Orchis purpurea. 15 l, Epipactis helleborine.

2017, Jan. 25 Litho. Perf. 13¼

5896 A1737	2.20 l multi	1.10	.55
a.	Sheet of 4	4.50	2.25
5897 A1737	4.50 l multi	2.10	1.10
a.	Sheet of 4	8.50	4.50
5898 A1737	8 l multi	3.75	1.90
a.	Sheet of 4	15.00	7.75
5899 A1737	15 l multi	7.25	3.75
a.	Sheet of 4	29.00	15.00
Nos. 5896-5899 (4)		14.20	7.30

A souvenir sheet of 4 containing Nos. 5896-5899 was printed in limited quantities.

Romania in European Union, 10th Anniv. — A1738

2017, Jan. 27   Litho.   Perf. 13¼

5900	A1738	8 l multi	3.75	1.90
a.		Sheet of 6	22.50	11.50

Birds
A1739

Designs: 2.50 l, Corvus monedula. 4.50 l, Garrulus glandarius. 8 l, Corvus frugilegus. 15 l, Pica pica.

2017, Feb. 10   Litho.   Perf. 13¼

5901	A1739	2.50 l multi	1.25	.60
a.		Sheet of 5 + label	6.25	3.00
5902	A1739	4.50 l multi	2.10	1.10
a.		Sheet of 5 + label	10.50	5.50
5903	A1739	8 l multi	3.75	1.90
a.		Sheet of 5 + label	19.00	9.50
5904	A1739	15 l multi	7.00	3.50
a.		Sheet of 5 + label	35.00	17.50
		Nos. 5901-5904 (4)	14.10	7.10

A souvenir sheet of 4 containing Nos. 5901-5904 was produced in limited quantities.

National Brukenthal Museum, 200th Anniv. — A1740

Baron Samuel von Brukenthal (1721-1803), governor of Transylvania, and: 2.20 l, Pocket watch. 2.50 l, Brukenthal Palace. 8 l, Brukenthal family crest. 15 l, Pocket watch, diff.

2017, Feb. 17   Litho.   Perf. 13¼

5905	A1740	2.20 l multi	1.10	.55
a.		Sheet of 5 + label	5.50	2.75
5906	A1740	2.50 l multi	1.25	.60
a.		Sheet of 5 + label	6.25	3.00
5907	A1740	8 l multi	3.75	1.90
a.		Sheet of 5 + label	19.00	9.50
5908	A1740	15 l multi	7.00	3.50
a.		Sheet of 5 + label	35.00	17.50
		Nos. 5905-5908 (4)	13.10	6.55

Postcrossing — A1741

2017, Feb. 24   Litho.   Perf. 13¼

5909	A1741	4 l multi	1.90	.95
a.		Sheet of 8 + central label	15.50	7.75

A1742

Easter
A1743

Design: 12 l, The Resurrection - The Harrowing of Hell.

2017, Mar. 10   Litho.   Perf. 13¼

5910	A1742	1.30 l multi	.60	.30
a.		Sheet of 8 + central label	5.00	2.40
5911	A1743	1.30 l multi	.60	.30
a.		Sheet of 8 + central label	5.00	2.40
b.		Sheet of 8, 4 each #5910-5911	5.00	2.40

Souvenir Sheet

5912	A1743	12 l multi	5.75	3.00

Two souvenir sheets of 3 containing No. 5912 and imperforate examples of Nos. 5190-5911, and the other containing Nos. 5910-5911 and one imperforate example of No. 5912 were printed in limited quantities.

National Flowers, Flags and Maps — A1744

Designs: 1.50 l, Paeonia peregrina, flag and map of Romania. 4.50 l, Ocimum basilicum, flag and map of Moldova. 8 l, Iris croatica, flag and map of Croatia. 15 l, Rosa damascena, flag and map of Bulgaria.

2017, Mar. 17   Litho.   Perf. 13¼

5913	A1744	1.50 l multi	.70	.35
a.		Sheet of 5 + label	3.50	1.75
5914	A1744	4.50 l multi	2.10	1.10
a.		Sheet of 5 + label	10.50	5.50
5915	A1744	8 l multi	3.75	1.90
a.		Sheet of 5 + label	19.00	9.50
5916	A1744	15 l multi	7.00	3.50
a.		Sheet of 5 + label	35.00	17.50
		Nos. 5913-5916 (4)	13.55	6.85

Decorated Weapons of the 18th Century — A1745

Designs: 2.50 l, Persian gun. 4.50 l, Italian flintlock pistol. 8 l, Turkish flintlock pistol. 15 l, Turkish pistol, diff.

2017, Mar. 24   Litho.   Perf. 14x13¼

5917	A1745	2.50 l multi	1.25	.60
a.		Sheet of 5 + label	6.25	3.00
5918	A1745	4.50 l multi	2.10	1.10
a.		Sheet of 5 + label	10.50	5.50
5919	A1745	8 l multi	3.75	1.90
a.		Sheet of 5 + label	19.00	9.50
5920	A1745	15 l multi	7.00	3.50
a.		Sheet of 5 + label	35.00	17.50
		Nos. 5917-5920 (4)	14.10	7.10

Corkscrews Type of 2016

Designs: 1.60 l, Pocket corkscrew, France, 18th cent. 2.70 l, Agate & gold corkscrew, France, 18th cent. 3.50 l, Bell type corkscrew, England, 19th cent. 4 l, Single lever corkscrew, France, 20th cent. 4.50 l, Zig-zag corkscrew, England, 19th cent. 8 l, Pistol corkscrew, France, 19th cent.

16 l, Corkscrew from Denmark, 20th cent., horiz.

2017, Mar. 29   Litho.   Perf. 13¼

5921	A1730	1.60 l multi	.75	.35
a.		Sheet of 8 + central label	6.00	3.00
b.		Sheet of 13 + 2 labels	9.75	4.75
5922	A1730	2.70 l multi	1.25	.65
a.		Sheet of 8 + central label	10.00	5.25
b.		Sheet of 13 + 2 labels	16.50	8.50

5923	A1730	3.50 l multi	1.75	.85
a.		Sheet of 8 + central label	14.00	7.00
b.		Sheet of 13 + 2 labels	23.00	11.50
5924	A1730	4 l multi	1.90	.95
a.		Sheet of 8 + central label	15.50	7.75
b.		Sheet of 13 + 2 labels	25.00	12.50
5925	A1730	4.50 l multi	2.10	1.10
a.		Sheet of 8 + central label	17.00	9.00
b.		Sheet of 13 + 2 labels	27.50	14.50
5926	A1730	8 l multi	3.75	1.90
a.		Sheet of 8 + central label	30.00	15.50
b.		Sheet of 13 + 2 labels	49.00	25.00
		Nos. 5921-5926 (6)	11.50	5.80

Souvenir Sheet
Imperf

5927	A1730	16 l multi	7.50	3.75

No. 5927 contains one 52x42mm stamp.

Symphony of Tulips Floral Exhibition, Pitesti — A1746

Tulips and: 2.50 l, Pitesti City Hall. 4 l, County Museum. 4.50 l, Rudolf Schwietzer-Cumpana Art Gallery. 16 l, Court of Appeals.

2017, Apr. 7   Litho.   Perf. 13¼

5928	A1746	2.50 l multi	1.25	.60
a.		Sheet of 5 + label	6.25	3.00
5929	A1746	4 l multi	2.00	1.00
a.		Sheet of 5 + label	10.00	5.00
5930	A1746	4.50 l multi	2.25	1.10
a.		Sheet of 5 + label	11.50	5.50
5931	A1746	16 l multi	7.75	4.00
a.		Sheet of 5 + label	39.00	20.00
		Nos. 5928-5931 (4)	13.25	6.70

Europa — A1747

Designs: 4.50 l, Hunyadi Castle, Hunedoara. 15 l, Károlyi Castle, Carei.

2017, Apr. 12   Litho.   Perf. 13¼

5932	A1747	4.50 l multi	2.25	1.10
a.		Sheet of 5 + label	11.50	5.50
5933	A1747	15 l multi	7.25	3.75
a.		Sheet of 5 + label	37.00	18.00
b.		Souvenir sheet of 4, 2 each #5932-5933, #5932 at UL	19.00	9.75
c.		As "b," #5933 at UL	19.00	9.75

Recently Extinct Animals — A1748

Designs: 2.70 l, Ectopistes migratorius, 1914. 3.50 l, Thylacinus cynocephalus, 1936. 8 l, Panthera tigris sondaica, 1976. 15 l, Lipotes vexillifer, 2002.

2017, Apr. 21   Litho.   Perf. 13¼

5934	A1748	2.70 l multi	1.40	.70
a.		Sheet of 5 + label	7.00	3.50
5935	A1748	3.50 l multi	1.75	.85
a.		Sheet of 5 + label	8.75	4.25
5936	A1748	8 l multi	4.00	2.00
a.		Sheet of 5 + label	20.00	10.00
5937	A1748	15 l multi	7.25	3.75
a.		Sheet of 5 + label	37.00	19.00
		Nos. 5934-5937 (4)	14.40	7.30

Iasi
A1749

Iasi coat of arms and: 2.50 l, Ghica-Comanesti House. 4.50 l, National Theater. 8 l, University of Iasi. 15 l, Rosetti-Roznovanu Palace.

16 l, Iasi coat of arms, vert.

2017, Apr. 26   Litho.   Perf. 13¼

5938	A1749	2.50 l multi	1.25	.60
a.		Sheet of 6	7.50	3.75
5939	A1749	4.50 l multi	2.25	1.10
a.		Sheet of 6	13.50	6.75
5940	A1749	8 l multi	4.00	2.00
a.		Sheet of 6	24.00	12.00
5941	A1749	15 l multi	7.25	3.75
a.		Sheet of 6	43.50	22.50
		Nos. 5938-5941 (4)	14.75	7.45

Souvenir Sheet

5942	A1749	16 l multi	7.75	4.00

No. 5942 contains one 27x42mm stamp. A souvenir sheet of 4 containing Nos. 5938-5941 was printed in limited quantities.

Endangered Species — A1750

Designs: 2.20 l, Aquila heliaca. 2.50 l, Falco columbarius. 2.70 l, Lutra lutra. 16 l, Huso huso.

2017, May 11   Litho.   Perf. 13¼

5943	A1750	2.20 l multi	1.10	.55
a.		Sheet of 5 + label	5.50	2.75
5944	A1750	2.50 l multi	1.25	.60
a.		Sheet of 5 + label	6.25	3.00
5945	A1750	2.70 l multi	1.40	.70
a.		Sheet of 5 + label	7.00	3.50
5946	A1750	16 l multi	8.00	4.00
a.		Sheet of 5 + label	40.00	20.00
b.		Souvenir sheet of 4, #5943-5946	12.00	6.00
		Nos. 5943-5946 (4)	11.75	5.85

National Museum of Romanian Literature, 60th Anniv. — A1751

Designs: 8 l, Dumitru Panaitescu (Perpessicius) (1891-1971), poet, and museum emblem. 16 l, Museum emblem, vert.

2017, May 17   Litho.   Perf. 13¼

5947	A1751	8 l multi	4.00	2.00
a.		Sheet of 8 + central label	32.00	16.00

Souvenir Sheet

5948	A1751	16 l multi	8.00	4.00

Ancient Jewelry — A1752

Designs: 4 l, Earrings, 7th cent. 4.50 l, Bell pendants, 5th cent., vert. 8 l, Earrings, 5th cent., vert. 12 l, Spiral bracelet, 1st cent. B.C. 15 l, Tubular bracelet, 4th cent. B.C.

2017, May 26   Litho.   Perf. 13¼

5949	A1752	4 l multi	2.00	1.00
a.		Sheet of 5 + label	10.00	5.00
5950	A1752	4.50 l multi	2.25	1.10
a.		Sheet of 5 + label	11.50	5.50
5951	A1752	8 l multi	4.00	2.00
a.		Sheet of 5 + label	20.00	10.00
5952	A1752	12 l multi	6.00	3.00
a.		Sheet of 5 + label	30.00	15.00
		Nos. 5949-5952 (4)	14.25	7.10

Souvenir Sheet

5953	A1752	15 l multi	7.50	3.75

Children at Play — A1753

Children: 3.50 l, Cycling. 4 l, Playing with balls. 4.50 l, Playing with balls. 4.50 l, Playing hopscotch. 15 l, Sledding and building snowman.

2017, May 31	Litho.	Perf. 13¼	
5954 A1753 3.50 l multi		1.75	.85
a. Sheet of 5 + label		1.75	.85
5955 A1753 4 l multi		2.00	1.00
a. Sheet of 5 + label		10.00	5.00
5956 A1753 4.50 l multi		2.25	1.10
a. Sheet of 5 + label		11.50	5.50
5957 A1753 15 l multi		7.50	3.75
a. Sheet of 5 + label		37.50	19.00

Steaua Soccer Team, 70th Anniv. — A1754

2017, June 6	Litho.	Perf. 13¼	
5958 A1754 8 l multi		4.00	2.00
a. Sheet of 8 + central label		32.00	16.00

Titu Maiorescu (1840-1937), Literary Critic — A1755

Designs: 4.50 l, Maiorescu and cover of Convorbiri Literare. 8 l, Maiorescu, vert.

2017, June 21	Litho.	Perf. 13¼	
5959 A1755 4.50 l multi		2.25	1.10
a. Sheet of 5 + label		11.50	5.50
5960 A1755 8 l multi		4.00	2.00
a. Sheet of 5 + label		20.00	10.00

Bucharest Municipality Museums — A1756

Designs: 2.50 l, 14th cent. Wallachian coin, Greek vase, 500 B.C., George Severeanu Museum. 2.70 l, Cherries, by Theodore Aman (1831-91), and his bust, Theodor Aman Museum. 3.50 l, Decorated plate, Nicolae Minovici Museum. 4 l, Stained-glass window, Vasile Urseanu Astronomical Observatory. 4.50 l, Microscope, paper on bacteriology, Victor Babes (1854-1926), bacteriologist, Victor Babes Museum. 15 l, Sign and Filipescu-Cesianu House. 16 l, Sutu Palace.

2017, June 29	Litho.	Perf. 13¼	
5961 A1756 2.50 l multi		1.25	.60
a. Sheet of 4		5.00	2.40
5962 A1756 2.70 l multi		1.40	.70
a. Sheet of 4		5.75	3.00
5963 A1756 3.50 l multi		1.75	.85
a. Sheet of 4		7.00	3.50
5964 A1756 4 l multi		2.00	1.00
a. Sheet of 4		8.00	4.00
5965 A1756 4.50 l multi		2.25	1.10
a. Sheet of 4		9.00	4.50
5966 A1756 15 l multi		7.50	3.75
a. Sheet of 4		30.00	15.00
Nos. 5961-5966 (6)		16.15	8.00

Souvenir Sheet

5967 A1756 16 l multi		8.00	4.00

No. 5967 contains one 96x33mm stamp.

Seascape Paintings — A1757

Designs: 2.20 l, City by Sea (Naples), by Nicolae Grigorescu (1838-1907). 2.70 l, Balchik, by Cecelia Citescu-Storck (1879-1969). 8 l, Balchik, by Dumitru Ghiata (1888-1972). 15 l, Shipwreck, by Ivan Aivazovsky (1817-1900), vert.

2017, July 7	Litho.	Perf. 13¾x13¼	
5968 A1757 2.20 l multi		1.25	.60
a. Sheet of 5 + label		6.25	3.00
5969 A1757 2.70 l multi		1.40	.70
a. Sheet of 5 + label		7.00	3.50
5970 A1757 8 l multi		4.25	2.10
a. Sheet of 5 + label		21.50	10.50

	Perf. 13¼x13¾		
5971 A1757 15 l multi		7.75	4.00
a. Sheet of 5 + label		39.00	20.00
Nos. 5968-5971 (4)		14.65	7.40

Heroes of World War I — A1758

Flag, soldiers and: 4.50 l, Ecaterina Teodoroiu (1894-1917), and cannon. 8 l, General Eremia Grigorescu (1863-1919), and fortress.

2017, July 14	Litho.	Perf. 13¼	
5972 A1758 4.50 l multi		2.40	1.25
a. Sheet of 5 + label		12.00	6.25
5973 A1758 8 l multi		4.25	2.10
a. Sheet of 5 + label		21.50	10.50

Stamp Day. A souvenir sheet of 2 containing Nos. 5972-5973 was printed in limited quantities.

Tourism — A1759

Designs: 2.50 l, Egret at Danube River Delta. 2.70 l, Pitcher, Clock Tower, Sighisoara, vert. 3.50 l, Deer, Bigar Waterfall. 4 l, Blouse, Voronet Monastery. 4.50 l, Woodpecker, train on Mocanita Narrow-Gauge Railway, vert. 15 l, Rugs from Oltenia, Horezu ceramics.

2017, July 26	Litho.	Perf. 13¼	
5974 A1759 2.50 l multi		1.40	.70
a. Sheet of 5 + label		7.00	3.50
5975 A1759 2.70 l multi		1.40	.70
a. Sheet of 5 + label		7.00	3.50
5976 A1759 3.50 l multi		1.90	.95
a. Sheet of 5 + label		9.50	4.75
5977 A1759 4 l multi		2.10	1.10
a. Sheet of 5 + label		10.50	5.50
5978 A1759 4.50 l multi		2.40	1.25
a. Sheet of 5 + label		12.00	6.25
5979 A1759 15 l multi		7.75	4.00
a. Sheet of 5 + label		39.00	20.00
b. Souvenir sheet of 6, #5974-5979, imperf.		17.00	8.75
Nos. 5974-5979 (6)		16.95	8.70

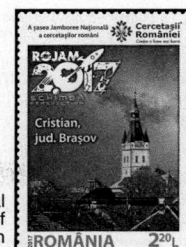

Sixth National Jamboree of Romanian Scouts — A1760

Jamboree emblem and: 2.20 l, Church tower, Cristian. 3.50 l, Tents at Jamboree site. 8 l, Scouts around campfire. 15 l, Scout salute.

2017, Aug. 4	Litho.	Perf. 13¼	
5980 A1760 2.20 l multi		1.25	.60
a. Sheet of 5 + label		6.25	3.00
5981 A1760 3.50 l multi		1.90	.95
a. Sheet of 5 + label		9.50	4.75
5982 A1760 8 l multi		4.25	2.10
a. Sheet of 5 + label		21.50	10.50
5983 A1760 15 l multi		7.75	4.00
a. Sheet of 5 + label		39.00	20.00
Nos. 5980-5983 (4)		15.15	7.65

Medias, 750th Anniv. of Mention in Document A1761

Arms and: 2.50 l, Stephan Ludwig Roth High School and its Gemini symbol. 4 l, Orthodox Cathedral, Tailor's Bastion Tower, statue of spinner. 4.50 l, Franciscan Architectural Complex, bas-relief. 16 l, Church of St. Margaret, sculpture of lion at Schuller House.

2017, Aug. 11	Litho.	Perf. 13¼	
5984 A1761 2.50 l multi		1.40	.70
a. Sheet of 5 + label		7.00	3.50
5985 A1761 4 l multi		2.10	1.10
a. Sheet of 5 + label		10.50	5.50
5986 A1761 4.50 l multi		2.40	1.25
a. Sheet of 5 + label		12.00	6.25
5987 A1761 16 l multi		8.25	4.25
a. Sheet of 5 + label		41.50	21.50
Nos. 5984-5987 (4)		14.15	7.30

A souvenir sheet of 4 containing Nos. 5984-5987 was printed in limited quantities.

Antique Automobiles in Ion Tiriac Collection — A1762

Designs: 2.20 l, 1899 Hurtu 3 ½ Quadricycle. 3.50 l, 1920 Delage Type CO. 8 l, 1930 Duesenberg Model J Torpedo Berline Convertible. 15 l, 1937 Cord 812 Custom Berverly.

	Perf. 13¾x13¼		
2017, Aug. 30		Litho.	
5988 A1762 2.20 l multi		1.25	.60
a. Sheet of 5 + label		6.25	3.00
5989 A1762 3.50 l multi		1.90	.95
a. Sheet of 5 + label		9.50	4.75
5990 A1762 8 l multi		4.25	2.10
a. Sheet of 5 + label		21.50	10.50
5991 A1762 15 l multi		7.75	4.00
a. Sheet of 5 + label		39.00	20.00
Nos. 5988-5991 (4)		15.15	7.65

A souvenir sheet of 4 containing Nos. 5988-5991 was printed in limited quantities.

No. 4335 Surcharged in Metallic Magenta

Method and Perf. As Before

2017, Aug. 31			
5992 A1221 8 l on 6000 l #4335 (MR)		4.25	2.10

Mihail Kogalniceanu (1817-91), Prime Minister — A1763

Designs: 4.50 l, Kogalniceanu and Danube Star newspaper. 8 l, Portrait of Kogalniceanu, vert.

2017, Sept. 6	Litho.	Perf. 13¼	
5993 A1763 4.50 l multi		2.40	1.25
a. Sheet of 5 + label		12.00	6.25
5994 A1763 8 l multi		4.25	2.10
a. Sheet of 5 + label		21.50	10.50

Cacti A1764

Flowers of: 3.50 l, Lophocereus schottii forma Monstruosus. 4 l, Opuntia aciculata. 4.50 l, Coryphantha sulcata. 15 l, Echinocactus horizonthaonius.

2017, Sept. 15	Litho.	Perf. 13¼	
5995 A1764 3.50 l multi		1.90	.95
a. Sheet of 4		7.75	4.00
5996 A1764 4 l multi		2.10	1.10
a. Sheet of 4		8.50	4.50
5997 A1764 4.50 l multi		2.40	1.25
a. Sheet of 4		9.75	5.00
5998 A1764 15 l multi		7.75	4.00
a. Sheet of 4		31.00	16.00
Nos. 5995-5998 (4)		14.15	7.30

A souvenir sheet of 4 containing Nos. 5995-5998 was printed in limited quantities.

Statue of Ion Heliade Radulescu and Bucharest University Building — A1765

Alexandru Ioan Cuza (1820-73),
Domnitor of Romania — A1766

2017, Sept. 20   Litho.   *Perf. 13¼*
5999 A1765 8 l multi   4.25   2.10
  a. Sheet of 8 + central label 34.00 17.00

Souvenir Sheet
Perf. 13¼x13¾
6000 A1766 16 l multi + 2 la-
    bels   8.25   4.25

Bucharest as capital of Romania, 155th
anniv.

Berries
A1767

Designs: 2.20 l, Hippophae rhamnoides.
3.50 l, Crategus monogyna. 8 l, Rosa canina.
15 l, Fragaria vesca.

2017, Sept. 29   Litho.   *Perf. 13¼*
6001 A1767 2.20 l multi   1.10   .55
  a. Sheet of 5 + label   5.50   2.75
6002 A1767 3.50 l multi   1.90   .95
  a. Sheet of 5 + label   9.50   4.75
6003 A1767 8 l multi   4.25   2.10
  a. Sheet of 5 + label   21.50 10.50
6004 A1767 15 l multi   7.75   4.00
  a. Sheet of 5 + label   39.00 20.00
    Nos. 6001-6004 (4)   15.00   7.60

Mushrooms
A1768

Designs: 2.50 l, Amanita caesarea. 4.50 l,
Amanita rubescens. 8 l, Leccinum aurantiacum. 15 l, Macrolepiota procera.

2017, Oct. 6   Litho.   *Perf. 13¼*
6005 A1768 2.50 l multi   1.25   .65
  a. Sheet of 5 + label   6.25   3.25
6006 A1768 4.50 l multi   2.25   1.10
  a. Sheet of 5 + label   11.50   5.50
6007 A1768 8 l multi   4.00   2.00
  a. Sheet of 5 + label   20.00 10.00
6008 A1768 15 l multi   7.75   4.00
  a. Sheet of 5 + label   39.00 20.00
    Nos. 6005-6008 (4)   15.25   7.75

A souvenir sheet of 4 containing Nos. 6005-
6008 was printed in limited quantities.

Sheep Breeds
A1769

Designs: 3.50 l, Merinos de Palas. 4 l,
Tigaie Ruginie. 4.50 l, Teleorman Black Head.
16 l, Turcana.

2017, Oct. 13   Litho.   *Perf. 13¼*
6009 A1769 3.50 l multi   1.75   .90
  a. Sheet of 5 + label   8.75   4.50
6010 A1769 4 l multi   2.00   1.00
  a. Sheet of 5 + label   10.00   5.00
6011 A1769 4.50 l multi   2.25   1.10
  a. Sheet of 5 + label   11.50   5.50
6012 A1769 16 l multi   8.25   4.25
  a. Sheet of 5 + label   42.00 21.50
    Nos. 6009-6012 (4)   14.25   7.25

Royal Tableware — A1770

Designs: 3.50 l, Goody & Co. porcelain fruit
dish. 4 l, Martin Hall & Co. egg service, vert.
4.50 l, Baccarat crystal punch bowl, vert. 15 l,
Meissen candy dish.

Perf. 14x13¼, 13¼x14
2017, Oct. 20   Litho.
6013 A1770 3.50 l multi   1.75   .90
  a. Sheet of 5 + label   8.75   4.50
6014 A1770 4 l multi   2.00   1.00
  a. Sheet of 5 + label   10.00   5.00
6015 A1770 4.50 l multi   2.25   1.10
  a. Sheet of 5 + label   11.50   5.50
6016 A1770 15 l multi   7.75   4.00
  a. Sheet of 5 + label   39.00 20.00
    Nos. 6013-6016 (4)   13.75   7.00

A souvenir sheet of 4 containing Nos. 6013-
6016 was printed in limited quantities.

Mosaics
Depicting Saints
From
Patriarchal
Cathedral
A1771

Designs: 1.80 l, St. Luke. 4 l, St. John
Chrysostom. 16 l, St. Demetrius the New.

2017, Oct. 27   Litho.   *Perf. 13¼*
6017 A1771 1.80 l multi   .90   .45
  a. Sheet of 5 + label   4.50   2.25
6018 A1771 4 l multi   2.00   1.00
  a. Sheet of 5 + label   10.00   5.00

Size: 42x52mm
Perf. 13¼x14
6019 A1771 16 l multi   8.25   4.25
  a. Sheet of 5 + label   42.00 21.50
    Nos. 6017-6019 (3)   11.15   5.70

Conference of Francophone Women,
Bucharest — A1772

2017, Nov. 1   Litho.   *Perf. 13¼*
6020 A1772 8 l multi   4.00   2.00
  a. Sheet of 8 + label   32.00 16.00

Bucharest
Circus
A1773

Designs: 3.50 l, Clown with "Star Circus"
drum. 4 l, Horse show. 4.50 l, Contortionist
acrobat. 15 l, Clown face and trapeze act.

2017, Nov. 6   Litho.   *Perf. 13¼x13¾*
6021 A1773 3.50 l multi   1.75   .90
  a. Sheet of 5 + label   8.75   4.50
6022 A1773 4 l multi   2.00   1.00
  a. Sheet of 5 + label   10.00   5.00
6023 A1773 4.50 l multi   2.25   1.10
  a. Sheet of 5 + label   11.50   5.50
6024 A1773 15 l multi   7.50   3.75
  a. Sheet of 5 + label   37.50 19.00
    Nos. 6021-6024 (4)   13.50   6.75

Geraniums
A1774

Designs: 2.20 l, Pelargonium peltatum.
2.50 l, Red Pelargonium zonale. 8 l, Pelargonium grandiflorum. 15 l, Pink Pelargonium
zonale.

2017, Nov. 17   Litho.   *Perf. 13¼*
6025 A1774 2.20 l multi   1.10   .55
  a. Sheet of 5 + label   5.50   2.75
6026 A1774 2.50 l multi   1.25   .65
  a. Sheet of 5 + label   6.50   3.25
6027 A1774 8 l multi   4.00   2.00
  a. Sheet of 5 + label   20.00 10.00
6028 A1774 15 l multi   7.50   3.75
  a. Sheet of 5 + label   37.50 19.00
    Nos. 6025-6028 (4)   13.85   6.95

A souvenir sheet of 4 containing Nos. 6025-
6028 was printed in limited quantities.

The Holy
Family
Recieving the
Shepherds
A1775

Madona and
Child
A1776

2017, Nov. 21   Litho.   *Perf. 13¼*
6029 A1775 1.30 l multi   .65   .35
  a. Sheet of 9, #6030, 8 #6029   6.00   3.25
6030 A1776 1.30 l multi   .65   .35
  a. Sheet of 9, #6029, 8 #6030   6.00   3.25

A souvenir sheet of 2 containing Nos. 6029-
6030 was printed in limited quantities.

Trees — A1777

Designs: No. 6031, Sorbus aucuparia. No.
6032, Picea abies.

2017, Nov. 24   Litho.   *Perf. 13¼*
6031 A1777 8 l multi   4.00   2.00
  a. Sheet of 5 + label   20.00 10.00
6032 A1777 8 l multi   4.00   2.00
  a. Sheet of 5 + label   20.00 10.00

Joint Issue between Romania and Estonia.
See Estonia Nos. 855-856.

Venomous
Animals
A1778

Designs: 3.50 l, Hapalochlaena maculosa.
4 l, Phyllobates terribilis. 4.50 l, Chironex fleck-
eri. 16 l, Oxyuranus microlepidotus.

2017, Dec. 7   Litho.   *Perf. 13¼*
6033 A1778 3.50 l multi   1.75   .90
  a. Sheet of 5 + label   8.75   4.50
6034 A1778 4 l multi   2.00   1.00
  a. Sheet of 5 + label   10.00   5.00
6035 A1778 4.50 l multi   2.25   1.10
  a. Sheet of 5 + label   11.50   5.50
6036 A1778 16 l multi   8.25   4.25
  a. Sheet of 5 + label   42.00 21.50
    Nos. 6033-6036 (4)   14.25   7.25

A souvenir sheet of 4 containing Nos. 6033-
6036 was printed in limited quantities.

King Michael I (1921-2017) — A1779

2017, Dec. 13   Litho.   *Perf. 13¼*
6037 A1779 8 l multi   4.00   2.00
  a. Sheet of 7 + 2 labels 28.00 14.00

Heroes of World
War I — A1780

Designs: 3.50 l, Ioan Dragalina (1860-
1916), general. 4 l, David Praporgescu (1865-
1916), general. 4.50 l, Radu R. Rosetti (1877-
1949), general. 16 l, Constantin Nazarie
(1865-1926), army archpriest.

2017, Dec. 14   Litho.   *Perf. 13¼*
6038 A1780 3.50 l multi   1.75   .90
  a. Sheet of 5 + label   8.75   4.50
6039 A1780 4 l multi   2.00   1.00
  a. Sheet of 5 + label   10.00   5.00
6040 A1780 4.50 l multi   2.25   1.10
  a. Sheet of 5 + label   11.50   5.50
6041 A1780 16 l multi   8.25   4.25
  a. Sheet of 5 + label   42.00 21.50
    Nos. 6038-6041 (4)   14.25   7.25

Stars of the
Stage and
Screen
A1781

Designs: No. 6042, Maia Morgenstern. No. 6043, Oana Pellea. No. 6044, Luminita Gheorghiu. No. 6045, George Mihaita. No. 6046, Horatiu Malaele. No. 6047, Marcel Iures.

2017, Dec. 20   Litho.   Perf. 13¼

6042	A1781	8 l	multi	4.00	2.00
a.		Sheet of 4		16.00	8.00
6043	A1781	8 l	multi	4.00	2.00
a.		Sheet of 4		16.00	8.00
6044	A1781	8 l	multi	4.00	2.00
a.		Sheet of 4		16.00	8.00
6045	A1781	8 l	multi	4.00	2.00
a.		Sheet of 4		16.00	8.00
6046	A1781	8 l	multi	4.00	2.00
a.		Sheet of 4		16.00	8.00
6047	A1781	8 l	multi	4.00	2.00
a.		Sheet of 4		16.00	8.00
b.		Souvenir sheet of 6, #6042-6047		24.00	12.00
		Nos. 6042-6047 (6)		24.00	12.00

Monument, Central Military Cemetery of the Royal Romanian Army, Zvolen, Slovakia — A1782

2018, Jan. 5   Litho.   Perf. 13¼

6048	A1782	8 l	multi	4.25	2.10
a.		Sheet of 5 + label		21.50	10.50

Diplomatic relations between Romania and Slovakia, 25th anniv. See Slovakia No. 783.

Cranes — A1783

Designs: 3.50 l, Antigone rubicunda. 4 l, Grus japonensis, horiz. 4.50 l, Anthropoides virgo, horiz. 15 l, Leucogeranus leucogeranus. 16 l, Balearica pavonina, horiz.

2018, Jan. 12   Litho.   Perf. 13¼

6049	A1783	3.50 l	multi	1.75	.90
a.		Sheet of 5 + label		8.75	4.50
6050	A1783	4 l	multi	2.00	1.00
a.		Sheet of 5 + label		10.00	5.00
6051	A1783	4.50 l	multi	2.25	1.10
a.		Sheet of 5 + label		11.50	5.50
6052	A1783	15 l	multi	7.75	4.00
a.		Sheet of 5 + label		39.00	20.00
		Nos. 6049-6052 (4)		13.75	7.00

Souvenir Sheet

6053	A1783	16 l	multi	8.25	4.25

A souvenir sheet of 4 containing Nos. 6049-6052, was issued in limited quantities. No. 6053 contains a 48x33mm stamp.

Braila, 650th Anniv. of Documented Existence A1784

Designs: 2.20 l, Baroque clock. 3.50 l The Nativity of Our Lord Cathedral. 4 l, Kinetic Fountain, horiz. 4.50 l, Maria Filotti Theater, horiz. 15 l, Panait Istrati Memorial House, horiz.

2018, Jan. 19   Litho.   Perf. 13¼

6054	A1784	2.20 l	multi	1.10	.60
a.		Sheet of 5 + label		5.50	2.75
6055	A1784	3.50 l	multi	1.75	.90
a.		Sheet of 5 + label		9.00	4.50
6056	A1784	4 l	multi	2.00	1.00
a.		Sheet of 5 + label		10.00	5.00
6057	A1784	4.50 l	multi	2.25	1.10
a.		Sheet of 5 + label		11.50	5.50
6058	A1784	15 l	multi	7.75	4.00
a.		Sheet of 5 + label		39.00	20.00
		Nos. 6054-6058 (5)		14.85	7.60

A souvenir sheet of 5 containing Nos. 6054-6058 was issued in limited quantities.

Mircea the Elder — A1785

Designs: 8 l, Statue. 16 l, Fresco from Bradetu Church.

2018, Jan. 31   Litho.   Perf. 13¼

6059	A1785	8 l	multi	4.25	2.10
a.		Sheet of 8 + central label		34.00	17.00

Souvenir Sheet
Perf. 13¼x14

6060	A1785	16 l	multi	8.50	4.25

No. 6060 contains one 42x52mm stamp.

2018 Winter Olympics, PyeongChang, South Korea — A1786

Designs: 2.50 l, Bobsled. 4.50 l, Alpine skiing. 8 l, Cross country skiing. 15 l, Ski jumping.

2018, Feb. 9   Litho.   Perf. 13¼

6061	A1786	2.50 l	multi	1.25	.60
a.		Sheet of 5 + label		6.25	3.00
6062	A1786	4.50 l	multi	2.40	1.25
a.		Sheet of 5 + label		12.00	6.25
6063	A1786	8 l	multi	4.25	2.10
a.		Sheet of 5 + label		21.50	10.50
6064	A1786	15 l	multi	8.00	4.00
a.		Sheet of 5 + label		40.00	20.00
b.		Souvenir sheet of 4, #6061-6064		16.00	8.00
		Nos. 6061-6064 (4)		15.90	7.95

The Romanian Renaissance, by Gheorghe Tattarescu (1818-94) A1787

Self-portrait, by Tattarescu — A1788

2018, Feb. 16   Litho.   Perf. 13¼

6065	A1787	8 l	multi	4.25	2.10
a.		Sheet of 8 + central label		34.00	17.00

Souvenir Sheet
Imperf

6066	A1788	15 l	multi	8.00	4.00

No. 3070 Surcharged in Gold

Method and Perf. As Before
2018, Feb. 19

6067	A887	31 l	on 10 l multi	16.50	8.25

Marin Constantin (1925-2011), Founder of Madrigal Choir — A1789

2018, Feb. 27   Litho.   Perf. 13¼

6068	A1789	8 l	multi	4.25	2.10
a.		Sheet of 8 + central label		34.00	17.00

Madrigal Choir, 55th anniv.

Easter A1790

Alba Iulia Cathedral icons: No. 6069, The Entrance to Jerusalem. No. 6070, The Resurrection of Jesus Christ. 12 l, The Crucifixion of Lord Jesus Christ.

2018, Mar. 9   Litho.   Perf. 13¼

6069	A1790	1.30 l	multi	.70	.35
a.		Sheet of 8 + central label		5.75	3.00
6070	A1790	1.30 l	multi	.70	.35
a.		Sheet of 8 + central label		5.75	3.00

---

b.		Sheet of 10, 5 each #6069-6070 + 2 labels		7.00	3.50

Souvenir Sheet

6071	A1790	12 l	multi	6.25	3.25

A souvenir sheet of 3 containing Nos. 6069-6071, and a souvenir sheet containing No. 6071 and imperforate examples of Nos. 6069-6070, were printed in limited quantities.

Famous Romanians — A1791

Romanian Coat of Arms — A1792

Designs: 2.60 l, Miron Cristea (1868-1939), patriarch of Romanian Orthodox church. 4.50 l, Bishop Iuliu Hossu (1885-1970). 8 l, Iuliu Maniu (1873-1953), Prime Minister. 15 l, Ion I. C. Bratianu (1864-1927), Prime Minister.

2018, Mar. 20   Litho.   Perf. 13¼

6072	A1791	2.60 l	multi	1.40	.70
a.		Sheet of 6 + 6 labels		8.50	4.25
6073	A1791	4.50 l	multi	2.40	1.25
a.		Sheet of 6 + 6 labels		14.50	7.50
6074	A1791	8 l	multi	4.25	2.10
a.		Sheet of 6 + 6 labels		25.50	13.00
6075	A1791	15 l	multi	8.00	4.00
a.		Sheet of 6 + 6 labels		48.00	24.00
		Nos. 6072-6075 (4)		16.05	8.05

Souvenir Sheet
Imperf

6076	A1792	16 l	multi	8.50	4.25

No. 6076 contains one 30mm diameter stamp. See Nos. 6178-6182.

Unification of Bessarabia and Romania, Cent. — A1793

Designs: 4 l, Alexandru Marghiloman (1854-1925), politician. 8 l, Ion Inculet (1884-1940), politician. 16 l, Pantelimon Halippa (1883-1979), journalist and politician.

2018, Mar. 27   Litho.   Perf. 13¼

6077	A1793	4 l	multi	2.10	1.10
a.		Sheet of 5 + label		10.50	5.50
6078	A1793	8 l	multi	4.25	2.10
a.		Sheet of 5 + label		21.50	10.50

Souvenir Sheet

6079	A1793	16 l	multi	8.50	4.25

No. 6079 contains one 24x33mm stamp.

Household Items to Hold Hot Objects A1794

Designs: 2.20 l, Iron rest. 2.50 l, Iron protection. 2.70 l, Ornamental plate. 3.50 l, Support with grate. 4 l, Plate with floral motif. 15 l, Plate with central foot plate.
16 l, Detail of plate with central foot plate.

2018, Mar. 29	Litho.	Perf. 13¼		
6080	A1794	2.20 l multi	1.25	.60
a.		Sheet of 8 + central label	10.00	5.00
b.		Sheet of 13 + 2 labels	16.50	8.00
6081	A1794	2.50 l multi	1.40	.70
a.		Sheet of 8 + central label	11.50	5.75
b.		Sheet of 13 + 2 labels	18.50	9.25
6082	A1794	2.70 l multi	1.50	.75
a.		Sheet of 8 + central label	12.00	6.00
b.		Sheet of 13 + 2 labels	19.50	9.75
6083	A1794	3.50 l multi	1.90	.95
a.		Sheet of 8 + central label	15.50	7.75
b.		Sheet of 13 + 2 labels	25.00	12.50
6084	A1794	4 l multi	2.10	1.10
a.		Sheet of 8 + central label	17.00	9.00
b.		Sheet of 13 + 2 labels	27.50	14.50
6085	A1794	15 l multi	8.00	4.00
a.		Sheet of 8 + central label	64.00	32.00
b.		Sheet of 13 + 2 labels	105.00	52.50
		Nos. 6080-6085 (6)	16.15	8.10

Souvenir Sheet
Imperf

6086	A1794	16 l multi	8.50	4.25

No. 6086 contains one 55x45mm stamp, with detail of object illustrated in No. 6085.
No. 6086 with gold foil embellishment was printed in limited quantities.
See Nos. 6235-6241.

Europa — A1795

Designs: 3.50 l, Bridge of Lies, Sibiu. 16 l, Anghel Saligny Bridge.

2018, Apr. 12	Litho.	Perf. 13¼		
6087	A1795	3.50 l multi	1.90	.95
a.		Sheet of 6	11.50	5.75
6088	A1795	16 l multi	8.50	4.25
a.		Sheet of 6	51.00	25.50
b.		Sheet of 4, 2 each #6087-6088, #6087 in UL	21.00	10.50
c.		As "b," #6088 in UL	21.00	10.50

A sheet of 2 containing imperforate examples of Nos. 6087-6088 was produced in limited quantities.

Famous Men — A1796

Romanian Athenaeum, Bucharest, and: 4 l, George Enescu (1881-1955), composer. 4.50 l, Eduard Wachmann (1836-1908), conductor. 8 l, Albert Galleron (1846-1930), architect of Romanian Athenaeum.

2018, Apr. 20	Litho.	Perf. 13¼		
6089	A1796	4 l multi	2.10	1.10
a.		Sheet of 5 + label	10.50	5.50
6090	A1796	4.50 l multi	2.40	1.25
a.		Sheet of 5 + label	12.00	6.25
6091	A1796	8 l multi	4.25	2.10
a.		Sheet of 5 + label	21.50	11.00
		Nos. 6089-6091 (3)	8.75	4.45

George Enescu Festival, 60th anniv. (No. 6089); George Enescu Philharmonic, 150th anniv. (No. 6090); Romanian Athenaeum building, 150th anniv. (No. 6091).

A1797

Comic Opera for Children, 20th Anniv. — A1798

2018, Apr. 25	Litho.	Perf. 13¼		
6092	A1797	8 l multi	4.25	2.10
a.		Sheet of 5 + 5 labels	21.50	10.50

Souvenir Sheet
Perf. 14x13¼

6093	A1798	16 l multi	8.50	4.25

Bucharest Municipality Pinacotheque, 85th Anniv. — A1799

Paintings: 4 l, Zinnias, by Gheorghe Petrascu. 4.50 l, Cornflowers, by Stefan Luchian. 8 l, Peasant Women, by Theodor Pallady, vert. 12 l, Woman with Red Scar, by Nicolae Grigorescu, vert.

2018, Apr. 27	Litho.	Perf. 14x13¼		
6094	A1799	4 l multi	2.10	1.10
a.		Sheet of 5 + label	10.50	5.50
6095	A1799	4.50 l multi	2.40	1.25
a.		Sheet of 5 + label	12.00	6.25

Perf. 13¼x14

6096	A1799	8 l multi	4.25	2.10
a.		Sheet of 5 + label	21.50	10.50
6097	A1799	12 l multi	6.50	3.25
a.		Sheet of 5 + label	32.50	16.50
		Nos. 6094-6097 (4)	15.25	7.70

World War I Medals and Decorations — A1800

Designs: 2.90 l, Star of Romania National Order. 3 l, Crown of Romania National Order. 4.50 l, Military Virtue Medal. 16 l, Commemorative Cross of the 1916-1918 War Medal.

2018, May 7	Litho.	Perf. 13¼x14		
6098	A1800	2.90 l multi	1.50	.75
a.		Sheet of 6	9.00	4.50
6099	A1800	3 l multi	1.60	.80
a.		Sheet of 6	9.75	5.00
6100	A1800	4.50 l multi	2.40	1.25
a.		Sheet of 6	14.50	7.50
6101	A1800	16 l multi	8.25	4.25
a.		Sheet of 6	50.00	25.50
		Nos. 6098-6101 (4)	13.75	7.05

Contemorary Art — A1801

Designs: 2.90 l, Dantesca I, sculpture by Daniela Fainis. 3 l, The Kiss, painting by Vladimir Zamfirescu. 15 l, Germination, sculpture by Ioan Nemtoi.

2018, May 11	Litho.	Perf. 13¼x14		
6102	A1801	2.90 l multi	1.50	.75
a.		Sheet of 5 + label	7.50	3.75
6103	A1801	3 l multi	1.60	.80
a.		Sheet of 5 + label	8.00	4.00
6104	A1801	15 l multi	7.75	4.00
a.		Sheet of 5 + label	39.00	20.00
		Nos. 6102-6104 (3)	10.85	5.55

Romanian Judo Federation, 50th Anniv. A1802

Designs: 2.90 l, Judoka in white on top. 12 l, Judoka in blue on top.

2018, May 18	Litho.	Perf. 13¼		
6105	A1802	2.90 l multi	1.50	.75
a.		Sheet of 5 + label	7.50	3.75
6106	A1802	12 l multi	6.25	3.00
a.		Sheet of 5 + label	31.50	15.00

Church Art Miniatures A1803

Designs: 2.90 l, The Last Supper, by unknown artist. 3 l, Holy Trinity, by Picu Patrut (1818-1872). 15 l, Christ Pantocrator, by Patrut.

2018, May 25	Litho.	Perf. 13¼		
6107	A1803	2.90 l multi	1.50	.75
a.		Sheet of 6	9.00	4.50
6108	A1803	3 l multi	1.60	.80
a.		Sheet of 6	9.75	5.00
6109	A1803	15 l multi	7.75	4.00
a.		Sheet of 6	46.50	24.00
		Nos. 6107-6109 (3)	10.85	5.55

Vertical pairs are tête-bêche on Nos. 6107a-6109a.

Romanian Man, Woman and Flag — A1804

Thailand Man, Woman and Flag — A1805

2018, May 31	Litho.	Perf. 13¼		
6110		Pair	1.50	.70
a.		A1804 1.50 l multi	.75	.35
b.		A1805 1.50 l multi	.75	.35
c.		Sheet of 8, 4 each #6110a-6110b	6.00	3.00

Diplomatic relations between Romania and Thailand, 45th anniv. See Thailand No. 3010.

2018 World Cup Soccer Championships, Russia — A1806

Designs: 2018 World Cup emblem and various players.

2018, June 7	Litho.	Perf. 13¼		
6111	A1806	1.70 l multi	.85	.40
a.		Sheet of 6	5.25	2.60
6112	A1806	2 l multi	1.00	.50
a.		Sheet of 6	6.00	3.00
6113	A1806	3 l multi	1.50	.75
a.		Sheet of 6	9.00	4.50
6114	A1806	8.50 l multi	4.25	2.10
a.		Sheet of 6	25.50	13.00
b.		Souvenir sheet of 4, #6111-6114	7.75	3.75
		Nos. 6111-6114 (4)	7.60	3.75

Famous Romanians — A1807

Designs: 1 l, Sofia Ionescu-Ogrezeanu (1920-2008), neurosurgeon. 1.20 l, Dimitrie Gusti (1880-1955), sociologist. 1.50 l, Ion Cantacuzino (1863-1934), microbiologist. 1.70 l, Nichita Stanescu (1933-83), writer. 2 l, Aurel Vlaicu (1882-1913), aviator. 3 l, Lucian Blaga (1895-1961), writer. 7 l, Traian Vuia (1872-1950), airplane designer. 8.50 l, Spiru Haret (1851-1912), mathematician and educator. 28.50 l, Henri Coanda (1886-1972), inventor.

2018, June 15	Litho.	Perf. 13¼		
6115	A1807	1 l multi	.50	.25
a.		Sheet of 3 + label	1.50	.75
6116	A1807	1.20 l multi	.60	.30
a.		Sheet of 3 + label	1.90	.90
6117	A1807	1.50 l multi	.75	.35
a.		Sheet of 3 + label	2.25	1.10
6118	A1807	1.70 l multi	.85	.40
a.		Sheet of 3 + label	2.60	1.25
6119	A1807	2 l multi	1.00	.50
a.		Sheet of 3 + label	3.00	1.50
6120	A1807	3 l multi	1.50	.75
a.		Sheet of 3 + label	4.50	2.25
6121	A1807	7 l multi	3.50	1.75
a.		Sheet of 3 + label	10.50	5.25
6122	A1807	8.50 l multi	4.25	2.10
a.		Sheet of 3 + label	13.00	6.50
6123	A1807	28.50 l multi	14.50	7.25
a.		Sheet of 3 + label	44.00	22.00
		Nos. 6115-6123 (9)	27.45	13.65

A booklet containing a pane of Nos. 6115-6123 was produced in limited quantities. See Nos. 6137-6145.

Traditional Embroidered
Blouses — A1808

Blouses from: 3 l, Bihor and Oas. 5 l,
Suceava and Vrancea. 7 l, Lugoj and
Padureni. 11.50 l, Mehedinti and Râmnicu
Sarat.

Perf. 13¾x13¼

		2018, June 22		Litho.	
6124	A1808	3 l multi		1.50	.75
a.		Sheet of 4		6.00	3.00
6125	A1808	5 l multi		2.50	1.25
a.		Sheet of 4		10.00	5.00
6126	A1808	7 l multi		3.50	1.75
a.		Sheet of 4		14.00	7.00
6127	A1808	11.50 l multi		5.75	3.00
a.		Sheet of 4		23.00	12.00
b.		Souvenir sheet of 4, #6124-6127		13.50	6.75
		Nos. 6124-6127 (4)		13.25	6.75

Minerals
A1809

Designs: 2 l, Pyrite and quartz. 5 l, Galena
and semseyite. 8.50 l, Gypsum and calcite.
12 l, Quartz and calcite.

		2018, June 29		Litho.	Perf. 13¼
6128	A1809	2 l multi		1.00	.50
a.		Sheet of 5 + label		5.00	2.50
6129	A1809	5 l multi		2.50	1.25
a.		Sheet of 5 + label		12.50	6.25
6130	A1809	8.50 l multi		4.25	2.10
a.		Sheet of 5 + label		21.50	10.50
6131	A1809	12 l multi		6.00	3.00
a.		Sheet of 5 + label		30.00	15.00
		Nos. 6128-6131 (4)		13.75	6.85

A sheet containing Nos. 6128-6131 was
printed in limited quantities.

Stamp Day — A1810

Horse-drawn mail coach and: 1.50 l,
Romania #1. 2 l, Romania #5. 3 l, Romania
#7. 5 l, Romania #34. 19 l, Romania #51.

		2018, July 13		Litho.	Perf. 13¼
6132	A1810	1.50 l multi		.75	.40
a.		Sheet of 5 + label		3.75	2.00
b.		Sheet of 3, imperf.		2.25	1.25
6133	A1810	2 l multi		1.00	.50
a.		Sheet of 5 + label		5.00	2.50
b.		Sheet of 3, imperf.		3.00	1.50
6134	A1810	3 l multi		1.50	.75
a.		Sheet of 5 + label		7.50	3.75
b.		Sheet of 3, imperf.		4.50	2.25
6135	A1810	5 l multi		2.50	1.25
a.		Sheet of 5 + label		12.50	6.25
b.		Sheet of 3, imperf.		7.50	3.75
6136	A1810	19 l multi		9.75	4.75
a.		Sheet of 5 + label		49.00	24.00
b.		Sheet of 3, imperf.		30.00	14.50
		Nos. 6132-6136 (5)		15.50	7.65

A sheet containing Nos. 6132-6136 was
printed in limited quantities.

Famous Romanians Type of 2018

Designs: 1.10 l, Cella Delavrancea (1887-
1991), pianist. 1.40 l, Dimitrie Paciurea (1873-
1932), sculptor. 1.60 l, Victor Brauner (1903-
66), painter. 2.60 l, George Apostu (1934-86),
sculptor. 2.90 l, Elvira Popesco (1894-1993),
actress. 5 l, Marcel Iancu (1895-1984), architect. 11.50 l, Dimitrie Cantemir (1673-1723),
historian. 12 l, Nicolae Iorga (1871-1940),
Prime Minister. 19 l, Nicolae Titulescu (1882-
1941), minister of foreign affairs.

		2018, July 17		Litho.	Perf. 13¼
6137	A1807	1.10 l multi		.55	.30
a.		Sheet of 3 + label		1.65	.90
6138	A1807	1.40 l multi		.70	.35
a.		Sheet of 3 + label		2.10	1.10
6139	A1807	1.60 l multi		.80	.40
a.		Sheet of 3 + label		2.40	1.25
6140	A1807	2.60 l multi		1.40	.70
a.		Sheet of 3 + label		4.25	2.10
6141	A1807	2.90 l multi		1.50	.75
a.		Sheet of 3 + label		4.50	2.25
6142	A1807	5 l multi		2.50	1.25
a.		Sheet of 3 + label		7.50	3.75
6143	A1807	11.50 l multi		6.00	3.00
a.		Sheet of 3 + label		18.00	9.00
6144	A1807	12 l multi		6.25	3.25
a.		Sheet of 3 + label		19.00	9.75
6145	A1807	19 l multi		9.75	4.75
a.		Sheet of 3 + label		30.00	14.50
		Nos. 6137-6145 (9)		29.45	14.75

A booklet containing a pane of Nos. 6137-
6145 was produced in limited quantities.

Queen Marie
(1875-1938)
A1811

Lilies and Queen Marie wearing: 3 l, Crown.
11.50 l, Tiara.
19 l, Queen Marie with arm on pedestal.

		2018, July 20		Litho.	Perf. 13¼
6146	A1811	3 l multi		1.50	.75
a.		Sheet of 6		9.00	4.50
6147	A1811	11.50 l multi		6.00	3.00
a.		Sheet of 6		36.00	18.00

Souvenir Sheet
Imperf

6148	A1811	19 l multi		9.75	4.75

No. 6148 contains one 42x56mm stamp. A
sheet of 2 containing imperforate examples of
Nos. 6146-6147 was printed in limited
quantities.

Writers — A1812

Designs: 2 l, Urmuz (1883-1923). 3 l, Geo
Bogza (1908-93). 19 l, Gellu Naum (1915-
2001).

		2018, July 27		Litho.	Perf. 13¼
6149	A1812	2 l multi		1.00	.50
a.		Sheet of 5 + label		5.00	2.50
6150	A1812	3 l multi		1.50	.75
a.		Sheet of 5 + label		7.50	3.75
6151	A1812	19 l multi		9.75	4.75
a.		Sheet of 5 + label		49.00	24.00
		Nos. 6149-6151 (3)		12.25	6.00

Emblem of
Romanian
Records
Museum
A1813

Emblem of
Romanian
Philatelic
Collection
A1814

Emblem of
International
Federation of
Philately
A1815

		2018, Aug. 3		Litho.	Perf. 13¼
6152	A1813	1.60 l multi		.80	.40
a.		Sheet of 8 + central label		6.50	3.25
6153	A1814	2 l multi		1.00	.50
a.		Sheet of 8 + central label		8.00	4.00
6154	A1815	11.50 l multi		5.75	3.00
a.		Sheet of 8 + central label		46.00	24.00
		Nos. 6152-6154 (3)		7.55	3.90

Souvenir Sheet
Imperf

6155	A1813	19 l multi		9.50	4.75

Romania
Breaking Off
Her Chains on
the Field of
Liberty, by
Constantin
Daniel
Rosenthal
(1820-51)
A1816

Revolutionary Romania, by
Rosenthal — A1817

		2018, Aug. 10		Litho.	Perf. 13¼
6156	A1816	5 l multi		2.50	1.25
a.		Sheet of 5 + label		12.50	6.25

Souvenir Sheet
Imperf

6157	A1817	28.50 l multi		14.50	7.25

Flora and Fauna of Domogled-Cerna
Valley National Park — A1818

Designs: 1.60 l, Edraianthus graminifolius
ssp. kitaibelii. 2 l, Primula auricula ssp. serratifolia. 5 l, Testudo hermanni, horiz. 19 l,
Lucanus cervus, horiz.
28.50 l, Zamenis longissimus, horiz.

		2018, Aug. 17		Litho.	Perf. 13¼
6158	A1818	1.60 l multi		.80	.40
a.		Sheet of 5 + label		4.00	2.00
6159	A1818	2 l multi		1.00	.50
a.		Sheet of 5 + label		5.00	2.50
6160	A1818	5 l multi		2.50	1.25
a.		Sheet of 5 + label		12.50	6.25
6161	A1818	19 l multi		9.50	4.75
a.		Sheet of 5 + label		47.50	24.00
		Nos. 6158-6161 (4)		13.80	6.90

Souvenir Sheet

6162	A1818	28.50 l multi		14.50	7.25

A sheet containing Nos. 6158-6161 was
printed in limited quantities.

Narrow-Gauge Steam
Locomotives — A1819

Locomotive on: 1.60 l, Brad-Criscior line. 7 l,
Moldovita line. 8.50 l, Sovata line. 12 l, Vaser
Valley line.
19 l, Sovata-Comandau line.

		2018, Aug. 24		Litho.	Perf. 13¼
6163	A1819	1.60 l multi		.80	.40
a.		Sheet of 5 + label		4.00	2.00
6164	A1819	7 l multi		3.50	1.75
a.		Sheet of 5 + label		17.50	8.75
6165	A1819	8.50 l multi		4.25	2.10
a.		Sheet of 5 + label		21.50	10.50
6166	A1819	12 l multi		6.00	3.00
a.		Sheet of 5 + label		30.00	15.00
		Nos. 6163-6166 (4)		14.55	7.25

Souvenir Sheet

6167	A1819	19 l multi		9.50	4.75

A sheet containing Nos. 6163-6166 was
printed in limited quantities.

Simona Halep, 2018 French Open
Women's Singles Champion — A1820

Designs: 5 l, Halep playing tennis. 28.50 l,
Halep lifting trophy, vert.

		2018, Aug. 29		Litho.	Perf. 13¼
6168	A1820	5 l multi		2.50	1.25
a.		Sheet of 4		10.00	5.00

Souvenir Sheet

6169	A1820	28.50 l multi		14.50	7.25

Winning Art in Children's Olympic
Games Stamp Design
Contest — A1821

Designs: 2 l, Chromatic Dynamics, by
Gabriel roman. 3 l, Tennis, by Sofia Fluerasu,
vert. 5 l, Young Hopes, by Anna Rocsana
Adumitroaie. 19 l, Grace and Elegance, by
Diana Aveloiu, vert.

Perf. 13¾x13¼, 13¼x13¾

		2018, Sept. 4		Litho.	
6170	A1821	2 l multi		1.00	.50
a.		Sheet of 4		4.00	2.00
6171	A1821	3 l multi		1.50	.75
a.		Sheet of 4		6.00	3.00
6172	A1821	5 l multi		2.50	1.25
a.		Sheet of 4		10.00	5.00
6173	A1821	9.50 l multi		9.50	4.75
a.		Sheet of 4		38.00	19.00
		Nos. 6170-6173 (4)		14.50	7.25

Camouflage of Birds — A1822

Designs: 2 l, Burhinus oedicnemus facing right. 3 l, Dendrocopos syriacus facing right. 5 l, Caprimulgus europaeus facing right. 19 l, Picus viridis facing left.

Perf. 13¼x13¾

			Litho.	
2018, Sept. 14				
6174	A1822	2 l multi	1.00	.50
a.		Bird facing left	1.00	.50
b.		Sheet of 5, #6174a, 4 #6174 + label	5.00	2.50
6175	A1822	3 l multi	1.50	.75
a.		Bird facing left	1.50	.75
b.		Sheet of 5, #6175a, 4 #6175 + label	7.50	3.75
6176	A1822	5 l multi	2.50	1.25
a.		Bird facing left	2.50	1.25
b.		Sheet of 5, #6176a, 4 #6176 + label	12.50	6.25
6177	A1822	19 l multi	9.50	4.75
a.		Bird facing right	9.50	4.75
b.		Sheet of 5, #6177a, 4 #6177 + label	47.50	24.00
		Nos. 6174-6177 (4)	14.50	7.25

A sheet containing Nos. 6174-6177 was printed in limited quantities.

Famous Romanians and Romanian Coat of Arms Types of 2018

Designs: 2 l, Gheorghe Pop de Basesti (1835-1919), politician. 5 l, Alexandru Vaida-Voevod (1872-1950), prime minister. 8.50 l, Iancu Flondor (1865-1924), politician. 11.50 l, Take Ionescu (1858-1922), prime minister. 19 l, Coat of arms of the Union of Transylvania and Romania.

			Litho.	Perf. 13¼
2018, Sept. 17				
6178	A1791	1.00 l multi	1.00	.50
a.		Sheet of 6 + 6 labels	6.00	3.00
6179	A1791	5 l multi	2.50	1.25
a.		Sheet of 6 + 6 labels	15.00	7.50
6180	A1791	8.50 multi	4.25	2.10
a.		Sheet of 6 + 6 labels	25.50	13.00
6181	A1791	11.50 l multi	5.75	3.00
a.		Sheet of 6 + 6 labels	34.50	18.00
		Nos. 6178-6181 (4)	13.50	6.85

Souvenir Sheet
Imperf

6182	A1792	19 l multi	9.50	4.75

No. 6182 contains one 30mm diameter stamp.

Rights of the Child
A1823

			Litho.	Perf. 13¼
2018, Sept. 28				
6183	A1823	5 l multi	2.50	1.25
a.		Sheet of 8 + central label	20.00	10.00

Birds
A1824

Designs: 2 l, Haliaeetus albicilla. 5 l, Dryocopus martius, vert. 8.50 l, Bubo bubo. 12 l, Pelecanus crispus, vert.

			Litho.	Perf. 13¼
2018, Oct. 5				
6184	A1824	2 l multi	1.00	.50
a.		Sheet of 5 + label	5.00	2.50
6185	A1824	5 l multi	2.50	1.25
a.		Sheet of 5 + label	12.50	6.25
6186	A1824	8.50 l multi	4.25	2.10
a.		Sheet of 5 + label	21.50	10.50
6187	A1824	12 l multi	6.00	3.00
a.		Sheet of 5 + label	30.00	15.00
		Nos. 6184-6187 (4)	13.75	6.85

A sheet containing Nos. 6184-6187 was printed in limited quantities.

Monuments in Bucharest
A1825

Designs: 1.40 l, Monument to Railway Heroes. 1.60 l, Monument to the Sanitary Heroes. 2 l, Tomb of the Unknown Soldier. 8.50 l, Monument to Air Heroes. 19 l, Monument to Military Engineers.

			Litho.	Perf. 13¼
2018, Oct. 12				
6188	A1825	1.40 l multi	.70	.35
a.		Sheet of 5 + label	3.50	1.75
6189	A1825	1.60 l multi	.80	.40
a.		Sheet of 5 + label	4.00	2.00
6190	A1825	2 l multi	1.00	.50
a.		Sheet of 5 + label	5.00	2.50
6191	A1825	8.50 l multi	4.25	2.10
a.		Sheet of 5 + label	21.50	10.50
6192	A1825	19 l multi	9.25	4.75
a.		Sheet of 5 + label	46.50	24.00
		Nos. 6188-6192 (5)	16.00	8.10

Beatification of Vladimir Ghika (1873-1954), 5th Anniv. — A1826

Designs: 5 l, Ghika. 28.50 l, Postage stamp design drawn by Ghika in 1918.

			Litho.	Perf. 13¼
2018, Oct. 15				
6193	A1826	5 l multi	2.50	1.25
a.		Sheet of 8 + central label	20.00	10.00

Souvenir Sheet

6194	A1826	28.50 l multi	14.00	7.00

Nicoae Minovici (1868-1941), Medical Examiner
A1827

Designs: 2 l, Minovici. 12 l, Minovici and Dr. Nicolae Minovici Folk Art Museum, Bucharest, horiz.

			Litho.	Perf. 13¼
2018, Oct. 23				
6195	A1827	2 l multi	1.00	.50
a.		Sheet of 5 + label	5.00	2.50
6196	A1827	12 l multi	6.00	3.00
a.		Sheet of 5 + label	30.00	15.00

Souvenir Sheet

Romanian Radio Broadcasting Company, 90th Anniv. — A1828

			Litho.	Imperf.
2018, Nov. 1				
6197	A1828	28.50 l multi	14.00	7.00

Annunciation Icon From Bucharest Patriarchal Residence Chapel
A1829

Nativity Icon From Bucharest Patriarchal Residence Chapel
A1830

			Litho.	Perf. 13¼
2018, Nov. 9				
6198	A1829	1.50 l multi	.75	.35
6199	A1830	1.50 l multi	.75	.35
a.		Sheet of 8, 4 each #6198-6199, + central label, #6198 at UR	6.00	3.00
b.		As "a," with #6199 at UR	6.00	3.00

Christmas. Perforate and imperforare sheets of 2 of Nos. 6198-6199 were printed in limited quantites.

Souvenir Sheet

Vase of Flowers and Hands of Queen Marie and King Ferdinand — A1831

Perf. 13¼x13¾

			Litho.	
2018, Nov. 16				
6200	A1831	28.50 l multi	14.00	7.00

Union of Transylvania With Romania, cent. Imperforate examples of No. 6200 were printed in limited quantities.

General Henri M. Berthelot (1861-1931) — A1832

Berthelot: 5 l, Decorating Romanian officers, 1917. 8.50 l, And his house in Hunedoara.

			Litho.	Perf. 13¼
2018, Nov. 27				
6201	A1832	5 l multi	2.50	1.25
a.		Sheet of 8 + central label	20.00	10.00
6202	A1832	8.50 l multi	4.25	2.10
a.		Sheet of 8 + central label	34.00	17.00

See France Nos. 5568-5569.

Consecration of the Altar of Salvation National Cathedral — A1833

Designs: 5 l, Cathedral and icon of the Apostle Andrew. 28.50 l, Icon of the Ascension.

Perf. 13¼x13¾

			Litho.	
2018, Nov. 29				
6203	A1833	5 l gold & multi	2.50	1.25
a.		Sheet of 5 + label	12.50	6.25

Souvenir Sheet
Perf. 13¾x13¼

6204	A1833	28.50 l gold & multi	14.00	7.00

No. 6204 contains one 52x84mm stamp.

Holiday Season Traditions
A1834

Designs: 2 l, Child mailing letter to Santa Claus. 3 l, Boy giving gift to girl. 11.50 l, People singing carols. 12 l, Snowman with Sorcova stick, skiers.

			Litho.	Perf. 13¼
2018, Dec. 7				
6205	A1834	2 l multi	1.00	.50
a.		Sheet of 5 + label	5.00	2.50
6206	A1834	3 l multi	1.50	.75
a.		Sheet of 5 + label	7.50	3.75
6207	A1834	11.50 l multi	5.75	3.00
a.		Sheet of 5 + label	29.00	15.00
6208	A1834	12 l multi	6.00	3.00
a.		Sheet of 5 + label	30.00	15.00
		Nos. 6205-6208 (4)	14.25	7.25

Souvenir Sheet

Gen. Nicolae Condeescu (1876-1936), Head of Intelligence Office — A1835

			Litho.	Perf. 13¼
2018, Dec. 14				
6209	A1835	28.50 l multi + 2 labels	14.00	7.00

Romanian Presidency of the Council of the European Union — A1836

2019, Jan. 4   Litho.   Perf. 13¼
6210	A1836	5 l multi	2.40	1.25
a.		Sheet of 10	24.00	12.50

Romanian Treasures — A1837

Designs: 2 l, Constantin Brancusi (1876-1957), sculptor, and his sculptures. 2.60 l, Romanian Athenaeum Concert Hall, coat of arms of Bucharest. 2.90 l, Henri Coanda (1886-1972), and Coanda 1910 airplane. 3 l, Birds and Danube Delta. 8.50 l. Palace of Culture, coat of arms of Iasi. 12 l, Eagle and Retezat National Park.

2019, Jan. 16   Litho.   Perf. 13¾x13¼
6211	A1837	2 l multi	1.00	.50
a.		Sheet of 5 + label	5.00	2.50
6212	A1837	2.60 l multi	1.25	.60
a.		Sheet of 5 + label	6.25	3.00
6213	A1837	2.90 l multi	1.40	.70
a.		Sheet of 5 + label	7.00	3.50
6214	A1837	3 l multi	1.50	.75
a.		Sheet of 5 + label	7.50	3.75
6215	A1837	8.50 l multi	4.25	2.10
a.		Sheet of 5 + label	21.50	10.50
6216	A1837	12 l multi	5.75	3.00
a.		Sheet of 5 + label	29.00	15.00
b.		Souvenir sheet of 6, #6211-6216	15.50	7.75
		Nos. 6211-6216 (6)	15.15	7.65

Souvenir Sheet

Alexandru Ioan Cuza (1820-73), Ruling Prince of United Principalities of Moldavia and Wallachia — A1838

2019, Jan. 23   Litho.   Perf. 13¼x13¾
6217	A1838	28.50 l multi	14.00	7.00

United Provinces of Moldavia and Wallachia, 160th Anniv.

Adult and Juvenile Animals A1839

Adult and juvenile: 3 l, Loxondonta africana, map of Africa. 5 l, Phascolarctos cinereus, map of Australia and New Zealand, horiz. 7 l, Panthera uncia, map of Asia. 12 l, Ursus arctos, map of Europe, horiz.

2019, Feb. 8   Litho.   Perf. 13¼
6218	A1839	3 l multi	1.50	.75
a.		Sheet of 5 + label	7.50	3.75
6219	A1839	5 l multi	2.40	1.25
a.		Sheet of 5 + label	12.00	6.25
6220	A1839	7 l multi	3.50	1.75
a.		Sheet of 5 + label	17.50	8.75
6221	A1839	12 l multi	5.75	3.00
a.		Sheet of 5 + label	29.00	15.00
		Nos. 6218-6221 (4)	13.15	6.75

Paintings of Nudes by Nicolae Grigorescu (1838-1907) — A1840

Designs: 2 l, Bacanta. 3 l, After the Bath. 5 l, Entering the Bath. 19 l, Before the Bath.

Perf. 13¼x13¾
2019, Feb. 15   Litho.
6222	A1840	2 l gold & multi	.95	.50
a.		Sheet of 4	4.00	2.00
6223	A1840	3 l gold & multi	1.50	.75
a.		Sheet of 4	6.00	3.00
6224	A1840	5 l gold & multi	2.40	1.25
a.		Sheet of 4	9.75	5.00
6225	A1840	19 l gold & multi	9.00	4.50
a.		Sheet of 4	36.00	18.00
		Nos. 6222-6225 (4)	13.85	7.00

Dog Breeds A1841

Designs: 3 l, Romanian Mioritic shepherd. 5 l, Romanian Carpathian shepherd. 8.50 l, Romanian Bucovina shepherd. 12 l, Romanian Raven shepherd.

2019, Feb. 22   Litho.   Perf. 13¼
6226	A1841	3 l multi	1.50	.75
a.		Sheet of 5 + label	7.50	3.75
6227	A1841	5 l multi	2.40	1.25
a.		Sheet of 5 + label	12.00	6.25
6228	A1841	8.50 l multi	4.00	2.00
a.		Sheet of 5 + label	20.00	10.00
6229	A1841	12 l multi	5.75	3.00
a.		Sheet of 5 + label	29.00	15.00
		Nos. 6226-6229 (4)	13.65	7.00

A sheet containing Nos. 6226-6229 was printed in limited quantities.

Cecilia Cutescu-Storck (1879-1969), Painter — A1842

Designs: 5 l, Self-portrait. 28.50 l, Sculpture of Cutescu-Storck, by her husband, Frederic Storck (1872-1942).

2019, Mar. 14   Litho.   Perf. 13¼
6230	A1842	5 l multi	2.40	1.25
a.		Sheet of 8 + central label	19.50	10.00

Souvenir Sheet
6231	A1842	28.50 l multi	13.50	6.75

Crucifixion A1843

Resurrection of Jesus Christ A1844

Crucifixion — A1845

2019, Mar. 22   Litho.   Perf. 13¼
6232	A1843	1.50 l multi	.70	.35
a.		Sheet of 8 + central label	5.75	3.00
6233	A1844	1.50 l multi	.70	.35
a.		Sheet of 8 + central label	5.75	3.00

Souvenir Sheet
Perf. 13¼x13¾
6234	A1845	28.50 l multi	13.50	6.75

Perforated and imperforate sheets of 2 containing Nos. 6232-6233 were printed in limited quantities, as was a perforated sheet of 3 containing Nos. 6232-6234 and a label.

Household Items to Hold Hot Objects Type of 2018

Designs: 1.40 l, Saint Valentine trivet (hearts), 19th cent. 1.60 l, Musical symbols support, 19th cent. 1.70 l, Trivet with grape bunch design, 20th cent. 7 l, Trivet with legs, 19th cent. 8.50 l, Artistic leaf-shaped support, 20th cent. 12 l, 19 l, Trivet with horseshoe and Masonic emblems, 19th cent.

2019, Mar. 29   Litho.   Perf. 13¼
6235	A1794	1.40 l multi	.65	.30
a.		Sheet of 8 + central label	5.25	2.40
b.		Sheet of 13 + 2 labels	8.50	4.00
6236	A1794	1.60 l multi	.75	.40
a.		Sheet of 8 + central label	6.00	3.25
b.		Sheet of 13 + 2 labels	9.75	5.25
6237	A1794	1.70 l multi	.80	.40
a.		Sheet of 8 + central label	6.50	3.25
b.		Sheet of 13 + 2 labels	10.50	5.25
6238	A1794	7 l multi	3.25	1.60
a.		Sheet of 8 + central label	26.00	13.00
b.		Sheet of 13 + 2 labels	42.50	21.00
6239	A1794	8.50 l multi	4.00	2.00
a.		Sheet of 8 + central label	32.00	16.00
b.		Sheet of 13 + 2 labels	52.00	26.00
6240	A1794	12 l multi	5.75	3.00
a.		Sheet of 8 + central label	46.00	24.00
b.		Sheet of 13 + 2 labels	75.00	39.00
		Nos. 6235-6240 (6)	15.20	7.70

Souvenir Sheet
Imperf
6241	A1794	19 l multi	9.00	4.50

No. 6241 contains one 55x45mm stamp. An embellished example of No. 6241 was printed in limited quantities.

Articles of the Romanian Constitution — A1846

Designs: 1.70 l, Article 12 regarding flag and national symbols. 1.80 l, Article 32 regarding right to education. 1.90 l, Article 34 regarding right to health and welfare. 2.40 l, Article 35 regarding right to healthy environment. 2.50 l, Article 21 regarding right to seek justice. 2.80 l, Article 30 regarding freedom of expression. 3.10 l, Article 25 regarding right to free movement. 7 l, Article 24 regarding right to defend oneself at trial. 19 l, Article 38 regarding right to be elected to Eueopean Parliament.

2019, Apr. 8   Litho.   Perf. 13¼
6242	A1846	1.70 l multi	.75	.40
a.		Sheet of 5 + label	3.75	2.00
6243	A1846	1.80 l multi	.85	.40
a.		Sheet of 5 + label	4.25	2.00
6244	A1846	1.90 l multi	.90	.45
a.		Sheet of 5 + label	4.50	2.25
6245	A1846	2.40 l multi	1.10	.55
a.		Sheet of 5 + label	5.50	2.75
6246	A1846	2.50 l multi	1.25	.60
a.		Sheet of 5 + label	6.25	3.00
6247	A1846	2.80 l multi	1.40	.70
a.		Sheet of 5 + label	7.00	3.50
6248	A1846	3.10 l multi	1.50	.75
a.		Sheet of 5 + label	7.50	3.75
6249	A1846	7 l multi	3.25	1.60
a.		Sheet of 5 + label	16.50	8.00
6250	A1846	19 l multi	9.00	4.50
a.		Sheet of 5 + label	45.00	22.50
b.		Sheet of 9, #6242-6250 + 9 labels	20.00	10.00
		Nos. 6242-6250 (9)	20.00	9.95

A booklet containing Nos. 6242-6250 was printed in limited quantities.

Europa A1847

Designs: 1.80 l, Alauda arvensis. 19 l, Aquila chrysaetos.

2019, Apr. 12   Litho.   Perf. 13¼
6251	A1847	1.80 l multi	.85	.40
a.		Sheet of 6	5.25	2.40
6252	A1847	19 l multi	9.00	4.50
a.		Sheet of 6	54.00	27.00
b.		Souvenir sheet of 4, 2 each #6251-6252, #6251 at UL	20.00	10.00
c.		Souvenir sheet of 4, 2 each #6251-6252, #6252 at UL	20.00	10.00

A sheet of 2 containing imperforate examples of Nos. 6251-6252 was printed in limited quantities.

Grampet Group Rail Company, 20th Anniv. — A1848

Locomotive and: 3.10 l, Tanker cars. 5 l, Shipping containers on flat cars. 7 l, Freight cars. 12 l, Automobile carrier cars. 28.50 l, Train and overhead wires.

2019, Apr. 19   Litho.   Perf. 13¼
6253	A1848	3.10 l multi	1.50	.75
a.		Sheet of 5 + label	7.50	3.75
6254	A1848	5 l multi	2.40	1.25
a.		Sheet of 5 + label	12.00	6.25
6255	A1848	7 l multi	3.25	1.60
a.		Sheet of 5 + label	16.50	8.00
6256	A1848	12 l multi	5.75	3.00
a.		Sheet of 5 + label	29.00	15.00
		Nos. 6253-6256 (4)	12.90	6.60

Souvenir Sheet
6257	A1848	28.50 l multi	13.50	6.75

Protected
Animals
A1849

Designs: 1.60 l, Lyruris tetrix. 1.90 l, Lynx lynx. 2.90 l, Ursus arctos. 5 l, Cervus elaphus. 7 l, Tetrao urogsallus. 12 l, Rupicapra rupicapra.
28.50 l, Bison bonasus, horiz.

2019, Apr. 25　Litho.　Perf. 13¼

6258	A1849	1.60 l multi	.75	.40
a.		Sheet of 5 + label	3.75	2.00
6259	A1849	1.90 l multi	.90	.45
a.		Sheet of 5 + label	4.50	2.25
6260	A1849	2.90 l multi	1.40	.70
a.		Sheet of 5 + label	7.00	3.50
6261	A1849	5 l multi	2.40	1.25
a.		Sheet of 5 + label	12.00	6.25
6262	A1849	7 l multi	3.25	1.60
a.		Sheet of 5 + label	16.50	8.00
6263	A1849	12 l multi	5.75	3.00
a.		Sheet of 5 + label	29.00	15.00
		Nos. 6258-6263 (6)	14.45	7.40

Souvenir Sheet

6264	A1849	28.50 l multi	13.50	6.75

A souvenir sheet containing Nos. 6258-6263 was printed in limited quantities.

Souvenir Sheet

Alexandru Romalo (1819-75),
Judge — A1850

2019, May 7　Litho.　Perf. 13¼

6265	A1850	28.50 l multi + 2 labels	13.50	6.75

Tourist Attractions — A1851

Designs: 1.60 l, Sturdza Castle, Miclauseni. 1.80 l, Hunyad Castle, Hunedoara. 1.90 l, Peles Castle, Sinaia. 5 l, Barsana Monastery, Barsana. 8.50 l, Rupea Fortress, Rupea. 12 l, Neamt Monastery, Targu Neamt.
28.50 l, City Hall, Sibiu, vert.

2019, May 9　Litho.　Perf. 13¾x13¼

6266	A1851	1.60 l multi	.75	.40
a.		Sheet of 5 + label	3.75	2.00
6267	A1851	1.80 l multi	.85	.45
a.		Sheet of 5 + label	4.25	2.25
6268	A1851	1.90 l multi	.90	.45
a.		Sheet of 5 + label	4.50	2.25
6269	A1851	5 l multi	2.40	1.25
a.		Sheet of 5 + label	12.00	6.25
6270	A1851	8.50 l multi	4.00	2.00
a.		Sheet of 5 + label	20.00	10.00

6271	A1851	12 l multi	5.75	3.00
a.		Sheet of 5 + label	29.00	15.00
b.		Souvenir sheet of 6, #6266-6271, imperf.	15.00	7.75
		Nos. 6266-6271 (6)	14.65	7.55

Souvenir Sheet
Perf. 13¼x13¾

6272	A1851	28.50 l multi	13.50	6.75

Peafowl — A1852

Designs: No. 6273, Afropavo congensis facing left. No. 6273A, Afropavo congensis facing right. No. 6274, Pavo muticus, with beak at right. No. 6274A, Pavo muticus, with beak at left. No. 6275, Pavo cristatus (white bird), with beak at right. No. 6275A, Pavo cristatus (white bird), with beak at left. No. 6276, Pavo cristatus (multicolored bird), with beak at left. No. 6276A, Pavo cristatus (multicolored bird), with beak at right.

2019, May 17　Litho.　Perf. 13¼

6273	A1852	1.80 l multi	.85	.45
6273A	A1852	1.80 l multi	.85	.45
b.		Sheet of 5, #6273A, 4 #6273 + label	4.25	2.25
6274	A1852	5 l multi	2.40	1.25
6274A	A1852	5 l multi	2.40	1.25
b.		Sheet of 5, #6274A, 4 #6274 + label	12.00	6.25
6275	A1852	8.50 l multi	4.00	2.00
6275A	A1852	8.50 l multi	4.00	2.00
b.		Sheet of 5, #6275A, 4 #6275 + label	20.00	10.00
6276	A1852	12 l multi	5.75	3.00
6276A	A1852	12 l multi	5.75	3.00
b.		Sheet of 5, #6276A, 4 #6276 + label	29.00	15.00
		Nos. 6273-6276A (8)	26.00	13.40

A souvenir sheet containing Nos. 6273, 6274, 6275 and 6276 was printed in limited quantities.

Souvenir Sheet

Visit to Romania of Pope
Francis — A1853

2019, May 31　Litho.　Perf. 13¼

6277	A1853	11.50 l multi	5.50	2.75

See Vatican City No. 1720.

Souvenir Sheet

Cross and Seven Stars — A1854

2019, June 2　Litho.　Perf. 13¼

6278	A1854	28.50 l multi + 8 labels	13.50	6.75

Beatification of seven Romanian Greek martyrs.

Melliferous Flowers — A1855

Designs: 1.90 l, Tilia tomentosa. 2.80 l, Robinia pseudoacacia. 5 l, Helianthus annuus. 8.50 l, Brassica rapa subsp. oleifera. 12 l, Malus domestica.

2019, June 11　Litho.　Perf. 13¼

6279	A1855	1.90 l multi	.90	.45
a.		Sheet of 5 + label	4.50	2.25
6280	A1855	2.80 l multi	1.40	.70
a.		Sheet of 5 + label	7.00	3.50
6281	A1855	5 l multi	2.40	1.25
a.		Sheet of 5 + label	12.00	6.25
6282	A1855	8.50 l multi	4.25	2.10
a.		Sheet of 5 + label	21.50	10.50
6283	A1855	12 l multi	5.75	3.00
a.		Sheet of 5 + label	29.00	15.00
		Nos. 6279-6283 (5)	14.70	7.50

A souvenir sheet containing Nos. 6279-6283 was printed in limited quantities.

Souvenir Sheet

Bust of Gheorghe Lazar (1779-1823),
Founder of First Romanian Technical
School — A1856

Perf. 13¾x13¼

6284	A1856	28.50 l multi	14.00	7.00

Politehnica University of Bucharest, 200th anniv. (in 2018).

Paintings of the Danube
River — A1857

Designs: 2.80 l, Danube Reaching the Cauldrons Area, by Marius Bunescu (1881-1971). 5 l, Landscape on the Danube, by Petre Iorgulescu Yor (1890-1939). 8.50 l, Danube at Turtucaia, by Gheorghe Petrascu (1872-1949). 12 l, Danube Landscape at Turtucaia, by Iosif Iser (1881-1958).

Perf. 13¾x13¼

2019, June 28　　　　Litho.

6285	A1857	2.80 l multi	1.40	.70
a.		Sheet of 4	5.75	3.00
6286	A1857	5 l multi	2.40	1.25
a.		Sheet of 4	9.75	5.00
6287	A1857	8.50 l multi	4.25	2.10
a.		Sheet of 4	17.00	8.50
6288	A1857	12 l multi	5.75	3.00
a.		Sheet of 4	23.00	12.00
		Nos. 6285-6288 (4)	13.80	7.05

Souvenir Sheet

Visit of King Ferdinand and Queen
Mary to Oradea, Cent. — A1858

2019, July 9　Litho.　Perf. 13¾x13¼

6289	A1858	28.50 l multi	13.50	6.75

End of World War I, cent. (in 2018).

First Man on the Moon, 50th
Anniv. — A1859

Designs: 5 l, Launch of Apollo 11, Command and Lunar Modules above Moon. 8.50 l, Astronaut on ladder of Lunar Module, Apollo 11 patch, Hermann Oberth (1894-1989) and Wernher von Braun (1912-77), aerospace engineers.

2019, July 11　Litho.　Perf. 13¾x13¼

6290	A1859	5 l multi	2.40	1.25
a.		Sheet of 5 + label	12.00	6.25
6291	A1859	8.50 l multi	4.00	2.00
a.		Sheet of 5 + label	20.00	10.00

Romanian Rulers and Their
Seals — A1860

Portrait and seal of: 3.10 l, Alexander the Good (c. 1375-1432). 7 l, Stephen the Great (c. 1433-1504). 8.50 l, Petru Rares (c. 1483-1546). 11.50 l, Vasile Lupu (1595-1661).

2019, July 15　Litho.　Perf. 13¼

6293	A1860	3.10 l multi	1.50	.75
a.		Sheet of 5 + label	7.50	3.75
6294	A1860	7 l multi	3.25	1.60
a.		Sheet of 5 + label	16.50	8.00
6295	A1860	8.50 l multi	4.00	2.00
a.		Sheet of 5 + label	20.00	10.00
6296	A1860	11.50 l multi	5.50	2.75
a.		Sheet of 5 + label	27.50	14.00
		Nos. 6293-6296 (4)	14.25	7.10

A sheet containing imperforate examples of Nos. 6293-6296 was printed in limited quantities.

Souvenir Sheets

A1861

Simona Halep, 2019 Wimbledon Women's Singles Champion — A1862

2019, July 26   Litho.   Perf. 13¼
6297 A1861 28.50 l multi   13.50 6.75

Litho., Sheet Margin Litho. With Foil Application
Imperf
6298 A1862 53.50 l multi   25.00 12.50

Flowers
A1863

Designs: 1.40 l, Daphne blagayana. 1.60 l, Fritillaria meleagris. 1.70 l, Aster alpinus. 3.10 l, Trollius europaeus. 5 l, Silene nivalis. 19 l, Linaria alpina.

2019, Aug. 8   Litho.   Perf. 13¼
6299 A1863 1.40 l multi   .65   .30
  a.   Sheet of 5 + label   3.25   1.50
6300 A1863 1.60 l multi   .75   .35
  a.   Sheet of 5 + label   3.75   1.75
6301 A1863 1.70 l multi   .80   .40
  a.   Sheet of 5 + label   4.00   2.00
6302 A1863 3.10 l multi   1.50   .75
  a.   Sheet of 5 + label   7.50   3.75
6303 A1863   5 l multi   2.40   1.25
  a.   Sheet of 5 + label   12.00   6.25
6304 A1863   19 l multi   8.75   4.50
  a.   Sheet of 5 + label   44.00 22.50
        Nos. 6299-6304 (6)   14.85   7.55

Exotic Birds
A1864

Designs: 1.40 l, Paradisaea apoda. 1.60 l, Pharomachrus mocinno, vert. 1.70 l,

Ramphastos dicolorus, vert. 3.10 l, Onychorhynchus mexicanus, vert. 5 l, Phoenicopterus ruber, vert. 19 l, Ptiloris magnificus.

2019, Aug. 14   Litho.   Perf. 13¼
6305 A1864 1.40 l multi   .65   .30
  a.   Sheet of 5 + label   3.25   1.50
6306 A1864 1.60 l multi   .75   .35
  a.   Sheet of 5 + label   3.75   1.75
6307 A1864 1.70 l multi   .80   .40
  a.   Sheet of 5 + label   4.00   2.00
6308 A1864 3.10 l multi   1.50   .75
  a.   Sheet of 5 + label   7.50   3.75
6309 A1864   5 l multi   2.40   1.25
  a.   Sheet of 5 + label   12.00   6.25
6310 A1864   19 l multi   8.75   4.50
  a.   Sheet of 5 + label   44.00 22.50
        Nos. 6305-6310 (6)   14.85   7.55

A sheet containing imperforate examples of Nos. 6305-6310 was printed in limited quantities.

Flowers on Mount Cozia
A1865

Designs: 1.40 l, Leontopodium alpinium. 1.60 l, Hypericum richeri. 1.70 l, Erythronium dens-canis. 7 l, Primula elatior. 8.50 l, Gentiana acaulis. 11.50 l, Dictammus albus.

2019, Aug. 23   Litho.   Perf. 13¼
6311 A1865 1.40 l multi   .65   .30
  a.   Sheet of 4   2.60   1.25
6312 A1865 1.60 l multi   .75   .35
  a.   Sheet of 4   3.00   1.40
6313 A1865 1.70 l multi   .80   .40
  a.   Sheet of 4   3.25   1.60
6314 A1865   7 l multi   3.25   1.60
  a.   Sheet of 4   13.00   6.50
6315 A1865 8.50 l multi   4.00   2.00
  a.   Sheet of 4   16.00   8.00
6316 A1865 11.50 l multi   5.50   2.75
  a.   Sheet of 4   22.00 11.00
        Nos. 6311-6316 (6)   14.95   7.40

A sheet containing imperforate examples of Nos. 6311-6316 was printed in limited quantities.

Romanian Lottery, 113th Anniv.
A1866

2019, Sept. 13   Litho.   Perf. 13¼
6317 A1866 8.50 l multi   4.00   2.00
  a.   Sheet of 5 + label   20.00 10.00

EFIRO 2019 Philatelic Exhibition, Bucharest
A1867

EFIRO emblem and: 1.70 l, Romania #C71. 3.10 l, 1858 cover, two examples of Romania #1. 12 l, Globe, letters, modes of mail transport.

2019, Sept. 19   Litho.   Perf. 13¼
6318 A1867 1.70 l multi   .80   .40
  a.   Sheet of 8 + central label 6.50   3.25
  b.   Sheet of 13 + 2 labels   10.50   5.25
6319 A1867 3.10 l multi   1.50   .75
  a.   Sheet of 8 + central label 12.00   6.00
  b.   Sheet of 13 + 2 labels   19.50   9.75
6320 A1867   12 l multi   5.50   2.75
  a.   Sheet of 8 + central label 44.00 12.00
  b.   Sheet of 13 + 2 labels   71.50 36.00
        Nos. 6318-6320 (3)   7.80   3.90

Souvenir Sheet
Imperf
6321 A1867 28.50 l multi   13.00 6.50

No. 6321 contains one 55x45mm stamp.

Ferdinand Magellan (c. 1480-1521), Explorer, His Ship, Victoria, and World Map — A1868

Design: 28.50 l, Magellan and ship's wheel.

2019, Sept. 24   Litho.   Perf. 13¼
6322 A1868   7 l multi   3.25   .60
  a.   Sheet of 8 + central label 26.00 13.00

Souvenir Sheet
Imperf
6323 A1868 28.50 l multi   13.00 6.50

Start of Magellan's circumnavigatory expedition, 500th anniv. No. 6323 contains one 34x24mm stamp.

Sibiu, 2019 Region of European Gastronomy — A1869

Designs: 1.40 l, Carpenter's Tower, glass of wine, and cheeses. 3.10 l, Turmul Sfatului, sausages and pork bellies. 5 l, Evangelical Church, red onions, bean and sausage stew. 19 l, Council Square, tray of meats, cheeses, vegetables and spreads.

2019, Oct. 1   Litho.   Perf. 13¼x13¾
6324 A1869 1.40 l multi   .65   .30
  a.   Sheet of 5 + label   3.25   1.50
6325 A1869 3.10 l multi   1.50   .75
  a.   Sheet of 5 + label   7.50   3.75
6326 A1869   5 l multi   2.40   1.25
  a.   Sheet of 5 + label   12.00   6.25
6327 A1869   19 l multi   8.75   4.50
  a.   Sheet of 5 + label   44.00 22.50
        Nos. 6324-6327 (4)   13.30   6.80

Paintings of Romanian Rulers
A1870

Portrait of: 1.50 l, Constantin Brancoveanu (1654-1714), by unknown artist. 1.60 l, Grigore II Ghica (1695-1752), by Theodor Aman. 7 l, Michael the Brave (1558-1601), by Misu Popp. 19 l, Stephen the Great (c. 1433-1504), by Constantin Lecca.

2019, Oct. 11   Litho.   Perf. 13¼x13¾
6328 A1870 1.50 l multi   .70   .35
  a.   Sheet of 4   3.00   1.40
6329 A1870 1.60 l multi   .75   .35
  a.   Sheet of 4   3.00   1.40
6330 A1870   7 l multi   3.25   1.60
  a.   Sheet of 4   13.00   6.50
6331 A1870   19 l multi   9.00   4.50
  a.   Sheet of 4   36.00 18.00
        Nos. 6328-6331 (4)   13.70   6.80

Palaces — A1871

Flags of Romania and Malta and: 1.70 l, Mogosoaia Palace, Romania. 8.50 l, Verdala Palace, Malta.

2019, Oct. 14   Litho.   Perf. 13¼
6332 A1871 1.70 l multi   .80   .40
  a.   Sheet of 5 + label   4.00   2.00
6333 A1871 8.50 l multi   4.00   2.00
  a.   Sheet of 5 + label   20.00 10.00

Joint Issue between Romania and Malta.
A sheet containing imperforate examples of Nos. 6332-6333 was printed in limited quantities. See Malta No. 1672.

Romanian Higher Education in Cluj-Napoca, Cent. — A1872

Designs: 3.10 l, Babes-Bolyai University building and emblem. 12 l, Cluj-Napoca University of Medicine and Pharmacy building and emblem, Iuliu Hatieganu (1885-1959), first dean (72x33mm).
28.50 l, Emblem of Babes-Bolyai University, spray from fountain in its botanical garden.

2019, Nov. 1   Litho.   Perf. 13¼
6334 A1872 3.10 l multi   1.50   .75
  a.   Sheet of 8   12.00   6.00
6335 A1872   12 l multi   5.75   3.00
  a.   Sheet of 8   46.00 24.00

Souvenir Sheet
Imperf
6336 A1872 28.50 l multi   13.50 6.75

No. 6336 contains one 36x36mm stamp.

Parks of Romania and Gibraltar — A1873

Designs: 7 l, Retezat National Park, Romania. 8 l, Upper Rock Nature Reserve, Gibraltar.

2019, Nov. 12   Litho.   Perf. 13¼
6337 A1873   7 l multi   3.25   1.60
  a.   Sheet of 5 + label   16.50   8.00
6338 A1873   8 l multi   4.00   2.00
  a.   Sheet of 5 + label   20.00 10.00

Joint Issue between Romania and Gibraltar.
A sheet containing imperforate examples of Nos. 6337-6338 was printed in limited quantities. See Gibraltar No. 1740.

Christmas — A1874

No. 6339 — Images from *Akathist Hymn of the Mother of God*: a, Nativity scene (denomination in green). b, Magi (denomination in red).
28.50 l, Madonna and Child, vert.

2019, Nov. 15 Litho. Perf. 13¼
6339	A1874	1.70 l	Pair, #a-b	1.60	.80
c.	Sheet of 8, 4 each #6339a-6339b, + central label, #6339a at UL			13.00	6.50
d.	As "c," #6339b at UL			13.00	6.50

Souvenir Sheet
Perf. 13¾x13¼
6340	A1874	28.50 l	multi	13.50	6.75

No. 6340 contains one 52x84mm stamp.

Animals and Thought Balloons
A1875

Designs: 1.60 l, Polar bears and "Ocretire" (protection) in balloon. 3.10 l, Berber macaque and "Nostalgie" (nostalgia) in balloon. 5 l, St. Bernard, kittens and "Prietenie" (friendliness) in balloon. 19 l, Elephants and "Bucurie" (joy) in balloon.

2019, Nov. 19 Litho. Perf. 13¼
6341	A1875	1.60 l	multi	.75	.35
a.	Sheet of 5 + label			3.75	1.75
6342	A1875	3.10 l	multi	1.50	.75
a.	Sheet of 5 + label			7.50	3.75
6343	A1875	5 l	multi	2.40	1.25
a.	Sheet of 5 + label			12.00	6.25
6344	A1875	19 l	multi	8.75	4.50
a.	Sheet of 5 + label			44.00	22.50
	Nos. 6341-6344 (4)			13.40	6.85

A sheet containing imperforate examples of Nos. 6341-6344 was printed in limited quantities.

Romanian Legal Education, 160th Anniv. — A1876

Designs: 8.50 l, University of Bucharest Faculty of Law emblem. 28.50 l, Emblem and building of University of Bucharest Faculty of Law, horiz.

2019, Nov. 21 Litho. Perf. 13¼
6345	A1876	8.50 l	multi	4.00	2.00
a.	Sheet of 5 + label			20.00	10.00

Souvenir Sheet
6346	A1876	28.50 l	multi	13.50	6.75

No. 6346 contains one 108x36mm stamp.

Romanian Royalty in Uniforms
A1877

Designs: 3.10 l, King Carol I (1839-1914). 7 l, King Ferdinand (1865-1927). 8.50 l, King Carol II (1893-1953). 11.50 l, King Michael (1921-2017). 28.50 l, King Carol I riding horse, horiz.

2019, Dec. 5 Litho. Perf. 13¼
6347	A1877	3.10 l	multi	1.50	.75
a.	Sheet of 4			6.00	3.00
6348	A1877	7 l	multi	3.25	1.60
a.	Sheet of 4			13.00	6.50
6349	A1877	8.50 l	multi	4.00	2.00
a.	Sheet of 4			16.00	8.00
6350	A1877	11.50 l	multi	5.50	2.75
a.	Sheet of 4			22.00	11.00
	Nos. 6347-6350 (4)			14.25	7.10

Souvenir Sheet
Perf. 13¼x13¾
6351	A1877	28.50 l	multi	13.50	6.75

No. 6351 contains one 84x52mm stamp. A sheet containing imperforate examples of Nos. 6347-6350 was printed in limited quantities.

Souvenir Sheet

Industrial and Aesthetic Design Education in Romania, 50th Anniv. — A1878

2019, Dec. 11 Litho. Perf. 13¼
6352	A1878	28.50 l	multi	13.50	6.75

Gramophones
A1879

Gramophone from: 1.40 l, Germany, 1908. 1.60 l, United States, 1900. 1.80 l, Germany, 1910. 7 l, Switzerland, 1907. 8.50 l, Germany, 1903. 12 l, Germany, 1908, diff. 28.50 l, Germany, 1910, horiz.

2019, Dec. 12 Litho. Perf. 13¼
6353	A1879	1.40 l	multi	.65	.35
a.	Sheet of 8 + central label			5.25	3.00
b.	Sheet of 13 + 2 labels			8.50	4.75
6354	A1879	1.60 l	multi	.75	.35
a.	Sheet of 8 + central label			6.00	3.00
b.	Sheet of 13 + 2 labels			9.75	4.75
6355	A1879	1.80 l	multi	.85	.40
a.	Sheet of 8 + central label			7.00	3.25
b.	Sheet of 13 + 2 labels			11.50	5.25
6356	A1879	7 l	multi	3.25	1.60
a.	Sheet of 8 + central label			26.00	13.00
b.	Sheet of 13 + 2 labels			42.50	21.00
6357	A1879	8.50 l	multi	4.00	2.00
a.	Sheet of 8 + central label			32.00	16.00
b.	Sheet of 13 + 2 labels			52.00	26.00
6358	A1879	12 l	multi	5.75	3.00
a.	Sheet of 8 + central label			46.00	24.00
b.	Sheet of 13 + 2 labels			75.00	39.00
	Nos. 6353-6358 (6)			15.25	7.70

Souvenir Sheet
Imperf
6359	A1879	28.50 l	multi	13.50	6.75

No. 6359 contains one 54x44mm stamp.

SEMI-POSTAL STAMPS

Queen Elizabeth Spinning — SP1

Perf. 11½, 11½x13½

1906, Jan. 14 Typo. Unwmk.
B1	SP1	3b (+ 7b) brown	6.00	3.75
B2	SP1	5b (+ 10b) lt grn	6.00	3.75
B3	SP1	10b (+ 10b) rose red	29.00	11.00
B4	SP1	15b (+ 10b) violet	20.00	7.50
	Nos. B1-B4 (4)		61.00	26.00

The Queen Weaving — SP2

1906, Mar. 18
B5	SP2	3b (+ 7b) org brn	6.00	3.75
B6	SP2	5b (+ 10b) bl grn	6.00	3.75
B7	SP2	10b (+ 10b) car	29.00	11.00
B8	SP2	15b (+ 10b) red vio	20.00	7.50
	Nos. B5-B8 (4)		61.00	26.00

Queen as War Nurse SP3

1906, Mar. 23 Perf. 11½, 13½x11½
B9	SP3	3b (+ 7b) org brn	6.00	3.75
B10	SP3	5b (+ 10b) bl grn	6.00	3.75
B11	SP3	10b (+ 10b) car	29.00	11.00
B12	SP3	15b (+ 10b) red vio	20.00	7.50
	Nos. B9-B12 (4)		61.00	26.00
	Nos. B1-B12 (12)		183.00	78.00

Booklet panes of 4 exist of Nos. B1-B3, B5-B7, B9-B12.
Counterfeits of Nos. B1-B12 are plentiful. Examples of Nos. B1-B12 with smooth, even gum are counterfeits.

SP4

1906, Aug. 4 Perf. 12
B13	SP4	3b (+ 7b) ol brn, buff & bl	3.25	1.50
B14	SP4	5b (+ 10b) grn, rose & buff	3.25	1.50
B15	SP4	10b (+ 10b) rose red, buff & bl	5.00	3.00
B16	SP4	15b (+ 10b) vio, buff & bl	13.00	3.75
	Nos. B13-B16 (4)		24.50	9.75

Guardian Angel Bringing Poor to Crown Princess Marie SP5

1907, Feb. Engr. Perf. 11
Center in Brown
B17	SP5	3b (+ 7b) org brn	4.00	1.50
B18	SP5	5b (+ 10b) dk grn	4.00	1.50
B19	SP5	10b (+ 10b) dk car	4.00	1.50
B20	SP5	15b (+ 10b) dl vio	4.00	1.50
	Nos. B17-B20 (4)		16.00	6.00

Nos. B1-B20 were sold for more than face value. The surtax, shown in parenthesis, was for charitable purposes.

Map of Romania SP9

Stephen the Great SP10

Michael the Brave SP11

Kings Carol I and Ferdinand SP12

Adam Clisi Monument — SP13

1927, Mar. 15 Typo. Perf. 13½
B21	SP9	1 l + 9 l lt vio	4.25	1.60
B22	SP10	2 l + 8 l Prus grn	4.25	1.60
B23	SP11	3 l + 7 l dp rose	4.25	1.60
B24	SP12	5 l + 5 l dp bl	4.25	1.60
B25	SP13	6 l + 4 l ol grn	6.25	2.50
	Nos. B21-B25 (5)		23.25	8.90

50th anniv. of the Royal Geographical Society. The surtax was for the benefit of that society. The stamps were valid for postage only from 3/15-4/14.

Boy Scouts in Camp — SP15

The Rescue — SP16

Prince Nicholas Chief Scout — SP16a

Designs: 3 l+3 l, Swearing in a Tenderfoot. 6 l+6 l, King Carol II in Scout's Uniform.

1931, July 15 Photo. Wmk. 225
B26	SP15	1 l + 1 l car rose	3.75	2.50
B27	SP16	2 l + 2 l dp grn	5.00	3.00
B28	SP15	3 l + 3 l ultra	6.00	3.00
B29	SP16a	4 l + 4 l ol gray	7.50	8.00
B30	SP16a	6 l + 6 l red brn	10.00	8.00
	Nos. B26-B30 (5)		32.25	24.50

The surtax was for the benefit of the Boy Scout organization.

Boy Scout Jamboree Issue

Scouts in Camp
SP20

Semaphore
Signaling
SP21

Trailing — SP22

Camp Fire — SP23

King Carol
II — SP24

King Carol II
and Prince
Michael — SP25

1932, June 8   **Wmk. 230**

B31	SP20	25b + 25b pck grn	3.00	1.10
B32	SP21	50b + 50b brt bl	4.00	2.25
B33	SP22	1 l + 1 l ol grn	4.50	3.25
B34	SP23	2 l + 2 l org red	7.50	4.50
B35	SP24	3 l + 3 l Prus bl	14.00	9.00
B36	SP25	6 l + 6 l blk brn	16.00	11.50
	Nos. B31-B36 (6)		49.00	31.60

For overprints see Nos. B44-B49.

Tuberculosis Sanatorium — SP26

Memorial Tablet to
Postal Employees
Who Died in World
War I — SP27

Carmen Sylva
Convalescent
Home — SP28

1932, Nov. 1

B37	SP26	4 l + 1 l dk grn	5.00	4.00
B38	SP27	6 l + 1 l chocolate	5.50	4.75
B39	SP28	10 l + 1 l dp bl	10.00	8.00
	Nos. B37-B39 (3)		20.50	16.75

The surtax was given to a fund for the employees of the postal and telegraph services.

Philatelic Exhibition Issue
Souvenir Sheet

King Carol II — SP29

1932, Nov. 20   **Unwmk.**   *Imperf.*

B40	SP29	6 l + 5 l dk ol grn	50.00	50.00

Intl. Phil. Exhib. at Bucharest, Nov. 20-24, 1932. Each holder of a ticket of admission to the exhibition could buy an example of No. B40. The ticket cost 20 lei.

Roadside Shrine
SP31

Woman Spinning
SP33

Woman
Weaving
SP32

1934, Apr. 16   **Wmk. 230**   *Perf. 13½*

B41	SP31	1 l + 1 l dk brn	1.00	.90
B42	SP32	2 l + 1 l blue	1.25	1.10
B43	SP33	3 l + 1 l slate grn	1.75	1.50
	Nos. B41-B43 (3)		4.00	3.50

Weaving Exposition.

Boy Scout Mamaia Jamboree Issue

Semi-Postal Stamps
of 1932 Overprinted
in Black or Gold

1934, July 8

B44	SP20	25b + 25b pck grn	3.75	2.50
B45	SP21	50b + 50b brt bl (G)	5.00	3.00
B46	SP22	1 l + 1 l ol grn	6.00	4.75
B47	SP23	2 l + 2 l org red	7.50	5.50
B48	SP24	3 l + 3 l Prus bl		
		(G)	16.00	7.00
B49	SP25	6 l + 6 l blk brn		
		(G)	18.00	9.50
	Nos. B44-B49 (6)		56.25	32.25

Sea Scout
Saluting
SP34

Scout Bugler
SP35

Sea and Land
Scouts
SP36

King Carol
II — SP37

Sea, Land and Girl
Scouts — SP38

1935, June 8

B50	SP34	25b ol blk	1.25	1.00
B51	SP35	1 l violet	2.75	2.25
B52	SP36	2 l green	3.50	3.00
B53	SP37	6 l + 1 l red brn	5.00	4.50
B54	SP38	10 l + 2 l dk ultra	14.00	13.00
	Nos. B50-B54 (5)		26.50	23.75

Fifth anniversary of accession of King Carol II, and a national sports meeting held June 8. Surtax aided the Boy Scouts. Nos. B50-B54 exist imperf. Value $250.

King Carol
II — SP39

1936, May

B55	SP39	6 l + 1 l rose car	.75	.55

Bucharest Exhibition and 70th anniversary of the dynasty. Exists imperf. Value $125

Girl of
Oltenia — SP40

Girl of
Saliste — SP42

Youth from
Gorj — SP44

Designs: 1 l+1 l, Girl of Banat. 3 l+1 l, Girl of Hateg. 6 l+3 l, Girl of Neamt. 10 l+5 l, Youth and girl of Bucovina.

1936, June 8

B56	SP40	50b + 50b brown	.60	.60
B57	SP40	1 l + 1 l violet	.60	.60
B58	SP42	2 l + 1 l Prus grn	.60	.70
B59	SP42	3 l + 1 l car rose	.60	.90
B60	SP44	4 l + 2 l red org	1.00	.90
B61	SP40	6 l + 3 l ol gray	1.00	1.20
B62	SP42	10 l + 5 l brt bl	2.25	2.40
	Nos. B56-B62 (7)		6.65	7.30

6th anniv. of accession of King Carol II. The surtax was for child welfare. Exist imperf. Value $300, unused or used.

Insignia of Boy Scouts
SP47   SP48

Jamboree
Emblem — SP49

1936, Aug. 20

B63	SP47	1 l + 1 l brt bl	3.00	5.25
B64	SP48	3 l + 3 l ol gray	4.50	5.25
B65	SP49	6 l + 6 l car rose	6.00	5.25
	Nos. B63-B65 (3)		13.50	15.75

Boy Scout Jamboree at Brasov (Kronstadt). Exist imperf. Value $350, unused or used.

Submarine
"Delfinul"
SP50

Designs: 3 l+2 l, Training ship "Mircea." 6 l+3 l, Steamship "S.M.R."

1936, Oct.

B66	SP50	1 l + 1 l pur	2.75	2.50
B67	SP50	3 l + 2 l ultra	2.50	3.00
B68	SP50	6 l + 3 l car rose	3.50	4.25
	Nos. B66-B68 (3)		8.75	9.75

Marine Exhibition at Bucharest. Exist imperf. Value $325, unused or used.

Soccer
SP53

Swimming
SP54

Throwing the
Javelin — SP55

Skiing — SP56

King Carol II
Hunting — SP57

Rowing
SP58

Horsemanship
SP59

Founding of
the U.F.S.R.
SP60

1937, June 8   Wmk. 230   Perf. 13½

B69	SP53	25b + 25b ol blk	1.00	.35
B70	SP54	50b + 50b brown	1.00	.45
B71	SP55	1 l + 50b violet	1.20	.50
B72	SP56	2 l + 1 l slate grn	1.50	.55
B73	SP57	3 l + 1 l rose lake	2.20	.70
B74	SP58	4 l + 1 l red org	3.60	1.10
B75	SP59	6 l + 2 l dp claret	4.25	1.90
B76	SP60	10 l + 4 l brt blue	5.25	2.25
	Nos. B69-B76 (8)		20.00	7.80

25th anniversary of the Federation of Romanian Sports Clubs (U.F.S.R.); 7th anniversary of the accession of King Carol II. Exist imperf. Value $200, unused or used.

Start of
Race — SP61

Javelin
Thrower — SP62

Designs: 4 l+1 l, Hurdling. 6 l+1 l, Finish of race. 10 l+1 l, High jump.

1937, Sept. 1   Wmk. 230   Perf. 13½

B77	SP61	1 l + 1 l purple	.75	.70
B78	SP62	2 l + 1 l green	.95	1.25
B79	SP61	4 l + 1 l vermilion	1.25	1.75
B80	SP62	6 l + 1 l maroon	1.40	1.90
B81	SP61	10 l + 1 l brt bl	4.25	3.50
	Nos. B77-B81 (5)		8.60	9.30

8th Balkan Games, Bucharest. Exist imperf. Value $200, unused or used.

> **Catalogue values for unused stamps in this section, from this point to the end of the section, are for Never Hinged items.**

King Carol
II — SP66

1938, May 24

B82	SP66	6 l + 1 l deep magenta	1.50	.45

Bucharest Exhibition (for local products), May 19-June 19, celebrating 20th anniversary of the union of Rumanian provinces. Exists imperf. Value $200, unused or used.

Dimitrie
Cantemir — SP67

Maria
Doamna — SP68

Mircea the Great
SP69

Constantine
Brancoveanu
SP70

Stephen the
Great — SP71

Prince
Cuza — SP72

Michael the
Brave — SP73

Queen
Elizabeth — SP74

King Carol
II — SP75

King Ferdinand
I — SP76

King Carol
I — SP77

1938, June 8   Perf. 13½

B83	SP67	25b + 25b ol blk	.80	.35
B84	SP68	50b + 50b brn	1.25	.35
B85	SP69	1 l + 1 l blk vio	1.25	.35
B86	SP70	2 l + 2 l dk yel grn	1.40	.35
B87	SP71	3 l + 2 l dp mag	1.40	.35
B88	SP72	4 l + 2 l scarlet	1.40	.35
B89	SP73	6 l + 2 l vio brn	1.50	.45
B90	SP74	7.50 l gray bl	1.75	.60
B91	SP75	10 l brt bl	2.25	.60
B92	SP76	16 l dk slate grn	3.50	2.00
B93	SP77	20 l vermilion	4.75	2.00
	Nos. B83-B93 (11)		21.25	7.75

8th anniv. of accession of King Carol II. Surtax was for Straja Tarii, a natl. org. for boys. Exist imperf. Value $175, unused or used.

"The Spring" — SP78

"Escorting
Prisoners"
SP79

"Rodica, the
Water Carrier"
SP81

Nicolae
Grigorescu
SP82

Design: 4 l+1 l, "Returning from Market."

1938, June 23   Perf. 13½

B94	SP78	1 l + 1 l brt bl	2.25	.70
B95	SP79	2 l + 1 l yel grn	2.25	1.25
B96	SP79	4 l + 1 l vermilion	2.25	1.25
B97	SP81	6 l + 1 l lake	3.00	2.25
B98	SP82	10 l + 1 l brt bl	6.75	2.50
	Nos. B94-B98 (5)		16.50	7.95

Birth centenary of Nicolae Grigorescu, Romanian painter. Exist imperf. Value $200, unused or used.

St. George and the
Dragon — SP83

1939, June 8   Photo.

B99	SP83	25b + 25b ol gray	.60	.45
B100	SP83	50b + 50b brn	.60	.45
B101	SP83	1 l + 1 l pale vio	.60	.45
B102	SP83	2 l + 2 l lt grn	.60	.45
B103	SP83	3 l + 2 l red vio	1.00	.45
B104	SP83	4 l + 2 l red org	1.40	.55
B105	SP83	6 l + 2 l car rose	1.50	.55
B106	SP83	8 l gray vio	1.75	.55
B107	SP83	10 l brt bl	1.90	.70
B108	SP83	12 l brt ultra	2.10	1.40
B109	SP83	16 l bl grn	2.25	1.75
	Nos. B99-B109 (11)		14.30	7.75

9th anniv. of accession of King Carol II. Exist imperf. Value $175, unused or used.

King Carol II
SP87

SP88

SP89

SP90

SP91

Wmk. 230

1940, June 8   Photo.   Perf. 13½

B113	SP87	1 l + 50b dl pur	.75	.30
B114	SP88	4 l + 1 l fawn	.75	.45
B115	SP89	6 l + 1 l blue	.75	.45
B116	SP90	8 l rose brn	1.10	.65
B117	SP89	16 l ultra	1.25	.90
B118	SP91	32 l dk vio brn	2.00	1.25
	Nos. B113-B118 (6)		6.60	4.00

10th anniv. of accession of King Carol II. Exist imperf. Value $200, unused or used.

King Carol II

SP92

SP93

1940, June 1

B119	SP92	1 l + 50b dk grn	.25	.25
B120	SP92	2.50 l + 50b Prus grn	.25	.25
B121	SP93	3 l + 1 l rose car	.35	.25
B122	SP92	3.50 l + 50b choc	.35	.35
B123	SP93	4 l + 1 l org brn	.50	.35
B124	SP93	6 l + 1 l sapphire	.75	.25
B125	SP93	9 l + 1 l brt bl	.85	.70
B126	SP93	14 l + 1 l dk bl grn	1.10	.90
	Nos. B119-B126 (8)		4.40	3.30

Surtax was for Romania's air force. Exist imperf. Value $200, unused or used.

View of
Danube
SP94

Greco-Roman
Ruins — SP95

Designs: 3 l+1 l, Hotin Castle. 4 l+1 l, Hurez Monastery. 5 l+1 l, Church in Bucovina. 8 l+1 l, Tower. 12 l+2 l, Village church, Transylvania. 16 l+2 l, Arch in Bucharest.

Inscribed: "Straja Tarii 8 Junie 1940"

1940, June 8   Perf. 14½x14, 14x14½

B127	SP94	1 l + 1 l dp vio	.40	.25
B128	SP95	2 l + 1 l red brn	.45	.30
B129	SP94	3 l + 1 l yel grn	.50	.35
B130	SP94	4 l + 1 l grnsh blk	.55	.40
B131	SP95	5 l + 1 l org ver	.60	.45
B132	SP95	8 l + 1 l brn car	.85	.60
B133	SP95	12 l + 2 l ultra	1.75	1.10
B134	SP95	16 l + 2 l dk bl gray	3.00	2.00
	Nos. B127-B134 (8)		8.10	5.45

Issued to honor Straja Tarii, a national organization for boys. Exist imperf. Value $140, unused or used.

King Michael — SP102

1940-42   Photo.   Wmk. 230

B138	SP102	1 l + 50b yel grn		
B138A	SP102	2 l + 50b yel grn	.25	.25
B139	SP102	2.50 l + 50b dk bl grn	.25	.25
B140	SP102	3 l + 1 l pur	.25	.25
B141	SP102	3.50 l + 50b rose pink	.25	.25
B141A	SP102	4 l + 50b org ver	.25	.25
B142	SP102	4 l + 1 l brn	.25	.25
B142A	SP102	5 l + 1 l dp plum	1.25	
B143	SP102	6 l + 1 l lt ultra	.25	.25
B143A	SP102	7 l + 1 l sl grn	.50	.25
B143B	SP102	8 l + 1 l dp vio	.50	
B143C	SP102	12 l + 1 l brn vio	.50	.25
B144	SP102	14 l + 1 l brt bl	.50	.25
B144A	SP102	19 l + 1 l lil rose	1.00	.25
	Nos. B138-B144A (14)		6.00	3.50

Issue years: Nos. B138A, B141A, B142A, B143A, B143B, B143C, B144A, 1942; others, 1940.

Corneliu Codreanu — SP103

1940, Nov. 8   Unwmk.   Perf. 13½

B145	SP103	7 l + 30 l dk grn	6.00	9.00

13th anniv. of the founding of the Iron Guard by Corneliu Codreanu.

Vasile Marin — SP104

Design: 15 l+15 l, Ion Mota.

1941, Jan. 13

B146	SP104	7 l + 7 l rose brn	3.50	6.00
B147	SP104	15 l + 15 l slate bl	5.00	9.00

Souvenir Sheet

Imperf

B148		Sheet of 2	75.00	125.00
a.	SP104	7 l + 7 l Prus bl	15.00	35.00
b.	SP104	15 l + 15 l Prus green		15.00	35.00

Vasile Marin and Ion Mota, Iron Guardists who died in the Spanish Civil War. No. B148 sold for 300 lei.

Crown, Leaves and Bible — SP107

Designs: 2 l+43 l, Library shelves. 7 l+38 l, Carol I Foundation, Bucharest. 10 l+35 l, King Carol I. 16 l+29 l, Kings Michael and Carol I.

Inscribed: "1891 1941"

Wmk. 230

1941, May 9   Photo.   Perf. 13½

B149	SP107	1.50 l + 43.50 l pur	1.60	2.50
B150	SP107	2 l + 43 l rose brn	1.60	2.50
B151	SP107	7 l + 38 l rose	1.60	2.50
B152	SP107	10 l + 35 l ol blk	1.60	2.50
B153	SP107	16 l + 29 l brown	1.60	2.50
	Nos. B149-B153 (5)		8.00	12.50

50th anniv. of the Carol I Foundation, established to endow research and stimulate the arts.

Same Overprinted in Red or Black

1941, Aug.

B154	SP107	1.50 l + 43.50 l (R)	2.00	4.00
B155	SP107	2 l + 43 l	2.00	4.00
B156	SP107	7 l + 38 l	2.00	4.00
B157	SP107	10 l + 35 l (R)	2.00	4.00
B158	SP107	16 l + 29 l	2.00	4.00

Occupation of Cernauti, Bucovina.

Same Overprinted in Red or Black

1941, Aug.

B159	SP107	1.50 l + 43.50 l (R)	2.00	4.00
B160	SP107	2 l + 43 l	2.00	4.00
B161	SP107	7 l + 38 l	2.00	4.00
B162	SP107	10 l + 35 l (R)	2.00	4.00
B163	SP107	16 l + 29 l	2.00	4.00
	Nos. B154-B163 (10)		20.00	40.00

Occupation of Chisinau, Bessarabia.

Romanian Red Cross — SP111

1941, Aug.   Perf. 13½

B164	SP111	1.50 l + 38.50 l	1.20	2.00
B165	SP111	2 l + 38 l	1.20	2.00
B166	SP111	5 l + 35 l	1.20	2.00
B167	SP111	7 l + 33 l	1.20	2.00
B168	SP111	10 l + 30 l	1.50	2.00
	Nos. B164-B168 (5)		6.30	10.00

Souvenir Sheet

Imperf

Without Gum

B169		Sheet of 2	20.00	20.00
a.	SP111	7 l + 33 l brown & red	2.75	3.50
b.	SP111	10 l + 30 l brt blue & red	2.75	3.50

The surtax on Nos. B164-B169 was for the Romanian Red Cross. No. B169 sold for 200 l.

King Michael and Stephen the Great SP113

Hotin and Akkerman Castles SP114

Romanian and German Soldiers SP115

Soldiers SP116

SP118

1941, Oct. 11   Perf. 14½x13½

B170	SP113	10 l + 30 l ultra	2.25	3.00
B171	SP114	12 l + 28 l dl org red	2.25	3.00
B172	SP115	16 l + 24 l lt brn	2.50	3.00
B173	SP116	20 l + 20 l dk vio	2.50	3.00
	Nos. B170-B173 (4)		9.50	12.00

Souvenir Sheet

Imperf

Without Gum

B174	SP118	Sheet of 2	12.00	17.50
a.		16 l blue gray	1.50	4.50
b.		20 l brown carmine	1.50	4.50

No. B174 sold for 200 l. The surtax aided the Anti-Bolshevism crusade.

Nos. B170-B174 Overprinted

1941, Oct.   Perf. 14½x13½

B175	SP113	10 l + 30 l ultra	2.00	3.00
B176	SP114	12 l + 28 l dl org red	2.00	3.00
B177	SP115	16 l + 24 l lt brn	2.50	3.00
B178	SP116	20 l + 20 l dk vio	2.50	3.00
	Nos. B175-B178 (4)		9.00	12.00

Souvenir Sheet

Imperf

Without Gum

B178A	SP118	Sheet of 2	17.50	25.00

Occupation of Odessa, Russia.

Types of Regular Issue, 1941

Designs: 3 l+50b, Sucevita Monastery, Bucovina. 5.50 l+50b, Rughi Monastery, Soroca, Bessarabia. 5.50 l+1 l, Tighina Fortress, Bessarabia. 6.50 l+1 l, Soroca Fortress, Bessarabia. 8 l+1 l, St. Nicholas Monastery, Suceava, Bucovina. 9.50 l+1 l, Milisauti Monastery, Bucovina. 10.50 l+1 l, Putna Monastery, Bucovina. 16 l+1 l, Cetatea Alba Fortress, Bessarabia. 25 l+1 l, Hotin Fortress, Bessarabia.

1941, Dec. 1   Wmk. 230   Perf. 13½

B179	A179	3 l + 50b rose brn	.45	.25
B180	A179	5.50 l + 50b red org	.60	.50
B181	A179	5.50 l + 1 l blk	.60	.50
B182	A179	6.50 l + 1 l dk brn	.75	.75
B183	A179	8 l + 1 l lt bl	.60	.40
B184	A177	9.50 l + 1 l gray bl	.75	.60
B185	A179	10.50 l + 1 l dk bl	.80	.40
B186	A179	16 l + 1 l vio	.90	.65
B187	A179	25 l + 1 l gray blk	1.00	.70
	Nos. B179-B187 (9)		6.45	4.75

Titu Maiorescu SP128

1942, Oct. 5

B188	SP128	9 l + 11 l dl vio	.70	1.00
B189	SP128	20 l + 20 l yel brn	1.75	2.50
B190	SP128	20 l + 30 l blue	2.00	3.00
	Nos. B188-B190 (3)		4.45	6.50

Souvenir Sheet

Imperf

Without Gum

B191	SP128	Sheet of 3	9.00	15.00

The surtax aided war prisoners.

No. B191 contains one each of Nos. B188-B190, imperf. Sold for 200 l.

Statue of Miron Costin at Jassy — SP130

1942, Dec.   Perf. 13½

B192	SP130	6 l + 44 l sepia	1.75	2.75
B193	SP130	12 l + 38 l violet	1.75	2.75
B194	SP130	24 l + 26 l blue	1.75	2.75
	Nos. B192-B194 (3)		5.25	8.25

Anniv. of the conquest of Transdniestria, and for use only in this territory which includes Odessa and land beyond the Duiester.

Michael, Antonescu, Hitler, Mussolini and Bessarabia Map SP131

Michael, Antonescu and (inset) Stephen of Moldavia SP132

Romanian Troops Crossing Pruth River to Retake Bessarabia — SP133

1942   Wmk. 230   Photo.   Perf. 13½

B195	SP131	9 l + 41 l red brn	2.75	3.50
B196	SP132	18 l + 32 l ol gray	2.75	3.50
B197	SP133	20 l + 30 l brt ultra	2.75	3.50
	Nos. B195-B197 (3)		8.25	10.50

First anniversary of liberation of Bessarabia.

Bucovina Coats of Arms
SP134   SP135

Design: 20 l+30 l, Bucovina arms with triple-barred cross.

1942, Nov. 1

B198	SP134	9 l + 41 l brt ver	2.75	3.50
B199	SP135	18 l + 32 l blue	2.75	3.50
B200	SP135	20 l + 30 l car rose	2.75	3.50
	Nos. B198-B200 (3)		8.25	10.50

First anniversary of liberation of Bucovina.

Andrei Muresanu
SP137

1942, Dec. 30
B201 SP137 5 l + 5 l violet   1.00 *1.75*
80th death anniv. of Andrei Muresanu, writer.

Avram Jancu, National
Hero — SP138

1943, Feb. 15
B202 SP138 16 l + 4 l brown   1.00 *1.75*

Nurse Aiding Wounded Soldier SP139

1943, Mar. 1   **Perf. 14½x14**
B203 SP139 12 l + 88 l red brn &
                              ultra   1.00 *1.25*
B204 SP139 16 l + 84 l brt ultra
                              & red   1.00 *1.25*
B205 SP139 20 l + 80 l ol gray &
                              red   1.00 *1.25*
      Nos. B203-B205 (3)   3.00 *3.75*

Souvenir Sheet
           Imperf
B206   Sheet of 2   8.00 *9.00*
   a. SP139 16 l + 84 l bright ultra &
               red   2.00 *2.50*
   b. SP139 20 l + 80 l olive gray &
               red   2.00 *2.50*

Surtax on Nos. B203-B206 aided the Romanian Red Cross.
No. B206 sold for 500 l.

Sword Hilt — SP141   Sword Severing Chain — SP142

Soldier and Family, Guardian Angel — SP143

           Perf. 14x14½
1943, June 22   **Wmk. 276**
B207 SP141 36 l + 164 l brn   3.75 *4.50*
B208 SP142 62 l + 138 l brt bl   3.75 *4.50*
B209 SP143 76 l + 124 l ver   3.75 *4.50*
      Nos. B207-B209 (3)   11.25 *13.50*

Souvenir Sheet
           Imperf
B210   Sheet of 2   20.00 *20.00*
   a. SP142 62 l + 138 l deep blue 5.75 *5.75*
   b. SP143 76 l + 124 l red org   5.75 *5.75*

2nd anniv. of Romania's entrance into WWII. No. B210 sold for 600 l.

Petru Maior — SP145

Horea, Closca and Crisan SP148

32 l+118 l, Gheorghe Sincai. 36 l+114 l, Timotei Cipariu. 91 l+109 l, Gheorghe Cosbuc.

Perf. 13½; 14½x14 (No. B214)
1943, Aug. 15   Photo.   Wmk. 276
B211 SP145 16 l + 134 l red org   .70 *1.40*
B212 SP145 32 l + 118 l lt bl   .70 *1.40*
B213 SP145 36 l + 114 l vio   .70 *1.40*
B214 SP145 62 l + 138 l car rose .70 *1.40*
B215 SP145 91 l + 109 l dk brn   .70 *1.40*
      Nos. B211-B215 (5)   3.50 *7.00*
      See Nos. B219-B223.

King Michael and Ion Antonescu
SP150

1943, Sept. 6
B216 SP150 16 l + 24 l blue   2.50 *3.50*
3rd anniv. of the government of King Michael and Marshal Ion Antonescu.

Symbols of Sports — SP151

1943, Sept. 26   **Perf. 13½**
B217 SP151 16 l + 24 l ultra   .75 *1.00*
B218 SP151 16 l + 24 l red brn   .75 *1.00*
Surtax for the benefit of Romanian sports.

Portrait Type of 1943
Designs: 16 l+134 l, Samuel Micu. 51 l+99 l, George Lazar. 56 l+144 l, Octavian Goga. 76 l+ 124 l, Simeon Barnutiu. 77 l+123 l, Andrei Saguna.

1943, Oct. 1
B219 SP145 16 l + 134 l red vio   .60 *1.20*
B220 SP145 51 l + 99 l orange   .60 *1.20*
B221 SP145 56 l + 144 l rose car .60 *1.20*
B222 SP145 76 l + 124 l slate bl .60 *1.20*
B223 SP145 77 l + 123 l brown   .60 *1.20*
      Nos. B219-B223 (5)   3.00 *6.00*
      The surtax aided refugees.

Calafat, 1877 — SP157

Designs: 2 l +2 l, World War I scene. 3.50 l+3.50 l, Stalingrad, 1943. 4 l+4 l, Tisza, 1919. 5 l+5 l, Odessa, 1941. 6.50 l+6.50 l, Caucasus, 1942. 7 l+7 l, Sevastopol, 1942. 20 l+20 l, Prince Ribescu and King Michael.

1943, Nov. 10   Photo.   Perf. 13½
B224 SP157 1 l + 1 l red brn   .30 *.50*
B225 SP157 2 l + 2 l dl vio   .30 *.50*
B226 SP157 3.50 l + 3.50 l lt ul-
                            tra   .30 *.50*
B227 SP157 4 l + 4 l mag   .30 *.50*
B228 SP157 5 l + 5 l red org   .70 *1.25*
B229 SP157 6.50 l + 6.50 l bl   .70 *1.25*

B230 SP157 7 l + 7 l dp vio   .80 *2.25*
B231 SP157 20 l + 20 l crim   1.25 *3.75*
      Nos. B224-B231 (8)   4.65 *10.50*
Centenary of Romanian Artillery.

Emblem of Romanian Engineers' Association — SP165

1943, Dec. 19   **Perf. 14**
B232 SP165 21 l + 29 l sepia   1.10 *1.75*
Society of Romanian Engineers, 25th anniv.

Motorcycle, Truck and Post Horn — SP166

Post Wagon SP167

Roman Post Chariot SP168

Post Rider — SP169

1944, Feb. 1   Wmk. 276   Perf. 14
B233 SP166 1 l + 49 l org
                            red   2.00 *3.00*
B234 SP167 2 l + 48 l lil rose   2.00 *3.00*
B235 SP168 4 l + 46 l ultra   2.00 *3.00*
B236 SP169 10 l + 40 l dl vio   2.00 *3.00*
      Nos. B233-B236 (4)   8.00 *12.00*

Souvenir Sheets
           Perf. 14
B237   Sheet of 3   8.00 *12.50*
   a. SP166 1 l + 49 l orange red .80 *1.20*
   b. SP167 2 l + 48 l orange red .80 *1.20*
   c. SP168 4 l + 46 l orange red .80 *1.20*
           Imperf
B238   Sheet of 3   8.00 *12.50*
   a. SP166 1 l + 49 l dull violet .80 *1.20*
   b. SP167 2 l + 48 l dull violet .80 *1.20*
   c. SP168 4 l + 46 l dull violet .80 *1.20*

The surtax aided communications employees.
No. B238 is imperf. between the stamps.
Nos. B237-B238 each sold for 200 l.

Nos. B233-B238 Overprinted

1944, Feb. 28
B239 SP166 1 l + 49 l org
                            red   4.50 *6.50*
B240 SP167 2 l + 48 l lil rose   4.50 *6.50*

B241 SP168 4 l + 46 l ultra   4.50 *6.50*
B242 SP169 10 l + 40 l dl vio   4.50 *6.50*
      Nos. B239-B242 (4)   18.00 *26.00*

Souvenir Sheets
     Perf. 14
B243   Sheet of 3   17.50 *25.00*
       Imperf
B244   Sheet of 3   17.50 *25.00*

Rugby Player — SP171

1944, Mar. 16   **Perf. 15**
B245 SP171 16 l + 184 l crimson 4.75 *7.50*
30th anniv. of the Romanian Rugby Assoc. The surtax was used to encourage the sport.

Dr. N. Cretzulescu SP172

1944, Mar. 1   Photo.   Perf. 13½
B246 SP172 35 l + 65 l brt ultra 1.10 *1.75*
Centenary of medical teaching in Romania.

Queen Mother Helen — SP173

1945, Feb. 10
B247 SP173 4.50 l + 5.50 l multi .35 *.70*
B248 SP173 10 l + 40 l multi   .45 *.90*
B249 SP173 15 l + 75 l multi   .70 *1.40*
B250 SP173 20 l + 80 l multi   1.00 *2.00*
      Nos. B247-B250 (4)   2.50 *5.00*
The surtax aided the Romanian Red Cross.

Kings Ferdinand and Michael and Map SP174

1945, Feb.   **Perf. 14**
B251 SP174 75 l + 75 l dk ol brn .50 *.75*
Romania's liberation.

Stefan Tomsa Church, Radaseni SP175

Municipal Home SP176

Gathering
Fruit — SP177

School
SP178

1944   Wmk. 276   Photo.   Perf. 14
B252 SP175   5 l + 145 l brt bl   1.00 1.00
B253 SP176 12 l + 138 l car rose   1.00 1.00
B254 SP177 15 l + 135 l red org   1.00 1.00
B255 SP178 32 l + 118 l dk brn   1.00 1.00
   Nos. B252-B255 (4)   4.00 4.00

King Michael and Carol I Foundation,
Bucharest — SP179

Design: 200 l, King Carol I and Foundation.

1945, Feb. 10   Perf. 13
B256 SP179 20 l + 180 l dp
                 org   .50   .75
B257 SP179 25 l + 175 l slate   .50   .75
B258 SP179 35 l + 165 l cl brn   .50   .75
B259 SP179 75 l + 125 l pale
                 vio   .50   .75
   Nos. B256-B259 (4)   2.00 3.00
Souvenir Sheet
Imperf
Without Gum
B260 SP179 200 l blue   7.50 15.00
Surtax was to aid in rebuilding the Public
Library, Bucharest.
#B256-B259 were printed in sheets of 4.
No. B260 sold for 1200 l.

Ion G.
Duca
SP181

16 l+184 l, Virgil Madgearu. 20 l+180 l,
Nikolai Jorga. 32 l+168 l, Ilie Pintilie.
35 l+165 l, Bernath Andrei. 36 l+164 l, Filimon
Sarbu.

1945, Apr. 30   Perf. 13
B261 SP181 12 l + 188 l dk bl   .70 1.00
B262 SP181 16 l + 184 l cl brn   .70 1.00
B263 SP181 20 l + 180 l blk
                 brn   .70 1.00
B264 SP181 32 l + 168 l brt
                 red   .70 1.00
B265 SP181 35 l + 165 l Prus
                 bl   .70 1.00
B266 SP181 36 l + 164 l lt vio   .70 1.00
   Nos. B261-B266 (6)   4.20 6.00
Souvenir Sheet
Imperf
B267   Sheet of 2   24.00 40.00
  a.   SP181 32 l + 168 l mag   4.75 7.50
  b.   SP181 35 l + 165 l mag   4.75 7.50
Honoring six victims of Nazi terrorism.
No. B267 sold for 1,000 l.

Books and
Torch — SP188

Designs: #B269, Flags of Russia and
Romania. #B270, Kremlin, Moscow. #B271,
Tudor Vladimirescu and Alexander Nevsky.

1945, May 20   Perf. 14
B268 SP188 20 l + 80 l ol grn   .40   .60
B269 SP188 35 l + 165 l brt
                 rose   .40   .60
B270 SP188 75 l + 225 l blue   .40   .60
B271 SP188 80 l + 420 l cl brn   .40   .60
   Nos. B268-B271 (4)   1.60 2.40
Souvenir Sheet
Imperf
Without Gum
B272   Sheet of 2   8.50 17.50
  a.   SP189 35 l + 165 l bright
                 red   2.00 3.50
  b.   SP190 75 l + 225 l bright
                 red   2.00 3.50
1st Soviet-Romanian Cong., May 20, 1945.
No. B272 sold for 900 l.

Karl
Marx — SP193

120 l+380 l, Friedrich Engels. 155 l+445 l,
Lenin.

1945, June 30   Perf. 13½
B273 SP193 75 l + 425 l car
                 rose   3.00 6.00
B274 SP193 120 l + 380 l bl   3.00 6.00
B275 SP193 155 l + 445 l dk
                 vio brn   3.00 6.00
Imperf
B276 SP193 75 l + 425 l bl   8.50 15.00
B277 SP193 120 l + 380 l dk
                 vio brn   8.50 15.00
B278 SP193 155 l + 445 l car
                 rose   8.50 15.00
   Nos. B273-B278 (6)   34.50 63.00
Nos. B276-B278 were printed in sheets of 4.

Woman Throwing
Discus — SP196

Designs: 16 l+184 l, Diving. 20 l+180 l, Skiing. 32 l+168 l, Volleyball. 35 l+165 l, Worker
athlete.

Wmk. 276
1945, Aug. 5   Photo.   Perf. 13
B279 SP196 12 l +188 l ol
                 gray   2.00 4.00
B280 SP196 16 l +184 l lt ultra   2.00 4.00
B281 SP196 20 l +180 l dp grn   2.00 4.00
B282 SP196 32 l +168 l mag   2.00 4.00
B283 SP196 35 l +165 l brt bl   2.00 4.00
Imperf
B284 SP196 12 l +188 l org
                 red   2.00 4.00
B285 SP196 16 l +184 l vio
                 brn   2.00 4.00
B286 SP196 20 l +180 l dp vio   2.00 4.00
B287 SP196 32 l +168 l yel   2.00 4.00
B288 SP196 35 l +165 l dk ol
                 grn   2.00 4.00
   Nos. B279-B288 (10)   20.00 40.00
Printed in sheets of 9.

Mail Plane
and Bird
Carrying
Letter
SP201

1945, Aug. 5   Perf. 13½
B289 SP201 200 l + 1000 l bl
                 & dk bl   25.00 45.00
  a.   With label   67.50 160.00
The surtax on Nos. B279-B289 was for the
Office of Popular Sports.
Issued in sheets of 30 stamps and 10
labels, arranged 10x4 with second and fourth
horizontal rows each having five alternating
labels.

Agriculture and Industry
United — SP202

King
Michael
SP203

1945, Aug. 23   Perf. 14
B290 SP202 100 l + 400 l red   .80 2.00
B291 SP203 200 l + 800 l blue   .85 2.00
The surtax was for the Farmers' Front.
For surcharges see Nos. B318-B325.

Political
Amnesty
SP204

Military
Amnesty
SP205

Agrarian
Amnesty
SP206

Tudor
Vladimirescu
SP207

Nicolae Horia
SP208

Reconstruction — SP209

1945, Aug.   Perf. 13
B292 SP204 20 l + 580 l
                 choc   10.00 10.00
B293 SP204 20 l + 580 l
                 mag   10.00 10.00
B294 SP205 40 l + 560 l
                 blue   10.00 10.00
B295 SP205 40 l + 560 l sl
                 grn   10.00 10.00
B296 SP206 55 l + 545 l
                 red   10.00 10.00
B297 SP206 55 l + 545 l
                 dk vio
                 brn   10.00 10.00
B298 SP207 60 l + 540 l
                 ultra   10.00 10.00
B299 SP207 60 l + 540 l
                 choc   10.00 10.00
B300 SP208 80 l + 520 l
                 red   10.00 10.00
B301 SP208 80 l + 520 l
                 mag   10.00 10.00
B302 SP209 100 l + 500 l sl
                 grn   10.00 10.00
B303 SP209 100 l + 500 l
                 red brn   10.00 10.00
   Nos. B292-B303 (12)   120.00 120.00
1st anniv. of Romania's armistice with Rus-
sia. Issued in panes of four.
Nos. B292-B303 also exist on coarse gray-
ish paper, ungummed (same value).

Electric
Train
SP210

Coats of
Arms
SP211

Truck on
Mountain
Road
SP212

Oil Field
SP213

"Agriculture" — SP214

1945, Oct. 1   Perf. 14
B304 SP210 10 l + 490 l ol
                 grn   .70   .70
B305 SP211 20 l + 480 l red
                 brn   .70   .70
B306 SP212 25 l + 475 l brn
                 vio   .70   .70
B307 SP213 55 l + 445 l ultra   .70   .70
B308 SP214 100 l + 400 l brn   .70   .70
Imperf
B309 SP210 10 l + 490 l blue   .70   .70
B310 SP211 20 l + 480 l vio   .70   .70
B311 SP212 25 l + 475 l bl
                 grn   .70   .70
B312 SP213 55 l + 445 l gray   .70   .70
B313 SP214 100 l + 400 l dp
                 mag   .70   .70
   Nos. B304-B313 (10)   7.00 7.00
16th Congress of the General Assoc. of
Romanian Engineers.

"Brotherhood" — SP215

160 l+1840 l, "Peace." 320 l+1680 l, Hammer crushing Nazism. 440 l+2560 l, "World Unity."

1945, Dec. 5   *Perf. 14*
B314	SP215	80 l + 920 l mag	17.50	25.00
B315	SP215	160 l + 1840 l org brn	17.50	25.00
B316	SP215	320 l + 1680 l vio	17.50	25.00
B317	SP215	440 l + 2560 l yel grn	17.50	25.00
	Nos. B314-B317 (4)		70.00	100.00

World Trade Union Congress at Paris, Sept. 25-Oct. 10, 1945.

Nos. B290 and B291 Surcharged in Various Colors

1946, Jan. 20
B318	SP202	10 l + 90 l (Bk)	.85	1.75
B319	SP203	10 l + 90 l (R)	.85	1.75
B320	SP202	20 l + 80 l (G)	.85	1.75
B321	SP203	20 l + 80 l (Bk)	.85	1.75
B322	SP202	80 l + 120 l (Bl)	.85	1.75
B323	SP203	80 l + 120 l (Bk)	.85	1.75
B324	SP202	100 l + 150 l (Bk)	.85	1.75
B325	SP203	100 l + 150 l (R)	.85	1.75
	Nos. B318-B325 (8)		6.80	14.00

Re-distribution of Land — SP219

Sower SP220

Ox Team Drawing Hay SP221

Old and New Plowing Methods SP222

1946, Mar. 6
B326	SP219	50 l + 450 l red	.40	.75
B327	SP220	100 l + 900 l purple	.40	.75
B328	SP221	200 l + 800 l orange	.40	.75
B329	SP222	400 l + 1600 l dk grn	.40	.75
	Nos. B326-B329 (4)		1.60	3.00

Agrarian reform law of Mar. 23, 1945.

Philharmonic Types of Regular Issue
Perf. 13, 13½x13
1946, Apr. 26   Photo.   Wmk. 276
B330	A211	200 l + 800 l brt red	.80	1.50
a.		Sheet of 12	22.50	25.00
B331	A213	350 l + 1650 l dk bl	.90	1.75
a.		Sheet of 12	22.50	25.00

Issued in sheets containing 12 stamps and 4 labels, with bars of music in the margins.

Agriculture SP223

Designs: 10 l+200 l, Hurdling. 80 l+200 l, Research. 80 l+300 l, Industry. 200 l+400 l, Workers and flag.

Wmk. 276
1946, July 28   Photo.   *Perf. 11½*
B332	SP223	10 l + 100 l dk org brn & red	.40	.75
B333	SP223	10 l + 200 l bl & red brn	.40	.75
B334	SP223	80 l + 200 l brn vio & brn	.40	.75
B335	SP223	80 l + 300 l dk org brn & rose lil	.40	.75
B336	SP223	200 l + 400 l Prus bl & red	.40	.75
	Nos. B332-B336 (5)		2.00	3.75

Issued in panes of 4 stamps with marginal inscription.

Dove — SP228

1946, Oct. 20   *Perf. 13½x13, Imperf.*
B338	SP228	300 l + 1200 l scar	.70	1.25

Souvenir Sheet
Perf. 14x14½
B339	SP228	1000 l scarlet	5.00	10.00

Romanian-Soviet friendship. No. B339 sold for 6000 lei.

Skiing — SP230

1946, Sept. 1   *Perf. 11½, Imperf.*
B340	SP230	160 l + 1340 l dk grn	.50	.75

Surtax for Office of Popular Sports.

Spinning SP231   Reaping SP232

Riding — SP233   Water Carrier SP234

1946, Nov. 20   *Perf. 14*
B342	SP231	80 l + 320 l brt red	.35	.75
B343	SP232	140 l + 360 l dp org	.35	.75
B344	SP233	300 l + 450 l brn ol	.35	.75
B345	SP234	600 l + 900 l ultra	.35	.75
	Nos. B342-B345 (4)		1.40	3.00

Democratic Women's Org. of Romania.

Angel with Food and Clothing SP235   Bread for Hungry Family SP236

Care for Needy — SP237

1947, Jan. 15   *Perf. 13½x14*
B346	SP235	1500 l + 3500 l red org	.30	.60
B347	SP236	3700 l + 5300 l dp vio	.30	.60

Miniature Sheet
Imperf
Without Gum
B348	SP237	5000 l + 5000 l ultra	7.50	15.00

Surtax helped the social relief fund. No. B348 is miniature sheet of one.

Student Reciting SP238

Allegory of Education — SP242

SP243

#B350, Weaving class. #B351, Young machinist. #B352, Romanian school.

Perf. 14x13½
1947, Mar. 5   Photo.   Wmk. 276
B349	SP238	200 l + 200 l vio bl	.25	.35
B350	SP238	300 l + 300 l red brn	.25	.35
B351	SP238	600 l + 600 l Prus grn	.25	.35
B352	SP238	1200 l + 1200 l ultra	.25	.35
B353	SP242	1500 l + 1500 l dp rose	.25	.35
	Nos. B349-B353 (5)		1.25	1.75

Souvenir Sheet
Imperf
B354	SP243	3700 l + 3700 l dl brn & dl bl	2.25	5.00

Romania's vocational schools, 50th anniv.

Victor Babes — SP244

#B356, Michael Eminescu. #B357, Nicolae Grigorescu. #B358, Peter Movila. #B359, Aleksander S. Pushkin. #B360, Mikhail V. Lomonosov. #B361, Peter I. Tchaikovsky. #B362, Ilya E. Repin.

1947, Apr. 18   *Perf. 14*
B355	SP244	1500 l + 1500 l red org	.25	.25
B356	SP244	1500 l + 1500 l dk ol grn	.25	.25
B357	SP244	1500 l + 1500 l dk bl	.25	.25
B358	SP244	1500 l + 1500 l dp plum	.25	.25
B359	SP244	1500 l + 1500 l scar	.25	.25
B360	SP244	1500 l + 1500 l rose brn	.25	.25
B361	SP244	1500 l + 1500 l ultra	.25	.25
B362	SP244	1500 l + 1500 l choc	.25	.25
	Nos. B355-B362 (8)		2.00	2.00

Transportation — SP252

Labor Day: No. B364, Farmer. No. B365, Farm woman. No. B366, Scientist and Romanian Academy of Sciences. No. B367, Laborer and factory.

1947, May 1
B363	SP252	1000 l + 1000 l dk ol brn	.30	.50
B364	SP252	1500 l + 1500 l red brn	.30	.50
B365	SP252	2000 l + 2000 l blue	.30	.50
B366	SP252	2500 l + 2500 l red vio	.30	.50
B367	SP252	3000 l + 3000 l crim rose	.30	.50
	Nos. B363-B367 (5)		1.50	2.50

No. 650 Surcharged in Carmine

1947, Sept. 6   *Perf. 13½*
B368	A234	2 l + 3 l on 36,000 l vio	1.00	2.00

Balkan Games of 1947, Bucharest.

Type of 1947 Surcharged in Carmine

Design: Cathedral of Curtea de Arges.

1947, Oct. 30   *Imperf.*
B369 A235 5 l + 5 l brt ultra .70 1.00
Soviet-Romanian Congress, Nov. 1-7.

Plowing — SP257

Perf. 14x14½
1947, Oct. 5   Photo.   Wmk. 276
B370 SP257 1 l + 1 l shown .25 .25
B371 SP257 2 l + 2 l Sawmill .25 .25
B372 SP257 3 l + 3 l Refinery .25 .25
B373 SP257 4 l + 4 l Steel mill .25 .25
Nos. B370-B373,CB12 (5) 1.70 1.70
17th Congress of the General Assoc. of Romanian Engineers.

Allegory of Industry, Science and Agriculture — SP258

Winged Man Holding Hammer and Sickle SP259

1947, Nov. 10   Perf. 14½x14
B374 SP258 2 l + 10 l rose lake .30 .30
B375 SP259 7 l + 10 l bluish blk .30 .30
2nd Trade Union Conf., Nov. 10.

SP260

SP264

Designs: 1 l+1 l, Convoy of Food for Moldavia. 2 l+2 l, "Everything for the Front-Everything for Victory." 3 l+3 l, Woman, child and hospital. 4 l+4 l, "Help the Famine-stricken Regions." 5 l+5 l, "Three Years of Action."

1947, Nov. 7   Perf. 14
B376 SP260 1 l + 1 l dk gray bl .30 .35
B377 SP260 2 l + 2 l dk brn .30 .35
B378 SP260 3 l + 3 l rose lake .30 .35

B379 SP260 4 l + 4 l brt ultra .30 .35
B380 SP264 5 l + 5 l red .30 .35
Nos. B376-B380 (5) 1.50 1.75
Issued in sheets of eight.

Discus Thrower — SP265

Balkan Games of 1947: 2 l+2 l, Runner. 5 l+5 l, Boy and girl athletes.

Wmk. 276
1948, Feb.   Photo.   Perf. 13½
B381 SP265 1 l + 1 l dk brn .45 .50
B382 SP265 2 l + 2 l car lake .60 .65
B383 SP265 5 l + 5 l blue 1.00 1.25
Nos. B381-B383,CB13-CB14 (5) 5.05 4.10

Labor — SP266

Youths Following Filimon Sarbu Banner — SP269

3 l+3 l, Agriculture. 5 l+5 l, Education.

1948, Mar. 15
B384 SP266 2 l + 2 l dk sl bl .35 .70
B385 SP266 3 l + 3 l gray grn .40 .70
B386 SP266 5 l + 5 l red brn .50 .70
Imperf
B387 SP269 8 l + 8 l dk car rose .70 .70
Nos. B384-B387,CB15 (5) 3.05 3.40
No. B387 issued in triangular sheets of 4.

Gliders — SP270

Sailboat Race SP271

Designs: No. B389, Early plane. No. B390, Plane over farm. No. B391, Transport plane. B393, Training ship, Mircea. B394, Danube ferry. B395, S.S. Transylvania.

1948, July 26   Perf. 14x14½
B388 SP270 2 l + 2 l blue 1.50 1.50
B389 SP270 5 l + 5 l pur 1.50 1.50
B390 SP270 8 l + 8 l dk car rose 2.50 2.50
B391 SP270 10 l + 10 l choc 3.25 3.25
B392 SP271 2 l + 2 l dk grn 1.50 1.50
B393 SP271 5 l + 5 l slate 1.50 1.50
B394 SP271 8 l + 8 l brt bl 2.50 2.50
B395 SP271 10 l + 10 l ver 3.25 3.25
Nos. B388-B395 (8) 17.50 17.50
Air and Sea Communications Day.

Type of Regular Issue and

Torch, Pen, Ink and Flag SP272

Alexandru Sahia — SP273

Perf. 14x13½, 13½x14
1948, Sept. 12
B396 A241 5 l + 5 l crimson .70 .70
B397 SP272 10 l + 10 l violet 1.10 1.10
B398 SP273 15 l + 15 l blue 1.50 1.50
Nos. B396-B398 (3) 3.30 3.30
Week of the Democratic Press, Sept. 12-19.
Nos. B396-B398 were also issued imperf. Value, unused $4.50, used $7.
1,500 sets of Nos. 695, B396-B398 perf and B396-B398 imperf were overprinted at "The Week of the Democratic Press" exposition. These stamps were not recognized by the Romanian PTT, although some examples were used on items mailed from the exposition post office.

Romanian-Soviet Association Emblem — SP274

Design: 15 l+15 l, Spasski Tower, Kremlin.

1948, Oct. 29   Perf. 14
B399 SP274 10 l + 10 l gray grn 2.50 3.00
B400 SP274 15 l + 15 l dp ultra 3.00 4.50
No. B399 was issued in sheets of 50 stamps and 50 labels.

Symbols of United Labor SP275

Agriculture SP276

Industry — SP277

1948, May 1   Perf. 14x13½, 13½x14
B401 SP275 8 l + 8 l red 1.50 2.00
B402 SP276 10 l + 10 l ol grn 1.75 2.50
B403 SP277 12 l + 12 l red brn 3.00 3.75
Nos. B401-B403 (3) 6.25 8.25
Labor Day, May 1. See No. CB17.

Automatic Riflemen — SP278

Soldiers Cutting Barbed Wire SP279

No. B406, Field Artillery. No. B407, Tank. No. B408, Warship.

Flags and Dates: 23 Aug 1944-9 Mai 1945
1948, May 9
B404 SP278 1.50 l + 1.50 l shown .35 .35
B405 SP279 2 l + 2 l shown .35 .35
B406 SP279 4 l + 4 l multi .65 .65
B407 SP279 7.50 l + 7.50 l multi 1.25 1.25
B408 SP279 8 l + 8 l multi 1.40 1.40
Nos. B404-B408,CB18-CB19 (7) 18.00 18.00
Honoring the Romanian Army.

Nicolae Balcescu — SP280

Balcescu and Revolutionists SP281

Balcescu, Sandor Petöfi and Revolutionists — SP282

Revolution of 1848: #B412, Balcescu and revolutionists.

1948, June 1   Perf. 13x13½
B409 SP280 2 l + 2 l car lake .40 .60
B410 SP281 5 l + 5 l dk vio .55 .70
B411 SP282 10 l + 10 l dk ol brn .75 1.25
B412 SP280 36 l + 18 l dp bl 1.75 2.25
Nos. B409-B412 (4) 3.45 4.80
For surcharges see Nos. 856-859.

Loading Freighter SP283

Designs: 3 l+3 l, Lineman. 11 l+11 l, Transport plane. 15 l+15 l, Railroad train.

Wmk. 289
1948, Dec. 10   Photo.   Perf. 14
Center in Black
B413 SP283 1 l + 1 l dk grn .65 1.10
B414 SP283 3 l + 3 l redsh brn .75 1.10
B415 SP283 11 l + 11 l dp bl 3.50 3.00

B416 SP283 15 l + 15 l red   4.00 4.50
  a.   Sheet of 4   20.00 25.00
        Nos. B413-B416 (4)   8.90 9.70

No. B416a contains four imperf. stamps
similar to Nos. B413-B416 in changed colors,
center in brown. No gum.

Runners — SP284

Parade of
Athletes
SP285

1948, Dec. 31   Perf. 13x13½, 13½x13
B421 SP284 5 l + 5 l grn   3.50 3.50
B422 SP285 10 l + 10 l brn vio   5.75 5.75
Imperf
B423 SP284 5 l + 5 l brown   3.50 3.50
B424 SP285 10 l + 10 l red   5.75 5.75
Nos. B421-B424,CB20-CB21 (6) 48.50 48.50

Nos. B421-B424 were issued in sheets of 4.

Souvenir Sheet

SP286

1950, Jan. 27
B425 SP286 10 l carmine   5.00 3.25

Philatelic exhib., Bucharest. Sold for 50 lei.

Crossing the Buzau, by Denis Auguste
Marie Raffet — SP287

1967, Nov. 15   Engr.   Perf. 13½
B426 SP287 55b + 45b ocher &
             indigo   .90   .45
             Stamp Day.

Old Bucharest, 18th Century
Painting — SP288

1968, Nov. 15   Photo.   Perf. 13½
B427 SP288 55b + 45b label   1.10   .60

Stamp Day. Simulated label has printed perforations. See Nos. 2386A, B428-B429.

1969, Nov. 15

Design: Courtyard, by M. Bouquet.
B428 SP288 55b + 45b label   1.00   .60

Stamp Day. Simulated label at right of
stamp has printed perforations.

1970, Nov. 15

Mail Coach in the Winter, by Emil Volkers.
B429 SP288 55b + 45b multi   1.10   .70

Stamp Day. No simulated label.

Lady with
Letter, by
Sava Hentia
SP289

1971, Nov. 15   Photo.   Perf. 13½
B430 SP289 1.10 l + 90b multi   1.25   .75

Stamp Day. Label portion below stamp has
printed perforations and shows Romania No.
12.

Portrait Type of Regular Issue

Designs: 4 l+2 l, Aman at his Desk, by B.
Iscovescu. 6 l+2 l, The Poet Alecsandri with
his Family, by N. Livaditti.

1973, June 20   Photo.   Perf. 13½
B432 A728 4 l + 2 l multi   1.50   .60
Souvenir Sheet
B433 A728 6 l + 2 l multi   3.00 3.00

No. B433 contains one 38x50mm stamp.

Map of
Europe
with
Emblem
Marking
Bucharest
SP291

1974, June 25   Photo.   Perf. 13½
B435 SP291 4 l + 3 l multi   1.50   .50

EUROMAX, European Exhibition of Maximaphily, Bucharest, Oct. 6-13.

Marketplace, Sibiu — SP292

1974, Nov. 15   Photo.   Perf. 13½
B436 SP292 2.10 l + 1.90 l multi 1.10 .40

Stamp Day.

**No. B436 Overprinted in Red:
"EXPOZITIA FILATELICA
'NATIONALA '74' / 15-24 noiembrie /
Bucuresti"**

1974, Nov. 15
B437 SP292 2.10 l + 1.90 l multi 2.25 2.25

NATIONALA '74 Philatelic Exhibition,
Bucharest, Nov. 15-24.

Post
Office,
Bucharest
SP293

Stamp Day: 2.10 l+1.90 l, like No. B438,
side view.

1975, Nov. 15   Photo.   Perf. 13½
B438 SP293 1.50 l + 1.50 l multi .85   .45
B439 SP293 2.10 l + 1.90 l multi 1.40 .65

**No. 2612 Surcharged and
Overprinted "EXPOZITIA
FILATELICA / BUCURESTI / 12-
19.IX.1976"**

1976, Sept. 12   Photo.   Perf. 13½
B440 A787 3.60 l + 1.80 l   4.00 3.25

Philatelic Exhibition, Bucharest, Sept. 12-19.

Elena Cuza, by
Theodor
Aman — SP294

1976, Nov. 15   Photo.   Perf. 13½
B441 SP294 2.10 l + 1.90 l multi 1.10 .70

Stamp Day.

Independence Type of 1977

Stamp Day: Battle of Rahova, after etching.

1977, May 9   Photo.   Perf. 13½
B442 A806 4.80 l + 2 l multi   1.50   .40

Dispatch Rider
Handing Letter to
Officer — SP295

1977, Nov.   Photo.   Perf. 13½
B443 SP295 2.10 l + 1.90 l multi 1.25 .85

Socflex Type of 1979

Flower Paintings by Luchian: 4 l+2 l, Field
flowers. 10 l+5 l, Roses.

1979, July 27   Photo.   Perf. 13½
B445 A847 4 l + 2 l multi   1.10 1.10
Souvenir Sheet
B446 A847 10 l + 5 l multi   3.00 3.00

Socflex Intl. Phil. Exhib., Bucharest, Oct.
26-Nov. 1. #B446 contains one 50x38mm
stamp.

Stamp
Day
SP297

1979, Dec. 12   Photo.   Perf. 13½
B447 SP297 2.10 l + 1.90 l multi .80   .25

Souvenir Sheet

Stamp Day — SP298

1980, July 1   Photo.   Perf. 13½
B448 SP298 5 l + 5 l multi   2.00 2.00

December 1989 Revolution — SP299

Designs: 50b+50b, Palace on fire,
Bucharest. 1 l+ 1 l, Crowd, Timisoara.
1.50 l+1 l, Soldiers & crowd, Tirgu Mures.
2 l+1 l, Soldiers in Bucharest, vert. 3 l+1 l,
Funeral, Timisoara. 3.50 l+1 l, Crowd celebrat-
ing, Brasov, vert. 4 l+1 l, Crowd with flags,
Sibiu. No. B456, Cemetery, Bucharest. No.
B457, Foreign aid.

1990, Oct. 1   Photo.   Perf. 13½
B449 SP299 50b +50b multi   .25   .25
B450 SP299 1 l +1 l multi   .25   .25
B451 SP299 1.50 l +1 l multi   .25   .25
B452 SP299 2 l +1 l multi   .30   .25
B453 SP299 3 l +1 l multi   .35   .25
B454 SP299 3.50 l +1 l multi   .40   .25
B455 SP299 4 l +1 l multi   .45   .25
B456 SP299 5 l +2 l multi   .60   .25
      Nos. B449-B456 (8)   2.85 2.00
Souvenir Sheet
B457 SP299 5 l +2 l multi   1.25 1.25

No. B457 contains one 54x42mm stamp.

Stamp Day — SP300

1992, July 15   Photo.   Perf. 13½
B458 SP300 10 l +4 l multi   .25   .25

For surcharge see No. B460.

Stamp
Day — SP301

1993, Apr. 26   Photo.   Perf. 13½
B459 SP301 15 l +10 l multi   .25   .25

No. B458 Surcharged in Red

1993, Nov. 9   Photo.   Perf. 13½
B460 SP300 70 l +45 l on 10 l+4 l   .50 .50

National History Museum, Bucharest SP302

1994, July 15   Photo.   Perf. 13½
B461 SP302 90 l +60 l multi   .30 .25
Stamp Day.

Souvenir Sheet

Romanian Olympic Committee, 90th Anniv. — SP303

No. B462: a, Pierre de Coubertin. b, Greece #125 (54x42mm). c, George V. Bibescu.

2004, Mar. 25   Photo.   Perf. 13¼
B462 SP303 16,000 l +5000 l   Sheet of 3, #a-c   4.25 4.25

First Romanian Philatelic Exhibition, 80th Anniv. — SP304

2004, July 15   Photo.   Perf. 13¼
B463 SP304 21,000 l +10,000 l multi   2.40 2.40
Litho.
Imperf
B464 SP304 21,000 l +10,000 l multi   2.40 2.40

AIR POST STAMPS

Capt. C. G. Craiu's Airplane AP1

Wmk. 95 Vertical
1928   Photo.   Perf. 13½
C1 AP1 1 l red brown   3.00 2.50
C2 AP1 2 l brt blue   3.00 2.50
C3 AP1 5 l carmine rose   3.00 2.50
Wmk. 95 Horizontal
C4 AP1 1 l red brown   4.00 3.25
C5 AP1 2 l brt blue   4.00 3.25
C6 AP1 5 l carmine rose   4.00 3.25
    Nos. C1-C6 (6)   21.00 17.25
Nos. C4-C6 also come with white gum.

Nos. C4-C6 Overprinted

1930
C7 AP1 1 l red brown   8.00 6.75
C8 AP1 2 l brt blue   8.00 6.75
  a.   Vert. pair, imperf. btwn.   175.00
C9 AP1 5 l carmine rose   8.00 6.75
    Nos. C7-C9 (3)   24.00 20.25
Same Overprint on Nos. C1-C3
Wmk. 95 Vertical
C10 AP1 1 l red brown   50.00 50.00
C11 AP1 2 l brt blue   50.00 50.00
C12 AP1 5 l carmine rose   50.00 50.00
    Nos. C10-C12 (3)   150.00 150.00
    Nos. C7-C12 (6)   174.00 170.25

Nos. C7-C12 for the accession of King Carol II.
Excellent connterfeits are known of Nos. C10-C12.

King Carol II — AP2

Bluish Paper
1930, Oct. 4   Unwmk.
C13 AP2 1 l dk violet   2.00 3.50
C14 AP2 2 l gray green   2.50 3.50
C15 AP2 5 l red brown   5.00 3.50
C16 AP2 10 l brt blue   9.00 3.50
    Nos. C13-C16 (4)   18.50 14.00
    Set, never hinged   36.50

Junkers Monoplane AP3

Monoplanes AP7

Designs: 3 l, Monoplane with biplane behind. 5 l, Biplane. 10 l, Monoplane flying leftward.

1931, Nov. 4   Wmk. 230
C17 AP3 2 l dull green   1.50 1.25
C18 AP3 3 l carmine   2.00 1.75
C19 AP3 5 l red brown   2.50 2.00
C20 AP3 10 l blue   6.00 4.50
C21 AP7 20 l dk violet   15.00 6.00
    Nos. C17-C21 (5)   27.00 15.50
    Set, never hinged   40.00

Exist imperforate. Value $350, unused or used.

Souvenir Sheets

Plane over Resita — AP8

Plane over Sinaia — AP9

Wmk. 276
1945, Oct. 1   Photo.   Perf. 13
Without Gum
C22 AP8 80 l slate green   17.50 25.00
Imperf
C23 AP9 80 l magenta   10.00 17.50

16th Congress of the General Assoc. of Romanian Engineers.

> **Catalogue values for unused stamps in this section, from this point to the end of the section, are for Never Hinged items.**

Plane AP10

Design: 500 l, Aviator and planes.

1946, Sept. 5   Perf. 13½x13
C24 AP10 200 l yel grn & bl   3.00 6.00
C25 AP10 500 l org red & dl bl   3.00 6.00

Sheets of four with marginal inscription.

Lockheed 12 Electra — AP12

1946, Oct.   Perf. 11½
C26 AP12 300 l crimson   1.00 1.00
  a.   Pair, #C26, CB6   2.25 2.25

Sheet contains 8 each of Nos. C26 and CB6, arranged so se-tenant or normal pairs are available.

CGM Congress Emblem — AP13

1947, Mar.   Wmk. 276   Perf. 13x14
C27 AP13 1100 l blue   .50 1.00

Congress of the United Labor Unions ("CGM"). Printed in sheets of 15.

"May 1" Supported by Parachutes AP14

Designs: No. C29, Air Force monument. No. C30, Plane over rural road.

1947, May 4   Perf. 11½
C28 AP14 3000 l vermilion   .30 .60
C29 AP14 3000 l grnsh gray   .30 .60
C30 AP14 3000 l blk brown   .30 .60
    Nos. C28-C30 (3)   .90 1.80

Printed in sheets of four with marginal inscriptions.

Plane and Conference Banner — AP17

1947, Nov. 10   Perf. 14
C31 AP17 11 l bl & dp car   1.25 1.25

2nd Trade Union Conference, Nov. 10.

Emblem of the Republic and Factories AP18

Industry and Agriculture — AP19

Transportation — AP20

**   Perf. 14x13½**
1948, Nov. 22   Wmk. 289   Photo.
C32 AP18 30 l cerise   .75 .25
  a.   30 l carmine ('50)   .85 .45
C33 AP19 50 l dk slate grn   1.25 .50
C34 AP20 100 l ultra   3.75 1.50
    Nos. C32-C34 (3)   5.75 2.25

No. C32a issued May 10. For surcharges see Nos. C37-C39.

Agriculture — AP21

Design: 50 l, Transportation.

1951-52   Wmk. 358   Perf. 13½
C35 AP21 30 l dk green ('52)   3.75 3.00
C36 AP21 50 l red brown   3.00 2.50

1951-55 Five Year Plan.
For surcharges see Nos. C40-C41.

Nos. C32-C36 Surcharged with New Values in Blue or Carmine
1952   Wmk. 289   Perf. 14x13½
C37 AP18 3b on 30 l car (Bl)   3.00 2.25
  a.   3b on 30 l cerise (Bl)   12.00 8.50
C38 AP19 3b on 50 l dk sl grn   1.00 .70
C39 AP20 3b on 100 l ultra   1.00 .70

Perf. 13½
Wmk. 358

C40	AP21	1 l on 30 l dk grn	8.00	1.50
C41	AP21	1 l on 50 l red brn	8.00	1.50
		Nos. C37-C41 (5)	21.00	6.65

Nos. 706 and 707
Surcharged in
Blue or Carmine

1953   Wmk. 289   Perf. 13½, 14

C43	A250	3 l on 20 l org brn	35.00	25.00
C44	A251	5 l on 30 l brt bl (C)	45.00	32.50

Plane facing right and surcharge arranged
to fit design on No. C44.

Plane over
City — AP22

Designs: 55b, Plane over Mountains. 1.75 l,
over Harvest fields. 2.25 l, over Seashore.

Perf. 14½x14
1956, Dec. 15   Photo.   Wmk. 358

C45	AP22	20b brt bl, org &		
		grn	.55	.80
C46	AP22	55b brt bl, grn &		
		ocher	1.25	.80
C47	AP22	1.75 l brt bl & red org	3.75	1.25
C48	AP22	2.55 l brt bl & red org	5.25	2.00
		Nos. C45-C48 (4)	10.80	4.85

Sputnik 1 and
Earth — AP23

3.75 l, Sputniks 1 and 2 circling globe.

1957, Nov. 6   Perf. 14

C49	AP23	25b brt ultra	.65	.25
C50	AP23	25b dk bl grn	.65	.25
C51	AP23	3.75 l brt ultra	3.50	.60
a.		Pair, #C49, C51 + label	6.00	3.75
C52	AP23	3.75 l dk bl grn	3.50	.60
a.		Pair, #C50, C52 + label	6.00	3.75
		Nos. C49-C52 (4)	8.30	1.70

Each sheet contains 27 triptychs with the
center rows arranged tete-beche.
In 1958 Nos. C49-C52 were overprinted: 1.)
"Expozitia Universal a Bruxelles 1958" and
star. 2.) Large star. 3.) Small star. Value, both
pairs: unused $30, used $20. Exist imperf.
Value, both pairs: unused $60 used $50.

Animal Type of Regular Issue, 1957

Birds: 3.30 l, Black-headed gull, horiz. 5 l,
Sea eagle, horiz.

Perf. 14x13½
1957, Dec. 27   Wmk. 358

C53	A445	3.30 l ultra & gray	4.00	1.00
C54	A445	5 l carmine & org	5.75	1.25

**Armed Forces Type of Regular
Issue**

Design: Flier and planes.

Perf. 13½x13
1958, Oct. 2   Unwmk.   Photo.

C55	A458	3.30 l brt violet	1.60	.50

Day of the Armed Forces, Oct. 2.

Earth and
Sputnik 3
Orbit
AP24

1958, Sept. 20   Perf. 14x13½

C56	AP24	3.25 l indigo & ocher	3.75	.75

Launching of Sputnik 3, May 15, 1958.

Type of Regular Issue, 1958
Souvenir Sheet

Design: Tête bêche pair of 27pa of 1858.

Perf. 11½
1958, Nov. 15   Unwmk.   Engr.

C57	A462	10 l blue, bluish	35.00	35.00

A similar sheet, printed in dull red and
imperf., exists. Values, unused $45; used
$22.50.
No. C57 on bluish and white papers was
overprinted in 1959 in vermilion to commemorate the 10th anniv. of the State Philatelic
Trade. Values: unused $100; used $125.

Lunik I
Leaving
Earth
AP25

1959, Feb. 4   Photo.   Perf. 14

C58	AP25	3.25 l vio bl, *pnksh*	15.00	2.00

Launching of the "first artificial planet of the
solar system."
For surcharge see No. C70.

Frederic Joliot-
Curie — AP26

1959, Apr. 25   Perf. 13½x14

C59	AP26	3.25 l ultra	4.00	.60

Frederic Joliot-Curie; 10th anniv. of the
World Peace Movement.

Rock Thrush
AP27

Birds: 20b, European golden oriole. 35b,
Lapwing. 40b, Barn swallow. No. C64, Goldfinch. No. C65, Great spotted woodpecker.
No. C66, Great tit. 1 l, Bullfinch. 1.55 l, Long-
tailed tit. 5 l, Wall creeper. Nos. C62-C67
vertical.

1959, June 25   Litho.   Perf. 14
Birds in Natural Colors

C60	AP27	10b gray, *cr*	.25	.25
C61	AP27	20b gray, *grysh*	.25	.25
C62	AP27	35b gray, *grysh*	.30	.25
C63	AP27	40b gray & red,		
		pnksh	.40	.25
C64	AP27	55b gray, *buff*	.55	.25
C65	AP27	55b gray, *grnsh*	.55	.25
C66	AP27	55b gray & ol,		
		grysh	.55	.25
C67	AP27	1 l gray and red,		
		cr	2.00	.25
C68	AP27	1.55 l gray & red,		
		pnksh	2.50	.25
C69	AP27	5 l gray, *grnsh*	6.00	2.25
		Nos. C60-C69 (10)	13.35	4.50

No. C58
Surcharged
in Red

1959, Sept. 14   Photo.   Unwmk.

C70	AP25	5 l on 3.25 l	13.50	3.75

1st Russian rocket to reach the moon,
9/14/59.

Miniature Sheet

Prince Vlad Tepes and
Document — AP28

1959, Sept. 15   Engr.   Perf. 11½x11

C71	AP28	20 l violet brn	150.00	150.00

500th anniv. of the founding of Bucharest.

Sport Type of Regular Issue, 1959

1959, Oct. 5   Litho.   Perf. 13½

C72	A474	2.80 l Boating	2.50	.50

Soviet Rocket,
Globe, Dog and
Rabbit — AP29

Photograph of Far Side of the
Moon — AP30

Design: 1.75 l, Trajectory of Lunik 3, which
hit the moon.

Perf. 14, 13½ (AP30)
1959, Dec.   Photo.   Wmk. 358

C73	AP29	1.55 l dk blue	3.00	.35
C74	AP30	1.60 l dk vio bl, *buff*	3.50	.55
C75	AP29	1.75 l dk blue	3.50	.55
		Nos. C73-C75 (3)	10.00	1.45

Soviet conquest of space.

Animal Type of Regular Issue, 1960.

Designs: 1.30 l, Golden eagle. 1.75 l, Black
grouse. 2 l, Lammergeier.

Unwmk.
1960, Mar. 3   Engr.   Perf. 14

C76	A480	1.30 l dk blue	1.75	.40
C77	A480	1.75 l olive grn	1.75	.40
C78	A480	2 l dk carmine	1.75	.50
		Nos. C76-C78 (3)	5.25	1.30

Aurel
Vlaicu and
Plane of
1910
AP31

Bucharest Airport and Turbo-
Jet — AP32

Designs: 20b, Plane and Aurel Vlaicu. 35b,
Amphibian ambulance plane. 40b, Plane
spraying crops. 55b, Pilot and planes, vert.
1.75 l, Parachutes at aviation sports meet.

1960, June 15   Litho.   Unwmk.

C79	AP31	10b yellow & brn	.25	.25
C80	AP31	20b red org & brn	.25	.25
		Photo. Wmk. 358		
C81	AP31	35b crimson	.40	.25
C82	AP31	40b violet	.55	.25
C83	AP31	55b blue	.80	.25
		Litho. Unwmk.		
C84	AP32	1.60 l vio bl, yel & em-		
		er	2.00	.40
C85	AP32	1.75 l bl, red, brn &		
		pale grn	2.50	.55
		Nos. C79-C85 (7)	6.75	2.20

50th anniv. of the first Romanian airplane
flight by Aurel Vlaicu.
For surcharge see No. C145.

Bucharest
Airport — AP33

1960   Wmk. 358   Photo.   Perf. 14

C86	AP33	3.20 l brt ultra	1.50	.25

Type of Regular Issue, 1960

Black Sea Resort: 2 l, Beach at Mamaia.

1960, Aug. 2   Litho.   Unwmk.

C87	A491	2 l grn, org & lt bl	1.50	.50

Sputnik 4
Flying into
Space
AP34

1960, June 8   Photo.   Wmk. 358

C88	AP34	55b deep blue	2.50	.25

Launching of Sputnik 4, May 15, 1960.

Saturnia Pyri
AP35

Papilio Machaon
AP36

Limenitis Populi — AP37

Designs: 40b, Chrisophanus virgaureae.
1.60 l, Acherontia atropos. 1.75 l, Apatura iris.

Perf. 13, 14x12½, 14

1960, Oct. 10   Typo.   Unwmk.
C89	AP35	10b multi	.25	.25
C90	AP37	20b multi	.25	.25
C91	AP37	40b multi	.35	.25
C92	AP36	55b multi	.65	.25
C93	AP36	1.60 l multi	2.00	.35
C94	AP36	1.75 l multi, horiz.	2.75	.35
	Nos. C89-C94 (6)		6.25	1.70

Compass Rose and Jet — AP38

Perf. 13½x14

1960, Nov. 1   Photo.   Wmk. 358
C95	AP38	55b brt bl + 45b label	.50	.25

Stamp Day.

Skier AP39

Slalom — AP40

Designs: 25b, Skiers going up. 40b, Bobsled. 55b, Ski jump. 1 l, Mountain climber. 1.55 l, Long-distance skier.

Perf. 14x13½, 13½x14

1961, Mar. 18   Litho.   Unwmk.
C96	AP39	10b olive & gray	.25	.25
C97	AP40	20b gray & dk red	.25	.25
C98	AP40	25b gray & bl grn	.35	.25
C99	AP40	40b gray & pur	.35	.25
C100	AP39	55b gray & ultra	.45	.25
C101	AP40	1 l gray & brn lake	.75	.25
C102	AP39	1.55 l gray & brn	1.10	.25
	Nos. C96-C102 (7)		3.50	1.75

Exist imperf. with changed colors. Value, set $5.

Maj. Yuri A. Gagarin — AP41

Design: 3.20 l, Gagarin in space capsule and globe with orbit, horiz.

Perf. 14x14½, 14½x14

1961, Apr. 19   Photo.   Unwmk.
C103	AP41	1.35 l brt blue	1.00	.30
C104	AP41	3.20 l ultra	2.25	.60

No. C104 exists imperf. in dark carmine rose. Value unused $7.50, canceled $3.25.

Eclipse over Republic Palace Place, Bucharest AP42

1.75 l, Total Eclipse, Scinteia House, telescope.

Perf. 14x13½

1961, June 13   Wmk. 358
C106	AP42	1.60 l ultra	1.25	.30
C107	AP42	1.75 l dk blue	1.50	.30

Total solar eclipse of Feb. 15, 1961.

Maj. Gherman S. Titov — AP43

55b, "Peace" and Vostok 2 rocket. 1.75 l, Yuri A. Gagarin and Gherman S. Titov, horiz.

Perf. 13½x14

1961, Sept. 11   Unwmk.
C108	AP43	55b dp blue	.55	.25
C109	AP43	1.35 l dp purple	.80	.25
C110	AP43	1.75 l dk carmine	1.25	.25
	Nos. C108-C110 (3)		2.60	.75

Issued to honor the Russian space navigators Y. A. Gagarin and G. S. Titov.

Globe and Stamps — AP44

1961, Nov. 15   Litho.   Perf. 13½x14
C111	AP44	55b multi + 45b label	1.00	.25

Stamp Day.

Railroad Station, Constanta AP45

Buildings: 20b, Tower, RPR Palace place, vert. 55b, Congress hall, Bucharest. 75b, Mill, Hunedoara. 1 l, Apartment houses, Bucharest. 1.20 l, Circus, Bucharest. 1.75 l, Worker's Club, Mangalia.

Perf. 13½x14, 14x13½

1961, Nov. 20   Typo.
C112	AP45	20b multi	.25	.25
C113	AP45	40b multi	.25	.25
C114	AP45	55b multi	.25	.25
C115	AP45	75b multi	.30	.25
C116	AP45	1 l multi	.40	.25
C117	AP45	1.20 l multi	.75	.25
C118	AP45	1.75 l multi	1.10	.25
	Nos. C112-C118 (7)		3.30	1.75

Space Exploration Stamps and Dove AP46

Design: Each stamp shows a different group of Romanian space exploration stamps.

1962, July 27   Perf. 14x13½
C119	AP46	35b yellow brn	.25	.25
C120	AP46	55b green	.30	.25
C121	AP46	1.35 l blue	.60	.25
C122	AP46	1.75 l rose red	1.10	.25
a.		Sheet of 4	3.00	1.50
	Nos. C119-C122 (4)		2.25	1.00

Peaceful space exploration.
No. C122a contains four imperf. stamps similar to Nos. C119-C122 in changed colors and with one dove covering all four stamps. Stamps are printed together without space between.

Andrian G. Nikolaev — AP47

Designs: 1.60 l, Globe and trajectories of Vostoks 3 and 4. 1.75 l, Pavel R. Popovich.

Perf. 13½x14

1962, Aug. 20   Photo.   Unwmk.
C123	AP47	55b purple	.30	.25
C124	AP47	1.60 l dark blue	.90	.30
C125	AP47	1.75 l rose claret	1.25	.30
	Nos. C123-C125 (3)		2.45	.85

1st Russian group space flight of Vostoks 3 and 4, Aug. 11-15, 1962.

Exhibition Hall — AP48

1962, Oct. 12   Litho.   Perf. 14x13
C126	AP48	1.60 l bl, vio bl & org	1.50	.25

4th Sample Fair, Bucharest.

The Coachmen by Szatmary — AP49

1962, Nov. 15   Perf. 13½x14
C127	AP49	55b + 45b label	1.25	.35

Stamp Day. Alternating label shows No. 14 on cover.

No. C127 Overprinted in Violet

1963, Mar. 30
C128	AP49	55b + 45b label	3.50	2.00

Romanian Philatelists' Assoc. meeting at Bucharest, Mar. 30.

Sighisoara Glass and Crockery Factory AP50

Industrial Plants: 40b, Govora soda works. 55b, Tirgul-Jiu wood processing factory. 1 l, Savinesti chemical plant (synthetic fibers). 1.55 l, Hunedoara metal factory. 1.75 l, Brazi thermal power station.

Perf. 14x13

1963, Apr. 10   Unwmk.   Photo.
C129	AP50	30b dk bl & red	.30	.25
C130	AP50	40b sl grn & pur	.30	.25
C131	AP50	55b brn red & dp bl	.30	.25
C132	AP50	1 l vio & brn	.30	.25
C133	AP50	1.55 l ver & dk bl	.70	.25

C134	AP50	1.75 l dk bl & magenta	1.00	.25
	Nos. C129-C134 (6)		2.90	1.50

Industrial achievements.

Lunik 4 Approaching Moon — AP51

1963, Apr. 29   Perf. 13½x14
C135	AP51	55b dk ultra & red	.45	.25

Imperf
C136	AP51	1.75 l vio & red	1.00	.25

Moon flight of Lunik 4, Apr. 2, 1963.

Steam Locomotive AP52

Designs: 55b, Diesel locomotive. 75b, Trolley bus. 1.35 l, Passenger ship. 1.75 l, Plane.

1963, July 10   Litho.   Perf. 14½x13
C137	AP52	40b multi	.35	.25
C138	AP52	55b multi	.40	.25
C139	AP52	75b multi	.60	.25
C140	AP52	1.35 l multi	1.00	.30
C141	AP52	1.75 l multi	1.40	.25
	Nos. C137-C141 (5)		3.75	1.30

Valeri Bykovski AP53

Designs: 1.20 l, Bykovski, vert. 1.60 l, Tereshkova, vert. 1.75 l, Valentina Tereshkova.

1963   Photo.
C142	AP53	55b blue	.30	.25
C143	AP53	1.40 l rose red	1.40	.30

Souvenir Sheet
Perf. 13
C144		Sheet of 2	2.75	.80
a.	AP53	1.20 l ultra	.60	.30
b.	AP53	1.60 l ultra	.75	.40

Space flights of Valeri Bykovski, June 14-19, and Valentina Tereshkova, first woman cosmonaut, June 16-19, 1963.

No. C79 Surcharged and Overprinted "1913-1963 50 ani de la moarte"
Unwmk.

1963, Sept. 15   Litho.   Perf. 14
C145	AP31	1.75 l on 10b	2.50	.95

50th death anniv. of Aurel Vlaicu, aviation pioneer.
Exists with "i" of "lei," missing.

Centenary Stamp of 1958 AP54

Stamps on Stamps: 40b, Sputnik 2 and Laika, No. 1200. 55b, Yurl A. Gagarin, No. C104a. 1.20 l, Nikolayev and Popovich, Nos. C123, C125. 1.55 l, Postal Administration Bldg. and letter carrier, No. 965.

1963, Nov. 15   Photo.   Perf. 14x13½
Size: 38x26mm
C146	AP54	20b lt bl & dk brn	.25	.25
C147	AP54	40b brt pink & dk bl	.25	.25
C148	AP54	55b lt ultra & dk car rose	.25	.25
C149	AP54	1.20 l ocher & pur	.45	.25

C150 AP54 1.55 l sal pink & ol
　　　　gray　　　　　　.65　.25
Nos. C146-C150,CB22 (6)　　4.60　1.75
15th UPU Congress, Vienna.

Pavel R.
Popovich
AP55

Astronauts and flag: 5b, Yuri A. Gagarin. 10b, Gherman S. Titov. 20b, John H. Glenn, Jr. 35b, M. Scott Carpenter. 40b, Andrian G. Nikolayev. 60b, Walter M. Schirra. 75b, L. Gordon Cooper. 1 l, Valeri Bykovski. 1.40 l, Valentina Tereshkova. (5b, 10b, 20b, 35b, 60b and 75b are diamond shaped).

Perf. 13½
1964, Jan. 15　Litho.　Unwmk.
Light Blue Background
C151	AP55	5b red, yel & vio bl	.30　.25
C152	AP55	10b red, yel & pur	.30　.25
C153	AP55	20b red, ultra & ol gray	.30　.25
C154	AP55	35b red, ultra & sl bl	.30　.25
C155	AP55	40b red, yel & ultra	.30　.25
C156	AP55	55b red, yel & ultra	.60　.25
C157	AP55	60b ultra, red & sep	.60　.25
C158	AP55	75b red, ultra & dk bl	.65　.25
C159	AP55	1 l red, yel & mar	.95　.25
C160	AP55	1.40 l red, yel & mar	1.10　.25

Nos. C151-C160 (10)　　5.40　2.50

Nos. C151-C160 exist imperf. in changed colors. Value, set $8 unused, $3 used.
A miniature sheet contains one imperf. horizontal 2 l ultramarine and yellow stamp. Size of stamp: 59½x43mm. Value unused $8.50, canceled $4.25.

Modern and 19th Century Post Office Buildings AP56

Engr. & Typo.
1964, Nov. 15　　　　Perf. 13½
C161 AP56 1.60 l ultra + 40b label　　1.25　.50

Stamp Day. Stamp and label are imperf. between.

Plane Approaching Airport and Coach Leaving Gate — AP57

Engr. & Typo.
1966, Oct. 20　　　　Perf. 13½
C162 AP57 55b + 45b label　　.90　.50
Stamp Day.

Space Exploration Type of Regular Issue

US Achievements in Space: 1.20 l, Early Bird satellite and globe. 1.55 l, Mariner 4 transmitting pictures of the moon. 3.25 l, Gemini 6 & 7, rendezvous in space. 5 l, Gemini 8 meeting Agena rocket, and globe.

1967, Feb. 15　Photo.　Perf. 13½
C163	A595	1.20 l silver & multi	.60　.25
C164	A595	1.55 l silver & multi	.75　.25
C165	A595	3.25 l silver & multi	1.00　.35
C166	A595	5 l silver & multi	1.50　.75

Nos. C163-C166 (4)　　3.85　1.50

10 years of space exploration.

Plane Spraying Crops — AP58

Designs: 55b, Aerial ambulance over river, horiz. 1 l, Red Cross and plane. 2.40 l, Biplane and Mircea Zorileanu, aviation pioneer.

Perf. 12x12½, 12½x12
1968, Feb. 28　Litho.　Unwmk.
C167	AP58	40b bl grn, blk & yel brn	.25　.25
C168	AP58	55b multicolored	.30　.25
C169	AP58	1 l ultra, pale grn & red org	.30　.25
C170	AP58	2.40 l brt rose lil & multi	.75　.30

Nos. C167-C170 (4)　　1.60　1.05

Moon, Earth and Path of Apollo 8 — AP59

Design: No. C172, Soyuz 4 and 5 over globe with map of Russia.

1969　Photo.　Perf. 13½
C171	AP59	3.30 l multi	1.60　1.60
C172	AP59	3.30 l multi	1.60　1.60

1st manned flight around the Moon, Dec. 21-27, 1968, and the first team flights of the Russian spacecrafts Soyuz 4 and 5, Jan. 16, 1969. See note after Hungary No. C284.
Issued in sheets of 4.
Issued: #C171, Jan. 17, #C172, Mar. 28.

Apollo 9 and Lunar Landing Module over Earth AP60

Design: 2.40 l, Apollo 10 and lunar landing module over moon, vert.

1969, June 15　Photo.　Perf. 13½
C173	AP60	60b multi	.25　.25
C174	AP60	2.40 l multi	1.75　.35

US space explorations, Apollo 9 and 10.

First Man on Moon — AP61

1969, July 24　Photo.　Perf. 13½
C175 AP61 3.30 l multi　　1.90　1.90

Man's first landing on the moon July 20, 1969, US astronauts Neil A. Armstrong and Col. Edwin E. Aldrin, Jr., with Lieut. Col. Michael Collins piloting Apollo 11. Printed in sheets of 4.

1970, June 29

1.50 l, Apollo 13 capsule splashing down in Pacific.

C176 AP61 1.50 l multi　　.75　.60

Flight and safe landing of Apollo 13, Apr. 11-17, 1970. Printed in sheets of 4.

BAC 1-11 Jet AP62

Design: 2 l, Fuselage BAC 1-11 and control tower, Bucharest airport.

1970, Apr. 6
C177	AP62	60b multi	.35　.25
C178	AP62	2 l multi	.80　.25

50th anniv. of Romanian civil aviation.

Flood Relief Type of Regular Issue
Design: 60b, Rescue by helicopter.

1970, Sept. 25　Photo.　Perf. 13½
C179 A671 60b bl gray, blk & olive　　.25　.25

Publicizing the plight of victims of the Danube flood. See No. 2207a.

Henri Coanda's Model Plane AP63

1970, Dec. 1
C180 AP63 60b multicolored　　1.10　.30
Henri Coanda's first flight, 60th anniversary.

Luna 16 on Moon AP64

No. C182, Lunokhod 1, unmanned vehicle on moon. No. C183, US astronaut & vehicle on moon.

1971, Mar. 5　Photo.　Perf. 13½
C181	AP64	3.30 l silver & multi	1.00　1.00
C182	AP64	3.30 l silver & multi	1.00　1.00
a.		Pair, #C181-C182 + 2 labels	2.75　2.75
C183	AP64	3.30 l silver & multi	1.50　1.50

Nos. C181-C183 (3)　　3.50　3.50

No. C181 commemorates Luna 16 Russian unmanned, automatic moon mission, Sept. 12-24, 1970 (labels are incorrectly inscribed Oct. 12-24). No. C182 commemorates Lunokhod 1 (Luna 17), Nov. 10-17, 1970. Nos. C181-C182 printed in sheets of 4 stamps, arranged checkerwise, and 4 labels. No. C183 commemorates Apollo 14 moon landing, Jan. 31-Feb. 9. Printed in sheets of 4 with 4 labels showing portraits of US astronauts Alan B. Shepard, Edgar D. Mitchell, Stuart A. Roosa, and Apollo 14 emblem.

Souvenir Sheet

Cosmonauts Patsayev, Dobrovolsky and Volkov — AP65

1971, July 26　Litho.　Perf. 13½
C184 AP65 6 l black & ultra　　6.50　5.00

In memory of Russian cosmonauts Viktor I. Patsayev, Georgi T. Dobrovolsky and Vladislav N. Volkov, who died during Soyuz 11 space mission, June 6-30, 1971.
No. C184 exists imperf. in black & blue green; Size: 130x90mm. Value, unused or used, $150.

Lunar Rover on Moon AP66

1971, Aug. 26　　　　Photo.
C185 AP66 1.50 l blue & multi　　1.50　1.50

US Apollo 15 moon mission, July 26-Aug. 7, 1971. No. C185 printed in sheets of 4 stamps and 4 labels showing astronauts David Scott, James Irwin, Alfred Worden and Apollo 15 emblem with dates.
No. C185 exists imperf. in green & multicolored. The sheet has a control number. Values: unused $150; used $110.

Olympics Type of Regular Issue
Souvenir Sheets

Designs: No. C186, Torchbearer and map of Romania. No. C187, Soccer.

1972　　Photo.　Perf. 13½
C186	A699	6 l pale grn & multi	7.50　7.50
C187	A699	6 l blue & multi	7.50　7.50

20th Olympic Games, Munich, Aug. 26-Sept. 11. No. C186 contains one stamp 50x38mm. No. C187 contains one stamp 48½x37mm.
Issued: #C186, Apr. 25; #C187, Sept. 29.
Two imperf. 6 l souvenir sheets exist, one showing equestrian, the other a satellite over globe. Value for either sheet, unused or used, $80.

Lunar Rover on Moon — AP67

1972, May 10　Photo.　Perf. 13½
C188 AP67 3 l vio bl, rose & gray grn　　1.10　.85

Apollo 16 US moon mission, Apr. 15-27, 1972. No. C188 printed in sheets of 4 stamps and 4 gray green and black labels showing Capt. John W. Young, Lt. Comdr. Thomas K. Mattingly 2nd, Col. Charles M. Duke, Jr., and Apollo 16 badge.

Aurel Vlaicu and Monoplane — AP68

Romanian Aviation Pioneers: 3 l, Traian Vuia and his flying machine.

1972, Aug. 15
C189 AP68 60b multicolored .25 .25
C190 AP68 3 l multicolored 1.00 .40

Olympic Medals Type of Regular Issue
Souvenir Sheet

Olympic silver and gold medals, horiz.

1972, Sept. 29   Litho.   Perf. 13½
C191 A714 6 l multicolored 7.50 7.50

Romanian medalists at 20th Olympic Games. An imperf. 6 l souvenir sheet exists showing gold medal. Value, unused or used, $70.

Apollo Type of Regular Issue
Souvenir Sheet

Design: 6 l, Lunar rover, landing module, rocket and astronauts on moon, horiz.

1972, Dec. 27   Photo.   Perf. 13½
C192 A715 6 l vio bl, bis & dl grn 10.00 10.00

No. C192 contains one stamp 48½x36mm. An imperf. 6 l souvenir sheet exists showing surface of moon with landing sites of last 6 Apollo missions and landing capsule. Value, unused or used, $80.

Type of Regular Issue, 1972

Design: Otopeni Airport, horiz.

1972, Dec. 20   Photo.   Perf. 13
Size: 29x21mm
C193 A710 14.60 l brt blue 1.50 .40

Apollo and Soyuz Spacecraft — AP69

3.25 l, Apollo and Soyuz after link-up.

1975, July 14   Photo.   Perf. 13½
C196 AP69 1.75 l vio bl, red & ol 1.25 1.25
C197 AP69 3.25 l vio bl, red & ol 1.25 1.25

Apollo Soyuz space test project (Russo-American cooperation), launching July 15; link-up, July 17. Nos. C196-C197 printed in sheets of 4 stamps, arranged checkerwise, and 4 rose lilac labels showing Apollo-Soyuz emblem.

European Security and Cooperation Conference — AP70

1975, July 30   Photo.   Perf. 13½
C198 AP70 Sheet of 4 2.50 2.50
  a. 2.75 l Map of Europe .35 .35
  b. 2.75 l Peace doves .35 .35
  c. 5 l Open book .75 .75
  d. 5 l Children playing .75 .75

European Security and Cooperation Conference, Helsinki, July 30-Aug. 1. No. C198b inscribed "posta aeriana."
An imperf. 10 l souvenir sheet exists showing Helsinki on map of Europe. Value, unused or used, $95.

Red Cross Type of 1976

Design: Blood donors, Red Cross plane.

1976, Apr. 20   Photo.   Perf. 13½
C199 A790 3.35 l multi .70 .25

De Havilland DH-9 — AP71

Airplanes: 40b, I.C.A.R. Comercial. 60b, Douglas DC-3. 1.75 l, AN-24. 2.75 l, IL-62. 3.60 l, Boeing 707.

1976, June 24   Photo.   Perf. 13½
C200 AP71 20b blue & multi .25 .25
C201 AP71 40b blue & multi .25 .25
C202 AP71 60b multi .25 .25
C203 AP71 1.75 l multi .40 .25
C204 AP71 2.75 l blue & multi .55 .25
C205 AP71 3.60 l multi .85 .30
  Nos. C200-C205 (6) 2.55 1.55

Romanian Airline, 50th anniversary.

Glider I.C.A.R.-1 — AP72

Gliders: 40b, I.S.-3d. 55b, R.G.-5. 1.50 l, I.S.-11. 3 l, I.S.-29D. 3.40 l, I.S.-28B.

1977, Feb. 20   Photo.   Perf. 13
C206 AP72 20b multi .25 .25
C207 AP72 40b multi .25 .25
C208 AP72 55b multi .25 .25
C209 AP72 1.50 l bl & multi .25 .25
C210 AP72 3 l multi .60 .25
C211 AP72 3.40 l multi .95 .25
  Nos. C206-C211 (6) 2.55 1.50

Souvenir Sheet

Boeing 707 over Bucharest Airport and Pioneers — AP73

1977, June 28   Photo.   Perf. 13½
C212 AP73 10 l multi 2.50 2.50

European Security and Cooperation Conference, Belgrade.
An imperf. 10 l souvenir sheet exists showing Boeing 707, map of Europe and buildings. Value, unused or used, $35.

Woman Letter Carrier, Mailbox AP74

30 l, Plane, newspapers, letters, packages.

1977   Photo.   Perf. 13½
C213 AP74 20 l multicolored 3.50 1.00
C214 AP74 30 l multicolored 5.50 1.75

Issue dates: 20 l, July 25, 30 l, Sept. 10.

LZ-1 over Friedrichshafen, 1900 — AP75

Airships: 1 l, Santos Dumont's dirigible over Paris, 1901. 1.50 l, British R-34 over New York and Statue of Liberty, 1919. 2.15 l, Italia over North Pole, 1928. 3.40 l, Zeppelin LZ-127 over Brasov, 1929. 4.80 l, Zeppelin over Sibiu, 1929. 10 l, Zeppelin over Bucharest, 1929.

1978, Mar. 20   Photo.   Perf. 13½
C215 AP75 60b multi .25 .25
C216 AP75 1 l multi .25 .25
C217 AP75 1.50 l multi .35 .25
C218 AP75 2.15 l multi .40 .25
C219 AP75 3.40 l multi .75 .25
C220 AP75 4.80 l multi 1.10 .25
  Nos. C215-C220 (6) 3.10 1.50

Souvenir Sheet

C221 AP75 10 l multi 2.50 2.50

History of airships. No. C221 contains one 50x37½mm stamp.

Soccer Type of 1978
Souvenir Sheet

10 l, 2 soccer players, Argentina '78 emblem.

1978, Apr. 15   Photo.   Perf. 13½
C222 A818 10 l blue & multi 3.00 3.00

11th World Cup Soccer Championship, Argentina, June 1-25. No. C222 contains one stamp 37x50mm. A 10 l imperf souvenir sheet exists showing goalkeeper. Values: unused $30; used $20.

Wilbur and Orville Wright, Flyer A — AP76

Aviation History: 1 l, Louis Blériot and his plane over English Channel, 1909. 1.50 l, Anthony Fokker and Fokker F-VII trimotor, 1926. 2.15 l, Andrei N. Tupolev and ANT-25 monoplane, 1937. 3 l, Otto Lilienthal and glider, 1891-96. 3.40 l, Traian Vuia and his plane, Montesson, France, 1906. 4.80 l, Aurel Vlaicu and 1st Romanian plane, 1910. 10 l, Henri Coanda and his "jet," 1910.

1978, Dec. 18   Photo.   Perf. 13½
C223 AP76 55b multi .25 .25
C224 AP76 1 l multi .25 .25
C225 AP76 1.50 l multi .25 .25
C226 AP76 2.15 l multi .35 .25
C227 AP76 3 l multi .35 .25
C228 AP76 3.40 l multi .40 .25
C229 AP76 4.80 l multi .45 .25
  Nos. C223-C229 (7) 2.30 1.75

Souvenir Sheet

C230 AP76 10 l multi 2.25 2.25

No. C230 contains one stamp 50x38mm.

Inter-Europa Type of 1979

3.40 l, Jet, mail truck and motorcycle.

1979, May 3   Photo.   Perf. 13
C231 A835 3.40 l multi .40 .40

Issued in sheets of 4.

Animal Type of 1980
Souvenir Sheet

1980, Mar. 25   Photo.   Perf. 13½
C232 A852 10 l Pelicans 2.25 2.25

No. C232 contains one stamp 38x50mm.

Mercury AP77

1981, June 30   Photo.   Perf. 13½
C233 AP77 55b shown .25 .25
C234 AP77 1 l Venus, Earth, Mars .25 .25
C235 AP77 1.50 l Jupiter .25 .25
C236 AP77 2.15 l Saturn .30 .25
C237 AP77 3.40 l Uranus .60 .25
C238 AP77 4.80 l Neptune, Pluto .75 .30
  Nos. C233-C238 (6) 2.40 1.55

Souvenir Sheet

C239 AP77 10 l Earth 2.25 2.25

No. C239 contains one stamp 37x50mm. An imperf. 10 l souvenir sheet exists showing planets in orbit. Value, unused or used, $30.

Romanian-Russian Space Cooperation — AP78

55b, Soyuz 40. 3.40 l, Salyut 6, Soyuz 40. 10 l, Cosmonauts, spacecraft.

1981   Photo.   Perf. 13½
C240 AP78 55b multicolored .25 .25
C241 AP78 3.40 l multicolored .50 .25

Souvenir Sheet

C242 AP78 10 l multicolored 2.25 2.25

No. C242 contains one stamp 50x39mm.
Issued: 55b, 3.40 l, May 14; 10 l, June 30.

An imperforate souvenir sheet titled "C.S.C.E. in EUROPA" was issued with limited distribution 1981, Oct. 28. The souvenir sheet contains three stamps showing a map of Europe, an airplane over a globe, and Madrid, respectively. Each stamp has a face value of 5 l. Value for sheet, $16.

Children's Games Type of 1981
1981, Nov. 25
C243 A880 4.80 l Flying model planes .70 .70

Standard Glider — AP79

1982, June 20   Photo.   Perf. 13½
C244 AP79 50b shown .25 .25
C245 AP79 1 l Excelsior D .25 .25
C246 AP79 1.50 l Dedal l .25 .25
C247 AP79 2.50 l Enthusiast .45 .25
C248 AP79 4 l AK-22 .60 .25
C249 AP79 5 l Grifrom .75 .30
  Nos. C244-C249 (6) 2.55 1.55

Agriculture Type of 1982
1982, June 29
C250 A888 4 l Helicopter spraying insecticide .60 .25

Vlaicu's Glider, 1909 — AP80

Aurel Vlaicu (1882-19), Aviator: 1 l, Memorial, Banesti-Prahova, vert. 2.50 l, Hero Aviators Memorial, by Kotzebue and Fekete, vert. 3 l, Vlaicu-1 glider, 1910.

1982, Sept. 27   Photo.   Perf. 13½
C251 AP80   50b multi   .25   .25
C252 AP80   1 l multi   .25   .25
C253 AP80   2.50 l multi   .40   .25
C254 AP80   3 l multi   .45   .25
  Nos. C251-C254 (4)   1.35 1.00

25th Anniv. of Space Flight AP81

Designs: 50b, H. Coanda, reaction motor, 1910. 1 l, H. Oberth, rocket, 1923. 1.50 l, Sputnik I, 1957. 2.50 l, Vostok I, 1961. 4 l, Apollo 11, 1969. 5 l, Columbia space shuttle, 1982. 10 l, Globe.

1983, Jan. 24
C255 AP81   50b multi   .25   .25
C256 AP81   1 l multi   .25   .25
C257 AP81   1.50 l multi   .30   .25
C258 AP81   2.50 l multi   .45   .25
C259 AP81   4 l multi   .70   .25
C260 AP81   5 l multi   .90   .25
  Nos. C255-C260 (6)   2.85 1.50

Souvenir Sheet
C261 AP81   10 l multi   2.50 2.50
No. C261 contains one stamp 41x53mm.

First Romanian-built Jet Airliner — AP82

1983, Jan. 25   Photo.   Perf. 13½
C262 AP82   11 l Rombac 1-11   2.75   .40

World Communications Year — AP83

1983, July 25   Photo.   Perf. 13½
C263 AP83   2 l Boeing 707, Postal van   .40   .25

An imperf. 10 l souvenir sheet showing a dove above the Palacic de Congresos de Madrid building was issued 1983, nov. 28 with limited distribution for EUROPA. Value, $20.

40th Anniv., Intl. Civil Aviation Organization — AP84

1984, Aug. 15   Photo.   Perf. 13½
C265 AP84   50b Lockheed L-14   .25   .25
C266 AP84   1.50 l BN-2 Islander   .35   .25
C267 AP84   3 l Rombac   .70   .25
C268 AP84   6 l Boeing 707   1.25   .35
  Nos. C265-C268 (4)   2.55 1.10

Halley's Comet — AP85

1986, Jan. 27   Photo.   Perf. 13½
C269 AP85   2 l shown   .60   .40
C270 AP85   4 l Space probes   1.50   .65

An imperf. 10 l air post souvenir sheet exists showing comet and space probes, red control number. Value, unused or used, $10. For surcharge, see No. C302.

Souvenir Sheet

Plane of Alexandru Papana, 1936 — AP86

1986, May 15   Photo.   Perf. 13½
C271 AP86   10 l multi   2.25 2.25
AMERIPEX '86.

Aircraft AP87

50b, Henri Auguste glider, 1909. 1 l, Sky diver, IS-28 B2 glider. 2 l, IS-29 D-2 glider. 3 l, IS-32 glider. 4 l, IAR-35 glider. 5 l, IS-28 M2, route.

1987, Aug. 10
C272 AP87   50b multi   .25   .25
C273 AP87   1 l multi   .25   .25
C274 AP87   2 l multi   .35   .25
C275 AP87   3 l multi   .55   .25
C276 AP87   4 l multi   .80   .25
C277 AP87   5 l multi   1.00   .30
  Nos. C272-C277 (6)   3.20 1.55

1st Moon Landing, 20th Anniv. — AP88

Designs: 50b, C. Haas. 1.50 l, Konstantin Tsiolkovski (1857-1935), Soviet rocket science pioneer. 2 l, H. Oberth and equations. 3 l, Robert Goddard and diagram on blackboard. 4 l, Sergei Korolev (1906-66), Soviet aeronautical engineer. 5 l, Wernher von Braun (1912-77), lunar module.

1989, Oct. 25   Photo.   Perf. 13½
C278 AP88   50b multicolored   .25   .25
C279 AP88   1.50 l multicolored   .35   .25
C280 AP88   2 l multicolored   .45   .25
C281 AP88   3 l multicolored   .65   .25
C282 AP88   4 l multicolored   .85   .25
C283 AP88   5 l multicolored   1.10   .25
  Nos. C278-C283 (6)   3.65 1.50

A 10 l souvenir sheet picturing Armstrong and *Eagle* lunar module was also issued. Value, unused or used, $22.50.

Souvenir Sheet

World Stamp Expo '89, Washington, DC, Nov. 17-Dec. 3 — AP89

1989, Nov. 17   Photo.   Perf. 13½
C284 AP89   5 l Postal coach   1.75 1.75

Captured Balloons — AP90

Balloons captured by Romanian army: 30 l, German balloon, Draken, 1903. 90 l, French balloon, Caquot, 1917.

1993, Feb. 26   Photo.   Perf. 13½
C285 AP90   30 l multicolored   .25   .25
C286 AP90   90 l multicolored   .70   .25

Souvenir Sheet

European Inventions, Discoveries — AP91

Europa: a, 240 l, Hermann Oberth (1894-1989), rocket scientist. b, 2100 l, Henri Coanda (1886-1972), aeronautical engineer.

1994, May 25   Photo.   Perf. 13
C287 AP91   Sheet of 2, #a.-b. + 2 labels   4.50 4.50

ICAO, 50th Anniv. AP92

Aircraft: 110 l, Traian Vuia, 1906. 350 l, Rombac 1-11. 500 l, Boeing 737-300. 635 l, Airbus A310.

1994, Aug. 12   Photo.   Perf. 13
C288 AP92   110 l multicolored   .25   .25
C289 AP92   350 l multicolored   .60   .25
C290 AP92   500 l multicolored   1.00   .25
C291 AP92   635 l multicolored   1.25   .25
  Nos. C288-C291 (4)   3.10 1.00

For surcharges see #C294-C297.

French-Romanian Aeronautical Agreement, 75th Anniv. — AP93

1995, Mar. 31   Photo.   Perf. 13x13¼
C292 AP93   60 l shown   .25   .25
C293 AP93   960 l Biplane Potez IX   1.25   .25

No. C291 Surcharged in Red

Methods and Perfs as Before
2000, May 19
C294 AP92 1700 l on 635 l multi .25   .25
C295 AP92 2000 l on 635 l multi .40   .25
C296 AP92 3900 l on 635 l multi .65   .25
C297 AP92 9050 l on 635 l multi 1.40   .60
  Nos. C294-C297 (4)   2.70 1.35

No. C293 Surcharged in Red

2000, Oct. 27   Photo.   Perf. 13¼
C298 AP93 2000 l on 960 l multi .25   .25
C299 AP93 4200 l on 960 l multi .45   .25
C300 AP93 4600 l on 960 l multi .45   .25
C301 AP93 6500 l on 960 l multi .65   .25
  Nos. C298-C301 (4)   1.80 1.00

Souvenir Sheet Footnoted Under No. C270 Surcharged in Gold

Litho. With Foil Application
2016, Apr. 22   Imperf.
C302 AP85   31 l on 10 l multi   16.00 8.00

AIR POST SEMI-POSTAL STAMPS

Catalogue values for unused stamps in this section are for Never Hinged items.

Corneliu Codreanu SPAP1

Unwmk.
1940, Dec. 1   Photo.   Perf. 14
CB1 SPAP1 20 l + 5 l Prus grn   4.50 3.25

Propaganda for the Rome-Berlin Axis. No. CB1 exists with overprint "1 Mai 1941 Jamboreea Nationala." This was a private overprint, not authorized by the Romanian Postal Service.

Plane over Sinaia — SPAP2

200 l+800 l, Plane over Mountains.

1945, Oct. 1   Wmk. 276   Imperf.
CB2 SPAP2   80 l + 420 l gray   2.50   2.50
CB3 SPAP2   200 l + 800 l ultra   2.50   2.50
16th Congress of the General Assoc. of Romanian Engineers.

Souvenir Sheet

Re-distribution of Land — SPAP4

1946, May 4   Photo.   Perf. 14
CB4 SPAP4   80 l blue   14.00   25.00
Agrarian reform law of Mar. 23, 1945. The sheet sold for 100 lei.

Souvenir Sheet

Plane Skywriting — SPAP5

1946, May 1   Perf. 13
CB5 SPAP5   200 l bl & brt red   12.00   22.50
Labor Day. The sheet sold for 10,000 lei.

Lockheed 12 Electra — SPAP6

1946, Sept. 1   Perf. 11½
CB6 SPAP6   300 l + 1200 l dp bl   1.00   1.25
For se-tenant see No. C26a and note after No. C26.
The surtax was for the Office of Popular Sports.

Miniature Sheet

Women of Wallachia, Transylvania and Moldavia — SPAP7

1946, Dec. 20   Wmk. 276   Imperf.
CB7 SPAP7   500 l + 9500 l choc   6.00   6.00
              & red
Democratic Women's Org. of Romania.

SPAP8

1946, Oct.   Imperf.
CB8 SPAP8   300 l deep plum   17.50   17.50
The surtax was for the Office of Popular Sports. Sheets of four. Stamp sold for 1300 l.

Laborer with Torch — SPAP9

1947, Mar. 1
CB9 SPAP9   3000 l + 7000 l choc   .80   1.50
Sheets of four with marginal inscription.

Plane — SPAP10

1947, June 27   Imperf.
CB10 SPAP10   15,000 l + 15,000   .80   .80
               l
Sheets of four with marginal inscription.

Plane above Shore Line — SPAP11

1947, May 1   Perf. 14x13
CB11 SPAP11   3000 l + 12,000 l   .60   .60
               bl

Planes over Mountains SPAP12

1947, Oct. 5   Perf. 14x14½
CB12 SPAP12   5 l + 5 l blue   .70   .70
17th Congress of the General Assoc. of Romanian Engineers.

Plane over Athletic Field — SPAP13

Wmk. 276
1948, Feb. 20   Photo.   Perf. 13½
CB13 SPAP13   7 l + 7 l vio   1.00   .70
Imperf
CB14 SPAP13   10 l + 10 l Prus   2.00   1.00
               grn
Balkan Games. Sheets of four with marginal inscription.

Swallow and Plane SPAP14

1948, Mar. 15   Perf. 14x13½
CB15 SPAP14   12 l + 12 l blue   1.10   .60

Bucharest-Moscow Passenger Plane, Douglas DC-3 Dakota — SPAP15

1948, Oct. 29   Perf. 14
CB16 SPAP15   20 l + 20 l dp bl   10.00   10.00
Printed in sheets of 8 stamps and 16 small, red brown labels. Sheet yields 8 triptychs, each comprising 1 stamp flanked by label with Bucharest view and label with Moscow view.

Douglas DC-4 — SPAP16

1948, May 1   Perf. 13½x14
CB17 SPAP16   20 l + 20 l blue   10.00   8.00
Issued to publicize Labor Day, May 1, 1948.

Pursuit Plane and Victim — SPAP17

1948, May 9   Perf. 13
CB18 SPAP17   3 l + 3 l shown   6.00   6.00
CB19 SPAP17   5 l + 5 l Bomber   8.00   8.00
Issued to honor the Romanian army.

Launching Model Plane — SPAP18

1948, Dec. 31   Perf. 13x13½
CB20 SPAP18   20 l + 20 l dp   15.00   15.00
               ultra
Imperf
CB21 SPAP18   20 l + 20 l Prus   15.00   15.00
               bl
Nos. CB20 and CB21 were issued in sheets of four stamps, with ornamental border and "1948" in contrasting color.

UPU Type of Air Post Issue, 1963

Design: 1.60 l+50b, Globe, map of Romania, planes and UPU monument.

Perf. 14x13½
1963, Nov. 15   Litho.   Unwmk.
Size: 75x27mm
CB22 AP54   1.60 l + 50b multi   2.75   .50
Surtax for the Romanian Philatelic Federation.

POSTAGE DUE STAMPS

D1

Perf. 11, 11½, 13½ and Compound
1881   Typo.   Unwmk.
J1   D1   2b brown   4.00   1.50
J2   D1   5b brown   22.50   2.50
  a.   Tête bêche pair   190.00   75.00
J3   D1   10b brown   30.00   1.50
J4   D1   30b brown   32.50   1.50
J5   D1   50b brown   26.00   2.75
J6   D1   60b brown   21.00   4.00
    Nos. J1-J6 (6)   136.00   13.75

1885
J7   D1   10b pale red brown   8.00   .50
J8   D1   30b pale red brown   8.00   .50

1887-90
J9   D1   2b gray green   4.00   1.00
J10   D1   5b gray green   8.00   3.50
J11   D1   10b gray green   8.00   3.50
J12   D1   30b gray green   8.00   1.00
    Nos. J9-J12 (4)   28.00   9.00

1888
J14   D1   2b green, yellowish   .90   .75
J15   D1   5b green, yellowish   2.25   2.25
J16   D1   10b green, yellowish   32.50   2.75
J17   D1   30b green, yellowish   17.50   1.25
    Nos. J14-J17 (4)   53.15   7.00

1890-96   Wmk. 163
J18   D1   2b emerald   1.60   .45
J19   D1   5b emerald   .80   .45
J20   D1   10b emerald   1.25   .45
J21   D1   30b emerald   2.00   .45
J22   D1   50b emerald   6.50   .95
J23   D1   60b emerald   8.75   3.25
    Nos. J18-J23 (6)   20.90   6.00

1898   Wmk. 200
J24   D1   2b blue green   .70   .45
J25   D1   5b blue green   .90   .30
J26   D1   10b blue green   1.40   .30
J27   D1   30b blue green   1.90   .30
J28   D1   50b blue green   4.75   .90
J29   D1   60b blue green   5.50   1.75
    Nos. J24-J29 (6)   15.15   4.00

1902-10   Thin Paper, Tinted Rose on Back   Unwmk.

J30	D1	2b green	.85	.50
J31	D1	5b green	.50	.25
J32	D1	10b green	.40	.25
J33	D1	30b green	.50	.25
J34	D1	50b green	2.50	.90
J35	D1	60b green	5.25	2.25
		Nos. J30-J35 (6)	10.00	4.15

1908-11   White Paper

J36	D1	2b green	.80	.50
J37	D1	5b green	.60	.50
a.		Tête bêche pair	12.00	12.00
J38	D1	10b green	.40	.30
a.		Tête bêche pair	12.00	12.00
J39	D1	30b green	.50	.30
a.		Tête bêche pair	12.00	12.00
J40	D1	50b green	2.00	1.25
		Nos. J36-J40 (5)	4.30	2.85

D2

1911   Wmk. 165

J41	D2	2b dark blue, *green*	.25	.25
J42	D2	5b dark blue, *green*	.25	.25
J43	D2	10b dark blue, *green*	.25	.25
J44	D2	15b dark blue, *green*	.25	.25
J45	D2	20b dark blue, *green*	.25	.25
J46	D2	30b dark blue, *green*	.25	.25
J47	D2	50b dark blue, *green*	.50	.30
J48	D2	60b dark blue, *green*	.60	.40
J49	D2	2 l dark blue, *green*	1.00	.80
		Nos. J41-J49 (9)	3.60	3.00

The letters "P.R." appear to be embossed instead of watermarked. They are often faint or entirely invisible.

The 20b, type D2, has two types, differing in the width of the head of the "2." This affects Nos. J52-J77, J82, J87-J88. For overprints see Nos. J78-J81, RAJ1-RAJ2, RAJ20-RAJ21, 3NJ1-3NJ7.

See Nos. J52-J77, J82, J87-J88. For overprints see Nos. J78-J81, RAJ1-RAJ2, RAJ20-RAJ21, 3NJ1-3NJ7.

Regular Issue of 1908 Overprinted

1918   Unwmk.

J50	A46	5b yellow green	1.40	.40
a.		Inverted overprint	5.00	5.00
J51	A46	10b rose	1.40	.40
a.		Inverted overprint	3.75	3.75

Postage Due Type of 1911

1920   Wmk. 165

J52	D2	5b black, *green*	.25	.25
J53	D2	10b black, *green*	.25	.25
J54	D2	20b black, *green*	4.00	.60
J55	D2	30b black, *green*	1.10	.40
J55A	D2	50b black, *green*	3.00	.90
		Nos. J52-J55A (5)	8.60	2.40

Perf. 11½, 13½ and Compound

1919   Unwmk.

J56	D2	5b black, *green*	.30	.25
J57	D2	10b black, *green*	.30	.25
J58	D2	20b black, *green*	1.00	.25
J59	D2	30b black, *green*	.90	.25
J60	D2	50b black, *green*	2.25	.40
		Nos. J56-J60 (5)	4.75	1.40

1920-26   White Paper

J61	D2	5b black	.25	.25
J62	D2	10b black	.25	.25
J63	D2	20b black	.25	.25
J64	D2	30b black	.25	.25
J65	D2	50b black	.40	.40
J66	D2	60b black	.25	.25
J67	D2	1 l black	.30	.30
J68	D2	2 l black	.25	.25
J69	D2	3 l black ('26)	.25	.25
J70	D2	6 l black ('26)	.30	.30
		Nos. J61-J70 (10)	2.75	2.75

1923-24

J74	D2	1 l black, *pale green*	.25	.25
J75	D2	2 l black, *pale green*	.45	.25
J76	D2	3 l black, *pale green* ('24)	1.25	.60
J77	D2	6 l blk, *pale green* ('24)	1.75	.60
		Nos. J74-J77 (4)	3.70	1.70

Postage Due Stamps of 1920-26 Overprinted

1930   *Perf. 13½*

J78	D2	1 l black	.25	.25
J79	D2	2 l black	.25	.25
J80	D2	3 l black	.35	.25
J81	D2	6 l black	.60	.30
		Nos. J78-J81 (4)	1.45	1.05

Accession of King Carol II.

> **Catalogue values for unused stamps in this section, from this point to the end of the section, are for Never Hinged items.**

Type of 1911 Issue

1931   Wmk. 225

J82	D2	2 l black	.90	.35

D3

1932-37   Wmk. 230

J83	D3	1 l black	.25	.25
J84	D3	2 l black	.25	.25
J85	D3	3 l black ('37)	.25	.25
J86	D3	6 l black ('37)	.25	.25
		Nos. J83-J86 (4)	1.00	1.00

See Nos. J89-J98.

Type of 1911 Issue

1942   Typo.   *Perf. 13½*

J87	D2	50 l black	.35	.25
J88	D2	100 l black	.50	.25

Type of 1932

1946-47   Unwmk.   *Perf. 14*

J89	D3	20 l black	.60	.55
J90	D3	100 l black ('47)	.45	.25
J91	D3	200 l black	1.10	.55
		Nos. J89-J91 (3)	2.15	1.35

1946-47   Wmk. 276

J92	D3	20 l black	.25	.25
J93	D3	50 l black	.25	.25
J94	D3	80 l black	.25	.25
J95	D3	100 l black	.25	.25
J96	D3	200 l black	.60	.35
J97	D3	500 l black	.90	.50
J98	D3	5000 l black ('47)	2.50	1.25
		Nos. J92-J98 (7)	5.00	3.10

Crown and King Michael — D3a

Perf. 14½x13½

1947   Typo.   Wmk. 276

J98A	D3a	2 l carmine	.40	.25
J98B	D3a	4 l gray blue	.75	.30
J98C	D3a	5 l black	1.10	.45
J98D	D3a	10 l violet brown	2.00	.75
		Nos. J98A-J98D (4)	4.25	1.75

Nos. J98A-J98D Overprinted

1948

J98E	D3a	2 l carmine	.30	.25
J98F	D3a	4 l gray blue	.75	.25
J98G	D3a	5 l black	1.00	.30
J98H	D3a	10 l violet brown	1.75	.55
		Nos. J98E-J98H (4)	3.80	1.35

In use, Nos. J98A-J106 and following issues were torn apart, one half being affixed to the postage due item and the other half being pasted into the postman's record book. Values are for unused and canceled-to-order pairs.

Communications Badge and Postwoman — D4

1950   Unwmk.   Photo.   *Perf. 14½x14*

J99	D4	2 l orange vermilion	.75	.75
J100	D4	4 l deep blue	.75	.75
J101	D4	5 l dark gray green	1.25	1.25
J102	D4	10 l orange brown	1.50	1.50

Wmk. 358

J103	D4	2 l orange vermilion	7.50	7.50
J104	D4	4 l deep blue	7.50	7.50
J105	D4	5 l dark gray green	3.50	3.50
J106	D4	10 l orange brown	2.00	2.00
		Nos. J99-J106 (8)	24.75	24.75

Postage Due Stamps of 1950 Surcharged with New Values in Black or Carmine

1952   Unwmk.

J107	D4	4b on 2 l	.40	.40
J108	D4	10b on 4 l (C)	.40	.40
J109	D4	20b on 5 l (C)	1.00	1.00
J110	D4	50b on 10 l	1.50	1.50
		Nos. J107-J110 (4)	3.30	3.30

Wmk. 358

J111	D4	4b on 2 l		
J112	D4	10b on 4 l (C)		
J113	D4	20b on 5 l (C)	7.50	7.50
J114	D4	50b on 10 l	7.50	7.50

The existence of Nos. J111-J112 has been questioned.

See note after No. J98H.

General Post Office and Post Horn — D5

1957   Wmk. 358   *Perf. 14*

J115	D5	3b black	.25	.25
J116	D5	5b red orange	.25	.25
J117	D5	10b red lilac	.25	.25
J118	D5	20b brt red	.25	.25
J119	D5	40b lt bl grn	.50	.25
J120	D5	1 l brt ultra	2.00	.40
		Nos. J115-J120 (6)	3.50	1.65

See note after No. J98H.

General Post Office and Post Horn — D6

1967, Feb. 25   Photo.   *Perf. 13*

J121	D6	3b brt grn	.25	.25
J122	D6	5b brt bl	.25	.25
J123	D6	10b lilac rose	.25	.25
J124	D6	20b vermilion	.25	.25
J125	D6	40b brown	.25	.25
J126	D6	1 l violet	.55	.25
		Nos. J121-J126 (6)	1.80	1.50

See note after No. J98H.

1970, Mar. 10   Unwmk.

J127	D6	3b brt grn	.25	.25
J128	D6	5b brt bl	.25	.25
J129	D6	10b lilac rose	.25	.25
J130	D6	20b vermilion	.25	.25
J131	D6	40b brown	.25	.25
J132	D6	1 l violet	.35	.25
		Nos. J127-J132 (6)	1.60	1.50

See note after No. J98H.

Symbols of Communications — D7

Designs: 10b, Like 5b. 20b, 40b, Pigeons, head of Mercury and post horn. 50b, 1 l, General Post Office, post horn and truck.

1974, Jan. 1   Photo.   *Perf. 13*

J133	D7	5b brt bl	.25	.25
J134	D7	10b olive	.25	.25
J135	D7	20b lilac rose	.25	.25
J136	D7	40b purple	.25	.25
J137	D7	50b brown	.25	.25
J138	D7	1 l orange	.35	.25
		Nos. J133-J138 (6)	1.60	1.50

See #J139-J144. For surcharges see #J147-J151.

1982, Dec. 23   Photo.   *Perf. 13½*

J139	D7	25b like #J135	.25	.25
J140	D7	50b like #J133	.25	.25
J141	D7	1 l like #J135	.25	.25
J142	D7	2 l like #J137	.45	.25
J143	D7	3 l like #J133	.70	.25
J144	D7	4 l like #J137	1.00	.25
		Nos. J139-J144 (6)	2.90	1.50

See note after No. J98H.

Post Horn — D8

1992, Feb. 3   Photo.   *Perf. 13½*

J145	D8	4 l red	.50	.25
J146	D8	8 l blue	.50	.25

See note after No. J98H.

D9

1994, Dec. 10   Photo.   *Perf. 13¼*

J146A	D9	10 l brown	.25	.25
J146B	D9	45 l orange	.40	.25

See note after No. J98H.

Nos. J140-J142, J144 Surcharged in Green, Deep Blue, or Black

1999, Mar. 12   Photo.   *Perf. 13½*

J147	D7	50 l on 50b #J140 (G)	.25	.25
J148	D7	50 l on 1 l #J141 (DBl)	.25	.25
J149	D7	100 l on 2 l #J142	.25	.25
J150	D7	700 l on 1 l #J141	.30	.25
J151	D7	1100 l on 4 l #J144	.45	.25
		Nos. J147-J151 (5)	1.50	1.25

Nos. J145, J146B Surcharged

2001, Jan. 17   Photo.   *Perf. 13¼*

J152	D8	500 l on 4 l red	.25	.25
J153	D8	1000 l on 4 l red	.25	.25
J154	D9	2000 l on 45 l org	.25	.25
		Nos. J152-J154 (3)	.75	.75

See note after No. J98H.

OFFICIAL STAMPS

Catalogue values for unused stamps in this section are for Never Hinged items.

Eagle Carrying National Emblem — O1

1929	Photo.	Wmk. 95	Perf. 13½	
O1	O1	25b red orange	.25	.25
O2	O1	50b dk brown	.25	.25
O3	O1	1 l dk violet	.30	.25
O4	O1	2 l olive grn	.30	.25
O5	O1	3 l rose car	.45	.25
O6	O1	4 l dk olive	.45	.25
O7	O1	6 l Prus blue	2.50	.25
O8	O1	10 l deep blue	.80	.25
O9	O1	25 l carmine brn	1.60	1.25
O10	O1	50 l purple	4.75	3.50
		Nos. O1-O10 (10)	11.65	6.75

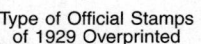

Type of Official Stamps of 1929 Overprinted

1930			Unwmk.	
O11	O1	25b red orange	.25	.25
O12	O1	50b dk brown	.25	.25
O13	O1	1 l dk violet	.35	.25
O14	O1	3 l rose carmine	.50	.25
		Nos. O11-O14 (4)	1.35	1.00

Nos. O11-O14 were not placed in use without overprint.

Same Overprint on Nos. O1-O10
Wmk. 95

O15	O1	25b red orange	.25	.25
O16	O1	50b dk brown	.25	.25
O17	O1	1 l dk violet	.25	.25
O18	O1	2 l dp green	.25	.25
O19	O1	3 l rose carmine	.60	.25
O20	O1	4 l olive black	.75	.25
O21	O1	6 l Prus blue	2.00	.25
O22	O1	10 l deep blue	.80	.25
O23	O1	25 l carmine brown	3.00	2.50
O24	O1	50 l purple	4.00	3.50
		Nos. O15-O24 (10)	12.15	8.00

Accession of King Carol II to the throne of Romania (Nos O11-O24).

Coat of Arms — O2

Perf. 13½, 13½x14½

1931-32		Typo.	Wmk. 225	
O25	O2	25b black	.30	.25
O26	O2	1 l lilac	.30	.25
O27	O2	2 l emerald	.60	.40
O28	O2	3 l rose	1.00	.70
		Nos. O25-O28 (4)	2.20	1.60

1932		Wmk. 230	Perf. 13½	
O29	O2	25b black	.30	.25
O30	O2	1 l violet	.40	.35
O31	O2	2 l emerald	.65	.55
O32	O2	3 l rose	.80	.65
O33	O2	6 l red brown	1.25	1.00
		Nos. O29-O33 (5)	3.40	2.80

PARCEL POST STAMPS

PP1

Perf. 11½, 13½ and Compound

1895		Wmk. 163	Typo.	
Q1	PP1	25b brown red	12.50	2.25

1896				
Q2	PP1	25b vermilion	10.00	1.25

Perf. 13½ and 11½x13½

1898		Wmk. 200		
Q3	PP1	25b brown red	7.00	1.25
a.		Tête bêche pair		
Q4	PP1	25b vermilion	7.00	.90

Thin Paper
Tinted Rose on Back

1905		Unwmk.	Perf. 11½	
Q5	PP1	25b vermilion	7.50	1.25

1911			White Paper	
Q6	PP1	25b pale red	7.50	1.25

No. 263 Surcharged in Carmine

1928			Perf. 13½	
Q7	A54	5 l on 10b yellow green	1.50	.30

POSTAL TAX STAMPS

Regular Issue of 1908 Overprinted

Perf. 11½, 13½, 11½x13½

1915			Unwmk.	
RA1	A46	5b green	.25	.25
RA2	A46	10b rose	.40	.25

The "Timbru de Ajutor" stamps represent a tax on postal matter. The money obtained from their sale was turned into a fund for the assistance of soldiers' families.

Until 1923 the only "Timbru de Ajutor" stamps used for postal purposes were the 5b and 10b. Stamps of higher values with this inscription were used to pay the taxes on railway and theater tickets and other fiscal taxes. In 1923 the postal rate was advanced to 25b.

The Queen Weaving — PT1

1916-18			Typo.	
RA3	PT1	5b gray blk	.25	.25
RA4	PT1	5b green ('18)	.70	.40
RA5	PT1	10b brown	.40	.25
RA6	PT1	10b gray blk ('18)	1.00	.45
		Nos. RA3-RA6 (4)	2.35	1.35

For overprints see Nos. RA7-RA8, RAJ7-RAJ9, 3NRA1-3NRA8.

Stamps of 1916 Overprinted in Red or Black

1918			Perf. 13½	
RA7	PT1	5b gray blk (R)	.70	.25
a.		Double overprint	5.00	
c.		Black overprint	5.00	
RA8	PT1	10b brn (Bk)	.70	.25
a.		Double overprint	5.00	
b.		Double overprint, one inverted	5.00	
c.		Inverted overprint	5.00	

Same Overprint on RA1 and RA2

1919				
RA11	A46	5b yel grn (R)	19.00	12.50
RA12	A46	10b rose (Bk)	19.00	12.50

Charity — PT3

Perf. 13½, 11½, 13½x11½

1921-24		Typo.	Unwmk.	
RA13	PT3	10b green	.25	.25
RA14	PT3	25b blk ('24)	.25	.25

Type of 1921-24 Issue

1928		Wmk. 95		
RA15	PT3	25b black	1.00	.45

Nos. RA13, RA14 and RA15 are the only stamps of type PT3 issued for postal purposes. Other denominations were used fiscally.

Catalogue values for unused stamps in this section, from this point to the end of the section, are for Never Hinged items.

Airplane — PT4

1931		Photo.	Unwmk.	
RA16	PT4	50b Prus bl	.45	.25
a.		Double impression	15.00	
RA17	PT4	1 l dk red brn	.75	.25
RA18	PT4	2 l ultra	1.00	.25
		Nos. RA16-RA18 (3)	2.20	.75

The use of these stamps, in addition to the regular postage, was obligatory on all postal matter on postal matter for the interior of the country. The money thus obtained was to augment the National Fund for Aviation. When the stamps were not used to prepay the special tax, it was collected by means of Postal Tax Due stamps Nos. RAJ20 and RAJ21.

Nos. RA17 and RA18 were also used for other than postal tax.

Head of Aviator — PT5

1932		Wmk. 230	Perf. 14 x 13½	
RA19	PT5	50b Prus bl	.30	.25
RA20	PT5	1 l red brn	.45	.25
RA21	PT5	2 l ultra	.70	.25
		Nos. RA19-RA21 (3)	1.45	.75

See notes after No. RA18.
After 1937 use of Nos. RA20-RA21 was limited to other than postal matter.
Nos. RA19-RA21 exist imperf.
Four stamps similar to type PT5 were issued in 1936: 10b sepia, 20b violet, 3 l green and 5 l red. These were used for purposes other than postal tax.

Aviator — PT5A

1936-37			Perf. 13¾x14½	
RA19A	PT5A	10b orange	1.00	.25
RA20A	PT5A	20b reddish pur ('37)	1.00	.25
RA21A	PT5A	50b rose	1.50	.45
		Nos. RA19A-RA21A (3)	3.50	.95

Aviator — PT6

1937			Perf. 13½	
RA22	PT6	50b Prus grn	.25	.25
RA23	PT6	1 l red brn	.35	.25
RA24	PT6	2 l brn	.45	.25
		Nos. RA22-RA24 (3)	1.05	.75

Stamps overprinted or inscribed "Fondul Aviatiei" other than Nos. RA22, RA23 or RA24 were used to pay taxes on other than postal matters.

King Michael — PT7

1943	Wmk. 276	Photo.	Perf. 14	
RA25	PT7	50b org ver	.25	.25
RA26	PT7	1 l lil rose	.25	.25
RA27	PT7	2 l brown	.25	.25
RA28	PT7	4 l lt ultra	.25	.25
RA29	PT7	5 l dull lilac	.25	.25
RA30	PT7	8 l yel grn	.25	.25
RA31	PT7	10 l blk brn	.25	.25
		Nos. RA25-RA31 (7)	1.75	1.75

The tax was obligatory on domestic mail. Examples of these stamps with an overprint consisting of a red cross and text are unissued franchise stamps.

Protection of Homeless Children — PT8

1945				
RA32	PT8	40 l Prus bl	.35	.25

PT9

Black Surcharge

1947	Unwmk.	Typo.	Perf. 14x14½	
RA33	PT9	1 l on 2 l + 2 l pink	.30	.25
a.		Inverted surcharge	25.00	25.00
RA34	PT9	5 l on 1 l + 1 l gray grn	2.50	2.50

"Hope" — PT10

1948			Perf. 14	
RA35	PT10	1 l rose	.90	.35
RA36	PT10	1 l rose violet	1.00	.35

A 2 lei blue and 5 lei ocher in type PT10 were issued primarily for revenue purposes.

POSTAL TAX DUE STAMPS

Catalogue values for unused stamps in this section are for Never Hinged items.

Postage Due Stamps of 1911 Overprinted

1915				Unwmk.
RAJ1	D2	5b dk bl, *grn*	.75	.25
RAJ2	D2	10b dk bl, *grn*	.75	.25
a.		Wmk. 165	10.00	1.00

PTD1

1916		Typo.		Unwmk.
RAJ3	PTD1	5b brn, *grn*	.40	.25
RAJ4	PTD1	10b red, *grn*	.40	.25

See Nos. RAJ5-RAJ6, RAJ10-RAJ11. For overprint see No. 3NRAJ1.

1918				
RAJ5	PTD1	5b red, *grn*	.25	.25
a.		Wmk. 165	1.00	.25
RAJ6	PTD1	10b brn, *grn*	.25	.25
a.		Wmk. 165	1.75	.25

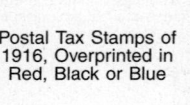

Postal Tax Stamps of 1916, Overprinted in Red, Black or Blue

RAJ7	PT1	5b gray blk (R)	.40	.25
a.		Inverted overprint	7.50	
RAJ8	PT1	10b brn (Bk)	.80	.25
a.		Inverted overprint	7.50	
RAJ9	PT1	10b brn (Bl)	5.00	5.00
a.		Vertical overprint	20.00	15.00
		Nos. RAJ7-RAJ9 (3)	6.20	5.50

Type of 1916

1921				
RAJ10	PTD1	5b red	.50	.25
RAJ11	PTD1	10b brown	.50	.25

PTD2

1922-25		Greenish Paper		Typo.
RAJ12	PTD2	10b brown	.25	.25
RAJ13	PTD2	20b brown	.25	.25
RAJ14	PTD2	25b brown	.25	.25
RAJ15	PTD2	50b brown	.25	.25
		Nos. RAJ12-RAJ15 (4)	1.00	1.00

1923-26				
RAJ16	PTD2	10b lt brn	.25	.25
RAJ17	PTD2	20b brown	.25	.25
RAJ18	PTD2	25b brown ('26)	.25	.25
RAJ19	PTD2	50b brown ('26)	.25	.25
		Nos. RAJ16-RAJ19 (4)	1.00	1.00

J82 and Type of 1911 Postage Due Stamps Overprinted in Red

1931		Wmk. 225		Perf. 13½
RAJ20	D2	1 l black	.25	.25
RAJ21	D2	2 l black	.25	.25

When the Postal Tax stamps for the Aviation Fund issue (Nos. RA16 to RA18) were not used to prepay the obligatory tax on letters, etc., it was collected by affixing Nos. RAJ20 and RAJ21.

OCCUPATION STAMPS

ISSUED UNDER AUSTRIAN OCCUPATION

Austria Military Stamps Nos. M51-M67 Surcharged

No. M51

No. M65

1917		Unwmk. Engr.		Perf. 12½
1N1	M3	3b on 3h ol gray	2.00	3.00
1N2	M3	5b on 5h ol gray	2.00	3.00
1N3	M3	6b on 6h violet	2.00	3.00
1N4	M3	10b on 10h org brn	.40	.70
1N5	M3	12b on 12h dp blue	1.50	2.50
1N6	M3	15b on 15h brt rose	1.50	2.50
1N7	M3	20b on 20h red brn	.40	.70
1N8	M3	25b on 25h ultra	.40	.70
1N9	M3	30b on 30h grnsh slate	.70	1.00
1N10	M3	40b on 40h ol bis	.70	1.00
a.		Perf. 11½	100.00	175.00
b.		Perf. 11½x12½	100.00	175.00
1N11	M3	50b on 50h dp grn	.40	.70
1N12	M3	60b on 60h car rose	.40	.70
1N13	M3	80b on 80h dl bl	.35	.65
1N14	M3	90b on 90h dk vio	.70	1.00
1N15	M4	2 l on 2k rose, *straw*	1.10	1.60
1N16	M4	3 l on 3k grn, *bl*	1.10	2.00
1N17	M4	4 l on 4k rose, *grn*	1.50	2.50
		Nos. 1N1-1N17 (17)	17.15	27.25

Nos. 1N1-1N14 have "BANI" surcharged in red.

Nos. 1N1-1N17 also exist imperforate. Value, set $125.

OS3　　　　OS4

1918				
1N18	OS3	3b ol gray	.35	.85
1N19	OS3	5b ol grn	.35	.85
1N20	OS3	6b violet	.35	.85
1N21	OS3	10b org brn	.35	.85
1N22	OS3	12b dp bl	.35	.85
1N23	OS3	15b brt rose	.35	.85
1N24	OS3	20b red brn	.35	.85
1N25	OS3	25b ultra	.35	.85
1N26	OS3	30b slate	.35	.85
1N27	OS3	40b ol bis	.35	.85
1N28	OS3	50b dp grn	.35	.85
1N29	OS3	60b rose	.35	.85
1N30	OS3	80b dl bl	.35	.85
1N31	OS3	90b dk vio	.35	.85
1N32	OS4	2 l rose, *straw*	.35	.85
1N33	OS4	3 l grn, *bl*	.75	2.25
1N34	OS4	4 l rose, *grn*	1.00	2.25
		Nos. 1N18-1N34 (17)	7.00	17.25

Exist. imperf. Value, set $80.

The complete series exists with "BANI" or "LEI" inverted, also with those words and the numerals of value inverted. Neither of these sets was regularly issued.

Austrian Nos. M69-M82 Overprinted In Black

1918		Typo.		Perf. 12½
1N35	M5	1h grnsh blue	40.00	
1N36	M5	2h orange	25.00	
1N37	M5	3h olive gray	47.50	
1N38	M5	5h yellow green	25.00	
1N39	M5	10h dark brown	70.00	
1N40	M5	20h red	70.00	
1N41	M5	25h blue	27.50	
1N42	M5	30h bister	47.50	
1N43	M5	45h dark slate	52.50	
1N44	M5	50h deep green	60.00	
1N45	M5	60h violet	80.00	
1N46	M5	80h rose	1,000.	
1N47	M5	90h brown violet	80.00	
		Nos. 1N35-1N47 (13)	1,625.	

Nos. 1N35-1N47 were on sale at the Vienna post office for a few days before the Armistice signing. They were never issued at the Army Post Offices.

ISSUED UNDER BULGARIAN OCCUPATION

Dobruja District

Bulgarian Stamps of 1915-16 Overprinted in Red or Blue

1916		Unwmk.	Perf. 11½, 14	
2N1	A20	1s dk blue grn (R)	.25	.25
2N2	A23	5s grn & vio brn (R)	3.00	1.75
2N3	A24	10s brn & brnsh blk (Bl)	.30	.25
2N4	A26	25s indigo & blk (Bl)	.30	.25
		Nos. 2N1-2N4 (4)	3.85	2.50

Many varieties of overprint exist.

ISSUED UNDER GERMAN OCCUPATION

German Stamps of 1905-17 Surcharged

1917		Wmk. 125		Perf. 14
3N1	A22	15b on 15pf dk vio (R)	1.00	1.00
3N2	A16	25b on 20pf ultra (Bk)	1.00	1.00
3N3	A16	40b on 30pf org & blk, *buff* (R)	17.50	17.50
		Nos. 3N1-3N3 (3)	19.50	19.50

"M.V.iR." are the initials of "Militär Verwaltung in Rumänien" (Military Administration of Romania).

German Stamps of 1905-17 Surcharged

1917-18				
3N4	A16	10b on 10pf car	1.10	1.40
3N5	A22	15b on 15pf dk vio	5.50	4.50
3N6	A16	25b on 20pf ultra	3.00	4.00
3N7	A16	40b on 30pf org & blk, *buff*	1.00	1.40
a.		"40" omitted	90.00	350.00
		Nos. 3N4-3N7 (4)	10.60	11.30

German Stamps of 1905-17 Surcharged

1918				
3N8	A16	5b on 5pf grn	.60	1.75
3N9	A16	10b on 10pf car	.60	1.50
3N10	A22	15b on 15pf dk vio	.25	.40
3N11	A16	25b on 20pf bl vio	.60	1.50
a.		25b on 20pf blue	2.50	8.00

3N12	A16	40b on 30pf org & blk, *buff*	.30	.35
		Nos. 3N8-3N12 (5)	2.35	5.50

German Stamps of 1905-17 Overprinted

1918				
3N13	A16	10pf carmine	8.75	40.00
3N14	A22	15pf dk vio	13.00	35.00
3N15	A16	20pf blue	1.25	1.75
3N16	A16	30pf org & blk, *buff*	13.00	22.50
		Nos. 3N13-3N16 (4)	36.00	99.25

POSTAGE DUE STAMPS ISSUED UNDER GERMAN OCCUPATION

Postage Due Stamps and Type of Romania Overprinted in Red

Perf. 11½, 13½ and Compound				
1918				**Wmk. 165**
3NJ1	D2	5b dk bl, *grn*	20.00	60.00
3NJ2	D2	10b dk bl, *grn*	20.00	60.00

The 20b, 30b and 50b with this overprint are fraudulent.

				Unwmk.
3NJ3	D2	5b dk bl, *grn*	8.00	10.50
3NJ4	D2	10b dk bl, *grn*	8.00	10.50
3NJ5	D2	20b dk bl, *grn*	3.00	2.75
3NJ6	D2	30b dk bl, *grn*	3.00	2.75
3NJ7	D2	50b dk bl, *grn*	3.00	2.75
		Nos. 3NJ1-3NJ7 (7)	65.00	149.25

POSTAL TAX STAMPS ISSUED UNDER GERMAN OCCUPATION

Romanian Postal Tax Stamps and Type of 1916

Overprinted in Red or Black

Perf. 11½, 13½ and Compound				
1917				**Unwmk.**
3NRA1	PT1	5b gray blk (R)	.80	2.75
3NRA2	PT1	10b brown (Bk)	.80	2.75

Same, Overprinted

1917-18				
3NRA3	PT1	5b gray blk (R)	1.50	3.50
a.		Black overprint	57.00	750.00
3NRA4	PT1	10b brown (Bk)	9.00	19.00
3NRA5	PT1	10b violet (Bk)	1.50	5.00
		Nos. 3NRA3-3NRA5 (3)	12.00	27.50

Same, Overprinted in Red or Black

1918				
3NRA6	PT1	5b gray blk (R)	45.00	30.00
3NRA7	PT1	10b brown (Bk)	45.00	30.00

Same, Overprinted

1918

3NRA8	PT1	10b violet (Bk)	.80	2.75

POSTAL TAX DUE STAMP ISSUED UNDER GERMAN OCCUPATION

Type of Romanian Postal Tax Due Stamp of 1916 Overprinted

Perf. 11½, 13½, and Compound

			Wmk. 165	
1918				
3NRAJ1	PTD1	10b red, *green*	2.50	3.00

ROMANIAN POST OFFICES IN THE TURKISH EMPIRE

40 Paras = 1 Piaster
Romania Nos. 120, 122 & 126 Surcharged

Perf. 11½, 13½ and Compound

		Wmk. 200	**Black Surcharge**	
1896				
1	A1910pa on 5b blue		32.50	30.00
2	A2020pa on 10b emer		24.00	22.50
3	A19 1pa on 25b violet		24.00	22.50
	Nos. 1-3 (3)		80.50	75.00

Violet Surcharge

4	A1910pa on 5b blue		17.00	15.00
5	A2020pa on 10b emer		17.00	15.00
6	A19 1pa on 25b violet		17.00	15.00
	Nos. 4-6 (3)		51.00	45.00

Romanian Stamps of 1908-18 Overprinted in Black or Red

1919		**Typo.**	**Unwmk.**	
7	A46	5b yellow grn	.50	.50
8	A46	10b rose	.65	.65
9	A46	15b red brown	.75	.75
10	A19	25b dp blue (R)	1.00	1.00
11	A19	40b gray brn (R)	2.75	2.75
		Nos. 7-11 (5)	5.65	5.65

All values exist with inverted overprint.

ROMANIAN POST OFFICES IN THE TURKISH EMPIRE POSTAL TAX STAMP

Romanian Postal Tax Stamp of 1918 Overprinted

1919 Unwmk.	**Perf. 11½, 11½x13½**			
RA1	PT1	5b green	2.50	2.50

ROUAD, ILE

ēl-ru-ad

(Arwad)

LOCATION — An island in the Mediterranean, off the coast of Latakia, Syria
GOVT. — French Mandate

In 1916, while a French post office was maintained on Ile Rouad, stamps were issued by France.

25 Centimes = 1 Piaster

French Offices in the Levant 1902-06 Stamps Ovptd.

Perf. 14x13½

			Unwmk.	
1916, Jan. 12				
1	A2	5c green	550.00	275.00
2	A3	10c rose red	550.00	275.00
3	A5	1pi on 25c blue	550.00	275.00

Dangerous counterfeits exist.
A 40c and 2pi-on-50c exist but were not regularly issued. Most examples have favor cancels. Value so canceled, $700 each.

Stamps of French Offices in the Levant, 1902-06, Overprinted Horizontally

1916, Dec.				
4	A2	1c gray	1.40	1.40
5	A2	2c lilac brown	1.50	1.50
6	A2	3c red orange	1.60	1.60
a.	Double overprint		210.00	
7	A2	5c green	1.75	1.75
8	A3	10c rose	2.00	2.00
9	A3	15c pale red	2.00	2.00
10	A3	20c brown violet	3.75	3.75
11	A5	1pi on 25c blue	2.75	2.75
12	A3	30c violet	2.50	2.50
13	A4	40c red & pale bl	6.00	6.00
14	A6	2pi on 50c bis brn & lavender	9.00	9.00
15	A6	4pi on 1fr cl & ol grn	16.00	16.00
16	A6	20pi on 5fr dk bl & buff	40.00	40.00
		Nos. 4-16 (13)	90.25	90.25

There is a wide space between the two words of the overprint on Nos. 13 to 16 inclusive. Nos. 4, 5 and 6 are on white and coarse, grayish (G. C.) papers.
(Note on G. C. paper follows France No. 184.)

RUANDA-URUNDI

rü-ˌän-də ü'rün-dē

(Belgian East Africa)

LOCATION — In central Africa, bounded by Congo, Uganda and Tanganyika
GOVT. — Former United Nations trusteeship administered by Belgium
AREA — 20,540 sq. mi.
POP. — 4,700,000 (est. 1958)
CAPITAL — Usumbura

See German East Africa in Vol. 3 for stamps issued under Belgian occupation.

In 1962 the two parts of the trusteeship became independent states, the Republic of Rwanda and the Kingdom of Burundi.

100 Centimes = 1 Franc

Stamps of Belgian Congo, 1923-26, Overprinted

			Perf. 12	
1924-26				
6	A32	5c orange yel	.25	.25
7	A32	10c green	.25	.25
a.	Double overprint		70.00	70.00
8	A32	15c olive brn	.25	.25
9	A32	20c olive grn	.25	.25
10	A44	20c green ('26)	.25	.25
11	A44	25c red brown	.40	.25
12	A44	30c rose red	.35	.35
13	A44	30c olive grn ('25)	.25	.25
14	A32	40c violet ('25)	.35	.35
a.	Inverted overprint		95.00	95.00
15	A44	50c gray blue	.35	.35
16	A44	50c buff ('25)	.40	.35
17	A44	75c red org	.65	.60
18	A44	75c gray blue ('25)	.60	.45
19	A44	1fr bister brown	.70	.60
20	A44	1fr dull blue ('26)	.75	.50
21	A44	3fr gray brown	6.00	2.50
22	A44	5fr gray	12.00	8.50
23	A44	10fr gray black	25.00	19.00
		Nos. 6-23 (18)	49.05	35.30
	Set, never hinged		160.00	

Belgian Congo Nos. 112-113 Overprinted in Red or Black

			Perf. 12½	
1925-27				
24	A44	45c dk vio (R) ('27)	.30	.30
25	A44	60c car rose (Bk)	.50	.50
	Set, never hinged		1.75	

Stamps of Belgian Congo, 1923-1927, Overprinted

1927-29				
26	A32	10c green ('29)	.60	.60
27	A32	15c ol brn ('29)	1.60	1.60
28	A44	35c green	.35	.35
29	A44	75c salmon red	.50	.45
30	A44	1fr rose red	.60	.50
31	A32	1.25fr dull blue	.85	.75
32	A32	1.50fr dull blue	.85	.75
33	A32	1.75fr dull blue	3.00	1.90

No. 32 Surcharged

34	A32	1.75fr on 1.50fr dl bl	.85	.75
		Nos. 26-34 (9)	9.20	7.65
	Set, never hinged		23.50	

No. 30 Surcharged

No. 33 Surcharged

1931				
35	A44	1.25fr on 1fr rose red	3.50	1.75
36	A32	2fr on 1.75fr dl bl	5.50	2.50
	Set, never hinged		20.00	

Porter — A1

Mountain Scene — A2

Designs: 5c, 60c, Porter. 15c, Warrior. 25c, Kraal. 40c, Cattle herders. 50c, Cape buffalo. 75c, Bahutu greeting. 1fr, Urundi women. 1.25fr, Bahutu mother. 1.50fr, 2fr, Making wooden vessel. 2.50fr, 3.25fr, Preparing hides. 4fr, Watuba potter. 5fr, Mututsi dancer. 10fr, Watusi warriors. 20fr, Urundi prince.

		Engr.	**Perf. 11½**	
1931-38				
37	A1	5c dp lil rose ('38)	.25	.25
38	A2	10c gray	.25	.25
39	A2	15c pale red	.25	.25
40	A2	25c brown vio	.25	.25
41	A1	40c green	.50	.50
42	A2	50c gray lilac	.25	.25
43	A1	60c lilac rose	.25	.25
44	A1	75c gray black	.25	.25
45	A2	1fr rose red	.40	.25
46	A1	1.25fr red brown	.40	.25
47	A1	1.50fr brown vio ('37)	.25	.25
48	A2	2fr deep blue	.50	.25
49	A2	2.50fr dp blue ('37)	.60	.60
50	A2	3.25fr brown vio	.65	.30
51	A2	4fr rose	.65	.45
52	A1	5fr gray	.65	.50
53	A1	10fr brown violet	.90	.90
54	A1	20fr brown	3.25	3.00
		Nos. 37-54 (18)	10.50	9.00
	Set, never hinged		25.00	

King Albert Memorial Issue

King Albert — A16

			Photo.	
1934				
55	A16	1.50fr black	.65	.65
	Never hinged		2.50	

Stamps of 1931-38 Surcharged in Black

1941				
56	A1	5c on 40c green	8.25	8.25
57	A2	60c on 50c gray lil	4.50	4.50
58	A2	2.50fr on 1.50fr brn vio	4.50	4.50
59	A2	3.25fr on 2fr dp bl	19.00	19.00
		Nos. 56-59 (4)	36.25	36.25
	Set, never hinged		110.00	

Belgian Congo No. 173 Overprinted in Black

1941   *Perf. 11*
60   A70   10c light gray   10.00   10.00
     Never hinged   27.50

    Inverts exist. Value $45.

Belgian Congo Nos. 179, 181 Overprinted in Black

1941
61   A70   1.75fr orange   6.00   6.00
62   A70   2.75fr vio bl   6.00   6.00
     Set, never hinged   52.50

    For surcharges see Nos. 64-65.

Belgian Congo No. 168 Surcharged in Black

1941   *Perf. 11½*
63   A66   5c on 1.50fr dp red brn
           & blk   .25   .25
     Never hinged   .35

    Inverts exist. Value $19.

Nos. 61-62 Surcharged with New Values and Bars in Black
1942
64   A70   75c on 1.75fr org   1.75   1.75
65   A70   2.50fr on 2.75fr vio bl   5.75   5.75
     Set, never hinged   27.50

    Inverts exist. Value $55.

Belgian Congo Nos. 167, 183 Surcharged in Black

1942   *Perf. 11, 11½*
66   A65   75c on 90c car & brn   1.25   1.25
  a.   Inverted surcharge   25.00   25.00
67   A70   2.50fr on 10fr rose red   2.50   1.90
  a.   Inverted surcharge   22.00   22.00
     Set, never hinged   7.50
    Nos. 66a-67a, never hinged   90.00

Oil Palms — A17

Oil Palms — A18

Watusi Chief — A19

Leopard A20

Askari — A21

Zebra — A22

Askari — A23

    Design: 100fr, Watusi chief.

1942-43   **Engr.**   *Perf. 12½*
68   A17   5c red   .25   .25
69   A18   10c ol grn   .25   .25
70   A18   15c brn car   .25   .25
71   A18   20c dp ultra   .25   .25
72   A18   25c brn vio   .25   .25
73   A18   30c dull blue   .25   .25
74   A18   50c dp grn   .25   .25
75   A18   60c chestnut   .25   .25
76   A18   75c dl lil & blk   .25   .25
77   A19   1fr dk brn & blk   .35   .25
78   A19   1.25fr rose red & blk   .40   .40
79   A20   1.75fr dk gray brn   1.00   .75
80   A20   2fr ocher   1.00   .50
81   A20   2.50fr carmine   1.00   .25
82   A21   3.50fr dk ol grn   .65   .35
83   A21   5fr orange   .80   .50
84   A21   6fr brt ultra   .80   .50
85   A21   7fr black   .80   .50
86   A21   10fr dp brn   1.00   .65
87   A22   20fr org brn & blk   2.50   2.50
88   A23   50fr red & blk ('43)   2.50   2.50
89   A23   100fr grn & blk ('43)   7.50   7.50
     Nos. 68-89 (22)   22.55   19.40
     Set, never hinged   45.00

    Nos. 68-89 exist imperforate, but have no franking value. Value, set never hinged $225, value set hinged $110.
    Miniature sheets of Nos. 72, 76, 77 and 83 were printed in 1944 by the Belgian Government in London and given to the Belgian political review, "Message," which distributed them to its subscribers, one a month. Values, each: $65 hinged; $130 never hinged.
    See note after Belgian Congo No. 225.
    For surcharges see Nos. B17-B20.

Baluba Mask — A25

    Carved Figures and Masks of Baluba Tribe: 10c, 50c, 2fr, 10fr, "Ndoha," figure of tribal king. 15c, 70c, 2.50fr, "Tshimanyi," an idol. 20c, 75c, 3.50fr, "Buangakokoma," statue of a kneeling beggar. 25c, 1fr, 5fr, "Mbuta," sacred double cup carved with two faces, Man and Woman. 40c, 1.25fr, 6fr, "Ngadimuashi," female mask. 1.50fr, 50fr, "Buadi-Muadi," mask with squared features (full face). 20fr, 100fr, "Mbowa," executioner's mask with buffalo horns.

1948-50   **Unwmk.**   *Perf. 12x12½*
90   A25   10c dp org   .25   .25
91   A25   15c ultra   .25   .25
92   A25   20c brt bl   .25   .25
93   A25   25c rose car   .30   .25
94   A25   40c violet   .25   .25
95   A25   50c ol brn   .25   .25
96   A25   70c yel grn   .25   .25
97   A25   75c magenta   .25   .25
98   A25   1fr yel org & dk
           vio   .30   .25
99   A25   1.25fr lt bl grn &
           mag   .30   .25
100   A25   1.50fr ol & mag ('50)   1.00   .75
101   A25   2fr org & mag   .30   .25
102   A25   2.50fr brn red & bl
           grn   .40   .25
103   A25   3.50fr lt bl & blk   .50   .30
104   A25   5fr bis & mag   1.00   .30
105   A25   6fr brn org & ind   1.00   .25
106   A25   10fr pale vio & red
           brn   1.25   .50
107   A25   20fr red org & vio
           brn   1.90   .80
108   A25   50fr dp org & blk   3.75   2.00
109   A25   100fr crim & blk brn   7.00   5.25
     Nos. 90-109 (20)   20.75   13.15
     Set, never hinged   100.00

Nos. 102 and 105 Surcharged with New Value and Bars in Black
1949
110   A25   3fr on 2.50fr   .40   .30
111   A25   4fr on 6fr   .45   .35
112   A25   6.50fr on 6fr   .60   .50
     Nos. 110-112 (3)   1.45   1.15
     Set, never hinged   2.75

St. Francis Xavier — A26

1953, Apr. 9   *Perf. 12½x13*
113   A26   1.50fr ultra & gray blk   .60   .60
     Never hinged   .90

    Death of St. Francis Xavier, 400th anniv.

Dissotis — A27

    Flowers: 15c, Protea. 20c, Vellozia. 25c, Littonia. 40c, Ipomoea. 50c, Angraecum. 60c, Euphorbia. 75c, Ochna. 1fr, Hibiscus. 1.25fr, Protea. 1.50fr, Schizoglossum. 2fr, Ansellia. 3fr, Costus. 4fr, Nymphaea. 5fr, Thunbergia. 7fr, Gerbera. 8fr, Gloriosa. 10fr, Silene. 20fr, Aristolochia.

Flowers in Natural Colors
1953   **Unwmk.**   **Photo.**   *Perf. 11½*
114   A27   10c plum & ocher   .25   .25
115   A27   15c red & yel grn   .25   .25
116   A27   20c green & gray   .25   .25
117   A27   25c dk grn & dl org   .25   .25
118   A27   40c grn & sal   .25   .25
119   A27   50c dk car & aqua   .25   .25
120   A27   60c bl grn & pink   .25   .25
121   A27   75c dp plum & gray   .25   .25
122   A27   1fr car & yel   .45   .25

---

123   A27   1.25fr dk grn & bl   .70   .65
124   A27   1.50fr vio & ap grn   .25   .25
125   A27   2fr ol grn & buff   2.25   .25
126   A27   3fr ol grn & pink   .70   .25
127   A27   4fr choc & lil   .70   .25
128   A27   5fr dp plum & lt bl
           grn   1.00   .25
129   A27   7fr dk grn & fawn   1.10   .65
130   A27   8fr grn & lt yel   1.75   .90
131   A27   10fr dp plum & pale
           ol   3.00   1.10
132   A27   20fr vio bl & dl sal   4.75   2.50
     Nos. 114-132 (19)   18.65   9.30
     Set, never hinged   47.50

    For overprints see Burundi Nos. 1-8.

King Baudouin and Tropical Scene A28

    Designs: Various African Views.

1955   **Engr. & Photo.**
Portrait Photo. in Black
133   A28   1.50fr rose carmine   2.75   1.25
134   A28   3fr green   2.75   1.25
135   A28   4.50fr ultra   2.75   1.25
136   A28   6.50fr deep claret   3.75   1.25
     Nos. 133-136 (4)   12.00   5.00
     Set, never hinged   27.50

    Nos. 133-136 exist imperf. Value, set $110.

Mountain Gorilla — A29

Cape Buffaloes A30

    Animals: 40c, 2fr, Black-and-white colobus (monkey). 50c, 6.50fr, Impalas. 1fr, Mountain gorilla. 3fr, 8fr, Elephants. 5fr, 10fr, Eland and Zebras. 20fr, Leopard. 50fr, Lions.

1959-61   **Unwmk.**   **Photo.**   *Perf. 11½*
Granite Paper
Size: 23x33mm, 33x23mm
137   A29   10c brn, crim, & blk
           brn   .25   .25
138   A30   20c blk, gray & ap
           grn   .25   .25
139   A29   40c mag, blk & gray
           grn   .25   .25
140   A30   50c grn, org yel &
           brn   .25   .25
141   A29   1fr brn, ultra & blk   .25   .25
142   A30   1.50fr blk, gray & org   .25   .25
143   A29   2fr grnsh bl, ind &
           brn   .25   .25
144   A30   3fr brn, dp car & blk   .25   .25
145   A30   5fr brn, dl yel, grn &
           blk   .25   .25
146   A30   6.50fr red, org yel &
           brn   .40   .45
147   A29   8fr bl, mag & blk   .50   .60
148   A30   10fr multi   .50   .60
Size: 45x26½mm
149   A30   20fr multi ('61)   .90   .90
150   A30   50fr multi ('61)   1.25   1.60
     Nos. 137-150 (14)   5.80   6.40
     Set, never hinged   8.00

    Nos. 137-150 exist imperf. Value, set $150.
    For surcharge see No. 153.
    For overprints see Burundi Nos. 9-24.

> **Catalogue values for unused stamps in this section, from this point to the end of the section, are for Never Hinged items.**

Map of Africa and Symbolic Honeycomb A31

1960, Feb.19   Unwmk.   Perf. 11½
Inscription in French
151 A31 3fr ultra & red   .50   .25
Inscription in Flemish
152 A31 3fr ultra & red   .50   .25

10th anniversary of the Commission for Technical Co-operation in Africa South of the Sahara (C. T. A.).
Nos. 151-152 exist imperf. Value, set $27.50.
For surcharges and overprints see Burundi Nos. 34-39.

No. 144 Surcharged with New Value and Bars

1960
153 A30 3.50fr on 3fr red, blk, brn   .40   .25

SEMI-POSTAL STAMPS

Belgian Congo Nos. B10-B11 Overprinted

1925   Unwmk.   Perf. 12½
B1 SP1 25c + 25c car & blk   .75   .50
B2 SP1 25c + 25c car & blk   .75   .50
    Set, never hinged   2.75

No. B2 inscribed "BELGISCH CONGO."
Commemorative of the Colonial Campaigns in 1914-1918. Nos. B1 and B2 alternate in the sheet.

Belgian Congo Nos. B12-B20 Overprinted in Blue or Red

1930   Perf. 11½
B3   SP3 10c + 5c ver   1.00   1.00
B4   SP3 20c + 10c dk brn   1.50   1.50
B5   SP5 35c + 15c dp grn   2.00   2.00
B6   SP5 60c + 30c dl vio   2.25   2.25
B7   SP3 1fr + 50c dk car   3.75   3.75
B8   SP5 1.75fr + 75c dp bl   9.75   9.75
          (R)
B9   SP5 3.50fr + 1.50fr rose
          lake   15.00 15.00
B10 SP5 5fr + 2.50fr red
          brn   15.00 15.00
B11 SP5 10fr + 5fr gray blk   16.00 16.00
     Nos. B3-B11 (9)   66.25 66.25
     Set, never hinged   170.00

On Nos. B3, B4 and B7 there is a space of 26mm between the two words of the overprint. The surtax was for native welfare.

Queen Astrid with Native Children — SP1

1936   Photo.
B12 SP1 1.25fr + 5c dk brn   .65   .65
B13 SP1 1.50fr + 10c dl rose   .65   .65
B14 SP1 2.50fr + 25c dk bl   1.25 1.25
     Nos. B12-B14 (3)   2.55 2.55
     Set, never hinged   7.50

Issued in memory of Queen Astrid. The surtax was for the National League for Protection of Native Children.

Lion of Belgium and Inscription "Belgium Shall Rise Again" — SP2

1942   Engr.   Perf. 12½
B15 SP2 10fr + 40fr blue   2.50 2.50
B16 SP2 10fr + 40fr dark red   2.50 2.50
     Set, never hinged   9.00

Nos. 74, 78, 79 and 82 Surcharged in Red

a

b

c

1945   Unwmk.   Perf. 12½
B17 A18 (a) 50c + 50fr   2.00 1.50
B18 A19 (b) 1.25fr + 100fr   2.00 1.50
B19 A20 (c) 1.75fr + 100fr   2.00 1.50
B20 A21 (b) 3.50fr + 100fr   2.00 1.50
     Nos. B17-B20 (4)   8.00 6.00
     Set, never hinged   22.50

Mozart at Age 7 — SP3

Queen Elizabeth and Mozart Sonata — SP4

1956   Engr.   Perf. 11½
B21 SP3 4.50fr + 1.50fr bluish
          vio   1.50 *1.50*
B22 SP4 6.50fr + 2.50fr claret   3.50 *3.50*
     Set, never hinged   10.00

200th anniv. of the birth of Wolfgang Amadeus Mozart.
Surtax for the Pro-Mozart Committee.

Nurse and Children — SP5

Designs: 4.50fr+50c, Patient receiving injection. 6.50fr+50c, Patient being bandaged.

1957   Photo.   Perf. 13x10½
Cross in Carmine
B23 SP5 3fr + 50c dk blue   .30   .30
B24 SP5 4.50fr + 50c dk grn   .50   .50
B25 SP5 6.50fr + 50c red brn   .75   .75
     Nos. B23-B25 (3)   1.55 1.55
     Set, never hinged   3.00

The surtax was for the Red Cross.

> **Catalogue values for unused stamps in this section, from this point to the end of the section, are for Never Hinged items.**

Soccer SP6

Sports: #B26, High Jumper. #B27, Hurdlers. #B29, Javelin thrower. #B30, Discus thrower.

1960   Unwmk.   Perf. 13½
B26 SP6 50c + 25c int bl &
          maroon   .40   .25
B27 SP6 1.50fr + 50c dk car &
          blk   .55   .25
B28 SP6 2fr + 1fr blk & dk car   .60   .25
B29 SP6 3fr + 1.25fr org ver &
          grn   1.90 1.25
B30 SP6 6.50fr + 3.50fr ol grn &
          red   2.10 1.25
     Nos. B26-B30 (5)   5.55 3.25

17th Olympic Games, Rome, Aug. 25-Sept. 11. The surtax was for the youth of Ruanda-Urundi.

Usumbura Cathedral — SP7

Designs: 1fr+50c, 5fr+2fr, Cathedral, sideview. 1.50fr+75c, 6.50fr+3fr, Stained glass window.

1961, Dec. 18   Perf. 11½
B31 SP7 50c + 25c brn & buff   .25   .25
B32 SP7 1fr + 50c grn & pale
          grn   .25   .25
B33 SP7 1.50fr + 75c multi   .25   .25
B34 SP7 3.50fr + 1.50fr lt bl & brt
          bl   .25   .25
B35 SP7 5fr + 2fr car & sal   .30   .30
B36 SP7 6.50fr + 3fr multi   .45   .35
     Nos. B31-B36 (6)   1.75 1.65

The surtax went for the construction and completion of the Cathedral at Usumbura.

POSTAGE DUE STAMPS

Belgian Congo Nos. J1-J7 Overprinted

1924-27   Unwmk.   Perf. 14
J1   D1 5c black brn   .25   .25
  a.   Double overprint   75.00 75.00
J2   D1 10c deep rose   .25   .25
J3   D1 15c violet   .30   .25
  a.   Double overprint   75.00 75.00
J4   D1 30c green   .50   .30
J5   D1 50c ultra   .50   .40

J6   D1 50c brt blue ('27)   .80   .45
J7   D1 1fr gray   .70   .55
     Nos. J1-J7 (7)   3.30 2.45
     Set, never hinged   5.50

> **Catalogue values for unused stamps in this section, from this point to the end of the section, are for Never Hinged items.**

Belgian Congo Nos. J8-J12 Overprinted in Carmine

1943   Perf. 14x14½, 12½
J8   D2 10c olive green   .25   .25
J9   D2 20c dk ultra   .25   .25
J10 D2 50c green   .25   .25
J11 D2 1fr dark brown   .45   .40
J12 D2 2fr yellow orange   .55   .50
     Nos. J8-J12 (5)   1.75 1.65

Nos. J8-J12 values are for stamps perf. 14x14½. Value, set perf. 12½ $10.

Belgian Congo Nos. J13-J19 Overprinted

1959   Engr.   Perf. 11½
J13 D3 10c olive brown   .25   .25
J14 D3 20c claret   .25   .25
J15 D3 50c green   .25   .25
J16 D3 1fr lt blue   .25   .25
J17 D3 2fr vermilion   .40   .35
J18 D3 4fr purple   .80   .70
J19 D3 6fr violet blue   .85   .75
     Nos. J13-J19 (7)   3.05 2.80

Both capital and lower-case U's are found in this overprint.

RUSSIA
ˈrəsh-ə

(Union of Soviet Socialist Republics)

LOCATION — Eastern Europe and Northern Asia
GOVT. — Republic
AREA — 6,592,691 sq. mi.
POP. — 147,100,000 (1999 est.)
CAPITAL — Moscow

An empire until 1917, the government was overthrown in that year and a socialist union of republics was formed under the name of the Union of Soviet Socialist Republics. The USSR includes the following autonomous republics which have issued their own stamps: Armenia, Azerbaijan, Georgia and Ukraine.

With the breakup of the Soviet Union on Dec. 26, 1991, eleven former Soviet republics established the Commonwealth of Independent States. Stamps inscribed "Rossija" are issued by the Russian Republic.

100 Kopecks = 1 Ruble

Catalogue values for unused stamps in this country are for Never Hinged items, beginning with Scott 1021 in the regular postage section, Scott B58 in the semi-postal section, and Scott C82 in the airpost section.

Watermarks

Wmk. 166 — Colorless Numerals ("1" for Nos. 1-2, "2" for No. 3, "3" for No. 4)

Wmk. 168 — Cyrillic EZGB & Wavy Lines

Wmk. 169 — Lozenges   Wmk. 171 — Diamonds

Wmk. 170 — Greek Border and Rosettes

Wmk. 226 — Diamonds Enclosing Four Dots

Wmk. 293 — Hammer and Sickle, Multiple

Wmk. 383 — Cyrillic Letters in Shield

Empire

Coat of Arms — A1

Wmk. 166
1857, Dec. 10   Typo.   Imperf.

1	A1 10k brown & blue	62,500.	950.	
	No gum	21,000.		
	Pen cancellation		475.	
	Penmark & postmark		475.	
	Straight line town cancellation, from		650.	
	Circular datestamp cancellation, from		900.	

Genuine unused examples of No. 1 are exceedingly rare. Most of those offered are used with pen cancellation removed. The unused value is for an example without gum. The very few known stamps with original gum sell for much more.

See Poland for similar stamp inscribed "ZALOT KOP. 10."

1858, Jan. 10   Perf. 14½, 15

2	A1 10k brown & blue	14,000.	175.
	No gum	4,400.	
3	A1 20k blue & orange	13,000.	1,700.
	No gum	4,250.	
4	A1 30k carmine & green	18,500.	2,500.
	No gum	5,750.	

Coat of Arms — A2

Wove Paper
1858-64   Unwmk.   Perf. 12½

5	A2 1k blk & yel ('64)	170.00	67.50
a.	1k black & orange	340.00	55.00
6	A2 3k blk & grn ('64)	1,100.	100.00
7	A2 5k blk & lil ('64)	1,000.	90.00
8	A1 10k brown & blue	275.00	13.50
9	A1 20k blue & orange	1,000.	80.00
a.	Half used as 10k on cover		
10	A1 30k car & grn	1,175.	125.00
	Nos. 5-10 (6)	4,720.	476.00

Coat of Arms — A3

1863

11	A3 5k black & blue	30.00	160.00

No. 11 was issued to pay local postage in St. Petersburg and Moscow. It is known to have been used in other cities. In Aug. 1864 it was authorized for use on mail addressed to other destinations.

1865, June 2   Perf. 14½, 15

12	A2 1k black & yellow	375.00	37.50
a.	1k black & orange	400.00	42.50
13	A2 3k black & green	350.00	17.50
14	A2 5k black & lilac	375.00	40.00
15	A1 10k brown & blue	925.00	3.00
a.	Thick paper	975.00	7.50
17	A1 20k blue & orange	2,750.	40.00
a.	Thick paper	3,000.	45.00
18	A1 30k car & grn	1,950.	40.00
a.	Thick paper	2,100.	45.00
	Nos. 12-18 (6)	6,725.	178.00

Horizontally Laid Paper
1866-70   Wmk. 168

19	A2 1k blk & yel	10.00	1.10
a.	1k black & orange	12.00	1.25
b.	Imperf.		3,000.
c.	Vertically laid	315.00	45.00
d.	Groundwork inverted	5,500.	5,500.
e.	Thick paper	75.00	55.00
f.	As "c," imperf.	7,500.	7,250.
g.	As "b," "c" & "d"	11,000.	17,000.
h.	1k blk & org, vert. laid paper	350.00	42.50
20	A2 3k blk & dp grn	12.50	1.50
a.	3k black & yellow green	12.50	1.50
b.	Imperf.		3,400.
c.	Vertically laid	400.00	50.00
d.	V's in groundwork (error) ('70)	2,000.	40.00
e.	3k black & blue green	12.50	1.50
22	A2 5k black & lilac	15.00	2.00
a.	5k black & gray	240.00	32.50
b.	Imperf.		4,250.
c.	Vertically laid	10,000.	160.00
d.	As "c," imperf.		
23	A1 10k brn & blue	45.00	1.75
a.	Vertically laid	525.00	16.50
b.	Center inverted		50,000.
c.	Imperf.		22,500.

24	A1 20k blue & org	100.00	15.00
a.	Vertically laid	5,250.	160.00
25	A1 30k car & grn	100.00	30.00
a.	Vertically laid	1,000.	120.00
	Nos. 19-25 (6)	282.50	51.35

Arms — A4

1875-82   Horizontally Laid Paper

26	A2 2k black & red	25.00	1.60
a.	Vertically laid	6,750.	160.00
b.	No gum	1,275.	
c.	Groundwork inverted		57,500.
27	A4 7k gray & rose ('79)	20.00	1.00
a.	Imperf.		8,500.
b.	Vertically laid	2,000.	65.00
	No gum	600.00	
c.	Wmkd. hexagons ('79)		170,000.
d.	Center inverted	—	—
e.	Center omitted	—	—
f.	7k black & carmine ('80)	21.00	.85
g.	7k pale gray & carmine ('82)	21.00	.85
28	A4 8k gray & rose	25.00	1.60
a.	Vertically laid	2,500.	82.50
	No gum	600.00	
b.	Imperf.		22,500.
c.	"C" instead of "B" in "Bocem"	650.00	250.
29	A4 10k brn & blue	50.00	5.75
a.	Center inverted		60,000.
30	A4 20k blue & org	67.50	10.00
a.	Cross-shaped "T" in bottom word	170.00	27.50
b.	Center inverted		75,000.
c.	Center double		90,000.
d.	As "a," center inverted		
	Nos. 26-30 (5)	187.50	19.95

The hexagon watermark of No. 27c is that of revenue stamps. No. 27c exists with Perm and Riga postmarks.

See Finland for stamps similar to designs A4-A15, which have "dot in circle" devices or are inscribed "Markka," "Markkaa," "Pen.," or "Pennia."

Imperial Eagle and Post Horns
A5   A6

Perf. 14 to 15 and Compound
1883-88   Wmk. 168
Horizontally Laid Paper

31	A5 1k orange	10.00	1.20
a.	Imperf.	62,500.	
b.	Groundwork inverted		9,000.
c.	1k yellow	6.75	1.20
32	A5 2k dark green	4.00	1.20
a.	2k yellow green ('88)	32.50	4.00
b.	Imperf.	1,100.	700.00
c.	Wove paper	—	
d.	Groundwork inverted		31,500.
33	A5 3k carmine	12.50	1.20
a.	Imperf.		
b.	Groundwork inverted		30,000.
c.	Wove paper		
34	A5 5k red violet	8.00	.90
a.	Groundwork inverted		8,500.
35	A5 7k blue	10.00	.90
a.	Imperf.	800.00	475.00
b.	Groundwork inverted	2,000.	1,900.
c.	Double impression of frame and center	—	
36	A6 14k blue & rose	85.00	2.50
a.	Center inverted	4,000.	3,000.
b.	Center inverted		6,250.
c.	Diagonal half surcharge "7" in red, on cover ('84)		—
37	A6 35k vio & grn	60.00	6.50
38	A6 70k brn & org	67.50	9.50
	Nos. 31-38 (8)	257.00	23.90

Before 1882 the 1, 2, 3 and 5 kopecks had small numerals in the background; beginning with No. 31 these denominations have a background of network, like the higher values.

No. 36c is handstamped. It is known with cancellations of Tiflis and Kutais, both in Georgia. It is believed to be of philatelic origin.

A7

1884 **Perf. 13½, 13½x11½**
Vertically Laid Paper

39	A7	3.50r blk & gray	1,200.	625.
a.		Horiz. laid	175,000.	15,000.
b.		Inverted center	—	—
40	A7	7r blk & org	800.	675.

Forgeries exist, both unused and used.

A8

Imperial Eagle and Post Horns with Thunderbolts — A9

With Thunderbolts Across Post Horns
Perf. 14 to 15 and Compound
1889, May 14
Horizontally Laid Paper

41	A8	4k rose	12.00	.45
a.		Groundwork inverted		16,000.
b.		Double impression of center	—	—
c.		Double impression of frame	—	—
42	A8	10k dark blue	20.00	.45
43	A8	20k blue & carmine	21.00	1.20
a.		Groundwork inverted		
44	A8	50k violet & green	16.00	1.50

Perf. 13½

45	A9	1r lt brn, brn & org	47.50	2.50
a.		Horiz. pair, imperf. btwn.	900.00	450.00
b.		Vert. pair, imperf. btwn.	850.00	425.00
c.		Center omitted	—	—
		Nos. 41-45 (5)	116.50	6.10

See #57C, 60, 63, 66, 68, 82, 85, 87, 126, 129, 131. For surcharges see #216, 219, 223, 226.

A10

A11

A12

With Thunderbolts Across Post Horns
1889-92 **Perf. 14½x15**
Horizontally Laid Paper

46	A10	1k orange	3.25	.50
a.		Imperf.	850.00	
47	A10	2k green	4.00	.50
a.		Imperf.	800.00	
b.		Groundwork inverted	800.00	17,000.
48	A10	3k carmine	8.00	.50
a.		Imperf.	425.00	350.00
49	A10	5k red vio	8.00	.60
b.		Groundwork omitted or inverted	850.00	650.00
50	A10	7k dk blue	5.25	.50
a.		Imperf.	425.00	9,000.
b.		Groundwork inverted	16,000.	11,250.
c.		Groundwork omitted	250.00	200.00
51	A11	14k blue & rose	16.00	.50
a.		Center inverted	6,750.	4,500.
b.		Center omitted	850.00	

52	A11	35k vio & grn	67.50	6.00

Perf. 13½

53	A12	3.50r blk & gray	50.00	8.00
a.		Center inverted	—	12,750.
54	A12	7r blk & yel	190.00	11.00
a.		Dbl. impression of black	—	45,000.
		Nos. 46-54 (9)	352.00	28.10

Perf. 14 to 15 and Compound
1902-05 **Vertically Laid Paper**

55	A10	1k orange	4.50	.35
a.		Imperf.	1,100.	1,100.
b.		Groundwork inverted	—	—
c.		Groundwork omitted	—	—
56	A10	2k yel grn	4.50	.35
a.		2k deep green	8.00	.70
b.		Groundwork inverted	—	—
c.		Groundwork omitted	—	—
d.		Groundwork double	375.00	375.00
57	A10	3k rose red	10.50	.35
a.		Groundwork omitted	—	—
b.		Double impression	275.00	250.00
d.		Imperf.	1,350.	—
e.		Groundwork inverted	—	—
f.		Groundwork double	275.00	
57C	A8	4k rose red ('04)	9.00	.85
f.		Double impression	340.00	275.00
g.		Groundwork inverted	—	16,500.
58	A10	5k red vio	19.00	.60
a.		5k dull violet	12.50	2.25
b.		Groundwork inverted	—	30,000.
c.		Imperf.	—	—
d.		Groundwork omitted	675.00	150.00
e.		Groundwork double	1,350.	100.00
59	A10	7k dk blue	10.50	.35
a.		Groundwork omitted	315.00	275.00
b.		Imperf.	675.00	600.00
c.		Groundwork inverted	—	—
60	A8	10k dk blue ('04)	4.00	.50
a.		Groundwork inverted	42.50	17.50
b.		Groundwork omitted	600.00	85.00
c.		Groundwork double	175.00	85.00
61	A11	14k blue & rose	22.50	.80
a.		Center inverted	—	4,000.
b.		Center omitted	1,100.	700.00
62	A11	15k brn vio & blue ('05)	20.00	2.00
a.		Center omitted	700.	
b.		Center inverted	4,500.	4,000.
63	A8	20k blue & car ('04)	11.00	.85
64	A11	25k dull grn & lil ('05)	45.00	2.50
a.		Center inverted	7,250.	6,000.
b.		Center omitted	—	—
65	A11	35k dk vio & grn	55.00	1.80
a.		Center inverted	2,500.	2,000.
b.		Center omitted	—	—
66	A8	50k vio & grn ('05)	35.00	1.00
67	A11	70k brn & org	45.00	3.25

Perf. 13½

68	A9	1r lt brn, brn & org	90.00	2.00
a.		Perf. 11½	700.00	50.00
b.		Perf. 13½x11½, 11½x13½	340.00	525.00
c.		Imperf.	—	—
d.		Center inverted	—	—
e.		Center omitted	675.00	250.00
f.		Horiz. pair, imperf. btwn.	1,100.	350.00
g.		Vert. pair, imperf. btwn.	900.00	340.00
69	A12	3.50r blk & gray	50.00	4.00
a.		Center inverted	—	14,000.
b.		Imperf., pair	2,000.	2,000.
70	A12	7r blk & yel	14.00	4.75
a.		Center inverted	7,000.	13,500.
b.		Horiz. pair, imperf. btwn.	3,000.	1,450.
d.		Imperf., pair	—	—

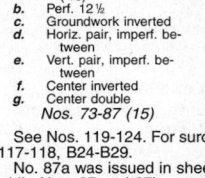

A13

1906 **Perf. 13½**

71	A13	5r dk blue, grn & pale blue	50.00	4.50
a.		Perf. 11½	500.00	275.00
72	A13	10r car rose, yel & gray	350.00	10.50
		Nos. 55-72 (19)	849.50	41.30

The design of No. 72 differs in many details from the illustration. Nos. 71-72 were printed in sheets of 25.

See Nos. 80-81, 83-84, 86, 108-109, 125, 127-128, 130, 132-135, 137-138. For surcharges see Nos. 217-218, 220-222, 224-225, 227-229.

A14

A15

Vertical Lozenges of Varnish on Face
1909-12 **Unwmk.** **Perf. 14x14½**
Wove Paper

73	A14	1k dull org yel	.45	.45
a.		1k orange yellow ('09)	2.50	.45
c.		Double impression	90.00	—
74	A14	2k dull green	.25	.25
a.		2k green ('09)	1.60	.25
b.		Double impression	100.00	—
75	A14	3k carmine	.25	.25
a.		3k rose red ('09)	1.40	.25
76	A15	4k carmine	.25	.25
a.		4k carmine rose ('09)	1.40	.25
77	A14	5k claret	2.50	.25
a.		5k lilac ('12)	.25	.25
b.		Double impression	95.00	—
78	A14	7k blue	.25	.25
a.		7k light blue ('09)	2.50	.45
b.		Imperf.	1,250.	
79	A15	10k dark blue	.25	.25
a.		10k light blue ('09)	80.00	8.00
b.		10k pale blue	8.00	2.00
80	A11	14k dk blue & car	.85	.25
a.		14k blue & rose ('09)	1.40	.25
81	A11	15k red brn & dp blue	.25	.25
a.		15k dull violet & blue ('09)	1.40	.25
c.		Center omitted	170.00	—
d.		Center double	50.00	—
82	A8	20k dull bl & dk car	.25	.25
a.		20k blue & carmine ('10)	1.40	.45
b.		Groundwork omitted	42.50	
c.		Center double	175.00	—
d.		Center and value omitted	—	—
83	A11	25k dl grn & dk vio	.25	.25
a.		25k green & violet ('09)	1.40	.45
b.		Center omitted	170.00	—
c.		Center double	175.00	—
84	A11	35k red brn & grn	.25	.25
a.		35k brown vio & yel green	.55	.40
b.		35k violet & green ('09)	1.40	.25
c.		Center double	25.00	—
85	A8	50k red brn & grn	.25	.25
a.		50k violet & green ('09)	3.25	.45
b.		Groundwork omitted	30.00	—
c.		Center double	175.00	—
d.		Center and value omitted	325.00	—
86	A11	70k brn & red	.25	.25
a.		70k lt brown & orange ('09)	2.50	.45
b.		Center double	175.00	—
c.		Center omitted	115.00	115.00

Perf. 13½

87	A9	1r pale brn, dk brn & org	.50	.35
a.		1r pale brn, brn & org ('10)	1.65	.45
b.		Perf. 12½	80.00	—
c.		Groundwork inverted	25.00	—
d.		Horiz. pair, imperf. between	25.00	—
e.		Vert. pair, imperf. between	25.00	—
f.		Center inverted	40.00	—
g.		Center double	25.00	—
		Nos. 73-87 (15)	7.05	4.05

See Nos. 119-124. For surcharges see Nos. 117-118, B24-B29.

No. 87a was issued in sheets of 40 stamps, while Nos. 87 and 87b came in sheets of 50. Nos. 87g-87k are listed below No. 138a.

Nearly all values of this issue are known without the lines of varnish.

The 7k has two types:

I — The scroll bearing the top inscription ends at left with three short lines of shading beside the first letter. Four pearls extend at lower left between the leaves and denomination panel.

II — Inner lines of scroll at top left end in two curls; three pearls at lower left.

Three clichés of type II (an essay) were included by mistake in the plate used for the first printing. Value of pair, type I with type II, unused $4,500.

SURCHARGES

Russian stamps of types A6-A15 with various surcharges may be found listed under Armenia, Batum, Far Eastern Republic, Georgia, Latvia, Siberia, South Russia, Transcaucasian Federated Republics, Ukraine, Russian Offices in China, Russian Offices in the Turkish Empire and Army of the Northwest.

Peter I — A16

Alexander II — A17

Alexander III — A18

Peter I — A19

Nicholas II
A20 A21

Catherine II — A22

Nicholas I — A23

Alexander I — A24

Alexis
Mikhailovich
A25

Paul I
A26

Elizabeth
Petrovna
A27

Michael
Feodorovich
A28

The
Kremlin — A29

Winter
Palace — A30

Romanov
Castle — A31

Nicholas II — A32

Without Lozenges of Varnish

1913, Jan. 2   Typo.   Perf. 13½

88	A16	1k brn org	1.60	.25
89	A17	2k yellow green	4.25	.25
90	A18	3k rose red	4.25	.25
b.		Double impression	600.00	
91	A19	4k dull red	1.60	.25
92	A20	7k brown	1.60	.25
b.		Double impression	675.00	
93	A21	10k deep blue	4.25	.25
94	A22	14k blue green	4.25	.40
95	A23	15k yellow brown	8.00	.60
96	A24	20k olive green	26.50	.70
97	A25	25k red violet	8.00	1.10
98	A26	35k gray vio & dk grn	2.50	.70
99	A27	50k brn & slate	10.75	1.90
100	A28	70k yel grn & brn	8.00	1.90

Engr.

101	A29	1r deep green	40.00	6.25
102	A30	2r red brown	65.00	11.00
103	A31	3r dark violet	50.00	11.00
104	A32	5r black brown	40.00	19.00
		Nos. 88-104 (17)	280.55	56.05
		Set, never hinged	650.00	

Imperf

88a	A16	1k brown orange	800.00	—
89a	A17	2k yellow green	800.00	—
90a	A18	3k rose red	800.00	—
91a	A19	4k dull red	1,900.	
92a	A20	7k brown	425.00	
93a	A21	10k deep blue	800.00	
94a	A22	14k blue green	1,900.	
101a	A29	1r deep green	1,600.	
102a	A30	2r red brown	800.00	
103b	A31	3r dark violet	800.00	
104a	A32	5r dark violet	1,900.	

Tercentenary of the founding of the Romanov dynasty.

See Nos. 105-107, 112-116, 139-141. For surcharges see Nos. 110-111, Russian Offices in the Turkish Empire 213-227.

Arms and 5-line Inscription on Back

No. 107 Back

Thin Cardboard
Without Gum

1915, Oct.   Typo.   Perf. 13½

105	A21	10k blue	2.50	32.50
106	A23	15k brown	2.50	32.50
107	A24	20k olive green	2.50	32.50
		Nos. 105-107 (3)	7.50	97.50

Imperf

105a	A21	10k	550.00	—
106a	A23	15k	200.00	—
107a	A24	20k	175.00	—

Nos. 105-107, 112-116 and 139-141 were issued for use as paper money, but contrary to regulations were often used for postal purposes. Back inscription means: "Having circulation on par with silver subsidiary coins."

Types of 1906 Issue
Vertical Lozenges of Varnish on Face

1915   Perf. 13½, 13½x13

108	A13	5r ind, grn & lt blue	1.40	.50
a.		5r dk bl, grn & pale bl ('15)	13.50	1.60
b.		Perf. 12½	20.00	6.75
c.		Center double	60.00	
d.		Pair, imperf. between	100.00	—

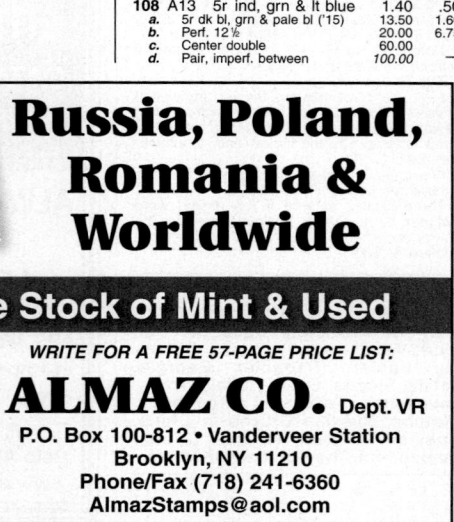

109	A13	10r car lake, yel & gray	2.00	.50
a.		10r carmine, yel & light gray	2.00	.50
b.		10r rose red, yel & gray ('15)	6.75	.85
c.		10r car, yel & gray blue (error)	2,700.	
d.		Groundwork inverted	450.00	
e.		Center double	60.00	—

Nos. 108a and 109b were issued in sheets of 25. Nos. 108, 108b, 109 and 109a came in sheets of 50. Chemical forgeries of No. 109c exist. Genuine examples usually are centered to upper right.

Nos. 92, 94
Surcharged

1916

110	A20	10k on 7k brown	.85	.50
a.		Inverted surcharge	210.00	
111	A22	20k on 14k bl grn	.85	.45

Imperf

110b	A20	10k on 7k brown	425.00	—
111a	A22	20k on 14k bl grn	425.00	—

Types of 1913 Issue
Arms, Value & 4-line inscription on Back
Surcharged Large Numerals on Nos. 112-113
Thin Cardboard

1916-17   Without Gum

112	A16	1 on 1k brn org ('17)	2.50	40.00
113	A17	2 on 2k yel green ('17)	2.50	40.00

Without Surcharge

114	A16	1k brown orange	50.00	—
115	A17	2k yellow green	52.50	—
116	A18	3k rose red	2.50	32.50

See note after No. 107.

Nos. 78a, 80a Surcharged

   a   b

1917   Perf. 14x14½

117	A14	10k on 7k lt blue	.85	.45
a.		Inverted surcharge	150.00	—
b.		Double surcharge	60.00	—
c.		Imperforate	375.00	—
118	A11	20k on 14k bl & rose	1.20	.45
a.		Inverted surcharge	250.00	

Provisional Government
Civil War
Type of 1889-1912 Issues
Vertical Lozenges of Varnish on Face

Two types of 7r:
Type I — Single outer frame line.
Type II — Double outer frame line.

Wove Paper

1917   Typo.   Imperf.

119	A14	1k orange	1.10	.25
120	A14	2k gray green	.25	.25
121	A14	3k red	.25	.25
122	A15	4k carmine	.85	2.50
123	A14	5k claret	.25	.25
124	A15	10k dark blue	20.00	20.00
125	A11	15k red brn & dp blue	.40	.25
a.		Center omitted	175.00	
126	A8	20k blue & car	.35	.35
a.		Groundwork omitted	42.50	—
127	A11	25k grn & gray vio	.50	1.00
128	A11	35k red brn & grn	.50	.35
129	A8	50k brn vio & grn	.45	.25
a.		Groundwork omitted	42.50	—
130	A11	70k brn & org	.45	.35
a.		Center omitted	100.00	
131	A9	1r pale brn, brn & red org	.35	.25
a.		Center inverted	25.00	
b.		Center omitted	25.00	
c.		Center double	25.00	
d.		Groundwork double	150.00	—
e.		Groundwork inverted	60.00	—
f.		Groundwork omitted	60.00	—
g.		Frame double	25.00	—

132	A12	3.50r mar & lt grn	1.10	.25
133	A13	5r dk blue, grn & pale blue	1.25	.35
a.		5r dk bl, grn & yel (error)	900.00	
b.		Groundwork inverted	3,600.	
134	A12	7r dk grn & pink (I)	1.20	1.15
a.		Center inverted	30,000.	
135	A13	10r scar, yel & gray	45.00	35.00
a.		10r scarlet, green & gray (error)	1,125.	
		Nos. 119-135 (17)	74.25	63.05

Beware of trimmed examples of No. 109 offered as No. 135.

Vertical Lozenges of Varnish on Face

1917   Perf. 13½, 13½x13

137	A12	3.50r mar & lt grn	.50	.25
138	A12	7r dk grn & pink (II)	2.50	.50
d.		Type I	40.00	6.75

Perf. 12½

137a	A12	3.50r maroon & lt grn	14.00	2.75
138a	A12	7r dk grn & pink (II)	17.00	4.75

Horizontal Lozenges of Varnish on Face

Perf. 13½x13

87h	A9	1r pale brown, brn & red orange	1.35	.30
i.		Imperf.	17.50	—
j.		As "i," center omitted	45.00	—
k.		As "i," center inverted	22.50	—
m.		As "i," center double	22.50	—
137b	A12	3.50r mar & lt green	2.50	.50
d.		Imperf.	2,250.	
138b	A12	7r dk grn & pink (II)	1.35	.25
c.		Imperf.	1,550.	

Nos. 87g, 137b and 138b often show the eagle with little or no embossing.

Types of 1913 Issue

No. 88 Surcharged
Large Numeral

No. 139 Back   No. 140 Back

The backside of Nos. 139-140 have surcharge & 4-line inscription.

1917

Thin Cardboard, Without Gum

139	A16	1 on 1k brown org	3.00	40.00
140	A17	2 on 2k yel green	3.00	40.00
a.		Imperf.	525.00	—
		Pair	1,700.	

Without Surcharge

141	A18	3k rose red	3.00	40.00
		Nos. 139-141 (3)	9.00	120.00

See note after No. 107.
Stamps overprinted with a Liberty Cap on Crossed Swords or with reduced facsimiles of pages of newspapers were a private speculation and without official sanction.

RUSSIAN TURKESTAN

Russian stamps of 1917-18 surcharged as above are frauds.

Russian Soviet Federated Socialist Republic

Severing Chain of Bondage — A33

1918	**Typo.**		**Perf. 13½**	
149	A33	35k blue	.45	6.25
a.		Imperf., pair	1,600.	
150	A33	70k brown	.50	7.25
a.		Imperf., pair	16,500.	

For surcharges see Nos. B18-B23, J1-J9 and note following No. B17.

A 15k stamp exists but was not regularly issued. Value, $30,000.

During 1918-22, the chaotic conditions of revolution and civil war brought the printing of stamps by the central government to a halt. Stocks of old tsarist Arms type stamps and postal stationery remained in use, and postal savings and various revenue stamps were authorized for postage use. During this period, stamps were sold and used at different rates at different times: 1918-20, sold at face value; from March, 1920, sold at 100 times face value; from Aug. 15, 1921, sold at 250r each, regardless of face value; from April, 1922, sold at 10,000r per 1k or 1r. In Oct. 1922, these issues were superseded by gold currency stamps.

See Nos. AR1-AR25 for fiscal stamps used as postage stamps during this period.

Symbols of Agriculture — A40

Symbols of Industry — A41

Soviet Symbols of Agriculture and Industry — A42

Science and Arts — A43

1921	**Unwmk.**	**Litho.**		**Imperf.**
177	A40	1r orange	1.00	140.00
178	A40	2r lt brown	1.00	140.00
a.		Double impression	800.00	
179	A41	5r dull ultra	2.25	140.00
a.		Double impression	—	
180	A42	20r blue	2.60	140.00
a.		Double impression	240.00	
b.		Pelure paper	10.00	175.00
c.		As "b," double impression	275.00	
181	A40	100r orange	.25	.25
a.		Double impression	200.00	
b.		Pelure paper	.25	.45
c.		As "b," double impression	200.00	
182	A40	200r lt brown	.50	.25
a.		Double impression	180.00	
b.		Triple impression	150.00	
c.		200r gray brown	25.00	
183	A43	250r dull violet	.25	.25
a.		Tête bêche pair	25.00	
b.		Double impression	90.00	
c.		Pelure paper	.25	.45
d.		As "c," tête bêche pair	32.50	
e.		As "c," double impression	100.00	
f.		Chalk surfaced paper	12.50	5.00
184	A40	300r green	.60	1.10
a.		Double impression	425.00	
b.		Pelure paper	12.00	22.50

185	A41	500r blue	1.00	.30
a.		Double impression	—	
186	A41	1000r carmine	.25	.30
a.		Double impression	110.00	
b.		Triple impression	135.00	
c.		Pelure paper	.85	.30
d.		As "c," double impression	90.00	
e.		Thick paper	2.50	2.75
f.		Chalk surfaced paper	.25	.50
		Nos. 177-186 (10)	9.70	562.45

Nos. 177-180 were on sale only in Petrograd, Moscow and Kharkov. Used values are for cancelled-to-order stamps. Postally used examples are worth substantially more.

Nos. 183a and 183d are from printings in which one of the two panes of 25 in the sheet were inverted. Thus, they are horizontal pairs, with a vertical gutter.

See Nos. 203, 205. For surcharges see Nos. 191-194, 196-199, 201, 210, B40, B43-B47, J10.

New Russia Triumphant A44

Type I — 37½mm by 23½mm.
Type II — 38½mm by 23¼mm.

1921, Aug. 10		**Wmk. 169**	**Engr.**	
187	A44	40r slate, type II	1.90	160.00
a.		Type I	1.90	160.00

The types are caused by paper shrinkage. One type has the watermark sideways in relation to the other.

For surcharges see Nos. 195, 200.

Initials Stand for Russian Federated Socialist Republic — A45

1921		**Litho.**	**Unwmk.**	
188	A45	100r orange	.85	.85
189	A45	250r violet	.85	.85
190	A45	1000r carmine rose	1.75	1.40
		Nos. 188-190 (3)	3.45	3.10

4th anniversary of Soviet Government.
A 200r was not regularly issued. Values: unused $60, never hinged $100.

Nos. 177-179 Surcharged in Black

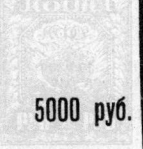

1922				
191	A40	5000r on 1r org	3.00	.80
a.		Inverted surcharge	140.00	32.50
b.		Double surch., red & blk	800.00	
c.		Pair, one without surcharge	250.00	
192	A40	5000r on 2r lt brn	3.00	1.10
a.		Inverted surcharge	110.00	90.00
b.		Double surcharge	145.00	
193	A41	5000r on 5r ultra	3.00	
a.		Inverted surcharge	—	450.00
b.		Double surcharge	145.00	

Beware of digitally created forgeries of the errors of Nos. 191-193 and 196-199.

No. 180 Surcharged

194	A42	5000r on 20r blue	2.10	2.25
a.		Pelure paper	16.50	3.25
b.		Pair, one without surcharge	125.00	

Nos. 177-180, 187-187a Surcharged in Black or Red

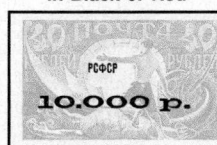

Wmk. Lozenges (169)

195	A44	10,000r on 40r, type I	70.00	50.00
a.		Inverted surcharge	225.00	
b.		Type II	67.50	50.00
c.		"1.0000" instead of "10.000"	2,750.	
d.		Double surcharge	8,500.	

Red Surcharge
Unwmk.

196	A40	5000r on 1r org	5.75	5.75
a.		Inverted surcharge	50.00	25.00
197	A40	5000r on 2r lt brn	5.75	5.75
a.		Inverted surcharge	125.00	30.00
198	A41	5000r on 5r ultra	5.75	5.75
199	A42	5000r on 20r blue	3.00	2.25
a.		Inverted surcharge	200.00	50.00
b.		Pelure paper	4.00	5.00

Wmk. Lozenges (169)

200	A44	10,000r on 40r, type I (R)	2.25	1.25
a.		Inverted surcharge	160.00	40.00
b.		Double surcharge	125.00	—
c.		With periods after Russian letters	1,100.	450.00
d.		Type II	2.25	2.75
e.		As "a," type II	125.00	40.00
f.		As "c," type II	200.00	

No. 183 Surcharged in Black or Blue Black

1922, Mar.			**Unwmk.**	
201	A43	7500r on 250r (Bk)	.25	.25
a.		Pelure paper	.25	.25
b.		Chalk surfaced paper	.45	.45
c.		Blue black surcharge	.50	.25
d.		Surch. typographed	250.00	
e.		As "c," surch. lithographed	850.00	
f.		As "d," surch. inverted	3,250.	
		Nos. 191-201 (11)	103.85	75.15

Nos. 201, 201a and 201b exist with surcharge inverted (value about $20 each), and double (about $25 each).

The horizontal surcharge was prepared but not issued. Values: $11 unused, $20 never hinged. The horizontal surcharge also exists on pelure paper. Values: $70 unused, $175 never hinged.

Type of 1921 and

"Workers of the World Unite" A46

1922		**Litho.**	**Wmk. 171**	
202	A46	5000r dark violet	1.90	.60
203	A42	7500r blue	.50	.50
204	A46	10,000r blue	17.50	3.00
			Unwmk.	
205	A42	7500r blue, *buff*	.50	.50
a.		Double impression	250.00	
206	A46	22,500r dk vio, *buff*	.50	.60
		Nos. 202-206 (5)	20.90	5.20

For surcharges see Nos. B41-B42.

No. 183 Surcharged Diagonally

1922	A43	**Unwmk.**		**Imperf.**
210	A43	100,000r on 250r	.50	.50
a.		Inverted surcharge	200.00	.50
b.		Pelure paper	.50	.50
c.		Chalk surfaced paper	2.25	1.65
d.		As "b," inverted surcharge	225.00	—

Marking 5th Anniversary of October Revolution — A48

1922			**Typo.**	
211	A48	5r ocher & black	.60	.25
212	A48	10r brown & black	.60	.25
213	A48	25r violet & black	1.60	.60
214	A48	27r rose & black	5.50	2.00
215	A48	45r blue & black	3.60	2.00
		Nos. 211-215 (5)	11.90	5.10

Pelure Paper

211a	A48	5r ocher & black	82.50
212a	A48	10r brown & black	120.00
213a	A48	25r violet & black	82.50
214a	A48	27r rose & black	82.50
215a	A48	45r blue & black	60.00

5th anniv. of the October Revolution. Sold in the currency of 1922 which was valued at 10,000 times that of the preceding years.
For surcharges see Nos. B38-B39.

Nos. 81, 82a, 85-86, 125-126, 129-130 Surcharged

1922-23			**Perf. 14½x15**	
216	A8	5r on 20k	.45	6.00
a.		Inverted surcharge	50.00	90.00
b.		Double surcharge	100.00	
c.		Pair, one without surch.	165.00	
217	A11	20r on 15k	1.90	2.00
a.		Inverted surcharge	120.00	90.00
b.		Pair, one without surch.	165.00	

218	A11	20r on 70k	.25	.35
	a.	Inverted surcharge	60.00	45.00
	b.	Double surcharge	50.00	50.00
	c.	Pair, one without surch.	165.00	
219	A8	30r on 50k	1.75	.50
	a.	Inverted surcharge	67.50	67.50
	c.	Groundwork omitted	50.00	50.00
	d.	Double surcharge	100.00	100.00
220	A11	40r on 15k	1.00	.35
	a.	Inverted surcharge	67.50	67.50
	b.	Double surcharge	90.00	90.00
	c.	Pair, one without surch.	165.00	
221	A11	100r on 15k	1.00	.35
	a.	Inverted surcharge	90.00	67.50
	b.	Double surcharge	90.00	67.50
	c.	Pair, one without surch.	225.00	
222	A11	200r on 15k	2.75	.35
	a.	Inverted surcharge	57.50	45.00
	b.	Double surcharge	67.50	45.00
	c.	Pair, one without surch.	225.00	

Nos. 221-222 exist with triple surcharge; No. 221 with double surcharge, one inverted. Value, each $100.

Imperf

223	A8	5r on 20k	32.50	25.00
224	A11	20r on 15k	9,500.	
225	A11	20r on 70k	.90	1.75
	a.	Inverted surcharge	82.50	
226	A8	30r on 50k brn vio & grn	.50	1.00
227	A11	40r on 15k	.30	.30
	a.	Inverted surcharge	140.00	
	b.	Double surcharge	100.00	
228	A11	100r on 15k	1.00	.50
	a.	Inverted surcharge	190.00	
229	A11	200r on 15k	.75	.50
	a.	Inverted surcharge	140.00	
	b.	Double surcharge	140.00	
	Nos. 216-223,225-229 (13)		45.05	38.95

Forgeries of No. 223-229 exist, including a dangerous digital forgery of No. 224.

Worker A49 / Soldier A50

1922-23	**Typo.**			**Imperf.**
230	A49	10r blue	.25	.25
231	A50	50r brown	.25	.25
232	A50	70r brown violet	.25	.25
233	A50	100r red	.25	.25
	Nos. 230-233 (4)		1.00	1.00

1923				**Perf. 14x14½**
234	A49	10r dp bl, perf. 13½	.25	2.75
	a.	Perf. 14	32.50	4.00
	b.	Perf. 12½	1.40	2.75
235	A50	50r brown	.25	2.75
	a.	Perf. 12½	7.50	3.25
	b.	Perf. 13½	2.25	2.75
236	A50	70r brown violet	.25	2.75
	a.	Perf. 12½	4.00	2.75
237	A50	100r red	.25	.25
	a.	Cliché of 70r in plate of 100r	50.00	30.00
	b.	Corrected cliché	—	
	Nos. 234-237 (4)		1.00	8.50

No. 237b has extra broken line at right.
Nos. 230-233 were surcharged for use in Far Eastern Republic. See Far Eastern Republic Nos. 66-70.

Soldier — A51 / Worker — A52 / Peasant — A53

1923				**Perf. 14½x15**
238	A51	3r rose	.25	.25
239	A52	4r brown	.25	.25
240	A53	5r light blue	.25	.25
	a.	Double impression	82.50	
241	A51	10r gray	.25	.25
	e.	Double impression	95.00	
241A	A51	20r brown violet	.50	.35
	b.	Double impression	140.00	
	Nos. 238-241A (5)		1.50	1.35

Imperf

238a	A51	3r rose	12.50	—
239a	A52	4r brown	30.00	—
	b.	As "a," double impression	150.00	—
240b	A53	5r light blue	8.00	—
241d	A51	10r gray	8.00	—
	f.	As "d," double impression	115.00	—
241c	A51	100r dark brown violet	275.00	—

Stamps of 1r buff, type A52, and 2r green, type A53, perf. 12 and imperf. were prepared but not put in use.
The imperfs of Nos. 238-241A were sold only by the philatelic bureau in Moscow.

Stamps of 20r, type A51, printed in gray black or dull violet are essays. Value, $200 each.
The stamps of this and the following issues were sold for the currency of 1923, one ruble of which was equal to 100 rubles of 1922 and 1,000,000 rubles of 1921.

Union of Soviet Socialist Republics

Reaping — A54

Sowing — A55

Fordson Tractor A56

Symbolical of the Exhibition — A57

1923, Aug. 19		**Litho.**		**Imperf.**
242	A54	1r brown & orange	4.50	2.50
243	A55	2r dp grn & pale grn	5.00	2.00
244	A56	5r dp bl & pale blue	5.00	3.75
245	A57	7r rose & pink	5.00	4.50

		Perf. 12½, 13½		
246	A54	1r brown & orange	5.00	3.75
	a.	Perf. 12½	42.50	37.50
247	A55	2r dp grn & pale grn, perf. 12½	6.00	3.75
248	A56	5r dp bl & pale bl	14.00	3.75
	a.	Perf. 13½	13.50	8.00
249	A57	7r rose & pink	5.00	6.00
	a.	Perf. 12½	24.00	12.50
	Nos. 242-249 (8)		49.50	30.00

1st Agriculture and Craftsmanship Exhibition, Moscow.

Worker — A58 / Soldier — A59 / Peasant — A60

1923		**Unwmk.**	**Litho.**	**Imperf.**
250	A58	1k orange	2.50	.45
251	A59	2k green	2.50	.45
252	A59	3k red brown	2.50	1.40
253	A58	4k deep rose	24.00	1.25
254	A58	5k lilac	2.50	.65
255	A60	6k light blue	2.75	.45
256	A59	10k dark blue	35.00	3.75
257	A58	20k yellow green	12.00	.75
258	A60	50k dark brown	19.00	2.50
259	A59	1r red & brown	50.00	5.00
	Nos. 250-259 (10)		152.75	16.65

1924				**Perf. 14½x15**
261	A58	4k deep rose	110.00	—
262	A59	10k dark blue	165.00	—
263	A59	30k violet	25.00	4.00
264	A59	40k slate gray	25.00	4.00
	Nos. 261-264 (4)		325.00	8.00

See Nos. 273-290, 304-321. For surcharges see Nos. 349-350.

Vladimir Ilyich Ulyanov (Lenin) — A61

1924				**Imperf.**
265	A61	3k red & black	8.25	2.40
266	A61	6k red & black	7.00	2.00
267	A61	12k red & black	5.50	2.00
268	A61	20k red & black	11.50	2.00
	Nos. 265-268 (4)		32.25	8.40

Three printings of Nos. 265-268 differ in size of red frame.

		Perf. 13½		
269	A61	3k red & black	6.75	4.00
270	A61	6k red & black	6.75	2.00
271	A61	12k red & black	12.00	2.00
272	A61	20k red & black	8.00	2.50
	Nos. 269-272 (4)		33.50	10.50
	Nos. 265-272 (8)		65.75	18.90

Death of Lenin (1870-1924). Forgeries of Nos. 265-272 exist.

Types of 1923

Worker — A62

There are small differences between the lithographed stamps of 1923 and the typographed of 1924-25. On a few values this may be seen in the numerals.
Type A58: Lithographed. The two white lines forming the outline of the ear are continued across the cheek. Typographed. The outer lines of the ear are broken where they touch the cheek.
Type A59: Lithographed. At the top of the right shoulder a white line touches the frame at the left. Counting from the edge of the visor of the cap, lines 5, 6 and sometimes 7 touch at their upper ends. Typographed. The top line of the shoulder does not reach the frame. On the cap lines 5, 6 and 7 run together and form a white spot.
Type A60: In the angle above the first letter "C" there is a fan-shaped ornament enclosing four white dashes. On the lithographed stamps these dashes reach nearly to the point of the angle. On the typographed stamps the dashes are shorter and often only three are visible.
On unused examples of the typographed stamps the raised outlines of the designs can be seen on the backs of the stamps.

1924-25		**Typo.**		**Imperf.**
273	A59	3k red brown	6.75	1.40
274	A58	4k deep rose	3.00	1.50
275	A59	10k dark blue	4.00	1.25
275A	A60	50k brown	6,750.	25.00

Other typographed and imperf. values include: 2k green, 5k lilac, 6k light blue, 20k green and 1r red and brown. Value, unused: $150, $100, $150, $200 and $1,000, respectively.
Nos. 273-275A were regularly issued. The 7k, 8k, 9k, 30k, 40k, 2r, 3r, and 5r also exist imperf. Value, set of 8, $75.

		Perf. 14½x15		
		Typo.		
276	A58	1k orange	175.00	8.00
277	A60	2k green	2.00	.45
278	A59	3k red brown	2.00	.45
279	A58	4k deep rose	2.00	.45
280	A58	5k lilac	160.00	5.00
281	A60	6k lt blue	2.00	.45
282	A59	7k chocolate	2.00	.45
283	A58	8k brn ol	1.80	.45
284	A60	9k orange red	4.50	.45
285	A59	10k dark blue	4.00	.45
286	A58	14k slate blue	225.00	2.50
287	A60	15k yellow	25,000.	210.00
288	A59	20k gray green	5.25	.45
288A	A60	30k violet	400.00	4.00
288B	A59	40k slate gray	800.00	4.00
289	A60	50k brown	225.00	10.00

290	A59	1r red & brn	19.00	1.00
291	A62	2r grn & rose	12.00	2.00
	Nos. 276-286,288-291 (17)		2,042.	40.55

See No. 323. Forgeries of No. 287 exist.

1925				**Perf. 12**
276a	A58	1k orange	2.50	1.00
277a	A60	2k green	21.50	1.00
278a	A59	3k red brown	3.50	9.00
279a	A58	4k deep rose	275.00	25.00
280a	A58	5k lilac	5.50	1.00
282a	A59	7k chocolate	10.00	1.00
283a	A58	8k brown olive	1,375.	5.00
284a	A60	9k orange red	20.00	2.50
285a	A59	10k dark blue	5.00	2.00
286a	A58	14k slate blue	2.50	1.00
287a	A60	15k yellow	6.75	1.00
288c	A58	20k gray green	27.50	1.00
288d	A60	30k violet	22.50	1.50
288e	A59	40k slate gray	110.00	2.50
289a	A60	50k brown	16.50	1.00
290a	A59	1r red & brown	2,000.	3,000.
	Nos. 276a-290a (16)		3,904.	3,056.

Soldier — A63 / Worker — A64

1924-25				**Perf. 13½**
292	A63	3r blk brn & grn	19.00	2.50
	a.	Perf. 10	5,500.	145.00
	b.	Perf. 13½x10	2,750.	
293	A64	5r dk bl & gray brn	200.00	12.50
	a.	Perf. 10½	70.00	

See Nos. 324-325.

Lenin Mausoleum, Moscow — A65

		Wmk. 170		
1925, Jan.		**Photo.**		**Imperf.**
294	A65	7k deep blue	9.00	2.50
295	A65	14k dark green	25.00	4.00
296	A65	20k carmine rose	14.00	5.00
297	A65	40k red brown	25.00	7.00
	Nos. 294-297 (4)		73.00	18.50

		Perf. 13½x14		
298	A65	7k deep blue	5.50	4.50
299	A65	14k dark green	25.00	6.75
300	A65	20k carmine rose	20.00	5.25
301	A65	40k red brown	26.00	6.25
	Nos. 298-301 (4)		76.50	22.75
	Nos. 294-301 (8)		149.50	41.25

First anniversary of Lenin's death.
Nos. 294-301 are found on both ordinary and thick paper. Those on thick paper sell for twice as much, except for No. 301, which is scarcer on ordinary paper.

Lenin — A66

		Wmk. 170		
1925, July		**Engr.**		**Perf. 13½**
302	A66	5r red brown	40.00	6.75
	a.	Perf. 12½	165.00	25.00
	b.	Perf. 10½ ('26)	82.50	11.00
303	A66	10r indigo	40.00	10.00
	a.	Perf. 12½	1,250.	175.00
	b.	Perf. 10½ ('26)	200.00	11.00

Imperfs. exist. Value, set $75.
See Nos. 407-408, 621-622

Types of 1923 Issue

1925-27	**Wmk. 170**	**Typo.**		**Perf. 12**
304	A58	1k orange	1.60	.35
305	A60	2k green	1.60	.35
306	A59	3k red brown	1.60	.35
307	A58	4k deep rose	1.60	.35
308	A58	5k lilac	1.60	.35
309	A60	6k lt blue	1.60	.75

310	A59	7k chocolate	3.25	.75
311	A58	8k brown olive	17.00	1.40
a.		Perf. 14½x15	325.00	27.50
312	A60	9k red	6.50	.75
313	A59	10k dark blue	3.50	.75
a.		10k pale blue ('27)	9.00	4.50
314	A58	14k slate blue	4.00	1.25
315	A60	15k yellow	9.50	1.25
316	A59	18k violet	17.00	1.75
317	A58	20k gray green	9.50	1.25
318	A60	30k violet	17.00	1.25
319	A59	40k slate gray	17.00	1.75
320	A60	50k brown	17.00	1.75
321	A59	1r red & brown	19.00	4.00
a.		Perf. 14½x15	325.00	50.00
323	A62	2r grn & rose red	75.00	11.00
a.		Perf. 14½x15	18.00	5.00

Perf. 13½

324	A63	3r blk brn & grn	27.50	9.50
a.		Perf. 12½	475.00	82.50
325	A64	5r dk blue & gray brn	35.00	12.50
		Nos. 304-325 (21)	287.35	53.40

Nos. 304-315, 317-325 exist imperf. Value, set $125.

Mikhail V. Lomonosov and Academy of Sciences — A67

1925, Sept.   Photo.   Perf. 12½, 13½

326	A67	3k orange brown	7.50	2.00
a.		Perf. 12½x12	40.00	6.75
c.		Perf. 13½	50.00	9.00
327	A67	15k dk olive green	14.00	2.25
a.		Perf. 12½	20.00	5.00

Russian Academy of Sciences, 200th anniv. Exist unwatermarked, on thick paper with yellow gum, perf. 13½. These are essays, later perforated and gummed. Value, each $50.

Prof. Aleksandr S. Popov (1859-1905), Radio Pioneer — A68

1925, Oct.   Perf. 13½

328	A68	7k deep blue	6.25	1.00
329	A68	14k green	10.00	1.50

For surcharge see No. 353.

Decembrist Exiles — A69   Street Rioting in St. Petersburg — A70

Revolutionist Leaders — A71

1925, Dec. 28   Imperf.

330	A69	3k olive green	5.00	1.00
331	A70	7k brown	32.50	3.50
332	A71	14k carmine lake	19.00	5.00

Perf. 13½

333	A69	3k olive green	4.50	1.25
a.		Perf. 12½	100.00	50.00
334	A70	7k brown	16.50	3.50
335	A71	14k carmine lake	19.50	5.50
		Nos. 330-335 (6)	97.00	19.75

Centenary of Decembrist revolution. For surcharges see Nos. 354, 357.

Revolters Parading — A72   Speaker Haranguing Mob — A73

Street Barricade, Moscow — A74

1925, Dec. 20   Imperf.

336	A72	3k olive green	5.00	7.50
337	A73	7k brown	17.50	8.75
338	A74	14k carmine lake	12.50	2.75

Perf. 12½, 12x12½

339	A72	3k olive green	5.50	3.00
a.		Perf. 13½	37.50	8.00
340	A73	7k brown	35.00	5.00
a.		Perf. 13½	17.50	5.25
b.		Horiz. pair, imperf. btwn.		
341	A74	14k carmine lake	6.75	3.75
a.		Perf. 13½	40.00	7.50
		Nos. 336-341 (6)	82.25	30.75

20th anniversary of Revolution of 1905. For surcharges see Nos. 355, 358.

Lenin — A75

1926   Wmk. 170   Engr.   Perf. 10½

342	A75	1r dark brown	37.50	4.00
a.		Perf. 12½	2,250.	—
343	A75	2r black violet	35.00	5.75
a.		Perf. 12½	2,250.	—
344	A75	3r dark green	37.50	5.75
a.		Perf. 12½	4,250.	—
b.		Horiz. pair, imperf. btwn.		5,000.
		Nos. 342-344 (3)	110.00	15.50

Nos. 342-343 exist imperf. See Nos. 406, 620.

Liberty Monument, Moscow — A76

1926, July   Litho.   Perf. 12x12½

347	A76	7k blue green & red	10.00	2.75
348	A76	14k blue green & vio	12.50	2.75

6th International Esperanto Congress at Leningrad. Exist perf. 11½. Value, set $8,500. For surcharge see No. 356.

Nos. 282, 282a and 310 Surcharged in Black

Two types of overprint: Type I, 2mm space between lines of surcharge; Type II, .7mm space between lines of surcharge.

1927, June   Unwmk.   Perf. 14½x15

349	A59	8k on 7k choc (I)	22.50	4.00
a.		Perf. 12x12¼	27.50	3.75
b.		Inverted surcharge	300.00	
c.		Type II	2,750.	140.00
d.		As "b," surcharge inverted	275.00	

Perf. 12
Wmk. 170

350	A59	8k on 7k chocolate	8.00	2.50
a.		Inverted surcharge	150.00	
b.		Type II	10,500.	70.00
c.		As "b," surcharge inverted	350.00	

The surcharge on Nos. 349-350 comes in two types: With space of 2mm between lines, and with space of ¾mm. The latter is much scarcer.

Same Surcharge on Stamps of 1925-26 in Black or Red
Perf. 13½, 12½, 12x12½

353	A68	8k on 7k dp bl (R)	6.75	2.25
a.		Inverted "8"	110.00	50.00
354	A70	8k on 7k brown	12.50	4.75
355	A73	8k on 7k brown	20.00	6.25
356	A76	8k on 7k bl grn & red	21.50	8.50

Imperf

357	A70	8k on 7k brown	11.00	4.00
358	A73	8k on 7k brown	19.00	7.00
		Nos. 349-350,353-358 (8)	121.25	39.25

Postage Due Stamps of 1925 Surcharged

Two settings: A's aligned (shown), bottom A to left.

Lithographed or Typographed
1927, June   Unwmk.   Perf. 12

359	D1	8k on 1k red, typo.	4.50	2.00
a.		Litho.	2,750.	150.00
360	D1	8k on 2k violet	4.50	2.00
a.		Inverted surcharge	275.00	

Perf. 12, 14½x14

361	D1	8k on 3k lt blue	4.50	2.00
a.		Inverted surcharge	275.00	
362	D1	8k on 7k orange	4.25	1.25
363	D1	8k on 8k green	4.50	2.00
a.		Inverted surcharge	—	1,750.
364	D1	8k on 10k dk blue	4.00	1.25
a.		Inverted surcharge	275.00	
365	D1	8k on 14k brown	3.75	4.00
a.		Inverted surcharge	350.00	
		Nos. 359-365 (7)	30.00	14.50

Wmk. 170
1927, June   Typo.   Perf. 12

366	D1	8k on 1k red	4.50	1.00
367	D1	8k on 2k violet	4.50	1.00
368	D1	8k on 3k lt blue	4.50	1.00
369	D1	8k on 7k orange	4.50	1.00
370	D1	8k on 8k green	4.50	1.00
371	D1	8k on 10k dk blue	4.50	1.00
372	D1	8k on 14k brown	4.50	1.00
a.		Inverted surcharge	—	1,750.
		Nos. 366-372 (7)	31.50	7.00

Nos. 366, 368-370 exist with inverted surcharge.

Dr. L. L. Zamenhof A77

1927   Photo.   Perf. 10½

373	A77	14k yel grn & brn	11.00	2.25

Unwmk.

374	A77	14k yel grn & brn	11.00	2.25
a.		Perf. 10	325.00	52.50
b.		Perf. 10x10½	175.00	75.00
c.		Imperf.	950.00	
d.		Vert. pair, imperf. btwn., never hinged	8,250.	

40th anniversary of creation of Esperanto.

Worker, Soldier, Peasant — A78   Worker and Sailor — A81

Lenin in Car Guarded by Soldiers A79

Smolny Institute, Leningrad A80

Map of the USSR A82

Men of Various Soviet Republics — A83

Workers of Different Races; Kremlin in
Background — A84

**Typo. (3k, 8k, 18k), Engr. (7k), Litho.
(14k), Photo. (5k, 28k)**
Perf. 13½, 12½x12, 11

1927, Oct.   **Unwmk.**
375	A78	3k bright rose	5.50	1.10
a.		Imperf., pair	5,000.	
376	A79	5k deep brown	14.00	2.25
a.		Imperf.	1,650.	500.00
b.		Perf. 12½	125.00	12.50
c.		Perf. 12½x10½	55.00	5.00
377	A80	7k myrtle green	14.00	4.00
a.		Perf. 11½	32.50	7.50
b.		Imperf., pair	1,500.	
378	A81	8k brown & black	8.00	1.50
a.		Perf. 10½x12½	42.50	2.75
379	A82	14k dull blue &		
		red	6.75	2.75
380	A83	18k blue	4.75	1.25
a.		Imperf.	275.00	
381	A84	28k olive brown	18.00	5.00
a.		Perf. 10	45.00	8.00
		Nos. 375-381 (7)	71.00	17.85

10th anniversary of October Revolution.
The paper of No. 375 has an overprint of
pale yellow wavy lines.
No. 377b exists with watermark 170. Value,
$1,000.

Worker — A85

Peasant — A86

Lenin — A87

1927-28   Typo.   *Perf. 13½*
Chalk Surfaced Paper
382	A85	1k orange	1.10	.35
a.		Imperf.	1,750.	
383	A86	2k apple green	4.25	.35
a.		Imperf.	1,750.	
385	A85	4k bright blue	1.10	.35
386	A86	5k brown	1.10	.35
a.		Imperf.	1,750.	—
388	A86	7k dark red ('28)	1.10	.35
a.		Double impression	475.00	
389	A85	8k green	7.00	.60
391	A85	10k light brown	5.00	.35
a.		Imperf.	1,325.	
392	A87	14k dark green ('28)	10.75	4.00
393	A87	18k olive green	12.00	1.25
a.		Imperf.	3,750.	
394	A87	18k dark blue ('28)	11.00	1.70
395	A86	20k dark gray green	16.50	.35
396	A85	40k rose red	20.00	2.00
397	A86	50k bright blue	24.00	1.10
399	A85	70k gray green	11.00	2.00
400	A86	80k orange	15.00	2.75
		Nos. 382-400 (15)	140.90	17.85

Soldier and
Kremlin — A88

Sailor and
Flag — A89

Cavalryman
A90

Aviator
A91

1928, Feb. 6
Chalk Surfaced Paper
402	A88	8k light brown	4.75	.85
a.		Imperf.	1,200.	—
403	A89	14k deep blue	12.00	1.50
404	A90	18k carmine rose	6.50	1.60
405	A91	28k yellow green	15.00	2.25
a.		Imperf.	7,000.	
		Nos. 402-405 (4)	38.25	6.20

10th anniversary of the Soviet Army.

Lenin Types of 1925-26
Wmk. 169
1928-29   Engr.   *Perf. 10½*
406	A75	3r dark green		
		('29)	52.50	3.50
a.		Perf. 10	52.50	6.75
b.		Imperf.	3,250.	—
407	A66	5r red brown	19.00	3.75
a.		Perf. 10	105.00	14.00
b.		Imperf.	20,000.	—
408	A66	10r indigo	19.00	4.50
a.		Perf. 10	27.50	6.75
b.		Imperf.	20,000.	—
		Nos. 406-408 (3)	90.50	11.75

Bugler Sounding Assembly
A92   A93

Perf. 12½x12
1929, Aug. 18   Photo.   Wmk. 170
411	A92	10k olive brown	32.50	6.25
a.		Perf. 10½	140.00	27.50
b.		Perf. 12½x12x10½x12	140.00	75.00
412	A93	14k slate	5.50	2.75
a.		Perf. 12½x12x10½x12	425.00	95.00

First All-Soviet Assembly of Pioneers.

Factory
Worker
A95

Peasant
A96

Farm Worker
A97

Soldier
A98

Worker,
Soldier,
Peasant
A100

Worker
A103

Lenin
A104

Peasant
A107

Factory
Worker
A109

Farm
Worker
A111

Perf. 12x12½
1929-31   Typo.   Wmk. 170
413	A103	1k orange	1.25	.25
a.		Perf. 10½	19.00	4.00
b.		Perf. 12x12¼	8.00	1.60
414	A95	2k yellow green	1.25	.25
415	A96	3k blue	2.75	.25
a.		Perf. 12x12¼	82.50	25.00
416	A97	4k claret	2.75	.45
417	A98	5k orange brown	2.75	.45
a.		Perf. 10½	190.00	25.00
418	A100	7k scarlet	2.75	.90
419	A103	10k olive green	2.75	.50
a.		Perf. 10½	400.00	40.00

Unwmk.
420	A104	14k indigo	5.50	1.00
a.		Perf. 10½	17.50	3.25

Wmk. 170
421	A100	15k dk ol grn ('30)	2.75	.85
422	A107	20k green	2.75	.85
a.		Imperf.	—	—
423	A109	30k dk violet	14.00	1.75
424	A111	50k dp brown	14.00	2.50
425	A98	70k dk red ('30)	8.00	2.50
426	A107	80k red brn ('31)	8.00	2.50
		Nos. 413-426 (14)	71.25	15.00

Nos. 422, 423, 424 and 426 have a background of fine wavy lines in pale shades of the
colors of the stamps.
See Nos. 456-466, 613A-619A. For
surcharge see No. 743.

Symbolical
of Industry
A112

Tractors
Issuing from
Assembly
Line — A113

Iron Furnace
(Inscription
reads, "More
Metal More
Machines")
A114

Blast Furnace
and Chart of
Anticipated Iron
Production
A115

1929-30   *Perf. 12x12½*
427	A112	5k orange brown	3.25	.90
428	A113	10k olive green	9.50	1.80

Perf. 12½x12
429	A114	20k dull green	9.50	3.00
a.		Perf. 10¾	8,000.	400.00
430	A115	28k violet black	4.25	2.00
		Nos. 427-430 (4)	26.50	7.70

Publicity for greater industrial production.
No. 429 exists perf. 10½. Value $4,000.

Red Cavalry
in Polish
Town after
Battle
A116

Cavalry
Charge
A117

Staff Officers
of 1st
Cavalry Army
A118

Plan of
Action for 1st
Cavalry
Army — A119

1930, Feb.   *Perf. 12x12½*
431	A116	2k yellow green	3.25	1.80
432	A117	5k light brown	7.00	1.80
433	A118	10k olive gray	14.00	2.75
434	A119	14k indigo & red	5.50	2.50
		Nos. 431-434 (4)	29.75	8.85

1st Red Cavalry Army, 10th anniversary.

Students
Preparing a
Poster
Newspaper
A120

1930, Aug. 15
435	A120	10k olive green	8.00	1.80

Educational Exhibition, Leningrad, 7/1-
8/15/30.

Telegraph
Office,
Moscow
A121

Lenin
Hydroelectric
Power
Station on
Volkhov
River
A122

1930 Photo. Wmk. 169 *Perf. 12¼*
436	A121	1r deep blue	19.00	5.00

Wmk. 170
437	A122	3r yel grn & blk brn	10.50	5.00

See Nos. 467, 469.

Battleship
Potemkin
A123

Inside
Presnya
Barricade
A124

Moscow Barricades
in 1905 — A125

1930 Typo. Perf. 12x12½, 12½x12
438	A123	3k red	1.75 .50
439	A124	5k blue	3.25 .70
440	A125	10k dk green & red	9.50 1.75
	Nos. 438-440 (3)		14.50 2.95

1931 Imperf.
452	A123	3k red	11.00 5.00
453	A124	5k deep blue	11.00 9.00
454	A125	10k dk green & red	22.00 17.50
	Nos. 452-454 (3)		44.00 31.50
	Nos. 438-454 (6)		58.50 34.45

Revolution of 1905, 25th anniversary.

Types of 1929-31 Regular Issue
1931-32 Imperf.
456	A103	1k orange	4.00 1.00
457	A95	2k yellow green	4.00 1.00
458	A96	3k blue	5.50 1.00
459	A97	4k claret	47.50 14.00
460	A98	5k orange brown	5.50 2.50
462	A103	10k olive green	55.00 22.50
464	A100	15k dk olive green	35.00 25.00
466	A109	30k dull violet	40.00 35.00
467	A121	1r dark blue	200.00 35.00
	Nos. 456-467 (9)		396.50 137.00

Nos. 459, 462-467 were sold only by the philatelic bureau.

Type of 1930 Issue
1931 Wmk. 170 Perf. 12x12½
469	A121	1r dark blue	8.00 1.50
	Never hinged		12.00

Maxim
Gorki — A133

1932-33 Photo.
470	A133	15k dark brown	8.00 1.75
a.		Imperf.	140.00 67.50
471	A133	35k dp ultra ('33)	35.00 14.50
	Set, never hinged		90.00

40th anniversary of Gorki's literary activity.

Lenin Addressing
the People
A134

Revolution in
Petrograd
(Leningrad)
A135

Dnieper
Hydroelectric
Power Station
A136

Asiatics Saluting
the Soviet
Flag — A139

Designs (dated 1917 1932): 15k, Collective farm. 20k, Magnitogorsk metallurgical plant in Urals. 30k, Radio tower and heads of 4 men.

1932-33 Perf. 12½x12; 12½ (30k)
472	A134	3k dark violet	4.25 1.25
473	A135	5k dark brown	4.25 1.25
474	A136	10k ultra	7.00 4.25
475	A136	15k dark green	4.25 1.50
476	A136	20k lake ('33)	4.25 1.50
477	A136	30k dk gray ('33)	55.00 15.00
478	A139	35k gray black	95.00 55.00
	Nos. 472-478 (7)		174.00 79.75
	Set, never hinged		325.00

October Revolution, 15th anniversary.

Breaking Prison
Bars — A140

1932, Nov. Litho. Perf. 12½x12
479	A140	50k dark red	32.50 9.50
	Never hinged		67.50

Intl. Revolutionaries' Aid Assoc., 10th anniv.

Trier,
Birthplace of
Marx — A141

Grave, Highgate
Cemetery,
London — A142

35k, Portrait & signature of Karl Marx (1818-83).

Perf. 12x12½, 12½x12
1933, Mar. Photo.
480	A141	3k dull green	4.00 1.80
481	A142	10k black brown	10.00 2.25
482	A142	35k brown violet	67.50 14.50
	Nos. 480-482 (3)		81.50 18.55
	Set, never hinged		145.00

Fine Arts Museum, Moscow — A145

1932, Dec. Perf. 12½
485	A145	15k black brown	5.00 6.00
486	A145	35k ultra	90.00 52.50
a.		Perf. 10½	67.50 32.50
	Set, never hinged		240.00

Moscow Philatelic Exhibition, 1932.
Nos. 485 and 486 were also issued in imperf. sheets of 4 containing 2 of each value, on thick paper for presentation purposes. They were not valid for postage. Value, from $19,500. Replicas of the sheet were made for Moscow 97 by the Canadian Society of Russian Philately.

Nos. 485 and 486a Surcharged

1933, Mar. Perf. 12½
487	A145	30k on 15k blk brn	50.00 15.00

Perf. 10½
488	A145	70k on 35k ultra	275.00 200.00
	Set, never hinged		500.00

Leningrad Philatelic Exhibition, 1933.

Peoples of the Soviet Union

Kazaks
A146

Lezghians
A147

Tungus
A150

Crimean
Tartars
A148

Jews,
Birobidzhan
A149

Buryats — A151

Yakuts — A156

Chechens
A152

Abkhas
A153

Georgians
A154

Nientzians
A155

Great Russians — A157

Tadzhiks — A158

Transcaucasians — A159

Turkmen — A160

Ukrainians — A161

Uzbeks — A162

Byelorussians — A163

Koryaks
A164

Bashkirs
A165

Chuvashes
A166

Perf. 12, 12x12½, 12½x12, 11x12, 12x11

1933, Apr.				Photo.
489	A146	1k black brown	9.00	2.00
490	A147	2k ultra	5.00	2.00
491	A148	3k gray green	18.00	2.00
492	A149	4k gray black	5.00	2.00
493	A150	5k brown violet	5.00	2.00
494	A151	6k indigo	5.00	2.00
495	A152	7k black brown	5.00	2.00
496	A153	8k rose red	11.00	2.00
497	A154	9k ultra	35.00	2.00
498	A155	10k black brown	5.00	2.00
499	A156	14k olive green	5.00	2.00
500	A157	15k orange	16.00	2.00
501	A158	15k ultra	13.00	2.00
502	A159	15k dark brown	13.00	2.00
503	A160	15k rose red	13.00	2.00
504	A161	15k violet brown	16.00	2.00
505	A162	15k gray black	13.00	2.00
506	A163	15k dull green	16.00	2.00
507	A164	20k dull blue	18.00	*2.00*
508	A165	30k brown violet	15.00	*3.00*
509	A166	35k black	15.00	*3.00*
		Nos. 489-509 (21)	256.00	44.00
		Set, never hinged	495.00	

V. V. Vorovsky
A169

3k, V. M. Volodarsky. 5k, M. S. Uritzky.

1933, Oct.			Perf. 12x12½
514	A169	1k dull green	4.00	1.00
515	A169	3k blue black	8.00	1.25
516	A169	5k olive brown	9.00	2.00
		Nos. 514-516 (3)	21.00	4.25
		Set, never hinged	42.50	

10th anniv. of the murder of Soviet Representative Vorovsky; 15th anniv. of the murder of the Revolutionists Volodarsky and Uritzky. See Nos. 531-532, 580-582.

Order of the Red Banner, 15th Anniv. — A173

1933, Nov. 17			Unwmk.	Perf. 14
518	A173	20k black, red & yel	15.00	3.50
		Never hinged	40.00	

No. 518, perf. 9½, is a proof. Values: unused, $4,000; never hinged, $8,000.

Commissar Schaumyan A174

Commissar Prokofii A. Dzhaparidze A175

Commissars Awaiting Execution — A176

Designs: 35k, Monument to the 26 Commissars. 40k, Worker, peasant and soldier dipping flags in salute.

1933, Dec. 1			
519	A174	4k brown	30.00	2.00
520	A175	5k dark gray	25.00	2.00
521	A176	20k purple	8.00	2.00

522	A176	35k ultra	80.00	17.50
523	A176	40k carmine	25.00	*7.00*
		Nos. 519-523 (5)	168.00	30.50
		Set, never hinged	440.00	

15th anniv. of the execution of 26 commissars at Baku. No. 521 exists imperf. Many part-perf varieties exist on all values of this issue, including imperf between pairs of several values.

Lenin's Mausoleum A179

1934, Feb. 7			Engr.	Perf. 14
524	A179	5k brown	20.00	2.50
a.		Imperf.	675.00	—
525	A179	10k slate blue	90.00	10.00
a.		Imperf.	675.00	—
526	A179	15k dk carmine	32.50	7.00
527	A179	20k green	6.00	5.25
528	A179	35k dark brown	32.50	8.00
		Nos. 524-528 (5)	181.00	32.75
		Set, never hinged	360.00	

10th anniversary of Lenin's death.

Ivan Fedorov A180

1934, Mar. 5			
529	A180	20k carmine rose	55.00	10.00
a.		Imperf.	675.00	—
530	A180	40k indigo	17.50	10.00
a.		Imperf.	675.00	—
		Set, never hinged	150.00	

350th anniv. of the death of Ivan Fedorov, founder of printing in Russia.

Portrait Type of 1933

Designs: 10k, Yakov M. Sverdlov. 15k, Victor Pavlovich Nogin.

1934, Mar.			Photo.	Wmk. 170
531	A169	10k ultra	27.50	6.00
532	A169	15k red	200.00	37.50
		Set, never hinged	475.00	

Deaths of Yakov M. Sverdlov, chairman of the All-Russian Central Executive Committee of the Soviets, 15th anniv., Victor Pavlovich Nogin, chairman Russian State Textile Syndicate, 10th anniv.

A184

Dmitri Ivanovich Mendeleev A185

1934, Sept. 15			Wmk. 170	Perf. 14
536	A184	5k emerald	22.00	3.00
537	A185	10k black brown	100.00	13.00
538	A185	15k vermilion	140.00	18.00
539	A184	20k ultra	22.00	5.50
		Nos. 536-539 (4)	284.00	39.50
		Set, never hinged	525.00	

Prof. D. I. Mendeleev (1834-1907), chemist who discovered the Periodic Law of Classification of the Elements.

Imperfs. exist of 5k (value $400) and 15k (value $400).

Lenin as Child and Youth
A186   A187

Demonstration before Lenin Mausoleum — A190

Designs: 5k, Lenin in middle age. 10k, Lenin the orator. 30k, Lenin and Stalin.

1934, Nov. 23			Unwmk.	Perf. 14
540	A186	1k indigo & black	22.00	4.00
541	A187	3k indigo & black	11.00	4.00
a.		Horiz. pair, imperf. btwn.	—	5,000.
542	A187	5k indigo & black	50.00	3.00
543	A187	10k indigo & black	16.50	2.50
544	A190	20k brn org & ultra	11.00	8.50
545	A190	30k brn org & car	240.00	35.00
		Nos. 540-545 (6)	350.50	57.00
		Set, never hinged	760.00	

First decade without Lenin.
See Nos. 931-935, 937.

Bombs Falling on City A192

"Before War and Afterwards" A194

Designs: 10k, Refugees from burning town. 20k, "Plowing with the sword." 35k, "Comradeship."

1935, Jan. 1			Wmk. 170	Perf. 14
546	A192	5k violet black	28.00	3.00
547	A192	10k ultra	130.00	15.00
548	A194	15k green	150.00	20.00
549	A194	20k dark brown	19.00	3.75
550	A194	35k carmine	220.00	30.00
		Nos. 546-550 (5)	547.00	71.75
		Set, never hinged	1,050.	

Anti-war propaganda, the designs symbolize the horrors of modern warfare.

Subway Tunnel A197

Subway Station Cross Section A198

Subway Station A199

Train in Station — A200

1935, Feb. 25			Wmk. 170	Perf. 14
551	A197	5k orange	42.50	7.50
552	A198	10k dark ultra	32.50	8.50
553	A199	15k rose carmine	300.00	32.50
554	A200	20k emerald	32.50	10.00
		Nos. 551-554 (4)	407.50	58.50
		Set, never hinged	815.00	

Completion of Moscow subway.

Friedrich Engels (1820-1895), German Socialist and Collaborator of Marx — A201

1935, May			Wmk. 170	Perf. 14
555	A201	5k carmine	14.00	4.00
556	A201	10k dark green	25.00	6.00
557	A201	15k dark blue	70.00	14.00
558	A201	20k brown black	13.50	6.00
		Nos. 555-558 (4)	122.50	30.00
		Set, never hinged	230.00	

Running — A202

Designs: 2k, Diving. 3k, Rowing. 4k, Soccer. 5k, Skiing. 10k, Bicycling. 15k, Tennis. 20k, Skating. 35k, Hurdling. 40k, Parade of athletes.

1935, Apr. 22			Unwmk.	Perf. 14
559	A202	1k org & ultra	20.00	4.25
560	A202	2k black & ultra	16.00	2.50
561	A202	3k grn & blk brn	22.00	3.00
562	A202	4k rose red & ultra	17.00	5.25
563	A202	5k pur & blk	20.00	2.50
564	A202	10k rose red & vio	20.00	5.25
565	A202	15k blk & blk brn	190.00	42.50
566	A202	20k blk brn & ultra	22.00	5.00
567	A202	35k ultra & blk brn	125.00	35.00
568	A202	40k blk brn & car	20.00	8.50
		Nos. 559-568 (10)	472.00	113.75
		Set, never hinged	925.00	

International Spartacist Games, Moscow. The games never took place.

Silver Plate of Sassanian Dynasty A212

1935, Sept. 10 — Wmk. 170

569	A212	5k orange red		57.50	3.50
570	A212	10k dk yel grn		22.50	5.25
571	A212	15k dark violet		22.50	8.50
572	A212	35k black brown		57.50	10.00
		Nos. 569-572 (4)		160.00	27.25
		Set, never hinged		300.00	

3rd International Congress of Persian Art, Leningrad, Sept. 12-18, 1935.

Kalinin, the Worker — A213

Mikhail Kalinin — A216

Kalinin as: 5k, farmer. 10k, orator.

1935, Nov. 20 — Unwmk. — Perf. 14

573	A213	3k rose lilac		3.75	1.25
a.		Horiz. pair, imperf. btwn.		—	4,500.
574	A213	5k green		3.75	1.25
575	A213	10k blue slate		7.50	1.75
576	A216	20k brown black		16.00	3.50
a.		Imperf.		1,500.	
		Nos. 573-576 (4)		31.00	7.75
		Set, never hinged		52.50	

60th birthday of Mikhail Kalinin, chairman of the Central Executive Committee of the USSR.

A217

Leo Tolstoy — A218

Design: 20k, Statue of Tolstoy.

1935, Dec. 4 — Perf. 14

577	A217	3k ol black & vio		7.00	2.50
b.		Horiz. pair, imperf. btwn.		—	2,000.
578	A218	10k vio blk & blk brn		11.00	1.50
b.		Vert. pair, imperf. btwn.		—	2,250.
579	A217	20k dk grn & blk brn		12.50	3.00
		Nos. 577-579 (3)		30.50	7.00
		Set, never hinged		57.50	

Perf. 11

577a	A217	3k		7.00	4.00
c.		Horiz. pair, imperf. btwn.		2,000.	850.00
578a	A218	10k		26.00	3.00
579a	A217	20k		9.00	4.50
b.		Vert. pair, imperf. btwn.		1,600.	1,100.
		Nos. 577a-579a (3)		42.00	11.50
		Set, never hinged		80.00	

25th anniv. of the death of Count Leo N. Tolstoy (1828-1910).

Portrait Type of 1933

Designs: 2k, Mikhail V. Frunze. 4k, N. E. Bauman. 40k, Sergei M. Kirov.

1935, Nov. — Wmk. 170 — Perf. 11

580	A169	2k purple		11.00	5.50
581	A169	4k brown violet		7.00	5.00
582	A169	40k black brown		19.00	5.00
		Nos. 580-582 (3)		37.00	15.50
		Set, never hinged		65.00	

Perf. 14

580a	A169	2k		10.00	1.50
b.		Vert. pair, imperf. btwn.		2,250.	
581a	A169	4k		22.50	3.00
582a	A169	40k		60.00	4.00
b.		Vert. pair, imperf. btwn.		—	2,750.
		Nos. 580a-582a (3)		92.50	8.50
		Set, never hinged		200.00	

Death of three revolutionary heroes.

Nos. 580-582 exist imperf. but were not regularly issued. Values: set: unused, $1,800; never hinged, $3,250.

Pioneers Preventing Theft from Mailbox A223

Designs: 3k, 5k, Pioneers preventing destruction of property. 10k, Helping recover kite. 15k, Girl Pioneer saluting.

1936, Apr. — Unwmk. — Perf. 14

583	A223	1k yellow green		2.00	1.00
b.		Vert. pair, imperf. btwn.		—	1,650.
584	A223	2k copper red		2.50	.85
b.		Vert. pair, imperf. btwn.		1,750.	1,650.
585	A223	3k slate blue		2.75	.85
586	A223	5k rose lake		4.50	1.40
587	A223	10k gray blue		6.75	2.50
b.		Horiz. pair, imperf. btwn.		2,650.	—
588	A223	15k brown olive		40.00	10.00
		Nos. 583-588 (6)		58.50	16.60
		Set, never hinged		135.00	

Perf. 11

583a	A223	1k		2.00	1.00
c.		Vert. pair, imperf. btwn.		—	1,200.
584a	A223	2k		2.50	1.00
c.		Vert. pair, imperf. btwn.		1,750.	1,900.
585a	A223	3k		2.25	1.00
b.		Vert. pair, imperf. btwn.		1,750.	1,650.
586a	A223	5k		22.50	2.25
587a	A223	10k		11.50	3.00
c.		Vert. pair, imperf. btwn.		—	2,750.
d.		Horiz. pair, imperf. btwn.		1,750.	1,650.
588a	A223	15k		17.50	5.50
		Nos. 583a-588a (6)		58.25	13.75
		Set, never hinged		105.00	

Nikolai A. Dobrolyubov, Writer and Critic, Birth Cent. — A227

1936, Aug. 13 — Typo. — Perf. 11½

589	A227	10k rose lake		10.50	5.50
		Never hinged		20.00	
a.		Perf. 14		8.50	3.50
		Never hinged		17.00	

Aleksander Sergeyevich Pushkin — A228

Statue of Pushkin, Moscow — A229

Chalky Paper

1937, Feb. 1

Line Perf 12¼

590	A228	10k yellow brown		3.50	.75
591	A228	20k Prus green		3.50	.75
592	A228	40k rose lake		3.50	.75
593	A229	50k blue		8.25	2.00
594	A229	80k carmine rose		42.50	6.00
595	A229	1r green		82.50	8.50
		Set, never hinged		120.00	

Chalky or Ordinary Paper
Comb Perf 12¼x11¾

590A	A228	10k yellow brown		7.00	2.00
591A	A228	20k Prus green		7.00	3.00
592A	A228	40k rose lake		12.00	3.00
593A	A229	50k blue		21.00	7.00
594A	A229	80k carmine rose		7.00	2.00
		Set, never hinged		120.00	

Line Perf 13¾x12¼

590B	A228	10k yellow brown		9.50	.75
591B	A228	20k Prus green		6.00	.75
592B	A228	40k rose lake		2.00	1.75
593B	A229	50k blue		27.00	4.75
594B	A229	80k carmine rose		22.50	6.00
595B	A229	1r green		52.50	8.50
		Set, never hinged		120.00	

Line Perf 11x12¼

590C	A228	10k yellow brown		37.50	2.25
591C	A228	20k Prus green		165.00	14.50
592C	A228	40k rose lake		145.00	14.50
593C	A229	50k blue		37.50	11.00
594C	A229	80k carmine rose		35.00	2.25
595C	A229	1r green		42.50	5.50
		Set, never hinged		120.00	

Line Perf 13¾

590D	A228	10k yellow brown		82.50	—
591D	A228	20k Prus green		60.00	—
592D	A228	40k rose lake		82.50	—
		Set, never hinged		120.00	

Line Perf 11

590E	A228	10k yellow brown		187.50	22.50
592E	A228	40k rose lake		140.00	22.50
		Set, never hinged		120.00	

Souvenir Sheet
Imperf

596		Sheet of 2		25.00	75.00
		Never hinged		50.00	
a.		10k brown		4.00	20.00
b.		50k brown		4.00	27.50

Pushkin (1799-1837), writer and poet.

Tchaikovsky Concert Hall — A230

Hotel Moscow — A231

Designs: 5k, 15k, Telegraph Agency House. 10k, Tchaikovsky Concert Hall. 20k, 50k, Red Army Theater. 40k, Palace of the Soviets.

Nos. 697-601, 604 Sizes: 41.25mm x 25mm
Nos. 602-603 Sizes: 44.5mm x 27mm

Unwmk.

1937, June — Photo. — Perf. 12

597	A230	3k brown violet		5.75	.75
b.		Imperf.		285.00	145.00
598	A230	5k henna brown		2.90	1.75
b.		Imperf.		285.00	105.00
599	A230	10k dark brown		6.00	.75
b.		Imperf.		700.00	285.00
600	A230	15k black		65.00	.75
b.		Imperf.		1,050.	475.00
601	A230	20k olive green		11.50	1.75
b.		Imperf.		82.50	325.00
602	A231	30k gray black		8.25	2.25
a.		Perf. 11		82.50	12.50
603	A231	40k violet		11.50	1.75
a.		Souv. sheet of 4, imperf.		29.00	25.00
b.		Imperf.		1,425.	—
604	A230	50k dark brown		11.50	6.00
b.		Imperf.		1,650.	425.00
		Nos. 597-604 (8)		122.40	15.75
		Set, never hinged		450.00	

First Congress of Soviet Architects. The 30k is watermarked Greek Border and Rosettes (170).

Nos. 602-603 are sized 44½x27mm, rest in set are sized 41¼x25mm.

Values for No. 603b are for stamps with large margins to ensure that they are from No. 603a.

Feliks E. Dzerzhinski — A235

1937, July 27 — Typo. — Perf. 12

606	A235	10k yellow brown		3.00	1.20
a.		Imperf.		1,500.	
607	A235	20k Prus green		6.75	1.20
a.		Imperf.		1,500.	
608	A235	40k rose lake		14.00	2.25
a.		Imperf.		1,500.	

609	A235	80k carmine		12.00	3.75
a.		Imperf.		1,500.	
		Nos. 606-609 (4)		35.75	8.40
		Set, never hinged		80.00	

Dzerzhinski, organizer of Soviet secret police, 10th death anniv.

Shota Rustaveli — A236

Line Perf 12¼

1938, Feb. — Unwmk. — Photo.

610	A236	20k deep green		7.25	1.00
		Never hinged		13.00	
a.		Comb perf. 12½x12		1,450.	375.00
b.		Imperf.		2,100.	

750th anniversary of the publication of the poem "Knight in the Tiger Skin," by Shota Rustaveli, Georgian poet.

Statue Surmounting Pavilion A237

Soviet Pavilion at Paris Exposition A238

1938 — Typo.

611	A237	5k red		1.25	.60
a.		Imperf.		1,650.	
612	A238	20k rose		1.75	.50
613	A237	50k dark blue		19.50	3.75
		Nos. 611-613 (3)		22.50	4.85
		Set, never hinged		42.50	

USSR participation in the 1937 International Exposition at Paris.

Types of 1929-32 and Lenin Types of 1925-26

1937-52 — Unwmk. — Perf. 11½x12, 12

613A	A103	1k dull org ('40)		7.50	2.50
614	A95	2k yel grn ('39)		6.75	1.00
615	A97	4k claret ('40)		65.00	3.50
b.		Imperf.		950.00	
615A	A98	5k org brn ('46)		65.00	10.00
616	A109	10k blue ('38)		1.25	.50
b.		Imperf.		725.00	
616A	A103	10k olive ('40)		145.00	12.50
b.		Imperf.		1,875.	
616B	A109	10k black ('52)		.25	.25
617	A97	20k dull green		1.25	.40
b.		Imperf.		2,950.	
617A	A107	20k green ('39)		100.00	6.25
b.		Imperf.		600.00	
618	A109	30k claret ('39)		45.00	1.75
b.		Imperf.		600.00	
619	A104	40k indigo ('38)		6.50	.75
b.		Imperf.		375.00	
619A	A111	50k dp brn ('40)		6.50	1.00

Engr.

620	A75	3r dk grn ('39)		2.50	.50
a.		Horiz. pair, imperf. btwn.		2,850.	
621	A66	5r red brn ('39)		8.50	2.50
622	A66	10r indigo ('39)		3.75	1.50
		Nos. 613A-622 (15)		464.75	44.90
		Set, never hinged		800.00	

No. 616B was re-issued in 1954-56 in slightly smaller format, 14½x21mm, and in gray black. See note after No. 738.

Airplane Route from Moscow to North Pole — A239

Soviet Flag and Airplanes at North Pole — A240

1938, Feb. 25   Litho.   Perf. 12
625 A239 10k brn & black .... 3.75 .75
626 A239 20k blue gray & blk .. 7.25 2.25
Typo.
627 A240 40k dl grn & car 18.00 3.75
   a.   Imperf. .... 1,450.
628 A240 80k rose car & car .... 4.00 .80
   a.   Imperf. 150.00
   b.   Double impression of flag ... 2,000.
      Nos. 625-628 (4) 33.00 7.55
      Set, never hinged 57.50

Soviet flight to the North Pole.

Infantryman A241

Soldier A242

Stalin Reviewing Cavalry A246

Chapayev and Boy — A247

Designs: 30k, Sailor, 40k, Aviator. 50k, Antiaircraft soldier.

1938, Mar.   Unwmk.
Photo.   Perf. 12
629 A241 10k gray blk & dk
        red .... 5.50 .75
630 A242 20k gray blk & dk
        red .... 8.25 .80
631 A242 30k gray blk & dk
        red 10.50 1.20
632 A242 40k gray blk & dk
        red 14.50 1.90
633 A242 50k gray blk & dk
        red 14.50 1.90
634 A246 80k gray blk & dk
        red 19.00 3.75
Typo.
Perf. 12x12½
635 A247 1r blk & car 6.00 2.00
   a.   Imperf. .... 1,150. —
      Nos. 629-635 (7) 78.25 12.30
      Set, never hinged 140.00

Workers' & Peasants' Red Army, 20th anniv.

Aviators Chkalov, Baidukov, Beliakov and Flight Route — A248

1938, Apr. 10   Photo.
636 A248 10k black & red .... 8.25 .75
   a.   Imperf. .... 5,250. 3,600.
637 A248 20k brn blk & red .... 12.00 .75
   a.   Imperf. 1,050. 375.00
638 A248 40k brown & red 12.00 2.00
   a.   Imperf. 1,050. 375.00
639 A248 50k brn vio & red 15.00 3.75
   a.   Imperf. 1,050. 375.00
      Nos. 636-639 (4) 47.25 7.25
      Set, never hinged 95.00

First Trans-Polar flight, June 18-20, 1937, from Moscow to Vancouver, Wash.

Aviators Gromov, Danilin, Yumashev and Flight Route — A249

1938, Apr. 13
640 A249 10k claret .... 10.00 .75
   a.   Imperf. 825.00
641 A249 20k brown black 12.00 1.75
   a.   Imperf. 725.00
642 A249 50k dull violet 13.00 5.00
   a.   Imperf. .... 23,000.
      Nos. 640-642 (3) 35.00 7.50
      Set, never hinged 60.00

First Trans-Polar flight, July 12-14, 1937, from Moscow to San Jacinto, Calif.

Arrival of the Rescuing Ice-breakers Taimyr and Murmansk A250

Ivan Papanin and His Men Aboard Ice-breaker Yermak — A251

1938, June 21   Typo.   Perf. 12, 12½
643 A250 10k violet brown 6.00 1.25
   a.   Imperf. .... 2,250.
644 A250 20k dark blue 8.25 1.50
   a.   Imperf. .... 2,250.
Photo.
645 A251 30k olive brown 21.00 3.75
   a.   Imperf. .... 3,250.
646 A251 50k ultra 16.50 6.00
   a.   Imperf. .... 2,350.
      Nos. 643-646 (4) 51.75 12.50
      Set, never hinged 110.00

Rescue of Papanin's North Pole Expedition.

Arms of Armenia — A252

Arms of USSR A253

No. 650

No. 651

No. 652

No. 653

No. 654

No. 655

No. 656

Designs: Different arms on each stamp.

Perf. 12, 12½
1937-38   Unwmk.   Typo.
647 A252 20k dp bl (Armenia) .. 10.50 2.00
648 A252 20k dl vio (Azerbai-
       jan) 10.50 2.00
649 A252 20k brn org (By-
       elorussia) 10.50 2.00
650 A252 20k car rose (Geor-
       gia) 10.50 2.00
651 A252 20k bl grn (Kazakh) .. 10.50 2.00
652 A252 20k emer (Kirghiz) ... 10.50 2.00
653 A252 20k yel org (Uzbek) .. 10.50 2.00
654 A252 20k bl (R.S.F.S.R.) ... 10.50 2.00
655 A252 20k claret (Tadzhik) . 10.50 2.00
656 A252 20k car (Turkmen) ... 10.50 2.00
657 A252 20k red (Ukraine) 10.50 2.00
Engr.
658 A253 40k brown red 9.25 2.00
      Nos. 647-658 (12) 124.75 24.00
      Set, never hinged 240.00

Constitution of USSR. No. 649 has inscriptions in Yiddish, Polish, Byelorussian and Russian.
   Issue dates: 40k, 1937. Others, 1938. See Nos. 841-842.

Nurse Weighing Child — A264

Children at Lenin's Statue — A265

Biology Lesson A266

Health Camp A267

Young Model Builders A268

1938, Sept. 15   Unwmk.   Perf. 12
659 A264 10k dk blue green 12.00 2.00
660 A265 15k dk blue green 3.50 3.50
661 A266 20k violet brown 13.00 2.50
662 A267 30k claret 13.00 2.50
663 A266 40k light brown 13.00 2.50
664 A268 50k deep blue 12.00 5.00
665 A268 80k light green 13.00 4.50
      Nos. 659-665 (7) 79.50 22.50
      Set, never hinged 145.00

Child welfare.

View of Yalta A269

Crimean Shoreline — A272

Designs: No. 667, View along Crimean shore. No. 668, Georgian military highway. No, 670, View near Yalta. No. 671, "Swallows' Nest" Castle. 20k, Dzerzhinski Rest House for workers. 30k, Sunset in Crimea. 40k, Alupka. 50k, Gursuf. 80k, Crimean Gardens. 1r, "Swallows' Nest" Castle, horiz.

1938, Sept. 21   Unwmk.
Photo.   Perf. 12
666 A269 5k brown 4.75 1.00
667 A269 5k black brown 4.75 1.00
668 A269 10k slate green 4.75 1.00
669 A272 10k brown 4.75 1.00
670 A269 15k black brown ... 6.00 1.75
671 A272 15k black brown ... 6.00 1.75
672 A269 20k dark brown 10.00 1.75
673 A272 30k black brown ... 12.00 1.75
674 A269 40k brown 12.00 1.75
675 A272 50k slate green 12.00 1.75
   a.   Horiz. pair, imperf. btwn. .. 2,175.
   b.   Vert. pair, imperf. btwn. ... 2,175.
676 A269 80k brown 12.00 1.75
677 A269 1r slate green 120.00 20.00
      Nos. 666-677 (12) 209.00 36.25
      Set, never hinged 400.00

Children Flying Model Plane A281

Glider A282

Captive Balloon — A283

Dirigible over Kremlin — A284

Parachute Jumpers — A285

Hydroplane A286

Balloon in Flight — A287

Balloon Ascent — A288

Four-motor Plane A289

Unwmk.
1938, Oct. 7   Typo.   Perf. 12
678	A281	5k violet brown	3.75	1.50
679	A282	10k olive gray	3.75	1.50
680	A283	15k pink	6.00	1.50
681	A284	20k deep blue	6.00	1.50
682	A285	30k claret	12.00	1.50
683	A286	40k deep blue	14.50	1.50
684	A287	50k blue green	12.00	2.50
685	A288	80k brown	14.50	2.50
686	A289	1r blue green	82.50	10.00
	Nos. 678-686 (9)		155.00	24.00
	Set, never hinged		270.00	

For overprints see Nos. C76-C76D.

Mayakovsky Station, Moscow Subway — A290

Sokol Terminal — A291

Kiev Station — A292

Dynamo Station A293

Train in Tunnel A294

Revolution Square Station A295

Unwmk.
1938, Nov. 7   Photo.   Perf. 12
687	A290	10k dp red vio	3.00	2.00
a.	Vert. pair, imperf. btwn.		2,175.	
688	A291	15k dark brown	6.00	2.00
689	A292	20k black brown	14.50	2.50
690	A293	30k dark red violet	21.00	4.75
a.	Vert. pair, imperf. btwn.		—	3,600.
691	A294	40k black brown	21.00	4.75
692	A295	50k dark brown	24.00	7.25
	Nos. 687-692 (6)		89.50	23.25
	Set, never hinged		155.00	

Second line of the Moscow subway opening.

Girl with Parachute A296

Young Miner A297

Harvesting A298

Designs: 50k, Students returning from school. 80k, Aviator and sailor.

1938, Dec. 7   Typo.   Perf. 12
693	A296	20k deep blue	13.00	2.50
694	A297	30k deep claret	13.00	2.50
695	A298	40k violet brown	10.50	2.50
696	A296	50k deep rose	35.00	8.25
697	A298	80k deep blue	8.25	2.50
	Nos. 693-697 (5)		79.75	21.75
	Set, never hinged		140.00	

20th anniv. of the Young Communist League (Komsomol).

Diving — A301

Discus Thrower — A302

Designs: 15k, Tennis. 20k, Acrobatic motorcyclists. 30k, Skier. 40k, Runners. 50k, Soccer. 80k, Physical culture.

Unwmk.
1938, Dec. 28   Photo.   Perf. 12
698	A301	5k scarlet	3.50	1.25
699	A302	10k black	3.50	1.25
700	A302	15k brown	6.00	1.75
701	A302	20k green	6.00	1.75
702	A302	30k dull violet	30.00	2.00
703	A302	40k deep green	15.00	2.00
704	A302	50k blue	82.50	10.00
705	A302	80k deep blue	10.50	5.00
	Nos. 698-705 (8)		157.00	25.00
	Set, never hinged		290.00	

Gorki Street, Moscow — A309

Dynamo Subway Station A315

Moscow scenes: 20k, Council House & Hotel Moscow. 30k, Lenin Library. 40k, Crimea Bridge. 50k, Bridge over Moscow River. 80k, Khimki River Terminal.

Paper with network as in parentheses
1939, Mar.   Typo.   Perf. 12
706	A309	10k brn (red brown)	1.25	1.25
707	A309	20k dk sl grn (lt blue)	1.50	1.50
708	A309	30k brn vio (red brn)	2.25	1.50
709	A309	40k blue (lt blue)	5.00	2.50
710	A309	50k rose lake (red brn)	5.00	3.00
711	A309	80k gray ol (lt blue)	47.50	5.75
712	A315	1r dk blue (lt blue)	47.50	7.50
	Nos. 706-712 (7)		110.00	23.00
	Set, never hinged		250.00	

"New Moscow." On 30k, denomination is at upper right.

Foundry-man — A316

1939, Mar.
713	A316	15k dark blue	7.50	.75
	Never hinged		14.50	
a.	Imperf.		2,000.	
	Never hinged		3,000.	

Statue on USSR Pavilion — A317

USSR Pavilion A318

1939, May   Photo.
714	A317	30k indigo & red	2.75	1.00
a.	Imperf. ('40)		3.00	1.00
715	A318	50k blue & bister brn	5.50	1.00
a.	Imperf. ('40)		6.00	1.25
	Set, never hinged		15.00	

Russia's participation in the NY World's Fair.

Paulina Osipenko A318a

Marina Raskova A318b

Design: 60k, Valentina Grizodubova.

1939, Mar.
718	A318a	15k green	8.25	2.00
719	A318b	30k brown violet	14.50	3.75
720	A318b	60k red	14.50	7.50
	Nos. 718-720 (3)		37.25	13.25
	Set, never hinged		65.00	

Non-stop record flight from Moscow to the Far East.
Exist imperf. Value, each unused $2,100.

Shevchenko, Early Portrait — A319

Monument at Kharkov — A321

30k, Shevchenko portrait in later years.

1939, Mar. 9
721	A319	15k black brn & blk	7.50	1.50
722	A319	30k dark red & blk	13.00	2.25
723	A321	60k green & dk brn	14.50	3.00
	Nos. 721-723 (3)		35.00	6.75
	Set, never hinged		80.00	

Taras G. Shevchenko (1814-1861), Ukrainian poet and painter.

Milkmaid with Prize Cow — A322

Tractor-plow at Work on Abundant Harvest A323

Designs: 20k, Shepherd tending sheep. No. 727, Fair pavilion. No. 728, Fair emblem. 45k, Turkmen picking cotton. 50k, Drove of horses. 60k, Symbolizing agricultural wealth. 80k, Kolkhoz girl with sugar beets. 1r, Hunter with Polar foxes.

1939, Aug.
724	A322	10k rose pink	3.50	.45
725	A323	15k red brown	3.50	.45
726	A323	20k slate black	9.50	2.00
727	A323	30k purple	5.75	1.00
728	A322	30k red orange	3.50	.45
729	A323	45k dark green	9.50	1.25
a.	Horiz. pair, imperf. btwn.		1,750.	
730	A322	50k copper red	2.00	.45
a.	Horiz. pair, imperf. btwn.		1,500.	
731	A322	60k bright purple	7.00	1.00
732	A322	80k dark violet	7.00	1.00
733	A322	1r dark blue	19.00	2.00
a.	Horiz. pair, imperf. btwn.		2,350.	
b.	Vert. pair, imperf. btwn.		1,500.	
	Nos. 724-733 (10)		70.25	10.05
	Set, never hinged		128.00	

Soviet Agricultural Fair.

Worker A331

Soldier A332

Aviator — A333

Perf. 11¾x12¼

Arms of USSR
A334   A335

Perf. 11¾x12¼

1939-43   **Unwmk.**   **Typo.**

734	A331	5k red	.40	.25
735	A332	15k dark green	.45	.25
736	A333	30k deep blue	.80	.25
737	A334	60k fawn ('43)	5.25	9.00

Photo.

738	A335	60k rose carmine	.80	.50
		Nos. 734-738 (5)	7.70	10.25
		Set, never hinged		15.00

No. 734 was re-issued in 1954-56 in slightly smaller format: 14x21½mm, instead of 14¾x22¼mm. Other values reissued in smaller format: 10k, 15k, 20k, 25k, 30k, 40k and 1r. (See notes following Nos. 622, 1260, 1347 and 1689.)

No. 416 Surcharged with New Value in Black

1939   **Wmk. 170**   **Perf. 12x12½**

743	A97	30k on 4k claret	25.00	12.50
a.		Unwmkd.	250.00	37.50

M.E. Saltykov (N. Shchedrin)
A336   A337

Unwmk.

1939, Sept.   **Typo.**   **Perf. 12**

745	A336	15k claret	3.00	.75
746	A337	30k dark green	3.75	.75
747	A337	45k olive gray	8.75	1.50
748	A337	60k dark blue	8.75	2.25
		Nos. 745-748 (4)	24.25	5.25
		Set, never hinged		80.00

Mikhail E. Saltykov (1826-89), writer & satirist who used pen name of N. Shchedrin.

Sanatorium of the State Bank — A338

Designs: 10k, 15k, Soviet Army sanatorium. 20k, Rest home, New Afyon. 30k, Clinical Institute. 50k, 80k, Sanatorium for workers in heavy industry. 60k, Rest home, Sukhumi.

1939, Nov.   **Photo.**   **Perf. 12**

749	A338	5k dull brown	2.00	.25
750	A338	10k carmine	2.00	.25
751	A338	15k yellow green	3.50	.45
752	A338	20k dk slate green	7.00	.45
753	A338	30k bluish black	3.50	.45
a.		Horiz. pair, imperf. between	2,500.	
754	A338	50k gray black	3.50	1.75
755	A338	60k brown violet	9.50	1.75
756	A338	80k orange red	7.00	1.75
		Nos. 749-756 (8)	38.00	7.10
		Set, never hinged		125.00

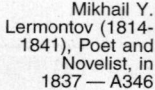

Mikhail Y. Lermontov (1814-1841), Poet and Novelist, in 1837 — A346

Portrait in 1838 — A347   Portrait in 1841 — A348

1939, Dec.

757	A346	15k indigo & sepia	8.25	1.25
a.		Vert. pair, imperf. between	—	1,650.

758	A347	30k dk grn & dull blk	12.00	3.00
a.		Vert. pair, imperf. between	—	1,650.
759	A348	45k brk red & indigo	8.25	1.25
		Nos. 757-759 (3)	28.50	5.50
		Set, never hinged		60.00

Nikolai Chernyshevski
A349

1939, Dec.   **Photo.**

760	A349	15k dark green	9.50	1.25
761	A349	30k dull violet	14.50	1.25
762	A349	60k Prus green	14.50	3.00
		Nos. 760-762 (3)	38.50	5.50
		Set, never hinged		50.00

50th anniversary of the death of Nikolai Chernyshevski, scientist and critic.

Anton Chekhov — A350

Design: 20k, 30k, Portrait with hat.

1940, Feb.   **Unwmk.**   **Perf. 12**

763	A350	10k dark yellow green	2.00	1.50
764	A350	15k ultra	3.75	1.50
765	A350	20k violet	3.75	1.50
766	A350	30k copper brown	14.50	1.50
		Nos. 763-766 (4)	24.00	6.00
		Set, never hinged		40.00

Chekhov (1860-1904), playwright.

Welcome to Red Army by Western Ukraine and Western Byelorussia A352

Designs: 30k, Villagers welcoming tank crew. 50k, 60k, Soldier giving newspapers to crowd. 1r, Crowd waving to tank column.

1940, Apr.

767	A352	10k deep rose	1.90	.75
768	A352	30k myrtle green	3.25	1.00
769	A352	50k gray black	3.75	1.25
770	A352	60k indigo	13.00	2.50
771	A352	1r red	9.75	2.00
		Nos. 767-771 (5)	31.65	7.50
		Set, never hinged		60.00

Liberation of the people of Western Ukraine and Western Byelorussia.

Ice-breaker "Josef Stalin," Captain Beloussov and Chief Ivan Papanin A356

Badigin and Papanin A358

Map of the Drift of the Sedov and Crew Members — A359

Design: 30k, Icebreaker Georgi Sedov, Captain Vadygin and First Mate Trofimov.

1940, Apr.

772	A356	15k dull yel green	3.50	.75
773	A356	30k dull purple	10.50	1.25
b.		Vert. pair, imperf. between	—	7,250.
774	A358	50k copper brown	6.50	1.50
775	A359	1r dark ultra	12.50	2.50
		Nos. 772-775 (4)	33.00	6.00
		Set, never hinged		57.50

Heroism of the Sedov crew which drifted in the Polar Basin for 812 days.

A360

Vladimir V. Mayakovsky — A361

1940, June   **Line Perf. 12¼**

776	A360	15k deep red	4.75	1.25
777	A360	30k copper brown	4.75	1.25
778	A361	60k dark gray blue	12.00	2.00
779	A361	80k bright ultra	9.50	1.25
		Nos. 776-779 (4)	31.00	5.75
		Set, never hinged		57.50

Mayakovsky, poet (1893-1930).

K.A. Timiryazev and Academy of Agricultural Sciences A362

In the Laboratory of Moscow University A363

Last Portrait A364

Monument in Moscow — A365

1940, June

780	A362	10k indigo	3.00	1.25
781	A363	15k purple	12.00	1.25
782	A364	30k dk violet brown	4.75	1.75
783	A365	60k dark green	4.75	2.50
		Nos. 780-783 (4)	24.50	6.75
		Set, never hinged		40.00

20th anniversary of the death of K. A. Timiryasev, scientist and professor of agricultural and biological sciences.

Relay Race A366

Sportswomen Marching — A367

Children's Sport Badge — A368

Skier — A369

Throwing the Grenade — A370

1940, July 21   **Line Perf. 12½**

784	A366	15k carmine rose	4.25	.75
785	A367	30k sepia	8.25	3.00
786	A368	50k dk violet blue	4.75	.75
787	A369	60k dk violet blue	12.00	3.00
788	A370	1r grayish green	14.50	.75
		Nos. 784-788 (5)	43.75	8.25
		Set, never hinged		85.00

Tchaikovsky Museum at Klin A371   Tchaikovsky & Passage from his Fourth Symphony A372

Peter Ilich Tchaikovsky and Excerpt from Eugene Onegin — A373

Comb Perf. 12¼x11¾

1940, Aug.   **Unwmk.**   **Typo.**

789	A371	15k Prus green	5.50	1.50
790	A372	20k brown	6.00	1.50
791	A371	30k dark blue	5.50	2.00
792	A371	50k rose lake	14.50	3.50
793	A373	60k red	12.00	7.00
		Nos. 789-793 (5)	43.50	15.50
		Set, never hinged		85.00

Tchaikovsky (1840-1893), composer.

Volga Provinces Pavilion A374

Northeast Provinces Pavilion — A376

ПАВИЛЬОН МОСКОВСКОЙ, РЯЗАНСКОЙ И ТУЛЬСКОЙ ОБЛ.
No. 797

ПАВИЛЬОН УКРАИНСКОЙ ССР
No. 798

ПАВИЛЬОН БЕЛОРУССКОЙ ССР
No. 799

ПАВИЛЬОН АЗЕРБАЙДЖАНСКОЙ ССР
No. 800

ПАВИЛЬОН ГРУЗИНСКОЙ ССР
No. 801

ПАВИЛЬОН АРМЯНСКОЙ ССР
No. 802

У ВХОДА В ПАВИЛЬОН УЗБЕКСКОЙ ССР
No. 803

ПАВИЛЬОН ТУРКМЕНСКОЙ ССР
No. 804

ПАВИЛЬОН ТАДЖИКСКОЙ ССР
No. 805

ПАВИЛЬОН КИРГИЗСКОЙ ССР
No. 806

ПАВИЛЬОН КАЗАХСКОЙ ССР
No. 807

ПАВИЛЬОН КАРЕЛО-ФИНСКОЙ ССР
No. 808

No. 795, Far East Provinces. No. 797, Central Regions. No. 798, Ukrainian. No. 799, Byelorussian. No. 800, Azerbaijan. No. 801, Georgian. No. 802, Armenian. No. 803, Uzbek. No. 804, Turkmen. No. 805, Tadzhik. No. 806, Kirghiz. No. 807, Kazakh. No. 808, Karelian Finnish. No. 809, Main building. No. 810, Mechanizaton Pavilion, Stalin statue.

1940, Oct.		Typo.	Line Perf. 12¼	
794	A374	10k shown	9.50	.55
795	A374	15k multicolored	9.50	.55
796	A376	30k shown	12.00	.55
797	A376	30k multicolored	14.50	.55
798	A376	30k multicolored	3.50	.55
799	A376	30k multicolored	3.50	.55
800	A374	30k multicolored	3.50	.55
801	A376	30k multicolored	7.00	.55
802	A376	30k multicolored	7.00	.55
803	A374	30k multicolored	3.50	.55
804	A376	30k multicolored	9.50	.55
805	A376	30k multicolored	3.50	.55
806	A376	30k multicolored	3.50	.55
807	A376	30k multicolored	3.50	.55
808	A376	30k multicolored	9.50	.55
809	A376	50k multicolored	16.50	1.50
810	A376	60k multicolored	19.00	2.50
		Nos. 794-810 (17)	138.50	12.25
		Set, never hinged	215.00	

All-Union Agricultural Fair.
Nos. 796-808 printed in three sheet formats with various vertical and horizontal se-tenant combinations.

Monument to Red Army Heroes — A391

Map of War Operations and M. V. Frunze — A393

Heroic Crossing of the Sivash A394

Designs: 15k, Grenade thrower. 60k, Frunze's headquarters, Stroganovka. 1r, Victorious soldier.

1940			Imperf.	
811	A391	10k dark green	2.25	.55
812	A391	15k orange ver	2.25	.55
813	A393	30k dull brown & car	6.25	1.50
814	A394	50k violet brn	3.50	1.00
815	A391	60k indigo	3.50	1.00
816	A391	1r gray black	4.25	1.50
		Nos. 811-816 (6)	22.00	6.10
		Set, never hinged	35.00	

			Perf. 12	
811A	A391	10k dark green	2.75	.55
812A	A391	15k orange ver	2.75	.55
813A	A393	30k dull brown & car	3.75	1.00
814A	A394	50k violet brn	2.75	.65
815A	A394	60k indigo	3.75	1.00
816A	A391	1r gray black	3.75	1.00
		Nos. 811A-816A (6)	19.50	4.75
		Set, never hinged	32.50	

20th anniversary of battle of Perekop.

Coal Miners — A397

Blast Furnace — A398

Bridge over Moscow-Volga Canal — A399

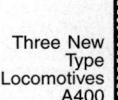

Three New Type Locomotives A400

Workers on a Collective Farm — A401

Automobiles and Planes A402

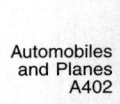

Oil Derricks — A403

1941, Jan.			Perf. 12	
817	A397	10k deep blue	2.00	1.00
818	A398	15k dark violet	2.25	1.25
819	A399	20k deep blue	2.75	1.50
820	A400	30k dark brown	3.00	1.50
821	A401	50k olive brown	3.75	1.75
822	A402	60k olive brown	4.50	2.50
823	A403	1r dark blue green	6.75	6.00
		Nos. 817-823 (7)	25.00	15.50
		Set, never hinged	60.00	

Soviet industries.

Troops on Skis — A404

Sailor — A405

Soldiers with Cannon A406

20k, Cavalry. 30k, Machine gunners. 45k, Army horsemen. 50k, Aviator. 1r, 3r, Marshal's Star.

1941-43				
824	A404	5k dark violet	2.00	.25
825	A405	10k deep blue	2.00	.25
826	A406	15k brt yellow green	1.00	.25
827	A404	20k vermilion	1.00	.25
828	A404	30k dull brown	1.00	.25
829	A406	45k gray green	4.00	.50
830	A404	50k dull blue	1.50	.75
831	A404	1r dull blue green	2.50	1.00
831A	A404	3r myrtle grn ('43)	10.00	1.75
		Nos. 824-831A (9)	25.00	5.25
		Set, never hinged	70.00	

Army & Navy of the USSR, 23rd anniv.

Battle of Ismail — A412

Field Marshal Aleksandr Suvorov — A413

1941		Unwmk.	Perf. 12	
832	A412	10k dark green	3.00	.25
833	A412	15k carmine rose	3.00	.30
834	A413	30k blue black	1.00	.70
835	A413	1r olive brown	3.00	3.00
		Nos. 832-835 (4)	10.00	4.25
		Set, never hinged	25.00	

150th anniversary of the capture of the Turkish fortress, Ismail.

Kirghiz Horse Breeder A414

Kirghiz Miner A415

1941, Mar.		Perf. 12, 12x12½		
836	A414	15k dull brown	2.50	.45
837	A415	30k dull purple	3.50	.60
		Set, never hinged	15.00	

15th anniversary of the Kirghizian Soviet Socialist Republic.

Prof. N. E. Zhukovski A416

Zhukovski Lecturing A418

Military Air Academy A417

1941, Mar.				
838	A416	15k deep blue	3.50	.35
839	A417	30k carmine rose	3.00	.65
840	A418	50k brown violet	3.50	1.00
		Nos. 838-840 (3)	10.00	2.00
		Set, never hinged	20.00	

Prof. Zhukovski, scientist (1847-1921).

Arms Type of 1938

Karelian-Finnish Soviet Socialist Republic.

1941, Mar.				
841	A252	30k rose	2.75	.75
842	A252	45k dark blue green	3.25	1.25
		Set, never hinged	15.00	

1st anniversary of the Karelian-Finnish Soviet Socialist Republic.

Spasski Tower, Kremlin — A420

Kremlin and Moscow River A421

1941, May		Typo.	Unwmk.	
843	A420	1r dull red	.75	.50
844	A421	2r brown orange	1.25	1.00
		Set, never hinged	5.00	

"Suvorov's March through the Alps, 1799" A422

Vasili Ivanovich Surikov, Self-portrait A424

"Stepan Rasin on the Volga" A423

1941, June		Photo.	Perf. 12	
845	A422	20k black	12.00	1.25
846	A423	30k scarlet	6.00	2.75
847	A422	50k dk vio brn	45.00	8.00
848	A423	1r gray green	45.00	11.00
849	A424	2r brown	45.00	13.00
		Nos. 845-849 (5)	153.00	36.00
		Set, never hinged	250.00	

Surikov (1848-1916), painter.

Mikhail Y. Lermontov, Poet, Death Centenary — A425

1941, July

850	A425	15k	Prus green	20.00	4.00
851	A425	30k	dark violet	25.00	6.00
		Set, never hinged		125.00	

Visitors in Lenin Museum A426

Lenin Museum A427

1941-42

852	A426	15k	rose red	14.00	6.00
853	A427	30k	dark violet ('42)	40.00	18.00
854	A426	45k	Prus green	21.00	9.00
855	A427	1r	org brn ('42)	45.00	17.00
		Nos. 852-855 (4)		120.00	50.00
		Set, never hinged		250.00	

Fifth anniversary of Lenin Museum.

Mother's Farewell to a Soldier Son ("Be a Hero!") — A428

1941, Aug.

856	A428	30k	carmine	15.00	15.00
		Never hinged		35.00	

Alisher Navoi — A429

1942, Jan.

857	A429	30k	brown	90.00	25.00
858	A429	1r	dark violet	60.00	25.00
		Set, never hinged		300.00	

Alisher Navoi, Uzbekian poet, 500th birth anniv.

People's Militia — A430

1941, Dec.   **Typo.**

859	A430	30k	dull blue	125.00	75.00
		Never hinged		300.00	

Junior Lieutenant Talalikhin Ramming German Plane in Midair A431

Captain Gastello and Burning Plane Diving into Enemy Gasoline Tanks A432

Major General Dovator and Cossack Cavalry in Action A433

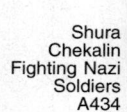

Shura Chekalin Fighting Nazi Soldiers A434

Nazi Soldiers Leading Zoya Kosmodemjanskaja to her Death — A435

1942-44   Unwmk.   Photo.   Perf. 12

860	A431	20k	bluish black	2.50	1.75
860A	A431	30k	Prus grn ('44)	2.50	1.75
861	A432	30k	bluish black	2.50	1.75
861A	A432	30k	dp ultra ('44)	2.50	1.75
862	A433	30k	black	2.50	1.75
863	A434	30k	black	2.50	1.75
863A	A434	30k	brt yel grn ('44)	2.50	1.75
864	A435	30k	black	2.50	1.75
864A	A435	30k	sewing vio ('44)	2.50	1.75
865	A434	1r	slate green	32.50	11.00
866	A435	2r	slate green	45.00	30.00
		Nos. 860-866 (11)		100.00	56.75
		Set, never hinged		200.00	

Issued to honor Soviet heroes.
For surcharges see Nos. C80-C81.

Anti-tank Artillery A436

Signal Corps in Action A437

Defense of Leningrad A440

Guerrilla Fighters A438

War Worker A439

Red Army Scouts A441

1942-43

867	A436	20k	black	2.50	1.50
868	A437	30k	sapphire	2.50	1.50
869	A438	30k	Prus grn ('43)	2.50	1.50
870	A439	30k	dull red brn ('43)	2.50	1.50
871	A440	60k	blue black	30.00	10.00
872	A441	1r	black brown	30.00	6.00
		Nos. 867-872 (6)		70.00	22.00
		Set, never hinged		120.00	

Women Workers and Soldiers A442

Flaming Tank A443

Women Preparing Food Shipments A444

Sewing Equipment for Red Army — A445

Anti-Aircraft Battery in Action — A446

1942-43   Typo.   Unwmk.

873	A442	20k	dark blue	1.25	1.00
874	A443	20k	dull rose violet	1.25	1.00
875	A444	30k	brn vio ('43)	1.75	1.75
876	A445	45k	dull rose red	7.00	5.00
877	A446	45k	dp dl blue ('43)	7.00	5.00
		Nos. 873-877 (5)		18.25	13.75
		Set, never hinged		30.00	

Manufacturing Explosives — A447

Designs: 10k, Agriculture. 15k, Group of Fighters. 20k, Storming the Palace. 30k, Lenin and Stalin. 60k, Tanks. 1r, Lenin. 2r, Revolution scene.

Inscribed: "1917 XXV 1942"

1943, Jan.   Photo.   Perf. 12

878	A447	5k	black brown	1.00	.50
879	A447	10k	black brown	1.00	.50
880	A447	15k	blue black	1.00	.50
881	A447	20k	blue black	1.50	.50
882	A447	30k	black brown	2.25	.60
883	A447	60k	black brown	3.50	1.50

884	A447	1r	dull red brown	4.00	2.00
885	A447	2r	black	11.00	3.50
		Nos. 878-885 (8)		25.25	9.60
		Set, never hinged		65.00	

25th anniversary of October Revolution.

Mount St. Elias, Alaska A455

Bering Sea and Bering's Ship — A456

1943, Apr.

886	A455	30k	chalky blue	.90	.50
887	A456	60k	Prus green	1.75	.65
888	A455	1r	yellow green	4.00	.80
889	A456	2r	bister brown	8.00	1.25
		Nos. 886-889 (4)		14.65	3.20
		Set, never hinged		25.00	

200th anniv. of the death of Vitus Bering, explorer (1681-1741).

Medical Corpsmen and Wounded Soldier A457

Trench Mortar A458

Army Scouts A459

Repulsing Enemy Tanks A460

Snipers A461

1943

890	A457	30k	blue gray	1.25	1.00
891	A458	30k	brown bister	1.25	1.00
892	A459	30k	blue gray	1.25	1.00
893	A460	60k	myrtle green	2.00	1.90
894	A461	60k	chalky blue	2.00	1.90
		Nos. 890-894 (5)		7.75	6.80
		Set, never hinged		20.00	

Maxim Gorki (1868-1936), Writer A462

1943, June

895	A462	30k	green	.80	.40
896	A462	60k	slate black	1.25	.50
		Set, never hinged		5.00	

Patriotic War Medal A463

Order of Field Marshal Suvorov A464

1943, July   **Engr.**
897 A463 1r black   1.00 1.00
898 A464 10r dk olive green   4.00 4.00
   Set, never hinged   8.00

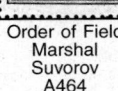

Sailors A465

Designs: 30k, Navy gunner and warship. 60k, Soldiers and tank.

1943, Oct.   **Photo.**
899 A465 20k golden brown   .35 .30
900 A465 30k dark myrtle green   .35 .30
901 A465 60k brt yellow green   .75 .60
902 A465 3r chalky blue   2.50 1.75
   Nos. 899-902 (4)   3.95 2.95
   Set, never hinged   7.00

25th anniv. of the Red Army and Navy.

Karl Marx — A468

1943, Sept.
903 A468 30k blue black   1.50 .25
904 A468 60k dk slate green   2.50 .25
   Set, never hinged   8.00

125th anniv. of the birth of Karl Marx.

Vladimir V. Mayakovsky — A469

1943, Oct.
905 A469 30k red orange   1.50 .40
906 A469 60k deep blue   1.50 .60
   Set, never hinged   6.00

Mayakovsky, poet, 50th birth anniv.

Flags of US, Britain, and USSR A470

1943, Nov.
907 A470 30k blk, dp red & dk bl   .40 .30
908 A470 3r sl blue, red & lt blue   2.60 .85
   Set, never hinged   5.00

The Tehran conference.

Ivan Turgenev (1818-83), Poet — A471

1943, Oct.
909 A471 30k myrtle green   20.00 20.00
910 A471 60k dull purple   25.00 25.00
   Set, never hinged   125.00

Map of Stalingrad A472

Harbor of Sevastopol and Statue of Lenin A473

Leningrad A474

Odessa A475

1944, Mar.   **Perf. 12**
911 A472 30k dull brown & car   1.75 .50
912 A473 30k dark blue   1.75 .50
913 A474 30k dk slate green   1.75 .50
914 A475 30k yel green   1.75 .50
   Nos. 911-914 (4)   7.00 2.00
   Set, never hinged   22.50

Honoring the defenders of Stalingrad, Leningrad, Sevastopol and Odessa. See No. 959.

No. 911 measures 33x22mm and also exists in smaller size: 32x21½mm.

USSR War Heroes A476

1944, Apr.
915 A476 30k deep ultra   .50 .25
   Never hinged   2.00

Sailor Loading Gun — A477

Tanks — A478

Soldier Bayoneting a Nazi A479

Infantryman A480

Soldier Throwing Hand Grenade — A481

1943-44   **Photo.**
916 A477 15k deep ultra   .30 .25
917 A478 20k red orange ('44)   .30 .25
918 A479 30k dull brn & dk red ('44)   .30 .25
919 A480 1r brt yel green   2.00 .40
920 A481 2r blue gray ('44)   2.00 1.00
   Nos. 916-920 (5)   4.90 2.15
   Set, never hinged   15.00

25th anniversary of the Young Communist League (Komsomol).

Flags of US, USSR, Great Britain — A482

1944, May 30   **Unwmk.**   **Perf. 12**
921 A482 60k black, red & blue   .50 .30
922 A482 3r dk bl, red & lt bl   2.75 1.10
   Set, never hinged   5.00

Day of the Nations United Against Germany, June 14, 1944.

Patriotic War Order — A483

Order of Prince Alexander Nevsky — A484

Order of Field Marshal Suvorov — A485

Order of Field Marshal Kutuzov — A486

Paper with network as in parenthesis
1944   **Typo.**   **Perf. 12**
923 A483 15k dull red (rose)   .35 .25
924 A484 20k blue (lt blue)   .35 .25
925 A485 30k green (green)   .50 .25
926 A486 60k dull red (rose)   .75 .40
   Nos. 923-926 (4)   1.95 1.15
   Set, never hinged   10.00

Imperf
923A A483 15k dull red (rose)   .35 .25
924A A484 20k blue (lt blue)   .35 .25
925A A485 30k green (green)   .50 .25
926A A486 60k dull red (rose)   .75 .40
   Nos. 923A-926A (4)   1.95 1.15
   Set, never hinged   10.00

Beware of bogus perforation "errors" created from imperfs.

Order of Patriotic War — A487

Order of Prince, Alexander Nevski — A488

Order of Field Marshal Kutuzov A489

Order of Field Marshal Suvorov A490

1944, June   **Unwmk.**   **Engr.**   *Perf. 12*
927 A487 1r black   .50 .40
928 A488 3r blue black   1.10 1.00
929 A489 5r dark olive green   1.75 1.25
930 A490 10r dark red   3.50 2.00
   Nos. 927-930 (4)   6.85 4.65
   Set, never hinged   20.00

Types of 1934, Inscribed 1924-1944 and

Lenin's Mausoleum — A491

30k (#931), 3r, Lenin & Stalin. 50k, Lenin in middle age. 60k, Lenin, the orator.

1944, June   **Photo.**
931 A190 30k orange & car   .30 .25
932 A186 30k slate & black   .30 .25
933 A187 45k slate & black   .50 .30
934 A187 50k slate & black   .50 .30
935 A187 60k slate & black   .50 .40
936 A491 1r indigo & brn blk   2.50 .75
937 A190 3r bl blk & dull org   3.00 1.25
   Nos. 931-937 (7)   7.60 3.50
   Set, never hinged   30.00

20 years without Lenin.

Nikolai Rimski-Korsakov A492   A493

1944, June   *Perf. 12*
938 A492 30k gray black   .25 .25
939 A493 60k slate green   .25 .25
940 A492 1r brt blue green   .55 .35
941 A493 3r purple   1.25 .40
   Nos. 938-941 (4)   2.30 1.25
   Set, never hinged   4.00

Imperf

938A	A492	30k gray black	.25	.25
939A	A493	60k slate green	.25	.25
940A	A492	1r brt blue green	.55	.35
941A	A493	3r purple	1.25	.40
		Nos. 938A-941A (4)	2.30	1.25
		Set, never hinged	5.00	

Rimski-Korsakov (1844-1909), composer.

N.A. Shchors — A494

Heroes of the 1918 Civil War: No. 943, V.I. Chapayev. No. 944, S.G. Lazo.

1944, Sept.   **Perf. 12**

942	A494	30k gray black	.35	.30
943	A494	30k dark slate green	.35	.30
944	A494	30k brt yellow green	.35	.30
		Nos. 942-944 (3)	1.05	.90
		Set, never hinged	3.00	

See Nos. 1209-1211, 1403.

Sergei A. Chaplygin — A497

1944, Sept.

945	A497	30k gray	.50	.30
946	A497	1r lt brown	1.50	.75
		Set, never hinged	3.00	

75th anniversary of the birth of Sergei A. Chaplygin, scientist and mathematician.

Khanpasha Nuradilov A498

A. Matrosov A499

F. Louzan A500

M. S. Polivanova and N. V. Kovshova A501

Pilot B. Safonov — A502

1944, July

947	A498	30k slate green	1.00	.60
948	A499	60k dull purple	1.75	.60
949	A500	60k dull blue	1.75	.60

950	A501	60k bright green	3.00	.60
951	A502	60k slate black	3.00	.60
		Nos. 947-951 (5)	10.50	3.00
		Set, never hinged	20.00	

Soviet war heroes.

Ilya E. Repin — A503

Ivan A. Krylov — A505

"Cossacks' Reply to Sultan Mohammed IV" — A504

1944, Nov.   **Perf. 12½**

952	A503	30k slate green	.65	.30
953	A504	50k dk blue green	.75	.30
954	A504	60k chalky blue	.75	.30
955	A503	1r dk org brn	1.00	.30
956	A504	2r dark purple	2.00	.60
		Nos. 952-956 (5)	5.15	1.80
		Set, never hinged	14.00	

Imperf

952A	A503	30k slate green	.65	.30
953A	A504	50k dk blue green	.75	.30
954A	A504	60k chalky blue	.75	.30
955A	A503	1r dk org brn	1.00	.30
956A	A504	2r dark purple	2.00	.60
		Nos. 952A-956A (5)	5.15	1.80
		Set, never hinged	14.00	

I. E. Repin (1844-1930), painter.

1944, Nov.   **Perf. 12**

957	A505	30k yellow brown	.50	.25
958	A505	1r dk violet blue	.50	.25
		Set, never hinged	3.00	

Krylov, fable writer, death centenary.

Leningrad Type of 1944
Souvenir Sheet

1944, Dec. 6   **Imperf.**

959	Sheet of 4	10.00	4.75
	Never hinged	25.00	
a.	Marginal inscriptions invert-ed		6,500.
b.	Marginal inscriptions double, one inverted		30,000.
c.	A474 30k dark slate green	1.00	.60

Relief of the siege of Leningrad, Jan. 27, 1944.

Partisan Medal — A507

Order for Bravery — A508

Order of Bogdan Chmielnicki A509

Order of Victory A510

Order of Ushakov A511

Order of Nakhimov A512

Paper with network as in parenthesis
Perf. 12½

1945, Jan.   **Unwmk.**

960	A507	15k black *(green)*	.25	.30
961	A508	30k dp blue *(lt blue)*	.35	.30
962	A509	45k dk blue	.35	.30
963	A510	60k dl rose *(pale rose)*	.45	.30
964	A511	1r dull blue *(green)*	.80	.40
965	A512	1r yel green *(blue)*	.80	.40
		Nos. 960-965 (6)	3.00	2.00
		Set, never hinged	7.00	

Imperf

960A	A507	15k black *(green)*	.25	.30
961A	A508	30k dp blue *(lt blue)*	.35	.30
962A	A509	45k dk blue	.35	.30
963A	A510	60k dl rose *(pale rose)*	.45	.30
964A	A511	1r dull blue *(green)*	.80	.40
965A	A512	1r yel green *(blue)*	.80	.40
		Nos. 960A-965A (6)	3.00	2.00
		Set, never hinged	5.00	

Beware of bogus perforation "errors" created from imperfs.

Aleksandr S. Griboedov — A513

1945, Jan.   **Photo.**   **Perf. 12½**

966	A513	30k dk slate green	.35	.25
967	A513	60k gray brown	.65	.30
		Set, never hinged	4.00	

Griboedov (1795-1829), poet & statesman.

Red Army Soldier — A514

1945, Mar.

968	A514	60k gray blk & henna	.50	.55
969	A514	3r gray blk & henna	1.50	1.10
		Set, never hinged	3.00	

Souvenir Sheet
Imperf

970	Sheet of 4	60.00	40.00
	Never hinged	100.00	
a.	A514 3r gray brown & henna	9.00	7.50
	Never hinged	15.00	

Second anniv. of victory at Stalingrad.

Order for Bravery A516

Order of Bogdan Chmielnicki A517

Order of Victory — A518

1945   **Engr.**   **Perf. 12**

971	A516	1r indigo	.50	.35
972	A517	2r black	1.75	.90
973	A518	3r henna	1.60	.75
		Nos. 971-973 (3)	3.85	2.00
		Set, never hinged	7.50	

See Nos. 1341-1342. For overprints see Nos. 992, 1709.

A519

A520

A521

A522

A523

Battle Scenes A524

1945, Apr.   **Photo.**   **Perf. 12½**

974	A519	20k sl grn, org red & black	.75	.60
975	A520	30k bl blk & dull org	.75	.60
976	A521	30k blue black	.75	.60
977	A522	60k orange red	1.50	.60
978	A523	1r sl grn & org red	6.00	2.75
979	A524	1r slate green	6.00	2.75
		Nos. 974-979 (6)	15.75	8.80
		Set, never hinged	25.00	

Red Army successes against Germany.

Parade in Red Square, Nov. 7, 1941 — A525

Designs: 60k, Soldiers and Moscow barricade, Dec. 1941. 1r, Air battle, 1941.

1945, June
980	A525	30k dk blue violet	.30	.25
981	A525	60k olive black	.70	.35
982	A525	1r black brown	2.00	1.40
		Nos. 980-982 (3)	3.00	2.00
		Set, never hinged	5.00	

3rd anniversary of the victory over the Germans before Moscow.

Elite Guard Badge and Cannons — A528

1945, Apr.   Typo.
983	A528	60k red	1.00	.50
		Never hinged	4.00	

Motherhood Medal — A529   Motherhood Glory Order — A530

Mother-Heroine Order — A531

Paper with network as in parenthesis
1945   Size: 22x33¼mm   Perf. 12½
984	A529	20k brown (lt blue)	.40	.40
985	A530	30k yel brown (green)	.50	.40
986	A531	60k dull rose (pale rose)	.80	.40

Imperf
984A	A529	20k brown (lt blue)	.40	.40
985A	A530	30k yel brown (green)	.50	.40
986D	A531	60k dull rose (pale rose)	.80	.40

Perf. 12½
Engr.
Size: 20x38mm
986A	A529	1r blk brn (green)	.80	.40
986B	A530	2r dp bl (lt blue)	1.75	.70
986C	A531	3r brn red (lt blue)	2.00	1.20
		Nos. 984-986D (9)	7.95	4.70
		Set, never hinged	20.00	

Academy Building, Moscow — A532

Academy at Leningrad and M. V. Lomonosov A533

1945, June   Photo.   Perf. 12½
987	A532	30k blue violet	.50	.30
a.		Horiz. pair, imperf. between	90.00	
988	A533	2r grnsh black	1.50	.65
		Set, never hinged	4.00	

Academy of Sciences, 220th anniv.

Popov and his Invention A534   Aleksandr S. Popov A535

1945, July   Unwmk.
989	A534	30k dp blue violet	.50	.25
990	A534	60k dark red	1.00	.35
991	A535	1r yellow brown	1.75	.50
		Nos. 989-991 (3)	3.25	1.10
		Set, never hinged	5.00	

"Invention of radio" by A. S. Popov, 50th anniv.

No. 973 Overprinted in Blue

1945, Aug.   Perf. 12
992	A518	3r henna	2.00	1.00

Victory of the Allied Nations in Europe.

Yakovlev-3 Fighter — A536

Petliakov-2 Dive Bombers — A537

Ilyushin-2 Bombers A538

#992A, 995, Yakovlev-3 Fighter. #992B, 1000, Petliakov-2 dive bombers. #992C, 996, Ilyushin-2 bombers. #992D, 993, Petliakov-8 heavy bomber. #992E, 1001, Tupolev-2 bombers. #992F, 997, Ilyushin-4 bombers. #992G, 999, Polikarpov-2 biplane. #992H, 998, Lavochkin-7 fighters. #992I, 994, Yakovlev-3 fighter in action.

1945-46   Unwmk.   Photo.   Perf. 12
992A	A536	5k dk violet ('46)	.40	.25
992B	A537	10k hen brn ('46)	.40	.25
992C	A537	15k hen brn ('46)	.80	.25
992D	A536	15k Prus grn ('46)	.80	.25
992E	A538	20k gray brn ('46)	.80	.50
992F	A538	30k violet ('46)	1.60	.50
992G	A538	30k brown ('46)	1.60	.50
992H	A538	50k blue vio ('46)	2.25	1.25
992I	A536	60k dl bl vio ('46)	3.00	1.50
993	A536	1r gray black	3.50	.60
994	A536	1r henna brown	3.50	.60
995	A536	1r brown	3.50	.60
996	A538	1r deep brown	3.50	.60
997	A538	1r intense black	3.50	.60
998	A538	1r orange ver	3.50	.60
999	A538	1r bright green	3.50	.60
1000	A538	1r deep brown	3.50	.60
1001	A538	1r violet blue	3.50	.60
		Nos. 992A-1001 (18)	43.15	10.65
		Set, never hinged	75.00	

Issued: #992A-992I, 3/26; #993-1001, 8/19.

A545

Lenin, 75th Birth Anniv. — A546

Various Lenin portraits.

Dated "1870-1945"
1945, Sept.   Perf. 12½
1002	A545	30k bluish black	.60	.35
1003	A546	50k gray brown	.75	.35
1004	A546	60k orange brown	.85	.35
1005	A546	1r greenish black	2.00	.35
1006	A546	3r sepia	6.00	1.25
		Nos. 1002-1006 (5)	10.20	2.65
		Set, never hinged	25.00	

Prince M. I. Kutuzov — A550

1945, Sept. 16
1007	A550	30k blue violet	.60	.40
1008	A550	60k brown	1.40	.60
		Set, never hinged	4.00	

Field Marshal Prince Mikhail Illarionovich Kutuzov (1745-1813).

Aleksandr Ivanovich Herzen A551

1945, Oct. 26
1009	A551	30k dark brown	.50	.40
1010	A551	2r black	1.50	.60
		Set, never hinged	5.00	

Herzen, author, revolutionist, 75th death anniv.

Ilya Mechnikov — A552

1945, Nov. 27
1011	A552	30k brown	.65	.40
1012	A552	1r greenish black	1.25	.60

Ilya I. Mechnikov, zoologist and bacteriologist (1845-1916).

Friedrich Engels — A553

1945, Nov.   Unwmk.   Perf. 12½
1013	A553	30k dark brown	1.00	.40
1014	A553	60k Prussian green	2.00	.60
		Set, never hinged	5.00	

125th anniversary of the birth of Friedrich Engels, collaborator of Karl Marx.

Tank Leaving Assembly Line — A554

Designs: 30k, Harvesting wheat. 60k, Airplane designing. 1r, Moscow fireworks.

1945, Dec. 25   Photo.
1015	A554	20k indigo & brown	1.00	.25
1016	A554	30k blk & org brn	1.00	.40
1017	A554	60k brown & green	1.75	.60
1018	A554	1r dk blue & org	2.25	.90
		Nos. 1015-1018 (4)	6.00	2.15
		Set, never hinged	15.00	

Artillery Observer and Guns A558

Heavy Field Pieces A559

1945, Dec.
1019	A558	30k brown	1.00	.50
1020	A559	60k sepia	2.00	.75
		Set, never hinged	7.00	

Artillery Day, Nov. 19, 1945.

Catalogue values for unused stamps in this section, from this point to the end of the section, are for Never Hinged items.

Victory Medal — A560   Soldier with Victory Flag — A561

1946, Jan. 23
1021	A560	30k dk violet	.75	.25
1022	A560	30k brown	.75	.25
1023	A560	60k greenish black	1.10	.25
1024	A560	60k henna	1.10	.25
1025	A561	60k black & dull red	3.75	1.10
		Nos. 1021-1025 (5)	7.45	2.10

Arms of USSR — A562   Red Square — A563

1946, Feb. 10
1026	A562	30k henna	1.00	.25
1027	A563	45k henna	1.50	.25
1028	A562	60k greenish black	2.50	.50
		Nos. 1026-1028 (3)	5.00	1.00

Elections to the Supreme Soviet of the USSR, Feb. 10, 1946.

Artillery in Victory Parade — A564

Victory Parade A565

1946, Feb. 23
1029	A564	60k dark brown	5.00	.50
1030	A564	2r dull violet	15.00	1.00
1031	A565	3r black & red	15.00	1.50
	Nos. 1029-1031 (3)		35.00	3.00

Victory Parade, Moscow, June 24, 1945.

Order of Lenin — A566   Order of Red Star — A567

Medal of Hammer and Sickle A568   Order of Token of Veneration A569

Gold Star Medal — A570   Order of Red Banner — A571

Order of the Red Workers' Banner — A572

Paper with network as in parenthesis

1946 Unwmk. Typo. Perf. 12½x12
1032	A566	60k myr grn (green)	1.40	1.10
1033	A567	60k dk vio brn (brown)	1.40	1.10
1034	A568	60k plum (pink)	1.40	1.10
1035	A569	60k dp blue (green)	1.40	1.10
1036	A570	60k dk car (salmon)	1.40	1.10
1037	A571	60k red (salmon)	1.40	1.10
1038	A572	60k dk brn vio (buff)	1.40	1.10
	Nos. 1032-1038 (7)		9.80	7.70

See Nos. 1650-1654.

Workers' Achievement of Distinction A573   Workers' Gallantry A574

Marshal's Star — A575   Defense of Soviet Trans-Arctic Regions — A576

Meritorious Service in Battle A577   Defense of Caucasus A578

Defense of Moscow — A579   Bravery — A580

Paper with network as in parenthesis

1946
1039	A573	60k choc (salmon)	3.00	1.25
1040	A574	60k brown (salmon)	3.00	1.25
1041	A575	60k blue (pale blue)	3.00	1.25
1042	A576	60k dk grn (green)	3.00	1.25
1043	A577	60k dk blue (green)	3.00	1.25
1044	A578	60k dk yel grn (grn)	3.00	1.25
1045	A579	60k carmine (pink)	3.00	1.25
1046	A580	60k dk violet (blue)	3.00	1.25
	Nos. 1039-1046 (8)		24.00	10.00

A581

Maxim Gorki A582

1946, June 18   Photo.
1047	A581	30k brown	1.50	.25
1048	A582	60k dark green	2.50	.25

10th anniversary of the death of Maxim Gorki (Alexei M. Peshkov).

Kalinin — A583

1946, June
1049	A583	20k sepia	2.00	.60

Mikhail Ivanovich Kalinin (1875-1946).

Chebyshev — A584

1946, May 25
1050	A584	30k brown	1.25	.35
1051	A584	60k gray brown	1.75	.65

Pafnuti Lvovich Chebyshev (1821-94), mathematician.

View of Sukhumi A585

Sanatorium at Sochi — A587

Designs: #1053, Promenade at Gagri. 45k, New Afyon Sanatorium.

1946, June 18
1052	A585	15k dark brown	1.25	.25
1053	A585	30k dk slate green	2.50	.25
1054	A585	30k dark green	2.50	.25
1055	A587	45k chestnut brown	3.75	.50
	Nos. 1052-1055 (4)		10.00	1.25

All-Union Parade of Physical Culturists — A589

1946, July 21
1056	A589	30k dark green	6.00	2.00

Tank Divisions in Red Square A590

1946, Sept. 8
1057	A590	30k dark green	1.50	.40
1058	A590	60k brown	2.50	.60

Honoring Soviet tankmen.

Belfry of Ivan the Great, Kremlin — A591   Bolshoi Theater, Moscow — A592

Hotel Moscow A593

Red Square — A597

Spasski Tower and Statues of Minin and Pozharski — A598

Moscow scenes: 20k, Bolshoi Theater, Sverdlov Square. 45k, View of Kremlin. 50k, Lenin Museum.

1946, Sept. 5
1059	A591	5k brown	1.00	.25
1060	A592	10k sepia	1.00	.25
1061	A593	15k chestnut	1.00	.25
1062	A593	20k light brown	2.00	.25
1063	A593	45k dark green	4.50	.45
1064	A593	50k brown	4.50	.50
1065	A597	60k blue violet	10.00	.60
1066	A598	1r chestnut brown	15.00	1.00
	Nos. 1059-1066 (8)		39.00	3.55

Workers' Achievement of Distinction A599   Workers' Gallantry A600

Partisan of the Patriotic War — A601   Defense of Soviet Trans-Arctic Regions — A602

Meritorious Service in Battle A603

Defense of Caucasus A604

Defense of Moscow — A605

Bravery — A606

1946, Sept. 5 Engr.

1067	A599	1r dark violet brown	3.75	1.50
1068	A600	1r dark carmine	3.75	1.50
1069	A601	1r carmine	3.75	1.50
1070	A602	1r blue black	3.75	1.50
1071	A603	1r black	3.75	1.50
1072	A604	1r black brown	3.75	1.50
1073	A605	1r olive black	3.75	1.50
1074	A606	1r deep claret	3.75	1.50
	Nos. 1067-1074 (8)		30.00	12.00

See Nos. 1650-1654.

Give the Country Each Year: 127 Million Tons of Grain A607

60 Million Tons of Oil — A608

60 Million Tons of Steel — A610

500 Million Tons of Coal — A609

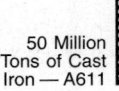

50 Million Tons of Cast Iron — A611

Perf. 12½x12

1946, Oct. 6		Photo.	Unwmk.	
1075	A607	5k olive brown	.25	.25
1076	A608	10k dk slate green	.50	.25
1077	A609	15k brown	.75	.25
1078	A610	20k dk blue violet	1.50	.25
1079	A611	30k brown	3.00	.25
	Nos. 1075-1079 (5)		6.00	1.25

Symbols of Transportation, Map and Stamps — A612

Early Soviet Stamp A613

Stamps of Soviet Russia — A614

1946, Nov. 6 Perf. 12½

1080	A612	15k blk & dk red	2.00	.55
a.		Sheet of 4, imperf.	100.00	50.00
1081	A613	30k dk grn & brn	3.00	.60
a.		Sheet of 4, imperf.	100.00	50.00
1082	A614	60k dk grn & blk	5.00	.85
a.		Sheet of 4, imperf.	100.00	50.00
	Nos. 1080-1082 (3)		10.00	2.00

1st Soviet postage stamp, 25th anniv.

Lenin and Stalin — A615

1946		Photo.	Perf. 12½	
1083	A615	30k dp brown org	2.00	1.00
a.		Sheet of 4, imperf.	75.00	35.00
b.		Single, imperf	5.00	1.50
1084	A615	30k dk green	2.00	1.00
a.		Single, imperf	5.00	1.50

October Revolution, 29th anniv.
Issued: #1083b-1084a, 11/6; #1083-1084, 12/18; #1083a, 6/47.

Dnieprostroy Dam and Power Station — A616

1946, Dec. 23 Perf. 12½

1085	A616	30k sepia	2.00	.60
1086	A616	60k chalky blue	4.00	.90

Aleksandr P. Karpinsky — A617

1947, Jan. 17 Unwmk.

1087	A617	30k dark green	1.25	.75
1088	A617	50k sepia	2.75	1.00

Karpinsky (1847-1936), geologist.

Canceled to Order
Canceled sets of new issues have long been sold by the government. Values in the second ("used") column are for these canceled-to-order stamps. Postally used stamps are worth more.

Nikolai A. Nekrasov — A618

1946, Dec. 4

1089	A618	30k sepia	1.50	.25
1090	A618	60k brown	2.50	.75

Nikolai A. Nekrasov (1821-1878), poet.

Lenin's Mausoleum A619

Lenin — A620

1947, Jan. 21

1091	A619	30k slate blue	2.50	.65
1092	A619	30k dark green	2.50	.65
1093	A620	50k dark brown	5.00	1.25
	Nos. 1091-1093 (3)		10.00	2.55

23rd anniversary of the death of Lenin. See Nos. 1197-1199.

F. P. Litke and Sailing Vessel A621

N. M. Przewalski, Mare and Foal — A622

1947, Jan. 27

1094	A621	20k blue violet	4.75	1.10
1095	A621	20k sepia	4.75	1.10
1096	A622	60k olive brown	10.50	1.40
1097	A622	60k sepia	10.50	1.40
	Nos. 1094-1097 (4)		30.50	5.00

Soviet Union Geographical Society, cent.

Nikolai E. Zhukovski (1847-1921), Scientist A623

1947, Jan. 17

1098	A623	30k sepia	1.50	.30
1099	A623	60k blue violet	2.25	.45

Stalin Prize Medal — A624

1946, Dec. 21 Photo.

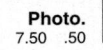

1100	A624	30k black brown	7.50	.50

Russian Soldier A625

Military Instruction A626

Aviator, Sailor and Soldier A627

Perf. 12x12½, 12½x12

1947, Feb. 23			Unwmk.	
1101	A625	20k sepia	2.50	.50
1102	A626	30k slate blue	3.75	.75
1103	A627	30k brown	3.75	.75
	Nos. 1101-1103 (3)		10.00	2.00

Imperf

1101A	A625	20k sepia	2.50	.50
1102A	A626	30k slate blue	3.75	.75
1103A	A627	30k brown	3.75	.75
	Nos. 1101A-1103A (3)		10.00	2.00

29th anniversary of the Soviet Army.

Reprints
From here through 1953 many sets exist in two distinct printings from different plates.

Arms of

Russian Socialist Federated Soviet Republic — A628

Armenian SSR — A629

Azerbaijan SSR — A630

Byelorussian SSR — A631

Estonian SSR — A632

Georgian SSR — A633

Karelo Finnish SSR — A634

Kazakh SSR — A635

Kirghiz
SSR — A636

Latvian
SSR — A637

Lithuanian
SSR — A638

Moldavian
SSR — A639

Tadzhkistan
SSR — A640

Turkmen
SSR — A641

Ukrainian
SSR — A642

Uzbek
SSR — A643

Soviet Union — A644

1947   Unwmk.   Photo.   Perf. 12½

1104	A628	30k henna brown	3.25	.50
1105	A629	30k chestnut	3.25	.50
1106	A630	30k olive brown	3.25	.50
1107	A631	30k olive green	3.25	.50
1108	A632	30k violet black	3.25	.50
1109	A633	30k dark vio brown	3.25	.50
1110	A634	30k dark violet	3.25	.50
1111	A635	30k deep orange	3.25	.50
1112	A636	30k dark violet	3.25	.50
1113	A637	30k yellow brown	3.25	.50
1114	A638	30k dk ol grn	3.25	.50
1115	A639	30k dk vio brn	3.25	.50
1116	A640	30k dark green	3.25	.50
1117	A641	30k gray black	3.25	.50
1118	A642	30k blue violet	3.25	.50
1119	A643	30k brown	3.25	.50

Litho.

1120	A644	1r dk brn, bl, gold & red	8.00	2.00
		Nos. 1104-1120 (17)	60.00	10.00

Aleksander S. Pushkin
(1799-1837),
Poet — A645

1947, Feb.   Photo.   Perf. 12

1121	A645	30k sepia	2.00	.35
1122	A645	50k dk yellow green	3.00	.75

Classroom
A646

Parade of
Women — A647

1947, Mar. 11

1123	A646	15k bright blue	2.00	.60
1124	A647	30k red	3.00	.90

Intl. Day of Women, Mar. 8, 1947.

Moscow
Council
Building
A648

1947   Perf. 12½

1125	A648	30k sep, gray blue & brick red	3.00	1.00

30th anniversary of the Moscow Soviet. Exists imperf. The imperf. exists also with gray blue omitted.
    Both perf. and imperf. stamps exist in two sizes: 40x27mm and 41x27mm.

May Day Parade in Red
Square — A649

1947, June 10   Perf. 12½

1126	A649	30k scarlet	1.50	.60
1127	A649	1r dk olive green	4.50	2.00

Labor Day, May 1, 1947.

Nos. 1062, 1064-1066 Ovptd. in Red

1947, Sept.   Perf. 12½x12

1128	A593	20k lt brown	2.00	.40
1129	A593	50k brown	4.00	1.00
1130	A597	60k blue violet	6.00	1.20
1131	A598	1r chestnut brown	8.00	1.40
		Nos. 1128-1131 (4)	20.00	4.00

Overprint arranged in 4 lines on No. 1131.

Crimea Bridge, Moscow — A650

Gorki Street,
Moscow
A651

View of Kremlin, Moscow — A652

Designs: No. 1134, Central Telegraph Building. No. 1135, Kiev Railroad Station. No. 1136, Kazan Railroad Station. No. 1137, Kaluga St. No. 1138, Pushkin Square. 50k, View of Kremlin. No. 1141, Grand Kremlin Palace. No. 1142, "Old Moscow," by Vasnetsov. No. 1143, St. Basil Cathedral. 2r, View of Kremlin. 3r, View of Kremlin. 5r, Hotel Moscow and government building.

1947   Photo.   Perf. 12½
Various Frames, Dated 1147-1947

1132	A650	5k dk bl & dk brn	.50	.50
1133	A651	10k red brn & brn blk	.50	.50
1134	A650	30k brown	1.20	.80
1135	A650	30k dk Prus blue	1.20	.80
1136	A650	30k ultra	1.20	.80
1137	A650	30k dp yel green	1.20	.80
1138	A651	30k yel green	1.20	.80
1139	A650	50k dp yel green	1.80	1.00
1140	A652	60k red brn & brn blk	1.90	1.20
1141	A651	60k gray blue	2.75	1.50
1142	A651	1r dark violet	4.25	2.50

Typo.
Colors: Blue, Yellow and Red

1143	A651	1r multicolored	4.25	2.50
1144	A651	2r multicolored	8.50	6.00
1145	A650	3r multicolored	15.00	8.00
a.		Souv. sheet of 4, imperf.	35.00	20.00
1146	A650	5r multicolored	25.00	16.00
		Nos. 1132-1146 (15)	70.45	43.70

Nos. 1128-1146 for founding of Moscow, 800th anniv.
Nos. 1143-1146 were printed in a single sheet containing a row of each denomination plus a row of labels.

Karamyshevsky Dam — A653

Map Showing
Moscow-Volga
Canal — A654

Designs: No. 1148, Direction towers, Yakromsky Lock. 45k, Yakromsky Pumping Station. 50k, Khimki Terminal. 1r, Lock #8.

1947, Sept. 7   Photo.

1147	A653	30k sepia	2.50	.50
1148	A653	30k red brown	2.50	.50
1149	A653	45k henna brown	3.25	.50
1150	A653	50k bright ultra	3.75	.50
1151	A654	60k bright rose	4.25	.50
1152	A653	1r violet	7.75	1.00
		Nos. 1147-1152 (6)	24.00	3.50

Moscow-Volga Canal, 10th anniversary.

Elektrozavodskaya Station — A655

Mayakovsky
Station — A656

Moscow Subway scenes: No. 1154, Ismailovsky Station. No. 1155, Sokol Station. No. 1156, Stalinsky Station. No. 1158, Kiev Station.

1947, Sept.

1153	A655	30k sepia	2.40	.55
1154	A655	30k blue black	2.40	.55
1155	A655	45k yellow brown	3.00	.60
1156	A655	45k deep violet	3.00	.60
1157	A656	60k henna brown	4.50	.80
1158	A656	60k deep yel grn	4.50	.80
		Nos. 1153-1158 (6)	19.80	3.90

Planes and
Flag — A657

1947, Sept. 1

1159	A657	30k deep violet	3.00	.40
1160	A657	1r bright ultra	7.00	.60

Day of the Air Fleet. For overprints see Nos. 1246-1247.

Spasski Tower,
Kremlin — A658

**   Perf. 12½**
1947, Nov.   Unwmk.   Typo.

1161	A658	60k dark red	18.00	4.50

See No. 1260.

Agave Plant at
Sukhumi — A659

Gullripsh
Sanatorium,
Sukhumi
A660

Peasants',
Livadia
A661

New Riviera
A662

Russian sanatoria: No. 1166, Abkhasia,
New Afyon. No. 1167, Kemeri, near Riga. No.
1168, Kirov Memorial, Kislovodsk. No. 1169,
Voroshilov Memorial, Sochi. No. 1170, Riza,
Gagri. No. 1171, Zapadugol, Sochi.

1947, Nov.			Photo.	
1162	A659	30k dark green	3.50	.50
1163	A660	30k violet	3.50	.50
1164	A661	30k olive	3.50	.50
1165	A662	30k brown	3.50	.50
1166	A660	30k red brown	3.50	.50
1167	A660	30k black violet	3.50	.50
1168	A660	30k bright ultra	3.50	.50
1169	A660	30k dk brown violet	3.50	.50
1170	A659	30k dk yel green	3.50	.50
1171	A660	30k sepia	3.50	.50
		Nos. 1162-1171 (10)	35.00	5.00

Blast
Furnaces,
Constantine
A663

Tractor Plant,
Kharkov
A664

Tractor Plant,
Stalingrad
A665

Maxim Gorki
Theater,
Stalingrad
A666

20k, No. 1180, Kirov foundry, Makeevka.
Nos. 1175, 1179, Agricultural machine plant,
Rostov.

1947, Nov.			Perf. 12½	
1172	A663	15k yellow brown	.35	.25
1173	A663	20k sepia	.60	.25
1174	A663	30k violet brown	.85	.25
1175	A663	30k dark green	.85	.25
1176	A664	30k brown	.85	.25
1177	A665	30k black brown	.85	.25
1178	A666	60k violet brown	1.60	.70
1179	A663	60k yellow brown	1.60	.70

1180	A663	1r orange red	3.50	1.40
1181	A664	1r red	3.50	1.40
1182	A665	1r violet	3.50	1.40
		Nos. 1172-1182 (11)	18.05	7.10
		Imperf		
1172A	A663	15k yellow brown	.35	.25
1173A	A663	20k sepia	.60	.25
1174A	A663	30k violet brown	.85	.25
1175A	A663	30k dark green	.85	.25
1176A	A664	30k brown	.85	.25
1177A	A665	30k black brown	.85	.25
1178A	A666	60k violet brown	1.60	.70
1179A	A663	60k yellow brown	1.60	.70
1180A	A663	1r orange red	3.50	1.40
1181A	A664	1r red	3.50	1.40
1182A	A665	1r violet	3.50	1.40
		Nos. 1172A-1182A (11)	18.05	7.10

Reconstruction of war-damaged cities and
factories, and as Five-Year-Plan publicity.

Revolutionists — A667

Designs: 30k, No. 1185, Revolutionists. 50k,
1r, Industry. No. 1186, 2r, Agriculture.

1947, Nov.			Perf. 12½	
		Frame in Dark Red		
1183	A667	30k greenish black	2.00	.30
1184	A667	50k blue black	3.00	.40
1185	A667	60k brown black	5.00	.55
1186	A667	60k brown	5.00	.55
1187	A667	1r black	8.00	.95
1188	A667	2r greenish black	15.00	1.50
		Nos. 1183-1188 (6)	38.00	4.25
		Imperf		
1183A	A667	30k greenish black	1.00	.30
1184A	A667	50k blue black	1.50	.40
1185A	A667	60k brown black	2.50	.55
1186A	A667	60k brown	2.50	.55
1187A	A667	1r black	4.00	.95
1188A	A667	2r greenish black	7.50	1.50
		Nos. 1183A-1188A (6)	19.00	4.25

30th anniversary of October Revolution.

Palace of the
Arts (Winter
Palace)
A668

Peter I
Monument — A669

Designs (Leningrad in 1947): 60k, Sts. Peter
and Paul Fortress. 1r, Smolny Institute.

1948, Jan. 10			Perf. 12½	
1189	A668	30k violet	3.00	1.10
1190	A669	50k dk slate green	5.00	1.25
1191	A668	60k sepia	6.00	2.40
1192	A669	1r dk brown violet	11.00	3.25
		Nos. 1189-1192 (4)	25.00	8.00

5th anniversary of the relief of the siege of
Leningrad from the German blockade.

Government
Building,
Kiev — A670

50k, Dnieprostroy Dam. 60k, Wheat field,
granary. 1r, Steel mill, coal mine.

1948, Jan. 25			Perf. 12½	
1193	A670	30k indigo	2.00	.40
1194	A670	50k violet	2.75	.50
1195	A670	60k golden brown	4.00	.85
1196	A670	1r sepia	6.25	2.25
		Nos. 1193-1196 (4)	15.00	4.00

Ukrainian SSR, 30th anniv.

Lenin Types of 1947
Inscribed "1924-1948"

1948, Jan. 21			Unwmk.	
1197	A619	30k brown violet	8.00	3.00
1198	A619	60k dark gray blue	8.00	3.00
1199	A620	60k dp yel grn	8.00	3.00
		Nos. 1197-1199 (3)	24.00	9.00

24th anniversary of the death of Lenin.

Vasili I.
Surikov — A672

1948, Feb. 15			Photo.	Perf. 12	
1201	A672	30k red brown	3.50	.75
1202	A672	60k dark green	6.50	1.25

Vasili Ivanovich Surikov, artist, birth cent.

Soviet Soldier and
Artillery — A675

Fliers and
Planes
A676

No. 1206, Soviet sailor. 60k, Military class.

1948, Feb. 23				
1205	A675	30k brown	2.50	.65
1206	A675	30k gray	2.50	.65
1207	A676	30k violet blue	2.50	.65
1208	A676	60k red brown	7.50	2.00
		Nos. 1205-1208 (4)	15.00	3.95

Hero Types of 1944

Designs: No. 1209, N.A. Shchors. No. 1210,
V.I. Chapayev. No. 1211, S.G. Lazo.

1948, Feb. 23				
1209	A494	60k deep green	6.50	1.75
1210	A494	60k yellow brown	6.50	1.75
1211	A494	60k violet blue	6.50	1.75
		Nos. 1209-1211 (3)	19.50	5.25

Nos. 1205-1211 for Soviet army, 30th anniv.

Karl Marx,
Friedrich Engels
and Communist
Manifesto
A677

1948, Apr.				
1212	A677	30k black	1.50	.25
1213	A677	50k henna brown	3.50	.30

Centenary of the Communist Manifesto.

Miner
A678

Marine
A679

Aviator
A680

Woman
Farmer
A681

Arms of
USSR
A682

Scientist
A683

Spasski
Tower,
Kremlin
A684

Soldier
A685

1948			Photo.	
1214	A678	5k sepia	.50	.30
1215	A679	10k violet	.85	.30
1216	A680	15k bright blue	1.25	.85
1217	A681	20k brown	1.50	.75
1218	A682	30k henna brown	2.50	1.25
1219	A683	45k brown violet	5.00	1.90
1220	A684	50k bright blue	7.00	3.00
1221	A685	60k bright green	8.50	4.25
		Nos. 1214-1221 (8)	27.10	12.60

See Nos. 1306, 1343-1347, 1689.

May Day Parade in Red
Square — A686

1948, June 5			Perf. 12	
1222	A686	30k deep car rose	5.00	.80
1223	A686	60k bright blue	15.00	1.25

Labor Day, May 1, 1948.

Vissarion G. Belinski
(1811-48), Literary
Critic — A687

1948, June 7			Unwmk.	Perf. 12	
1224	A687	30k brown	5.00	1.00
1225	A687	50k dark green	7.50	2.00
1226	A687	60k purple	15.00	2.00
		Nos. 1224-1226 (3)	27.50	5.00

Aleksandr N. Ostrovski
A690   A691

1948, June 10   Photo.   Perf. 12
1227	A690	30k bright green	4.50	2.50
1228	A691	60k brown	9.00	4.50
1229	A691	1r brown violet	15.00	8.00
	Nos. 1227-1229 (3)		28.50	15.00

Ostrovski (1823-1886), playwright.
Exist imperf. Value, set $250.

Ivan I. Shishkin
(1832-1898),
Painter — A692

"Field of
Rye," by
Shishkin
A693

60k, "Bears in a Forest," by Shishkin.

Photo. (30k, 1r), Typo. (50k, 60k)
1948, June 12
1230	A692	30k dk grn & vio brn	13.00	3.50
1231	A693	50k multicolored	20.00	7.50
1232	A693	60k multicolored	30.00	8.00
1233	A692	1r brn & bl blk	37.50	21.00
	Nos. 1230-1233 (4)		100.50	40.00

Industrial
Expansion
A694

Public Gathering at Leningrad — A695

Photo., Frames Litho. in Carmine
1948, June 25
1234	A694	15k red brown	3.50	1.00
1235	A695	30k slate	4.50	1.50
1236	A694	60k brown black	7.00	2.75
	Nos. 1234-1236 (3)		15.00	5.25

Industrial five-year plan.

Planting
Crops
A696

Nos. 1238, 1243, Gathering vegetables.
Nos. 1239, 1241, Baling cotton. No. 1240,
Planting Crops. No. 1242, Harvesting grain.

1948, July 12   Photo.
1237	A696	30k carmine rose	.75	.30
1238	A696	30k blue green	.75	.30
1239	A696	45k red brown	1.50	.70
1240	A696	50k brown black	2.25	.70
1241	A696	60k dark green	2.10	.80

1242	A696	60k dk blue green	2.10	.80
1243	A696	1r purple	5.50	1.40
	Nos. 1237-1243 (7)		14.95	5.00

Agricultural five-year plan.

Arms and Citizens
of USSR — A697

Photo., Frames Litho. in Carmine
1948, July 25
1244	A697	30k slate	10.00	2.50
1245	A697	60k greenish black	15.00	5.00

25th anniv. of the USSR.

Nos. 1159 and
1160 Overprinted in
Red

1948, Aug. 24   Perf. 12½
1246	A657	30k deep violet	3.00	2.50
1247	A657	1r bright ultra	10.00	2.50

Air Fleet Day, 1948. On sale one day.

Soviet
Miners — A698

Miner's Day, Aug. 29: 60k, Scene in mine.
1r, Miner's badge.

1948, Aug.   Photo.   Perf. 12½x12
1248	A698	30k blue	3.00	.35
1249	A698	60k purple	6.00	.45
1250	A698	1r green	11.00	1.20
	Nos. 1248-1250 (3)		20.00	2.00

A. A.
Zhdanov — A699

1948, Sept. 3
1251	A699	40k slate	4.00	2.00

Andrei A. Zhdanov, statesman, 1896-1948.

Soviet
Sailor — A700

1948, Sept. 12   Perf. 12
1252	A700	30k blue green	6.00	3.00
1253	A700	60k bright blue	14.00	5.00

Navy Day, Sept. 12.

Slalom
A701

Motorcyclist — A702

Designs: No. 1254, Foot race. 30k, Soccer
game. 45k, Motorboat race. 50k, Diving.

1948, Sept. 15   Perf. 12½x12
1253A	A701	15k dark blue	2.50	.25
1254	A702	15k violet	1.00	.25
1254A	A702	20k dk slate blue	3.50	.55
1255	A701	30k brown	2.00	.25
1256	A701	45k sepia	3.00	.35
1257	A702	50k blue	3.00	.35
	Nos. 1253A-1257 (6)		15.00	2.00

Tankmen
Group
A703

Design: 1r, Tank parade.

1948, Sept. 25
1258	A703	30k sepia	4.50	1.50
1259	A703	1r rose	10.50	3.50

Day of the Tankmen, Sept. 25.

Spasski Tower Type of 1947
1948   Litho.   Perf. 12x12½
1260	A658	1r brown red	2.00	.25

No. 1260 was re-issued in 1954-56 in
slightly smaller format: 14½x21½mm, instead
of 14¾x22mm and in a paler shade. See note
after No. 738.

Train — A704

Transportation 5-year plan: 60k, Auto and
bus at intersection. 1r, Steamships at anchor.

1948, Sept. 30   Photo.   Perf. 12½x12
1261	A704	30k brown	30.00	7.50
1262	A704	50k dark green	60.00	10.00
1263	A704	60k blue	100.00	12.50
1264	A704	1r blue violet	100.00	20.00
	Nos. 1261-1264 (4)		290.00	50.00

Horses
A705

Livestock 5-year plan: 60k, Dairy farm.

1948, Sept. 30   Perf. 12
1265	A705	30k slate gray	11.00	4.00
1266	A705	60k bright green	19.00	6.50
1267	A705	1r brown	35.00	9.50
	Nos. 1265-1267 (3)		65.00	20.00

Pouring
Molten Metal
A706

Designs: 60k, 1r, Iron pipe manufacture.

1948, Oct. 14   Perf. 12½
1268	A706	30k purple	3.00	.75
1269	A706	50k brown	3.00	1.00
1270	A706	60k carmine	3.00	1.25
1271	A706	1r dull blue	3.00	2.00
	Nos. 1268-1271 (4)		12.00	5.00

Heavy
Machinery
Plant
A707

Design: 60k, Pump station interior.

1948, Oct. 14
1272	A707	30k purple	10.00	.75
1273	A707	50k sepia	5.00	1.25
1274	A707	60k brown	10.00	1.40
	Nos. 1272-1274 (3)		25.00	3.40

Nos. 1268-1274 publicize the 5-year plan for
steel, iron and machinery industries.

Khachatur Abovian
(1809-1848),
Armenian Writer
and Poet — A708

1948, Oct. 16   Perf. 12x12½
1275	A708	40k purple	7.00	2.50
1276	A708	50k deep green	8.00	2.50

Farkhatz
Hydroelectric
Station
A709

Design: 60k, Zouiev Hydroelectric Station.

1948, Oct. 24   Perf. 12½
1277	A709	30k green	15.00	5.00
1278	A709	60k red	15.00	5.00
1279	A709	1r carmine rose	15.00	5.00
	Nos. 1277-1279 (3)		45.00	15.00

Electrification five-year plan.

Coal
Mine — A710

Designs: Nos. 1282, 1283, Oil field and tank
cars.

1948, Oct. 24
1280	A710	30k sepia	25.00	1.25
1281	A710	60k brown	35.00	2.50
1282	A710	60k red brown	35.00	2.50
1283	A710	1r blue green	115.00	3.75
	Nos. 1280-1283 (4)		210.00	10.00

Coal mining and oil production 5-year plan.

Flying Model
Planes — A712

Marching
Pioneers
A713

Pioneers Saluting — A714

60k, Pioneer bugler. 1r, Pioneers at campfire.

1948, Oct. 26			Perf. 12½	
1284	A712	30k dark bl grn	30.00	4.25
1285	A713	45k dark violet	40.00	5.50
1286	A714	45k deep carmine	32.50	4.75
1287	A714	60k deep ultra	45.00	7.25
1288	A713	1r deep blue	100.00	13.00
		Nos. 1284-1288 (5)	247.50	34.75

Young Pioneers, a Soviet youth organization, and governmental supervision of children's summer vacations.

Marching Youths A715

Farm Girl — A716   League Members and Flag — A717

Designs: 50k, Communist students. 1r, Flag and badges. 2r, Young worker.

Inscribed: "1918 1948 XXX"

1948, Oct. 29			Perf. 12½	
1289	A715	20k violet brown	12.50	1.25
1290	A716	25k rose red	13.50	1.60
1291	A717	40k brown & red	22.50	2.00
1292	A715	50k blue green	29.00	3.25
1293	A717	1r multicolored	95.00	14.50
1294	A716	2r purple	50.00	11.00
		Nos. 1289-1294 (6)	222.50	33.60

30th anniversary of the Young Communist League (Komsomol).

Stage of Moscow Art Theater A719

K. S. Stanislavski, V. I. Nemirovich Danchenko A720

1948, Nov. 1			Perf. 12½	
1295	A719	40k gray blue	6.50	3.50
1296	A720	1r violet brown	9.50	4.50

Moscow Art Theater, 50th anniv.

Flag and Moscow Buildings — A721

1948, Nov. 7			Perf. 12½	
1297	A721	40k red	5.00	2.25
1298	A721	1r green	10.00	2.75

31st anniversary of October Revolution.

House of Unions, Moscow A722

Player's Badge (Rook and Chessboard) A723

1948, Nov. 20			Perf. 12½	
1299	A722	30k greenish blue	2.50	.35
1300	A723	40k violet	6.25	.50
1301	A722	50k orange brown	6.25	.90
		Nos. 1299-1301 (3)	15.00	1.75

16th Chess Championship.

Artillery Salute A724

1948, Nov. 19			Perf. 12½	
1302	A724	30k blue	30.00	10.00
1303	A724	1r rose carmine	70.00	25.00

Artillery Day, Nov. 19, 1948.

Vasili Petrovich Stasov — A725

Stasov and Barracks of Paul's Regiment, Petrograd A726

1948, Nov. 27			Unwmk.	
1304	A725	40k brown	6.50	1.75
1305	A726	1r sepia	13.50	3.25

Stasov (1769-1848), architect.

Arms Type of 1948

1948		Litho.	Perf. 12x12½	
1306	A682	40k brown red	50.00	3.00

See No. 1689.

Y. M. Sverdlov Monument A727

Design: 40k, Lenin Street, Sverdlovsk.

1948		Photo.	Perf. 12½	
1307	A727	30k blue	1.00	.25
1308	A727	40k purple	1.25	.35
1309	A727	1r bright green	2.50	.60
		Nos. 1307-1309 (3)	4.75	1.20

225th anniv. of the city of Sverdlovsk (before 1924, Ekaterinburg). Exist imperf. Value, set $20.00.

"Swallow's Nest," Crimea A729   Hot Spring, Piatigorsk A730

Shoreline, Sukhumi A731   Tree-lined Walk, Sochi A732

Formal Gardens, Sochi A733

Stalin Highway, Sochi — A734

Colonnade, Kislovodsk A735

Seascape, Gagri A736

1948, Dec. 30			Perf. 12½	
1310	A729	40k brown	6.25	.60
1311	A730	40k bright red violet	6.25	.60
1312	A731	40k dark green	6.25	.60
1313	A732	40k violet	6.25	.60
1314	A733	40k dark purple	6.25	.60
1315	A734	40k dark blue green	6.25	.60
1316	A735	40k bright blue	6.25	.60
1317	A736	40k dark blue green	6.25	.60
		Nos. 1310-1317 (8)	50.00	4.80

Byelorussian S.S.R. Arms — A737

1949, Jan. 4				
1318	A737	40k henna brown	6.00	2.00
1319	A737	1r blue green	9.00	3.00

Byelorussian SSR, 30th anniv.

Mikhail V. Lomonosov — A738

Lomonosov Museum, Leningrad A739

1949, Jan. 10				
1320	A738	40k red brown	7.00	3.50
1321	A738	50k green	9.00	3.50
1322	A739	1r deep blue	20.00	8.00
		Nos. 1320-1322 (3)	36.00	15.00

Cape Dezhnev (East Cape) A740

Design: 1r, Map and Dezhnev's ship.

1949, Jan. 30				
1323	A740	40k olive green	12.50	5.00
1324	A740	1r gray	27.50	10.00

300th anniv. of the discovery of the strait between Asia and America by S. I. Dezhnev.

Souvenir Sheet

A741

1949, Dec.			Imperf.	
1325	A741	Sheet of 4	500.00	300.00
		Hinged	200.00	
a.		40k Stalin's birthplace, Gorki	25.00	35.00
b.		40k Lenin & Stalin, Leningrad, 1917	25.00	35.00
c.		40k Lenin & Stalin, Gorki	25.00	35.00
d.		40k Marshal Stalin	25.00	35.00

70th birthday of Joseph V. Stalin.

Lenin Mausoleum — A742

1949, Jan. 21			Perf. 12½	
1326	A742	40k ol grn & org brn	15.00	7.50
1327	A742	1r gray blk & org brn	25.00	12.50
a.		Sheet of 4	600.00	500.00

25th anniversary of the death of Lenin. No. 1327a exists imperf. Value $975 mint, $3,000 used.

Admiral S. O.
Makarov — A743

1949, Mar. 15

1328	A743	40k blue	8.00	4.00
1329	A743	1r red brown	17.00	6.00

Centenary of the birth of Admiral Stepan Osipovich Makarov, shipbuilder.

Kirov Military Medical Academy A744

Professors Botkin, Pirogov and Sechenov A745

1949, Mar. 24

1330	A744	40k red brown	6.00	3.00
1331	A745	50k blue	12.00	5.00
1332	A744	1r blue green	12.00	6.50
		Nos. 1330-1332 (3)	30.00	14.50

150th anniversary of the foundation of Kirov Military Medical Academy, Leningrad.

Soviet Soldier A746

1949, Mar. 16   **Photo.**

1333	A746	40k rose red	20.00	10.00

31st anniversary of the Soviet army.

Textile Weaving A747

Political Leadership — A748

Designs: 25k, Preschool teaching. No. 1337, School teaching. No. 1338, Farm women. 1r, Women athletes.

Inscribed: "8 МАРТА 1949г"

1949, Mar. 8   **Perf. 12½**

1334	A747	20k dark violet	.45	.25
1335	A747	25k blue	.60	.25
1336	A748	40k henna brown	.80	.25
1337	A747	50k slate gray	1.50	.35
1338	A747	50k brown	1.50	.35
1339	A747	1r green	4.00	.50
1340	A748	2r copper red	6.00	1.50
		Nos. 1334-1340 (7)	14.85	3.45

International Women's Day, Mar. 8.

Medal Types of 1945

1948-49   **Engr.**

1341	A517	2r green ('49)	12.00	5.00
1341A	A517	2r violet brown	11.00	5.25
1342	A518	3r brown car ('49)	8.00	.75
		Nos. 1341-1342 (3)	31.00	11.00

For overprint see No. 1709.

Types of 1948

1949   **Litho.**   **Perf. 12x12½**

1343	A678	15k black	2.00	1.00
1344	A681	20k green	3.00	1.25
1345	A680	25k dark blue	2.50	1.00
1346	A683	30k brown	3.50	1.50
1347	A684	50k deep blue	90.00	20.00
		Nos. 1343-1347 (5)	101.00	24.75

The 20k, 25k and 30k were re-issued in 1954-56 in slightly smaller format. The 20k measures 14x21mm, instead of 15x22mm; 25k, 14½x21mm, instead of 14½x21¾mm; and 30k, 14½x21mm, instead of 15x22mm.

The smaller-format 20k is olive green, the 25k, slate blue. The 15k was reissued in 1959 (?) in smaller format: 14x21mm, instead of 14½x22mm. See note after No. 738.

Vasili R. Williams (1863-1939), Agricultural Scientist A749

1949, Apr. 18   **Photo.**   **Perf. 12½**

1348	A749	25k blue green	5.00	2.75
1349	A749	50k brown	10.00	4.25

Russian Citizens and Flag — A750

1949, Apr. 30   **Perf. 12½**

1350	A750	40k scarlet	3.00	1.00
1351	A750	1r blue green	16.00	6.00

Labor Day, May 1, 1949.

A. S. Popov and Radio — A751

Popov Demonstrating Radio to Admiral Makarov — A752

1949, May   **Unwmk.**

1352	A751	40k purple	8.00	3.25
1353	A752	50k brown	16.00	6.25
1354	A751	1r blue green	16.00	10.00
		Nos. 1352-1354 (3)	40.00	19.50

54th anniversary of Popov's discovery of the principles of radio.

Soviet Publications A753

Reading Pravda A754

1949, May 4

1355	A753	40k crimson	11.00	3.75
1356	A754	1r dark violet	29.00	8.00

Soviet Press Day.

Ivan V. Michurin — A755

1949, July 28

1357	A755	40k blue gray	7.00	1.50
1358	A755	1r bright green	13.00	3.50

Michurin (1855-1925), agricultural scientist.

A. S. Pushkin, 1822 — A756

Pushkin Reading Poem A757

No. 1360, Pushkin portrait by Kiprensky, 1827. 1r, Pushkin Museum, Boldino.

1949, June   **Unwmk.**

1359	A756	25k indigo & sepia	3.75	.75
1360	A756	40k org brn & sep	8.75	1.75
a.		Souv. sheet of 4, 2 each #1359, 1360, imperf.	200.00	40.00
1361	A757	40k brn red & dk violet	8.75	2.00
1362	A757	1r choc & slate	21.00	4.00
1363	A757	2r brn & vio bl	32.50	6.50
		Nos. 1359-1363 (5)	74.75	15.00

150th anniversary of the birth of Aleksander S. Pushkin.

Horizontal rows of Nos. 1361 and 1363 contain alternate stamps and labels.

No. 1360a issued July 20.

River Tugboat A758

1r, Freighter, motorship "Bolshaya Volga."

1949, July, 13

1364	A758	40k slate blue	25.00	5.00
1365	A758	1r red brown	50.00	15.00

Centenary of the establishment of the Sormovo Machine and Boat Works.

VCSPS No. 3, Kislovodsk A759

State Sanatoria for Workers: No. 1367, Communications, Khosta. No. 1368, Sanatorium No. 3, Khosta. No. 1369, Electric power, Khosta. No. 1370, Sanatorium No. 1, Kislovodsk. No. 1371, State Theater, Sochi. No. 1372, Frunze Sanatorium, Sochi. No. 1373, Sanatorium at Machindzhaury. No. 1374, Clinical, Chaltubo. No. 1375, Sanatorium No. 41, Zheleznovodsk.

1949, Sept. 10   **Photo.**   **Perf. 12½**

1366	A759	40k violet	1.00	.25
1367	A759	40k black	1.00	.25
1368	A759	40k carmine	1.00	.25
1369	A759	40k blue	1.00	.25
1370	A759	40k violet brown	1.00	.25
1371	A759	40k red orange	1.00	.25
1372	A759	40k dark brown	1.00	.25
1373	A759	40k green	1.00	.25
1374	A759	40k red brown	1.00	.25
1375	A759	40k blue green	1.00	.25
		Nos. 1366-1375 (10)	10.00	2.50

Regatta A760

Sports, "1949": 25k, Kayak race. 30k, Swimming. 40k, Bicycling. No. 1380, Soccer. 50k, Mountain climbing. 1r, Parachuting. 2r, High jump.

1949, Aug. 7

1376	A760	20k bright blue	.70	.25
1377	A760	25k blue green	.70	.25
1378	A760	30k violet	1.20	.25
1379	A760	40k red brown	1.20	.25
1380	A760	40k green	1.20	.25
1381	A760	50k dk blue gray	1.50	.25
1382	A760	1r carmine rose	4.50	.70
1383	A760	2r gray black	8.75	1.10
		Nos. 1376-1383 (8)	19.75	3.30

V. V. Dokuchayev and Fields A761

1949, Aug. 8

1384	A761	40k brown	1.00	.30
1385	A761	1r green	2.00	.45

Vasili V. Dokuchayev (1846-1903), pioneer soil scientist.

Vasili Bazhenov and Lenin Library, Moscow A762

1949, Aug. 14   **Photo.**   **Perf. 12½**

1386	A762	40k violet	4.00	.35
1387	A762	1r red brown	6.00	.45

Bazhenov, architect, 150th death anniv.

A. N. Radishchev — A763

1949, Aug. 31

1388	A763	40k blue green	15.00	6.00
1389	A763	1r gray	35.00	9.00

200th anniversary of the birth of Aleksandr N. Radishchev, writer.

Ivan P. Pavlov A764

1949, Sept. 30   **Unwmk.**

1390	A764	40k deep brown	5.00	.75
1391	A764	1r gray black	10.00	1.25

Pavlov (1849-1936), Russian physiologist.

Globe Encircled by Letters A765

1949, Oct.   **Perf. 12½**
1392	A765	40k org brn & indigo	2.50	.30
a.		Imperf.	25.00	5.00
1393	A765	50k indigo & gray vio	2.50	.30
a.		Imperf.	25.00	5.00

75th anniv. of the UPU.

Cultivators A766

Map of European Russia — A767

Designs: No. 1395, Peasants in grain field. 50k, Rural scene. 2r, Old man and children.

1949, Oct. 18   **Perf. 12½**
1394	A766	25k green	31.00	12.50
1395	A766	40k violet	7.75	2.75
1396	A767	40k gray grn & blk	9.00	5.50
1397	A766	50k deep blue	8.00	4.50
1398	A766	1r gray black	20.00	9.00
1399	A766	2r dark brown	25.00	12.50
		Nos. 1394-1399 (6)	100.75	46.75

Encouraging agricultural development. Nos. 1394, 1398, 1399 measure 33x19mm. Nos. 1395, 1397 measure 33x22mm.

Maly (Little) Theater, Moscow A768

M. N. Ermolova, I. S. Mochalov, A. N. Ostrovski, M. S. Shchepkin and P. M. Sadovsky A769

1949, Oct. 27
1400	A768	40k green	2.50	.25
1401	A768	50k red orange	3.75	.40
1402	A769	1r deep brown	8.75	.85
		Nos. 1400-1402 (3)	15.00	1.50

125th anniversary of the Maly Theater (State Academic Little Theater).

Chapayev Type of 1944

1949, Oct. 22   **Photo.**
1403	A494	40k brown orange	75.00	30.00

30th anniversary of the death of V. I. Chapayev, a hero of the 1918 civil war.

Portrait and outer frame same as type A494. Dates "1919 1949" are in upper corners. Other details differ.

125th Anniv. of the Birth of Ivan Savvich Nikitin, Russian Poet (1824-1861) — A770

1949, Oct. 24   **Unwmk.**
1404	A770	40k brown	1.50	.25
1405	A770	1r slate blue	2.50	.35

Spasski Tower and Russian Citizens A771

1949, Oct. 29   **Perf. 12½**
1406	A771	40k brown orange	6.00	4.00
1407	A771	1r deep green	10.00	6.00

October Revolution, 32nd anniversary.

Sheep, Cattle and Farm Woman — A772

1949, Nov. 2
1408	A772	40k chocolate	8.00	.40
1409	A772	1r violet	12.00	.60

Encouraging better cattle breeding in Russia.

Arms and Flag of USSR — A773

1949, Nov. 30   **Engr.**   **Perf. 12**
1410	A773	40k carmine	20.00	6.00

Constitution Day.

Electric Trolley Car — A774

40k, 1r, Diesel train. 50k, Steam train.

1949, Nov. 19   **Photo.**   **Perf. 12½**
1411	A774	25k red	4.00	.50
1412	A774	40k violet	7.00	.50
1413	A774	50k brown	9.00	.75
1414	A774	1r Prus green	30.00	1.25
		Nos. 1411-1414 (4)	50.00	3.00

Ski Jump — A775

Designs: 40k, Girl on rings. 50k, Ice hockey. 1r, Weight lifter. 2r, Wolf hunt.

1949, Nov. 12   **Unwmk.**
1415	A775	20k dark green	1.20	.55
1416	A775	40k orange red	2.40	.65
1417	A775	50k deep blue	3.00	.80
1418	A775	1r red	6.00	.90
1419	A775	2r violet	12.00	1.10
		Nos. 1415-1419 (5)	24.60	4.00

Textile Mills — A776

Designs: 25k, Irrigation system. 40k, 1r, Government buildings, Stalinabad. 50k, University of Medicine.

"Russia" versus "War" — A777

1949, Dec. 7   **Photo.**   **Perf. 12**
1420	A776	20k blue	3.00	.25
1421	A776	25k green	3.00	.25
1422	A776	40k red orange	4.50	.25
1423	A776	50k violet	7.50	.40
1424	A776	1r gray black	12.00	1.00
		Nos. 1420-1424 (5)	30.00	2.15

Tadzhik Republic, 20th anniv.

1949, Dec. 25
1425	A777	40k rose carmine	3.00	.25
1426	A777	50k blue	4.00	.75

Issued to portray Russia as the defender of world peace.

Byelorussians and Flag — A778

Design: No. 1428, Ukrainians and flag.

Inscribed: "1939 1949"

1949, Dec. 23   **Unwmk.**
1427	A778	40k orange red	37.50	5.00
1428	A778	50k deep orange	37.50	5.00

Return of western territories to the Byelorussian and Ukrainian Republics, 10th anniv.

Teachers College A779

25k, State Theater. #1431, Government House. #1432, Navol Street, Tashkent. 1r, Fergana Canal. 2r, Kuigonyarsk Dam.

1950, Jan. 3
1429	A779	20k blue	1.00	.25
1430	A779	25k gray black	1.00	.25
1431	A779	40k red orange	2.00	.25
1432	A779	40k violet	1.50	.25
1433	A779	1r green	4.00	1.00
1434	A779	2r brown	6.00	1.00
		Nos. 1429-1434 (6)	15.50	3.00

Uzbek Republic, 25th anniversary.

Lenin at Razliv — A780

Lenin's Office, Kremlin A781

Design: 1r, Lenin Museum.

1950, Jan.   **Unwmk.**   **Litho.**   **Perf. 12**
1435	A780	40k dk grn & dk brn	3.00	.50
1436	A781	50k dk brn, red brn & grn	4.00	.50

1437	A781	1r dk brn, dk grn & cream	9.00	2.00
		Nos. 1435-1437 (3)	16.00	3.00

26th anniversary of the death of Lenin.

Textile Factory, Ashkhabad A782

Designs: 40k, 1r, Power dam and Turkmenian arms. 50k, Rug making.

1950, Jan. 7   **Photo.**
1438	A782	25k gray black	3.50	1.00
1439	A782	40k brown	5.00	.75
1440	A782	50k green	6.50	1.25
1441	A782	1r purple	15.00	2.50
		Nos. 1438-1441 (4)	30.00	5.50

Turkmen Republic, 25th anniversary.

Motion Picture Projection A783

1950, Feb.
1442	A783	25k brown	40.00	25.00

Soviet motion picture industry, 30th anniv.

Voter — A784   Kremlin — A785

1950, Mar. 8
1443	A784	40k green, *yellow*	20.00	4.00
1444	A785	1r rose carmine	40.00	6.00

Supreme Soviet elections, Mar. 12, 1950.

Morozov Monument, Moscow — A786

1950, Mar. 16   **Perf. 12½**
1445	A786	40k black brn & red	20.00	3.25
1446	A786	1r dk green & red	30.00	7.50

Unveiling of a monument to Pavlik Morozov, Pioneer.

Globes and Communication Symbols — A787

1950, Apr. 1
1447	A787	40k deep green, *blue*	10.00	4.50
1448	A787	50k deep blue, *blue*	12.00	5.50

Meeting of the Post, Telegraph, Telephone and Radio Trade Unions.

State Polytechnic Museum A788

State Museum of Oriental Cultures A789

State University Museum — A790

Pushkin Museum A791

Museums: No. 1451, Tretiakov Gallery. No. 1452, Timiryazev Biology Museum. No. 1453, Lenin Museum. No. 1454, Museum of the Revolution. No. 1456, State History Museum.

Inscribed: "МОСКВА 1949" in Top Frame

Multicolored Centers

1950, Mar. 28		Litho.	Perf. 12½	
1449	A788	40k dark blue	6.00	.50
1450	A789	40k dark blue	6.00	.50
1451	A789	40k green	6.00	.50
1452	A789	40k dark brown	6.00	.50
1453	A789	40k olive brown	6.00	.50
1454	A789	40k claret	6.00	.50
1455	A790	40k red	6.00	.50
1456	A790	40k chocolate	6.00	.50
1457	A791	40k brown violet	6.00	.50
		Nos. 1449-1457 (9)	54.00	4.50

Soviets of Three Races — A792

1r, 4 Russians and communist banner, horiz.

1950, May 1		Photo.	Perf. 12½	
1458	A792	40k org red & gray	15.00	2.25
1459	A792	1r red & gray black	20.00	5.00

Labor Day, May 1, 1950.

A. S. Shcherbakov A793

1950, May			Unwmk.	
1460	A793	40k black, pale blue	8.00	1.00
1461	A793	1r dk green, buff	12.50	2.00

Shcherbakov, political leader (1901-1945).

Monument A794   Victory Medal A795

Perf. 12x12½

1950		Photo.	Wmk. 293	
1462	A794	40k dk brown & red	37.50	4.00

Unwmk.

| 1463 | A795 | 1r carmine rose | 37.50 | 8.00 |

5th Intl. Victory Day, May 9, 1950.

A. V. Suvorov — A796

50k, Suvorov crossing Alps, 32½x47mm. 60k, Badge, flag and marchers, 24x39½mm. 2r, Suvorov facing left, 19x33½mm.

Various Designs and Sizes Dated "1800 1950"

1950			Perf. 12, 12½x12	
1464	A796	40k blue, pink	15.00	4.00
1465	A796	50k brown, pink	19.00	8.00
1466	A796	60k gray black, pale gray	19.00	8.00
1467	A796	1r dk brn, lemon	23.00	12.00
1468	A796	2r greenish blue	50.00	18.00
		Nos. 1464-1468 (5)	126.00	50.00

Field Marshal Count Aleksandr V. Suvorov (1730-1800).

Farmers Studying Agronomic Techniques A797

No. 1470, 1r, Sowing on collective farm.

1950, June			Perf. 12½	
1469	A797	40k dk grn, pale grn	7.50	2.00
1470	A797	40k gray black, buff	7.50	2.00
1471	A797	1r blue, lemon	15.00	4.00
		Nos. 1469-1471 (3)	30.00	8.00

George M. Dimitrov — A798

1950, July 2				
1472	A798	40k gray blk, citron	6.00	3.00
1473	A798	1r gray blk, salmon	14.00	6.00

Dimitrov (1882-1949), Bulgarian-born revolutionary leader and Comintern official.

Opera and Ballet Theater, Baku — A799

Designs: 40k, Azerbaijan Academy of Science. 1r, Stalin Avenue, Baku.

1950, July		Photo.	Perf. 12½	
1474	A799	25k dp grn, citron	15.00	1.50
1475	A799	40k brn, pink	10.00	5.00
1476	A799	1r gray blk, buff	15.00	8.50
		Nos. 1474-1476 (3)	40.00	15.00

Azerbaijan SSR, 30th anniversary.

Victory Theater — A800

Lenin Street A801

Designs: 50k, Gorky Theater. 1r, Monument marking Stalingrad defense line.

1950, June				
1477	A800	20k dark blue	5.00	1.50
1478	A801	40k green	5.00	2.25
1479	A801	50k red orange	10.00	3.50
1480	A801	1r gray	10.00	6.00
		Nos. 1477-1480 (4)	30.00	13.25

Restoration of Stalingrad.

Moscow Subway Stations: "Park of Culture" A802

#1482, Kaluzskaya station. #1483, Taganskaya. #1484, Kurskaya. #1485, Paveletskaya. #1486, Park of Culture. #1487, Taganskaya.

1950, July 30		Size: 33½x23mm		
1481	A802	40k deep carmine	5.50	.90
1482	A802	40k dk grn, buff	5.50	.90
1483	A802	40k deep blue, buff	5.50	.90
1484	A802	1r dark brn, citron	8.25	3.00
1485	A802	1r purple	8.25	3.00
1486	A802	1r dark grn, citron	8.25	3.00

Size: 33x18½mm

1487	A802	1r black, pink	8.25	3.25
		Nos. 1481-1487 (7)	49.50	14.95

Socialist Peoples and Flags A803

1950, Aug. 4		Unwmk.	Perf. 12½	
1488	A803	40k multicolored	1.75	.25
1489	A803	50k multicolored	3.50	.30
1490	A803	1r multicolored	4.75	.50
		Nos. 1488-1490 (3)	10.00	1.05

Trade Union Building, Riga — A804

Opera and Ballet Theater, Riga — A805

Designs: 40k, Latvian Cabinet building. 50k, Monument to Jan Rainis. 1r, Riga State Univ. 2r, Latvian Academy of Sciences.

1950		Photo.	Perf. 12½	
1491	A804	25k dark brown	3.00	1.50
1492	A804	40k scarlet	5.00	2.50
1493	A804	50k dark green	10.00	3.50
1494	A805	60k deep blue	12.00	4.00
1495	A805	1r lilac	15.00	6.00
1496	A804	2r sepia	30.00	10.00
		Nos. 1491-1496 (6)	75.00	27.50

Latvian SSR, 10th anniv.

Lithuanian Academy of Sciences A806

Marite Melnik — A807

Design: 1r, Cabinet building.

1950				
1497	A806	25k dp bl, bluish	6.00	2.50
1498	A807	40k brown	12.00	7.50
1499	A806	1r scarlet	42.00	15.00
		Nos. 1497-1499 (3)	60.00	25.00

Lithuanian SSR, 10th anniv.

Stalingrad Square, Tallinn A808

Victor Kingisepp — A809

Designs: 40k, Government building, Tallinn. 50k, Estonia Theater, Tallinn.

1950				
1500	A808	25k dark green	5.00	2.00
1501	A808	40k scarlet	5.00	3.00
1502	A808	50k blue, yellow	10.00	5.00
1503	A809	1r brown, blue	30.00	12.00
		Nos. 1500-1503 (4)	50.00	22.00

Estonian SSR, 10th anniv.

Citizens Signing Appeal for Peace A810

Children and Governess — A811

Design: 50k, Peace Demonstration.

1950, Oct. 16   Photo.
1504 A810 40k red, *salmon*   4.00   3.00
1505 A811 40k black   4.00   3.00
1506 A811 50k dark red   8.50   5.00
1507 A810 1r brown, *salmon*   24.00   9.00
Nos. 1504-1507 (4)   40.50   20.00

F. G. Bellingshausen, M. P. Lazarev and Globe — A812

Route of Antarctic Expedition — A813

Blue Paper
1950, Oct. 25   Unwmk.   Perf. 12½
1508 A812 40k dark carmine   35.00   15.00
1509 A813 1r purple   65.00   35.00
130th anniversary of the Bellingshausen-Lazarev expedition to the Antarctic.

M. V. Frunze — A814

1950, Oct. 31
1510 A814 40k blue, *buff*   10.00   3.00
1511 A814 1r brown, *blue*   30.00   12.00
Frunze, military strategist, 25th death anniv.

M. I. Kalinin — A815

1950, Nov. 20   Engr.
1512 A815 40k deep green   10.00   1.50
1513 A815 1r reddish brown   10.00   2.50
1514 A815 5r violet   35.00   6.00
Nos. 1512-1514 (3)   55.00   10.00
75th anniversary of the birth of M. I. Kalinin, Soviet Russia's first president.

Gathering Grapes A816

G. M. Sundukian — A818

1950, Nov. 29   Photo.   Perf. 12½
1515 A816 20k dp blue, *buff*   5.00   1.00
1516 A817 40k red org, *blue*   32.50   8.50
1517 A818 1r ol gray, *yellow*   7.50   3.50
Nos. 1515-1517 (3)   45.00   13.00
Armenian Republic, 30th anniv. 1r also for birth of Sundukian, playwright.

Apartment Building, Koteljnicheskaya Quay — A819

Hotel, Kalanchevkaya Square — A820

Various Buildings
Inscribed: "Mockba, 1950"
1950, Dec. 2   Unwmk.
1518 A819 1r red brn, *buff*   57.50   22.00
1519 A819 1r gray black   57.50   22.00
1520 A819 1r brown, *blue*   57.50   22.00
1521 A819 1r dk green, *blue*   57.50   22.00
1522 A820 1r dp blue, *buff*   57.50   22.00
1523 A820 1r black, *buff*   57.50   22.00
1524 A820 1r red orange   57.50   22.00
1525 A820 1r dk grn, *yellow*   57.50   22.00
Nos. 1518-1525 (8)   460.00   176.00
Set, hinged   250.00
Skyscrapers planned for Moscow.

Spasski Tower, Kremlin — A821

1950, Dec. 4
1526 A821 1r dk grn, red brn & yel brown   75.00   5.00
October Revolution, 33rd anniversary.

Golden Autumn by Levitan A822

I. I. Levitan (1861-90), Painter A823

1950, Dec. 6   Litho.   Perf. 12½
1527 A822 40k multicolored   10.00   .55
     Perf. 12
     Photo.
1528 A823 50k red brown   15.00   .55

Black Sea by Aivazovsky — A824

Ivan K. Aivazovsky (1817-1900) Painter A825
Design: 50k, "Ninth Surge."

1950, Dec. 6   Litho.
Multicolored Centers
1529 A824 40k chocolate   3.50   .30
1530 A824 50k chocolate   4.50   .50
1531 A825 1r indigo   8.50   1.25
Nos. 1529-1531 (3)   16.50   2.05

Flags and Newspapers Iskra and Pravda — A826
1r, Flag and profiles of Lenin and Stalin.

1950, Dec. 23   Photo.
1532 A826 40k gray blk & red   50.00   15.00
1533 A826 1r dk brn & red   100.00   35.00
1st issue of the newspaper Iskra, 50th anniv.

Presidium of Supreme Soviet, Alma-Ata A827
Design: 1r, Opera and Ballet Theater.

Inscribed: "ALMA-ATA" in Cyrillic
1950, Dec. 27
1534 A827 40k gray black, *blue*   10.00   7.50
1535 A827 1r red brn, *yellow*   25.00   7.50
Kazakh Republic, 30th anniversary. Cyrillic charcters for "ALMA-ATA" are above building in vignette on 40k, immediately below building on right on 1r.

Decembrists and Senatskaya Square, Leningrad — A828

1950, Dec. 30   Unwmk.
1536 A828 1r blk brn, *yellow*   30.00   10.00
Decembrist revolution of 1825.

Lenin at Razliv A829
Design: 1r, Lenin and young communists.

Multicolored Centers
1951, Jan. 21   Litho.   Perf. 12½
1537 A829 40k olive green   7.00   .30
1538 A829 1r indigo   13.00   .70
27th anniversary of the death of Lenin.

Mountain Pasture A830

Government Building, Frunze A831

1951, Feb. 2   Photo.   Perf. 12½
1539 A830 25k dk brown, *blue*   10.00   3.50
1540 A831 40k dp green, *blue*   20.00   6.50
Kirghiz Republic, 25th anniv.

Government Building, Tirana A832

1951, Jan. 6   Unwmk.   Perf. 12
1541 A832 40k green, *bluish*   50.00   40.00
Honoring the Albanian People's Republic.

Bulgarians Greeting Russian Troops A833

Lenin Square, Sofia — A834
Design: 60k, Monument to Soviet soldiers.

1951, Jan. 13
1542 A833 25k gray blk, *bluish*   12.00   5.00
1543 A834 40k org red, *sal*   17.50   10.00
1544 A834 60k blk brn, *sal*   30.00   15.00
Nos. 1542-1544 (3)   59.50   30.00
Honoring the Bulgarian People's Republic.

Choibalsan State University — A835

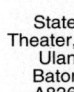
State Theater, Ulan Bator A836

Mongolian Republic Emblem and Flag — A837

1951, Mar. 12
1545 A835 25k purple, *salmon* .55 .65
1546 A836 40k dp orange, *yellow* 1.25 1.00
1547 A837 1r multicolored 3.25 1.50
Nos. 1545-1547 (3) 5.05 3.15

Honoring the Mongolian People's Republic.

D. A. Furmanov (1891-1926) Writer — A838

Furmanov at Work A839

1951, Mar. 17 **Perf. 12½**
1548 A838 40k brown 22.50 2.00
1549 A839 1r gray black, *buff* 27.50 3.00

Russian War Memorial, Berlin — A840

1951, Mar. 21 **Perf. 12**
1550 A840 40k dk gray grn & dk red 40.00 6.00
1551 A840 1r brn blk & red 50.00 14.00

Stockholm Peace Conference.

Kirov Machine Works A841

1951, May 19 **Photo.** **Perf. 12½**
1552 A841 40k brown, *cream* 17.50 3.00

Kirov Machine Works, 150th anniv.

Bolshoi Theater, Moscow — A842

Russian Composers A843

1951, May **Unwmk.**
1553 A842 40k multicolored 10.00 1.00
1554 A843 1r multicolored 10.00 1.25

Bolshoi Theater, Moscow, 175th anniv.

Liberty Bridge, Budapest A844

Monument to Liberators — A845

Budapest Buildings: 40k, Parliament. 60k, National Museum.

1951, June 9 **Perf. 12**
1555 A844 25k emerald 5.00 4.00
1556 A844 40k bright blue 5.00 4.00
1557 A844 60k sepia 10.00 6.00
1558 A845 1r sepia, *salmon* 20.00 10.00
Nos. 1555-1558 (4) 40.00 24.00

Honoring the Hungarian People's Republic.

Harvesting Wheat A846

Designs: 40k, Apiary. 1r, Gathering citrus fruits. 2r, Cotton picking.

1951, June 25
1559 A846 25k dark green 6.50 3.50
1560 A846 40k green, *bluish* 6.50 3.50
1561 A846 1r brown, *yellow* 6.50 6.00
1562 A846 2r dk grn, *sal* 30.00 14.00
Nos. 1559-1562 (4) 49.50 26.00

Kalinin Museum, Moscow — A847

Mikhail I. Kalinin — A848

Design: 1r, Kalinin statue.

1951, Aug. 4 **Perf. 12x12½, 12½x12**
1563 A847 20k org brn & black 1.50 .25
1564 A848 40k dp green & choc 3.00 .50
1565 A848 1r vio blue & gray 5.50 .75
Nos. 1563-1565 (3) 10.00 1.50

5th anniv. of the death of Kalinin.

F. E. Dzerzhinski, 25th Death Anniv. — A849

Design: 1r, Profile of Dzerzhinski.

1951, Aug. 4 **Engr.** **Perf. 12x12½**
1566 A849 40k brown red 12.00 3.00
1567 A849 1r gray black 18.00 5.00

Aleksandr M. Butlerov — A850

A. Kovalevski A850a

P. K. Kozlov A850b

N. S. Kurnakov — A850c

P. N. Lebedev A850d

N. I. Lobachevski A850e

A. N. Lodygin A850f

A. N. Severtsov A850g

K. E. Tsiolkovsky A850h

Russian Scientists: No. 1570 Sonya Kovalevskaya. No. 1572, S. P. Krashenin-nikov. No. 1577, D. I. Mendeleev. No. 1578, N. N. Miklukho-Maklai. No. 1580, A. G. Stoletov. No. 1581, K. A. Timiryasev. No. 1583, P. N. Yablochkov.

1951, Aug. 15 **Photo.** **Perf. 12½**
1568 A850 40k org red, *bluish* 12.50 1.25
1569 A850a 40k dk blue, *sal* 4.75 .50
1570 A850 40k pur, *salmon* 4.75 .50
1571 A850b 40k orange red 4.75 .50
1572 A850 40k purple 4.75 .50
1573 A850c 40k brn, *sal* 4.75 .50
1574 A850 40k blue 4.75 .50
1575 A850e 40k brown 4.75 .50
1576 A850f 40k green 4.75 .50
1577 A850 40k deep blue 4.75 .50
1578 A850g 40k org red, *sal* 4.75 .50
1579 A850 40k sepia, *sal* 4.75 .50
1580 A850 40k grn, *sal* 4.75 .50
1581 A850 40k brn, *sal* 4.75 .50
1582 A850h 40k gray blk, *blue* 20.00 1.40
1583 A850 40k sepia 4.75 .50
Nos. 1568-1583 (16) 99.00 9.65

Two printings exist in differing stamp sizes of most of this issue.

A. A. Aliabiev — A851

Design: No. 1585, V. S. Kalinnikov.

1951, Aug. 28
1584 A851 40k brown, *salmon* 50.00 15.00
1585 A851 40k gray, *salmon* 50.00 15.00

Russian composers.

Opera and Ballet Theater, Tbilisi — A852

Gathering Citrus Fruit — A853

40k, Principal street, Tbilisi. 1r, Picking tea.

1951 **Unwmk.** **Perf. 12½**
1586 A852 20k dp grn, *yellow* 5.00 1.60
1587 A853 25k pur, org & brn 5.00 1.60
1588 A853 40k dk brn, *blue* 22.50 3.50
1589 A853 1r red brn & dk grn 17.50 8.00
Nos. 1586-1589 (4) 50.00 14.70

Georgian Republic, 30th anniversary.

Emblem of
Aviation
Society — A854

Planes and Emblem — A855

60k, Flying model planes. 1r, Parachutists.

1951, Sept. 19   Litho.   Perf. 12½
Dated: "1951"
1590 A854 40k multicolored   3.00   .25
1591 A854 60k emer, lt bl & brn   10.00   .45
1592 A854 1r blue, sal & lilac   12.50   .45
1593 A855 2r multicolored   22.50   1.00
    Nos. 1590-1593 (4)   48.00   2.15
    Promoting interest in aviation.

Victor M.
Vasnetsov (1848-
1926),
Painter — A856

Three Heroes, by Vasnetsov — A857

1951, Oct. 15
1594 A856 40k dk bl, brn & buff   12.00   .75
1595 A857 1r multicolored   18.00   1.25

Hydroelectric
Station, Lenin
and
Stalin — A858

Design: 1r, Spasski Tower, Kremlin.

1951, Nov. 6   Photo.   Perf. 12½
Dated: "1917-1951"
1596 A858 40k blue vio & red   35.00 10.00
1597 A858 1r dk brown & red   65.00 35.00
    34th anniversary of October Revolution.

Map, Dredge
and
Khakhovsky
Hydroelectric
Station
A859

Map, Volga Dam and Tugboat — A860

Designs (each showing map): 40k, Stalingrad Dam. 60k, Excavating Turkmenian canal.
1r, Kuibyshev dam.

1951, Nov. 28   Perf. 12½
1598 A859 20k multicolored   18.00   3.00
1599 A860 30k multicolored   27.00   4.50
1600 A860 40k multicolored   32.50   6.50
1601 A860 60k multicolored   55.00   9.50
1602 A860 1r multicolored   115.00   15.00
    Nos. 1598-1602 (5)   247.50   38.50

Flag and
Citizens Signing
Peace
Appeal — A861

1951, Nov. 30   Perf. 12½
1603 A861 40k gray & red   20.00   7.00
    Third All-Union Peace Conference.

Mikhail V.
Ostrogradski,
Mathematician,
150th Birth
Anniv. — A862

1951, Dec. 10   Unwmk.
1604 A862 40k black brn, *pink* 17.50 10.00

Monument to Jan
Zizka,
Prague — A863

Monument to
Soviet
Liberators
A864

25k, Monument to Soviet Soldiers, Ostrava.
40k, Julius Fucik. 60k, Smetana Museum,
Prague.

1951, Dec. 10   Perf. 12½
1605 A863 20k vio blue, *sal*   16.00   3.00
1606 A863 25k copper red,
              yel   35.00   12.50
1607 A863 40k red org, *sal*   60.00   7.50

1608 A863 60k brnsh gray,
              buff   35.00   6.00
1609 A864 1r brnsh gray,
              buff   30.00   9.00
    Nos. 1605-1609 (5)   176.00   38.00
    Soviet-Czechoslovakian friendship.

Volkhovski Hydroelectric Station and
Lenin Statue — A865

1951, Dec. 19
1610 A865 40k dk bl, gray & yel   6.00   .25
1611 A865 1r pur, gray & yel   14.00   .55
    25th anniv. of the opening of the Lenin
Volkhovski hydroelectric station.

Lenin as a
Schoolboy
A866

Horizontal Designs: 60k, Lenin among children. 1r, Lenin and peasants.

1952, Jan. 24   Photo.   Perf. 12½
Multicolored Centers
1612 A866 40k dk blue green   2.25   .55
1613 A866 60k violet blue   3.25   .55
1614 A866 1r orange brown   4.50   .65
    Nos. 1612-1614 (3)   10.00   1.75
    28th anniversary of the death of Lenin.

Semenov — A867

1952, Feb. 1
1615 A867 1r sepia, *blue*   15.00   8.00
    Petr Petrovich Semenov-Tianshanski (1827-
1914), traveler and geographer who explored
the Tian Shan mountains.

Kovalevski — A868

1952, Mar. 3   Unwmk.
1616 A868 40k sepia, *yellow*   25.00   10.00
    V. O. Kovalevski (1843-1883), biologist and
palaeontologist.

Skaters
A869

1952, Mar. 3
1617 A869 40k shown   4.00   .40
1618 A869 60k Skiers   6.00   .60

N. V. Gogol and Characters from
"Taras Bulba" — A870

Designs: 60k, Gogol and V. G. Belinski. 1r,
Gogol and Ukrainian peasants.

1952, Mar. 4   Dated: "1852-1952"
1619 A870 40k sepia, *blue*   5.00   .50
1620 A870 60k multicolored   5.00   .50
1621 A870 1r multicolored   15.00   1.00
    Nos. 1619-1621 (3)   25.00   2.00
    Death centenary of N. V. Gogol, writer.

G. K. Ordzhonikidze
A871

1952, Apr. 23   Photo.   Perf. 12½
1622 A871 40k dp green, *pink* 19.00   8.50
1623 A871 1r sepia, *blue*   11.00   3.50
    15th anniv. of the death of Grigori K.
Ordzhonikidze, Georgian party worker.

Workers and
Soviet
Flag — A872

Workers'
Rest Home
A873

No. 1626, Aged citizens. No. 1627,
Schoolgirl.

1952, May 15   Unwmk.
1624 A872 40k red & blk,
              cream   40.00   10.00
1625 A873 40k red & dk grn,
              pale gray   80.00   18.00
1626 A873 40k red & brown,
              pale gray   40.00   10.00
1627 A872 40k red & black,
              pale gray   40.00   10.00
    Nos. 1624-1627 (4)   200.00   48.00
    Adoption of Stalin constitution., 15th anniv

A. S. Novikov-Priboy and Ship — A874

1952, June 5
1628 A874 40k blk, pale cit & bl
              grn   1.00   .30
    Novikov-Priboy, writer, 75th birthanniv.

150th anniv. of Birth of Victor Hugo (1802-1855), French Writer — A875

1952, June 5   Unwmk.   Perf. 12½
1629 A875 40k brn org, gray & black   2.00 .25

Julaev — A876

1952, June 28
1630 A876 40k rose red, *pink*   1.00 .25
200th anniversary of the birth of Salavat Julaev, Bashkir hero who took part in the insurrection of 1773-1775.

Sedov — A877

1952, July 4
1631 A877 40k dk bl, dk brn & blue green   37.50 8.00
Georgi J. Sedov, Arctic explorer (1877-1914).

Arms and Flag of Romania — A878

University Square, Bucharest A879

Design: 60k, Monument to Soviet soldiers.

1952, July 26
1632 A878 40k multicolored   4.50 1.00
1633 A878 60k dk green, *pink*   7.50 2.50
1634 A879 1r bright ultra   13.00 5.00
      Nos. 1632-1634 (3)   25.00 8.50

Zhukovski — A880

Design: No. 1636, K. P. Bryullov.

1952, July 26   Pale Blue Paper
1635 A880 40k gray black   10.00 .50
1636 A880 40k brt blue green   10.00 .50
V. A. Zhukovski, poet, and Bryullov, painter (1799-1852).

Ogarev — A881

1952, Aug. 29
1637 A881 40k deep green   .75 .25
75th anniversary of the death of N. P. Ogarev, poet and revolutionary.

Uspenski — A882

1952, Sept. 4
1638 A882 40k indigo & dk brn   2.00 .50
Gleb Ivanovich Uspenski (1843-1902), writer.

Nakhimov — A883

1952, Sept. 9
1639 A883 40k multicolored   5.00 2.00
Adm. Paul S. Nakhimov (1802-1855).

University Building, Tartu — A884

1952, Oct. 2
1640 A884 40k black brn, *sal*   20.00 3.00
150th anniversary of the enlargement of the University of Tartu, Estonia.

Kajum Nasyri — A885

1952, Nov. 5
1641 A885 40k brown, *yellow*   15.00 5.00
Nasyri (1825-1902), Tartar educator.

A. N. Radishchev — A886

1952, Oct. 23
1642 A886 40k blk, brn & dk red   6.00 1.00
Radishchev, writer, 150th death anniv.

M.S. Joseph Stalin at Entrance to Volga-Don Canal — A887

Design: 1r, Lenin, Stalin and red banners.

1952, Nov. 6   Perf. 12½
1643 A887 40k multicolored   15.00 6.00
1644 A887 1r brown, red & yel   25.00 9.00
35th anniversary of October Revolution.

Pavel Andreievitch Fedotov (1815-52), Artist — A888

1952, Nov. 26
1645 A888 40k red brn & black   2.00 .50

V. D. Polenov, Artist, 25th Death Anniv. — A889

"Moscow Courtyard" — A890

1952, Dec. 6
1646 A889 40k red brown & buff   3.50 .35
1647 A890 1r multicolored   4.50 .65

A. I. Odoyevski (1802-39) Poet — A891

1952, Dec. 8
1648 A891 40k gray blk & red org 5.00 .50

D. N. Mamin-Sibiryak — A892

1952, Dec. 15
1649 A892 40k dp green, *cream* 2.00 .50
Centenary of the birth of Dimitrii N. Mamin-Sibiryak (1852-1912), writer.

Composite Medal Types of 1946 Frames as A599-A606 Centers as Indicated

Medals: 1r, Token of Veneration. 2r, Red Star. 3r, Red Workers' Banner. 5r, Red Banner. 10r, Lenin.

1952-59		Engr.	Perf. 12½	
1650	A569	1r dark brown	9.00	7.00
1651	A567	2r red brown	1.40	.55
1652	A572	3r dp blue violet	2.00	.95
1653	A571	5r dk car ('53)	2.50	.95
1654	A566	10r bright rose	4.50	1.90
a.		10r dull red ('59)	5.00	2.00
		Nos. 1650-1654 (5)	19.40	11.35

Vladimir M. Bekhterev (1857-1927), Neuropathologist A893

1952, Dec. 24   Photo.
1655 A893 40k vio bl, slate & blk 3.00 .50

Byelorusskaya Station — A894

Designs (Moscow Subway stations): 40k, Botanical Garden Station. 40k, Novoslobodskaya Station. 40k, Komsomolskaya Station.

1952, Dec. 30   Multicolored Centers
1656 A894 40k dull violet 3.50 .50
1657 A894 40k light ultra 3.50 .50
1658 A894 40k blue gray 3.50 .50
1659 A894 40k dull green 3.50 .50
a.   Horiz. strip of 4, #1656-1659 15.00 4.00

USSR Emblem and Flags of 16 Union Republics — A895

1952, Dec. 30
1660 A895 1r grn, dk red & brn 25.00 4.50
30th anniversary of the USSR.

Lenin — A896

1953, Jan. 26
1661 A896 40k multicolored   10.00 4.00
29 years without Lenin.

Stalin Peace
Medal — A897

1953, Apr. 30   *Perf. 12½*
1662 A897 40k red brn, bl &
     dull yel   12.00 6.00

Valerian V.
Kuibyshev
A898

1953, June 6
1663 A898 40k red brn & black   3.00 .55
Kuibyshev (1888-1935), Bolshevik leader.

A899

1953, July 21
1664 A899 40k buff & dk brown   20.00 1.25
Nikolai G. Chernyshevski (1828-1889),
writer and radical leader; exiled to Siberia for
24 years.

A900

1953, July 19
1665 A900 40k ver & gray brown   8.00 2.00
60th anniv. of the birth of Vladimir V.
Mayakovsky, poet.

Tsymijanskaja Dam — A901

Volga-Don Canal: No. 1666, Lock No. 9,
Volga-Don Canal. No. 1667, Lock 13. No.
1668, Lock 15. No. 1669, Volga River lighthouse. No. 1671, M. S. "Joseph Stalin" in
canal.

1953, Aug. 29   **Litho.**
1666 A901 40k multicolored   4.00 1.00
1667 A901 40k multicolored   4.00 2.00
1668 A901 40k multicolored   4.00 1.00
1669 A901 40k multicolored   4.00 2.00
1670 A901 40k multicolored   4.00 1.00
1671 A901   1r multicolored   5.00 1.00
   Nos. 1666-1671 (6)   25.00 8.00

V. G.
Korolenko
(1853-1921),
Writer — A902

1953, Aug. 29   Photo.   *Perf. 12x12½*
1672 A902 40k brown   2.00 .25

Count Leo N.
Tolstoy (1828-1910),
Writer — A903

1953, Sept.   *Perf. 12*
1673 A903   1r dark brown   15.00 5.00

Moscow
University and
Two
Youths — A904

1r, Komsomol badge and four orders.

1953, Oct. 29   *Perf. 12½x12*
1674 A904 40k multicolored   12.50 2.00
1675 A904   1r multicolored   22.50 3.00
35th anniversary of the Young Communist
League (Komsomol).

Nationalities of
the Soviet
Union — A905

60k, Lenin and Stalin at Smolny.

1953, Nov. 6
1676 A905 40k multicolored   30.00 10.00
1677 A905 60k multicolored   50.00 15.00
36th anniversary of October Revolution.
No. 1676 measures 25½x38mm; No. 1677,
25½x42mm.

Lenin and His
Writings — A906

1r, Lenin facing left and pages of "What to
Do."

1953
1678 A906 40k multicolored   8.00 4.00
1679 A906   1r dk brn, org brn
     & red   14.00 8.50
Communist Party formation, 50th anniv.
(40k). 2nd cong. of the Russian Socialist
Party, 50th anniv. (1r).
   Issued: 40k, 11/12; 1r, 12/14.

Lenin
Statue — A907

Peter I Statue, Decembrists'
Square — A908

Leningrad Views: Nos. 1681 & 1683, Admiralty building. Nos. 1685 & 1687, Smolny
Institute.

1953, Nov. 23
1680 A907 40k brn blk, *yellow*   8.00 4.00
1681 A907 40k vio brn, *yellow*   8.00 4.00
1682 A907 40k dk brn, *pink*   6.00 3.00
1683 A907 40k brn blk, *cream*   6.00 3.00
1684 A908   1r dk brn, *blue*   17.50 10.00
1685 A908   1r dk green, *pink*   17.50 10.00
1686 A908   1r violet, *yellow*   14.00 9.00
1687 A908   1r blk brn, *blue*   14.00 9.00
   Nos. 1680-1687 (8)   91.00 52.00
See Nos. 1944-1945, 1943a.

"Pioneers" and
Model of
Lomonosov Moscow
University — A909

1953, Dec. 22   **Litho.**   *Perf. 12*
1688 A909 40k dk sl grn, dk brn
     & red   5.00 1.75

Arms Type of 1948

1954-57
1689 A682 40k scarlet   1.00 .50
   a.   8 ribbon turns on wreath at left
     ('54)   4.25 1.65
No. 1689 was re-issued in 1954-56 typographed in slightly smaller format:
14½x21¾mm, instead of 14¾x21¾mm, and in
a lighter shade. See note after No. 738.
No. 1689 has 7 ribbon turns on left side of
wreath.

Aleksandr S.
Griboedov, Writer
(1795-1829)
A910

1954, Mar. 4   **Photo.**
1690 A910 40k dp claret, *cream*   2.25 .75
1691 A910   1r black, *green*   5.75 2.00

Kremlin
View — A911

1954, Mar. 7   Litho.   *Perf. 12½x12*
1692 A911 40k red & gray   12.00 3.00
1954 elections to the Supreme Soviet.

V. P.
Chkalov — A912

1954, Mar. 16   *Perf. 12*
1693 A912   1r gray, vio bl & dk
     brown   20.00 10.00
50th anniversary of the birth of Valeri P.
Chkalov (1904-1938), airplane pilot.

Lenin — A913

Lenin at
Smolny
A914

Designs: No. 1696, Lenin's home (later
museum), Ulyanovsk. No. 1697, Lenin
addressing workers. No. 1698, Lenin among
students, University of Kazan.

1954, Apr. 16   **Photo.**
1694 A913 40k multicolored   6.00 2.00
   Size: 38x27½mm
1695 A914 40k multicolored   6.00 2.00
1696 A914 40k multicolored   6.00 2.00
   Size: 48x35mm
1697 A914 40k multicolored   6.00 2.00
1698 A914 40k multicolored   6.00 2.00
   Nos. 1694-1698 (5)   30.00 10.00
30th anniversary of the death of Lenin.
For overprint see No. 2060.

Joseph V. Stalin — A915

1954, Apr. 30   Unwmk.   *Perf. 12*
1699 A915 40k dark brown   15.00 2.00
First anniversary of the death of Stalin.

Supreme Soviet Buildings in Kiev and Moscow A916

T. G. Shevchenko Statue, Kharkov — A917

Designs: No. 1701, University building, Kiev. No. 1702, Opera, Kiev. No. 1703, Ukranian Academy of Science. No. 1705, Bogdan Chmielnicki statue, Kiev. No. 1706 Flags of Soviet Russia and Ukraine. No. 1707, T. G. Shevchenko statue, Kanev. No. 1708, Chmielnicki proclaming reunion of Ukraine and Russia, 1654.

1954, May 10   Litho.
Size: 37½x26mm, 26x37½mm
1700 A916 40k red brn, sal, cream & black   2.50 .25
1701 A916 40k ultra, vio bl & brn 2.50 .25
1702 A916 40k red brn, buff, blue brown   2.50 .25
1703 A916 40k org brn, cream & grn   2.50 .25
1704 A917 40k rose red, blk, yel & brown   2.25 .25
1705 A917 60k multicolored   3.00 .30
1706 A917 1r multicolored   5.00 .50
Size: 42x28mm
1707 A916 1r multicolored   3.50 .75
Size: 45x29½mm
1708 A916 1r multicolored, pink 5.00 .75

No. 1341 Overprinted in Carmine

1709 A517 2r green   9.00 1.75
Nos. 1700-1709 (10)   37.75 5.30
300th anniversary of the union between the Ukraine and Russia.

Sailboat Race A918

Basketball A919

No. 1711, Hurdle race. No. 1712, Swimmers. No. 1713, Cyclists. No. 1714, Track. No. 1715, Skier. No. 1716, Mountain climbing.

1954, May 29
Frames in Orange Brown
1710 A918 40k blue & black   2.25 .35
1711 A918 40k vio gray & blk   2.25 .35
1712 A918 40k dk blue & black   2.25 .35
1713 A918 40k dk brn & buff   2.25 .35
1714 A918 40k black brn & buff   2.25 .35
1715 A918 1r blue & black   5.50 .95
1716 A918 1r blue & black   5.50 .90
1717 A919 1r dk brn & brn   7.50 1.50
Nos. 1710-1717 (8)   29.75 5.10

For overprint see No. 2170.

Cattle A920

No. 1719, Potato planting and cultivation. No. 1720, Kolkhoz hydroelectric station.

1954, June 8
1718 A920 40k brn, cream, ind & blue gray   3.75 1.00
1719 A920 40k gray grn, buff & brown   3.75 1.00
1720 A920 40k blk, bl grn & vio bl   3.75 1.00
Nos. 1718-1720 (3)   11.25 3.00

Anton P. Chekhov, Writer, 50th Death Anniv. — A921

1954, July 15
1721 A921 40k green & black brn 5.00 .50

F. A. Bredichin, V. J. Struve, A. A. Belopolski and Observatory — A922

1954, July 26
1722 A922 40k vio bl, blk & blue 10.00 1.00
Restoration of Pulkov Observatory.

Mikhail I. Glinka, Composer, 150th Birth Anniv. — A923

Pushkin and Zhukovsky Visiting Glinka A924

1954, July 26
1723 A923 40k dp cl, pink & blk brown   6.00 1.00
1724 A924 60k multicolored   9.00 2.00

Nikolai A. Ostrovsky (1904-36), Blind Writer — A925

1954, Sept. 29 Photo. Perf. 12½x12
1725 A925 40k brn, dark red & yel   7.00 1.00

Monument to Sunken Ships — A926

Defenders of Sevastopol — A927

Design: 1r, Admiral P. S. Nakhimov.

1954, Oct. 17   Perf. 12½
1726 A926 40k blue grn, blk & ol brown   4.00 1.10
1727 A927 60k org brn, blk & brn   5.50 1.60
1728 A926 1r brn, blk & ol green   10.50 2.25
Nos. 1726-1728 (3)   20.00 4.95
Centenary of the defense of Sevastopol during the Crimean War.

Sculpture at Exhibition Entrance — A928

Agriculture Pavilion — A929

Cattle Pavilion A929a

Designs: No. 1732, Machinery pavilion. No. 1733, Main entrance. No. 1734, Main pavilion.

Perf. 12½, 12½x12, 12x12½
1954, Nov. 5   Litho.
Size: 26x37mm
1729 A928 40k multicolored   2.00 .50
Size: 40x29mm
1730 A929 40k multicolored   2.00 .50
1731 A929a 40k multicolored   2.00 .50
1732 A929 40k multicolored   2.00 .50
Size: 40½x33mm
1733 A929 1r multicolored   6.00 2.00
Size: 28½x40½mm
1734 A928 1r multicolored   6.00 2.00
Nos. 1729-1734 (6)   20.00 6.00

1954 Agricultural Exhibition.

Marx, Engels, Lenin and Stalin — A930

1954, Nov. 6   Photo.   Perf. 12½x12
1735 A930 1r dk brn, pale org & red   6.00 2.50
37th anniversary of October Revolution.

Kazan University Building A931

1954, Nov. 11   *Perf. 12x12½*
1736 A931 40k deep blue   1.75 .50
1737 A931 60k claret   3.25 1.00
Founding of Kazan University, 150th anniv.

Salome Neris A932

1954, Nov. 17   *Perf. 12½x12*
1738 A932 40k red org & ol gray 4.00 1.50
50th anniversary of the birth of Salome Neris (1904-1945), Lithuanian poet.

Vegetables and Garden A933

Cultivating Flax — A934

Designs: No. 1741, Tractor plowing field. No. 1742, Loading ensilage.

1954, Dec. 12   Litho.   *Perf. 12x12½*
1739	A933	40k multicolored	1.60	.50
1740	A934	40k multicolored	1.60	.50
1741	A933	40k multicolored	1.60	.50
1742	A934	60k multicolored	7.25	.50
		Nos. 1739-1742 (4)	12.05	2.00

Joseph Stalin, 75th Birth Anniv. — A935

1954, Dec. 21   Engr.   *Perf. 12½x12*
| 1743 | A935 | 40k rose brown | 1.50 | .50 |
| 1744 | A935 | 1r dark blue | 3.50 | .60 |

Anton G. Rubinstein (1829-94), Composer A936

1954, Dec. 30   Photo.
| 1745 | A936 | 40k claret, gray & blk | 4.00 | 1.00 |

Vsevolod M. Garshin (1855-1888), Writer — A937

Lithographed and Photogravure
1955, Mar. 2   Unwmk.   *Perf. 12*
| 1746 | A937 | 40k buff, blk brn & green | 2.00 | .50 |

K. A. Savitsky and Painting A938

1955, Mar. 21   Photo.
1747	A938	40k multicolored	3.00	.30
a.		Sheet of 4, black inscription	35.00	35.00
b.		As "a," red brown inscription	35.00	35.00

K. A. Savitsky (1844-1905), painter. Size: Nos. 1747a, 1747b, 152x108mm.

Globe and Clasped Hands — A939

1955, Apr. 9   Litho.
| 1748 | A939 | 40k multicolored | 2.00 | .50 |

International Conference of Public Service Unions, Vienna, April 1955.

Poets Pushkin and Mickiewicz — A940

Brothers in Arms Monument, Warsaw — A941

Palace of Culture and Science, Warsaw A942

Copernicus, Painting by Jan Matejko (in Medallion) — A943

Unwmk.
1955, Apr. 22   Photo.   *Perf. 12*
1749	A940	40k chalky blue, vio & black	2.50	.35
1750	A941	40k violet black	2.50	.35
1751	A942	1r brt red & gray black	5.50	1.25
1752	A943	1r multicolored	5.50	1.25
		Nos. 1749-1752 (4)	16.00	3.20

Polish-USSR treaty of friendship, 10th anniv.

Lenin at Shushinskoe — A944

Lenin at Secret Printing House — A945

Design: 1r, Lenin and Krupskaya with peasants at Gorki, 1921.

1955, Apr. 22
Frame and Inscription in Dark Red
1753	A944	60k multicolored	1.50	.50
1754	A944	1r multicolored	3.00	.75
1755	A945	1r multicolored	3.00	.75
		Nos. 1753-1755 (3)	7.50	2.00

85th anniversary of the birth of Lenin.

Friedrich von Schiller — A946

1955, May 10
| 1756 | A946 | 40k chocolate | 2.00 | .50 |

150th anniversary of the death of Friedrich von Schiller, German poet.

A. G. Venezianov and "Spring on the Land" — A947

1955, June 21   Photo.
| 1757 | A947 | 1r multicolored | 5.00 | .50 |
| a. | | Souvenir sheet of 4 | 45.00 | 25.00 |

Venezianov, painter, 175th birth anniv.

Anatoli K. Liadov (1855-1914), Composer — A948

1955, July 5   Litho.
| 1758 | A948 | 40k red brn, blk & lt brn | 2.50 | .50 |

Aleksandr Popov — A949

1955, Nov. 5
Portraits Multicolored
| 1759 | A949 | 40k light ultra | 1.75 | .50 |
| 1760 | A949 | 1r gray brown | 3.25 | .50 |

60th anniv. of the construction of a coherer for detecting Hertzian electromagnetic waves by A. S. Popov, radio pioneer.

Lenin — A950

Storming the Winter Palace — A951

Design: 1r, Lenin addressing the people.

1955, Nov. 6
1761	A950	40k multicolored	3.00	1.00
1762	A951	40k multicolored	3.00	1.00
1763	A951	1r multicolored	7.50	2.00
		Nos. 1761-1763 (3)	13.50	4.00

38th anniversary of October Revolution.

Apartment Houses, Magnitogorsk — A952

1955, Nov. 29
| 1764 | A952 | 40k multicolored | 3.00 | 1.00 |

25th anniversary of the founding of the industrial center, Magnitogorsk.

Arctic Observation Post — A953

Design: 1r, Scientist at observation post.

1955, Nov. 29   *Perf. 12½x12*
1765	A953	40k multicolored	6.00	2.00
1766	A953	60k multicolored	6.00	2.00
1767	A953	1r multicolored	6.00	2.00
a.		Souvenir sheet of 4 ('58)	35.00	50.00
		Nos. 1765-1767 (3)	18.00	6.00

Publicizing the Soviet scientific drifting stations at the North Pole.

In 1962, No. 1767a was overprinted in red "1962" on each stamp and, in the lower sheet margin, a three-line Russian inscription meaning "25 years from the beginning of the work of "NP-1" station."

Sheet value, $75 unused, $100 canceled.

Fedor Ivanovich Shubin (1740-1805), Sculptor — A954

1955, Dec. 22   *Perf. 12*
| 1768 | A954 | 40k green & multi | 1.00 | .35 |
| 1769 | A954 | 1r brown & multi | 1.00 | .35 |

Federal Socialist Republic Pavilion (R.S.F.S.R.) — A955

ПАВИЛЬОН ТАДЖИКСКОЙ ССР
No. 1771

ПАВИЛЬОН БЕЛОРУССКОЙ ССР
No. 1772

ПАВИЛЬОН АЗЕРБАЙДЖАНСКОЙ ССР
No. 1773

ПАВИЛЬОН ГРУЗИНСКОЙ ССР
No. 1774

ПАВИЛЬОН АРМЯНСКОЙ ССР
No. 1775

ПАВИЛЬОН ТУРКМЕНСКОЙ ССР
No. 1776

(ПАВИЛЬОН УЗБЕКСКОЙ ССР)
No. 1777

(ПАВИЛЬОН УКРАИНСКОЙ ССР)
No. 1778

(ПАВИЛЬОН КАЗАХСКОЙ ССР)
No. 1779

(ПАВИЛЬОН КИРГИЗСКОЙ ССР)
No. 1780

(ПАВИЛЬОН КАРЕЛО-ФИНСКОЙ ССР)
No. 1781

(ПАВИЛЬОН МОЛДАВСКОЙ ССР)
No. 1782

(ПАВИЛЬОН ЭСТОНСКОЙ ССР)
No. 1783

(ПАВИЛЬОН ЛАТВИЙСКОЙ ССР)
No. 1784

(ПАВИЛЬОН ЛИТОВСКОЙ ССР)
No. 1785

Designs: Pavilions.

1955   **Litho.**   **Unwmk.**
Centers in Natural Colors; Frames
in Blue Green and Olive

1770	A955	40k shown	1.00	.50
a.		Sheet of 4	15.00	15.00
1771	A955	40k Tadzhik	1.00	.50
1772	A955	40k Byelorussian	1.00	.50
a.		Sheet of 4	15.00	15.00
1773	A955	40k Azerbaijan	1.00	.50
1774	A955	40k Georgian	1.00	.50
1775	A955	40k Armenian	1.00	.50
1776	A955	40k Turkmen	1.00	.50
1777	A955	40k Uzbek	1.00	.50
1778	A955	40k Ukrainian	1.00	.50
a.		Sheet of 4	15.00	15.00
1779	A955	40k Kazakh	1.00	.50
1780	A955	40k Kirghiz	1.00	.50
1781	A955	40k Karelo-Finnish	1.00	.50
1782	A955	40k Moldavian	1.00	.50
1783	A955	40k Estonian	1.00	.50
1784	A955	40k Latvian	1.00	.50
1785	A955	40k Lithuanian	1.00	.50
		Nos. 1770-1785 (16)	16.00	8.00

All-Union Agricultural Fair.
Nos. 1773-1785 were printed in sheets containing various stamps, providing a variety of horizontal se-tenant pairs and strips. Value, $50 per sheet.

Lomonosov Moscow State University,
200th Anniv. — A956

Design: 1r, New University buildings.

1955, June 9   **Perf. 12**

1786	A956	40k multicolored	2.00	.25
a.		Sheet of 4 ('56)	10.00	10.00
1787	A956	1r multicolored	4.00	.50
a.		Sheet of 4 ('56)	20.00	20.00

Vladimir V. Mayakovsky — A957

1955, May 31
1788   A957   40k multicolored   2.00   .50
Mayakovsky, poet, 25th death anniv.

Race
Horse — A958

Trotter
A959

1956, Jan. 9

1789	A958	40k dark brown	3.00	.40
1790	A958	60k Prus grn & blue green	4.50	.60
1791	A959	1r dull pur & blue vio	7.50	1.00
		Nos. 1789-1791 (3)	15.00	2.00

International Horse Races, Moscow, Aug. 14-Sept. 4, 1955.

Alexei N. Krylov
(1863-1945),
Mathematician,
Naval
Architect — A960

1956, Jan. 9
1792   A960   40k gray, brown & black   2.00   .50

Symbol of
Spartacist
Games, Stadium
and
Factories — A961

1956, Jan. 18
1793   A961   1r red vio & lt grn   2.00   .50
5th All-Union Spartacist Games of Soviet Trade Union sport clubs, Moscow, Aug. 12-18, 1955.

Atomic
Power
Station
A962

Design: 60k, Atomic Reactor.

1956, Jan. 31

1794	A962	25k multicolored	1.25	.40
1795	A962	60k multicolored	3.25	1.00
1796	A962	1r multicolored	5.50	1.75
		Nos. 1794-1796 (3)	10.00	3.15

Establishment of the first Atomic Power Station of the USSR Academy of Science. Inscribed in Russian: "Atomic Energy in the service of the people."

Statue of
Lenin,
Kremlin and
Flags
A963

1956, Feb.
1797   A963   40k multicolored   5.00   .50
1798   A963   1r ol, buff & red org   7.00   1.50
20th Congress of the Communist Party of the Soviet Union.

Khachatur
Abovian,
Armenian Writer,
150th Birth
Anniv. — A964

1956, Feb. 25   **Unwmk.**   **Perf. 12**
1799   A964   40k black brn, *bluish*   5.00   .50

Workers with Red
Flag — A965

1956, Mar. 14
1800   A965   40k multicolored   6.00   .75
Revolution of 1905, 50th anniversary.

Nikolai A.
Kasatkin — A966

1956, Apr. 30
1801   A966   40k carmine lake   2.00   .50
Kasatkin (1859-1930), painter.

"On the
Oka
River"
A967

1956, Apr. 30
     Center Multicolored
1802   A967   40k bister & black   5.00   .40
1803   A967   1r ultra & black   7.00   .60
A. E. Arkhipov, painter.

I. P. Kulibin,
Inventor, 220th
Birth
Anniv. — A968

1956, May 12
1804   A968   40k multicolored   2.00   .25

Vassili
Grigorievitch
Perov (1833-82),
Painter — A969

"Birdcatchers" — A970

Painting: No. 1807, "Hunters at Rest."

1956, May 12
     Multicolored Centers
1805   A969   40k green   3.00   .40
1806   A970   1r brown   6.00   .80
1807   A970   1r orange brown   6.00   .80
     Nos. 1805-1807 (3)   15.00   2.00

Ural
Pavilion
A971

(ПАВИЛЬОН ТАТАРСКОЙ АССР)
No. 1809

(ПАВИЛЬОН "ПОВОЛЖЬЕ")
No. 1810

(ПАВИЛЬОН ЦЕНТРАЛЬНЫХ ЧЕРНОЗЕМНЫХ ОБЛАСТЕЙ)
No. 1811

(ПАВИЛЬОН СЕВЕРО-ВОСТОЧНЫХ ОБЛАСТЕЙ)
No. 1812

(ПАВИЛЬОН СЕВЕРНОГО КАВКАЗА)
No. 1813

(ПАВИЛЬОН БАШКИРСКОЙ АССР)
No. 1814

(ПАВИЛЬОН ДАЛЬНЕГО ВОСТОКА)
No. 1815

(ПАВИЛЬОН ЦЕНТРАЛЬНЫХ ОБЛАСТЕЙ)
No. 1816

(ПАВИЛЬОН ЮНЫХ НАТУРАЛИСТОВ)
No. 1817

(ПАВИЛЬОН "СИБИРЬ")
No. 1818

(ПАВИЛЬОН "ЛЕНИНГРАД-СЕВЕРО-ЗАПАД")
No. 1819

No. 1820

Pavilions: No. 1809, Tatar Republic. No. 1810, Volga District. No. 1811, Central Black Earth Area. No. 1812, Northeastern District. No. 1813, Northern Caucasus. No. 1814, Bashkir Republic. No. 1815, Far East. No. 1816, Central Asia. No. 1817, Young Naturalists. No. 1818, Siberia. No. 1819, Leningrad and Northwestern District. No. 1820, Moscow, Tula, Kaluga, Ryazan and Bryansk Districts.

1956, Apr. 25
Multicolored Centers

1808	A971	1r yel green & pale yel	3.00	.50
1809	A971	1r blue grn & pale yel	3.00	.50
1810	A971	1r dk blue grn & pale yel	3.00	.50
1811	A971	1r dk bl grn & yel grn	3.00	.50
1812	A971	1r dk blue grn & buff	3.00	.50
1813	A971	1r ol gray & pale yel	3.00	.50
1814	A971	1r olive & yellow	3.00	.50
1815	A971	1r olive grn & lemon	3.00	.50
1816	A971	1r olive brn & lemon	3.00	.50
1817	A971	1r olive brn & lemon	3.00	.50
1818	A971	1r brown & yellow	3.00	.50
1819	A971	1r redsh brown & yel	3.00	.50
1820	A971	1r dk red brn & yel	3.00	.50
		Nos. 1808-1820 (13)	39.00	6.50

All-Union Agricultural Fair, Moscow.
Six of the Pavilion set were printed se-tenant in one sheet of 30 (6x5), the strip containing Nos. 1809, 1816, 1817, 1813, 1818 and 1810 in that order. Two others, Nos. 1819-1820, were printed se-tenant in one sheet of 35. Value, $50 per sheet.

Lenin — A972

1956, May 25
1821	A972	40k lilac & multi	6.00	1.00

86th anniversary of the birth of Lenin.

Lobachevski A973

1956, June 4
1822	A973	40k black brown	2.00	.25

Nikolai Ivanovich Lobachevski (1793-1856), mathematician.

Nurse and Textile Factory A974

No. 1824, First aid instruction.

1956, June 4   **Unwmk.**
1823	A974	40k lt ol grn, grnsh bl & red	3.00	.25
1824	A974	40k red brn, lt bl & red	3.00	.25

Red Cross and Red Crescent. No. 1823 measures 37x25mm; No. 1824, 40x28mm.

V. K. Arseniev (1872-1930), Explorer and Writer — A975

1956, June 15   **Litho.**   **Perf. 12**
1825	A975	40k violet, black & rose	3.00	.50

I. M. Sechenov (1829-1905), Physiologist A976

1956, June 15
1826	A976	40k multicolored	2.00	.50

A. K. Savrasov, Painter — A977

1956, June 22
1827	A977	1r dull yel & brown	3.00	.50

I. V. Michurin, Scientist, Birth Centenary A978

Design: 60k, I. V. Michurin with Pioneers.

1956, June 22
Center Multicolored
1828	A978	25k dark brown	.55	.25
1829	A978	60k green & lt blue	1.10	.40
1830	A978	1r light blue	2.25	.55
		Nos. 1828-1830 (3)	3.90	1.20

Nos. 1828 and 1830 measure 32x25mm. No. 1829 measures 47x26mm.

Nadezhda K. Krupskaya A979

1956, June 28
1831	A979	40k brn, lt blue & pale brown	8.00	2.00

Krupskaya (1869-1939), teacher and wife of Lenin.
See Nos. 1862, 1886, 1983, 2028.

S. M. Kirov (1886-1934), Revolutionary A980

1956, June 28
1832	A980	40k red, buff & brown	2.00	.50

Nikolai S. Leskov (1831-1895), Novelist — A981

1956, July 10
1833	A981	40k olive bister & brn	1.50	.25
1834	A981	1r green & dk brown	3.50	.75

Aleksandr A. Blok (1880-1921), Poet — A982

1956, July 10
1835	A982	40k olive & brn, cream	2.00	.50

Farm Machinery Factory A983

1956, July 23   **Perf. 12½x12**
1836	A983	40k multicolored	2.00	.50

Rostov Farm Machinery Works, 25th anniv.

A984

1956, July 23   **Unwmk.**
1837	A984	40k brown & rose vio	5.00	.50

G. N. Fedotova (1846-1925), actress. See No. 2026.

P. M. Tretiakov and Art Gallery A985

"The Rooks Have Arrived" by A. K. Savrasov A986

1956, July 31   **Perf. 12**
1838	A985	40k multicolored	5.00	1.00
1839	A986	40k multicolored	5.00	1.00

Tretiakov Art Gallery, Moscow, cent.

Relay Race A987

Volleyball — A988

#1842, Rowing. #1843, Swimming. #1844, Medal with heads of man and woman. #1845, Tennis. #1846, Soccer. #1847, Fencing. #1848, Bicycle race. #1849, Stadium and flag. #1850, Diving. #1851, Boxing. #1852, Gymnast. 1r, Basketball.

1956, Aug. 5
1840	A987	10k carmine rose	.40	.25
1841	A988	25k dk orange brn	.60	.25
1842	A988	25k brt grnsh blue	.60	.25
1843	A988	25k grn, blue & lt brn	.60	.25
1844	A988	40k org, pink, bis & yellow	1.25	.25
1845	A988	40k orange brown	1.25	.25
1846	A987	40k brt yel grn & dk brown	1.25	.25
1847	A987	40k grn, brt grn & dk brn, grnsh	1.25	.25
1848	A987	40k blue green	1.25	.25
1849	A988	40k brt yel grn & red	1.25	.25
1850	A988	40k greenish blue	1.25	.25
1851	A988	60k violet	1.75	.25
1852	A987	60k brt violet	1.75	.25
1853	A987	1r red brown	2.50	.40
		Nos. 1840-1853 (14)	16.95	3.65

All-Union Spartacist Games, Moscow, Aug. 5-16.

Parachute Landing — A989

1956, Aug. 5   **Perf. 12x12½**
1854	A989	40k multicolored	2.00	1.00

Third World Parachute Championships, Moscow, July 1956.

Building under Construction A990

Builders' Day: 60k, Building a factory. 1r, Building a dam.

1956 **Photo.** *Perf. 12*
1855 A990 40k deep orange 1.50 .50
1856 A990 60k dark carmine 1.00 .50
1857 A990 1r intense blue 2.50 .50
　Nos. 1855-1857 (3) 5.00 1.50

Ivan Franko — A991

1956, Aug. 27
1858 A991 40k deep claret 1.25 .25
1859 A991 1r bright blue 1.75 .30
　Franko, writer (1856-1916).

Makhmud Aivazov — A992

Type I　　Type II

Two types:
I — Three lines in panel with "148."
II — Two lines in panel with "148."

1956, Aug. 27
1860 A992 40k emerald (II) 5.00 3.00
　a. Type I 21.00 18.00
　148th birthday of Russia's oldest man, an Azerbaijan collective farmer.

Robert Burns, Scottish Poet, 160th Death Anniv. — A993

1956-57 **Photo.**
1861 A993 40k yellow brown 6.00 2.00
　Engr.
1861A A993 40k lt ultra & brn ('57) 4.00 1.00
　For overprint see No. 2174.

Portrait Type of 1956
　Lesya Ukrainka (1871-1913), Ukrainian writer.

1956, Aug. 27 **Litho.**
1862 A979 40k olive, blk & brown 4.00 1.00

Statue of Nestor — A995

1956, Sept. 22 *Perf. 12x12½*
1863 A995 40k multicolored 1.50 .25
1864 A995 1r multicolored 3.50 .50
　900th anniversary of the birth of Nestor, first Russian historian.

Aleksandr Andreevich Ivanov (1806-58), Painter — A996

1956, Sept. 22 **Unwmk.**
1865 A996 40k gray & brown 2.00 .25

I. E. Repin and "Volga River Boatmen" — A997

"Cossacks Writing a Letter to the Turkish Sultan" — A998

1956, Aug. 21
Multicolored Centers
1866 A997 40k org brn & black 7.00 1.00
1867 A998 1r chalky blue & blk 13.00 3.00
　Ilya E. Repin (1844-1930), painter.

Chicken Farm A999

　Designs: No. 1869, Harvest. 25k, Harvesting corn. No. 1871, Women in corn field. No. 1872, Farm buildings. No. 1873, Cattle. No. 1874, Farm workers, inscriptions and blast furnances.

1956, Oct. 7
1868 A999 10k multicolored .50 .25
1869 A999 10k multicolored .50 .25
1870 A999 25k multicolored 1.00 .25
1871 A999 40k multicolored 2.25 .50
1872 A999 40k multicolored 2.25 .50
1873 A999 40k multicolored 2.25 .50
1874 A999 40k multicolored 2.25 .50
　Nos. 1868-1874 (7) 11.00 2.75

#1868, 1872, 1873 measure 37x25½mm; #1869-1871 37x27½mm; #1874 37x21mm.

Benjamin Franklin — A1000

G. B Shaw A1000a

Dostoevski A1000b

　Portraits: #1876 Sesshu (Toyo Oda). #1877, Rembrandt. #1879, Mozart. #1880, Heinrich Heine. #1882, Ibsen. #1883, Pierre Curie.

1956, Oct. 17 **Photo.**
　Size: 25x37mm
1875 A1000 40k copper brn 3.75 1.60
1876 A1000 40k brt orange 3.75 1.60
1877 A1000 40k black 3.75 1.60
1878 A1000a 40k black 3.75 1.60
　Size: 21x32mm
1879 A1000 40k grnsh blue 3.75 1.60
1880 A1000 40k violet 3.75 1.60
1881 A1000b 40k green 3.75 1.60
1882 A1000 40k brown 3.75 1.60
1883 A1000 40k brt green 3.75 1.60
　Nos. 1875-1883 (9) 33.75 14.40
　Great personalities of the world.

Antarctic Bases — A1001

1956, Oct. 22 **Litho.** *Perf. 12x12½*
1884 A1001 40k slate, grnsh bl & red 2.00 .50
　Soviet Scientific Antarctic Expedition.

G. I. Kotovsky (1881-1925), Military Commander A1002

1956, Oct. 30
1885 A1002 40k magenta 2.50 1.00

Portrait Type of 1956
　Portrait: Julia A. Zemaite (1845-1921), Lithaunian novelist.

1956, Oct. 30 *Perf. 12*
1886 A979 40k lt ol green & brn 3.00 1.00

Fedor A. Bredichin (1831-1904), Astronomer — A1004

1956, Oct. 30
1887 A1004 40k sepia & ultra 3.00 .75

Field Marshal Count Aleksandr V. Suvorov (1730-1800) A1005

1956, Nov. 17 **Engr.**
1888 A1005 40k org & maroon .75 .25
1889 A1005 1r ol & dk red brn 1.75 .30
1890 A1005 3r lt red brn & black 2.50 .75
　Nos. 1888-1890 (3) 5.00 1.30

Shatura Power Station A1006

1956 **Litho.** *Perf. 12½x12*
1891 A1006 40k multicolored 6.00 .50
　30th anniv. of the Shatura power station.

Kryakutni's Balloon, 1731 — A1007

1956, Nov. 17
1892 A1007 40k lt brn, sepia & yel 5.00 .50
　225th anniv. of the 1st balloon ascension of the Russian inventor, Kryakutni.

A1008

1956, Dec. 3 **Unwmk.** *Perf. 12*
1893 A1008 40k ultra & brown 1.00 .50
　Yuli M. Shokalski (1856-1940), oceanographer and geodesist.

Apollinari M. Vasnetsov and "Winter Scene" A1009

1956, Dec. 30
1894 A1009 40k multicolored 2.00 .50
　Vasnetsov (1856-1933), painter.

Indian Building and Books — A1010

1956, Dec. 26
1895 A1010 40k deep carmine 2.00 .50
　Kalidasa, 5th century Indian poet.

Ivan Franko, Ukrainian Writer — A1011

1956, Dec. 26   **Engr.**
1896 A1011 40k dk slate green   2.00   .50
     See Nos. 1858-1859.

Leo N. Tolstoy A1012

Portraits of Writers: No. 1898, Mikhail V. Lomonosov. No. 1899, Aleksander S. Pushkin. No. 1900, Maxim Gorki. No. 1901, Shota Rustaveli. No. 1902, Vissarion G. Belinski. No. 1903, Mikhail Y. Lermontov, poet, and Darjal Ravine in Caucasus.

1956-57   **Litho.**   **Perf. 12½x12**
     Size: 37½x27½mm
1897 A1012 40k brt grnsh blue
       & brown   2.10   .25
1898 A1012 40k dk red, ol &
       brn olive   2.10   .25
     Size: 35½x25½mm
1899 A1012 40k dk gray blue &
       brown   2.10   .25
1900 A1012 40k black & brn car   2.10   .25
1901 A1012 40k ol, brn & ol
       gray   2.10   .25
1902 A1012 40k bis, dl vio &
       brn ('57)   2.10   .25
1903 A1012 40k indigo & ol
       ('57)   2.10   .25
     Nos. 1897-1903 (7)   14.70   1.75
     Famous Russian writers.
     See Nos. 1960-1962, 2031, 2112.

Fedor G. Volkov and Theater A1013

1956, Dec. 31   **Unwmk.**
1904 A1013 40k mag, gray & yel   1.00   .30
     200th anniversary of the founding of the St. Petersburg State Theater.

Vitus Bering and Map of Bering Strait A1016

1957, Feb. 6
1905 A1016 40k brown & blue   2.00   .50
     275th anniversary of the birth of Vitus Bering, Danish navigator and explorer.

Dmitri I. Mendeleev A1017

1957, Feb. 6   **Perf. 12x12½**
1906 A1017 40k gray & gray brn   3.00   1.00
     D. I. Mendeleev (1834-1907), chemist.

Mikhail I. Glinka — A1018

Design: 1r, Scene from opera Ivan Susanin.

1957, Feb. 23   **Perf. 12**
1907 A1018 40k dk red, buff &
       sep   1.50   .30
1908 A1018 1r multicolored   2.50   .50
     Mikhail I. Glinka (1804-1857), composer.

All-Union Festival of Soviet Youth, Moscow — A1019

1957, Feb. 23
1909 A1019 40k dk blue, red &
       ocher   .75   .35

23rd Ice Hockey World Championship, Moscow — A1020

Designs: 25k, Emblem. 40k, Player. 60k, Goalkeeper.

1957, Feb. 24   **Photo.**
1910 A1020 25k deep violet   1.00   .25
1911 A1020 40k bright blue   1.00   .25
1912 A1020 60k emerald   1.00   .35
     Nos. 1910-1912 (3)   3.00   .85

Dove and Festival Emblem — A1021

1957   **Litho.**   **Perf. 12**
1913 A1021 40k multicolored   .40   .25
1914 A1021 60k multicolored   .60   .25
     6th World Youth Festival, Moscow. Exist imperf. Value, each $30.

Assembly Line — A1022

1957, Mar. 15
1915 A1022 40k Prus grn & dp
       org   3.00   .75
     Moscow Machine Works centenary.

Black Grouse A1023

Axis Deer — A1024

No. 1916, Gray partridge. No. 1918, Polar bear. No. 1920, Bison. No. 1921, Mallard. No. 1922, European elk. No. 1923, Sable.

1957, Mar. 28
     Center in Natural Colors
1916 A1024 10k yel brown   .85   .35
1917 A1023 15k brown   .85   .35
1918 A1023 15k slate blue   .90   .35
1919 A1024 20k red orange   .90   .35
1920 A1023 30k ultra   .90   .35
1921 A1023 30k dk olive grn   .90   .35
1922 A1023 40k dk olive grn   2.25   .40
1923 A1024 40k violet blue   2.25   .40
     Nos. 1916-1923 (8)   9.80   2.90
     See Nos. 2213-2219, 2429-2431.

Wooden Products, Hohloma A1025

National Handicrafts: No. 1925, Lace maker, Vologda. No. 1926, Bone carver, North Russia. No. 1927, Woodcarver, Moscow area. No. 1928, Rug weaver, Turkmenistan. No. 1929, Painting.

1957-58   **Unwmk.**
1924 A1025 40k red org, yel &
       black   3.00   .80
1925 A1025 40k brt car, yel &
       brown   3.00   .80
1926 A1025 40k ultra, buff &
       gray   3.00   .80
1927 A1025 40k brn, pale yel &
       hn brown   3.00   .80
1928 A1025 40k buff, brn, bl &
       org ('58)   1.50   .90
1929 A1025 40k multicolored
       ('58)   1.50   .90
     Nos. 1924-1929 (6)   15.00   5.00

Aleksei Nikolaievitch Bach (1857-1946), Biochemist A1026

1957, Apr. 6   **Litho.**   **Perf. 12**
1930 A1026 40k ultra, brn & buff   5.00   .30

Georgi Valentinovich Plekhanov (1856-1918), Political Philosopher A1027

1957, Apr. 6   **Engr.**
1931 A1027 40k dull purple   .60   .30

Leonhard Euler A1028

1957, Apr. 17   **Litho.**
1932 A1028 40k lilac & gray   2.00   .50
     Leonhard Euler (1707-1783), Swiss mathematician and physicist.

Lenin, 87th Birth Anniv. — A1029

Designs: No. 1934, Lenin talking to soldier and sailor. No. 1935, Lenin participating in a subbotnik, a voluntary neighborhood clean-up.

1957, Apr. 22
     Multicolored Centers
1933 A1029 40k magenta & bis   3.00   1.00
1934 A1029 40k magenta & bis   3.00   1.00
1935 A1029 40k magenta & bis   3.00   1.00
     Nos. 1933-1935 (3)   9.00   3.00

Youths of All Races Carrying Festival Banner — A1030

Design: 20k, Sculptor with motherhood statue. 40k, Young couples dancing. 1r, Festival banner and fireworks over Moscow University.

1957, May 27   **Perf. 12x12½**
1936 A1030 10k emer, pur & yel   .25   .25
1937 A1030 20k multicolored   .60   .25
1938 A1030 25k emer, pur & yel   .90   .25
1939 A1030 40k rose, bl grn &
       bis brn   .90   .25
1940 A1030 1r multicolored   1.40   .25
     Nos. 1936-1940 (5)   4.05   1.25
     6th World Youth Festival in Moscow. The 10k, 20k, and 1r exist imperf. Value: 10k, 20k, each $20; 1r $200.

Marine Museum Place and Neva — A1031

Designs: No. 1942, Lenin monument. No. 1943, Nevski Prospect and Admiralty.

1957, May 27 Photo. Perf. 12
1941 A1031 40k blue green 1.50 .40
1942 A1031 40k reddish brown 1.50 .40
1943 A1031 40k bluish violet 1.50 .40
  a. Souv. sheet of 3, red border 35.00 20.00
  Nos. 1941-1943 (3) 4.50 1.20
  250th anniversary of Leningrad.
  No. 1943a contains imperf. stamps similar to #1941, 1680 (in reddish brown), 1943, and is for 40th anniv. of the October Revolution. Issued Nov. 7, 1957. A similar sheet is listed as No. 2002a.

Type of 1953 Overprinted in Red

No. 1944

No. 1945

Designs: No. 1944, Peter I Statue, Decembrists' Square. No. 1945, Smolny Institute.

1957, May 27 Perf. 12½x12
1944 A908 1r black brn, *greenish* 1.50 .25
1945 A908 1r green, *pink* 1.50 .25
  250th anniversary of Leningrad. The overprint is in one line on No. 1945.

Henry Fielding — A1032

1957, June 20 Litho.
1946 A1032 40k multicolored 1.00 .50
  Fielding (1707-54), English playwright, novelist.

William Harvey — A1033

1957, May 20 Photo.
1947 A1033 40k brown 1.00 .50
  300th anniversary of the death of the English physician William Harvey, discoverer of blood circulation.

M. A. Balakirev (1836-1910), Composer A1034

1957, May 20 Engr.
1948 A1034 40k bluish black 2.00 .50

A. I. Herzen and N. P. Ogarev A1035

1957, May 20 Litho.
1949 A1035 40k blk vio & dk ol gray 1.00 .50
  Centenary of newspaper Kolokol (Bell).

Kazakhstan Workers' Medal — A1036

1957, May 20
1950 A1036 40k lt blue, blk & yel 1.00 .35

A1037 A1037a A1037b

Portraits: No. 1951, A. M. Liapunov. No. 1952, V. Mickevicius Kapsukas, writer. No. 1953, G. Bashindchagian, Armenian painter. No. 1954, Yakub Kolas, Byelorussian poet. No. 1955, Carl von Linné, Swedish botanist.

1957 Various Frames Photo.
1951 A1037 40k dull red brown 6.50 1.00
1952 A1037a 40k sepia 5.00 1.00
1953 A1037 40k sepia 5.00 1.00
1954 A1037b 40k gray 5.00 1.00
1955 A1037 40k brown black 5.00 1.00
  Nos. 1951-1955 (5) 26.50 5.00
  See Nos. 2036-2038, 2059.

Bicyclist A1038

1957, June 20 Litho.
1956 A1038 40k claret & vio blue 1.00 .50
  10th Peace Bicycle Race.

Telescope A1039

Designs: No. 1958, Comet and observatory. No. 1959, Rocket leaving earth.

1957, July 4 Size: 25½x37mm
1957 A1039 40k brn, ocher & blue 2.00 .35
1958 A1039 40k indigo, lt bl & yel 2.00 .35
  Size: 14½x21mm
1959 A1039 40k blue violet 2.00 .35
  Nos. 1957-1959 (3) 6.00 1.05
  International Geophysical Year, 1957-58. See Nos. 2089-2091.

Folksinger A1040

1957, May 20
1960 A1040 40k multicolored 5.00 1.00
  "The Song of Igor's Army," Russia's oldest literary work.

Taras G. Shevchenko, Ukrainian Poet — A1041

Design: No. 1962, Nikolai G. Chernyshevski, writer and politician.

1957, July 20
1961 A1041 40k grn & dk red brn 1.00 .35
1962 A1041 40k orange brn & grn 1.00 .35

Woman Gymnast — A1043

25k, Wrestling. No. 1965, Stadium. No. 1966, Youths of three races. 60k, Javelin thrower.

1957, July 15 Litho. Perf. 12
1963 A1043 20k bluish vio & org brn .60 .25
1964 A1043 25k brt grn & claret .75 .25
1965 A1043 40k Prus bl, ol & red 1.20 .25
1966 A1043 40k crimson & violet 1.20 .25
1967 A1043 60k ultra & brown 1.60 .40
  Nos. 1963-1967 (5) 5.35 1.40
  Third International Youth Games, Moscow.

Javelin Thrower — A1044

Designs: No. 1969, Sprinter. 25k, Somersault. No. 1971, Boxers. No. 1972, Soccer players, horiz. 60k, Weight lifter.

1957, July 20 Unwmk.
1968 A1044 20k lt ultra & ol blk .45 .25
1969 A1044 20k brt grn, red vio & black .45 .25

1970 A1044 25k orange, ultra & blk .60 .25
1971 A1044 40k rose vio & blk .90 .30
1972 A1044 40k dp pink, bl, buff & black .90 .30
1973 A1044 60k lt violet & brn 1.50 .40
  Nos. 1968-1973 (6) 4.80 1.75
  Success of Soviet athletes at the 16th Olympic Games, Melbourne.

Kupala — A1045

1957, July 27 Photo.
1974 A1045 40k dark gray 10.00 5.00
  Yanka Kupala (1882-1942), poet.

Kremlin A1046

Moscow Views: No. 1976, Stadium. No. 1977, University. No. 1978, Bolshoi Theater.

Center in Black

1957, July 27 Litho.
1975 A1046 40k dull red brown .35 .25
1976 A1046 40k brown violet .35 .25
1977 A1046 1r red 1.10 .25
1978 A1046 1r brt violet blue 1.10 .25
  Nos. 1975-1978 (4) 2.90 1.00
  Sixth World Youth Festival, Moscow.

Lenin Library A1047

1957, July 27 Photo.
1979 A1047 40k brt grnsh blue .75 .35
  a. Souvenir sheet of 2, light blue, imperf. 20.00 20.00
  Intl. Phil. Exhib., Moscow, July 29-Aug. 11. No. 1979 exists imperf. Value $7.50.

Pierre Jean de Beranger(1780-1857), French Song Writer — A1048

1957, Aug. 9
1980 A1048 40k brt blue green .75 .35

Globe, Dove and Olive Branch — A1049

1957, Aug. 8 Litho.
1981 A1049 40k bl, grn & bis brn 2.50 1.00
1982 A1049 1r violet, grn & brn 5.50 2.00
  Publicity for world peace.

Portrait Type of 1956

Portrait: 40k, Clara Zetkin (1857-1933), German communist.

1957, Aug. 9
1983 A979 40k gray blue, brn & blk ... 5.00 1.00

Krenholm Factory, Narva A1050

1957, Sept. 8 Photo.
1984 A1050 40k black brown ... 2.00 .50

Centenary of Krenholm textile factory, Narva, Estonia.

Carrier Pigeon and Globes A1051

1957, Sept. 26 Unwmk. Perf. 12
1985 A1051 40k blue ... .40 .25
1986 A1051 60k lilac ... .60 .25

Intl. Letter Writing Week, Oct. 6-12.

Vyborzhets Factory, Lenin Statue A1052

1957, Sept. 23 Litho.
1987 A1052 40k dark blue ... 2.00 1.00

Krasny Vyborzhets factory, Leningrad, cent.

Vladimir Vasilievich Stasov (1824-1906), Art and Music Critic — A1053

1957, Sept. 23 Engr.
1988 A1053 40k brown ... .50 .30
1989 A1053 1r bluish black ... 1.00 .30

Congress Emblem A1054

1957, Oct. 7 Litho. Perf. 12
1990 A1054 40k gray blue & blk, bluish ... 1.00 .35

4th International Trade Union Congress, Leipzig, Oct. 4-15.

Konstantin E. Tsiolkovsky and Rockets A1055

1957, Oct. 7
1991 A1055 40k dk blue & pale brown ... 3.50 .50

Tsiolkovsky (1857-1935), rocket and astronautics pioneer.
For overprint see No. 2021.

Sputnik 1 Circling Globe — A1056

1957 Photo.
1992 A1056 40k indigo, bluish ... 1.40 .50
1993 A1056 40k bright blue ... 1.40 .50

Launching of first artificial earth satellite, Oct. 4. Issue dates: No. 1992, Nov. 5; No. 1993, Dec. 28.

Turbine Wheel, Kuibyshev Hydroelectric Station — A1057

1957, Nov. 20 Litho.
1994 A1057 40k red brown ... 1.00 .35

All-Union Industrial Exhib. See #2030.

Meteor — A1058

1957, Nov. 20
1995 A1058 40k multicolored ... 10.00 1.00

Falling of Sikhote Alinj meteor, 10th anniv.

Lenin — A1059

Design: 60k, Lenin reading Pravda, horiz.

1957, Oct. 30 Engr.
1996 A1059 40k blue ... 1.00 .25
1997 A1059 60k rose red ... 1.00 .25

40th anniversary of October Revolution.

Students and Moscow University — A1060

Miner and Railroad A1061

No. 1999, Red flag, Lenin. No. 2000, Lenin addressing workers and peasants. No. 2002, Harvester.

Perf. 12½x12, 12x12½, 12½

1957, Oct. 15 Litho.
1998 A1060 10k buff, sepia & red ... .40 .25
1999 A1060 40k buff, red, sep & yel ... .80 .25
2000 A1060 40k red, black & yel ... .80 .25
2001 A1061 40k red, yel & green ... .80 .25
2002 A1061 60k red, ocher & vio brn ... 1.25 .25
　　a. Souvenir sheet of 3, #2000-2002, imperf. ... 50.00 25.00
　Nos. 1998-2002 (5) ... 4.05 1.25

40th anniv. of the October Revolution. A similar sheet is listed as No. 1943a.
Nos. 1998-2002 exist imperf. Value, set $12.50.

Federal Socialist Republic A1062

Uzbek Republic — A1063

Republic: No. 2005, Tadzhik (building, peasant girl). No. 2006, Byelorussia (truck). No. 2007, Azerbaijan (buildings). No. 2008, Georgia (valley, palm, couple). No. 2009, Armenia, (fruit, power line, mountains). No. 2010, Turkmen (couple, lambs). No. 2011, Ukraine (farmers). No. 2012, Kazakh (harvester, combine). No. 2013, Kirghiz (horseback rider, building). No. 2014, Moldavia (automatic sorting machine). No. 2015, Estonia (girl in national costume). No. 2016, Latvia (couple, sea, field). No. 2017, Lithuania (farm, farmer couple).

1957, Oct. 25
2003 A1062 40k multicolored ... 1.00 .35
2004 A1063 40k multicolored ... 1.00 .35
2005 A1062 40k multicolored ... 1.00 .35
2006 A1062 40k multicolored ... 1.00 .35
2007 A1062 40k multicolored ... 1.00 .35
2008 A1062 40k multicolored ... 1.00 .35
2009 A1062 40k multicolored ... 1.00 .35
2010 A1062 40k multicolored ... 1.00 .35
2011 A1063 40k multicolored ... 1.00 .35
2012 A1062 40k multicolored ... 1.00 .35
2013 A1062 40k multicolored ... 1.00 .35
2014 A1062 40k multicolored ... 1.00 .35
2015 A1063 40k multicolored ... 1.00 .35
2016 A1062 40k multicolored ... 1.00 .35
2017 A1062 40k multicolored ... 1.00 .35
　Nos. 2003-2017 (15) ... 15.00 5.25

40th anniversary of the October Revolution.

Artists and Academy of Art — A1064

Red Army Monument, Berlin — A1065

1r, Worker and Peasant monument, Moscow.

1957, Dec. 16
2018 A1064 40k black, pale salmon ... .60 .25
2019 A1064 60k black ... .90 .30
2020 A1065 1r black, pink ... 1.50 .45
　Nos. 2018-2020 (3) ... 3.00 1.00

200th anniversary of the Academy of Arts, Leningrad. Artists on 40k are K. P. Bryulov, Ilya Repin and V. I. Surikov.

No. 1991 Overprinted in Black

1957, Nov. 28
2021 A1055 40k ... 40.00 5.00

Launching of Sputnik 1.

Ukrainian Arms, Symbolic Figures A1066

1957, Dec. 24
2022 A1066 40k yel, red & blue ... .75 .35

Ukrainian Soviet Republic, 40th anniv.

Edvard Grieg — A1067

1957, Dec. 24 Photo.
2023 A1067 40k black, buff ... 3.00 1.00

Grieg, Norwegian composer, 50th death anniv.

Giuseppe Garibaldi — A1068

1957, Dec. 24 Litho.
2024 A1068 40k plum, lt grn & blk ... 1.00 .35

Garibaldi, (1807-1882) Italian patriot.

Vladimir Lukich Borovikovsky (1757-1825), Painter — A1069

1957, Dec. 24 Photo.
2025 A1069 40k brown ... 1.00 .50

Portrait Type of 1956

Portrait: 40k, Mariya Nikolayevna Ermolova (1853-1928), actress.

1957, Dec. 28 Litho.
2026 A984 40k red brn & brt vio ... 1.00 .30

Kuibyshev Hydroelectric Station and Dam A1070

1957, Dec. 28
2027 A1070 40k dark blue, buff ... 3.00 .50

Type of 1956

Portrait: 40k, Rosa Luxemburg (1870-1919), German socialist.

1958, Jan. 8
2028 A979 40k blue & brown 1.50 .60

Chi Pai-shih — A1070a

1958, Jan. 8 Photo.
2029 A1070a 40k deep violet 10.00 1.00
Chi Pai-shih (1864-1957), Chinese painter.

Flag and Symbols of Industry A1070b

1958, Jan. 8 Litho.
2030 A1070b 60k gray vio, red & black 2.00 .50
All-Union Industrial Exhib. Exists imperf. Value, $250.

Aleksei N. Tolstoi, Novelist & Dramatist (1883-1945) A1071

1958, Jan. 28 Photo. *Perf. 12*
2031 A1071 40k brown olive 1.00 .30
See Nos. 2112, 2175-2178C.

Symbolic Figure Greeting Sputnik 2 — A1072

1957-58 **Figure in Buff** **Litho.**
2032 A1072 20k black & rose .75 .25
2033 A1072 40k black & grn ('58) 1.00 .25
2034 A1072 60k blk & lt brn ('58) 1.25 .25
2035 A1072 1r black & blue 2.00 .50
  Nos. 2032-2035 (4) 5.00 1.25
Launching of Sputnik 2, Nov. 3, 1957.

Small Portrait Type of 1957

No. 2036, Henry W. Longfellow, American poet. No. 2037, William Blake, English artist, poet, mystic. No. 2038, E. Charents, Armenian poet.

1958, Mar. **Unwmk.** *Perf. 12*
Various Frames
2036 A1037 40k gray black 5.00 2.25
2037 A1037 40k gray black 5.00 2.25
2038 A1037 40k sepia 5.00 2.25
  Nos. 2036-2038 (3) 15.00 6.75

Victory at Pskov A1073

Soldier and Civilian — A1074

Designs: No. 2040, Airman, sailor and soldier. No. 2042, Sailor and soldier. 60k, Storming of Berlin Reichstag building.

1958, Feb. 21
2039 A1073 25k multicolored .50 .40
2040 A1073 40k multicolored 1.00 .40
2041 A1074 40k multicolored 1.00 .40
2042 A1074 40k multicolored 1.00 .40
2043 A1073 60k multicolored 1.50 .40
  Nos. 2039-2043 (5) 5.00 2.00
40th anniversary of Red Armed Forces.

Peter Ilich Tchaikovsky A1075

Swan Lake Ballet A1076

Design: 1r, Tchaikovsky, pianist and violinist.

1958, Mar. 18
2044 A1075 40k grn, bl, brn & red .60 .25
2045 A1076 40k grn, ultra, red & yel .60 .25
2046 A1075 1r lake & emerald 2.00 .50
  Nos. 2044-2046 (3) 3.20 1.00
Honoring Tchaikovsky and for the Tchaikovsky competitions for pianists and violinists. Exist imperf. Value, set $10.
Nos. 2044-2045 were printed in sheets of 30, including 15 stamps of each value and 5 se-tenant pairs. Value, pairs $10.

V. F. Rudnev — A1077

1958, Mar. 25 **Unwmk.**
2047 A1077 40k green, blk & ocher 1.00 .50
Rudnev, naval commander.

Maxim Gorki — A1078

1958, Apr. 3 **Litho.** *Perf. 12*
2048 A1078 40k multicolored .75 .50
Gorki, writer, 90th birth anniv.

Spasski Tower — A1079

1958, Apr. 9
2049 A1079 40k dp violet, *pinkish* .75 .25
2050 A1079 60k rose red 1.25 .25
13th Congress of the Young Communist League (Komsomol).

Russian Pavilion, Brussels A1080

1958, Apr.
2051 A1080 10k multicolored .45 .25
2052 A1080 40k multicolored .55 .25
Universal and International Exhibition at Brussels. Exist imperf. Value $5.

Lenin — A1081

1958, Apr. 22 **Engr.**
2053 A1081 40k dk blue gray 1.00 .65
2054 A1081 60k rose brown 1.50 .65
2055 A1081 1r brown 2.50 .65
  Nos. 2053-2055 (3) 5.00 1.95
88th anniversary of the birth of Lenin.

1958, May 5
Portrait: Nos. 2056-2058, Karl Marx.
2056 A1081 40k brown 1.00 .25
2057 A1081 60k dark blue 1.50 .25
2058 A1081 1r dark red 2.50 .40
  Nos. 2056-2058 (3) 5.00 .90
140th anniversary of the birth of Marx.

Jan A. Komensky (Comenius) — A1082

1958, Apr. 17 **Photo.**
2059 A1082 40k green 3.00 1.00

No. 1695 Overprinted in Blue

1958, Apr. 22
2060 A914 40k multicolored 4.50 1.00
Academy of Arts, Moscow, 200th anniv.

Lenin Order — A1083

1958, Apr. 30 **Litho.**
2061 A1083 40k brn, yel & red 1.00 .50

Carlo Goldoni — A1084

1958, Apr. 28 **Photo.**
2062 A1084 40k blue & dk gray .75 .35
Carlo Goldoni, Italian dramatist.

Radio Tower, Ship and Planes A1085

1958, May 7
2063 A1085 40k blue grn & red 5.00 .50
Issued for Radio Day, May 7.

Globe and Dove — A1086

1958, May 6 **Litho.**
2064 A1086 40k blue & black .40 .25
2065 A1086 60k ultra & black .60 .25
4th Congress of the Intl. Democratic Women's Federation, June, 1958, at Vienna.

Ilya Chavchavadze A1087

1958, May 12 **Photo.**
2066 A1087 40k black & blue .80 .35
50th anniversary of the death of Ilya Chavchavadze, Georgian writer.

Flags and Communication Symbols — A1088

1958-59 **Litho.**
2067 A1088 40k blue, red, yel & blk 8.00 3.00
a. Red half of Czech flag at bottom 8.00 3.00
Communist ministers' meeting on social problems in Moscow, Dec. 1957.

On No. 2067, the Czech flag (center flag in vertical row of five) is incorrectly pictured with red stripe on top. This error is corrected on No. 2067a.

Bugler — A1089

Pioneers: 25k, Boy with model plane.

1958, May 29   Unwmk.   Perf. 12
2068 A1089 10k ultra, red & red brn   .50 .25
2069 A1089 25k ultra, yel & red brn   .50 .25

Children of Three Races — A1090

Design: No. 2071, Child and bomb.

1958, May 29
2070 A1090 40k car, ultra & brn   .50 .25
2071 A1090 40k car & brn   .50 .25

Intl. Day for the Protection of Children.

Soccer Players and Globe — A1091

1958, June 5
2072 A1091 40k blue, red & buff   .75 .25
2073 A1091 60k blue, red & buff 2.25 .30

6th World Soccer Championships, Stockholm, June 8-29. Exist imperf. Value $5.

Rimski-Korsakov A1092

1958, June 5   Photo.
2074 A1092 40k blue & brown   3.00 .50

Nikolai Andreevich Rimski-Korsakov (1844-1908), composer.

Girl Gymnast — A1093

No. 2076, Gymnast on rings and view.

1958, June 24   Litho.
2075 A1093 40k ultra, red & buff   1.00 .25
2076 A1093 40k blue, red buff & grn   1.00 .25

14th World Gymnastic Championships, Moscow, July 6-10.

Bomb, Globe, Atom, Sputniks, Ship A1094

1958, July 1
2077 A1094 60k dk blue, blk & org   9.00 1.00

Conference for peaceful uses of atomic energy, held at Stockholm.

Street Fighters — A1095

1958, July 5
2078 A1095 40k red & violet blk   2.00 .30

Communist Party in the Ukraine, 40th anniv.

Moscow State University A1096

Congress Emblem — A1097

1958, July 8   Perf. 12
2079 A1096 40k red & blue   .75 .25
2080 A1097 60k lt grn, blue & red   1.25 .30
  a.   Souvenir sheet of 2   10.00 7.00

5th Congress of the International Architects' Organization, Moscow.
No. 2080a contains Nos. 2079-2080, imperf., with background design in yellow, brown, blue and red. Issued Sept. 8, 1958.

Young Couple A1098

1958, June 25
2081 A1098 40k blue & ocher   .75 .30
2082 A1098 60k yel green & ocher   1.25 .45

Day of Soviet Youth.

Sputnik 3 Leaving Earth A1099

1958, June 16
2083 A1099 40k vio blue, grn & rose   2.50 .35

Launching of Sputnik 3, May 15. Printed in sheets with alternating labels, giving details of launching.

Sadriddin Aini — A1100

1958, July 15
2084 A1100 40k rose, black & buff   3.00 .50

80th birthday of Aini, Tadzhik writer.

Emblem A1101

1958, July 21   Typo.   Perf. 12
2085 A1101 40k lilac & blue   .75 .35

1st World Trade Union Conference of Working Youths, Prague, July 14-20.

Type of 1958-59 and

TU-104 and Globe A1102

Design: 1r, Turbo-propeller liner AN-10.

1958, Aug.   Litho.
2086 A1102 60k blue, red & bis   .75 .25
2087 A1123 1r yel, red & black   1.25 .25

Soviet civil aviation. Exist imperf. Value, set $5.50. See Nos. 2147-2151.

L. A. Kulik A1103

1958, Aug. 12
2088 A1103 40k sep, bl, yel & claret   2.00 .50

50th anniv. of the falling of the Tungus meteor and the 75th anniv. of the birth of L. A. Kulik, meteorist.

IGY Type of 1957

Designs: No. 2089, Aurora borealis and camera. No. 2090, Schooner "Zarja" exploring's earth magnetism. No. 2091, Weather balloon and radar.

1958, July 29   Size: 25½x37mm
2089 A1039 40k blue & brt yel   1.40 .35
2090 A1039 40k blue green   1.40 .35
2091 A1039 40k bright blue   1.40 .35
    Nos. 2089-2091 (3)   4.20 1.05

International Geophysical Year, 1957-58.

Crimea Observatory A1104

Moscow University A1105

Design: 1r, Telescope.

1958, Aug.   Photo.
2092 A1104 40k brn & brt grnsh bl   2.00 .35
2093 A1105 60k lt blue, vio & yel   2.50 .35
2094 A1104 1r dp blue & org brn   3.50 .35
    Nos. 2092-2094 (3)   8.00 1.05

10th Congress of the International Astronomical Union, Moscow.

Postilion, 16th Century A1106

Designs: No. 2095, 15th cent. letter writer. No. 2097, A. L. Ordyn-Natshokin and sleigh mail coach, 17th cent. No. 2098, Mail coach and post office, 18th cent. No. 2099, Troika, 19th cent. No. 2100, Lenin stamp, ship and Kremlin. No. 2101, Jet plane and troika. No. 2102, Leningrad Communications Museum, vert. No. 2103, V. N. Podbielski and letter carriers. No. 2104, Mail train. No. 2105, Loading mail on plane. No. 2106, Ship, plane, train and globe.

1958, Aug. Unwmk. Litho. Perf. 12
2095 A1106 10k red, blk, yel & lil   .25 .25
2096 A1106 10k multicolored   .25 .25
2097 A1106 25k ultra & slate   .60 .30
2098 A1106 25k black & ultra   .60 .30
2099 A1106 40k car lake & brn blk   1.20 .45
2100 A1106 40k blk, mag & brn   1.20 .45
2101 A1106 40k red, org & gray   1.20 .45
2102 A1106 40k sal & brn   1.20 .45
2103 A1106 60k grnsh blue & red lil 1.50 .35
2104 A1106 60k grnsh bl & lilac   1.50 .35
2105 A1106 1r multicolored   3.25 .70
2106 A1106 1r multicolored   3.25 .70
    Nos. 2095-2106 (12)   16.00 5.00

Centenary of Russian postage stamps.
Two imperf. souvenir sheets exist, measuring 155x106mm. One contains one each of Nos. 2095-2099, with background design in red, ultramarine, yellow and brown. The other contains one each of Nos. 2100, 2103-2106, with background design in blue, gray, ocher, pink and brown. Value for both, $50 unused, $10 canceled.
Nos. 2096, 2100-2101 exist imperf. Value for both, $20 unused, $10 canceled.

M. I. Chigorin, Chess Player, 50th Death Anniv. — A1107

1958, Aug. 30   Photo.
2107 A1107 40k black & emerald   2.00 .50

Golden Gate, Vladimir A1108

60k, Gorki Street with trolley bus and truck.

1958, Aug. 23   Litho.
2108 A1108 40k multicolored   .80 .40
2109 A1108 60k lt violet, yel & blk 1.20 .60

850th anniv. of the city of Vladimir.

Nurse Bandaging Man's Leg — A1109

No. 2111, Hospital, & people of various races.

1958, Sept. 15
2110 A1109 40k multicolored .75 .30
2111 A1109 40k ol, lem & red .75 .30
40 years of Red Cross-Red Crescent work.

Portrait Type of 1958
Mikhail E. Saltykov (Shchedrin), writer.

1958, Sept. 15
2112 A1071 40k brn black & mar 5.00 1.00

Rudagi — A1110

1958, Oct. 10   **Litho.**   **Perf. 12**
2113 A1110 40k multicolored 2.00 .50
1100th anniversary of the birth of Rudagi, Persian poet.

V. V. Kapnist — A1111

1958, Sept. 30
2114 A1111 40k blue & gray 1.00 .50
200th anniversary of the birth of V. V. Kapnist, poet and dramatist.

Book, Torch, Lyre, Flower A1112

1958, Oct. 4
2115 A1112 40k red org, ol & blk 2.00 .50
Conf. of Asian & African Writers, Tashkent.

Chelyabinsk Tractor Factory A1113

Designs: No. 2117, Zaporozstal foundry. No. 2118, Ural machine building plant.

1958, Oct. 20   **Photo.**
2116 A1113 40k green & yellow 1.50 .30
2117 A1113 40k brown red & yel 1.50 .30
2118 A1113 40k blue 1.50 .30
   Nos. 2116-2118 (3) 4.50 .90
Pioneers of Russian Industry.

Ancient Georgian on Horseback A1114

1958, Oct. 18   **Litho.**
2119 A1114 40k ocher, ultra & red 2.00 .50
1500th anniv. of Tbilisi, capital of Georgia.

Red Square, Moscow — A1115

АЛМА-АТА · ПЛОЩАДЬ им. В. И. ЛЕНИНА
No. 2121

ТБИЛИСИ · ПРОСПЕКТ РУСТАВЕЛИ
No. 2125

ФРУНЗЕ · УНИВЕРСИТЕТСКАЯ ПЛОЩАДЬ
No. 2127

ОБЩИЙ ВИД ГОРОДА ЕРЕВАН
No. 2128

МИНСК · КРУГЛАЯ ПЛОЩАДЬ
No. 2131

Capitals of Soviet Republics: No. 2121, Lenin Square, Alma Ata. No. 2122, Lenin statue, Ashkhabad. No. 2123, Lenin statue, Tashkent. No. 2124, Lenin Square, Stalinabad. No. 2125, Rustaveli Ave., Tbilisi. No. 2126, View from Dvina River, Riga. No. 2127, University Square, Frunze. No. 2128, View, Yerevan. No. 2129, Communist Street, Baku. No. 2130, Lenin Prospect, Kishinev. No. 2131, Round Square, Minsk. No. 2132, Viru Gate, Tallinn. No. 2133, Main Street, Kiev. No. 2134, View, Vilnius.

1958   **Engr.**
2120 A1115 40k violet 1.00 .45
2121 A1115 40k brt blue green 1.00 .45
2122 A1115 40k greenish gray 1.00 .45
2123 A1115 40k dark gray 1.00 .45
2124 A1115 40k blue 1.00 .45
2125 A1115 40k violet blue 1.00 .45
2126 A1115 40k brown red 1.00 .45
2127 A1115 40k dk blue gray 1.00 .45
2128 A1115 40k brown 1.00 .45
2129 A1115 40k purple 1.00 .45
2130 A1115 40k olive 1.00 .45
2131 A1115 40k gray brown 1.00 .45
2132 A1115 40k emerald 1.00 .45
2133 A1115 40k lilac rose 1.00 .45
2134 A1115 40k orange ver 1.00 .45
   Nos. 2120-2134 (15) 15.00 6.75
See No. 2836.

Young Civil War Soldier, 1919 — A1116

20k, Industrial brigade. 25k, Youth in World War II. 40k, Girl farm worker. 60k, Youth building new towns. 1r, Students, fighters for culture.

1958, Oct. 25   **Litho.**
2135 A1116 10k multicolored .40 .25
2136 A1116 20k multicolored .75 .25
2137 A1116 25k multicolored .90 .25
2138 A1116 40k multicolored 1.50 .25
2139 A1116 60k multicolored 2.25 .25
2140 A1116 1r multicolored 4.50 1.00
   Nos. 2135-2140 (6) 10.30 2.25
40th anniversary of the Young Communist League (Komsomol).

Marx and Lenin — A1117

Lenin, Intellectual, Peasant and Miner A1118

1958, Oct. 31
2141 A1117 40k multicolored .50 .25
2142 A1118 1r multicolored 1.50 .30
41st anniversary of Russian Revolution.

Torch, Wreath and Family A1119

1958, Nov. 5
2143 A1119 60k blk, beige & dull bl 1.00 .50
10th anniversary of the Universal Declaration of Human Rights.

Sergei Esenin (1895-1925), Poet — A1120

1958, Nov. 29
2144 A1120 40k multicolored 1.00 .50

G. K. Ordzhonikidze A1121

1958, Dec. 12   **Perf. 12**
2145 A1121 40k multicolored 1.00 .50
G. K. Ordzhonikidze (1886-1937), Georgian party worker.

Kuan Han-ching — A1122

1958, Dec. 5
2146 A1122 40k dk blue & gray 3.00 1.00
700th anniversary of the theater of Kuan Han-ching, Chinese dramatist.

Airliner IL-14 and Globe A1123

Soviet civil aviation: No. 2148, Jet liner TU-104. No. 2149, Turbo-propeller liner TU-114. 60k, Jet liner TU-110. 2r, Turbo-propeller liner IL-18.

1958-59
2147 A1123 20k ultra, blk & red .40 .25
2148 A1123 40k bl grn, blk & red .60 .25
2149 A1123 40k brt bl, blk & red .60 .25
2150 A1123 60k rose car & black .60 .25
2151 A1123 2r plum, red & black ('59) 1.75 .25
   Nos. 2147-2151 (5) 3.95 1.25
Exist imperf.; value $10.
See Nos. 2086-2087.

Eleonora Duse — A1124

1958, Dec. 26
2152 A1124 40k blue grn & gray 1.00 .50
Duse, Italian actress, birth cent.

John Milton — A1125

1958, Dec. 17
2153 A1125 40k brown 1.00 .50
John Milton (1608-1674), English poet.

K. F. Rulye — A1126

1958, Dec. 26
2154 A1126 40k ultra & black 1.00 .50
Rulye, educator, death cent.

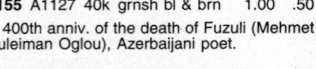

Fuzuli — A1127

1958, Dec. 23   **Photo.**
2155 A1127 40k grnsh bl & brn 1.00 .50
400th anniv. of the death of Fuzuli (Mehmet Suleiman Oglou), Azerbaijani poet.

Census Emblem and Family — A1128

Design: No. 2157, Census emblem.

1958, Dec.		Litho.	
2156	A1128	40k multicolored	.75	.25
2157	A1128	40k yel, gray, bl & red	.75	.25

1959 Soviet census.

Lunik and Sputniks over Kremlin — A1129

Designs: 40k, Lenin and view of Kremlin. 60k, Workers and Lenin power plant on Volga.

1959, Jan.		Unwmk.	*Perf. 12*	
2158	A1129	40k multicolored	1.50	.25
2159	A1129	60k multicolored	2.50	.75
2160	A1129	1r red, yel & vio bl	7.00	1.50
	Nos. 2158-2160 (3)		11.00	2.50

21st Cong. of the Communist Party and "the conquest of the cosmos by the Soviet people."

Lenin Statue, Minsk Buildings — A1130

1958, Dec. 20
2161 A1130 40k red, buff & brn   .75 .35
Byelorussian Republic, 40th anniv.

Atomic Icebreaker "Lenin" A1131

Design: 60k, Diesel Locomotive "TE-3."

1958, Dec. 31				
2162	A1131	40k multicolored	1.75	1.00
2163	A1131	60k multicolored	2.75	1.25

Shalom Aleichem — A1132

1959, Feb. 10
2164 A1132 40k chocolate   .75 .35
Aleichem, Yiddish writer, birth cent.

Evangelista Torricelli — A1133

Scientists: No. 2166, Charles Darwin, English biologist. No. 2167, N. F. Gamaleya, microbiologist.

1959, Feb.		Various Frames	
2165	A1133	40k blue green & blk	.75	.25
2166	A1133	40k chalky blue & brn	.75	.25
2167	A1133	40k dk red & black	.75	.25
	Nos. 2165-2167 (3)		2.25	.75

Woman Skater — A1134

1959, Feb. 5
2168 A1134 25k ultra, black & ver   .75 .25
2169 A1134 40k ultra & black   1.25 .30
Women's International Ice Skating Championships, Sverdlovsk.

No. 1717 Overprinted in Orange Brown

1959, Feb. 12
2170 A919 1r dk brn & brn   7.50 5.00
"Victory of the USSR Basketball Team — Chile 1959." However, the 3rd World Basketball Championship honors went to Brazil when the Soviet team was disqualified for refusing to play Nationalist China.

Frederic Joliot-Curie A1135

1959, Mar. 3   Litho.   *Perf. 12*
2171 A1135 40k turq bl & gray brn, *beige*   1.00 .25
Joliot-Curie (1900-58), French scientist.

Selma Lagerlöf — A1136

1959, Feb. 26
2172 A1136 40k red brn & blk   .75 .35
Lagerlöf (1858-1940), Swedish writer.

Peter Zwirka — A1137

1959, Mar. 3
2173 A1137 40k hn brn & blk, *yel*   .75 .35
Zwirka (1909-1947), Lithuanian writer.

No. 1861A Overprinted in Red: "1759 1959"

1959, Feb. 26   Engr.
2174 A993 40k lt ultra & brown   10.00 10.00
200th anniversary of the birth of Robert Burns, Scottish poet.

Type of 1958

Russian Writers: No. 2175, A. S. Griboedov. No. 2176, A. N. Ostrovski. No. 2177, Anton Chekhov. No. 2178, I. A. Krylov. No. 2178A, Nikolai V. Gogol. No. 2178B, S. T. Aksakov. No. 2178C, A. V. Koltzov. poet, and reaper.

1959			Litho.	
2175	A1071	40k buff, cl, blk & vio	.75	.40
2176	A1071	40k vio & brown	.75	.40
2177	A1071	40k slate & hn brn	.75	.40
2178	A1071	40k ol bister & brn	.75	.40
2178A	A1071	40k ol, gray & bis	.75	.40
2178B	A1071	40k brn, vio & bis	.75	.40
2178C	A1071	40k violet & black	.75	.40
	Nos. 2175-2178C (7)		5.25	2.80

No. 2178A for the 150th birth anniv. of Nikolai V. Gogol, writer. No. 2178B the centenary of the death of S. T. Aksakov, writer.

A. S. Popov and Rescue from Ice Float A1138

60k, Radio broadcasting "Peace" in 5 languages.

1959, Mar. 13				
2179	A1138	40k brn, blk & dk blue	.75	.25
2180	A1138	60k multicolored	1.25	.25

Centenary of the birth of A. S. Popov, pioneer in radio research.

M.S. Rossija at Odessa A1139

Ships: 10k, Steamer, Vladivostok-Petropavlovsk-Kamchatka line. 20k, M.S. Feliks Dzerzhinski, Odessa-Latakia line. No. 2184, Ship, Murmansk-Tyksi line. 60k, M.S. Mikhail Kalinin at Leningrad. 1r, M.S. Baltika, Leningrad-London line.

1959		Litho.	Unwmk.	
2181	A1139	10k multicolored	.30	.25
2182	A1139	20k red, lt grn & dk bl	.40	.25
2183	A1139	40k multicolored	.75	.25
2184	A1139	40k blue, buff & red	1.25	.25
2185	A1139	60k bl grn, red & buff	1.50	.30
2186	A1139	1r ultra, red & yel	1.75	1.00
	Nos. 2181-2186 (6)		5.95	2.30

Honoring the Russian fleet.

Globe and Luna 1 A1140

Luna 1, launched Jan. 2, 1959: No. 2188, Globe and route of Luna 1.

1959, Apr. 13				
2187	A1140	40k red brown & rose	2.50	.50
2188	A1140	40k ultra & blue	2.50	.50

Saadi and "Gulistan" A1141

1959, Mar. 20   Photo.
2189 A1141 40k dk blue & black   .75 .35
Persian poet Saadi (Muslih-ud-Din) and 700th anniv. of his book, "Gulistan" (1258).

Sulhan S. Orbeliani — A1142

1959, Apr. 2
2190 A1142 40k dull rose & black   .75 .35
Orbeliani (1658-1725), Georgian writer.

Drawing by Korin — A1143

1959, Apr. 10   Litho.
2191 A1143 40k multicolored   5.00 1.50
Ogata Korin (1653?-1716), Japanese artist.

Lenin — A1144

1959, Apr. 17   Engr.
2192 A1144 40k sepia   1.00 .50
89th anniversary of the birth of Lenin.

Cachin — A1146

1959, Apr. 27   Photo.
2194 A1146 60k dark brown   1.00 .30
Marcel Cachin (1869-1958), French Communist Party leader.

Joseph Haydn — A1147

1959, May 8
2195 A1147 40k dk bl, gray & brn black   5.00 .50
Sesquicentennial of the death of Joseph Haydn, Austrian composer.

Alexander von Humboldt — A1148

1959, May 6
2196 A1148 40k violet & brown   .75   .35
Alexander von Humboldt, German naturalist and geographer, death centenary.

Three Races Carrying Flag of Peace — A1149

1959, Apr. 30   **Litho.**
2199 A1149 40k multicolored   1.00   .25
10th anniv. of World Peace Movement.

Mountain Climber — A1150

Sports and Travel: No. 2201, Tourists reading map. No. 2202, Canoeing, horiz. No. 2203, Skiers.

1959, May 15
2200 A1150 40k multicolored   .50   .25
2201 A1150 40k multicolored   .50   .25
2202 A1150 40k multicolored   .50   .25
2203 A1150 40k multicolored   .50   .25
   Nos. 2200-2203 (4)   2.00 1.00

I. E. Repin Statue, Moscow — A1151

Statues: No. 2205, Lenin, Ulyanovsk. 20k, V. V. Mayakovsky, Moscow. 25k, Alexander Pushkin, Leningrad. 60k, Maxim Gorki, Moscow. 1r, Tchaikovsky, Moscow.

1959   **Photo.**   **Unwmk.**
2204 A1151 10k ocher & sepia   .25   .25
2205 A1151 10k red & black   .25   .25
2206 A1151 20k violet & sepia   .35   .25
2207 A1151 25k grnsh blue &
              blk   .45   .25
2208 A1151 60k lt green & slate .75   .25
2209 A1151 1r lt ultra & gray 1.75   .45
   Nos. 2204-2209 (6)   3.80 1.70

N. Y. Coliseum and Spasski Tower — A1152

1959, June 25   Litho.   Perf. 12
2210 A1152 20k multicolored   .30   .25
2211 A1152 40k multicolored   .70   .25
   a.   Souv. sheet of 1, imperf. 5.00 .50
Soviet Exhibition of Science, Technology and Culture, New York, June 20-Aug. 10. No. 2211a issued July 20.

Animal Types of 1957

No. 2213, Hare. No. 2214, Siberian horse. No. 2215, Tiger. No. 2216, Red squirrel. No. 2217, Pine marten. No. 2218, Hazel hen. No. 2219, Mute swan.

1959-60   Litho.   Perf. 12
Center in Natural Colors
2213 A1023 20k vio blue ('60)   .60   .25
2214 A1023 25k blue black   .60   .25
2215 A1023 25k brown   .60   .25
2216 A1023 40k deep green   .80   .25
2217 A1023 40k dark green   .80   .25
2218 A1024 60k dark green   1.25   .40
2219 A1023 1r bright blue   1.75   .85
   Nos. 2213-2219 (7)   6.40 2.50

Louis Braille — A1153

1959, July 16
2220 A1153 60k blue grn, bis &
              brn   .75   .35
150th anniversary of the birth of Louis Braille, French educator of the blind.

Musa Djalil — A1154

1959, July 16   Photo.
2221 A1154 40k violet & black 1.75   .35
Musa Djalil, Tatar poet.

Sturgeon A1155

1959, July 16
2222 A1155 40k shown   .75   .25
2223 A1155 60k Chum salmon   1.25   .25
   See Nos. 2375-2377.

Gymnast A1156

Athletes Holding Spartacist Games emblem — A1157

Designs: 25k, Runner. 60k, Water polo.

1959, Aug. 7
2224 A1156 15k lilac rose & gray .30 .25
2225 A1156 25k yel green & red
              brn   .60   .25
2226 A1157 30k brt red & gray   .75   .25
2227 A1156 60k blue & org yel 1.25   .25
   Nos. 2224-2227 (4)   2.90 1.00
2nd National Spartacist Games.

Globe and Hands — A1158

1959, Aug. 12   Litho.
2228 A1158 40k yel, blue & red .75   .35
2nd Intl. Conf. of Public Employees Unions.

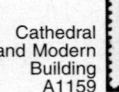

Cathedral and Modern Building A1159

1959, Aug. 21   Unwmk.   Perf. 12
2229 A1159 40k blue, ol, yel &
              red   1.00   .25
1100th anniv. of the city of Novgorod.

Schoolboys in Workshop — A1160

Design: 1r, Workers in night school.

1959, Aug. 27   Photo.
2230 A1160 40k dark purple   .25   .25
2231 A1160 1r dark blue   .50   .25
Strengthening the connection between school and life.

Glacier Survey — A1161

Rocket and Observatory A1162

Designs: 25k, Oceanographic ship "Vityaz" and map. 40k, Plane over Antarctica, camp and emperor penguin.

1959
2232 A1161 10k blue green   .25   .25
2233 A1161 25k brt blue & red   .30   .25
2234 A1161 40k ultra & red   .50   .25
2235 A1162 1r ultra & buff   1.50   .30
   Nos. 2232-2235 (4)   2.55 1.05
Intl. Geophysical Year. 1st Russian rocket to reach the moon, Sept. 14, 1959 (#2235).

Workers and Farmers Holding Atom Symbol — A1163

1959, Sept. 23   Litho.
2236 A1163 40k red org & bister .75 .35
All-Union Economic Exhibition, Moscow.

Russian and Chinese Students A1164

40k, Russian miner and Chinese steel worker.

1959, Sept. 25   Litho.   Perf. 12
2237 A1164 20k multicolored   .80   .30
2238 A1164 40k multicolored   1.20   .45
People's Republic of China, 10th anniv.

Letter Carrier A1165

1959, Sept.
2239 A1165 40k dk car rose &
              black   .40   .25
2240 A1165 60k blue & black   .60   .25
Intl. Letter Writing Week, Oct. 4-10.

Makhtumkuli A1166

1959, Sept. 30   Photo.
2241 A1166 40k brown   1.00   .25
225th anniversary of the birth of Makhtumkuli, Turkmen writer.

East German Emblem and Workers A1167

City Hall, East Berlin — A1168

1959, Oct. 6   Litho.
2242 A1167 40k multicolored   .35   .25
Photo.
2243 A1168 60k dp claret & buff .45 .25
German Democratic Republic, 10th anniv.

Steel Production — A1169

7-Year Production Plan (Industries): No. 2244, Chemicals. No. 2245, Spasski Tower, hammer and sickle. No. 2246, Home building. No. 2247, Meat production, woman with farm animals. No. 2248, Man working machinery. No. 2249, Grain production, woman tractor driver. No. 2250, Oil. No. 2251, Textiles. No. 2252, Steel. No. 2253, Coal. No. 2254, Iron. No. 2255, Electric power.

1959-60			**Litho.**
2244	A1169	10k vio, grnsh blue & maroon	.50 .25
2245	A1169	10k orange & dk car	.50 .25
2246	A1169	15k brn, yel & red	.50 .25
2247	A1169	15k brn, grn & mar	.50 .25
2248	A1169	20k bl grn, yel & red	.50 .25
2249	A1169	20k green, yel & red	.50 .25
2250	A1169	30k lilac, sal & red	.50 .25
2251	A1169	30k gldn brn, lil, red & green ('60)	.50 .25
2252	A1169	40k vio bl, yel & org	.50 .25
2253	A1169	40k dk blue, pink & dp rose	.50 .25
2254	A1169	60k org red, yel, bl & maroon	.50 .25
2255	A1169	60k ultra, buff & red	.50 .25
Nos. 2244-2255 (12)			6.00 3.00

Arms of Tadzhikistan A1170

1959, Oct. 13
2258 A1170 40k red, emer, ocher & black   .75   .35
Tadzhikistan statehood, 30th anniversary.

Path of Luna 3 and Electronics Laboratory A1171

1959, Oct. 12
2259 A1171 40k violet   1.50   .50
Flight of Luna 3 around the moon, Oct. 4, 1959.

Red Square, Moscow A1172

1959, Oct. 26   Engr.
2260 A1172 40k dark red   1.00   .50
42nd anniversary of October Revolution.

US Capitol, Globe and Kremlin — A1173

1959, Oct. 27   Photo.
2261 A1173 60k blue & yellow   1.00   .50
Visit of Premier Nikita Khrushchev to the US, Sept., 1959.

Helicopter — A1174

25k, Diver. 40k, Motorcyclist. 60k, Parachutist.

1959, Oct. 28
2262 A1174 10k vio blue & mar   .25   .25
2263 A1174 25k blue & brown   .60   .25
2264 A1174 40k red brn & indigo   1.00   .25
2265 A1174 60k blue & ol bister   1.25   .25
Nos. 2262-2265 (4)   3.10   1.00
Honoring voluntary aides of the army.

Moon, Earth and Path of Rocket A1175

No. 2267, Kremlin and diagram showing rocket and positions of moon and earth.

1959, Nov. 1   Litho.
2266 A1175 40k bl, dk bl, red & bis   1.50   .25
2267 A1175 40k gray, pink & red   1.50   .25
Landing of the Soviet rocket on the moon, Sept. 14, 1959.

Sandor Petőfi A1176

Victory Statue and View of Budapest — A1177

1959, Nov. 9   Perf. 12x12½, 12½x12
2268 A1176 20k gray & ol bister   .50   .25
2269 A1177 40k multicolored   1.50   .50
Soviet-Hungarian friendship.
For overprint see No. 2308.

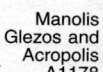

Manolis Glezos and Acropolis A1178

1959, Nov. 12   Photo.   Perf. 12x12½
2270 A1178 40k ultra & brown   9.00   3.00
Manolis Glezos, Greek communist.

A. A. Voskresensky, Chemist, 150th Birth Anniv. — A1179

1959, Dec. 7   Perf. 12½x12
2271 A1179 40k ultra & brown   .75   .35

Chusovaya River, Ural — A1180

No. 2273, Lake Ritza, Caucasus. No. 2274, Lena River, Siberia. No. 2275, Seashore, Far East. No. 2276, Lake Iskander, Central Asia. No. 2277, Lake Baikal, Siberia. No. 2278, Belukha Mountain, Altai range. No. 2279, Khibiny Mountains. No. 2280, Gursuf region, Crimea.

1959, Dec.		**Engr.**	**Perf. 12½**
2272	A1180	10k purple	.25 .25
2273	A1180	10k rose carmine	.25 .25
2274	A1180	25k dark blue	.65 .25
2275	A1180	25k olive	.65 .25
2276	A1180	25k dark red	.65 .25
2277	A1180	40k claret	1.50 .25
2278	A1180	60k Prus blue	2.25 .35
2279	A1180	1r olive green	4.50 .75
2280	A1180	1r deep orange	4.50 .75
Nos. 2272-2280 (9)			15.20 3.35

"Trumpeters of 1st Cavalry" by M. Grekov — A1181

1959, Dec. 30   Litho.   Perf. 12½x12
2283 A1181 40k multicolored   2.00   1.00
40th anniversary of the 1st Cavalry.

Farm Woman — A1182

Designs: 25k, Architect. 60k, Steel worker.

1958-60		**Engr.**	**Perf. 12½**
2286	A1182	20k slate grn ('59)	7.00 3.75
2287	A1182	25k sepia ('59)	3.25 1.60
2288	A1182	60k carmine	9.25 4.25
Perf. 12x12½			
Litho.			
2290	A1182	20k green ('60)	.25 .25
2291	A1182	25k sepia ('60)	.75 .25
2292	A1182	60k vermilion ('59)	.25 .25
2293	A1182	60k blue ('60)	1.50 .25
Nos. 2286-2293 (7)			22.25 10.60

Mikhail V. Frunze (1885-1925), Revolutionary A1183

1960, Jan. 25   Photo.   Perf. 12½
2295 A1183 40k dark red brown   1.00   .35

G.N. Gabrichevsky, Microbiologist, Birth Cent. — A1184

Perf. 12½x12
1960, Jan. 30   Unwmk.
2296 A1184 40k brt vio & brn   1.00   .35

Anton Chekhov and Moscow Home A1185

40k, Chekhov in later years, Yalta home.

1960, Jan. 20   Litho.   Perf. 12x12½
2297 A1185 20k red, gray & vio bl   .40   .25
2298 A1185 40k dk blue, buff & brn   .70   .25
Anton P. Chekhov (1860-1904), playwright.

Vera Komissar-zhevskaya (1864-1910), Actress — A1186

1960, Feb. 5   Photo.   Perf. 12½x12
2299 A1186 40k chocolate   1.00   .50

8th Olympic Winter Games, Squaw Valley, Calif., Feb. 18-29 A1187

Sports: 10k, Ice hockey. 25k, Speed skating. 40k, Skier. 60k, Woman figure skater. 1r, Ski jumper.

1960, Feb. 18		**Litho.**	**Perf. 11½**
2300	A1187	10k ocher & vio blue	.25 .25
2301	A1187	25k multicolored	.50 .25
2302	A1187	40k org, rose lil & vio blue	.75 .25
2303	A1187	60k vio, grn & buff	1.25 .25
2304	A1187	1r bl, grn & brn	2.25 .35
Nos. 2300-2304 (5)			5.00 1.35

Sword into Plowshare Statue, UN, NY — A1188

1960   **Perf. 12x12½**
2305 A1188 40k grnsh bl, yel & brown   1.00   .50
     a.   Souvenir sheet, imperf.   2.00   .50

No. 2305a for Premier Nikita Khrushchev's visit to the 15th General Assembly of the UN in NYC.

Women of Various Races A1189

1960, Mar. 8
2306 A1189 40k multicolored   1.00   .35

50 years of Intl. Woman's Day, Mar. 8.

Planes in Combat and Timur Frunze A1190

1960, Feb. 23   **Perf. 12½x12**
2307 A1190 40k multicolored   2.00 1.50

Lieut. Timur Frunze, World War II hero.

No. 2269 Overprinted in Red

1960, Apr. 4
2308 A1177 40k multicolored   4.50 2.50

15th anniversary of Hungary's liberation from the Nazis.

Lunik 3 Photographing Far Side of Moon — A1191

Design: 60k, Far side of the moon.

1960   **Photo.**   **Perf. 12x12½**
2309 A1191 40k pale bl, dk bl & yel   1.75   .30
     Litho.
2310 A1191 60k lt bl, dk bl & citron   2.25   .30

Photographing of the far side of the moon, Oct. 7, 1959.

Lenin as Child A1192

Various Lenin Portraits and: 20k, Lenin with children and Christmas tree. 30k, Flag, workers and ship. 40k, Kremlin, banners and marchers. 60k, Map of Russia, buildings and ship. 1r, Peace proclamation and globe.

1960, Apr. 10   **Litho.**   **Perf. 12½x12**
2311 A1192 10k multicolored   .25   .25
2312 A1192 20k red, green & blk   .30   .25
2313 A1192 30k multicolored   .30   .25
2314 A1192 40k multicolored   .75   .25

2315 A1192 60k multicolored   1.00   .30
2316 A1192 1r red, vio bl & brn   2.00   .45
     Nos. 2311-2316 (6)   4.80 1.75

90th anniversary of the birth of Lenin.

Steelworker A1193

1960, Apr. 30   **Photo.**
2317 A1193 40k brown & red   1.00   .50

Industrial overproduction by 50,000,000r during the 1st year of the 7-year plan.

Government House, Baku A1194

1960, Apr.   **Litho.**   **Perf. 12½x12½**
2318 A1194 40k bister & brown   1.00   .30

Azerbaijan, 40th anniv.
For surcharge see #2898.

Brotherhood Monument, Prague — A1195

Design: 60k, Charles Bridge, Prague.

1960, Apr. 29   **Photo.**   **Perf. 12½x12**
2319 A1195 40k brt blue & blk   .25   .25
2320 A1195 60k blk brn & yel   .75   .30

Czechoslovak Republic, 15th anniv.

Radio Tower and Popov Central Museum of Communications, Leningrad — A1196

1960, May 6   **Litho.**
2321 A1196 40k blue, ocher & brn   1.00   .50

Radio Day.

   Gen. I. D. Tcherniakovski and Soldiers — A1197

1960, May 4
2322 A1197 1r multicolored   1.00   .50

Gen. I. D. Tcherniakovski, World War II hero and his military school.

Robert Schumann (1810-56), German Composer A1198

1960, May 20   **Photo.**   **Perf. 12x12½**
2323 A1198 40k ultra & black   1.00   .50

Yakov M. Sverdlov (1885-1919), 1st USSR Pres. — A1199

1960, May 24   **Perf. 12½x12**
2324 A1199 40k dk brn & org brn   1.00   .50

Stamp of 1957 Under Magnifying Glass A1200

1960, May 28   **Litho.**   **Perf. 11½**
2325 A1200 60k multicolored   1.00   .50

Stamp Day.

Karl Marx Avenue, Petrozavodsk, Karelian Autonomous Republic — A1201

No. 2327

No. 2329

No. 2330

No. 2332

No. 2333

No. 2341

No. 2342

Capitals, Soviet Autonomous Republics: No. 2327, Lenin street, Batum, Adzhar. No. 2328, Cultural Palace, Izhevsk, Udmurt. No. 2329, August street, Grozny, Chechen-Ingush. No. 2330, Soviet House, Cheboksary, Chuvash. No. 2331, Buinak Street, Makhachkala, Dagestan. No. 2332, Soviet street, Ioshkar Ola, Mari. No. 2333, Chkalov street, Dzaudzhikau, North Ossetia. No. 2334, October street, Yakutsk, Yakut. No. 2335, House of Ministers, Nukus, Kara-Kalpak.

1960   **Engr.**   **Perf. 12½**
2326 A1201 40k Prus green   1.10   .50
2327 A1201 40k violet blue   1.10   .50
2328 A1201 40k green   1.10   .50
2329 A1201 40k maroon   1.10   .50
2330 A1201 40k dull red   1.10   .50
2331 A1201 40k carmine   .90   .30
2332 A1201 40k dark brown   .90   .30
2333 A1201 40k orange brown   .90   .30
2334 A1201 40k dark blue   .90   .30
2335 A1201 40k brown   .90   .30
     Nos. 2326-2335 (10)   10.00 4.00

See Nos. 2338-2344C. For overprints see Nos. 2336-2337.

No. 2326 Overprinted in Red

1960, June 4
2336 A1201 40k Prus green   5.00 3.00

Karelian Autonomous Rep., 40th anniv.

No. 2328 Overprinted in Red

1960, Nov. 4
2337 A1201 40k green   5.00 3.00

Udmurt Autonomous Rep., 40th anniv.

1961-62   **Perf. 12½, 12½x12**

Capitals, Soviet Autonomous Republics: No. 2338, Rustaveli Street, Sukhumi, Abkhazia. No. 2339, House of Soviets, Nalchik, Kabardino-Balkar. No. 2340, Lenin Street, Ulan-Ude, Buriat. No. 2341, Soviet Street, Syktyvkar, Komi. No. 2342, Lenin Street, Nakhichevan, Nakhichevan. No. 2343, Elista, Kalmyk. No. 2344, Ufa, Bashkir. No. 2344A, Lobachevsky Square, Kazan, Tartar. No. 2344B, Kizil, Tuvinia. No. 2344C, Saransk, Mordovia.

2338   A1201 4k orange ver   .30   .25
2339   A1201 4k dark violet   .30   .25
2340   A1201 4k dark blue   .30   .25
2341   A1201 4k gray   .30   .25
2342   A1201 4k dk car rose   .30   .25
2343   A1201 4k olive green   .30   .25
2344   A1201 4k dull purple   .30   .25
2344A A1201 4k grnsh blk ('62)   .40   .25
2344B A1201 4k claret ('62)   .40   .25
2344C A1201 4k deep grn ('62)   .40   .25
     Nos. 2338-2344C (10)   3.30 2.50

Denominations of Nos. 2338-2344C are in the revalued currency.

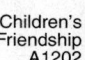

Children's Friendship A1202

Drawings by Children: 20k, Collective farm, vert. 25k, Winter joys. 40k, "In the Zoo."

Perf. 12x12½, 12½x12

1960, June 1		**Litho.**		
2345	A1202	10k multicolored	.50	.25
2346	A1202	20k multicolored	.50	.25
2347	A1202	25k multicolored	.50	.25
2348	A1202	40k multicolored	.50	.25
	Nos. 2345-2348 (4)		*2.00*	*1.00*

Lomonosov University and Congress Emblem — A1203

1960, June 17 Photo. Perf. 12½x12
2349 A1203 60k yel & dk brn 1.25 .40

1st congress of the International Federation for Automation Control, Moscow.

Sputnik 4 and Globe — A1204

1960, June 17 Perf. 12x12½
2350 A1204 40k vio blue & dp org 3.00 .55

Launching on May 15, 1960, of Sputnik 4, which orbited the earth with a dummy cosmonaut.

Kosta Hetagurov (1859-1906), Ossetian Poet — A1205

1960, June 20 Litho. Perf. 12½
2351 A1205 40k gray blue & brn 1.00 .50

Flag and Tallinn, Estonia A1206

Soviet Republics, 20th Annivs.: No. 2353, Flag and Riga, Latvia. No. 2354, Flag and Vilnius, Lithuania.

Perf. 12x12½, 12½ (#2353)

1960			**Photo.**	
2352	A1206	40k red & ultra	.65	.25
		Typo.		
2353	A1206	40k blue, gray & red	.65	.25
		Litho.		
2354	A1206	40k blue, red & grn	.65	.25
	Nos. 2352-2354 (3)		*1.95*	*.75*

Cement Factory, Belgorod A1207

Design: 40k, Factory, Novy Krivoi.

1960, June 28 Perf. 12½x12
2355 A1207 25k ultra & black .40 .25
2356 A1207 40k rose brn & blk .60 .25

"New buildings of the 1st year of the 7-year plan."

Automatic Production Line and Roller Bearing A1208

No. 2358, Automatic production line and gear.

1960, June 13 Perf. 11½
2357 A1208 40k rose violet .50 .25
2358 A1208 40k Prus green .50 .25

Publicizing mechanization and automation of factories.

Running A1209

Sports: 10k, Wrestling. 15k, Basketball. 20k, Weight lifting. 25k, Boxing. No. 2364, Fencing. No. 2365, Diving. No. 2366, Women's gymnastics. 60k, Canoeing. 1r, Steeplechase.

1960, Aug. 1		**Litho.**	**Perf. 11½**	
2359	A1209	5k multicolored	.25	.25
2360	A1209	10k brn, blue & yel	.25	.25
2361	A1209	15k multicolored	.25	.25
2362	A1209	20k blk, crim & sal	.30	.25
2363	A1209	25k lake, sl & rose	.30	.25
2364	A1209	40k vio bl, bl & bis	.40	.25
2365	A1209	40k vio, gray & pink	.40	.25
2366	A1209	40k multicolored	.50	.25
2367	A1209	60k multicolored	.60	.25
2368	A1209	1r brn, lil & pale grn	.90	.45
	Nos. 2359-2368 (10)		*4.15*	*2.70*

17th Olympic Games, Rome, 8/25-9/11.

No. 2365 Overprinted in Red

1960, Aug. 23
2369 A1209 40k vio, gray & pink 10.00 7.50

12th San Marino-Riccione Stamp Fair.

Kishinev, Moldavian Republic A1210

1960, Aug. 2 Perf. 12x12½
2370 A1210 40k multicolored 1.00 .50

20th anniversary of Moldavian Republic.

Tractor and Factory A1211

Book Museum, Hanoi — A1212

Perf. 12x12½, 12½x12
1960, Aug. 25
2371 A1211 40k green, ocher & blk .60 .25
2372 A1212 60k blue, lilac & brn .90 .25

15th anniversary of North Viet Nam.

Gregory N. Minkh, Microbiologist, 125th Birth Anniv. — A1213

1960, Aug. 25 Photo. Perf. 12½x12
2373 A1213 60k bister brn & dk brn 1.00 .50

"March," by I. I. Levitan A1214

1960, Aug. 29
2374 A1214 40k ol bister & black .75 .30

I. I. Levitan, painter, birth cent.

Fish Type of 1959

Designs: 20k, Pikeperch. 25k, Fur seals. 40k, Ludogan whitefish.

1960, Sept. 3 Perf. 12½
2375 A1155 20k blue & black .40 .25
2376 A1155 25k vio gray & red brn .40 .25
2377 A1155 40k rose lil & pur .75 .25
  Nos. 2375-2377 (3) *1.55* *.75*

Forest by I. I. Shishkin — A1215

1960, Aug. 29 Engr.
2378 A1215 1r red brown 2.00 .50

5th World Forestry Congress, Seattle, Wash., Aug. 29-Sept. 10.

Globe with USSR and Letter A1216

1960, Sept. 10 Litho. Perf. 12x12½
2379 A1216 40k multicolored .40 .25
2380 A1216 60k multicolored .50 .30

Intl. Letter Writing Week, Oct. 3-9.

Farmer, Worker, Scientist A1217

1960, Oct. 4 Typo. Perf. 12½
2381 A1217 40k multicolored .60 .25

Kazakh SSR, 40th anniv.

Globes and Olive Branch — A1218

1960, Sept. 29 Litho. Perf. 12½x12
2382 A1218 60k pale vio, bl & gray .70 .25

World Federation of Trade Unions, 15th anniv.

Kremlin, Sputnik 5 and Dogs Belka and Strelka A1219

1960, Sept. 29 Photo.
2383 A1219 40k brt pur & yellow .75 .30
2384 A1219 1r blue & salmon 2.25 .40

Flight of Sputnik 5, Aug. 19-20, 1960.

Passenger Ship "Karl Marx" A1220

Ships: 40k, Turbo-electric ship "Lenin." 60k, Speedboat "Raketa" (Rocket).

1960, Oct. 24 Litho. Perf. 12x12½
2385 A1220 25k bl, blk & yel .40 .25
2386 A1220 40k blue, black & red .60 .25
2387 A1220 60k blue, blk & rose 1.00 .35
  Nos. 2385-2387 (3) *2.00* *.85*

A. N. Voronikhin and Kasansky Cathedral, Leningrad A1221

1960, Oct. 24 Photo.
2388 A1221 40k gray & brn black 1.00 .50

Voronikhin, architect, 200th birth anniv.

J. S. Gogebashvili A1222

1960, Oct. 29
2389 A1222 40k dk gray & mag 1.00 .50

120th anniversary of the birth of J. S. Gogebashvili, Georgian teacher and publicist.

Red Flag, Electric
Power Station
and
Factory — A1223

1960, Oct. 29   **Litho.**
2390 A1223 40k red, yel & brown .70 .25
43rd anniversary of October Revolution.

Leo Tolstoy
A1224

Designs: 40k, Tolstoy in Yasnaya Polyana.
60k, Portrait, vert.

Perf. 12x12½, 12½x12
1960, Nov. 14
2391 A1224 20k violet & brown .30 .25
2392 A1224 40k blue & lt brown .70 .25
2393 A1224 60k dp clar & sep 1.00 .35
   Nos. 2391-2393 (3) 2.00 .85
50th anniversary of the death of Count Leo
Tolstoy, writer.

Yerevan,
Armenian
Republic
A1225

1960, Nov. 14   **Perf. 12x12½**
2394 A1225 40k bl, red, buff &
    brn 1.00 .50
Armenian Soviet Rep., 40th anniv.

Friedrich Engels,
140th Birth
Anniv. — A1226

1960, Nov. 25 **Engr.** **Perf. 12½**
2395 A1226 60k slate 1.00 .50

Badge of Youth
Federation
A1227

1960, Nov. 2   **Litho.**
2396 A1227 60k brt pink, blk &
    yel .50 .25
Intl. Youth Federation, 15th anniv.

40-ton Truck
MAL-530
A1228

Automotive Industry: 40k, "Volga" car. 60k,
"Moskvitch 407" car. 1r, "Tourist LAS-697"
Bus.

1960, Oct. 29 **Photo.** **Perf. 12x12½**
2397 A1228 25k ultra & gray .40 .25
2398 A1228 40k ol bister & ultra .60 .25
2399 A1228 60k Prus green & dp
    car .90 .25

Litho.
2400 A1228 1r multicolored 1.40 .35
   Nos. 2397-2400 (4) 3.30 1.10

N. I.
Pirogov — A1229

1960, Dec. 13 **Photo.** **Perf. 12½x12**
2401 A1229 40k grn & brn blk 1.00 .50
Pirogov, surgeon, 125th birth anniv.

Friendship
University and
Students
A1230

1960, Nov.   **Perf. 12x12½**
2402 A1230 40k brown carmine 1.00 .50
Completion of Friendship of Nations University in Moscow.
For surcharge see No. 2462.

Mark
Twain
A1231

1960, Nov. 30   **Perf. 12½x12**
2403 A1231 40k dp org & brown 2.00 .90
Mark Twain, 125th birth anniv.

Dove and
Globe — A1232

1960, Oct. 29   **Photo.**
2404 A1232 60k maroon & gray 1.00 .50
Intl. Democratic Women's Fed, 15th anniv.

Akaki
Tsereteli — A1233

1960, Dec. 27
2405 A1233 40k vio & blk brn 1.00 .30
Tsereteli, Georgian poet, 120th birth anniv.

Frederic
Chopin, after
Delacroix
A1234

1960, Dec. 24   **Perf. 12x11½**
2406 A1234 40k bister & brown 1.10 .25
Chopin, Polish composer, 150th birth anniv.

North Korean Flag
and Flying
Horse — A1235

1960, Dec. 24 **Litho.** **Perf. 12½x12**
2407 A1235 40k multicolored 1.00 .50
15th anniversary of "the liberation of the
Korean people by the Soviet army."

Crocus — A1236

Asiatic Flowers: No. 2409, Tulip. No. 2410,
Trollius. No. 2411, Tulip. No. 2412, Ginseng.
No. 2413, Iris. No. 2414, Hypericum. 1r, Dog
rose.

1960   **Perf. 12x12½**
Flowers in Natural Colors
2408 A1236 20k green & violet .30 .25
2409 A1236 20k vio blue & black .30 .25
2410 A1236 25k gray .35 .25
2411 A1236 40k ol bister & black .40 .25
2412 A1236 40k grn & blk,
    wmkd. .40 .25
2413 A1236 60k yel, green & red .75 .25
2414 A1236 60k bluish grn & blk .75 .25
2415 A1236 1r slate grn & blk 1.25 .25
   Nos. 2408-2415 (8) 4.50 2.00
The watermark on No. 2412 consists of vertical rows of chevrons.

Lithuanian
Costumes
A1237

Regional Costumes: 60k, Uzbek.

Perf. 12½ (10k), 11½ (60k)
1960, Dec. 24 **Typo.** **Unwmk.**
2416 A1237 10k multicolored .25 .25
2417 A1237 60k multicolored 1.00 .40

Currency Revalued
1961-62 **Litho.** **Perf. 11½**
Regional Costumes: No. 2418, Moldavia.
No. 2419, Georgia. No. 2420, Ukrainia. No.
2421, White Russia. No. 2422, Kazakhstan.
No. 2422A, Latvia. 4k, Koryak. 6k, Russia.
10k, Armenia. 12k, Estonia.
2418 A1237 2k buff, brn & ver .25 .25
2419 A1237 2k red, brn, ocher
    · & black .25 .25
2420 A1237 3k ultra, buff, red
    & brown .30 .25
2421 A1237 3k red org, ocher
    & black .30 .25
2422 A1237 3k buff, brn, grn &
    red .30 .25
2422A A1237 3k org red, gray ol
    & blk ('62) .30 .25
2423 A1237 4k multicolored .50 .25
2424 A1237 6k multicolored .60 .30
2425 A1237 10k brn, ol bis &
    vermilion .90 .35
2426 A1237 12k red, ultra &
    black 1.25 .45
   Nos. 2418-2426 (10) 4.95 2.85
See Nos. 2723-2726.

Lenin and Map Showing
Electrification — A1238

1961   **Perf. 12½x12**
2427 A1238 4k blue, buff &
    brown .50 .25
2428 A1238 10k red org & blue
    blk 1.00 .35
State Electrification Plan, 40th anniv. (in
1960).

Animal Types of 1957
1961, Jan. 7   **Perf. 12½**
2429 A1024 1k Brown bear .75 .25
2430 A1023 6k Beaver 2.25 .70
2431 A1023 10k Roe deer 3.00 .95
   Nos. 2429-2431 (3) 6.00 1.90

Georgian
Flag and
Views
A1239

1961, Feb. 15   **Perf. 12½x12**
2432 A1239 4k multicolored .40 .25
40th anniv. of Georgian SSR.

Nikolai D.
Zelinski,
Chemist,
Birth Cent.
A1240

1961, Feb. 6 **Photo.** **Perf. 12x12½**
2433 A1240 4k rose violet .50 .25

Nikolai A.
Dobrolyubov (1836-
61), Journalist and
Critic — A1241

1961, Feb. 5   **Perf. 11½x12**
2434 A1241 4k brt blue & brown .55 .25

A1242

Designs: 3k, Cattle. 4k, Tractor in cornfield.
6k, Mechanization of Grain Harvest. 10k,
Women picking apples.

1961   **Perf. 12x12½, 12x11½**
2435 A1242 3k blue & magenta .30 .25
2436 A1242 4k green & dk gray .30 .25
2437 A1242 6k vio blue & brn .70 .25
2438 A1242 10k maroon & ol grn 1.00 .40
   Nos. 2435-2438 (4) 2.30 1.15
Agricultural development.

A1243

Designs: 1k, "Labor" Holding Peace Flag. 2k, Harvester and silo. 3k, Space rockets. 4k, Arms and flag of USSR. 6k, Kremlin tower. 10k, Workers' monument. 12k, Minin and Pozharsky Monument and Spasski tower. 16k, Plane over power station and dam.

Perf. 12x12½; 12x11½ (Nos. 2439A, 2442 & 12k)

1961-65   Engr.   Unwmk.
2439	A1243	1k olive bister	1.00	.25

Litho.
2439A	A1243	1k olive bister	1.00	.25
2440	A1243	2k green	.35	.30
2441	A1243	3k dk violet	2.50	.25

Engr.
2442	A1243	3k dk violet	5.25	2.50

Litho.
2443	A1243	4k red	.75	.25
2443A	A1243	4k org brn ('65)	13.00	9.00
2444	A1243	6k vermilion	6.00	.90
2445	A1243	6k dk car rose	2.00	.25
2446	A1243	10k orange	3.75	.25

Photo.
2447	A1243	12k brt magenta	3.50	.30

Litho.
2448	A1243	16k ultra	4.50	.80
	Nos. 2439-2448 (12)		43.60	15.30

V. P. Miroshnitchenko — A1244

1961, Feb. 23   Photo.   Perf. 12½x12
2449 A1244 4k violet brn & slate .75 .40
Soldier hero of World War II.
See Nos. 2570-2571.

Taras G. Shevchenko and Birthplace — A1245

Shevchenko Statue, Kharkov — A1246

6k, Book, torch and Shevchenko with beard.

Perf. 12½, 11½x12
1961, Mar.   Litho.; Photo. (4k)
2450	A1245	3k brown & violet	.50	.25
2451	A1246	4k red org & gray	.40	.25
2452	A1245	6k blk, grn & red brn	.85	.25
	Nos. 2450-2452 (3)		1.75	.80

Shevchenko, Ukrainian poet, death cent. No. 2452 was printed with alternating green and black label, containing a quotation.
See No. 2852.

Andrei Rubljov — A1247

1961, Mar. 13   Litho.   Perf. 12½x12
2453 A1247 4k ultra, bister & brn 1.00 .50
Rubljov, painter, 600th birth anniv.

N. V. Sklifosovsky A1248

1961, Mar. 26   Photo.   Perf. 11½x12
2454 A1248 4k ultra & black 1.00 .35
Sklifosovsky, surgeon, 125th birth anniv.

Robert Koch — A1249

1961, Mar. 26
2455 A1249 6k dark brown 2.00 .50
Koch, German microbiologist, 59th death anniv.

Globe and Sputnik 8 — A1250

10k, Venera 1 space probe and its path to Venus.

1961, Apr.   Litho.   Perf. 11½
2456 A1250 6k dk & lt blue & org .65 .25

Photo.
2457 A1250 10k vio blue & yel .90 .35
Launching of the Venera 1 space probe, 2/12/61.

Open Book and Globe A1251

1961, Apr. 7   Litho.   Perf. 12½x12
2458 A1251 6k ultra & sepia .75 .25
Centenary of the magazine "Around the World."

Musician, Dancers and Singers A1252

1961, Apr. 7   Unwmk.
2459 A1252 4k yel, red & black .50 .25
Russian National Choir, 50th anniv.

African Breaking Chains and Map — A1253

6k, Globe, torch & black & white handshake.

1961, Apr. 15   Perf. 12½
2460	A1253	4k multicolored	.60	.25
2461	A1253	6k blue, pur & org	.60	.25

Africa Day and 3rd Conference of Independent African States, Cairo, Mar. 25-31.

No. 2402 Surcharged in Red

1961, Apr. 15   Photo.   Perf. 12x12½
2462 A1230 4k on 40k brn car 1.00 .40
Naming of Friendship University, Moscow, in memory of Patrice Lumumba, Premier of Congo.

Maj. Yuri A. Gagarin A1254

6k, Kremlin, rockets and radar equipment. 10k, Rocket, Gagarin with helmet and Kremlin.

1961, Apr.   Perf. 11½ (3k), 12½x12½
2463 A1254 3k Prus blue .35 .25

Litho.
2464	A1254	6k blue, vio & red	.70	.25
2465	A1254	10k red, blue grn & brn	1.20	.25
	Nos. 2463-2465 (3)		2.25	.75

1st man in space, Yuri A. Gagarin, Apr. 12, 1961. No. 2464 printed with alternating light blue and red label.
Nos. 2463-2465 exist imperf. Value $5.

Lenin — A1255

1961, Apr. 22   Litho.   Perf. 12x12½
2466 A1255 4k dp car, sal & blk .75 .25
91st anniversary of Lenin's birth.

Rabindranath Tagore — A1256

1961, May 8   Engr.   Perf. 11½x12
2467 A1256 6k bis, maroon & blk 1.00 .25
Tagore, Indian poet, birth cent.

The Hunchbacked Horse — A1257

Fairy Tales: 1k, The Geese and the Swans. 3k, Fox, Hare and Cock. 6k, The Peasant and the Bear. 10k, Ruslan and Ludmilla.

1961   Litho.   Perf. 12½
2468	A1257	1k multicolored	.25	.25
2469	A1257	3k multicolored	.75	.35
2470	A1257	4k multicolored	.50	.25
2471	A1257	6k multicolored	.90	.40
2472	A1257	10k multicolored	1.10	.45
	Nos. 2468-2472 (5)		3.50	1.70

"Man Conquering Space" A1258

Design: 6k, Giuseppe Garibaldi.

1961, May 24   Photo.
2481	A1258	4k orange brown	.40	.30
2482	A1258	6k lilac & salmon	.60	.30

International Labor Exposition, Turin.

Lenin — A1259

Various portraits of Lenin.

1961   Photo.   Perf. 12½x12½
Olive Bister Frame
2483	A1259	20k dark green	1.75	1.00
2484	A1259	30k dark blue	2.75	2.00
2485	A1259	50k rose red	8.00	6.00
	Nos. 2483-2485 (3)		12.50	9.00

Patrice Lumumba — A1260

1961, May 29   **Litho.**
2486 A1260 2k yellow & brown   .50 .25
Lumumba (1925-61), premier of Congo.

Kindergarten — A1261

Children's Day: 3k, Young Pioneers in camp. 4k, Young Pioneers, vert.

    Perf. 12½x12, 12x12½
1961, May 31   **Photo.**
2487 A1261 2k orange & ultra   .25 .25
2488 A1261 3k ol bister & purple   .60 .30
2489 A1261 4k red & gray   1.00 .25
   Nos. 2487-2489 (3)   1.85 .80

Dog Zvezdochka and Sputnik 10 — A1263

Sputniks 9 and 10: 4k, Dog Chernushka and Sputnik 9, vert.

1961, June 8 Litho. Perf. 12½, 11½
2491 A1263 2k vio, Prus blue & blk   5.00 2.50
      Photo.
2492 A1263 4k Prus blue & brt grn   5.00 2.50

Vissarion G. Belinski, Author, 150th Birth. Anniv. — A1265

Engraved and Photogravure
1961, June 13   **Perf. 11½x12**
2493 A1265 4k carmine & black   .75 .35

Lt. Gen. D.M. Karbishev A1266

1961, June 22 Litho. Perf. 12½
2494 A1266 4k black, red & yel   .35 .25
Karbishev was tortured to death in the Nazi prison camp at Mauthausen, Austria.

Hydro-meteorological Map and Instruments — A1267

1961, June 21   **Perf. 12x12½**
2495 A1267 6k ultra & green   .50 .35
40th anniversary of hydro-meteorological service in Russia.

Gliders A1268

6k, Motorboat race. 10k, Motorcycle race.

1961, July 5 Photo. Perf. 12½
2497 A1268 4k dk slate grn & crim   .30 .25
     Litho.
2498 A1268 6k slate & vermilion .45 .25
2499 A1268 10k slate & vermilion 1.40 .35
   Nos. 2497-2499 (3)   2.15 .85
USSR Technical Sports Spartakiad.

Javelin Thrower A1269

1961, Aug. 8 Photo. Perf. 12½x12
2500 A1269 6k dp car & pink   .50 .25
7th Trade Union Spartacist Games.

S. I. Vavilov — A1270

1961, July 25
2501 A1270 4k lt green & sepia   .60 .25
Vavilov, president of Academy of Science.

Vazha Pshavela — A1271

1961   **Photo.**   **Perf. 11½x12**
2502 A1271 4k dk brn & cream   .75 .35
Pshavela, Georgian poet, birth cent.

Scientists at Control Panel for Rocket — A1272

Globe and Youth Activities A1273

Design: 2k, Men pushing tank into river.

1961   **Unwmk.**   **Perf. 11½**
2503 A1273 2k orange & sepia   .25 .25
2504 A1272 4k lilac & dk green   .60 .40
2505 A1273 6k ultra & citron   1.00 .60
   Nos. 2503-2505 (3)   1.85 1.25
International Youth Forum, Moscow.

Arms of Mongolian Republic and Sukhe Bator Statue A1274

1961, July 25 Litho. Perf. 12½x12
2506 A1274 4k multicolored   1.00 .50
Mongol national revolution, 40th anniv.

Knight Kalevipoeg A1275

1961, July 31
2507 A1275 4k black, blue & yel   .75 .35
1st publication of "Kalevipoeg," Estonian national saga, recorded by R. K. Kreutzwald, Estonian writer, cent.

Symbols of Biochemistry A1276

1961, July 31
2508 A1276 6k multicolored   .75 .35
5th Intl. Biochemistry Congress, Moscow.

Major Titov and Vostok 2 — A1277

4k, Globe with orbit and cosmonaut.

1961, Aug.   **Photo.**   **Perf. 11½**
2509 A1277 4k vio blue & dp plum   .35 .25
2510 A1277 6k brown, grn & org   .65 .25
1st manned space flight around the world, Maj. Gherman S. Titov, Aug. 6-7, 1961. Nos. 2509-2510 exist imperf. Value, set $10.

A. D. Zacharov and Admiralty Building, Leningrad A1278

1961, Aug. 8   **Perf. 12x11½**
2511 A1278 4k blue, dk brn & buff   .50 .25
Zacharov (1761-1811), architect.

Defense of Brest, 1941 A1279

Designs: No. 2512, Defense of Moscow. No. 2514, Defense of Odessa. No. 2514A, Defense of Sevastopol. No. 2514B, Defense of Leningrad. No. 2514C, Defense of Kiev. No. 2514D, Battle of the Volga (Stalingrad).

1961-63   **Photo.**   **Perf. 12½x12**
2512 A1279 4k blk & red brn (Moscow)   .50 .25
      Litho.
2513 A1279 4k (Brest)   .50 .25
2514 A1279 4k (Odessa)   .50 .25
2514A A1279 4k (Sevastopol; '62)   .50 .25
2514B A1279 4k brn, dl bl & bis (Leningrad; '63)   .50 .25
2514C A1279 4k blk & multi (Kiev; '63)   .50 .25
2514D A1279 4k dl org & multi (Volga; '63)   .50 .25
   Nos. 2512-2514D (7)   3.50 1.75
"War of Liberation," 1941-1945. See Nos. 2757-2758.

Students' Union Emblem A1280

1961, Aug. 8 Litho. Perf. 12½
2515 A1280 6k ultra & red   .75 .35
15th anniversary of the founding of the International Students' Union.

Soviet Stamps A1281

Stamps and background different on each denomination.

1961, Aug.   **Perf. 12½x12**
2516 A1281 2k multicolored   .40 .25
2517 A1281 4k multicolored   .75 .30
2518 A1281 6k multicolored   1.25 .35
2519 A1281 10k multicolored   2.00 .50
   Nos. 2516-2519 (4)   4.40 1.40
40 years of Soviet postage stamps.

Nikolai A. Schors Statue, Kiev — A1282

Statue: 4k, Gregori I. Kotovski, Kishinev.

1961 Photo. Perf. 11½x12
2520 A1282 2k lt ultra & sepia .50 .25
2521 A1282 4k rose vio & sepia .50 .25

Letters and Means of
Transportation — A1283

1961, Sept. 15 Perf. 11½
2522 A1283 4k dk car & black .50 .25
International Letter Writing Week.

Angara
River
Bridge,
Irkutsk
A1284

1961, Sept. 15 Litho. Perf. 12½x12
2523 A1284 4k ol bis, lil & blk 2.00 .50
300th anniversary of Irkutsk.

Lenin, Marx, Engels and
Marchers — A1285

3k, Obelisk commemorating conquest of
space and Moscow University. #2526, Harvester combine. #2527, Industrial control
center. #2528, Worker pointing to globe.

1961 Litho.
2524 A1285 2k ver, yel & brown .40 .25
2525 A1285 3k org & deep blue 2.25 .40
2526 A1285 4k mar, bis & red
brown .75 .40
2527 A1285 4k car rose, brn, org
& blue .75 .40
2528 A1285 4k red & dk brown .75 .40
Nos. 2524-2528 (5) 4.90 1.85
22nd Congress of the Communist Party of
the USSR, Oct. 17-31.

Soviet Soldier
Monument,
Berlin — A1286

1961, Sept. 28 Photo. Perf. 12x12½
2529 A1286 4k red & gray violet .75 .30
10th anniversary of the International Federation of Resistance, FIR.

Workers Studying
Mathematics — A1287

Designs: 2k, Communist labor team. 4k,
Workers around piano.

1961, Sept. 28 Litho. Perf. 12½x12
2530 A1287 2k plum & red,
cream .50 .35
2531 A1287 3k brn & red, yellow 1.00 .50
2532 A1287 4k vio blue & red, cr 1.50 .65
Nos. 2530-2532 (3) 3.00 1.50
Publicizing Communist labor teams in their
efforts for labor, education and relaxation.

Rocket and Stars — A1288

Engraved on Aluminum Foil
1961, Oct. 17 Perf. 12½
2533 A1288 1r black & red 25.00 25.00
Soviet scientific and technical achievements
in exploring outer space.

Overprinted in Red

1961, Oct. 23
2534 A1288 1r black & red 27.50 27.50
Communist Party of the USSR, 22nd cong.

Amangaldi
Imanov — A1289

1961, Oct. 25 Photo. Perf. 11½x12
2535 A1289 4k green, buff & brn .75 .25
Amangaldi Imanov (1873-1919), champion
of Soviet power in Kazakhstan.

Franz Liszt
(1811-86),
Composer
A1290

1961, Oct. 31 Perf. 12x11½
2536 A1290 4k mar, dk brn &
ocher 5.00 2.00

Flags and
Slogans
A1291

1961, Nov. 4 Perf. 11½
2537 A1291 4k red, yel & dark
red .75 .35
44th anniversary of October Revolution.

Hand Holding
Hammer — A1292

Congress
Emblem
A1293

Designs: Nos. 2538, 2542, Congress
emblem. Nos. 2539, 2543, African breaking
chains. No. 2541, Three hands holding globe.

1961, Nov. Perf. 12, 12½, 11½
2538 A1293 2k scarlet & bister .25 .25
2539 A1293 2k dk purple & gray .25 .25
2540 A1292 4k plum, org & blue .60 .25
2541 A1292 4k blk, lt blue & pink .75 .25
2542 A1293 4k grn, bister & red .75 .25
2543 A1293 6k ind, dull yel & red .75 .25
Nos. 2538-2543 (6) 3.35 1.50
Fifth World Congress of Trade Unions, Moscow, Dec. 4-16.

Lomonosov
Statue — A1294

Designs: 6k, Lomonosov at desk. 10k,
Lomonosov, his birthplace and Leningrad
Academy of Science, horiz.

Perf. 11½x12, 12x11½
1961, Nov. 19 Photo. & Engr.
2544 A1294 4k Prus blue, yel
grn & brown .60 .25
2545 A1294 6k grn, yel & blk 1.00 .35
2546 A1294 10k mar, slate & brn 1.25 .60
Nos. 2544-2546 (3) 2.85 1.20
250th anniversary of the birth of M. V.
Lomonosov, scientist and poet.

Hands Holding
Hammer and
Sickle — A1295

1961, Nov. 27 Litho. Perf. 12x12½
2547 A1295 4k red & yellow .60 .30
USSR constitution, 25th anniv.

Romeo and Juliet
Ballet — A1296

Ballets: 2k, Red Flower. 3k, Paris Flame.
10k, Swan Lake.

1961-62 Perf. 12x12½
2548 A1296 2k brn, car & lt
green ('62) .25 .25
2549 A1296 3k multi ('62) .45 .25
2550 A1296 6k dk brn, bis & vio .65 .25

2551 A1296 10k blue, pink & dk
brn 1.00 .30
Nos. 2548-2551 (4) 2.35 1.05
Honoring the Russian Ballet.

Linemen
A1297

1961 Perf. 12½
2552 A1297 3k shown .75 .25
2553 A1297 4k Welders .75 .25
2554 A1297 6k Surveyor 1.50 .35
Nos. 2552-2554 (3) 3.00 .85
Honoring self-sacrificing work of youth in the
7-year plan.

Andrejs
Pumpurs
(1841-1902),
Latvian Poet
and Satirist
A1298

1961, Dec. 20 Perf. 12x11½
2555 A1298 4k gray & claret 2.00 .50

Bulgarian
Couple,
Flag,
Emblem
and
Building
A1299

1961, Dec. 28 Perf. 12½x12
2556 A1299 4k multicolored 1.00 .50
Bulgarian People's Republic, 15th anniv.

Fridtjof
Nansen
A1300

1961, Dec. 30 Photo. Perf. 11½
2557 A1300 6k dk blue & brown 2.00 .60
Centenary of the birth of Fridtjof Nansen,
Norwegian Polar explorer.

Mihael Ocipovich Dolivo-
Dobrovolsky — A1301

1962, Jan. 25 Perf. 12x11½
2558 A1301 4k bister & dark blue .50 .25
Dolivo-Dobrovolsky, scientist and electrical
engineer, birth cent.

Woman
and
Various
Activities
A1302

1962, Jan. 26 Perf. 11½
2559 A1302 4k bister, blk & dp
org .50 .25
Honoring Soviet Women.

Aleksander S. Pushkin, 125th Death Anniv. — A1303

1962, Jan. 26   Litho.   Perf. 12½x12
2560 A1303 4k buff, dk brn & ver   .50   .25

Dancers A1304

1962, Feb. 6   Perf. 12x12½
2561 A1304 4k bister & ver   .50   .25
State ensemble of folk dancers, 25th anniv.

Speed Skating, Luzhniki Stadium A1305

Perf. 11½
1962, Feb. 17   Unwmk.   Photo.
2562 A1305 4k orange & ultra   .60   .25
Intl. Winter Sports Championships, Moscow.

No. 2562 Overprinted

1962, Mar. 3
2563 A1305 4k orange & ultra   2.40 1.50
Victories of I. Voronina and V. Kosichkin, world speed skating champions, 1962.

Ski Jump A1305a

10k, Woman long distance skier, vert.

1962, May 31   Perf. 11½
2564 A1305a 2k ultra, brn & red   .30   .25
2565 A1305a 10k org, ultra & black   .70   .25
Intl. Winter Sports Championships, Zakopane.

Hero Type of 1961

4k, V. S. Shalandin. 6k, Magomet Gadgiev.

1962, Feb. 22   Perf. 12½x12
2570 A1244 4k dk blue & brown   3.00   .80
2571 A1244 6k brn & slate grn   1.00   .80
Soldier heroes of World War II.

Skier A1306

1962, Mar. 3   Perf. 11½
2572 A1306 4k shown   .40   .25
2573 A1306 6k Ice hockey   .50   .25
2574 A1306 10k Ice skating   1.00   .40
    Nos. 2572-2574 (3)   1.90   .90
First People's Winter Games, Sverdlovsk.
For overprints see Nos. 2717, 3612.

Aleksandr Ivanovich Herzen (1812-70), Political Writer A1307

1962, Mar. 28   Litho.   Perf. 12x12½
2575 A1307 4k ultra, black & buff   .50   .25

Lenin — A1308

Design: 6k, Lenin, horiz.

1962, Mar. 28   Perf. 12x12½, 12½x12
2576 A1308 4k brown, red & yel   .30   .25
2577 A1308 6k blue, org & brn   .50   .25
14th congress of the Young Communist League (Komsomol).

Vostok 1 — A1309

1962, Apr.   Unwmk.   Perf. 11x11½
2578 A1309 10k multicolored   .50   .35
1st anniv. of Yuri A. Gagarin's flight into space.
    No. 2578 was printed in sheets of 20 stamps alternating with 20 labels.
    No. 2578 was also issued imperf. Value $2.25.

Bust of Tchaikovsky A1310

1962, Apr. 19 Photo.   Perf. 11½x12
2579 A1310 4k blue, blk & bis   1.00   .30
Second International Tchaikovsky Competition in Moscow.

Youths of 3 Races, Broken Chain, Globe A1311

1962, Apr. 19   Perf. 11½
2580 A1311 6k black, brn & yel   .50   .25
International Day of Solidarity of Youth against Colonialism.

Ulyanov (Lenin) Family Portrait A1312

Lenin A1313

1962, Apr. 21   Perf. 12x11½
2581 A1312 4k gray, red & dk brn   .40   .25

Typographed and Embossed
Perf. 12½
2582 A1313 10k dk red, gray & blk   .90   .35
a.   Souv. sheet of 2, perf. 12   5.00 3.00
92nd anniversary of the birth of Lenin. No. 2582a for 94th anniv. of the birth of Lenin. Issued Nov. 6, 1964.

Cosmos 3 Satellite — A1314

1962, Apr. 26   Litho.   Perf. 12½x12
2586 A1314 6k blk, lt blue & vio   .50   .25
Cosmos 3 earth satellite launching, Apr. 24.

Charles Dickens — A1315

No. 2589, Jean Jacques Rousseau.

1962, Apr. 29
2588 A1315 6k blue, brn & pur   .50   .25
Perf. 11½x12
Photo.
2589 A1315 6k gray, lilac & brn   .50   .25
Charles Dickens, English writer, 150th birth anniv., and Jean Jacques Rousseau, French writer, 250th birth anniv.

Karl Marx Monument, Moscow — A1316

1962, Apr. 29   Perf. 12x12½
2590 A1316 4k deep ultra & gray   .50   .25

Pravda, Lenin, Revolutionists A1317

Lenin Reading Pravda — A1318

No. 2592, Pravda, Lenin and rocket.

1962, May 4   Litho.
2591 A1317 4k blk, bis & red   .65   .25
2592 A1317 4k red, blk & ocher   .65   .25
Perf. 11½
Photo.
2593 A1318 4k ocher, dp clar & red   .65   .25
    Nos. 2591-2593 (3)   1.95   .75
50th anniversary of Pravda, Russian newspaper founded by Lenin.

Malaria Eradication Emblem and Mosquito A1319

1962
2594 A1319 4k Prus blue, red & blk   .50   .25
2595 A1319 6k ol grn, red & blk   .50   .35
WHO drive to eradicate malaria.
Issue dates: 4k, May 6; 6k, June 23.
No. 2595 exists imperf. Value $1.75.

Pioneers Taking Oath before Lenin and Emblem A1320

Designs (Emblem and): 3k, Lenja Golikov and Valja Kotik. No. 2598, Pioneers building rocket model. No. 2599, Red Cross, Red Crescent and nurse giving health instruction. 6k, Pioneers of many races and globe.

1962, May 19   Litho.   Perf. 12½x12
2596 A1320 2k green, red & brn   .30   .25
2597 A1320 3k multicolored   .30   .25
2598 A1320 4k multicolored   .50   .25
2599 A1320 4k multicolored   .50   .25
2600 A1320 6k multicolored   .80   .25
    Nos. 2596-2600 (5)   2.40 1.25
All-Union Lenin Pioneers, 40th anniv.

Mesrob — A1321

1962, May 27 Photo. Perf. 12½x12
2601 A1321 4k yel & dk brn 1.00 .25

"1600th" anniversary of the birth of Bishop Mesrob (350?-439), credited as author of the Armenian and Georgian alphabets.

Ivan A. Goncharov A1322

1962, June 18
2602 A1322 4k gray & brown .75 .35

Ivan Aleksandrovich Goncharov (1812-91), novelist, 150th birth anniv.

Volleyball — A1323

2k, Bicyclists, horiz. 10k, Eight-man shell. 12k, Goalkeeper, soccer, horiz. 16k, Steeplechase.

1962, June 27 Perf. 11½
2603 A1323 2k lt brn, blk & ver .25 .25
2604 A1323 4k brn org, black & buff .30 .25
2605 A1323 10k ultra, black & yel .85 .25
2606 A1323 12k lt blue, brn & yel .95 .25
2607 A1323 16k lt green, blk & red 1.10 .45
Nos. 2603-2607 (5) 3.45 1.55

Intl. Summer Sports Championships, 1962.

Louis Pasteur — A1324

1962, June 30 Perf. 12½x12
2608 A1324 6k blk & brn org .60 .25

Invention of the sterilization process by Louis Pasteur, French chemist, cent.

Library, 1862 A1325

Design: No. 2610, New Lenin Library.

1962, June 30 Photo.
2609 A1325 4k slate & black .40 .25
2610 A1325 4k slate & black .40 .25
a. Pair, #2609-2610 2.00 .75

Centenary of the Lenin Library, Moscow.

Auction Building and Ermine — A1326

1962, June 30 Litho.
2611 A1326 6k multicolored 1.00 .25

International Fur Auction, Leningrad.

Young Couple, Lenin, Kremlin — A1327

Workers of Three Races and Dove — A1328

1962, June 30 Perf. 12x12½
2612 A1327 2k multicolored .40 .30
2613 A1328 4k multicolored .60 .30

Program of the Communist Party of the Soviet Union for Peace and Friendship among all people.

Hands Breaking Bomb A1329

1962, July 7 Perf. 11½
2614 A1329 6k blue, blk & olive .50 .35

World Congress for Peace and Disarmament, Moscow, July 9-14.

Yakub Kolas and Yanka Kupala A1330

1962, July 7 Photo. Perf. 12½x12
2615 A1330 4k henna brn & buff .50 .35

Byelorussian poets. Kolas (1882-1956), and Kupala (1882-1942).

Alekper Sabir (1862-1911), Azerbaijani Poet, Satirist — A1331

1962, July 16 Perf. 11½
2616 A1331 4k buff, dk brn & blue .70 .35

Examples inscribed "Azerbajanyn" were withdrawn before release. Value, $250.

Cancer Congress Emblem A1332

1962, July 16 Litho. Perf. 12½
2617 A1332 6k grnsh blue, blk & red .50 .35

8th Anti-Cancer Cong., Moscow, July 1962.

N. N. Zinin, Chemist, 150th Birth Anniv. A1333

1962, July 16 Photo. Perf. 12x11½
2618 A1333 4k violet & dk brown .35 .25

I. M. Kramskoy, Painter — A1334

I. D. Shadr, Sculptor A1335

M. V. Nesterov, Painter A1336

1962, July 28 Perf. 11½x12, 12x12½
2619 A1334 4k gray, mar & dk brn .50 .30
2620 A1335 4k blk & red brn .50 .30
2621 A1336 4k multicolored .50 .30
Nos. 2619-2621 (3) 1.50 .90

Vostok 2 Going into Space — A1337

Perf. 11½
1962, Aug. 7 Unwmk. Photo.
2622 A1337 10k blk, lilac & blue .50 .25
2623 A1337 10k blk, org & blue .50 .25

1st anniv. of Gherman Titov's space flight. Issued imperf. on Aug. 6. Value, set $4.

Friendship House, Moscow A1338

1962, Aug. 15 Perf. 12x12½
2624 A1338 6k ultra & gray .50 .25

Moscow State University and Atom Symbol — A1339

Design: 6k, Map of Russia, atom symbol and "Peace" in 10 languages.

1962, Aug. 15 Litho. Perf. 12½x12
2625 A1339 4k multicolored .50 .25
2626 A1339 6k multicolored .50 .25

Use of atomic energy for peace.

Andrian G. Nikolayev A1340

Cosmonauts in Space Helments — A1341

"To Space" Monument by G. Postnikov — A1342

Design: No. 2628, Pavel R. Popovich, with inscription at left and dated "12-15-VIII, 1962." 1r, Monument and portraits of Gagarin, Titov, Nikolayev and Popovich.

1962 Photo. Perf. 11½
2627 A1340 4k blue, brn & red .40 .25
2628 A1340 4k blue, brn & red .40 .25

Perf. 12½x12
Litho.
2629 A1341 6k dk bl, lt bl, org & yellow 1.00 .30

Perf. 11½
Photo.
2630 A1342 6k brt blue & multi .70 .25
2631 A1342 10k violet & multi .90 .35
Nos. 2627-2631 (5) 3.40 1.40

Souvenir Sheet
1962, Nov. 27 Litho. Perf. 12½
2631A A1342 1r brt bl, blk & sil 35.00 5.00

Nos. 2627-2631A honor the four Russian "conquerors of space," with Nos. 2627-2629 for the 1st group space flight, by Vostoks 3 and 4, Aug. 11-15, 1962. Also issued imperf. Value, set $6, souvenir sheet $50. For overprint see No. 2662.

Carp and Bream — A1343

Design: 6k, Freshwater salmon.

1962, Aug. 28 Photo. Perf. 11½x12
2632 A1343 4k blue & orange .45 .25
2633 A1343 6k blue & orange .60 .30
Fish preservation in USSR.

Feliks E. Dzerzhinski — A1344

1962, Sept. 6 Litho. Perf. 12½x12
2634 A1344 4k ol grn & dk blue .50 .25
Dzerzhinski (1877-1926), organizer of Soviet secret police, 85th birth anniv.

O. Henry and New York Skyline A1345

1962, Sept. 10 Photo. Perf. 12x11½
2635 A1345 6k yel, red brn & black .55 .35
O. Henry (William Sidney Porter, 1862-1910), American writer.

Barclay de Tolly, Mikhail I. Kutuzov, Petr I. Bagration A1346

4k, Denis Davidov leading partisans. 6k, Battle of Borodino. 10k, Wasilisa Kozhina and partisans.

1962, Sept. 25 Perf. 12½x12
2636 A1346 3k orange brown .30 .25
2637 A1346 4k ultra .30 .25
2638 A1346 6k blue gray .65 .25
2639 A1346 10k violet .75 .25
    Nos. 2636-2639 (4) 2.00 1.00
War of 1812 against the French, 150th anniv.

Street in Vinnitsa A1347

1962, Sept. 25 Photo.
2640 A1347 4k yel bister & black .50 .25
Town of Vinnitsa, Ukraine, 600th anniv.

"Mail and Transportation" — A1348

1962, Sept. 25 Perf. 11½
2641 A1348 4k blue grn, blk & lil .50 .25
Intl. Letter Writing Week, Oct. 7-13.

Cedar — A1349

4k, Canna. 6k, Arbutus. 10k, Chrysanthemum.

1962, Sept. 27 Engr. & Photo.
2642 A1349 3k ver, black & grn .75 .25
2643 A1349 4k multicolored .75 .25
2644 A1349 6k multicolored 1.25 .25
2645 A1349 10k multicolored 2.25 .25
    Nos. 2642-2645 (4) 5.00 1.00
Nikitsky Botanical Gardens, 150th anniv.

Construction Worker — A1350

Designs: No. 2647, Hiker. No. 2648, Surgeon. No. 2649, Worker and lathe. No. 2650, Agricultural worker. No. 2651, Textile worker. No. 2652, Modern home.

1962, Sept. 29 Litho. Perf. 12x12½
2646 A1350 4k org, gray & vio blue .25 .25
2647 A1350 4k yel, gray, grn & blue .25 .25
2648 A1350 4k grn, gray & lilac rose .25 .25
2649 A1350 4k ver, gray & lilac .25 .25
2650 A1350 4k bl, gray & emer .25 .25
2651 A1350 4k brt pink, gray & vio .25 .25
2652 A1350 4k yel, gray, dp vio, red & brown .25 .25
    Nos. 2646-2652 (7) 1.75 1.75

Sputnik and Stars A1351

1962, Oct. 4 Perf. 12½x12
2653 A1351 10k multicolored .80 .30
5th anniversary, launching of Sputnik 1.

M. F. Ahundov, Azerbaijan Poet and Philosopher, 150th Birth Anniv. — A1352

1962, Oct. 2 Photo.
2654 A1352 4k lt grn & dk brn .50 .25

Farm and Young Couple with Banner A1353

Designs: No. 2656, Tractors, map and surveyor. No. 2657, Farmer, harvester and map.

1962, Oct. 18 Litho. Perf. 12½x12
2655 A1353 4k multicolored .75 .25
2656 A1353 4k multicolored .75 .25
2657 A1353 4k brown, yel & red .75 .25
    Nos. 2655-2657 (3) 2.25 .75
Honoring pioneer developers of virgin soil.

N. N. Burdenko   V. P. Filatov
A1354   A1355

1962, Oct. 20 Perf. 12½x12
2658 A1354 4k red brn, lt brn & blk .50 .25
2659 A1355 4k multicolored .50 .25
Scientists and academicians.

Lenin Mausoleum, Red Square — A1356

1962, Oct. 26 Litho.
2660 A1356 4k multicolored .60 .25
92nd anniversary of Lenin's birth.

Worker, Flag and Factories A1357

1962, Oct. 29 Perf. 12x12½
2661 A1357 4k multicolored .50 .25
45th anniv. of the October Revolution.

No. 2631 Overprinted in Dark Violet

1962, Nov. 3 Photo. Perf. 11½
2662 A1342 10k violet & multi 3.00 2.50
Launching of a rocket to Mars.

Togolok Moldo (1860-1942), Kirghiz Poet A1358

Sajat Nova (1712-1795), Armenian Poet A1359

1962, Nov. 17 Perf. 12x12½
2663 A1358 4k brn red & black 1.00 .25
2664 A1359 4k ultra & black 1.00 .25

Arms, Hammer & Sickle and Map of USSR A1360

1962, Nov. 17 Perf. 11½
2665 A1360 4k red, org & dk red .50 .25
USSR founding, 40th anniv.

Space Rocket, Earth and Mars — A1361

1962, Nov. 17 Perf. 12½x12
Size: 73x27mm
2666 A1361 10k purple & org red 1.00 .40
Launching of a space rocket to Mars, Nov. 1, 1962.

Electric Power Industry — A1362

Designs: No. 2668, Machines. No. 2669, Chemicals and oil. No. 2670, Factory construction. No. 2671, Transportation. No. 2672, Telecommunications and space. No. 2673, Metals. No. 2674, Grain farming. No. 2675, Dairy, poultry and meat.

1962 Litho. Perf. 12½x12
2667 A1362 4k ultra, red, blk & gray .60 .25
2668 A1362 4k ultra, gray, yel & cl .60 .25
2669 A1362 4k yel, pink, blk, gray & brown .60 .25
2670 A1362 4k yel, blue, red brn & gray .45 .25
2671 A1362 4k mar, yel, red & blue .45 .25
2672 A1362 4k brt yel, blue & brn .45 .25
2673 A1362 4k lil, org, yel & dk brn .45 .25
2674 A1362 4k vio, bis, org red & dk brown .45 .25
2675 A1362 4k emer, dk brn, brn & gray .45 .25
    Nos. 2667-2675 (9) 4.50 2.25
"Great decisions of the 22nd Communist Party Congress" and Russian people at work. Issued: #2667-2669, 11/19; others, 12/28.

Queen, Rook and Knight — A1363

Perf. 12½
1962, Nov. 24   Unwmk.   Photo.
2676 A1363 4k org yel & blk   .60 .40
30th Russian Chess Championships.

Gen. Vasili Blucher A1364

1962, Nov. 27   Perf. 11½
2677 A1364 4k multicolored   3.00 .25
General Vasili Konstantinovich Blucher (1889-1938).

V. N. Podbelski (1887-1920), Minister of Posts — A1365

1962, Nov. 27   Perf. 12½x12
2678 A1365 4k red brn, gray & blk   .60 .25

Makarenko A1366   Gaidar A1367

1962, Nov. 30   Perf. 11½x12
2679 A1366 4k multicolored   .65 .45
2680 A1367 4k multicolored   .65 .45
A. S. Makharenko (1888-1939) and Arkadi Gaidar (1904-1941), writers.

Dove and Globe — A1368

1962, Dec. 22   Litho.   Perf. 12½x12
2681 A1368 4k multicolored   1.00 .50
New Year 1963. Has alternating label inscribed "Happy New Year!" Issued imperf. on Dec. 20. Value $2.

D. N. Prjanishnikov A1369

1962, Dec. 22   Perf. 12x12½
2682 A1369 4k multicolored   1.00 .25
Prjanishnikov, founder of Russian agricultural chemistry.

Rose-colored Starlings — A1370

4k, Red-breasted geese. 6k, Snow geese. 10k, White storks. 16k, Greater flamingos.

1962, Dec. 26   Photo.   Perf. 11½
2683 A1370 3k grn, blk & pink   .35 .25
2684 A1370 4k brn, blk & dp org   .50 .25
2685 A1370 6k gray, blk & red   .60 .25
2686 A1370 10k blue, blk & red   .90 .30
2687 A1370 16k lt bl, rose & blk   1.50 .50
    Nos. 2683-2687 (5)   3.85 1.55

FIR Emblem A1371

1962, Dec. 26   Perf. 12x12½
2688 A1371 4k violet & red   .45 .25
2689 A1371 6k grnsh blue & red   .45 .25
4th Cong. of the Intl. Federation of Resistance.

Map of Russia, Bank Book and Number of Savings Banks A1372

Design: 6k, as 4k, but with depositors.

1962, Dec. 30   Litho.   Perf. 12½x12
2690 A1372 4k multicolored   .75 .25
2691 A1372 6k multicolored   1.25 .30
40th anniv. of Russian savings banks.

Rustavsky Fertilizer Plant — A1373

Hydroelectric Power Stations: No. 2693, Bratskaya. No. 2964, Volzhskaya.

1962, Dec. 30   Photo.   Perf. 12½
2692 A1373 4k ultra, lt blue & black   .70 .25
2693 A1373 4k yel grn, bl grn & blk   .70 .25
2694 A1373 4k gray bl, brt bl & blk   .70 .25
    Nos. 2692-2694 (3)   2.10 .75

Stanislavski A1374

Perf. 12½
1963, Jan. 15   Unwmk.   Engr.
2695 A1374 4k slate green   .50 .25
Stanislavski (professional name of Konstantin Sergeevich Alekseev, 1863-1938), actor, producer and founder of the Moscow Art Theater.

A. S. Serafimovich (1863-1949), Writer — A1375

1963, Jan. 19   Photo.   Perf. 11½
2696 A1375 4k mag, dk brn & gray   .50 .25

Children in Nursery A1376

Designs: No. 2698, Kindergarten. No. 2699, Pioneers marching and camping. No. 2700, Young people studying and working.

1963, Jan. 31
2697 A1376 4k brn org, org red & black   .70 .25
2698 A1376 4k blue, mag & org   .70 .25
2699 A1376 4k brt grn, red & brn   .70 .25
2700 A1376 4k multicolored   .70 .25
    Nos. 2697-2700 (4)   2.80 1.00

Wooden Dolls and Toys, Russia — A1377

National Handicrafts: 6k, Pottery, Ukraine. 10k, Bookbinding, Estonia. 12k, Metalware, Dagestan.

1963, Jan. 31   Litho.   Perf. 12½x12½
2701 A1377 4k multicolored   .45 .25
2702 A1377 6k multicolored   .60 .25
2703 A1377 10k multicolored   .90 .35
2704 A1377 12k ultra, org & black   1.00 .40
    Nos. 2701-2704 (4)   2.95 1.25

Gen. Mikhail N. Tukhachevski — A1378

Designs: No. 2706, U. M. Avetisian. No. 2707, A. M. Matrosov. No. 2708, J. V. Panfilov. No. 2709, Y. F. Fabrisciuss.

Perf. 12½x12
1963, Feb.   Photo.   Unwmk.
2705 A1378 4k blue grn & slate grn   .60 .25
2706 A1378 4k org brown & blk   .60 .25
2707 A1378 4k ultra & dk brown   .60 .25
2708 A1378 4k dp rose & black   .60 .25
2709 A1378 4k rose lil & vio bl   .60 .25
    Nos. 2705-2709 (5)   3.00 1.25
45th anniv. of the Soviet Army and honoring its heroes. No. 2705 for Gen. Mikhail Nikolaevich Tukhachevski (1893-1937).

M. A. Pavlov — A1379   E. O. Paton and Dnieper Bridge, Kiev — A1379a

Portraits: No. 2711, I. V. Kurchatov. No. 2712, V. I. Vernadski. No. 2713, Aleksei N. Krylov. No. 2714, V. A. Obrutchev, geologist.

1963   Perf. 11½x12
Size: 21x32mm
2710 A1379 4k gray, buff & dk bl   .50 .25
2711 A1379 4k slate & brown   .50 .25
Perf. 12
2712 A1379 4k lil gray & lt brn   .50 .25
Perf. 11½
Size: 23x34½mm
2713 A1379 4k dk blue, sep & red   .50 .25
2714 A1379 4k brn ol, gray & red   .50 .25
2715 A1379a 4k grnsh bl, blk & red   .50 .25
    Nos. 2710-2715 (6)   3.00 1.50
Members of the Russian Academy of Science. No. 2715 for Eugene Oskarovich Paton (1870-1953), bridge building engineer.

Winter Sports A1380

1963, Feb. 28   Perf. 11½
2716 A1380 4k brt blue, org & blk   .50 .25
5th Trade Union Spartacist Games. Printed in sheets of 50 (5x10) with every other row inverted.

No. 2573 Overprinted

1963, Mar. 20
2717 A1306 6k Prus blue & plum 3.00 1.00
Victory of the Soviet ice hockey team in the World Championships, Stockholm. For overprint see No. 3612.

Victor Kingisepp A1381

1963, Mar. 24   Perf. 12x12½
2718 A1381 4k blue gray & choc   .50 .25
75th anniversary of the birth of Victor Kingisepp, communist party leader. Exists imperf.

Rudolfs Blaumanis
(1863-1908),
Latvian
Writer — A1382

1963, Mar. 24   *Perf. 12½x12*
2719 A1382 4k ultra & dk red brn   .50   .25

Flower and
Globe — A1383

Designs: 6k, Atom diagram and power line.
10k, Rocket in space.

1963, Mar. 26   *Perf. 11½*
2720 A1383 4k red, ultra & grn   .50   .25
2721 A1383 6k grn & lilac   1.00   .35
2722 A1383 10k red, vio & lt blue   1.50   .45
    Nos. 2720-2722 (3)   3.00   1.05

"World without Arms and Wars."
The 10k exists imperf. Value: $2 mint; $1
used.
For overprint see No. 2754.

Costume Type of 1960-62

Regional Costumes: 3k, Tadzhik. No. 2724,
Kirghiz. No. 2725, Azerbaijan. No. 2726,
Turkmen.

1963, Mar. 31   **Litho.**   *Perf. 11½*
2723 A1237 3k blk, red, ocher &
       org   1.25   .30
2724 A1237 4k brown, ver, ocher
       & ultra   1.25   .30
2725 A1237 4k blk, ocher, red &
       grn   1.25   .30
2726 A1237 4k red, lil, ocher &
       blk   1.25   .30
    Nos. 2723-2726 (4)   5.00   1.20

Lenin
A1384

1963, Mar. 30   **Engr.**   *Perf. 12*
2727 A1384 4k red & brown   3.50   1.00

93rd anniversary of the birth of Lenin.

Luna 4
Approaching
Moon — A1385

1963, Apr. 2   **Photo.**
2728 A1385 6k black, lt blue &
       red   1.00   .25

Soviet rocket to the moon, Apr. 2, 1963.
Exists imperforate. Values: unused, $2; used,
$1.
For overprint see No. 3160.

Woman
and
Beach
Scene
A1386

Designs: 4k, Young man's head and factory.
10k, Child's head and kindergarden.

1963, Apr. 7   **Litho.**   *Perf. 12½x12*
2729 A1386 2k multicolored   .35   .25
2730 A1386 4k multicolored   .40   .30
2731 A1386 10k multicolored   .70   .40
    Nos. 2729-2731 (3)   1.45   .95

15th anniversary of World Health Day.

A1387

No. 2732: a, d, Sputnik & Earth. b, e, Vostok
1, earth & moon. c, f, Rocket & Sun.

1963, Apr. 12
2732   Block of 6   5.00   1.50
 a.   A1387 10k "10k" blk, blue & lil
       rose   .70   .25
 b.   A1387 10k "10k" lil rose, blue &
       blk   .70   .25
 c.   A1387 10k "10k" black, red &
       yel   .70   .25
 d.   A1387 10k "10k" blue   .70   .25
 e.   A1387 10k "10k" lilac rose   .70   .25
 f.   A1387 10k "10k" yellow   .70   .25

Cosmonauts' Day.

Demian Bednii
(1883-1945),
Poet — A1388

1963, Apr. 13   **Photo.**
2735 A1388 4k brown & black   .50   .25

Soldiers on
Horseback and
Cuban
Flag — A1389

Soviet-Cuban friendship: 6k, Cuban flag,
hands with gun and book. 10k, Cuban and
USSR flags and crane lifting tractor.

1963, Apr. 25   *Perf. 11½*
2736 A1389 4k blk, red & ultra   .30   .25
2737 A1389 6k blk, red & ultra   .40   .25
2738 A1389 10k red, ultra & blk   .80   .25
    Nos. 2736-2738 (3)   1.50   .75

Karl
Marx — A1390

1963, May 9   *Perf. 12x12½*
2739 A1390 4k dk red brn & blk   .50   .25

145th anniversary of the birth of Marx.

Hasek — A1391

1963, Apr. 29   *Perf. 11½x12*
2740 A1391 4k black   .75   .25

Jaroslav Hasek (1883-1923), Czech writer.

Moscow
P.O. for
Foreign
Mail
A1392

1963, May 9   *Perf. 11½*
2741 A1392 6k brt vio & red brn   .50   .25

5th Conference of Communications Ministers of Socialist countries, Budapest.

King and
Pawn
A1393

6k, Queen, bishop. 16k, Rook, knight.

1963, May 22   **Photo.**
2742 A1393 4k multicolored   .60   .25
2743 A1393 6k ultra, brt pink &
       grnsh blue   1.00   .30
2744 A1393 16k brt plum, brt
       pink & black   2.40   .55
    Nos. 2742-2744 (3)   4.00   1.10

25th Championship Chess Match, Moscow.
Exists imperf., issued May 18. Value $6.

Richard
Wagner — A1394

Design: No. 2745A, Giuseppe Verdi.

1963   **Unwmk.**   *Perf. 11½x12*
2745 A1394 4k black & red   1.50   .50
2745A A1394 4k red & violet brn   1.50   .50

150th annivs. of the births of Wagner and
Verdi, German and Italian composers.

15th European
Boxing
Championships,
Moscow
A1395

4k, Boxers. 6k, Referee proclaiming victor.

1963, May 29   **Litho.**   *Perf. 12½*
2746 A1395 4k multicolored   .60   .25
2747 A1395 6k multicolored   .90   .35

A1396

Valentina Tereshkova — A1397

Designs: No. 2748, Valeri Bykovski. No.
2749, Valentina Tereshkova. No. 2751, Bykovski. No. 2752, Symbolic man and woman fliers. No. 2753, Valentina Tereshkova, vert.

Litho. (A1396); Photo. (A1397)
1963   *Perf. 12½x12, 12x12½*
2748   4k multicolored   .90   .25
2749   4k multicolored   .90   .25
 a.   A1396 Pair #2748-2749   1.80   .80
2750 A1397 6k grn & dk car
       rose   .75   .25
2751 A1397 6k purple & brown   .75   .25
2752 A1397 10k blue & red   1.50   .40
2753 A1396 10k multicolored   2.10   .50
    Nos. 2748-2753 (6)   6.90   1.90

Space flights of Valeri Bykovski, June 14-19,
and Valentina Tereshkova, 1st woman cosmonaut, June 16-19, 1963, in Vostoks 5 and 6.
No. 2749a has continuous design.
Nos. 2750-2753 exist imperf. Value $9.

No. 2720
Overprinted in Red

1963, June 24   **Photo.**   *Perf. 11½*
2754 A1383 4k red, ultra & green   .90   .50

Intl. Women's Cong., Moscow, June 24-29.

Globe,
Camera
and Film
A1398

1963, July 7   **Photo.**   *Perf. 11½*
2755 A1398 4k gray & ultra   .90   .35

3rd International Film Festival, Moscow.

Vladimir V.
Mayakovsky, Poet,
70th Birth
Anniv. — A1399

1963, July 19   **Engr.**   *Perf. 12½*
2756 A1399 4k red brown   .90   .25

Tanks and
Map
A1400

Design: 6k, Soldier, tanks and flag.

1963, July   **Litho.**   *Perf. 12½x12*
2757 A1400 4k sepia & orange   .75   .25
2758 A1400 6k org, slate green &
       blk   1.00   .35

20th anniversary of the Battle of Kursk in the
"War of Liberation," 1941-1945.

Bicyclist — A1401

Sports: 4k, Long jump. 6k, Women divers, horiz. 12k, Basketball. 16k, Soccer.

1963, July 27   Perf. 12½x12, 12x12½

2759	A1401	3k multicolored	.25	.25
2760	A1401	4k multicolored	.25	.25
2761	A1401	6k multicolored	.40	.25
2762	A1401	12k multicolored	.85	.25
2763	A1401	16k multicolored	1.25	.30
a.		Souvenir sheet of 4, imperf.	15.00	3.00
	Nos. 2759-2763 (5)		3.00	1.30

3rd Spartacist Games.
Exist imperf. Value $5.
No. 2763a contains stamps similar to the 3k, 4k, 12k and 16k, with colors changed. Issued Dec. 22.

Ice Hockey — A1402

1963, July 27   Photo.
2764 A1402 6k red & gray blue   .50   .25

World Ice Hockey Championship, Stockholm. For overprint see No. 3012.

Lenin — A1403

1963, July 29
2765 A1403 4k red & black   .50   .25

60th anniversary of the 2nd Congress of the Social Democratic Labor Party.

Freighter and Relief Shipment — A1404

Design: 12k, Centenary emblem.

1963, Aug. 8   Perf. 12½

2766	A1404	6k Prus green & red	.35	.25
2767	A1404	12k dark blue & red	.90	.25

Centenary of International Red Cross.

Lapp Reindeer Race A1405

Designs: 4k, Pamir polo, vert. 6k, Burjat archery. 10k, Armenian wrestling, vert.

1963, Aug. 8   Perf. 11½

2768	A1405	3k lt vio bl, brn & red	.45	.25
2769	A1405	4k bis brn, red & blk	.60	.25
2770	A1405	6k yel, black & red	.75	.25
2771	A1405	10k sepia, blk & dk red	1.25	.35
	Nos. 2768-2771 (4)		3.05	1.10

A. F. Mozhaisky (1825-1890), Pioneer Airplane Builder — A1406

Aviation Pioneers: 10k, P. N. Nesterov (1887-1914), pioneer stunt flyer. 16k, N. E. Zhukovski (1847-1921), aerodynamics pioneer, and pressurized air tunnel.

1963, Aug. 18   Engr. & Photo.

2772	A1406	6k black & brt blue	.30	.25
2773	A1406	10k black & brt blue	.60	.25
2774	A1406	16k black & brt blue	1.00	.25
	Nos. 2772-2774 (3)		1.90	.75

Alexander S. Dargomyzhski and Scene from "Rusalka" — A1408

S. S. Gulak-Artemovsky and Scene from "Cossacks on the Danube" — A1409

No. 2777, Georgi O. Eristavi and theater.

Perf. 11½x12, 12x12½

1963, Sept. 10   Photo.

2776	A1408	4k violet & black	.50	.25
2777	A1408	4k gray violet & brn	.60	.25
2778	A1409	4k red & black	.50	.25
	Nos. 2776-2778 (3)		1.60	.75

Dargomyzhski, Ukrainian composer; Eristavi, Georgian writer, and Gulak-Artemovsky, Ukrainian composer, 150th birth annivs.

Map of Antarctica, Penguins, Research Ship and Southern Lights — A1410

Designs: 4k, Map, southern lights and snocats (trucks). 6k, Globe, camp and various planes. 12k, Whaler and whales.

1963, Sept. 16   Litho.   Perf. 12½x12

2779	A1410	3k multicolored	.40	.25
2780	A1410	4k multicolored	.60	.30
2781	A1410	6k vio, blue & red	1.00	.40
2782	A1410	12k multicolored	2.00	.75
	Nos. 2779-2782 (4)		4.00	1.70

"The Antarctic - Continent of Peace."

Letters, Globe, Plane, Train and Ship A1411

1963, Sept. 20   Photo.   Perf. 11½
2783 A1411 4k violet, black & org .75 .25

International Letter Writing Week.

Denis Diderot — A1412

1963, Oct. 10   Unwmk.   Perf. 11½
2784 A1412 4k dk blue, brn & yel bister .75 .25

Denis Diderot (1713-84), French philosopher and encyclopedist.

Gleb Uspenski — A1414

Portraits: No. 2787, N. P. Ogarev. No. 2788, V. Brusov. No. 2789, F. Gladkov.

1963, Oct. 10

2786	A1414	4k buff, red brn & dk brown	.75	.25
2787	A1414	4k blk & pale grn	.75	.25
2788	A1414	4k car, brown & gray	.75	.25
2789	A1414	4k car, ol brn & gray	.75	.25
	Nos. 2786-2789 (4)		3.00	1.00

Gleb Ivanovich Uspenski (1843-1902), historian and writer; Ogarev, politician, 150th birth anniv.; Brusov, poet, 90th birth anniv.; Fyodor Gladkov (1883-1958), writer.

"Peace" Worker, Student, Astronaut and Lenin — A1415

Designs: No. 2794, "Labor," automatic controls. No. 2795, "Liberty," painter, lecturer, woman reading newspaper. No. 2796, "Equality," elections, regional costumes. No. 2797, "Brotherhood," Recognition of achievement. No. 2798, "Happiness," Family.

1963, Oct. 15   Litho.   Perf. 12½x12

2793	A1415	4k dk red, red & blk	.55	.35
2794	A1415	4k red, dk red & blk	.55	.35
2795	A1415	4k dk red, red & blk	.55	.35
2796	A1415	4k dk red, red & blk	.55	.35
2797	A1415	4k dk red, red & blk	.55	.35
2798	A1415	4k dk red, red & blk	.55	.35
a.		Strip of 6, #2793-2798	4.00	3.00

Proclaiming Peace, Labor, Liberty, Equality, Brotherhood and Happiness.

Kirghiz Academy and Moscow State University A1416

1963, Oct. 22   Perf. 12x12½
2799 A1416 4k red, yel & vio blue .50 .25

Russia's annexation of Kirghizia, cent.

Lenin and Young Workers A1417

Design: No. 2801, Lenin and Palace of Congresses, the Kremlin.

1963, Oct. 24   Photo.   Perf. 11½

2800	A1417	4k crimson & black	.50	.25
2801	A1417	4k carmine & black	.50	.25

13th Congr. of Soviet Trade Unions, Moscow.

Olga Kobylyanskaya, Ukrainian Novelist, Birth Cent. — A1418

1963, Oct. 24   Perf. 11½x12
2802 A1418 4k tan & dk car rose .60 .30

Ilya Mechnikov A1419

6k, Louis Pasteur. 12k, Albert Calmette.

1963, Oct. 28   Perf. 12

2803	A1419	4k green & bister	.50	.35
2804	A1419	6k purple & bister	.70	.35
2805	A1419	12k blue & bister	1.40	.35
	Nos. 2803-2805 (3)		2.60	1.05

Pasteur Institute, Paris, 75th anniv; 12k for Albert Calmette (1863-1933), bacteriologist.

Cruiser Aurora and Rockets A1420

1963, Nov. 1

2806	A1420	4k mar, blk, gray & red orange	.45	.25
2807	A1420	4k mar, blk, gray & brt rose red	.55	.25

Development of the Armed Forces, and 46th anniv. of the October Revolution. The bright rose red ink of No. 2807 is fluorescent.

Mausoleum Gur Emir, Samarkand A1421

Architecture in Samarkand, Uzbekistan: #2809, Shakhi-Zinda Necropolis. 6k, Registan Square.

1963, Nov. 14   Litho.   Perf. 12
Size: 27½x27½mm
2808 A1421 4k bl, yel & red brn   .50   .25
2809 A1421 4k bl, yel & red brn   .50   .25
Size: 55x27½mm
2810 A1421 6k bl, yel & red brn   1.00   .25
    Nos. 2808-2810 (3)   2.00   .75

Proclamation, Spasski Tower and Globe A1422

1963, Nov. 15   Photo.   Perf. 12x11½
2811 A1422 6k purple & lt blue   .50   .25
Signing of the Nuclear Test Ban Treaty between the US and the USSR.

Pushkin Monument, Kiev — A1423

M. S. Shchepkin A1424

Portrait: No. 2814, V. L. Durov (1863-1934), circus clown.

1963   Engr.   Perf. 12x12½
2812 A1423 4k dark brown   1.50   .25
2813 A1424 4k brown   1.50   .25
2814 A1424 4k brown black   2.00   .25
    Nos. 2812-2814 (3)   5.00   .75
No. 2813 for M. S. Shchepkin, actor, 75th birth anniv.

Yuri M. Steklov, 1st Editor of Izvestia, 90th Birth Anniv. A1425

1963, Nov. 17   Photo.   Perf. 11½
2815 A1425 4k black & lilac rose   .60   .25

Vladimir G. Shuhov and Moscow Radio Tower — A1426

1963, Nov. 17   Perf. 12½x12
2816 A1426 4k green & black   .50   .30
Shuhov, scientist, 110th birth anniv.

USSR and Czech Flags, Kremlin and Hradcany A1427

1963, Nov. 25   Perf. 11½
2817 A1427 6k red, ultra & brown   .50   .25
Russo-Czechoslovakian Treaty, 20th anniv.

Fyodor A. Poletaev — A1428

1963, Nov. 25   Litho.   Perf. 12½x12
2818 A1428 4k multicolored   .50   .30
F. A. Poletaev, Hero of the Soviet Union, National Hero of Italy, and holder of the Order of Garibaldi.

Julian Grimau and Worker Holding Flag — A1429

1963, Nov. 29   Photo.   Perf. 11½
Flag and Name Panel Embossed
2819 A1429 6k vio black, red & buff   1.00   .25
Spanish anti-fascist fighter Julian Grimau.

Rockets, Sky and Tree — A1430

1963, Dec. 12   Litho.   Perf. 12x12½
2820 A1430 6k multicolored   1.00   .25

"Happy New Year!" — A1431

Photogravure and Embossed
1963, Dec. 20   Perf. 11½
2821 A1431 4k grn, dk blue & red   .50   .25
2822 A1431 6k grn, dk bl & fluor. rose red   .60   .30
Nos. 2820-2822 issued for New Year 1964.

Mikas J. Petrauskas, Lithuanian Composer, 90th Birth Anniv. A1432

1963, Dec. 20   Photo.   Perf. 11½x12
2823 A1432 4k brt grn & brn   .75   .35

Topaz — A1433

Precious stones of the Urals: 4k, Jasper. 6k, Amethyst. 10k, Emerald. 12k, Rhodonite. 16k, Malachite.

1963, Dec. 26   Litho.   Perf. 12
2824 A1433 2k brn, yel & blue   .30   .25
2825 A1433 4k multicolored   .40   .25
2826 A1433 6k red & purple   .50   .30
2827 A1433 10k multicolored   .80   .40
2828 A1433 12k multicolored   1.10   .50
2829 A1433 16k multicolored   1.40   .60
    Nos. 2824-2829 (6)   4.50   2.35

Coat of Arms and Sputnik A1434

Rockets: No. 2831, Luna I. No. 2832, Rocket around the moon. No. 2833, Vostok I, first man in space. No. 2834, Vostok III & IV. No. 2835, Vostok VI, first woman astronaut.

1963, Dec. 27   Litho. & Embossed
2830 A1434 10k red, gold & gray   .80   .30
2831 A1434 10k red, gold & gray   .80   .30
2832 A1434 10k red, gold & gray   .80   .30
2833 A1434 10k red, gold & gray   .80   .30
2834 A1434 10k red, gold & gray   .80   .30
2835 A1434 10k red, gold & gray   .80   .30
    a.   Vert. strip of 6, #2830-2835   5.50   2.50
Soviet achievements in space.

Dyushambe, Tadzhikistan — A1435

1963, Dec. 30   Engr.
2836 A1435 4k dull blue   .60   .30
No. 2836 was issued after Stalinabad was renamed Dyushambe.
For overprint see No. 2943.

Flame, Broken Chain and Rainbow A1436

1963, Dec. 30   Litho.
2837 A1436 6k multicolored   .75   .25
15th anniversary of the Universal Declaration of Human Rights.

F. A. Sergeev A1437

1963, Dec. 30   Photo.   Perf. 12x12½
2838 A1437 4k gray & red   .50   .25
80th anniversary of the birth of the revolutionist Artjem (F. A. Sergeev).

Sun and Radar A1438

6k, Sun, Earth, vert. 10k, Earth, Sun.

1964, Jan. 1   Photo.   Perf. 11½
2839 A1438 4k brt mag, org & blk   .45   .35
2840 A1438 6k org yel, red & bl   .60   .35
2841 A1438 10k blue, vio & org   .90   .35
    Nos. 2839-2841 (3)   1.95   1.05
International Quiet Sun Year, 1964-65.

Christian Donalitius A1439

1964, Jan. 1   Unwmk.   Perf. 12
2842 A1439 4k green & black   .50   .25
Lithuanian poet Christian Donalitius (Donelaitis), 250th birth anniv.

Women's Speed Skating A1440

Designs: 4k, Women's cross country skiing. 6k, 1964 Olympic emblem and torch. 10k, Biathlon. 12k, Figure skating pair.

1964, Feb. 4   Perf. 11½, Imperf.
2843 A1440 2k ultra, blk & lil rose   .25   .25
2844 A1440 4k lil rose, blk & ultra   .40   .25
2845 A1440 6k dk bl, red & blk   .50   .25
2846 A1440 10k grn, lil & blk   .90   .30
2847 A1440 12k lil, blk & grn   .90   .30
    Nos. 2843-2847 (5)   2.95   1.40

9th Winter Olympic Games, Innsbruck Jan. 29-Feb. 9, 1964. Exists imperf. Values: unused, $4; used, $3. See Nos. 2865, 2867-2870.

Anna S. Golubkina (1864-1927),
Sculptor — A1441

1964, Feb. 4   **Photo.**
2848 A1441 4k gray, brn & buff   .50   .25

No. 2450 Overprinted

and

Taras G.
Shevchenko
A1443

Designs: 4k, Shevchenko statue, Kiev. 10k, Shevchenko by Ilya Repin. (Portrait on 6k by I. Kramskoi.)

1964   **Litho.**   **Perf. 12**
2852 A1245 3k brown & violet   3.00 2.00
      Engr.
2853 A1443 4k magenta   .30   .25
2854 A1443 4k deep green   .30   .25
2855 A1443 6k red brown   .40   .25
2856 A1443 6k indigo   .40   .25
      Photo.
2857 A1443 10k bister & brown   .50   .25
2858 A1443 10k buff & dull violet   .50   .25
   Nos. 2852-2858 (7)   5.40 3.50

Shevchenko, Ukrainian poet, 150th birth anniv.
   Issued: #2852, 2857-2858, 2/22; Others, 3/1.

K. S.
Zaslonov
A1444

Soviet Heroes: No. 2860, N. A. Vilkov. No. 2861, J. V. Smirnov. No. 2862, V. S. Khorujaia (heroine). No. 2862A, I. M. Sivko. No. 2862B, I. S. Polbin.

1964-65   **Photo.**
2859 A1444 4k hn brn & brn
            blk   .50   .35
2860 A1444 4k Prus bl & vio
            blk   .50   .35
2861 A1444 4k brn red & ind   .50   .35
2862 A1444 4k bluish gray &
            dk brown   .50   .35
2862A A1444 4k lil & blk ('65)   .50   .35
2862B A1444 4k blue & dk brn
            ('65)   .50   .35
   Nos. 2859-2862B (6)   3.00 2.10

Printer
Inking
Form,
16th
Century
A1445

6k, Statue of Ivan Fedorov, 1st Russian printer.

1964, Mar. 1   **Litho.**   **Unwmk.**
2863 A1445 4k multicolored   .60   .25
2864 A1445 6k multicolored   .80   .25
   400th anniv. of book printing in Russia.

Nos. 2843-
2847
Overprinted

and

Ice Hockey
A1446

Olympic
Gold
Medal, "11
Gold, 8
Silver, 6
Bronze"
A1447

Design: 3k, Ice hockey.

1964, Mar. 9   **Photo.**   **Perf. 11½**
2865 A1440 2k ultra, blk & lilac
           rose   .25   .25
2866 A1446 3k blk, bl grn & red   .30   .25
2867 A1440 4k lil rose, blk & ul-
           tra   .35   .25
2868 A1440 6k dk bl, red & blk   .75   .25
2869 A1440 10k grn, lil & blk   .85   .30
2870 A1440 12k lilac, blk & grn   .95   .35
           Perf. 12
2871 A1447 16k org red & gldn
           brown   1.40   .40
   Nos. 2865-2871 (7)   4.85 2.05

Soviet victories at the 9th Winter Olympic Games.
   On Nos. 2865, 2867-2870 the black overprints commemorate victories in various events and are variously arranged in 3 to 6 lines, with "Innsbruck" in Russian added below "1964" on 2k, 4k, 10k and 12k.

Rubber
Industry — A1448

Designs: No. 2873, Textile industry. No. 2874, Cotton, wheat, corn and helicopter spraying land.

1964   **Litho.**   **Perf. 12x12½**
2872 A1448 4k org, lilac, ultra &
           blk   .65   .25
2873 A1448 4k org, blk, grn & ul-
           tra   .65   .25
2874 A1448 4k dull yel, ol, red &
           bl   .65   .25
   Nos. 2872-2874 (3)   1.95   .75

Importance of the chemical industry to the Soviet economy.
   Issued: #2872, 2/10; #2873-2874, 3/27.

Regular and
Volunteer
Militiamen
A1449

1964, Mar. 27   **Photo.**   **Perf. 12**
2875 A1449 4k red & deep ultra   .75   .35
   Day of the Militia.

Sailor and Odessa
Lighthouse — A1450

No. 2877, Lenin statue and Leningrad.

1964   **Litho.**   **Perf. 12½x12**
2876 A1450 4k red, lt grn, ultra &
           black   .80   .35
2877 A1450 4k red, yel, grn, brn
           & black   .80   .35
2878 A1451 4k bl, gray, red &
           emer   .80   .35
   Nos. 2876-2878 (3)   2.40 1.05

Liberation of Odessa (#2876), Leningrad (#2877), Byelorussia (#2878), 20th anniv.
   Issued: #2876, 4/10; #2877, 5/9; #2878, 6/30.

First Soviet
Sputniks
A1452

F. A.
Tsander — A1453

Designs: 6k, Mars 1 spacecraft. No. 2886, Konstantin E. Tsiolkovsky. No. 2887, N. I. Kibaltchitch. No. 2888, Statue honoring 3 balloonists killed in 1934 accident. 12k, Gagarin and satellite.

     Perf. 11½, Imperf.
1964, Apr.   **Photo.**
2883 A1452 4k red org, blk &
           blue green   .40   .25
2884 A1452 6k dk bl & org red   .65   .25
2885 A1453 10k grn, blk & fluor.
           pink   .80   .30
2886 A1453 10k dk bl grn, blk &
           fluor. pink   .80   .30
2887 A1453 10k lilac, blk & lt grn   .80   .30
2888 A1453 10k blue & black   .80   .30
2889 A1452 12k blue grn, org
           brn & black   1.25   .40
   Nos. 2883-2889 (7)   5.50 2.10

Leaders in rocket theory and technique.

Lenin, 94th
Birth Anniv.
A1454

Engraved and Photogravure
1964-65   **Perf. 12x11½**
2890 A1454 4k blk, buff & lilac
           rose   4.50 3.50
   a.   Re-engraved ('65)   3.50 3.50

On No. 2890a, the portrait shading is much heavier. Lines on collar are straight and unbroken, rather than dotted.
   For souvenir sheet see No. 2582a.

William Shakespeare, 400th Birth
Anniv. — A1455

1964, Apr. 23   **Perf. 11½**
2891 A1455 10k gray & red brn   1.00   .40
   See Nos. 2985-2986.

"Irrigation" — A1456

1964, May 12   **Litho.**   **Perf. 12x12½**
2892 A1456 4k multicolored   .65   .25

A1457

      Perf. 12½x11½
1964, May 12   **Photo.**
2893 A1457 4k blue & gray brn   .50   .25
   Y. B. Gamarnik, army commander, 70th birth anniv.

D. I. Gulia
A1458

Portraits: No. 2895, Hamza Hakim-Zade Nijazi. No. 2896, Saken Seifullin. No. 2896A, M. M. Kotsyubinsky. No. 2896B, Stepanos Nazaryan. No. 2896C, Toktogil Satyiganov.

Engraved and Photogravure
1964   **Unwmk.**   **Perf. 12x11½**
2894 A1458 4k grn, buff & blk   .80   .35
2895 A1458 4k red, buff & blk   .80   .35
2896 A1458 4k brn, ocher, buff
           & black   .80   .35
2896A A1458 4k brn lake, blk &
           buff   .80   .35
2896B A1458 4k blue, pale bl, blk
           & buff   .80   .35
2896C A1458 4k red brn & blk   .80   .35
   Nos. 2894-2896C (6)   4.80 2.10

Abkhazian poet Gulia, 90th birth anniv.; Uzbekian writer and composer Nijazi, 75th birth anniv.; Kazakian poet Seifullin, 70th birth anniv.; Ukrainian writer Kotsyubinsky (1864-1913); Armenian writer Nazaryan (1814-1879); Kirghiz poet Satylganov (1864-1933).

Arkadi
Gaidar
(1904-41)
A1459

Writers: No. 2897A, Nikolai Ostrovsky (1904-36) and battle scene (portrait at left).

1964　　Photo.　　Perf. 12
2897 A1459 4k red orange & gray .50 .25
Engr.
2897A A1459 4k brn lake & blk .50 .25

No. 2318
Surcharged

1964, May 27　Litho.　Perf. 12
2898 A1194 4k on 40k bis & brn 4.00 2.00
Azerbaijan's joining Russia, 150th anniv.

"Romania" A1460

No. 2900, "Poland," (map, Polish eagle, industrial and agricultural symbols). No. 2901, "Bulgaria" (flag, rose, industrial and agricultural symbols). No. 2902, Soviet and Yugoslav soldiers and embattled Belgrade. No. 2903, "Czechoslovakia" (view of Prague, arms, Russian soldier and woman). No. 2903A, Map and flag of Hungary, Liberty statue. No. 2903B, Statue of Russian Soldier and Belvedere Palace, Vienna. No. 2904, Buildings under construction, Warsaw; Polish flag and medal.

1964-65　Litho.　Perf. 12
2899 A1460 6k gray & multi .60 .25
2900 A1460 6k ocher, red & brn .60 .25
2901 A1460 6k tan, grn & red .60 .25
2902 A1460 6k gray, blk, dl bl, ol & red .60 .25
2903 A1460 6k ultra, black & red ('65) .60 .25
2903A A1460 6k brn, red & green ('65) .60 .25
2903B A1460 6k dp org, gray bl & black ('65) .60 .25
2904 A1460 6k blue, red, yel & bister ('65) .60 .25
　Nos. 2899-2904 (8) 4.80 2.00

20th anniversaries of liberation from German occupation of Romania, Poland, Bulgaria, Belgrade, Czechoslovakia, Hungary, Vienna and Warsaw.

Elephant A1461

Designs: 2k, Giant panda, horiz. 4k, Polar bear. 6k, European elk. 10k, Pelican. 12k, Tiger. 16k, Lammergeier.

Perf. 12x12½, 12½x12, Imperf.
1964　　　　　　Photo.
Size: 25x36mm, 36x25mm
2905 A1461 1k red & black .25 .25
2906 A1461 2k tan & black .25 .25
Perf. 12
Size: 26x28mm
2907 A1461 4k grnsh gray, black & tan .25 .25
Perf. 12x12½
Size: 25x36mm
2908 A1461 6k ol, dk brn & tan .60 .25
Perf. 12
Size: 26x28mm
2909 A1461 10k ver, gray & blk .90 .40

Perf. 12½x12, 12x12½
Size: 36x25mm, 25x36mm
2910 A1461 12k brn, ocher & blk 1.25 .40
2911 A1461 16k ultra, blk, bis & yellow 1.60 .60
　Nos. 2905-2911 (7) 5.10 2.40
100th anniv. of the Moscow zoo.
Issue dates: Perf., June 18. Imperf., May.

Leningrad Post Office A1462

1964, June 30　Litho.　Perf. 12
2912 A1462 4k citron, blk & red .75 .25
Leningrad postal service, 250th anniv.

Corn — A1463

1964　　Photo.　Perf. 11½, Imperf.
2913 A1463 2k shown .25 .25
2914 A1463 3k Wheat .35 .25
2915 A1463 4k Potatoes .35 .25
2916 A1463 6k Beans .55 .25
2917 A1463 10k Beets .90 .25
2918 A1463 12k Cotton 1.10 .30
2919 A1463 16k Flax 1.50 .35
　Nos. 2913-2919 (7) 5.00 1.90
Issue dates: Perf., July 10. Imperf., June 25.

Thorez — A1464

1964, July 31
2920 A1464 4k black & red .60 .40
Maurice Thorez, chairman of the French Communist party.

Equestrian and Russian Olympic Emblem A1465

Designs: 4k, Weight lifter. 6k, High jump. 10k, Canoeing. 12k, Girl gymnast. 16k, Fencing.

1964, July　　Perf. 11½, Imperf.
2921 A1465 3k lt yel grn, red, brn & black .25 .25
2922 A1465 4k yel, black & red .25 .25
2923 A1465 6k lt blue, blk & red .35 .25
2924 A1465 10k bl grn, red & blk .50 .25
2925 A1465 12k gray, blk & red .70 .25
2926 A1465 16k lt ultra, blk & red .90 .25
　Nos. 2921-2926 (6) 2.95 1.50

18th Olympic Games, Tokyo, 10/10-25/64. Two 1r imperf. souvenir sheets exist, showing emblem, woman gymnast and stadium. Size: 91x71mm.
Value, red sheet, $7 unused, $3 canceled; green sheet, $200 unused, $300 canceled.

Three Races — A1466

1964, Aug. 8　Photo.　Perf. 12
2929 A1466 6k orange & black .50 .40
International Congress of Anthropologists and Ethnographers, Moscow.

Indian Prime Minister Jawaharlal Nehru (1889-1964) A1467

1964, Aug. 20　　　　Perf. 11½
2930 A1467 4k brown & black .75 .25

Souvenir Sheet

Conquest of Space

1964, Aug. 20　　　Perf. 11½x12
2930A Sheet of 6 5.00 3.00
　b. On glossy paper 15.00 5.00

Marx and Engels — A1468

Designs: No. 2932 Lenin and title page of "CPSS Program." No. 2933, Worker breaking chains around the globe. No. 2934, Title pages of "Communist Manifesto" in German and Russian. No. 2935, Globe and banner inscribed "Workers of the World Unite."

1964, Aug. 27　Photo.　Perf. 11½x12
2931 A1468 4k red, dk red & brown .60 .25
2932 A1468 4k red, brn & slate .60 .25
2933 A1468 4k blue, fluor. brt rose & black .60 .25
Perf. 12½x12
Litho.
2934 A1468 4k ol blk, blk & red .60 .25
2935 A1468 4k bl, red & ol bis .60 .25
　Nos. 2931-2935 (5) 3.00 1.25
Centenary of First Socialist International.

A. V. Vishnevsky A1469

Portraits: No. 2937, N. A. Semashko. No. 2938, D. Ivanovsky.

Size: 23½x35mm
1964　　Photo.　Perf. 11½
2936 A1469 4k gray & brown .65 .30
2937 A1469 4k buff, sepia & red .65 .30
Litho.
Size: 22x32½mm
2938 A1469 4k tan, gray & brown .65 .30
　Nos. 2936-2938 (3) 1.95 .90
90th birth anniv. Vishnevsky, surgeon, and Semashko, founder of the Russian Public Health Service; Ivanovsky (1864-1920), biologist.

Palmiro Togliatti (1893-1964), General Secretary of the Italian Communist Party — A1470

1964, Sept. 15　　Perf. 12½x12
2939 A1470 4k black & red .50 .25

Letter, Aerogram and Globe A1471

1964, Sept. 20　　　　Litho.
2940 A1471 4k tan, lil rose & ultra .50 .25
Intl. Letter Writing Week, Oct. 5-11.

Arms of German Democratic Republic, Factories, Ship and Train — A1472

1964, Oct. 7　　　　Perf. 12
2942 A1472 6k blk, yel, red & bis .50 .25
German Democratic Republic, 15th anniv.

No. 2836 Overprinted in Red

1964, Oct. 7　　　　Engr.
2943 A1435 4k dull blue 5.00 5.00
40th anniversary of Tadzhik Republic.

Woman Holding Bowl of Grain and Fruit A1473

Uzbek Farm Couple and Arms — A1474

Turkmen Woman Holding Arms — A1475

1964, Oct.   **Litho.**
2944 A1473 4k red, green & brn   .75 .25
2945 A1474 4k red yel & claret   .75 .25
2946 A1475 4k red, black & red brn   .75 .25
Nos. 2944-2946 (3)   2.25 .75

40th anniv. of the Moldavian, Uzbek and Turkmen Socialist Republics.
Issue dates: #2944, Oct. 7; others, Oct. 26.

Soldier and Flags A1476

1964, Oct. 14
2947 A1476 4k red, bis, dk brn & bl .75 .25
Liberation of the Ukraine, 20th anniv.

Mikhail Y. Lermontov (1814-41), Poet — A1477

Designs: 4k, Birthplace of Tarchany. 10k, Lermontov and Vissarion G. Belinski.

1964, Oct. 14   **Engr.; Litho. (10k)**
2948 A1477 4k violet black   .40 .25
2949 A1477 6k black   .50 .25
2950 A1477 10k dk red brn & buff   1.10 .30
Nos. 2948-2950 (3)   2.00 .80

Hammer and Sickle A1478

1964, Oct. 14   **Litho.**
2951 A1478 4k dk blue, red, ocher & yellow   .50 .25
47th anniversary of October Revolution.

Col. Vladimir M. Komarov A1479

Komarov, Feoktistov and Yegorov — A1480

Designs: No. 2953, Boris B. Yegorov, M.D. No. 2954, Konstantin Feoktistov, scientist. 10k, Spacecraft Voskhod I and cosmonauts. 50k, Red flag with portraits of Komarov, Feoktistov and Yegorov, and trajectory around earth.

Perf. 11½ (A1479), 12½x12
1964   **Photo.**
2952 A1479 4k bl grn, blk & org   .45 .25
2953 A1479 4k bl grn, blk & org   .45 .25
2954 A1479 4k bl grn, blk & org   .45 .25
     Size: 73x23mm
2955 A1480 6k vio & dk brn   .80 .25
2956 A1480 10k dp ultra & pur   1.25 .25
     Imperf
     Litho.
     Size: 90x45½mm
2957 A1480 50k vio, red & gray   5.00 2.50
Nos. 2952-2957 (6)   8.40 3.75

3-men space flight of Komarov, Yegorov and Feoktistov, Oct. 12-13. Issued: #2952-2954, 10/19; #2955, 10/17; #2956, 10/13; #2957, 11/20.

A. I. Yelizarova-Ulyanova — A1482

Portrait: No. 2961, Nadezhda K. Krupskaya.

1964, Nov. 6   **Photo.**   **Perf. 11½**
2960 A1482 4k brn, org & indigo   .50 .25
2961 A1482 4k indigo, red & brn   .50 .25

Yelizarova-Ulyanova, Lenin's sister, birth cent. & Krupskaya, Lenin's wife, 95th birth anniv.

Farm Woman, Sheep, Flag of Mongolia A1483

1964, Nov. 20   **Litho.**   **Perf. 12**
2962 A1483 6k multicolored   .50 .25
Mongolian People's Republic, 40th anniv.

Mushrooms A1484

Designs: Various mushrooms.

1964, Nov. 25   **Litho.**   **Perf. 12**
2963 A1484 2k ol grn, red brn & yellow   .25 .25
2964 A1484 4k green & yellow   .50 .25
2965 A1484 6k bluish grn, brn & yellow   .75 .25
2966 A1484 10k grn, org red & brn   1.20 .40
2967 A1484 12k ultra, yel & grn   2.25 .50
Nos. 2963-2967 (5)   4.95 1.65

Nos. 2963-2967 exist varnished, printed in sheets of 25 with 10 labels in outside vertical rows. Issued Nov. 30. Value, set: mint $7.50; used $3.

A. P. Dovzhenko — A1485

Design: 6k, Scene from "Chapayev" (man and boy with guns).

1964, Nov. 30   **Photo.**   **Perf. 12**
2968 A1485 4k gray & dp ultra   1.00 .35
2968A A1485 6k pale olive & blk   1.00 .35

Dovzhenko (1894-1956), film producer, and 30th anniv. of the production of the film "Chapayev."

"Happy New Year" — A1486

Photogravure and Engraved
1964, Nov. 30   **Perf. 11½**
2969 A1486 4k multicolored   1.00 .50
New Year 1965. The bright rose ink is fluorescent.

V. J. Struve — A1487

Portraits: No. 2971, N. P. Kravkov. No. 2971A, P. K. Sternberg. No. 2971B, Ch. Valikhanov. No. 2971C, V. A. Kistjakovski.

1964-65   **Photo.**   **Perf. 12½x11½**
2970   A1487 4k sl bl & dk brn   .55 .25
     Litho.
2971   A1487 4k brn, red & blk   .55 .25
     Photo.
     Perf. 11½
2971A A1487 4k dk bl & dk brn   .55 .25
     Perf. 12
2971B A1487 4k rose vio & blk   .55 .25
2971C A1487 4k brn vio, blk & cit   .55 .25
Nos. 2970-2971C (5)   2.75 1.25

Astronomer Struve (1793-1864), founder of Pulkov Observatory; Kravkov (1865-1924), pharmacologist; Sternberg (1865-1920), astronomer; Valikhanov (1835-1865), Kazakh scientist; Kistjakovski (1865-1952), chemist.
Issued: #2970, 11/30; #2971, 1/31/65; #2971A-2971B, 9/21/65; #2971C, 12/24.

S. V. Ivanov and Skiers A1488

1964, Dec. 22   **Engr.**   **Perf. 12½**
2972 A1488 4k black & brown   .75 .35
S. V. Ivanov (1864-1910), painter.

Chemical Industry: Fertilizers and Pest Control — A1489

Importance of the chemical industry for the national economy: 6k, Synthetics factory.

1964, Dec. 25   **Photo.**   **Perf. 12**
2973 A1489 4k olive & lilac rose   .50 .25
2974 A1489 6k dp ultra & black   .50 .25

European Cranberries A1490

Wild Berries: 3k, Huckleberries. 4k, Mountain ash. 10k, Blackberries. 16k, Cranberries.

1964, Dec. 25   **Perf. 11½x12**
2975 A1490 1k pale grn & car   .25 .25
2976 A1490 3k gray, vio bl & grn   .30 .25
2977 A1490 4k gray, org red & brown   .30 .25
2978 A1490 10k lt grn, dk vio blue & claret   .90 .25
2979 A1490 16k gray, brt green & car rose   1.25 .25
Nos. 2975-2979 (5)   3.00 1.25

Academy of Science Library A1491

1964, Dec. 25   **Typo.**   **Perf. 12x12½**
2980 A1491 4k blk, pale grn & red   .75 .35

250th anniv. of the founding of the Academy of Science Library, Leningrad.

Congress Palace, Kremlin — A1492

1964, Dec. 25
2981 A1492 1r dark blue   4.50 1.25

Khan Tengri — A1493

Mountains: 6k, Kazbek, horiz. 12k, Twin peaks of Ushba.

1964, Dec. 29   **Photo.**   **Perf. 11½**
2982 A1493 4k grnsh bl, vio bl & buff   .70 .35
2983 A1493 6k yel, dk brn & ol   .75 .35
2984 A1493 12k lt yel, grn & pur   1.50 .35
Nos. 2982-2984 (3)   2.95 1.05

Development of mountaineering in Russia.

Portrait Type of 1964
Design: 6k, Michelangelo. 12k, Galileo.

Engraved and Photogravure
1964, Dec. 30   **Perf. 11½**
2985 A1455 6k sep, red brn & org   .75 .25
2986 A1455 12k dk brn & green   2.25 .30

Michelangelo Buonarotti, artist, 400th death anniv. and Galileo Galilei, astronomer and physicist, 400th birth anniv.

Helmet
A1494

Treasures from Kremlin Treasury: 6k, Quiver. 10k, Jeweled fur crown. 12k, Gold ladle. 16k, Bowl.

1964, Dec. 30   **Litho.**
2987	A1494	4k multicolored	.25	.25
2988	A1494	6k multicolored	.35	.25
2989	A1494	10k multicolored	.50	.25
2990	A1494	12k multicolored	1.25	.25
2991	A1494	16k multicolored	1.40	.25
		Nos. 2987-2991 (5)	3.75	1.25

Dante Alighieri (1265-1321), Italian Poet — A1495

1965, Jan. 29   **Photo.**   **Perf. 11½**
2995 A1495 4k dk red brn & ol bis .50 .25

Blood Donor — A1496

Honoring blood donors: No. 2997, Hand holding carnation, and donors' emblem.

1965, Jan. 31   **Perf. 12**
2996	A1496	4k dk car, red, vio bl & bl	.60	.25
2997	A1496	4k brt grn, red & dk grn	.60	.25

Bandy — A1497

6k, Figure skaters and Moscow Sports Palace.

1965, Feb.   **Photo.**   **Perf. 11½x12**
2998	A1497	4k blue, red & yellow	.50	.25
2999	A1497	6k green, blk & red	.50	.25

4k issued Feb. 21, for the victory of the Soviet team in the World Bandy Championship, Moscow, Feb. 21-27; 6k issued Feb. 12, for the European Figure Skating Championship. For overprint see No. 3017.

Police Dog — A1498

Dogs: 1k, Russian hound. 2k, Irish setter. No. 3003, Pointer. No. 3004, Fox terrier. No. 3005, Sheepdog. 3006, Borzoi. 10k, Collie. 12k, Husky. 16k, Caucasian sheepdog. (1k, 2k, 4k, 12k and No. 3006 horiz.)

Perf. 12x11½, 11½x12 (Photo. stamps); 12x12½, 12½x12 (Litho.)
Photo., Litho. (1k, 10k, 12k, 16k)
1965, Feb. 26
3000	A1498	1k blk, yel & mar	.25	.25
3001	A1498	2k ultra, blk & red brown	.45	.25
3002	A1498	3k blk, ocher & org red	.45	.25
3003	A1498	4k org, yel grn & blk	.70	.25
3004	A1498	4k brn, blk & lt grn	.70	.25
3005	A1498	6k chalky blue, sep & red	1.20	.25
3006	A1498	6k chalky bl, org brn & black	1.20	.25
3007	A1498	10k yel green, ocher & red	1.90	.35
3008	A1498	12k gray, blk & ocher	2.10	.45
3009	A1498	16k multicolored	2.75	.60
		Nos. 3000-3009 (10)	11.70	3.15

Richard Sorge (1895-1944), Soviet spy and Hero of the Soviet Union — A1499

1965, Mar. 6   **Photo.**   **Perf. 12x12½**
3010 A1499 4k hn brn & blk 3.00 1.00

Communications Symbols — A1500

1965, Mar. 6   **Perf. 12½x12**
3011 A1500 6k grnsh blue, vio & brt purple .60 .30

Intl. Telecommunication Union, cent.

No. 2764 Overprinted

1965, Mar. 20   **Photo.**   **Perf. 12**
3012 A1402 6k red & gray blue 2.50 1.00

Soviet victory in the European and World Ice Hockey Championships.

Lt. Col. Alexei Leonov Taking Movies in Space — A1501

1r, Leonov walking in space and Voskhod 2.

1965, Mar. 23   **Photo.**   **Perf. 12**
Size: 73x23mm
3015 A1501 10k brt ultra, org & gray .75 .35

First man walking in space, Lt. Col. Alexei Leonov, Mar. 17, 1965 ("18 March" on stamp). Exists imperf. Value $2.

Souvenir Sheet

1965, Apr. 12   **Litho.**
3016 A1501 1r multicolored 6.00 2.00

Space flight of Voskhod 2. No. 3016 contains one 81x27mm stamp.

No. 2999 Overprinted

1965, Mar. 26   **Perf. 11½x12**
3017 A1497 6k grn, blk & red 3.00 1.00

Soviet victory in the World Figure Skating Championships.

Flags of USSR and Poland A1502

1965, Apr. 12   **Photo.**   **Perf. 12**
3018 A1502 6k bister & red .50 .25

20th anniversary of the signing of the Polish-Soviet treaty of friendship, mutual assistance and postwar cooperation.

Tsiolkovsky Monument, Kaluga; Globe and Rockets — A1503

Rockets, Radio Telescope, TV Antenna A1504

Designs: 12k, Space monument, Moscow. 16k, Cosmonauts' monument, Moscow. No. 3023, Globe with trajectories, satellite and astronauts.

1965, Apr. 12   **Perf. 11½**
3019	A1503	4k pale grn, black & brt rose	.25	.25
3020	A1503	12k vio, pur & brt rose	.55	.25
3021	A1503	16k multicolored	.85	.25

Lithographed on Aluminum Foil
Perf. 12½x12
3022	A1504	20k black & red	5.00	4.00
3023	A1504	20k blk, blue & red	5.00	4.00
		Nos. 3019-3023 (5)	11.65	8.75

National Cosmonauts' Day. On Nos. 3019-3021 the bright rose is fluorescent.

Lenin — A1505

1965, Apr. 16   **Engr.**   **Perf. 12**
3024 A1505 10k tan & indigo .75 .25

95th anniversary of the birth of Lenin.

Poppies — A1506

Flowers: 3k, Daisies. 4k, Peony. 6k, Carnation. 10k, Tulips.

1965, Apr. 23   **Photo.**   **Perf. 11**
3025	A1506	1k mar, red & grn	.25	.25
3026	A1506	3k dk brn, yel & grn	.40	.25
3027	A1506	4k blk, grn & lilac	.75	.25
3028	A1506	6k dk sl grn, grn & red	1.00	.25
3029	A1506	10k dk plum, yel & grn	1.50	.25
		Nos. 3025-3029 (5)	3.90	1.25

Soviet Flag, Broken Swastikas, Fighting in Berlin A1507

Designs: 2k, "Fatherland Calling!" (woman with proclamation) by I. Toidze. 3k, "Attack on Moscow" by V. Bogatkin. No. 3033, "Rest after the Battle" by Y. Neprintsev. No. 3034, "Mother of Partisan" by S. Gerasimov. 6k, "Our Flag — Symbol of Victory" (soldiers with banner) by V. Ivanov. 10k, "Tribute to the Hero" (mourners at bier) by F. Bogorodsky. 12k, "Invincible Nation and Army" (worker and soldier holding shell) by V. Koretsky. 16k, "Victory celebration on Red Square" by K. Yuan. 20k, Soldier and symbols of war.

1965   **Perf. 11½**
3030	A1507	1k red, blk & gold	.25	.25
3031	A1507	2k crim, blk & gold	.25	.25
3032	A1507	3k ultra & gold	.40	.25
3033	A1507	4k green & gold	.45	.25
3034	A1507	4k violet & gold	.45	.25
3035	A1507	6k dp claret & gold	.75	.25
3036	A1507	10k plum & gold	1.10	.25
3037	A1507	12k blk, red & gold	1.40	.35
3038	A1507	16k lilac rose & gold	1.90	.40
3039	A1507	20k red, blk & gold	2.25	.50
		Nos. 3030-3039 (10)	9.20	3.00

20th anniv. of the end of World War II. Issued Apr. 25-May 1.

Souvenir Sheet

From Popov's Radio to Space Telecommunications — A1508

1965, May 7   **Litho.**   **Perf. 11½**
3040 A1508 1r blue & multi 5.00 1.00

70th anniv. of Aleksandr S. Popov's radio pioneer work. No. 3040 contains 6 labels without denominations or country name.

Marx, Lenin and Crowd with Flags — A1509

1965, May 9 Photo. Perf. 12x12½
3041 A1509 6k red & black .50 .25
6th conference of Postal Ministers of Communist Countries, Peking, June 21-July 15.

Bolshoi Theater, Moscow — A1510

1965, May 20 Perf. 11x11½
3042 A1510 6k grnsh blue, bis & blk 1.00 .25
International Theater Day.

Col. Pavel Belyayev A1511

Design: No. 3044, Lt. Col. Alexei Leonov.

1965, May 23 Perf. 12x11½
3043 A1511 6k magenta & silver .60 .25
3044 A1511 6k purple & silver .60 .25
Space flight of Voskhod 2, Mar. 18-19, 1965, and the 1st man walking in space, Lt. Col. Alexei Leonov.

Sverdlov — A1512

Portrait: No. 3046, Juldash Akhunbabaev.

Photogravure and Engraved
1965, May 30 Perf. 11½x12
3045 A1512 4k orange brn & blk 1.50 .35
3046 A1512 4k lt violet & blk 1.50 .35
Yakov M. Sverdlov, 1885-1919, 1st pres. of USSR, and J. Akhunbabaev, 1885-1943, pres. of Uzbek Republic.

Grotewohl — A1513

1965, June 12 Photo. Perf. 12
3051 A1513 4k black & magenta .50 .25
Otto Grotewohl, prime minister of the German Democratic Republic (1894-1964).

Maurice Thorez — A1514

1965, June 12
3052 A1514 6k brown & red .50 .25
Maurice Thorez (1900-1964), chairman of the French Communist party.

Communication by Satellite — A1515

Designs: No. 3054, Pouring ladle, steel mill and map of India. No. 3055, Stars, satellites and names of international organizations.

1965, June 15 Litho.
3053 A1515 3k olive, blk & gold .50 .30
3054 A1515 6k emer, dk grn & gold .50 .30
3055 A1515 6k vio blue, gold & blk .50 .30
Nos. 3053-3055 (3) 1.50 .90
Emphasizing international cooperation through communication, economic cooperation and international organizations.

Symbols of Chemistry A1516

1965, June 15 Photo. Perf. 11½
3056 A1516 4k blk, brt rose & brt bl .45 .25
20th Cong. of the Intl. Union of Pure and Applied Chemistry (IUPAC), Moscow. The bright rose ink is fluorescent.

V. A. Serov A1517

Design: 6k, Full-length portrait of Feodor Chaliapin, the singer, by Serov.

1965, June 25 Typo. Perf. 12½
3057 A1517 4k red brn, buff & blk .50 .25
3058 A1517 6k ol bis & blk .50 .25
Serov (1865-1911), historical painter.

Abay Kunanbaev, Kazakh Poet — A1518

Designs (writers and poets): No. 3060, Vsevolod Ivanov (1895-1963). No. 3060A,

Eduard Vilde, Estonian writer. No. 3061, Mark Kropivnitsky, Ukrainian playwright. No. 3062, Manuk Apeghyan, Armenian writer and critic. No. 3063, Musa Djalil, Tartar poet. No. 3064, Hagop Hagopian, Armenian poet. No. 3064A, Djalil Mamedkulizade, Azerbaijan writer.

1965-66 Photo. Perf. 12½x12
3059 A1518 4k lt violet & blk .55 .30
3060 A1518 4k rose lilac & blk .55 .30
3060A A1518 4k gray & black .55 .30
3061 A1518 4k black & org brn .55 .30
Perf. 12½
Typo.
3062 A1518 4k crim, blue grn & blk .55 .30
Perf. 11½
Photogravure and Engraved
3063 A1518 4k black & org brn ('66) .55 .30
3064 A1518 4k grn & blk ('66) .55 .30
Photo.
3064A A1518 4k Prus green & blk ('66) .55 .30
Nos. 3059-3064A (8) 4.40 2.40
Sizes: Nos. 3059-3062, 38x25mm. Nos. 3063-3064A, 35x23mm.

Jan Rainis A1518a

1965, Sept. 8 Photo. Perf. 12½x12
3064B A1518a 4k dl blue & blk .50 .25
Rainis (1865-1929), Latvian playwright. "Rainis" was pseudonym of Jan Plieksans.

Film, Screen, Globe and Star A1519

1965, July 5 Litho. Perf. 12
3065 A1519 6k brt blue, gold & blk .50 .25
4th Intl. Film Festival, Moscow: "For Humanism in Cinema Art, for Peace and Friendship among Nations."

Concert Bowl, Tallinn A1520

"Lithuania" A1521

"Latvia" A1522

1965, July Perf. 12x11½, 11½x12
3066 A1520 4k ultra, blk, red & ocher 1.00 .25
3067 A1521 4k red & brown 1.00 .25
3068 A1522 4k yel, red & blue 1.00 .25
Nos. 3066-3068 (3) 3.00 .75
25th anniversaries of Estonia, Lithuania and Latvia as Soviet Republics. Issued: #3066, 7/7; #3067, 7/14; #3068, 7/16.

"Keep Peace" — A1523

1965, July 10 Photo. Perf. 11x11½
3069 A1523 6k yel, blk & blue .55 .25

Protesting Women and Czarist Eagle A1524

Designs: No. 3071, Soldier attacking distributor of handbills. No. 3072, Fighters on barricades with red flag. No. 3073, Monument for sailors of Battleship "Potemkin," Odessa.

1965, July 20 Litho. Perf. 11½
3070 A1524 4k blk, red & ol grn .50 .25
3071 A1524 4k red, ol grn & blk .50 .25
3072 A1524 4k red, black & brn .50 .25
3073 A1524 4k red & violet blue .50 .25
Nos. 3070-3073 (4) 2.00 1.00
60th anniversary of the 1905 revolution.

Gheorghe Gheorghiu-Dej (1901-1965), President of Romanian State Council (1961-1965) A1525

1965, July 26 Photo. Perf. 12
3074 A1525 4k black & red .40 .25

Relay Race A1526

Sport: No. 3076, Bicycle race. No. 3077, Gymnast on vaulting horse.

1965, Aug. 5 Litho. Perf. 12½x12
3075 A1526 4k vio blue, bis brn & red brown 1.00 .25
3076 A1526 4k buff, red brn, gray & maroon 1.00 .25
3077 A1526 4k bl, mar, buff & lt brn 1.00 .25
Nos. 3075-3077 (3) 3.00 .75
8th Trade Union Spartacist Games.

Electric Power A1527

Designs: 2k, Metals in modern industry. 3k, Modern chemistry serving the people. 4k, Mechanization, automation and electronics.

6k, New materials for building industry. 10k, Mechanization and electrification of agriculture. 12k, Technological progress in transportation. 16k, Application of scientific discoveries to industry.

1965, Aug. 5   Photo.   Perf. 12x11½
3078	A1527	1k olive, bl & blk	.25	.25
3079	A1527	2k org, blk & yel	.25	.25
3080	A1527	3k yel, vio & bister	.25	.25
3081	A1527	4k ultra, ind & red	.25	.25
3082	A1527	6k ultra & bister	.40	.25
3083	A1527	10k yel, org & red brn	.75	.25
3084	A1527	12k Prus blue & red	.60	.25
3085	A1527	16k rose lilac, blk & violet blue	1.00	.25
		Nos. 3078-3085 (8)	3.75	2.00

Creation of the material and technical basis of communism.

Gymnast — A1528

Design: 6k, Bicycling.

1965, Aug. 12   Perf. 11½
3086	A1528	4k multi & red	1.00	.25
3087	A1528	6k grnsh bl, red & brn	1.00	.25

9th Spartacist Games for school children.

Javelin and Running — A1529

Designs: 6k, High jump and shot put. 10k, Hammer throwing and hurdling.

1965, Aug. 27
3088	A1529	4k brn, lilac & red	.50	.25
3089	A1529	6k brn, yel green & red	.50	.25
3090	A1529	10k brn, chlky bl & red	1.00	.25
		Nos. 3088-3090 (3)	2.00	.75

US-Russian Track and Field Meet, Kiev.

Worker and Globe — A1530

Designs: No 3092, Heads of three races and torch. No. 3093, Woman with dove.

1965, Sept. 1
3091	A1530	6k dk purple & tan	.35	.25
3092	A1530	6k brt bl, brn & red org	.35	.25
3093	A1530	6k Prus green & tan	.35	.25
		Nos. 3091-3093 (3)	1.05	.75

Intl. Fed. of Trade Unions (#3091), Fed. of Democratic Youth (#3092), Democratic Women's Fed. (#3093), 20th annivs.

Flag of North Viet Nam, Factory and Palm — A1531

1965, Sept. 1   Litho.   Perf. 12
3094	A1531	6k red, yel, brn & gray	.35	.25

Republic of North Viet Nam, 20th anniv.

Scene from Film "Potemkin" A1532

Film Scenes: 6k, "Young Guard." 12k, "Ballad of a Soldier."

1965, Sept. 29   Litho.   Perf. 12½x12
3095	A1532	4k blue, blk & red	1.25	.25
3096	A1532	6k multicolored	1.50	.25
3097	A1532	12k multicolored	2.25	.25
		Nos. 3095-3097 (3)	5.00	.75

Post Rider, 16th Century — A1533

History of the Post: No. 3099, Mail coach, 17th-18th centuries. 2k, Train, 19th century. 4k, Mail truck, 1920. 6k, Train, ship and plane. 12k, New Moscow post office, helicopter, automatic sorting and canceling machines. 16k, Lenin, airport and map of USSR.

1965   Photo.   Unwmk.   Perf. 11½x12
3098	A1533	1k org brn, dk gray & dk green	.50	.25
3099	A1533	1k gray, ocher & dk brown	.50	.25
3100	A1533	2k dl lil, brt bl & brn	.35	.25
3101	A1533	4k bis, rose lake & blk	.55	.25
3102	A1533	6k pale brn, Prus grn & black	.65	.25
3103	A1533	12k lt ultra, lt brn & blk	1.50	.25
3104	A1533	16k gray, rose red & vio black	1.50	.25
		Nos. 3098-3104 (7)	5.55	1.75

For overprint see No. 3175.

Scientific Conquests of the Arctic and Antarctic — A1534

No. 3106, Icebreakers "Taimir" and "Vaigitch." No. 3107, Atomic Icebreaker "Lenin." 6k, Dickson Settlement. 10k, Sailing ships "Vostok" and "Mirni," Bellinghausen-Lazarev expedition & icebergs. 16k, Vostok South Pole station.

1965, Oct. 23   Litho.   Perf. 12
Size: 37x25mm
3106		4k bl, blk & org	.45	.25
3107		4k bl, blk & org	.45	.25
a.		A1534 Pair #3106-3107	1.00	.50
3108	A1534	6k sepia & dk vio	1.10	.25

Size: 33x33mm
3109	A1534	10k red, black & buff	1.40	.25

Size: 37x25mm
3110	A1534	16k vio blk & red brn	1.60	.50
		Nos. 3106-3110 (5)	5.00	1.50

Souvenir Sheet

Basketball, Map of Europe and Flags — A1535

1965, Oct. 29   Litho.   Imperf.
3111	A1535	1r multicolored	5.00	1.50

14th European Basketball Championship, Moscow.

Timiryazev Agriculture Academy, Moscow — A1536

1965, Oct. 30   Photo.   Perf. 11
3112	A1536	4k brt car, gray & vio bl	.50	.25

Agriculture Academy, Moscow, cent.

Souvenir Sheet

Lenin — A1537

Lithographed and Engraved
1965, Oct. 30   Imperf.
3113	A1537	10k sil, blk & dp org	10.00	1.25

48th anniv. of the October Revolution.

Nicolas Poussin (1594-1665), French Painter — A1538

1965, Nov. 16   Photo.   Perf. 11½
3114	A1538	4k gray blue, dk bl & dk brown	.50	.25

Kremlin A1539

1965, Nov. 16   Perf. 12x11½
3115	A1539	4k black, ver & silver	1.00	.25

New Year 1966.

Mikhail Ivanovich Kalinin (1875-1946), USSR President (1923-1946) A1540

1965, Nov. 19   Perf. 12½
3116	A1540	4k dp claret & red	.35	.25

Klyuchevskaya Sopka — A1541

Kamchatka Volcanoes: 12k, Karumski erupting, vert. 16k, Koryakski snowcovered.

1965, Nov. 30   Litho.   Perf. 12
3117	A1541	4k multicolored	.60	.25
3118	A1541	12k multicolored	1.60	.30
3119	A1541	16k multicolored	2.75	.45
		Nos. 3117-3119 (3)	4.95	1.00

October Subway Station, Moscow — A1542

Subway Stations: No. 3121, Lenin Avenue, Moscow. No. 3122, Moscow Gate, Leningrad. No. 3123, Bolshevik Factory, Kiev.

1965, Nov. 30   Engr.
3120	A1542	6k indigo	.75	.30
3121	A1542	6k brown	.75	.30
3122	A1542	6k gray brown	.75	.30
3123	A1542	6k slate green	.75	.30
		Nos. 3120-3123 (4)	3.00	1.20

Buzzard — A1543

Birds: 2k, Kestrel. 3k, Tawny eagle. 4k, Red kite. 10k, Peregrine falcon. 12k, Golden eagle, horiz. 14k, Lammergeier, horiz. 16k, Gyrfalcon.

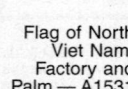

1965 **Photo.** **Perf. 11½x12**
3124 A1543 1k gray grn & black .25 .25
3125 A1543 2k pale brn & blk .25 .25
3126 A1543 3k lt ol grn & black .25 .25
3127 A1543 4k lt gray brn & blk .35 .25
3128 A1543 10k lt vio brn & blk 1.00 .25
3129 A1543 12k blue & black 1.25 .25
3130 A1543 14k bluish gray & blk 1.40 .25
3131 A1543 16k dl red brn & blk 1.75 .30
Nos. 3124-3131 (8) 6.50 2.05
Issued: 4k, 10k, Nov.; 1k, 2k, 12k, 14k, 12/24; 3k, 16k, 12/29.

Red Star Medal, War Scene and View of Kiev A1544

Red Star Medal, War Scene and view of: No. 3133, Leningrad. No. 3134, Odessa. No. 3135, Moscow. No. 3136, Brest Litovsk. No. 3137, Volgograd (Stalingrad). No. 3138, Sevastopol.

1965, Dec. **Perf. 11½**
Red, Gold and
3132 A1544 10k brown .50 .25
3133 A1544 10k dark blue .50 .25
3134 A1544 10k Prussian blue .50 .25
3135 A1544 10k dark violet .50 .25
3136 A1544 10k dark brown .50 .25
3137 A1544 10k black .50 .25
3138 A1544 10k gray .50 .25
Nos. 3132-3138 (7) 3.50 1.75
Honoring the heroism of various cities during World War II. Issued: #3136-3138, 12/30; others, 12/20.

Map and Flag of Yugoslavia, and National Assembly Building A1545

1965, Dec. 30 **Litho.** **Perf. 12**
3139 A1545 6k vio blue, red & bis .70 .25
Republic of Yugoslavia, 20th anniv.

Collective Farm Watchman by S.V. Gerasimov A1547

Painting: 16k, "Major's Courtship" by Pavel Andreievitch Fedotov, horiz.

1965, Dec. 31 **Engr.**
3145 A1547 12k red & sepia 1.50 .35
3146 A1547 16k red & dark blue 2.50 .65
Painters: Gerasimov, 80th birth anniv; Pavel A. Fedotov (1815-52).

Turkeys, Geese, Chicken and Globe A1548

Congress Emblems: No. 3147, Microscope and Moscow University. No. 3149, Crystals. No. 3150, Oceanographic instruments and ship. No. 3151, Mathematical symbols.

1966 **Photo.** **Perf. 11½**
3147 A1548 6k dull bl, blk & red .60 .25
3148 A1548 6k gray, pur & black .60 .25
3149 A1548 6k ol bis, blk & bl .60 .25

3150 A1548 6k grnsh blue & blk .60 .25
3151 A1548 6k dull yel, red
brn & blk .60 .25
Nos. 3147-3151 (5) 3.00 1.25
Intl. congresses to be held in Moscow: 9th Cong. of Microbiology (#3147); 13th Cong. on Poultry Raising (#3148); 7th Cong. on Crystallography (#3149); 2nd Intl. Cong. of Oceanography (#3150); Intl. Cong. of Mathematicians (#3151).
See Nos. 3309-3310.

Mailman and Milkmaid, 19th Century Figurines — A1549

1966, Jan. 28 **Litho.**
3152 A1549 6k shown .40 .25
3153 A1549 10k Tea set .60 .25
Bicentenary of Dimitrov Porcelain Works.

Romain Rolland (1866-1944), French Writer — A1550

Portrait: No. 3155, Eugène Pottier (1816-1887), French poet and author of the "International."

1966 **Photo. & Engr.** **Perf. 11½**
3154 A1550 4k dk blue & brn org .75 .25
3155 A1550 4k sl, red & dk red brn .75 .25

Horseback Rider, and Flags of Mongolia and USSR — A1551

1966, Jan. 31 **Litho.** **Perf. 12½x12**
3159 A1551 4k red, ultra & vio brn .50 .25
20th anniversary of the signing of the Mongolian-Soviet treaty of friendship and mutual assistance.

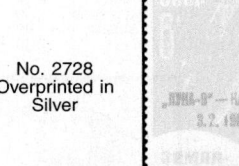

No. 2728 Overprinted in Silver

1966, Feb. 5 **Photo.** **Perf. 12**
3160 A1385 6k blk, lt blue & red 5.00 4.00
1st soft landing on the moon by Luna 9, Feb. 3, 1966.

Map of Antarctica With Soviet Stations — A1552

Diesel Ship "Ob" and Emperor Penguins — A1553

No. 3164, Snocat tractors and aurora australis.

1966, Feb. 14 **Photo.** **Perf. 11**
3162 A1552 10k sky bl, sil & dk car 1.50 1.00
3163 A1553 10k silver & dk car 1.50 1.00
3164 A1553 10k dk car, sil & sky bl 1.50 1.00
a. Strip of 3, #3162-3164 5.00 5.00
10 years of Soviet explorations in Antarctica. No. 3162 has horizontal rows of perforation extending from either mid-side up to the map.

Lenin A1554

1966, Feb. 22 **Photo.** **Perf. 12x11½**
3165 A1554 10k grnsh black & gold 1.00 .50
3166 A1554 10k dk red & silver 1.00 .25
96th anniversary of the birth of Lenin.

N.Y. Iljin, Guardsman A1555

Soviet Heroes: #3168, Lt. Gen. G. P. Kravchenko. #3169, Pvt. Anatoli Uglovsky.

1966 **Perf. 11½x12**
3167 A1555 4k dp org & vio black .65 .25
3168 A1555 4k grnsh bl & dk pur .65 .25
3169 A1555 4k green & brown .65 .25
Nos. 3167-3169 (3) 1.95 .75

Kremlin Congress Hall — A1556

1966, Feb. 28 **Typo.** **Perf. 12**
3172 A1556 4k gold, red & lt ultra .50 .25
23rd Communist Party Congress.

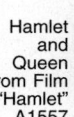

Hamlet and Queen from Film "Hamlet" A1557

Film Scene: 4k, Two soldiers from "The Quick and the Dead."

1966, Feb. 28 **Litho.**
3173 A1557 4k red, blk & ol 1.00 .25
3174 A1557 10k ultra & black 1.00 .25

No. 3104 Overprinted

1966, Mar. 10 Photo. **Perf. 11½x12**
3175 A1533 16k multicolored 5.00 2.50
Constituent assembly of the All-Union Society of Philatelists, 1966.

Emblem and Skater — A1558

Designs: 6k, Emblem and ice hockey. 10k, Emblem and slalom skier.

1966, Mar. 11 **Perf. 11**
3176 A1558 4k ol, brt ultra & red .35 .25
3177 A1558 6k bluish lilac, red & dk brown .60 .25
3178 A1558 10k lt bl, red & dk brn .95 .25
Nos. 3176-3178 (3) 1.90 .75
Second Winter Spartacist Games, Sverdlovsk. The label-like upper halves of Nos. 3176-3178 are separated from the lower halves by a row of perforations.

Electric Locomotive — A1559

Designs: 6k, Map of the Lenin Volga-Baltic Waterway, Admiralty, Leningrad, and Kremlin. 10k, Ship passing through lock in waterway, vert. 12k, M.S. Aleksander Pushkin. 16k, Passenger liner and globe.

1966   Litho.   Perf. 12½x12, 12x12½
3179	A1559	4k multicolored	.65	.25
3180	A1559	6k gray, ultra, red & black	.65	.25
3181	A1559	10k Prus bl, gray brn & black	.90	.25
3182	A1559	12k blue, ver & blk	1.40	.25
3183	A1559	16k blue & multi	1.40	.25
		Nos. 3179-3183 (5)	5.00	1.25

Modern transportation.
Issued: #3179-3181, 8/6; #3182-3183, 3/25.

Supreme Soviet Building, Frunze — A1560

1966, Mar. 25   Photo.   Perf. 12
3184	A1560	4k deep red	.50	.25

40th anniv. of the Kirghiz Republic.

Sergei M. Kirov — A1561

Portraits: No. 3186, Grigori Ordzhonikidze. No. 3187, Ion Yakir.

1966   Engr.   Perf. 12
3185	A1561	4k dk red brown	1.00	.30
3186	A1561	4k slate green	1.00	.30
3187	A1561	4k dark gray violet	1.00	.30
		Nos. 3185-3187 (3)	3.00	.90

Kirov (1886-1934), revolutionist and Secretary of the Communist Party Central Committee; Ordzhonikidze (1886-1937), a political leader of the Red Army and government official; Yakir, military leader in October Revolution, 70th birth anniv.
Issued: #3185, 3/27; #3186, 6/22; #3187, 7/30.

Souvenir Sheet

Lenin — A1563

Embossed and Typographed
1966, Mar. 29   Imperf.
3188	A1563	50k red & silver	5.00	1.00

23rd Communist Party Congress.

Aleksandr E. Fersman (1883-1945), Mineralogist A1564

Soviet Scientists: No. 3190, D. K. Zabolotny (1866-1929), microbiologist. No. 3191, M. A. Shatelen (1866-1957), physicist. No. 3191A, Otto Yulievich Schmidt (1891-1956), scientist and arctic explorer.

1966, Mar. 30   Litho.   Perf. 12½x12
3189	A1564	4k vio blue & multi	.75	.30
3190	A1564	4k red brn & multi	.75	.30
3191	A1564	4k lilac & multi	.75	.30
3191A	A1564	4k Prus bl & brn	.75	.30
		Nos. 3189-3191A (4)	3.00	1.20

Overprinted in Red

1966, Apr. 3   Typo.   Imperf.
3192	A1565	10k gold, blk, brt bl & brt rose	2.00	1.50

Launching of the 1st artificial moon satellite, Luna 10. The bright rose ink is fluorescent on Nos. 3192-3194.

Luna 10 Automatic Moon Station — A1565

Design: 12k, Station on moon.

1966, Apr. 12   Perf. 12
3193	A1565	10k multicolored	.80	.30
3194	A1565	12k multicolored	1.20	.30

Day of Space Research, Apr. 12, 1966.

Molniya 1 and Television Screens A1566

1966, Apr. 12   Litho.   Perf. 12½
3195	A1566	10k gold, blk, brt bl & red	1.00	.30

Launching of the communications satellite "Lightning 1," Apr. 23, 1965.

Ernst Thälmann — A1567

Portraits: No. 3197, Wilhelm Pieck. No. 3198, Sun Yat-sen. No. 3199, Sen Katayama.

1966-67   Engr.   Perf. 12½x12
3196	A1567	6k rose claret	1.25	.25
3197	A1567	6k blue violet	1.25	.25
3198	A1567	6k reddish brown	1.25	.25

Photo.
3199	A1567	6k gray green ('67)	1.25	.25
		Nos. 3196-3199 (4)	5.00	1.00

Thälmann (1886-1944), German Communist leader; Pieck (1876-1960), German Dem. Rep. Pres.; Sun Yat-sen (1866-1925), leader of the Chinese revolution; Katayama (1859-1933), founder of Social Democratic Party in Japan in 1901.
Issued: No. 3196, 4/16; No. 3197-3198, 6/22; No. 3199, 11/2/67.

Soldier, 1917, and Astronaut A1568

1966, Apr. 30   Litho.   Perf. 11½
3200	A1568	4k brt rose & black	.50	.25

15th Congress of the Young Communist League (Komsomol).

Ice Hockey Player — A1569

1966, Apr. 30
3201	A1569	10k red, ultra, gold & black	.50	.25

Soviet victory in the World Ice Hockey Championships. For souvenir sheet see No. 3232. For overprint see No. 3315.

Nicolai Kuznetsov A1570

Heroes of Guerrilla Warfare during WWII (Gold Star of Hero of the Soviet Union and): No. 3203, Imant Sudmalis. No. 3204, Anya Morozova. No. 3205, Filipp Strelets. No. 3206, Tikhon Bumazhkov.

1966, May 9   Photo.   Perf. 12x12½
3202	A1570	4k green & black	.60	.25
3203	A1570	4k ocher & black	.60	.25
3204	A1570	4k blue & black	.60	.25
3205	A1570	4k brt rose & black	.60	.25
3206	A1570	4k violet & black	.60	.25
		Nos. 3202-3206 (5)	3.00	1.25

Peter I. Tchaikovsky A1571

4k, Moscow State Conservatory, Tchaikovsky monument. 16k, Tchaikovsky House, Klin.

1966, May 26   Typo.   Perf. 12½
3207	A1571	4k red, yel & black	1.00	.25
3208	A1571	6k yel, red & black	1.25	.25
3209	A1571	16k red, bluish gray & black	3.00	.35
		Nos. 3207-3209 (3)	5.25	.90

Third International Tchaikovsky Contest, Moscow, May 30-June 29.

Runners — A1572

Designs: 6k, Weight lifters. 12k, Wrestlers.

1966, May 26   Photo.   Perf. 11x11½
3210	A1572	4k emer, olive & brn	.50	.25
3211	A1572	6k org, blk & lt brn	.75	.25
3212	A1572	12k grnsh bl, brn ol & black	1.00	.25
		Nos. 3210-3212 (3)	2.25	.75

No. 3210, Znamensky Brothers Intl. Track Competitions; No. 3211, Intl. Weightlifting Competitions; No. 3212, Intl. Wrestling Competitions for Ivan Poddubny Prize.

Jules Rimet World Soccer Cup, Ball and Laurel — A1573

Chessboard, Gold Medal, Pawn and King A1574

Designs: No. 3214, Soccer. 12k, Fencers. 16k, Fencer, mask, foil and laurel branch.

1966, May 31   Litho.   Perf. 11½
3213	A1573	4k rose red, gold & blk	.30	.25
3214	A1573	6k emer, tan, blk & red	.45	.25
3215	A1574	6k brn, gold, blk & white	1.75	.75
3216	A1573	12k brt bl, ol & blk	1.10	.25
3217	A1573	16k multicolored	1.40	.25
		Nos. 3213-3217 (5)	5.00	1.80

Nos. 3213-3214 for World Cup Soccer Championship, Wembley, England, July 11-30; No. 3215 the World Chess Title Match between Tigran Petrosian and Boris Spassky; Nos. 3216-3217 the World Fencing Championships. For souvenir sheet see No. 3232.

Sable and Lake Baikal, Map of Barguzin Game Reserve — A1575

Design: 6k, Map of Lake Baikal region and Game Reserve, brown bear on lake shore.

1966, June 25   Photo.   Perf. 12
3218	A1575	4k steel blue & black	1.50	.25
3219	A1575	6k rose lake & black	1.50	.25

Barguzin Game Reserve, 50th anniv.

Pink Lotus — A1576

6k, Palms and cypresses. 12k, Victoria cruziana.

1966, June 30   **Perf. 11½**
3220 A1576 3k grn, pink & yel   .25   .25
3221 A1576 6k grnsh bl, ol brn
     & dk brn   1.00   .25
3222 A1576 12k multicolored   1.75   .25
     Nos. 3220-3222 (3)   3.00   .75

Sukhum Botanical Garden, 125th anniv.

Dogs Ugolek and Veterok after Space Flight A1577

Designs: No. 3224, Diagram of Solar System, globe and medal of Venera 3 flight. No. 3225, Luna 10, earth and moon.

1966, July 15   **Perf. 12x11½**
3223 A1577 6k ocher, ind & org
     brn   1.00   .25
3224 A1577 6k crim, blk & silver   1.00   .25
     Perf. 12x12½
3225 A1577 6k dk blue & bis brn   1.00   .25
     Nos. 3223-3225 (3)   3.00   .75

Soviet achievements in space.

Itkol Hotel, Mount Cheget and Map of USSR A1578

Arch of General Headquarters, Winter Palace and Alexander Column A1579

Resort Areas: 4k, Ship on Volga River and Zhigul Mountain. 10k, Castle, Kislovodsk. 12k, Ismail Samani Mausoleum, Bukhara, Uzbek. 16k, Hotel Caucasus, Sochi.

1966 Litho.   **Perf. 12½x12, 12½ (6k)**
3226 A1578 1k multicolored   .25   .25
3227 A1578 4k multicolored   .35   .25
3228 A1578 6k multicolored   .40   .25
3229 A1578 10k multicolored   .65   .25
3230 A1578 12k multicolored   .90   .25
3231 A1578 16k multicolored   1.40   .30
     Nos. 3226-3231 (6)   3.95   1.55

Issue dates: 10k, Sept. 14; others, July 20.

Souvenir Sheet

A1580

1966, July 26   **Litho.**   **Perf. 11½**
3232 A1580   Sheet of 4   10.00   2.00
   a.   10k Fencers   2.00   .40
   b.   10k Chess   2.00   .40
   c.   10k Soccer cup   2.00   .40
   d.   10k Ice hockey   2.00   .40

World fencing, chess, soccer and ice hockey championships.
See Nos. 3201, 3213-3217.

Congress Emblem, Congress Palace and Kremlin Tower — A1581

1966, Aug. 6   Photo.   Perf. 11½x12
3233 A1581 4k brown & yellow   .35   .25
Consumers' Cooperative Societies, 7th Cong.

Dove, Crane, Russian and Japanese Flags A1582

1966, Aug. 9   **Perf. 12½x11½**
3234 A1582 6k gray & red   1.00   .25
Soviet-Japanese friendship, and 2nd meeting of Russian and Japanese delegates at Khabarovsk.

"Knight Fighting with Tiger" by Rustaveli A1583

Designs: 4k, Shota Rustaveli, bas-relief. 6k, "Avtandil at a Mountain Spring." 50k, Shota Rustaveli Monument and design of 3k stamp.

1966, Aug. 31   Engr.   Perf. 11½x12½
3235 A1583 3k blk, *olive green*   .75   .25
3236 A1583 4k brown, *yellow*   .90   .25
3237 A1583 6k bluish black, *lt*
     ultra   1.40   .25
     Nos. 3235-3237 (3)   3.05   .75

Souvenir Sheet
Imperf
Engraved and Photogravure
3238 A1583 50k slate grn & bis   4.00   1.25

800th anniv. of the birth of Shota Rustaveli, Georgian poet, author of "The Knight in the Tiger's Skin." No. 3238 contains one 32x49mm stamp; dark green margin with design of 6k stamp.

Coat of Arms and Fireworks over Moscow A1584

Lithographed (Lacquered)
1966, Sept. 14   **Perf. 11½**
3239 A1584 4k multicolored   .50   .25
49th anniversary of October Revolution.

Grayling A1585

Designs (Fish and part of design of 6k stamp): 4k, Sturgeon. 6k, Trawler, net and map of Lake Baikal, vert. 10k, Two Baikal cisco. 12k, Two Baikal whitefish.

1966, Sept. 25   **Photo. & Engr.**
3240 A1585 2k multicolored   .25   .25
3241 A1585 4k multicolored   .25   .25
3242 A1585 6k multicolored   .35   .25
3243 A1585 10k multicolored   .50   .25
3244 A1585 12k gray, dk grn &
     red brown   .75   .25
     Nos. 3240-3244 (5)   2.10   1.25

Fish resources of Lake Baikal.

Map of USSR and Symbols of Transportation and Communication — A1586

Designs (map of USSR and): No. 3246, Technological education. No. 3247, Agriculture and mining. No. 3248, Increased productivity through five-year plan. No. 3249, Technology and inventions.

1966, Sept. 29   Photo.   Perf. 11½x12
3245 A1586 4k ultra & silver   .60   .25
3246 A1586 4k car & silver   .60   .25
3247 A1586 4k red brn & silver   .60   .25
3248 A1586 4k red & silver   .60   .25
3249 A1586 4k dp green & silver   .60   .25
     Nos. 3245-3249 (5)   3.00   1.25

23rd Communist Party Congress decisions.

Government House, Kishinev, and Moldavian Flag — A1587

1966, Oct. 8   Litho.   Perf. 12½x12
3250 A1587 4k multicolored   .50   .50
500th anniversary of Kishinev.

Symbolic Water Cycle A1588

1966, Oct. 12   **Perf. 11½**
3251 A1588 6k multicolored   1.00   .25
Hydrological Decade (UNESCO), 1965-1974.

Nikitin Monument in Kalinin, Ship's Prow and Map — A1589

1966, Oct. 12   **Photo.**
3252 A1589 4k multicolored   .50   .25
Afanasii Nikitin's trip to India, 500th anniv.

Scene from Opera "Nargiz" by M. Magomayev — A1590

No. 3254, Scene from opera "Kerogli" by Y. Gadjubekov (knight on horseback and armed men).

1966, Oct. 12
3253 A1590 4k black & ocher   .75   .25
3254 A1590 4k blk & blue green   .75   .25
   a.   Pair, #3253-3254   2.00   .50

Azerbaijan opera. Printed in checkerboard arrangement.

Fighters A1591

1966, Oct. 26
3255 A1591 6k red, blk & ol bister   .50   .25
30th anniversary of Spanish Civil War.

National Militia — A1592

1966, Oct. 26   Litho.   Perf. 12x12½
3256 A1592 4k red & dark brown   .50   .25
25th anniv. of the National Militia.

Protest Rally — A1592a

1966, Oct. 26   **Perf. 12**
3256A A1592a 6k yel, black & red   .50   .30

"Hands off Viet Nam!"

Soft Landing on Moon, Luna 9 — A1593

Symbols of Agriculture and Chemistry A1594

Designs: 1k, Congress Palace, Moscow, and map of Russia. 3k, Boy, girl and Lenin banner. 4k, Flag. 6k, Plane and Ostankino Television Tower. 10k, Soldier and Soviet star. 12k, Steel worker. 16k, "Peace," woman with dove. 20k, Demonstrators in Red Square, flags, carnation and globe. 50k, Newspaper, plane, train and Communications Ministry. 1r, Lenin and industrial symbols.

Inscribed "1966"

1966		**Litho.**	**Perf. 12**
3257	A1593	1k dk red brown	.25 .25
3258	A1593	2k violet	.25 .25
3259	A1593	3k red lilac	.25 .25
3260	A1593	4k bright red	.25 .25
3261	A1593	6k ultra	.25 .25
3262	A1593	10k olive	.40 .25
3263	A1593	12k red brown	1.10 .25
3264	A1593	16k violet blue	1.40 .25
		Perf. 11½	
		Photo.	
3265	A1594	20k bis, red & dk bl	2.00 .25
3266	A1594	30k dp grn & green	2.50 .30
3267	A1594	50k blue & violet bl	4.50 .35
3268	A1594	1r black & red	7.00 .55
		Nos. 3257-3268 (12)	20.15 3.45

No. 3260 was issued on fluorescent paper in 1969.
See Nos. 3470-3481.

Ostankino Television Tower, Molniya 1 Satellite and Kremlin A1595

1966, Nov. 19   **Litho.**   **Perf. 12**
3273 A1595 4k multicolored   1.00 .25

New Year, 1967, the 50th anniversary of the October Revolution.

Diagram of Luna 9 Flight — A1596

Arms of Russia and Pennant Sent to Moon — A1597

No. 3276, Luna 9 & photograph of moonscape.

1966, Nov. 25		**Typo.**	**Perf. 12**
3274	A1596	10k black & silver	.65 .25
3275	A1597	10k red & silver	.65 .25
3276	A1596	10k black & silver	.65 .25
a.		Strip of 3, #3274-3276	2.00 1.00

Soft landing on the moon by Luna 9, Jan. 31, 1966, and the television program of moon pictures on Feb. 2.

Battle of Moscow, 1941 — A1598

Details from "Defense of Moscow" Medal and Golden Star Medal A1599

25th anniv. of Battle of Moscow: 10k, Sun rising over Kremlin. Ostankino Tower, chemical plant and rockets.

Perf. 12, 11½ (A1599)

1966, Dec. 1			**Photo.**
3277	A1598	4k red brown	.25 .25
3278	A1599	6k bister & brown	1.00 .25
3279	A1598	10k dp bister & yel	1.75 .25
		Nos. 3277-3279 (3)	3.00 .75

Cervantes and Don Quixote A1600

1966, Dec. 15   **Photo.**   **Perf. 11½**
3280 A1600 6k gray & brown   .50 .25

Miguel Cervantes Saavedra (1547-1616), Spanish writer.

Bering's Ship and Map of Voyage to Commander Islands — A1601

Far Eastern Territories: 2k, Medny Island and map. 4k, Petropavlosk-Kamchatski Harbor. 6k, Geyser, Kamchatka, vert. 10k, Avachinskaya Bay, Kamchatka. 12k, Fur seals, Bering Island. 16k, Guillemots in bird sanctuary, Kuril Islands.

1966, Dec. 25		**Litho.**	**Perf. 12**
3281	A1601	1k bister & multi	.45 .25
3282	A1601	2k bister & multi	.50 .25
3283	A1601	4k dp blue & multi	.60 .25
3284	A1601	6k multicolored	.75 .25
3285	A1601	10k dp blue & multi	1.00 .25
3286	A1601	12k olive & multi	1.00 .40
3287	A1601	16k lt blue & multi	1.25 .75
		Nos. 3281-3287 (7)	5.55 2.40

Communications Satellite, Molniya 1 — A1602

Design: No. 3289, Luna 11 moon probe, moon, earth and Soviet emblem.

1966, Dec. 29	**Photo.**		**Perf. 12x11½**
3288	A1602	6k blk, vio bl & brt rose	1.00 .30
3289	A1602	6k black & brt rose	1.00 .30

Space explorations. The bright rose is fluorescent.

Golden Stag, Scythia, 6th Century B.C. — A1603

Treasures from the Hermitage, Leningrad: 6k, Silver jug, Persia, 5th Century A.D. 10k, Statue of Voltaire by Jean Antoine Houdon. 12k, Malachite vase, Ural, 1840. 16k, "The Lute Player," by Michelangelo de Caravaggio. (6k, 10k, 12k are vertical).

1966, Dec. 29		**Engr.**	**Perf. 12**
3290	A1603	4k yellow & black	.45 .25
3291	A1603	6k gray & black	.60 .25
3292	A1603	10k dull vio & black	.90 .25
3293	A1603	12k emer & black	1.25 .30
3294	A1603	16k ocher & black	1.75 .35
		Nos. 3290-3294 (5)	4.95 1.40

Sea Water Converter and Pavilion at EXPO '67 A1604

Pavilion and: 6k, Splitting atom, vert. 10k, "Proton" space station. 30k, Soviet pavilion.

1967, Jan. 25		**Litho.**	**Perf. 12**
3295	A1604	4k multicolored	.75 .25
3296	A1604	6k multicolored	.75 .25
3297	A1604	10k multicolored	1.50 .25
		Nos. 3295-3297 (3)	3.00 .75
		Souvenir Sheet	
3298	A1604	30k multicolored	3.00 1.25

EXPO '67, Intl. Exhib., Montreal, 4/28-10/27.

1st Lieut. B. I. Sizov A1605

Design: No. 3300, Sailor V. V. Khodyrev.

1967, Feb. 16	**Photo.**		**Perf. 12x11½**
3299	A1605	4k dull yel & ocher	.40 .25
3300	A1605	4k gray & dk gray	.40 .25

Heroes of World War II.

Woman's Head and Pavlov Shawl — A1606

1967, Feb. 16   **Perf. 11**
3301 A1606 4k vio, red & grn   1.00 .25

International Woman's Day, Mar. 8.

Movie Camera and Film — A1607

1967, Feb. 16   **Photo.**   **Perf. 11½**
3302 A1607 6k multicolored   .50 .25

5th Intl. Film Festival, Moscow, July 5-20.

Trawler Fish Factory and Fish — A1608

Designs: No. 3304, Refrigerationship. No. 3305, Crab canning ship. No. 3306, Fishing trawler. No. 3307, Black Sea seiner.

1967, Feb. 28		**Litho.**	**Perf. 12x11½**
Ships in Black and Red			
3303	A1608	6k blue & gray	.60 .25
3304	A1608	6k blue & gray	.60 .25
3305	A1608	6k blue & gray	.60 .25
3306	A1608	6k blue & gray	.60 .25
3307	A1608	6k blue & gray	.60 .25
a.		Vert. strip of 5, #3303-3307	3.25 1.50

Soviet fishing industry.

Newspaper Forming Hammer and Sickle, Red Flag — A1609

1967, Mar. 13   **Litho.**   **Perf. 12x12½**
3308 A1609 4k cl brn, red, yel & brn   .40 .25

50th anniversary of newspaper Izvestia.

Congress Type of 1966

Congress Emblems and: No. 3309, Moscow State University, construction site and star. No. 3310, Pile driver, mining excavator, crossed hammers, globe and "V."

1967, Mar. 10		**Photo.**	**Perf. 11½**
3309	A1548	6k ultra, brt blue & blk	.50 .25
3310	A1548	6k blk, org red & blue	.50 .25

Intl. congresses to be held in Moscow: 7th General Assembly Session of the Intl. Standards Association (#3309); 5th Intl. Mining Cong. (#3310).

International Tourist Year Emblem and
Travel Symbols — A1610

1967, Mar. 10   **Perf. 11**
3314 A1610 4k blk, sky bl & sil   .50   .25
International Tourist Year, 1967.

No. 3201 Overprinted

1967, Mar. 29   Litho.   Perf. 11½
3315 A1569 10k multicolored   2.00 1.00
Victory of the Soviet team in the Ice Hockey
Championships, Vienna, Mar. 18-29. Overprint reads: "Vienna-1967."

Space Walk — A1611

Designs: 10k, Rocket launching from satellite. 16k, Spaceship over moon, and earth.

1967, Mar. 30   Litho.   Perf. 12
3316 A1611   4k bister & multi   .50   .25
3317 A1611 10k black & multi   1.00   .25
3318 A1611 16k lilac & multi   1.50   .30
  Nos. 3316-3318 (3)   3.00   .80
National Cosmonauts' Day.

Lenin as
Student, by
V. Tsigal
A1612

Sculptures of Lenin: 3k, Monument at Ulya-
novsk by M. Manizer. 4k, Lenin in Razliv, by V.
Pinchuk, horiz. 6k, Head, by G. Neroda. 10k,
Lenin as Leader, statue, by N. Andreyev.

1967   Photo.   Perf. 12x11½, 11½x12
3319   A1612   2k ol grn, sepia &
                  buff   .30   .25
3320   A1612   3k maroon & brn   .30   .25
3321   A1612   4k ol black & gold   .45   .25
3322   A1612   6k dk bl, sil & blk   .60   .25
3323   A1612 10k sil, gray bl &
                  blk   1.10   .25
3323A A1612 10k gold, gray &
                  black   1.10   .25
  Nos. 3319-3323A (6)   3.85 1.50

97th anniversary of the birth of Lenin.
Issued: #3323A, Oct. 25; others, Apr. 22.

Lt. M. S. Kharchenko and Battle
Scenes — A1613

Designs: No. 3325, Maj. Gen. S. V. Rudnev.
No. 3326, M. Shmyrev.

1967, Apr. 24   Perf. 12x11½
3324 A1613 4k brt pur & ol bis   .40   .25
3325 A1613 4k ultra & ol bister   .40   .25
3326 A1613 4k org brn & ol bis-
                  ter   .40   .25
  Nos. 3324-3326 (3)   1.20   .75
Partisan heroes of WWII.

Marshal S. S.
Biryuzov, Hero of
the Soviet
Union — A1614

1967, May 9   Photo.   Perf. 12
3327 A1614 4k ocher & sl grn   .35   .25

Driver
Crossing
Lake
Ladoga
A1615

1967, May 9   Perf. 11½
3328 A1615 4k plum & blue gray   .35   .25
25th anniversary of siege of Leningrad.

Views of
Old and
New Minsk
A1616

1967, May 9
3329 A1616 4k sl grn & blk   .35   .25
900th anniversary of Minsk.

Red Cross and
Tulip — A1617

1967, May 15   Perf. 12
3330 A1617 4k yel brn & red   .50   .25
Centenary of the Russian Red Cross.

Stamps of 1918 and 1967 — A1618

1967   Photo.   Perf. 11½
3331 A1618 20k blue & black   1.00   .30
  a.   Souv. sheet of 2, imperf.   3.00 1.25

All-Union Philatelic Exhibition "50 Years of
the Great October," Moscow, Oct. 1-10. Se-
tenant with label showing exhibition emblem.
Issue dates: 20k, May 25. Sheet, Oct. 1.
No. 3331 was re-issued Oct. 3 with "Oct. 1-
10" printed in blue on the label. Value $2.

Komsomolsk-on-Amur and Map of
Amur River — A1619

1967, June 12   Perf. 12x12½
3332 A1619 4k red & brown   .60   .25

35th anniv. of the Soviet youth town, Komsomolsk-on-Amur. Printed with label showing
boy and girl of Young Communist League and
tents.

Souvenir Sheet

Sputnik Orbiting Earth — A1620

1967, June 24   Litho.   Perf. 13x12
3333 A1620 30k black & multi   7.50 6.00
10th anniv. of the launching of Sputnik 1,
the 1st artificial satellite, Oct. 4, 1957.

Motorcyclist
A1621

Photogravure and Engraved
1967, June 24   Perf. 12x11½
3334 A1621 10k multicolored   .35   .25
Intl. Motor Rally, Moscow, July 19.

G. D. Gai (1887-
1937), Corps
Commander of
the First Cavalry,
1920 — A1622

1967, June 30   Photo.   Perf. 12
3335 A1622 4k red & black   .35   .25

Children's
Games
Emblem
and Trophy
A1623

1967, July 8   Perf. 11½
3336 A1623 4k silver, red & black   .35   .25
10th National Athletic Games of School
Children, Leningrad, July, 1967.

Games
Emblem
and Trophy
A1624

No. 3338, Cup and gymnast. No. 3339, Cup
and bicyclists. No. 3340, Cup and diver.

1967, July 20
3337 A1624 4k silver, red & black   .25   .25
3338 A1624 4k silver, red & black   .25   .25
  a.   Pair, #3337-3338   1.00   .35
3339 A1624 4k silver, red & black   .25   .25
3340 A1624 4k silver, red & black   .25   .25
  a.   Pair, #3339-3340   1.00   .35
4th Natl. Spartacist Games, & USSR 50th
anniv.
Se-tenant in checkerboard arrangement.

V. G. Klochkov (1911-41), Hero of the
Soviet Union — A1625

1967, July 20   Perf. 12½x12
3341 A1625 4k red & black   .75   .30
Alternating label shows citation.

Soviet
Flag,
Arms and
Moscow
Views
A1626

Arms of USSR and Laurel — A1627

АРМЯНСКАЯ ССР
ՀԱՅԿԱԿԱՆ ՍՍՀ

No. 3343

АЗЕРБАЙДЖАНСКАЯ ССР
АЗӘРБАЈЧАН ССР

No. 3344

БЕЛОРУССКАЯ ССР
БЕЛАРУСКАЯ ССР

No. 3345

ГРУЗИНСКАЯ ССР
 საქართველოს სსრ

No. 3347

КИРГИЗСКАЯ ССР
КЫРГЫЗ ССР

No. 3349

Молдавская ССР
РСС Молдовеняскэ

No. 3352

Таджикская ССР
РСС Точикистон

No. 3353

Туркменская ССР
Туркменистан ССР

No. 3354

Украинская ССР
Українська Р.С.Р

No. 3355

Узбекская ССР
Ўзбекистон ССР

No. 3356

Flag, Crest and Capital of Republic.

1967, Aug. 4   Litho.   Perf. 12½x12

3342	A1626	4k shown	.60	.25
3343	A1626	4k Armenia	.60	.25
3344	A1626	4k Azerbaijan	.60	.25
3345	A1626	4k Byelorussia	.60	.25
3346	A1626	4k Estonia	.60	.25
3347	A1626	4k Georgia	.60	.25
3348	A1626	4k Kazakhstan	.60	.25
3349	A1626	4k Kirghizia	.60	.25
3350	A1626	4k Latvia	.60	.25
3351	A1626	4k Lithuania	.60	.25
3352	A1626	4k Moldavia	.60	.25
3353	A1626	4k Tadzhikistan	.60	.25
3354	A1626	4k Turkmenistan	.60	.25
3355	A1626	4k Ukraine	.60	.25
3356	A1626	4k Uzbekistan	.60	.25
3357	A1627	4k red, gold & black	.60	.25
		Nos. 3342-3357 (16)	9.60	4.00

50th anniversary of October Revolution.

Communication Symbols — A1628

1967, Aug. 16   Photo.   Perf. 12
3358 A1628 4k crimson & silver   1.00 .50
Development of communications in USSR.

Flying Crane, Dove and Anniversary
Emblem — A1629

1967, Aug. 20   Perf. 12½x12
3359 A1629 16k silver, red & blk   1.00 .30
Russo-Japanese Friendship Meeting, held at Khabarovsk. Emblem is for 50th anniv. of October Revolution.

Karl Marx and Title Page of "Das Kapital" — A1630

1967, Aug. 22   Engr.   Perf. 12½x12
3360 A1630 4k sepia & dk red   3.00 .30
Centenary of the publication of "Das Kapital" by Karl Marx.

Russian Checkers Players A1631

Design: 6k, Woman gymnast.

Photogravure and Engraved
1967, Sept. 9   Perf. 12x11½
3361 A1631 1k lt brn, dp brn & sl   .50 .25
3362 A1631 6k ol bister & maroon   .50 .25

World Championship of Russian Checkers (Shashki) at Moscow, and World Championship of Rhythmic Gymnastics.

Javelin A1632

1967, Sept. 9   Engr.   Perf. 12x12½
3363 A1632 2k shown   .65 .25
3364 A1632 3k Running   .65 .25
3365 A1632 4k Jumping   .65 .25
Nos. 3363-3365 (3)   1.95 .75

Europa Cup Championships, Kiev, Sept. 15-17.

Ice Skating and Olympic Emblem A1633

Designs: 3k, Ski jump. 4k, Emblem of Winter Olympics, vert. 10k, Ice hockey. 12k, Long-distance skiing.

Photogravure and Engraved
1967, Sept. 20   Perf. 11½
3366 A1633 2k gray, blk & bl   .25 .25
3367 A1633 3k bis, ocher, blk & green   .25 .25
3368 A1633 4k gray, bl, red & blk   .25 .25
3369 A1633 10k bis, brn, bl & blk   .75 .25
3370 A1633 12k gray, blk, lil & grn   1.50 .25
Nos. 3366-3370 (5)   3.00 1.25

10th Winter Olympic Games, Grenoble, France, Feb. 6-18, 1968.

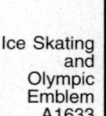

Arctic Blue Fox A1634

Fur-bearing Animals: 4k, Silver Fox. 6k, Red fox, horiz. 10k, Muskrat, horiz. 12k, Ermine. 16k, Sable. 20k, Mink, horiz.

1967, Sept. 20   Photo.
3371 A1634 2k brn, blk & gray blue   .25 .25
3372 A1634 4k tan, dk brn & gray blue   .30 .25
3373 A1634 6k gray grn, ocher & black   .45 .25

3374 A1634 10k yel grn, dk brn & ocher   .65 .25
3375 A1634 12k lilac, blk & bis   .75 .25
3376 A1634 16k org, brn & black   .80 .25
3377 A1634 20k gray blue, blk & dk brown   1.00 .30
Nos. 3371-3377 (7)   4.20 1.80

International Fur Auctions in Leningrad.

Young Guards Memorial — A1635

1967, Sept. 23
3378 A1635 4k magenta, org & blk   .50 .25
25th anniv. of the fight of the Young Guards at Krasnodon against the Germans.

Map of Cedar Valley Reservation and Snow Leopard — A1636

1967, Oct. 14   Perf. 12
3379 A1636 10k ol bister & black   1.00 .25
Far Eastern Cedar Valley Reservation.

Planes and Emblem A1637

1967, Oct. 14   Perf. 11½
3380 A1637 6k dp blue, red & gold   .50 .25
French Normandy-Neman aviators, who fought on the Russian Front, 25th anniv.

Militiaman and Soviet Emblem A1638

1967, Oct. 14   Perf. 12½x12
3381 A1638 4k ver & ultra   .35 .25
50th anniversary of the Soviet Militia.

Space Station Orbiting Moon — A1639

Science Fiction: 6k, Explorers on the moon, horiz. 10k, Rocket flying to the stars. 12k, Landscape on Red Planet, horiz. 16k, Satellites from outer space.

1967   Litho.   Perf. 12x12½, 12½x12
3382 A1639 4k multicolored   .25 .25
3383 A1639 6k multicolored   .35 .25
3384 A1639 10k multicolored   .45 .25
3385 A1639 12k multicolored   .60 .25
3386 A1639 16k multicolored   .65 .25
Nos. 3382-3386 (5)   2.30 1.25

Emblem of USSR and Red Star — A1640

Lenin Addressing 2nd Congress of Soviets, by V. A. Serov — A1641

Builders of Communism, by L. M. Merpert and Y. N. Skripkov — A1641a

Paintings: No. 3389, Lenin pointing to Map, by L. A. Schmatjko, 1957. No. 3390, The First Cavalry Army, by M. B. Grekov, 1924. No. 3391, Working Students on the March, by B. V. Yoganson, 1928. No. 3392, Russian Friendship for the World, by S. M. Karpov, 1924. No. 3393, Five-Year Plan Morning, by Y. D. Romas, 1934. No. 3394, Farmers' Holiday, by S. V. Gerasimov, 1937. No. 3395, Victory in the Great Patriotic War, by Y. K. Korolev, 1965.

Lithographed and Embossed
1967, Oct. 25   Perf. 11½
3387 A1640 4k gold, yel, red & dk brown   .50 .25
3388 A1641 4k gold & multi   .50 .25
3389 A1641 4k gold & multi   .50 .25
3390 A1641 4k gold & multi   .50 .25
3391 A1641 4k gold & multi   .50 .25
3392 A1641 4k gold & multi   .50 .25
3393 A1641 4k gold & multi   .50 .25
3394 A1641 4k gold & multi   .50 .25
3395 A1641 4k gold & multi   .50 .25
3396 A1641a 4k gold & multi   .50 .25
a. Souvenir sheet of 2   4.25 1.00
Nos. 3387-3396 (10)   5.00 2.50

50th anniversary of October Revolution, No. 3396a contains two 40k imperf. stamps similar to Nos. 3388 and 3396. Issued Nov. 5.

Souvenir Sheet

Hammer, Sickle and Sputnik — A1642

1967, Nov. 5   Engr.   Perf. 12½x12
3397 A1642 1r lake   5.00 2.00
50th anniv. of the October Revolution. Margin contains "50" as a watermark.

Ostankino Television Tower — A1643

1967, Nov. 5   Litho.   Perf. 11½
3398 A1643 16k gray, org & black   .35 .25

Jurmala Resort and Hepatica A1644

Health Resorts of the Baltic Region: 6k, Narva-Joesuu and Labrador tea. 10k, Druskininkai and cranberry blossoms. 12k, Zelenogradsk and Scotch heather, vert. 16k, Svetlogorsk and club moss, vert.

Perf. 12½x12, 12x12½
1967, Nov. 30   Litho.
Flowers in Natural Colors
3399 A1644 4k blue & black   .25 .25
3400 A1644 6k ocher & black   .35 .25
3401 A1644 10k green & black   .60 .25
3402 A1644 12k gray olive & blk .75 .25
3403 A1644 16k brown & black   1.10 .25
   Nos. 3399-3403 (5)   3.05 1.25

Emergency Commission Emblem — A1645

1967, Dec. 11   Photo.   Perf. 11½
3404 A1645 4k ultra & red   .75 .25
All-Russia Emergency Commission (later the State Security Commission), 50th anniv.

Hotel Russia and Kremlin A1646

1967, Dec. 14
3405 A1646 4k silver, dk brn & brt
              pink   2.00 .25
New Year 1968. The pink is fluorescent.

Soldiers, Sailors, Congress Building, Kharkov, and Monument to the Men of Arsenal — A1647

Designs: 6k, Hammer and sickle and scenes from industry and agriculture. 10k, Ukrainians offering bread and salt, monument of the Unknown Soldier, Kiev, and Lenin monument in Zaporozhye.

1967, Dec. 20   Litho.   Perf. 12½
3406 A1647 4k multicolored   .30 .25
3407 A1647 6k multicolored   .65 .25
3408 A1647 10k multicolored   .80 .25
   Nos. 3406-3408 (3)   1.75 .75
50th anniv. of the Ukrainian SSR.

Three Kremlin Towers A1648

Kremlin: 6k, Cathedral of the Annunciation, horiz. 10k, Konstantin and Elena, Nabatnaya and Spasski towers. 12k, Ivan the Great bell tower. 16k, Kutafya and Troitskaya towers.

Engraved and Photogravure
1967, Dec. 25   Perf. 12x11½, 11½x12
3409 A1648 4k dk brn & claret .25 .25
3410 A1648 6k dk brn, yel &
               grn   .35 .25
3411 A1648 10k maroon & slate .65 .25
3412 A1648 12k sl grn, yel & vio .90 .25
3413 A1648 16k brn, pink & red 1.00 .25
   Nos. 3409-3413 (5)   3.15 1.25

Coat of Arms, Lenin's Tomb and Rockets A1649

Designs: No. 3415, Agricultural Progress: Wheat, reapers and silo. No. 3416, Industrial Progress: Computer tape, atom symbol, cogwheel and factories. No. 3417, Scientific Progress: Radar, microscope, university buildings. No. 3418, Communications progress: Ostankino TV tower, railroad bridge, steamer and Aeroflot emblem, vert.

1967, Dec. 25   Engr.   Perf. 12½
3414 A1649 4k maroon   .30 .25
3415 A1649 4k green   .30 .25
3416 A1649 4k red brown   .30 .25
3417 A1649 4k violet blue   .30 .25
3418 A1649 4k dark blue   .30 .25
   Nos. 3414-3418 (5)   1.50 1.25
Material and technical basis of Russian Communism.

Monument to the Unknown Soldier, Moscow — A1650

1967, Dec. 25
3419 A1650 4k carmine   .50 .25
Dedication of the Monument of the Unknown Soldier of WWII in the Kremlin Wall.

Seascape by Ivan Aivazovsky — A1651

Paintings: 3k, Interrogation of Communists by B. V. Yoganson, 1933. No. 3422, The

Lacemaker, by V. A. Tropinin, 1823, vert. No. 3423, Bread-makers, by T. M. Yablonskaya, 1949. No. 3424, Alexander Nevsky, by P. D. Korin, 1942-43, vert. No. 3425, The Boyar Morozov Going into Exile by V. I. Surikov, 1887. No. 3426, The Swan Maiden, by M. A. Vrubel, 1900, vert. No. 3427, The Arrest of a Propagandist by Ilya E. Repin, 1878. 16k, Moscow Suburb in February by G. G. Nissky, 1957.

Perf. 12½x12, 12x12½, 12, 11½
1967, Dec. 29   Litho.
Size: 47x33mm, 33x47mm
3420 A1651 3k multicolored   .25 .25
3421 A1651 4k multicolored   .30 .25
3422 A1651 4k multicolored   .30 .25
Size: 60x35mm, 35x60mm
3423 A1651 6k multicolored   .40 .25
3424 A1651 6k multicolored   .40 .25
3425 A1651 6k multicolored   .40 .25
Size: 47x33mm, 33x47mm
3426 A1651 10k multicolored   .70 .25
3427 A1651 10k multicolored   .70 .25
3428 A1651 16k multicolored   1.10 .40
   Nos. 3420-3428 (9)   4.55 2.40
Tretiakov Art Gallery, Moscow.

Globe, Wheel and Workers of the World — A1652

1968, Jan. 18   Photo.   Perf. 12
3429 A1652 6k ver & green   .50 .25
14th Trade Union Congress.

Lt. S. Baikov and Velikaya River Bridge A1653

Heroes of WWII (War Memorial and): No. 3431. Lt. A. Pokalchuk. No. 3432, P. Gutchenko.

1968, Jan. 20   Perf. 12½x12
3430 A1653 4k blue gray & black .35 .25
3431 A1653 4k rose & black   .35 .25
3432 A1653 4k gray green & black .35 .25
   Nos. 3430-3432 (3)   1.05 .75

Thoroughbred and Horse Race — A1654

Horses: 6k, Arab mare and dressage, vert. 10k, Orlovski trotters. 12k, Altekin horse performing, vert. 16k, Donskay race horse.

1968, Jan. 23   Perf. 11½
3433 A1654 4k ultra, blk & red
               lil   .40 .25
3434 A1654 6k crim, blk & ultra .65 .25
3435 A1654 10k grnsh blue, blk
               & orange   .95 .40
3436 A1654 12k org brn, black &
               apple green   1.25 .50
3437 A1654 16k ol grn, blk & red 1.75 .70
   Nos. 3433-3437 (5)   5.00 2.10
Horse breeding.

Maria I. Ulyanova (1878-1937), Lenin's Sister — A1655

1968, Jan. 30   Perf. 12x12½
3438 A1655 4k indigo & pale green .50 .25

Soviet Star and Flags of Army, Air Force and Navy A1656

Lenin Addressing Troops in 1919 — A1657

No. 3441, Dneprostroi Dam & sculpture "On Guard." No. 3442, 1918 poster & marching volunteers. No. 3443, Red Army entering Vladivostok, 1922, & soldiers' monument in Primorie. No. 3444, Poster "Red Army as Liberator," Western Ukraine. No. 3445, Poster "Westward," defeat of German army. No. 3446, "Battle of Stalingrad" monument & German prisoners of war. No. 3447, Victory parade on Red Square, May 24, 1945, & Russian War Memorial, Berlin. Nos. 3448-3449, Modern weapons and Russian flag.

1968, Feb. 20   Typo.   Perf. 12x12½
3439 A1656 4k gold & multi   .30 .25
Photo.
Perf. 11½x12
3440 A1657 4k blk, red, pink &
               silver   .30 .25
3441 A1657 4k gold, black & red .30 .25
Litho.
Perf. 12½x12
3442 A1657 4k yel grn, blk, red &
               buff   .30 .25
3443 A1657 4k grn, dk brn, red &
               bis   .30 .25
3444 A1657 4k green & multi   .30 .25
3445 A1657 4k yel green & multi .30 .25
Perf. 11½x12, 12x11½
Photo.
3446 A1657 4k blk, silver & red .30 .25
3447 A1657 4k gold, blk, pink &
               red   .30 .25
3448 A1656 4k blk, red & silver .30 .25
   Nos. 3439-3448 (10)   3.00 2.50

Souvenir Sheet
1968, Feb. 23   Litho.   Imperf.
3449 A1656 1r blk, silver & red 4.50 1.50
50th anniv. of the Armed Forces of the USSR. No. 3449 contains one 25x37½mm stamp with simulated perforations.

Maxim Gorki
(1868-1936),
Writer — A1658

1968, Feb. 29   Photo.   *Perf. 12*
3450 A1658 4k gray ol & dk brown   .50   .25

Fireman, Fire
Truck and
Boat — A1659

1968, Mar. 30   Photo.   *Perf. 12x12½*
3451 A1659 4k red & black   .60   .25
50th anniversary of Soviet Fire Guards.

Link-up of Cosmos
186 and 188
Satellites — A1660

1968, Mar. 30   *Perf. 11½*
3452 A1660 6k blk, dp lilac rose &
              gold   .50   .25
First link-up in space of two satellites, Cosmos 186 and Cosmos 188, Oct. 30, 1967.

N. N. Popudrenko — A1661

Design: No. 3454, P. P. Vershigora.

1968, Mar. 30   *Perf. 12½x12*
3453 A1661 4k gray green & black   .30 .25
3454 A1661 4k lt purple & black   .30 .25
Partisan heroes of World War II.

Globe and
Hand
Shielding
from War
A1662

1968, Apr. 11   *Perf. 11½*
3455 A1662 6k sil, mar, ver &
              black   .60   .35
Emergency session of the World Federation
of Trade Unions and expressing solidarity with
the people of Vietnam.

Space Walk
A1663

6k, Docking operation of Kosmos 186 &
Kosmos 188. 10k, Exploration of Venus.

1968, Apr. 12   Litho.
3456 A1663 4k multicolored   .50   .25
3457 A1663 6k multicolored   .50   .25
3458 A1663 10k multicolored   1.00 .25
  a. Block of 3, #3456-3458 + 3 la-
        bels   3.50 .50
National Astronauts' Day.

Lenin, 1919
A1664

Lenin Portraits: No. 3460, Addressing crowd
on Red Square, Nov. 7, 1918. No. 3461, Full-
face portrait, taken in Petrograd, Jan. 1918.

Engraved and Photogravure
1968, Apr. 16   *Perf. 12x11½*
3459 A1664 4k gold, brown & red   1.00 .25
3460 A1664 4k gold, red & black   1.00 .25
3461 A1664 4k gold, brn, buff &
              red   1.00 .25
  Nos. 3459-3461 (3)   3.00 .75
98th anniversary of the birth of Lenin.

Alisher Navoi,
Uzbek Poet,
525th Birth
Anniv. — A1665

1968, Apr. 29   Photo.   *Perf. 12x12½*
3462 A1665 4k deep brown   .50   .25

Karl Marx
(1818-83)
A1666

1968, May 5   Engr.   *Perf. 11½x12*
3463 A1666 4k black & red   .50   .25

Frontier
Guard — A1667

Jubilee
Badge — A1668

1968, May 22   Photo.   *Perf. 11½*
3464 A1667 4k sl grn, ocher & red 1.00 .25
3465 A1668 6k sl grn, blk & red
              brn   1.00 .25
Russian Frontier Guards, 50th anniv.

Crystal and
Congress
Emblem
A1669

Congress Emblems and: No. 3467, Power
lines and factories. No. 3468, Ground beetle.
No. 3469, Roses and carbon rings.

1968, May 30
3466 A1669 6k blue, dk blue &
              grn   .50   .25
3467 A1669 6k org, gold & dk
              brn   .50   .25
3468 A1669 6k red brn, gold &
              blk   .50   .25
3469 A1669 6k lil rose, org & blk .50   .25
  Nos. 3466-3469 (4)   2.00 1.00
Intl. congresses, Leningrad: 8th Cong. for
Mineral Research; 7th World Power Conf.;
13th Entomological Cong.; 4th Cong. for the
Study of Volatile Oils.

Types of 1966
Designs as before.

1968, June 20   Engr.   *Perf. 12*
3470 A1593 1k dk red brown   .45   .25
3471 A1593 2k deep violet   .45   .25
3472 A1593 3k plum   .55   .25
3473 A1593 4k bright red   .60   .25
3474 A1593 6k blue   .80   .25
3475 A1593 10k olive   1.00 .40
3476 A1593 12k red brown   1.10 .45
3477 A1593 16k violet blue   1.40 .60

**   *Perf. 12½***
3478 A1594 20k red   1.60 .75
3479 A1594 30k bright green   2.75 .90
3480 A1594 50k violet blue   5.75 1.10

**   *Perf. 12x12½***
3481 A1594 1r gray, red brn &
              black   8.50 2.75
  Nos. 3470-3481 (12)   24.95 8.25

Sadriddin
Aini
A1670

1968, June 30   Photo.   *Perf. 12½x12*
3482 A1670 4k olive bister & mar   .50   .25
Aini (1878-1954), Tadzhik poet.

Post
Rider and
C.C.E.P.
Emblem
A1671

#3484, Modern means of communications
(train, ship, planes and C.C.E.P. emblem).

1968, June 30
3483 A1671 6k gray & red brown   .50   .25
3484 A1671 6k org brn & bis   .50   .25
Annual session of the Council of the Consultative Commission on Postal Investigation
of the UPU (C.C.E.P.), Moscow, 9/20-10/5.

Bolshevik Uprising,
Kiev — A1672

1968, July 5   *Perf. 11½*
3485 A1672 4k gold, red & plum   .50   .25
Ukrainian Communist Party, 50th anniv.

Athletes
A1673

1968, July 9
3486 A1673 4k yel, dp car & bis   .50   .25
1st Youth Summer Sports Games for 50th
anniv. of the Leninist Young Communists
League.

Field
Ball — A1674

Table
Tennis
A1675

Designs: 6k, 20th Baltic Regatta. 10k, Soccer player and cup. 12k, Scuba divers.

**   *Perf. 12x12½, 12½x12***
1968, July 18   Litho.
3487 A1674 2k red & multi   .25   .25
3488 A1675 4k purple & multi .30   .25
3489 A1674 6k blue & multi   .60   .25
3490 A1674 10k multicolored   .90   .25
3491 A1675 12k green & multi 1.00 .25
  Nos. 3487-3491 (5)   3.05 1.25
European youth sports competitions.

Rhythmic
Gymnast
A1676

6k, Weight lifting. 10k, Rowing. 12k,
Women's hurdling. 16k, Fencing. 40k,
Running.

1968, July 31   Photo.   *Perf. 11½*
**   Gold Background**
3492 A1676 4k blue & green   .30   .25
3493 A1676 6k dp rose & pur   .45   .25
3494 A1676 10k yel grn & grn .60   .25
3495 A1676 12k org & red brn .75   .25
3496 A1676 16k ultra & pink   1.00 .25
  Nos. 3492-3496 (5)   3.10 1.25

Souvenir Sheet
Perf. 12½x12
Lithographed and Photogravure
3497 A1676 40k gold, grn, org & gray   3.00 1.00

19th Olympic Games, Mexico City, 10/12-27.

Gediminas Tower, Vilnius — A1677

1968, Aug. 14   Photo.   Perf. 11½
3498 A1677 4k mag, tan & red   .50 .25

Soviet power in Lithuania, 50th anniv.

Tbilisi State University A1678

1968, Aug. 14   Perf. 12
3499 A1678 4k slate grn & lt brn   .50 .25

Tbilisi State University, Georgia, 50th anniv.

Laocoon — A1679

1968, Aug. 16   Perf. 11½
3500 A1679 6k sepia, blk & mar   3.50 .50

"Promote solidarity with Greek democrats."

Red Army Man, Cavalry Charge and Order of the Red Banner of Battle — A1680

Designs: 3k, Young man and woman, Dneprostroi Dam and Order of the Red Banner of Labor. 4k, Soldier, storming of the Reichstag, Berlin, and Order of Lenin. 6k, "Restoration of National Economy" (workers), and Order of Lenin. 10k, Young man and woman cultivating virgin land and Order of Lenin. 50k, like 2k.

1968, Aug. 25   Litho.   Perf. 12½x12
3501 A1680   2k gray, red & ocher   .25 .25
3502 A1680   3k multicolored   .50 .25
3503 A1680   4k org, ocher & rose car   .50 .25
3504 A1680   6k multicolored   .75 .25
3505 A1680   10k olive & multi   1.25 .25
   Nos. 3501-3505 (5)   3.25 1.25

Souvenir Sheet
Imperf
3506 A1680 50k ultra, red & bister   2.00 .50

50th anniv. of the Lenin Young Communist League, Komsomol.

Chemistry Institute and Dimeric Molecule A1681

1968, Sept. 3   Photo.   Perf. 11½
3507 A1681 4k vio bl, dp lil rose & black   .50 .25

50th anniversary of Kurnakov Institute for General and Inorganic Chemistry.

Letter, Compass Rose, Ship and Plane A1682

Compass Rose and Stamps of 1921 and 1965 A1683

1968, Sept. 16   Photo.   Perf. 11½
3508 A1682 4k dk car rose, brn & brt red   .50 .25
3509 A1683 4k dk blue, blk & bister   .50 .25

No. 3508 for Letter Writing Week, Oct. 7-13, and No. 3509 for Stamp Day and the Day of the Collector.

The 26 Baku Commissars, Sculpture by Merkurov — A1684

1968, Sept. 20
3510 A1684 4k multicolored   .50 .25

50th anniversary of the shooting of the 26 Commissars, Baku, Sept. 20, 1918.

Toyvo Antikaynen (1898-1941), Finnish Workers' Organizer — A1685

1968, Sept. 30   Perf. 12
3511 A1685 6k gray & sepia   .60 .25

Russian Merchant Marine Emblem A1686

1968, Sept. 30   Perf. 12x11½
3512 A1686 6k blue, red & indigo   .50 .25

Russian Merchant Marine.

Order of the October Revolution — A1687

Typographed and Embossed
1968, Sept. 30   Perf. 12x12½
3513 A1687 4k gold & multi   .50 .25

51st anniv. of the October Revolution. Printed with alternating label.

Pavel P. Postyshev — A1688

Designs: No. 3515, Stepan G. Shaumyan (1878-1918). No. 3516, Akmal Ikramov (1898-1938). No. 3516A, N. G. Markin (1893-1918). No. 3516B, P. E. Dybenko (1889-1938). No. 3516C, S. V. Kosior (1889-1939). No. 3516D, Vasili Kikvidze (1895-1919).

Size: 21½x32½mm

1968-70   Engr.   Perf. 12½x12
3514   A1688   4k bluish black   .65 .25
3515   A1688   4k bluish black   .65 .25
3516   A1688   4k gray black   .65 .25
3516A   A1688   4k black   .65 .25
3516B   A1688   4k dark car ('69)   .65 .25
3516C   A1688   4k indigo ('69)   .65 .25
3516D   A1688   4k dk brown ('70)   .65 .25
   Nos. 3514-3516D (7)   4.55 1.75

Honoring outstanding workers for the Communist Party and the Soviet State.
Issued: #3514-3516, 9/30/68; #3516A, 12/31/68; #3516D, 9/24/70; others, 5/15/69.
See #3782.

American Bison and Zebra A1689

Designs: No. 3518, Purple gallinule and lotus. No. 3519, Great white egrets, vert. No. 3520, Ostrich and golden pheasant, vert. No. 3521, Eland and guanaco. No. 3522, European spoonbill and glossy ibis.

Perf. 12½x12, 12x12½
1968, Oct. 16   Litho.
3517 A1689   4k ocher, brn & blk   .65 .30
3518 A1689   4k ocher & multi   .65 .30
3519 A1689   6k olive & black   .75 .30
3520 A1689   6k gray & multi   .75 .30
3521 A1689   10k dp grn & multi   1.10 .40
3522 A1689   10k emerald & multi   1.10 .40
   Nos. 3517-3522 (6)   5.00 2.00

Askania Nova and Astrakhan state reservations.

Ivan S. Turgenev (1818-83), Writer — A1690

1968, Oct. 10   Engr.   Perf. 12x12½
3523 A1690 4k green   4.50 .50

Warrior, 1880 B.C. and Mt. Ararat — A1691

Design: 12k, David Sasountsi monument, Yerevan, and Mt. Ararat.

Engraved and Photogravure
1968, Oct. 18   Perf. 11½
3524 A1691 4k blk & dk blue, gray   .35 .25
3525 A1691 12k dk brn & choc, bis   .45 .25

Yerevan, capital of Armenia, 2,750th anniv.

First Radio Tube Generator and Laboratory A1692

1968, Oct. 26   Photo.   Perf. 11½
3526 A1692 4k dk bl, dp bis & blk   .50 .25

50th anniversary of Russia's first radio laboratory at Gorki (Nizhni Novgorod).

Prospecting Geologist and Crystals A1693

6k, Prospecting for metals: seismographic test apparatus with shock wave diagram, plane, truck. 10k, Oil derrick in the desert.

1968, Oct. 31   Litho.   Perf. 11½
3527 A1693   4k blue & multi   .50 .25
3528 A1693   6k multicolored   .30 .25
3529 A1693   10k multicolored   .70 .25
   Nos. 3527-3529 (3)   1.50 .75

Geology Day. Printed with alternating label.

Borovoe, Kazakhstan — A1694

Landscapes: No. 3531, Djety-Oguz, Kirghizia, vert. No. 3532, Issyk-kul Lake, Kirghizia. No. 3533, Borovoe, Kazakhstan, vert.

Perf. 12½x12, 12x12½
1968, Nov. 20   Typo.
3530 A1694   4k dk red brn & multi   .35 .25
3531 A1694   4k gray & multi   .35 .25
3532 A1694   6k dk red brn & multi   .35 .25
3533 A1694   6k black & multi   .35 .25
   Nos. 3530-3533 (4)   1.40 1.00

Recreational areas in the Kazakh and Kirghiz Republics.

Medals and Cup, Riccione, 1952, 1961 and 1965 — A1695

4k, Medals, Eiffel Tower and Arc de Triomphe, Paris, 1964. 6k, Porcelain plaque, gold medal and Brandenburg Gate, Debria, Berlin, 1950, 1959. 12k, Medal and prize-winning stamp #2888, Buenos Aires. 16k, Cups and medals, Rome, 1952, 1954. 20k, Medals, awards and views, Vienna, 1961, 1965. 30k, Trophies, Prague, 1950, 1955, 1962.

1968, Nov. 27   Photo.   Perf. 11½x12
3534	A1695	4k dp cl, sil & blk	.25	.25
3535	A1695	6k dl bl, gold & blk	.25	.25
3536	A1695	10k lt ultra, gold & blk	.30	.35
3537	A1695	12k blue, sil & blk	.35	.25
3538	A1695	16k red, gold & blk	.55	.25
3539	A1695	20k brt blue, gold & blk	.60	.25
3540	A1695	30k org brn, gold & blk	.90	.30
	Nos. 3534-3540 (7)		3.20	1.90

Awards to Soviet post office at foreign stamp exhibitions.

Worker with Banner — A1696

1968, Nov. 29   Perf. 12x12½
3541 A1696 4k red & black .50 .35
Estonian Workers' Commune, 50th anniv.

V. K. Lebedinsky and Radio Tower — A1697

1968, Nov. 29   Perf. 11½x12
3542 A1697 4k gray grn, blk & gray .50 .25
V. K. Lebedinsky (1868-1937), scientist.

Souvenir Sheet

Communication via Satellite — A1698

1968, Nov. 29   Litho.   Perf. 12
3543	A1698	Sheet of 3	3.00	.75
a.		16k Molniya I	.70	.25
b.		16k Map of Russia	.70	.25
c.		16k Ground Station "Orbite"	.70	.25

Television transmission throughout USSR with the aid of the earth satellite Molniya I.

Sprig, Spasski Tower, Ministry of Foreign Affairs and Library A1699

1968, Dec. 1   Perf. 11½
3544 A1699 4k ultra, sil, grn & red .25 .30
New Year 1969.

Maj. Gen. Georgy Beregovoi A1700

1968, Dec. 14   Photo.   Perf. 11½
3545 A1700 10k Prus blue, blk & red .50 .25
Flight of Soyuz 3, Oct. 26-30.

Rail-laying and Casting Machines A1701

Soviet railroad transportation: 4k, Railroad map of the Soviet Union and Train.

1968, Dec. 14   Perf. 12½x12
3546 A1701 4k rose mag & org .60 .25
3547 A1701 10k brown & emerald .60 .25

Newspaper Banner and Monument A1702

1968, Dec. 23   Perf. 11½
3548 A1702 4k tan, red & dk brn 1.00 .25
Byelorussian communist party, 50th anniv.

The Reapers, by A. Venetzianov A1703

Knight at the Crossroads, by Viktor M. Vasnetsov — A1704

Paintings: 2k, The Last Day of Pompeii, by Karl P. Bryullov. 4k, Capture of a Town in Winter, by Vasili I. Surikov. 6k, On the Lake, by I.I. Levitan. 10k, Alarm, 1919 (family), by K. Petrov-Vodkin. 16k, Defense of Sevastopol, 1942, by A. Deineka. 20k, Sculptor with a Bust of Homer, by G. Korzhev. 30k, Celebration on Uritsky Square, 1920, by G. Koustodiev. 50k, Duel between Peresvet and Chelubey, by Avilov.

Perf. 12x12½, 12½
1968, Dec. 25   Litho.
3549	A1703	1k multicolored	.25	.25
3550	A1704	2k multicolored	.25	.25
3551	A1704	3k multicolored	.25	.25
3552	A1704	4k multicolored	.25	.25
3553	A1704	6k multicolored	.40	.25
3554	A1703	10k multicolored	.70	.25
3555	A1704	16k multicolored	1.10	.25
3556	A1703	20k multicolored	1.25	.25
3557	A1704	30k multicolored	2.00	.40
3558	A1704	50k multicolored	3.50	.80
	Nos. 3549-3558 (10)		9.95	3.20

Russian State Museum, Leningrad.

House, Zaoneje, 1876 — A1705

Russian Architecture: 4k, Carved doors, Gorki Oblast, 1848. 6k, Church, Kizhi Pogost, 1714. 10k, Fortress wall, Rostov-Yaroslav, 16th-17th centuries. 12k, Gate, Tsaritsino, 1785. 16k, Architect Rossi Street, Leningrad.

1968, Dec. 27   Engr.   Perf. 12x12½
3559	A1705	3k dp brown, *ocher*	.35	.25
3560	A1705	4k green, *yellow*	.35	.25
3561	A1705	6k vio, *gray violet*	.60	.25
3562	A1705	10k dl bl, *grnsh gray*	.95	.30
3563	A1705	12k car, *gray*	1.20	.40
3564	A1705	16k black, *yellowish*	1.50	.50
	Nos. 3559-3564 (6)		4.95	1.95

Banners of Young Communist League, October Revolution Medal — A1707

1968, Dec. 31   Litho.   Perf. 12
3566 A1707 12k red, yel & black .60 .30
Award of Order of October Revolution to the Young Communist League on its 50th anniversary.

Soldiers on Guard — A1708

1969, Jan. 1   Perf. 12x12½
3567 A1708 4k orange & claret .40 .25
Latvian Soviet Republic, 50th anniv.

Revolutionaries and Monument — A1709

Designs: 4k, Partisans and sword. 6k, Workers and Lenin Medals.

1969, Jan.   Photo.   Perf. 11½
3568	A1709	2k ocher & rose clar	.30	.25
3569	A1709	4k ocher & red	.30	.25
3570	A1709	6k dk ol, mag & red	.30	.25
	Nos. 3568-3570 (3)		.90	.75

Byelorussian Soviet Republic, 50th anniv.

Souvenir Sheet

Vladimir Shatalov, Boris Volynov, Alexei S. Elisseyev, Evgeny Khrunov — A1710

1969, Jan. 22   Imperf.
3571 A1710 50k dp bis & dk brn 2.00 .75
1st team flights of Soyuz 4 and 5, 1/16/69.

Leningrad University A1711

1969, Jan. 23   Photo.   Perf. 12½x12
3572 A1711 10k black & maroon .40 .25
University of Leningrad, 150th anniv.

Ivan A. Krylov (1769?-1844), Fable Writer — A1712

1969, Feb. 13   Litho.   Perf. 12x12½
3573 A1712 4k black & multi .50 .30

Nikolai Filchenkov A1713

Designs: No. 3575, Alexander Kosmodemiansky. No. 3575A, Otakar Yarosh, member of Czechoslovak Svoboda Battalion.

1969   Photo.
3574	A1713	4k dl rose & blk	.25	.25
3575	A1713	4k emer & dk brn	.25	.25
3575A	A1713	4k blue & black	.25	.25
	Nos. 3574-3575A (3)		.75	.75

Heroes of World War II. Issued: #3575A, May 9; others, Feb. 23.

"Shoulder to the Wheel," Parliament, Budapest A1714

Design: "Shoulder to the Wheel" is a sculpture by Zigmond Kisfaludi-Strobl.

1969, Mar. 21   Typo.   Perf. 11½
3576 A1714 6k black, ver & lt grn .50 .25
Hungarian Soviet Republic, 50th anniv.

Oil Refinery and Salavat Tualeyev
Monument — A1715

1969, Mar. 22   Litho.   Perf. 12
3577 A1715 4k multicolored .40 .25
50th anniv. of the Bashkir Autonomous
Socialist Republic.

Sergei P. Korolev, Sputnik 1, Space
Monument, Moscow — A1716

Vostok on
Launching
Pad — A1717

Natl. Cosmonauts' Day: No. 3579, Zond 2 orbiting moon, and photograph of earth made by Zond 5. 80k, Spaceship Soyuz 3.

Perf. 12½x12, 12x12½
1969, Apr. 12   Litho.
3578 A1716 10k black, vio & grn .65 .25
3579 A1716 10k dk brn, yel &
                      brn red .65 .25
3580 A1717 10k multicolored .65 .25
       Nos. 3578-3580 (3) 1.95 .75

Souvenir Sheet
Perf. 12
3581 A1716 80k vio, green & red 2.00 .75
No. 3581 contains one 37x24mm stamp.

Lenin
University,
Kazan, and
Kremlin
A1718

Lenin
House,
Kuibyshev
A1718a

Lenin
House,
Pskov
A1718b

Lenin House, Shushensko — A1718c

Smolny
Institute,
Leningrad
A1718d

Places Connected with Lenin: #3586, Straw Hut, Razliv. #3587, Lenin Museum, Gorki. #3589, Lenin's room, Kremlin. #3590, Lenin Museum, Ulyanovsk. #3591, Lenin House, Ulyanovsk.

1969   Photo.   Perf. 11½
3582 A1718 4k pale rose &
                      multi .35 .25
3583 A1718a 4k beige & multi .35 .25
3584 A1718b 4k bis brn & multi .35 .25
3585 A1718c 4k gray vio & multi .35 .25
3586 A1718 4k violet & multi .35 .25
3587 A1718 4k blue & multi .35 .25
3588 A1718d 4k brick red &
                      multi .35 .25
3589 A1718 4k rose red &
                      multi .35 .25
3590 A1718 4k lt red brn &
                      multi .35 .25
3591 A1718 4k dull grn & multi .35 .25
       Nos. 3582-3591 (10) 3.50 2.50
99th anniv. of the birth of Lenin.

Telephone, Transistor Radio and
Trademark — A1719

1969, Apr. 25   Perf. 12½x12
3592 A1719 10k sepia & dp org .50 .25
50th anniversary of VEF Electrical Co.

ILO Emblem and Globe — A1720

1969, May 9   Perf. 11
3593 A1720 6k car rose & gold .40 .25
50th anniversary of the ILO.

Suleiman
Stalsky
A1721

1969, May 15   Photo.   Perf. 12½x12
3595 A1721 4k tan & ol green .40 .25
Stalsky (1869-1937), Dagestan poet.

Yasnaya
Polyana
Rose
A1722

4k, "Stroynaya" lily. 10k, Cattleya orchid. 12k, "Listopad" dahlia. 14k, "Ural Girl" gladioli.

1969, May 15   Litho.   Perf. 11½
3596 A1722 2k multicolored .25 .25
3597 A1722 4k multicolored .45 .25
3598 A1722 10k multicolored 1.10 .25
3599 A1722 12k multicolored 1.40 .25
3600 A1722 14k multicolored 1.50 .25
       Nos. 3596-3600 (5) 4.70 1.25
Work of the Botanical Gardens of the Academy of Sciences.

Ukrainian
Academy
of
Sciences
A1723

1969, May 22   Photo.   Perf. 12½x12
3601 A1723 4k brown & yellow .50 .25
Ukrainian Academy of Sciences, 50th anniv.

Film, Camera
and Medal
A1724

Ballet
Dancers
A1725

1969, June 3   Litho.   Perf. 12x12½
3602 A1724 6k rose car, blk &
                      gold .30 .25
3603 A1725 6k dk brown & multi .30 .25
Intl. Film Festival in Moscow, and 1st Intl. Young Ballet Artists' Competitions.

Congress Emblem
and Cell
Division — A1726

1969, June 10   Photo.   Perf. 11½
3605 A1726 6k dp clar, lt bl & yel .50 .30
Protozoologists, 3rd Intl. Cong., Leningrad.

Estonian Singer
and Festival
Emblem — A1727

1969, June 14   Perf. 12x12½
3606 A1727 4k ver & bister .90 .25
Centenary of the Estonian Song Festival.

Mendeleev and Formula with Author's
Corrections — A1728

30k, Dmitri Ivanovich Mendeleev, vert.

Engraved and Lithographed
1969, June 20   Perf. 12
3607 A1728 6k brown & rose .90 .30

Souvenir Sheet
3608 A1728 30k carmine rose 5.00 1.25
Cent. of the Periodic Law (classification of elements), formulated by Dimitri I. Mendeleev (1834-1907). No. 3608 contains one engraved 29x37mm stamp.

Hand
Holding
Peace
Banner
and World
Landmarks
A1729

1969, June 20   Photo.   Perf. 11½
3609 A1729 10k bl, dk brn & gold .40 .25
20th anniversary of the Peace Movement.

Laser Beam
Guiding Moon
Rocket — A1730

1969, June 20
3610 A1730 4k silver, black & red .50 .25
Soviet scientific inventions, 50th anniv.

Ivan Kotlyarevski (1769-1838),
Ukrainian Writer — A1731

Typographed and Photogravure
1969, June 25   Perf. 12½x12
3611 A1731 4k blk, olive & lt brn .50 .25

No. 2717 Overprinted in Vermilion

1969, June 25   Photo.   *Perf. 11½*
3612 A1306 6k Prus blue & plum   4.00 1.50
Soviet victory in the Ice Hockey World Championships, Stockholm, 1969.

"Hill of Glory" Monument and Minsk Battle Map A1732

1969, July 3   Litho.   *Perf. 12x12½*
3613 A1732 4k red & olive   .40 .25
25th anniv. of the liberation of Byelorussia from the Germans.

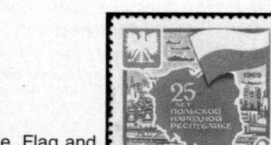

Eagle, Flag and Map of Poland A1733

No. 3615, Hands holding torch, flags of Bulgaria, USSR, Bulgarian coat of arms.

1969, July 10   Photo.   *Perf. 12*
3614 A1733 6k red & bister   .60 .25
Litho.
3615 A1733 6k bis, red, grn & blk   .60 .25
25th anniv. of the Polish Republic; liberation of Bulgaria from the Germans.

Monument to 68 Heroes — A1734

1969, July 15   Photo.   *Perf. 12*
3616 A1734 4k red & maroon   .50 .30
25th anniversary of the liberation of Nikolayev from the Germans.

Old Samarkand A1735

Design: 6k, Intourist Hotel, Samarkand.

1969, July 15   Typo.
3617 A1735 4k multicolored   .35 .25
3618 A1735 6k multicolored   .35 .25
2500th anniversary of Samarkand.

Volleyball — A1736

Design: 6k, Kayak race.

Photogravure and Engraved
1969, July 20   *Perf. 11½*
3619 A1736 4k dp org & red brn   .35 .25
3620 A1736 6k multicolored   .35 .25
Championships: European Junior Volleyball; European Rowing.

Munkascy & "Woman Churning Butter" — A1737

1969, July 20   Photo.
3621 A1737 6k dk brn, blk & org   .40 .25
Mihaly von Munkascy (1844-1900), Hungarian painter.

Miners' Monument A1738

1969, July 30
3622 A1738 4k silver & magenta   .40 .25
Centenary of the founding of the city of Donetsk, in the Donets coal basin.

Machine Gun Cart, by Mitrofan Grekov — A1739

1969, July 30   Engr.   *Perf. 12½x12*
3623 A1739 4k red brn & brn red   1.00 .25
First Mounted Army, 50th anniv.

Barge Pullers Along the Volga, by Repin — A1740

Ilya E. Repin (1844-1930), Self-portrait A1741

Repin Paintings: 6k, "Not Expected." 12k, Confession. 16k, Dnieper Cossacks.

Perf. 12½x12, 12x12½
1969, Aug. 5   Litho.
3624 A1740 4k multicolored   .75 .25
3625 A1740 6k multicolored   .75 .25
3626 A1741 10k bis, red brn & blk   1.00 .25
3627 A1740 12k multicolored   1.50 .25
3628 A1740 16k multicolored   2.00 .25
   Nos. 3624-3628 (5)   6.00 1.25

Runner — A1742

Design: 10k, Athlete on rings.

1969, Aug. 9   *Perf. 12x12½*
3629 A1742 4k red, green & blk   .30 .25
3630 A1742 10k grn, lt bl & blk   .30 .25
Souvenir Sheet
Imperf
3631 A1742 20k red, bister & blk   2.50 .60
9th Trade Union Spartakiad, Moscow.

Komarov — A1743

1969, Aug. 22   Photo.   *Perf. 12x11½*
3632 A1743 4k olive & brown   .40 .25
V. L. Komarov (1869-1945), botanist.

Hovannes Tumanian, Armenian Landscape — A1744

1969, Sept. 1   Typo.   *Perf. 12½x12*
3633 A1744 10k blk & peacock blue   1.50 .25
Tumanian (1869-1923), Armenian poet.

Turkmenian Wine Horn, 2nd Century — A1745

Designs: 6k, Persian Simurg vessel (giant anthropomorphic bird), 13th century. 12k, Head of goddess Kannon, Korea, 8th century. 16k, Bodhisattva, Tibet, 7th century. 20k, Statue of Ebisu and fish (tai), Japan, 17th century.

1969, Sept. 3   Litho.   *Perf. 12x12½*
3634 A1745 4k blue & multi   .25 .25
3635 A1745 6k lilac & multi   .25 .25
3636 A1745 12k red & multi   .40 .25
3637 A1745 16k blue vio & multi   .55 .25
3638 A1745 20k pale grn & multi   .70 .25
   Nos. 3634-3638 (5)   2.15 1.30
Treasures from the State Museum of Oriental Art.

Mahatma Gandhi (1869-1948) A1746

1969, Sept. 10   Engr.
3639 A1746 6k deep brown   .90 .35

Black Stork Feeding Young A1747

Belovezhskaya Forest reservation: 6k, Doe and fawn (red deer). 10k, Fighting bison. 12k, Lynx and cubs. 16k, Wild pig and piglets.

1969, Sept. 10   Photo.   *Perf. 12*
Size: 75x23mm, 10k; 35x23mm, others
3640 A1747 4k blk, yel grn & red   .50 .25
3641 A1747 6k blue grn, dk brn & ocher   .75 .25
3642 A1747 10k dk brn, dull org & dp org   1.50 .25
3643 A1747 12k dk & yel green, brn & gray   1.50 .25
3644 A1747 16k gray, yel grn & dk brown   2.00 .25
   Nos. 3640-3644 (5)   6.25 1.25

Komitas A1748

1969, Sept. 18   Typo.   *Perf. 12½x12*
3645 A1748 6k blk, gray & sal   .50 .30
Komitas (S. N. Sogomonian, 1869-1935), Armenian composer.

Lisa Chaikina A1749

A. Cheponis, J. Aleksonis and G. Borisa A1750

#3647, Major S. I. Gritsevets & fighter planes.

1969, Sept. 20   Photo.   *Perf. 12½x12*
3646 A1749 4k olive & brt green   .35 .25
3647 A1749 4k gray & black   .35 .25

Perf. 11½

3648 A1750 4k hn brn, brn & buff .35 .25
   Nos. 3646-3648 (3) 1.05 .75
    Heroes of the Soviet Union.

Ivan Petrovich
Pavlov (1849-
1936), Physiologist
A1751

1969, Sept. 26

3649 A1751 4k multicolored .50 .25

East German
Arms, TV Tower
and
Brandenburg
Gate — A1752

1969, Oct. 7   Litho.   Perf. 12

3650 A1752 6k red, black & yel .60 .25
    German Democratic Republic, 20th anniv.

Aleksei
Vasilievich
Koltsov (1809-
42),
Poet — A1753

1969, Oct. 14   Photo.   Perf. 12x12½

3652 A1753 4k lt blue & brown .50 .25

National
Emblem
A1754

1969, Oct. 14   Perf. 12x11½

3653 A1754 4k gold & red .50 .30
    25th anniversary of the liberation of the
Ukraine from the Nazis.

Stars,
Hammer and
Sickle
A1755

1969, Oct. 21   Typo.   Perf. 11½

3654 A1755 4k vio blue, gold, yel
      & red .50 .25
    52nd anniversary of October Revolution.

Georgy
Shonin
and
Valery
Kubasov
A1756

Designs: No. 3656, Anatoly Filipchenko,
Vladislav Volkov and Viktor Gorbatko. No.
3657, Vladimir Shatalov and Alexey Elisyev.

1969, Oct. 22   Photo.   Perf. 12½x12

3655 A1756 10k black & gold .65 .25
3656 A1756 10k black & gold .65 .25
3657 A1756 10k black & gold .65 .25
  a. Strip of 3, #3655-3657 2.00 .60
    Group flight of the space ships Soyuz 6,
Soyuz 7 and Soyuz 8, Oct. 11-13.

Lenin
as a
Youth
A1757

1969, Oct. 25   Engr.   Perf. 11½

3658 A1757 4k dark red, *pink* .50 .30
    1st Soviet Youth Philatelic Exhibition, Kiev,
dedicated to Lenin's 100th birthday.

Emblem of
Communications
Unit of
Army — A1758

1969, Oct. 30   Photo.

3659 A1758 4k dk red, red & bis-
      ter .50 .25
    50th anniversary of the Communications
Troops of Soviet Army.

Souvenir Sheet

Lenin and Quotation — A1759

Lithographed and Embossed

1969, Nov. 6   Imperf.

3660 A1759 50k red, gold & pink 3.00 .75
    52nd anniv. of the October Revolution.

Cover of "Rules of the Kolkhoz" and
Farm Woman's Monument — A1760

1969, Nov. 18   Photo.   Perf. 12½x12

3661 A1760 4k brown & gold .50 .25
    3rd All Union Collective Farmers' Congress,
Moscow, Nov.-Dec.

Vasilissa,
the Beauty,
by Ivan Y.
Bilibin
A1761

Designs (Book Illustrations by Ivan Y.
Bilibin): 10k, Marya Morevna. 16k, Finist, the
Fine Fellow, horiz. 20k, Tale of the Golden
Cockerel. 50k, The Tale of Tsar Sultan. The
inscriptions on the 16k and 20k are transposed. 4k, 10k, 16k are fairy tales; 20k and
50k are tales by Pushkin.

1969, Nov. 20   Litho.   Perf. 12

3662 A1761 4k gray & multi .25 .25
3663 A1761 10k gray & multi .60 .50
3664 A1761 16k gray & multi .75 .75
3665 A1761 20k gray & multi .85 .85
3666 A1761 50k gray & multi 3.00 1.40
  a. Strip of 5, #3662-3666 6.50 5.50
    Illustrator and artist Ivan Y. Bilibin.

USSR
Emblems
Dropped on
Venus, Radar
Installation
and Orbits
A1762

    6k, Interplanetary station, space capsule,
orbits.

1969, Nov. 25   Photo.   Perf. 12x11½

3667 A1762 4k bis, blk & red .35 .25
3668 A1762 6k gray, lil rose & blk .35 .25
    Completion of the fights of the space sta-
tions Venera 5 and Venera 6.

Flags of USSR and
Afghanistan — A1763

1969, Nov. 30   Photo.   Perf. 11½

3669 A1763 6k red, blk & grn .50 .25
    50th anniversary of diplomatic relations
between Russia and Afghanistan.

Russian State Emblem
and Star — A1764

Coil Stamp

1969, Nov. 13   Perf. 11x11½

3670 A1764 4k red 2.00 .30

MiG Jet and First MiG Fighter
Plane — A1765

1969, Dec. 12   Perf. 11½x12

3671 A1765 6k red, black & gray .60 .25
    Soviet aircraft builders.

Lenin and
Flag
A1766

Typographed and Lithographed

1969, Dec. 25   Perf. 11½

3672 A1766 4k gold, blue, red &
      blk .40 .25
    Happy New Year 1970, birth cent. of Lenin.

Antonov 2 — A1767

    Aircraft: 3k, PO-2. 4k, ANT-9. 6k, TsAGI 1-
EA. 10k, ANT-20 "Maxim Gorki." 12k, Tupolev-
104. 16k, Mi-10 helicopter. 20k, Ilyushin-62.
50k, Tupolev-144.

Photogravure and Engraved

1969   Perf. 11½x12

3673 A1767 2k bister & multi .25 .25
3674 A1767 3k multicolored .25 .25
3675 A1767 4k multicolored .25 .25
3676 A1767 6k multicolored .30 .25
3677 A1767 10k lt vio & multi .50 .25
3678 A1767 12k multicolored .70 .25
3679 A1767 16k multicolored .85 .25
3680 A1767 20k multicolored .90 .25
    Nos. 3673-3680 (8) 4.00 2.00

Souvenir Sheet
Imperf

3681 A1767 50k blue & multi 3.00 1.00

    History of national aeronautics and aviation.
No. 3681 margin contains signs of the zodiac,
partly overlapping the stamp.
    Issued: #3679, 3681, 12/31; others 12/25.

Photograph
of Earth by
Zond
7 — A1768

Designs: No. 3683a, same as 10k. No.
3683b, Photograph of moon.

1969, Dec. 26   Photo.   Perf. 12x11½

3682 A1768 10k black & multi .40 .30

Souvenir Sheet

Litho. **Imperf.**

3683 Sheet of 2 4.00 1.50
  a. A1768 50k indigo & multi 1.65 .90
  b. A1768 50k dark brown & multi 1.65 .90

Space explorations of the automatic stations Zond 6, Nov. 10-17, 1968, and Zond 7, Aug. 8-14, 1969. No. 3683 contains 27x40mm stamps with simulated perforations.

Model Aircraft — A1769

Technical Sports: 4k, Motorboats. 6k, Parachute jumping.

1969, Dec. 26 **Engr.** **Perf. 12½x12**
3684 A1769 3k bright magenta .45 .25
3685 A1769 4k dull blue green .45 .25
3686 A1769 6k red orange .45 .25
  Nos. 3684-3686 (3) 1.35 .75

Romanian Arms and Soviet War Memorial, Bucharest A1770

1969, Dec. 31 **Photo.** **Perf. 11½**
3687 A1770 6k rose red & brown .60 .35

25th anniversary of Romania's liberation from fascist rule.

Ostankino Television Tower, Moscow A1771

1969, Dec. 31 **Typo.** **Perf. 12**
3688 A1771 10k multicolored 1.00 .35

Conversation with Lenin, by A. Shirokov (in front of red table) — A1772

Paintings: No. 3689, Lenin, by N. Andreyev. No. 3690, Lenin at Marxist Meeting, St. Petersburg, by A. Moravov (behind table). No. 3691, Lenin at Second Party Congress, by Y. Vinogradov (next to table). No. 3692, First Day of Soviet Power, by N. Babasyuk (leading crowd). No. 3694, Farmers' Delegation Meeting Lenin, by F. Modorov (seated at desk). No. 3695, With Lenin, by V. A. Serov (with cap, in background). No. 3696, Lenin on May 1, 1920, by I. Brodsky (with cap, in foreground). No. 3697, Builder of Communism, by a group of painters (in red). No. 3698, Mastery of Space, by A. Deyneka (rockets).

1970, Jan. 1 **Litho.** **Perf. 12**
3689 A1772 4k multicolored .35 .25
3690 A1772 4k multicolored .35 .25
3691 A1772 4k multicolored .35 .25
3692 A1772 4k multicolored .35 .25

3693 A1772 4k multicolored .35 .25
3694 A1772 4k multicolored .35 .25
3695 A1772 4k multicolored .35 .25
3696 A1772 4k multicolored .35 .25
3697 A1772 4k multicolored .35 .25
3698 A1772 4k multicolored .35 .25
  Nos. 3689-3698 (10) 3.50 2.50

Centenary of birth of Lenin (1870-1924).

Map of Antarctic, "Mirny" and "Vostok" A1773

Design: 16k, Camp and map of the Antarctic with Soviet Antarctic bases.

1970, Jan. 27 **Photo.** **Perf. 11½**
3699 A1773 4k multicolored .30 .25
3700 A1773 16k multicolored 1.50 .25

150th anniversary of the Bellingshausen-Lazarev Antarctic expedition.

F. W. Sychkov and "Tobogganing" — A1774

1970, Jan. 27 **Perf. 12½x12**
3701 A1774 4k sepia & vio blue .50 .25

F. W. Sychkov (1870-1958), painter.

Col. V. B. Borsoyev A1775

Design: No. 3703, Sgt. V. Peshekhonov.

1970, Feb. 10 **Perf. 12x12½**
3702 A1775 4k brown olive & brn .30 .25
3703 A1775 4k dark gray & plum .30 .25

Heroes of the Soviet Union.

Geographical Society Emblem and Globes — A1776

1970, Feb. 26 **Photo.** **Perf. 11½**
3704 A1776 6k bis, Prus bl & dk brn .50 .30

Russian Geographical Society, 125th anniv.

Torch of Peace — A1777

1970, Mar. 3 **Litho.** **Perf. 12**
3705 A1777 6k blue green & tan .50 .25

Intl. Women's Solidarity Day, Mar. 8.

Symbols of Russian Arts and Crafts — A1778

Lenin — A1779

Designs: 6k, Russian EXPO '70 pavilion. 10k, Boy holding model ship.

1970, Mar. 10 **Photo.** **Perf. 11½**
3706 A1778 4k dk blue grn, red & black .25 .25
3707 A1778 6k blk, silver & red .25 .25
3708 A1778 10k vio bl, sil & red .25 .25
  Nos. 3706-3708 (3) .75 .75

Souvenir Sheet
Engr. & Litho.
Perf. 12x12½
3709 A1779 50k dark red 2.00 1.00

EXPO '70 Intl. Exhibition, Osaka, Japan, 3/15-4/13.

Lenin — A1780

1970, Mar. 14 **Photo.** **Perf. 11½**
3710 A1780 4k red, blk & gold .50 .30

Souvenir Sheet
Photogravure and Embossed
Imperf
3711 A1780 20k red, blk & gold 5.00 2.00

USSR Philatelic Exhibition dedicated to the centenary of the birth of Lenin.

Friendship Tree, Sochi — A1781

1970, Mar. 18 **Litho.** **Perf. 11½**
3712 A1781 10k multicolored .50 .25

Friendship among people. Printed with alternating label.

National Emblem, Hammer and Sickle, Oil Derricks A1782

1970, Mar. 18 **Photo.** **Perf. 11½**
3713 A1782 4k dk car rose & gold .75 .25

Azerbaijan Republic, 50th anniversary.

Ice Hockey Players A1783

1970, Mar. 18
3714 A1783 6k blue & slate green .35 .25

World Ice Hockey Championships, Sweden.

Overprinted in Red

1970, Apr. 1 **Photo.** **Perf. 11½**
3715 A1783 6k blue & slate green 1.00 .25

Soviet hockey players as the tenfold world champions.

D. N. Medvedev A1784

Portrait: No. 3717, K. P. Orlovsky.

1970, Mar. 26 **Engr.** **Perf. 12x12½**
3716 A1784 4k chocolate .30 .25
3717 A1784 4k dk redsh brown .30 .25

Heroes of the Soviet Union.

Worker, Books, Globes and UNESCO Symbol A1785

1970, Mar. 26 **Photo.** **Perf. 12½x12**
3718 A1785 6k car lake & ocher .50 .25

UNESCO-sponsored Lenin Symposium, Tampere, Finland, Apr. 6-10.

Hungarian Arms, Budapest Landmarks A1786

1970, Apr. 4   Typo.   Perf. 11½
3719 A1786 6k multicolored   .50 .25
Liberation of Hungary, 25th anniv.
See No. 3738.

Cosmonauts' Emblem A1787

1970, Apr. 12   Litho.   Perf. 11½
3720 A1787 6k buff & multi   .50 .25
Cosmonauts' Day.

Lenin, 1891 — A1788

Designs: Various portraits of Lenin.

Lithographed and Typographed
1970, Apr. 15   Perf. 12x12½
3721 A1788 2k green & gold   .25 .25
3722 A1788 2k ol gray & gold   .25 .25
3723 A1788 4k vio blue & gold   .25 .25
3724 A1788 4k lake & gold   .25 .25
3725 A1788 6k red brn & gold   .25 .25
3726 A1788 6k lake & gold   .25 .25
3727 A1788 10k dk brn & gold   .25 .25
3728 A1788 10k dk rose brn &
                gold   .35 .25
3729 A1788 12k blk, sil & gold   .45 .25
Photo.
3730 A1788 12k red & gold   .45 .25
Nos. 3721-3730 (10)   3.00 2.50

Souvenir Sheet
1970, Apr. 22   Litho. & Typo.
3731 A1788 20k blk, silver & gold 3.00 1.50
Cent. of the birth of Lenin. Issued in sheets of 8 stamps surrounded by 16 labels showing Lenin-connected buildings, books, coats of arms and medals. Value, $50. No. 3731 contains one stamp in same design as No. 3729.

Order of Victory — A1789

Designs: 2k, Monument to the Unknown Soldier, Moscow. 3k, Victory Monument, Berlin-Treptow. 4k, Order of the Great Patriotic War. 10k, Gold Star of the Order of Hero of the Soviet Union and Medal of Socialist Labor. 30k, like 1k.

1970, May 8   Photo.   Perf. 11½
3732 A1789 1k red lil, gold &
                gray   .25 .25
3733 A1789 2k dark brn, gold &
                red   .25 .25
3734 A1789 3k dark brn, gold &
                red   .40 .25
3735 A1789 4k dark brn, gold &
                red   .70 .25

3736 A1789 10k red lil, gold &
                red   1.40 .25
Nos. 3732-3736 (5)   3.00 1.25
Souvenir Sheet
Imperf
3737 A1789 30k dk red, gold &
                gray   2.00 .60
25th anniv. of victory in WWII. No. 3737 has simulated perforations.

Arms-Landmark Type of 1970
Czechoslovakia arms and view of Prague.

1970, May 8   Typo.   Perf. 12½
3738 A1786 6k dk brown & multi   .50 .25
25th anniversary of the liberation of Czechoslovakia from the Germans.

Young Fighters, and Youth Federation Emblem A1791

1970, May 20   Litho.   Perf. 12
3739 A1791 6k blue & black   .50 .25
25th anniversary of the World Federation of Democratic Youth.

Lenin A1792

1970, May 20   Photo.   Perf. 11½
3740 A1792 6k red   .50 .25
Intl. Youth Meeting dedicated to the cent. of the birth of Lenin, UN, NY, June 1970.

Komsomol Emblem with Lenin — A1793

1970, May 20   Litho.   Perf. 12
3741 A1793 4k red, yel & purple   .50 .25
16th Congress of the Young Communist League, May 26-30.

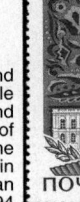

Hammer and Sickle Emblem and Building of Supreme Soviet in Kazan A1794

No. 3744

No. 3744B

No. 3744C

Designs (Hammer-Sickle Emblem and Supreme Soviet Building in): No. 3743,

Petrozavodsk. No. 3744, Cheboksary. No. 3744A, Elista. No. 3744B, Izhevsk. No. 3744C, Yoshkar-Ola.

1970   Engr.   Perf. 12x12½
3742 A1794 4k violet blue   .50 .25
3743 A1794 4k green   .50 .25
3744 A1794 4k dark carmine   .50 .25
3744A A1794 4k red   .50 .25
3744B A1794 4k dark green   .50 .25
3744C A1794 4k dark carmine   .50 .25
Nos. 3742-3744C (6)   3.00 1.50
50th annivs. of the Tatar (#3742), Karelian (#3743), Chuvash (#3744), Kalmyk (#3744A), Udmurt (#3744B) and Mari (#3744C) autonomous SSRs.
Issued: #3742, 5/27; #3743, 6/5; #3744, 6/24; #3744A-3744B, 10/22; #3744C, 11/4.
See Nos. 3814-3823, 4286, 4806.

9th World Soccer Championships for the Jules Rimet Cup, Mexico City, May 29-June 21 — A1795

10k, Woman athlete on balancing bar.

1970, May 31   Photo.   Perf. 11½
3745 A1795 10k lt gray & brt rose   .40 .25
3746 A1795 16k dk grn & org brn   .65 .25
17th World Gymnastics Championships, Ljubljana, Oct. 22-27 (#3745).

Sword into Plowshare Statue, UN, NY — A1796

1970, June 1   Litho.   Perf. 12x12½
3747 A1796 12k gray & lake   .50 .25
25th anniversary of the United Nations.

Soyuz 9, Andrian Nikolayev, Vitaly Sevastyanov A1797

1970, June 7   Photo.   Perf. 12x11½
3748 A1797 10k multicolored   .50 .25
424 hour space flight of Soyuz 9, June 1-19.

Friedrich Engels A1798

1970, June 16   Engr.   Perf. 12x12½
3749 A1798 4k chocolate & ver   .50 .25
Friedrich Engels (1820-1895), German socialist, collaborator with Karl Marx.

Armenian Woman and Symbols of Agriculture and Industry A1799

Design: No. 3751, Kazakh woman and symbols of agriculture and industry.

1970, June 16   Photo.   Perf. 11½
3750 A1799 4k red brn & silver   .30 .30
3751 A1799 4k brt rose lilac & gold   .30 .30
50th anniv. of the Armenian & Kazakh Soviet Socialist Republics.

Missile Cruiser "Grozny" — A1800

Soviet Warships: 3k, Cruiser "Aurora." 10k, Cruiser "October Revolution." 12k, Missile cruiser "Varyag." 20k, Atomic submarine "Leninsky Komsomol."

1970, July 26   Photo.   Perf. 11½x12
3752 A1800 3k lilac, pink & blk   .25 .25
3753 A1800 4k yellow & black   .25 .25
3754 A1800 10k rose & black   .45 .25
3755 A1800 12k buff & dk brown   .45 .25
3756 A1800 20k blue grn, dk brn
                & vio blue   .90 .25
Nos. 3752-3756 (5)   2.30 1.25
Navy Day.

Soviet and Polish Workers and Flags — A1801

1970, July 26   Perf. 12
3757 A1801 6k red & slate   .50 .25
25th anniversary of the Treaty of Friendship, Collaboration and Mutual Assistance between USSR and Poland.

"History," Petroglyphs, Sputnik and Emblem — A1802

1970, Aug. 16   Perf. 11½
3758 A1802 4k red brn, buff & blue .50 .25
13th International Congress of Historical Sciences in Moscow.

Mandarin Ducks A1803

Animals from the Sikhote-Alin Reserve: 6k, Pine marten. 10k, Asiatic black bear, vert. 16k, Red deer. 20k, Ussurian tiger.

Perf. 12½x12, 12x12½

1970, Aug. 19			Litho.
3759	A1803	4k multicolored	.55 .25
3760	A1803	6k multicolored	.65 .25
3761	A1803	10k multicolored	.80 .30
3762	A1803	16k ultra & multi	1.25 .45
3763	A1803	20k gray & multi	1.75 .60
		Nos. 3759-3763 (5)	5.00 1.85

Magnifying Glass
over Stamp, and
Covers — A1804

1970, Aug. 31	Photo.	Perf. 12x12½
3764	A1804	4k red & silver	.50 .25

2nd All-Union Philatelists' Cong., Moscow.

Pioneers'
Badge — A1805

Soviet general education: 2k, Lenin and Children, monument. 4k, Star and scenes from play "Zarnitsa."

1970, Sept. 24	Photo.	Perf. 11½
3765	A1805	1k gray, red & gold	.35 .25
3766	A1805	2k brn, red & slate grn	.35 .25
3767	A1805	4k lt ol, car & gold	.35 .25
		Nos. 3765-3767 (3)	1.05 .75

Yerevan
University
A1806

1970, Sept. 24	Photo.	Perf. 12½x12
3768	A1806	4k ultra & salmon pink	.50 .25

Yerevan State University, 50th anniv.

Library Bookplate,
Vilnius University
A1807

1970, Oct.	Typo.	Perf. 12x12½
3772	A1807	4k silver, gray & blk	.50 .25

Vilnius University Library, 400th anniv.

Woman Holding
Flowers — A1808

1970, Oct. 30		Photo.
3773	A1808	6k blue & lt brown	.50 .25

25th anniversary of the International Democratic Federation of Women.

Farm Woman, Cattle Farm — A1809

Designs: No. 3775, Farmer and mechanical farm equipment. No. 3776, Farmer, fertilization equipment and plane.

1970, Oct. 30		Perf. 11½x12
3774	A1809	4k olive, yellow & red	.35 .25
3775	A1809	4k ocher, yellow & red	.35 .25
3776	A1809	4k lt vio, yellow & red	.35 .25
		Nos. 3774-3776 (3)	1.05 .75

Aims of the new agricultural 5-year plan.

Lenin — A1810

Lithographed and Embossed
1970, Nov. 3		Perf. 12½x12
3777	A1810	4k red & gold	.50 .25

Souvenir Sheet
| 3778 | A1810 | 30k red & gold | 2.00 .75 |

53rd anniv. of the October Revolution.

No. 3389 Overprinted in Gold

1970, Nov. 3		Perf. 11½
3779	A1641	4k gold & multi	1.00 .50

50th anniversary of the GOELRO Plan for the electrification of Russia.

Spasski Tower
and Fir
Branch — A1811

1970, Nov. 23	Litho.	Perf. 12½x12
3780	A1811	6k multicolored	.50 .25

New Year, 1971.

A. A.
Baykov — A1812

1970, Nov. 25	Photo.	Perf. 12½x12
3781	A1812	4k sepia & golden brn	.50 .25

Baykov (1870-1946), metallurgist and academician.

Portrait Type of 1968

Portrait: No. 3782, A. D. Tsyurupa.

1970, Nov. 25	Photo.	Perf. 12x12½
3782	A1688	4k brown & salmon	.50 .25

Tsyurupa (1870-1928), First Vice Chairman of the Soviet of People's Commissars.

Vasily
Blazhenny
Church, Red
Square
A1813

Tourist publicity: 6k, Performance of Swan Lake. 10k, Two deer. 12k, Folk art. 14k, Sword into Plowshare statue, by E. Vouchetich, and museums. 16k, Automobiles and woman photographer.

Photogravure and Engraved
1970, Nov. 29		Perf. 12x11½
	Frame in Brown Orange	
3783	A1813	4k multicolored	.25 .25
3784	A1813	6k multicolored	.25 .25
3785	A1813	10k brn org & sl green	.35 .25
3786	A1813	12k multicolored	.45 .25
3787	A1813	14k multicolored	.50 .25
3788	A1813	16k multicolored	.65 .25
		Nos. 3783-3788 (6)	2.45 1.50

Daisy — A1814

1970, Nov. 29	Litho.	Perf. 11½
3789	A1814	4k shown	.25 .25
3790	A1814	6k Dahlia	.25 .25
3791	A1814	10k Phlox	.40 .25
3792	A1814	12k Aster	.50 .25
3793	A1814	16k Clementis	.85 .25
		Nos. 3789-3793 (5)	2.25 1.25

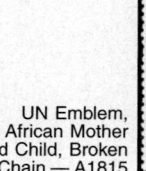

UN Emblem,
African Mother
and Child, Broken
Chain — A1815

1970, Dec. 10	Photo.	Perf. 12x12½
3794	A1815	10k blue & dk brown	.50 .25

United Nations Declaration on Colonial Independence, 10th anniversary.

Ludwig van Beethoven (1770-1827),
Composer — A1816

1970, Dec. 16	Engr.	Perf. 12½x12
3795	A1816	10k deep claret, *pink*	.50 .30

Skating — A1817

Design: 10k, Skiing.

1970, Dec. 18	Photo.	Perf. 11½
3796	A1817	4k lt gray, ultra & dk red	.35 .25
3797	A1817	10k lt gray, brt grn & brn	.65 .25

1971 Trade Union Winter Games.

Luna 16 — A1818

Designs: No. 3799, 3801b, Luna 16 leaving moon. No. 3800, 3801c, Capsule landing on earth. No. 3801a, like No. 3798.

1970, Dec.	Photo.	Perf. 11½
3798	A1818	10k gray blue	.40 .25
3799	A1818	10k dk purple	.40 .25
3800	A1818	10k gray blue	.40 .25
		Nos. 3798-3800 (3)	1.20 .75

Souvenir Sheet
3801		Sheet of 3	4.00 1.00
a.	A1818	20k blue	1.00 .25
b.	A1818	20k dark purple	1.00 .25
c.	A1818	20k blue	1.00 .25

Luna 16 unmanned, automatic moon mission, Sept. 12-24, 1970.
Nos. 3801a-3801c have attached labels (no perf. between vignette and label). Issue dates: No. 3801. Dec. 18; Nos. 3798-3800, Dec. 28.

The
Conestabile
Madonna, by
Raphael
A1819

Paintings: 4k, Apostles Peter and Paul, by El Greco. 10k, Perseus and Andromeda, by Rubens, horiz. 12k, The Prodigal Son, by Rembrandt. 16k, Family Portrait, by van Dyck. 20k, The Actress Jeanne Samary, by Renoir. 30k, Woman with Fruit, by Gauguin. 50k, The Little Madonna, by da Vinci. All paintings from the Hermitage in Leningrad, except 20k from Pushkin Museum, Moscow.

Perf. 12x12½, 12½x12
1970, Dec. 23		Litho.
3802	A1819	3k gray & multi	.25 .25
3803	A1819	4k gray & multi	.25 .25
3804	A1819	10k gray & multi	.60 .25
3805	A1819	12k gray & multi	.60 .25
3806	A1819	16k gray & multi	.70 .25
3807	A1819	20k gray & multi	.85 .25
3808	A1819	30k gray & multi	1.75 .25
		Nos. 3802-3808 (7)	5.00 1.75

Souvenir Sheet
Imperf
| 3809 | A1819 | 50k gold & multi | 3.00 .90 |

Harry Pollitt and Shipyard
A1820

1970, Dec. 31   Photo.   Perf. 12
3810 A1820 10k maroon & brown   .40 .30
Pollitt (1890-1960), British labor leader.

International Cooperative Alliance
A1821

1970, Dec. 31   Perf. 11½x12
3811 A1821 12k yel green & red   .50 .30
Intl. Cooperative Alliance, 75th anniv.

Lenin — A1822

1971, Jan. 1   Perf. 12
3812 A1822 4k red & gold   .50 .25
Year of the 24th Congress of the Communist Party of the Soviet Union.

Georgian Republic Flag
A1823

1971, Jan. 12   Litho.   Perf. 11½
3813 A1823 4k ol bister & multi   .50 .25
Georgian SSR, 50th anniversary.

Republic Anniversaries Type of 1970

No. 3816

No. 3818

Designs (Hammer-Sickle Emblem and): No. 3814, Supreme Soviet Building, Makhachkala. No. 3815, Fruit, ship, mountain, conveyor. No. 3816, Grapes, refinery, ship. No. 3817, Supreme Soviet Building, Nalchik. No. 3818, Supreme Soviet Building, Syktyvkar, and lumber industry. No. 3819, Natural resources, dam, mining. No. 3820, Industrial installations and natural products. No. 3821, Ship, "industry." No. 3822, Grapes, pylons and mountains. No. 3823, Kazbek Mountain, industrial installations, produce.

Engraved; Litho. (#3815, 3823)
1971-74   Perf. 12x12½
3814 A1794 4k dk blue green   1.00 .25
3815 A1794 4k rose red   1.00 .25
3816 A1794 4k red   1.00 .25
3817 A1794 4k blue   1.00 .25
3818 A1794 4k green   1.00 .25
3819 A1794 4k brt bl ('72)   1.00 .25
3820 A1794 4k car rose ('72)   1.00 .25
3821 A1794 4k brt ultra ('73)   1.00 .25

3822 A1794 4k golden brn ('74)   1.00 .25
3823 A1794 4k dark red ('74)   1.00 .25
   Nos. 3814-3823 (10)   10.00 2.50

50th annivers. of Dagestan (No. 3814), Abkazian (No. 3815), Adzhar (No. 3816), Kabardino-Balkarian (No. 3817), Komi (No. 3818), Yakut (No. 3819), Checheno-Ingush (No. 3820), Buryat (No. 3821), Nakhichevan (No. 3822), and North Ossetian (No. 3823) autonomous SSRs.

No. 3823 also for bicentenary of Ossetia's union with Russia.

Issued: No. 3814, 1/20; No. 3815, 3/3; No. 3816, 6/16; Nos. 3817-3818, 8/17; No. 3819, 4/20; No. 3820, 11/22; No. 3821, 5/24; No. 3822, 2/6; No. 3823, 7/7.

Tower of Genoa, Cranes, Hammer and Sickle
A1824

1971, Jan. 28   Typo.   Perf. 12
3824 A1824 10k dk red, gray & yel   .50 .25
Founding of Feodosiya, Crimea, 2500th anniv.

Palace of Culture, Kiev — A1825

1971, Feb. 16   Photo.   Perf. 11½
3825 A1825 4k red, bister & blue   .50 .25
Ukrainian Communist Party, 24th cong.

N. Gubin, I. Chernykh, S. Kosinov
A1826

1971, Feb. 16   Perf. 12½x12
3826 A1826 4k slate grn & vio brn   .50 .25
Heroes of the Soviet Union.

"Industry and Agriculture"
A1827

1971, Feb. 16   Perf. 12x12½
3827 A1827 6k olive bister & red   .50 .25
State Planning Organization, 50th anniv.

Lesya Ukrayinka (1871-1913), Ukrainian Poet — A1828

1971, Feb. 25
3828 A1828 4k orange red & bister   .50 .25

"Summer" Dance — A1829

Dancers of Russian Folk Dance Ensemble: No. 3830, "On the Skating Rink." No. 3831, Ukrainian dance "Hopak." No. 3832, Adzharian dance. No. 3833, Gypsy dance.

1971, Feb. 25   Litho.   Perf. 12½x12
3829 A1829 10k bister & multi   .40 .25
3830 A1829 10k olive & multi   .40 .25
3831 A1829 10k olive bis & multi   .40 .25
3832 A1829 10k gray & multi   .40 .25
3833 A1829 10k grnsh gray & multi   .40 .25
   Nos. 3829-3833 (5)   2.00 1.25

Luna 17 on Moon
A1830

Designs: No. 3835, Ground control. No. 3836, Separation of Lunokhod 1 and carrier. 16k, Lunokhod 1 in operation.

1971, Mar. 16   Photo.   Perf. 11½
3834 A1830 10k dp vio & sepia   .35 .25
3835 A1830 12k dk blue & sepia   .50 .25
3836 A1830 12k dk blue & sepia   .50 .25
3837 A1830 16k dp vio & sepia   .65 .25
   a.   Souv. sheet of 4   2.50 1.00
   Nos. 3834-3837 (4)   2.00 1.00

Luna 17 unmanned, automated moon mission, Nov. 10-17, 1970.
No. 3837a contains Nos. 3834-3837, size 32x21mm each.

Paris Commune, Cent. — A1831

1971, Mar. 18   Litho.   Perf. 12
3838 A1831 6k red & black   .50 .25

Industry, Science, Culture
A1832

1971, Mar. 29   Perf. 11½
3839 A1832 6k bister, brn & red   .50 .25
24th Communist Party Cong., 3/30-4/3.

Yuri Gagarin Medal
A1833

1971, Mar. 30   Photo.   Perf. 11½
3840 A1833 10k brown & lemon   .50 .25
10th anniv. of man's first flight into space.

Space Research
A1834

1971, Mar. 30
3841 A1834 12k slate bl & vio brn   .50 .25
Cosmonauts' Day, Apr. 12.

E. Birznieks-Upitis (1871-1960), Latvian Writer — A1835

1971, Apr. 1   Perf. 12x12½
3842 A1835 4k red brown & gray   .35 .25

Bee and Blossom — A1836

1971, Apr. 1   Perf. 11½
3843 A1836 6k olive & multi   .90 .25
23rd International Beekeeping Congress, Moscow, Aug. 22-Sept. 2.

Souvenir Sheet

Cosmonauts and Spacecraft — A1837

Designs: 10k, Vostok. No. 3844b, Yuri Gagarin. No. 3844c, First man walking in space. 16k, First orbital station.

1971, Apr. 12   Litho.   Perf. 12
3844 A1837 Sheet of 4   2.50 1.00
   a.   10k violet brown   .45 .25
   b.-c.   12k Prussian green   .45 .25
   d.   16k violet brown   .50 .25

10th anniv. of man's 1st flight into space. Size of stamps: 26x19mm.

Lenin Memorial, Ulyanovsk — A1838

1971, Apr. 16   **Photo.**   *Perf. 12*
3845   A1838   4k cop red & ol bister   .40   .25

Lenin's birthday. Memorial was built for centenary celebration of his birth.

Lt. Col. Nikolai I. Vlasov — A1839

1971, May 9   **Photo.**   *Perf. 12x12½*
3846   A1839   4k gray olive & brn   .40   .25

Hero of the Soviet Union.

Khafiz Shirazi, Tadzhik-Persian Poet, 650th Birth Anniv. — A1840

1971, May 9   **Litho.**
3847   A1840   4k olive, brn & black   .50   .25

GAZ-66 — A1841

Soviet Cars: 3k, BelAZ-540 truck. No. 3850, Moskvich-412. No. 3851, ZAZ-968. 10k, Volga.

1971, May 12   **Photo.**   *Perf. 11x11½*
3848   A1841   2k yellow & multi   .25   .25
3849   A1841   3k lt blue & multi   .25   .25
3850   A1841   4k lt blue & multi   .25   .25
3851   A1841   4k lt gray & multi   .25   .25
3852   A1841   10k lt lilac & multi   .25   .25
   Nos. 3848-3852 (5)   1.25   1.25

Bogomolets A1842

1971, May 24   **Photo.**   *Perf. 12*
3853   A1842   4k orange & black   .50   .25

A. A. Bogomolets, physician, 90th birth anniv.

Satellite — A1843

1971, June 9   *Perf. 11½*
3854   A1843   6k blue & multi   .60   .25

15th General Assembly of the International Union of Geodesics and Geophysics.

Symbols of Science and History A1844

1971, June 9   *Perf. 12*
3855   A1844   6k green & gray   .50   .25

13th Congress of Science History.

Oil Derrick & Symbols A1845

1971, June 9   *Perf. 11½*
3856   A1845   6k multicolored   .60   .25

8th World Oil Congress.

Sukhe Bator Monument — A1846

1971, June 16   **Typo.**   *Perf. 12*
3857   A1846   6k red, gold & black   .60   .25

50th anniversary of Mongolian revolution.

Monument of Defenders of Liepaja A1847

1971, June 21   **Photo.**
3858   A1847   4k gray, black & brn   .50   .25

30th anniversary of the defense of Liepaja (Libau) against invading Germans.

Map of Antarctica and Station — A1848

Engraved and Photogravure
1971, June 21   *Perf. 11½*
3859   A1848   6k black, grn & ultra   1.25   .30

Antarctic Treaty pledging peaceful uses of & scientific co-operation in Antarctica, 10th anniv.

Weather Map, Plane, Ship and Satellite — A1849

1971, June 21
3860   A1849   10k black, red & ultra   .50   .30

50th anniversary of Soviet Hydrometeorological service.

FIR Emblem, "Homeland" by E. Vouchetich A1850

1971, June 21   **Photo.**   *Perf. 12x12½*
3861   A1850   6k dk red & slate   .50   .25

International Federation of Resistance Fighters (FIR), 20th anniversary.

Discus and Running A1851

Designs: 4k, Archery (women). 6k, Dressage. 10k, Basketball. 12k, Wrestling.

Lithographed and Engraved
1971, June 24   *Perf. 11½*
3862   A1851   3k vio blue, *rose*   .25   .25
3863   A1851   4k slate grn, *pale pink*   .25   .25
3864   A1851   6k red brn, *apple grn*   .25   .25
3865   A1851   10k dk pur, *gray blue*   .35   .25
3866   A1851   12k red brn, *yellow*   .40   .25
   Nos. 3862-3866 (5)   1.50   1.25

5th Summer Spartakiad.

Benois Madonna, by da Vinci A1852

Paintings: 4k, Mary Magdalene, by Titian. 10k, The Washerwoman, by Jean Simeon Chardin, horiz. 12k, Portrait of a Young Man, by Frans Hals. 14k, Tancred and Arminia, by Nicolas Poussin, horiz. 16k, Girl with Fruit, by Murillo. 20k, Girl with Ball, by Picasso.

Perf. 12x12½, 12½x12
1971, July 7   **Litho.**
3867   A1852   2k bister & multi   .25   .25
3868   A1852   4k bister & multi   .25   .25
3869   A1852   10k bister & multi   .40   .25
3870   A1852   12k bister & multi   .45   .25
3871   A1852   14k bister & multi   .55   .25
3872   A1852   16k bister & multi   .65   .25
3873   A1852   20k bister & multi   .75   .25
   Nos. 3867-3873 (7)   3.30   1.75

Foreign master works in Russian museums.

Kazakhstan Flag, Lenin Badge — A1853

1971, July 7   **Photo.**   *Perf. 11½*
3874   A1853   4k blue, red & brown   .50   .25

50th anniversary of the Kazakh Communist Youth League.

Star Emblem and Letters A1854

1971, July 14
3875   A1854   4k oliver, blue & black   .50   .25

International Letter Writing Week.

Nikolai A. Nekrasov, by Ivan N. Kramskoi A1855

Portraits: No. 3877, Aleksandr Spendiarov, by M. S. Saryan. 10k, Fedor M. Dostoevski, by Vassili G. Perov.

1971, July 14   **Litho.**   *Perf. 12x12½*
3876   A1855   4k citron & multi   .25   .25
3877   A1855   4k gray blue & multi   .25   .25
3878   A1855   10k multicolored   .40   .25
   Nos. 3876-3878 (3)   .90   .75

Nikolai Alekseevitch Nekrasov (1821-1877), poet, Fedor Mikhailovich Dostoevski (1821-1881), novelist, Spendiarov (1871-1928), Armenian composer. See Nos. 4056-4057.

Zachary Paliashvili (1871-1933), Georgian Composer and Score — A1856

1971, Aug. 3   **Photo.**   *Perf. 12x12½*
3879   A1856   4k brown   .50   .25

Gorki Kremlin, Stag and Hydrofoil A1857

1971, Aug. 3   **Litho.**   *Perf. 12*
3880   A1857   16k multicolored   .50   .25

Gorki (formerly Nizhni Novgorod), 750th anniv. See Nos. 3889, 3910-3914.

Federation Emblem and Students A1858

1971, Aug. 3 Photo. Perf. 11½
3881 A1858 6k ultra & multi .50 .25
Intl. Students Federation, 25th anniv.

Common Dolphins A1859

Sea Mammals: 6k, Sea otter. 10k, Narwhals. 12k, Walrus. 14k, Ribbon seals.

Photogravure and Engraved
1971, Aug. 12 Perf. 11½
3882 A1859 4k silver & multi .40 .25
3883 A1859 6k silver & multi .40 .25
3884 A1859 10k silver & multi .60 .25
3885 A1859 12k silver & multi .70 .25
3886 A1859 14k silver & multi .90 .25
Nos. 3882-3886 (5) 3.00 1.25

Miner's Star of Valor — A1860

1971, Aug. 17 Photo. Perf. 11½
3887 A1860 4k bister, black & red .50 .25
250th anniversary of the discovery of coal in the Donets Basin.

Ernest Rutherford and Diagram of Movement of Atomic Particles A1861

1971, Aug. 24 Photo. Perf. 12
3888 A1861 6k magenta & dk ol .75 .25
Rutherford (1871-1937), British physicist.

Gorki and Gorki Statue — A1862

1971, Sept. 14 Perf. 11½
3889 A1862 4k steel blue & multi .50 .25
Gorki (see No. 3880).

Troika and Spasski Tower A1863

1971, Sept. 14
3890 A1863 10k black, red & gold .50 .25
New Year 1972.

Automatic Production Center — A1864

#3892, Agricultural development. #3893, Family in shopping center. #3894, Hydro-generators, thermoelectric station. #3895, Marchers, flags, books inscribed Marx and Lenin.

1971, Sept. 29 Photo. Perf. 12x11½
3891 A1864 4k purple, red & blk .40 .25
3892 A1864 4k ocher, red & brn .40 .25
3893 A1864 4k yel, olive & red .40 .25
3894 A1864 4k bister, red & brn .40 .25
3895 A1864 4k ultra, red & slate .40 .25
Nos. 3891-3895 (5) 2.00 1.25
Resolutions of 24th Soviet Union Communist Party Congress.

The Meeting, by Vladimir Y. Makovsky A1865

Ivan N. Kramskoi, Self-portrait — A1866

Paintings: 4k, Woman Student, by Nikolai A. Yaroshenko. 6k, Woman Miner, by Nikolai A. Kasatkin. 10k, Harvest, by G. G. Myasoyedov, horiz. 16k, Country Road, by A. K. Savrasov. 20k, Pine Forest, by I. I. Shishkin, horiz.

Perf. 12x12½, 12½x12
1971, Oct. 14 Litho.
Frame in Light Gray
3896 A1865 2k multicolored .25 .25
3897 A1865 4k multicolored .25 .25
3898 A1865 6k multicolored .25 .25
3899 A1865 10k multicolored .50 .25
3900 A1865 16k multicolored .55 .25
3901 A1865 20k multicolored 1.10 .25
Nos. 3896-3901 (6) 2.90 1.50

Souvenir Sheet
Lithographed and Gold Embossed
3902 A1866 50k dk green & multi 2.00 .60
History of Russian painting.

V. V. Vorovsky, Bolshevik Party Leader and Diplomat, Birth Cent. — A1867

1971, Oct. 14 Engr. Perf. 12
3903 A1867 4k red brown .50 .25

Cosmonauts Dobrovolsky, Volkov and Patsayev — A1868

1971, Oct. 20 Photo. Perf. 11½x12
3904 A1868 4k black, lilac & org .50 .25
In memory of cosmonauts Lt. Col. Georgi T. Dobrovolsky, Vladislav N. Volkov and Viktor I. Patsayev, who died during the Soyuz 11 space mission, June 6-30, 1971.

Order of October Revolution — A1869

1971, Oct. 20 Litho. Perf. 12
3905 A1869 4k red, yel & black .50 .25
54th anniversary of October Revolution.

E. Vakhtangov and "Princess Turandot" A1870

Designs: No. 3907, Boris Shchukin and scene from "Man with Rifle (Lenin)," horiz. No. 3908, Ruben Simonov and scene from "Cyrano de Bergerac," horiz.

Perf. 12x12½, 12½x12
1971, Oct. 26 Photo.
3906 A1870 10k mar & red brn .35 .25
3907 A1870 10k brown & dull yel .35 .25
3908 A1870 10k red brn & ocher .35 .25
Nos. 3906-3908 (3) 1.05 .75
Vakhtangov Theater, Moscow, 50th anniv.

Dzhambul Dzhabayev(1846-1945), Kazakh Poet — A1871

1971, Nov. 16 Perf. 12x12½
3909 A1871 4k orange & brown .50 .25

Gorki Kremlin Type, 1971
Designs: 3k, Pskov Kremlin and Velikaya River. 4k, Novgorod Kremlin and eternal flame memorial. 6k, Smolensk Fortress and liberation monument. 10k, Kolomna Kremlin and buses. 50k, Moscow Kremlin.

1971, Nov. 16 Litho. Perf. 12
3910 A1857 3k multicolored .75 .25
3911 A1857 4k multicolored .75 .25
3912 A1857 6k gray & multi .75 .25
3913 A1857 10k olive & multi .75 .25
Nos. 3910-3913 (4) 3.00 1.00

Souvenir Sheet
Engraved and Lithographed
Perf. 11½
3914 A1857 50k yellow & multi 1.50 .75
Historic buildings. No. 3914 contains one 21½x32mm stamp.

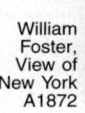

William Foster, View of New York A1872

1971 Litho. Perf. 12
3915 A1872 10k brn & blk ("-1961") 1.00 .25
a. "-1964" 20.00 7.25
William Foster (1881-1961), chairman of Communist Party of US.
No. 3915a was issued Nov. 16 with incorrect death date (1964). No. 3915, with corrected date (1961), was issued Dec. 8.

Aleksandr Fadeyev and Cavalrymen — A1873

1971, Nov. 25 Photo. Perf. 12½x12
3916 A1873 4k slate & orange .50 .25
Aleksandr Fadeyev (1901-1956), writer.

Amethyst and Diamond Brooch A1874

Precious Jewels: No. 3918, Engraved Shakh diamond, India, 16th cent. No. 3919, Diamond daffodils, 18th cent. No. 3920, Amethyst & diamond pendant. No. 3921, Diamond rose made for centenary of Lenin's birth. No. 3922, Diamond & pearl pendant.

1971, Dec. 8 Litho. Perf. 11½
3917 A1874 10k brt blue & multi .35 .25
3918 A1874 10k dk red & multi .35 .25
3919 A1874 10k grnsh black & multi .35 .25
3920 A1874 20k grnsh black & multi .70 .30
3921 A1874 20k rose red & multi .70 .30
3922 A1874 30k black & multi 1.00 .45
Nos. 3917-3922 (6) 3.45 1.80

Souvenir Sheet

Workers with Banners, Congress Hall and Spasski Tower — A1875

1971, Dec. 15 Photo. Perf. 11x11½
3923 A1875 20k red, pale grn & brn 2.00 1.00
See note after No. 3895. No. 3923 contains one partially perforated stamp.

Vanda Orchid — A1876

Flowers: No. 3924, No. 3929b, shown. No. 3925, Anthurium. No. 3926, No. 3929c, Flowering crab cactus. No. 3927, No. 3929a, Amaryllis. No. 3928, No. 3929d, Medinilla magnifica.

1971, Dec. 15   Litho.   Perf. 12x12½
3924 A1876 1k olive & multi .25 .25
3925 A1876 2k green & multi .25 .25
3926 A1876 4k blue & multi .40 .25
3927 A1876 12k multicolored .50 .25
3928 A1876 14k multicolored .65 .25
    Nos. 3924-3928 (5) 2.05 1.25

Miniature Sheet
Perf. 12
3929   Sheet of 4 1.50 .75
a.-d.   A1876 10k any single .40 .25

Nos. 3929a-3929d have white background, black frame line and inscription. Size of stamps 19x57mm.

Issued: Nos. 3924-3928, 12/15; No. 3929, 12/30.

Peter I Reviewing Fleet, 1723 — A1877

History of Russian Fleet: 4k, Oriol, first ship built in Eddinovo, 1668, vert. 10k, Battleship Poltava, 1712, vert. 12k, Armed ship Ingermanland, 1715, vert. 16k, Frigate Vladimir, 1848.

Perf. 11½x12, 12x11½
1971, Dec. 15   Engr. & Photo.
3930 A1877 1k multicolored .30 .25
3931 A1877 4k brown & multi .45 .30
3932 A1877 10k multicolored 1.20 .75
3933 A1877 12k multicolored 1.40 .75
3934 A1877 16k lt green & multi 1.90 1.00
    Nos. 3930-3934 (5) 5.25 3.05

Ice Hockey A1878

1971, Dec. 15   Litho.   Perf. 12½
3935 A1878 6k multicolored .50 .25

25th anniversary of Soviet ice hockey.

A1879

Oil rigs and causeway in Caspian Sea.

1971, Dec. 30   Perf. 11½
3936 A1879 4k dp blue, org & blk .50 .25

Baku oil industry.

A1880

1972, Jan. 5   Engr.   Perf. 12
3937 A1880 4k yellow brown .50 .25

G. M. Krzhizhanovsky (1872-1959), scientist and co-worker with Lenin.

Alexander Scriabin (1872-1915), Composer A1881

1972, Jan. 6   Photo.   Perf. 12x12½
3938 A1881 4k indigo & olive .50 .25

Bering's Cormorant A1882

Birds: 6k, Ross' gull, horiz. 10k, Barnacle geese. 12k, Spectacled eiders, horiz. 16k, Mediterranean gull.

1972, Jan. 12   Perf. 11½
3939 A1882 4k dk grn, blk & yel .30 .25
3940 A1882 6k ind, pink & blk .50 .25
3941 A1882 10k grnsh blue, blk
    & brown .80 .35
3942 A1882 12k multicolored .95 .45
3943 A1882 16k ultra, gray & red 1.25 .60
    Nos. 3939-3943 (5) 3.80 1.90

Waterfowl of the USSR.

11th Winter Olympic Games, Sapporo, Japan, Feb. 3-13 — A1883

Designs (Olympic Rings and): 4k, Speed skating. 6k, Women's figure skating. 10k, Ice hockey. 12k, Ski jump. 16k, Long-distance skiing. 50k, Sapporo '72 emblem.

1972, Jan. 20   Litho.   Perf. 12x12½
3944 A1883 4k bl grn, red & brn .25 .25
3945 A1883 6k yel grn, blue &
    dp orange .25 .25
3946 A1883 10k vio, bl & dp org .40 .25
3947 A1883 12k light blue, blue
    & brick red .50 .25
3948 A1883 16k gray, bl & brt
    rose .60 .25
    Nos. 3944-3948 (5) 2.00 1.25

Souvenir Sheet
3949 A1883 50k multicolored 1.50 .75

For overprint see No. 3961.

Heart, Globe and Exercising Family — A1884

1972, Feb. 9   Photo.
3950 A1884 4k brt grn & rose
    red .50 .25

Heart Month sponsored by the WHO.

Leipzig Fair Emblem and Soviet Pavilion — A1885

1972, Feb. 22   Perf. 11½
3951 A1885 16k red & gold .75 .25

50th anniversary of the participation of the USSR in the Leipzig Trade Fair.

Hammer, Sickle and Cogwheel Emblem — A1886

1972, Feb. 29   Perf. 12x12½
3952 A1886 4k rose red & lt brn .50 .25

15th USSR Trade Union Congress, Moscow, March 1972.

Aloe — A1887

Medicinal Plants: 2k, Horn poppy. 4k, Groundsel. 6k, Orthosiphon stamineus. 10k, Nightshade.

1972, Mar. 14   Litho.   Perf. 12x12½
Flowers in Natural Colors
3953 A1887 1k olive bister .80 .25
3954 A1887 2k slate green .80 .25
3955 A1887 4k brt purple .80 .25
3956 A1887 6k violet blue .80 .25
3957 A1887 10k dk brown .80 .25
    Nos. 3953-3957 (5) 4.00 1.25

Aleksandra Kollontai — A1888

No. 3959, Georgy Chicherin. No. 3960, Kamo (pseudonym of S.A. Ter-Petrosyan).

1972, Mar. 20   Engr.   Perf. 12½x12
3958 A1888 4k red brown .35 .25
3959 A1888 4k claret .35 .25
3960 A1888 4k olive bister .35 .25
    Nos. 3958-3960 (3) 1.05 .75

Outstanding workers of the Communist Party of the Soviet Union and for the State.

No. 3949 Overprinted
Souvenir Sheet

1972, Mar. 20   Litho.   Perf. 12x12½
3961 A1883 50k multicolored 4.00 2.00

Victories of Soviet athletes in the 11th Winter Olympic Games (8 gold, 5 silver, 3 bronze medals).

For similar overprints see Nos. 4028, 4416.

Orbital Station Salyut and Spaceship Soyuz Docking Above Earth — A1889

Designs: No. 3963, Mars 2 approaching Mars, and emblem dropped on Mars. 16k, Mars 3, which landed on Mars, Dec. 2, 1971.

1972, Apr. 5   Photo.   Perf. 11½x12
3962 A1889 6k vio, blue & silver .40 .25
3963 A1889 6k pur, ocher & sil .40 .25
3964 A1889 16k pur, blue & sil 1.20 .25
    Nos. 3962-3964 (3) 2.00 .75

Cosmonauts' Day.

Shield and Products of Izhory Factory A1890

1972, Apr. 20   Perf. 12½x12
3965 A1890 4k purple & silver .50 .25

250th anniversary of Izhory Factory, founded by Peter the Great.

Leonid Sobinov in "Eugene Onegin," by Tchaikovsky — A1891

1972, Apr. 20
3966 A1891 10k dp brown & buff .50 .25

Sobinov (1872-1934), opera singer.

Book,
Torch,
Children
and Globe
A1892

1972, May 5   **Perf. 11½**
3967 A1892 6k brn, grnsh bl &
              buff   .35   .25
International Book Year 1972.

Girl in
Laboratory
and
Pioneers
A1893

Designs: 1k, Pavlik Morosov (Pioneer hero),
Pioneers saluting and banner. 3k, Pioneers
with wheelbarrow, Chukchi boy, and Chukotka
Pioneer House. 4k, Pioneer Honor Guard and
Parade. 30k, Pioneer Honor Guard, vert.

1972, May 10
3968 A1893 1k red & multi   .50   .25
3969 A1893 2k multicolored   .50   .25
3970 A1893 3k multicolored   .50   .25
3971 A1893 4k gray & multi   .50   .25
       Nos. 3968-3971 (4)   2.00 1.00
Souvenir Sheet
Perf. 12x12½
3972 A1893 30k multicolored   1.50   .75
50th anniversary of the Lenin Pioneer
Organization of the USSR.

Pioneer
Bugler
A1894

1972, May 27   Photo.   Perf. 11½
3973 A1894 4k red, ocher & plum   .50 .25
2nd Youth Philatelic Exhibition, Minsk, and
50th anniv. of Lenin Pioneer Org.

M. S. Ordubady
(1872-1950),
Azerbaijan Writer
and Social
Worker — A1895

1972, May 25   **Perf. 12x12½**
3974 A1895 4k orange & rose brn   .50 .25

Globe
A1896

1972, May 25   **Perf. 11½**
3975 A1896 6k multicolored   .50 .30
European Safety and Cooperation Conference, Brussels.

Cossack
Leader, by
Ivan Nikitin
A1897

Paintings: 4k, Fedor G. Volkov (actor), by
Anton Losenko. 6k, V. Majkov (poet), by Fedor
Rokotov. 10k, Nikolai I. Novikov (writer), by
Dimitri Levitsky. 12k, Gavriil R. Derzhavin
(poet, civil servant), by Vladimir Borovikovsky.
16k, Peasants' Supper, by Mikhail Shibanov,
horiz. 20k, View of Moscow, by Fedor Alexeyev, horiz.

Perf. 12x12½, 12½x12
1972, June 7   **Litho.**
3976 A1897 2k gray & multi   .25   .25
3977 A1897 4k gray & multi   .25   .25
3978 A1897 6k gray & multi   .25   .25
3979 A1897 10k gray & multi   .30   .25
3980 A1897 12k gray & multi   .30   .25
3981 A1897 16k gray & multi   .45   .25
3982 A1897 20k gray & multi   .60   .25
       Nos. 3976-3982 (7)   2.40 1.75
History of Russian painting. See Nos. 4036-
4042, 4074-4080, 4103-4109.

George Dimitrov
(1882-1949),
Bulgarian
Communist Party
Leader — A1898

1972, June 15 Photo. Perf. 12½x12
3983 A1898 6k brown & ol bister   .50 .25

20th Olympic
Games,
Munich,
8/26-9/11
A1899

Olympic Rings and: 4k, Fencing. 6k,
Women's gymnastics. 10k, Canoeing. 14k,
Boxing. 16k, Running. 50k, Weight lifting.

1972, July 1   **Perf. 12x11½**
3984 A1899 4k brt mag & gold   .25   .25
3985 A1899 6k dp green & gold   .25   .25
3986 A1899 10k brt blue & gold   .55   .25
3987 A1899 14k Prus bl & gold   .60   .25
3988 A1899 16k red & gold   .85   .25
       Nos. 3984-3988 (5)   2.50 1.25
Souvenir Sheet
Perf. 11½
3989 A1899 50k gold & multi   1.50   .60
No. 3989 contains one 25x35mm stamp.
For overprint see No. 4028.

Congress
Palace,
Kiev
A1900

1972, July 1   **Photo. & Engr.**
3990 A1900 6k Prus blue & bister   .50 .25
9th World Gerontology Cong., Kiev, 7/2-7.

Roald
Amundsen,
"Norway,"
Northern
Lights
A1901

1972, July 13   Photo.   Perf. 11½
3991 A1901 6k vio blue & dp bis-
              ter   1.00 .25
Roald Amundsen (1872-1928), Norwegian
polar explorer.

17th
Century
House,
Chernigov
A1902

Designs: 4k, Market Square, Lvov, vert. 10k,
Kovnirov Building, Kiev. 16k, Fortress,
Kamenets-Podolski, vert.

Perf. 12x12½, 12½x12
1972, July 18   **Litho.**
3992 A1902 4k citron & multi   .25   .25
3993 A1902 6k gray & multi   .25   .25
3994 A1902 10k ocher & multi   .60   .25
3995 A1902 16k salmon & multi   .80   .25
       Nos. 3992-3995 (4)   1.90 1.00
Historic and architectural treasures of the
Ukraine.

Asoka
Pillar,
Indian
Flag, Red
Fort, New
Delhi
A1903

1972, July 27   Photo.   Perf. 11½
3996 A1903 6k dk blue, emer & red .50 .25
25th anniversary of India's independence.

Miners'
Emblem
A1904

1972, Aug. 10
3997 A1904 4k violet gray & red   .50 .25
25th Miners' Day.

Far East Fighters'
Monument
A1905

Designs: 4k, Monument for Far East Civil
War heroes, industrial view. 6k, Vladivostok
rostral column, Pacific fleet ships.

1972, Aug. 10
3998 A1905 3k red org, car &
              black   .50 .25
3999 A1905 4k yel, sepia & blk   .50 .25
4000 A1905 6k pink, dk car &
              black   .50 .25
       Nos. 3998-4000 (3)   1.50 .75
50th anniversary of the liberation of the Far
Eastern provinces.

Boy with
Dog, by
Murillo
A1906

Paintings from the Hermitage, Leningrad:
4k, Breakfast, Velazquez. 6k, Milkmaid's Family, Louis Le Nain. 16k, Sad Woman, Watteau.
20k, Moroccan Saddling Steed, Delacroix.
50k, Self-portrait, Van Dyck. 4k, 6k horiz.

Perf. 12½x12, 12x12½
1972, Aug. 15   **Litho.**
4001 A1906 4k multicolored   .25   .25
4002 A1906 6k multicolored   .25   .25
4003 A1906 10k multicolored   .40   .25
4004 A1906 16k multicolored   .60   .25
4005 A1906 20k multicolored   .90   .25
       Nos. 4001-4005 (5)   2.40 1.25
Souvenir Sheet
Perf. 12
4006 A1906 50k multicolored   2.50 1.00

Sputnik 1 — A1907

No. 4008, Launching of Vostok 2. No. 4009,
Lenov floating in space. No. 4010, Lunokhod
on moon. No. 4011, Venera 7 descending to
Venus. No. 4012, Mars & descending to Mars.

1972, Sept. 14 Litho. Perf. 12x11½
4007 A1907 4k shown   .35   .25
4008 A1907 6k multicolored   .35   .25
4009 A1907 6k multicolored   .35   .25
4010 A1907 6k multicolored   .35   .25
4011 A1907 6k multicolored   .35   .25
4012 A1907 6k multicolored   .35   .25
       Nos. 4007-4012 (6)   2.10 1.50
15 years of space era. Sheets of 6.

Konstantin
Aleksandrovich
Mardzhanishvili
(1872-1933),
Theatrical
Producer
A1908

1972, Sept. 20   Engr.   Perf. 12x12½
4013 A1908 4k slate green   .50 .25

Museum Emblem, Communications
Symbols — A1909

1972, Sept. 20   Photo.   Perf. 11½
4014 A1909 4k slate green & multi .50 .25
Centenary of the A. S. Popov Central
Museum of Communications.

"Stamp" and Topical Collecting Symbols A1910

Engraved and Lithographed

1972, Oct. 4　　**Perf. 12**
4015 A1910 4k yel, black & red .50 .25
Philatelic Exhibition in honor of 50th anniversary of the USSR.

Lenin A1911

1972, Oct. 12　**Photo.**　**Perf. 11½**
4016 A1911 4k gold & red .50 .25
55th anniversary of October Revolution.

Militia Badge — A1912

1972, Oct. 12
4017 A1912 4k gold, red & dk brn .30 .25
55th anniv. of the Militia of the USSR.

Arms of USSR A1913

USSR, 50th anniv.: No. 4019, Arms and industrial scene. No. 4020, Arms, Supreme Soviet, Kremlin. No. 4021, Lenin. No. 4022, Arms, worker, book (Constitution).
30k, Coat of arms and Spasski Tower, horiz.

1972, Oct. 28　　**Perf. 12x11½**
4018 A1913 4k multicolored .30 .25
4019 A1913 4k multicolored .30 .25
4020 A1913 4k multicolored .30 .25
4021 A1913 4k multicolored .30 .25
4022 A1913 4k multicolored .30 .25
　　Nos. 4018-4022 (5) 1.50 1.25

Souvenir Sheet
Lithographed; Embossed
Perf. 12
4023 A1913 30k red & gold 1.50 .40

Kremlin and Snowflake A1914

Engraved and Photogravure
1972, Nov. 15　　**Perf. 11½**
4024 A1914 6k multicolored 1.00 .25
New Year 1973.

Savings Bank Book — A1915

1972, Nov. 15 Photo.　**Perf. 12x12½**
4025 A1915 4k lilac & slate .50 .25
50th anniv. of savings banks in the USSR.

Soviet Olympic Emblem and Laurel A1916

Design: 30k, Soviet Olympic emblem and obverse of gold, silver and bronze medals.

1972, Nov. 15　　**Perf. 11½**
4026 A1916 20k brn ol, red & gold .50 .40
4027 A1916 30k dp car, gold & brn 1.00 .60

No. 3989 Overprinted in Red
Souvenir Sheet

1972, Nov. 15
4028 A1899 50k gold & multi 2.50 1.25
Soviet medalists at 20th Olympic Games.

Battleship Peter the Great, 1872 — A1917

History of Russian Fleet: 3k, Cruiser Varyag, 1899. 4k, Battleship Potemkin, 1900. 6k, Cruiser Ochakov, 1902. 10k, Mine layer Amur, 1907.

Engraved and Photogravure
1972, Nov. 22　　**Perf. 11½x12**
4029 A1917 2k multicolored .35 .25
4030 A1917 3k multicolored .35 .25
4031 A1917 4k multicolored .45 .25
4032 A1917 6k multicolored .70 .25
4033 A1917 10k multicolored 1.10 .25
　　Nos. 4029-4033 (5) 2.95 1.25

Grigory S. Skovoroda (1722-1794), Ukrainian Philosopher and Humanist A1918

1972, Dec. 7　**Engr.**　**Perf. 12**
4034 A1918 4k dk violet blue .50 .25

Child Reading Traffic Rules — A1919

1972, Dec. 7　**Photo.**　**Perf. 11½**
4035 A1919 4k Prus blue, blk & red .50 .25
Traffic safety campaign.

Russian Painting Type of 1972

2k, Meeting of Village Party Members, by E. M. Cheptsov, horiz. 4k, Pioneer Girl, by Nicolai A. Kasatkin. 6k, Woman Delegate, by G. G. Ryazhsky. 10k, Winter's End, by K. F. Yuon, horiz. 16k, The Partisan A. G. Lunev, by N. I. Strunnikov. 20k, Igor E. Grabar, self-portrait. 50k, Blue Space (seascape with flying geese), by Arcadi A. Rylov, horiz.

Perf. 12x12½, 12½x12
1972, Dec. 7　　**Litho.**
4036 A1897 2k olive & multi .25 .25
4037 A1897 4k olive & multi .25 .25
4038 A1897 6k olive & multi .25 .25
4039 A1897 10k olive & multi .25 .25
4040 A1897 16k olive & multi .40 .25
4041 A1897 20k olive & multi .60 .25
　　Nos. 4036-4041 (6) 2.00 1.50

Souvenir Sheet
Perf. 12
4042 A1897 50k multicolored 1.75 1.25
History of Russian painting.

Symbolic of Theory and Practice — A1920

Engraved and Photogravure
1972, Dec. 7　　**Perf. 11½**
4043 A1920 4k sl grn, yel & red brn .50 .25
Centenary of Polytechnic Museum, Moscow.

Venera 8 and Parachute A1921

1972, Dec. 28　**Photo.**　**Perf. 11½**
4044 A1921 6k dl claret, bl & blk .50 .25

Souvenir Sheet
Imperf
4045 　　Sheet of 2 7.00 2.00
a. A1921 50k Venera 8 3.00 .90
b. A1921 50k Mars 3 3.00 .90
Soviet space research. No. 4045 contains 2 40x20mm stamps with simulated perforations.

Globe, Torch and Palm — A1922

1973, Jan. 5　　**Perf. 11x11½**
4046 A1922 10k tan, vio blue & red .50 .30
15th anniversary of Afro-Asian Peoples' Solidarity Organization (AAPSO).

I. V. Babushkin — A1923

1973, Jan. 10　**Engr.**　**Perf. 12**
4047 A1923 4k greenish black .50 .25
Babushkin (1873-1906), revolutionary.

"30," Map and Admiralty Tower, Leningrad A1924

1973, Jan. 10　**Photo.**　**Perf. 11½**
4048 A1924 4k pale brn, ocher & blk .50 .25
30th anniversary of the breaking of the Nazi blockade of Leningrad.

TU-154 Turbojet Passenger Plane — A1925

1973, Jan. 10　**Litho.**　**Perf. 12**
4049 A1925 6k multicolored .75 .25
50th anniversary of Soviet Civil Aviation.

Gediminas Tower, Flag, Modern Vilnius A1926

1973, Jan. 10　**Photo.**　**Perf. 11½**
4050 A1926 10k gray, red & green .50 .30
650th anniversary of Vilnius.

Heroes' Memorial, Stalingrad — A1927

Designs (Details from Monument): 3k, Man with rifle and "Mother Russia," vert. 10k, Mourning mother and child. 12k, Arm with torch, vert. No. 4055a, Red star, hammer and sickle emblem and statuary like 3k. No. 4055b, "Mother Russia," vert.

1973, Feb. 1   Litho.   Perf. 11½

4051	A1927	3k dp org & blk	1.25	.25
4052	A1927	4k dp yel & blk	1.25	.25
4053	A1927	10k olive & multi	1.25	.25
4054	A1927	12k dp car & black	1.25	.25
		Nos. 4051-4054 (4)	5.00	1.00

Souvenir Sheet
Perf. 12x12½, 12½x12

4055		Sheet of 2	3.00	1.00
a.-b.	A1927 20k any single		.75	.25

30th anniv. of the victory over the Germans at Stalingrad. #4055 contains 2 40x18mm stamps.

Large Portrait Type of 1971

Designs: 4k, Mikhail Prishvin (1873-1954), author. 10k, Fedor Chaliapin (1873-1938), opera singer, by K. Korovin.

1973   Litho.   Perf. 11½x12

4056	A1855	4k pink & multi	.50	.25
4057	A1855	10k lt blue & multi	.50	.25

Issue dates: 4k, Feb. 1; 10k, Feb. 8.

"Mayakovsky   "Mossovet
Theater" — A1928   Theater" — A1929

1973, Feb. 1   Photo.   Perf. 11½

4058	A1928	10k red, gray & indigo	.50	.25
4059	A1929	10k red, mag & gray	.50	.25

50th anniversary of the Mayakovsky and Mossovet Theaters in Moscow.

Copernicus and Solar System A1930

1973, Feb. 8   Engr. & Photo.

| 4060 | A1930 | 10k ultra & sepia | .75 | .25 |

500th anniversary of the birth of Nicolaus Copernicus (1473-1543), Polish astronomer.

Ice Hockey A1931

Design: 50k, Two players, vert.

1973, Mar. 14   Photo.   Perf. 11½

| 4061 | A1931 | 10k gold, blue & sep | .50 | .25 |

Souvenir Sheet

| 4062 | A1931 | 50k bl grn, gold & sep | 2.00 | 1.00 |

European and World Ice Hockey Championships, Moscow.
See No. 4082.

Athletes and Banners of Air, Land and Naval Forces — A1932

1973, Mar. 14

| 4063 | A1932 | 4k bright blue & multi | .50 | .25 |

Sports Society of Soviet Army, 50th anniv.

Tank, Red Star and Map of Battle of Kursk — A1933

1973, Mar. 14

| 4064 | A1933 | 4k gray, black & red | .50 | .25 |

30th anniversary of Soviet victory in the Battle of Kursk during World War II.

Nikolai E. Bauman (1873-1905), Bolshevist Revolutionary A1934

1973, Mar. 20   Engr.   Perf. 12½x12

| 4065 | A1934 | 4k brown | .50 | .25 |

Red Cross and Red Crescent — A1935

6k, Theater curtain & mask. 16k, Youth Festival emblem & young people.

1973, Mar. 20   Photo.   Perf. 11

4066	A1935	4k gray grn & red	.45	.25
4067	A1935	6k violet blue & red	.45	.25
4068	A1935	16k multicolored	1.10	.25
		Nos. 4066-4068 (3)	2.00	.75

Union of Red Cross and Red Crescent Societies of the USSR, 50th annivs.; 15th Cong. of the Intl. Theater Institute; 10th World Festival of Youth and Students, Berlin.

Aleksandr N. Ostrovsky, by V. Perov A1936

1973, Apr. 5   Litho.   Perf. 12x12½

| 4069 | A1936 | 4k tan & multi | .50 | .25 |

Ostrovsky (1823-1886), dramatist.

Earth Satellite   Lunokhod 2 on
"Interkosmos"   Moon and Lenin
A1937   Moon Plaque
                       A1938

1973, Apr. 12   Photo.   Perf. 11½

4070	A1937	6k brn ol & dull cl	.25	.25
4071	A1938	6k vio blue & multi	.25	.25

Souvenir Sheets
Perf. 12x11½

4072		Sheet of 3, purple & multi	1.50	.75
a.	A1938 20k Lenin plaque		.40	.25
b.	A1938 20k Lunokhod 2		.40	.25
c.	A1938 20k Telecommunications		.40	.25
4073		Sheet of 3, slate grn & multi	1.50	.75
a.	A1938 20k Lenin plaque		.40	.25
b.	A1938 20k Lunokhod 2		.40	.25
c.	A1938 20k Telecommunications		.40	.25

Cosmonauts' Day. No. 4070 for cooperation in space research by European communist countries.
Souvenir sheets contain 3 50x21mm stamps.

Russian Painting Type of 1972

Paintings: 2k, Guitarist, V. A. Tropinin. 4k, Young Widow, by P. A. Fedotov. 6k, Self-portrait, by O. A. Kiprensky. 10k, Woman with Grapes ("An Afternoon in Italy") by K. P. Bryullov. 12k, Boy with Dog ("That was my Father's Dinner"), by A. Venetsianov. 16k, "Lower Gallery of Albano," by A. A. Ivanov. 20k, Soldiers ("Conquest of Siberia"), by V. I. Surikov, horiz.

Perf. 12x12½, 12½x12

1973, Apr. 18   Litho.

4074	A1897	2k gray & multi	.25	.25
4075	A1897	4k gray & multi	.25	.25
4076	A1897	6k gray & multi	.25	.25
4077	A1897	10k gray & multi	.25	.25
4078	A1897	12k gray & multi	.45	.25
4079	A1897	16k gray & multi	.60	.25
4080	A1897	20k gray & multi	.70	.25
		Nos. 4074-4080 (7)	2.75	1.75

Athlete, Ribbon of Lenin Order — A1939

1973, Apr. 18   Photo.   Perf. 11½

| 4081 | A1939 | 4k blue, red & ocher | .50 | .25 |

50th anniversary of Dynamo Sports Society.

No. 4062 with Blue Green Inscription and Ornaments Added in Margin
Souvenir Sheet

1973, Apr. 26   Photo.   Perf. 11½

| 4082 | A1931 | 50k multicolored | 5.00 | 2.00 |

Soviet victory in European and World Ice Hockey Championships, Moscow.

"Mikhail Lermontov," Route Leningrad to New York — A1940

1973, May 20   Photo.   Perf. 11½

| 4083 | A1940 | 16k multicolored | .60 | .25 |

Inauguration of transatlantic service Leningrad to New York.

Ernest E. T. Krenkel, Polar Stations and Ship Chelyuskin A1941

1973, May 20   Litho. & Engr.

| 4084 | A1941 | 4k dull blue & olive | 1.00 | .30 |

Krenkel (1903-1971), polar explorer.

Emblem and Sports — A1942

1973, May 20   Litho.   Perf. 12x12½

| 4085 | A1942 | 4k multicolored | .65 | .25 |

Sports Association for Labor and Defense.

Latvian Song Festival, Cent. — A1943

1973, May 24

| 4086 | A1943 | 10k Singers | .65 | .25 |

Throwing the Hammer — A1944

Designs: 3k, Athlete on rings. 4k, Woman diver. 16k, Fencing. 50k, Javelin.

1973, June 14   Litho.   Perf. 11½

4087	A1944	2k lemon & multi	.25	.25
4088	A1944	3k blue & multi	.25	.25
4089	A1944	4k citron & multi	.25	.25
4090	A1944	16k lilac & multi	.35	.25
		Nos. 4087-4090 (4)	1.10	1.00

Souvenir Sheet

| 4091 | A1944 | 50k gold & multi | 1.75 | 1.25 |

Universiad, Moscow, 1973.

Souvenir Sheet

Valentina Nikolayeva-Tereshkova — A1945

1973, June 14   Photo.   Perf. 12x11½

4092	A1945	Sheet of 3 + label	3.00	1.25
a.	20k as cosmonaut		.55	.25
b.	20k with Indian and African women		.55	.25
c.	20k with daughter		.55	.25

Flight of the 1st woman cosmonaut, 10th anniv.

European Bison — A1946

1973, July 26 Photo. Perf. 11x11½
4093 A1946 1k shown .25 .25
4094 A1946 3k Ibex .25 .25
4095 A1946 4k Caucasian
snowcock .25 .25
4096 A1946 6k Beaver .25 .25
4097 A1946 10k Deer and fawns .25 .25
Nos. 4093-4097 (5) 1.25 1.25

Caucasus and Voronezh wildlife reserves.

Party Membership Card with Lenin Portrait — A1947

1973, July 26 Litho. Perf. 11½
4098 A1947 4k multicolored .50 .25

70th anniversary of 2nd Congress of the Russian Social Democratic Workers' Party.

Abu-al-Rayhan al-Biruni (973-1048), Arabian (Persian) Scholar and Writer — A1948

1973, Aug. 9 Engr. Perf. 12x12½
4099 A1948 6k red brown .50 .25

White House, Spasski Tower, Hemispheres — A1949

#4101, Eiffel Tower, Spasski Tower, globe. #4102, Schaumburg Palace, Bonn, Spasski Tower, globe. Stamps show representative buildings of Moscow, Washington, New York, Paris & Bonn.

1973, Aug. 10 Photo. Perf. 11½x12
4100 A1949 10k magenta & multi 1.00 .50
4101 A1949 10k brown & multi 1.00 .50
4102 A1949 10k dp car & multi 1.00 .50
 a. Souv. sheet of 3 + 3 labels 4.50 2.50
Nos. 4100-4102 (3) 3.00 1.50

Visit of General Secretary Leonid I. Brezhnev to Washington, Paris and Bonn. Nos. 4100-4102 each printed with se-tenant label with different statements by Brezhnev in Russian and English, French and German, respectively.
No. 4102a contains 4k stamps similar to Nos. 4100-4102 in changed colors. Issued Nov. 26.
See Nos. 4161-4162.

Russian Painting Type of 1972

2k, S. T. Konenkov, sculptor, by P. D. Korin. 4k, Tractor Operators at Supper, by A. A. Plastov. 6k, Letter from the Front, by A. I. Laktionov. 10k, Mountains, by M. S. Saryan. 16k, Wedding on a Future Street, by Y. I. Pimenov. 20k, Ice Hockey, mosaic by A. A. Deineka. 50k, Lenin at 3rd Congress of Young Communist League, by B. V. Yoganson.

1973, Aug. 22 Litho. Perf. 12x12½
Frame in Light Gray
4103 A1897 2k multicolored .25 .25
4104 A1897 4k multicolored .25 .25
4105 A1897 6k multicolored .25 .25
4106 A1897 10k multicolored .25 .25

4107 A1897 16k multicolored .45 .25
4108 A1897 20k multicolored .55 .25
Nos. 4103-4108 (6) 2.00 1.50
Souvenir Sheet
Perf. 12
4109 A1897 50k multicolored 3.00 1.50

History of Russian Painting.

Museum, Tashkent A1950

1973, Aug. 23 Photo. Perf. 12x12½
4110 A1950 4k multicolored .50 .25

Lenin Central Museum, Tashkent branch.

Y. M. Steklov — A1951

1973, Aug. 27 Photo. Perf. 11½x12
4111 A1951 4k multicolored .50 .25

Steklov (1873-1941), party worker, historian, writer.

Book, Pen and Torch — A1952

1973, Aug. 31 Perf. 11½
4112 A1952 6k multicolored .50 .25

Conf. of Writers of Asia & Africa, Alma-Ata.

Echinopanax Elatum — A1953

Medicinal Plants: 2k, Ginseng. 4k, Orchis maculatus. 10k, Arnica montana. 12k, Lily of the valley.

1973, Sept. 5 Litho. Perf. 12x12½
4113 A1953 1k yellow & multi .25 .25
4114 A1953 2k lt blue & multi .25 .25
4115 A1953 4k gray & multi .25 .25
4116 A1953 10k sepia & multi .25 .25
4117 A1953 12k green & multi .25 .25
Nos. 4113-4117 (5) 1.25 1.25

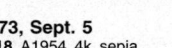

Imadeddin Nasimi, Azerbaijani Poet, 600th Birth Anniv. — A1954

1973, Sept. 5 Engr.
4118 A1954 4k sepia .50 .25

Cruiser Kirov — A1955

Soviet Warships: 4k, Battleship October Revolution. 6k, Submarine Krasnogvardeyets. 10k, Torpedo boat Soobrazitelny. 16k, Cruiser Red Caucasus.

Engraved and Photogravure
1973, Sept. 12 Perf. 11½x12
4119 A1955 3k violet & multi .25 .25
4120 A1955 4k green & multi .25 .25
4121 A1955 6k multicolored .25 .25
4122 A1955 10k blue grn & multi .40 .25
4123 A1955 16k multicolored .60 .25
Nos. 4119-4123 (5) 1.75 1.25

Globe and Red Flag Emblem — A1956

1973, Sept. 25 Photo. Perf. 11½
4124 A1956 6k gold, buff & red .50 .25

15th anniversary of the international communist review "Problems of Peace and Socialism," published in Prague.

Emelyan I. Pugachev and Peasant Army — A1957

Engraved and Photogravure
1973, Sept. 25 Perf. 11½x12
4125 A1957 4k brn, bister & red .75 .25

Bicentenary of peasant revolt of 1773-75 led by Emelyn Ivanovich Pugachev.

Crystal, Institute Emblem and Building A1958

1973, Oct. 5 Perf. 11½
4126 A1958 4k black & multi .50 .25

Leningrad Mining Institute, 150th anniv.

Palm, Globe, Flower — A1959

1973, Oct. 5 Photo.
4127 A1959 6k red, gray & dk blue .50 .25

World Cong. of Peace-loving Forces, Moscow.

Elena Stasova — A1960

1973, Oct. 5 Perf. 11½x12
4128 A1960 4k deep claret .50 .25

Elena Dmitriyevna Stasova (1873-1966), communist party worker.
See Nos. 4228-4229.

Order of Friendship — A1961

1973, Oct. 5 Litho. Perf. 12
4129 A1961 4k red & multi .75 .25

56th anniv. of the October Revolution. Printed se-tenant with coupon showing Arms of USSR and proclamation establishing Order of Friendship of People, in 1972, on the 50th anniv. of the USSR.

Marshal Malinovsky A1962

1973, Oct. 5 Engr.
4130 A1962 4k slate .50 .25

Rodion Y. Malinovsky (1898-1967).
See Nos. 4203-4205.

Ural Man, Red Guard, Worker — A1963

1973, Oct. 17 Photo. Perf. 11½
4131 A1963 4k red, gold & black .50 .25

250th anniversary of the city of Sverdlovsk.

Dimitri Cantemir
(1673-1723),
Prince of
Moldavia,
Writer — A1964

1973, Oct. 17   Engr.   Perf. 12x12½
4132 A1964 4k rose claret   .50 .25

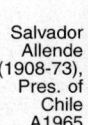

Salvador
Allende
(1908-73),
Pres. of
Chile
A1965

1973, Nov. 26   Photo.   Perf. 11½
4133 A1965 6k rose brn & black   .50 .25

Spasski Tower,
Kremlin — A1966

1973, Nov. 30   Litho.   Perf. 12x12½
4134 A1966 6k brt blue & multi   1.00 .25
New Year 1974.

Nariman Narimanov
A1967

1973, Nov. 30   Engr.   Perf. 12
4135 A1967 4k slate green   .50 .25
Nariman Narimanov (1870-1925), Chairman
of Executive Committee of USSR.

Russo-Balt, 1909 — A1968

Designs: 3k, AMO-F15 truck, 1924. 4k,
Spartak, NAMI-1 car, 1927. 12k, Ya-6 autobus, 1929. 16k, GAZ-A car, 1932.

1973, Nov. 30   Photo.   Perf. 12x11½
4136 A1968   2k purple & multi   .25 .25
4137 A1968   3k olive & multi   .25 .25
4138 A1968   4k ocher & multi   .25 .25
4139 A1968 12k vio blue & multi   .40 .25
4140 A1968 16k red & multi   .50 .25
    Nos. 4136-4140 (5)   1.65 1.25

Development of Russian automotive industry. See Nos. 4216-4220, 4325-4329, 4440-
4444.

Still Life, by Frans Snyders — A1969

Paintings: 6k, Woman Trying on Earrings, by
Rembrandt, vert. 10k, Sick Woman and Physi-
cian, by Jan Steen, vert. 12k, Still Life with
Sculpture, by Jean-Baptiste Chardin. 14k,
Lady in Garden, by Claude Monet. 16k, Young
Love, by Jules Bastien-Lepage, vert. 20k Girl
with Fan, by Auguste Renoir, vert. 50k, Flora,
by Rembrandt, vert.

Perf. 12x11½, 11½x12
1973, Dec. 12   Litho.
4141 A1969   4k bister & multi   .25 .25
4142 A1969   6k bister & multi   .25 .25
4143 A1969 10k bister & multi   .40 .25
4144 A1969 12k bister & multi   .45 .25
4145 A1969 14k bister & multi   .50 .25
4146 A1969 16k bister & multi   .55 .25
4147 A1969 20k bister & multi   .70 .25
    Nos. 4141-4147 (7)   3.10 1.75

Souvenir Sheet
Perf. 12
4148 A1969 50k multicolored   2.00 1.00
Foreign paintings in Russian museums.

Pablo
Picasso
(1881-1973),
Painter
A1970

1973, Dec. 20   Photo.   Perf. 12x11½
4149 A1970 6k gold, slate grn &
             red   .75 .25

Organ Pipes and
Dome,
Riga — A1971

No. 4151, Small Trakai Castle, Lithuania.
No. 4152, Great Sea Gate, Tallinn, Estonia.
10k, Town Hall and "Old Thomas" weather
vane, Tallinn.

1973, Dec. 20   Engr.   Perf. 12x12½
4150 A1971   4k blk, red & slate
              grn   .25 .25
4151 A1971   4k gray, red & buff   .25 .25
4152 A1971   4k black, red & grn   .25 .25
4153 A1971 10k sep, grn, red &
              blk   .25 .25
    Nos. 4150-4153 (4)   1.00 1.00
Architecture of the Baltic area.

I. G. Petrovsky   L. A. Artsimovich
A1972   A1973

No. 4154, I. G. Petrovsky (1901-73), mathematician, rector of Moscow State University.

No. 4155, L. A. Artsimovich (1909-73), physicist, academician. No. 4156, K. D. Ushinsky
(1824-71), teacher. No. 4157, M. D. Million-
schikov (1913-73), vice president of Academy
of Sciences.

1973-74   Photo.   Perf. 11½
4154 A1972 4k orange & multi   .50 .25
4155 A1973 4k blk brn & olive   .50 .25
Engr.
Perf. 12½x12
4156 A1973 4k multicolored   .50 .25
Litho.
Perf. 12
4157 A1973 4k multicolored   .50 .25
    Nos. 4154-4157 (4)   2.00 1.00
Issued: #4154, 12/28/73; others, 2/6/74.

Flags of India and USSR, Red Fort,
Taj Mahal and Kremlin — A1974

Design: No. 4162, Flags of Cuba and
USSR, José Marti Monument, Moncada Barracks and Kremlin.

1973-74   Litho.   Perf. 12
4161 A1974 4k lt ultra & multi   1.00 .25
4162 A1974 4k lt grn & multi ('74) 1.00 .25

Visit of General Secretary Leonid I.
Brezhnev to India and Cuba. Nos. 4161-4162
each printed with se-tenant label with different
statements by Brezhnev in Russian and Hindi,
and Russian and Spanish respectively.

Red Star, Soldier,
Newspaper
A1975

1974, Jan. 1   Photo.   Perf. 11x11½
4166 A1975 4k gold, red & black .50 .25
50th anniversary of the Red Star newspaper.

Victory Monument, Peter-Paul
Fortress, Statue of Peter I — A1976

1974, Jan. 16   Litho.   Perf. 11½
4167 A1976 4k multicolored   1.00 .25
30th anniversary of the victory over the
Germans near Leningrad.

Oil Workers,
Refinery — A1977

1974, Jan. 16   Photo.   Perf. 11½
4168 A1977 4k dull blue, red & blk .50 .25
10th anniversary of the Tyumen oilfields.

Comecon
Building — A1978

1974, Jan. 16   Photo.   Perf. 11½
4169 A1978 16k red brn, ol & red .50 .25
25th anniversary of the Council for Mutual
Economic Assistance.

Skaters
and Rink,
Medeo
A1979

1974, Jan. 28
4170 A1979 6k slate, brn red & bl .50 .25
European Women's Skating Championships, Medeo, Alma-Ata.

Art Palace,
Leningrad,
Academy,
Moscow
A1980

1974, Jan. 30   Photo. & Engr.
4171 A1980 10k multicolored   .50 .25
25th anniversary of the Academy of Sciences of the USSR.

3rd Winter
Spartiakad
Emblem — A1981

1974, Mar. 20   Photo.   Perf. 11½
4172 A1981 10k gold & multi   .50 .25
Third Winter Spartiakad.

Young People and
Emblem — A1982

1974, Mar. 20   Photo. & Engr.
4173 A1982 4k multicolored   .50 .25
Youth scientific-technical work.

Azerbaijan
Theater — A1983

1974, Mar. 20 Photo. Perf. 11½
4174 A1983 6k org, red brn & brn .50 .25
Centenary of Azerbaijan Theater.

Meteorological Satellite
"Meteor" — A1984

Cosmonauts V. G. Lazarev and O. G.
Makarov and Soyuz 12 — A1985

Design: No. 4177, Cosmonauts P. I. Klimuk
and V. V. Lebedev, and Soyuz 13.

1974, Mar. 27 Perf. 11½
4175 A1984 6k violet & multi .60 .25
Perf. 12x11½
4176 A1985 10k grnsh bl & multi .70 .25
4177 A1985 10k dull yel & multi .70 .25
Nos. 4175-4177 (3) 2.00 .75
Cosmonauts' Day.

Odessa by Moonlight, by
Aivazovski — A1986

Seascapes by Aivazovski: 4k, Battle of
Chesma, 1848, vert. 6k, St. George's Monastery. 10k, Stormy Sea. 12k, Rainbow (shipwreck). 16k, Shipwreck. 50k, Portrait of
Aivazovski, by Kramskoy, vert.

Perf. 12x11½, 11½x12
1974, Mar. 30 Litho.
4178 A1986 2k gray & multi .25 .25
4179 A1986 4k gray & multi .25 .25
4180 A1986 6k gray & multi .25 .25
4181 A1986 10k gray & multi .30 .25
4182 A1986 12k gray & multi .45 .25
4183 A1986 16k gray & multi .70 .25
Nos. 4178-4183 (6) 2.20 1.50
Souvenir Sheet
4184 A1986 50k gray & multi 2.00 .90

Ivan Konstantinovich Aivazovski (1817-
1900), marine painter. Sheets of Nos. 4178-
4183 each contain 2 labels with commemorative inscriptions.
See Nos. 4230-4234.

Young
Man and
Woman,
Banner
A1987

1974, Mar. 30 Litho. Perf. 12½x12
4185 A1987 4k red, yel & brown .50 .25
17th Cong. of the Young Communist League.

Lenin, by
V. E.
Tsigal
A1988

1974, Mar. 30
4186 A1988 4k yel, red & brown .50 .25
50th anniversary of naming the Komsomol
(Young Communist League) after Lenin.

Souvenir Sheet

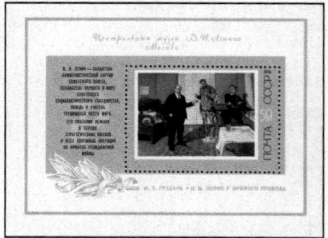

Lenin at the Telegraph, by Igor E.
Grabar — A1989

1974, Apr. 16 Litho. Perf. 12
4187 A1989 50k multicolored 2.00 .90
104th anniv. of the birth of Lenin.

Rainbow, Swallow
over
Clouds — A1990

6k, Fish in water. 10k, Crystal. 16k, Rose.
20k, Fawn. 50k, Infant.

1974, Apr. 24 Photo. Perf. 11½
4188 A1990 4k lilac & multi .25 .25
4189 A1990 6k multicolored .25 .25
4190 A1990 10k multicolored .35 .25
4191 A1990 16k blue & multi .55 .25
4192 A1990 20k citron & multi .60 .25
Nos. 4188-4192 (5) 2.00 1.25
Souvenir Sheet
Litho.
Perf. 12x12½
4193 A1990 50k blue & multi 2.00 .80

EXPO '74 World's Fair, theme "Preserve the
Environment," Spokane, WA, May 4-Nov. 4.

Congress Emblem
and
Clover — A1991

1974, May 7 Photo. Perf. 11½
4194 A1991 4k green & multi .50 .25
12th International Congress on Meadow
Cultivation, Moscow, 1974.

"Cobblestones, Weapons of the
Proletariat," by I. D. Shadr — A1992

1974, May 7
4195 A1992 4k gold, red & olive .50 .25
50th anniversary of the Lenin Central Revolutionary Museum of the USSR.

Saiga — A1993

Fauna of USSR: 3k, Koulan (wild ass). 4k,
Desman. 6k, Sea lion. 10k, Greenland whale.

1974, May 22 Litho. Perf. 11½
4196 A1993 1k olive & multi .40 .25
4197 A1993 3k green & multi .80 .35
4198 A1993 4k multicolored .80 .35
4199 A1993 6k multicolored 1.10 .50
4200 A1993 10k multicolored 1.90 .60
Nos. 4196-4200 (5) 5.00 2.05

Peter Ilich Tchaikovsky — A1994

1974, May 22 Photo. Perf. 11½
4201 A1994 6k multicolored .50 .25
5th International Tchaikovsky Competition,
Moscow.

Souvenir Sheet

Aleksander S. Pushkin, by O. A.
Kiprensky — A1995

1974, June 4 Litho. Imperf.
4202 A1995 50k multicolored 2.00 .80
Aleksander S. Pushkin (1799-1837).

Marshal Type of 1973

Designs: No. 4203, Marshal F. I. Tolbukhin
(1894-1949); No. 4204, Admiral I. S. Isakov
(1894-1967); No. 4205, Marshal S. M.
Budenny (1883-1973).

1974 Engr. Perf. 12
4203 A1962 4k olive green .50 .25
4204 A1962 4k indigo .50 .25
4205 A1962 4k slate green .50 .25
Nos. 4203-4205 (3) 1.50 .75
Issued: #4203, 6/5; #4204, 7/18; #4205,
8/20.

Stanislavski and Nemirovich-
Danchenko — A1996

1974, June 12 Litho. Perf. 12
4211 A1996 10k yel, black & dk red .50 .25
75th anniv. of the Moscow Arts Theater.

Runner,
Track,
Open Book
A1997

1974, June 12 Photo. Perf. 11½
4212 A1997 4k multicolored .50 .25
13th Natl. School Spartakiad, Alma-Ata.

Railroad
Car
A1998

1974, June 12
4213 A1998 4k multicolored 1.00 .25
Egorov Railroad Car Factory, cent.

Victory Monument,
Minsk — A1999

No. 4215, Monument & Government House,
Kiev.

1974, June 20
4214 A1999 4k violet, black & yel .50 .25
4215 A1999 4k blue, black & yel .50 .25
30th anniversary of liberation of Byelorussia
(No. 4214), and of Ukraine (No. 4215).
Issued: #4214, June 20; #4215, July 18.

Automotive Type of 1973

Designs: 2k, GAZ AA truck, 1932. 3k, GAZ
03-30 bus, 1933. 4k, Zis 5 truck, 1933. 14k,
Zis 8 bus, 1934. 16k, Zis 101 car, 1936.

1974, June 20 Perf. 12x11½
4216 A1968 2k brown & multi .25 .25
4217 A1968 3k multicolored .25 .25
4218 A1968 4k orange & multi .25 .25
4219 A1968 14k multicolored .50 .25
4220 A1968 16k multicolored .60 .25
Nos. 4216-4220 (5) 1.85 1.25
Soviet automotive industry.

Liberation
Monument,
Poltava — A2000

1974, July 7 Perf. 11½
4221 A2000 4k dull red & sepia .50 .25
800th anniversary of city of Poltava.

Nike Monument, Warsaw and Polish Flag — A2001

1974, July 7   Litho.   Perf. 12½x12
4222 A2001 6k olive & red   .50 .25
Polish People's Republic, 30th anniversary.

Mine Layer — A2002

Soviet Warships: 4k, Landing craft. 6k, Anti-submarine destroyer and helicopter. 16k, Anti-submarine cruiser.

Engraved and Photogravure
1974, July 25   Perf. 11½x12
4223 A2002 3k multicolored   .25 .25
4224 A2002 4k multicolored   .70 .25
4225 A2002 6k multicolored   1.00 .25
4226 A2002 16k multicolored   2.00 .25
     Nos. 4223-4226 (4)   3.95 1.00

Pentathlon A2003

1974, Aug. 7   Photo.   Perf. 11½
4227 A2003 16k gold, blue & brown .50 .25
World Pentathlon Championships, Moscow.

Portrait Type of 1973
No. 4228, Dimitri Ulyanov (1874-1943). Soviet official and Lenin's brother. No. 4229, V. Menzhinsky (1874-1934), Soviet official.

1974, Aug. 7   Engr.   Perf. 12½x12
4228 A1960 4k slate green   .50 .25

Litho.
Perf. 12x11½
4229 A1960 4k rose lake   .50 .25

Painting Type of 1974
Russian paintings: 4k, Lilac, by W. Kontchalovski. 6k, "Towards the Wind" (sailboats), by E. Kalnins. 10k, "Spring" (girl and landscape), by O. Zardaryan. 16k, Northern Harbor, G. Nissky. 20k, Kirghiz Girl, by S. Chuikov, vert.

Perf. 12x11½, 11½x12
1974, Aug. 20   Litho.
4230 A1986 4k gray & multi   .25 .25
4231 A1986 6k gray & multi   .25 .25
4232 A1986 10k gray & multi   .55 .25
4233 A1986 16k gray & multi   .80 .25
4234 A1986 20k gray & multi   1.10 .25
     Nos. 4230-4234 (5)   2.95 1.25
Printed in sheets of 18 stamps and 2 labels.

Page of First Russian Primer — A2004

1974, Aug. 20   Photo.   Perf. 11½
4235 A2004 4k black, red & gold .50 .25
1st printed Russian primer, 400th anniv.

Monument, Russian and Romanian Flags — A2005

1974, Aug. 23
4236 A2005 6k dk blue, red & yel .50 .25
Romania's liberation from Fascist rule, 30th anniversary.

Vitebsk A2006

1974, Sept. 4   Litho.   Perf. 12
4237 A2006 4k dk car & olive   .50 .25
Millennium of city of Vitebsk.

Kirghiz Republic A2007

50th Anniv. of Founding of Republics (Flags, industrial and agricultural themes): No. 4239, Moldavia. No. 4240, Turkmen. No. 4241, Uzbek. No. 4242, Tadzhik.

1974, Sept. 4   Perf. 11½x11
4238 A2007 4k vio blue & multi   1.00 .25
4239 A2007 4k maroon & multi   1.00 .25
4240 A2007 4k yellow & multi   1.00 .25
4241 A2007 4k green & multi   1.00 .25
4242 A2007 4k lt blue & multi   1.00 .25
     Nos. 4238-4242 (5)   5.00 1.25

Arms and Flag of Bulgaria — A2008

Photogravure and Engraved
1974, Sept. 4   Perf. 11½
4243 A2008 6k gold & multi   .50 .25
30th anniv. of the Bulgarian revolution.

Arms of DDR and Soviet War Memorial, Treptow A2009

1974, Sept. 4   Photo.
4244 A2009 6k multicolored   .50 .25
German Democratic Republic, 25th anniv.

Souvenir Sheet

Soviet Stamps and Exhibition Poster — A2010

1974, Sept. 4   Litho.   Perf. 12x12½
4245 A2010 50k multicolored   7.50 3.00
3rd Cong. of the Phil. Soc. of the USSR.

Maly State Theater — A2011

1974, Oct. 3   Photo.   Perf. 11x11½
4246 A2011 4k red, black & gold .50 .25
150th anniversary of the Lenin Academic Maly State Theater, Moscow.

"Guests from Overseas," by N. K. Roerich — A2012

1974, Oct. 3   Litho.   Perf. 12
4247 A2012 6k multicolored   .50 .25
Nicholas Konstantin Roerich (1874-1947), painter and sponsor of Roerich Pact and Banner of Peace.

UPU Monument, Bern, and Arms of USSR A2013

Development of Postal Service — A2014

UPU Cent.: No. 4248, Ukrainian coat of arms, letters, UPU emblem and headquarters, Bern. No. 4249, Arms of Byelorussia, UPU emblem, letters, stagecoach and rocket.

Photogravure and Engraved
1974, Oct. 9   Perf. 12x11½
4248 A2013 10k red & multi   .35 .25
4249 A2013 10k red & multi   .35 .25
4250 A2013 10k red & multi   .35 .25
     Nos. 4248-4250 (3)   1.05 .75

Souvenir Sheet
Typo.
Perf. 11½x12
4251 A2014 Sheet of 3   5.00 2.50
  a.   30k Jet and UPU emblem   1.25 .75
  b.   30k Mail coach, UPU emblem 1.25 .75
  c.   40k UPU emblem   1.25 .75

Order of Labor, 1st, 2nd and 3rd Grade A2015

KAMAZ Truck Leaving Kama Plant — A2016

Design: No. 4254, Nurek Hydroelectric Plant.

1974, Oct. 16   Litho.   Perf. 12½x12
4252 A2015 4k multicolored   .65 .25
4253 A2016 4k multicolored   .65 .25
4254 A2016 4k multicolored   .65 .25
     Nos. 4252-4254 (3)   1.95 .75

Space Stations Mars 4-7 over Mars A2017

P. R. Popovich, Y. P. Artyukhin and Soyuz 14 — A2018

Design: No. 4257, Cosmonauts G. V. Sarafanov and L. S. Demin, Soyuz 15, horiz.

Perf. 12x11½, 11½
1974, Oct. 28   Photo.
4255 A2017 6k multicolored   .25 .25
4256 A2018 10k multicolored   .40 .25
4257 A2018 10k multicolored   .40 .25
     Nos. 4255-4257 (3)   1.05 .75
Russian explorations of Mars (6k); flight of Soyuz 14 (No. 4256) and of Soyuz 15, Aug. 26-28 (No. 4257).

Mongolian Flag and Arms A2019

1974, Nov. 14   Photo.   Perf. 11½
4258 A2019 6k gold & multi   .50 .25
Mongolian People's Republic, 50th anniv.

Guards' Ribbon, Estonian Government Building, Tower — A2020

1974, Nov. 14
4259 A2020 4k multicolored .50 .25
Liberation of Estonia, 30th anniversary.

Tanker, Passenger and Cargo Ships — A2021

1974, Nov. 14 Typo. Perf. 12½x12
4260 A2021 4k multicolored .50 .25
USSR Merchant Marine, 50th anniversary.

Spasski Tower Clock — A2022

1974, Nov. 14 Litho. Perf. 12
4261 A2022 4k multicolored .50 .25
New Year 1975.

The Fishmonger, by Pieters A2023

Paintings: 4k, The Marketplace, by Beuckelaer, 1564, horiz. 10k, A Drink of Lemonade, by Gerard Terborch. 14k, Girl at Work, by Gabriel Metsu. 16k, Saying Grace, by Jean Chardin. 20k, The Spoiled Child, by Jean Greuze. 50k, Self-portrait, by Jacques Louis David.

Perf. 12x12½, 12½x12
1974, Nov. 20 Litho.
4262 A2023 4k bister & multi .25 .25
4263 A2023 6k bister & multi .25 .25
4264 A2023 10k bister & multi .25 .25
4265 A2023 14k bister & multi .50 .25
4266 A2023 16k bister & multi .55 .25
4267 A2023 20k bister & multi .70 .25
Nos. 4262-4267 (6) 2.50 1.50

Souvenir Sheet
Perf. 12
4268 A2023 50k multicolored 2.00 .75
Foreign paintings in Russian museums. Printed in sheets of 16 stamps and 4 labels.

Morning Glory — A2024

Designs: Flora of the USSR.

1974, Nov. 20 Perf. 12x12½
4269 A2024 1k red brn & multi .25 .25
4270 A2024 2k green & multi .25 .25
4271 A2024 4k multicolored .25 .25
4272 A2024 10k brown & multi .25 .25
4273 A2024 12k dk blue & multi .25 .25
Nos. 4269-4273 (5) 1.25 1.25

Ivan S. Nikitin (1824-1861), Poet — A2025

1974, Dec. 11 Photo. Perf. 11½
4274 A2025 4k gray grn, grn & blk .50 .25

Leningrad Mint — A2026

Photogravure and Engraved
1974, Dec. 11 Perf. 11
4275 A2026 6k silver & multi .50 .25
250th anniversary of the Leningrad Mint.

Mozhajsky Plane, 1882 — A2027

Early Russian Aircraft: No. 4277, Grizidubov-N biplane, 1910. No. 4278, Russia-A, 1910. No. 4279, Russian Vityaz (Sikorsky), 1913. No. 4280, Grigorovich flying boat, 1914.

1974, Dec. 25 Photo. Perf. 11½x12
4276 A2027 6k olive & multi .60 .25
4277 A2027 6k ultra & multi .60 .25
4278 A2027 6k magenta & multi .60 .25
4279 A2027 6k red & multi .60 .25
4280 A2027 6k brown & multi .60 .25
Nos. 4276-4280 (5) 3.00 1.25
Russian aircraft history, 1882-1914.

Souvenir Sheet

Sports and Sport Buildings, Moscow — A2028

1974, Dec. 25 Perf. 11½
4281 A2028 Sheet of 4 1.00 .50
a. 10k Woman gymnast .25 .25
b. 10k Running .25 .25
c. 10k Soccer .25 .25
d. 10k Canoeing .25 .25
Moscow preparing for Summer Olympic Games, 1980.

Rotary Press, Masthead A2029

1975, Jan. 20
4282 A2029 4k multicolored .50 .25
Komsomolskaya Pravda newspaper, 50th anniv.

Masthead and Pioneer Emblems — A2030

1975, Jan. 20
4283 A2030 4k red, blk & silver .50 .25
Pioneers' Pravda newspaper, 50th anniv.

Spartakiad Emblem and Skiers — A2031

1975, Jan. 20
4284 A2031 4k blue & multi .50 .25
8th Winter Spartakiad of USSR Trade Unions.

Games' Emblem, Hockey Player and Skier A2032

1975, Jan. 20
4285 A2032 16k multicolored .50 .25
5th Winter Spartakiad of Friendly Armies, Feb. 23-Mar. 1.

Republic Anniversaries Type of 1970

Design (Hammer-Sickle Emblem and): No. 4286, Landscape and produce.

1975, Jan. 24 Engr. Perf. 12x12½
4286 A1794 4k green .50 .25
50th anniversary of Karakalpak Autonomous Soviet Socialist Republic.

David, by Michelangelo — A2033

Michelangelo, Self-portrait — A2034

Works by Michelangelo: 6k, Squatting Boy. 10k, Rebellious Slave. 14k, The Creation of Adam. 20k, Staircase, Laurentian Library, Florence. 30k, The Last Judgment.

Lithographed and Engraved
1975, Feb. 27 Perf. 12½x12½
4296 A2033 4k slate grn & grn .25 .25
4297 A2033 6k red brn & bister .25 .25
4298 A2033 10k slate grn & grn .30 .25
a. Min. sheet, 2 ea #4296-4298 5.00 5.00
4299 A2033 14k red brn & bister .50 .25
4300 A2033 20k slate grn & grn .70 .25
4301 A2033 30k red brn & bister 1.00 .25
a. Min. sheet, 2 ea #4299-4301 5.00 2.00
Nos. 4296-4301 (6) 3.00 1.50

Souvenir Sheet
Perf. 12x11½
4302 A2034 50k gold & multi 4.00 .80
Michelangelo Buonarroti (1475-1564), Italian sculptor, painter and architect. Issued only in the min. sheets of 6.

Mozhajski, Early Plane and Supersonic Jet TU-144 — A2035

1975, Feb. 27 Photo. Perf. 12x11½
4303 A2035 6k violet blue & ocher .50 .25
A. F. Mozhajski (1825-1890), pioneer aircraft designer, birth sesquicentennial.

"Metric System" A2036

1975, Mar. 14 Perf. 11½
4304 A2036 6k blk, vio blue & org .50 .25
Intl. Meter Convention, Paris, 1875, cent.

Spartakiad Emblem and Sports A2037

1975, Mar. 14
4305 A2037 6k red, silver & black .50 .25
6th Summer Spartakiad.

Liberation Monument, Parliament, Arms — A2038

Charles Bridge Towers, Arms and Flags — A2039

1975, Mar. 14
4306 A2038 6k gold & multi .25 .25
4307 A2039 6k gold & multi .25 .25
30th anniv. of liberation from fascism, Hungary (#4306) & Czechoslovakia (#4307).

Flags of France and USSR — A2040

1975, Mar. 25   Litho.   Perf. 12
4308 A2040 6k lilac & multi .50 .25
50th anniv. of the establishment of diplomatic relations between France and USSR, 1st foreign recognition of Soviet State.

Yuri A. Gagarin, by L. Kerbel — A2041

A. V. Filipchenko, N.N. Rukavishnikov, Russo-American Space Emblem, Soyuz 16 — A2042

Cosmonauts' Day: 10k, A. A. Gubarev, G. M. Grechko aboard Soyuz 17 & orbital station Salyut 4.

Perf. 11½x12, 12x11½
1975, Mar. 28   Photo.
4309 A2041 6k blue, sil & red .25 .25
4310 A2042 10k blk, blue & red .50 .25
4311 A2042 16k multicolored .75 .25
Nos. 4309-4311 (3) 1.50 .75

Warsaw Treaty Members' Flags — A2043

1975, Apr. 16   Litho.   Perf. 12
4312 A2043 6k multicolored .50 .25
Signing of the Warsaw Treaty (Bulgaria, Czechoslovakia, German Democratic Rep.,

Hungary, Poland, Romania, USSR), 20th anniv.

Lenin on Steps of Winter Palace, by V. G. Zyplakow A2044

1975, Apr. 22   Perf. 12x12½
4313 A2044 4k multicolored .60 .25
105th anniversary of the birth of Lenin.

Communications Emblem and Exhibition Pavilion — A2045

1975, Apr. 22   Perf. 11½
4314 A2045 6k ultra, red & silver .50 .25
International Communications Exhibition, Sokolniki Park, Moscow, May 1975.

Lenin and Red Flag — A2046

Order of Victory — A2047

No. 4316, Eternal Flame and guard. No. 4317, Woman munitions worker. No. 4318, Partisans. No. 4319, Soldier destroying swastika. No. 4320, Soldier with gun and banner.

1975, Apr. 22   Typo.   Perf. 12
4315 A2046 4k shown .25 .25
4316 A2046 4k multicolored .25 .25
4317 A2046 4k multicolored .25 .25
4318 A2046 4k multicolored .25 .25
4319 A2046 4k multicolored .25 .25
4320 A2046 4k multicolored .25 .25
Nos. 4315-4320 (6) 1.50 1.50

Souvenir Sheet
Litho., Typo. & Photo.
Imperf
4321 A2047 50k multicolored 2.00 1.00
World War II victory, 30th anniversary.

War Memorial, Berlin-Treptow A2048

1975, Apr. 25   Litho.   Perf. 12x12½
4322 A2048 6k buff & multi .50 .25

Souvenir Sheet
4323 A2048 50k dull blue & multi 2.00 .60
Socflex 75 Intl. Phil. Exhib. honoring 30th anniv. of WWII victory, Moscow, May 8-18.

Soyuz-Apollo Docking Emblem and Painting by Cosmonaut A. A. Leonov — A2049

1975, May 23   Photo.   Perf. 12x11½
4324 A2049 20k multicolored .50 .30
Russo-American space cooperation.

Automobile Type of 1973
2k, GAZ-M-I car, 1936. 3k, 5-ton truck, YAG-6, 1936. 4k, ZIZ-16, autobus, 1938. 12k, KIM-10 car, 1940. 16k, GAZ-67B jeep, 1943.

1975, May 23   Photo.   Perf. 12x11½
4325 A1968 2k dp org & multi .25 .25
4326 A1968 3k green & multi .25 .25
4327 A1968 4k dk green & multi .25 .25
4328 A1968 12k maroon & multi .30 .25
4329 A1968 16k olive & multi .45 .25
Nos. 4325-4329 (5) 1.50 1.25

Canal, Emblem, Produce — A2050

1975, May 23   Perf. 11½
4330 A2050 6k multicolored .50 .25
9th Intl. Congress on Irrigation and Drainage, Moscow, and International Commission on Irrigation and Drainage, 25th anniv..

Flags and Arms of Poland and USSR, Factories A2051

1975, May 23
4331 A2051 6k multicolored .50 .25
Treaty of Friendship, Cooperation and Mutual Assistance between Poland & USSR, 30th anniv.

Man in Space and Earth A2052

1975, May 23
4332 A2052 6k multicolored .50 .25
First man walking in space, Lt. Col. Alexei Leonov, 10th anniversary.

Yakov M. Sverdlov (1885-1919), Organizer and Early Member of Communist Party — A2053

1975, June 4
4333 A2053 4k multicolored .50 .25

Congress, Emblem, Forest and Field A2054

1975, June 4
4334 A2054 6k multicolored .50 .25
8th International Congress for Conservation of Plants, Moscow.

Symbolic Flower with Plants and Emblem A2055

1975, June 20   Litho.   Perf. 11½
4335 A2055 6k multicolored .50 .25
12th International Botanical Congress.

Souvenir Sheet

UN Emblem — A2056

1975, June 20   Photo.   Perf. 11½x12
4336 A2056 50k gold & blue 2.00 1.00
30th anniversary of United Nations.

Globe and Film A2057

1975, June 20   Photo.   Perf. 11½
4337 A2057 6k multicolored .50 .25
9th Intl. Film Festival, Moscow, 1975.

Soviet and American Astronauts and
Flags — A2058

Apollo and Soyuz After Link-up and
Earth — A2059

Soyuz Launch
A2060

Designs: No. 4340, Spacecraft before link-
up, earth and project emblem. 50k, Soviet Mission Control Center.

1975, July 15   Litho.   Perf. 11½
4338	A2058	10k multicolored	.35	.25
4339	A2059	12k multicolored	.45	.25
4340	A2059	12k multicolored	.45	.25
a.		Vert. pair, #4339-4340	1.50	.50
4341	A2060	16k multicolored	.75	.40
		Nos. 4338-4341 (4)	2.00	1.15

Souvenir Sheet
Photo.
Perf. 12x11½
| 4342 | A2058 | 50k multicolored | 3.00 | 1.25 |

Apollo-Soyuz space test project (Russo-
American space cooperation), launching, July
15; link-up July 17.
No. 4342 contains one 50x21mm stamp.
See US Nos. 1569-1570.

Sturgeon, Caspian Sea, Oceanexpo
75 Emblem — A2061

Designs (Oceanexpo 75 Emblem and): 4k,
Salt-water shell, Black Sea. 6k, Eel, Baltic
Sea. 10k, Sea duck, Arctic Sea. 16k, Crab,
Far Eastern waters. 20k, Chrisipther (fish),
Pacific Ocean.

1975, July 22   Photo.   Perf. 11
4343	A2061	3k multicolored	.25	.25
4344	A2061	4k multicolored	.25	.25
4345	A2061	6k green & multi	.25	.25
4346	A2061	10k dk blue & multi	.35	.25
4347	A2061	16k purple & multi	.65	.25
4348	A2061	20k multicolored	1.50	.25
		Nos. 4343-4348 (6)	3.25	1.50

Souvenir Sheet
Perf. 12x11½
4349		Sheet of 2	2.00	.90
a.	A2061	30k Dolphin rising	.75	.30
b.	A2061	30k Dolphin diving	.75	.30

Oceanexpo 75, 1st Intl. Oceanographic
Exhib., Okinawa, July 20, 1975-Jan. 1976. No.
4349 contains 55x25mm stamps.

Parade, Red Square, 1941, by K. F.
Yuon — A2062

Paintings: 2k, Morning of Industrial Moscow,
by Yuon. 6k, Soldiers Inspecting Captured
Artillery, by Lansere. 10k, Excavating Metro
Tunnel, by Lansere. 16k, Pushkin and His
Wife at Court Ball, by Ulyanov, vert. 20k, De
Lauriston at Kutuzov's Headquarters, by
Ulyanov.

1975, July 22   Litho.   Perf. 12½x11½
4350	A2062	1k gray & multi	.25	.25
4351	A2062	2k gray & multi	.25	.25
4352	A2062	6k gray & multi	.25	.25
4353	A2062	10k gray & multi	.25	.25
4354	A2062	16k gray & multi	.50	.25
4355	A2062	20k gray & multi	.70	.25
		Nos. 4350-4355 (6)	2.20	1.50

Konstantin F. Yuon (1875-1958), Yevgeni Y.
Lansere (1875-1946), Nikolai P. Ulyanov
(1875-1949).
Nos. 4350-4355 issued in sheets of 16 plus
4 labels.

Finlandia Hall, Map of Europe,
Laurel — A2063

1975, Aug. 18   Photo.   Perf. 11½
| 4356 | A2063 | 6k brt blue, gold & blk | .50 | .25 |

European Security and Cooperation Conference, Helsinki, July 30-Aug. 1. Printed se-tenant with label with quotation by Leonid I.
Brezhnev, first secretary of Communist party.

Ciurlionis, Waves
and Lighthouse
A2064

1975, Aug. 20   Photo. & Engr.
| 4357 | A2064 | 4k grn, indigo & gold | .50 | .25 |

M. K. Ciurlionis, Lithuanian composer, birth
centenary.

Avetik
Isaakyan, by
Martiros
Saryan
A2065

1975, Aug. 20   Litho.   Perf. 12x12½
| 4358 | A2065 | 4k multicolored | .50 | :25 |

Isaakyan (1875-1957), Armenian poet.

Jacques
Duclos — A2066

1975, Aug. 20   Photo.   Perf. 11½x12
| 4359 | A2066 | 6k maroon & silver | .50 | .25 |

Duclos (1896-1975), French labor leader.

al-Farabi — A2067

1975, Aug. 20   Perf. 11½
| 4360 | A2067 | 6k grnsh blue, brn & bis | .50 | .25 |

Nasr al-Farabi (870?-950), Arab philosopher.

Male
Ruffs
A2068

1975, Aug. 25   Litho.   Perf. 12½x12
4361	A2068	1k shown	.25	.25
4362	A2068	4k Altai roebuck	.25	.25
4363	A2068	6k Siberian marten	.25	.25
4364	A2068	10k Old squaw (duck)	.40	.25
4365	A2068	16k Badger	.55	.25
		Nos. 4361-4365 (5)	1.70	1.25

Berezina River and Stolby wildlife reservations, 50th anniversary.

A2069   A2070

Designs: No. 4366, Flags of USSR, North
Korea, arms of N. K., Liberation monument,
Pyongyang. No. 4367, Flags of USSR, North
Viet Nam, arms of N.V., industrial
development.

1975, Aug. 28   Perf. 12
| 4366 | A2069 | 6k multicolored | .30 | .25 |
| 4367 | A2070 | 6k multicolored | .30 | .25 |

Liberation of North Korea from Japanese
occupation (#4366); and establishment of
Democratic Republic of Viet Nam (#4367),
30th anniversary.

P. Klimuk and V. Sevastyanov, Soyuz
18 and Salyut 4 Docking — A2071

1975, Sept. 12   Photo.   Perf. 12x11½
| 4368 | A2071 | 10k ultra, blk & dp org | .50 | .25 |

Docking of space ship Soyuz 18 and space
station Salyut 4.

S. A.
Esenin and
Birches
A2072

Photogravure and Engraved
1975, Sept. 12   Perf. 11½
| 4369 | A2072 | 6k brown & ocher | .50 | .25 |

Sergei A. Esenin (1895-1925), poet.

Standardization Symbols — A2073

1975, Sept. 12   Photo.   Perf. 11½
| 4370 | A2073 | 4k red & multi | .50 | .25 |

USSR Committee for Standardization of
Communications Ministry, 50th anniversary.

Karakul
Lamb
A2074

1975, Sept. 22   Photo.   Perf. 11½
| 4371 | A2074 | 6k black, yel & grn | .50 | .25 |

3rd International Symposium on astrakhan
production, Samarkand, Sept. 22-27.

Dr. M. P.
Konchalovsky
A2075

1975, Sept. 30   Perf. 11½x12
| 4372 | A2075 | 4k brown & red | .50 | .25 |

Konchalovsky (1875-1942), physician.

Exhibition Emblem — A2076

1975, Sept. 30   *Perf. 11½*
4373 A2076 4k deep blue & red   .50 .25
3rd All-Union Youth Phil. Exhib., Yerevan.

IWY Emblem and Rose — A2077

1975, Sept. 30 Litho. *Perf. 12x11½*
4374 A2077 6k multicolored   .50 .25
International Women's Year 1975.

Yugoslavian Flag and Parliament A2078

1975, Sept. 30 Photo. *Perf. 11½*
4375 A2078 6k gold, red & blue   .50 .25
Republic of Yugoslavia, 30th anniv.

Illustration from 1938 Edition, by V. A. Favorsky — A2079

1975, Oct. 20 Typo. *Perf. 12*
4376 A2079 4k buff, red & black   .50 .25
175th anniversary of the 1st edition of the old Russian saga "Slovo o polku Igoreve."

Mikhail Ivanovich Kalinin — A2080

No. 4378, Anatoli Vasilievich Lunacharski.

1975, Oct. 20 Engr. *Perf. 12*
4377 A2080 4k sepia   .25 .25
4378 A2080 4k sepia   .25 .25
Kalinin (1875-1946), chairman of Central Executive Committee and Presidium of Supreme Soviet; Lunacharski (1875-1933), writer, commissar for education.

Hand Holding Torch and Lenin Quotation — A2081

1975, Oct. 20   Engr.
4379 A2081 4k red & olive   .50 .25
First Russian Revolution (1905), 70th anniv.

Building Baikal-Amur Railroad — A2082

Novolipetsk Metallurgical Plant — A2083

Nevynomyssk Chemical Plant, Fertilizer Formula — A2084

1975, Oct. 30 Photo. *Perf. 11½*
4380 A2082 4k gold & multi   .40 .25
4381 A2083 4k red, gray & sl grn   .40 .25
4382 A2084 4k red, blue & silver   .40 .25
     Nos. 4380-4382 (3)   1.20 .75
58th anniversary of October Revolution.

Bas-relief of Decembrists and "Decembrists at the Senate Square," by D. N. Kardovsky — A2085

1975, Nov. 12   Litho. & Engr.
4383 A2085 4k gray & multi   .50 .25
Sesquicentennial of Decembrist rising.

Star and "1976" — A2086

1975, Nov. 12 Litho. *Perf. 12x12½*
4384 A2086 4k green & multi   .50 .25
New Year 1976.

Village Street, by F. A. Vasilev A2087

Paintings by Vasilev: 4k, Road in Birch Forest. 6k, After the Thunderstorm. 10k, Swamp, horiz. 12k, In the Crimean Mountains. 16k, Meadow, horiz. 50k, Portrait, by Kramskoi.

Perf. 12x12½, 12½x12
1975, Nov. 25
4385 A2087 2k gray & multi   .25 .25
4386 A2087 4k gray & multi   .25 .25
4387 A2087 6k gray & multi   .25 .25
4388 A2087 10k gray & multi   .30 .25
4389 A2087 12k gray & multi   .55 .25
4390 A2087 16k gray & multi   .60 .25
     Nos. 4385-4390 (6)   2.20 1.50

Souvenir Sheet
Perf. 12
4391 A2087 50k gray & multi   2.00 .90
Fedor Aleksandrovich Vasilev (1850-1873), landscape painter. Nos. 4385-4390 printed in sheets of 7 stamps and one label.

Landing Capsule, Venus Surface, Lenin Banner A2088

1975, Dec. 8 Photo. *Perf. 11½*
4392 A2088 10k multicolored   .50 .25
Flights of Soviet interplanetary stations Venera 9 and Venera 10.

Gabriel Sundoukian — A2089

1975, Dec. 8 Litho. *Perf. 12*
4393 A2089 4k multicolored   .50 .30
Sundoukian (1825-1912), Armenian playright.

Polar Poppies, Taiga A2090

Regional Flowers: 6k, Globeflowers, tundra. 10k, Buttercups, oak forest. 12k, Wood anemones, steppe. 16k, Eminium Lehmannii, desert.

Photogravure and Engraved
1975, Dec. 25   *Perf. 12x11½*
4394 A2090 4k black & multi   .25 .25
4395 A2090 6k black & multi   .50 .25
4396 A2090 10k black & multi   .60 .25
4397 A2090 12k black & multi   1.20 .25
4398 A2090 16k black & multi   1.75 .25
     Nos. 4394-4398 (5)   4.30 1.25

A. L. Mints (1895-1974), Academician A2091

1975, Dec. 31 Photo. *Perf. 11½x12*
4399 A2091 4k dp brown & gold   .50 .25

Demon, by A. Kochupalov A2092

Paintings: 6k, Vasilisa the Beautiful, by I. Vakurov. 10k, Snow Maiden, by T. Zubkova. 16k, Summer, by K. Kukulieva. 20k, The Fisherman and the Goldfish, by I. Vakurov, horiz.

1975, Dec. 31 Litho. *Perf. 12*
4400 A2092 4k bister & multi   .25 .25
4401 A2092 6k bister & multi   .35 .25
4402 A2092 10k bister & multi   .60 .25
4403 A2092 16k bister & multi   .75 .25
4404 A2092 20k bister & multi   1.00 .25
  a.   Strip of 5, #4400-4404   5.00 1.25
Palekh Art State Museum, Ivanov Region.

Wilhelm Pieck (1876-1960), Pres. of German Democratic Republic — A2093

1976, Jan. 3 Engr. *Perf. 12½x12*
4405 A2093 6k greenish black   .50 .25

M. E. Saltykov-Shchedrin, by I.N. Kramskoi — A2094

1976, Jan. 14 Litho. *Perf. 12x12½*
4406 A2094 4k multicolored   .50 .25
Mikhail Evgrafovich Saltykov-Shchedrin (1826-1889), writer and revolutionist.

Congress Emblem — A2095

1976, Feb. 2 Photo. *Perf. 11½*
4407 A2095 4k red, gold & mar   .50 .25

Souvenir Sheet
Perf. 11½x12
4408 A2095 50k red, gold & mar   1.75 .65
25th Congress of the Communist Party of the Soviet Union.

Lenin Statue, Kiev — A2096

1976, Feb. 2   Perf. 11½
4409 A2096 4k red, black & blue   .50 .25
Ukrainian Communist Party, 25th Congress.

Ice Hockey, Games' Emblem A2097

Designs (Winter Olympic Games' Emblem and): 4k, Cross-country skiing. 6k, Figure skating, pairs. 10k, Speed skating. 20k, Luge. 50k, Winter Olympic Games' emblem, vert.

1976, Feb. 4   Litho.   Perf. 12½x12
4410 A2097 2k multicolored   .25 .25
4411 A2097 4k multicolored   .25 .25
4412 A2097 6k multicolored   .25 .25
4413 A2097 10k multicolored   .35 .25
4414 A2097 20k multicolored   .90 .30
  Nos. 4410-4414 (5)   2.00 1.30

Souvenir Sheet
Perf. 12x12½
4415 A2097 50k vio bl, org & red   2.00 1.00
12th Winter Olympic Games, Innsbruck, Austria, Feb. 4-15. No. 4415 contains one stamp; silver and violet blue margin showing designs of Nos. 4410-4414. Size: 90x80mm.

No. 4415 Overprinted in Red
Souvenir Sheet

1976, Mar. 24
4416 A2097 50k multicolored   3.00 2.00
Success of Soviet athletes in 12th Winter Olympic Games. Translation of overprint: "Glory to Soviet Sport! The athletes of the USSR have won 13 gold, 6 silver and 8 bronze medals."

K.E. Voroshilov A2098

1976, Feb. 4   Engr.   Perf. 12
4417 A2098 4k slate green   .50 .25
Kliment Efremovich Voroshilov (1881-1969), pres. of revolutionary military council, commander of Leningrad front, USSR pres. 1953-60. See Nos. 4487-4488, 4545-4548.

Flag over Kremlin Palace of Congresses, Troitskaya Tower A2099

Photogravure on Gold Foil
1976, Feb. 24   Perf. 12x11½
4418 A2099 20k gold, grn & red   3.50 1.00
25th Congress of the Communist Party of the Soviet Union (CPSU).

Lenin on Red Square, by P. Vasiliev — A2100

1976, Mar. 10   Litho.   Perf. 12½x12
4419 A2100 4k yellow & multi   .50 .25
106th anniversary of the birth of Lenin.

Atom Symbol and Dubna Institute — A2101

1976, Mar. 10   Photo.   Perf. 11½
4420 A2101 6k vio bl, red & silver   .50 .25
Joint Institute of Nuclear Research, Dubna, 20th anniversary.

Bolshoi Theater — A2102

1976, Mar. 24   Litho.   Perf. 11x11½
4421 A2102 10k yel, blue & dk brn   .50 .25
Bicentenary of Bolshoi Theater.

Back from the Fair, by Konchalovsky — A2103

Paintings by P. P. Konchalovsky: 2k, The Green Glass. 6k, Peaches. 16k, Meat, Game and Vegetables. 20k, Self-portrait, 1943, vert.

1976, Apr. 6   Perf. 12½x12, 12x12½
4422 A2103 1k yellow & multi   .25 .25
4423 A2103 2k yellow & multi   .25 .25
4424 A2103 6k yellow & multi   .30 .25
4425 A2103 16k yellow & multi   .60 .25
4426 A2103 20k yellow & multi   .75 .30
  Nos. 4422-4426 (5)   2.15 1.30
Birth centenary of P. P. Konchalovsky.

Vostok, Salyut-Soyuz Link-up — A2104

Yuri A. Gagarin — A2105

Designs: 6k, Meteor and Molniya Satellites, Orbita Ground Communications Center. 10k, Cosmonauts on board Salyut space station and Mars planetary station. 12k, Interkosmos station and Apollo-Soyuz linking.

Lithographed and Engraved
1976, Apr. 12   Perf. 11½
4427 A2104 4k multicolored   .25 .25
4428 A2104 6k multicolored   .35 .25
4429 A2104 10k multicolored   .50 .25
4430 A2104 12k multicolored   .90 .25
  Nos. 4427-4430 (4)   2.00 1.00

Souvenir Sheet
Engr.   Perf. 12
4431 A2105 50k black   10.00 2.00
1st manned flight in space, 15th anniv.

I. A. Dzhavakhishvili A2106

1976, Apr. 20   Photo.   Perf. 11½x12
4432 A2106 4k multicolored   .50 .25
Dzhavakhishvili (1876-1940), scientist.

Samed Vurgun and Derrick — A2107

1976, Apr. 20   Perf. 11½
4433 A2107 4k multicolored   .50 .25
Vurgun (1906-56), natl. poet of Azerbaijan.

1st All-Union Festival of Amateur Artists — A2108

USSR Flag, Worker and Farmer Monument.

1976, May 12   Litho.   Perf. 11½x12
4434 A2108 4k multicolored   .50 .25

Intl. Federation of Philately, 50th Anniv. — A2109

1976, May 12   Photo.   Perf. 11½
4435 A2109 6k FIP Emblem   .50 .25

Souvenir Sheet

V. A. Tropinin, Self-portrait — A2110

1976, May 12   Litho.   Perf. 12
4436 A2110 50k multicolored   1.50 1.00
Vasily Andreevich Tropinin (1776-1857), painter.

Emblem, Dnieper Bridge — A2111

1976, May 20   Photo.   Perf. 11½
4437 A2111 4k Prus blue, gold & blk   .50 .25
Bicentenary of Dnepropetrovsk.

Dr. N. N.
Burdenko — A2112

1976, May 20   *Perf. 11½x12*
4438 A2112 4k deep brown & red   .50 .25
Burdenko (1876-1946), neurosurgeon.

K. A. Trenev
(1876-1945),
Playwright
A2113

1976, May 20   *Perf. 11½*
4439 A2113 4k black & multi   .50 .25

Automobile Type of 1973

2k, ZIS-110 passenger car. 3k, GAZ-51 Gorky truck. 4k, GAZ-M-20 Pobeda passenger car. 12k, ZIS-150 Moscow Motor Works truck. 16k, ZIS-154 Moscow Motor Works bus.

1976, June 15   *Photo.*   *Perf. 12x11½*
4440 A1968   2k grnsh bl & multi   .25   .25
4441 A1968   3k bister & multi   .25   .25
4442 A1968   4k dk blue & multi   .25   .25
4443 A1968   12k brown & multi   .55   .25
4444 A1968   16k deep car & multi   .70   .25
    Nos. 4440-4444 (5)   2.00 1.25

Canoeing
A2114

USSR National Olympic Committee Emblem and: 6k, Basketball, vert. 10k, Greco-Roman wrestling. 14k, Women's discus, vert. 16k, Target shooting. 50k, Olympic medal, obverse and reverse.

    Perf. 12½x12, 12x12½
1976, June 23   *Litho.*
4445 A2114   4k red & multi   .25   .25
4446 A2114   6k red & multi   .25   .25
4447 A2114   10k red & multi   .35   .25
4448 A2114   14k red & multi   .25   .25
4449 A2114   16k red & multi   .25   .25
    Nos. 4445-4449 (5)   1.35 1.25

Souvenir Sheet
4450 A2114 50k red & multi   3.00   .75
21st Olympic Games, Montreal, Canada, July 17-Aug. 1.
For overprint see No. 4472.

Electric
Trains,
Overpass
A2115

1976, June 23   *Photo.*   *Perf. 11½*
4451 A2115 4k multicolored   1.00 .25
Electrification of USSR railroads, 50th anniversary.

L. Emilio Recabarren — A2116

1976, July 6
4452 A2116 6k gold, red & blk   .50 .25
Luis Emilio Recabarren (1876-1924), founder of Chilean Communist Party.

Ljudmilla
Mikhajlovna
Pavlichenko (1916-
1974), WWII
Heroine — A2117

1976, July 6
4453 A2117 4k dp brn, silver & yel   .50 .25

Pavel
Andreevich
Fedotov
(1815-1852),
Painter
A2118

Paintings: 2k, New Partner, by P. A. Fedotov. 4k, The Fastidious Fiancée, horiz. 6k, Aristocrat's Breakfast. 10k, Gamblers, horiz. 16k, The Outing. 50k, Self-portrait.

    Perf. 12x12½, 12½x12
1976, July 15   *Litho.*
4454 A2118   2k black & multi   .25   .25
4455 A2118   4k black & multi   .25   .25
4456 A2118   6k black & multi   .25   .25
4457 A2118   10k black & multi   .50   .25
4458 A2118   16k black & multi   .75   .25
    Nos. 4454-4458 (5)   2.00 1.25

Souvenir Sheet
    Perf. 12
4459 A2118 50k multicolored   1.50   .75
Nos. 4454-4458 each printed in sheets of 20 stamps and center label with black commemorative inscription.

S. S.
Nametkin — A2119

1976, July 20   *Photo.*   *Perf. 11½x12*
4460 A2119 4k blue, black & buff   .50 .25
Sergei Semenovich Nametkin (1876-1950), organic chemist.

Squacco
Heron — A2120

Waterfowl: 3k, Arctic loon. 4k, European coot. 6k, Atlantic puffin. 10k, Slender-billed gull.

1976, Aug. 18   *Litho.*   *Perf. 12x12½*
4465 A2120   1k dk green & multi   .25   .25
4466 A2120   3k ol green & multi   .50   .50
4467 A2120   4k orange & multi   .80   .80
4468 A2120   6k purple & multi   1.10 1.10
4469 A2120   10k brt blue & multi   2.40 2.40
    Nos. 4465-4469 (5)   5.05 5.05
Nature protection.

Peace
Dove
A2121

1976, Aug. 25   *Photo.*   *Perf. 11½*
4470 A2121 4k salmon, gold & blue .50 .25
2nd Stockholm appeal and movement to stop arms race.

Resistance
Movement
Emblem
A2122

1976, Aug. 25
4471 A2122 6k dk bl, blk & gold   .50 .25
Intl. Resistance Movement Fed., 25th anniv.

No. 4450 Overprinted in Gold
Souvenir Sheet

1976, Aug. 25   *Litho.*   *Perf. 12½x12*
4472 A2114 50k red & multi   3.00   .75
Victories of Soviet athletes in 21st Olympic Games (47 gold, 43 silver and 35 bronze medals).

Flags of India and
USSR — A2123

1976, Sept. 8   *Perf. 12*
4473 A2123 4k multicolored   .50 .25
Friendship and cooperation between USSR and India.

UN, UNESCO
Emblems, Open
Book — A2124

1976, Sept. 8   *Engr.*   *Perf. 12x12½*
4474 A2124 16k multicolored   .50 .30
UNESCO, 30th anniv.

B. V. Volynov, V. M. Zholobov, Star
Circling Globe — A2125

1976, Sept. 8   *Photo.*   *Perf. 12x11½*
4475 A2125 10k brn, blue & black   .50 .35
Exploits of Soyuz 21 and Salyut space station.

"Industry" — A2126

1976, Sept. 17
4476 A2126   4k shown   .40   .25
4477 A2126   4k Farm industry   .40   .25
4478 A2126   4k Science   .40   .25
4479 A2126   4k Transport & com-
         munications   .40   .25
4480 A2126   4k Intl. cooperation   .40   .25
    Nos. 4476-4480 (5)   2.00 1.25
25th Congress of the Communist Party of the Soviet Union.

Victory, by I.
I. Vakurov
A2127

Paintings: 2k, Plower, by I. I. Golikov, horiz. 4k, Au (woman), by I. V. Markichev. 12k, Firebird, by A. V. Kotuhin, horiz. 14k, Festival, by A. I. Vatagin.

    Perf. 12½x12, 12x12½
1976, Sept. 22   *Litho.*
4481 A2127   2k black & multi   .25   .25
4482 A2127   4k black & multi   .25   .25
4483 A2127   12k black & multi   1.25   .25
4484 A2127   14k black & multi   1.40   .25
4485 A2127   20k black & multi   1.75   .35
    Nos. 4481-4485 (5)   4.90 1.35
Palekh Art State Museum, Ivanov Region.

Shostakovich, Score from 7th
Symphony, Leningrad — A2128

1976, Sept. 25 Engr. Perf. 12½x12
4486 A2128 6k dk vio blue .50 .25

Dimitri Dimitrievich Shostakovich (1906-1975), composer.

Voroshilov Type of 1976

No. 4487, Zhukov. No. 4488, Rokossovsky.

1976, Oct. 7 Engr. Perf. 12
4487 A2098 4k slate green .25 .25
4488 A2098 4k brown .25 .25

Marshal Georgi Konstantinovich Zhukov (1896-1974), commander at Stalingrad and Leningrad and Deputy of Supreme Soviet; Marshal Konstantin K. Rokossovsky (1896-1968), commander at Stalingrad.

Intercosmos-14
A2129

10k, India's satellite Arryabata. 12k, Soyuz-19 and Apollo before docking. 16k, French satellite Aureole and Northern Lights. 20k, Docking of Soyuz-Apollo, Intercosmos-14 and Aureole.

1976, Oct. 15 Photo. Perf. 11½
4489 A2129 6k black & multi .25 .25
4490 A2129 10k black & multi .30 .25
4491 A2129 12k black & multi .40 .25
4492 A2129 16k black & multi .45 .25
4493 A2129 20k black & multi .60 .25
Nos. 4489-4493 (5) 2.00 1.25

Interkosmos Program for Scientific and Experimental Research.

Vladimir I.
Dahl
A2130

Photogravure and Engraved
1976, Oct. 15 Perf. 11½
4494 A2130 4k green & dk grn .50 .25

Vladimir I. Dahl (1801-1872), physician, writer, compiled Russian Dictionary.

Electric
Power
Industry
A2131

No. 4496, Balashovo textile mill. No. 4497, Laying of drainage pipes and grain elevator.

1976, Oct. 20 Photo. Perf. 11½
4495 A2131 4k dk blue & multi .50 .25
4496 A2131 4k rose brn & multi .50 .25
4497 A2131 4k slate grn & multi .50 .25
Nos. 4495-4497 (3) 1.50 .75

59th anniversary of the October Revolution.

Petrov
Tumor
Research
Institute
A2132

M. A.
Novinski — A2133

1976, Oct. 28
4498 A2132 4k vio blue & gold .50 .25

Perf. 11½x12
4499 A2133 4k dk brn, buff & blue .50 .25

Petrov Tumor Research Institute, 50th anniversary, and 135th birth anniversary of M. A. Novinski, cancer research pioneer.

Aviation
Emblem,
Gakkel VII,
1911
A2134

Russian Aircraft (Russian Aviation Emblem and): 6k, Gakkel IX, 1912. 12k, I. Steglau No. 2, 1912. 14k, Dybovski's Dolphin, 1913. 16k, Iliya Muromets, 1914.

Lithographed and Engraved
1976, Nov. 4 Perf. 12x12½
4500 A2134 3k multicolored .25 .25
4501 A2134 6k multicolored .25 .25
4502 A2134 12k multicolored .50 .35
4503 A2134 14k multicolored .55 .35
4504 A2134 16k multicolored .60 .50
Nos. 4500-4504 (5) 2.15 1.70

See Nos. C109-C120.

Saffron
A2135

Flowers of the Caucasus: 2k, Pasqueflowers. 3k, Gentian. 4k, Columbine. 6k, Checkered lily.

1976, Nov. 17 Perf. 12x11½
4505 A2135 1k multicolored .40 .40
4506 A2135 2k multicolored .40 .40
4507 A2135 3k multicolored .40 .40
4508 A2135 4k multicolored .40 .40
4509 A2135 6k multicolored .40 .40
Nos. 4505-4509 (5) 2.00 2.00

Spasski
Tower
Clock,
Greeting
Card
A2136

1976, Nov. 25 Litho. Perf. 12½x12
4510 A2136 4k multicolored .60 .25

New Year 1977.

Parable of the Workers in the
Vineyard, by Rembrandt — A2137

Rembrandt Paintings in Russian Museums: 6k, Danae. 10k, David and Jonathan, vert. 14k, Holy Family, vert. 20k, Rembrandt's brother Adrian, 1654, vert. 50k, Artaxerxes, Esther and Haman.

Perf. 12½x12, 12x12½
1976, Nov. 25 Photo.
4511 A2137 4k multicolored .25 .25
4512 A2137 6k multicolored .35 .25
4513 A2137 10k multicolored .60 .25
4514 A2137 14k multicolored .90 .25
4515 A2137 20k multicolored 1.40 .25
Nos. 4511-4515 (5) 3.50 1.25

Souvenir Sheet
4516 A2137 50k multicolored 6.50 2.00

Rembrandt van Rijn (1606-69). Nos. 4511 and 4515 printed in sheets of 7 stamps and decorative label.

Armed
Forces
Order
A2138

Worker and
Farmer, by
V. I. Muhina
A2139

Marx and Lenin,
by Fridman and
Belostotsky
A2140

Council for
Mutual Economic
Aid Building
A2141

Lenin, 1920
Photograph
A2142

Globe and
Sputnik Orbits
A2143

Designs: 2k, Golden Star and Hammer and Sickle medals. 4k, Coat of arms and "CCCP." 6k, TU-154 plane, globe and airmail envelope. 10k, Order of Labor. 12k, Space exploration medal with Gagarin portrait. 16k, Lenin Prize medal.

1976 Engr. Perf. 12x12½
4517 A2138 1k greenish black .25 .25
4518 A2138 2k brt magenta .25 .25
4519 A2138 3k red .25 .25
4520 A2138 4k brick red .25 .25
4521 A2138 6k Prus blue .25 .25
4522 A2138 10k olive green .45 .25
4523 A2139 12k violet blue .50 .25
4524 A2139 16k deep green .60 .25

Perf. 12½x12
4525 A2140 20k brown red .80 .25
4526 A2141 30k brick red 1.10 .25
4527 A2142 50k brown 1.90 .25
4528 A2143 1r dark blue 4.00 .25
Nos. 4517-4528 (12) 10.60 3.00

Issued: Nos. 4517-4524, 12/17; Nos. 4525-4528, 8/10.
See Nos. 4596-4607. For overprint see No. 5720.

Luna 24
Emblem
and Moon
Landing
A2144

1976, Dec. 17 Photo. Perf. 11½
4531 A2144 10k multicolored .50 .25

Moon exploration of automatic station Luna 24.

Icebreaker "Pilot" — A2145

Icebreakers: 6k, Ermak, vert. 10k, Fedor Litke. 16k, Vladimir Ilich, vert. 20k, Krassin.

Perf. 12x11½, 11½x12
1976, Dec. 22 Litho. & Engr.
4532 A2145 4k multicolored .25 .25
4533 A2145 6k multicolored .35 .25
4534 A2145 10k multicolored .55 .25
4535 A2145 16k multicolored .75 .25
4536 A2145 20k multicolored 1.10 .30
Nos. 4532-4536 (5) 3.00 1.30

See Nos. 4579-4585.

Soyuz 22 Emblem, Cosmonauts V. F.
Bykovsky and V. V. Aksenov — A2146

1976, Dec. 28 Photo. Perf. 12x11½
4537 A2146 10k multicolored .50 .25

Soyuz 22 space flight, Sept. 15-23.

Society
Emblem — A2147

1977, Jan. 1 Perf. 11½
4538 A2147 4k multicolored .50 .25

Red Banner Voluntary Soc., supporting Red Army, Navy & Air Force, 50th anniv.

S. P. Korolev, Vostok Rocket and Satellite A2148

1977, Jan. 12
4539 A2148 4k multicolored .50 .25

Sergei Pavlovich Korolev (1907-1966), creator of first Soviet rocket space system.

Globe and Palm A2149

1977, Jan. 12
4540 A2149 4k multicolored .50 .25

World Congress of Peace Loving Forces, Moscow, Jan. 1977.

Sedov and "St. Foka" A2150

1977, Jan. 25 Photo. Perf. 11½
4541 A2150 4k multicolored .50 .25

G.Y. Sedov (1877-1914), polar explorer and hydrographer.

Worker and Farmer Monument and Izvestia Front Page — A2151

1977, Jan. 25
4542 A2151 4k silver, black & red .50 .25

60th anniversary of newspaper Izvestia.

Ship Sailing Across the Oceans — A2152

1977, Jan. 25
4543 A2152 6k deep blue & gold .50 .25

24th Intl. Navigation Cong., Leningrad.

Congress Hall and Troitskaya Tower, Kremlin — A2153

1977, Feb. 9 Photo. Perf. 11½
4544 A2153 4k red, gold & black .50 .25

16th Congress of USSR Trade Unions.

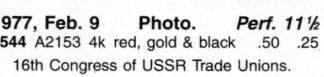

Voroshilov Type of 1976

Marshals of the Soviet Union: No. 4545, Leonid A. Govorov (1897-1955). No. 4546, Ivan S. Koniev. No. 4547, K. A. Merezhkov. No. 4548, W. D. Sokolovsky.

1977		**Engr.**	**Perf. 12**	
4545	A2098	4k brown	.40	.25
4546	A2098	4k slate green	.40	.25
4547	A2098	4k brown	.40	.25
4548	A2098	4k black	.40	.25
	Nos. 4545-4548 (4)		1.60	1.00

Issue dates: #4545, Feb. 9; others, June 7.

Academy, Crest, Anchor and Ribbons A2155

Photogravure and Engraved
1977, Feb. 9 Perf. 11½
4549 A2155 6k multicolored .50 .25

A. A. Grechko Naval Academy, Leningrad, sesquicentennial.

Jeanne Labourbe — A2156

1977, Feb. 25 Photo. Perf. 11½
4550 A2156 4k multicolored .50 .25

Jeanne Labourbe (1877-1919), leader of French communists in Moscow.

Queen and Knights — A2157

1977, Feb. 25
4551 A2157 6k multicolored .50 .25

4th European Chess Championships.

Cosmonauts V. D. Zudov and V. I. Rozhdestvensky — A2158

1977, Feb. 25 Perf. 12x11½
4552 A2158 10k multicolored .50 .25

Soyuz 23 space flight, Oct. 14-16, 1976.

A. S. Novikov-Priboy (1877-1944), Writer — A2159

1977, Mar. 16 Photo. Perf. 11½
4553 A2159 4k multicolored .50 .25

Welcome, by M. N. Soloninkin A2160

Folk Tale Paintings from Fedoskino Artists' Colony: 6k, Along the Street, by V. D. Antonov, horiz. 10k, Northern Song, by J. V. Karapaev. 12k, Tale of Tsar Saltan, by A. I. Kozlov. 14k, Summer Troika, by V. A. Nalimov, horiz. 16k, Red Flower, by V. D. Lipitsky.

		Perf. 12x12½, 12½x12		
1977, Mar. 16				**Litho.**
4554	A2160	4k black & multi	.45	.25
4555	A2160	6k black & multi	.45	.25
4556	A2160	10k black & multi	.65	.25
4557	A2160	12k black & multi	.95	.25
4558	A2160	14k black & multi	1.10	.25
4559	A2160	16k black & multi	1.40	.30
	Nos. 4554-4559 (6)		5.00	1.55

Lenin on Red Square, by K.V. Filatov — A2161

1977, Apr. 12 Perf. 12½x11½
4560 A2161 4k multicolored .50 .25

107th anniversary of the birth of Lenin.

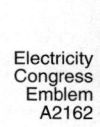

Electricity Congress Emblem A2162

1977, Apr. 12 Photo. Perf. 11½
4561 A2162 6k blue, red & gray .50 .25

World Electricity Congress, Moscow 1977.

Yuri Gagarin, Sputnik, Soyuz and Salyut — A2163

1977, Apr. 12 Perf. 12x11½
4562 A2163 6k multicolored .50 .25

Cosmonauts' Day.

N. I. Vavilov — A2164

1977, Apr. 26 Photo. Perf. 11½
4563 A2164 4k multicolored .50 .25

Vavilov (1887-1943), agricultural geneticist.

Feliks E. Dzerzhinski A2165

1977, May 12 Engr. Perf. 12½x12
4564 A2165 4k black .50 .25

Feliks E. Dzerzhinski (1877-1926), organizer and head of secret police (OGPU).

Saxifraga Sibirica — A2166

Siberian Flowers: 3k, Dianthus repena. 4k, Novosieversia glactalis. 6k, Cerasticum maxinicem. 16k, Golden rhododendron.

1977, May 12		**Litho. Perf. 12x12½**		
4565	A2166	2k multicolored	.25	.25
4566	A2166	3k multicolored	.25	.25
4567	A2166	4k multicolored	.25	.25
4568	A2166	5k multicolored	.35	.25
4569	A2166	16k multicolored	.90	.25
	Nos. 4565-4569 (5)		2.00	1.25

V. V. Gorbatko, Y. N. Glazkov, Soyuz 24 Rocket A2167

1977, May 16 Photo. Perf. 12x11½
4570 A2167 10k multicolored .50 .25

Space explorations of cosmonauts on Salyut 5 orbital station, launched with Soyuz 24 rocket.

Film and Globe — A2168

1977, June 21 Photo. Perf. 11½
4571 A2168 6k multicolored .50 .25

10th Intl. Film Festival, Moscow 1977.

Lion Hunt, by Rubens — A2169

Rubens Paintings, Hermitage, Leningrad: 4k, Lady in Waiting, vert. 10k, Workers in Quarry. 12k, Alliance of Water and Earth, vert. 20k, Landscape with Rainbow. 50k, Self-portrait.

Perf. 12x12½, 12½x12

1977, June 24   **Litho.**
4572	A2169	4k yellow & multi	.30 .25
4573	A2169	6k yellow & multi	.30 .25
4574	A2169	10k yellow & multi	.60 .25
4575	A2169	12k yellow & multi	.75 .25
4576	A2169	20k yellow & multi	1.00 .30
		Nos. 4572-4576 (5)	2.95 1.30

Souvenir Sheet
4577 A2169 50k yellow & multi   2.00 .60

Peter Paul Rubens (1577-1640), painter. Sheets of No. 4575 contain 2 labels with commemorative inscriptions and Atlas statue from Hermitage entrance.

Souvenir Sheet

Judith, by Giorgione — A2170

1977, July 15   **Litho.**   **Perf. 12x12½**
4578 A2170 50k multicolored   2.00 1.00

Il Giorgione (1478-1511), Venetian painter.

Icebreaker Type of 1976

Icebreakers: 4k, Aleksandr Sibiryakov. 6k, Georgi Sedov. 10k, Sadko. 12k, Dezhnev. 14k, Siberia. 16k, Lena. 20k, Amguyema.

Lithographed and Engraved

1977, July 27   **Perf. 12x11½**
4579	A2145	4k multicolored	.25 .25
4580	A2145	6k multicolored	.40 .25
4581	A2145	10k multicolored	.75 .25
4582	A2145	12k multicolored	1.00 .25
4583	A2145	14k multicolored	1.25 .25
4584	A2145	16k multicolored	1.50 .35
4585	A2145	20k multicolored	1.75 .45
		Nos. 4579-4585 (7)	6.90 2.05

Souvenir Sheet

Icebreaker Arctica — A2171

Lithographed and Engraved

1977, Sept. 15   **Perf. 12½x12**
4586 A2171 50k multicolored   5.00 3.00

Arctica, first ship to travel from Murmansk to North Pole, Aug. 9-17.

View and Arms of Stavropol — A2172

1977, Aug. 16   **Photo.**   **Perf. 11½**
4587 A2172 6k multicolored   .50 .25

200th anniversary of Stavropol.

Stamps and Exhibition Emblem — A2173

1977, Aug. 16
4588 A2173 4k multicolored   .50 .25

October Revolution Anniversary Philatelic Exhibition, Moscow.

Yuri A. Gagarin and Spacecraft — A2174

No. 4590, Alexei Leonov floating in space. No. 4591, Orbiting space station, cosmonauts at control panel. Nos. 4592-4594, Various spacecraft: No. 4592, International cooperation for space research. No. 4593, Interplanetary flights. No. 4594, Exploring earth's atmosphere. 50k, "XX," laurel, symbolic Sputnik with Red Star.

1977, Oct. 4   **Photo.**   **Perf. 11½x12**
4589	A2174	10k sepia & multi	.25 .25
4590	A2174	10k gray & multi	.25 .25
4591	A2174	10k gray green & multi	.25 .25
4592	A2174	20k green & multi	.45 .35
4593	A2174	20k vio bl & multi	.45 .35
4594	A2174	20k bister & multi	.45 .35
		Nos. 4589-4594 (6)	2.10 1.80

Souvenir Sheet
4595 A2174 50k claret & gold   5.00 5.00

20th anniv. of space research. No. 4595 contains one stamp, size: 22x32mm.

Types of 1976

Designs: 15k, Communications emblem and globes; others as before.

1977-78   **Litho.**   **Perf. 12x12½**
4596	A2138	1k olive green	.25 .25
4597	A2138	2k lilac rose	.25 .25
4598	A2139	3k brick red	.25 .25
4599	A2138	4k vermilion	.25 .25
4600	A2139	6k Prus blue	.30 .25
4601	A2138	10k gray green	.50 .25
4602	A2139	12k vio blue	.65 .25
4602A	A2139	15k blue ('78)	5.00 .35
4603	A2139	16k slate green	.80 .25

Perf. 12½x12
4604	A2140	20k brown red	.80 .25
4605	A2141	30k dull brick red	1.10 .25
4606	A2142	50k brown	1.25 .25
4607	A2143	1r dark blue	3.75 .25
		Nos. 4596-4607 (13)	15.15 3.25

Nos. 4596-4602A, 4604-4607 were printed on dull and shiny paper.
For overprint see No. 5720. For surcharges see Uzbekistan Nos. 16-17, 23, 27-29, 61A.

Souvenir Sheet

Bas-relief, 12th Century, Cathedral of St. Dimitri, Vladimir — A2175

6k, Necklace, Ryazan excavations, 12th cent. 10k, Mask, Cathedral of the Nativity, Suzdal, 13th cent. 12k, Archangel Michael, 15th cent. icon. 16k, Chalice by Ivan Fomin,

1449. 20k, St. Basil's Cathedral, Moscow, 16th cent.

1977, Oct. 12   **Litho.**   **Perf. 12**
4608		Sheet of 6	3.00 1.25
a.		A2175 4k gold & black	.25 .25
b.		A2175 6k gold & multi	.25 .25
c.		A2175 10k gold & multi	.25 .25
d.		A2175 12k gold & multi	.25 .25
e.		A2175 16k gold & multi	.35 .25
f.		A2175 20k gold & multi	.35 .25

Masterpieces of old Russian culture.

Fir, Snowflake, Molniya Satellite — A2176

1977, Oct. 12   **Perf. 12x12½**
4609 A2176 4k multicolored   1.00 .25

New Year 1978.

Cruiser Aurora and Torch A2177

1977, Oct. 26   **Photo.**   **Perf. 12x11½**
4610	A2177	4k gold, red & blk	.25 .25
4611	A2177	4k gold, red & blk	.25 .25
4612	A2177	4k gold, red & blk	.25 .25
4613	A2177	4k gold, red & blk	.25 .25
		Nos. 4610-4613 (4)	1.00 1.00

Souvenir Sheet   **Perf. 11½**

60th Anniversary of Revolution Medal — A2178

4614 A2178 30k gold, red & blk   1.50 .60

60th Anniv. of October Revolution: No. 4611, Lenin speaking at Finland Station (monument), 1917. No. 4612, 1917 Peace Decree, Brezhnev's book about Lenin. No. 4613, Kremlin tower with star and fireworks.

Flag of USSR, Constitution (Book) with Coat of Arms — A2179

Designs: No. 4616, Red banner, people and cover of constitution. 50k, Constitution, Kremlin and olive branch.

1977, Oct. 31   **Litho.**   **Perf. 12½x12**
4615	A2179	4k red, black & yel	.25 .25
4616	A2179	4k red, black & yel	.25 .25

Souvenir Sheet   Perf. 11½x12½

Lithographed and Embossed
4617 A2179 50k red, gold & yel   2.00 1.00

Adoption of new constitution. No. 4617 contains one 70x50mm stamp.

Souvenir Sheet   Perf. 11½x12½

Leonid Brezhnev — A2180

Lithographed and Embossed
1977, Nov. 2   **Perf. 11½x12**
4618 A2180 50k gold & multi   4.00 1.00

Adoption of new constitution, General Secretary Brezhnev, chairman of Constitution Commission.

Postal Official and Postal Code — A2181

Mail Processing (Woman Postal Official and): No. 4620, Mail collection and Moskvich 430 car. No. 4621, Automatic letter sorting machine. No. 4622, Mail transport by truck, train, ship and planes. No. 4623, Mail delivery in city and country.

Lithographed and Engraved
1977, Nov. 16   **Perf. 12½x12**
4619	A2181	4k multicolored	.35 .25
4620	A2181	4k multicolored	.35 .25
4621	A2181	4k multicolored	.35 .25
4622	A2181	4k multicolored	.35 .25
4623	A2181	4k multicolored	.35 .25
		Nos. 4619-4623 (5)	1.75 1.25

Capital, Asoka Pillar, Red Fort — A2182

1977, Dec. 14   **Photo.**   **Perf. 11½**
4624 A2182 6k maroon, gold & red   .60 .25

30th anniversary of India's independence.

Proclamation Monument, Charkov A2183

1977, Dec. 14   **Litho.**   **Perf. 12x12½**
4625 A2183 6k multicolored   .50 .25

60th anniv. of Soviet power in the Ukraine.

Lebetina Viper — A2184

Protected Fauna: 1k to 12k, Venomous snakes, useful for medicinal purposes. 16k, Polar bear and cub. 20k, Walrus and calf. 30k, Tiger and cub.

Photogravure and Engraved
1977, Dec. 16   *Perf. 11½x12*
4626 A2184 1k black & multi   .25   .25
4627 A2184 4k black & multi   .25   .25
4628 A2184 6k black & multi   .25   .25
4629 A2184 10k black & multi   .35   .25
4630 A2184 12k black & multi   .45   .25
4631 A2184 16k black & multi   .55   .25
4632 A2184 20k black & multi   .75   .25
4633 A2184 30k black & multi   1.00   .35
    Nos. 4626-4633 (8)   3.85 2.10

Wheat, Combine, Silos — A2185

1978, Jan. 27   Photo.   Perf. 11½
4634 A2185 4k multicolored   .50   .25
    Gigant collective grain farm, Rostov Region, 50th anniversary.

Congress Palace, Spasski Tower — A2186

1978, Jan. 27   Litho.   Perf. 12x12½
4635 A2186 4k multicolored   .50   .25
    Young Communist League, Lenin's Komsomol, 60th anniv. and its 25th Cong.

Liberation Obelisk, Emblem, Dove — A2187

1978, Jan. 27   Photo.   Perf. 11½
4636 A2187 6k multicolored   .50   .25
    8th Congress of International Federation of Resistance Fighters, Minsk, Belorussia.

Soldiers Leaving for the Front — A2188

Designs: No. 4638, Defenders of Moscow Monument, Lenin banner. No. 4639, Soldier as defender of the people.

1978, Feb. 21   Litho.   Perf. 12½x12
4637 A2188 4k red & multi   .50   .25
4638 A2188 4k red & multi   .50   .25
4639 A2188 4k red & multi   .50   .25
    Nos. 4637-4639 (3)   1.50   .75
    60th anniversary of USSR Military forces.

Celebration in Village — A2189

Kustodiev Paintings: 6k, Shrovetide (winter landscape). 10k, Morning, by Kustodiev. 12k, Merchant's Wife Drinking Tea. 20k, Bolshevik. 50k, Self-portrait, vert.

1978, Mar. 3   Perf. 11½
            Size: 70x33mm
4640 A2189 4k lilac & multi   .25   .25
4641 A2189 6k lilac & multi   .30   .25
            Size: 47x32mm
            Perf. 12½x12
4642 A2189 10k lilac & multi   .50   .25
4643 A2189 12k lilac & multi   .65   .25
4644 A2189 20k lilac & multi   .85   .25
    Nos. 4640-4644 (5)   2.55 1.25
            Souvenir Sheet
            Perf. 11½x12½
4644A A2189 50k lilac & multi   2.00   .75
    Boris Mikhailovich Kustodiev (1878-1927), painter. Nos. 4642-4644 have se-tenant label showing museum where painting is kept. No. 4644A has label giving short biography.

Docking in Space, Intercosmos Emblem A2190

Designs: 6k, Rocket, Soviet Cosmonaut Aleksei Gubarev and Czechoslovak Capt. Vladimir Remek on launching pad. 32k, Parachute, helicopter, Intercosmos emblem, USSR and Czechoslovakian flags.

1978, Mar. 10   Litho.   Perf. 12x12½
4645 A2190 6k multicolored   .25   .25
4646 A2190 15k multicolored   .60   .25
4647 A2190 32k multicolored   1.20   .40
    Nos. 4645-4647 (3)   2.05   .90
    Intercosmos, Soviet-Czechoslovak cooperative space program.

Festival Emblem — A2191

1978, Mar. 17   Litho.   Perf. 12x12½
4648 A2191 4k blue & multi   .50   .25
    11th Youth & Students' Cong., Havana.

Tulip, Bolshoi Theater A2192

Moscow Flowers: 2k, Rose "Moscow morning" and Lomonosov University. 4k, Dahlia "Red Star" and Spasski Tower. 10k, Gladiolus "Moscovite" and VDNH Building. 12k, Ilich anniversary iris and Lenin Central Museum.

1978, Mar. 17   Perf. 12½x12
4649 A2192 1k multicolored   .40   .25
4650 A2192 2k multicolored   .40   .25
4651 A2192 4k multicolored   .40   .25
4652 A2192 10k multicolored   .40   .25
4653 A2192 12k multicolored   .40   .25
    Nos. 4649-4653 (5)   2.00 1.25

IMCO Emblem and Waves — A2193

1978, Mar. 17   Litho.   Perf. 12x12½
4654 A2193 6k multicolored   .50   .25
    Intergovernmental Maritime Consultative Org., 20th anniv., and World Maritime Day.

Spaceship, Orbits of Salyut 5, Soyuz 26 and 27 — A2194

1978, Apr. 12   Photo.   Perf. 12
4655 A2194 6k blue, dk blue & gold   .50   .25
    Cosmonauts' Day, Apr. 12.

World Federation of Trade Unions Emblem — A2195

1978, Apr. 16   Perf. 12
4656 A2195 6k multicolored   .50   .25
    9th World Trade Union Congress, Prague.

2-2-0 Locomotive, 1845, Petersburg and Moscow Stations — A2196

Locomotives: 1k, 1st Russian model by E. A. and M. W. Cherepanov, vert. 2k, 1-3-0 freight, 1845. 16k, Aleksandrov 0-3-0, 1863. 20k, 2-2-0 passenger and Sergievsk Pustyn platform, 1863.

1978, Apr. 20   Litho.   Perf. 11½
4657 A2196 1k orange & multi   .25   .25
4658 A2196 2k ultra & multi   .25   .25
4659 A2196 3k yellow & multi   .30   .25

4660 A2196 16k green & multi   1.20   .25
4661 A2196 20k rose & multi   1.00   .25
    Nos. 4657-4661 (5)   3.00 1.25
            Souvenir Sheet

Lenin, by V. A. Serov — A2197

1978, Apr. 22   Perf. 12x12½
4662 A2197 50k multicolored   2.00   .75
    108th anniversary of the birth of Lenin.

A2198

No. 4663, Soyuz and Salyut 6 docking in space. No. 4664, Y. V. Romanenko and G. M. Grechko.

1978, June 15   Perf. 12
4663 15k multicolored   .40   .25
4664 15k multicolored   .40   .25
   a. A2198 Pair, #4663-4664   1.00   .40
    Photographic survey and telescopic observations of stars by crews of Soyuz 26, Soyuz 27 and Soyuz 28, Dec. 10, 1977-Mar. 16, 1978. Nos. 4663-4664 printed se-tenant with label showing schematic pictures of various experiments.

Space Meteorology, Rockets, Spaceship, Earth — A2200

No. 4665, Natural resources of earth and Soyuz. No. 4667, Space communications, "Orbita" Station and Molnyia satellite. No. 4668, Man, earth and Vostok. 50k, Study of magnetosphere, Prognoz over earth.

1978, June 23   Perf. 12x12½
4665 A2200 10k green & multi   .50   .25
4666 A2200 10k blue & multi   .50   .25
4667 A2200 10k violet & multi   .50   .25
4668 A2200 10k rose lil & multi   .50   .25
    Nos. 4665-4668 (4)   2.00 1.00
            Souvenir Sheet
            Perf. 11½x12½
4669 A2200 50k multicolored   2.00   .75
    Space explorations of the Intercosmos program. #4669 contains one 36x51mm stamp.

Soyuz Rocket on Carrier — A2201

Designs (Flags of USSR and Poland, Intercosmos Emblem): 15k, Crystal, spaceship (Sirena, experimental crystallogenesis in space). 32k, Research ship "Cosmonaut Vladimir Komarov," spaceship, world map and paths of Salyut 6, Soyuz 29-30.

1978,	Litho.	Perf. 12½x12		
4670	A2201	6k multicolored	.25	.25
4671	A2201	15k multicolored	.40	.25
4672	A2201	32k multicolored	.80	.40
		Nos. 4670-4672 (3)	1.45	.90

Intercosmos, Soviet-Polish cooperative space program. Issued: 6k, 6/28; 15k, 6/30; 32k, 7/5.

Lenin, Awards Received by Komsomol A2202

Kamaz Car, Train, Bridge, Hammer and Sickle — A2203

1978, July 5		Perf. 12x12½		
4673	A2202	4k multicolored	.25	.25
4674	A2203	4k multicolored	.25	.25

Leninist Young Communist League (Komsomol), 60th anniv. (#4673); Komsomol's participation in 5-year plan (#4674).
For overprint see No. 4703.

M. V. Zaharov (1898-1972), Marshal of the Soviet Union — A2204

1978, July 5	Engr.		Perf. 12	
4675	A2204	4k sepia	.50	.25

Torch, Flags of Participants A2205

1978, July 25 Litho.		Perf. 12x12½		
4676	A2205	4k multicolored	.50	.25

Construction of Soyuz gas-pipeline (Friendship Line), Orenburg. Flags of participating countries shown: Bulgaria, Hungary, German Democratic Republic, Poland, Romania, USSR, Czechoslovakia.

Dr. William Harvey (1578-1657), Discoverer of Blood Circulation — A2206

1978, July 25		Perf. 12		
4677	A2206	6k blue, blk & dp grn	.50	.25

Nikolai Gavilovich Chernyshevsky (1828-1889), Revolutionary — A2207

1978, July 30	Engr.		Perf. 12x12½	
4678	A2207	4k brown, yellow	.50	.25

Whitewinged Petrel A2208

Antarctic Fauna: 1k, Crested penguin, horiz. 4k, Emperor penguin and chick. 6k, White-blooded pikes. 10k, Sea elephant, horiz.

Perf. 12x11½, 11½x12				
1978, July 30			Litho.	
4679	A2208	1k multicolored	1.00	.25
4680	A2208	3k multicolored	1.00	.25
4681	A2208	4k multicolored	1.00	.25
4682	A2208	6k multicolored	1.00	.25
4683	A2208	10k multicolored	1.00	.25
		Nos. 4679-4683 (5)	5.00	1.25

The Red Horse, by Petrov-Votkin — A2209

Paintings by Petrov-Votkin: 6k, Mother and Child, Petrograd, 1918. 10k, Death of the Commissar. 12k, Still-life with Fruit. 16k, Still-life with Teapot and Flowers. 50k, Self-portrait, 1918, vert.

1978, Aug. 16 Litho.		Perf. 12½x12		
4684	A2209	4k silver & multi	.25	.25
4685	A2209	6k silver & multi	.35	.25
4686	A2209	10k silver & multi	.55	.25
4687	A2209	12k silver & multi	.85	.25
4688	A2209	16k silver & multi	1.00	.25
		Nos. 4684-4688 (5)	3.00	1.25

Souvenir Sheet
Perf. 11½x12

4689	A2209	4k silver & multi	1.50	.75

Kozma Sergeevich Petrov-Votkin (1878-1939), painter. Nos. 4684-4688 have se-tenant labels. No. 4689 has label the size of stamp.

Soyuz 31 in Shop, Intercosmos Emblem, USSR and DDR Flags A2210

Designs (Intercosmos Emblem, USSR and German Democratic Republic Flags and): 15k, Pamir Mountains photographed from space; 32k, Salyut 6, Soyuz 29 and 31 complex and spectrum. 32k, Soyuz 31 docking, photographed from Salyut 6.

1978	Litho.	Perf. 12x12½		
4690	A2210	6k multicolored	.25	.25
4691	A2210	15k multicolored	.40	.25
4692	A2210	32k multicolored	1.00	.45
		Nos. 4690-4692 (3)	1.65	.95

Intercosmos, Soviet-East German cooperative space program.
Issued: 6k, 8/27; 15k, 8/31; 32k, 9/3.

PRAGA '78 Emblem, Plane, Radar, Spaceship A2211

Photogravure and Engraved

1978, Aug. 29		Perf. 11½		
4693	A2211	6k multicolored	.50	.25

PRAGA '78 International Philatelic Exhibition, Prague, Sept. 8-17.

Leo Tolstoi (1828-1910), Novelist and Philosopher A2212

1978, Sept. 7	Engr.		Perf. 12x12½	
4694	A2212	4k slate green	1.40	.90

Stag, Conference Emblem — A2213

1978		Photo.	Perf. 11½	
4695	A2213	4k multicolored	.25	.25

14th General Assembly of the Society for Wildlife Preservation, Ashkhabad.

Bronze Figure, Erebuni, 8th Century A2214

Armenian Architecture: 6k, Etchmiadzin Cathedral, 4th century. 10k, Stone crosses, Dzaghkatzor, 13th century. 12k, Library, Erevan, horiz. 16k, Lenin statue, Lenin Square, Erevan, horiz.

1978	Litho.	Perf. 12x12½, 12½x12		
4696	A2214	4k multicolored	.25	.25
4697	A2214	6k multicolored	.25	.25
4698	A2214	10k multicolored	.30	.25
4699	A2214	12k multicolored	.40	.25
4700	A2214	16k multicolored	.50	.25
		Nos. 4696-4700 (5)	1.70	1.25

Issued: 4k, 10k, 16k, 9/12; others, 10/14.

Memorial, Messina, Russian Warships A2215

1978, Sept. 12	Photo.		Perf. 11½	
4701	A2215	6k multicolored	.50	.25

70th anniversary of aid given by Russian sailors during Messina earthquake.

Communications Emblem, Ostankino TV Tower — A2216

1978, Sept. 20	Photo.		Perf. 11½	
4702	A2216	4k multicolored	.50	.25

Organization for Communication Cooperation of Socialist Countries, 20th anniv.

No. 4673 Overprinted

1978, Sept. 20	Litho.		Perf. 12x12½	
4703	A2202	4k multicolored	2.00	.70

Philatelic Exhibition for the Leninist Young Communist League.

Souvenir Sheet

Diana, by Paolo Veronese — A2217

1978, Sept. 28	Litho.		Perf. 12x11½	
4704	A2217	50k multicolored	2.00	1.00

Veronese (1528-88), Italian painter.

Souvenir Sheet

Kremlin, Moscow — A2218

Lithographed and Embossed
1978, Oct. 7   *Perf. 11½x12*
4705 A2218 30k gold & multi   2.00 .65
Russian Constitution, 1st anniversary.

Stepan Georgevich
Shaumyan (1878-
1918), Communist
Party Functionary
A2219

1978, Oct. 11   **Engr.**   *Perf. 12½x12*
4706 A2219 4k slate green   .50 .25

Ferry, Russian and
Bulgarian
Colors — A2220

1978, Oct. 14   **Photo.**   *Perf. 11½*
4707 A2220 6k multicolored   .50 .25
Opening of Ilychovsk-Varna Ferry.

Hammer and
Sickle,
Flags — A2221

1978, Oct. 26   **Photo.**   *Perf. 11½*
4708 A2221 4k gold & multi   .50 .25
61st anniversary of October Revolution.

Silver Gilt Cup, Novgorod, 12th
Century — A2222

Old Russian Art: 10k, Pokrowna Nerli
Church, 12th century, vert. 12k, St. George
Slaying the Dragon, icon, Novgorod, 15th cen-
tury, vert. 16k, The Czar, cannon, 1586.

Perf. 12½x12, 12x12½
1978, Nov. 28   **Litho.**
4709 A2222 6k multicolored   .25 .25
4710 A2222 10k multicolored   .45 .25
4711 A2222 12k multicolored   .50 .25
4712 A2222 16k multicolored   .75 .25
   Nos. 4709-4712 (4)   1.95 1.00

Oncology Institute,
Emblem — A2223

1978, Dec. 1   **Photo.**   *Perf. 11½*
4713 A2223 4k multicolored   .50 .25
P.A. Herzen Tumor Institute, 75th anniv.

Savior Tower,
Kremlin — A2224

1978, Dec. 20   **Litho.**   *Perf. 12x12½*
4714 A2224 4k silver, blue & red   .50 .25
     New Year 1979.

Nestor Pechersky, Chronicler, c.
885 — A2225

History of Postal Service: 6k, Birch bark letter and stylus. 10k, Messenger with trumpet
and staff, from 14th century Psalm book. 12k,
Winter traffic, from 16th century book by
Sigizmund Gerberstein. 16k, Prikaz post
office, from 17th century icon.

Lithographed and Engraved
1978, Dec. 20   *Perf. 12½x12*
4715 A2225 4k multicolored   .25 .25
4716 A2225 6k multicolored   .25 .25
4717 A2225 10k multicolored   .50 .25
4718 A2225 12k multicolored   .55 .25
4719 A2225 16k multicolored   .65 .25
   Nos. 4715-4719 (5)   2.20 1.25

Kovalenok and Ivanchenkov, Salyut 6-
Soyuz — A2226

1978, Dec. 20   **Photo.**   *Perf. 11½x12*
4720 A2226 10k multicolored   .50 .25
Cosmonauts V. V. Kovalenok and A. S.
Ivanchenkov spent 140 days in space, June
15-Nov. 2, 1978.

Vasilii Pronchishchev — A2227

Icebreakers: 6k, Captain Belousov, 1954,
vert. 10k, Moscow. 12k, Admiral Makarov,

1974. 16k, Lenin, 1959, vert. 20k, Nuclear-
powered Arctica.

Perf. 11½x12, 12x11½
1978, Dec. 20   **Photo. & Engr.**
4721 A2227 4k multicolored   .25 .25
4722 A2227 6k multicolored   .35 .25
4723 A2227 10k multicolored   .45 .25
4724 A2227 12k multicolored   .60 .25
4725 A2227 16k multicolored   .70 .25
4726 A2227 20k multicolored   .80 .25
   Nos. 4721-4726 (6)   3.15 1.50

Souvenir Sheet

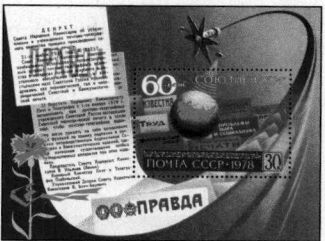

Mastheads and Globe with
Russia — A2228

1978, Dec. 28   **Litho.**   *Perf. 12*
4727 A2228 30k multicolored   1.50 .35
Distribution of periodicals through the Post
and Telegraph Department, 60th anniversary.

Cuban Flags
Forming
Star — A2229

1979, Jan. 1   **Photo.**   *Perf. 11½*
4728 A2229 6k multicolored   .50 .25
Cuban Revolution, 20th anniversary.

Russian and Byelorussian Flags,
Government Building, Minsk — A2230

1979, Jan. 1
4729 A2230 4k multicolored   .50 .25
Byelorussian SSR and Byelorussian Communist Party, 60th annivs.

Ukrainian and
Russian Flags,
Reunion
Monument
A2231

1979, Jan. 16
4730 A2231 4k multicolored   .50 .25
Reunion of Ukraine & Russia, 325th anniv.

Old and
New
Vilnius
University
Buildings
A2232

1979, Jan. 16   **Photo. & Engr.**
4731 A2232 4k black & salmon   .50 .25
400th anniversary of University of Vilnius.

Bulgaria
No. 1 and
Exhibition
Hall
A2233

1979, Jan. 25   **Litho.**   *Perf. 12½x12*
4732 A2233 15k multicolored   .50 .25
Filaserdica '79 Philatelic Exhibition, Sofia,
for centenary of Bulgarian postal service.

Sputniks, Soviet
Radio Hams
Emblem — A2234

1979, Feb. 23   **Photo.**   *Perf. 11½*
4733 A2234 4k multicolored   .50 .25
Sputnik satellites Radio 1 and Radio 2,
launched, Oct. 1978.

1-3-0 Locomotive, 1878 — A2235

Locomotives: 3k, 1-4-0, 1912. 4k, 2-3-1,
1915. 6k, 1-3-1, 1925. 15k, 1-5-0, 1947.

1979, Feb. 23   **Litho.**   *Perf. 11½*
4734 A2235 2k multicolored   .25 .25
4735 A2235 3k multicolored   .25 .25
4736 A2235 4k multicolored   .25 .25
4737 A2235 6k multicolored   .40 .25
4738 A2235 15k multicolored   1.00 .25
   Nos. 4734-4738 (5)   2.15 1.25

Souvenir Sheet

Medal for Land Development — A2236

1979, Mar. 14   *Perf. 11½x12½*
4739 A2236 50k multicolored   2.00 .75
25th anniv. of drive to develop virgin lands.

Venera 11 and 12 over Venus — A2237

1979, Mar. 16   Photo.   *Perf. 11½*
4740 A2237 10k multicolored   .50   .25
Interplanetary flights of Venera 11 and Venera 12, December 1978.

Albert Einstein, Equation and Signature A2238

1979, Mar. 16
4741 A2238 6k multicolored   .50   .25
Einstein (1879-1955), theoretical physicist.

Congress Emblem A2239

1979, Mar. 16
4742 A2239 6k multicolored   .50   .25
21st World Veterinary Congress, Moscow.

"To Arms," by Robert Berény (1887-1953) — A2240

1979, Mar. 21
4743 A2240 4k multicolored   .50   .25
Soviet Republic of Hungary, 60th anniv.

Salyut 6, Soyuz, Research Ship, Letters — A2241

1979, Apr. 12   Litho.   *Perf. 11½x12*
4744 A2241 15k multicolored   .50   .25
Cosmonauts' Day.

Souvenir Sheet

Ice Hockey — A2242

1979, Apr. 14   Photo.   *Perf. 12x11½*
4745 A2242 50k multicolored   2.00   .75
World and European Ice Hockey Championships, Moscow, Apr. 14-27.
For overprint see No. 4751.

Souvenir Sheet

Lenin — A2243

1979, Apr. 18
4746 A2243 50k red, gold & brn   1.50   .75
109th anniversary of the birth of Lenin.

Astronauts' Training Center A2244

Design: 32k, Astronauts, landing capsule, radar, helicopter and emblem.

1979, Apr. 12   Litho.   *Perf. 11½*
4747 A2244 6k multicolored   .30   .25
4748 A2244 32k multicolored   .70   .40
Joint Soviet-Bulgarian space flight.

Exhibition Emblem — A2245

1979, Apr. 18   Photo.   *Perf. 11½*
4749 A2245 15k sil, red & vio
             blue   1.00   .25
National USSR Exhibition in the United Kingdom. Se-tenant label with commemorative inscription.

Blast Furnace, Pushkin Theater, "Tent" Sculpture — A2246

1979, May 24   Photo.   *Perf. 11½*
4750 A2246 4k multicolored   .50   .25
50th anniversary of Magnitogorsk City.

No. 4745 Overprinted in Red

1979, May 24   *Perf. 12x11½*
4751 A2242 50k multicolored   2.00   .80
Victory of Soviet team in World and European Ice Hockey Championships.

Infant, Flowers, IYC Emblem — A2247

1979, June 1   Litho.   *Perf. 12x12½*
4752 A2247 4k multicolored   .50   .25
International Year of the Child.

Horn Player and Bears Playing Balalaika, Bogorodsk Wood Carvings — A2248

Folk Art: 3k, Decorated wooden bowls, Khokhloma. 4k, Tray decorated with flowers, Zhestovo. 6k, Carved bone boxes, Kholmogory. 15k, Lace, Vologda.

1979, June 14   Litho.   *Perf. 12½x12*
4753 A2248 2k multicolored   .25   .25
4754 A2248 3k multicolored   .25   .25
4755 A2248 4k multicolored   .25   .25
4756 A2248 6k multicolored   .25   .25
4757 A2248 15k multicolored   .25   .25
      Nos. 4753-4757 (5)   1.25 1.25
Nos. 4753-4757 printed in sheets of 7 stamps and decorative label. Value, set with attached labels, $3.

V. A. Djanibekov, O. G. Makarov, Spacecraft A2249

1979, June   *Perf. 12x11½*
4758 A2249 4k multicolored   .50   .25
Flights of Soyuz 26-27 and work on board of orbital complex Salyut 6.

COMECON Building, Members' Flags — A2250

1979, June 26   *Perf. 12*
4759 A2250 16k multicolored   .50   .25
Council for Mutual Economic Aid of Socialist Countries, 30th anniversary.

Scene from "Potemkin" and Festival Emblem — A2251

Photogravure and Engraved
1979, July   *Perf. 11½*
4760 A2251 15k multicolored   .50   .25
11th International Film Festival, Moscow, and 60th anniversary of Soviet film industry.

Lenin Square Station, Tashkent A2252

1979, July   Litho.   *Perf. 12*
4761 A2252 4k multicolored   .50   .25
Tashkent subway.

Souvenir Sheets

Atom Symbol, Factories, Dam — A2253

1979, July 23   Photo.   *Perf. 11½x12*
4762 A2253 30k multicolored   2.00 .45
50th anniversary of 1st Five-Year Plan.

USSR Philatelic Society Emblem — A2254

1979, July 25   Litho.   *Perf. 12x12½*
4763 A2254 50k gray grn & red   2.00 .70
4th Cong. of USSR Phil. Soc., Moscow.

Exhibition Hall, Scene from "Chapayev" A2255

1979, Aug. 8   Photo.   *Perf. 11½*
4764 A2255 4k multicolored   .50 .25
60th anniversary of Soviet Film and Exhibition of History of Soviet Film.

Roses, by P. P. Konchalovsky, 1955 — A2256

Russian Flower Paintings: 1k, Flowers and Fruit, by I. F. Khrutsky, 1830. 2k, Phlox, by I. N. Kramskoi, 1884. 3k, Lilac, by K. A. Korovin, 1915. 15k, Bluebells, by S. V. Gerasimov, 1944. 2k, 3k, 15k, vert.

Perf. 12½x12, 12x12½
1979, Aug. 16   **Litho.**
4765 A2256 1k multicolored   .25 .25
4766 A2256 2k multicolored   .25 .25
4767 A2256 3k multicolored   .25 .25
4768 A2256 15k multicolored   .30 .25
4769 A2256 32k multicolored   .45 .30
    Nos. 4765-4769 (5)   1.50 1.30

John Maclean — A2257

1979, Aug. 29   Litho.   *Perf. 11½*
4770 A2257 4k red & black   .50 .25
John Maclean (1879-1923), Scottish Communist labor leader.

Soviet Circus Emblem — A2258

1979, Sept.
4771 A2258 4k multicolored   .50 .25
Soviet Circus, 60th anniversary.

Friendship — A2259

Children's Drawings: 3k, Children and Horses. 4k, Dances. 15k, The Excursion.

1979, Sept. 10   *Perf. 12½x12*
4772 A2259 2k multicolored   .50 .25
4773 A2259 3k multicolored   .50 .25
4774 A2259 4k multicolored   .50 .25
4775 A2259 15k multicolored   .50 .25
    Nos. 4772-4775 (4)   2.00 1.00
International Year of the Child. Exist imperf. Value, $50 each.

Oriolus oriolus — A2260

Birds: 3k, Dendrocopus minor. 4k, Parus cristatus. 10k, Tyto alba. 15k, Caprimulgus europaeus.

1979, Sept. 18
4776 A2260 2k multicolored   .25 .25
4777 A2260 3k multicolored   .25 .25
4778 A2260 4k multicolored   .45 .25
4779 A2260 10k multicolored   .90 .25
4780 A2260 15k multicolored   1.40 .25
    Nos. 4776-4780 (5)   3.25 1.25

German Arms, Marx, Engels, Lenin, Berlin A2261

1979, Oct. 7   Photo.   *Perf. 11½*
4781 A2261 6k multicolored   .50 .25
German Democratic Republic, 30th anniv.

Valery Ryumin, Vladimir Lyakhov, Salyut 6 — A2262

Design: No. 4783, Spacecraft.

1979, Oct. 10   *Perf. 12x11½*
4782 A2262 15k multicolored   .50 .25
4783 A2262 15k multicolored   .50 .25
a. Pair, #4782-4783   1.25 .75
175 days in space, Feb. 25-Aug. 19. No. 4783a has continuous design.

Star — A2264

1979, Oct. 18   *Perf. 11½*
4784 A2264 4k multicolored   .50 .25
USSR Signal Troops, 60th anniversary.

Hammer and Sickle — A2265

1979, Oct. 18
4785 A2265 4k multicolored   .50 .25
October Revolution, 62nd anniversary.

Katherina, by T. G. Shevchenko A2266

Ukrainian Paintings: 3k, Working Girl, by K.K. Kostandi. 4k, Lenin's Return to Petrograd, by A.M. Lopuhov. 10k, Soldier's Return, by N.V. Kostetsky. 15k, Going to Work, by M.G. Belsky.

1979, Nov. 18   Litho.   *Perf. 12x12½*
4786 A2266 2k multicolored   .25 .25
4787 A2266 3k multicolored   .25 .25
4788 A2266 4k multicolored   .25 .25
4789 A2266 10k multicolored   .50 .25
4790 A2266 15k multicolored   .75 .25
    Nos. 4786-4790 (5)   2.00 1.25

Shabolovka Radio Tower, Moscow — A2267

1979, Nov. 28   Photo.   *Perf. 12*
4791 A2267 32k multicolored   .50 .35
Radio Moscow, 50th anniversary.

Mischa Holding Stamp — A2268

1979, Nov. 28   *Perf. 12x12½*
4792 A2268 4k multicolored   .90 .25
New Year 1980.

Hand Holding Peace Message — A2269

Peace Program in Action: No. 4794, Hands holding cultural symbols. No. 4795, Hammer and sickle, flag.

1979, Dec. 5   Litho.   *Perf. 12*
4793 A2269 4k multicolored   .65 .25
4794 A2269 4k multicolored   .65 .25
4795 A2269 4k multicolored   .65 .25
    Nos. 4793-4795 (3)   1.95 .75

Policeman, Patrol Car, Helicopter A2270

Traffic Safety: 4k, Car, girl and ball. 6k, Speeding cars.

1979, Dec. 20   *Perf. 12x12½*
4796 A2270 3k multicolored   .50 .25
4797 A2270 4k multicolored   .50 .25
4798 A2270 6k multicolored   .50 .25
    Nos. 4796-4798 (3)   1.50 .75

Vulkanolog — A2271

Research Ships and Portraits: 2k, Professor Bogorov. 4k, Ernst Krenkel. 6k, Vladislav Volkov. 10k, Cosmonaut Yuri Gagarin. 15k, Academician E.B. Kurchatov.

Lithographed and Engraved
1979, Dec. 25   *Perf. 12x11½*
4799 A2271 1k multicolored   .25 .25
4800 A2271 2k multicolored   .25 .25
4801 A2271 4k multicolored   .25 .25
4802 A2271 6k multicolored   .30 .25
4803 A2271 10k multicolored   .35 .25
4804 A2271 15k multicolored   .60 .25
    Nos. 4799-4804 (6)   2.00 1.50

See Nos. 4881-4886.

Souvenir Sheet

Explorers Raising Red Flag at North Pole — A2272

1979, Dec. 25   Photo.   Perf. 11½x12
4805 A2272 50k multicolored   2.00   .75
Komsomolskaya Pravda North Pole expedition.

Type of 1970

4k, Coat of arms, power line, factories.

1980, Jan. 10   Litho.   Perf. 12x12½
4806 A1794 4k carmine   .50   .25
Mordovian Autonomous SSR, 50th anniv.

Freestyle Skating A2273

1980, Jan. 22   Perf. 12x12½, 12½x12
4807 A2273 4k Speed skating, vert.   .25   .25
4808 A2273 6k shown   .25   .25
4809 A2273 10k Ice hockey   .25   .25
4810 A2273 15k Downhill skiing   .35   .25
4811 A2273 20k Luge, vert.   .50   .35
    Nos. 4807-4811 (5)   1.60   1.35

Souvenir Sheet

4812 A2273 50k Cross-country skiing, vert.   2.00   1.00
13th Winter Olympic Games, Lake Placid, NY, Feb. 12-24.
Nos. 4808, 4809 exist imperf. Value, $50 for both.

Nikolai Ilyitch Podvoiski (1880-1948), Revolutionary A2274

1980, Feb. 16   Engr.   Perf. 12½x12
4813 A2274 4k claret brown   1.00   .25

Rainbow, by A.K. Savrasov — A2275

No. 4815, Summer Harvest, by A.G. Venetsianov, vert. No. 4816, Old Erevan, by M.S. Saryan.

1980, Mar. 4   Litho.   Perf. 11½
4814 A2275 6k multicolored   .35   .25
4815 A2275 6k multicolored   .35   .25
4816 A2275 6k multicolored   .35   .25
    Nos. 4814-4816 (3)   1.05   .75

Souvenir Sheet

Cosmonaut Alexei Leonov — A2276

1980, Mar. 18   Litho.   Perf. 12½x12
4817 A2276 50k multicolored   1.50   .75
Man's first walk in space (Voskhod 2, Mar. 18-19, 1965).

Georg Ots, Estonian Artist — A2277

1980, Mar. 21   Engr.
4818 A2277 4k slate blue   .50   .25

Lenin Order, 50th Anniversary A2278

1980, Apr. 6   Photo.   Perf. 11½
4819 A2278 4k multicolored   .50   .25

Souvenir Sheet

Cosmonauts, Salyut 6 and Soyuz — A2279

1980, Apr. 12   Litho.   Perf. 12
4820 A2279 50k multicolored   1.50   1.00
Intercosmos cooperative space program.

Flags and Arms of Azerbaijan, Government House — A2280

1980, Apr. 22   Photo.
4821 A2280 4k multicolored   .50   .25
Azerbaijan Soviet Socialist Republic, Communist Party of Azerbaijan, 60th anniv.

Souvenir Sheet

Lenin, 110th Birth Anniversary — A2281

1980, Apr. 22   Perf. 12x11½
4822 A2281 30k multicolored   1.50   .75

"Mother Russia," Fireworks over Moscow — A2282

No. 4824, Soviet War Memorial, Berlin, raising of Red flag. No. 4825, Parade, Red Square, Moscow.

1980, Apr. 25   Litho.
4823 A2282 4k multicolored   .35   .25
4824 A2282 4k multicolored   .35   .25
4825 A2282 4k multicolored   .35   .25
    Nos. 4823-4825 (3)   1.05   .75
35th anniv. of victory in World War II. Nos. 4823, 4824 exist imperf. Value, $25 for both.

Workers' Monument A2283

1980, May 12   Litho.   Perf. 12
4826 A2283 4k multicolored   .50   .25
Workers' Delegates in Ivanovo-Voznesensk, 75th anniversary.

"XXV" — A2284

1980, May 14   Photo.   Perf. 11½
4827 A2284 32k multicolored   .50   .35
Signing of Warsaw Pact (Bulgaria, Czechoslovakia, German Democratic Rep., Hungary, Poland, Romania, USSR), 25th anniv.

YaK-24 Helicopter, 1953 — A2285

1980, May 15   Litho.   Perf. 12½x12
4828 A2285 1k shown   .25   .25
4829 A2285 2k MI-8, 1962   .25   .25
4830 A2285 3k KA-26, 1965   .25   .25
4831 A2285 6k MI-6, 1957   .25   .25
4832 A2285 15k MI-10   .35   .25
4833 A2285 32k V-12   .65   .40
    Nos. 4828-4833 (6)   2.00   1.65
Nos. 4832-4833 exist imperf. Value, $50 for both.

David Anhaght, Illuminated Manuscript A2286

1980, May 16   Perf. 12
4834 A2286 4k multicolored   .50   .25
David Anacht, Armenian philosopher, 1500th birth anniversary.

Emblem, Training Lab — A2287

15k, Cosmonauts meeting. 32k, Press conference.

1980, June 4
4835 A2287 6k shown   .25   .25
4836 A2287 15k multicolored   .40   .25
4837 A2287 32k multicolored   .85   .55
    Nos. 4835-4837 (3)   1.50   1.05
Intercosmos cooperative space program (USSR-Hungary).

Polar Fox A2288

2k, Dark silver fox, vert. 6k, Mink. 10k, Azerbaijan nutria, vert. 15k, Black sable.

1980, June 25   Litho.   Perf. 12x12½
4838 A2288 2k multicolored   .25   .25
4839 A2288 4k shown   .25   .25
4840 A2288 6k multicolored   .25   .25
4841 A2288 10k multicolored   .25   .25
4842 A2288 15k multicolored   .25   .25
    Nos. 4838-4842 (5)   1.25   1.25

Factory, Buildings, Arms of Tatar A.S.S.R. A2289

1980, June 25   Perf. 12
4843 A2289 4k multicolored   .50   .25
Tatar Autonomous SSR, 60th anniv.

College — A2290

1980, July 1   Photo.   Perf. 11½
4844 A2290 4k multicolored   .50   .25
 Bauman Technological College, Moscow, 150th anniversary.

Ho Chi Minh — A2291

1980, July 7
4845 A2291 6k multicolored   .50   .25

Red Flag, Lithuanian Arms, Flag, Red Guards Monument A2292

1980, July 12   Litho.   Perf. 12
4846 A2292 4k multicolored   .50   .25
 Lithuanian SSR, 40th anniv.

Russian Flag and Arms, Latvian Flag, Monument, Buildings A2293

 Design: No. 4848, Russian flag and arms, Estonian flag, monument, buildings.

1980, July 21   Litho.   Perf. 12
4847 A2293 4k multicolored   .35   .25
4848 A2293 4k multicolored   .35   .25
 Restoration of Soviet power.

Cosmonauts Boarding Soyuz A2294

1980, July 24   Perf. 12x12½
4849 A2294 6k shown   .25   .25
4850 A2294 15k Working aboard
                spacecraft   .45   .25
4851 A2294 32k Return flight   .80   .55
     Nos. 4849-4851 (3)   1.50 1.05
 Center for Cosmonaut Training, 20th anniv.

Avicenna (980-1037), Philosopher and Physician — A2295

**Photogravure and Engraved
1980, Aug. 16   Perf. 11½**
4852 A2295 4k multicolored   .50   .25

Soviet Racing Car KHADI-7 — A2296

1980, Aug. 25   Litho.   Perf. 12
4853 A2296 2k shown   .25   .25
4854 A2296 6k KHADI-10   .25   .25
4855 A2296 15k KHADI-113   .25   .25
4856 A2296 32k KHADI-133   .25   .25
     Nos. 4853-4856 (4)   1.00 1.00
 No. 4856 exists imperf. Value, $50.

Kazakhstan Republic, 60th Anniversary A2297

1980, Aug. 26
4857 A2297 4k multicolored   .50   .25

Ingres, Self-portrait, and Nymph A2298

1980, Aug. 29   Perf. 12x12½
4858 A2298 32k multicolored   .50   .35
 Jean Auguste Dominique Ingres (1780-1867), French painter.
 Exists imperf. Value, $25.

Morning on the Field of Kulikovo, by A. Bubnov — A2299

1980, Sept. 6   Litho.   Perf. 12
4859 A2299 4k multicolored   .50   .25
 Battle of Kulikovo, 600th anniversary.

Town Hall, Tartu — A2300

1980, Sept. 15   Photo.   Perf. 11½
4860 A2300 4k multicolored   .50   .25
 Tartu, 950th anniversary.

Y.V. Malyshev, V.V. Aksenov A2301

1980, Sept. 15   Litho.   Perf. 12x12½
4861 A2301 10k multicolored   .50   .25
 Soyuz T-2 space flight.

Flight Training, Yuri Gagarin — A2302

1980, Sept. 15   Photo.   Perf. 11½x12
4862 A2302 6k shown   .25   .25
4863 A2302 15k Space walk   .40   .25
4864 A2302 32k Endurance test   .85   .45
     Nos. 4862-4864 (3)   1.50   .95
 Gagarin Cosmonaut Training Center, 20th anniversary.

Intercosmos A2303

 6k, Intercosmos Emblem, Flags of USSR and Cuba, and Cosmonauts training. 15k, Inside weightless cabin. 32k, Landing.

1980, Sept. 15   Litho.   Perf. 12x12½
4865 A2303 6k multicolored   .25   .25
4866 A2303 15k multicolored   .40   .25
4867 A2303 32k multicolored   .85   .45
     Nos. 4865-4867 (3)   1.50   .95
 Intercosmos cooperative space program (USSR-Cuba).

October Revolution, 63rd Anniversary A2304

1980, Sept. 20   Photo.   Perf. 11½
4868 A2304 6k multicolored   .50   .25

David Guramishvili (1705-1792), Poet — A2305

1980, Sept. 20
4869 A2305 6k multicolored   .50   .25

Family with Serfs, by N.V. Nevrev (1830-1904) — A2305a

 Design: No. 4869B, Countess Tarakanova, by K.D. Flavitsky (1830-1866), vert.

1980, Sept. 25   Litho.   Perf. 11½
4869A A2305a 6k multicolored   .50   .25
4869B A2305a 6k multicolored   .50   .25

A.F. Ioffe (1880-1960), Physicist — A2306

1980, Sept. 29
4870 A2306 4k multicolored   .50   .25

Siberian Pine A2307

1980, Sept. 29   Litho.   Perf. 12½x12
4871 A2307 2k shown   .25   .25
4872 A2307 4k Oak   .25   .25
4873 A2307 6k Lime tree, vert.   .25   .25
4874 A2307 10k Sea bucthorn   .50   .25
4875 A2307 15k European ash   .75   .25
     Nos. 4871-4875 (5)   2.00 1.25

A.M. Vasilevsky (1895-1977), Soviet Marshal — A2308

1980, Sept. 30   Engr.   Perf. 12
4876 A2308 4k dark green   .50   .25

Souvenir Sheet

Mischa Holding Olympic Torch — A2309

1980, Nov. 24   **Perf. 12x12½**
4877   A2309   1r multicolored   5.00   1.75
    Completion of 22nd Summer Olympic Games, Moscow, July 19-Aug. 3.

A.V. Suvorov (1730-1800), General and Military Theorist A2310

1980, Nov. 24   **Engr.**
4878   A2310   4k slate   .50   .25

A2311

1980, Nov. 24   **Litho.**   **Perf. 12**
4879   A2311   4k multicolored   .50   .25
    Armenian SSR & Armenian Communist Party, 60th annivs.

Aleksandr Blok (1880-1921), Poet — A2312

1980, Nov. 24
4880   A2312   4k multicolored   .50   .25

Research Ship Type of 1979
Lithographed and Engraved
1980, Nov. 24   **Perf. 12x11½**
4881   A2271   2k Aju Dag, Fleet
         arms   .25   .25
4882   A2271   3k Valerian
         Uryvaev   .25   .25
4883   A2271   4k Mikhail Somov   .25   .25
4884   A2271   6k Sergei Korolev   .25   .25
4885   A2271   10k Otto Schmidt   .25   .25
4886   A2271   15k Mstislav Keldysh   .25   .25
    Nos. 4881-4886 (6)   1.50   1.50
    For overprint see No. 5499.

Russian Flag — A2313

1980, Dec. 1   **Engr.**   **Perf. 12x12½**
4887   A2313   3k orange red   2.00   .25

Soviet Medical College, 50th Anniversary A2314

1980, Dec. 1   **Photo.**   **Perf. 11½**
4888   A2314   4k multicolored   .50   .25

New Year 1981 A2315

1980, Dec. 1   **Litho.**   **Perf. 12**
4889   A2315   4k multicolored   .50   .25

Lenin, Electrical Plant A2316

1980, Dec. 18
4890   A2316   4k multicolored   .50   .25
    60th anniversary of GOELRO (Lenin's electro-economic plan).

A.N. Nesmeyanov (1899-1980), Chemist — A2317

1980, Dec. 19   **Perf. 12½x12**
4891   A2317   4k multicolored   .50   .25

Nagatinski Bridge, Moscow — A2318

Photogravure and Engraved
1980, Dec. 23   **Perf. 11½x12**
4892   A2318   4k shown   .25   .25
4893   A2318   6k Luzhniki Bridge   .25   .25
4894   A2318   15k Kalininski Bridge   .25   .25
    Nos. 4892-4894 (3)   .75   .75

S.K. Timoshenko (1895-1970), Soviet Marshal — A2319

1980, Dec. 25   **Engr.**   **Perf. 12**
4895   A2319   4k rose lake   .50   .25

Flags of India and USSR, Government House, New Delhi A2320

1980, Dec. 30   **Litho.**   **Perf. 12x12½**
4896   A2320   4k multicolored   .50   .35
    Visit of Pres. Brezhnev to India. Printed se-tenant with inscribed label.

Mirny Base — A2321

    6k, Earth station, rocket. 15k, Map, supply ship.

1981, Jan. 5   **Perf. 12**
4897   A2321   4k shown   .25   .25
4898   A2321   6k multicolored   .35   .25
4899   A2321   15k multicolored   .90   .25
    Nos. 4897-4899 (3)   1.50   .75
    Soviet Antarctic research, 25th anniv.

Dagestan Soviet Socialist Republic, 60th Anniversary A2322

1981, Jan. 20
4900   A2322   4k multicolored   .50   .25

Bandy World Championship, Khabarovsk — A2323

1981, Jan. 20
4901   A2323   6k multicolored   .50   .25

26th Congress of Ukrainian Communist Party A2324

1981, Jan. 23   **Photo.**   **Perf. 11½**
4902   A2324   4k multicolored   .50   .25

Lenin, "XXVI" A2325

1981   **Photo.**   **Perf. 11½**
4903   A2325   4k multicolored   .50   .25

Lenin and Congress Building — A2326

Banner and Kremlin — A2327

Photogravure and Embossed
1982   **Perf. 11½x12**
4904   A2326   20k multicolored   1.50   .75
Souvenir Sheet
Litho.
Perf. 12x12½
4905   A2327   50k multicolored   1.50   .75
    26th Communist Party Congress. Issue dates: 4k, 20k, Jan. 22; 50k, Feb. 16.

Mstislav V. Keldysh — A2328

Photogravure and Engraved
1981, Feb. 10   **Perf. 11½x12**
4906   A2328   4k multicolored   .50   .25
    Mstislav Vsevolodovich Keldysh (1911-1978), mathematician.

Freighter, Flags of USSR and India — A2329

1981, Feb. 10   **Litho.**   **Perf. 12**
4907   A2329   15k multicolored   .50   .30
    Soviet-Indian Shipping Line, 25th anniv.

Baikal-Amur Railroad and Map — A2330

    10th Five-Year Plan Projects (1976-1980): No. 4909, Gas plant, Urengoi (spherical tanks). No. 4910, Enisei River power station (dam). No. 4911, Atomic power plant. No. 4912, Paper mill. No. 4913, Coal mining, Ekibstyi.

1981, Feb. 18   **Perf. 12½x12**
4908   A2330   4k multicolored   .25   .25
4909   A2330   4k multicolored   .25   .25
4910   A2330   4k multicolored   .25   .25
4911   A2330   4k multicolored   .25   .25

4912	A2330	4k multicolored	.25	.25
4913	A2330	4k multicolored	.25	.25
		Nos. 4908-4913 (6)	1.50	1.50

Georgian Soviet Socialist Republic, 60th Anniv. A2331

1981, Feb. 25   *Perf. 12*
| 4914 | A2331 | 4k multicolored | .50 | .25 |

Abkhazian Autonomous Soviet Socialist Republic, 60th Anniv. — A2332

1981, Mar. 4
| 4915 | A2332 | 4k multicolored | .50 | .25 |

Exists imperf.

Communications Institute — A2333

1981, Mar. 12   *Photo.*   *Perf. 11½*
| 4916 | A2333 | 4k multicolored | .50 | .25 |

Moscow Electrotechnical Institute of Communications, 60th anniv.

Satellite, Radio Operator — A2334

1981, Mar. 12
| 4917 | A2334 | 4k multicolored | .50 | .25 |

30th All-Union Amateur Radio Designers Exhibition.

Cosmonauts L.I. Popov and V.V. Ryumin A2335

1981, Mar. 20   *Litho.*   *Perf. 12*
4918	A2335	15k shown	.25	.25
4919	A2335	15k Spacecraft complex	.25	.25
a.		Pair, #4918-4919 + label	1.00	.50

185-day flight of Cosmos 35-Salyut 6-Cosmos 37 complex, Apr. 9-Oct. 11, 1980. No. 4919a has a continuous design.

Cosmonauts O. Makarov, L. Kizim and G. Strekalov — A2336

1981, Mar. 20   *Perf. 12½x12*
| 4920 | A2336 | 10k multicolored | .50 | .25 |

Soyuz T-3 flight, Nov. 27-Dec. 10, 1980.

Lift-Off, Baikonur Base — A2337

15k, Mongolians watching flight on TV. 32k, Re-entry.

1981, Mar. 23
4921	A2337	6k shown	.25	.25
4922	A2337	15k multicolored	.40	.25
4923	A2337	32k multicolored	.85	.50
		Nos. 4921-4923 (3)	1.50	1.00

Intercosmos cooperative space program (USSR-Mongolia).

Vitus Bering A2338

1981, Mar. 25   *Engr.*   *Perf. 12x12½*
| 4924 | A2338 | 4k dark blue | .50 | .25 |

Bering (1680-1741), Danish navigator.

Yuri Gagarin and Earth — A2339

Yuri Gagarin — A2340

1981, Apr. 12   *Photo.*   *Perf. 11½x12*
4925	A2339	6k shown	.25	.25
4926	A2339	15k S.P. Korolev (craft designer)	.40	.25
4927	A2339	32k Monument	.65	.25
		Nos. 4925-4927 (3)	1.30	.75

Souvenir Sheet
| 4928 | A2340 | 50k shown | 5.00 | 1.00 |

Soviet space flights, 20th anniv. Nos. 4925-4927 each se-tenant with label.

Salyut Orbital Station, 10th Anniv. of Flight A2341

1981, Apr. 19   *Litho.*   *Perf. 12x12½*
| 4929 | A2341 | 32k multicolored | .50 | .35 |

Souvenir Sheet

111th Birth Anniv. of Lenin — A2342

1981, Apr. 22   *Perf. 11½x12½*
| 4930 | A2342 | 50k multicolored | 1.50 | .60 |

Sergei Prokofiev (1891-1953), Composer A2343

1981, Apr. 23   *Engr.*   *Perf. 12*
| 4931 | A2343 | 4k dark violet | .50 | .25 |

New Hofburg Palace, Vienna — A2344

1981, May 5   *Litho.*
| 4932 | A2344 | 15k multicolored | .50 | .25 |

WIPA 1981 Phil. Exhib., Vienna, May 22-31.

Adzhar Autonomous Soviet Socialist Republic, 60th Anniv. — A2345

1981, May 7
| 4933 | A2345 | 4k multicolored | .50 | .25 |

Centenary of Welding (Invented by N.N. Benardos) A2346

Lithographed and Engraved
1981, May 12   *Perf. 11½*
| 4934 | A2346 | 6k multicolored | .50 | .25 |

Intl. Architects Union, 14th Congress, Warsaw — A2347

1981, May 12   *Photo.*
| 4935 | A2347 | 15k multicolored | .50 | .25 |

Albanian Girl, by A.A. Ivanov A2348

No. 4937, Horseman, by F.A. Roubeau. No. 4938, The Demon, by M.A. Vrubel, horiz. No. 4939, Sunset over the Sea, by N.N. Ge, horiz.

1981, May 15   *Litho.*   *Perf. 12x12½*
4936	A2348	10k multicolored	.50	.25
4937	A2348	10k multicolored	.50	.25
4938	A2348	10k multicolored	.50	.25
4939	A2348	10k multicolored	.50	.25
		Nos. 4936-4939 (4)	2.00	1.00

Cosmonauts in Training A2349

1981, May 15
4940	A2349	6k shown	.25	.25
4941	A2349	15k In space	.40	.25
4942	A2349	32k Return	.85	.50
		Nos. 4940-4942 (3)	1.50	1.00

Intercosmos cooperative space program (USSR-Romania).

Dwarf Primrose — A2350

Flowers of the Carpathian Mountains: 6k, Great carline thistle. 10k, Mountain parageum. 15k, Alpine bluebell. 32k, Rhododendron kotschyi.

1981, May 20   *Perf. 12*
4943 A2350 4k multicolored   .25 .25
4944 A2350 6k multicolored   .25 .25
4945 A2350 10k multicolored   .25 .25
4946 A2350 15k multicolored   .40 .25
4947 A2350 32k multicolored   .85 .50
     Nos. 4943-4947 (5)   2.00 1.50

Luigi Longo, Italian Labor Leader, 1st Death Anniv. — A2351

1981, May 24   **Photo.**   *Perf. 11½*
4948 A2351 6k multicolored   .50 .25

Nizami Gjanshevi (1141-1209), Azerbaijan Poet — A2352

1981, May 25   **Photo. & Engr.**
4949 A2352 4k multicolored   .50 .25

A2353

1981, June 18   **Litho.**   *Perf. 12*
4950 A2353 4k Running   .25 .25
4951 A2353 6k Soccer   .25 .25
4952 A2353 10k Discus throwing   .25 .25
4953 A2353 15k Boxing   .30 .25
4954 A2353 32k Diving   .45 .35
     Nos. 4950-4954 (5)   1.50 1.35

Mongolian Revolution, 60th anniv. — A2354

1981, July 6
4955 A2354 6k multicolored   .75 .25

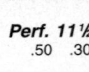

12th Intl. Film Festival, Moscow — A2355

1981, July 6   **Photo.**   *Perf. 11½*
4956 A2355 15k multicolored   .50 .30

River Tour Boat Lenin A2356

6k, Cosmonaut Gagarin. 15k, Valerian Kuibyshev. 32k, Freighter Baltijski.

1981, July 9   **Litho.**   *Perf. 12½*
4957 A2356 4k shown   .25 .25
4958 A2356 6k multicolored   .25 .25
4959 A2356 15k multicolored   .35 .25
4960 A2356 32k multicolored   .65 .45
     Nos. 4957-4960 (4)   1.50 1.20

Icebreaker Maligin — A2357

Photogravure and Engraved
1981, July 9   *Perf. 11½x12*
4961 A2357 15k multicolored   .50 .30

26th Party Congress Resolutions (Intl. Cooperation) — A2358

1981, July 15   **Photo.**   *Perf. 12x11½*
4962 A2358 4k shown   .25 .25
4963 A2358 4k Industry   .25 .25
4964 A2358 4k Energy   .25 .25
4965 A2358 4k Agriculture   .25 .25
4966 A2358 4k Communications   .25 .25
4967 A2358 4k Arts   .25 .25
     Nos. 4962-4967 (6)   1.50 1.50

I.N. Ulyanov (Lenin's Father), 150th Anniv. of Birth — A2359

1981, July 25   **Engr.**   *Perf. 11½*
4968 A2359 4k multicolored   .50 .25

Leningrad Theater, 225th Anniv. — A2360

1981, Aug. 12   **Photo.**   *Perf. 11½*
4969 A2360 6k multicolored   .50 .25

A.M. Gerasimov, Artist, Birth Centenary A2361

1981, Aug. 12   **Litho.**   *Perf. 12*
4970 A2361 4k multicolored   .50 .25

Physical Chemistry Institute, Moscow Academy of Science, 50th Anniv. A2362

1981, Aug. 12   **Photo.**   *Perf. 11½*
4971 A2362 4k multicolored   .50 .25

Siberian Tit A2363

Song birds — 10k, Tersiphone paradisi, vert. 15k, Emberiza jankovski. 20k, Sutora webbiana, vert. 32k, Saxicola torquata, vert.

Perf. 12½x12, 12x12½
1981, Aug. 20   **Litho.**
4972 A2363 6k shown   .25 .25
4973 A2363 10k multicolored   .30 .25
4974 A2363 15k multicolored   .40 .25
4975 A2363 20k multicolored   .45 .30
4976 A2363 32k multicolored   .60 .35
     Nos. 4972-4976 (5)   2.00 1.40

60th Anniv. of Komi Autonomous Soviet Socialist Republic — A2364

1981, Aug. 22   *Perf. 12*
4977 A2364 4k multicolored   .50 .25

Svyaz-'81 Intl. Communications Exhibition — A2365

Photogravure and Engraved
1981, Aug. 22   *Perf. 11½*
4978 A2365 4k multicolored   .50 .25

60th Anniv. of Kabardino-Balkar Autonomous Soviet Socialist Republic — A2366

1981, Sept. 1   **Litho.**   *Perf. 12*
4979 A2366 4k multicolored   .50 .25

War Veterans' Committee, 25th Anniv. — A2367

1981, Sept. 1   **Photo.**   *Perf. 11½*
4980 A2367 4k multicolored   .50 .25

Schooner Kodor — A2368

Training ships — 4k, 4-masted bark Tovarich I. 6k, Barkentine Vega I. 15k, 3-masted bark Tovarich. 20k, 4-masted bark Kruzenstern. 32k, 4-masted bark Sedov.
4k, 6k, 15k, 20k, horiz.

Perf. 12½x12, 12x12½
1981, Sept. 18   **Litho.**
4981 A2368 4k multicolored   .25 .25
4982 A2368 6k multicolored   .25 .25
4983 A2368 10k shown   .25 .25
4984 A2368 15k multicolored   .30 .25
4985 A2368 20k multicolored   .45 .25
4986 A2368 32k multicolored   .60 .30
     Nos. 4981-4986 (6)   2.10 1.55

A2369

1981, Oct. 10   *Perf. 12*
4987 A2369 4k multicolored   .50 .25

Kazakhstan's Union with Russia, 250th Anniv.

A2370

1981, Oct. 10   **Photo.**   *Perf. 11½*
4988 A2370 4k multicolored   .50 .25

Mikhail Alekseevich Lavrentiev (1900-80), mathematician. Exists imperf.

64th Anniv. of October
Revolution — A2371

1981, Oct. 15   **Litho.**
4989 A2371 4k multicolored   .50   .25

Ekran Satellite TV Broadcasting
System — A2372

1981, Oct. 15   **Perf. 12**
4990 A2372 4k multicolored   .50   .25

Salyut 6-Soyuz
flight of V.V.
Kovalionok and
V.P. Savinykh
A2373

1981, Oct. 15
4991   10k Text   .40   .25
4992   10k Cosmonauts   .40   .25
    a.   A2373   Pair, #4991-4992   1.00   .30

Souvenir Sheet

Birth Centenary of Pablo
Picasso — A2375

1981, Oct. 25   **Perf. 12x12½**
4993 A2375 50k multicolored   2.00   .75

A2376

Photogravure and Engraved
1981, Nov. 5   **Perf. 11½**
4994 A2376 4k multicolored   .50   .25
   Sergei Dmitrievich Merkurov (1881-1952),
artist.

Autumn, by Niko Piromanashvili,
1913 — A2377

   Paintings: 6k, Gurian Woman, by S.G.
Kikodze, 1921. 10k, Fellow Travelers, by U.M.
Dzhaparidze, 1936, horiz. 15k, Shota Rustaveli, by S.S. Kobuladze, 1938. 32k, Collecting Tea, by V.D. Gudiashvili, 1964, horiz.

Perf. 12x12½, 12½x12
1981, Nov. 5   **Litho.**
4995 A2377   4k multicolored   .25   .25
4996 A2377   6k multicolored   .25   .25
4997 A2377   10k multicolored   .30   .25
4998 A2377   15k multicolored   .40   .25
4999 A2377   32k multicolored   1.00   .40
    Nos. 4995-4999 (5)   2.20   1.40

New Year
1982 — A2378

1981, Dec. 2   **Litho.**   **Perf. 12**
5000 A2378 4k multicolored   1.00   .25

Public Transportation 19th-20th
Cent. — A2379

Photogravure and Engraved
1981, Dec. 10   **Perf. 11½x12**
5001 A2379 4k Sled   .25   .25
5002 A2379 6k Horse-drawn
        trolley   .25   .25
5003 A2379 10k Coach   .25   .25
5004 A2379 15k Taxi, 1926   .25   .25
5005 A2379 20k Bus, 1926   .35   .30
5006 A2379 32k Trolley, 1912   .50   .40
    Nos. 5001-5006 (6)   1.85   1.70

Souvenir Sheet

Kremlin and New Delhi
Parliament — A2380

1981, Dec. 17   **Photo.**
5007 A2380 50k multicolored   1.50   .75
   1st direct telephone link with India.

A2381

A2382

1982, Jan. 11   **Litho.**   **Perf. 12**
5008 A2381 4k multicolored   .50   .25
5009 A2382 4k multicolored   .50   .25
   60th anniv. of Checheno-Ingush Autonomous SSR and of Yakutsk Autonomous SSR.

1500th Anniv. of Kiev — A2383

1982, Jan. 12   **Photo.**   **Perf. 11½x12**
5010 A2383 10k multicolored   .50   .25

S.P. Korolev
(1907-66), Rocket
Designer — A2384

1982, Jan. 12   **Perf. 11½**
5011 A2384 4k multicolored   .50   .25

Nazym Khikmet
(1902-1963),
Turkish
Poet — A2385

1982, Jan. 20   **Litho.**   **Perf. 12**
5012 A2385 6k multicolored   .50   .25

10th World Trade Union Congress,
Havana — A2386

1982, Feb. 1   **Photo.**   **Perf. 11½**
5013 A2386 15k multicolored   .50   .25

17th Soviet Trade
Union Congress
A2387

1982, Feb. 10   **Litho.**
5014 A2387 4k multicolored   .50   .25

Edouard
Manet (1832-
1883)
A2388

1982, Feb. 10   **Perf. 12x12½**
5015 A2388 32k multicolored   1.00   .45

Equestrian
Sports
A2389

1982, Feb. 16   **Photo.**   **Perf. 11½**
5016 A2389   4k Hurdles   .25   .25
5017 A2389   6k Riding   .30   .25
5018 A2389   15k Racing   .45   .25
    Nos. 5016-5018 (3)   1.00   .75
   No. 5016 exists imperf. Value, $25.

2nd Death Anniv.
of Marshal Tito of
Yugoslavia
A2390

1982, Feb. 25   **Litho.**   **Perf. 12**
5019 A2390 6k olive black   .50   .25

350th
Anniv. of
State
University
of Tartu
A2392

1982, Mar. 4   **Photo.**   **Perf. 11½**
5020 A2392 4k multicolored   .50   .25

9th Intl. Cardiologists Congress,
Moscow — A2393

1982, Mar. 4
5021 A2393 15k multicolored   .50   .25

Souvenir Sheet

Biathlon, Speed Skating — A2394

1982, Mar. 6　Litho.　Perf. 12½x12
5022　A2394　50k multicolored　　1.50　.70
　　5th Natl. Athletic Meet.

Blueberry
Bush — A2395

4k, Cloudberries. 10k, Brambles. 15k, Cornelian cherries. 32k, Wild strawberries.

1982, Mar. 10　Litho.　Perf. 12x12½
5023　A2395　4k multicolored　　.25　.25
5024　A2395　6k shown　　　　　.25　.25
5025　A2395　10k multicolored　　.25　.25
5026　A2395　15k multicolored　　.25　.25
5027　A2395　32k multicolored　　.50　.25
　　Nos. 5023-5027 (5)　　　1.50　1.25

Venera 13 and
Venera 14
Flights — A2396

1982, Mar. 10　Photo.　Perf. 11½
5028　A2396　10k multicolored　　.50　.25

Marriage
Ceremony,
by V.V.
Pukirev
(1832-1890)
A2397

Paintings: No. 5030, M.I. Lopukhina, by V.L. Borovikovsky (1757-1825). No. 5031, E.V. Davidov, by O.A. Kiprensky (1782-1836). No. 5032, Oak Trees, by I.I. Shishkin (1832-1898).

1982, Mar. 18　　　　Perf. 12
5029　A2397　6k multicolored　　.25　.25
5030　A2397　6k multicolored　　.25　.25
5031　A2397　6k multicolored　　.25　.25
5032　A2397　6k multicolored　　.25　.25
　　Nos. 5029-5032 (4)　　　1.00　1.00

K.I. Chukovsky
(1882-1969),
Writer — A2398

1982, Mar. 31　　　　Engr.
5033　A2398　4k gray & black　　.50　.25

Cosmonauts' Day — A2399

1982, Apr. 12　Photo.　Perf. 12x11½
5034　A2399　6k multicolored　　.50　.25

Souvenir Sheet

112th Birth Anniv. of Lenin — A2400

1982, Apr. 22　Photo.　Perf. 11½x12
5035　A2400　50k multicolored　　1.50　.70

V.P. Soloviev-
Sedoi (1907-79),
Composer
A2401

1982, Apr. 25　Engr.　Perf. 12
5036　A2401　4k brown　　　　.50　.25

G. Dimitrov (1882-
1949), 1st
Bulgarian Prime
Minister — A2402

1982, Apr. 25
5037　A2402　6k green　　　　.50　.25

Kremlin Tower,
Moscow — A2403

1982　　Litho.　Perf. 12½x12
5038　A2403　45k brown　　　1.00　.65
　a.　Engraved　　　　　　1.00　.65
　　Issued: #5038, Apr. 25. #5038a, Oct. 12.

70th Anniv.
of Pravda
Newspaper
A2404

1982, May 5　Photo.　Perf. 12x11½
5039　A2404　4k multicolored　　.50　.25

UN Conf. on
Human
Environment, 10th
anniv. — A2405

1982, May 10　　　　Perf. 11½
5040　A2405　6k multicolored　　.50　.25

Pioneers' Org.,
60th
anniv. — A2406

1982, May 19
5041　A2406　4k multicolored　　.50　.25

Communist Youth
Org., 19th
Cong. — A2407

1982, May 19
5042　A2407　4k multicolored　　.50　.25

ITU Delegates
Conf.,
Nairobi — A2408

1982, May 19
5043　A2408　15k multicolored　　.50　.25

TUL-80 Electric Locomotive — A2409

1982, May 20　　　　Perf. 12x11½
5044　A2409　4k shown　　　　　.25　.25
5045　A2409　6k TEP-75 diesel　　.25　.25
5046　A2409　10k TEP-7 diesel　　.30　.25
5047　A2409　15k WL-82m electric　.45　.45
5048　A2409　32k EP-200 electric　.95　.45
　　Nos. 5044-5048 (5)　　2.20　1.50

1982 World Cup — A2410

1982, June 4　　　　Perf. 11½x12
5049　A2410　20k olive & purple　　.50　.30

Rare
Birds — A2411

18th Ornithological Cong., Moscow — 2k, Grus Monacha. 4k, Haliaeetus pelagicus. 6k, Eurynorhynchus. 10k, Eulabeia indica. 15k, Chettusia gregaria. 32k, Ciconia boyciana.

1982, June 10　Litho.　Perf. 12x12½
5050　A2411　2k multicolored　　.25　.25
5051　A2411　4k multicolored　　.25　.25
5052　A2411　6k multicolored　　.25　.25
5053　A2411　10k multicolored　　.25　.25
5054　A2411　15k multicolored　　.30　.25
5055　A2411　32k multicolored　　.70　.35
　　Nos. 5050-5055 (6)　　2.00　1.60

Komomolsk-on-Amur City, 50th
Anniv. — A2412

Photogravure and Engraved
1982, June 10　　　　Perf. 11½
5056　A2412　4k multicolored　　.50　.25

Tatchanka, by M.B. Grekov (1882-
1934) — A2413

1982, June 15　Litho.　Perf. 12½x12
5057　A2413　6k multicolored　　.50　.25

2nd UN
Conference on
Peaceful Uses of
Outer Space,
Vienna, Aug. 9-
21 — A2414

1982, June 15　Photo.　Perf. 11½
5058　A2414　15k multicolored　　.50　.25
　　Exists in a miniature sheet of 8. Value, $75.

Intercosmos Cooperative Space
Program (USSR-France) — A2415

1982		Litho.	Perf. 12½x12	
5059	A2415	6k Cosmonauts	.25	.25
a.		Miniature sheet of 8	75.00	
5060	A2415	20k Rocket, globe	.35	.25
a.		Miniature sheet of 8	75.00	
5061	A2415	45k Satellites	.80	.40
a.		Miniature sheet of 8	75.00	
		Nos. 5059-5061 (3)	1.40	.90

Souvenir Sheet

| 5062 | A2415 | 50k Emblem, satel-
lite | 1.50 | .75 |

No. 5062 contains one 41x29mm stamp.
Issue dates: 6k, 50k, June 24. 20k, 45k, July 2.

The Tale of the Golden Cockerel, by
P. Sosin, 1968 — A2416

Lacquerware Paintings, Ustera: 10k, Minin's
Appeal to Count Posharski, by J. Fomichev,
1953. 15k, Two Peasants, by A. Kotyagin,
1933. 20k, The Fisherman, by N. Klykov,
1933, 32k, The Arrest of the Propagandists, by
N. Shishakov, 1968.

1982, July 6		Litho.	Perf. 12½x12	
5063	A2416	6k multicolored	.25	.25
5064	A2416	10k multicolored	.25	.25
5065	A2416	15k multicolored	.30	.25
5066	A2416	20k multicolored	.50	.25
5067	A2416	32k multicolored	.75	.30
		Nos. 5063-5067 (5)	2.05	1.30

Telephone
Centenary
A2417

1982, July 13			Perf. 12	
5068	A2417	4k Phone, 1882	.50	.25

P. Schilling's Electro-magnetic
Telegraph Sesquicentennial — A2418

Photogravure and Engraved

1982, July 16			Perf. 11½	
5069	A2418	6k Voltaic cells	.50	.25

Intervision
Gymnastics
Contest
A2419

1982, Aug. 10			Photo.	
5070	A2419	15k multicolored	.50	.30

Gliders
A2420

4k, Mastjahart Glider, 1923. 6k, Red Star,
1930. 10k, ZAGI-2, 1934.
20k, Stakhanovets, 1939. 32k, Troop carrier
GR-29, 1941.

1982, Aug. 20		Litho.	Perf. 12½x12	
5071	A2420	4k multicolored	.25	.25
5072	A2420	6k multicolored	.25	.25
5073	A2420	10k multicolored	.30	.25

Size: 60x28mm
Perf. 11½x12

5074	A2420	20k multicolored	.60	.25
5075	A2420	32k multicolored	.75	.35
		Nos. 5071-5075 (5)	2.15	1.35

See Nos. 5118-5122.

Garibaldi (1807-
1882)
A2421

1982, Aug. 25		Photo.	Perf. 11½	
5076	A2421	6k multicolored	.50	.25

Exists imperf. Value, $25.

Intl. Atomic Energy
Authority, 25th
Anniv. — A2422

1982, Aug. 30

| 5077 | A2422 | 20k multicolored | .50 | .25 |

Marshal B.M.
Shaposhnikov
(1882-1945)
A2423

1982, Sept. 10		Engr.	Perf. 12	
5078	A2423	4k red brown	.50	.25

World Chess
Championship
A2424

1982, Sept. 10		Photo.	Perf. 11½	
5079	A2424	6k King	.50	.25
5080	A2424	6k Queen	.50	.25

See #5084.

African Natl.
Congress, 70th
Anniv. — A2425

1982, Sept. 10

| 5081 | A2425 | 6k multicolored | .50 | .25 |

S.P. Botkin (1832-
89),
Physician — A2426

1982, Sept. 17		Engr.	Perf. 12½x12	
5082	A2426	4k green	.50	.25

Souvenir Sheet

25th Anniv. of Sputnik — A2427

1982, Sept. 17		Litho.	Perf. 12x12½	
5083	A2427	50k multicolored	2.00	.65

**No. 5079 Overprinted in Gold for
Karpov's Victory**

1982, Sept. 22		Photo.	Perf. 11½	
5084	A2424	6k multicolored	1.00	.30

World War II Warships — A2428

4k, Submarine S-56. 6k, Minelayer
Gremjashtsky. 15k, Mine sweeper T-205. 20k,
Cruiser Red Crimea. 45k, Sebastopol.

Photogravure and Engraved

1982, Sept. 22			Perf. 11½x12	
5085	A2428	4k multicolored	.25	.25
5086	A2428	6k multicolored	.25	.25
5087	A2428	15k multicolored	.30	.25
5088	A2428	20k multicolored	.40	.25
5089	A2428	45k multicolored	.80	.45
		Nos. 5085-5089 (5)	2.00	1.45

65th Anniv. of
October Revolution
A2429

1982, Oct. 12		Litho.	Perf. 12	
5090	A2429	4k multicolored	.50	.25

House of the Soviets,
Moscow — A2430

60th Anniv. of USSR: No. 5092, Dnieper
Dam, Komosomol Monument, Statue of
worker. No. 5093, Soviet War Memorial, resistance poster. No. 5094, Worker at podium,
decree text. No. 5095, Workers' Monument,
Moscow, Rocket, jet. No. 5096, Arms, Kremlin.

1982, Oct. 25		Photo.	Perf. 11½x12	
5091	A2430	10k multicolored	.50	.25
5092	A2430	10k multicolored	.50	.25
5093	A2430	10k multicolored	.50	.25
5094	A2430	10k multicolored	.50	.25
5095	A2430	10k multicolored	.50	.25
5096	A2430	10k multicolored	.50	.25
		Nos. 5091-5096 (6)	3.00	1.50

**No. 5095 Overprinted in Red for All-
Union Philatelic Exhibition, 1984**

1982, Nov. 10

| 5097 | A2430 | 10k multicolored | 1.00 | .25 |

Portrait of an
Actor, by
Domenico
Fetti
A2431

Paintings from the Hermitage: 10k, St.
Sebastian, by Perugino. 20k, Danae, by Titian,
horiz. 45k, Portrait of a Woman, by Correggio.
No. 5102, Self-portrait, by Capriolo. No.
5103a, Portrait of a Young Woman, by Melzi.

		Perf. 12x12½		
1982, Nov. 25		Litho.	Wmk. 383	
5098	A2431	4k multicolored	.25	.25
5099	A2431	10k multicolored	.25	.25
5100	A2431	20k multicolored	.30	.25
5101	A2431	45k multicolored	.50	.40
5102	A2431	50k multicolored	.75	.55
		Nos. 5098-5102 (5)	2.05	1.70

Souvenir Sheet

| 5103 | | Sheet of 2 | 2.50 | 1.65 |
| a. | A2431 | 50k multicolored | 1.00 | .65 |

Printed in sheets of 24 stamps + label and
15 stamps + label. Value, sheet of 15 stamps
+ label, $75.

See Nos. 5129-5134, 5199-5204, 5233-
5238, 5310-5315, 5335-5340.

New Year
1983 — A2432

1982, Dec. 1   **Unwmk.**
5104 A2432 4k multicolored   .50   .25
  a.   Miniature sheet of 8   100.00
    Exists imperf. Value, $50.

Souvenir Sheet

60th Anniv. of USSR — A2433

1982, Dec. 3   **Perf. 12½x12**
5105 A2433 50k multicolored   2.00   .90

Souvenir Sheet

Mountain Climbers Scaling Mt. Everest — A2434

1982, Dec. 20   **Photo.**   **Perf. 11½x12**
5106 A2434 50k multicolored   2.00   .90

Lighthouses A2435

1982, Dec. 29   **Litho.**   **Perf. 12**
5107 A2435 6k green & multi   .50   .25
5108 A2435 6k lilac & multi   .50   .25
5109 A2435 6k salmon & multi   .50   .25
5110 A2435 6k lt gldn brn & multi   .50   .25
5111 A2435 6k lt brown & multi   .50   .25
    Nos. 5107-5111 (5)   2.50 1.25
    No. 5111 exists imperf. Value, $25.
    See Nos. 5179-5183, 5265-5269.

Mail Transport — A2436

1982, Dec. 22   **Perf. 12**
5112 A2436 5k greenish blue   5.00 1.00

1983, May 20   **Litho.**   **Perf. 12**
5113 A2436 5k blue   1.75   .25
    For surcharge see Uzbekistan #61E.

Iskra Newspaper Masthead A2438

1983, Jan. 5   **Litho.**   **Perf. 12x12½**
5114 A2438 4k multicolored   .50   .25
    80th anniv. of 2nd Congress of Social-Democratic Workers' Party.

Fedor P. Tolstoi (1783-1873), Painter — A2439

1983, Jan. 5   **Photo.**   **Perf. 11½**
5115 A2439 4k multicolored   .50   .25

65th Anniv. of Armed Forces — A2440

1983, Jan. 25   **Litho.**   **Perf. 12**
5116 A2440 4k multicolored   .50   .25
    Exists imperf. Value, $25.

Souvenir Sheet

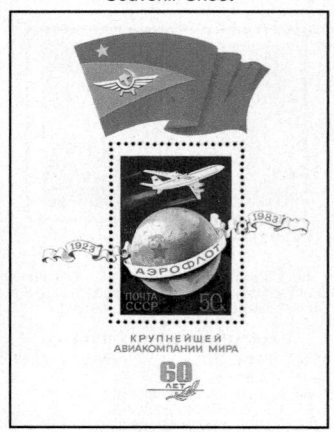

60th Anniv. of Aeroflot Airlines — A2441

1983, Feb. 9   **Perf. 12x12½**
5117 A2441 50k multicolored   1.50 1.00

Glider Type of 1982

1983, Feb. 10   **Perf. 12½x12**
5118 A2420 2k A-9, 1948   .25   .25
5119 A2420 4k KAJ-12, 1957   .25   .25
5120 A2420 6k A-15, 1960   .25   .25
5121 A2420 20k SA-7, 1970   .40   .25
5122 A2420 45k LAJ-12, 1979   .75   .60
    Nos. 5118-5122 (5)   1.90 1.60

Tashkent Bimillennium — A2442

1983, Feb. 17   **Perf. 12½x12**
5123 A2442 4k View   .50   .25

B.N. Petrov (1913-1980), Scientist — A2443

1983, Feb. 17
5124 A2443 4k multicolored   .50   .25

Holy Family, by Raphael A2444

1983, Feb. 17   **Perf. 12x12½**
5125 A2444 50k multicolored   .50   .25
  a.   Miniature sheet of 15 + label   20.00

Soyuz T-7-Salyut 7-Soyuz T-5 Flight A2445

    10k, L. Popov, A. Serebrov, S. Savitskaya.

1983, Mar. 10   **Perf. 12x12½**
5126 A2445 10k multicolored   .50   .25

Souvenir Sheet

World Communications Year — A2446

1983, Mar. 10   **Photo.**   **Perf. 11½**
5127 A2446 50k multicolored   2.00 1.25

A.W. Aleksandrov, Natl. Anthem Composer — A2447

1983, Mar. 22   **Litho.**   **Perf. 12**
5128 A2447 4k multicolored   .50   .25
    Exists imperf. Value, $50.

Hermitage Type of 1982

    Rembrandt Paintings, Hermitage, Leningrad: 4k, Portrait of an Old Woman. 10k, Portrait of a Learned Man. 20k, Old Warrior. 45k, Portrait of Mrs. B. Martens Doomer. No. 5133, Sacrifice of Abraham. No. 5134a, Portrait of an Old Man in a Red Garment.

     Perf. 12x12½
1983, Mar. 25   **Wmk. 383**
5129 A2431 4k multicolored   .25   .25
5130 A2431 10k multicolored   .25   .25
5131 A2431 20k multicolored   .70   .35
5132 A2431 45k multicolored   1.40   .70
5133 A2431 50k multicolored   1.50   .75
    Nos. 5129-5133 (5)   4.10 2.30

Souvenir Sheet
Lithographed and Embossed

5134   Sheet of 2 + label   2.00 1.50
  a.   A2431 50k multicolored   .75   .75

    Nos. 5129-5133 printed in sheets of 24 + label and in miniature sheets of 15 + label. Value, set of miniature sheets, $75.

Souvenir Sheet

Cosmonauts' Day — A2449

Perf. 12½x12
1983, Apr. 12   Litho.   Unwmk.
5135 A2449 50k Soyuz T   2.00 2.00

Souvenir Sheet

113th Birth Anniv. of Lenin — A2450

Photogravure and Engraved
1983, Apr. 22   Perf. 11½x12
5136 A2450 50k multicolored   1.50 .80

A. Berezovoy, V. Lebedev — A2451

Salyut 7-Soyuz T Spacecraft — A2452

1983, Apr. 25   Litho.   Perf. 12½x12½
5137 A2451 10k multicolored   .50 .25
5138 A2452 10k multicolored   .50 .25
  a. Pair, #5137-5138   1.00 .50
Salyut 7-Soyuz T 211-Day Flight. Exists se-tenant with label.

Karl Marx
(1818-1883)
A2453

1983, May 5   Perf. 12x12½
5139 A2453 4k multicolored   .50 .25

View of Rostov-on-Don — A2454

1983, May 5   Photo.   Perf. 11½
5140 A2454 4k multicolored   .50 .25
Exists imperf. Value, $50.

Buriat Autonomous Soviet Socialist
Republic, 60th Anniv. — A2455

1983, May 12   Litho.   Perf. 12
5141 A2455 4k multicolored   .50 .25

Kirov Opera and Ballet Theater,
Leningrad, 200th Anniv. — A2456

Photogravure and Engraved
1983, May 12   Perf. 11½x12
5142 A2456 4k multicolored   .50 .25

Emblem of Motorcycling, Auto Racing,
Shooting, Motorboating, Parachuting
Organization — A2457

1983, May 20   Litho.   Perf. 11½
5143 A2457 6k multicolored   .50 .25

A.I. Khachaturian (1903-1978),
Composer — A2458

1983, May 25   Engr.   Perf. 12½x12
5144 A2458 4k violet brown   1.00 .30

Chelyabinsk Tractor Plant, 50th
Anniv. — A2459

1983, June 1   Photo.   Perf. 11½
5145 A2459 4k multicolored   .50 .25

Simon
Bolivar
Bicentenary
A2460

Photogravure and Engraved
1983, June 10   Perf. 12
5146 A2460 6k brown & dk
              brown   .50 .25

City of Sevastopol, 200th
Anniv. — A2461

1983, June 14 Photo. Perf. 11½x12
5147 A2461 5k multicolored   .50 .25

Spring
Flowers — A2462

1983, June 14   Litho.   Perf. 12x12½
5148 A2462 4k multicolored   .25 .25
5149 A2462 6k multicolored   .25 .25
5150 A2462 10k multicolored   .30 .25
5151 A2462 15k multicolored   .50 .30
5152 A2462 20k multicolored   .70 .35
  Nos. 5148-5152 (5)   2.00 1.40

Valentina Tereshkova's Spaceflight,
20th Anniv. — A2463

1983, June 16   Litho.   Perf. 12
5153 A2463 10k multicolored   .50 .25
  a. Miniature sheet of 8   200.00

P.N. Pospelov
(1898-1979),
Academician
A2464

Photogravure and Engraved
1983, June 20   Perf. 11½
5154 A2464 4k multicolored   .50 .25

10th European
Cong. of
Rheumatologists
A2465

1983, June 21   Photo.   Perf. 11½
5155 A2465 4k multicolored   .50 .25

13th International Film Festival,
Moscow — A2466

1983, July 7   Litho.   Perf. 12
5156 A2466 20k multicolored   .50 .25

Ships of the Soviet Fishing
Fleet — A2467

4k, Two trawlers. 6k, Refrigerated trawler.
10k, Large trawler. 15k, Large refrigerated
ship. 20k, Base ship.

Photogravure and Engraved
1983, July 20   Perf. 12x11½
5157 A2467 4k multicolored   .25 .25
5158 A2467 6k multicolored   .25 .25
5159 A2467 10k multicolored   .35 .25
5160 A2467 15k multicolored   .50 .25
5161 A2467 20k multicolored   .65 .25
  Nos. 5157-5161 (5)   2.00 1.25

E.B. Vakhtangov (1883-1922), Actor
and Producer — A2468

1983, July 20   Photo.   Perf. 11½
5162 A2468 5k multicolored   .50 .25

"USSR-1"
Stratospheric Flight,
50th
Anniv. — A2469

1983, July 25   Photo.   Perf. 12
5163 A2469 20k multicolored   .50 .40
  a. Miniature sheet of 8   100.00

Food Fish
A2470

4k, Oncorhynchus nerka. 6k, Perciformes.
15k, Anarhichas minor. 20k, Neogobius fluviatilis, 45k, Platichthys stellatus.

1983, Aug. 5   Litho.   Perf. 12½x12
5164 A2470 4k multicolored   .25 .25
5165 A2470 6k multicolored   .25 .25
5166 A2470 15k multicolored   .25 .25
5167 A2470 20k multicolored   .30 .30
5168 A2470 45k multicolored   .50 .60
  Nos. 5164-5168 (5)   1.55 1.65

A2471

SOZPHILEX '83 Philatelic Exhibition — A2472

1983, Aug. 18   Photo.   Perf. 11½
5169 A2471 6k multicolored   .50 .25
Souvenir Sheet
5170 A2472 50k Moscow Skyline   2.00 .80

Miniature Sheet

First Russian Postage Stamp, 125th Anniv. — A2473

Photogravure and Engraved
1983, Aug. 25   Perf. 11½x12
5171 A2473 50k pale yel & black   2.00 .70

No. 5171 Ovptd. in Red for the 5th Philatelic Society Congress

1984, Oct. 1
5171A A2473 50k pale yel & blk   4.00 3.50

Namibia Day — A2474

1983, Aug. 26   Photo.   Perf. 11½
5172 A2474 5k multicolored   .50 .25

Palestinian Solidarity — A2475

1983, Aug. 29   Photo.   Perf. 11½
5173 A2475 5k multicolored   .50 .25

1st European Championship of Radio-Telegraphy, Moscow — A2476

1983, Sept. 1   Photo.   Perf. 11½
5174 A2476 6k multicolored   .50 .25
Exists imperf. Value, $50.

4th UNESCO Council on Communications Development — A2477

1983, Sept. 2   Photo.   Perf. 12x11½
5175 A2477 10k multicolored   .50 .25

Muhammad Al-Khorezmi, Uzbek Mathematician, 1200th Birth Anniv. — A2478

Photogravure and Engraved
1983, Sept. 6   Perf. 11½
5176 A2478 4k multicolored   .50 .25

Marshal A.I. Egorov (1883-1939) A2479

1983, Sept. 8   Engr.   Perf. 12
5177 A2479 4k brown violet   .50 .25

October Revolution, 66th anniv. — A2484

1983, Oct. 12   Litho.   Perf. 12
5193 A2484 4k multicolored   .50 .25

Union of Georgia and Russia, 200th Anniv. — A2480

1983, Sept. 8   Photo.   Perf. 11½
5178 A2480 6k multicolored   .50 .25

Lighthouse Type of 1982
Baltic Sea lighthouses.
1983, Sept. 19   Litho.   Perf. 12
5179 A2435 1k Kipu   .25 .25
5180 A2435 5k Keri   .25 .25
5181 A2435 10k Stirsudden   .30 .25
5182 A2435 12k Tahkun   .50 .25
5183 A2435 20k Tallinn   .70 .30
    Nos. 5179-5183 (5)   2.00 1.30

Early Spring, by V.K. Bialynicki-Birula, 1912 — A2481

Belorussian Paintings: 4k, Portrait of the Artist's Wife with Fruit and Flowers, by J.F. Khrutzky, 1838. 15k, Young Partisan, by E.A. Zaitsev, 1943. 20k, Partisan Madonna, by M.A. Savitsky, 1967. 45k, Harvest, by V.K. Tsvirko, 1972. 15k, 20k, vert.

Perf. 12½x12, 12x12½
1983, Sept. 28
5184 A2481 4k multicolored   .25 .25
5185 A2481 6k multicolored   .25 .25
5186 A2481 15k multicolored   .25 .25
5187 A2481 20k multicolored   .30 .25
5188 A2481 45k multicolored   .40 .25
    Nos. 5184-5188 (5)   1.45 1.25

Hammer and Sickle Steel Mill, Moscow, Centenary A2482

1983, Oct. 1   Photo.   Perf. 11½
5189 A2482 4k multicolored   .50 .25

Natl. Food Program A2483

1983, Oct. 10
5190 A2483 5k Wheat production   .50 .25
5191 A2483 5k Cattle, dairy
                products   .50 .25
5192 A2483 5k Produce   .50 .25
    Nos. 5190-5192 (3)   1.50 .75

Ivan Fedorov — A2485

1983, Oct. 12   Engr.   Perf. 12x12½
5194 A2485 4k dark brown   .50 .25
Ivan Fedorov, first Russian printer (Book of the Apostles), 400th death anniv.

Urengoy-Uzgorod Transcontinental Gas Pipeline Completion — A2486

1983, Oct. 12   Photo.   Perf. 12x11½
5195 A2486 5k multicolored   .50 .25

A.W. Sidorenko (1917-82), Geologist — A2487

1983, Oct. 19   Litho.   Perf. 12
5196 A2487 4k multicolored   .50 .25

Campaign Against Nuclear Weapons — A2488

1983, Oct. 19   Photo.   Perf. 11½
5197 A2488 5k Demonstration   .50 .25
Exists imperf. Value $50.

Maktumkuli, Turkmenistan Poet, 250th Birth Anniv. — A2489

1983, Oct. 27
5198 A2489 5k multicolored   .50 .25

Hermitage Painting Type of 1982
Paintings by Germans: 4k, Madonna and Child with Apple Tree, by Lucas Cranach the Elder. 10k, Self-portrait, by Anton R. Mengs. 20k, Self-portrait, by Jürgen Ovens. 45k, Sailboat, by Caspar David Friedrich. No. 5203, Rape of the Sabines, by Johann Schoenfeld, horiz. No. 5204a, Portrait of a Young Man, by Ambrosius Holbein.

Perf. 12x12½, 12½x12
1983, Nov. 10   Litho.   Wmk. 383
5199 A2431 4k multicolored   .25 .25
5200 A2431 10k multicolored   .25 .25
5201 A2431 20k multicolored   .30 .25
5202 A2431 45k multicolored   .60 .40
5203 A2431 50k multicolored   .70 .50
    Nos. 5199-5203 (5)   2.10 1.65

Souvenir Sheet

5204	Sheet of 2 + label	3.00 1.50
a.	A2431 50k multicolored	1.50 .50

Nos. 5199-5203 with labels, value $5.
Printed in sheets of 24+label and 15+label.
Value, each $75.

Physicians Against Nuclear War Movement — A2490

Perf. 11½

1983, Nov. 17   Photo.   Unwmk.
5205 A2490 5k Baby, dove, sun   .50 .25

Sukhe Bator (1893-1923), Mongolian People's Rep. Founder — A2491

1983, Nov. 17
5206 A2491 5k Portrait   .50 .25

New Year 1984 A2492

1983, Dec. 1
5207 A2492 5k Star, snowflakes   .50 .25

Exists imperf; Value, $50.
Printed in sheets of 50. Also exist in miniature sheets of 16. Value, $150.

Newly Completed Buildings, Moscow — A2493

3k, Children's Musical Theater. 4k, Tourist Hotel, vert. 6k, Council of Ministers. 20k, Ismaelovo Hotel. 45k, Novosti Press Agency.

Perf. 12½x12, 12x12½

			Engr.
1983, Dec. 15			
5208	A2493	3k multicolored	.25 .25
5209	A2493	4k multicolored	.25 .25
5210	A2493	6k multicolored	.25 .25
5211	A2493	20k multicolored	.40 .30
5212	A2493	45k multicolored	.75 .50
	Nos. 5208-5212 (5)		1.90 1.55

Souvenir Sheet

Environmental Protection Campaign — A2494

1983, Dec. 20   Photo.   Perf. 11½
5213 A2494 50k multicolored   1.50 1.50

Moscow Local Broadcasting Network, 50th anniv. — A2495

1984, Jan. 1
5214 A2495 4k multicolored   .50 .25

European Women's Skating Championships — A2496

1984, Jan. 1   Perf. 12x11½
5215 A2496 5k multicolored   .50 .25

Exists imperf. Value, $50.

Cuban Revolution, 25th Anniv. A2497

1984, Jan. 1   Perf. 11½
5216 A2497 5k Flag, "25"   .50 .25

Exists imperf. Value, $50.

World War II Tanks — A2498

1984, Jan. 25   Litho.   Perf. 12½x12

5217	A2498	10k KW	.60 .25
5218	A2498	10k IS-2	.60 .25
5219	A2498	10k T-34	.60 .25
5220	A2498	10k ISU-152	.60 .25
5221	A2498	10k SU-100	.60 .25
	Nos. 5217-5221 (5)		3.00 1.25

No. 5220 exists imperf. Value, $50.

1984 Winter Olympics — A2499

1984, Feb. 8   Photo.   Perf. 11½x12

5222	A2499	5k Biathlon	.25 .25
a.		Miniature sheet of 8	45.00
5223	A2499	10k Speed skating	.25 .25
a.		Miniature sheet of 8	45.00
5224	A2499	20k Hockey	.25 .25
a.		Miniature sheet of 8	45.00
5225	A2499	45k Figure skating	.25 .25
a.		Miniature sheet of 8	45.00
	Nos. 5222-5225 (4)		1.00 1.00

Exist imperf. Value, each $50.

Moscow Zoo, 120th Anniv. — A2500

1984, Feb. 16   Litho.   Perf. 12½x12

5226	A2500	2k Mandrill	.25 .25
5227	A2500	3k Gazelle	.25 .25
5228	A2500	4k Snow leopard	.25 .25
5229	A2500	5k Crowned crane	.25 .25
5230	A2500	20k Macaw	.25 .25
	Nos. 5226-5230 (5)		1.25 1.25

Yuri Gagarin (1934-68) — A2501

1984, Mar. 9   Engr.   Perf. 12½x12
5231 A2501 15k Portrait, Vostok   .50 .25
a.   Miniature sheet of 8   150.00

Souvenir Sheet

Mass Development of Virgin and Unused Land, 30th Anniv. — A2502

1984, Mar. 14   Photo.   Perf. 11½x12
5232 A2502 50k multicolored   1.50 .75

Hermitage Painting Type of 1982

Paintings by English Artists: 4k, E.K. Vorontsova, by George Hayter. 10k, Portrait of Mrs. Greer, by George Romney. 20k, Before a Thunderstorm, by George Morland, horiz. 45k, Portrait of an Unknown Man, by Marcus Gheeraerts Jr. No. 5237, Cupid and Venus, by Joshua Reynolds. No. 5238a, Portrait of a Lady in Blue, by Thomas Gainsborough.

Perf. 12x12½, 12½x12

1984, Mar. 20   Litho.   Wmk. 383

5233	A2431	4k multicolored	.25 .25
5234	A2431	10k multicolored	.25 .25
5235	A2431	20k multicolored	.30 .25
5236	A2431	45k multicolored	.70 .40
5237	A2431	50k multicolored	.80 .45
	Nos. 5233-5237 (5)		2.30 1.60

Souvenir Sheet

5238	Sheet of 2	2.00 1.00
a.	A2431 50k multicolored	.50 .40

Nos. 5233-5237 each se-tenant with label showing text and embossed emblem. Value, set of pairs with label, $5. Exists also in miniature sheets of 15 + label. Value, set, $75.

S.V. Ilyushin — A2503

Perf. 11½

1984, Mar. 23   Photo.   Unwmk.
5239 A2503 5k Aircraft designer, (1894-1977)   .50 .25

Andrei S. Bubnov — A2504

1984, Apr. 3   Perf. 11½x12
5240 A2504 5k Statesman, (1884-1940)   .50 .25

Intercosmos Cooperative Space Program (USSR-India) — A2505

Designs: 5k, Weather Station M-100 launch. 20k, Geodesy (satellites, observatory). 45k, Rocket, satellites, dish antenna. 50k, Flags, cosmonauts.

1984   Perf. 12x11½

5241	A2505	5k multicolored	.25 .25
5242	A2505	20k multicolored	.35 .25
5243	A2505	45k multicolored	.40 .25
	Nos. 5241-5243 (3)		1.00 .75

Souvenir Sheet

5244	A2505 50k multicolored	1.50 .75

No. 5244 contains one 25x36mm stamp. Issue dates: 50k, Apr. 5; others, Apr. 3.

Cosmonauts' Day — A2506

1984, Apr. 12   Perf. 11½x12
5245 A2506 10k Futuristic spaceman   .50 .25

Tchelyuskin Arctic Expedition, 50th Anniv. — A2507

Photogravure and Engraved

1984, Apr. 13   Perf. 11½x12
5246 A2507 6k Ship   .25 .25
a.   Miniature sheet of 8   40.00

5247	A2507	15k Shipwreck	.50	.25

5247 A2507 15k Shipwreck .50 .25
a. Miniature sheet of 8 40.00
5248 A2507 45k Rescue 1.50 .70
a. Miniature sheet of 8 40.00
Nos. 5246-5248 (3) 2.25 1.20

Souvenir Sheet
Photo.

5249 A2507 50k Hero of Soviet Union medal 1.50 .70

First HSU medal awarded to rescue crew. No. 5249 contains one 27x39mm stamp.

Souvenir Sheet

114th Birth Anniv. of Lenin — A2508

1984, Apr. 22   Litho.   Perf. 11½x12½
5250 A2508 50k Portrait 1.50 .70

Aquatic Plants — A2509

1k, Lotus. 2k, Euriola. 3k, Water lilies, horiz. 10k, White nymphaea, horiz. 20k, Marshflowers, horiz.

1984, May 5   Perf. 12x12½, 12½x12
5251 A2509 1k multicolored .25 .25
5252 A2509 2k multicolored .25 .25
5253 A2509 3k multicolored .25 .25
5254 A2509 10k multicolored .25 .25
a. Miniature sheet of 8 30.00
5255 A2509 20k multicolored .45 .25
Nos. 5251-5255 (5) 1.45 1.25

Soviet Peace Policy — A2510

No. 5256, Marchers, banners (at left). No. 5257, Text. No. 5258, Marchers, banners (at right).

1984, May 8   Photo.   Perf. 11½
5256 A2510 5k multicolored .35 .25
5257 A2510 5k multicolored .35 .25
5258 A2510 5k multicolored .35 .25
a. Strip of 3, #5256-5258 2.00 .50

A2511

1984, May 15   Photo.   Perf. 11½
5259 A2511 10k multicolored .50 .25

E.O. Paton Institute of Electric Welding, 50th anniv.

A2512

1984, May 21
5260 A2512 10k multicolored .50 .30

25th Conf. for Electric and Postal Communications Cooperation.

A2513

1984, May 29
5261 A2513 5k violet brown .50 .25

Maurice Bishop, Grenada Prime Minister (1944-83).

A2514

1984, May 31
5262 A2514 5k multicolored 1.00 .25

V.I. Lenin Central Museum, 60th anniv.

City of Archangelsk, 400th Anniv. — A2515

1984, June 1   Photo. & Engr.
5263 A2515 5k multicolored .50 .25

European Youth Soccer Championship — A2516

1984, June 1   Photo.   Perf. 12x11½
5264 A2516 15k multicolored .50 .30

Lighthouse Type of 1982

Far Eastern seas lighthouses.

1984, June 14   Litho.   Perf. 12
5265 A2435 1k Petropavlovsk .40 .25
5266 A2435 2k Tokarev .40 .25
5267 A2435 4k Basargin .40 .25

5268 A2435 5k Kronitsky .40 .25
5269 A2435 10k Marekan .40 .25
Nos. 5265-5269 (5) 2.00 1.25

Salyut 7-Soyuz T-9 150-Day Flight — A2517

1984, June 27   Litho.   Perf. 12
5270 A2517 15k multicolored .50 .25

A2518

Photogravure and Engraved
1984, July 1   Perf. 11½
5271 A2518 10k multicolored .50 .25

Morflot, Merchant & Transport Fleet, 60th anniv.

60th Anniv. of Awarding V.I. Lenin Name to Youth Communist League — A2519

1984, July 1   Photo.   Perf. 11½x12
5272 A2519 5k multicolored .50 .25

Liberation of Byelorussia, 40th Anniv. A2520

1984, July 3   Photo.   Perf. 12x11½
5273 A2520 5k multicolored .50 .25

CMEA Conference, Moscow — A2521

1984, June 12   Photo.   Perf. 11½
5274 A2521 5k CMEA Building & Kremlin .50 .25

A2522

1984, July 20   Photo.   Perf. 11½
5275 A2522 5k Convention seal .50 .25

27th Intl. Geological Cong., Moscow.

A2523

1984, July 22   Photo.   Perf. 11½
5276 A2523 5k Arms, draped flag .50 .25

People's Republic of Poland, 40th anniv.

B. V. Asafiev (1884-1949), Composer — A2524

1984, July 25   Engr.   Perf. 12½x12
5277 A2524 5k greenish black .50 .25

Relations with Mexico, 60th Anniv. A2525

1984, Aug. 4   Litho.   Perf. 12
5278 A2525 5k USSR, Mexican flags .50 .25

Miniature Sheet

Russian Folk Tales A2526

Designs: a, 3 archers. b, Prince and frog. c, Old man and prince. d, Crowd and swans. e, Wolf and men. f, Bird and youth. g, Youth on white horse. h, Couple with Tsar. i, Village scene. j, Man on black horse. k, Old man. l, Young woman.

1984, Aug. 10   Litho.   Perf. 12x12½
5279 Sheet of 12 5.00 2.00
a.-l. A2526 5k, any single .30 .25

Friendship '84 Games A2527

1984, Aug. 15   Photo.   Perf. 11½
5280	A2527	1k	Basketball	.25	.25
5281	A2527	5k	Gymnastics, vert.	.25	.25
5282	A2527	10k	Weightlifting	.25	.25
5283	A2527	15k	Wrestling	.25	.25
5284	A2527	20k	High jump	.25	.25
		Nos. 5280-5284 (5)		1.25	1.25

A2528

1984, Aug. 23   Litho.   Perf. 12
5285	A2528	5k	Flag, monument	.50	.25

Liberation of Romania, 40th anniv.

A2529

Designs: 35k, Sable. 2r, Ship, arctic map. 3r, Child and globe. 5r, Palm frond and globe. Subjects: 35k, 3r, Environmental protection. 2r, Arctic development. 5r, World peace.

1984, Sept. 5   Litho.   Perf. 12½x12
5286	A2529	35k	multicolored	.65	.35
5287	A2529	2r	multicolored	.80	.45

Engr.
5288	A2529	3r	multicolored	4.00	1.10
5289	A2529	5r	multicolored	5.00	1.90
		Nos. 5286-5289 (4)		10.45	3.80

Nos. 5286 and 5287 were issued in 1984 on chalky paper, which fluoresces under UV light. Reprints on ordinary paper were made in 1988 and 1991, respectively. Values above are for the later printings. The 1984 printings are valued, mint or used, at 90c for No. 5286, and $3 for No. 5287.
See Nos. 6016B-6017A.

World Chess Championships
A2530

No. 5290, Motherland statue, Volgograd. No. 5291, Spasski Tower, Moscow.

1984, Sept. 7   Photo.   Perf. 11½
5290	A2530	15k	multicolored	.50	.30
5291	A2530	15k	multicolored	.50	.30

Bulgarian Revolution, 40th Anniv. — A2531

1984, Sept. 9   Photo.   Perf. 11½
5292	A2531	5k	Bulgarian arms	.50	.25

Ethiopian Revolution, 10th Anniv. A2532

1984, Sept. 12   Litho.   Perf. 12
5293	A2532	5k	Ethiopian flag, seal	.50	.25

Novokramatorsk Machinery Plant, 50th Anniv. — A2533

Photogravure and Engraved
1984, Sept. 20   Perf. 11½
5294	A2533	5k	Excavator	.50	.25

Nakhichevan ASSR, 60th Anniv. — A2534

1984, Sept. 20   Litho.   Perf. 12
5295	A2534	5k	Arms	.50	.25

Television from Space, 25th Anniv. A2535

1984, Oct. 4   Photo.   Perf. 11½
5296	A2535	5k	Luna 3	.25	.25
5297	A2535	20k	Venera 9	.35	.25
5298	A2535	45k	Meteor satellite	.40	.25
		Nos. 5296-5298 (3)		1.00	.75

Souvenir Sheet
Perf. 11½x12
5299	A2535	50k	Camera, space walker, vert.	1.50	.75

No. 5299 contains one 26x37mm stamp.

German Democratic Republic, 35th Anniv. A2536

1984, Oct. 7   Photo.   Perf. 11½
5300	A2536	5k	Flag, arms	.50	.25

Ukrainian Liberation, 40th Anniv. A2537

1984, Oct. 8   Photo.   Perf. 12x11½
5301	A2537	5k	Motherland statue, Kiev	.50	.25

Soviet Republics and Parties, 60th Anniv. A2538

SSR Flags & Arms: No. 5302, Moldavian. No. 5303, Kirgiz. No. 5304, Tadzhik. No. 5305, Uzbek. No. 5306, Turkmen.

1984   Litho.   Perf. 12
5302	A2538	5k	multicolored	.25	.25
5303	A2538	5k	multicolored	.25	.25
5304	A2538	5k	multicolored	.25	.25
5305	A2538	5k	multicolored	.25	.25
5306	A2538	5k	multicolored	.25	.25
		Nos. 5302-5306 (5)		1.25	1.25

Issued: No. 5302, 10/12; Nos. 5303-5304, 10/14; Nos. 5305-5306, 10/27.

Kremlin, 1917 Flag — A2539

1984, Oct. 23   Photo.   Perf. 11½
5307	A2539	5k	multicolored	.50	.25

October Revolution, 67th anniv.

Aircraft, Spacecraft A2540

1984, Nov. 6   Photo.   Perf. 11½
5308	A2540	5k	multicolored	.50	.25

M. Frunze Inst. of Aviation & Cosmonautics.

Baikal — Amur Railway Completion A2541

5k, Workers, map, engine.

1984, Nov. 7   Photo.   Perf. 11½
5309	A2541	5k	multicolored	.50	.25

Hermitage Type of 1982

Paintings by French Artists: 4k, Girl in a Hat, by Jean Louis Voille. 10k, A Stolen Kiss, by Jean-Honore Fragonard. 20k, Woman Combing her Hair, by Edgar Degas. 45k, Pigmalion and Galatea, by Francois Boucher. 50k, Landscape with Polyphenus, by Nicholas Poussin. No. 5315a, Child with a Whip, by Pierre-Auguste Renoir.

Perf. 12x12½, 12½x12
1984, Nov. 20   Litho.   Wmk. 383
5310	A2431	4k	multicolored	.25	.25
5311	A2431	10k	multi, horiz.	.35	.25
5312	A2431	20k	multicolored	.55	.45
5313	A2431	45k	multi, horiz.	.85	.55
5314	A2431	50k	multi, horiz.	1.00	.65
		Nos. 5310-5314 (5)		3.00	2.15

Souvenir Sheet
5315			Sheet of 2	3.00	1.50
a.	A2431	50k	multicolored	1.00	.50

Nos. 5310-5314 exist se-tenant with label. Value, set, $5. Also exists in miniature sheets of 15 + label. Value, set of sheets, $75.

Mongolian Peoples' Republic, 60th Anniv. — A2542

5k, Mongolian flag, arms.

Perf. 11½
1984, Nov. 26   Photo.   Unwmk.
5316	A2542	5k	multicolored	.50	.25

New Year 1985 — A2543

5k, Kremlin, snowflakes.

1984, Dec. 4   Litho.   Perf. 11½
5317	A2543	5k	multicolored	.50	.25
a.			Miniature sheet of 8	110.00	

Souvenir Sheet

Environmental Protection — A2544

50k, Leaf, pollution sources.

1984, Dec. 4   Litho.   Perf. 12½x12
5318	A2544	50k	multicolored	2.00	.75

Russian Fire Vehicles — A2545

3k, Crew wagon, 19th cent. 5k, Pumper, 19th cent. 10k, Ladder truck, 1904. 15k, Pumper, 1904. 20k, Ladder truck, 1913.

Photogravure and Engraved
1984, Dec. 12   Perf. 12x11½
5319	A2545	3k	multicolored	.25	.25
5320	A2545	5k	multicolored	.25	.25
5321	A2545	10k	multicolored	.55	.25
5322	A2545	15k	multicolored	.75	.25
5323	A2545	20k	multicolored	1.20	.25
		Nos. 5319-5323 (5)		3.00	1.25

See Nos. 5410-5414.

Intl. Venus-Halley's Comet Project — A2546

15k, Satellite, flight path.

1984, Dec. 15   Photo.   Perf. 12x11½
5324	A2546	15k	multicolored	1.00	.25
a.			Miniature sheet of 8	75.00	

Indira Gandhi (1917-1984), Indian Prime Minister — A2547

1984, Dec. 28   Litho.   Perf. 12
5325 A2547 5k Portrait   .50 .25

1905 Revolution A2548

5k, Flag, Moscow memorial.

1985, Jan. 22   Photo.   Perf. 11½
5326 A2548 5k multicolored   .50 .25

A2549

1985, Jan. 24
5327 A2549 5k multicolored   .50 .25
Patrice Lumumba Peoples' Friendship University, 25th Anniv.

Mikhail Vasilievich Frunze (1885-1925), Party Leader — A2550

1985, Feb. 2
5328 A2550 5k bluish, blk & ocher   .50 .25

Karakalpak ASSR, 60th Anniv. A2551

1985, Feb. 16   Perf. 12
5329 A2551 5k Republic arms   .50 .25

10th Winter Spartakiad of Friendly Armies — A2552

1985, Feb. 23   Perf. 11½
5330 A2552 5k Hockey player, emblem   .50 .25

Kalevala, 150th Anniv. A2553

1985, Feb. 25   Litho.   Perf. 12
5331 A2553 5k Rune singer, frontispiece   .50 .25
Finnish Kalevala, collection of Karelian epic poetry compiled by Elias Lonrot.

Yakov M. Sverdlov (1885-1919), Party Leader — A2554

1985, Mar. 3   Engr.   Perf. 12½x12
5332 A2554 5k rose lake   .50 .25
Yakov M. Sverdlov (1885-1919), party leader.

Pioneer Badge, Awards — A2555

1985, Mar. 6   Photo.   Perf. 11½
5333 A2555 5k multicolored   .50 .25
Pionerskaya Pravda, All-Union children's newspaper, 60th Anniv.

Maria Alexandrovna Ulyanova (1835-1916), Lenin's Mother — A2556

1985, Mar. 6   Engr.   Perf. 12½x12
5334 A2556 5k black   .50 .25

Hermitage Type of 1982

Paintings by Spanish artists: 4k, The Young Virgin Praying, vert., by Francisco de Zurbaran (1598-1664). 10k, Still-life, by Antonio Pereda (c. 1608-1678). 20k, The Immaculate Conception, vert., by Murillo (1617-1682). 45k, The Grinder, by Antonio Puga. No. 5339, Count Olivares, vert., by Diego Velazques (1599-1660). No. 5340a, Portrait of the actress Antonia Zarate, vert., by Goya (1746-1828).

Perf. 12x12½, 12½x12
1985, Mar. 14   Litho.   Wmk. 383
5335 A2431 4k multicolored   .25 .25
5336 A2431 10k multicolored   .30 .25
5337 A2431 20k multicolored   .50 .40
5338 A2431 45k multicolored   1.25 .90
5339 A2431 50k multicolored   1.40 .95
    Nos. 5335-5339 (5)   3.70 2.75
Souvenir Sheet
Lithographed and Embossed
5340   Sheet of 2 + label   3.00 2.00
    a. A2431 50k multicolored   1.10 .75
    Nos. 5335-5339 exist in miniature sheets of 15 + label. Value, set of sheets, $75.

EXPO '85, Tsukuba, Japan A2557

Soviet exhibition, Expo '85 emblems and: 5k, Cosmonauts in space. 10k, Communications satellite. 20k, Alternative energy sources development. 45k, Future housing systems. 50k, Soviet exhibition emblem, globe.

Perf. 12x11½
1985, Mar. 17   Photo.   Unwmk.
5341 A2557 5k multicolored   .25 .25
5342 A2557 10k multicolored   .25 .25
5343 A2557 20k multicolored   .50 .35
5344 A2557 45k multicolored   1.00 .70
    Nos. 5341-5344 (4)   2.00 1.55
Souvenir Sheet
5345 A2557 50k multicolored   1.50 .90
Nos. 5341-5344 issued in sheets of 25. Miniature sheets of 8 exist. Value, set, $100.

Souvenir Sheet

Johann Sebastian Bach (1685-1750), Composer — A2558

Photogravure and Engraved
1985, Mar. 21   Perf. 12x11½
5346 A2558 50k black   1.50 1.00

Natl. Crest, Budapest Memorial — A2559

1985, Apr. 4   Litho.   Perf. 12
5347 A2559 5k multi   .50 .25
Hungary liberated from German occupation, 40th Anniv.

Emblem — A2560

1985, Apr. 5   Photo.   Perf. 11½
5348 A2560 15k multi   .50 .30
Society for Cultural Relations with Foreign Countries, 60th anniv.

Victory over Fascism, 40th Anniv. A2561

#5349, Battle of Moscow, soldier, Kremlin, portrait of Lenin. #5350, Soldier, armed forces. #5351, Armaments production, worker. #5352, Partisan movement, cavalry. #5353, Berlin-Treptow war memorial, German Democratic Republic. #5354, Order of the Patriotic War, second class.

1985, Apr. 20   Perf. 12x11½
5349 A2561 5k multicolored   .25 .25
5350 A2561 5k multicolored   .25 .25
5351 A2561 5k multicolored   .25 .25
5352 A2561 5k multicolored   .25 .25
5353 A2561 5k multicolored   .25 .25
    Nos. 5349-5353 (5)   1.25 1.25
Souvenir Sheet
Perf. 11½
5354 A2561 50k multicolored   1.50 .50
No. 5354 contains one 28x40mm stamp. Issued in sheets of 25. Exists in miniature sheets of 8. Value, set, $25.

No. 5353 Ovptd. in Red for 40th Year Since World War II Victory All-Union Philatelic Exhibition

1985, Apr. 29   Photo.   Perf. 12x11½
5354A A2561 5k brn lake, gold & vermilion   2.00 .50

Yuri Gagarin Center for Training Cosmonauts, 25th Anniv. — A2562

Cosmonauts day: Portrait, cosmonauts, Soyuz-T spaceship.

1985, Apr. 12   Photo.   Perf. 11½x12
5355 A2562 15k multicolored   .50 .25
    a.   Miniature sheet of 8   125.00

12th World Youth Festival, Moscow — A2563

1985, Apr. 15   Litho.   Perf. 12x12½
5356	A2563	1k	Three youths	.25	.25
5357	A2563	3k	African girl	.25	.25
5358	A2563	5k	Girl, rainbow	.25	.25
a.			Miniature sheet of 8	10.00	
5359	A2563	20k	Asian youth, camera	.35	.35
5360	A2563	45k	Emblem	.75	.35
			Nos. 5356-5360 (5)	1.85	1.45

Souvenir Sheet
1985, July 4
5361	A2563	30k	Emblem	1.50	1.00

115th Birth Anniv. of Lenin — A2564

Portrait and: No. 5362, Lenin Museum, Tampere, Finland. No. 5363, Memorial apartment, Paris, France.

1985, Apr. 22   Photo.   Perf. 11½x12
5362	A2564	5k	multicolored	.25	.25
5363	A2564	5k	multicolored	.25	.25

Souvenir Sheet
Litho.
Perf. 12x12½
5364	A2564	30k	Portrait	1.50	1.00

No. 5364 contains one 30x42mm stamp.

Order of Victory — A2565

Photogravure and Engraved
1985, May 9   Perf. 11½
5365	A2565	20k	sil, royal bl, dk red & gold	.60	.35

Allied World War II victory over Germany and Japan, 40th anniv.

Arms — A2566

1985, May 9   Litho.   Perf. 12½x12
5366	A2566	5k	multicolored	.50	.25

Liberation of Czechoslovakia from German occupation, 40th Anniv.

Flags of Member Nations — A2567

1985, May 14   Photo.   Perf. 11½
5367	A2567	5k	multicolored	.50	.25

Warsaw Treaty Org., 30th anniv.

Mikhail Alexandrovich Sholokhov (1905-1984), Novelist & Nobel Laureate — A2568

Portraits and book covers: No. 5368, Tales from the Don, Quiet Flows the Don, A Human Tragedy. No. 5369, The Quiet Don, Virgin Lands Under the Plow, Thus They Have Fought for Their Homeland. No. 5370, Portrait.

1985, May 24   Photo.   Perf. 12½x12
5368	A2568	5k	Portrait at left	.35	.25
5369	A2568	5k	Portrait at right	.35	.25

Photo.
Perf. 12x11½
Size: 37x52mm
5370	A2568	5k	brn, gold & black	.35	.25
			Nos. 5368-5370 (3)	1.05	.75

INTERCOSMOS Project Halley-Venus — A2570

15k, Spacecraft, satellites, Venus.

1985, June 11   Litho.   Perf. 12
5372	A2570	15k	multicolored	.50	.25
a.			Miniature sheet of 8	125.00	

Artek Pioneer Camp, 60th Anniv. A2571

4k, Camp, badges, Lenin Pioneers emblem.

1985, June 14   Photo.   Perf. 11½
5373	A2571	4k	multicolored	.50	.25

Mutiny on the Battleship Potemkin, 80th Anniv. — A2572

Photogravure and Engraved
1985, June 16   Perf. 11½x12
5374	A2572	5k	dk red, gold & black	.50	.25

Miniature Sheet

Soviet Railways Rolling Stock — A2573

Designs: a, Electric locomotive WL 80-R (grn). b, Tanker car (bl). c, Refrigerator car (bl). d, Sleeper car (brn). e, Tipper car (brn). f, Box car (brn). g, Shunting diesel locomotive (bl). h, Mail car (grn).

1985, June 15   Engr.   Perf. 12½x12
5375	A2573		Sheet of 8	3.00	1.65
a.-h.		10k	any single	.35	.25

Cosmonauts L. Kizim, V. Soloviov, O. Atkov and Salyut-7 Spacecraft — A2574

1985, June 25   Litho.
5376	A2574	15k	multicolored	.50	.25
a.			Miniature sheet of 8	50.00	

Soyuz T-10, Salyut-7 and Soyuz T-11 flights, Feb. 8-Oct. 2, 1984.

Beating Sword into Plowshares, Sculpture Donated to UN Hdqtrs. by USSR — A2575

Photogravure and Engraved
1985, June 26   Perf. 11½
5377	A2575	45k	multicolored	.50	.35

UN 40th anniv.

Intl. Youth Year A2576

1985, June 26   Photo.   Perf. 12
5378	A2576	10k	multicolored	.50	.25

Medicinal Plants from Siberia — A2577

2k, O. dictiocarpum. 3k, Thermopsis lanceolata. 5k, Rosa acicularis lindi. 20k, Rhaponticum carthamoides. 45k, Bergenia crassifolia fritsch.

1985, July 10   Litho.   Perf. 12½x12
5379	A2577	2k	multicolored	.25	.25
5380	A2577	3k	multicolored	.25	.25
5381	A2577	5k	multicolored	.25	.25
5382	A2577	20k	multicolored	.50	.25
a.			Miniature sheet of 8	35.00	
5383	A2577	45k	multicolored	.75	.50
			Nos. 5379-5383 (5)	2.00	1.60

Cosmonauts V. A. Dzhanibekov, S. E. Savistskaya, and I. P. Volk, Soyuz T-12 Mission, July 17-29, 1984 — A2578

1985, July 17
5384	A2578	10k	multicolored	.50	.25
a.			Miniature sheet of 8	100.00	

1st woman's free flight in space.

A2579

Caecilienhof Palace, Potsdam, Flags of UK, USSR, & US.

1985, July 17
5385	A2579	15k	multicolored	.50	.25

Potsdam Conference, 40th anniv.

Finlandia Hall, Helsinki — A2580

1985, July 25   Photo.   Perf. 11½
5386	A2580	20k	multicolored	.50	.30
a.			Miniature sheet of 8	100.00	

Helsinki Conference on European security and cooperation, 10th anniv.

Flags of USSR, North Korea, Liberation Monument in Pyongyang A2581

1985, Aug. 1
5387	A2581	5k	multicolored	.50	.25

Socialist Rep. of North Korea, 40th anniv.

Endangered Wildlife — A2582

Designs: 2k, Sorex bucharensis, vert. 3k, Cardiocranius paradoxus. 5k, Selevinia betpakdalensis, vert. 20k, Felis caracal. 45k, Gazella subgutturosa. 50k, Panthera pardus.

Perf. 12x12½, 12½x12
1985, Aug. 15   Litho.
5388	A2582	2k	multicolored	.25	.25
5389	A2582	3k	multicolored	.25	.25
5390	A2582	5k	multicolored	.25	.25

Size: 47x32mm

5391 A2582 20k multicolored .60 .30
a.   Miniature sheet of 8   100.00
5392 A2582 45k multicolored 1.20 .60
   Nos. 5388-5392 (5)   2.55 1.65

Souvenir Sheet

5393 A2582 50k multicolored 2.50 .75

Youth World Soccer Cup Championships, Moscow — A2583

1985, Aug. 24   *Perf. 12*
5394 A2583 5k multicolored .50 .25

Alexander G. Stakhanov, Coal Miner & Labor Leader A2584

1985, Aug. 30 Photo.   *Perf. 11½*
5395 A2584 5k multicolored .50 .25
   Stakhanovite Movement for high labor productivity, 50th anniv.

Bryansk Victory Memorial, Buildings, Arms A2585

1985, Sept. 1
5396 A2585 5k multicolored .50 .25
   Millennium of Bryansk.

Socialist Republic of Vietnam, 40th Anniv. — A2586

1985, Sept. 2 Litho.   *Perf. 12½x12*
5397 A2586 5k Arms .50 .25

A2587

1985, Sept. 2 Photo.   *Perf. 11½*
5398 A2587 10k multicolored .50 .25
   1985 World Chess Championship match, A. Karpov Vs. G. Kasparov, Moscow.

Lutsk City, Ukrainian SSR, 900th Anniv. — A2588

1985, Sept. 14
5399 A2588 5k Lutsk Castle .50 .25

Open Book, the Weeping Jaroslavna and Prince Igor's Army — A2589

Photogravure and Engraved
1985, Sept. 14   *Perf. 11½x12*
5400 A2589 10k multicolored .50 .25
   The Song of Igor's Campaign, epic poem, 800th anniv.

Sergei Vasilievich Gerasimov (1885-1964), Painter A2590

1985, Sept. 26   *Perf. 12x11½*
5401 A2590 5k Portrait .50 .25

October Revolution, 68th Anniv. — A2591

1985, Oct. 10 Photo.   *Perf. 11½*
5402 A2591 5k multicolored .50 .25

UN 40th Anniv. — A2592

1985, Oct. 24
5403 A2592 15k multicolored .50 .25

Krisjanis Barons (1835-1923), Latvian Folklorist — A2593

Lithographed and Engraved
1985, Oct. 31
5404 A2593 5k beige & black .50 .25

Lenin, Laborer Breaking Chains A2594

1985, Nov. 20   **Photo.**
5405 A2594 5k multicolored .50 .25
   Petersburg Union struggle for liberation of the working classes, founded by Lenin, 90th anniv.

Largest Soviet Telescope, 10th Anniv. — A2595

1985, Nov. 20 Engr.   *Perf. 12½x12*
5406 A2595 10k dark blue .50 .25
   Soviet Observatory inauguration.

A2596

1985, Nov. 25   **Photo.**
5407 A2596 5k multicolored .50 .25
   Angolan Independence, 10th anniv.

A2597

1985, Nov. 29   *Perf. 11½*
5408 A2597 5k multicolored .50 .25
   Socialist Federal Republic of Yugoslavia, 40th anniv.

New Year — A2598

1985, Dec. 3 Litho.   *Perf. 12*
5409 A2598 5k multicolored 1.00 .25
a.   Miniature sheet of 8   22.50

Vehicle Type of 1984
1985, Dec. 18 Photo.   *Perf. 12x11½*
5410 A2545 3k AMO-F15, 1926 .25 .25
5411 A2545 5k PMZ-1, 1933 .25 .25
5412 A2545 10k AC-40, 1977 .35 .25
5413 A2545 20k AL-30, 1970 .55 .35
5414 A2545 45k AA-60, 1978 1.10 .70
   Nos. 5410-5414 (5)   2.50 1.80

Samantha Smith — A2599

1985, Dec. 25   *Perf. 12*
5415 A2599 5k vio blue, choc & ver .50 .25
   American student invited to meet with Soviet leaders in 1984.

A2600

1985, Dec. 30   **Litho.**
5416 A2600 5k multicolored .50 .25
   N.M. Emanuel (1915-1984), chemist.

A2601

1985, Dec. 30
5417 A2601 5k Sightseeing .50 .25
5418 A2601 5k Sports .50 .25
   Family leisure activities.

Intl. Peace Year — A2602

1986, Jan. 2 Photo.   *Perf. 11½*
5419 A2602 20k brt blue, bluish grn & silver .50 .30

Flags, Congress Palace, Carnation A2603

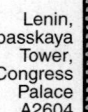

Lenin, Spasskaya Tower, Congress Palace A2604

Lenin — A2605

1986, Jan. 3
5420 A2603 5k multicolored .25 .25
Photogravure and Engraved
Perf. 12x11½
5421 A2604 20k multicolored 1.00 .30
Souvenir Sheet
Photo.
Perf. 11½
5422 A2605 50k multicolored 2.50 .70
27th Communist Party Congress.

A2606

1986, Jan. 10 **Perf. 11½x12**
5423 A2606 15k multicolored .50 .25
a. Miniature sheet of 8 20.00
Modern Olympic Games, 90th anniv.

A2607

Flora of Russian Steppes, different.

Perf. 12½x12, 12x12½

1986, Jan. 15 **Litho.**
5424 A2607 4k multicolored .25 .25
5425 A2607 5k multi, horiz. .25 .25
5426 A2607 10k multicolored .35 .25
5427 A2607 15k multicolored .50 .30
5428 A2607 20k multicolored .60 .35
a. Miniature sheet of 8 32.50
Nos. 5424-5428 (5) 1.95 1.40

A2608

Vodovzvodnaya Tower, Grand Kremlin Palace.

1986, Jan. 20 **Perf. 12½x12**
5429 A2608 50k grayish green 1.50 .70

A2609

1986, Feb. 20 **Perf. 11½**
5430 A2609 5k multicolored .50 .25
Voronezh City, 400th anniv.

A2610

1986, Feb. 20 **Engr.** **Perf. 12**
5431 A2610 10k bluish black .50 .25
Bela Kun (1886-1939), Hungarian party leader.

A2611

1986, Feb. 28 **Perf. 12½x12**
5432 A2611 5k grayish black .50 .25
Karolis Pozhela (1896-1926), Lithuanian party founder.

Intercosmos Project Halley, Final Stage — A2612

15k, Vega probe, comet. 50k, Vega I, comet.

1986, Mar. 6 **Litho.** **Perf. 12**
5433 A2612 15k multi .50 .25
a. Miniature sheet of 8 125.00
Souvenir Sheet
Perf. 12½x12
5434 A2612 50k multi 5.00 .75
No. 5434 contains one 42x30mm stamp.

Butterflies
A2613

4k, Utetheisa pulchella. 5k, Allancastria caucasica. 10k, Zegris eupheme. 15k, Catocala sponsa. 20k, Satyrus bischoffi.

1986, Mar. 18 **Perf. 12x12½**
5435 A2613 4k multicolored .25 .25
5436 A2613 5k multicolored .25 .25
5437 A2613 10k multicolored .40 .25
5438 A2613 15k multicolored .50 .50
5439 A2613 20k multicolored .65 .55
a. Miniature sheet of 8 60.00
Nos. 5435-5439 (5) 2.05 1.80

EXPO '86, Vancouver
A2614

1986, Mar. 25 **Photo.** **Perf. 12x11½**
5440 A2614 20k Globe, space station .50 .30
a. Miniature sheet of 8 20.00

S.M. Kirov (1886-1934), Party Leader — A2615

1986, Mar. 27 **Engr.** **Perf. 12½x12**
5441 A2615 5k black .50 .25

Cosmonauts' Day — A2616

Designs: 5k, Konstantin E. Tsiolkovsky (1857-1935), aerodynamics innovator, and futuristic space station. 10k, Sergei P. Korolev (1906-1966), rocket scientist, and Vostok spaceship, vert. 15k, Yuri Gagarin, 1st cosmonaut, Sputnik I and Vega probe.

Perf. 12½x12, 12x12½

1986, Apr. 12 **Litho.**
5442 A2616 5k multicolored .50 .25
a. Miniature sheet of 8 50.00
5443 A2616 10k multicolored .50 .25
a. Miniature sheet of 8 50.00
5444 A2616 15k multicolored .75 .25
a. Miniature sheet of 7 + label 50.00
Nos. 5441-5444 (4) 2.25 1.00

No. 5444 printed se-tenant with label picturing Vostok and inscribed for the 25th anniv. of first space flight.

1986 World Ice Hockey Championships, Moscow — A2617

1986, Apr. 12 **Photo.** **Perf. 11½**
5445 A2617 15k multicolored .50 .25

Ernst Thalmann (1886-1944), German Communist Leader — A2618

1986, Apr. 16 **Engr.** **Perf. 12½x12**
5446 A2618 10k dark brown .35 .25
5447 A2618 10k reddish brown .35 .25

Lenin, 116th Birth Anniv. — A2619

Portraits and architecture: No. 5448, Socialist-Democratic People's House, Prague. No. 5449, Lenin Museum, Leipzig. No. 5450, Lenin Museum, Poronino, Poland.

1986, Apr. 22 **Photo.** **Perf. 11½x12**
5448 A2619 5k multicolored .35 .25
5449 A2619 5k multicolored .35 .25
5450 A2619 5k multicolored .35 .25
Nos. 5448-5450 (3) 1.05 .75

Tambov City, 350th Anniv.
A2620

1986, Apr. 27 **Perf. 11½**
5451 A2620 5k Buildings, city arms .50 .25

Soviet Peace Fund, 25th Anniv.
A2621

1986, Apr. 27
5452 A2621 10k lt chalky bl, gold & brt ultra .50 .25

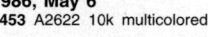

29th World Cycle Race, May 6-22 — A2622

1986, May 6
5453 A2622 10k multicolored .50 .25

Toadstools
A2623

No. 5454, Amanita phalloides. No. 5455, Amanita muscaria. No. 5456, Amanita pantherina. No. 5457, Tylopilus felleus. No. 5458, Hypholoma fasciculare.

1986, May 15 **Litho.** **Perf. 12**
5454 A2623 4k multi .25 .25
a. Miniature sheet of 8 10.00
5455 A2623 5k multi .25 .25
a. Miniature sheet of 8 10.00
5456 A2623 10k multi .45 .25
a. Miniature sheet of 8 10.00
5457 A2623 15k multi .50 .30
a. Miniature sheet of 8 10.00
5458 A2623 20k multi .65 .35
a. Miniature sheet of 8 10.00
Nos. 5454-5458 (5) 2.10 1.40

A2624

1986, May 19   Photo.   Perf. 11½
5459 A2624 10k multicolored   .50   .25
UNESCO Campaign, Man and Biosphere.

A2625

1986, May 20
5460 A2625 10k multicolored   .50   .25
9th Soviet Spartakiad.

A2626

Design: Lenin's House, Eternal Glory and V. I. Chapaiev monuments, Gorky State Academic Drama Theater.

1986, May 24
5461 A2626 5k multicolored   .50   .25
City of Kuibyshev, 400th anniv.

A2627

1986, May 25
5462 A2627 5k multicolored   .50   .25
"COMMUNICATION '86, Moscow."

1986 World Cup Soccer
Championships, Mexico — A2628

5k, 10k, Various soccer plays. 15k, World Cup on FIFA commemorative gold medal.

1986, May 31
5463 A2628   5k multicolored   .25   .25
   a.   Miniature sheet of 8   15.00
5464 A2628 10k multicolored   .30   .25
   a.   Miniature sheet of 8   15.00
5465 A2628 15k multicolored   .45   .25
   a.   Miniature sheet of 8   15.00
    Nos. 5463-5465 (3)   1.00   .75

Paintings in the Tretyakov Gallery,
Moscow — A2629

Designs: 4k, Lane in Albano. 1837, by M.I. Lebedev, vert. 5k, View of the Kremlin in Foul Weather, 1851, by A.K. Savrasov. 10k, Sunlit Pine Trees, 1896, by I.I. Shishkin, vert. 15k, Return, 1896, by A.E. Arkhipov. 45k, Wedding Procession in Moscow, the 17th Century, 1901, by A.P. Ryabushkin.

Perf. 12x12½, 12½x12
1986, June 11   Litho.
5466 A2629   4k multicolored   .25   .25
   a.   Miniature sheet of 8   10.00
5467 A2629   5k multicolored   .25   .25
   a.   Miniature sheet of 8   10.00
5468 A2629 10k multicolored   .35   .25
   a.   Miniature sheet of 8   10.00

Size: 74x37mm
Perf. 11½
5469 A2629 15k multicolored   .40   .30
   a.   Miniature sheet of 8   10.00
5470 A2629 45k multicolored   1.10   .75
   a.   Miniature sheet of 8   10.00
    Nos. 5466-5470 (5)   2.35   1.80

Irkutsk City, 300th
Anniv. — A2630

1986, June 28   Photo.   Perf. 11½
5471 A2630 5k multicolored   .50   .25

Goodwill
Games,
Moscow,
July 5-20
A2631

1986, July 4   Photo.   Perf. 11½
5472 A2631 10k Prus bl, gold & blk   .50   .25
5473 A2631 10k brt blue, gold & blk   .50   .25

UNESCO Projects
in Russia — A2632

Designs: 5k, Information sciences. 10k, Geological correlation. 15k, Inter-governmental oceanographic commission. 35k, Intl. hydrologic program.

1986, July 15
5474 A2632   5k multicolored   .25   .25
5475 A2632 10k multicolored   .40   .25
5476 A2632 15k multicolored   .50   .30
5477 A2632 35k multicolored   .95   .55
    Nos. 5474-5477 (4)   2.10   1.35

Tyumen,
400th
Anniv.
A2633

1986, July 27
5478 A2633 5k multicolored   .50   .25

A2634

1986, Aug. 1   Photo.   Perf. 11½
5479 A2634 10k multicolored   .50   .25
Olof Palme (1927-86), Prime Minister of Sweden.

A2635

1986, Aug. 8
5480 A2635 15k multicolored   .50   .25
10th World Women's Basketball Championships, Moscow, Aug. 15-17.

Natl. Sports Committee Intl. Alpinist
Camps — A2636

4k, Mt. Lenin. 5k, Mt. E. Korzhenevskaya. 10k, Mt. Belukha. 15k, Mt. Communism. 30k, Mt. Elbrus.

1986, Sept. 5   Litho.   Perf. 12
5481 A2636   4k multi   .25   .25
5482 A2636   5k multi   .25   .25
   a.   Miniature sheet of 8   35.00
5483 A2636 10k multi   .35   .25
5484 A2636 15k multi   .40   .25
5485 A2636 30k multi   .70   .30
    Nos. 5481-5485 (5)   1.95   1.30

See Nos. 5532-5535.

Souvenir Sheet

Red Book, Rainbow, Earth — A2637

1986, Sept. 10   Perf. 11½
5486 A2637 50k multicolored   2.00   .75
Nature preservation.

A2638

1986, Sept. 13   Photo.
5487 A2638 5k multicolored   .50   .25
Chelyabinsk, 250th anniv.

A2639

1986, Sept. 23
5488 A2639 15k multicolored   .50   .25
Mukran, DDR to Klaipeda, Lithuania, Train Ferry, inauguration.

A2640

1986, Sept. 26
5489 A2640 5k multicolored   .50   .25
Siauliai, Lithuanian SSR, 750th anniv.

Trucks — A2641

No. 5490, Ural-375D, 1964. No. 5491, GAZ-53A, 1965. No. 5492, KrAZ-256B, 1966. No.

5493, MAZ-515B, 1974. No. 5494, ZIL-133GY, 1979.

1986, Oct. 15   *Perf. 11½x12*
5490 A2641 4k multicolored .25 .25
5491 A2641 5k multicolored .25 .25
5492 A2641 10k multicolored .60 .25
  a.   Miniature sheet of 8   25.00
5493 A2641 15k multicolored .75 .30
5494 A2641 20k multicolored 1.25 .35
   Nos. 5490-5494 (5)   3.10 1.40

October Revolution, 69th anniv. — A2642

Design: Lenin Monument in October Square, Kremlin, Moscow.

1986, Oct. 1   Litho.   *Perf. 12*
5495 A2642 5k multicolored .50 .25

A2643

5k, Icebreaker, helicopters. 10k, Mikhail Somov port side.

1986, Oct. 10   Photo.   *Perf. 11½*
5496   5k multicolored .40 .25
5497   10k multicolored .40 .25
  a.   A2643 Pair, #5496-5497 1.00 .25
  b.   Miniature sheet of 8, 4 each   75.00

Souvenir Sheet
           Perf. 12½x11½
5498 A2643 50k Trapped in ice 3.00 .65

Mikhail Somov trapped in the Antarctic. No. 5497a has a continuous design. No. 5498 contains one 51½x36½mm stamp.

No. 4883 Ovptd. in Black for Rescue of the Mikhail Somov

Lithographed & Engraved
1986, Oct. 10   *Perf. 12x11½*
5499 A2271 4k multicolored 1.00 .25

Locomotives — A2644

4k, EU 684-37, 1929. 5k, FD 21-3000, 1941. 10k, OV-5109, 1907. 20k, C017-1613, 1944. 30k, FDP 20-578, 1941.

1986, Oct. 15   Litho.   *Perf. 12*
5500 A2644 4k multi .25 .25
5501 A2644 5k multi .25 .25
5502 A2644 10k multi .55 .25
  a.   Miniature sheet of 8   25.00
5503 A2644 20k multi .85 .40
5504 A2644 30k multi 1.10 .65
   Nos. 5500-5504 (5)   3.00 1.80

Grigori Konstantinovich Ordzhonikidze (1886-1937), Communist Party Leader — A2645

1986, Oct. 18   Engr.   *Perf. 12½x12*
5505 A2645 5k dark blue green .50 .25

A.G. Novikov (1896-1984), Composer — A2646

1986, Oct. 30
5506 A2646 5k dark brown 1.00 .25

A2647

1986, Nov. 4   Photo.   *Perf. 11½*
5507 A2647 10k blue & silver .50 .25

UNSECO, 40th anniv.

A2648

1986, Nov. 12
5508 A2648 5k lt grnsh gray & blk   .50 .25

Sun Yat-sen (1866-1925), Chinese statesman.

Mikhail Vasilyevich Lomonosov, Scientist A2649

1986, Nov. 19   Engr.   *Perf. 12x12½*
5509 A2649 5k dk violet brown .50 .25

Aircraft by A.S. Yakovlev — A2650

1986, Nov. 25   Photo.   *Perf. 11½x12*
5510 A2650 4k 1927 .25 .25
5511 A2650 5k 1935 .25 .25
  a.   Miniature sheet of 8   50.00
5512 A2650 10k 1946 .40 .25
5513 A2650 20k 1972 .65 .35
5514 A2650 30k 1981 .95 .50
   Nos. 5510-5514 (5)   2.50 1.60

New Year 1987 A2651

1986, Dec. 4   Litho.   *Perf. 11½*
5515 A2651 5k Kremlin towers .50 .25
  a.   Miniature sheet of 8   35.00

27th Communist Party Cong., 2/25-3/6 — A2652

Red banner and: No. 5516, Computers. No. 5517, Engineer, computer, dish receivers. No. 5518, Aerial view of city. No. 5519, Council for Mutual Economic Assistance building, workers. No. 5520, Spasski Tower, Kremlin Palace.

1986, Dec. 12   Photo.   *Perf. 11½x12*
5516 A2652 5k multicolored .25 .25
5517 A2652 5k multicolored .25 .25
5518 A2652 5k multicolored .25 .25
5519 A2652 5k multicolored .25 .25
5520 A2652 5k multicolored .25 .25
   Nos. 5516-5520 (5)   1.25 1.25

A2653

1986, Dec. 24   Engr.   *Perf. 12½x12*
5521 A2653 5k black .50 .25

Alexander Yakovlevich Parkhomenko (1886-1921), revolution hero.

A2654

1986, Dec. 25   Photo.   *Perf. 11½*
5522 A2654 5k brown & buff .50 .25

Samora Moises Machel (1933-1986) Pres. of Mozambique.

Miniature Sheet

Palace Museums in Leningrad — A2655

1986, Dec. 25   Engr.   *Perf. 12*
5523 A2655   Sheet of 5 + label 3.00 1.40
  a.   5k State Museum, 1898 .25 .25
  b.   10k The Hermitage, 1764 .35 .25
  c.   15k Petrodvorets, 1728 .45 .30
  d.   20k Yekaterininsky, 1757 .55 .35
  e.   50k Pavlovsk, restored c. 1945 1.25 .75

18th Soviet Trade Unions Congress, Feb. 24-28 — A2656

1987, Jan. 7   Photo.   *Perf. 11½*
5524 A2656 5k multicolored .50 .25

Butterflies A2657

4k, Atrophaneura alcinous. 5k, Papilio machaon. 10k, Papilio alexanor. 15k, Papilio maackii. 30k, Iphiclides podalirius.

1987, Jan. 15   Litho.   *Perf. 12x12½*
5525 A2657 4k multicolored .25 .25
5526 A2657 5k multicolored .25 .25
5527 A2657 10k multicolored .30 .25
5528 A2657 15k multicolored .40 .30
5529 A2657 30k multicolored .80 .50
   Nos. 5525-5529 (5)   2.00 1.55

A2658

1987, Jan. 31   *Perf. 12½x12*
5530 A2658 5k multicolored .50 .25

Karlis Miyesniyek (1887-1977), Artist.

A2659

1987, Feb. 4   *Perf. 12*
5531 A2659 5k buff & lake   .50   .25

Stasis Shimkus (1887-1943), composer.

Alpinist Camps Type of 1986

4k, Chimbulak Gorge. 10k, Shavla Gorge. 20k, Mts. Donguz-orun, Nakra-tau. 35k, Mt. Kazbek.

1987, Feb. 4
5532 A2636   4k multicolored   .25   .25
5533 A2636 10k multicolored   .30   .25
  a.   Miniature sheet of 8   15.00
5534 A2636 20k multicolored   .40   .25
5535 A2636 35k multicolored   .65   .40
       Nos. 5532-5535 (4)   1.60 1.15

Vasily Ivanovich Chapayev (1887-1919), Revolution Hero — A2660

1987, Feb. 9   Engr.
5536 A2660 5k dark red brown   .50   .25

Heino Eller (1887-1970), Estonian Composer — A2661

1987, Mar. 7   Litho.   *Perf. 12*
5537 A2661 5k buff & brown   .50   .25

A2662

1987, Mar. 8   Photo.   *Perf. 11½*
5538 A2662 5k multicolored   .40   .25

Souvenir Sheet
Perf. 11½x12
5539 A2662 50k "XX," and
                    colored bands   2.00   .75

All-Union Leninist Young Communist League 20th Congress, Moscow. No. 5539 contains one 26x37mm stamp.

A2663

Photogravure and Engraved
1987, Mar. 20   *Perf. 11½*
5540 A2663 5k buff & sepia   .50   .25

Iosif Abgarovich Orbeli (1887-1961), first president of the Armenian Academy of Sciences.

World Wildlife Fund — A2664

Polar bears.

1987, Mar. 25   Photo.   *Perf. 11½x12*
5541 A2664   5k multicolored   .30   .25
  a.   Miniature sheet of 8   150.00
5542 A2664 10k multicolored   .40   .25
  a.   Miniature sheet of 8   150.00
5543 A2664 20k multicolored   .90   .40
  a.   Miniature sheet of 8   150.00
5544 A2664 35k multicolored   1.40   .75
  a.   Miniature sheet of 8   150.00
       Nos. 5541-5544 (4)   3.00 1.65

Cosmonauts' Day — A2665

1987, Apr. 12   *Perf. 11½*
5545 A2665 10k Sputnik, 1957   .35   .25
5546 A2665 10k Vostok 3 and
                    4, 1962   .35   .25
5547 A2665 10k Mars 1, 1962   .35   .25
  a.   Miniature sheet of 8   50.00
       Nos. 5545-5547 (3)   1.05   .75

UN Emblem, ESCAP Headquarters, Bangkok — A2666

1987, Apr. 21
5548 A2666 10k multicolored   .50   .25

UN Economic and Social Commission for Asia and the Pacific, 40th anniv.

Lenin, 117th Birth Anniv. — A2667

Paintings: No. 5549, Lenin's Birthday, by N.A. Sysoyev. No. 5550, Lenin with Delegates at the 3rd Congress of the Soviet Young Communist League, by P.O. Belousov. No. 5551a, Lenin's Underground Activity (Lenin, lamp), by D.A. Nalbandyan. No. 5551b, Before the Assault (Lenin standing at table), by S.P. Viktorov. No. 5551c, We'll Show the Earth the New Way (Lenin, soldiers, flags), by A.G. Lysenko. No. 5551d, Lenin in Smolny, October 1917 (Lenin seated), by M.G. Sokolov. No. 5551e, Lenin, by N.A. Andreyev.

1987, Apr. 22   Litho.   *Perf. 12½x12*
5549 A2667 5k multicolored   .50   .25
5550 A2667 5k multicolored   .50   .25

Souvenir Sheet
Perf. 12
5551   Sheet of 5   2.00   .75
  a.-e.   A2667 10k any single   .30   .25

Sizes: Nos. 5551a-5551d, 40x28mm; No. 5551e, 40x56mm.

A2668

1987, May 5   Photo.   *Perf. 11½*
5552 A2668 10k multicolored   .50   .25

European Gymnastics Championships, Moscow, May 18-26.

Bicycle Race — A2669

1987, May 6
5553 A2669 10k multicolored   .50   .25

40th Peace Bicycle Race, Poland-Czechoslovakia-German Democratic Republic, May.

Fauna — A2670

5k, Menzbira marmot. 10k, Bald badger, horiz. 15k, Snow leopard.

Perf. 12½x12 (#5554), 12x12½
1987, May 15   Litho.
5554 A2670   5k multicolored   .50   .25
  a.   Miniature sheet of 8   35.00
5555 A2670 10k multicolored   .60   .25

Size: 32x47mm
5556 A2670 15k multicolored   .90   .25
       Nos. 5554-5556 (3)   2.00   .75

Passenger Ships — A2671

5k, Maxim Gorki. 10k, Alexander Pushkin. 30k, The Soviet Union.

1987, May 20   Photo.   *Perf. 12x11½*
5557 A2671   5k multicolored   .25   .25
5558 A2671 10k multicolored   .50   .25
  a.   Miniature sheet of 8   125.00
5559 A2671 30k multicolored   1.25   .45
       Nos. 5557-5559 (3)   2.00   .95

Paintings by Foreign Artists in the Hermitage Museum — A2672

4k, Portrait of a Woman, by Lucas Cranach Sr. (1472-1553). 5k, St. Sebastian, by Titian. 10k, Justice, by Durer. 30k, Adoration of the Magi, by Pieter Brueghel the Younger (c. 1564-1638). 50k, Ceres, by Rubens.

Perf. 12x12½, 12½x12
1987, June 5   Litho.
5560 A2672   4k multicolored   .25   .25
5561 A2672   5k multicolored   .25   .25
  a.   Miniature sheet of 8   175.00
5562 A2672 10k multicolored   .25   .25
  a.   Miniature sheet of 8   175.00
5563 A2672 30k multicolored   .60   .40
5564 A2672 50k multicolored   .75   .50
       Nos. 5560-5564 (5)   2.10 1.65

Tolyatti City, 250th Anniv. — A2673

Design: Zhiguli car, Volga Motors factory, Lenin Hydroelectric plant.

1987, June 6   Photo.   *Perf. 11½*
5565 A2673 5k multicolored   .50   .25

Aleksander Pushkin (1799-1837), Poet — A2674

1987, June 6   Litho.
5566 A2674 5k buff, yel brn &
                    deep brown   .50   .25

Printed se-tenant with label. Value pair, stamp + label, $1.

A2675

1987, June 7   Engr.   *Perf. 12½x12*
5567 A2675 5k black   .50   .25

Maj.-Gen. Sidor A. Kovpak (1887-1967), Vice-Chairman of the Ukranian SSR.

A2676

1987, June 23   Photo.   *Perf. 11½*
5568 A2676 10k multicolored   .50   .25

Women's World Congress on Nuclear Disarmament, Moscow, June 23-27.

Tobolsk City, 400th Anniv. — A2677

Design: Tobolsk kremlin, port, theater and Ermak Monument.

1987, June 25
5569 A2677 5k multicolored   .50   .25

Mozambique-USSR Treaty of Friendship and Cooperation, 10th anniv. — A2678

No. 5570, Flag of Frelimo, man. No. 5571, Flags of Mozambique, USSR.

1987, June 25
5570   5k multicolored   .40   .25
5571   5k multicolored   .40   .25
a.   A2678 Pair, #5570-5571   1.00   .30

Ferns — A2679

4k, Scolopendrium vulgare. 5k, Ceterach officinarum. 10k, Salvinia natans, horiz. 15k, Matteuccia struthiopteris. 50k, Adiantum pedatum.

1987, July 2   Litho.   Perf. 12
5572 A2679   4k multicolored   .25   .25
5573 A2679   5k multicolored   .25   .25
5574 A2679 10k multicolored   .30   .25
5575 A2679 15k multicolored   .30   .30
5576 A2679 50k multicolored   1.00   .75
   Nos. 5572-5576 (5)   2.10 1.80

A2680

No. 5577, Kremlin and 2000 Year-old Coin of India. No. 5578, Red Fort, Delhi, Soviet hammer & sickle.

1987, July 3
5577 A2680   5k shown   .40   .25
5578 A2680   5k muticolored   .40   .25
a.   Pair, #5577-5578   1.00   .30

Festivals 1987-88: India in the USSR (No. 5577) and the USSR in India (No. 5578).

15th Intl. Film Festival, July 16-17, Moscow — A2681

1987, July 6   Photo.   Perf. 11½
5579 2681 10k multicolored   .50   .25

Joint Soviet-Syrian Space Flight A2682

Mir Space Station — A2683

Flags, Intercosmos emblem and: 5k, Cosmonaut training and launch. 10k, Mir space station, Syrian parliament and cosmonauts. 15k, Gagarin Memorial, satellite dishes and cosmonauts wearing space suits.

1987   Litho.   Perf. 12x12½
5580 A2682   5k multicolored   .25   .25
5581 A2682 10k multicolored   .50   .25
5582 A2682 15k multicolored   .75   .25
   Nos. 5580-5582 (3)   1.50   .75
Souvenir Sheet
5583 A2683 50k multicolored   1.50   .75
Issued: 5k, 7/22; 10k, 7/24; 15k, 50k 7/30.

Intl. Atomic Energy Agency, 30th Anniv. A2684

1987, July 29   Photo.   Perf. 11½
5584 A2684 20k multicolored   .50   .25

14th-16th Century Postrider — A2685

Designs: 5k, 17th cent. postman and 17th cent. kibitka (sled). 10k, 16th-17th cent. ship and 18th cent. packet. 30k, Railway station and 19th cent. mailcars. 35k, AMO-F-15 bus and car, 1905. 50k, Postal headquarters, Moscow, and modern postal delivery trucks.

Photo. & Engr.
1987, Aug. 25   Perf. 11½x12
5585 A2685   4k buff & black   .25   .25
5586 A2685   5k buff & black   .25   .25
5587 A2685 10k buff & black   .35   .25
5588 A2685 30k buff & black   .75   .25
5589 A2685 35k buff & black   1.00   .40
   Nos. 5585-5589 (5)   2.60 1.40

Souvenir Sheet
5590 A2685 50k pale yel, dull gray grn & blk   2.00   .90

A2686

October Revolution, 70th Anniv. — A2687

Paintings by Russian artists: No. 5591, Long Live the Socialist Revolution! by V.V. Kuznetsov. No. 5592, V.I. Lenin Proclaims the Soviet Power (Lenin pointing), by V.A. Serov. No. 5593, V.I. Lenin (with pencil), by P.V. Vasiliev. No. 5594, On the Eve of the Storm (Lenin, Trotsky, Dzerzhinski), by V.V. Pimenov. No. 5595, Taking the Winter Palace by Storm, by V.A. Serov.

1987, Aug. 25   Litho.   Perf. 12½x12
5591 A2686   5k shown   .30   .25
a.   Miniature sheet of 8   5.00
5592 A2686   5k multicolored   .30   .25
a.   Miniature sheet of 8   5.00
5593 A2686   5k multicolored   .30   .25
a.   Miniature sheet of 8   5.00
Size: 70x33mm
Perf. 11½
5594 A2686   5k multicolored   .30   .25
a.   Miniature sheet of 8   5.00
5595 A2686   5k multicolored   .30   .25
a.   Miniature sheet of 8   5.00
   Nos. 5591-5595 (5)   1.50 1.25
Souvenir Sheet
Photo. & Engr.
Perf. 12x11½
5596 A2687 30k gold & black   1.50   .45
   For overprint see No. 5604.

Souvenir Sheet

Battle of Borodino, 175th Anniv. — A2688

1987, Sept. 7   Litho.   Perf. 12½x12
5597 A2688 1r blk, yel brn & blue gray   3.00 1.50

A2689

1987, Sept. 18   Engr.
5598 A2689   5k intense blue   .50   .25
Pavel Petrovich Postyshev (1887-1939), party leader.

Moscow, 840th Anniv. — A2690

Design: 5k, Monument to founder Yuri Dolgoruki, by sculptor S. Orlov, A. Antropov, N. Stamm and architect V. Andreyev, in Sovetskaya Square, and buildings in Moscow.

1987, Sept. 19   Photo.   Perf. 11½
5599 A2690   5k dk red brn, cr & dk org   .50   .25

Scientists — A2691

Designs: No. 5600, Muhammed Taragai Ulugh Begh (1394-1449), Uzbek astronomer and mathematician. No. 5601, Sir Isaac Newton (1642-1727), English physicist and mathematician. No. 5602, Marie Curie (1867-1934), physicist, chemist, Nobel laureate.

1987, Oct. 3   Photo. & Engr.
5600 A2691   5k dk bl, org brn & blk   .50   .25
5601 A2691   5k dull grn, blk & dk ultra   .50   .25
5602 A2691   5k brn & dp blue   .50   .25
   Nos. 5600-5602 (3)   1.50   .75

Nos. 5600-5602 each printed se-tenant with inscribed label.

Souvenir Sheet

COSPAS-SARSAT Intl. Satellite System for Tracking Disabled Planes and Ships — A2692

1987, Oct. 15   Photo.
5603 A2692 50k multicolored   3.00   .75

No. 5595 Overprinted in Gold

1987, Oct. 17   **Litho.**
5604 A2686 5k multicolored   1.50 .40

All-Union Philatelic Exhibition and the 70th Anniv. of the October Revolution.

Sheet of 8 No. 5595 has the overprint in the margin.

My Quiet Homeland, by V.M. Sidorov — A2693

The Sun Above Red Square, by P.P. Ossovsky — A2694

Paintings by Soviet artists exhibited at the 7th Republican Art Exhibition, Moscow, 1985: 4k, There Will be Cities in the Taiga, by A.A. Yakovlev. 5k, Mother, by V.V. Shcherbakov. 30k, On Jakutian Soil, by A.N. Osipov. 35k, Ivan's Return, by V.I. Yerofeyev.

1987, Oct. 20   **Perf. 12x12½, 12½x12**
5605	A2693	4k multi, vert.	.25 .25
5606	A2693	5k multi, vert.	.25 .25
5607	A2693	10k multicolored	.35 .25
5608	A2693	30k multicolored	.75 .45
5609	A2693	35k multicolored	.85 .50
	Nos. 5605-5609 (5)		2.45 1.70

Souvenir Sheet
Perf. 11½x12½
5610 A2694 50k multicolored   3.00 1.00

John Reed (1887-1920), American Journalist — A2695

1987, Oct. 22   **Perf. 11½**
5611 A2695 10k buff & dk brn   .50 .25

Samuil Yakovlevich Marshak (1887-1964), Author — A2696

1987, Nov. 3   **Engr.**   **Perf. 12½x12**
5612 A2696 5k deep claret   .50 .25

A2697

1987, Nov. 8
5613 A2697 5k slate blue   .50 .25
Ilja Grigorjevich Chavchavadze (1837-1907), Georgian author.

Indira Gandhi (1917-1984) A2698

1987, Nov. 19   **Photo.**   **Perf. 11½**
5614 A2698 5k black & brown   .50 .25

A2699

1987, Nov. 25   **Perf. 12½x12**
5615 A2699 5k black   .50 .25
Vadim Nikolaevich Podbelsky (1887-1920), revolution leader.

A2700

1987, Nov. 25
5616 A2700 5k dark blue gray   .50 .25
Nikolai Ivanovich Vavilov (1887-1943), botanist.

A2701

Modern Science: 5k, TOKAMAK, a controlled thermonuclear reactor. 10k, Kola Project (Earth strata study). 20k, RATAN-600 radiotelescope.

Photo. & Engr.
1987, Nov. 25   **Perf. 11½**
5617	A2701	5k grnsh gray & brn	.25 .25
5618	A2701	10k dull grn, lt blue gray & dark blue	.35 .25
5619	A2701	20k gray olive, blk & buff	.50 .30
	Nos. 5617-5619 (3)		1.10 .80

U.S. and Soviet Flags, Spasski Tower and US Capitol — A2702

1987, Dec. 17   **Photo.**
5620 A2702 10k multicolored   .50 .25
INF Treaty (eliminating intermediate-range nuclear missiles) signed by Gen.-Sec. Gorbachev and Pres. Reagan, Dec. 8.

New Year 1988 A2703

1987, Dec. 2   **Litho.**   **Perf. 12x12½**
5621	A2703	5k Kremlin	.50 .25
a.		Miniature sheet of 8	17.50

Marshal Ivan Khristoforovich Bagramyan (1897-1982) A2704

1987, Dec. 2   **Engr.**   **Perf. 12½x12**
5622 A2704 5k black   .50 .25

Miniature Sheet

18th-19th Cent. Naval Commanders and War Ships — A2705

Designs: 4k, Adm. Grigori Andreyevich Spiridov (1713-1790), Battle of Chesmen. 5k, Fedor Fedorovich Ushakov (1745-1817), Storming of Corfu. 10k, Adm. Dimitiri Nikolayevich Senyavin (1763-1831) and flagship at the Battle of Afon off Mt. Athos. 25k, Mikhail Petrovich Lazarev (1788-1851), Battle of Navarin. 30k, Adm. Pavel Stepanovich Nakhimov (1802-1855), Battle of Sinop.

1987, Dec. 22
5623	A2705	Sheet of 5 + label	5.00 1.25
a.		4k dark blue & indigo	.35 .25
b.		5k maroon & indigo	.35 .25
c.		10k maroon & indigo	.50 .25
d.		25k dark blue & indigo	1.00 .40
e.		30k dark blue & indigo	1.25 .50

No. 5623 contains corner label (LR) picturing ensign of period Russian Navy vessels and anchor.

See No. 5850.

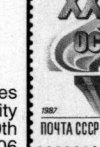

Asia-Africa Peoples Solidarity Organization, 30th Anniv. — A2706

1987, Dec. 26   **Photo.**   **Perf. 11½**
5624 A2706 10k multicolored   .50 .25

1st Soviet Postage Stamp, 70th Anniv. — A2707

1988, Jan. 4   **Photo.**   **Perf. 11½**
5625	A2707	10k #149, #150 UR	.50 .25
5626	A2707	10k #150, #149 UR	.50 .25
a.		Pair, #5625-5626	1.00 .30

Lettering in brown on No. 5625, in blue on No. 5626.

A2708

5k, Biathlon. 10k, Cross-country skiing. 15k, Slalom. 20k, Pairs figure skating. 30k, Ski jumping.
50k, Ice hockey, horiz.

1988, Jan. 4
5627	A2708	5k multi	.25 .25
a.		Miniature sheet of 8	80.00
5628	A2708	10k multi	.30 .25
a.		Miniature sheet of 8	80.00
5629	A2708	15k multi	.40 .30
a.		Miniature sheet of 8	80.00
5630	A2708	20k multi	.50 .35
a.		Miniature sheet of 8	80.00
5631	A2708	30k multi	.70 .50
a.		Miniature sheet of 8	80.00
	Nos. 5627-5631 (5)		2.15 1.65

Souvenir Sheet
5632 A2708 50k multi   2.00 1.00
1988 Winter Olympics, Calgary.
For overprint see No. 5665.

A2709

1988, Jan. 7
5633 A2709 35k blue & gold   1.00 .65
World Health Org., 40th anniv.

Lord Byron (1788-1824), English Poet A2710

Photo. & Engr.
1988, Jan. 22   **Perf. 12x11½**
5634 A2710 15k Prus blue, blk & grn black   .50 .30

A2711

1988, Jan. 27   **Photo.**   **Perf. 11½**
5635 A2711 20k multicolored   .50 .40

Cultural, Technical and Educational Agreement with the US, 30th anniv.

A2712

1988, Feb. 5
5636 A2712 5k black & tan   .50 .25

G.I. Lomov-Oppokov (1888-1938), party leader. See Nos. 5649, 5660, 5666, 5673, 5700, 5704, 5721, 5812.

Animated Soviet Cartoons — A2713

1k, Little Humpback Horse, 1947. 3k, Winnie-the-Pooh, 1969. 4k, Gena, the Crocodile, 1969. 5k, Just you Wait! 1969. 10k, Hedgehog in the Mist, 1975.
30k, Post, 1929.

1988, Feb. 18   **Litho.**   **Perf. 12½x12**
5637 A2713 1k multicolored   .25 .25
5638 A2713 3k multicolored   .25 .25
5639 A2713 4k multicolored   .25 .25
5640 A2713 5k multicolored   .25 .25
5641 A2713 10k multicolored   .30 .25
    Nos. 5637-5641 (5)   1.30 1.25
Souvenir Sheet
5642 A2713 30k multicolored   2.00 .60

A2714

1988, Feb. 21   **Photo.**   **Perf. 11½**
5643 A2714 10k buff & black   .50 .25

Mikhail Alexandrovich Bonch-Bruevich (1888-1940), broadcast engineer.

A2715

1988, Feb. 25
5644 A2715 15k blk, brt bl & dk red   .50 .30
   a.   Miniature sheet of 8   40.00

Intl. Red Cross and Red Crescent Organizations, 125th anniv.

World Speed Skating Championships, Mar. 5-6, Alma-Ata — A2716

1988, Mar. 13   **Photo.**   **Perf. 11½**
5645 A2716 15k blk, vio & brt blue   .50 .30

No. 5645 printed se-tenant with label picturing Alma-Ata skating rink, Medeo.

A2717

1988, Mar. 13   **Litho.**   **Perf. 12½x12**
5646 A2717 10k dark olive green   .50 .25

Anton Semenovich Makarenko (1888-1939), teacher, youth development expert.

Franzisk Skorina (b. 1488), 1st Printer in Byelorussia A2718

1988, Mar. 17   **Engr.**   **Perf. 12x12½**
5647 A2718 5k gray black   .50 .25

Labor Day — A2719

1988, Mar. 22   **Photo.**   **Perf. 11½**
5648 A2719 5k multicolored   .50 .25

Party Leader Type of 1988
1988, Mar. 24   **Engr.**   **Perf. 12**
5649 A2712 5k dark green   .50 .25

Victor Eduardovich Kingisepp (1888-1922).

Organized Track and Field Events in Russia, Cent. A2721

1988, Mar. 24   **Photo.**   **Perf. 11½**
5650 A2721 15k multicolored   .50 .30

Marietta Sergeyevna Shaginyan (1888-1982), Author — A2722

1988, Apr. 2   **Litho.**   **Perf. 12½x12**
5651 A2722 10k brown   .50 .25

Soviet-Finnish Peace Treaty, 40th Anniv. — A2723

1988, Apr. 6   **Photo.**   **Perf. 11½**
5652 A2723 15k multicolored   .50 .30

Cosmonaut's Day — A2724

MIR space station, Soyuz TM transport ship, automated cargo ship *Progress* & *Quant* module.

1988, Apr. 12   **Perf. 11½x12**
5653 A2724 15k multicolored   .50 .30
   a.   Miniature sheet of 8   40.00

Victory, 1948, Painted by P.A. Krivonogov A2725

1988, Apr. 20   **Litho.**   **Perf. 12x12½**
5654 A2725 5k multicolored   .50 .25

Victory Day (May 9).

Sochi City, 150th Anniv. A2726

1988, Apr. 20   **Photo.**   **Perf. 11½**
5655 A2726 5k multicolored   .50 .25

Branches of the Lenin Museum — A2727

Portrait of Lenin and: No. 5656, Central museum, Moscow, opened May 15, 1926. No. 5657, Branch, Leningrad, opened in 1937. No. 5658, Branch, Kiev, opened in 1938. No. 5659, Branch, Krasnoyarsk, opened in 1987.

1988, Apr. 22   **Perf. 12**
5656 A2727 5k vio brown & gold   .25 .25
5657 A2727 5k brn vio, vio brown & gold   .25 .25
5658 A2727 5k dp brn ol & gold   .25 .25
5659 A2727 5k dark green & gold   .25 .25
   a.   Block of 4, Nos. 5656-5659   1.00 .40
    See Nos. 5765-5767, 5885-5887.

Party Leader Type of 1988
1988, Apr. 24   **Photo.**   **Perf. 11½**
5660 A2712 5k blue black   .50 .25

Ivan Alexeyevich Akulov (1888-1939).

EXPO '88, Brisbane, Australia — A2729

1988, Apr. 30
5661 A2729 20k multicolored   .50 .35

Karl Marx — A2730

1988, May 5   **Engr.**   **Perf. 12**
5662 A2730 5k chocolate   .50 .25

Social and Economic
Reforms — A2731

Designs: No. 5663, Cruiser *Aurora*, revolutionary soldiers, workers and slogans Speeding Up, Democratization, and Glasnost against Kremlin Palace. No. 5664, Worker, agriculture and industries.

1988, May 5   Photo.   Perf. 12x11½
5663 A2731 5k multicolored   .25   .25
5664 A2731 5k multicolored   .25   .25

No. 5632 Ovptd. in Dark Red
Souvenir Sheet

1988, May 12   Photo.   Perf. 11½
5665 A2708 50k multicolored   2.00   1.25
Victory of Soviet athletes at the 1988 Winter Olympics, Calgary. No. 5665 overprinted below stamp on souvenir sheet margin. Soviet sportsmen won 11 gold, 9 silver and 9 bronze medals.

Party Leader Type of 1988
1988, May 19   Engr.   Perf. 12
5666 A2712 5k black   .50   .25
Nikolai Mikhailovich Shvernik (1888-1970).

Hunting Dogs — A2733

Designs: 5k, Russian borzoi, fox hunt. 10k, Kirghiz greyhound, falconry. 15k, Russian retrievers. 20k, Russian spaniel, duck hunt. 35k, East Siberian husky, bear hunt.

1988, May 20   Litho.
5667 A2733   5k multicolored   .25   .25
5668 A2733 10k multicolored   .40   .25
5669 A2733 15k multicolored   .55   .25
5670 A2733 20k multicolored   .75   .40
5671 A2733 35k multicolored   1.00   .50
     Nos. 5667-5671 (5)   2.95   1.65

A2734

1988, May 29   Photo.   Perf. 11½
5672 A2734 5k multicolored   .50   .25
Soviet-US Summit Conf., May 29-June 2, Moscow.

Party Leader Type of 1988
1988, June 6   Engr.   Perf. 12
5673 A2712 5k brown black   .50   .25
Valerian Vladimirovich Kuibyshev (1888-1935).

A2736

Design: Flags, Mir space station and Soyuz TM spacecraft.

1988, June 7   Photo.   Perf. 11½
5674 A2736 15k multicolored   .50   .35
Shipka '88, USSR-Bulgarian joint space flight, June 7.

A2737

Design: Natl. & Canadian flags, skis & obe.

1988, June 16
5675 A2737 35k multicolored   .50   .35
Soviet-Canada transarctic ski expedition, May-Aug.

A2738

1988, June 16
5676 A2738 5k multicolored   .50   .25
For a world without nuclear weapons.

A2739

A2740

**19th All-union Communist Party
Conference, Moscow — A2741**

1988, June 16   Litho.   Perf. 12
5677 A2739 5k multicolored   .25   .25
Photo.
Perf. 11½
5678 A2740 5k multicolored   .25   .25
Souvenir Sheet
Perf. 11½x12
5679 A2741 50k multicolored   2.00   .75

1988
Summer
Olympics,
Seoul
A2742

1988, June 29   Litho.   Perf. 12
5680 A2742   5k Hurdling   .25   .25
5681 A2742 10k Long jump   .25   .25
  a.   Miniature sheet of 8   25.00
5682 A2742 15k Basketball   .40   .30
  a.   Miniature sheet of 8   25.00
5683 A2742 20k Rhythmic gym-
             nastics   .50   .35
  a.   Miniature sheet of 8   25.00
5684 A2742 30k Swimming   .60   .50
  a.   Miniature sheet of 8   25.00
     Nos. 5680-5684 (5)   2.00   1.65
Souvenir Sheet
5685 A2742 50k Soccer   1.50   1.00
For overprint see No. 5722.

Phobos Intl. Space
Project — A2743

10k, Satellite, space probe.

1988, July 7   Photo.   Perf. 11½x12
5686 A2743 10k multicolored   .50   .25
For the study of Phobos, a satellite of Mars.

Flowers Populating
Deciduous
Forests — A2744

5k, Campanula latifolia. 10k, Orobus vernus, horiz. 15k, Pulmonaria obscura. 20k, Lilium martagon. 35k, Ficaria verna.

1988, July 7   Litho.   Perf. 12
5687 A2744   5k multicolored   .25   .25
5688 A2744 10k multicolored   .35   .25
5689 A2744 15k multicolored   .50   .35
5690 A2744 20k multicolored   .65   .45
5691 A2744 35k multicolored   1.10   .75
     Nos. 5687-5691 (5)   2.85   2.05

A2745

1988, July 14   Photo.   Perf. 11½
5692 A2745 5k multicolored   .50   .25
Leninist Young Communist League (Komsomol), 70th anniv. For overprint see No. 5699.

A2746

1988, July 18
5693 A2746 10k multicolored   .50   .25
Nelson Mandela (1918-2013), South African anti-apartheid leader.

Paintings in the Timiriazev Equestrian
Museum of the Moscow Agricultural
Academy — A2747

Paintings: 5k, *Light Gray Arabian Stallion*, by N.E. Sverchkov, 1860. 10k, *Konvoets, a Kabardian*, by M.A. Vrubel, 1882, vert. 15k, *Horsewoman Riding an Orlov-Rastopchinsky*, by N.E. Sverchkov. 20k, *Letuchya, a Gray Orlov Trotter*, by V.A. Serov, 1886, vert. 30k, *Sardar, an Akhaltekinsky Stallion*, by A.B. Villevalde, 1882.

1988, July 20   Litho.   Perf. 12½x12
5694 A2747   5k multicolored   .25   .25
5695 A2747 10k multicolored   .25   .25
5696 A2747 15k multicolored   .40   .25
5697 A2747 20k multicolored   .55   .35
5698 A2747 30k multicolored   .90   .65
     Nos. 5694-5698 (5)   2.35   1.75

No. 5692 Ovptd.
for the All-Union
Philatelic
Exhibition,
Moscow, Aug. 10-
17

1988, Aug. 10   Photo.   Perf. 11½
5699 A2745 5k multicolored   .50   .30

Party Leader Type of 1988
1988, Aug. 13   Engr.   Perf. 12½x12
5700 A2712 5k black   .50   .25
Petr Lazarevich Voykov (1888-1927), economic and trade union plenipotentiary.

Intl. Letter-Writing Week — A2749

1988, Aug. 25   Photo.   *Perf. 11½*
5701 A2749 5k blue grn & dark
blue green   .50   .25

Earth, Mir space
station and Soyuz-
TM
A2750

1988, Aug. 29
5702 A2750 15k multicolored   .50   .30
Soviet-Afghan joint space flight.

A2751

1988, Sept. 1   Photo.   *Perf. 11½*
5703 A2751 10k multicolored   .50   .25
Problems of Peace and Socialism magazine, 30th anniv.

Party Leader Type of 1988
1988, Sept. 13   Engr.   *Perf. 12*
5704 A2712 5k black   .50   .25
Emmanuil Ionovich Kviring (1888-1937).

A2753

A2753a

A2753b

A2753c

A2753d

Designs: No. 5705, *Ilya Muromets*, Russian
lore. No. 5706, *Ballad of the Cossack Golota*,
Ukrainian lore. No. 5707, *Musician-Magician*,
a Byelorussian fairy tale. No. 5708, *Koblandy-
batyr*, a poem from Kazakh. No. 5709,
Alpamysh, a fairy tale from Uzbek.

Perf. 12x12½, 12½x12
1988, Sept. 22   Litho.
5705 A2753 10k multicolored   .25   .25
5706 A2753a 10k multicolored   .25   .25
5707 A2753b 10k multicolored   .25   .25
5708 A2753c 10k multicolored   .25   .25
5709 A2753d 10k multicolored   .25   .25
  Nos. 5705-5709 (5)   1.25   1.25

Nos. 5705-5709 each printed se-tenant with
inscribed labels. See design A2795.

*Appeal of the
Leader,*
1947, by I.M.
Toidze
A2754

1988, Oct. 5   *Perf. 12x12½*
5710 A2754 5k multicolored   .40   .25
October Revolution, 71st anniv.

A2755

1988, Oct. 18   Engr.   *Perf. 12*
5711 A2755 10k black   .50   .25
Andrei Timofeyevich Bolotov (1738-1833),
agricultural scientist, publisher.

A2756

1988, Oct. 18
5712 A2756 10k steel blue   .50   .25
Andrei Nikolayevich Tupolev (1888-1972),
aeronautical engineer.

A2757

20k, Map of expedition route, atomic icebreaker *Sibirj* & expedition members.

1988, Oct. 25   Litho.
5713 A2757 20k multicolored   .50   .35
North Pole expedition (in 1987).
Exists imperf. Value, $35.

A2758

1988, Oct. 30   Engr.
5714 A2758 5k brown black   .40   .25
Dmitry F. Ustinov (1908-84), minister of
defense.

Soviet-Vietnamese Treaty, 10th
Anniv. — A2759

1988, Nov. 3   Photo.   *Perf. 11½*
5715 A2759 10k multicolored   .50   .25

State Broadcasting and Sound
Recording Institute, 50th
Anniv. — A2760

1988, Nov. 3
5716 A2760 10k multicolored   .50   .25

UN
Declaration
of Human
Rights, 40th
Anniv.
A2761

1988, Nov. 21
5717 A2761 10k multicolored   .50   .25

New Year
1989 — A2762

Design: Preobrazhensky Regiment body-
guard riding to announce Peter the Great's
decree to celebrate new year's eve as of January 1, 1700.

1988, Nov. 24   Litho.   *Perf. 12x11½*
5718 A2762 5k multicolored   .50   .25

Soviet-French Joint Space
Flight — A2763

1988, Nov. 26   Photo.   *Perf. 11½*
5719 A2763 15k Space walkers   .50   .30

No. 4607
Overprinted in Red

1988, Dec. 16   Litho.   *Perf. 12½x12*
5720 A2143 1r dark blue   5.00   2.25
Space mail.

Party Leader Type of 1988
1988, Dec. 16   Engr.
5721 A2712 5k slate green   .50   .25
Martyn Ivanovich Latsis (1888-1938).

No. 5685 Overprinted in Bright Blue
Souvenir Sheet

1988, Dec. 20   Litho.   *Perf. 12*
5722 A2742 50k multicolored   2.00   1.00
Victory of Soviet athletes at the 1988 Summer Olympics, Seoul. Overprint on margin of
No. 5722 specifies that Soviet athletes won 55
gold, 31 silver and 46 bronze medals.

Post Rider — A2765

Designs: 3k, Cruiser *Aurora*. 4k, Spasski
Tower, Lenin Mausoleum. 5k, Natl. flag, crest.
10k, *The Worker and the Collective Farmer*,
1935, sculpture by V.I. Mukhina. 15k, Satellite
dish. 20k, Lyre, art tools, quill pen, parchment
(arts and literature). 25k, *Discobolus*, 5th cent.
sculpture by Myron (c. 480-440 B.C.). 30k,
Map of the Antarctic, penguins. 35k, *Mercury*,
sculpture by Giambologna (1529-1608). 50k,
White cranes (nature conservation). 1r, UPU
emblem.

1988, Dec. 22   Engr.   *Perf. 12x11½*
5723 A2765 1k dark brown   .25   .25
5724 A2765 3k dark blue green   .25   .25
5725 A2765 4k indigo   .25   .25
5726 A2765 5k red   .25   .25
5727 A2765 10k claret   .25   .25
5728 A2765 15k deep blue   .30   .25
5729 A2765 20k olive gray   .35   .30
5730 A2765 25k dark green   .40   .35
5731 A2765 30k dark blue   .50   .40
5732 A2765 35k dark red brown   .60   .50
5733 A2765 50k sapphire   .80   .50

Perf. 12x12½
5734 A2765 1r blue gray   1.60   1.25
  Nos. 5723-5734 (12)   5.80   4.80

See Nos. 5838-5849, 5984-5987. For
surcharges see Uzbekistan #15, 22, 25-26,
61B, 61D, 61F.

Fountains of Petrodvorets
A2766

Designs: 5k, Samson Fountain, 1723, and Great Cascade. 10k, Adam Fountain, 1722, and sculptures, 1718, by D. Bonazza. 15k, Golden Mountain Cascade, by N. Miketti (1721-1723) and M.G. Zemtsov. 30k, Roman Fountains, 1763. 50k, Oak Tree Fountain, 1735.

1988, Dec. 25   Engr.   Perf. 11½x12
5735 A2766 5k myrtle green   .25   .25
5736 A2766 10k myrtle green   .25   .25
5737 A2766 15k myrtle green   .30   .25
5738 A2766 30k myrtle green   .60   .40
5739 A2766 50k myrtle green   1.00   .70
  a.   Pane of 5, #5735-5739   5.00 1.50

Panes have photogravure margin. Panes are printed bilaterally and separated in the center by perforations so that stamps in the 2nd pane are arranged in reverse order from the 1st pane.

19th Communist Party Congress — A2767

1988, Dec. 30   Photo.   Perf. 12x11½
Multicolored and
5740 A2767 5k deep car (power)   .50   .25
5741 A2767 5k dp bl vio (indus-
                try)   .50   .25
5742 A2767 5k green (land)   .50   .25
  Nos. 5740-5742 (3)   1.50   .75

Souvenir Sheet

Inaugural Flight of the *Buran* Space Shuttle, Nov. 15 — A2768

1988, Dec. 30   Perf. 11½x12
5743 A2768 50k multicolored   2.00   .75

Luna 1, 30th Anniv. — A2769

1989, Jan. 2   Photo.   Perf. 11½
5744 A2769 15k multicolored   .50   .30

Jalmari Virtanen (1889-1939), Karelian Poet — A2770

1989, Jan. 8
5745 A2770 5k olive brown   .50   .25

Council for Mutual Economic Assistance, 40th Anniv.
A2771

1989, Jan. 8
5746 A2771 10k multicolored   .50   .25

Environmental Protection — A2772

1989, Jan. 18   Litho.   Perf. 12½x12
5747 A2772 5k Forest   .30   .25
5748 A2772 10k Arctic deer   .50   .25
5749 A2772 15k Stop desert en-
                croachment   .70   .30
  Nos. 5747-5749 (3)   1.50   .80

Nos. 5747-5749 printed se-tenant with inscribed labels picturing maps.

Samovars A2773

Samovars in the State Museum, Leningrad: 5k, Pear-shaped urn, late 18th cent. 10k, Barrel-shaped urn by Ivan Listisin, early 19th cent. 20k, "Kabachok" urn by the Sokolov Bros., Tula, c. 1830. 30k, Vase-shaped urn by the Nikolari Malikov Studio, Tula, c. 1840.

1989, Feb. 8   Photo.   Perf. 11½
5750 A2773 5k multicolored   .25   .25
5751 A2773 10k multicolored   .30   .25
5752 A2773 20k multicolored   .60   .30
5753 A2773 30k multicolored   .85   .45
  Nos. 5750-5753 (4)   2.00 1.25

Modest Petrovich Mussorgsky (1839-1881), Composer — A2774

1989, Feb. 15   Litho.   Perf. 12½x12
5754 A2774 10k dull vio & vio
                brn   1.00   .25

P.E. Dybenko (1889-1938), Military Commander
A2775

1989, Feb. 28   Engr.   Perf. 12
5755 A2775 5k black   .50   .25

T.G. Shevchenko (1814-1861), Poet
A2776

1989, Mar. 6   Litho.   Perf. 11½
5756 A2776 5k pale grn, blk &
                brn   .50   .25
  Exists imperf. Value, $25.

Cultivated Lilies — A2777

1989, Mar. 15   Perf. 12½x12
5757 A2777 5k Lilium speci-
                osum   .25   .25
5758 A2777 10k African queen   .25   .25
5759 A2777 15k Eclat du soir   .30   .25
5760 A2777 30k White tiger   .80   .55
  Nos. 5757-5760 (4)   1.60 1.30

Souvenir Sheet

Labor Day, Cent. — A2778

1989, Mar. 25   Perf. 11½x12
5761 A2778 30k multicolored   2.00   .60

Victory Banner, by P. Loginov and V. Pamfilov
A2779

1989, Apr. 5   Litho.   Perf. 12x12½
5762 A2779 5k multicolored   .50   .25
  World War II Victory Day.

Cosmonauts' Day — A2780

1989, Apr. 12   Photo.   Perf. 11x11½
5763 A2780 15k Mir space sta-
                tion   .50   .30

A2781

1989, Apr. 14   Perf. 11½
5764 A2781 10k multicolored   .75   .25

Bering Bridge Soviet-American Expedition, Anadyr and Kotzebue.

Type of 1988

Portraits and branches of the Lenin Central Museum: No. 5765, Kazan. No. 5766, Kuibyshev. No. 5767, Frunze.

1989, Apr. 14   Litho.   Perf. 12
5765 A2727 5k rose brown &
                multi   .25   .25
5766 A2727 5k olive gray & multi   .25   .25
5767 A2727 5k deep brown &
                multi   .25   .25
  Nos. 5765-5767 (3)   .75   .75

Lenin's 119th Birth Anniv.

Souvenir Sheet

Launch of Interplanetary Probe *Phobos* — A2783

1989, Apr. 24   Perf. 11½x12
5768 A2783 50k multicolored   1.75   .85

A2784

1989, May 5   Photo.   Perf. 11½
5769 A2784 5k multicolored   .50   .25

Hungarian Soviet Republic, 70th anniv.

A2785

1989, May 5   Photo. & Engr.
5770 A2785 5k multicolored   .40   .25

Volgograd, 400th anniv.

Honeybees A2786

No. 5771, Drone. No. 5772, Workers, flowers, man-made hive. No. 5773, Worker collecting pollen. No. 5774, Queen, drones, honeycomb.

1989, May 18   Litho.   Perf. 12
5771 A2786 5k multi   .25 .25
5772 A2786 10k multi   .25 .25
5773 A2786 20k multi   .50 .50
5774 A2786 35k multi   .90 .50
     Nos. 5771-5774 (4)   1.90 1.25

No. 5771 exists imperf. Value, $30.

Photography, 150th Anniv. — A2787

1989, May 24   Photo.   Perf. 11½
5775 A2787 5k multicolored   .50 .25

I.A. Kuratov (1839-1875),
Author — A2788

1989, June 26   Litho.   Perf. 12½x12
5776 A2788 5k dk golden brn   .40 .25

Jean Racine
(1639-1699),
French
Dramatist
A2789

Photo. & Engr.
1989, June 16   Perf. 12x11½
5777 A2789 15k multicolored   .50 .25

Europe, Our
Common
Home — A2790

Designs: 5k, Map of Europe, stylized bird. 10k, Crane, two men completing a bridge, globe. 15k, Stork's nest, globe.

1989, June 20   Photo.   Perf. 11½
5778 A2790 5k multicolored   .25 .25
5779 A2790 10k multicolored   .30 .25
5780 A2790 15k multicolored   .50 .35
     Nos. 5778-5780 (3)   1.05 .85

Mukhina, by
Nesterov
A2791

1989, June 25   Litho.   Perf. 12x12½
5781 A2791 5k chalky blue   .50 .25

Vera I. Mukhina (1889-1953), sculptor.

13th World Youth
and Student
Festival,
Pyongyang
A2792

1989, July 1   Litho.   Perf. 12
5782 A2792 10k multicolored   .40 .25

Ducks
A2793

No. 5783, Tadorna tadorna. No. 5784, Anas crecca. No. 5785, Tadorna ferruginea.

1989, July 1
5783 A2793 5k multicolored   .25 .25
5784 A2793 15k multicolored   .35 .25
5785 A2793 20k multicolored   .40 .30
  a.   Min. sheet, 2 5k, 4 15k, 3 20k 5.00 3.00
     Nos. 5783-5785 (3)   1.00 .80

French
Revolution,
Bicent.
A2794

Designs: 5k, PHILEXFRANCE '89 emblem and Storming of the Bastille. 15k, Marat, Danton, Robespierre. 20k, "La Marseillaise," from the Arc de Triomphe carved by Francois Rude (1784-1855).

Photo. & Engr., Photo. (15k)
1989, July 7   Perf. 11½
5786 A2794 5k multicolored   .25 .25
5787 A2794 15k multicolored   .35 .25
5788 A2794 20k multicolored   .40 .30
  a.   Miniature sheet of 8   9.00
     Nos. 5786-5788 (3)   1.00 .80

A2795

A2795a

A2795b

A2795c

Folklore and
Legends
A2795d

Designs: No. 5789, Amiraniani, Georgian lore. No. 5790, Koroglu, Azerbaijan lore. No. 5791, Fir, Queen of the Grass-snakes, Lithuanian lore. No. 5792, Mioritsa, Moldavian lore. No. 5793, Lachplesis, Latvian lore.

1989, July 12   Litho.   Perf. 12x12½
5789 A2795 10k multicolored   .40 .25
5790 A2795a 10k multicolored   .40 .25
5791 A2795b 10k multicolored   .40 .25
5792 A2795c 10k multicolored   .40 .25
5793 A2795d 10k multicolored   .40 .25
     Nos. 5789-5793 (5)   2.00 1.25

Each printed with a se-tenant label. See types A2753-A2753d & #5890-5894.

Tallinn Zoo, 50th
Anniv. — A2796

1989, July 20   Photo.   Perf. 11½
5794 A2796 10k Lynx   .50 .25

Intl. Letter Writing
Week — A2797

1989, July 20   Litho.   Perf. 12
5795 A2797 5k multicolored   .40 .25

Exists imperf. Value, $35.

Pulkovskaya Observatory, 150th
Anniv. — A2798

Photo. & Engr.
1989, July 20   Perf. 11½
5796 A2798 10k multicolored   .50 .25

Souvenir Sheet

Peter the Great and Battle
Scene — A2799

1989, July 27   Photo.   Perf. 11½x12
5797 A2799 50k dk bl & dk brn   1.50 1.00

Battle of Hango, 275th anniv.

City of
Nikolaev,
Bicent.
A2800

1989, Aug. 3   Photo.   Perf. 11½
5798 A2800 5k multicolored   .50 .25

80th Birth Anniv.
of Kwame
Nkrumah, 1st
Pres. of
Ghana — A2801

1989, Aug. 9
5799 A2801 10k multicolored   .40 .25

6th
Congress
of the All-
Union
Philatelic
Soc.,
Moscow
A2802

1989, Aug. 9   Perf. 12
5800 A2802 10k bl, blk & pink   .50 .25

Printed se-tenant with label picturing simulated stamps and congress emblem.

James
Fenimore
Cooper
(1789-1851),
American
Novelist
A2803

Photo. & Engr.
1989, Aug. 19   Perf. 12x11½
5801 A2803 15k multicolored   .50 .35

A2804

Soviet Circus Performers — A2805

Performers and scenes from their acts: 1k, V.L. Durov, clown and trainer. 3k, M.N. Rumyantsev, clown. 4k, V.I. Filatov, bear trainer. 5k, E.T. Kio, magician. 10k, V.E. Lazarenko, acrobat and clown. 30k, Moscow Circus, Tsvetnoi Boulevard.

1989, Aug. 22   Litho.   Perf. 12
5802	A2804	1k multicolored	.40	.25
5803	A2804	3k multicolored	.40	.25
5804	A2804	4k multicolored	.40	.25
5805	A2804	5k multicolored	.40	.25
5806	A2804	10k multicolored	.40	.25
		Nos. 5802-5806 (5)	2.00	1.25

Souvenir Sheet
Perf. 12x12½
5807	A2805	30k multicolored	2.00	.70

Nos. 5802-5806 exist imperf. Value, $30 each.

5th World Boxing
Championships,
Moscow — A2806

1989, Aug. 25   Photo.   Perf. 11½
5808	A2806	15k multicolored	.50	.35

Aleksandr Popov
(1859-1905),
Inventor of Radio
in
Russia — A2807

Design: *Demonstration of the First Radio Receiver, 1895, by N. Sysoev.*

1989, Oct. 5   Litho.   Perf. 12x12½
5809	A2807	10k multicolored	.50	.25

A2808

1989, Oct. 7   Photo.   Perf. 11½
5810	A2808	5k multicolored	.40	.25

German Democratic Republic, 40th anniv.

Polish
People's
Republic,
45th Anniv.
A2809

1989, Oct. 7
5811	A2809	5k multicolored	.50	.25

Party Leader Type of 1988
1989, Oct. 10   Engr.   Perf. 12
5812	A2712	5k black	.40	.25

S.V. Kosior (1889-1939).

A2811

1989, Oct. 10
5813	A2811	15k dark red brown	.60	.25

Jawaharlal Nehru, 1st prime minister of independent India.

Guardsmen of October, by M.M. Chepik — A2812

1989, Oct. 14   Litho.   Perf. 12½x12
5814	A2812	5k multicolored	.40	.25

October Revolution, 72nd anniv.
Exists imperf. Value, $30.

Kosta Khetagurov (1859-1906),
Ossetic Poet — A2813

1989, Oct. 14
5815	A2813	5k dark red brown	.40	.25

Exists imperf.

A2814

1989, Oct. 14   Photo.   Perf. 11½
5816	A2814	5k buff, sepia & black	.50	.25

Li Dazhao (1889-1927), communist party leader of China.

A2815

1989, Oct. 20   Engr.   Perf. 12
5817	A2815	5k black	.40	.25

Jan Karlovich Berzin (1889-1938), army intelligence leader.

Russian — A2816

Musical Instruments: No. 5819, Byelorussian. No. 5820, Ukrainian. No. 5821, Uzbek.

Photo. & Engr.
1989, Oct. 20   Perf. 12x11½
Denomination Color
5818	A2816	10k blue	.25	.25
5819	A2816	10k brown	.25	.25
5820	A2816	10k lemon	.25	.25
5821	A2816	10k blue green	.25	.25
		Nos. 5818-5821 (4)	1.00	1.00

See Nos. 5929-5932, 6047-6049.

Scenes from
Novels by
James
Fenimore
Cooper
A2817

Designs: No. 5822, *The Hunter,* (settlers, canoe). No. 5823, *Last of the Mohicans* (Indians, settlers). No. 5824, *The Pathfinder* (couple near cliff). No. 5825, *The Pioneers* (women, wild animals). No. 5826, *The Prairie* (injured Indians, horse).

1989, Nov. 17   Litho.   Perf. 12x12½
5822	A2817	20k multicolored	.60	.40
5823	A2817	20k multicolored	.60	.40
5824	A2817	20k multicolored	.60	.40
5825	A2817	20k multicolored	.60	.40
5826	A2817	20k multicolored	.60	.40
a.		Strip of 5, #5822-5826	3.00	2.00

Printed in a continuous design.

Monuments
A2818

No. 5827, Pokrovsky Cathedral, St. Basil's, statue of K. Minin and D. Pozharsky, Moscow. No. 5828, Petropavlovsky Cathedral, statue of Peter the Great, Leningrad. No. 5829, Sofiisky Cathedral, Bogdan Chmielnicki monument, Kiev. No. 5830, Khodzha Akhmed Yasavi Mausoleum, Turkestan. No. 5831, Khazret-Khyzr Mosque, Samarkand.

1989, Nov. 20   Perf. 11½
Color of "Sky"
5827	A2818	15k tan	.40	.30
5828	A2818	15k gray green	.40	.30
5829	A2818	15k blue green	.40	.30
5830	A2818	15k violet blue	.40	.30
5831	A2818	15k bright blue	.40	.30
		Nos. 5827-5831 (5)	2.00	1.50

New
Year
1990
A2819

1989, Nov. 22   Perf. 12
5832	A2819	5k multicolored	.50	.25

Space
Achievements
A2820

Designs: Nos. 5833, 5837a, Unmanned Soviet probe on the Moon. Nos. 5834, 5837b, American astronaut on Moon, 1969. Nos. 5835, 5837c, Soviet cosmonaut and American astronaut on Mars. Nos. 5836, 5837d, Mars, planetary body, diff.

1989, Nov. 24
5833	A2820	25k multicolored	.75	.55
5834	A2820	25k multicolored	.75	.55
5835	A2820	25k multicolored	.75	.55
5836	A2820	25k multicolored	.75	.55
a.		Block of 4, #5833-5836	3.00	2.20

Souvenir Sheet
Imperf
5837		Sheet of 4	2.25	1.50
a.-d.		A2820 25k any single	.50	.35

World Stamp Expo '89, Washington DC, Nov. 17-Dec. 3; 20th UPU Cong. See US No. C126.

Type of 1988
Dated 1988
1989, Dec. 25   Litho.   Perf. 12x12½
5838	A2765	1k dark brown	.25	.25
5839	A2765	3k dark blue green	.25	.25
5840	A2765	4k indigo	.25	.25
5841	A2765	5k red	.25	.25
5842	A2765	10k claret	.30	.25
5843	A2765	15k deep blue	.45	.30
5844	A2765	20k olive gray	.60	.40
5845	A2765	25k dark green	.75	.50
5846	A2765	30k dark blue	.90	.60
5847	A2765	35k dark red brown	1.00	.70
5848	A2765	50k sapphire	1.50	1.00
5849	A2765	1r blue gray	3.50	2.00
		Nos. 5838-5849 (12)	10.00	6.75

For surcharges see Uzbekistan #15, 22, 25-26, 61B, 61D, 61F.

Admirals Type of 1987
Miniature Sheet

Admirals & battle scenes: 5k, V.A. Kornilov (1806-54). 10k, V.I. Istomin (1809-55). 15k, G.I. Nevelskoi (1813-76). 20k, G.I. Butakov (1820-82). 30k, A.A. Popov (1821-98). 35k, Stepan O. Makarov (1849-1904).

1989, Dec. 28   Engr.   Perf. 12½x12
5850		Sheet of 6	6.00	2.00
a.	A2705	5k brown & Prus blue	.25	.25
b.	A2705	10k brown & Prus blue	.25	.25
c.	A2705	15k dark blue & Prus blue	.40	.25
d.	A2705	20k dark blue & Prus blue	.50	.35
e.	A2705	30k brown & Prus blue	.85	.50
f.	A2705	35k brown & Prus blue	1.00	.60

Global
Ecology — A2821

10k, Flower dying, industrial waste entering the environment. 15k, Bird caught in industrial waste, Earth. 20k, Sea of chopped trees.

1990, Jan. 5   Photo.   Perf. 11½
5851	A2821	10k multicolored	.35	.25
5852	A2821	15k multicolored	.50	.35
5853	A2821	20k multicolored	.65	.45
		Nos. 5851-5853 (3)	1.50	1.05

Capitals of the Republics

A2822

A2822a

A2822b

A2822c

A2822d

A2822e

A2822f

A2822g

A2822h

A2822i

A2822j

A2822k

A2822l

A2822m

A2822n

1990, Jan. 18   Litho.   Perf. 12x12½

5854	A2822	5k	Moscow	.30	.25
5855	A2822a	5k	Tallinn	.30	.25
5856	A2822b	5k	Riga	.30	.25
5857	A2822c	5k	Vilnius	.30	.25
5858	A2822d	5k	Minsk	.30	.25
5859	A2822e	5k	Kiev	.30	.25
5860	A2822f	5k	Kishinev	.30	.25
5861	A2822g	5k	Tbilisi	.30	.25
5862	A2822h	5k	Yerevan	.30	.25
5863	A2822i	5k	Baku	.30	.25
5864	A2822j	5k	Alma-Ata	.30	.25
5865	A2822k	5k	Tashkent	.30	.25
5866	A2822l	5k	Frunze	.30	.25
5867	A2822m	5k	Ashkhabad	.30	.25
5868	A2822n	5k	Dushanbe	.30	.25

Nos. 5854-5868 (15)   4.50 3.75

A2823

1990, Feb. 3   Perf. 11½
5869 A2823 10k black & brown   .50 .25
Ho Chi Minh (1890-1969).

A2824

1990, Feb. 3   Photo.
5870 A2824 5k multicolored   .50 .25
Vietnamese Communist Party, 60th anniv.

Owls
A2825

Perf. 12x12½, 12½x12
1990, Feb. 8   Litho.
5871 A2825 10k Nyctea scandia-ca   .30 .25
a.   Miniature sheet of 8   6.00
5872 A2825 20k Bubo bubo, vert.   .60 .40
5873 A2825 35k Asio otus   1.60 1.00
Nos. 5871-5873 (3)   2.50 1.65

Penny Black, 150th Anniv. A2826

Emblems and various Penny Blacks: No. 5875, Position TP. No. 5876, Position TF. No. 5877, Position AH. No. 5878, Position VK. No. 5879, Position AE.

1990, Feb. 15   Photo.   Perf. 11½
5874 A2826 10k shown   .35 .25
5875 A2826 20k gold & black   .50 .35
a.   Miniature sheet of 8   6.50
5876 A2826 20k gold & black   .50 .35
a.   Miniature sheet of 8   6.50
5877 A2826 35k multicolored   .85 .55
5878 A2826 35k multicolored   .85 .55
Nos. 5874-5878 (5)   3.05 2.05

Souvenir Sheet
Perf. 12x11½
5879 A2826   1r dk green & blk   4.00 2.00
Stamp World London '90 (35k).
No. 5879 contains one 37x26mm stamp.

ITU, 125th Anniv. A2827

1990, Feb. 20   Photo.   Perf. 11½
5880 A2827 20k multicolored   .50 .35

Labor Day A2828

1990, Mar. 28   Photo.   Perf. 11½
5881 A2828 5k multicolored   .40 .25

Victory, 1945, by A. Lysenko A2829

1990, Mar. 28   Litho.   Perf. 12x12½
5882 A2829 5k multicolored   .50 .25
End of World War II, 45th anniv.

Mir Space Station, Cosmonaut A2830

1990, Apr. 12
5883 A2830 20k multicolored   .50 .35
a.   Miniature sheet of 8   5.00
Cosmonauts' Day.

Lenin, 120th Birth Anniv. — A2831

1990, Apr. 14   Engr.   Perf. 11½
5884 A2831 5k red brown   .40 .25
LENINIANA '90 all-union philatelic exhibition.

Lenin Birthday Type of 1988
Portrait of Lenin and: No. 5885, Lenin Memorial (birthplace), Ulyanovsk. No. 5886, Branch of the Central Lenin Museum, Baku. No. 5887, Branch of the Central Lenin Museum, Tashkent.

1990, Apr. 14   Litho.   Perf. 12
5885 A2727 5k dark car & multi   .30 .25
5886 A2727 5k rose vio & multi   .30 .25
5887 A2727 5k dark grn & multi   .30 .25
Nos. 5885-5887 (3)   .90 .75
Lenin, 120th Birth Anniv.

Tchaikovsky, Scene from *Iolanta* — A2832

1990, Apr. 25   Engr.   Perf. 12½x12
5888 A2832 15k black   1.00 .35
Tchaikovsky (1840-1893), composer.

Kalmyk Legend *Dzhangar,* 550th Anniv. — A2833

1990, May 22   Litho.   Perf. 12x12½
5889 A2833 10k blk & blk brn   .50 .25

Folklore Type of 1989
Designs: No. 5890, *Manas,* Kirghiz legend (Warrior with saber leading battle). No. 5891, *Guraguli,* Tadzhik legend (Armored warriors and elephant). No. 5892, *David Sasunsky,* Armenian legend (Men, arches), vert. No. 5893, *Gerogly,* Turkmen legend (Sleeping woman, man with lute), vert. No. 5894, *Kalevipoeg,* Estonian legend (Man with boards), vert. Nos. 5890-5894 printed se-tenant with descriptive label.

1990, May 22   Perf. 12½x12, 12x12½
5890 A2795 10k multicolored   .40 .25
5891 A2795 10k multicolored   .40 .25
5892 A2795 10k multicolored   .40 .25
5893 A2795 10k multicolored   .40 .25
5894 A2795 10k multicolored   .40 .25
Nos. 5890-5894 (5)   2.00 1.25

World Cup Soccer Championships, Italy 1990 — A2834

Various soccer players.

1990, May 25   Perf. 12x12½
5895 A2834 5k multicolored   .25 .25
a.   Miniature sheet of 8   4.00
5896 A2834 10k multicolored   .30 .25
a.   Miniature sheet of 8   6.00
5897 A2834 15k multicolored   .40 .30
5898 A2834 25k multicolored   .70 .55
5899 A2834 35k multicolored   .90 .75
a.   Strip of 5, #5895-5899   3.00 2.00

A2835

1990, June 5   Litho.   Perf. 11½
5900 A2835 15k multicolored   .50 .30
Final agreement, European Conference on Security and Cooperation, 15th anniv.

45th World Shooting Championships, Moscow — A2836

1990, June 5   Photo.
5901 A2836 15k multicolored   .50 .30

Cooperation in Antarctic Research A2837

1990, June 13   Litho.   Perf. 12x12½
5902 A2837 5k Scientists on ice   .35 .25
5903 A2837 50k Krill   1.60 1.00
a.   Souv. sheet of 2, #5902-5903   2.00
See Australia Nos. 1182-1183.

Goodwill Games A2838

1990, June 14   Litho.   Perf. 11½
5904 A2838 10k multicolored   .50 .25

Souvenir Sheet

Battle of the Neva River, 750th Anniv. — A2839

1990, June 20   Litho.   Perf. 12½x12
5905 A2839 50k multicolored   2.00 1.25

Duck Conservation — A2840

5k, Anas platyrhychos. 15k, Bucephala clangula. 20k, Netta rufina.

1990, July 1   Litho.   Perf. 12
5906 A2840 5k multicolored   .25 .25
5907 A2840 15k multicolored   .30 .25
5908 A2840 20k multicolored   .45 .25
a.   Miniature sheet of 9   4.00
Nos. 5906-5908 (3)   1.00 .75
Nos. 5906-5908 exists imperf.

Poultry A2841

5k, Obroshinsky geese. 10k, Adler rooster & hen. 15k, North Caucasian turkeys.

1990, July 1   Perf. 12x12½
5909 A2841 5k multicolored   .30 .25
5910 A2841 10k multicolored   .30 .25
5911 A2841 15k multicolored   .30 .25
Nos. 5909-5911 (3)   .90 .85

Spaso-Efrosinievsky Monastery, Polotsk — A2842

Statue of Nicholas Baratashvili and Pantheon, Mtsaminda A2843 — Palace of Shirvanshahs, Baku A2844

Statue of Stefan III the Great, Kishinev — A2845 — St. Nshan's Church, Akhpat — A2846

Historic Architecture: No. 5915, Cathedral, Vilnius. No. 5917, St. Peter's Church, Riga. No. 5919, Niguliste Church, Tallinn.

1990, Aug. 1   Litho.   Perf. 11½
5912 A2842 15k multicolored   .40 .25
5913 A2843 15k multicolored   .40 .25
5914 A2844 15k multicolored   .40 .25
5915 A2845 15k multicolored   .40 .25
5916 A2845 15k multicolored   .40 .25
5917 A2842 15k multicolored   .40 .25
5918 A2846 15k multicolored   .40 .25
5919 A2842 15k multicolored   .40 .25
Nos. 5912-5919 (8)   3.20 2.00
See Nos. 5968-5970.

Prehistoric Animals — A2847

1990, Aug. 15
5920 A2847 1k Sordes   .25 .25
5921 A2847 3k Chalicotherium   .25 .25
5922 A2847 5k Indricotherium   .25 .25
5923 A2847 10k Saurolophus   .25 .25
5924 A2847 20k Thyestes   .50 .35
Nos. 5920-5924 (5)   1.50 1.35
Nos. 5921-5923 vert.

Indian Child's Drawing of the Kremlin A2848

No. 5926, Russian child's drawing of India.

1990, Aug. 15   Perf. 12
5925 A2848 10k multicolored   .40 .25
5926 A2848 10k multicolored   .40 .25
a.   Pair, #5925-5926   1.00 .50
See India Nos. 1318-1319.

Letter Writing Week — A2849

1990, Sept. 12   Engr.   Perf. 12x11½
5927 A2849 5k blue   .50 .25

Traffic Safety — A2850

1990, Sept. 12   Litho.   Perf. 11½
5928 A2850 5k multicolored   .50 .25

Musical Instruments Type of 1989

#5929, Kazakh. #5930, Georgian. #5931, Azerbaijanian. #5932, Lithuanian.

Photo. & Engr.
1990, Sept. 20   Perf. 12x11½

		Denomination	Color		
5929	A2816	10k	brown	.35	.25
5930	A2816	10k	green	.35	.25
5931	A2816	10k	orange	.35	.25
5932	A2816	10k	blue	.35	.25
		Nos. 5929-5932 (4)		1.40	1.00

Killer Whales A2855

Northern Sea Lions A2856

Sea Otter A2857

Common Dolphin A2858

1990, Oct. 3   Litho.   Perf. 12x11½
5933 A2855 25k multicolored   .45 .30
5934 A2856 25k multicolored   .45 .30
5935 A2857 25k multicolored   .45 .30
5936 A2858 25k multicolored   .45 .30
a.   Block of 4, #5933-5936   2.00 1.50
See US Nos. 2508-2511.

October Revolution, 73rd Anniv. — A2859

Design: Lenin Among the Delegates to the 2nd Congress of Soviets, by S.V. Gerasimov.

1990, Oct. 10   Litho.   Perf. 12x12½
5937 A2859 5k multicolored   .50 .25

Nobel Laureates in Literature — A2860

#5938, Ivan A. Bunin (1870-1953). #5939, Boris Pasternak (1890-1960). #5940, Mikhail A. Sholokov (1905-1984).

1990, Oct. 22   Perf. 12
5938 A2860 15k brown olive   .50 .25
5939 A2860 15k bluish black   .50 .25
5940 A2860 15k black   .50 .25
Nos. 5938-5940 (3)   1.50 .75

Submarines — A2861

1990, Nov. 14   Litho.   Perf. 12
5941 A2861 5k Sever-2   .25 .25
5942 A2861 10k Tinro-2   .25 .25
5943 A2861 15k Argus   .25 .25
5944 A2861 25k Paisis   .60 .45
5945 A2861 35k Mir   .75 .50
Nos. 5941-5945 (5)   2.10 1.70

A2862

Armenia-Mother Monument by E. Kochar.

1990, Nov. 27   Litho.   Perf. 11½
5946 A2862 10k multicolored   .50 .25
Armenia '90 Philatelic Exhibition.

A2863

Soviet Agents: #5947, Rudolf I. Abel (1903-71). #5948, Kim Philby (1912-88). #5949, Konon T. Molody (1922-70). #5950, S.A. Vaupshasov (1899-1976). #5951, I.D. Kudrya (1912-42).

1990, Nov. 29   Photo.   Perf. 11½
5947 A2863 5k black & brown   .40 .25
5948 A2863 5k black & bluish blk   .40 .25
5949 A2863 5k black & yel brown   .40 .25
5950 A2863 5k black & yel green   .40 .25
5951 A2863 5k black & brown   .40 .25
Nos. 5947-5951 (5)   2.00 1.25

Joint Soviet-Japanese Space Flight — A2864

1990, Dec. 2   Litho.   Perf. 12
5952 A2864 20k multicolored   .75 .50

Happy New Year — A2865

1990, Dec. 3   Perf. 11½
5953 A2865 5k multicolored   .50 .25
b.   Miniature sheet of 8   4.00

Charter for a New Europe — A2865a

1990, Dec. 31   Litho.   Perf. 11½
5953A A2865a 30k Globe, Eiffel Tower   .75   .50

Marine Life A2866

4k, Rhizostoma pulmo. 5k, Anemonia sulcata. 10k, Squalus acanthias. 15k, Engraulis encrasicolus. 20k, Tursiops truncatus.

1991, Jan. 4   Perf. 12
5954 A2866 4k multicolored   .25   .25
5955 A2866 5k multicolored   .25   .25
5956 A2866 10k multicolored   .35   .25
5957 A2866 15k multicolored   .50   .35
5958 A2866 20k multicolored   .65   .45
  Nos. 5954-5958 (5)   2.00   1.45

Chernobyl Nuclear Disaster, 5th Anniv. A2867

1991, Jan. 22   Perf. 11½
5959 A2867 15k multicolored   .50   .25

Sorrento Coast with View of Capri, 1826, by S.F. Shchedrin (1791-1830) — A2868

Evening in the Ukraine, 1878, by A.I. Kuindzhi (1841-1910) — A2869

Paintings: No. 5961, New Rome, St. Angel's Castle, 1823, by Shchedrin. No. 5963, Birch Grove, 1879, by Kuindzhi.

1991, Jan. 25   Perf. 12½x12
5960 A2868 10k multicolored   .35   .25
5961 A2868 10k multicolored   .35   .25
  a. Pair, #5960-5961+label   .75   .50
5962 A2869 10k multicolored   .35   .25
5963 A2869 10k multicolored   .35   .25
  a. Pair, #5962-5963+label   .75   .50
  Nos. 5960-5963 (4)   1.40   1.00

Paul Keres (1916-1975), Chess Grandmaster — A2870

1991, Jan. 7   Litho.   Perf. 11½
5964 A2870 15k dark brown   .50   .35

Environmental Protection — A2871

Designs: 10k, Bell tower near Kaliazin, Volga River region. 15k, Lake Baikal. 20k, Desert zone of former Aral Sea.

1991, Feb. 5   Perf. 11½
5965 A2871 10k multicolored   .35   .25
5966 A2871 15k multicolored   .50   .35
5967 A2871 20k multicolored   .65   .45
  Nos. 5965-5967 (3)   1.50   1.05

Moslem Tower, Uzgen, Kirghizia A2872

Mukhammed Bashar Mausoleum, Tadzhikstan A2873

Talkhatan-baba Mosque, Turkmenistan A2874

1991, Mar. 5
5968 A2872 15k multicolored   .30   .25
5969 A2873 15k multicolored   .30   .25
5970 A2874 15k multicolored   .30   .25
  Nos. 5968-5970 (3)   .90   .75
  See Nos. 5912-5919.

Russian Settlements in America — A2875

Designs: 20k, G. I. Shelekhov (1747-1795), Alaska colonizer. 30k, A. A. Baranov, (1746-1819), first governor of Russian America. 50k, I. A. Kuskov, founder of Fort Ross, California.

1991, Mar. 14   Perf. 12x11½
5971 A2875 20k brt blue & black   .35   .25
5972 A2875 30k olive brn & blk   .65   .45
5973 A2875 50k red brn & black   1.10   .60
  Nos. 5971-5973 (3)   2.10   1.30

Yuri A. Gagarin A2876

Inscription, Nos. 5977c, 5977e

1991, Apr. 6   Perf. 11½x12
5974 A2876 25k Pilot   .75   .50
5975 A2876 25k Cosmonaut   .75   .50
5976 A2876 25k Pilot, wearing hat   .75   .50
5977 A2876 25k As civilian   .75   .50
  a. Block of 4, #5974-5977   3.00   2.50
  b. Sheet of 4, #5974-5977, imperf.   4.00   2.80
  c. As "b," inscribed   10.00   5.00
  d. Sheet, 2 each, #5974-5977, Perf. 12x11½   10.00   6.00
  e. As "d," inscribed   10.00   6.00
  Nos. 5977b-5977c have simulated perforations.

May 1945 by A. and S. Tkachev A2877

1991, Apr. 10   Perf. 12
5978 A2877 5k multicolored   .50   .25
  World War II Victory Day.

Asia and Pacific Transport Network, 10th Anniv. — A2878

1991, Apr. 15   Perf. 11½
5979 A2878 10k multicolored   .50   .25

Type of 1988 Dated 1991

Designs: 2k, Early ship, train, and carriage. 7k, Airplane, helicopter, ocean liner, cable car, van. 12k, Space shuttle. 13k, Space station.

1991, Apr. 15   Litho.   Perf. 12x12½
5984 A2765 2k orange brown   .50   .25
  a. Imperf   .50   .25
5985 A2765 7k bright blue   .50   .25
  a. Perf. 12x11½, photo.   .50   .25
5986 A2765 12k dk lilac rose   .90   .30
5987 A2765 13k deep violet   1.00   .35
  Nos. 5984-5987 (4)   2.90   1.15

Nos. 5984-5987 were also issued on chalky paper. Vaue, $4.
For surcharges see Tadjikistan #10-11, Uzbekistan #18, 61C.

Lenin, 121st Birth Anniv. A2879

Painting: Lenin working on "Materialism and Empirical Criticism" by P.P. Belousov.

1991, Apr. 22   Litho.   Perf. 12
5992 A2879 5k multicolored   .50   .25

Sergei Prokofiev (1891-1953), Composer — A2880

1991, Apr. 23   Perf. 12½x12
5993 A2880 15k brown   .60   .40

Orchids — A2881

3k, Cypripedium calceolus. 5k, Orchis purpurea. 10k, Ophrys apifera. 20k, Calypso bulbosa. 25k, Epipactis palustris.

1991, May 7   Perf. 12
5994 A2881 3k multicolored   .25   .25
5995 A2881 5k multicolored   .25   .25
5996 A2881 10k multicolored   .25   .25
5997 A2881 20k multicolored   .30   .25
5998 A2881 25k multicolored   .45   .25
  Nos. 5994-5998 (5)   1.50   1.25

A2882

Nobel Prize Winners: No. 5999, Ivan P. Pavlov (1849-1936), 1904, Physiology. No. 6000, Elie Metchnikoff (1845-1916), 1908, Physiology. No. 6001, Andrei D. Sakharov, (1921-89), 1975, Peace.

1991, May 14
5999 A2882 15k black   .50   .30
6000 A2882 15k black   .50   .30
6001 A2882 15k blue black   .50   .30
  Nos. 5999-6001 (3)   1.50   .90

William Saroyan (1908-1981), American Writer — A2883

1991, May 22   Perf. 11½
6002 A2883 1r multicolored   3.00   2.25
  See United States No. 2538.

Russia-Great Britain Joint Space Mission — A2884

1991, May 18　　Litho.　　Perf. 12
6003　A2884　20k multicolored　　　.75　.50

Cultural Heritage A2885

Designs: 10k, Miniature from "Ostomirov Gospel," by Sts. Cyril & Methodius, 1056-1057. 15k, "Russian Truth," manuscript, 11th-13th century by Jaroslav Mudrin. 20k, Sergei Radonezhski by Troitse Sergeiev Lavra, 1424. 25k, Trinity, icon by Andrei Rublev, c. 1411. 30k, Illustration from "Book of the Apostles," by Ivan Feodorov and Petr Mstislavetz, 1564.

1991, June 20　Litho.　Perf. 12x12½
6004　A2885　10k multicolored　　　.35　.25
6005　A2885　15k multicolored　　　.55　.35
6006　A2885　20k multicolored　　　.70　.50
　a.　　Miniature sheet of 8　　4.00
6007　A2885　25k multicolored　　　.90　.60
　a.　　Miniature sheet of 8　　4.00
6008　A2885　30k multicolored　　1.00　.80
　a.　　Strip of #6004-6008　　5.00　3.00

Ducks A2886

Designs: 5k, Anas acuta. 15k, Aythya marila. 20k, Oxyura leucocephala.

1991, July 1　　　　　　　Perf. 12
6009　A2886　5k multicolored　　　.25　.25
6010　A2886　15k multicolored　　　.35　.35
6011　A2886　20k multicolored　　　.45　.45
　a.　　Min. sheet of 9, 2 #6009, 4
　　　#6010, 3 #6011　　4.25　3.25
　　　Nos. 6009-6011 (3)　　1.05　1.05

Airships A2887

Designs: 1k, Albatross, 1910, vert. 3k, GA-42, 1987, vert. 4k, Norge, 1923. 5k, Victory, 1944. 20k, Graf Zeppelin, 1928.

1991, July 18
6012　A2887　1k multicolored　　　.40　.25
6013　A2887　3k multicolored　　　.40　.25
6014　A2887　4k multicolored　　　.40　.25
6015　A2887　5k multicolored　　　.40　.25
6016　A2887　20k multicolored　　　.40　.25
　a.　　Miniature sheet of 8　　4.00
　　　Nos. 6012-6016 (5)　　2.00　1.25

Types of 1984

2r, Ship, Arctic map. 3r, Child & globe. 5r, Palm frond and globe.

1991-92　　Litho.　　Perf. 12½x12
6016B　A2529　2r multicolored　　　.50　.25
　c.　　Imperf　　1.00　.50
6017　A2529　3r multicolored　　5.00　2.50
6017A　A2529　5r multicolored　　4.00　1.50
　　　Nos. 6016B-6017A (3)　　9.50　4.25

Issued: 3r, 6/25; 5r, 11/10; No. 6016B, 8/22/91; No. 6016Bc, 4/20/92.

Conf. on Security and Cooperation in Europe — A2888

1991, July 1　　Photo.　　Perf. 11½
6018　A2888　10k multicolored　　　.50　.25

Bering & Chirikov's Voyage to Alaska, 250th Anniv. — A2889

Design: No. 6020, Sailing ship, map.

1991, July 27　　　　　Perf. 12x11½
6019　A2889　30k multicolored　　　.50　.25
6020　A2889　30k multicolored　　　.50　.25

A2890

1991, Aug. 1　　　　　　Perf. 12
6021　A2890　30k multicolored　　　.50　.25
Ukrainian declaration of sovereignty.

A2891

1991, Aug. 1　　　　　Perf. 12x11½
6022　A2891　7k brown　　　1.00　.25
Letter Writing Week.

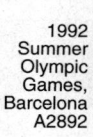

1992 Summer Olympic Games, Barcelona A2892

1991, Sept. 4　　Litho.　　Perf. 12x12½
6023　A2892　10k Canoeing　　　.25　.25
　a.　　Miniature sheet of 8　　5.00
6024　A2892　20k Running　　　.30　.25
　a.　　Miniature sheet of 8　　5.00
6025　A2892　30k Soccer　　　.45　.25
　a.　　Miniature sheet of 8　　5.00
　　　Nos. 6023-6025 (3)　　1.00　.75

Victims of Aug. 1991 Failed Coup — A2893

Citizens Protecting Russian "White House" — A2893a

No. 6026, Vladimir Usov, b. 1954. No. 6027, Illya Krichevsky, b. 1963. No. 6028, Dmitry Komar, b. 1968.

1991, Oct. 11　　Litho.　　Perf. 11½
6026　A2893　7k multicolored　　　.30　.25
6027　A2893　7k multicolored　　　.30　.25
6028　A2893　7k multicolored　　　.30　.25
　　　Nos. 6026-6028 (3)　　.90　.75
Souvenir Sheet
6029　A2893a　50k multicolored　　2.00　.50

USSR-Austria Joint Space Mission — A2894

1991, Oct. 2　　Litho.　　Perf. 11½
6030　A2894　20k multicolored　　　.50　.25

Folk Holidays

Ascension, Armenia A2895

New Year, Azerbaijan A2895a

Ivan Kupala Day, Byelorussia A2895b

New Year, Estonia A2895c

Berikaoba, Georgia A2895d

Kazakhstan — A2895e

Kys Kumai, Kirgizia — A2895f

Ivan Kupala Day, Latvia — A2895g

Palm Sunday, Lithuania A2895h

Plugushorul, Moldavia A2895i

Shrovetide, Russia — A2895j

New Year, Tadzhikistan A2895k

Harvest, Turkmenistan — A2895l

Christmas, Ukraine — A2895m

Spring Tulips,
Uzbekistan
A2895n

Perf. 12x12½, 12½x12

1991, Oct. 4				**Litho.**
6031	A2895	15k multicolored	.25	.25
6032	A2895a	15k multicolored	.25	.25
6033	A2895b	15k multicolored	.25	.25
6034	A2895c	15k multicolored	.25	.25
6035	A2895d	15k multicolored	.25	.25
6036	A2895e	15k multicolored	.25	.25
6037	A2895f	15k multicolored	.25	.25
6038	A2895g	15k multicolored	.25	.25
6039	A2895h	15k multicolored	.25	.25
6040	A2895i	15k multicolored	.25	.25
6041	A2895j	15k multicolored	.25	.25
6042	A2895k	15k multicolored	.25	.25
6043	A2895l	15k multicolored	.25	.25
6044	A2895m	15k multicolored	.25	.25
6045	A2895n	15k multicolored	.25	.25
a.	Min. sheet, 2 each #6031-6045		10.00	
	Nos. 6031-6045 (15)		3.75	3.75

A2896

1991, Oct. 29   Litho.   Perf. 11½
6046 A2896 7k multicolored   .50 .25

Election of Boris Yeltsin, 1st president of Russian Republic, June 12, 1991.

Musical Instruments Type of 1989

Musical Instruments: No. 6047, Moldavia. No. 6048, Latvia. No. 6049, Kirgiz.

Photo. & Engr.

1991, Nov. 19   Perf. 12x11½
Denomination   Color

6047	A2816	10k red	.50	.25
6048	A2816	10k brt greenish bl	.50	.25
6049	A2816	10k red lilac	.50	.25
	Nos. 6047-6049 (3)		1.50	.75

New Year
1992
A2897

1991, Dec. 8   Litho.   Perf. 12x12½
6050 A2897 7k multicolored   .50 .25
a.   Miniature sheet of 8   4.00

A2899

Russian Historians: No. 6052, V. N. Tatischev (1686-1750). No. 6053, N. M. Karamzin (1766-1826). No. 6054, S. M. Soloviev (1820-79). No. 6055, Vasili O. Klyuchevsky (1841-1911).

1991, Dec. 12   Photo. & Engr.

6052	A2899	10k multicolored	.50	.25
6053	A2899	10k multicolored	.50	.25
6054	A2899	10k multicolored	.50	.25
6055	A2899	10k multicolored	.50	.25
	Nos. 6052-6055 (4)		2.00	1.00

With the breakup of the Soviet Union on Dec. 26, 1991, eleven former Soviet republics established the Commonwealth of Independent States. Stamps inscribed "Rossija" are issued by the Russian Republic.

1992 Winter
Olympics,
Albertville — A2900

14k, Cross-country skiing, ski jumping. 1r, Freestyle skiing. 2r, Bobsleds.

1992, Jan. 10   Litho.   Perf. 11½x12

6056	A2900	14k multicolored	.45	.25
a.	Miniature sheet of 8		2.75	
6057	A2900	1r multicolored	.50	.25
a.	Miniature sheet of 8		3.25	
6058	A2900	2r multicolored	1.00	.25
a.	Miniature sheet of 8		5.00	
	Nos. 6056-6058 (3)		1.95	.75

Souvenir Sheet

Battle on the Ice, 750th
Anniv. — A2901

1992, Feb. 20   Litho.   Perf. 12½x12
6059 A2901 50k multicolored   1.00 .65

A2902

Designs: 10k, Golden Portal, Vladimir. 15k, Kremlin, Pskov. 20k, St. George Slaying the Dragon. 25k, 55k, Triumph Gate, Moscow. 30k, 80k, "Millennium of Russia," by M.O. Mikeshin, Novgorod. 60k, Minin-Posharsky Monument, Moscow. 1r, Church, Kizhi. 1.50r, Monument to Peter the Great, St. Petersburg. 2r, St. Basil's Cathedral, Moscow. 3r, Tretyakov Gallery, Moscow. 5r, Morosov House, Moscow. 10r, St. Isaac's Cathedral, St. Petersburg. 25r, Monument to Yuri Dolgoruky, Moscow. 100r, Kremlin, Moscow.

Perf. 12½x12, 11½x12 (15k, 25k, 3r)

1992				**Litho.**
6060	A2902	10k salmon	.45	.25
6060A	A2902	15k dark brn	.45	.25
6061	A2902	20k red	.45	.25
6062	A2902	25k red brown	.45	.25
6063	A2902	30k black	.45	.25
6064	A2902	50k dark blue	.45	.25
6065	A2902	55k dark bl grn	.45	.25
6066	A2902	60k blue green	.45	.25
6066A	A2902	80k lake	.45	.25
6067	A2902	1r yel brown	.45	.25
6067A	A2902	1.50r olive	.50	.25
6068	A2902	2r blue	.45	.25
6068A	A2902	3r red	.45	.25
6069	A2902	5r dark brn	.75	.25
6070	A2902	10r bright blue	.80	.25
6071	A2902	25r dark red	3.00	.50
6071A	A2902	100r brt olive	4.50	1.00
	Nos. 6060-6071A (17)		14.95	5.25

Issued: 20k, 30k, 2/26; 10k, 60k, 2r, 4/20; 25r, 5/25; 10r, 100r, May; 1r, 1.50r, 5r, 6/25; 55k, 8/11; 50k, 80k, 8/18; 15k, 25k, 3r, 9/10.
Nos. 6060-6071A were also issued on chalky paper. Value, same.
See Nos. 6109-6124.

Victory by N. N.
Baskakov
A2903

1992, Mar. 5   Perf. 12x12½
6072 A2903 5k multicolored   .50 .25

End of World War II, 47th anniv.

Prioksko-Terrasny Nature
Reserve — A2904

1992, Mar. 12   Perf. 12
6073 A2904 50k multicolored   .25 .25

Russia-Germany
Joint Space
Mission — A2905

1992, Mar. 17
6074 A2905 5r multicolored   1.00 .30

Souvenir Sheet

Discovery of America, 500th
Anniv. — A2906

1992, Mar. 18   Perf. 12x11½
6075 A2906 3r Ship, Columbus   1.00 .80

Characters
from
Children's
Books
A2907

1992, Apr. 22   Litho.   Perf. 12

6076	A2907	25k Pinocchio	.50	.25
6077	A2907	30k Cipollino	.50	.25
6078	A2907	35k Dunno	.50	.25
6079	A2907	50k Karlson	.50	.25
	Nos. 6076-6079 (4)		2.00	1.00

Space
Accomplishments
A2908

Designs: No. 6081, Astronaut, Russian space station and space shuttle. No. 6082, Sputnik, Vostok, Apollo Command and Lunar modules. No. 6083, Soyuz, Mercury and Gemini spacecraft.

1992, May 29   Litho.   Perf. 11½x12

6080	A2908	25r multicolored	.60	.25
6081	A2908	25r multicolored	.60	.25
6082	A2908	25r multicolored	.60	.25
6083	A2908	25r multicolored	.60	.25
a.	Block of 4, #6080-6083		3.00	1.25

See US Nos. 2631-2634.

1992
Summer
Olympics,
Barcelona
A2909

Perf. 11½x12, 12x11½

1992, June 5				**Photo.**
6084	A2909	1r Team handball, vert.	.25	.25
a.	Miniature sheet of 8		1.50	1.50
6085	A2909	2r Fencing	.30	.25
a.	Miniature sheet of 8		3.50	2.00
6086	A2909	3r Judo	.50	.25
a.	Miniature sheet of 8		5.00	2.00
	Nos. 6084-6086 (3)		1.05	.75

Explorers — A2910

Designs: 55r, L. A. Zagoskin, Alaska-Yukon. 70r, N. N. Miklucho-Maklai, New Guinea. 1r, G. I. Langsdorf, Brazil.

1992, June 23   Litho.   Perf. 12x11½

6087	A2910	55k multicolored	.30	.25
6088	A2910	70k multicolored	.30	.25
6089	A2910	1r multicolored	.30	.25
	Nos. 6087-6089 (3)		.90	.75

Ducks
A2911

1992, July 1   Perf. 12

6090	A2911	1r Anas querquedula	.30	.25
6091	A2911	2r Aythya ferina	.30	.25
6092	A2911	3r Anas falcata	.30	.25
a.	Min. sheet of 9, 3 #6090, 4 #6091, 2 #6092		3.00	2.10
	Nos. 6090-6092 (3)		.90	.75

The Saviour,
by Andrei
Rublev
A2912

1992, July 3   *Perf. 12x12½*
6093 A2912 1r multicolored .50 .25
  a.   Miniature sheet of 8   3.00 1.60

The Taj Mahal Mausoleum in Agra, by
Vasili Vereshchagin (1842-
1904) — A2913

Design: No. 6095, Let Me Approach (detail),
by Vereshchagin.

1992, July 3   *Perf. 12½x12*
6094 A2913 1.50r multicolored .30 .25
6095 A2913 1.50r multicolored .30 .25
  a.   Pair, #6094-6095 + label   .90 .30

Cathedral of
the
Assumption,
Moscow
A2914

Cathedral of the
Annunciation,
Moscow
A2915

No. 6098, Archangel Cathedral, Moscow.

1992, Sept. 3   **Litho.**   *Perf. 11½*
6096 A2914 1r multicolored .30 .25
  a.   Miniature sheet of 9   3.00
6097 A2915 1r multicolored .30 .25
  a.   Miniature sheet of 9   3.00
6098 A2915 1r multicolored .30 .25
  a.   Miniature sheet of 9   3.00
     Nos. 6096-6098 (3)   .90 .75

The Nutcracker, by Tchaikovsky,
Cent. — A2916

Designs: No. 6099, Nutcrackers, one hold-
ing rifle. No. 6100, Nutcrackers, diff. No. 6101,
Pas de deux before Christmas tree. No. 6102,
Ballet scene.

1992, Nov. 4   **Litho.**   *Perf. 12½x12*
6099 A2916 10r multicolored .50 .25
6100 A2916 10r multicolored .50 .25
6101 A2916 25r multicolored 1.00 .50
6102 A2916 25r multicolored 1.00 .50
  a.   Block of 4, #6099-6102   4.00 2.00

A2917   A2918

A2919   Icons — A2920

Christmas: No. 6103, Joachim and Anna,
16th cent. No. 6104, Madonna and Child, 14th
cent. No. 6105, Archangel Gabriel, 12th cent.
No. 6106, St. Nicholas, 16th cent.

1992, Nov. 27   *Perf. 11½*
6103 A2917 10r multicolored .40 .25
6104 A2918 10r multicolored .40 .25
6105 A2919 10r multicolored .40 .25
6106 A2920 10r multicolored .40 .25
  a.   Block of 4, #6103-6106   2.25 1.25

See Sweden Nos. 1979-1982.

New Year
1993
A2921

1992, Dec. 2   **Litho.**   *Perf. 12x12½*
6107 A2921 50k multicolored .30 .25
  a.   Miniature sheet of 9   3.00

Discovery of
America, 500th
Anniv. — A2922

1992, Dec. 29   *Perf. 11½x12*
6108 A2922 15r Flags, sculpture .50 .35

Monuments Type of 1992

Designs: 4r, Church, Kizhi. 6r, Monument to
Peter the Great, St. Petersburg. 15r, 45r, The
Horsebreaker, St. Petersburg. 50r, Kremlin,
Rostov. 75r, Monument to Yuri Dolgoruky,
Moscow. 150r, Golden Gate of Vladimir. 250r,
Church, Bogolyubovo. 300r, Monument of
Minin and Pozharsky. 500r, Lomonosov Uni-
versity, Moscow. 750r, State Library, Moscow.
1000r, Fortress of St. Peter and St. Paul, St.
Petersburg. 1500r, Pushkin Museum, Mos-
cow. 2500r, Admiralty, St. Petersburg. 5000r,
Bolshoi Theater, Moscow.

Litho., Photo. (50r, 250r, 500r)
Perf. 12½x12, 12x11½ (1000r)
1992-95
6109 A2902   4r red brown .25 .25
6110 A2902   6r gray blue .25 .25
6111 A2902   15r brown .30 .25
  a.   Photo.   .30 .25
6112 A2902   45r slate 1.40 .45
6113 A2902   50r purple .40 .25
6114 A2902   75r red brown 2.75 .70
6115 A2902   150r blue .35 .25
6116 A2902   250r green 4.00 .30
6117 A2902   300r red brown .70 .45
6118 A2902   500r violet 8.00 .60
6119 A2902   750r olive grn .60 .35
6120 A2902 1000r slate .70 .50
6121 A2902 1500r green 1.10 .60
6122 A2902 2500r olive brn 1.75 1.00
6123 A2902 5000r blue grn 3.50 2.00
     Nos. 6109-6123 (15) 26.05 8.20

Issued: #6111a, 6113, 6116, 6118,
12/25/92; #6109-6110, 6/4/93; #6112, 6114,
1/25/93; 150r, 300r, 12/30/93; 1000r, 1/27/95;
750r, 1500r, 2500r, 5000r, 2/21/95.
For surcharge see #6529.

Marius Petipa (1818-1910),
Choreographer — A2923

Ballets: No. 6126, Paquita (1847). No. 6127,
Sleeping Beauty (1890). No. 6128, Swan Lake
(1895). No. 6129, Raymonda (1898).

1993, Jan. 14   **Litho.**   *Perf. 12½x12*
6126 A2923 25r multicolored .75 .25
6127 A2923 25r multicolored .75 .25
6128 A2923 25r multicolored .75 .25
6129 A2923 25r multicolored .75 .25
  a.   Block of 4, #6126-6129   4.00 2.00

A2924

Characters from Children's Books: a, 2r,
Scrub and Rub. b, 3r, Big Cockroach. c, 10r,
The Buzzer Fly. d, 15r, Doctor Doolittle. e, 25r,
Barmalei.

1993, Feb. 25   **Litho.**   *Perf. 12½x12*
6130 A2924 Strip of 5, #a.-e. 1.00 .75

No. 6130 printed in continuous design.

A2925

1993, Mar. 18   **Photo.**   *Perf. 11½x12*
6131 A2925 10r Vyborg Castle .50 .25

City of Vyborg, 700th anniv.

Battle of
Kursk, 50th
Anniv.
A2926

1993, Mar. 25   *Perf. 12x12½*
6132 A2926 10r multicolored .50 .25

Victory Day.

Flowers — A2927

10r, Saintpaulia ionantha. 15r, Hibiscus
rosa-sinensis. 25r, Cyclamen persicum. 50r,
Fuchsia hybrida. 100r, Begonia
semperflorens.

1993, Mar. 25   *Perf. 12½x12*
6133 A2927 10r multicolored .25 .25
6134 A2927 15r multicolored .25 .25
6135 A2927 25r multicolored .25 .25
6136 A2927 50r multicolored .40 .30
  a.   Miniature sheet of 8   5.00
6137 A2927 100r multicolored .85 .60
  a.   Miniature sheet of 8   10.00
     Nos. 6133-6137 (5)   2.00 1.65

See Nos. 6196-6200.

Communications
Satellites — A2928

1993, Apr. 12   **Photo.**   *Perf. 11½*
6138 A2928 25r Molniya-3 .25 .25
6139 A2928 45r Ekran-M .30 .25
6140 A2928 50r Gorizont .30 .25
6141 A2928 75r Luch .50 .35
6142 A2928 100r Express .65 .50
     Nos. 6138-6142 (5) 2.00 1.60

Souvenir Sheet
Perf. 12x11½
6143 A2928 250r Ground station,
             horiz.   2.00 1.40

No. 6143 contains one 37x26mm stamp.

Antique
Silver
A2929

15r, Snuff box, 1820, mug, 1849. 25r, Tea
pot, 1896-1908. 45r, Vase, 1896-1908. 75r,
Tray, candlestick holder, 1896-1908. 100r,
Coffee pot, cream and sugar set, 1852. 250r,
Sweet dish, 1896-1908, biscuit dish, 1844.

1993, May 5   **Litho.**   *Perf. 11½*
6144 A2929 15r multicolored .25 .25
6145 A2929 25r multicolored .25 .25
  a.   Miniature sheet of 9   3.50
6146 A2929 45r multicolored .30 .25
6147 A2929 75r multicolored .50 .35
6148 A2929 100r multicolored .70 .45
  a.   Miniature sheet of 9   6.50
     Nos. 6144-6148 (5) 2.00 1.55

Souvenir Sheet
Perf. 12½x12
6149 A2929 250r multicolored 2.50 1.25

No. 6149 contains one 52x37mm stamp.

A2930

Novgorod
Kremlin
A2931

Designs: No. 6150, Kremlin towers, 14th-
17th cent. No. 6151, St. Sofia's Temple, 11th
cent. No. 6152, Belfry of St. Sophia's, 15th-
18th cent. 250r, Icon, "Sign of the Virgin," 12th
cent.

1993, June 4   **Litho.**   *Perf. 12*
6150 A2930 25r multicolored .50 .25
6151 A2931 25r multicolored .50 .25
6152 A2931 25r multicolored .50 .25
  a.   Sheet, 3 each #6150-6152   5.00 3.00
     Nos. 6150-6152 (3)   1.50 .75

Souvenir Sheet
Perf. 12½x12
6153 A2930 250r multicolored 3.00 1.75

No. 6153 contains one 42x30mm stamp.

Russian-Danish Relations, 500th Anniv. — A2932

1993, June 17   *Perf. 11½*
6154 A2932 90r grn & light grn   .75   .25
See Denmark No. 985.

Ducks A2933

90r, Somateria stelleri. 100r, Somateria mollissima. 250r, Somateria spectabilis.

1993, July 1   **Litho.**   *Perf. 12*
6155 A2933   90r multicolored   .50   .25
6156 A2933 100r multicolored   .50   .25
6157 A2933 250r multicolored   1.00   .30
   a.   Min. sheet, 4 each #6155-
       6156, 1 #6157   4.50
    Nos. 6155-6157 (3)   2.00   .80

Sea Life A2934

50r, Pusa hispida. 60r, Paralithodes brevipes. 90r, Todarodes pacificus. 100fr, Oncorhynchus masu. 250r, Fulmarus glacialis.

1993, July 6
6158 A2934   50r multicolored   .25   .25
6159 A2934   60r multicolored   .25   .25
6160 A2934   90r multicolored   .40   .25
6161 A2934 100r multicolored   .40   .25
6162 A2934 250r multicolored   1.10   .75
   a.   Sheet, #6162, 2 each #6158-
       6161   5.00
    Nos. 6158-6162 (5)   2.40 1.75

Natl. Museum of Applied Arts and Folk Crafts, Moscow — A2935

Designs: No. 6163, Skopino earthenware candlestick. No. 6164, Painted tray, horiz. No. 6165, Painted box, distaff. No. 6166, Enamel icon of St. Dmitry of Solun. 250r, Fedoskino lacquer miniature Easter egg depicting the Resurrection.

Perf. 12x12½, 12½x12
1993, Aug. 11   **Litho.**
6163 A2935   50r multicolored   .25   .25
6164 A2935   50r multicolored   .25   .25
6165 A2935 100r multicolored   .35   .25
6166 A2935 100r multicolored   .35   .25
6167 A2935 250r multicolored   .75   .45
    Nos. 6163-6167 (5)   1.95 1.45

Goznak (Bank Note Printer and Mint), 175th Anniv. A2936

1993, Sept. 2   **Litho.**   *Perf. 12*
6168 A2936 100r multicolored   1.00   .25

Shipbuilders — A2937

No. 6169, Peter the Great (1672-1725), Goto Predestinatsia. No. 6170, K.A. Shilder (1786-1854), first all-metal submarine. No. 6171, I.A. Amosov (1800-78), screw steamship Archimedes. No. 6172, I.G. Bubnov (1872-1919), submarine Bars. No. 6173, B.M. Malinin (1889-1949), submarine Dekabrist. No. 6174, A.I. Maslov (1894-1968), cruiser Kirov.

1993, Sept. 7
6169 A2937 100r multicolored   .50   .25
6170 A2937 100r multicolored   .50   .25
6171 A2937 100r multicolored   .50   .25
6172 A2937 100r multicolored   .50   .25
6173 A2937 100r multicolored   .50   .25
6174 A2937 100r multicolored   .50   .25
   a.   Block of 6, #6169-6174   5.00 1.50

A2938

Moscow Kremlin A2939

No. 6175, Granovitaya Chamber (1487-91). No. 6176, Church of Rizpolozheniye (1484-88). No. 6177, Teremnoi Palace (1635-36).

1993, Oct. 28   **Litho.**   *Perf. 12*
6175 A2938 100r multicolored   .45   .25
   a.   Miniature sheet of 9   4.50
6176 A2939 100r multicolored   .45   .25
   a.   Miniature sheet of 9   4.50
6177 A2939 100r multicolored   .45   .25
   a.   Miniature sheet of 9   4.50
    Nos. 6175-6177 (3)   1.35   .75

Panthera Tigris A2940

Designs: 100r, Adult in woods. 250r, Two cubs. 500r, Adult in snow.

1993, Nov. 25   **Litho.**   *Perf. 12½x12*
6178 A2940   50r multicolored   .35   .25
6179 A2940 100r multicolored   .35   .25
6180 A2940 250r multicolored   .50   .25
6181 A2940 500r multicolored   1.25   .60
   a.   Block of 4, #6178-6181   3.00 1.75
   b.   Miniature sheet, 2 #6181a   6.00

World Wildlife Fund.

New Year 1994 — A2941

1993, Dec. 2   **Photo.**   *Perf. 11½*
6182 A2941 25r multicolored   1.00   .25
   a.   Sheet of 8   50.00

A2942

1993, Nov. 25   **Photo.**   *Perf. 11½x12*
6183 A2942 90r gray, blk & red   .75   .25
Prevention of AIDS.

Wildlife — A2943

No. 6184, Phascolarctos cinereus. No. 6185, Monachus schauinslandi. No. 6186, Haliaeetus leucocephalus. No. 6187, Elephas maximus. No. 6188, Grus vipio. No. 6189, Ailuropoda melanoleuca. No. 6190, Phocoenoides dalli. No. 6191, Eschrichtius robustus.

1993, Dec. 30   **Litho.**   *Perf. 12½x12*
6184 A2943 250r multicolored   .50   .25
6185 A2943 250r multicolored   .50   .25
6186 A2943 250r multicolored   .50   .25
6187 A2943 250r multicolored   .50   .25
6188 A2943 250r multicolored   .50   .25
6189 A2943 250r multicolored   .50   .25
6190 A2943 250r multicolored   .50   .25
6191 A2943 250r multicolored   .50   .25
   a.   Min. sheet of 8, #6184-6191   7.50
    Nos. 6184-6191 (8)   4.00 2.00

Nikolai Rimsky-Korsakov (1844-1908), Scene from "Sadko" — A2944

Scenes from operas: No. 6193, "Golden Cockerel," 1907. No. 6194, "The Czar's Bride," 1898. No. 6195, "The Snow Maiden," 1881.

1994, Jan. 20   **Litho.**   *Perf. 12½x12*
6192 A2944 250r multicolored   1.25   .50
6193 A2944 250r multicolored   1.25   .50
6194 A2944 250r multicolored   1.25   .50
6195 A2944 250r multicolored   1.25   .50
   a.   Block of 4, #6192-6195   5.00 2.00

Flower Type of 1993

Designs: 50r, Epiphyllum peacockii. No. 6197, Mammillaria swinglei. No. 6198, Lophophora williamsii. No. 6199, Opuntia basilaris. No. 6200, Selenicereus grandiflorus.

1994, Feb. 25   **Litho.**   *Perf. 12½x12*
6196 A2927   50r multicolored   .25   .25
6197 A2927 100r multicolored   .35   .25
   a.   Min. sheet of 8   7.50 4.00
6198 A2927 100r multicolored   .35   .25
   a.   Min. sheet of 8   7.50 4.00
6199 A2927 250r multicolored   .50   .25
6200 A2927 250r multicolored   .50   .25
    Nos. 6196-6200 (5)   1.95 1.25

Cathedral of St. Peter, York, Great Britain — A2945

Metropolis Church, Athens — A2946

Gothic Church, Roskilde, Denmark A2947

Notre Dame Cathedral, Paris — A2948

St. Peter's Basilica, Vatican City — A2949

Cologne Cathedral, Germany A2950

St. Basil's Cathedral, Moscow — A2951

Seville Cathedral,
Spain — A2952

No. 6207, St. Patrick's Cathedral, NYC, US.

1994, Mar. 24   Litho.   Perf. 12x12½
6201	A2945	150r multicolored	.25	.25
6202	A2946	150r multicolored	.25	.25
6203	A2947	150r multicolored	.25	.25
6204	A2948	150r multicolored	.25	.25
6205	A2949	150r multicolored	.25	.25
6206	A2950	150r multicolored	.25	.25
6207	A2950	150r multicolored	.25	.25
6208	A2951	150r multicolored	.25	.25
a.		Min. sheet of 9	5.00	5.00
6209	A2952	150r multicolored	.25	.25
a.		Min. sheet of 9, #6201-6209	5.00	5.00
		Nos. 6201-6209 (9)	2.25	2.25

Space
Research
A2953

Designs: 100r, TS-18 Centrifuge, Soyuz
landing module during re-entry. 250r, Soyuz
spacecraft docked at Mir space station. 500r,
Training in hydrolaboratory, cosmonaut during
space walk.

1994, Apr. 12   Litho.   Perf. 12x11½
6210	A2953	100r multicolored	.25	.25
6211	A2953	250r multicolored	.30	.25
6212	A2953	500r multicolored	.45	.25
		Nos. 6210-6212 (3)	1.00	.75

Liberation
of Soviet
Areas,
50th
Anniv.
A2954

Battle maps and: a, Katyusha rockets, liber-
ation of Russia. b, Fighter planes, liberation of
Ukraine. c, Combined offensive, liberation of
Belarus.

1994, Apr. 26   Perf. 12
6213	A2954	100r Block of 3, #a.-		
		c., + label	2.00	.45

See Belarus No. 78, Ukraine No. 195.

Russian Architecture
A2955

Structure, architect: 50r, Krasniye Vorota,
Moscow, Prince D.V. Ukhtomsky (1719-74).
100r, Academy of Science, St. Petersburg,
Giacomo Quarenghi (1744-1817). 150r, Trinity
Cathedral, St. Petersburg, V.P. Stasov (1769-
1848). 300r, Church of Christ the Saviour,
Moscow, K.A. Ton (1794-1881).

1994, May 25   Litho.   Perf. 12½x12
6214	A2955	50r lt brown & blk	.50	.25
6215	A2955	100r red brn & blk	.50	.25
6216	A2955	150r olive grn & blk	.50	.25
6217	A2955	300r gray vio & blk	.50	.25
		Nos. 6214-6217 (4)	2.00	1.00

Painting Type of 1992

Paintings by V. D. Polenov (1844-1927): No.
6218, Christ and the Adultress, 1886-87. No.
6219, Golden Autumn, 1893.

1994, June 1   Litho.   Perf. 12½x12
6218	A2913	150r multicolored	.25	.25
6219	A2913	150r multicolored	.25	.25
a.		Pair, #6218-6219 + label	.50	.35

Ducks
A2956

1994, July 1   Perf. 12
6220	A2956	150r Anas pene-		
		lope	.30	.25
6221	A2956	250r Aythya fuligula	.40	.25
6222	A2956	300r Anas formosa	.60	.25
a.		Min. sheet, 3 #6220, 4		
		#6221, 2 #6222	5.00	2.00
b.		As "a," overprinted	10.00	2.00
		Nos. 6220-6222 (3)	1.30	.75

No. 6222b is overprinted in sheet margin:
"World Philatelic Exhibition Moscow-97" in
Cyrillic and Latin with four exhibition emblems.

A2957

1994, July 5   Photo.   Perf. 11½x12
6223	A2957	100r multicolored	1.00	.25

1994 Goodwill Games, St. Petersburg.

A2958

Nobel Prize Winners in Physics: No. 6224,
P.L. Kapitsa (1894-1984). No. 6225, P.A.
Cherenkov (1904-90).

1994, July 5   Litho.   Perf. 12
6224	A2958	150r sepia	.50	.25
6225	A2958	150r sepia	.50	.25

Intl.
Olympic
Committee,
Cent.
A2959

1994, July 5
6226	A2959	250r multicolored	1.00	.25

Russian Postal
Day — A2960

1994, July 8   Perf. 11½x12
6227	A2960	125r multicolored	1.00	.25

Porcelain
A2961

Designs: 50r, Snuff box, 1752. 100r, Candlestick, 1750-1760. 150r, Statue of watercar-
rier, 1818. 250r, Vase, 19th cent. 300r, Statue
of lady with mask, 1910. 500r, Monogramed
dinner service, 1848.

1994, Aug. 10   Litho.   Perf. 11½
6228	A2961	50r multicolored	.40	.25
a.		Min. sheet of 9	5.00	2.50
b.		As "a," overprinted	5.00	3.00
6229	A2961	100r multicolored	.40	.25
6230	A2961	150r multicolored	.40	.25
6231	A2961	250r multicolored	.40	.25
6232	A2961	300r multicolored	.40	.25
		Nos. 6228-6232 (5)	2.00	1.25

Souvenir Sheet
6233	A2961	500r multicolored	3.00	1.00

No. 6228b is overprinted in sheet margin:
"World Philatelic Exhibition Moscow 97" in
Cyrillic and Latin with four exhibition logos.

Integration of Tuva
into Russia, 50th
Anniv. — A2962

1994, Oct. 13   Photo.   Perf. 11½12
6234	A2962	125r multicolored	1.00	.25

Russian Voyages of
Exploration — A2963

Sailing ships and: No. 6235, V.M. Golovnin,
Kurile Islands expedition, 1811. No. 6236, I.F.
Kruzenstern, trans-global expedition, 1803-06.
No. 6237, F.P. Wrangel, North American
expedition, 1829-35. No. 6238, F.P. Litke,
Novaya Zemlya expedition, 1821-24.

Photo. & Engr.
1994, Nov. 22   Perf. 12x11½
6235	A2963	250r multicolored	.50	.25
6236	A2963	250r multicolored	.50	.25
a.		Miniature sheet of 8	5.00	1.10
6237	A2963	250r multicolored	.50	.25
6238	A2963	250r multicolored	.50	.25
		Nos. 6235-6238 (4)	2.00	1.00

Russian Fleet, 300th anniv. (#6236a).

New Year 1995 — A2964

1994, Dec. 6   Photo.   Perf. 12x11½
6239	A2964	125r multicolored	1.00	.25
a.		Min. sheet of 8	8.00	2.00

Alexander
Griboedov
(1795-1829),
Poet,
Diplomat
A2965

1995, Jan. 5   Litho.   Perf. 11½
6240	A2965	250r sepia & black	.75	.25

No. 6240 printed se-tenant with label.

A2966

Mikhail Fokine (1880-1942),
Choreographer — A2967

Scenes from ballets: No. 6241, Scheher-
azade. No. 6242, The Fire Bird. No. 6243,
Petrouchka.

1995, Jan. 18   Litho.   Perf. 12½x12
6241	A2966	500r multicolored	.50	.25
6242	A2967	500r multicolored	.50	.25
6243	A2967	500r multicolored	.50	.25
a.		Block of 3 + label	5.00	1.00

Mikhail Kutuzov (1745-1813), Field
Marshal — A2968

1995, Jan. 20
6244	A2968	300r multicolored	.50	.25
a.		Miniature sheet of 8	4.00	3.00

16th-17th
Cent.
Architecture,
Moscow
A2969

Designs: 125r, English Yard, Varvarka St.
250r, Áverki Kirillov's house, Bersenevskaya
Embankment. 300r, Volkov's house,
Kharitonievsky Lane.

1995, Feb. 15   Litho.   Perf. 12½x12
6245	A2969	125r multicolored	1.00	.25
6246	A2969	250r multicolored	1.00	.25
6247	A2969	300r multicolored	1.00	.25
a.		Min. sheet, 2 #6245, 4		
		#6246, 3 #6247	15.00	15.00
b.		Min. sheet, as "a," diff. mar-		
		gin	55.00	55.00
		Nos. 6245-6247 (3)	3.00	.75

Sheet margin on No. 6247b has emblems
and inscriptions in Cyrillic and Latin for "World
Philatelic Exhibition Moscow '97."

UN Fight Against Drug Abuse — A2970

1995, Mar. 1   *Perf. 12½x12*
6248   A2970   150r multicolored   .60   .25

Endangered Species — A2971

a, Shoreline. b, Pusa hispida. c, Lynx. d, River, trees.

1995, Mar. 1   *Perf. 12x12½*
6249   A2971   250r Block of 4, #a.-
    d.   1.50   .75

Nos. 6249a-6249b, 6249c-6249d are continuous designs. See Finland No. 960.

End of World War II, 50th Anniv. A2972

#6250, Churchill, Roosevelt, Stalin at Yalta. #6251, Ruins of Reichstag, Berlin. #6252, Monument to concentration camp victims. #6253, Tomb of the Unknown Soldier, Moscow, vert. #6254, Potsdam Conference, map of divided Germany, vert. #6255, Russian planes over Manchuria. #6256, Victory parade, Moscow, vert.

1995, Apr. 7   *Perf. 12x12½, 12½x12*
6250   A2972   250r multicolored   .35   .25
6251   A2972   250r multicolored   .35   .25
6252   A2972   250r multicolored   .35   .25
6253   A2972   250r multicolored   .35   .25
6254   A2972   250r multicolored   .35   .25
6255   A2972   250r multicolored   .35   .25

    Size: 37x52mm
6256   A2972   500r multicolored   .35   .25
  a.   Souv. sheet of 1, perf 11½x12   2.25   1.50
    Nos. 6250-6256 (7)   2.45   1.75

MIR-Space Shuttle Docking, Apollo-Soyuz Link-Up — A2973

a, Space shuttle Atlantis. b, MIR space station. c, Apollo command module. d, Soyuz spacecraft.

1995, June 29   *Litho.*   *Perf. 12x12½*
6257   A2973   1500r Block of 4,
    #a.-d.   5.00   3.00

No. 6257 is a continuous design.

Radio, Cent. A2974

Design: 250r, Alexander Popov (1859-1905), radio-telegraph.

1995, May 3   *Litho.*   *Perf. 11½*
6258   A2974   250r multicolored   .50   .25

Flowers — A2975

No. 6259, Campanula patula. No. 6260, Leucanthemum vulgare. No. 6261, Trifolium pratense. No. 6262, Centaurea jacea. 500r, Geranium pratense.

1995, May 18   *Litho.*   *Perf. 12½x12*
6259   A2975   250r multicolored   .60   .25
6260   A2975   250r multicolored   .60   .25
6261   A2975   300r multicolored   .60   .25
  a.   Min. sheet of 8   5.00
  b.   As "a," different margin   5.00
6262   A2975   300r multicolored   .60   .25
6263   A2975   500r multicolored   .60   .25
    Nos. 6259-6263 (5)   3.00   1.25

No. 6261b has emblems and inscriptions in Cyrillic and Latin for "World Philatelic Exhibition Moscow '97."

Songbirds — A2976

No. 6264, Alauda arvensis. No. 6265, Turdus philomelos. No. 6266, Carduelis carduelis. No. 6267, Cyanosylvia svecica. No. 6268, Luscinia luscinia.

1995, June 15   *Litho.*   *Perf. 12½x12*
6264   A2976   250r multicolored   .40   .25
6265   A2976   250r multicolored   .40   .25
6266   A2976   500r multicolored   .40   .25
6267   A2976   500r multicolored   .40   .25
6268   A2976   750r multicolored   .40   .25
  a.   Min. sheet, 2 each #6264-
     6265, 1 #6268 + label   5.00   1.10
  b.   Min. sheet, 2 each #6266-
     6267, 1 #6268 + label   5.00   1.50
    Nos. 6264-6268 (5)   2.00   1.25

St. Trinity, Jerusalem A2977

Sts. Peter & Paul, Karlovy Vary — A2978

St. Nicholas, Vienna — A2979

St. Nicholas, New York — A2980

Russian Orthodox Churches abroad: 750r, St. Alexei, Leipzig.

1995, July 5   *Litho.*   *Perf. 12x12½*
6269   A2977   300r multicolored   .35   .25
6270   A2978   300r multicolored   .35   .25
6271   A2979   500r multicolored   .35   .25
6272   A2980   500r multicolored   .35   .25
6273   A2980   750r multicolored   .35   .25
  a.   Min. sheet, 2 ea #6269-6273   4.00   4.00
    Nos. 6269-6273 (5)   1.75   1.25

Principality of Ryazan, 900th Anniv. — A2981

1995, July 20   *Photo.*   *Perf. 11½*
6274   A2981   250r Kremlin Cathedral   .50   .25

Fabergé Jewelry in Kremlin Museums A2982

Designs: 150r, Easter egg, 1909, St. Petersburg. 250r, Goblet, 1899-1908, Moscow. 300r, Cross, 1899-1908, St. Petersburg. 600r, Ladle, 1890, Moscow. 750r, Easter egg, 1910, St. Petersburg. 1500r, Easter egg, 1904-06, St. Petersburg.

1995, Aug. 15   *Litho.*   *Perf. 11½*
6275   A2982   150r multicolored   .40   .25
6276   A2982   250r multicolored   .40   .25
6277   A2982   300r multicolored   .40   .25
6278   A2982   500r multicolored   .40   .25
6279   A2982   750r multicolored   .40   .30
    Nos. 6275-6279 (5)   2.00   1.30

    Souvenir Sheet
6280   A2982   1500r multicolored   1.00   1.00

No. 6280 contains one 37x51mm stamp.

    Souvenir Sheet

Singapore '95 — A2983

1995, Sept. 1   *Perf. 12½x12*
6281   A2983   2500r multicolored   2.00   1.75

Ducks A2984

Designs: 500r, Histrionicus histrionicus. 750r, Aythya baeri. 1000r, Mergus merganser.

1995, Sept. 1   *Perf. 12*
6284   A2984   500r multicolored   .40   .25
6285   A2984   750r multicolored   .60   .25
6286   A2984   1000r multicolored   1.00   .40
  a.   Miniature sheet, 2 #6284, 4
     #6285, 3 #6286   4.00   4.00
    Nos. 6284-6286 (3)   2.00   .90

Russian Fleet, 300th Anniv. — A2985

Paintings: 250r, Battle of Grengam, 1720. 300r, Bay of Cesme, 1770. 500r, Battle of Revel Roadstead, 1790. 750r, Kronstadt Roadstead, 1840.

1995, Sept. 14   *Litho.*   *Perf. 12*
6287   A2985   250r multicolored   .25   .25
6288   A2985   300r multicolored   .25   .25
6289   A2985   500r multicolored   .30   .25
6290   A2985   750r multicolored   .40   .25
    Nos. 6287-6290 (4)   1.20   1.00

Arms & Flag of the Russian Federation — A2986

1995, Oct. 4   *Litho.*   *Perf. 12x12½*
6291   A2986   500r multicolored   .50   .25

No. 6291 is printed with se-tenant label.

UN, 50th Anniv. — A2987

1995, Oct. 4
6292   A2987   500r multicolored   .50   .30

Peace and Freedom — A2988

Europa: No. 6293, Storks in nest, countryside. No. 6294, Stork in flight.

1995, Nov. 15   *Litho.*   *Perf. 12x12½*
6293   1500r multicolored   1.00   .75
6294   1500r multicolored   1.00   .75
  a.   A2988   Pair, Nos. 6293-6294   2.25   1.75

No. 6294a is a continuous design.

Christmas A2989

1995, Dec. 1 — Perf. 12

6295	A2989 500r multicolored	.50	.25
a.	Miniature sheet of 9	5.00	

A2990

A2990a

A2990b

Early Russian Dukes — A2990c

Designs: No. 6296, Yuri Dolgorouki (1090-1157), Duke of Souzdal, Grand Duke of Kiev, founder of Moscow. No. 6297, Alexander Nevski (1220-63), Duke of Novgorod, Grand Duke of Vladimir. No. 6298, Michael Alexandrovitsch (1333-39), Prince of Tver. No. 6299, Dimitri Donskoi (1350-89), Duke of Moscow, Vladimir. No. 6300, Ivan III (1440-1505), Grand Duke of Moscow.

Litho. & Engr.
1995, Dec. 21 — Perf. 12

6296	A2990 1000r multicolored	.60	.40
6297	A2990a 1000r multicolored	.60	.40
6298	A2990b 1000r multicolored	.60	.40
6299	A2990c 1000r multicolored	.60	.40
6300	A2990c 1000r multicolored	.60	.40
	Nos. 6296-6300 (5)	3.00	2.00

See #6359-6362.

A2991

1996, Jan. 31 — Litho. — Perf. 12

6301	A2991 750r dull olive black	.50	.25

Nikolai N. Semenov (1896-1986), chemist.

A2992

Flowers: 500r, Viola wittrockiana. No. 6303, Dianthus barbatus. No. 6304, Lathyrus odoratus. No. 6305, Fritillaria imperialis. No. 6306, Antirrhinum majus.

1996, Feb. 22 — Litho. — Perf. 12

6302	A2992 500r multicolored	.35	.25
6303	A2992 750r multicolored	.45	.25
6304	A2992 750r multicolored	.45	.25
6305	A2992 1000r multicolored	.55	.30
6306	A2992 1000r multicolored	.55	.30
a.	Min. sheet of 20, 4 each #6302-6306 + 4 labels	12.00	12.00
	Nos. 6302-6306 (5)	2.35	1.35

Domestic Cats A2993

Designs: No. 6307, European tiger. No. 6308, Russian blue. No. 6309, Persian white. No. 6310, Siamese. No. 6311, Siberian.

1996, Mar. 21
Color of Background

6307	A2993 1000r orange	.60	.30
6308	A2993 1000r brown	.60	.30
6309	A2993 1000r red	.60	.30
6310	A2993 1000r blue violet	.60	.30
6311	A2993 1000r green	.60	.30
a.	Sheet, 2 ea #6307-6311	7.00	7.00
	Nos. 6307-6311 (5)	3.00	1.50

Souvenir Sheet

Modern Olympic Games, Cent. — A2994

1996, Mar. 27

6312	A2994 5000r multicolored	3.00	2.00

Victory Day — A2995

Design: Painting, "Plunged Down Banners," by A. S. Mikhailov.

1996, Apr. 19 — Litho. — Perf. 12

6313	A2995 1000r multicolored	.60	.25
a.	Sheet of 8 + label	8.00	

Value of No. 6313 single + label, $2.

Tula, 850th Anniv. A2996

1996, May 14 — Perf. 12½x12

6314	A2996 1500r Tula Kremlin	.75	.40

Russian Trams A2997

Designs: 500r, Putilovsky plant. No. 6316, Sormovo, 1912. No. 6317, "X" series, 1928. No. 6318, "KM" series, 1931. No. 6319, LM-57, 1957. 2500r, Model 71-608 K, 1993.

1996, May 16 — Photo. — Perf. 11½

6315	A2997 500r multicolored	.25	.25
6316	A2997 750r multicolored	.30	.25
6317	A2997 750r multicolored	.30	.25
6318	A2997 1000r multicolored	.45	.30
6319	A2997 1000r multicolored	.45	.30
6320	A2997 2500r multicolored	1.25	.90
a.	Souvenir sheet	2.00	2.00
b.	Sheet of 6	7.50	7.50
	Nos. 6315-6320 (6)	3.00	2.25

A2998

Europa (Famous Women): No. 6321, E.R. Daschkova (1744-1810), scientist. No. 6322, S.V. Kovalevskaya (1850-91), mathematician.

1996, May 20 — Litho. — Perf. 12x12½

6321	A2998 1500r green & black	1.50	.75
6322	A2998 1500r lilac & black	1.50	.75

A2999

1996, June 1 — Litho. — Perf. 12½x12

6323	A2999 1000r multicolored	.60	.35

UNICEF, 50th anniv.

Summer, by P.P. Sokolov A3000

Post Troika, by P.N. Gruzinsky A3001

Design: No. 6326, Winter, by Sokolov.

1996, June 14

6324	A3000 1500r multicolored	.65	.50
6325	A3001 1500r multicolored	.65	.50
6326	A3000 1500r multicolored	.65	.50
	Nos. 6324-6326 (3)	1.95	1.50

Moscow, 850th Anniv. — A3002

Paintings of urban views: No. 6327, Yauza River, 1790's. No. 6328, Kremlin Palace, 1797. No. 6329, Kamenny Bridge, 1811. No. 6330, Volkhonka Steet, 1830's. No. 6331, Vorvarka St. 1830-40's. No. 6332, Petrovsky Park, troikas.

1996, June 20 — Litho. — Perf. 12

6327	A3002 500r multicolored	.25	.25
6328	A3002 500r multicolored	.25	.25
6329	A3002 750r multicolored	.35	.25
6330	A3002 750r multicolored	.35	.25
6331	A3002 1000r multicolored	.40	.25
a.	Sheet, 2 ea #6327, 6330-6331	5.00	
6332	A3002 1000r multicolored	.40	.25
a.	Sheet, 2 ea #6328-6329, 6332	5.00	
b.	Sheet of 6, #6327-6332	5.00	
	Nos. 6327-6332 (6)	2.00	1.50

No. 6332b has emblems and inscriptions in Cyrillic and Latin for "World Philatelic Exhibition Moscow '97."

Traffic Police, 60th Anniv. A3003

a, Pedestrian crossing guard. b, Children receiving traffic safety education. c, Officer writing citation.

1996, July 3 — Litho. — Perf. 12x12½

6333	A3003 1500r Sheet of 3, #a.-c.	3.00	1.50

1996 Summer Olympic Games, Atlanta — A3004

1996, July 10 — Perf. 12

6334	A3004 500r Basketball	.25	.25
6335	A3004 1000r Boxing	.35	.25
6336	A3004 1000r Swimming	.35	.25
6337	A3004 1500r Women's gymnastics	.60	.30
6338	A3004 1500r Hurdles	.60	.30
a.	Sheet of 8	5.00	
	Nos. 6334-6338 (5)	2.15	1.35

A3005

Russian Navy, 300th Anniv. A3006

Ships: 750r, Yevstafy, 1762. No. 6340, Petropavlovsk, 1894. No. 6341, Novik, 1913. Nos. 6342, 6346a, Galera, 1696. Nos. 6343, 6346d, Aircraft carrier Admiral Kuznetzov, 1985. No. 6344, Tashkent, 1937. No. 6345, Submarine C-13, 1939.

No. 6346: b, Atomic submarine, 1981. c, Sailing ship Azov, 1826.

Litho. & Engr.
1996, July 26 — Perf. 12

6339	A3005 750r multicolored	.50	.25
6340	A3005 1000r multicolored	.80	.25
6341	A3005 1000r multicolored	.80	.25
6342	A3006 1000r multicolored	.80	.25
6343	A3006 1000r multicolored	.80	.25
a.	Sheet, 3 each #6342-6343	10.00	10.00
6344	A3005 1500r multicolored	.65	.40
6345	A3005 1500r multicolored	.65	.40
	Nos. 6339-6345 (7)	5.00	2.05

Souvenir Sheet

6346	A3006 1000r Sheet of 4, #a.-d. + label	2.00	1.25

No. 6346 has blue background.

Aleksandr Gorsky (1871-1924), Choreographer — A3006a

a, 750r, Portrait, scenes from "The Daughter of Gudule," "Salambo." b, 1500r, Don Quixote. c, 1500r, Giselle. d, 750r, La Bayadere.

1996, Aug. 7   Litho.   Perf. 12½x12
6347 A3006a Block of 4, #a.-d.   2.00 1.00
e.   Sheet of 6, #6347b   10.00 5.00

Treaty Between Russia and Belarus A3006b

1996, Aug. 27   Perf. 12x12½
6348 A3006b 1500r Natl. flags   .50 .30

17th-20th Cent. Enamelwork — A3007

Designs: No. 6349, Chalice, 1679. No. 6350, Aromatic bottle, 17th cent. No. 6351, Ink pot, ink set, 17th-18th cent. No. 6352, Coffee pot, 1750-1760. No. 6353, Perfume bottle, 19th-20th cent.
5000r, Icon, Our Lady of Kazan, 1894.

1996, Sept. 10   Perf. 11½
6349 A3007 1000r multicolored   .50 .25
6350 A3007 1000r multicolored   .50 .25
a.   Sheet of 9   5.00 2.50
6351 A3007 1000r multicolored   .50 .25
6352 A3007 1500r multicolored   .50 .30
6353 A3007 1500r multicolored   .50 .30
a.   Sheet of 9   5.00 2.50
Nos. 6349-6353 (5)   2.50 1.35

Souvenir Sheet
6354 A3007 1000r multicolored   2.00 1.00
No. 6353a inscribed in sheet margin for Moscow '97.
No. 6354 contains one 35x50mm stamp.

UNESCO, 50th Anniv. A3008

1996, Oct. 15   Perf. 12x12½
6355 A3008 1000r multicolored   .50 .25
No. 6355 issued in sheets of 8.

Icons, Religious Landmarks A3009

Designs: a, Icon of Our Lady of Iverone, Moscow. b, Holy Monastery of Stavrovouni, Cyprus. c, Icon of St. Nicholas, Cyprus. d, Resurrection (Iverone), Gate, Moscow.

1996, Nov. 13   Perf. 11½
6356 A3009 1500r Block of 4, #a.-d.   3.25 1.60
See Cyprus Nos. 893-896.

New Year 1997 — A3010

Design: Chiming Clock of Moscow, Kremlin.

1996, Dec. 5
6357 A3010 1000r multicolored   .50 .25
a.   Sheet of 8   5.00 2.50

Natl. Ice Hockey Team, 50th Anniv. A3011

Action scenes: a, Two players. b, Three players. c, Three players, referee.

1996, Dec. 5   Perf. 12
6358 A3011 1500r Strip of 3, #a.-c.   3.00 1.10

Basil III — A3012

Ivan IV (the Terrible) — A3013

Feodor Ivanovich — A3014

Boris Godunov — A3015

Litho. & Engr.
1996, Dec. 20   Perf. 12
6359 A3012 1500r multicolored   .75 .35
6360 A3013 1500r multicolored   .75 .35
6361 A3014 1500r multicolored   .75 .35
6362 A3015 1500r multicolored   .75 .35
Nos. 6359-6362 (4)   3.00 1.40
See #6296-6300.

Flowers — A3016

Designs: No. 6363, Chaenomeles japonica. No. 6364, Amygdalus triloba. No. 6365, Cytisus scoparius. No. 6366, Rosa pimpinellifolia. No. 6367, Philadelphus coronarius.

1997, Jan. 21   Litho.   Perf. 12½x12
6363 A3016 500r multicolored   .75 .25
6364 A3016 500r multicolored   .75 .25
6365 A3016 1000r multicolored   1.25 .55
6366 A3016 1000r multicolored   1.25 .55
6367 A3016 1000r multicolored   1.25 .55
Nos. 6363-6367 (5)   5.25 2.15

Souvenir Sheet

Moscow, 850th Anniv. — A3017

1997, Feb. 20   Perf. 12x12½
6368 A3017 3000r Coat of arms   2.00 1.00

Shostakovich Intl. Music Festival — A3018

Dmitri D. Shostakovich (1906-75), composer.

1997, Feb. 26   Perf. 12
6369 A3018 1000r multicolored   .50 .25

Souvenir Sheet

Coat of Arms of Russia, 500th Anniv. — A3019

1997, Mar. 20
6370 A3019 3000r multicolored   2.00 .70

Post Emblem — A3020

Designs: 100r, Agriculture. 150r, Oil rig. 250r, Cranes (birds). 300r, Radio/TV tower. 500r, Russian Post emblem. 750r, St. George slaying dragon. 1000r, Natl. flag, arms. 1500r, Electric power. 2000r, Train. 2500r, Moscow Kremlin. 3000r, Satellite. 5000r, Fine arts.

1997   Chalky Paper   Perf. 12½x12
6371 A3020 100r blk & yel brn   .25 .25
6372 A3020 150r blk & red lilac   .25 .25
6373 A3020 250r blk & olive   .35 .25
6374 A3020 300r blk & dk grn   .65 .25
6375 A3020 500r blk & dk bl   .55 .25
6376 A3020 750r blk & brown   1.10 .25
6377 A3020 1000r blue & red   1.10 .25
6378 A3020 1500r blk & grn bl   1.60 .30
6379 A3020 2000r blk & green   1.25 .40
6380 A3020 2500r blk & red   2.25 .45
6381 A3020 3000r blk & purple   2.25 .60
6382 A3020 5000r blk & brown   3.25 1.00
Nos. 6371-6382 (12)   14.85 4.50

Nos. 6371-6382 exist on normal (glossy) paper. Values, same.
Issued: 500r, 750r, 1000r, 1500r, 2500r, 3/31; 100r, 150r, 250r, 300r, 2000r, 3000r, 5000r, 4/30.
See Nos. 6423-6433, 6550-6560, 6617-6620.

A3021

1997, Mar. 31   Litho.   Perf. 12
6383 A3021 1000r multicolored   10.00 .25
City of Vologda, 850th anniv.

A3022

Europa (Stories and Legends): Legend of Volga.

1997, May 5   Litho.   Perf. 12½x12
6384 A3022 1500r multicolored   3.50 .80

Moscow, 850th Anniv. — A3023

Historic buildings: a, Cathedral of Christ the Savior. b, Turrets and roofs of the Kremlin. c, Grand Palace of the Kremlin, cathedral plaza. d, St. Basil's Cathedral. e, Icon, St. George slaying the Dragon. f, Text of first chronicled record of Moscow, 1147. g, Prince Aleksandr Nevski, Danilov Monastery. h, 16th cent. miniature of Moscow Kremlin. i, Miniature of coronation of Czar Ivan IV. j, 16th cent. map of Moscow.

1997, May 22
6385 A3023 1000r Sheet of 10, #a.-j.   12.00 12.00
Nos. 6385c, 6385h are 42x42mm.

Helicopters — A3024

1997, May 28   Litho.   Perf. 12½x12
6386 A3024 500r Mi-14   6.00 2.50
6387 A3024 1000r Mi-24   6.00 2.50
6388 A3024 1500r Mi-26   6.00 2.50
6389 A3024 2000r Mi-28   6.00 2.50
a.   Sheet of 6   45.00
6390 A3024 2500r Mi-34   6.00 2.50
Nos. 6386-6390 (5)   30.00 12.50

Fairy Tales by Aleksander S. Pushkin — A3025

Designs: 500r, Man holding rope beside lake, devil running, from "The Tale of the Priest and his Workman Balda." 1000r, Two women, two men, from "The Tale of Tsar Saltan." 1500r, Man fishing, fish, man, castle, from "The Tale of the Fisherman and the Fish." 2000r, Princess on steps, old woman holding apple, from "The Tale of the Dead Princess." 3000r, Woman, King bowing while holding scepter, rooster up in air, from "The Tale of the Golden Cockerel."

Photo. & Engr.

				1997, June 6	**Perf. 12x12½**
6391	A3025	500r multicolored		.60	.25
6392	A3025	1000r multicolored		1.25	.25
6393	A3025	1500r multicolored		1.75	.30
6394	A3025	2000r multicolored		2.50	.40
6395	A3025	3000r multicolored		3.50	.60
a.		Strip of 5, #6391-6395		15.00	12.00
b.		Sheet of 2 #6395a		40.00	40.00

Diplomatic Relations Between Russia and Thailand A3026

Design: St. Petersburg, Russian flag, Bangkok, Thailand flag.

1997, June 20   Litho.   Perf. 12½x12
6396 A3026 1500r multicolored   1.00 .30

Wildlife A3027

Designs: a, 500r, Pteromys volans. b, 750r, Felix lynx. c, 1000r, Tetrao urogallus. d, 2000r, Lutra lutra. e, 3000r, Numenius arguata.

1997, July 10   Perf. 12
6397 A3027 Block of 5. #a.-e., + label   3.00 1.50

Russian Regions A3028

No. 6398, Winter scene, Archangel Oblast. No. 6399, Ocean, beach, Kaliningrad Oblast, vert. No. 6400, Ship, Krasnodarsky Krai. No. 6401, Mountains, Yakutia, vert. No. 6402, Mountain, sailing ship monument, Kamchatka Oblast.

			1997, July 15	**Perf. 12½x12, 12x12½**
6398	A3028	1500r multicolored	.55	.30
6399	A3028	1500r multicolored	.55	.30
6400	A3028	1500r multicolored	.55	.30
6401	A3028	1500r multicolored	.55	.30
6402	A3028	1500r multicolored	.55	.30
		Nos. 6398-6402 (5)	2.75	1.50

Cartoon Character Kljopa A3029

Kljopa and: 500r, Rainbow, balloons. 1000r, Hang glider. 1500r, Troika.

			1997, July 25	**Perf. 11½**
6403	A3029	500r multicolored	.50	.25
6404	A3029	1000r multicolored	1.00	.25

Size: 45x33mm
Perf. 12
| 6405 | A3029 | 1500r multicolored | 1.50 | .40 |
| | | Nos. 6403-6405 (3) | 3.00 | .90 |

World Philatelic Exhibition, Moscow 97 — A3030

Designs: a, No. 1, No. 35. b, No. 6061.

1997, Aug. 5   Perf. 11½
6406 A3030 1500r Pair, #a.-b.   1.00 .50
c.   Sheet of 6 stamps   9.00 9.00

A3031

History of Russia, Peter I: No. 6407, Planning new capital. No. 6408, Reforming the military. No. 6409, In Baltic Sea naval battle. No. 6410, Ordering administrative reform. No. 6411, Advocating cultural education. 5000r, Peter I (1672-1725).

			1997, Aug. 15	**Perf. 12x12½**
6407	A3031	2000r multicolored	1.10	.50
6408	A3031	2000r multicolored	1.10	.50
6409	A3031	2000r multicolored	1.10	.50
6410	A3031	2000r multicolored	1.10	.50
6411	A3031	2000r multicolored	1.10	.50
		Nos. 6407-6411 (5)	5.50	2.50

Souvenir Sheet
Litho. & Engr.
6411A A3031 5000r multicolored   4.00 1.50

Indian Independence, 50th Anniv. — A3032

1997, Aug. 15   Perf. 12
6412 A3032 500r multicolored   .50 .25

Russian Pentathlon, 50th Anniv. — A3033

1997, Sept. 1   Perf. 12½x12
6413 A3033 1000r multicolored   .50 .25

Russian Soccer, Cent. A3034

1997, Sept. 4
6414 A3034 2000r multicolored   .75 .35

World Ozone Layer Day A3035

1997, Sept. 16   Perf. 12x12½
6415 A3035 1000r multiocolored   .50 .25

A3036

1997, Oct. 1
6416 A3036 1000r multicolored   1.00 .50
Russia's admission to European Council. No. 6416 printed with se-tenant label.

Souvenir Sheet

Pushkin's "Eugene Onegin," Translated by Abraham Shlonsky — A3038

1997, Nov. 19   Litho.   Perf. 12
6418 A3038 3000r multicolored   2.00 1.60
See Israel No. 1319.

Russian State Museum, St. Petersburg, Cent. — A3039

500r, Boris and Gleb, 14th cent. icon. 1000r, "The Volga Boatmen," by I. Repin. 1500r, "A Promenade," by Marc Chagall. 2000r, "A Merchant's Wife Having Tea," by Kustodiyev.

			1997, Nov. 12	**Litho.**	**Perf. 12**
6419	A3039	500r multi, vert.		.25	.25
6420	A3039	1000r multi, vert.		.40	.25
6421	A3039	1500r multi		.60	.30
6422	A3039	2000r multi		.80	.40
		Nos. 6419-6422 (4)		2.05	1.20

Nos. 6419-6422 were each issued in sheets of 8 + label. See Nos. 6446-6450.

Post Emblem Type of 1997

			1998, Jan. 1	**Litho.**	**Perf. 12x12½**
6423	A3020	10k like #6371		.25	.25
6424	A3020	15k like #6372		.25	.25
6425	A3020	25k like #6373		.25	.25
6426	A3020	30k like #6374		.25	.25
6427	A3020	50k like #6375		.30	.25
6428	A3020	1r like #6377		.60	.30
6429	A3020	1.50r like #6378		.90	.45
6430	A3020	2r like #6379		1.25	.60
6431	A3020	2.50r like #6380		1.40	.70
6432	A3020	3r like #6381		1.75	.90
6433	A3020	5r like #6382		3.00	1.40
		Nos. 6423-6433 (11)		10.20	5.60

Nos. 6423-6433 were printed on chalky paper and normal (glossy) paper. Values, same.

Vasily Surikov (1848-1916), V. Vasnetsov (1848-1926), Painters — A3040

Entire paintings or details by Surikov: No. 6434, Menshikov in Berezovo, 1887. No. 6435, Boyarynya Morozova, 1887.
By Vasnetsov, vert.: No. 6436, The Struggle of Slavs with the Nomads, 1881. No. 6437, Ivan Tsarevitch on a Wolf, 1889.

			1998, Jan. 24	**Perf. 12**
6434	A3040	1.50r multicolored	.90	.45
6435	A3040	1.50r multicolored	.90	.45
a.		Pair, #6434-6435 + label	3.00	.90
6436	A3040	1.50r multicolored	.90	.45
6437	A3040	1.50r multicolored	.90	.45
a.		Pair, #6436-6437 + label	3.00	.90

1998 Winter Olympic Games, Nagano — A3041

50k, Cross country skiing. 1r, Pairs figure skating. 1.50r, Biathlon.

			1998, Jan. 27	**Litho.**	**Perf. 12**
6438	A3041	50k multicolored		.40	.25
6439	A3041	1r multicolored		1.00	.30
6440	A3041	1.50r multicolored		1.60	.45
a.		Sheet, 2 each #6438-6440		10.00	3.00
		Nos. 6438-6440 (3)		3.00	1.00

Aquarium Fish A3042

Designs: No. 6441, Hyphessobrycon callistus. No. 6442, Epalzeorhynchus bicolor. 1r, Synodontis galinae. No. 6444, Botia kristinae. No. 6445, Cichlasoma labiatum.

			1998, Feb. 25	**Litho.**	**Perf. 12½x12**
6441	A3042	50k multicolored		.35	.25
6442	A3042	50k multicolored		.35	.25
6443	A3042	1r multicolored		.60	.25
a.		Sheet of 6		25.00	12.50
6444	A3042	1.50r multicolored		.90	.30
6445	A3042	1.50r multicolored		.90	.30
		Nos. 6441-6445 (5)		3.10	1.35

Russian State Museum, St. Petersburg, Cent., Type of 1997

Designs: No. 6446, The Last Day of Pompeii, by K.P. Bryullov, 1833. No. 6447, Our Lady of Malevolent Hearts Tenderness, by K.S. Petrov-Vodkin, 1914-15. No. 6448, Mast Pine Grove, by I.I. Shishkin, 1898. No. 6449, The Ninth Wave, by I.K. Aivazovsky, 1850.
3r, The Mihailovksy Palace (detail), by K.P. Beggrov, 1832.

1998, Mar. 17   **Perf. 12x12½**
6446	A3039	1.50r multicolored	1.20	.30
6447	A3039	1.50r multicolored	1.20	.30
6448	A3039	1.50r multicolored	1.20	.30
6449	A3039	1.50r multicolored	1.20	.30
a.		Sheet, 2 each #6446-6449 + label	10.00	5.00

Nos. 6446-6449 (4)   4.80   1.20

Souvenir Sheet

6450	A3039	3r multicolored	2.00	1.00

Souvenir Sheet

Expo '98, Lisbon — A3043

1998, Apr. 15   **Perf. 12½x12**
6451	A3043	3r Emblem, dolphins	2.00	.75

Theater of Arts, Moscow, Cent. — A3044

1998, Apr. 24   **Perf. 12**
6452	A3044	1.50r multicolored	1.00	.40

No. 6452 was printed se-tenant with label.

Shrove-tide Natl. Festival — A3045

1998, May 5   **Litho.**   **Perf. 12½x12**
6453	A3045	1.50r multicolored	1.00	.50

Europa.

A3046

A3046a

A3046b

Aleksander S. Pushkin (1799-1837), Poet — A3046c

Pushkin's drawings: No. 6454, Lyceum where Puskin studied 1811-17. No. 6455, A. N. Wolf, contemporary of Pushkin's. No. 6456, Tatyana, heroine of novel, "Eugene Onegin." No. 6457, Cover of 1830 manuscript. No. 6458, Self-portrait.

Litho. & Engr.

1998, May 28   **Perf. 12x12½**
6454	A3046	1.50r multicolored	.60	.30
6455	A3046a	1.50r multicolored	.60	.30
6456	A3046b	1.50r multicolored	.60	.30
6457	A3046c	1.50r multicolored	.60	.30
6458	A3046c	1.50r multicolored	.60	.30
a.		Sheet, 2 each #6454-6458	20.00	5.00

Nos. 6454-6458 (5)   3.00   1.50

City of Ulyanovsk (Simbirsk), 350th Anniv. — A3047

1998, May 28   **Litho.**   **Perf. 12½x12**
6459	A3047	1r multicolored	3.00	.30

Czar Nicholas II (1868-1918) — A3048

1998, June 30   **Litho.**   **Perf. 11½**
6460	A3048	3r multicolored	1.00	.60

Printed se-tenant with label.

City of Taganrog, 300th Anniv. — A3049

1998, June 10   **Litho.**   **Perf. 12½x12**
6461	A3049	1r multicolored	.75	.25

Souvenir Sheet

1998 World Youth Games, Moscow — A3049a

1998, June 25   **Litho.**   **Perf. 12½x12**
6461A	A3049a	3r multicolored	1.25	.75

A3050

Wild Berries: 50k, Vitis amurensis. 75k, Rubus idaeus. 1r, Schisandra chinensis. 1.50r, Vaccinium vitis-idaea. 2r, Rubus arcticus.

1998, July 10
6462	A3050	50k multicolored	.25	.25
6463	A3050	75k multicolored	.40	.25
6464	A3050	1r multicolored	.50	.25
6465	A3050	1.50r multicolored	.75	.30
6466	A3050	2r multicolored	1.00	.40

Nos. 6462-6466 (5)   2.90   1.45

A3051

1998, July 15
6467	A3051	1r multicolored	1.00	.25

Ekaterinburg, 275th anniv.

Soviet Intelligence Agents — A3052

No. 6468, L. R. Kvasnikov (1905-93). No. 6469, Morris Cohen (1910-95). No. 6470, Leontina Cohen (1913-92). No. 6471, A.A. Yatskov (1913-93).

1998, Aug. 10   **Litho.**   **Perf. 12**
6468	A3052	1r green & black	.75	.25
6469	A3052	1r brn, bister & blk	.75	.25
6470	A3052	1r slate & black	.75	.25
6471	A3052	1r claret & black	.75	.25

Nos. 6468-6471 (4)   3.00   1.00

Orders of Russia — A3053

1r, St. Andrey Pervozvanny. 1.50r St. Catherine. 2r, St. Alexander Nevsky. 2.50r, St. George.

1998, Aug. 20   **Litho.**   **Perf. 12x12½**
6472	A3053	1r multi	.35	.25
6472A	A3053	1.50r multi	.55	.25
6472B	A3053	2r multi	.70	.35
6472C	A3053	2.50r multi	.90	.45
d.		Block of 4, #6472-6472C	3.50	1.75
e.		Souvenir sheet of 4, #6472-6472C + label	25.00	10.00

See #6496-6500.

Murmansk Oblast A3054

Khabarovsk Krai — A3055

Karelia Republic — A3056   Buryat Republic — A3057

1998, Sept. 15   **Litho.**   **Perf. 12**
6473	A3054	1.50r multicolored	.60	.30
6474	A3055	1.50r multicolored	.60	.30
6475	A3056	1.50r multicolored	.60	.30
6476	A3057	1.50r multicolored	.60	.30
6477	A3054	1.50r Primorski Krai	.60	.30

Nos. 6473-6477 (5)   3.00   1.50

World Stamp Day A3058

1998, Oct. 9   **Litho.**   **Perf. 12**
6478	A3058	1r multicolored	.75	.25

Universal Declaration of Human Rights, 50th Anniv. — A3059

1998, Oct. 15
6479	A3059	1.50r multicolored	.50	.30

No. 6479 released with se-tenant label.

Menatep Bank, 10th Anniv. — A3060

1998, Oct. 29
6480 A3060 2r multicolored   1.00 .40

A sheet of eight was withdrawn from sale because the Menatep Bank went bankrupt. Value, $50.

20th Cent. Achievements — A3061

1998, Nov. 12
6481 A3061 1r Aviation   .50 .25
6482 A3061 1r Space   .50 .25
6483 A3061 1r Television   .50 .25
6484 A3061 1r Genetics   .50 .25
6485 A3061 1r Nuclear power   .50 .25
6486 A3061 1r Computers   .50 .25
    Nos. 6481-6486 (6)   3.00 1.50

M.I. Koshkin (1898-1940), Tank Designer — A3062

1998, Nov. 20
6487 A3062 1r multicolored   1.00 .25

New Year — A3063

1998, Dec. 1   Litho.   Perf. 11½
6488 A3063 1r multicolored   .50 .25
  a.   Sheet of 9   12.00 5.00

Moscow-St. Petersburg Telephone Line, Cent. — A3064

1999, Jan. 13
6489 A3064 1r multicolored   .50 .25

Hunting A3065

1999, Jan. 29   Litho.   Perf. 11¼
6490 A3065 1r Wild turkey   .25 .25
6491 A3065 1.50r Ducks   .45 .25
6492 A3065 2r Releasing raptor .55 .25
6493 A3065 2.50r Wolves   .75 .30
6494 A3065 3r Bear   .90 .35
    Nos. 6490-6494 (5)   2.90 1.40

Souvenir Sheet

Mediterranean Cruise of Feodor F. Ushakov, Bicent. — A3066

1999, Feb. 19   Perf. 12½x12
6495 A3066 5r multicolored   2.00 .55

Order of Russia Type of 1998
    1r, St. Vladimir, 1782. 1.50r, St. Anne, 1797.
2r, St. John of Jerusalem, 1798. 2.50r, White
Eagles, 1815. 3r, St. Stanislas, 1815.

1999, Feb. 25   Litho.   Perf. 12x12¼
6496 A3053 1r multicolored   .35 .25
6497 A3053 1.50r multicolored .45 .25
6498 A3053 2r multicolored   .60 .25
6499 A3053 2.50r multicolored .75 .30
6500 A3053 3r multicolored   .90 .40
  a.   Sheet of 5, #6496-6500 40.00 25.00

Children's Paintings — A3067

Designs: No. 6501, Family picnic. No. 6502, City, bridge, boats on water, helicopter. No. 6503, Stylized city, vert.

1999, Mar. 24   Litho.   Perf. 12¼x12
6501 A3067 1.20r multicolored .65 .25
6502 A3067 1.20r multicolored .65 .25
6503 A3067 1.20r multicolored .65 .25
    Nos. 6501-6503 (3)   1.95 .75

Souvenir Sheet

Russian Navy's Use of Flag with St. Andrew's Cross, 300th Anniv. — A3068

1999, Mar. 24   Litho.   Perf. 12½x12
6504 A3068 7r multicolored   2.50 1.00

Souvenir Sheet

Intl. Space Station — A3069

1999, Apr. 12   Perf. 11½x12½
6505 A3069 7r multicolored   5.00 .60

IBRA '99 World Philatelic Exhibition, Nuremberg — A3070

1999, Apr. 27   Perf. 12½x12
6506 A3070 3r multicolored   .50 .25

Fishermen and Fishing Gear — A3071

1999, Apr. 30   Perf. 11¾
6507 A3071 1r Raft   .25 .25
6508 A3071 2r Three fishermen .40 .25
6509 A3071 2r Fisherman, boat .40 .25
6510 A3071 3r Spear fishing   .50 .25
6511 A3071 3r Ice fishermen   .50 .25
    Nos. 6507-6511 (5)   2.05 1.25

Council of Europe, 50th Anniv. A3072

1999, May 5   Perf. 12x12¼
6512 A3072 3r multicolored   .50 .25

Europa A3073

1999, May 5   Perf. 12½x12
6513 A3073 5r Bison, Oka Natl. Nature Reserve 2.25 .60

Red Deer — A3074

Designs: a, Bucks. b, Does.

1999, May 18   Perf. 12½x12
6514 A3074 2.50r Pair, #a.-b. 3.00 .35
       Complete booklet #6514   3.00

See People's Republic of China #2958-2959.

Aleksander Pushkin (1799-1837), Poet A3075

Paintings of Pushkin by: 1r, S. G. Chirikov, 1815. 3r, J. E. Vivien, 1826. 5r, Karl P. Bryulov, 1836.
    7r, Vasily A. Tropinin, 1827

Litho. & Engr.
1999, May 27   Perf. 12
6515 A3075 1r multicolored   .35 .25
6516 A3075 3r multicolored   .55 .25
6517 A3075 5r multicolored   1.10 .35
  a.   Min. sheet, 2 ea #6515-6517 9.00 3.75
    Nos. 6515-6517 (3)   2.00 .85

Souvenir Sheet
Perf. 12x12½
6518 A3075 7r multicolored   2.00 .60

No. 6518 contains one 30x41mm stamp.

North Ossetia Republic A3076

Stavropol Kray A3077

Evenki Autonomous Okrug — A3078   Bashkir Republic — A3079

1999, June 2   Litho.   Perf. 12
6519 A3076 2r multicolored   .30 .25
6520 A3077 2r multicolored   .30 .25
6521 A3078 2r multicolored   .30 .25
6522 A3079 2r multicolored   .30 .25
6523 A3076 2r Kirov Oblast   .30 .25
    Nos. 6519-6523 (5)   1.50 1.25

Roses — A3080

1999, June 10   Perf. 12¼x11¾
Color of Rose
6524 A3080 1.20r pink   .25 .25
6525 A3080 1.20r yellow   .25 .25
6526 A3080 2r red & yellow   .30 .25
6527 A3080 3r white   .45 .25
6528 A3080 4r red   .60 .30
  a.   Min. sheet of 5, #6524-6528 10.00 4.50
  b.   Strip of 5, #6524-6528   5.00 2.50
    Nos. 6524-6528 (5)   1.85 1.30

No. 6123 Surcharged
1999, June 22   Litho.   Perf. 12½x12
6529 A2902 1.20r on 5000r   1.00 .30

Rostov-on-Don, 250th Anniv. — A3081

1999, July 8   Litho.   Perf. 11¾x12¼
6530 A3081 1.20r multi   2.50 .25

UPU, 125th Anniv. — A3082

1999, Aug. 23   *Perf. 11¾*
6531 A3082 3r multi   .55 .30

Paintings of Karl P. Bryullov (1799-1852) — A3083

Paintings: a, Horsewoman, 1832. b, Portrait of Y. P. Samoilova and Amacillia Paccini.

1999, Aug. 25   Litho.   *Perf. 11¾x12*
6532 A3083 2.50r Pair, #a-b, + central label   2.00 .35

Motorcycles — A3084

Designs: a, 1r, IZ-1, 1929. b, 1.50r, L-300, 1930. c, 2r, M-72, 1941. d, 2.50r, M-1A, 1945. e, 5r, IZ Planet 5, 1987.

1999, Sept. 9   Litho.   *Perf. 11¾*
6533 A3084 Block of 5, #a.-e., + label   3.00 .85
    Booklet #6533   5.50

The booklet also contains an unfranked cacheted envelope with First Day Cancel.

Field Marshal Aleksandr Suvorov's Alpine Campaign, Bicent. A3085

Designs: No. 6534, Suvorov and soldiers, monument at Schöllenen Gorge. No. 6535, Suvorov's vanguard at Lake Klöntal.

1999, Sept. 24   Litho.   *Perf. 12x11½*
6534 A3085 2.50r multi   .40 1.50
   a.   Miniature sheet of 8   40.00
6535 A3085 2.50r multi   .40 1.50
   a.   Miniature sheet of 8   40.00

See Switzerland Nos. 1056-1057.

Native Sports — A3086

#6536, Kalmyk wrestling. #6537, Horse racing. #6538, Stick tossing. #6539, Reindeer racing. #6540, Weight lifting.

Perf. 11¾x11½, 11½x11¾
1999, Sept. 30   Litho.
6536 A3086 2r multi   .40 .25
6537 A3086 2r multi   .40 .25
6538 A3086 2r multi   .40 .25
6539 A3086 2r multi   .40 .25
6540 A3086 2r multi, vert.   .40 .25
   Nos. 6536-6540 (5)   2.00 1.25

Popular Singers A3087

Designs: No. 6542, Leonid Utesov (1895-1982). No. 6543, Mark Bernes (1911-69). No. 6544, Claudia Shulzhenko (1906-84). No. 6545, Lidia Ruslanova (1900-73). No. 6546, Bulat Okudzhava (1924-97). No. 6547, Vladimir Vysotsky (1938-80). No. 6548, Viktor Tsoi (1962-90). No. 6549, Igor Talkov (1956-91).

1999, Oct. 6   Litho.   *Perf. 12x12¼*
6542 A3087 2r multi   .40 .25
6543 A3087 2r multi   .40 .25
6544 A3087 2r multi   .40 .25
6545 A3087 2r multi   .40 .25
6546 A3087 2r multi   .40 .25
6547 A3087 2r multi   .40 .25
6548 A3087 2r multi   .40 .25
6549 A3087 2r multi   .40 .25
   a.   Miniature sheet, #6542-6549   10.00
   Nos. 6542-6549 (8)   3.20 2.00

Types of 1997 Redrawn with Microprinting Replacing Vertical Lines
1999, Oct. 26   Litho.   *Perf. 12x12¼*
Granite Paper
6550 A3020 10k Like #6371   .50 .25
6551 A3020 15k Like #6372   .50 .25
6552 A3020 25k Like #6373   .50 .25
6553 A3020 30k Like #6374   .50 .25
6554 A3020 50k Like #6375   .50 .25
6555 A3020 1r Like #6377   .50 .25
6556 A3020 1.50r Like #6378   .50 .25
6557 A3020 2r Like #6379   .50 .25
6558 A3020 2.50r Like #6380   .50 .25
6559 A3020 3r Like #6381   .50 .30
6560 A3020 5r Like #6382   .50 .40
   Nos. 6550-6560 (11)   5.50 2.95

Dated 1998.

Spartak, Russian Soccer Champions A3088

1999, Nov. 27   *Perf. 12x12¼*
6561 A3088 2r multi   .60 .25

New Year 2000 — A3089

Designs: a, Grandfather Frost, planets. b, Tree, earth in shell.

1999, Dec. 1   *Perf. 11½x11¾*
6562 A3089 1.20r Pair, #a-b   2.25 .25
   c.   Sheet of 6 #6562a   15.00
   d.   Sheet of 6 #6562b   20.00

No. 6562 printed in sheets of 30 stamps.

Christianity, 2000th Anniv. — A3090

Paintings: No. 6563, The Raising of the Daughter of Jairus, by Vassili D. Polenov, 1871. No. 6564, Christ in the Wilderness, by Ivan N. Kramskoy, 1872. No. 6565, Christ in the House of Mary and Martha, by G. I.

Semiradsky, 1886. No. 6566, What is Truth?, by Nikolai N. Gay, 1890, vert.
7r, Appearance of the Risen Christ, by Alexander A. Ivanov, 1837-57.

2000, Jan. 1   Litho.   *Perf. 12*
6563 A3090 3r multi   .50 .25
6564 A3090 3r multi   .50 .25
6565 A3090 3r multi   .50 .25
6566 A3090 3r multi   .50 .25
   Nos. 6563-6566 (4)   2.00 1.00
Souvenir Sheet
Perf. 12¼x12
6567 A3090 7r multi   2.00 1.00

No. 6567 contains one 52x37mm stamp.

Souvenir Sheet

Christianity, 2000th Anniv. — A3091

No. 6568: a, Mother of God mosaic, St. Sofia Cathedral, Kiev, 11th cent. b, Christ Pantocrator fresco, Church of the Savior's Transfiguration, Polotsk, Belarus, 12th cent. c, Volodymyr Madonna, Tretiakov Gallery, Moscow, 12th cent.

2000, Jan. 5   *Perf. 12x12¼*
6568 A3091 3r Sheet of 3, #a-c   3.00 1.25

See Belarus No. 330, Ukraine No. 370.

Nikolai D. Psurtsev (1900-80), Communications Minister — A3092

Litho. & Engr.
2000, Feb. 1   *Perf. 12x12¼*
6569 A3092 2.50r multi   .50 .25

Souvenir Sheet

Christianity, 2000th Anniv. — A3093

2000, Feb. 10   Litho.   *Perf. 12¼*
6570 A3093 10r Kremlin Cathedrals   5.00 .70

No. 6570 contains two 37x52mm labels.

Polar Explorers — A3094

Designs: No. 6571, R. L. Samoilovich (1881-1940). No. 6572, V. Y. Vize (1886-1954). No. 6573, Mikhail M. Somov (1908-73). No. 6574, P. A. Gordienko (1913-82). No. 6575, A. F. Treshnikov (1914-91).

2000, Feb. 24   *Perf. 11¾*
6571 A3094 2r multi   .80 .25
6572 A3094 2r multi   .80 .25
6573 A3094 2r multi   .80 .25
6574 A3094 2r multi   .80 .25
6575 A3094 2r multi   .80 .25
   a.   Miniature sheet of 5, #6571-6575, + label   60.00 60.00
   Nos. 6571-6575 (5)   4.00 1.25

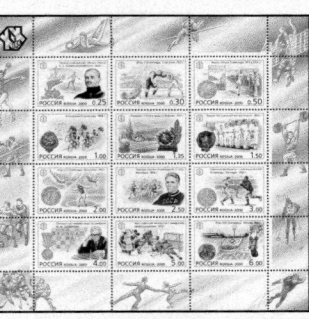

National Sporting Milestones of the 20th Century — A3095

No. 6576: a, 25k, N. A. Panin-Kolomenkin, 1st Olympic champion, 1908. b, 30k, Stockholm Olympics, 1912. c, 50k, All-Russian Olympiad, 1913-14. d, 1r, All-Union Spartacist Games, 1928. e, 1.35r, Sports Association for Labor & Defense, 1931. f, 1.50r, Honored Master of Sport award, 1934. g, 2r, Helsinki Olympics, 1952. h, 2.50r, Vladimir P. Kuts, gold medalist at Melbourne Olympics, 1956. i, 3r, Gold medalist soccer team at Melbourne, 1956. j, 4r Mikhail M. Botvinnik, chess champion. k, 5r, Hockey series between Canada and Soviet Union, 1972. l, 6r, Moscow Olympics, 1980.

2000, Mar. 15   *Perf. 12¼x12*
6576 A3095 Sheet of 12, #a-l   7.50 2.50

Souvenir Sheet

World Meteorological Organization, 50th Anniv. — A3096

2000, Mar. 20
6577 A3096 7r multi   2.00 .45

A3097   A3098

End of World War II, 55th Anniv. — A3099

War effort posters: No. 6581, Soldier holding child.
5r, Soldier and medal.

2000, Apr. 10
6578 A3097 1.50r multi   .50 .25
6579 A3098 1.50r multi   .50 .25
6580 A3099 1.50r multi   .50 .25
6581 A3099 1.50r multi   .50 .25
   Nos. 6578-6581 (4)   2.00 1.00
Souvenir Sheet
6582 A3099 5r multi   3.00 .75
   a.   Miniature sheet, #6578-6581, 2 #6582   20.00 10.00

International Space Cooperation A3100

2r, Apollo-Soyuz mission. 3r, Intl. Space Station. 5r, Sea-based launching station.

2000, Apr. 12				**Perf. 12**	
6583	A3100	2r multi, vert.		.65	.25
a.		Miniature sheet of 6		20.00	10.00
6584	A3100	3r multi		.75	.25
6585	A3100	5r multi, vert.		1.60	.25
	Nos. 6583-6585 (3)			3.00	.75

Traffic Safety Week — A3101

2000, Apr. 20	Litho.		**Perf. 12x12½**	
6586	A3101	1.75r multi	.50	.25

Holocaust A3102

2000, May 5			**Perf. 12**	
6587	A3102	2r multi	7.50	2.50

Election of Vladimir V. Putin as President — A3103

2000, May 7	Litho.		**Perf. 12**	
6588	A3103	1.75r multi	2.00	.35

Europa, 2000
Common Design Type

2000, May 9	Litho.		**Perf. 12½x12½**	
6589	CD17	7r multi	4.00	.85
	Booklet, #6589		10.00	

Souvenir Sheet

Expo 2000, Hanover — A3104

2000, May 17	Litho.		**Perf. 12½x12½**	
6590	A3104	10r multi	3.00	.60

Yamalo-Nenets Autonomous Okrug — A3105

Kalmykia Republic — A3106   Mari El Republic — A3107

Tatarstan Republic — A3108

2000, May 25			**Perf. 12**	
6591	A3105	3r shown	1.00	.50
6592	A3105	3r Chuvash Republic	1.00	.50
6593	A3106	3r shown	1.00	.50
6594	A3107	3r shown	1.00	.50
6595	A3108	3r shown	1.00	.50
6596	A3108	3r Udmurtia Republic	1.00	.50
	Nos. 6591-6596 (6)		6.00	3.00

National Scientific Milestones in the 20th Century — A3109

No. 6597: a, 1.30r, Observation of ferromagnetic resonance by V. K. Arkadjev, 1913. b, 1.30r, Botanical diversity studies by N. I. Vavilov, 1920. c, 1.30r, Moscow Mathematical School, N. N. Luzin, 1920-30. d, 1.75r, Theories on light wave emissions by I. Y. Tamm, 1929. e, 1.75r, Discovery of superfluidity of liquid helium, by P. L. Kapitsa, 1938. f, 1.75r, Research in chemical chain reactions by N. N. Semenov, 1934. g, 2r, Phase stability in particle accelerators, by V. I. Veksler, 1944-45. h, 2r, Translation of Mayan texts by Y. V. Knorozov, 1950s. i, 2r, Research into pogonophorans by A. V. Ivanov. j, 3r, Photographing of the dark side of the moon by Luna 3, 1959. k, 3r, Research in quantum electronics by N. G. Basov and A. M. Prokhorov, 1960s. l, 3r, Slavic ethnolinguistic dictionary by N. I. Tolstoi, 1995.

2000, June 20			**Perf. 12½x12**	
6597	A3109	Sheet of 12, #a-l	15.00	3.50

Dogs — A3110

2000, July 20		**Perf. 12x11¾**	
6598	Horiz. strip of 5	3.00	1.00
a.	A3110 1r Chihuahua	.45	.25
b.	A3110 1.50r Toy terrier	.45	.25
c.	A3110 2r Miniature poodle	.45	.25
d.	A3110 2.50r French bulldog	.50	.25
e.	A3110 3r Japanese chin	.60	.25
f.	Souvenir sheet, #6598e, 2 each #6598a-6598d, perf. 11¾	14.00	14.00

2000 Summer Olympics, Sydney — A3111

Designs: 2r, Fencing. 3r, Synchronized swimming. 5r, Volleyball.

2000, Aug. 15	Litho.		**Perf. 12**	
6599-6601	A3111	Set of 3	2.00	.65

Geological Service, 300th Anniv. — A3112

Minerals: 1r, Charoite. 2r, Hematite. 3r, Rock crystals. 4r, Gold.

2000, Aug. 22			**Perf. 11¾**	
6602-6605	A3112	Set of 4	1.50	.60

National Cultural Milestones in the 20th Century — A3113

No. 6606: a, 30k, Tours of Russian ballet and opera companies, 1908-14. b, 50k, Black Square on White, by Kazimir S. Malevich, 1913. c, 1r, Battleship Potemkin, movie by Sergein Eisenstein, 1925. d, 1.30r, Maxim Gorki, writer. e, 1.50r, Symbols of socialism. f, 1.75r, Vladimir V. Mayakovsky, poet, and propaganda posters. g, 2r, Vsevolod V. Meyerhold, Konstantin S. Stanislavsky, actors. h, 2.50r, Dmitry D. Shostakovich, composer. i, 3r, Galina S. Ulanova, ballet dancer. j, 4r, A. T. Tvardovsky, poet. k, 5r, Restoration of historical monuments and buildings. l, 6r, D. S. Likhachev, literary critic.

2000, Sept. 20	Litho.		**Perf. 12½x12**	
6606	A3113	Sheet of 12, #a-l	6.00	2.00

Fish in Lake Peipus — A3114

No. 6607: a, Stizostedion lucioperka, Coregonus lauaretus manaenoides. b, Osmerus eperlanus spirinchus, Coregonus albula.

2000, Oct. 25			**Perf. 12x12¼**	
6607	A3114	Horiz. pair + central label	2.00	.50
a.-b.		2.50r Any single	.50	.25
		Booklet, #6607	2.50	

See Estonia No. 403.

National Technological Milestones in the 20th Century — A3115

No. 6608: a, 1.50r, Medicine. b, 1.50r, Construction. c, 1.50r, Motor transport. d, 2r, Power generation. e, 2r, Communications. f, 2r, Space technology. g, 3r, Aviation. h, 3r, Rail transport. i, 3r, Sea transport. j, 4r, Metallurgy. k, 4r, Oil refining. l, 4r, Mineral extraction.

2000, Nov. 28			**Perf. 12½x12**	
6608	A3115	Sheet of 12, #a-l	5.00	2.50

Happy New Millennium — A3116

2000, Dec. 1			**Perf. 12**	
6609	A3116	2r multi	1.00	.35
a.		Sheet of 6	6.00	2.50

Foreign Intelligence Service, 80th Anniv. — A3117

2000, Dec. 14	Litho.		**Perf. 12x12½**	
6610	A3117	2.50r multi	.50	.25

Kabardino-Balkaria Republic — A3118

Dagestan Republic A3119

Samara Oblast A3120

2001, Jan. 10			**Perf. 12**	
6611	A3118	3r shown	1.00	.50
6612	A3119	3r shown	1.00	.50
6613	A3120	3r shown	1.00	.50
6614	A3118	3r Chita Oblast	1.00	.50
6615	A3118	3r Komi Republic, vert.	1.00	.50
	Nos. 6611-6615 (5)		5.00	2.50

Souvenir Sheet

Naval Education in Russia, 300th Anniv. — A3121

No. 6616: a, 1.50r, Mathematics and Navigation School, Moscow. b, 2r, Geographical expeditions. c, 8r, St. Petersburg Naval Institute.

2001, Jan. 10   **Perf. 12x12¼**
6616 A3121   Sheet of 3, #a-c   5.00   1.00

Type of 1997 With Lines of Microprinting for Vertical Lines

Designs: 10r, Ballerina. 25r, Rhythmic gymnast. 50r, Earth and computer. 100r, UPU emblem.

2001, Jan. 24   **Litho.**   **Perf. 11¾x12¼**
6617	A3020	10r multi	.75	.45
6618	A3020	25r blk & yel brn	3.00	1.10
6619	A3020	50r blk & blue	5.00	2.00
6620	A3020	100r blk & claret	9.00	3.50
		Nos. 6617-6620 (4)	17.75	7.05

A3122

A3123

A3124

A3124a

Tulips — A3125

2001, Feb. 2   **Litho.**   **Perf. 12¼x12**
6625		Horiz. strip of 5	3.00	.75
a.	A3122	2r Happy Birthday	.40	.25
b.	A3123	2r Be Happy	.40	.25
c.	A3124	2r Congratulations	.40	.25
d.	A3124a	2r Good luck	.40	.25
e.	A3125	2r With Love	.40	.25
f.		Sheet, #6625a-6625e + label	10.00	2.00

Paintings — A3126

No. 6626, 3r (brown background): a, Portrait of P. A. Bulakhov, by Vasily Andreevich Tropinin, 1823. b, Portrait of E. I. Karzinkina, by Tropinin, 1838.

No. 6627, 3r (tan and white background): a, Portrait of I. A. Galitsin, by A. M. Matveev, 1728 . b, Portrait of A. P. Galitsina, by Matveev, 1728.

2001, Feb. 15   **Litho.**   **Perf. 12**
Pairs, #a-b, + Central Label
6626-6627 A3126   Set of 2   3.00   .60

St. Petersburg, 300th Anniv. — A3127

Paintings: 1r, Senate Square and Peter the Great Monumnet, by B. Patersen, 1799. 2r, English Embankment Near senate, by Patersen, 1801. 3r, View of Mikhailovsky Castle From Fontanka Embankment, by Patersen, 1801. 4r, View of the River Moika Near the Stable Department Building, by A. E. Martynov, 1809. 5r, View of the Neva River From the Peter and Paul Fortress, by K. P. Beggrov, 19th cent.

2001, Mar. 15   **Perf. 12x11¾**
| 6628-6632 | A3127 | Set of 5 | 2.00 | .80 |
| 6632a | | Sheet, #6628-6632, + label | 7.50 | 3.00 |

Dragonflies — A3128

No. 6633: a, 1r, Pyrrhosoma nymphula. b, 1.50r, Epitheca bimaculata. c, 2r, Aeschna grandis. d, 3r, Libellula depressa. e, 5r, Coenagrion hastulatum.

2001, Apr. 5   **Perf. 12x12¼**
6633 A3128   Block of 5, #a-e, + label   3.00   .75

First Manned Space Flight, 40th Anniv. — A3129

No. 6634: a, Cosmonaut Yuri Gagarin and rocket designer Sergei Korolev. b, Gagarin saluting.

2001, Apr. 12   **Litho.**   **Perf. 12½x12**
| 6634 | A3129 | 3r Horiz. pair, #a-b | 2.00 | .60 |
| c. | | Sheet, 3 #6634 | 6.00 | 2.75 |

Europa — A3130

2001, May 9   **Litho.**   **Perf. 11¾**
| 6635 | A3130 | 8r multi | 1.00 | .50 |
| a. | | Sheet of 6 | 10.00 | 5.00 |

Intl. Federation of Philately, 75th Anniv. — A3131

2001, May 17   **Perf. 11½**
6636 A3131 2.50r multi   .50   .25

Declaration of State Sovereignty Day — A3132

Litho. & Embossed

2001, June 5   **Perf. 13¼**
6637 A3132 5r multi   2.00   1.00

Russian Emblems A3133

Designs: No. 6638a, Flag. No. 6638b, National anthem. Nos. 6638c, 6639a, Arms.

Litho. & Embossed

2001, June 5   **Perf. 13¼**
6638		Horiz. strip of 3	2.00	.75
a.-b.	A3133	2.50r Any single	.30	.25
c.		A3133 5r multi	.60	.30
d.		Booklet pane of 1, #6638a	—	—
e.		Booklet pane of 1, #6638b	—	—

Souvenir Sheet

6639		Sheet of 3, #6638a-6638b, 6639a	35.00	15.00
a.		A3133 100r multi	30.00	8.00
b.		Booklet, #6639a	100.00	
		Booklet, #6638d, 6638e, 6639b	100.00	

A souvenir booklet, produced in a quantity of 3,000, exists. It comprises a pane of No. 6639 and panes of 4 each of Nos. 6638a, 6638b and 6639a. Booklets were issued with red, blue or white borders. Value, each $500.

A3134

Houses of Worship — A3135

Designs: No. 6640, Cathedral, Vladimir, 1189. No. 6641, Cathedral, Zvenigorod, 1405. No. 6642, Cathedral, Moscow, 1792. No. 6643, Cathedral, Rostov-on-Don, 1792. No. 6644, Mosque, Ufa, 1830. No. 6645, Church, St, Petersburg, 1838. No. 6646, Mosque, Kazan, 1849. No. 6647, Synagogue, Moscow, 1891. No. 6648, Synagogue, St. Petersburg, 1893. No. 6649, Cathedral, Moscow, 1911. No. 6650, Temple, Ulan-Ude, 1976. No. 6651, Church, Bryansk, 1996. No. 6652, Church, Ryazan, 1996. No. 6653, Church, Lesosibirsk, 1999.

2001, July 12   **Litho.**   **Perf. 11½**
6640	A3134	2.50r multi	.35	.25
6641	A3134	2.50r multi	.35	.25
6642	A3134	2.50r shown	.35	.25
6643	A3134	2.50r multi	.35	.25
6644	A3134	2.50r multi	.35	.25
6645	A3134	2.50r multi	.35	.25
6646	A3134	2.50r multi	.35	.25
6647	A3134	2.50r multi	.35	.25
6648	A3134	2.50r multi	.35	.25
6649	A3134	2.50r multi	.35	.25
6650	A3134	2.50r multi	.35	.25
6651	A3135	2.50r shown	.35	.25
6652	A3134	2.50r multi	.35	.25
6653	A3134	2.50r multi	.35	.25
		Nos. 6640-6653 (14)	4.90	3.50

Souvenir Sheet

First Russian Railroad, 150th Anniv. — A3136

2001, July 25   **Perf. 12**
6654 A3136 12r multi   2.00   .50

Flight of Gherman Titov on Vostok 2, 40th Anniv. — A3137

2001, Aug. 6   **Litho.**   **Perf. 12¼x12**
| 6655 | A3137 | 3r multi | 1.00 | .25 |
| a. | | Sheet of 6 | 6.00 | 3.00 |

Film Stars A3138

Designs: No. 6656, 2.50r, Mikhail Zharov (1899-1981). No. 6657, 2.50r, Faina Ranevskaya (1896-1984). No. 6658, 2.50r, Nikolai Kryuchkov (1910-94). No. 6659, 2.50r, Nikolai Rybnikov (1930-90). No. 6660, 2.50r, Lubov Orlova (1902-75). No. 6661, 2.50r, Yuri Nikulin (1921-97). No. 6662, 2.50r, Evgeny Leonov (1926-94). No. 6663, 2.50r, Anatoly Papanov (1922-87). No. 6664, 2.50r, Andrei Mironov (1941-87).

2001, Sept. 20   **Perf. 12**
| 6656-6664 | A3138 | Set of 9 | 2.00 | 1.25 |
| 6664a | | Sheet, #6656-6664 | 10.00 | 5.00 |

Ivan Lazarev (1735-1801) and Institute of Eastern Languages — A3139

2001, Sept. 26   **Perf. 11¾**
6665 A3139 2.50r multi   .50   .35

See Armenia No. 635.

Arkady Raikin (1911-87), Comedian — A3140

2001, Oct. 9   *Perf. 12*
6666 A3140 2r gray & black   .50 .25

Year of Dialogue Among Civilizations A3141

2001, Oct. 9
6667 A3141 5r multi   .50 .35

Souvenir Sheet

Vladimir Dal (1801-72), Author — A3142

2001, Oct. 16   *Perf. 12x12½*
6668 A3142 10r multi   2.00 .75

Constitutional Court, 10th Anniv. A3143

2001, Nov. 1   *Perf. 11¾x12*
6669 A3143 3r multi   .50 .25

Savings Bank of Russia, 160th Anniv. — A3144

2001, Nov. 2   *Perf. 12x11¾*
6670 A3144 2.20r multi   .50 .25

Souvenir Sheet

Defense of Moscow, 60th Anniv. — A3145

2001, Nov. 15   *Perf. 12x12½*
6671 A3145 10r multi   3.00 .60

Commonwealth of Independent States, 10th Anniv. — A3146

2001, Nov. 28   *Perf. 12*
6672 A3146 2r multi   2.00 .75
   a.   Miniature sheet of 10   20.00

Happy New Year — A3147

2001, Dec. 4   *Perf. 12x12¼*
6673 A3147 2.50r multi   .50 .25
   a.   Sheet of 6   10.00 5.00

Amur Oblast A3148

Khakassia Republic A3149

Karachay-Cherkessia Republic — A3150

Sakhalin Oblast A3151

Altai Republic — A3152

2002, Jan. 2   *Perf. 12x12¼, 12¼x12*
6674 A3148 3r multi   1.00 .50
6675 A3149 3r multi   1.00 .50
6676 A3150 3r multi   1.00 .50
6677 A3151 3r multi   1.00 .50
6678 A3152 3r multi   1.00 .50
   Nos. 6674-6678 (5)   5.00 2.50

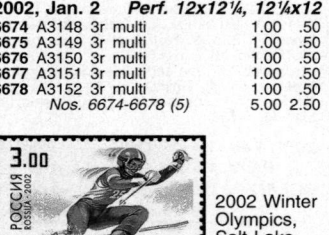

2002 Winter Olympics, Salt Lake City A3153

Designs: 3r, Skier. 4r, Figure skater. 5r, Ski jumper.

2002, Jan. 24   *Perf. 12x12¼*
6679-6681 A3153   Set of 3   1.50 .75

World Unity Against Terrorism A3154

2002, Jan. 30
6682 A3154 5r multi   .50 .35

Souvenir Sheet

Trans-Siberian Railway, Cent. — A3155

2002, Jan. 30   *Perf. 12¼x12*
6683 A3155 12r multi   3.00 .60

New Hermitage, 150th Anniv. A3156

Designs: No. 6684, Ecce Homo, by Peter Paul Rubens, before 1612. No. 6685, Courtesan, by Hendrik Goltzius, 1606. No. 6686, Helmet, by Philippo Negroli, 1530s. No. 6687, Gonzaga Cameo, 3rd Cent. B.C.
   15r, New Hermitage, 1861, by Luigi Premazzi.

Litho. & Embossed
2002, Feb. 15   *Perf. 13¼*
6684 A3156 2.50r multi   .75 .30
   a.   Booklet pane of 1   20.00
6685 A3156 2.50r multi   .75 .30
   a.   Booklet pane of 1   20.00
6686 A3156   5r multi   1.50 .60
   a.   Booklet pane of 1   40.00
6687 A3156   5r multi   1.50 .60
   a.   Booklet pane of 1   40.00
   Nos. 6684-6687 (4)   4.50 1.80

Souvenir Sheet
6688 A3156   15r multi   3.00 1.00
   a.   Booklet pane of 1   125.00
   Booklet, #6684a-6688a   350.00

Lilies
A3157   A3158

Flower color: No. 6690, White. No. 6692, White with red spots. No. 6693, Red and white with red spots.

Perf. 12¼x11¾
2002, Feb. 20   Litho.
6689 A3157 2.50r multi   .50 .25
6690 A3157 2.50r multi   .50 .25
6691 A3158 2.50r multi   .50 .25
6692 A3157 2.50r multi   .50 .25
6693 A3157 2.50r multi   .50 .25
   b.   Miniature sheet, #6689-6693 + label   5.00 2.00
   Nos. 6689-6693 (5)   2.50 1.25

Dogs — A3159

2002, Mar. 15   *Perf. 11¾*
6694   Horiz. strip of 5   4.00 2.00
   a.   A3159 1r Cane Corso   .60 .25
   b.   A3159 2r Shar-pei   .60 .25
   c.   A3159 3r Bull mastiff   .60 .25
   d.   A3159 4r Fila Brasileiro   .60 .25
   e.   A3159 5r Neapolitan mastiff   .60 .25
   f.   Miniature sheet of 9, #6694c, 6694d, 6694e, 2 # 6694a, 4 #6694b   5.00 2.00

St. Petersburg, 300th Anniv. (in 2003) — A3160

Designs: No. 6695, Kazan Cathedral (semicircular colonnade), monument to Marshal Barclay de Tolly. No. 6696, St. Isaac's Cathedral and sculpture. No. 6697, Cathedral of the Resurrection, bridge, griffin. No. 6698, St. Peter and Paul Cathedral, angel and cross steeple, vert. No. 6699, Admiralty and ship steeple, vert.

Litho. & Embossed
2002, Apr. 25   *Perf. 13¼*
6695 A3160   5r multi   5.00 1.50
   a.   Booklet pane of 1   20.00
6696 A3160   5r multi   5.00 1.50
   a.   Booklet pane of 1   20.00
6697 A3160 25r multi   20.00 6.50
   a.   Booklet pane of 1   52.50
6698 A3160 25r multi   20.00 6.50
   a.   Booklet pane of 1   52.50
6699 A3160 25r multi   20.00 6.50
   a.   Booklet pane of 1   52.50
   Booklet, #6695a-6699a   200.00
   Nos. 6695-6699 (5)   70.00 22.50

The embossed portions of the designs of the 25r values bear 22k gold applications.

Security Services, 80th Anniv. — A3161

No. 6700: a, A. K. Artuzov (1891-1937). b, N. I. Demidenko (1896-1934). c, J. K. Olsky (1898-1937). d, S. V. Puzitsky (1895-1937). e,

V. A. Styrne (1897-1937). f, G. S. Syroezhkin (1900-37).

2002, Apr. 30   Litho.   Perf. 12x12¼
6700 A3161   2r Sheet of 6, #a-f   5.00 1.75

Europa
A3162

2002, May 9   **Perf. 12½x12**
6701 A3162   8r multi   1.00   .50
a.   Miniature sheet of 6   6.00 3.00

Admiral P. S. Nakhimov (1802-55) — A3163

2002, May 24   **Perf. 12x11¾**
6702 A3163   2r multi   .50   .25
a.   Miniature sheet of 8   5.00 2.00

European Organization of Supreme Audit Institutions, 5th Congress — A3164

2002, May 24   **Perf. 12x12¼**
6703 A3164   2r multi   .50   .25

Kamchatka Peninsula Volcanos — A3165

No. 6704: a, 1r, Steaming geysers. b, 2r, Mud hole. c, 3r, Karymski Volcano. d, 5r, Crater lake.

2002, June 20   Litho.   Perf. 12
6704 A3165   Block of 4, #a-d   1.50   .60

Carriages
A3166

Designs: No. 6705a, Russian carriage, 1640s. No. 6705b, Closed sleigh, 1732. Nos. 6705c, 6706a, Coupe carriage, 1746. Nos. 6705d, 6706b, 25r, English calash, 1770s. Nos. 6705e, 6706c, Berline carriage, 1769.

Litho. & Embossed
2002, July 25   **Perf. 13x13¼**
6705 Block of 5 + label   3.00   .95
a.-b.   A3166 2.50r Any single   .25   .25
c.-e.   A3166 5r Any single   .40   .40
f.   Booklet pane, #6705a   27.50
g.   Booklet pane, #6705b   27.50
h.   Booklet pane, #6705c   57.50
i.   Booklet pane, #6705d   57.50
j.   Booklet pane, #6705e   57.50

Booklet, #6705f-6705j   250.00

Souvenir Sheet
6706 A3166   25r Sheet of 3, #a-c   6.00 6.00

Kamov Helicopters — A3167

2002, Aug. 8   Litho.   Perf. 12½x12
6707 Block of 5 + label   3.00 1.00
a.   A3167 1r KA-10   .45   .25
b.   A3167 1.50r KA-22   .45   .25
c.   A3167 2r KA-26   .45   .25
d.   A3167 2.50r KA-27   .45   .25
e.   A3167 5r KA-50   .45   .25

Anatoly A. Sobchak, Mayor of St. Petersburg (1937-2000)
A3168

2002, Aug. 10   **Perf. 12x12½**
6708 A3168   3.25r multi   5.00   .35

Birds — A3169

No. 6709: a, Anthropoides virgo. b, Larus ichthyaetus.

2002, Aug. 29   **Perf. 12¼x12**
6709 A3169   2.50r Horiz. pair, #a-b   .50   .50

See Kazakhstan No. 385.

Kostroma, 850th Anniv. A3170

2002, Sept. 2   Litho.   Perf. 12x12¼
6710 A3170   2r multi   1.00   .25

Government Ministries, 200th Anniv. — A3171

Arms and/or Russian flag and ministry buildings or symbols: No. 6711, 3r, Defense (light green background, dark green frame). No. 6712, 3r, Foreign Affairs (light blue background, dark green frame). No. 6713, 3r, Internal Affairs (light blue background, dark blue frame). No. 6714, 3r, Education (pink background, red frame). No. 6715, 3r, Finance (lilac background, dark blue frame). No. 6716, 3r, Justice (light yellow background, gray blue frame).

2002, Sept. 2   **Perf. 12**
6711-6716 A3171   Set of 6   2.00   .85

Russian State, 1140th Anniv. — A3172

2002, Sept. 17   **Perf. 11½x11¾**
6717 A3172   3r multi   .50   .25

2002 Census — A3173

Litho. & Embossed
2002, Sept. 17   **Perf. 13¼x13**
Stamp + label
6718 A3173   4r shown   5.00   .75
a.   Booklet pane of 4, no labels   650.00
Complete booklet, #6718a   750.00

Litho.
Self-Adhesive
Serpentine Die Cut 10¾x11
6719 A3173   3r Emblem, people   4.50   .50
a.   Booklet pane of 8, no labels   45.00
Complete booklet, #6719a   50.00

Customs Service — A3174

No. 6720: a, 2r, Customs house, Arkhangelsk, 18th cent. b, 3r, Customs officers, St. Petersburg, 1830s. c, 5r, Kalanchovsky customs warehouse, Moscow, 19th cent.

2002, Sept. 25   Litho.   Perf. 12x12¼
6720 A3174   Sheet of 3, #a-c   5.00 1.00

Souvenir Sheet

Battle of Stalingrad, 60th Anniv. — A3175

2002, Oct. 4
6721 A3175   10r multi   3.00 1.00

Eyes Displaying Interest
A3176

Eyes Displaying Gladness
A3177

Eyes Displaying Astonishment
A3178

Eyes Displaying Grief — A3179

Eyes Displaying Anger — A3180

Eyes Displaying Disgust
A3181

Eyes Displaying Shame — A3182

Eyes Displaying
Contempt
A3183

Eyes Displaying
Guilt — A3184

Eyes Displaying
Fear — A3185

2002, Oct. 17   **Perf. 12x11¾**
6722   Sheet of 10   5.00   2.50
a.   A3176 1.50r multi   .40   .25
b.   A3177 1.50r multi   .40   .25
c.   A3178 1.50r multi   .40   .25
d.   A3179 1.50r multi   .40   .25
e.   A3180 1.50r multi   .40   .25
f.   A3181 1.50r multi   .40   .25
g.   A3182 1.50r multi   .40   .25
h.   A3183 1.50r multi   .40   .25
i.   A3184 1.50r multi   .40   .25
j.   A3185 1.50r multi   .40   .25

Emperor
Alexander I (1777-
1825)
A3186

Alexander I: No. 6723, 4r, And Manifesto of
March 12, 1801 (blue frame). No. 6724, 4r,
Taking over codification of laws from his secre-
tary Mikhail M. Speransky, Oct. 1809 (green
frame). No. 6725, 7r, Receiving historian N. M.
Karamzin (red frame). No. 6726, 7r, Entering
Paris with troops, Mar. 1814 (brown frame).
10r, Portrait of Alexander I, by Francois
Gérard.

Litho. & Engr.
2002, Nov. 12   **Perf. 12x12½**
6723-6726 A3186 Set of 4   8.00   1.50
Souvenir Sheet
6727 A3186 10r multi   6.00   1.60

Russian Orthodox
Monasteries — A3187

Designs: No. 6728, 5r, Monastery of St.
Daniel, 1282. No. 6729, 5r, Sergii Lavra, 1337.
No. 6730, 5r, Valaam Monastery, 14th cent.
No. 6731, 5r, Monastery of Reverend Savva,
1398. No. 6732, 5r, Pskov Cave Monastery,
1470.

Litho. & Embossed
2002, Nov. 26   **Perf. 12½**
6728-6732 A3187 Set of 5   10.00   3.50
6732a   Souvenir sheet, #6728-
           6732 + label   8.00   4.00

Nos. 6728-6732 each were issued in sheets
of 9 stamps + label. The labels on these
sheets differ from the label on No. 6732a.
Value, set of 5 sheets $100.
See Nos. 6756-6761, 6818-6822.
A limited edition booklet exists containing
booklet panes of one of each of Nos. 6728-
6732 and 6756-6761. Value, $350.

Happy New
Year — A3188

2002, Dec. 2 Litho.   **Perf. 12¼x11¾**
6733 A3188 3.50r multi   .50   .25
a.   Sheet of 6   7.00   3.50

Sculpture
and Buildings
A3189

Designs: 2r, Sculpture "Artemis with Deer,"
Palace, Arkhangelskoye. 2.50r, Sculpture
"Omphala," Chinese Palace, Oranienbaum. 3r,
Sculpture of griffin, mansion, Marfino. 4r,
Sculpture "Erminia," Grand Palace, Pavlovsk.
5r, Allegorical sculpture of Scamander River,
Palace, Kuskovo.

Town name Panels with Colored Backgrounds
Denomination Color
Serpentine Die Cut 11
2002, Dec. 16   **Self-Adhesive**
6734 A3189   2r brown   .50   .25
6735 A3189 2.50r blue   .75   .25
6736 A3189   3r indigo   1.00   .25
6737 A3189   4r violet   1.25   .60
6738 A3189   5r purple   1.50   .60
      Nos. 6734-6738 (5)   5.00   1.95

See also Nos. 6802-6805, 6823-6827.

Nuclear
Physicists
A3190

Reactor diagrams and: No. 6739, 2.50r,
Anatoly P. Alexandrov (1903-94). No. 6740,
2.50r, Igor V. Kurchatov (1903-60).

2003, Jan. 8   **Perf. 12½x12**
6739-6740 A3190 Set of 2   2.00   .25

Souvenir Sheet

Antarctic Research — A3191

No. 6741: a, Ice borings, map. b, Vostok
research station.

2003, Jan. 8   **Perf. 11½x12¼**
6741 A3191 5r Sheet of 2, #a-b   3.00   1.10

Kemerovo
Oblast
A3192

Kurgan
Oblast
A3193

Magadan
Oblast
A3194

Perm Oblast
A3195

Ulyanovsk
Oblast
A3196

Astrakhan
Oblast — A3197

2003, Jan. 10 Perf. 12x12¼, 12¼x12
6742 A3192 3r multi   1.00   .50
6743 A3193 3r multi   1.00   .50
6744 A3194 3r multi   1.00   .50
6745 A3195 3r multi   1.00   .50
6746 A3196 3r multi   1.00   .50
6747 A3197 3r multi   1.00   .50
      Nos. 6742-6747 (6)   6.00   3.00

Commonwealth of
Independent
States
Intergovernmental
Communications
by Courier, 10th
Anniv. — A3198

2003, Jan. 16   **Perf. 12x12½**
6748 A3198 3r multi   .50   .25

Victory at 2002 Davis Cup Tennis
Championships — A3199

Designs: 4r, Fans with signs and Russian
flags. 8r, Ball and net, fans with Russian flags.
50r, Davis Cup.

2003, Feb. 19 Litho.   **Perf. 13¼**
6749-6750 A3199 Set of 2   1.50   .45
Souvenir Sheet
Litho. with Foil Application & Embossed
                                      Perf. 13¼x13
6751 A3199 50r silver & multi   8.00   2.10
a.   Miniature sheet, Nos 6749-
           6751   50.00

No. 6751 contains one 51x39mm stamp.

Yaroslav Mudry (the Wise) (978-1054),
Grand Prince of Kiev — A3200

Vladimir II Monomakh (1053-1125),
Grand Prince of Kiev — A3201

Daniel Aleksandrovich Moscowsky
(1261-1303), Grand Prince of
Moscow — A3202

Ivan II Ivanovich Krasny (the Red)
(1320-1359), Grand Prince of
Moscow — A3203

Litho. & Engr.
2003, Mar. 4   **Perf. 11¾**
6752 A3200 8r multi   1.00   .40
6753 A3201 8r multi   1.00   .40
6754 A3202 8r multi   1.00   .40
6755 A3203 8r multi   1.00   .40
      Nos. 6752-6755 (4)   4.00   1.60

Monasteries Type of 2002

Designs: No. 6756, 5r, Yuriev Monastery,
Novgorod, 1030. No. 6757, 5r, Tolgsky Nunnery, 1314. No. 6758, 5r, Kozelsk Optina Pustyn Monastery, 14th-15th cent. No. 6759, 5r,
Solovetsky Zosima and Savvatii Monastery,
15th cent. No. 6760, 5r, Novodevichy Nunnery, 1524. No. 6761, 5r, Seraphim Nunnery,
Diveyevo, 1780.

Litho. & Embossed
2003, Mar. 26   **Perf. 12½**
6756-6761 A3187 Set of 6   5.00   1.10
6761a   Souvenir sheet, #6756-
           6761   10.00   2.00

Nos. 6756-6761 each were issued in sheets
of 9 stamps + label. A limited edtion booklet
exists containing booklet panes of one of each
of Nos. 6728-6732 and 6756-6761. Value,
$450.

Petrozavodsk, 300th
Anniv. — A3204

                                      Perf. 12¼x11¾
2003, Mar. 26   **Litho.**
6762 A3204 3r multi   .50   .25

Novosibirsk, Cent. A3205

2003, Apr. 15   Perf. 11¾x12¼
6763   A3205   3r multi   .50   .25

Souvenir Sheet

Baltic Fleet, 300th Anniv. — A3206

2003, Apr. 15   Perf. 12¼x11¾
6764   A3206   12r multi   4.00   2.00

Aram Khatchaturian (1903-78), Composer — A3207

2003, Apr. 23   Perf. 12
6765   A3207   2.50r multi   1.00   .35

Europa — A3208

2003, May 5   Perf. 12¼x11¾
6766   A3208   8r multi   .75   .50
   a.   Sheet of 6   9.50   4.75

Carillons — A3209

No. 6767: a, St. Rombout's Cathedral, Mechelen, Belgium, and bells (denomination at left). b, Sts. Peter and Paul Cathedral, St. Petersburg, and bells (denomination at right).

Litho. & Engr.

2003, May 15   Perf. 12
6767   A3209   5r Horiz. pair, #a-b   1.00   .50
   c.   Sheet, 3 #6767   5.00   2.00

See Belgium No. 1956.

Anichkov Bridge — A3210

Neva River Drawbridge — A3211

Vasilievsky Island — A3212

Palace Square — A3213

Winter Palace — A3214

Summer Garden — A3215

Peter I Monument — A3216

Designs: 75r, 100r, Peter I Monument.

Litho. & Embossed

2003, May 15   Perf. 13x13¼
6768   A3210   5r multi   2.50   .80
6769   A3211   5r multi   2.50   .80
6770   A3212   5r multi   2.50   .80
6771   A3213   5r multi   2.50   .80
6772   A3214   5r multi   2.50   .80
6773   A3215   5r multi   2.50   .80
   Nos. 6768-6773 (6)   15.00   4.80

Souvenir Sheet
Perf. 13¼

6774   A3216   50r multi   15.00   3.50
6775   A3216   75p multi   15.00   3.25
6776   A3216   100p multi   20.00   4.25

St. Petersburg, 300th anniv.
Nos. 6775 and 6776 contain one 37x51mm stamp.
A booklet exists containing one pane of Nos. 6768-6773 and one pane of No. 6774 with an extended margin. Value, $500.

Space Flight of Valentina Tereshkova, 40th Anniv. — A3217

2003, May 20   Litho.   Perf. 12¼x11¾
6777   A3217   3r multi   .50   .25
   a.   Sheet of 6   7.00   1.50

Second World Anti-Narcotics Congress A3218

2003, May 25   Litho.   Perf. 12x12½
6778   A3218   3r multi   .50   .25

Pskov, 1100th Anniv. A3219

2003, June 3   Perf. 11¾x12¼
6779   A3219   3r multi   1.00   .25

Krasnoyarsk, 375th Anniv. A3220

2003, June 10
6780   A3220   4r multi   1.00   .25

Symbols of Industry, 5 Ruble Coin A3221

2003, June 10   Perf. 12½x12
6781   A3221   5r multi   .50   .25
Promotion of "Transparent Economy."

Souvenir Sheet

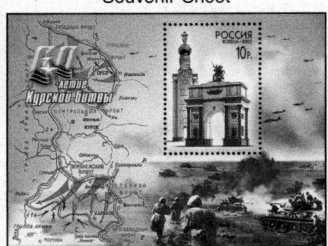

Battle of Kursk, 60th Anniv. — A3222

2003, June 10   Perf. 12x12½
6782   A3222   10r multi   3.00   1.25

Komi Republic Forests — A3223

No. 6783: a, 2r, Stone pillars, Man-Pupuner Mountain. b, 3r, Kozhim River. c, 5r, Upper Pechora River.

2003, June 25   Perf. 12x12¼
6783   A3223   Block of 3, #a-c, +   label   5.00   .50

Souvenir Sheet

St. Petersburg Postal Service, 300th Anniv. — A3224

2003, June 29   Perf. 12¼x12
6784   A3224   12r multi   3.00   .60

Beetles A3225

No. 6785: a, Lucanus cervus. b, Calosoma sycophanta. c, Carabus lopatini. d, Carabus constricticollis. e, Carabus caucasicus.

2003, July 22   Perf. 12
6785   Horiz. strip of 5   3.00   .85
   a.   A3225   1r multi   .40   .25
   b.   A3225   2r multi   .40   .25
   c.   A3225   3r multi   .50   .25
   d.   A3225   4r multi   .65   .25
   e.   A3225   5r multi   .85   .25
   f.   Sheet, #6785a-6785e, + label   7.00   3.50

Intl. Association of Academies of Science, 10th Anniv. A3226

2003, July 30   Perf. 11¼
6786   A3226   2.50r multi   .50   .25

Chita, 350th Anniv. A3227

2003, Aug. 14   Perf. 12x12¼
6787   A3227   3r multi   1.00   .25

World Conference on Climate Fluctuations, Moscow — A3228

2003, Aug. 14   Perf. 11¾
6788   A3228   4r multi   1.00   .45

Mushrooms A3229

Various mushrooms.

2003, July 22   Perf. 11¾
6789   Horiz. strip of 5   3.00   .85
   a.   A3229   2r multi   .40   .25
   b.   A3229   2.50r multi   .40   .25

c. A3229 3r multi .50 .25
d. A3229 4r multi .70 .25
e. A3229 5r multi .90 .25
f. Sheet, #6789a-6789e, + label 7.00 3.00

Fruit
A3230

Designs: No. 6790, 5r, Melon. No. 6791, 5r, Apples. No. 6792, 5r, Pear. No. 6793, 5r, Pineapple. No. 6794, 5r, Strawberries.

2003, Aug. 27 *Perf. 13½*
6790-6794 A3230 Set of 5 3.50 2.50

Nos. 6790-6794 are impregnated with fruit scents. Values are for stamps with surrounding selvage.

Caspian Sea Fauna — A3231

No. 6795: a, Phoca caspica. b, Huso huso.

2003, Sept. 9 *Perf. 12½x12*
6795 A3231 2.50r Horiz. pair,
#a-b 2.00 .45
c. Sheet, 3 each #6795a-
6795b 35.00 10.00

See Iran No. 2873.

Souvenir Sheet

Russian Journalism, 300th
Anniv. — A3232

2003, Sept. 12 *Perf. 12x12¼*
6796 A3232 10r multi 3.00 .35

Automobiles — A3233

Designs: a, 3r, 1911 Russo-Balt K 12/20. b, 4r, 1929 NAMI-1. c, 4r, 1939 GAZ-M1. d, 5r, 1946 GAZ-67b. e, 5r, 1954 GAZ-M20 Pobeda.

2003, Sept. 17 *Perf. 11¾x11½*
6797 A3233 Block of 5, #a-e, +
label 5.00 1.25

Constitution, 10th Anniv. — A3234

2003, Oct. 15 *Perf. 12½x12*
6798 A3234 3r multi .50 .25

E. T. Krenkel (1903-71), Polar
Explorer — A3235

2003, Oct. 15 *Perf. 12x12½*
6799 A3235 4r multi .60 .30

Souvenir Sheet

Battle of Sinop, 150th Anniv. — A3236

2003, Nov. 5 *Perf. 12¼x12*
6800 A3236 12r multi 3.00 .55

Happy New
Year — A3237

2003, Dec. 1 *Perf. 12½*
Flocked Paper
6801 A3237 7r multi .50 .25

**Sculpture and Buildings Type of
2002**

Designs: 1r, Ostankino Palace. 1.50r, Gatchinsky Palace. 6r, Grand Palace, Petrodvorets. 10r, Empress Catherine's Palace, Tsarskoye Selo.

2003, Dec. 5 *Serpentine Die Cut 11*
Self-Adhesive
6802 A3189 1r multi .75 .25
6803 A3189 1.50r multi .75 .25
6804 A3189 6r multi 1.25 .25
6805 A3189 10r multi 2.25 .35
Nos. 6802-6805 (4) 5.00 1.10

Legislative
Bodies,
10th Anniv.
A3238

No. 6806: a, Federation Council (denomination at right). b, State Duma (denomination at left).

2003, Dec. 10 *Perf. 12¼x12*
6806 Horiz. pair + central label 1.00 .25
a.-b. A3238 2.50r Either single .40 .25

Belgorod
Oblast
A3239

Ivanovo
Oblast
A3240

Lipetsk
Oblast
A3241

Moscow
Oblast
A3242

Nenetsky
Okrug
A3243

Nizhny
Novgorod
Oblast
A3244

2004, Jan. 6 *Perf. 12x12¼*
6807 A3239 5r multi 1.00 .50
6808 A3240 5r multi 1.00 .50
6809 A3241 5r multi 1.00 .50
6810 A3242 5r multi 1.00 .50
6811 A3243 5r multi 1.00 .50
6812 A3244 5r multi 1.00 .50
Nos. 6807-6812 (6) 6.00 3.00

Souvenir Sheet

World War II Offensives of 1944, 60th
Anniv. — A3245

2004, Jan. 16 *Litho.* *Perf. 12x12¼*
6813 A3245 10r multi 3.00 .75

V. P. Chkalov (1904-38), Test
Pilot — A3246

2004, Jan. 23 *Perf. 11¾x12*
6814 A3246 3r multi .50 .25
a. Miniature sheet of 8 8.00

Tales by P. P. Bazhov (1879-
1950) — A3247

No. 6815: a, 2r, The Stone Flower. b, 4r, The Malachite Box. c, 6r, The Golden Hair.

2004, Jan. 27 *Perf. 12x11¾*
6815 A3247 Horiz. strip of 3,
#a-c 1.50 .60
d. Miniature sheet, 2 #6815 7.50 2.75

Yuly B. Khariton (1904-66),
Physicist — A3248

2004, Feb. 12 *Litho.* *Perf. 12¼x12*
6816 A3248 3r multi .50 .25

Yuri Gagarin (1934-68), First Man in
Space — A3249

2004, Feb. 20 *Perf. 12*
6817 A3249 3r multi .50 .25
a. Miniature sheet of 8 10.00

Monasteries Type of 2002

Designs: No. 6818, 8r, St. Panteleimon Monastery, Mt. Athos, Greece, 11th cent. No. 6819, 8r, Holy Assumption Kiev-Pecherskaya Lavra, Ukraine, 1051. No. 6820, 8r, Convent of the Savior and Efrosinia, Polotsk, Belarus, 1128. No. 6821, 8r, Gorney Convent, Israel, 1886. No. 6822, 8r, Pyukhtitsky Convent of the Assumption, Estonia.

Litho. & Embossed
2004, Mar. 16 *Perf. 12½*
6818-6822 A3187 Set of 5 5.00 2.25
6822a Miniature sheet, #6818-
6822 + label 10.00 3.00

A limited edition booklet exists containing booklet panes of one of each of Nos. 6818-6822. Value, $250.

**Sculptures and Buildings Type of
2002 Redrawn**

Designs as before.

**Town Name Panels At Bottom With
White Background
Denomination Color**

2004 *Litho.* *Serpentine Die Cut 11*
Self-Adhesive
6823 A3189 2r brown .50 .25
6824 A3189 2.50r blue .50 .25
6825 A3189 3r indigo .50 .25
6826 A3189 4r violet .70 .25
6827 A3189 5r purple .80 .25
Nos. 6823-6827 (5) 3.00 1.25

Issued: 2r, 4r, 4/5; 2.50r, 5r, 4/12; 3r, 4/15. Nos. 6823-6827 have a crest with stronger lines and vignettes in slightly different shades than Nos. 6734-6738. The background of the town name panels on Nos. 6734-6738 have dots of color, which on some stamps are faint, but are easily seen under magnification.

Kronshtadt, 300th Anniv. — A3250

2004, Apr. 15   **Perf. 12½x12**
6828 A3250 4r multi   .50 .25

Zodiac Signs A3251

No. 6829: a, Aries. b. Leo. c, Sagittarius.
No. 6830: a, Gemini. b. Aquarius. c, Libra.
No. 6831: a, Capricorn. b, Taurus. c, Virgo.
No. 6832: a, Pisces. b, Cancer. c, Scorpio.

Litho. & Embossed
2004, Apr. 21   **Perf. 13¼x13**
6829   Horiz. strip of 3   2.50 .65
   a.-c.   A3251 5r Any single   .50 .25
6830   Horiz. strip of 3   2.50 .65
   a.-c.   A3251 5r Any single   .50 .25
6831   Horiz. strip of 3   2.50 .65
   a.-c.   A3251 5r Any single   .50 .25
6832   Horiz. strip of 3   2.50 .65
   a.-c.   A3251 5r Any single   .50 .25
   d.   Miniature sheet, #6829a-6829c,   6830a-6830c, 6831a-6831c, 6832a-6832c   15.00 5.00

Empress Catherine II (1729-96) A3252

Catherine the Great: 6r, Watching scientific presentation of Mikhail Lomonosov. 7r, Giving money to support education, vert. 8r, At legislative commission meeting, vert. 9r, Viewing ships at Inkerman Palace, Crimea. 15r, Portrait.

Perf. 12½x12, 12x12½
2004, Apr. 27   **Litho. & Engr.**
6833-6836 A3252   Set of 4   3.50 1.60
Souvenir Sheet
Perf. 11¾x12¼
6837 A3252 15r multi   3.50 1.00
No. 6837 contains one 33x47mm stamp.

Europa A3253

2004, May 5   **Litho.**   **Perf. 11¾x12¼**
6838 A3253 8r multi   1.25 .50
   a.   Miniature sheet of 8   10.00 5.00

Souvenir Sheet

Defense of Port Arthur (Lüshun, China) in Russo-Japanese War, Cent. — A3254

2004, May 12   **Perf. 11¼**
6839 A3254 10r multi   3.00 1.00

Mikhail I. Glinka (1804-57), Composer — A3255

No. 6840: a, Portrait. b, Scene from opera "Life for the Tsar," 1836. c, Scene from opera "Ruslan and Ludmila," 1842.

2004, May 20   **Perf. 12**
6840 A3255 4r Block of 3, #a-c, + label   3.00 .60

Russian Crown — A3256

Carved Head — A3257

Treasures from the Amber Room, State Museum, St. Petersburg: No. 6842, Cameo depicting Moses and Pharaoh, vert. 25r, Touch and Smell, Florentine mosaic.

Litho. & Embossed
2004, May 25   **Perf. 13¼**
6841 A3256 5r multi   1.00 .50
   a.   Miniature sheet of 10   17.50
6842 A3256 5r multi   1.00 .50
   a.   Miniature sheet of 10   17.50
6843 A3257 5r multi   1.00 .50
   a.   Miniature sheet of 10   17.50
Nos. 6841-6843 (3)   3.00 1.50
Souvenir Sheet
Perf. 13
6844 A3257 25r multi   3.00 1.50
A limited edition booklet exists containing booklet panes of one of each of Nos. 6841-6844. Value, $150.

German-Russian Youth Meeting A3258

2004, June 3   **Litho.**   **Perf. 11¼**
6845 A3258 8r multi   1.00 .50
See Germany No. 2287.

Vladimir K. Kokkinaki (1904-85), Test Pilot — A3259

2004, June 8   **Perf. 12**
6846 A3259 3r multi   .50 .25
   a.   Miniature sheet of 8   10.00

Victory — A3260

Who Comes With the Sword Will Die by the Sword — A3261

Patriotic paintings by S. Prisekin: No. 6848, Marshal Zhukov. No. 6850, And the Oath of Allegiance We Have Honored, Smolensk, 1812.

2004, June 8   **Perf. 11¾x11½**
6847 A3260 5r shown   .50 .25
6848 A3260 5r multi   .50 .25
Perf. 11¾
6849 A3261 5r shown   .50 .25
6850 A3261 5r multi   .50 .25
Nos. 6847-6850 (4)   2.00 1.00

Women's Riding Habits — A3262

Designs: No. 6851, 4r, Three women, horse. No. 6852, 4r, Three women, horse, dog. No. 6853, 4r, Two women, horse, two dogs.

2004, July 15   **Perf. 12x11¾**
6851-6853 A3262   Set of 3   2.00 .75
6853a   Miniature sheet, 2 each #6851-6853   8.00 4.00

2004 Summer Olympics, Athens — A3267

2004, July 20   **Perf. 12**
6854 A3267 Horiz. pair with central label   1.00 .50
   a.   3r Running   .25 .25
   b.   8r Wrestling   .75 .35

Souvenir Sheet

Admiralty Shipyard, 300th Anniv. — A3268

2004, July 22   **Perf. 12x12¼**
6855 A3268 12r multi   3.00 .60

Miniature Sheet

Children and Road Safety — A3269

No. 6856: a, Ducks crossing street at pedestrian crossing. b, Boy and turtle crossing street with green light. c, Driver near fenced garden. d, Girl playing in street. e, Accident showing eggs flying out of car.

2004, Aug. 5   **Perf. 12**
6856 A3269 4r Sheet of 5, #a-e, + label   5.00 1.00

Worldwide Fund for Nature (WWF) — A3270

Gulo gulo: a, With pine branches. b, With dead bird. c, On tree branch. d, With young.

2004, Aug. 12   **Perf. 11¼**
6857 A3270 Block of 4   3.00 1.10
   a.-d.   8r Any single   .75 .25
   e.   Miniature sheet, #6857a, 2 each #6857b-6857c, 3 #6857d + label   10.00 5.00

Tomsk, 400th
Anniv. — A3271

2004, Aug. 20   *Perf. 12¼x12*
6858 A3271 4r multi   .50 .25

ITAR-TASS News
Agency,
Cent. — A3272

2004, Aug. 20   *Perf. 12*
6859 A3272 4r multi   .50 .25
    a.   Miniature sheet of 10   10.00

Famous
Men — A3273

Designs: No. 6860, 5r, B. G. Muzrukov
(1904-79), organizer of defense industry. No.
6861, 5r, N. L. Dukhov (1904-64), rocket
designer.

2004, Sept. 8
6860-6861 A3273   Set of 2   1.00 .50

Tsar Paul I
(1754-1801)
A3274

Designs: No. 6862, 10r, Seated. No. 6863,
10r, Standing.
20p, Wearing hat.

Litho. & Engr.
2004, Sept. 10   *Perf. 12*
6862-6863 A3274   Set of 2   1.00 .50
    Souvenir Sheet
6864 A3274 20r multi   3.00 1.00

S. N. Rerikh (1904-93),
Painter — A3275

    Perf. 11¾x11½
2004, Sept. 16   Litho.
6865 A3275 4r multi   .50 .25

Vsevolod III (1154-1212), Grand
Prince of Novgorod — A3276

Litho. & Engr.
2004, Oct. 7   *Perf. 11¾*
6866 A3276 12r multi   2.00 .55

Kazan State University, 200th
Anniv. — A3277

2004, Oct. 20   Litho.   *Perf. 12x11¾*
6867 A3277 5r multi   1.00 .25

Silver Containers — A3278

Designs: No. 6868, 4.70r, Bowl, c. 1880-
1890. No. 6869, 4.70r, Milk container, 1900.
No. 6870, 4.70r, Ladle, 1910. No. 6871, 4.70r,
Vase, c. 1900-08, vert.

Litho. & Embossed
2004, Oct. 26   *Perf. 13¼*
6868-6871 A3278   Set of 4   4.00 1.00

Happy New
Year — A3279

    Serpentine Die Cut
2004, Nov. 12   Litho.
    Self-Adhesive
6872 A3279 5r multi   8.00 4.00
    a.   Miniature sheet of 8   75.00

Altai Republic Landscapes — A3280

No. 6873: a, 2r, Belukha Mountain. b, 3r,
Katun River. c, 5r, Teletskoye Lake.

2004, Nov. 18   *Perf. 12*
6873 A3280   Block of 3, #a-c, +
        label   2.00 .50

Baikonur
Cosmodrome,
50th
Anniv. — A3281

2004, Dec. 1
6874   Horiz. strip of 4   3.00 1.00
    a.   A3281 2.50r R-7 missile   .35 .25
    b.   A3281 3.50r Proton rocket   .40 .25
    c.   A3281 4r Soyuz rocket   .50 .25
    d.   A3281 6r Zenit rocket   .75 .30
    e.   Miniature sheet, 2 #6874   10.00 5.00

Mordovian
Republic
A3282

Smolensk
Oblast
A3283

Tver
Oblast
A3284

Chukotsky Autonomous
Okrug — A3285

Koryak Autonomous Okrug — A3286

Taimyr Autonomous Okrug — A3287

2005, Jan. 10
6875 A3282 5r multi   1.00 .40
6876 A3283 5r multi   1.00 .40
6877 A3284 5r multi   1.00 .40
6878 A3285 5r multi   1.00 .40
6879 A3286 5r multi   1.00 .40
6880 A3287 5r multi   1.00 .40
    Nos. 6875-6880 (6)   6.00 2.40

Moscow M. V. Lomonosov State
University, 250th Anniv. — A3288

2005, Jan. 12
6881 A3288 5r multi   1.00 .25
    a.   Miniature sheet of 9   10.00

    Souvenir Sheet

Expo 2005, Aichi, Japan — A3289

2005, Feb. 21   Litho.   *Perf. 12½x12*
6882 A3289 15r multi   5.50 2.75

Archaeological Treasures of
Sarmatia — A3290

Designs: No. 6883, 5r, Silver bowl with bull
design (shown). No. 6884, 5r, Gold and wood
bowl with bear design. No. 6885, 7r, Gold
ornament with camel design. No. 6886, 7r,
Gold ornament with deer design, vert.

Litho. & Embossed
2005, Feb. 25   *Perf. 13¼*
6883-6886 A3290   Set of 4   8.00 4.00

Submarine
Force,
Cent.
A3291

Submarines: 2r, Type M, VI-bis series. 3r,
Type S, IX-bis series. 5r, Type Sch, X-bis
series. 8r, Type K.

2005, Mar. 3   Litho.   *Perf. 12x12¼*
6887-6890 A3291   Set of 4   *25.00 12.50*

Kazan,
1000th
Anniv.
A3292

Designs: No. 6891, 5r, Suyumbike Tower
(shown). No. 6892, 5r, Kul Sharif Mosque. 7r,
Cathedral of the Annunciation.

2005, Mar. 10   *Perf. 11¾x12*
6891-6893 A3292   Set of 3   2.50 .60
6893a   Souvenir sheet, #6891-
        6893   20.00 7.00

Emperor Alexander II (1818-81) A3293

Alexander II and: No. 6894, 10r, Educator Vasily Zhukovsky, pillar (blue frame). No. 6895, 10r, Coronation (red frame). No. 6896, 10r, At desk (green frame). No. 6897, 10r, On horse (brown frame).
25r, Portrait.

Litho. & Engr.

2005, Mar. 28   *Perf. 12x12½*
6894-6897 A3293   Set of 4   5.00   2.00
Souvenir Sheet
6898 A3293 25r multi   3.50   1.25

Victory in World War II, 60th Anniv. — A3294

Designs: No. 6899, 2r, Soldier at column with grafitti. No. 6900, 2r, Soldiers and tank. No. 6901, 3r, Soldier watching pigeons eat. No. 6902, 3r, Jubilant soldiers return to Moscow. 5r, Soldiers and captured Nazi banners.
10r, Soldiers saluting Soviet flag over Reichstag building.

2005, Apr. 5   **Litho.**   *Perf. 12*
6899-6903 A3294   Set of 5   2.00   .55
6899a   Sheet of 9 + label   15.00   6.00
6903a   Souvenir sheet, #6899-6903, + label   5.00   2.50

Souvenir Sheet
Perf. 12x12¼
6904 A3294 10r multi   3.00   1.50

Liberation of Vienna by Soviet Troops, 60th Anniv. A3295

2005, Apr. 13   **Litho.**   *Perf. 12*
6905 A3295 6r multi   1.00   .30

Souvenir Sheet

Fauna — A3296

No. 6906: a, Aquila danga (eagle). b, Catocala sponsa (butterflies). c, Castor fiber (beaver). d, Meles meles (badger).

2005, Apr. 15
6906 A3296 5r Sheet of 4, #a-d, + label   3.00   1.00

See Belarus No. 554.

Souvenir Sheet

Opening of First Line of Moscow Metro, 70th Anniv. — A3297

No. 6907: a, 5r, Old train, stations, map of first line. b, 10r, Modern train, modern Metro map.

2005, Apr. 25   *Perf. 11½x12¼*
6907 A3297   Sheet of 2, #a-b   2.50   .75

Bid of Moscow to Host 2012 Summer Olympics A3298

2005, May 5   *Perf. 12*
6908 A3298 4r multi   1.00   .25

Europa — A3299

2005, May 5   *Perf. 12¼x12¼*
6909 A3299 8r multi   1.50   .75
a.   Sheet of 6   9.50   4.75

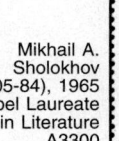

Mikhail A. Sholokhov (1905-84), 1965 Nobel Laureate in Literature A3300

2005, May 20   *Perf. 11¾*
6910 A3300 5r multi   1.00   .25

Fauna A3301

No. 6911: a, Martes zibellina. b, Panthera tigris altaica.

2005, June 1   *Perf. 12*
6911   Horiz. pair, #a-b, + central label   2.50   .75
a.-b.   A3301 8r Either single   1.00   .35

See North Korea Nos. 4436-4437.

Bees A3302

2005, June 15   *Perf. 11¼*
6912   Horiz. strip of 5   3.50   1.25
a.   A3302 3r Bombus armeniacus   .40   .25
b.   A3302 4r Bombus fragrans   .60   .25
c.   A3302 5r Bombus anachoreta   .75   .30
d.   A3302 6r Bombus unicus   .60   .30
e.   A3302 7r Bombus czerskii   .80   .35
f.   Souvenir sheet, #6912a-6912e, + label   10.00   5.00

Kaliningrad, 750th Anniv. — A3303

2005, June 23   *Perf. 12¼x12*
6913 A3303 5r multi   1.00   .45

N. E. Bauman Moscow State Technical University, 175th Anniv. — A3304

2005, July 1   *Perf. 12*
6914 A3304 5r multi   1.00   .35

Lighthouses — A3305

Map and: 5r, Mudyugsky Lighthouse. 6r, Solovetsky Lighthouse. 8r, Svyatonossky Lighthouse.

2005, July 4   **Litho.**
6915-6917 A3305   Set of 3   2.00   1.00

MiG Fighters A3306

Designs: No. 6918, 5r, MiG-3. No. 6919, 5r, MiG-15. No. 6920, 5r, MiG-21. No. 6921, 5r, MiG-25. No. 6922, 5r, MiG-29.

2005, July 6
6918-6922 A3306   Set of 5   3.00   1.25
6922a   Souvenir sheet, #6918-6922, + label   10.00   5.00

Souvenir Sheet

Battle of Kulikovo, 625th Anniv. — A3307

2005, Aug. 2   *Perf. 12½x12*
6923 A3307 15r multi   2.50   .75

Souvenir Sheet

Water — A3308

No. 6924: a, 3r, Hands in water. b, 3.50r, Ocean wave. c, 4r, Iceberg. d, 4.50r, Waterfall. e, 5r, Water droplets on leaf.

2005, Aug. 16   *Perf. 12*
6924 A3308   Sheet of 5, #a-e, + label   3.50   1.00

Field Marshal Aleksandr V. Suvorov (1729-1800) — A3309

2005, Sept. 15   **Litho.**   *Perf. 12x11¾*
6925 A3309 4r multi   .90   .25
a.   Miniature sheet of 8   9.50   3.25

Sea Infantry, 300th Anniv. — A3310

No. 6926 — Sea infantrymen from: a, 2r, 18th cent. b, 3r, 19th cent. c, 4r, 20th cent. d, 5r, 21st cent.

2005, Oct. 19   **Litho.**   *Perf. 11¾*
6926 A3310   Block of 4, #a-d   2.50   .75

Santa Claus (Ded Moroz) A3311

2005, Oct. 26   *Perf. 12*
6927 A3311 5r multi   .75   .25

Printed in sheets of 8.

UNESCO, 60th Anniv. A3312

2005, Nov. 1   *Perf. 11¼*
6928 A3312 5.60r multi   .75   .25

Christmas and New Year's Day A3313

2005, Dec. 1
6929 A3313 5.60r multi .80 .30
a. Sheet of 9 7.50 3.00

Antonov
Airplanes
A3314

Designs: No. 6930, 5.60r, An-3T. No. 6931, 5.60r, An-12. No. 6932, 5.60r, An-24. No. 6933, 5.60r, An-74. No. 6934, 5.60r, An-124.

2006, Jan. 12 **Litho.** **Perf. 12**
6930-6934 A3314 Set of 5 3.50 1.50
6934a Sheet, #6930-6934, + label 10.00 5.00

2006
Winter
Olympics,
Turin
A3315

Designs: No. 6935, 4r, Luge. No. 6936, 4r, Speed skating. No. 6937, 4r, Snowboarding.

2006, Jan. 18
6935-6937 A3315 Set of 3 1.50 .70

Armenia Day in Russia — A3316

2006, Jan. 22 **Perf. 11¼**
6938 A3316 10r multi 1.25 .60
See Armenia No. 723.

Antarctic
Research,
50th
Anniv.
A3317

Designs: No. 6939, 7r, Underwater researcher, transport vehicle. No. 6940, 7r, Scientific ship, airplane. No. 6941, 7r, Icebreaker, penguins.

2006, Jan. 26 **Perf. 12**
6939-6941 A3317 Set of 3 2.50 1.25
6941a Sheet of 6 #6941 6.50 3.25

Peter I Interrogating Tsarevich Aleksei,
by N. N. Ge (1831-94) — A3318

Design: No. 6943, 5.60r, Portrait of N. N. Ge, by I. E. Repin, vert.

2006, Feb. 16
6942-6943 A3318 Set of 2 2.50 1.00

Paintings by
M. A. Vrubel
(1856-1910)
A3319

Designs: No. 6944, 5.60r, Tsarevna-Swan (shown). No. 6945, 5.60r, Self-portrait.

2006, Feb. 27 **Litho.** **Perf. 12**
6944-6945 A3319 Set of 2 2.50 1.00

Russian
Submarine
Fleet,
Cent.
A3320

Submarine: 3r, 667A. 4r, 671. 6r, 941. 7r, 949A.

2006, Feb. 28 **Perf. 12**
6946-6949 A3320 Set of 4 12.00 5.00

Moscow
Kremlin
Museums,
Bicent.
A3321

Designs: No. 6950, 5r, No. 6954b, 20r, Throne of Ivan IV. No. 6951, 5r, No. 6954c, 20r, Orb of Tsar Michael. No. 6952, 5r, No. 6954d, 20r, Helmet of Tsar Michael. No. 6953, 5r, No. 6954e, 20r, State sword and shield. No. 6954a, 20r, No. 6955, 15r, Monomakh's cap.

Litho., Litho. & Embossed (#6954)
2006, Mar. 6 **Perf. 11¾x12**
6950-6953 A3321 Set of 4 2.50 1.00
6954 Horiz. strip of 5 45.00 45.00
a.-e. A3321 20r Any single 8.25 8.25
Souvenir Sheet
Perf. 11¾x12¼
6955 A3321 15r multi 1.50 .75

Airplanes
Designed
by
Aleksandr
S.
Yakovlev
(1906-89)
A3322

Designs: No. 6956, 5r, AIR-1. No. 6957, 5r, Yak-42. No. 6958, 5r, Yak-54. No. 6959, 5r, Yak-130. No. 6960, 5r, Yak-141.

2006, Mar. 20 **Litho.** **Perf. 12¼x12**
6956-6960 A3322 Set of 5 3.25 1.25
6960a Souvenir sheet, #6956-6960 10.00 5.00

Duma, Cent. — A3323

2006, Apr. 8 **Perf. 12½x12**
6961 A3323 15p multi 2.00 1.00

Arms
A3324

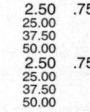

Flag
A3325

2006, Apr. 20 **Perf. 14**
6962 A3324 5.60r multi 2.50 .75
Booklet, 10 #6962 25.00
Booklet, 15 #6962 37.50
Booklet, 20 #6962 50.00
6963 A3325 5.60r multi 2.50 .75
Booklet, 10 #6963 25.00
Booklet, 15 #6963 37.50
Booklet, 20 #6963 50.00

Paintings In
Tretyakov
Gallery,
Moscow
A3326

Tretyakov Gallery and Statue of Pavel
M. Tretyakov — A3327

Designs: No. 6964, 5.60r, Trinity, by Anrrej Roubljov, c. 1420. No. 6965, 5.60r, Girl with Peaches, by V. A. Serov, 1887. No. 6966, 5.60r, Beyond the Eternal Calm, by I. I. Levitan, 1894, horiz. No. 6967, 5.60r, Three Heroes, by V. M. Vasnetsov, 1898, horiz.

Perf. 11¾x12, 12x11¾
2006, Apr. 26 **Litho.**
6964-6967 A3326 Set of 4 2.75 1.25
Souvenir Sheet
Perf. 12½x12
6968 A3327 15r multi 1.90 .85

Emperor
Alexander III
(1845-94)
A3328

Designs: No. 6970, 10r, Alexander III and map. No. 6971, 10r, Alexander III, flag and ship.
25r, Alexander III.

Litho. & Engr.
2006, May 4 **Perf. 12x12½**
6970-6971 A3328 Set of 2 5.00 2.00
Souvenir Sheet
Perf. 12x12¼
6972 A3328 25r multi 3.00 1.50

Blagoveschensk, 150th
Anniv. — A3329

2006, May 11 **Litho.** **Perf. 12x12¼**
6973 A3329 5r multi .80 .25

Baltic Shipyards, 150th
Anniv. — A3330

2006, May 22 **Perf. 12x12½**
6974 A3330 12p multi 2.00 .75

Luzhniki
Olympic
Stadium,
50th Anniv.
A3331

2006, May 29 **Perf. 12**
6975 A3331 6r multi .75 .35

Flowers — A3332

No. 6976: a, Spring flowers (denomination at UL). b, Summer flowers (denomination at UR). c, Fall flowers (denomination at LL). d, Winter flowers (denomination at LR).

2006, June 6 **Perf. 11½**
6976 A3332 7r Block of 4, #a-d 4.00 2.00

Altai Territories as Part of Russia,
250th Anniv. — A3333

Litho. & Embossed

2006, June 15		Perf. 11¼	
6977	A3333	5r multi	.80	.25
a.	Miniature sheet of 9		10.00	

Adygeya
Republic — A3334

Vladimir
Oblast — A3335

Ryazan
Oblast
A3336

Kostroma
Oblast
A3337

Pskov
Oblast
A3338

Tula Oblast
A3339

2006, June 20	Litho.	Perf. 12	
6978	A3334 6r multi	.75	.35
6979	A3335 6r multi	.75	.35
6980	A3336 6r multi	.75	.35
6981	A3337 6r multi	.75	.35
6982	A3338 6r multi	.75	.35
6983	A3339 6r multi	.75	.35
	Nos. 6978-6983 (6)	4.50	2.10

Circumnavigation by the Kruzenshtern,
2005-06 — A3340

2006, June 29			
6984	A3340 4r multi	1.00	.50

Arcticcoal,
75th Anniv.
A3341

2006, July 12		Perf. 11¼	
6985	A3341 4r multi	.70	.35

Souvenir Sheet

Bolshoi Tsarskoselski Palace, 250th
Anniv. — A3342

No. 6986: a, 5r, Left portion. b, 6r, Central
portion. c, 7r, Right portion.

2006, July 17		Perf. 12x11¾	
6986	A3342	Sheet of 3, #a-c	3.00	1.00

Branch, by A. A. Ivanov (1806-
58) — A3343

Design: No. 6988, 6r, Portrait of A. A. Ivanov, by S. P. Postnikov, vert.

2006, July 17		Perf. 12	
6987-6988	A3343	Set of 2	1.25	.60

Novodevichy Monastery, by A. M.
Vasnetsov (1856-1933) — A3344

Design: No. 6990, 6r, Portrait of A. M. Vasnetsov, by N.D. Kuznetsov, vert.

2006, July 24			
6989-6990	A3344	Set of 2	1.25	.60

Barents Sea Lighthouses — A3345

Designs: 5r, Kaninsky Lighthouse. 6r, Kildin-
sky North Lighthouse. 8r, Vaidagubsky Lighthouse, vert.

2006, Aug. 10			
6991-6993	A3345	Set of 3	2.50	1.25

Souvenir Sheet

Russian State Theater, 250th
Anniv. — A3346

2006, Aug. 16		Perf. 12¼x12	
6994	A3346 15r multi	1.75	.75

Fauna of
Sakha
Republic
A3347

Designs: 3r, Rhodostethia rosea. 4r, Grus
leucogeranus. 5r, Ursus maritimus. 6r, Equus
caballus. 7r, Rangifer tarandus.

2006, Aug. 29		Perf. 11½x11¼	
6995-6999	A3347	Set of 5	2.75	1.40
6999a		Souvenir sheet, #6995-6999, + label	3.75	1.90

Russian Language Development
International Youth Project — A3348

2006, Sept. 5	Litho.	Perf. 11¼	
7000	A3348 7r multi	1.50	.75

D. S. Likhachev
(1906-99), Literary
Critic — A3349

2006, Sept. 19		Perf. 12	
7001	A3349 5r multi	.60	.35
a.	Sheet of 6 + 2 labels	3.75	2.00

Nature of the Caucausus
Region — A3350

No. 7002: a, 6r, Mountain. b, 7r, Stream. c,
8r, Bison.

2006, Sept. 22		Perf. 12	
7002	A3350	Block of 3, #a-c, + label	2.50	1.00

Television
Broadcasting
In Russia,
75th Anniv.
A3351

2006, Oct. 5		Perf. 11¼	
7003	A3351 7r multi	.95	.35

Mobile Telephone Communications in
Russia, 15th Anniv. — A3352

2006, Oct. 12		Perf. 12	
7004	A3352 7r multi	.80	.35

Admission to European Council, 10th
Anniv. — A3353

2006, Oct. 18		Perf. 12x12¼	
7005	A3353 8r multi	.95	.45

Savings Banks, 165th Anniv. — A3354

Designs: 7r, N. A. Kristofari (1802-81), bank
founder, and bank building. 15r, Kristofari,
vert.

2006, Oct. 18		Perf. 12	
7006	A3354 7r multi	1.00	.50

Souvenir Sheet
Perf. 12x12½

7007	A3354 15r multi	1.75	.85

No. 7007 contains one 30x42mm stamp.

Regional
Communications
Commonwealth, 15th
Anniv. — A3355

2006, Nov. 9 — **Perf. 12¼x12**
7008 A3355 5r multi — 1.25 .30

Ded Moroz
(Russian Santa
Claus) — A3356

2006, Nov. 29 — **Perf. 11¾**
7009 A3356 7r multi — .95 .35
Printed in sheets of 6.

Russian National Atlas — A3357

2006, Dec. 7 — **Perf. 12x11¾**
7010 A3357 6r multi — .95 .30

New Year
2007
A3358

2006, Dec. 12 — **Perf. 12**
7011 A3358 7r multi — .95 .35
a. Souvenir sheet of 6 — 6.00 3.00

Vladimir M. Bekhterev (1857-1927),
Psychoneurologist — A3359

2007, Jan. 15 — **Litho.** — **Perf. 12**
7012 A3359 5r multi — .70 .30

Ivan I.
Shishkin
(1832-98),
Painter
A3360

Designs: No. 7013, 7r, Portrait of Shishkin,
by I. N. Kramskoy (shown). No. 7014, 7r, In the
North Wild, by Shishkin

2007, Jan. 25
7013-7014 A3360 Set of 2 — 1.75 .85

Order of St.
George,
200th Anniv.
A3361

2007, Feb. 7 — **Litho.**
7015 A3361 10r multi — 1.25 .60

Souvenir Sheet
Litho. & Embossed
7016 A3361 50r multi — 7.00 3.00
No. 7015 was printed in sheets of 8 + label.
No. 7016 contains one diamond-shaped
57x57mm stamp.

Russian G. V. Plekhanov Economic
Academy, Cent. — A3362

2007, Feb. 9 Litho. — **Perf. 13¾x13½**
7017 A3362 5r multi — .70 .30

Orest A.
Kiprensky
(1782-1836),
Painter
A3363

Paintings by Kiprensky: No. 7018, 7r, Self-
portrait (shown). No. 7019, 7r, Poor Eliza.

Perf. 12, 13½x13¾ (#7019)
2007, Mar. 2
7018-7019 A3363 Set of 2 — 1.75 .85

Russian Post
Emblem — A3364

2007, Mar. 12 — **Perf. 12¼x12**
7020 A3364 6.50r blue — 1.00 .50
Complete booklet, 10 #7020 — 15.00
Complete booklet, 20 #7020 — 30.00
Compare with type A3827.

Souvenir Sheet

Intl. Polar Year — A3365

No. 7021: a, 6r, Icebreaker, scientific station. b, 7r, Glacier. c, 8r, Wildlife and cultural
heritage.

2007, Mar. 21 — **Perf. 12**
7021 A3365 Sheet of 3, #a-c — 5.00 1.25

Souvenir Sheet

Famous Men — A3366

No. 7022: a, Arkady Tarkovsky (1907-89),
poet. b, Andrei Tarkovsky (1932-86), film
director.

2007, Apr. 4 — **Perf. 12¼x12**
7022 A3366 8r Sheet of 2, #a-b — 2.00 1.00

Souvenir Sheet

Space Exploration, 50th
Anniv. — A3367

No. 7023: a, 10r, Sputnik 1. b, 20r, Sergei P.
Korolev (1907-66), aeronautical engineer. c,
20r, Konstantin E. Tsiolkovsky (1857-1935),
scientist.

2007, Apr. 12 — **Perf. 11¾**
7023 A3367 Sheet of 3, #a-c — 6.00 3.00

Bashkiria as Part of Russia, 450th
Anniv. — A3368

2007, Apr. 24 — **Perf. 11¼**
7024 A3368 6.50r multi — .80 .35

Pavel P.
Chistyakov
(1832-1919),
Painter
A3369

Paintings of Chistyakov by: No. 7025, 7r, I.
E. Repin (shown). No. 7026, 7r, V. A. Serov.

2007, May 11 — **Perf. 12**
7025-7026 A3369 Set of 2 — 1.50 .85

Vladimir L.
Borovikovsky
(1757-1825),
Painter
A3370

Designs: No. 7027, 7r, Portrait of Borovikovsky, by I. V. Bugaevsky-Blagodatny (shown).
No. 7028, 7r, Portrait of Sisters Anna and Barbara Gavrilovna.

2007, May 15
7027-7028 A3370 Set of 2 — 1.50 .85

Souvenir Sheet

First Russian Postage Stamps, 150th
Anniv. — A3371

2007, May 24 — **Perf. 12¼x12**
7029 A3371 10r multi — 1.50 .60

Telephones in Russia, 125th
Anniv. — A3372

2007, June 14 — **Perf. 14**
7030 A3372 5r multi — .70 .30

Souvenir Sheet

Russian Academy of Arts, 250th
Anniv. — A3373

Litho. & Engr.
2007, June 15   *Perf. 12¼x12*
7031   A3373   25r multi   3.00   1.50

Emblem of 2007
St. Petersburg
World Stamp
Exhibition
A3374

2007, June 19   **Litho.**   *Perf. 12x12½*
7032   A3374   5r multi   .70   .30
   a.   Perf. 12   1.00   .50
    No. 7032a was printed in sheets of 8 + central label.

Souvenir Sheet

Plesetsk Cosmodrome, 50th
Anniv. — A3375

2007, July 2   *Perf. 12¼x12*
7033   A3375   12r multi   1.50   .75

Khakassia as Part of Russia, 300th
Anniv. — A3376

2007, July 12   **Litho.**   *Perf. 11¼*
7034   A3376   6.50r multi   .70   .45

N. A. Lunin (1907-70),
Submariner — A3377

M. I. Gadzhiev (1907-42),
Submariner — A3378

2007, July 25   *Perf. 12x12¼*
7035   Horiz. pair + central label   3.00   .85
   a.   A3377   7r multi   .75   .40
   b.   A3378   7r multi   .75   .40

S. P. Botkin
(1832-89),
Physician
A3379

2007, Aug. 14   *Perf. 12x12½*
7036   A3379   5r blue & black   .65   .30

Irkutsk
Oblast
A3380

Orel
Oblast
A3381

Altai Kray
A3382

Vologda
Oblast
A3383

Rostov
Oblast
A3384

Novosibirsk Oblast — A3385

2007, Aug. 21   *Perf. 12x12¼*
7037   A3380   7r multi   1.00   .50
7038   A3381   7r multi   1.00   .50
7039   A3382   7r multi   1.00   .50
7040   A3383   7r multi   1.00   .50
7041   A3384   7r multi   1.00   .50
7042   A3385   7r multi   1.00   .50
     Nos. 7037-7042 (6)   6.00   3.00

Souvenir Sheet

Biblio-Globus Bookstore, 50th
Anniv. — A3386

2007, Aug. 24
7043   A3386   12r multi   1.75   .70

Souvenir Sheet

Russian Language Year — A3387

2007, Sept. 14   *Perf. 12¼x12*
7044   A3387   12r multi   1.60   .70

Souvenir Sheet

Flowers — A3388

    No. 7045: a, Gladiolus gandavensis. b, Iris ensata. c, Rosa hybrida. d, Nelumbo nucifera.

2007, Sept. 26   **Litho.**
7045   A3388   6r Sheet of 4, #a-d   3.00   1.50
    See North Korea No. 4689.

Worldwide Fund for Nature
(WWF) — A3389

    Designs: 5r, Ciconia boyciana. 6r, Uncia uncia. 7r, Bison bonasus.

2007, Oct. 1   *Perf. 11¼*
7046-7048   A3389   Set of 3   2.25   1.10
7048a   Miniature sheet of 8, 2 #7048, 3 each #7046-7047, + label   5.75   2.75

Trucks — A3390

    No. 7049: a, 1924 AMO-F-15. b, 1932 GAZ-AA (MM). c, 1942 ZIS-5V.

2007, Oct. 25   *Perf. 11¾x11½*
7049   A3390   Horiz. strip of 3   3.00   1.50
   a.-c.   8r Any single   1.00   .50
   d.   Miniature sheet of 8, 2 #7049a, 3 each #7049b-7049c, + label   7.75   3.75

Russian
House of
Science
and
Culture,
Berlin
A3391

2007, Oct. 29   *Perf. 12*
7050   A3391   8r multi   .90   .45
    Russian Language Year.

Horses — A3392

    Horse's head and: 6r, Vladimir horse pulling wagon. No. 7052, 7r, Orlov Trotter pulling sulky. No. 7053, 7r, Don horse with rider. 8r, Vyatsky horse jumping.

2007, Nov. 7   *Perf. 11¾*
7051-7054   A3392   Set of 4   2.75   1.25
7054a   Souvenir sheet, #7051-7054   2.75   1.25

Arctic
Deep Sea
Exploration
A3393

    No. 7055: a, Mir-1 bathyscaphe. b, Russian flag on North Pole on map.

2007, Dec. 7   **Litho.**   *Perf. 12*
7055   A3393   8r Vert. pair, #a-b, + label   1.75   1.00

New Year's Day — A3394

2007, Dec. 7   *Perf. 11¾x11½*
7056   A3394   8r multi   .85   .45
   a.   Miniature sheet of 6   6.00   3.00

First Russian Postage Stamps, 150th Anniv. — A3395

2008, Jan. 10 **Perf. 12x11¼**
7057 A3395 8r No. 1 .90 .45

Count Alexei N. Tolstoy (1883-1945), Writer — A3396

2008, Jan. 10 **Perf. 12**
7058 A3396 6r multi .70 .30

Nobel Laureates in Physics A3397

Designs: No. 7059, 6r, Ilya M. Frank (1908-90), 1958 laureate. No. 7060, 6r, Lev D. Landau (1908-68), 1962 laureate.

2008, Jan. 22 **Perf. 11¾**
7059-7060 A3397 Set of 2 1.25 .70

Agustín de Betancourt (1758-1824), Engineer — A3398

2008, Feb. 1 **Litho.** **Perf. 12½x12**
7061 A3398 9r multi 1.00 .50
See note under No. 7097.

Astrakhan, 450th Anniv. — A3399

2008, Feb. 22 **Perf. 11¾**
7062 A3399 9r multi 1.00 .50

Valentin P. Glushko (1908-89), Spacecraft Designer — A3400

2008, Mar. 17 **Perf. 12¼x12**
7063 A3400 8r multi .90 .45

Miniature Sheet

Archaeology — A3401

No. 3401 — Metal plates featuring: a, Mythological beast, 2nd cent. B.C.- 1st cent. A.D. b, Two oxen, 2nd cent. B.C.- 1st cent. A.D. c, Deer, 4th-3rd cents. B.C.

Litho. & Embossed
2008, Mar. 25 **Perf. 12½x12**
7064 A3401 12r Sheet of 3, #a-c 4.00 2.00

2008 Summer Olympics, Beijing — A3402

No. 7065 — Various athletes with stripe at upper right corner in: a, Gray. b, Blue. c, Black.

2008, Apr. 15 **Litho.** **Perf. 11¾**
7065 A3402 8r Horiz. strip of 3, #a-c 2.75 1.50
d. Souvenir sheet, #7065 2.75 1.50

Souvenir Sheet

Black Sea Naval Fleet, 225th Anniv. — A3403

2008, Apr. 29 **Perf. 12x12¼**
7066 A3403 15r multi 2.00 1.00

Europa A3404

2008, May 5 **Perf. 12¼x12**
7067 A3404 8r multi .70 .35
a. Miniature sheet of 6 4.50 2.10

Election of Pres. Dmitry Medvedev A3405

2008, May 7 **Perf. 12x12¼**
7068 A3405 7r multi 1.00 .35

Krasnoyarsk Kray — A3406

Sverdlovsk Oblast — A3407

Penza Oblast A3408

Volgograd Oblast A3409

Yaroslavl Oblast A3410

2008, May 20 **Perf. 12¼x12, 12x12¼**
7069 A3406 8r multi .75 .35
7070 A3407 8r multi .75 .35
7071 A3408 8r multi .75 .35
7072 A3409 8r multi .75 .35
7073 A3410 8r multi .75 .35
Nos. 7069-7073 (5) 3.75 1.75

Cathedrals — A3411

No. 7074: a, St. Demetrius's Cathedral, Vladimir, Russia, 12th cent., and winged beast. b, St. George's Cathedral, Voronets Monastery, Romania, 15th cent., and chrismon.

2008, June 23 **Perf. 11½**
7074 A3411 Horiz. pair, #a-b, + central label 2.75 1.50
a.-b. 12r Either single 1.50 .75
c. Miniature sheet, 3 #7074 9.00 4.50
See Romania Nos. 5057-5058.

Helicopter Sports in Russia, 50th Anniv. — A3412

2008, July 12 **Litho.** **Perf. 11¾**
7075 A3412 5r multi .50 .25

Pokrovsk Cathedral — A3413

2008, July 25 **Perf. 11¾x12¼**
7076 A3413 7.50r multi .80 .35
Complete booklet, 10 #7076 10.00
Complete booklet, 20 #7076 22.50

Souvenir Sheet

Northern Navy, 75th Anniv. — A3414

2008, July 26 **Perf. 12x12½**
7077 A3414 15r multi 4.00 1.00

Udmurtia as Part of Russia, 450th Anniv. — A3415

2008, July 28 **Perf. 11½**
7078 A3415 7.50r multi .80 .35

Souvenir Sheet

Kizhi UNESCO World Heritage Site — A3416

No. 7079: a, Church, 1714. b, Bell tower, 1862. c, Church, 1694-1764.

2008, July 31 **Perf. 11¾x12¼**
7079 A3416 10r Sheet of 3, #a-c 3.50 1.75

Souvenir Sheet

Emperor Nicholas I (1796-
1855) — A3417

Litho. & Engr.

2008, Aug. 8		**Perf. 12x12½**
7080 A3417	35r multi	4.00 2.00

Souvenir Sheet

International Polar Year — A3418

No. 7081 — Map of Northern Russia and
various ships: a, 6r. b, 7r. c, 8r.

2008, Aug. 28	**Litho.**	**Perf. 12x11½**
7081 A3418	Sheet of 3, #a-c	5.00 1.25

Wildlife — A3419

Perf. 12¼x12 Syncopated

			Litho.
2008, Aug. 29			**Litho.**
7082 A3419	10k Hare	.25	.25
7083 A3419	15k Hare	.25	.25
7084 A3419	25k Hare	.25	.25
7085 A3419	30k Fox	.25	.25
7086 A3419	50k Fox	.25	.25
7087 A3419	1r Fox	.25	.25
7088 A3419	1.50r Lynx	.25	.25
7089 A3419	2r Lynx	.25	.25
7090 A3419	2.50r Lynx	.25	.25
7091 A3419	3r Elk	.30	.25
7092 A3419	4r Elk	.40	.25
7093 A3419	5r Elk	.45	.25
7094 A3419	6r Bear	.50	.25
7095 A3419	10r Bear	.85	.40
7096 A3419	25r Bear	2.10	1.00
	Nos. 7082-7096 (15)	6.85	4.65

Souvenir Sheet

Goznak (State Currency Printers),
190th Anniv. — A3420

**Litho. & Embossed With Foil
Application**

		Perf.
2008, Sept. 1		**Perf.**
7097 A3420	20r black & gold	3.00 1.10

No. 7097 contains one 33mm diameter
stamp.
A booklet containing booklet panes of 1 of
Nos. 7061 and 7097 exists. Value, $55.

Flora and Fauna — A3421

No. 7098: a, Woodpecker and squirrel in
birch tree. b, Fawn. c, Mushrooms, evergreens
and birch tree.

2008, Sept. 12	**Litho.**	**Perf. 12x12¼**
7098 A3421	7r Block of 3, #a-c, + label	3.00 1.25

Leningrad
Oblast
A3422

2008, Sept. 17		
7099 A3422	8r multi	.80 .40

Souvenir Sheet

History of the Cossacks — A3423

No. 7100: a, Silver medal. b, Crossed
swords and wreath. c, Sword hilt.

2008, Sept. 17		**Perf. 11¾x12¼**
7100 A3423	10r Sheet of 3, #a-c	4.00 1.60

Helicopters — A3424

2008, Oct. 2		**Perf. 12¼x12**
7101 A3424	7r Ka-226	1.00 .40
7102 A3424	7r Ka-32	1.00 .40
a.	Miniature sheet, 3 each #7101-7102	5.50 2.75

Central Sikhote-Alin UNESCO World
Heritage Site — A3425

No. 7103 — Various forest views: a, 7r. b,
8r. c, 9r.

2008, Oct. 15	**Litho.**	**Perf. 12**
7103 A3425	Block of 3, #a-c, + label	3.00 1.25

Federation Council, 15th
Anniv. — A3426

State
Duma,
15th
Anniv.
A3427

2008, Nov. 13		**Perf. 12½x12**
7104 A3426	10r multi	1.10 .50
7105 A3427	10r multi	1.10 .50

Nos. 7104-7105 each were printed in sheets
of 14 + label.

Bridges — A3428

Bridges over: 6r, Moscow River, Moscow.
7r, Volga River, Kimry. 8r, Ob River, Surgut.
9r, Neva River, St. Petersburg.

2008, Nov. 28		**Perf. 12x12¼**
7106-7109 A3428	Set of 4	3.00 1.50
7109a	Miniature sheet of 8, 2 each #7106-7109	6.50 3.00

Shuvalov
Swimming
School,
Cent.
A3429

2008, Dec. 5		
7110 A3429	8r multi	.85 .40

Russia,
2008
World Ice
Hockey
Champions
A3430

2008, Dec. 5		
7111 A3430	8r multi	.85 .40

For surcharge, see No. 7375.

Bicycles — A3431

Designs: No. 7112, 7r, 1946 bicycle, derail-
leur. No. 7113, 7r, 1954 bicycle, front chain
ring, chain guard and pedals. No. 7114, 7r,
1917 bicycle, saddle. No. 7115, 7r, 1938 bicycle, handlebars.

2008, Dec. 11	**Litho.**	**Perf. 12x11½**
7112-7115 A3431	Set of 4	3.00 1.50
7115a	Miniature sheet, 2 each # 7112-7115	5.75 2.75

Nos. 7112-7115 each were printed in sheets
of 8 + central label.

A3432

A3433

A3434

Traditional
Dagestan
Costumes
and
Decorations
A3435

2008, Dec. 18		**Perf. 11½x12**
7116 A3432	7.50r multi	.75 .30
7117 A3433	7.50r multi	.75 .30
7118 A3434	7.50r multi	.75 .30
7119 A3435	7.50r multi	.75 .30
a.	Miniature sheet, 2 each #7116-7119	6.50 3.00
	Nos. 7116-7119 (4)	3.00 1.20

Nos. 7116-7119 each were printed in sheets
of 11 + label.

New Year 2009 — A3436

2008, Dec. 18　　　　**Perf. 11¾**
7120　A3436　7.50r multi　　　　.80　.35

Voronezh Oblast A3437

Chelyabinsk Oblast — A3438

Saratov Oblast A3439

2009, Jan. 17　　　　**Perf. 12**
7121　A3437　9r multi　　　　.90　.35
7122　A3438　9r multi　　　　.90　.35
7123　A3439　9r multi　　　　.90　.35
　　　Nos. 7121-7123 (3)　　2.70　1.05

Ernesto "Che" Guevara and Cuban Flag — A3440

2009, Jan. 19　　　　**Perf. 12x12¼**
7124　A3440　10r multi　　　　2.25　.75

Cuban Revolution, 50th anniv. See Cuba No. 4924A.

Naval Museum, 300th Anniv. — A3441

2009, Jan. 22　Litho.　Perf. 12x11½
7125　A3441　7r multi　　　　.75　.30

Vasily G. Perov (1834-82), Painter A3442

Designs: No. 7126, 9r, Self-portrait, 1851. No. 7127, 9r, Drinking of Tea in Mytischi, Near Moscow, 1862, horiz.

2009, Jan. 28　Perf. 11½x12, 12x11½
7126-7127　A3442　Set of 2　1.75　.75

Souvenir Sheet

Dmitri Mendeleev (1834-1907), Chemist — A3443

2009, Feb. 6　　　　**Perf. 12x12¼**
7128　A3443　15r multi　　　　1.50　.60

No. 7128 with an 80r surcharge and an overprint in the sheet margin marking 2019 as International Year of the Periodic Table was produced in limited quantities and issues on Mar. 19, 2019.

G. Bakhchivandji (1909-43), Test Pilot — A3444

2009, Feb. 16　　　**Perf. 12¼x12**
7129　A3444　10r multi　　　　.80　.45

Yuri Gagarin (1934-68), First Cosmonaut A3445

2009, Mar. 6　　　　**Perf. 12x12¼**
7130　A3445　10r multi　　　　.80　.45
Printed in sheets of 10 + 2 central labels.

Souvenir Sheet

Aleksandr S. Popov (1859-1905), Electrical Engineer — A3446

2009, Mar. 16　Litho.　Perf.
7131　A3446　20r multi　　　　2.00　.85

Scenes From Novels By Nikolai V. Gogol (1809-52) — A3447

Gogol — A3448

No. 7132 — Scenes from: a, 6r, The Inspector General. b, 7r, Dead Souls. c, 8r, The Overcoat. d, 9r, Taras Bulba.

2009, Apr. 1　　　　**Perf. 12**
7132　A3447　Sheet of 4, #a-d　3.00　1.40

Souvenir Sheet
Perf. 12x12¼
7133　A3448　15r multi　　　　1.75　.60

Weapons of World War II — A3449

Designs: 7r, SRT-40 and ARS-36 rifles. 8r, 1895 Nagan revolver and 1933 Tokarev pistol. 9r, PPS-43 and PPSh-41 machine guns. 10r, DP and SG-43 machine guns.

2009, Apr. 27　　　　**Perf. 11¾**
7134-7137　A3449　Set of 4　3.50　1.50
7137a　　Sheet of 8, 2 each #7134-
　　　　7137　　　　　　6.00　3.00

A booklet containing four panes of one of Nos. 7134-7137 sold for 225r. Value, $30.

Europa A3450

2009, May 5　　　　**Perf. 12**
7138　A3450　9r multi　　　　.90　.40
　a.　　Miniature sheet of 9　8.50　3.50

Intl. Year of Astronomy.

Hydrometeorological Service, 175th Anniv. — A3451

Weather map and: 8r, Weather measuring equipment, A. Y. Kupfer (1799-1865), weather scientist. 9r, Weather satellite.

2009, May 15　　　　**Perf. 12x12¼**
7139-7140　A3451　Set of 2　1.75　.85
7140a　　Sheet of 8, 4 each #7139-
　　　　7140　　　　　　8.00　3.25

Souvenir Sheet

Empress Catherine I (1684-1727) — A3452

Litho. & Engr.
2009, May 21　　　**Perf. 12x12¼**
7141　A3452　35r multi　　　　3.25　1.60

Kalmykia as Part of Russia, 400th Anniv. — A3453

2009, June 2　Litho.　Perf. 11½x11¼
7142　A3453　7r multi　　　　.75　.30

Atomic-powered Icebreakers — A3454

Ships: 7r, Lenin. 8r, Taimyr. 9r, Yamal. 10r, 50 Let Pobedy.

2009, June 18　Litho.　Perf. 12x11½
7143-7146　A3454　Set of 4　3.25　1.60

Nos. 7143-7146 each were printed in sheets of 8 + 2 labels.

Souvenir Sheet

Battle of Poltava, 300th
Anniv. — A3455

2009, June 26 **Perf. 11¾x12¼**
7147 A3455 30r multi 3.00 1.40

Youth Year — A3456

2009, June 27 **Perf. 12¼x12**
7148 A3456 8r multi .90 .40

Ingushetia
Republic
A3457

Chechen
Republic
A3458

Tomsk
Oblast
A3459

2009, July 7 **Perf. 12**
7149 A3457 9r multi .85 .40
7150 A3458 9r multi .85 .40
7151 A3459 9r multi .85 .40
Nos. 7149-7151 (3) 2.55 1.20

Miniature Sheet

Helicopters Designed by M. L. Mil
(1909-70) — A3460

No. 7152: a, 5r, Mi-1. b, 6r, Mi-4. c, 7r, Mi-8.
d, 8r, Mi-34. e, 9r, Mi-28.

2009, July 10 **Perf. 12¼x12**
7152 A3460 Sheet of 5, #a-e, +
label 3.50 1.75

Zinaida E. Serebryakova (1884-1967),
Painter — A3461

Paintings by Serebryakova: No. 7153, 9r,
Self-portrait in Dressing Room (shown). No.
7154, 9r, Autumn Field.

2009, July 15 **Perf. 11½x12**
7153-7154 A3461 Set of 2 1.75 .85

Andrei A.
Gromyko
(1909-89),
Foreign
Affairs
Minister of
Soviet Union
A3462

2009, July 17 **Litho.** **Perf. 11½**
7155 A3462 7r multi .65 .30

Miniature Sheet

Solovetski Islands — A3463

No. 7156 — Map and: a, St. Troitsky
Church, 17th cent., and horse. b, St. Sergiev
Church, 19th cent., and cow. c, Solovetski
Monastery, 15th cent. d, Andrei Pervozvannyi
Church, 18th cent.

2009, July 27 **Perf. 12**
7156 A3463 12r Sheet of 4, #a-d 5.00 2.25

Emblem of St.
Petersburg
A3464

Emblem of Moscow
A3465

2009, Aug. 6 **Litho.** **Perf. 11¾x12¼**
7157 A3464 6.60r multi .65 .30
Complete booklet, 10 #7157 6.50
Complete booklet, 20 #7157 13.00
7158 A3465 9r multi .85 .45
Complete booklet, 10 #7158 8.50
Complete booklet, 20 #7158 17.00

Bridges — A3466

Designs: 6r, Oka River Bridge, Nizhni
Novgorod. 7r, Irtysh River Bridge, Khanty-
Mansiysk. 8r, Matsesta River Bridge, Sochi.
9r, Don River Bridge, Rostov-na-Donu.

2009, Aug. 12 **Litho.** **Perf. 12x12¼**
7159-7162 A3466 Set of 4 2.75 1.40
7162a Miniature sheet of 8, 2
each #7159-7162 5.75 2.75

Miniature Sheet

Towns of Military Glory — A3467

No. 7163 — City names at top: a, Belgorod
(8 letters in city name, tanks). b, Kursk. c, Orel
(4 letters in city name, tanks and guns). d,
Polyarny (8 letters in city name, ships). e,
Rzhev (4 letters in city name, tanks and
trucks).

Litho. With Foil Application
2009, Aug. 24 **Perf. 11¼**
7163 A3467 10r Sheet of 5, #a-e,
+ label 4.75 2.40

Souvenir Sheet

Great Novgorod, 1150th
Anniv. — A3468

Litho. & Embossed
2009, Sept. 4 **Perf. 12½x12**
7164 A3468 50r multi 4.75 2.70

Souvenir Sheet

Famous Cossacks — A3469

No. 7165: a, Ermak Timofeevich (c. 1540-
1585), explorer of Siberia (with helmet). b,
Semen Ivanovich Dezhnev (c. 1605-72),
explorer of Siberia (with beard). c, Count
Matvei Ivanovich Platov (1757-1818), general
(with mustache).

Perf. 11¾x12¼
2009, Sept. 15 **Litho.**
7165 A3469 10r Sheet of 3, #a-c 2.75 1.40

19th Century
Headdresses
A3470

Designs: No. 7166, 9r, Tver region man
wearing hat. No. 7167, 9r, Moscow region
woman wearing headdress with blue ribbon
(blue background). No. 7168, 9r, Nizhny
Novgorod region woman wearing veiled headdress (red background). No. 7169, 9r, Yaroslavl region woman wearing veiled headdress
(blue green background).

2009, Sept. 23 **Perf. 11¼x12**
7166-7169 A3470 Set of 4 3.50 1.75
7169a Miniature sheet of 8, 2
each #7166-7169 7.00 3.50

Nos. 7166-7169 each were printed in sheets
of 11 + label.

Kremlins
A3471

Kremlins in: 1r, Astrakhan. 1.50r, Zaraisk.
2r, Kazan. 2.50r, Kolomna. 3r, Rostov. 4r,
Nizhny Novgorod. 5r, Novgorod. 6r, Pskov.
10r, Moscow. 25r, Ryazan. 50r, Tobolsk. 100r,
Tula.

2009, Oct. 1 **Serpentine Die Cut 11**
Self-Adhesive
7170 A3471 1r multi .30 .25
7171 A3471 1.50r multi .30 .25
7172 A3471 2r multi .30 .25
7173 A3471 2.50r multi .30 .25
7174 A3471 3r multi .30 .25
7175 A3471 4r multi .35 .25
7176 A3471 5r multi .50 .25
7177 A3471 6r multi .55 .25
7178 A3471 10r multi .90 .45
7179 A3471 25r multi 2.50 1.25
a. Sheet of 10, #7170-7179 3.50
7180 A3471 50r multi 5.00 2.50
7181 A3471 100r multi 9.50 4.75
a. Miniature sheet of 12,
#7170-7181 21.00
Nos. 7170-7181 (12) 20.80 10.95

Issued: No. 7179a, 1/24/14. See Nos. 7847-
7848, 7932.

World Food Program — A3472

2009, Oct. 7   *Perf. 11¾*
7182 A3472 10r multi   1.00 .50

Admiral Vladimir Ivanovich Istomin
(1809-55) — A3473

2009, Oct. 14   *Perf. 12x11½*
7183 A3473 10r multi   1.00 .50

Traffic
Safety
A3474

2009, Oct. 22   *Perf. 12½x12*
7184 A3474 9r multi   .90 .45

Order of the Hero
of the Soviet
Union, 75th
Anniv. — A3475

**Litho. & Embossed With Foil
Application**
2009, Oct. 29   *Perf. 12x12¼*
7185 A3475 9r multi   .90 .45

Souvenir Sheet

Empress Elizabeth Petrovna (1709-
62) — A3476

Litho. & Engr.
2009, Nov. 6   *Perf. 12x12¼*
7186 A3476 40r multi   4.00 2.00

Department of Transportation, 200th
Anniv. — A3477

2009, Nov. 9   **Litho.**   *Perf. 12¼x12*
7187 A3477 9r multi   .90 .45

Shchepkin
Drama
School,
200th
Anniv.
A3478

2009, Nov. 25
7188 A3478 10r multi   1.00 .50

Antarctic
Treaty,
50th
Anniv.
A3479

2009, Nov. 30   **Litho.**
7189 A3479 15r multi   1.50 .75

New Year's
Day — A3480

2009, Dec. 1   *Die Cut*
    Self-Adhesive
7190 A3480 10r multi   1.00 .50

Strategic
Rocket
Forces, 50th
Anniv.
A3481

2009, Dec. 10   *Perf. 11¼x12*
7191 A3481 9r multi   1.00 .45

Fountains
A3482

Fountain in: 9r, Verkhnyaya Pyshma. 10r,
Nizhny Novgorod. 12r, Novy Urengoi, vert.
15r, Yaroslavl.

Serpentine Die Cut 11¼
2009, Dec. 15   **Self-Adhesive**
7192-7195 A3482   Set of 4   4.50 2.25

Anatoly K.
Serov
(1910-39),
Pilot
A3483

Valentina S. Grizodubova (1910-93),
Pilot — A3484

2010, Jan. 14   **Litho.**   *Perf. 12½x12*
7196 A3483 10r multi   1.00 .50
7197 A3484 10r multi   1.00 .50

A3485

Anton P. Chekhov (1860-1904),
Writer — A3486

No. 7198 — Characters from: a, 8r, Lady
with the Dog. b, 10r, The Seagull. c, 12r, The
Artist's Story (The House with the Mezzanine).
20r, Chekhov.

2010, Jan. 29   **Litho.**   *Perf. 11¾x12¼*
7198 A3485   Sheet of 3, #a-c   4.00 2.00
    Souvenir Sheet
    Perf.
7199 A3486 20r multi   3.00 1.50

Peoples' Friendship University,
Moscow, 50th Anniv. — A3487

2010, Feb. 5   **Litho.**   *Perf. 12x11½*
7200 A3487 10r multi   1.00 .50

2010 Winter Olympics,
Vancouver — A3488

Litho. & Embossed
2010, Feb. 11   *Perf. 11½*
7201 A3488 15r multi   1.25 .60

Paintings by
Fedor S.
Rokotov (c.
1735-1808)
A3489

Portraits of: No. 7202, 10.50r, Prince D. M.
Golitsyn. No. 7203, 10.50r, Countess E. A.
Musina-Pushkina.

2010, Mar. 19   **Litho.**   *Perf. 11¼x12*
7202-7203 A3489   Set of 2   2.00 1.00

Orenburg
Oblast
A3490

Tuva
Republic
A3491

2010, Mar. 24   *Perf. 12x12¼*
7204 A3490 10.50r multi   1.00 .50
7205 A3491 10.50r multi   1.00 .50

Evgeny K. Fedorov (1910-81), Polar
Explorer — A3492

2010, Apr. 9   *Perf. 12x12¼*
7206 A3492 12r multi   1.25 .40

Miniature Sheet

Towns of Military Glory — A3493

No. 7207 — City names at top: a, Malgobek
(8 letters in city name, airplanes, cannons and
cavalry). b, Elnja (5 letters in city name,

bazookas, cannons and tanks). c, Elets (4 letters in city name, trucks, cannons and tanks). d, Voronezh (7 letters in city name, airplanes and cannons). e, Luga (4 letters in city name, cannons and tanks).

Litho. With Foil Application
2010, Apr. 15   Perf. 11¼
7207 A3493 10r Sheet of 5, #a-e,
      + label   4.25 1.75

World War II Tanks — A3494

Designs: 9r, BT-7M. 10r, T-70. 11r, T-34-85. 12r, IS-2.

2010, Apr. 20   Litho.   Perf. 13½
7208-7211 A3494 Set of 4   4.00 1.50
7211a   Sheet of 8, 2 each #7208-
         7211   8.00 3.00

Souvenir Sheet

Soviet Union Order of
Victory — A3495

Litho. & Embossed
2010, Apr. 26   Perf. 12
7212 A3495 50r multi   4.25 1.75
Victory in World War II, 65th anniv.

Europa — A3496

2010, May 5   Litho.   Perf. 12x12½
7213 A3496 10.50r multi   .70   .35
a.   Miniature sheet of 6   5.00 2.10

Modernization of Cyrillic Alphabet,
300th Anniv. — A3497

2010, May 18   Perf. 12x12¼
7214 A3497 7.70r multi   .75   .25

Souvenir Sheet

Ivan Fedorov (c. 1510-83),
Printer — A3498

Litho. & Engr.
2010, May 18   Perf. 12½x12
7215 A3498 50r multi   4.50 1.60

Miniature Sheet

Watches — A3499

No. 7216 — Watch from: a, 6r, Wooden pocket watch by M. S. Bronnikov and Son. 9r, Pobeda wrist watch, 1946. 12r, Shturmanskie wrist watch, 1949. 15r, Chaika wrist watch, 1990.

2010, May 28   Litho.   Perf. 12¼
7216 A3499 Sheet of 4, #a-d 3.75 1.40

Dmitry Levitzky (c.1735-1822),
Painter — A3500

Designs: No. 7217, 10.50r, Self-portrait (detail), 1783. No. 7218, 10.50r, Portrait of G. I. Alymova, 1776.

2010, June 7   Perf. 11½x12
7217-7218 A3500 Set of 2   2.00   .70

Souvenir Sheet

Valaam Archipelago — A3501

2010, June 8   Perf. 12
7219 A3501 25r multi   1.60   .80

Souvenir Sheet

Tsarskoye Selo (Tsar's Village)
UNESCO World Heritage Site, 300th
Anniv. — A3502

No. 7220: a, Egyptian Gates. b, Pushkin Monument, vert. c, Alexander Palace.

                Perf. 12x12¼, 12¼x12
2010, June 18
7220 A3502 15r Sheet of 3, #a-c 4.25 1.50

Icons of Russia and Serbia — A3503

No. 7221: a, Archangel Michael, by Andrei Rublev, 15th cent., Russia. b, Odigitria Virgin, Belgrade, Serbia, 14th cent.

2010, June 28   Perf. 11½
7221 A3503 15r Pair, #a-b   2.75 1.00
See Serbia No. 515.

Vladivostok, 150th Anniv. — A3504

2010, July 2   Perf. 13½
7222 A3504 15r multi   1.40   .50

Bryansk
Oblast
A3505

Jewish Autonomous Oblast — A3506

2010, July 14   Perf. 12x12¼
7223 A3505 10.50r multi   .90   .35
7224 A3506 10.50r multi   .90   .35

Curonian Spit UNESCO World
Heritage Site — A3507

No. 7225 — Spit with denomination at: a, Left. b, Right.

2010, June 26   Litho.   Perf. 13½
7225   Horiz. pair + central la-
        bel   4.00 1.00
a.-b. A3507 15r Either single 1.75   .50
A gritty substance is affixed to the areas of the stamps and labels showing sand.

A3508

A3509

A3510

Headdresses
of Tatarstan
A3511

2010, July 30   Litho.   Perf. 11½x12
7226 A3508 11r multi   1.00   .35
7227 A3509 11r multi   1.00   .35
7228 A3510 11r multi   1.00   .35
7229 A3511 11r multi   1.00   .35
a.   Miniature sheet of 8, 2 each
      #7226-7229   7.50 3.00
      Nos. 7226-7229 (4)   3.00 1.40

Nos. 7226-7229 each were printed in sheets of 11 + label.

Souvenir Sheet

Ferapontov Monastery UNESCO
World Heritage Site — A3512

2010, Aug. 2   *Perf. 12½x12*
7230 A3512 30r multi   3.00 1.00

Nikolai N. Zubov (1885-1960), Arctic
Explorer, and Icebreaker
Sadko — A3513

2010, Aug. 12   *Perf. 12x12¼*
7231 A3513 12r multi   1.25 .40

Souvenir Sheet

Cossacks — A3514

No. 7232: a, Don Cossacks, brown horse. b,
Kuban Cossacks, white horse. c, Terek Cossacks, black horse.

2010, Aug. 20
7232 A3514 12r Sheet of 3, #a-c   3.50 1.25

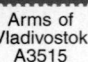

Arms of   Arms of
Vladivostok   Yaroslavl
A3515   A3516

2010, Aug. 27   *Perf. 11¾x12¼*
7233 A3515 7.70r multi   .75 .25
    Complete booklet, 10 #7233   7.50
    Complete booklet, 20 #7233   15.00
7234 A3516 10.50r multi   1.25 .35
    Complete booklet, 10 #7234   12.50
    Complete booklet, 20 #7234   25.00

Souvenir Sheet

Fresh Wind, Volga, by Isaac I. Levitan
(1860-1900) — A3517

2010, Aug. 30   *Perf. 12½x12*
7235 A3517 25r multi   2.50 .85

Memorial to
End of World
War II,
Moscow
A3518

2010, Sept. 2   *Perf. 11½*
7236 A3518 15r multi   1.50 .50
End of World War II, 65th anniv.

Gherman Titov
(1935-2000),
Cosmonaut
A3519

2010, Sept. 10   *Perf. 13½*
7237 A3519 10.50r multi   1.10 .35
No. 7237 was printed in sheets of 6 + 2
labels. For surcharge, see No. 7754.

Souvenir Sheet

Yaroslavl, 1000th Anniv. — A3520

Serpentine Die Cut 10
2010, Sept. 10   **Self-Adhesive**
7238 A3520 50r multi   5.00 1.60

Bridges — A3521

Designs: 9r, Jubilee Bridge, Yaroslavl. 10r,
Matsesta Valley Bridge, Sochi. 11r, Moscow
Canal Bridge, Khlebnikovo, Moscow Oblast.
12r, Kola Bay Bridge, Murmansk.

2010, Sept. 15   *Perf. 12x12¼*
7239-7242 A3521   Set of 4   4.00 1.40
7242a   Miniature sheet of 8, 2
      each #7239-7242   8.00 2.75

Miniature Sheet

Bank of Russia, 150th Anniv. — A3522

No. 7243: a, 10r, 1855 copper half-kopeck
coin. b, 15r, 1895 one-ruble coin. c, 20r, 1924
fifty-kopeck coin. d, 25r, 2006 gold fifty-ruble
coin.

Litho. & Embossed
2010, Sept. 22   *Perf. 12¼*
7243 A3522   Sheet of 4, #a-d   7.00 2.40

Teacher's
Year
A3523

Serpentine Die Cut 10
2010, Oct. 5   **Self-Adhesive**   **Litho.**
7244 A3523 10.50r multi   1.25 .35

2010 Census — A3524

2010, Oct. 14   ***Serpentine Die Cut 10***
         Self-Adhesive
7245 A3524 12r red & blue   1.25 .40

Shokan
Valikhanov (1835-
65), Diplomat,
Ethnologist
A3525

2010, Oct. 21   *Perf. 12x12½*
7246 A3525 15r multi   1.50 .50
See Kazakhstan No. 628.

Sputnik 5 Spaceflight Carrying Dogs
Belka and Strelka, 50th
Anniv. — A3526

2010, Oct. 29   *Perf. 12x12¼*
7247 A3526 10r multi   .90 .35

Khanty-Mansi Autonomous
Okrug — A3527

Kursk
Oblast
A3528

2010, Nov. 1
7248 A3527 10.50r multi   .70 .35
7249 A3528 10.50r multi   .70 .35

Soviet Union Victory in UEFA
European Soccer Championships,
50th Anniv. — A3529

2010, Nov. 10   *Perf. 11½*
7250 A3529 12r multi   .80 .40
Printed in sheets of 8 + central label.

Souvenir Sheet

Nikolai I. Pirogov (1810-81),
Surgeon — A3530

2010, Nov. 25   *Perf. 12x12½*
7251 A3530 20r multi   1.75 .70

Kachino Aviation School, Cent. — A3531

2010, Nov. 29   *Perf. 11½*
7252   A3531   15r multi   1.50   .50
Printed in sheets of 8 + central label.

New Year's Day A3532

2010, Dec. 1   **Self-Adhesive**   *Die Cut*
7253   A3532   10.50r multi   1.25   .35

Mstislav Keldysh (1911-78), Mathematician and Space Propulsion Pioneer — A3533

2011, Jan. 25   *Perf. 12½x12*
7254   A3533   12r multi   .85   .40

Souvenir Sheet

Princess Maria Alexandrovna (1824-80) — A3534

2011, Feb. 21   *Perf.*
7255   A3534   40r multi   4.00   1.50
City of Mariehamn, Aland Islands, 150th anniv. See Finland (Aland Islands) No. 313.

Souvenir Sheet

Sochi, Host City of 2014 Winter Olympics — A3535

2011, Mar. 15   *Perf. 12½x12*
7256   A3535   25r multi   1.90   .95

Novgorod Oblast — A3536

Tyumen Oblast — A3537

Tambov Oblast — A3538

2011, Mar. 30   *Perf. 12¼x12*
7257   A3536   11.80r multi   1.25   .40
7258   A3537   11.80r multi   1.25   .40
7259   A3538   11.80r multi   1.25   .40
    Nos. 7257-7259 (3)   3.75   1.20

Souvenir Sheet

Yuri Gagarin, First Man in Space, 50th Anniv. — A3539

2011, Apr. 12   **Litho.**   *Perf. 12x12¼*
7260   A3539   50r multi   5.00   1.90

Miniature Sheet

Towns of Military Glory — A3540

No. 7261 — City names at top: a, Vyborg (6 letters in city name, airplanes and tanks). b, Rostov-on-Don (city name with hyphens, cannons). c, Tuapse (6 letters in city name, airplanes, cannons and ships). d, Vladikavkaz (11 letters in name, airplanes and cannons). e, Veliki Novgorod (15 letters in city name, vehicle on skis, cannons and tanks). f, Velikiye Luki (10 letters in city name, biplanes, cannons and tanks).

Litho. With Foil Application
2011, Apr. 20   *Perf. 11¼*
7261   A3540   12r Sheet of 6, #a-f   6.50   2.60

Russian Peace Fund, 50th Anniv. A3541

2011, Apr. 27   **Litho.**   *Perf. 13½*
7262   A3541   8.50r multi   .90   .30

World War II Military Aircraft — A3542

Designs: 9r, Yakovlev Yak-3 fighter. 10r, Lavochkin La-5 fighter. 11r, Ilyushin Il-2 attack plane. 12r, Petlyakov Pe-2 bomber.

2011, Apr. 29
7263-7266   A3542   Set of 4   4.00   1.50
7266a   Sheet of 8, 2 each #7263-7266   8.00   3.00

A booklet containing panes of one of each of the stamps was produced in limited quantities. Value, $30.

Europa A3543

2011, May 5   *Perf. 11¼*
7267   A3543   15r multi   1.50   .55
Intl. Year of Forests.

Miniature Sheet

Clocks — A3544

No. 7268 — Clock at: a, 9r, Central Telegraph Office, Moscow. b, 12r, Admiralty Building, St. Petersburg. c, 15r, Moscow State University. d, 25r, Railway Station, Sochi.

2011, May 16   *Perf. 12¼*
7268   A3544   Sheet of 4, #a-d   6.00   2.25

Kiril I. Shchelkin (1911-68), Physicist A3545

2011, May 17   *Perf. 12x12½*
7269   A3545   12r multi   1.25   .45

Irkutsk Arms A3546

Komi Republic Arms A3547

2011, May 26   *Perf. 11¾x12¼*
7270   A3546   8.50r multi   .75   .30
    Complete booklet, 10 #7270   7.50
    Complete booklet, 20 #7270   15.00
7271   A3547   11.80r multi   1.00   .40
    Complete booklet, 10 #7271   10.00
    Complete booklet, 20 #7271   20.00

Kazansky Cathedral, St. Petersburg — A3548

Russian Diplomatic Mission, Cetinje, Montenegro — A3549

2011, May 26   *Perf. 12½x12*
7272   Horiz. pair + central label   3.00   1.10
  a.   A3548 15r multi   1.40   .55
  b.   A3549 15r multi   1.40   .55
See Montenegro Nos. 285-286.

Famous Men — A3550

Designs: No. 7273, 12r, Valery Bryusov (1873-1924), painter. No. 7274, 12r, Hovannes Tumanian (1869-1923), poet.

2011, June 1   *Perf. 12x12½*
7273-7274   A3550   Set of 2   2.25   .85
Nos. 7273-7274 each were printed in sheets of 14 + label. See Armenia Nos. 877-878.

Independence of Venezuela, Bicent. — A3551

2011, June 20   *Perf. 12½x12*
7275   A3551   12r multi   1.25   .45

Irkutsk, 350th Anniv. — A3552

2011, June 24   *Perf. 12x11½*
7276   A3552   15r multi   1.40   .55

Buryatia as Part of Russia, 350th
Anniv. — A3553

2011, June 27   *Perf. 11½*
7277   A3553   11.80r multi   1.25   .40

State Road
Inspection,
75th Anniv.
A3554

2011, June 27   *Litho.*
7278   A3554   15r multi   1.50   .55

Souvenir Sheet

Order of St. Andrew the
Apostle — A3555

2011, July 1   *Perf. 12x12½*
7279   A3555   50r multi   4.50   1.90

Souvenir Sheet

Pechora-Ilych Nature
Reserve — A3556

2011, July 29   *Perf. 12x12¼*
7280   A3556   25r multi   2.25   .85

Souvenir Sheet

Malye Korely Museum of Wooden
Architecture — A3557

No. 7281: a, 10r, Chapel of St. Makary, 18th
cent. b, 15r, Resurrection Church, 17th cent.
c, 20r, Windmill, 20th cent.

2011, Aug. 1
7281   A3557   Sheet of 3, #a-c   4.25   1.60

Bridges — A3558

Designs: 9r, Pochtamtsky Bridge, St.
Petersburg. 10r, Patriarshy Bridge, Moscow.
12r, Kena River Bridge, Arkhangelsk Oblast.
15r, Vezelka River Bridge, Belgorod.

2011, Aug. 15   *Litho.*
7282-7285   A3558   Set of 4   4.25   1.60
   7285a   Souvenir sheet of 8, 2
        each #7282-7285   8.50   3.25

Souvenir Sheet

Cossacks — A3559

No. 7286: a, Amur Cossacks (woman holding pail). b, Astrakhan Cossacks (man on
horse). c, Volga Cossacks (woman holding
jar).

2011, Aug. 29   *Perf. 12x12¼*
7286   A3559   15r Sheet of 3, #a-c   4.00   1.50

Recipients of the Order of St. Andrew
the Apostle — A3560

Designs: No. 7287, 15r, Dmitry S.
Likhachev (1906-99), Russian language and
literature scholar. No. 7288, 15r, Lyudmila G.
Zykina (1929-2009), singer. No. 7289, 15r,
Boris V. Petrovsky (1908-2004), Health
minister.

2011, Sept. 1   *Perf. 12x11¼*
7287-7289   A3560   Set of 3   4.25   1.50
   See Nos. 7369-7371, 7442, 7457, 7478,
   7578, 7846, 7995.

Field Marshal Michael Barclay de Tolly
(1761-1818) — A3561

2011, Sept. 9
7290   A3561   15r multi   1.50   .50
   Printed in sheets of 8 + central label.

Modern Art — A3562

Designs: No. 7291, 14r, Monument to Yuri
Nikulin, sculpture by A. I. Rukavishnikov,
2000. No. 7292, 14r, View of Borisoglebsky
Monastery, painting by N. I. Borovskoy, 2001.
No. 7293, 14r, Seascape, by A. V. Adamov,
2007. No. 7294, 14r, Gymnasts of the
U.S.S.R., painting by D.D. Zhilinsky, 1964-65,
vert. No. 7295, 14r, Aidan, painting by T.T.
Salakhov, 1967, vert. No. 7296, 14r, Akinshino
Village, painting by V. Y. Yukin, 1995
(50x50mm).

   Perf. 12x11¼, 11¼x12, 12 (#7296)
2011, Sept. 12
7291-7296   A3562   Set of 6   8.00   2.75

Souvenir Sheet

Derbent Citadel UNESCO World
Heritage Site — A3563

2011, Sept. 13   *Perf. 12½x12*
7297   A3563   50r multi   4.50   1.75

A3564

A3565

A3566

Traditional
19th and
20th Century
Headdresses
of Northern
Russia
A3567

2011, Sept. 15   *Perf. 12*
7298   A3564   12r multi   1.25   .40
7299   A3565   12r multi   1.25   .40
7300   A3566   12r multi   1.25   .40
7301   A3567   12r multi   1.25   .40
   a.   Souvenir sheet of 8, 2 each
       #7298-7301, perf. 11½x12   10.00   3.25
   Nos. 7298-7301 (4)   5.00   1.60

Worldwide
Fund for
Nature
(WWF),
50th Anniv.
A3568

2011, Sept. 26   *Perf. 11¼*
7302   A3568   15r multi   1.50   .50

Tourist Sites in Sochi — A3569

Designs: 15r, Krasnaya Polyana Ski Resort.
20r, Marine Terminal Building. 25r, Watch-
tower on Bolshoy Akhun Mountain. 30r,
Volkonskiy dolmen.

2011, Sept. 27   Perf. 12½x12
Dated "2011"

7303	A3569	15r multi + label	1.25	.50
7304	A3569	20r multi + label	2.00	.65
7305	A3569	25r multi + label	2.25	.80
7306	A3569	30r multi + label	3.00	.95
a.		Souvenir sheet of 4, #7303-7306, + 4 labels	7.50	3.00
		Nos. 7303-7306 (4)	8.50	2.90

Sochi, host city of 2014 Winter Olympics. Nos. 7303-7306 each were printed in sheets of 6 + 6 labels, with each label being in one of six languages (Russian, English, Chinese, French, Spanish, German). No. 7306a was printed in six versions, with the inscriptions on the labels in the sheet all being in one of the six languages.

See Nos. 7348-7351.

Eurasian Econonim Community Innovative Biotechnologies Program — A3570

2011, Sept. 30   Perf. 13½
7307	A3570	9r multi	1.00	.30

Sports of the 2014 Winter Olympics, Sochi A3571

Designs: No. 7308, 25r, Cross-country skiing. No. 7309, 25r, Ski jumping. No. 7310, 25r, Short-track speed skating.

Litho. & Embossed
2011, Oct. 3   Perf. 11¼
7308-7310	A3571	Set of 3	7.00	2.40
7308a		Dated "2014" at right	2.00	.70
7309a		Dated "2014" at right	2.00	.70
7310a		Dated "2014" at right	2.00	.70

Nos. 7308-7310 each were printed in sheets of 8 + label.

Issued: Nos. 7308a, 7309a, 7310a, 1/24/14.

Regional Communications Commonwealth, 20th Anniv. — A3572

2011, Oct. 10   Litho.   Perf. 12x12½
7311	A3572	12r multi	1.25	.40

Arsenal Factory, 300th Anniv. A3573

2011, Oct. 14   Perf. 11¼
7312	A3573	15r multi	1.50	.50

A3574

Moscow Post Office, 300th Anniv. — A3575

No. 7313: a, Afanasy L. Ordin-Naschokin (c. 1605-80), founder of Russian postal system, horse-drawn mail sleigh, sealed and rolled document . b, Russia #1, 19th cent. stagecoach. c, Russia #856, 5795, postal card, mail box, Moskvich 400-422 mail vehicle. d, Russia #7178, postal cards, Moscow Post Office, mail van.

50r, Wax seal with 300th anniversary emblem.

2011, Oct. 21   Litho.   Perf. 12½x12
7313		Horiz. strip of 4	4.50	1.60
a.-d.	A3574	11.80r Any single	.90	.40

Souvenir Sheet
Litho. & Embossed
Perf.
7314	A3575	50r multi	5.00	1.60

State Kremlin Palace (Kremlin Palace of Congresses), 50th Anniv. — A3576

2011, Oct. 24   Litho.   Perf. 12x12¼
7315	A3576	12r multi	1.25	.40

Constitutional Court, 20th Anniv. — A3577

2011, Oct. 27
7316	A3577	12r multi	1.25	.40

Petr G. Sobolevsky (1782-1841) and People Near Gas Streetlight — A3578

2011, Oct. 28   Perf. 12½x12
7317	A3578	12r multi	1.25	.40

Gas use in Russia, 200th anniv.

Commonweath of Independent States, 20th Anniv. — A3579

2011, Nov. 3   Perf. 12x11½
7318	A3579	11.80r multi	1.25	.40

Souvenir Sheet

Mikhail V. Lomonosov (1711-65), Scientist — A3580

Litho. & Engr.
2011, Nov. 17   Perf. 12¼x12
7319	A3580	100r multi	10.00	3.25
a.		Booklet pane of 1	15.00	
		Complete booklet, #7319a	15.00	

No. 7319a is rectangular. Complete booklet sold for 200r.

Souvenir Sheet

Moskvoretsky Bridge, Painting by Konstantin A. Korovin (1861-1939) — A3581

2011, Nov. 21   Litho.   Perf. 12x12½
7320	A3581	45r multi	4.50	1.50

Empress Catherine II (1729-96) — A3582

2011, Nov. 25   Perf. 12x11½
7321	A3582	8.50r multi	1.00	.30

Insurance in Russia, 225th anniv.

Russian Olympic Committee, Cent. — A3583

2011, Nov. 25   Perf. 12½x12
7322	A3583	15r multi	1.25	.50

Kaluga Oblast A3584

Omsk Oblast A3585

2011   Litho.   Perf. 12x12¼
7323	A3584	11.80r multi	1.25	.40
7324	A3585	11.80r multi	1.25	.40

Issued: No. 7323, 11/30; No. 7324, 12/12.

New Year's Day A3586

Litho. With Foil Application
2011, Dec. 1   Perf. 11¼
7325	A3586	20r multi	2.00	.70

Russian-Italian Year of Culture — A3587

2011, Dec. 10   Litho.   Perf. 12¼x12
7326	A3587	15r multi	1.50	.50

See Italy No. 3110.

Lace — A3588

Lace from: No. 7327, 15r, Belev (brown background). No. 7328, 15r, Elets (red brown background). No. 7329, 15r, Vyatka (purple background). No. 7330, 15r, Vologda (blue background).

Perf. 11¼x11½
2011, Dec. 12   Litho. & Engr.
7327-7330	A3588	Set of 4	5.50	1.90

Souvenir Sheet

Tula Small Arms Factory, 300th Anniv. — A3589

2012, Feb. 1   Litho.   Perf. 12
7331 A3589 50r multi   5.00 1.75

Whales — A3590

No. 7332: a, 15r, Orcinus orca. b, 20r, Megaptera novaeangliae.

2012, Feb. 8   Perf. 13½
7332 A3590 Vert. pair, #a-b   3.25 1.25

Pyotr N. Nesterov (1887-1914), Aeronautical Pioneer — A3591

2012, Feb. 13   Perf. 12½x12
7333 A3591 15r multi   1.50   .55

No. 7333 was printed in sheets of 10 + 2 central labels.

Souvenir Sheet

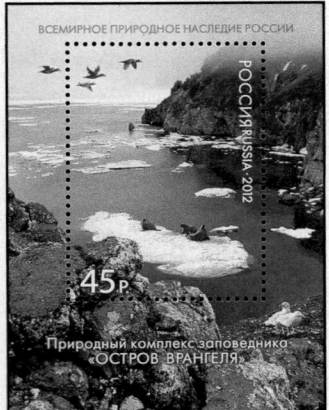

Wrangel Island — A3592

2012, Feb. 27   Perf. 12
7334 A3592 45r multi   4.50 1.60

Mascots for 2014 Winter Olympics, Sochi — A3593

No. 7335: a, Snow Leopard (48x53mm). b, Zaya the Hare (28x44mm). c, Polar Bear (44x59mm).

2012, Feb. 27   Die Cut
Self-Adhesive
7335 A3593 15r Sheet of 3, #a-c   4.25 1.60

Snowflake and Fire Boy, Mascots for 2014 Winter Paralympics, Sochi — A3594

2012, Feb. 27   Die Cut
Self-Adhesive
7336 A3594 30r multi   3.25 1.10

Gold Star Medal A3596

Order of St. George A3597

Order of Merit for the Fatherland A3598

Litho. & Embossed
2012, Mar. 2   Perf. 11¾
7337 A3596 25r multi   2.50   .85
7338 A3597 25r multi   2.50   .85
7339 A3598 25r multi   2.50   .85
      Nos. 7337-7339 (3)   7.50 2.55

Nos. 7337-7339 each were printed in sheets of 7 + label.

Marina M. Raskova (1912-43), Combat Pilot — A3599

2012, Mar. 21 Litho. Perf. 12½x12
7340 A3599 15r multi   1.50   .50

No. 7540 was pritned in sheets of 10 + central label.

Pyotr A. Stolypin (1862-1911), Prime Minister A3600

2012, Apr. 6   Perf. 11½
7341 A3600 15r multi   1.50   .50

World War II Military Vehicles — A3601

Designs: 10r, GAZ-AA truck. 12r, ZIS-5B truck. 14r, GAZ-67B general personnel carrier. 15r, GAZ-M1 automobile.

2012, Apr. 16   Perf. 13½
7342-7345 A3601 Set of 4   5.00 1.75
7345a   Souvenir sheet of 8, 2 each
           #7342-7345   7.00 3.50

A booklet containing panes of one of each of Nos. 7342-7345 was produced in limited quantities. Value, $30.

Miniature Sheet

Towns of Military Glory — A3602

No. 7346 — City names at top: a, Pskov (5 letters in city name with last letter "B," airplanes, cannons and tanks). b, Vyazma (6 letters in city name, airplanes, cannons, artillery launchers). c, Naro-Fominsk (10 letters and hyphen in city name, airplanes, cannons and tanks). d, Tver (5 letters in city name with last letter "b", airplanes, cannons and tanks). e, Kronshtadt (9 letters in city name, cannons, airplanes and ships). f, Dmitrov (7 letters in city name, airplanes, cannons, machine guns).

Litho. With Foil Application
2012, Apr. 20   Perf. 11¼
7346 A3602 15r Sheet of 6, #a-f   9.00 3.25

Emblem of Russian War Veteran's Association — A3603

2012, Apr. 26 Litho. Perf. 11½
7347 A3603 10r multi   1.10   .35

Tourist Sites in Sochi Type of 2011

Designs: 15r, Sail Rock, near Gelendzhik. 20r, Sochi Railway Station. 25r, Gazebo in Botanical Gardens, Sochi. 30r, Orehovsky Waterfall, Sochi.

2012, Apr. 27   Perf. 12½x12
Dated "2012"
7348 A3569 15r multi + label   1.40   .50
7349 A3569 20r multi + label   1.75   .70
7350 A3569 25r multi + label   2.25   .85
7351 A3569 30r multi + label   2.75 1.10
 a.   Souvenir sheet of 4, #7348-
      7351 + 4 labels   8.50 3.25
      Nos. 7348-7351 (4)   8.15 3.15

Nos. 7348-7351 each were printed in sheets of 6 + 6 labels, with each label being in one of six languages (Russian, English, Chines, French, Spanish, German). No. 7351a was printed in six versions, with the inscriptions on the labels in the sheet all being in one of the six languages.

Europa A3604

2012, May 4   Perf. 11½
7352 A3604 15r multi   1.50   .45

Third Inauguration of Pres. Vladimir Putin — A3605

2012, May 7   **Litho. & Embossed**
7353 A3605 15r multi   1.50 .45

Heroes A3606

Gold Star Medal and: No. 7354, 15r, V. V. Zamaryev (1959-2004). No. 7355, 15r, D. A. Razumovsky (1968-2004). No. 7356, 15r, Irina Janina (1966-99). No. 7357, 15r, A. V. Putsykin (1980-2008). No. 7358, 15r, A. B. Tsydenzhapov (1991-2010).

2012, May 7   **Litho.**   **Perf. 12½x12**
7354-7358 A3606   Set of 5   7.00 2.40
Nos. 7354-7358 each were printed in sheets of 5 + label.

Souvenir Sheet

Mikhail V. Nesterov (1862-1942), Painter — A3607

2012, May 17   **Perf. 12x12½**
7359 A3607 30r multi   3.00 .95

Ivan N. Kramskoi (1837-87), Painter A3608

Designs: No. 7360, 15r, Self-portrait (detail), 1867. No. 7361, 15r, Portrait of an Unknown Woman, 1883, horiz.

2012, May 29   **Perf. 11½x12, 12x11½**
7360-7361 A3608   Set of 2   3.00 .95

Souvenir Sheet

Ivan A. Goncharov (1812-91), Writer — A3609

2012, June 4   **Perf.**
7362 A3609 30r multi   3.00 .95

First Non-stop Transpolar Flight, 75th Anniv. A3610

2012, June 6   **Perf. 11½**
7363 A3610 13r multi   1.25 .40
No. 7363 was printed in sheets of 8 + central label.

Souvenir Sheet

Pushkin Museum of Fine Arts, Moscow, Cent. — A3611

2012, June 6   **Perf. 12½x12**
7364 A3611 30r multi   3.00 .95

Monument to Minin and Pozharsky, Moscow A3612

Triumphal Arch, Moscow A3613

2012, June 14   **Perf. 11¾x12¼**
7365 A3612 9.20r multi   .90 .30
   Complete booklet, 10 #7365   9.00
   Complete booklet, 20 #7365   18.00
7366 A3613 13r multi   1.40 .40
   Complete booklet, 10 #7366   14.00
   Complete booklet, 20 #7366   28.00

Newts — A3614

No. 7367: a, Lissotriton vulgaris. b, Triturus cristatus.

2012, June 25   **Perf. 11¼x12**
7367 A3614 13r Pair, #a-b   2.50 .80
See Belarus Nos. 829-830.

Oleg E. Kutafin (1937-2008), Lawyer, and Order of Merit for the Fatherland — A3615

2012, June 26   **Perf. 12½x12**
7368 A3615 15r multi   1.50 .45
Printed in sheets of 14 + label.

Recipients of the Order of St. Andrew Type of 2011

Order of St. Andrew and: No. 7369, 15r, Patriarch Aleksei II (1929-2008). No. 7370, 15r, Irina K. Arkhipova (1925-2010), opera singer. No. 7371, 15r, Valeri I. Shumakov (1931-2008), transplant surgery pioneer.

2012, June 29   **Perf. 12x11½**
7369-7371 A3560   Set of 3   4.50 1.40
Nos. 7369-7371 each were printed in sheets of 11 + label.

Souvenir Sheet

Belozersk, 1050th Anniv. — A3617

2012, July 4   **Perf. 12**
7372 A3617 30r multi   3.00 .95

Souvenir Sheet

Izborsk, 1150th Anniv. — A3618

2012, July 4   **Perf. 12¼x12**
7373 A3618 30r multi   3.00 .95

Record Non-stop Transpolar Flight, 75th Anniv. A3619

2012, July 6   **Perf. 11¼**
7374 A3619 13r multi   1.25 .40
Printed in sheets of 8 + central label.

No. 7111 Srchd.

Method and Perf. As Before
2012, July 6
7375 A3430 12r on 8r #7111   6.00 3.00
Victory of Russian men's ice hockey team in 2012 World Championships.

Churches — A3620

No. 7376: a, Church of the Savior on Spilled Blood, St. Petersburg, Russia. b, Episcopal Palace, Astorga, Spain.

2012, July 17   **Litho.**   **Perf. 11¼**
7376 A3620 13r Pair, #a-b   2.50 .85
No. 7376 was printed in sheets containing 4 pairs + central label. See Spain No. 3863.

Mordovia, 1000th Anniv. — A3621

2012, July 20
7377　A3621　13r multi　　　　1.25　.40

Souvenir Sheet

2012 Summer Olympics,
London — A3622

2012, July 26　　　　*Perf. 11½*
7378　A3622　50r multi　　　4.25　1.60

A3623

A3624

Modern Art — A3625

Designs: No. 7379, Warm Day, by Georgy
A. Leman, 1996. No. 7380, Cossacks' Send
Off, by Sergei A. Gavrilyachenko, 1999. No.
7381, Autumn Interior, by Aleksei N.
Sukhovetsky, 1992. No. 7382, Monument to F.
I. Shalyapin in Kazan, by Andrei V. Balashov,
1999. No. 7383, Russian Madonna, by Vasily
I. Nestorenko, 1992. No. 7384, Mammoths in
Khanty-Mansiysk, by Andrei N. Kovalchuk,
2007.

2012, July 30　　　　*Perf. 12x11½*
7379　A3623　15r multi　　　1.50　.70
7380　A3623　15r multi　　　1.50　.70

　　　　　　Perf. 11½x12
7381　A3624　15r multi　　　1.50　.70
7382　A3624　15r multi　　　1.50　.70
　　　　　　Perf. 11¼
7383　A3625　15r multi　　　1.50　.70
7384　A3625　15r multi　　　1.50　.70
　　　Nos. 7379-7384 (6)　　9.00　4.20

Gleb E. Kotelnikov (1872-1944),
Inventor of Packable
Parachute — A3626

2012, Aug. 2　　　　*Perf. 12½x12*
7385　A3626　13r multi　　　1.00　.40

Friedrich A. Tsander (1887-1933),
Rocketry Pioneer — A3627

2012, Aug. 9　　　　*Litho.*
7386　A3627　9.20r multi　　1.00　.30

Russian Air Force, Cent. — A3628

2012, Aug. 10　　　　*Perf. 13½*
7387　A3628　15r multi　　　1.50　.45

Souvenir Sheet

Rostov, 1150th Anniv. — A3629

2012, Aug. 20　　　　*Perf. 11¾*
7388　A3629　30r multi　　　3.00　.95

Souvenir Sheet

Cossacks — A3630

No. 7389: a, Enisei Cossacks (woman
touching horse). b, Orenburg Cossacks
(woman seated). c, Ussuriisk Cossacks (man
on horse).

2012, Aug. 22　　　　*Perf. 12x12¼*
7389　A3630　15r Sheet of 3, #a-c　4.50　1.50

Souvenir Sheet

War of 1812, Bicent. — A3631

2012, Aug. 27　　　　*Perf. 12*
7390　A3631　50r multi　　　5.00　1.60

Souvenir Sheet

Trinity Monastery of St.
Sergius — A3632

2012, Aug. 30　　　　*Perf. 12x12¼*
7391　A3632　45r multi　　　4.50　1.50

Asia-Pacific Economic Cooperation
Summit, Vladivostok — A3633

2012, Aug. 31　　　　*Perf. 13½*
7392　A3633　13r multi　　　1.25　.40
　A booklet containing one pane of two No.
7392 was printed in a limited edition. Value,
$20.

Souvenir Sheet

On a Visit, Painting by Abram E.
Arkhipov (1862-1930) — A3634

2012, Sept. 7　　　　*Perf. 12x12½*
7393　A3634　50r multi　　　5.00　1.60

Lawyers
A3635

Designs: No. 7394, 15r, Gavrila R.
Derzhavin (1741-1816). No. 7395, 15r, Mikhail
M. Speransky (1772-1839). No. 7396, 15r,
Anatoly F. Koni (1844-1927).

2012, Sept. 7　　　　*Perf. 11½*
7394-7396　A3635　Set of 3　4.50　1.50
　Nos. 7394-7396 each were printed in sheets
of 8 + label. See Nos. 7499-7500, 7588-7590,
7629, 7702-7704, 7791-7793, 7882-7884,
7975-7977.

Fort Ross, Russian Outpost on
California Coast, 200th
Anniv. — A3636

2012, Sept. 11　　　　*Perf. 12x12¼*
7397　A3636　13r multi　　　1.25　.40

Quick
Response
Code and
Emblem of
2014 Winter
Olympics,
Sochi
A3637

Serpentine Die Cut 10
2012, Sept. 18　　　*Self-Adhesive*
7398　A3637　25r multi　　　2.50　.80

Russian Statehood (Founding of Rurik
Dynasty), 1150th Anniv. — A3638

2012, Sept. 19　　　　*Perf. 12x11¼*
7399　A3638　10r multi　　　1.25　.30

Vologda
Region
Costumes
A3639

2012, Sept. 21　　　　*Perf. 11½x12*
7400　A3639　15r multi　　　1.50　.50

Souvenir Sheet

Russian Railways, 175th
Anniv. — A3640

2012, Sept. 30 **Perf. 11¾**
7401 A3640 50r multi 5.00 1.60

North
Shipyard,
Saint
Petersburg,
Cent.
A3641

2012, Oct. 1 **Perf. 11¼**
7402 A3641 15r multi 1.50 .50

Souvenir Sheet

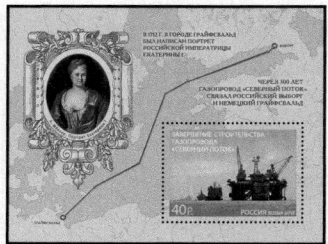

Completion of Gas Pipeline Between
Vyborg and Greifswald,
Germany — A3642

2012, Oct. 5 **Perf. 12**
7403 A3642 40r multi 4.00 1.40

Border
Guards,
500th
Anniv.
A3643

2012, Oct. 10 **Perf. 12¼x12**
7404 A3643 13r multi 1.50 .40

No. 7404 was printed in sheets of 11 + 4
labels.

Sports of the
2014 Winter
Olympics,
Sochi
A3644

Designs: No. 7405, 25r, Freestyle skiing.
No. 7406, 25r, Alpine (downhill) skiing. No.
7407, 25r, Snowboarding. No. 7408, 25r, Skeleton. No. 7409, 25r, Luge. No. 7410, 25r,
Speed skating.

Litho. & Embossed
2012, Oct. 19 **Perf. 11¼**
7405-7410 A3644 Set of 6 15.00 4.75
7405a Dated "2014" at right 2.25 .70
7406a Dated "2014" at right 2.25 .70
7407a Dated "2014" at right 2.25 .70
7408a Dated "2014" at right 2.25 .70
7409a Dated "2014" at right 2.25 .70

7409b Booklet pane of 3, #7309a,
  7408a, 7409a 7.00 —
7410a Dated "2014" at right 2.25 .70
Nos. 7405-7410 each were printed in sheets
of 8 + central label.
Issued: Nos. 7405a, 7406a, 7407a, 7408a,
7409a, 7409b, 7410a, 1/24/14.

Souvenir Sheet

Restoration of National Unity After
"Time of Troubles," 400th
Anniv. — A3645

2012, Nov. 2 Litho. Perf. 12x12½
7411 A3645 40r multi 4.00 1.40

A3646

A3647

A3648

A3649

Cast Iron Moldings From
Kasli — A3649

Litho. & Thermography
2012, Nov. 15
7412 A3646 20r blk & green 2.00 1.00
7413 A3647 20r blk & blue 2.00 1.00
7414 A3648 20r blk & rose brn 2.00 1.00
7415 A3649 20r blk & lilac 2.00 1.00
  Nos. 7412-7415 (4) 8.00 4.00
Nos. 7412-7415 each were printed in sheets
of 4.

Souvenir Sheets

Moscow Coat of Arms — A3650

Saint Petersburg Coat of
Arms — A3651

Litho. & Embossed
2012, Nov. 30 **Perf. 12**
7416 A3650 50r multi 5.00 1.60
7417 A3651 50r multi 5.00 1.60

A booklet containing a pane of No. 7416
and a pane of No. 7417 sold for 226.50r.

Russian Animated Films — A3652

No. 7418: a, Winnie the Pooh (Winnie,
Piglet with umbrella, bees). b, Mowgli (Mowgli, with wolf, bear and panther). c, A Kid and
Karlson (Man, boy sitting in chair, cat and
dog). d, Vovka in the Far-Away Kingdom (boy
sitting, two men in polka-dot clothing).

2012, Dec. 3 Litho. Perf. 12x12¼
7418 A3652 10r Block of 4, #a-d 4.00 1.40

New Year 2013 — A3653

2012, Dec. 3 **Perf. 11¼**
7419 A3653 13r blue 1.25 .40

Souvenir Sheet

Konstantin Stanislavsky (1863-1938),
Theater Director — A3654

2013, Jan. 17 **Perf.**
7420 A3654 50r multi 5.00 1.75

Georgy
Flyorov
(1913-90),
Nuclear
Physicist
A3655

2013, Jan. 21 **Perf. 12¼x12**
7421 A3655 15r multi 1.50 .50
Adoption of name of Flevorium (in honor of
Flyorov) for element 114.

Rams — A3656

No. 7422: a, Ovis ammon. b, Capra caucasica. c, Capra aegagrus. d, Ovis nivicola.

2013, Jan. 30 **Perf. 11½**
7422 A3656 15r Block or strip of
  4, #a-d 6.00 2.00

Miniature Sheet

Towns of Military Glory — A3657

No. 7423 — City names at top: a, Arkhangelsk (11 letters in city name, airplanes, artillery and ships). b, Bryansk (6 letters in city
name, airplanes, mortars on tripods, and
trucks). c, Volokolamsk (11 letters in city
name, biplanes, cannons, and tanks). d,
Kalach-na-Donu (hyphenated city name, airplanes and tanks). e, Kozelsk (8 letters in city
name, biplanes, cannons, and armored locomotives). f, Nalchik (7 letters in city name,
mortars and artillery).

Litho. With Foil Application
2013, Jan. 30
7423 A3657 15r Sheet of 6, #a-f 9.00 3.00

Penza, 350th
Anniv. — A3658

2013, Feb. 8   Litho.   Perf. 12x12¼
7424 A3658 15r multi   1.50   .50

Russian
Orders — A3659

Designs: No. 7425, 25r, Order of Suvorov
(name at top on one line). No. 7426, 25r,
Order of Alexander Nevsky (name at top on
two lines). No. 7427, 25r, Order of St. Catherine the Great (name at top on three lines).

Litho. & Embossed
2013, Feb. 18   Perf. 11¾
7425-7427 A3659 Set of 3   7.50   2.50
Nos. 7425-7427 each were printed in sheets
of 7 + label.

Alexander I. Pokryshkin (1913-85),
Soviet Air Force Marshal — A3660

2013, Feb. 22   Litho.   Perf. 12½x12
7428 A3660 15r multi   1.50   .50
No. 7428 was printed in sheets of 10 + central label.

Military
Heroes
A3661

Designs: No. 7429, 15r, Nikolai S. Maidanov
(1956-2000). No. 7430, 15r, Valery I. Shkurny
(1959-2000). No. 7431, 15r, Evgeny N.
Chernyshev (1963-2010). No. 7432, 15r, Oleg
G. Ilyin (1967-2004). No. 7433, 15r, Yuri A.
Dmitriev (1978-2002).

2013, Feb. 22
7429-7433 A3661 Set of 5   7.00   2.50
Nos. 7429-7433 each were printed in sheets
of 5 + label.

Souvenir Sheet

Uvs Nuur Basin UNESCO World
Heritage Site — A3662

2013, Feb. 27
7434 A3662 45r multi   4.50   1.50
A gritty substance was applied to portions of
the design.

Conifers — A3663

No. 7435: a, Juniperus davurica. b, Microbi-
ota decussata. c, Larix cajanderi. d, Picea
obovata.

**2013, Mar. 4   Serpentine Die Cut 11
Self-Adhesive**
7435 A3663 15r Block of 4, #a-d   6.00   2.00

Souvenir Sheet

General Mikhail D. Skobolev on Horse,
by Nikolai D. Dmitriev-
Orenburgsky — A3664

2013, Mar. 5   Perf. 12x12½
7436 A3664 35r multi   3.50   1.10
Russo-Turkish War, 135th anniv. See Bulgaria No. 4626.

Viktor S. Chernomyrdin (1938-2010),
Prime Minister — A3665

2013, Mar. 14   Perf. 12½x12
7437 A3665 15r multi   1.50   .50
Printed in sheets of 14 + label.

Obukhov
State Plant,
St.
Petersburg,
150th Anniv.
A3666

2013, Mar. 26   Perf. 11¼
7438 A3666 15r multi   1.50   .50
A booklet containing a pane containing one
No. 7438 was printed in limited quantities.
Value, $30.

Diplomatic Relations Between Russia
and Algeria, 50th Anniv. — A3667

2013, Apr. 1   Perf. 12½x12
7439 A3667 10r multi   1.25   .30

Europa — A3668

2013, Apr. 26   Perf. 13½
7440 A3668 15r multi   1.50   .50

Winter Palace — A3669

Admiralty and St. Isaac's
Cathedral — A3670

Old Stock Exchange, Vasilyevsky
Island — A3671

2013, Apr. 26   Perf. 12x12¼
7441   Horiz. strip of 3   4.50   1.50
  a. A3669 10r multi   .90   .30
  b. A3670 15r multi   1.25   .50
  c. A3671 20r multi   1.75   .70
Historic Center of St. Petersburg UNESCO
World Heritage Site.

**Recipients of Order of St. Andrew
Type of 2011**

Design: Order of St. Andrew and Heidar
Aliyev (1923-2003), Pres. of Azerbaijan.

2013, May 6   Perf. 12x11¼
7442 A3560 15r multi   .95   .50
No. 7442 was printed in sheets of 11 +
label. Compare with No. 7457. See Azerbaijan
No. 1022.

World War II Ships — A3672

Designs: 10r, Mine sweeper "Mina." 12r,
Escort ship "Metel." 15r, Armored boat "BKA-
75." 20r, Gunboat "Usyskin."

2013, May 8   Perf. 13½
7443-7446 A3672 Set of 4   5.50   1.90
  7446a   Sheet of 8, 2 each
                #7443-7446   11.00   4.00
A booklet containing panes of one of each
of the stamps was produced in limited quantities. Value, $35.

Souvenir Sheet

Alexandrovskaya Sloboda, 500th
Anniv. — A3673

2013, May 18   Perf. 12x12½
7447 A3673 50r multi   5.00   1.60

Souvenir Sheet

Mission of Saints Cyril and Methodius
to Slavic Lands, 1150th
Anniv. — A3674

2013, May 24   Perf. 12¼x12
7448 A3674 40r multi   4.00   1.25

Scientific Research Ship "Vyacheslav
Tikhonov" — A3675

Oil Tanker "Timofey
Guzhenko" — A3676

2013, June 5   **Perf. 12x11¾**
7449 A3675 14.25r multi   1.50   .45
7450 A3676 14.25r multi   1.50   .45
   Nos. 7449-7450 each were printed in sheets of 8 + label.

A3677

Modern Art — A3678

Designs: No. 7451, On the Trubezh River, by V. P. Polotnov, 2008. No. 7452, Indian Summer, by D. A. Belyukin, 2003. No. 7453, The Girl and the City, by A. A. Lubavin, 2005.

2013, June 17   **Perf. 11¼x12**
7451 A3677 15r multi   1.50   .45
         Perf. 11¼
7452 A3678 15r multi   1.50   .45
7453 A3678 15r multi   1.50   .45
   Nos. 7451-7453 (3)   4.50 1.35

Arms of   Arms of
Aleksandrov   Kazan
A3679   A3680

2013, June 18   **Perf. 11¾x12¼**
7454 A3679 10r multi   1.00   .30
    Complete booklet, 10 #7454   10.00
    Complete booklet, 20 #7454   20.00
7455 A3680 14.25r multi   1.50   .45
    Complete booklet, 10 #7455   15.00
    Complete booklet, 20 #7455   30.00

Souvenir Sheet

27th Summer Universiade,
Kazan — A3681

2013, June 25   **Perf. 12x12¼**
7456 A3681 25r multi   2.50   .80
   A booklet containing one example of No. 7456 sold for 255r. Value, $25.

Order of St. Andrew and Rasul G.
Gamzatov (1923-2003), Poet — A3682

2013, June 28   **Perf. 12x11½**
7457 A3682 15r multi   1.50   .45
   No. 7457 was printed in sheets of 11 + label. Compare with No. 7442.

Sports of the
2014 Winter
Olympics,
Sochi
A3683

Designs: No. 7458, 25r, Nordic combined skiing. No. 7459, 25r, Bobsled. No. 7460, 25r, Pairs figure skating.

Litho. & Embossed
2013, June 29   **Perf. 11¼**
7458-7460 A3683   Set of 3   7.50 2.40
7458a   Dated "2014" at right   2.50   .70
7459a   Dated "2014" at right   2.50   .70
7460a   Dated "2014" at right   2.50   .70
7460b   Booklet pane of 3, #7407a,   7410a, 7460a   7.50   —
   Nos. 7458-7460 each were printed in sheets of 8 + central label.
   Issued: Nos. 7458a, 7459a, 7460a, 7460b, 1/24/14.

Gull and Russia
No.
2753 — A3684

2013, July 5   **Litho.**   **Perf. 11¾**
7461 A3684 14.25r multi   1.50   .45
   Space flight of Valentina Tereshkova, first woman in space, 50th anniv.

Kerchief From Karabanovo — A3685

Kerchief From Trekhgorny Factory,
Moscow — A3686

Kerchief From Orenburg — A3687

Shawl From Pavlovsky
Posad — A3688

2013, July 5   **Perf. 11½**
7462 A3685 15r multi   1.50   .45
7463 A3686 15r multi   1.50   .45
7464 A3687 15r multi   1.50   .45
7465 A3688 15r multi   1.50   .45
   Nos. 7462-7465 (4)   6.00 1.80
   Nos. 7462-7465 each were printed in sheets of 4.

Souvenir Sheet

Christianization of Russia, by V. M.
Vasnetsov — A3689

2013, July 28   **Litho.**   **Perf. 12**
7466 A3689 30r multi   3.00   .95
   Christianization of Russia, 1025th anniv. See Belarus No. 870, Ukraine No. 930.

Souvenir Sheet

Penza Coat of Arms — A3690

2013, Aug. 2   **Litho.**   **Perf. 12x12½**
7467 A3690 50r multi   5.00 1.50

MS Princess Anastasia — A3691

2013, Aug. 5   **Litho.**   **Perf. 12**
7468 A3691 14.25r multi   1.50   .45
   See Finland (Aland Islands) No. 347.

18th Intl. Track and Field
Championships, Moscow — A3692

2013, Aug. 10   **Litho.**   **Perf. 12¼x12**
7469 A3692 14.25r multi   1.50   .45

Miniature Sheet

Aircraft Designed by Andrei N. Tupolev
(1888-1972) — A3693

   No. 7470: a, 10r, Tu-2. b, 13r, Tb-7. c, 15r, Tu-16. d, 17r, Tu-22M3. e, 20r, Tu-95.

2013, Aug. 13   **Litho.**   **Perf. 12¼x12**
7470 A3693   Sheet of 5, #a-e, +   label   7.50 2.10

Kolomna
Locomotive
Works, 150th
Anniv.
A3694

2013, Aug. 15   **Litho.**   **Perf. 11¼**
7471 A3694 15r multi   1.50   .45

Communications Satellite, Arrows and
Map of Russia — A3695

2013, Aug. 21   **Litho.**   **Perf. 12¼x12**
7472 A3695 14.25r multi   1.50   .45

Paintings by Ivan Myasoyedov (Eugen
Zotow) (1881-1953) — A3696

   No. 7473: a, Voyage of the Argonauts, 1909. b, Silum, 1945.

2013, Sept. 2   **Litho.**   **Perf. 12x11¼**
7473 A3696 15r Pair, #a-b   3.50   .95
   Printed in sheets of 10 containing 5 each #7473a-7473b, + 2 labels. See Liechtenstein No. 1592.

Souvenir Sheet

Discovery of Severnaya Zemlya
Archipelago, Cent. — A3697

No. 7474: a, Icebreaker Vaigach (ship facing
left). b, Boris A. Vilkitsky (1885-1961), hydrographer and expedition leader, vert. c, Icebreaker Taimyr (ship facing right).

Perf. 12x12¼, 12¼x12 (#7474b)
2013, Sept. 4
7474 A3697 15r Sheet of 3, #a-c 4.00 1.40

A booklet containing three panes, each containing one each of Nos. 7474a-7474c sold for 284r. Value, $35.

18th Conference
of Intl.
Association
of
Prosecutors,
Moscow — A3698

2013, Sept. 6 Litho. Perf. 12x12¼
7475 A3698 15r multi 1.50 .45

Souvenir Sheet

Smolensk, 1150th Anniv. — A3699

2013, Sept. 21 Litho. Perf. 12¼x12
7476 A3699 50r multi 5.00 1.60

Souvenir Sheet

Olympic Flame — A3700

2013, Oct. 7 Litho. Perf. 12
7477 A3700 50r multi 5.00 1.60

2014 Winter Olympics, Sochi.

**Recipients of the Order of St.
Andrew Type of 2012**

Design: Order of St. Andrew and Sergey V.
Mikhalkov (1913-2009), writer.

2013, Oct. 9 Litho. Perf. 12x11¼
7478 A3560 15r multi 1.50 .45

No. 7478 was printed in sheets of 11 + label.

Souvenir Sheet

Coat of Arms of Yaroslavl — A3701

2013, Oct. 11 Litho. Perf. 12x12½
7479 A3701 50r multi 5.00 1.60

Souvenir Sheet

Battle of Leipzig, by Carl
Rechlin — A3702

2013, Oct. 19 Litho. Perf. 12x12½
7480 A3702 50r multi 5.00 1.60
Battle of Leipzig, 200th anniv.

Modern
Art — A3703

Designs: No. 7481, 15r, Monument to A. I.
Pokryshkin, by M. V. Pereyaslavets, 2005. No.
7482, 15r, Bouquet, by V. M. Malyi, 2005. No.
7483, 15r, Kerosene, by A. L. Bobykin, 2012,
horiz.

Perf. 11½x12, 12x11½
2013, Oct. 25 Litho.
7481-7483 A3703 Set of 3 4.50 1.40

Sports of the
2014 Winter
Olympics,
Sochi
A3704

Designs: No. 7484, Biathlon. No. 7485,
Curling. No. 7486, Ice hockey.

Litho. & Embossed
2013-14 Perf. 11¼
Dated "2013" at Right
7484 A3704 25r multi 2.50 .75
  a. Dated "2014" at right 2.50 .70
  b. Booklet pane of 3, #7406a,
    7459a, 7484a 7.50 —
7485 A3704 25r multi 2.50 .75
  a. Dated "2014" at right 2.50 .70
  b. Booklet pane of 3, #7308a,
    7458a, 7485a 7.50 —
7486 A3704 25r multi 2.50 .75
  a. Dated "2014" at right 2.50 .70
  b. Sheet of 15, #7308a,
    7309a, 7310a, 7405a,
    7406a, 7407a, 7408a,
    7409a, 7410a, 7458a,
    7459a, 7460a, 7484a,
    7485a, 7486a, + label 37.50 10.50
  c. Booklet pane of 3, #7310a,
    7405a, 7486a 7.50 —

Complete booklet, #7409b,
  7460b, 7484b, 7485b,
  7486c 37.50
  Nos. 7484-7486 (3) 7.50 2.25

Issued: Nos. 7484-7486, 11/1; Nos. 7484a,
7484b, 7485a, 7485b, 7486a, 7486b, 7486c,
1/24/14.
Nos. 7484-7486 were each printed in sheets
of 8 + central label. Complete booklet sold for
595r.

Sambo, 75th
Anniv. — A3705

2013, Nov. 1 Litho. Perf. 12x12½
7487 A3705 10r multi 1.25 .30

Police Uniforms
A3706

Designs: No. 7488, 15r, Dragoon and police
officer, 1718. No. 7489, 15r, Police officer and
captain, 19th cent. No. 7490, 15r, Traffic
policeman and militia foreman, 1934. No.
7491, 15r, Police lieutenant and major general, 2012.

2013, Nov. 8 Litho. Perf. 11¾
7488-7491 A3706 Set of 4 6.00 1.90
7491a Souvenir sheet of 8, 2
  each #7488-7491 12.00 3.75

Miniature Sheets

A3707

Sports Legends — A3708

No. 7492: a, Yevgeny Grishin (1931-2005),
speed skater. b, Lyudmila Pakhomova (1946-86), ice dancer. c, Vladimir Melanin (1933-94),
biathlete. d, Alexander Ragulin (1941-2004),
ice hockey player. e, Anatoly Firsov (1941-2000), ice hockey player.
No. 7493: a, Klavdiya Boyarskikh (1939-2009), cross-country skier. b, Vsevolod
Bobrov (1922-79), soccer and ice hockey
player. c, Tatyana Averina (1950-2001), speed
skater. d, Pierre de Coubertin (1863-1937),
founder of the Modern Olympic Games. e,
Ludwig Guttman (1899-1980), founder of the
Paralympic Games.

2013 Litho. Perf. 11¾
7492 A3707 15r Sheet of 5, #a-e 7.50 2.40
7493 A3708 15r Sheet of 5, #a-e 7.50 2.40

2014 Winter Olympics, Sochi. Issued: No.
7492, 11/15; No. 7493, 12/14.

New Year
2014
A3709

Mascots of the 2014 Winter Olympics,
Sochi: No. 7494, 20r, Leopard. No. 7495, 20r,
Hare. No. 7496, 20r, Polar Bear. No. 7497,
20r, Snowflake and Ray of Light.

Serpentine Die Cut 11
2013, Nov. 29 Litho.
Self-Adhesive
7494-7497 A3709 Set of 4 8.00 2.50
7497a Sheet of 8, 2 each
  #7494-7497 16.00

Miniature Sheet

Venues of the 2014 Winter Olympics
and Paralympics, Sochi — A3710

No. 7498: a, Crowd outside of Fisht Olympic
Stadium. b, Biathletes at Laura Biathlon and
Ski Complex. c, Ski jumps at Russki Gorki
Jumping Center. d, Crowds and flagpoles
outside of Bolshoi Ice Dome. e, Iceberg Skating Palace at night. f, Photographer and crowd
outside of Shayba Arena.

2013, Nov. 30 Litho. Perf. 11¾
7498 A3710 20r Sheet of 6, #a-f 12.50 3.75

Lawyers Type of 2012

Designs: No. 7499, 15r, Alexander N. Radishchev (1749-1802). No. 7500, 15r, Fedor N.
Plevako (1842-1909).

2013, Dec. 3 Litho. Perf. 11½
7499-7500 A3635 Set of 2 3.00 .95

Nos. 7499-7500 each were printed in sheets
of 8 + label.

Automobiles
A3711

No. 7501: a, ZiL-111B. b, Sunbeam Alpine.

2013, Dec. 5 Litho. Perf. 11½
7501 A3711 15r Pair, #a-b 3.00 .95

Printed in sheets containing four each
#7501a-7501b + central label. See Monaco
No. 2740.

State Duma, 20th Anniv. — A3712

Federation Council, 20th Anniv. — A3713

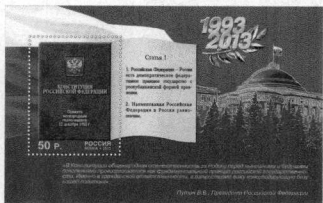

Constitution, 20th Anniv. — A3714

2013, Dec. 12   Litho.   Perf. 11½
7502 A3712 20r multi   2.00 .60
7503 A3713 20r multi   2.00 .60

Souvenir Sheet
Perf. 12
7504 A3714 50r multi   5.00 1.60

Vladimir A. Steklov (1864-1926), Mathematician — A3715

2014, Jan. 9   Litho.   Perf. 12½x12
7505 A3715 15r multi   1.50 .45

Order of Zhukov A3716

Order of Kutuzov A3717

Order of Ushakov A3718

Litho. & Embossed
2014, Jan. 31   Perf. 11¾
7506 A3716 25r multi   2.50 .70
7507 A3717 25r multi   2.50 .70
7508 A3718 25r multi   2.50 .70
    Nos. 7506-7508 (3)   7.50 2.10

Nos. 7506-7508 each were printed in sheets of 7 + label.

Souvenir Sheet

Medals of the 2014 Winter Olympics, Sochi — A3719

No. 7509: a, 25r, Bronze medal. b, 50r, Silver medal. c, 75r, Gold medal, vert.

Perf. 12x12¼, 12¼x12 (75r)
2014, Feb. 7   Litho. & Embossed
7509 A3719   Sheet of 3, #a-c 15.00 4.25
  d.   As #7509, overprinted with
        Cyrillic text in red in sheet
        margin   15.00 4.25

Issued: No. 7509d, 4/25. Overprint on No. 7509d gives medal count of Russian team (13 gold, 11 silver, 9 bronze) at 2014 Winter Olympics.

Souvenir Sheet

Moscow Zoo, 150th Anniv. — A3720

2014, Feb. 13   Litho.   Perf. 12
7510 A3720 40r multi   4.00 1.10

Military Heroes A3721

Designs: No. 7511, 15r, Aleksandr V. Perov (1975-2004) (shown). No. 7512, 15r, Andrei A. Turkin (1975-2004). No. 7513, 15r, Andrei N. Rozhkov (1961-98). No. 7514, 15r, Viktor S. Chechviy (1960-99). No. 7515, 15r, Mikhail Y. Malofeev (1956-2000).

2014, Feb. 21   Litho.   Perf. 12½x12
7511-7515 A3721   Set of 5   7.50 2.10

Nos. 7511-7515 were each printed in sheets of 5 + label.

Souvenir Sheet

Medals of the 2014 Winter Paralympics, Sochi — A3722

No. 7516: a, 25r, Bronze medal. b, 50r, Silver medal. c, 75r, Gold medal, vert.

Perf. 12x12¼, 12¼x12 (75r)
2014   Litho. & Embossed
7516 A3722   Sheet of 3, #a-c 12.00 4.25
  d.   As #7516, overprinted with
        Cyrillic text in red in sheet
        margin   12.00 4.25

Issued: No. 7516, 3/7; No. 7516d, 4/25. Overprint on No. 7516d gives medal count of Russian team (30 gold, 28 silver, 22 bronze) at 2014 Winter Paralympics.

Souvenir Sheet

Summer Garden, by Aleksei Mikhailovich Gritsai (1914-98) — A3723

2014, Mar. 7   Litho.   Perf. 12x12¼
7517 A3723 50r multi   5.00 1.50

Flowers — A3724

No. 7518: a, Chamaenerion angustifolium. b, Lupinus polyphyllus. c, Cichorium intybus. d, Matricaria recutita.

2014, Mar. 14   Litho.   Perf. 11¼
7518 A3724 15r Block of 4, #a-d 6.50 1.75

Mark L. Gallai (1914-98), Test Pilot, and M-3 Bomber A3725

2014, Mar. 28   Litho.   Perf. 12½x12
7519 A3725 15r multi   1.50 .40

No. 7519 was printed in sheets of 10 + central label.

Souvenir Sheet

Liberation of Russia, Belarus and Ukraine From Nazi Occupation, 70th Anniv. — A3726

2014, Apr. 18   Litho.   Perf. 12x12¼
7520 A3726 50r multi   5.00 1.50

See Belarus No. 898.

Ekaterina I. Zelenko (1916-41), World War II Pilot — A3727

Boris I. Kovzan (1922-85), World War II Pilot — A3728

Alexei S. Khlobystov (1918-43), World War II Pilot — A3729

Petr V. Eremeyev (1911-41), World War II Pilot — A3730

2014, Apr. 18   Litho.   Perf. 13½
7521 A3727 15r multi   1.50 .40
7522 A3728 15r multi   1.50 .40
7523 A3729 15r multi   1.50 .40
7524 A3730 15r multi   1.50 .40
  a.   Sheet of 8, 2 each #7521-
        7524   12.00 3.50
    Nos. 7521-7524 (4)   6.00 1.60

Nos. 7521-7524 were each printed in sheets of 7 + label.

World War II Artillery — A3731

Designs: 12r, 53-K 45-mm anti-tank gun.
15r, ZIS-3 76-mm divisional gun. 18r, 52-K 85-
mm anti-aircraft gun. 20r, M-30 122-mm
howitzer.

2014, Apr. 25   Litho.   Perf. 13½
7525-7528 A3731   Set of 4   7.00 1.90
7528a   Sheet of 8, 2 each   14.00 4.00
#7525-7528

A booklet containing four panes of one of
each of Nos. 7525-7528 sold for 350r. Value,
$40.

Musicians
Playing
Balalaika and
Accordion
A3732

2014, Apr. 30   Litho.   Perf. 12
7529 A3732 18r multi   1.90 .50

Europa.

Yakov B.
Zeldovich
(1914-87),
Physicist
A3733

2014, May 5   Litho.   Perf. 12¼x12
7530 A3733 15r multi   1.50 .45

Clock Towers and Clocks — A3734

No. 7531: a, 15r, Zytglogge, Bern, Switzerland. b, 20r, Kazansky Tower, Moscow.

2014, May 21   Litho.   Perf. 11¼
7531 A3734   Pair, #a-b   3.50 1.00

No. 7531 was printed in sheets of 8 (4 of
each stamp) + central label. See Switzerland
Nos. 1528-1529.

Concord Tower, Magas — A3735

2014, June 4   Litho.   Perf. 11¼
7532 A3735 15r multi   1.50 .45

Souvenir Sheet

St. Petersburg Post Office, 300th
Anniv. — A3736

2014, June 10   Litho.   Perf.
7533 A3736 50r multi   5.00 1.50

Crimean
Republic
A3737

Sevastopol
A3738

2014   Litho.   Perf. 12x12¼
7534 A3737 15r multi   1.50 .45
Perf. 12¼x12
7535 A3738 15r multi   1.50 .45

Issued: No. 7534, 6/19; No. 7535, 6/20.

Souvenir Sheet

Hermitage Museum, 250th
Anniv. — A3739

2014, June 20   Litho.   Perf. 11¾
7536 A3739 50r multi   5.00 1.50

Arms of Sergiev
Posad — A3740

Perf. 11¾x12¼
2014, June 24   Litho.
7537 A3740 10.50r multi   1.10 .30
  Complete booklet, 10 #7537   10.00
  Complete booklet, 20 #7537   20.00

Topol-M Missile Launcher and
Barricades Manufacturing
Plant — A3741

2014, June 26   Litho.   Perf. 11¼
7538 A3741 15r multi   1.60 .45

Barricades Manufacturing Plant, Volgograd,
cent.

Vladimir
N.
Chelomey
(1914-84).
Missile
Engineer
A3742

2014, June 27   Litho.   Perf. 12¼x12
7539 A3742 15r multi   1.50 .45

Tuva as Part of Russia,
Cent. — A3743

2014, June 27   Litho.   Perf. 11¼
7540 A3743 15r multi   1.50 .45

Souvenir Sheet

Approval of Construction of Baikal-
Amur Mainline Railway, 40th
Anniv. — A3744

2014, July 2   Litho.   Perf. 12
7541 A3744 40r multi   4.00 1.25

Diplomatic Relations Between Russia
and Bulgaria, 135th Anniv.
A3745

2014, July 7   Litho.   Perf. 12¼x12
7542 A3745 15r multi   1.50 .40

See Bulgaria No. 4684.

Hero of Labor of
the Russian
Federation
Medal — A3746

Medal for the
Defense of
Leningrad
A3747

Medal for the
Defense of
Sevastopol
A3748

Medal for the
Defense of
Stalingrad
A3749

Medal for the
Defense of
Moscow
A3750

Litho. & Embossed
2014, July 7   Perf. 11¾
7543 A3746 25r multi   2.50 .70
7544 A3747 25r multi   2.50 .70
7545 A3748 25r multi   2.50 .70
7546 A3749 25r multi   2.50 .70
7547 A3750 25r multi   2.50 .70
  Nos. 7543-7547 (5)   12.50 3.50

Nos. 7543-7547 were each printed in sheets
of 7 + label.

Hugo Chávez (1954-2013), President of Venezuela — A3751

2014, July 28   Litho.   Perf. 12x12¼
7548 A3751 15r multi   .85   .40

World War I, Cent. — A3752

Designs: No. 7549, 20r, Soldiers charging with rifles with bayonets, map of battle for Osovets Fortress. No. 7550, 20r, Soldiers and cannon, map of battle for Erzum Fortress. No. 7551, 20r, General Aleksei A. Brusilov (seated) and his officers, map of Brusilov Offensive. No. 7552, 20r, Russian Expeditionary Corps in France (with flag), map of Europe and Asia.

2014, July 31   Litho.   Perf. 12
7549-7552 A3752 Set of 4   8.00 2.25

Nos. 7549-7552 were each printed in sheets of 11 + label. A booklet containing panes of one of each of the stamps was produced in limited quantities. Value, $40.

Souvenir Sheet

Battle of Gangut, 300th Anniv. — A3753

2014, Aug. 1   Litho.   Perf. 11¾
7553 A3753 50r multi   5.00 1.40

Wild Cats — A3754

No. 7554: a, 15r, Otocolobus manul. b, 16r, Felis silvestris. c, 17r, Prionailurus bengalensis euptilurus. d, 18r, Felis chaus.

2014, Aug. 1   Litho.   Perf. 13½
7554 A3754 Block or vert. strip
              of 4, #a-d   7.00 1.90
              See No. 7581.

Medal for the Defense of the Caucasus A3755

Medal for the Defense of Kiev — A3756

Medal for the Defense of Odessa A3757

Medal for the Defense of the Arctic — A3758

Litho. & Embossed
2014, Aug. 8   Perf. 11¾
7555 A3755 25r multi   2.50   .70
7556 A3756 25r multi   2.50   .70
7557 A3757 25r multi   2.50   .70
7558 A3758 25r multi   2.50   .70
        Nos. 7555-7558 (4)   10.00 2.80

Nos. 7555-7558 were each printed in sheets of 7 + label.

Kyzyl, Cent. A3759

2014, Aug. 23   Litho.   Perf. 12½x12
7559 A3759 15r multi   1.50   .40

Icebreaker Vitus Bering — A3760

Tugboat Sadko — A3761

2014, Aug. 26   Litho.   Perf. 12
7560 A3760 15r multi   1.50   .40
7561 A3761 15r multi   1.50   .40

Battles of Khakhin Gol, 75th Anniv. — A3762

2014, Aug. 28   Litho.   Perf. 11½
7562 A3762 15r multi   1.50   .40
        See Mongolia No. 2816.

Miniature Sheet

Towns of Military Glory — A3763

No. 7563 — City names at top: a, Anapa (5 letters in city name, airplanes, guns and ships). b, Vladivostok (11 letters in city name, airplanes, trucks and ships). c, Kovrov (6 letters in city name, guns and tanks). d, Kolpino (7 letters in city name, airplanes and tanks). e, Stary Oscol (2 words in city name, airplanes, guns and tanks). f, Tikhvin (6 letters in city name, airplanes and tanks).

Litho. With Foil Application
2014, Aug. 28   Perf. 11½
7563 A3763 20r Sheet of 6, #a-f 12.50 3.25

Uniforms of Postal and Communications Workers A3764

Designs: No. 7564, 15r, Clerk and postman of Yamskoi Post Office, 1671. No. 7565, 15r, Postman and official from Yamskoi Post Office, 1767. No. 7566, 15r, Official and telegraph operator, 1870. No. 7567, 15r, Postman and operator, 1950.

2014, Sept. 1   Litho.   Perf. 13½
7564-7567 A3764 Set of 4   6.00 1.60
7567a   Souvenir sheet of 8, 2
            each #7564-7567   12.00 3.25

Printing in Russia, 450th Anniv. — A3765

2014, Sept. 3   Litho.   Perf. 12x11¼
7568 A3765 15r multi   1.50   .40

Souvenir Sheet

Kolomenskoye Church of the Ascenscion UNESCO World Heritage Site — A3766

2014, Sept. 5   Litho.   Perf. 12x12½
7569 A3766 45r multi   4.50 1.10

Souvenir Sheet

St. Sergius of Radonezh (1314-92), Monk — A3767

Litho. & Silk-Screened
2014, Sept. 16   Perf. 12
7570 A3767 70r multi   7.00 1.75

Special Communications Center and Vehicles — A3768

2014, Sept. 18   Litho.   Perf. 12½x12
7571 A3768 18r multi   1.90   .45

Souvenir Sheet

Coat of Arms of City of
Krasnodar — A3769

2014, Sept. 25   Litho.   *Perf. 12x12½*
7572 A3769 50r multi   5.00 1.25

Ice Hockey — A3770

2014, Oct. 7   Litho.   *Perf. 13½*
7573 A3770 20r multi   2.10 .45

Formula 1 Race Cars — A3771

2014, Oct. 12   Litho.   *Perf. 13½*
7574 A3771 15r multi   1.50 .30
2014 Sochi Grand Prix.

Birds — A3772

2014, Oct. 12   Litho.   *Perf. 12½x12*
7575 A3772 Horiz. pair   3.50 .70
  a.   15r Accipiter nisus   1.50 .30
  b.   18r Pandion haliaetus   2.00 .40
See North Korea No.

Souvenir Sheet

Mikhail Lermontov (1814-41),
Writer — A3773

2014, Oct. 15   Litho.   *Perf. 12½x12*
7576 A3773 50r multi   2.25 1.10

Arms of Sochi — A3774

2014, Oct. 21   Litho.   *Perf. 11¾x12¼*
7577 A3774 15r multi   1.50 .30
  Complete booklet, 10 #7577   15.00
  Complete booklet, 20 #7577   30.00

Recipients of the Order of St. Andrew Type of 2011

Design: Order of St. Andrew and General Mikhail Kalashnikov (1919-2013), arms designer.

2014, Oct. 24   Litho.   *Perf. 12x11¼*
7578 A3560 15r multi   1.50 .30
No. 7578 was printed in sheets of 11 + label.

Galina Vishnevskaya (1926-2012),
Opera Singer — A3775

2014, Oct. 24   Litho.   *Perf. 12½x12*
7579 A3775 15r multi   1.50 .30
No. 7579 was printed in sheets of 14 + label.

Souvenir Sheet

Imperial Orthodox Palestine
Society — A3776

No. 7580: a, Grand Duchess Elizabeth (1864-1918), holy martyr of Russian Orthodox Church. b, Society emblem. c, Sergei Imperial Hospice, Russian Compound, Jerusalem.

2014, Oct. 29   Litho.   *Perf. 12x12¼*
7580 A3776 20r Sheet of 3, #a-c   6.00 1.40

Wild Cats Type of 2014

No. 7581: a, 15r, Uncia uncia. b, 18r, Panthera pardus orientalis. c, 20r, Panthera tigris altaica.

2014, Nov. 7   Litho.   *Perf. 11¾*
7581 A3754 Horiz. strip of 3,
              #a-c   6.50 1.25

Georgi N. Babakin (1914-71), Designer of Spacecraft A3777

2014, Nov. 13   Litho.   *Perf. 12½x12*
7582 A3777 15r multi   1.50 .30

Souvenir Sheet

2014 World Cup Soccer
Championships, Brazil — A3778

2014, Nov. 25   Litho.   *Perf.*
7583 A3778 50r multi   5.00 .95

Kerzhensky Nature Reserve — A3779

2014, Nov. 25   Litho.   *Perf. 12x12¼*
7584 A3779 15r multi   1.50 .30

Carved Wooden Door Trim From
Nizhny Novgorod — A3780

Carved Wooden Door Trim From
Pskov — A3781

Nos. 7585 and 7586: a, Denomination at left. b, Denomination at right.

2014, Nov. 28   Litho.   *Perf. 11½*
7585 A3780 20r Horiz. pair, #a-b   4.25 .75
7586 A3781 20r Horiz. pair, #a-b   4.25 .75
A varnish applied to parts of the vignette has a rough feel.

Souvenir Sheet

Coat of Arms of City of Tver — A3782

2014, Dec. 2   Litho.   *Perf. 12x12½*
7587 A3782 50r multi   5.00 .95

Lawyers Type of 2012

Designs: No. 7588, 15r, Count Pavel I. Yaguzhinsky (1683-1736). No. 7589, 15r, Fedor F. Martens (1845-1909). No. 7590, 15r, Sergei A. Muromtsev (1850-1910).

2014, Dec. 3   Litho.   *Perf. 11½*
7588-7590 A3635 Set of 3   5.00 .80
Nos. 7588-7590 were each printed in sheets of 8 + label.

Modern Art — A3783

Designs: No. 7591, 15r, Peresvet's Victory, by Pavel V. Ryzhenko, 2005. No. 7592, 15r, Lilacs, by Polina V. Mineeva, 2010. No. 7593, 15r, Pskov Kremlin, by Sergei N. Troshin, 2011. No. 7594, 15r, Spring in Kolomenskoe, by Ivan Krivshinko, 2002 (50x38mm). No. 7595, 15r, River Vorya Near Radonezh, by Aleksandr K. Sytov, 2005 (50x38mm). No. 7596, 15r, Statue of Alexander Nevsky, by Alexei I. Ignatov, 2013 (33x65mm).

Perf. 11¼, 12x11½ (#7594-7595), 13½ (#7596)
2014, Dec. 12   Litho.
7591-7596 A3783 Set of 6   9.50 1.60

New Year 2015 — A3784

2014, Dec. 12   Litho.   *Perf. 12x11½*
7597 A3784 15r multi   1.25 .25

Europa A3785

2015, Jan. 16   Litho.   *Perf. 11½x12*
7598 A3785 23r multi   2.50 .35

Souvenir Sheet

October, Domotkanovo, by Valentin A.
Serov (1865-1911) — A3786

2015, Jan. 22   Litho.   *Perf. 12½x12*
7599 A3786 50r multi   5.00 .75

Postcrossing A3787

Serpentine Die Cut 10
2015, Jan. 27   Litho.
Self-Adhesive
7600 A3787 23r multi   2.50 .35

Souvenir Sheet

Lena Pillars Nature Park UNESCO
World Heritage Site — A3788

2015, Feb. 10   Litho.   *Perf. 12½x12*
7601 A3788 50r multi   5.00 .80

Sergei P. Kapitsa (1928-2012), Physicist and Host of Television Science Shows A3789

2015, Feb. 12   Litho.   Perf. 11½x12
7602 A3789 15r multi   1.50   .25

Miniature Sheet

Towns of Military Glory — A3790

No. 7603 — City names at top: a, Lomonosov (9 letters in city name, trucks, tanks, ships). b, Maloyaroslavets (13 letters in city name, artillery). c, Mozhaisk (7 letters in city name, airplanes, cannons, barricades). d, Petropavlovsk-Kamchatsky (23 letters in city name, airplanes, guns, submarines). e, Taganrog (8 letters in city name, airplanes, tanks, submarines). f, Khabarovsk (9 letters in city name, airplanes, trucks, ships).

Litho. With Foil Application
2015, Feb. 15   Perf. 11½
7603 A3790 20r Sheet of 6, #a-f 12.50 2.00

Order of Nakhimov A3791

Order of Courage A3792

Order of Friendship A3793

Litho. & Embossed
2015, Feb. 19   Perf. 11¾
7604 A3791 25r multi   2.50   .40
7605 A3792 25r multi   2.50   .40
7606 A3793 25r multi   2.50   .40
      Nos. 7604-7606 (3)   7.50   1.20

Nos. 7604-7606 were each printed in sheets of 7 + label.

Spies A3794

Designs: No. 7607, 16r, Alexander I. Galushkin (1903-42). No. 7608, 16r, Pavel M. Silaev (1916-42).

2015, Mar. 18   Litho.   Perf. 11½
7607-7608 A3794 Set of 2   3.25   .60

Nos. 7607-7608 were each printed in sheets of 8 + label.

Submariners — A3795

No. 7609: a, Captain Evgeni Y. Osipov (1913-43), denomination at LR. b, Captain Alexander I. Marinesco (1913-63), denomination at LL.

2015, Mar. 19   Litho.   Perf. 12
7609 A3795 Horiz. pair + central label   3.25   .60
a.-b. 16r Either single   1.50   .30

Felix Dzerzhinsky Independent Operational Purpose Division — A3796

2015, Mar. 21   Litho.   Perf. 13½
7610 A3796 17r multi   1.75   .30

Zemstvo Post, 150th Anniv. A3797

2015, Mar. 26   Litho.   Perf. 12½x12
7611 A3797 20r multi   1.50   .35

Liberation of Warsaw Medal — A3798

Liberation of Prague Medal — A3799

Liberation of Belgrade Medal — A3800

Litho. & Embossed
2015, Apr. 2   Perf. 11¾
7612 A3798 30r multi   3.00   2.00
7613 A3799 30r multi   3.00   2.00
7614 A3800 30r multi   3.00   2.00
      Nos. 7612-7614 (3)   9.00   6.00

Nos. 7612-7614 were each printed in sheets of 7 + label.

First Spacewalk, 50th Anniv. — A3801

2015, Apr. 10   Litho.   Perf. 12x12½
7615 A3801 17r multi   1.50   .35

Blood Donation Program — A3802

2015, Apr. 16   Litho.   Perf. 12½x12
7616 A3802 17r multi   1.50   .35

Trees — A3803

No. 7617: a, Pinus stankewiczii. b, Juniperus excelsa. c, Acer platanoides. d, Quercus robur.

Serpentine Die Cut 11
2015, Apr. 16   Litho.
Self-Adhesive
7617 A3803 20r Block of 4, #a-d 8.00 1.60

Russian Federation Accounting Bureau — A3804

2015, Apr. 17   Litho.   Perf. 12x11½
7618 A3804 20r multi   2.00   .40

Penny Black, 175th Anniv. — A3805

2015, Apr. 23   Litho.   Perf. 12x11½
7619 A3805 26.50r multi   2.50   .55

World War II Armored Trains — A3806

Train named: 12r, Moscow Metro. 17r, Fighter of the German Invaders. 19r, Moskvich. 27r, Kozma Minin.

2015, Apr. 30   Litho.   Perf. 13½
7620-7623 A3806 Set of 4   5.50   1.50
7623a   Souvenir sheet of 8, 2 each #7620-7623   11.00   3.00

A booklet containing panes of one of each of the stamps was produced in limited quantities. Value, $40.

Souvenir Sheet

Victory in Europe in World War II, 70th Anniv. — A3807

2015, May 5   Litho.   Perf. 11¾
7624 A3807 70r multi   6.00   1.50

Liberation of Konigsberg Medal — A3808

Liberation of Vienna Medal — A3809

Liberation of Berlin Medal — A3810

Liberation of Budapest Medal — A3811

Litho. & Embossed

2015, May 5		Perf. 11¾	
7625	A3808 30r multi	2.50	.60
7626	A3809 30r multi	2.50	.60
7627	A3810 30r multi	2.50	.60
7628	A3811 30r multi	2.50	.60
	Nos. 7625-7628 (4)	10.00	2.40

Nos. 7625-7628 were each printed in sheets of 7 + label.

Lawyers Type of 2012

Design: 17r, Roman A. Rudenko (1907-81).

2015, May 6		Perf. 11½	
7629	A3635 17r multicolored	1.75	.35

No. 7629 was printed in sheets of 8 + label.

International Telecommunication Union, 150th Anniv. — A3812

2015, May 7	Litho.	Perf. 12½x12	
7630	A3812 17r dull blue	1.75	.30

Sviaz-Expocomm 2015 Intl. Telecommunications Exhibition, Moscow — A3813

2015, May 12	Litho.	Perf. 13½	
7631	A3813 19r multi	2.00	.35

Eurasian Economic Union — A3814

2015, May 21	Litho.	Perf. 12x11½	
7632	A3814 17r multi	1.25	.30

Joseph Brodsky (1940-96), 1987 Nobel Literature Laureate A3815

2015, May 22	Litho.	Perf. 13½	
7633	A3815 17r multi	1.25	.30

Dogs — A3816

No. 7634: a, 16r, South Russian shepherds. b, 18r, Caucasian shepherds. c, 20r, Central Asian shepherds. d, 26.50r, Black Russian terriers.

2015, May 28	Litho.	Perf. 13½	
7634	A3816	Block or vert. strip of 4, #a-d	8.00 1.50

Souvenir Sheet

Pyotr Ilyich Tchaikovsky (1840-93), Composer — A3817

Litho. & Engr.

2015, May 28		Perf. 12	
7635	A3817 150r multi	15.00	3.00

Norilsk Nickel Mining Company, 80th Anniv. — A3818

Litho. & Embossed

2015, June 2		Perf. 13½	
7636	A3818 26.50r multi	2.00	.50

Souvenir Sheet

Bank of Russia, 155th Anniv. — A3819

No. 7637: a, Evgeny I. Lamansky (1825-1902), bank governor. b, Russian coins. c, Bank building, Moscow.

Litho., Litho. & Embossed (#7637b)

2015, June 4		Perf. 12	
7637	A3819 40r Sheet of 3, #a-c	9.00	2.10

Artek International Children's Center, 90th Anniv. — A3820

2015, June 16	Litho.	Perf. 11¼	
7638	A3820 26.50r multi	2.00	.45

Arms of Derbent A3821

Arms of Nizhny Novgorod A3822

Perf. 11¾x12¼

2015, June 16		Litho.	
7639	A3821 12r multi	1.00	.25
	Complete booklet, 10 #7639	10.00	
	Complete booklet, 20 #7639	20.00	
7640	A3822 17r multi	1.50	.30
	Complete booklet, 10 #7640	15.00	
	Complete booklet, 20 #7640	30.00	

Paintings by Pavel A. Fedotov (1815-52) — A3823

Designs: No. 7641, 25r, Encore! Encore! No. 7642, 25r, Portrait of N. P. Zhdanovich at the Harpsichord, vert.

Perf. 12x11½, 11½x12

2015, June 23		Litho.	
7641-7642	A3823	Set of 2	3.50 .90

Silhouettes of Alexander Pushkin, Nikolai Gogol and Anna Akhmatova A3824

2015, June 25	Litho.	Perf. 11¼	
7643	A3824 17r multi	1.25	.30

Literature Year in Russia.

International Summits in Ufa — A3825

2015, July 7	Litho.	Perf. 12x12½	
7644	A3825 19r multi	1.25	.30

Prince Pyotr Bagration (1765-1812), General — A3826

2015, July 10	Litho.	Perf. 12x11½	
7645	A3826 21r multi	1.50	.35

No. 7645 was printed in sheets of 8 + central label.

Russian Post Emblem A3827

Emblem of the Russian Geographical Society A3828

Serpentine Die Cut 14½x15

2015, July 23		Litho.	
		Self-Adhesive	
7646	A3827 17r multi	1.00	.25
7647	A3828 35r multi	3.00	.55

Compare type A3827 to type A3364.

2015 Intl. Swimming Federation World Championships, Kazan — A3829

2015, July 24	Litho.	Perf. 13½	
7648	A3829 17r multi	1.25	.25

World War I Heroes A3830

Designs: No. 7649, 21r, Konstantin I. Nedorubov (1889-1978). No. 7650, 21r, Ivan V. Tyulenev (1892-1978). No. 7651, 21r, Nikolai I. Ulanov (1881-1948). No. 7652, 21r, Ivan L. Khizhnyak (1893-1980).

2015, Aug. 3   Litho.   Perf. 11½x12
7649-7652 A3830   Set of 4   6.00 1.40
Nos. 7649-7652 were each printed in sheets of 11 + label.

19th-20th Cent. Porcelain Tile From Moscow — A3831

19th-20th Cent. Porcelain Tile From Abramtsevo — A3832

19th-20th Cent. Porcelain Tile From Turygino — A3833

17th-18th Cent. Porcelain Tile From Yaroslavl — A3834

2015, Aug. 4   Litho.   Perf. 11½
7653 A3831 20r multi   1.60   .30
7654 A3832 20r multi   1.60   .30
7655 A3833 20r multi   1.60   .30
7656 A3834 20r multi   1.60   .30
    Nos. 7653-7656 (4)   6.40 1.20

Uniforms of Railway Employees A3835

Uniforms of: No. 7657, 17r, General and Conductor of Officer of Lines of Communications, 1843. No. 7658, 17r, Head of Depot and second-class driver, 1952. No. 7659, 17r, Head of Railways and conductor, 1979. No. 7660, 17r, Trainmaster and conductor, 2015.

2015, Aug. 11   Litho.   Perf. 13½
7657-7660 A3835   Set of 4   5.00 1.00
7660a   Souvenir sheet of 8, 2
    each #7657-7660   10.00 2.00

Admiral Gennady Nevelskoy Monument, Nikolayevsk-on-Amur — A3836

2015, Aug. 14   Litho.   Perf. 12x12½
7661 A3836 17r multi   1.25   .25

Leningrad Zoo, St. Petersburg, 150th Anniv. — A3837

2015, Aug. 14   Litho.   Perf. 13½
7662 A3837 19r multi   1.25   .30

Vysokopetrovsky Monastery, 700th Anniv. — A3838

St. Laurentius Monastery, 500th Anniv. — A3839

2015, Aug. 23   Litho.   Perf. 13½
7663 A3838 19r multi   1.25   .30
7664 A3839 19r multi   1.25   .30
Nos. 7663-7664 were each printed in sheets of 9 + label.

Boris F. Safonov (1915-42), Military Pilot A3840

2015, Aug. 26   Litho.   Perf. 12½x12
7665 A3840 12r multi   .75   .25
No. 7665 was printed in sheets of 10 + central label.

Arch of Triumph, Pyongyang A3841

2015, Aug. 28   Litho.   Perf. 11¼
7666 A3841 19r multi   1.25   .30
Liberation of Korea, 70th anniv. See North Korea No.

Souvenir Sheet

Kazan Coat of Arms — A3842

2015, Aug. 28   Litho.   Perf. 12x12½
7667 A3842 50r gold & multi   3.50   .75

End of World War II, 70th Anniv. — A3843

2015, Sept. 2   Litho.   Perf. 13½
7668 A3843 17r multi   1.25   .25

Souvenir Sheet

Nizhny Novgorod Stone Kremlin, 500th Anniv. — A3844

2015, Sept. 9   Litho.   Perf. 11¾
7669 A3844 35r multi   2.50   .55

World War I Military Equipment — A3845

Designs: No. 7670, 21r, Mosin-Nagant 7.62mm rifle. No. 7671, 21r, 76.2mm rapid firing gun. No. 7672, 21r, Destroyer "Novik." No. 7673, 21r, Sikorsky S-22 Ilya Muroments bomber.

2015, Sept. 10   Litho.   Perf. 12
7670-7673 A3845   Set of 4   5.00 1.40
Nos. 7670-7673 were each printed in sheets of 11 + label.

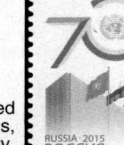

United Nations, 70th Anniv. A3846

Serpentine Die Cut 10
2015, Sept. 15   Litho.
Self-Adhesive
7674 A3846 26.50r multi   1.75   .40

Souvenir Sheet

World Cup Trophy — A3847

2015, Sept. 18   Litho.   Perf. 12
7675 A3847 100r multi   6.50 1.60
2018 World Cup Soccer Championships, Russia.

Federal Anti-Monopoly Service, 25th Anniv. — A3848

2015, Sept. 21   Litho.   Perf. 12x11½
7676 A3848 21r multi   1.50   .30

Architecture A3849

No. 7677: a, Kremlin, Moscow (denomination at LR). b, Maiden's Tower, Baku, Azerbaijan (denomination at LL).

2015, Sept. 22   Litho.   Perf. 11½
7677   Pair   2.50   .60
a.-b. A3849 19r Either single   1.00   .30
Russia and Azerbaijan joint issue.
Printed in sheets containing 4 pairs + central label. See Azerbaijan No. 1092.

Arctic Oil Production — A3850

No. 7678: a, Prirazlomnaya Oil Platform (denomination at LL). b, Mikhail Ulyanov tanker (denomination at LR).

2015, Sept. 23   Litho.   Perf. 11½
7678 A3850 19r Horiz. pair, #a-b 2.50   .60

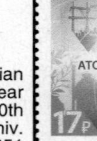

Russian Nuclear Industry, 70th Anniv. A3851

2015, Sept. 24   Litho.   Perf. 11½
7679 A3851 17r multi   1.25   .25

St. Vladimir the Great (c. 958-1015), Christianizer of Kievan Rus' — A3852

2015, Sept. 25   Litho.   Perf. 13½
7680 A3852 21r multi   1.50   .30

Miniature Sheet

Russian Stamps Commemorating the World Cup Soccer Championships — A3853

No. 7681: a, Russia #2073 (green panel). b, Russia #2606 (orange panel). c, Russia #3214 (purple panel). d, Russia #3746 (dark blue panel). e, Russia #5049 (Prussian blue panel). f, Russia #5463 (red panel).

2015, Oct. 1   Litho.   Perf. 11¼
7681 A3853 26.50r Sheet of 6,
           #a-f   10.00 2.50

Victor Vasnetsov House Museum, Moscow A3854

2015, Oct. 2   Litho.   Perf. 12½x12
7682 A3854 19r multi   1.50   .30

Souvenir Sheet

Derbent, 2000th Anniv. — A3855

2015, Oct. 2   Litho.   Perf. 12
7683 A3855 35r gold & multi   2.50   .55

All-Russian Society for Protection of Monuments of History and Culture, 50th Anniv. — A3856

2015, Oct. 14   Litho.   Perf. 12½x12
7684 A3856 26.50r multi   1.75   .40

Diplomatic Relations Between Russia and Mexico, 125th Anniv. — A3857

No. 7685: a, Saints Peter and Paul Cathedral, St. Petersburg. b, Chapultepec Castle, Mexico City.

2015, Oct. 19   Litho.   Perf. 11½
7685 A3857 19r Pair, #a-b   2.50   .60
  Printed in sheets containing 4 pairs + central label. See Mexico Nos. 2955-2956.

Souvenir Sheet

Ancient City of Tauric Chersonese and its Chora UNESCO World Hereitage Site — A3858

2015, Oct. 23   Litho.   Perf. 12
7686 A3858 35r multi   2.50   .55

Disaster Risk Reduction A3859

Serpentine Die Cut 11
2015, Oct. 28   Litho.
Self-Adhesive
7687 A3859 19r multi   1.25   .30

Sobibor Monument, by Mieczyslaw Welter — A3860

2015, Oct. 30   Litho.   Perf. 12x12½
7688 A3860 21r multi   1.50   .30
  Uprising at Sobibor Death Camp, 72nd anniv.

St. Tikhon of Moscow (1865-1925), 11th Patriarch of Moscow A3861

2015, Nov. 5   Litho.   Perf. 11½x12
7689 A3861 19r multi   1.25   .30

Souvenir Sheet

Kostroma Coat of Arms — A3862

2015, Nov. 5   Litho.   Perf. 12x12½
7690 A3862 50r gold & multi   3.00   .75

Ashot L. Badalov (1915-2011), Founder of State Commission for Radio Frequencies — A3863

2015, Nov. 10   Litho.   Perf. 12½x12
7691 A3863 19r multi   1.25   .30

Heroes of the Russian Federation A3864

Designs: No. 7692, 17r, Vladimir V. Maksimchuk (1947-94). No. 7693, 17r, Valeriy A. Tinkov (1957-95). No. 7694, 17r, Ivan Y. Shelohvostov (1978-2003). No. 7695, 17r, Sergey A. Solnechnikov (1980-2012). No. 7696, 17r, Vitaly V. Maiboroda (1981-2013).

2015, Nov. 10   Litho.   Perf. 12½x12
7692-7696 A3864 Set of 5   5.00   1.40
  Nos. 7692-7696 were each printed in sheets of 5 + label.

Cathedral of the Intercession of the Holy Virgin, Bogolyubovo A3865

Pha That Luang, Vientiane, Laos A3866

Serpentine Die Cut 10
2015, Nov. 11   Litho.
Self-Adhesive
7697 Pair   3.00   .60
  a. A3865 21r multi   1.50   .30
  b. A3866 21r multi   1.50   .30
  Printed in sheets containing 4 pairs + central label. See Laos Nos. 1907-1908.

Zlatoust Arms Factory, 200th Anniv. A3867

2015, Nov. 17   Litho.   Perf. 11½
7698 A3867 17r multi   1.25   .25

Stadiums for 2018 World Cup Soccer Championships — A3868

No. 7699: a, Luzhniki Stadium, Moscow (blue panel). b, Fisht Stadium, Sochi (orange panel). c, Kazan Arena, Kazan (red panel). d, Spartak Stadium, Moscow (green panel).

2015, Nov. 17   Litho.   Perf. 13½
7699 A3868 21r Block or vert.
           strip of 4, #a-d   6.00   1.25

Ministry for Civil Defense, Emergencies and Natural Disasters, 25th Anniv. — A3869

2015, Nov. 27   Litho.   Perf. 12x11½
7700 A3869 21r multi   1.25   .30

Timiryazev State Agrarian University, 150th Anniv. A3870

Serpentine Die Cut 10
2015, Dec. 3   Litho.
Self-Adhesive
7701 A3870 17r multi   1.25   .25

Lawyers Type of 2012

Designs: No. 7702, 17r, Nikolai V. Muraviev (1850-1908). No. 7703, 17r, Konstantin P. Pobedonostsev (1827-1907). No. 7704, 17r, Nikolai S. Tagantsev (1843-1923).

2015, Dec. 3   Litho.   Perf. 11½
7702-7704 A3635 Set of 3   3.50   .70
  Nos. 7702-7704 were each printed in sheets of 8 + label.

Miniature Sheet

Russian Soccer Players — A3871

No. 7705: a, Gavriil D. Kachalin (1911-95). b, Valentin B. Bubukin (1933-2008). c, Yuriy M. Voynov (1931-2003). d, Valentin K. Ivanov (1934-2011). e, Sergei S. Salnikov (1925-84). f, Eduard A. Streltsov (1937-90). g, Lev I. Yashin (1929-90).

2015, Dec. 9   Litho.   Perf. 12½x12
7705 A3871 26.50r Sheet of 7,
#a-g, + 9
labels   12.50 2.60

2018 World Cup Soccer Championships, Russia.

New Year 2016 — A3872

2015, Dec. 10   Litho.   Perf. 13½
7706 A3872 35r multi   2.50 .50

Russian Cuisine A3873

2016, Jan. 13   Litho.   Perf. 11½x12
7707 A3873 21r multi   1.25 .25

Souvenir Sheet

Night on the Dnieper River, by Arkhip Kuindzhi (1841-1910) — A3874

2016, Jan. 27   Litho.   Perf. 12x12½
7708 A3874 50r multi   3.50 .65

Historians — A3875

No. 7709 — History books and: a, Nikolai M. Karamzin (1766-1826). b, Vasily O. Klyuchevsky (1841-1911).

2016, Jan. 28   Litho.   Perf. 12x12½
7709   Horiz. pair + central label   3.00 .60
a.-b. A3875 25r Either single   1.25 .30

Miniature Sheet

Towns of Military Glory — A3876

No. 7710: a, Gatchina (7 letters in city name, artillery and tanks). b, Grozny (8 letters in city name, airplanes, mortars, locomotives). c, Petrozavodsk (12 letters in city name, airplanes, trucks with guns and tanks). d, Staraya Russa (two words in city name, airplanes, snow vehicles, trucks with guns). e, Feodosia (8 letters in city name, airplanes, tanks and ships).

Litho. With Foil Application
2016, Feb. 18   Perf. 11¼
7710 A3876 20r Sheet of 5, #a-e,
+ label   6.50 1.40

Ice Hockey Players and Gagarin Cup — A3877

2016, Feb. 20   Litho.   Perf. 11½
7711 A3877 19r multi   1.25 .25

Miniature Sheet

Russian Medals and Orders — A3878

No. 7712: a, Gold Star Medal (like #7337). b, Hero of Labor of the Russian Federation Medal (like #7543). c, Order of St. Andrew (double-headed eagle with crucifix at top). d, Order of St. George (like #7338). e, Order of Merit for the Fatherland (like #7339). f, Order of St. Catherine the Great (like #7427). g, Order of Alexander Nevsky (like #7426). h, Order of Suvorov (like #7425). i, Order of Ushakov (like #7508). j, Order of Zhukov (like #7506). k, Order of Kutuzov (like #7507). l, Order of Nakhimov (like #7604). m, Order of Courage (like #7605). n, Order of Military Merit (blue ribbon with central red stripe). o, Order of Naval Merit (white ribbon with three blue stripes). p, Order of Honor (blue ribbon with one white stripe). q, Order of Friendship (like #7606). r, Order of Parental Glory (white ribbon with two blue stripes).

Litho. & Embossed
2016, Feb. 20   Perf. 12¼x12
Dated "2016" Above "Russia"
7712 A3878 25r Sheet of 18,
#a-r   35.00 6.25

A booklet containing 18 panes of one of each of Nos. 7712a-7712r sold for 1500r. Value, $110.

Russian Membership in Council of Europe, 20th Anniv. — A3879

2016, Feb. 26   Litho.   Perf. 12x12¼
7713 A3879 21r multi   1.50 .30

Regional Communications Commonwealth, 25th Anniv. — A3880

2016, Mar. 3   Litho.   Perf. 12½x12
7714 A3880 17r multi   1.25 .25

Heroes of the Russian Federation A3881

Designs: No. 7715, 19r, Viktor M. Adamishin (1962-95). No. 7716, 19r, Alexei V. Balandin (1961-2009). No. 7717, 19r, Dmitri A. Serkov (1981-2007).

2016, Mar. 24   Litho.   Perf. 12½x12
7715-7717 A3881   Set of 3   3.50 .85

Nos. 7715-7717 were each printed in sheets of 5 + label. See Nos. 7773-7774, 7804-7805, 7811-7812, 7855-7856, 7899-7900, 7906-7907, 7955, 7985-7986, 8003-8004, 8095=8097.

Postcrossing A3882

Serpentine Die Cut 10
2016, Mar. 25   Litho.
Self-Adhesive
7718 A3882 31r multi   2.00 .45

Armed Forces Courier Corps, 300th Anniv. — A3884

2016, Apr. 15   Litho.   Perf. 13½
7720 A3884 21r multi   1.25 .30

Kislovodsk Health Resort Park — A3885

2016, Apr. 22   Litho.   Perf. 13½
7721 A3885 23r multi   1.40 .35

No. 7721 was printed in sheets of 7 + label.

Notaries Institute of Russia, 150th Anniv. A3886

2016, Apr. 27   Litho.   Perf. 12½x12
7722 A3886 19r multi   1.25 .30

No. 7722 was printed in sheets of 14 + label.

2016 World Ice Hockey Championships, Russia — A3887

2016, May 6   Litho.   Perf. 11¼
7723 A3887 19r multi   1.25 .30

Alexey P. Maresyev (1916-2001), Pilot — A3888

2016, May 20   Litho.   Perf. 12½x12
7724 A3888 21.50r multi   1.50 .30

No. 7724 was printed in sheets of 10 + central label.

Paintings by Nicholas P. Krasnoff (1864-1939) A3889

No. 7725: a, View from Vittoriosa Gate, Malta. b, Dulber Palace, Crimea.

2016, May 24   Litho.   Perf. 11¼x12
7725 A3889 21r Pair, #a-b   2.75   .65

No. 7725 was printed in sheets of 10, containing 5 each Nos. 7725a-7725b, + 2 labels. See Malta Nos. 1562-1563.

Rosa Khutor Alpine Resort — A3890

2016, May 26   Litho.   Perf. 11¾
7726 A3890 31r multi   1.75   .45

Chapel Near Vrsic, Slovenia Built by Russian World War I Prisoners of War, Cent. — A3891

2016, May 27   Litho.   Perf. 13½
7727 A3891 21r multi   1.25   .30

No. 7727 was printed in sheets of 7 + label. See Slovenia No. 1171.

Monument to Minin and Pozharsky, Moscow — A3892

Serpentine Die Cut 15x14½
2016, June 2   Litho.
Self-Adhesive
7728 A3892 19r multi   1.25   .30
Russian Historical Society, 150th anniv.

Emblem of Union of Philatelists of Russia — A3893

Serpentine Die Cut 15x14½
2016, June 2   Litho.
Self-Adhesive
7729 A3893 37r multi   2.50   .60

Souvenir Sheet

Mikhail Bulgakov (1891-1940), Writer — A3894

2016, June 3   Litho.   Perf. 12
7730 A3894 90r multi   6.00 1.50

Pushkin State Russian Language Institute, 50th Anniv. — A3895

2016, June 6   Litho.   Perf. 13½
7731 A3895 24r multi   1.50   .40
For surcharge, see No. 8070.

Commonwealth of Independent States, 25th Anniv. — A3896

2016, June 9   Litho.   Perf. 11½
7732 A3896 17r multi   1.25   .25

20th St. Petersburg International Economic Forum — A3897

2016, June 16   Litho.   Perf. 12¼
7733 A3897 20r multi   1.50   .30

Soldiers Defending Brest Fortress — A3898

Litho. & Embossed
2016, June 22   Perf. 11¾
7734 A3898 35r multi   2.25   .55
No. 7734 was printed in sheets of 7 + label. See Belarus No. 986.

Dogs — A3899

2016, June 23   Litho.   Perf. 13½
7735   Pair   3.25   .80
a.   A3899 19r Collie   1.25   .30
b.   A3899 31r German shepherd   2.00   .50

Rzhev, 800th Anniv. A3900

2016, June 23   Litho.   Perf. 12
7736 A3900 24r multi   1.50   .40

Yuri Levitan (1914-83), Radio Announcer A3901

2016, June 24   Litho.   Perf. 12x12½
7737 A3901 19r multi   1.25   .30

Russian International News Agency, 75th Anniv.

Count Dmitri A. Milyutin (1816-1912), Minister of War — A3902

2016, June 28   Litho.   Perf. 12x11½
7738 A3902 21.50r multi   1.40   .35
No. 7738 was printed in sheets of 8 + central label.

Traffic Safety A3903

2016, June 28   Litho.   Perf. 11¼
7739 A3903 14r multi   .90   .25

2016 All-Russian Agricultural Census A3904

Serpentine Die Cut 10
2016, July 1   Litho.
Self-Adhesive
7740 A3904 20r multi   1.25   .30

Global Navigation Satellite System A3905

Serpentine Die Cut 11
2016, July 5   Litho.
Self-Adhesive
7741 A3905 19r multi   1.25   .30

Velikiye Luki, 850th Anniv. A3906

2016, July 14   Litho.   Perf. 11¼
7742 A3906 24r multi   .75   .35

Order of Military Merit — A3907

Order of Naval Merit — A3908

Order of Honor — A3909

Order of Parental Glory — A3910

Litho, & Embossed

2016, July 19			**Perf. 11¾**	
7743	A3907	25r multi	1.50	.35
7744	A3908	25r multi	1.50	.35
7745	A3909	25r multi	1.50	.35
7746	A3910	25r multi	1.50	.35
	Nos. 7743-7746 (4)		6.00	1.40

Nos. 7743-7746 were each printed in sheets of 7 + label.

World War I Military Equipment — A3911

Designs: No. 7747, 24r, Fedorov Avtomat 6.5mm rifle. No. 7748, 24r, Imperatritsa Ekaterina Velikaya ship. No. 7749, 24r, Grigorovich M-5 flying boat. No. 7750, 24r, Mgebrov-Isotta-Fraschini armored vehicle.

2016, July 28		Litho.	**Perf. 12**	
7747-7750	A3911	Set of 4	6.00	1.50

Nos. 7747-7750 were each printed in sheets of 11 + label. A booklet containing eight panes of one of each of Nos. 7670-7673, 7525-7528 sold for 500r. Value, $40.

Russian Stamps Commemorating the World Cup Soccer Championships — A3912

No. 7751: a, Russia #5896 (blue panel). b, Label commemorating 1994 World Cup (red panel). c, Label commemorating 2002 World

Cup (orange red panel). d, Russia #7583 (purple panel).

2016, July 29		Litho.	**Perf. 11¼**	
7751	A3912	21.50r Sheet of 4,		
		#a-d	5.00	1.40

Likhachov Automotive Plant, Moscow, Cent. A3913

2016, Aug. 2		Litho.	**Perf. 11¼**	
7752	A3913	21.50r multi	1.50	.35

Orel, 450th Anniv. A3914

2016, Aug. 5		Litho.	**Perf. 12½x12**	
7753	A3914	24r multi	1.50	.35

No. 7237 Surcharged in Silver

Method and Perf. As Before

2016, Aug. 5				
7754	A3519	31r on 10.50r		
		#7237	30.00	30.00

No. 7754 was printed in sheets of 6 + 2 labels.

Omsk, 300th Anniv. A3915

2016, Aug. 6		Litho.	**Perf. 12½x12**	
7755	A3915	24r multi	1.50	.35

Russian Presence at Mount Athos, 1000th Anniv. — A3916

2016, Aug. 9		Litho.	**Perf. 11¼**	
7756	A3916	31r multi	2.00	.45

Souvenir Sheet

Kizhi Ethnographic Museum, 50th Anniv. — A3917

No. 7757: a, Church of the Intercession (9 domes) and buildings. b, Transfiguration Church (22 domes) and buildings. c, Bell tower and windmill.

Litho. & Engr.

2016, Aug. 19			**Perf. 12**	
7757	A3917	50r Sheet of 3, #a-		
		c	10.00	2.25

A booklet containing one pane of Nos. 7757 sold for 365r.

Arms of Velikiye Luki A3918

Arms of Murmansk A3919

Perf. 11¾x12¼

2016, Aug. 23		Litho.		
7758	A3918	14r multi	.90	.25
	Complete booklet, 10 #7758		9.00	
	Complete booklet, 20 #7758		18.00	
7759	A3919	19r multi	1.25	.30
	Complete booklet, 10 #7759		12.50	
	Complete booklet, 20 #7759		25.00	

Stadiums for 2018 World Cup Soccer Championships — A3920

No. 7760: a, Volgograd Arena (green panel). b, Ekaterinburg Arena (blue panel). c, Rostov Arena (orange panel). d, Samara Arena (red panel).

2016, Aug. 26		Litho.	**Perf. 13½**	
7760	A3920	21.50r Block or vert.		
		strip of 4,		
		#a-d	5.00	1.40

Souvenir Sheet

Russian Arctic National Park — A3921

2016, Aug. 30		Litho.	**Perf. 11¾**	
7761	A3921	80r multi	5.50	1.25

A booklet containing one pane of No. 7761 sold for 350r. Value, $37.50.

Ulan-Ude, 350th Anniv. A3922

2016, Sept. 1		Litho.	**Perf. 12½x12**	
7762	A3922	24r multi	1.50	.35

Lukoil Oil Company — A3923

2016, Sept. 6		Litho.	**Perf. 13½**	
7763	A3923	24r multi	1.50	.40

Unified State Exam A3924

Serpentine Die Cut 10

2016, Sept. 14			Litho.	
		Self-Adhesive		
7764	A3924	19r multi	1.25	.30

Souvenir Sheets

Magas Coat of Arms — A3925

Perm Coat of Arms — A3926

2016, Sept. 16		Litho.	**Perf. 12x12½**	
7765	A3925	50r multi	3.50	.80
7766	A3926	50r multi	3.50	.80

Russian Presidential Academy of National Economy and Public Administration — A3927

2016, Sept. 20		Litho.	**Perf. 12x11½**	
7767	A3927	19r multi	1.25	.30

Alexander M. Prokhorov (1916-2002), 1964 Nobel Laureate in Physics A3928

2016, Sept. 22		Litho.	**Perf. 11¾**	
7768	A3928	21.50r multi	1.50	.35

Vasily A. Degtyaryov Munitions Plant, Kovrov, Cent. A3929

2016, Sept. 27		Litho.	**Perf. 11½**	
7769	A3929	21.50r multi	1.50	.35

Tarkhankut Lighthouse — A3930

Chersonesus Lighthouse — A3931

2016, Sept. 29 Litho. Perf. 12½x12
7770 A3930 14r multi   .90   .25
7771 A3931 14r multi   .90   .25

Murmansk, Cent. — A3932

2016, Oct. 4 Litho. Perf. 12½x12
7772 A3932 24r multi   1.50   .40

Heroes Type of 2016

Designs: No. 7773, 19r, Mark N. Yevtyukhin (1964-2000). No. 7774, 19r, Nikolai V. Skrypnik (1944-96).

2016, Oct. 5 Litho. Perf. 12½x12
7773-7774 A3881 Set of 2   2.50   .60

Nos. 7773-7774 were each printed in sheets of 5 + label.

Metropolitan Macarius of Moscow and Kolomna (1816-82), Church Historian A3933

2016, Oct. 7 Litho. Perf. 11¾x12
7775 A3933 24r multi   1.50   .40

Yelnya Offensive, 75th Anniv. — A3934

Battle of Hanko, 75th Anniv. — A3935

Litho. & Embossed
2016, Oct. 11 Perf. 11¾
7776 A3934 35r multi   2.25   .55
7777 A3935 35r multi   2.25   .55

Nos. 7776-7777 were each printed in sheets of 7 + label.

Souvenir Sheet

Abramtsevo Museum Reserve — A3936

No. 7778 — Owners of Museum building: a, Sergey T. Aksakov (1791-1859), writer. b, Savva I. Mamontov (1841-1918), industrialist.

2016, Oct. 25 Litho. Perf. 12
7778 A3936 25r Sheet of 2, #a-b 4.50 .80

No. 7778 with a fluorescent overprint of a quotation by Aksakov in the sheet margin was printed in limited quantities and sold for 300r. Value, $25.

Federal Customs Service — A3937

2016, Oct. 25 Litho. Perf. 12x11½
7779 A3937 24r multi   1.50   .40

Souvenir Sheet

Sable — A3938

2016, Oct. 27 Litho. Perf. 12¼x12
7780 A3938 70r multi   4.50 1.10

Barguzinsky State Biosphere Nature Reserve, cent. No. 7780 with an Ecology Year 2017 emblem overprinted in the sheet margin in green was issued on Aug. 1, 2017 and sold for 150r. Value, $10.

Miniature Sheet

Russian Soccer Players — A3939

No. 7781: a, Viktor M. Bannikov (1938-2001). b, Konstantin I. Beskov (1920-2006). c, Nikolay G. Latyshev (1913-99). d, Slava K. Metreveli (1936-98). e, Nikolai P. Morozov (1916-81). f, Igor A. Netto (1930-99). g, Galimzyan S. Khusainov (1937-2010).

2016, Oct. 28 Litho. Perf. 12½x12
7781 A3939 29r Sheet of 7, #a-
            g, + 9 labels   14.00 3.25

2018 World Cup Soccer Championships, Russia.

Russkaya Pravda, Law Code of Kievan Rus, 1000th Anniv. A3940

2016, Oct. 31 Litho. Perf. 12½x12
7782 A3940 19r multi   1.25   .30

Djamaldin K. Yandiev (1916-79), Poet — A3941

2016, Nov. 10 Litho. Perf. 11¾
7783 A3941 19r multi   1.25   .30

Caffeinated Beverages of Russia and Argentina — A3942

No. 7784: a, Tea and tea service, Russia (denomination at LL). b, Mate and mate service, Argentina (denomination at LR).

2016, Nov. 14 Litho. Perf. 12x12½
7784 A3942 29r Horiz. pair, #a-b 3.50 .95

See Argentina Nos. 2809-2810.

Battle of Moscow, 75th Anniv. — A3943

Litho. & Embossed
2016, Nov. 16 Perf. 11¾
7785 A3943 35r multi   2.25   .55

No. 7785 was printed in sheets of 7 + label. A booklet containing panes of one of Nos. 7734, 7776, 7777 and 7785 sold for 800r. See Kazakhstan No. 794.

Modern Art — A3944

Designs: No. 7786, 31r, We Serve the Fatherland and the Special Forces, by Yuri Orlov, 2002. No. 7787, 31r, Dawn, Chersonesus, by Nikolai Morgun, 2002 (50x50mm). No. 7788, 31r, Monument to Alexander Suvorov, by Dmitry Tugarinov, 1999, Switzerland (50x50mm). No. 7789, 31r, Golden Balls, Stavropol, by Valery Arzumanov, 2012 (50x50mm).

Perf. 12x11½ (#7786), 11¼
2016, Nov. 29 Litho.
7786-7789 A3944 Set of 4   8.00 2.00

New Year 2017 — A3945

2016, Dec. 1 Litho. Perf. 11½x11¼
7790 A3945 19r multi   1.25   .30

No. 7790 was printed in sheets of 4. Lithographed examples of No. 7790 with holographic foil were printed in sheets of 4 that sold for 255r.

Lawyers Type of 2012

Designs: No. 7791, 19r, Gabriel F. Shershenevich (1863-1912). No. 7792, 19r, Konstantin I. Palen (1833-1912). No. 7793, 19r, Vladimir A. Tumanov (1926-2011).

2016, Dec. 2 Litho. Perf. 11½
7791-7793 A3635 Set of 3   4.00   .95

Nos. 7791-7793 were each printed in sheets of 8 + label.

F-1 Nuclear Reactor, Moscow, 70th Anniv. A3946

2016, Dec. 8 Litho. Perf. 11½
7794 A3946 19r multi   1.25   .30

Miniature Sheet

Russian Soccer Players — A3947

No. 7795: a, Anatoliy A. Banishevskiy (1946-97). b, Valery I. Voronin (1939-98). c, Anatoli M. Ilyin (1931-2016). d, Yevgeniy V. Rudakov (1942-2011). e, Pavel F. Sadyrin (1942-2001). f, Igor L. Chislenko (1939-94). g, Albert A. Shesternyov (1941-94).

2016, Dec. 9 Litho. Perf. 12½x12
7795 A3947 29r Sheet of 7, #a-
            g, + 9 labels   14.00 3.50

2018 World Cup Soccer Championships, Russia. A six-pane booklet containing one each of Nos. 7705a-7705g, 7781a-7781g, and 7795a-7795g sold for 1200r. Value, $100.

Churches A3948

No. 7796: a, Church of St. John the Theologian, Ohrid, Macedonia (brown building). b,

Trinity Cathedral, St. Petersburg (white building with blue domes).

2016, Dec. 13 Litho.   Perf. 12½x12
7796 A3948 21.50r Pair, #a-b   2.50 .75

Printed in sheets of 8 containing 4 each Nos. 7796a-7796b, + central label. See Macedonia No. 734.

Souvenir Sheet

Nuremberg War Crimes Trials, 70th Anniv. — A3949

2016, Dec. 14 Litho.   Perf. 12
7797 A3949 70r multi   5.00 1.25

Uniforms of the Diplomatic Service A3950

Uniforms of: No. 7798, 19r, Privy counselor and chancellor, 1834. No. 7799, 19r, State counselor and collegiate registrar, 1904. No. 7800, 19r, USSR ambassador extraordinary and plenipotentiary and attaché of the People's commisariat of Foreign Affairs, 1945. No. 7801, 19r, Russian Federation ambassadors extraordinary and plenipotentiary, 2001.

2016, Dec. 20 Litho.   Perf. 13½
7798-7801 A3950 Set of 4   5.00 1.25
7801a   Souvenir sheet of 8, 2   10.00 2.50
         each #7798-7801

Yevgeny Zababakhin (1917-84), Nuclear Physicist and Weapons Designer — A3951

2017, Jan. 16 Litho.   Perf. 12½x12
7802 A3951 19r multi   1.25 .30

Bast Shoes — A3952

2017, Jan. 24 Litho.   Perf. 12x12½
7803 A3952 29r multi   2.00 .50

Heroes Type of 2016

Designs: No. 7804, 19r, Andrey G. Karlov (1954-2016). No. 7805, 19r, Sulom-Beck Oskanov (1943-92).

2017, Feb. 7 Litho.   Perf. 12½x12
Dated "2017"
7804-7805 A3881 Set of 2   2.75 .70

Nos. 7804-7805 were each printed in sheets of 5 + label.

Souvenir Sheet

Zabivaka, Mascot of 2018 World Cup Soccer Championships — A3953

2017, Feb. 7 Litho.   Perf. 12x12½
7806 A3953 100r multi   6.50 1.75

Emblem of the High Commissioner for Human Rights in the Russian Federation — A3954

2017, Feb. 27 Litho.   Perf. 12½x12
7807 A3954 19r multi   1.25 .35

Miniature Sheet

October Revolution, Cent. — A3955

No. 7808: a, Abdication of Tsar Nicholas II, Mar. 15, 1917 (Mar. 2, old style). b, Proclamation of Russian Republic, Sept. 14, 1917 (Sept. 1, old style). c, Election of Constituent Assembly, Nov. 25, 1917 (Nov. 12, old style). d, Assault on the Winter Palace by Cruiser Aurora, Nov. 7, 1917 (Oct. 27, old style).

2017, Mar. 2 Litho.   Perf. 11¾
7808 A3955 35r Sheet of 4, #a-d 9.00 2.50

A booklet containing a pane of stamps like No. 7808 sold for 505r. Value, $50.

2017 Confederations Cup Soccer Tournament, Russia — A3956

Litho. & Embossed
2017, Mar. 9   Perf. 11¾
7809 A3956 35r multi   2.25 .60

For surcharge, see No. 7861.

St. Michael's Castle, St. Petersburg — A3957

2017, Mar. 15 Litho.   Perf. 12½x12
7810 A3957 24r multi   1.50 .45

Europa.

Heroes Type of 2016

Designs: No. 7811, 19r, Sergey A. Ashikhmin (1977-2012). No. 7812, 19r, Vadim K. Yermakov (1972-96).

2017, Mar. 23 Litho.   Perf. 12½x12
7811-7812 A3881 Set of 2   2.75 .70

Nos. 7811-7812 were each printed in sheets of 5 + label.

Commonwealth of Independent States Interparliamentary Assembly — A3958

2017, Mar. 27 Litho.   Perf. 12½x12
7813 A3958 35r multi   2.50 .60

Flowers — A3959

No. 7814: a, Galanthus woronowii. b, Erythronium caucasicum. c, Diospyros lotus. d, Cyclamen coum ssp. caucasicum.

Serpentine Die Cut 11
2017, Mar. 29   Litho.
Self-Adhesive
7814 A3959 Block of 4   7.50 4.00
a.-d.   29r Any single   1.50 1.00

Icebreaker Krasin, Cent. — A3960

2017, Mar. 31 Litho.   Perf. 12½x12
7815 A3960 24r multi   1.75 .45
No. 7815 was printed in sheets of 14 + label.

Miniature Sheet

Turtles — A3961

No. 7816: a, Emys orbicularis. b, Pelodiscus sinensis. c, Mauremys caspica. d, Testudo graeca.

2017, Apr. 4 Litho.   Perf. 11¾x12¼
7816 A3961 35r Sheet of 4, #a-d 9.00 2.50

Mechanical Engineering Design Bureau, Kolomna, 75th Anniv. A3962

2017, Apr. 11 Litho.   Perf. 11¼
7817 A3962 19r multi   1.40 .35

Souvenir Sheet

Association of Combat Veterans of Internal Affairs Agencies and Internal Troops, 25th Anniv. — A3963

Litho. & Embossed
2017, Apr. 21   Perf. 12x12½
7818 A3963 100r multi   6.50 1.75

Souvenir Sheet

The Battle on the Ice, by Valentin Serov — A3964

2017, Apr. 26 Litho.   Perf. 12x11¾
7819 A3964 90r multi   6.50 1.60

Battle on the Ice, 775th anniv.

Sailors in Northern Convoys of World War II — A3965

Litho. & Embossed
2017, May 4   Perf. 11¾
7820 A3965 41r multi   2.75 .75

No. 7820 was printed in sheets of 7 + label.

Emblem of Russian Student Spring Festival A3966

Serpentine Die Cut 10

2017, May 15   Litho.

Self-Adhesive

7821 A3966 22r multi   1.50   .40

Fables A3967

No. 7822: a, The Fox and the Grapes. b, The Tortoise and the Hare. c, The Rooster and the Pearl. d, The Wolf and the Crane.

2017, May 17   Litho.   Perf. 11¼x12

7822   Horiz. strip of 4   9.00 2.50
a.-d. A3967 35r Any single   2.00   .60

Souvenir Sheet

Cape Fiolent Near Sevastopol, by Vasily Vereshchagin (1842-1904) — A3968

2017, May 24   Litho.   Perf. 12x12½

7823   A3968 95r multi   6.50 1.75

Souvenir Sheet

Astrakhan Coat of Arms — A3969

2017, May 30   Litho.   Perf. 12x12½

7824   A3969 60r multi   4.00 1.10

Izvestia Newspaper, Cent. — A3970

2017, June 1   Litho.   Perf. 11¾

7825   A3970 27r multi   1.75   .50

Flag of Republic of Ingushetia — A3971

2017, June 4   Litho.   Perf. 12¼x12

7826   A3971 25r multi   1.75   .40

Republic of Ingushetia, 25th anniv.

Ecology Year A3972

2017, June 5   Litho.   Perf. 11½

7827   A3972 22r multi   1.25   .35

Russian Defense Sport and Technology Organization A3973

Designs: No. 7828, 22r, Rifle shooting. No. 7829, 22r, Radio direction finding.

2017, June 28   Litho.   Perf. 12x12½

7828-7829 A3973   Set of 2   3.00   .75

Russian State Shipbuilding, 350th Anniv. A3974

2017, June 29   Litho.   Perf. 11¼

7830   A3974 33r multi   2.00   .55

Arms of Azov A3975

Arms of Orekhovo-Zuyevo A3976

2017, June 29   Litho.   Perf. 12x12¼

7831   A3975 16r multi   1.10   .25
      Complete booklet, 10 #7831   11.00
      Complete booklet, 20 #7831   22.00
7832   A3976 22r multi   1.50   .35
      Complete booklet, 10 #7832   15.00
      Complete booklet, 20 #7832   30.00

Resurrection Cathedral, Omsk — A3977

2017, June 30   Litho.   Perf. 12x12½

7833   A3977 27r multi   1.75   .45

1897 Meeting of King Chulalongkorn of Thailand and Tsar Nicholas II of Russia — A3978

2017, July 3   Litho.   Perf. 12x12¼

7834   A3978 22r multi   1.50   .35

Diplomatic relations between Russia and Thailand, 120th anniv. No. 7834 was printed in sheets of 14 + central label. See Thailand No. 2964.

Souvenir Sheet

Kaliningrad Coat of Arms — A3979

2017, July 10   Litho.   Perf. 12x12¼

7835   A3979 60r gold & multi   4.00 1.00

Bakhchysarai Museum, Cent. — A3980

2017, July 12   Litho.   Perf. 12x12½

7836   A3980 100r multi   6.50 1.75

Pyotr Vyazemsky (1792-1878), Poet — A3981

2017, July 21   Litho.   Perf. 12x11¼

7837   A3981 22r multi   1.50   .35

No. 7837 was printed in sheets of 11 + label.

Souvenir Sheet

Entrance to Sevastopol Bay, by Ivan Aivazovsky (1817-1900) — A3982

2017, July 25   Litho.   Perf. 12x12¼

7838   A3982 95r multi   6.50 1.60

A self-adhesive imperforate sheet like No. 7838 was issued on Oct. 10 and sold for 240r.

Souvenir Sheet

Ivangorod Fortress, 525th Anniv. — A3983

2017, July 28   Litho.   Perf. 12¼x12

7839   A3983 90r multi   6.00 1.50

19th World Festival of Youth and Students, Moscow and Sochi — A3984

No. 7840 — Stamps commemorating previous festivals: a, Russia #1914. b, Russia #5360. c, Pair of Russia #4068. d, Russia #4648. e, Russia #5782.

2017, Aug. 3   Litho.   Perf. 11¼

7840   A3984 35r Sheet of 5, #a-
      e, + label   10.00 3.25

Battle of Crimea and Defense of Sevastopol, 75th Anniv. — A3985

World War II Guerilla Fighters — A3986

Normandie-Niemen French Air
Regiment — A3987

2017 Litho. & Embossed Perf. 11¾
7841 A3985 41r multi 2.50 .75
7842 A3986 41r multi 2.50 .75
7843 A3987 41r multi 2.50 .75
Nos. 7841-7843 (3) 7.50 2.25

Issued: No. 7841, 8/4; No. 7842, 8/24; No.
7843, 9/1. Nos. 7841-7843 were each printed
in sheets of 7 + label. See France No. 5302.

Stadiums for 2018 World Cup Soccer
Championships — A3988

No. 7844: a, Nizhny Novgorod Stadium
(green panel). b, Kaliningrad Stadium (blue
panel). c, Mordovia Arena, Saransk (red
panel). d, St. Petersburg Stadium (orange
panel).

2017, Aug. 23 Litho. Perf. 11¾
7844 A3988 22r Block or vert.
strip of 4, #a-d 6.00 1.60

Archimandrite Antonin Kapustin (1817-
94), Head of Russian Orthodox
Ecclesiastical Mission in
Jerusalem — A3989

2017, Aug. 23 Litho. Perf. 11¾
7845 A3989 27r multi 2.00 .45

**Recipients of the Order of St,
Andrew Type of 2011**

Design: Order of St. Andrew and Fazu
Aliyeva (1932-2016), poet.

2017, Aug. 29 Litho. Perf. 12x11¼
7846 A3560 27r multi 1.75 .45
No. 7846 was printed in sheets of 11 + label.

Kremlins Type of 2009

Kremlins in: 22r, Alexandrov. 41r, Vologda.

Serpentine Die Cut 11
2017, Aug. 30 Litho.
Self-Adhesive
7847 A3471 22r multi 1.50 .40
7848 A3471 41r multi 2.50 .75

Modern Art — A3990

Designs: No. 7849, 35r, The Sower, by N.V.
Kolupaev, 2008. No. 7850, 35r, Autumn Evening, by A. I. Telik, 2009. No. 7851, 35r, Conversation, sculpture by Vladimir I. Koshelev,
2007. No. 7852, 35r, Missing, 1946, by Andrei
P. Gorsky, 1962 (50x38mm).

Perf. 11¼, 12x11¼ (#7852)
2017, Sept. 13 Litho.
7849-7852 A3990 Set of 4 9.00 2.50

Indira Gandhi
(1917-84), Prime
Minister of India,
and Flag of
India — A3991

2017, Sept. 21 Litho. Perf. 12x12½
7853 A3991 35r multi 2.50 .60

Military Academy of the General Staff
of the Armed Forces — A3992

2017, Sept. 27 Litho. Perf. 12x11½
7854 A3992 27r multi 2.00 .45

Heroes Type of 2016

Designs: No. 7855, 22r, Vladislav A. Dolonin
(1969-95). No. 7856, 22r, Viktor V. Matveyev
(1963-2001).

2017, Sept. 28 Litho. Perf. 12½x12
7855-7856 A3881 Set of 2 3.00 .80
Nos. 7855-7856 were each printed in sheets
of 5 + label.

Civil Defense
of the
Russian
Federation
A3993

2017, Oct. 3 Litho. Perf. 11½
7857 A3993 27r multi 2.00 .45

Investigative Committee of
Russia — A3994

2017, Oct. 6 Litho. Perf. 12x11½
7858 A3994 27r multi 2.00 .45

19th World Festival of Youth and
Students — A3995

2017, Oct. 14 Litho. Perf.
7859 A3995 100r multi 7.00 1.75

137th Assembly of Inter-Parliamentary
Union, St. Petersburg — A3996

2017, Oct. 14 Litho. Perf. 11½
7860 A3996 35r sil & dk blue 2.50 .60

No. 7809
Surcharged in
Bluish Violet

Method and Perf. As Before
2017, Oct. 17
7861 A3956 50r on 35r #7809 7.50 7.50
No. 7861 was printed in a sheet of 9 that
sold for 700r.

Zhostovo Painting, 1976 — A3997

Zhostovo Painting, 1957 — A3998

Zhostovo Painting, 1980 — A3999

No. 7862: a, Bird facing left. b, Bird facing
right.

2017, Oct. 23 Litho. Perf. 11½x11¼
7862 Horiz. pair 3.00 .80
a.-b. A3997 22r Either single 1.50 .40
7863 A3998 22r multi 1.50 .40
7864 A3999 22r multi 1.50 .40
Nos. 7862-7864 (3) 6.00 1.60

No. 7862 was printed in sheets containing
two pairs. Nos. 7863-7864 were each printed
in sheets of 4.

Uniforms of
Customs
Officials
A4000

Designs: No. 7865, 22r, Customs guard and
manager, 1827. No. 7866. 22r, Controller and
customs manager, 1904. No. 7867, 22r, Controller and customs chief, 1952. No. 7868, 22r,
Dog training specialist and department head,
2017.

2017, Oct. 25 Litho. Perf. 11¾
7865-7868 A4000 Set of 4 6.00 1.50
7868a Souvenir sheet of 8, 2
each #7865-7868 12.00 3.00

Dancers
A4001

No. 7869: a, Seven Beryozka dancers, Russia. b, Bhavai dancer, India.

2017, Oct. 26 Litho. Perf. 11½
7869 A4001 35r Pair, #a-b 4.50 1.25
Joint issue between Russia and India.
No. 7869 was printed in sheets containing 4
pairs and a central label. See India Nos. 2969-
2970.

Mir Interstate
Television
and Radio
Company,
25th Anniv.
A4002

Serpentine Die Cut 11¼
2017, Oct. 31 Litho.
Self-Adhesive
7870 A4002 27r multi 2.00 .45
See Belarus No. 1065, Kazakhstan No. 830.

Russian Satellite Communication
Company, 50th Anniv. — A4003

2017, Nov. 1 Litho. Perf. 12½x12
7871 A4003 22r multi 1.50 .40

Souvenir Sheet

Ostankino Television Tower and Television Center, 50th Anniv. — A4004

No. 7872: a, Television tower. b, Television Center, horiz.

2017, Nov. 7   **Litho.**   *Perf. 11¾*
7872   A4004   50r Sheet of 2, #a-b   6.50   3.00

Gorny Convent, Ein Karem, Israel A4005

2017, Nov. 14   **Litho.**   *Perf. 12½x12*
7873   A4005   35r multi   2.25   1.60

No. 7873 was printed in sheets of 8 + central label. See Israel No. 2160.

Treasures of Russia A4006

Designs: No. 7874, 22r, Orlov diamond on scepter (cerise background). No. 7875, 22r, Emerald and diamond brooch (yellow brown background). No. 7876, 22r, Orb with sapphire and diamonds (dark emerald background). No. 7877, 22r, Tourmaline pendant carved into bunch of grapes.

2017, Nov. 16   **Litho.**   *Perf. 11½*
7874-7877   A4006   Set of 4   6.00   3.00

Diamond Fund of Russia. A booklet containing four panes of 1 of litho. and embossed examples of Nos. 7874-7877 was released on Dec. 19 and sold for 1200r. Value, $90.

Maya Plisetskaya (1925-2015), Ballet Dancer — A4007

2017, Nov. 20   **Litho.**   *Perf. 12½x12*
7878   A4007   27r multi   2.00   .45

Printed in sheets of 14 + label.

Prosecutor General's Office — A4008

2017, Nov. 23   **Litho.**   *Perf. 12x11½*
7879   A4008   27r multi   1.75   .45

Saint Tikhon of Moscow (1865-1925), 11th Patriarch of Moscow A4009

2017, Nov. 29   **Litho.**   *Perf. 11½*
7880   A4009   41r multi   2.75   .70

Re-establishment of Patriarchate in Russia, cent. No. 7880 was printed in sheets of 8 + central label.

New Year 2018 A4010

No. 7881 — 2018 World Cup mascot, Zabivaka: a, Kicking soccer ball. b, Heading soccer ball. c, Chasing soccer ball.

Serpentine Die Cut 11¼
2017, Dec. 1   **Litho.**
         Self-Adhesive
7881   Strip of 3   6.00   4.00
   a.   A4010 22r multi   1.50   .70
   b.   A4010 33r multi   2.25   1.10
   c.   A4010 35r multi   2.50   .90

Lawyers Type of 2012

Designs: No. 7882, 22r, Ivan I. Dmitriev (1760-1837). No. 7883, 22r, Nikolai M. Korkunov (1853-1904). No. 7884, 22r, Sergei S. Alexeyev (1924-2013).

2017, Dec. 4   **Litho.**   *Perf. 11½*
7882-7884   A3635   Set of 3   4.00   3.00

Nos. 7882-7884 were each printed in sheets of 8 + label.

Federal Treasury — A4011

2017, Dec. 7   **Litho.**   *Perf. 12x11½*
7885   A4011   27r multi   2.00   .45

Monument to Evpaty Kolovrat, by Oleg Sedov — A4012

2017, Dec. 8   **Litho.**   *Perf. 11¼*
7886   A4012   35r multi   2.50   1.75

Yevgeny Primakov (1929-2015), Prime Minister — A4013

2017, Dec. 18   **Litho.**   *Perf. 12½x12*
7887   A4013   27r multi   2.00   .45

Printed in sheets of 14 + label.

Religious Buildings — A4014

No. 7888: a, Bakhchisaray Assumption Monastery, Russia (denomination at LL). b, Golden Temple of Dambulla, Sri Lanka (denomination at LR).

2017, Dec. 18   **Litho.**   *Perf. 12½x12*
7888   A4014   35r Horiz. pair, #a-b   4.50   3.25

Joint issue between Russia and Sri Lanka. See Sri Lanka No.

Federal Security Service, Cent. A4015

2017, Dec. 20   **Litho.**   *Perf. 11½*
7889   A4015   27r multi   1.75   .80

Soccer in Art — A4016

Designs: No. 7890, 22r, Monument to Vsevolod Bobrov, by Anatoly Dyoma and Sergey Mikhailov, 2002. No. 7891, 22r, Soccer Player, bas-relief in Moscow Metro by Elena Yanson-Manizer, 1953. No. 7892, 22r, Soccer, by Aleksandr Deyneka, 1928. No. 7893, 22r, Soccer, by Yuri Pimenov, 1926.

2017, Dec. 20   **Litho.**   *Perf. 12x12½*
7890-7893   A4016   Set of 4   6.00   4.00
7893a   Souvenir sheet of 8, 2 each
     #7890-7893   12.00   8.00

Miniature Sheet

Woodpeckers — A4017

No. 7894: a, Picus viridis. b, Dendrocopos major. c, Dryocopus martius. d, Dendrocopos minor.

2018, Jan. 18   **Litho.**   *Perf. 12x12½*
7894   A4017   35r Sheet of 4, #a-d   9.00   5.00

Nikolai Lavyorov (1930-2016), Geologist — A4018

Vladimir Zeldin (1915-2016), Actor — A4019

2018   **Litho.**   *Perf. 12½x12*
7895   A4018   27r multi   1.75   1.50
7896   A4019   27r multi   1.75   1.50

Full Cavalier of the Order of Merit of the Motherland.
Issued: No. 7895, 1/18; No. 7896, 1/22. No. 7895 was printed in sheets of 14 + label. No. 7896 was printed in sheets of 18 + label.

Battle of Stalingrad, 75th Anniv. — A4020

Litho. & Embossed
2018, Feb. 2   *Perf. 11¾*
7897   A4020   41r multi   2.50   2.00

Printed in sheets of 7 + label.

Kontinental Hockey League, 10th Anniv. — A4021

2018, Feb. 15   **Litho.**   *Perf. 11½*
7898   A4021   22r multi   1.50   .80

Heroes Type of 2016

Designs: No. 7899, 22r, Anatoly V. Lebed (1963-2012). No. 7900, 22r, Alexander V. Krasikov (1958-2005).

2018, Feb. 20   **Litho.**   *Perf. 12½x12*
            Dated "2018"
7899-7900   A3881   Set of 2   2.50   1.50

Nos. 7899-7900 were each printed in sheets of 5.

Floating Bridge, Moscow — A4022

2018, Feb. 21   Litho.   Perf. 11¾
7901 A4022 28r multi   1.75 1.00
Europa.

Great Arctic State Nature
Reserve — A4023

2018, Feb. 28   Litho.   Perf. 11¾
7902 A4023 30r multi   2.00 1.25

2019 Winter Universiade,
Krasnoyarsk — A4024

No. 7903: a, Bobrovy Log Fun Park (22mm long blue panel). b, Platinum Arena, Krasnoyarsk Sports and Entertainment Complex (51mm long magenta panel). c, Ivan Yarygin Sports Palace (32mm long magenta panel). d, Biathlon Academy Multi-purpose Complex (46mm long blue panel)

2018, Mar. 2   Litho.   Perf. 11¾
7903 A4024 40r Block of 4, #a-d 10.00 6.00

Souvenir Sheet

Liberation of Bulgaria and End of
Russo-Turkish War, 140th
Anniv. — A4025

No. 7904: a, Nikolai Grigoryevich Stoletov (1831-1912), Russian commander. b, Count Iosif Vladimirovich Gurko (1828-1901), Russian general. c, Eduard Ivanovich Totleben (1818-84), Russian general.

Litho. & Embossed
2018, Mar. 20   Perf. 12
7904 A4025 60r Sheet of 3, #a-c 12.00 8.00

See Bulgaria No. 4841.

Lilac Varieties — A4026

No. 7905: a, Nadezhda. b, Krasavitsa Moskvy. c, Gortenziya. d, Dzhambul.

Serpentine Die Cut 11
2018, Mar. 21   Litho.
Self-Adhesive
7905 A4026 Block of 4   7.50 4.00
a.-d.   30r Any single   2.00 1.00

Heroes Type of 2016
Designs: 22r, Alexey B. Bukhanov (1965-2003). 27r, Dmitry E. Gorshkov (1971-99).

2018   Litho.   Perf. 12½x12
7906-7907 A3881 Set of 2   3.00 2.00
Issued: 22r, 3/22; 27r, 5/4.

Souvenir Sheet

Portrait of Maxim Gorky, by Nikolai
Bogdanov-Belsky — A4027

2018, Mar. 28   Litho.   Perf. 12
7908 A4027 100r multi   6.50 4.50
Gorky (1868-1936), writer.

Military Commissariats,
Cent. — A4028

2018, Mar. 29   Litho.   Perf. 11¼
7909 A4028 25r multi   1.75 .90

A4029

Designs: Kurchatov Institute (National Nuclear Energy Research Center), 75th Anniv.

2018, Apr. 12   Litho.   Perf. 12½x12
7910 A4029 30r multi   2.50 1.00

30th International Exhibition for
Information and Communication
Technology, Moscow — A4030

2018, Apr. 24   Litho.   Perf. 11½
7911 A4030 40r multi   2.50 1.25

Karl Marx (1818-83), Political
Theorist — A4031

2018, May 4   Litho.   Perf. 12x11¼
7912 A4031 27r multi   1.75 .90

Inauguration
of Pres.
Vladimir Putin
A4032

2018, May 7   Litho.   Perf. 11½
7913 A4032 22r multi   1.40 .70

Battle of the Caucasus, 75th
Anniv. — A4033

Litho. & Embossed
2018, May 8   Perf. 11¾
7914 A4033 41r multi   2.75 1.40

Printed in sheets of 7 + label.

2018 World Cup Soccer
Championships, Russia — A4034

Soccer players and flags of countries in competition in Group: No. 7915, 40r, A (Russia, Saudia Arabia, Egypt, Uruguay). No. 7916, 40r, B (Portugal, Spain, Morocco, Iran). No. 7917, 40r, C (France, Australia, Peru, Denmark). No. 7918, 40r, D (Argentina, Iceland, Croatia, Nigeria). No. 7919, 40r, E (Brazil, Switzerland, Costa Rica, Serbia). No. 7920, 40r, F (Germany, Mexico, Sweden, South Korea). No. 7921, 40r, G (Belgium, Panama, Tunisia, England). No. 7922, 40r, H (Poland, Senegal, Colombia, Japan).

2018, May 10   Litho.   Perf. 12½x12
7915-7922 A4034 Set of 8   20.00 14.00
7922a   Souvenir sheet of 8,
             #7915-7922   20.00 14.00

Flowers — A4035

No. 7923: a, Chrysanthemums and cherry blossoms, red and white polka-dotted ribbon.

b, Daisies and rhododendrons, white, red and blue striped ribbon.

2018, May 16   Litho.   Perf. 12x12½
7923 A4035 27r Pair, #a-b   3.50 1.75

Printed in sheets of 14 containing 7 each Nos. 7923a- 7923b + label. See Japan Nos. 4204-4205.

Miniature Sheet

Beekeeping — A4036

No. 7924 — Apiarist: a, Putting hand in bee colony in tree. b, Applying smoke to bee colony in tree. c, Holding honey from box hives with slanted roofs. d, Holding frame above hive.

2018, May 17   Litho.   Perf. 11¼
7924 A4036 40r Sheet of 4, #a-d, + label 10.00 7.00

Souvenir Sheet

Russian Police, 300th Anniv. — A4037

2018, May 25   Litho.   Perf. 11¼
7925 A4037 95r multi   6.50 3.25

Souvenir Sheets

Novosibirsk Coat of Arms — A4038

Salekhard Coat of Arms — A4039

Ivanovo Coat of Arms — A4040

Grozny Coat of Arms — A4041

2018   **Litho.**   **Perf. 12x12½**
7926	A4038 70r multi	4.50	2.25
7927	A4039 70r multi	4.50	2.25
7928	A4040 70r multi	4.50	2.25
7929	A4041 70r multi	4.50	2.25
	Nos. 7926-7929 (4)	18.00	9.00

Issued: Nos. 7926-7927, 5/29; Nos. 7928-7929, 6/20.

Souvenir Sheet

World Cup Trophy — A4042

2018, June 14   **Litho.**   **Perf. 11¼**
7931	A4042 100r multi	6.50	3.25
a.	As #7931, with Cyrillic overprint in sheet margin	6.50	3.25

Issued: No. 7931a, 8/7. Cyrillic overprint on No. 7931a gives July 15, 2018 date and France 4 - Croatia 2 results of World Cup final match.

Kremlins Type of 2009
Serpentine Die Cut 11
2018, June 25   **Litho.**
Self-Adhesive
7932	A3471 46r Vologda Kremlin	2.75 1.50

Gardens by the Bay, Singapore — A4043

Covered Amphitheater, Zaryadye Park, Moscow — A4044

2018, June 25   **Litho.**   **Perf. 11¾**
7933	Pair	5.00	2.50
a.	A4043 40r multi	2.50	1.25
b.	A4044 40r multi	2.50	1.25

Russia and Singapore Joint Issue.

See Singapore Nos. 1892-1893.

Russian Radio and Electronic Reconnaissance, Cent. — A4045

2018, June 29   **Litho.**   **Perf. 11¾**
7934	A4045 32r multi	2.00	1.00

Victory in the War of 1812, by Z. K. Tsereteli, and Park Pobedy Metro Station — A4046

The Church of St. Tryphon, by S. V. Goryaev, and Maryina Roshcha Metro Station — A4047

24-Hour Soviet Sky, by A. A. Deineka, and Mayakovskaya Metro Station — A4048

Alexander Nevsky, by P. D. Korin, and Komsomolskaya Metro Station — A4049

2018, June 29   **Litho.**   **Perf. 12x11¼**
7935	Vert. strip of 4	10.00	5.00
a.	A4046 40r multi	2.50	1.25
b.	A4047 40r multi	2.50	1.25
c.	A4048 40r multi	2.50	1.25
d.	A4049 40r multi	2.50	1.25

Mosaic art in Moscow Metro.

Kemerovo, Cent. A4050

2018, July 6   **Litho.**   **Perf. 12½x12**
7936	A4050 27r multi	1.75	.90

Novokuznetsk, 400th Anniv. — A4051

2018, July 7   **Litho.**   **Perf. 12x12½**
7937	A4051 27r multi	1.75	.90

Grigory Kisunko (1918-98), Developer of Soviet Missile Defense System A4052

2018, July 10   **Litho.**   **Perf. 12½x12**
7938	A4052 22r multi	1.40	.70

Church on the Blood, Yekaterinburg A4053

2018, July 17   **Litho.**   **Perf. 12x12½**
7939	A4053 27r multi	1.75	.90

Assumption Cathedral, Omsk — A4054

2018, July 25   **Litho.**   **Perf. 12x12½**
7940	A4054 32r multi	2.00	1.00

Gold Saltcellar by Jewelry Firm of Ivan P. Khlebnikov A4055

Troika Sculpture by Jewelry Firm of Ignatii P. Sazikov A4056

Silver Drinking Bowl by Jewelry Firm of Carl Fabergé A4057

Basket by Jewelry Firm of Pavel A. Ovchinnikov A4058

2018, July 26   **Litho.**   **Perf. 11¼**
7941	A4055 27r multi	1.75	.90
7942	A4056 27r multi	1.75	.90
7943	A4057 27r multi	1.75	.90
7944	A4058 27r multi	1.75	.90
	Nos. 7941-7944 (4)	7.00	3.60

Nos. 7941-7944 were each printed in sheets of 8 + label.

Souvenir Sheet

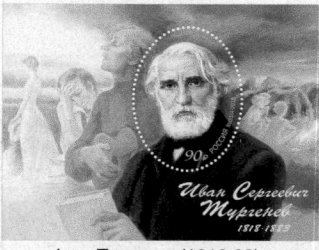

Ivan Turgenev (1818-83), Writer — A4059

2018, Aug. 10   **Litho.**   **Perf.**
7945	A4059 90r multi	6.50	3.00

Federal Public Registration, Cadastre and Cartography Service — A4060

2018, Aug. 20   **Litho.**   **Perf. 12x11½**
7946	A4060 27r multi	1.75	.80

Battle of Kursk, 75th Anniv. — A4061

Litho. & Embossed
2018, Aug. 23   **Perf. 11¾**
7947	A4061 41r multi	2.50	1.25

Printed in sheets of 7 + label.

Tver Carriage Works, 120th Anniv. A4062

2018, Aug. 24   **Litho.**   **Perf. 11½**
7948	A4062 27r multi	1.50	.80

Diplomatic and Courier
Communication, Cent. — A4063

2018, Aug. 27   Litho.   Perf. 11½
7949 A4063 27r multi   1.60   .80

Miniature Sheet

Enameled Arts and Crafts — A4064

No. 7950: a, Vologda enamel piece (blue green background). b, Krasnoselskaya enamel piece (red background). c, Kubachi enamel pitcher and cup (blue background). d, Rostov enamel plate and cup (purple background).

2018, Aug. 30   Litho.   Perf. 11½
7950 A4064 25r Sheet of 4, #a-d 6.50 3.00

New Wave International Contest for
Young Popular Music
Performers — A4065

2018, Aug. 31   Litho.   Perf. 11¾
7951 A4065 22r multi   1.40   .60

Souvenir Sheet

Goznak Factory — A4066

Litho. & Engr.
2018, Sept. 4   Perf. 11¾
7952 A4066 200r multi   12.00 6.00

Goznak, state security printer and producer
of stamps, coins and banknotes, 200th anniv.

Tutayev
Motor Plant,
50th Anniv.
A4067

2018, Sept. 5   Litho.   Perf. 11½
7953 A4067 27r multi   1.75   .80

Abram F. Ioffe (1880-196), Physicist,
and A. F. Ioffe Physical Technical
Institute, St. Petersburg — A4068

2018, Sept. 5   Litho.   Perf. 12x12¼
7954 A4068 32r multi   2.00 1.00
A. F. Ioffe Physical-Technical Institute, Cent.

Heroes Type of 2016
Design: 27r, Oleg N. Dolgov (1976-96).

2018, Sept. 6   Litho.   Perf. 12½x12
Dated "2018"
7955 A3881 27r multi   1.50   .80
Printed in sheets of 5 + label.

Modern Art — A4069

Designs: No. 7956, 37r, In the Fields, painting by N. N. Plastov, 2003. No. 7957, 37r, The Painter M. V. Nesterov, sculpture by A. A. Mironov, 2008, vert. No. 7958, 37r, Monument to Soldiers Who Died in Local Wars and Military Conflicts, sculpture by G. Z. Dolmogombetov, 2007 (33x65mm). No. 7959, 37r, Office Clock with Calendar, by P. N. Radimov, 2005, (33x65mm).

**Perf. 12x11½ (#7956), 11½x12
(#7957), 11¾**
2018, Sept. 20   Litho.
7956-7959 A4069 Set of 4   9.50 4.50

Souvenir Sheet

Moscow Oblast Coat of
Arms — A4070

Litho. & Embossed
2018, Oct. 4   Perf. 12
7960 A4070 120r multi   7.50 4.00

Mosque and Skyscrapers,
Grozny — A4071

2018, Oct. 5   Litho.   Perf. 12x11½
7961 A4071 46r multi   2.75 1.40
Grozny, 200th anniv.

NTV
Broadcasting
Company
Emblem
A4072

Serpentine Die Cut 11¼
2018, Oct. 10   Litho.
Self-Adhesive
7962 A4072 32r multi   2.00 1.00

Komsomol (All-Union Leninist Young
Communist League), Cent. — A4073

Litho. & Embossed
2018, Oct. 25   Perf. 11¾
7963 A4073 46r multi   2.75 1.40

Main
Directorate of
the General
Staff of the
Armed
Forces, Cent.
A4074

2018, Nov. 5   Litho.   Perf. 11½
7964 A4074 27r multi   1.50   .75

Opening of Crimean Bridge — A4075

2018, Nov. 6   Litho.   Perf. 12¼x12
7965 A4075 46r multi + 2 flank-
              ing labels   2.75 1.40

Central Research Institute of
Communications, Cent. — A4076

2018, Nov. 9   Litho.   Perf. 12¼x12
7966 A4076 27r multi   1.25   .60

State Secret
Services of
the Armed
Forces, Cent.
A4077

2018, Nov. 13   Litho.   Perf. 11½
7967 A4077 27r multi   1.25   .60

General V. F.
Margelov
Higher
Airborne
Command
School,
Ryazan,
Cent.
A4078

2018, Nov. 13   Litho.   Perf. 11½
7968 A4078 27r multi   1.25   .60

Federal Service for the Supervision of
Communications, Information
Technology and Mass Media — A4079

2018, Nov. 15   Litho.   Perf. 12x11½
7969 A4079 27r multi   1.25   .60

Battle of the Dnieper, 75th
Anniv. — A4080

Litho. & Embossed
2018, Nov. 15   Perf. 11¾
7970 A4080 41r multi   2.00 1.00
No. 7970 was printed in sheets of 7 + label.

Ordzhonikidze Higher Military
Command School, Cent. — A4081

2018, Nov. 16   Litho.   Perf. 12x12¼
7971 A4081 32r multi   1.50   .75

Souvenir Sheet

Khabarovsk Coat of Arms — A4082

2018, Nov. 22   Litho.   Perf. 12x12¼
7972 A4082 70r gold & multi   3.00 1.50

Combined Arms Academy of the
Armed Forces — A4083

2018, Nov. 27   Litho.   Perf. 12x11¼
7973 A4083 27r multi   1.25   .60

Nikolai E. Zhukovsky Central Aerohydrodynamic Institute, Cent. — A4084

2018, Nov. 30   Litho.   Perf. 11¾
7974 A4084 32r multi   1.50 .75

Lawyers Type of 2012

Designs: No. 7975, 27r, Dmitry N. Zamyatnin (1805-81). No. 7976, 27r, Olympiad S. Ioffe (1920-2005). No. 7977, 27r, Yury P. Novitsky (1882-1922).

2018, Dec. 4   Litho.   Perf. 11¼
7975-7977 A3635   Set of 3   3.75 2.00

Nos. 7975 were each printed in sheets of 8 + label.

New Year 2019 A4085

Serpentine Die Cut 11¼
2018, Dec. 4   Litho.
Self-Adhesive
7978 A4085 22r multi   1.25 .60

Prince Mikhail of Tver (1271-1318) — A4086

2018, Dec. 5   Litho.   Perf. 11¾
7979 A4086 32r multi   1.50 .75

Financial and Economic Service of the Armed Services, Cent. A4087

2018, Dec. 7   Litho.   Perf. 11¼
7980 A4087 27r multi   1.25 .60

Alexander Solzhenitsyn (1918-2008), 1970 Nobel Literature Laureate A4088

2018, Dec. 11   Litho.   Perf. 11¾
7981 A4088 27r multi   1.25 .60

Miniature Sheet

Constitution, 25th Anniv. — A4089

No. 7982: a, Constitution. b, Russian Federation Council Building with fence in front, Federal Assembly (Duma) Building. c, Government Building of the Russian Federation (Russian White House) with one flag. d, Court buildings.

2018, Dec. 12   Litho.   Perf. 12¼x12
7982 A4089 40r Sheet of 4, #a-d   8.00 5.00

Dmitrov Kremlin Museum-Reserve, Cent. — A4090

2018, Dec. 13   Litho.   Perf. 11¾
7983 A4090 40r multi   2.00 1.25

Federal Service for Alcohol Market Regulation — A4091

2018, Dec. 14   Litho.   Perf. 12x11¼
7984 A4091 32r multi   1.50 .75

Heroes Type of 2016

Designs: No. 7985, 27r, Sergey S. Gromov (1966-95). No. 7986, 27r, German A. Ugryumov (1948-2001).

2018, Dec. 17   Litho.   Perf. 12¼x12
Dated "2018"
7985-7986 A3881   Set of 2   2.75 1.60

Nos. 7985-7986 were each printed in sheets of 5 + label.

Spies A4092

Designs: No. 7987, 27r, Vasily M. Chebotaryov (1918-44). No. 7988, 27r, Mikhail P. Krygin (1918-45).

2018, Dec. 17   Litho.   Perf. 11¼
7987-7988 A4092   Set of 2   2.75 1.60

Nos. 7987-7988 were each printed in sheets of 8 + label.

St.George Cross A4093

Award for Kindness A4094

Award for Mentoring A4095

Award for 30 Years of Irreproachable Service — A4096

Award for 50 Years of Irreproachable Service — A4097

Litho. & Embossed
2018, Dec. 20   Perf. 11¾x12
7989 A4093 51r multi   2.50 1.00
7990 A4094 51r multi   2.50 1.00
7991 A4095 51r multi   2.50 1.00
7992 A4096 51r multi   2.50 1.00
7993 A4097 51r multi   2.50 1.00
  Nos. 7989-7993 (5)   12.50 5.00

Nos. 7989-7993 were each printed in sheets of 8 + central label.

Cathedral of the Nativity of Christ, Omsk — A4098

2019, Jan. 9   Litho.   Perf. 12x12¼
7994 A4098 37r multi   2.00 1.00

Recipients of the Order of St. Andrew Type of 2011

Design: Order of St. Andrew and Daniil A. Granin (1919-2017), writer.

2019, Jan. 11   Litho.   Perf. 12x11¼
7995 A3560 40r multi   2.00 1.00

No. 7995 was printed in sheets of 11 + label.

Siberian Crane and Chick — A4099

2019, Jan. 22   Litho.   Perf. 12x11¼
7996 A4099 45r multi   2.00 1.00

Europa.

End of the Siege of Leningrad, 75th Anniv. — A4100

Litho. & Embossed
2019, Jan. 25   Perf. 11¾
7997 A4100 46r multi   2.00 1.00

No. 7997 was printed in sheets of 7 + label.

Venues for ther 2019 Winter Universiade, Krasnoyarsk — A4101

No. 7998: a, Sopka Sports Complex with parked cars at left (blue panel at LR). b, Crystal Arena Ice Palace with blue, red and yellow roof tiles (magenta panel at LR). c, Yenisei Stadium with red brown curved entrance arch (magenta panel at LR). d, Congress Hall of 2019 Winter Universiade (blue panel at LR).

2019, Feb. 1   Litho.   Perf. 11¾
7998 A4101 45r Block of 4, #a-d   8.00 4.00

Uniforms of Courier Service A4102

Designs: No. 7999, 22r, Officer and courier of the Courier Corps, 1797. No. 8000, 22r, Officer and senior courier of the Courier Corps, 1862. No. 8001, 22r, Head of feldpost & felgeger by Special Commissions, 1924. No. 8002, 22r, Officer of Field Communications and Deputy Director of SFS of Russia, 2011.

2019, Feb. 12	Litho.	Perf. 11¾
7999-8002 A4102	Set of 4	4.00 2.00
8002a	Souvenir sheet of 8, 2 each #7999-8002	8.00 4.00

Heroes Type of 2016

Designs: No. 8003, 27r, Roman A. Kitanin (1978-2007). No. 8004, 27r, Oleg V. Tereshkin (1971-95).

2019, Feb. 22	Litho.	Perf. 12¼x12

Dated "2019"

8003-8004 A3881	Set of 2	2.50 1.25

Nos. 8003-8004 were each printed in sheets of 5 + label.

Dogs — A4103

No. 8005: a, Yorkshire terriers with bows. b, Shorthaired Petit Brabançons. c. Pugs playing with ball. d, Russian toy terriers in snow.

2019, Feb. 28	Litho.	Perf. 11¾
8005 A4103 35r Block or vert.		
	strip of 4, #a-d	6.50 3.25

Souvenir Sheet

2019 Winter Universiade, Krasnoyarsk — A4104

2019, Mar. 2	Litho.	Perf. 12x12¼
8006 A4104 100r multi		4.50 2.25

No. 8006 with a serial number and an inscription in the sheet margin giving the medal count of the Russian team was produced in limited quantities and issued on Apr. 16, 2019. Value, $30.

Secret Intelligence Officers A4105

Designs: No. 8007, 27r, Africa de las Heras (1909-88). No. 8008, 27r, Zoya Ivanovna Voskresenskaya-Rybkina (1907-92).

2019, Mar. 12	Litho.	Perf. 11½
8007-8008 A4105	Set of 2	2.50 1.25

Nos. 8007-8008 were each printed in sheets of 8 + central label.

Examples of No. 7128 with an 80r surcharge and an added Cyrillic inscription in the sheet margin commemorating 2019 as the International Year of the Periodic Table were produced in limited quantities and issued on Mar. 16, 2019.

Apple Varieties — A4106

No. 8009: a, Bogatyr. b, Belyi Naliv. c, Antonovka Obyknovennaya. d, Orlik.

Serpentine Die Cut 11¼

2019, Mar. 26		Litho.

Self-Adhesive

8009 A4106	Block of 4	9.00 4.50
a.-d.	45r Any single	2.00 1.00

Souvenir Sheets

Tyumen Coat of Arms — A4107

Ufa Coat of Arms — A4108

2019, Mar. 28	Litho.	Perf. 12x12¼
8010 A4107 70r multi		3.25 1.60
8011 A4108 80r multi		3.50 1.75

Alexey I. Fatyanov (1919-59), Song Writer A4109

2019, Mar. 29	Litho.	Perf. 11¼x12
8012 A4109 29r multi		1.50 .75

Internet Country Code Top Level Domain ".ru," 25th Anniv. A4110

2019, Apr. 5	Litho.	Perf. 11½
8013 A4110 32r multi		1.25 .60

Marcial Waters Resort Spa, 300th Anniv. — A4111

2019, Apr. 5	Litho.	Perf. 11¾
8014 A4111 50r multi		2.00 1.00

Crimean Offensive, 75th Anniv. — A4112

Litho. & Embossed

2019, Apr. 18	Litho.	Perf. 11¾
8015 A4112 46r multi		2.00 1.00

No. 8015 was printed in sheets of 7 + label.

Federal Communications Agency — A4113

2019, Apr. 24	Litho.	Perf. 12x11½
8016 A4113 32r multi		1.50 .75

Medal of Ushakov A4114

Order of Merit for the Fatherland A4115

Medal for Bravery A4116

Medal of Suvarov A4117

Litho. & Embossed

2019, Apr. 26		Perf. 12
8017 A4114 50r multi		2.50 1.25
8018 A4115 50r multi		2.50 1.25
8019 A4116 50r multi		2.50 1.25
8020 A4117 50r multi		2.50 1.25
Nos. 8017-8020 (4)		10.00 5.00

Nos. 8017-8020 were each printed in sheets of 8 + central label.

Boris Rosing (1869-1933), Inventor of Early Television Components — A4118

2019, May 6	Litho.	Perf. 12½x12
8021 A4118 32r multi		1.25 .60

No. 8021 was printed in sheets of 10 + central label.

Mustai Karim (1919-2005), Poet — A4119

2019, May 15	Litho.	Perf. 11¾
8022 A4119 35r multi		1.25 .60

No. 8022 was printed in sheets of 8 + central label.

Cup, Bowl and Owl Vessel From Alexandrovskaya Sloboda Museum — A4120

2019, May 18	Litho.	Perf. 11½x12
8023 A4120 32r multi		1.50 .75

Alexandrovskaya Sloboda Museum, Alexandrov, cent.

Souvenir Sheet

Overgrown Pond, by Vasily D. Polenov
(1844-1927) — A4121

2019, May 29   Litho.   *Perf. 12*
8024 A4121 100r gold & multi   5.00 2.50

Souvenir Sheet

The Ceremonial Meeting of the State
Council on May 7, 1901, by Ilya E.
Repin (1844-1930) — A4122

2019, May 29   Litho.   *Perf. 11¾*
8025 A4122 100r gold & multi   5.00 2.50

Arkhangelsk State Museum,
Cent. — A4123

2019, May 30   Litho.   *Perf. 11¾*
8026 A4123 35r multi   1.50 .75

Yeniseysk, 400th Anniv. — A4124

2019, June 7   Litho.   *Perf. 11¾*
8027 A4124 40r multi   1.25 .65

Emblem of Russian
Postal
Service — A4125

Serpentine Die Cut 11½ Syncopated
2019, June 11   Litho.
Self-Adhesive
Frame Color
8028 A4125 23r blue   1.25 .60
        See Nos. 8051-8053.

Petr L. Kapitsa
(1894-1984),
1978 Nobel
Laureate in
Physics
A4126

2019, June 14   Litho.   *Perf. 11¾*
8029 A4126 32r multi   1.25 .60

Central Armed Forces Museum,
Moscow, Cent. — A4127

2019, June 18   Litho.   *Perf. 12x11¼*
8030 A4127 40r multi   1.25 .65

A-50 Radar
Detection
Airplane and
Building of
Vega Radio
Engineering
Company
A4128

2019, June 20   Litho.   *Perf. 11½*
8031 A4128 50r multi   1.60 .80

Birdhouse, Sculpture by Matvey G.
Manizer, and Revolution Square Metro
Station — A4129

Sympathy, Sculpture by Vladimir
Tsigal, and Mendeleevskaya Metro
Station — A4130

Defenders of the Fatherland, Sculpture
by Georgii I. Motovilov, and
Smolenskaya Metro Station — A4131

Young Family, Sculpture by S. A.
Goryainov, and Polyanka Metro
Station — A4132

2019, Mar. 26 Litho. *Perf. 12x11¼*
8032   Vert. strip of 4   8.00 4.00
  a. A4129 45r multi   2.00 1.00
  b. A4130 45r multi   2.00 1.00
  c. A4131 45r multi   2.00 1.00
  d. A4132 45r multi   2.00 1.00
     Sculptures in the Moscow Metro.

Bird With
Woman's
Head and "I
Love Russia"
Inscription
A4133

Serpentine Die Cut 11¼
2019, June 27   Litho.
Self-Adhesive
8033 A4133 18r multi   .60 .30

International Day of
Parliamentarism — A4134

2019, June 27   Litho.   *Perf. 11½*
8034 A4134 53r multi   1.75 .85

Bellflower Varieties — A4135

No. 8035: a, Campaenula bononiensis. b,
Campanula persicifolia. c, Campanula ciliata.
d, Campanula pendula.

Serpentine Die Cut 11
2019, June 28   Litho.
Self-Adhesive
8035 A4135   Block of 4   8.00 4.00
  a.-d.   45r Any single   2.00 1.00

Operation Bagration (Belarussian
Strategic Offensive Operation), 75th
Anniv. — A4136

Litho. & Embossed
2019, July 3   *Perf. 11¾*
8036 A4136 50r multi   1.60 .80
No. 8036 was printed in sheets of 7 + label.
See Belarus No. 1145.

Ammeter, Measuring Tape, Stopwatch
and Platinum-Iridium Cylinder Under
Glass Cap — A4137

2019, July 9   Litho.   *Perf. 11½*
8037 A4137 53r multi   1.75 .85
     International System of Units.

Grape Harvesting — A4138

No. 8038 — Woman with basket of: a, Russian floral (green) grapes. b, Bulgarian Ruby
Kaliskin (purple) grapes.

2019, July 15 Litho. *Perf. 12¼x12*
8038 A4138 45r Horiz. pair, #a-b 4.00 2.00
     See Bulgaria No. 4907.

Souvenir Sheet

Ships of the Discovery of
Antarctica — A4139

No. 8039: a, Mirny (denominaation at LR).
b, Vostok (denomination at LL).

2019, July 16 Litho. *Perf. 12¼x12*
8039 A4139 50r Sheet of 2, #a-b 3.25 1.60
Discovery of Antarctica, 200th anniv. (in
2020).

Miniature Sheet

Endangered Animals — A4140

No. 8040: a, Cuon alpinus. b, Monodon
monoceros. c, Vulpes lagopus semenovi. d,
Lagenorhynchus albirostris.

2019, July 23 Litho. *Perf. 11½x11¼*
8040 A4140 50r Sheet of 4, #a-d 6.25 3.25

Souvenir Sheet

Fifth Army International
Games — A4141

No. 8041: a, Tank biathlon. b, Aviadarts.

2019, July 26   Litho.   *Perf. 11¼*
8041 A4141 45r Sheet of 2, #a-b,
             + central label   3.00 1.50

Souvenir Sheet

Exhibition of Achievements of National Economy, Moscow, 80th Anniv. — A4142

No. 8042: a, Space Pavilion and rocket. b, Friendship of Nations Fountain. c, Northern Entrance Gate.

2019, July 31   Litho.   Perf. 11¼
8042 A4142 50r Sheet of 3, #a-c,
              + label   4.75 2.40

Emblem of Russian Postal Service Type of 2019 and

A4143   A4144

Emblem of Russian Postal Service

A4145   A4146

Serpentine Die Cut 11½ Syncopated
2019, Aug. 7   Litho.

Self-Adhesive
Frame Color
8043 A4143 50k blue   .25   .25
8044 A4143 1r brown   .25   .25
8045 A4143 2r brn carmine   .25   .25
8046 A4143 2.50r gray green   .25   .25
8047 A4143 3r blue grn   .25   .25
8048 A4143 4r carmine   .25   .25
8049 A4144 5r blue   .25   .25
8050 A4144 6r violet   .25   .25
8051 A4145 10r violet brown   .30   .25
8052 A4125 25r purple   .75   .35

Size: 26x35mm
8053 A4125 50r gray green   1.50   .75
8054 A4146 100r lt blue   3.00 1.50
     Nos. 8043-8054 (12)   7.55 4.85

Eurasian Economic Union, 5th Anniv. A4147

2019, Aug. 9   Litho.   Perf. 11½
8055 A4147 50r gold & multi   1.50   .75

Vyborg-Petrozavodsk Offensive, 75th Anniv. — A4148

Litho. & Embossed
2019, Aug. 9   Perf. 11¾
8056 A4148 50r multi   1.50   .75

No. 8056 was printed in sheets of 7 + label. A booklet containing panes of 1 of Nos. 7997, 8015, 8036 and 8056 and panes of 1 of imperforate gold stamps similar to those stamps was produced in limited quantities.

Tolbukhin Lighthouse — A4149

2019, Aug. 13   Litho.   Perf. 12½x12
8057 A4149 32r multi   .95   .50

Spasskaya Tower International Military Music Festival — A4150

Perf. 11¾x11¼
2019, Aug. 22   Litho.
8058 A4150 53r multi   1.60   .80

2019 World Skills Championships, Kazan — A4151

Serpentine Die Cut 11¼
2019, Aug. 22   Litho.
8059 A4151 53r brt yel green 1.60   .80

Academic Archaelogy in Russia, Cent. — A4152

No. 8060: a, Carved fish figurine. b, Figure of a woman. c, White Sea petroglyphs. d, Bison.

Perf. 11¾x11¼
2019, Aug. 26   Litho.
8060 A4152 40r Block or vert.
              strip of 4, #a-d 4.75 2.40

Motorcycles — A4153

Designs: No. 8061, 32r, 1934 PMZ A-750. No. 8062, 32r, 1938 IZh-8. No. 8063, 32r, 2009 Ural-Sakhara.

2019, Aug. 29   Litho.   Perf. 12½x12
8061-8063 A4153 Set of 3   3.00 1.50
8063a   Sheet of 12, 4 each
             #8061-8063, + 3 labels 12.00 6.00

Nos. 8061-8063 were each printed in sheets of 8 + central label.

Breastplate with Portrait of Tsar Peter I — A4154

Diadem A4155

Port Bouquet A4156

Rattle-Whistle — A4157

2019, Sept. 3   Litho.   Perf. 11½
8064 A4154 40r multi   1.25   .60
8065 A4155 40r multi   1.25   .60
8066 A4156 40r multi   1.25   .60
8067 A4157 40r multi   1.25   .60
     Nos. 8064-8067 (4)   5.00 2.40

A booklet containing panes of 1 of lithographed and embossed stamps similar to Nos. 8064-8067 was printed in limited quantities.

Oleg P. Tabakov (1935-2018), Artistic Director of the Moscow Art Theater — A4158

2019, Sept. 4   Litho.   Perf. 12½x12
8068 A4158 40r multi   1.25   .60

No. 8068 was printed in sheets of 14 + label.

Mohandas K. Gandhi (1869-1948), Indian Nationalist Leader — A4159

2019, Sept. 4   Litho.   Perf. 12x12½
8069 A4159 40r multi   1.25   .60

No. 7731 Surcharged in Gold

Method and Perf. As Before
2019, Sept. 5
8070 A3895 45r on 24r #7731
              (G)   1.40   .70

Kazan Kremlin, Site of 2019 Aga Khan Architecture Award Ceremony — A4160

2019, Sept. 12   Litho.   Perf. 12½x12
8071 A4160 53r multi   1.60   .80

Political Organizations in the Armed Forces, Cent. — A4161

2019, Sept. 16   Litho.   Perf. 12½x12
8072 A4161 40r multi   1.25   .60

General S. M. Shtemenko Higher Military School, Krasnodar — A4162

2019, Sept. 17   Litho.   Perf. 12¼x12
8073 A4162 40r multi   1.25   .60

Souvenir Sheet

Mikhail T. Kalashnikov (1919-2013), Firearms Designer — A4163

2019, Sept. 18   Litho.   Perf. 12¼x12
8074 A4163 100r multi   3.25 1.60

Moscow Kremlin, Sunny, by Evgeny V. Romashko — A4164

Chameleon Rock at Sunset, by Elena S. Brazhunenko — A4165

Lyalyh, by V. O. Umarsultanov A4166

Statue of Alexander S. Pushkin, Nur-Sultan, Kazakhstan, by Andrey N. Kovalchuk A4167

I Love My Horse, by V. A. Glukhov — A4168

2019, Sept. 20　Litho.　Perf. 12x11¾
8075　A4164　50r multi　　1.60　.80
8076　A4165　50r multi　　1.60　.80
Perf. 11¾x12
8077　A4166　50r multi　　1.60　.80
8078　A4167　50r multi　　1.60　.80
Perf. 11¼
8079　A4168　50r multi　　1.60　.80
　　Nos. 8075-8079 (5)　8.00　4.00

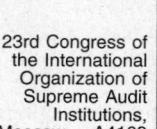

23rd Congress of the International Organization of Supreme Audit Institutions, Moscow — A4169

2019, Sept. 23　Litho.　Perf. 12x12¼
8080　A4169　40r multi　　1.25　.60

Souvenir Sheet

Evgraf F. Komarovsky (1769-1843), Military Leader and Memoir Writer — A4170

2019, Sept. 25　Litho.　Perf.
8081　A4170　100r multi　　3.25　1.60

M. V. Frunze Higher Combined Arms School, Omsk — A4171

2019, Oct. 1　Litho.　Perf. 12¼x12
8082　A4171　35r multi　　1.10　.55

World Post Day, 50th Anniv. — A4172

Serpentine Die Cut 11
2019, Oct. 9　　　　Litho.
Self-Adhesive
8083　A4172　23r multi　　.75　.35
With Blue Frame
8084　A4172　50r multi　　1.60　.80

Universal Postal Union, 145th Anniv. A4173

2019, Oct. 9　Litho.　Perf. 12½x12
8085　A4173　45r multi　　1.40　.70

Souvenir Sheet

Women, by Filipp A. Malyavin (1869-1940) — A4174

2019, Oct. 10　Litho.　Perf. 12
8086　A4174　110r multi　　3.50　1.75

Moscow Expocenter, 60th Anniv. — A4175

2019, Oct. 17　Litho.　Perf. 12½x12
8087　A4175　32r multi　　1.00　.50

Communications Troops, Cent. — A4176

2019, Oct. 18　Litho.　Perf. 11½
8088　A4176　50r multi　　1.60　.80

St. Andrew's Hall, Grand Kremlin Palace, Moscow — A4177

2019, Oct. 21　Litho.　Perf. 12x11½
8089　A4177　53r multi　　1.75　.85

Masha A4178

Bear A4179

Masha and the Bear A4180

Serpentine Die Cut 11
2019, Oct. 22　　　　Litho.
Self-Adhesive
8090　　Horiz. strip of 3　3.25
　a.　A4178　23r multi　　.75　.35
　b.　A4179　23r multi　　.75　.35
　c.　A4180　50r multi　　1.60　.80
　　Masha and the Bear cartoon series, 10th anniv.

Miniature Sheet

Airplanes Designed by Sergey V. Ilyushin (1894-1977) — A4181

　No. 8091: a, Il-2. b, Il-28. c, Il-14. d, Il-18. e, Il-62.

2019, Oct. 23　Litho.　Perf. 12¼x12
8091　A4181　50r Sheet of 5, #a-e,
　　　　+ label　　8.00　4.00

Souvenir Sheet

Russian State Circuses, Cent. — A4182

2019, Oct. 30　Litho.　Perf.
8092　A4182　100r multi　　3.25　1.60

Military University of the Ministry of Defense of the Russian Federation, Moscow, Cent. — A4183

2019, Nov. 5　Litho.　Perf. 12¼x12
8093　A4183　40r multi　　1.25　.60

Marshal S. M. Budyonny Military Academy of the Signal Corps, Cent. — A4184

2019, Nov. 8　Litho.　Perf. 12¼x12
8094　A4184　43r multi　　1.40　.70

Heroes Type of 2016

　Designs: No. 8095, 27r, Alexander A. Prokhorenko (1990-2016). No. 8096, 27r, Leonid G. Valov (1947-95). No. 8097, 27r, Mikhail A. Myasnikov (1975-2008).

2019, Nov. 8　Litho.　Perf. 12½x12
Dated "2019"
8095-8097　A3881　Set of 3　　2.50　1.25
　　Nos. 8095-8097 were each printed in sheets of 5 + label.

Ivan D. Papanin (1894-1986), Polar
Explorer — A4185

2019, Nov. 14   Litho.   Perf. 12¼x12
8098 A4185 53r multi   1.75   .85

Ministry of Transport Building — A4186

2019, Nov. 20   Litho.   Perf. 12x11½
8099 A4186 40r multi   1.25   .60

Souvenir Sheet

St. Petersburg — A4187

No. 8100: a, Lakhta Center. b, Gazprom
Arena, horiz.

2019, Nov. 22   Litho.   Perf. 11¾
8100 A4187 60r Sheet of 2, #a-b 3.75 1.90

Souvenir Sheet

In the House, by Sergei Vinogradov
(1869-1938) — A4188

2019, Nov. 29   Litho.   Perf. 12
8101 A4188 150r multi   4.75 2.40

Mining and
Industrial
Supervision,
300th Anniv.
A4189

2019, Dec. 2   Litho.   Perf. 11½
8102 A4189 50r multi   1.60   .80

New Year
2020
A4190

Serpentine Die Cut 11
2019, Dec. 5   Litho.
Self-Adhesive
8103 A4190 23r multi   .75   .35

Foreign Intelligence Service
Building — A4191

2019, Dec. 6   Litho.   Perf. 12x11½
8104 A4191 40r multi   1.40   .70

A4192

A4193

A4194

Kholmogorsk Bone Carvings — A4195

Litho. & Embossed
2019, Dec. 10   Perf. 12¼x12
8105 A4192 56r multi   1.90   .95
8106 A4193 56r multi   1.90   .95
8107 A4194 56r multi   1.90   .95
8108 A4195 56r multi   1.90   .95
     Nos. 8105-8108 (4)   7.60 3.80

Kholmogory
Post Road From
Arkhangelsk to
Moscow
A4196

2020, Jan. 15   Litho.   Perf. 11¾
8110 A4196 53r multi   1.75   .85
     Europa.

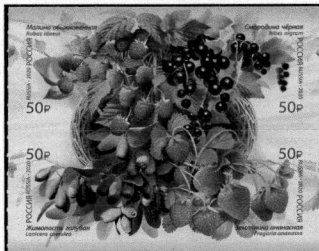

Berries — A4197

No. 8111: a, Rubus idaeus. b, Ribes nigrum.
c, Lonicera caerulea. d, Fragaria ananassa.

Serpentine Die Cut 11
2020, Jan. 17   Litho.
Self-Adhesive
8111 A4197 50r Block of 4, #a-d 6.25 3.25

Souvenir Sheet

Tula Kremlin, 500th Anniv. — A4198

2020, Jan. 21   Litho.   Perf. 12x12½
8112 A4198 120r multi   3.75 1.90

Souvenir Sheet

Ruskeala Mountain Park, Karelia,
Cent. — A4199

2020, Jan. 23   Litho.   Perf. 12
8113 A4199 100r multi   3.25 1.60

Souvenir Sheet

Discovery of Antarctica, 200th
Anniv. — A4200

No. 8114: a, Fabian von Bellingshausen
(1778-1852), explorer. b, Mikhail P. Lazarev
(1788-1851), explorer.

2020, Jan. 28   Litho.   Perf. 12x12½
8114 A4200 50r Sheet of 2, #a-b 3.25 1.60
Joint issue between Russia and Estonia.
See Estonia No. 914.

Vistula-Oder Offensive, 75th
Anniv. — A4201

Litho. & Embossed
2020, Jan. 30   Perf. 11¾
8115 A4201 60r multi   1.90   .95
No. 8115 was printed in sheets of 7 + label.

Souvenir Sheet

Midday, by Arkady A. Plastov (1893-
1972) — A4202

2020, Jan. 31   Litho.   Perf. 12x11¾
8116 A4202 150r multi   4.75 2.40

Jewel
Encrusted
Bow
A4203

Jewel
Encrusted
Flower
Bouquet
A4204

Bracelet With
Portrait
A4205

Spinel of
Grand
Imperial
Crown
A4206

2020, Feb. 3   Litho.   Perf. 11¼
8117 A4203 50r multi   1.60   .80
8118 A4204 50r multi   1.60   .80
8119 A4205 50r multi   1.60   .80
8120 A4206 50r multi   1.60   .80
     Nos. 8117-8120 (4)   6.40 3.20

Ivan A. Bunin
(1870-1953),
1933 Nobel
Laureate in
Literature
A4207

2020, Feb. 7   Litho.   Perf. 11¾
8121 A4207 50r multi   1.50   .75

Sculpture of Winston Churchill, Franklin D. Roosevelt and Joseph Stalin at Yalta Conference, by Zurab Tsereteli — A4208

2020, Feb. 10   **Litho.**   **Perf. 11**
8122   A4208   50r multi   1.50   .75

Yalta Conference, 75th Anniv.

Pushkin Medal A4209

Zhukov Medal A4210

Nesterov Medal A4211

Defender of Free Russia Medal A4212

Litho. & Embossed
2020, Feb. 12   **Perf. 11½x12**
8123	A4209	60r multi	1.90	.95
8124	A4210	60r multi	1.90	.95
8125	A4211	60r multi	1.90	.95
8126	A4212	60r multi	1.90	.95
	Nos. 8123-8126 (4)		7.60	3.80

POSTAL-FISCAL STAMPS

During 1918-22, Postal Savings stamps and Control stamps were authorized for postal use. Because of hyper-inflation during 1920-22, Russian

---

Arms stamps and these postal-fiscal stamps were sold and used at different rates at different times: 1918-20, sold at face value; from March, 1920, sold at 100 times face value; from Aug. 15, 1921, sold at 250r each, regardless of face value; from April, 1922, sold at 10,000r per 1k or 1r. In Oct. 1922, these issues were superseded by gold currency stamps.

Postal Savings Stamps

PF1

Perf. 14½x14¾
1918, Jan. 12   **Wmk. 171**   **Typo.**
AR1	PF1	1k dp red, *buff*	.60	1.00
AR2	PF1	5k green, *buff*	.60	1.00
AR3	PF1	10k chocolate, *buff*	1.20	1.00
	Nos. AR1-AR3 (3)		2.40	3.00

Nos. AR1-AR14 have a faint burelé background, which is noted as the paper color in these listings.

For surcharges of Nos. AR1-AR3, see Armenia Nos. 250-253, Far Eastern Republic Nos. 35 and 36, South Russia Nos. 47-49 and numerous Ukraine issues beginning with Nos. 45e-47e.

Postal Savings Stamps

PF2

PF3

1918, June 5   **Litho.**   **Perf. 13**
AR4	PF2	25k black, *rose*	11.00	37.50
AR5	PF2	50k brn, *pale brn*	24.00	50.00
AR6	PF3	50k brn, *pale brn*	35.00	62.50
	Nos. AR4-AR6 (3)		70.00	150.00

Control Stamps

PF4

PF5

PF6

PF7

PF8

1918, June 5   **Litho.**   **Perf. 13**
AR7	PF4	25k blk, *pale brn*	24.00	32.50
AR8	PF4	50k brn, *buff*	17.50	50.00
AR9	PF5	1r org, *buff*	1.50	3.50
AR10	PF5	3r grn, *buff*	1.50	3.50
AR11	PF5	5r dp blue, *buff*	1.50	3.75
AR12	PF6	10r dp red, *buff*	1.50	3.75
AR13	PF7	25r dp brn, *buff*	5.00	15.00
AR14	PF8	100r blk, *blue & car*	3.75	6.25
	Nos. AR7-AR14 (8)		56.25	118.25

General Revenue Stamps

PF9

1918   **Litho.**   **Perf. 12x12½**
AR15	PF9	5k lil brn, *buff*	1.50	—
AR16	PF9	10k ol brn, *lt blue*	1.50	—
AR17	PF9	15k dp blue, *pink*	1.50	—
AR18	PF9	20k reddish brn, *buff*	1.50	—
AR19	PF9	50k org red, *gray*	1.50	—
AR20	PF9	75k ol grn, *buff*	3.25	—
AR21	PF9	1r red, *pale blue*	6.25	—
AR22	PF9	1.25r dk brn, *redsh brn*	30.00	—
AR23	PF9	2r vio, *dk grn*	30.00	—
AR24	PF9	3r dp vio blue, *rose lil*	3.50	—
AR25	PF9	5r dp blue grn, *lt grn*	6.50	—
	Nos. AR15-AR25 (11)		87.00	

Nos. AR15-AR25 exist in tête-bêche vertical pairs and in tête-bêche vertical gutter pairs.

SEMI-POSTAL STAMPS

Empire

Admiral Kornilov Monument, Sevastopol SP1

Pozharski and Minin Monument, Moscow SP2

Statue of Peter the Great, Leningrad SP3

Alexander II Memorial and Kremlin, Moscow SP4

1905 Typo. Unwmk. Perf. 12x12½
B1	SP1	3k red, brn & grn	24.00	5.25
		Never hinged	140.00	
B2	SP2	5k lil, vio & straw	5.00	3.50
		Never hinged	20.00	

B3	SP3	7k lt bl, dk bl & pink	5.00	3.50
		Never hinged	20.00	
B4	SP4	10k lt blue, dk bl & yel	7.50	.50
		Never hinged	25.00	
	Nos. B1-B4 (4)		41.50	12.75

Line Perf. 13¼
B1a	SP3	3k red, brn & grn	40.00	1.25
B3a	SP3	7k lt bl, dk bl & pink	82.50	1.25
B4a	SP4	10k lt bl, dk bl & yel	7.50	.50
B1b	SP1	3k red, brn & grn	16.50	5.00
B1c	SP1	3k red, brn & grn	200.00	200.00
B1d	SP1	3k red, brn & grn	200.00	200.00

These stamps were sold for 3 kopecks over face value. The surtax was donated to a fund for the orphans of soldiers killed in the Russo-Japanese war.

Ilya Murometz Legendary Russian Hero — SP5

Designs: 3k, Don Cossack Bidding Farewell to His Sweetheart. 7k, Symbolical of Charity. 10k, St. George Slaying the Dragon.

1914 Colored Papers Perf. 11½
B5	SP5	1k red brn & dk grn, *straw*	2.00	2.00
B6	SP5	3k mar & gray grn, *pink*	3.00	3.00
B7	SP5	7k dk brn & dk grn, *buff*	3.50	2.00
B8	SP5	10k dk bl & brn, *blue*	12.00	4.50
	Nos. B5-B8 (4)		20.50	11.50

Perf. 12½
B5a	SP5	1k red brn & dk grn, *straw*	3.75	3.25
B6a	SP5	3k mar & gray grn, *pink*	4.25	3.25
B7a	SP5	7k dk brn & dk grn, *buff*	9.50	7.50
B8a	SP5	10k dk bl & brn, *blue*	21.00	7.50
	Nos. B5a-B8a (4)		38.50	21.50

Perf. 13¼
B5b	SP5	1k red brn & dk grn, *straw*	8.50	2.00
B6b	SP5	3k mar & gray grn, *pink*	225.00	45.00
B7b	SP5	7k dk brn & dk grn, *buff*	3.75	3.75
B8b	SP5	10k dk bl & brn, *blue*	24.00	5.50

1915 White Paper Perf. 11½
B9	SP5	1k org brn & gray	2.25	2.00
B10	SP5	3k car & gray blk	2.25	2.00
B12	SP5	10k dk bl & dk brn	4.25	2.25
	Nos. B9-B12 (3)		8.75	

Perf. 12½
B9a	SP5	1k org brn & gray	3.50	2.00
B10a	SP5	3k car & gray blk	3.50	2.00
d.		Horiz. pair, imperf. between	175.00	
B11	SP5	7k dk brn & dk grn	12.00	
B12a	SP5	10k dk bl & dk brn	4.25	2.25

Perf. 13¼
B9b	SP5	1k org brn & gray	2.25	2.00
B10b	SP5	3k car & gray blk	2.25	2.00
B12b	SP5	10k dk bl & dk brn	5.00	2.25
	Nos. B9b-B12b (3)		9.50	6.25

Imperf
B9c	SP5	1k org brn & gray	425.00	225.00
B10c	SP5	3k car & gray blk	425.00	225.00
B11	SP5	B11 dk brn & dk grn	425.00	225.00
B12c	SP5	10k dk bl & dk brn	425.00	225.00
	Nos. B9c-B12c (3)		1,275.	675.00

These stamps were sold for 1 kopeck over face value. The surtax was donated to charities connected with the war of 1914-17.

No. B11 not regularly issued. It exists only perf 11½ (with Specimen overprint) and 12½.

For surcharges of Nos. B5-B13, see Armenia Nos. 255-265 and Siberia No. 64.

Russian Soviet Federated Socialist Republic
Volga Famine Relief Issue

Relief Work on Volga River — SP9

Administering Aid to Famine Victim — SP10

Genuine

Forgery

Characteristics between the genuine and forgery stamps:

Genuine: Shadow of the old man's stick at bottom left joins the base of the stick. At top in the second line of text within the second word, the lower serifs of the fifth letter and the A in the word just merge together. Word under denomination is clear on left side. The paper is whitish.

Forgery: Shadow and stick has a clear gap the base of the stick. At top in the second line of text within the second word the lower serifs of the fifth letter and the A there is a clear gap. Word under denomination has a deformed "y" on the left side. The paper is pale cream and thicker, the design is less detailed and blurry.

			1921	**Litho.**	**Imperf.**
B14	SP9	2250r green		3.75	6.00
a.		Pelure paper		165.00	125.00
B15	SP9	2250r deep red		2.00	11.00
a.		Pelure paper		19.00	15.00
B16	SP9	2250r brown		3.75	11.00
B17	SP10	2250r dark blue		9.50	30.00
a.		2250r dark blue		20.00	—
		Nos. B14-B17 (4)		19.00	58.00

Forged cancels and counterfeits of Nos. B14-B17 are plentiful.

Stamps of type A33 with this overprint were not charity stamps nor did they pay postage in any form.

They represent taxes paid on stamps exported from or imported into Russia. In 1925 the semi-postal stamps of 1914-15 were surcharged for the same purpose. Stamps of the regular issues

1918 and 1921 have also been surcharged with inscriptions and new values, to pay the importation and exportation taxes.

Nos. 149-150 Surcharged in Black, Red, Blue or Orange

			1922, Feb.	**Perf. 13½**	
B18	A33	100r + 100r on 70k		1.60	1.25
c.		"100 p. + p. 100"		225.00	290.00
B19	A33	100r + 100r on 70k			
		(R)		1.60	1.25
B20	A33	100r + 100r on 70k		1.00	1.25
		(Bl)			
B21	A33	250r + 250r on 35k		.50	.75
B22	A33	250r + 250r on 35k			
		(R)		1.00	2.00
B23	A33	250r + 250r on 35k			
		(O)		1.60	5.00
		Nos. B18-B23 (6)		7.30	11.50

Surcharge Inverted

B18a	A33	100r + 100r on 70k		160.00	1.00
B19a	A33	100r + 100r on 70k		140.00	60.00
B20a	A33	100r + 100r on 70k			
		(Bl)		70.00	45.00
B21a	A33	250r + 250r on 35k		70.00	—
B22a	A33	250r + 250r on 35k			
		(R)		200.00	45.00
B23a	A33	250r + 250r on 35k		225.00	100.00

Surcharge Double

B18b	A33	100r + 100r on 70k		200.00	—
B19b	A33	100r + 100r on 70k			
		(R)		200.00	—
B21b	A33	250r + 250r on 35k		200.00	
B22b	A33	250r + 250r on 35k			
		(R)		200.00	—

Issued to raise funds for Volga famine relief.

Regular Issues of 1909-18 Overprinted

			1922, Aug. 19	**Perf. 14**	
B24	A14	1k orange		350.00	350.00
B25	A14	2k green		22.50	35.00
B26	A14	3k red		22.50	35.00
B27	A14	5k claret		22.50	35.00
B28	A15	10k dark blue		22.50	35.00
			Imperf		
B29	A14	1k orange		350.00	350.00
		Nos. B24-B29 (6)		790.00	840.00

Overprint Inverted (Reading Up)

B24a	A14	1k orange		825.00	
B25a	A14	2k green		325.00	
B26a	A14	3k red		825.00	
		Never hinged		1,750.	
B27a	A14	5k claret		825.00	
		Never hinged		1,750.	
B28a	A15	10k dark blue		825.00	
		Never hinged		1,900.	
B29a	A14	1k orange		825.00	
		Never hinged		1,750.	

Double Overprint

B25b	A14	2k green		600.00	900.00
B26b	A14	3k red		1,450.	
B27b	A14	5k claret		725.00	
B28b	A15	10k dark blue		1,200.	
B29b	A14	1k orange		2,400.	

The overprint means "Philately for the Children". The stamps were sold at five million times their face values and 80% of the amount was devoted to child welfare. The stamps were sold only at Moscow and for one day.

Nos. B24-B26 were reprinted ("second issue"). Values are for the second issue. The 1k from the first issue are worth about 3 times the values shown. Expertization is recommended to distinguish the two printings.

Worker and Peasant (Industry and Agriculture) — SP11

Allegory: Agriculture Will Help End Distress SP12

Star of Hope, Wheat and Worker-Peasant Handclasp — SP13

Sower — SP14

		1922	**Litho.**	**Imperf.**	
		Without Gum			
B30	SP11	2t (2000r) green		15.00	250.00
B31	SP12	2t (2000r) rose		29.00	125.00
B32	SP13	4t (4000r) rose		42.50	125.00
B33	SP14	6t (6000r) green		22.50	125.00
		Nos. B30-B33 (4)		109.00	625.00
		Double Impression			
B30a	SP11	(2000r) green		475.00	
B31a	SP12	(2000r) rose		650.00	
B32a	SP13	(4000r) rose		725.00	
B33a	SP14	(6000r) green		575.00	
		Triple Impression			
B30b	SP11	(2000r) green		450.00	
B31b	SP12	(2000r) rose		600.00	
B32b	SP13	(4000r) rose		675.00	
B33b	SP14	(6000r) green		500.00	

Nos. B30-B33 exist with double impression. Counterfeits of Nos. B30-B33 exist; beware also of forged cancellations.

Miniature examples of Nos. B30-B33 exist, taken from the 1933 Soviet catalogue.

Automobile SP15

Steamship SP16

Railroad Train SP17

Airplane SP18

		1922		**Imperf.**	
B34	SP15	(20r+5r) light violet		.40	.75
B35	SP16	(20r+5r) violet		.50	.75
B36	SP17	(20r+5r) gray blue		.40	.75
B37	SP18	(20r+5r) blue gray		2.25	4.25
		Nos. B34-B37 (4)		3.55	6.50

Inscribed "For the Hungry." Each stamp was sold for 200,000r postage and 50,000r charity. Counterfeits of Nos. B34-B37 exist.

Nos. 212, 183, 202 Surcharged in Bronze, Gold or Silver

		1923		**Imperf.**	
B38	A48	1r +1r on 10r		500.00	500.00
a.		Inverted surcharge		1,250.	1,000.
B39	A48	1r +1r on 10r			
		(G)		50.00	30.00
a.		Inverted surcharge		325.00	225.00
B40	A43	2r +2r on 250r		50.00	40.00
a.		Pelure paper		40.00	25.00
b.		Inverted surcharge		325.00	200.00
c.		Double surcharge		—	
		Wmk. 171			
B41	A46	4r +4r on 5000r		30.00	25.00
a.		Date spaced "1 923"		425.00	375.00
b.		Inverted surcharge		1,150.	1,150.
B42	A46	4r +4r on 5000r			
		(S)		1,000.	500.00
a.		Inverted surcharge		4,750.	2,500.
b.		Date spaced "1 923"		2,500.	1,850.
c.		As "b," inverted surch.		22,500.	8,000.
		Nos. B38-B42 (5)		1,630.	1,095.

The inscriptions mean "Philately's Contribution to Labor." The stamps were on sale only at Moscow and for one day. The surtax was for charitable purposes.

Counterfeits of No. B42 exist.

Leningrad Flood Issue

Nos. 181-182, 184-186 Surcharged

		1924	**Unwmk.**	**Imperf.**	
B43	A40	3k + 10k on 100r		3.50	3.50
a.		Pelure paper		2.50	4.00
b.		Inverted surcharge		250.00	
B44	A40	7k + 20k on 200r		3.75	3.75
a.		Inverted surcharge		300.00	
B45	A40	14k + 30k on 300r		3.75	3.75
a.		Pelure paper		625.00	

Similar Surcharge in Red or Black

B46	A41	12k + 40k on 500r			
		(R)		3.75	3.75
a.		Double surcharge		1,600.	—
b.		Inverted surcharge		1,550.	
B47	A41	20k + 50k on			
		1000r		3.00	3.00
a.		Thick paper		20.00	25.00
b.		Pelure paper		10.00	10.00
c.		Chalk surface paper		60.00	25.00
		Nos. B43-B47 (5)		17.75	17.75

The surcharge on Nos. B43 to B45 reads: "S.S.S.R. For the sufferers by the inundation at Leningrad." That on Nos. B46 and B47 reads: "S.S.S.R. For the Leningrad Proletariat, 23, IX, 1924."

No. B46 is surcharged vertically, reading down, with the value as the top line.

Orphans
SP19

Lenin as a
Child
SP20

1926		**Typo.**	**Perf. 13½**	
B48	SP19	10k brown	14.50	8.75
B49	SP20	20k deep blue	60.00	16.00

Wmk. 170

B50	SP19	10k brown	3.00	1.50
B51	SP20	20k deep blue	7.50	3.50
		Nos. B48-B51 (4)	85.00	29.75

Two kopecks of the price of each of these
stamps was donated to organizations for the
care of indigent children.

Types of 1926 Issue

1927

B52	SP19	8k + 2k yel green	1.75	.50
B53	SP20	18k + 2k deep rose	15.00	5.00

Surtax was for child welfare.

Industrial
Training
SP21

Agricultural
Training
SP22

		Perf. 10, 10½, 12½		
1929-30		**Photo.**		**Unwmk.**
B54	SP21	10k +2k ol brn & org brn	14.50	3.00
a.		Perf. 10½	200.00	25.00
B55	SP21	10k +2k ol grn ('30)	6.00	1.50
B56	SP22	20k +2k blk brn & bl, perf. 10	10.00	2.25
a.		Perf. 12½	125.00	25.00
b.		Perf. 10	20.00	5.00
B57	SP22	20k +2k bl grn ('30)	8.50	2.25
		Nos. B54-B57 (4)	39.00	9.00

Surtax was for child welfare.

> Catalogue values for unused
> stamps in this section, from this
> point to the end of the section, are
> for Never Hinged items.

"Montreal Passing
Torch to
Moscow" — SP23

Moscow '80
Olympic Games
Emblem — SP24

22nd Olympic Games, Moscow, 1980:
16k+6k, like 10k+5k. 60k+30k, Aerial view of
Kremlin and Moscow '80 emblem.

1976, Dec. 28		**Litho.**	**Perf. 12x12½**	
B58	SP23	4k + 2k multi	.50	.25
B59	SP24	10k + 5k multi	.70	.35
B60	SP24	16k + 6k multi	.80	.40
		Nos. B58-B60 (3)	2.00	1.00

Souvenir Sheet
Photo.
Perf. 11½

B61	SP23	60k + 30k multi	2.25	1.65

Greco-Roman Wrestling — SP25

Moscow '80 Emblem and: 6k+3k, Free-style
wrestling. 10k+5k, Judo. 16k+6k, Boxing.
20k+10k, Weight lifting.

1977, June 21		**Litho.**	**Perf. 12½x12**	
B62	SP25	4k + 2k multi	.25	.25
B63	SP25	6k + 3k multi	.25	.25
B64	SP25	10k + 5k multi	.25	.30
B65	SP25	16k + 6k multi	.40	.35
B66	SP25	20k + 10k multi	.60	.45
		Nos. B62-B66 (5)	1.75	1.60

Perf. 12½x12, 12x12½

1977, Sept. 22

Designs: 4k+2k, Bicyclist. 6k+3k, Woman
archer, vert. 10k+5k, Sharpshooting. 16k+6k,
Equestrian. 20k+10k, Fencer. 50k+25k,
Equestrian and fencer.

B67	SP25	4k + 2k multi	.25	.25
B68	SP25	6k + 3k multi	.25	.25
B69	SP25	10k + 5k multi	.40	.30
B70	SP25	16k + 6k multi	.55	.35
B71	SP25	20k + 10k multi	.70	.45
		Nos. B67-B71 (5)	2.15	1.60

Souvenir Sheet
Perf. 12½x12

B72	SP25	50k + 25k multi	2.00	1.65

1978, Mar. 24			**Perf. 12½x12**	

Designs: 4k+2k, Swimmer at start. 6k+3k,
Woman diver, vert. 10k+5k, Water polo.
16k+6k, Canoeing. 20k+10k, Canadian single.
50k+25k, Start of double scull race.

B73	SP25	4k + 2k multi	.25	.25
B74	SP25	6k + 3k multi	.25	.25
B75	SP25	10k + 5k multi	.30	.25
B76	SP25	16k + 6k multi	.40	.30
B77	SP25	20k + 10k multi	.60	.45
		Nos. B73-B77 (5)	1.80	1.50

Souvenir Sheet

B78	SP25	50k + 25k grn & blk	2.00	2.00

Star-class
Yacht — SP26

Keel Yachts and Moscow '80 Emblem:
6k+3k, Soling class. 10k+5k, Centerboarder
470. 16k+6k, Finn class. 20k+10k, Flying
Dutchman class. 50k+25k, Catamaran Tornado, horiz.

1978, Oct. 26		**Litho.**	**Perf. 12x12½**	
B79	SP26	4k + 2k multi	.25	.25
B80	SP26	6k + 3k multi	.25	.25
B81	SP26	10k + 5k multi	.30	.25
B82	SP26	16k + 6k multi	.40	.30
B83	SP26	20k + 10k multi	.60	.40
		Nos. B79-B83 (5)	1.80	1.45

Souvenir Sheet
Perf. 12½x12

B84	SP26	50k + 25k multi	2.00	1.40

Women's
Gymnastics
SP27

Designs: 6k+3k, Man on parallel bars.
10k+5k, Man on horizontal bar. 16k+6k,
Woman on balance beam. 20k+10k, Woman
on uneven bars. 50k+25k, Man on rings.

1979, Mar. 21		**Litho.**	**Perf. 12x12½**	
B85	SP27	4k + 2k multi	.25	.25
B86	SP27	6k + 3k multi	.25	.25
B87	SP27	10k + 5k multi	.30	.25
B88	SP27	16k + 6k multi	.40	.30
B89	SP27	20k + 10k multi	.60	.40
		Nos. B85-B89 (5)	1.80	1.45

Souvenir Sheet
Perf. 12½x12

B90	SP25	50k + 25k multi	2.00	1.40

1979, June			**Perf. 12½x12, 12x12½**	

Designs: 4k+2k, Soccer. 6k+3k, Basketball.
10k+5k, Women's volleyball. 16k+6k, Handball. 20k+10k, Field hockey.

B91	SP25	4k + 2k multi	.25	.25
B92	SP27	6k + 3k multi	.25	.25
B93	SP27	10k + 5k multi	.30	.25
B94	SP25	16k + 6k multi	.40	.30
B95	SP25	20k + 10k multi	.60	.40
		Nos. B91-B95 (5)	1.80	1.45

22nd Olympic Games, Moscow, July 19-
Aug. 3, 1980.

Running,
Moscow
'80
Emblem
SP27a

No. B97, Pole vault. No. B98, Discus. No.
B99, Hurdles. No. B100, Javelin. No. B101,
Walking, vert. No. B102, Hammer throw. No.
B103, High jump. No. B104, Shot put. No.
B105, Long jump.
No. B106, Relay race.

1980		**Litho.**	**Perf. 12½x12, 12x12½**	
B96	SP27a	4k + 2k shown	.25	.25
B97	SP27a	4k + 2k multi	.25	.25
B98	SP27a	6k + 3k multi	.25	.25
B99	SP27a	6k + 3k multi	.25	.25
B100	SP27a	10k + 5k multi	.40	.25
B101	SP27a	10k + 5k multi	.40	.25
B102	SP27a	16k + 6k multi	.70	.30
B103	SP27a	16k + 6k multi	.70	.30
B104	SP27a	20k + 10k multi	.90	.40
B105	SP27a	20k + 10k multi	.90	.40
		Nos. B96-B105 (10)	5.00	2.90

Souvenir Sheet

B106	SP27a	50k + 25k multi	2.00	1.00

22nd Olympic Games, Moscow, July 19-
Aug. 3. Issued: Nos. B96, B99, B101, B103,
B105, Feb. 6; others, Mar. 12.

Moscow '80 Emblem, Relief from St.
Dimitri's Cathedral, Arms of
Vladimir — SP28

Moscow '80 Emblem and: No. B108, Bridge
over Klyazma River and Vladimir Hotel. No.
B109, Relief from Nativity Cathedral and coat
of arms (falcon), Suzdal. No. B110, Tourist
complex and Pozharski Monument, Suzdal.
No. B111, Frunze Monument, Ivanovo, torch
and spindle. No. B112, Museum of First Soviets, Fighters of the Revolution Monument,
Ivanovo.

Photogravure and Engraved

1977, Dec. 30			**Perf. 11½x12**	
B107	SP28	1r + 50k multi	1.40	1.00
B108	SP28	1r + 50k multi	1.40	1.00
B109	SP28	1r + 50k multi	1.40	1.00
B110	SP28	1r + 50k multi	1.40	1.00
B111	SP28	1r + 50k multi	1.40	1.00
B112	SP28	1r + 50k multi	1.40	1.00
		Nos. B107-B112 (6)	8.40	6.00

"Tourism around the Golden Ring."

Fortifications
and Arms of
Zagorsk
SP29

Moscow '80 Emblem and (Coat of Arms
design): No. B114, Gagarin Palace of Culture
and new arms of Zagorsk (building & horse).
No. B115, Rostov Kremlin with St. John the
Divine Church and No. B116, View of Rostov
from Nero Lake (deer). No. B117, Alexander
Nevski and WWII soldiers' monuments, Pereslav-Zalesski and No. B118, Peter the Great
monument, Pereslav-Zalesski (lion & fish). No.
B119, Tower and wall of Monastery of the
Transfiguration, Yaroslavl and No. B120, Dock
and monument for Soviet heroes, Yaroslava
(bear).

1978			**Perf. 12x11½**	
		Multicolored and		
B113	SP29	1r + 50k gold	2.00	1.00
B114	SP29	1r + 50k silver	2.00	1.00
B115	SP29	1r + 50k silver	2.00	1.00
B116	SP29	1r + 50k silver	2.00	1.00
B117	SP29	1r + 50k gold	2.00	1.00
B118	SP29	1r + 50k silver	2.00	1.00
B119	SP29	1r + 50k gold	2.00	1.00
B120	SP29	1r + 50k silver	2.00	1.00
		Nos. B113-B120 (8)	16.00	8.00

Issued: #B113-B116, 10/16; #B117-B120,
12/25.

1979			**Perf. 12x11½**	

Moscow '80 Emblem and: No. B121,
Narikaly Fortress, Tbilisi, 4th century. No.
B122, Georgia Philharmonic Concert Hall,
"Muse" sculpture, Tbilisi. No. B123, Chir-Dor
Mosque, 17th century, Samarkand. No. B124,
Peoples Friendship Museum, "Courage" mon-
ument, Tashkent. No. B125, Landscape,
Erevan. B126, Armenian State Opera and Bal-
let Theater, Erevan.

Multicolored and

B121	SP29	1r+50k sil, bl circle	1.75	1.25
B122	SP29	1r+50k gold, yel circle	1.75	1.25
B123	SP29	1r+50k sil, bl 8-point star	1.75	1.25
B124	SP29	1r+50k gold, red 8-point star	1.75	1.25
B125	SP29	1r+50k sil, bl diamond	1.75	1.25
B126	SP29	1r+50k gold, red diamond	1.75	1.25
		Nos. B121-B126 (6)	10.50	7.50

Issued: #B121-B124, 9/5; #B125-B126, Oct.

Kremlin
SP29a

Kalinin Prospect, Moscow
SP29b

Admiralteistvo, St. Isaak Cathedral, Leningrad — SP29c

World War II Defense Monument, Leningrad SP29d

Bogdan Khmelnitisky Monument, St. Sophia's Monastery Kiev SP29e

Metro Bridge, Dnieper River, Kiev — SP29f

Palace of Sports, Obelisk, Minsk SP29g

Republican House of Cinematography, Minsk — SP29h

Vyshgorodsky Castle, Town Hall, Tallinn SP29i

Viru Hotel, Tallinn SP29j

Moscow '80 Emblem, Coat of Arms.

1980		Perf. 12x11½	
B127	SP29a	1r + 50k multi	1.50 1.25
B128	SP29b	1r + 50k multi	1.50 1.25
B129	SP29c	1r + 50k multi	1.50 1.25
B130	SP29d	1r + 50k multi	1.50 1.25
B131	SP29e	1r + 50k multi	1.50 1.25
B132	SP29f	1r + 50k multi	1.50 1.25
B133	SP29g	1r + 50k multi	1.50 1.25
B134	SP29h	1r + 50k multi	1.50 1.25
B135	SP29i	1r + 50k multi	1.50 1.25
B136	SP29j	1r + 50k multi	1.50 1.25
	Nos. B127-B136 (10)		15.00 12.50

Tourism. Issue dates: #B127-B128, Feb. 29. #B129-B130, Mar. 25; #B131-B136, Apr. 30.

Soviet Culture Fund — SP30

Art treasures: No. B137, *O.K. Lansere*, 1910, by Z.E. Serebriakova, vert. No. B138, *Boyar's Wife Examining an Embroidery Design*, 1905, by K.V. Lebedev. No. B139, *Talent*, 1910, by N.P. Bogdanov-Belsky, vert. No. B140, *Trinity*, 15th-16th cent., Novgorod School, vert.

		Perf. 12x12½, 12½x12	
1988, Aug. 22		Litho.	
B137	SP30	10k +5k multi	.35 .25
B138	SP30	15k +7k multi	.45 .35
B139	SP30	30k +15k multi	1.25 .75
	Nos. B137-B139 (3)		2.05 1.35

Souvenir Sheet

B140	SP30	1r +50k multi	2.00 1.00

SP31

1988, Oct. 20		Litho.	*Perf. 12*	
B141	SP31	10k +5k Bear	.25	.25
B142	SP31	10k +5k Wolf	.25	.25
B143	SP31	20k +10k Fox	.40	.35
B144	SP31	20k +10k Boar	.40	.35
B145	SP31	20k +10k Lynx	.40	.35
a.		Block of 5+label	2.00	1.60

Zoo Relief Fund. See #B152-B156, B166-B168.

Lenin Children's Fund SP32

Children's drawings and fund emblem: No. B146, Skating Rink. No. B147, Rooster. No. B148, May (girl and flowers).

1988, Dec. 12		Litho.	*Perf. 12*	
B146	SP32	5k +2k multi	.25	.25
B147	SP32	5k +2k multi	.25	.25
B148	SP32	5k +2k multi	.25	.25
a.		Block of 3+label, #B146-B148	2.00	1.00

See Nos. B169-B171.

SP33

#B149, Tigranes I (c. 140-55 B.C.), king of Armenia, gold coin. #B150, St. Ripsime Temple, c. 618. #B151, *Virgin and Child*, fresco (detail) by Ovnat Ovnatanyan, 18th cent., Echmiadzin Cathedral.

1988, Dec. 27			*Perf. 12½x12*	
B149	SP33	20k +10k multi	.40	.25
B150	SP33	30k +15k multi	.50	.30
B151	SP33	50k +25k multi	1.00	.50
a.		Block of 3+label, #B149-B151	2.00	1.00

Armenian earthquake relief. For surcharges see Nos. B173-B175.

Zoo Relief Type of 1988

Nos. B152-B156 are horiz. stamps.

1989, Mar. 20		Litho.	*Perf. 12*	
B152	SP31	10k+5k Marten	.40	.30
B153	SP31	10k+5k Squirrel	.40	.30
B154	SP31	20k+10k Hare	.75	.50
B155	SP31	20k+10k Hedgehog	.75	.50
B156	SP31	20k+10k Badger	.75	.50
a.		Block of 5+label, #B152-B156	3.00	2.00

Lenin Children's Fund Type of 1988

Fund emblem and children's drawings: No. B157, Rabbit. No. B158, Cat. No. B159, Doctor. Nos. B157-B159 vert.

1989, June 14		Litho.	*Perf. 12*	
B157	SP32	5k +2k multi	.50	.25
B158	SP32	5k +2k multi	.50	.25
B159	SP32	5k +2k multi	.50	.25
a.		Block of 3+label, #B157-B159	2.00	.75

Surtax for the fund.

Soviet Culture Fund SP34

Paintings and porcelain: No. B160, *Village Market*, by A. Makovsky. No. B161, *Lady Wearing a Hat*, by E. Zelenin. No. B162, *Portrait of the Actress Bazhenova*, by A. Sofronova. No. B163, *Two Women*, by H. Shaiber. No. B164, Popov porcelain coffee pot and plates, 19th cent.

1989		Litho.	*Perf. 12x12½*	
B160	SP34	4k +2k multi	.25	.25
B161	SP34	5k +2k multi	.25	.25
B162	SP34	10k +5k multi	.30	.25
B163	SP34	20k +10k multi	.50	.30
B164	SP34	30k +15k multi	.85	.50
	Nos. B160-B164 (5)		2.15	1.55

Souvenir Sheet

Nature Conservation — SP35

1989, Dec. 14		Photo.	*Perf. 11½*	
B165	SP35	20k + 10k Swallow	5.00	5.00

Surtax for the Soviet Union of Philatelists.

Zoo Relief Type of 1988

No. B166, Aquila chrysaetos. No. B167, Falco cherrug. No. B168,

1990, May 4		Litho.	*Perf. 12*	
B166	SP31	10k +5k multi	.45	.30
B167	SP31	20k +10k multi	1.00	.65
B168	SP31	20k +10k multi	1.00	.65
a.		Block of 3 + label, #B166-B168	3.00	1.65

Nos. B166-B168 horiz.

Lenin's Children Fund Type of 1988

No. B169, Clown. No. B170, Group of women. No. B171, Group of children. No. B169-B171, vert.

1990, July 3		Litho.	*Perf. 12*	
B169	SP32	5k +2k multi	.65	.25
B170	SP32	5k +2k multi	.65	.25
B171	SP32	5k +2k multi	.65	.25
a.		Block of 3, #B169-B171 + label	2.00	.45

Nature Conservation — SP36

1990, Sept. 12   Litho.   *Perf. 12*
B172 SP36 20k +10k multi   1.10 1.10
Surtax for Soviet Union of Philatelists.

Nos. B149-B151 Overprinted

No. B173   Nos. B174-B175

1990, Nov. 24   Litho.   *Perf. 12x12½*
B173 SP33 20k +10k multi   .90   .65
B174 SP33 30k +15k multi   1.40   .90
B175 SP33 50k +25k multi   2.25 1.50
a.   Block of 3+label, #B173-B175 4.00 3.00
Armenia '90 Philatelic Exhibition.

Soviet Culture Fund — SP37

Paintings by N. K. Roerich: 10k+5k, Unkrada, 1909. 20k+10k, Pskovo-Pechorsky Monastery, 1907.

1990, Dec. 20   Litho.   *Perf. 12½x12*
B176 SP37 10k +5k multi   .40   .25
B177 SP37 20k +10k multi   .60   .35

Souvenir Sheet

Joys of All Those Grieving, 18th Cent. — SP38

1990, Dec. 23   *Perf. 12½x12*
B178 SP38 50k +25k multi   2.00 1.00
Surtax for Charity and Health Fund.

Ciconia Ciconia SP39

1991, Feb. 4   Litho.   *Perf. 12*
B179 SP39 10k +5k multi   .55   .35
Surtax for the Zoo Relief Fund.

Souvenir Sheet

USSR Philatelic Society, 25th Anniv. — SP40

1991, Feb. 15   *Perf. 12x12½*
B180 SP40 20k +10k multi   1.10 1.10

The Universe by V. Lukianets SP41

No. B182, Another Planet by V. Lukianets.

1991, June 1   Litho.   *Perf. 12½x12*
B181 SP41 10k +5k multi   .50   .25
B182 SP41 10k +5k multi   .50   .25
Lenin's Children's Fund.

SP42

1991, July 10   *Perf. 12½x12*
B183 SP42 20k +10k multi   .50   .25
Surtax for Soviet Culture Fund.

SP43

1991, July 10   *Perf. 12*
B184 SP43 20k +10k multi   .50   .25
Surtax for Soviet Charity & Health Fund

Souvenir Sheet

SP44

1992, Jan. 22   Litho.   *Perf. 12½x12*
B185 SP44 3r +50k multi   1.00   .70
Surtax for Nature Preservation.

AIR POST STAMPS

AP1

Plane Overprint in Red

1922   Unwmk.   *Imperf.*
C1   AP1 45r green & black   10.00   —
a.   Translucent paper   85.00

5th anniversary of October Revolution. No. C1 was on sale only at the Moscow General Post Office. Counterfeits exist.

Fokker F-111 — AP2

1923   Photo.
C2   AP2 1r red brown   20.00
C3   AP2 3r deep blue   20.00
C4   AP2 5r green   5.00
a.   Wide "5"   40,000.
C5   AP2 10r carmine   5.00
     Nos. C2-C5 (4)   50.00

Nos. C2-C5 were not placed in use.

Nos. C2-C5 Surcharged

1924
C6   AP2 5k on 3r dp
              blue   5.50   2.00
C7   AP2 10k on 5r green   2.50   .60
a.   Wide "5"   1,250. 700.00
b.   Inverted surcharge   2,750.   —
C8   AP2 15k on 1r red
              brown   10.00   2.00
a.   Inverted surcharge   1,400. 500.00
C9   AP2 20k on 10r car   2.50   .50
a.   Inverted surcharge   4,000. 2,500.
     Nos. C6-C9 (4)   20.50   5.10

Airplane over Map of World AP3

1927, Sept. 1   Litho.   *Perf. 13x12*
C10 AP3 10k dk bl & yel brn   25.00 15.00
C11 AP3 15k dp red & ol grn   50.00 20.00
1st Intl. Air Post Cong. at The Hague, initiated by the USSR.

Graf Zeppelin and "Call to Complete 5-Year Plan in 4 Years" — AP4

1930   Photo.   Wmk. 226   *Perf. 12½*
C12 AP4 40k dark blue   40.00 20.00
a.   Perf. 10½   40.00 20.00
b.   Imperf.   1,650. 1,325.
C13 AP4 80k carmine   40.00 20.00
a.   Perf. 10½   40.00 20.00
b.   Imperf.   1,650. 1,325.

Flight of the Graf Zeppelin from Friedrichshafen to Moscow and return.

Symbolical of Airship Communication from the Tundra to the Steppes — AP5

Airship over Dneprostroi Dam — AP6

Airship over Lenin Mausoleum — AP7

Airship Exploring Arctic Regions — AP8

Constructing an Airship AP9

1931-32   Wmk. 170   Photo.   *Imperf.*
C15 AP5 10k dark violet   40.00 30.00
Litho.
C16 AP6 15k gray blue   40.00 30.00
Typo.
C17 AP7 20k dk carmine   40.00 30.00
Photo.
C18 AP8 50k black brown   40.00 30.00
a.   50k gray blue (error)   85,000.
C19 AP9 1r dark green   40.00 32.50
     Nos. C15-C19 (5)   200.00 152.50

Perf. 12x12¼, 12¼x12½x12 (#C21, C23)
C20 AP5 10k dark violet   3.00   1.75
Litho.
C21 AP6 15k gray blue   120.00 19.00
Typo.
C22 AP7 20k dk carmine   3.00   1.75
a.   20k light red   3.00
Photo.
C23 AP8 50k black brown   14.50   4.00
a.   50k gray blue (error)   500.00 300.00
C24 AP9 1r dark green   15.00   2.50

Perf. 12½

			Unwmk.	Engr.
C25	AP6	15k gray blk ('32)	6.00	1.25
a.		Perf. 10½	2,000.	135.00
b.		Perf. 14	17.50	22.50
c.		Imperf.	—	3,250.
		Nos. C20-C25 (6)	161.50	30.25

The 11½ perforation on Nos. C20-C25 is of private origin; beware also of bogus perforation "errors."

North Pole Issue

Graf Zeppelin and Icebreaker "Malygin" Transferring Mail — AP10

1931   Wmk. 170   Imperf.

C26	AP10	30k dark violet	35.00	17.50
C27	AP10	35k dark green	7.25	4.25
C28	AP10	1r gray black	48.00	17.50
C29	AP10	2r deep ultra	24.00	17.50
		Nos. C26-C29 (4)	114.25	56.75

Perf. 12x12¼

C30	AP10	30k dark violet	45.00	15.00
C31	AP10	35k dark green	60.00	12.50
C32	AP10	1r gray black	105.00	35.00
C33	AP10	2r deep ultra	45.00	15.00
		Nos. C30-C33 (4)	255.00	77.50

Perf. 12¼

C30a	AP10	30k dark violet	40.00	17.50
C31a	AP10	35k dark green	37.50	25.00
C32a	AP10	1r gray black	60.00	60.00
C33a	AP10	2r deep ultra	45.00	20.00

Map of Polar Region, Airplane and Icebreaker "Sibiryakov" — AP11

Perf. 12, 10½

1932, Aug. 26   Wmk. 170

C34	AP11	50k car rose	100.00	15.00
a.		Perf. 10½	30,000.	14,000.
b.		Perf. 10½x12		20,000.
C35	AP11	1r green	50.00	30.00
a.		Perf. 12		37.50

2nd International Polar Year in connection with proposed flight from Franz-Josef Land to Archangel which, being impossible, actually went from Archangel to Moscow to destinations.

Stratostat "U.S.S.R." — AP12

1933   Photo.   Perf. 14

C37	AP12	5k ultra	210.00	10.00
C38	AP12	10k carmine	70.00	10.00
C39	AP12	20k violet	30.00	9.50
		Nos. C37-C39 (3)	310.00	29.50

Pairs, Imperf. Between

C37a	Vert. pair, imperf. between	11,250.	—
C37b	Horiz. pair, imperf. between	6,500.	2,500.
C38a	Horiz. pair, imperf. between	—	12,750.
C39a	Vert. pair, imperf. between	11,500.	—

Ascent into the stratosphere by Soviet aeronauts, Sept. 30th, 1933.

Furnaces of Kuznetsk AP13

Designs: 10k, Oil wells. 20k, Collective farm. 50k, Map of Moscow-Volga Canal project. 80k, Arctic cargo ship.

1934, Feb.   Wmk. 170   Perf. 14

C40	AP13	5k ultra	35.00	6.00
C41	AP13	10k green	35.00	6.75
C42	AP13	20k carmine	100.00	7.50
C43	AP13	50k dull blue	250.00	35.00
C44	AP13	80k purple	80.00	9.00
		Nos. C40-C44 (5)	500.00	64.25

Unwmk.

C45	AP13	5k ultra	35.00	4.00
C46	AP13	10k green	35.00	3.75
a.		Horiz. pair, imperf. btwn.	2,000.	1,250.
C47	AP13	20k carmine	45.00	6.00
C48	AP13	50k dull blue	260.00	28.50
C49	AP13	80k purple	28.00	6.00
		Nos. C45-C49 (5)	403.00	48.25

10th anniversary of Soviet civil aviation and airmail service. Counterfeits exist, perf 11½.

I. D. Usyskin AP18

10k, A. B. Vasenko. 20k, P. F. Fedosenko.

1934   Wmk. 170   Perf. 11

C50	AP18	5k vio brown	17.50	6.00
C51	AP18	10k brown	115.00	6.00
C52	AP18	20k ultra	27.50	8.25
		Nos. C50-C52 (3)	160.00	20.25

Perf. 13¾

C50a	AP18	5k	135.	
C51a	AP18	10k		4,500.
C52a	AP18	20k	10,000.	
		Nos. C50a-C52a (3)	10,135.	4,500.

Honoring victims of the stratosphere disaster. See Nos. C77-C79.
Beware of examples of Nos. C50-C52 reperforated to resemble Nos. C50a-C52a.

Airship "Pravda" — AP19

Airship Landing — AP20

Airship "Voroshilov" — AP21

Sideview of Airship — AP22

Airship "Lenin" — AP23

1934   Perf. 14

C53	AP19	5k red orange	25.00	2.40
C54	AP20	10k claret	27.50	3.75
C55	AP21	15k brown	75.00	10.00
C56	AP22	20k black	15.00	7.50
C57	AP23	30k ultra	375.00	55.00
		Nos. C53-C57 (5)	517.50	78.65

Capt. V. Voronin and "Chelyuskin" — AP24

Prof. Otto Y. Schmidt — AP25

A. V. Lapidevsky AP26

S. A. Levanevsky AP27

"Schmidt Camp" — AP28

Designs: 15k, M. G. Slepnev. 20k, I. V. Doronin. 25k, M. V. Vodopianov. 30k, V. S. Molokov. 40k, N. P. Kamanin.

1935   Perf. 14

C58	AP24	1k red orange	12.50	2.25
C59	AP25	3k rose car	12.50	2.25
C60	AP26	5k emerald	7.50	2.25
C61	AP27	10k dark brown	17.50	2.25
C62	AP27	15k black	17.50	3.75
C63	AP27	20k deep claret	22.50	3.75
C64	AP27	25k indigo	120.00	17.50
C65	AP27	30k dull green	750.00	50.00
C66	AP27	40k purple	22.00	12.00
C67	AP28	50k dark ultra	50.00	30.00
		Nos. C58-C67 (10)	1,032.	126.00

Aerial rescue of ice-breaker Chelyuskin crew and scientific expedition.

No. C61 Surcharged in Red

1935, Aug.

C68	AP27	1r on 10k dk brn	500.00	475.00
a.		Inverted surcharge	90,000.	
b.		Lower case Cyrillic "F"	1,500.	1,450.
c.		As "b," inverted surcharge	600,000.	

Moscow-San Francisco flight. Counterfeits exist.

Single-Engined Monoplane — AP34

Five-Engined Transport — AP35

20k, Twin-engined cabin plane. 30k, 4r-motored transport. 40k, Single-engined amphibian. 50k, Twin-motored transport. 80k, 8-motored transport.

1937   Unwmk.   Perf. 12

C69	AP34	10k yel brn & blk	3.00	1.00
a.		Imperf.		
C70	AP34	20k gray grn & blk	3.00	1.00
C71	AP34	30k red brn & blk	3.00	1.00
C72	AP34	40k vio brn & blk	5.25	1.00
C73	AP34	50k dk vio & blk	16.50	2.00
C74	AP35	80k bl vio & brn	16.50	6.00
C75	AP35	1r blk, brn & buff	45.00	8.50
a.		Sheet of 4, imperf.	175.00	215.00

Vertical Pairs, Imperf. Between

C69b	AP34	10k yel brn & blk	—	62.50
C70a	AP34	20k gray grn & blk	3,250.	3,250.
C71a	AP34	30k red brn & blk	—	4,250.
C72a	AP34	40k vio brn & blk	3,250.	3,250.
C73a	AP34	50k dk vio & blk	—	4,500.
		Nos. C69-C75 (7)	92.25	20.50
		Set, never hinged	168.00	

Jubilee Aviation Exhib., Moscow, Nov. 15-20.
Vertical pairs, imperf. between, exist for No. C71, value $4,000; No. C72, value $5,750; No. C73, value $2,300.

Types of 1938 Regular Issue Overprinted in Various Colors

1939   Typo.

C76	A282	10k red (C)	4.00	1.25
C76A	A285	30k blue (R)	6.75	1.25
C76B	A286	40k dl grn (Br)	8.25	1.50
C76C	A287	50k dl vio (R)	6.75	2.50

C76D A289 1r brown (Bl)   12.50 3.50
    a.   Double overprint   1,500.
    Nos. C76-C76D (5)   38.25 10.00
    Set, never hinged   100.00
    Soviet Aviation Day, Aug. 18, 1939.

Types of 1934 with "30.1.1944" Added at Lower Left

Designs: No. C77, P. F. Fedosenko. No. C78, I. D. Usyskin. No. C79, A. B. Vasenko.

1944   **Photo.**   **Perf. 12**
C77 AP18 1r deep blue   5.00 .75
C78 AP18 1r slate green   5.00 .75
C79 AP18 1r brt yellow green   5.00 .75
    Nos. C77-C79 (3)   15.00 2.25
    Set, never hinged   30.00
    1934 stratosphere disaster, 10th anniv.

Nos. 860A and 861A Surcharged in Red

1944, May 25
C80 A431 1r on 30k Prus green   .50 .25
C81 A432 1r on 30k deep ultra   .50 .25
    Set, never hinged   2.00

Catalogue values for unused stamps in this section, from this point to the end of the section, are for Never Hinged items.

Planes and Soviet Air Force Flag — AP42

1948, Dec. 10   **Litho.**   **Perf. 12½**
C82 AP42 1r dark blue   10.00 .75
    Air Force Day.

Plane over Zages, Caucasus — AP43

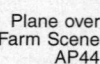

Plane over Farm Scene AP44

Map of Russian Air Routes and Transport Planes — AP45

No. C85, Sochi, Northern Caucasus. No. C86, Far East. No. C87, Leningrad. 2r, Moscow. 3r, Arctic.

          Perf. 12x12½
1949, Nov. 9   **Photo.**   **Unwmk.**
C83 AP43 50k red brn, lemon   4.50 .80
C84 AP44 60k sepia, pale
        buff   8.50 1.00
C85 AP44 1r org brn, yelsh   8.50 1.40
C86 AP43 1r blue, bluish   8.50 1.40

C87 AP43 1r red brn, pale
        fawn   8.50 1.40
C88 AP45 1r blk, ultra &
        red, gray   17.50 4.00
C89 AP43 2r org brn, bluish   26.00 11.00
C90 AP43 3r dk green, blu-
        ish   42.50 4.00
    Nos. C83-C90 (8)   124.50 25.00

Plane and Mountain Stream — AP46

Design: 1r, Like No. C86.

1955   **Litho.**   **Perf. 12½x12**
C91 AP46 1r multicolored   5.00 .50
C92 AP46 2r black & yel grn   10.00 .50
    For overprints see Nos. C95-C96.

Globe and Plane — AP47

1955, May 31   **Photo.**
C93 AP47 2r chocolate   1.25 .25
C94 AP47 2r deep blue   1.25 .25

Nos. C91 and C92 Overprinted in Red

        Perf. 12x12½
1955, Nov. 22   **Litho.**   **Unwmk.**
C95 AP46 1r multicolored   8.00 2.00
C96 AP46 2r black & yel grn   12.00 3.00

    Issued for use at the scientific drifting stations North Pole-4 and North Pole-5. The inscription reads "North Pole-Moscow, 1955." Counterfeits exist.

Arctic Camp AP48

1956, June 8   **Perf. 12½x12**
C97 AP48 1r blue, grn, brn, yel &
       red   1.50 .50
    Opening of scientific drifting station North Pole-6.

Helicopter over Kremlin — AP49

1960, Mar. 5   **Photo.**   **Perf. 12**
C98 AP49 60k ultra   1.00 .25

Surcharged with New Value, Bars and "1961"

1961, Dec. 20
C99 AP49 6k on 60k ultra   .50 .25

Air Force Emblem and Arms of Normandy — AP50

1962, Dec. 30   **Unwmk.**   **Perf. 11½**
C100 AP50 6k blue grn, ocher &
       car   .35 .25
    French Normandy-Neman Escadrille, which fought on the Russian front, 20th anniv.

Jet over Map Showing Airlines in USSR AP51

Designs: 12k, Aeroflot emblem and globe. 16k, Jet over map showing Russian international airlines.

1963, Feb.
C101 AP51 10k red, blk & tan   .75 .25
C102 AP51 12k blue, red, tan &
       blk   1.00 .25
C103 AP51 16k blue, blk & red   1.25 .25
    Nos. C101-C103 (3)   3.00 .75
    Aeroflot, the civil air fleet, 40th anniv.

Tupolev 134 at Sheremetyevo Airport, Moscow — AP52

Civil Aviation: 10k, An-24 (Antonov) and Vnukovo Airport, Moscow. 12k, Mi-10 (Mil helicopter) and Central Airport, Moscow. 16k, Be-10 (Beriev) and Chinki Riverport, Moscow. 20k, Antei airliner and Domodedovo Airport, Moscow.

1965, Dec. 31
C104 AP52 6k org, red & vio   .30 .25
C105 AP52 10k lt grn, org red &
       gray   .50 .25
C106 AP52 12k lil, dk sep & lt
       grn   .50 .25
C107 AP52 16k lil, lt brn, red &
       grn   .75 .25
C108 AP52 20k org red, pur &
       gray   .95 .25
    Nos. C104-C108 (5)   3.00 1.25

Aviation Type of 1976

Aviation 1917-1930 (Aviation Emblem and): 4k, P-4 BIS biplane, 1917. 6k, AK-1 monoplane, 1924. 10k, R-3 (ANT-3) biplane, 1925. 12k, TB-1 (ANT-4) monoplane, 1925. 16k, R-5 biplane, 1929. 20k, Shcha-2 amphibian, 1930.

Lithographed and Engraved
1977, Aug. 16   **Perf. 12x11½**
C109 A2134 4k multicolored   .25 .25
C110 A2134 6k multicolored   .25 .25
C111 A2134 10k multicolored   .25 .25
C112 A2134 12k multicolored   .35 .25
C113 A2134 16k multicolored   .45 .25
C114 A2134 20k multicolored   .60 .25
    Nos. C109-C114 (6)   2.15 1.50

1978, Aug. 10

4k, PO-2 biplane, 1928. 6k, K-5 passenger plane, 1929. 10k, TB-3, cantilever monoplane, 1930. 12k, Stal-2, 1931. 16k, MBR-2 hydroplane, 1932. 20k, I-16 fighter plane, 1934.

C115 A2134 4k multicolored   .25 .25
C116 A2134 6k multicolored   .25 .25
C117 A2134 10k multicolored   .30 .25
C118 A2134 12k multicolored   .30 .25
C119 A2134 16k multicolored   .40 .25
C120 A2134 20k multicolored   .50 .30
    Nos. C115-C120 (6)   2.00 1.55
    Aviation 1928-1934.

Jet and Compass Rose — AP53

1978, Aug. 4   **Litho.**   **Perf. 12**
C121 AP53 32k dark blue   3.00 .35

Aeroflot Plane AH-28 — AP54

Designs: Various Aeroflot planes.

Photogravure and Engraved
1979   **Perf. 11½x12**
C122 AP54 2k shown   .25 .25
C123 AP54 3k YAK-42   .25 .25
C124 AP54 10k T4-154   .30 .25
C125 AP54 15k IL76 transport   .45 .25
C126 AP54 32k IL86 jet liner   .85 .45
    Nos. C122-C126 (5)   2.10 1.45

AIR POST OFFICIAL STAMPS

    Used on mail from Russian embassy in Berlin to Moscow. Surcharged on Consular Fee stamps. Currency: the German mark.

OA1

Surcharge in Carmine Bicolored Burelage
1922, July   **Litho.**   **Perf. 13½**
CO1 OA1 12m on 2.25r   150.00 —
    a.   Inverted surcharge   7,500. —
CO2 OA1 24m on 3r   175.00 —
    a.   Inverted surcharge   7,500. —
CO3 OA1 120m on 2.25r   195.00 —
CO4 OA1 600m on 3r   260.00 —
CO5 OA1 1200m on 10k   975.00 —
CO6 OA1 1200m on 50k   37,500. —
CO7 OA1 1200m on 2.25r   1,950. —
CO8 OA1 1200m on 3r   2,250. —

    Three types of each denomination, distinguished by shape of "C" in surcharge and length of second line of surcharge. Used stamps have pen or crayon cancel. Forgeries exist.

SPECIAL DELIVERY STAMPS

Motorcycle Courier — SD1

Express
Truck — SD2

Design: 80k, Locomotive.

Perf. 12½x12, 12x12½

			Wmk. 170	
1932		**Photo.**		
E1	SD1	5k dull brown	10.00	3.00
E2	SD2	10k violet brown	35.00	10.00
E3	SD2	80k dull green	80.00	8.50
		Nos. E1-E3 (3)	125.00	21.50
		Set, never hinged	250.00	

Used values are for c-t-o.

POSTAGE DUE STAMPS

Regular Issue of 1918
Surcharged in Red or
Carmine

1924-25		**Unwmk.**	**Perf. 13½**	
J1	A33	1k on 35k blue	2.00	.50
J2	A33	3k on 35k blue	2.00	.50
J3	A33	5k on 35k blue	2.00	.50
a.		Imperf.	450.00	
J4	A33	8k on 35k blue	2.00	.50
		('25)		
a.		Imperf.	450.00	
J5	A33	10k on 35k blue	2.00	.50
a.		Pair, one without surcharge	550.00	
J6	A33	12k on 70k brown	2.00	.50
J7	A33	14k on 35k blue	2.00	.50
		('25)		
a.		Imperf.	450.00	
J8	A33	32k on 35k blue	2.50	.50
J9	A33	40k on 35k blue	2.50	.50
a.		Imperf.	450.00	
c.		Pair, one without surcharge	675.00	
		Nos. J1-J9 (9)	19.00	4.50

Inverted Surcharge

J1b	A33	1k on 35k blue	150.00	—
J2b	A33	3k on 35k blue	150.00	—
J3b	A33	5k on 35k blue	150.00	—
J4b	A33	8k on 35k blue	150.00	—
J6b	A33	12k on 70k brown	200.00	—
J7b	A33	14k on 35k brown	150.00	—
J8b	A33	32k on 35k brown	150.00	—
J9b	A33	40k on 35k brown	175.00	—

Regular Issue of
1921 Surcharged in
Violet

1924			**Imperf.**	
J10	A40	1k on 100r orange	6.75	8.00
a.		1k on 100r yellow	8.75	8.00
b.		Pelure paper	6.75	8.00
c.		Inverted surcharge	225.00	

D1

Lithographed or Typographed

1925			**Perf. 12**	
J11	D1	1k red	2.00	.75
J12	D1	2k violet	2.00	.75
J13	D1	3k light blue	2.00	.75
J14	D1	7k orange	2.00	.75
J15	D1	8k green	2.00	.75
J16	D1	10k dark blue	2.00	.75
J17	D1	14k brown	2.00	.75
		Nos. J11-J17 (7)	14.00	5.25

Perf. 14½x14

J13a	D1	3k	12.50	1.00
J14a	D1	7k	20.00	1.00
J16a	D1	10k	—	—
J17a	D1	14k	5.00	1.00
		Nos. J13a-J17a (4)	37.50	3.00

Value of No. J16a unused is based on 2012
auction realization.

1925	**Wmk. 170**	**Typo.**	**Perf. 12**	
J18	D1	1k red	1.60	.40
J19	D1	2k violet	1.75	.40
J20	D1	3k light blue	1.75	.40
J21	D1	7k orange	1.75	.40
J22	D1	8k green	1.75	.40
J23	D1	10k dark blue	1.75	.40
J24	D1	14k brown	1.75	.40
		Nos. J18-J24 (7)	12.10	2.80

For surcharges see Nos. 359-372.

WENDEN (LIVONIA)

A former district of Livonia, a province
of the Russian Empire, which became
part of Latvia, under the name of
Vidzeme.

Used values for Nos. L2-L12 are for
pen-canceled stamps. Postmarked
examples sell for considerably more.

A1

1862		**Unwmk.**	**Imperf.**	
L1	A1	(2k) blue	45.00	
a.		Tête bêche pair	350.00	

No. L1 may have been used for a short
period of time but withdrawn because of small
size. Some consider it an essay.

A2

A3

1863				
L2	A2	(2k) rose & black	240.00	240.00
a.		Background inverted	600.00	600.00
L3	A3	(4k) blue grn & blk	175.00	150.00
a.		(4k) yellow green & black	300.00	300.00
b.		Half used as 2k on cover		2,500.
c.		Background inverted	950.00	500.00
d.		As "a," background inverted	650.00	400.00

The official imitations of Nos. L2 and L3
have a single instead of a double hyphen after
"WENDEN." Value, each $25.

Coat of Arms
A4 A5 A6

1863-71				
L4	A4	(2k) rose & green	90.00	90.00
a.		Yellowish paper		
b.		Green frame around central oval	95.00	60.00
c.		Tête bêche pair	2,500.	
L5	A5	(2k) rose & grn ('64)	125.00	100.00
L6	A6	(2k) rose & green	125.00	75.00
		Nos. L4-L6 (3)	340.00	265.00

Official imitations of Nos. L4b and L5 have a
rose instead of a green line around the central
oval. The first official imitation of No. L6 has
the central oval 5½mm instead of 6¼mm wide;
the second imitation is less clearly printed
than the original and the top of the "f" of
"Briefmarke" is too much hooked. Value, each
$25.

Coat of Arms
A7 A8

1872-75			**Perf. 12½**	
L7	A7	(2k) red & green	85.00	50.00
L8	A8	2k yel grn & red ('75)	8.50	11.00
a.		Numeral in upper right corner resembles an inverted "3"	30.00	30.00

Reprints of No. L8 have no horizontal lines
in the background. Those of No. L8a have the
impression blurred and only traces of the horizontal lines. Value, $25.

A9

1878-80				
L9	A9	2k green & red	15.00	7.00
a.		Imperf.		
L10	A9	2k blk, grn & red ('80)	10.00	10.00
a.		Imperf., pair	35.00	

No. L9 has been reprinted in blue green and
yellow green with perforation 11½ and in gray
green with perforation 12½ or imperforate.

1884			**Perf. 11½**	
L11	A9	2k black, green & red	3.00	3.00
a.		Green arm omitted	21.00	
b.		Arm inverted	21.00	
c.		Arm double	27.50	
d.		Imperf., pair	150.00	

Wenden
Castle — A10

1901			**Litho.**	
L12	A10	2k dk green & brown	12.00	10.00
a.		Tête bêche pair	45.00	
b.		Imperf., pair	100.00	

OCCUPATION STAMPS

ISSUED UNDER GERMAN OCCUPATION

German Stamps
Overprinted in Black

On Stamps of 1905-17

1916-17	**Wmk. 125**		**Perf. 14, 14½**	
N1	A22	2½pf gray	.65	1.00
N2	A16	3pf brown	.25	.25
N3	A16	5pf green	.65	1.00
N4	A22	7½pf orange	.65	1.00
N5	A16	10pf carmine	.65	1.00
N6	A22	15pf yel brn	3.00	2.00
N7	A22	15pf dk vio ('17)	.65	1.00
N8	A16	20pf ultra	1.00	1.00
N9	A16	20pf org & blk, yel	.50	.50
N10	A16	40pf lake & blk	1.00	3.75
N11	A16	50pf vio & blk, buff	1.00	1.50
N12	A17	1m car rose	12.00	3.50
		Nos. N1-N12 (12)	22.00	17.50
		Set, never hinged	65.00	

These stamps were used in the former Russian provinces of Suvalki, Vilnius, Kaunas,
Kurland, Estland and Lifland.

ISSUED UNDER FINNISH OCCUPATION

Finnish Stamps of 1917-
18 Overprinted

1919		**Unwmk.**	**Perf. 14**	
N13	A19	5p green	12.50	15.00
N14	A19	10p rose	12.50	15.00
N15	A19	20p buff	12.50	15.00
N16	A19	40p red violet	12.50	15.00
N17	A19	50p orange brn	125.00	150.00
N18	A19	1m dl rose & blk	140.00	140.00

N19	A19	5m violet & blk	425.00	425.00
N20	A19	10m brown & blk	725.00	725.00
		Nos. N13-N20 (8)	1,465.	1,500.
		Set, never hinged	3,000.	

"Aunus" is the Finnish name for Olonets, a
town of Russia.

Counterfeits overprints exist.

> Catalogue values for unused
> stamps in this section, from this
> point to the end of the section, are
> for Never Hinged items.

Issued under German Occupation

Germany Nos. 506 to
523 Overprinted in
Black

1941-43		**Unwmk.**	**Typo.**	**Perf. 14**	
N21	A115	1pf gray black	.25	.25
N22	A115	3pf light brown	.25	.25
N23	A115	4pf slate	.25	.25
N24	A115	5pf dp yellow green	.25	.25
N25	A115	6pf purple	.25	.25
N26	A115	8pf red	.25	.25
N27	A115	10pf dk brown ('43)	.65	3.25
N28	A115	12pf carmine ('43)	.65	2.75

Engr.

N29	A115	10pf dark brown	1.25	1.40
N30	A115	12pf brt carmine	1.25	1.40
N31	A115	15pf brown lake	.25	.25
N32	A115	16pf peacock grn	.25	.25
N33	A115	20pf blue	.25	.25
N34	A115	24pf orange brown	.25	.25
N35	A115	25pf brt ultra	.25	.25
N36	A115	30pf olive green	.25	.25
N37	A115	40pf brt red violet	.25	.25
N38	A115	50pf myrtle green	.25	.25
N39	A115	60pf dk red brown	.25	.25
N40	A115	80pf indigo	.25	.65
		Nos. N21-N40 (20)	7.80	13.20

Issued for use in Estonia, Latvia and
Lithuania.

Same Overprinted in
Black

		Typo.		
N41	A115	1pf gray black	.25	.25
N42	A115	3pf lt brown	.25	.25
N43	A115	4pf slate	.25	.25
N44	A115	5pf dp yel green	.25	.25
N45	A115	6pf purple	.25	.25
N46	A115	8pf red	.25	.25
N47	A115	10pf dk brown ('43)	.55	2.40
N48	A115	12pf carmine ('43)	.55	2.40

Engr.

N49	A115	10pf dk brown	1.00	1.60
N50	A115	12pf brt carmine	1.00	1.60
N51	A115	15pf brown lake	.25	.25
N52	A115	16pf peacock green	.25	.25
N53	A115	20pf blue	.25	.25
N54	A115	24pf orange brown	.25	.25
N55	A115	25pf bright ultra	.25	.25
N56	A115	30pf olive green	.25	.25
N57	A115	40pf brt red violet	.25	.25
N58	A115	50pf myrtle green	.25	.25
N59	A115	60pf dk red brown	.25	.25
N60	A115	80pf indigo	.25	.25
		Nos. N42-N60 (20)	7.10	12.00

ARMY OF THE NORTHWEST

(Gen. Nicolai N. Yudenich)

Russian Stamps of 1909-
18 Overprinted in Black
or Red

On Stamps of 1909-12

Perf. 14 to 15 and Compound

1919, Aug. 1				
1	A14	2k green	5.00	20.00
2	A14	5k claret	5.00	10.00
3	A15	10k dk blue (R)	10.00	25.00
4	A11	15k red brn & bl	5.00	15.00
5	A8	20k blue & car	10.00	15.00

6	A11	25k grn & gray vio	15.00	25.00
7	A8	50k brn vio & grn	10.00	15.00

Perf. 13½

8	A9	1r pale brn, dk brn & org	25.00	50.00
9	A13	10r scar, yel & gray	150.00	200.00

On Stamps of 1917
Imperf

10	A14	3k red	5.00	10.00
11	A12	3.50r mar & lt grn	17.50	35.00
12	A13	5r dk blue, grn & pale bl	17.50	30.00
13	A12	7r dk grn & pink	150.00	200.00

No. 2 Surcharged
Perf. 14, 14½x15

14	A14	10k on 5k claret	5.00	20.00
		Nos. 1-14 (14)	430.00	670.00

Nos. 1-14 exist with inverted overprint or surcharge. The 1, 3½, 5, 7 and 10 rubles with red overprint are trial printings (value $150 each). The 20k on 14k, perforated, and the 1, 2, 5, 15, 70k and 1r imperforate were overprinted but never placed in use. Value: $300, $30, $45, $45, $45, $45 and $65.

These stamps were in use from Aug. 1 to Oct. 15, 1919.

Counterfeits of Nos. 1-14 abound.

ARMY OF THE NORTH

A1

A2

A3

A4

A5

1919, Sept.   Typo.   Imperf.

1	A1	5k brown violet	.60	1.00
2	A2	10k blue	.60	1.00
3	A3	15k yellow	.60	1.00
4	A4	20k rose	.60	1.00
5	A5	50k green	.60	1.00
		Nos. 1-5 (5)	3.00	5.00

The letters OKCA are the initials of Russian words meaning "Special Corps, Army of the North." The stamps were in use from about the end of September to the end of December, 1919.

Used values are for c-t-o stamps.

(General Miller)

A set of seven stamps of this design was prepared in 1919, but not issued. Value, set $35. Counterfeits exist.

RUSSIA OFFICES ABROAD

For various reasons the Russian Empire maintained Post Offices to handle its correspondence in several foreign countries. These were similar to the Post Offices in foreign countries maintained by other world powers.

OFFICES IN CHINA

100 Kopecks = 1 Ruble
100 Cents = 1 Dollar (1917)

Russian Stamps Overprinted in Blue or Red

On Issues of 1889-92
Horizontally Laid Paper
1899-1904   Wmk. 168   Perf. 14½x15

1	A10	1k orange (Bl)	.75	1.00
2	A10	2k yel green (R)	.75	1.00
3	A10	3k carmine (Bl)	.75	1.00
4	A10	5k red violet (Bl)	.75	1.00
5	A10	7k dk blue (R)	1.50	2.50
a.		Inverted overprint	500.00	
6	A8	10k dk blue (R)	1.50	2.50
7	A8	50k vio & grn (Bl) ('04)	12.00	8.50

Perf. 13½

8	A9	1r lt brn, brn & org (Bl) ('04)	150.00	150.00
		Nos. 1-8 (8)	168.00	167.50

On Issues of 1902-05
Overprinted in Black, Red or Blue
Perf. 14½ to 15 and Compound
1904-08   Vertically Laid Paper

9	A8	4k rose red (Bl)	6.00	3.50
10	A10	7k dk blue (R)	15.00	15.00
11	A8	10k dk blue (R)	1,500.	1,300.
a.		Groundwork inverted	14,500.	
12	A11	14k bl & rose (R)	10.00	10.00
13	A11	15k brn vio & blue (Bl) ('08)	35.00	30.00
14	A8	20k blue & car (Bl)	5.00	5.00
15	A11	25k dull grn & lil (R) ('08)	50.00	50.00
16	A11	35k dk vio & grn (R)	10.00	10.00
17	A8	50k vio & grn (Bl)	100.00	125.00
18	A11	70k brn & org (Bl)	15.00	13.00

Perf. 13½

19	A9	1r lt brn, brn & org (Bl)	25.00	25.00
20	A12	3.50r blk & gray (R)	5.00	5.00
21	A13	5r dk bl, grn & pale bl (R) ('07)	8.50	12.00
a.		Inverted overprint	2,500.	
22	A12	7r blk & yel (Bl)	25.00	12.00
23	A13	10r scar, yel & gray (Bl) ('07)	100.00	100.00
		Nos. 9-10,12-23 (14)	409.50	415.50

On Issues of 1909-12
Wove Paper
Lozenges of Varnish on Face
1910-16   Unwmk.   Perf. 14x14½

24	A14	1k orange yel (Bl)	.50	.50
25	A14	1k org yel (Bl Bk)	6.00	5.00
26	A14	2k green (Bk)	1.00	1.00
27	A14	2k green (Bl)	7.50	15.00
a.		Double ovpt. (Bk and Bl)		
28	A14	3k rose red (Bl)	2.00	5.00
29	A14	3k rose red (Bk)	12.00	12.00
30	A15	4k carmine (Bl)	1.00	2.00
31	A15	4k carmine (Bk)	10.00	10.00
32	A14	7k lt blue (Bk)	1.00	1.00
33	A15	10k blue (Bk)	1.00	1.00
34	A11	14k blue & rose (Bk)	10.00	5.00
35	A11	14k blue & rose (Bl)		
36	A11	15k dl vio & bl (Bk)	1.00	1.25
37	A8	20k blue & car (Bk)	5.00	7.00
38	A11	25k green & vio (Bl)	3.50	6.00
39	A11	25k grn & vio (Bk)	1.00	1.60
40	A11	35k vio & grn (Bk)	1.00	1.00
42	A8	50k vio & grn (Bl)	2.00	2.00
43	A8	50k brn vio & grn (Bk)	18.00	20.00
44	A11	70k lt brn & org (Bl)	1.00	2.00

Perf. 13½

45	A9	1r pale brn, brn & org (Bl)	1.25	2.40
47	A13	5r dk bl, grn & pale bl (R)	25.00	15.00
		Nos. 24-34,36-47 (21)	110.75	115.75

The existence of #35 is questioned.

Russian Stamps of 1902-12
Surcharged

a

b

c

On Stamps of 1909-12
1917   Perf. 11½, 13½, 14, 14½x15

50	A14(a)	1c on 1k dl org yel	.60	5.50
51	A14(a)	2c on 2k dull grn	.60	5.50
a.		Inverted surcharge	100.00	
52	A14(a)	3c on 3k car	.60	5.50
a.		Inverted surcharge	100.00	
b.		Double surcharge	150.00	
53	A15(a)	4c on 4k car	1.25	4.25
54	A14(a)	5c on 5k claret	1.25	15.00
55	A15(b)	10c on 10k dk blue	1.25	15.00
a.		Inverted surcharge	100.00	100.00
b.		Double surcharge	115.00	
56	A11(a)	14c on 14k dk blue & car	1.25	10.00
a.		Imperf.	6.00	
b.		Inverted surcharge	100.00	
57	A11(a)	15c on 15k brn lil & dp blue	1.25	15.00
a.		Inverted surcharge	50.00	
58	A8(b)	20c on 20k bl & car	1.25	15.00
59	A11(a)	25c on 25k grn & vio	1.25	15.00
60	A11(a)	35c on 35k brn vio & grn	1.50	15.00
a.		Inverted surcharge	50.00	
61	A8(a)	50c on 50k brn vio & grn	1.25	15.00
62	A11(a)	70c on 70k brn & red org	1.25	15.00
63	A9(c)	$1 on 1r pale brn, brn & org	1.25	15.00
		Nos. 50-63 (14)	15.80	

On Stamps of 1902-05
Vertically Laid Paper
Perf. 11½, 13, 13½, 13½x11½
Wmk. Wavy Lines (168)

64	A12	$3.50 on 3.50r blk & gray	20.00	40.00
65	A13	$5 on 5r dk bl, grn & pale blue	20.00	40.00
66	A12	$7 on 7r blk & yel	10.00	32.50

On Stamps of 1915
Wove Paper
Unwmk.   Perf. 13½

68	A13	$5 on 5r ind, grn & lt blue	25.00	50.00
a.		Inverted surcharge	500.00	
70	A13	$10 on 10r car lake, yel & gray	50.00	100.00
		Nos. 64-70 (5)	125.00	262.50

The surcharge on Nos. 64-70 is in larger type than on the $1.

Russian Stamps of 1909-18 Surcharged in Black or Red

On Stamps of 1909-12
1920   Perf. 14, 14½x15

72	A14	1c on 1k dull org yel	175.00	275.00
73	A14	2c on 2k dull grn (R)	16.00	27.50
74	A14	3c on 3k car	16.00	37.50
75	A15	4c on 4k car	18.00	22.50
a.		Inverted surcharge	130.00	150.00
76	A14	5c on 5k claret	60.00	90.00
77	A15	10c on 10k dk bl (R)	150.00	225.00
78	A14	10c on 10k on 7k blue (R)	125.00	190.00

On Stamps of 1917-18
Imperf

79	A14	1c on 1k orange	42.50	37.50
a.		Inverted surcharge	125.00	150.00
80	A14	5c on 5k claret	35.00	55.00
a.		Inverted surcharge	150.00	
b.		Double surcharge	250.00	
c.		Surcharged "Cent" only	95.00	
		Nos. 72-80 (9)	637.50	960.00

OFFICES IN THE TURKISH EMPIRE

Various powers maintained post offices in the Turkish Empire before World War I by authority of treaties which ended with the signing of the Treaty of Lausanne in 1923. The foreign post offices were closed Oct. 27, 1923.

100 Kopecks = 1 Ruble
40 Paras = 1 Piaster (1900)

The editors recommend that the stamps of Russian Offices in the Turkish Empire, 1863-1879, be purchased accompanied by certificates of authenticity issued by the competent authorities and committees.

Coat of Arms
A1

1863		Unwmk.	Typo.		Imperf.
1	A1	6k blue		325.00	3,000.
a.		6k light blue, thin paper		350.00	3,000.
b.		6k light blue, medium paper		325.00	3,000.
c.		6k dark blue, chalky paper ('66)		165.00	

Values are for stamps without faults. Most stamps from this set have faults. Forgeries exist.
No. 1c was unissued.

A2 · A3

1865				Litho.	
2	A2	(2k) brown & blue		800.00	750.00
3	A3	(20k) blue & red		900.00	850.00

Twenty-eight varieties of each.

A4 · A5

1866		Horizontal Network		
4	A4	(2k) rose & pale bl	25.00	30.00
5	A5	(20k) deep blue & rose	40.00	50.00

1867		Vertical Network		
6	A4	(2k) rose & pale bl	75.00	100.00
7	A5	(20k) dp blue & rose	200.00	100.00

The initials inscribed on Nos. 2 to 7 are those of the Russian Company of Navigation and Trade.
The official imitations of Nos. 2 to 7 are on yellowish white paper. The colors are usually paler than those of the originals and there are minor differences in the designs.

A6

Horizontally Laid Paper

1868		Typo.	Wmk. 168		Perf. 11½
8	A6	1k brown		50.00	20.00
9	A6	3k green		60.00	25.00
10	A6	5k blue		60.00	25.00
11	A6	10k car & green		75.00	25.00
		Nos. 8-11 (4)		245.00	95.00

Colors of Nos. 8-11 dissolve in water.

1872-90					Perf. 14½x15
12	A6	1k brown		10.00	2.00
13	A6	3k green		25.00	3.00
14	A6	5k blue		5.00	1.00
15	A6	10k pale red & grn		1.25	.60
		('90)			
b.		10k carmine & green		24.00	3.75
		Nos. 12-15 (4)		41.25	6.60

Vertically Laid Paper

12a	A6	1k		75.00	18.00
13a	A6	3k		75.00	18.00
14a	A6	5k		75.00	18.00
15a	A6	10k		190.00	47.50
		Nos. 12a-15a (4)		415.00	101.50

Nos. 12-15 exist imperf.

No. 15 Surcharged in Black or Blue

a · b

c

1876					
16	A6(a)	8k on 10k (Bk)		75.00	45.00
a.		Vertically laid			2,750.
b.		Inverted surcharge		400.00	
17	A6(a)	8k on 10k (Bl)		90.00	75.00
a.		Vertically laid			
b.		Inverted surcharge			

1879					
18	A6(b)	7k on 10k (Bk)		80.00	65.00
a.		Vertically laid		750.00	750.00
b.		Inverted surcharge			
19	A6(b)	7k on 10k (Bl)		125.00	85.00
a.		Vertically laid		1,750.	1,750.
b.		Inverted surcharge		500.00	
19C	A6(c)	7k on 10k (Bl)		1,250.	1,250.
19D	A6(c)	7k on 10k (Bk)		1,250.	1,250.

Nos. 16-19D have been extensively counterfeited.

1879					Perf. 14½x15
20	A6	1k black & yellow		3.00	1.00
a.		Vertically laid		10.00	5.00
21	A6	2k black & rose		5.00	3.00
a.		Vertically laid		10.00	5.00
22	A6	7k carmine & gray		9.00	1.00
a.		Vertically laid		42.50	15.00
		Nos. 20-22 (3)		17.00	5.00

1884					
23	A6	1k orange		.75	.50
24	A6	2k green		1.00	.75
25	A6	5k pale red violet		4.00	2.00
26	A6	7k blue		2.00	1.50
		Nos. 23-26 (4)		7.75	4.75

Nos. 23-26 imperforate are believed to be proofs.
No. 23 surcharged "40 PARAS" is bogus, though some examples were postally used.

Russian Company of Navigation and Trade

This overprint, in two sizes, was privately applied in various colors to Russian Offices in the Turkish Empire stamps of 1900-1910.

A7 · A8

Surcharged in Blue, Black or Red

1900		Horizontally Laid Paper			
27	A7	4pa on 1k orange (Bl)		1.25	1.25
a.		Inverted surcharge		30.00	30.00
28	A7	4pa on 1k orange (Bk)		1.25	1.25
a.		Inverted surcharge		30.00	30.00
29	A7	10pa on 2k green		.25	.25
30	A8	1pi on 10k dk blue		.50	.60
a.		Inverted surcharge			
		Nos. 27-30 (4)		3.25	3.35

A9 · A10

A11

1903-05		Vertically Laid Paper			
31	A7	10pa on 2k yel green		.60	.40
a.		Inverted surcharge		75.00	
32	A8	20pa on 4k rose red (Bl)		.60	.40
a.		Inverted surcharge		95.00	
33	A8	1pi on 10k dk blue		.60	.40
a.		Groundwork inverted		50.00	15.00
34	A8	2pi on 20k blue & car (Bk)		1.40	.75
35	A8	5pi on 50k brn vio & grn		3.50	1.25
36	A9	7pi on 70k brn & org (Bl)		4.00	2.00
					Perf. 13½
37	A10	10pi on 1r lt brn, brn & org (Bl)		6.50	4.00
38	A11	35pi on 3.50r blk & gray		20.00	10.00
39	A11	70pi on 7r blk & yel		24.00	12.50
		Nos. 31-39 (9)		61.20	31.70

A12 · A13

A14

Wove Paper
Lozenges of Varnish on Face

1909		Unwmk.		Perf. 14½x15	
40	A12	5pa on 1k orange		.30	.40
41	A12	10pa on 2k green		.35	.65
a.		Inverted surcharge		30.00	30.00
42	A12	20pa on 4k carmine		.70	1.00
43	A12	1pi on 10k blue		.75	1.20
44	A12	5pi on 50k vio & grn		1.40	1.60
45	A12	7pi on 70k brn & org		2.00	2.75
				Perf. 13½	
46	A13	10pi on 1r brn & org		3.00	5.00
47	A14	35pi on 3.50r mar & lt grn		12.00	14.00
48	A14	70pi on 7r dk grn & pink		20.00	25.00
		Nos. 40-48 (9)		40.50	51.60

50th anniv. of the establishing of the Russian Post Offices in the Levant.

Nos. 40-48 Overprinted with Names of Various Cities Overprinted "Constantinople" in Black

1909-10					Perf. 14½x15
61	A12	5pa on 1k		.40	.40
c.		Inverted overprint		50.00	
62	A12	10pa on 2k		.40	.40
c.		Inverted overprint		30.00	
63	A12	20pa on 4k		.75	.75
c.		Inverted overprint		30.00	
64	A12	1pi on 10k		.75	.75
65	A12	5pi on 50k		1.50	1.50
66	A12	7pi on 70k		3.00	3.00
					Perf. 13½
67	A13	10pi on 1r		15.00	15.00
a.		"Constanttnople"		100.00	100.00
68	A14	35pi on 3.50r		50.00	30.00
c.		"Constautinople"		100.00	100.00
d.		"Constantjnople"		100.00	100.00
69	A14	70pi on 7r		45.00	42.50
c.		"Constantinople"		100.00	100.00
d.		"Constantjnople"		100.00	100.00

Blue Overprint
Perf. 14½x15

70	A12	5pa on 1k		8.00	8.00
		Nos. 61-70 (10)		124.80	102.30

"Consnantinople"

61a	A12	5pa on 1k		10.00	
62a	A12	10pa on 2k		10.00	
63a	A12	20pa on 4k		10.00	
64a	A12	1pi on 10k		10.00	
65a	A12	5pi on 50k		10.00	
66a	A12	7pi on 70k		12.00	
68a	A14	35pi on 3.50r		50.00	
69a	A14	70pi on 7r		90.00	
70a	A12	5pa on 1k		90.00	
		Nos. 61a-70a (9)		212.00	

"Constantinopie"

61b	A12	5pa on 1k		25.00	
d.		Inverted overprint		50.00	
62b	A12	10pa on 2k		25.00	
d.		Inverted overprint		50.00	
63b	A12	20pa on 4k		30.00	
d.		Inverted overprint		60.00	
64b	A12	1pi on 10k		30.00	
65b	A12	5pi on 50k		30.00	
66b	A12	7pi on 70k		30.00	
68b	A14	35pi on 3.50r		60.00	
69b	A14	70pi on 7r		90.00	
		Nos. 61b-69b (8)		320.00	

Overprinted "Jaffa"
Black Overprint

71	A12	5pa on 1k		2.10	3.75
a.		Inverted overprint		75.00	
72	A12	10pa on 2k		2.50	4.00
a.		Inverted overprint		50.00	
73	A12	20pa on 4k		3.00	5.25
a.		Inverted overprint		60.00	
74	A12	1pi on 10k		3.75	5.25
a.		Double overprint		95.00	
75	A12	5pi on 50k		9.00	10.50
76	A12	7pi on 70k		11.00	14.00
				Perf. 13½	
77	A13	10pi on 1r		50.00	50.00
78	A14	35pi on 3.50r		100.00	100.00
79	A14	70pi on 7r		125.00	150.00

Blue Overprint
Perf. 14½x15

80	A12	5pa on 1k		12.00	12.00
		Nos. 71-80 (10)		318.35	354.75

Overprinted "Ierusalem" in Black
Black Overprint

81	A12	5pa on 1k		2.10	2.75
a.		Inverted overprint		60.00	
b.		"erusalem"		25.00	
c.		As "b," overprint inverted		50.00	
82	A12	10pa on 2k		2.75	4.25
a.		Inverted overprint		30.00	
b.		"erusalem"		25.00	
c.		As "b," overprint inverted		50.00	
83	A12	20pa on 4k		4.25	5.50
a.		Inverted overprint		30.00	
b.		"erusalem"		25.00	
c.		As "b," overprint inverted		50.00	
84	A12	1pi on 10k		4.25	5.50
a.		"erusalem"		30.00	
85	A12	5pi on 50k		7.25	11.00
a.		"erusalem"		35.00	
86	A12	7pi on 70k		14.00	17.50
a.		"erusalem"		35.00	
				Perf. 13½	
87	A13	10pi on 1r		50.00	50.00
88	A14	35pi on 3.50r		125.00	125.00
89	A14	70pi on 7r		125.00	150.00

Blue Overprint
Perf. 14½x15

90	A12	5pa on 1k		15.00	25.00
		Nos. 81-90 (10)		349.60	396.50

Overprinted "Kerassunde"
Black Overprint

91	A12	5pa on 1k		.60	.80
a.		Inverted overprint		50.00	
92	A12	10pa on 2k		.60	.80
a.		Inverted overprint		50.00	

93	A12	20pa on 4k	1.00 1.10
a.		Inverted overprint	50.00
94	A12	1pi on 10k	1.25 1.25
95	A12	5pi on 50k	2.25 2.50
96	A12	7pi on 70k	3.50 4.00

Perf. 13½

97	A13	10pi on 1r	13.00 15.00
98	A14	35pi on 3.50r	42.50 42.50
99	A14	70pi on 7r	65.00 52.50

Blue Overprint
Perf. 14½x15

100	A12	5pa on 1k	15.00 15.00
		Nos. 91-100 (10)	144.70 135.45

Overprinted "Mont Athos"

Black Overprint

101	A12	5pa on 1k	1.25 1.50
b.		Inverted overprint	100.00
102	A12	10pa on 2k	1.25 1.50
b.		Inverted overprint	100.00
103	A12	20pa on 4k	1.75 3.00
b.		Inverted overprint	100.00
104	A12	1pi on 10k	2.25 4.00
b.		Double overprint	125.00
105	A12	5pi on 50k	7.00 7.50
106	A12	7pi on 70k	8.00 8.50
b.		Pair, one without "Mont Athos"	125.00

Perf. 13½

107	A13	10pi on 1r	35.00 35.00
108	A14	35pi on 3.50r	80.00 80.00
109	A14	70pi on 7r	145.00 150.00

Blue Overprint
Perf. 14½x15

110	A12	5pa on 1k	12.50 17.00
		Nos. 101-110 (10)	294.00 308.00

"Mont Atho"

101a	A12	5pa on 1k	35.00
102a	A12	10pa on 2k	35.00
103a	A12	20pa on 4k	35.00
c.		Inverted overprint	125.00
104a	A12	1pi on 10k	35.00
c.		As "a," double overprint	150.00
105a	A12	5pi on 50k	35.00
106a	A12	7pi on 70k	35.00
110a	A12	5pa on 1k	65.00

"M nt Athos"

101d	A12	5pa on 1k	35.00
102d	A12	10pa on 2k	35.00
103d	A12	20pa on 4k	35.00
105d	A12	5pi on 50k	65.00
106d	A12	7pi on 70k	90.00

Overprinted

111	A12	5pa on 1k	1.50 2.00
a.		Pair, one without overprint	125.00
112	A12	10pa on 2k	1.50 2.00
a.		Pair, one without overprint	125.00
113	A12	20pa on 4k	2.50 3.50
a.		Pair, one without overprint	125.00
114	A12	1pi on 10k	4.50 6.00
a.		Pair, one without overprint	125.00
115	A12	5pi on 50k	7.00 9.50
a.		Pair, one without overprint	150.00
116	A12	7pi on 70k	13.00 17.50
a.		Pair, one without overprint	125.00

Perf. 13½

117	A13	10pi on 1r	80.00 80.00
		Nos. 111-117 (7)	110.00 120.50

The overprint is larger on No. 117.

Overprinted "Salonique"
Black Overprint
Perf. 14½x15

131	A12	5pa on 1k	1.50 2.00
a.		Inverted overprint	55.00
b.		Pair, one without overprint	60.00
132	A12	10pa on 2k	2.00 4.00
a.		Inverted overprint	55.00
b.		Pair, one without overprint	60.00
133	A12	20pa on 4k	2.50 5.00
a.		Inverted overprint	55.00
b.		Pair, one without overprint	60.00
134	A12	1pi on 10k	3.00 6.00
a.		Inverted overprint	75.00
135	A12	5pi on 50k	3.50 8.00
136	A12	7pi on 70k	5.00 10.00

Perf. 13½

137	A13	10pi on 1r	32.50 40.00
138	A14	35pi on 3.50r	80.00 85.00
139	A14	70pi on 7r	100.00 115.00

Blue Overprint
Perf. 14½x15

140	A12	5pa on 1k	15.00 15.00
		Nos. 131-140 (10)	245.00 290.00

Overprinted "Smyrne"
Black Overprint

141	A12	5pa on 1k	.65 1.25
a.		Double overprint	10.00
b.		Inverted overprint	25.00
142	A12	10pa on 2k	.65 1.25
a.		Inverted overprint	25.00
143	A12	20pa on 4k	1.40 1.60
a.		Inverted overprint	17.50
144	A12	1pi on 10k	1.40 1.75
145	A12	5pi on 50k	3.00 3.00
146	A12	7pi on 70k	4.50 6.00

Perf. 13½

147	A13	10pi on 1r	18.00 22.50
148	A14	35pi on 3.50r	37.50 40.00
149	A14	70pi on 7r	55.00 62.50

Blue Overprint
Perf. 14½x15

150	A12	5pa on 1k	11.00 11.00
		Nos. 141-150 (10)	133.10 150.85

"Smyrn"

141c	A12	5pa on 1k	18.00 20.00
142b	A12	10pa on 2k	18.00 20.00
143b	A12	20pa on 4k	18.00 20.00
144a	A12	1pi on 10k	20.00 25.00
145a	A12	5pi on 50k	20.00 25.00
146a	A12	7pi on 70k	20.00 25.00
		Nos. 141c-146a (6)	114.00 135.00

Overprinted "Trebizonde"
Black Overprint

151	A12	5pa on 1k	.80 1.00
a.		Inverted overprint	25.00
b.		Pair, one without overprint	60.00
152	A12	10pa on 2k	.80 1.00
a.		Inverted overprint	25.00
b.		Pair, one without "Trebizonde"	60.00
153	A12	20pa on 4k	.95 .95
a.		Inverted overprint	25.00
b.		Pair, one without overprint	100.00
154	A12	1pi on 10k	.95 1.50
a.		Pair, one without "Trebizonde"	35.00
155	A12	5pi on 50k	2.10 2.50
156	A12	7pi on 70k	4.25 5.50

Perf. 13½

157	A13	10pi on 1r	19.00 20.00
158	A14	35pi on 3.50r	37.50 37.50
159	A14	70pi on 7r	52.50 55.00

Blue Overprint
Perf. 14½x15

160	A12	5pa on 1k	6.25 7.50
		Nos. 151-160 (10)	125.10 132.45

On Nos. 158 and 159 the overprint is spelled "Trebisonde".

Overprinted "Beyrouth"
Black Overprint
1910

161	A12	5pa on 1k	.50 .85
162	A12	10pa on 2k	.50 .85
a.		Inverted overprint	25.00
163	A12	20pa on 4k	.80 1.10
164	A12	1pi on 10k	.80 1.40
165	A12	5pi on 50k	1.90 2.75
166	A12	7pi on 70k	4.00 5.50

Perf. 13½

167	A13	10pi on 1r	19.00 21.00
168	A14	35pi on 3.50r	40.00 42.50
169	A14	70pi on 7r	55.00 60.00
		Nos. 161-169 (9)	122.50 135.95

Overprinted "Dardanelles"
Perf. 14½x15

171	A12	5pa on 1k	1.25 2.50
a.		Pair, one without overprint	60.00
172	A12	10pa on 2k	1.25 2.50
a.		Pair, one without overprint	60.00
173	A12	20pa on 4k	3.25 3.25
a.		Inverted overprint	25.00
174	A12	1pi on 10k	3.50 3.50
175	A12	5pi on 50k	6.50 7.50
176	A12	7pi on 70k	14.00 14.00

Perf. 13½

177	A13	10pi on 1r	21.00 21.00
178	A14	35pi on 3.50r	37.50 40.00
a.		Center and ovpt. inverted	5,000. 2,750.
179	A14	70pi on 7r	60.00 65.00
		Nos. 171-179 (9)	148.25 159.25

Overprinted "Metelin"
Perf. 14½x15

181	A12	5pa on 1k	1.25 2.00
a.		Inverted overprint	65.00
182	A12	10pa on 2k	2.25 4.25
a.		Inverted overprint	65.00
183	A12	20pa on 4k	2.25 5.25
a.		Inverted overprint	65.00
184	A12	1pi on 10k	4.50 6.50
185	A12	5pi on 50k	5.50 8.50
186	A12	7pi on 70k	8.50 11.50

Perf. 13½

187	A13	10pi on 1r	30.00 32.50
188	A14	35pi on 3.50r	72.50 75.00
189	A14	70pi on 7r	82.50 87.50

Blue Overprint
Perf. 14½x15

190	A12	5pa on 1k	12.50 17.00
		Nos. 181-190 (10)	221.75 250.00

Overprinted "Rizeh"
Perf. 14½x15

191	A12	5pa on 1k	.65 1.00
a.		Inverted overprint	30.00
192	A12	10pa on 2k	.65 1.00
a.		Inverted overprint	30.00
193	A12	20pa on 4k	1.10 1.40
a.		Inverted overprint	30.00
194	A12	1pi on 10k	1.10 1.40
195	A12	5pi on 50k	1.75 3.75
196	A12	7pi on 70k	3.25 6.00

Perf. 13½

197	A13	10pi on 1r	17.50 21.00
198	A14	35pi on 3.50r	27.50 35.00
199	A14	70pi on 7r	44.00 52.50
		Nos. 191-199 (9)	97.50 123.05

Nos. 61-199 for the establishing of Russian Post Offices in the Levant, 50th anniv.

A15

Vertically Laid Paper

1910   Wmk. 168   Perf. 14½x15

200	A15	20pa on 5k red violet (Bl)	.60 .60

A16   A17

Wove Paper
Vertical Lozenges of Varnish on Face

1910   Unwmk.   Perf. 14x14½

201	A16	5pa on 1k org yel (Bl)	.40 .50
202	A16	10pa on 2k green (R)	.40 .50
a.		Inverted overprint	25.00
203	A17	20pa on 4k car rose (Bl)	.40 .50
204	A17	1pi on 10k blue (R)	.40 .50
a.		Inverted overprint	25.00
205	A8	5pi on 50k vio & grn (Bl)	.75 1.20
206	A9	7pi on 70k lt brn & org (Bl)	1.00 1.25

Perf. 13½

207	A10	10pi on 1r pale brn, brn & org (Bl)	1.40 1.50
		Nos. 201-207 (7)	4.75 5.95

Russian Stamps of 1909-12 Surcharged in Black

No. 208   Nos. 209-212

1912   Perf. 14x14½

208	A14	20pa on 5k claret	.80 .60
209	A11	1½pi on 15k dl vio & blue	.80 .75
210	A8	2pi on 20k bl & car	.80 .90
211	A11	2½pi on 25k grn & vio	1.00 1.25
a.		Double surcharge	150.00 150.00
212	A11	3½pi on 35k vio & grn	1.60 1.60
		Nos. 208-212 (5)	5.00 5.10

Russia Nos. 88-91, 93, 95-104 Surcharged

c   d

e   f

g

1913   Perf. 13½

213	A16(c)	5pa on 1k	.25 .25
214	A17(d)	10pa on 2k	.25 .25
215	A18(c)	15pa on 3k	.25 .25
216	A19(c)	20pa on 4k	.25 .25
217	A21(e)	1pi on 10k	.25 .25
218	A23(f)	1½pi on 15k	.50 .50
219	A24(f)	2pi on 20k	.50 .50
220	A25(f)	2½pi on 25k	.75 .75
221	A26(f)	3½pi on 35k	1.60 1.60
222	A27(e)	5pi on 50k	2.00 2.00
223	A28(f)	7pi on 70k	8.00 15.00
224	A29(e)	10pi on 1r	9.00 15.00
225	A30(e)	20pi on 2r	1.60 8.00
226	A31(g)	30pi on 3r	2.75 250.00
227	A32(e)	50pi on 5r	150.00 500.00
		Nos. 213-227 (15)	177.95 794.60

Romanov dynasty tercentenary.
Forgeries exist of overprint on No. 227.

Russia Nos. 75, 71, 72 Surcharged

h   i

Perf. 14x14½
Wove Paper

228	A14(h)	15pa on 3k	.25 .25

Perf. 13, 13½

230	A13(i)	50pi on 5r	3.00 10.00

Vertically Laid Paper
Wmk. Wavy Lines (168)

231	A13(i)	100pi on 10r	7.00 20.00
a.		Double surcharge	750.00
		Nos. 228-231 (3)	10.25 30.25

No. 228 has lozenges of varnish on face but No. 230 has not.

Wrangel Issues

For the Posts of Gen. Peter Wrangel's army and civilian refugees from South Russia, interned in Turkey, Serbia, etc.

Very few of the Wrangel overprints were actually sold to the public, and many of the covers were made up later with the original cancels. Reprints abound. Values probably are based on sales of reprints in most cases.

Russian Stamps of 1902-18 Surcharged in Blue, Red or Black

On Russia Nos. 69-70
Vertically Laid Paper
1921   **Wmk. 168**   *Perf. 13½*

232	A12	10,000r on 3.50r	250.00	250.00
233	A12	10,000r on 7r	250.00	250.00
234	A12	20,000r on 3.50r	250.00	250.00
235	A12	20,000r on 7r	250.00	250.00
	Nos. 232-235 (4)		1,000.	1,000.

On Russia Nos. 71-86, 87a, 117-118, 137-138
Wove Paper
Perf. 14x14½, 13½
Unwmk.

236	A14	1000r on 1k	3.25	3.25
237	A14	1000r on 2k (R)	3.25	3.25
237A	A14	1000r on 2k (Bk)	47.50	47.50
238	A14	1000r on 3k	1.10	1.10
a.		Inverted surcharge	10.00	10.00
239	A15	1000r on 4k	1.10	1.10
a.		Inverted surcharge	10.00	10.00
240	A14	1000r on 5k	1.10	1.10
a.		Inverted surcharge	10.00	10.00
241	A14	1000r on 7k	1.10	1.10
a.		Inverted surcharge	10.00	10.00
242	A15	1000r on 10k	1.10	1.10
a.		Inverted surcharge	10.00	10.00
243	A14	1000r on 10k on 7k	1.10	1.10
244	A14	5000r on 3k	1.10	1.10
245	A11	5000r on 14k	10.00	10.00
246	A11	5000r on 15k	1.10	1.10
a.		"PYCCKIN"	12.00	12.00
247	A8	5000r on 20k	3.50	3.50
a.		"PYCCKIN"	12.00	12.00
248	A11	5000r on 20k on 14k	3.50	3.50
249	A11	5000r on 25k	1.10	1.10
250	A11	5000r on 35k	1.10	1.10
a.		Inverted surcharge	10.00	10.00
b.		New value omitted	10.00	10.00
251	A8	5000r on 50k	1.10	1.10
a.		Inverted surcharge	10.00	10.00
252	A11	5000r on 70k	1.10	1.10
a.		Inverted surcharge	10.00	10.00
253	A9	10,000r on 1r (Bl)	1.10	1.10
254	A9	10,000r on 1r (Bk)	8.25	8.25
255	A12	10,000r on 3.50r	3.50	3.50
256	A12	10,000r on 5r	45.00	45.00
257	A13	10,000r on 10r	4.25	4.25
258	A9	20,000r on 1r	2.50	2.50
259	A12	20,000r on 3.50r	2.50	2.50
a.		Inverted surcharge	10.00	10.00
b.		New value omitted	20.00	20.00
260	A12	20,000r on 7r	92.50	92.50
261	A13	20,000r on 10r	2.50	2.50
	Nos. 236-261 (27)		246.30	246.30

On Russia No. 104

261A	A32	20,000r on 5r	950.00	

On Russia Nos. 119-123, 125-135
Imperf

262	A14	1000r on 1k	1.20	1.20
263	A14	1000r on 2k (R)	1.20	1.20
263A	A14	1000r on 2k (Bk)	1.50	1.50
264	A14	1000r on 3k	1.20	1.20
265	A15	1000r on 4k	40.00	40.00
266	A14	1000r on 5k	1.50	1.50
267	A14	5000r on 3k	1.20	1.20
268	A11	5000r on 15k	1.50	1.50
268A	A8	5000r on 20k	60.00	
268B	A11	5000r on 25k	60.00	
269	A11	5000r on 35k	3.00	3.00
270	A8	5000r on 50k	3.00	3.00
271	A11	5000r on 70k	1.20	1.20
272	A9	10,000r on 1r (Bl)	1.20	1.20
a.		Inverted surcharge	10.00	10.00
273	A9	10,000r on 1r (Bk)	1.20	1.20
274	A12	10,000r on 3.50r	1.20	1.20
275	A13	10,000r on 5r	10.00	10.00
276	A12	10,000r on 7r	60.00	60.00
276A	A13	10,000r on 10r	200.00	
277	A9	20,000r on 1r (Bl)	1.20	1.20
a.		Inverted surcharge	10.00	10.00
278	A9	20,000r on 1r (Bk)	1.20	1.20
279	A12	20,000r on 3.50r	10.00	10.00
280	A13	20,000r on 5r	1.20	1.20
281	A12	20,000r on 7r	47.50	47.50
281A	A13	20,000r on 10r	275.00	
	Nos. 262-268,269-276,277-281 (21)		191.20	191.20

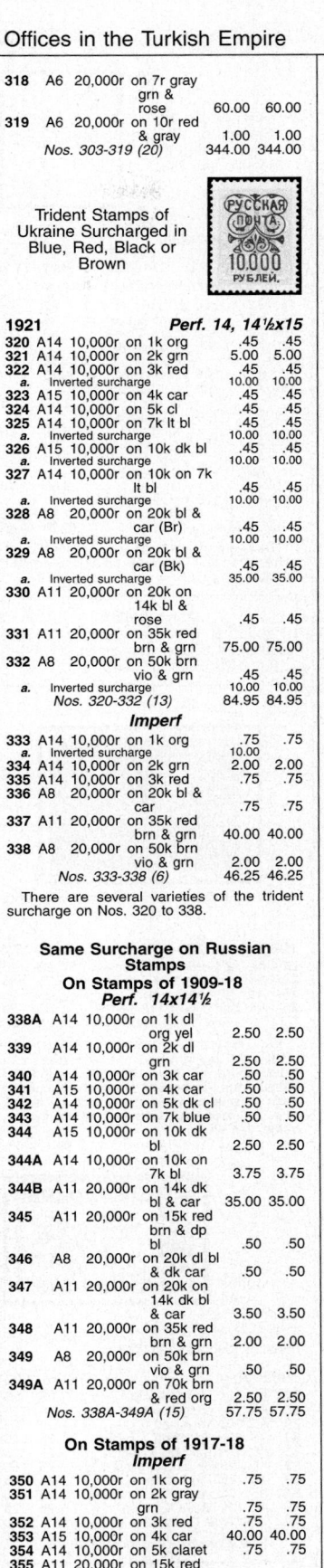

A18   A19

On Russia AR1-AR3
Perf. 14½x15
Wmk. 171

282	A18	10,000r on 1k red, buff	6.50	6.50
283	A19	10,000r on 5k grn, buff	6.50	6.50
a.		Inverted surcharge	10.00	
284	A19	10,000r on 10k brn, buff	6.50	6.50
a.		Inverted surcharge	10.00	
	Nos. 282-284 (3)		19.50	19.50

On Stamps of Russian Offices in Turkey On No. 38-39
Vertically Laid Paper
Wmk. Wavy Lines (168)

284B	A11	20,000r on 35pi on 3.50r	300.00	
284C	A11	20,000r on 70pi on 7r	400.00	

On Nos. 200-207
Vertically Laid Paper

284D	A15	1000r on 20pa on 5k	5.00	5.00

Wove Paper
Unwmk.

285	A16	1000r on 5pa on 1k	2.50	2.50
286	A16	1000r on 10pa on 2k	2.50	2.50
287	A17	1000r on 20pa on 4k	2.50	2.50
288	A17	1000r on 1pi on 10k	2.50	2.50
289	A8	5000r on 5pi on 50k	2.50	2.50
290	A9	5000r on 7pi on 70k	2.50	2.50
291	A10	10,000r on 10pi on 1r	12.50	12.50
a.		Inverted surcharge	25.00	25.00
b.		Pair, one without surcharge	20.00	20.00
292	A10	20,000r on 10pi on 1r	2.50	2.50
a.		Inverted surcharge	25.00	25.00
b.		Pair, one without surcharge	25.00	25.00
	Nos. 284D-292 (9)		35.00	35.00

On Nos. 208-212

293	A14	1000r on 20pa on 5k	2.50	2.50
294	A11	5000r on 1½pi on 15k	2.50	2.50
295	A8	5000r on 2pi on 20k	2.50	2.50
296	A11	5000r on 2½pi on 25k	2.50	2.50
297	A11	5000r on 3½pi on 35k	2.50	2.50
	Nos. 293-297 (5)		12.50	12.50

On Nos. 228, 230-231

298	A14	1000r on 15pa on 3k	1.00	1.00
299	A13	10,000r on 50pi on 5r	65.00	65.00
300	A13	10,000r on 100pi on 10r	92.50	92.50
301	A13	20,000r on 50pi on 5r	1.00	1.00
302	A13	20,000r on 100pi on 10r	92.50	92.50
	Nos. 298-302 (5)		252.00	252.00

On Stamps of South Russia
Denikin Issue
Imperf

303	A5	5000r on 5k org	1.00	1.00
a.		Inverted surcharge	10.00	
304	A5	5000r on 10k green	1.00	1.00
305	A5	5000r on 15k red	1.00	1.00
306	A5	5000r on 35k lt bl	1.00	1.00
307	A5	5000r on 70k dk blue	1.00	1.00
307A	A5	10,000r on 70k dk blue	50.00	50.00
308	A6	10,000r on 1r brn & red	1.00	1.00
309	A6	10,000r on 2r gray vio & yel	1.00	1.00
a.		Inverted surcharge	30.00	30.00
310	A6	10,000r on 3r dull rose & grn	3.50	3.50
311	A6	10,000r on 5r slate & vio	2.50	2.50
312	A6	10,000r on 7r gray grn & rose	100.00	100.00
313	A6	10,000r on 10r red & gray	2.00	2.00
314	A6	20,000r on 1r brn & red	1.00	1.00
315	A6	20,000r on 2r gray vio & yel (Bl)	35.00	35.00
a.		Inverted surcharge	30.00	30.00
315B	A6	20,000r on 2r gray vio & yel (Bk)	1.00	1.00
316	A6	20,000r on 3r dull rose & grn (Bl)	50.00	50.00
316A	A6	20,000r on 3r dull rose & grn (Bk)	30.00	30.00
317	A6	20,000r on 5r slate & vio	1.00	1.00

318	A6	20,000r on 7r gray grn & rose	60.00	60.00
319	A6	20,000r on 10r red & gray	1.00	1.00
	Nos. 303-319 (20)		344.00	344.00

Trident Stamps of Ukraine Surcharged in Blue, Red, Black or Brown

1921   *Perf. 14, 14½x15*

320	A14	10,000r on 1k org	.45	.45
321	A14	10,000r on 2k grn	5.00	5.00
322	A14	10,000r on 3k red	.45	.45
a.		Inverted surcharge	10.00	10.00
323	A15	10,000r on 4k car	.45	.45
324	A14	10,000r on 5k cl	.45	.45
325	A14	10,000r on 7k lt bl	.45	.45
a.		Inverted surcharge	10.00	10.00
326	A15	10,000r on 10k dk bl	.45	.45
327	A14	10,000r on 10k on 7k lt bl	.45	.45
a.		Inverted surcharge	10.00	10.00
328	A8	20,000r on 20k bl & car (Br)	.45	.45
a.		Inverted surcharge	10.00	10.00
329	A8	20,000r on 20k bl & car (Bk)	.45	.45
a.		Inverted surcharge	35.00	35.00
330	A11	20,000r on 20k on 14k bl & rose	.45	.45
331	A11	20,000r on 35k red brn & grn	75.00	75.00
332	A8	20,000r on 50k brn vio & grn	.45	.45
a.		Inverted surcharge	10.00	10.00
	Nos. 320-332 (13)		84.95	84.95

Imperf

333	A14	10,000r on 1k org	.75	.75
a.		Inverted surcharge	10.00	
334	A14	10,000r on 2k grn	2.00	2.00
335	A14	10,000r on 3k red	.75	.75
336	A8	20,000r on 20k bl & car	.75	.75
337	A11	20,000r on 35k red brn & grn	40.00	40.00
338	A8	20,000r on 50k brn vio & grn	2.00	2.00
	Nos. 333-338 (6)		46.25	46.25

There are several varieties of the trident surcharge on Nos. 320 to 338.

Same Surcharge on Russian Stamps
On Stamps of 1909-18
Perf. 14x14½

338A	A14	10,000r on 1k dl org yel	2.50	2.50
339	A14	10,000r on 2k dl grn	2.50	2.50
340	A14	10,000r on 3k car	.50	.50
341	A15	10,000r on 4k car	.50	.50
342	A14	10,000r on 5k dk cl	.50	.50
343	A14	10,000r on 7k blue	.50	.50
344	A15	10,000r on 10k dk bl	2.50	2.50
344A	A14	10,000r on 10k on 7k bl	3.75	3.75
344B	A11	20,000r on 14k dk bl & car	35.00	35.00
345	A11	20,000r on 15k red brn & dp bl	.50	.50
346	A8	20,000r on 20k dl bl & dk car	.50	.50
347	A11	20,000r on 20k on 14k dk bl & car	3.50	3.50
348	A11	20,000r on 35k red brn & grn	2.00	2.00
349	A8	20,000r on 50k brn vio & grn	.50	.50
349A	A11	20,000r on 70k brn & red org	2.50	2.50
	Nos. 338A-349A (15)		57.75	57.75

On Stamps of 1917-18
Imperf

350	A14	10,000r on 1k org	.75	.75
351	A14	10,000r on 2k gray grn	.75	.75
352	A14	10,000r on 3k red	.75	.75
353	A15	10,000r on 4k car	40.00	40.00
354	A14	10,000r on 5k claret	.75	.75
355	A11	20,000r on 15k red brn & dp bl	.75	.75
356	A8	20,000r on 50k brn vio & grn	2.00	2.00
357	A11	20,000r on 70k brn & org	.75	.75
	Nos. 350-357 (8)		46.50	46.50

Same Surcharge on Stamps of Russian Offices in Turkey
On Nos. 40-45
Perf. 14½x15

358	A12	10,000r on 5pa on 1k	5.00	5.00
359	A12	10,000r on 10pa on 2k	5.00	5.00
360	A12	10,000r on 20pa on 4k	5.00	5.00
361	A12	10,000r on 1pi on 10k	5.00	5.00
362	A12	20,000r on 5pi on 50k	5.00	5.00
363	A12	20,000r on 7pi on 70k	5.00	5.00
	Nos. 358-363 (6)		30.00	30.00

On Nos. 201-206

364	A16	10,000r on 5pa on 1k	6.00	6.00
365	A16	10,000r on 10pa on 2k	6.00	6.00
366	A17	10,000r on 20pa on 4k	6.00	6.00
367	A17	10,000r on 1pi on 10k	6.00	6.00
368	A8	20,000r on 5pi on 50k	6.00	6.00
369	A9	20,000r on 7pi on 70k	6.00	6.00
	Nos. 364-369 (6)		36.00	36.00

On Nos. 228, 208-212, Stamps of 1912-13

370	A14	10,000r on 15pa on 3k	5.00	5.00
371	A14	10,000r on 20pa on 5k	5.00	5.00
372	A11	20,000r on 1½pi on 15k	5.00	5.00
373	A8	20,000r on 2pi on 20k	5.00	
374	A11	20,000r on 2½pi on 25k	5.00	
375	A11	20,000r on 3½pi on 35k	5.00	

Same Surcharge on Stamp of South Russia, Crimea Issue

376	A8	20,000r on 5r on 20k bl & car	750.00	
	Nos. 370-376 (7)		780.00	15.00

RWANDA

ru-ˈän-də

(Rwandaise Republic)

LOCATION — Central Africa, adjoining the ex-Belgian Congo, Tanganyika, Uganda and Burundi
GOVT. — Republic
AREA — 10,169 sq. mi.
POP. — 8,154,933(?) (1999 est.)
CAPITAL — Kigali

Rwanda was established as an independent republic on July 1, 1962. With Burundi, it had been a UN trusteeship territory administered by Belgium. See Ruanda-Urundi.

100 Centimes = 1 Franc

Catalogue values for all unused stamps in this country are for Never Hinged items.

Watermark

Wmk. 368 — JEZ Multiple

Gregoire Kayibanda and Map of Africa — A1

Design: 40c, 1.50fr, 6.50fr, 20fr, Rwanda map spotlighted, "R" omitted.

Perf. 11½

			Photo.	
1962, July 1		Unwmk.		
1	A1	10c brown & gray grn	.25	.25
2	A1	40c brown & rose lil	.25	.25
3	A1	1fr brown & blue	.65	.40
4	A1	1.50fr brown & lt brn	.25	.25
5	A1	3.50fr brown & dp org	.25	.25
6	A1	6.50fr brown & lt vio bl	.25	.25
7	A1	10fr brown & citron	.30	.25
8	A1	20fr brown & rose	.40	.40
		Nos. 1-8 (8)	2.60	2.30

Map of Africa and Symbolic Honeycomb A2

Ruanda-Urundi Nos. 151-152 Overprinted with Metallic Frame Obliterating Previous Inscription and Denomination. Black Commemorative Inscription and "REPUBLIQUE RWANDAISE." Surcharged with New Value.

1963, Jan. 28		Unwmk.	Perf. 11½	
9	A2	3.50fr sil, blk, ultra & red	.25	.25
10	A2	6.50fr brnz, blk, ultra & red	1.25	1.10
11	A2	10fr stl bl, blk, ultra & red	.30	.25
12	A2	20fr sil, blk, ultra & red	.75	.50
		Nos. 9-12 (4)	2.55	2.10

Rwanda's admission to UN, Sept. 18, 1962.

Ruanda-Urundi Stamps of 1953 Overprinted in Metallic and Black

Designs as before.

1963, Mar. 21		Unwmk.	Perf. 11½	
Flowers in Natural Colors				
13	A27	25c dk grn & dl org	.40	.25
14	A27	40c green & salmon	.40	.25
15	A27	60c bl grn & pink	.40	.25
16	A27	1.25fr dk green & blue	1.60	1.25
17	A27	1.50fr vio & apple grn	1.40	1.00
18	A27	2fr on 1.50fr vio & ap grn	2.50	1.25
19	A27	4fr on 1.50fr vio & ap grn	3.00	1.25
20	A27	5fr dp plum & lt bl grn	3.00	1.50
21	A27	7fr dk green & fawn	3.00	1.50
22	A27	10fr dp plum & pale ol	4.50	2.00
		Nos. 13-22 (10)	20.20	10.50

The overprint consists of silver panels with black lettering. The panels on No. 19 are bluish gray.

Imperforates exist of practically every issue, starting with Nos. 1-8, except Nos. 9-12, 13-22, 36 and 55-69.

Wheat Emblem, Bow, Arrow, Hoe and Billhook — A4

1963, June 25		Photo.	Perf. 13½	
23	A4	2fr brown & green	.25	.25
24	A4	4fr magenta & ultra	.25	.25
25	A4	7fr red & gray	.25	.25
26	A4	10fr olive grn & yel	.50	.30
		Nos. 23-26 (4)	1.25	1.05

FAO "Freedom from Hunger" campaign.
The 20fr leopard and 50fr lion stamps of Ruanda-Urundi, Nos. 149-150, overprinted "Republique Rwandaise" at top and "Contre la Faim" at bottom, were intended to be issued Mar. 21, 1963, but were not placed in use. Value, set $200.

Coffee A5

Designs: 10c, 40c, 4fr, Coffee. 20c, 1fr, 7fr, Bananas. 30c, 2fr, 10fr, Tea.

1963, July 1			Perf. 11½	
27	A5	10c violet bl & brn	.25	.25
28	A5	20c slate & yellow	.25	.25
29	A5	30c vermilion & grn	.25	.25
30	A5	40c dp green & brown	.25	.25
31	A5	1fr maroon & yellow	.25	.25
32	A5	2fr dk blue & green	.75	.50
33	A5	4fr red & brown	.25	.25
34	A5	7fr yellow grn & yellow	.25	.25
35	A5	10fr violet & green	.25	.25
		Nos. 27-35 (9)	2.75	2.50

First anniversary of independence.

Common Design Types pictured following the introduction.

African Postal Union Issue
Common Design Type

1963, Sept. 8		Unwmk.	Perf. 12½	
36	CD114	14fr black, ocher & red	1.00	.75

Post Horn and Pigeon — A6

1963, Oct. 25		Photo.	Perf. 11½	
37	A6	50c ultra & rose	.25	.25
38	A6	1.50fr brown & blue	.65	.40
39	A6	3fr dp plum & gray	.45	.25
40	A6	20fr green & yellow	.45	.25
		Nos. 37-40 (4)	1.60	1.15

Rwanda's admission to the UPU, Apr. 6.

Scales, UN Emblem and Flame A7

1963, Dec. 10		Unwmk.	Perf. 11½	
41	A7	5fr crimson	.25	.25
42	A7	6fr brt purple	.70	.35
43	A7	10fr brt blue	.30	.25
		Nos. 41-43 (3)	1.25	.85

15th anniversary of the Universal Declaration of Human Rights.

Children's Clinic — A8

Designs: 20c, 7fr, Laboratory examination, horiz. 30c, 10fr, Physician examining infant. 40c, 20fr, Litter bearers, horiz.

1963, Dec. 30		Photo.		
44	A8	10c yel org, red & brn blk	.25	.25
45	A8	20c grn, red & brn blk	.25	.25
46	A8	30c bl, red & brn blk	.25	.25
47	A8	40c red lil, red & brn	.25	.25
48	A8	2fr bl grn, red brn & blk	.95	.65
49	A8	7fr ultra, red & blk	.25	.25
50	A8	10fr red brn, red & brn blk	.30	.25
51	A8	20fr dp org, red & brn	.65	.25
		Nos. 44-51 (8)	3.15	2.40

Centenary of the International Red Cross.

Map of Rwanda and Woman at Water Pump — A9

1964, May 4		Unwmk.	Perf. 11½	
52	A9	3fr lt grn, dk brn & ultra	.25	.25
53	A9	7fr pink, dk brn & ultra	.35	.25
54	A9	10fr yel, dk brn & ultra	.50	.30
		Nos. 52-54 (3)	1.10	.80

Souvenir Sheet
Imperf

54A	A9	25fr lilac, bl, brn & blk	8.50	8.50

UN 4th World Meteorological Day, Mar. 23.

Overprinted & Surcharged in Silver and Black

Ruanda-Urundi Nos. 138, 142

Ruanda-Urundi Nos. 139, 141, 143, 149-150

Ruanda-Urundi Nos. 140, 144-148

Ruanda-Urundi No. 153

Designs: 10c, 20c, 30c, Buffaloes. 40c, 2fr, Black-and-white colobus (monkey). 50c, 7.50fr, Impalas. 1fr, Mountain gorilla. 3fr, 4fr, 8fr, African elephants. 5fr, 10fr, Eland and zebras. 20fr, Leopard. 50fr, Lions. 40c, 1fr and 2fr are vertical.

1964, June 29		Photo.	Perf. 11½	
Size: 33x23mm, 23x33mm				
55	A30	10c on 20c gray, ap grn & blk	.25	.25
56	A30	20c blk, gray & ap grn	.25	.25
57	A30	30c on 1.50fr blk, gray & org	.25	.25
58	A29	40c mag, blk & gray grn	.25	.25
59	A30	50c grn, org yel & brn	.25	.25
60	A29	1fr ultra, blk & brn	.30	.25
61	A29	2fr grnsh bl, ind & brn	.30	.25
62	A30	3fr brn, dp car & blk	.40	.25
63	A30	4fr on 3.50fr on 3fr brn, dp car & blk	.50	.25
64	A30	5fr brn, dl yel, grn & blk	.50	.25
65	A30	7.50fr on 6.50fr red, org yel & brn	.90	.25
66	A30	8fr blue, mag & blk	8.00	3.75
67	A30	10fr brn, dl yel, brt pink & blk	1.75	.35
Size: 45x26½mm				
68	A30	20fr hn brn, ocher & blk	2.75	.65
69	A30	50fr dp blue & brown	4.25	2.00
		Nos. 55-69 (15)	20.90	9.50

Inverted overprints/surcharges exist. Value, each $10.

Boy with Crutch and Gatagara Home — A11

Designs: 40c, 8fr, Girls with sewing machines, horiz. 4fr, 10fr, Girl on crutches, map of Rwanda and Gatagara Home.

1964, Nov. 10		Photo.	Perf. 11½	
70	A11	10c lilac blk brn	.25	.25
71	A11	40c blue & blk brn	.25	.25
72	A11	4fr org red & blk brn	.35	.25
73	A11	7.50fr yel grn & blk brn	.55	.25
74	A11	8fr bister & blk brn	1.60	.90
75	A11	10fr magenta & blk brn	.85	.40
		Nos. 70-75 (6)	3.85	2.30

Gatagara Home for handicapped children.

Basketball — A12

Sport: 10c, 4fr, Runner, horiz. 30c, 20fr, High jump, horiz. 40c, 50fr, Soccer.

Size: 26x38mm

1964, Dec. 8		**Litho.**	*Perf.*	*13½*
76	A12	10c gray, sl & dk grn	.25	.25
77	A12	20c pink, sl & rose red	.25	.25
78	A12	30c lt grn, sl & grn	.25	.25
79	A12	40c buff, sl & brn	.25	.25
80	A12	4fr vio gray, sl & vio	.25	.25
81	A12	5fr pale grn, sl & yel grn	1.40	1.25
82	A12	20fr pale lil, sl & red lil	.45	.35
83	A12	50fr gray, sl & dk gray	.90	.75
a.		Souvenir sheet of 4	7.25	7.25
		Nos. 76-83 (8)	4.00	3.60

18th Olympic Games, Tokyo, Oct. 10-25. No. 83a contains 4 stamps (10fr, soccer; 20fr, basketball; 30fr, high jump; 40fr, runner). Size of stamps: 28x38mm.

Quill, Books, Radical and Retort — A13

Medical School and Student with Microscope — A14

30c, 10fr, Scales, hand, staff of Mercury and globe. 40c, 12fr, View of University.

1965, Feb. 22		**Engr.**	*Perf.*	*11½*
84	A13	10c multicolored	.25	.25
85	A13	20c multicolored	.25	.25
86	A13	30c multicolored	.25	.25
87	A14	40c multicolored	.25	.25
88	A13	5fr multicolored	.25	.25
89	A14	7fr multicolored	.25	.25
90	A13	10fr multicolored	.90	.90
91	A14	12fr multicolored	.35	.25
		Nos. 84-91 (8)	2.75	2.65

National University of Rwanda at Butare.

Abraham Lincoln, Death Cent. A15

1965, Apr. 15		**Photo.**	*Perf.*	*13½*
92	A15	10c emerald & dk red	.25	.25
93	A15	20c red brn & dk bl	.25	.25
94	A15	30c brt violet & red	.25	.25
95	A15	40c brt grnsh bl & red	.25	.25
96	A15	9fr orange brn & pur	.25	.25
97	A15	40fr black & brt grn	2.00	.80
		Nos. 92-97 (6)	3.25	2.05

Souvenir Sheet

98	A15	50fr red lilac & red	3.75	3.75

Nos. 92-96 exist without figure of value. Value, set $700.

Marabous — A16

Zebras A17

30c, Impalas. 40c, Crowned cranes, hippopotami & cattle egrets. 1fr, Cape buffalos. 3fr, Cape hunting dogs. 5fr, Yellow baboons. 10fr, Elephant & map of Rwanda with location of park. 40fr, Anhinga, great & reed cormorants. 100fr, Lions.

1965, Apr. 28		**Photo.**	*Perf.*	*11½*
		Size: 32x23mm		
99	A16	10c multicolored	.25	.25
100	A17	20c multicolored	.25	.25
101	A16	30c multicolored	.25	.25
102	A17	40c multicolored	.25	.25
103	A16	1fr multicolored	.60	.35
104	A17	3fr multicolored	.60	.35
105	A16	5fr multicolored	8.50	2.50
106	A17	10fr multicolored	.75	.35
		Size: 45x26mm		
107	A17	40fr multicolored	2.50	.50
108	A17	100fr multicolored	4.50	.50
		Nos. 99-108 (10)	18.45	5.55

Kagera National Park publicity.

Telstar and ITU Emblem A18

Designs: 40fr, 50fr, Syncom satellite. 60fr, old and new communications equipment.

1965		**Unwmk.**	*Perf.*	*13½*
109	A18	10c red brn, ultra & car	.25	.25
110	A18	40c violet, emer & yel	.25	.25
111	A18	4.50fr blk, car & dk bl	1.50	.55
112	A18	50fr dk brn, yel grn & brt grn	1.50	.40
		Nos. 109-112 (4)	3.50	1.45

Souvenir Sheet

113	A18	60fr blk brn, org brn & bl	4.00	4.00

ITU, cent. Issued: No. 113, 7/19; others, 5/17.

Papilio Bromius Chrapkowskii Suffert — A19

Various butterflies and moths in natural colors.

1965-66		**Photo.**	*Perf.*	*12½*
114	A19	10c black & yellow	.25	.25
115	A19	15c blk & dp org ('66)	.25	.25
116	A19	20c black & lilac	.25	.25
117	A19	30c black & red lil	.25	.25
118	A19	35c dk brn & dk bl ('66)	.25	.25
119	A19	40c black & Prus bl	.35	.25
120	A19	1.50fr black & grn ('66)	.50	.25
121	A19	3fr dk brn & ol grn ('66)	5.50	1.50
122	A19	4fr black & red brn	4.50	2.00
123	A19	10fr black & pur ('66)	1.00	.30
124	A19	50fr black & brown	4.00	1.75
125	A19	100fr dk brn & bl ('66)	5.75	1.50
		Nos. 114-125 (12)	22.85	8.80

The 15c, 20c, 40c, 1.50fr, 10fr and 50fr are horizontal.

Cattle, ICY Emblem and Map of Africa — A20

Map of Africa and: 40c, Tree & lake. 4.50fr, Gazelle under tree. 45fr, Mount Ruwenzori.

1965, Oct. 25		**Unwmk.**	*Perf.*	*12*
126	A20	10c olive bis & bl grn	.25	.25
127	A20	40c lt ultra, red brn & grn	.25	.25
128	A20	4.50fr brt grn, yel & brn	1.25	.50
129	A20	45fr rose claret	1.00	.30
		Nos. 126-129 (4)	2.75	1.30

John F. Kennedy (1917-1963) — A21

1965, Nov. 22		**Photo.**	*Perf.*	*11½*
130	A21	10c brt grn & dk brn	.25	.25
131	A21	40c brt pink & dk brn	.25	.25
132	A21	50c dk blue & dk brn	.25	.25
133	A21	1fr gray ol & dk brn	.25	.25
134	A21	8fr violet & dk brn	2.25	1.25
135	A21	50fr gray & dk brn	1.75	1.00
		Nos. 130-135 (6)	5.00	3.25

Souvenir Sheet

136		Sheet of 2	11.00	11.00
a.	A21	40fr org & dark brown	4.50	4.50
b.	A21	60fr ultra & dark brown	5.00	5.00

Madonna — A22

1965, Dec. 20				
137	A22	10c gold & dk green	.25	.25
138	A22	40c gold & dk brn red	.25	.25
139	A22	50c gold & dk blue	.25	.25
140	A22	4fr gold & slate	.80	.55
141	A22	6fr gold & violet	.30	.25
142	A22	30fr gold & dk brown	.65	.50
		Nos. 137-142 (6)	2.50	2.05

Christmas.

Father Joseph Damien and Lepers — A23

Designs: 40c, 45fr, Dr. Albert Schweitzer and Hospital, Lambarene.

1966, Jan. 31			*Perf.*	*11½*
143	A23	10c ultra & red brn	.25	.25
144	A23	40c dk red & vio bl	.25	.25
145	A23	4.50fr slate & brt grn	.25	.25
146	A23	45fr brn & hn brn	2.00	1.10
		Nos. 143-146 (4)	2.75	1.85

Issued for World Leprosy Day.

Pope Paul VI, St. Peter's, UN Headquarters and Statue of Liberty — A24

Design: 40c, 50fr, Pope Paul VI, Papal arms and UN emblem.

1966, Feb. 28		**Photo.**	*Perf.*	*12*
147	A24	10c henna brn & slate	.25	.25
148	A24	40c brt blue & slate	.25	.25
149	A24	4.50fr lilac & slate	1.75	1.00
150	A24	50fr brt green & slate	1.25	.45
		Nos. 147-150 (4)	3.50	1.95

Visit of Pope Paul VI to the UN, New York City, Oct. 4, 1965.

Globe Thistle — A25

Flowers: 20c, Blood lily. 30c, Everlasting. 40c, Natal plum. 1fr, Tulip tree. 3fr, Rendle orchid. 5fr, Aloe. 10fr, Ammocharis tinneana. 40fr, Coral tree. 100fr, Caper. (20c, 40c, 1fr, 3fr, 5fr, 10fr are vertical).

1966, Mar. 14			*Perf.*	*11½*
		Granite Paper		
151	A25	10c lt blue & multi	.25	.25
152	A25	20c orange & multi	.25	.25
153	A25	30c car rose & multi	.25	.25
154	A25	40c green & multi	.25	.25
155	A25	1fr multicolored	.25	.25
156	A25	3fr indigo & multi	.25	.25
157	A25	5fr multicolored	7.00	2.25
158	A25	10fr blue grn & multi	.35	.25
159	A25	40fr brown & multi	1.75	.50
160	A25	100fr dk bl grn & multi	3.50	1.50
a.		Miniature sheet	9.00	9.00
		Nos. 151-160 (10)	14.10	6.00

No. 160a contains one 100fr stamp in changed color, bright blue and multicolored.

Opening of WHO Headquarters, Geneva — A26

1966, May 1		**Litho.**	*Perf.*	*12½x12*
161	A26	2fr lt olive green	.25	.25
162	A26	3fr vermilion	.25	.25
163	A26	5fr violet blue	.25	.25
		Nos. 161-163 (3)	.75	.75

Soccer — A27

20c, 9fr, Basketball. 30c, 50fr, Volleyball.

1966, May 30		**Photo.**	*Perf.*	*15x14*
164	A27	10c dl grn, ultra & blk	.25	.25
165	A27	20c crimson, grn & blk	.25	.25
166	A27	30c bl, brt rose lil & blk	.25	.25
167	A27	40c yel bis, grn & blk	.25	.25
168	A27	9fr gray, red lil & blk	.25	.25

169 A27 50fr rose lil, Prus bl &
    blk   .90   .70
Nos. 164-169 (6)   2.15 1.95
National Youth Sports Program.

Mother and
Child, Planes
Dropping
Bombs — A28

1966, June 29   **Perf. 13½**
**Design and Inscription Black and
Red**
170 A28 20c rose lilac   .25   .25
171 A28 30c yellow green   .25   .25
172 A28 50c lt ultra   .25   .25
173 A28 6fr yellow   .25   .25
174 A28 15fr blue green   .80   .45
175 A28 18fr lilac   .80   .45
Nos. 170-175 (6)   2.60 1.90
Campaign against nuclear weapons.

A29

Global soccer ball.

1966, July   **Perf. 11½**
176 A29 20c org & indigo   .25   .25
177 A29 30c lilac & indigo   .25   .25
178 A29 50c brt grn & indigo .25   .25
179 A29 6fr brt rose & indigo .90   .25
180 A29 12fr lt vio brn & ind 2.00 .40
181 A29 25fr ultra & indigo 2.50 .65
Nos. 176-181 (6)   6.15 2.05
World Soccer Cup Championship, Wembley, England, July 11-30.

A30

Designs: 10c, Mikeno Volcano and crested shrike, horiz. 40c, Nyamilanga Falls. 50c, Gahinga and Muhabura volcanoes and lobelias, horiz. 55fr, Rusumu Falls.

1966, Oct. 24   **Engr.**   **Perf. 14**
182 A30 10c green   .25   .25
183 A30 40c brown carmine .30   .25
184 A30 4.50fr violet blue .50   .40
185 A30 55fr red lilac   .70   .55
Nos. 182-185 (4)   1.75 1.45

UNESCO Emblem, African Artifacts
and Musical Clef — A31

UNESCO 20th Anniv.: 30c, 10fr, Hands holding primer showing giraffe and zebra. 50c, 15fr, Atom symbol and power drill. 1fr, 50fr, Submerged sphinxes and sailboat.

1966, Nov. 4   **Photo.**   **Perf. 12**
186 A31 20c brt rose & dk bl .25   .25
187 A31 30c grnsh blue & blk .25   .25
188 A31 50c ocher & blk   .25   .25
189 A31 1fr violet & blk   .25   .25

190 A31 5fr yellow grn & blk .25   .25
191 A31 10fr brown & blk   .25   .25
192 A31 15fr red lilac & dk bl .30   .30
193 A31 50fr dull bl & blk   .40   .40
Nos. 186-193 (8)   2.20 2.20

Rock
Python — A32

Snakes: 20c, 20fr, Jameson's mamba. 30c, 3fr, Rock python. 50c, Gaboon viper. 1fr, Black-lipped spitting cobra. 5fr, African sand snake. 70fr, Egg-eating snake. (20c, 50c, 3fr and 20fr are horizontal.)

1967, Jan. 30   **Photo.**   **Perf. 11½**
194 A32 20c red & black   .25   .25
195 A32 30c bl, dk brn & yel .25   .25
196 A32 50c yel grn & multi .25   .25
197 A32 1fr lt lil, blk & bis .25   .25
198 A32 3fr lt vio, dk brn & yel .40   .25
199 A32 5fr yellow & multi   .60   .25
200 A32 20fr pale pink & multi 2.25 1.00
201 A32 70fr pale vio, brn & blk 3.00 1.25
Nos. 194-201 (8)   7.25 3.75

Ntaruka Hydroelectric Station and Tea
Flowers — A33

Designs: 30c, 25fr, Transformer and chrysanthemums (pyrethrum). 50c, 50fr, Sluice and coffee.

1967, Mar. 6   **Photo.**   **Perf. 13½**
202 A33 20c maroon & dp bl .25   .25
203 A33 30c black & red brn .25   .25
204 A33 50c brown & violet   .25   .25
205 A33 4fr dk grn & dp plum .25   .25
206 A33 25fr violet & sl grn .50   .30
207 A33 50fr dk blue & brn 1.10   .65
Nos. 202-207 (6)   2.60 1.95
Ntaruka Hydroelectric Station.

Souvenir Sheets

Cogwheels — A34

1967, Apr. 15   **Engr.**   **Perf. 11½**
208 A34 100fr dk red brown 4.50 4.50
209 A34 100fr brt rose lilac 4.50 4.50
7th "Europa" Phil. Exhib. and the Philatelic Salon of African States, Naples, Apr. 8-16.

Souvenir Sheet

African Dancers and EXPO '67
Emblem — A35

1967, Apr. 28   **Perf. 11½**
210 A35 180fr dark purple 4.75 4.75
EXPO '67, Intl. Exhib., Montreal, Apr. 28-Oct. 27.
A similar imperf. sheet has the stamp in violet brown.

St. Martin, by
Van Dyck and
Caritas
Emblem
A36

Paintings: 40c, 15fr, Rebecca at the Well, by Murillo, horiz. 60c, 18fr, St. Christopher, by Dierick Bouts. 80c, 26fr, Job and his Friends, by Il Calabrese (Mattia Preti), horiz.

Perf. 13x11, 11x13
1967, May 8   **Photo.**
Black Inscription on Gold Panel
211 A36 20c dark purple   .25   .25
212 A36 40c blue green   .25   .25
213 A36 60c rose carmine   .25   .25
214 A36 80c deep blue   .25   .25
215 A36 9fr redsh brown   .85   .45
216 A36 15fr orange ver   .30   .25
217 A36 18fr dk olive grn   .35   .25
218 A36 26fr dk carmine rose .40   .35
Nos. 211-218 (8)   2.90 2.30
Issued to publicize the work of Caritas-Rwanda, Catholic welfare organization.

Round Table Emblem and
Zebra — A37

Round Table Emblem and: 40c, Elephant. 60c, Cape buffalo. 80c, Antelope. 18fr, Wheat. 100fr, Palm tree.

1967, July 31   **Photo.**   **Perf. 14**
219 A37 20c gold & multi   .25   .25
220 A37 40c gold & multi   .25   .25
221 A37 60c gold & multi   .25   .25
222 A37 80c gold & multi   .25   .25
223 A37 18fr gold & multi   .40   .25
224 A37 100fr gold & multi 2.00 1.00
Nos. 219-224 (6)   3.40 2.25
Rwanda Table No. 9 of Kigali, a member of the Intl. Round Tables Assoc.

EXPO '67 Emblem, Africa Place and
Dancers and Drummers — A38

EXPO '67 Emblem, Africa Place and: 30c, 3fr, Drum and vessels. 50c, 40fr, Two dancers. 1fr, 34fr, Spears, shields and bow.

1967, Aug. 10   **Photo.**   **Perf. 12**
225 A38 20c brt blue & sepia .25   .25
226 A38 30c brt rose lil & sepia .25   .25
227 A38 50c orange & sepia .25   .25
228 A38 1fr green & sepia   .25   .25
229 A38 3fr violet & sepia   .25   .25
230 A38 15fr emerald & sepia .25   .25
231 A38 34fr rose red & sepia .40   .35
232 A38 40fr grnsh bl & sepia .60   .45
Nos. 225-232 (8)   2.50 2.30

Lions Emblem,
Globe and
Zebra — A39

1967, Oct. 16   **Photo.**   **Perf. 13½**
233 A39 20c lilac, bl & blk   .25   .25
234 A39 80c lt grn, bl & blk   .25   .25
235 A39 1fr rose car, bl & blk .25   .25
236 A39 8fr bister, bl & blk   .30   .25
237 A39 10fr ultra, bl & blk   .40   .25
238 A39 50fr yel grn, bl & blk 1.75 1.00
Nos. 233-238 (6)   3.20 2.25
50th anniversary of Lions International.

Woodland Kingfisher — A40

Birds: 20c, Red bishop, vert. 60c, Red-billed quelea, vert. 80c, Double-toothed barbet. 2fr, Pin-tailed whydah, vert. 3fr, Solitary cuckoo. 18fr, Green wood hoopoe, vert. 25fr, Blue-collared bee-eater. 80fr, Regal sunbird, vert. 100fr, Red-shouldered widowbird.

1967, Dec. 18   **Perf. 11½**
239 A40 20c multicolored   .25   .25
240 A40 40c multicolored   .25   .25
241 A40 60c multicolored   .25   .25
242 A40 80c multicolored   .25   .25
243 A40 2fr multicolored   .35   .30
244 A40 3fr multicolored   .40   .30
245 A40 18fr multicolored   1.50   .75
246 A40 25fr multicolored   2.00 1.00
247 A40 80fr multicolored   4.50 3.25
248 A40 100fr multicolored 6.25 4.75
Nos. 239-248 (10)   16.00 11.35

Souvenir Sheet

Ski Jump, Speed Skating — A41

1968, Feb. 12   **Photo.**   **Perf. 11½**
249 A41   Sheet of 2   11.00 11.00
  a. 50fr bl, blk & grn (skier) 3.50 3.50
  b. 50fr grn, blk & bl (skater) 3.50 3.50
  c. Souv. sheet of 2, #249a at
     right   12.00 12.00
10th Winter Olympic Games, Grenoble, France, Feb. 6-18.

Runner, Mexican Sculpture and
Architecture — A42

Sport and Mexican Art: 40c, Hammer throw,
pyramid and animal head. 60c, Hurdler and
sculptures. 80c, Javelin and sculptures.

1968, May 27	**Photo.**		**Perf. 11½**	
250 A42	20c ultra & multi		.35	.25
251 A42	40c multicolored		.35	.25
252 A42	60c lilac & multi		.35	.25
253 A42	80c orange & multi		.35	.25
	Nos. 250-253 (4)		1.40	1.00

19th Olympic Games, Mexico City, 10/12-27.

Souvenir Sheet

19th Olympic Games, Mexico
City — A43

a, 8fr, Soccer. b, 10fr, Mexican horseman,
cactus. c, 12fr, Field hockey. d, 18fr, Cathedral, Mexico City. e, 20fr, Boxing. f, 30fr, Modern buildings, musical instruments, vase.

1968, May 27		**Perf. 11½**	
	Granite Paper		
254 A43	Sheet of 6, #a.-f.	11.00	11.00

Three sets of circular gold "medal" overprints with black inscriptions were applied to
the six stamps of No. 254 to honor 18 Olympic
winners. Issued Dec. 12, 1968. Value $70.

Souvenir Sheet

Martin Luther King, Jr. — A44

1968, July 29	**Engr.**	**Perf. 13½**	
255 A44	100fr sepia	3.00	1.75

Rev. Dr. Martin Luther King, Jr. (1929-68),
American civil rights leader. See No. 406.

Diaphant
Orchid — A45

Flowers: 40c, Pharaoh's scepter. 60c,
Flower of traveler's-tree. 80c, Costus afer. 2fr,
Banana tree flower. 3fr, Flower and fruit of
papaw tree. 18fr, Clerodendron. 25fr, Sweet

---

potato flowers. 80fr, Baobab tree flower. 100fr,
Passion flower.

1968, Sept. 9	**Litho.**		**Perf. 13**	
256 A45	20c lilac & multi		.25	.25
257 A45	40c multicolored		.25	.25
258 A45	60c bl grn & multi		.25	.25
259 A45	80c multicolored		.25	.25
260 A45	2fr brt yellow & multi		.25	.25
261 A45	3fr multicolored		.25	.25
262 A45	18fr multicolored		.40	.25
263 A45	25fr gray & multi		.70	.30
264 A45	80fr multicolored		2.50	.75
265 A45	100fr multicolored		2.75	1.25
	Nos. 256-265 (10)		7.85	4.05

Equestrian
and
"Mexico
1968"
A46

Designs: 40c, Judo and "Tokyo 1964." 60c,
Fencing and "Rome 1960." 80c, High jump
and "Berlin 1936." 38fr, Women's diving and
"London 1908 and 1948." 60fr, Weight lifting
and "Paris 1900 and 1924."

1968, Oct. 24	**Litho.**		**Perf. 14x13**	
266 A46	20c orange & sepia		.25	.25
267 A46	40c grnsh bl & sepia		.25	.25
268 A46	60c car rose & sepia		.25	.25
269 A46	80c ultra & sepia		.25	.25
270 A46	38fr red & sepia		.55	.25
271 A46	60fr emerald & sepia		1.30	.55
	Nos. 266-271 (6)		2.85	1.80

19th Olympic Games, Mexico City, 10/12-27.

Tuareg,
Algeria — A47

African National Costumes: 40c, Musicians,
Upper Volta. 60c, Senegalese women. 70c,
Girls of Rwanda going to market. 8fr, Women
married couple from Morocco. 20fr, Nigerian
officials in state dress. 40fr, Man and women
from Zambia. 50fr, Man and woman from
Kenya.

1968, Nov. 4	**Litho.**		**Perf. 13**	
272 A47	30c multicolored		.25	.25
273 A47	40c multicolored		.25	.25
274 A47	60c multicolored		.25	.25
275 A47	70c multicolored		.25	.25
276 A47	8fr multicolored		.25	.25
277 A47	20fr multicolored		.75	.25
278 A47	40fr multicolored		1.40	.45
279 A47	50fr multicolored		1.60	.85
	Nos. 272-279 (8)		5.00	2.80

Souvenir Sheet

Nativity, by Giorgione — A48

1968, Dec. 16	**Engr.**	**Perf. 11½**	
280 A48	100fr green	7.00	7.00

Christmas.
See Nos. 309, 389, 422, 494, 564, 611, 713,
787, 848, 894.

Singing Boy,
by Frans
Hals — A49

Paintings and Music: 20c, Angels' Concert,
by van Eyck. 40c, Angels' Concert, by Matthias Grunewald. 60c, No. 283a, Singing Boy,
by Frans Hals. 80c, Lute Player, by Gerard
Terborch. 2fr, The Fifer, by Manet. 6fr, No.
286a, Young Girls at the Piano, by Renoir.

1969, Mar. 31	**Photo.**		**Perf. 13**	
281 A49	20c gold & multi		.25	.25
282 A49	40c gold & multi		.25	.25
283 A49	60c gold & multi		.25	.25
a.	Souvenir sheet, 75fr		3.50	3.50
284 A49	80c gold & multi		.25	.25
285 A49	2fr gold & multi		.25	.25
286 A49	6fr gold & multi		.25	.25
a.	Souvenir sheet, 75fr		3.50	3.50
	Nos. 281-286,C6-C7 (8)		6.50	5.25

Tuareg
Men — A50

African Headdresses: 40c, Ovambo woman,
South West Africa. 60c, Guinean man and
Congolese woman. 80c, Dagger dancer,
Guinean forest area. 8fr, Mohammedan Niger-
ians. 20fr, Luba dancer, Kabondo, Congo.
40fr, Senegalese and Gambian women. 80fr,
Rwanda dancer.

1969, May 29	**Litho.**		**Perf. 13**	
287 A50	20c multicolored		.25	.25
288 A50	40c multicolored		.25	.25
289 A50	60c multicolored		.25	.25
290 A50	80c multicolored		.25	.25
291 A50	8fr multicolored		.40	.25
292 A50	20fr multicolored		.75	.25
293 A50	40fr multicolored		1.75	.45
294 A50	80fr multicolored		4.00	.85
	Nos. 287-294 (8)		7.90	2.80

See #398-405. For overprints see #550-557.

The Moneylender and his Wife, by
Quentin Massys — A51

Design: 70fr, The Moneylender and his
Wife, by Marinus van Reymerswaele.

1969, Sept. 10	**Photo.**		**Perf. 13**	
295 A51	30fr silver & multi		1.00	.75
296 A51	70fr gold & multi		2.50	1.50

5th anniv. of the African Development Bank.
Printed in sheets of 20 stamps and 20 labels
with commemorative inscription.
For overprints see Nos. 612-613.

Souvenir Sheet

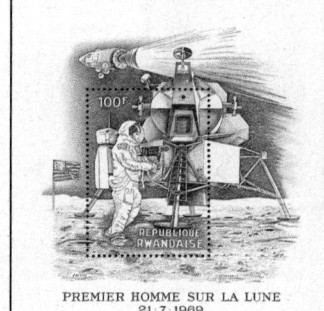

First Man on the Moon — A52

1969, Oct. 9	**Engr.**	**Perf. 11½**	
297 A52	100fr blue gray	4.25	4.25

See note after Mali No. C80. See No. 407.

Camomile and
Health
Emblem — A53

Medicinal Plants and Health Emblem: 40c,
Aloe. 60c, Cola. 80c, Coca. 3fr, Hagenia abis-
sinica. 75fr, Cassia. 80fr, Cinchona. 100fr,
Tephrosia.

1969, Nov. 24	**Photo.**		**Perf. 13**	
	Flowers in Natural Colors			
298 A53	20c gold, blue & blk		.25	.25
299 A53	40c gold, yel grn &			
	blk		.25	.25
300 A53	60c gold, pink & blk		.25	.25
301 A53	80c gold, green & blk		.25	.25
302 A53	3fr gold, org & blk		.25	.25
303 A53	75fr gold, yel & blk		2.75	1.25
304 A53	80fr gold, lilac & blk		3.25	1.40
305 A53	100fr gold, dl yel & blk		3.75	1.75
	Nos. 298-305 (8)		11.00	5.65

For overprints and surcharge, see Nos. 534-
539, B1.

Worker with Pickaxe
and Flag — A54

1969, Nov.	**Photo.**		**Perf. 11½**	
306 A54	6fr brt pink & multi		.45	.25
307 A54	18fr ultra & multi		.95	.45
308 A54	40fr brown & multi		1.60	.95
	Nos. 306-308 (3)		3.00	1.65

10th anniversary of independence.
For overprints see Nos. 608-610.

Christmas Type of 1968
Souvenir Sheet

Design: "Holy Night" (detail), by Correggio.

1969, Dec. 15	**Engr.**	**Perf. 11½**	
309 A48	100fr ultra	4.50	4.50

The Cook, by Pierre Aertsen — A55

Paintings: 20c, Quarry Worker, by Oscar Bonnevalle, horiz. 40c, The Plower, by Peter Brueghel, horiz 60c, Fisherman, by Constantin Meunier. 80c, Slipway, Ostende, by Jean van Noten, horiz. 10fr, The Forge of Vulcan, by Velasquez, horiz. 50fr, "Hiercheuse" (woman shoveling coal), by Meunier. 70fr, Miner, by Pierre Paulus.

1969, Dec. 22		Photo.	Perf. 13½	
310	A55	20c gold & multi	.25	.25
311	A55	40c gold & multi	.25	.25
312	A55	60c gold & multi	.25	.25
313	A55	80c gold & multi	.25	.25
314	A55	8fr gold & multi	.25	.25
315	A55	10fr gold & multi	.25	.25
316	A55	50fr gold & multi	1.40	.45
317	A55	70fr gold & multi	1.90	.80
		Nos. 310-317 (8)	4.80	2.75

ILO, 50th anniversary.

Napoleon Crossing St. Bernard, by Jacques L. David — A56

Paintings of Napoleon Bonaparte (1769-1821): 40c, Decorating Soldier before Tilsit, by Jean Baptiste Debret. 60c, Addressing Troops at Augsburg, by Claude Gautherot. 80c, First Consul, by Jean Auguste Ingres. 8fr, Battle of Marengo, by Jacques Auguste Pajou. 20fr, Napoleon Meeting Emperor Francis II, by Antoine Jean Gros. 40fr, Gen. Bonaparte at Arcole, by Gros. 80fr Coronation, by David.

1969, Dec. 29				
318	A56	20c gold & multi	.25	.25
319	A56	40c gold & multi	.25	.25
320	A56	60c gold & multi	.25	.25
321	A56	80c gold & multi	.25	.25
322	A56	8fr gold & multi	.30	.25
323	A56	20fr gold & multi	.85	.40
324	A56	40fr gold & multi	1.75	.85
325	A56	80fr gold & multi	3.25	1.40
		Nos. 318-325 (8)	7.15	3.90

Epsom Derby, by Gericault — A57

Paintings of Horses: 40c, Horses Emerging from the Sea, by Delacroix. 60c, Charles V at Muhlberg, by Titian, vert. 80c, Amateur Jockeys, by Edgar Degas, 8fr, Horsemen at Rest, by Philips Wouwerman. 20fr, Imperial Guards Officer, by Géricault, vert. 40fr, Friends of the Desert, by Oscar Bonnevalle. 80fr, Two Horses (detail from the Prodigal Son), by Rubens.

1970, Mar. 31		Photo.	Perf. 13½	
326	A57	20c gold & multi	.25	.25
327	A57	40c gold & multi	.25	.25
328	A57	60c gold & multi	.25	.25
329	A57	80c gold & multi	.25	.25
330	A57	8fr gold & multi	.25	.25
331	A57	20fr gold & multi	1.25	.25
332	A57	40fr gold & multi	2.00	.45
333	A57	80fr gold & multi	3.25	.80
		Nos. 326-333 (8)	7.75	2.75

Souvenir Sheet

Fleet in Bay of Naples, by Peter Brueghel, the Elder — A58

1970, May 2		Engr.	Perf. 11½	
334	A58	100fr brt rose lilac	15.00	15.00

10th Europa Phil. Exhib., Naples, Italy, May 2-10.

Examples of No. 334 were trimmed to 68x58mm and overprinted in silver or gold "NAPLES 1973" on the stamp, and "Salon Philatelique des Etats Africains / Exposition du Timbre-Poste Europa" in October, 1973.

Soccer and Mexican Decorations A59

Designs: Various scenes from soccer game and pre-Columbian decorations.

1970, June 15		Photo.	Perf. 13	
335	A59	20c gold & multi	.25	.25
336	A59	30c gold & multi	.25	.25
337	A59	50c gold & multi	.25	.25
338	A59	1fr gold & multi	.25	.25
339	A59	6fr gold & multi	.25	.25
340	A59	18fr gold & multi	.85	.25
341	A59	30fr gold & multi	1.10	.45
342	A59	90fr gold & multi	2.25	.90
		Nos. 335-342 (8)	5.45	2.85

9th World Soccer Championships for the Jules Rimet Cup, Mexico City, 5/30-6/21.

Tharaka Meru Woman, East Africa — A60

African National Costumes: 30c, Musician with wooden flute, Niger. 50c, Woman water carrier, Tunisia. 1fr, Ceremonial costumes, North Nigeria. 3fr, Strolling troubadour "Griot," Mali. 5fr, Quipongos women, Angola. 50fr, Man at prayer, Mauritania. 90fr, Sinehatiali dance costumes, Ivory Coast.

1970, June 1		Litho.		
343	A60	20c multi	.25	.25
344	A60	30c multi	.25	.25
345	A60	50c multi	.25	.25
346	A60	1fr multi	.25	.25
347	A60	3fr multi	.25	.25
348	A60	5fr multi	.30	.25
349	A60	50fr multi	2.00	.45
350	A60	90fr multi	3.00	.90
		Nos. 343-350 (8)	6.55	2.85

For overprints and surcharges see Nos. 693-698, B2-B3.

Flower Arrangement, Peacock, EXPO '70 Emblem — A61

EXPO Emblem and: 30c, Torii and Camellias, by Yukihiko Yasuda. 50c, Kabuki character and Woman Playing Samisen, by Nampu Katayama. 1fr, Tower of the Sun, and Warrior Riding into Water. 3fr, Pavilion and Buddhist deity. 5fr, Pagoda and modern painting by Shuho Yamakawa. 20fr, Japanese inscription "Omatsuri" and Osaka Castle. 70fr, EXPO '70 emblem and Warrior on Horseback.

1970, Aug. 24		Photo.	Perf. 13	
351	A61	20c gold & multi	.25	.25
352	A61	30c gold & multi	.25	.25
353	A61	50c gold & multi	.25	.25
354	A61	1fr gold & multi	.25	.25
355	A61	3fr gold & multi	.25	.25
356	A61	5fr gold & multi	.30	.25
357	A61	20fr gold & multi	.70	.35
358	A61	70fr gold & multi	2.00	.90
		Nos. 351-358 (8)	4.25	2.75

EXPO '70 International Exhibition, Osaka, Japan, Mar. 15-Sept. 13.

Young Mountain Gorillas — A62

Various Gorillas. 40c, 80c, 2fr, 100fr are vert.

1970, Sept. 7				
359	A62	20c olive & blk	.25	.25
360	A62	40c brt rose lil & blk	.25	.25
361	A62	60c blue, brn & blk	.25	.25
362	A62	80c org brn & blk	.30	.25
363	A62	1fr dp car & blk	.85	.25
364	A62	2fr black & multi	1.25	.45
365	A62	15fr sepia & blk	2.75	1.25
366	A62	100fr brt bl & blk	16.00	3.50
		Nos. 359-366 (8)	21.90	6.45

Pierre J. Pelletier and Joseph B. Caventou A63

Designs: 20c, Cinchona flower and bark. 80c, Quinine powder and pharmacological vessels. 1fr, Anopheles mosquito. 3fr, Malaria patient and nurse. 25fr, "Malaria" (mosquito).

1970, Oct. 27		Photo.	Perf. 13	
367	A63	20c silver & multi	.25	.25
368	A63	80c silver & multi	.25	.25
369	A63	1fr silver & multi	.25	.25
370	A63	3fr silver & multi	.25	.25
371	A63	25fr silver & multi	.75	.25
372	A63	70fr silver & multi	1.75	.60
		Nos. 367-372 (6)	3.50	1.85

150th anniv. of the discovery of quinine by Pierre Joseph Pelletier (1788-1842) and Joseph Bienaimé Caventou (1795-1877), French pharmacologists.

Apollo Spaceship A64

Apollo Spaceship: 30c, Second stage separation. 50c, Spaceship over moon surface. 1fr, Landing module and astronauts on moon. 3fr, Take-off from moon. 5fr, Return to earth. 10fr, Final separation of nose cone. 80fr, Splashdown.

1970, Nov. 23		Photo.	Perf. 13	
373	A64	20c silver & multi	.25	.25
374	A64	30c silver & multi	.25	.25
375	A64	50c silver & multi	.25	.25
376	A64	1fr silver & multi	.25	.25
377	A64	3fr silver & multi	.25	.25
378	A64	5fr silver & multi	.25	.25
379	A64	10fr silver & multi	.75	.30
380	A64	80fr silver & multi	3.00	1.25
		Nos. 373-380 (8)	5.25	3.05

Conquest of space.

Franklin D. Roosevelt and Brassocattleya Olympia Alba — A65

Portraits of Roosevelt and various orchids.

1970, Dec. 21		Photo.	Perf. 13	
381	A65	20c blue, blk & brn	.25	.25
382	A65	30c car rose, blk & brn	.25	.25
383	A65	50c dp org, blk & brn	.25	.25
384	A65	1fr green, blk & brn	.30	.25
385	A65	2fr maroon, blk & grn	.35	.25
386	A65	6fr lilac & multi	.40	.25
387	A65	30fr bl, blk & sl grn	1.25	.60
388	A65	60fr lil rose, blk & sl grn	2.50	.80
		Nos. 381-388 (8)	5.55	2.90

Pres. Roosevelt, 25th death anniv.

Christmas Type of 1968
Souvenir Sheet

Design: 100fr, Adoration of the Shepherds, by José de Ribera, vert.

1970, Dec. 24		Engr.	Perf. 11½	
389	A48	100fr Prus blue	4.50	4.50

Pope Paul VI — A66

Popes: 20c, John XXIII, 1958-1963. 30c, Pius XII, 1939-1958. 40c, Pius XI, 1922-39. 1fr, Benedict XV, 1914-22. 18fr, St. Pius X, 1903-14. 20fr, Leo XIII, 1878-1903. 60fr, Pius IX, 1846-78.

1970, Dec. 31		Photo.	Perf. 13	
390	A66	10c gold & dk brn	.25	.25
391	A66	20c gold & dk grn	.25	.25
392	A66	30c gold & dp claret	.25	.25
393	A66	40c gold & indigo	.30	.25
394	A66	1fr gold & dk pur	.35	.25
395	A66	18fr gold & purple	.80	.25
396	A66	20fr gold & org brn	1.10	.40
397	A66	60fr gold & blk brn	2.50	.80
		Nos. 390-397 (8)	5.80	2.70

Centenary of Vatican I, Ecumenical Council of the Roman Catholic Church, 1869-70. For overprints see Nos. 644-651.

Headdress Type of 1969

African Headdresses: 20c, Rendille woman. 30c, Young Toubou woman, Chad. 50c, Peul man, Niger. 1fr, Young Masai man, Kenya. 5fr, Young Peul girl, Niger. 18fr, Rwanda woman. 25fr, Man, Mauritania. 50fr, Rwanda women with pearl necklaces.

1971, Feb. 15		Litho.	Perf. 13	
398	A50	20c multi	.25	.25
399	A50	30c multi	.25	.25
400	A50	50c multi	.25	.25
401	A50	1fr multi	.25	.25
402	A50	5fr multi	.30	.25
403	A50	18fr multi	.75	.25
404	A50	25fr multi	1.75	.30
405	A50	50fr multi	3.25	.60
		Nos. 398-405 (8)	7.05	2.40

For overprints see Nos. 550-557.

M. L. King Type of 1968
Souvenir Sheet

Design: 100fr, Charles de Gaulle (1890-1970), President of France.

1971, Mar. 15   Engr.   Perf. 13½
406 A44 100fr ultra   4.25 4.25

Astronaut Type of 1969 Inscribed in Dark Violet with Emblem and: "APOLLO / 14 / SHEPARD / ROOSA / MITCHELL"

1971, Apr. 15   Engr.   Perf. 11½
Souvenir Sheet
407 A52 100fr brown orange   12.00 12.00

Apollo 14 US moon landing, Jan. 31-Feb. 9.

Beethoven, by Christian Horneman A67

Beethoven Portraits: 30c, Joseph Stieler. 50c, by Ferdinand Schimon. 3fr, by H. Best. 6fr, by W. Fassbender. 90fr, Beethoven's Funeral Procession, by Leopold Stöber.

1971, July 5   Photo.   Perf. 13
408 A67 20c gold & multi   .25 .25
409 A67 30c gold & multi   .25 .25
410 A67 50c gold & multi   .25 .25
411 A67 3fr gold & multi   .25 .25
412 A67 6fr gold & multi   .50 .25
413 A67 90fr gold & multi   2.50 1.75
    Nos. 408-413 (6)   4.00 3.00

Ludwig van Beethoven (1770-1827), composer.

Equestrian — A68

Olympic Sports: 30c, Runner at start. 50c, Basketball. 1fr, High jump. 8fr, Boxing. 10fr, Pole vault. 20fr, Wrestling. 60fr, Gymnastics (rings).

1971, Oct. 25   Photo.   Perf. 13
414 A68 20c gold & black   .25 .25
415 A68 30c gold & dp rose lil   .25 .25
416 A68 50c gold & vio bl   .25 .25
417 A68 1fr gold & dp grn   .25 .25
418 A68 8fr gold & henna brn   .25 .25
419 A68 10fr gold & purple   .30 .25
420 A68 20fr gold & dp brn   .50 .25
421 A68 60fr gold & Prus bl   1.50 .60
    Nos. 414-421 (8)   3.55 2.35

20th Summer Olympic Games, Munich, Aug. 26-Sept. 10, 1972.

Christmas Type of 1968
Souvenir Sheet

100fr, Nativity, by Anthony van Dyck, vert.

1971, Dec. 20   Engr.   Perf. 11½
422 A48 100fr indigo   5.75 5.75

Adam by Dürer — A69

Paintings by Albrecht Dürer (1471-1528), German painter and engraver: 30c, Eve. 50c, Hieronymus Holzschuher, Portrait. 1fr, Lamentation of Christ. 3fr, Madonna with the Pear. 5fr, St. Eustace. 20fr, Sts. Paul and Mark. 70fr, Self-portrait, 1500.

1971, Dec. 31   Photo.   Perf. 13
423 A69 20c gold & multi   .25 .25
424 A69 30c gold & multi   .25 .25
425 A69 50c gold & multi   .25 .25
426 A69 1fr gold & multi   .25 .25
427 A69 3fr gold & multi   .25 .25
428 A69 5fr gold & multi   .35 .25
429 A69 20fr gold & multi   .70 .25
430 A69 70fr gold & multi   1.50 1.35
    Nos. 423-430 (8)   3.80 3.10

A 600fr stamp on gold foil honoring Apollo 15 was issued Jan. 15, 1972. Value $160.

Guardsmen Exercising — A70

National Guard Emblem and: 6fr, Loading supplies. 15fr, Helicopter ambulance. 25fr, Health Service for civilians. 50fr, Guardsman and map of Rwanda, vert.

1972, Feb. 7   Perf. 13½x14, 14x13½
431 A70 4fr dp org & multi   .25 .25
432 A70 6fr yellow & multi   .25 .25
433 A70 15fr lt blue & multi   .35 .25
434 A70 25fr red & multi   .90 .45
435 A70 50fr multicolored   2.00 1.20
    Nos. 431-435 (5)   3.75 2.40

"The National Guard serving the nation."
For overprints see Nos. 559-563.

Ice Hockey, Sapporo Olympics Emblem A71

1972, Feb. 12   Perf. 13x13½
436 A71 20c shown   .25 .25
437 A71 30c Speed skating   .25 .25
438 A71 50c Ski jump   .25 .25
439 A71 1fr Men's figure skating   .25 .25
440 A71 6fr Cross-country ski-
          ing   .25 .25
441 A71 12fr Slalom   .25 .25
442 A71 20fr Bobsledding   .40 .25
443 A71 60fr Downhill skiing   1.30 1.25
    Nos. 436-443 (8)   3.20 3.00

11th Winter Olympic Games, Sapporo, Japan, Feb. 3-13.

Antelopes and Cercopithecus — A72

1972, Mar. 20   Photo.   Perf. 13
444 A72 20c shown   .25 .25
445 A72 30c Buffaloes   .25 .25
446 A72 50c Zebras   .30 .25
447 A72 1fr Rhinoceroses   .35 .30
448 A72 2fr Wart hogs   .45 .35

449 A72 6fr Hippopotami   .60 .45
450 A72 18fr Hyenas   1.10 .60
451 A72 32fr Guinea fowl   2.00 .85
452 A72 60fr Antelopes   2.75 1.40
453 A72 80fr Lions   4.00 2.25
    Nos. 444-453 (10)   12.05 6.95

Akagera National Park.

A73

Family raising flag of Rwanda.

1972, Apr. 4   Perf. 13x12½
454 A73 6fr dk red & multi   .25 .25
455 A73 18fr green & multi   .45 .25
456 A73 60fr brown & multi   1.40 1.10
    Nos. 454-456 (3)   2.10 1.60

10th anniversary of the Referendum establishing Republic of Rwanda.

A74

Birds: 20c, Common Waxbills and Hibiscus. 30c, Collared sunbird. 50c, Variable sunbird. 1fr, Greater double-collared sunbird. 4fr, Ruwenzori puff-back flycatcher. 6fr, Red-billed fire finch. 10fr, Scarlet-chested sunbird. 18fr, Red-headed quelea. 60fr, Black-headed gonolek. 100fr, African golden oriole.

1972, May 17   Photo.   Perf. 13
457 A74 20c dl grn & multi   .25 .25
458 A74 30c buff & multi   .25 .25
459 A74 50c yellow & multi   .25 .25
460 A74 1fr lt blue & multi   .25 .25
461 A74 4fr dl rose & multi   .30 .25
462 A74 6fr lilac rose & multi   .35 .25
463 A74 10fr pink & multi   .40 .25
464 A74 18fr gray & multi   1.00 .30
465 A74 60fr multicolored   3.25 1.25
466 A74 100fr violet & multi   4.75 2.25
    Nos. 457-466 (10)   11.05 5.55

Belgica '72 Emblem, King Baudouin, Queen Fabiola, Pres. and Mrs. Kayibanda — A75

1972, June 24   Photo.   Perf. 13
Size: 37x34mm
467 A75 18fr Rwanda landscape   1.00 .35
468 A75 22fr Old houses, Bruges   1.25 .35
Size: 50x34mm
469 A75 40fr shown   2.50 .50
    a. Strip of 3, #467-469   6.50 6.50

Belgica '72 Intl. Phil. Exhib., Brussels, June 24-July 9.

Pres. Kayibanda Addressing Meeting — A76

Pres. Grégoire Kayibanda: 30c, promoting officers of National Guard. 50c, with wife and children. 6fr, casting vote. 10fr, with wife and dignitaries at Feast of Justice. 15fr, with Cabinet and members of Assembly. 18fr, taking oath of office. 50fr, Portrait, vert.

1972, July 4   Perf. 13
470 A76 20c gold & slate grn   .25 .25
471 A76 30c gold & dk pur   .25 .25
472 A76 50c gold & choc   .25 .25
473 A76 6fr gold & Prus bl   .25 .25
474 A76 10fr gold & dk pur   .25 .25
475 A76 15fr gold & dk bl   .35 .25
476 A76 18fr gold & brn   .45 .40
477 A76 50fr gold & Prus bl   1.10 .85
    Nos. 470-477 (8)   3.15 2.75

10th anniversary of independence.

Equestrian, Olympic Emblems A77

Stadium, TV Tower and: 30c, Hockey. 50c, Soccer. 1fr, Broad jump. 6fr, Bicycling. 18fr, Yachting. 30fr, Hurdles. 44fr, Gymnastics, women's.

1972, Aug. 16   Photo.   Perf. 14
478 A77 20c dk brn & gold   .25 .25
479 A77 30c vio bl & gold   .25 .25
480 A77 50c dk green & gold   .25 .25
481 A77 1fr dp claret & gold   .25 .25
482 A77 6fr black & gold   .25 .25
483 A77 18fr brown & gold   .40 .25
484 A77 30fr dk vio & gold   .75 .55
485 A77 44fr Prus bl & gold   1.25 .80
    Nos. 478-485 (8)   3.65 2.85

20th Olympic Games, Munich, 8/26-9/11.

Relay (Sport) and UN Emblem A78

1972, Oct. 23   Photo.   Perf. 13
486 A78 20c shown   .25 .25
487 A78 30c Musicians   .25 .25
488 A78 50c Dancers   .25 .25
489 A78 1fr Operating room   .25 .25
490 A78 6fr Weaver & painter   .25 .25
491 A78 18fr Classroom   .35 .30
492 A78 24fr Laboratory   .55 .45
493 A78 50fr Hands of 4 races
          reaching for equal-
          ity   1.10 .85
    Nos. 486-493 (8)   3.25 2.85

Fight against racism.

Christmas Type of 1968
Souvenir Sheet

Design: 100fr, Adoration of the Shepherds, by Jacob Jordaens, vert.

1972, Dec. 11   Perf. 11½
494 A48 100fr red brown   4.50 4.50

Phymateus Brunneri — A79

Various insects. 30c, 1fr, 6fr, 22fr, 100fr, vert.

1973, Jan. 31   **Photo.**   **Perf. 13**
495	A79	20c multi	.25	.25
496	A79	30c multi	.25	.25
497	A79	50c multi	.25	.25
498	A79	1fr multi	.25	.25
499	A79	2fr multi	.25	.25
500	A79	6fr multi	.40	.25
501	A79	18fr multi	.80	.40
502	A79	22fr multi	1.25	.70
503	A79	70fr multi	3.50	2.25
504	A79	100fr multi	5.00	3.50
		Nos. 495-504 (10)	12.20	8.35

Souvenir Sheet
Perf. 14

505	A79	80fr like 20c	11.00	11.00

No. 505 contains one stamp 43½x33½mm.

Emile Zola,
by Edouard
Manet — A80

Paintings Connected with Reading, and Book Year Emblem: 30c, Rembrandt's Mother. 50c, St. Jerome Removing Thorn from Lion's Paw, by Colantonio. 1fr, Apostles Peter and Paul, by El Greco. 2fr, Virgin and Child with Book, by Roger van der Weyden. 6fr, St. Jerome in his Cell, by Antonella de Messina. 40fr, St. Barbara, by Master of Flemalle. No. 513, Don Quixote, by Oscar Vonnevalle. No. 514, Pres. Kayibanda reading book.

1973, Mar. 12   **Photo.**   **Perf. 13**
506	A80	20c gold & multi	.25	.25
507	A80	30c gold & multi	.25	.25
508	A80	50c gold & multi	.25	.25
509	A80	1fr gold & multi	.25	.25
510	A80	2fr gold & multi	.25	.25
511	A80	6fr gold & multi	.25	.25
512	A80	40fr gold & multi	1.00	.80
513	A80	100fr gold & multi	2.50	2.00
		Nos. 506-513 (8)	5.00	4.30

Souvenir Sheet
Perf. 14

514	A80	100fr gold, bl & ind	4.00	4.00

International Book Year.

Longombe
A81

Musical instruments of Central & West Africa.

1973, Apr. 9   **Photo.**   **Perf. 13½**
515	A81	20c shown	.25	.25
516	A81	30c Horn	.25	.25
517	A81	50c Xylophone	.25	.25
518	A81	1fr Harp	.25	.25
519	A81	4fr Alur horns	.25	.25
520	A81	6fr Drum, bells and horn	.25	.25
521	A81	18fr Large drums (Ngoma)	.50	.25
522	A81	90fr Toba	3.00	1.60
		Nos. 515-522 (8)	5.00	3.35

Rubens and
Isabella Brandt,
by Rubens — A82

Paintings from Old Pinakothek, Munich (IBRA Emblem and): 30c, Young Man, by Cranach. 50c, Woman Peeling Turnips, by Chardin. 1fr, The Abduction of Leucippa's Daughters, by Rubens. 2fr, Virgin and Child, by Filippo Lippi. 6fr, Boys Eating Fruit, by Murillo. 40fr, The Lovesick Woman, by Jan Steen. No. 530, Jesus Stripped of His Garments, by El Greco. No. 531, Oswolt Krel, by Dürer.

1973, May 11
523	A82	20c gold & multi	.25	.25
524	A82	30c gold & multi	.25	.25
525	A82	50c gold & multi	.25	.25
526	A82	1fr gold & multi	.25	.25
527	A82	2fr gold & multi	.25	.25
528	A82	6fr gold & multi	.25	.25
529	A82	40fr gold & multi	1.00	.75
530	A82	100fr gold & multi	2.75	2.00
		Nos. 523-530 (8)	5.25	4.25

Souvenir Sheet

531	A82	100fr gold & multi	4.00	4.00

IBRA München 1973 Intl. Phil. Exhib., Munich, May 11-20. No. 531 contains one 40x56mm stamp.

Map of
Africa and
Peace
Doves
A83

Design: 94fr, Map of Africa and hands.

1973, July 23   **Photo.**   **Perf. 13½**
532	A83	6fr gold & multi	.30	.25
533	A83	94fr gold & multi	2.75	2.50

Org. for African Unity, 10th anniv. For overprints see Nos. 895-896.

Nos. 298-303 Overprinted in Blue, Black, Green or Brown: "SECHERESSE / SOLIDARITE AFRICAINE"

1973, Aug. 23   **Photo.**   **Perf. 13**
534	A53	20c multi (Bl)	.25	.25
535	A53	40c multi (Bk)	.25	.25
536	A53	60c multi (Bl)	.25	.25
537	A53	80c multi (G)	.25	.25
538	A53	3fr multi (G)	.45	.25
539	A53	75fr multi (Br)	3.00	1.00
		Nos. 534-539,B1 (7)	10.45	8.25

African solidarity in drought emergency.

African Postal Union Issue
Common Design Type
1973, Sept. 12   **Engr.**   **Perf. 13**
540	CD137	100fr dp brn, bl & brn	4.00	2.00

Six-lined Distichodus — A84

African Fish: 30c, Little triggerfish. 50c, Spotted upside-down catfish. 1fr, Nile mouthbreeder. 2fr, African lungfish. 6fr, Pareutropius mandevillei. 40fr, Congo characin. 100fr, Like 20c. 150fr, Julidochromis ornatus.

1973, Sept. 3   **Photo.**   **Perf. 13**
541	A84	20c gold & multi	.25	.25
542	A84	30c gold & multi	.25	.25
543	A84	50c gold & multi	.25	.25
544	A84	1fr gold & multi	.25	.25
545	A84	2fr gold & multi	.25	.25
546	A84	6fr gold & multi	.35	.25
547	A84	40fr gold & multi	1.75	.75
548	A84	150fr gold & multi	6.00	3.25
		Nos. 541-548 (8)	9.35	5.50

Souvenir Sheet

549	A84	100fr gold & multi	6.50	6.50

No. 549 contains one stamp 48x29mm.

Nos. 398-405
Overprinted in
Black, Silver,
Green or Blue

1973, Sept. 15   **Litho.**
550	A50	20c multi (Bk)	.25	.25
551	A50	30c multi (S)	.25	.25
552	A50	50c multi (Bk)	.25	.25
553	A50	1fr multi (G)	.25	.25
554	A50	5fr multi (S)	.25	.25
555	A50	18fr multi (Bk)	.75	.25
556	A50	25fr multi (Bk)	1.50	.50
557	A50	50fr multi (Bl)	3.00	1.00
		Nos. 550-557 (8)	6.50	3.00

Africa Weeks, Brussels, Sept. 15-30, 1973. On the 30c, 1fr and 25fr the text of the overprint is horizontal.

Nos. 431-435 Overprinted in Gold

Perf. 13½x14, 14x13½
1973, Oct. 31   **Photo.**
559	A70	4fr dp org & multi	.25	.25
560	A70	6fr yellow & multi	.25	.25
561	A70	15fr lt blue & multi	.50	.30
562	A70	25fr red & multi	.90	.40
563	A70	50fr multicolored	1.75	.95
		Nos. 559-563 (5)	3.65	2.15

25th anniv. of the Universal Declaration of Human Rights.

Christmas Type of 1968
Souvenir Sheet
Adoration of the Shepherds, by Guido Reni.

1973, Dec. 15   **Engr.**   **Perf. 11½**
564	A48	100fr brt violet	4.75	4.75

Copernicus
and Astrolabe
A85

Designs: 30c, 18fr, 100fr, Portrait. 50c, 80fr, Copernicus and heliocentric system. 1fr, like 20c.

1973, Dec. 26   **Photo.**   **Perf. 13**
565	A85	20c silver & multi	.25	.25
566	A85	30c silver & multi	.25	.25
567	A85	50c silver & multi	.25	.25
568	A85	1fr gold & multi	.25	.25
569	A85	18fr gold & multi	1.00	.50
570	A85	80fr gold & multi	3.00	2.25
		Nos. 565-570 (6)	5.00	3.75

Souvenir Sheet

571	A85	100fr gold & multi	5.50	5.50

Nicolaus Copernicus (1473-1543).

Pres. Juvénal
Habyarimana — A86

1974, Apr. 8   **Photo.**   **Perf. 11½**
Black Inscriptions
572	A86	1fr bister & sepia	.25	.25
573	A86	2fr ultra & sepia	.25	.25
574	A86	5fr rose red & sep	.25	.25
575	A86	6fr grnsh bl & sep	.25	.25
576	A86	26fr lilac & sepia	.55	.30
577	A86	60fr ol grn & sepia	1.50	1.25
		Nos. 572-577 (6)	3.05	2.55

Souvenir Sheet

Christ Between the Thieves (Detail),
by Rubens — A87

1974, Apr. 12   **Engr.**   **Perf. 11½**
578	A87	100fr sepia	13.00	13.00

Easter.

Yugoslavia-Zaire Soccer Game — A88

Games' emblem and soccer games.

1974, July 6   **Photo.**   **Perf. 13½**
579	A88	20c shown	.25	.25
580	A88	40c Netherlands-Sweden	.25	.25
581	A88	60c Germany (Fed.)-Australia	.25	.25
582	A88	80c Haiti-Argentina	.25	.25
583	A88	2fr Brazil-Scotland	.25	.25
584	A88	6fr Bulgaria-Uruguay	.30	.25
585	A88	40fr Italy-Poland	1.25	.60
586	A88	50fr Chile-Germany (DDR)	1.75	1.25
		Nos. 579-586 (8)	4.55	3.35

World Cup Soccer Championship, Munich, June 13-July 7.

Marconi's Laboratory Yacht
"Elletra" — A89

Designs: 30c, Marconi and steamer "Carlo Alberto." 50c, Marconi's wireless apparatus and telecommunications satellites. 4fr, Marconi and globes connected by communications waves. 35fr, Marconi's radio, and radar. 60fr, Marconi and transmitter at Poldhu, Cornwall. 50fr, like 20c.

1974, Aug. 19   **Photo.**   **Perf. 13½**
587	A89	20c violet, blk & grn	.25	.25
588	A89	30c green, blk & vio	.25	.25
589	A89	50c yellow, blk & lil	.25	.25
590	A89	4fr salmon, blk & bl	.25	.25
591	A89	35fr lilac, blk & yel	.80	.50
592	A89	60fr blue, blk & brnz	1.50	1.00
		Nos. 587-592 (6)	3.30	2.50

Souvenir Sheet

593	A89	50fr gold, blk & lt bl	3.00	3.00

Guglielmo Marconi (1874-1937), Italian electrical engineer and inventor.

The Flute Player,
by J.
Leyster — A90

Paintings: 20c, Diane de Poitiers, Fontaine-
bleau School. 50c, Virgin and Child, by David.
1fr, Triumph of Venus, by Boucher. 10fr,
Seated Harlequin, by Picasso. 18fr, Virgin and
Child, 15th century. 20fr, Beheading of St.
John, by Hans Fries. 50fr, Daughter of Anders-
dotter, by J. F. Höckert.

1974, Sept. 23   Photo.   Perf. 14x13
594	A90	20c gold & multi	.25	.25
595	A90	30c gold & multi	.25	.25
596	A90	50c gold & multi	.25	.25
597	A90	1fr gold & multi	.25	.25
598	A90	10fr gold & multi	.25	.25
599	A90	18fr gold & multi	.50	.30
600	A90	20fr gold & multi	.50	.40
601	A90	50fr gold & multi	1.50	1.25
		Nos. 594-601 (8)	3.75	3.20

INTERNABA 74 Intl. Phil. Exhib., Basel,
June 7-10, and Stockholmia 74, Intl. Phil.
Exhib., Stockholm, Sept. 21-29.
Six multicolored souvenir sheets exist containing two 15fr stamps each in various combinations of designs of Nos. 594-601. Value, set
$12.
One souvenir sheet of four 25fr stamps
exists with designs of Nos. 595, 597, 599 and
601. Value, $8.50.

Messenger
Monk — A91

UPU Emblem and Messengers: 30c, Inca.
50c, Morocco. 1fr, India. 18fr, Polynesia. 80fr,
Rwanda.

1974, Oct. 9   Perf. 14
602	A91	20c gold & multi	.25	.25
603	A91	30c gold & multi	.25	.25
604	A91	50c gold & multi	.25	.25
605	A91	1fr gold & multi	.25	.25
606	A91	18fr gold & multi	.60	.40
607	A91	80fr gold & multi	2.25	1.75
		Nos. 602-607 (6)	3.85	3.15

Centenary of Universal Postal Union.

Nos. 306-308
Overprinted

1974, Dec. 16   Photo.   Perf. 11½
608	A54	6fr brt pink & multi	5.50	3.75
609	A54	18fr ultra & multi	5.50	3.75
610	A54	40fr brn & multi	5.50	3.75
		Nos. 608-610 (3)	16.50	11.25

15th anniversary of independence.

Christmas Type of 1968
Souvenir Sheet

Adoration of the Kings, by Joos van Cleve.

1974, Dec. 23   Engr.   Perf. 11½
611	A48	100fr slate green	15.00 15.00

**Nos. 295-296 Overprinted: "1974 /
10e Anniversaire"**

1974, Dec. 30   Photo.   Perf. 13
612	A51	30fr sil & multi	1.25	.85
613	A51	70fr gold & multi	2.25	1.75

African Development Bank, 10th anniversary.

Uganda
Kob — A92

Antelopes: 30c, Bongos, horiz. 50c,
Rwanda antelopes. 1fr, Young sitatungas,
horiz. 4fr, Greater kudus. 10fr, Impalas, horiz.
34fr, Waterbuck. 40fr, Impalas. 60fr, Greater
kudu. 100fr, Derby's elands, horiz.

1975, Mar. 17   Photo.   Perf. 13
614	A92	20c multi	.25	.25
615	A92	30c multi	.30	.25
616	A92	50c multi	.45	.25
617	A92	1fr multi	.75	.25
618	A92	4fr multi	.90	.30
619	A92	10fr multi	1.75	.60
620	A92	34fr multi	3.75	1.10
621	A92	100fr multi	7.50	2.25
		Nos. 614-621 (8)	15.65	5.25

Miniature Sheets
622	A92	40fr multi	26.00	26.00
623	A92	60fr multi	26.00	26.00

Miniature Sheets

Pietá, by Cranach the Elder — A93

20fr, The Burial of Jesus, by Raphael. 50fr,
By van der Weyden. 100fr, By Bellini.

1975, Apr. 1   Photo.   Perf. 13x14
624	A93	20fr multicolored	3.00	3.00
625	A93	30fr shown	3.00	3.00
626	A93	50fr multicolored	3.00	3.00
627	A93	100fr multicolored	3.00	3.00
		Nos. 624-627 (4)	12.00	12.00

Easter. Size of stamps: 40x52mm.
See Nos. 681-684.

Souvenir Sheets

Prince Balthazar Charles, by
Velazquez — A94

Paintings: 30fr, Infanta Margaret of Austria,
by Velazquez. 50fr, The Divine Shepherd, by
Murillo. 100fr, Francisco Goya, by V. Lopez y
Portana.

1975, Apr. 4   Photo.   Perf. 13
628	A94	20fr multi	4.00	4.00
629	A94	30fr multi	4.00	4.00
630	A94	50fr multi	4.00	4.00
631	A94	100fr multi	4.00	4.00
		Nos. 628-631 (4)	16.00	16.00

Espana 75 Intl. Phil. Exhib., Madrid, Apr. 4-
13. Size of stamps: 38x48mm. See Nos. 642-
643. For overprints see Nos. 844-847.

Pyrethrum (Insect
Powder) — A95

1975, Apr. 14   Perf. 13
632	A95	20c shown	.25	.25
633	A95	30c Tea	.25	.25
634	A95	50c Coffee (beans and pan)	.25	.25
635	A95	4fr Bananas	.25	.25
636	A95	10fr Corn	.25	.25
637	A95	12fr Sorghum	.30	.25
638	A95	26fr Rice	.75	.35
639	A95	47fr Coffee (workers and beans)	1.50	.75
		Nos. 632-639 (8)	3.80	2.60

Souvenir Sheets
Perf. 13½
640	A95	25fr like 50c	1.75	1.75
641	A95	75fr like 47fr	3.50	3.50

Year of Agriculture and 10th anniversary of
Office for Industrialized Cultivation.

Painting Type of 1975
Souvenir Sheets

75fr, Louis XIV, by Hyacinthe Rigaud. 125fr,
Cavalry Officer, by Jean Gericault.

1975, June 6   Photo.   Perf. 13
642	A94	75fr multi	6.00	6.00
643	A94	125fr multi	8.00	8.00

ARPHILA 75, Intl. Philatelic Exhibition,
Paris, June 6-16. Size of stamps: 38x48mm.

**Nos. 390-397 Overprinted: "1975 /
ANNEE / SAINTE"**

1975, June 23   Photo.   Perf. 13
644	A66	10c gold & dk brn	.25	.25
645	A66	20c gold & dk grn	.25	.25
646	A66	30c gold & dp claret	.25	.25
647	A66	40c gold & indigo	.25	.25
648	A66	1fr gold & dk pur	.25	.25
649	A66	18fr gold & purple	.45	.40
650	A66	20fr gold & org brn	.75	.60
651	A66	60fr gold & blk brn	2.25	1.75
		Nos. 644-651 (8)	4.70	4.00

Holy Year 1975.

White Pelicans — A96

African birds — 30c, Malachite kingfisher.
50c, Goliath herons. 1fr, Saddle-billed storks.
4fr, African jacana. 10fr, African anhingas.
34fr, Sacred ibis. 80fr, Hartlaub ducks.
40fr, Flamingoes. 60fr, Crowned cranes.

1975, June 20
652	A96	20c shown	.25	.25
653	A96	30c multicolored	.25	.25
654	A96	50c multicolored	.25	.25
655	A96	1fr multicolored	.25	.25
656	A96	4fr multicolored	.40	.25
657	A96	10fr multicolored	.75	.25
658	A96	34fr multicolored	2.25	1.00
659	A96	80fr multicolored	5.50	2.00
		Nos. 652-659 (8)	9.90	4.50

Miniature Sheets
660	A96	40fr multicolored	17.50	17.50
661	A96	60fr multicolored	22.50	22.50

Globe
Representing
Races and WPY
Emblem — A97

World Population Year: 26fr, Population
graph and emblem. 34fr, Globe with open
door and emblem.

1975, Sept. 1   Photo.   Perf. 13½x13
662	A97	20fr dp bl & multi	.60	.40
663	A97	26fr dl red brn & multi	.70	.55
664	A97	34fr yel & multi	1.00	.80
		Nos. 662-664 (3)	2.30	1.75

The Bath, by
Mary Cassatt
and IWY
Emblem — A98

IWY Emblem and: 30c, Mother and Infant
Son, by Julius Gari Melchers. 50c, Woman
with Milk Jug, by Jan Vermeer. 1fr, Water Carrier, by Goya. 8fr, Rwanda woman cotton
picker. 12fr, Scientist with microscope. 18fr,
Mother and child. 25fr, Empress Josephine,
by Pierre-Paul Prud'hon. 40fr, Madame
Vigee-Lebrun and Daughter, self-portrait.
60fr, Woman carrying child on back and water
jug on head.

1975, Sept. 15   Perf. 13
665	A98	20c gold & multi	.25	.25
666	A98	30c gold & multi	.25	.25
667	A98	50c gold & multi	.25	.25
668	A98	1fr gold & multi	.25	.25
669	A98	8fr gold & multi	.25	.25
670	A98	12fr gold & multi	.30	.25
671	A98	18fr gold & multi	.65	.30
672	A98	60fr gold & multi	2.40	1.25
		Nos. 665-672 (8)	4.60	3.05

Souvenir Sheets
Perf. 13½
673	A98	25fr multi	90.00	90.00
674	A98	40fr multi	90.00	90.00

International Women's Year. Nos. 673-674
each contain one stamp 37x49mm.

Owl, Quill and
Book — A99

30c, Hygiene emblem. 1.50fr, Kneeling
woman holding scales of Justice. 18fr, Chemist in laboratory. 26fr, Symbol of commerce &
chart. 34fr, University Building.

1975, Sept. 29   Perf. 13
675	A99	20c pur & multi	.25	.25
676	A99	30c ultra & multi	.25	.25
677	A99	1.50fr lilac & multi	.25	.25
678	A99	18fr blue & multi	.35	.25
679	A99	26fr olive & multi	.55	.40
680	A99	34fr blue & multi	1.00	.70
		Nos. 675-680 (6)	2.65	2.10

National Univ. of Rwanda, 10th anniv.

Painting Type of 1975
Souvenir Sheets

Paintings by Jan Vermeer (1632-1675): 20fr,
Man and Woman Drinking Wine. 30fr, Woman
in Blue Reading Letter. 50fr, Painter in his
Studio. 100fr, Young Woman Playing Virginal.

1975, Oct. 13　Photo.　Perf. 13x14
681	A93	20fr multi	3.25	3.25
682	A93	30fr multi	3.25	3.25
683	A93	50fr multi	3.25	3.25
684	A93	100fr multi	3.25	3.25
		Nos. 681-684 (4)	13.00	13.00

Size of stamps: 40x52mm.

Waterhole and Impatiens
Stuhlmannii — A100

Designs: 30c, Antelopes, zebras, candelabra cactus. 50c, Brush fire, and tapinanthus prunifolius. 5fr, Bulera Lake and Egyptian white lotus. 8fr, Erosion prevention and protea madiensis. 10fr, Marsh and melanthera brownei. 26fr, Landscape, lobelias and senecons. 100fr, Sabyinyo Volcano and polystachya kermesina.

1975, Oct. 25　　　　　　Perf. 13
685	A100	20c blk & multi	.25	.25
686	A100	30c blk & multi	.25	.25
687	A100	50c blk & multi	.25	.25
688	A100	5fr blk & multi	.25	.25
689	A100	8fr blk & multi	.25	.25
690	A100	10fr blk & multi	.25	.25
691	A100	26fr blk & multi	1.00	.75
692	A100	100fr blk & multi	3.00	2.25
		Nos. 685-692 (8)	5.50	4.50

Nature protection.
For overprints see Nos. 801-808.

Nos. 343-348
Overprinted

1975, Nov. 10　Litho.　Perf. 13
693	A60	20c multi	.25	.25
694	A60	30c multi	.25	.25
695	A60	50c multi	.25	.25
696	A60	1fr multi	.25	.25
697	A60	3fr multi	.25	.25
698	A60	5fr multi	.25	.25
		Nos. 693-698,B2-B3 (8)	6.75	6.00

African solidarity in drought emergency.

Fork-lift
Truck on
Airfield
A101

Designs: 30c, Coffee packing plant. 50c, Engineering plant. 10fr, Farmer with hoe, vert. 35fr, Coffee pickers, vert. 54fr, Mechanized harvester.

Wmk. JEZ Multiple (368)
1975, Dec. 1　Photo.　Perf. 14x13½
699	A101	20c gold & multi	.25	.25
700	A101	30c gold & multi	.25	.25
701	A101	50c gold & multi	.25	.25
702	A101	10fr gold & multi	.25	.25
703	A101	35fr gold & multi	.65	.45
704	A101	54fr gold & multi	1.30	.85
		Nos. 699-704 (6)	2.95	2.30

Basket Carrier
and Themabelga
Emblem — A102

Themabelga Emblem and: 30c, Warrior with shield and spear. 50c, Woman with beads. 1fr, Indian woman. 5fr, Male dancer with painted body. 7fr, Woman carrying child on back. 35fr, Male dancer with spear. 51fr, Female dancers.

1975, Dec. 8　　Unwmk.　Perf. 13½
705	A102	20c blk & multi	.25	.25
706	A102	30c blk & multi	.25	.25
707	A102	50c blk & multi	.25	.25
708	A102	1fr blk & multi	.25	.25
709	A102	5fr blk & multi	.25	.25
710	A102	7fr blk & multi	.35	.25
711	A102	35fr blk & multi	.90	.45
712	A102	51fr blk & multi	1.75	1.10
		Nos. 705-712 (8)	4.25	3.05

THEMABELGA Intl. Topical Philatelic Exhibition, Brussels, Dec. 13-21.

Christmas Type of 1968

Adoration of the Kings, by Peter Paul Rubens.

1975, Dec. 22　Engr.　Perf. 11½
713	A48	100fr brt rose lil	9.50	9.50

Dr. Schweitzer, Keyboard,
Score — A103

Albert Schweitzer and: 30c, 5fr, Lambaréné Hospital. 50c, 10fr, Organ pipes from Strassbourg organ, and score. 1fr, 80fr, Dr. Schweitzer's house, Lambaréné. 3fr, like 20c.

1976, Jan. 30　Photo.　Perf. 13½
714	A103	20c maroon & pur	.25	.25
715	A103	30c grn & pur	.25	.25
716	A103	50c brn org & pur	.25	.25
717	A103	1fr red lil & pur	.25	.25
718	A103	3fr vio bl & pur	.25	.25
719	A103	5fr brn & pur	.25	.25
720	A103	10fr bl & pur	.30	.25
721	A103	80fr ver & pur	2.10	1.25
		Nos. 714-721 (8)	3.90	3.00

World Leprosy Day.
For overprints see Nos. 788-795.

Surrender
at Yorktown
A104

American Bicentennial (Paintings): 30c, Instruction at Valley Forge. 50c, Presentation of Captured Colors at Yorktown. 1fr, Washington at Fort Lee. 18fr, Washington Boarding British Warship. 26fr, Washington Studying Battle Plans at Night. 34fr, Washington Firing Cannon. 40fr, Washington Crossing the Delaware. 100fr, Sailing Ship "Bonhomme Richard," vert.

1976, Mar. 22　Photo.　Perf. 13x13½
722	A104	20c gold & multi	.25	.25
723	A104	30c gold & multi	.25	.25
724	A104	50c gold & multi	.25	.25
725	A104	1fr gold & multi	.25	.25
726	A104	18fr gold & multi	.55	.25
727	A104	26fr gold & multi	.60	.30
728	A104	34fr gold & multi	.90	.55
729	A104	40fr gold & multi	1.25	1.00
		Nos. 722-729 (8)	4.30	3.10

Souvenir Sheet
Perf. 13½
730	A104	100fr gold & multi	5.00	5.00

See Nos. 754-761.

Sister Yohana,
First Nun — A105

30c, Abdon Sabakati, one of first converts. 50c, Father Alphonse Brard, first Superior of Save Mission. 4fr, Abbot Balthazar Gafuku, one of first priests. 10fr, Msgr. Bigirumwami, first bishop. 25fr, Save Church, horiz. 60fr, Kabgayi Cathedral, horiz.

Perf. 13x13½, 13½x13
1976, Apr. 26　　　　　　Photo.
731	A105	20c multi	.25	.25
732	A105	30c multi	.25	.25
733	A105	50c multi	.25	.25
734	A105	4fr multi	.25	.25
735	A105	10fr multi	.25	.25
736	A105	25fr multi	.50	.30
737	A105	60fr multi	1.25	.45
		Nos. 731-737 (7)	3.00	2.00

50th anniv. of the Roman Catholic Church of Rwanda.

Yachting — A106

Montreal Games Emblem and: 30c, Steeplechase. 50c, Long jump. 1fr, Hockey. 10fr, Swimming. 18fr, Soccer. 29fr, Boxing. 51fr, Vaulting.

1976, May 24　Photo.　Perf. 13x13½
738	A106	20c gray & dk car	.25	.25
739	A106	30c gray & Prus bl	.25	.25
740	A106	50c gray & blk	.25	.25
741	A106	1fr gray & pur	.25	.25
742	A106	10fr gray & ultra	.30	.25
743	A106	18fr gray & dk brn	.40	.25
744	A106	29fr gray & blk	.70	.35
745	A106	51fr gray & slate grn	1.10	.75
		Nos. 738-745 (8)	3.50	2.60

21st Olympic Games, Montreal, Canada, July 17-Aug. 1.

First Message, Manual
Switchboard — A107

Designs: 30c, Telephone, 1876 and interested crowd. 50c, Telephone c. 1900, and woman making a call. 1fr, Business telephone exchange, c. 1905. 4fr, "Candlestick" phone, globe and A. G. Bell. 8fr, Dial phone and Rwandan man making call. 26fr, Telephone, 1976, satellite and radar. 60fr, Push-button telephone, Rwandan international switchboard operator.

1976, June 21　Photo.　Perf. 14
746	A107	20c dl red & indigo	.25	.25
747	A107	30c grnsh bl & indigo	.25	.25
748	A107	50c brn & indigo	.25	.25
749	A107	1fr org & indigo	.25	.25
750	A107	4fr lilac & indigo	.25	.25
751	A107	8fr grn & indigo	.30	.25
752	A107	26fr dl red & indigo	.75	.40
753	A107	60fr vio & indigo	1.60	.85
		Nos. 746-753 (8)	3.90	2.75

Centenary of first telephone call by Alexander Graham Bell, Mar. 10, 1876.

Type of 1976 Overprinted in Silver with Bicentennial Emblem and "Independence Day"

Designs as before.

1976, July 4　　　　　Perf. 13x13½
754	A104	20c silver & multi	.25	.25
755	A104	30c silver & multi	.25	.25
756	A104	50c silver & multi	.25	.25
757	A104	1fr silver & multi	.25	.25
758	A104	18fr silver & multi	.60	.30
759	A104	26fr silver & multi	.80	.35
760	A104	34fr silver & multi	.90	.60
761	A104	40fr silver & multi	1.10	.80
		Nos. 754-761 (8)	4.40	3.05

Independence Day.

Soccer, Montreal
Olympic
Emblem — A108

30c, Shooting. 50c, Woman canoeing. 1fr, Gymnast. 10fr, Weight lifting. 12fr, Diving. 26fr, Equestrian. 50fr, Shot put.

1976, Aug. 1　Photo.　Perf. 13½x13
762	A108	20c multi	.25	.25
763	A108	30c multi	.25	.25
764	A108	50c multi	.25	.25
765	A108	1fr multi	.25	.25
766	A108	10fr multi	.25	.25
767	A108	12fr multi	.25	.25
768	A108	26fr multi	.75	.50
769	A108	50fr multi	1.75	1.00
		Nos. 762-769 (8)	4.00	3.00

Souvenir Sheet

Various phases of hurdles race, horiz.

770		Sheet of 4	5.50	5.50
a.	A108	20fr Start	.55	.55
b.	A108	30fr Sprint	.90	.90
c.	A108	40fr Hurdle	1.10	1.10
d.	A108	60fr Finish	1.75	1.75

21st Olympic Games, Montreal, Canada, July 17-Aug. 1.

Apollo and
Soyuz Take-
offs, Project
Emblem
A109

Designs: 30c, Soyuz in space. 50c, Apollo in space. 1fr, Apollo. 2fr, Spacecraft before docking. 12fr, Spacecraft after docking. 30fr, Astronauts visiting in docked spacecraft. 54fr, Apollo splashdown.

1976, Oct. 29　Photo.　Perf. 13½x14
771	A109	20c multi	.25	.25
772	A109	30c multi	.25	.25
773	A109	50c multi	.25	.25
774	A109	1fr multi	.25	.25
775	A109	2fr multi	.25	.25
776	A109	12fr multi	.75	.35
777	A109	30fr multi	2.50	.90
778	A109	50fr multi	3.50	1.50
		Nos. 771-778 (8)	8.00	4.00

Apollo Soyuz space test program (Russo-American cooperation), July 1975.
For overprints see Nos. 836-843.

Eulophia
Cucullata — A110

Orchids: 30c, Eulophia streptopetala. 50c, Disa Stairsii. 1fr, Aerangis kotschyana. 10fr, Eulophia abyssinica. 12fr, Bonatea steudneri. 26fr, Ansellia gigantea. 50fr, Eulophia angolensis.

1976, Nov. 22　Photo.　Perf. 14x13½
779	A110	20c multi	.25	.25
780	A110	30c multi	.25	.25
781	A110	50c multi	.25	.25
782	A110	1fr multi	.25	.25
783	A110	10fr multi	.45	.25
784	A110	12fr multi	.70	

785	A110	26fr multi	1.75 .60
786	A110	50fr multi	3.50 1.10
		Nos. 779-786 (8)	7.40 3.25

Christmas Type of 1968
Souvenir Sheet
Design: Nativity, by Francois Boucher.

1976, Dec. 20 Engr. Perf. 11½

787	A48	100fr brt ultra	8.00 8.00

Nos. 714-721 Overprinted: "JOURNEE / MONDIALE / 1977"

1977, Jan. 29 Photo. Perf. 13½

788	A103	20c mar & pur	.25 .25
789	A103	30c grn & pur	.25 .25
790	A103	50c brn org & pur	.25 .25
791	A103	1fr red lil & pur	.25 .25
792	A103	3fr vio bl & pur	.25 .25
793	A103	5fr brn & pur	.25 .25
794	A103	10fr bl & pur	.35 .25
795	A103	80fr ver & pur	2.50 1.50
		Nos. 788-795 (8)	4.35 3.25

World Leprosy Day.

Hands and Symbols of Learning — A111

Designs: 26fr, Hands and symbols of science. 64fr, Hands and symbols of industry.

1977, Feb. 7 Litho. Perf. 12½

796	A111	10fr multi	.25 .25
797	A111	26fr multi	.70 .45
798	A111	64fr multi	1.40 .85
		Nos. 796-798 (3)	2.35 1.55

10th Summit Conference of the African and Malagasy Union, Kigali, 1976.

Souvenir Sheets

Descent from the Cross, by Rubens — A112

Easter: 25fr, Crucifixion, by Rubens.

1977, Apr. 27 Photo. Perf. 13

799	A112	25fr multi	9.00 9.00
800	A112	75fr multi	11.00 11.00

Size of stamp: 40x40mm.

Nos. 685-692 Overprinted

1977, May 2

801	A100	20c blk & multi	.25 .25
802	A100	30c blk & multi	.25 .25
803	A100	50c blk & multi	.25 .25
804	A100	5fr blk & multi	.25 .25
805	A100	8fr blk & multi	.40 .30
806	A100	10fr blk & multi	.50 .40
807	A100	26fr blk & multi	1.75 1.00
808	A100	100fr blk & multi	6.25 3.50
		Nos. 801-808 (8)	9.90 6.20

World Water Conference.

Roman Fire Tower, African Tom-tom A113

ITU Emblem and: 30c, Chappe's optical telegraph and postilion. 50c, Morse telegraph and code. 1fr, Tug Goliath laying cable in English Channel. 4fr, Telephone, radio, television. 18fr, Kingsport (US space exploration ship) and Marots communications satellite. 26fr, Satellite tracking station and O.T.S. satellite. 50fr, Mariner II, Venus probe.

1977, May 23 Litho. Perf. 12½

809	A113	20c multi	.25 .25
810	A113	30c multi	.25 .25
811	A113	50c multi	.25 .25
812	A113	1fr multi	.25 .25
813	A113	4fr multi	.25 .25
814	A113	18fr multi	.50 .25
815	A113	26fr multi	.75 .50
816	A113	50fr multi	1.40 1.00
		Nos. 809-816 (8)	3.90 3.00

World Telecommunications Day.

Souvenir Sheets

Amsterdam Harbor, by Willem van de Velde, the Younger — A114

40fr, The Night Watch, by Rembrandt.

1977, May 26 Photo. Perf. 13½

817	A114	40fr multi	7.00 7.00
818	A114	60fr multi	7.00 7.00

AMPHILEX '77 Intl. Philatelic Exhibition, Amsterdam, May 27-June 5. Size of stamp: 38x49mm.

Road to Calvary, by Rubens — A115

Paintings by Peter Paul Rubens (1577-1640): 30c, Judgment of Paris, horiz. 50c, Marie de Medicis. 1fr, Heads of Black Men, horiz. 4fr, 26fr, Details from St. Ildefonso triptych. 8fr, Helene Fourment and her Children, horiz. 60fr, Helene Fourment.

1977, June 13 Perf. 14

819	A115	20c gold & multi	.25 .25
820	A115	30c gold & multi	.25 .25
821	A115	50c gold & multi	.35 .25
822	A115	1fr gold & multi	.40 .25
823	A115	4fr gold & multi	.45 .25
824	A115	8fr gold & multi	.50 .30
825	A115	26fr gold & multi	1.10 .75
826	A115	60fr gold & multi	1.75 1.50
		Nos. 819-826 (8)	5.05 3.80

Souvenir Sheet

Viking on Mars — A116

1977, June 27 Photo. Perf. 13

827	A116	100fr multi	60.00 60.00

US Viking landing on Mars, first anniv.

Crested Eagle — A117

Birds of Prey: 30c, Snake eagle. 50c, Fish eagle. 1fr, Monk vulture. 3fr, Red-tailed buzzard. 5fr, Yellow-beaked kite. 20fr, Swallow-tailed kite. 100fr, Bateleur.

1977, Sept. 12 Litho. Perf. 14

828	A117	20c multi	.25 .25
829	A117	30c multi	.25 .25
830	A117	50c multi	.25 .25
831	A117	1fr multi	.25 .25
832	A117	3fr multi	.30 .25
833	A117	5fr multi	.60 .25
834	A117	20fr multi	2.25 .90
835	A117	100fr multi	6.75 3.25
		Nos. 828-835 (8)	10.90 5.65

Nos. 771-778 Overprinted: "in memoriam / WERNHER VON BRAUN / 1912-1977"

1977, Sept. 19 Photo. Perf. 13½x14

836	A109	20c multi	.25 .25
837	A109	30c multi	.25 .25
838	A109	50c multi	.25 .25
839	A109	1fr multi	.25 .25
840	A109	2fr multi	.25 .25
841	A109	12fr multi	.30 .25
842	A109	30fr multi	2.25 1.40
843	A109	54fr multi	4.25 2.25
		Nos. 836-843 (8)	8.05 5.15

Wernher von Braun (1912-1977), space and rocket expert.

Nos. 628-631 Gold Embossed "ESPAMER '77" and ESPAMER Emblem
Souvenir Sheets

1977, Oct. 3 Photo. Perf. 13

844	A94	20fr multi	6.25 6.25
845	A94	30fr multi	6.25 6.25
846	A94	50fr multi	6.25 6.25
847	A94	100fr multi	6.25 6.25
		Nos. 844-847 (4)	25.00 25.00

ESPAMER '77, International Philatelic Exhibition, Barcelona, Oct. 7-13.

Christmas Type of 1968
Souvenir Sheet
100fr, Nativity, by Peter Paul Rubens.

1977, Dec. 12 Engr. Perf. 13½

848	A48	100fr violet blue	5.75 5.75

Marginal inscription typographed in red.

Boy Scout Playing Flute — A118

Designs: 30c, Campfire. 50c, Bridge building. 1fr, Scouts with unit flag. 10fr, Map reading. 18fr, Boating. 26fr, Cooking. 44fr, Lord Baden-Powell.

1978, Feb. 20 Litho. Perf. 12½

849	A118	20c yel grn & multi	.25 .25
850	A118	30c blue & multi	.25 .25
851	A118	50c lilac & multi	.25 .25
852	A118	1fr blue & multi	.25 .25
853	A118	10fr pink & multi	.40 .25
854	A118	18fr lt grn & multi	.90 .35
855	A118	26fr orange & multi	1.50 .60
856	A118	44fr salmon & multi	2.25 1.25
		Nos. 849-856 (8)	6.05 3.45

10th anniversary of Rwanda Boy Scouts.

Chimpanzees A119

Designs: 30c, Gorilla. 50c, Colobus monkey. 3fr, Galago. 10fr, Cercopithecus monkey (mone). 26fr, Potto. 60fr, Cercopithecus monkey (griuet). 150fr, Baboon.

1978, Mar. 20 Photo. Perf. 13½x13

857	A119	20c multi	.25 .25
858	A119	30c multi	.25 .25
859	A119	50c multi	.25 .25
860	A119	3fr multi	.25 .25
861	A119	10fr multi	.65 .50
862	A119	26fr multi	1.50 1.25
863	A119	60fr multi	4.00 3.00
864	A119	150fr multi	7.00 7.00
		Nos. 857-864 (8)	14.15 12.75

Euporus Strangulatus — A120

Coleoptera: 30c, Rhina afzelii, vert. 50c, Pentalobus palini. 3fr, Corynodes dejeani, vert. 10fr, Mecynorhina torquata. 15fr, Mecocerus rhombeus, vert. 20fr, Macrotoma serripes. 25fr, Neptunides stanleyi, vert. 26fr, Petrognatha gigas. 100fr, Eudicella gralli, vert.

1978, May 22 Litho. Perf. 14

865	A120	20c multi	.25 .25
866	A120	30c multi	.25 .25
867	A120	50c multi	.25 .25
868	A120	3fr multi	.30 .25
869	A120	10fr multi	.40 .25
870	A120	15fr multi	.60 .30
871	A120	20fr multi	.85 .35
872	A120	25fr multi	1.10 .50
873	A120	26fr multi	1.50 .55
874	A120	100fr multi	4.50 2.25
		Nos. 865-874 (10)	10.00 5.20

Crossing "River of Poverty" A121

Emblem and: 10fr, 60fr, Men poling boat, facing right. 26fr, like 4fr.

1978, May 29 Perf. 12½

875	A121	4fr multi	.25 .25
876	A121	10fr multi	.25 .25
877	A121	26fr multi	.60 .40
878	A121	60fr multi	1.25 .80
		Nos. 875-878 (4)	2.35 1.70

Natl. Revolutionary Development Movement (M.R.N.D.).

Soccer, Rimet Cup, Flags of
Netherlands and Peru — A122

11th World cup, Argentina, June 1-25, (Various Soccer Scenes and Flags of): 30c, Sweden & Spain. 50c, Scotland & Iran. 2fr, Germany & Tunisia. 3fr, Italy & Hungary. 10fr, Brazil and Austria. 34fr, Poland & Mexico. 100fr, Argentina & France.

1978, June 19   *Perf. 13*
879	A122	20c multi	.25	.25
879A	A122	30c multi	.25	.25
879B	A122	50c multi	.25	.25
880	A122	2fr multi	.25	.25
881	A122	3fr multi	.25	.25
882	A122	10fr multi	.35	.25
883	A122	34fr multi	1.25	.70
884	A122	100fr multi	2.75	1.90
	Nos. 879-884 (8)		5.60	4.10

Wright
Brothers,
Flyer
I — A123

History of Aviation: 30c, Santos Dumont and Canard 14, 1906. 50c, Henry Farman and Voisin No. 1, 1908. 1fr, Jan Olieslaegers and Bleriot, 1910. 3fr, Marshal Balbo and Savoia S-17, 1919. 10fr, Charles Lindbergh and Spirit of St. Louis, 1927. 55fr, Hugo Junkers and Junkers JU52/3, 1932. 60fr, Igor Sikorsky and Sikorsky VS 300, 1939. 130fr, Concorde over New York.

1978, Oct. 30   **Litho.**   *Perf. 13½x14*
885	A123	20c multi	.25	.25
886	A123	30c multi	.25	.25
887	A123	50c multi	.25	.25
888	A123	1fr multi	.25	.25
889	A123	3fr multi	.25	.25
890	A123	10fr multi	.35	.25
891	A123	55fr multi	1.40	.75
892	A123	60fr multi	1.60	.85
	Nos. 885-892 (8)		4.60	3.10

Souvenir Sheet
Perf. 13x13½
893	A123	130fr multi	6.50	6.50

No. 893 contains one stamp 47x35mm.

Christmas Type of 1968
Souvenir Sheet

Design: 200fr, Adoration of the Kings, by Albrecht Dürer, vert.

1978, Dec. 11   **Engr.**   *Perf. 11½*
894	A48	200fr brown	8.00	8.00

Nos. 532-533, Overprinted "1963 1978" in Black or Blue

1978, Dec. 18   **Photo.**   *Perf. 13½*
895	A83	6fr multi (Bk)	.25	.25
896	A83	94fr multi (Bl)	2.50	2.00

Org. for African Unity, 15th anniv.

Goats
A124

20c, Ducks, vert. 50c, Cock and chickens, vert. 4fr, Rabbits. 5fr, Pigs, vert. 15fr, Turkey. 50fr, Sheep and cattle, vert. 75fr, Bull.

1978, Dec. 28   **Litho.**   *Perf. 14*
897	A124	20c multi	.25	.25
898	A124	30c multi	.25	.25
899	A124	50c multi	.25	.25
900	A124	4fr multi	.30	.25
901	A124	5fr multi	.30	.25
902	A124	15fr multi	.70	.35

903	A124	50fr multi	2.25	.95
904	A124	75fr multi	4.00	1.60
	Nos. 897-904 (8)		8.30	4.15

Husbandry Year.

Papilio
Demodocus
A125

Butterflies: 30c, Precis octavia. 50c, Charaxes smaragdalis. 4fr, Charaxes guderiana. 15fr, Colotis evippe. 30fr, Danaus limniace. 50fr, Byblia acheloia. 150fr, Utetheisa pulchella.

1979, Feb. 19   **Photo.**   *Perf. 14½*
905	A125	20c multi	.25	.25
906	A125	30c multi	.30	.25
907	A125	50c multi	.35	.25
908	A125	4fr multi	.50	.25
909	A125	15fr multi	.90	.30
910	A125	30fr multi	2.25	.45
911	A125	50fr multi	3.00	.90
912	A125	150fr multi	7.50	2.50
	Nos. 905-912 (8)		15.05	5.15

Euphorbia
Grantii,
Weavers
A126

Design: 60fr, Drummers and Intelsat IV-A.

1979, June 8   **Photo.**   *Perf. 13*
913	A126	40fr multi	1.25	1.00
914	A126	60fr multi	2.50	1.50

Philexafrique II, Libreville, Gabon, June 8-17.

Entandrophragma Excelsum — A127

Trees and Shrubs: 20c, Polyscias fulva. 50c, Ilex mitis. 4fr, Kigelia Africana. 15fr, Ficus thonningi. 20fr, Acacia Senegal. 50fr, Symphonia globulifera. 110fr, Acacia sieberana. 20c, 50c, 15fr, 50fr, vertical.

1979, Aug. 27   *Perf. 14*
915	A127	20c multi	.25	.25
916	A127	30c multi	.25	.25
917	A127	50c multi	.25	.25
918	A127	4 fr multi	.30	.25
919	A127	15fr multi	.45	.25
920	A127	20fr multi	.65	.40
921	A127	50fr multi	1.50	.80
922	A127	110fr multi	3.25	2.00
	Nos. 915-922 (8)		6.90	4.45

Black and
White
Boys, IYC
Emblem
A128

26fr, 100fr, Children of various races, diff., vert.

Perf. 13½x13, 13x13½
1979, Nov. 19   **Photo.**
923	A128	Block of 8	10.00	7.50
a.		26fr, any single	.90	.45
924	A128	42fr multi	1.50	.90

Souvenir Sheet
925	A128	100fr multi	6.00	6.00

Intl. Year of the Child. No. 923 printed in sheets of 16 (4x4).

Basket
Weaving
A129

Perf. 12½x13, 13x12½
1979, Dec. 3   **Litho.**
926	A129	50c shown	.25	.25
927	A129	1.50fr Wood carving, vert.	.25	.25
928	A129	2fr Metal working, vert.	.25	.25
929	A129	10fr Jewelry, vert.	.25	.25
930	A129	20fr Straw plaiting	.30	.25
931	A129	26fr Wall painting, vert.	.65	.45
932	A129	40fr Pottery	1.50	1.00
933	A129	100fr Smelting, vert.	3.25	1.50
	Nos. 926-933 (8)		6.70	4.20

Souvenir Sheet

Children of Different Races, Christmas
Tree — A130

1979, Dec. 24   **Engr.**   *Perf. 12*
934	A130	200fr ultra & dp mag	9.00	9.00

Christmas; Intl. Year of the Child.

German
East
Africa
#N5, Hill
A131

Sir Rowland Hill (1795-1879), originator of penny postage, and Stamps of Ruanda-Urundi or: 30c, German East Africa #N23. 50c, German East Africa #NB9. 3fr, #25. 10fr, #42. 26fr, #123. 100fr, #B28.

1979, Dec. 31   **Litho.**   *Perf. 14*
935	A131	20c multi	.25	.25
936	A131	30c multi	.25	.25
937	A131	50c multi	.25	.25
938	A131	3fr multi	.25	.25
939	A131	10fr multi	.25	.25
940	A131	26fr multi	.65	.35
941	A131	60fr multi	1.75	.90
942	A131	100fr multi	3.00	1.25
	Nos. 935-942 (8)		6.65	3.65

Sarothrura
Pulchra
A132

Birds of the Nyungwe Forest: 20c Ploceus alienus, vert. 30c, Regal sunbird, vert. 3fr, Tockus alboterminatus. 10fr, Pygmy owl, vert. 26fr, Emerald cuckoo. 60fr, Finch, vert. 100fr, Stepanoaetus coronatus, vert.

Perf. 13½x13, 13x13½
1980, Jan. 7   **Photo.**
943	A132	20c multi	.25	.25
944	A132	30c multi	.25	.25
945	A132	50c multi	.25	.25
946	A132	3fr multi	.25	.25
947	A132	10fr multi	.60	.40
948	A132	26fr multi	1.50	.80
949	A132	60fr multi	3.75	1.25
950	A132	100fr multi	5.50	2.75
	Nos. 943-950 (8)		12.35	6.20

First
Footstep
on Moon,
Spacecraft
A133

Spacecraft and Moon Exploration: 1.50fr, Descent onto lunar surface. 8fr, American flag. 30fr, Solar panels. 50fr, Gathering soil samples. 60fr, Adjusting sun screen. 200fr, Landing craft.

1980, Jan. 31   **Photo.**   *Perf. 13x13½*
951	A133	50c multi	.25	.25
952	A133	1.50fr multi	.25	.25
953	A133	8fr multi	.25	.25
954	A133	30fr multi	1.00	.50
955	A133	50fr multi	1.75	.80
956	A133	60fr multi	2.00	.90
	Nos. 951-956 (6)		5.50	2.95

Souvenir Sheet
957	A133	200fr multi	7.50	7.50

Apollo 11 moon landing, 10th anniv. (1979).

Globe, Butare
and 1905
Chicago Club
Emblems
A134

Rotary Intl., 75th Anniv. (Globe, Emblems of Butare or Kigali Clubs and): 30c, San Francisco, 1908. 50c, Chicago, 1910. 4fr, Buffalo, 1911. 15fr, London, 1911. 20fr, Glasgow, 1912. 50fr, Bristol, 1917. 60fr, Rotary Intl., 1980.

1980, Feb. 23   **Litho.**   *Perf. 13*
958	A134	20c multi	.25	.25
959	A134	30c multi	.25	.25
960	A134	50c multi	.25	.25
961	A134	4fr multi	.25	.25
962	A134	15fr multi	.35	.25
963	A134	20fr multi	.50	.25
964	A134	50fr multi	.90	.40
965	A134	60fr multi	1.50	.65
	Nos. 958-965 (8)		4.25	2.55

Gymnast,
Moscow '80
Emblem
A135

1980, Mar. 10   *Perf. 12½*
966	A135	20c shown	.25	.25
967	A135	30c Basketball	.25	.25
968	A135	50c Bicycling	.25	.25
969	A135	3fr Boxing	.25	.25
970	A135	20fr Archery	.55	.25
971	A135	26fr Weight lifting	.75	.30
972	A135	50fr Javelin	1.50	.65
973	A135	100fr Fencing	2.75	1.25
	Nos. 966-973 (8)		6.55	3.45

22nd Summer Olympic Games, Moscow, July 19-Aug. 3.

Souvenir Sheet

Amalfi Coast, by Giacinto
Gigante — A136

1980, Apr. 28   Photo.   Perf. 13½
974 A136 200fr multi   7.50 7.50

20th Intl. Philatelic Exhibition, Europa '80,
Naples, Apr. 26-May 4.

Geaster
Mushroom
A137

30c, Lentinus atrobrunneus. 50c, Gomphus
stereoides. 4fr, Cantharellus cibarius. 10fr,
Stilbothamnium dybowskii. 15fr, Xeromphalina
tenuipes. 70fr, Podoscypha elegans. 100fr,
Mycena.

1980, July 21   Photo.   Perf. 13½
975	A137	20c	shown	.30	.25
976	A137	30c	multicolored	.45	.25
977	A137	50c	multicolored	.55	.25
978	A137	4fr	multicolored	.90	.25
979	A137	10fr	multicolored	1.50	.50
980	A137	15fr	multicolored	3.25	.75
981	A137	70fr	multicolored	9.00	2.00
982	A137	100fr	multicolored	15.00	4.00
		Nos. 975-982 (8)		30.95	8.05

Still Life, by Renoir — A138

Impressionist Painters: 30c, 26fr, At the
Theater, by Toulouse-Lautrec, vert. 50c, 10fr,
Seaside Garden, by Monet. 4fr, Mother and
Child, by Mary Cassatt, vert. 5fr, Starry Night,
by Van Gogh. 10fr, Dancers at their Toilet, by
Degas, vert. 50fr, The Card Players, by
Cezanne. 70fr, Tahitian Women, by Gauguin,
vert. 75fr, like 20c. 100fr, In the Park, by
Seurat.

1980, Aug. 4   Litho.   Perf. 14
983	A138	20c	multi	.25	.25
984	A138	30c	multi	.25	.25
985	A138	50c	multi	.25	.25
986	A138	4fr	multi	.25	.25
a.		Sheet of 2, 4fr, 26fr		3.00	3.00
987	A138	5fr	multi	.30	.25
a.		Sheet of 2, 5fr, 75fr		3.00	3.00
988	A138	10fr	multi	.40	.25
a.		Sheet of 2, 10fr, 70fr		3.00	3.00
989	A138	50fr	multi	1.50	.55
a.		Sheet of 2, 50fr, 10fr		3.00	3.00
990	A138	70fr	multi	2.25	.85
991	A138	100fr	multi	3.50	1.25
		Nos. 983-991 (9)		8.95	4.15

Souvenir Sheet

Virgin of the Harpies, by Andrea Del
Sarto — A139

Photogravure and Engraved
1980, Dec. 22   Perf. 11½
992 A139 200fr multi   8.00 8.00

Christmas.

Belgian War of Independence,
Engraving — A140

Belgian Independence Sesquicentennial:
Engravings of War of Independence.

1980, Dec. 29   Litho.   Perf. 12½
993	A140	20c	pale grn & brn	.25	.25
994	A140	30c	brn org & brn	.25	.25
995	A140	50c	lt bl & brn	.25	.25
996	A140	9fr	yel & brn	.25	.25
997	A140	10fr	brt lil & brn	.25	.25
998	A140	20fr	ap grn & brn	.45	.25
999	A140	70fr	pink & brn	1.90	.65
1000	A140	90fr	lem & brn	2.75	1.50
		Nos. 993-1000 (8)		6.35	3.65

Swamp
Drainage
A141

1980, Dec. 31   Photo.   Perf. 13½
1001	A141	20c	shown	.25	.25
1002	A141	30c	Fertilizer shed	.25	.25
1003	A141	1.50fr	Rice fields	.25	.25
1004	A141	8fr	Tree planting	.30	.25
1005	A141	10fr	Terrace plant-ing	.40	.25
1006	A141	40fr	Farm buildings	1.25	.50
1007	A141	90fr	Bean cultiva-tion	2.50	.90
1008	A141	100fr	Tea cultivation	2.75	1.10
		Nos. 1001-1008 (8)		7.95	3.75

Soil Conservation Year.

Pavetta Rwandensis — A142

30c, Cyrtorchis praetermissa. 50c, Pavonia
urens. 4fr, Cynorkis kassnerana. 5fr, Gardenia
ternifolia. 10fr, Leptactina platyphylla. 20fr,
Lobelia petiolata. 40fr, Tapinanthus brunneus.
70fr, Impatiens niamniamensis. 150fr, Dissotis
rwandensis.

1981, Apr. 6   Photo.   Perf. 13x13½
1009	A142	20c	shown	.25	.25
1010	A142	30c	multicolored	.25	.25
1011	A142	50c	multicolored	.25	.25
1012	A142	4fr	multicolored	.25	.25
1013	A142	5fr	multicolored	.25	.25
1014	A142	10fr	multicolored	.35	.25
1015	A142	20fr	multicolored	.60	.30
1016	A142	40fr	multicolored	1.50	.75
1017	A142	70fr	multicolored	2.75	1.25
1018	A142	150fr	multicolored	5.50	2.25
		Nos. 1009-1018 (10)		11.95	6.05

Girl
Knitting — A143

SOS Children's Village: Various children.

1981, Apr. 27   Perf. 13
1019	A143	20c	multi	.25	.25
1020	A143	30c	multi	.25	.25
1021	A143	50c	multi	.25	.25
1022	A143	1fr	multi	.25	.25
1023	A143	8fr	multi	.25	.25
1024	A143	10fr	multi	.30	.25
1025	A143	70fr	multi	1.75	.80
1026	A143	150fr	multi	4.25	1.60
		Nos. 1019-1026 (8)		7.55	3.90

Carolers, by
Norman
Rockwell
A144

Designs: Saturday Evening Post covers by
Norman Rockwell.

1981, May 11   Litho.   Perf. 13½x14
1027	A144	20c	multi	.25	.25
1028	A144	30c	multi	.25	.25
1029	A144	50c	multi	.25	.25
1030	A144	1fr	multi	.25	.25
1031	A144	8fr	multi	.40	.25
1032	A144	20fr	multi	.80	.25
1033	A144	50fr	multi	2.00	.95
1034	A144	70fr	multi	2.75	1.25
		Nos. 1027-1034 (8)		6.95	3.70

Cerval
A145

Meat-eating animals — 30c, Jackals. 2fr,
Genet. 2.50fr, Banded mongoose. 10fr, Zorille.
15fr, White-cheeked otter. 70fr, Golden wild
cat. 200fr, Hunting dog, vert.

1981, June 29   Photo.   Perf. 13½x14
1035	A145	20c	shown	.25	.25
1036	A145	30c	multicolored	.25	.25
1037	A145	2fr	multicolored	.30	.25
1038	A145	2.50fr	multicolored	.35	.25
1039	A145	10fr	multicolored	.60	.30
1040	A145	15fr	multicolored	1.25	.65
1041	A145	70fr	multicolored	4.25	2.25
1042	A145	200fr	multicolored	7.50	5.00
		Nos. 1035-1042 (8)		14.75	9.20

Drummer Sending Message — A146

30c, Map, communication waves. 2fr, Jet,
radar screen. 2.50fr, Satellite, teletape. 10fr,
Dish antenna. 15fr, Ship, navigation devices.
70fr, Helicopter. 200fr, Satellite with solar
panels.

1981, Sept. 1   Litho.   Perf. 13
1043	A146	20c	shown	.25	.25
1044	A146	30c	multicolored	.25	.25
1045	A146	2fr	multicolored	.25	.25
1046	A146	2.50fr	multicolored	.25	.25
1047	A146	10fr	multicolored	.30	.25
1048	A146	15fr	multicolored	.40	.25
1049	A146	70fr	multicolored	2.00	1.50
1050	A146	200fr	multicolored	6.25	3.50
		Nos. 1043-1050 (8)		9.95	6.50

1500th
Birth
Anniv. of
St.
Benedict
A147

Paintings and Frescoes of St. Benedict:
20c, Leaving his Parents, Mt. Oliveto Monastery, Maggiore. 30c, Oldest portrait, 10th
cent., St. Chrisogone Church, Rome, vert.
50c, Portrait, Virgin of the Misericord polyp-
tich, Borgo San Sepolcro. 4fr, Giving the
Rules of the order to his Monks, Mt. Oliveto
Monastery. 5fr, Monks at their Meal, Mt.
Oliveto Monastery. 20fr, Portrait, 13th cent.,
Lower Chruch of the Holy Spirit, Subiaco, vert.
70fr, Our Lady in Glory with Sts. Gregory and
Benedict, San Gimigniao, vert. 100fr, Priest
Carrying Easter Meal to St. Benedict, by Jan
van Coninxloo, 16th cent.

Perf. 13½x13, 13x13½
1981, Nov. 30   Photo.
1051	A147	20c	multi	.25	.25
1052	A147	30c	multi	.25	.25
1053	A147	50c	multi	.30	.25
1054	A147	4fr	multi	.30	.25
1055	A147	5fr	multi	.40	.25
1056	A147	20fr	multi	1.00	.50
1057	A147	70fr	multi	2.25	1.25
1058	A147	100fr	multi	3.25	2.50
		Nos. 1051-1058 (8)		8.00	5.50

Intl. Year of the
Disabled
A148

1981, Dec. 7   Litho.   Perf. 13
1059	A148	20c	Painting	.25	.25
1060	A148	30c	Soccer	.25	.25
1061	A148	4.50fr	Crocheting	.25	.25
1062	A148	5fr	Painting vase	.25	.25
1063	A148	10fr	Sawing	.30	.25
1064	A148	60fr	Sign language	1.40	.55
1065	A148	70fr	Doing puzzle	1.90	.65
1066	A148	100fr	Juggling	2.75	1.25
		Nos. 1059-1066 (8)		7.35	3.70

Souvenir Sheet

Noël 1981

RWANDA 200F

L'ADORATION DES MAGES
HUGO VANDER GOES
1440-1482
GALERIE DE DAHLEM - BERLIN

Christmas — A149

200fr, Adoration of the Kings, by van der Goes.

Photo. & Engr.

1981, Dec. 21			Perf. 13½	
1067	A149	200fr multicolored	7.50	7.50

Natl. Rural
Water
Supply
Year
A150

20c, Deer drinking. 30c, Women carrying water, vert. 50c, Pipeline. 10fr, Filing pan, vert. 19fr, Drinking. 70fr, Mother, child, vert. 100fr, Lake pumping station, vert.

1981, Dec. 28		Litho.	Perf. 12½	
1068	A150	20c multicolored	.25	.25
1069	A150	30c multicolored	.25	.25
1070	A150	50c multicolored	.25	.25
1071	A150	10fr multicolored	.25	.25
1072	A150	19fr multicolored	.55	.30
1073	A150	70fr multicolored	1.75	.80
1074	A150	100fr multicolored	2.75	1.10
		Nos. 1068-1074 (7)	6.05	3.20

World
Food
Day,
Oct. 16,
1981
A151

1982, Jan. 25		Litho.	Perf. 13	
1075	A151	20c Cattle	.25	.25
1076	A151	30c Bee	.25	.25
1077	A151	50c Fish	.25	.25
1078	A151	1fr Avocados	.25	.25
1079	A151	8fr Boy eating banana	.25	.25
1080	A151	20fr Sorghum	.60	.30
1081	A151	70fr Vegetables	2.00	.85
1082	A151	100fr Balanced diet	3.25	1.50
		Nos. 1075-1082 (8)	7.10	3.90

Hibiscus Berberidifolius — A152

No. 1084, Hypericum lanceolatum, vert. No. 1085, Canarina eminii. No. 1086, Polygala ruwenxoriensis. No. 1087, Kniphofia grantii, vert. No. 1088, Euphorbia candelabrum, vert. No. 1089, Disa erubescens, vert. No. 1090, Gloriosa simplex.

1982, June 14		Litho.	Perf. 13	
1083	A152	20c multi	.25	.25
1084	A152	30c multi	.25	.25
1085	A152	50c multi	.25	.25
1086	A152	4fr multi	.30	.25
1087	A152	35fr multi	.45	.25
1088	A152	35fr multi	1.40	.50
1089	A152	70fr multi	2.50	.90
1090	A152	80fr multi	3.00	1.60
		Nos. 1083-1090 (8)	8.40	4.25

20th Anniv. of Independence — A153

1982, June 28				
1091	A153	10fr Flags	.25	.25
1092	A153	20fr Hands releasing doves	.40	.25
1093	A153	30fr Flag, handshake	.70	.40
1094	A153	50fr Govt. buildings	1.50	.65
		Nos. 1091-1094 (4)	2.85	1.55

1982 World
Cup — A154

Designs: Various soccer players.

1982, July 6			Perf. 14x14½	
1095	A154	20c multi	.25	.25
1096	A154	30c multi	.25	.25
1097	A154	1.50fr multi	.25	.25
1098	A154	8fr multi	.25	.25
1099	A154	10fr multi	.25	.25
1100	A154	20fr multi	.65	.40
1101	A154	70fr multi	2.25	.90
1102	A154	90fr multi	3.00	1.25
		Nos. 1095-1102 (8)	7.15	3.80

TB Bacillus Centenary — A155

1982, Nov. 22		Litho.	Perf. 14½	
1103	A155	10fr Microscope, slide	.30	.25
1104	A155	20fr Serum, slide	.60	.25
1105	A155	70fr Lungs, slide	3.00	1.00
1106	A155	100fr Koch	3.50	1.75
		Nos. 1103-1106 (4)	7.40	3.25

Souvenir Sheets

Madam Recamier, by David — A156

PHILEXFRANCE '82 Intl. Stamp Exhibition, Paris, June 11-21: No. 1108, St. Anne and Virgin and Child with Franciscan Monk, by H. van der Goes. No. 1109, Liberty Guiding the People, by Delacroix. No. 1110, Pygmalion, by P. Delvaux.

1982, Dec. 11			Perf. 13½	
1107	A156	40fr multi	3.00	3.00
1108	A156	40fr multi	3.00	3.00
1109	A156	60fr multi	3.00	3.00
1110	A156	60fr multi	3.00	3.00
		Nos. 1107-1110 (4)	12.00	12.00

Souvenir Sheet

NOËL 1982

RWANDA 200F

REPOS PENDANT LA FUITE
B. E. MURILLO
1618 - 1682
ERMITAGE - LENINGRAD

Rest During the Flight to Egypt, by Murillo — A157

1982, Dec. 20			Photo. & Engr.	
1111	A157	200fr carmine rose	8.00	8.00

Christmas.

10th Anniv. of UN Conference on
Human Environment — A158

1982, Dec. 27		Litho.	Perf. 14	
1112	A158	20c Elephants	.25	.25
1113	A158	30c Lion	.25	.25
1114	A158	50c Flower	.25	.25
1115	A158	4fr Bull	.25	.25
1116	A158	5fr Deer	.25	.25
1117	A158	10fr Flower, diff.	.30	.25
1118	A158	20fr Zebras	.60	.30
1119	A158	40fr Crowned cranes	1.25	.65
1120	A158	50fr Bird	1.75	.85
1121	A158	70fr Woman pouring coffee beans	2.60	1.10
		Nos. 1112-1121 (10)	7.75	4.40

Scouting
Year
A159

20c, Animal first aid. 30c, Camp. 1.50fr, Campfire. 8fr, Scout giving sign. 10fr, Knot. 20fr, Camp, diff. 70fr, Chopping wood. 90fr, Sign, map.

		Perf. 13½x14½		
1983, Jan. 17			Photo.	
1122	A159	20c multicolored	.25	.25
1123	A159	30c multicolored	.25	.25
1124	A159	1.50fr multicolored	.25	.25
1125	A159	8fr multicolored	.50	.25
1126	A159	10fr multicolored	.60	.30
1127	A159	20fr multicolored	1.40	.65
1128	A159	70fr multicolored	4.75	2.25
1129	A159	90fr multicolored	7.00	2.75
		Nos. 1122-1129 (8)	15.00	6.95

For overprints see Nos. 1234-1241.

Nectar-sucking
Birds — A160

20c, Angola nectar bird. 30c, Royal nectar birds. 50c, Johnston's nectar bird. 4fr, Bronze nectar birds. 5fr, Collared souimangas. 10fr, Blue-headed nectar bird. 20fr, Purple-bellied nectar bird. 40fr, Copper nectar birds. 50fr, Olive-bellied nectar birds. 70fr, Red-breasted nectar bird.

		Perf. 14x14½, 14½x14		
1983, Jan. 31			Litho.	
1130	A160	20c multicolored	.25	.25
1131	A160	30c multicolored	.25	.25
1132	A160	50c multicolored	.25	.25
1133	A160	4fr multicolored	.30	.25
1134	A160	5fr multicolored	.40	.25
1135	A160	10fr multicolored	.85	.35
1136	A160	20fr multicolored	1.50	.50
1137	A160	40fr multicolored	2.75	1.10
1138	A160	50fr multicolored	3.50	1.50
1139	A160	70fr multicolored	5.50	2.25
		Nos. 1130-1139 (10)	15.55	6.95

30c, 4fr, 10fr, 40fr, 70fr horiz. Inscribed 1982.

Soil Erosion
Prevention
A161

20c, Driving cattle. 30c, Pineapple field. 50c, Interrupted ditching. 9fr, Hedges, ditches. 10fr, Reafforestation. 20fr, Anti-erosion barriers. 30fr, Contour planting. 50fr, Terracing. 60fr, Protection of river banks. 70fr, Fallow, planted strips.

1983, Feb. 14			Perf. 14½	
1140	A161	20c multicolored	.25	.25
1141	A161	30c multicolored	.25	.25
1142	A161	50c multicolored	.25	.25
1143	A161	9fr multicolored	.30	.25
1144	A161	10fr multicolored	.35	.30
1145	A161	20fr multicolored	.50	.25
1146	A161	30fr multicolored	.80	.60
1147	A161	50fr multicolored	1.60	1.00
1148	A161	60fr multicolored	1.90	1.10
1149	A161	70fr multicolored	2.75	1.25
		Nos. 1140-1149 (10)	8.95	5.60

For overprints & surcharges see Nos. 1247-1255.

Cardinal Cardijn
(1882-1967)
A162

Young Catholic Workers Movement Activities. Inscribed 1982.

1983, Feb. 22			Perf. 12½x13	
1150	A162	20c Feeding ducks	.25	.25
1151	A162	30c Harvesting bananas	.25	.25
1152	A162	50c Carrying melons	.25	.25
1153	A162	10fr Teacher	.30	.25
1154	A162	19fr Shoemakers	.40	.25
1155	A162	20fr Growing millet	.50	.25
1156	A162	70fr Embroidering	2.00	.75
1157	A162	80fr shown	2.25	1.00
		Nos. 1150-1157 (8)	6.20	3.25

Gorilla — A163

Various gorillas. Nos. 1158-1163 horiz.

1983, Mar. 14			Perf. 14	
1158	A163	20c multi	.25	.25
1159	A163	30c multi	.25	.25
1160	A163	9.50fr multi	.35	.25
1161	A163	10fr multi	.45	.35
1162	A163	20fr multi	1.25	.65
1163	A163	30fr multi	1.75	.85
1164	A163	60fr multi	3.00	1.50
1165	A163	70fr multi	3.25	2.00
		Nos. 1158-1165 (8)	10.55	6.10

Souvenir Sheet

The Granduca Madonna, by Raphael — A164

1983, Dec. 19   **Perf. 11½**
Typo. & Engr.
1166 A164 200fr multi   8.00 8.00
Christmas.

Local Trees — A165

No. 1167, Hagenia abyssinica. No. 1168, Dracaena steudneri. No. 1169, Phoenix reclinata. No. 1170, Podocarpus milanjianus. No. 1171, Entada abyssinica. No. 1172, Parinari excelsa. No. 1173, Newtonia buchananii. No. 1174, Acacia gerrardi, vert.

1984, Jan. 15   **Litho.**   **Perf. 13½x13**
1167	A165	20c multicolored	.25	.25
1168	A165	30c multicolored	.25	.25
1169	A165	50c multicolored	.25	.25
1170	A165	10fr multicolored	.30	.25
1171	A165	19fr multicolored	.75	.30
1172	A165	70fr multicolored	2.00	.80
1173	A165	100fr multicolored	3.25	1.10
1174	A165	200fr multicolored	5.00	2.25
		Nos. 1167-1174 (8)	12.05	5.45

World Communications Year — A166

1984, May 21   **Litho.**   **Perf. 12½**
1175	A166	20c Train	.25	.25
1176	A166	30c Ship	.25	.25
1177	A166	4.50fr Radio	.25	.25
1178	A166	10fr Telephone	.30	.25
1179	A166	15fr Mail	.40	.25
1180	A166	50fr Jet	1.40	.50
1181	A166	70fr Satellite, TV screen	1.90	.75
1182	A166	100fr Satellite	3.00	1.00
		Nos. 1175-1182 (8)	7.75	3.50

1st Manned Flight Bicent. — A167

Historic flights: 20c, Le Martial, Sept. 19, 1783. 30c, La Montgolfiere, Nov. 21, 1783. 50c, Charles and Robert, Dec. 1, 1783, and Blanchard, Mar. 2, 1784. 9fr, Jean-Pierre

Blanchard and wife in balloon. 10fr, Blanchard and Jeffries, 1785. 50fr, E. Demuyter, 1937. 80fr, Propane gas balloons. 200fr, Abruzzo, Anderson and Newman, 1978.

1984, June 4   **Litho.**   **Perf. 13**
1183	A167	20c multi	.25	.25
1184	A167	30c multi	.25	.25
1185	A167	50c multi	.25	.25
1186	A167	9fr multi	.30	.25
1187	A167	10fr multi	.35	.25
1188	A167	50fr multi	1.60	.75
1189	A167	80fr multi	2.25	1.00
1190	A167	200fr multi	6.50	3.00
		Nos. 1183-1190 (8)	11.75	6.00

1984 Summer Olympics — A168

1984, July 16   **Perf. 14**
1191	A168	20c Equestrian	.25	.25
1192	A168	30c Wind surfing	.25	.25
1193	A168	50c Soccer	.30	.25
1194	A168	9fr Swimming	.70	.35
1195	A168	10fr Field hockey	.80	.40
1196	A168	40fr Fencing	2.00	1.50
1197	A168	80fr Running	3.25	2.50
1198	A168	200fr Boxing	8.00	4.75
		Nos. 1191-1198 (8)	15.55	10.25

Zebras and Buffaloes — A169

20c, Zebra with colt. 30c, Buffalo with calf, vert. 50c, Two zebras, vert. 9fr, Zebras fighting. 10fr, Buffalo, vert. 80fr, Zebra herd. 100fr, Zebra, vert. 200fr, Buffalo.

1984, Nov. 26   **Litho.**   **Perf. 13**
1199	A169	20c multicolored	.25	.25
1200	A169	30c multicolored	.25	.25
1201	A169	50c multicolored	.25	.25
1202	A169	9fr multicolored	.60	.25
1203	A169	10fr multicolored	.70	.30
1204	A169	80fr multicolored	3.00	1.50
1205	A169	100fr multicolored	4.00	2.25
1206	A169	200fr multicolored	8.50	4.00
		Nos. 1199-1206 (8)	17.55	9.05

Souvenir Sheet

Christmas 1984 — A170

Design: Virgin and Child, by Correggio.

1984, Dec. 24   **Typo. & Engr.**
1207 A170 200fr multicolored   7.50 7.50

Gorilla Gorilla Beringei — A171

10fr, Adults and young. 15fr, Adults. 25fr, Female holding young. 30fr, Three adults. 200fr, Baby climbing branch, vert.

1985, Mar. 25   **Litho.**   **Perf. 13**
1208	A171	10fr multi	2.75	1.75
1209	A171	15fr multi	4.50	2.75
1210	A171	25fr multi	9.00	5.00
1211	A171	30fr multi	11.00	5.00
		Nos. 1208-1211 (4)	27.25	15.00

Souvenir Sheet
Perf. 11½x12
1212 A171 200fr multi   15.00 15.00
No. 1212 contains one 37x52mm stamp.

Self-Sufficiency in Food Production — A172

Designs: 20c, Raising chickens and turkeys. 30c, Pineapple harvest. 50c, Animal husbandry. 9fr, Grain products. 10fr, Education. 50fr, Sowing grain. 80fr, Food reserves. 100fr, Banana harvest.

1985, Mar. 30
1213	A172	20c multi	.25	.25
1214	A172	30c multi	.25	.25
1215	A172	50c multi	.25	.25
1216	A172	9fr multi	.25	.25
1217	A172	10fr multi	.30	.25
1218	A172	50fr multi	1.10	.60
1219	A172	80fr multi	1.75	1.10
1220	A172	100fr multi	2.50	2.25
		Nos. 1213-1220 (8)	6.65	5.20

Natl. Redevelopment Movement, 10th Anniv. — A173

1985, July 5
1221	A173	10fr multi	.25	.25
1222	A173	30fr multi	1.00	.25
1223	A173	70fr multi	2.00	1.00
		Nos. 1221-1223 (3)	3.25	1.50

UN, 40th Anniv. A174

1985, July 25
1224	A174	50fr multi	1.75	1.50
1225	A174	100fr multi	3.25	2.50

Audubon Birth Bicent. — A175

Illustrations of North American bird species by John J. Audubon — 10fr, Barn owl. 20fr, White-faced owl. 40fr, Red-breasted hummingbird. 80fr, Warbler.

1985, Sept. 18
1226	A175	10fr multicolored	2.50	1.00
1227	A175	20fr multicolored	3.00	2.00
1228	A175	40fr multicolored	6.00	4.00
1229	A175	80fr multicolored	10.00	7.00
		Nos. 1226-1229 (4)	21.50	14.00

Intl. Youth Year A176

1985, Oct. 14
1230	A176	7fr Education and agriculture	.25	.25
1231	A176	9fr Bicycling	.25	.25
1232	A176	44fr Construction	1.25	.70
1233	A176	80fr Schoolroom	2.25	1.40
		Nos. 1230-1233 (4)	4.00	2.60

Nos. 1122-1129 Ovptd. in Green or Rose Violet with the Girl Scout Trefoil and "1910/1985"

1985, Nov. 25   **Perf. 13½x14½**
1234	A159	20c multi	.25	.25
1235	A159	30c multi (RV)	.25	.25
1236	A159	1.50fr multi	.50	.25
1237	A159	8fr multi (RV)	1.00	.25
1238	A159	10fr multi	1.50	.75
1239	A159	20fr multi	3.00	1.25
1240	A159	70fr multi (RV)	8.00	2.50
1241	A159	90fr multi	12.00	5.00
		Nos. 1234-1241 (8)	26.50	10.50

Natl. Girl Scout Movement, 75th anniv.

Souvenir Sheet

Adoration of the Magi, by Titian — A177

Photo. & Engr.
1985, Dec. 24   **Perf. 11½**
1242 A177 200fr violet   8.50 8.50

Christmas.

Transportation and Communication — A178

1986, Jan. 27   Litho.   Perf. 13
1243 A178 10fr Articulated truck .30 .25
1244 A178 30fr Hand-canceling
letters 1.00 .45
1245 A178 40fr Kigali Satellite
Station 1.50 .70
Size: 52x34mm
1246 A178 80fr Kayibanda Airport, Kigali 2.00 1.50
Nos. 1243-1246 (4) 4.80 2.90

Nos. 1141-1149 Surcharged or Ovptd. with Silver Bar and "ANNEE 1986 / INTENSIFICATION AGRICOLE"

1986, May 5   Litho.   Perf. 14½
1247 A161 9fr #1143 1.25 .50
1248 A161 10fr on 30c #1141 1.25 .50
1249 A161 10fr on 50c #1142 1.50 .50
1250 A161 10fr #1144 1.50 .50
1251 A161 20fr #1145 2.50 1.00
1252 A161 30fr #1146 3.75 1.50
1253 A161 50fr #1147 5.00 2.25
1254 A161 60fr #1148 7.00 3.50
1255 A161 70fr #1149 8.00 4.50
Nos. 1247-1255 (9) 31.75 14.75

1986 World Cup Soccer
Championships, Mexico — A179

Various soccer plays, natl. flags.

1986, June 16   Perf. 13
1256 A179 2fr Morocco, England .50 .25
1257 A179 4fr Paraguay, Iraq .75 .25
1258 A179 5fr Brazil, Spain 1.00 .50
1259 A179 10fr Italy, Argentina 1.75 .75
1260 A179 40fr Mexico, Belgium 6.00 1.75
1261 A179 45fr France, USSR 8.00 2.50
Nos. 1256-1261 (6) 18.00 6.00

For overprints see Nos. 1360-1365.

Akagera Natl. Park — A180

1986, Dec. 15   Litho.   Perf. 13
1262 A180 4fr Antelopes .80 .25
1263 A180 7fr Shoebills .80 .30
1264 A180 9fr Cape elands 1.10 .30
1265 A180 10fr Giraffe 1.10 .30
1266 A180 80fr Elephants 6.50 3.00
1267 A180 90fr Crocodiles 7.75 3.00
Size: 48x34mm
1268 A180 100fr Weaver birds 7.75 5.00
1269 A180 100fr Pelican,
zebras 7.75 5.00
a. Pair, #1268-1269 + label 25.00 25.00
Nos. 1262-1269 (8) 33.55 17.15

No. 1269a has continuous design.
A souvenir sheet containing five No. 1269a
exists. Value $210.

Christmas, Intl. Peace Year — A181

1986, Dec. 24   Litho.   Perf. 13
1270 A181 10fr shown .25 .25
1271 A181 15fr Dove, Earth .75 .50
1272 A181 30fr like 10fr 1.00 .80
1273 A181 70fr like 15fr 2.25 2.25
Nos. 1270-1273 (4) 4.25 3.80

UN Child
Survival
Campaign
A182

1987, Feb. 13
1274 A182 4fr Breast feeding .25 .25
1275 A182 6fr Rehydration therapy .30 .25
1276 A182 10fr Immunization .50 .30
1277 A182 70fr Growth monitoring 3.25 1.75
Nos. 1274-1277 (4) 4.30 2.55

Year of Natl. Self-sufficiency in Food
Production — A183

1987, June 15   Litho.   Perf. 13
1278 A183 5fr Farm .25 .25
1279 A183 7fr Storing produce .25 .25
1280 A183 40fr Boy carrying basket of fish, pro-
duce 1.50 .80
1281 A183 60fr Tropical fruit 2.00 1.25
Nos. 1278-1281 (4) 4.00 2.55

Nos. 1279-1281 vert.

Natl. Independence, 25th
Anniv. — A184

10fr, Pres. Habyarimana, soldiers, farmers.
40fr, Pres. officiating government session.
70fr, Pres., Pope John Paul II. 100fr, Pres.

1987, July 1
1283 A184 10fr multi .50 .30
1284 A184 40fr multi 1.60 1.25
1285 A184 70fr multi 2.75 2.25
1286 A184 100fr multi, vert. 3.75 3.25
Nos. 1283-1286 (4) 8.60 7.05

A 5fr value exists but was not officially
issued. Value $100.

Fruit
A185

1987, Sept. 28
1287 A185 10fr Bananas,
vert. .40 .25
1288 A185 40fr Pineapples 1.25 1.00
1289 A185 80fr Papayas 2.75 2.25
1290 A185 90fr Avocados 3.25 2.50
1291 A185 100fr Strawberries,
vert. 4.25 3.00
Nos. 1287-1291 (5) 11.90 9.00

Leopards — A186

No. 1292, Female, cub. No. 1293, Three
cubs playing. No. 1294, Adult attacking
gazelle. No. 1295, In tree. No. 1296, Leaping
from tree.

1987, Nov. 18   Litho.   Perf. 13
1292 A186 50fr multi 6.00 3.00
1293 A186 50fr multi 6.00 3.00
1294 A186 50fr multi 6.00 3.00
1295 A186 50fr multi 6.00 3.00
1296 A186 50fr multi 6.00 3.00
a. Strip of 5, Nos. 1292-1296 30.00 15.00
Nos. 1292-1296 (5) 30.00 15.00

A souvenir sheet containing five No. 1296a
exists. Value $200.

Intl. Year of the Volunteer — A187

5fr, Constructing village water system. 12fr,
Education, vert. 20fr, Modern housing, vert.
60fr, Animal husbandry, vert.

1987, Dec. 12
1297 A187 5fr multicolored .25 .25
1298 A187 12fr multicolored .50 .25
1299 A187 20fr multicolored 1.00 .50
1300 A187 60fr multicolored 2.75 2.00
Nos. 1297-1300 (4) 4.50 3.00

Souvenir Sheet

Virgin and Child, by Fra Angelico
(c. 1387-1455) — A188

1987, Dec. 24   Engr.   Perf. 11½
1301 A188 200fr deep mag &
dull blue 9.00 9.00

Christmas.

Maintenance of the Rural Economy
Year — A189

1988, June 13   Litho.   Perf. 13
1302 A189 10fr Furniture store .35 .25
1303 A189 40fr Dairy farm 1.00 1.00
1304 A189 60fr Produce market 1.75 1.25
1305 A189 80fr Fruit market 2.50 2.00
Nos. 1302-1305 (4) 5.60 4.50

Primates, Nyungwe Forest — A190

2fr, Chimpanzee. 3fr, Black and white
colobus. 10fr, Pygmy galago. 90fr,
Cercopithecidae ascagne.

1988, Sept. 15   Litho.   Perf. 13
1306 A190 2fr multicolored .50 .25
1307 A190 3fr multicolored .70 1.25
1308 A190 10fr multicolored 2.00 .75
1309 A190 90fr multicolored 10.50 4.50
Nos. 1306-1309 (4) 13.70 6.75

1988 Summer Olympics,
Seoul — A191

1988, Sept. 19
1310 A191 5fr Boxing .35 .25
1311 A191 7fr Relay .40 .25
1312 A191 8fr Table tennis .50 .25
1313 A191 10fr Women's running 1.50 .50
1314 A191 90fr Hurdles 5.75 2.50
Nos. 1310-1314 (5) 8.50 3.75

Organization of
African Unity,
25th
Anniv. — A192

1988, Nov. 30   Litho.   Perf. 13
1315 A192 5fr shown .25 .25
1316 A192 7fr Handshake, map .25 .25
1317 A192 8fr "OAU" in brick,
map .25 .25
1318 A192 90fr Slogan 3.00 2.25
Nos. 1315-1318 (4) 3.75 3.00

Souvenir Sheet

Detail of The Virgin and the Soup, by
Paolo Veronese — A193

1988, Dec. 23   Engr.   Perf. 13½
1319 A193 200fr multicolored 7.00 7.00

Christmas. Margin is typographed.

Intl. Red Cross and Red Crescent
Organizations, 125th Annivs. — A194

1988, Dec. 30   Litho.   Perf. 13
1320	A194	10fr Refugees	.40	.25
1321	A194	30fr First aid	1.00	.75
1322	A194	40fr Elderly	1.35	1.00
1323	A194	100fr Travelling doctor	3.25	2.50
	Nos. 1320-1323 (4)		6.00	4.50

Nos. 1322-1323 vert.

Medicinal
Plants — A195

5fr, Plectranthus barbatus. 10fr, Tetradenia
riparia. 20fr, Hygrophila auriculata. 40fr,
Datura stramonium. 50fr, Pavetta ternifolia.

1989, Feb. 15   Litho.   Perf. 13
1324	A195	5fr multicolored	*1.00*	*.50*
1325	A195	10fr multicolored	*2.00*	*1.00*
1326	A195	20fr multicolored	*4.00*	*2.00*
1327	A195	40fr multicolored	*8.00*	*4.00*
1328	A195	50fr multicolored	*14.00*	*7.00*
	Nos. 1324-1328 (5)		*29.00*	*14.50*

Interparliamentary Union,
Cent. — A196

1989, Oct. 20   Litho.   Perf. 13
1329	A196	10fr shown	.35	.25
1330	A196	30fr Hills, lake	1.00	.75
1331	A196	70fr Hills, stream	2.25	2.00
1332	A196	90fr Sun rays, hills	2.75	2.25
	Nos. 1329-1332 (4)		6.35	5.25

Souvenir Sheet

Christmas — A197

Adoration of the Magi by Rubens.

1989, Dec. 29   Engr.   Perf. 11½
1333	A197	100fr blk, red & grn	8.75	8.75

Rural Organization Year — A198

Designs: 10fr, Making pottery. 70fr, Carrying produce to market. 90fr, Firing clay pots.
100fr, Clearing land.

1989, Dec. 29   Litho.   Perf. 13½x13
1334	A198	10fr multi	.50	.25
1335	A198	70fr multi, vert.	2.00	1.50
1336	A198	90fr multi	2.50	2.00
1337	A198	200fr multi	6.00	4.75
	Nos. 1334-1337 (4)		11.00	8.50

Revolution, 30th Anniv. (in
1989) — A199

Designs: 10fr, Improved living conditions.
60fr, Couple, farm tools. 70fr, Modernization.
100fr, Flag, map, native.

1990, Jan. 22   Perf. 13
1338	A199	10fr multi	.40	.40
1339	A199	60fr multi, vert.	2.00	1.25
1340	A199	70fr multi	2.25	1.75
1341	A199	100fr multi	4.00	2.50
	Nos. 1338-1341 (4)		8.65	5.90

Inscribed 1989.

French Revolution, Bicent. (in
1989) — A200

Paintings of the Revolution: 10fr, Triumph of
Marat by Boilly. 60fr, Rouget de Lisle singing
La Marseillaise by Pils. 70fr, Oath of the Ten-
nis Court by David. 100fr, Trial of Louis XVI by
Court.

1990, Jan. 22
1342	A200	10fr multicolored	.40	.40
1343	A200	60fr multicolored	2.00	2.00
1344	A200	70fr multicolored	2.25	2.25
1345	A200	100fr multicolored	4.00	4.00
	Nos. 1342-1345 (4)		8.65	8.65

Inscribed 1989.

African Development Bank, 25th
Anniv. (in 1989) — A201

1990, Feb. 22   Perf. 13½x13
1346	A201	10fr Building con-
struction	.45	.25
1347	A201	20fr Harvesting	.80	.75
1348	A201	40fr Cultivation	1.50	1.00
1349	A201	90fr Building, truck,
harvesters	3.25	2.50
	Nos. 1346-1349 (4)		6.00	4.50

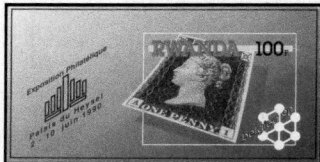

Belgica '90, Intl. Philatelic
Exhibition — A202

No. 1350, Great Britain #1. No. 1351,
Belgium #B1011. No. 1352, Rwanda #516.

1990, May 21   Litho.   Imperf.
1350	A202	100fr multi	4.25	4.25
1351	A202	100fr multi	4.25	4.25
1352	A202	100fr multi	4.25	4.25
	Nos. 1350-1352 (3)		12.75	12.75

Visit of
Pope
John
Paul II
A203

1990, Aug. 27   Litho.   Perf. 13½x13
1353	A203	10fr shown	3.00	3.00
1354	A203	70fr Holding cruci-
fix	17.00	17.00

Souvenir Sheet
Perf. 11½
1355	A203	100fr Hands to-
gether	30.00	30.00

No. 1355 contains one 36x51mm stamp.

Intl.
Literacy
Year
A204

Designs: 10fr, Teacher at blackboard. 20fr,
Teacher seated at desk. 50fr, Small outdoor
class. 90fr, Large outdoor class.

1991, Jan. 25   Litho.   Perf. 13½x13
1356	A204	10fr multicolored	.50	.25
1357	A204	20fr multicolored	.75	.40
1358	A204	50fr multicolored	1.75	1.25
1359	A204	90fr multicolored	3.25	1.75
	Nos. 1356-1359 (4)		6.25	3.65

Nos. 1256-
1261 Ovptd.
in Black on Silver

1990, May 25   Litho.   Perf. 13
1360	A179	2fr on No. 1256	3.00	3.00
1361	A179	4fr on No. 1257	4.00	4.00
1362	A179	5fr on No. 1258	5.00	5.00
1363	A179	10fr on No. 1259	9.00	9.00
1364	A179	40fr on No. 1260	25.00	25.00
1365	A179	45fr on No. 1261	30.00	30.00
	Nos. 1360-1365 (6)		76.00	76.00

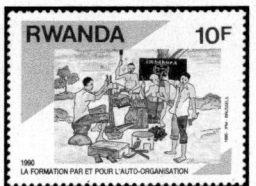

Self-help Organizations — A205

No. 1366, Tool making. No. 1367, Animal
husbandry. No. 1368, Textile manufacturing.
No. 1369, Road construction.

1991, Jan. 25   Litho.   Perf. 13½x13
1366	A205	10fr multicolored	.60	.30
1367	A205	20fr multicolored	1.25	.60
1368	A205	50fr multicolored	2.00	1.25
1369	A205	90fr multicolored	4.00	2.50
	Nos. 1366-1369 (4)		7.85	4.65

Dated 1990.

A206

5fr, Statue of Madonna. 15fr, One of the
Order's nuns. 70fr, Group photo, vert. 110fr,
Cardinal Lavigerie.

1992, Oct. 1   Litho.   Perf. 14
1370	A206	5fr multi, vert.	1.75	1.75
1371	A206	15fr multi, vert.	6.25	6.25
1372	A206	70fr multi	20.00	20.00
1373	A206	110fr multi, vert.	37.50	37.50
	Nos. 1370-1373 (4)		65.50	65.50

Cardinal Lavigerie, Founder of the Order of
White Fathers and Sisters, Death Cent.

1992 Summer Olympic Games,
Barcelona — A207

Designs: a, 20fr, Runners. b, 30fr, Swimmer. c, 90fr, Soccer players.

1993, Feb. 1
1374	A207	Sheet of 3, #a.-c.	40.00	40.00

Protection
of
Vegetable
Crops
A208

Designs: 10fr, Removing parasites and
weeds. 15fr, Spraying pesticides. 70fr,
Zonocerus elegans on plants. 110fr,
Phenacoccus manihoti.

1993, June 15   Litho.   Perf. 14
1375	A208	10fr multi	5.00	5.00
1376	A208	15fr multi	8.50	8.50
1377	A208	70fr multi	37.50	37.50
1378	A208	110fr multi	62.50	62.50
	Nos. 1375-1378 (4)		113.50	113.50

World Conference on Nutrition,
Rome — A209

Designs: 15fr, Man fishing. 50fr, People at fruit market. 100fr, Man milking cow. 500fr, Mother breastfeeding.

1992, Dec.		Litho.	Perf. 14	
1381	A209	15fr multicolored	1.25	1.25
1382	A209	50fr multicolored	4.00	4.00
1383	A209	100fr multicolored	6.50	6.50
1384	A209	500fr multicolored	40.00	40.00
		Nos. 1381-1384 (4)	51.75	51.75

Wildlife
A210

1998		Litho.	Perf. 14	
1385	A210	15fr Toad	3.00	3.00
1386	A210	100fr Snail	5.00	5.00
1387	A210	150fr Porcupine	6.00	6.00
1388	A210	300fr Chameleon	8.00	8.00
a.		Souvenir sheet, #1385-1388, Imperf.	24.00	24.00
		Nos. 1385-1388 (4)	22.00	22.00

Plants
A211

15fr, Opuntia. 100fr, Gloriosa superba. 150fr, Markhamia lutea. 300fr, Hagenia abyssinica.

1998		Litho.	Perf. 14	
1389	A211	15fr multi, vert.	3.00	3.00
1390	A211	100fr multi, vert.	5.00	5.00
1391	A211	150fr multi, vert.	6.00	6.00
1392	A211	300fr multi	8.00	8.00
a.		Souvenir sheet, #1389-1392, imperf.	26.00	26.00
		Nos. 1389-1392 (4)	22.00	22.00

Remembrance of Genocide
Victims — A212

20fr, Map, coffins, horiz. 30fr, Orphans, horiz. 400fr, People protesting.

1999 (?)		Litho.	Perf. 14	
1392B	A212	20fr multi	1.50	1.50
1392C	A212	30fr multi	2.50	2.50
1393	A212	200fr multi	11.50	11.50
1394	A212	400fr multi	20.00	20.00

Rwandan postal officials have declared "illegal" sets depicting: Millennium (eleven sheets of 9 with various subjects), Pornography (two sheets of 9), Chess (sheet of 9 unoverprinted, and also overprinted in Russian), Double-decker buses (sheet of 9), Butterflies (sheet of 9), Hot air balloons (sheet of 9), Old automobiles (sheet of 9), Motorcycle racing (sheet of 9), Trains (sheet of 9), Fungi (sheet of 6), Cats (sheet of 6), Roses (sheet of 6).

Sheet of six stamps of various values depicting Wildlife Trusts (Snakes).

Souvenir sheet of two 500fr stamps depicting Mother Teresa.

Souvenir sheet of one 500fr stamp depicting Wildlife Trusts (Snakes).

AIDS
Prevention
for
Children
A213

AIDS Prevention for Children — A214

Designs: 20fr, Children, red ribbon, tree. 30fr, Red ribbon, hands, children, vert. 200fr, Children, hand, red ribbon.

Perf. 13½x13¾, 13¾x13½

2003, Jan. 1			Litho.	
1395	A213	20fr multi	—	—
1396	A213	100fr multi	—	—
1397	A214	200fr multi	—	—
1398	A214	500fr multi	—	—

Art and
Culture — A215

Designs: 34fr, Two dancers. 300fr, People dancing. 500fr, Basket weaving. 600fr, Face looking through torn fabric. 1000fr, Containers, horiz.

Perf. 13¾x13¼, 13¼x13¾

2010, Nov. 15			Litho.	
1399	A215	34fr multi	2.10	2.10
1400	A215	300fr multi	4.25	4.25
1401	A215	500fr multi	8.50	8.50
1402	A215	600fr multi	11.00	11.00
1403	A215	1000fr multi	19.00	19.00

Mountain Gorilla — A216

Design: 30fr, Gorilla and foliage. 40fr, Adults and juveniles. 2000fr, Side view of gorilla. 5000fr, Gorilla sitting in front of trees.

Perf. 13¼x13¾

2010, Nov. 15			Litho.	
1404	A216	30fr multi	1.60	1.60
1405	A216	40fr multi	2.10	2.10
1406	A216	2000fr multi	25.00	25.00
1407	A216	5000fr multi	50.00	50.00

SEMI-POSTAL STAMPS

No. 305 Srchd. in Black and Ovptd. in Brown:
"SECHERESSE/SOLIDARITE AFRICAINE"

1973, Aug. 23		Photo.	Perf. 13	
B1	A53	100fr + 50fr multi	6.00	6.00

African solidarity in drought emergency.

Nos. 349-350 Srchd. and Ovptd. Like Nos. 693-698

1975, Nov. 10		Litho.	Perf. 13	
B2	A60	50fr + 25fr multi	2.25	2.00
B3	A60	90fr + 25fr multi	3.00	2.50

African solidarity in drought emergency.

AIR POST STAMPS

African Postal Union Issue, 1967
Common Design Type

1967, Sept. 18		Engr.	Perf. 13	
C1	CD124	6fr brn, rose cl & gray	.30	.25
C2	CD124	18fr brt lil, ol brn & plum	.60	.35
C3	CD124	30fr grn, dp bl & red	1.40	.65
		Nos. C1-C3 (3)	2.30	1.25

PHILEXAFRIQUE Issue

Alexandre Lenoir, by Jacques L. David
AP1

1968, Dec. 30		Photo.	Perf. 12½	
C4	AP1	100fr emerald & multi	3.25	1.75

Issued to publicize PHILEXAFRIQUE, Philatelic exhibition in Abidjan, Feb. 14-23, 1969. Printed with alternating emerald label.

2nd PHILEXAFRIQUE Issue

Ruanda-Urundi No. 123, Cowherd and Lake Victoria — AP2

1969, Feb. 14		Litho.	Perf. 14	
C5	AP2	50fr multicolored	1.75	1.25

Opening of PHILEXAFRIQUE, Abidjan, 2/14.

Painting Type of Regular Issue

Paintings and Music: 50fr, The Music Lesson, by Fragonard. 100fr, Angels' Concert, by Memling, horiz.

1969, Mar. 31		Photo.	Perf. 13	
C6	A49	50fr gold & multi	1.75	1.25
C7	A49	100fr gold & multi	3.25	2.50

African Postal Union Issue, 1971
Common Design Type

Design: Woman and child of Rwanda and UAMPT Building, Brazzaville, Congo.

1971, Nov. 13			Perf. 13x13½	
C8	CD135	100fr blue & multi	2.75	2.50

No. C8 Overprinted in Red

a

b

1973, Sept. 17		Photo.	Perf. 13x13½	
C9	CD135(a)	100fr multi	4.50	4.50
C10	CD135(b)	100fr multi	4.50	4.50
a.		Pair, #C9-C10	11.00	11.00

3rd Conference of French-speaking countries, Liège, Sept. 15-Oct. 14. Overprints alternate checkerwise in same sheet.

Sassenage Castle, Grenoble — AP3

1977, June 20		Litho.	Perf. 12½	
C11	AP3	50fr multi	2.00	1.25

Intl. French Language Council, 10th anniv.

Philexafrique II-Essen Issue
Common Design Types

Designs: No. C12, Okapi, Rwanda #239. No. C13, Woodpecker, Oldenburg #4.

1978, Nov. 1		Litho.	Perf. 12½	
C12	CD138	30fr multi	1.50	1.50
C13	CD139	30fr multi	1.50	1.50
a.		Pair, #C12-C13	4.00	4.00

SAAR

'sär

LOCATION — On the Franco-German border southeast of Luxembourg
POP. — 1,400,000 (1959)
AREA — 991 sq. mi.
CAPITAL — Saarbrücken

A former German territory, the Saar was administered by the League of Nations 1920-35. After a January 12, 1935, plebiscite, it returned to Germany, and the use of German stamps was resumed. After World War II, France occupied the Saar and later established a protectorate. The provisional semi-independent State of Saar was established Jan. 1, 1951. France returned the Saar to the German Federal Republic Jan. 1, 1957.

Saar stamps were discontinued in 1959 and replaced by stamps of the German Federal Republic.

100 Pfennig = 1 Mark
100 Centimes = 1 Franc (1921)

Catalogue values for unused stamps in this country are for Never Hinged items, beginning with Scott 221 in the regular postage section, and Scott B85 in the semi-postal section.

Watermark

Wmk. 285 — Marbleized Pattern

German Stamps of 1906-19 Overprinted

Perf. 14, 14½

1920, Jan. 30   **Wmk. 125**

1	A22	2pf gray	1.60	4.50
c.		Inverted overprint	325.00	550.00
d.		Double overprint	2,000.	2,600.
1A	A16	2pf blue gray (ovptd. on Germany #80)	8,500.	
2	A22	2½pf gray	9.50	27.50
c.		Inverted overprint	350.00	650.00
3	A16	3pf brown	1.00	2.75
c.		Inverted overprint	325.00	550.00
4	A16	5pf deep green	.50	1.00
c.		Inverted overprint	600.00	—
f.		Double overprint	800.00	1,450.
5	A22	7½pf orange	.65	1.75
c.		Inverted overprint	—	800.00
6	A16	10pf carmine	.55	1.25
c.		Inverted overprint	550.00	1,050.
d.		Double overprint	725.00	1,200.
7	A22	15pf dk violet	.50	1.00
c.		Double overprint	800.00	1,450.
8	A16	20pf blue violet	.50	1.00
c.		Double overprint	600.00	950.00
9	A16	25pf red org & blk, *yellow*	9.50	20.00
c.		Inverted overprint	800.00	2,400.
10	A16	30pf org & blk, *yel buff*	17.50	35.00
11	A22	35pf red brown	.55	1.25
c.		Inverted overprint	475.00	1,050.
12	A16	40pf dp lake & blk	.55	1.25
c.		Inverted overprint	475.00	1,050.
13	A16	50pf pur & blk, *yel buff*	.55	1.60
c.		Inverted overprint	400.00	725.00
14	A16	60pf dp gray lilac	.55	1.25
15	A16	75pf green & blk	.55	1.25
c.		Inverted overprint	240.00	400.00
16	A16	80pf lake & blk, *rose*	190.00	275.00

Overprinted

Type I

17	A17	1m carmine rose	27.50	40.00
a.		Inverted overprint	725.00	1,450.
b.		Double overprint	800.00	1,450.

Type II

17f	A17	1m carmine rose	40.00	80.00
		Nos. 1-17 (17)	262.05	417.35

Three types of overprint exist on Nos. 1-5, 12, 13; two types on Nos. 6-11, 14-16. For detailed listings, see the *Scott Classic Specialized Catalogue*.

The 3m type A19 exists overprinted like No. 17, but was not issued. Values: unused $16,000; never hinged $33,000.
Overprint forgeries exist.

Bavarian Stamps of 1914-16 Overprinted

Perf. 14x14½

1920, Mar. 1   **Wmk. 95**

19	A10	2pf gray	900.00	4,750.
20	A10	3pf brown	80.00	650.00
21	A10	5pf yellow grn	.75	1.60
a.		Double overprint	800.00	
22	A10	7½pf green	32.50	275.00
23	A10	10pf carmine rose	.75	1.60
a.		Double overprint	325.00	650.00
24	A10	15pf vermilion	.95	1.90
a.		Double overprint	400.00	800.00
25	A10	15pf carmine	7.25	16.00
26	A10	20pf blue	.65	1.60
a.		Double overprint	325.00	650.00
27	A10	25pf gray	11.00	16.00
28	A10	30pf orange	6.50	11.00
30	A10	40pf olive green	10.50	16.00
31	A10	50pf red brown	2.00	4.50
a.		Double overprint	350.00	650.00
32	A10	60pf dark green	3.25	8.00

Overprinted

Perf. 11½

35	A11	1m brown	24.00	35.00
a.		1m dark brown	16.00	32.50
36	A11	2m dk gray violet	60.00	140.00
37	A11	3m scarlet	120.00	160.00
		Nos. 35-37 (3)	204.00	335.00

Overprinted

38	A12	5m deep blue	800.00	875.00
39	A12	10m yellow green	140.00	250.00

Nos. 19, 20 and 22 were not officially issued, but were available for postage. Examples are known legitimately used on cover. The 20m type A12 was also overprinted in small quantity. Values: unused $125,000; never hinged $200,000.
No. 21a is valued without gum.
Overprint forgeries exist.

German Stamps of 1906-20 Overprinted

Perf. 14, 14½

1920, Mar. 26   **Wmk. 125**

41	A16	5pf green	.25	.50
a.		Inverted overprint	16.00	160.00
42	A16	5pf red brown	.50	.80
43	A16	10pf carmine	.25	.50
a.		Inverted overprint	47.50	325.00
44	A16	10pf orange	.45	.50
a.		Inverted overprint	16.00	
45	A22	15pf dk violet	.25	.50
a.		Inverted overprint	27.50	240.00
46	A16	20pf blue violet	.25	.50
a.		Inverted overprint	35.00	—
47	A16	20pf green	.95	.50
a.		Double overprint, never hinged	80.00	
48	A16	30pf org & blk, *buff*	.40	.50
a.		Double overprint	65.00	
b.		Inverted overprint	—	
49	A16	30pf dull blue	.55	.75
50	A16	40pf lake & blk	.30	.50
51	A16	40pf car rose	1.00	.75
52	A16	50pf pur & blk, *buff*	.55	.50
a.		Double overprint	65.00	400.00
53	A16	60pf red violet	.65	.50
a.		Inverted overprint	80.00	325.00
54	A16	75pf green & blk	.75	.50
a.		Double overprint	110.00	400.00
b.		Inverted overprint	110.00	
55	A17	1.25m green	2.75	1.25
a.		Inverted overprint	95.00	
56	A17	1.50m yellow brn	2.00	1.25
a.		Inverted overprint	95.00	800.00
57	A21	2.50m lilac red	4.75	13.50
58	A16	4m black & rose	8.75	22.50
a.		Double overprint	110.00	
		Nos. 41-58 (18)	25.35	46.30

On No. 57 the overprint is placed vertically at each side of the stamp.
No. 58a is valued never hinged.
Counterfeit overprints exist.

Germany No. 90 Surcharged in Black

1921, Feb.

65	A16	20pf on 75pf grn & blk	.40	1.25
a.		Inverted surcharge	24.00	72.50
b.		Double surcharge	55.00	125.00

Germany No. 120 Surcharged

66	A22	5m on 15pf vio brn	5.50	16.00
67	A22	10m on 15pf vio brn	6.00	19.00
		Nos. 65-67 (3)	11.90	36.25

Forgeries exist of Nos. 66-67.

Old Mill near Mettlach — A3

Miner at Work — A4

Entrance to Reden Mine — A5

Saar River Traffic — A6

Saar River near Mettlach — A7

Slag Pile at Völklingen — A8

Signal Bridge, Saarbrücken — A9

Church at Mettlach — A10

"Old Bridge," Saarbrücken A11

Cable Railway at Ferne — A12

Colliery Shafthead — A13

Saarbrücken City Hall — A14

Pottery at Mettlach — A15

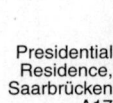

St. Ludwig's Cathedral — A16

Presidential Residence, Saarbrücken A17

Burbach Steelworks, Dillingen A18

1921   **Unwmk.**   **Typo.**   **Perf. 12½**

68	A3	5pf ol grn & vio	.35	.50
a.		Tête bêche pair	3.50	20.00
c.		Center inverted	100.00	340.00
69	A4	10pf org & ultra	.35	.50
70	A5	20pf grn & slate	.35	1.00
a.		Tête bêche pair	6.50	40.00
c.		Perf. 10½	22.50	225.00
d.		As "c," tête bêche pair	140.00	675.00
71	A6	25pf brn & dk bl	.40	.80
a.		Tête bêche pair	7.25	40.00

72	A7	30pf gray grn & brn	.40	.75
a.		Tête bêche pair	12.00	60.00
c.		30pf ol grn & blk	2.40	22.50
d.		As "c," tête bêche pair	12.50	72.50
e.		As "c," imperf., pair	120.00	
73	A8	40pf vermilion		.50
a.		Tête bêche pair	19.00	80.00
74	A9	50pf gray & blk	.95	4.00
75	A10	60pf red & dk brn	1.60	3.50
76	A11	80pf deep blue	.75	1.00
a.		Tête bêche pair	21.00	110.00
77	A12	1m lt red & blk	.80	1.60
a.		1m grn & blk	450.00	
78	A13	1.25m lt brn & dk grn	.95	2.00
79	A14	2m red & blk	2.40	4.00
80	A15	3m brn & dk ol	3.25	9.50
a.		Center inverted	125.00	
81	A16	5m yel & vio	12.00	24.00
82	A17	10m grn & red brn	12.00	24.00
83	A18	25m ultra, red & blk	32.50	80.00
		Nos. 68-83 (16)	69.45	157.65

Values for tête bêche pairs are for vertical pairs. Horizontal pairs sell for about twice as much.

The ultramarine ink on No. 69 appears to be brown where it overlays the orange.

Exist imperf but were not regularly issued. Value $1,400. (hinged).

Nos. 70-83 Surcharged in Red, Blue or Black

a

b

c

1921, May 1

85	A5(a)	3c on 20pf (R)	.40	.50
a.		Tête bêche pair	4.75	32.50
b.		Inverted surcharge	95.00	
d.		Perf. 10½	4.75	160.00
e.		As "d," tête bêche pair	21.00	—
86	A6(a)	5c on 25pf (R)	.40	.50
a.		Tête bêche pair	95.00	400.00
87	A7(a)	10c on 30pf (Bl)	.40	.50
a.		Tête bêche pair	4.75	25.00
b.		Inverted surcharge	95.00	450.00
c.		Double surcharge	95.00	475.00
88	A8(a)	15c on 40pf (Bk)	.50	.50
a.		Tête bêche pair	95.00	400.00
b.		Inverted surcharge	95.00	450.00
89	A9(a)	20c on 50pf (R)	.40	.50
90	A10(a)	25c on 60pf (Bl)	.50	.50
91	A11(a)	30c on 80pf (Bk)	1.60	1.00
a.		Tête bêche pair	12.50	60.00
c.		Inverted surcharge	140.00	600.00
d.		Double surcharge	140.00	600.00
92	A12(a)	40c on 1m (Bl)	2.00	.50
a.		Inverted surcharge	110.00	450.00
b.		Double surcharge	140.00	600.00
93	A13(a)	50c on 1.25m (Bk)	3.25	1.00
a.		Double surcharge	275.00	950.00
b.		Perf. 10½	72.50	140.00
94	A14(a)	75c on 2m (Bl)	4.75	2.00
a.		Inverted surcharge	110.00	
95	A15(b)	1fr on 3m (Bl)	4.50	2.40
96	A16(b)	2fr on 5m (Bl)	12.00	6.50
97	A17(b)	3fr on 10m (Bk)	17.50	25.00
b.		Double surcharge	200.00	800.00

98	A18(c)	5fr on 25m (Bl)	17.50	35.00
		Nos. 85-98 (14)	65.70	76.40

In these surcharges the period is occasionally missing and there are various wrong font and defective letters.

Values for tête bêche pairs are for vertical pairs. Horizontal pairs sell for about twice as much.

Nos. 85-89, 91, 93, 97-98 exist imperforate but were not regularly issued.

Cable Railway, Ferne — A19

Miner at Work — A20

"Old Bridge," Saarbrücken A21

Saarbrücken City Hall — A22

Slag Pile at Völklingen A23

Pottery at Mettlach — A24

Saar River Traffic — A25

St. Ludwig's Cathedral A26

Colliery Shafthead A27

Mettlach Church — A28

Burbach Steelworks, Dillingen A29

Perf. 12½x13½, 13½x12½

				Typo.
1922-23				
99	A19	3c ol grn & straw	.40	.65
100	A20	5c orange & blk	.40	.40
101	A21	10c blue green	.40	.40
102	A19	15c deep brown	1.25	.40
103	A19	15c orange ('23)	2.40	.40
104	A22	20c dk bl & lem	13.50	.40
105	A22	20c brt bl & straw ('23)	4.00	.40
106	A22	25c red & yellow	6.50	2.25
107	A22	25c mag & straw ('23)	2.40	.40
108	A23	30c carmine & yel	2.00	2.10
109	A24	40c brown & yel	1.60	.40
110	A24	50c dk bl & straw	.95	.40
111	A24	75c dp grn & straw	13.50	24.00
112	A24	75c blk & straw ('23)	32.50	3.25
113	A26	1fr brown red	2.40	.80
114	A27	2fr deep violet	6.50	3.25
115	A28	3fr org & dk grn	24.00	6.50
116	A29	5fr brn & red brn	24.00	45.00
		Nos. 99-116 (18)	138.70	91.40

Nos. 99-116 exist imperforate but were not regularly issued.
For overprints see Nos. O1-O15.

Madonna of Blieskastel — A30

1925, Apr. 9 Photo. Perf. 13½x12½
Size: 23x27mm

118	A30	45c lake brown	2.75	5.25

Size: 31½x36mm
Perf. 12

119	A30	10fr black brown	16.00	24.00

Nos. 118-119 exist imperforate but were not regularly issued.
For overprint see No. 154.

Market Fountain, St. Johann — A31

View of Saar Valley A32

Colliery Shafthead A35

Burbach Steelworks A36

Designs: 15c, 75c, View of Saar Valley. 20c, 40c, 90c, Scene from Saarlouis fortifications. 25c, 50c, Tholey Abbey.

1927-32			**Perf. 13½**	
120	A31	10c deep brown	.75	.50
121	A32	15c olive black	.40	1.10
122	A32	20c brown org	.40	.50
123	A32	25c bluish slate	.75	.50
124	A31	30c olive green	.95	.50
125	A32	40c olive brown	.75	.50
126	A35	50c magenta	.95	.50
127	A35	60c red org ('30)	4.00	.55
128	A35	75c brown violet	.75	.50
129	A35	80c red orange	2.40	8.75
130	A32	90c dp red ('32)	12.00	17.50
131	A35	1fr violet	2.40	.50
132	A36	1.50fr sapphire	6.50	.50
133	A36	2fr brown red	6.50	.50
134	A36	3fr dk olive grn	14.50	1.25
135	A36	5fr deep brown	14.50	7.25
		Nos. 120-135 (16)	68.50	41.40

For surcharges and overprints see Nos. 136-153, O16-O26.

Nos. 126 and 129 Surcharged

1930-34

136	A32	40c on 50c mag ('34)	1.60	1.60
137	A35	60c on 80c red orange	2.00	2.40

Plebiscite Issue

Stamps of 1925-32 Ovptd. in Various Colors

1934, Nov. 1			**Perf. 13½**	
139	A31	10c brown (Br)	.40	.55
140	A32	15c black grn (G)	.40	.55
141	A32	20c brn org (O)	.65	1.40
142	A32	25c bluish sl (Bl)	.65	1.40
143	A31	30c olive grn (G)	.40	.55
144	A32	40c olive brn (Br)	.40	.75
145	A32	50c magenta (R)	.75	1.40
146	A35	60c red orange (O)	.65	.55
147	A32	75c brown vio (V)	.75	1.25
148	A32	90c deep red (R)	.75	1.40
149	A35	1fr violet (V)	.75	1.60
150	A36	1.50fr sapphire (Bl)	1.25	3.25
151	A36	2fr brn red (R)	2.00	4.75
152	A36	3fr dk ol grn (G)	4.75	9.50
153	A36	5fr dp brn (Br)	20.00	32.50

Size: 31½x36mm
Perf. 12

154	A30	10fr blk brn (Br)	24.00	60.00
		Nos. 139-154 (16)	58.55	121.40

French Administration

Miner A37

Steel Workers A38

Harvesting Sugar Beets — A39

Mettlach Abbey — A40

Marshal Ney — A41

Saar River near Mettlach A42

1947   Unwmk.   Photo.   Perf. 14

155	A37	2pf gray	.25	.40
156	A37	3pf orange	.25	.50
157	A37	6pf dk Prus grn	.25	.40
158	A37	8pf scarlet	.25	.35
159	A37	10pf rose violet	.25	.40
160	A38	15pf brown	.25	6.50
161	A38	16pf ultra	.25	.40
162	A38	20pf brown rose	.25	.40
163	A38	24pf dp brown org	.25	.40
164	A39	25pf cerise	.25	22.50
165	A39	30pf lt olive grn	.25	.80
166	A39	40pf orange brn	.25	1.20
167	A39	50pf blue violet	.25	22.50
168	A40	60pf violet	.25	22.50
169	A40	80pf dp orange	.25	.40
170	A41	84pf brown	.25	.40
171	A42	1m gray green	.25	.50
		Nos. 155-171 (17)	4.25	80.55
		Set, never hinged	5.50	

Nos. 155-162, 164-171 exist imperf.

Types of 1947

1947   Wmk. 285

172	A37	12pf olive green	.25	.40
173	A39	45pf crimson	.25	16.00
174	A40	75pf brt blue	.25	.40
		Nos. 172-174 (3)	.75	16.80
		Set, never hinged	1.00	

Nos. 172-174 exist imperf.

Types of 1947 Surcharged in Black or Red

Printing II

1947, Nov. 27   Unwmk.

175	A37	10c on 2pf gray	.25	.55
176	A37	60c on 3pf org	.25	1.10
177	A37	1fr on 10pf rose vio	.25	.55
178	A37	2fr on 12pf ol grn, wmk. 285	.25	1.50
179	A38	3fr on 15pf brn	.25	1.50
180	A38	4fr on 16pf ultra	.25	8.00
181	A38	5fr on 20pf brn rose	.25	1.10
182	A38	6fr on 24pf dp brn org	.25	.65
183	A39	9fr on 30pf lt ol grn	.25	13.50
184	A39	10fr on 50pf bl vio (R)	.25	20.00
185	A40	14fr on 60pf vio	.25	13.50
186	A41	20fr on 84pf brn	.35	21.00
187	A42	50fr on 1m gray grn	.50	21.00
		Nos. 175-187 (13)	3.60	103.95
		Set, never hinged	5.50	

Printing I

175a	A37	10c on 2pf gray	35.00	360.00
176a	A37	60c on 3pf org	29.00	800.00
177a	A37	1fr on 10pf rose vio	2.40	16.00
178a	A37	2fr on 12pf ol grn, wmk. 285	.75	4.00
179a	A38	3fr on 15pf brn	350.00	2,400.
180a	A38	4fr on 16pf ultra	7.25	110.00
181a	A38	5fr on 20pf brn rose	80.00	4,750.
182a	A38	6fr on 24pf dp brn org	.25	4.75
183a	A39	9fr on 30pf lt ol grn	45.00	800.00
184a	A39	10fr on 50pf bl vio (R)	550.00	4,750.
185a	A40	14fr on 60pf violet	87.50	950.00
186a	A41	20fr on 84pf brn	2.00	8.00

187a	A42	50fr on 1m gray grn	55.00	350.00
		Nos. 175a-187a (13)	1,244.	15,303.
		Set, never hinged	2,800.	

Printing I was surcharged on Nos. 155-171, which was printed on yellowish paper with brownish gum. The crossbar of the A's in SAAR is high on the 10c, 60c, 1fr, 2fr, 9fr and 10fr; numeral "1" has no base serif on the 3fr and 4fr, 5fr, 6fr; 14fr, 14fr, wide space between vignette and SAAR panel; 1m inscribed "1M."

Printing II was surcharged on a special printing of the basic stamps, on white paper with white gum, and with details of design that differ on each denomination. The "A" crossbar is low on 10c, 60c, 1fr, 2fr, 9fr, 10fr; numeral "1" has base serif on 3fr, 4fr, 5fr, 6fr; 14fr, narrow space between vignette and SAAR panel; 20fr, minor retouches; 1m inscribed "1SM."

Inverted surcharges exist on Nos. 175-187 and 175a-187a.

French Protectorate

Clasped Hands — A43

Colliery Shafthead — A44

2fr, 3fr, Worker. 4fr, 5fr, Girl gathering wheat. 6fr, 9fr, Miner. 14fr, Smelting. 20fr, Reconstruction. 50fr, Mettlach Abbey portal.

Perf. 14x13, 13

1948, Apr. 1   Engr.   Unwmk.

188	A43	10c henna brn	.35	2.00
189	A43	60c dk Prus grn	.35	2.00
190	A43	1fr brown blk	.25	.30
191	A43	2fr rose car	.25	.30
192	A43	3fr black brn	.25	.30
193	A43	4fr red	.25	.30
194	A43	5fr red violet	.25	.30
195	A43	6fr henna brown	.35	.30
196	A43	9fr dk Prus grn	2.00	.50
197	A44	10fr dark blue	1.25	.80
198	A44	14fr dk vio brn	1.60	1.10
199	A44	20fr henna brn	3.25	1.10
200	A44	50fr blue blk	6.50	2.75
		Nos. 188-200 (13)	16.90	12.05
		Set, never hinged	35.00	

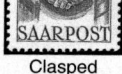

Map of the Saar A45

1948, Dec. 15   Photo.   Perf. 13½x13

201	A45	10fr dark red	.75	4.00
202	A45	25fr deep blue	1.25	8.00
		Set, never hinged	4.75	

French Protectorate establishment, 1st anniv.

Caduceus, Microscope, Bunsen Burner and Book — A46

1949, Apr. 2   Perf. 13x13½

203	A46	15fr carmine	2.75	.50
		Never hinged	7.25	

Issued to honor Saar University.

Ludwig van Beethoven A47

Laborer Using Spade A51

Saarbrücken — A52

Designs: 10c, Building trades. 1fr, 3fr, Gears, factories. 5fr, Dumping mine waste. 6fr, 15fr, Coal mine interior. 8fr, Communications symbols. 10fr, Emblem of printing. 12fr, 18fr, Pottery. 25fr, Blast furnace worker. 45fr, Rock formation "Great Boot." 60fr, Reden Colliery, Landsweiler. 100fr, View of Weibelskirchen.

1949-51   Unwmk.   Perf. 13x13½

204	A47	10c violet brn	.25	2.00
205	A47	60c gray ('51)	.25	2.00
206	A47	1fr carmine lake	.50	.35
207	A47	3fr brown ('51)	3.25	.40
208	A47	5fr dp violet ('50)	.80	.35
209	A47	6fr Prus grn ('51)	4.75	.40
210	A47	8fr olive grn ('51)	.50	.65
211	A47	10fr orange ('50)	2.00	.35
212	A47	12fr dk green	6.50	.35
213	A47	15fr red ('50)	2.75	.35
214	A47	18fr brn car ('51)	1.25	5.25

Perf. 13½

215	A51	20fr gray ('50)	.80	.35
216	A51	25fr violet blue	9.50	.35
217	A52	30fr red brown ('51)	6.50	.50
218	A52	45fr rose lake ('51)	1.60	.55
219	A51	60fr deep grn ('51)	3.25	2.00
220	A51	100fr brown	4.75	2.40
		Nos. 204-220 (17)	49.20	18.60
		Set, never hinged	125.00	

Catalogue values for unused stamps in this section, from this point to the end of the section, are for Never Hinged items.

Peter Wust — A54

1950, Apr. 3

221	A54	15fr carmine rose	12.50	7.25

Wust (1884-1940), Catholic philosopher.

St. Peter — A55

1950, June 29   Engr.   Perf. 13

222	A55	12fr deep green	3.25	10.00
223	A55	15fr red brown	4.75	9.50
224	A55	25fr blue	8.00	21.00
		Nos. 222-224 (3)	16.00	40.50

Holy Year, 1950.

Street in Ottweiler — A56

1950, July 10   Photo.   Perf. 13x13½

225	A56	10fr orange brown	6.00	8.00

Founding of Ottweiler, 400th anniv.

Symbols of the Council of Europe A57

1950, Aug. 8   Perf. 13½

226	A57	25fr deep blue	35.00	12.00

Issued to commemorate the Saar's admission to the Council of Europe. See No. C12.

Post Rider and Guard — A62

1951, Apr. 29   Engr.   Perf. 13

227	A62	15fr dk violet brn	8.75	19.00

Issued to publicize Stamp Day, 1951.

"Agriculture and Industry" and Fair Emblem — A63

1951, May 12   Photo.   Perf. 13x13½

228	A63	15fr dk gray grn	2.75	6.50

1951 Fair at Saarbrücken.

Tower of Mittelbexbach and Flowers — A67

1951, June 9   Engr.   Perf. 13

229	A67	15fr dark green	2.75	1.75

Exhibition of Gardens & Flowers, Bexbach, 1951.

Refugees — A68

1952, May 2   Unwmk.   Perf. 13

230	A68	15fr bright red	3.50	1.40

Issued to honor the Red Cross.

Globe & Stylized Fair Building — A69

1952, Apr. 26
231 A69 15fr red brown   2.50 1.40
   1952 Fair at Saarbrücken.

Mine Shafts A70

Ludwig's Gymnasium A71

General Post Office A72

Reconstruction of St. Ludwig's Cathedral — A73

3fr, 18fr, Bridge building. 6fr, Transporter bridge, Mettlach. 30fr, Saar University Library.

			Engr.	
1952-55				
232	A70	1fr dk bl grn ('53)	.25	.25
233	A71	2fr purple ('53)	.25	.25
234	A72	3fr dk car rose ('53)	.25	.25
235	A72	5fr dk grn (no inscription)	4.75	.25
236	A72	5fr dk grn ("Hauptpostamt Saarbrücken") ('54)	.25	.25
237	A72	6fr vio brn ('53)	.40	.25
238	A71	10fr brn ol ('53)	.40	.25
239	A72	12fr green ('53)	.75	.25
240	A70	15fr blk brn (no inscription)	8.00	.25
241	A70	15fr blk brn ("Industrie-Land-schaft") ('53)	3.50	.25
242	A70	15fr dp car ('55)	.35	.25
243	A72	18fr dk rose brn ('55)	2.75	4.75
244	A72	30fr ultra ('53)	.95	.95
245	A73	500fr brn car ('53)	16.00	65.00
		Nos. 232-245 (14)	38.85	73.45

   For overprints see Nos. 257-259.

"SM" Monogram — A74

1953, Mar. 23
246 A74 15fr dark ultra   2.10 1.60
   1953 Fair at Saarbrücken.

Bavarian and Prussian Postilions A75

1953, May 3
247 A75 15fr deep blue   6.75 13.00
   Stamp Day.

Fountain and Fair Buildings — A76

1954, Apr. 10
248 A76 15fr deep green   2.10 .95
   1954 International Fair at Saarbrücken.

Post Coach and Post Bus of 1920 — A77

1954, May 9   **Engr.**
249 A77 15fr red   9.50 13.50
   Stamp Day, May 9, 1954.

Madonna and Child, Holbein A78

   Designs: 10fr, Sistine Madonna, Raphael. 15fr, Madonna and Child with pear, Durer.

1954, Aug. 14
250 A78 5fr deep carmine   2.40 3.25
251 A78 10fr dark green   2.40 3.25
252 A78 15fr dp violet bl   3.25 5.50
   Nos. 250-252 (3)   8.05 12.00
   Centenary of the promulgation of the Dogma of the Immaculate Conception.

Cyclist and Flag — A79

1955, Feb. 28 Photo.   **Perf. 13x13½**
253 A79 15fr multicolored   .40 .75
   World championship cross country bicycle race.

Symbols of Industry and Rotary Emblem — A80

1955, Feb. 28
254 A80 15fr orange brown   .40 .95
   Rotary International, 50th anniversary.

Flags of Participating Nations — A81

1955, Apr. 18 Photo.   **Perf. 13x13½**
255 A81 15fr multicolored   .40 .75
   1955 International Fair at Saarbrücken.

Postman at Illingen A82

Unwmk.
1955, May 8   Engr.   Perf. 13
256 A82 15fr deep claret   2.00 2.40
   Issued to publicize Stamp Day, 1955.

Nos. 242-244 Overprinted "VOLKSBEFRAGUNG 1955"

1955, Oct. 22
257 A70 15fr deep carmine   .45 .70
258 A72 18fr dk rose brn   .45 .55
259 A72 30fr ultra   .65 .70
   Nos. 257-259 (3)   1.55 1.95
   Plebiscite, Oct. 23, 1955.

Symbols of Industry and the Fair — A83

1956, Apr. 14 Photo.   **Perf. 11½**
260 A83 15fr dk brn red & yel grn   .40 .95
   Intl. Fair at Saarbrücken, Apr. 14-29, 1956.

Radio Tower, Saarbrücken — A84

1956, May 6   **Granite Paper**
261 A84 15fr grn & grnsh bl   .40 .95
   Stamp Day.

German Administration

Arms of Saar — A85

Perf. 13x13½
1957, Jan. 1   Litho.   Wmk. 304
262 A85 15fr brick red & blue   .25 .40
   Return of the Saar to Germany.

Pres. Theodor Heuss — A86

1957		**Typo.**	**Perf. 14**	
		Size: 18x22mm		
263	A86	1(fr) brt green	.25	.25
264	A86	2(fr) brt violet	.25	.25
265	A86	3(fr) bister brown	.25	.25
266	A86	4(fr) red violet	.35	.80
267	A86	5(fr) lt olive green	.25	.25
268	A86	6(fr) vermilion	.25	.50
269	A86	10(fr) gray	.25	.35
270	A86	12(fr) deep orange	.25	.25
271	A86	15(fr) lt blue green	.25	.25
272	A86	18(fr) carmine rose	.65	2.40
273	A86	25(fr) brt lilac	.45	
		Engr.		
274	A86	30(fr) pale purple	.45	.80
275	A86	45(fr) gray olive	1.10	2.75
276	A86	50(fr) violet brn	1.10	1.25
277	A86	60(fr) dull rose	1.60	3.25
278	A86	70(fr) red orange	2.90	4.75
279	A86	80(fr) olive green	.95	3.75
280	A86	90(fr) dark gray	2.75	6.50
		Size: 24x29mm		
281	A86	100(fr) dk carmine	2.40	8.00
282	A86	200(fr) violet	6.50	25.00
		Nos. 263-282 (20)	23.20	62.40

   See Nos. 289-308.

Steel Industry — A87

Perf. 13x13½

1957, Apr. 20   Litho.   Wmk. 304
284 A87 15fr gray & magenta   .25   .40
The 1957 Fair at Saarbrücken.

Merzig Arms and St. Peter's Church — A88

1957, May 25   Perf. 14
285 A88 15fr blue   .25   .40
Centenary of the town of Merzig.

"United Europe" — A89

Lithographed; Tree Embossed
Perf. 14x13½

1957, Sept. 16   Unwmk.
286 A89 20fr orange & yel   .40   1.00
287 A89 35fr violet & pink   .95   1.20
Europa, publicizing a united Europe for peace and prosperity.

Carrier Pigeons — A90

Wmk. 304

1957, Oct. 5   Litho.   Perf. 14
288 A90 15fr dp carmine & blk   .25   .40
Intl. Letter Writing Week, Oct. 6-12.

Redrawn Type of 1957; "F" added after denomination
1957   Wmk. 304   Litho.   Perf. 14
Size: 18x22mm

289	A86	1fr gray green	.25	.25
290	A86	3fr blue	.25	.25
291	A86	5fr olive	.25	.25
292	A86	6fr lt brown	.25	.50
293	A86	10fr violet	.25	.25
294	A86	12fr brown org	.25	.25
295	A86	15fr dull green	.40	.25
296	A86	18fr gray	2.00	4.75
297	A86	20fr lt olive grn	1.25	3.25
298	A86	25fr orange brn	.40	.40
299	A86	30fr rose lilac	.95	.40
300	A86	35fr brown	2.40	3.25
301	A86	45fr lt blue grn	2.00	4.00
302	A86	50fr dk red brown	.95	2.00
303	A86	70fr brt green	4.75	5.50
304	A86	80fr chalky blue	2.40	5.25
305	A86	90fr rose carmine	5.50	6.50

Engr.
Size: 24x29mm

306	A86	100fr orange	5.50	7.25
307	A86	200fr brt green	8.75	25.00
308	A86	300fr blue	9.50	29.00
		Nos. 289-308 (20)	48.25	98.55

"Max and Moritz" — A91

Design: 15fr, Wilhelm Busch.

Perf. 13½x13
1958, Jan. 9   Litho.   Wmk. 304
309 A91 12fr lt grn & blk   .25   .25
310 A91 15fr red & black   .25   .40
Death of Wilhelm Busch, humorist, 50th anniv.

"Prevent Forest Fires" — A92

1958, Mar. 5   Perf. 14
311 A92 15fr brt red & blk   .25   .40
Issued to aid in the prevention of forest fires.

Rudolf Diesel A93

1958, Mar. 18   Engr.
312 A93 12fr dk blue grn   .25   .40
Centenary of the birth of Rudolf Diesel, inventor.

Fair Emblem and City Hall, Saarbrücken A94

1958, Apr. 10   Litho.   Perf. 14
313 A94 15fr dull rose   .25   .40
1958 Fair at Saarbrücken.

View of Homburg A95

1958, June 14   Engr.   Wmk. 304
314 A95 15fr gray green   .25   .40
400th anniversary of Homburg.

Turner Emblem — A96

1958, July 21   Litho.   Perf. 13½x14
315 A96 12fr gray, blk & dl grn   .25   .40
150 years of German Gymnastics and the 1958 Gynastic Festival.

Herman Schulze-Delitzsch A97

1958, Aug. 29   Engr.   Wmk. 304
316 A97 12fr yellow green   .25   .40
150th anniv. of the birth of Schultze-Delitzsch, founder of German trade organizations.

Common Design Types pictured following the introduction.

Europa Issue, 1958
Common Design Type
1958, Sept. 13   Litho.
Size: 24½x30mm
317 CD1 12fr yellow grn & bl   .45   .80
318 CD1 30fr lt blue & red   .60   1.50
Issued to show the European Postal Union at the service of European integration.

Jakob Fugger — A98

Perf. 13x13½
1959, Mar. 6   Wmk. 304
319 A98 15fr dk red & blk   .25   .40
500th anniv. of the birth of Jakob Fugger the Rich, businessman and banker.

Old and New City Hall and Burbach Mill — A99

1959, Apr. 1   Engr.   Perf. 14x13½
320 A99 15fr light blue   .25   .40
Greater Saarbrucken, 50th anniversary.

Hands Holding Merchandise A100

1959, Apr. 1   Litho.
321 A100 15fr deep rose   .25   .40
1959 Fair at Saarbrucken.

Alexander von Humboldt — A101

1959, May 6   Engr.   Perf. 13½x14
322 A101 15fr blue   .40   .40
Cent. of the death of Alexander von Humboldt, naturalist and geographer.

SEMI-POSTAL STAMPS

Red Cross Dog Leading Blind Man — SP1

Maternity Nurse with Child — SP4

Designs: No. B2, Nurse and invalid. No. B3, Children getting drink at spring.

Perf. 13½
1926, Oct. 25   Photo.   Unwmk.

B1	SP1	20c + 20c dk ol grn	8.00	20.00
B2	SP1	40c + 40c dk brn	8.00	20.00
B3	SP1	50c + 50c red org	8.00	20.00
B4	SP4	1.50fr + 1.50fr brt bl	19.00	47.50
		Nos. B1-B4 (4)	43.00	107.50

Nos. B1-B4 Overprinted

1927, Oct. 1

B5	SP1	20c + 20c dk ol grn	12.50	35.00
B6	SP1	40c + 40c dk brn	12.50	35.00
B7	SP1	50c + 50c red org	11.00	32.50
B8	SP4	1.50fr + 1.50fr brt bl	17.50	72.50
		Nos. B5-B8 (4)	53.50	175.00

"The Blind Beggar" by Dyckmans SP5

"Almsgiving" by Schiestl SP6

"Charity" by Raphael — SP7

1928, Dec. 23   Photo.

B9	SP5	40c (+40c) blk brn	12.00	72.50
B10	SP5	50c (+50c) brn rose	12.00	72.50
B11	SP5	1fr (+1fr) dl vio	12.00	72.50
B12	SP6	1.50fr (+1.50fr) cob bl	12.00	72.50
B13	SP6	2fr (+2fr) red brn	14.00	100.00
B14	SP6	3fr (+3fr) dk ol grn	14.00	135.00
B15	SP7	10fr (+10fr) dk brn	360.00	4,000.
		Nos. B9-B15 (7)	436.00	4,525.

"Orphaned" by Kaulbach SP8

"St. Ottilia" by Feuerstein SP9

"Madonna" by Ferruzzio — SP10

1929, Dec. 22
B16	SP8	40c (+15c) ol grn	2.00	5.50
B17	SP8	50c (+20c) cop red	4.00	9.50
B18	SP8	1fr (+50c) vio brn	4.00	11.00
B19	SP9	1.50fr (+75c) Prus bl	4.00	11.00
B20	SP9	2fr (+1fr) brn car	4.00	11.00
B21	SP9	3fr (+2fr) sl grn	8.00	25.00
B22	SP10	10fr (+8fr) blk	47.50	135.00
	Nos. B16-B22 (7)		73.50	208.00

"The Safety-Man" SP11

"The Good Samaritan" SP12

"In the Window" — SP13

1931, Jan. 20
B23	SP11	40c (+15c) dk org brn	8.00	24.00
B24	SP11	60c (+20c) dk org red	8.00	24.00
B25	SP12	1fr (+50c) mag	8.00	47.50
B26	SP11	1.50fr (+75c) sapphire	8.00	47.50
B27	SP12	2fr (+1fr) dk org brn	8.00	47.50
B28	SP12	3fr (+2fr) ol grn	20.00	47.50
B29	SP13	10fr (+10fr) dk org brn	95.00	290.00
	Nos. B23-B29 (7)		155.00	528.00

St. Martin of Tours — SP14

Nos. B33-B35, Charity. No. B36, The Widow's Mite.

1931, Dec. 23
B30	SP14	40c (+15c) dp brn	12.50	35.00
B31	SP14	60c (+20c) ver	12.50	35.00
B32	SP14	1fr (+50c) dk redsh brn	16.00	55.00
B33	SP14	1.50fr (+75c) sapphire	19.00	55.00
B34	SP14	2fr (+1fr) dp red	22.50	55.00
B35	SP14	3fr (+2fr) ol grn	27.50	95.00
B36	SP14	5fr (+5fr) red brn	95.00	325.00
	Nos. B30-B36 (7)		205.00	655.00

Ruins at Kirkel — SP17

Illingen Castle, Kerpen SP23

Designs: 60c, Church at Blie. 1fr, Castle Ottweiler. 1.50fr, Church of St. Michael, Saarbrucken. 2fr, Statue of St. Wendel. 3fr, Church of St. John, Saarbrucken.

1932, Dec. 20
B37	SP17	40c (+15c) dp brn	9.50	22.50
B38	SP17	60c (+20c) dk org red	9.50	22.50
B39	SP17	1fr (+50c) dp pur	14.00	40.00
B40	SP17	1.50fr (+75c) ol grn	20.00	47.50
B41	SP17	2fr (+1fr) dp red	20.00	55.00
B42	SP17	3fr (+2fr) ol grn	55.00	175.00
B43	SP23	5fr (+5fr) red	125.00	290.00
	Nos. B37-B43 (7)		253.00	652.50

Scene of Neunkirchen Disaster — SP24

1933, June 1
B44	SP24	60c (+ 60c) org red	16.00	20.00
B45	SP24	3fr (+ 3fr) ol grn	35.00	72.50
B46	SP24	5fr (+ 5fr) org brn	35.00	72.50
	Nos. B44-B46 (3)		86.00	165.00

The surtax was for the aid of victims of the explosion at Neunkirchen, Feb. 10.

"Love" — SP25

Designs: 60c, "Anxiety." 1fr, "Peace." 1.50fr, "Solace." 2fr, "Welfare." 3fr, "Truth." 5fr, Figure on Tomb of Duchess Elizabeth of Lorraine

1934, Mar. 15   **Photo.**
B47	SP25	40c (+15c) blk brn	5.50	16.00
B48	SP25	60c (+20c) red org	5.50	16.00
B49	SP25	1fr (+50c) dl vio	7.25	20.00
B50	SP25	1.50fr (+75c) blue	14.00	35.00
B51	SP25	2fr (+1fr) car rose	12.50	35.00
B52	SP25	3fr (+2fr) ol grn	14.00	35.00
B53	SP25	5fr (+5fr) red brn	32.50	87.50
	Nos. B47-B53 (7)		91.25	244.50

Nos. B47-B53 Overprinted like Nos. 139-154 in Various Colors Reading up

1934, Dec. 1   **Perf. 13x13½**
B54	SP25	40c (+15c) (Br)	3.50	14.00
B55	SP25	60c (+20c) (R)	3.50	14.00
B56	SP25	1fr (+50c) (V)	11.00	25.00
B57	SP25	1.50fr (+75c) (Bl)	7.25	25.00
B58	SP25	2fr (+1fr) (R)	11.00	35.00
B59	SP25	3fr (+2fr) (G)	10.00	32.50
B60	SP25	5fr (+5fr) (Br)	15.00	40.00
	Nos. B54-B60 (7)		61.25	185.50

French Protectorate

SP32

Various Flood Scenes — SP33

Inscribed "Hochwasser-Hilfe 1947-48"

Perf. 13½x13, 13x13½

1948, Oct. 12   **Photo.**
B61	SP32	5fr + 5fr dl grn	2.25	35.00
B62	SP33	6fr + 4fr dk vio	2.25	32.50
B63	SP32	12fr + 8fr red	3.00	47.50
B64	SP33	18fr + 12fr bl	4.00	47.50
a.		Souv. sheet of 4, #B61-B64, imperf.	325.00	2,750.
	Nos. B61-B64,CB1 (5)		22.50	402.50
	Set, never hinged		47.50	

The surtax was for flood relief.

Hikers and Ludweiler Hostel SP34

No. B66, Hikers approaching Weisskirchen Hostel.

1949, Jan. 11   **Perf. 13½x13**
B65	SP34	8fr + 5fr dk grn	1.00	105.00
B66	SP34	10fr + 7fr dk grn	1.40	105.00
	Set, never hinged		8.00	

The surtax aided youth hostels.

Mare and Foal SP35

Design: No. B68, Jumpers.

1949, Sept. 25   **Perf. 13½**
B67	SP35	15fr + 5fr brn red	5.50	32.50
B68	SP35	25fr + 15fr blue	6.75	35.00
	Set, never hinged		27.50	

Day of the Horse, Sept. 25, 1949.

Detail from "Moses Striking the Rock" — SP36

No. B70, "Christ at the Pool of Bethesda." No. B71, "The Sick Child." No. B72, "St. Thomas of Villeneuve." No. B73, Madonna of Blieskastel.

1949, Dec. 20   **Engr.**   **Perf. 13**
B69	SP36	8fr + 2fr indigo	3.50	40.00
B70	SP36	12fr + 3fr dk grn	4.00	47.50
B71	SP36	15fr + 5fr brn lake	6.00	80.00
B72	SP36	25fr + 10fr dp ultra	10.00	125.00
B73	SP36	50fr + 20fr choc	15.00	225.00
	Nos. B69-B73 (5)		38.50	517.50
	Set, never hinged		87.50	

Adolph Kolping — SP37

1950, Apr. 3   **Photo.**   **Perf. 13x13½**
B74	SP37	15fr + 5fr car rose	13.00	80.00
	Never hinged		25.00	

Relief for the Hungry — SP38

Engraved and Typographed

1950, Apr. 28   **Perf. 13**
B75	SP38	25fr + 10fr dk brn car & red	12.50	65.00
	Never hinged		27.50	

Stagecoach — SP39

1950, Apr. 22   **Engr.**
B76	SP39	15fr + 5fr brn red & dk brn	30.00	110.00
	Never hinged		67.50	

Stamp Day, Apr. 27, 1950. Sold at the exhibition and to advance subscribers.

Lutwinus Seeking Admission to Abbey SP40

Designs: 12fr+3fr, Lutwinus Building Mettlach Abbey. 15fr+5fr, Lutwinus as Abbot. 25fr+10fr, Bishop Lutwinus at Rheims. 50fr+20fr, Aid to the poor and sick.

1950, Nov. 10   **Unwmk.**   **Perf. 13**
B77	SP40	8fr + 2fr dk brn	4.00	32.50
B78	SP40	12fr + 3fr dk grn	4.00	32.50
B79	SP40	15fr + 5fr red brn	4.25	52.50
B80	SP40	25fr + 10fr blue	6.50	72.50
B81	SP40	50fr + 20fr brn car	9.00	125.00
	Nos. B77-B81 (5)		27.75	315.00
	Set, never hinged		60.00	

The surtax was for public assistance.

Mother and Child — SP41

1951, Apr. 28
B82	SP41	25fr + 10fr dk grn & car	10.00	65.00
	Never hinged		19.00	

The surtax was for the Red Cross.

John Calvin and Martin Luther — SP42

1951, Oct. 31
B83 SP42 15fr + 5fr blk brn   1.60 *7.25*
  Never hinged   3.50
  Reformation in Saar, 375th anniv.

"Mother" — SP43

15fr+5fr, "Before the Theater." 18fr+7fr, "Sisters of Charity." 30fr+10fr, "The Good Samaritan." 50fr+ 20fr, "St. Martin and Beggar."

1951, Nov. 3
B84 SP43 12fr + 3fr dk grn   3.00 *19.00*
B85 SP43 15fr + 5fr pur   3.00 *19.00*
B86 SP43 18fr + 7fr dk red   3.25 *19.00*
B87 SP43 30fr + 10fr dp bl   5.25 *35.00*
B88 SP43 50fr + 20fr blk brn   10.50 *72.50*
  Nos. B84-B88 (5)   25.00 *164.50*
  Set, never hinged   52.50

> **Catalogue values for unused stamps in this section, from this point to the end of the section, are for Never Hinged items.**

Runner with Torch — SP44

30fr+5fr, Hand with olive branch, and globe.

1952, Mar. 29   **Unwmk.**   **Perf. 13**
B89 SP44 15fr + 5fr dp grn   6.00 *12.00*
B90 SP44 30fr + 5fr dp bl   6.00 *13.50*
  XV Olympic Games, Helsinki, 1952.

Postrider Delivering Mail SP45

1952, Mar. 30
B91 SP45 30fr + 10fr dark blue   12.00 *27.50*
  Stamp Day, Mar. 29, 1952.

Count Stroganoff as a Boy — SP46

Portraits: 18fr+7fr, The Holy Shepherd by Murillo. 30fr+10fr, Portrait of a Boy by Georg Melchior Kraus.

1952, Nov. 3
B92 SP46 15fr + 5fr dk brn   3.25 *11.00*
B93 SP46 18fr + 7fr brn lake   4.75 *14.00*
B94 SP46 30fr + 10fr dp bl   6.50 *16.00*
  Nos. B92-B94 (3)   14.50 *41.00*
  The surtax was for child welfare.

Henri Dunant — SP47

1953, May 3   **Cross in Red**
B95 SP47 15fr + 5fr blk brn   2.75 *7.25*

Clarice Strozzi by Titian — SP48

Children of Rubens SP49

Portrait: 30fr+10fr, Rubens' son.

1953, Nov. 16
B96 SP48 15fr + 5fr purple   3.25 *5.50*
B97 SP49 18fr + 7fr dp claret   3.50 *6.00*
B98 SP48 30fr + 10fr dp ol grn   4.75 *9.50*
  Nos. B96-B98 (3)   11.50 *21.00*
  The surtax was for child welfare.

St. Benedict Blessing St. Maurus — SP50

1953, Dec. 18   **Litho.**
B99 SP50 30fr + 10fr black   2.50 *8.00*
  The surtax was for the abbey at Tholey.

Child and Cross — SP51

1954, May 10   **Engr.**
B100 SP51 15fr + 5fr chocolate   3.25 *7.25*
  The surtax was for the Red Cross.

Street Urchin with Melon, Murillo — SP52

Paintings: 10fr+5fr, Maria de Medici, Bronzino. 15fr+7fr, Baron Emil von Maucler, Dietrich.

1954, Nov. 15
B101 SP52 5fr + 3fr red   .95 *1.40*
B102 SP52 10fr + 5fr dk red   .95 *1.40*
B103 SP52 15fr + 7fr purple   .95 *2.00*
  Nos. B101-B103 (3)   2.85 *4.80*
  The surtax was for child welfare.

Nurse Holding Baby — SP53

  Perf. 13x13½
1955, May 5   **Photo.**   **Unwmk.**
B104 SP53 15fr + 5fr blk & red   .55 *1.00*
  The surtax was for the Red Cross.

Dürer's Mother, Age 63 — SP54

Etchings by Dürer: 10fr+5fr, Praying hands. 15fr+7fr, Old man of Antwerp.

1955, Dec. 10   **Engr.**   **Perf. 13**
B105 SP54 5fr + 3fr dk grn   .50 *1.25*
B106 SP54 10fr + 5fr ol grn   .80 *1.60*
B107 SP54 15fr + 7fr ol bis   1.10 *1.90*
  Nos. B105-B107 (3)   2.40 *4.75*
  The surtax was for public assistance.

First Aid Station, Saarbrücken, 1870 — SP55

1956, May 7
B108 SP55 15fr + 5fr dk brn   .40 *.95*
  The surtax was for the Red Cross.

"Victor of Benevent" — SP56

1956, July 25   **Unwmk.**   *Perf. 13*
B109 SP56 12fr + 3fr dk yel grn &
  bl grn   .55 *.75*
B110 SP56 15fr + 5fr brn vio & brn   .55 *.75*
  Melbourne Olympics, 11/22-12/8/56.

Winterberg Monument — SP57

1956, Oct. 29
B111 SP57 5fr + 2fr green   .30 *.50*
B112 SP57 12fr + 3fr red lilac   .30 *.50*
B113 SP57 15fr + 5fr brown   .30 *.65*
  Nos. B111-B113 (3)   .90 *1.65*
  The surtax was for the rebuilding of monuments.

"La Belle Ferronnière" by da Vinci — SP58

Designs: 10fr + 5fr, "Saskia" by Rembrandt. 15fr+7fr, "Family van Berchem," by Frans Floris. (Detail: Woman playing Spinet.)

1956, Dec. 10
B114 SP58 5fr + 3fr deep blue   .30 *.30*
B115 SP58 10fr + 5fr deep claret   .30 *.50*
B116 SP58 15fr + 7fr dark green   .30 *.80*
  Nos. B114-B116 (3)   .90 *1.60*
  The surtax was for charitable works.

German Administration

Miner with Drill — SP59

6fr+4fr, Miner. 15fr+7fr, Miner and conveyor. 30fr+10fr, Miner and coal elevator.

  Wmk. 304
1957, Oct. 1   **Litho.**   **Perf. 14**
B117 SP59 6fr + 4fr bis brn &
  blk   .25 *.25*
B118 SP59 12fr + 6fr blk & yel
  grn   .25 *.35*
B119 SP59 15fr + 7fr blk & red   .35 *.40*
B120 SP59 30fr + 10fr blk & bl   .40 *.75*
  Nos. B117-B120 (4)   1.25 *1.75*
  The surtax was to finance young peoples' study trip to Berlin.

"The Fox who Stole the Goose" — SP60

15fr+7fr, "A Hunter from the Palatinate."

1958, Apr. 1　Wmk. 304　Perf. 14

B121 SP60 12fr + 6fr brn red, grn & blk　.25　.30
B122 SP60 15fr + 7fr grn, red, blk & gray　.25　.40

The surtax was to finance young peoples' study trip to Berlin.

Friedrich Wilhelm Raiffeisen SP61 — Dairy Maid SP62

Designs: 15fr+7fr, Girl picking grapes. 30fr+10fr, Farmer with pitchfork.

1958, Oct. 1　Wmk. 304　Perf. 14

B123 SP61 6fr + 4fr gldn brn & dk brn　.25　.25
B124 SP62 12fr + 6fr grn, red & yel　.25　.25
B125 SP62 15fr + 7fr red, yel & bl　.50　.50
B126 SP62 30fr + 10fr bl & ocher　.65　.75
　Nos. B123-B126 (4)　1.65　1.75

AIR POST STAMPS

Airplane over Saarbrücken — AP1

Perf. 13½

1928, Sept. 19　Unwmk.　Photo.

C1 AP1 50c brown red　4.00　4.00
C2 AP1 1fr dark violet　6.50　4.75

For overprints see Nos. C5, C7.

Saarbrücken Airport and Church of St. Arnual — AP2

1932, Apr. 30

C3 AP2 60c orange red　6.50　4.75
C4 AP2 5fr dark brown　45.00　95.00

For overprints see Nos. C6, C8.

Nos. C1-C4 Overprinted like Nos. 139-154 in Various Colors

1934, Nov. 1　Perf. 13½, 13½x13

C5 AP1 50c brn red (R)　4.00　7.25
C6 AP2 60c org red (O)　3.25　2.75
C7 AP1 1fr dk vio (V)　7.25　9.50
C8 AP2 5fr dk brn (Br)　9.50　14.00
　Nos. C5-C8 (4)　24.00　33.50

French Protectorate

Shadow of Plane over Saar River AP3

Unwmk.

1948, Apr. 1　Engr.　Perf. 13

C9 AP3 25fr red　2.00　3.25
C10 AP3 50fr dk vio grn　1.25　2.40
C11 AP3 200fr rose car　12.00　35.00
　Nos. C9-C11 (3)　15.25　40.65
Set, never hinged　35.00

Symbols of the Council of Europe AP4

1950, Aug. 8　Photo.　Perf. 13½

C12 AP4 200fr red brown　65.00　210.00
　Never hinged　140.00

Saar's admission to the Council of Europe.

AIR POST SEMI-POSTAL STAMP

French Protectorate

Flood Scene SPAP1

Perf. 13½x13

1948, Oct. 12　Photo.　Unwmk.

CB1 SPAP1 25fr + 25fr sep　11.00　240.00
　Never hinged　24.00
　Souvenir sheet of 1　325.00　2,700.
　Never hinged　800.00

The surtax was for flood relief.

OFFICIAL STAMPS

Regular Issue of 1922-1923 Ovptd. Diagonally in Red or Blue

Perf. 12½x13½, 13½x12½

1922-23　　　　　Unwmk.

O1 A19 3c ol grn & straw (R)　.95　35.00
O2 A20 5c org & blk (R)　.40　.40
　a. Pair, one without overprint　275.00
O3 A21 10c bl grn (R)　.40　.35
　a. Inverted overprint　32.50
O4 A19 15c dp brn (Bl)　.40　.35
　a. Pair, one without overprint　290.00
　b. Double overprint　65.00
O5 A19 15c org (Bl) ('23)　2.40　.50
O6 A22 20c dk bl & lem (R)　.40　.35
　a. Inverted overprint　32.50
　b. Double overprint　65.00
O7 A22 20c brt bl & straw (R) ('23)　2.40　.50
O8 A22 25c red & yel (Bl)　4.00　1.20
O9 A22 25c mag & straw (Bl) ('23)　2.40　.50
O10 A23 30c car & yel (Bl)　.40　.35
　a. Inverted overprint　52.50
O11 A24 40c brn & yel (Bl)　.55　.35
O12 A25 50c dk bl & straw (R)　.55　.35
　a. Inverted overprint　32.50
O13 A24 75c dp grn & straw (R)　24.00　27.50
O14 A24 75c blk & straw (R) ('23)　4.75　2.40
O15c A26 1fr brn red (Bl)　12.00　2.40
　Nos. O1-O15 (15)　56.00　72.50

The set (Type I) exists imperf. Value, hinged $1850. No. O15c (Type II) exists imperf. Value, hinged $325.

Regular Issue of 1927-30 Overprinted in Various Colors

1927-34　　　　　Perf. 13½

O16 A31 10c dp brn (Bl) ('34)　2.00　2.40
O17 A32 15c ol blk (Bl) ('34)　2.00　6.50

O18 A32 20c brn org (Bk) ('31)　2.00　1.60
O19 A32 25c bluish sl (Bl)　2.40　6.50
O20a A31 30c ol grn (Org red)　2.00　.50
O21b A32 40c olive brn (C)　2.00　.35
O22b A32 50c mag (Bl)　4.00　.40
O23 A35 60c red org (Bk) ('30)　1.20　.35
O24b A32 75c brn vio (C)　2.40　.80
O25b A35 1fr vio (RO)　2.40　.40
O26b A32 2fr brn red (Bl)　2.40　.40
　Nos. O16-O26 (11)　24.80　20.20

The overprint exists in two types: at a 32 degree angle, applied to O20-O22, O24-O26 in 1927; and at a 23-25 degree angle, applied to all values 1929/1934. The less expensive varieties are listed. For detailed listings, see the Scott Classic Specialized Catalogue.

The overprint on Nos. O16 and O20 is known only inverted. Nos. O21-O26 exist with double overprint.

French Protectorate

Arms — O1

1949, Oct. 1　Engr.　Perf. 14x13

O27 O1 10c deep carmine　.25　19.00
O28 O1 30c blue black　.25　22.50
O29 O1 1fr Prus green　.25　1.00
O30 O1 2fr orange red　.55　1.20
O31 O1 5fr blue　.75　1.00
O32 O1 10fr black　.35　1.00
O33 O1 12fr red violet　3.25　11.00
O34 O1 15fr indigo　.35　1.00
O35 O1 20fr green　.75　1.20
O36 O1 30fr violet rose　3.25　4.75
O37 O1 50fr purple　.75　4.00
O38 O1 100fr red brown　32.50　300.00
　Nos. O27-O38 (12)　43.25　367.65
Set, never hinged　120.00

ST. CHRISTOPHER

sänt ˈkris-tə-fər

LOCATION — Island in the West Indies, southeast of Puerto Rico
GOVT. — A Presidency of the former Leeward Islands Colony
AREA — 68 sq. mi.
POP. — 18,578 (estimated)
CAPITAL — Basseterre

Stamps of St. Christopher were discontinued in 1890 and replaced by those of Leeward Islands. For later issues, inscribed "St. Kitts-Nevis" or "St. Christopher-Nevis-Anguilla," see St. Kitts-Nevis.

12 Pence = 1 Shilling

Queen Victoria — A1

Wmk. Crown and C C (1)
1870, Apr. 1　Typo.　Perf. 12½

1 A1 1p dull rose　95.00　52.50
2 A1 1p lilac rose　82.50　35.00
3 A1 6p green ('71)　140.00　8.75
　Nos. 1-3 (3)　317.50　96.25

1875-79　　　　　Perf. 14

4 A1 1p lilac rose　80.00　8.00
　b. Half used as ½p on cover (2½p rate)　2,500.
5 A1 2½p red brown ('79)　200.00　275.00
6 A1 4p blue ('79)　225.00　16.00
7 A1 6p green　60.00　6.00
　a. Horiz. pair, imperf. vert.　—
　Nos. 4-7 (4)　565.00　305.00

For surcharges see Nos. 18-20.

1882-90　　Wmk. Crown and C A (2)

8 A1 ½p green　6.75　4.25
9 A1 1p rose　3.50　2.25
　a. Half used as ½p on cover
10 A1 1p lilac rose　600.00　77.50
　a. Diagonal half used as ½p on cover

11 A1 2½p red brown　200.00　67.50
　a. 2½p deep red brown　210.00　72.50
12 A1 2½p ultra ('84)　5.75　2.00
13 A1 4p blue　550.00　27.50
14 A1 4p gray ('84)　1.75　1.10
15 A1 6p olive brn ('90)　95.00　425.00
16 A1 1sh violet ('87)　105.00　75.00
　a. 1sh bright mauve ('90)　95.00　180.00
　Nos. 8-16 (9)　1,568.　682.10

For surcharges see Nos. 17, 21-23.

No. 9 Bisected and Handstamp Surcharged in Black

1885, Mar.

17 A1 ½p on half of 1p　29.00　45.00
　b. Inverted surcharge　250.00　125.00
　c. Unsevered pair　140.00　140.00
　d. As "c," one surcharge inverted　450.00　325.00
　e. Double surcharge
　f. As "b," unsevered pair　1,100.

No. 7 Surcharged in Black

No. 18 — No. 19

No. 20

1884-86　　　　　Wmk. 1

18 A1 1p on 6p grn ('86)　22.50　50.00
　a. Inverted surcharge　10,000.
　b. Double surcharge　2,600.
19 A1 4p on 6p green　75.00　57.50
　a. Period after "PENCE"　75.00　57.50
　b. Double surcharge　3,000.
20 A1 4p on 6p grn ('86)　60.00　105.00
　a. Without period after "d"　250.00　325.00
　b. Double surcharge　2,750.　3,000.
　Nos. 18-20 (3)　157.50　212.50

The line through original value on Nos. 18 and 20 was added by hand. Value for No. 18b is for stamp with pen cancellation or with violet handstamp (revenue cancels).

Nos. 8 and 12 Surcharged in Black Like No. 18 or

No. 21 — No. 22

1887-88　　　　　Wmk. 2

21 A1 1p on ½p green　50.00　60.00
22 A1 1p on 2½p ('88)　72.50　72.50
　a. Inverted surcharge　27,500.　11,000.
23 A1 1p on ½p, no line over original value ('88)　22,000.　15,000.

Nos. 18 and 21 have the same type of One Penny surcharge. The line through the original value on Nos. 21 and 22 were added by hand. No. 23 probably is a sheet that was meant to be No. 22 but was missed when the bars were added.

Antigua No. 18 was used in St. Christopher in 1890. It is canceled "A12" instead of "A02." Values: used $140, on cover $850.

POSTAL FISCAL ISSUES

Nevis Nos. 22 and 28 Overprinted "REVENUE" Horizontally and "Saint Christopher" Diagonally

1883

AR1 A5 1p violet　425.00
AR2 A5 6p green　130.00　170.00

**Stamps of St. Christopher Ovptd.
"SAINT KITTS / NEVIS / REVENUE"
in 3 Lines**

1885

AR3	A1	1p rose	3.00	19.00
AR4	A1	3p violet	17.50	72.50
AR5	A1	6p orange brown	22.00	55.00
AR6	A1	1sh olive	4.25	47.50

Other values exist with the above overprints but were not available for postal purposes.

ST. HELENA

sānt ˈhe-lə-nə

LOCATION — Island in the Atlantic Ocean, 1,200 miles west of Angola
GOVT. — British Crown Colony
AREA — 47 sq. mi.
POP. — 7,145 (?) (1999 est.)
CAPITAL — Jamestown

12 Pence = 1 Shilling
20 Shillings = 1 Pound
100 Pence = 1 Pound (1971)

> Catalogue values for unused stamps in this country are for Never Hinged items, beginning with Scott 128 in the regular postage section, Scott B1 in the semi-postal section and Scott J1 in the postage due section.

Values for unused stamps are for examples with original gum as defined in the catalogue introduction. Very fine examples of Nos. 2-7, 11-39a and 47-47b will have perforations touching the design on one or more sides due to the narrow spacing of the stamps on the plates. Stamps with perfs clear of the design on all four sides are scarce and will command higher prices.

Watermark

Wmk. 6 — Star

Queen Victoria — A1

1856, Jan. Wmk. 6 Engr. Imperf.

1	A1	6p blue	600.00	225.00

For types surcharged see Nos. 8-39, 47.

1861 Clean-Cut Perf. 14 to 15½

2	A1	6p blue	2,100.	325.00

1863 Rough Perf. 14 to 15½

2B	A1	6p blue	525.00	160.00

1871-74 Wmk. 1 Perf. 12½

3	A1	6p dull blue	900.00	125.00
4	A1	6p ultra ('73)	575.00	97.50

1879 Perf. 14x12½

5	A1	6p gray blue	575.00	60.00

1889 Perf. 14

6	A1	6p gray blue	550.00	60.00

1889 Wmk. Crown and C A (2)

7	A1	6p gray	42.50	6.00

Type of 1856 Surcharged

a b

Long Bar, 16, 17, 18 or 19mm

1863 Wmk. 1 Imperf.

8	A1(a)	1p on 6p brn red (srch. 17mm)	150.00	250.00
a.		Double surcharge	6,750.	4,250.
b.		Surcharge omitted	23,000.	
9	A1(a)	1p on 6p brn red (srch. 19mm)	150.00	275.00
10	A1(b)	4p on 6p car	600.00	300.00
a.		Double surcharge	16,000.	10,000.

1864-73 Perf. 12½

11	A1(a)	1p on 6p brn red	70.00	35.00
a.		Double surcharge	12,000.	
12	A1(b)	1p on 6p brn red ('71)	140.00	21.00
a.		Blue black surcharge	1,200.	675.00
13	A1(b)	3p on 6p yel ('73)	160.00	50.00
a.		Blue black surcharge	4,800.	2,700.
14	A1(b)	3p on 6p dk vio ('73)	140.00	72.50
15	A1(b)	4p on 6p car	175.00	60.00
a.		Double surcharge		6,750.
16	A1(b)	1sh on 6p grn (bar 16 to 17mm)	450.00	35.00
a.		Double surcharge		24,000.
17	A1(b)	1sh on 6p dp grn (bar 18mm) ('73)	750.00	20.00
a.		Blue black surcharge		—

1868 Short Bar, 14 or 15mm

18	A1(a)	1p on 6p brn red	225.00	67.50
a.		Imperf., pair	6,000.	
b.		Double surcharge		—
19	A1(b)	2p on 6p yel	200.00	72.50
a.		Imperf	12,000.	
20	A1(b)	3p on 6p dk vio	120.00	60.00
a.		Double surcharge		7,250.
b.		Imperf., pair	2,000.	
c.		3p on 6p pale purple	3,300.	900.00
21	A1(b)	4p on 6p car (words 18mm)	140.00	72.50
a.		Double surcharge		6,000.
b.		Imperf, single	14,500.	
22	A1(b)	4p on 6p car (words 19mm)	325.00	150.00
a.		Words double, 18mm and 19mm	26,000.	11,000.
b.		Imperf.		—
c.		Surcharge omitted		6,000.
23	A1(a)	1sh on 6p yel grn	750.00	160.00
a.		Double surcharge	19,500.	
b.		Pair, one without surcharge	19,500.	
c.		Imperf	17,000.	
24	A1(a)	5sh on 6p org	67.50	77.50

1882 Perf. 14x12½

25	A1(a)	1p on 6p brown red	90.00	18.00
26	A1(b)	2p on 6p yellow	140.00	60.00
27	A1(b)	3p on 6p violet	350.00	85.00
28	A1(b)	4p on 6p carmine (words 16½mm)	170.00	72.50

1883 Perf. 14

29	A1(a)	1p on 6p brown red	120.00	22.50
30	A1(b)	2p on 6p yellow	150.00	37.50
31	A1(a)	1sh on 6p yel grn	25.00	15.00

Long Bar, 18mm

1882 Perf. 14x12½

32	A1(b)	1sh on 6p dp grn	900.00	30.00

Short Bar, 14 or 14½mm

1884-94 Wmk. 2 Perf. 14

33	A1(b)	½p on 6p grn (words 17mm)	12.00	22.50
a.		½p on 6p emer, blurred print (words 17mm) ('84)	20.00	23.00
b.		Double surcharge	1,450.	1,575.
34	A1(b)	½p on 6p grn (words 15mm) ('94)	3.25	3.50
35	A1(a)	1p on 6p red ('87)	5.75	4.50
36	A1(b)	2p on 6p yel ('94)	3.25	9.50

37	A1(b)	3p on 6p dp vio ('87)	9.00	5.00
a.		3p on 6p red violet	7.75	12.00
b.		Double surcharge,#37a	11,500.	7,250.
c.		Double surcharge, #37		11,000.
38	A1(b)	4p on 6p pale brn (words 16½mm; '90)	47.50	42.50
a.		4p on 6p dk brn (words 17mm; '94)	30.00	21.00
b.		With thin bar below thick one	850.00	850.00

1894 Long Bar, 18mm

39	A1(b)	1sh on 6p yel grn	65.00	30.00
a.		Double surcharge	5,750.	

See note after No. 47.

Queen Victoria — A3

1890-97 Typo. Perf. 14

40	A3	½p green ('97)	3.25	7.75
41	A3	1p rose ('96)	20.00	2.40
42	A3	1½p red brn & grn ('96)	5.50	15.00
43	A3	2p yellow ('96)	6.00	14.50
44	A3	2½p ultra ('96)	18.00	14.50
45	A3	5p violet ('96)	13.50	37.50
46	A3	10p brown ('96)	29.00	72.50
		Nos. 40-46 (7)	95.25	164.15

Type of 1856 Surcharged

1893 Engr. Wmk. 2

47	A1	2½p on 6p blue	3.75	6.75
a.		Double surcharge	25,000.	
b.		Double impression	11,500.	

In 1905 remainders of Nos. 34-47 were sold by the postal officials. They are canceled with bars, arranged in the shape of diamonds, in purple ink. No such cancellation was ever used on the island and the stamps so canceled are of slight value. With this cancellation removed, these remainders are sometimes offered as unused. Some have been recanceled with a false dated postmark.

King Edward VII — A5

1902 Typo. Wmk. 2

48	A5	½p green	2.00	3.00
49	A5	1p carmine rose	13.00	.85

Government House — A6

"The Wharf" — A7

1903, June Wmk. 1

50	A6	½p gray grn & brn	2.40	4.00
51	A7	1p carmine & blk	1.90	1.00
52	A6	2p ol grn & blk	14.00	1.50
53	A7	8p brown & blk	26.50	37.50
54	A6	1sh org buff & brn	27.50	47.50
55	A7	2sh violet & blk	65.00	100.00
		Nos. 50-55 (6)	137.30	191.00

A8

1908, May Wmk. 3

56	A8	2½p ultra	2.00	1.90
57	A8	4p black & red, yel	8.00	21.00
58	A8	6p dull violet	14.00	17.00
		Nos. 56-58 (3)	24.00	39.90

Wmk. 2

60	A8	10sh grn & red, grn	275.00	325.00

Nos. 57 and 58 exist on both ordinary and chalky paper; No. 56 on ordinary and No. 60 on chalky paper.

Government House — A9

"The Wharf" — A10

1912-16 Ordinary Paper Wmk. 3

61	A9	½p green & blk	3.25	12.00
62	A10	1p carmine & blk	5.75	2.00
a.		1p scarlet & black ('16)	14.50	24.00
63	A10	1½p orange & blk	4.25	9.00
64	A9	2p gray & black	7.50	2.00
65	A10	2½p ultra & blk	4.25	7.25
66	A9	3p vio & blk, yel	4.25	6.00
67	A10	8p dull vio & blk	12.00	60.00
68	A9	1sh black, green	11.00	42.50
69	A10	2sh ultra & blk, bl	50.00	100.00
70	A10	3sh violet & blk	75.00	160.00
		Nos. 61-70 (10)	177.25	400.75

See Nos. 75-77.

King Edward VII — A11

For description of dies I and II see "Dies of British Colonial Stamps" in the front of the catalogue.

Die I

1912 Chalky Paper

71	A11	4p black & red, yel	15.00	30.00
72	A11	6p dull vio & red vio	4.75	6.00

A12

1913 Ordinary Paper

73	A12	4p black & red, yel	10.00	3.25
74	A12	6p dull vio & red vio	16.00	35.00

1922 Wmk. 4

75	A10	1p green	3.25	55.00
76	A10	1½p rose red	12.00	52.50
77	A9	3p ultra	25.00	95.00
		Nos. 75-77 (3)	40.25	202.50

Badge of the
Colony — A13

1922-27		Chalky Paper		Wmk. 4	
79	A13	½p blk & gray		4.00	4.00
80	A13	1p grn & blk		4.25	2.00
81	A13	1½p rose red		3.75	15.00
82	A13	2p pale gray & gray		4.50	2.40
83	A13	3p ultra		2.40	4.75
84	A13	5p red & grn, emer		6.50	6.75
85	A13	6p red vio & blk		7.50	9.75
86	A13	8p vio & blk		4.50	8.50
87	A13	1sh dk brn & blk		7.75	11.00
88	A13	1sh6p grn & blk, emer		18.00	60.00
89	A13	2sh ultra & vio, bl		22.50	55.00
90	A13	2sh6p car & blk, yel		17.00	77.50
91	A13	5sh grn & blk, yel		45.00	90.00
92	A13	7sh6p org & blk		160.00	200.00
93	A13	10sh ol grn & blk		170.00	250.00
94	A13	15sh vio & blk, bl		1,100.	2,750.
		Nos. 79-93 (15)		477.65	796.65

Nos. 88, 90, and 91 are on ordinary paper.

		Wmk. 3 Chalky Paper			
95	A13	4p black, yel		15.00	7.25
96	A13	1sh6p bl grn & blk, grn		26.50	72.50
97	A13	2sh6p car & blk, yel		30.00	77.50
98	A13	5sh grn & blk, yel		50.00	120.00
99	A13	£1 red vio & blk, red		475.00	700.00
		Nos. 95-99 (5)		596.50	977.25

Issue dates: ½p, 1½p, 2p, 3p, 4p, 8p, February, 1923; 5p, Nos. 88-91, 1927; others, June 1922.

Centenary Issue

Lot and Lot's
Wife — A14

Plantation; Queen Victoria and Kings
William IV, Edward VII, George V
A15

Map of the
Colony
A16

Quay,
Jamestown
A17

View of
James
Valley — A18

View of
Jamestown
A19

View of
Mundens
A20

St. Helena — A21

View of High
Knoll — A22

Badge of
the Colony
A23

		Perf. 12			
1934, Apr. 23		Engr.		Wmk. 4	
101	A14	½p dk vio & blk		1.25	1.00
102	A15	1p green & blk		.80	1.00
103	A16	1½p red & blk		3.00	4.00
104	A17	2p orange & blk		3.75	1.50
105	A18	3p blue & blk		1.75	5.50
106	A19	6p lt blue & blk		4.00	3.75
107	A20	1sh dk brn & blk		8.00	22.50
108	A21	2sh6p car & blk		50.00	60.00
109	A22	5sh choc & blk		100.00	100.00
110	A23	10sh red vio & blk		300.00	350.00
		Nos. 101-110 (10)		472.55	549.25
		Set, never hinged		800.00	

Common Design Types
pictured front of this volume.

Silver Jubilee Issue
Common Design Type

1935, May 6			Perf. 13½x14		
111	CD301	1½p car & dk blue		1.25	7.25
112	CD301	2p gray blk & ultra		2.40	1.50
113	CD301	6p indigo & grn		8.50	4.75
114	CD301	1sh brt vio & ind		19.00	23.00
		Nos. 111-114 (4)		31.15	36.50
		Set, never hinged		52.50	

Coronation Issue
Common Design Type

1937, May 19					
115	CD302	1p deep green		.45	.90
116	CD302	2p deep orange		.40	.55
117	CD302	3p bright ultra		.60	.60
		Nos. 115-117 (3)		1.45	2.05
		Set, never hinged		2.00	

Badge of the
Colony — A24

1938-40				Perf. 12½	
118	A24	½p purple		.25	.75
119	A24	1p dp green		7.00	2.40
119A	A24	1p org yel ('40)		.25	.30
120	A24	1½p carmine		.30	.40
121	A24	2p orange		.25	.25
122	A24	3p ultra		55.00	18.00
122A	A24	3p gray ('40)		.35	.30
122B	A24	4p ultra ('40)		1.10	.85
123	A24	6p gray blue		1.10	1.40
123A	A24	8p olive ('40)		1.75	1.00

124	A24	1sh sepia		1.10	.35
125	A24	2sh6p deep claret		11.00	6.75
126	A24	5sh brown		11.00	12.50
127	A24	10sh violet		11.00	18.00
		Nos. 118-127 (14)		101.45	63.25
		Set, never hinged		160.00	

Issue dates: May 12, 1938, July 8, 1940.
See Nos. 136-138.

> Catalogue values for unused stamps in this section, from this point to the end of the section, are for Never Hinged items.

Peace Issue
Common Design Type

		Perf. 13½x14			
1946, Oct. 21		Wmk. 4		Engr.	
128	CD303	2p deep orange		.30	.40
129	CD303	4p deep blue		.35	.30

Silver Wedding Issue
Common Design Types

1948, Oct. 20	Photo.		Perf. 14x14½		
130	CD304	3p black		.30	.30
		Perf. 11½x11			
		Engr.; Name Typo.			
131	CD305	10sh blue violet		32.50	42.50

UPU Issue
Common Design Types
Engr.; Name Typo. on 4p, 6p

1949, Oct. 10		Perf. 13½, 11x11½			
132	CD306	3p rose carmine		.30	1.00
133	CD307	4p indigo		3.50	1.60
134	CD308	6p olive		.65	3.25
135	CD309	1sh slate		.40	1.25
		Nos. 132-135 (4)		4.85	7.10

George VI Type of 1938

1949, Nov. 1	Engr.		Perf. 12½		
		Center in Black			
136	A24	1p blue green		1.40	1.50
137	A24	1½p carmine rose		1.40	1.50
138	A24	2p carmine		1.40	1.50
		Nos. 136-138 (3)		4.20	4.50

Coronation Issue
Common Design Type

1953, June 2			Perf. 13½x13		
139	CD312	3p purple & black		1.25	1.25

Badge of the
Colony
A25

A26

Designs: 1p, Flax plantation. 1½p, Heart-shaped waterfall. 2p, Lace making. 2½p, Drying flax. 3p, Wire bird. 4p, Flagstaff and barn. 6p, Donkeys carrying flax. 7p, Map. 1sh, Entrance, government offices. 2sh 6p, Cutting flax. 5sh, Jamestown. 10sh, Longwood house.

1953, Aug. 4	Perf. 13½x14, 14x13½				
		Center and Denomination in Black			
140	A25	½p emerald		.45	.30
141	A25	1p dark green		.25	.25
142	A26	1½p red violet		3.00	1.25
143	A25	2p rose lake		.75	.30
144	A25	2½p red		.60	.30
145	A25	3p brown		4.25	.30
146	A25	4p deep blue		.60	.90
147	A25	6p purple		.60	.35
148	A25	7p gray		.95	1.60
149	A25	1sh dk car rose		.60	.85
150	A25	2sh 6p violet		17.00	7.25
151	A25	5sh chocolate		21.00	12.00
152	A25	10sh orange		42.50	27.00
		Nos. 140-152 (13)		92.55	52.65

A27

		Perf. 11½			
1956, Jan. 3		Wmk. 4		Engr.	
153	A27	3p dk car rose & blue		.25	.25
154	A27	4p redsh brown & blue		.25	.25
155	A27	6p purple & blue		.25	.25
		Nos. 153-155 (3)		.75	.75

Cent. of the 1st St. Helena postage stamp.

Arms of
East India
Company
A28

Designs: 6p, Dutton's ship "London" off James Bay. 1sh, Memorial stone from fort built by Governor Dutton.

		Perf. 12½x13			
1959, May 5				Wmk. 314	
156	A28	3p rose & black		.25	.25
157	A28	6p gray & yellow green		.35	.65
158	A28	1sh orange & black		.40	.65
		Nos. 156-158 (3)		1.00	1.55

300th anniv. of the landing of Capt. John Dutton on St. Helena and of the 1st settlement.

Cape Canary
A29

Elizabeth II
A30

Queen and
Prince
Andrew
A31

Designs: 1p, Cunning fish, horiz. 2p, Brittle starfish, horiz. 4½p, Redwood flower. 6p, Red fody (Madagascar weaver). 7p, Trumpetfish, horiz. 10p, Keeled feather starfish, horiz. 1sh, Gumwood flowers. 1sh6p, Fairy tern. 2sh6p, Orange starfish, horiz. 5sh, Night-blooming cereus. 10sh, Deepwater bull's-eye, horiz.

		Perf. 11½x12, 12x11½			
1961, Dec. 12		Photo.		Wmk. 314	
159	A29	1p multicolored		.40	.25
160	A29	1½p multicolored		.50	.25
161	A29	2p gray & red		.25	.25
162	A30	3p dk blue, rose & grnsh blue		.50	.40
163	A29	4½p slate, brn & grn		.65	.60
164	A29	6p cit, brn & dp car		4.00	.75
165	A29	7p vio, blk & red brn		.50	.75
166	A29	10p blue & dp cl		.90	.75
167	A29	1sh red brn, grn & yel		.90	1.25
168	A29	1sh6p gray bl & blk		10.00	5.00
169	A29	2sh6p grnsh bl, yel & red		5.00	2.75
170	A29	5sh grn, brn & yel		12.00	4.50
171	A29	10sh gray bl, blk & sal		15.00	10.50

Perf. 14x14½
172 A31 £1 turq blue &
   choc   22.50   22.50
Nos. 159-172 (14)   73.10   50.50
For overprints see Nos. 176-179.

Freedom from Hunger Issue
Common Design Type
1963, Apr. 4   **Perf. 14x14½**
173 CD314 1sh6p ultra   2.25   1.10

Red Cross Centenary Issue
Common Design Type
      Wmk. 314
1963, Sept. 2   **Litho.**   **Perf. 13**
174 CD315   3p black & red   .30   .30
175 CD315 1sh6p ultra & red   1.40   2.00

Nos. 159, 162, 164 and 168
Overprinted: "FIRST LOCAL POST /
4th JANUARY 1965"
Perf. 11½x12, 12x11½
1965, Jan. 4   **Photo.**   **Wmk. 314**
176 A29   1p multicolored   .25   .25
177 A30   3p dk bl, rose &
    grnsh bl   .25   .25
178 A29   6p cit, brn & dp car   .25   .30
179 A29 1sh6p gray blue & blk   .60   .35
Nos. 176-179 (4)   1.35   1.15
Establishment of the 1st internal postal service on the island.

ITU Issue
Common Design Type
      Perf. 11x11½
1965, May 17   **Litho.**   **Wmk. 314**
180 CD317 3p ultra & gray   .30   .30
181 CD317 6p red lil & blue grn   .50   .30

Intl. Cooperation Year Issue
Common Design Type
1965, Oct. 25   **Litho.**   **Perf. 14½**
182 CD318 1p blue grn & claret   .25   .25
183 CD318 6p lt violet & green   .70   .25

Churchill Memorial Issue
Common Design Type
1966, Jan. 24   **Photo.**   **Perf. 14**
Design in Black, Gold and Carmine Rose
184 CD319   1p bright blue   .25   .25
185 CD319   3p green   .35   .35
186 CD319   6p brown   .50   .50
187 CD319 1sh6p violet   .75   .85
Nos. 184-187 (4)   1.85   1.95

World Cup Soccer Issue
Common Design Type
1966, July 1   **Litho.**   **Perf. 14**
188 CD321 3p multicolored   .35   .30
189 CD321 6p multicolored   .90   .30

WHO Headquarters Issue
Common Design Type
1966, Sept. 20   **Litho.**   **Perf. 14**
190 CD322   3p multicolored   1.00   .25
191 CD322 1sh6p multicolored   2.50   1.25

UNESCO Anniversary Issue
Common Design Type
1966, Dec. 1   **Litho.**   **Perf. 14**
192 CD323   3p "Education"   .75   .50
193 CD323   6p "Science"   1.25   .90
194 CD323 1sh6p "Culture"   3.25   2.25
Nos. 192-194 (3)   5.25   3.65

Badge of St.
Helena — A32

Perf. 14½x14
1967, May 5   **Photo.**   **Wmk. 314**
195 A32   1sh dk grn & multi   .25   .25
196 A32 2sh6p blue & multi   .40   .40
   a. Carmine omitted   1,100.
St. Helena's New Constitution.

The
Great
Fire of
London
A33

3p, Three-master Charles. 6p, Boats bringing new settlers to shore. 1sh6p, Settlers at work.

Perf. 13½x13
1967, Sept. 4   **Engr.**   **Wmk. 314**
197 A33   1p black & carmine   .25   .25
198 A33   3p black & vio blue   .25   .25
199 A33   6p black & dull violet   .25   .25
200 A33 1sh6p black & ol green   .25   .25
Nos. 197-200 (4)   1.00   1.00
Tercentenary of the arrival of settlers from London after the Great Fire of Sept. 2-4, 1666.

Maps of
Tristan da
Cunha
and St.
Helena
A34

Designs: 8p, 2sh3p, Maps of St. Helena and Tristan da Cunha.

Perf. 14x14½
1968, June 4   **Photo.**   **Wmk. 314**
Maps in Sepia
201 A34   4p dp red lilac   .25   .25
202 A34   8p olive   .25   .30
203 A34 1sh9p deep ultra   .25   .40
204 A34 2sh3p Prus blue   .25   .40
Nos. 201-204 (4)   1.00   1.35
30th anniv. of Tristan da Cunha as a Dependency of St. Helena.

Sir
Hudson
Lowe
A35

1sh6p, 2sh6p, Sir George Bingham.

Perf. 13½x13
1968, Sept. 4   **Litho.**   **Wmk. 314**
205 A35   3p multicolored   .25   .25
206 A35   9p multicolored   .25   .25
207 A35 1sh6p multicolored   .25   .30
208 A35 2sh6p multicolored   .25   .45
Nos. 205-208 (4)   1.00   1.25
Abolition of slavery in St. Helena, 150th anniv.

Road Construction — A36

Designs: 1p, Electricity development. 1½p, Dentist. 2p, Pest control. 3p, Apartment houses in Jamestown. 4p, Pasture and livestock improvement. 6p, School children listening to broadcast. 8p, Country cottages. 10p, New school buildings. 1sh, Reforestation. 1sh6p, Heavy lift crane. 2sh6p, Playing children in Lady Field Children's Home. 5sh, Agricultural training. 10sh, Ward in New General Hospital. £1, Lifeboat "John Dutton."

      Wmk. 314
1968, Nov. 4   **Litho.**   **Perf. 13½**
209 A36   ½p multicolored   .25   .25
210 A36   1p multicolored   .25   .25
211 A36   1½p multicolored   .25   .25
212 A36   2p multicolored   .25   .25
213 A36   3p multicolored   .30   .25
214 A36   4p multicolored   .25   .25
215 A36   6p multicolored   .30   .25
216 A36   8p multicolored   .30   .30
217 A36   10p multicolored   .30   .30
218 A36   1sh multicolored   .30   .70
219 A36 1sh6p multicolored   .60   3.00
220 A36 2sh6p multicolored   .75   3.50

221 A36   5sh multicolored   1.30   3.50
222 A36   10sh multicolored   2.75   5.25
223 A36   £1 multicolored   7.50   14.00
Nos. 209-223 (15)   15.65   32.50
See Nos. 244-256.

Brig Perseverance, 1819 — A37

Ships: 8p, M.S. Dane, 1857. 1sh9p, S.S. Llandovery Castle, 1925. 2sh3p, M.S. Good Hope Castle, 1969.

1969, Apr. 19   **Litho.**   **Perf. 13½**
224 A37   4p violet & multi   .25   .25
225 A37   8p ocher & multi   .25   .45
226 A37 1sh9p ver & multi   .30   .60
227 A37 2sh3p dk blue & multi   .35   .75
Nos. 224-227 (4)   1.15   2.05
Issued in recognition of St. Helena's dependence on sea mail.

Surgeon and
Officer (Light
Company) 20th
Foot, 1816 — A38

British Uniforms: 6p, Warrant Officer and Drummer, 53rd Foot, 1815. 1sh8p, Drum Major, 66th Foot, 1816, and Royal Artillery Officer, 1820. 2sh6p, Private 91st Foot and 2nd Corporal, Royal Sappers and Miners, 1832.

Perf. 14x14½
1969, Sept. 3   **Litho.**   **Wmk. 314**
228 A38   6p red & multi   .35   .35
229 A38   8p blue & multi   .45   .45
230 A38 1sh8p green & multi   .45   .45
231 A38 2sh6p gray & multi   .45   .55
Nos. 228-231 (4)   1.70   1.80

Charles
Dickens,
"The
Pickwick
Papers"
A39

Dickens and: 8p, "Oliver Twist." 1sh6p, "Martin Chuzzlewit." 2sh6p, "Bleak House."

Perf. 13½x13
1970, June 9   **Litho.**   **Wmk. 314**
232 A39   4p dk brown & multi   .35   .25
233 A39   8p slate & multi   .45   .25
234 A39 1sh6p multicolored   .70   .25
235 A39 2sh6p multicolored   1.50   .35
Nos. 232-235 (4)   3.00   1.10
Charles Dickens (1812-70), English novelist.

Mouth to Mouth Resuscitation — A40

Centenary of British Red Cross Society: 9p, Girl in wheelchair and nurse. 1sh9p, First aid. 2sh3p, British Red Cross Society emblem.

1970, Sept. 15   **Perf. 14½**
236 A40   6p bister, red & blk   .25   .25
237 A40   9p lt blue grn, red &
    blk   .25   .25
238 A40 1sh9p gray, red & blk   .25   .30
239 A40 2sh3p pale vio, red &
    blk   .30   .45
Nos. 236-239 (4)   1.05   1.25

A41

Regimental Emblems: 4p, Officer's Shako Plate, 20th Foot, 1812-16. 9p, Officer's breast plate, 66th Foot, before 1818. 1sh3p, Officer's full dress shako, 91st Foot, 1816. 2sh11p, Ensign's shako, 53rd Foot, 1815.

      Wmk. 314
1970, Nov. 2   **Litho.**   **Perf. 14½**
240 A41   4p multicolored   .25   .25
241 A41   9p red & multi   .25   .25
242 A41 1sh3p dk gray & multi   .40   .40
243 A41 2sh11p dk gray grn &
    multi   .70   .70
Nos. 240-243 (4)   1.60   1.60
See Nos. 263-270, 273-276.

Type of 1968
"P" instead of "d"
1971, Feb. 15   **Litho.**   **Perf. 13½**
244 A36   ½p like #210   .25   .25
245 A36   1p like #211   .25   .25
246 A36   1½p like #212   .25   .25
247 A36   2p like #213   2.00   1.00
   a. Perf. 14½ ('75)   .75   7.50
248 A36   2½p like #214   .30   .30
249 A36   3½p like #215   .45   .35
250 A36   4½p like #216   .45   .45
251 A36   5p like #217   .55   .55
252 A36   7½p like #218   .70   .70
253 A36   10p like #219   .80   .80
254 A36   12½p like #220   1.00   1.00
255 A36   25p like #221   1.60   1.60
256 A36   50p like #222   2.00   2.00
Nos. 244-256 (13)   10.60   9.50
The paper of Nos. 244-256 is thinner than the paper of Nos. 209-223 and No. 223 (£1) has been reprinted in slightly different colors. Value $16.

A42

St. Helena, from Italian Miniature, 1460

Perf. 14x14½
1971, Apr. 5   **Litho.**   **Wmk. 314**
257 A42   2p violet blue & multi   .25   .25
258 A42   5p multicolored   .25   .25
259 A42   7½p multicolored   .25   .25
260 A42 12½p olive & multi   .25   .25
Nos. 257-260 (4)   1.00   1.00
Easter 1971.

Napoleon,
after
J. L. David,
and Tomb in
St. Helena
A43

34p, Napoleon, by Hippolyte Paul Delaroche

1971, May 5   **Perf. 13½**
261 A43   2p multicolored   .25   .25
262 A43 34p multicolored   1.25   1.00
Sesquicentennial of the death of Napoleon Bonaparte (1769-1821).

Military Type of 1970

1½p, Sword Hilt, Artillery Private, 1815. 4p, Baker rifle, socket bayonet, c. 1816. 6p, Infantry officer's sword hilt, 1822. 22½p, Baker rifle, light sword bayonet, c. 1823.

1971, Nov. 10　　　　Perf. 14½

263	A41	1½p green & multi	.25	.25
264	A41	4p gray & multi	.50	.35
265	A41	6p purple & multi	.50	.45
266	A41	22½p multicolored	1.00	1.25
		Nos. 263-266 (4)	2.25	2.30

1972, June 19

Designs: 2p, Royal Sappers and Miners breastplate, 1823. 5p, Infantry sergeant's pike, 1830. 7½p, Royal Artillery officer's breastplate, 1830. 12½p, English military pistol, 1800.

267	A41	2p multicolored	.25	.25
268	A41	5p plum & black	.35	.45
269	A41	7½p dp blue & multi	.40	.55
270	A41	12½p olive & multi	.40	1.00
		Nos. 267-270 (4)	1.40	2.25

Silver Wedding Issue, 1972
Common Design Type

Design: Queen Elizabeth II, Prince Philip, St. Helena plover and white fairy tern.

1972, Nov. 20　Photo.　Perf. 14x14½

271	CD324	2p sl grn & multi	.25	.35
272	CD324	16p rose brn & multi	.35	.85

Military Type of 1970

Designs: 2p, Shako, 53rd Foot, 1815. 5p, Band and Drums sword hilt, 1830. 7½p, Royal Sappers and Miners officers' hat, 1830. 12½p, General's sword hilt, 1831.

1973, Sept. 20　Litho.　Perf. 14½

273	A41	2p dull brown & multi	.25	.55
274	A41	5p multicolored	.30	1.00
275	A41	7½p olive grn & multi	.50	1.25
276	A41	12½p lilac & multi	.75	1.50
		Nos. 273-276 (4)	1.80	4.30

Princess Anne's Wedding Issue
Common Design Type

1973, Nov. 14　Wmk. 314　Perf. 14

277	CD325	2p multicolored	.25	.25
278	CD325	18p multicolored	.25	.25

Westminster and Claudine Beached During Storm, 1849 — A45

Designs: 4p, East Indiaman True Briton, 1790. 6p, General Goddard in action off St. Helena, 1795. 22½p, East Indiaman Kent burning in Bay of Biscay, 1825.

Perf. 14½x14

1973, Dec. 17　Litho.　Wmk. 314

279	A45	1½p multicolored	.25	.40
280	A45	4p multicolored	.35	.60
281	A45	6p multicolored	.35	.60
282	A45	22½p multicolored	1.40	1.75
		Nos. 279-282 (4)	2.35	3.35

Tercentenary of the East India Company Charter.

UPU Emblem, Ships A46

Design: 25p, UPU emblem and letters.

1974, Oct. 15　　　　Perf. 14½x14

283	A46	5p blue & multi	.25	.25
284	A46	25p red & multi	.40	.50
a.		Souvenir sheet of 2, #283-284	1.05	1.50

Centenary of Universal Postal Union.

Churchill and Blenheim Palace — A47

25p, Churchill, Tower Bridge & Thames.

1974, Nov. 30　Wmk. 373　Perf. 14½

285	A47	5p black & multi	.25	.25
286	A47	25p black & multi	.40	.60
a.		Souvenir sheet of 2, #285-286	1.20	2.00

Sir Winston Churchill (1874-1965).

Capt. Cook and Jamestown — A48

5p, Capt. Cook and "Resolution," vert.

Perf. 14x13½, 13½x14

1975, July 14　　　　Litho.

287	A48	5p multicolored	.40	.25
288	A48	25p multicolored	.80	1.00

Return of Capt. James Cook to St. Helena, bicent.

Mellissia Begonifolia — A49

Designs: 5p, Mellissius adumbratus (insect). 12p, Aegialitis St. Helena (bird), horiz. 25p, Scorpaenia mellissii (fish), horiz.

1975, Oct. 20　Wmk. 373　Perf. 13

289	A49	2p gray & multi	.25	.25
290	A49	5p gray & multi	.25	.25
291	A49	12p gray & multi	.40	.75
292	A49	25p gray & multi	.40	.90
		Nos. 289-292 (4)	1.30	2.15

Centenary of the publication of "St. Helena," by John Charles Melliss.

Pound Note A50

Design: 33p, 5-pound note.

1976, Apr. 15　Wmk. 314　Perf. 13½

293	A50	8p claret & multi	.30	.30
294	A50	33p multicolored	.80	.80

First issue of St. Helena bank notes.

St. Helena No. 8 — A51

Designs: 8p, St. Helena No. 80, vert. 25p, Freighter Good Hope Castle.

Perf. 13½x14, 14x13½

1976, May 4　　　　Litho.　Wmk. 373

295	A51	5p buff, brown & blk	.25	.25
296	A51	8p lt grn, grn & blk	.25	.25
297	A51	25p multicolored	.40	.60
		Nos. 295-297 (3)	.90	1.10

Festival of stamps 1976. See Tristan da Cunha #208a for souvenir sheet that contains one each of Ascension #214, St. Helena #297 and Tristan da Cunha #208.

High Knoll, by Capt. Barnett A52

Views on St. Helena, lithographs: 3p, Friar Rock, by G. H. Bellasis, 1815. 5p, Column Lot, by Bellasis. 6p, Sandy Bay Valley, by H. Salt, 1809. 8p, View from Castle terrace, by Bellasis. 9p, The Briars, 1815. 10p, Plantation House, by J. Wathen, 1821. 15p, Longwood House, by Wathen, 1821. 18p, St. Paul's Church, by Vincent Brooks. 26p, St. James's Valley, by Wathen, 1815. 40p, St. Matthew's Church, Longwood, by Brooks. £1, St. Helena and sailing ship, by Bellasis. £2, Sugar Loaf Hill, by Wathen, 1821.

Wmk. 373

1976, Nov. 28　Litho.　Perf. 14

No Date Imprint Below Design

Size: 38½x25mm

298	A52	1p multicolored	.30	1.15
a.		Inscribed "1982"	.30	1.15
299	A52	3p multicolored	.35	1.15
300	A52	5p multicolored	.30	1.15
301	A52	6p multicolored	.30	1.15
302	A52	8p multicolored	.30	1.15
303	A52	9p multicolored	.30	1.15
304	A52	10p multicolored	.50	.60
a.		Inscribed "1982"	.50	.60
305	A52	15p multicolored	.45	.55
306	A52	18p multicolored	.45	1.50
307	A52	26p multicolored	.65	1.50
308	A52	40p multicolored	.85	1.75

Size: 47½x35mm

Perf. 13½

309	A52	£1 multicolored	2.00	4.00
310	A52	£2 multicolored	3.00	5.50
a.		Inscribed "1982"	4.00	5.50
		Nos. 298-310 (13)	9.75	22.30

Issue dates: 1p, 3p, 5p, 8p, 10p, 18p, 26p, 40p, £1, Sept. 28; others Nov. 23. Nos. 298a, 304a, 310a, 5/10/82.
For overprints see Nos. 376-377.

Royal Party Leaving St. Helena, 1947 — A53

15p, Queen's scepter, dove. 26p, Prince Philip paying homage to the Queen.

1977, Feb. 7　Wmk. 373　Perf. 13

311	A53	8p multicolored	.25	.25
312	A53	15p multicolored	.25	.30
313	A53	26p multicolored	.25	.40
		Nos. 311-313 (3)	.75	.95

25th anniv. of the reign of Elizabeth II.

Halley's Comet, from Bayeux Tapestry A54

8p, 17th cent. sextant. 27p, Edmund Halley and Halley's Mount, St. Helena.

1977, Aug. 23　Litho.　Perf. 14

314	A54	5p multicolored	.45	.45
315	A54	8p multicolored	.60	.45
316	A54	27p multicolored	1.25	1.25
		Nos. 314-316 (3)	2.30	2.15

Edmund Halley's visit to St. Helena, 300th anniv.

Elizabeth II Coronation Anniversary Issue
Common Design Types
Souvenir Sheet
Unwmk.

1978, June 2　Litho.　Perf. 15

317	Sheet of 6	1.75	1.75
a.	CD326 25p Black dragon of Ulster	.30	.30
b.	CD327 25p Elizabeth II	.30	.30
c.	CD328 25p Sea Lion	.30	.30

No. 317 contains 2 se-tenant strips of Nos. 317a-317c, separated by horizontal gutter.

St. Helena, 17th Century Engraving — A55

Designs: 5p, 9p, 15p, Various Chinese porcelain and other utensils salvaged from wreck. 8p, Bronze cannon. 20p, Dutch East Indiaman.

Wmk. 373

1978, Aug. 14　Litho.　Perf. 14½

318	A55	3p multicolored	.25	.25
319	A55	5p multicolored	.25	.25
320	A55	8p multicolored	.25	.30
321	A55	9p multicolored	.30	.35
322	A55	15p multicolored	.40	.50
323	A55	20p multicolored	.55	.65
		Nos. 318-323 (6)	2.00	2.30

Wreck of the Witte Leeuw, 1613.

"Discovery" A56

Capt. Cook's voyages: 8p, Cook's portable observatory. 12p, Pharnaceum acidum (plant), after sketch by Joseph Banks. 25p, Capt. Cook, after Flaxman/Wedgwood medallion.

1979, Feb. 19　Litho.　Perf. 11

324	A56	3p multicolored	.25	.25
325	A56	8p multicolored	.25	.25
326	A56	12p multicolored	.40	.35

Litho.; Embossed

327	A56	25p multicolored	.50	.90
		Nos. 324-327 (4)	1.40	1.75

St. Helena No. 176 A57

5p, Rowland Hill and his signature. 20p, St. Helena No. 8. 32p, St. Helena No. 49.

1979, Aug. 20　Litho.　Perf. 14

328	A57	5p multi, vert.	.25	.25
329	A57	8p multi	.25	.25
330	A57	20p multi	.25	.25
331	A57	32p multi	.25	.25
		Nos. 328-331 (4)	1.00	1.00

Sir Rowland Hill (1795-1879), originator of penny postage.

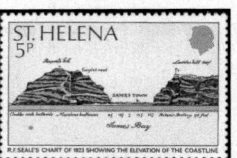

Seale's Chart, 1823 — A58

8p, Jamestown & Inclined Plane, 1829. 50p, Inclined Plane (stairs), 1979.

1979, Dec. 10   Litho.   Perf. 14
332 A58 5p multi .25 .25
333 A58 8p multi .25 .25
334 A58 50p multi, vert. .40 .70
 Nos. 332-334 (3) .90 1.20

Inclined Plane, 150th anniversary.

Tomb of Napoleon I, 1848 — A59

Empress Eugenie: 8p, Landing at St. Helena. 62p, Visiting Napoleon's tomb.

1980, Feb. 23   Litho.   Perf. 14½
335 A59 5p multicolored .25 .25
336 A59 8p multicolored .25 .25
337 A59 62p multicolored .75 .75
 a. Souvenir sheet of 3, #335-337 1.10 1.10
 Nos. 335-337 (3) 1.25 1.25

Visit of Empress Eugenie (widow of Napoleon III) to St. Helena, centenary.

East Indiaman, London 1980 Emblem — A60

8p, "Dolphin" postal stone. 47p, Jamestown castle postal stone.

1980, May 6   Litho.   Perf. 14½
338 A60 5p shown .25 .25
339 A60 8p multicolored .25 .25
340 A60 47p multicolored .50 .50
 a. Souvenir sheet of 3, #338-340 1.00 1.00
 Nos. 338-340 (3) 1.00 1.00

London 1980 Intl. Stamp Exhib., May 6-14.

Queen Mother Elizabeth Birthday Issue
Common Design Type
1980, Aug. 18   Litho.   Perf. 14
341 CD330 24p multicolored .50 .50

The Briars, 1815 A61

30p, Wellington, by Goya, vert.

1980, Nov. 17   Litho.   Perf. 14
342 A61 9p shown .25 .25
343 A61 30p multicolored .45 .45

Duke of Wellington's visit to St. Helena, 175th anniv. Nos. 342-343 issued in sheets of 10 with gutter giving historical background.

Redwood Flower A62

8p, Old father-live-forever. 15p, Gumwood. 27p, Black cabbage.

1981, Jan. 5   Perf. 13½
344 A62 5p shown .25 .25
345 A62 8p multicolored .25 .25
346 A62 15p multicolored .25 .25
347 A62 27p multicolored .35 .35
 Nos. 344-347 (4) 1.10 1.10

John Thornton's Map of St. Helena, 1700 — A63

5p, Reinel Portolan Chart, 1530. 20p, St. Helena, 1815. 30p, St. Helena, 1817. 24p, Gastaldi's map of Africa, 16th cent.

1981, May 22   Litho.   Perf. 14½
348 A63 5p multicolored .25 .25
349 A63 8p shown .25 .25
350 A63 20p multicolored .30 .30
351 A63 30p multicolored .50 .50
 Nos. 348-351 (4) 1.30 1.30

Souvenir Sheet
352 A63 24p multicolored .70 .70

Royal Wedding Issue
Common Design Type
Wmk. 373
1981, July 22   Litho.   Perf. 14
353 CD331 14p Bouquet .25 .25
354 CD331 29p Charles .30 .30
355 CD331 32p Couple .30 .30
 Nos. 353-355 (3) .85 .85

Charonia Variegata — A64

1981, Sept. 10   Litho.   Perf. 14
356 A64 7p shown .25 .25
357 A64 10p Cypraea spurca sanctahelenae .25 .25
358 A64 25p Janthina janthina .50 .50
359 A64 53p Pinna rudis .90 .90
 Nos. 356-359 (4) 1.90 1.90

Traffic Guards Taking Oath — A65

1981, Nov. 5
360 A65 7p shown .25 .25
361 A65 11p Posting signs .25 .25
362 A65 25p Animal care .30 .30
363 A65 50p Duke of Edinburgh .60 .60
 Nos. 360-363 (4) 1.40 1.40

Duke of Edinburgh's Awards, 25th anniv.

St. Helena Dragonfly — A66

1982, Jan. 4   Litho.   Perf. 14½
364 A66 7p shown .25 .25
365 A66 10p Burchell's beetle .25 .25
366 A66 25p Cockroach wasp .50 .50
367 A66 32p Earwig .65 .65
 Nos. 364-367 (4) 1.65 1.65

See Nos. 386-389.

Sesquicentennial of Charles Darwin's Visit — A67

7p, Portrait. 14p, Flagstaff Hill, hammer. 25p, Ring-necked pheasants. 29p, Beagle.

1982, Apr. 19   Litho.   Perf. 14
368 A67 7p multicolored .25 .25
369 A67 14p multicolored .35 .35
370 A67 25p multicolored .60 .60
371 A67 29p multicolored .75 .75
 Nos. 368-371 (4) 1.95 1.95

Princess Diana Issue
Common Design Type
1982, July 1   Litho.   Perf. 14
372 CD333 7p Arms .25 .25
373 CD333 11p Honeymoon .25 .25
374 CD333 29p Diana .50 .50
375 CD333 55p Portrait 1.00 1.00
 Nos. 372-375 (4) 2.00 2.00

Nos. 305, 307 Overprinted "1st PARTICIPATION / COMMONWEALTH GAMES 1982"
1982, Oct. 25   Litho.   Perf. 14
376 A52 15p multicolored .30 .30
377 A52 26p multicolored .40 .40

Scouting Year A68

1982, Nov. 29
378 A68 3p Baden-Powell, vert. .25 .25
379 A68 11p Campfire .25 .25
380 A68 29p Canon Walcott, vert. .40 .40
381 A68 59p Thompsons Wood camp .80 .80
 Nos. 378-381 (4) 1.70 1.70

Coastline from Jamestown — A69

1983, Jan. 14
382 A69 7p King and Queen Rocks, vert. .25 .25
383 A69 11p Turk's Cap, vert. .25 .25
384 A69 29p shown .40 .40
385 A69 59p Munden's Point .80 .80
 Nos. 382-385 (4) 1.70 1.70

Insect Type of 1982
1983, Apr. 22   Litho.   Perf. 14½
386 A66 11p Death's-head hawkmoth .25 .25
387 A66 15p Saldid-shore bug .25 .25
388 A66 29p Click beetle .40 .40
389 A66 59p Weevil .90 .90
 Nos. 386-389 (4) 1.80 1.80

Local Fungi A70

11p, Coriolus versicolor, vert. 15p, Pluteus brunneisucus, vert. 29p, Polyporus induratus. 59p, Coprinus angulatus, vert.

Wmk. 373
1983, June 16   Litho.   Perf. 14
390 A70 11p multicolored .30 .30
391 A70 15p multicolored .35 .35
392 A70 29p multicolored .60 .60
393 A70 59p multicolored .90 .90
 Nos. 390-393 (4) 2.15 2.15

Local Birds — A71

1983, Sept. 12   Litho.   Perf. 14x14½
394 A71 7p Padda oryzivora .25 .25
395 A71 15p Foudia madagascariensis .40 .35
396 A71 33p Estrilda astrild 1.00 .80
397 A71 59p Serinus flaviventris 1.70 1.50
 Nos. 394-397 (4) 3.35 2.90

Souvenir Sheet

Christmas 1983 — A72

Stained Glass, Parish Church of St. Michael.

1983, Oct. 17   Litho.   Perf. 14x13½
398 A72 Sheet of 10 4.00 3.00
 a. 10p multicolored .25 .25
 b. 15p multicolored .45 .35

Sheet contains strips of 5 of 10p and 15p with center margin telling St. Helena story. See Nos. 424-427, 442-445.

150th Anniv. of the Colony — A73

1984, Jan. 3   Litho.   Perf. 14
399 A73 1p No. 101 .25 .25
400 A73 3p No. 102 .25 .25
401 A73 6p No. 103 .25 .25
402 A73 7p No. 104 .25 .25
403 A73 11p No. 105 .25 .25
404 A73 15p No. 106 .25 .30
405 A73 29p No. 107 .40 .50
406 A73 33p No. 109 .45 .55
407 A73 59p No. 110 .75 .85
408 A73 £1 No. 108 1.40 1.60
409 A73 £2 New coat of arms 2.75 3.25
 Nos. 399-409 (11) 7.25 8.30

Visit of Prince Andrew A74

1984, Apr. 4   Litho.   Perf. 14
410 A74 11p Andrew, Invincible .25 .25
411 A74 60p Andrew, Herald 1.15 1.15

Lloyd's List Issue
Common Design Type
1984, May 14   Perf. 14½x14
412 CD335 10p St. Helena, 1814 .25 .25
413 CD335 18p Solomon's facade .40 .40
414 CD335 25p Lloyd's Coffee House .55 .55
415 CD335 50p Papanui, 1898 1.20 1.20
 Nos. 412-415 (4) 2.40 2.40

New Coin Issue A75

1984, July 23   **Perf. 14**
416	A75	10p 2p, Donkey	.25	.25
417	A75	15p 5p, Wire bird	.25	.35
418	A75	29p 1p, Yellowfin tuna	.55	.70
419	A75	50p 10p, Arum lily	1.00	1.20
		Nos. 416-419 (4)	2.05	2.50

Centenary of Salvation Army in St. Helena — A76

7p, Secretary Rebecca Fuller, vert. 11p, Meals on Wheels service. 25p, Jamestown SA Hall. 60p, Hymn playing, clock tower, vert.

1984, Oct. 14   Litho.   Wmk. 373
420	A76	7p multicolored	.25	.25
421	A76	11p multicolored	.25	.25
422	A76	25p multicolored	.25	.50
423	A76	60p multicolored	.75	1.25
		Nos. 420-423 (4)	1.50	2.25

Stained Glass Windows Type of 1983

6p, St. Helena visits prisoners. 10p, Betrothal of St. Helena. 15p, Marriage of St. Helena & Constantius. 33p, Birth of Constantine.

1984, Nov. 9
424	A72	6p multicolored	.25	.25
425	A72	10p multicolored	.25	.30
426	A72	15p multicolored	.30	.40
427	A72	33p multicolored	.75	.90
		Nos. 424-427 (4)	1.55	1.85

Queen Mother 85th Birthday Issue
Common Design Type

11p, Portrait, age 2. 15p, Queen Mother, Elizabeth II. 29p, Attending ballet, Covent Garden. 55p, Holding Prince Henry.

70p, Queen Mother and Ford V8 Pilot.

Perf. 14½x14

1985, June 7   Litho.   Wmk. 384
428	CD336	11p multicolored	.25	.25
429	CD336	15p multicolored	.30	.30
430	CD336	29p multicolored	.60	.60
431	CD336	55p multicolored	1.10	1.10
		Nos. 428-431 (4)	2.25	2.25

Souvenir Sheet
432	CD336	70p multicolored	3.00	3.00

Marine Life — A78

Perf. 13x13½

1985, July 12   Litho.   Wmk. 373
433	A78	7p Rock bullseye	.25	.25
434	A78	11p Mackerel	.25	.25
435	A78	15p Skipjack tuna	.25	.40
436	A78	33p Yellowfin tuna	.75	1.00
437	A78	50p Stump	1.00	1.50
		Nos. 433-437 (5)	2.50	3.40

Audubon Birth Bicent. A79

Portrait of naturalist and his illustrations of American bird species.

1985, Sept. 2   **Perf. 14**
438	A79	11p John Audubon, vert.	.25	.30
439	A79	15p Common gallinule	.30	.40
440	A79	25p Tropic bird	.55	.70
441	A79	60p Noddy tern	1.50	1.75
		Nos. 438-441 (4)	2.60	3.15

Stained Glass Windows Type of 1983

Christmas: 7p, St. Helena journeys to the Holy Land. 10p, Zambres slays the bull. 15p, The bull restored to life, conversion of St. Helena. 60p, Resurrection of the corpse, the true cross identified.

1985, Oct. 14
442	A72	7p multicolored	.25	.30
443	A72	10p multicolored	.25	.35
444	A72	15p multicolored	.30	.40
445	A72	60p multicolored	1.25	1.50
		Nos. 442-445 (4)	2.05	2.55

Society Banners A80

Designs: 10p, Church Provident Society for Women. 11p, Working Men's Christian Assoc. 25p, Church Benefit Society for Children. 29p, Mechanics & Friendly Benefit Society. 33p, Ancient Order of Foresters.

Perf. 13x13½

1986, Jan. 7   Wmk. 384
446	A80	10p multicolored	.25	.25
447	A80	11p multicolored	.25	.25
448	A80	25p multicolored	.40	.60
449	A80	29p multicolored	.50	.70
450	A80	33p multicolored	.60	.80
		Nos. 446-450 (5)	2.00	2.60

Queen Elizabeth II 60th Birthday
Common Design Type

Designs: 10p, Making 21st birthday broadcast, royal tour of South Africa, 1947. 15p, In robes of state, Throne Room, Buckingham Palace, Silver Jubilee, 1977. 20p, Onboard HMS Implacable, en route to South Africa, 1947. 50p, State visit to US, 1976. 65p, Visiting Crown Agents' offices, 1983.

1986, Apr. 21   **Perf. 14½**
451	CD337	10p scarlet, blk & sil	.25	.25
452	CD337	15p ultra & multi	.25	.30
453	CD337	20p green, blk & sil	.25	.35
454	CD337	50p violet & multi	.75	.95
455	CD337	65p rose vio & multi	1.00	1.20
		Nos. 451-455 (5)	2.50	3.05

For overprints see Nos. 488-492.

Halley's Comet — A81

Designs: 9p, Site of Halley's observatory on St. Helena. 12p, Edmond Halley, astronomer. 20p, Halley's planisphere of the southern stars. 65p, Voyage to St. Helena on the Unity.

1986, May 15   Wmk. 373   Perf. 14½
456	A81	9p multicolored	.55	.55
457	A81	12p multicolored	.65	.65
458	A81	20p multicolored	.90	.90
459	A81	65p multicolored	2.00	2.00
		Nos. 456-459 (4)	4.10	4.10

Royal Wedding Issue, 1986
Common Design Type

Designs: 10p, Informal portrait. 40p, Andrew in dress uniform at parade.

Wmk. 384

1986, July 23   **Perf. 14**
460	CD338	10p multicolored	.25	.25
461	CD338	40p multicolored	.80	.80

Explorers and Ships — A82

Designs: 1p, James Ross (1800-62), Erebus. 3p, Robert FitzRoy (1805-65), Beagle. 5p, Adam Johann von Krusenstern (1770-1846), Nadezhda, Russia. 9p, William Bligh (1754-1817), Resolution. 10p, Otto von Kotzebue (1786-1846), Rurik, Germany. 12p, Philip Carteret (1639-82), Swallow. 15p, Thomas Cavendish (c.1560-92), Desire. 20p, Louis-Antoine de Bougainville (1729-1811), La Boudeuse, France. 25p, Fyodor Petrovitch Litke (1797-1882), Seniavin, Russia. 40p, Louis Isidore Duperrey (1786-1865), La Coquille, France. 60p, John Byron (1723-86), Dolphin. £1, James Cook, Endeavour. £2, Jules Dumont d'Urville (1790-1842), L'Astrolabe, France.

Wmk. 384

1986, Sept. 22   Litho.   Perf. 14½
462	A82	1p red brown	.40	1.50
463	A82	3p bright ultra	.40	1.50
464	A82	5p olive green	.40	1.50
465	A82	9p deep claret	.50	1.50
466	A82	10p sepia	.55	1.50
467	A82	12p brt blue green	.55	1.50
468	A82	15p brown lake	.65	1.50
469	A82	20p sapphire	.85	1.50
470	A82	25p red brown	.90	1.50
471	A82	40p myrtle green	1.40	2.00
472	A82	60p brown	1.75	2.75
473	A82	£1 Prussian blue	2.75	4.50
474	A82	£2 bright violet	5.50	8.00
		Nos. 462-474 (13)	16.60	30.75

Ships of Royal Visitors A83

Portraits and vessels: 9p, Prince Edward, HMS Repulse, 1925. 13p, King George VI, HMS Vanguard, 1947. 38p, Prince Philip, HMY Britannia, 1957. 45p, Prince Andrew, HMS Herald, 1984.

1987, Feb. 16   Wmk. 373   Perf. 14
475	A83	9p multicolored	1.50	1.25
476	A83	13p multicolored	2.25	1.50
477	A83	38p multicolored	3.50	3.50
478	A83	45p multicolored	4.00	4.00
		Nos. 475-478 (4)	11.25	10.25

Rare Plants — A84

1987, Aug. 3   **Perf. 14½x14**
479	A84	9p St. Helena tea plant	.70	.70
480	A84	13p Baby's toes	1.10	1.10
481	A84	38p Salad plant	2.10	2.10
482	A84	45p Scrubwood	2.60	2.60
		Nos. 479-482 (4)	6.50	6.50

Marine Mammals A85

Wmk. 384

1987, Oct. 24   Litho.   Perf. 14
483	A85	9p Lesser rorqual	1.50	1.50
484	A85	13p Risso's dolphin	1.60	1.60
485	A85	45p Sperm whale	4.00	4.00
486	A85	60p Euphrosyne dolphin	5.75	5.75
		Nos. 483-486 (4)	12.85	12.85

Souvenir Sheet
487	A85	75p Humpback whale	10.50	10.50

Nos. 451-455 Ovptd. "40TH WEDDING ANNIVERSARY" in Silver
Wmk. 384

1987, Dec. 9   Litho.   Perf. 14½
488	CD337	10p scarlet, blk & sil	.25	.25
489	CD337	15p ultra & multi	.25	.25
490	CD337	20p green, blk & sil	.25	.40
491	CD337	50p violet & multi	.50	.85
492	CD337	65p rose vio & multi	.85	1.10
		Nos. 488-492 (5)	2.10	2.85

Australia Bicentennial A86

Ships and signatures: 9p, HMS Defence, 1691, and William Dampier. 13p, HMS Resolution, 1775, and James Cook. 45p, HMS Providence, 1792, and William Bligh. 60p, HMS Beagle, 1836, and Charles Darwin.

Wmk. 384

1988, Mar. 1   Litho.   Perf. 14½
493	A86	9p multicolored	2.25	2.00
494	A86	13p multicolored	3.00	3.00
495	A86	45p multicolored	4.75	4.75
496	A86	60p multicolored	6.25	6.25
		Nos. 493-496 (4)	16.25	16.00

Christmas — A87

Religious paintings by unknown artists: 5p, The Holy Family with Child. 20p, Madonna. 38p, The Holy Family with St. John. 60p, The Holy Virgin with the Child.

Wmk. 373

1988, Oct. 11   Litho.   Perf. 14
497	A87	5p multicolored	.25	.25
498	A87	20p multicolored	.65	.65
499	A87	38p multicolored	1.20	1.20
500	A87	60p multicolored	1.75	1.75
		Nos. 497-500 (4)	3.85	3.85

Lloyds of London, 300th Anniv.
Common Design Type

Designs: 9p, Underwriting room, 1886. 20p, Edinburgh Castle. 45p, Bosun Bird. 60p, Spangereid on fire off St. Helena, 1920.

Wmk. 384

1988, Nov. 1   Litho.   Perf. 14
501	CD341	9p multi	.45	.40
502	CD341	20p multi, horiz.	2.00	1.25
503	CD341	45p multi, horiz.	2.75	2.50
504	CD341	60p multi	3.50	3.00
		Nos. 501-504 (4)	8.70	7.15

Rare Plants — A88

1989, Jan. 6   **Perf. 14**
505	A88	9p Ebony	.45	.45
506	A88	20p St. Helena lobelia	1.10	1.10
507	A88	45p Large bellflower	2.00	2.00
508	A88	60p She cabbage tree	2.60	2.60
		Nos. 505-508 (4)	6.15	6.15

Flags and Military Uniforms, 1815 — A89

Designs: 9p, Soldier, 53rd Foot. 13p, Officer, 53rd Foot. 20p, Royal marine. 45p, Officer, 66th Foot. 60p, Soldier, 66th Foot.

1989, June 5   Litho.

509		Strip of 5	7.50	10.00
a.	A89	9p multicolored	.55	.55
b.	A89	13p multicolored	.65	.65
c.	A89	20p multicolored	1.05	1.05
d.	A89	45p multicolored	2.10	2.10
e.	A89	60p multicolored	2.75	2.75

Nos. 509a-509e Overprinted

1989, July 7   Litho.   Perf. 14

510		Strip of 5	8.50	11.00
a.	A89	9p multicolored	.85	.85
b.	A89	13p multicolored	.90	.90
c.	A89	20p multicolored	1.10	1.10
d.	A89	45p multicolored	2.25	2.25
e.	A89	60p multicolored	3.00	3.00

PHILEXFRANCE '89.

New Central (Prince Andrew) School A90

1989, Aug. 24   Perf. 14½

511	A90	13p Agriculture	.80	.75
512	A90	20p Literacy	1.25	1.10
513	A90	25p Building exterior	1.60	1.60
514	A90	60p Campus	3.75	3.75
		Nos. 511-514 (4)	7.40	7.20

Christmas — A91

10p, The Madonna with the Pear, by Durer. 20p, The Holy Family Under the Apple Tree, by Rubens. 45p, The Virgin in the Meadow, by Raphael. 60p, The Holy Family with Saint John, by Raphael.

1989, Oct. 10   Wmk. 373   Perf. 14

515	A91	10p multicolored	.65	.50
516	A91	20p multicolored	1.10	1.10
517	A91	45p multicolored	2.60	2.60
518	A91	60p multicolored	3.50	3.50
		Nos. 515-518 (4)	7.85	7.70

Early Vehicles A92

1989, Dec. 1   Wmk. 384   Perf. 14½

519	A92	9p 1930 Chevrolet	.90	.90
520	A92	20p 1929 Austin Seven	1.60	1.60
521	A92	45p 1929 Morris Cowley	3.00	3.00
522	A92	60p 1932 Sunbeam	4.25	4.25
		Nos. 519-522 (4)	9.75	9.75

Souvenir Sheet

523	A92	£1 Ford Model A	9.50	9.50

Farm Animals — A93

1990, Feb. 1   Litho.   Perf. 14

524	A93	9p Sheep	.70	.70
525	A93	13p Pigs	.90	.90
526	A93	45p Cow, calf	2.60	2.60
527	A93	60p Geese	3.25	3.25
		Nos. 524-527 (4)	7.45	7.45

Great Britain No. 2 A94

Exhibition emblem and: 20p, Great Britain No. 1. 38p, Mail delivery to branch p.o. 45p, Main p.o., mail van.

1990, May 3   Wmk. 373

528	A94	13p shown	.70	.70
529	A94	20p multicolored	1.05	1.05
530	A94	38p multicolored	2.00	2.00
531	A94	45p multicolored	2.25	2.25
		Nos. 528-531 (4)	6.00	6.00

Stamp World London '90, 150th anniv. of the Penny Black.

Queen Mother, 90th Birthday
Common Design Types

25p, As Duchess of York, 1923. £1, Visiting communal feeding center, 1940.

1990, Aug. 4   Wmk. 384   Perf. 14x15

532	CD343	25p multicolored	1.25	1.25

Perf. 14½

533	CD344	£1 multicolored	4.00	4.00

Telecommunications — A95

1990, July 28   Wmk. 373   Perf. 14

534	A95	Block of 4	4.25	4.25
a.-d.		20p any single	.95	.95

Dane, 1857 — A96

Designs: 20p, RMS St. Helena offloading cargo. 38p, Launching new RMS St. Helena, 1989. 45p, Duke of York launching new RMS St. Helena. £1, New RMS St. Helena.

1990, Sept. 13   Perf. 14½

535	A96	13p multicolored	1.25	1.25
536	A96	20p multicolored	2.00	2.00
537	A96	38p multicolored	4.00	4.00
538	A96	45p multicolored	4.25	4.25
		Nos. 535-538 (4)	11.50	11.50

Souvenir Sheet

539	A96	£1 multicolored	12.50	12.50

See Ascension Nos. 493-497, Tristan da Cunha Nos. 482-486.

Christmas — A97

Parish Churches — 10p, Baptist Chapel, Sandy Bay. 13p, St. Martin in the Hills. 20p, St. Helena and the Cross. 38p, St. James Church. 45p, St. Paul's Church.

1990, Oct. 18   Perf. 13

540	A97	10p multicolored	.50	.50
541	A97	13p multicolored	.60	.60
542	A97	20p multicolored	.90	.90
543	A97	38p multicolored	1.75	1.75
544	A97	45p multicolored	2.00	2.00
		Nos. 540-544 (5)	5.75	5.75

Removal of Napoleon's Body from St. Helena, 150th Anniv. — A98

Designs: 13p, Funeral cortege, Jamestown wharf. 20p, Moving coffin to *Belle Poule*, James Bay. 38p, Transfer of coffin from *Belle Poule* to *Normandie*, Cherbourg. 45p, Napoleon's Tomb, St. Helena.

1990, Dec. 15   Wmk. 373   Perf. 14

545	A98	13p green & black	1.50	1.25
546	A98	20p blue & black	2.10	2.00
547	A98	38p violet & black	3.75	3.75
548	A98	45p multicolored	4.50	4.50
		Nos. 545-548 (4)	11.85	11.50

A99

Military Uniforms 1897: 13p, Officer, Leicestershire Regiment. 15p, Officer, York and Lancaster Regiment. 20p, Color Sergeant, Leicestershire Regiment. 38p, Drummer/Flautist, York and Lancaster Regiment. 45p, Lance Corporal, York and Lancaster Regiment.

1991, May 2

549	A99	13p multicolored	1.40	1.40
550	A99	15p multicolored	1.60	1.60
551	A99	20p multicolored	2.00	2.00
552	A99	38p multicolored	3.25	3.25
553	A99	45p multicolored	4.25	4.25
		Nos. 549-553 (5)	12.50	12.50

Elizabeth & Philip, Birthdays
Common Design Types

1991, July 1   Wmk. 384   Perf. 14½

554	CD345	25p multicolored	1.20	1.20
555	CD346	25p multicolored	1.20	1.20
a.		Pair, #554-555 + label	2.75	2.75

A100

Christmas (Paintings): 10p, Madonna and Child, Titian. 13p, Holy Family, Mengs. 20p, Madonna and Child, Dyce. 38p, Two Trinities, Murillo. 45p, Virgin and Child, Bellini.

1991, Nov. 2   Wmk. 373   Perf. 14

556	A100	10p multicolored	1.00	1.00
557	A100	13p multicolored	1.10	1.10
558	A100	20p multicolored	1.75	1.75
559	A100	38p multicolored	3.25	3.25
560	A100	45p multicolored	3.75	3.75
		Nos. 556-560 (5)	10.85	10.85

Phila Nippon '91 — A101

Motorcycles: 13p, Matchless 346cc (ohv), 1947. 20p, Triumph Tiger 100, 500cc, 1950. 38p, Honda CD 175cc, 1967. 45p, Yamaha DTE 400, 1976. 65p, Suzuki RM 250cc, 1984.

Perf. 14x14½

1991, Nov. 16   Litho.   Wmk. 384

561	A101	13p multicolored	1.25	1.25
562	A101	20p multicolored	2.00	2.00
563	A101	38p multicolored	3.25	3.25
564	A101	45p multicolored	4.00	4.00
		Nos. 561-564 (4)	10.50	10.50

Souvenir Sheet

565	A101	65p multicolored	9.50	9.50

Discovery of America, 500th Anniv. — A102

15p, STV Eye of the Wind. 25p, STV Soren Larsen. 35p, Santa Maria, Nina & Pinta. 50p, Columbus, Santa Maria.

Wmk. 373

1992, Jan. 24   Litho.   Perf. 14

566	A102	15p multicolored	2.00	2.00
567	A102	25p multicolored	2.75	2.75
568	A102	35p multicolored	3.75	3.75
569	A102	50p multicolored	4.50	4.50
		Nos. 566-569 (4)	13.00	13.00

World Columbian Stamp Expo '92, Chicago and Genoa '92 Intl. Philatelic Exhibitions.

Queen Elizabeth II's Accession to the Throne, 40th Anniv.
Common Design Type

1992, Feb. 6

570	CD349	11p multicolored	.45	.45
571	CD349	15p multicolored	.65	.65
572	CD349	25p multicolored	1.10	1.10
573	CD349	35p multicolored	1.50	1.50
574	CD349	50p multicolored	2.00	2.00
		Nos. 570-574 (5)	5.70	5.70

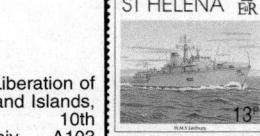

Liberation of Falkland Islands, 10th Anniv. — A103

Designs: No. 579a, 13p + 3p, like No. 575. b, 20p + 4p, like No. 576. c, 38p + 8p, like No. 577. d, 45p + 8p, like No. 578.

1992, June 12

575	A103	13p HMS Ledbury	1.00	1.00
576	A103	20p HMS Brecon	1.50	1.50
577	A103	38p RMS St. Helena	2.50	2.50
578	A103	45p First mail drop, 1982	3.00	3.00
		Nos. 575-578 (4)	8.00	8.00

Souvenir Sheet

579	A103	Sheet of 4, #a.-d.	8.50	8.50

Surtax for Soldiers', Sailors' and Airmens' Families Association.

Christmas — A104

Children in scenes from Nativity plays: 13p, Angel, shepherds. 15p, Magi, shepherds. 20p, Joseph, Mary. 45p, Nativity scene.

1992, Oct. 12   Wmk. 384

580	A104	13p multicolored	1.25	1.25
581	A104	15p multicolored	1.40	1.40
582	A104	20p multicolored	1.90	1.90
583	A104	45p multicolored	4.25	4.25
		Nos. 580-583 (4)	8.80	8.80

Anniversaries — A105

Designs: 13p, Man broadcasting at radio station. 20p, Scouts marching in parade. 38p, Breadfruit, HMS Providence, 1792. 45p, Governor Colonel Brooke, Plantation House.

1992, Dec. 4   Wmk. 373   Perf. 14½

584	A105	13p multicolored	1.25	1.25
585	A105	20p multicolored	1.75	1.75
586	A105	38p multicolored	3.25	3.25
587	A105	45p multicolored	3.75	3.75
		Nos. 584-587 (4)	10.00	10.00

Radio St. Helena, 25th anniv. (#584). Scouting on St. Helena, 75th anniv. (#585). Captain Bligh's visit, 200th anniv. (#586). Plantation House, 200th anniv. (#587).

Flowers — A106

9p, Moses in the bulrush. 13p, Periwinkle. 20p, Everlasting flower. 38p, Cigar plant. 45p, Lobelia erinus.

Perf. 14½x14

1993, Mar. 19   Litho.   Wmk. 384

588	A106	9p multicolored	.90	.90
589	A106	13p multicolored	1.30	1.30
590	A106	20p multicolored	1.75	1.75
591	A106	38p multicolored	3.00	3.00
592	A106	45p multicolored	3.50	3.50
		Nos. 588-592 (5)	10.45	10.45

See Nos. 636-640.

Wirebird A107

3p, Adult with eggs. 5p, Male, brooding female. 12p, Downy young, adult. 25p, Two immature birds. 40p, Adult in flight. 60p, Immature bird.

Wmk. 373

1993, Aug. 16   Litho.   Perf. 13½

593	A107	3p multicolored	1.15	1.15
594	A107	5p multicolored	1.40	1.40
595	A107	12p multicolored	2.25	2.25
596	A107	25p multicolored	4.50	4.50
597	A107	40p multicolored	1.75	1.75
598	A107	60p multicolored	2.75	2.75
		Nos. 593-598 (6)	13.80	13.80

Birds A108

1p, Swainson's canary. 3p, Chuckar partridge. 11p, Pigeon. 12p, Waxbill. 15p, Common myna. 18p, Java sparrow. 25p, Red-billed tropicbird. 35p, Maderian storm petrel. 75p, Madagascar fody. £1, Common fairy tern. £2, Southern giant petrel. £5, Wirebird.

1993, Aug. 26   Perf. 14½

599	A108	1p multicolored	.25	.65
600	A108	3p multicolored	.25	.65
601	A108	11p multicolored	.40	.65
602	A108	12p multicolored	.45	.65
603	A108	15p multicolored	.55	.70
604	A108	18p multicolored	.70	.85
605	A108	25p multicolored	.80	1.10
606	A108	35p multicolored	1.10	1.50
607	A108	75p multicolored	2.25	3.00
a.		Souvenir sheet of 1	3.00	3.25
608	A108	£1 multicolored	3.00	3.50
609	A108	£2 multicolored	6.25	7.00
610	A108	£5 multicolored	15.50	18.00
		Nos. 599-610 (12)	31.50	38.25

Nos. 599-604, 607, 610 are vert.
No. 607a for Hong Kong '97. Issued: 2/3/97. See No. 691.

Christmas — A109

Toys: 12p, Teddy bear, soccer ball. 15p, Sailboat, doll. 18p, Paint palette, rocking horse. 25p, Kite, airplane. 60p, Guitar, roller skates.

1993, Oct. 1   Perf. 13½x14

611	A109	12p multicolored	1.00	1.00
612	A109	15p multicolored	1.10	1.10
613	A109	18p multicolored	1.20	1.20
614	A109	25p multicolored	1.75	1.75
615	A109	60p multicolored	3.50	3.50
		Nos. 611-615 (5)	8.55	8.55

Flowers — A110

Photographs: No. 616a, Arum lily. No. 617a, Ebony. No. 618a, Shell ginger.
Nos. 616b-618b: Child's painting of same flower as in "a."

1994, Jan. 6   Wmk. 384   Perf. 14

616	A110	12p Pair, #a.-b.	1.50	1.50
617	A110	25p Pair, #a.-b.	2.50	2.50
618	A110	35p Pair, #a.-b.	3.00	3.00

Pets — A111

Designs: 12p, Abyssinian guinea pig. 25p, Common tabby cat. 53p, Plain white, black rabbits. 60p, Golden labrador.

1994, Feb. 18   Wmk. 373   Perf. 14½

619	A111	12p multicolored	.90	.90
620	A111	25p multicolored	2.10	2.10
621	A111	53p multicolored	4.00	4.00
622	A111	60p multicolored	4.25	4.25
		Nos. 619-622 (4)	11.25	11.25

Hong Kong '94.

Fish — A112

12p, Springer's blenny. 25p, Bastard five finger. 53p, Deepwater gurnard. 60p, Green fish.

1994, June 6   Wmk. 384   Perf. 14

623	A112	12p multicolored	.90	.90
624	A112	25p multicolored	1.75	1.75
625	A112	53p multicolored	4.00	4.00
626	A112	60p multicolored	4.25	4.25
		Nos. 623-626 (4)	10.90	10.90

Butterflies A113

12p, Lampides boeticus. 25p, Cynthia cardui. 53p, Hypolimnas bolina. 60p, Danaus chrysippus.

1994, Aug. 9   Wmk. 373

627	A113	12p multicolored	1.25	1.25
628	A113	25p multicolored	2.25	2.25
629	A113	53p multicolored	3.50	3.50
630	A113	60p multicolored	4.00	4.00
		Nos. 627-630 (4)	11.00	11.00

Christmas Carols — A114

Designs: 12p, "Silent night, holy night..." 15p, "While shepherds watched..." 25p, "Away in a manger..." 38p, "We three kings..." 60p, Angels from the realms of glory.

1994, Oct. 6

631	A114	12p multicolored	.60	.70
632	A114	15p multicolored	.80	.90
633	A114	25p multicolored	1.25	1.40
634	A114	38p multicolored	2.00	2.25
635	A114	60p multicolored	3.25	3.75
		Nos. 631-635 (5)	7.90	9.00

Flower Type of 1993
Wmk. 384

1994, Dec. 15   Litho.   Perf. 14½

636	A106	12p Honeysuckle	.55	.55
637	A106	15p Gobblegheer	.70	.70
638	A106	25p African lily	1.00	1.00
639	A106	38p Prince of Wales feathers	1.60	1.60
640	A106	60p St. Johns lily	2.50	2.50
		Nos. 636-640 (5)	6.35	6.35

Emergency Services — A115

12p, Fire engine. 25p, Inshore rescue craft. 53p, Police, rural patrol. 60p, Ambulance.

Designs: 12p, Abyssinian guinea pig. 25p, Common tabby cat. 53p, Plain white, black rabbits. 60p, Golden labrador.

Harpers Earth Dam Project A116

Wmk. 384

1995, Feb. 2   Litho.   Perf. 14

641	A115	12p multicolored	1.00	1.00
642	A115	25p multicolored	2.25	2.25
643	A115	53p multicolored	4.00	4.00
644	A115	60p multicolored	4.75	4.75
		Nos. 641-644 (4)	12.00	12.00

Designs: a, Site clearance. b, Earthworks in progress. c, Laying the outlet pipe. d, Revetment block protection. e, Completed dam, June 1994.

Wmk. 373

1995, Apr. 6   Litho.   Perf. 14½

645	A116	25p Strip of 5, #a.-e.	6.75	6.75

No. 645 is a continuous design.

End of World War II, 50th Anniv.
Common Design Types

Designs: No. 646, CS Lady Denison Pender. No. 647, HMS Dragon. No. 648, RFA Darkdale. No. 649, HMS Hermes. No. 650, St. Helena Rifles on parade. No. 651, Gov. Maj. W.J. Bain Gray during Victory Parade. No. 652, 6-inch gun, Ladder Hill. No. 653, Signal Station, flag hoist signalling VICTORY. No. 654, Reverse of War Medal 1939-45.

1995, May 8   Wmk. 373   Perf. 14

646	CD351	5p multicolored	1.20	1.20
647	CD351	5p multicolored	1.20	1.20
a.		Pair, #646-647	2.75	2.75
648	CD351	12p multicolored	2.10	2.10
649	CD351	12p multicolored	2.10	2.10
a.		Pair, #648-649	4.75	4.75
650	CD351	25p multicolored	3.00	3.00
651	CD351	25p multicolored	3.00	3.00
a.		Pair, #650-651	7.25	7.25
652	CD351	53p multicolored	3.50	3.50
653	CD351	53p multicolored	3.50	3.50
a.		Pair, #652-653	9.00	9.00
		Nos. 646-653 (8)	19.60	19.60

Souvenir Sheet

654	CD352	£1 multicolored	6.50	6.50

Invertebrates — A117

Designs: 12p, Blushing snail. 25p, Golden sail spider. 53p, Spiky yellow woodlouse. 60p, St. Helena shore crab. £1, Giant earwig.

1995, Aug. 29   Wmk. 373   Perf. 14

655	A117	12p multicolored	1.30	1.40
656	A117	25p multicolored	2.00	2.25
657	A117	53p multicolored	3.25	3.75
658	A117	60p multicolored	3.75	4.25
		Nos. 655-658 (4)	10.30	11.65

Souvenir Sheet

659	A117	£1 multicolored	7.50	8.00

Souvenir Sheet

Orchids — A118

a, Epidendrum ibaguense. b, Vanda Miss Joaquim.

Perf. 14½x14

1995, Sept. 1   Wmk. 384

660	A118	50p Sheet of 2, #a.-b.	8.50	8.50

Singapore '95.

Christmas
A119

Children's drawings: 12p, Christmas Eve in Jamestown. 15p, Santa, musicians. 25p, Party at Blue Hill Community Center. 38p, Santa walking in Jamestown. 60p, RMS St. Helena.

Perf. 14x14½
1995, Oct. 17   Litho.   Wmk. 373

661	A119 12p multicolored	.55	.55
662	A119 15p multicolored	.65	.65
663	A119 25p multicolored	1.10	1.10
664	A119 38p multicolored	1.60	1.60
665	A119 60p multicolored	2.25	2.25
	Nos. 661-665 (5)	6.15	6.15

Union
Castle
Mail
Ships
A120

12p, Walmer Castle, 1915. 25p, Llangibby Castle, 1934. 53p, Stirling Castle, 1940. 60p, Pendennis Castle, 1965.

Wmk. 384
1996, Jan. 8   Litho.   Perf. 14

666	A120 12p multicolored	1.40	1.40
667	A120 25p multicolored	2.50	2.50
668	A120 53p multicolored	5.25	5.25
669	A120 60p multicolored	5.75	5.75
	Nos. 666-669 (4)	14.90	14.90

See Nos. 707-710.

Radio,
Cent.
A121

Designs: 60p, Telecommunications equipment on St. Helena. £1, Marconi aboard yacht, Elettra.

Wmk. 373
1996, Mar. 28   Litho.   Perf. 13½

670	A121 60p multicolored	3.00	3.00
671	A121 £1 multicolored	5.00	5.00

Queen Elizabeth II, 70th Birthday
Common Design Type

Various portraits of Queen, scenes of St. Helena: 15p, Jamestown. 25p, Prince Andrew School. 53p, Castle entrance. 60p, Plantation house.
£1.50, Queen wearing tiara, formal dress.

Perf. 14x14½
1996, Apr. 22   Litho.   Wmk. 384

672	CD354 15p multicolored	.70	.70
673	CD354 25p multicolored	1.10	1.10
674	CD354 53p multicolored	2.25	2.25
675	CD354 60p multicolored	2.40	2.40
	Nos. 672-675 (4)	6.45	6.45

Souvenir Sheet

676	CD354 £1.50 multicolored	6.00	6.25

CAPEX
'96
A122

Postal transport: 12p, Mail airlifted to HMS Protector, 1964. 25p, First local post delivery, motorscooter, 1965. 53p, Mail unloaded at Wideawake Airfield, Ascension Island. 60p, Mail received at St. Helena.
£1, LMS Jubilee Class 4-6-0 locomotive No. 5624 "St. Helena."

Wmk. 384
1996, June 8   Litho.   Perf. 14

677	A122 12p multicolored	.60	.60
678	A122 25p multicolored	1.25	1.25
679	A122 53p multicolored	2.50	2.50
680	A122 60p multicolored	2.75	2.75
	Nos. 677-680 (4)	7.10	7.10

Souvenir Sheet

681	A122 £1 multicolored	6.00	6.00

Napoleonic
Sites
A123

12p, Mr. Porteous' House. 25p, Briars Pavillion. 53p, Longwood House. 60p, Napoleon's Tomb.

Wmk. 373
1996, Aug. 12   Litho.   Perf. 14½

682	A123 12p multicolored	1.10	1.10
683	A123 25p multicolored	2.40	2.40
684	A123 53p multicolored	4.75	4.75
685	A123 60p multicolored	5.50	5.50
	Nos. 682-685 (4)	13.75	13.75

Christmas
A124

Flowers: 12p, Frangipani. 15p, Bougainvillaea. 25p, Jacaranda. £1, Pink periwinkle.

Wmk. 373
1996, Oct. 1   Litho.   Perf. 14½

686	A124 12p multicolored	.60	.60
687	A124 15p multicolored	.80	.80
688	A124 25p multicolored	1.30	1.30
689	A124 £1 multicolored	4.50	4.50
	Nos. 686-689 (4)	7.20	7.20

Endemic
Plants — A125

Designs: a, Black cabbage tree. b, Whitewood. c, Tree fern. d, Dwarf jellico. e, Lobelia. f, Dogwood.

1997, Jan. 17   Perf. 14½x14

690	A125 25p Sheet of 6, #a.- f.	13.00	13.00

Bird Type of 1993
Souvenir Sheet
Wmk. 373
1997, June 20   Litho.   Perf. 14½

691	A108 75p like No. 610	3.00	3.50

Return of Hong Kong to China, July 1, 1997.

Discovery of St.
Helena, 500th
Anniv. (in
2002) — A126

20p, Discovery by Joao da Nova, May 21, 1502. 25p, 1st inhabitant, Don Fernando

Lopez, 1515. 30p, Landing by Thomas Cavendish, 1588. 80p, Ship, Royal Merchant, 1591.

1997, May 29   Perf. 14

692	A126 20p multicolored	1.40	1.40
693	A126 25p multicolored	1.75	1.75
694	A126 30p multicolored	1.90	1.90
695	A126 80p multicolored	5.00	5.00
	Nos. 692-695 (4)	10.05	10.05

See Nos. 712-715, 736-739, 755-758, 769-772.

Queen Elizabeth II and Prince Philip,
50th Wedding Anniv. — A127

No. 696, Queen, Prince coming down steps, royal visit, 1947. No. 697, Wedding portrait. No. 698, Wedding portrait, diff. No. 699, Queen receiving flowers, royal visit, 1947. No. 700, Royal visit, 1957. No. 701, Queen, Prince waving from balcony on wedding day.
£1.50, Queen, Prince riding in open carriage.

Wmk. 384
1997, July 10   Litho.   Perf. 13½

696	10p multicolored	1.00	1.00
697	10p multicolored	1.00	1.00
a.	A127 Pair, #696-697	2.50	2.50
698	15p multicolored	1.25	1.25
699	15p multicolored	1.25	1.25
a.	A127 Pair, #698-699	3.00	3.00
700	50p multicolored	2.25	2.25
701	50p multicolored	2.25	2.25
a.	A127 Pair, #700-701	5.50	5.50
	Nos. 696-701 (6)	9.00	9.00

Souvenir Sheet
Perf. 14x14½

702	A127 £1.50 multi, horiz.	10.00	10.00

Christmas — A128

Perf. 13½x14
1997, Sept. 29   Litho.   Wmk. 384

703	A128 15p Flowers	.95	.95
704	A128 20p Calligraphy	1.35	1.35
705	A128 40p Camping	2.40	2.40
706	A128 75p Entertaining	4.75	4.75
	Nos. 703-706 (4)	9.45	9.45

Duke of Edinburgh's Award in St. Helena, 25th anniv.

Union Castle Mail Ships Type of 1996

20p, Avondale Castle, 1900. 25p, Dunnottar Castle, 1936. 30p, Llandovery Castle, 1943. 80p, Good Hope Castle, 1977.

Wmk. 384
1998, Jan. 2   Litho.   Perf. 14

707	A120 20p multicolored	2.75	2.25
708	A120 25p multicolored	3.00	2.25
709	A120 30p multicolored	3.25	2.25
710	A120 80p multicolored	6.50	6.50
	Nos. 707-710 (4)	15.50	13.25

Diana, Princess of Wales (1961-97)
Common Design Type

a, Wearing hat. b, In white pin-striped suit jacket. c, In green jacket. d, Wearing choker necklace.

Perf. 14½x14
1998, Apr. 4   Litho.   Wmk. 373

711	CD355 30p Sheet of 4, #a.-d.	4.25	4.25

No. 711 sold for £1.20 + 20p, with surtax from international sales being donated to Princess Diana Memorial Fund and surtax from national sales being donated to designated local charity.

Discovery of St. Helena, 500th Anniv. Type of 1997

17th Century events, horiz.: 20p, Fortifying and planting, 1659. 25p, Dutch invasion, 1672. 30p, English recapture, 1673. 80p, Royal Charter, 1673.

Wmk. 384
1998, July 2   Litho.   Perf. 14
Size: 39x26mm

712	A126 20p multicolored	1.15	1.15
713	A126 25p multicolored	1.60	1.60
714	A126 30p multicolored	2.10	2.10
715	A126 80p multicolored	4.00	4.00
	Nos. 712-715 (4)	8.85	8.85

Maritime Heritage — A129

Ships: 10p, HMS Desire, 1588. 15p, Dutch ship, "White Leeuw," 1602. 20p, HMS Swallow, HMS Dolphin, 1751. 25p, HMS Endeavour, 1771. 30p, HMS Providence, 1792. 35p, HMS St. Helena, 1815. 40p, HMS Northumberland, 1815. 50p, Russian brig, "Rurik," 1815. 75p, HMS Erebus, 1826. 80p, Pole junk, "Keying," 1847. £2, La Belle Poule, 1840. £5, HMS Rattlesnake, 1861.

Perf. 13½x14
1998, Aug. 25   Litho.   Wmk. 373

716	A129 10p multicolored	.65	.90
717	A129 15p multicolored	.70	.90
718	A129 20p multicolored	.75	.90
719	A129 25p multicolored	.90	1.35
720	A129 30p multicolored	1.25	1.45
721	A129 35p multicolored	1.35	1.60
722	A129 40p multicolored	1.75	2.00
723	A129 50p multicolored	2.25	3.00
724	A129 75p multicolored	3.25	4.00
725	A129 80p multicolored	3.75	4.50
726	A129 £2 multicolored	9.00	11.00
727	A129 £5 multicolored	21.00	22.00
	Nos. 716-727 (12)	46.60	53.60

Christmas
A130

Island crafts: 15p, Metal work. 20p, Wood turning. 30p, Inlaid woodwork. 85p, Hessian and seedwork.

1998, Sept. 28   Perf. 14

728	A130 15p multicolored	.55	.55
729	A130 20p multicolored	.75	.75
730	A130 30p multicolored	1.30	1.30
731	A130 85p multicolored	3.00	3.00
	Nos. 728-731 (4)	5.60	5.60

Souvenir Sheet

H. M. Bark Endeavour at Anchor,
1771 — A131

Perf. 13½x14
1999, Mar. 5   Litho.   Wmk. 373

732	A131 £1.50 multicolored	9.75	9.75

Australia '99 World Stamp Expo.

Wedding of Prince Edward and Sophie Rhys-Jones
Common Design Type
Perf. 13¾x14
1999, June 15   **Litho.**   **Wmk. 384**

733	CD356	30p	Separate portraits	1.00 1.00
734	CD356	£1.30	Couple	4.00 4.00

Souvenir Sheet

PhilexFrance '99, World Philatelic Exhibition — A132

1999, July 2   **Perf. 14**

735	A132	£1.50 #261	8.00 8.00

Discovery of St. Helena, 500th Anniv. Type of 1997
Designs, horiz: 20p, Jamestown fortification. 25p, First safe roadway up Ladder Hill, 1718. 30p, Governor Skottowe with Captain Cook. 80p, Presentation of sword of honor to Governor Brooke, 1799.

Perf. 14¼x14
1999, July 12   **Litho.**   **Wmk. 373**

736	A126	20p	multicolored	1.90 1.90
737	A126	25p	multicolored	2.25 2.25
738	A126	30p	multicolored	2.75 2.75
739	A126	80p	multicolored	5.75 5.75
		Nos. 736-739 (4)		12.65 12.65

Queen Mother's Century
Common Design Type
Queen Mother: 15p, With King George VI visiting St. Helena. 25p, With King George VI inspecting bomb damage at Buckingham Palace. 30p, With Prince Andrew, 97th birthday. 80p, As commandant-in-chief of Royal Air Force Central Flying School. £1.50, With family at coronation of King George VI.

Wmk. 384
1999, Sept. 3   **Litho.**   **Perf. 13½**

740	CD358	15p	multicolored	.75 .75
741	CD358	25p	multicolored	1.40 1.40
742	CD358	30p	multicolored	1.75 1.75
743	CD358	80p	multicolored	4.25 4.25
		Nos. 740-743 (4)		8.15 8.15

Souvenir Sheet

744	CD358	£1.50 multicolored	8.00 8.00

Cable & Wireless, Cent. A133

Wmk. 373
1999, Nov. 26   **Litho.**   **Perf. 14**

745	A133	20p	Cable, communication equipment	1.50 1.50
746	A133	25p	CS Seine	1.75 1.75
747	A133	30p	CS Anglia	2.10 2.10
748	A133	80p	Headquarters	5.75 5.75
		Nos. 745-748 (4)		11.10 11.10

Souvenir Sheet

Union-Castle Line Centenary Voyage — A134

1999, Dec. 23   **Perf. 13x13¾**

749	A134	£2 multicolored	14.00 14.00

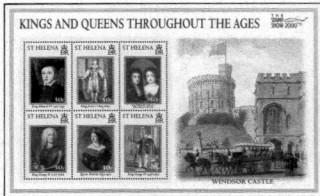

British Monarchs — A135

Designs: a, Edward VI. b, James I. c, William III, Mary II. d, George II. e, Victoria. f, George VI.

Wmk. 373
2000, Feb. 29   **Perf. 14**

750	A135	30p Sheet of 6, #a.-f.	12.00 12.00

The Stamp Show 2000, London.

Boer War, Cent. A136

Designs: 15p, Distillation plant, Ruperts. 25p, Camp, Broadbottom. 30p, Committee of Boer prisoners. 80p, Boer General Piet Cronjé, prisoner at Kent Cottage.

Wmk. 373
2000, Apr. 10   **Litho.**   **Perf. 14**

751-754	A136	Set of 4	12.50 12.50

Discovery of St. Helena, 500th Anniv. Type of 1997
Designs: 20p, Withdrawal of the East India Company, 1833, horiz. 25p, Abolition of slavery, 1832, horiz. 30p, Napoleon arrives in 1815, departs in 1840, horiz. 80p, Chief Dinizulu, 1890, horiz.

2000, May 23   **Wmk. 373**   **Perf. 13¾**

755-758	A126	Set of 4	11.50 11.50

Souvenir Sheet

Royal Birthdays — A137

No. 759: a, Princess Margaret, 70th birthday. b, Prince Andrew, 40th birthday. c, Prince William, 18th birthday. d, Princess Anne, 50th birthday. e, Queen Mother, 100th birthday.

2000, Aug. 4   **Wmk. 384**   **Perf. 14**

759	A137	Sheet of 5	37.50 37.50
a.-d.		25p Any single	5.25 5.25
e.		50p multi	10.50 10.50

No. 759e is 42x56mm.

Christmas Pantomimes A138

a, Beauty and the Beast. b, Puss in Boots. c, Little Red Riding Hood. d, Jack and the Beanstalk. e, Snow White and the Seven Dwarfs.

Wmk. 373
2000, Oct. 10   **Litho.**   **Perf. 13**

760		Strip of 5	7.00 7.00
a.-e.		A138 20p Any single	1.10 1.10

Souvenir Sheet

New Year 2001 (Year of the Snake) — A139

No. 761: a, 30p, Chinese white dolphin. b, 40p, Striped dolphin.

Wmk. 373
2001, Feb. 1   **Litho.**   **Perf. 14½**

761	A139	Sheet of 2, #a-b	10.00 10.00

Hong Kong 2001 Stamp Exhibition.

Age of Victoria — A140

Designs: 10p, St. Helena #1. 15p, Visit of HMS Beagle, 1836. 20p, Jamestown, horiz. 25p, Queen Victoria, horiz. 30p, Diamond Jubilee, horiz. 50p, Lewis Carroll. £1.50, Coffee receives award at the Great Exhibition.

Wmk. 373
2001, May 24   **Litho.**   **Perf. 14**

762-767	A140	Set of 6	10.50 10.50

Souvenir Sheet

768	A140	£1.50 multi	7.00 8.00

Discovery of St. Helena, 500th Anniv. Type of 1997
Designs, horiz.: 20p, World Wars I and II. 25p, Schools. 30p, Flax industry. 80p, RMS St. Helena.

2001, July 19   **Perf. 14x14¾**

769-772	A126	Set of 4	11.50 11.50

World War II Royal Navy Ships A141

HMS: 15p, Dunedin. 20p, Repulse. 25p, Nelson. 30p, Exmoor. 40p, Eagle. 50p, Milford.

2001, Sept. 20   **Perf. 14**

773-778	A141	Set of 6	14.00 14.00

Tammy Wynette (1942-98), American Singer A142

Wynette and Christmas carols: 10p, It Came Upon a Midnight Clear. 15p, Joy to the World. 20p, Away in the Manger. 30p, Silent Night.

Wmk. 373
2001, Oct. 11   **Litho.**   **Perf. 14**

779-782	A142	Set of 4	4.50 4.50

Souvenir Sheet

783	A142	£1.50 Portrait, vert.	7.00 7.00

Napoleon Bonaparte's Early Years — A143

Napoleon: 20p, As young man. 25p, At military school. 30p, At dance. 80p, With family.

2001, Nov. 1   **Perf. 13¾x14**

784-787	A143	Set of 4	12.00 12.00

Reign Of Queen Elizabeth II, 50th Anniv. Issue
Common Design Type
Designs: Nos. 788, 792a, 20p, Princess Elizabeth with Princess Margaret. Nos. 789, 792b, 25p, Wearing tiara. Nos. 790, 792c, 30p, With Princes Andrew and Edward, 1967. Nos. 791, 792d, 80p, In 1999. No. 792e, 50p, 1955 portrait by Annigoni (38x50mm).

Perf. 14¼x14½, 13¾ (#792e)
2002, Feb. 6   **Litho.**   **Wmk. 373**
With Gold Frames

788	CD360	20p	multicolored	.50 .50
789	CD360	25p	multicolored	1.60 1.60
790	CD360	30p	multicolored	1.90 1.90
791	CD360	80p	multicolored	4.75 4.75
		Nos. 788-791 (4)		8.75 8.75

Souvenir Sheet
Without Gold Frames

792	CD360	Sheet of 5, #a-e	11.00 11.00

Birdlife International A144

Wirebird: 10p, With beak open. 15p, Running, vert. 25p, Looking left with beak closed, vert. 30p, In flight. 80p, Looking right with beak closed.

Perf. 14¼x13¾, 13¾x14¼
2002, Apr. 15   **Litho.**

793	A144	10p	multi	.90 .90
a.		Perf. 14¼		.60 .60
794	A144	15p	multi	1.25 1.25
a.		Perf. 14¼		.85 .85
795	A144	30p	multi	1.75 1.75
a.		Perf. 14¼		1.40 1.40
796	A144	80p	multi	4.25 4.25
a.		Perf. 14¼		3.50 3.50
		Nos. 793-796 (4)		8.15 8.15

Souvenir Sheet
Perf. 14¼

797	A144	Sheet, #793a-796a, 797a	9.00 9.00
a.		25p multi	2.60 2.60

Discovery of St. Helena, 500th Anniv. A145

View of island and: 20p, Sir William W. Doveton (1753-1843), council member, military officer. 25p, Canon Lawrence C. Walcott

(1880-1951). 30p, Governor Hudson R. Janisch (1824-84). 80p, Dr. Wilberforce J. J. Arnold (1867-1925), colonial surgeon.

Wmk. 373

2002, May 21	Litho.		Perf. 14
798-801	A145	Set of 4	8.25 8.25

Ships of the Falkland Islands War A146

Designs: 15p, HMS Hermes. 20p, HMS Leeds Castle. 25p, HMS Intrepid. 30p, HMS Glasgow. 40p, RMS St. Helena, HMS Brecon, HMS Ledbury. 50p, HMS Courageous.

Wmk. 373

2002, June 14	Litho.		Perf. 14
802-807	A146	Set of 6	9.50 9.50

Queen Mother Elizabeth (1900-2002)
Common Design Type

Designs: 20p, Holding baby (black and white photograph). 25p, Wearing red hat. 30p, As young woman, without hat (black and white photograph). 50p, Wearing blue hat.
No. 812: a, 35p, Without hat, diff. (black and white photo). b, £1, Wearing blue hat and scarf.

Wmk. 373

2002, Aug. 5	Litho.		Perf. 14¼
		With Purple Frames	
808	CD361	20p multicolored	.50 .50
809	CD361	25p multicolored	1.00 1.00
810	CD361	30p multicolored	1.50 1.50
811	CD361	50p multicolored	2.50 2.50
		Nos. 808-811 (4)	5.50 5.50

Souvenir Sheet
Without Purple Frames
Perf. 14½x14¼

812	CD361	Sheet of 2, #a-b	6.50 6.50

Worldwide Fund for Nature (WWF) A147

Sperm whales: 10p, Three underwater. 15p, One surfacing. 20p, Two underwater. 30p, One with tail out of water.

Wmk. 373

2002, Oct. 3	Litho.		Perf. 14
813-816	A147	Set of 4	5.00 5.00
816a		Strip of 4, #813-816	5.25 5.25

Souvenir Sheet

Visit of Princess Royal (Princess Anne) — A148

Wmk. 373

2002, Nov. 15	Litho.		Perf. 14
817	A148	£2 multi	9.00 9.00

Tourism A149

Design: No. 818, Ship Queen Elizabeth 2 visits St. Helena.
No. 819: a, Plantation House. b, RMS St. Helena in Jamestown harbor. c, Napoleon's Tomb, Briars Pavilion. d, Ebony flower, Diana's Peak. e, Wirebird, Napoleon's House. f, Broadway House. g, St. Helena Golf Course. h, St. Helena Yacht Club. i, Sport fishing. j, Diving Club. k, St. Helena Heritage Society Museum.

Perf. 13½x13¼

818	A149	25p multi	2.00 2.00
819	A149	25p Sheet of 12, #a-k, 818 + 4 labels	15.50 15.50

Head of Queen Elizabeth II
Common Design Type

Wmk. 373

2003, June 2	Litho.		Perf. 13¾
820	CD362	£2.50 multi	9.00 9.00

Coronation of Queen Elizabeth II, 50th Anniv.
Common Design Type

Designs: Nos. 821, 823a, 30p, Queen with scepter. Nos. 822, 824b, 50p, Queen in carriage.

Perf. 14¼x14½

2003, June 2	Litho.	Wmk. 373
	Vignettes Framed, Red Background	
821	CD363	30p multicolored	1.50 1.50
822	CD363	50p multicolored	2.00 2.00

Souvenir Sheet
Vignettes Without Frame, Purple Panel

823	CD363	Sheet of 2, #a-b	3.75 3.75

Wild Flowers — A150

Designs: 10p, Monkey toe. 15p, Buddleia madagascariensis. 20p, Lady's petticoat. 25p, Fuchsia boliviana. 30p, Tallowvine. 40p, Elderberry. 50p Yellow pops. 75p, Lucky leaf. 80p, Ginger. £1, Lily shot. £2, Waxy ginger. £5, Lantana camara.

Wmk. 373

2003, June 10	Litho.		Perf. 14
824	A150	10p multi	.45 .45
825	A150	15p multi	.60 .60
826	A150	20p multi	.80 .80
827	A150	25p multi	1.00 1.00
828	A150	30p multi	1.25 1.25
829	A150	40p multi	1.60 1.60
830	A150	50p multi	2.00 2.00
831	A150	75p multi	3.00 3.50
832	A150	80p multi	3.25 4.00
833	A150	£1 multi	4.00 5.00
834	A150	£2 multi	7.75 10.00
835	A150	£5 multi	19.00 22.50
		Nos. 824-835 (12)	44.70 52.70

Powered Flight, Cent. — A151

Designs: 10p, Westland-Aerospatiale Lynx Helicopter. 15p, Douglas C-124 Globemaster. 20p, British Aerospace Nimrod AEW Mk3. 25p, Lockheed C-130 Hercules. 30p, Lockheed Tristar. 50p, Wright Flyer. £1.80, Supermarine Walrus.

Wmk. 373

2003, Aug. 12		Wmk. 373
	Stamp + Label	
836-841	A151	Set of 6	11.00 11.00

Souvenir Sheet

842	A151	£1.80 multi	9.00 9.00

Christmas — A152

Astronomical photos: 10p, Large Magellanic Cloud. 15p, Small Magellanic Cloud. 20p, Omega Centauri. 25p, Eta Carinae. 30p, Southern Cross.

Wmk. 373

2003, Oct. 6	Litho.		Perf. 13½
843-847	A152	Set of 5	8.00 8.00

Medical Pioneers A153

Designs: 10p, Christiaan Barnard (1922-2001). 25p, Marie Curie (1867-1934). 30p, Louis Pasteur (1822-95). 50p, Sir Alexander Fleming (1881-1955).

Wmk. 373

2004, Mar. 19	Litho.		Perf. 14¼
848-851	A153	Set of 4	9.00 9.00

Royal Horticultural Society, Bicent. — A154

Flowers: 10p, Freesia. 15p, Bottle brush. 30p, Ebony. 50p, Olive. £1, Maurandya.

Wmk. 373

2004, May 25	Litho.		Perf. 14
852-855	A154	Set of 4	5.00 5.00

Souvenir Sheet

856	A154	£1 multi	4.00 4.00

Merchant Ships A155

Designs: 20p, SS Umtata. 30p, SS Umzinto. 50p, SS Umtali. 80p, SS Umbilo.

Wmk. 373

2004, Nov. 4	Litho.		Perf. 13¼
857-860	A155	Set of 4	12.00 11.50

Christmas — A156

Stained-glass windows: 10p, St. Matthew. 15p, St. John. 20p, St. Peter. 30p, St. James. 50p, St. Paul.

Wmk. 373

2004, Oct. 5	Litho.		Perf. 14
861-865	A156	Set of 5	7.50 7.50

Rock Formations — A157

Wmk. 373

2005, Jan. 14	Litho.		Perf. 14
866		Horiz. strip of 4	11.00 11.00
a.	A157	35p The Friar	1.60 1.60
b.	A157	40p Sugar Loaf	1.90 1.90
c.	A157	50p The Turk's Cap	2.10 2.10
d.	A157	£1 Lot's Wife	4.25 4.25

Battle of Trafalgar, Bicent. — A158

Designs: 10p, HMS Bellerophon in action against the Aigle and Monarca. 20p, British 18-pounder naval pattern cannon. 30p, HMS Victory. 50p, Royal Navy first lieutenant, 1805, vert. 60p, HMS Conquerer, vert. 80p, Portrait of Admiral Horatio Nelson, vert.
No. 873, vert.: a, Portrait of Admiral Cuthbert Collingwood. b, HMS Royal Sovereign.

Wmk. 373, Unwmkd. (30p)

2005, May 10	Litho.		Perf. 13½
867-872	A158	Set of 6	16.00 16.00

Souvenir Sheet

873	A158	75p Sheet of 2, #a-b	9.00 9.00

No. 869 has particles of wood from the HMS Victory embedded in the areas covered by a thermographic process that produces a raised, shiny effect.

Miniature Sheet

End of World War II, 60th Anniv. — A159

No. 874: a, 20p, HMS Milford. b, 20p, HMS Nelson. c, 20p, RFA Darkdale. d, 20p, HMS St. Helena. e, 20p, Ship and Atlantic Star Medal. f, 30p, Codebreaker Alan M. Turing and Enigma code machine. g, 30p, Capt. Johnnie Walker, HMS Starling. h, 30p, British Prime Minister Winston Churchill. i, 30p, Churchill infantry tank. j, 30p, Hawker Hurricanes.

Wmk. 373

2005, June 24	Litho.		Perf. 13¾
874	A159	Sheet of 10, #a-j	16.50 16.50

Pope John Paul II (1920-2005) A160

Wmk. 373

2005, Aug. 31	Litho.		Perf. 14
875	A160	50p multi	3.00 3.00

England's Elizabethan Era — A161

No. 876, 10p: a, Sir Francis Drake. b, Golden Hind.
No. 877, 15p: a, Sir Walter Raleigh. b, Ark Royal.
No. 878, 25p: a, Queen Elizabeth I. b, Spanish Armada.
No. 879, £1: a, William Shakespeare. b, Old Globe Theater.

2005, Sept. 7   Perf. 13¾
Horiz. Pairs, #a-b
876-879 A161   Set of 4   15.00 15.00

Christmas — A162

Stories by Hans Christian Andersen (1805-75): 10p, The Little Fir Tree. 25p, The Ugly Duckling. 30p, The Snow Queen. £1, The Little Mermaid.

Wmk. 373
2005, Oct. 4   Litho.   Perf. 14
880-883 A162   Set of 4   7.25 7.25

Battle of Trafalgar, Bicent. — A163

Designs: 50p, HMS Victory. 80p, Ships in battle, horiz. £1.20, Admiral Horatio Nelson.

2005, Oct. 18   Unwmk.   Perf. 13¼
884-886 A163   Set of 3   12.00 12.00

Stamps in the British Library Collection — A164

Designs: 10p, St. Helena #B2-B4. 20p, Cape of Good Hope #6. 25p, US #C3a. 30p, St. Helena #1. 80p, Great Britain #1. £1.20, Mauritius #2.
£2, Like 30p.

Perf. 14¼x14¾
2006, Jan. 16   Litho.   Wmk. 373
887-892 A164   Set of 6   18.00 18.00
Souvenir Sheet
893 A164   £2 multi   11.00 11.00
St. Helena postage stamps, 150th anniv. (Nos. 890, 893).

Europa Stamps, 50th Anniv. A165

Designs: 10p, Five stars, European Union flag. 30p, Five stars, letter. 80p, Four stars, ball. £1.20, Star painting stamp, three stars in circle.

2006, Feb. 6   Unwmk.   Perf. 14
894-897 A165   13.00 13.00
897a   Souvenir sheet, #894-897   12.50 12.50

Queen Elizabeth II, 80th Birthday A166

Queen: 10p, As young girl. 30p, As young woman, wearing tiara. 80p, As older woman, wearing tiara. £1.20, With gray hair.
No. 902: a, Wearing tiara. b, Without head covering.

Wmk. 373
2006, Apr. 21   Litho.   Perf. 14
898-901 A166   Set of 4   13.00 13.00
Souvenir Sheet
902 A166   £1 Sheet of 2, #a-b   11.00 11.00

Miniature Sheet

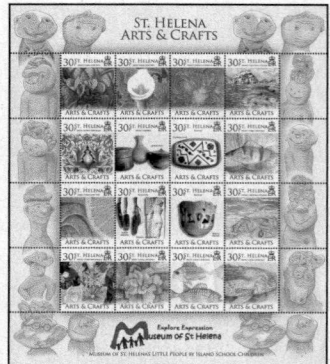

Arts and Crafts — A167

No. 903: a, Painting of red flower, by Emma-Jane Yon. b, Painting of white lily, by Yon. c, Painting of red flower, by Christina Stroud. d, Painting of dolphins, by Stroud. e, Painting of flowers, by Muriel Gardener. f, Turned wood objects, by Jackie Essex. g, Pottery by Corinda Essex. h, Painting of striped fish, by Laura Lawrence. i, Painting of orange and peel, by Yon. j, Sculptures by Sandy Walters and Johnny Drummond. k, Pottery by Serena Thorpe. l, Painting of shells, by Stroud. m, Painting of flowers, by Stroud. n, Painting of flower, by Lawrence. o, Painting of two fish, by Lawrence. p, Painting of red fish, by Lawrence.

2006, May 20   Perf. 13¾
903 A167   30p Sheet of 16, #a-p   22.50 22.50

Christmas — A168

Designs: 10p, Partridge in a pear tree. 15p, Two turtle doves. 25p, Three French hens. 30p, Four calling birds. 50p, Five golden rings. £1, Six geese a-laying.

Perf. 13¾x13½
2006, Aug. 31   Litho.   Wmk. 373
904-909 A168   Set of 6   10.50 10.50
Values are for stamps with surrounding selvage.
See Nos. 931-936.

Anniversaries — A169

No. 910, 20p: a, Queen Victoria at first investiture of Victoria Cross. b, Charge of the Light Brigade, Victoria Cross.
No. 911, 25p: a, Charles Darwin. b, Wirebird.
No. 912, 30p: a, Isambard Kingdom Brunel, coal cars at Cardiff docks. b, RMS St. Helena at Cardiff docks.
No. 913, £1: a, Charles Dickens, Dingley Dell cricket match. b, Samuel Pickwick, cricket match.

Wmk. 373
2006, Nov. 16   Litho.   Perf. 13¾
Horiz. Pairs, #a-b
910-913 A169   Set of 4   24.00 24.00
Victoria Cross, 150th anniv.; Darwin's visit to St. Helena, 170th anniv.; Birth of Brunel, 200th anniv.; Publishing of Dickens' Pickwick Papers, 170th anniv.

Bonapartes A170

Designs: 25p, Napoleon II (1811-32). 30p, Napoleon I (1769-1821). £1, Napoleon III (1808-73).

2007, Jan. 16   Perf. 15x14¼
914-916 A170   Set of 3   7.75 7.75
916a   Souvenir sheet, #914-916   7.75 7.75

Wedding of Queen Elizabeth II and Prince Philip, 60th Anniv. — A171

Designs: 25p, Couple. 35p, Queen in wedding gown. 40p, Couple, Queen in Wedding gown. No. 920, £2, Couple and coach.
No. 921, £2, Couple, Queen in wedding gown, diff.

Wmk. 373
2007, Apr. 26   Litho.   Perf. 13¾
917-920 A171   Set of 4   15.00 15.00
Souvenir Sheet
Perf. 14¼
921 A171   £2 multi   10.00 10.00
No. 921 contains one 43x57mm stamp.

BirdLife International — A172

Designs: 15p, Black noddies. 30p, Madeiran storm petrels. 50p, Masked boobies. £2, Sooty terns.

2007, June 12   Perf. 12½x13
922-925 A172   Set of 4   15.00 15.00

Scouting, Cent. A173

Designs: 15p, Scout patches, neckerchief. 30p, Lord Robert Baden-Powell inspecting Scouts, 1936, trumpeter. 50p, Baden-Powell and Rev. L. C. Walcott, compass. No. 929, £1, Baden-Powell, rope lashing.
No. 930, £1, vert.: a, Emblem of 1st Jamestown Scout Group. b, Baden-Powell.

2007, July 9   Perf. 13¾
926-929 A173   Set of 4   9.00 9.00
Souvenir Sheet
930 A173   £1 Sheet of 2, #a-b   9.00 9.00

Christmas Type of 2006

Designs: 10p, Seven swans a-swimming. 15p, Eight maids a-milking. 25p, Nine ladies dancing. 30p, Ten lords a-leaping. 50p, Eleven pipers piping. £1, Twelve drummers drumming.

Perf. 13¾x13½
2007, Sept. 3   Litho.   Wmk. 373
931-936 A168   Set of 6   10.50 10.50
Values are for stamps with surrounding selvage.

Atlantic Ocean Navigation and Aviation Firsts — A174

Designs: 25p, SS Savannah, first steamship to cross the Atlantic, 1819. 40p, Airplane of Alcock & Brown, first pilots to cross the Atlantic, 1919. 45p, Sailboat of Alain Gerbault, first man to sail solo east to west across the Atlantic, 1923. £1.20, Charles Lindbergh's Spirit of St. Louis, first solo flight across the Atlantic, 1927.

Wmk. 373
2007, Nov. 6   Litho.   Perf. 14
937-940 A174   Set of 4   12.00 12.00

Royal Air Force, 90th Anniv. A175

Airplanes: 15p, Airco D. H. 9. 25p, Hawker Hurricane. 35p, Handley Page Hastings. 40p, English Electric Lightning. 50p, Harrier GR7. £1.50, Berlin Airlift airplane.

Wmk. 373
2008, Apr. 1   Litho.   Perf. 14
941-945 A175   Set of 5   10.00 10.00
Souvenir Sheet
946 A175   £1.50 multi   7.50 7.50
Nos. 941-945 each printed in sheets of 8 + label.

Souvenir Sheet

Napoleonic Sites on St. Helena — A176

No. 947: a, 90p, Longwood House in 1821. b, £1, Napoleon's tomb. c, £1.25, Longwood House in 2008.

Perf. 13¼x13¾

2008, May 7   Litho.   Wmk. 373
947 A176   Sheet of 3, #a-c   15.00 15.00

Bird Type of 2007 Without BirdLife International Emblem

Designs: 15p, Brown boobies. 35p, Brown noddies. 40p, Fairy terns. £1.25, Red-billed tropicbirds.

2008, July 17   Perf. 12½x13
948-951 A172   Set of 4   10.00 10.00

Fish A177

Designs: 5p, Deepwater bullseye. 10p, Five finger. 15p, Deepwater greenfish. 20p, Hardback soldier. 25p, Deepwater gurnard. 35p, Red mullet. 40p, Softback soldier. 50p, Rock bullseye. 80p, Gurnard. £1, Cunningfish. £2, Hogfish. £5, Marmalade razorfish.

2008, Aug. 19   Perf. 13¾
952 A177   5p multi   .30 .30
953 A177   10p multi   .45 .45
954 A177   15p multi   .65 .65
955 A177   20p multi   .90 .90
956 A177   25p multi   1.05 1.05
957 A177   35p multi   1.60 1.60
958 A177   40p multi   1.75 1.75
959 A177   50p multi   2.10 2.10
960 A177   80p multi   3.50 3.50
961 A177   £1 multi   4.50 4.50
962 A177   £2 multi   8.50 8.50
963 A177   £5 multi   21.00 21.00
a.   Sheet of 12, #952-963   47.50 47.50
    Nos. 952-963 (12)   46.30 46.30

Flag — A178

2008, Aug. 19   Unwmk.   Die Cut
Booklet Stamp
Self-Adhesive

964 A178   35p multi   2.00 2.00
a.   Booklet pane of 12   24.00

Christmas A179

Flowers: 15p, African lily. 25p, Christmas cactus. 35p, Honeysuckle. 40p, St. John's lily. £1, Crucifix orchid.

Perf. 13x12½

2008, Sept. 1   Litho.   Wmk. 373
965-969 A179   Set of 5   8.50 8.50

End of World War I, 90th Anniv. — A180

Poetry about World War I: 10p, "The Soldier," by Rupert Brooke. 15p, "Aftermath," by Siegfried Sassoon. 25p, "Anthem for Doomed Youth," by Wilfred Owen. 35p, "For the Fallen," by Laurence Binyon. 40p, "In Flanders Fields," by John McCrae. 50p, "In Memoriam," by Edward Thomas. £2, Cenotaph, St. Helena.

2008, Sept. 16   Wmk. 406   Perf. 14
970-975 A180   Set of 6   9.00 9.00
Souvenir Sheet
976 A180   £2 multi   8.50 8.50

Miniature Sheet

Ascension to Throne of King Henry VIII (1491-1547), 500th Anniv. — A181

No. 977: a, Henry VIII holding scroll. b, Catherine of Aragon (1485-1536), first wife. c, Anne Boleyn (c. 1507-36), second wife. d, Jane Seymour (c. 1509-37), third wife. e, Henry VIII, diff. f, Ship Mary Rose. g, Anne of Cleves (1515-57), fourth wife. h, Catherine Howard (c. 1520-42), fifth wife. i, Catherine Parr (1512-48), sixth wife. j, Hampton Court.

Wmk. 373
2009, Jan. 9   Litho.   Perf. 14
977 A181   50p Sheet of 10, #a-j   22.50 22.50

Naval Aviation, Cent. A182

Designs: 15p, Westland Sea King helicopter and Royal Navy ship. 35p, Fairey Swordfish and Royal Navy ships. 40p, BAe Harrier. 50p, Blackburn Buccaneer and Royal Navy ship. £1.50, Lieutenant E. L. Gerrard in airplane at Central Flying School, 1913.

Wmk. 406
2009, Apr. 17   Litho.   Perf. 14
978-981 A182   Set of 4   9.50 9.50
Souvenir Sheet
982 A182   £1.50 multi   8.00 8.00

Nos. 978-981 each were printed in sheets of 8 + central label.

Souvenir Sheet

Donation of the Briars Pavilion, 50th Anniv. — A183

No. 983: a, 90p, Briars Pavilion, c. 1857. b, £1, Napoleon Bonaparte and Betsy Balcombe. c, £1.25, Briars Pavilion, 2008.

2009, May 26   Litho.   Perf. 13¼x13¾
983 A183   Sheet of 3, #a-c   15.00 15.00

Space Exploration A184

Designs: 15p, Deep Space Tracking Station, Ascension Island. 35p, Early rocketry experiment by Dr. Robert Goddard. 40p, Launch of Apollo 11. 90p, Space Shuttle Discovery landing. No. 988, £1.20, Astronauts working on International Space Station. No. 989, £1.20, Astronauts on Moon, painting by Capt. Alan Bean, vert.

Wmk. 406
2009, July 20   Litho.   Perf. 13¼
984-988 A184   Set of 5   11.50 11.50
Souvenir Sheet
Perf. 13x13½
989 A184   £1.20 multi   5.00 5.00

First man on the Moon, 40th anniv. No. 989 contains one 40x60mm stamp.

Christmas — A185

Designs: 15p, Christmas parade. 25p, Christmas pageant in church. 40p, Church at night. £1, Christmas lights on buildings.

Wmk. 406
2009, Sept. 1   Litho.   Perf. 14
990-993 A185   Set of 4   7.00 7.00

Anglican Diocese of St. Helena, 150th Anniv. — A186

Designs: 15p, St. Paul's Cathedral. 35p, St. Matthew's Church. 40p, St. James' Church. £1, Piers Calveley Claughton (1814-84), first bishop of St. Helena.

2009, Oct. 1
994-997 A186   Set of 4   7.00 7.00

Miniature Sheet

History of 17th Century England — A187

No. 998: a, King Charles I (1600-49). b, King Charles II (1630-85). c, Prince Rupert (1619-82). d, Oliver Cromwell (1599-1658). e, Richard Cromwell (1626-1712). f, King Charles I arrests members of Parliament. g, New Model Army. h, Execution of King Charles I. i, Dissolution of Parliament. j, Coronation of King Charles II.

Wmk. 406
2010, Jan. 29   Litho.   Perf. 14
998 A187   50p Sheet of 10, #a-j   22.50 22.50

Battle of Britain, 70th Anniv. — A188

Designs: 15p, Children in bunker. 25p, Fire fighters. 35p, Milkman delivering through rubble. 40p, Bus in bomb crater. 90p, Contrails. £1, Lookout. £1.50, Sir Douglas Bader (1910-82), flying ace.

Wmk. 406
2010, Mar. 18   Litho.   Perf. 13
999-1004 A188   Set of 6   14.00 14.00
Souvenir Sheet
1005 A188   £1.50 black & gray   7.50 7.50

Nos. 999-1004 each were printed in sheets of 6.

Souvenir Sheet

Great Britain No. 154 — A189

Wmk. 406

2010, May 8   Litho.   Perf. 14
1006 A189   £1.50 multi   6.50 6.50
  Reign of King George V, cent. London 2010
Festival of Stamps.

World of
Soccer — A190

  Designs: No. 1007, 40p, Soccer player and
ball. No. 1008, 40p, Map of Africa and St.
Helena. No. 1009, 40p, Two soccer players
and ball.

2010, May 14   Perf. 14x14¾
1007-1009 A190   Set of 3   5.00 5.00
1009a   Souvenir sheet of 3,
          #1007-1009   5.00 5.00

Girl
Guides,
Cent.
A191

  Designs: 15p, Rainbows. 25p, Brownies.
40p, Girl Guides. 90p, Lord Robert Baden-
Powell and wife, Olave.

2010, Aug. 23   Perf. 14
1010-1013 A191   Set of 4   7.00 7.00

Christmas
A192

  Sites and flowers: 15p, Jacob's Ladder, Crucifix orchid. 25p, Diana's Peak, St. John's lily.
40p, High Knoll Fort, Agapanthus. £1, Heart-
shaped Waterfall, Honeysuckle.

2010, Oct. 25   Perf. 13¾
1014-1017 A192   Set of 4   7.50 7.50

RMS St. Helena, 20th Anniv. — A193

  Designs: 15p, Ship in 2010. 35p, Arrival on
maiden voyage in St. Helena. 40p, Launch of
ship, 1990. 90p, Captain's table.

2010, Nov. 19   Perf. 14x14¾
1018-1021 A193   Set of 4   7.50 7.50

Service of Queen Elizabeth II and
Prince Philip — A194

  Designs: 15p, Queen Elizabeth II. 25p,
Queen and Prince Philip. 35p, Queen and
Prince Philip, diff. No. 1025, 40p, Queen and
Prince Philip, Queen wearing yellow dress.
No. 1026, 40p, Queen and Prince Philip,
Queen wearing blue hat. 90p, Prince Philip.
£1.50, Queen and Prince Philip, diff.

Perf. 13¼
2011, Mar. 1   Litho.   Unwmk.
1022-1027 A194   Set of 6   9.50 9.50
1027a   Sheet of 6, #1022-1027, +
          3 labels   9.50 9.50
Souvenir Sheet
1028 A194   £1.50 multi   6.00 6.00

Souvenir Sheet

Wedding of Prince William and
Catherine Middleton — A195

Perf. 14¾x14¼
2011, Apr. 29   Litho.   Wmk. 406
1029 A195   £3 multi   11.50 11.50

Photographs of Wedding of Prince
William and Catherine
Middleton — A196

  Designs: 15p, Bride and her sister, Pippa.
35p, Couple in coach waving. 40p, Couple
standing, holding hands, vert. 60p, Couple
standing and waving, vert. £1, Couple kissing,
vert.

2011, Sept. 1   Perf. 14¼x14, 14x14¼
1030-1034 A196   Set of 5   9.00 9.00

Worldwide Fund for Nature
(WWF) — A197

  Island hogfish: 35p, Male. 40p, Juvenile.
50p, Immature female. £1.20, £1.50, Male
near rocks.

2011, Oct. 31   Perf. 14¼x14
1035-1038 A197   Set of 4   8.00 8.00
1038a   Sheet of 16, 4 each #1035-
          1038   32.00 32.00
Souvenir Sheet
1039 A197   £1.50 multi   5.00 5.00

Christmas
A198

  Royal Fleet auxiliary ships: 35p, RFA Gold
Rover. 50p, RFA Black Rover. 60p, RFA Lyme
Bay. £1.20, RFA Darkdale.

2011, Nov. 14   Perf. 13¾
1040-1043 A198   Set of 4   8.50 8.50

Commonwealth
Parliamentary
Association,
Cent. — A199

  Centenary emblem and: No. 1044, 50p,
Court House, Jamestown. No. 1045, 50p,
Royal Charter. No. 1046, 50p, Commonwealth
Parliamentary Association Headquarters,
London.

2011, Nov. 28   Perf. 13¾x13¼
1044-1046 A199   Set of 3   4.75 4.75
1046a   Souvenir sheet of 3,
          #1044-1046   4.75 4.75

Reign of Queen Elizabeth II, 60th
Anniv. — A200

  Various photographs of Queen Elizabeth II:
20p, 35p, 40p, 50p, 60p, £1.
£1.50, Queen Elizabeth II wearing tiara.

2012, Feb. 6   Perf. 13½
1047-1052 A200   Set of 6   9.75 9.75
1052a   Souvenir sheet, #1047-
          1052 + 3 labels   9.75 9.75
Souvenir Sheet
1053 A200   £1.50 multi   4.75 4.75

Children's Art — A201

  Various children's drawings commemorating
the 60th anniversary of the reign of Queen
Elizabeth II: 20p, 35p, 50p, £1.

2012, June 12   Wmk. 406   Perf. 14
1054-1057 A201   Set of 4   6.50 6.50

Falkland
Islands
War,
30th
Anniv.
A202

  1982 photographs of RMS St Helena: 20p,
Crew. 35p, At Grytviken. 40p, At Ascension
Island. 50p, At Grytviken, diff. £1, Under
escort.

2012, June 26
1058-1062 A202   Set of 5   7.75 7.75

Christmas
A203

  Titles of Chirstmas hymns: 20p, O Little
Town of Bethlehem. 35p, While Shepherds
Watched. 50p, Away in a Manger. £1, Silent
Night, Holy Night.

2012, Nov. 5   Wmk. 406
1063-1066 A203   Set of 4   6.75 6.75

Items Commemorating British
Coronations — A204

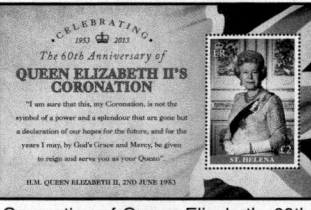

Coronation of Queen Elizabeth, 60th
Anniv. — A205

  Various items commemorating the coronation of: 20p, Queen Victoria. 35p, King Edward
VII. 40p, King George V. 50p, King George VI.
£1, Queen Elizabeth II.

2013, Feb. 6   Perf. 14
1067-1071 A204   Set of 5   7.50 7.50
Souvenir Sheet
Perf. 14¾x14
1072 A205   £2 multi   6.00 6.00

Lady
Margaret
Thatcher
(1925-2013),
British Prime
Minister
A206

  Various photographs: 40p, 50p, 60p, £1.

2013, Aug. 8   Perf. 13¾
1073-1076 A206   Set of 4   8.00 8.00
1076a   Souvenir sheet of 4, #1073-
          1076   8.00 8.00

Birth of Prince
George of
Cambridge
A207

  Designs: 25p, Duke of Cambridge holding
Prince George. 40p, Duchess of Cambridge
holding Prince George. 60p, Prince George.
£1, Duke and Duchess of Cambridge, Prince
George.

Perf. 13½x13¼
2013, Nov. 6   Litho.   Wmk. 406
1077-1080 A207   Set of 4   7.25 7.25

Airport
Project
A208

  Designs: 25p, NP Glory 4 docked at
Rupert's. 40p, Haul Road. 50p, Bradley's
Camp. 60p, Dry Gut.
£2, Plant machinery.

Wmk. 406
2014, June 27   Litho.   Perf. 14
1081-1084 A208   Set of 4   6.00 6.00
Souvenir Sheet
1085 A208   £2 multi   7.00 7.00

Miniature Sheet

Brownies, Cent. — A209

No. 1086: a, 25p, Emblem (48x54mm). b, 40p, Jamestown Brownies, 1970 (48x27mm). c, 60p, Pat Benjamin presenting bouquet to Princess Margaret (24x54mm). d, 70p, Brownie pack, 1960 (24x54mm). e, £1, Brownie pack Thinking Day, 2014 (48x27mm).

Perf. 14x14¾

2014, Oct. 15		Litho.		Wmk. 406
1086	A209	Sheet of 5, #a-e	9.50	9.50

Christmas A210

Designs: 25p, Whale shark. 30p, Sea slug. 40p, St. Helena Gregory. 50p, Cunning fish. 60p, Silver eel. £1, Orange cup coral.

Wmk. 406

2014, Oct. 15		Litho.	**Perf. 14**
1087-1092	A210	Set of 6	9.75 9.75

St. Helena's Participation in the Commonwealth Games — A211

Designs: 30p, Team members at Brisbane Commonwealth Games, 1982. 50p, RMS St. Helena crew holding Queen's baton, 2014. 60p, St. Helena National Amateur Sports Association, 2014. £1, Team members at Glasgow Commonwealth Games, 2014.

Wmk. 406

2014, Oct. 20		Litho.	**Perf. 14**
1093-1096	A211	Set of 4	7.75 7.75

Launch of the RMS St. Helena, 25th Anniv. A212

Designs: 25p, Laying of the keel. 30p, Hull construction. 50p, Hull on launch day. 60p, Sea trials.

Wmk. 406

2014, Oct. 31		Litho.	**Perf. 14**
1097-1099	A212		3.50 3.50

Souvenir Sheet

1100	A212	60p multi	1.90 1.90

Paintings of Jamestown Main Street Buildings, by Andy Crowe A213

Various buildings. 50p, 80p are 20x36mm.

Wmk. 406

2015, May 21		Litho.	**Perf. 13¼**	
1101		Horiz. strip of 4	7.25	7.25
a.	A213 40p multi		1.25	1.25
b.	A213 50p multi		1.60	1.60
c.	A213 60p multi		1.90	1.90
d.	A213 80p multi		2.50	2.50

Birds A214

Designs: 5p, Fairy tern. 10p, Zebra dove. 15p, Chukar partridge. 20p, Brown booby. 30p, Java sparrow. 40p, Wilson's storm petrel. 50p, Red-billed tropicbird. 60p, Masked booby. 80p, Sooty tern. £1, Yellow canary. £2, Red fody. £5, Wirebird.

Wmk. 406

2015, Nov. 11		Litho.	**Perf. 13¾**	
1102	A214	5p multi	.25	.25
1103	A214	10p multi	.30	.30
1104	A214	15p multi	.45	.45
1105	A214	20p multi	.60	.60
1106	A214	30p multi	.90	.90
1107	A214	40p multi	1.25	1.25
1108	A214	50p multi	1.50	1.50
1109	A214	60p multi	1.90	1.90
1110	A214	80p multi	2.40	2.40
1111	A214	£1 multi	3.00	3.00
1112	A214	£2 multi	6.00	6.00
1113	A214	£5 multi	15.00	15.00
a.	Souvenir sheet of 12, #1102-1113		33.50	33.50
	Nos. 1102-1113 (12)		33.55	33.55

Christmas — A215

Santa Claus: 25p, In sleigh. 40p, Holding Christmas tree and bag of gifts. 50p, By Christmas tree. 60p, On chimney. £1, Holding Christmas pudding.

Wmk. 406

2015, Nov. 21		Litho.	**Perf. 14**
1114-1118	A215	Set of 5	8.25 8.25

Airport Project A216

Designs: 25p, Students burying time capsule. 40p, Final rock blast. 50p, Permanent wharf, Rupert's. 60p, Control tower construction. £2, Runway construction.

Wmk. 406

2016, Jan. 1		Litho.	**Perf. 14**
1119-1122	A216	Set of 4	5.25 5.25

Souvenir Sheet

1123	A216	£2 multi	6.00 6.00

Souvenir Sheet

Napoleon Bonaparte (1769-1821), Emperor of France — A217

Wmk. 406

2016, Feb. 1		Litho.	**Perf. 14**
1124	A217	£2 multi	5.75 5.75

Napoleon's exile on St. Helena, 200th anniv.

Christmas — A218

Designs: 25p, Orchestra and Salvation Army Band playing music. 50p, Salvation Army Band playing music. 60p, Pilling Primary School Choir.

Wmk. 406

2016, Nov. 1		Litho.	**Perf. 14**
1125-1127	A218	Set of 3	3.50 3.50

Flowers A219

Designs: 15p, Poinsettia. 25p, Amaryllis. 60p, Agapanthus. £1, St. John's lily.

Perf. 13x13½

2017, Sept. 30		Litho.	Wmk. 406
1128-1131	A219	Set of 4	5.50 5.50

Christmas.

Island Scenery A220

Designs: 40p, Shark's Valley. 50p, Lot. 60p, Diana's Peak. £1, Longwood Barn. £1.50, Lot's Wife's Ponds.

Perf. 13¼x13¾

2017, Oct. 16		Litho.	Wmk. 406
1132-1135	A220	Set of 4	6.75 6.75

Souvenir Sheet
Perf. 13½

1136	A220	£1.50 multi	4.00 4.00

No. 1136 contains one 40x40mm stamp.

Final Voyage of RMS St. Helena A221

Designs: 25p, Launch of RMS St. Helena, 1989. 40p, Farewell celebrations, Cape Town. 50p, Final departure from St. Helena. 60p, Capt. Rodney Young, first captain from St. Helena. £2, RMS St. Helena leaving James' Bay.

Perf. 13¼x13½

2018, Feb. 10		Litho.	Wmk. 406
1137-1140	A221	Set of 4	5.00 5.00

Souvenir Sheet

1141	A221	£2 multi	5.50 5.50

Wedding of Prince Harry and Meghan Markle A222

Various photographs of couple: 15p, 25p, 60p, £1.
£1.50, Couple, diff.

Perf. 14¼x14

2018, May 19	A222	Litho.	Wmk. 406
1142-1145		Set of 4	5.50 5.50

Souvenir Sheet
Perf. 14¼

1146	A222	£1.50 multi	4.00 4.00

Airport Project A223

Designs: 25p, Sept. 15, 2015 calibration flight crew. 40p, First calibration flight on runway. 50p, Control tower. 60p, First helicopter landing.
£2, E190-100IGW airplane landing, Oct. 14, 2017.

Perf. 13¼x13½

2018, May 21	A223	Litho.	Wmk. 406
1147-1150		Set of 4	4.75 4.75

Souvenir Sheet

1151	A223	£2 multi	5.50 5.50

Festival of Lights A224

Christmas parade: 15p, Floats. 50p, At the seafront. 60p, At Market Square. £1, Participants and viewers.

Perf. 14x14¼

2018, Sept. 17		Litho.	Wmk. 406
1152-1155	A224	Set of 4	6.00 6.00

Jonathan, the Seychelles Giant Tortoise — A225

Various depictions of Jonathan, the oldest land animal: 50p, 60p, 80p, £1.30.

Wmk. 406

2019, Sept. 15		Litho.	**Perf. 14¼**
1156-1159	A225	Set of 4	8.00 8.00

SEMI-POSTAL STAMPS

Catalogue values for unused stamps in this section are for Never Hinged items.

Tristan da Cunha Nos. 46, 49-51 Ovptd. "ST. HELENA / Tristan Relief" and Srchd. with New Value and "+"

Perf. 12½x13

1961, Oct. 12		**Wmk. 314**	**Engr.**
B1	A3 2½c + 3p	1,500.	600.00
B2	A3 5c + 6p	1,600.	650.00
B3	A3 7½c + 9p	2,250.	900.00
B4	A3 10c + 1sh	2,250.	1,100.
	Nos. B1-B4 (4)	7,600.	3,250.

Withdrawn from sale Oct. 19.

POSTAGE DUE STAMPS

Catalogue values for unused stamps in this section are for Never Hinged items.

Map — D1

Perf. 15x14

1986, June 9		**Litho.**		**Wmk. 384**
		Background Color		
J1	D1	1p tan	.25	.45
J2	D1	2p orange	.25	.45
J3	D1	5p vermilion	.25	.45
J4	D1	7p violet	.25	.45
J5	D1	10p chalky blue	.25	.55
J6	D1	25p dull yellow grn	.70	1.50
		Nos. J1-J6 (6)	1.95	3.85

WAR TAX STAMPS

No. 62a Surcharged

1916		**Wmk. 3**		**Perf. 14**
MR1	A10	1p + 1p scar & blk	3.00	4.00
a.	Double surcharge			20,000.

No. 62 Surcharged

1919				
MR2	A10	1p + 1p car & blk	2.10	5.50

ST. KITTS

sānt 'kits

LOCATION — West Indies southeast of Puerto Rico
GOVT. — With Nevis, Associated State in British Commonwealth
AREA — 65 sq. mi.
POP. — 31,824 (1991)
CAPITAL — Basseterre

See St. Christopher for stamps used in St. Kitts until 1890. From 1890 until 1903, stamps of the Leeward Islands were used. From 1903 until 1956, stamps of St. Kitts-Nevis and Leeward Islands were used concurrently. See St. Kitts-Nevis for stamps used through June 22, 1980, after which St. Kitts and

---

Nevis pursued separate postal administrations.

100 Cents = 1 Dollar

Catalogue values for all unused stamps in this country are for Never Hinged items.

Watermark

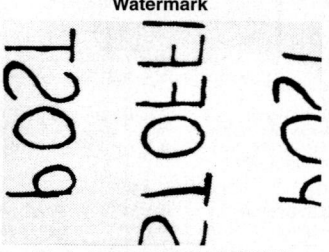

Wmk. 380 — "POST OFFICE"

St. Kitts-Nevis Nos. 357-369 Ovptd.

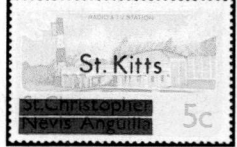

Perf. 14½x14

1980, June 23		**Litho.**		**Wmk. 373**
25	A61	5c multicolored	.25	.25
26	A61	10c multicolored	.25	.25
27	A61	12c multicolored	.35	.80
28	A61	15c multicolored	.25	.25
29	A61	25c multicolored	.25	.25
30	A61	30c multicolored	.25	.25
31	A61	40c multicolored	.25	.25
32	A61	45c multicolored	.50	.25
33	A61	50c multicolored	.25	.25
34	A61	55c multicolored	.25	.25
35	A61	$1 multicolored	.25	.25
36	A61	$5 multicolored	.30	1.00
37	A61	$10 multicolored	.45	1.75
		Nos. 25-37 (13)	3.85	6.05

All but 12c, 45c, 50c, exist unwatermarked. About the same values.

Ships — A2

4c, HMS Vanguard, 1762. 10c, HMS Boreas, 1787. 30c, HMS Druid, 1827. 55c, HMS Winchester, 1831. $1.50, Philosopher, 1857. $2, S.S. Contractor, 1930.

1980, Aug. 8				**Perf. 13½**
38	A2	4c multicolored	.25	.25
39	A2	10c multicolored	.25	.25
40	A2	30c multicolored	.25	.25
41	A2	55c multicolored	.25	.25
42	A2	$1.50 multicolored	.30	.35
43	A2	$2 multicolored	.35	.45
		Nos. 38-43 (6)	1.65	1.80

Nos. 38-43 not issued without overprint. The 4c, and possibly others, exist without the overprint.

Queen Mother, 80th Birthday — A3

1980, Sept. 4			**Perf. 14**
44	A3 $2 multicolored	.40	.60

Christmas — A4

1980, Nov. 10			**Perf. 14½**
45	A4 5c Magi following star	.25	.25
46	A4 15c Shepherds, star	.25	.25
47	A4 30c Bethlehem, star	.25	.25
48	A4 $4 Adoration of the Magi	.60	.50
	Nos. 45-48 (4)	1.35	1.25

Birds — A5

1c, Frigatebird. 4c, Rusty-tailed flycatcher. 5c, Purple-throated carib. 6c, Burrowing owl. 8c, Purple martin. 10c, Yellow-crowned night heron. 15c, Bananaquit. 20c, Scaly-breasted thrasher. 25c, Grey kingbird. 30c, Green-throated carib. 40c, Ruddy turnstone. 45c, Black-faced grassquit. 50c, Cattle egret. 55c, Brown pelican. $1, Lesser Antillean bullfinch. $2.50, Zenaida dove. $5, Sparrow hawk. $10, Antillean crested hummingbird.

No Date Imprint Below Design

1981		**Wmk. 373**		**Perf. 13½x14**
49	A5	1c multicolored	.25	.25
50	A5	4c multicolored	.35	.25
51	A5	5c multicolored	.25	.25
52	A5	6c multicolored	.60	.25
53	A5	8c multicolored	.45	.25
54	A5	10c multicolored	.30	.25

Perf. 14
Size: 38x25mm

55	A5	15c multicolored	.30	.25
56	A5	20c multicolored	.30	.25
57	A5	25c multicolored	.30	.25
58	A5	30c multicolored	.30	.25
59	A5	40c multicolored	.35	.30
60	A5	45c multicolored	.40	.40
61	A5	50c multicolored	.40	.40
62	A5	55c multicolored	.40	.40
63	A5	$1 multicolored	.75	.75
64	A5	$2.50 multicolored	1.7	2.25
65	A5	$5 multicolored	3.00	3.50
66	A5	$10 multicolored	5.00	6.00
		Nos. 49-66 (18)	15.40	16.50

Issued: Nos. 51, 54-66, Feb. 5; others, May 30.

"1982" Imprint Below Design

1982, June 8				
49a	A5	1c multicolored	.50	.35
50a	A5	4c multicolored	.50	.30
51a	A5	5c multicolored	.60	.30
52a	A5	6c multicolored	.65	.40
53a	A5	8c multicolored	.70	.30
54a	A5	10c multicolored	.70	.30

Perf. 14
Size: 38x25mm

55a	A5	15c multicolored	.75	.30
56a	A5	20c multicolored	.80	.30
57a	A5	25c multicolored	.80	.30
58a	A5	30c multicolored	.80	.35
59a	A5	40c multicolored	1.00	.40
60a	A5	45c multicolored	1.25	.45
61a	A5	50c multicolored	1.50	.50
62a	A5	55c multicolored	1.75	.75
63a	A5	$1 multicolored	2.75	1.00
64a	A5	$2.50 multicolored	4.50	3.00
65a	A5	$5 multicolored	7.00	6.50
66a	A5	$10 multicolored	11.50	10.00
		Nos. 49a-66a (18)	38.05	25.80

"1983" Imprint Below Design

1983				
55b	A5	15c multicolored	2.75	.50
56b	A5	20c multicolored	2.75	.50
57b	A5	25c multicolored	2.75	.50
58b	A5	30c multicolored	2.75	.50
59b	A5	40c multicolored	4.25	.60
60b	A5	45c multicolored	4.50	1.25
63b	A5	$1 multicolored	10.50	2.50
64b	A5	$2.50 multicolored	18.00	5.00
		Nos. 55b-64b (8)	48.25	11.35

For overprints see Nos. 112-122.

Military Uniforms — A6

Foot Regiments: 5c, Battalion Company sergeant, 3rd Regiment, c. 1801. 15c, Light Company private, 15th Regiment, c. 1814. No. 69, Battalion Company officer, 45th Regiment, 1796-7. No. 70, Officer, 15th Regiment, c. 1780. No. 71, Officer, 9th Regiment, 1790. No. 72, Light Company officer, 5th Regiment, c. 1822. No. 73, Grenadier, 38th Regiment, 1751. No. 74, Battalion Company officer, 11th Regiment, c. 1804.

1981-83				**Perf. 14½**
67	A6	5c multi	.25	.25
68	A6	15c multi ('83)	.25	.25
69	A6	30c multi	.25	.25
70	A6	30c multi ('83)	.25	.25
71	A6	55c multi	.25	.25
72	A6	55c multi ('83)	.35	.35
73	A6	$2.50 multi	.55	.55
74	A6	$2.50 multi ('83)	.80	1.60
		Nos. 67-74 (8)	2.95	3.75

Issued: 3/5/81; 5/25/83.

Prince Charles, Lady Diana, Royal Yacht Charlotte A6a

Prince Charles and Lady Diana — A6b

1981, June 23				**Perf. 14**
75	A6a	55c Saudadoes	.25	.25
76	A6b	55c Couple	.25	.25
a.	Bklt. pane of 4, perf. 12½x12, unwmkd.			.90
77	A6a	$2.50 The Royal George	.40	.40
78	A6b	$2.50 like 55c	.75	.75
a.	Bklt. pane of 2, perf. 12½x12, unwmkd.		1.75	1.75
79	A6a	$4 HMY Britannia	1.00	1.00
80	A6b	$4 like 55c	1.25	1.25
		Nos. 75-80 (6)	3.90	3.90

Souvenir Sheet

1981, Dec. 14			**Perf. 12½x12**
81	A6b $5 like 55c	2.00	2.00

Wedding of Prince Charles and Lady Diana Spencer. Nos. 76a, 78a issued Nov. 19, 1981.

Natl. Girl Guide Movement, 50th Anniv. — A7

Designs: 5c, Miriam Pickard, 1st Guide commissioner. 30c, Lady Baden-Powell's visit, 1964. 55c, Visit of Princess Alice, 1960. $2, Thinking-Day Parade, 1980s.

1981, Sept. 21				
82	A7	5c multicolored	.25	.25
83	A7	30c multicolored	.25	.25
84	A7	55c multicolored	.25	.25
85	A7	$2 multicolored	.25	.35
		Nos. 82-85 (4)	1.00	1.10

Christmas — A8

Stained-glass windows — 5c, Annunciation. 30c, Nativity, baptism. 55c, Last supper, crucifixion. $3, Appearance before Apostles, ascension to heaven.

1981, Nov. 30

86	A8	5c multicolored	.25	.25
87	A8	30c multicolored	.25	.25
88	A8	55c multicolored	.25	.25
89	A8	$3 multicolored	.40	.50
		Nos. 86-89 (4)	1.15	1.25

Brimstone Hill Siege, Bicent. — A9

1982, Mar. 15

90	A9	15c Adm. Samuel Hood	.25	.25
91	A9	55c Marquis de Bouille	.25	.25

Souvenir Sheet

92	A9	$5 Battle scene	1.40	1.40

No. 92 has multicolored margin picturing battle scene. Size: 96x71mm.

21st Birthday of Princess Diana, July 1 — A10

15c, Alexandra of Denmark, Princess of Wales, 1863. 55c, Paternal arms of Alexandra. $6, Diana.

1982, June 22   **Perf. 13½x14**

93	A10	15c multicolored	.25	.25
94	A10	55c multicolored	.25	.25
95	A10	$6 multicolored	.50	.75
		Nos. 93-95 (3)	1.00	1.25

Nos. 93-95 Ovptd.

1982, July 12

96	A10	15c multicolored	.25	.25
97	A10	55c multicolored	.25	.25
98	A10	$6 multicolored	.45	.75
		Nos. 96-98 (3)	.95	1.25

Birth of Prince William of Wales.

Scouting, 75th Anniv. — A11

Merit badges.

1982, Aug. 18   **Perf. 14x13½**

99	A11	5c Nature	.25	.25
100	A11	55c Rescue	.35	.35
101	A11	$2 First aid	1.00	1.00
		Nos. 99-101 (3)	1.60	1.60

Christmas — A12

Children's drawings.

1982, Oct. 20

102	A12	5c shown	.25	.25
103	A12	55c Nativity	.25	.25
104	A12	$1.10 Three Kings	.25	.25
105	A12	$3 Annunciation	.30	.40
		Nos. 102-105 (4)	1.05	1.15

A13

Commonwealth Day: 55c, Cruise ship Stella Oceanis docked. $2, RMS Queen Elizabeth 2 anchored in harbor off St. Kitts.

1983, Mar. 14   **Perf. 14**

106	A13	55c multicolored	.25	.25
107	A13	$2 multicolored	.40	.40

Boys' Brigade, Cent. — A14

Designs: 10c, Sir William Smith, founder. 45c, Brigade members outside Sandy Point Methodist Church. 50c, Drummers. $3, Badge.

1983, July 27

108	A14	10c multicolored	.35	.30
109	A14	45c multicolored	.45	.40
110	A14	50c multicolored	.45	.40
111	A14	$3 multicolored	.75	2.00
		Nos. 108-111 (4)	2.00	3.10

Nos. 51//66 Overprinted

a

1983, Nov. 7

127	A16	15c shown	.25	.25
128	A16	30c Shepherds	.25	.25
129	A16	55c Mary, Joseph	.25	.25
130	A16	$2.50 Nativity	.30	.30
a.		Souvenir sheet of 4, #127-130	1.00	1.10
		Nos. 127-130 (4)	1.05	1.05

b

Without Date Imprint Below Design

1983, Sept. 19

112	A5(a)	5c multicolored	.25	.25
c.		Local overprint	10.00	10.00
113c	A5(b)	15c multicolored	7.00	1.25
116c	A5(b)	30c multicolored	27.50	27.50
118c	A5(b)	55c multicolored	.65	.65
119c	A5(b)	$1 multicolored	11.00	11.00
120	A5(b)	$2.50 multicolored	2.75	2.75
121c	A5(b)	$5 multicolored	4.75	4.75
122c	A5(b)	$10 multicolored	6.50	6.50
		Nos. 112-122c (8)	60.40	54.65

No. 112c has serifed letters and reads down. Exists reading up. Value $25.

Nos. 51a//65a Overprinted "1982" Imprint Below Design

1983, Sept. 19

112a	A5(a)	5c multicolored	.45	.25
d.		Local overprint	2.25	2.25
113a	A5(b)	15c multicolored	2.00	2.00
115a	A5(b)	25c multicolored	2.00	2.00
116a	A5(b)	30c multicolored	2.00	2.00
121a	A5(b)	$5 multicolored	5.50	5.50
		Nos. 112a-121a (5)	11.95	11.75

No. 112a exists with inverted overprint. Value $32.50. No. 113a exists with double overprint. Value $8.50. No. 115a exists with inverted overprint. Value $14.

No. 112d has serifed letters and reads down. Exists reading up. Value $7.50.

Nos. 52b//66b Overprinted "1983" Imprint Below Design

113	A5(b)	15c multicolored	.35	.25
114	A5(b)	20c multicolored	.35	.25
115	A5(b)	25c multicolored	.55	.25
116	A5(b)	30c multicolored	.55	.25
117	A5(b)	40c multicolored	.60	.25
118	A5(b)	55c multicolored	.65	.30
119	A5(b)	$1 multicolored	1.25	.60
120b	A5(b)	$2.50 multicolored	2.50	2.50
121	A5(b)	$5 multicolored	3.75	4.50
122	A5(b)	$10 multicolored	4.50	6.50
		Nos. 113-122 (10)	15.05	15.65

No. 118 exists with inverted overprint. Value $10.

Manned Flight Bicent. — A15

Designs: 10c, *Montgolfiere*, 1783, vert. 45c, Sikorsky *Russian Knight*, 1913. 50c, Lockheed TriStar. $2.50, Bell XS-1, 1947.

1983, Sept. 28   **Wmk. 380**

123	A15	10c multicolored	.25	.25
124	A15	45c multicolored	.25	.25
125	A15	50c multicolored	.25	.25
126	A15	$2.50 multicolored	.75	.75
a.		Souvenir sheet of 4, #123-126	1.60	1.60
		Nos. 123-126 (4)	1.50	1.50

1st Flight of a 4-engine aircraft, May 1913 (45c); 1st manned supersonic aircraft, 1947 ($2.50).

Christmas — A16

Batik Art A17

1984-85

131	A17	15c Country bus	.25	.25
132	A17	40c Donkey cart	.30	.25
133	A17	45c Parrot, vert.	.25	.25
134	A17	50c Man under palm tree, vert.	.25	.25
135	A17	60c Rum shop, cyclist	.60	.25
136	A17	$1.50 Fruit seller, vert.	.45	.70
137	A17	$3 Butterflies, vert.	.70	1.75
138	A17	$3 S.V. Polynesia	1.25	2.25
		Nos. 131-138 (8)	4.05	5.95

Issued: 15c, 40c, 60c, No. 138, 2/6/85; others, 1/30/84.

Marine Life A18

5c, Cushion star. 10c, Rough file shell. 15c, Red-lined cleaning shrimp. 20c, Bristleworm. 25c, Flamingo tongue. 30c, Christmas tree worm. 40c, Pink-tipped anemone. 50c, Smallmouth grunt. 60c, Glasseye snapper. 75c, Reef squirrelfish. $1, Sea fans, flamefish. $2.50, Reef butter-flyfish. $5, Black soldierfish. $10, Cocoa damselfish.

1984, July 4

139	A18	5c multicolored	.25	.25
140	A18	10c multicolored	.25	.25
a.		Wmk. 384 "1986"	1.50	1.00
b.		As "a," "1988" imprint	1.25	1.00
141	A18	15c multicolored	.25	.25
142	A18	20c multicolored	.25	.25
143	A18	25c multicolored	.25	.25
144	A18	30c multicolored	.40	.35
145	A18	40c multicolored	.55	.40
146	A18	50c multicolored	.60	.40
147	A18	60c multicolored	1.10	1.10
a.		Wmk. 384 ('88)	1.25	1.40
148	A18	75c multicolored	2.50	.75
149	A18	$1 multicolored	1.00	1.00
150	A18	$2.50 multicolored	3.00	3.75
151	A18	$5 multicolored	7.00	15.00
a.		Wmk. 384 ('88)	9.00	11.00
152	A18	$10 multicolored	11.00	15.00
a.		Wmk. 384 ('88)	14.00	15.00
		Nos. 139-152 (14)	28.40	39.00

Nos. 149-152 vert.
Nos. 147a, 151a, 152a have "1988" imprint.

4-H in St. Kitts, 25th Anniv. A19

1984, Aug. 15

153	A19	30c Agriculture	.25	.25
154	A19	55c Animal husbandry	.30	.30
155	A19	$1.10 Pledge, flag, youths	.50	.60
156	A19	$3 Parade	1.00	1.25
		Nos. 153-156 (4)	2.05	2.40

1st Anniv. of Independence — A20

15c, Construction of Royal St. Kitts Hotel. 30c, Folk dancers. $1.10, O Land of Beauty, vert. $3, Sea, palm trees, map, vert.

1984, Sept. 18

157	A20	15c multicolored	.25	.25
158	A20	30c multicolored	.30	.30
159	A20	$1.10 multicolored	.50	.60
160	A20	$3 multicolored	1.00	1.40
		Nos. 157-160 (4)	2.05	2.55

Christmas — A21

1984, Nov. 1
161	A21	15c Opening gifts	.25	.25
162	A21	60c Caroling	.55	.55
163	A21	$1 Nativity	.75	.75
164	A21	$2 Leaving church	1.25	1.25
		Nos. 161-164 (4)	2.80	2.80

Ships
A22

1985, Mar. 27   **Perf. 13½x14**
165	A22	40c Tropic Jade	1.00	1.00
166	A22	$1.20 Atlantic Clipper	2.00	2.00
167	A22	$2 M.V. Cunard Countess	2.75	2.75
168	A22	$2 Mandalay	3.25	3.25
		Nos. 165-168 (4)	9.00	9.00

Mt. Olive Masonic
Lodge, 150th
Anniv. — A23

Designs: 15c, James Derrick Cardin (1871-1954). 75c, Lodge banner. $1.20, Compass, Bible, square, horiz. $3, Charter, 1835.

1985, Nov. 9   **Perf. 15**
169	A23	15c multicolored	.65	.40
170	A23	75c multicolored	1.40	1.40
171	A23	$1.20 multicolored	1.40	2.75
172	A23	$3 multicolored	1.75	4.50
		Nos. 169-172 (4)	5.20	9.05

Christmas — A24

1985, Nov. 27   **Unwmk.**
173	A24	10c Map of St. Kitts	.30	.25
174	A24	40c Golden Hind	.60	.40
175	A24	60c Sir Francis Drake	.60	.50
176	A24	$3 Drake's shield of arms	.80	4.00
		Nos. 173-176 (4)	2.30	5.15

Visit of Sir Francis Drake to St. Kitts, 400th anniv.

Queen Elizabeth
II, 60th
Birthday — A25

Designs: 10c, With Prince Philip. 20c, Walking with government officials. 40c, Riding horse in parade. $3, Portrait.

1986, July 9   **Perf. 14**
177	A25	10c multicolored	.25	.25
178	A25	20c multicolored	.35	.25
179	A25	40c multicolored	.60	.45
180	A25	$3 multicolored	2.40	3.00
		Nos. 177-180 (4)	3.60	3.95

For overprints see Nos. 185-188.

Common Design Types
pictured following the introduction.

Royal Wedding Issue, 1986
Common Design Type

Designs: 15c, Prince Andrew and Sarah Ferguson, formal engagement announcement. $2.50, Prince Andrew in military dress uniform.

1986, July 23   **Wmk. 384**
Perf. 14½x14
| 181 | CD338 | 15c multicolored | .25 | .25 |
| 182 | CD338 | $2.50 multicolored | 1.25 | 2.00 |

Agriculture Exhibition — A26

Children's drawings: 15c, Family farm, by Kevin Tatem, age 14. $1.20, Striving for growth, by Alister Williams, age 19.

1986, Sept. 18   **Perf. 13½x14**
| 183 | A26 | 15c multicolored | .25 | .25 |
| 184 | A26 | $1.20 multicolored | 1.25 | 1.50 |

**Nos. 177-180 Ovptd. "40th
ANNIVERSARY / U.N. WEEK 19-26
OCT." in Gold**

1986, Oct. 22   Unwmk.   Perf. 14
185	A25	10c multicolored	.25	.25
186	A25	20c multicolored	.25	.25
187	A25	40c multicolored	.40	.40
188	A25	$3 multicolored	1.90	3.00
		Nos. 185-188 (4)	2.80	3.90

World Wildlife
Fund — A27

Various green monkeys, Cercopithecus aethiops sabaeus.

1986, Dec. 1
189	A27	15c multi	5.00	.75
190	A27	20c multi, diff.	5.50	.75
191	A27	60c multi, diff.	8.50	3.00
192	A27	$1 multi, diff.	11.50	5.00
		Nos. 189-192 (4)	30.50	9.50

Auguste
Bartholdi — A28

Statue of Liberty, Cent. — A29

60c, Torch, head, 1876-78. $1.50, Warship Isere, France. $3, Delivering statue, 1884. $3.50, Head.

1986, Dec. 17 Perf. 14x14½, 14½x14
193	A28	40c shown	.30	.30
194	A28	60c multicolored	.40	.60
195	A28	$1.50 multicolored	1.10	1.75
196	A28	$3 multicolored	1.25	3.00
		Nos. 193-196 (4)	3.05	5.65

Souvenir Sheet
| 197 | A29 | $3.50 multicolored | 2.50 | 3.50 |
| | | Nos. 194-195 horiz. | | |

British and French
Uniforms — A30

Designs: No. 198, Officer, East Norfolk Regiment, 1792. No. 199, Officer, De Neustrie Regiment, 1779. No. 200, Sergeant, Third Foot the Buffs, 1801. No. 201, Artillery officer, 1812. No. 202, Private, Light Company, 5th Foot Regiment, 1778. No. 203, Grenadier, Line Infantry, 1796.

1987, Feb. 25   **Perf. 14½**
198	A30	15c multicolored	.45	.30
199	A30	15c multicolored	.45	.30
200	A30	40c multicolored	.75	.55
201	A30	40c multicolored	.75	.55
202	A30	$2 multicolored	1.75	3.00
203	A30	$2 multicolored	1.75	3.00
a.		Souvenir sheet of 6, #198-203	9.00	9.00
		Nos. 198-203 (6)	5.90	7.70

Sugar Cane
Industry — A31

No. 204: a, Warehouse. b, Barns. c, Steam emitted by processing plant. d, Processing plant. e, Field hands.
No. 205a, Locomotive. b, Locomotive and tender. c, Open cars. d, Empty and loaded cars, tractor. e, Loading sugar cane.

1987, Apr. 15   **Perf. 14**
204		Strip of 5	1.00	1.50
a.-e.		A31 15c any single	.25	.30
205		Strip of 5	2.00	3.50
a.-e.		A31 75c any single	.30	.70

Visiting
Aircraft
A32

40c, L-1011-500 Tri-Star. 60c, BAe Super 748. $1.20, DHC-6 Twin Otter. $3, Aerospatiale ATR-42.

Perf. 14x14½
1987, June 24   **Wmk. 373**
206	A32	40c multicolored	.70	.50
207	A32	60c multicolored	1.00	1.00
208	A32	$1.20 multicolored	1.60	2.75
209	A32	$3 multicolored	3.75	4.75
		Nos. 206-209 (4)	7.05	9.00

Fungi — A33

15c, Hygrocybe occidentalis. 40c, Marasmius haemato-cephalus. $1.20, Psilocybe cubensis. $2, Hygrocybe acutoconica. $3, Boletellus cubensis.

1987, Aug. 26   Wmk. 384   Perf. 14
210	A33	15c multicolored	.70	.30
211	A33	40c multicolored	1.60	.40
212	A33	$1.20 multicolored	3.25	3.25
213	A33	$2 multicolored	4.00	4.00
214	A33	$3 multicolored	5.00	5.00
		Nos. 210-214 (5)	14.55	12.95

Carnival
Clowns — A34

1987, Oct. 28   **Perf. 14½**
215	A34	15c multi	.25	.25
216	A34	40c multi, diff.	.60	.60
217	A34	$1 multi, diff.	1.50	1.50
218	A34	$3 multi, diff.	3.00	4.25
		Nos. 215-218 (4)	5.35	6.60

Christmas 1987. See Nos. 235-238.

Flowers — A35

1988, Jan. 20
219	A35	15c Ixora	.25	.25
220	A35	40c Shrimp plant	.50	.50
221	A35	$1 Poinsettia	1.10	1.40
222	A35	$3 Honolulu rose	3.75	4.25
		Nos. 219-222 (4)	5.60	6.40

Tourism
A36

No. 223, Ft. Thomas Hotel. No. 224, Fairview Inn. No. 225, Frigate Bay Beach Hotel. No. 226, Ocean Terrace Inn. No. 227, The Golden Lemon. No. 228, Royal St. Kitts Casino and Jack Tar Village. No. 229, Rawlins Plantation Hotel and Restaurant.

1988, Apr. 20   **Wmk. 373**
223	A36	60c multicolored	.95	.95
224	A36	60c multicolored	.95	.95
225	A36	60c multicolored	.95	.95
226	A36	60c multicolored	.95	.95
227	A36	$3 multicolored	2.50	2.75
228	A36	$3 multicolored	2.50	2.75
229	A36	$3 multicolored	2.50	2.75
		Nos. 223-229 (7)	11.30	12.05

See Nos. 239-244.

Leeward Islands Cricket Tournament, 75th Anniv. — A37

Designs: 40c, Leeward Islands Cricket Assoc. emblem, ball and wicket. $3, Cricket match at Warner Park.

1988, July 13   *Perf. 13x13½*
230	A37	40c multicolored	2.00	.30
231	A37	$3 multicolored	4.00	4.00

Independence, 5th Anniv. — A38

Designs: 15c, Natl. flag. 60c, Natl. coat of arms. $5, Princess Margaret presenting the Nevis Constitution Order to Prime Minister Simmonds, Sept. 19, 1983.

1988, Sept. 19   **Wmk. 384**   *Perf. 14½*
232	A38	15c shown	1.25	.45
233	A38	60c multicolored	1.60	1.00

Souvenir Sheet
234	A38	$5 multicolored	5.50	5.50

Christmas Type of 1987
Carnival clowns.

1988, Nov. 2   **Wmk. 373**
235	A34	15c multi	.25	.25
236	A34	40c multi, diff.	.25	.25
237	A34	80c multi, diff.	.40	.55
238	A34	$3 multi, diff.	1.60	2.50
		Nos. 235-238 (4)	2.50	3.55

Tourism Type of 1988
Wmk. 384

1989, Jan. 25   **Litho.**   *Perf. 14*
239	A36	20c Old Colonial House	.25	.25
240	A36	20c Georgian House	.25	.25
241	A36	$1 Romney Manor	.65	.90
242	A36	$1 Lavington Great House	.65	.90
243	A36	$2 Treasury Building	1.00	1.75
244	A36	$2 Government House	1.00	1.75
		Nos. 239-244 (6)	3.80	5.80

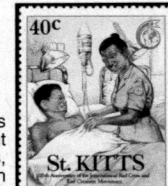

Intl. Red Cross and Red Crescent Organizations, 125th Anniv. (in 1988) — A39

1989, May 8   **Litho.**   **Wmk. 384**
Perf. 14x14½
245	A39	40c shown	.30	.30
246	A39	$1 Ambulance	.80	.80
247	A39	$3 Anniv. emblem	2.50	3.25
		Nos. 245-247 (3)	3.60	4.35

Moon Landing, 20th Anniv.
Common Design Type

Apollo 13: 10c, Lunar rover at Taurus-Littrow landing site. 20c, Fred W. Haise Jr., John L. Swigert Jr., and James A. Lovell Jr. $1, Mission emblem. $2, Splashdown in the South Pacific. $5, Buzz Aldrin disembarking from the lunar module, Apollo 11 mission.

1989, July 20   *Perf. 14*
Size of Nos. 249-250: 29x29mm
248	CD342	10c multicolored	.25	.25
249	CD342	20c multicolored	.25	.25
250	CD342	$1 multicolored	.75	.75
251	CD342	$2 multicolored	1.25	1.50
		Nos. 248-251 (4)	2.50	2.75

Souvenir Sheet
252	CD342	$5 multicolored	5.50	5.50

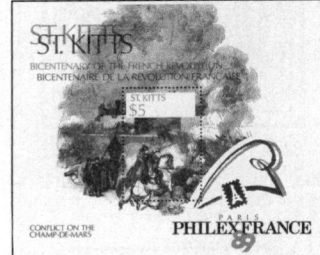

Conflict on the Champ-de-Mars — A40

1989, July 7
253	A40	$5 multicolored	4.25	4.25

PHILEXFRANCE '89, French revolution bicent.

Outline Map of St. Kitts — A41

1989   *Perf. 15x14*
255	A41	10c purple & blk	.25	.25
256	A41	15c red & blk	.25	.25
257	A41	20c org brn & blk	.25	.25
259	A41	40c bister & blk	.60	.25
261	A41	60c blue & blk	.80	.50
265	A41	$1 green & blk	1.40	1.40
		Nos. 255-265 (6)	3.55	2.90

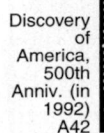

Discovery of America, 500th Anniv. (in 1992) A42

Designs: 15c, Galleon passing St. Kitts during Columbus's 2nd voyage, 1493. 80c, Coat of arms and map of 4th voyage. $1, Navigational instruments, c. 1500. $5, Exploration of Cuba and Hispaniola during Columbus's 2nd voyage, 1493-1496.

1989, Nov. 8   **Wmk. 384**   *Perf. 14*
269	A42	15c multicolored	2.25	.30
270	A42	80c multicolored	4.00	2.00
271	A42	$1 multicolored	4.50	2.00
272	A42	$5 multicolored	13.00	14.00
		Nos. 269-272 (4)	23.75	18.30

World Stamp Expo '89 A43

Exhibition emblem, flags and: 15c, Poinciana tree. 40c, Ft. George Citadel, Brimstone Hill. $1, Light Company private, 5th Foot Regiment, 1778. $3, St. George's Anglican Church.

1989, Nov. 17   **Wmk. 373**
273	A43	15c multicolored	.50	.25
274	A43	40c multicolored	.90	.40
275	A43	$1 multicolored	2.25	1.60
276	A43	$3 multicolored	3.75	5.00
		Nos. 273-276 (4)	7.40	7.25

Butterflies A45

15c, Junonia evarete. 40c, Anartia jatrophae. 60c, Heliconius charitonius. $3, Biblis hyperia.

1990, June 6   **Litho.**   *Perf. 13½*
277	A45	15c multicolored	1.25	.75
278	A45	40c multicolored	2.25	1.25
279	A45	60c multicolored	2.25	1.25
280	A45	$3 multicolored	6.50	6.50
		Nos. 277-280 (4)	12.25	9.75

Nos. 277-280 with EXPO '90 Emblem Added to Design

1990, June 6
281	A45	15c multicolored	1.50	.75
282	A45	40c multicolored	2.50	2.00
283	A45	60c multicolored	2.50	1.25
284	A45	$3 multicolored	7.00	7.00
		Nos. 281-284 (4)	13.50	9.75

Expo '90, International Garden and Greenery Exposition, Osaka, Japan.

Cannon on Brimstone Hill, 300th Anniv. — A46

15c, 40c, View of Brimstone Hill. 60c, Fort Charles under bombardment. $3, Men firing cannon.

1990 June 30   **Wmk. 384**   *Perf. 14*
285	A46	15c multicolored	.35	.25
286	A46	40c multicolored	.65	.35
287	A46	60c multicolored	1.25	1.00
288		Pair	7.00	7.00
a.		A46 60c multicolored	1.25	1.00
b.		A46 $3 multicolored	3.50	3.50
		Nos. 285-288 (4)	9.25	8.60

No. 288 has a continuous design.

Souvenir Sheet

Battle of Britain, 50th Anniv. — A47

1990, Sept. 15
289	A47	Sheet of 2	24.00	24.00
a.-b.		$3 any single	9.50	9.50

Ships A48

1990, Oct. 10   **Wmk. 373**
294	A48	10c Romney	.75	.50
a.		Wmk. 384	.75	.60
295	A48	15c Baralt	.75	.30
296	A48	20c Wear	1.00	.35
297	A48	25c Sunmount	1.00	.35
298	A48	40c Inanda	1.00	.35
299	A48	50c Alcoa Partner	1.00	.35
300	A48	60c Dominica	1.40	.35
301	A48	80c CGM Provence	1.50	.50
302	A48	$1 Director	1.50	.90
303	A48	$1.20 Typical barque, 1860-1880	2.00	1.50
304	A48	$2 Chignecto	2.50	2.50
305	A48	$3 Berbice	3.50	4.25
a.		Souvenir sheet of 1	3.00	3.00
306	A48	$5 Vamos	5.50	6.50
307	A48	$10 Federal Maple	9.00	11.00
		Nos. 294-307 (14)	32.40	29.70

No. 305a issued 2/3/97 for Hong Kong '97.

Christmas — A49

Traditional games.

1990, Nov. 14   *Perf. 14*
308	A49	10c Single fork	.25	.25
309	A49	15c Boulder breaking	.25	.25
310	A49	40c Double fork	.40	.40
311	A49	$3 Run up	2.50	3.75
		Nos. 308-311 (4)	3.40	4.65

Flowers — A50

10c, White periwinkle, horiz. 40c, Pink oleander, horiz. 60c, Pink periwinkle. $2, White oleander.

Perf. 14x13½, 13½x14
1991, May 8   **Litho.**   **Wmk. 373**
312	A50	10c multicolored	.75	.30
313	A50	40c multicolored	1.50	.45
314	A50	60c multicolored	2.00	.90
315	A50	$2 multicolored	3.50	4.50
		Nos. 312-315 (4)	7.75	6.15

Natl. Census — A51

1991, May 13   **Wmk. 384**   *Perf. 14*
316	A51	15c multicolored	.25	.25
317	A51	$2.40 multicolored	3.50	3.50

Elizabeth & Philip, Birthdays
Common Design Types
Wmk. 384

1991, June 17   **Litho.**   *Perf. 14½*
318	CD346	$1.20 multicolored	1.00	1.00
319	CD345	$1.80 multicolored	1.50	1.50
a.		Pair, #318-319 + label	3.00	3.00

Fish A52

1991, Aug. 28   **Wmk. 373**   *Perf. 14*
320	A52	10c Nassau grouper	.75	.35
321	A52	60c Hogfish	1.50	.75
322	A52	$1 Red hind	2.50	2.50
323	A52	$3 Porkfish	4.25	5.25
		Nos. 320-323 (4)	9.00	8.85

University of the West Indies A53

Designs: 15c, Chancellor Sir Shridath Ramphal, School of Continuing Studies, St. Kitts. 50c, Administration Bldg., Cave Hill Campus, Barbados. $1, Engineering Bldg., St. Augustine Campus, Trinidad & Tobago. $3, Ramphal, Mona Campus, Jamaica.

1991, Sept. 25   **Wmk. 384**
324 A53 15c multicolored   .40   .35
325 A53 50c multicolored   .80   .80
326 A53 $1 multicolored   1.60   1.40
327 A53 $3 multicolored   4.50   5.00
      Nos. 324-327 (4)   7.30   7.55

Christmas — A54

Various scenes of traditional play, "The Bull."

1991, Nov. 6   **Wmk. 373**
328 A54 10c multicolored   .40   .40
329 A54 15c multicolored   .40   .40
330 A54 60c multicolored   1.25   1.25
331 A54 $3 multicolored   4.75   4.75
      Nos. 328-331 (4)   6.80   6.80

Queen Elizabeth II's Accession to the Throne, 40th Anniv.
Common Design Type

1992, Feb. 6   **Wmk. 384**
332 CD349 10c multicolored   .30   .25
333 CD349 40c multicolored   1.25   .55
334 CD349 60c multicolored   .80   .45
335 CD349 $1 multicolored   1.25   1.25

                                      Wmk. 373
336 CD349 $3 multicolored   3.00   3.00
      Nos. 332-336 (5)   6.60   5.50

St. Kitts and Nevis Red Cross Society, 50th Anniv. — A55

10c, Map of St. Kitts & Nevis. 20c, St. Kitts & Nevis flag. 50c, Red Cross House, St. Kitts. $2.40, Jean-Henri Dunant, founder of Red Cross.

                                      Perf. 13½x14
1992, May 8   **Litho.**   **Wmk. 373**
337 A55 10c multicolored   1.50   .75
338 A55 20c multicolored   2.25   .60
339 A55 50c multicolored   2.00   1.00
340 A55 $2.40 multicolored   4.50   5.25
      Nos. 337-340 (4)   10.25   7.60

Discovery of America, 500th Anniv. — A56

1992, July 6   **Perf. 13**
341 A56 $1 Coming ashore   2.00   1.25
342 A56 $2 Natives, ships   4.00   4.00

Organization of East Caribbean States.

A57

Designs: 25c, Fountain, Independence Square. 50c, Berkeley Memorial drinking fountain and clock. 80c, Sir Thomas Warner's tomb. $2, War Memorial.

1992, Aug. 19   **Perf. 12½x13**
343 A57 25c multicolored   .25   .25
344 A57 50c multicolored   .45   .45
345 A57 80c multicolored   .75   .75
346 A57 $2 multicolored   1.75   2.50
      Nos. 343-346 (4)   3.20   3.95

Christmas — A58

Stained glass windows: 20c, Mary and Joseph. 25c, Shepherds. 80c, Three Wise Men. $3, Mary, Joseph and Christ Child.

1992, Oct. 28 **Wmk. 384** **Perf. 14½**
347 A58 20c multicolored   .30   .25
348 A58 25c multicolored   .30   .25
349 A58 80c multicolored   .70   .70
350 A58 $3 multicolored   3.00   3.75
      Nos. 347-350 (4)   4.30   4.95

Royal Air Force, 75th Anniv.
Common Design Type

Designs: 25c, Short Singapore III. 50c, Bristol Beaufort. 80c, Westland Whirlwind. $1.60, English Electric Canberra.
No. 355a, Handley Page 0/400. b, Fairey Long Range Monoplane. c, Vickers Wellesley. d, Sepecat Jaguar.

                   Wmk. 373
1993, Apr. 1   **Litho.**   **Perf. 14**
351 CD350 25c multicolored   .85   .85
352 CD350 50c multicolored   1.60   1.60
353 CD350 80c multicolored   2.10   2.10
354 CD350 $1.60 multicolored   4.25   5.00
      Nos. 351-354 (4)   8.80   9.55

                   Miniature Sheet
355 CD350 $2 Sheet of 4,
              #a.-d.   14.00 14.00

Diocese of the Northeastern Caribbean and Aruba, 150th Anniv. — A59

Designs: 25c, Diocesan Conference, Basseterre, horiz. 50c, Cathedral of St. John the Divine. 80c, Diocesan coat of arms and motto, horiz. $2, First Bishop, Right Reverend Daniel G. Davis.

              Perf. 13½x14, 14x13½
1993, May 21   **Litho.**   **Wmk. 384**
356 A59 25c multicolored   .30   .30
357 A59 50c multicolored   .50   .50
358 A59 80c multicolored   1.00   1.00
359 A59 $2 multicolored   2.25   3.00
      Nos. 356-359 (4)   4.05   4.80

Coronation of Queen Elizabeth II, 40th Anniv. — A60

Royal regalia and stamps of St. Kitts-Nevis: 10c, Eagle-shaped ampulla, No. 119. 25c, Anointing spoon, No. 334. 80c, Tassels, No. 333. $2, Staff of Scepter with the Cross, No. 354a-354c.

1993, June 2   **Perf. 14½x14**
360 A60 10c multicolored   .50   .40
361 A60 25c multicolored   .70   .55
362 A60 80c multicolored   1.25   1.25
363 A60 $2 multicolored   2.25   2.75
      Nos. 360-363 (4)   4.70   4.95

Girls' Brigade Intl., Cent. — A61

1993, July 1   **Perf. 13½x14**
364 A61 80c Flags   2.50   1.00
365 A61 $3 Badge, coat of arms   4.25   4.25

Independence, 10th Anniv. — A62

Designs: 20c, Flag, map of St. Kitts and Nevis, plane, ship and island scenes. 80c, Natl. arms, independence emblem. $3, Natl. arms, map.

                                      Wmk. 373
1993, Sept. 10   **Litho.**   **Perf. 14**
366 A62 20c multicolored   1.00   .25
367 A62 80c multicolored   1.25   .80
368 A62 $3 multicolored   4.00   4.75
      Nos. 366-368 (3)   6.25   5.80

Christmas — A63

                                      Perf. 13½x14
1993, Nov. 16   **Litho.**   **Wmk. 373**
369 A63 25c Roselle   .50   .50
370 A63 50c Poinsettia   .75   .75
371 A63 $1.60 Snow on the
              Mountain   2.50   3.00
      Nos. 369-371 (3)   3.75   4.25

Prehistoric Aquatic Reptiles — A64

Designs: a, Mesosaurus. b, Placodus. c, Liopleurodon. d, Hydrotherosaurus. e, Caretta.

                   Wmk. 384
1994, Feb. 18   **Litho.**   **Perf. 14**
372 A64 $1.20 Strip of 5, #a.-
              e.   10.00 10.00
373 A64 $1.20 #372 ovptd.
              with Hong
              Kong '94 em-
              blem   11.50 11.50

                   Souvenir Sheet

Treasury Building, Cent. — A65

                                      Wmk. 373
1994, Mar. 21   **Litho.**   **Perf. 13½**
374 A65 $10 multicolored   11.00 11.00

Order of the Caribbean Community — A66

First award recipients: Nos. 375a, 376a, Sir Shridath Ramphal, statesman, Guyana. Nos. 375b, 376b, Emblem of the Order. Nos. 375c, 376c, Derek Walcott, writer, St. Lucia. Nos. 375d, 376d, William Demas, economist, Trinidad and Tobago.

                   Wmk. 373
1994, July 13   **Litho.**   **Perf. 14**
375 A66 10c Strip of 5, #a, b, c,
              d   1.25   1.25
376 A66 $1 Strip of 5, #a, b, c,
              d   6.75   6.75

CARICOM, 20th anniv. (Nos. 375b, 376b).

Christmas — A67

1994, Oct. 31
377 A67 25c Carol singing   .25   .25
378 A67 25c Opening presents   .25   .25
379 A67 80c Carnival   .75   .75
380 A67 $2.50 Nativity   2.75   2.75
      Nos. 377-380 (4)   4.00   4.00

         Intl. Year of the Family.

Green Turtle A68

                                      Wmk. 373
1995, Feb. 27   **Litho.**   **Perf. 14**
381 A68 10c shown   .75   .75
382 A68 40c On beach   .90   .90
383 A68 50c Laying eggs   1.10   1.10
384 A68 $1 Hatchlings   1.50   1.50
  a.   Strip of 4, #381-384   6.50   6.50

         World Wildlife Fund.
No. 384a issued in sheets of 16 stamps.

First St. Kitts Postage Stamp, 125th Anniv. A69

St. Christopher #1 at left and: 25c, St. Christopher #1. 80c, St. Kitts-Nevis #72. $2.50, St. Kitts-Nevis #91. $3, St. Kitts-Nevis #119.

                   Wmk. 373
1995, Apr. 10   **Litho.**   **Perf. 13½**
385 A69 25c multicolored   .25   .25
386 A69 80c multicolored   .60   .50
387 A69 $2.50 multicolored   2.50   2.50
388 A69 $3 multicolored   3.00   3.00
      Nos. 385-388 (4)   6.35   6.25

End of World War II, 50th Anniv.
Common Design Types

Designs: 20c, Caribbean Regiment, North Africa. 50c, TBM Avengers on anti-submarine patrol. $2, Spitfire MkVb. $8, US destroyer escort on anti-submarine duty.
$3, Reverse of War Madal 1939-45.

                   Wmk. 373
1995, May 8   **Litho.**   **Perf. 13½**
389 CD351 20c multicolored   .25   .25
390 CD351 50c multicolored   .65   .65
391 CD351 $2 multicolored   2.50   2.50
392 CD351 $8 multicolored   8.00   8.00
      Nos. 389-392 (4)   11.40 11.40

                   Souvenir Sheet
                    Perf. 14
393 CD352 $3 multicolored   5.00   5.00

SKANTEL, 10th
Anniv. — A70

Designs: 10c, Satellite transmission. 25c,
Telephones, computer. $2, Transmission
tower, satellite dish. $3, Satellite dish silhouetted against sun.

1995, Sept. 27   **Perf. 13½x14**
394 A70 10c multicolored .25 .25
395 A70 25c multicolored .35 .35
396 A70 $2 multicolored 2.50 2.50
397 A70 $3 multicolored 3.00 3.75
    Nos. 394-397 (4) 6.10 6.85

UN, 50th Anniv.
Common Design Type

Designs: 40c, Energy, clean environment.
50c, Coastal, ocean resources. $1.60, Solid
waste management. $2.50, Forestry reserves.

1995, Oct. 24   **Perf. 13½x13**
398 CD353 40c multicolored .50 .50
399 CD353 50c multicolored .65 .65
400 CD353 $1.60 multicolored 2.00 2.25
401 CD353 $2.50 multicolored 3.00 3.75
    Nos. 398-401 (4) 6.15 7.15

FAO, 50th
Anniv.
A71

Designs: 25c, Vegetables. 50c, Glazed carrots, West Indian peas & rice. 80c, Tania, Cassava plants. $1.50, Waterfall, Green Hill Mountain.

1995, Nov. 13   **Perf. 13½**
402 A71 25c multicolored .25 .25
403 A71 50c multicolored .50 .50
404 A71 80c multicolored .85 .85
405 A71 $1.50 multicolored 1.75 2.75
    Nos. 402-405 (4) 3.35 4.35

Sea
Shells — A72

a, Flame helmet. b, Triton's trumpet. c, King
helmet. d, True tulip. e, Queen conch.

Wmk. 373
1996, Jan. 10   **Litho.**   **Perf. 13**
406 A72 $1.50 Strip of 5, #a.-
    e. 8.75 8.75

CAPEX
'96 — A73

Leeward Islands LMS Jubilee Class 4-6-0
Locomotives: 10c, No. 45614. $10, No. 5614.

Perf. 13½x14
1996, June 8   **Litho.**   **Wmk. 373**
407 A73 10c multicolored .90 .90
    Souvenir Sheet
    Perf. 14x15
408 A73 $10 multicolored 9.00 9.00
    No. 408 is 48x31mm.

A74

Modern Olympic Games, Cent.: 10c, Runner, St. Kitts & Nevis flag. 25c, High jumper, US flag. 80c, Runner, Olympic flag. $3, Athens Games poster, 1896. $6, Olympic torch.

Wmk. 384
1996, June 30   **Litho.**   **Perf. 14**
409 A74 10c multicolored .25 .25
410 A74 25c multicolored .25 .25
411 A74 80c multicolored .75 .75
412 A74 $3 multicolored 2.50 2.50
    Nos. 409-412 (4) 3.75 3.75

    Souvenir Sheet
413 A74 $6 multicolored 5.25 5.25
    Olymphilex '96 (#413).

A75

Defense Force, Cent.: 10c, Volunteer rifleman, 1896. 50c, Mounted infantry, 1911. $2, Bandsman, 1940-60. $2.50, Modern uniform, 1996.

1996, Nov. 1   **Wmk. 373**
414 A75 10c multicolored .25 .25
415 A75 50c multicolored .45 .45
416 A75 $2 multicolored 1.75 1.75
417 A75 $2.50 multicolored 2.00 2.00
    Nos. 414-417 (4) 4.45 4.45

Christmas — A76

Paintings: 15c, Holy Virgin and Child, by Anais Colin, 1844. 25c, Holy Family, After Rubens. 50c, Madonna with the Goldfinch, by Krause on porcelain after Raphael, 1507. 80c, Madonna on Throne with Angels, by unknown Spanish, 17th cent.

1996, Nov. 29
418 A76 15c multicolored .25 .25
419 A76 25c multicolored .35 .25
420 A76 50c multicolored .80 .65
421 A76 80c multicolored 1.00 1.25
    Nos. 418-421 (4) 2.40 2.40

Fish — A77

a, Princess parrot fish. b, Yellowbelly hamlet. c, Coney. d, Clown wrasse. e, Doctor fish. f, Squirrelfish. g, Queen angelfish. h, Spanish hogfish. i, Red hind. j, Red grouper. k, Yellowtail snapper. l, Mutton hamlet.

1997, Apr. 24   **Perf. 13½**
422 A77 $1 Sheet of 12, #a.-l. 14.50 14.50

Queen Elizabeth II and Prince Philip,
50th Wedding Anniv. — A78

Designs: No. 423, Queen. No. 424, Prince riding with Royal Guard. No. 425, Queen riding in carriage. No. 426, Prince Philip. No. 427, Early photo of Queen, Prince. No. 428, Prince riding horse.
    Queen, Prince riding in open carriage, horiz.

Wmk. 373
1997, July 10   **Litho.**   **Perf. 13½**
423   10c multicolored .50 .50
424   10c multicolored .50 .50
  a.   A78 Pair, #423-424 1.35 1.35
425   25c multicolored .75 .75
426   25c multicolored .75 .75
  a.   A78 Pair, #425-426 1.75 1.75
427   $3 multicolored 2.25 2.25
428   $3 multicolored 2.25 2.25
  a.   A78 Pair, #427-428 6.00 6.00
    Nos. 423-428 (6) 7.00 7.00

    Souvenir Sheet
    Perf. 14x14½
429 A78 $6 multicolored 8.50 8.50

Christmas — A79

Churches: No. 430, Zion Moravian. No. 431, Wesley Methodist. $1.50, St. Georges Anglican. $15, Co-Cathedral of the Immaculate Conception.

Perf. 13½x14
1997, Oct. 31   **Litho.**   **Wmk. 384**
430 A79 10c multi .25 .25
431 A79 10c multi .25 .25
432 A79 $1.50 multi, vert. 1.40 1.40
433 A79 $15 multi, vert. 12.00 12.00
    Nos. 430-433 (4) 13.90 13.90

Natl. Heroes' Day — A80

No. 434, Robert L. Bradshaw (1916-78), 1st premier of St. Kitts, Nevis, & Anguilla. No. 435, Joseph N. France, trade unionist. No. 436, C.A. Paul Southwell (1913-79), 1st chief minister of St. Kitts, Nevis, & Anguilla. $3, France, Bradshaw, & Southwell.

1997, Sept. 16   **Perf. 13½**
434 A80 25c multi, vert. .25 .25
435 A80 25c multi, vert. .25 .25
436 A80 25c multi, vert. .25 .25
437 A80 $3 multi 2.25 2.25
    Nos. 434-437 (4) 3.00 3.00

Diana, Princess of Wales (1961-97)
Common Design Type

No. 438: a, like No. 437A. b, Wearing red jacket. c, Wearing white dress. d, Holding flowers.

Perf. 14½x14
1998, Mar. 31   **Litho.**   **Wmk. 373**
437A CD355 30c Wearing
       white hat .40 .40

Sheet of 4
438 CD355 $1.60 Sheet of 4,
    #a.-d. 4.75 4.75

No. 438 sold for $6.40 + 90c, with surtax from international sales being donated to Princess Diana Memorial Fund and surtax from national sales being donated to designated local charity.

Butterflies
A81

Designs: 10c, Common long-tail skipper. 15c, White peacock. 25c, Caribbean buckeye. 30c, Red rim. 40c, Cassius blue. 50c, Flambeau. 60c, Lucas's blue. 90c, Cloudless sulphur. $1, Monarch. $1.20, Fiery skipper. $1.60, Zebra. $3, Southern dagger tail. $5, Polydamus swallowtail. $10, Tropical checkered skipper.

Perf. 14¼x14½
1997, Dec. 29   **Litho.**   **Wmk. 373**
439   A81   10c multicolored .25 .25
  a.   "S" in "Proteus" to left of midline of leaf above .45 .45
440   A81   15c multicolored .30 .30
441   A81   25c multicolored .40 .40
442   A81   30c multicolored .40 .40
443   A81   40c multicolored .40 .40
444   A81   50c multicolored .60 .60
445   A81   60c multicolored .70 .70
446   A81   90c multicolored 1.10 1.10
447   A81 $1 multicolored 1.10 1.10
448   A81 $1.20 multicolored 1.40 1.40
449   A81 $1.60 multicolored 1.75 1.75
450   A81 $3 multicolored 2.75 2.75
  a.   "S" in "$" same size as numeral 4.00 4.00
451   A81 $5 multicolored 4.00 4.00
  a.   Inscribed "Polydamas" 6.00 6.00
452   A81 $10 multicolored 7.00 7.00
  a.   "S" in "$" same size as numeral 10.00 10.00
    Nos. 439-452 (14) 22.15 22.15

Nos. 439a, 450a, 451a and 452a have other minor design differences.

University
of West
Indies,
50th
Anniv.
A82

Perf. 13½x13
1998, July 20   **Litho.**   **Wmk. 373**
453 A82 80c shown .70 .70
454 A82 $2 Arms, mortarboard 1.90 1.90

Carnival
Santa
A83

Wmk. 373
1998, Oct. 30   **Litho.**   **Perf. 14**
455 A83 80c shown .65 .65
456 A83 $1.20 With two dancers 1.00 1.00

UPU, 125th
Anniv. — A84

Wmk. 373
1999, Mar. 5   **Litho.**   **Perf. 14**
457 A84 30c shown .40 .40
458 A84 90c Map of St. Kitts 1.00 1.00

Birds of the Eastern Caribbean A85

Designs: a, Caribbean martin. b, Spotted sandpiper. c, Sooty tern. d, Red-tailed hawk. e, Trembler. f, Belted kingfisher. g, Black-billed duck. h, Yellow warbler. i, Blue-headed hummingbird. j, Antillean euphonia. k, Fulvous whistling duck. l, Mangrove cuckoo. m, Carib grackle. n, Caribbean elaenia. o, Common ground dove. p, Forest thrush.

Wmk. 373

1999, Apr. 27	**Litho.**		*Perf. 14*		
459	A85	80c	Sheet of 16, #a.-		
			p.	13.00	13.00

IBRA '99.

1st Manned Moon Landing, 30th Anniv.
Common Design Type

Designs: 80c, Lift-off. 90c, In lunar orbit. $1, Aldrin deploying scientific equipment. $1.20, Heat shield burns on re-entry. $10, Earth as seen from moon.

Perf. 14x13¾

1999, July 20	**Litho.**		**Wmk. 384**		
460	CD357	80c	multicolored	.75	.75
461	CD357	90c	multicolored	.90	.90
462	CD357	$1	multicolored	1.00	1.00
463	CD357	$1.20	multicolored	.95	1.25
		Nos. 460-463 (4)		3.60	3.90

Souvenir Sheet
Perf. 14

464	CD357	$10	multicolored	7.75	7.75

No. 464 contains one 40mm circular stamp.

Christmas — A86

Wmk. 373

1999, Oct. 29	**Litho.**		*Perf. 13¾*		
465	A86	10c	shown	.25	.25
466	A86	30c	3 musicians	.25	.25
467	A86	80c	6 musicians	.70	.70
468	A86	$2	4 musicians, diff.	1.90	2.25
		Nos. 465-468 (4)		3.10	3.45

Children's Drawings Celebrating the Millennium — A87

1999, Dec. 29	**Litho.**		*Perf. 14*		
469	A87	10c	by Adom Taylor	.35	.35
470	A87	30c	by Travis Liburd	.35	.35
471	A87	50c	by Darren Moses	.90	.90
472	A87	$1	by Pierre Liburd	1.60	1.60
		Nos. 469-472 (4)		3.20	3.20

Carifesta VII — A88

Designs: 30c, Festival participants. 90c, Emblem. $1.20, Dancer, vert.

Wmk. 373

2000, Aug. 30	**Litho.**		*Perf. 14*		
473	A88	30c	multi	.25	.25
474	A88	90c	multi	.75	.75
475	A88	$1.20	multi	1.15	1.15
		Nos. 473-475 (3)		2.15	2.15

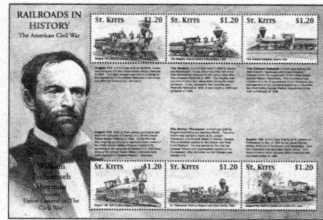

Railroads in American Civil War — A89

No. 476, $1.20, horiz.: a, Engine 133. b, Quigley. c, Colonel Holobird. d, Engine 150. e, Doctor Thompson. f, Engine 156.
No. 477, $1.20, horiz.: a, Governor Nye. b, Engine 31. c, C. A. Henry. d, Engine 152. e, Engine 116. f, Job Terry.
No. 478, $1.60, horiz.: a, Dover. b, Scout. c, Baltimore & Ohio Railroad locomotive. d, John M. Forbes. e, Edward Kidder. f, William W. Wright.
No. 479, $1.60, horiz.: a, Engine 83. b, General. c, Engine 38. d, Texas. e, Engine 162. f, Christopher Adams, Jr.
No. 480, $5, Ulysses S. Grant. No. 481, $5, George B. McClellan. No. 482, $5, Herman Haupt. No. 483, $5, Robert E. Lee.

Unwmk.

2001, Feb. 19	**Litho.**		*Perf. 14*		
Sheets of 6, #a-f					
476-479	A89	Set of 4		35.00	35.00
Souvenir Sheets					
480-483	A89	Set of 4		35.00	35.00

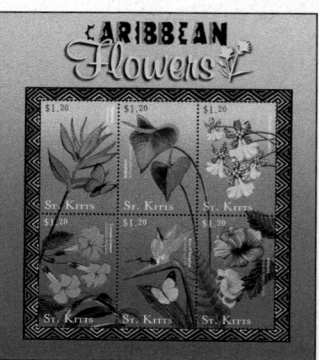

Flora & Fauna — A90

No. 484, $1.20 — Flowers: a, Heliconia. b, Anthurium. c, Oncidium splendidum. d, Trumpet creeper. e, Bird of paradise. f, Hibiscus.
No. 485, $1.20: a, Bananaquit. b, Anthurium (hills and clouds in background). c, Common dolphin. d, Horse mushroom. e, Green anole. f, Monarch butterfly.
No. 486, $1.60 — Birds: a, Laughing gull. b, Sooty tern. c, White-tailed tropicbird. d, Painted bunting. e, Belted kingfisher. f, Yellow-bellied sapsucker.
No. 487, $1.60 — Butterflies: a, Figure-of-eight. b, Banded king shoemaker. c, Orange theope. d, Grecian shoemaker. e, Clorinde. f, Small lace-wing.
No. 488, $1.60, horiz.: a, Beaugregory. b, Banded butterflyfish. c, Cherubfish. d, Rock beauty. e, Red snapper. f, Leatherback turtle.
No. 489, $5, Leochilus carinatus. No. 490, $5, Iguana, horiz. No. 491, $5, Ruby-throated hummingbird, horiz. No. 492, $5, Common morpho, horiz.
No. 493, $5, Redband parrotfish, horiz.

2001, Mar. 12			*Perf. 14*		
Sheets of 6, #a-f					
484-488	A90	Set of 5		37.50	37.50
Souvenir Sheets					
489-493	A90	Set of 5		28.00	28.00

Compare No. 491 with No. 520.

2001 Census — A91

Designs: 30c, People in house. $3, People, barn, silos.

2001, Apr. 18	**Litho.**		*Perf. 14½x14¼*		
494-495	A91	Set of 2		3.50	3.50

Queen Victoria (1819-1901) — A92

No. 496: a, At coronation. b, In wedding gown. c, With Prince Albert visiting wounded Crimean War veterans. d, With Prince Albert, 1854.
$5, Wearing crown.

2001, Apr. 26			*Perf. 14*		
496	A92	$2	Sheet of 4, #a-d	8.25	8.25
Souvenir Sheet					
497	A92	$5	black	5.75	5.75

No. 496 contains four 28x42mm stamps.

Monet Paintings — A93

No. 498, horiz.: a, On the Coast of Trouville. b, Vétheuil in Summer. c, Field of Yellow Iris Near Giverny. d, Coastguard's Cottage at Varengeville.
$5, Poplars on the Banks of the Epte, Seen From the Marshes.

2001, July 16			*Perf. 13¾*		
498	A93	$2	Sheet of 4, #a-d	10.00	10.00
Souvenir Sheet					
499	A93	$5	multi	5.25	5.25

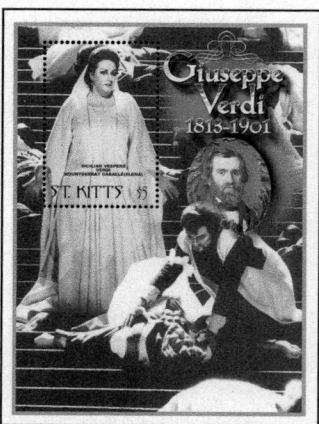

Giuseppe Verdi (1813-1901), Opera Composer — A94

No. 500 — Scenes from the Sicilian Vespers: a, French soldiers in Palermo (all standing). b, French soldiers in Palermo (some seated). c, Costume design. d, Sicilian people and French soldiers

$5, Montserrat Caballé.

2001, July 16			*Perf. 14*		
500	A94	$2	Sheet of 4, #a-d	8.50	8.50
Souvenir Sheet					
501	A94	$5	multi	5.75	5.75

Royal Navy Submarines, Cent. — A95

No. 502, horiz.: a, A Class submarine. b, HMS Dreadnaught battleship. c, HMS Amethyst. d, HMS Barnham. e, HMS Exeter. f, HMS Eagle.
$5, HMS Dreadnaught submarine.

2001, July 16			*Perf. 14*		
502	A95	$1.40	Sheet of 6, #a-f	19.00	19.00
Souvenir Sheet					
503	A95	$5	multi	10.00	10.00

No. 502 contains six 42x28mm stamps.

Queen Elizabeth II, 75th Birthday — A96

No. 504: a, In blue hat, holding flowers. b, In flowered hat, looking right. c, In blue hat and coat. d, In flowered hat, looking left.
$5, On horse.

2001, July 16					
504	A96	$2	Sheet of 4, #a-d	8.50	8.50
Souvenir Sheet					
505	A96	$5	multi	5.50	5.50

Phila Nippon '01, Japan — A97

Woodcuts: 50c, Hatsufunedayu as a Tatebina, by Shigenobu. 80c, Yamagawa Samurai Kodenji as Tsuyu No Mae, by Kiyonobu I. $1, Senya Nakamura as Tokonatsu, by Kiyomasu I. $1.60, Sumida River, by Shunsho. $2, Wrestler, Kuemon Yoba, by Shun-ei. $3, Two Actors in Roles, by Kiyonobu Torii I. $5, Full Length Actor Protraits, by Shun-ei.

2001, July 16			*Perf. 12x12¼*		
506-511	A97	Set of 6		9.00	9.00
Souvenir Sheet					
512	A97	$5	multi	6.00	6.00

Mao Zedong (1893-1976) — A98

No. 514: a, In 1926. b, In 1945 (green background). c, In 1945 (lilac background).
$3, Undated picture.

2001, July 16   **Litho.**   **Perf. 13¾**
513 A98 $2 Sheet of 3, #a-c   9.00 9.00
Souvenir Sheet
514 A98 $3 multi   4.50 4.50

Flora & Fauna — A99

No. 515, $1.20 — Birds: a, Trembler. b, White-tailed tropicbird. c, Red-footed booby. d, Red-legged thrush. e, Painted bunting. f, Bananaquit.
No. 516, $1.20 — Orchids: a, Maxillaria cucullata. b, Cattleya dowiana. c, Rossioglossum grande. d, Aspasia epidendroides. e, Lycaste skinneri. f, Cattleya perciviliana.
No. 517, $1.60 — Butterflies: a, Orange-barred sulphur. b, Giant swallowtail. c, Orange theope. d, Blue night. e, Grecian shoemaker. f, Cramer's mesene.
No. 518, $1.60 — Mushrooms: a, Pholiota spectabilis. b, Flammula penetrans. c, Ungulina iocephala. e, Amanita muscaria. f, Corinus comatus.
No. 519, $1.60, horiz. — Whales: a, Killer.whale b, Cuvier's beaked whale. c, Humpback whale. d, Sperm whale. e, Blue whale. f, Whale shark.
No. 520, $5, Ruby-throated hummingbird. No. 521, $5, Psychilis atropurpurea. No. 522, $5, Figure-of-eight butterfly. No. 523, $5, Lepiota procera. No. 524, $5, Sei whale, horiz.

2001, Sept. 18   **Perf. 14**
Sheets of 6, #a-f
515-519 A99   Set of 5   35.00 35.00
Souvenir Sheets
520-524 A99   Set of 5   25.00 25.00
Compare No. 520 with No. 490.

Christmas and
Carnival — A100

Designs: 10c, Angel, Christmas tree. 30c, Fireworks. 80c, Wreath, dove, bells, candy cane. $2, Steel drums.

2001, Nov. 26
525-528 A100   Set of 4   4.00 4.00

Reign of Queen Elizabeth II, 50th
Anniv. — A101

No. 529: a, Ceremonial coach. b, Prince Philip. c, Queen and Queen Mother. d, Queen wearing tiara.
$5, Queen and Prince Philip.

2002, Feb. 6   **Perf. 14¼**
529 A101 $2 Sheet of 4, #a-d   6.50 6.50
Souvenir Sheet
530 A101 $5 multi   4.75 4.75

United We
Stand — A102

Perf. 13½x13¼
2002, June 17   **Litho.**
531 A102 80c multi   1.90 1.90
Printed in sheets of 4.

2002
Winter
Olympics,
Salt Lake
City
A103

Designs: No. 532, $3, Cross-country skiing. No. 533, $3, Alpine skiing.

2002, June 17   **Perf. 13¼x13½**
532-533 A103   Set of 2   5.75 5.75
533a   Souvenir sheet, #532-533   5.75 5.75
Souvenir Sheet

New Year 2002 (Year of the
Horse) — A104

Details of Wen-Gi's Returning to Han, by Chang Yu: a, Horse and rider, dog. b, Group of horses and riders. c, Horse and rider, two attendants. d, Standard bearer on horse.

2002, June 17   **Perf. 12½**
534 A104 $1.60 Sheet of 4, #a-d   5.00 5.00

Intl. Year of Mountains — A105

No. 535: a, Mt. Sakura, Japan. b, Mount Assiniboine, Canada. c, Mt. Asgard, Canada. d, Bugaboo Spire, Canada.
$6, Mt. Owen, Wyoming.

2002, June 17   **Perf. 13¼x13½**
535 A105 $2 Sheet of 4, #a-d   6.50 6.50
Souvenir Sheet
536 A105 $6 multi   6.00 6.00

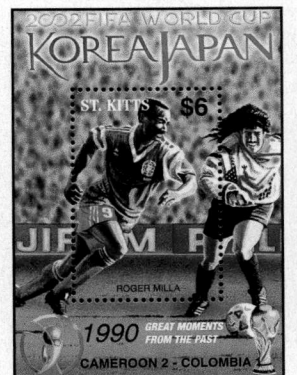

2002 World Cup Soccer
Championships, Japan and
Korea — A106

No. 537 — World Cup trophy and: a, $1.65, 1982 World Cup poster. b, $1.65, Just Fontaine, French flag. c, $1.65, U.S. player and flag. d, $1.65, Swedish player and flag. e, $6, Daegu Sports Complex, Korea (55x41mm).
$6, Roger Milla.

2002, June 17   **Perf. 13½x13¼**
537 A106   Sheet of 5, #a-e   10.50 10.50
Souvenir Sheet
538 A106 $6 multi   5.50 5.50

20th World Scout Jamboree,
Thailand — A107

No. 539, horiz.: a, Scout sign. b, Silver Award 2. c, Council patch. d, Scout with sword.
$6, Environmental Studies merit badge.

2002, June 17   **Perf. 13¼x13½**
539 A107 $2 Sheet of 4, #a-d   7.50 7.50
Souvenir Sheet
Perf. 13½x13¼
540 A107 $6 multi   5.75 5.75

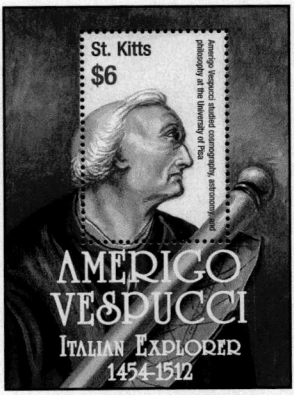

Amerigo Vespucci (1454-1512),
Explorer — A108

No. 541, horiz.: a, Vespucci with feathered hat. b, 1507 World map by Martin Waldseemüller. c, Vespucci with beard.
$6, Vespucci with bald head.

2002, June 17   **Perf. 13¼x13½**
541 A108 $3 Sheet of 3, #a-c   7.50 7.50
Souvenir Sheet
Perf. 13½x13¼
542 A108 $6 multi   5.75 5.75

Kim Collins,
Sprinter — A109

Collins: 30c, Running. 90c, Wearing 2001 IAAF bronze medal.

2002, July 2   **Perf. 14**
543-544 A109   Set of 2   2.50 2.50

Christmas — A110

Fruits: 10c, Soursop. 80c, Passion fruit. $1, Sugar apple. $2, Custard apple.

2002, Oct. 14   **Litho.**
545-548 A110   Set of 4   5.75 5.75

Queen Mother Elizabeth (1900-
2002) — A111

No. 549: a, Wearing green dress. b, Wearing yellow dress and hat.

2002, Nov. 18   **Litho.**   **Perf. 14**
549 A111 $2 Pair, #a-b   4.50 4.50
No. 549 printed in sheets containing 2 pairs.

First Non-stop Solo Transatlantic Flight, 75th Anniv. — A112

Charles Lindbergh: a, In suit, denomination in white. b, And Spirit of St. Louis, denomination in blue violet. c, In suit, looking right, denomination in blue violet. d, And Spirit of St. Louis, denomination in white. e, Wearing pilot's headgear. f, Wearing overcoat.

2002, Nov. 18
550 A112 $1.50 Sheet of 6,
#a-f 10.00 10.00

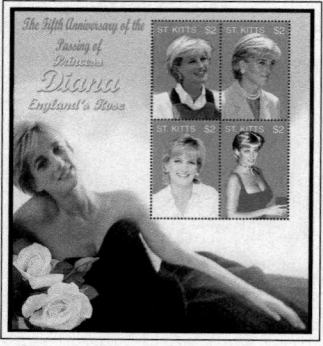

Princess Diana (1961-97) — A113

No. 551, $2: a, Wearing bulletproof vest. b, Wearing gray suit with pearls. c, Wearing yellow blouse. d, Wearing red dress and necklace.
No. 552, $2: a, Wearing white coat with purple piping. b, With hands clasped. c, Wearing red dress without necklace. d, Wearing white dress.

2002, Nov. 18 Litho.
Sheets of 4, #a-d
551-552 A113 Set of 2 14.00 14.00

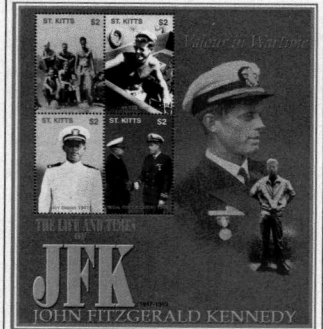

Pres. John F. Kennedy (1917-63) — A114

No. 553, $2: a, With sailors, Solomon Islands, 1942. b, On PT109, 1942. c, As Navy Ensign, 1941. d, Receiving medal for gallantry, 1944.
No. 554, $2: a, Peace Corps. b, Space program. c, Civil rights. d, Nuclear disarmament.

2002, Nov. 18 Perf. 14
Sheets of 4, #a-d
553-554 A114 Set of 2 14.00 14.00

New Year 2003 (Year of the Ram) — A115

No. 555: a, Piebald ram. b, Ram with long coat. c, Ram sculpture, looking right.

2003, Jan. 27 Perf. 14¼x13¾
555 A115 $1 Vert. strip of 3, #a-c 4.50 4.50
No. 555 printed in sheets containing 2 strips.

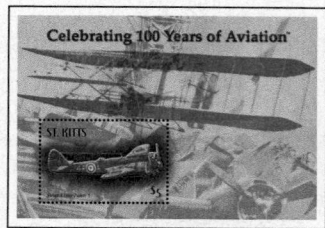

Powered Flight, Cent. — A116

No. 556: a, Voisin LA5. b, Gotha G.V. c, Polikarpov I-16. d, Bell YFM-1.
$5, Bristol Blenheim 1.

2003, June 17 Litho. Perf. 14
556 A116 $2 Sheet of 4, #a-d 6.50 6.50
Souvenir Sheet
557 A116 $5 multi 3.50 3.50

Tour de France Bicycle Race, Cent. — A117

No. 558: a, Miguel Indurain, 1994. b, Indurain, 1995. c, Bjarne Riis, 1996. d, Jan Ullrich, 1997.
$5, Indurain, 1991-95.

2003, June 17 Perf. 13½x13¼
558 A117 $2 Sheet of 4, #a-d 6.00 6.00
Souvenir Sheet
559 A117 $5 multi 3.75 3.75

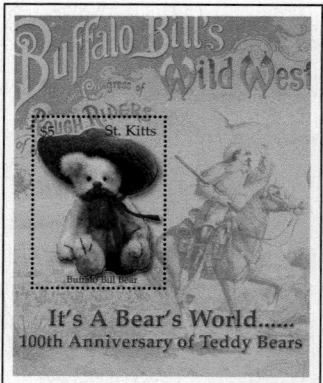

Teddy Bears, Cent. — A118

No. 560: a, Queen Victoria Bear. b, Teddy Roosevelt Bear. c, George Washington Bear. d, General Patton Bear.
$5, Buffalo Bill Bear.

2003, June 17 Perf. 13¾
560 A118 $2 Sheet of 4, #a-d 6.50 6.50
Souvenir Sheet
561 A118 $5 multi 4.00 4.00

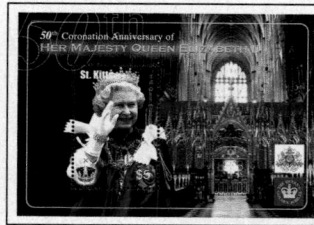

Coronation of Queen Elizabeth II, 50th Anniv. — A119

No. 562: a, Wearing tiara as young woman. b, Wearing tiara and red sash. c, Wearing tiara and blue sash.
$5, Queen waving.

2003, June 17 Litho. Perf. 14
562 A119 $3 Sheet of 3, #a-c 6.50 6.50
Souvenir Sheet
563 A119 $5 multi 4.00 4.00

Caribbean Community, 30th Anniv. — A120

2003, June 23
564 A120 30c multi 1.10 1.10

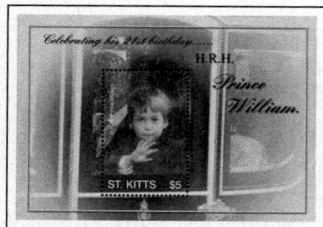

Prince William, 21st Birthday — A121

No. 565: a, As toddler, in jacket. b, As young boy, in striped shirt. c, Wearing sports shirt.
$5, As child, waving.

2003, July 1
565 A121 $3 Sheet of 3, #a-c 6.25 6.25
Souvenir Sheet
566 A121 $5 multi 3.75 3.75

Norman Rockwell Paintings of Boy Scouts from Boy Scout Calendars — A122

No. 567: a, Scout and Sailors, 1937. b, Scouts with Camping Gear, 1937. c, Boy and Dog at Window, 1968. d, Scout at Attention, 1932.
$5, Boy Scout and Cub Scout, 1950.

2003, Aug. 18 Perf. 14
567 A122 $2 Sheet of 4, #a-d 5.75 5.75
Souvenir Sheet
568 A122 $5 multi 3.75 3.75

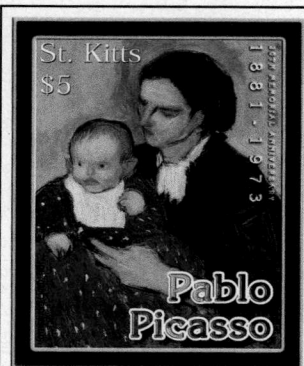

Painting by Pablo Picasso — A123

No. 569: a, Child with Wooden Horse. b, Child with a Ball. c, The Butterfly Catcher. d, Boy with a Lobster. e, Baby Wearing Polka Dot Dress. f, El Bobo, After Murillo.
$5, Untitled painting.

2003, Aug. 18 Perf. 14
569 A123 $1.60 Sheet of 4, #a-d 6.75 6.75
Souvenir Sheet
Imperf
570 A123 $5 multi 3.75 3.75
No. 569 contains six 28x42mm stamps.

Rembrandt Paintings A124

Designs: 50c, A Family Group. $1, Portrait of Cornelis Claesz Anslo and Aetje Gerritsor Schouten, horiz. $1.60, Portrait of a Young Woman. $3, Man in Military Costume.
No. 575: a, An Old Woman Reading. b, Hendrickje Stoffels. c, Rembrandt's Mother. d, Saskia.
$5, Judas Returning the Thirty Pieces of Silver.

2003, Aug. 18   **Perf. 14¼**
571-574 A124   Set of 4   4.25 4.25
575 A124 $2 Sheet of 4, #a-d   5.50 5.50
Souvenir Sheet
576 A124 $5 multi   3.50 3.50

Japanese Art — A125

Designs: 90c, Tokiwa Gozen with Her Son in the Snow, by Hokumei Shunkyokusai. $1, Courtesan and Asahina, attributed to Choki Eishosai. $1.50, Parody of Sugawara No Michizane Seated on an Ox, by Toyokuni Utagawa. $3, Visiting a Flower Garden, by Kunisada Utagawa.

No. 581 — Akugenta Yoshihira, by Kunisada Utagawa: a, Man with bow. b, Man with sword at waist. c, Man holding scarf. d, Man with sword on shoulder.

$6, The Courtesan Katachino Under a Cherry Tree, by Toyoharu Utagawa.

2003, Aug. 18
577-580 A125   Set of 4   5.00 5.00
581 A125 $2 Sheet of 4, #a-d   6.25 6.25
Souvenir Sheet
582 A125 $6 multi   4.50 4.50

White Gibbon, by Giuseppe Castiglione A126

2004, Jan. 15   **Perf. 13¾x13½**
583 A126 $1.60 shown   1.40 1.40
Souvenir Sheet
Perf. 13¼
584 A126 $3 Painting detail   2.75 2.75

New Year 2004 (Year of the Monkey). No. 583 printed in sheets of 4. No. 584 contains one 30x37mm stamp.

D-Day, 60th Anniv. — A127

No. 585, horiz.: a, 12th Panzer Division moves into position. b, German heavy tank. c, British and Germans clash (soldiers). d, British and Germans clash (soldiers, tank).
$5, Allied cemetery, Normandy.

2004, Sept. 21   **Litho.**   **Perf. 14**
585 A127 $2 Sheet of 4, #a-d   6.00 6.00
Souvenir Sheet
586 A127 $5 multi   4.00 4.00

2004 Summer Olympics, Athens A128

Designs: 50c, Jiri Guth Jarkovsky, member of first International Olympic Committee. 90c, Poster for 1972 Munich Olympics. $1, Poster for 1900 Paris Olympics. $3, Sculpture of wrestlers.

2004, Sept. 21   **Perf. 14¼**
587-590 A128   Set of 4   3.50 3.50

Souvenir Sheet

Deng Xiaoping (1904-97), Chinese Leader — A129

2004, Sept. 21   **Litho.**   **Perf. 14**
591 A129 $5 multi   4.00 4.00

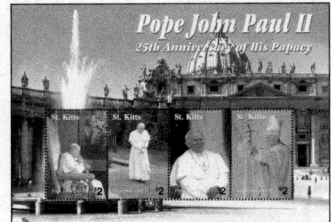

Election of Pope John Paul II, 25th Anniv. (in 2003) — A130

No. 592: a, Seated. b, Walking in garden. c, With arms clasped. d, Holding crucifix.

2004, Sept. 21
592 A130 $2 Sheet of 4, #a-d   6.50 6.50

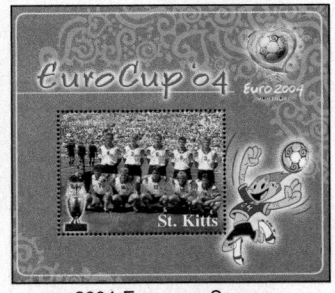

2004 European Soccer Championships, Portugal — A131

No. 593, vert.: a, Berti Vogts. b, Patrik Berger. c, Oliver Bierhoff. d, Empire Stadium. $5, 1996 German team.

2004, Sept. 21   **Perf. 14¼**
593 A131 $2 Sheet of 4, #a-d   6.00 6.00
Souvenir Sheet
594 A131 $5 multi   3.50 3.50

No. 593 contains four 28x42mm stamps.

Locomotives, 200th Anniv. — A132

No. 595, $2: a, Italian State Railways Class 685 2-8-2. b, Swiss Federal Railways 4-6-0. c, BESA Class 4-6-0. d, Great Western City Class 4-4-0.
No. 596, $2: a, Northumbrian 0-2-2. b, Prince Class 2-2-2. c, Adler 2-2-2. d, L&NWR Webb Compound 2-4-0.
No. 597, $2: a, American Standard 4-4-0. b, New South Wales Government Class 79 4-4-0. c, Johnson Midland Single 4-2-2. d, Union Pacific FEF-3 Class 4-8-4.
No. 598, $5, Crampton Type 4-2-0. No. 599, $5, CN Class U-2 4-8-4. No. 600, $5, Baldwin 2-8-2, vert.

Perf. 13¼x13½, 13½x13¼
2004, Sept. 21
Sheets of 4, #a-d
595-597 A132   Set of 3   18.00 18.00
Souvenir Sheets
598-600 A132   Set of 3   11.50 11.50

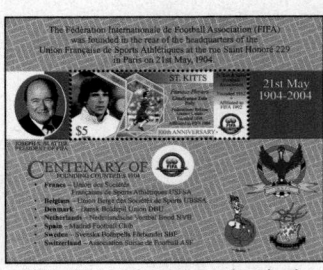

FIFA (Fédération Internationale de Football Association), Cent. — A133

No. 601: a, Demetrio Albertini. b, Romario. c, Gerd Muller. d, Danny Blanchflower. $5, Gianfranco Zola.

2004, Nov. 8   **Perf. 12¾x12½**
601 A133 $2 Sheet of 4, #a-d   5.50 5.50
Souvenir Sheet
602 A133 $5 multi   3.50 3.50

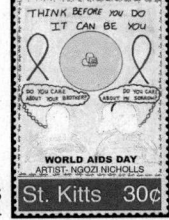

World AIDS Day — A134

Posters by: 30c, Ngozi Nicholls. 80c, Travis Liburd. 90c, Darren Kelly, horiz. $1, Shane Berry.

2004, Dec. 1   **Perf. 14**
603-606 A134   Set of 4   3.75 3.75

New Year 2005 (Year of the Rooster) A135

Mother Hen and Her Brood, by unknown artist: $1.60, Detail. $5, Entire painting.

2005, Feb. 7   **Perf. 12**
607 A135 $1.60 multi   1.50 1.50
Souvenir Sheet
608 A135 $5 multi   4.75 4.75

Wildcats — A136

No. 609, vert.: a, Ocelot. b, Bengal leopard. c, Tiger. d, Leopard.
$5, Sumatran tiger.

2005, Feb. 7   **Perf. 12¾**
609 A136 $2 Sheet of 4, #a-d   6.00 6.00
Souvenir Sheet
610 A136 $5 multi   4.50 4.50

Prehistoric Animals — A137

No. 611, horiz.: a, Triceratops. b, Deinonychus. c, Apatosaurus.
No. 612, horiz.: a, Dimetrodon. b, Homalocephale. c, Stegosaurus.
No. 613, horiz.: a, Sabre-toothed tiger. b, Edmontosaurus. c, Tyrannosaurus rex.
No. 614: $5, Brontosaurus. No. 615, $5, Woolly mammoth. No. 616, $5, Andrewsarchus, horiz.

2005, Feb. 7
611 A137 $3 Sheet of 3, #a-c   6.75 6.75
612 A137 $3 Sheet of 3, #a-c   6.75 6.75
613 A137 $3 Sheet of 3, #a-c   6.75 6.75
Souvenir Sheet
614 A137 $5 multi   3.75 3.75
615 A137 $5 multi   3.75 3.75
616 A137 $5 multi   3.75 3.75

Parrots — A138

No. 617, vert.: a, Australian king parrot. b, Rose-breasted cockatoo. c, Pale-headed rosella. d, Eastern rosella.
$5, Rainbow lorikeets.

2005, Feb. 7   **Litho.**   **Perf. 12¾**
617 A138 $2 Sheet of 4, #a-d   6.00 6.00
Souvenir Sheet
618 A138 $5 multi   4.50 4.50

Insects and Butterflies — A139

No. 619, vert.: a, Papilio demoleus. b, Ephemeroptera. c, Hamadryas februa. d, Aphylla caraiba.
$5, Small blue butterfly.

2005, Feb. 7
619 A139 $2 Sheet of 4, #a-d   6.75 6.75
Souvenir Sheet
620 A139 $5 multi   4.25 4.25

Ducks
A140

Designs: 25c, White-cheeked pintails. $1, Fulvous whistling ducks. $2, White-faced whistling duck. $3, Black-bellied whistling ducks.

2005, Feb. 7
621-624 A140   Set of 4   5.00 5.00

Souvenir Sheet

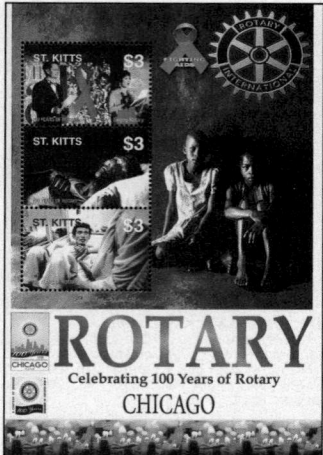

Rotary International, Cent. — A141

No. 625: a, Beijing Rotary meeting. b, Sick man. c, Sick man and visitor.

2005, May 11
625 A141 $3 Sheet of 3, #a-c   7.00 7.00

Hans Christian Andersen (1805-75), Author — A142

No. 626 — Book covers: a, Hans Christian Andersen's Fairy Tales. b, The Emperor's New Clothes. c, The Nutcracker.
$5, The Emperor's New Clothes, diff.

2005, May 11
626 A142 $3 Sheet of 3, #a-c   6.25 6.25
Souvenir Sheet
627 A142 $5 multi   3.50 3.50

Jules Verne (1828-1905), Writer — A143

No. 628, vert.: a, Verne. b, Sea monster attack. c, Rouquayrol. d, Modern Aqualung.
$5, Atomic submarine.

2005, May 11
628 A143 $3 Sheet of 4, #a-d   6.50 6.50
Souvenir Sheet
629 A143 $5 multi   4.00 4.00

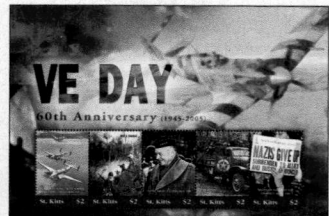

End of World War II, 60th Anniv. — A144

No. 630, $2: a, US Navy Hudson PDB-1 patrol bombers. b, World War II combat. c, Gen. Dwight D. Eisenhower. d, Transporting German prisoners of war. e, Newspaper announcing Nazi surrender.
No. 631, $2: a, USS Arizona under attack. b, USS Arizona Captain Franklin Van Valkenburgh. c, Hiroshima atomic blast. d, Historic marker of first atomic bomb loading pit, Tinian Island. e, Memorial Cenotaph, Hiroshima Peace Park.

2005, May 11   Litho.
Sheets of 5, #a-e
630-631 A144   Set of 2   18.00 18.00

Battle of Trafalgar, Bicent. — A145

Ships: 50c, Montagne. 90c, San Jose. $2, Imperieuse. $3, San Nicolas.
$5, British Navy gun crew on HMS Victory.

2005, May 11   Perf. 12¾
632-635 A145   Set of 4   5.50 5.50
Souvenir Sheet
636 A145 $5 multi   4.50 4.50

Pope John Paul II (1920-2005) and Nelson Mandela — A146

2005, July 19   Perf. 13½
637 A146 $3 multi   2.50 2.50
Printed in sheets of 4.

Souvenir Sheet

Taipei 2005 Stamp Exhibition — A147

No. 638 — Various Chinese junks with denominations in: a, Red. b, Blue. c, Gray. d, Yellow orange.

2005, Aug. 19   Perf. 14
638 A147 $2 Sheet of 4, #a-d   6.50 6.50

Christmas — A148

Paintings: 30c, Virgin and Child, by Gerard David. 50c, Virgin and Child, by David, diff. 90c, Virgin and Child, by David, diff. $2, Virgin and Child, by Bartolomeo Suardi Bramentine.
$5, Nativity, by Martin Schongauer.

2005, Dec. 6   Litho.   Perf. 13¾x13½
639-642 A148   Set of 4   2.75 2.75
Souvenir Sheet
643 A148 $5 multi   3.75 3.75

Treaty of Basseterre, 25th Anniv. — A149

Designs: 30c, Eastern Caribbean Central Bank. 90c, 25th anniversary emblem of Organization of Eastern Caribbean States. $2.50, Heads of government of Organization of Eastern Caribbean States, vert.

2006, Sept. 11   Litho.   Perf. 12¾
644-645 A149   Set of 2   1.00 1.00
Souvenir Sheet
Perf. 12
646   Sheet of 2 #646a   3.50 3.50
  a. A149 $2.50 multi   1.50 1.50

Rembrandt (1606-69), Painter A150

Paintings or painting details: 50c, Bathsheba with King David's Letter. 80c, Isaac and Rebecca (Rebecca). 90c, Isaac and Rebecca (Isaac). $1, Samson Threatening His Father-in-Law (father-in-law). $1.60, Samson Threatening His Father-in-Law (Samson). $2, Equestrian Portrait.
$6, Landscape with a Stone Bridge, horiz.

2006, Nov. 15   Perf. 12
647-652 A150   Set of 6   5.50 5.50
Imperf
Size: 101x70mm
653 A150 $6 multi   4.50 4.50

Christmas — A151

Paintings or painting details by Peter Paul Rubens: 25c, Mary In Adoration Before the Sleeping Infant. 60c, The Holy Family Under the Apple Tree (Madonna and Child). $1, The Holy Family Under the Apple Tree (cherub). $1.20, St. Francis of Assisi Receives the Infant Jesus from Mary.
No. 658: a, Like 25c. b, Like 60c. c, Like $1. d, Like $1.20.

2006, Dec. 27   Perf. 13½
654-657 A151   Set of 4   2.40 2.40
Souvenir Sheet
658 A151 $2 Sheet of 4, #a-d   6.25 6.25

Souvenir Sheet

Christopher Columbus (1451-1506), Explorer — A152

2007, Jan. 3   Perf. 13¼
659 A152 $6 multi   4.25 4.25

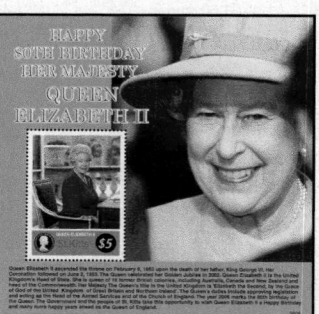

Queen Elizabeth II, 80th Birthday (in 2006) — A153

No. 660: a, Wearing beige and brown hat. b, Wearing tiara. c, Wearing light blue hat. d, Wearing crown.
$5, Seated at desk.

2007, Jan. 3
660 A153 $2 Sheet of 4, #a-d   5.50 5.50
Souvenir Sheet
661 A153 $5 multi   3.50 3.50

Betty Boop — A154

No. 662 — Betty Boop in spotlight with background color of: a, Red. b, Green. c, White. d, Purple. e, Blue. f, Yellow.
No. 663 — Betty Boop in: a, Green heart. b, Purple heart.

2007, Jan. 3
662 A154 $1.60 Sheet of 6, #a-f 7.25 7.25
Souvenir Sheet
663 A154 $3 Sheet of 2, #a-b 4.25 4.25

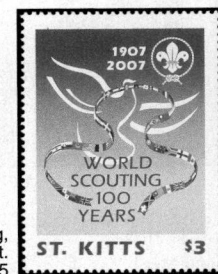

Scouting, Cent. A155

Dove with flags, Scouting emblem, text and: $3, Years "1907" and "2007." $5, No years, horiz.

2007, Jan. 3
664 A155 $3 multi 2.25 2.25
Souvenir Sheet
665 A155 $5 multi 3.50 3.50
No. 664 was printed in sheets of 4.

Space Achievements — A156

No. 666 — Giotto Comet Probe: a, Pre-launch test at Kourou launch site. b, Halley's Comet (black sky). c, Halley's Comet above cloud. d, Giotto Comet Probe. e, Giotto spacecraft mounted on Ariane rocket. f, Halley's Comet (blue sky).
No. 667, vert. — Launching of Luna 9: a, Molniya launch vehicle. b, Luna 9 flight apparatus. c, Luna 9 soft lander. d, Photograph of Ocean of Storms taken by Luna 9.
$5, Space Station Mir.

2007, Jan. 3 Litho. Perf. 13¼
666 A156 $1.60 Sheet of 6, #a-f 6.75 6.75
667 A156 $2 Sheet of 4, #a-d 5.75 5.75
Souvenir Sheet
668 A156 $5 multi 3.50 3.50
Miniature Sheets

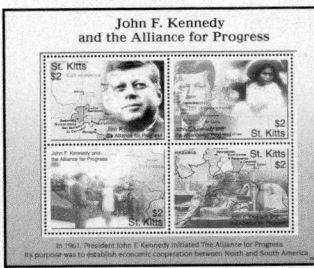

Pres. John F. Kennedy (1917-63) — A157

No. 669, $2: a, Kennedy and map of Central America. b, Kennedy, woman and child, map of Caribbean. c, Kennedy addressing group, map of Western South America. d, Kennedy shaking hands with man, map of Eastern South America.
No. 670, $2: a, Kennedy greeting Peace Corps volunteers (inscription in black). b, Peace Corps volunteer Ida Shoatz and Peruvians. c, R. Sargent Shriver, Peace Corps Director. d, Kennedy greeting Peace Corps volunteers, diff. (inscription in white).

2007, Jan. 3
Sheets of 4, #a-d Litho.
669-670 A157 Set of 2 11.50 11.50

A158

Elvis Presley (1935-77) — A159

No. 672 — Denomination color: a, Blue. b, Red. c, Black. d, Lilac.

2007, Feb. 15 Perf. 14
671 A158 $2 multi 1.60 1.60
672 A159 $2 Sheet of 4, #a-d 5.75 5.75
No. 671 was printed in sheets of 4.

Miniature Sheet

Marilyn Monroe (1926-62), Actress — A160

No. 673 — Monroe with: a, Pinkie in mouth. b, Glasses. c, Strapless gown. d, Hand on cheek.

2007, Feb. 15 Perf. 13½
673 A160 $2 Sheet of 4, #a-d 5.75 5.75

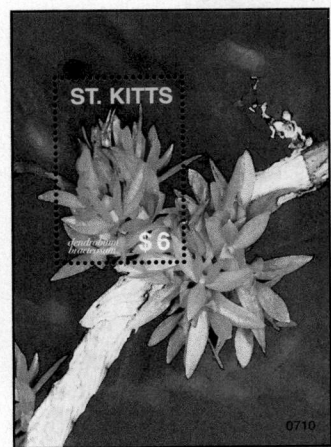

Orchids — A161

No. 674: a, Rhynchostele cervantesii. b, Oerstedella wallisii. c, Disa uniflora. d, Pleione formosana.
$6, Dendrobium bracteosum.

2007, June 18 Perf. 12¾
674 A161 $2 Sheet of 4, #a-d 6.50 6.50
Souvenir Sheet
675 A161 $6 multi 4.50 4.50

Birds — A162

No. 676, horiz.: a, Brown noddy. b, Royal albatross. c, Masked booby. d, Cormorant. $6, Rock cormorant.

2007, June 18 Perf. 12¾
676 A162 $2 Sheet of 4, #a-d 5.75 5.75
Souvenir Sheet
677 A162 $6 multi 4.25 4.25

Worldwide Fund for Nature (WWF) — A163

Tiger sharks: a, Three sharks. b, Two sharks. c, Two sharks and sunlight. d, One shark.

2007, June 18
678 Strip or block of 4 3.75 3.75
a.-d. A163 $1.20 Any single .85 .85
e. Sheet, 2 each #a-d 7.25 7.25
Souvenir Sheets

National Basketball Association Players and Team Emblems — A164

No. 679, $8: a, Steve Nash. b, Phoenix Suns emblem.
No. 680, $8: a, Shaquille O'Neal. b, Miami Heat emblem, denomination in black.
No. 681, $8: a, Dwyane Wade. b, Miami Heat emblem, denomination in orange.
No. 682, $8: a, Yao Ming. b, Houston Rockets emblem.

Litho. (Margin Embossed)
2007, Aug. 16 Imperf.
Without Gum
Sheets of 2, #a-b
679-682 A164 Set of 4 47.50 47.50

Fruit — A165

2007, Oct. 16 Litho. Perf. 13¼x12½
683 A165 10c Cherries .25 .25
684 A165 15c Coconuts .25 .25
685 A165 30c Watermelons .25 .25
686 A165 40c Pineapples .30 .30
687 A165 50c Guava .40 .40
688 A165 60c Sugar apples .45 .45
689 A165 80c Passion fruit .60 .60
690 A165 90c Starfruit .70 .70
691 A165 $1 Tangerines .75 .75

692 A165 $5 Noni fruit 3.75 3.75
693 A165 $10 Papayas 7.50 7.50
Nos. 683-693 (11) 15.20 15.20
Miniature Sheet

Elvis Presley (1935-77) — A166

No. 694 — Presley wearing: a, White shirt. b, Jacket with bird design. c, Black shirt. d, Blue jacket. e, Red and white shirt. f, White jacket and red shirt, holding microphone.

2007, Oct. 26 Perf. 13¼
694 A166 $1.60 Sheet of 6, #a-f 7.00 7.00

Pope Benedict XVI — A167

2007, Nov. 26
695 A167 $1.10 multi 1.10 1.10

Wedding of Queen Elizabeth II and Prince Philip, 60th Anniv. A168

No. 696: a, Queen Elizabeth II. b, Couple on wedding day. $6, Couple waving.

2007, Nov. 26
696 A168 $1.60 Pair, #a-b 2.25 2.25
Souvenir Sheet
697 A168 $6 multi 4.25 4.25
No. 696 printed in sheets containing three of each stamp.

Concorde A169

No. 698, $1.60: a, Concorde flying left. b, Concorde flying right.
No. 699, $1.60: a, Concorde over Singapore. b, Concorde at Melbourne, Australia airport.

2007, Nov. 26 Pairs, #a-b Litho.
698-699 A169 Set of 2 4.50 4.50
Nos. 698-699 each printed in sheets containing three of each stamp in pairs.

Princess Diana (1961-97) — A170

No. 700 — Various depictions of Princess Diana: a, Country name in black, "Princess Diana" at right. b, Country name in white, "Princess Diana" at left. c, Country name in white, "Princess Diana" at right. d, Country name in black, "Princess Diana" at left.
$6, Like #700c, gray background.

2007, Nov. 26   **Perf. 13¼**
700 A170 $2 Sheet of 4, #a-d   5.75 5.75

Souvenir Sheet
701 A170 $6 multi   4.25 4.25

Christmas
A171

Various ribboned wreaths: 10c, 30c, 60c, $1.

2007, Dec. 3   **Perf. 12½**
702-705 A171   Set of 4   1.50 1.50

Miniature Sheet

2008 Summer Olympics, Beijing — A172

No. 706 — 2008 Summer Olympics emblem and: a, Paris World's Fair, 1900. b, 1900 Olympics poster. c, Charlotte Cooper. d, Alvin Kraenzlein.

2008, June 18   **Litho.**   **Perf. 12¾**
706 A172 $1.40 Sheet of 4, #a-d   5.50 5.50

Robert L. Bradshaw (1916-78), Chief Minister — A173

Perf. 11¼x11½
2008, Sept. 19   **Litho.**
707 A173 10c multi   .40 .40
St. Kitts Labor Party, 75th anniv.

Moravian Churches
A174

Designs: 10c, Bethel Church. $3, Zion Church. $10, Bethesda Church, vert.

Perf. 11½x11¼, 11¼x11½
2008, Sept. 19
708-710 A174   Set of 3   12.00 12.00
Moravian Church in St. Kitts, 230th anniv.

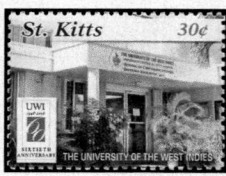

University of the West Indies, 60th Anniv. A175

Designs: 30c, University Center, St. Kitts. 90c, 60th anniv. emblem. $5, 60th anniv. emblem, horiz.

2008, Sept. 19
711-713 A175   Set of 3   6.00 6.00

Independence, 25th Anniv. — A176

Designs: 30c, Stars, lines and "25." $1, Agriculture. $5, Sailing Towards Our Future, vert.

2008, Sept. 19
714-716 A176   Set of 3   5.50 5.50

Miniature Sheet

Visit to Lourdes of Pope Benedict XVI — A177

No. 717 — Pope Benedict, statue of St. Bernadette with: a, Leaves at top. b, Cathedral spires at UR. c, Cathedral roof and side of spire at UR. d, Gray triangle at LR.

2008, Sept. 26   **Perf. 13¼**
717 A177 $2 Sheet of 4, #a-d   8.00 8.00

Miniature Sheet

Elvis Presley (1935-77) — A178

No. 718 — Presley wearing: a, Brown shirt. b, Leather jacket. c, Red shirt and black vest. d, Blue shirt. e, Olive green shirt. f, White shirt.

2008, Sept. 26
718 A178 $1.60 Sheet of 6, #a-f   7.00 7.00

Christmas
A179

Designs: 10c, Palm trees with Christmas ornaments. 50c, Palm trees and beach house. 60c, Star and palm trees. $1, Christmas ornaments and palm fronds.

2008, Dec. 29   **Litho.**   **Perf. 14x14¾**
719-722 A179   Set of 4   2.00 2.00

Inauguration of U.S. Pres. Barack Obama — A180

Obama with: $3, Blue gray tie. $10, Red tie.

Perf. 12½x11¾
2009, Feb. 24   **Litho.**
723 A180 $3 multi   5.00 5.00

Souvenir Sheet
Perf.
724 A180 $10 multi   8.00 8.00
No. 723 was printed in sheets of 4. No. 724 contains one 38mm diameter stamp.

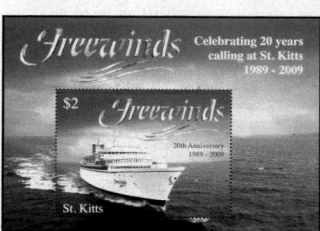

Freewinds Docking at St. Kitts, 20th Anniv. — A181

No. 725: a, 30c, Freewinds at night (42x28mm). b, 90c, Freewinds and yacht near harbor (42x28mm). c, $3, Bow of Freewinds, vert. (42x57mm).

2009, July 20   **Litho.**   **Perf. 13¼**
725 A181   Sheet of 3, #a-c   2.75 2.75
Souvenir Sheet
Perf. 11½x12
726 A181 $2 shown   1.40 1.40

Miniature Sheet

Princess Diana (1961-97) — A182

No. 727 — Color of gown: a, Red. b, Purple. c, White. d, Blue.

2009, Sept. 7   **Perf. 13½x13¼**
727 A182 $2 Sheet of 4, #a-d   5.25 5.25

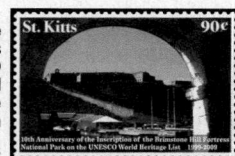

Brimstone Hill as UNESCO World Heritage Site, 10th Anniv. A183

2009, Dec. 7   **Litho.**   **Perf. 13¼**
728 A183 90c multi   .80 .80

Miniature Sheet

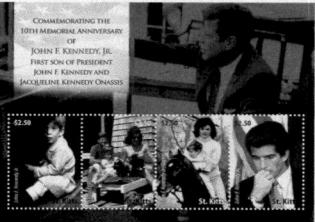

John F. Kennedy, Jr. (1960-99), Magazine Publisher — A184

No. 729: a, As child, sitting under father's desk. b, As child with father, mother and dogs. c, As child, with mother on horse. d, As adult.

2009, Dec. 15   **Perf. 11½**
729 A184 $2.50 Sheet of 4, #a-d   6.50 6.50

Miniature Sheets

A185

Michael Jackson (1958-2009),
Singer — A186

No. 730: a, With arms extended, denomination in green. b, Wearing hat, denomination in green. c, With arms extended, denomination in blue. d, Wearing hat, denomination in blue.
No. 731: a, Wearing red jacket, without yellow spot in background at left center. b, With snake, yellow spot in background at left center. c, Wearing red jacket, yellow spot in background at left center. d, With snake, without yellow spot in background at left center.

2009, Dec. 15
730 A185 $2.50 Sheet of 4, #a-d 7.00 7.00
731 A186 $2.50 Sheet of 4, #a-d 7.00 7.00

First Man on the Moon, 40th
Anniv. — A187

No. 732: a, Saturn V rocket. b, Bootprint on Moon. c, Pres. John F. Kennedy, eagle, Moon and Earth. d, Apollo 11 command module.
$6, Command module, diff.

2009, Dec. 30   **Perf. 11½x12**
732 A187 $2.50 Sheet of 4, #a-d 7.00 7.00
            Souvenir Sheet
733 A187 $6 multi   4.00 4.00

Christmas
A188

Designs: 10c, "Merry Christmas" on flag of St. Kitts & Nevis. 30c, Candy canes. $1.20, Christmas trees on map of St. Kitts. $3, Christmas tree and candles on box showing flag.

2009, Dec. 30   **Perf. 14¾x14**
734-737 A188   Set of 4   3.25 3.25

Miniature Sheet

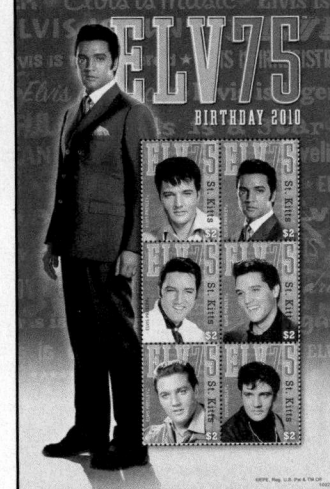

Elvis Presley (1935-77) — A189

No. 738 — Presley wearing: a, Shirt with open collar. b, Suit and tie. c, Shirt with neckerchief. d, Black jacket. e, Shirt with open collar and jacket. f, Black shirt, guitar strap over shoulder.

2010, Jan. 8   **Perf. 11½**
738 A189 $2 Sheet of 6, #a-f   9.25 9.25

Butterflies
A190

Designs: 30c, Scarlet peacock. 90c, Gulf fritillary. No. 741, $3, White peacock. $5, Painted lady.
No. 743: a, Ruddy daggerwing. b, Danaid eggfly. c, Mangrove buckeye. d, Black swallowtail.
No. 744, $3: a, Owl butterfly. b, Giant swallowtail.

2010, Mar. 15   **Litho.**   **Perf. 12**
739-742 A190   Set of 4   7.00 7.00
743 A190 $2.50 Sheet of 4, #a-d 7.50 7.50
            Souvenir Sheet
744 A190 $3 Sheet of 2, #a-b 5.00 5.00

Birds
A191

Designs: 30c, Solitary sandpiper. 90c, Piping plover. No. 747, $3, Prairie warbler. $5, Western sandpiper.
No. 749, vert.: a, Masked booby. b, Sooty tern. c, Brown booby. d, Black noddy.
No. 750, $3: a, Long-billed dowitcher. b, Willet.

2010, Mar. 22
745-748 A191   Set of 4   7.00 7.00
749 A191 $2.50 Sheet of 4, #a-d 7.50 7.50
            Souvenir Sheet
750 A191 $3 Sheet of 2, #a-b 5.00 5.00

Pres. Abraham
Lincoln (1809-
65)
A192

2010, May 11
751 A192 $2.50 black   1.90 1.90
     Printed in sheets of 4.

Fish
A193

Designs: 30c, Red lionfish. 90c, Stoplight parrotfish. $3, Black jack. $5, Bermuda blue angelfish.
No. 756: a, Banggai cardinalfish. b, Barrier reef anemonefish. c, Crevelle jack. d, Lookdown.
No. 757, $3: a, Red Sea clownfish. b, Saddleback clownfish.

2010, June 7   Litho.   Perf. 14¾x14¼
752-755 A193   Set of 4   7.00 7.00
756 A193 $2.50 Sheet of 4, #a-d 7.50 7.50
            Souvenir Sheet
757 A193 $3 Sheet of 2, #a-b 5.00 5.00

A194

Mushrooms — A195

Designs: 25c, Alboleptonia stylophora. 80c, Cantharellus cibarius. $1, Armillaria puiggarii. $5, Battarrea phalloides.
No. 762: a, Cantharellus cinnabarinus. b, Collybia aurea. c, Collybia biformis. d, Amanita ocreata. e, Calocybe cyanea. f, Chroogomphus rutilus.

2010, June 7   **Perf. 14¼x14¾**
758-761 A194   Set of 4   5.25 5.25
            Perf. 14¾x14¼
762 A195 $2 Sheet of 6, #a-f   9.00 9.00
     Antverpia 2010 National and European Championship of Philately, Antwerp (#762).

Miniature Sheets

Boy Scouts of America, Cent. — A196

No. 763, $2.50: a, Cub Scouting. b, Boy Scouting. c, Varsity Scouting. d, Venturing.
No. 764, $2.50: a, Eagle Scout emblem. b, Order of the Arrow. c, Alpha Phi Omega. d, National Eagle Scout Association.

2010, June 30   **Perf. 13¼**
            Sheets of 4, #a-d
763-764 A196   Set of 2   15.00 15.00

Arctic Animals — A197

No. 765: a, Ermine. b, Arctic fox. c, Harp seal. d, Arctic wolf. e, Arctic hare. f, Snowy owl.
$6, Polar bear.

2010, Aug. 4   **Perf. 11½**
765 A197 $2 Sheet of 6, #a-f   9.00 9.00
            Souvenir Sheet
766 A197 $6 multi   4.50 4.50

HENRI
DUNANT
Founder
of the
RED CROSS

Henri Dunant (1828-1910), Founder of
the Red Cross — A198

No. 767 — Dunant, Red Cross and: a, Czar Nicholas II of Russia. b, Henri Dufour. c, Frédéric Passy. d, Victor Hugo.
$6, Red Cross nurse.

2010, Sept. 1   **Perf. 11½x12**
767 A198 $2.50 Sheet of 4, #a-d 7.50 7.50
            Souvenir Sheet
            Perf. 11½
768 A198 $6 multi   4.50 4.50

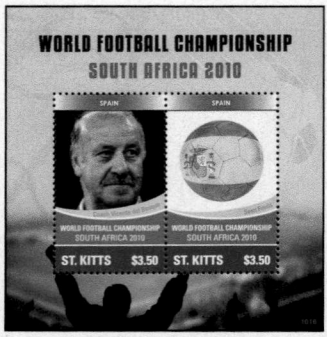

2010 World Cup Soccer
Championships, South Africa — A199

No. 769: a, Pedro. b, Miroslav Klose. c,
Xavi. d, Piotr Trochowski. e, Carlos Puyol. f,
Philipp Lahm.
No. 770, $3.50: a, Spain Coach Vicente del
Bosque. b, Soccer ball with Spanish flag.
No. 771, $3.50: Germany Coach Joachim
Loew. b, Soccer ball with German flag.

2010, Oct. 6			Perf. 12
769	A199	$1.50 Sheet of 6,	
		#a-f	6.75 6.75
Souvenir Sheets of 2, #a-b			
770-771	A199	Set of 2	10.50 10.50

Souvenir Sheets

A200

A201

A202

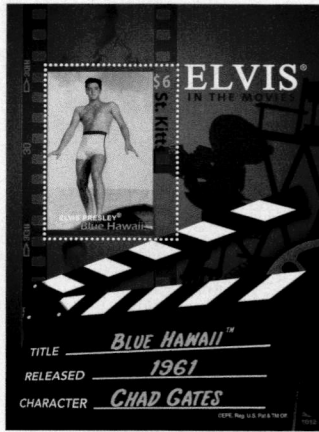

Elvis Presley (1935-77) — A203

2010, Oct. 6			Perf. 13½
772	A200	$6 multi	4.50 4.50
773	A201	$6 multi	4.50 4.50
774	A202	$6 multi	4.50 4.50
775	A203	$6 multi	4.50 4.50
		Nos. 772-775 (4)	18.00 18.00

A204

Princess Diana (1961-97) — A205

No. 776 — Princess Diana wearing: a,
Beige hat. b, Rose lilac and white hat.
No. 777: a, Princess Diana wearing red hat,
area below line shaded. b, Princess Diana
wearing strapless gown, area below line
shaded. c, Princess Diana wearing tiara,
entire dress below line. d, As "c," strap of
dress above line above denomination. e, As
"a," area below line not shaded. f, As "b," area
below line not shaded.

2010, Dec. 8			Perf. 12
776	A204	$2.75 Pair, #a-b	4.25 4.25
777	A205	$2 Sheet of 6, #a-f	9.00 9.00

No. 776 was printed in sheets containing
two pairs.

Christmas
2010 — A206

Paintings: 10c, Journey of the Magi, by Fra
Angelico. 25c, Madonna Worshiping the
Child and an Angel, by Biagio d'Antonio. 30c,
The Nativity, by Master of Vyssi Brod. 90c,
The Journey of the Magi, by James Tissot.
$1.80, Worship of the Shepherds, by Agnolo di
Cosimo. $3, Madonna with Child, by Carlo
Crivelli.

**Perf. 11½ (10c, 25c), 12¾x13
Syncopated**

2011, Feb. 21			Litho.
778-783	A206	Set of 6	4.75 4.75

Pope John Paul
II (1920-2005)
A207

Pope John Paul II wearing: No. 784, $2.50,
Zucchetto. No. 785, $2.50, Miter.

2011, Feb. 21			Perf. 12
784-785	A207	Set of 2	3.75 3.75

Nos. 784-785 each were printed in sheets of
4.

Visit of
Pope
Benedict
XVI to
Portugal
A208

Designs: No. 786, Pope Benedict XVI and
buildings. No. 787 — Arms of Portugal, Pope
Benedict XVI and background color of: a, Red.
b, Green.

2011, Feb. 21			Perf. 12
786	A208	$2.75 multi	2.10 2.10
Perf. 13 Syncopated			
787	A208	$2.75 Sheet of 4,	
		#787a, 3 #787b	8.25 8.25

No. 786 was printed in sheets of 4.

Paintings by Sandro Botticelli (1445-
1510) — A209

No. 788: a, Giovanna Albizi with Venus and
the Graces. b, Lemmi Fresco. c, Portrait of a
Young Woman. d, St. Sebastian.
$6, The Last Communion of St. Jerome,
horiz.

2011, Feb. 21			Perf. 12
788	A209	$2.50 Sheet of 4, #a-d	7.50 7.50
Souvenir Sheet			
Perf. 13 Syncopated			
789	A209	$6 multi	4.50 4.50

Miniature Sheets

A210

Pres. Barack Obama — A211

Nos. 790 and 791 — Pres. Obama and one-
quarter of Presidential seal at: a, LR. b, LL. c,
UR. d, UL.

2011, Feb. 21			Perf. 12
790	A210	$2.50 Sheet of 4, #a-d	7.50 7.50
791	A211	$2.50 Sheet of 4, #a-d	7.50 7.50

Dolphins — A212

No. 792: a, Pantropical spotted dolphin. b,
Killer whale. c, Tucuxi. d, Clymene dolphin.
No. 793, $6, Rough-toothed dolphin. No.
794, $6, Bottlenose dolphin.

2011, Feb. 21			Perf. 13 Syncopated
792	A212	$2.50 Sheet of 4, #a-d	7.50 7.50
Souvenir Sheets			
Perf. 12			
793-794	A212	Set of 2	9.00 9.00

Engagement of Prince William and
Catherine Middleton — A213

No. 795, $2.50 — Red background: a,
Couple, Middleton standing in front of door. b,
Prince William. c, Middleton. d, Couple, diff.
No. 796, $2.50 — Blue background: a,
Couple, Middleton wearing hat. b, Prince Wil-
liam. c, Middleton. d, Couple, diff.
No. 797, $6, Couple, red background, vert.
No. 798, $6, Couple, blue background, vert.

2011, Feb. 21   **Perf. 12**
Sheets of 4, #a-d
795-796 A213   Set of 2   15.00 15.00
Souvenir Sheets
Perf. 13 Syncopated
797-798 A213   Set of 2   9.00 9.00

Miniature Sheet

Cricket World Cup, India, Sri Lanka
and Bangladesh — A214

No. 799 — Cricket players: a, Ricky Ponting, Australia. b, Shakib Al Hasan (incorrectly identified as Shahid Afridi), Bangladesh. c, Ashish Bagai, Canada. d, Mahendra Singh Dhoni, India. e, Andrew Strauss (incorrectly identified as Ricky Ponting), England. f, William Porterfield, Ireland. g, Maurice Ouma, Kenya. h, Daniel Vettori, New Zealand. i, Shahid Afridi, Pakistan. j, Graeme Smith, South Africa. k, Kumar Sangakkara, Sri Lanka. l, Peter Borren, Netherlands. m, Elton Chigumbura, Zimbabwe. n, Darren Sammy, West Indies.

2011, Apr. 2   **Litho.**   **Perf.**
799 A214 $1.90 Sheet of 14,
    #a-n   20.00 20.00

No. 799 exists with inscriptions corrected. Values, same.

Souvenir Sheets

PhilaNippon '11, Yokohama,
Japan — A215

Designs: No. 800, $6, Tokyo. No. 801, $6, Okinawa. No. 802, $6, Mt. Fuji.

2011, May 18   **Perf. 11½x11¼**
800-802 A215   Set of 3   13.50 13.50

St. Kitts-Nevis-Anguilla National Bank,
40th Anniv. — A216

Designs: 10c, Bank building. $3, Anniversary emblem and olive branch, vert.

Perf. 14¾x14¼, 14¼x14¾
2011, June 27
803-804 A216   Set of 2   2.40 2.40

Miniature Sheets

Mother Teresa (1910-97,
Humanitarian — A217

No. 805, $2.75 — Stamps with purple and maroon panels: a, Mother Teresa with Ronald and Nancy Reagan. b, Mother Teresa with Sister of Charity at doorway. c, Mother Teresa

---

holding child. d, Mother Teresa and Paris Mayor Jacques Chirac.
No. 806, $2.75 — Stamps with blue and olive green panels and flower: a, Mother Tereesa. b, Mother Teresa and Prince Charles. c, Mother Teresa holding baby. d, Mother Teresa touching baby held by Sister of Charity.

2011, July 5   **Perf. 13 Syncopated**
Sheets of 4, #a-d
805-806 A217   Set of 2   16.50 16.50

Miniature Sheets

A218

Elvis Presley (1935-77) — A219

No. 807: a, Presley in decorated jacket, seen from back. b, Presley with blue face. c, Presley with pink face. d, Presley with arms raised.
No. 808: a, Presley at piano. b, Presley splaying guitar. c, Prelsy holding microphone, facing right. d, Presley holding microphone, facing left.

2011, July 14   **Perf. 12½x12¾**
807 A218 $3 Sheet of 4, #a-d   9.00 9.00
Perf. 12¾x12½
808 A219 $3 Sheet of 4, #a-d   9.00 9.00

Princess Diana (1961-97) — A220

No. 809 — Princess Diana: a, Greeting crowd. b, Holding baby. c, Wearing red and white dress. d, Wearing checked overcoat.
$6, Princess Diana wearing white sweater, horiz.

2011, July 14   **Perf. 13 Syncopated**
809 A220 $2.75 Sheet of 4, #a-d   8.25 8.25
Souvenir Sheet
Perf. 12½
810 A220 $6 multi   4.50 4.50
No. 810 contains one 51x38mm stamp.

A221

Wedding of Prince William and
Catherine Middleton — A222

No. 811: a, $2, Bride facing right (40x30mm). b, $2, Groom facing left (40x30mm). c, $2, Couple facing right (40x30mm). d, $2, Couple facing left (40x30mm). e, $4, Bride facing left (40x60mm).
No. 812: a, Couple facing right, wall in background. b, Couple facing forward, wall in background. c, As "b," horse in background. d, As "a," horse in background.
$6, Couple facing right.

2011, July 14   **Perf. 11½**
811 A221   Sheet of 5, #a-e   9.00 9.00
Perf. 12½x12
812 A222 $2.75 Sheet of 4, #a-d   8.25 8.25
Souvenir Sheet
Perf. 13½x13¼
813 A221 $6 multi   4.50 4.50
No. 813 contains one 51x38mm stamp.

Miniature Sheets

U.S. Civil War, 150th Anniv. — A223

No. 814, $2.50 — Eagle, shield, Union and Confederate flags, General Robert E. Lee and General George G. Meade from Battle of Gettysburg, July 1-3, 1863, and: a, Union positions near Cemetery Ridge (image in green). b, Union artillery, Hazlitt's Battery in action. c, Union positions near Cemetery Ridge (images in brown). d, Union artillery, Cemetery hill in the distance.
No. 815, $2.50 — Eagle, shield, Union and Confederate flags, Lieutenant General James Longstreet and Major General Oliver O. Howard from Battle of Gettysburg, July 1-3, 1863, and: a, Behind the breastworks on Culp's Hill. b, Jubal Early's attack on East Cemetery Hill. c, Confederate Army's 2nd Maryland Infantry at Culp's Hill. d, Confederate pickets on Culp's Hill.
No. 816, $2.50 — Eagle, shield, Union and Confederate flags, Lieutenant General Richard S. Ewell and Brigadier General George S. Greene from Battle of Gettysburg, July 1-3, 1863, and: a, Cavalry engagement. b, Battle of Gettysburg. c, Hand to hand combat. d, Battery A, 1st Rhode Island, at Cemetery Ridge.

2011, July 14   **Perf. 13 Syncopated**
Sheets of 4, #a-d
814-816 A223   Set of 3   22.50 22.50

Flowers — A224

No. 817, horiz.: a, Bird of paradise. b, Gardenia. c, Dutch amaryllis. d, Ginger flower. e, Lobster claw. f, Bleeding heart.
No. 818: a, Cockscomb. b, Passion flower. c, Prairie Blue Eyes day lily. d, Blue water lily.
No. 819, $6, Painted feather. No. 820, $6, Cuban lily, horiz.

2011, July 14   **Perf. 12**
817 A224 $2 Sheet of 6, #a-f   9.00 9.00
818 A224 $2.75 Sheet of 4, #a-d   8.25 8.25
Souvenir Sheets
819-820 A224   Set of 2   9.00 9.00
No. 817 contains six 64x32mm triangular stamps.

Miniature Sheet

2012 Summer Olympics,
London — A225

No. 821 — Scenes from 1948 Summer Olympics, London: a, Crowd at Wembley Stadium. b, Robert Mathias. c, Maureen Gardner and Fanny Blankers-Koen. d, Poster for 1948 Summer Olympics.

2011, Nov. 14   **Perf. 13 Syncopated**
821 A225 $3 Sheet of 4, #a-d   9.00 9.00

Commonwealth Games Federation
General Assembly, St. Kitts &
Nevis — A226

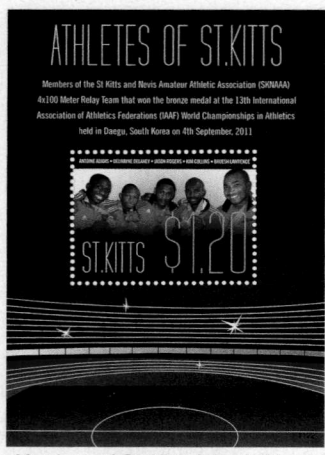

Members of St. Kitts & Nevis Men's
4x100 Meter Relay Team — A227

2011, Dec. 8   **Perf. 14**
822 A226 25c multi   .25   .25
Souvenir Sheet
Perf. 12
823 A227 $1.20 multi   .90   .90

Princess Diana
(1961-97)
A228

Princess Diana: $3, Wearing tiara. $9, Without tiara.

2012, Oct. 1   **Perf. 13¾**
824 A228 $3 multi   2.25 2.25
Souvenir Sheet
825 A228 $9 multi   6.75 6.75
No. 824 was printed in sheets of 4. No. 825 contains one 49x49mm diamond-shaped stamp.

A229

A230

Reign of Queen Elizabeth II, 60th
Anniv. — A231

Children's drawings: No. 826, 10c, Child's drawing for £2 stamp. No. 827, 10c, Diamond, crown, arrow, flags of St. Christopher, Nevis and Anguilla and St. Kitts and Nevis. 25c, Crown. 30c, Wreath of flags and "60." $1.20, Flags of St. Kitts and Nevis and Great Britain, "60" clock towers, handshake.
No. 831 — Queen Elizabeth II: a, Wearing hat. b, Without head covering. c, Wearing crown. d, Wearing tiara.
$9, Sketch of Queen Elizabeth II.

2012, Oct. 1   **Perf. 14**
826-830 A229   Set of 5   1.50 1.50
Perf. 13¾
831 A230 $3.50 Sheet of 4,
     #a-d   10.50 10.50
Souvenir Sheet
Perf. 12¾
832 A231 $9 multi   6.75 6.75

Pres. Abraham Lincoln (1809-
65) — A233

No. 833 — Photographs of Lincoln: a, Blue field of flag across top in background. b, Blue field of flag at UL. c, Red stripe of flag across top, Lincoln's arms visible to country name. d, Red stripe of flag across top, Lincoln's arms not visible.
$6, Sculpture of Lincoln in Lincoln Memorial.

2012, Oct. 1   **Perf. 14**
833 A233 $2.75 Sheet of 4, #a-
     d   8.25 8.25
Souvenir Sheet
834 A233 $6 multi   4.50 4.50

A234

Fish — A235

No. 835: a, French angelfish. b, Barracuda. c, Spotted trunkfish. d, Trumpetfish. e, Orange-lined triggerfish. f, Eagle ray.
$6, Butterflyfish.

2012, Oct. 1   **Perf. 13 Syncopated**
835 A234 $2.50 Sheet of 6,
     #a-f   11.00 11.00
Souvenir Sheet
836 A235 $6 multi   4.50 4.50

Parrots — A236

No. 837: a, Green-winged macaw. b, St. Vincent Amazon. c, Yellow-headed Amazon. d, Orange-winged Amazon.
$6, Blue and gold macaw, horiz.

2012, Oct. 1   **Perf. 14**
837 A236 $2.75 Sheet of 4, #a-d   8.25 8.25
Souvenir Sheet
Perf. 12¾
838 A236 $6 multi   4.50 4.50
No. 838 contains one 51x38mm stamp.

Shells — A237

No. 839: a, Turbo petholatus. b, Mitra stictica. c, Muricanthus radix. d, Murex bicolor.
$6, Haliotis asinina, vert.

2012, Oct. 1   **Perf.**
839 A237 $2.75 Sheet of 4, #a-d   8.25 8.25
Souvenir Sheet
Perf. 12
840 A237 $6 multi   4.50 4.50
No. 840 contains one 30x80mm rectangular stamp.

Souvenir Sheets

A238

A239

A240

Elvis Presley (1935-77) — A241

2012, Oct. 1   **Perf. 12¾**
841 A238 $9 multi   6.75   6.75
842 A239 $9 multi   6.75   6.75
843 A240 $9 multi   6.75   6.75
844 A241 $9 multi   6.75   6.75
     Nos. 841-844 (4)   27.00 27.00

Antioch Baptist
Church, 50th
Anniv. — A242

Designs: 10c, Reverend Dr. William Manasseh Connor. 30c, Church building.

2013, June 3   **Perf. 13¼x12½**
845-846 A242   Set of 2   .30   .30

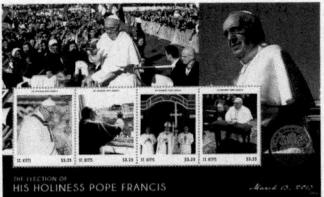

Election of Pope Francis — A243

No. 847 — Pope Francis: a, Carrying censer. b, Waving from window. c, Holding crucifix. d, Kneeling in prayer.
$9, Pope Francis waving from window, diff.

2013, Aug. 7   **Litho.**   **Perf. 14**
847 A243 $3.25 Sheet of 4, #a-d   9.75 9.75

Souvenir Sheet
Perf. 12½
848 A243 $9 multi   6.75 6.75
No. 848 contains one 38x51mm stamp.

Miniature Sheet

Butterflies — A244

No. 849: a, Bates olivewing butterfly. b, Orange-barred sulphur butterfly. c, Blue satyr butterfly. d, Red flasher butterfly. e, Nymphalid butterfly. f, Hypolereia ocalea. g, Isamia carpenteri. h, Blue morpho butterfly. i, Variable cattleheart butterfly. j, Heliconius aoede.

2013, Aug. 12   **Litho.**   **Perf. 14**
849 A244 $1.60 Sheet of 10, #a-j   12.00 12.00

Miniature Sheet

Moths — A245

No. 850: a, Athis clitarcha. b, Oryba kadeni. c, Copaxa denda. d, Citheronia azteca.

2013, Aug. 12   **Litho.**   **Perf. 12**
850 A245 $3 Sheet of 4, #a-d   9.00 9.00

Souvenir Sheets

Elvis Presley (1935-77) — A246

Various photographs of Presley with frame color of: No. 851, $9, Black. No. 852, $9, Gray. No. 853, $9, Red (color photograph of Presley). No. 854, $9, Purple. No. 855, $9, Red (black-and-white photograph of Presley).

2013, Aug. 12   **Litho.**   **Perf. 13¼**
851-855 A246   Set of 5   34.00 34.00

Orchids — A247

No. 856: a, Bletilla striata. b, Phaius hybrid. c, Cymbidium "Showgirl." d, Dendrobium nobile. e, Zygopetalum crinitum.
$9, Cuitlauzina pendula.

2013, Aug. 26   **Litho.**   **Perf. 14**
856 A247 $2.75 Sheet of 5, #a-e   10.50 10.50

Souvenir Sheet
Perf. 12½
857 A247 $9 multi   6.75 6.75
No. 857 contains one 38x51mm stamp.

Birth of Prince George of
Cambridge — A248

No. 858: a, Duchess of Cambridge holding Prince George. b, Duke of Cambridge holding Prince George. c, Duke and Duchess of Cambridge, Prince George. d, Prince George.
$9, Duke and Duchess of Cambridge, horiz.

2013, Sept. 10   **Litho.**   **Perf. 13¾**
858 A248 $3.25 Sheet of 4, #a-d   9.75 9.75

Souvenir Sheet
Perf. 12½
859 A248 $9 multi   6.75 6.75
No. 859 contains one 51x38mm stamp.

A249

Nelson Mandela (1918-2013),
President of South Africa — A250

No. 860: a, People holding signs with pictures of Mandela. b, Black-and-white photograph of Mandela, "Mandela" at left in orange.
No. 861: a, Mandela in red shirt, waving. b, Mandela in suit, seated. c, Like #860b, "Mandela" at left in red.

2013-14   **Litho.**   **Perf. 13¾**
860 A249 $4.75 Horiz. pair, #a-b   7.00 7.00
861 A250 $4.75 Sheet of 4, #861a, 861b, 2 #861c   14.00 14.00
Issued: No. 860, 2/19/14; No. 861, 12/19. No. 860 was printed in sheets containing two pairs.

Miniature Sheet

Hummingbirds — A251

No. 862: a, Lophornis regulus. b, Lophornis delattrei. c, Calothorax fanny. d, Lophornis ornatus. e, Lophornis helenae. f, Selaphorus platycerus.

2014, Feb. 19   **Litho.**   **Perf. 13¾**
862 A251 $2.50 Sheet of 6, #a-f   11.00 11.00

Reptiles — A252

No. 863: a, Anolis carolinensis. b, Anolis cristatellus. c, Hemidactylus mabouia. d, Iguana iguana.
$9, Sphaerodactylus sabanus, vert.

2014, Feb. 19   **Litho.**   **Perf. 13¾**
863 A252 $3.25 Sheet of 4, #a-d   9.75 9.75

Souvenir Sheet
Perf. 12¾
864 A252 $9 multi   6.75 6.75
No. 864 contains one 38x51mm stamp.

Marine Mammals — A253

No. 865: a, Pygmy killer whale. b, Short-finned pilot whale. c, Dwarf sperm whale. d, Humpback whale.
$9, West Indian manatee.

2014, Feb. 19   **Litho.**   **Perf. 14**
865 A253 $3.50 Sheet of 4, #a-d   10.50 10.50

Souvenir Sheet
Perf. 12
866 A253 $9 multi   6.75 6.75

Pres. John F. Kennedy (1917-63) — A254

No. 867 — Various photos of Pres. Kennedy at lectern, with denomination at: a, UL. b, UR. c, LL, d, LR.
No. 868, $9, Black-and-white photograph of Pres. Kennedy. No. 869, $9, Color photograph of Pres. Kennedy at White House.

Perf. 13 Syncopated
2014, Feb. 19   **Litho.**
867 A254 $3 Sheet of 4, #a-d   9.00 9.00
Souvenir Sheets
868-869 A254   Set of 2   13.50 13.50

Miniature Sheets

A255

Exploration of Mars — A256

No. 870 — Inscriptions: a, Mars Reconnaissance Orbiter. b, Phobos. c, Mars Orbiter. d, Mars Climate.
No. 871 — Inscriptions: a, Mars Reconnaissance Orbiter, diff. b, Mariner 7. c, Mars Rover. d, Viking.

Perf. 13 Syncopated
2014, Feb. 19   **Litho.**
870 A255 $3.25 Sheet of 4, #a-d   9.75 9.75
871 A256 $3.25 Sheet of 4, #a-d   9.75 9.75

Yuri Gagarin (1934-68), First Man in Space — A257

No. 872 — Gagarin with: a, His daughters. b, Cosmonaut Valentina Tereshkova and United Nations Secretary General U Thant. c, Indian Prime Minister Jawaharlal Nehru. d, Rocket designer Sergei Korolev.
$9, Gagarin and Vostok 1.

2014, Feb. 19   **Litho.**   **Perf. 12**
872 A257 $2.75 Sheet of 4, #a-d   8.25 8.25
Souvenir Sheet
873 A257 $9 multi   6.75 6.75

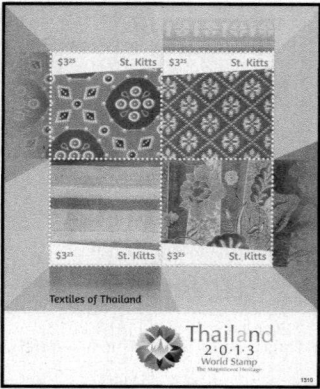

Thailand 2013 World Stamp Exhibition, Bangkok — A258

No. 874 — Textile designs: a, Circles and diamonds in red and pink. b, White geometric in diamond with blue background. c, Stripes. d, Flowers.
$9, Blue flower.

2014, Feb. 19   **Litho.**   **Perf. 13¾**
874 A258 $3.25 Sheet of 4, #a-d   9.75 9.75
Souvenir Sheet
875 A258 $9 multi   6.75 6.75

Children's Art — A259

Winning art in Human Rights Sensitization Project for Persons with Disabilities stamp design contest by: 10c, Xouria Jefferson. 15c, Nijaunte David. 30c, Nyiel Mayen. $50, Shernel Evans.

2014, Aug. 18   **Litho.**   **Perf. 13¼**
876-879 A259   Set of 4   37.50 37.50

Cactus Flowers — A260

No. 880: a, Echinocactus quehlianus. b, Cereus chalybaeus. c, Cereus rhodoleucanthus. d, Cereus hankeanus. e, Phyllocactus gordonianus. f, Cereus peruvianus.
$9, Echinocactus damsii.

2014, Sept. 4   **Litho.**   **Perf. 14**
880 A260 $2.25 Sheet of 6,
              #a-f   10.00 10.00
Souvenir Sheet
Perf.
881 A260 $9 multi   6.75 6.75
No. 881 contains one 38mm diameter stamp.

World War I, Cent. — A261

No. 882, $3.25: a, Dove with olive branch. b, Jigsaw puzzle pieces. c, Helmet on rifle. d, Highway bridge.
No. 883, $3.25, horiz.: a, U.S. M1917 tank. b, German Stürmpanzerwagen A7V-U tank. c, British Mark A Whippet tank. d, French Renault FT-17 tank.
No. 884, $5, horiz. — U.S. President Woodrow Wilson: a, With handkerchief in pocket of suit. b, Without handkerchief in pocket of suit.
No. 885, $5: a, British Mark IV tank. b, German A7V tank.

2014, Sept. 4   **Litho.**   **Perf. 14**
Sheets of 4, #a-d
882-883 A261   Set of 2   19.50 19.50
Souvenir Sheets of 2, #a-b
884-885 A261   Set of 2   15.00 15.00
No. 884 contains two 51x38mm stamps. No. 885 contains two 38x51mm stamps.

Christmas A262

Paintings by Raphael: $2.20, Reading Madonna and Child. $2.25, The Sistine Madonna. $3.50, Madonna Del Granduca. $5, The Virgin and Child.

2014, Dec. 15   **Litho.**   **Perf. 12¾**
886-889 A262   Set of 4   9.75 9.75

Trains — A263

No. 890: a, Light rail. b, Monorail. c, Steam engine train. d, Diesel train.
No. 891: a, Electric train. b, Maglev train.

Perf. 13 Syncopated
2014, Dec. 31   **Litho.**
890 A263 $3.25 Sheet of 4, #a-d   9.75 9.75
Souvenir Sheet
891 A263 $5 Sheet of 2, #a-b   7.50 7.50

A264

A265

A266

Sunflowers — A267

Various sunflowers, as shown.

2014, Dec. 31   **Litho.**   **Perf. 13¾**
892 A264 $3.25 Sheet of 4, #a-d   9.75 9.75
893 A265 $3.25 Sheet of 4, #a-d   9.75 9.75
Souvenir Sheets
Perf.
894 A266 $10 multi   7.50 7.50
895 A267 $10 multi   7.50 7.50

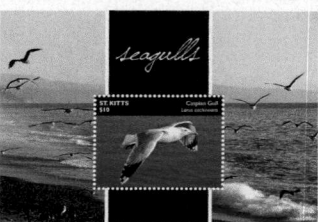

Seagulls — A268

No. 896, $3.25: a, Black-tailed gull. b, California gull. c, Gray-headed gull. d, European herring gull.
No. 897, $3.25: a, Yellow-legged gull. b, Common gull. c, Audouin's gull. d, Iceland gull.
No. 898, $10, Caspian gull. No. 899, $10, Dolphin gull.

2014, Dec. 31   **Litho.**   **Perf. 14**
Sheets of 4, #a-d
896-897 A268   Set of 2   19.50 19.50
Souvenir Sheets
898-899 A268   Set of 2   15.00 15.00

Tropical Fish — A269

No. 900, $3.25: a, French angelfish. b, Queen parrotfish. c, Rock beauty. d, Spotted drum.
No. 901, $3.25: a, Fairy basslet. b, Four-eyed butterflyfish. c, Glasseye snapper. d, Spotted eagle ray.
No. 902, $10, Queen angelfish. No. 903, $10, Smooth trunkfish, vert.

2014, Dec. 31   Litho.   Perf. 14
Sheets of 4, #a-d
900-901 A269 Set of 2   19.50 19.50
Souvenir Sheets
Perf. 12
902-903 A269 Set of 2   15.00 15.00

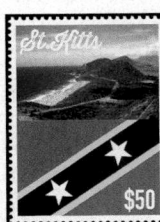

National
Symbols — A270

Designs: $50, Aerial view of St. Kitts, flag of St. Kitts and Nevis. $100, Coat of arms of St. Kitts and Nevis.

2015, Jan. 5   Litho.   Perf. 14x14¼
904 A270 $50 multi   37.50 37.50
905 A270 $100 multi   75.00 75.00

Marine Life of Taiwan — A271

No. 906: a, Warty frogfish. b, White-margin sea slug. c, Blue-ringed angelfish. d, Maroon clownfish. e, Huang Ze gray crab. f, Hawksbill sea turtle.
No. 907: a, Head of Peacock mantis shrimp. b, Body of Peacock mantis shrimp.

2015, Mar. 24   Litho.   Perf. 14
906 A271 $3.15 Sheet of 6,
#a-f   14.00 14.00
Souvenir Sheet
Perf. 12
907 A271 $5 Sheet of 2,
#a-b   7.50 7.50

World War I Posters — A272

No. 908, $3.15 — Posters from United States depicting: a, Old woman and flag. b, Soldier with bugle, flag. c, Marines attacking, flag in background. d, Soldiers landing on shore, ships in background. e, Bald eagle attacking black eagle, airplanes in background. f, Statue of Liberty pointing.
No. 909, $3.15 — Posters from Great Britain depicting: a, Picture of soldier on pendant. b, Airplane and soldiers. c, Soldier with pipe in mouth marching. d, Crowd watching soldiers marching past British flag. e, Soldier pulling on airplane propeller. f, Woman holding British flag.
No. 910, $10, Uncle Sam pointing. No. 911, $10, British Army hat.

2015, Mar. 24   Litho.   Perf. 12½
Sheets of 6, #a-f
908-909 A272 Set of 2   28.00 28.00
Souvenir Sheets
910-911 A272 Set of 2   15.00 15.00

Palm Trees — A273

No. 912: a, Coconut palm, denomination in pink. b, Petticoat palm. c, Coconut palm, denomination in pale yellow. d, Royal palm, denomination in light blue. e, Royal palm, denomination in pink. f, Palmetto palm.
$10, Cococnut palm, horiz.

2015, Apr. 1   Litho.   Perf. 13¼x13
912 A273 $3.15 Sheet of 6,
#a-f   14.00 14.00
Souvenir Sheet
Perf. 13¼
913 A273 $10 multi   7.50 7.50
No. 913 contains one 51x38mm stamp.

Green-throated Carib Hummingbird and Other Birds — A274

Design: $10, Green-throated Carib hummingbird.

2015, June 1   Litho.   Perf. 14
914 A274 $1 multi   .75 .75
Souvenir Sheet
Perf. 12¾
915 A274 $10 multi   7.50 7.50
No. 915 contains one 51x38mm stamp.

Singapore 2015 World Stamp
Exhibition — A275

No. 916 — Tourist attractions in Singapore: a, Sentosa Island. b, Singapore Flyer. c, Tiger Sky Tower. d, Kusu Island.
$10, Flower at Botanic Gardens, vert.

2015, Aug. 3   Litho.   Perf. 12
916 A275 $3.25 Sheet of 4, #a-d   9.75 9.75
Souvenir Sheet
917 A275 $10 multi   7.50 7.50

Cats — A276

No. 918: a, Birman. b, Devon Rex. c, Selkirk Rex. d, American Curl. e, Scottish Fold. f, Exotic shorthair.
$10, Bengal cat, vert.

2015, Aug. 3   Litho.   Perf. 14
918 A276 $3.15 Sheet of 6,
#a-f   14.00 14.00
Souvenir Sheet
Perf. 12
919 A276 $10 multi   7.50 7.50

Battle of Waterloo, 200th
Anniv. — A277

No. 920 — Paintings: a, Scotland Forever!, by Lady Butler. b, The Battle of Waterloo, by Jan Willem Pieneman. c, Wellington at Waterloo, by Robert Alexander Hillingford. d, The Last Grenadier at Waterloo, by Horace Vernet.
$10, The Battle of Waterloo, by William Sadler.

2015, Aug. 3   Litho.   Perf. 12½
920 A277 $3.25 Sheet of 4, #a-d   9.75 9.75
Souvenir Sheet
Perf. 12
921 A277 $10 multi   7.50 7.50
No. 921 contains one 80x30mm stamp.

Birth of Princess Charlotte of
Cambridge — A278

No. 922: a, Duke and Duchess of Cambridge, Duchess carrying Princess Charlotte. b, Duke and Duchess of Cambridge, Duke holding Princess Charlotte's baby carrier. c, Duke of Cambridge putting baby carrier in automobile. d, Duke of Cambridge and Prince George.
$10, Duchess of Cambridge and Princess Charlotte, vert.

2015, Aug. 10   Litho.   Perf. 12
922 A278 $3.25 Sheet of 4, #a-d   9.75 9.75
Souvenir Sheet
923 A278 $10 multi   7.50 7.50

Owls — A279

No. 924, $3.25 — Owl and feather, white background: a, Barn owl. b, Burrowing owl. c, Central American pygmy owl. d, Great horned owl.
No. 925, $3.25 — Owl, black frame: a, Barred owl. b, Burrowing owl. c, Bare-legged owls. d, Barn owl.
No. 926, $10, Ashy-faced owl. No. 927, $10, Short-eared owl.

2015, Sept. 8   Litho.   Perf. 12
Sheets of 4, #a-d
924-925 A279 Set of 2   19.50 19.50
Souvenir Sheets
926-927 A279 Set of 2   15.00 15.00

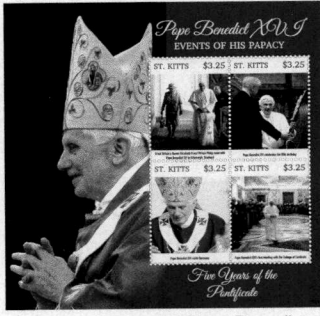

Events of Reign of Pope Benedict
XVI — A280

No. 928 — Pope Benedict XVI: a, Meeting Queen Elizabeth II and Prince Philip. b, Celebrating 85th birthday. c, Visiting Germany. d, At first meeting with College of Cardinals.
$10, Pope Benedict XVI giving Urbi et Orbi Easter blessing, horiz.

2015, Sept. 8   Litho.   Perf. 12x12½
928 A280 $3.25 Sheet of 4, #a-d   9.75 9.75
Souvenir Sheet
Perf. 12
929 A280 $10 multi   7.50 7.50
No. 929 contains one 50x30mm stamp.

Christmas
A281

Paintings by Raphael: 30c, Small Cowper Madonna. $2.25, The Tempi Madonna. $3.50, Madonna with Beardless Saint Joseph. $5, Sistine Madonna.

2015, Nov. 2   Litho.   Perf. 13½
930-933 A281   Set of 4   8.25 8.25

Worldwide Fund
for Nature
(WWF) — A282

No. 934 — West Indian mahogany tree: a, Seeds in opened fruit. b, Foliage, c, Forest. d, Fruit on tree.

2016, Apr. 14   Litho.   Perf. 14
934   Strip of 4, #a-d   9.75 9.75
a.-d. A282 $3.25 Any single   2.40 2.40
e.   Souvenir sheet of 8, 2 each
      #934a-934d   19.50 19.50

Paintings — A283

No. 935, $3.50: a, Blue House, by Boris Kustodiev. b, Dog Lying in the Snow, by Marc Liegender. c, A Girl with a Watering Can, by Pierre-Auguste Renoir.
No. 936, $3.50: a, Mandolin on a Chair, by Paul Gauguin. b, Bouquet of Flowers, by Henri Rousseau. c, Girl at a Sewing Machine, by Edward Hopper.
No. 937, $10, Murnau, A Village Street, by Wassily Kandinsky. No. 938, $10, Bedroom in Arles, by Vincent van Gogh.

2016, May 26   Litho.   Perf. 12½
Sheets of 3, #a-c
935-936 A283   Set of 2   15.50 15.50
Size: 100x100mm
Imperf
937-938 A283   Set of 2   15.00 15.00
No. 938 "Arles" is spelled incorrectly on stamp.

Seaplanes — A284

No. 939: a, Ambrosini SAL 10 Grifone. b, Savoia-Marchetti S65. c, Macchi-Castoldi MC72. d, Savoia-Marchetti S51. $10, Savoia-Marchetti S55X.

2016, May 26   Litho.   Perf. 14
939 A284 $3.25 Sheet of 4, #a-d 9.75 9.75
Souvenir Sheet
940 A284 $10 multi   7.50 7.50

Characters From Star Trek (2009 Movie) — A285

No. 941: a, Spock. b, Kirk. c, Elder Spock. d, Sulu. e, Uhura. f, Bones McCoy. $10, Spock and Elder Spock.

2016, May 26   Litho.   Perf. 12
941 A285 $3 Sheet of 6, #a-f   13.50 13.50
Souvenir Sheet
Perf. 14
942 A285 $10 multi   7.50 7.50

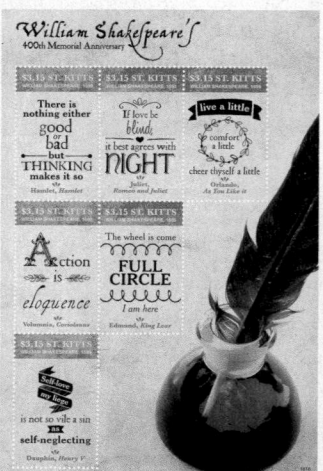

Lines From Plays by William Shakespeare (1564-1616) — A286

No. 943 — Line from: a, Hamlet. b, Romeo and Juliet. c, Orlando's line, As You Like It. d, Coriolanus. e, King Lear. f, Henry V. $13, Roslind's line from, As You Like It, diff.

2016, May 26   Litho.   Perf. 12
943 A286 $3.15 Sheet of 6, #a-f 14.00 14.00
Souvenir Sheet
944 A286 $13 multi   9.75 9.75

Queen Elizabeth II, Longest-Reigning British Monarch — A287

No. 945 — Queen Elizabeth II: a, Wearing gray raincoat and head scarf. b, Wearing black jacket, camera and binoculars around neck. c, Wearing dark blue jacket, arms folded. d, Wearing head scarf, taking photograph. e, Wearing blue vest jacket. f, Wearing dark green raincoat and head scarf, with camera. $10, Taking photogaph, horiz.

2016, May 26   Litho.   Perf. 14
945 A287 $3.15 Sheet of 6, #a-f 14.00 14.00
Souvenir Sheet
Perf. 12
946 A287 $10 multi   7.50 7.50
No. 946 contains one 80x30mm stamp.

New York City Landmarks — A288

No. 947: a, Statue of Lion, New York Public Library. b, Statue of Prometheus, Rockefeller Center c, Glory of Commerce statue, Grand Central Terminal. d, Angel of the Waters statue (Bethesda Fountain), Central Park. $12, Statue of Liberty, vert.

2016, May 26   Litho.   Perf. 12
947 A288 $3.50 Sheet of 4, #a-d 10.50 10.50
Souvenir Sheet
Perf. 12½
948 A288 $12 multi   9.00 9.00
2016 World Stamp Show, New York. No. 948 contains one 38x51mm stamp.

A289

September 11, 2001 Terrorist Attacks, 15th Anniv. — A290

No. 949: a, Soldier saluting at Flight 93 National Memorial. b, Aerial view of Pentagon. c, Pentagon Sept. 11 Memorial. d, Sept. 11 Memorial, Liberty State Park, New Jersey. e, Sept. 11 Fire Department of New York Memorial Wall. f, Sept. 11 Memorial, Bayonne, New Jersey.
No. 950: a, World Trade Center, denomination in white. b, World Trade Center tower, denomination partly over sky. c, World Trade Center tower, country name partly over sky. d, Tribute in Light. $13, World Trade Center, horiz.

2016, May 26   Litho.   Perf. 14
949 A289 $3.15 Sheet of 6, #a-f 14.00 14.00
Perf. 12
950 A290 $3.25 Sheet of 4, #a-d 9.75 9.75
Souvenir Sheet
951 A290 $13 multi   9.75 9.75
No. 951 contains one 40x30mm stamp.

Mammals — A291

No. 952: a, Dhole. b, Jaguar. c, Ring-tailed lemur. d, Orangutan. e, Lion. f, Malayan tapir.
No. 953: a, Red panda. b, Hippopotamus. c, Black rhinoceros. d, Bengal tiger. $10, Mohol bushbaby.

2016, May 26   Litho.   Perf. 14
952 A291 $3.15 Sheet of 6, #a-f 14.00 14.00
953 A291 $3.25 Sheet of 4, #a-d 9.75 9.75
Souvenir Sheet
954 A291 $10 multi   7.50 7.50

Flowers — A292

No. 955: a, Damask rose. b, Moss rose. c, Blue passion flower. d, Common sunflower. e, Paperflower. f, Windflower.
No. 956: a, Elegant zinnia. b, Asian globeflower. c, Creeping zinnia. d, Blackeyed Susan. $10, Persian carpet.

2016, May 26   Litho.   Perf. 14
955 A292 $3.15 Sheet of 6, #a-f 14.00 14.00
956 A292 $3.25 Sheet of 4, #a-d 9.75 9.75
Souvenir Sheet
957 A292 $10 multi   7.50 7.50

Miniature Sheets

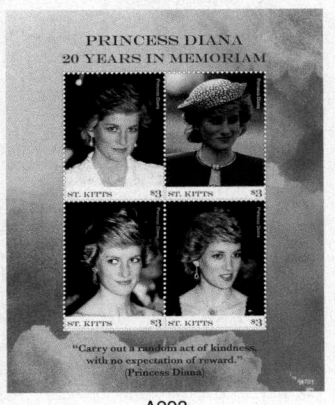

PRINCESS DIANA
20 YEARS IN MEMORIAM

"Carry out a random act of kindness,
with no expectation of reward."
(Princess Diana)

A293

Princess Diana (1961-97) — A294

No. 958 — Princess Diana wearing: a, White dress and pendant earrings. b, Blue and white hat. c, Strapless gown. d, Black dress and pendant earrings.

No. 959: a, Princess Diana, in silver and white, holding Prince William. b, Princess Diana, in green and white dress, holding Prince William. c, Princess Diana with arms around head of Prince William. d, Prince William holding infant Prince George. e, Prince William holding toddler Prince George. f, Princes William and George walking.

				2017, June 7	**Litho.**	**Perf. 14**	
958	A293	$3 Sheet of 4, #a-d				9.00	9.00
959	A294	$3 Sheet of 6, #a-f				13.50	13.50

Queen Elizabeth II, 90th Birthday (in 2016) — A295

No. 960 — Queen Elizabeth II: a, As toddler (30x40mm). b, With Prince Philip (30x40mm). c, With Princes Philip and Charles and Princess Anne (30x40mm). d, With Princes Philip, William and George, Duchess of Cambridge and Princess Charlotte (30x90mm).

No. 961 — Queen Elizabeth II wearing: a, Magenta jacket and hat. b, Apple green and white jacket and hat, holding flowers. $10, Queen Elizabeth II wearing apple green and white jacket, waving.

			2017, June 7	**Litho.**	**Perf. 14**	
960	A295	$3 Sheet of 4, #a-d			9.00	9.00

Souvenir Sheets
Perf. 12

961	A295	$5 Sheet of 2, #a-b		7.50	7.50

Perf. 13¾

962	A295	$10 multi		7.50	7.50

No. 961 contains two 30x50mm stamps. No. 962 contains one 50x50mm diamond-shaped stamp.

Animals — A296

No. 963: a, Greater mouse deer. b, Flightless steamer duck. c, Arctic cookie stars. d, Florida bark scorpion.
$10, Silverstone's poison frog.

			2017, June 7	**Litho.**	**Perf. 12½**	
963	A296	$5 Sheet of 4, #a-d			5.00	15.00

Souvenir Sheet

964	A296	$10 multi		7.50	7.50

OFFICIAL STAMPS

Nos. 28-37 Ovptd. "OFFICIAL"
Perf. 14½x14

			1980, June 23	**Litho.**	**Wmk. 373**	
O1	A61	15c multicolored			.25	.25
O2	A61	25c multicolored			.25	.25
O3	A61	30c multicolored			.25	.25
O4	A61	40c multicolored			.25	.25
O5	A61	45c multicolored			.25	.25
O6	A61	50c multicolored			.25	.25
O7	A61	55c multicolored			.25	.25
O8	A61	$1 multicolored			.30	.30
O9	A61	$5 multicolored			1.00	1.50
O10	A61	$10 multicolored			1.50	2.75
		Nos. O1-O10 (10)			4.55	6.30

No. O7 exists with inverted overprint. Value $22. No. O10 exists with inverted overprint. Value $100.

Unwmk.

O2a	A61	25c		.30	.25
O3a	A61	30c		.60	.40
O4a	A61	40c		11.50	12.50
O7a	A61	55c		.85	1.00
O8a	A61	$1		1.40	1.25
O9a	A61	$5		3.25	5.00
O10a	A61	$10		4.25	7.00
		Nos. O2a-O10a (7)		22.15	27.40

Nos. 55-66 Ovptd. "OFFICIAL"

			1981, Feb. 5		**Perf. 14**	
O11	A5	15c multicolored			.25	.25
O12	A5	20c multicolored			.25	.25
O13	A5	25c multicolored			.25	.25
O14	A5	30c multicolored			.25	.25
O15	A5	40c multicolored			.40	.25
O16	A5	45c multicolored			.45	.25
O17	A5	50c multicolored			.45	.25
O18	A5	55c multicolored			.55	.30
O19	A5	$1 multicolored			.90	.70
O20	A5	$2.50 multicolored			2.00	1.25
O21	A5	$5 multicolored			3.25	2.50
O22	A5	$10 multicolored			5.50	4.50
		Nos. O11-O22 (12)			14.50	11.00

Nos. 75-80 Ovptd. or Surcharged "OFFICIAL" in Ultra or Black

		1983, Feb. 2			
O23	A6a	45c on $2.50 No. 77			
		(U)		.35	.35
a.		Black surcharge			
O24	A6b	45c on $2.50 No. 78			
		(U)		.45	.45
a.		Black surcharge			
O25	A6a	55c on 55c No. 75		.35	.35
O26	A6b	55c on 55c No. 76		.60	.60
O27	A6a	$1.10 on $4 No. 79			
		(B)		.60	.60
a.		Ultra surcharge		3.00	
O28	A6b	$1.10 on $4 No. 80			
		(B)		1.10	1.10
a.		Ultra surcharge		25.00	
		Nos. O23-O28 (6)		3.45	3.45

No. O23 exists with double surcharge and inverted surcharge. Values, $16 and $3, respectively. No. O24 exists with double surcharge and inverted surcharge. Values, $60 and $20, respectively. No. O25 exists with double surcharge and inverted surcharge. Values, $18 and $6, respectively. No. O26 exists with double surcharge and inverted surcharge. Values, $60 and $19, respectively. No. O27 exists with double surcharge. Value $15. No. O28 exists with double surcharge. Value $45. Nos. O27a and O28a exist with inverted surcharge.

Nos. 141-152 Ovptd. "OFFICIAL"

			1984, July 4		**Wmk. 380**	
O29	A18	15c multicolored			.70	1.50
O30	A18	20c multicolored			.80	1.50
O31	A18	25c multicolored			.80	1.50
O32	A18	30c multicolored			.90	1.50
O33	A18	40c multicolored			1.00	1.50
O34	A18	50c multicolored			1.00	1.50
O35	A18	60c multicolored			1.25	2.00
O36	A18	75c multicolored			1.60	2.00
O37	A18	$1 multicolored			2.50	2.50
O38	A18	$2.50 multicolored			4.50	6.00
O39	A18	$5 multicolored			8.00	3.00
O40	A18	$10 multicolored			14.50	6.00
		Nos. O29-O40 (12)			37.55	30.50

ST. KITTS-NEVIS

sānt ˈkits-ˈnē-vəs

(St. Christopher-Nevis-Anguilla)

LOCATION — West Indies southeast of Puerto Rico
GOVT. — Associated State in British Commonwealth
AREA — 153 sq. mi.
POP. — 43,309, excluding Anguilla (1991)
CAPITAL — Basseterre, St. Kitts

St. Kitts-Nevis was one of the presidencies of the former Leeward Islands colony until it became a colony itself in 1956. In 1967 Britain granted internal self-government.

See "St. Christopher" for stamps used in St. Kitts before 1890. From 1890 until 1903, stamps of the Leeward Islands were used. From 1903 until 1956, stamps of St. Kitts-Nevis and Leeward Islands were used concurrently.

Starting in 1967, issues of Anguilla are listed under that heading. Starting in 1980 stamps inscribed St. Kitts or Nevis are listed under those headings.

12 Pence = 1 Shilling
20 Shillings = 1 Pound
100 Cents = 1 Dollar (1951)

Catalogue values for unused stamps in this country are for Never Hinged items, beginning with Scott 91 in the regular postage section and Scott O1 in the officials section.

Columbus Looking for Land — A1

Medicinal Spring — A2

Wmk. Crown and C A (2)

			1903	**Typo.**	**Perf. 14**	
1	A1	½p grn & vio			2.00	.80
2	A2	1p car & black			5.25	.25
3	A1	2p brn & vio			3.50	12.00
4	A2	2½p ultra & black			20.00	6.00
5	A2	3p org & green			25.00	32.50
6	A1	6p red vio & blk			8.00	47.50
7	A1	1sh org & grn			7.75	12.00
8	A2	2sh blk & grn			13.50	22.50
9	A1	2sh6p violet & blk			20.00	50.00
10	A2	5sh ol grn & gray vio			70.00	246.05
		Nos. 1-10 (10)			175.00	

			1905-18		**Wmk. 3**	
11	A1	½p green & violet			16.50	8.25
12a	A1	½p dl blue grn ('16)			1.00	3.25
13	A2	1p carmine & blk			9.50	.30
14a	A2	1p scarlet ('16)			1.00	.25
15	A1	2p brn & vio, ordinary paper			11.00	9.00
16	A1	2½p ultra & blk			40.00	6.00
17	A1	2½p ultra			3.00	.60
18	A2	3p org & grn, chalky paper			3.50	3.00
19	A1	6p red violet & gray blk ('16)			12.00	35.00
a.		6p purple & gray, chalky paper ('08)			24.00	27.50

20	A1	1sh org & grn, chalky paper ('09)		4.00	35.00
21	A2	5sh ol grn & gray vio ('18)		47.50	120.00
		Nos. 11-21 (11)		149.00	220.65

Nos. 13, 19a and 21 are on chalky paper only and Nos. 15, 18 and 20 are on both ordinary and chalky paper.
For stamp and type overprinted see #MR1-MR2.

King George V — A3

A4

			1920-22		**Ordinary Paper**	
24	A3	½p green			4.25	6.00
25	A4	1p carmine			4.00	6.50
26	A3	1½p orange			1.40	2.00
27	A4	2p gray			3.25	7.50
28	A3	2½p ultramarine			8.25	10.00
a.		"A" missing from watermark			600.00	

Chalky Paper

29	A4	3p vio & dull vio, yel		2.00	12.00
30	A3	6p red vio & dull vio		4.00	12.00
31	A4	1sh blk, gray grn		4.00	4.50
32	A3	2sh ultra & dull vio, bl		28.00	57.50
33	A4	2sh6p red & blk, bl		5.50	45.00
34	A3	5sh red & grn, yel		5.50	45.00
35	A4	10sh red & grn, grn		14.50	52.50
36	A3	£1 blk & vio, red		300.00	375.00
		Nos. 24-36 (13)		384.65	635.50

			1921-29	**Ordinary Paper**		**Wmk. 4**
37	A3	½p yel green			2.50	1.50
38	A4	1p rose red			1.25	.25
39	A4	1p dp violet ('22)			7.50	1.10
40	A3	1½p rose red ('25)			7.50	1.50
41	A3	1½p fawn ('28)			2.25	.35
42	A4	2p gray			1.00	.65
43	A3	2½p pale bright blue ('22)			1.75	2.50
44	A3	2½p brown ('22)			4.75	12.50

Chalky Paper

43a	A3	2½p ultra ('27)		1.75	1.50
45	A4	3p ultra ('22)		1.60	4.00
46	A4	3p vio & dl vio, yel		2.40	2.75
47	A3	6p red vio & dl vio ('24)		8.50	6.75
48	A4	1sh blk, grn ('29)		6.50	4.00
49	A3	2sh ultra & vio, bl ('22)		15.00	40.00
50	A4	2sh6p red & blk, bl ('27)		25.00	30.00
51	A3	5sh red & grn, yel ('29)		55.00	100.00
		Nos. 37-51 (16)		144.25	209.35
		Set, ovptd. "SPECIMEN"		450.00	

No. 43 exists on ordinary and chalky paper.

Caravel in Old Road Bay — A5

			1923		**Wmk. 4**	
52	A5	½p green & blk			2.50	9.25
53	A5	1p violet & blk			5.00	3.25
54	A5	1½p car & blk			5.00	11.00
55	A5	2p dk gray & blk			4.25	1.75
56	A5	2½p brown & blk			6.50	35.00
57	A5	3p ultra & blk			6.50	16.00
58	A5	6p red vio & blk			10.50	35.00
59	A5	1sh ol grn & blk			15.00	35.00
60	A5	2sh ultra & blk, bl			52.50	85.00
61	A5	2sh6p red & blk, blue			52.50	100.00
62	A5	10sh red & blk, emer			325.00	600.00

Wmk. 3

63	A5	5sh red & blk, yel		92.50	250.00
64	A5	£1 vio & blk, red		825.00	1,775.
		Nos. 52-63 (12)		577.75	1,181.

Tercentenary of the founding of the colony of St. Kitts (or St. Christopher).

Common Design Types pictured following the introduction.

Silver Jubilee Issue
Common Design Type
Inscribed "St. Christopher and Nevis"

Perf. 11x12

				Wmk. 4
1935, May 6		**Engr.**		
72	CD301	1p car & dk blue	1.00	.75
73	CD301	1½p gray blk & ultra	.80	1.00
74	CD301	2½p ultra & brown	1.00	.90
75	CD301	1sh brn vio & ind	8.00	16.00
		Nos. 72-75 (4)	10.80	18.65
		Set, never hinged	18.50	

Coronation Issue
Common Design Type
Inscribed "St. Christopher and Nevis"

				Perf. 13½x14
1937, May 12				
76	CD302	1p carmine	.25	.30
77	CD302	1½p brown	.30	.25
78	CD302	2½p bright ultra	.40	1.60
		Nos. 76-78 (3)	.95	2.15
		Set, never hinged	1.25	

George VI
A6

Medicinal Spring
A7

Columbus Looking for Land — A8

Map Showing Anguilla
A9

Perf. 13½x14 (A6, A9), 14 (A7, A8)

1938-48				**Typo.**
79	A6	½p green	.25	.25
80	A6	1p carmine	1.00	.55
81	A6	1½p orange	.25	.30
82	A7	2p gray & car	.90	1.40
83	A6	2½p ultra	.50	.35
84	A7	3p car & pale lilac	2.75	5.50
85	A8	6p rose lil & dl grn	5.00	1.60
86	A7	1sh green & gray blk	3.00	1.00
87	A7	2sh6p car & gray blk	8.50	4.50
88	A8	5sh car & dull grn	17.50	12.00

Typo., Center Litho.
Chalky Paper

89	A9	10sh brt ultra & blk	9.50	20.00
90	A9	£1 brown & blk	9.50	22.50
		Nos. 79-90 (12)	58.65	69.95
		Set, never hinged	85.00	

Issued: ½, 1, 1½, 2½p, 8/15/38; 2p, 1941; 3, 6p, 2sh6p, 5sh, 1942; 1sh, 1943; 10sh, £1, 9/1/48.

For types overprinted see Nos. 99-104.

1938, Aug. 15			**Perf. 13x11½**
82a	A7	2p	18.00	3.00
84a	A7	3p	16.00	8.25
85a	A8	6p	6.50	3.00
86a	A7	1sh	8.50	2.25
87a	A7	2sh6p	22.50	10.00
88a	A8	5sh	47.50	25.00
		Nos. 82a-88a (6)	119.00	51.50

> Catalogue values for unused stamps in this section, from this point to the end of the section, are for Never Hinged items.

Peace Issue
Common Design Type
Inscribed "St. Kitts-Nevis"

1946, Nov. 1		**Engr.**		**Perf. 13½x14**
91	CD303	1½p deep orange	.25	.25
92	CD303	3p carmine	.25	.25

Silver Wedding Issue
Common Design Types
Inscribed: "St. Kitts-Nevis"

1949, Jan. 3		**Photo.**		**Perf. 14x14½**
93	CD304	2½p bright ultra	.25	.50

Perf. 11½x11
Engraved; Name Typographed

94	CD305	5sh rose carmine	11.00	10.00

UPU Issue
Common Design Types
Inscribed: "St. Kitt's-Nevis"

Engr.; Name Typo. on 3p, 6p

1949, Oct. 10			**Perf. 13½, 11x11½**
95	CD306	2½p ultra	.25	.35
96	CD307	3p deep carmine	2.50	2.75
97	CD308	6p red lilac	.25	2.00
98	CD309	1sh blue green	.35	.45
		Nos. 95-98 (4)	3.35	5.55

Types of 1938 Overprinted in Black or Carmine

On A6

On A7-A8

Perf. 13½x14, 13x12½

1950, Nov. 10			**Wmk. 4**
99	A6	1p carmine	.25	.25
100	A6	1½p orange	.25	.55
a.		Wmk. 4a (error)	1,450.	
b.		Wmk. 4, no crown (error)	3,400.	
101	A6	2½p ultra	.25	.25
102	A7	3p car & pale lilac	.80	.85
103	A8	6p rose lil & dl grn	.45	.25
104	A7	1sh grn & gray blk (C)	1.50	.40
		Nos. 99-104 (6)	3.50	2.55

300th anniv. of the settlement of Anguilla.

University Issue
Common Design Types
Inscribed: "St. Kitts-Nevis"

Perf. 14x14½

1951, Feb. 16		**Engr.**		**Wmk. 4**
105	CD310	3c org yel & gray blk	.45	.25
106	CD311	12c red violet & aqua	.45	2.00

St. Christopher-Nevis-Anguilla

Bath House and Spa, Nevis — A10

Map — A11

Designs: 2c, Warner Park, St. Kitts. 4c, Brimstone Hill, St. Kitts. 5c, Nevis. 6c, Pinney's Beach, Nevis. 12c, Sir Thomas Warner's Tomb. 24c, Old Road Bay, St. Kitts. 48c, Picking Cotton. 60c, Treasury, St. Kitts. $1.20, Salt Pond, Anguilla. $4.80, Sugar Mill, St. Kitts.

1952, June 14			**Perf. 12½**
107	A10	1c ocher & dp grn	.25	3.00
108	A10	2c emerald	1.00	1.00
109	A11	3c purple & red	.40	1.25
110	A10	4c red	.25	.25
111	A10	5c gray & ultra	.40	.25
112	A10	6c deep ultra	.40	.25
113	A11	12c redsh brn & dp blue	1.25	.25
114	A10	24c car & gray blk	.40	.25
115	A10	48c vio brn & ol bis	3.00	6.50
116	A10	60c dp grn & och	2.25	4.50
117	A10	$1.20 dp ultra & dp green	8.00	6.50
118	A10	$4.80 car & emer	15.00	20.00
		Nos. 107-118 (12)	32.60	44.00

Coronation Issue
Common Design Type

1953, June 2			**Perf. 13½x13**
119	CD312	2c brt green & blk	.35	.25

Types of 1952 with Portrait of Queen Elizabeth II

½c, Salt Pond, Anguilla. 8c, Sombrero Lighthouse. $2.40, Map of Anguilla & Dependencies.

1954-57		**Engr.**		**Perf. 12½**
120	A10	½c gray olive ('56)	.40	.25
121	A10	1c ocher & dp grn	.25	.25
a.		Horiz. pair, imperf. vert.		9,000.
122	A10	2c emerald	1.00	.25
123	A11	3c purple & red	.80	.25
124	A10	4c red	.25	.25
125	A10	5c gray & ultra	.25	.25
126	A10	6c deep ultra	1.50	.25
127	A11	8c dark gray ('57)	3.00	.30
128	A11	12c redsh brn & dp blue	.25	.25
129	A10	24c carmine & blk	.25	.25
130	A10	48c brn & ol bister	1.50	.65
131	A10	60c dp grn & ocher	5.25	7.50
132	A10	$1.20 dp ultra & dp green	18.00	4.00
133	A10	$2.40 red org & blk ('57)	16.00	16.00
134	A10	$4.80 car & emer	19.00	11.00
		Nos. 120-134 (15)	67.70	41.70

Issued: 24c-$1.20, $4.80, 12/1/54; ½c, 7/3/56; 8c, $2.40, 2/1/57; others, 3/1/54.

Alexander Hamilton and Nevis Scene
A12

1957, Jan. 11			**Perf. 12½**
135	A12	24c dp ultra & yel grn	.55	.25

Bicent. of the birth of Alexander Hamilton.

West Indies Federation
Common Design Type

Perf. 11½x11

1958, Apr. 22		**Engr.**		**Wmk. 314**
136	CD313	3c green	.75	.35
137	CD313	6c blue	1.00	2.25
138	CD313	12c carmine rose	1.25	.50
		Nos. 136-138 (3)	3.00	3.10

Federation of the West Indies, Apr. 22, 1958.

Stamp of Nevis, 1861
A13

Designs (Stamps of Nevis, 1861 issue): 8c, 4p stamp. 12c, 6p stamp. 24c, 1sh stamp.

1961, July 15			**Perf. 14**
139	A13	2c green & brown	.25	.25
140	A13	8c blue & pale brown	.30	.25
141	A13	12c carmine & gray	.35	.25
142	A13	24c orange & green	.50	.50
		Nos. 139-142 (4)	1.40	1.25

Centenary of the first stamps of Nevis.

Red Cross Centenary Issue
Common Design Type

1963, Sept. 2		**Litho.**		**Perf. 13**
143	CD315	3c black & red	.25	.25
144	CD315	12c ultra & red	.65	.65

New Lighthouse, Sombrero — A14

Loading Sugar Cane, St. Kitts
A15

Designs: 2c, Pall Mall Square, Basseterre. 3c, Gateway, Brimstone Hill Fort, St. Kitts. 4c, Nelson's Spring, Nevis. 5c, Grammar School, St. Kitts. 6c, Mt. Misery Crater, St. Kitts. 10c, Hibiscus. 15c, Sea Island cotton, Nevis. 20c, Boat building, Anguilla. 25c, White-crowned pigeon. 50c, St. George's Church tower, Basseterre. 60c, Alexander Hamilton. $1, Map of St. Kitts-Nevis. $2.50, Map of Anguilla. $5, Arms of St. Christopher-Nevis-Anguilla.

1963, Nov. 20		**Photo.**		**Perf. 14**
145	A14	½c blue & dk brn	.25	.25
146	A15	1c multicolored	.25	.25
147	A14	2c multicolored	.25	.25
a.		Yellow omitted	300.00	
148	A14	3c multicolored	.25	.25
149	A14	4c multicolored	.25	.25
150	A15	5c multicolored	3.00	.25
151	A15	6c multicolored	.25	.25
152	A14	10c multicolored	.25	.25
153	A14	15c multicolored	.70	.25
154	A14	20c multicolored	.30	.25
155	A14	25c multicolored	2.25	.25
156	A15	50c multicolored	.60	.35
157	A14	60c multicolored	1.10	.40
158	A14	$1 multicolored	2.50	.55
159	A15	$2.50 multicolored	2.75	2.75
160	A15	$5 multicolored	7.00	7.00
		Nos. 145-160 (16)	21.95	13.80

For overprints see Nos. 161-162.

1967-69			**Wmk. 314 Sideways**
145a	A14	½c ('69)	.25	2.00
147b	A14	2c	1.75	.25
148a	A14	3c ('68)	.35	.25
153a	A14	15c ('68)	.90	.45
155a	A14	25c ('68)	2.50	.25
158a	A14	$1 ('68)	6.00	4.00
		Nos. 145a-158a (6)	11.75	7.20

Nos. 148 and 155 Overprinted: "ARTS / FESTIVAL / ST. KITTS / 1964"

1964, Sept. 14				
161	A14	3c multicolored	.25	.25
162	A14	25c multicolored	.25	.25

ITU Issue
Common Design Type

Perf. 11x11½

1965, May 17		**Litho.**		**Wmk. 314**
163	CD317	2c bister & rose red	.25	.25
164	CD317	50c grnsh blue & ol	.35	.35

Intl. Cooperation Year Issue
Common Design Type

1965, Oct. 25			**Perf. 14½**
165	CD318	2c blue grn & claret	.25	.30
166	CD318	25c lt violet & green	.55	.30

Churchill Memorial Issue
Common Design Type

1966, Jan. 24		**Photo.**		**Perf. 14**

Design in Black, Gold and Carmine Rose

167	CD319	½c bright blue	.25	.85
a.		Denomination omitted	500.00	
168	CD319	3c green	.25	.25
169	CD319	15c brown	.40	.30
170	CD319	25c violet	.60	.30
		Nos. 167-170 (4)	1.50	1.70

Royal Visit Issue
Common Design Type

1966, Feb. 14		**Litho.**		**Perf. 11x12**
171	CD320	3c violet blue	.25	.35
172	CD320	25c dk carmine rose	.65	.40

World Cup Soccer Issue
Common Design Type

1966, July 1		**Litho.**		**Perf. 14**
173	CD321	6c multicolored	.35	.40
174	CD321	25c multicolored	.50	.40

Festival Emblem
With
Dolphins — A16

Unwmk.
1966, Aug. 15   Photo.   Perf. 14
175 A16 3c gold, grn, yel & blk .25 .25
176 A16 25c silver, grn, yel & blk .30 .30

Arts Festival of 1966.

WHO Headquarters Issue
Common Design Type
1966, Sept. 20   Litho.   Perf. 14
177 CD322 3c multicolored .25 .25
178 CD322 40c multicolored .35 .35

UNESCO Anniversary Issue
Common Design Type
1966, Dec. 1   Litho.   Perf. 14
179 CD323 3c "Education" .25 .25
180 CD323 6c "Science" .25 .25
181 CD323 40c "Culture" .40 .40
Nos. 179-181 (3) .90 .90

Independent State

Government Headquarters,
Basseterre — A17

Designs: 10c, Flag and map of Anguilla, St. Christopher and Nevis. 25c, Coat of Arms.

Wmk. 314
1967, July 1   Photo.   Perf. 14½
182 A17 3c multicolored .25 .25
183 A17 10c multicolored .25 .25
184 A17 25c multicolored .25 .25
Nos. 182-184 (3) .75 .75

Achievement of independence, Feb. 27, 1967.

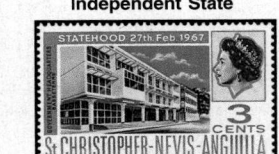

Charles Wesley,
Cross and
Palm — A18

3c, John Wesley. 40c, Thomas Coke.

1967, Dec. 1   Litho.   Perf. 13x13½
185 A18 3c dp lilac, dp car & blk .25 .25
186 A18 25c ultra, grnsh blue & blk .25 .25
187 A18 40c ocher, yellow & blk .25 .25
Nos. 185-187 (3) .75 .75

Attainment of autonomy by the Methodist Church in the Caribbean and the Americas, and for the opening of headquarters near St. John's, Antigua, May 1967.

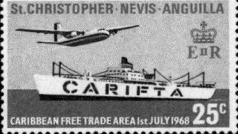

Cargo
Ship
and
Plane
A19

Perf. 13½x13
1968, July 30   Litho.   Wmk. 314
188 A19 25c multicolored .25 .25
189 A19 50c brt blue & multi .45 .45

Issued to publicize the organization of the Caribbean Free Trade Area, CARIFTA.

Martin Luther King,
Jr. — A20

Perf. 12x12½
1968, Sept. 30   Litho.   Wmk. 314
190 A20 50c multicolored .45 .35

Dr. Martin Luther King, Jr. (1929-68), American civil rights leader.

Mystical Nativity,
by Botticelli — A21

Christmas (Paintings): 25c, 50c, The Adoration of the Magi, by Rubens.

Perf. 14½x14
1968, Nov. 27   Photo.   Wmk. 314
191 A21 12c brt violet & multi .25 .25
192 A21 25c multicolored .25 .25
193 A21 40c gray & multi .25 .25
194 A21 50c crimson & multi .25 .25
Nos. 191-194 (4) 1.00 1.00

Snook
A22

Fish: 12c, Needlefish (gar). 40c, Horse-eye jack. 50c, Red snapper. The 6c is misinscribed "tarpon."

Perf. 14x14½
1969, Feb. 25   Photo.   Wmk. 314
195 A22 6c brt green & multi .25 .25
196 A22 12c blue & multi .30 .25
197 A22 40c gray blue & multi .30 .25
198 A22 50c multicolored .40 .30
Nos. 195-198 (4) 1.25 1.05

Arms of Sir Thomas Warner and Map
of Islands — A23

Designs: 25c, Warner's tomb in St. Kitts. 40c, Warner's commission from Charles I.

1969, Sept. 1   Litho.   Perf. 13½
199 A23 20c multicolored .25 .25
200 A23 25c multicolored .25 .25
201 A23 40c multicolored .25 .25
Nos. 199-201 (3) .75 .75

Issued in memory of Sir Thomas Warner, first Governor of St. Kitts-Nevis, Barbados and Montserrat.

Adoration of the
Kings, by Jan
Mostaert — A24

Christmas (Painting): 40c, 50c, Adoration of the Kings, by Geertgen tot Sint Jans.

1969, Nov. 17   Perf. 13½
202 A24 10c olive & multi .25 .25
203 A24 25c violet & multi .25 .25
204 A24 40c yellow grn & multi .25 .25
205 A24 50c maroon & multi .25 .25
Nos. 202-205 (4) 1.00 1.00

Pirates Burying
Treasure, Frigate
Bay — A25

Caravels,
16th
Century
A26

Designs: 1c, English two-decker, 1650. 2c, Flags of England, Spain, France, Holland and Portugal. 3c, Hilt of 17th cent. rapier. 5c, Henry Morgan and fire boats. 6c, The pirate L'Ollonois and a carrack (pirate vessel). 10c, Smugglers' ship. 15c, Spanish 17th cent. piece of eight and map of Caribbean. 20c, Garrison and ship cannon and map of Spanish Main. 25c, Humphrey Cole's astrolabe, 1574. 50c, Flintlock pistol and map of Spanish Main. 60c, Dutch Flute (ship). $1, Capt. Bartholomew Roberts and document with death sentence for his crew. $2.50, Railing piece (small cannon), 17th cent. and map of Spanish Main. $5, Francis Drake, John Hawkins and ships. $10, Edward Teach (Blackbeard) and his capture.

Wmk. 314 Upright (A25), Sideways (A26)
1970, Feb. 1   Litho.   Perf. 14
206 A25 ½c multicolored .25 .25
207 A25 1c multicolored .40 .25
208 A25 2c multicolored .25 .25
209 A25 3c multicolored .25 .25
210 A26 4c multicolored .25 .25
211 A26 5c multicolored .40 .25
212 A26 6c multicolored .40 .25
213 A26 10c multicolored .40 .25
214 A25 15c Hispanianum 2.25 .50
215 A25 15c Hispaniarum 4.50 .25
216 A26 20c multicolored .45 .25
217 A25 25c multicolored .40 .25
218 A26 50c multicolored .85 .90
219 A25 60c multicolored 1.50 .80
220 A25 $1 multicolored 1.50 .80
221 A26 $2.50 multicolored 1.50 4.50
222 A26 $5 multicolored 2.75 5.00
Nos. 206-222 (17) 18.30 15.25

Coin inscription was misspelled on No. 214, corrected on No. 215 (issued Sept. 8).

Wmk. 314 Sideways (A25), Upright (A26)
1973-74
206a A25 ½c multicolored .25 2.00
208a A25 2c multicolored .25 2.00
209a A25 3c multicolored .25 1.50
211a A26 5c multicolored .35 1.75
212a A26 6c multicolored .40 .80
213a A26 10c multicolored .50 .80
215a A25 15c multicolored .85 .85
216a A26 20c multicolored 1.00 1.40
217a A25 25c multicolored 1.25 1.75
218a A26 50c multicolored 1.75 1.75
220a A25 $1 multicolored 3.25 3.75
222A A26 $10 multi ('74) 21.00 13.00
Nos. 206a-220a,222A (12) 31.10 31.35

Issue dates: $10, Nov. 16; others, Sept. 12.

1975-77   Wmk. 373
207b A25 1c multi ('77) .40 .25
209b A25 3c multi ('76) .25 .25
210b A26 4c multi ('76) .25 .25
211b A26 5c multicolored .30 .35

212b A26 6c multicolored 1.00 .25
213b A26 10c multi ('76) .45 .25
215b A25 15c multi ('76) .55 .25
216b A26 20c multicolored 2.75 8.00
219b A25 60c multi ('76) 9.50 2.00
220b A25 $1 multi ('77) 8.00 3.00
Nos. 207b-220b (10) 23.45 14.85

Pip Meeting Convict, from "Great
Expectations" — A27

Designs: 20c, Miss Havisham from "Great Expectations." 25c, Dickens' birthplace, Portsmouth, vert. 40c, Charles Dickens, vert.

Perf. 13x13½, 13½x13
1970, May 1   Litho.   Wmk. 314
223 A27 4c gold, Prus blue & brn .25 .80
224 A27 20c gold, claret & brn .25 .25
225 A27 25c gold, violet & brn .25 .25
226 A27 40c dk blue, gold & brn .25 .35
Nos. 223-226 (4) 1.00 1.65

Charles Dickens (1812-70), English novelist.

Local
Steel
Band
A28

25c, Local string band. 40c, "A Midsummer Night's Dream," 1963 performance.

1970, Aug. 1   Perf. 13½
227 A28 20c multicolored .25 .25
228 A28 25c multicolored .25 .25
229 A28 40c multicolored .25 .25
Nos. 227-229 (3) .75 .75

Issued to publicize the 1970 Arts Festival.

St. Christopher No. 1 and St. Kitts
Post Office, 1970 — A29

Designs: 20c, 25c, St. Christopher Nos. 1 and 3. 50c, St. Christopher No. 3 and St. Kitts postmark, Sept. 2, 1871.

Wmk. 314
1970, Sept. 14   Litho.   Perf. 14½
230 A29 ½c green & rose .25 .25
231 A29 20c vio bl, rose & grn .25 .25
232 A29 25c brown, rose & grn .25 .25
233 A29 50c black, grn & dk red .30 .45
Nos. 230-233 (4) 1.05 1.20

Centenary of stamps of St. Christopher.

Holy Family, by
Anthony van
Dyck — A30

Christmas: 3c, 40c, Adoration of the Shepherds, by Frans Floris.

1970, Nov. 16   Perf. 14
234 A30 3c multicolored .25 .25
235 A30 20c ocher & multi .25 .25
236 A30 25c dull red & multi .25 .25
237 A30 40c green & multi .25 .25
Nos. 234-237 (4) 1.00 1.00

Monkey Fiddle A31

Flowers: 20c, Mountain violets. 30c, Morning glory. 50c, Fringed epidendrum.

1971, Mar. 1　Litho.　Perf. 14
238 A31 ½c multicolored .25 .40
239 A31 20c multicolored .25 .25
240 A31 30c multicolored .25 .25
241 A31 50c multicolored .30 1.00
　Nos. 238-241 (4) 1.05 1.90

Chateau de Poincy, St. Kitts — A32

Designs: 20c, Royal poinciana. 50c, De Poincy's coat of arms, vert.

1971, June 1　Litho.　Wmk. 314
242 A32 20c green & multi .25 .25
243 A32 30c dull yellow & multi .25 .25
244 A32 50c brown & multi .25 .25
　Nos. 242-244 (3) .75 .75

Philippe de Longvilliers de Poincy became first governor of French possessions in the Antilles in 1639.

East Yorks A33

Designs: 20c, Royal Artillery. 30c, French Infantry. 50c, Royal Scots.

1971, Sept. 1　　　　Perf. 14
245 A33 ½c black & multi .25 .25
246 A33 20c black & multi .30 .25
247 A33 30c black & multi .35 .25
248 A33 50c multicolored .45 .25
　Nos. 245-248 (4) 1.35 1.00

Siege of Brimstone Hill, 1782.

Crucifixion, by Quentin Massys — A34

**　　　　Perf. 14x13½**
1972, Apr. 1　Litho.　Wmk. 314
249 A34 4c brick red & multi .25 .25
250 A34 20c gray green & multi .25 .25
251 A34 30c dull blue & multi .25 .25
252 A34 40c lt brown & multi .25 .25
　Nos. 249-252 (4) 1.00 1.00

Easter 1972.

Madonna and Child, by Bergognone A35

Paintings: 20c, Adoration of the Kings, by Jacopo da Bassano, horiz. 25c, Adoration of the Shepherds, by Il Domenichino. 40c, Madonna and Child, by Fiorenzo di Lorenzo.

1972, Oct. 2　Perf. 13½x14, 14x13½
253 A35 3c gray green & multi .25 .25
254 A35 20c deep plum & multi .25 .25
255 A35 25c sepia & multi .25 .25
256 A35 40c red & multi .25 .25
　Nos. 253-256 (4) 1.00 1.00

Christmas 1972.

Silver Wedding Issue, 1972
Common Design Type
Queen Elizabeth II, Prince Philip, pelicans.

1972, Nov. 20　Photo.　Perf. 14x14½
257 CD324 20c car rose & multi .30 .25
258 CD324 25c ultra & multi .35 .25

Warner Landing at St. Kitts — A36

Designs: 25c, Settlers growing tobacco. 40c, Building fort at "Old Road." $2.50, Warner's ship off St. Kitts, Jan. 28, 1623.

1973, Jan. 28　Litho.　Perf. 14x13½
259 A36 4c pink & multi .25 .25
260 A36 25c brown & multi .25 .25
261 A36 40c blue & multi .25 .25
262 A36 $2.50 multicolored .85 1.10
　Nos. 259-262 (4) 1.60 1.85

350th anniversary of the landing of Sir Thomas Warner at St. Kitts.
For overprints see Nos. 266-269.

The Last Supper, by Juan de Juanes — A37

Easter (The Last Supper), by): 4c, Titian, vert. 25c, ascribed to Roberti, vert.

**　　Perf. 14x13½, 13½x14**
1973, Apr. 16　Photo.　Wmk. 314
263 A37 4c blue black & multi .25 .25
264 A37 25c multicolored .25 .25
265 A37 $2.50 purple & multi .80 .60
　Nos. 263-265 (3) 1.30 1.10

Nos. 259-262 Overprinted

1973, May 31　Litho.　Perf. 14x13½
266 A36 4c pink & multi .25 .25
267 A36 25c brown & multi .25 .25
268 A36 40c blue & multi .25 .25
269 A36 $2.50 multicolored .30 .30
　Nos. 266-269 (4) 1.05 1.05

Visit of Prince Charles, May 1973.

Harbor Scene and St. Kitts-Nevis No. 3 — A38

25c, Sugar mill and #2. 40c, Unloading of boat and #1. $2.50, Rock carvings and #5.

1973, Oct. 1　Litho.　Perf. 13½x14
270 A38 4c salmon & multi .25 .25
271 A38 25c lt blue & multi .40 .30
272 A38 40c multicolored .60 .50
273 A38 $2.50 multicolored 1.50 1.00
　a.　Souvenir sheet of 4, #270-273 2.75 4.50
　Nos. 270-273 (4) 2.75 2.05

70th anniv. of 1st St. Kitts-Nevis stamps.

Princess Anne's Wedding Issue
Common Design Type

1973, Nov. 14　　　　Perf. 14
274 CD325 25c brt green & multi .25 .25
275 CD325 40c citron & multi .25 .25

Virgin and Child, by Murillo — A39

Christmas (Paintings): 40c, Holy Family, by Anton Raphael Mengs. 60c, Holy Family, by Sassoferrato. $1, Holy Family, by Filippino Lippi, horiz.

1973, Dec. 1　Litho.　Perf. 14x13½
276 A39 4c brt blue & multi .25 .25
277 A39 40c orange & multi .25 .25
278 A39 60c multicolored .25 .25
279 A39 $1 multicolored .35 .35
　Nos. 276-279 (4) 1.10 1.10

Christ Carrying Cross, by Sebastiano del Piombo — A40

Easter: 25c, Crucifixion, by Goya. 40c, Trinity, by Diego Ribera. $2.50, Burial of Christ, by Fra Bartolomeo, horiz.

1974, Apr. 8　　　　Perf. 13
280 A40 4c olive & multi .25 .25
281 A40 25c lt blue & multi .25 .25
282 A40 40c purple & multi .25 .25
283 A40 $2.50 gray & multi .90 1.00
　Nos. 280-283 (4) 1.65 1.75

University Center, St. Kitts, Chancellor Hugh Wooding — A41

1974, June 1　　　　Perf. 13½
284 A41 10c blue & multi .25 .25
285 A41 $1 pink & multi .25 .25
　a.　Souvenir sheet of 2, #284-285 .55 .65

University of the West Indies, 25th anniv.

Nurse Explaining Family Planning — A42

Designs: 4c, Globe and hands reaching up, vert. 40c, Family, vert. $2.50, WPY emblem and scale balancing embryo and world.

**　　　　Wmk. 314**
1974, Aug. 5　Litho.　Perf. 14
286 A42 4c blk, blue & brn .25 .25
287 A42 25c multicolored .25 .25
288 A42 40c multicolored .25 .25
289 A42 $2.50 lilac & multi .30 .25
　Nos. 286-289 (4) 1.05 1.30

Family planning and World Population Week, Aug. 4-10.

Churchill as Lieutenant, 21st Lancers — A43

Knight of the Garter — A44

Designs: 25c, Churchill as Prime Minister. 60c, Churchill Statue, Parliament Square, London.

1974, Nov. 30
290 A43 4c dull violet & multi .25 .25
291 A43 25c yellow & multi .25 .25
292 A44 40c lt blue & multi .25 .25
293 A44 60c lt blue & multi .25 .25
　a.　Souvenir sheet of 4, #290-293 1.05 1.25
　Nos. 290-293 (4) 1.00 1.00

Sir Winston Churchill (1874-1965).

Souvenir Sheets

Boeing 747 over St. Kitts-Nevis — A45

1974, Dec. 16   *Perf. 14x13½*
294 A45 40c multicolored   .90 .90
295 A45 45c multicolored   1.00 1.00

Opening of Golden Rock Intl. Airport.

The Last Supper, by Doré — A46

Easter: 25c, Jesus mocked. 40c, Jesus falling beneath the Cross. $1, Raising the Cross. Designs based on Bible illustrations by Paul Gustave Doré (1833-1883).

1975, Mar. 24   *Perf. 14½*
296 A46 4c ultra & multi   .25 .25
297 A46 25c lt blue & multi   .25 .25
298 A46 40c bister & multi   .25 .25
299 A46 $1 salmon pink & multi   .25 .25
    Nos. 296-299 (4)   1.00 1.00

ECCA Headquarters, Basseterre, and Map of St. Kitts — A47

Designs: 25c, Specimen of $1 note, issued by ECCA. 40c, St. Kitts half dollar, 1801, and $4 coin, 1875. 45c, Nevis "9 dogs" coin, 1801, and 2c, 5c, coins, 1975.

**   *Perf. 13½x14***
1975, June 2   **Wmk. 373**
300 A47 12c orange & multi   .25 .25
301 A47 25c olive & multi   .25 .25
302 A47 40c vermilion & multi   .25 .25
303 A47 45c brt blue & multi   .25 .25
    Nos. 300-303 (4)   1.00 1.00

East Caribbean Currency Authority Headquarters, Basseterre, opening.

Evangeline Booth, Salvation Army — A48

Designs (IWY Emblem and): 25c, Sylvia Pankhurst, suffragette. 40c, Marie Curie, scientist. $2.50, Lady Annie Allen, teacher.

**   *Perf. 14x14½***
1975, Sept. 15   **Litho.**   **Wmk. 314**
304 A48 4c orange brn & blk   .40 .25
305 A48 25c lilac pur & blk   .50 .25
306 A48 40c blue, vio bl & blk   2.40 .80
307 A48 $2.50 yellow brn & blk   1.75 4.25
    Nos. 304-307 (4)   5.05 5.55

International Women's Year 1975.

Golfer Swinging Club — A49

1975, Nov. 1   *Perf. 14*
308 A49 4c rose red & blk   .85 .25
309 A49 25c yellow & blk   1.15 .25
310 A49 40c emerald & blk   1.35 .40
311 A49 $1 blue & blk   2.10 2.50
    Nos. 308-311 (4)   5.45 3.40

Opening of Frigate Bay Golf Course.

St. Paul, by Sacchi Pier Francesco A50

Christmas (Paintings, details): 40c, St. James, by Bonifazio di Pitati. 45c, St. John, by Pier Francesco Mola. $1, Virgin Mary, by Raphael.

**   Wmk. 373**
1975, Dec. 1   **Litho.**   *Perf. 14*
312 A50 25c ultra & multi   .30 .25
313 A50 40c multicolored   .45 .40
314 A50 45c red brown & multi   .50 .45
315 A50 $1 gold & multi   1.25 2.25
    Nos. 312-315 (4)   2.50 3.35

The Crucifixion — A51

The Last Supper — A52

Stained Glass Windows: No. 316, Virgin Mary. No. 317, Christ on the Cross. No. 318, St. John. 40c, The Last Supper (different). $1, Baptism of Christ.

**   *Perf. 14x13½***
1976, Apr. 14   **Litho.**   **Wmk. 373**
316 A51 4c black & multi   .25 .25
317 A51 4c black & multi   .25 .25
318 A51 4c black & multi   .25 .25
    a. A51 Triptych, #316-318   1.00 1.50
**   *Perf. 14½***
319 A52 25c black & multi   .30 .30
320 A52 40c black & multi   .35 .30
321 A52 $1 black & multi   .70 .80
    Nos. 319-321 (3)   1.35 1.40

Easter 1976. No. 318a has continuous design.

Map of West Indies, Bats, Wicket and Ball A52a

Prudential Cup — A52b

**   Unwmk.**
1976, July 8   **Litho.**   *Perf. 14*
322 A52a 12c lt blue & multi   .40 .35
323 A52b 40c lilac rose & blk   1.25 .75
    a. Souvenir sheet of 2, #322-323 5.00 5.00

World Cricket Cup, won by West Indies Team, 1975.

Crispus Attucks and Boston Massacre — A53

Designs: 40c, Alexander Hamilton and Battle of Yorktown. 45c, Thomas Jefferson and Declaration of Independence. $1, George Washington and Crossing of the Delaware.

1976, July 26   **Litho.**   **Wmk. 373**
324 A53 20c gray & multi   .25 .25
325 A53 40c gray & multi   .30 .25
326 A53 45c gray & multi   .30 .25
327 A53 $1 gray & multi   .65 .85
    Nos. 324-327 (4)   1.50 1.60

American Bicentennial.

Nativity, Sforza Book of Hours — A54

Christmas (Paintings): 40c, Virgin and Child, by Bernardino Pintoricchio. 45c, Our Lady of Good Children, by Ford Maddox Brown. $1, Christ Child, by Margaret W. Tarrant.

1976, Nov. 1   *Perf. 14*
328 A54 20c purple & multi   .25 .25
329 A54 40c dk blue & multi   .25 .25
330 A54 45c multicolored   .25 .25
331 A54 $1 multicolored   .30 .50
    Nos. 328-331 (4)   1.05 1.25

Queen Planting Tree, 1966 Visit — A55

Designs: 55c, The scepter. $1.50, Bishops paying homage to the Queen.

1977, Feb. 7   **Litho.**   *Perf. 14x13½*
332 A55 50c multicolored   .25 .25
333 A55 55c multicolored   .25 .25
334 A55 $1.50 multicolored   .25 .50
    Nos. 332-334 (3)   .75 1.00

25th anniv. of the reign of Elizabeth II.

Christ on the Cross, by Niccolo di Liberatore — A56

Easter: 30c, Resurrection (Imitator of Mantegna). 50c, Resurrection, by Ugolino, horiz. $1, Christ Rising from Tomb, by Gaudenzio.

**   Wmk. 373**
1977, Apr. 1   **Litho.**   *Perf. 14*
335 A56 25c yellow & multi   .25 .25
336 A56 30c deep blue & multi   .25 .25
337 A56 50c olive green & multi   .25 .25
338 A56 $1 red & multi   .25 .25
    Nos. 335-338 (4)   1.00 1.00

Estridge Mission A57

20c, Mission emblem. 40c, Basseterre Mission.

1977, June 27   **Litho.**   *Perf. 12½*
339 A57 4c blue & black   .25 .25
340 A57 20c multicolored   .25 .25
341 A57 40c orange yel & blk   .25 .25
    Nos. 339-341 (3)   .75 .75

Bicentenary of Moravian Mission.

Microscope, Flask, Syringe — A58

12c, Blood, fat, nerve cells. 20c, Symbol of community participation. $1, Inoculation.

1977, Oct. 11   **Litho.**   *Perf. 14*
342 A58 3c multicolored   .25 .25
343 A58 12c multicolored   .40 .60
344 A58 20c multicolored   .45 .25
345 A58 $1 multicolored   1.10 1.40
    Nos. 342-345 (4)   2.20 2.50

Pan American Health Organization, 75th anniversary (PAHO).

Nativity, West Window — A59

Christmas, Stained-glass Windows, Chartres Cathedral: 6c, Three Kings. 40c, Virgin and Child. $1, Virgin and Child, Rose Window.

1977, Nov. 15				Wmk. 373	
346	A59	4c multicolored		.25	.25
347	A59	6c multicolored		.25	.25
348	A59	40c multicolored		.35	.25
349	A59	$1 multicolored		.65	.45
		Nos. 346-349 (4)		1.50	1.20

Green Monkey and Young — A60

Green Monkeys: 5c, $1.50, Mother and young sitting on branch. 55c, like 4c.

		Wmk. 373			
1978, Apr. 15		Litho.	Perf. 14½		
350	A60	4c multicolored		.25	.25
351	A60	5c multicolored		.25	.25
352	A60	55c multicolored		.75	.30
353	A60	$1.50 multicolored		1.75	1.50
		Nos. 350-353 (4)		3.00	2.30

Elizabeth II Coronation Anniversary Issue

Common Design Types

Souvenir Sheet

		Unwmk.			
1978, Apr. 21		Litho.	Perf. 15		
354		Sheet of 6		1.00	1.00
a.	CD326	$1 Falcon of Edward III		.25	.25
b.	CD327	$1 Elizabeth II		.25	.25
c.	CD328	$1 Pelican		.25	.25

No. 354 contains 2 se-tenant strips of Nos. 354a-354c, separated by horizontal gutter with commemorative and descriptive inscriptions and showing central part of coronation procession with coach.

Tomatoes A61

Designs: 2c, Defense Force band. 5c, Radio and TV station. 10c, Technical College. 12c, TV assembly plant. 15c, Sugar cane harvest. 25c, Craft Center. 30c, Cruise ship. 40c, Sea crab and lobster. 45c, Royal St. Kitts Hotel and golf course. 50c, Pinneys Beach, Nevis. 55c, New Runway at Golden Rock. $1, Cotton pickers. $5, Brewery. $10, Pineapples and peanuts.

		Perf. 14½x14			
1978, Sept. 8				Wmk. 373	
355	A61	1c multicolored		.25	.25
356	A61	2c multicolored		.25	.25
357	A61	5c multicolored		.25	.25
358	A61	10c multicolored		.25	.25
359	A61	12c multicolored		.25	.75
360	A61	15c multicolored		.25	.25
361	A61	25c multicolored		.25	.25
362	A61	30c multicolored		1.50	1.50
363	A61	40c multicolored		.45	.25
364	A61	45c multicolored		2.75	1.25
365	A61	50c multicolored		.35	.25
366	A61	55c multicolored		1.25	.25
367	A61	$1 multicolored		.40	.40
368	A61	$5 multicolored		.75	1.25
369	A61	$10 multicolored		1.25	1.75
		Nos. 355-369 (15)		10.45	9.15

For overprints see Nevis Nos. 100-112, O1-O10.

Investiture — A62

Designs: 10c, Map reading. 25c, Pitching tent. 40c, Cooking. 50c, First aid. 55c, Rev. W. A. Beckett, founder of Scouting in St. Kitts.

		Wmk. 373			
1978, Oct. 9		Litho.	Perf. 13½		
370	A62	5c multicolored		.25	.25
371	A62	10c multicolored		.25	.25
372	A62	25c multicolored		.35	.35
373	A62	40c multicolored		.45	.50
374	A62	50c multicolored		.50	.60
375	A62	55c multicolored		.60	.65
		Nos. 370-375 (6)		2.40	2.60

50th anniversary of St. Kitts-Nevis Scouting.

King Bringing Gift — A63

Christmas: 15c, 30c, King bringing gift, diff. $2.25, Three Kings paying homage to Infant Jesus.

1978, Dec. 1			Perf. 14x13½		
376	A63	5c multicolored		.25	.25
377	A63	15c multicolored		.25	.25
378	A63	30c multicolored		.25	.25
379	A63	$2.25 multicolored		.25	.50
		Nos. 376-379 (4)		1.00	1.25

Canna Coccinea — A64

Flowers: 30c, Heliconia bihai. 55c, Ruellia tuberosa. $1.50, Gesneria ventricosa.

1979, Mar. 19			Perf. 14		
380	A64	5c multicolored		.25	.25
381	A64	30c multicolored		.40	.40
382	A64	55c multicolored		.50	.50
383	A64	$1.50 multicolored		.85	1.60
		Nos. 380-383 (4)		2.00	2.75

See Nos. 393-396.

Rowland Hill and St. Christopher No. 1 — A65

Rowland Hill and: 15c, St. Kitts-Nevis #233. 50c, Great Britain #4. $2.50, St. Kitts-Nevis #64.

1979, July 2		Litho.	Perf. 14½		
384	A65	5c multicolored		.25	.25
385	A65	15c multicolored		.25	.25
386	A65	50c multicolored		.30	.35
387	A65	$2.50 multicolored		.65	1.10
		Nos. 384-387 (4)		1.45	1.95

Sir Rowland Hill (1795-1879), originator of penny postage.

The Woodman's Daughter, by Millais — A66

Paintings by John Everett Millais and IYC Emblem: 25c, Cherry Ripe. 30c, The Rescue, horiz. 55c, Bubbles. $1, Christ in the House of His Parents.

1979, Nov. 12		Litho.	Perf. 14		
388	A66	5c multicolored		.25	.25
389	A66	25c multicolored		.30	.30
390	A66	30c multicolored		.30	.30
391	A66	55c multicolored		.40	.40
		Nos. 388-391 (4)		1.25	1.25

Souvenir Sheet

392	A66	$1 multicolored		1.25	1.25

Christmas 1979; Intl. Year of the Child.

Flower Type of 1979

Flowers: 4c, Clerodendrum aculeatum. 55c, Inga laurina. $1.50, Epidendrum difforme. $2, Salvia serontina.

1980, Feb. 4		Litho.	Perf. 14		
393	A64	4c multicolored		.40	.25
394	A64	55c multicolored		.50	.30
395	A64	$1.50 multicolored		1.75	1.75
396	A64	$2 multicolored		.90	2.25
		Nos. 393-396 (4)		3.55	4.55

Nevis Lagoon, London 1980 Emblem — A67

30c, Fig Tree Church, vert. 55c, Nisbet Plantation. $3, Lord Nelson, by Fuger, vert. 75c, Nelson Falling, by D. Dighton.

1980, May 6		Litho.	Perf. 13½		
397	A67	5c shown		.25	.25
398	A67	30c multicolored		.30	.30
399	A67	55c multicolored		.50	.50
400	A67	$3 multicolored		2.50	2.50
		Nos. 397-400 (4)		3.55	3.55

Souvenir Sheet

401	A67	75c multicolored		2.50	2.00

London 80 Intl. Phil. Exhib., May 6-14; Lord Nelson, (1758-1805).

WAR TAX STAMPS

No. 12 Overprinted

1916		Wmk. 3	Perf. 14		
MR1	A1	½p deep green		1.10	.55

Type of 1905-18 Issue Overprinted

WAR STAMP

1918					
MR2	A1	1½p orange		1.75	1.00

OFFICIAL STAMPS

Catalogue values for unused stamps in this section are for Never Hinged items.

Nos. 359, 361, 363-369 Overprinted: **OFFICIAL**

		Perf. 14½x14			
1980		Litho.		Wmk. 373	
O1	A61	12c multicolored		.80	1.25
O2	A61	25c multicolored		.25	.25
O3	A61	40c multicolored		.55	.50
O4	A61	45c multicolored		3.50	2.00
O5	A61	50c multicolored		.40	.45
O6	A61	55c multicolored		1.45	.50
O7	A61	$1 multicolored		.75	2.25
O8	A61	$5 multicolored		.85	2.50
O9	A61	$10 multicolored		1.50	3.50
		Nos. O1-O9 (9)		10.05	13.20

ST. LUCIA

sānt ˈlü-shə

LOCATION — Island in the West Indies, one of the Windward group
GOVT. — Independent state in British Commonwealth
AREA — 240 sq. mi.
POP. — 154,020 (1999 est.)
CAPITAL — Castries

The British colony of St. Lucia became an associated state March 1, 1967, and independent in 1979.

12 Pence = 1 Shilling
100 Cents = 1 Dollar (1949)

> Catalogue values for unused stamps in this country are for Never Hinged items, beginning with Scott 127 in the regular postage section, Scott C1 in the air post section, Scott J3 in the postage due section, and Scott O1 in the officials section.

Watermarks

Wmk. 5 — Small Star

Wmk. 380 — "POST OFFICE"

Values for unused stamps are for examples with original gum as defined in the catalogue introduction. Very fine examples of Nos. 1-26 will have perforations touching the design on at least one side due to the narrow spacing of the stamps on the plates. Stamps with perfs clear of the framelines on all four sides are very scarce and will command higher prices.

Queen Victoria — A1

Perf. 14 to 16

			Engr.	Wmk. 5
1860, Dec. 18				
1	A1	(1p) rose red	110.00	75.00
a.	Double impression		2,500.	
b.	Horiz. pair, imperf vert.			

2	A1	(4p) blue	250.00	175.00
a.	Horiz. pair, imperf vert.			
3	A1	(6p) green	325.00	225.00
a.	Horiz. pair, imperf vert.			
	Nos. 1-3 (3)		685.00	475.00

For types overprinted see Nos. 15, 17, 19-26.

1863		**Wmk. 1**	**Perf. 12½**	
4	A1	(1p) lake	95.00	110.00
5	A1	(4p) slate blue	140.00	150.00
6	A1	(6p) emerald	225.00	225.00
	Nos. 4-6 (3)		460.00	485.00

Nos. 4-6 exist imperforate on stamp paper, from proof sheets.

1864				
7	A1	(1p) black	30.00	14.00
8	A1	(4p) yellow	210.00	50.00
a.	(4p) olive yellow		425.00	100.00
b.	(4p) lemon yellow		1,750.	
9	A1	(6p) lilac	140.00	42.50
a.	(6p) lilac		210.00	32.50
b.	(6p) deep lilac		160.00	42.50
10	A1	(1sh) red orange	250.00	32.50
a.	(1sh) orange		275.00	32.50
c.	Horiz. pair, imperf between		—	
	Nos. 7-10 (4)		630.00	139.00

Nos. 7-10 exist imperforate on stamp paper, from proof sheets.

Perf. 14

11	A1	(1p) deep black	50.00	22.00
a.	Horiz. pair, imperf between		—	
12	A1	(4p) yellow	130.00	24.00
a.	(4p) olive yellow		325.00	105.00
13	A1	(6p) pale lilac	125.00	24.00
a.	(6p) deep lilac		125.00	45.00
b.	(6p) violet		275.00	57.50
14	A1	(1sh) deep orange	175.00	19.00
a.	(1sh) orange		250.00	25.00
	Nos. 11-14 (4)		480.00	89.00

Type of 1860 Surcharged in Black or Red

a   b

1881				
15	A1(a)	½p green	85.00	120.00
17	A1(b)	2½p scarlet	60.00	27.50

1883-84		**Wmk. Crown and CA (2)**		
19	A1(a)	½p green	37.50	50.00
20	A1(a)	1p black (R)	52.50	16.00
a.	Half used as ½p on cover			
21	A1(a)	4p yellow	325.00	24.00
22	A1(a)	6p violet	50.00	50.00
23	A1(a)	1sh orange	310.00	190.00
	Nos. 19-23 (5)		775.00	330.00

1884			**Perf. 12**	
24	A1(a)	4p yellow	300.00	32.50

Nos. 5 & 6 Surcharged

1885		**Wmk. 1**	**Perf. 12½**	
25	A1	½p emerald	77.50	
26	A1	6p slate blue	1,500.	

Nos. 25 and 26 were prepared for use but not issued.

A5

For explanation of dies A and B see "Dies of British Colonial Stamps…" in the catalogue Table of Contents.

1883-98		**Typo.**	**Wmk. 2**	**Perf. 14**	
27	A5	½p green ('91)		4.00	1.25
a.	Die A ('83)			17.50	10.00
28	A5	1p rose		55.00	19.00
29	A5	1p lilac ('91)		7.00	.35
a.	Die A ('86)			15.00	7.25
b.	Imperf., pair			900.00	
30	A5	2p ultra & brn org ('98)		6.00	1.25
31	A5	2½p ultra ('91)		14.00	1.25
a.	Die A ('83)			75.00	3.00
32	A5	3p lilac & grn ('91)		10.00	6.50
a.	Die A ('86)			150.00	20.00
33	A5	4p brown ('93)		8.00	3.00
a.	Die A ('85)			50.00	1.50
b.	Imperf., pair			1,050.	
34	A5	6p violet ('86)		300.00	240.00
a.	Imperf., pair			2,000.	
35	A5	6p lilac & blue ('87)		7.00	18.00
a.	Die A ('87)			40.00	29.00
36	A5	1sh brn org ('85)		450.00	175.00
37	A5	1sh lil & red ('91)		14.00	6.00
a.	Die A ('87)			150.00	37.50
38	A5	5sh lil & org ('91)		60.00	175.00
39	A5	10sh lil & blk ('91)		110.00	175.00
	Nos. 27-39 (13)			1,043.	821.60

Nos. 32, 32a, 35a and 33a Surcharged in Black

No. 40   No. 41   No. 42

1892					
40	A5	½p on 3p lil & grn		95.00	30.00
b.	Double surcharge			1,000.	800.00
c.	Inverted surcharge			2,450.	800.00
d.	Triple surcharge, one on back			1,350.	1,500.
41	A5	½p on half of 6p lilac & blue		32.50	4.00
a.	Slanting serif			240.00	150.00
c.	Without the bar of "½"			325.00	160.00
d.	"2" of "½" omitted			575.00	600.00
e.	Surcharged sideways			1,700.	
f.	Double surcharge			725.00	725.00
g.	Triple surcharge			1,450.	
42	A5	1p on 4p brown		9.00	4.75
b.	Double surcharge			275.00	
c.	Inverted surcharge			1,100.	950.00
d.	Thick diagonal stroke in first "N"			30.00	24.00
e.	Thick diagonal stroke in second "N"			30.00	24.00
	Nos. 40-42 (3)			136.50	38.75

No. 40 is found with wide or narrow "O" in "ONE," and large or small "A" in "HALF." For more detailed listings, see the *Scott Classic Specialized Catalogue of Stamps and Covers.*

Edward VII — A9

Numerals of 3p, 6p, 1sh and 5sh of type A9 are in color on plain tablet.

1902-03			**Typo.**	
43	A9	½p violet & green	4.50	1.90
44	A9	1p violet & car rose	6.50	.90
46	A9	2½p violet & ultra	40.00	8.00

47	A9	3p violet & yellow	9.50	10.00
48	A9	1sh green & black	17.00	50.00
	Nos. 43-48 (5)		77.50	70.80

The Pitons — A10

Wmk. 1 sideways

1902, Dec. 16			**Engr.**	
49	A10	2p brown & green	16.00	2.50

Fourth centenary of the discovery of the island by Columbus.

1904-05		**Typo.**	**Wmk. 3**	
50	A9	½p violet & green	11.50	.65
a.	Chalky paper		13.00	1.40
51	A9	1p violet & car rose	9.00	1.40
a.	Chalky paper		12.00	1.40
52	A9	2½p violet & ultra	40.00	2.75
a.	Chalky paper		18.00	5.00
53	A9	3p violet & yellow	13.00	3.25
54	A9	6p vio & dp vio ('05)	27.50	35.00
a.	Chalky paper		21.00	47.50
55	A9	1sh green & blk ('05)	50.00	32.50
56	A9	5sh green & car ('05)	85.00	200.00
	Nos. 50-56 (7)		236.00	275.55

No. 55 is on chalky paper only.

1907-10				
57	A9	½p green	2.00	1.10
58	A9	1p carmine	4.75	.35
59	A9	2½p ultra	4.25	2.00

Chalky Paper

60	A9	3p violet, yel ('09)	3.25	19.00
61	A9	6p violet & red vio ('10)	9.25	40.00
a.	6p violet & dull vio ('10)	75.00	90.00
62	A9	1sh black, grn ('09)	5.25	8.75
63	A9	5sh grn & red, yel ('05)	67.50	77.50
	Nos. 57-63 (7)		96.25	148.70

King George V
A11   A12

Numerals of 3p, 6p, 1sh and 5sh of type A11 are in color on plain tablet.

For description of dies I and II see "Dies of British Colonial Stamps" in Table of Contents.

Die I

1912-19			**Ordinary Paper**	
64	A11	½p deep green	.75	.50
65	A11	1p scarlet	9.00	.25
a.	1p carmine		2.00	.25
66	A12	2p gray ('13)	1.60	4.50
67	A11	2½p bright blue	4.50	3.00

Chalky Paper
Numeral on White Tablet

68	A11	3p violet, yel	1.40	2.50
a.	Die II		30.00	60.00
69	A11	6p vio & red vio	2.25	21.00
70	A11	1sh black, green	7.00	5.50
a.	1sh black, bl grn, ol back	17.50	19.00
71	A11	1sh fawn	20.00	50.00
72	A11	5sh grn & red, yel	26.50	85.00
	Nos. 64-72 (9)		73.00	172.25

A13   A14

1913-14   **Chalky Paper**
73 A13 4p scar & blk, yel 1.00 2.25
74 A14 2sh6p blk & red, bl 25.00 50.00

Surface-colored Paper
75 A13 4p scarlet & blk, yel .75 1.60

Die II
1921-24 Wmk. 4 Ordinary Paper
76 A11 ½p green 1.25 .55
77 A11 1p carmine 14.50 20.00
78 A11 1p dk brn ('22) 1.60 .25
79 A13 1½p rose red ('22) .85 2.75
80 A12 2p gray .85 .25
81 A11 2½p ultra 7.50 3.00
82 A11 2½p orange ('24) 16.00 60.00
83 A11 3p dull blue ('24) 7.00 12.00

Chalky Paper
84 A11 3p violet, yel 3.75 13.50
85 A13 4p scar & blk, yel ('24) 1.40 2.75
86 A11 6p vio & red vio 2.50 5.25
87 A11 1sh fawn 7.50 3.50
88 A14 2sh6p blk & red, bl ('24) 20.00 36.00
89 A11 5sh grn & red, yel 60.00 95.00
    Nos. 76-89 (14) 144.70 254.80

Common Design Types pictured following the introduction.

Silver Jubilee Issue
Common Design Type
1935, May 6 Engr. Perf. 13½x14
91 CD301 ½p green & blk .30 2.00
92 CD301 2p gray blk & ultra .95 1.40
93 CD301 2½p blue & brn 1.25 1.40
94 CD301 1sh brt vio & ind 13.50 16.00
    Nos. 91-94 (4) 16.00 20.80
    Set, never hinged 26.00

Port Castries A15

Columbus Square, Castries A16

Ventine Falls A17

Soldiers' Monument A19

Fort Rodney, Pigeon Island A18

Government House A20

Seal of the Colony A21

Center in Black
1936, Mar. 1 Perf. 14
95 A15 ½p light green .35 .55
a. Perf. 13x12 5.50 26.00
96 A16 1p dark brown .45 .25
a. Perf. 13x12 10.00 4.25
97 A17 1½p carmine .70 .35
a. Perf. 12x13 17.50 2.50
98 A15 2p gray .60 .25
99 A16 2½p blue .60 .25
100 A17 3p dull green 1.50 .75
101 A15 4p brown 2.00 1.25
102 A16 6p orange 2.00 1.25
103 A18 1sh lt bl, perf. 13x12 3.50 2.50
104 A19 2sh6p ultra 15.00 14.00
105 A20 5sh violet 19.00 25.00
106 A21 10sh car rose, perf. 13x12 60.00 100.00
    Nos. 95-106 (12) 105.70 146.40
    Set, never hinged 225.00

Nos. 95a, 96a and 97a are coils.
Issue date: Nos. 95a, 96a, Apr. 8.

Coronation Issue
Common Design Type
1937, May 12 Perf. 11x11½
107 CD302 1p dark purple .25 .40
108 CD302 1½p dark carmine .40 .25
109 CD302 2½p deep ultra .40 1.40
    Nos. 107-109 (3) 1.05 2.05
    Set, never hinged 1.50

King George VI — A22

Columbus Square, Castries A23

Government House A24

The Pitons A25

Loading Bananas A26

Arms of the Colony — A27

Perf. 12½ (#110-111, 1½p-3½p, 8p, 3sh, 5sh, £1), 12 (6p, 1sh, 2sh, 10sh)
1938-48
110 A22 ½p green ('43) .25 .25
a. Perf. 14½x14 1.40 .25
111 A22 1p deep violet .25 .25
a. Perf. 14½x14 2.00 .85

112 A22 1p red, Perf. 14½x14 ('47) .25 .25
a. Perf. 12½ .65 .85
113 A22 1½p carmine ('43) 1.00 1.40
a. Perf. 14½x14 1.40 .50
114 A22 2p gray ('43) .25 .25
a. Perf. 14½x14 2.25 1.75
115 A22 2½p ultra ('43) .25 .25
a. Perf. 14½x14 3.00 .25
116 A22 2½p violet ('47) .85 .25
117 A22 3p red org ('43) .25 .25
a. Perf. 14½x14 1.00 .25
118 A22 3½p brt ultra ('47) .85 .25
119 A23 6p magenta ('48) 6.50 1.75
a. Perf. 13½ 2.00 .50
120 A22 8p choc ('46) 2.75 .40
121 A24 1sh lt brn ('48) .75 .40
a. Perf. 13½ 1.10 .40
122 A25 2sh red vio & sl bl 3.50 1.50
123 A22 3sh brt red vio ('46) 6.75 2.00
124 A26 5sh rose vio & blk 10.00 11.00
125 A27 10sh black, yel 7.50 9.00
126 A22 £1 sepia ('46) 9.00 8.00
    Nos. 110-126 (17) 50.95 37.45
    Set, never hinged 75.00

See Nos. 135-148.

Catalogue values for unused stamps in this section, from this point to the end of the section, are for Never Hinged items.

Peace Issue
Common Design Type
Perf. 13½x14
1946, Oct. 8 Wmk. 4 Engr.
127 CD303 1p lilac .25 .30
128 CD303 3½p deep blue .25 .30

Silver Wedding Issue
Common Design Types
1948, Nov. 26 Photo. Perf. 14x14½
129 CD304 1p scarlet .25 .25

Perf. 11½x11
Engraved; Name Typographed
130 CD305 £1 violet brown 22.00 40.00

UPU Issue
Common Design Types
Engr.; Name Typo. on 6c, 12c.
Perf. 13½, 11x11½
1949, Oct. 10 Wmk. 4
131 CD306 5c violet .25 .85
132 CD307 6c deep orange 1.60 2.50
133 CD308 12c red lilac .30 .25
134 CD309 24c blue green .40 .25
    Nos. 131-134 (4) 2.55 3.85

Types of 1938
Values in Cents and Dollars
1949, Oct. 1 Engr. Perf. 12½
135 A22 1c green .35 .25
a. Perf. 14 3.25 .50
136 A22 2c rose lilac 1.25 .25
a. Perf. 14½x14 4.50 1.25
137 A22 3c red 1.60 2.50
138 A22 4c gray .95 .25
a. Perf. 14½x14 18,800.
139 A22 5c violet 1.75 .25
140 A22 6c red orange 1.25 3.50
141 A22 7c ultra 4.00 3.00
142 A22 12c rose lake 6.75 4.00
a. Perf. 14½x14 ('50) 750.00 550.00
143 A22 16c brown 5.75 .65

Perf. 11½
144 A27 24c Prus blue .75 .25
145 A27 48c olive green 1.75 1.60
146 A27 $1.20 purple 2.75 10.00
147 A27 $2.40 blue green 4.50 20.00
148 A27 $4.80 dk car rose 11.50 21.00
    Nos. 135-148 (14) 44.90 67.50

Nos. 144 to 148 are of a type similar to A27, but with the denomination in the top corners and "St. Lucia" at the bottom.
For overprints see Nos. 152-155.

University Issue
Common Design Types
Perf. 14x14½
1951, Feb. 16 Wmk. 4
149 CD310 3c red & gray black .55 .75
150 CD311 12c brn car & blk .85 .75

Phoenix Rising from Burning Buildings — A28

Engr. & Typo.
1951, June 19 Perf. 13½x13
151 A28 12c dp blue & car .50 1.10
Reconstruction of Castries.

Nos. 136, 138, 139 and 142 Overprinted in Black

1951, Sept. 25 Perf. 12½
152 A22 2c rose lilac .25 .85
153 A22 4c gray .25 .60
154 A22 5c violet .25 .85
155 A22 12c rose lilac .45 .85
    Nos. 152-155 (4) 1.20 2.90

Adoption of a new constitution for the Windward Islands, 1951.

Coronation Issue
Common Design Type
1953, June 2 Engr. Perf. 13½x13
156 CD312 3c carmine & black .70 .35

Queen Elizabeth II A29

Arms of St. Lucia A30

1953-54 Engr. Perf. 14½x14
157 A29 1c green .25 .25
158 A29 2c rose lilac .25 .25
159 A29 3c red .25 .25
160 A29 4c gray .25 .25
161 A29 5c violet .25 .25
162 A29 6c orange .25 .25
163 A29 8c rose lake .40 .25
164 A29 10c ultra .25 .25
165 A29 15c brown .35 .25

Perf. 11x11½
166 A30 25c Prus blue .40 .25
167 A30 50c brown olive 5.00 .50
168 A30 $1 blue green 4.75 2.50
169 A30 $2.50 dark car rose 6.00 4.75
    Nos. 157-169 (13) 18.65 10.25

Issued: 2c, 10/28; 4c, 1/7/54; 1c, 5c, 4/1/54; others, 9/2/54.

West Indies Federation
Common Design Type
Perf. 11½x11
1958, Apr. 22 Wmk. 314
170 CD313 3c green .40 .25
171 CD313 6c blue .65 1.75
172 CD313 12c carmine rose 1.00 .80
    Nos. 170-172 (3) 2.05 2.80

16th Century Ship and Pitons — A31

1960, Jan. 1 Perf. 12½x13
173 A31 8c carmine rose .40 .40
174 A31 10c orange .50 .50
175 A31 25c dark blue .60 .60
    Nos. 173-175 (3) 1.50 1.50

Granting of new constitution.

St. Lucia Stamp
of 1860 — A32

1960, Dec. 18   Engr.   Perf. 13½
176 A32 5c ultra & red brown   .25   .25
177 A32 16c yel grn & blue blk   .30   .75
178 A32 25c carmine & green   .30   .25
    Nos. 176-178 (3)   .85 1.25
Centenary of St. Lucia's first postage
stamps.

Freedom from Hunger Issue
Common Design Type
1963, June 4   Photo.   Perf. 14x14½
179 CD314 25c green   .40   .40

Red Cross Centenary Issue
Common Design Type
Wmk. 314
1963, Sept. 2   Litho.   Perf. 13
180 CD315 4c black & red   .25   .25
181 CD315 25c ultra & red   1.00 1.00

A33

A34

Fishing
Boats,
Soufrière
Bay — A35

Designs: 15c, Pigeon Island. 25c, Reduit
Beach. 35c, Castries Harbor. 50c, The Pitons.
$1, Vigie Beach, vert. $2.50, Queen Elizabeth
II, close-up.

Wmk. 314
1964, Mar. 1   Photo.   Perf. 14½
182 A33 1c dark car rose   .30   .25
183 A33 2c violet   .50   .60
184 A33 4c brt blue green   1.30   .35
185 A33 5c slate blue   .40   .25
186 A33 6c brown   1.30 2.00
187 A34 8c lt blue & multi   .30   .25
188 A34 10c multicolored   .60   .25
189 A35 12c multicolored   .70 1.25
190 A35 15c blue & ocher   .30   .25
    a. Wmkd. sideways ('68)   .30   .25
191 A35 25c multicolored   .50   .25
192 A35 35c dk blue & buff   1.75   .25
193 A35 50c brt blue, blk &
        yel   2.10 .25
194 A35 $1 multicolored   2.75 2.00
195 A35 $2.50 blue & buff   4.25 2.25
    Nos. 182-195 (14)   17.05 10.45
For overprints see Nos. 215-225.

Shakespeare Issue
Common Design Type
1964, Apr. 23   Perf. 14x14½
196 CD316 10c bright green   .45   .25

ITU Issue
Common Design Type
Perf. 11x11½
1965, May 17   Litho.   Wmk. 314
197 CD317 2c red lil & brt pink   .25   .25
198 CD317 50c lilac & yel grn   1.00 1.00

Intl. Cooperation Year Issue
Common Design Type
1965, Oct. 25   Wmk. 314   Perf. 14½
199 CD318 1c blue grn & claret   .25   .25
200 CD318 25c lt violet & grn   .30   .30

Churchill Memorial Issue
Common Design Type
1966, Jan. 24   Photo.   Perf. 14
**Design in Black, Gold and Carmine
Rose**
201 CD319 4c bright blue   .25   .25
202 CD319 6c green   .25   .25
203 CD319 25c brown   .40   .40
204 CD319 35c violet   .60   .60
    Nos. 201-204 (4)   1.50 1.50

Royal Visit Issue
Common Design Type
1966, Feb. 4   Litho.   Perf. 11x12
205 CD320 4c violet blue   .40   .35
206 CD320 25c dk carmine rose   1.10 1.00

World Cup Soccer Issue
Common Design Type
1966, July 1   Litho.   Perf. 14
207 CD321 4c multicolored   .30   .25
208 CD321 25c multicolored   .85   .65

WHO Headquarters Issue
Common Design Type
1966, Sept. 20   Litho.   Perf. 14
209 CD322 4c multicolored   .25   .25
210 CD322 25c multicolored   .55   .55

UNESCO Anniversary Issue
Common Design Type
1966, Dec. 1   Litho.   Perf. 14
211 CD323 4c "Education"   .25   .25
212 CD323 12c "Science"   .35   .35
213 CD323 25c "Culture"   .55   .55
    Nos. 211-213 (3)   1.15 1.15

Associated State
**Nos. 183, 185-194 Overprinted in
Red: "STATEHOOD / 1st MARCH
1967"**
Wmk. 314
1967, Mar. 1   Photo.   Perf. 14½
215 A33 2c violet   .35   .35
216 A33 5c slate blue   .25   .25
217 A33 6c brown   .25   .25
218 A34 8c lt blue & multi   .35   .25
219 A34 10c multicolored   .50   .25
220 A35 12c multicolored   1.10   .30
221 A35 15c blue & ocher   1.40 1.40
222 A35 25c multicolored   1.40 1.10
223 A35 35c dk blue & buff   1.40 1.60
224 A35 50c multicolored   1.40 1.75
225 A35 $1 multicolored   1.40 2.00
    Nos. 215-225 (11)   9.80 9.50
    The 1c and $2.50, similarly overprinted,
were not sold to the public at the post office
but were acknowledged belatedly (May 10) by
the government and declared valid. Values for
both stamps: unused $6; used $9.
    The 1c, 6c and $2.50 overprints exist in
black as well as red. No. 213 also exists with
this overprint in blue and in black.

Madonna and
Child with St.
John, by
Raphael — A36

1967, Oct. 16   Wmk. 314   Perf. 14½
227 A36 4c black, gold & multi   .25   .25
228 A36 25c multicolored   .25   .25
    Christmas 1967.

Cricket Batsman
and Gov.
Frederick
Clarke — A37

Perf. 14½x14
1968, Mar. 8   Photo.   Wmk. 314
229 A37 10c multicolored   .25   .25
230 A37 35c multicolored   .40   .40
    Visit of the Marylebone Cricket Club to the
West Indies, Jan.-Feb. 1968.

"Noli me Tangere,"
by Titian — A38

Easter: 10c, 25c, The Crucifixion, by
Raphael.

1968, Mar. 25   Perf. 14½
231 A38 10c multicolored   .25   .25
232 A38 15c multicolored   .25   .25
233 A38 25c multicolored   .25   .25
234 A38 35c multicolored   .25   .25
    Nos. 231-234 (4)   1.00 1.00

Martin Luther
King, Jr. — A39

Perf. 13½x14
1968, July 4   Photo.   Wmk. 314
235 A39 25c dp blue, blk & brn   .25   .25
236 A39 35c violet, blk & brn   .25   .25
    Dr. Martin Luther King, Jr. (1929-68), Ameri-
can civil rights leader.

Virgin and Child in
Glory, by
Murillo — A40

Christmas: 10c, 35c, Virgin and Child, by
Bartolomé E. Murillo.

Perf. 14½x14
1968, Oct. 17   Photo.   Wmk. 314
237 A40 5c dark blue & multi   .25   .25
238 A40 10c multicolored   .25   .25
239 A40 25c red brown & multi   .25   .25
240 A40 35c deep blue & multi   .25   .25
    Nos. 237-240 (4)   1.00 1.00

Purple-throated Carib — A41

Birds: 15c, 35c, St. Lucia parrot.

1969, Jan. 10   Litho.   Perf. 14½
241 A41 10c multicolored   .70   .70
242 A41 15c multicolored   .90   .90
243 A41 25c multicolored   1.10 1.10
244 A41 35c multicolored   1.25 1.25
    Nos. 241-244 (4)   3.95 3.95

Ecce Homo, by
Guido Reni — A42

Painting: 15c, 35c, The Resurrection, by Il
Sodoma (Giovanni Antonio de Bazzi).

Perf. 14½x14
1969, Mar. 20   Photo.   Wmk. 314
245 A42 10c purple & multi   .25   .25
246 A42 15c green & multi   .25   .25
247 A42 25c black & multi   .25   .25
248 A42 35c ocher & multi   .25   .25
    Nos. 245-248 (4)   1.00 1.00
    Easter 1969.

Map of Caribbean — A43

Design: 25c, 35c, Clasped hands and
arrows with names of CARIFTA members.

1969, May 29   Wmk. 314   Perf. 14
249 A43 5c violet blue & multi   .25   .25
250 A43 10c deep plum & multi   .25   .25
251 A43 25c ultra & multi   .25   .25
252 A43 35c green & multi   .25   .25
    Nos. 249-252 (4)   1.00 1.00
    First anniversary of CARIFTA (Caribbean
Free Trade Area).

Silhouettes of Napoleon and
Josephine — A44

Perf. 14½x13
1969, Sept. 22   Photo.   Unwmk.
**Gold Inscription; Gray and Brown
Medallions**
253 A44 15c dull blue   .25   .25
254 A44 25c deep claret   .25   .25
255 A44 35c deep green   .25   .25
256 A44 50c yellow brown   .25   .55
    Nos. 253-256 (4)   1.00 1.30
    Napoleon Bonaparte, 200th birth anniv.

Madonna and
Child, by Paul
Delaroche — A45

Christmas: 10c, 35c, Holy Family, by
Rubens.

Perf. 14½x14
1969, Oct. 27   Photo.   Wmk. 314
Center Multicolored
257 A45 5c dp rose lil & gold   .25   .25
258 A45 10c Prus blue & gold   .25   .25
259 A45 25c maroon & gold   .25   .25
260 A45 35c dp yel grn & gold   .25   .25
    Nos. 257-260 (4)   1.00 1.00

House of Assembly — A46

Queen
Elizabeth II, by
A. C. Davidson-
Houston
A47

2c, Roman Catholic Cathedral. 4c, Castries Boulevard. 5c, Castries Harbor. 6c, Sulphur springs. 10c, Vigie Airport. 12c, Reduit beach. 15c, Pigeon Island. 25c, The Pitons & sailboat. 35c, Marigot Bay. 50c, Diamond Waterfall. $1, St. Lucia flag & motto. $2.50, Coat of arms. $10, Map of St. Lucia.

Wmk. 314 Sideways, Upright (#271-274)

1970-73		Litho.	Perf. 14½	
261	A46	1c multicolored	.25	.25
262	A46	2c multicolored	.25	.25
a.		Wmk. upright	.90	.90
263	A46	4c multicolored	1.00	.25
a.		Wmk. upright	1.75	1.75
264	A46	5c multicolored	1.50	.25
265	A46	6c multicolored	.25	.25
266	A46	10c multicolored	2.00	.25
267	A46	12c multicolored	.30	.25
268	A46	15c multicolored	.40	.25
269	A46	25c multicolored	1.00	.25
270	A46	35c multicolored	.50	.25
271	A47	50c multicolored	.85	.80
272	A47	$1 multicolored	.50	.70
273	A47	$2.50 multicolored	.75	1.75
274	A47	$5 multicolored	1.75	4.00
274A	A47	$10 multicolored	5.50	9.00
		Nos. 261-274A (15)	16.80	18.75

Issued: #261-274, Feb. 1, 1970; #274A, Dec. 3, 1973; #262a, 263a, Mar. 15, 1974.

1975, July 28			Wmk. 373	
263b	A46	4c multicolored	1.10	2.10
264a	A46	5c multicolored	1.40	1.00
266a	A46	10c multicolored	2.00	1.75
268a	A46	15c multicolored	3.00	2.25
		Nos. 263b-268a (4)	7.50	7.10

The Three Marys
at the Tomb, by
Hogarth — A48

35c, The Sealing of the Tomb. $1, The Ascension. The designs are from the altarpiece painted by William Hogarth for the Church of St. Mary Redcliffe in Bristol, 1755-56.

Roulette 8½xPerf. 12½

1970, Mar. 7		Litho.	Wmk. 314	
		Size: 27x54mm		
275	A48	25c dark brown & multi	.25	.25
276	A48	35c dark brown & multi	.25	.25
		Size: 38x54mm		
277	A48	$1 dark brown & multi	.40	.40
a.		Triptych (#275-277)	1.20	1.20

Easter 1970.
Nos. 275-277 printed se-tenant in sheets of 30 (10 triptychs) with the center $1 stamp 10mm raised compared to the flanking 25c and 35c stamps.

Charles Dickens and Characters from his Works — A49

1970, June 8		Wmk. 314	Perf. 14	
278	A49	1c brown & multi	.25	.25
279	A49	25c Prus blue & multi	.30	.25
280	A49	35c brown red & multi	.35	.30
281	A49	50c red lilac & multi	.40	1.00
		Nos. 278-281 (4)	1.30	1.80

Charles Dickens (1812-70), English novelist.

Nurse Holding Red Cross Emblem A50

15c, 35c, British, St. Lucia & Red Cross flags.

Perf. 14½x14

1970, Aug. 18		Litho.	Wmk. 314	
282	A50	10c multicolored	.25	.25
283	A50	15c multicolored	.25	.25
284	A50	25c buff & multi	.35	.40
285	A50	35c multicolored	.45	.40
		Nos. 282-285 (4)	1.30	1.30

Centenary of British Red Cross Society.

Madonna with the Lilies, by Luca della Robbia A51

Lithographed and Embossed

1970, Nov. 16		Unwmk.	Perf. 11	
286	A51	5c dark blue & multi	.25	.25
287	A51	10c violet blue & multi	.25	.25
288	A51	35c car lake & multi	.30	.25
289	A51	40c deep green & multi	.30	.30
		Nos. 286-289 (4)	1.10	1.05

Christmas 1970.

Christ on the Cross, by Rubens — A52

Easter: 15c, 40c, Descent from the Cross, by Peter Paul Rubens.

Perf. 14x13½

1971, Mar. 29		Litho.	Wmk. 314	
290	A52	10c dull green & multi	.25	.25
291	A52	15c dull red & multi	.25	.25
292	A52	35c brt blue & multi	.30	.25
293	A52	40c multicolored	.30	.40
		Nos. 290-293 (4)	1.10	1.15

Moule à Chique Lighthouse — A53

Design: 25c, Beane Field Airport.

1971, Apr. 30			Perf. 14½x14	
294	A53	5c olive & multi	.35	.25
295	A53	25c bister & multi	.55	.25

Opening of Beane Field Airport.

View of Morne Fortune (Old Days) — A54

The "a" stamp shows an old print (as shown) and the "b" stamp a contemporary photograph of the same view (plain frame). 10c, Castries City. 25c, Pigeon Island. 50c, View from Government House.

Perf. 13½x14

1971, Aug. 10		Litho.	Wmk. 314	
296	A54	5c Pair, #a.-b.	.40	.40
297	A54	10c Pair, #a.-b.	.50	.50
298	A54	25c Pair, #a.-b.	.60	.60
299	A54	50c Pair, #a.-b.	1.10	1.10
		Nos. 296-299 (4)	2.60	2.60

Virgin and Child, by Verrocchio — A55

Virgin and Child painted by: 10c, Paolo Moranda. 35c, Giovanni Battista Cima. 40c, Andrea del Verrocchio.

1971, Oct. 15			Perf. 14	
304	A55	5c green & multi	.25	.25
305	A55	10c brown & multi	.25	.25
306	A55	35c ultra & multi	.25	.25
307	A55	40c red & multi	.25	.25
		Nos. 304-307 (4)	1.00	1.00

Christmas 1971.

St. Lucia, School of Dolci, and Arms — A56

1971, Dec. 13			Perf. 14x14½	
308	A56	5c gray & multi	.25	.25
309	A56	10c lt green & multi	.25	.25
310	A56	25c tan & multi	.35	.25
311	A56	50c lt blue & multi	.75	.75
		Nos. 308-311 (4)	1.60	1.50

National Day.

Lamentation, by Carracci A57

Easter: 25c, 50c, Angels Weeping over Body of Jesus, by Guercino.

1972, Feb. 15			Wmk. 314	
312	A57	10c lt violet & multi	.25	.25
313	A57	25c ocher & multi	.25	.25
314	A57	35c ultra & multi	.35	.25
315	A57	50c lt green & multi	.45	.45
		Nos. 312-315 (4)	1.30	1.20

Teachers' College and Science Building — A58

15c, University Center and coat of arms. 25c, Secondary School. 35c, Technical College.

1972, Apr. 18		Litho.	Perf. 14	
316	A58	5c multicolored	.25	.25
317	A58	15c multicolored	.25	.25
318	A58	25c multicolored	.25	.25
319	A58	35c multicolored	.25	.25
		Nos. 316-319 (4)	1.00	1.00

Opening of Morne Educational Complex.

Steam Conveyance Co. Stamp and Map of St. Lucia — A59

Designs: 10c, Castries Harbor and 3c stamp. 35c, Soufriere Volcano and 1c stamp. 50c, One cent, 3c, 6c stamps.

1972, June 22			Perf. 14½	
320	A59	5c yellow & multi	.25	.25
321	A59	10c violet blue & multi	.25	.25
322	A59	35c car rose & multi	.65	.25
323	A59	50c emerald & multi	1.10	1.25
		Nos. 320-323 (4)	2.25	2.00

Centenary of St. Lucia Steam Conveyance Co. Ltd. postal service.

Holy Family, by Sebastiano Ricci — A60

1972, Oct. 18			Perf. 14½x14	
324	A60	5c dk brown & multi	.25	.25
325	A60	10c green & multi	.25	.25
326	A60	35c carmine & multi	.25	.25
327	A60	40c dk blue & multi	.30	.25
		Nos. 324-327 (4)	1.05	1.00

Christmas 1972.

Silver Wedding Issue
Common Design Type

Design: Queen Elizabeth II, Prince Philip, St. Lucia coat of arms and St. Lucia parrot.

1972, Nov.		Photo.	Perf. 14x14½	
328	CD324	15c car rose & multi	.30	.30
329	CD324	35c olive & multi	.45	.45

Weekday Headdress A61

Women's Headdresses: 10c, For church wear. 25c, Unmarried girl. 50c, Formal occasions.

1973, Feb. 1		Wmk. 314	Perf. 13	
330	A61	5c multicolored	.25	.25
331	A61	10c dark gray & multi	.25	.25
332	A61	25c multicolored	.25	.25
333	A61	50c slate blue & multi	.25	.85
		Nos. 330-333 (4)	1.00	1.60

Arms of
St. Lucia — A62

Coil Stamps

1973, Apr. 19   Litho.   Perf. 14½x14
334	A62	5c gray olive	.35	.70
a.		Watermark sideways ('76)	.80	2.00
335	A62	10c blue	.35	.70
a.		Watermark sideways ('76)	.80	2.00
336	A62	25c claret	.35	.70
a.		Watermark sideways ('76)	14.00	
		Nos. 334-336 (3)	1.05	2.10

H.M.S.
St. Lucia
A63

Designs: Old Sailing ships.

1973, May 24   Litho.   Perf. 13½x14
337	A63	15c shown	.25	.25
338	A63	35c "Prince of Wales"	.35	.35
339	A63	50c "Oliph Blossom"	.50	.50
340	A63	$1 "Rose"	1.10	1.10
a.		Souv. sheet of 4, #337-340, perf. 15	2.50	2.50
		Nos. 337-340 (4)	2.20	2.20

Banana Plantation and Flower — A64

Designs: 15c, Aerial spraying. 35c, Washing and packing bananas. 50c, Loading.

1973, July 26   Litho.   Perf. 14
341	A64	5c multicolored	.25	.25
342	A64	15c multicolored	.25	.25
343	A64	35c multicolored	.25	.25
344	A64	50c multicolored	.55	.55
		Nos. 341-344 (4)	1.30	1.30

Banana industry.

Madonna and
Child, by Carlo
Maratta — A65

Christmas (Paintings): 15c, Virgin in the Meadow, by Raphael. 35c, Holy Family, by Angelo Bronzino. 50c, Madonna of the Pear, by Durer.

1973, Oct. 17   Litho.   Perf. 14x13½
345	A65	5c citron & multi	.25	.25
346	A65	15c ultra & multi	.25	.25
347	A65	35c dp green & multi	.25	.25
348	A65	50c red & multi	.25	.25
		Nos. 345-348 (4)	1.00	1.00

Princess Anne's Wedding Issue
Common Design Type

1973, Nov. 14   Wmk. 314   Perf. 14
349	CD325	40c gray green & multi	.25	.25
350	CD325	50c lilac & multi	.25	.25

The Betrayal of Christ, by
Ugolino — A66

Easter (Paintings by Ugolino, 14th Cent.): 35c, The Way to Calvary. 80c, Descent from the Cross. $1, Resurrection.

1974, Apr. 1   Perf. 13½x13
351	A66	5c ocher & multi	.25	.25
352	A66	35c ocher & multi	.25	.25
353	A66	80c ocher & multi	.25	.25
354	A66	$1 ocher & multi	.25	.30
a.		Souvenir sheet of 4, #351-354	1.75	1.75
		Nos. 351-354 (4)	1.00	1.05

3 Escalins,
1798 — A67

Pieces of Eight: 35c, 6 escalins, 1798. 40c, 2 livres 5 sols, 1813. $1, 6 livres 15 sols, 1813.

1974, May 20   Perf. 13½
355	A67	15c lt olive & multi	.25	.25
356	A67	35c multicolored	.25	.25
357	A67	40c green & multi	.35	.35
358	A67	$1 brown & multi	.65	.65
a.		Souvenir sheet of 4, #355-358	2.00	2.00
		Nos. 355-358 (4)	1.50	1.50

Coins of Old St. Lucia.

Baron de Laborie,
1784 — A68

Portraits: 35c, Sir John Moore, Lieutenant Governor, 1796-97. 80c, Major General Sir Dudley St. Leger Hill, 1834-37. $1, Sir Frederick Joseph Clarke, 1967-71.

Wmk. 314
1974, Aug. 29   Litho.   Perf. 14½
359	A68	5c ocher & multi	.25	.25
360	A68	35c brt blue & multi	.25	.25
361	A68	80c violet & multi	.25	.25
362	A68	$1 multicolored	.25	.25
a.		Souvenir sheet of 4, #359-362	1.00	1.00
		Nos. 359-362 (4)	1.00	1.00

Past Governors of St. Lucia.

Virgin and Child,
by
Verrocchio — A69

Christmas (Virgin and Child): 35c, by Andrea della Robbia. 80c, by Luca della Robbia. $1, by Antonio Rossellino.

1974, Nov. 13   Wmk. 314   Perf. 13½
363	A69	5c gray & multi	.25	.25
364	A69	35c pink & multi	.25	.25
365	A69	80c brown & multi	.25	.25
366	A69	$1 olive & multi	.25	.25
a.		Souvenir sheet of 4, #363-366	1.25	2.25
		Nos. 363-366 (4)	1.00	1.00

Churchill and Gen.
Montgomery — A70

Design: $1, Churchill and Pres. Truman.

1974, Nov. 30   Perf. 14
367	A70	5c multicolored	.25	.25
368	A70	$1 multicolored	.30	.35

Sir Winston Churchill (1874-1965).

Crucifixion, by
Van der
Weyden — A71

Easter: 35c, "Noli me Tangere," by Julio Romano. 80c, Crucifixion, by Fernando Gallego. $1, "Noli me Tangere," by Correggio.

Perf. 14x13½
1975, Mar. 27   Wmk. 314
369	A71	5c brown & multi	.25	.25
370	A71	35c ultra & multi	.25	.25
371	A71	80c red brown & multi	.25	.25
372	A71	$1 green & multi	.25	.35
		Nos. 369-372 (4)	1.00	1.10

Nativity — A72   Adoration of the
                      Kings — A73

No. 375, Virgin & Child. No. 376, Adoration of the Shepherds. 40c, Nativity. $1, Virgin & Child with Sts. Catherine of Alexandria and Siena.

Wmk. 314
1975, Dec.   Litho.   Perf. 14½
373	A72	5c lilac rose & multi	.25	.25
374	A73	10c yellow & multi	.25	.25
375	A73	10c yellow & multi	.25	.25
376	A73	10c yellow & multi	.25	.25
a.		Strip of 3, #374-376	.40	.40
377	A72	40c yellow & multi	.30	.30
378	A72	$1 blue & multi	.70	.70
a.		Souv. sheet of 3, #373, 377-378	1.10	1.25
		Nos. 373-378 (6)	2.00	2.00

Christmas 1975.

"Hanna," First US Warship — A74

Revolutionary Era Ships: 1c, "Prince of Orange," British packet. 2c, "Edward," British sloop. 5c, "Millern," British merchantman. 15c, "Surprise," Continental Navy lugger. 35c, "Serapis," British warship. 50c, "Randolph," first Continental Navy frigate. $1, Frigate "Alliance."

Perf. 14½
1976, Jan. 26   Litho.   Unwmk.
379-386	A74	Set of 8	3.50	3.50
386a		Souv. sheet, #383-386, perf. 13	3.50	3.50

American Bicentennial.

Laughing
Gull — A75

Birds: 2c, Little blue heron. 4c, Belted kingfisher. 5c, St. Lucia parrot. 6c, St. Lucia oriole. 8c, Brown trembler. 10c, American kestrel. 12c, Red-billed tropic bird. 15c, Common gallinule. 25c, Brown noddy. 35c, Sooty tern. 50c, Osprey. $1, White-breasted thrasher. $2.50, St. Lucia black finch. $5, Rednecked pigeon. $10, Caribbean elaenia.

Wmk. 314 (1c); 373 (others)
1976, May 7   Litho.   Perf. 14½
387	A75	1c gray & multi	.30	1.40
388	A75	2c gray & multi	.30	1.40
389	A75	4c gray & multi	.35	1.40
390	A75	5c gray & multi	1.60	1.10
391	A75	6c gray & multi	1.10	1.10
392	A75	8c gray & multi	1.25	2.25
393	A75	10c gray & multi	1.10	.40
394	A75	12c gray & multi	1.75	2.50
395	A75	15c gray & multi	1.10	.25
396	A75	25c gray & multi	1.60	1.00
397	A75	35c gray & multi	2.75	1.40
398	A75	50c gray & multi	5.25	3.75
399	A75	$1 gray & multi	3.25	3.75
400	A75	$2.50 gray & multi	6.00	6.75
401	A75	$5 gray & multi	6.50	4.75
402	A75	$10 gray & multi	6.00	8.00
		Nos. 387-402 (16)	40.20	41.20

Map of
West
Indies,
Bats,
Wicket
and Ball
A75a

Prudential
Cup — A75b

1976, July 19   Unwmk.   Perf. 14
403	A75a	50c lt blue & multi	.90	.90
404	A75b	$1 lilac rose & black	1.75	1.75
a.		Souvenir sheet of 2, #403-404	5.00	5.50

World Cricket Cup, won by West Indies Team, 1975.

Arms of H.M.S.
Ceres — A76

Coats of Arms of Royal Naval Ships: 20c, Pelican. 40c, Ganges. $2, Ariadne.

1976, Sept. 6   Wmk. 373   Perf. 14½
405	A76	10c gold & multi	.35	.30
406	A76	20c gold & multi	.65	.60
407	A76	40c gold & multi	.95	.85
408	A76	$2 gold & multi	2.40	2.40
		Nos. 405-408 (4)	4.35	4.15

Madonna and Child, by Murillo — A77

Paintings: 20c, Virgin and Child, by Lorenzo Costa. 50c, Madonna and Child, by Adriaea Isenbrandt. $2, Madonna and Child with St. John, by Murillo. $2.50, Like 10c.

1976, Nov. 15   Litho.   Perf. 14½

409	A77	10c multicolored	.25	.25
410	A77	20c multicolored	.25	.25
411	A77	50c multicolored	.25	.25
412	A77	$2 multicolored	.70	.70
		Nos. 409-412 (4)	1.45	1.45

Souvenir Sheet

413	A77	$2.50 multicolored	1.40	1.40

Christmas.

Elizabeth II, "Palms and Water" — A78

Wmk. 373

1977, Feb. 7   Litho.   Perf. 14½

414	A78	10c multicolored	.25	.25
415	A78	20c multicolored	.25	.25
416	A78	40c multicolored	.25	.25
417	A78	$2 multicolored	.25	.25
		Nos. 414-417 (4)	1.00	1.00

Souvenir Sheet

418	A78	$2.50 multicolored	.75	1.00

25th anniv. of the reign of Elizabeth II.

Scouts of Tapion School — A79

1c, Sea Scouts, St. Mary's College. 2c, Scout giving oath. 10c, Tapion School Cub Scouts. 20c, Venture Scout, Soufrière. 50c, Scout from Gros Islet Division. $1, $2.50, Boat drill, St. Mary's College.

1977, Oct. 17   Unwmk.   Perf. 15

419	A79	½c multicolored	.25	.25
420	A79	1c multicolored	.25	.25
421	A79	2c multicolored	.25	.25
422	A79	10c multicolored	.25	.25
423	A79	20c multicolored	.25	.25
424	A79	50c multicolored	.40	.40
425	A79	$1 multicolored	.90	.90
		Nos. 419-425 (7)	2.55	2.55

Souvenir Sheet

426	A79	$2.50 multicolored	2.00	2.00

6th Caribbean Boy Scout Jamboree, Kingston, Jamaica, Aug. 5-14.

Nativity, by Giotto — A80

Christmas (Virgin and Child by): 1c, Fra Angelico. 2c, El Greco. 20c, Caravaggio. 50c,

Velazquez. $1, Tiepolo. $2.50, Adoration of the Kings, by Tiepolo.

1977, Oct. 31   Litho.   Perf. 14

427-433	A80	Set of 7	2.00	2.00

Suzanne Fourment in Velvet Hat, by Rubens — A81

Rubens Paintings: 35c, Rape of the Sabine Women (detail). 50c, Ludovicus Nonnius, portrait. $2.50, Minerva Protecting Pax from Mars (detail).

Perf. 14x14½

1977, Nov. 28   Litho.   Wmk. 373

434	A81	10c multicolored	.25	.25
435	A81	35c multicolored	.25	.25
436	A81	50c multicolored	.30	.30
437	A81	$2.50 multicolored	1.60	1.60
a.		Souv. sheet, #434-437, perf. 15	3.00	3.00
		Nos. 434-437 (4)	2.40	2.40

Peter Paul Rubens (1577-1640).

Yeoman of the Guard and Life Guard A82

Dress Uniforms: 20c, Groom and postilion. 50c, Footman and coachman. $3, State trumpeter and herald. $5, Master of the Queen's House and Gentleman at Arms.

Unwmk.

1978, June 2   Litho.   Perf. 14

438	A82	15c multicolored	.25	.25
439	A82	20c multicolored	.25	.25
440	A82	50c multicolored	.30	.30
441	A82	$3 multicolored	.50	.50
		Nos. 438-441 (4)	1.30	1.30

Souvenir Sheet

442	A82	$5 multicolored	.90	.90

25th anniv. of coronation of Elizabeth II. Nos. 438-441 exist in miniature sheets of 3 plus label, perf. 12.

Queen Angelfish A83

Tropical Fish: 20c, Four-eyed butterflyfish. 50c, French angelfish. $2, Yellowtail damselfish. $2.50, Rock beauty.

1978, June 19   Litho.   Perf. 14½

443	A83	10c multicolored	.25	.25
444	A83	20c multicolored	.40	.25
445	A83	50c multicolored	.70	.50
446	A83	$2 multicolored	2.25	2.25
		Nos. 443-446 (4)	3.60	3.25

Souvenir Sheet

447	A83	$2.50 multicolored	3.75	3.75

French Grenadier, Map of Battle — A84

30c, British Grenadier & Bellin map of St. Lucia, 1762. 50c, British fleet opposing French landing & map of coast from Gros Islet to Cul-de-Sac. $2.50, Light infantrymen & Gen. James Grant.

1978, Nov. 15   Litho.   Perf. 14

448	A84	10c multicolored	.50	.25
449	A84	30c multicolored	.75	.35
450	A84	50c multicolored	1.00	.60
451	A84	$2.50 multicolored	2.50	2.50
		Nos. 448-451 (4)	4.75	3.70

Bicent. of Battle of St. Lucia (Cul-de-Sac).

Annunciation A85

Christmas: 55c, 80c, Adoration of the Kings.

Perf. 14x14½

1978, Dec. 4   Wmk. 373

452	A85	30c multicolored	.25	.25
453	A85	50c multicolored	.25	.25
454	A85	55c multicolored	.30	.30
455	A85	80c multicolored	.40	.40
		Nos. 452-455 (4)	1.20	1.20

Independent State

Hewanorra Airport A86

Independence: 30c, New coat of arms. 50c, Government house and Allen Lewis, first Governor General. $2, Map of St. Lucia, French, St. Lucia and British flags.

1979, Feb. 22   Litho.   Perf. 14

456	A86	10c multicolored	.25	.25
457	A86	30c multicolored	.25	.25
458	A86	50c multicolored	.25	.25
459	A86	$2 multicolored	.50	.50
a.		Souvenir sheet of 4, #456-459	1.50	1.50
		Nos. 456-459 (4)	1.25	1.25

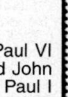

Paul VI and John Paul I A87

Pope Paul VI and: 30c, Pres. Anwar Sadat of Egypt. 50c, Secretary General U Thant and UN emblem. 55c, Prime Minister Golda Meir of Israel. $2, Martin Luther King, Jr.

1979, May 7   Litho.   Perf. 14

460	A87	10c multicolored	.25	.25
461	A87	30c multicolored	.30	.25
462	A87	50c multicolored	.40	.40
463	A87	55c multicolored	.50	.45
464	A87	$2 multicolored	1.50	1.50
		Nos. 460-464 (5)	2.95	2.85

In memory of Popes Paul VI and John Paul I.

Jersey Cows A88

Agricultural Diversification: 35c, Fruits and vegetables. 50c, Waterfall (water conservation). $3, Coconuts, copra industry.

1979, July 2   Litho.   Perf. 14

465	A88	10c multicolored	.25	.25
466	A88	35c multicolored	.25	.25
467	A88	50c multicolored	.25	.25
468	A88	$3 multicolored	.60	.60
		Nos. 465-468 (4)	1.35	1.35

Lindbergh's Route over St. Lucia, Puerto Rico-Paramaribo — A89

1979, Nov.   Litho.   Perf. 14

469	A89	10c Lindbergh, hydro-plane	.40	.25
470	A89	30c shown	.45	.25
471	A89	50c Landing at La Toc	.60	.40
472	A89	$2 Flight covers	1.65	1.65
		Nos. 469-472 (4)	3.10	2.55

Lindbergh's inaugural airmail flight (US-Guyana) via St. Lucia, 50th anniversary.

Prince of Saxony, by Cranach the Elder — A90

IYC (Emblem and): 50c, Infanta Margarita, by Velazquez. $2, Girl Playing Badminton, by Jean Baptiste Chardin. $2.50, Mary and Francis Wilcox, by Stock. $5, Two Children, by Pablo Picasso.

1979, Dec. 17   Litho.   Perf. 14

473	A90	10c multicolored	.25	.25
474	A90	50c multicolored	.25	.25
475	A90	$2 multicolored	.50	.50
476	A90	$2.50 multicolored	.50	.50
		Nos. 473-476 (4)	1.50	1.50

Souvenir Sheet

477	A90	$5 multicolored	2.00	2.00

A91

Maltese Cross Cancels and: 10c, Penny Post notice, 1839. 50c, Hill's original stamp design. $2, St. Lucia #1. $2.50, Penny Black. $5, Hill portrait.

1979, Dec. 27

478	A91	10c multicolored	.25	.25
479	A91	50c multicolored	.25	.25
480	A91	$2 multicolored	.25	.50
481	A91	$2.50 multicolored	.40	.60
		Nos. 478-481 (4)	1.15	1.60

Souvenir Sheet

482	A91	$5 multicolored	1.25	1.25

Sir Rowland Hill (1793-1879), originator of penny postage. Nos. 478-481 also issued in sheets of 5 plus label, perf. 12x12½.

A92

IYC Emblem, Virgin and Child Paintings by: 10c, Virgin and Child, by Bernardino Fungi, IYC emblem. 50c, Carlo Dolci. $2, Titian. $2.50, Giovanni Bellini.

1980, Jan. 14

483	A92	10c multicolored	.25	.25
484	A92	50c multicolored	.25	.25
485	A92	$2 multicolored	.75	.75
486	A92	$2.50 multicolored	1.00	1.00
a.		Souvenir sheet of 4, #483-486	2.50	2.50
		Nos. 483-486 (4)	2.25	2.25

Christmas 1979; Intl. Year of the Child.

St. Lucia
Conveyance
Co. Ltd.
Stamp,
1873
A92a

London 1980 Emblem and Covers: 30c, "Assistance" 1p postmark, 1879. 50c, Postage due handstamp, 1929. $2, Postmarks on 1844 cover.

Wmk. 373

1980, May 6   Litho.   Perf. 14

487	A92a	10c multicolored	.25	.25
488	A92a	30c multicolored	.25	.25
489	A92a	50c multicolored	.25	.25
490	A92a	$2 multicolored	.25	.25
a.		Souvenir sheet of 4, #487-490	.80	.80
		Nos. 487-490 (4)	1.00	1.00

London 1980 Intl. Stamp Exhib., May 6-14.

Intl. Year of
the
Child — A93

½c, Mickey on rocket. 1c, Donald Duck spacewalking. 2c, Minnie Mouse on moon. 3c, Goofy hitch hiking. 4c, Goofy on moon. 5c, Pluto digging on moon. 10c, Donald Duck, space creature. $2, Donald Duck paddling satellite. $2.50, Mickey Mouse in lunar rover. $5, Goofy on moon.
Space scenes. 1c, 4c, 5c, 10c, $2, $2.50 horiz.

1980, May 29   Litho.   Perf. 11

491	A93	½c multicolored	.25	.25
492	A93	1c multicolored	.25	.25
493	A93	2c multicolored	.25	.25
494	A93	3c multicolored	.25	.25
495	A93	4c multicolored	.25	.25
496	A93	5c multicolored	.25	.25
497	A93	10c multicolored	.25	.25
498	A93	$2 multicolored	1.75	1.75
499	A93	$2.50 multicolored	1.75	1.75
		Nos. 491-499 (9)	5.25	5.25

Souvenir Sheet

500	A93	$5 multicolored	4.50	4.50

Queen
Mother
Elizabeth,
80th
Birthday
A94

1980, Aug. 4   Litho.   Perf. 14

501	A94	10c multicolored	.25	.25
502	A94	$2.50 multicolored	.40	1.00

Souvenir Sheet
Perf. 12½x12

503	A94	$3 multicolored	.80	.80

HS-748 on Runway, St. Lucia Airport,
Hewanorra — A95

10c, DC-10, St. Lucia Airport. 15c, Bus, Castries. 20c, Refrigerator ship. 25c, Islander

plane. 30c, Pilot boat. 50c, Boeing 727. 75c, Cruise ship. $1, Lockheed Tristar, Piton Mountains. $2, Cargo ship. $5, Boeing 707. $10, Queen Elizabeth 2.

Wmk. 373

1980, Aug. 11   Litho.   Perf. 14½

504	A95	5c shown	.30	.30
505	A95	10c multicolored	.50	.30
506	A95	15c multicolored	.35	.40
507	A95	20c multicolored	.35	.40
508	A95	25c multicolored	.50	.40
509	A95	30c multicolored	.40	.45
510	A95	50c multicolored	.75	.75
511	A95	75c multicolored	.60	1.75
512	A95	$1 multicolored	.75	1.50
513	A95	$2 multicolored	1.40	2.40
514	A95	$5 multicolored	3.50	6.00
515	A95	$10 multicolored	6.75	10.00
		Nos. 504-515 (12)	16.15	24.65

For surcharges see Nos. 531-533.

1984, May 15   Wmk. 380

507a	A95	20c	2.50	2.50
508a	A95	25c	3.25	3.25
509a	A95	30c	3.25	3.25
512a	A95	$1	6.50	6.50
513a	A95	$2	7.50	7.50
515a	A95	$10	15.00	15.00
		Nos. 507a-515a (6)	38.00	38.00

Shot Put, Moscow '80 Emblem — A96

1980, Sept. 22   Litho.   Perf. 14

516	A96	10c shown	.25	.25
517	A96	50c Swimming	.25	.25
518	A96	$2 Gymnastics	.90	.90
519	A96	$2.50 Weight lifting	1.10	1.10
		Nos. 516-519 (4)	2.50	2.50

Souvenir Sheet

520	A96	$5 Passing the torch	2.00	2.00

22nd Summer Olympic Games, Moscow, July 19-Aug. 3.

A97

1980, Sept. 30   Perf. 14

521	A97	10c Palms, coast at dusk	.25	.25
522	A97	50c Rocky shore	.25	.25
523	A97	$2 Sand beach	.40	.40
524	A97	$2.50 Pitons at sunset	.50	.50
		Nos. 521-524 (4)	1.40	1.40

Souvenir Sheet

525	A97	$5 Two-master	1.75	1.75

Rotary International, 75th Anniversary.

A98

Nobel Prize Winners: 10c, Sir Arthur Lewis, Economics. 50c, Martin Luther King, Jr., peace, 1964. $2, Ralph Bunche, peace, 1950. $2.50, Albert Schweitzer, peace, 1952. $5, Albert Einstein, physics, 1921.

1980, Oct. 23   Litho.   Perf. 14

526	A98	10c multicolored	.25	.25
527	A98	50c multicolored	.25	.25
528	A98	$2 multicolored	.60	.60
529	A98	$2.50 multicolored	1.00	1.00
		Nos. 526-529 (4)	2.10	2.10

Souvenir Sheet

530	A98	$5 multicolored	2.75	2.75

Nos. 506-507, 510 Surcharged

1980, Nov. 3   Litho.   Perf. 14½

531	A95	$1.50 on 15c multi	.35	.35
532	A95	$1.50 on 20c multi	.35	.35
533	A95	$1.50 on 50c multi	.35	.35
		Nos. 531-533 (3)	1.05	1.05

Nativity, by
Battista — A99

Angel and Citizens of St.
Lucia — A100

Christmas: 30c, Adoration of the Kings, by Bruegel the Elder. $2, Adoration of the Shepherds, by Murillo.

1980, Dec. 1   Perf. 14

534	A99	10c multicolored	.25	.25
535	A99	30c multicolored	.25	.25
536	A99	$2 multicolored	.45	.45
		Nos. 534-536 (3)	.95	.95

Souvenir Sheet

537	A100	Sheet of 3	1.00	1.00
a.		$1 any single	.30	.30

Agouti — A101

1981, Jan. 19   Litho.   Perf. 14

538	A101	10c shown	.25	.25
539	A101	50c St. Lucia parrot	.75	.25
540	A101	$2 Purple-throated carib	2.25	1.30
541	A101	$2.50 Fiddler crab	1.75	1.75
		Nos. 538-541 (4)	5.00	3.55

Souvenir Sheet

542	A101	$5 Monarch butterfly	4.00	4.00

Royal Wedding Issue
Common Design Type

1981, June 16   Litho.   Perf. 14

543	CD331	25c Couple	.25	.25
544	CD331a	50c Clarence House	.25	.25
545	CD331a	$4 Charles	.30	.30
		Nos. 543-545 (3)	.80	.80

Nos. 543-545 also printed in sheets of 5 plus label, perf. 12, in changed colors.

Souvenir Sheet

546	CD331	$5 Glass coach	.70	.70
549	CD331	Booklet	5.50	5.50
a.		Pane of 1, $5, Couple	2.00	2.00
b.		Pane of 6 (3x50c, Diana, 3x$2, Charles)	3.50	3.50

A102

Picasso Birth Centenary: 30c, The Cock. 50c, Man with Ice Cream. 55c, Woman Dressing her Hair. $3, Seated Woman. $5, Night Fishing at Antibes.

1981, May   Litho.   Perf. 14

550	A102	30c multicolored	.25	.25
551	A102	50c multicolored	.30	.30
552	A102	55c multicolored	.35	.35
553	A102	$3 multicolored	1.75	1.75
		Nos. 550-553 (4)	2.65	2.65

Souvenir Sheet

554	A102	$5 multicolored	3.50	3.50

A103

10c, Industry. 35c, Community service. 50c, Hikers. $2.50, Duke of Edinburgh.

Wmk. 373

1981, Sept. 28   Litho.   Perf. 14½

555	A103	10c multicolored	.25	.25
556	A103	35c multicolored	.25	.25
557	A103	50c multicolored	.25	.25
558	A103	$2.50 multicolored	.30	.30
		Nos. 555-558 (4)	1.05	1.05

Duke of Edinburgh's Awards, 25th anniv.

Intl. Year
of the
Disabled
A104

1981, Oct. 30   Litho.   Perf. 14

559	A104	10c Louis Braille	.25	.25
560	A104	50c Sarah Bernhardt	.25	.25
561	A104	$2 Joseph Pulitzer	.70	.70
562	A104	$2.50 Henri de Toulouse-Lautrec	1.10	1.10
		Nos. 559-562 (4)	2.30	2.30

Souvenir Sheet

563	A104	$5 Franklin D. Roosevelt	1.75	1.75

A105

Christmas: Adoration of the King Paintings.

1981, Dec. 15
564	A105	10c Sfoza	.25	.25
565	A105	30c Orcanga	.25	.25
566	A105	$1.50 Gerard	.50	.50
567	A105	$2.50 Foppa	1.00	1.00
		Nos. 564-567 (4)	2.00	2.00

A106

1981, Dec. 29   Unwmk.
568	A106	10c No. 1	.25	.25
569	A106	30c No. 251	.25	.25
570	A106	50c No. 459	.40	.40
571	A106	$2 UPU, St. Lucia flags	1.30	1.30
		Nos. 568-571 (4)	2.20	2.20

Souvenir Sheets
572	A106	$5 GPO, Castries	2.00	2.00

First anniv. of UPU membership.

A107

1980s Decade for Women (Paintings of Women by Women): 10c, Fanny Travis Cochran, by Cecilia Beaux. 50c, Women with Dove, by Marie Laurencin. $2, Portrait of a Young Pupil of David. $2.50, Self-portrait, by Rosalba Carriera. $5, Self-portrait, by Elisabeth Vigee-Le Brun.

Unwmk.
1981, Dec. 1   Litho.   Perf. 14
573	A107	10c multicolored	.25	.25
574	A107	50c multicolored	.25	.25
575	A107	$2 multicolored	.75	.50
576	A107	$2.50 multicolored	1.00	1.00
		Nos. 573-576 (4)	2.25	2.00

Souvenir Sheet
577	A107	$5 multicolored	1.50	1.50

1982 World Cup Soccer A108

Designs: Various soccer players.

1982, Feb. 15   Litho.   Perf. 14½
578	A108	10c multicolored	.40	.40
579	A108	50c multicolored	1.40	1.40
580	A108	$2 multicolored	1.75	1.75
581	A108	$2.50 multicolored	2.00	2.00
		Nos. 578-581 (4)	5.55	5.55

Souvenir Sheet
582	A108	$5 multicolored	4.00	4.00

Battle of the Saints
Bicentenary — A109

10c, Pigeon Island 35c, Battle. 50c, Admirals Rodney, DeGrasse. $2.50, Map.

Wmk. 373
1982, Apr. 13   Litho.   Perf. 14
583	A109	10c multicolored	.40	.40
584	A109	35c multicolored	.80	.80
585	A109	50c multicolored	1.20	1.20
586	A109	$2.50 multicolored	4.25	4.25
a.		Souvenir sheet of 4, #583-586	8.50	8.50
		Nos. 583-586 (4)	6.65	6.65

Scouting Year — A110

1982, Aug. 4   Litho.   Perf. 14
587	A110	10c Map reading	.25	.25
588	A110	50c First aid	.25	.25
589	A110	$1.50 Camping	1.25	1.25
590	A110	$2.50 Campfire sing	2.00	2.00
		Nos. 587-590 (4)	3.75	3.75

Princess Diana Issue
Common Design Type
Perf. 14½x14
1982, Sept. 1   Unwmk.
591	CD332	50c Leeds Castle	.30	.30
592	CD332	$2 Diana	1.50	1.50
593	CD332	$4 Wedding	2.40	2.40
		Nos. 591-593 (3)	4.20	4.20

Souvenir Sheet
594	CD332	$5 Diana, diff.	4.50	4.50

Christmas 1982 — A111

Paintings: 10c, Adoration of the Kings, by Brueghel the Elder. 30c, Nativity, by Lorenzo Costa. 50c, Virgin and Child, Fra Filippo Lippi. 80c, Adoration of the Shepherds, by Nicolas Poussin.

Wmk. 373
1982, Nov. 10   Litho.   Perf. 14
595	A111	10c multicolored	.25	.25
596	A111	30c multicolored	.25	.25
597	A111	50c multicolored	.40	.40
598	A111	80c multicolored	.70	.70
		Nos. 595-598 (4)	1.60	1.60

A111a

1983, Mar. 14   Litho.
599	A111a	10c Twin Peaks	.30	.30
600	A111a	30c Beach	.40	.40
601	A111a	50c Banana harvester	.30	.30
602	A111a	$2 Flag	1.75	1.75
		Nos. 599-602 (4)	2.75	2.75

Commonwealth day.

Crown Agents
Sesquicentennial
A112

Wmk. 373
1983, Apr. 1   Litho.   Perf. 14½
603	A112	10c Headquarters, London	.25	.25
604	A112	15c Road construction	.25	.25
605	A112	50c Map	.25	.25
606	A112	$2 First stamp	1.25	1.25
		Nos. 603-606 (4)	2.00	2.00

World Communications Year — A113

10c, Shipboard intercommunication. 50c, Air-to-air. $1.50, Satellite. $2.50, Computer communications. $5, Weather satellite.

Unwmk.
1983, July 12   Litho.   Perf. 15
607	A113	10c multicolored	.25	.25
608	A113	50c multicolored	.55	.55
609	A113	$1.50 multicolored	1.25	1.25
610	A113	$2.50 multicolored	2.00	2.00
		Nos. 607-610 (4)	4.05	4.05

Souvenir Sheet
611	A113	$5 multicolored	3.50	3.50

Coral Reef Fish A114

10c, Longspine squirrelfish. 50c, Banded butter-flyfish. $1.50, Blackbar soldierfish. $2.50, Yellowtail snappers. $5, Red hind.

1983, Aug. 23
612	A114	10c multicolored	.25	.25
613	A114	50c multicolored	.25	.25
614	A114	$1.50 multicolored	1.00	1.00
615	A114	$2.50 multicolored	1.50	1.50
		Nos. 612-615 (4)	3.00	3.00

Souvenir Sheet
616	A114	$5 multicolored	4.50	4.50

For overprint see No. 800.

Locomotives — A115

No. 617, Princess Coronation. No. 618, Duke of Sutherland. No. 619, Leeds United. No. 620, Lord Nelson. No. 621, Bodmin. No. 622, Eton. No. 623, Flying Scotsman. No. 624, Stephenson's Rocket.

Perf. 12½
1983, Oct. 13   Litho.   Unwmk.
Se-tenant Pairs, #a.-b.
a. — Side and front views.
b. — Action scene.
617	A115	35c multicolored	.25	.25
618	A115	35c multicolored	.25	.25
619	A115	50c multicolored	.25	.65
620	A115	50c multicolored	.25	.65
621	A115	$1 multicolored	.60	1.10
622	A115	$1 multicolored	.60	1.10
623	A115	$2 multicolored	1.25	2.10
624	A115	$2 multicolored	1.25	2.10
		Nos. 617-624 (8)	4.70	8.20

See Nos. 674-679, 711-718, 774-777, 807-814.

Virgin and Child Paintings by Raphael — A115a

10c, Niccolini-Cowper Madonna. 30c, Holy Family with a Palm Tree. 50c, Sistine Madonna. $5, Alba Madonna.

Wmk. 373
1983, Oct. 24   Litho.   Perf. 14
629	A115a	10c multicolored	.25	.25
630	A115a	30c multicolored	.25	.25
631	A115a	50c multicolored	.25	.25
632	A115a	$5 multicolored	1.60	1.60
		Nos. 629-632 (4)	2.35	2.35

Christmas.

Battle of Waterloo, King George III — A116

Nos. 633a, 633b, shown. No. 634a, George III, diff. No. 634b, Kew Palace. No. 635a, Arms of Elizabeth I. No. 635b, Elizabeth I. No. 636a, Arms of George III. No. 636b, George III, diff. No. 637a, Elizabeth I, diff. No. 637b, Hatfield Palace. No. 638a, Spanish Armada. No. 638b, Elizabeth, I, diff.

Perf. 12½
1984, Mar. 13   Litho.   Unwmk.
633	A116	5c Pair, #a.-b.	.25	.35
634	A116	10c Pair, #a.-b.	.25	.35
635	A116	35c Pair, #a.-b.	.25	.50
636	A116	60c Pair, #a.-b.	.40	.90
637	A116	$1 Pair, #a.-b.	.60	1.25
638	A116	$2.50 Pair, #a.-b.	1.75	3.50
		Nos. 633-638 (6)	3.50	6.85

Unissued 30c, 50c, $1, $2.50 and $5 values became available with the liquidation of the printer.

Colonial Building, Late 19th Cent. — A118

Local Architecture. 10c, Buildings, mid-19th cent., vert. 65c, Wooden chattel, early 20th cent. $2.50, Treasury, 1906.

Perf. 14x13½, 13½x14

1984, Apr. 6			Wmk. 380	
645	A118	10c multicolored	.25	.25
646	A118	45c shown	.40	.35
647	A118	65c multicolored	.55	.45
648	A118	$2.50 multicolored	2.00	1.75
		Nos. 645-648 (4)	3.20	2.80

For overprints see Nos. 796, 801.

Logwood Tree and Blossom — A118a

Perf. 13½x14, 14x13½

1984, June 12			Wmk. 380	
649	A118a	10c shown	.25	.25
650	A118a	45c Calabash	.25	.25
651	A118a	65c Gommier, vert.	.30	.30
652	A118a	$2.50 Rain tree	1.40	1.40
		Nos. 649-652 (4)	2.20	2.20

For overprint see No. 802.

Automobiles — A119

5c, Bugatti 57SC, 1939. 10c, Chevrolet Bel Air, 1957. $1, Alfa Romeo, 1930. $2.50, Duesenberg, 1932.

Perf. 12½

1984, June 25		Litho.		Unwmk.

Se-tenant Pairs, #a.-b.
a. — Side and front views.
b. — Action scene.

653	A119	5c multicolored	.25	.25
654	A119	10c multicolored	.25	.25
655	A119	$1 multicolored	.30	1.25
656	A119	$2.50 multicolored	.60	3.00
		Nos. 653-656 (4)	1.40	4.75

See Nos. 686-693, 739-742, 850-855.

Endangered Reptiles — A120

			Wmk. 380	
1984, Aug. 8		**Litho.**	***Perf. 14***	
661	A120	10c Pygmy gecko	.25	.25
662	A120	45c Maria Isld. ground lizard	.45	.45
663	A120	65c Green iguana	.60	.60
664	A120	$2.50 Couresse snake	1.25	1.25
		Nos. 661-664 (4)	2.55	2.55

For overprint see No. 797.

Leaders of the World, 1984
Olympics — A121

#665a, Volleyball. #665b, Volleyball, diff.. #666a, Women's hurdles. #666b, Men's hurdles. #667a, Showjumping. #667b, Dressage. #668a, Women's gymnastics. #668b, Men's gymnastics.

Perf. 12½

1984, Sept. 21		Litho.		Unwmk.
665	A121	5c Pair, #a.-b.	.25	.25
666	A121	10c Pair, #a.-b.	.25	.25
667	A121	65c Pair, #a.-b.	.25	.60
668	A121	$2.50 Pair, #a.-b.	1.00	2.00
		Nos. 665-668 (4)	1.75	3.10

Locomotive Type of 1983

1c, TAW 2-6-2T, 1897. 15c, Crocodile 1-C.C.-1, 1920. 50c, The Countess 0.6.0T, 1903. 75c, Class GE6/6C.C., 1921. $1, Class P8, 4.6.0, 1906. $2, Der Alder 2.2.2., 1835.

1984, Sept. 21		Litho.		*Perf. 12½*

Se-tenant Pairs, #a.-b.
a. — Side and front views.
b. — Action scene.

674	A115	1c multicolored	.25	.25
675	A115	15c multicolored	.25	.40
676	A115	50c multicolored	.30	.55
677	A115	75c multicolored	.30	.85
678	A115	$1 multicolored	.40	.60
679	A115	$2 multicolored	.50	.80
		Nos. 674-679 (6)	2.00	3.45

Automobile Type of 1983

10c, Panhard and Levassor, 1889. 30c, N.S.U. R0-80 Saloon, 1968. 55c, Abarth, Balbero, 1958. 65c, TVR Vixen 2500M, 1972. 75c, Ford Mustang Convertible, 1965. $1, Ford Model T, 1914. $2, Aston Martin DB3S, 1954. $3, Chrysler Imperial CG, 1931.

1984, Dec. 19		Litho.		*Perf. 12½*

Se-tenant Pairs, #a.-b.
a. — Side and front views.
b. — Action scene.

686	A119	10c multicolored	.25	.25
687	A119	30c multicolored	.25	.35
688	A119	55c multicolored	.25	.65
689	A119	65c multicolored	.25	.75
690	A119	75c multicolored	.25	.90
691	A119	$1 multicolored	.35	1.25
692	A119	$2 multicolored	1.00	2.50
693	A119	$3 multicolored	1.10	3.50
		Nos. 686-693 (8)	3.70	10.15

Christmas — A122

		Wmk. 380		
1984, Oct. 31		**Litho.**	***Perf. 14***	
702	A122	10c Wine glass	.25	.25
703	A122	35c Altar	.25	.25
704	A122	65c Creche	.25	.25
705	A122	$3 Holy family, abstract	.25	1.00
a.		Souvenir sheet of 4, #702-705	2.60	2.60
		Nos. 702-705 (4)	1.00	1.75

Abolition of Slavery, 150th Anniv. — A123

Engraving details, Natl. Archives, Castries: 10c, Preparing manioc. 35c, Working with cassava flour. 55c, Cooking, twisting and drying tobacco. $5, Tobacco production, diff.

1984, Dec. 12		Litho.		*Perf. 14*
706	A123	10c bright buff & blk	.25	.25
707	A123	35c bright buff & blk	.25	.25
708	A123	55c bright buff & blk	.25	.25
709	A123	$5 bright buff & blk	.75	2.50
		Nos. 706-709 (4)	1.50	3.25

Souvenir Sheet

710		Sheet of 4	2.50	2.50
a.		A123 10c like No. 706	.25	.25
b.		A123 35c like No. 707	.25	.25
c.		A123 55c like No. 708	.25	.25
d.		A123 $5 like No. 709	.70	.70

#710a-710d se-tenant in continuous design.

Locomotive Type of 1983

5c, J.N.R. Class C-53, 1928, Japan. 15c, Heavy L, 1885, India. 35c, QGR Class B18¼, 1926, Australia. 60c, Owain Glyndwr, 1923, U.K. 75c, Lion, 1838, U.K. $1, Coal Engine, 1873, U.K. $2, No. 2238 Class Q6, 1921, U.K. $2.50, Class H, 1920, U.K.

1985, Feb. 4		Unwmk.		*Perf. 12½*

Se-tenant Pairs, #a.-b.
a. — Side and front views.
b. — Action scene.

711	A115	5c multicolored	.25	.25
712	A115	15c multicolored	.25	.25
713	A115	35c multicolored	.25	.60
714	A115	60c multicolored	.25	.60
715	A115	75c multicolored	.25	.75
716	A115	$1 multicolored	.30	.80
717	A115	$2 multicolored	.50	1.20
718	A115	$2.50 multicolored	.70	1.50
		Nos. 711-718 (8)	2.75	5.95

Girl Guides, 75th Anniv. — A124

1985, Feb. 21		Wmk. 380		*Perf. 14*
727	A124	10c multicolored	.40	.25
728	A124	35c multicolored	1.00	.25
729	A124	65c multicolored	2.25	.75
730	A124	$3 multicolored	4.25	5.50
		Nos. 727-730 (4)	7.90	6.75

For overprint see No. 795.

Butterflies — A125

No. 731a, Clossiana selene. No. 731b, Inachis io. No. 732a, Philaethria werneckei. No. 732b, Catagramma sorana. No. 733a, Kallima inachus. No. 733b, Hypanartia paullus. No. 734a, Morpho rhetenor helena. No. 734b, Ornithoptera meridionalis.

1985, Feb. 28		Unwmk.		*Perf. 12½*
731	A125	15c Pair, #a.-b.	.25	.25
732	A125	40c Pair, #a.-b.	.25	.25
733	A125	60c Pair, #a.-b.	.25	.25
734	A125	$2.25 Pair, #a.-b.	1.50	1.50
		Nos. 731-734 (4)	2.25	2.25

Automobile Type of 1983

15c, 1940 Hudson Eight, US. 50c, 1937 KdF, Germany. $1, 1925 Kissel Goldbug, US. $1.50, 1973 Ferrari 246GTS, Italy.

1985, Mar. 29		Se-tenant Pairs		
739	A119	15c multicolored	.25	.25
740	A119	50c multicolored	.40	.60
741	A119	$1 multicolored	.40	.60
742	A119	$1.50 multicolored	.80	1.50
		Nos. 739-742 (4)	1.85	2.95

Military Uniforms — A126

Designs: 5c, Grenadier, 70th Foot Reg., c. 1775. 10c, Grenadier Co. Officer, 14th Foot Reg., 1780. 20c, Battalion Co. Officer, 46th Foot Reg., 1781. 25c, Officer, Royal Artillery Reg., c. 1782. 30c, Officer, Royal Engineers Corps., 1782. 35c, Battalion Co. Officer, 54th Foot Reg., 1782. 45c, Grenadier Co. Private, 14th Foot Reg., 1782. 50c, Gunner, Royal Artillery Reg., 1796. 65c, Battalion Co. Private, 85th Foot Reg., c. 1796. 75c, Battalion Co. Private, 76th Foot Reg., 1796. 90c, Battalion Co. Private, 81st Foot Reg., c. 1796. $1, Sergeant, 74th (Highland) Foot Reg., 1796. $2.50, Private, Light Co., 93rd Foot Reg., 1803. $5, Battalion Co. Private, 1st West India Reg., 1803. $15, Officer, Royal Artillery Reg., 1850.

1985, May 7		Wmk. 380		*Perf. 15*

"1984" Imprint Below Design

747	A126	5c multicolored	.35	.65
748	A126	10c multicolored	.45	.25
749	A126	20c multicolored	.50	.35
a.		"1986" Imprint	.65	.65
750	A126	25c multicolored	.65	.25
a.		"1986" Imprint	.65	.65
751	A126	30c multicolored	.80	.35
752	A126	35c multicolored	.75	.25
753	A126	45c multicolored	.85	.50
754	A126	50c multicolored	1.00	.50
755	A126	65c multicolored	1.10	.65
756	A126	75c multicolored	1.25	1.00
757	A126	90c multicolored	1.50	1.00
758	A126	$1 multicolored	1.60	1.00
759	A126	$2.50 multicolored	4.00	6.50
760	A126	$5 multicolored	6.25	13.00
761	A126	$15 multicolored	17.00	26.00
		Nos. 747-761 (15)	38.05	52.25

See Nos. 876-879.

1987				**Unwmk.**

1986 Imprint Below Design

747a	A126	5c	.40	.75
748a	A126	10c	.60	.40
751a	A126	30c	.85	.65
753a	A126	45c	.95	.75
754a	A126	50c	1.00	.90
759a	A126	$2.50	5.00	6.00
760a	A126	$5	6.50	11.00
		Nos. 747a-760a (7)	15.30	20.45

Issued: No. 747a-748a, 2/24; No. 751a-760a, 3/16.

1989			**Wmk. 384**	
747b	A126	5c "1988" Imprint	.85	1.25
748b	A126	10c "1989 " Imprint	1.10	.65
749a	A126	20c "1989" Imprint	1.50	1.25
750b	A126	25c "1988" Imprint	1.00	1.25
750c	A126	25c "1989" Imprint	1.00	1.25

No. 750b issued 9/88.

World War II Aircraft A127

5c, Messerschmitt 109-E. 55c, Avro 683 Lancaster Mark I Bomber. 60c, North American P.51-D Mustang. $2, Supermarine Spitfire Mark II.

1985, May 30   Unwmk.   Perf. 12½
Se-tenant Pairs, #a.-b.
a. — Action scene.
b. — Bottom, front and side views.

762	A127	5c multicolored	.25	.40
763	A127	55c multicolored	.60	.90
764	A127	60c multicolored	.60	.90
765	A127	$2 multicolored	.80	1.60
		Nos. 762-765 (4)	2.25	3.80

Nature Reserves A128

Birds in habitats: 10c, Frigate bird, Frigate Island Sanctuary. 35c, Mangrove cuckoo, Savannes Bay, Scorpion Island. 65c, Yellow sandpiper, Maria Island. $3, Audubon's shearwater, Lapins Island.

1985, June 20   Wmk. 380   Perf. 15

770	A128	10c multicolored	.35	.25
771	A128	35c multicolored	.65	.40
772	A128	65c multicolored	.75	.75
773	A128	$3 multicolored	2.40	2.40
		Nos. 770-773 (4)	4.15	3.80

Locomotive Type of 1983

10c, No. 28 Tender engine, 1897, U.K. 30c, No. 1621 Class M, 1893, U.K. 75c, Class Dunalastair, 1896, U.K. $2.50, Big Bertha No. 2290, 1919, U.K.

1985, June 26   Unwmk.   Perf. 12½
Se-tenant Pairs, #a.-b.
a. — Side and front views.
b. — Action scene.

774	A115	10c multicolored	.25	.25
775	A115	30c multicolored	.40	.40
776	A115	75c multicolored	.40	.60
777	A115	$2.50 multicolored	1.00	1.60
		Nos. 774-777 (4)	2.05	2.85

Queen Mother, 85th Birthday — A129

Nos. 782a, 787a, Facing right. Nos. 782b, 787b, Facing left. No. 783a, Facing right. No. 783b, Facing left. Nos. 784a, 788a, Facing right. Nos. 784b, 788b, Facing front. No. 785a, Facing front. No. 785b, Facing right. No. 786a, Facing right. No. 786b, Facing left.

1985, Aug. 16

782	A129	40c Pair, #a.-b.	.25	.50
783	A129	75c Pair, #a.-b.	.40	.60
784	A129	$1.10 Pair, #a.-b.	.40	1.00
785	A129	$1.75 Pair, #a.-b.	.50	1.50
		Nos. 782-785 (4)	1.55	3.60

Souvenir Sheets of 2

786	A129	$2 #a.-b.	1.00	1.00
787	A129	$3 #a.-b.	2.50	2.50
788	A129	$6 #a.-b.	3.50	3.50

For overprints see No. 799.

Intl. Youth Year — A130

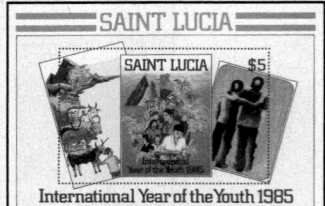

Abstracts, by Lyndon Samuel — A131

Illustrations by local artists: 10c, Youth playing banjo, by Wayne Whitfield. 45c, Riding tricycle, by Mark D. Maragh. 75c, Youth against landscape, by Bartholemew Eugene. $3.50, Abstract, by Lyndon Samuel.

1985, Sept. 5   Wmk. 380   Perf. 15

791	A130	10c multicolored	.25	.25
792	A130	45c multicolored	.50	.25
793	A130	75c multicolored	.50	.50
794	A130	$3.50 multicolored	1.10	1.00
		Nos. 791-794 (4)	2.35	4.00

Souvenir Sheet

795	A131	$5 multicolored	2.25	2.25

Intl. Youth Year.

Stamps of 1983-85 Ovptd.
"CARIBBEAN ROYAL VISIT 1985" in
Two or Three Lines
Perfs. as Before

1985, Nov.   Wmk. as Before

796	A124	35c #728	6.00	3.00
797	A118	65c #647	1.50	2.75
798	A120	65c #663	5.50	4.00
799	A129	$1.10 #784a-784b	12.50	17.50
800	A114	$2.50 #615	10.00	8.00
801	A118	$2.50 #648	2.00	7.00
802	A119	$2.50 #652	2.00	7.00
		Nos. 796-802 (7)	39.50	49.25

Masquerade Figures — A132

Madonna and Child, by Dunstan St. Omer — A133

Unwmk.
1985, Dec. 23   Litho.   Perf. 15

803	A132	10c Papa Jab	.25	.25
804	A132	45c Paille Bananne	.25	.25
805	A132	65c Cheval Bois	.75	.75
		Nos. 803-805 (3)	1.25	1.25

Miniature Sheet

806	A133	$4 multi	1.75	1.75

Christmas 1985.

Locomotive Type of 1983

5c, 1983 MWCR Rack Loco Tip Top, US. 15c, 1975 BR Class 87 Stephenson Bo-Bo, UK. 30c, 1901 Class D No. 737, UK. 60c, 1922 No. 13 2-Co-2, UK. 75c, 1954 BR Class EM2 Electra Co-Co, UK. $1, 1922 City of Newcastle, UK. $2.25, 1930 DRG Von Kruckenberg, Propeller-driven Rail Car, Germany. $3, 1893 JNR No. 860, Japan.

1986, Jan. 17   Perf. 12½x13
Se-tenant Pairs, #a.-b.
a. — Side and front views.
b. — Action scene.

807	A115	5c multicolored	.25	.40
808	A115	15c multicolored	.25	.25
809	A115	30c multicolored	.40	.60
810	A115	60c multicolored	.50	.80
811	A115	75c multicolored	.60	1.00
812	A115	$1 multicolored	.80	1.20
813	A115	$2.25 multicolored	1.20	1.60
814	A115	$3 multicolored	1.20	1.60
		Nos. 807-814 (8)	5.20	7.45

Miniature Sheets

Cook-out — A134

Designs: No. 823b, Scout sign. No. 824a, Wicker basket, weavings. No. 824b, Lady Olave Baden-Powell, Girl Guides founder.

1986, Mar. 3   Litho.   Perf. 13x12½

823	A134	Sheet of 2	2.25	3.50
a.-b.		$4 any single	1.25	1.75
824	A134	Sheet of 2	3.75	4.00
a.-b.		$6 any single	2.00	2.00

Scouting anniv., Girl Guides 75th anniv. Values are for sheets with plain border. Exist with decorative border. Value, set, $8.50.

A135

Queen Elizabeth II, 60th Birthday — A136

Various photographs: 5c, Pink hat. 10c, Visiting Marian Home. 45c, Mindoo Phillip Park speech. 50c, Opening Leon Hess School. $1, Princess Elizabeth. $3.50, Blue hat. $5, Government House. $6, Canberra, 1982, vert. $7, HMY Britannia, Castries Harbor. $8, Straw hat.

Perf. 13x12½, 12½x13, 14x15 (A136)
1986

825	A135	5c multicolored	.25	.25
826	A136	10c multicolored	.25	.25
827	A136	45c multicolored	.30	.30
828	A136	50c multicolored	.35	.35
829	A135	75c multicolored	.25	.30
830	A135	$3.50 multicolored	.50	1.25
831	A136	$5 multicolored	3.25	3.25
832	A135	$6 multicolored	.60	1.75
		Nos. 825-832 (8)	5.75	7.70

Souvenir Sheets

833	A136	$7 multicolored	5.00	5.00
834	A135	$8 multicolored	4.00	5.50

Issue dates: Nos. 825, 829-830, 832, Apr. 21; Nos. 826-828, 831, 833, June 14.

State Visit of Pope John Paul II A137

55c, Kissing the ground. 60c, St. Joseph's Convent. 80c, Cathedral, Castries. $6, Pope.

1986, July 7   Perf. 14x15, 15x14

835	A137	55c multicolored	1.50	1.00
836	A137	60c multicolored	1.60	1.00
837	A137	80c multicolored	2.00	2.00
		Nos. 835-837 (3)	5.10	4.00

Souvenir Sheet

838	A137	$6 multicolored	12.00	12.00
		Nos. 837-838 vert.		

Wedding of Prince Andrew and Sarah Ferguson — A138

No. 839a, Sarah. No. 839b, Prince Andrew. No. 840a, Couple, horiz. No. 840b, Prince Andrew, Nancy Reagan, horiz.

1986, July 23   Perf. 12½

839	A138	80c Pair, #a.-b.	1.00	1.00
840	A138	$2 Pair, #a.-b.	2.50	2.50

#840a-840b show Westminster Abbey in LR.

US Peace Corps in St. Lucia, 25th Anniv. A139

80c, Technical instruction. $2, Pres. Kennedy, vert. $3.50, Natl. crests, corps emblem.

1986, Sept. 25   Litho.   Perf. 14

843	A139	80c multicolored	.40	.50
844	A139	$2 multicolored	1.10	1.50
845	A139	$3.50 multicolored	1.75	2.60
		Nos. 843-845 (3)	3.25	4.60

Wedding of Prince Andrew and Sarah Ferguson — A140

1986, Oct. 15   Perf. 15

846	A140	50c Andrew	.40	.40
847	A140	80c Sarah	.60	.60
848	A140	$1 At altar	.75	.75
849	A140	$3 In open carriage	1.50	1.50
		Nos. 846-849 (4)	3.25	3.25

Souvenir Sheet

849A	A140	$7 Andrew, Sarah	4.50	4.50

Automobile Type of 1983

20c, 1969 AMC AMX, US. 50c, 1912 Russo-Baltique, Russia. 60c, 1932 Lincoln KB, US. $1, 1933 Rolls Royce Phantom II Continental, UK. $1.50, 1939 Buick Century, US. $3, 1957 Chrysler 300 C, US.

1986, Oct. 23   Litho.   Perf. 12½x13
Se-tenant Pairs, #a.-b.
a. — Side and front views.
b. — Action scene.

850	A119	20c multicolored	.30	.35
851	A119	50c multicolored	.30	.60
852	A119	60c multicolored	.30	.60
853	A119	$1 multicolored	.50	1.25
854	A119	$1.50 multicolored	.70	1.75
855	A119	$3 multicolored	1.40	3.50
		Nos. 850-855 (6)	3.50	8.05

Chak-Chak Band — A141

1986, Nov. 7   Perf. 15

862	A141	15c shown	.25	.25
863	A141	45c Folk dancing	.35	.25
864	A141	80c Steel band	.60	.60
865	A141	$5 Limbo dancer	1.00	3.00
		Nos. 862-865 (4)	2.20	4.10

Souvenir Sheet

866	A141	$10 Gros Islet	5.25	5.25

Christmas A142

Churches: 10c, St. Ann Catholic, Mon Repos. 40c, St. Joseph the Worker Catholic, Gros Islet. 80c, Holy Trinity Anglican, Castries. $4, Our Lady of the Assumption Catholic, Soufriere, vert. $7, St. Lucy Catholic, Micoud.

1986, Nov.

867	A142	10c multicolored	.25	.25
868	A142	40c multicolored	.25	.25
869	A142	80c multicolored	.50	.50
870	A142	$4 multicolored	.80	2.75
		Nos. 867-870 (4)	1.80	3.75

Souvenir Sheet

871	A142	$7 multicolored	3.50	3.50

Map of St. Lucia — A143

Perf. 14x14½
1987, Feb. 24   Litho.   Wmk. 373
No Date Imprint Below Design

872	A143	5c beige & blk	.25	.25
a.		Imprint "1988"	.25	.25
b.		Wmk. 384, "1989" imprint	.25	.25
873	A143	10c pale yel grn & blk	.25	.25
a.		Imprint "1988"	.25	.25
b.		Wmk. 384, "1989" imprint	.25	.25
874	A143	45c orange & blk	.60	.60
a.		Imprint "1992"	.60	.60
875	A143	50c pale violet & blk	.60	.60
a.		Imprint "1989"	.60	.60
		Nos. 872-875 (4)	1.70	1.70

Issued: #872a, 873a, 9/88; #875a, 3/17/89; #872b, 873b, 4/12/89.
See #937.

Uniforms Type of 1985

Designs: 15c, Battalion company private, 2nd West India Regiment, 1803. 60c, Battalion company officer, 5th Regiment of Foot, 1778. 80c, Battalion company officer, 27th (or Inniskilling) Regiment of Foot, c. 1780. $20, Grenadier company private, 46th Regiment of Foot, 1778.

1987, Mar. 16   Unwmk.   Perf. 15
"1986" Imprint Date Below Design

876	A126	15c multicolored	.45	.25
877	A126	60c multicolored	1.00	.75
878	A126	80c multicolored	1.50	1.00

879	A126	$20 multicolored	17.50	25.00
b.		Imprint "1987"	—	—
		Nos. 876-879 (4)	20.45	27.00
		Dated 1986.		

1988   Wmk. 384
Imprint Date Below Design As Noted

876a	A126	15c "1988"	1.25	.90
b.		Imprint "1989"	1.25	.90
877a	A126	60c "1988"	2.50	2.00
878a	A126	80c "1988"	2.75	2.25
879a	A126	$20 "1989"	24.50	35.00
		Nos. 876a-879a (4)	31.00	40.15

A144

Statue of Liberty, Cent. — A145

1987, Apr. 29   Wmk. 373   Perf. 14½

880	A144	15c Statue, flags	.45	.45
881	A144	80c Statue, ship	.95	.95
882	A144	$1 Statue, Concorde jet	1.50	1.50
883	A144	$5 Statue, flying boat	5.00	5.00
		Nos. 880-883 (4)	7.90	7.90

Souvenir Sheet

884	A145	$6 Statue, New York City	4.50	4.50

Maps, Surveying Instruments A147

Wmk. 384
1987, Aug. 31   Litho.   Perf. 14

888	A147	15c 1775	.50	.50
889	A147	60c 1814	1.30	1.30
890	A147	$1 1888	2.00	2.00
891	A147	$2.50 1987	4.25	4.25
		Nos. 888-891 (4)	8.05	8.05

First cadastral survey of St. Lucia.

Victoria Hospital, Cent. — A148

No. 894a, Ambulance, nurse, 1987. No. 894b, Nurse, hammock, 1913. No. 895a, Hospital, 1987. No. 895b, Hospital, 1887.

Wmk. 384
1987, Nov. 4   Litho.   Perf. 14½

894	A148	$1 Pair, #a.-b.	4.50	4.50
895	A148	$2 Pair, #a.-b.	8.00	8.00

Souvenir Sheet

896	A148	$4.50 Main gate, 1987	9.50	9.50

Christmas A149

Paintings (details) by unidentified artists — 15c, The Holy Family. 50c, Adoration of the Shepherds. 60c, Adoration of the Magi. 90c, Madonna and Child. $6, Holy Family.

1987, Nov. 30

897	A149	15c multicolored	.40	.40
898	A149	50c multicolored	.85	.85
899	A149	60c multicolored	1.10	1.10
900	A149	90c multicolored	1.30	1.30
		Nos. 897-900 (4)	3.65	3.65

Souvenir Sheet

901	A149	$6 multicolored	5.75	5.75

World Wildlife Fund — A150

Amazonian parrots, Amazona versicolor.

Wmk. 384
1987, Dec. 18   Litho.   Perf. 14

902	A150	15c multi	2.50	2.50
903	A150	35c multi, diff.	3.25	3.25
904	A150	60c multi, diff.	4.50	4.50
905	A150	$1 multi, diff.	7.00	7.00
		Nos. 902-905 (4)	17.25	17.25

American Indian Artifacts — A151

25c, Carib clay zemi. 30c, Troumassee cylinder. 80c, Three-pointer stone. $3.50, Dauphine petroglyph.

Wmk. 384
1988, Feb. 24   Litho.   Perf. 14½

906	A151	25c multicolored	.25	.25
907	A151	30c multicolored	.25	.25
908	A151	50c multicolored	.50	.50
909	A151	$3.50 multicolored	2.75	2.75
		Nos. 906-909 (4)	3.75	3.75

St. Lucia Cooperative Bank, 50th Anniv. — A152

Perf. 15x14
1988, Apr. 29   Litho.   Wmk. 373

910	A152	10c Coins, banknotes	.45	.45
911	A152	45c Branch in Castries	.80	.80
912	A152	60c like 45c	.90	.90
913	A152	80c Branch in Vieux Fort	1.40	1.40
		Nos. 910-913 (4)	3.55	3.55

Cable and Wireless in St. Lucia, 50th Anniv. A153

Designs: 15c, Rural telephone exchange. 25c, Antique and modern telephones. 80c, St. Lucia Teleport (satellite dish). $2.50, Map of Eastern Caribbean microwave communications system.

Wmk. 384
1988, June 10   Litho.   Perf. 14

914	A153	15c multicolored	.40	.40
915	A153	25c multicolored	.40	.40
916	A153	80c multicolored	.95	.95
917	A153	$2.50 multicolored	3.75	3.75
		Nos. 914-917 (4)	5.50	5.50

Cent. of the Methodist Church in St. Lucia — A154

Wmk. 384
1988, Aug. 15   Litho.   Perf. 14½

918	A154	15c Altar, window	.25	.25
919	A154	80c Chancel	.60	.60
920	A154	$3.50 Exterior	2.25	2.25
		Nos. 918-920 (3)	3.10	3.10

Tourism — A155

Lagoon and: 10c, Tourists, gourmet meal. 30c, Beverage, tourists. 80c, Tropical fruit. $2.50, Fish and chef. $5.50, Market.

Perf. 14x13½
1988, Sept. 15   Wmk. 384

921	A155	Strip of 4	6.50	6.50
a.		10c multicolored	.60	.60
b.		30c multicolored	.60	.60
c.		80c multicolored	1.60	1.60
d.		$2.50 multicolored	4.50	4.50

Souvenir Sheet

922	A155	$5.50 multicolored	4.00	4.00

Lloyds of London, 300th Anniv.
Common Design Type

Designs: 10c, San Francisco earthquake, 1906. 60c, Castries Harbor, horiz. 80c, *Lady Nelson*, sunk off Castries Harbor, 1942, horiz. $2.50, Castries on fire, 1948.

Wmk. 373
1988, Oct. 17   Litho.   Perf. 14

923	CD341	10c multicolored	.60	.60
924	CD341	60c multicolored	1.60	1.60
925	CD341	80c multicolored	2.10	2.10
926	CD341	$2.50 multicolored	4.50	4.50
		Nos. 923-926 (4)	8.80	8.80

A156

Christmas: Flowers — 15c, Snow on the mountain. 45c, Christmas candle. 60c, Balisier. 80c, Poinsettia. $5.50, Flower arrangement.

Perf. 14½x14
1988, Nov. 22   Litho.   Wmk. 384

927	A156	15c multicolored	.40	.40
928	A156	45c multicolored	.75	.75
929	A156	60c multicolored	.90	.90
930	A156	80c multicolored	1.10	1.10
		Nos. 927-930 (4)	3.15	3.15

Souvenir Sheet

931	A156	$5.50 multicolored	3.50	3.50

A157

Natl. Independence, 10th Anniv.: 15c, Princess Alexandra presenting constitution to Prime Minister Compton. 80c, Sulfur springs geothermal well. $1, Sir Arthur Lewis Community College. $2.50, Pointe Seraphine tax-free shopping center. $5, Emblem.

Perf. 13½x13

1989, Feb. 22			**Wmk. 373**	
932	A157	15c Nationhood	.25	.25
933	A157	80c Development	.70	.70
934	A157	$1 Education	1.00	1.00
935	A157	$2.50 Progress	2.00	2.00
		Nos. 932-935 (4)	3.95	3.95

Souvenir Sheet

936	A157	$5 With Confidence We Progress	3.50	3.50

Map Type of 1987
Perf. 14x14½

1989, Mar. 17		**Litho.**	**Wmk. 373**	
937	A143	$1 scarlet & black	1.25	1.25

Indigenous Mushrooms A158

15c, Gerronema citrinum. 25c, Lepiota spiculata. 50c, Calocybe cyanocephala. $5, Russula puiggarii.

Perf. 14½x14

1989, May 31		**Litho.**	**Wmk. 384**	
938	A158	15c multicolored	1.00	.50
939	A158	25c multicolored	1.40	.50
940	A158	50c multicolored	2.25	1.00
941	A158	$5 multicolored	8.50	11.00
		Nos. 938-941 (4)	13.15	13.00

PHILEXFRANCE '89, French Revolution Bicent. — A159

Views of St. Lucia and text: 10c, Independence day announcement, vert. 60c, French revolutionary flag at Morne Fortune, 1791. $1, "Men are born and live free and equal in rights," vert. $3.50, Captain La Crosse's arrival at Gros Islet, 1792.

Wmk. 373

1989, July 14			**Perf. 14**	
942	A159	10c multicolored	.50	.25
943	A159	60c multicolored	2.75	.75
944	A159	$1 multicolored	3.00	1.25
945	A159	$3.50 multicolored	10.00	10.00
		Nos. 942-945 (4)	16.25	12.25

Intl. Red Cross, 125th Anniv. A160

50c, Natl. headquarters. 80c, Seminar in Castries, 1987. $1, Ambulance.

1989, Oct. 10		**Wmk. 384**	**Perf. 14½**	
946	A160	50c multicolored	1.60	1.60
947	A160	80c multicolored	2.00	2.25
948	A160	$1 multicolored	2.50	2.50
		Nos. 946-948 (3)	6.10	6.35

Christmas Lanterns Shaped Like Buildings A161

1989, Nov. 17			**Perf. 14x14½**	
949	A161	10c multi	.25	.25
950	A161	50c multi, diff.	.60	.60
951	A161	90c multi, diff.	1.25	1.25
952	A161	$1 multi, diff.	1.40	1.40
		Nos. 949-952 (4)	3.50	3.50

Trees In Danger of Extinction — A162

10c, Chinna. 15c,

"1990" Imprint Date Below Design

1990		**Wmk. 384**	**Perf. 14**	
953	A162	10c multi	.60	.60
954	A162	15c Latanier	.60	.25
955	A162	20c Gwi gwi	.60	.60
956	A162	25c L'encens	.30	.25
957	A162	50c Bois lele	.45	.45
958	A162	80c Bois d'amande	1.15	.50
959	A162	95c Mahot piman grand bois	2.10	1.15
960	A162	$1 Balata	1.40	1.40
961	A162	$1.50 Pencil cedar	2.50	2.50
962	A162	$2.50 Bois cendre	5.00	5.00
963	A162	$5 Lowye cannelle	7.50	7.50
964	A162	$25 Chalantier grand bois	19.50	22.00
		Nos. 953-964 (12)	41.70	42.20

Issued: 20c, 25c, 50c, $25, 2/21; 10c, 15c, 80c, $1.50, 4/12; 95c, $1, $2.50, $5, 6/25.
For overprints see Nos. 971, O28-O39.

Year Imprint Dates as Noted

1992-95		**Wmk. 373**	**Perf. 14**	
953a	A162	10c "1992"	2.00	2.00
b.		"1993"	2.00	2.00
c.		"1994"	2.00	2.00
954a	A162	15c "1992"	2.00	2.00
b.		"1994"	2.00	2.00
955a	A162	20c "1995"	2.00	2.00
956a	A162	25c "1994"	2.00	2.00
957a	A162	50c "1992"	4.00	4.00
b.		"1993"	4.00	4.00
c.		"1994"	4.00	4.00
		Nos. 953a-957a (5)	12.00	12.00

Centenary of St. Mary's College, Intl. Literacy Year — A163

Designs: 30c, Father Tapon, original building. 45c, Rev. Brother Collins, current building. 75c, Students in literacy class. $2, Door to knowledge, children.

1990, June 6		**Wmk. 373**		
965	A163	30c multicolored	.35	.35
966	A163	45c multicolored	.55	.55
967	A163	75c multicolored	.85	.85
968	A163	$2 multicolored	2.25	2.25
		Nos. 965-968 (4)	4.00	4.00

Queen Mother, 90th Birthday
Common Design Types

1990, Aug. 3		**Wmk. 384**	**Perf. 14x15**	
969	CD343	50c Coronation, 1937	.60	.60

Perf. 14½

970	CD344	$5 Arriving at theater, 1949	4.00	4.00

No. 963 Overprinted

1990, Aug. 13			**Perf. 14**	
971	A162	$5 multicolored	4.75	4.75

Intl. Garden and Greenery Exposition, Osaka, Japan.

Christmas — A164

Paintings: 10c, Adoration of the Magi by Rubens. 30c, Adoration of the Shepherds by Murillo. 80c, Adoration of the Magi by Rubens, diff. $5, Adoration of the Shepherds by Champaigne.

1990, Dec. 3			**Perf. 14**	
972	A164	10c multicolored	.50	.50
973	A164	30c multicolored	1.15	1.15
974	A164	80c multicolored	1.75	1.75
975	A164	$5 multicolored	8.00	8.00
		Nos. 972-975 (4)	11.40	11.40

Boats A165

Various boats.

1991, Mar. 27		**Wmk. 373**	**Perf. 14½**	
976	A165	50c multicolored	2.00	2.00
977	A165	80c multicolored	2.25	2.25
978	A165	$1 multicolored	2.75	2.75
979	A165	$2.50 multicolored	7.00	7.00
		Nos. 976-979 (4)	14.00	14.00

Souvenir Sheet

980	A165	$5 multicolored	12.50	12.50

Butterflies — A166

60c, Polydamas swallowtail. 80c, St. Christopher's hairstreak. $1, St. Lucia mestra. $2.50, Godman's hairstreak.

Wmk. 373

1991, Aug. 15		**Litho.**	**Perf. 14**	
981	A166	60c multicolored	2.75	1.00
982	A166	80c multicolored	3.00	1.50
983	A166	$1 multicolored	3.25	1.75
984	A166	$2.50 multicolored	6.50	8.25
		Nos. 981-984 (4)	15.50	12.50

Christmas A167

10c, Jacmel Church. 15c, Red Madonna, vert. 80c, Monchy Church. $5, Blue Madonna, vert.

Perf. 14x14½

1991, Nov. 20		**Litho.**	**Wmk. 384**	
985	A167	10c multicolored	.50	.25
986	A167	15c multicolored	.70	.25
987	A167	80c multicolored	2.75	2.75
988	A167	$5 multicolored	6.00	6.00
		Nos. 985-988 (4)	9.95	9.25

Atlantic Rally for Cruisers A168

Designs: 60c, Cruisers crossing Atlantic, map. 80c, Cruisers tacking.

1991, Dec. 10		**Wmk. 384**	**Perf. 14**	
989	A168	60c multicolored	2.25	2.25
990	A168	80c multicolored	3.00	3.00

Discovery of America, 500th Anniv. — A169

Wmk. 373

1992, July 6		**Litho.**	**Perf. 13**	
991	A169	$1 Coming ashore	2.25	2.25
992	A169	$2 Natives, ships	4.50	4.50

Organization of East Caribbean States.

Contact with New World A170

15c, Amerindians. 40c, Juan de la Cosa, 1499. 50c, Columbus, 1502. $5, Gimie, Dec. 13th.

1992, Aug. 4			**Perf. 13½**	
993	A170	15c multicolored	.50	.25
994	A170	40c multicolored	2.25	.50
995	A170	50c multicolored	3.00	.75
996	A170	$5 multicolored	9.00	9.00
		Nos. 993-996 (4)	14.75	10.50

Christmas A171

Paintings: 10c, Virgin and Child, by Delaroche. 15c, The Holy Family, by Rubens. 60c, Virgin and Child, by Luini. 80c, Virgin and Child, by Sassoferrato.

Wmk. 373

1992, Nov. 9		**Litho.**	**Perf. 14½**	
997	A171	10c multicolored	.70	.25
998	A171	15c multicolored	.70	.40
999	A171	60c multicolored	2.75	1.75
1000	A171	80c multicolored	2.75	2.25
		Nos. 997-1000 (4)	6.90	4.65

Anti-Drugs
Campaign — A172

Perf. 13½x14

1993, Feb. 1   Litho.   Wmk. 373
1001 A172 $5 multicolored   9.00 9.00

Gros Piton
from Delcer,
Choiseul, by
Dunstan St.
Omer
A173

Paintings: 75c, Reduit Bay, by Derek
Walcott. $5, Woman and Child at River, by
Nancy Cole Auguste.

1993, Nov. 1   Wmk. 373   Perf. 13
1002 A173 20c multicolored   .35 .25
1003 A173 75c multicolored   1.25 1.00
1004 A173 $5 multicolored   6.25 7.00
   Nos. 1002-1004 (3)   7.85 8.25

Christmas
A174

Details of paintings: 15c, The Madonna of
the Rosary, by Murillo. 60c, The Madonna and
Child, by Van Dyck. 95c, The Annunciation, by
Champaigne.

1993, Dec. 6   Perf. 14
1005 A174 15c multicolored   .25 .25
1006 A174 60c multicolored   1.00 .60
1007 A174 95c multicolored   1.75 1.75
   Nos. 1005-1007 (3)   3.00 2.60

A175

1994, July 25   Perf. 13
1008 A175 20c multicolored   1.00 .75
Souvenir Sheet
1009 A175 $5 multicolored   7.50 7.50
Abolition of Slavery on St. Lucia, bicent.

A176

Christmas (Flowers): 20c, Euphorbia
pulcherrima. 75c, Heliconia rostrata. 95c,
Alpinia purpurata. $5.50, Anthurium
andreanum.

1994, Dec. 9   Perf. 12½x13
1010 A176 20c multicolored   .25 .25
1011 A176 75c multicolored   1.00 1.00
1012 A176 95c multicolored   1.40 1.40
1013 A176 $5.50 multicolored   5.75 5.75
   Nos. 1010-1013 (4)   8.40 8.40

Battle of
Rabot,
Bicent.
A177

1995, Apr. 28   Perf. 13½
1014 A177 20c Map of island   .45 .25
1015 A177 75c Rebelling
        slaves   1.10 1.10
1016 A177 95c Battle scene   1.60 1.60
   Nos. 1014-1016 (3)   3.15 2.95
Souvenir Sheet
Perf. 13
1017 A177 $5.50 Battle map   6.00 6.00

End of World War II, 50th Anniv.
Common Design Types

Designs: 20c, ATS women in Britain. 75c,
German U-boat off St. Lucia. 95c, Caribbean
regiment, North Africa. $1.10, Presentation
Spitfire Mk V.
$5.50, Reverse of War Medal 1939-45.

Wmk. 373
1995, May 8   Litho.   Perf. 13½
1018 CD351 20c multi   .50 .25
1019 CD351 75c multi   1.75 1.00
1020 CD351 95c multi   2.00 1.40
1021 CD351 $1.10 multi   2.50 2.00
   Nos. 1018-1021 (4)   6.75 4.65
Souvenir Sheet
Perf. 14
1022 CD352 $5.50 multi   5.50 5.50

UN, 50th Anniv.
Common Design Type

10c, Puma helicopter. 65c, Renault truck.
$1.35, Transall C160. $5, Douglas DC3.

Wmk. 373
1995, Oct. 24   Litho.   Perf. 14
1023 CD353 10c multi   .25 .25
1024 CD353 65c multi   .75 .50
1025 CD353 $1.35 multi   1.50 1.50
1026 CD353 $5 multi   5.00 5.00
   Nos. 1023-1026 (4)   7.50 7.25

Christmas — A178

Flowers: 15c, Eranthemum nervosum. 70c,
Bougainvillea. $1.10, Allamanda cathartica.
$3, Hibiscus rosa sinensis.

Wmk. 373
1995, Nov. 20   Litho.   Perf. 13
1027 A178 15c multicolored   .25 .25
1028 A178 70c multicolored   .60 .50
1029 A178 $1.10 multicolored   .95 .95
1030 A178 $3 multicolored   2.40 2.40
   Nos. 1027-1030 (4)   4.20 4.10

Carnival — A179

1996, Feb. 16   Wmk. 384
**   Litho.   Perf. 14**
1031 A179 20c Calypso king   .85 .85
1032 A179 65c Carnival band   2.00 2.00
1033 A179 95c King of the
        band   2.75 2.75
1034 A179 $3 Carnival queen   5.25 5.25
   Nos. 1031-1034 (4)   10.85 10.85

Water — A180

1996, Mar. 5   Wmk. 373
1035 A180 20c Muddy stream   .25 .25
1036 A180 65c Clear stream   .50 .50
1037 A180 $5 Modern dam   4.00 5.00
   Nos. 1035-1037 (3)   4.75 5.75

Tourism
A181

Designs: 65c, Market. 75c, Riding horses on
beach. 95c, Outdoor wedding ceremony. $5,
Annual Intl. Jazz Festival.

Wmk. 373
1996, May 13   Litho.   Perf. 14
1038-1041 A181 Set of 4   7.00 7.00

Modern Olympic Games,
Cent. — A182

No. 1042a, Early runner. No. 1042b, Modern runner. No. 1043a, Two sailboats. No.
1043b, Four sailboats.

Wmk. 373
1996, July 19   Litho.   Perf. 14
1042 A182 15c Pair, #a.-b.   1.60 1.60
1043 A182 75c Pair, #a.-b.   4.75 4.75
Nos. 1042-1043 have continuous designs.

Flags
&
Ships
A183

Flag, ship: 10c, Spanish Royal banner,
1502, Spanish caravel. 15c, Skull & cross-
bones, 1550, pirate carrack. 20c, Royal
Netherlands, 1660, Dutch 80-gun ship. 25c,
Union flag, 1739, Royal Navy 64-gun ship.
40c, French Imperial, 1750, French 74-gun
ship. 50c, Martinique & St. Lucia, 1766,
French brig. 55c, British White Ensign, 1782,
Royal Navy Frigate Squadron. 65c, British Red
Ensign, 1782, Battle of the Saints. 75c, British
Blue Ensign, 1782, RN brig. 95c, Fench Tri-
color, 1792, French 38-gun frigate. $1, British
Union, 1801, West Indies Grand Fleet. $2.50,
Confederate, 1861, CSA steam/sail armed
cruiser. $5, Canada, 1915-19, Canadian V &
W class destroyer. $10, US, 1942-48, Fletcher
class destroyer. $25, National, cruise ship.

Perf. 14x15
1996-97   Litho.   Wmk. 384
"1996" Date Imprint Below Design
1046 A183 10c multi   1.00 .30
   b.   Imprint "2000"   .40 .40
1047 A183 15c multi   1.70 .30
   b.   Imprint "2000"   .40 .40
1048 A183 20c multi   .70 .30
   b.   Imprint "2000"   .40 .40
1049 A183 25c multi   .75 .30
   b.   Imprint "2000"   .40 .40

1050 A183 40c multi   2.00 .50
1051 A183 50c multi   1.00 .50
1052 A183 55c multi   1.00 .50
1053 A183 65c multi   1.00 .55
1054 A183 75c multi   1.25 .65
1055 A183 95c multi   1.25 .65
1056 A183 $1 multi   1.25 .80
1057 A183 $2.50 multi   2.75 2.50
1058 A183 $5 multi   4.00 4.50
1059 A183 $10 multi   7.25 9.00
1060 A183 $25 multi   14.50 16.00
   Nos. 1046-1060 (15)   41.40 37.30

Issued: 10c, 15c, 20c, 25c, 40c, 9/16/96;
50c, 55c, 65c, 75c, 95c, 11/18/96; $1, $2.50,
$5, $10, $25, 1/8/97.

1998-2004   Wmk. 373
Date Imprint Below Design as Noted
1046a A183 10c multi, "1998"   .75 .40
1047a A183 15c multi, "1998"   .75 .40
1048a A183 20c multi, "1998"   .75 .40
   c.   Imprint "2001"   .40 .40
   d.   Imprint "2002"   .75 .30
   e.   Imprint "2003"   .40 .40
   f.   Imprint "2004"   .40 .40
1049a A183 25c multi, "2002"   .40 .40
1051a A183 50c multi, "1998"   1.00 .50
1053a A183 65c multi, "2001"   .70 .55
1054a A183 75c multi, "2003"   1.00 1.00
1056a A183 $1 multi, "2001"   1.40 1.40
1059a A183 $10 multi, "2001"   10.00 11.00
   Nos. 1046a-1059a (9)   16.75 16.05

#1046a, 1047a, 1048a, 1051a, 7/12/98;
#1053a, 1056a, 1059a, 4/2001. #1049a, 2002.
No. 1054a, May 2003.

Christmas — A184

Flowers: 20c, Cordia sebestena. 75c,
Cryptostegia grandiflora. 95c, Hibiscus elatus.
$5, Caularthron bicornutum.

Wmk. 384
1996, Dec. 1   Litho.   Perf. 14
1061-1064 A184 Set of 4   7.50 7.50

Queen Elizabeth II and Prince Philip,
50th Wedding Anniv. — A185

No. 1068a, Queen. No. 1068b, Prince with
horses. No. 1069a, Prince. No. 1069b, Queen
riding in carriage. No. 1070a, Queen, Prince.
No. 1070b, Princess Anne riding horse.
$5, Queen, Prince riding in open carriage,
horiz.

Perf. 14½x14
1997, July 10   Litho.   Wmk. 384
1068 A185 75c Pair, #a.-b.   2.25 2.25
1069 A185 95c Pair, #a.-b.   2.50 2.50
1070 A185 $1 Pair, #a.-b.   2.75 2.75
   Nos. 1068-1070 (3)   7.50 7.50
Souvenir Sheet
Perf. 14x14½
1071 A185 $5 multicolored   6.00 6.00

Disasters — A186

20c, MV St. George capsizes, 1935. 55c,
SS Belle of Bath founders. $1, SS Ethelgonda

runs aground, 1897. $2.50, Hurricane devastation, 1817.

1997, July 14   **Perf. 14x15**
1072-1075 A186   Set of 4   11.50 11.50

Events of 1797 — A187

Designs: 20c, Taking of Praslin. 55c, Battle of Dennery. 70c, Peace. $3, Brigands join 1st West India Regiment.

     Wmk. 373
1997, Aug. 15   **Litho.**   **Perf. 14**
1076-1079 A187   Set of 4   10.50 10.50

Christmas — A188

Church art: 20c, Roseau Church. 60c, Altarpiece, Regional Seminary, Trinidad. 95c, Our Lady of the Presentation, Trinidad. $5, The Four Days of Creation.

     Perf. 14x15
1997, Dec. 1   **Litho.**   **Wmk. 384**
1080-1083 A188   Set of 4   7.00 7.00

Diana, Princess of Wales (1961-97) — A189

1998, Jan. 19   **Litho.**   **Perf. 14**
1084 A189 $1 multicolored   .90 .90
No. 1084 was issued in sheets of 9.

CARICOM, 25th Anniv. — A190

20c, Errol Barrow, Forbes Burnham, Dr. Eric Williams, Michael Manley signing CARICOM Treaty, 1973. 75c, CARICOM flag, St. Lucia Natl. flag.

     Wmk. 373
1998, July 1   **Litho.**   **Perf. 13½**
1085 A190 20c multicolored   .25 .25
1086 A190 75c multicolored   1.25 1.25

Birds — A191

Designs: 70c, St. Lucia oriole. 75c, Lesser Antillean pewee. 95c, Bridled quail dove. $1.10, Semper's warbler.

1998, Oct. 23   **Wmk. 373**   **Perf. 14**
1087-1090 A191 70c Set of 4   9.50 9.50

Universal Declaration of Human Rights, 50th Anniv. — A192

Various butterflies, chains or rope.

1998, Oct. 28
1091 A192 20c multicolored   .75 .30
1092 A192 65c multicolored   1.50 .75
1093 A192 70c multicolored   1.60 .75
1094 A192 $5 multicolored   6.00 6.50
    Nos. 1091-1094 (4)   9.85 8.30

Christmas — A193

Flowers: 20c, Tabebuia serratifolia. 50c, Hibiscus sabdariffa. 95c, Euphorbia leucocephala. $2.50, Calliandra slaneae.

     Wmk. 373
1998, Nov. 27   **Litho.**   **Perf. 14**
1095-1098 A193 20c Set of 4   6.25 6.25

University of West Indies, 50th Anniv. A194

15c, The Black Prometheus. 75c, Sir Arthur Lewis, Sir Arthur Lewis College. $5, The Pitons.

1998, Nov. 30
1099 A194 15c multicolored   .25 .25
1100 A194 75c multicolored   .75 .50
1101 A194 $5 multicolored   4.50 5.25
    Nos. 1099-1101 (3)   5.50 6.00

Wildlife A195

Designs: 20c, Saint Lucia tree lizard. 75c, Boa constrictor. 95c, Leatherback turtle. $5, Saint Lucia whiptail.

     Wmk. 373
1999, July 15   **Litho.**   **Perf. 13½**
1102-1105 A195   Set of 4   7.50 7.50

UPU, 125th Anniv. A196

20c, Mail steamer "Tees". 65c, Sikorsky S.38. 95c, Mail ship "Lady Drake". $3, DC-10. $5, Heinrich von Stephan.

     Wmk. 373
1999, Oct. 9   **Litho.**   **Perf. 14**
1106 A196 20c multicolored   .70 .30
1107 A196 65c multicolored   1.40 .55
1108 A196 95c multicolored   1.60 .65
1109 A196 $3 multicolored   4.00 4.00
    Nos. 1106-1109 (4)   7.70 5.50

Souvenir Sheet
     Perf. 14¼
1110 A196 $5 multicolored   5.50 5.50
Stamp inscription on No. 1107 is misspelled. No. 1110 contains one 30x38mm stamp.

Christmas and Millennium — A197

Designs: 20c, Nativity. $1, Cathedral of the Immaculate Conception.

     Perf. 13¾x14
1999, Dec. 14   **Litho.**   **Wmk. 373**
1111 A197 20c multi   .25 .25
1112 A197 $1 multi   1.60 1.60

Independence, 21st Anniv. — A198

20c, Vintage badge of the colony. 75c, 1939 badge. 95c, 1967 arms. $1, 1979 arms.

     Perf. 14x13¾
2000, Feb. 29   **Litho.**   **Wmk. 373**
1113 A198 20c multi   .30 .30
1114 A198 75c multi   .75 .60
1115 A198 95c multi   .95 .85
1116 A198 $1 multi   1.25 1.00
    Nos. 1113-1116 (4)   3.25 2.75

Historical Views A199

Designs: 20c, Fort sugar factory, 1886-1941. 60c, Coaling at Port Castries, 1885-1940. $1, Fort Rodney, Pigeon Island, 1780-1861. $5, Military hospital ruins, Pigeon Island, 1824-1861.

     Wmk. 373
2000, Sept. 4   **Litho.**   **Perf. 14**
1117-1120 A199   Set of 4   6.50 6.50

First Municipality of Castries, 150th Anniv. — A200

Designs: 20c, Old Castries Market. 75c, Central Library. 95c, Port Castries. $5, Mayors Henry H. Breen, Joseph Desir.

     Perf. 13¼x13½
2000, Oct. 9   **Litho.**   **Wmk. 373**
1121-1124 A200   Set of 4   6.50 8.00

Girl Guides in St. Lucia, 75th Anniv. A201

Guides: 70c, Marching in brown uniforms. $1, Marching in blue uniforms. $2.50, At campground.

2000, Oct. 16
1125-1127 A201   Set of 3   5.50 6.00

Christmas — A202

Churches: 20c, Holy Trinity, Castries. 50c, St. Paul's, Vieux-Fort. 95c, Christ, Soufriere. $2.50, Grace, River D'Oree.

2000, Nov. 22   **Perf. 14**
1128-1131 A202   Set of 4   5.50 6.00

Worldwide Fund for Nature (WWF) — A203

Birds: No. 1132, 20c, White breasted thrasher. No. 1133, 20c, St. Lucia black finch. No. 1134, 95c, St. Lucia oriole. No. 1135, 95c, Forest thrush.

     Wmk. 373
2001, Feb. 1   **Litho.**   **Perf. 14**
1132-1135 A203   Set of 4   4.50 4.75
1135a   Strip of 4, #1132-1135   4.50 4.75

Jazz Festival, 10th Anniv. — A204

Designs: 20c, Crowd, stage. $1, Crowd, stage, ocean. $5, Musicians.

     Perf. 13¾x14
2001, May 3   **Litho.**   **Wmk. 373**
1136-1138 A204   Set of 3   7.00 7.50

Civil Administration, Bicent. — A205

Designs: 20c, British flag, island, ship. 65c, French flag, Napoleon Bonaparte, signing of the Treaty of Amiens. $1.10, British flag, King George III, ships. $3, Island map, King George IV.

     Perf. 14x13¾
2001, Sept. 24   **Litho.**   **Unwmk.**
1139-1142 A205   Set of 4   5.50 6.00

Christmas — A206

Various stained glass windows: 20c, 95c, $2.50.

2001, Dec. 7 **Wmk. 373** *Perf. 13½*
1143-1145 A206 Set of 3 5.25 5.25

Reign Of Queen Elizabeth II, 50th Anniv. Issue
Common Design Type

Designs: Nos. 1146, 1150a, 25c, Princess Elizabeth, 1927. Nos. 1147, 1150b, 65c, Wearing hat. Nos. 1148, 1150c, 75c, In 1947. Nos. 1149, 1150d, 95c, In 1996. No. 1150e, $5, 1955 portrait by Annigoni (38x50mm).

Perf. 14¼x14½, 13¾ (#1150e)
2002, Feb. 6 **Litho.** **Wmk. 373**
With Gold Frames
1146 CD360 25c multicolored .50 .50
1147 CD360 65c multicolored 1.25 1.25
1148 CD360 75c multicolored 1.45 1.45
1149 CD360 95c multicolored 1.80 1.80
Nos. 1146-1149 (4) 5.00 5.00

Souvenir Sheet
Without Gold Frames
1150 CD360 Sheet of 5, #a-e 7.25 7.25

Royal Navy Ships A207

Designs: 15c, HMS St. Lucia, 1803. 75c, HMS Thetis, 1781. $1, HMS Berwick, 1903. $5, HMS Victory, 1805.

Wmk. 373
2002, June 10 **Litho.** *Perf. 14*
1151-1154 A207 Set of 4 10.00 10.00

Queen Mother Elizabeth (1900-2002)
Common Design Type

Designs: 50c, Holding baby (black and white photograph). 65c, Wearing red hat. 95c, Wearing hat (black and white photograph). $1, Wearing blue hat.
No. 1159: a, $2, Wearing tiara. b, $2, Wearing blue hat, diff.

Perf. 13¾x14¼
2002, Aug. 5 **Litho.** **Wmk. 373**
With Purple Frames
1155 CD361 50c multicolored .80 .80
1156 CD361 65c multicolored 1.10 1.10
1157 CD361 95c multicolored 1.50 1.50
1158 CD361 $1 multicolored 1.60 1.60
Nos. 1155-1158 (4) 5.00 5.00

Souvenir Sheet
Without Purple Frames
Perf. 14½x14¼
1159 CD361 Sheet of 2, #a-b 7.00 7.00

Awarding of Nobel Literature Prize to Derek Walcott, 10th Anniv. — A208

Designs: 20c, Walcott. 65c, Men and children, horiz. 70c, Women. $5, People in boat.

Wmk. 373
2002, Oct. 11 **Litho.** *Perf. 13¾*
1160-1163 A208 Set of 4 8.00 8.00

Salvation Army in St. Lucia, Cent. A209

Designs: 20c, William and Catherine Booth, Salvation Army workers. $1, Early Salvation Army officers in parade. $2.50, Salvation Army shield, "Blood and Fire" crest.

Wmk. 373
2002, Nov. 27 **Litho.** *Perf. 14*
1164-1166 A209 Set of 3 8.00 8.00

Christmas — A210

Paintings: 20c, Adoration of the Shepherds, by Bernardino. 50c, Adoration of the Kings, by Girolamo, vert. 75c, Adoration of the Kings, by Foppa, vert. $5, Adoration of the Shepherds, by the Le Nain Brothers.

2002, Dec. 4 *Perf. 14x14¾, 14¾x14*
1167-1170 A210 Set of 4 9.00 9.00

Coronation of Queen Elizabeth II, 50th Anniv.
Common Design Type

Designs: Nos. 1171, 20c, 1173b, Queen with crown. Nos. 1172, 75c, 1173a, Queen's carriage.

Perf. 14¼x14½
2003, June 2 **Litho.** **Wmk. 373**
Vignettes Framed, Red Background
1171 CD363 20c multicolored .50 .50
1172 CD363 75c multicolored 1.75 1.75

Souvenir Sheet
Vignettes Without Frame, Purple Panel
1173 CD363 $2.50 Sheet of 2, #a-b 6.50 6.50

200 Years of Continuous Mail Service — A211

Designs: 20c, Letters from 1803 and 1844, 1822 fleuron postmark. 25c, St. Lucia #1-3. 65c, Map, mail ship Hewanorra. 75c, Post offices of 1900 and present time.

Wmk. 373
2003, July 14 **Litho.** *Perf. 14¼*
1174-1177 A211 Set of 4 3.75 3.75

Powered Flight, Cent. — A212

Designs: 20c, Sikorsky S-38. 70c, Consolidated PBY-5A Catalina. $1, Lockheed Lodestar. $5, Spitfire Mk V "St. Lucia."

Perf. 13¼x13¾
2003, Nov. 28 **Wmk. 373**
Stamps + Labels
1178-1181 A212 Set of 4 9.75 9.75

Parrot A213

Island A214

Perf. 14x14¼
2003, Nov. **Coil Stamps**
1182 A213 10c multicolored .25 .25
1183 A214 25c multicolored .40 .30

Christmas A215

Madonna and Child and: 20c, Sorrel flowers, ginger root. 75c, Sorrel drink, ginger ale. 95c, Masqueraders. $1, Christmas lanterns.

2003, Dec. 2 *Perf. 14*
1184-1187 A215 Set of 4 5.25 5.25

Independence, 25th Anniv. — A216

Designs: 20c, Flag raising ceremony, vert. 95c, People, book, airplane, ships, banana plant, vert. $1.10, "25" and leaves. $5, Harbor.

2004, Feb. 20 *Perf. 13¾*
1188-1191 A216 Set of 4 7.50 7.50

Caribbean Bird Festival — A217

No. 1192: a, Antillean crested hummingbird. b, St. Lucia pewee. c, Purple-throated carib. d, Gray trembler. e, Rufous-throated solitaire. f, St. Lucia warbler. g, Antillean euphonia. h, Semper's warbler.

Perf. 13¼x13
2004, June 30 **Litho.** **Wmk. 373**
1192 A217 Block of 8 10.00 10.00
a.-h. $1 Any single 1.25 1.25

Tourism A218

Designs: 45c, Sailing. 65c, Horse riding. 70c, Scuba diving. $1, Walking.

2004, Sept. 6 *Perf. 13¼*
1193-1196 A218 Set of 4 5.00 5.00

World AIDS Day A219

Designs: No. 1197, 30c, Condoms, syringe, couple. No. 1198, 30c, Children, woman.

Wmk. 373
2004, Dec. 1 **Litho.** *Perf. 14*
1197-1198 A219 Set of 2 2.25 2.25

Christmas — A220

Painting details: 30c, Adoration of the Kings, by Dosso Dossi. 75c, Adoration of the Shepherds, by Nicolas Poussin, vert. 95c, Adoration of the Kings, by Joos van Wassenhove, vert. $1, Adoration of the Shepherds, by Carel Fabritius.

2004, Dec. 14 *Perf. 14x14¾, 14¾x14*
1199-1202 A220 Set of 4 3.50 3.50

St. Joseph's Convent, 150th Anniv. A221

Nun and: 30c, Women. 95c, Convent and steps. $2.50, Building and street.

Wmk. 373
2005, Mar. 14 **Litho.** *Perf. 13¾*
1203-1205 A221 Set of 3 5.50 5.50

Battle of Trafalgar, Bicent. — A222

Designs: 30c, HMS Thunderer off St. Lucia. 75c, HMS Britannia in action against the Bucentaure. 95c, Admiral Horatio Nelson, vert. $5, HMS Victory.
$10, HMS Thunderer (44x44mm).

Wmk. 373, Unwmkd. ($5)
2005, June 13 **Litho.** *Perf. 13¼*
1206-1209 A222 Set of 4 8.75 8.75
Souvenir Sheet
Perf. 13¾
1210 A222 $10 multi 11.00 11.00

No. 1209 has particles of wood from the HMS Victory embedded in the areas covered by a thermographic process that produces a shiny, raised effect.

Pope John Paul II (1920-2005) A223

2005, Aug. 29 **Wmk. 373** *Perf. 14*
1211 A223 $2 multi 3.00 3.00

Christmas — A224

Designs: 30c, Church of the Purification of the Blessed Virgin, Castries. $5, Minor Basilica of the Immaculate Conception, Castries.

Wmk. 373
2005, Nov. 28   Litho.   Perf. 14
1212-1213 A224 Set of 2   5.00 5.00

Fruits and Nuts A225

Designs: 15c, Blighia sapida. 20c, Solanum melongena. 25c, Mangifera indica. 30c, Coccoloba uvifera. 50c, Carica papaya. 55c, Spondias mombin. 65c, Chrysobalanus icaco. 70c, Artocarpus altilis. 75c, Annona reticulata. 95c, Psidium guajava. $1, Musa sp. $2.50, Manilkara achras. $5, Anacardium occidentale. $25, Mammea americana.

2005, Dec. 5   **Perf. 14**
1214 A225 15c multi   .30   .30
1215 A225 20c multi   .30   .30
1216 A225 25c multi   .30   .30
1217 A225 30c multi   .30   .30
   a.   Wmk. 406, dated "2010"   .30   .30
   b.   Wmk. 406, dated "2013"   .25   .25
1218 A225 50c multi   .40   .40
1219 A225 55c multi   .45   .45
1220 A225 65c multi   .50   .50
1221 A225 70c multi   .55   .55
1222 A225 75c multi   .60   .60
1223 A225 95c multi   .80   .80
1224 A225 $1 multi   .85   .85
1225 A225 $2.50 multi   2.10 2.10
1226 A225 $5 multi   4.25 4.25
1227 A225 $25 multi   20.00 20.00
   Nos. 1214-1227 (14)   31.70 31.70
   Issued: No. 1217a, 4/7/10.

Art by Llewellyn Xavier — A226

Designs: 20c, Axe Head. 30c, Turtle. $2.50, Pre-Columbian Vase. $5, Pre-Columbian Zemi.

Wmk. 373
2006, Mar. 15   Litho.   Perf. 12¾
1228-1231 A226 Set of 4   6.00 6.00

2006 World Cup Soccer Championships, Germany — A227

Various soccer players: 95c, $2.

Wmk. 373
2006, June 9   Litho.   Perf. 14
1232-1233 A227 Set of 2   2.25 2.25
1233a   Souvenir sheet, #1232-1233   2.25 2.25

Leeward Islands Air Transport, 50th Anniv. A228

LIAT airplane: 30c, In flight. 75c, On ground.

Perf. 12½x13
2006, Oct. 16   Litho.   Wmk. 373
1234-1235 A228 Set of 2   .80   .80

Christmas A229

Designs: 95c, Choir and director. $2, Sesenne Descartes, folk singer, and musicians.

2006, Nov. 16
1236-1237 A229 Set of 2   2.25 2.25

Cricket — A230

Designs: 30c, Mindoo Phillip. 75c, Map and flag of St. Lucia. 95c, Beausejour Cricket Grounds, horiz.
$5, Beausejour Cricket Grounds, horiz. diff.

Perf. 13x12½, 12½x13
2007, Feb. 28   Litho.
1238-1240 A230 Set of 3   1.50 1.50
Souvenir Sheet
1241 A230 $5 multi   3.75 3.75
No. 1241 contains one 56x42mm stamp.

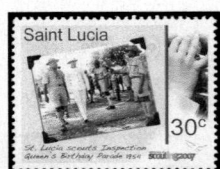

Scouting, Cent. A231

Designs: 30c, Inspection of St. Lucia Scouts, 1954 Queen's Birthday Parade, hands and trumpet. $5, St. Lucia Cub Scout laying wreath, 2005 Remembrance Day Parade, poppies.
No. 1244, vert.: a, St. Lucia Scout Association emblem. b, Lord Robert Baden-Powell and Chief Joe Big Plume.

Wmk. 373
2007, Aug. 20   Litho.   Perf. 13¾
1242-1243 A231 Set of 2   4.00 4.00
Souvenir Sheet
1244 A231 $2.50 Sheet of 2, #a-b   3.75 3.75

Christmas A232

Designs: 30c, Lantern Parade. $10, Nativity scene.

Perf. 12½x13
2007, Dec. 10   Litho.   Wmk. 373
1245-1246 A232 Set of 2   7.75 7.75

2008 Summer Olympics, Beijing A233

Designs: 75c, Bamboo, diving. 95c, Dragon, running. $1, Lanterns, running. $2.50, Fish, high jump.

Wmk. 373
2008, Apr. 30   Litho.   Perf. 13¼
1247-1250 A233 Set of 4   4.00 4.00

Worldwide Fund For Nature (WWF) — A234

Saint Lucia whiptail: 75c, On leaves. $2.50, On grass and rocks. $5, Two whiptails facing left. $10, Two whiptails facing left and right.

Wmk. 373
2008, Nov. 4   Litho.   Perf. 14
1251-1254 A234 Set of 4   14.00 14.00
1254a   Miniature sheet of 16, 4 each #1251-1254   56.00 56.00

University of the West Indies, 60th Anniv. A235

Wmk. 373
2008, Nov. 14   Litho.   Perf. 13
1255 A235 $5 multi   4.00 4.00

Christmas A236

Designs: 95c, Wreath, bell, ornaments, gift, rose. $5, Star, candle, Holy Family, holly.

2008, Nov. 25   Perf. 13¼
1256-1257 A236 Set of 2   4.75 4.75

Independence, 30th Anniv. — A237

Designs: 30c, Castries waterfront. $2.50, Roseau Dam. $5, Rodney Bay Marina. $10, Sir John G. M. Compton (1925-2007), prime minister, and flag.

Perf. 12½x13
2009, Feb. 20   Litho.   Wmk. 406
1258-1261 A237 Set of 4   13.50 13.50

Intl. Year of Biodiversity — A238

Designs: 30c, Lobelia. 75c, Iguana. 95c, Hercules beetle. $2.50, White-breasted thrasher.

Perf. 13x12¾
2010, June 11   Litho.   Wmk. 406
1262-1265 A238 Set of 4   3.50 3.50

Gros-Islets Township, 25th Anniv. — A239

Perf. 14x15
2010, Aug. 27   Litho.   Wmk. 406
1266 A239 95c multi   .70   .70

Service of Queen Elizabeth II and Prince Philip — A240

Designs: No. 1267, $1.50, Prince Philip. No. 1268, $1.50, Queen Elizabeth II and Prince Philip. No. 1269, $2, Queen and Prince Philip, color photograph, diff. No. 1270, $2, Queen and Prince Philip, black-and-white photograph. No. 1271, $2.50, Queen and Prince Philip, black-and-white photograph, diff. No. 1272, $2.50, Queen.
$6, Queen and Prince Philip, diff.

Perf. 13¼
2011, Mar. 1   Litho.   Unwmk.
1267-1272 A240 Set of 6   9.00 9.00
1272a   Sheet of 6, #1267-1272, + 3 labels   9.00 9.00
Souvenir Sheet
1273 A240 $6 multi   4.50 4.50

Campaign Against HIV and AIDS, 30th Anniv. — A241

Perf. 12¾x13
2011, Sept. 1   Litho.   Wmk. 406
1274 A241 30c multicolored   .25   .25

Bishop Charles Gachet (1911-84) and Church, Soufriere — A242

2011, Dec. 1   **Perf. 14**
1275 A242 30c multicolored   .25 .25
Christmas.

Reign of Queen Elizabeth II, 60th Anniv. — A243

Queen Elizabeth II: No. 1276, $1.50, Wearing blue green dress. No. 1277, $1.50, Wearing crown. No. 1278, $2, Without tiara. No. 1279, $2, Wearing tiara. No. 1280, $2.50, Without hat. No. 1281, $2.50, Wearing hat. $6, Wearing tiara.

2012, Feb. 6   **Unwmk.**   **Perf. 13½**
1276-1281 A243 Set of 6   9.00 9.00
1281a   Souvenir sheet, #1276-
     1281 + 3 labels   9.00 9.00
Souvenir Sheet
1282 A243 $6 multi   4.50 4.50

Paintings by Llewellyn Xavier A244

Designs: $5, Pitons. $10, The Spirit of Freedom, vert.

Perf. 13¼x13½, 13½x13¼
2013, Apr. 8   **Litho.**   **Unwmk.**
1283-1284 A244 Set of 2   11.50 11.50

Dragonflies — A245

Designs: 5c, Antillean skimmer. 20c, Spot-tailed dasher. 30c, Vermillion saddlebags. 50c, Tawny pennant. 75c, Great pondhawk. $1, Band-winged dragonlet. $1.50, Wandering glider. $2, Rambur's forktail.

2013, Apr. 8   **Litho.**   **Perf. 13½**
1285 A245 5c multi   .25 .25
1286 A245 20c multi   .25 .25
1287 A245 30c multi   .25 .25
1288 A245 50c multi   .35 .35
1289 A245 75c multi   .55 .55
1290 A245 $1 multi   .75 .75
1291 A245 $1.50 multi   1.10 1.10
1292 A245 $2 multi   1.50 1.50
   Nos. 1285-1292 (8)   5.00 5.00

Elevation to Cardinal of Archbishop Kelvin Edward Felix — A246

Designs: $3, Cardinal Felix. $5, Pope Francis and Cardinal Felix, horiz.

Perf. 13¾x13½, 13½x13¾
2014, Dec. 12   **Litho.**
1293-1294 A246 Set of 2   6.00 6.00

AIR POST STAMP

Catalogue values for unused stamps in this section are for Never Hinged items.

Map of St. Lucia — AP1

Perf. 14½x14
1967, Mar. 1   **Photo.**   **Unwmk.**
C1 AP1 15c blue   .50 .50
St. Lucia's independence.
Exists imperf. and also in souvenir sheet. Values: single, $10; souvenir sheet $40.

POSTAGE DUE STAMPS

D1

Type I — "No." 3mm wide (shown).
Type II — "No." 4mm wide.

Rough Perf. 12
1931   **Unwmk.**   **Typeset**
J1 D1 1p blk, *gray bl*, type I   10.00 20.00
  a.   Type II   24.00 47.50
J2 D1 2p blk, *yel*, type I   22.00 47.50
  a.   Type II   45.00 105.00
  b.   Vertical pair, imperf. btwn.   7,500.

The serial numbers are handstamped. Type II has round "o" and period. Type I has tall "o" and square period.

Catalogue values for unused stamps in this section, from this point to the end of the section, are for Never Hinged items.

D2

1933-47   **Typo.**   **Wmk. 4**   *Perf. 14*
Chalky Paper
J3 D2 1p black   15.00 8.00
J4 D2 2p black   40.00 10.00
J5 D2 4p black ('47)   11.00 50.00
J6 D2 8p black ('47)   11.00 60.00
  Nos. J3-J6 (4)   77.00 128.00
   Issue date: June 28, 1947.

Chalky Paper
1952, Nov. 27   **Values in Cents**
J7 D2 2c black   .25 9.50
  a.   Ordinary paper ('49)   1.90 30.00
J8 D2 4c black   .60 14.00
  a.   Ordinary paper ('49)   3.75 24.00
J9 D2 8c black   3.50 50.00
  a.   Ordinary paper ('49)   3.50 30.00
J10 D2 16c black   5.00 65.00
  a.   Ordinary paper ('49)   16.00 75.00
  Nos. J7-J10 (4)   9.35 138.50
   Nos. J7a-J10a issued 10/1/1949.

Wmk. 4a (error)
J7a D2 2c   40.00
J8a D2 4c   55.00
J9a D2 8c   350.00
J10a D2 16c   475.00
  Nos. J7a-J10a (4)   920.00

1965, Mar. 9   **Wmk. 314**
J11 D2 2c black   .75 10.00
J12 D2 4c black   1.00 11.00
In the 2c center the "c" is heavier and the period bigger.
  Nos. J9-J12 exist with overprint "Statehood/1st Mar. '67" in red. Values: unused $190; used $160.

Arms of St. Lucia — D3

1981, Aug. 4   **Litho.**   **Wmk. 373**
J13 D3 5c red brown   .25 .65
J14 D3 15c green   .25 .50
J15 D3 25c deep orange   .25 .50
J16 D3 $1 dark blue   .25 1.25
  Nos. J13-J16 (4)   1.00 2.90

1990   **Wmk. 384**   *Perf. 15x14*
J17 D3 5c red brown   .25 .25
J18 D3 15c green   .25 .25
J19 D3 25c deep orange   .25 .25
J20 D3 $1 dark blue   .50 1.00
  Nos. J17-J20 (4)   1.25 1.75

WAR TAX STAMPS

No. 65 Overprinted

1916   **Wmk. 3**   *Perf. 14*
MR1 A11 1p scarlet   13.00 19.00
  a.   Double overprint   550.00 650.00
  b.   1p carmine   67.50 55.00

Overprinted

MR2 A11 1p scarlet   1.40 .35

OFFICIAL STAMPS

Catalogue values for unused stamps in this section are for Never Hinged items.

Nos. 504-515 Overprinted

Wmk. 373
1983, Oct. 13   **Litho.**   *Perf. 14½*
O1 A95 5c multicolored   .30 .25
O2 A95 10c multicolored   .30 .25
O3 A95 15c multicolored   .30 .25
O4 A95 20c multicolored   .35 .25
O5 A95 25c multicolored   .50 .45
O6 A95 30c multicolored   .70 .45
O7 A95 50c multicolored   .80 .45
O8 A95 75c multicolored   1.10 .80
O9 A95 $1 multicolored   1.50 1.00
O10 A95 $2 multicolored   2.00 2.25
O11 A95 $5 multicolored   4.00 4.25
O12 A95 $10 multicolored   8.50 10.00
  Nos. O1-O12 (12)   20.35 20.65

Nos. 747-761 Overprinted

1985, May 7   **Litho.**   *Perf. 15*
O13 A126 5c multicolored   .65 1.00
O14 A126 10c multicolored   .65 1.00
O15 A126 20c multicolored   .75 1.00
O16 A126 25c multicolored   .75 .75
O17 A126 30c multicolored   .90 .90
O18 A126 35c multicolored   1.00 1.00
O19 A126 45c multicolored   1.10 1.10
O20 A126 50c multicolored   1.25 1.25
O21 A126 65c multicolored   1.40 1.50
O22 A126 75c multicolored   1.40 2.00
O23 A126 90c multicolored   1.50 2.10
O24 A126 $1 multicolored   2.00 2.25
O25 A126 $2.50 multicolored   3.25 4.00
O26 A126 $5 multicolored   5.00 5.50
O27 A126 $15 multicolored   10.50 12.00
  Nos. O13-O27 (15)   32.10 37.35

Nos. 953-964 Overprinted

1990, Feb. 21   **Wmk. 384**   *Perf. 14*
O28 A162 10c multicolored   .40 1.00
O29 A162 15c multicolored   .40 1.00
O30 A162 20c multicolored   .50 .50
O31 A162 25c multicolored   .50 .50
O32 A162 50c multicolored   .65 .65
O33 A162 80c multicolored   .75 .75
O34 A162 95c multicolored   1.25 1.25
O35 A162 $1 multicolored   1.40 1.40
O36 A162 $1.50 multicolored   2.00 2.50
O37 A162 $2.50 multicolored   3.25 3.75
O38 A162 $5 multicolored   6.00 6.50
O39 A162 $25 multicolored   16.00 18.00
  Nos. O28-O39 (12)   33.10 37.80

Issued: 20c, 25c, 50c, $25, 2/21; 10c, 15c, 80c, $1.50, 4/12; 95c, $1, $2.50, $5, 6/25.

STE. MARIE DE MADAGASCAR

sānt-mə-rē-də-ˌmad-ə-ˈgas-kər

LOCATION — An island off the east coast of Madagascar
GOVT. — French Possession
AREA — 64 sq. mi.
POP. — 8,000 (approx.)

In 1896 Ste.-Marie de Madagascar was attached to the colony of Madagascar for administrative purposes.

100 Centimes = 1 Franc

Navigation and Commerce — A1

1894 Unwmk. Typo. *Perf. 14x13½*
Name of Colony in Blue or Carmine

1	A1	1c black, *lil bl*	1.75	1.75
2	A1	2c brown, *buff*	2.75	2.75
3	A1	4c claret, *lavender*	5.00	5.00
4	A1	5c green, *grnsh*	12.00	11.00
5	A1	10c black, *lavender*	13.50	10.50
6	A1	15c blue	40.00	36.00
7	A1	20c red, *green*	30.00	28.00
8	A1	25c black, *rose*	25.00	22.00
9	A1	30c brown, *bister*	17.50	16.00
10	A1	40c red, *straw*	17.50	16.00
11	A1	50c carmine, *rose*	52.50	52.50
12	A1	75c violet, *org*	100.00	72.50
13	A1	1fr brnz grn, *straw*	52.50	47.50
		Nos. 1-13 (13)	370.00	321.50

Perf. 13½x14 stamps are counterfeits.

These stamps were replaced by those of Madagascar.

ST. MARTIN

sānt ˌmär-tən

LOCATION — The southern part of the island of St. Martin in the Caribbean Sea.
AREA — 13 sq. mi.
POP. — 33,119 (2007)
CAPITAL — Philipsburg

On Oct. 10, 2010, St. Martin, formerly part of Netherlands Antilles, became a constituent state within the Kingdom of the Netherlands.

100 Cents = 1 Florin (gulden)

Catalogue values for all unused stamps in this country are for Never Hinged items.

Flag, Arms, Map of Island and West Indies, Map of South America A1

** *Perf. 13¾***
2010, Oct. 10   Litho.   Unwmk.

1	A1	164c multi	2.00	2.00

25th Paper Money Fair, Maastricht, Nedtherlands — A2

No. 2: a, 80c, 50 koruna banknote, Slovakia, 1999. b, 112c, 100 franc banknote, New Hebrides, 1977. c, 145c, 20 pula banknote, Botswana, 1982. d, 195c, 50 dalasi banknote, Gambia, 1989. e, 240c, 10 rupee banknote, Sri Lanka, 1979. f, 285c, 10 riyal banknote, Qatar, 2003.

2011, Apr. 6   *Perf. 14*

2	A2	Block of 6, #a-f	12.00	12.00

Miniature Sheet

Peonies — A3

No. 3: a, Pink peony. b, Two white peonies and bud. c, White peony. d, Red peony and bud.
350c, Blue peonies.

2011, Apr. 28

3	A3	110c Sheet of 4, #a-d	5.00	5.00

Souvenir Sheet

4	A3	350c multi	4.00	4.00

Butterflies — A4

No. 5: a, 50c, Ornithoptera chimaera. b, 70c, Morpho cypris. c, 120c, Paralaxita lacoon. d, 145c, Eurytides iphitas. e, 166c, Dercas lycorias. f, 210c, Ancyluris jurgensenii.

2011, June 1   Litho.   *Perf. 14*

5	A4	Block of 6, #a-f	8.50	8.50

Flowers — A5

No. 6: a, 21c, Camellia "Yuletide." b, 25c, Cornus kousa. c, 30c, Magnolia "Vulcan." d, 34c, Bidens laevis. e, 40c, Syringa vulgaris. f, 60c, Rosa "Charmian." g, 80c, Philadelphus. h, 170c, Rhododendron arboreum. i, 190c, Hydrangea macrophylla. j, 220c, Magnolia grandiflora. k, 295c, Buddleja davidii. l, 335c, Ribes sanguineum.

2011, Aug. 24

6	A5	Block of 12, #a-l	17.00	17.00

Maps — A6

No. 7: a, 111c, Map of St. Martin. b, 145c, Map of Caribbean Sea with St. Martin highlighted, vert. c, 350c, Map of South America with St. Martin highlighted, vert.

2011, Oct. 5

7	A6	Vert. strip of 3, #a-c	7.00	7.00

A7

A8

Designs of stamps inscribed "A": No. 8, Clock. No. 9, Agraulis vanillae. No. 10, Salt pickers. No. 11, Mangos. No. 12, Coconuts.
Designs of denominated stamps: 115c, Princess Juliana International Airport. 145c, Ocean Liner *Allure of the Seas.* 195c, Flamboyant tree. 205c, Danaus plexippus. 240c, Winair airplane. 285c, Pelican. 405c, Aerial view of Philipsburg.
No. 20: a, Beach. b, Maho Beach Airport. c, Harbor.

2011   Litho.   *Perf. 14*
Stamps Inscribed "A"

8	A7	(115c) multi	1.40	1.40
9	A7	(204c) multi	2.25	2.25
10	A7	(205c) multi	2.40	2.40
11	A7	(285c) multi	3.25	3.25
12	A7	(380c) multi	4.25	4.25
		Nos. 8-12 (5)	13.55	13.55

Stamps With Denominations

13	A8	115c multi	1.40	1.40
14	A8	145c multi	1.75	1.75
15	A8	195c multi	2.25	2.25
16	A8	205c multi	2.40	2.40
17	A8	240c multi	2.75	2.75
18	A8	285c multi	3.25	3.25
19	A8	405c multi	4.50	4.50
		Nos. 13-19 (7)	18.30	18.30

Size: 19x15mm
** *Perf. 13¾x13¼***

20	Strip of 3, #a-c	5.75	5.75
a.-c.	A8 170c Any single	1.90	1.90

Issued: Nos. 8-12, 14-15, 17-19, 10/6; Nos. 13, 16, 11/15; No. 20, 11/11. See Nos. 26-27.

Ships — A9

No. 21: a, 50c, Skuldelev Knorr, c. 1030. b, 60c, Mataro, 1450. c, 80c, St. Micahel, 1669. d, 380c, Herring buss, 1700. e, 405c, Wendur, 1884. f, 525c, Pearling dhow, c. 1900.

2011, Nov. 30   *Perf. 14*

21	A9	Block of 6, #a-f	17.00	17.00

Butterflies — A10

No. 22: a, 25c, Boloria selene. b, 50c, Hesperia comma. c, 75c, Lysandra bellargus. d, 100c, Limenitis camilla. e, 150c, Erebia aethiops. f, 200c, Minois dryas. g, 250c, Vanessa atalanta. h, 300c, Zerynthia polyxena. i, 305c, Parnassius phoebus smintheus. j, 310c, Clossiana dia. k, 335c, Pieris rapae. l, 400c, Brenthis daphne.

2012, Feb. 29

22	A10	Block of 12, #a-l	30.00	30.00

Flowers — A11

No. 23: a, 10c, Anemone hupehensis. b, 25c, Caltha palustris. c, 50c, Helleborus thibetanus. d, 125c, Lobelia cardinalis. e, 125c, Osteospermum jucundum. f, 175c, Narcissus. g, 225c, Hemerocallis. h, 355c, Doronicum orientale. i, 455c, Catharanthus roseus. j, 500c, Alstromeria.

2012, Apr. 4
23 A11 Block of 10, #a-j 23.00 23.00

Women's Carnival Costumes — A12

No. 24 — Various costumes: a, 115c. b, 250c. c, 275c. d, 375c.

2012, May 2
24 A12 Horiz. strip of 4, #a-d 11.50 11.50

Historical Sites — A13

No. 25: a, 170c, Border Monument with two dates at Fort St. Louis. b, 200c, Border Monument with one date. c, 300c, Courthouse.

2012, May 30
25 A13 Horiz. strip of 3, #a-c 7.50 7.50

Type of 2011

Designs: 10c, Flamboyant tree in bloom. 175c, Princess Juliana International Airport.

2012, June 13   *Perf. 14*
26 A8 10c multi .25 .25
27 A8 175c multi 2.00 2.00

A14

Indonesia 2012 Intl. Stamp Exhibition, Jakarta — A15

No. 28: a, 120c, Prambanan Hindu Temple. b, 300c, Varanus komodoensis. c, 400c, Borobudur Buddhist Temple.
No. 29 — Rafflesia arnoldii flower with denomination at: a, 50c, LL. b, 100c, LR. c, 250c, UL. d, 400c, UR.

2012, June 13
28 A14 Vert. strip of 3, #a-c 9.25 9.25

Souvenir Sheet
29 A15 Sheet of 4, #a-d 9.00 9.00

2012 Summer Olympics, London — A16

No. 30: a, 25c, Handball. b, 50c, Running. c, 75c, Field hockey. d, 90c, Judo. e, 100c, Tennis. f, 120c, Soccer. g, 170c, Kayaking. h, 200c, Cycling. i, 220c, Gymnastics. j, 250c, Basketball. k, 300c, Beach volleyball. l, 400c, Triple jump.
No. 31: a, 125c, Archery. b, 225c, Diving. c, 350c, Weight lifting.

2012, July 18
30 A16 Block of 12, #a-l 22.50 22.50

Souvenir Sheet
31 A16 Sheet of 3, #a-c 8.00 8.00

Dutch Royalty — A17

No. 32: a, 100c, Queen Beatrix. b, 125c, Queen Beatrix at ship's wheel. c, 200c, Queen Beatrix holding infant. d, 275c, Prince Willem-Alexander. e, 325c, Princess Margriet. f, 475c, Princess Máxima.

2012, Sept. 12
32 A17 Block of 6, #a-f 17.00 17.00

Miniature Sheet

Final Position of 1948 Chess Match Between Mikhail Botvinnik and Max Euwe — A18

No. 33: a, 10c, Black rook. b, 20c, Black king. c, 30c, White pawn. d, 40c, Black rook. e, 55c, Black pawn. f, 75c, Black pawn. g, 85c, Black knight. h, 95c, Black pawn. i, 100c, Black pawn. j, 110c, Black pawn. k, 120c, White bishop. l, 135c, White pawn. m, 165c, White pawn. n, 185c, White bishop. o, 195c, White pawn. p, 210c, White rook. q, 230c, White pawn. r, 260c, White pawn. s, 380c, White king.

2012, Oct. 17
33 A18 Sheet of 19, #a-s, +
      45 labels 28.00 28.00

Local Scenes — A19

No. 34: a, 115c, Fort Amsterdam. b, 200c, Hoofdstraat. c, 250c, View of beach. d, 350c, Airplane on final approach over Maho Beach.

2012, Nov. 14
34 A19 Block of 4, #a-d 12.50 12.50

Birds — A20

No. 35: a, 10c, Amazilia leucogaster. b, 30c, Aulacorhynchus derbianus. c, 50c, Bubo virginianus. d, 75c, Jacamerops aurea. e, 100c, Pteroglossus aracari. f, 150c, Discosura longicauda. g, 175c, Accipiter bicolor. h, 200c, Gampsonyx swainsonii. i, 240c, Leptodon cayanensis. j, 300c, Topaza pella. k, 350c, Trogon violaceus. l, 400c, Cotinga cayana.

2012, Dec. 12
35 A20 Block of 12, #a-l 24.00 24.00

Churches — A21

No. 36: a, 110c, Cole Bay Seventh Day Adventist Church. b, 150c, Simpson Bay Catholic Church. c, 200c, Philipsburg Methodist Church, vert. d, 350c, South Reward Catholic Church, vert.

2013, Jan. 2   *Litho.*   *Perf. 14*
36 A21 Block of 4, #a-d 9.25 9.25

Miniature Sheet

Birds — A22

No. 37: a, 25c, Columba plumbea. b, 50c, Chlorostilbon mellisugus. c, 75c, Cyanocorax cyanomelas. d, 100c, Eucometis penicillata. e, 150c, Mionectes oleagineus. f, 200c, Hemithraupis flavicollis. g, 225c, Myrmotherula guttata. h, 250c, Piaya cayana. i, 300c, Piaya melanogaster. j, 350c, Piaya minuta. k, 400c, Pygiptila stellaris. l, 475c, Turdus fumigatus.

2013, Feb. 6   *Litho.*   *Perf. 14*
37 A22 Sheet of 12, #a-l, +
      3 labels 29.00 29.00

Politicians — A23

No. 38: a, 250c, Dr. Albert Claudius Wathey (1926-98). b, 300c, Vance James, Jr. (1949-2008).

2013, Mar. 6	Litho.	Perf. 14		
38	A23	Horiz. pair, #a-b	6.25	6.25

Cruise
Ships
A24

Designs: No. 39, 180c, Allure of the Seas. No. 40, 180c, Oasis of the Seas. No. 41, 180c, Ruby Princess. No. 42, 180c, Queen Victoria. No. 43, 180c, Carnival Dream. No. 44, 180c, Disney Fantasy.

2013		Litho.	Perf. 13¾	
39-44	A24	Set of 6	12.00	12.00

Issued: Nos. 39-40, 3/6; Nos. 41-42, 4/3; Nos. 43-44, 6/5.
Compare with type A43.

Local Scenes — A25

No. 45: a, 75c, A. C. Wathey Cruise Pier. b, 100c, Dr. A. C. Wathery Port Complex. c, 215c, Grote Bay. d, 325c, KLM airplane landing.

2013, Apr. 3	Litho.	Perf. 14		
45	A25	Block of 4, #a-d	8.00	8.00

Butterflies — A26

No. 46: a, 25c, Adelpha bredowii. b, 50c, Anteros carausias. c, 75c, Anthocharis sara. d, 100c, Asterocampa leilia. e, 150c, Calycopis cecrops. f, 175c, Charaxes jasius. g, 225c, Glaucosyche lygdamus. h, 250c,

Gonepteryx rhamni. i, 325c, Hamadryas feronia. j, 350c, Plebejus acmon. k, 375c, Pyrgus communis. l, 400c, Strymon melinus.

2013, May 2	Litho.	Perf. 14		
46	A26	Block of 12, #a-l	28.00	28.00

Miniature Sheet

Scouting — A27

No. 47: a, 175c, Scout holding St. Martin troop sign. b, 200c, Four Scouts. c, 250c, Two Scouts in kayaks, horiz. d, 350c, Four Scouts, horiz.

2013, June 5	Litho.	Perf. 14		
47	A27	Sheet of 4, #a-d	11.00	11.00

Dutch Royalty — A28

No. 48: a, 100c, King William I. b, 200c, King William II. c, 300c, King William III. d, 400c, Queen Wilhelmina. e, 450c, Queen Juliana. f, 550c, Queen Beatrix.
No. 49: a, 300c, Queen Máxima. b, 550c, King Willem-Alexander.

2013, July 10	Litho.	Perf. 14		
48	A28	Sheet of 6, #a-f, + 3 labels	22.50	22.50

Souvenir Sheet

| 49 | A28 | Sheet of 2, #a-b | 9.50 | 9.50 |

Ships — A29

No. 50: a, 125c, Savannah, 1819. b, 200c, Steam trawler, 1877. c, 275c, Alice M. Colburn, 1896. d, 325c, Muirneag, 1903. e, 350c, S.T.S. Lord Nelson, 1985. f, 350c, S.T.S. Young Endeavour, 1987.

2013, Sept. 4	Litho.	Perf. 14		
50	A29	Block of 6, #a-f	18.50	18.50

United States Lighthouses — A30

No. 51: a, 150c, Cape Hatteras Lighthouse, North Carolina. b, Portland Breakwater Lighthouse, Maine. c, 250c, Cape St. George Lighthouse, Florida. d, 300c, Molokai Lighthouse,

Hawaii. e, 400c, Pensacola Lighthouse, Florida. f, 450c, Rock of Ages Lighthouse, Michigan.

2013, Oct. 2	Litho.	Perf. 14		
51	A30	Block or vert. strip of 6, #a-f	19.50	19.50

Miniature Sheet

Final Position of 1972 Chess Match Between Boris Spassky and Bobby Fischer — A31

No. 52: a, 11c, Black king. b, 22c, Black pawn. c, 33c, Black pawn. d, 44c, Black pawn. e, 60c, White pawn. f, 70c, Black pawn. g, 80c, White pawn. h, 90c, Black pawn. i, 125c, White queen. j, 150c, Black pawn. k, 175c, Black queen. l, 200c, Black bishop. m, 215c, White pawn. n, 225c, White king. o, 300c, White pawn. p, 350c, White pawn. q, 350c, White bishop.

2013, Nov. 6	Litho.	Perf. 14		
52	A31	Sheet of 17, #a-q, + 47 labels	28.00	28.00

Miniature Sheet

Paintings by Johannes Vermeer — A32

No. 53: a, 100c, Girl with a Red Hat. b, 250c, The Milkmaid. c, 350c, Girl with a Pearl Earring. d, 500c, Woman in Blue Reading a Letter.

2013, Dec. 4	Litho.	Perf. 14		
53	A32	Sheet of 4, #a-d, + 2 labels	13.50	13.50

Miniature Sheet

Flowers — A33

No. 54: a, 10c, Costus speciosus. b, 20c, Cynara cardunculus. c, 50c, Dendrobium macrophyllum. d, 70c, Disa diores. e, 90c, Hibiscus rosa-sinensis. f, 100c, Kniphofia. g, 150c, Leontopodium alpinum. h, 210c, Phalaenopsis chibae. i, 300c, Phalaenopsis schilleriana. j, 350c, Rhynchostylis coelestis. k, 400c, Tillandsia cyanea. l, 650c, Vanda coerulea.

2014, Apr. 9	Litho.	Perf. 14		
54	A33	Sheet of 12, #a-l	27.00	27.00

Miniature Sheet

Paintings by Frans Hals (c. 1582-1666) — A34

No. 55: a, 150c, De Vrolijke Drinker (The Merry Drinker). b, 250c, Het Zigeunemeisje (Gypsy Girl). c, 450c, Malle Babbe. d, 550c, De Luitspeler (Jester with a Lute).

2014, May 14	Litho.	Perf. 14		
55	A34	Sheet of 4, #a-d, + 2 labels	16.00	16.00

Miniature Sheet

Birds — A35

No. 56: a, 10c, Celeus elegans. b, 20c, Celeus flavus. c, 50c, Coccyzus melacoryphus. d, 70c, Donacobius atricapillus. e, 90c, Elanoides forficatus. f, 100c, Eupetomena macroura. g, 150c, Gampsonyx swainsonii. h, 210c, Leptodon cayanensis. i, 300c, Mimus gilvus. j, 350c, Momotus momota. k, 400c, Piculus rubiginosus. l, 650c, Venilornis cassini.

2014, June 18	Litho.	Perf. 14		
56	A35	Sheet of 12, #a-l	27.00	27.00

Miniature Sheet

Fruits — A36

No. 57: a, 75c, Fragaria ananassa. b, 125c, Malus domestica. c, 275c, Nephelium lappaceum. d, 325c, Prunus armeniaca. e, 475c, Prunus persica. f, 525c, Pyrus.

2014, Aug. 20	Litho.	Perf. 14
57 A36	Sheet of 6, #a-f	20.00 20.00

Miniature Sheet

Soccer — A37

No. 58 — Soccer ball and: a, 150c, Two players chasing ball. b, 250c, Goalie diving for ball. c, 450c, Player dribbling ball. d, 550c, Player ready to kick ball.

2014, Sept. 17	Litho.	Perf. 14
58 A37	Sheet of 4, #a-d, + 2 labels	16.00 16.00

Miniature Sheet

Netherlands Stamps — A38

No. 59 — Canceled examples of stamps with incorrect perforations: a, 175c, Netherlands #47. b, 325c, Netherlands #154. c, 575c, Netherlands #5. d, 725c, Netherlands #70.

2014, Oct. 15	Litho.	Perf. 14
59 A38	Sheet of 4, #a-d	20.00 20.00

Miniature Sheet

Traditional Women's Dresses — A39

No. 60 — Various dresses: a, 150c. b, 250c. c, 450c. d, 550c.

2014, Nov. 19	Litho.	Perf. 14
60 A39	Sheet of 4, #a-d	16.00 16.00

Butterflies — A40

No. 61: a, 10c, Colias cesonia. b, 20c, Historis acheronta. c, 50c, Historis acheronta, diff. d, 70c, Issoria lathonia. e, 90c, Marpesia chiron. f, 100c, Ornithoptera paradisea. g, 150c, Papilio zelicaon. h, 210c, Polygonia interrogationis. i, 300c, Precis orithya. j, 350c, Speyeria diana. k, 400c, Speyeria idalia. l, 650c, Troides aeacus.

2014, Dec. 10	Litho.	Perf. 14
61 A40	Block of 12, #a-l	27.00 27.00

Birds — A41

No. 62: a, 10c, Micrastur semitorquatus. b, 30c, Brachygalba lugubris. c, 60c, Caprimulgus rufus. d, 90c, Caprimulgus nigrescens. e, 110c, Chondrohierax uncinatus. f, 150c, Colaptes campestris. g, 200c, Chordeiles acutipennis. h, 250c, Hydropsalis climacocerca. i, 300c, Otus atricapillus. j, 325c, Galbula dea. k, 475c, Zebrilus undulates. l, 500c, Eurypyga helias.

2015, Jan. 14	Litho.	Perf. 14
62 A41	Block of 12, #a-l	28.00 28.00

Miniature Sheet

Shells — A42

No. 63: a, 90c, Buccinum politum. b, 110c, Bulla striata. c, 270c, Cypraecassis testiculus. d, 330c, Neptunea contraria. e, 500c, Phos senticosus. f, 600c, Trigonostoma pellucida.

2015, Feb. 11	Litho.	Perf. 14
63 A42	Sheet of 6, #a-f	21.50 21.50

Allure of the Seas — A43

2015, Mar. 2	Litho.	Perf. 14
64 A43	180c multi	2.00 2.00

Compare with type A24.

Banknotes — A44

No. 65: a, 90c, Gabon 5000-franc note. b, 110c, Sri Lanka 2-rupee note. c, 270c, Oman 1-rial note. d, 330c, Zambia 50-kwacha note. e, 500c, Gambia 25-dalasi note. f, 600c, Tanzania 5000-shilling note.

2015, Mar. 18	Litho.	Perf. 14
65 A44	Block of 6, #a-f	21.50 21.50

Souvenir Sheet

Queen Wilhelmina (1880-1962) — A45

No. 66 — Various depictions of Queen Wilhelmina: a, 500c. b, 700c.

2015, Apr. 15	Litho.	Perf. 14
66 A45	Sheet of 2, #a-b	13.50 13.50

Cruise Ships — A46

No. 67: a, Norwegian Getaway. b, Jewel of the Seas. c, Freedom of the Seas. d, Royal Princess.

2015, June 17	Litho.	Perf. 14
67	Horiz. strip of 4	18.00 18.00
a.	A46 275c multi	3.25 3.25
b.	A46 325c multi	3.75 3.75
c.	A46 475c multi	5.25 5.25
d.	A46 525c multi	5.75 5.75

Miniature Sheets

A47

Tourism — A48

No. 68: a, Bottles on Guavaberry Emporium table and shelves. b, Exterior of Guavaberry Emporium. c. Macaws in St. Martin Zoo. d, Peacock in St. Martin Zoo. e, Flamboyant tree on Saunders Estate. f, Boardwalk Village, Philipsburg.

No. 69: a, Children's art on wall, Madam Estate Zoo. b, Mounted butterflies. c, Brown pelican. d, Sculpture. e, Bridge, Simpson Bay Lagoon. f, Iguana.

Serpentine Die Cut 14¼

2015, July 1   Self-Adhesive   Litho.

68	A47	Sheet of 6 + 6 labels	12.00	
a.-f.		180c Any single	2.00	2.00
69	A48	Sheet of 10, #68c-68f, 69a-69f + 10 labels	20.00	
a.-f.		180c Any single	2.00	2.00

Flowers — A49

No. 70: a, 25c, Antigonon leptopus. b, 50c, Fritillaria imperialis, c, 75c, Callistemom lanceolatus. d, 100c, Hibiscus schizopetalus. e, 150c, Canna generalis. f, 250c, Lilium pumilum. g, 350c, Hymenocallis caribaea. h, 400c, Narcissus tazetta. i, 500c, Pyrostegia venusta. j, 600c, Ricinus communis.

2015, Aug. 19   Litho.   Perf. 14

70	A49	Block of 10, #a-j	28.00	28.00

Miniature Sheets

Butterflies — A50

No. 71: a, 25c, Hypolimnas misippus. b, 50c, Papilio krishna. c, 75c, Euphydryas chalcedona. d, 100c, Feniseca tarquinius. e, 150c, Papilio demodocus.

No. 72: a, 250c, Brephidium exile. b, 350c, Pseudotergumia fidia. c, 400c, Satyrium titus. d, 500c, Papilio arcturus. e, 600c, Thessalia theona.

2015, Sept. 16   Litho.   Perf. 14

71	A50	Sheet of 5, #a-e	4.50	4.50
72	A50	Sheet of 5, #a-e	23.50	23.50

Fish — A51

No. 73: a, 25c, Acanthodoras spinosissimus. b, 50c, Acaronia nassa, c, 75c, Acestrorhynchus falcatus. d, 100c, Amphilophus citrinellus. e, 150c, Brochis splendens. f, 250c, Erythrinus erythrinus. g, 350c, Copeina arnoldi. h, 400c, Charax gibbosus. i, 500c,

---

Symphysodon aequifasciatus. j, 600c, Phractocephalus hemioliopterus.

2015, Oct. 14   Litho.   Perf. 14

73	A51	Block of 10, #a-j	28.00	28.00

Primates — A52

No. 74: a, 75c, Cebus capucinus. b, 125c, Ateles geoffroyi. c, 275c, Presbytis obscura. d, 325c, Ateles paniscus. e, 475c, Cebus apella. f, 525c, Callicebus torquatus.

2015, Nov. 18   Litho.   Perf. 14

74	A52	Block of 6, #a-f	20.00	20.00

Pilioko
Paintings — A53

No. 75 — Various paintings with frame color at bottom of: a, 275c, Lilac. b, 325c, Light blue. c, 475c, Dark blue. d, 525c, Ultramarine.

2015, Dec. 9   Litho.   Perf. 14

75	A53	Vert. strip of 4, #a-d	18.00	18.00

Butterflies — A54

No. 76: a, 25c, Achlyodes thraso. b, 100c, Amblyscirtes eos. c, 125c, Anartia jatrophae. d, 200c, Apodemia nais. e, 250c, Atrytonopsis

---

hianna. f, 300c, Biblis hyperia. g, 350c, Callicore hydaspes. h, 400c, Catocala amatrix. i, 450c, Chlosyne rosita. j, 500c, Erora latea.

No. 77, 500c, Tithorea harmonia. No. 78, 500c, Mechanitis polymnia. No. 79, 500c, Morpho anaxibia. No. 80, 500c, Strymon acis bartrami. No. 81, 500c, Perisama priene. No. 82, 500c, Eumaeus atala. No. 83, 500c, Prepona praeneste. No. 84, 500c, Greta andromica. No. 85, 500c, Nymphidium mantus. No. 86, 500c, Arawacus lincoides. No. 87, 500c, Morpho portis. No. 88, 500c, Archaeopropona demophon.

2016, Jan. 2   Litho.   Perf. 14

76	A54	Sheet of 10, #a-j, + 2 labels	30.00	30.00

Souvenir Sheets

77-88	A54	Set of 12	67.50	67.50

Birds — A55

No. 89: a, 25c, Amazonetta brasiliensis. b, 100c, Anhinga anhinga. c, 125c, Aramides saracura. d, 200c, Calidris bairdii. e, 250c, Cariama cristata. f, 300c, Cochlearicus cochlearicus. g, 350c, Crypturellus parvirostris. h, 400c, Cygnus melancoryphus. i, 450c, Gallinago paraguaiae. j, 500c, Jabiru mycteria.
Designs: No. 90, 500c, Amazona aestiva. No. 91, 500c, Amazona xanthops. No. 92, 500c, Anadorhynchus hyacinthinus. No. 93, 500c, Athene cunicularia. No. 94, 500c, Brotogeris chiriri. No. 95, 500c, Brotogeris tirica. No. 96, 500c, Columba picazuro. No. 97, 500c, Columbina picui. No. 98, 500c, Myiopsitta monachus. No. 99, 500c, Pionopsitta pileata. No. 100, 500c, Pyrrhura frontalis. No. 101, 500c, Scardafella squammata.

2016, Jan. 6   Litho.   Perf. 14

89	A55	Sheet of 10, #a-j, + 2 labels	30.00	30.00

Souvenir Sheets

90-101	A55	Set of 12	67.50	67.50

No. 89h "Melancoryphus" is spelled wrong. See No. 115.

Butterflies — A56

No. 102: a, 25c, Eurytides marcellus. b, 100c, Hamadryas laodamia. c, 125c, Heliconius melpomene. d, 200c, Hesperia leonardus. e, 250c, Mestra amymone. f, 300c, Myscelia ethusa. g, 350c, Neominois ridingsii. h, 400c, Papilio polyxenes. i, 450c, Phocides polybius. j, 500c, Riodina lysippus.
No. 103, 500c, Actias luna. No. 104, 500c, Arachnis picta. No. 105, 500c, Dismorphia fortunate. No. 106, 500c, Eumorphus pandorus. No. 107, 500c, Eurytides marchandi. No. 108, 500c, Eurytides philolaus. No. 109, 500c, Graphium agamemnon. No. 110, 500c, Hemaris diffinis. No. 111, 500c, Hyalophora cecropia. No. 112, 500c, Ithomia iphianassa. No. 113, 500c, Pteronymia artena. No. 114, 500c, Rothschildia cincta.

2016, Jan. 13   Litho.   Perf. 14

102	A56	Sheet of 10, #a-j, + 2 labels	30.00	30.00

Souvenir Sheets

103-114	A56	Set of 12	67.50	67.50

Birds Type of 2016
Miniature Sheet

No. 115: a, 25c, Mergus octocetaceus. b, 100c, Phaetusa simplex. c, 125c, Phimosus infuscatus. d, 200c, Podiceps major. e, 250c, Puffinus puffinus. f, 300c, Rhynchops niger. g, 350c, Sarcoramphus papa. h, 400c, Sterna maxima. i, 450c, Theristicus caudatus. j, 500c, Vanellus chilensis.

2016, Jan. 20   Litho.   Perf. 14

115	A55	Sheet of 10, #a-j, + 2 labels	30.00	30.00

Souvenir Sheets

Flowers — A57

Designs: No. 116, 500c, Corydalis aurea. No. 117, 500c, Corydalis sempervirens. No. 118, 500c, Dicentra chrysantha. No. 119, 500c, Dicentra cucullaria. No. 120, 500c, Eschscholzia californica. No. 121, 500c, Nuphar lutea. No. 122, 500c, Nuphar polysepala. No. 123, 500c, Nymphaea mexicana. No. 124, 500c, Silene acaulis. No. 125, 500c, Silene californica. No. 126, 500c, Silene virginica. No. 127, 500c, Romneya coulteri.

2016, Jan. 27   Litho.   Perf. 14

116-127	A57	Set of 12	67.50	67.50

See Nos. 152-159.

Souvenir Sheets

Parrots — A58

Designs: No. 128, 500c, Deroptyus accipitrinus. No. 129, 500c, Eclectus roratus. No. 130, 500c, Pionites leucogaster. No. 131, 500c, Pionites melanocephala. No. 132, 500c, Pionus senilis. No. 133, 500c, Poicephalus gulielmi. No. 134, 500c, Poicephalus senegalus. No. 135, 500c, Prioniturus mada. No. 136, 500c, Psittaculirostris edwardsii. No. 137, 500c, Psittacus erithacus. No. 138, 500c, Tanygnathus m. megalorhynchus. No. 139, 500c, Tanygnathus sumatranus.

2016, Feb. 3   Litho.   Perf. 14

128-139	A58	Set of 12	67.50	67.50

See Nos. 160-167.

Souvenir Sheets

Frogs — A59

Designs: No. 140, 500c, Bufo bufo. No. 141, 500c, Cochranella truebae. No. 142, 500c, Hyla arborea. No. 143, 500c, Hyla fasciata. No. 144, 500c, Limnodynastes ornatus. No. 145, 500c, Mantidactylus grandidieri. No. 146, 500c, Occidozyga baluensis. No. 147, 500c, Oophaga lehmanni. No. 148, 500c, Oophaga pumilio. No. 149, 500c, Osteocephalus buckleyi. No. 150, 500c, Rana temporaria. No. 151, 500c, Staurois natator.

2016, Feb. 10   Litho.   Perf. 14

140-151	A59	Set of 12	67.50	67.50

Flowers Type of 2016
Souvenir Sheets

Designs: No. 152, 500c, Agrostemma githago. No. 153, 500c, Aquilegia formosa. No. 154, 500c, Arctomecon merriamii. No. 155, 500c, Caltha leptosepala. No. 156, 500c, Chelidonium majus. No. 157, 500c, Clematis hirsutissima. No. 158, 500c, Clematis ligusticifolia. No. 159, 500c, Clematis virginiana.

2016, Feb. 17   Litho.   Perf. 14
152-159 A57   Set of 8   45.00 45.00

Parrots Type of 2016
Souvenir Sheets

Designs: No. 160, 500c, Amazona amazonica. No. 161, 500c, Amazona autumnalis. No. 162, 500c, Amazona guildingi. No. 163, 500c, Amazona ochrocephala. No. 164, 500c, Ara auricollis. No. 165, 500c, Cacatua moluccensis. No. 166, 500c, Calyptorhynchus magnificus. No. 167, 500c, Coracopsis vasa.

2016, Feb. 24   Litho.   Perf. 14
160-167 A58   Set of 8   45.00 45.00

Miniature Sheet

37th St. Martin Heineken
Regatta — A60

No. 168: a, Crew on two boats. b, Two dancers, musicians on stage in background. c, Stage lights pointing at people on stage. d, Boats in regatta. e, Two boats. f, Four women with beer bottles. g, Crowd with raised arms. h, Boat with red star on sail. i, Four crewmembers near boat's mast. j, Boat facing left.

Serpentine Die Cut 14
2017, Jan. 2   Self-Adhesive   Litho.
168 A60   190c Sheet of 10, #a-
          j, + 10 labels   21.50 21.50

Miniature Sheet

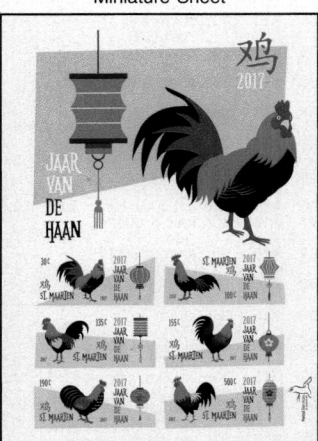

New Year 2017 (Year of the
Rooster) — A61

No. 169 — Rooster facing: a, 30c, Right. b, 100c, Left. c, 135c, Left. d, 155c, Right. e, 190c, Right. f, 500c, Left.

Serpentine Die Cut 14
2017, Jan. 27   Litho.
          Self-Adhesive
169 A61   Sheet of 6, #a-f, + 6
          labels   12.50 12.50

A62

Designs: 5c, Butterfly. 10c, Butterfly, diff. 20c, Butterfly on flower. 25c, Nerium oleander. 30c, Ixora coccinea. 55c, Ruellia brittoniana. 100c, Bougainvillea x buttiana. 135c, Fort Amsterdam, vert. 155c, Fort Amsterdam. 190c, Monument at Fort Amsterdam, vert. 305c, Cannons at Fort Amsterdam. 500c, Butterfly on flower. 10f, Cassia fistula.

Perf. 13¼x14, 14x13¼
2017, Mar. 1   Litho.
170 A62   5c multi   .25   .25
171 A62   10c multi   .25   .25
172 A62   20c multi   .25   .25
173 A62   25c multi   .30   .30
174 A62   30c multi   .35   .35
175 A62   55c multi   .60   .60
176 A62   100c multi   1.10   1.10
177 A62   135c multi   1.50   1.50
178 A62   155c multi   1.75   1.75
179 A62   190c multi   2.10   2.10
180 A62   305c multi   3.50   3.50
181 A62   500c multi   5.75   5.75
182 A62   10f multi   11.50   11.50
       Nos. 170-182 (13)   29.20 29.20

Miniature Sheet

Butterflies — A63

No. 183: a, 10c, Lycorea halia. b, 30c, Caligo bellerophon. c, 100c, Idea leuconoe. d, 135c, Siproeta stelenes. e, 165c, Lycorea halia, diff. f, 200c, Caligo bellerophon, diff. g, 205c, Idea leuconoe, diff. h, 260c, Siproeta stelenes, diff. i, 415c, Radena similis. j, 10f, Radena similis, diff.

2017, Mar. 1   Litho.   Perf. 13¼x14
183 A63   Sheet of 10, #a-j   28.00 28.00

Miniature Sheet

Birds — A64

No. 184: a, Granaatkolibrie (purple-throated Carib). b, Amerikaanse torenvalk (American kestrel). c, Bruine pelikan (brown pelican). d, Suikerdiefje (bananquit). e, Slechtvalk (peregrine falcon). f, Antilliaanse kuifkolibrie (Antillean crested hummingbird). g, Maskergrondvink (black-faced grassquit). h, Groenkeelkolibrie (green-throated Carib). i, Smelleken (merlin). j, Antillendikbekje (Lesser Antillean bullfinch). k, Coereba flaveola. l, Falco peregrinus. m, Eulampis jugularis. n, Falco sparverius. o, Pelecanus occidentalis. p, Falco columbarius. q, Loxigilla noctis. r, Orthorhynchus cristatus. s, Tiaris bicolor. t, Eulampis holosericeus.

2017, Aug. 31   Litho.   Perf. 13¼x14
184 A64   190c Sheet of 20,
          #a-t   42.50 42.50

A65

A66

A67

Marine
Life — A68

2018, July 20   Litho.   Perf. 13¼x14
185   Strip of 4   4.50 4.50
  a. A65 100c multi   1.10   1.10
  b. A66 100c multi   1.10   1.10
  c. A67 100c multi   1.10   1.10
  d. A68 100c multi   1.10   1.10

Miniature Sheet

Butterflies — A69

No. 186: a, Inachis io. b, Nymphalis antiopa. c, Celastrina argiolus. d, Aphantopus hyperantus. e, Lycaena phlaeas. f, Hamearis lucina. g, Hiparchia semele. h, Erynnis tages. i, Polyommatus icarus. j, Pontia daplidice. k, Thecla betulae. l, Anthocharis cardamines. m, Pieris brassicae. n, Vanessa atalanta. o, Pieris rapae. p, Carterocephalus palaemon. q, Boloria euphrosyne. r, Aglais urticae. s, Maculinea arion. t, Polygonia c-album. u, Maniola

---

jurtina. v, Cynthia cardui. w, Apatura iris. x, Papilio machaon.

2018, Oct. 29   Litho.   Perf. 13¼x14
186 A69   100c Sheet of 24, #a-
          x   27.00 27.00

Miniature Sheet

New Year 2019 (Year of the
Pig) — A70

No. 187 — Various depictions of pig and lantern: a, 85c. b, 135c. c, 165c. d, 260c. e, 305c. f, 420c.

Serpentine Die Cut 14
2019, Feb. 5   Self-Adhesive   Litho.
187 A70   Sheet of 6, #a-f, + 6
          labels   15.50 15.50

Miniature Sheet

St. Martin Carnival, 50th Anniv. — A71

No. 188: a, 85c, Woman wearing mask, facing right. b, 135c, Costume detail. c, 165c, Mask. d, 260c, Two women in costume. e, 305c, Woman's torso. f, 420c, Woman wearing mask, facing forward.

Serpentine Die Cut 14
2019, Apr. 20   Litho.
          Self-Adhesive
188 A71   Sheet of 6, #a-f, + 6
          labels   15.50 15.50

Miniature Sheet

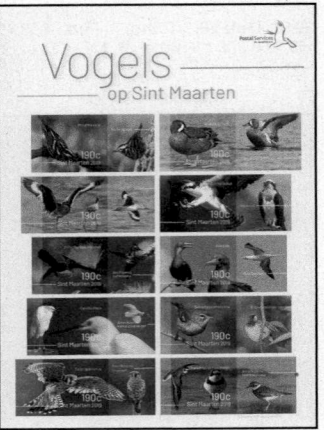

Birds — A72

No. 189: a, Mniotilta varia. b, Spatula discors. c, Tringa semipalmata. d, Pandion haliaetus. e, Orthorhyncus cristatus. f, Sula sula. g, Egretta thula. h, Setophaga americana. i, Falco sparverius. j, Charadrius semipalmatus.

Serpentine Die Cut 14

2019, June 24		Litho.
Self-Adhesive		
189	A72	190c Sheet of 10, #a-j, + 10 labels	21.50 21.50

ST. PIERRE & MIQUELON

sānt-ˈpi̯ə̯r and ˈmik-ə-ˌlän

LOCATION — Two small groups of islands off the southern coast of Newfoundland
GOVT. — Formerly a French colony, now a Department of France
AREA — 93 sq. mi.
POP. — 6,966 (1999 est.)
CAPITAL — St. Pierre

The territory of St. Pierre and Miquelon became a Department of France in July 1976.

100 Centimes = 1 Franc
100 Cents = 1 Euro (2002)

Catalogue values for unused stamps in this country are for Never Hinged items, beginning with Scott 300 in the regular postage section, Scott B13 in the semipostal section, Scott C1 in the airpost section, and Scott J68 in the postage due section.

Stamps of French Colonies Handstamp Surcharged in Black

1885		Unwmk.	Imperf.
1	A8	05c on 40c ver, *straw*	150.00 60.00
2	A8	10c on 40c ver, *straw*	45.00 35.00
a.		"M" inverted	375.00 350.00
3	A8	15c on 40c ver, *straw*	45.00 35.00
		Nos. 1-3 (3)	240.00 130.00

Nos. 2 and 3 exist with "SPM" 17mm wide instead of 15½mm.
Nos. 1-3 exist with surcharge inverted and with it doubled.

Handstamp Surcharged in Black

b c

d

1885				
4	A8 (b)	05c on 35c blk, *yel*	160.00	110.00
5	A8 (b)	05c on 75c car, *rose*	375.00	300.00
6	A8 (b)	05c on 1fr brnz grn, *straw*	40.00	32.50
7	A8 (c)	25c on 1fr brnz grn, *straw*	14,000.	2,800.
8	A8 (d)	25c on 1fr brnz grn, *straw*	2,700.	1,925.

Nos. 7 and 8 exist with surcharge inverted, and with it vertical. No. 7 exists with "S P M" above "25" (the handstamping was done in two steps). See the *Scott Specialized Catalogue of Stamps and Covers* for detailed listings.

1885			Perf. 14x13½
9	A9 (c)	5c on 2c brn, *buff*	7,250. 2,700.
10	A9 (d)	5c on 4c cl, *lav*	550.00 350.00
11	A9 (b)	05c on 20c red, *grn*	47.50 47.50

No. 9 surcharge is normally inverted. Nos. 10 and 11 exist with a variety of overprint errors. See the *Scott Specialized Catalogue of Stamps and Covers* for detailed listings.

A15

1886, Feb.		Typo.	Imperf.
Without Gum			
12	A15	5c black	1,500.
13	A15	10c black	1,600.
14	A15	15c black	1,400.
		Nos. 12-14 (3)	4,500.

"P D" are the initials for "Payé a destination."
Excellent forgeries exist.

Stamps of French Colonies Surcharged in Black

e f

1891			Perf. 14x13½
15	A9 (e)	15c on 30c brn, *bis*	52.50 40.00
a.		Inverted surcharge	310.00 260.00
16	A9 (e)	15c on 35c blk, *org*	725.00 575.00
a.		Inverted surcharge	875.00 700.00
17	A9 (f)	15c on 35c blk, *org*	2,000. 1,650.
a.		Inverted surcharge	— 2,100.
18	A9 (e)	15c on 40c red, *straw*	125.00 95.00
a.		Inverted surcharge	300.00 250.00

Stamps of French Colonies Overprinted in Black or Red

1891, Oct. 15			
19	A9	1c blk, *lil bl*	17.00 13.50
a.		Inverted overprint	40.00 40.00

20	A9	1c blk, *lil bl* (R)	17.00 15.00
a.		Inverted overprint	40.00 40.00
21	A9	2c brn, *buff*	17.00 13.50
a.		Inverted overprint	40.00 40.00
b.		"S" omitted in "ST"	110.00 110.00
22	A9	2c brn, *buff* (R)	32.50 30.00
a.		Inverted overprint	82.50 82.50
23	A9	4c claret, *lav*	17.00 13.50
a.		Inverted overprint	40.00 40.00
24	A9	4c claret, *lav* (R)	32.50 30.00
a.		Inverted overprint	65.00 65.00
25	A9	5c grn, *grnsh*	27.50 19.00
a.		Double surcharge	260.00
26	A9	10c blk, *lav*	47.50 40.00
a.		Inverted overprint	95.00 95.00
b.		"S" omitted in "ST"	160.00 160.00
27	A9	10c blk, *lav* (R)	32.50 30.00
a.		Inverted overprint	65.00 65.00
28	A9	15c blue	45.00 32.50
29	A9	20c red, *grn*	110.00 100.00
30	A9	25c blk, *rose*	40.00 27.50
31	A9	30c brn, *bis*	150.00 125.00
32	A9	35c vio, *org*	525.00 400.00
33	A9	40c red, *straw*	100.00 80.00
a.		Double surcharge	500.00
34	A9	75c car, *rose*	140.00 130.00
a.		Inverted overprint	240.00 225.00
35	A9	1fr brnz grn, *straw*	120.00 105.00
a.		Inverted overprint	220.00 220.00
		Nos. 19-35 (17)	1,471. 1,205.

Numerous varieties of mislettering occur in the preceding overprint: "ST," "P," "M," "ON," or "-" missing; "-" instead of "ON"; "=" instead of "-." These varieties command values double or triple those of normal stamps.

Surcharged in Black

1891-92			
36	A9	1c on 5c grn, *grnsh*	16.00 16.00
37	A9	1c on 10c blk, *lav*	18.00 16.50
38	A9	1c on 25c blk, *rose* ('92)	12.50 12.00
39	A9	2c on 10c blk, *lav*	16.00 16.00
a.		Double surcharge	170.00 170.00
b.		Triple surcharge	350.00 350.00
40	A9	2c on 15c bl	18.00 16.50
41	A9	2c on 25c blk, *rose* ('92)	12.50 12.00
42	A9	4c on 20c red, *grn*	16.00 16.00
43	A9	4c on 25c blk, *rose* ('92)	12.50 12.00
a.		Double surcharge	160.00 160.00
44	A9	4c on 30c brn, *bis*	32.50 26.00
45	A9	4c on 40c red, *straw*	32.50 26.00
		Nos. 36-45 (10)	186.50 169.00

See note after No. 35.

French Colonies 1881-86 Stamps Surcharged in Black

j k

1892, Nov. 4			
46	A9 (j)	1c on 5c grn, *grnsh*	16.00 14.00
47	A9 (j)	2c on 5c grn, *grnsh*	16.00 14.00
48	A9 (j)	4c on 5c grn, *grnsh*	16.00 14.00
49	A9 (k)	1c on 25c blk, *rose*	12.50 12.00
50	A9 (k)	2c on 25c blk, *rose*	12.50 12.00
51	A9 (k)	4c on 25c blk, *rose*	12.50 12.00
		Nos. 46-51 (6)	85.50 78.00

See note after No. 35.

Postage Due Stamps of French Colonies Overprinted in Red

1892, Dec. 1			Imperf.
52	D1	10c black	60.00 40.00
53	D1	20c black	40.00 35.00
54	D1	30c black	37.50 37.50
55	D1	40c black	32.50 32.50
56	D1	60c black	140.00 140.00

Black Overprint

57	D1	1fr brown	190.00 190.00
58	D1	2fr brown	325.00 325.00
59	D1	5fr brown	500.00 475.00
		Nos. 52-59 (8)	1,325. 1,275.

See note after No. 35. "T P" stands for "Timbre Poste."

Navigation and Commerce — A16

1892-1908		Typo.	Perf. 14x13½
60	A16	1c blk, *lil bl*	1.90 1.90
61	A16	2c brown, *buff*	1.90 1.90
62	A16	4c claret, *lav*	3.00 3.00
63	A16	5c green, *grnsh*	4.50 3.75
64	A16	5c yel grn ('08)	6.00 3.75
65	A16	10c black, *lav*	8.25 6.75
66	A16	10c red ('00)	6.00 3.75
67	A16	15c bl, quadrille paper	19.00 6.00
68	A16	15c gray, *lt gray* ('00)	100.00 65.00
69	A16	20c red, *grn*	30.00 24.00
70	A16	25c black, *rose*	13.50 3.75
71	A16	25c blue ('00)	25.00 15.00
72	A16	30c brown, *bis*	13.50 9.00
73	A16	35c blk, *yel* ('06)	8.00 7.25
74	A16	40c red, *straw*	9.75 9.00
75	A16	50c car, *rose*	52.50 42.50
76	A16	50c brown, *az* ('00)	40.00 37.50
77	A16	75c violet, *org*	35.00 30.00
78	A16	1fr brnz grn, *straw*	35.00 22.00
		Nos. 60-78 (19)	412.80 299.80

Perf. 13½x14 stamps are counterfeits.
For surcharges and overprints see Nos. 110-120, Q1-Q2.

Fisherman A17

Fulmar Petrel A18

Fishing Schooner A19

1909-30				
79	A17	1c org red & ol	.40	.50
80	A17	2c olive & dp bl	.40	.50
81	A17	4c violet & ol	.55	.75
a.		Perf 11	160.00	
82	A17	5c bl grn & ol grn	1.20	.75
83	A17	5c blue & blk ('22)	.55	.75
84	A17	10c car rose & red	1.20	1.10
85	A17	10c bl grn & ol grn ('22)	.75	.75
86	A17	10c bis & mag ('25)	.55	.75
86A	A17	15c dl vio & rose ('17)	.80	.75
87	A17	20c bis brn & vio brn	1.25	1.10
88	A18	25c dp blue & blue	4.50	3.00
89	A18	25c ol brn & bl grn ('22)	1.25	1.50
90	A18	30c org & vio brn	2.60	2.60
91	A18	30c rose & dull red ('22)	1.75	2.25
92	A18	30c red brn & bl ('25)	1.00	1.00
93	A18	30c gray grn & bl grn ('26)	1.50	2.25
94	A18	35c ol grn & vio brn	.80	.80
95	A18	40c vio brn & ol grn	4.00	3.00
96	A18	45c vio & ol grn	1.10	1.50
97	A18	50c ol & ol grn	2.25	2.25
98	A18	50c bl & pale bl ('22)	1.75	2.25
99	A18	50c yel brn & mag ('25)	1.60	2.25
100	A18	60c dk bl & ver ('25)	1.40	1.90
101	A18	65c vio & org brn ('28)	2.50	3.00
102	A18	75c brn & ol	1.90	2.25
103	A18	90c brn red & org red ('30)	35.00	37.50
104	A19	1fr ol grn & dp bl	5.00	3.75

105	A19	1.10fr bl grn & org red ('28)	5.50	7.50
106	A19	1.50fr bl & dp bl ('30)	15.00	15.00
107	A19	2fr violet & brn	6.00	4.50
108	A19	3fr red vio ('30)	18.00	22.50
109	A19	5fr vio brn & ol grn	13.50	12.50
		Nos. 79-109 (32)	135.55	142.75

For overprints and surcharges see Nos. 121-131, 206C-206D, B1-B2, Q3-Q5.

Stamps of 1892-1906 Surcharged in Carmine or Black

n   o

1912

110	A16	5c on 2c brn, buff	3.75	4.00
111	A16	5c on 4c claret, lav (C)	1.10	1.50
112	A16	5c on 15c blue (C)	1.10	1.50
113	A16	5c on 20c red, grn	.90	1.10
114	A16	5c on 25c blk, rose (C)	.90	1.10
115	A16	5c on 30c brn, bis (C)	1.10	1.50
116	A16	5c on 35c blk, yel (C)	1.90	2.25
117	A16	10c on 40c red, straw	1.50	1.90
118	A16	10c on 50c car, rose	1.50	1.90
119	A16	10c on 75c dp vio, org	3.75	4.50
120	A16	10c on 1fr brnz grn, straw	5.25	6.25
		Nos. 110-120 (11)	22.75	27.50

Two spacings between the surcharged numerals are found on Nos. 110 to 120. For detailed listings, see the *Scott Classic Specialized Catalogue of Stamps and Covers.*

Stamps and Types of 1909-17 Surcharged in Black, Blue (Bl) or Red

1924-27

121	A17	25c on 15c dl vio & rose ('25)	.55	.75
a.		Double surcharge	190.00	
b.		Triple surcharge	210.00	
122	A19	25c on 2fr vio & lt brn (Bl)	.80	1.10
123	A19	25c on 5fr brn & ol grn (Bl)	.90	1.10
a.		Triple surcharge	210.00	
124	A18	65c on 45c vio & ol grn ('25)	2.25	3.00
125	A18	85c on 75c brn & ol ('25)	2.25	3.00
126	A18	90c on 75c brn red & dp org ('27)	3.00	3.75
127	A19	1.25fr on 1fr dk bl & ultra (R) ('26)	3.00	3.75
128	A19	1.50fr on 1fr ultra & dk bl ('27)	4.00	4.50
129	A19	3fr on 5fr ol brn & red vio ('27)	5.25	6.00
130	A19	10fr on 5fr ver & ol grn ('27)	25.00	29.00
131	A19	20fr on 5fr vio & ver ('27)	32.50	40.00
		Nos. 121-131 (11)	79.50	95.95

Common Design Types pictured following the introduction.

Colonial Exposition Issue
Common Design Types

1931, Apr. 13		**Engr.**	**Perf. 12½**	
Name of Country in Black				
132	CD70	40c deep green	6.00	6.00
133	CD71	50c violet	6.00	6.00
134	CD72	90c red orange	6.00	6.00
135	CD73	1.50fr dull blue	6.00	6.00
		Nos. 132-135 (4)	24.00	24.00

Map and Fishermen — A20

Lighthouse and Fish — A21

Fishing Steamer and Sea Gulls A22

Perf. 13½x14, 14x13½

1932-33			**Typo.**	
136	A20	1c red brn & ultra	.25	.35
137	A21	2c blk & dk grn	.40	.50
138	A22	4c mag & ol brn	.40	.60
139	A22	5c vio & dk brn	.80	1.10
140	A21	10c red brn & blk	.80	1.10
141	A21	15c dk blue & vio	1.60	2.25
142	A20	20c blk & dk org	1.90	2.25
143	A20	25c lt vio & lt grn	1.90	2.25
144	A22	30c ol grn & bl grn	1.90	2.25
145	A22	40c dp bl & dk brn	1.90	2.25
146	A21	45c ver & dp grn	1.90	2.25
147	A21	50c dk brn & dk grn	2.25	2.60
148	A22	65c ol brn & org	2.60	3.00
149	A20	75c grn & red org	2.25	2.60
150	A20	90c dull red & red	2.75	3.75
151	A22	1fr org brn & org red	2.60	3.00
152	A20	1.25fr dp bl & lake ('33)	2.60	3.00
153	A20	1.50fr dp blue & blue	2.60	3.00
154	A22	1.75fr blk & dk brn ('33)	3.25	3.75
155	A22	2fr bl blk & Prus bl	12.00	13.50
156	A21	3fr dp grn & dk brn	15.00	19.00
157	A21	5fr brn red & dk brn	32.50	37.50
158	A22	10fr dk grn & vio	75.00	82.50
159	A20	20fr ver & dp grn	85.00	92.50
		Nos. 136-159 (24)	254.15	286.85

For overprints and surcharges see Nos. 160-164, 207-221.

Nos. 147, 149, 153-154, 157 Overprinted in Black, Red or Blue

p

q

1934, Oct. 18

160	A21(p)	50c (Bk)	6.50	7.50
161	A20(q)	75c (Bk)	9.50	10.50
162	A20(q)	1.50fr (Bk)	9.50	10.50
163	A22(p)	1.75fr (R)	10.00	12.50
164	A21(p)	5fr (Bl)	45.00	47.50
		Nos. 160-164 (5)	80.50	88.50

400th anniv. of the landing of Jacques Cartier.

Paris International Exposition Issue
Common Design Types

1937			**Perf. 13**	
165	CD74	20c deep violet	2.40	2.75
166	CD75	30c dark green	2.40	2.75
167	CD76	40c carmine rose	2.40	2.75
168	CD77	50c dk brn & bl	2.40	2.75
169	CD78	90c red	2.50	2.75
170	CD79	1.50fr ultra	2.50	2.75
		Nos. 165-170 (6)	14.60	16.50

Colonial Arts Exhibition Issue
Souvenir Sheet
Common Design Type

1937			**Imperf.**	
171	CD78	3fr dark ultra	35.00	47.50

Dog Team A23

Port St. Pierre A24

Tortue Lighthouse A25

Soldiers' Bay at Langlade A26

1938-40		**Photo.**	**Perf. 13½x13**	
172	A23	2c dk bl grn	.25	.35
a.		Value omitted	425.00	
173	A23	3c brown violet	.25	.35
174	A23	4c dk red violet	.30	.40
175	A23	5c carmine lake	.30	.40
176	A23	10c bister brown	.30	.40
177	A23	15c red violet	.75	.80
178	A23	20c blue violet	1.00	1.10
179	A23	25c Prus blue	3.00	3.00
180	A24	30c dk red violet	.75	.80
181	A24	35c deep green	1.00	1.10
182	A24	40c slate blue ('40)	.25	.35
183	A24	45c dp grn ('40)	.50	.60
a.		Value omitted	110.00	
184	A24	50c carmine rose	1.00	1.10
185	A24	55c Prus blue	4.50	4.50
186	A24	60c violet ('39)	.75	.90
187	A24	65c brown	7.00	7.00
188	A24	70c org yel ('39)	.75	1.00
189	A25	80c violet	1.75	1.90
190	A25	90c ultra ('39)	1.00	1.25
191	A25	1fr brt pink	15.00	15.00
192	A25	1fr pale ol grn ('40)	1.10	1.25
193	A25	1.25fr brt rose ('39)	2.50	2.75
194	A25	1.40fr dk brn ('40)	1.25	1.50
195	A25	1.50fr blue green	1.25	1.50
196	A25	1.60fr rose vio ('40)	1.25	1.50
197	A25	1.75fr deep blue	4.00	4.50
198	A26	2fr rose violet	.90	1.10
199	A26	2.25fr brt blue ('39)	1.25	1.60
200	A26	2.50fr org yel ('40)	1.25	1.50
201	A26	3fr gray brown	1.25	1.50
202	A26	5fr henna brown	1.25	1.50
203	A26	10fr dk bl, *bluish*	2.00	2.25
204	A26	20fr slate green	2.50	3.00
		Nos. 172-204 (33)	62.15	67.75

For overprints and surcharges see Nos. 222-255, 260-299, B9-B10.

New York World's Fair Issue
Common Design Type

1939, May 10		**Engr.**	**Perf. 12½x12**	
205	CD82	1.25fr carmine lake	2.40	3.00
206	CD82	2.25fr ultra	2.40	3.00

For overprints and surcharges see Nos. 256-259.

Lighthouse on Cliff — A27

1941		**Engr.**	**Perf. 12½x12**	
206A	A27	1fr dull lilac	2.00	
206B	A27	2.50fr blue	2.00	

Nos. 206A-206B were issued by the Vichy government in France, but were not placed on sale in St. Pierre & Miquelon.

For surcharges, see B11-B12.

Free French Administration
The circumstances surrounding the overprinting and distribution of these stamps were most unusual. Practically all of the stamps issued in small quantities, with the exception of Nos. 260-299, were obtained by speculators within a few days after issue. At a later date, the remainders were taken over by the Free French Agency in Ottawa, Canada, by whom they were sold at a premium for the benefit of the Syndicat des Oeuvres Sociales. Large quantities appeared on the market in 1991, including many "errors." More may exist.

Excellent counterfeits of these surcharges and overprints are known.

Nos. 86 & 92 Ovptd. in Black — a

1942		**Unwmk.**	**Perf. 14x13½**	
206C	A17	10c	1,600.	1,700.
206D	A18	30c	1,600.	1,700.

The letters "F. N. F. L." are the initials of "Forces Navales Francaises Libres" or "Free French Naval Forces."

Ovptd. in Black on Nos. 137-139, 145-148, 151, 154-155, 157

207	A21	2c	275.00	300.00
208	A22	4c	67.50	80.00
208A	A22	5c	1,000.	1,200.
209	A22	40c	17.50	21.00
210	A21	45c	210.00	250.00
211	A21	50c	17.50	21.00
212	A22	65c	60.00	67.50
213	A22	1fr	450.00	500.00
214	A22	1.75fr	17.50	21.00
215	A22	2fr	24.00	27.50
216	A22	5fr	425.00	475.00

Nos. 142, 149, 152-153 Overprinted in Black

Perf. 13½x14

216A	A20	20c	500.00	575.00
217	A20	75c	45.00	55.00
218	A20	1.25fr	40.00	47.50
218A	A20	1.50fr	600.00	675.00

On Nos. 152, 149 Surcharged with New Value and Bars

219	A20	10fr on 1.25fr	65.00	72.50
220	A20	20fr on 75c	65.00	72.50

No. 154
Srchd. in
Red

Perf. 14x13½

221	A22	5fr on		
		1.75fr	22.50	27.50

Stamps of
1938-40
Ovptd.

Perf. 13½x13

222	A23	2c dk bl grn	600.00	650.00
223	A23	3c brn vio	225.00	250.00
224	A23	4c dk red vio	110.00	140.00
225	A23	5c car lake	1,000.	1,200.
226	A23	10c bis brn	17.00	18.00
227	A23	15c red vio	1,900.	2,100.
228	A23	20c blue vio	210.00	210.00
229	A23	25c Prus blue	17.00	18.00
230	A24	35c dp grn	1,000.	1,100.
231	A24	40c slate blue	21.00	25.00
232	A24	45c dp grn	21.00	25.00
233	A24	55c Prus blue	11,000.	12,500.
234	A24	60c violet	675.00	775.00
235	A24	65c brown	25.00	30.00
236	A24	70c org yel	47.50	55.00
237	A25	80c violet	500.00	575.00
238	A25	90c ultra	21.00	25.00
239	A25	1fr pale ol grn	26.00	30.00
240	A25	1.25fr brt rose	22.50	26.00
241	A25	1.40fr dk brn	21.00	25.00
242	A25	1.50fr bl grn	950.00	1,100.
243	A25	1.60fr rose vio	21.00	25.00
244	A26	2fr rose vio	87.50	110.00
245	A26	2.25fr brt blue	21.00	25.00
246	A26	2.50fr org yel	26.00	30.00
247	A26	3fr gray brn	12,500.	13,000.
248	A26	5fr hen brn	2,500.	2,750.
248A	A26	20fr sl grn	1,200.	1,300.

Nos. 176,
190 Srchd.
in Black

249	A23	20c on 10c	14.50	17.00
250	A23	30c on 10c	12.00	13.50
251	A25	60c on 90c	13.50	16.00
252	A25	1.50fr on 90c	17.50	20.00
253	A23	2.50fr on 10c	22.50	25.00
254	A23	10fr on 10c	67.50	80.00
255	A25	20fr on 90c	75.00	87.50
		Nos. 249-255 (7)	222.50	259.00

New York World's Fair Issue
Overprinted type "a" in Black

Perf. 12½x12

256	CD82	1.25fr car lake	22.50	25.00
257	CD82	2.25fr ultra	21.00	24.00

Nos. 205-
206
Surcharged

258	CD82	2.50fr on 1.25fr	22.50	25.00
259	CD82	3fr on 2.25fr	22.50	25.00

Stamps of
1938-40
Ovptd. in
Carmine

1941			**Perf. 13½x13**	
260	A23	10c bister brn	47.50	55.00
261	A23	20c blue violet	47.50	55.00
262	A23	25c Prus blue	47.50	55.00
263	A24	40c slate blue	47.50	55.00
264	A24	45c dp grn	52.50	60.00
265	A24	65c brown	52.50	60.00
266	A24	70c org yel	52.50	60.00
267	A25	80c violet	52.50	60.00
268	A25	90c ultra	52.50	60.00
269	A25	1fr pale ol grn	52.50	60.00
270	A25	1.25fr brt rose	52.50	60.00
271	A25	1.40fr dk brown	52.50	60.00
272	A25	1.60fr rose violet	52.50	60.00
273	A25	1.75fr brt blue	52.50	60.00
274	A26	2fr rose violet	52.50	60.00
275	A26	2.25fr brt blue	52.50	60.00
276	A26	2.50fr org yel	52.50	60.00
277	A26	3fr gray brn	52.50	60.00

Same Surcharged in Carmine with New Values

278	A23	10fr on 10c bis brn	125.00	140.00
279	A25	20fr on 90c ultra	125.00	140.00
		Nos. 260-279 (20)	1,175.	1,340.

Stamps of 1938-40 Overprinted in Black

280	A23	10c bister brn	72.50	87.50
281	A23	20c blue violet	72.50	87.50
282	A23	25c Prus blue	72.50	87.50
283	A24	40c slate blue	72.50	87.50
284	A24	45c dp grn	72.50	87.50
285	A24	65c brown	72.50	87.50
286	A24	70c orange yel	72.50	87.50
287	A25	80c violet	72.50	87.50
288	A25	90c ultra	72.50	87.50
289	A25	1fr pale ol grn	72.50	87.50
290	A25	1.25fr brt rose	72.50	87.50
291	A25	1.40fr dk brown	72.50	87.50
292	A25	1.60fr rose violet	72.50	87.50
293	A25	1.75fr brt blue	950.00	1,100.
294	A26	2fr rose vio	72.50	87.50
295	A26	2.25fr brt blue	72.50	87.50
296	A26	2.50fr orange yel	72.50	87.50
297	A26	3fr gray brn	72.50	87.50

Same Surcharged in Black with New Values

298	A23	10fr on 10c bis brn	175.00	200.00
299	A25	20fr on 90c ultra	190.00	225.00
		Nos. 280-299 (20)	2,548.	3,013.

Christmas Day plebiscite ordered by Vice Admiral Emile Henri Muselier, commander of the Free French naval forces (Nos. 260-299).

Types of 1938-40 Without RF

1942		**Photo.**	**Perf. 13½**
299A	A23	4c dk red vio	.55
299B	A23	15c red violet	1.40
299C	A23	20c blue violet	1.40
299D	A26	10fr dk blue	2.10
299E	A26	20fr ol olive	2.50
		Nos. 299A-299E (5)	7.95

Nos. 299A-299E were issued by the Vichy government in France, but were not placed on sale in St. Pierre & Miquelon.

> **Catalogue values for unused stamps in this section, from this point to the end of the section, are for Never Hinged items.**

St. Malo
Fishing
Schooner
A28

1942		**Photo.**	**Perf. 14x14½**	
300	A28	5c dark blue	.55	.30
301	A28	10c dull pink	.50	.30
302	A28	25c brt green	.50	.30
303	A28	30c slate black	.50	.30
304	A28	40c brt grnsh blue	.50	.30
305	A28	60c brown red	.55	.40
306	A28	1fr dark violet	.80	.65
307	A28	1.50fr brt red	1.75	1.40
308	A28	2fr brown	1.10	.80
309	A28	2.50fr brt ultra	1.75	1.40
310	A28	4fr dk orange	1.40	1.00
311	A28	5fr dp plum	1.10	1.10

312	A28	10fr lt ultra	2.10	1.75
313	A28	20fr dark green	2.40	1.90
		Nos. 300-313 (14)	15.90	11.90

Nos. 300, 302, 309 Surcharged in Carmine or Black

1945				
314	A28	50c on 5c (C)	.50	.30
315	A28	70c on 5c (C)	.50	.30
316	A28	80c on 5c (C)	.55	.40
317	A28	1.20fr on 5c (C)	.70	.55
318	A28	2.40fr on 25c	.70	.55
319	A28	3fr on 25c	.95	.80
320	A28	4.50fr on 25c	1.60	1.25
321	A28	15fr on 2.50fr (C)	2.00	1.75
		Nos. 314-321 (8)	7.50	5.90

Eboue Issue
Common Design Type

1945		**Engr.**	**Perf. 13**	
322	CD91	2fr black	1.40	.95
323	CD91	25fr Prussian green	3.00	2.50

Nos. 322 and 323 exist imperforate. Value, set $47.50.

RF
POSTES
10c

Soldiers' Bay — A29

Fishing
Industry
Symbols
A30

Fishermen
A31

Weighing
the Catch
A32

Fishing
Boat and
Dinghy
A33

Storm-swept Coast — A34

1947, Oct. 6		**Engr.**	**Perf. 12½**	
324	A29	10c chocolate	.55	.40
325	A29	30c violet	.55	.40
326	A29	40c rose lilac	.55	.40
327	A29	50c intense blue	.55	.40
328	A30	60c carmine	1.25	.95
329	A30	80c brt ultra	1.25	.95
330	A31	1fr dk green	1.25	.95
331	A31	1.20fr blue grn	1.25	.95
332	A31	1.50fr black	1.25	.95

333	A31	2fr red brown	1.25	.95
334	A32	3fr rose violet	3.50	3.00
335	A32	3.60fr dp brown org	2.50	2.10
336	A32	4fr sepia	3.25	2.25
337	A33	5fr orange	3.50	2.50
338	A33	6fr blue	3.50	2.50
339	A33	10fr Prus green	4.50	3.25
340	A34	15fr dk slate grn	6.00	4.50
341	A34	20fr vermilion	8.50	6.50
342	A34	25fr dark blue	10.50	7.50
		Nos. 324-342 (19)	55.45	41.40

> **Imperforates**
> Most stamps of St. Pierre and Miquelon from 1947 onward exist imperforate in issued and trial colors, and also in small presentation sheets in issued colors.

Silver
Fox — A35

1952, Oct. 10		**Unwmk.**	**Perf. 13**	
343	A35	8fr dk brown	5.00	1.50
344	A35	17fr blue	6.75	2.10

Military Medal Issue
Common Design Type

1952, Dec. 15		**Engr. & Typo.**	
345	CD101	8fr multicolored	16.00	15.00

Fish
Freezing
Plant
A36

1955-56			**Engr.**	
346	A36	30c ultra & dk blue	.75	.75
347	A36	50c gray, blk & sepia	.75	.75
348	A36	3fr purple	1.40	1.40
349	A36	40fr Prussian blue	3.50	2.75
		Nos. 346-349 (4)	6.40	5.65

Issued: 40fr, July 4; others, Oct. 22, 1956.

FIDES Issue

Fish
Freezer "Le
Galantry"
A37

Perf. 13x12½

1956, Mar. 15			**Unwmk.**	
350	A37	15fr blk brn & chestnut	6.00	4.00

See note in Common Design section after CD103.

Codfish
A38

4fr, 10fr, Lighthouse and fishing fleet.

1957, Nov. 4			**Perf. 13**	
351	A38	40c dk brn & grnsh bl	.55	.55
352	A38	1fr brown & green	.65	.65
353	A38	2fr indigo & dull blue	1.00	1.00
354	A38	4fr maroon, car & pur	2.25	2.25
355	A38	10fr grnsh bl, dk bl & brn	2.60	2.60
		Nos. 351-355 (5)	7.05	7.05

Human Rights Issue
Common Design Type

1958, Dec. 10		**Engr.**	**Perf. 13**	
356	CD105	20fr red brn & dk blue	3.50	2.50

Flower Issue
Common Design Type
1959, Jan. 28 Photo. *Perf. 12½x12*
357 CD104 5fr Spruce 4.50 2.25

Ice Hockey
A39

1959, Oct. 7 Engr. *Perf. 13*
358 A39 20fr multicolored 3.75 1.75

Mink
A40

1959, Oct. 7 Engr. *Perf. 13*
359 A40 25fr ind, yel grn & brn 5.25 2.50

Cypripedium
Acaule — A41

Flower: 50fr, Calopogon pulchellus.

1962, Apr. 24 Unwmk. *Perf. 13*
360 A41 25fr grn, org & car
   rose 5.75 2.75
361 A41 50fr green & car lake 8.75 3.50
   Nos. 360-361,C24 (3) 27.50 11.25

Eider Ducks — A42

Birds: 1fr, Rock ptarmigan. 2fr, Ringed plovers. 6fr, Blue-winged teal.

1963, Mar. 4 *Perf. 13*
362 A42 50c blk, ultra & ocher 1.00 .60
363 A42 1fr red brn, ultra & rose 1.50 .90
364 A42 2fr blk, dk bl & bis 1.90 .90
365 A42 6fr multicolored 3.75 2.00
   Nos. 362-365 (4) 8.15 4.40

Albert
Calmette
A43

1963, Aug. 5 Engr.
366 A43 30fr dk brn & dk blue 10.00 6.75
Albert Calmette, bacteriologist, birth cent.

Red Cross Centenary Issue
Common Design Type
1963, Sept. 2 Unwmk. *Perf. 13*
367 CD113 25fr ultra, gray & car 12.00 5.50

Human Rights Issue
Common Design Type
1963, Dec. 10 Unwmk. *Perf. 13*
368 CD117 20fr org, bl & dk brn 7.00 3.50

Philatec Issue
Common Design Type
1964, Apr. 4 Engr.
369 CD118 60fr choc, grn & dk
   bl 11.00 8.00

Rabbits
A44

1964, Sept. 28 *Perf. 13*
370 A44 3fr shown 2.00 1.40
371 A44 4fr Fox 2.00 1.40
372 A44 5fr Roe deer 5.00 2.75
373 A44 34fr Charolais bull 15.00 8.00
   Nos. 370-373 (4) 24.00 13.55

Airport and
Map of St.
Pierre and
Miquelon
A45

40fr, Television tube and tower, map. 48fr, Map of new harbor of St. Pierre.

1967 Engr. *Perf. 13*
374 A45 30fr ind, bl & dk red 8.00 5.00
375 A45 40fr sl grn, ol & dk
   red 8.00 5.00
376 A45 48fr dk red, brn & sl
   bl 12.50 5.75
   Nos. 374-376 (3) 28.50 15.75

Issued: 30fr, 10/23; 40fr, 11/20; 48fr, 9/25.

WHO Anniversary Issue
Common Design Type
1968, May 4 Engr. *Perf. 13*
377 CD126 10fr multicolored 12.00 9.00

René de Chateaubriand and Map of
Islands — A46

Designs: 4fr, J. D. Cassini and map. 15fr, Prince de Joinville, Francois F. d'Orleans (1818-1900), ships and map. 25fr, Admiral Gauchet, World War I warship and map.

1968, May 20 Photo. *Perf. 12½x13*
378 A46 4fr multicolored 5.75 3.75
379 A46 6fr multicolored 6.50 4.50
380 A46 15fr multicolored 10.00 5.75
381 A46 25fr multicolored 14.00 6.50
   Nos. 378-381 (4) 36.25 20.50

Human Rights Year Issue
Common Design Type
1968, Aug. 10 Engr. *Perf. 13*
382 CD127 20fr bl, ver & org yel 8.00 5.50

Belle
Rivière,
Langlade
A47

Design: 15fr, Debon Brook, Langlade.

1969, Apr. 30 Engr. *Perf. 13*
Size: 36x22mm
383 A47 5fr bl, slate grn &
   brn 4.25 2.75
384 A47 15fr brn, bl & dl grn 5.75 3.50
   Nos. 383-384,C41-C42 (4) 50.00 27.25

Treasury
A48

Designs: 25fr, Scientific and Technical Institute of Maritime Fishing. 30fr, Monument to seamen lost at sea. 60fr, St. Christopher College.

1969, May 30 Engr. *Perf. 13*
385 A48 10fr brt bl, cl & blk 5.50 3.25
386 A48 25fr dk bl, brt bl & brn
   red 9.25 4.75
387 A48 30fr blue, grn & gray 10.00 6.25
388 A48 60fr brt bl, brn red &
   blk 17.00 10.00
   Nos. 385-388 (4) 41.75 24.25

Ringed
Seals
A49

Designs: 3fr, Sperm whales. 4fr, Pilot whales. 6fr, Common dolphins.

1969, Oct. 6 Engr. *Perf. 13*
389 A49 1fr lil, vio brn & red
   brn 2.75 1.75
390 A49 3fr bl grn, ind & red 2.75 1.75
391 A49 4fr ol, gray grn & mar 5.25 3.50
392 A49 6fr brt grn, pur & red 7.50 3.50
   Nos. 389-392 (4) 18.25 10.50

L'Estoile
and
Granville,
France
A50

40fr, "La Jolie" & St. Jean de Luz, France, 1750. 48fr, "Le Juste" & La Rochelle, France, 1860.

1969, Oct. 13 Engr. *Perf. 13*
393 A50 34fr grn, mar & slate
   grn 17.50 10.00
394 A50 40fr brn red, lem & sl
   grn 25.00 11.00
395 A50 48fr multicolored 35.00 12.50
   Nos. 393-395 (3) 80.00 33.50

Historic ships connecting St. Pierre and Miquelon with France.

ILO Issue
Common Design Type
1969, Nov. 24
396 CD131 20fr org, gray &
   ocher 10.00 5.50

UPU Headquarters Issue
Common Design Type
1970, May 20 Engr. *Perf. 13*
397 CD133 25fr dk car, brt bl &
   brn 14.00 7.75
398 CD133 34fr maroon, brn &
   gray 20.00 8.50

Rowers and
Globe
A51

1970, Oct. 13 Photo. *Perf. 12½x12*
399 A51 20fr lt grnsh bl & brn 18.00 7.50
World Rowing Championships, St. Catherine.

Blackberries
A52

1970, Oct. 20 Engr. *Perf. 13*
400 A52 3fr shown 1.75 1.40
401 A52 4fr Strawberries 1.90 1.75
402 A52 5fr Raspberries 2.75 1.75
403 A52 6fr Blueberries 5.25 2.25
   Nos. 400-403 (4) 11.65 7.15

Ewe and
Lamb
A53

30fr, Animal quarantine station. 34fr, Charolais bull. 48fr, Refrigeration ship slaughterhouse.

1970 Engr. *Perf. 13*
404 A53 15fr plum, grn & olive 11.00 4.50
405 A53 30fr sl, bis brn & ap
   grn 12.50 6.75
406 A53 34fr red lil, org brn &
   emer 20.00 8.75
407 A53 48fr multicolored 18.00 8.00
   Nos. 404-407 (4) 61.50 28.00

Issue dates: 48fr, Nov. 10; others, Dec. 8.

Saint
François
d'Assise
1900
A54

Ships: 35fr, Sainte Jehanne, 1920. 40fr, L'Aventure, 1950. 80fr, Commandant Bourdais, 1970.

1971, Aug. 25
408 A54 30fr Prus bl & hn
   brn 32.50 14.50
409 A54 35fr Prus bl, lt grn &
   ol brn 47.50 14.50
410 A54 40fr sl grn, bl & dk
   brn 52.50 11.00
411 A54 80fr dp grn, bl & blk 67.50 20.00
   Nos. 408-411 (4) 200.00 60.00

Deep-sea fishing fleet.

"Aconit" and Map of Islands — A55

1971, Sept. 27 Engr. *Perf. 13*
412 A55 22fr shown 30.00 13.00
413 A55 25fr Alysse 37.50 13.50
414 A55 50fr Mimosa 50.00 20.00
   Nos. 412-414 (3) 117.50 46.50

Rallying of the Free French forces, 30th anniv.

Ship's Bell — A56

St. Pierre Museum: 45fr, Old chart and sextants, horiz.

1971, Oct. 25 Photo. *Perf. 12½x13*
415 A56 20fr gray & multi 25.00 8.50
416 A56 45fr red brn & multi 40.00 15.00

De Gaulle Issue
Common Design Type
Designs: 35fr, Gen. de Gaulle, 1940. Pres. de Gaulle, 1970.

1971, Nov. 9 Engr. *Perf. 13*
417 CD134 35fr ver & blk 24.00 12.50
418 CD134 45fr ver & blk 32.50 18.50

Haddock
A57

Fish: 3fr, Hippoglossoides platessoides. 5fr, Sebastes mentella. 10fr, Codfish.

1972, Mar. 7
419	A57	2fr vio bl, ind & pink	5.00	2.50
420	A57	3fr grn & gray olive	6.00	3.75
421	A57	5fr Prus bl & brick red	7.00	3.50
422	A57	10fr grn & slate grn	13.00	6.00
		Nos. 419-422 (4)	31.00	15.75

Oldsquaws — A58

Birds: 10c, 70c, Puffins. 20c, 90c, Snow owl. 40c, like 6c. Identification of birds on oldsquaw and puffin stamps transposed.

1973, Jan. 1   **Engr.**   **Perf. 13**
423	A58	6c Prus bl, pur & brn	2.00	1.25
424	A58	10c Prus bl, blk & org	2.75	1.90
425	A58	20c ultra, bis & dk vio	3.25	2.50
426	A58	40c pur, sl grn & brn	4.50	3.00
427	A58	70c brt grn, blk & org	6.50	4.00
428	A58	90c Prus bl, bis & pur	12.00	6.00
		Nos. 423-428 (6)	31.00	18.65

Indoor Swimming Pool — A59

Design: 1fr, Cultural Center of St. Pierre.

1973, Sept. 25   Engr.   Perf. 13
429	A59	60c brn, brt bl & dk car	5.75	3.50
430	A59	1fr bl grn, ocher & choc	7.75	5.00

Opening of Cultural Center of St. Pierre.

Map of Islands, Weather Balloon and Ship, WMO Emblem A60

1974, Mar. 23   Engr.   Perf. 13
431	A60	1.60fr multicolored	13.50	6.50

World Meteorological Day.

Gannet Holding Letter — A61

1974, Oct. 9   Engr.   Perf. 13
432	A61	70c blue & multi	6.00	2.75
433	A61	90c red & multi	7.50	4.50

Centenary of Universal Postal Union.

Clasped Hands over Red Cross — A62

1974, Oct. 15   Photo.   Perf. 12½x13
434	A62	1.50fr multicolored	12.00 5.50

Honoring blood donors.

Hands Putting Money into Fish-shaped Bank — A63

1974, Nov. 15   Engr.   Perf. 13
435	A63	50c ocher & vio bl	6.50 4.00

St. Pierre Savings Bank centenary.

Church of St. Pierre and Seagulls A64

Designs: 10c, Church of Miquelon and fish. 20c, Church of Our Lady of the Sailors, and fishermen.

1974, Dec. 9   Engr.   Perf. 13
436	A64	6c multicolored	2.50	1.75
437	A64	10c multicolored	5.00	2.00
438	A64	20c multicolored	7.50	2.75
		Nos. 436-438 (3)	15.00	6.50

Danaus Plexippus A65

Design: 1fr, Vanessa atalanta, vert.

1975, July 17   Litho.   Perf. 12½
439	A65	1fr blue & multi	9.75 5.00
440	A65	1.20fr green & multi	14.50 5.50

Pottery — A66   Mother and Child, Wood Carving — A67

1975, Oct. 2   Engr.   Perf. 13
441	A66	50c ol, brn & choc	4.50 3.50
442	A67	60c blue & dull yel	6.50 3.50

Local handicrafts.

Pointe Plate Lighthouse and Murres A68

10c, Galantry lighthouse and Atlantic puffins. 20c, Cap Blanc lighthouse, whale and squid.

1975, Oct. 21
443	A68	6c vio bl, blk & lt grn	3.25	2.25
444	A68	10c lil rose, blk & dk ol	5.50	3.50
445	A68	20c blue, indigo & brn	8.25	6.75
		Nos. 443-445 (3)	17.00	12.50

Georges Pompidou (1911-74), Pres. of France — A68a

1976, Feb. 17   Engr.   Perf. 13
446	A68a	1.10fr brown & slate	7.00 4.00

Georges Pompidou (1911-1974), President of France.

Washington and Lafayette, American Flag — A69

1976, July 12   Photo.   Perf. 13
447	A69	1fr multicolored	6.00 3.50

American Bicentennial.

Woman Swimmer and Maple Leaf — A70

70c, Basketball and maple leaf, vert.

1976, Aug. 10   Engr.   Perf. 13
448	A70	70c multicolored	6.00 4.00
449	A70	2.50fr multicolored	12.50 5.00

21st Olympic Games, Montreal, Canada, July 17-Aug. 1.

Vigie Dam — A71

1976, Sept. 7   Engr.   Perf. 13
450	A71	2.20fr multicolored	8.00 4.50

Croix de Lorraine — A72

Fishing Vessels: 1.40fr, Goelette.

1976, Oct. 5   Photo.   Perf. 13
451	A72	1.20fr multicolored	9.00 3.50
452	A72	1.40fr multicolored	10.00 5.50

France Nos. 1783-1784, 1786-1789, 1794, 1882, 1799, 1885, 1802, 1889, 1803-1804 and 1891 Ovptd. "SAINT PIERRE / ET / MIQUELON"

1986, Feb. 4   Engr.   Perf. 13
453	A915	5c dark green	.45	.35
454	A915	10c dull red	.25	.25
455	A915	20c brt green	.25	.25
456	A915	30c orange	.25	.25
457	A915	40c brown	.25	.25
458	A915	50c lilac	.25	.25
459	A915	1fr olive green	.45	.35
460	A915	1.80fr emerald	.85	.70
461	A915	2fr brt yellow grn	.85	.75
462	A915	2.20fr red	.95	.80
463	A915	3fr chocolate brn	1.25	1.25
464	A915	3.20fr sapphire	1.50	1.25
465	A915	4fr brt carmine	1.60	1.40
466	A915	5fr gray blue	2.00	1.75
467	A915	10fr purple	4.00	3.00
		Nos. 453-467 (15)	15.15	12.85

Discovery of St. Pierre & Miquelon by Jacques Cartier, 450th Anniv. — A73

1986, June 11   Engr.   Perf. 13
476	A73	2.20fr sep, sage grn & redsh brn	1.50 .90

Statue of Liberty, Cent. — A74

1986, July 4
477	A74	2.50fr Statue, St. Pierre Harbor	2.00 1.25

Fishery Resources — A75

1986-89   Engr.   Perf. 13
478	A75	1fr bright red	.75	.40
479	A75	1.10fr brt orange	.65	.45
480	A75	1.30fr dark red	.75	.50
481	A75	1.40fr violet	1.00	.55
482	A75	1.40fr dark red	.75	.50
483	A75	1.50fr brt ultra	.90	.55
484	A75	1.60fr emerald grn	.90	.60
485	A75	1.70fr green	.95	.55
		Nos. 478-485 (8)	6.65	4.10

Issued: 1fr, #481, 10/22; 1.10fr, 1.50fr, 10/14/87; 1.30fr, 1.60fr, 8/7/88; #482, 1.70fr, 7/14/89.

Holy Family, Stained Glass by J. Balmet — A76

1986, Dec. 10   Litho.   Perf. 13
486	A76	2.20fr multicolored	1.75 1.00

Christmas.

Hygrophorus Pratensis — A77

No. 488, Russula paludosa britz. No. 489, Tricholoma virgatum. No. 490, Hydnum repandum.

	1987-90	Engr.	Perf. 12½	
487	A77	2.50fr multicolored	1.75	1.00
488	A77	2.50fr multicolored	1.40	.90
489	A77	2.50fr multicolored	1.00	.90
490	A77	2.50fr multicolored	1.00	.90
		Nos. 487-490 (4)	5.15	3.70

Issued: #487, Feb. 14; #488, Jan. 29, 1988; #489, Jan. 28, 1989; #490, Jan. 17, 1990.

Dr. François Dunan (1884-1961), Clinic — A78

	1987, Apr. 29	Engr.	Perf. 13	
491	A78	2.20fr brt bl, blk & dk red brn	1.25	.90

Transat Yacht Race, Lorient to St. Pierre to Lorient A79

	1987, May 16			
492	A79	5fr dp ultra, dk rose brn & brt bl	2.75	1.40

Visit of Pres. Mitterand A80

	1987, May 29	Litho.	Perf. 12½x13	
493	A80	2.20fr dull ultra, gold & scar	1.90	1.00

Marine Slip, Cent. A81

	1987, June 20	Litho.	Perf. 13	
494	A81	2.50fr pale sal & dk red brn	1.75	1.10

Stern Trawler La Normande — A82

	1987-91		Photo.	
495	A82	3fr shown	3.00	1.75
496	A82	3fr Le Marmouset	1.75	1.10
497	A82	3fr Tugboat Le Malabar	1.50	.80
498	A82	3fr St. Denis, St. Pierre	1.50	.90
499	A82	3fr Cryos	1.50	.90
		Nos. 495-499 (5)	9.25	5.45

Issued: #495, 10/14; #496, 9/28/88; #497, 10/11/89; #498, 10/24/90; #499, 11/6/91.

St. Christopher and the Christ Child, Stained Glass Window and Scout Emblem — A83

	1987, Dec. 9	Litho.	Perf. 13	
503	A83	2.20fr multicolored	1.75	1.00

Christmas, Scout movement in St. Pierre & Miquelon, 50th anniv.

The Great Barachoise Nature Reserve — A84

	1987, Dec. 16	Engr.	Perf. 13x12½	
504		3fr Horses, waterfowl	2.00	1.25
505		3fr Waterfowl, seals	2.00	1.25
a.		A84 Pair, #504-505 + label	4.50	3.25

No. 505a is in continuous design.

	1988, Nov. 2			
506	A84	2.20fr Ross Cove	1.50	.75
507	A84	13.70fr Cap Perce	5.50	4.75
a.		Pair, #506-507 + label	7.50	7.50

No. 507a is in continuous design.

1988 Winter Olympics, Calgary A86

	1988, Mar. 5	Engr.	Perf. 13	
508	A86	5fr brt ultra & dark red	2.50	1.60

Louis Thomas (1887-1976), Photographer — A87

	1988, May 4	Engr.	Perf. 13	
509	A87	2.20fr blk, dk ol bis & Prus bl	1.10	.70

France No. 2105 Overprinted "ST-PIERRE ET MIQUELON"

	1988, July 25	Engr.	Perf. 13	
510	A1107	2.20fr ver, blk & violet blue	1.75	.90

Seizure of Schooner Nellie J. Banks, 50th Anniv. A88

	1988, Aug. 7			
511	A88	2.50fr brn, vio blue & brt blue	1.75	1.10

The Nellie J. Banks was seized by Canada for carrying prohibited alcohol in 1938.

Christmas — A89

	1988, Dec. 17	Litho.	Perf. 13	
512	A89	2.20fr multicolored	1.25	.90

Judo Competitions in St. Pierre & Miquelon, 25th Anniv. — A90

	1989, Mar. 4	Engr.	Perf. 13	
513	A90	5fr brn org, blk & yel grn	2.25	1.40

French Revolution Bicent.; 40th Anniv. of the UN Declaration of Human Rights (in 1988) — A91

	1989	Engr.	Perf. 12½x13	
514	A91	2.20fr Liberty	1.10	.75
515	A91	2.20fr Equality	1.10	.75
516	A91	2.20fr Fraternity	1.10	.75
		Nos. 514-516 (3)	3.30	2.25

Issued: #514, 3/22; #515, 5/3; #516, 6/17.

Souvenir Sheet

French Revolution, Bicent. — A92

Designs: a, Bastille, liberty tree. b, Bastille, ship. c, Building, revolutionaries raising flag and liberty tree. d, Revolutionaries, building with open doors.

	1989, July 14	Engr.	Perf. 13	
517	A92	Sheet of 4 + 2 labels	10.00	10.00
a.-d.		5fr any single	2.25	2.25

Heritage of Ile aux Marins — A93

Designs: 2.20fr, Coastline, ships in harbor, girl in boat, fish. 13.70fr, Coastline, ships in harbor, boy flying kite from boat, map of Ile aux Marins.

	1989, Sept. 9	Engr.	Perf. 13x12½	
518		2.20fr multi	1.75	.70
519		13.70fr multi	5.75	4.25
a.		A93 Pair, #518-519 + label	8.50	8.50

Nos. 519a is in continuous design.

George Landry and Bank Emblem A95

	1989, Nov. 8	Engr.	Perf. 13	
520	A95	2.20fr bl & golden brn	1.10	.75

Bank of the Islands, cent.

Christmas — A96

	1989, Dec. 2	Litho.	Perf. 13	
521	A96	2.20fr multicolored	1.10	.75

France Nos. 2179-2182, 2182A-2186, 2188-2189, 2191-2194, 2204B, 2331, 2333-2334, 2336-2339, 2342 Ovptd.

	1990-96	Engr.	Perf. 13	
522	A1161	10c brn blk	.25	.25
523	A1161	20c light grn	.25	.25
524	A1161	50c bright vio	.25	.25
525	A1161	1fr orange	.50	.35
526	A1161	2fr apple grn	.90	.70
527	A1161	2fr blue	1.00	.75
528	A1161	2.10fr green	.95	.75
529	A1161	2.20fr green	1.10	.80
530	A1161	2.30fr red	1.10	.30
531	A1161	2.40fr emerald	1.25	.50
532	A1161	2.50fr red	1.25	.25
533	A1161	2.70fr emerald	1.25	1.10
534	A1161	3.20fr bright bl	1.75	1.10
535	A1161	3.40fr blue	1.75	.95
536	A1161	3.50fr apple grn	1.75	.75
537	A1161	3.80fr brt pink	2.00	.75
538	A1161	3.80fr blue	1.75	.75
539	A1161	4fr brt lil rose	2.25	.75
540	A1161	4.20fr rose lilac	2.25	.95
541	A1161	4.40fr blue	2.10	1.00
542	A1161	4.50fr magenta	2.40	1.90
543	A1161	5fr dull blue	2.00	1.00
544	A1161	10fr violet	4.00	1.00
544A	A1161	(2.50fr) red	1.50	.50
		Nos. 522-544A (24)	35.55	17.65

Booklet Stamps
Self-Adhesive
Die Cut

545	A1161	2.50fr red	1.60	1.00
a.		Booklet pane of 10	16.00	
545B	A1161	(2.80fr) red	1.75	1.10
a.		Booklet pane of 10	17.50	

Issued: 2.30fr, 1/2/90; 2.10fr, 2/5/90; 10c, 20c, 50c, 3.20fr, #537, 4/17/90; 1fr, 5fr, #526, 10fr, 7/16/90; #532, 2.20fr, 12/21/91; 3.40fr, 4fr, 1/8/92; #545, 2/8/92; 4.20fr, 1/13/93; #544A, 7/5/93; 2.40fr, 3.50fr, 4.40fr, #545B, 10/6/93; #527, 8/17/94; #538, 4/10/96; 2.70fr, 4.50fr, 6/12/96.

Gen. Charles de Gaulle's Call for French Resistance, 50th Anniv. — A97

1990, June 18 *Perf. 13*
546 A97 2.30fr red, claret & blue 1.40 .70

Charles de Gaulle (1890-1970) A98

Design: 1.70fr, De Gaulle as General. 2.30fr, De Gaulle as President of France.

1990, Nov. 22
547 A98 1.70fr red, claret & blue .75 .55
548 A98 2.30fr red, claret & blue 1.25 .80
a. Pair, #547-548 + central label 2.25 2.25

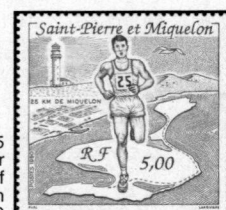

25 Kilometer Race of Miquelon A99

1990, June 23
549 A99 5fr Runner, map 2.75 1.10

Micmac Canoe, 1875 A100

1990, Aug. 15 *Engr.* *Perf. 13x13½*
550 A100 2.50fr multicolored 1.25 .70

Views of St. Pierre — A101

Harbor scene.

1990, Oct. 24 *Engr.* *Perf. 13x12½*
551 A101 2.30fr bl, grn & brn 1.00 .50
552 A101 14.50fr bl, grn & brn 6.50 3.50
a. Pair, #551-552 + label 9.00 9.00

No. 552a is in continous design.

Christmas — A103

1990, Dec. 15 *Litho.*
553 A103 2.30fr multicolored 1.25 .65

Papilio Brevicaudata A104

3.60fr, Aeshna Eremita, Nuphar Variegatum.

1991-92 *Litho.* *Perf. 13*
554 A104 2.50fr multicolored 1.50 .95
Perf. 12
555 A104 3.60fr multicolored 1.60 1.00
Issued: 2.50fr, Jan. 16; 3.60fr, Mar. 4, 1992.

Marine Tools, Sailing Ship A105

Litho. & Engr.
1991, Mar. 6 *Perf. 13*
559 A105 1.40fr yellow & green .75 .50
560 A105 1.70fr yellow & red .90 .55

Scenic Views A106

Designs: Nos. 548, 552, Saint Pierre. Nos. 549, 553, Ile aux Marins. Nos. 550, 554, Langlade. Nos. 551, 555, Miquelon.

1991, Apr. 17 *Engr.* *Perf. 13*
561 A106 1.70fr blue .80 .65
562 A106 1.70fr blue .80 .65
563 A106 1.70fr blue .80 .65
564 A106 1.70fr blue .80 .65
a. Strip of 4, #561-564 3.25 3.25
565 A106 2.50fr red 1.25 .95
566 A106 2.50fr red 1.25 .95
567 A106 2.50fr red 1.25 .95
568 A106 2.50fr red 1.25 .95
a. Strip of 4, #565-568 5.00 5.00
Nos. 561-568 (8) 8.20 6.40

Lyre Music Society, Cent. — A107

1991, June 21 *Engr.* *Perf. 13*
569 A107 2.50fr multicolored 1.50 .70

Newfoundland Crossing by Rowboat "Los Gringos" — A108

1991, Aug. 3 *Engr.* *Perf. 13x12½*
570 A108 2.50fr multicolored 1.50 .70

Basque Sports A109

1991, Aug. 24 *Perf. 13*
571 A109 5fr red & green 2.10 1.40

Natural Heritage — A110

2.50fr, Fishermen. 14.50fr, Shoreline, birds.

1991, Oct. 18 *Engr.* *Perf. 13x12½*
572 A110 2.50fr multicolored 1.50 .90
573 A110 14.50fr multicolored 6.50 5.00
a. Pair, #572-573 + label 8.50 8.50

No. 573a is in continuous design.

Central Economic Cooperation Bank, 50th Anniv. — A111

1991, Dec. 2 *Engr.* *Perf. 13x12½*
574 A111 2.50fr 1941 100fr note 1.40 .70

Christmas A112

1991, Dec. 21 *Litho.* *Perf. 13*
575 A112 2.50fr multicolored 1.40 .75
Christmas Day Plebiscite, 50th anniv.

Vice Admiral Emile Henri Muselier (1882-1965), Commander of Free French Naval Forces — A113

1992, Jan. 8 *Litho.* *Perf. 13*
576 A113 2.50fr multicolored 1.50 .75

1992 Winter Olympics, Albertville A114

1992, Feb. 8 *Engr.* *Perf. 13*
577 A114 5fr vio bl, blue & mag 2.10 1.25

Caulking Tools, Bow of Ship A115

Litho. & Engr.
1992, Apr. 1 *Perf. 13x12½*
578 A115 1.50fr pale bl gray & brn .75 .45
579 A115 1.80fr pale bl gray & bl .90 .45

Lighthouses — A116

Designs: a, Galantry. b, Feu Rouge. c, Pointe-Plate. d, Ile Aux Marins.

1992, July 8 *Litho.* *Perf. 13*
580 A116 2.50fr Strip of 4, #a.-d. 5.50 3.50

Natural Heritage — A117

1992, Sept. 9 *Engr.* *Perf. 13x12½*
581 A117 2.50fr Langlade 1.50 .75
582 A117 15.10fr Doulisie Valley 7.50 3.75
a. Pair, #581-582 + label 9.00 9.00

No. 582a is in continuous design.
See Nos. 593-594, 605-606.

Discovery of America, 500th Anniv. — A118

Photo. & Engr.
1992, Oct. 12 *Perf. 13x12½*
583 A118 5.10fr multicolored 2.50 1.25

Le Baron de L'Esperance — A119

1992, Nov. 18   Engr.   Perf. 13
584 A119 2.50fr claret, brn & bl   1.25   .75

Christmas — A120

1992, Dec. 9   Litho.   Perf. 13
585 A120 2.50fr multicolored   1.40   .80

Commander R. Birot (1906-1942) — A121

1993, Jan. 13
586 A121 2.50fr multicolored   1.50   .90

Deep Sea Diving A122

1993, Feb. 10   Engr.   Perf. 12
587 A122 5fr multicolored   2.75   1.25

A123

Monochamus Scutellatus, Cichorium Intybus.

1993, Mar. 10   Litho.   Perf. 13½x13
588 A123 3.60fr multicolored   1.75   .80
    See No. 599.

A124

Slicing cod.

1993, Apr. 7   Litho.   Perf. 13½x13
589 A124 1.50fr green & multi   .85   .50
590 A124 1.80fr red & multi   1.00   .55

Move to the Magdalen Islands, Quebec, by Miquelon Residents, Bicent. — A125

1993, June 9   Engr.   Perf. 13
591 A125 5.10fr brn, bl & grn   2.50   1.25

Fish A126

Designs: a, Capelin. b, Ray. c, Halibut (fletan). d, Toad fish (crapaud).

1993, July 30   Photo.   Perf. 13
592 A126 2.80fr Strip of 4, #a.-d.   6.00   6.00

Natl. Heritage Type of 1992
1993, Aug. 18   Engr.   Perf. 13x12½
593 A117 2.80fr Miquelon   1.75   1.00
594 A117 16fr Otter pool   7.00   5.75
a.   Pair, #593-594 + label   11.00   11.00

No. 594a is a continuous design.

Commissioner's Residence — A127

1993, Oct. 6   Engr.   Perf. 13
595 A127 3.70fr multicolored   1.60   .90

Christmas A128

1993, Dec. 13   Litho.   Perf. 13
596 A128 2.80fr multicolored   1.60   .80

Commander Louis Blaison (1906-1942), Submarine Surcouf — A129

1994, Jan. 12   Litho.   Perf. 13
597 A129 2.80fr multicolored   1.75   .80

Petanque World Championships — A130

1994, Feb. 9   Engr.   Perf. 12½x12
598 A130 5.10fr multicolored   2.50   1.75

Insect and Flower Type of 1993
Cristalis tenax, taraxacum officinale, horiz.

1994, Mar. 9   Litho.   Perf. 13x13½
599 A123 3.70fr multicolored   2.10   1.25

Drying Codfish, 1905 A131

1994   Litho.   Perf. 13
600 A131 1.50fr blk & bl grn   .90   .55
601 A131 1.80fr multicolored   1.20   .65
Issued: 1.50fr, 5/4/94; 1.80fr, 4/6/94.

Women's Right to Vote, 50th Anniv. A132

1994, Apr. 21
602 A132 2.80fr multicolored   1.60   .80

Hospital Ship St. Pierre, Cent. A133

1994, July 2
603 A133 2.80fr multicolored   1.75   .80

Souvenir Sheet

Ships — A134

Designs: a, Miquelon. b, Isle of St. Pierre. c, St. George XII. d, St. Eugene IV.

1994, July 6   Perf. 12
604 A134 Sheet of 4   8.50   8.50
a.-b.   2.80fr any single   1.50   1.25
c.-d.   3.70fr any single   2.00   1.75
    See No. 628.

Natl. Heritage Type of 1992
1994, Aug. 17   Engr.   Perf. 13
605 A117 2.80fr Woods   2.00   .90
606 A117 16fr "The Hat"   7.50   4.00
a.   Pair, #605-606 + label   10.50   10.00

Parochial School A135

1994, Oct. 5   Engr.   Perf. 13
607 A135 3.70fr multicolored   1.60   .95

Stamp Show A136

1994, Oct. 15
608 A136 3.70fr grn, yel & bl   1.75   1.10

Christmas A137

1994, Nov. 23   Litho.   Perf. 13
609 A137 2.80fr multicolored   1.60   .80

Louis Pasteur (1822-95) A138

1995, Jan. 11   Litho.   Perf. 13
610 A138 2.80fr multicolored   1.60   .80

Triathlon A139

1995, Feb. 8   Engr.   Perf. 12
611 A139 5.10fr multicolored   2.25   1.25

A140

Dicranum Scoparium & Cladonia Cristatella.

1995, Mar. 8   Litho.   Perf. 13
612 A140 3.70fr multicolored   1.75   1.10
    See Nos. 625, 635.

A141

Cooper and his tools.

1995, Apr. 5　　Litho.　　Perf. 13½x13
613　A141　1.50fr black & multi　　.75　.50
614　A141　1.80fr red & multi　　　.90　.55

Shellfish
A142

a, Snail. b, Crab. c, Scallop. d, Lobster.

1995, July 5　　Litho.　　Perf. 13
616　　　Strip of 4　　　　　　　6.00　6.00
　a.-d.　A142 2.80fr any single　　1.40　1.00

Geological Mission — A143

Designs: 2.80fr, Rugged terrain along shoreline, diagram of mineral location, zircon. 16fr, Geological map, terrain.

1995, Aug. 16　　Engr.　　Perf. 13x12½
617　A143　2.80fr multicolored　　2.00　1.00
618　A143　16fr multicolored　　　7.00　5.00
　a.　Pair, #617-618 + label　　9.50　9.50

Sister Cesarine (1845-1922), St. Joseph de Cluny — A144

1995, Sept. 6　　Litho.　　Perf. 13
619　A144　1.80fr multicolored　　1.10　.75

The Francoforum Public Building — A145

1995, Oct. 4　　　　　　　　Engr.
620　A145　3.70fr multicolored　　1.75　1.00

Christmas — A146

Design: 2.80fr, Toys in store window.

1995, Nov. 22　　Litho.　　Perf. 13
621　A146　2.80fr multicolored　　1.75　.90

Charles de Gaulle (1890-1970)
A147

1995, Nov. 9　　Litho.　　Perf. 13x13½
622　A147　14fr multicolored　　　5.75　3.50

Commandant Jean Levasseur (1909-47) — A148

1996, Jan. 10　　　　　　　　Perf. 13
623　A148　2.80fr multicolored　　1.75　.80

Boxing
A149

1996, Feb. 7　　Engr.　　Perf. 12x12½
624　A149　5.10fr multicolored　　2.50　1.25

Plant Type of 1995

Design: Cladonia verticillata and polytrichum juniperinum.

1996, Mar. 13　　Litho.　　Perf. 13
625　A140　3.70fr multicolored　　1.75　1.10

Blacksmiths and Their Tools
A150

1996, Apr. 10
626　A150　1.50fr black & multi　　.75　.35
627　A150　1.80fr red & multi　　　.85　.50

Ship Type of 1994

Designs: a, Radar II. b, SPM Roro. c, Pinta. d, Pascal Anne.

1996, July 10　　Litho.　　Perf. 13
628　　　Sheet of 4　　　　　　　7.00　7.00
　a.-d.　A134 3fr Any single　　1.50　1.00

Aerial View of Miquelon — A151

Designs: 3fr, "Le Cap," mountains, buildings. 15.50fr, "Le Village," buildings.

1996, Aug. 14　　Engr.　　Perf. 13x12½
629　　　3fr multicolored　　　　1.25　1.25
630　　　15.50fr multicolored　　6.00　6.00
　a.　A151 Pair, #629-630 + label　7.75　7.75

Customs House, Cent.
A152

1996, Oct. 9　　Engr.　　Perf. 12½x13
631　A152　3.80fr blue & black　　1.50　.90

Fall Stamp Show — A153

1996, Nov. 6　　Litho.　　Perf. 13
632　A153　1fr multicolored　　　.70　.45

Christmas — A154

1996, Nov. 20　　Litho.　　Perf. 13
633　A154　3fr multicolored　　　1.50　.90

Constant Colmay (1903-65)
A155

1997, Jan. 8　　Litho.　　Perf. 13
634　A155　3fr multicolored　　　1.50　.90

Plant Type of 1995

Design: Phalacrocorax carbo, sedum rosea.

1997, Mar. 12　　Litho.　　Perf. 13
635　A140　3.80fr multicolored　　1.50　.90

Maritime Heritage
A156

Designs: 1.70fr, Man in doorway of salt house. 2fr, Boat, naval architect's drawing.

1997, Apr. 9　　Litho.　　Perf. 13
636　A156　1.70fr multicolored　　.75　.50
637　A156　2fr multicolored　　　.90　.60

Volleyball
A157

Litho. & Engr.
1997, Apr. 9　　　　　　　　Perf. 12
638　A157　5.20fr multicolored　　2.25　1.10

Fish — A158

a, Shark. b, Salmon. c, Poule d'eau. d, Mackerel.

1997, July 9　　Litho.　　Perf. 13
639　A158　3fr Strip of 4, #a.-d.　　5.50　4.50

Bay, Headlands — A159

3fr, Basque Cape. 15.50fr, Diamant.

1997, Aug. 13　　　　　　　　Perf. 13x12
640　A159　3fr multicolored　　　1.50　1.00
641　A159　15.50fr multicolored　5.50　3.50
　a.　Pair #640-641 + label　　7.00　6.25

France Nos. 2589-2603 Ovptd.
"ST. PIERRE / ET / MIQUELON"

			1997-98	**Engr.**	**Perf. 13**
642	A1409	10c brown	.25	.25
643	A1409	20c brt blue grn	.25	.25
644	A1409	50c purple	.30	.30
645	A1409	1fr bright org	.35	.25
646	A1409	2fr bright blue	.80	.30
647	A1409	2.70fr bright green	1.10	.30
648	A1409	(3fr) red	1.40	.30
649	A1409	3.50fr apple green	1.50	.55
650	A1409	3.80fr blue	1.40	.65
651	A1409	4.20fr dark orange	1.60	.65
652	A1409	4.40fr blue	1.75	.65
653	A1409	4.50fr bright pink	1.75	.75
654	A1409	5fr brt grn bl	1.90	.80
655	A1409	6.70fr dark green	2.75	1.25
656	A1409	10fr violet	3.75	1.40
		Nos. 642-656 (15)	20.85	8.65

Issued: 2.70fr, (3fr), 3.80fr, 8/13/97; 10c, 20c, 50c, 3.50fr, 4.40fr, 10fr, 10/8/97; 1fr, 2fr, 4.20fr, 4.50fr, 5fr, 6.70fr, 1/7/98.
See No. 664 for self-adhesive (3fr).

Post Office Building
A160

1997, Oct. 8　　Engr.　　Perf. 13
657　A160　3.80fr multicolored　　1.60　.90

Christmas — A161

1997, Nov. 19　　Litho.　　Perf. 13
658　A161　3fr multicolored　　　1.50　.80

Alain Savary (1918-88), Governor, Territorial Deputy A162

1998, Jan. 7　　Litho.　　Perf. 13
659　A162　3fr multicolored　　　1.40　.70

1998
Winter
Olympic
Games,
Nagano
A163

1998, Feb. 11   Engr.   Perf. 12
660 A163 5.20fr Curling   2.25 1.10

Flora and
Fauna
A164

1998, Mar. 11   Photo.   Perf. 13
661 A164 3.80fr multicolored   1.75 .95

Ice
Workers
A165

1998, Apr. 8   Litho.
662 A165 1.70fr shown   .75 .65
663 A165 2fr Cutting ice from
          lake   .90 .65

**France Nos. 2604, 2620 Ovptd. "ST.
PIERRE / ET / MIQUELON"**
Die Cut x Serpentine Die Cut
1998, Apr. 8   Engr.
Self-Adhesive
664 A1409 (3fr) red   1.25 .60
 a.   Booklet pane of 10   15.00

No. 664a is a complete booklet. The peelable backing serves as a booklet cover.

1998, May 13   Perf. 13
665 A1424 3fr red & blue   1.25 .60

Houses — A166

a, Gray. b, Yellow, red roof. c, Pink. d, White,
red roof.

1998, July 8   Litho.   Perf. 13
666 A166 3fr Strip of 4, #a.-d.   5.00 2.50

French in North America — A167

1998, Sept. 30   Engr.   Perf. 13x12½
670 A167 3fr multicolored   1.25 .60

Cape Blue Natl. Park — A168

Designs: 3fr, Point Plate Lighthouse, shoreline. 15.50fr, Cape Blue.

1998, Sept. 30   Perf. 13x12
671 A168   3fr multicolored   1.25 .95
672 A168 15.50fr multicolored   6.50 3.50
 a.   Pair, #671-672 + label   8.75 8.75

France,
1998 World
Cup
Soccer
Champions
A169

1998, Oct. 21   Litho.   Perf. 13
673 A169 3fr multicolored   1.60 .60

Memorial to War
Dead — A170

1998, Nov. 11   Engr.
674 A170 3.80fr multicolored   1.60 .75

Christmas — A171

1998, Nov. 18   Litho.
675 A171 3fr multicolored   1.25 .60

Emile Letournel (1927-94), Orthopedic
Surgeon, Traumatologist — A172

1999, Jan. 6   Engr.   Perf. 13
676 A172 3fr multicolored   1.25 .60

Painting, "The Beach at Fisherman
Island," by Patrick Guillaume — A173

1999, Feb. 10   Litho.
677 A173 5.20fr multicolored   2.00 .95
         See No. 692.

La Plate-
Bière
A174

3.80fr, Rubus chamaemorus.

1999, Mar. 10   Litho.   Perf. 13
678 A174 3.80fr multicolored   1.60 .75
         See No. 693, 705, 736.

Horseshoeing — A175

1.70fr, Horse, blacksmith and his tools. 2fr,
Applying horseshoes in blacksmith's shop.

1999, Apr. 7   Litho.   Perf. 13
679 A175 1.70fr multicolored   .80 .50
680 A175   2fr multicolored   .95 .50

**France No. 2691 Ovptd. "ST.
PIERRE / ET / MIQUELON"**
1999, Apr. 7   Engr.
681 A1470 3fr red & blue   1.25 .60

Value is shown in both francs and euros on
No. 681.

**France No. 2691A Overprinted "ST.
PIERRE / ET / MIQUELON"**
Die Cux x Serpentine Die Cut 7
1999, Apr. 5   Engr.
Self-Adhesive
681A A1470 3fr red & blue   2.00 1.00
 b.   Booklet of 10   20.00

First
Stamps of
France,
150th
Anniv.
A176

a, France #3, St. Pierre & Miquelon #9, 79.
b, #145, 270. c, #C21, C36. d, #476, 676.

1999, June 23   Litho.   Perf. 13
682 A176 3fr Sheet of 4, #a.-d.   7.00 7.00
PhilexFrance '99, World Philatelic Exhibition.

Ships — A177

a, Bearn. b, Pro Patria. c, Erminie. d,
Colombier.

1999, July 7   Litho.   Perf. 13x13½
683 A177 3fr Sheet of 4, #a.-d.   6.00 6.00

General de Gaulle Place — A178

1999, Aug. 11   Engr.   Perf. 13x12¼
684   3fr Cars, yield sign   1.00 1.00
685   15.50fr Docked boats   5.50 5.50
 a.   A178 Pair, #684-685 + label 7.50 7.50

Visit of Pres.
Jacques Chirac,
Sept.
1999 — A179

1999, Sept. 7   Litho.   Perf. 13¼x13
686 A179 3fr multicolored   1.40 .60

Archives
A180

1999, Oct. 6   Engr.   Perf. 13x12¾
687 A180 5.40fr deep rose lilac   2.25 1.00

Christmas
A181

1999, Nov. 17   Litho.   Perf. 13
688 A181 3fr multi   1.50 .75

Year 2000 — A182

2000, Jan. 12   Litho.   Perf. 13¼x13
689 A182 3fr multi   1.50 .75

Whales
A183

Designs: 3fr, Megaptera novaeangliae.
5.70fr, Balaenoptera physalus.

2000, Jan. 26   Engr.   Perf. 13x12¾
690 A183   3fr blk & Prus bl   1.25 .60
691 A183 5.70fr Prus grn & blk   2.75 1.10
         See also Nos. 702-703.

Painting Type of 1999
2000, Feb. 9   Litho.   Perf. 13
692 A173 5.20fr Les Graves   2.25 1.00

Plant Type of 1999
2000, Mar. 8
693 A174 3.80fr Vaccinium vitis-
               idaea   1.50 .70

Wood
Gatherer
A184

Vignette colors: 1.70fr, Blue. 2fr, Brown.

2000, Apr. 5   **Engr.**
694-695 A184 Set of 2   2.00 1.00

Millennium
A185

No. 696: a, Lobstermen on Newfoundland coast, 1904. b, Women on shore, 1905. c, World War I conscripts on ship Chicago, 1915. d, Soldiers in action at Souain Hill, 1915. e, Men walking on ice, 1923. f, Unloading cases of champagne to be smuggled to US, 1925. g, St. Pierre & Miquelon Pavilion at Colonial Expostion in Paris, 1931. h, Alcohol smugglers, 1933. i, Adm. Emile Muselier inspecting troops on ship Mimosa, 1942. j, World War II soldiers crossing bridge, 1945.

No. 697: a, Fishery employees, 1951. b, Fishing trawler, 1960. c, Visit of Gen. Charles de Gaulle, 1967. d, First television images, 1967. e, Port facilities, 1970. f, New high school, 1977. g, Resumption of stamp issuing, 1986. h, Voyage fo Eric Tabarly, 1987. i, Exclusive Economic Zone, 1992. j, New airport, 1999.

2000   **Litho.**   *Perf. 13x13¼*
696   Sheet of 10   16.00 13.00
a.-j.   A185 3fr Any single   1.40   .75
697   Sheet of 10   14.00 11.00
a.-j.   A185 2fr Any single   1.25   .75

Issue: No. 696, 6/21; No. 697, 12/6.

The Inger — A186

2000, Oct. 4   **Engr.**   *Perf. 13x13¼*
698 A186 5.40fr green   3.00 1.40

Boathouses in November — A187

2000, Oct. 4   *Perf. 13x12¼*
699   Pair + central label   9.50 8.50
a.   A187 3fr Hill   1.50 1.00
b.   A187 15.50fr Church   7.50 5.00

Christmas — A188

2000, Nov. 15   **Litho.**   *Perf. 13¼x13*
700 A188 3fr multi   1.50   .80

New Year 2001 — A189

2001, Jan. 3   **Litho.**   *Perf. 13x12¾*
701 A189 3fr multi   2.00   .50

Whale Type of 2000

Designs: 3fr, *Orcinus orca*. 5.70fr, *Globicephala melaena*.

2001, Jan. 24   **Engr.**   *Perf. 13x12¾*
702-703 A183 Set of 2   3.50 1.50

Landscape
A190

2001, Feb. 21   **Litho.**   *Perf. 13*
704 A190 5.20fr multi   2.50 1.10

Plant Type of 1999

2001, Mar. 21   **Litho.**   *Perf. 13*
705 A174 3.80fr Vaccinium oxycoccos   1.75   .80

Hay
Gatherers
A191

Denomination colors: 1.70fr, Red brown. 2fr, Lilac.

2001, Apr. 18
706-707 A191 Set of 2   2.00   .95

Seasons
A192

Designs: No. 708, 3fr, Autumn. No. 709, 3fr, Winter.

2001, June 20
708-709 A192 Set of 2   3.00 1.50
      See Nos. 714-715.

Vestibules — A193

No. 710: a, Guillou House. b, Jugan House. c, Ile-aux-Marins town hall. d, Vogé House.

2001, July 25
710 A193   Horiz. strip of 4   5.75 5.00
a.-d.   3fr Any single   1.50 1.00

Anse du Gouvernement — A194

Houses and: a, Boat. b, Rocks near shore.

2001, Sept. 12   **Engr.**   *Perf. 13x12¼*
711   A194   Horiz. pair, #a-b,
           + central label   10.00 8.50
a.-b.   10fr Any single   4.75 3.25

Saint Pierre Pointe Blanche — A195

2001, Sept. 26   **Litho.**   *Perf. 13*
712 A195 5fr multi   2.40 1.40

The Marie-Thérèse — A196

2001, Sept. 26   **Engr.**   *Perf. 13x13¼*
713 A196 5.40fr green   2.60 1.40

Seasons Type of 2001

Designs: No. 714, 3fr, Spring. No. 715, 3fr, Summer.

2001, Oct. 17   **Litho.**   *Perf. 13*
714-715 A192 Set of 2   3.00 1.60

Commander
Jacques
Pepin
Lehalleur
(1911-2000)
A197

2001, Nov. 14
716 A197 3fr multi   1.80   .80

Christmas — A198

2001, Nov. 28
717 A198 3fr multi   1.50   .80

100 Cents = 1 Euro (€)

France Nos. 2849-2863
Overprinted

2002, Jan. 1   **Engr.**   *Perf. 13*
718 A1583   1c yellow   .25   .25
719 A1583   2c brown   .25   .25
720 A1583   5c brt bl grn   .25   .25
721 A1583   10c purple   .30   .25
722 A1583   20c brt org   .60   .50
723 A1583   41c brt green   1.40 1.00
724 A1583   50c dk blue   1.60 1.25
725 A1583   53c apple grn   1.75 1.25
726 A1583   58c blue   1.90 1.40
727 A1583   64c dark org   2.00 1.50
728 A1583   67c brt blue   2.10 1.60
729 A1583   69c brt pink   2.10 1.60
730 A1583   €1 Prus blue   3.00 2.40
731 A1583   €1.02 dk green   3.25 2.50
732 A1583   €2 violet   6.25 4.75
    Nos. 718-732 (15)   27.00 20.75

Introduction
of the Euro
A199

2002, Jan. 30   **Litho.**   *Perf. 13*
733 A199 €1 multi   3.00 1.50

Pinnipeds
A200

Designs: 46c, *Phoca vitulina*. 87c, *Halichoerus grypus*.

2002, Mar. 7   **Engr.**   *Perf. 13¼*
734-735 A200 Set of 2   4.00 2.00
      See Nos. 748-749.

Plant Type of 1999

2002, Mar. 20   **Litho.**   *Perf. 13*
736 A174 58c Pomme de pré   1.75   .90

Laranaga Farm, c. 1900 — A201

2002, Mar. 20   **Engr.**   *Perf. 13x12¾*
737 A201 79c green   2.50 1.25
      See also Nos. 751, 772.

Net Mender
A202

Colors: 26c, Orange brown. 30c, Blue.

2002, Apr. 15   **Engr.**   *Perf. 13x13¼*
738-739 A202 Set of 2   1.75   .90

West Point — A204

2002, June 24   **Litho.**   *Perf. 13*
741 A204 75c multi   2.40 1.10

Tiaude de Morue, Local Cod
Dish — A205

2002, July 10
742 A205 50c multi   1.60   .80

France No. 2835 Overprinted "ST. PIERRE / ET / MIQUELON"

2002, Sept. 11   **Engr.**   *Perf. 13*
743 A1409 (46c) red   1.50   .75

Arctic Hare
A206

2002, Sept. 11   **Litho.**   *Perf. 13*
744 A206 46c multi   1.50   .75

The Troutpool — A207

2002, Oct. 11   Engr.   Perf. 13x13¼
745 A207 84c green   2.75 1.40

Henry Cove — A208

No. 208: a, Gull and islands. b, Aerial view of St. Pierre.

2002, Nov. 6   Engr.   Perf. 13x12¼
746 A208 Horiz. pair +
           central label   13.50 11.00
a.-b. €2 Either single   6.25   3.25

Christmas
A209

2002, Nov. 27   Litho.   Perf. 13
747 A209 46c multi   1.50   .75

Pinnipeds Type of 2002
Designs: 46c, Phoca groenlandica. 87c, Cystophora cristata.

2003, Jan. 5   Engr.   Perf. 13¼
748-749 A200 Set of 2   4.25   2.25

Msgr. François Maurer (1922-2000) A210

2003, Jan. 8   Litho.   Perf. 13
750 A210 46c multi   1.50   .75

Farm Type of 2002
2003, Mar. 12   Engr.   Perf. 13x13¼
751 A201 79c Capandeguy Farm,
           c. 1910   2.50   1.25

France Nos. 2835A, 2921, and 2952-2957 Overprinted Like No. 718

2003		Engr.	Perf. 13	
752	A1409	(41c) brt green	1.40	.70
753	A1583	58c apple grn	1.90	.95
754	A1583	70c yellow grn	2.25	1.10
755	A1583	75c bright blue	2.40	1.25
756	A1583	90c dark blue	3.00	1.50
757	A1583	€1.11 red lilac	3.50	1.75
758	A1583	€1.90 vio brn	6.00	3.00
		Nos. 752-758 (7)	20.45	10.25

Booklet Stamp
Self-Adhesive
Serpentine Die Cut 6¾ Vert.

758A A1409 (46c) red   1.50   .75
b.   Booklet pane of 10   15.00

Issued: (46c), 3/12. (41c), 4/23. 58c, 70c, 75c, 90c, €1.11, €1.90, 9/24.

Blueberries — A211

2003, Apr. 23   Litho.   Perf. 13
759 A211 75c multi   2.40   1.25

Pulley Repairer A212

2003, May 14   Engr.
760 A212 30c blue gray   1.00   .70

Intl. Congress on Traditional Architecture — A213

No. 761: a, Patrice, Jézéquel and Jugan houses. b, Notre-Dame des Marins Church, Borotra house.

2003, May 22   Perf. 13x12¼
761 A213 Horiz. pair +
           central label   13.50 11.00
a.-b. €2 Either single   6.25   4.00

ASSP Soccer Team, Cent. A214

2003, Aug. 7   Litho.   Perf. 13
762 A214 50c multi   1.60   .80

Buck A215

2003, Sept. 10
763 A215 50c multi   1.75   1.75

Lions Club in St. Pierre & Miquelon, 50th Anniv. A216

2003, Oct. 29   Litho.   Perf. 13x13¼
764 A216 50c multi   1.75   1.75

Langlade Strawberry Preserves — A217

2003, Oct. 29   Perf. 13
765 A217 50c multi   1.75   1.75

The Afrique — A218

2003, Nov. 6   Engr.   Perf. 13x12½
766 A218 90c blue green   3.25   3.25

Christmas — A219

2003, Dec. 3   Litho.   Perf. 13
767 A219 50c multi   1.75   1.75

Joseph Lehuenen (d. 2001), Historian, Mayor — A220

2004, Feb. 25   Engr.   Perf. 13x13¼
768 A220 50c brown   1.75   1.75

Rodrigue Cove — A221

2004, Mar. 10   Litho.   Perf. 13
769 A221 75c multi   3.00   3.00

Marine Mammals A222

Designs: 50c, Lagenorhynchus acutus. €1.08, Phocoena phocoena.

2004, Mar. 24   Engr.   Perf. 13¼
770-771 A222 Set of 2   6.00   6.00
       See also Nos. 806-807.

Farm Type of 2002
2004, Apr. 7   Engr.   Perf. 13x12½
772 A201 90c Ollivier Farm, c.
           1920   3.00   3.00

Fishermen in Boat A223

2004, May 12   Litho.   Perf. 13
773 A223 30c multi   1.10   1.10

Port of St. Pierre — A224

No. 774: a, Ships, denomination at right. b, Ships and dock, denomination at left.

2004, June 26   Engr.   Perf. 13x12¼
774 A224 Horiz. pair +
           central label   13.50 13.50
a.-b. €2 Either single   6.25   6.25

Micmac Indians of Miquelon — A225

2004, July 17   Litho.   Perf. 13
775 A225 50c multi   1.75   1.75

No. 775 Overprinted

2004, Aug. 14
776 A225 50c multi   3.25   3.25

Red Fox A226

2004, Sept. 13
777 A226 50c multi   1.75   1.75

Dinner Table — A227

2004, Sept. 13
778 A227 90c multi   3.50   3.50

The Fulwood — A228

2004, Nov. 5   Engr.   Perf. 13x13¼
779 A228 75c dark purple   2.75   2.75

Souvenir Sheet

Ships — A229

No. 780: a, Cap Blanc. b, Lisabeth-C. c, Shamrock. d, Aldona.

2004, Nov. 17　Litho.　Perf. 13
780　A229　50c Sheet of 4, #a-d　8.00 8.00

SIAA Soccer Team, 50th Anniv. (in 2003) A230

2004, Nov. 24
781　A230　44c multi　1.60 1.60

Christmas — A231

2004, Dec. 8
782　A231　50c multi　1.75 1.75

France Nos. 3066, 3068-3070, 3072, 3074-3075, 3077-3079, 3081 and 3083 Overprinted

2005		**Engr.**		**Perf. 13**	
783	A1713	1c	yellow	.25	.25
784	A1713	5c	brown black	.25	.25
785	A1713	10c	violet	.30	.30
786	A1713	(45c)	green	1.40	1.40
787	A1713	(50c)	red	1.60	1.60
788	A1713	55c	dark blue	1.75	1.75
789	A1713	58c	olive green	1.90	1.90
790	A1713	64c	dark green	2.00	2.00
791	A1713	70c	dark green	2.25	2.25
792	A1713	75c	light blue	2.40	2.40
793	A1713	82c	fawn	2.60	2.60
794	A1713	90c	dark blue	3.00	3.00
795	A1713	€1	orange	3.25	3.25
796	A1713	€1.11	red violet	3.50	3.50
797	A1713	€1.22	red violet	3.75	3.75
798	A1713	€1.90	chocolate	6.00	6.00
799	A1713	€1.98	chocolate	6.25	6.25
Nos. 783-799 (17)				42.45	42.45

Booklet Stamp
Self-Adhesive
Serpentine Die Cut 6¾ Vert.

800　A1713　(50c) red　1.60 1.60
a.　Booklet pane of 10 (on France #3083a)　16.00

Issued: Nos. 1c, 10c, (45c), (50c), 58c, 70c, 75c, 90c, €1, €1.11, €1.90, 1/12. 5c, 55c, 64c, 82c, €1.22, €1.98, 3/23. Face values shown for Nos. 786, 787 and 800 are those the stamps sold for on the day of issue.

Henri Claireaux (1911-2001), Senator — A232

2005, Jan. 25　Engr.　Perf. 13x13¼
804　A232　50c lilac　1.75 1.75

Allumette Cove — A233

2005, Feb. 16　Litho.　Perf. 13
805　A233　75c multi　2.75 2.75

Marine Mammals Type of 2004

Designs: 53c, Delphinus delphis. €1.15, Lagenorhynchus albirostris.

2005, Mar. 9　Engr.　Perf. 13¼
806-807　A222　Set of 2　6.50 6.50

Horse Point Farm — A234

2005, Apr. 20　　Perf. 13x13¼
808　A234　90c olive green　3.50 3.50

Fog, Clouds and Houses A235

2005, May 11　Litho.　Perf. 13
809　A235　30c multi　1.10 1.10

Seven Ponds Valley — A236

No. 810: a, Bird at left. b, Rabbit at right.

2005, June 14　Engr.　Perf. 13x12¼
810　A236　Horiz. pair + central label　15.00 15.00
a.-b.　€2 Either single　6.25 2.00

Variable Hare A237

2005, Sept. 7　Litho.　Perf. 13
811　A237　53c multi　2.00 2.00

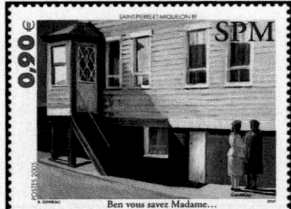

Local Expression "Ben Vous Savez Madame" — A238

2005, Sept. 29
812　A238　90c multi　3.00 2.75

The Transpacific — A239

2005, Oct. 12　Engr.　Perf. 13x13¼
813　A239　75c blue　2.50 2.50

Status as Territorial Collectivity, 20th Anniv. — A240

2005, Oct. 27　Litho.　Perf. 13
814　A240　53c multi　1.75 1.75

Christmas A241

2005, Dec. 7
815　A241　53c multi　1.75 1.00

Snow on Trees — A242

2006, Jan. 25
816　A242　53c multi　2.10 1.25

Sailors' Festival — A243

2006, Feb. 8
817　A243　53c multi　1.75 1.25

Albert Pen (1935-2003), President of General Council — A244

2006, Mar. 1　　Engr.
818　A244　53c henna brn　1.75 1.25

Whales A245

Designs: 53c, Little rorqual. €1.15, Physeter catodon.

2006, Apr. 12　Engr.　Perf. 13¼
819-820　A245　Set of 2　6.00 2.00

Houses on Clear Day A246

2006, June 7　Litho.　Perf. 13
821　A246　30c multi　1.00 .50

Sénat Archipelago — A247

2006, June 20
822　A247　53c multi　1.75 1.00

Prohibition, by Jean-Claude Girardin — A248

2006, July 19　Litho.　Perf. 13
823　A248　75c multi　2.25 1.50

Le Petit-Barachois — A249

No. 824: a, Houses. b, Houses and boats.

2006, July 26   Engr.   Perf. 13x12¾
824   A249   Horiz. pair with
              central label   13.50 13.50
a.-b.   €2 Either single   6.25   6.25

Zazpiak Bat Pelota Fronton,
Cent. — A250

2006, Aug. 23   Litho.   Perf. 13
825   A250   53c multi   1.60   1.60

Orchids — A251

No. 826: a, Spiranthe de Romanzoff. b, Arethusa. c, Habénaire papillon. d, Habénaire
lacérée.

2006, Sept. 6   Engr.   Perf. 13x13¼
826   Horiz. strip of 4   7.00   7.00
a.-d.   A251 53c Any single   1.60   1.60

Dugue Farm — A252

2006, Sept. 20   Engr.   Perf. 13x12½
827   A252   95c black   3.00   3.00

The Penny Fair — A253

2006, Oct. 4   Engr.   Perf. 13x12½
828   A253   95c black   3.00   3.00

Souvenir Sheet

Passenger Boats — A254

No. 829: a, Anahitra. b, Maria Galanta. c,
Saint-Eugène V. d, Atlantic Jet.

2006, Nov. 15   Litho.   Perf. 13
829   A254   54c Sheet of 4, #a-d   8.00   8.00

Christmas
A255

2006, Dec. 6
830   A255   54c multi   1.75   1.75

Sister Hilarion
(1913-2003)
A256

2007, Jan. 10   Engr.   Perf. 13
831   A256   54c multi   1.75   1.75

Horses — A257

2007, Feb. 21   Litho.   Perf. 13
832   A257   €1.01 multi   3.00   3.00

Plactopecten Magellanicus — A258

2007, Mar. 10   Engr.   Perf. 13¼
833   A258   €1 multi   3.50   3.50

Audit
Office,
Bicent.
A259

2007, Mar. 19
834   A259   54c multi   1.75   1.75

**France Nos. 3247-3251 Overprinted
Like No. 783**
2007, Mar. 28   Engr.   Perf. 13
835   A1713   10c gray   .25   .25
836   A1713   60c dark blue   1.60   1.60
837   A1713   70c yel green   1.90   1.90
838   A1713   85c purple   2.25   2.25
839   A1713   86c fawn   2.40   2.40
       Nos. 835-839 (5)   8.40   8.40

Yellow-beaked Warbler — A260

2007, Apr. 14   Litho.   Perf. 13
840   A260   44c multi   1.50   1.50

The Mi'kmaqs on Miquelon, by Jean-
Claude Roy — A261

2007, May 26
841   A261   80c multi   2.75   2.75

Fog and
House
A262

2007, June 9
842   A262   30c multi   1.00   1.00

**France Nos. 3252-3254 Overprinted
Like No. 783**
2007, June 20   Engr.   Perf. 13
843   A1713   €1.15 blue   3.75   3.75
844   A1713   €1.30 red violet   4.00   4.00
845   A1713   €2.11 chocolate   6.75   6.75
       Nos. 843-845 (3)   14.50 14.50

Entrance to the Port of St.
Pierre — A263

No. 846: a, Seagull and buoy. b, Ship and
lighthouses.

2007, June 30   Engr.   Perf. 13x12¼
846   Horiz. pair + central
       label   15.00 15.00
a.-b.   A263 €2.40 Either single 6.50   6.50

Delamaire Farm — A264

2007, Sept. 8   Engr.   Perf. 13x12½
847   A264   €1.06 black   3.00   3.00

Carnivorous
Plants — A265

No. 848: a, Sundew (Rossolis
intermédiaire). b, Bladderwort (Utriculaire
cornue). c, Butterwort (Grassette vulgaire). d,
Pitcher plant (Sarracénie pourpre).

Litho. & Engr.
2007, Sept. 29   Perf. 13x13¼
848   Horiz. strip of 4   7.00   7.00
a.-d.   A265 54c Any single   1.60   1.60

Deer Hunting — A266

2007, Oct. 20   Litho.   Perf. 13
849   A266   €1.65 multi   5.25   5.25

Miniature Sheet

Passenger Boats — A267

No. 850: a, Petit Miquelon. b, Marguerite II.
c, Ile-aux-Marins. d, Mousse.

2007, Nov. 10
850   A267   54c Sheet of 4, #a-d   7.00   7.00

Christmas — A268

2007, Dec. 1   Litho.   Perf. 13
851   A268   54c multi   1.75   1.75

René Autin (1921-
60), Soldier — A269

2008, Jan. 19   Engr.   Perf. 13
852   A269   54c blk & henna brn   1.75   1.75

Window — A270

2008, Feb. 23   Litho.   Perf. 13
853 A270 €1.01 multi   3.25 3.25

Cod Pens
A271

2008, Mar. 8   Engr.   Perf. 13¼
854 A271 €1 multi   3.25 3.25

Langlade Dune — A272

No. 855: a, Birds and butterfly. b, Bird.

2008, Mar. 29   Perf. 13x12¼
855 A272 Horiz. pair +
              central label   15.00 15.00
a.-b. €2.40 Either single   7.50 7.50

Black-throated Warbler — A273

2008, May 3   Litho.   Perf. 13
856 A273 47c multi   1.50 1.50

Local
Artisan
Crafts
A274

2008, May 17   Engr.
857 A274 33c black & olive   1.10 1.10

**France Nos. 3383-3388 Overprinted
Like No. 783**
2008, May 28   Engr.   Perf. 13
858 A1713 (65c) dark blue   2.10 2.10
859 A1713   72c yel green   2.25 2.25
860 A1713   88c fawn   2.75 2.75
861 A1713 €1.25 blue   4.00 4.00
862 A1713 €1.33 red violet   4.25 4.25
863 A1713 €2.18 chocolate   7.00 7.00
       Nos. 858-863 (6)   22.35 22.35

Return of the Fishermen, by Michelle
Foliot — A275

2008, June 7   Litho.   Perf. 13
864 A275 80c multi   2.50 2.50

Waves, Music and Guitar — A276

2008, July 12
865 A276 55c multi   1.75 1.75

Rowboat On Shore — A277

2008, Aug. 10   Litho.   Perf. 13
866 A277 55c multi   1.60 1.60

Taekwondo
A278

2008, Oct. 4   Litho. & Engr.   Perf. 13
867 A278 55c multi   1.50 1.50

Miniature Sheet

Ice Block Cutting — A279

No. 868: a, Workers pushing ice block up
ramp onto sled. b, Workers pulling up ice
blocks with tongs. c, Sleds awaiting ice blocks.
d, Ice cutters with saws.

2008, Oct. 22   Litho.
868 A279 €1 Sheet of 4, #a-d 10.50 10.50

France Nos. 3453-3465
Overprinted

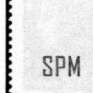

2008-09   Engr.   Perf. 13
869 A1912   1c yellow   .25   .25
870 A1912   5c gray brown   .25   .25
871 A1912   10c gray   .25   .25
872 A1912 (50c) green   1.25 1.25
873 A1912 (55c) red   1.40 1.40
874 A1912 (65c) dark blue   1.75 1.75
875 A1912   72c olive green 1.90 1.90
876 A1912   85c purple   2.25 2.25
877 A1912   88c fawn   2.25 2.25
878 A1912   €1   orange   2.75 2.75
879 A1912 €1.25 blue   3.50 3.50
880 A1912 €1.33 red violet   3.50 3.50
881 A1912 €2.18 chocolate   5.75 5.75
     Nos. 869-881 (13)   27.05 27.05

Issued: Nos. 869-873, 11/1; Nos. 874-877,
2/28/09; Nos. 878-881, 4/22/09.

Hare Hunting — A280

2008, Nov. 8   Litho.   Perf. 13
882 A280 €1.65 multi   4.25 4.25

Christmas
A281

2008, Nov. 26   Litho.   Perf. 13
883 A281 55c multi   1.40 1.40

Fox Sparrow — A282

2009, Jan. 14
884 A282 47c multi   1.25 1.25

Colors of Winter — A283

2009, Feb. 14
885 A283 €1 multi   2.60 2.60

Henri Morazé (1903-
86), Alcohol
Merchant — A284

2009, Mar. 14   Engr.
886 A284 56c blk & org brown   1.40 1.40

ATR 42 Airplane — A285

Litho. & Engr.
2009, Mar. 28   Perf. 13x13¼
887 A285 80c blue & black   2.25 2.25

Local
Artisan
Crafts
A286

2009, Apr. 8   Engr.   Perf. 13
888 A286 33c dp bl & bl grn   .90 .90

The Blue Bench, by Raphaele
Goineau — A287

2009, May 13   Litho.   Perf. 13
889 A287 56c multi   1.60 1.60

Place Monsigneur François
Maurer — A288

No. 890: a, Buildings. b, Buildings and park-
ing lot with two lampposts.

Perf. 13x12¼x13x13
2009, May 27   Engr.
890 A288 Horiz. pair +
              central label   14.00 14.00
a.-b. €2.50 Either single   7.00 7.00
No. 890b is upside-down in relation to No.
890a.

Tennis
A289

2009, June 10   Engr.   Perf. 12¼
891 A289 €1.05 multi   3.00 3.00

Pictorial
Stamps of
1909,
Cent.
A290

2009, June 27   Engr.   Perf. 13¼
892 A290 €1 multi   3.00 3.00

France No. 3471 Overprinted "SPM" Like No. 869

Serpentine Die Cut 6¾ Vert.

2009, Sept. 15   Engr.

Booklet Stamp
Self-Adhesive

893	A1912	(56c) red	1.75	1.75
a.		Booklet pane of 12	21.00	

Duck Hunting — A291

2009, Sept. 26   Litho.   *Perf. 13*

894 A291 €1.50 multi   4.50 4.50

Past and Present Radio Station Buildings A292

2009, Oct. 10   *Perf. 13x13¼*

895 A292 56c multi   1.75 1.75

Man at Window — A293

2009, Oct. 24   *Perf. 13*

896 A293 80c multi   2.40 2.40

Miniature Sheet

Winter Scenes of Port of St. Pierre — A294

No. 897: a, Men standing on ice in harbor, boats in background. b, Bull on ice near ship. c, Pointe-aux-Canons Lighthouse. d, Fishing boats in ice.

2009, Nov. 4   Litho.   *Perf. 13*

897 A294 56c Sheet of 4, #a-d   6.75 6.75

Christmas — A295

2009, Nov. 25

898 A295 56c multi   1.75 1.75

Richard Bartlett (1913-81), Member of French Resistance — A296

2010, Jan. 16   Engr.   *Perf. 13*

899 A296 56c blk & org brn   1.60 1.60

France Nos. 3612-3616 Overprinted "SPM" Like No. 869

2010   Engr.   *Perf. 13*

900	A1912	73c olive green	2.10	2.10
901	A1912	90c fawn	2.50	2.50
902	A1912	€1.30 blue	3.75	3.75
903	A1912	€1.35 red violet	3.75	3.75
904	A1912	€2.22 chocolate	6.00	6.00
		Nos. 900-904 (5)	18.10	18.10

Issued: Nos. 900-902, 1/27, Nos. 903-904, 2/24.

Black and White Warbler — A297

2010, Feb. 10   Litho.   *Perf. 13*

905 A297 47c multi   1.25 1.25

Crabber and Crab Pot — A298

2010, Mar. 13   Litho.   *Perf. 13*

906 A298 €1 multi   2.75 2.75

Miquelon Cape — A299

No. 907: a, Birds in flight. b, Cape, buoy.

2010, Apr. 10   Engr.   *Perf. 13x12¼*

907	A299	Horiz. pair + central label	13.50	13.50
a.-b.		€2.50 Either single	6.75	6.75

Helicopter Carrier Jeanne d'Arc — A300

Litho. & Engr.

2010, Apr. 24   *Perf. 13*

908 A300 €1 multi   2.75 2.75

Children's Art — A301

No. 909: a, Lighthouse, boat and bird, by Eric Coste. b, Ship, whale and houses, by Laura Caspar.

2010, Apr. 24   Litho.

909 A301 €1 Horiz. pair, #a-b   5.50 5.50

Reims F406 — A302

2010, May 15   Engr.   *Perf. 13x12½*

910 A302 80c multi   2.00 2.00

Telegraph Office and Morse Code A303

2010, June 19   Litho.   *Perf. 13x13¼*

911 A303 56c multi   1.40 1.40

Local Artisan Crafts A304

2010, June 26   Engr.

912 A304 33c multi   .85 .85

Swimming A305

2010, July 10   *Perf. 12¼*

913 A305 €1.05 multi   2.75 2.75

Hunt for 1927 Oiseau Blanc Transatlantic Flight — A306

Litho. & Engr.

2010, Sept. 1   *Perf. 13*

914 A306 €1.10 multi   3.00 3.00

Duck Hunting — A307

2010, Sept. 22   Litho.

915 A307 €1.65 multi   4.50 4.50

Children Sledding Past Side of Building — A308

2010, Oct. 20

916 A308 58c multi   1.75 1.75

Christmas A309

2010, Dec. 1   *Perf. 13x13¼*

917 A309 58c multi   1.60 1.60

Miniature Sheet

Festivals and Parades — A310

No. 918: a, Departing of the Fleet Festival. b, Assumption Day (August 15) Parade. c, Holy Child (Sainte-Enfance) Festival. d, Corpus Christi (Fête-Dieu) Parade.

2010, Nov. 6   Litho.   *Perf. 13*

918	A310	Sheet of 4	9.00	9.00
a.-b.		58c Either single	1.60	1.60
c.		€1 multi	2.75	2.75
d.		€1.05 multi	3.00	3.00

Cape May Warbler — A311

2011, Jan. 15

919 A311 47c multi   1.25 1.25

France Nos. 3871-3876 Overprinted "SPM" Like No. 869

2011   Engr.   *Perf. 13*

920	A1912	75c olive green	2.10	2.10
921	A1912	87c purple	2.50	2.50
922	A1912	95c fawn	2.60	2.60
923	A1912	€1.35 blue	3.75	3.75
924	A1912	€1.40 red violet	4.00	4.00
925	A1912	€2.30 chocolate	6.25	6.25
		Nos. 920-925 (6)	21.20	21.20

Issued: 75c, 95c, €2.30, 1/29. 87c, €1.35, €1.40, 2/26.

Larch
Cones — A312

2011, Feb. 12　　　　　　**Litho.**
926 A312 €1.05 multi　　　　3.00 3.00

Henriette Bonin
(1899-1985),
School
Teacher — A313

2011, Mar. 12　　　　　　**Engr.**
927 A313 58c blk & org brn　1.75 1.75

Notre Dame des
Marins Church,
Ile Aux
Marins — A314

2011, Apr. 9　**Litho.**　**Perf. 13¼x13**
928 A314 58c multi　　　　　1.75 1.75

St. Pierre
& Miquelon
Literary
Prize
A315

2011, Apr. 9　　　　**Perf. 13x13¼**
929 A315 58c multi　　　　　1.75 1.75

Miniature Sheet

A316

No. 930 — Old photographs of Ile aux
Chiens (Ile aux Marins): a, Fishing boats on
shore, houses close in background. b, Ile aux
Chiens Festival. c, Procession of fishermen
outside church. d, Fishermen preparing boats
at harbor, houses in distance.

2011, Apr. 20　　　　　　**Perf. 13**
930 A316 58c Sheet of 4, #a-d　6.75 6.75

Local
Artisan
Crafts
A317

2011, May 14　**Engr.**　**Perf. 13¼x13**
931 A317 33c multi　　　　　.95 .95

St. Pierre & Miquelon 2011 Philatelic
Exhibition — A318

2011, June 4　**Litho.**　**Perf. 13**
932 A318 85c multi　　　　　2.50 2.50

Man and Boy Throwing Rocks at
Cans — A319

2011, June 25
933 A319 58c multi　　　　　1.75 1.75

Sailing
A320

2011, July 10　**Engr.**　**Perf. 12¼**
934 A320 €1.05 multi　　　　3.00 3.00

L'Anse à Bertrand — A321

No. 935: a, White house with red trim. b,
Red house with white trim.

2011, Sept. 7　　　　　**Perf. 13x12¼**
935　A321　Horiz. pair +
　　　　　　　central label　14.00 14.00
a.-b.　€2.50 Either single　7.00 7.00

Miniature Sheet

Rescue Boats — A322

No. 936: a, P'tit Saint-Pierre. b, Jaro II. c,
Radar IV. d, Fulmar.

2011, Sept. 28　**Litho.**　**Perf. 13**
936 A322 60c Sheet of 4, #a-d　6.75 6.75

A323

A324

A325

A326

A327

Details From
"Sous le Vol
du Goéland, "
Painting by
Jean-Jacques
Oliviéro
A328

2011, Oct. 19　**Perf. 13x13½, 13½x13**
937　Sheet of 6　　　　10.50 10.50
a.　A323 60c multi　　　1.75 1.75
b.　A324 60c multi　　　1.75 1.75
c.　A325 60c multi　　　1.75 1.75
d.　A326 60c multi　　　1.75 1.75
e.　A327 60c multi　　　1.75 1.75
f.　A328 60c multi　　　1.75 1.75

Souvenir Sheet

Squadron Escort Forbin — A329

Litho. & Engr.
2011, Nov. 8　　　　　**Perf. 13½x13**
938 A329 €1.10 multi　　　3.00 3.00

See French Southern & Antarctic Territories
No. 449.

Christmas
A330

2011, Nov. 30　**Litho.**　**Perf. 13**
939 A330 60c multi　　　　　1.60 1.60

Birds and Birdhouse — A331

2012, Jan. 7　**Litho.**　**Perf. 13**
940 A331 47c multi　　　　　1.25 1.25

**France Nos. 4050-4056 Overprinted
"SPM" Like No. 869**
Methods and Perfs As Before

2012				
941	A2178	(55c)	gray	.95 .95
942	A2179	(60c)	red	1.60 1.60
943	A2180	(€1.07)	dark blue	3.00 3.00
944	A2181	(€1.07)	purple	3.00 3.00
945	A2182	(€1.25)	fawn	3.25 3.25
946	A2183	(€1.95)	red violet	5.25 5.25
947	A2184	(€3.65)	chocolate	9.75 9.75
	Nos. 941-947 (7)			26.80 26.80

Issued: Nos. 941, 942, 943, 946, 1/21;
others, 2/11.

Trawler Le Ravenel — A332

2012, Feb. 4　**Litho.**　**Perf. 13**
948 A332 60c multi　　　　　1.60 1.60

Church, Langlade — A333

2012, Mar. 10
949 A333 87c multi　　　　　2.25 2.25

Marine Life
A334

No. 950: a, Leptasterias polaris. b, Urticina
felina. c, Pagurus acadianus. d, Cynea
capilata.

2012, Mar. 24　　　　　　**Perf. 13x13¼**
950　Horiz. strip of 4　　6.50 6.50
a.-d.　A334 60c Any single　1.60 1.60

France Nos. 4079-4082 Overprinted
"SPM" Like No. 869
Methods and Perfs As Before

2012, Apr. 14

951	A2191	(33c)	green	.90	.90
952	A2192	(47c)	yellow green	1.25	1.25
953	A2193	(58c)	blue green	1.60	1.60
954	A2194	(85c)	dk bl green	2.25	2.25
	Nos. 951-954 (4)			6.00	6.00

A335

A336

A337

A338

A339

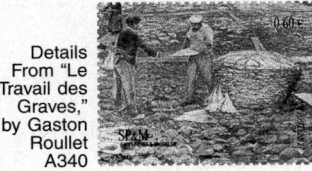

Details From "Le Travail des Graves," by Gaston Roullet — A340

Perf. 13¼x13, 13x13¼ (horiz. stamps)

2012, May 16   **Photo.**

955		Sheet of 6	9.00	9.00
a.	A335	60c multi	1.50	1.50
b.	A336	60c multi	1.50	1.50
c.	A337	60c multi	1.50	1.50
d.	A338	60c multi	1.50	1.50
e.	A339	60c multi	1.50	1.50
f.	A340	60c multi	1.50	1.50

Archipélitude Museum, 25th Anniv. — A341

Litho. & Engr.

2012, June 16   **Perf. 13x13¼**

956   A341   60c multi   1.50   1.50

André Paturel (1942-87), Designer of Local St. Pierre & Miquelon Flag — A342

2012, July 16   **Perf. 13**

957   A342   33c org brn & blk   .85   .85

2012 Summer Olympics, London A343

2012, July 28   **Perf. 12¼**

958   A343   €1.07 multi   2.75   2.75

Children's Art, Lighthouse, Swans and Puffins — A344

Litho. & Engr.

2012, Sept. 15   **Perf. 13x13¼**

959   A344   €1.15 multi   3.00   3.00

Child at Play — A345

2012, Sept. 29   **Litho.**   **Perf. 13**

960   A345   60c multi   1.60   1.60

Paintings of Boats — A346

No. 961: a, Le Béothuk, by Dirk Verdoorn. b, Esprit du Barachois, by François Bellec.

2012, Oct. 13

961   A346   60c Horiz. pair, #a-b   3.25   3.25

Chapeau de Miquelon — A347

No. 962: a, Seals on rocks. b, Chapeau de Miquelon and seal in water.

2012, Oct. 27   **Engr.**   **Perf. 13x12¼**

962	A347	Horiz. pair + central label	13.00	13.00
a.-b.		€2.50 Either single	6.50	6.50

Christmas — A348

2012, Dec. 1   **Litho.**   **Perf. 13**

963   A348   60c multi   1.60   1.60

Blue Jay — A349

2013, Jan. 12

964   A349   47c multi   1.25   1.25

Rock Formation — A350

2013, Jan. 26

965   A350   90c multi   2.50   2.50

Bulot, the Carnival King A351

2013, Feb. 16   **Engr.**   **Perf. 13¼**

966   A351   €1.13 multi   3.00   3.00

Maison Chartier A352

2013, Feb. 27   **Litho.**   **Perf. 13x13¼**

967   A352   63c multi   1.75   1.75

Miniature Sheet

Fishing — A353

No. 968: a, Workers processing cod on table. b, Fishermen in boats. c, Workers and stack of dried cod. d, Fishermen in water pulling in net.

2013, Mar. 13   **Perf. 13**

968   A353   63c Sheet of 4, #a-d   6.50   6.50

Trawler "Le Finlande" — A354

2013, Mar. 27   **Engr.**   **Perf. 13x13¼**

969   A354   €1.30 multi   3.50   3.50

Ship's Rigging A355

2013, Apr. 24   **Litho. & Engr.**

970   A355   €1.25 multi   3.25   3.25

Rugby A356

2013, May 15   **Engr.**   **Perf. 12x12¼**

971   A356   €1.13 multi   3.00   3.00

Miniature Sheet

Church of Miquelon Frescoes, by Yvette Detcheverry — A357

No. 972: a, Le sacrifice d'Abraham (The Sacrifice of Abraham). b, Le jugement de Salomon (The Judgment of Solomon). c, Présenation des tables de la loi (Moses Receiving the Law). d, Moise sur le mont Sinai (Moses on Mount Sinai). e, La nativité (Nativity). f, Le baptême du Christ (Baptism of Christ). g, La peche miraculeuse (The Miraculous Catch).

2013, June 1   Photo.   Perf. 13¼x13
972   A357   Sheet of 7   12.50 12.50
a.-g.   63c Any single   1.75   1.75
No. 972 has rows of rouletting between stamps.

Brother Sénier (1885-1978) A358

2013, June 15   Engr.   Perf. 13
973   A358   (33c) org brn & blk   .90   .90

Boys Playing Marbles — A359

2013, June 29   Litho.   Perf. 13
974   A359   63c multi   1.75   1.75

Miniature Sheet

Fire Trucks — A360

No. 975: a, 1961 Ford F600 (Le plateau). b, 2003 Freightliner FL80 4X4 (Le premier secours). c, 1992 Ford F350 4X4 (La garderobe). d, 1972 Ford F600 (Le camion dévidoir).

2013, July 13   Litho.   Perf. 13
975   A360   63c Sheet of 4, #a-d   6.75   6.75

Old and New Hospital Buildings A361

2013, Sept. 21   Litho.   Perf. 13x13¼
976   A361   63c multi   1.75   1.75

France Nos. 4411-4421 Overprinted

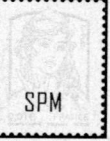

2013-14		Engr.	Perf. 13	
977	A2320	1c yellow	.25	.25
978	A2320	5c dk brown	.25	.25
979	A2320	10c brown	.30	.30
980	A2321	(56c) dk gray	1.50	1.50
981	A2322	(63c) red	1.75	1.75
982	A2320	€1 orange	2.75	2.75
983	A2323	(€1.13) blue	3.00	3.00

984	A2324	(€1.13) purple	3.00	3.00
985	A2322	(€1.30) fawn	3.50	3.50
986	A2322	(€2.15) red violet	6.00	6.00
987	A2322	(€3.90) chocolate	11.00	11.00
		Nos. 977-987 (11)	33.30	33.30

Issued: Nos. 977, 983-985, 10/26; Nos. 978-982, 10/5; Nos. 986-987, 3/15/14.

Doyen Lions Club, 60th Anniv. A362

Litho. & Engr.
2013, Oct. 19   Perf. 13x13¼
988   A362   (47c) multi   1.25   1.25

Anse à Ravenel — A363

No. 989: a, Horse-drawn carts on beach, houses. b, Shoreline and birds.

2013, Nov. 8   Engr.   Perf. 13x12¼
989   A363   Horiz. pair + central label   13.50 13.50
a.-b.   €2.50 Either single   6.75   6.75

Christmas — A364

2013, Dec. 7   Litho.   Perf. 13
990   A364   63c multi   1.75   1.75

Treaty of Utrecht, 300th Anniv. A365

2013, Dec. 18   Engr.   Perf. 12¾
991   A365   90c multi   2.50   2.50

Values are for stamps with surrounding selvage.

Bombycilla Garrulus — A366

2014, Jan. 16   Litho.   Perf. 13
992   A366   47c multi   1.25   1.25

Girl Blowing Bubbles — A367

2014, Feb. 1   Litho.   Perf. 13
993   A367   93c black   2.50   2.50

Trawler Shamrock III — A368

2014, Feb. 16   Engr.   Perf. 13
994   A368   €1.16 multi   3.25   3.25

Albert Briand (1909-66), Politician — A369

2014, Mar. 29   Engr.   Perf. 13
995   A369   33c org brn & blk   .90   .90

Ship's Rigging A370

Litho. & Engr.
2014, Feb. 26   Perf. 13x13¼
996   A370   €1.25 multi   3.50   3.50

Miniature Sheet

Working Dogs — A371

No. 997: a, Two dogs pulling sled carrying sticks. b, Two children with dog pulling four-wheeled wagon. c, One dog pulling sled carrying sticks. d, Dog pulling two-wheeled cart carrying tree.

2014, Apr. 19   Litho.   Perf. 13
997   A371   66c Sheet of 4, #a-d   7.50   7.50

Lebailly Forge — A372

2014, May 3   Engr.   Perf. 13¼
998   A372   66c multi   1.90   1.90

Les Voiles Blanches — A373

No. 999: a, 60c, House on Les Voiles Blanches (38x40mm). b, €1.40, Les Voiles Blanches, painting by Jean-Clause Girardin (62x40mm).

2014, May 24   Photo.   Perf. 13
999   A373   Horiz. pair, #a-b   5.50   5.50

Old and New Photographs of Court House — A374

2014, June 21   Litho.   Perf. 13x13¼
1000   A374   €1.35 multi   3.75   3.75

Miniature Sheet

Old Automobiles — A375

No. 1001: a, Three people in Ford Model T. b, Eugene Folquet standing next to automobile. c, Family of four in automobiles. d, Red Ford Model A.

2014, July 5   Litho.   Perf. 13
1001   A375   66c Sheet of 4, #a-d   7.25   7.25

Stamp Exhibitions — A376

No. 1002: a, 33c, Emblems of St. Pierre & Miquelon International Stamp Exhibition and Inter-American Federation of Philately (38x40mm). b, 66c, Emblems of Thailand 2013 World Stamp Exhibition and International Philatelic Federation, surcharged stamps of St. Pierre & Miquelon (62x40mm).

2014, Sept. 27   Photo.   Perf. 13
1002   A376   Horiz. pair, #a-b   2.50   2.50

Leatherback Turtle — A377

Litho. & Engr.
2014, Oct. 18   Perf. 13
1003   A377   69c multi   1.75   1.75

Savoyard Pond — A378

No. 1004: a, Runner, man flying kite. b, Fisherman, windsurfers on pond, rider on horse.

2014, Nov. 8   Engr.   Perf. 13x12¼
1004   Horiz. pair + central label   12.50 12.50
a.-b.   A378 €2.50 Either single   6.25   6.25

Departure of the Jeannette, Cent. — A379

Litho. & Engr.

2014, Nov. 15   **Perf. 13**
1005 A379 €1 multi   2.50 2.50

World War I, cent.

Christmas — A380

2014, Nov. 22   **Litho.**   **Perf. 13**
1006 A380 66c multi   1.75 1.75

Visit of French President François Hollande to St. Pierre & Miquelon — A381

2014, Dec. 27   **Litho.**   **Perf. 13**
1007 A381 76c multi   1.90 1.90

American Redstart — A382

2015, Jan. 17   **Engr.**   **Perf. 13**
1008 A382 38c multi   .90 .90

Painting of Blueberry Fields by Claude L'Espagnol — A383

2015, Feb. 6   **Engr.**   **Perf. 13**
1009 A383 76c multi   1.75 1.75

Francis Leroux (1908-82), Tourist Bureau President — A384

2015, Mar. 28   **Engr.**   **Perf. 13**
1010 A384 38c blk & org brn   .85 .85

Fishing Trawler Victor Pleven — A385

2015, Mar. 28   **Engr.**   **Perf. 13**
1011 A385 €1.05 dark blue & grn   2.40 2.40

Miniature Sheet

Animals at Work — A386

No. 1012: a, Map of St. Pierre & Miquelon, horse-drawn ice sled. b, Line of horse-drawn ice sleds. c, Horse-drawn ice sleds on ice with ice cutters. d, Ox-drawn cart.

2015, Apr. 18   **Litho.**   **Perf. 13**
1012 A386 76c Sheet of 4, #a-d   7.00 7.00

Renovation of Theater to Renaissance Fire Station — A387

2015, Apr. 28   **Litho.**   **Perf. 13x13¼**
1013 A387 €1.50 multi   3.50 3.50

Miniature Sheet

Automobiles of the 1950s — A388

No. 1014: a, 1958 Studebaker President. b, 1955 Mercury Custom. c, 1957 Citroen ID 19 Luxe. d, 1955 Renault 4 CV.

2015, June 6   **Litho.**   **Perf. 13**
1014 A388 76c Sheet of 4, #a-d   6.75 6.75

Souvenir Sheet

First Voyage of Reproduction of the Hermione — A389

No. 1015: a, €1.05, Marquis de Lafayette (1757-1834). b, €1.38, Lafayette's ship, Hermione, horiz.

Engr. (#1015a), Litho.

2015, July 22   **Perf. 13**
1015 A389   Sheet of 2, #a-b   5.50 5.50

The Laundrette of the Mountain A390

2015, Sept. 9   **Engr.**   **Perf. 13¼**
1016 A390 76c multi   1.75 1.75

Pointe aux Canons Lighthouse — A391

Litho. & Engr.

2015, Sept. 23   **Perf. 13**
1017 A391 76c multi   1.75 1.75

Lithobates Clamitans and Nuphar Variegata — A392

2015, Oct. 7   **Litho. & Engr.**   **Perf. 13**
1018 A392 76c multi   1.75 1.75

Miniature Sheet

Gendarmerie — A393

No. 1019 — Various emblems, map of St. Pierre & Miquelon and: a, 38c, Gendarme. b, 76c, Snowplow. c, €1.05, Boat. d, €1.38, Two officers.

Litho. & Embossed

2015, Nov. 5   **Perf. 13**
1019 A393   Sheet of 4, #a-d   7.75 7.75

Admiral Dominque Gauchet (1857-1931) — A394

2015, Nov. 11   **Engr.**   **Perf. 13x13¼**
1020 A394 €1 blk & dk bl   2.10 2.10

Christmas — A395

2015, Nov. 28   **Litho.**   **Perf. 13**
1021 A395 80c multi   1.75 1.75

Carpodacus Purpureus — A396

2016, Jan. 29   **Litho.**   **Perf. 13**
1022 A396 40c multi   .90 .90

Overturned Fishing Boat and Other Fishing Boat Equipment A397

2016, Feb. 19   **Litho.**   **Perf. 13x13¼**
1023 A397 80c multi   1.75 1.75

Fishing Trawler La Grande Hermine — A398

2016, Mar. 18   **Engr.**   **Perf. 13x13¼**
1024 A398 €1.10 multi   2.50 2.50

Map of St. Pierre & Miquelon — A399

2016, Mar. 21   **Litho.**   **Perf. 13**
Background Color
1025 A399 1c lt blue   .25 .25
1026 A399 2c yellow   .25 .25
1027 A399 3c lt green   .25 .25
1028 A399 5c gray   .25 .25
1029 A399 10c lilac   .25 .25
1030 A399 (40c) pink   .90 .90
    Nos. 1025-1030 (6)   2.15 2.15

No. 1030 is inscribed "20g." See No. 1041.

Notre Dame des Ardilliers Church, Miquelon A400

2016, Apr. 23   **Engr.**   **Perf. 13¼**
1031 A400 €1.40 multi   3.25 3.25

Renovated Prefecture Building, St. Pierre A401

2016, May 14   **Litho.**   **Perf. 13x13¼**
1032 A401 70c multi   1.60 1.60

Miniature Sheet

French National Gendarmerie in St. Pierre & Miquelon — A402

No. 1033 — Map of St. Pierre and Miquelon and gendarmes: a, 40c, Dusting for fingerprints. b, 80c, Standing near airplane. c, €1.10, With dog. d, €1.40, Wearing tactical armor.

Litho. & Embossed
2016, May 28   Perf. 13¼x13
1033 A402   Sheet of 4, #a-d   8.25 8.25

Dock, Rope and Pulley — A403

Litho. & Engr.
2016, June 11   Perf. 13¼x13
1034 A403 80c multi   1.90 1.90

Souvenir Sheet

Resettlement of St. Pierre and Miquelon Under French Rule, 200th Anniv. — A404

No. 1035: a, €1.10, Frigate La Revanche (28x37mm). b, €1.40, People watching ships, 1816 (56x37mm).

Litho. & Engr.
2016, June 22   Perf. 13x13¼
1035 A404   Sheet of 2, #a-b   5.75 5.75

Miniature Sheet

Ambulances — A405

No. 1036: a, Horse-drawn ambulance, 1934. b, Ambulance sleigh, 1948. c, Dodge WK60 ambulance, 1966. d, Chevrolet Model 3100 ambulance, 1949.

2016, July 8   Litho.   Perf. 13
1036 A405 80c Sheet of 4, #a-d   7.25 7.25

Sister Pierre Fontaine (1923-2012) — A406

2016, Sept. 9   Engr.   Perf. 13
1037 A406 (40c) blk & brn org   .90 .90

Ponte Plate Lighthouse — A407

2016, Oct. 7   Engr.   Perf. 13x13¼
1038 A407 80c multi   1.75 1.75

Battle of the Somme, Cent. — A408

2016, Nov. 11   Engr.   Perf. 13x12½
1039 A408 €1.10 multi   2.50 2.50

Christmas — A409

2016, Nov. 18   Litho.   Perf. 13
1040 A409 85c multi   1.90 1.90

Map Type of 2016
2017, Jan. 1   Litho.   Perf. 13
Background Color
1041 A399 (43c) dark blue   .90 .90
No. 1041 is inscribed "20g."

Geothlypis Trichas — A410

2017, Jan. 25   Litho.   Perf. 13
1042 A410 75c multi   1.60 1.60

A411

No. 1043: a, €1.17, House of Nature and the Environment (52x31mm). b, €1.49, Dandelion seed head and map of St. Pierre & Miquelon (31x31mm).

2017, Jan. 31   Photo.   Perf. 13
1043 A411   Horiz. pair, #a-b   5.75 5.75
International Year of Sustainable Tourism for Development (No. 1043b).

Fishing Trawler Le Dauphin — A412

2017, Mar. 15   Engr.   Perf. 13x12½
1044 A412 €1.20 multi   2.60 2.60

Miniature Sheet

Telephone Communications — A413

No. 1045: a, 43c, Dial telephone. b, 85c, Central switchboard and operators. c, €1.20, Radio Maritime operator. d, €1.40, Operator of modern phone system.

2017, Apr. 19   Litho.   Perf. 13
1045 A413   Sheet of 4, #a-d   8.50 8.50

Cod Filleting A414

2017, May 22   Litho.   Perf. 13x13¼
1046 A414 85c multi   1.90 1.90

Ropes and Bollards A415

Litho. & Engr.
2017, June 26   Perf. 13x13¼
1047 A415 85c multi   2.00 2.00

Miniature Sheet

Motorcycles — A416

No. 1048: a, 43c, George Blin, his daughter and Peugeot P55C motorcycle. b, 85c, Désiré Briand on Peugeot Model 125 Type 55 motorcycle. c, €1.20, Charles Guillaume on Peugeot 150cc motorcycle. d, €1.40, Son of François Detcheverry and Zündapp Combinette 50 moped.

2017, July 5   Litho.   Perf. 13
1048 A416   Sheet of 4, #a-d   9.25 9.25

Rowers at Ternua Basque Festival — A417

2017, Aug. 4   Engr.   Perf. 13
1049 A417 €1.40 multi   3.50 3.50

Father Jean-Marie-Roger Tillard (1927-2000), Theologian — A418

2017, Sept. 6   Engr.   Perf. 13
1050 A418 (43c) blk & chestnut   1.00 1.00

Cap Blanc Lighthouse A419

2017, Oct. 18   Engr.   Perf. 13
1051 A419 €1.20 multi   2.75 2.75

Souvenir Sheet

Yachting — A420

No. 1052: a, €1, André Paturel Sailing Center, 30th anniv. b, €2, Eric Tabarly (1931-98), naval officer and yachtsman, vert.

Litho. (€1), Litho. & Engr (€2)
2017, Nov. 9   Perf. 13
1052 A420   Sheet of 2, #a-b   7.25 7.25

Explosion of the Mont Blanc in Halifax Harbor, Cent. — A421

Litho. & Engr.
2017, Nov. 11   Perf. 13
1053 A421 €1.50 multi   3.75 3.75

Christmas
A422

2017, Nov. 15   Litho.   *Perf. 13¼x13*
1054   A422   85c multi   2.10   2.10

Souvenir Sheet

St. Pierre Cathedral, St.
Pierre — A423

2017, Dec. 1   Litho.   *Perf. 13¼x13*
1055   A423   €2 multi   4.75   4.75

Dendroica Palmarum — A424

2018, Jan. 17   Litho.   *Perf. 13*
1056   A424   80c multi   2.00   2.00

Yellow-bellied
Sapsucker
A425

2018, Feb. 14   Litho.   *Perf. 13*
1057   A425   95c multi   2.40   2.40

Fishing Vessel Le Névé — A426

2018, Mar. 14   Engr.   *Perf. 13x12½*
1058   A426   95c multi   2.40   2.40

Souvenir Sheet

French Patrol Ship "Fulmar," 20th
Anniv. — A427

2018, Apr. 6   Litho.   *Perf. 13*
1059   A427   €2 multi   4.75   4.75

Old St. Vincent Workhouse, 150th
Anniv. — A428

2018, Apr. 14   Engr.   *Perf. 13¼x13*
1060   A428   €1.40 blk & dp ultra   3.50   3.50

Cod Fishermen
A429

2018, May 19   Litho.   *Perf. 13¼x13*
1061   A429   46c multi   1.10   1.10

Ship Bel
Espoir
A430

Litho. & Engr.
2018, June 13   *Perf. 13x13¼*
1062   A430   €1.30 multi   3.00   3.00

Souvenir Sheet

Jules Verne (1828-1905),
Writer — A431

2018, July 7   Litho. & Engr.   *Perf. 13*
1063   A431   €2 multi   4.75   4.75

Miniature Sheet

Scooters — A432

No. 1064: a, 46c, Man looking at Cezeta
scooter. b, 95c, Man and woman on Lambretta
scooter. c, €1.30, Two men and Lambretta
scooter. d, €1.40, Man and woman on Lambretta scooter, diff.

2018, Aug. 7   Litho.   *Perf. 13*
1064   A432   Sheet of 4, #a-d   9.50   9.50

Pierre Hélène
(1907-93), and Diving
Helmet — A433

2018, Sept. 12   Engr.   *Perf. 13*
1065   A433   (95c) blk & lt brn   2.25   2.25

Île aux
Marins
Lighthouse
A434

Litho. & Engr.
2018, Oct. 13   *Perf. 13x13¼*
1066   A434   95c multi   2.25   2.25

Marasmius Oreades — A435

2018, Nov. 8   Engr.   *Perf. 13x13¼*
1067   A435   95c multi   2.25   2.25

Christmas — A436

2018, Nov. 8   Litho.   *Perf. 13¼x13*
1068   A436   95c multi   2.25   2.25

End of World War I, Cent. — A437

Litho. & Engr.
2018, Nov. 11   *Perf. 13x12¾*
1069   A437   €1.50 multi   3.50   3.50

Bay-breasted Warbler — A438

2019, Jan. 17   Litho.   *Perf. 13x12¾*
1070   A438   €1.05 multi   2.40   2.40

Wreck of a Schooner on
Langlade — A439

2019, Feb. 13   Litho.   *Perf. 13x12¾*
1071   A439   50c multi   1.25   1.25

**France No. 5478 Overprinted Like
No. 977**
2019, Feb. 20   Litho.   *Perf. 13*
1072   A2829   (€1.50) red   —   —

No. 1072 was originally put on sale in 2018
only at a stamp show in Paris.

Wrecked Ship "Le Victoria" — A440

2019, Mar. 18   Engr.   *Perf. 13¼*
1073   A440   €1.40 multi   3.25   3.25

Arche
Museum
A441

2019, Apr. 17   Engr.   *Perf. 13¼*
1074   A441   €1.40 multi   3.25   3.25

Docked
Dories
A442

2019, May 15   Litho.   *Perf. 13x13¼*
1075   A442   90c multi   2.10   2.10

Schooner
"Le Rara-
Avis"
A443

Litho. & Engr.
2019, June 12   *Perf. 13x13¼*
1076   A443   €1.05 multi   2.40   2.40

Souvenir Sheet

François-René de Chateaubriand
(1768-1848), Writer — A444

Litho. & Engr.

2019, July 10   *Perf. 13*
1077 A444 €2 multi   4.50 4.50

Georges Poulet
(1914-2008), Deputy
Mayor — A445

2019, Sept. 15   Engr.   *Perf. 13*
1078 A445 (€1.05) blk & lt brn   2.40 2.40

Miniature Sheet

Taxicabs — A446

No. 1079: a, Chevrolet Biscayne. b, Volkswagen Type 2. c, Pontiac Le Mans. d, Dodge Aries.

2019, Sept. 25   Litho.   *Perf. 13*
1079 A446 €1.05 Sheet of 4,
    #a-d   9.25 9.25

Souvenir Sheet

Gendarmerie Command Flag
Ceremony — A447

2019, Oct. 2   Litho.   *Perf. 13¼x13*
1080 A447 €3 multi   6.75 6.75

Galantry
Lighthouse
A448

Litho. & Engr.

2019, Oct. 13   *Perf. 13x13¼*
1081 A448 €1.40 multi   3.25 3.25

Boletus Chippewaensis — A449

Litho. & Engr.

2019, Nov. 7   *Perf. 13*
1082 A449 €1.50 multi   3.50 3.50

Shoemaker — A450

2019, Nov. 12   Engr.   *Perf. 13*
1083 A450 (€1.05) dk red brn   2.40 2.40

Souvenir Sheet

Cargo Vessel Hawaiki Nui — A451

Litho. & Engr.

2019, Nov. 12   *Perf. 13¼x13*
1084 A451 €4 multi   9.00 9.00

See French Polynesia No. 1240.

Christmas
A452

2019, Nov. 12   Litho.   *Perf. 13x13¼*
1085 A452 €1.05 multi   2.40 2.40

SEMI-POSTAL STAMPS

Regular
Issue of
1909-17
Surcharged
in Red

1915-17   Unwmk.   *Perf. 14x13½*
B1 A17   10c + 5c car rose
    & red   3.00 3.75
B2 A17   15c + 5c dl vio &
    rose ('17)   3.00 3.75

Curie Issue
Common Design Type

1938, Oct. 24   Engr.   *Perf. 13*
B3   CD80 1.75fr + 50c brt ul-
    tra   21.00 22.50

French Revolution Issue
Common Design Type

1939, July 5   Photo.
Name and Value Typo. in Black
B4   CD83   45c + 25c green   13.50 14.50
B5   CD83   70c + 30c brown   13.50 14.50
B6   CD83   90c + 35c red
    org   13.50 14.50
B7   CD83 1.25fr + 1fr rose
    pink   13.50 14.50
B8   CD83 2.25fr + 2fr blue   13.50 14.50
    Nos. B4-B8 (5)   67.50 72.50

Common Design Type and

Sailor of Landing
Force — SP1

Dispatch
Boat "Ville
d'Ys"
SP2

1941   Photo.   *Perf. 13½*
B8A   SP1   1fr + 1fr red   4.50
B8B   CD86 1.50fr + 3fr maroon   4.50
B8C   SP2   2.50fr + 1fr blue   4.50
    Nos. B8A-B8C (3)   13.50

Nos. B8A-B8C were issued by the Vichy government, and were not placed on sale in the colony.

Nos. 239,
246 Srchd.
in Carmine

1942   Unwmk.   *Perf. 13½x13*
B9   A25   1fr + 50c   75.00 75.00
B10   A26   2.50fr + 1fr   75.00 75.00

Petain Type
of 1941
Srchd. in
Black or
Red

1944   Engr.   *Perf. 12½x12*
B11   50c + 1.50fr on 2.50fr dp bl
    (R)   1.60
B12   + 2.50fr on 1fr vio   1.60

Colonial Development Fund.
Nos. B11-B12 were issued by the Vichy government in France, but were not placed on sale in St. Pierre & Miquelon.

Catalogue values for unused stamps in this section, from this point to the end of the section, are for Never Hinged items.

Red Cross Issue
Common Design Type

1944   *Perf. 14½x14*
B13   CD90 5fr + 20fr dp ultra   2.60 2.60

Surtax for the French Red Cross and national relief.

Tropical Medicine Issue
Common Design Type

1950, May 15   Engr.   *Perf. 13*
B14   CD100 10fr + 2fr red brn
    & red   16.00 15.00
The surtax was for charitable work.

Art School
Telethon — SP3

2007, Nov. 24   Litho.   *Perf. 13¼x13*
B15   SP3 54c +16c multi   2.50 2.50

AIR POST STAMPS

Catalogue values for unused stamps in this section are for Never Hinged items.

Common Design Type
Perf. 14½x14

1942, Aug. 17   Photo.   Unwmk.
C1   CD87   1fr dark orange   .80 .65
C2   CD87   1.50fr bright red   .85 .70
C3   CD87   5fr brown red   1.10 .95
C4   CD87   10fr black   1.60 1.40
C5   CD87   25fr ultra   1.75 1.25
C6   CD87   50fr dark green   2.50 2.10
C7   CD87   100fr plum   3.00 2.50
    Nos. C1-C7 (7)   11.60 9.40

Victory Issue
Common Design Type

1946, May 8   Engr.   *Perf. 12½*
C8   CD92 8fr deep claret   2.10 2.10

Chad to Rhine Issue
Common Design Types

1946, June 6
C9   CD93   5fr brown red   1.90 1.40
C10   CD94   10fr lilac rose   1.90 1.40
C11   CD95   15fr gray blk   2.75 2.40
C12   CD96   20fr violet   3.00 2.40
C13   CD97   25fr chocolate   3.75 3.25
C14   CD98   50fr grnsh blk   4.00 3.50
    Nos. C9-C14 (6)   17.30 14.35

Plane, Sailing Vessel and
Coast — AP2

AP3

AP4

1947, Oct. 6
C15   AP2   50fr yel grn & rose   10.00 4.50
C16   AP3   100fr dk blue grn   14.50 7.00
C17   AP4   200fr bluish blk & brt
    rose   16.00 8.75
    Nos. C15-C17 (3)   40.50 20.25

UPU Issue
Common Design Type

1949, Oct. 1   Engr.   *Perf. 13*
C18   CD99 25fr multicolored   20.00 12.00

Liberation Issue
Common Design Type

1954, June 8
C19 CD102 15fr sepia & red   19.00 12.00
10th anniversary of the liberation of France.

Plane over St. Pierre Harbor — AP6

1956, Oct. 22
C20 AP6 500fr ultra & indigo   55.00 22.50

Dog and Village — AP7

Design: 100fr, Caravelle over archipelago.

1957, Nov. 4   Unwmk.   Perf. 13
C21 AP7 50fr gray, brn blk &
            bl   52.50 22.50
C22 AP7 100fr black & gray   21.00 11.00

Anchors and Torches — AP8

1959, Sept. 14   Engr.   Perf. 13
C23 AP8 200fr dk pur, grn & cl   18.00 8.00
Approval of the constitution and the vote which confirmed the attachment of the islands to France.

Pitcher Plant — AP9

1962, Apr. 24   Unwmk.   Perf. 13
C24 AP9 100fr green, org & car   13.00 5.00

Gulf of St. Lawrence and Submarine "Surcouf" — AP10

Perf. 13½x12½
1962, July 24   Photo.
C25 AP10 500fr dk red & bl   130.00 100.00
20th anniv. of St. Pierre & Miquelon's joining the Free French.

Telstar Issue
Common Design Type

1962, Nov. 22   Engr.   Perf. 13
C26 CD111 50fr Prus grn & bis   7.25 4.50

Arrival of Governor Dangeac, 1763 — AP11

1963, Aug. 5   Unwmk.   Perf. 13
C27 AP11 200fr dk bl, sl grn &
            brn   26.00 12.00
Bicentenary of the arrival of the first French governor.

Jet Plane and Map of Maritime Provinces and New England — AP12

1964, Sept. 28   Engr.   Perf. 13
C28 AP12 100fr choc & Prus bl   14.00 8.00
Inauguration of direct airmail service between St. Pierre and New York City.

ITU Issue
Common Design Type

1965, May 17
C29 CD120 40fr org brn, dk bl
            & lil rose   24.00 11.50

French Satellite A-1 Issue
Common Design Type

Designs: 25fr, Diamant rocket and launching installations. 30fr, A-1 satellite.

1966, Jan. 24   Engr.   Perf. 13
C30 CD121 25fr dk brn, dk bl
            & rose cl   6.00 4.00
C31 CD121 30fr dk bl, rose cl
            & dk brn   7.50 6.00
a.   Strip of 2, #C30-C31 + label   14.50 14.50

French Satellite D-1 Issue
Common Design Type

1966, May 23   Engr.   Perf. 13
C32 CD122 48fr brt grn, ultra &
            rose claret   9.00 6.00

Arrival of Settlers — AP13

1966, June 22   Photo.   Perf. 13
C33 AP13 100fr multicolored   15.00 6.50
150th anniv. of the return of the islands of St. Pierre and Miquelon to France.

Front Page of Official Journal and Printing Presses — AP14

1966, Oct. 20   Engr.   Perf. 13
C34 AP14 60fr dk bl, lake & dk
            pur   13.50 6.75
Centenary of the Government Printers and the Official Journal.

Map of Islands, Old and New Fishing Vessels — AP15

Design: 100fr, Cruiser Colbert, maps of Brest, St. Pierre and Miquelon.

1967, July 20   Engr.   Perf. 13
C35 AP15 25fr dk bl, gray &
            crim   26.00 15.00
C36 AP15 100fr multicolored   42.50 27.50
Visit of President Charles de Gaulle.

Speed Skater and Olympic Emblem — AP16

60fr, Ice hockey goalkeeper.

1968, Apr. 22   Photo.   Perf. 13
C37 AP16 50fr ultra & multi   9.25 4.00
C38 AP16 60fr green & multi   11.00 5.75
10th Winter Olympic Games, Grenoble, France, Feb. 6-18.

War Memorial, St. Pierre — AP17

1968, Nov. 11   Photo.   Perf. 12½
C39 AP17 500fr multicolored   25.00 17.00
World War I armistice, 50th anniv.

Concorde Issue
Common Design Type

1969, Apr. 17   Engr.   Perf. 13
C40 CD129 34fr dk brn & olive   32.50 11.00

Scenic Type of Regular Issue, 1969

Designs: 50fr, Grazing horses, Miquelon. 100fr, Gathering driftwood on Mirande Beach, Miquelon.

1969, Apr. 30   Engr.   Perf. 13
Size: 47½x27mm
C41 A47 50fr ultra, brn & ol   15.00 7.00
C42 A47 100fr dk brn, bl & sl   25.00 14.00

L'Esperance Leaving Saint-Malo, 1600 — AP18

1969, June 16   Engr.   Perf. 13
C43 AP18 200fr blk, grn & dk
            red   52.50 22.50

Pierre Loti and Sailboats — AP19

1969, June 23
C44 AP19 300fr lemon, choc &
            Prus bl   60.00 27.50
Loti (1850-1923), French novelist and naval officer.

EXPO Emblem and "Mountains" by Yokoyama Taikan — AP20

34fr, Geisha, rocket and EXPO emblem, vert.

1970, Sept. 8   Engr.   Perf. 13
C45 AP20 34fr dp cl, ol & ind   24.00 8.75
C46 AP20 85fr org, ind & car   40.00 18.50
EXPO '70 Intl. Exposition, Osaka, Japan, Mar. 15-Sept. 13.

Etienne François Duke of Choiseul and his Ships — AP21

Designs: 50fr, Jacques Cartier, ship and landing party. 60fr, Sebastien Le Gonrad de Sourdeval, ships and map of islands.

1970, Nov. 25   Portrait in Lake
C47 AP21 25fr lilac & Prus bl   26.00 10.00
C48 AP21 50fr sl grn & red lil   32.00 12.00
C49 AP21 60fr red lil & sl grn   40.00 18.00
    Nos. C47-C49 (3)   98.00 40.00

De Gaulle, Cross of Lorraine, Sailor, Soldier, Coast Guard — AP22

1972, June 18   Engr.   Perf. 13
C50 AP22 100fr lil, brn & grn   30.00 16.00
Charles de Gaulle (1890-1970), French pres.

Louis Joseph de Montcalm — AP23

Designs: 2fr, Louis de Buade Frontenac, vert. 4fr, Robert de La Salle.

1973, Jan. 1
C51 AP23 1.60fr multicolored   9.50 4.00
C52 AP23 2fr multicolored   12.00 6.50
C53 AP23 4fr multicolored   21.00 11.00
    Nos. C51-C53 (3)   42.50 21.50

Transall C 160 over St. Pierre — AP24

1973, Oct. 16   Engr.   *Perf. 13*
C54 AP24 10fr multicolored   50.00 25.00

Arms and Map of Islands, Fish and Bird — AP25

1974, Nov. 5   Photo.   *Perf. 13*
C55 AP25 2fr gold & multi   16.00 6.50

Copernicus, Kepler, Newton and Einstein — AP26

1974, Nov. 26   Engr.
C56 AP26 4fr multicolored   18.50 9.00
Nicolaus Copernicus (1473-1543), Polish astronomer.

Type of 1909, Cod and ARPHILA Emblem AP27

1975, Aug. 5   Engr.   *Perf. 13*
C57 AP27 4fr ultra, red & indigo 21.00 9.50
ARPHILA 75, International Philatelic Exhibition, Paris, June 6-16.

Judo, Maple Leaf, Olympic Rings AP28

1975, Nov. 18   Engr.   *Perf. 13*
C58 AP28 1.90fr red, blue & vio   10.00 5.50
Pre-Olympic Year.

Concorde — AP29

1976, Jan. 21   Engr.   *Perf. 13*
C59 AP29 10fr red, blk & slate   32.50 16.00
1st commercial flight of supersonic jet Concorde from Paris to Rio, Jan. 21.

A. G. Bell, Telephone and Satellite AP30

1976, June 22   Litho.   *Perf. 12½*
C60 AP30 5fr vio bl, org & red   10.00 5.50
Centenary of first telephone call by Alexander Graham Bell, Mar. 10, 1876.

Aircraft — AP31

5fr, Hawker-Siddeley H. S. 748, 1987. 10fr, Latecoere 522, 1939.

1987, June 30   Engr.   *Perf. 13*
C61 AP31 5fr multicolored   2.75 1.40
C62 AP31 10fr multicolored   5.25 2.75

Hindenburg — AP32

10fr, Douglas DC3, 1948-1988. 20fr, Piper Aztec.

1988-89   Engr.   *Perf. 13*
C63 AP32 5fr multicolored   2.50 1.25
C64 AP32 10fr multicolored   5.00 2.75
C65 AP32 20fr multicolored   7.50 4.00
   Nos. C63-C65 (3)   15.00 8.00
Issued: 20fr, May 31, 1989; others, June 22.

Flying Flea, Bird — AP33

1990, May 16   Engr.
C66 AP33 5fr multicolored   2.10 1.25

Piper Tomahawk — AP34

1991, May 29   Engr.   *Perf. 13*
C67 AP34 10fr multicolored   4.00 2.50

Radio-controlled Model Airplanes — AP35

1992, May 6
C68 AP35 20fr brown, red & org   8.00 4.25

Migratory Birds — AP36

1993-97   *Perf. 13x12½*
C69 AP36 5fr Shearwater
           (Puffin)   2.00 1.40
C70 AP36 10fr Golden plover   4.00 2.25
       Perf. 13x13½
C71 AP36 10fr Arctic Tern   4.25 2.25
       Perf. 13
C72 AP36 15fr Courlis   6.25 3.50
C73 AP36 5fr Peregrine fal-
           con, vert.   2.50 1.40
   Nos. C69-C73 (5)   19.00 10.90
Issued: #C69-C70, 5/12; #C71, 5/10/95; #C72, 5/15/96; #C73, 5/28/97.

Disappearance of the Flight of Nungesser and Coli, 70th Anniv. — AP37

1997, June 11
C74 AP37 14fr blk, grn bl & brn 6.00 3.50

Bald Eagle — AP38

1998-2001   Engr.   *Perf. 13*
C74A AP38 5fr Buzzard   2.25 1.25
C75 AP38 10fr shown   4.75 3.00
C75A AP38 15fr Heron   5.25 3.00
C76 AP38 20fr Wild duck   7.25 5.00
   Issued: 5fr, 12/13/00; 10fr, 5/6; 15fr, 5/23/01; 20fr, 5/5/99.

Puffin — AP39

2002, Apr. 22
C77 AP39 €2.50 multi   8.75 4.50

Solan Goose — AP40

2003, June 18   Engr.   *Perf. 13x12½*
C78 AP40 €2.50 multi   8.75 5.75

Bustard — AP41

2004, July 7   Engr.   *Perf. 13x13¼*
C79 AP41 €2.50 multi   8.75 6.25

Piping Plover — AP42

2005, June 22   *Perf. 13x12½*
C80 AP42 €2.50 multi   8.75 6.00

Atlantic Sea Gull — AP43

2006, June 14   Engr.   *Perf. 13x12½*
C81 AP43 €2.53 multi   8.75 7.75

Eider — AP44

2007, May 5   Engr.   *Perf. 13x12½*
C82 AP44 €1.50 multi   4.00 4.00

Harlequin Ducks — AP45

2008, June 28   Engr.   Perf. 13x12¾
C83 AP45 €1.50 multi   4.75 4.75

AIR POST SEMI-POSTAL STAMPS

Bringing Children to Hospital — SPAP1

Perf. 13½x12½
1942, June 22   Unwmk.   Photo.
CB1 SPAP1 1.50fr + 3.50fr green   6.50
CB2 SPAP1 2fr + 6fr brown   6.50

Native children's welfare fund.
Nos. CB1-CB2 were issued by the Vichy government in France, but were not placed on sale in St. Pierre & Miquelon.

Colonial Education Fund
Common Design Type

1942, June 22
CB3 CD86a 1.20fr + 1.80fr blue
                 & red   7.00

No. CB3 was issued by the Vichy government in France, but was not placed on sale in St. Pierre & Miquelon.

POSTAGE DUE STAMPS

Postage Due Stamps of French Colonies Overprinted in Red

1892   Unwmk.   Imperf.
J1 D1 5c black   85.00   85.00
J2 D1 10c black   26.00   26.00
J3 D1 15c black   26.00   26.00
J4 D1 20c black   26.00   26.00
J5 D1 30c black   26.00   26.00
J6 D1 40c black   26.00   26.00
J7 D1 60c black   82.50   90.00

Black Overprint
J8 D1 1fr brown   200.00 200.00
J9 D1 2fr brown   200.00 200.00
    Nos. J1-J9 (9)   697.50 705.00

These stamps exist with and without hyphen. See note after No. 59.

Postage Due Stamps of France, 1893-1924, Overprinted

1925-27   Perf. 14x13½
J10 D2 5c blue   .75   1.10
J11 D2 10c dark brown   .75   1.10
J12 D2 20c olive green   .80   1.10
J13 D2 25c rose   1.10   1.50
J14 D2 30c red   1.90   2.25
J15 D2 45c blue green   2.25   2.25
J16 D2 50c brown vio   2.60   3.75
J17 D2 1fr red brn, straw 3.50 4.00
J18 D2 3fr magenta ('27) 12.00 15.00

Surcharged

J19 D2 60c on 50c buff   2.75   3.75
J20 D2 2fr on 1fr red   4.50   5.50
    Nos. J10-J20 (11)   32.55 41.30

Newfoundland Dog — D3

1932, Dec. 5   Typo.
J21 D3 5c dk blue & blk   1.50   1.90
J22 D3 10c green & blk   1.50   1.90
J23 D3 20c red & blk   1.75   2.25
J24 D3 25c red vio & blk   1.75   2.25
J25 D3 30c orange & blk   3.50   4.50
J26 D3 45c lt blue & blk   5.50   6.75
J27 D3 50c blue grn & blk 8.50 10.50
J28 D3 60c brt rose & blk 15.00 15.00
J29 D3 1fr yellow brn & blk 25.00 30.00
J30 D3 2fr dp violet & blk 35.00 37.50
J31 D3 3fr dk brown & blk 47.50 55.00
    Nos. J21-J31 (11)   146.50 167.55

For overprints and surcharge see Nos. J42-J46.

Codfish — D4

1938, Nov. 17   Photo.   Perf. 13
J32 D4 5c gray black   .40   .50
J33 D4 10c dk red violet   .40   .50
J34 D4 15c slate green   .50   .75
J35 D4 20c deep blue   .55   .75
J36 D4 30c rose carmine   .55   .75
J37 D4 50c dk blue green   .70   .80
J38 D4 60c dk blue   .95   1.10
J39 D4 1fr henna brown   1.90   2.25
J40 D4 2fr gray brown   4.50   5.25
J41 D4 3fr dull violet   4.75   6.00
    Nos. J32-J41 (10)   15.20 18.65

For overprints see Nos. J48-J67.

Postage Due Stamps of 1932 Overprinted in Black

1942   Unwmk.   Perf. 14x13½
J42 D3 25c red vio & blk 425.00 425.00
J43 D3 30c orange & blk   425.00 425.00
J44 D3 50c blue grn & blk 1,400. 1,400.
J45 D3 2fr dp vio & bl
              blk   60.00   60.00

Same Surcharged in Black

No. J46

No. J46a

J46 D3 3fr on 2fr dp vio &
            blk, "F.N.F.L."
            omitted   24.00   24.00
  a. With "F.N.F.L."   40.00   40.00
    Nos. J42-J46 (5)   2,334. 2,334.

Postage Due Stamps of 1938 Overprinted in Black

1942   Perf. 13
J48 D4 5c gray black   24.00   27.50
J49 D4 10c dk red violet 24.00   27.50
J50 D4 15c slate green   24.00   27.50
J51 D4 20c deep blue   24.00   27.50
J52 D4 30c rose carmine   24.00   27.50
J53 D4 50c dk blue green 47.50   52.50
J54 D4 60c dark blue   100.00 110.00
J55 D4 1fr henna brown   110.00 125.00
J56 D4 2fr gray brown   125.00 140.00
J57 D4 3fr dull violet   140.00 160.00
    Nos. J48-J57 (10)   642.50 725.00

Christmas Day plebiscite ordered by Vice Admiral Emile Henri Muselier, commander of the Free French naval forces.

Postage Due Stamps of 1938 Overprinted in Black

1942
J58 D4 5c gray black   52.50   60.00
J59 D4 10c dk red violet 11.00   12.00
J60 D4 15c slate green   11.00   12.00
J61 D4 20c deep blue   11.00   12.00
J62 D4 30c rose carmine   11.00   12.00
J63 D4 50c dk blue green 11.00   12.00
J64 D4 60c dark blue   11.00   12.00
J65 D4 1fr henna brown   27.50   32.50
J66 D4 2fr gray brown   32.50   35.00
J67 D4 3fr dull violet   575.00 625.00
    Nos. J58-J67 (10)   753.50 824.50

Catalogue values for unused stamps in this section, from this point to the end of the section, are for Never Hinged items.

Arms and Fishing Schooner — D5

1947, Oct. 6   Engr.   Perf. 13
J68 D5 10c deep orange   .30   .30
J69 D5 30c deep ultra   .30   .30
J70 D5 50c dk blue green   .50   .50
J71 D5 1fr deep carmine   .65   .65
J72 D5 2fr dk green   .90   .90
J73 D5 3fr violet   2.00   2.00
J74 D5 4fr chocolate   2.00   2.00
J75 D5 5fr yellow green   2.25   2.25
J76 D5 10fr black brown   3.00   3.00
J77 D5 20fr orange red   3.25   3.25
    Nos. J68-J77 (10)   15.15 15.15

Newfoundland Dog — D6

1973, Jan. 1   Engr.   Perf. 13
J78 D6 2c brown & blk   1.00   1.00
J79 D6 10c purple & blk   1.40   1.40
J80 D6 20c grnsh bl & blk 2.25   2.25
J81 D6 30c dk car & blk   4.50   4.50
J82 D6 1fr blue & blk   11.00 11.00
    Nos. J78-J82 (5)   20.15 20.15

France Nos. J106-J115 Overprinted "ST - PIERRE ET MIQUELON" Reading Up in Red

1986, Sept. 15   Engr.   Perf. 13
J83 D8 10c multicolored   .25   .25
J84 D8 20c multicolored   .25   .25
J85 D8 30c multicolored   .25   .25
J86 D8 40c multicolored   .25   .25
J87 D8 50c multicolored   .40   .40
J88 D8 1fr multicolored   .50   .50
J89 D8 2fr multicolored   .95   .95
J90 D8 3fr multicolored   1.40   1.40
J91 D8 4fr multicolored   1.75   1.75
J92 D8 5fr multicolored   2.50   2.50
    Nos. J83-J92 (10)   8.50   8.50

PARCEL POST STAMPS

No. 65 Overprinted

1901   Unwmk.   Perf. 14x13½
Q1 A16 10c blk, lav   140.00 140.00
  a. Inverted overprint   1,250. 1,250.

No. 66 Overprinted

Q2 A16 10c red   35.00   35.00

Nos. 84 and 87 Overprinted

1917-25
Q3 A17 10c car rose & red 4.50   6.00
  a. Double overprint   300.00
Q4 A17 20c bis brn & vio
              brn ('25)   3.75   5.25
  a. Double overprint   190.00

No. Q4 with Additional Overprint in Black

1942
Q5 A17 20c bis brn & vio
              brn   1,100. 1,200.

ST. THOMAS & PRINCE ISLANDS

sănt-'tăm-əs and 'prin̩ts 'ī-lənd

Democratic Republic of Sao Tome and Principe

LOCATION — Two islands in the Gulf of Guinea, 125 miles off the west coast of Africa
GOVT. — Republic
AREA — 387 sq. mi.
POP. — 154,878 (1999 est.)
CAPITAL — Sao Tome

This colony of Portugal became a province, later an overseas territory, and achieved independence on July 12, 1975.

1000 Reis = 1 Milreis
100 Centavos = 1 Escudo (1913)
100 Cents = 1 Dobra (1977)

> Catalogue values for unused stamps in this country are for Never Hinged items, beginning with Scott 353 in the regular postage section, Scott J52 in the postage due section, and Scott RA4 in the postal tax section.

Portuguese Crown — A1

5, 25, 50 REIS:
Type I — "5" is upright.
Type II — "5" is slanting.

10 REIS:
Type I — "1" has short serif at top.
Type II — "1" has long serif at top.

40 REIS:
Type I — "4" is broad.
Type II — "4" is narrow.

Perf. 12½, 13½

1869-75		Unwmk.		Typo.
1	A1	5r black, I	4.25	2.40
a.		Type II	4.25	2.40
2	A1	10r yellow, I	26.00	13.50
a.		Type II	26.00	13.50
3	A1	20r bister	5.50	3.50
4	A1	25r rose, I	3.00	1.75
a.		25r red	3.50	1.75
5	A1	40r blue ('75), I	9.00	6.00
a.		Type II	9.00	6.00
6	A1	50r gray grn, II	26.00	18.00
a.		Type I	26.00	18.00
7	A1	100r gray lilac	14.00	7.25
8	A1	200r red orange ('75)	17.00	12.00
9	A1	300r chocolate ('75)	15.00	9.00
		Nos. 1-9 (9)	119.75	73.40

1881-85				
10	A1	10r gray grn, I	12.00	7.75
a.		Perf. 13½, I	12.00	6.75
b.		Perf. 13½, I	15.00	9.00
11	A1	20r car rose ('85)	6.00	4.00
12	A1	25r vio ('85), II	5.00	3.00
13	A1	40r yel buff, II	9.75	6.75
a.		Perf. 13½	11.50	7.25
14	A1	50r dk blue, I	4.00	3.00
a.		Type II	4.00	3.00
		Nos. 10-14 (5)	36.75	24.50

For surcharges and overprints see Nos. 63-64, 129-129B, 154.
Nos. 1-14 have been reprinted on stout white paper, ungummed, with rough perforation 13½, also on ordinary paper with shiny white gum and clean-cut perforation 13½ with large holes.

King Luiz — A2

Typo., Head Embossed

1887			**Perf. 12½, 13½**	
15	A2	5r black	12.00	3.50
16	A2	10r green	12.00	3.75
17	A2	20r brt rose	13.50	4.00
a.		Perf. 12½	135.00	110.00
18	A2	25r violet	8.25	3.00
19	A2	40r brown	8.25	4.00
20	A2	50r blue	10.25	3.75
21	A2	100r yellow brn	7.25	3.75
22	A2	200r gray lilac	26.00	13.50
23	A2	300r orange	29.00	13.50
		Nos. 15-23 (9)	126.50	52.75

For surcharges and overprints see Nos. 24-26, 62, 65-72, 130-131, 155-158, 234-237.
Nos. 15, 16, 19, 21, 22, and 23 have been reprinted in paler colors than the originals, with white gum and cleancut perforation 13½. Value $1.50 each.

Nos. 16-17, 19 Surcharged

a   b

c

1889-91			**Without Gum**	
24	A2(a)	5r on 10r	60.00	45.00
25	A2(b)	5r on 20r	60.00	45.00
26	A2(c)	50r on 40r ('91)	330.00	150.00
		Nos. 24-26 (3)	450.00	240.00

Varieties of Nos. 24-26, including inverted and double surcharges, "5" inverted, "Cinoc" and "Cinco," were deliberately made and unofficially issued.

King Carlos — A6

1895		Typo.	**Perf. 11½, 12½**	
27	A6	5r yellow	1.60	1.50
28	A6	10r red lilac	2.25	1.25
29	A6	15r red brown	3.50	1.75
30	A6	20r lavender	3.50	2.00
31	A6	25r green	3.25	1.25
32	A6	50r light blue	3.25	1.25
a.		Perf. 13½	3.25	1.40
33	A6	75r rose	9.50	5.50
34	A6	80r yellow grn	19.00	14.00
35	A6	100r brn, yel	8.25	5.50
36	A6	150r car, rose	11.00	7.25
37	A6	200r dk bl, bl	14.50	11.00
38	A6	300r dk bl, sal	16.50	13.50
		Nos. 27-38 (12)	96.10	65.75

For surcharges and overprints see Nos. 73-84, 132-137, 159-165, 238-243, 262-264, 268-274.

King Carlos — A7

1898-1903			**Perf. 11½**	

Name and Value in Black except 500r

39	A7	2½r gray	.60	.25
40	A7	5r orange	.60	.25
41	A7	10r lt green	.60	.40
42	A7	15r brown	2.10	1.40
43	A7	15r gray grn ('03)	1.10	1.10
44	A7	20r gray violet	1.25	.50
45	A7	25r sea green	.75	.40
46	A7	25r carmine ('03)	1.10	.30
47	A7	50r blue	1.10	.50
48	A7	50r brown ('03)	4.50	4.50
49	A7	65r dull blue ('03)	22.50	9.00
50	A7	75r rose	18.00	9.75
51	A7	75r red lilac ('03)	2.50	1.40
52	A7	80r brt violet	9.50	9.00
53	A7	100r dk blue, bl	3.50	2.40

54	A7	115r org brn, pink ('03)	10.00	8.00
55	A7	130r brn, straw ('03)	10.00	6.00
56	A7	150r brn, buff	4.25	2.50
57	A7	200r red lil, pnksh	6.75	4.25
58	A7	300r dk blue, rose	10.00	5.25
59	A7	400r dull bl, straw ('03)	15.00	8.50
60	A7	500r blk & red, bl ('01)	13.00	7.25
61	A7	700r vio, yelsh ('01)	21.00	15.00
		Nos. 39-61 (23)	159.70	97.90

For overprints and surcharges see Nos. 86-105, 116-128, 138-153, 167-169, 244-249, 255-261, 265-267.

Stamps of 1869-95 Surcharged in Red or Black

1902		**On Stamp of 1887**		
62	A2	130r on 5r blk (R)	9.75	5.50
a.		Perf. 13½	70.00	45.00

		On Stamps of 1869		
63	A1	115r on 50r grn	19.00	6.50
64	A1	400r on 10r yel	85.00	60.00
a.		Double surcharge	250.00	180.00

		On Stamps of 1887		
65	A2	65r on 20r rose	14.50	6.00
a.		Perf. 13½	40.00	20.00
66	A2	65r on 25r violet	9.75	5.50
a.		Inverted surcharge	55.00	33.00
67	A2	65r on 100r yel brn	9.75	5.50
68	A2	115r on 10r blue grn	9.75	5.50
69	A2	115r on 300r orange	9.75	5.50
70	A2	130r on 200r gray lil	12.00	5.50
71	A2	400r on 40r brown	18.00	11.00
72	A2	400r on 50r blue	21.00	13.00
a.		Perf. 13½	600.00	450.00

		On Stamps of 1895		
73	A6	65r on 5r yellow	7.25	4.25
74	A6	65r on 10r red vio	7.25	4.25
75	A6	65r on 15r choc	7.25	4.25
76	A6	65r on 20r lav	7.25	4.25
77	A6	115r on 25r grn	7.25	4.25
78	A6	115r on 150r car, rose	7.25	4.25
79	A6	115r on 200r bl, bl	7.25	4.25
80	A6	130r on 75r rose	7.25	4.25
81	A6	130r on 100r brn, yel	9.00	5.50
a.		Double surcharge	40.00	30.00
82	A6	130r on 300r bl, sal	7.25	4.25
83	A6	400r on 50r lt blue	2.40	1.75
a.		Perf. 13½	5.00	3.00
84	A6	400r on 80r yel grn	2.40	1.75

On Newspaper Stamp No. P12

85	N3	400r on 2½r brown	3.75	3.00
a.		Double surcharge		
		Nos. 62-85 (24)	301.05	179.75

Reprints of Nos. 63, 64, 67, 71, and 72 have shiny white gum and clean-cut perf. 13½.

Stamps of 1898 Overprinted

1902				
86	A7	15r brown	3.75	1.75
87	A7	25r sea green	3.75	1.50
88	A7	50r blue	3.75	1.50
89	A7	75r rose	9.00	5.75
		Nos. 86-89 (4)	20.25	10.50

No. 49 Surcharged in Black

1905				
90	A7	50r on 65r dull blue	6.00	3.75

Stamps of 1898-1903 Overprinted in Carmine or Green

1911				
91	A7	2½r gray	.25	.25
a.		Inverted overprint	15.00	11.00
92	A7	5r orange	.25	.25
93	A7	10r lt green	.25	.25
a.		Inverted overprint	15.00	12.00
94	A7	15r gray green	.25	.25
95	A7	20r gray violet	.25	.25
96	A7	25r carmine (G)	.60	.25
97	A7	50r brown	.50	.25
a.		Inverted overprint	15.00	12.00
98	A7	75r red lilac	.50	.25
99	A7	100r dk bl, bl	.90	.75
a.		Inverted overprint	17.50	14.00
100	A7	115r org brn, pink	2.00	1.40
101	A7	130r brown, straw	2.00	1.40
102	A7	200r red lil, pnksh	10.00	6.00
103	A7	400r dull blue, straw	2.75	1.25
104	A7	500r blk & red, bl	2.75	1.25
105	A7	700r violet, yelsh	2.75	1.25
		Nos. 91-105 (15)	26.00	15.30

King Manuel II — A8

Overprinted in Carmine or Green

1912			**Perf. 11½, 12**	
106	A8	2½r violet	.25	.25
a.		Double overprint	16.00	16.00
b.		Double overprint, one inverted	25.00	
107	A8	5r black	.25	.25
108	A8	10r gray green	.25	.25
a.		Double overprint	14.00	14.00
109	A8	20r carmine (G)	2.00	1.10
110	A8	25r violet brn	1.40	.60
111	A8	50r dk blue	1.40	.60
112	A8	75r bister brn	1.40	.60
113	A8	100r brn, lt grn	2.10	.85
114	A8	200r dk grn, sal	3.00	2.40
115	A8	300r black, azure	4.00	2.10
		Nos. 106-115 (10)	16.05	9.00

Stamps of 1898-1905 Overprinted in Black

1913		**On Stamps of 1898-1903**		
116	A7	2½r gray	2.10	1.50
a.		Inverted overprint	20.00	20.00
b.		Double overprint	20.00	20.00
117	A7	5r orange	2.40	1.75
118	A7	15r gray green	52.50	33.00
a.		Inverted overprint	75.00	
119	A7	20r gray violet	3.00	1.75
a.		Inverted overprint	15.00	
120	A7	25r carmine	10.00	5.00
a.		Inverted overprint	30.00	
b.		Double overprint	30.00	
121	A7	75r red lilac	5.00	3.50
122	A7	100r bl, bluish	12.00	9.75
123	A7	115r org brn, pink	28.00	21.00
a.		Double overprint	75.00	60.00
124	A7	130r brn, straw	14.50	14.00
125	A7	200r red lil, pnksh	33.00	18.00
126	A7	400r dl bl, straw	16.00	14.00
127	A7	500r blk & red, gray	52.50	42.50
128	A7	700r vio, yelsh	72.50	55.00
		Nos. 116-128 (13)	303.50	220.75

On Provisional Issue of 1902

129	A1	115r on 50r grn	160.00	97.50
129B	A1	400r on 10r yel	700.00	600.00
130	A2	115r on 10r blue grn	5.50	3.00
a.		Inverted overprint	25.00	
131	A2	400r on 50r blue	130.00	80.00
132	A6	115r on 25r grn	4.00	3.00
a.		Inverted overprint	20.00	
133	A6	115r on 150r car, rose	72.50	60.00
a.		Inverted overprint	100.00	
134	A6	115r on 200r bl, bl	4.00	3.00
135	A6	130r on 75r rose	4.00	3.00
a.		Inverted overprint	50.00	
136	A6	400r on 50r lt bl	7.25	5.25
a.		Perf. 13½	18.50	11.00
137	A6	400r on 80r yel grn	9.75	5.00

Same Overprint on Nos. 86, 88, 90

138	A7	15r brown	4.75	3.00
139	A7	50r blue	4.75	4.00
140	A7	50r on 65r dl bl	18.00	13.50
		Nos. 138-140 (3)	27.50	19.50

No. 123-125, 130-131 and 137 were issued without gum.

Stamps of 1898-1905
Overprinted in Black

Ceres — A9

On Stamps of 1898-1903

141	A7	2½r gray	1.75	1.50
a.		Inverted overprint	9.00	
b.		Double overprint	20.00	20.00
c.		Double overprint inverted	30.00	
142	A7	5r orange	47.50	30.00
143	A7	15r gray green	3.50	2.75
a.		Inverted overprint	25.00	
144	A7	20r gray violet	140.00	85.00
a.		Inverted overprint	600.00	
145	A7	25r carmine	55.00	42.50
a.		Inverted overprint	75.00	
146	A7	75r red lilac	4.00	2.75
a.		Inverted overprint	5.00	
147	A7	100r blue, *bl*	5.00	3.50
148	A7	115r org brn, *pink*	13.50	9.25
a.		Inverted overprint	25.00	
149	A7	130r brown, *straw*	13.50	8.50
a.		Inverted overprint	25.00	
150	A7	200r red lil, *pnksh*	5.00	3.50
a.		Inverted overprint	10.00	
151	A7	400r dull bl, *straw*	14.50	8.50
152	A7	500r blk & red, *gray*	14.50	10.25
153	A7	700r violet, *yelsh*	17.50	14.00

On Provisional Issue of 1902

154	A1	115r on 50r green	275.00	200.00
155	A2	115r on 10r bl grn	5.00	3.75
156	A2	115r on 300r org	290.00	160.00
157	A2	130r on 5r black	300.00	160.00
158	A2	400r on 50r blue	140.00	100.00
159	A6	115r on 25r green	4.00	2.40
160	A6	115r on 150r car, *rose*	5.00	4.00
a.		"REPUBLICA" inverted	20.00	
161	A6	115r on 200r bl, *bl*	5.00	4.00
162	A6	130r on 75r rose	5.00	4.00
a.		Inverted surcharge	20.00	
163	A6	130r on 100r brn, *yel*	575.00	400.00
164	A6	400r on 50r lt bl	5.00	4.00
a.		Perf. 13½	29.00	21.00
165	A6	400r on 80r yel grn	5.25	4.00
166	N3	400r on 2½r brn	5.00	4.00

Same Overprint on Nos. 86, 88, 90

167	A7	15r brown	4.00	1.50
a.		Inverted overprint	20.00	
168	A7	50r blue	4.00	1.50
a.		Inverted overprint	20.00	
169	A7	50r on 65r dull bl	4.50	3.00
		Nos. 167-169 (3)	12.50	6.00

Most of Nos. 141-169 were issued without gum.

Common Design Types
pictured following the introduction.

Vasco da
Gama Issue of
Various
Portuguese
Colonies
Surcharged

On Stamps of Macao

170	CD20	¼c on ½a bl grn	2.00	1.60
171	CD21	½c on 1a red	2.00	1.60
172	CD22	1c on 2a red vio	2.00	1.60
173	CD23	2½c on 4a yel grn	2.00	1.60
174	CD24	5c on 8a dk bl	2.60	2.00
175	CD25	7½c on 12a vio brn	4.50	3.25
176	CD26	10c on 16a bis brn	2.60	1.75
177	CD27	15c on 24a bister	2.60	1.75
		Nos. 170-177 (8)	20.30	15.15

On Stamps of Portuguese Africa

178	CD20	¼c on ½a bl grn	1.50	1.25
179	CD21	½c on 5r red	1.50	1.25
180	CD22	1c on 10r red vio	1.50	1.25
181	CD23	2½c on 25r yel grn	1.50	1.25
182	CD24	5c on 50r dk bl	1.50	1.25
183	CD25	7½c on 75r vio brn	4.00	3.75
184	CD26	10c on 100r bis brn	2.10	1.75
185	CD27	15c on 150r bister	2.10	1.75
		Nos. 178-185 (8)	15.70	13.50

On Stamps of Timor

186	CD20	¼c on ½a bl grn	2.00	1.40
187	CD21	½c on 1a red	2.00	1.40
188	CD22	1c on 2a red vio	2.00	1.40
a.		Double surcharge	35.00	30.00
189	CD23	2½c on 4a yel grn	2.00	1.40
190	CD24	5c on 8a dk bl	2.60	2.00
191	CD25	7½c on 12a vio brn	4.50	3.25
192	CD26	10c on 16a bis brn	2.60	1.75
193	CD27	15c on 24a bister	2.60	1.75
		Nos. 186-193 (8)	20.30	14.35
		Nos. 170-193 (24)	56.30	43.00

Ceres — A9

Name and Value in Black
Chalky Paper

1914		Typo.	Perf. 15x14	
194	A9	¼c olive brown	.70	.50
195	A9	½c black	.70	.50
196	A9	1c blue green	1.00	.50
197	A9	1½c lilac brn	1.00	.50
198	A9	2c carmine	.70	.50
199	A9	2½c lt violet	.70	.50
200	A9	5c deep blue	.70	.50
201	A9	7½c yellow brn	1.75	1.10
202	A9	8c slate	1.75	1.10
203	A9	10c orange brn	2.00	1.00
204	A9	15c plum	3.00	1.25
205	A9	20c yellow green	2.00	1.10
206	A9	30c brown, *grn*	3.75	1.75
207	A9	40c brown, *pink*	3.75	1.75
208	A9	50c orange, *sal*	8.25	5.00
209	A9	1e green, *blue*	8.25	4.00
		Nos. 194-209 (16)	40.00	21.55

For surcharges see Nos. 250-253, 281-282.

1920
Ordinary Paper

210	A9	¼c olive brown	.75	.60
211	A9	1½c lilac brn	3.00	2.40
212	A9	7½c yellow brn	3.75	2.75
213	A9	10c orange brn	4.00	2.75
		Nos. 210-213 (4)	11.50	8.50

1922-26			Perf. 12x11½	
214	A9	¼c olive brown	.50	.40
215	A9	½c black	.50	.40
216	A9	1c yellow grn ('22)	.50	.40
217	A9	1½c lilac brn	.50	.40
218	A9	2c carmine	.50	.40
219	A9	2c gray ('26)	.25	.25
220	A9	2½c lt violet	.50	.40
221	A9	3c orange ('22)	.50	.40
222	A9	4c rose ('22)	.50	.40
223	A9	4½c gray ('22)	.50	.40
224	A9	5c brt blue ('22)	.70	.40
225	A9	6c lilac ('22)	.50	.40
226	A9	7c ultra ('22)	.55	.40
227	A9	7½c yellow brn	.70	.60
228	A9	8c slate	.70	.60
229	A9	10c orange brn	.70	.60
230	A9	12c blue green ('22)	.85	.60
231	A9	15c brn rose ('22)	1.00	.60
232	A9	20c yellow green	1.00	.60
233	A9	24c ultra ('26)	3.00	2.00
233A	A9	25c choc ('26)	3.00	2.00
233B	A9	30c gray ('22)		
233C	A9	40c turq bl ('22)	1.25	.75
233D	A9	50c lt violet ('26)	.40	.30
233E	A9	60c dk blue ('22)	1.40	.75
233F	A9	60c rose ('26)	3.00	.75
233G	A9	80c brt rose ('22)	3.50	.90

Glazed Paper

233H	A9	1e pale rose ('22)	4.00	2.10
233I	A9	1e blue ('26)	3.00	1.00
233J	A9	2e dk violet ('22)	5.00	2.50
233K	A9	5e buff ('26)	18.00	7.50
233L	A9	10e pink ('26)	30.00	14.00
233M	A9	20e pale turq ('26)	80.00	40.00
		Nos. 214-233M (33)	168.25	84.15

Preceding Issues
Overprinted in Bt.
Red

1915
On Provisional Issue of 1902

234	A2	115r on 10r green	4.00	2.75
235	A2	115r on 300r org	4.00	2.75
236	A2	130r on 5r black	9.00	4.25
237	A2	130r on 200r gray lil	2.75	1.75
238	A6	115r on 25r green	1.25	.75
239	A6	115r on 150r car, *rose*	1.25	.75
240	A6	115r on 200r bl, *bl*	1.25	.75
241	A6	130r on 75r rose	1.25	.75
242	A6	130r on 100r brn, *yel*	14.50	11.00
243	A6	130r on 300r bl, *sal*	2.10	1.20

Same Overprint on Nos. 88 and 90

244	A7	50r blue	1.40	1.00
245	A7	50r on 65r dull bl	1.40	1.00
		Nos. 234-245 (12)	44.15	28.70

No. 86 Overprinted in
Blue and Surcharged
in Black

1919

246	A7	2½c on 15r brown	1.40	1.00

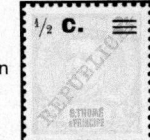

No. 91 Surcharged in
Black

247	A7	½c on 2½r gray	6.00	4.50
248	A7	1c on 2½r gray	4.25	2.75
249	A7	2½c on 2½r gray	2.10	1.50

No. 194 Surcharged in
Black

250	A9	½c on ¼c ol brn	5.50	4.00
251	A9	2c on ¼c ol brn	5.50	4.00
252	A9	2½c on ¼c ol brn	18.00	12.00

No. 199 Surcharged in
Black

253	A9	4c on 2½c lt vio	1.75	1.25
		Nos. 246-253 (8)	44.50	31.00

Nos. 246-253 were issued without gum.

Stamps of 1898-1905
Overprinted in Green
or Red

1920
On Stamps of 1898-1903

255	A7	75r red lilac (G)	1.20	.75
256	A7	100r blue, *blue* (R)	1.20	.85
257	A7	115r org brn, *pink* (G)	3.50	1.75
258	A7	130r brn, *straw* (G)	37.50	28.00
259	A7	200r red lil, *pnksh* (G)	3.50	1.75
260	A7	500r blk, & red, *gray* (G)	2.40	1.75
261	A7	700r vio, *yelsh* (G)	3.50	2.10

On Stamps of 1902

262	A6	115r on 25r grn (R)	2.10	1.20
263	A6	115r on 200r bl, *bl* (R)	2.40	1.75
264	A6	130r on 75r rose (G)	3.00	1.75

On Nos. 88-89

265	A7	50r blue (R)	2.50	2.10
266	A7	75r rose (R)	17.00	8.00

On No. 90

267	A7	50r on 65r dl bl (R)	17.00	7.75
		Nos. 255-257,259-267 (12)	59.30	31.50

Nos. 238-243
Surcharged in Blue
or Red

1923 | | | Without Gum | |

268	A6	10c on 115r on 25r (Bl)	1.25	.90
269	A6	10c on 115r on 150r (R)	1.25	.90
270	A6	10c on 115r on 200r (R)	1.25	.90
271	A6	10c on 130r on 75r (Bl)	1.25	.90

272	A6	10c on 130r on 100r (Bl)	1.50	1.25
273	A6	10c on 130r on 300r (R)	1.50	1.25
		Nos. 268-273 (6)	8.00	6.10

Nos. 268-273 are usually stained and discolored.

Nos. 84-85
Surcharged

1925

274	A6	40c on 400r on 80r yel grn	2.10	1.25
275	N3	40c on 400r on 2½r brn	2.10	1.25

Nos. 233H and 233J
Surcharged

1931

281	A9	70c on 1e pale rose	3.50	1.50
282	A9	1.40e on 2e dk vio	5.75	3.50

Ceres — A11

1934		Typo.	Wmk. 232	
		Perf. 12x11½		
283	A11	1c bister	.30	.25
284	A11	5c olive brown	.45	.25
285	A11	10c violet	.45	.25
286	A11	15c black	.40	.25
287	A11	20c gray	.40	.25
288	A11	30c dk green	.40	.25
289	A11	40c red orange	.40	.25
290	A11	45c brt blue	.60	.60
291	A11	50c brown	.50	.50
292	A11	60c olive vio	.80	.50
293	A11	70c brown org	.80	.50
294	A11	80c emerald	.85	.50
295	A11	85c deep rose	4.25	2.10
296	A11	1e maroon	1.15	.70
297	A11	1.40e dk blue	3.00	1.75
298	A11	2e dk violet	3.00	1.75
299	A11	5e apple green	10.00	5.25
300	A11	10e olive bister	22.00	11.00
301	A11	20e orange	72.50	40.00
		Nos. 283-301 (19)	122.25	66.90

Common Design Types
Inscribed "S. Tomé"

1938		Unwmk.	Perf. 13½x13	
		Name and Value in Black		
302	CD34	1c gray green	.25	.25
303	CD34	5c orange brown	.25	.25
304	CD34	10c dk carmine	.25	.25
305	CD34	15c dk violet brn	.25	.25
306	CD34	20c slate	.25	.25
307	CD35	30c rose violet	.25	.25
308	CD35	35c brt green	.50	.40
309	CD35	40c brown	.50	.40
310	CD35	50c brt red vio	.50	.40
311	CD36	60c gray black	.50	.40
312	CD36	70c brown violet	.50	.40
313	CD36	80c orange	.50	.40
314	CD36	1e red	1.25	1.00
315	CD37	1.75e blue	2.10	1.50
316	CD37	2e brown car	21.00	6.50
317	CD37	5e olive green	22.00	7.00
318	CD38	10e blue violet	25.00	8.75
319	CD38	20e red brown	45.00	11.50
		Nos. 302-319 (18)	120.85	40.15

Marble Column and
Portuguese Arms
with Cross — A12

1938   *Perf. 12½*
320	A12	80c blue green	3.00	2.40
321	A12	1.75e deep blue	11.50	6.00
322	A12	20e brown	60.00	29.00
	Nos. 320-322 (3)		74.50	37.40

Visit of the President of Portugal in 1938.

Common Design Types
Inscribed "S. Tomé e Principe"

1939   *Perf. 13½x13*
Name and Value in Black
323	CD34	1c gray grn	.25	.25
324	CD34	5c orange brn	.25	.25
325	CD34	10c dk carmine	.25	.25
326	CD34	15c dk vio brn	.25	.25
327	CD34	20c slate	.35	.25
328	CD35	30c rose violet	.25	.25
329	CD35	35c brt green	.25	.25
330	CD35	40c brown	.45	.40
331	CD35	50c brt red vio	.45	.40
332	CD36	60c gray black	.75	.50
333	CD36	70c brown violet	.80	.50
334	CD36	80c orange	.80	.50
335	CD36	1e red	1.00	.80
336	CD37	1.75e blue	2.10	1.00
337	CD37	2e brown car	3.50	1.75
338	CD37	5e olive green	6.75	4.00
339	CD38	10e blue violet	18.00	6.75
340	CD38	20e red brown	24.00	8.00
	Nos. 323-340 (18)		60.45	26.35

Cola Nuts — A13

Designs: 5c, Cola Nuts. 10c, Breadfruit. 30c, Annona. 50c, Cacao pods. 1e, Coffee. 1.75e, Dendem. 2e, Avocado. 5e, Pineapple. 10e, Mango. 20e, Coconuts.

1948   *Litho.*   *Perf. 14½*
341	A13	5c black & yellow	.80	.35
342	A13	10c black & buff	.85	.55
343	A13	30c indigo & gray	4.00	2.10
344	A13	50c brown & yellow	4.50	3.00
345	A13	1e red & rose	5.75	3.00
346	A13	1.75e blue & gray	9.00	6.00
347	A13	2e black & grn	8.50	3.00
348	A13	5e brown & lil rose	26.00	12.00
349	A13	10e black & pink	26.00	13.00
350	A13	20e black & gray	55.00	42.50
a.	Sheet of 10, #341-350		200.00	150.00
	Nos. 341-350 (10)		140.40	85.50

No. 350a sold for 42.50 escudos.

Lady of Fatima Issue
Common Design Type

1948, Dec.   *Unwmk.*
351	CD40	50c purple	8.50	7.00

Catalogue values for unused stamps in this section, from this point to the end of the section, are for Never Hinged items.

UPU Symbols — A14

1949   *Unwmk.*   *Perf. 14*
352	A14	3.50e black & gray	9.00	6.50

UPU, 75th anniv.

Holy Year Issue
Common Design Types

1950   *Perf. 13x13½*
353	CD41	2.50e blue	3.00	1.90
354	CD42	4e orange	4.75	3.00

Holy Year Extension Issue
Common Design Type

1951   *Perf. 14*
355	CD43	4e indigo & bl gray + label	3.00	2.00

Stamp without label attached sells for less.

Medical Congress Issue
Common Design Type

1952   *Perf. 13½*
356	CD44	10c Clinic	.35	.30

Joao de Santarem — A15

Portraits: 30c, Pero Escobar. 50c, Fernao de Po 1e, Alvaro Esteves. 2e, Lopo Goncalves. 3.50e, Martim Fernandes.

1952   *Unwmk.*   *Litho.*   *Perf. 14*
Centers Multicolored
357	A15	10c cream & choc	.25	.25
358	A15	30c pale grn & dk grn	.25	.25
359	A15	50c gray & dk gray	.25	.25
360	A15	1e gray bl & dk bl	.75	.25
361	A15	2e lil gray & vio brn	.50	.25
362	A15	3.50e buff & choc	.75	.25
	Nos. 357-362 (6)		2.75	1.50

For overprints and surcharges see Nos. 423, 425, 428-429, 432, 450-457, 474-481.

Jeronymos Convent A16

1953   *Perf. 13x13½*
363	A16	10c dk brown & gray	.25	.25
364	A16	50c brn org & org	.60	.40
365	A16	3e blue blk & gray blk	2.00	.80
	Nos. 363-365 (3)		2.85	1.45

Exhib. of Sacred Missionary Art, Lisbon, 1951.

Stamp Centenary Issue

Stamp of Portugal and Arms of Colonies — A17

1953   *Photo.*   *Perf. 13*
366	A17	50c multicolored	1.15	.80

Centenary of Portugal's first postage stamps.

Presidential Visit Issue

Map and Plane — A18

1954   *Typo. & Litho.*   *Perf. 13½*
367	A18	15c blk, bl, red & grn	.25	.25
368	A18	5e brown, green & red	1.00	.75

Visit of Pres. Francisco H. C. Lopes.

Sao Paulo Issue
Common Design Type

1954   *Litho.*
369	CD46	2.50e bl, gray bl & blk	.70	.50

Fair Emblem, Globe and Arms — A19

1958   *Unwmk.*   *Perf. 12x11½*
370	A19	2.50e multicolored	.80	.50

World's Fair at Brussels.

Tropical Medicine Congress Issue
Common Design Type

Design: Cassia occidentalis.

1958   *Perf. 13½*
371	CD47	5e pale grn, brn, yel, grn & red	2.75	2.00

Compass Rose — A20

1960   *Litho.*   *Perf. 13½*
372	A20	10e gray & multi	1.35	.65

500th death anniv. of Prince Henry the Navigator.

Going to Church — A21

1960   *Perf. 14½*
373	A21	1.50e multicolored	.55	.45

10th anniv. of the Commission for Technical Co-operation in Africa South of the Sahara (C.C.T.A.).

Sports Issue
Common Design Type

Sports: 50c, Angling. 1e, Gymnast on rings. 1.50e, Handball. 2e, Sailing. 2.50e, Sprinting. 20e, Skin diving.

1962, Jan. 18   *Litho.*   *Perf. 13½*
Multicolored Design
374	CD48	50c gray green	.25	.25
a.		"$50 CORREIOS" omitted	50.00	
375	CD48	1e lt lilac	.65	.25
376	CD48	1.50e salmon	.70	.25
377	CD48	2e blue	.80	.35
378	CD48	2.50e gray green	1.10	.50
379	CD48	20e dark blue	3.25	1.60
	Nos. 374-379 (6)		6.75	3.20

On No. 374a, the blue impression, including imprint, is missing.
For overprint see No. 449.

Anti-Malaria Issue
Common Design Type

Design: Anopheles gambiae.

1962   *Unwmk.*   *Perf. 13½*
380	CD49	2.50e multicolored	2.25	1.25

Airline Anniversary Issue
Common Design Type

1963   *Unwmk.*   *Perf. 14½*
381	CD50	1.50e pale blue & multi	.80	.50

National Overseas Bank Issue
Common Design Type

Design: Francisco de Oliveira Chamico.

1964, May 16   *Perf. 13½*
382	CD51	2.50e multicolored	.70	.50

ITU Issue
Common Design Type

1965, May 17   *Litho.*   *Perf. 14½*
383	CD52	2.50e tan & multi	2.00	1.00

Infantry Officer, 1788 — A22

35c, Sergeant with lance, 1788. 40c, Corporal with musket, 1788. 1e, Private with musket, 1788. 2.50e, Artillery officer, 1806. 5e, Private, 1811. 7.50e, Private, 1833. 10e, Lancer officer, 1834.

1965, Aug. 24   *Litho.*   *Perf. 13½*
384	A22	20c multicolored	.25	.25
385	A22	35c multicolored	.25	.25
386	A22	40c multicolored	.35	.25
387	A22	1e multicolored	1.25	.65
388	A22	2.50e multicolored	1.25	.65
389	A22	5e multicolored	2.00	1.40
390	A22	7.50e multicolored	3.00	2.00
391	A22	10e multicolored	3.75	2.55
	Nos. 384-391 (8)		12.10	7.55

For overprints and surcharges see Nos. 424, 426-427, 435, 458-463, 482-485, 489-490.

National Revolution Issue
Common Design Type

Design: 4e, Arts and Crafts School and Anti-Tuberculosis Dispensary.

1966, May 28   *Litho.*   *Perf. 11½*
392	CD53	4e multicolored	.80	.50

Navy Club Issue
Common Design Type

Designs: 1.50e, Capt. Campos Rodrigues and ironclad corvette Vasco da Gama. 2.50e, Dr. Aires Kopke, microscope and tsetse fly.

1967, Jan. 31   *Litho.*   *Perf. 13*
393	CD54	1.50e multicolored	1.30	.50
394	CD54	2.50e multicolored	2.00	.80

Valinhos Shrine, Children and Apparition — A23

1967, May 13   *Litho.*   *Perf. 12½x13*
395	A23	2.50e multicolored	.50	.25

50th anniv. of the apparition of the Virgin Mary to 3 shepherd children, Lucia dos Santos, Francisco and Jacinta Marto, at Fatima.

Cabral Medal, from St. Jerome's Convent — A24

1968, Apr. 22   *Litho.*   *Perf. 14*
396	A24	1.50e blue & multi	.65	.40

500th birth anniv. of Pedro Alvares Cabral, navigator who took possession of Brazil for Portugal.

Admiral Coutinho Issue
Common Design Type

Design: 2e, Adm. Coutinho, Cago Coutinho Island and monument, vert.

1969, Feb. 17   *Litho.*   *Perf. 14*
397	CD55	2e multicolored	.60	.35

Vasco da Gama's Fleet — A25

1969, Aug. 29   Litho.   Perf. 14
398 A25 2.50e multicolored   .65 .50
Vasco da Gama (1469-1524), navigator.

Administration Reform Issue
Common Design Type
1969, Sept. 25   Litho.   Perf. 14
399 CD56 2.50e multicolored   .45 .45
For overprint see No. 430.

Manuel Portal of Guarda Episcopal See — A26

1969, Dec. 1   Litho.   Perf. 14
400 A26 4e multicolored   .60 .35
500th birth anniv. of King Manuel I.

Pero Escobar, Joao de Santarem and Map of Islands — A27

1970, Jan. 25   Litho.   Perf. 14
401 A27 2.50e lt blue & multi   .50 .30
500th anniv. of the discovery of St. Thomas and Prince Islands.

Pres. Américo Rodrigues Thomaz — A28

1970   Litho.   Perf. 12½
402 A28 2.50e multicolored   .45 .40
Visit of Pres. Américo Rodrigues Thomaz of Portugal.

Marshal Carmona Issue
Common Design Type
Antonio Oscar Carmona in dress uniform.
1970, Nov. 15   Litho.   Perf. 14
403 CD57 5e multicolored   .75 .40

Coffee Plant and Stamps — A29

Designs: 1.50e, Postal Administration Building and stamp No. 1, horiz. 2.50e, Cathedral of St. Thomas and stamp No. 2.

1970, Dec.   Perf. 13½
404 A29 1e multicolored   .25 .25
405 A29 1.50e multicolored   .35 .25
406 A29 2.50e multicolored   .60 .25
   Nos. 404-406 (3)   1.20 .75
Centenary of St. Thomas and Prince Islands postage stamps.

Descent from the Cross — A30

1972, May 25   Litho.   Perf. 13
407 A30 20e lilac & multi   2.75 1.75
4th centenary of publication of The Lusiads by Luiz Camoens.

Olympic Games Issue
Common Design Type
Track and javelin, Olympic emblem.
1972, June 20   Perf. 14x13½
408 CD59 1.50e multicolored   .45 .25

Lisbon-Rio de Janeiro Flight Issue
Common Design Type
Design: 2.50e, "Lusitania" flying over warship at St. Peter Rocks.
1972, Sept. 20   Litho.   Perf. 13½
409 CD60 2.50e multicolored   .50 .25

WMO Centenary Issue
Common Design Type
1973, Dec. 15   Litho.   Perf. 13
410 CD61 5e dull grn & multi   .60 .50
For overprint see No. 434.

Republic

Flags of Portugal and St. Thomas & Prince A31

1975, July 12   Litho.   Perf. 13½
411 A31 3e gray & multi   .25 .25
412 A31 10e yellow & multi   .90 .45
413 A31 20e lt blue & multi   1.60 .95
414 A31 50e salmon & multi   3.75 2.25
   Nos. 411-414 (4)   6.50 3.90
Argel Agreement, granting independence, Argel, Sept. 26, 1974.
For overprints see Nos. 675-678.

Man and Woman with St. Thomas & Prince Flag A32

1975, Dec. 21
415 A32 1.50e pink & multi   .25 .25
416 A32 4e multicolored   .45 .40
417 A32 7.50e org & multi   .60 .50
418 A32 20e blue & multi   1.25 1.40
419 A32 50e ocher & multi   3.00 2.40
   Nos. 415-419 (5)   5.55 4.95
Proclamation of Independence, 12/7/75.

Chart and Hand — A33

1975, Dec. 21   Litho.   Perf. 13½
420 A33 1e ocher & multi   .25 .25
421 A33 1.50e multicolored   .25 .25
422 A33 2.50e orange & multi   .35 .25
   Nos. 420-422 (3)   .85 .75
National Reconstruction Fund.

Stamps of 1952-1973 Overprinted

1977   Litho.   Perf. 13½, 14, 13
423 A15 10c multi (#357)   .35 .25
424 A22 20c multi (#384)   .35 .25
425 A15 30c multi (#358)   .35 .25
426 A22 35c multi (#385)   .35 .25
427 A22 40c multi (#386)   .35 .25
428 A15 50c multi (#359)   .35 .25
429 A15 1e multi (#360)   .55 .45
430 CD56 2.50e multi (#399)   .40 .30
431 A27 2.50e multi (#401)   .40 .30
432 A15 3.50e multi (#362)   1.30 1.10
433 A26 4e multi (#400)   .70 .60
434 CD61 5e multi (#410)   .90 .60
435 A22 7.50e multi (#390)   1.60 1.30
436 A20 10e multi (#372)   2.40 2.00
   Nos. 423-436 (14)   10.35 8.35
The 10c, 30c, 50c, 1e, 3.50e, 10e issued with glassine interleaving stuck to back.

Pres. Manuel Pinto da Costa and Flag A34

Designs: 3.50e, 4.50e, Portuguese Governor handing over power. 12.50e, like 2e.

1977, Jan.   Perf. 13½
437 A34 2e yellow & multi   .25 .25
438 A34 3.50e blue & multi   .40 .25
439 A34 4.50e red & multi   .55 .40
440 A34 12.50e multicolored   1.00 .50
   Nos. 437-440 (4)   2.20 1.40
1st anniversary of independence.

Some of the sets that follow may not have been issued by the government.

Peter Paul Rubens (1577-1640), Painter — A35

Details from or entire paintings: 1e (60x44mm), Diana and Calixto, horiz. 5e (60x36mm), The Judgement of Paris, horiz. 10e (60x28mm), Diana and her Nymphs Surprised by Fauns, horiz. 15e (40x64mm), Andromeda and Perseus. 20e (40x64mm),

The Banquet of Tereo. 50e (32x64mm) Fortuna.
No. 447a, 20e, (30x40mm) like #445. No. 447b, 75e, (40x30mm) The Banquet of Tereo, diff.
1977, June 28   Litho.   Perf. 13½
441 A35 1e multicolored   .25 .25
442 A35 5e multicolored   .25 .25
443 A35 10e multicolored   .40 .30
444 A35 15e multicolored   2.00 1.25
445 A35 20e multicolored   3.00 2.00
446 A35 50e multicolored   5.50 4.75
   Nos. 441-446 (6)   11.40 8.80
Souvenir Sheet
Perf. 14
447 A35 Sheet of 2, #a.-b.   13.00 13.00
See type A40 for Rubens stamps without "$" in denomination.

Ludwig van Beethoven — A36

Designs: a, 20e, Miniature, 1802, by C. Hornemann. b, 30e, Life mask, 1812, by F. Klein. c, 50e, Portrait, 1818, by Ferdinand Schimon.

1977, June 28   Perf. 13½
448 A36 Strip of 3, #a.-c.   11.00 8.00
For overprint see No. 617.

No. 379 Ovptd. "Rep. Democr. / 12-7-77"
1977, July 12
449 CD48 20e multicolored   100.00

Pairs of Nos. 358-359, 357, 362, 384-386 Overprinted Alternately in Black

a   b

1977, Oct. 19   Litho.   Perf. 14, 13½
450 A15(a) 3e on 30c multi   3.50 1.25
451 A15(b) 3e on 30c multi   3.50 1.25
452 A15(a) 5e on 50c multi   1.00 .30
453 A15(b) 5e on 50c multi   1.00 .30
454 A15(a) 10e on 10c multi   1.75 .60
455 A15(b) 10e on 10c multi   1.75 .60
456 A15(a) 15e on 3.50e multi   4.50 1.00
457 A15(b) 15e on 3.50e multi   4.50 1.00
458 A22(a) 20e on 20c multi   5.50 1.40
459 A22(b) 20e on 20c multi   5.50 1.40
460 A22(a) 35e on 35c multi   8.00 1.90
461 A22(b) 35e on 35c multi   8.00 1.90
462 A22(a) 40e on 40c multi   9.00 3.25
463 A22(b) 40e on 40c multi   9.00 3.25
   Nos. 450-463 (14)   66.50 19.40
Centenary of membership in UPU. Overprints "a" and "b" alternate in sheets. Nos. 450-457 issued with glassine interleaving stuck to back.
These overprints exist in red on Nos. 452-453, 458-463 and on 1e on 10c, 3.50e and 30e on 30c. Value, set $125.

Mao Tse-tung
(1893-1976),
Chairman,
People's
Republic of
China — A37

1977, Dec.   Litho.   Perf. 13½x14
464 A37 50d multicolored   8.00 4.00
  a.   Souvenir sheet   8.00 4.00
    For overprint see No. 597.

Lenin — A38

Russian Supersonic Plane — A39

Designs: 40d, Rowing crew. 50d, Cosmonaut Yuri A. Gagarin.

1977, Dec.   Perf. 13½x14, 14x13½
465 A38 15d multicolored   1.60   .80
466 A39 30d multicolored   2.40 1.60
467 A39 40d multicolored   4.00 2.40
468 A38 50d red & black   6.50 3.25
  a.   Sheet of 4, #465-468   22.50 22.50
    Nos. 465-468 (4)   14.50 8.05
60th anniv. of Russian October Revolution.
For overprints see Nos. 592-595.

Paintings by
Rubens — A40

Designs: 5d, 70d, Madonna and Standing Child. 10d, Holy Family. 25d, Holy Family, diff. 50d, Madonna and Child.

1977, Dec.   Perf. 13½, 13½x14 (50d)
             Size: 31x47mm (50d)
469 A40 5d multicolored   1.60 1.00
470 A40 10d multicolored   3.25 1.75
471 A40 25d multicolored   7.25 4.00
472 A40 50d multicolored   8.00 4.50
473 A40 70d multicolored   12.00 7.50
  a.   Sheet of 4, #469-471, #473 30.00 30.00
    Nos. 469-473 (5)   32.10 18.75
No. 472 exists in souvenir sheets of 1, perf. and imperf.

Pairs of Nos. 357-359, 362, 384-385
             Surcharged

        c   #475

      #477   #479

      #481   #483, 485

1978, May 25   Perf. 14½, 13½
474 A15 (c) 3d on 30c #358   .40   .40
475 A15   3d on 30c #358   .40   .40
  a.   Pair, #474-475   1.00 1.00
476 A15 (c) 5d on 50c #359   .60   .60
477 A15   5d on 50c #359   .60   .60
  a.   Pair, #476-477   1.20 1.20
478 A15 (c) 10d on 10c #357   1.25 1.25
479 A15   10d on 10c #357   1.25 1.25
  a.   Pair, #478-479   2.60 2.60
480 A15   15d on 3.50e
                        #362   1.60 1.60
481 A15   15d on 3.50e
                        #362   1.60 1.60
  a.   Pair, #480-481   3.25 3.25
482 A22 (c) 20d on 20c #384   2.50 2.50
483 A22   20d on 20c #384   2.50 2.50
  a.   Pair, #482-483   5.25 5.25
484 A22 (c) 35d on 35c #385   4.50 4.50
485 A22   35d on 35c #385   4.50 4.50
  a.   Pair, #484-485   10.00 10.00
    Nos. 474-485 (12)   21.70 21.70
    Nos. 475a-485a (6)   23.30 23.30
Overprints for each denomination alternate on sheet. Nos. 474-481 issued with glassine interleaving stuck to back.

Flag of St. Thomas and Prince
Islands — A41

Designs: Nos. 487, 487a, Map of Islands, vert. No. 488, Coat of arms, vert.

1978, July 12   Perf. 14x13½, 13½x14
486 A41 5d multi   1.10 1.10
487 A41 5d multi   1.10 1.10
  a.   Souvenir sheet, 50d   24.00 24.00
488 A41 5d multi   1.10 1.10
  a.   Strip of 3, #486-488   3.75 3.75
Third anniversary of independence. Printed in sheets of 9. No. 487a contains one imperf. stamp.

No. 386 Surcharged

1978, Sept. 3   Litho.   Perf. 13½
489 A22 40d on 40e #386   3.00 3.00
490 A22 40d on 40e #386   3.00 3.00
  a.   Pair, #489-490   6.50 6.50
    Membership in United Nations, 3rd anniv.

Miniature Sheets

Intl. Philatelic Exhibition, 1978 — A42

No. 491: a, Tahitian Women with Fan, by Paul Gauguin. b, Still Life, by Matisse. c, Barbaric Tales, by Gauguin. d, Portrait of Armand Roulin, by Van Gogh. e, Abstract, by Georges Braque.
No. 492: a, 20d, like #491c. b, 30d, Horsemen on the Beach, by Gauguin.

1978, Nov. 1   Perf. 14
491 A42 10d Sheet of 9, #e., 2
              each #a.-d.   20.00
           Imperf
492 A42   Sheet of 3, #491a,
              492a-492b   10.00
Intl. Philatelic Exhibition, Essen.
No. 492 has simulated perfs and exists with green margin and without simulated perfs and stamps in different order.

                          UPU,
                          Centennial
                          A43

No. 493: a, Emblem, yellow & black. b, Emblem, green & black. c, Emblem, blue & black. d, Emblem, red & black. e, Concorde, balloon. f, Sailing ship, satellite. g, Monorail, stagecoach. h, Dirigible, steam locomotive. 50d, like #493h.

1978, Nov. 1   Perf. 14
493 A43 Sheet of 12, #a.-d.,
            2 each #e.-h.   40.00
  a.-d.   5d Any single   1.75
  e.-h.   15d Any single   4.00
           Souvenir Sheet
494 A43 50d multicolored   27.50
    For overprint see No. 706.

Miniature Sheets

New Currency, 1st Anniv. — A44

Obverse and reverse of bank notes: #a, 1000d. b, 50d. c, 500d. d, 100d. e, Obverse of 50c, 1d, 2d, 5d, 10d, 20d coins.

1978, Dec. 15   Perf. 13½
             Sheets of 9
495 A44 5d #e., 2 each #a.-d.   8.00
496 A44 8d #e., 2 each #a.-d.   10.00

World Cup Soccer Championships,
Argentina — A45

Various soccer plays: No. 497a, Two players in yellow shirts, one in blue. b, Two players in blue shirts, one in white. c, Six players, referee. d, Two players. No. 498a, Seven players. b, Two players at goal. c, Six players.

1978, Dec. 15   Perf. 14
497 A45 3d Block of 4, #a.-d.   4.50
498 A45 25d Strip of 3, #a.-c.   18.00
Souvenir sheets of one exist, also exist imperf.

**Overprinted with Names of Winning
Countries**

No. 499b, ITALIA, 1934/38. c, BRASIL, 1958/62/70. d, ALEMANIA 1954/74. No. 500a, INGLATERRA, 1966. b, Vencedores 1978 / 1o ARGENTINA / 2o HOLANDA / 3o BRASIL. c, ARGENTINA 1978.

1979, June 1   Litho.   Perf. 14
499 A45 3d Block of 4, #a.-d.   1.75
500 A45 25d Strip of 3, #a.-c.   8.25
Souvenir sheets of one exist.

Butterflies — A46

Flowers — A47

Designs: 50c, Charaxes odysseus. 1d, Crinum giganteum. No. 503a, Quisqualis indicia. b, Tecoma stans. c, Nerium oleander. d, Pyrostegia venusta. 10d, Hypolimnas salmacis thomensis. d, Crenis boisduvali insularis. 25d, Asystasia gangetica. No. 507, Charaxes varanes defulvata. Nos. 508, Hibiscus mutabilis.

Perf. 15, 15x14½ (#503), 14½x15 (#505)

1979, June 8
501	A46	50c multicolored	.80	.80
502	A47	1d multicolored	.60	.60
503	A47	8d Block of 4, #a.-d.	6.50	6.50
504	A46	10d multicolored	1.75	1.75
505	A47	11d Block of 4, #a.-d.	7.00	7.00
506	A47	25d multicolored	3.75	3.75
		Nos. 501-506 (6)	20.40	20.40

Souvenir Sheets
Perf. 15

507	A46	50d multicolored	13.50	13.50

Imperf

508	A47	50d multicolored	10.50	10.50

No. 508 contains one 30x46mm stamp with simulated perforations.

Intl. Communications Day — A48

1979, July 6   **Perf. 13**
509	A48	1d shown	.25	.25
510	A48	11d CCIR emblem	1.75	1.75
a.		Pair, #509-510 + label	2.10	2.10
511	A48	14d Syncom, 1963	2.10	2.10
512	A48	17d Symphony, 1975	2.75	2.75
a.		Pair, #511-512 + label	5.00	5.00
		Nos. 509-512 (4)	6.85	6.85

Intl. Advisory Council on Radio Communications (CCIR), 50th anniv. (#510).

Intl. Year of the Child A49

Designs: 1d, Child's painting of bird. 7d, Young Pioneers. 14d, Children coloring on paper. 17d, Children eating fruit. 50d, Children from different countries joining hands.

1979, July 6
513	A49	1d multicolored	.30	.30
514	A49	7d multicolored	1.80	1.80
515	A49	14d multicolored	2.25	2.25
516	A49	17d multicolored	3.25	3.25

Size: 100x100mm
Imperf

517	A49	50d multicolored	21.00	21.00
		Nos. 513-517 (5)	28.60	28.60

Souvenir Sheets

Sir Rowland Hill, 1795-1879 — A50

1979, Sept. 15   **Perf. 15**
518	A50	25d DC-3 Dakota	27.50

Perf. 14
519	A50	25d Graf Zeppelin, vert.	22.50

1st Air Mail Flight, Lisbon to St. Thomas & Prince, 30th anniv. (#518), Brasiliana '79 Intl. Philatelic Exhibition and 18th UPU Congress (#519).
See Nos. 528-533 for other stamps inscribed "Historia da Aviancao."
For overprint see No. 700.

Albrecht Durer, 450th Death Anniv. — A51

Portraits: No. 520, Willibald Pirckheimer. No. 521, Portrait of a Negro. 1d, Portrait of a Young Man, facing right. 7d, Adolescent boy. 8d, The Negress Catherine. No. 525, Girl with Braided Hair. No. 526, Self-portrait as a Boy. No. 527, Feast of the Holy Family.

1979   **Background Color**   **Perf. 14**
520	A51	50c blue green	.25	.25
521	A51	50c orange	.25	.25
522	A51	1d blue	.40	.40
523	A51	7d brown	1.75	1.75
524	A51	8d red	1.75	1.75
525	A51	25d lilac	7.25	7.25
		Nos. 520-525 (6)	11.65	11.65

Souvenir Sheets
Perf. 13½

526	A51	25d lil, buff & blk	20.00	20.00

Perf. 13½x14

527	A51	25d blk, lil & buff	20.00	20.00

Christmas, Intl. Year of the Child (#527). No. 527 contains one 35x50mm stamp.
Issued: #520-526, Nov. 29; #527, Dec. 25.
For overprint see No. 591.

History of Aviation A52

1979, Dec. 21   **Perf. 15**
528	A52	50c Wright Flyer I	.25	.25
529	A52	1d Sikorsky VS 300	.30	.30
530	A52	5d Spirit of St. Louis	1.25	1.25
531	A52	7d Dornier DO X	1.75	1.75
532	A52	8d Santa Cruz Fairey III D	1.75	1.75
533	A52	17d Space Shuttle	4.75	4.75
		Nos. 528-533 (6)	10.05	10.05

See No. 518 for souvenir sheet inscribed "Historia da Aviancao."

History of Navigation A53

50c, Caravel, 1460. 1d, Portuguese galleon, 1560. 3d, Sao Gabriel, 1497. 5d, Caravelao Navio Dos. 8d, Caravel Redonda, 1512. No. 539, Galley Fusta, 1540. No. 540, Map of St. Thomas & Prince, 1602.

1979, Dec. 21
534	A53	50c multicolored	.25	.25
535	A53	1d multicolored	.30	.30
536	A53	3d multicolored	.70	.70
537	A53	5d multicolored	1.25	1.25
538	A53	8d multicolored	1.75	1.75
539	A53	25d multicolored	5.50	5.50
		Nos. 534-539 (6)	9.75	9.75

Size: 129x98mm
Imperf

540	A53	25d multicolored	8.00	8.00

Birds — A54

No. 541, Serinus rufobrunneus. No. 542, Euplectes aureus. No. 543, Alcedo leucogaster nais. No. 544, Dreptes thomensis. No. 545, Textor grandis. No. 546, Speirops lugubris.
No. 547, Treron S. thomae.

1979, Dec. 21   **Perf. 14**
541	A54	50c multicolored	.25	.25
542	A54	50c multicolored	.25	.25
543	A54	1d multicolored	.25	.25
544	A54	7d multicolored	1.60	1.60
545	A54	8d multicolored	2.00	2.00
546	A54	100d multicolored	16.00	16.00
		Nos. 541-546 (6)	20.35	20.35

Souvenir Sheet
Perf. 14½

547	A54	25d multicolored	12.00	12.00

No. 546 is airmail.

Fish A55

50c, Cypselurus lineatus. 1d, Canthidermis maculatus. 5d, Diodon hystrix. 7d, Ostracion tricornis. 8d, Rhinecanthus aculeatus. 50d, Chaetodon striatus. 25d, Holocentrus axensionis.

1979, Dec. 28   **Perf. 14**
548	A55	50c multicolored	.25	.25
549	A55	1d multicolored	.25	.25
550	A55	5d multicolored	.30	.30
551	A55	7d multicolored	1.90	1.90
552	A55	8d multicolored	2.25	2.25
553	A55	50d multicolored	11.00	11.00
		Nos. 548-553 (6)	15.95	15.95

Souvenir Sheet
Perf. 14½

554	A55	25d multicolored	14.00	14.00

No. 553 is airmail.

Balloons — A56

Designs: 50c, Blanchard, 1784. 1d, Lunardi II, 1785. 3d, Von Lutgendorf, 1786. 7d, John Wise "Atlantic," 1859. 8d, Salomon Anree "The Eagle," 1896. No. 560, Stratospheric balloon of Prof. Piccard, 1931. No. 560A, Indoor demonstration of hot air balloon, 1709, horiz.

1979, Dec. 28   **Perf. 15**
555	A56	50c multicolored	.25	.25
556	A56	1d multicolored	.25	.25
557	A56	3d multicolored	.60	.60
558	A56	7d multicolored	1.40	1.40
559	A56	8d multicolored	1.50	1.50
560	A56	17d multicolored	5.25	5.25
		Nos. 555-560 (6)	9.25	9.25

Souvenir Sheet
Perf. 14

560A	A56	25d multicolored	10.00	10.00

No. 560A contains one 50x38mm stamp.

Dirigibles A57

Designs: 50c, Dupuy de Lome, 1872. 1d, Paul Hanlein, 1872. 3d, Gaston brothers, 1882. 7d, Willows II, 1909. 8d, Ville de Lucerne, 1910. 17d, Mayfly, 1910.

1979, Dec. 28   **Perf. 15**
561	A57	50c multicolored	.25	.25
562	A57	1d multicolored	.25	.25
563	A57	3d multicolored	.90	.90
564	A57	7d multicolored	1.60	1.60
565	A57	8d multicolored	1.75	1.75
566	A57	17d multicolored	4.00	4.00
		Nos. 561-566 (6)	8.75	8.75

1980 Olympics, Lake Placid & Moscow A58

Olympic Venues: 50c, Lake Placid, 1980. Nos. 568, 572a, Mexico City, 1968. Nos. 569, 572b, Munich, 1972. Nos. 570, 572c, Montreal, 1976. Nos. 571, 572d, Moscow, 1980.

1980, June 13   **Litho.**   **Perf. 15**
567	A58	50c multicolored	.50	.50
568	A58	11d multicolored	2.50	2.50
569	A58	11d multicolored	2.50	2.50
570	A58	11d multicolored	2.50	2.50
571	A58	11d multicolored	2.50	2.50
		Nos. 567-571 (5)	10.50	10.50

Souvenir Sheet

572	A58	7d Sheet of 4, #a.-d.	9.00	9.00

Proclamation Type of 1975 and

Sir Rowland Hill (1795-1879) — A59

Sir Rowland Hill and: 50c, #1. 1d, #415. 8d, #411. No. 576, #449. No. 577, #418.

1980, June 1   **Perf. 15**
573	A59	50c multicolored	.25	.25
574	A59	1d multicolored	.30	.30
575	A59	8d multicolored	2.00	2.00
576	A59	20d multicolored	5.50	5.50
		Nos. 573-576 (4)	8.05	8.05

Souvenir Sheet

Imperf

577 A32 20d multicolored   11.00 11.00

No. 577 contains one 38x32mm stamp with simulated perforations.

Moon Landing, 10th Anniv. (in 1979) — A60

50c, Launch of Apollo 11, vert. 1d, Astronaut on lunar module ladder, vert. 14d, Setting up research experiments. 17d, Astronauts, experiment. 25d, Command module during re-entry.

1980, June 13   **Perf. 15**
578	A60	50c multicolored	.40	.40
579	A60	1d multicolored	.55	.55
580	A60	14d multicolored	5.00	5.00
581	A60	17d multicolored	7.00	7.00
		Nos. 578-581 (4)	12.95	12.95

Souvenir Sheet

582 A60 25d multicolored   9.50 9.50

Miniature Sheet

Independence, 5th Anniv. — A61

#583: a, US #1283B. b, Venezuela #C942. c, Russia #3710. d, India #676. e, T. E. Lawrence (1888-1935). f, Ghana #106. g, Russia #2486. h, Algeria #624. i, Cuba #1318. j, Cape Verde #366. k, Mozambique #617. l, Angola #601. 25d, King Amador.

1980, July 12   **Perf. 13**
583 A61 5d Sheet of 12, #a.-
    l. + 13 labels   12.50 12.50

Souvenir Sheet

Perf. 14

584 A61 25d multicolored   9.50 9.50

No. 584 contains one 35x50mm stamp. For overprint see No. 596.

No. 527 Ovptd. "1980" on Stamp and Intl. Year of the Child emblem in Sheet Margin

1980, Dec. 25   **Perf. 14**
591 A51 25d on No. 527   20.00 20.00

Christmas.

Nos. 465-468a Overprinted in Black or Silver

1981, Feb. 2   **Perf. 13½x14, 14x13½**
592	A38	15d on #465 (S)	2.75	2.75
593	A39	30d on #466 (S)	3.75	3.75
594	A39	40d on #467	7.25	7.25
595	A38	50d on #468	9.00	9.00
a.		on No. 468a	50.00	
		Nos. 592-595 (4)	22.75	22.75

No. 584 Ovptd. with UN and Intl. Year of the Child emblems and Three Inscriptions

1981, Feb. 2   **Perf. 14**
596 A61 25d on No. 584   29.00 29.00

Nos. 464-464a Ovptd. in Silver and Black "UNIAO / SOVIETICA / VENCEDORA / 1980" with Olympic emblem and "JOGOS OLIMPICOS DE MOSCOVO 1980"

1981, May 15   **Perf. 13½x14**
597 A37 50d on #464   9.00 9.00
    a.   on #464a   9.00 9.00

Mammals — A65

No. 598, Crocidura thomensis. No. 599, Mustela nivalis. 1d, Viverra civetta. 7d, Hipposioleros fuliginosus. 8d, Rattus norvegicus. 14d, Eidolon helvum. 25d, Cercopithecus mona.

1981, May 22   **Perf. 14**
598	A65	50c multicolored	.25	.25
599	A65	50c multicolored	.25	.25
600	A65	1d multicolored	.40	.40
601	A65	7d multicolored	2.10	2.10
602	A65	8d multicolored	2.50	2.50
603	A65	14d multicolored	4.50	4.50
		Nos. 598-603 (6)	10.00	10.00

Souvenir Sheet

Perf. 14½

604 A65 25d multicolored   19.00 19.00

For surcharges see Nos. 1352-1353A.

Shells — A66

No. 605, Haxaplex hoplites. No. 606, Bolinus cornutus. 1d, Cassis tessellata. 1.50d, Harpa doris. 11d, Strombus latus. 17d, Cymbium glans.
No. 611: a, 10d, Bolinus cornutus, diff. b, 15d, Conus genuanus.

1981, May 22   **Perf. 14**
605	A66	50c multicolored	.25	.25
606	A66	50c multicolored	.25	.25
607	A66	1d multicolored	.40	.40
608	A66	1.50d multicolored	.60	.60
609	A66	11d multicolored	3.00	3.00
610	A66	17d multicolored	4.75	4.75
		Nos. 605-610 (6)	9.25	9.25

Souvenir Sheet

Perf. 14½

611 A66 Sheet of 2, #a.-b.   19.00 19.00

For surcharges, see Nos. 1987, 1990, 1993, 2014, 2017, 2020, 2041, 2044, 2047, 2068, 2071, 2074.

Johann Wolfgang von Goethe (1749-1832), Poet — A67

Design: 75d, Goethe in the Roman Campagna, by Johann Heinrich W. Tischbein.

1981, Nov. 14   **Perf. 14**
612 A67 25d multicolored   2.75 2.00

Souvenir Sheet

613 A67 75d multicolored   8.00 8.00

PHILATELIA '81, Frankfurt/Main, Germany.

Tito — A68

1981, Nov. 14   **Perf. 12½x13**
614	A68	17d Wearing glasses	1.40	1.40
615	A68	17d shown	1.40	1.40
a.		Sheet of 2, #614-615	7.75	7.75

Souvenir Sheet

Perf. 14x13½

616 A68 75d In uniform   6.75 6.75

Nos. 614-615 issued in sheets of 4 each plus label. For overprints see Nos. 644-646.

No. 448 Overprinted in White

1981, Nov. 28   **Perf. 13½**
617 A36   Strip of 3, #a.-c.   18.00 18.00

Wedding of Prince Charles and Lady Diana. On No. 617 the white overprint was applied by a thermographic process producing a shiny, raised effect.
Overprint exists in gold, $35 value.

World Chess Championships — A69

Chess pieces: No. 618, Egyptian. No. 619, Two Chinese, green. No. 620, Two Chinese, red. No. 621, English. No. 622, Indian. No. 623, Scandinavian. 75d, Khmer.
No. 624: a, Anatoly Karpov. b, Victor Korchnoi.

1981, Nov. 28   **Litho.**   **Perf. 14**
618	A69	1.50d multicolored	.30	.30
619	A69	1.50d multicolored	.30	.30
620	A69	1.50d multicolored	.30	.30
621	A69	1.50d multicolored	.30	.30
622	A69	30d multicolored	3.25	3.25
623	A69	30d multicolored	3.25	3.25
624	A69	30d Pair, #a.-b.	3.25	3.25
		Nos. 618-624 (7)	10.95	10.95

Souvenir Sheet

625 A69 75d multicolored   18.00 18.00

Nos. 618-623 exist in souvenir sheets of one. No. 624 exists in souvenir sheet with simulated perfs. Nos. 618-625 exist imperf.

No. 624 Ovptd. in red "ANATOLIJ KARPOV / Campeao Mundial / de Xadrez 1981"

1981, Dec. 10   **Perf. 14**
627 A69 30d Pair, #a.-b.   10.00 10.00

Exists in souvenir sheet with simulated perfs or imperf.

Pablo Picasso — A70

Paintings: 14d, The Old and the New Year. No. 629: a, Young Woman. b, Child with Dove. c, Paul as Pierrot with Flowers. d, Francoise, Claude, and Paloma.
No. 630: a, Girl. b, Girl with Doll. 75d, Father, Mother and Child.

1981, Dec. 10   **Perf. 14x13½**
628	A70	14d multicolored	1.25	1.25
629	A70	17d Strip of 4, #a.-d.	6.50	6.50
630	A70	20d Pair, #a.-b.	6.50	6.50
		Nos. 628-630 (3)	14.25	14.25

Souvenir Sheet

Perf. 13½

631 A70 75d multicolored   13.00 13.00

Intl. Year of the Child. Christmas (#628, 631). No. 630 is airmail.
Nos. 628, 629a-629d, 630a-630b exist in souvenir sheets of one. No. 631 contains one 50x60mm stamp.
See Nos. 683-685.

Intl. Year of the Child — A71

Paintings, No. 632, 1.50d: a, Girl with Dog, by Thomas Gainsborough. b, Miss Bowles, by Sir Joshua Reynolds. c, Sympathy, by Riviere. d, Master Simpson, by Devis. e, Two Boys with Dogs, by Gainsborough.
No. 633, 1.50d: a, Girl feeding cat. b, Girl wearing cat mask. c, White cat. d, Cat wearing red bonnet. e, Girl teaching cat to read.
No. 634, 50d: a, Boy and Dog, by Picasso. b, Clipper, by Picasso.
No. 635, 50d: a, Two white cats. b, Himalayan cat.

1981, Dec. 30   **Perf. 14**
632	A71	Strip of 5, #a.-e.	1.25	1.25
633	A71	Strip of 5, #a.-e.	1.25	1.25
634	A71	Pair, #a.-b.	9.00	9.00
635	A71	Pair, #a.-b. + label	9.00	9.00
		Nos. 632-635 (4)	20.50	20.50

Souvenir Sheets

Perf. 13½

636	A71	75d Girl with dog	8.50	8.50
637	A71	75d Girl with cat	8.50	8.50

Nos. 636-637 contain one 30x40mm stamp.

2nd Central Africa Games, Luanda, Angola — A73

No. 638: a, Shot put. b, Discus. c, High jump. d, Javelin.
50d, Team handball. 75d, Runner.

1981, Dec. 30   **Perf. 13½x14**
638 A73 17d Strip of 4, a.-d.   6.00 6.00
639 A73 50d multicolored   4.50 4.50
    Souvenir Sheet
640 A73 75d multicolored   8.00 8.00

World Food Day — A74

No. 641: a, Ananas sativus. b, Colocasia esculenta. c, Artocarbus altilis.
No. 642: a, Mangifera indica. b, Theobroma cacao. c, Coffea arabica.
75d, Musa sapientum (Bananas).

1981, Dec. 30
641 A74 11d Strip of 3, #a.-c.   3.00 3.00
642 A74 30d Strip of 3, #a.-c.   7.75 7.75
    Souvenir Sheet
643 A74 75d multicolored   7.00 7.00
    No. 643 also exist imperf.

Nos. 614-616 Ovptd. in Black

1982, May 25   **Perf. 12½x13**
644 A68 17d on #614   2.75 2.75
645 A68 17d on #615   2.75 2.75
  a.   On #615a   8.00 8.00
    Souvenir Sheet
    Perf. 14
646 A68 75d on #616   15.00 15.00

World Cup Soccer Championships, Spain — A75

Emblem and: No. 647: a, Goalie in blue shirt jumping to catch ball. b, Two players, yellow, red shirts. c, Two players, black shirts. d, Goalie in green shirtcatching ball.
No. 648: a, Player dribbling. b, Goalie facing opponent.
No. 649, Goalie catching ball from emblem in front of goal. No. 650, Like #649 with continuous design.

1982, June 21   **Perf. 13½x14**
647 A75 15d Strip of 4, #a.-d.   5.00 5.00
648 A75 25d Pair, #a.-b.   4.75 4.75

    Souvenir Sheets
649 A75 75d multicolored   —
650 A75 75d multicolored   8.00 8.00
    Nos. 648a-648b are airmail. Nos. 647a-647d, 648a-648b exist in souvenir sheets of one.

A76

Transportation: No. 651, Steam locomotive, TGV train. No. 652, Propeller plane and Concorde.

1982, June 21   **Perf. 12½x13**
651 A76 15d multicolored   4.75 2.00
652 A76 15d multicolored   4.75 2.00
  a.   Souv. sheet of 2, #651-652   12.00 12.00
    PHILEXFRANCE '82.

A77

1982, July 31
653 A77 25d multicolored   5.50 3.75
    Robert Koch, discovery of tuberculosis bacillus, cent.

Goethe, 150th Anniv. of Death A78

1982, July 31   **Perf. 13x12½**
654 A78 50d multicolored   6.50 6.00
    Souvenir Sheet
655 A78 10d like #654   11.00 11.00

A79

1982, July 31   **Perf. 12½x13**
656 A79 75d multicolored   6.25 6.25
    Souvenir Sheet
657 A79 10d Sheet of 1   5.50
657A A79 10d Sheet of 2, purple & multi   9.00
    Princess Diana, 21st birthday. No. 657A exists with red violet inscriptions and different central flower.

A80

Boy Scouts, 75th Anniv.: 15d, Cape of Good Hope #178-179. 30d, Lord Baden-Powell, founder of Boy Scouts.

1982, July 31
658 A80 15d multicolored   1.40 1.20
659 A80 30d multicolored   3.00 2.75
  a.   Souv. sheet, #658-659 + label   12.00
    Nos. 658-659 exits in sheets of 4 each plus label.

A81

Caricatures by Picasso — #660: a, Musicians. b, Stravinsky.

1982, July 31
660 A81 30d Pair, #a.-b.   4.50 4.50
    Souvenir Sheet
661 A81 5d like #660b   12.00 12.00
    Igor Stravinsky (1882-1971), composer.

A82

George Washington, 250th Anniv. of Birth: Nos. 662, 663b, Washington, by Gilbert Stuart. Nos. 663, 663c, Washington, by Roy Lichtenstein.

1982, July 31
662 A82 30d multicolored   2.10 2.10
663 A82 30d blk & pink   2.10 2.10
    Souvenir Sheet
663A A82 5d Sheet of 2, #b.-c.   9.00 9.00

Dinosaurs — A83

No. 664, Parasaurolophus. No. 665, Stegosaurus. No. 666, Triceratops. No. 667, Brontosaurus. No. 668, Tyrannosaurus rex. No. 669, Dimetrodon.
No. 670: a, 25d, Pteranodon. b, 50d, Stenopterygius.

1982, Nov. 30   **Perf. 14x13½**
664 A83 6d multicolored   .85 .70
665 A83 16d multicolored   2.25 2.00
666 A83 16d multicolored   2.25 2.00
667 A83 16d multicolored   2.25 2.00

668 A83 16d multicolored   2.25 2.00
669 A83 50d multicolored   7.25 6.00
    Nos. 664-669 (6)   17.10 14.70
    Souvenir Sheet
670 A83 Sheet of 2, #a.-b. 13.50 13.50
    Charles Darwin, cent. of death (#670).

Explorers A84

Departure of Marco Polo from Venice — A85

Explorers and their ships: 50c, Thor Heyerdahl, Kon-tiki.
No. 672: a, Magellan, Carrack. b, Drake, Golden Hind. c, Columbus, Santa Maria. d, Leif Eriksson, Viking longship.
50d, Capt. Cook, Endeavour.

1982, Dec. 21   **Litho.**
671 A84 50c multicolored   .25 .25
672 A84 18d Strip of 4, #a.-d.   6.25 6.25
673 A84 50d multicolored   4.75 4.75
    Nos. 671-673 (3)   11.25 11.25
    Souvenir Sheet
674 A85 75d multicolored   13.00 13.00

Nos. 411-414 Ovptd. with Assembly Emblem and "2o ANIVERSARIO DA 1a ASSEMBLEIA DA J.M.L.S.T.P." in Silver

1982, Dec. 24   **Perf. 13½x14**
675 A31 3d on #411   .40 .30
676 A31 10d on #412   1.00 1.00
677 A31 20d on #413   2.75 2.75
678 A31 50d on #414   5.00 5.00
    Nos. 675-678 (4)   9.15 9.05

MLSTP 3rd Assembly A86

1982, Dec. 24   **Perf. 13½x14**
679 A86 8d bl & multi   .65 .65
680 A86 12d grn & multi   .95 .95
681 A86 16d brn org & multi   1.25 1.25
682 A86 30d red lilac & multi   2.50 2.50
    Nos. 679-682 (4)   5.35 5.35

Picasso Painting Type of 1981

Designs: No. 683a, Lola. b, Aunt Pepa. c, Mother. d, Lola with Mantilla.
No. 684: a, Corina Romeu. b, The Aperitif. 75d, Holy Family in Egypt, horiz.

1982, Dec. 24
683 A70 18d Strip of 4, #a.-d.   7.00 7.00
684 A70 25d Pair, #a.-b.   4.50 4.50

Souvenir Sheet
Perf. 14x13½

685 A70 75d multicolored   27.50 27.50

Intl. Women's Year (#683-684), Christmas (#685).

Locomotives — A87

9d, Class 231K, France, 1941.

No. 687: a, 1st steam locomotive, Great Britain, 1825. b, Class 59, Africa, 1947. c, William Mason, US, 1850. d, Mallard, Great Britain, 1938.

50d, Henschel, Portugal, 1929. 75d, Locomotive barn, Swindon, Great Britain.

1982, Dec. 31   Perf. 14x13½
686	A87	9d multicolored	.50 .50
687	A87	16d Strip of 4, #a.-d.	6.00 6.00
688	A87	50d multicolored	4.25 4.25
		Nos. 686-688 (3)	10.75 10.75

Souvenir Sheet

689 A87 75d multicolored   10.50 10.50

Easter — A88

Paintings: No. 690: a, St. Catherine, by Raphael. b, St. Margaret, by Raphael.

No. 691: a, Young Man with a Pointed Beard, by Rembrandt. b, Portrait of a Young Woman, by Rembrandt.

No. 692: a, Rondo (Dance of the Italian Peasants), by Rubens, horiz. b, The Garden of Love, by Rubens, horiz.

No. 693, Samson and Delilah, by Rubens. No. 694, Descent from the Cross, by Rubens.

No. 695: a, Elevation of the Cross, by Rembrandt. b, Descent from the Cross, by Rembrandt.

Nos. 696a, 697, The Crucifixion, by Raphael. Nos. 696b, 698, The Transfiguration, by Raphael.

1983, May 9   Perf. 13½x14, 14x13½
690	A88	16d Pair, #a.-b.	3.25 3.25
691	A88	16d Pair, #a.-b.	3.25 3.25
692	A88	16d Pair, #a.-b.	3.25 3.25
693	A88	18d multicolored	2.00 2.00
694	A88	18d multicolored	2.00 2.00
695	A88	18d Pair, #a.-b.	4.00 4.00
696	A88	18d Pair, #a.-b.	4.00 4.00
		Nos. 690-696 (7)	21.75 21.75

Souvenir Sheets

697	A88	18d vio & multi	9.00
698	A88	18d multicolored	9.00

Souvenir sheets containing Nos. 690a-690b, 691a-691b, 692a-692b, 693, 694, 695a-695b exist.

BRASILIANA '83, Rio de Janeiro — A89

Santos-Dumont dirigibles: No. 699a, #5. b, #14 with airplane.

1983, July 29   Litho.   Perf. 13½
699 A89 25d Pair, #a.-b.   4.00 4.00

First manned flight, bicent.

No. 519 Overprinted with Various Designs

1983, July 29   Litho.   Perf. 14
Souvenir Sheet

700 A50 25d multicolored   40.00

BRASILIANA '83.

First Manned Flight, Bicent. — A90

No. 701: a, Wright Flyer No. 1, 1903. b, Alcock & Brown Vickers Vimy, 1919.

No. 702: a, Bleriot monoplane, 1909. b, Boeing 747, 1983.

No. 703: a, Graf Zeppelin, 1929. b, Montgolfiere brother's balloon, 1783. No. 704, Pierre Tetu-Brissy. 60d, Flight of Vincent Lunardi's second balloon, vert.

1983, Sept. 16   Perf. 14x13½
701	A90	18d Pair, #a.-b.	3.75 3.75
702	A90	18d Pair, #a.-b.	3.75 3.75
703	A90	20d Pair, #a.-b.	4.50 4.50
704	A90	20d multicolored	2.25 2.25
		Nos. 701-704 (4)	14.25 14.25

Souvenir Sheet
Perf. 13½x14

705 A90 60d multicolored   6.75 6.75

Individual stamps from Nos. 701-704 exist in souvenir sheets of 1. Value of 4 $50.

Nos. 493e, 493a, 493e (#706a) and 493g, 493c, 493g (#706b) Ovptd. in Gold with UPU and Philatelic Salon Emblems and:
"SALON DER PHILATELIE ZUM / XIX WELTPOSTKONGRESS / HAMBURG 1984" Across Strips of Three Stamps
Nos. 493f, 493b, 493f (#706c) 493h, 493d, 493h (#706d) Ovptd. in Gold with UPU and Philatelic Salon Emblems and:
"19TH CONGRESSO DA / UNIAO POSTAL UNIVERSAL / HAMBURGO 1984" Across Strips of Three Stamps

1983, Dec. 24   Perf. 14
706 A43 Sheet of 12, #a.-d.   30.00

Overprint is 91x30mm. Exists imperf with silver overprint.

Christmas — A91

Paintings: No. 707, Madonna of the Promenade, 1518, by Raphael. No. 708, Virgin of Guadalupe, 1959, by Salavador Dali.

1983, Dec. 24   Perf. 12½x13
707	A91	30d multicolored	2.75 2.75
708	A91	30d multicolored	2.75 2.75

Nos. 707-708 exist in souvenir sheets of 1.

Automobiles — A92

No. 709: a, Renault, 1912. b, Rover Phaeton, 1907.

No. 710: a, Morris, 1913. b, Delage, 1910.

No. 711: a, Mercedes Benz, 1927. b, Mercedes Coupe, 1936.

No. 712: a, Mercedes Cabriolet, 1924. b, Mercedes Simplex, 1902.

75d, Peugeot Daimler, 1894.

1983, Dec. 28   Perf. 14x13½
709	A92	12d Pair, #a.-b.	2.25 2.25
710	A92	12d Pair, #a.-b.	2.25 2.25
711	A92	20d Pair, #a.-b.	3.75 3.75
712	A92	20d Pair, #a.-b.	3.75 3.75
		Nos. 709-712 (4)	12.00 12.00

Souvenir Sheet
713 A92 75d multicolored   9.00 9.00

Nos. 709-712 exist as souvenir sheets. No. 713 contains one 50x41mm stamp.

Medicinal Plants — A93

50c, Cymbopogon citratus. 1d, Adenoplus breviflorus. 5.50d, Bryophillum pinatum. 15.50d, Buchholzia coriacea. 16d, Hiliotropium indicum. 20d, Mimosa pigra. 46d, Piperonia pallucila. 50d, Achyranthes aspera.

1983, Dec. 28   Perf. 13½
714	A93	50c multi	.25 .25
715	A93	1d multi	.25 .25
716	A93	5.50d multi	.45 .45
717	A93	15.50d multi	1.60 1.60
718	A93	16d multi	1.60 1.60
719	A93	20d multi	2.00 2.00
720	A93	46d multi	4.75 4.75
721	A93	50d multi	5.50 5.50
		Nos. 714-721 (8)	16.40 16.40

For surcharges, see Nos. 1355-1357, 1984, 1991, 1992, 2011, 2018, 2019, 2038, 2045, 2046, 2065, 2072, 2073.

1984 Olympics, Sarajevo and Los Angeles A94

No. 722, Pairs' figure skating.
No. 723: a, Downhill skiing. b, Speed skating. c, Ski jumping.
No. 724, Equestrian.
No. 725: a, Cycling. b, Rowing. c, Hurdling.
No. 726: a, Bobsled. b, Women's archery.

1983, Dec. 29   Perf. 13½x14
722	A94	16d multicolored	1.50 1.50
723	A94	16d Strip of 3, #a.-c.	4.50 4.50
724	A94	18d multicolored	1.75 1.75
725	A94	18d Strip of 3, #a.-c.	5.25 5.25
		Nos. 722-725 (4)	13.00 13.00

Souvenir Sheet
726 A94 30d Sheet of 2, #a.-b.   7.00 7.00

Souvenir sheets of 2 exist containing Nos. 722 and 723b, 723a and 723c, 724 and 725b, 725a and 725c.

Birds — A95

50c, Spermestes cucullatus. 1d, Xanthophilus princeps. 1.50d, Thomasophantes sanctithomae. 2d, Quelea erythrops. 3d, Textor velatus peixotoi. 4d, Anabathmis hartlaubii. 5.50d, Serinus mozambicus santhome. 7d, Estrilda astrild angolensis. 10d, Horizorhinus dohrni. 11d, Zosterops ficedulinus. 12d, Prinia molleri. 14d, Chrysococcyx cupreus insularum. 15.50d, Halcyon malimhicus dryas. 16d, Turdus olivaceofuscus. 17d, Oriolus crassirostris. 18.50d, Dicrurus modestus. 20d, Columba thomensis. 25d, Stigmatopelia senegalensis thome. 30d, Chaetura thomensis. 42d, Onychognatus fulgidus. 46d, Lamprotornis ornatus. 100d, Tyto alba thomensis.

1983, Dec. 30   Perf. 13½
727	A95	50c multi	.25 .25
728	A95	1d multi	.25 .25
729	A95	1.50d multi	.25 .25
730	A95	2d multi	.25 .25
731	A95	3d multi	.25 .25
732	A95	4d multi	.45 .45
733	A95	5.50d multi	.45 .45
734	A95	7d multi	.80 .80
735	A95	10d multi	1.05 1.05

Size: 30x43mm
736	A95	11d multi	1.30 1.30
737	A95	12d multi	1.30 1.30
738	A95	14d multi	1.45 1.45
739	A95	15.50d multi	1.60 1.60
740	A95	16d multi	1.75 1.75
741	A95	17d multi	1.75 1.75
742	A95	18.50d multi	1.90 1.90
743	A95	20d multi	2.00 2.00
744	A95	25d multi	2.75 2.75

Size: 31x47mm
Perf. 13½x14
745	A95	30d multi	3.25 3.25
746	A95	42d multi	4.50 4.50
747	A95	46d multi	5.25 5.25
748	A95	100d multi	10.00 10.00
		Nos. 727-748 (22)	42.80 42.80

For surcharges see Nos. 1295C-1300H, 1343-1351, 1361-1363, 1372-1373, 1988, 1994, 2015, 2042, 2069, 2092, C21.

Souvenir Sheet

ESPANA '84, Madrid — A96

Paintings: a, 15.50d, Paulo Riding Donkey, by Picasso. b, 16d, Abstract, by Miro. c, 18.50d, My Wife in the Nude, by Dali.

1984, Apr. 27   **Perf. 13½x14**
749 A96 Sheet of 3, #a.-c.   6.00   6.00

LUBRAPEX '84, Lisbon — A97

Children's drawings: 16d, Children watching play. 30d, Adults.

1984, May 9   **Perf. 13½**
750 A97 16d multicolored   1.50   1.50
751 A97 30d multicolored   2.50   2.50

Intl. Maritime Organization, 25th Anniv. — A98

Ships: Nos. 752a, 753a, Phoenix, 1869. 752b, 753b, Hamburg, 1893. 752c, 753c, Prince Heinrich, 1900.
No. 754: a, Leopold, 1840. b, Stadt Schaffhausen, 1851. c, Crown Prince, 1890. d, St. Gallen, 1905.
No. 755: a, Elise, 1816. b, De Zeeuw, 1824. c, Friedrich Wilhelm, 1827. d, Packet Hansa.
No. 756: a, Savannah, 1818. b, Chaperone, 1884. c, Alida, 1847. d, City of Worcester, 1881.
No. 757, Ferry, Lombard Bridge, Hamburg, c. 1900. No. 758, Train, coaches on bridge, c. 1880, vert. No. 759, Windmill, bridge, vert. No. 760, Queen of the West. No. 761, Bremen. No. 762, Union.

1984, June 19 Litho.   **Perf. 14x13½**
752 A98 50c Strip of 3, #a.-c.   3.50   3.50
753 A98 50c Strip of 3, #a.-c.   3.50   3.50
754 A98 7d Piece of 4, #a.-d.   4.25   4.25
   e.   Souv. sheet of 2, #754a-754b
   f.   Souv. sheet of 2, #754c-754d
755 A98 8d Piece of 4, #a.-d.   4.25   4.25
   e.   Souv. sheet of 2, #755a-755b
   f.   Souv. sheet of 2, #755c-755d
756 A98 15.50d Piece of 4,
     #a.-d.   7.50   7.50
   e.   Souv. sheet of 2, #756a, 756d
   f.   Souv. sheet of 2, #756b-756c
    Nos. 752-756 (5)   23.00 23.00
    Nos. 754e-754f, 755e-755f,
    756e-756f   72.50

Souvenir Sheets
Perf. 14x13½, 13½x14
757 A98 10d multicolored   8.50   8.50
758 A98 10d multicolored   8.50   8.50
759 A98 10d multicolored   8.50   8.50

Perf. 13½
760 A98 15d multicolored   12.00 12.00
761 A98 15d multicolored   12.00 12.00
762 A98 15d multicolored   12.00 12.00
    Nos. 757-762 (6)   61.50 61.50

Nos. 757-759 exist imperf in different colors. Nos. 760-762 contain one 60x33mm stamp each. Nos. 753a-753c have UPU and Hamburg Philatelic Salon emblems and are additionally inscribed "PARTICIPACAO DE S. TOME E PRINCIPE / NO CONGRESSO DA U.P.U. EM HAMBURGO."
Sheets containing Nos. 754-756 contain one label.

Natl. Campaign Against Malaria A99

1984, Sept. 30   **Perf. 13½**
764 A99 8d Malaria victim   1.10   1.10
765 A99 16d Mosquito, DDT,
    vert.   2.00   2.00
766 A99 30d Exterminator, vert.   3.50   3.50
    Nos. 764-766 (3)   6.60   6.60

A100

World Food Day: 8d, Emblem, animals, produce. 16d, Silhouette, animals. 46d, Plowed field, produce. 30d, Tractor, field, produce, horiz.

1984, Oct. 16
767 A100 8d multicolored   1.05   1.05
768 A100 16d multicolored   1.60   1.60
769 A100 46d multicolored   3.25   3.25
    Nos. 767-769 (3)   5.90   5.90

Souvenir Sheet
770 A100 30d multicolored   3.75   3.75
    For surcharges see No. 1366.

A101

Mushrooms: 10d, Coprinus micaceus. 20d, Amanita rubescens. 30d, Armillariella mellea. 50d, Hygrophorus chrysodon, horiz.

1984, Nov. 5
771 A101 10d multicolored   3.00   3.00
772 A101 20d multicolored   5.50   5.50
773 A101 30d multicolored   8.00   8.00
    Nos. 771-773 (3)   16.50 16.50

Souvenir Sheet
774 A101 50d multicolored   16.00 16.00

Christmas A102

Designs: 30d, Candles, offering, stable. 50d, Stable, Holy Family, Kings.

1984, Dec. 25
775 A102 30d multicolored   2.75   2.75

Souvenir Sheet
776 A102 50d multicolored   4.75   4.75
    No. 776 contains one 60x40mm stamp.

Conference of Portuguese Territories in Africa A103

1985, Feb. 14
777 A103 25d multicolored   2.75   2.75

Reinstatement of Flights from Lisbon to St. Thomas, 1st Anniv. — A104

Designs: 25d, Douglas DC-3, map of northwest Africa. 30d, Air Portugal Douglas DC-8. 50d, Fokker Friendship.

1985, Dec. 6 Litho.   **Perf. 13½**
778 A104 25d multicolored   2.25   2.25
779 A104 30d multicolored   2.50   2.50

Souvenir Sheet
779A A104 50d multicolored   8.00   8.00

Flowers — A105

1985, Dec. 30   **Perf. 11½x12**
780 A105 16d Flowering cactus   1.20   1.20
781 A105 20d Sunflower   1.90   1.90
782 A105 30d Porcelain rose   2.10   2.10
    Nos. 780-782 (3)   5.20   5.20

Mushrooms A106

6d, Fistulina hepatica. 25d, Collybia butyracea. 30d, Entoloma clypeatum. 75d, Cogumelos II.

1986, Sept. 18   **Perf. 13½**
783 A106 6d multicolored   .65   .65
784 A106 25d multicolored   2.40   2.40
785 A106 30d multicolored   2.50   2.50
    Nos. 783-785 (3)   5.55   5.55

Souvenir Sheet
786 A106 75d multicolored   10.00   8.00
    No. 786 exists with margins trimmed on four sides removing the control number.

Miniature Sheet

World Cup Soccer, Mexico A107

No. 787: a, Top of trophy. b, Bottom of trophy. c, Interior of stadium. d, Exterior of stadium.

1986, Oct. 1
787 A107 25d Sheet of 4, #a.-
    d.   10.00 10.00
    For overprints see Nos. 818-818A.

Miniature Sheet

1988 Summer Olympics, Seoul — A108

Seoul Olympic Games emblem, and: No. 788a, Map of North Korea. b, Torch. c, Olympic flag, map of South Korea. d, Text.

1986, Oct. 2
788 A108 25d Sheet of 4, #a.-
    d.   14.50 14.50

Halley's Comet — A109

Designs: No. 789a, 5d, Challenger space shuttle, 1st launch. b, 6d, Vega probe. c, 10d, Giotto probe. d, 16d, Comet over Nuremberg, A.D. 684.
90d, Comet, Giotto probe, horiz.

1986, Oct. 27
789 A109 Sheet of 4, #a.-
    d. + 5 labels   9.00   7.00

Souvenir Sheet
790 A109 90d multicolored   9.00   9.00

Automobiles — A110

Designs: No. 791a, 50c, Columbus Monument, Barcelona. b, 6d, Fire engine ladder truck, c. 1900. c, 16d, Fire engine, c. 1900. d, 30d, Fiat 18 BL Red Cross ambulance, c. 1916.

1986, Nov. 1
791 A110 Sheet of 4, #a.-d. +
    5 labels   10.00   8.00

Railway Stations and Signals A111

Designs: 50c, London Bridge Station, 1900. 6d, 100-300 meter warning signs. 20d, Signal lamp. 50d, St. Thomas & Prince Station.

1986, Nov. 2   *Perf. 13½*
792 A111 50c multicolored   .45 .45
793 A111 6d multicolored   1.10 1.10
794 A111 20d multicolored   3.75 3.75
    Nos. 792-794 (3)   5.30 5.30

Souvenir Sheet

795 A111 50d multicolored   6.50 6.50

LUBRAPEX '86, Brazil — A112

Exhibition emblem and: No. 796a, 1d, Line fisherman on shore. b, 1d, Line fisherman in boat. c, 2d, Net fisherman. d, 46d, Couple trap fishing, lobster.

1987, Jan. 15
796 A112 Sheet of 4, #a.-d. + 2 labels   7.00 7.00

Intl. Peace Year A113

Designs: 8d, Mahatma Gandhi. 10d, Martin Luther King, Jr. 16d, Red Cross, Intl. Peace Year, UN, UNESCO, Olympic emblems and Nobel Peace Prize medal. 20d, Albert Luthuli. 75d, Peace Dove, by Picasso.

1987, Jan. 15
797 A113 8d bl, blk & pur   .95 .95
798 A113 10d bl, blk & grn   1.10 1.10
799 A113 16d multicolored   2.00 2.00
800 A113 20d multicolored   2.50 2.50
    Nos. 797-800 (4)   6.55 6.55

Souvenir Sheet

801 A113 75d multicolored   6.50 6.50

Christmas 1986 — A114

Paintings by Albrecht Durer: No. 802a, 50c, Virgin and Child. b, 1d, Madonna of the Carnation. c, 16d, Virgin and Child, diff. d, 20d, The Nativity. 75d, Madonna of the Goldfinch.

1987, Jan. 15
802 A114 Strip of 4, #a.-d.   6.00 6.00

Souvenir Sheet

803 A114 75d multicolored   8.00 8.00

Fauna and Flora — A115

Birds: a, 1d, Agapornis fischeri. b, 2d, Psittacula krameri. c, 10d, Psittacus erithacus. d, 20d, Agapornis personata psittacidae.
Flowers: e, 1d, Passiflora caerulea. f, 2d, Oncidium nubigenum. g, 10d, Heliconia wagneriana. h, 20d, Guzmania liguiata.
Butterflies: i, 1d, Aglais urticae. j, 2d, Pieris brassicae. k, 10d, Fabriciana niobe. l, 20d, Zerynthia polyxena.
Dogs: m, 1d, Sanshu. n, 2d, Hamiltonstovare. o, 10d, Gran spitz. p, 20d, Chowchow.

1987, Oct. 15   *Perf. 14x13½*
804 A115 Sheet of 16, #a.-p.   20.00 20.00

Sports Institute, 10th Anniv. — A116

No. 805: a, 50c, Three athletes. b, 20d, Map of St. Thomas and Prince, torchbearers. c, 30d, Volleyball, soccer, team handball and basketball players.
50d, Bjorn Borg.

1987, Oct. 30
805 A116 Strip of 3, #a.-c.   4.25 4.25

Souvenir Sheet
Perf. 13½x14

806 A116 50d Sheet of 1 + label   6.50 6.50

Miniature Sheet

Discovery of America, 500th Anniv. (in 1992) — A117

Emblem and: No. 807: a, 15d, Columbus with globe, map and arms. b, 20d, Battle between Spanish galleon and pirate ship. c, 20d, Columbus landing in New World. 100d, Model ship, horiz.

1987, Nov. 3   *Perf. 13½x14*
807 A117 Sheet of 3, #a.-c. + 3 labels   8.00 8.00

Souvenir Sheet
Perf. 14x13½

808 A117 100d multicolored   9.00 9.00

Mushrooms — A118

Designs: No. 809a, 6d, Calocybe ionides. b, 25d, Hygrophorus coccineus. c, 30d, Boletus versipellis. 35d, Morchella vulgaris, vert.

1987, Nov. 10   *Perf. 14x13½*
809 A118 Strip of 3, #a.-c.   5.50 5.50

Souvenir Sheet
Perf. 13½x14

810 A118 35d multicolored   5.00 5.00

Locomotives — A119

No. 811: a, 5d, Jung, Germany. b, 10d, Mikado 2413. c, 20d, Baldwin, 1920. 50d, Pamplona Railroad Station, 1900.

1987, Dec. 1   *Litho.*   *Perf. 14x13½*
811 A119 Strip of 3, #a.-c.   6.00 6.00

Souvenir Sheet

812 A119 50d multicolored   7.25 7.25

Miniature Sheet

Christmas — A120

Paintings of Virgin and Child by: No. 813a, 1d, Botticelli. b, 5d, Murillo. c, 15d, Raphael. d, 20d, Memling.
50d, Unknown artist, horiz.

1987, Dec. 20   *Perf. 13½x14*
813 A120 Sheet of 4, #a.-d.   3.75 3.75

Souvenir Sheet
Perf. 14x13½

814 A120 50d multicolored   5.25 5.25

World Boy Scout Jamboree, Australia, 1987-88 — A121

1987, Dec. 30   *Perf. 14x13½*
815 A121 50c multicolored   3.00 .80

Russian October Revolution, 70th Anniv. A122

1988   *Litho.*   *Perf. 12*
816 A122 25d Lenin addressing revolutionaries   2.25 2.25

Souvenir Sheet

Lubrapex '88 — A123

1988, May   *Perf. 14x13½*
817 A123 80d Trolley   5.25 5.25

Nos. 787a-787d Ovptd.
"CAMPEONATO MUNDIAL / DE FUTEBOL MEXICO '86 / ALEMANHA / SUBCAMPIAO" in Silver (#818) or Same with "ARGENTINA / CAMPIAO" Instead in Gold (#818A) Across Four Stamps

1988, Aug. 15   *Perf. 13½*
818 A107 25d Block of 4 (S)   25.00 25.00
818A A107 25d Block of 4 (G)   25.00 25.00

Medicinal Plants — A123a

Mushrooms — A123b

Medicinal plants: No. 819a, 5d, Datura metel. b, 5d, Salaconta. c, 5d, Cassia occidentalis. d, 10d, Solanum ovigerum. e, 20d, Leonotis nepetifolia.
Mushrooms: No. 820a, 10d, Rhodopaxillus nudus. b, 10d, Volvaria volvacea. c, 10d, Psalliota bispora. d, 10d, Pleurotus ostreatus. e, 20d, Clitocybe geotropa.

1988, Oct. 26   *Perf. 13½x14*
819 A123a Strip of 5, #a.-e.   6.75 6.75
820 A123b Strip of 5, #a.-e.   8.00 8.00

Souvenir Sheets

821 A123a 35d Hiersas durero   6.25 6.25
822 A123b 35d Mushroom on wood   6.25 6.25

Miniature Sheets of 4

Passenger Trains — A123c

No. 823: a, Swiss Federal Class RE 6/6, left. b, Class RE 6/6, right.
No. 824: a, Japan Natl. Class EF 81, left. b, Class EF 81, right.
No. 825: a, German Electric E 18, 1930, left. b, E 18, 1930, right.
60d, Japan Natl. Class 381 Electric.

1988, Nov. 4 — Perf. 14x13½

823	A123c	10d 2 ea #a.-b. + 2 labels	5.50	5.50
824	A123c	10d 2 ea #a.-b. + 2 labels	5.50	5.50
825	A123c	10d 2 ea #a.-b. + 2 labels	5.50	5.50

Nos. 823-825 (3) 16.50 16.50

Souvenir Sheet

826	A123c	60d multicolored	8.00	8.00

Butterflies — A123d

Various flowers and: No. 827a, White and brown spotted butterfly. b, Dark brown and white butterfly, flower stigma pointing down. c, Brown and white butterfly, flower stigma pointing up.
50d, Brown, white and orange butterfly.

1988, Nov. 25 — Perf. 13½x14

827	A123d	10d Strip of 3, #a.-c.	4.50	4.00

Souvenir Sheet

828	A123d	50d multicolored	9.00	9.00

Ferdinand von Zeppelin (1838-1917)
A123e

Berlin, 750th Anniv. — A123f

No. 829: a, Sailing ship, dirigible L23. b, Dirigibles flying over British merchant ships. c, Rendezvous of zeppelin with Russian ice breaker Malygin.
No. 830: a, Airship Le Jeune at mooring pad, Paris, 1903, vert. b, von Zeppelin, vert.

Perf. 14x13½, 13½x14

1988, Nov. 25

829	A123e	10d Strip of 3, #a.-c.	7.75	7.75
830	A123e	10d Pair, #a.-b.	5.25	5.25

Souvenir Sheet

831	A123f	50d multicolored	8.00	8.00

Natl. Arms — A123g

Automatic Telephone Exchange Linking the Islands, 1st Anniv. — A123h

1988, Dec. 15 — Perf. 13½

832	A123g	10d multicolored	1.40	1.40
833	A123h	25d multicolored	3.00	3.00

Olympics Games, Seoul, Barcelona and Albertville — A123i

World Cup Soccer Championships, Italy, 1990 — A123j

No. 834, View of Barcelona, Cobi. No. 835, Barcelona Games emblem. No. 836, Gold medal from 1988 Seoul games. No. 837, Emblems of 1988 & 1992 games. No. 838, Bear on skis, Albertville, 1992. No. 839, Soccer ball. No. 840, Italy '90 Championships emblem. No. 841, World Cup Trophy. No. 842, Transfer of Olympic flag during Seoul closing ceremony. No. 843, Olympic pins. No. 844, like No. 838. No. 845, Soccer balls as hemispheres of globe.

1988, Dec. 15 — Perf. 14x13½, 13½x14

834	A123i	5d multi	1.60	1.60
835	A123i	5d multi, vert.	1.60	1.60
836	A123i	5d multi, vert.	1.60	1.60
837	A123i	5d multi	1.60	1.60
838	A123i	5d grn & multi	1.60	1.60
839	A123j	5d multi	1.60	1.60
840	A123j	5d multi, vert.	1.60	1.60
841	A123j	5d multi, vert.	1.60	1.60

Nos. 834-841 (8) 12.80 12.80

Souvenir Sheets — Perf. 14x13½

842	A123i	50d multi	10.00	10.00
843	A123i	50d multi	10.00	10.00
844	A123i	50d blue & multi	10.00	10.00
845	A123j	50d multi	10.00	10.00

No. 842 exists with Olympic emblems in gold or silver. No. 845 exists with marginal inscriptions in gold or silver. See Nos. 876-877 for souvenir sheets similar in design to No. 840.

Intl. Boy Scout Jamboree, Australia, 1987-88 — A123k

No. 846: a, Campfire. b, Scout emblem, pitched tents, flag. c, Scout emblem, tent flaps, flag, axe.
110d, Trefoil center point, horiz.

1988, Dec. 15 — Perf. 13½x14

846	A123k	10d Strip of 3, #a.-c.	6.75	6.75

Souvenir Sheet — Perf. 14x13½

847	A123k	110d multicolored	20.00	20.00

Intl. Red Cross, 125th Anniv. — A123m

No. 848: a, 50c, Patient in hospital. b, 5d, Transporting victims. c, 20d, Instructing workers. 50d, Early mail train, horiz.

1988, Dec. 15 — Perf. 13½x14

848	A123m	Strip of 3, #a.-c.	7.25	7.25

Souvenir Sheet — Perf. 14x13½

849	A123m	50d multicolored	10.50	10.50

No. 848c is airmail.

Miniature Sheet

Christmas — A123n

No. 850: a, 10d, Madonna and Child with St. Anthony Abbot and the Infant Baptism, by Titian. b, 10d, Madonna and Child with St. Catherine and a Rabbit, by Titian. c, 10d, Nativity Scene, by Rubens. d, 30d, Adoration of the Magi, by Rubens.
50d, The Annunciation (detail), by Titian, vert.

1988, Dec. 23 — Perf. 14x13½

850	A123n	Sheet of 4, #a.-d.	8.00	8.00

Souvenir Sheet — Perf. 13½x14

851	A123n	50d multicolored	6.75	6.75

Titian, 500th anniv. of birth. Country name does not appear on No. 850d.

French Revolution, Bicent. — A123o

Designs: No. 852, Eiffel Tower, Concorde, stylized doves, flag. No. 853 Eiffel Tower, flag, stylized doves. No. 854, Eiffel Tower, flag, stylized doves, TGV train, vert. 50d, TGV train.

Perf. 14x13½, 13½x14

1989, July 14 — Litho.

852	A123o	10d multicolored	1.50	1.50
853	A123o	10d multicolored	1.50	1.50
854	A123o	10d multicolored	1.50	1.50

Nos. 852-854 (3) 4.50 4.50

Souvenir Sheet

855	A123o	50d multicolored	6.50	6.50

Fruit — A123p

1989, Sept. 15 — Perf. 13½x14

856	A123p	50c Chapu-chapu	.25	.25
857	A123p	1d Guava	.25	.25
858	A123p	5d Mango	.25	.25
859	A123p	10d Carambola	.25	.25
860	A123p	25d Nona	.45	.45
861	A123p	50d Avacado	.90	.90
862	A123p	50d Cajamanga	.90	.90

Perf. 14x13½

863	A123p	60d Jackfruit	.95	.95
864	A123p	100d Cacao	1.50	1.50
865	A123p	250d Bananas	4.00	4.00
866	A123p	500d Papaya	8.75	8.75

Nos. 856-866 (11) 18.45 18.45

For surcharges see Nos. 1170B, 1170E-1170G, 1170J-1170K, 1170N, 1358-1360.

Souvenir Sheet — Perf. 13½x14

867	A123p	1000d Pomegranate	18.00	18.00

Nos. 863-866 are horiz.

Orchids A123q

Designs: No. 868, Dendrobium phalaenopsis. No. 869, Catteleya granulosa. 50d, Diothonea imbricata and maxillaria eburnea.

1989, Oct. 15 — Perf. 13½x14

868	A123q	20d multicolored	2.00	2.00
869	A123q	20d multicolored	2.00	2.00

Souvenir Sheet

870	A123q	50d multicolored	4.75	4.75

Hummingbirds — A124

Designs: No. 871, Topaza bella, Sappho sparganura, vert. No. 872, Petasophores anais. No. 873, Lophornis adorabilis, Chalcostigma herrani, vert. 50d, Oreotrochilus chimborazo.

1989, Oct. 15 — Perf. 13½x14, 14x13½

871	A124	20d multicolored	1.75	1.75
872	A124	20d multicolored	1.75	1.75
873	A124	20d multicolored	1.75	1.75

Nos. 871-873 (3) 5.25 5.25

Souvenir Sheet — Perf. 14x13½

874	A124	50d multicolored	5.25	5.25

Miniature Sheet

1990 World Cup Soccer
Championships, Italy — A125

Program covers: No. 875: a, 10d, Globe and
soccer ball, 1962. b, 10d, Foot kicking ball,
1950. c, 10d, Abstract design, 1982. d, 20d,
Player kicking ball, 1934.
No. 876: a, Character emblem, horiz. b,
USA 94, horiz. 50d, like #876a, horiz.

1989, Oct. 24   Perf. 13½x14
875 A125   Block of 4, #a.-
                    d.   7.25   7.25
Souvenir Sheets
Perf. 14x13½
876 A125 25d Sheet of 2, #a.-
                    b.   6.50   6.50
877 A125 50d blue & multi   6.50   6.50

1992 Summer Olympics,
Barcelona — A126

1989, Oct. 24   Perf. 13½x14, 14x13½
878 A126 5d Tennis, vert.   .90   .90
879 A126 5d Basketball, vert.   .90   .90
880 A126 5d Running   .90   .90
881 A126 35d Baseball, vert.   6.50   6.50
        Nos. 878-881 (4)   9.20   9.20
Souvenir Sheet
Perf. 14x13½
882 A126 50d Sailing   8.00   8.00
883 A126 50d Mosaic   8.00   8.00

Nos. 878-881 exist in souvenir sheets of
one. Value for 4 sheets, $22.50. The country
name on souvenir sheet of one of No. 878
appears in the margin, rather than on the
stamp itself.

Locomotives — A127

1989, Oct. 27   Perf. 14x13½, 13½x14
884 A127 20d Japan   2.25   2.25
885 A127 20d Philippines   2.25   2.25
886 A127 20d Spain, vert.   2.25   2.25
887 A127 20d India   2.25   2.25
888 A127 20d Asia   2.25   2.25
        Nos. 884-888 (5)   11.25 11.25
Souvenir Sheets
889 A127 50d Garratt, Africa   7.50   7.50
890 A127 50d Trans-Gabon,
                    vert.   7.50   7.50

Nos. 884-888 exist in souvenir sheets of one.

Ships
A128

#891, Merchant ships at sea, 16th cent.
#892, Caravels, merchant ships in harbor,
16th cent. #893, 3 merchant ships at sea, 18th
cent. #894, War ships, 18th cent. #895, 4
merchant ships, 18th cent. #896, Passenger
liner, Port of Hamburg. #897, German sailing
ship, 17th cent.

1989, Oct. 27   Perf. 14x13½
891 A128 20d multicolored   2.00   2.00
892 A128 20d multicolored   2.00   2.00
893 A128 20d multicolored   2.00   2.00
894 A128 20d multicolored   2.00   2.00
895 A128 20d multicolored   2.00   2.00
        Nos. 891-895 (5)   10.00 10.00
Souvenir Sheets
896 A128 50d multicolored   6.00   6.00
Perf. 13½x14
897 A128 50d multi, vert.   6.00   6.00

Discovery of America, 500th anniv., in 1992
(#891-895) and Hamburg, 800th anniv. (#891-
897).
Nos. 891-895 exist in souvenir sheets of
one. Value for 5 sheets, $15.

Butterflies
A129

1989, Dec. 20   Perf. 13½x14
898 A129 20d Tree bark   2.25   2.25
899 A129 20d Leaves   2.25   2.25
900 A129 20d Flowers   2.25   2.25
901 A129 20d Bird   2.25   2.25
902 A129 20d Blades of
                    grass   2.25   2.25
        Nos. 898-902 (5)   11.25 11.25
Souvenir Sheet
903 A129 100d yel, brn & multi 10.50 10.50

Nos. 898-902 exist in souvenir sheets of
one. Value for 5 sheets, $30.

25º ANIVERSÁRIO
BANCO AFRICANO DE
DESENVOLVIMIENTO

African
Development
Bank, 25th
Anniv. — A130

1989, Dec. 20   Perf. 13½x14
904 A130 25d blk, lt bl & grn 3.25   3.25

World Telecommunications
Day — A131

1989, Dec. 20   Perf. 14x13½
905 A131 60d multicolored   5.00   5.00

Souvenir Sheet
Perf. 13½x14
906 A131 100d Early Bird satel-
                lite, vert.   9.00   9.00

Christmas
A132

Paintings: No. 907, Adoration of the Magi
(detail), by Durer. No. 908, Young Virgin Mary,
by Titian. No. 909, Adoration of the King, by
Rubens. No. 910, Sistine Madonna, by
Raphael. 100d, Madonna and Child Surrounded by Garland and Boy Angels, by
Rubens.

1989, Dec. 23   Perf. 13½x14
907 A132 25d multicolored   2.50   2.50
908 A132 25d multicolored   2.50   2.50
909 A132 25d multicolored   2.50   2.50
910 A132 25d multicolored   2.50   2.50
        Nos. 907-910 (4)   10.00 10.00
Souvenir Sheet
911 A132 100d multicolored   10.00 10.00

Nos. 907-910 exist in souvenir sheets of
one. Value for 4 sheets, $13.50.

Expedition of Sir Arthur Eddington to
St. Thomas and Prince, 70th Anniv.
A133

Designs: No. 912, Albert Einstein with
Eddington. No. 913, Locomotive on Prince
Island. No. 914, Roca Sundy railway station.

1990   Litho.   Perf. 13½
912 A133 60d multicolored   5.25   5.25
913 A133 60d multicolored   5.25   5.25
914 A133 60d multicoloed   5.25   5.25
    a.   Souvenir sheet of 3, #912-
                914   18.00 18.00
        Nos. 912-914 (3)   15.75 15.75

For surcharge see No. 1295A-1295B.

Souvenir Sheet

Independence, 15th Anniv. — A134

Designs: a, Map, arms. b, Map, birds carrying envelope. c, Flag.

1990, July 12   Perf. 13½
916 A134 50d Sheet of 3, #a.-
                c.   14.00 14.00

Orchids — A135

1989, Dec. 20   Perf. 14x13½

No. 917, Eulophia guineensis. No. 918,
Ancistrochilus. No. 919, Oeceoclades macu-
lata. No. 920, Vanilla imperialis. No. 921,
Ansellia africana.
No. 922, Angraecum distichum, horiz. No.
923, Polystachya affinis, horiz.

1990, Sept. 15   Litho.   Perf. 13½
917 A135 20d multicolored   1.75   1.75
918 A135 20d multicolored   1.75   1.75
919 A135 20d multicolored   1.75   1.75
920 A135 20d multicolored   1.75   1.75
921 A135 20d multicolored   1.75   1.75
        Nos. 917-921 (5)   8.75   8.75
Souvenir Sheets
Perf. 14x13½
922 A135 50d multicolored   4.50   4.50
923 A135 50d multicolored   4.50   4.50

Expo '90, Intl. Garden and Greenery Exposition, Osaka.

Locomotives — A136

5d, Bohemia, 1923-41. 20d, W. Germany,
1951-56. No. 926, Mallet, 1896-1903. No. 927,
Russia, 1898-1910. No. 928, England, 1927-
30.
No. 929, Camden-Amboy, 1834-38. No.
930, Stockton-Darlington, 1825.

1990, Sept. 28   Perf. 14x13½
924 A136 5d multicolored   .45   .45
925 A136 20d multicolored   1.75   1.75
926 A136 25d multicolored   2.25   2.25
927 A136 25d multicolored   2.25   2.25
928 A136 25d multicolored   2.25   2.25
        Nos. 924-928 (5)   8.95   8.95
Souvenir Sheets
929 A136 50d multicolored   5.50   5.50
930 A136 50d multicolored   5.50   5.50

Souvenir Sheet

Iberoamericana '90 Philatelic
Exposition — A137

1990, Oct. 7
931 A137 300d Armas Castle   16.00 12.00

1990 World Cup
Soccer
Championships,
Italy — A138

No. 932, German team with World Cup Trophy. No. 933, 2 players with ball. No. 934, 3
players with ball. No. 935, Italian player. No.
936, US Soccer Federation emblem and team
members. No. 937, World Cup Trophy.

1990, Oct. 15   Perf. 13½
932 A138 25d multicolored   2.25   2.25
933 A138 25d multicolored   2.25   2.25
934 A138 25d multicolored   2.25   2.25
935 A138 25d multicolored   2.25   2.25
        Nos. 932-935 (4)   9.00   9.00
Souvenir Sheets
Perf. 14x13½
936 A138 50d multi, horiz.   4.50   4.50
937 A138 50d multi, horiz.   4.50   4.50

S. TOMÉ E PRÍNCIPE

BOLETUS AEREUS 1990

Db 20   Mushrooms
A139

No. 938, Boletus aereus. No. 939, Coprinus micaceus. No. 940, Pholiota spectabilis. No. 941, Krombholzia aurantiaca. No. 942, Stropharia aeruginosa.
No. 943, Hypholoma capnoides. No. 944, Pleurotus ostreatus.

1990, Nov. 2   *Perf. 13½x14*

938	A139	20d multicolored	2.00	2.00
939	A139	20d multicolored	2.00	2.00
940	A139	20d multicolored	2.00	2.00
941	A139	20d multicolored	2.00	2.00
942	A139	20d multicolored	2.00	2.00
	Nos. 938-942 (5)		10.00	10.00

Souvenir Sheets
Perf. 14x13½

943	A139	20d multicolored	6.00	6.00
944	A139	50d multicolored	6.00	6.00

Nos. 943-944 horiz. See Nos. 1014-1020.

S. TOMÉ E PRÍNCIPE

PAPILIO PARADIESA 1990

Db 25

Butterflies — A140

No. 945, Megistanis baeotus. No. 946, Ascia vamillae. No. 947, Danaus chrysippus. No. 948, Morpho menelaus. No. 949, Papilio rutulus, vert. No. 950, Papilio paradiesa.
No. 951, Parnassius clodius, vert. No. 952, Papilio macmaon, vert.

1990, Nov. 2   *Perf. 14x13½, 13½x14*

945	A140	15d multicolored	1.30	1.30
946	A140	15d multicolored	1.30	1.30
947	A140	15d multicolored	1.30	1.30
948	A140	15d multicolored	1.30	1.30
949	A140	15d multicolored	1.30	1.30
950	A140	25d multicolored	2.10	2.10
	Nos. 945-950 (6)		8.60	8.60

Souvenir Sheets

951	A140	50d multicolored	8.00	8.00
952	A140	50d multicolored	8.00	8.00

S. TOMÉ E PRÍNCIPE

NATAL · 1990

Db 25

Presenting
Gifts to the
Newborn
King — A141

Christmas: No. 954, Nativity scene. No. 955, Adoration of the Magi. No. 956, Flight into Egypt. No. 957, Adoration of the Magi, diff. No. 958, Portrait of Artist's Daughter Clara (detail), by Rubens, horiz.

1990, Nov. 30   *Perf. 13½x14*

953	A141	25d multicolored	2.25	2.25
954	A141	25d multicolored	2.25	2.25
955	A141	25d multicolored	2.25	2.25
956	A141	25d multicolored	2.25	2.25
	Nos. 953-956 (4)		9.00	9.00

Souvenir Sheets

957	A141	50d multicolored	4.75	4.75

Perf. 14x13½

958	A141	50d multicolored	4.75	4.75

Death of Rubens, 350th anniv. (#958).

Db 20

S. TOMÉ E PRÍNCIPE

DÜRER · 1990

Anniversaries
and Events
A142

No. 960, Oath of Confederation. No. 961, Pointed roof. No. 962, William Tell statue, vert. No. 963, Brandenburg Gate. No. 964, Penny Black. No. 965, 100d bank note.

1990, Dec. 15   *Perf. 13½x14*

959	A142	20d multicolored	1.75	1.75

Souvenir Sheets
Perf. 14x13½, 13½x14 (#962, 964)

960	A142	50d multicolored	4.50	4.50
961	A142	50d multicolored	4.50	4.50
962	A142	50d multicolored	4.50	4.50
963	A142	50d multicolored	4.50	4.50
964	A142	50d multicolored	4.50	4.50
965	A142	50d multicolored	4.50	4.50

Swiss Confederation, 700th anniv. (#959-962). Brandenburg Gate, 200th anniv. (#963). First postage stamp, 150th anniv. (#964). Independence of St. Thomas and Prince, 15th anniv. (#965).

S. TOMÉ E PRÍNCIPE   Db 20

100º ANIVERSARIO DA MORTE DE VAN GOGH · 1990

Paintings — A143

No. 966, The Bathers, by Renoir. No. 967, Girl Holding Mirror for Nude, by Picasso. No. 968, Nude, by Rubens. No. 969, Descent from the Cross (detail), by Rubens. No. 970, Nude, by Titian. No. 971, Landscape, by Durer. No. 972, Rowboats, by Van Gogh. No. 973, Nymphs, by Titian. No. 974, Bather, by Titian. No. 975, Postman Joseph Roulin (detail), by Van Gogh. No. 976, The Abduction of the Daughters of Leucippus, by Rubens. No. 977, Nude, by Titian, diff.

1990, Dec. 15   *Perf. 14x13½, 13½x14*

966	A143	10d multi	1.05	1.05
967	A143	10d multi, vert.	1.05	1.05
968	A143	10d multi, vert.	1.05	1.05
969	A143	10d multi, vert.	1.05	1.05
970	A143	10d multi, vert.	1.05	1.05
971	A143	20d multi	2.10	2.10
972	A143	20d multi, vert.	2.10	2.10
973	A143	25d multi, vert.	2.40	2.40
974	A143	25d multi, vert.	2.40	2.40
	Nos. 966-974 (9)		14.25	14.25

Souvenir Sheets
Perf. 13½x14

975	A143	50d multi, vert.	8.00	8.00
976	A143	50d multi, vert.	8.00	8.00
977	A143	50d multi, vert.	8.00	8.00

Rubens, 350th anniv. of death (Nos. 968-969, 976). Titian, 500th anniv. of death (Nos. 970, 973-974, 977). Van Gogh, centennial of death (Nos. 972, 975).
See No. 958 for other souvenir sheet for Rubens death anniv.

S. TOMÉ E PRÍNCIPE

LAGARTICHA 1991

Db 1

Flora and Fauna — A144

Designs: 1d, Gecko. 5d, Cobra. 10d, No. 980, Sea turtle. No. 981, Fresh water turtle. No. 982, Civet. 70d, Civet in tree. No. 984, Civet with young. No. 985, Civet in den.
Psittacus erithacus: 80d, In tree, vert. 100d, On branch with wings spread, vert. 250d, Feeding young, vert. No. 989, Three in flight, vert.

1991, Feb. 2   *Perf. 14x13½*

978	A144	1d multicolored	.25	.25
979	A144	5d multicolored	.25	.25
980	A144	10d multicolored	.25	.25
981	A144	50d multicolored	.70	.70
982	A144	50d multicolored	.70	.70
983	A144	70d multicolored	1.20	1.20
984	A144	75d multicolored	1.20	1.20
985	A144	75d multicolored	1.20	1.20

Perf. 13½x14

986	A144	80d multicolored	1.30	1.30
987	A144	100d multicolored	1.50	1.50
988	A144	250d multicolored	4.00	4.00
989	A144	500d multicolored	8.00	8.00
	Nos. 978-989 (12)		20.55	20.55

Souvenir Sheets

990	A144	500d multicolored Orchid, vert.	9.00	9.00
991	A144	500d multicolored Rose, vert.	9.00	9.00

See Nos. 1054I-1054N. For surcharges see Nos. 1170H-1170I, 1170L-1170M, 1307A.

S. TOMÉ E PRÍNCIPE   Db 75

COMBOIO 1991

Locomotives — A145

1991, May 7   *Perf. 14x13½, 13½x14*

992	A145	75d shown	1.00	1.00
993	A145	75d North America, vert.	1.00	1.00
994	A145	75d Germany, vert.	1.00	1.00
995	A145	75d New Delhi, vert.	1.00	1.00
996	A145	75d Brazil, vert.	1.00	1.00
997	A145	200d Two leaving terminal	2.50	2.50
	Nos. 992-997 (6)		7.50	7.50

Souvenir Sheets

998	A145	500d Engine 120, vert.	7.00	7.00
999	A145	500d Engine 151-001	7.00	7.00

Db 75

S. TOMÉ E PRÍNCIPE

PSITTACULA KUHLII 1991

Birds — A146

No. 1000, Psittacula kuhlii. No. 1001, Plydolophus rosaceus. No. 1002, Falco tinnunculus. No. 1003, Platycercus palliceps. No. 1004, Marcrocercus aracanga.
No. 1005, Ramphastos culmenatus. No. 1006, Strix nyctea.

1991, July 8   *Perf. 13½x14*

1000	A146	75d multicolored	1.20	1.20
1001	A146	75d multicolored	1.20	1.20
1002	A146	75d multicolored	1.20	1.20
1003	A146	75d multicolored	1.20	1.20
1004	A146	200d multicolored	3.25	3.25
	Nos. 1000-1004 (5)		8.05	8.05

Souvenir Sheets

1005	A146	500d multicolored	14.00	9.25
1006	A146	500d multicolored	9.25	9.25

Db 75

S. TOMÉ E PRÍNCIPE

RUBENS 1991

Paintings
A147

50d, Venus and Cupid, by Titian. #1008, Horse's Head (detail), by Rubens. #1009, Child's face (detail), by Rubens. 100d, Spanish Woman, by Picasso. 200d, Man with Christian Flag, by Titian. #1012, Study of a Negro, by Rubens. #1013, Madonna and Child, by Raphael.

1991, July 31

1007	A147	50d multicolored	.70	.70
1008	A147	75d multicolored	1.05	1.05
1009	A147	75d multicolored	1.05	1.05
1010	A147	100d multicolored	1.60	1.60
1011	A147	200d multicolored	3.25	3.25
	Nos. 1007-1011 (5)		7.65	7.65

Souvenir Sheets

1012	A147	500d multicolored	7.75	7.75
1013	A147	500d multicolored	7.75	7.75

Mushroom Type of 1990

No. 1014, Clitocybe geotropa. No. 1015, Lepiota procera. 75d, Boletus granulatus. 125d, Coprinus comatus. 200d, Amanita rubescens.
No. 1019, Armillariella mellea. No. 1020, Nictalis parasitica, horiz.

1991, Aug. 30

1014	A139	50d multicolored	.70	.70
1015	A139	50d multicolored	.70	.70
1016	A139	75d multicolored	1.05	1.05
1017	A139	125d multicolored	1.75	1.75
1018	A139	200d multicolored	3.25	3.25
	Nos. 1014-1018 (5)		7.45	7.45

Souvenir Sheets

1019	A139	500d multicolored	7.75	7.75

Perf. 14x13½

1020	A139	500d multicolored	7.75	7.75

Db 50

S. TOMÉ E PRÍNCIPE

Flowers
A148

No. 1022, Zan tedeschia elliotiana. No. 1023, Cyrtanthes pohliana. No. 1024, Phalaenopsis lueddemanniana. No. 1025, Haemanthus katharinae. 500d, Arundina graminifolia.

1991, Sept. 9   *Perf. 13½x14*

1021	A148	50d shown	.75	.75
1022	A148	50d multicolored	.75	.75
1023	A148	100d multicolored	1.60	1.60
1024	A148	100d multicolored	1.60	1.60
1025	A148	200d multicolored	3.50	3.50
	Nos. 1021-1025 (5)		8.20	8.20

Souvenir Sheet

1026	A148	500d multicolored	7.75	7.75

Souvenir Sheet

S. TOMÉ E PRÍNCIPE
BARCELONA
SEDE DOS XXV JOGOS
OLÍMPICOS DE VERÃO
XV CERTAME
FILATÉLICO
IBEROAMERICANO
BARCELONA
11 A 20 OUTUBRO 1991
TOMÉ E PRÍNCIPE
800 Db

Iberoamericano '92 Intl. Philatelic
Exhibition — A149

1991, Oct. 11   Litho.   *Perf. 14x13½*

1027	A149	800d multicolored	6.25	6.25

Discovery of America, 500th Anniv. (in 1992) — A150

No. 1028, Columbus. No. 1029, Sailing ship. No. 1030, Sailing ship, diff. No. 1031, Landing in New World. No. 1032, Pointing the way. No. 1033, Columbus' fleet, horiz.

1991, Oct. 12   **Perf. 13½x14**
1028	A150	50d multicolored	
1029	A150	50d multicolored	
1030	A150	75d multicolored	
1031	A150	125d multicolored	
1032	A150	200d multicolored	
	Nos. 1028-1032	10.00	

Souvenir Sheet
Perf. 14x13½
| 1033 | A150 | 500d multicolored | 10.00 |

Butterflies — A151

1991, Oct. 16   **Perf. 14x13½**
| 1034 | A151 | 125d Limentis popul | 3.50 3.50 |
| 1035 | A151 | 125d Pavon inachis io | 3.50 3.50 |

Souvenir Sheet
Perf. 13½x14
| 1036 | A151 | 500d Zerynthia polyxena | 7.25 7.25 |

Phila Nippon '91.

1991, Nov. 15   **Perf. 14x13½**
1037	A151	125d Macaon papilio machaon	2.00 2.00
1038	A151	125d Gran pavon	2.00 2.00
1039	A151	125d Pavon inachis io, diff.	2.00 2.00
1040	A151	125d Artia caja	2.00 2.00
	Nos. 1037-1040 (4)	8.00 8.00

Souvenir Sheet
Perf. 13½x14
| 1041 | A151 | 500d Unnamed butterfly, vert. | 8.00 8.00 |

Christmas.

Landmarks — A152

Landmarks of France: No. 1042, Ile de France, vert. No. 1043, Chenonceau Castle. No. 1044, Azay-le-Rideau Castle. No. 1045, Chambord Castle. No. 1046, Chaumont Castle. No. 1047, Fountainebleau Palace.

Perf. 13½x14, 14x13½
1991, Nov. 15
| 1042-1047 | A152 | 25d Set of 6 | 2.50 2.50 |

Souvenir Sheet
| 1048 | A152 | 500d Paris map, 1615 | 7.50 7.50 |

French National Exposition.

Souvenir Sheet

Fauna — A153

Animals and birds: a, Weasel, monkey. b, Civet, rats. c, Goat, cow. d, Rabbits, wildcat. e, Parrot, black bird. f, White bird, multicolored bird.

1991, Nov. 15   **Perf. 14x13½**
| 1049 | A153 | 25d Sheet of 6, #a.- f. | 8.00 8.00 |

French National Exposition.

Express Mail Service from St. Thomas and Prince — A154

1991   **Litho.**   **Perf. 14**
| 1050 | A154 | 3000d multicolored | 16.00 16.00 |

Souvenir Sheets

1991 Intl. Olympic Committee Session, Birmingham — A154a

Designs: No. 1050A, IOC emblem, Birmingham Session. No. 1050B, 1998 Winter Olympics emblem, Nagano. No. 1050C, 1998 Winter Olympics mascot.

1992   **Litho.**   **Perf. 14**
1050A	A154a	800d multi	10.00 10.00
1050B	A154a	800d multi	10.00 10.00
1050C	A154a	800d multi	10.00 10.00
	Nos. 1050A-1050C (3)	30.00 30.00

Souvenir Sheet

IBEREX '91 — A154b

1992
| 1050D | A154b | 800d multi | 10.00 10.00 |

Souvenir Sheets

1992 Winter Olympics, Albertville — A154c

Olympic medals.

1992   **Set of 4, a.-d.**
| 1050E | A154c | 50d multi | 40.00 25.00 |

No. 1050E exists as four souvenir sheets with pictures of different medalists in sheet margins: a., Blanca Fernandez, Spain; b., Alberto Tomba, Italy; c., Mark Kirchner, Germany; d., Torgny Mogren, Norway.

1992 Summer Olympics, Barcelona A154d

View of earth from space with: No. 1050F, High jumper. No. 1050G, Roller hockey player. No. 1050H, Equestrian. No. 1050I, Kayaker. No. 1050J, Weight lifter. No. 1050K, Archer. No. 1050L, Michael Jordan, horiz.

1992
| 1050F-1050K | A154d | 50d Set of 6 | 7.50 7.50 |

Souvenir Sheet
| 1050L | A154d | 50d multicolored | 8.00 8.00 |

Whales — A155

Designs: No. 1051, Orcinus orca. No. 1052, Orcinus orca, four on surface of water. No. 1053, Pseudoraca crassidens. No. 1054, Pseudoraca crassidens, three under water.

1992   **Litho.**   **Perf. 14**
| 1051-1054 | A155 | 450d Set of 4 | 6.00 6.00 |

World Wildlife Fund.

Visit of Pope John Paul II — A155a

c, Flags, Pope. d, Church with two steeples. e, Church, diff.
f, Pope, vert. g, Church, blue sky, vert. h, Church, closer view, vert.

1992, Apr. 19   **Litho.**   **Perf. 14**
Sheets of 4
| 1054A | A155a | 200d #d.-e., 2 #c | 10.00 10.00 |
| 1054B | A155a | 200d #g.-h., 2 #f | 10.00 10.00 |

Miniature Sheets

Pope John Paul II and Flower — A155c

Pope John Paul II and Bird — A155d

No. 1054C — Flower and Pope looking: t, Straight ahead. u, To right, three-quarters. v, Slightly to left. w, To right, profile.
No. 1054D — Bird and Pope looking: x, Straight ahead. y, To right, three-quarters. z, Slightly to left. aa, To right, profile.
No. 1054E — Flower, diff. and Pope looking: ab, Straight ahead. ac, To right, three-quarters. ad, Slightly to left. ae, To right, profile.
No. 1054F — Bird, diff. and Pope looking: af, Straight ahead. ag, To right, three-quarters. ah, Slightly to left. ai, To right, profile.
No. 1054G — Flower, diff. and Pope looking: aj, Straight ahead. ak, To right, three-quarters. al, Slightly to left. am, To right, profile.
No. 1054H — Bird, diff. and Pope looking: an, Straight ahead. ao, To right, three-quarters. ap, Slightly to left. aq, To right, profile.

1992, Apr. 19   **Perf. 13¾x14**
1054C	A155c	120d Sheet of 4, #t-w	— —
1054D	A155d	120d Sheet of 4, #x-aa	— —
1054E	A155c	150d Sheet of 4, #ab-ae	— —
1054F	A155d	150d Sheet of 4, #af-ai	— —
1054G	A155c	180d Sheet of 4, #aj-am	— —
1054H	A155d	250d Sheet of 4, #an-aq	— —
	Set of 6 sheets	85.00	

For surcharges see Nos. 1170C-1170D.

Flora and Fauna Type of 1991

Designs: No. 1054I, 1000d, Brown & white bird, vert. No. 1054J, 1500d, Yellow flower, vert. No. 1054K, 2000d, Red flower, vert. No. 1054L, 2500d, Black bird, vert.
No. 1054M, Sea turtle. No. 1054N, Yellow flowers.

1992, Apr. 19   *Perf. 14*
1054I-1054L A144 Set of 4   35.00 35.00
Souvenir Sheets
1054M A144 800d multi   — —
1054N A144 800d multi   — —

UN Conference on Environmental Development, Rio — A155b

Designs: 65d, Rain forest. 110d, Walruses. 150d, Raptor. 200d, Tiger. 275d, Elephants. Each 800d: No. 1054T, Panda, horiz. No. 1054U, Zebras, horiz.

1992, June 6   Litho.   *Perf. 14*
1054O-1054S A155b Set of 5 10.00
Souvenir Sheets
1054T-1054U A155b Set of 2 20.00

Souvenir Sheet

Olymphilex '92 — A156

Olympic athletes: a, Women's running. b, Women's gymnastics. c, Earvin "Magic" Johnson.

1992, July 29
1055 A156 300d Sheet of 3,
      #a.-c.   10.00 10.00

Mushrooms
A157

75d, Leccinum ocabrum. 100d, Amanita spissa, horiz. 125d, Strugilomyces floccopus. 200d, Suillus luteus. 500d, Agaricus siluaticus. #1061, Amanita pantherma, horiz. #1062, Agaricus campestre.

1992, Sept. 5   *Perf. 14*
1056 A157 75d multicolored   .70   .70
1057 A157 100d multicolored   .90   .90
1058 A157 125d multicolored   1.05 1.05
1059 A157 200d multicolored   1.75 1.75
1060 A157 500d multicolored   5.00 5.00
   Nos. 1056-1060 (5)   9.40 9.40
Souvenir Sheets
Perf. 14x13½, 13½x14
1061 A157 1000d multicolored 10.00 10.00
1062 A157 1000d multicolored 10.00 10.00

Birds — A158

Designs: 75d, Paradisea regie, pipra rupicole. 100d, Trogon pavonis. 125d, Paradisea apoda. 200d, Pavocriotctus. 500d, Ramphatos maximus. No. 1068, Woodpecker. No. 1069, Picus major.

1992, Sept. 15   *Perf. 14*
1063 A158 75d multicolored   .55   .55
1064 A158 100d multicolored   .80   .80
1065 A158 125d multicolored   .95   .95
1066 A158 200d multicolored   1.50 1.50
1067 A158 500d multicolored   3.75 3.75
   Nos. 1063-1067 (5)   7.55 7.55
Souvenir Sheets
Perf. 13½x14
1068 A158 1000d multicolored 9.00 9.00
1069 A158 1000d multicolored 9.00 9.00

Marcelo da Veiga (1892-1976),
Writer — A159

Designs: a, 10d. b, 40d. c, 50d. d, 100d.

1992, Oct. 3   *Perf. 13½*
1070 A159 Sheet of 4, #a.-d.   4.00 4.00

Locomotives — A160

Designs: 75d, 100d, 125d, 200d, 500d, Various locomotives. No. 1076, Steam train arriving at station. No. 1077, Engineer, stoker in locomotive cab.

1992, Oct. 3   *Perf. 14x13½*
1071 A160 75d black   .65   .65
1072 A160 100d black   .80   .80
1073 A160 125d black   1.05 1.05
1074 A160 200d black   1.75 1.75
1075 A160 500d black   5.00 5.00
   Nos. 1071-1075 (5)   9.25 9.25
Souvenir Sheets
1076 A160 1000d black   9.00 9.00
1077 A160 1000d black   9.00 9.00

Butterflies and Moths — A161

75d, Chelonia purpurea. 100d, Hoetera philocteles. 125d, Attacus pavonia major. 200d, Ornithoptera urvilliana. 500d, Acherontia atropos. No. 1083, Peridromia amphinome, vert. No. 1084, Uramia riphacus, vert.

1992, Oct. 18   *Perf. 14x13½*
1078 A161 75d multicolored   .60   .60
1079 A161 100d multicolored   .90   .90
1080 A161 125d multicolored   1.10 1.10

1081 A161 200d multicolored   1.75 1.75
1082 A161 500d multicolored   5.00 5.00
   Nos. 1078-1082 (5)   9.35 9.35
Souvenir Sheets
Perf. 13½x14
1083 A161 1000d multicolored 9.00 9.00
1084 A161 1000d multicolored 9.00 9.00

1992, 1996 Summer Olympics,
Barcelona and Atlanta — A162

50d, Wind surfing. No. 1086, Wrestling. No. 1087, Women's 4x100 meters relay. No. 1088, Swimming. No. 1089, Equestrian, vert. No. 1090, Field hockey. No. 1091, Men's 4x100 meters relay, vert. No. 1092, Mascots for Barcelona and Atlanta. No. 1093, Opening ceremony, Barcelona.
No. 1094, Atlanta '96 Emblem, vert. No. 1095, Archer lighting Olympic Flame with flaming arrow, vert. No. 1096, Transfer of Olympic Flag, closing ceremony, vert. No. 1097, Gymnastics. No. 1098, Tennis players.

1992, Oct. 1   Litho.   *Perf. 14*
1085 A162 50d multicolored   .65   .65
1086 A162 300d multicolored   2.00 2.00
1087 A162 300d multicolored   2.00 2.00
1088 A162 300d multicolored   2.00 2.00
1089 A162 300d multicolored   2.00 2.00
1090 A162 300d multicolored   2.00 2.00
1091 A162 300d multicolored   2.00 2.00
1092 A162 300d multicolored   2.00 2.00
1093 A162 300d multicolored   2.00 2.00
   Nos. 1085-1093 (9)   16.65 16.65
Souvenir Sheets
1094 A162 800d multicolored   9.00 9.00
1095 A162 1000d multicolored   7.00 7.00
1096 A162 1000d multicolored   7.00 7.00
Perf. 13½
1097 A162 1000d multicolored   7.25 7.25
Perf. 14
1098 A162 1000d multicolored   7.25 7.25

Butterflies
A163

Designs: No. 1099, White butterfly. No. 1100, Black and orange butterfly. No. 1101, Pink flower, black, white, red and blue butterfly. No. 1102, Black and white butterfly on right side of flower stem. No. 1103, Yellow and black butterfly. 2000d, Iris flower, black butterfly wing, horiz.

1993, May 26   Litho.   *Perf. 14*
1099-1103 A163 500d Set of 5   18.00 18.00
Souvenir Sheet
1104 A163 2000d multi   16.00 16.00

Flowers
A164

No. 1105, Fucinho de porco. No. 1106, Heliconia. No. 1107, Gravo nacional. No. 1108, Tremessura. No. 1109, Anturius. No. 1110, Girassol.

1993, June 18
1105 A164 500d multicolored   3.25 3.25
1106 A164 500d multicolored   3.25 3.25
1107 A164 500d multicolored   3.25 3.25
1108 A164 500d multicolored   3.25 3.25
1109 A164 500d multicolored   3.25 3.25
   Nos. 1105-1109 (5)   16.25 16.25
Souvenir Sheet
1110 A164 2000d multicolored   14.00 14.00

Miniature Sheet

Union of Portuguese Speaking
Capitals — A165

Designs: a, 100d, Emblem. b, 150d, Grotto. c, 200d, Statue of Christ the Redeemer, Rio de Janeiro. d, 250d, Skyscraper. e, 250d, Monument. f, 300d, Building with pointed domed roof. g, 350d, Municipal building. h, 400d, Square tower. i, 500d, Residence, flag, truck.

1993, July 30
1111 A165 Sheet of 9, #a.-i.   16.00 16.00
   Brasiliana '93.

Birds — A166

Designs: No. 1112, Cecia. No. 1113, Suisui. No. 1114, Falcon. No. 1115, Parrot. No. 1116, Heron.
No. 1117, Macaw, toucan, horiz.

1993, June 15   Litho.   *Perf. 14*
1112-1116 A166 500d Set of 5   17.50 17.50
Souvenir Sheet
1117 A166 1000d multi   8.50 8.50

Dinosaurs — A167

No. 1118, Lystrosaurus. No. 1119, Patagosaurus. No. 1120, Shonisaurus ictiosaurios, vert. No. 1121, Dilophosaurus, vert. No. 1122, Dicraeosaurus, vert. No. 1123, Tyrannosaurus rex, vert.

1993, July 21
1118-1123 A167 500d Set of 6   19.00 19.00
Souvenir Sheets
1124 A167 1000d Protoavis   9.00 9.00
1125 A167 1000d Brachi-
        osaurus   9.00 9.00

Mushrooms
A168

No. 1126, Agrocybe aegerita. No. 1127, Psalliota arvensis. No. 1128, Coprinus comatus. No. 1129, Hygrophorus psittacinus. No. 1130, Amanita caesarea.
No. 1131, Ramaria aurea. No. 1132, Pluteus murinus, horiz.

1993, May 25   **Litho.**   **Perf. 14**
1126-1130 A168   800d Set of
      5   20.00 20.00
Souvenir Sheets
1131-1132 A168 2000d Set of
      2   20.00 20.00

Locomotives — A169

Nos. 1133-1137, Various views of small diesel locomotive.
Nos. 1138-1139, Various steam locomotives, vert.

1993, June 16
1133-1137 A169   800d Set of
      5   20.00 20.00
Souvenir Sheets
1138-1139 A169 2000d Set of
      2   24.00 24.00

1994 World Cup Soccer
Championships, U.S. — A170

Designs: No. 1140, Team photo. No. 1141, Players in white uniforms. No. 1142, Two players in yellow uniforms, player in red, white and blue uniform. No. 1143, Players with yellow shirts and green shorts celebrating. No. 1144, Two players in red and white uniforms, one player in red, white and blue uniform. No. 1145, Player in yellow and blue uniform, player in red, white and blue uniform. No. 1146, Two players and official. No. 1147, Two players, vert.
No. 1148, Fans, faces painted as flags. No. 1149, Stylized player.

1993, July 6
1140-1147 A170   800d Set of
      8   25.00 25.00
Souvenir Sheets
1148-1149 A170 2000d Set of
      2   15.00 15.00

UPU Congress — A171

1993, Aug. 16
1150 A171 1000d shown   5.25   4.00
Souvenir Sheet
1151 A171 2000d Ship   9.00   9.00

1996 Summer Olympics,
Atlanta — A172

Each 800d: No. 1152, Fencing. No. 1153, Women's running. No. 1154, Water polo. No. 1155, Soccer. No. 1156, Men's running. No. 1157, Boxing. No. 1158, Wrestling. No. 1159, High jump.
Each 2000d: No. 1160, Shooting, vert. No. 1161, Sailing, vert. No. 1162, Equestrian, vert. No. 1163, Kayak, vert.

1993, Oct. 19   **Litho.**   **Perf. 13½x14**
1152-1159 A172   Set of 8   35.00 35.00
Souvenir Sheets
1160-1163 A172   Set of 4   35.00 35.00

1994 World Cup Soccer
Championships, U.S. — A173

1994, Jan. 12   **Perf. 14**
1164 A173 500d blk, bl & red   3.00 3.00
Issued in miniature sheets of 4.

Movie
Stars — A174

Each 10d: No. 1165a, James Dean. b, Bette Davis. c, Elvis Presley. d, Humphrey Bogart. e, John Lennon. f, Marilyn Monroe. g, Birthday cake. h, Audrey Hepburn.
Each 10d: No. 1166a-1166i, Various portraits of Elvis Presley.
Each 10d: No. 1167a-1167i, Various portraits of Marilyn Monroe.
Each 50d: No. 1168, James Dean, diff. No. 1169, Elvis Presley, diff.
No. 1169A: Marilyn Monroe.

1994, Feb. 15
1165 A174   Sheet of 8, #a.-h.   8.00   8.00
Sheets of 9, #a-i
1166-1167 A174   Set of 2   8.00   8.00
Souvenir Sheets
1168-1169 A174   Set of 2   8.00   8.00
1169A A174   2000d multi   15.00 15.00

Souvenir Sheet

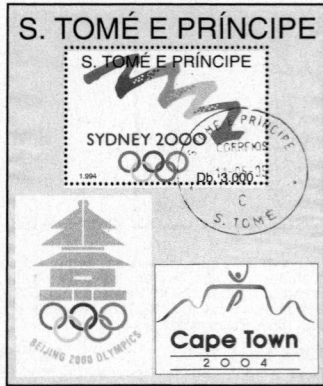

Sydney 2000 — A175

1994, June 8
1170 A175 3000d multicolored   15.00 15.00

Signing of
Argel
Accord,
20th Anniv.
A175a

1994   **Litho.**   **Perf. 14**
1170A A175a 250d multi   4.25   4.25

Nos. 978, 979 Surcharged

d

Nos. 856, 978-979 Surcharged

e

Nos. 856-858, 860 Surcharged

f - Type I

Two Types of Type "f":
Type I — "5" lacks ornaments.
Type II — "5" has an ornament on the tail.
No. 1170M exists in two types:
Type I — With a vertical comma composed of a dot and tail.
Type II — With a diagonally elongated dot as the comma.

Surcharge Typo.
1995, Mar. 2, 1996?
Printing Methods and Perfs as Before
1170B A123p(f)   100d on 25d
           #860   10.00   .50
1170C A155c   200d on 120d
           #1054C   —   —
o.-r.   any single   —   —

1170D A155d 300d on 120d		
#1054D	—	—
s.-v. any single	—	—
1170E A123p(e) 350d on 50c		
#856	—	—
1170F A123p(fI) 350d on 50c		
#856	—	—
1170G A123p(fII) 350d on 50c		
#856	—	—
1170H A144(e) 350d on 1d		
#978	10.00	1.00
1170I A144(d) 350d on 1d		
#978	10.00	1.00
1170J A123p(fI) 350d on 1d		
#857	—	—
1170K A123p(fII) 350d on 1d		
#857	—	—
1170L A144(d) 400d on 5d		
#979	10.00	1.00
1170M A144(e) 400d on 5d		
#979	10.00	1.00
1170N A123p(f) 400d on 5d		
#858	—	—

Butterflies
A176

No. 1171, Timeleoa maqulata-formosana. No. 1172, Morfho cypris. No. 1173, Thais polixena. No. 1174, Argema moenas. No. 1175, Leptocircus megus-ennius.
2000d, Armandia lidderdalei.

1995, May 10   **Litho.**   **Perf. 14**
1171-1175 A176 1200d Set of
      5   12.50 12.50
Souvenir Sheet
1176   A176 2000d multi   8.00   8.00

Flowering
Fruits, Orchids
A177

Flowering fruits: No. 1177, 350d, Pessego. No. 1178, 370d, Untue. No. 1179, 380d, Pitanga. No. 1180, 800d, Morango. No. 1181, 1000d, Izaquente.
Orchids, each 2000d: No. 1182, Max. houtteana. No. 1183, Max. marginata.

1995, June 6
1177-1181 A177   Set of 5   14.00 14.00
Souvenir Sheets
1182-1183 A177   Set of 2   16.00 16.00

Mushrooms
A179

Designs, each 1000d: No. 1185, Lactarius deliciosus. No. 1186, Marasmius oreades. No. 1187, Boletus edulis. No. 1188, Boletus aurantiacus. No. 1189, Lepiota procera. No. 1190, Cortinarius praestans.
Each 2000d: No. 1191, Chantharellus cibarius. No. 1192, Lycoperdon pyriforme, horiz.

1995, Nov. 2 **Litho.** *Perf. 14*
1185-1190 A179 Set of 6 14.00 14.00
Souvenir Sheets
1191-1192 A179 Set of 2 14.00 14.00

UN, 50th Anniv. — A180

Traditional handicrafts made from palm leaves: No. 1193, 350d, Baskets. No. 1194, 350d, Brooms. No. 1195, 400d, Lamp shades. No. 1196, 500d, Klissakli, mussuá. No. 1197, 500d, Pávu. No. 1198, 1000d, Vámplêgá.

1995, June 20 **Litho.** *Perf. 13½x14*
1193-1198 A180 Set of 6 7.50 7.50

Trains — A181

Locomotives, each 1000d: No. 1199, Steam, "#100." No. 1200, Steam, "#778." No. 1201, G. Thommen steam. No. 1202, Steam "#119," vert. No. 1203, Mt. Washington cog railway. No. 1204, Electric.
Each 2000d: No. 1205, Electric train on snow-covered mountain, vert. No. 1206, Electric train car with door open, vert.

1995, July 24 *Perf. 14x13½, 13½x14*
1199-1204 A181 Set of 6 22.50 22.50
Souvenir Sheets
1205-1206 A181 Set of 2 19.00 19.00
See Nos. 1280-1286.

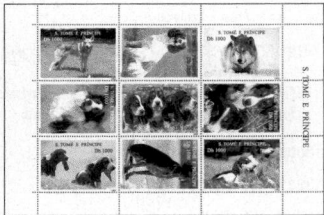

Dogs & Cats — A182

No. 1207, each 1000d: Various dogs. b, d, f, h, vert.
No. 1208, each 1000d: Various cats. b, d, f, h, vert.
Each 2000d: No. 1209, St. Bernard, German shepherd. No. 1210, Beagle, vert. No. 1211, Cat, kittens. No. 1212, Kitten on top of mother, vert.

1995, Aug. 12 *Perf. 14*
Sheets of 9, #a-i
1207-1208 A182 Set of 2 45.00 45.00
Souvenir Sheets
1209-1212 A182 Set of 5 37.50 37.50

New Year 1996 (Year of the Rat) A183

Various species of rats, mice, each 100d.

1995, Oct. 28
1213 A183 Sheet of 9, #a.-i. 5.50 5.50

Motion Pictures, Cent. — A184

Movie posters, each 1000d: No. 1214: a, Gone with the Wind. b, Stagecoach. c, Tarzan and His Mate. d, Oregon Trail. e, The Oklahoma Kid. f, King Kong. g, A Lady Fights Back. h, Steamboat Around the Bend. i, Wee Willie Winkie.
Each 2000d: No. 1215, Bring 'Em Back Alive. No. 1216 Indian chief.

1995, May 10 **Litho.** *Perf. 14*
1214 A184 Sheet of 9, #a.-i. 15.00 15.00
Souvenir Sheets
1215-1216 A184 Set of 2 15.00 15.00

Horses — A185

Designs: No. 1217, Various horses, each 1000d.
Each 2000d: No. 1218, Painting of Indian on horse, wild horses, horiz. No. 1219, City scene, horses, carriage, horiz.

1995, May 16
1217 A185 Sheet of 9, #a.-i. 16.00 16.00
Souvenir Sheets
1218-1219 A185 Set of 2 16.00 16.00
Nos. 1218-1219 each contain one 50x35mm stamp.

Souvenir Sheet

Euro '96, European Soccer Championships, Great Britain — A186

1995, July 2 *Perf. 13½x14*
1220 A186 2000d multicolored 7.50 7.50

Souvenir Sheet

Protection of World's Endangered Species — A187

1995, July 6 *Perf. 14*
1221 A187 2000d multicolored 8.00 8.00

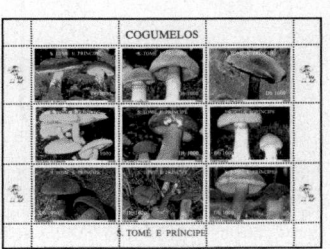

Mushrooms — A188

Designs, each 1000d: No. 1222a, Xerocomus rubellus. b, Rozites caperata. c, Cortinarius violaceus. d, Pholiota flammans. e, Lactarius volemus. f, Cortinarius (yellow). g, Cartinarius (blue). h, Higroforo. i, Boletus chrysenteron.
Each 2000d: No. 1223, Amanita muscaria, vert. No. 1224, Russula cyanoxantha, vert.

1995, Nov. 2
1222 A188 Sheet of 9, #a.-i. 18.00 18.00
Souvenir Sheets
1223-1224 A188 Set of 2 14.00 14.00

Details or Entire Paintings — A189

No. 1225, each 1000d: a, Aurora and Cefalo. b, Madonna and Child with St. John as a Boy. c, Romulus and Remus. d, Lamentation over the Dead Christ. e, Vison of All Saints Day. f, Perseus and Andromeda. g, The Scent. h, The Encounter in Lyon. i, The Art School of Rubens-Bildern.
Each 2000d: No. 1226, Statue of Ceres. No. 1227, Flight into Egypt, horiz.
All but #1225g (Jan Brueghel the Elder) and 1225i are by Rubens.

1995, Sept. 27 **Litho.** *Perf. 14*
1225 A189 Sheet of 9, #a.-i. 18.00 18.00
Souvenir Sheets
1226-1227 A189 Set of 2 18.00 18.00

Greenpeace, 25th Anniv. — A190

Designs: No. 1237, Potto. No. 1238, Iguana. No. 1239, Tiger. No. 1240, Lion. 50d, Elephant, horiz.

1996, Aug. 5 **Litho.** *Perf. 14*
1237-1240 A190 50d Set of 4 10.00 10.00
Souvenir Sheet
1241 A190 50d multicolored 4.25 4.25

Dogs & Cats — A191

Dogs — A191a

Nos. 1242a-1242i: Various pictures of dogs with cats, kittens.

Nos. 1243a-1243i: Various close-up pictures of different breeds of dogs.

No. 1244, Labrador retriever. No. 1245, Bird, woman's eye, vert. No. 1246, Two kittens. No. 1247, Collie, vert. No. 1248, Poodle, vert. No. 1249, Pit bull terrier, vert. No. 1250, Brown and white terrier, vert.

1995, Aug. 12　　Litho.　　Perf. 14
Sheets of 9, #a-i
1242	A191	1000d multi		22.50	22.50
1243	A191a	1000d multi		22.50	22.50

Souvenir Sheets
1244	A191	2000d multi		6.50	6.50
1245	A191	2000d multi		6.50	6.50
1246	A191	2000d multi		6.50	6.50
1247	A191	2000d multi		6.50	6.50
1248	A191a	2000d multi		6.50	6.50
1249	A191a	2000d multi		6.50	6.50
1250	A191a	2000d multi		6.50	6.50

Orchids
A192

No. 1251, each 1000d: a, Findlayanum. b, Stan. c, Cruentum. d, Trpla suavis. e, Lowianum. f, Gratiosissimum. g, Cyrtorchis monteirae. h, Sarcanthus birmanicus. i, Loddigesii.

Each 2000d: No. 1252, Barkeria Skinneri. No. 1253, Dendrobium nobile.

1995, Sept. 12
1251	A192	Sheet of 9, #a.-i.		19.00	19.00

Souvenir Sheets
1252-1253	A192	Set of 2		16.00	16.00

Paintings, Drawings by Durer,
Rubens — A193

Designs, each 750d: No. 1254, Soldier on Horseback, by Durer, vert. No. 1255, Archangel St. Michael Slaying Satan, by Rubens, vert. No. 1256, Nursing Madonna in Half Length, by Durer, vert. No. 1257, Head of a Deer, by Durer, vert. No. 1258, View of Innsbruck from the North, by Durer. No. 1259, Madonna Nursing on a Grassy Bench, by Durer, vert. No. 1260, Helene Fourment and Her Children, by Rubens, vert. No. 1261, Adam and Eve, by Durer, vert.

Each 2000d: No. 1262, A Young Hare, by Durer, vert. No. 1263, Mills on a River Bank,

by Durer. No. 1264, Holy Family with a Basket, by Rubens, vert. No. 1265, The Annunciation, by Rubens, vert.

1995, Dec. 16　　Litho.　　Perf. 14
1254-1261	A193	Set of 8		16.00	16.00

Souvenir Sheets
1262-1265	A193	Set of 4		32.50	32.50

Christmas.

Independence, 20th Anniv. — A194

1995, July 12　　Litho.　　Perf. 13½
1266	A194	350d multicolored		4.50	1.90

1996 Summer Olympic Games,
Atlanta — A195

Various shells, Nos. 1267-1271 each 1000d.

1996, Jan. 10　　Litho.　　Perf. 14
1267-1271	A195	Set of 5		18.00	18.00

Souvenir Sheet
1272	A195	2000d multicolored		9.00	9.00

Anniversaries and Events — A196

1996, Aug. 2　　　　Perf. 14x13½
1273	A196	500d multicolored		7.50	2.00

UNICEF, 50th anniv., Alfred Nobel, 150th anniv. of birth, Phila-Seoul 96, KOREA 2002, 1996 Summer Olympic Games, Atlanta.

UNESCO
A197

Butterflies, each 1000d: No. 1274, Papilio weiskei. No. 1275, Heliconius melpomene. No. 1276, Papilio arcas-mylotes. No. 1277, Mesomenia cresus. No. 1278, Catagramma iyca-satrana.

No. 1279, Lemonius sudias.

1996, Sept. 10　　　　Perf. 13½x14
1274-1278	A197	Set of 5		14.00	14.00

Souvenir Sheet
1279	A197	2000d multicolored		6.00	6.00

Train Type of 1995

Each 1000d: No. 1280, SNCF. No. 1281, CN. No. 1282, White locomotive. No. 1283, Green locomotive. No. 1284, Train in city.

Each 2000d: No. 1285, Modern train. No. 1286, Old train.

1996, Oct. 7　　　　　　Perf. 14
1280-1284	A181	Set of 5		14.00	14.00

Souvenir Sheets
1285-1286	A181	Set of 2		10.00	10.00

Beetles — A198

No. 1287, each 1500d: a, Grant's rhinoceros. b, Emerald-colored. c, California laurel borer. d, Giant stag.

Each 2000d: No. 1288, Maple borer. No. 1289, Arizona june.

1996, Nov. 7　　　　Perf. 13½x14
1287	A198	Sheet of 4, #a.-d.		16.00	16.00

Souvenir Sheets
1288-1289	A198	Set of 2		14.00	14.00

Plants, Orchids — A199

Each 1000d: No. 1290: a, Eryngium fortidum. b, Ocimum viride. c, Piper umbellatum. d, Phal. mariae. e, Odm. chiriquense. f, Phal. gigantea. g, Abutilon grandiflorum. h, Aframomium danielli. i, Chemopodium ambrosioides.

Each 2000d: No. 1291, Crinum jacus. No. 1292, Oncoba apinosa forsk. No. 1293, Z. mackai. No. 1294, Aspasia principissa.

1996, Oct. 14
1290	A199	Sheet of 9, #a.-i.		22.50	22.50

Souvenir Sheets
1291-1294	A199	Set of 4		35.00	35.00

Nos. 769, 912, 914 Surcharged

No. 1295B

1996-1997?　　Surcharge Typo.
Perfs. & Printing Methods as Before
1295	A100	500d on 46d #769	—	—
1295A	A133	500d on 60d #912	—	—
1295B	A133	500d on 60d #914	4.50	4.50

Nos. 1295A-1295B exist with four varieties of the letters "Db". Type I: "D" is rounded, and "b" has a very small hole. Type II: Bottom of "D" is higher than "b", and "b" has a small hole. Type III: "D" is slightly squared, and "b" has a

tall hole. Type IV: "D" is very rounded, and "b" has a large round hole.

Nos. 727-730, 733-734, 736-739, 744, 746, 748 Surcharged in Blue, Black, or Violet

No. 1296

No. 1298C

Surcharge Handstamped
1996-1997?
Printing Methods and Perfs as Before
1295C	A95	1000d on 5.50d #733	—	—
1296	A95	1000d on 11d #736 (dk bl)	—	—
1297	A95	1000d on 12d #737 (Bl)	—	—
b.		Black surcharge	—	—
1297A	A95	1000d on 15.50d #739	—	—
1298	A95	1000d on 42d #746	5.00	2.75
1298A	A95	2500d on 50c #727 (Bl)	—	—
1298B	A95	2500d on 1d #728 (Bl)	—	—
1298C	A95	2500d on 1.50d #729 (Bl)	8.00	6.75
g.		Violet surcharge	—	—
1298D	A95	2500d on 2d #730 (Bl)	—	—
1298E	A95	2500d on 7d #734 (Bl)	—	—
1298F	A95	2500d on 14d #738 (Bl)	—	—
h.		Violet surcharge	—	—
1299	A95	2500d on 25d #744 (Bl)	8.00	6.75
1300	A95	2500d on 100d #748 (Bl)	8.00	6.75
a.		Violet surcharge	—	—

Nos. 727, 733, 735, 742 Surcharged "Dbs." in Blue or Black

1997?　　Surcharge Handstamped
Printing Methods and Perfs as Before
1300B	A95	2500d on 50c #727 (Bl)	—	—
1300C	A95	2500d on 5.50d #733	—	—
1300D	A95	2500d on 10d #735	—	—
1300E	A95	2500d on 18.50d #742 (Bl)	—	—

Nos. 729, 742, 747 Surcharged Large "Dbs." in Blue, Black or Green

1997?　　Surcharge Handstamped
Printing Methods and Perfs as Before
1300F	A95	1500d on 18.50d #742	—	—
1300G	A95	1500d on 46d #747 (Bl)	—	—
1300H	A95	2500d on 1500d on 1.50d #729 (Gr on Bl)	—	—

The editors would like to examine an example of No. 1300H without the green surcharge.

Musicians, Musical Instruments A200

"The Beatles" — No. 1301, each 1500d: a, John Lennon. b, Paul McCartney. c, George Harrison. d, Ringo Starr.

Traditional instruments — No. 1302, each 1500d: a, Animal horn. b, Flutes. c, Tambourine, drum, sticks. d, Canza.

Each 2000d: No. 1303, Guitar, Elvis Presley (in sheet margin). No. 1304, Maraca, Antonio Machin.

1996, Nov. 19   Litho.   Perf. 13½x14
Sheets of 4, #a-d
1301-1302 A200 Set of 2   37.50 37.50
Souvenir Sheets
1303-1304 A200 Set of 2   19.00 19.00

Fish — A201

No. 1305, each 1500d: a, Sailfish. b, Barracuda. c, Cod. d, Atlantic mackerel.

Each 2000d: No. 1306, Bluefin tuna. No. 1307, Squirrelfish.

1996, Dec. 10   Perf. 14x13½
1305 A201 Sheet of 4, #a.-d.   18.00 18.00
Souvenir Sheets
1306-1307 A201 Set of 2   20.00 20.00

No. 988 Surcharged in Dark Blue

Methods and Perfs as Before **1997, Apr. 16   Surcharge Typo.**
1307A A144 1000d on 250d
               multi   35.00   8.00
  b.   "Dbs." normal
No. 1307A "Dbs." is in italics. No. 1307Ab "Dbs." is in regular font.

A202

Diana, Princess of Wales (1961-97) — A202a

No. 1308: Various portraits, vert.
100d, Diana talking with her sons (in sheet margin), vert. 500d, Portrait. 2000d, Diana, Mother Teresa (in sheet margin), vert.

1997   Litho.   Perf. 14
1308 A202   10d Sheet of 9,
                  #a.-i.   22.50 22.50
Souvenir Sheets
Perf. 13½x14, 14x13½
1309 A202   100d mul-
                  ticolored   12.00 12.00
1310 A202a 500d gold & mul-
                  ti   12.00 12.00
1311 A202a 2000d gold & mul-
                  ti   8.00   8.00
   Issued: No. 1308, 100d, 500d, 10/15/97; 2000d, 10/20/97.

Souvenir Sheet

Michael Schumacher, World Champion Formula I Driver — A203

1997, Dec. 12   Perf. 14
1312 A203 500d multicolored   9.00   9.00

Titanic — A205

No. 1317, 1000d — Titanic, White Star Line flag and inset image of: a, Captain Edward J. Smith. b, Titanic approaching icebergs. c, Titanic shooting flares. d, Distress codes. e, Titanic cruising in daylight. f, Titanic with icebergs at left. g, Lifeboats near sinking Titanic. h, Sinking Titanic. i, Map showing location of sinking.

No. 1318, 1000d: a, Construction of Titanic. b, Titanic leaving dock. c, Titanic and seagulls. d, Titanic shooting flares. e, Lifeboats near sinking Titanic. f, Sinking Titanic. g, Titanic, lifeboat, ship's officer. h, Bow of sunken Titanic. i, Stern of sunken Titanic.

No. 1319, 2000d, Captain and Titanic (multicolored). No. 1320, 2000d, Captain and Titanic (black).

1998, July 1   Litho.   Perf. 14x13¾
Sheets of 9, #a-i
1317-1318 A205   Set of 2   —   —
Souvenir Sheets
1319-1320 A205   Set of 2   15.00 15.00

Expo '98, Lisbon — A206

Sea around the islands, each 3500d: No. 1326, Man fishing from shore. No. 1327, Man in small sailboat, sharks in water below. No. 1328, Flying fish. No. 1329, Diver connecting line on sea bottom. No. 1330, Man paddling boat, turtle, fish below.
8000d, Map of St. Thomas & Prince, vert.

1998   Litho.   Perf. 14
1326-1330 A206 Set of 5   16.00 13.50
Souvenir Sheet
1331 A206 8000d multicolored 20.00   8.00

2nd AICEP Philatelic Exhibition — A207

Traditional food, each 3500d: No. 1332, Feijao de coco, coconuts. No. 1333, Cooked bananas, fruit, wine. No. 1334, Molho no fogo, fish, fruit, wine. No. 1335, Calulu, fruits, vegetables, wine. No. 1336, Izaquente de acucar, sugar beet.
7000d, Pot cooking over open fire, vert.

1998, Aug. 1
1332-1336 A207   Set of 5   16.00   7.00
Souvenir Sheet
1337 A207 7000d multicolored   8.00   8.00

Souvenir Sheet

Portugal 98 Stamp Exhibition — A210

1998, Sept. 4   Litho.   Perf. 14x13¾
1342 A210 7000d Ship on map 15.00   8.00
   Five stamps were issued with the souvenir sheet. The editors would like to examine them.

Nos. 731-732, 735-737, 739-742, 746-747 Surcharged in Blue or Violet
1997?   Surcharge Handstamped
Printing Methods and Perfs as Before
1343 A95 2500d on 3d #731
                       (V)   —   —
1344 A95 2500d on 4d #732
                       (BI)   —   —
1345 A95 2500d on 10d #735
                       (BI)   —   —
1345A A95 2500d on 11d #736
                       (BI)   —   —
1346 A95 2500d on 12d #737
                       (BI)   —   —
1346A A95 2500d on 15.50d
                       #739 (BI)   —   —
1347 A95 2500d on 16d #740
                       (BI)   —   —
1348 A95 2500d on 17d #741
                       (V)   —   —
1349 A95 2500d on 18.50d
                       #742 (BI),
                       value right
                       of oblitera-
                       tor   —   —
   a.   Value below obliterator   —   —
1350 A95 2500d on 42d #746
                       (BI)   —   —
1351 A95 2500d on 46d #747
                       (BI)   —   —

Nos. 599, 603 Surcharged in Black or Green
Surcharge Handstamped (Nos. 1352-1353), Typo. (No. 1353A)
1998?
Printing Methods and Perfs as Before
1352 A65 3000d on 50c
                  #599,
                  surch. at
                  bottom   —   —
1352A A65 3000d on 50c
                  #599,
                  surch. at
                  top (G)   —   —
1353 A65 3000d on 14d #603   —   —
1353A A65 3000d on 14d #603   —   —
   No. 1353 was handstamped, the letters are messy, the obliterator is one bar. No. 1353A was typographed, the letters are neat, the obliterator is two bars.
   Some sources indicate that No. 610 was surcharged 3000d and belongs in this set. The editors would like to see evidence of its existence.

Nos. 719-721 Surcharged in Blue
1999   Surcharge Handstamped
Printing Methods and Perfs as Before
1355 A63 3000d on 20d #719   —   —
1356 A63 3000d on 46d #720   —   —
1357 A63 3000d on 50d #721   —   —
   Nos. 1356 and 1357 do not have an obliterator.

Nos. 856-858 Surcharged in Black

1999   Surcharge Typo.
Printing Methods and Perfs as Before
1358 A123p 3000d on 50c #856 15.00 5.00
1359 A123p 3000d on 1d #857   15.00 5.00
1360 A123p 3000d on 5d #858   15.00 5.00
   Nos. 1358 and 1360 have various obliterators. No. 1359 has no obliterator.

Nos. 728, 735, 739 Surcharged

1999, Nov.   Surcharge Typo.
Printing Methods and Perfs as Before

1361	A95	5000d on 15.50d #739	10.00	10.00
1362	A95	7000d on 10d #735	15.00	15.00
1363	A95	10,000d on 1d #728	20.00	20.00
		Nos. 1361-1363 (3)	45.00	45.00

Christmas — A211

Designs: Nos. 1364, 1367, 5000d, Adoration of the Shepherds. Nos. 1365, 1368, 6000d, Presentation of Jesus in the Temple. Nos. 1366, 1369, 10,000d, Flight Into Egypt.

1999, Dec. 23   Litho.   Perf. 12¾x13
| 1364-1366 | A211 | Set of 3 | 9.50 | 9.50 |

Souvenir Sheets
| 1367-1369 | A211 | Set of 3 | 10.00 | 10.00 |

Stamps on Nos. 1367-1369 have continuous designs.

Souvenir Sheet

Independence, 25th Anniv. — A213

No. 1371: a, 5000d, Mountain, bird. b, 6000d, Stylized mountains, birds, flag. c, 7000d, Mountains, "25," flag. d, 10,000d, Mountain, bird, diff.

2000, July 12   Litho.   Perf. 12¾
| 1371 | A213 | Sheet of 4, #a-d | 13.00 | 13.00 |

Nos. 746, 748 Surcharged

2000, Aug. 7   Surcharge Typo.
Printing Methods and Perfs as Before
| 1372 | A95 | 5000d on 42d multi | 3.00 | 2.50 |
| 1373 | A95 | 5000d on 100d multi | 3.00 | 2.50 |

2000 Summer Olympics, Sydney — A214

Olympic rings and: 5000d, Runner, stadium, kangaroos, bird. 7000d, Runner, Sydney Opera House, kangaroos, emu.
15,000d, Sydney Harbour Bridge, Opera House, kangaroo, horiz.

2000, Sept. 14   Litho.   Perf. 12¾
| 1374-1375 | A214 | Set of 2 | 6.00 | 6.00 |

Souvenir Sheet
Perf. 13
| 1376 | A214 | 15,000d multi | 7.50 | 7.50 |

Souvenir Sheet

España 2000 Intl. Philatelic Exhibition — A215

2000, Oct. 6   Perf. 12¾
| 1377 | A215 | 15,000d multi | 9.00 | 9.00 |

Holy Year 2000 — A216

Designs: No. 1381a, 3000d, God, the Father. No. 1381b, 5000d, St. Anne, Virgin Mary, infant Jesus. Nos. 1378, 1381c, 6000d, St. Thomas. No. 1381d, 6000d, Processional cross. Nos. 1379, 1381e, 7000d, Altarpiece. Nos. 1380, 1381f, 8000d, Cathedral.

2000, Dec. 21   Perf. 12¾
With "Natal 2000" Inscription
| 1378-1380 | A216 | Set of 3 | 10.00 | 10.00 |

Without "Natal 2000" Inscription
| 1381 | A216 | Sheet of 6, #a-f | 17.00 | 17.00 |
| | g. | Souvenir sheet, #1381a-1381b, 1381d-1381e, perf. 12 | 10.00 | 10.00 |

Rosa de Porcellana A218

Flower in: Nos. 1391, 5000d, 1393a, 7000d, Pink. Nos. 1392, 5000d, 1393b, 8000d, Red.

2001, Apr. 12   Litho.   Perf. 13¾x14
| 1391-1392 | A218 | Set of 2 | 4.75 | 4.75 |

Souvenir Sheet
| 1393 | A218 | Sheet of 2, #a-b | 7.50 | 7.50 |

Butterflies A219

Designs: No. 1394, 3500d, Graphium leonidas (brown frame). No. 1395, 5000d, Acraea newtoni (bright red frame). No. 1396, 6000d, Papilio bromius (bright red frame). No. 1397, 7500d, Papilio dardanos (brown frame).
No. 1398: a, 3500d, Graphium leonidas (orange frame). b, 5000d, Acraea newtoni (dark red frame). c, 6000d, Papilio bromius (dark red frame). d, 7500d, Papilio dardanos (orange frame).
15,000d, Euchloron megaera serrei.

2001, July 15   Perf. 13¼x13½
| 1394-1397 | A219 | Set of 4 | 10.00 | 10.00 |

Souvenir Sheets
| 1398 | A219 | Sheet of 4, #a-d | 11.00 | 11.00 |
| 1399 | A219 | 15,000d multi | 7.50 | 7.50 |

Worldwide Fund for Nature (WWF) A220

Lepidochelys olivacea: 3500d, One swimming. 5000d, Two swimming. 6000d, Three leaving water. 7500d, Three hatchlings in sand.

2001, Oct.
| 1400-1403 | A220 | Set of 4 | 9.00 | 8.00 |

Nos. 1400-1403 were each issued in sheets of four. The margin of each of the four stamps on the sheets differs.
See No. 1431. For surcharges, see Nos. 2199-2201.

Souvenir Sheets

Famous Men — A221

Designs: No. 1404, 15,000d, Charlie Chaplin (1889-1977), comedian. No. 1405, 15,000d, Louis Armstrong (1900-71), musician. No. 1406, 15,000d, Walt Disney (1901-66), film producer. No. 1407, 15,000d, Giuseppe Verdi (1813-1901), composer, vert.

2002   Litho.   Perf. 13¼
| 1404-1407 | A221 | Set of 4 | 27.50 | 27.50 |

Issued: No. 1404, 3/11; No. 1405, 3/12; No. 1406, 3/13; No. 1407, 3/14.

Insects A222

Designs: No. 1408, 5000d, Euchroea clementi. No. 1409, 5000d, Dicranorrhina derbyana. No. 1410, 5000d, Stephanorrhina guttata. 8000d, Polybothris sumptuosa gemma.

2002, Mar. 15   Perf. 13¼x13½
| 1408-1411 | A222 | Set of 4 | 11.00 | 11.00 |

Souvenir Sheet

Henri de Toulouse-Lautrec (1865-1901), Painter — A223

Perf. 13¼x13¼x13¼x Rouletted
2002, Mar. 16
| 1412 | A223 | 15,000d Sheet of 2 | 13.00 | 13.00 |

Stamps in No. 1412 are tete-beche. The rouletting continues through the selvage allowing the sheet to be broken up into two half-sheets.

Souvenir Sheets

Chinese Zodiac Animals — A224

No. 1413, 15,000d: a, Rat. b, Tiger. c, Ox. d, Rabbit.
No. 1414, 15,000d: a, Dragon. b, Horse. c, Snake. d, Goat.
No. 1415, 15,000d: a, Monkey. b, Dog. c, Cock. d, Pig.

2002   Perf.
| 1413-1415 | A224 | Set of 3 | 75.00 | 75.00 |

Each sheet was rouletted into quadrants.

In Remembrance of Sept. 11, 2001 Terrorist Attacks — A225

2002, May 27   Perf. 13½x13¼
With White Frame
| 1416 | A225 | 5000d multi | 2.75 | 2.75 |

Souvenir Sheet
Without White Frame
| 1417 | A225 | 15,000d multi | 8.00 | 8.00 |

No. 1417 contains one 40x51mm stamp.

Souvenir Sheet

Barcelona Architecture of Antonio Gaudí — A226

No. 1418: a, 7000d, Casa Battló (dark brown building, 27x41mm). b, 7000d, Casa Mila (light building, 27x41mm). c, 20,000d, Church of Sagrada Familia (29x47mm).

Perf. 13½x13¼, 13¼ (#1418c)
2002, Sept. 28
| 1418 | A226 | Sheet, #a-c | 13.00 | 13.00 |

A column of rouletting separates the sheet into two halves, one containing Nos. 1418a-1418b, and the other containing No. 1418c. An additional column of rouletting is found at the left side of the half sheet containing No. 1418c.

Orchids — A227

Designs: 2000d, Phaius mannii. 6000d, Cyrtorchis arcuata. 9000d, Calanthe sylvatica. 10,000d, Bulbophyllum lizae. 20,000d, Bulbophyllum saltatorium.

Perf. 13½x13¼

2002, Nov. 19			Litho.
1419-1422 A227	Set of 4		14.00 14.00

Souvenir Sheet

1424 A227	20,000d multi	10.00 10.00

A number has been reserved for an additional item in this set.

Birds — A228

Designs: 1000d, Nectarinia newtonii. 7000d, Prinior molleri. 9000d, Neospiza concolor. 10,000d, Lanius newtoni. 20,000d, Otus hartlaubi.

Perf. 13½x13¼

2002, Nov. 20			Litho.
1425-1428 A228	Set of 4		13.00 13.00
1428a	Souvenir sheet, #1425-1428		13.00 13.00

Souvenir Sheet

1429 A228	20,000d multi	10.00 10.00

Miniature Sheet

Circus Animals — A229

No. 1430: a, 2000d, Horses (30x40mm). b, 6000d, Chimpanzees (30x40mm). c, 9000d, Seals (30x40mm). d, 10,000d, Tigers (30x40mm). e, 20,000d, Elephants (60x80mm).

2002, Nov. 22		Perf. 13¼x13
1430 A229	Sheet of 5, #a-e	14.00 14.00

A column of rouletting separates the sheet into two halves, one containing Nos. 1430a-1430d and the other containing No. 1430e.

Worldwide Fund for Nature Type of 2001
Souvenir Sheet

No. 1431 — Lepidochelys olivacea: a, 6000d, Two swimming. b, 6000d, Three hatchlings in sand. c, 7000d, One swimming. d, 7000d, Three leaving water.

2002, Dec. 31		Perf. 13¼x13½
1431 A220	Sheet of 4, #a-d	14.00 14.00

Space Travelers A230

Designs: 6000d, Laika. 7000d, Yuri Gagarin. 8000d, Dennis Tito.

2003, Feb. 20		Perf. 13x13¼
1432-1434 A230	Set of 3	9.00 9.00
1434a	Souvenir sheet, #1432-1434, perf. 12½x12¾	9.00 9.00

Souvenir Sheet

The Last Supper, by Leonardo da Vinci — A231

2003, Apr. 17		Perf. 13½x13¼
1435 A231	25,000d multi	11.00 11.00

Easter.

Crustaceans — A232

Designs: Nos. 1436, 1440a, 3500d, Coenobita perlatus. Nos. 1437, 1440b, 7000d, Carcinus maenas. Nos. 1438, 1440c, 8000d, Uca tetragonon. Nos. 1439, 1440d, 9000d, Ovalipes ocellatus. 20,000d, Panulirus pencillatus.

2003, Apr. 24		Perf. 13¼x13½
With White Frames		
1436-1439 A232	Set of 4	12.50 12.50
Without White Frames		
1440 A232	Sheet of 4, #a-d	12.50 12.50

Souvenir Sheet

1441 A232	20,000d multi	9.00 9.00

Vincent van Gogh (1853-90), Painter — A233

Paintings: No. 1442, 6000d, Young Peasant Woman with Straw Hat Sitting in the Wheat, 1890. No. 1443, 6000d, Head of a Peasant Woman with White Cap, 1885. No. 1444, 7000d, Patience Escalier. No. 1445, 7000d, Charles-Elzéard Trabuc.

No. 1446 — Self-portraits from: a, 6000d, 1886 (head at left). b, 6000d, 1886 (head at right). c, 7000d, 1888. d, 7000d, 1889.

2003, May 30		Litho. Perf. 13½x13
1442-1445 A233	Set of 4	10.50 10.50
Souvenir Sheet		
1446 A233	Sheet of 4, #a-d	10.50 10.50

Skull With Burning Cigarette, by Vincent van Gogh — A234

2003, May 31		
1447 A234	7000d multi	3.25 3.25

WHO anti-smoking campaign.

Personagens Célebres

A235

Personagens Célebres

A236

Personagens Célebres

Famous People — A237

No. 1448: a, Lord Robert Baden-Powell, dogs. b, Pres. George W. Bush, rescue workers. c, Pope John Paul II, Copernicus. d, Astronaut Neil Armstrong, Russian cosmonaut. e, Vincent van Gogh self-portrait, and painting. f, Louis Pasteur, cat. g, Sir Alexander Fleming, mushrooms. h, Elvis Presley on motorcylce, automobile. i, Walt Disney, dog.

No. 1449: a, Pope John Paul II, Pres. George W. Bush. b, Male chess player. c, Nelson Mandela, mineral. d, Charles Darwin, dinosaur. e, Tiger Woods, Rotary emblem. f, Dr. Albert Schweitzer, bird. g, Hector Berlioz. h, Pablo Picasso and painting. i, Pope John Paul II and Mother Teresa.

No. 1450: a, Pope John Paul II and UN Secretary General Kofi Annan. b, Formula I race car driver and car. c, Lady Olave Baden-Powell, cat. d, Female chess player. e, Sir Rowland Hill, train. f, Rotary emblem, Lions emblem and founders. g, Henri Dunant, Princess Diana. h, Paul Gauguin and painting. i, Pope John Paul II, Princess Diana.

2003	Litho.	Perf. 12¾x13¼
1448 A235	5000d Sheet of 9,	
	#a-i	10.00 10.00
1449 A236	5000d Sheet of 9,	
	#a-i	10.00 10.00
1450 A237	5000d Sheet of 9,	
	#a-i	10.00 10.00
Nos. 1448-1450 (3)		30.00 30.00

Each stamp exists in a souvenir sheet of 1.

25º Aniversário do Pontificado de João Paulo II 1978-2003

A238

25º Aniversário do Pontificado de João Paulo II 1978-2003

A239

A240

Reign of Pope John Paul II, 25th Anniv. — A241

Various photographs of Pope John Paul II.

2003		
1451 A238	5000d Sheet of 9,	
	#a-i	10.00 10.00
1452 A239	5000d Sheet of 9,	
	#a-i	10.00 10.00
Souvenir Sheets		
1453 A240	38,000d multi	8.50 8.50
1454 A241	38,000d multi	8.50 8.50

A242

A243

Marilyn Monroe (1926-62),
Actress — A245

Various Marilyn Monroe photographs and
magazine covers.

2003
1455	A242	5000d Sheet of 9,		
		#a-i	10.00	10.00
1456	A243	5000d Sheet of 9,		
		#a-i	10.00	10.00

Souvenir Sheets
1457	A244	38,000d multi	8.50	8.50
1458	A245	38,000d multi	8.50	8.50

A244

A246

A247

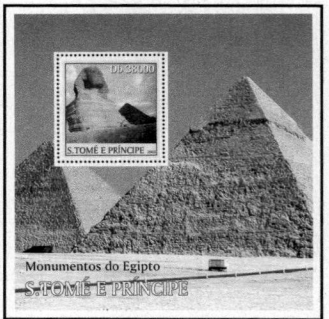

A248

Ancient Egyptian Monuments — A249

Various photographs.

2003
1459	A246	5000d Sheet of 9,		
		#a-i	10.00	10.00
1460	A247	5000d Sheet of 9,		
		#a-i	10.00	10.00

Souvenir Sheets
1461	A248	38,000d multi	8.50	8.50
1462	A249	38,000d multi	8.50	8.50

A250

A251

A252

A253

A254

St. Petersburg, Russia, 300th
Anniv. — A255

Various unnamed paintings or buildings.

2003
1463	A250	5000d Sheet of 9,		
		#a-i	10.00	10.00
1464	A251	5000d Sheet of 9,		
		#a-i	10.00	10.00
1465	A252	5000d Sheet of 9,		
		#a-i	10.00	10.00
		Nos. 1463-1465 (3)	30.00	30.00

Souvenir Sheets
1466	A253	38,000d multi	8.50	8.50
1467	A254	38,000d multi	8.50	8.50
1468	A255	38,000d multi	8.50	8.50

A256

Volcanoes, Minerals and
Firefighters — A257

A258

Fire Vehicles — A259

Nos. 1469 — Various pictures of volcanoes
and minerals: a, 1000d, With firefighter. b,
2000d, Without firefighter. c, 3000d, With
firefighter. d, 5000d, Without firefighter. e,

6000d, With firefighter. f, 15,000d, Without firefighter.

No. 1470 — Various pictures of volcanoes and minerals: a, 1000d, Without firefighter. b, 2000d, With firefighter. c, 3000d, Without firefighter. d, 5000d, With firefighter. e, 6000d, Without firefighter. f, 15,000d, With firefighter.

Nos. 1471 and 1472 — Various fire vehicles: a, 1000d. b, 2000d. c, 3000d. d, 5000d. e, 6000d. f, 15,000d.

No. 1473, Like #1469e. No. 1474, Like #1470d. No. 1475, Like #1471c. No. 1476, Like #1472f.

Perf. 12¾x13¼, 13¼x12¾ (#1474)

2003

1469	A256	Sheet of 6, #a-f	9.00	9.00
1470	A257	Sheet of 6, #a-f	9.00	9.00
1471	A258	Sheet of 6, #a-f	9.00	9.00
1472	A259	Sheet of 6, #a-f	9.00	9.00
		Nos. 1469-1472 (4)	36.00	36.00

Souvenir Sheets

1473	A256	38,000d multi	8.50	8.50
1474	A257	38,000d multi	8.50	8.50
1475	A258	38,000d multi	8.50	8.50
1476	A259	38,000d multi	8.50	8.50

A260

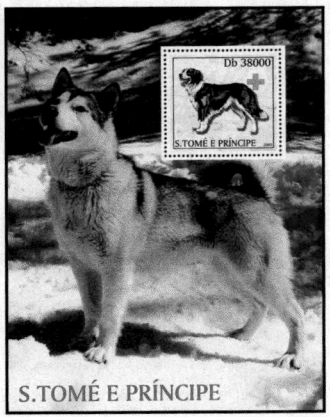

Red Cross Emblem and Dogs — A261

No. 1477 — Red Cross emblem and various dogs: a, 1000d. b, 2000d. c, 3000d. d, 5000d. e, 6000d. f, 15,000d.

Perf. 12¾x13¼, 13¼x12¾ (#1478)

2003

1477	A260	Sheet of 6, #a-f	10.00	10.00

Souvenir Sheet

1478	A261	38,000d multi	9.50	9.50

Pope John Paul II and Orchids — A262

No. 1479 — Pope and orchids: a, 1000d, Phalaenopsis bellina. b, 2000d, Rhynchostylis monachica. c, 3000d, Vanda bensonii. d, 5000d, Paphiopedilum hirsutissimum. e, 6000d, Liparis latifolia. f, 15,000d, Trichoglottis seidenfadenii.
38,000d, Like #1479a.

2003   **Perf. 12¾x13¼**

1479	A262	Sheet of 6, #a-f	10.00	10.00

Souvenir Sheet

1480	A262	38,000d multi	9.50	9.50

Marilyn Monroe and Orchids — A263

No. 1481 — Monroe and orchids: a, 1000d, Phalaenopsis amabilis. b, 2000d, Rhynchostylis retusa. c, 3000d, Phalaenopsis stuartiana. d, 5000d, Rhynchostylis gigantea. e, 6000d, Vanda coerulea. f, 15,000d, Trichoglottis brachiata.
38,000d, Like #1481b.

2003

1481	A263	Sheet of 6, #a-f	10.00	10.00

Souvenir Sheet

1482	A263	38,000d multi	9.50	9.50

Birds and Concorde — A264

No. 1483 — Concorde and penguins: a, 1000d. b, 2000d. c, 3000d. d, 5000d. e, 6000d. f, 15,000d.

No. 1484 — Birds: a, 1000d, Lybius torquatus, and Concorde. b, 2000d, Prinia subflava. c, 3000d, Tockus erythrorhynchus, and Concorde. d, 5000d, Poicephalus meyeri. e, 6000d, Uraeginthus angolensis, and Concorde. f, 15,000d, Laniarius atrococcineus.

No. 1485, 38,000d, Like #1483e. No. 1486, 38,000d, Like #1484c.

2003   **Sheets of 6, #a-f**

1483-1484	A264	Set of 2	18.00	18.00

Souvenir Sheets

1485-1486	A264	Set of 2	17.00	17.00

Birds — A265

No. 1487 — Various pheasants: a, 1000d. b, 2000d. c, 3000d. d, 5000d. e, 6000d. f, 15,000d.

No. 1488 — Birds and orchids: a, Polytelis alexandrae, Dendrochilum wenzelii. b, Neophena splendida, Dendrobium sulcatum. c, Pyrrhura calliptera, Dendrobium nobile. d, Aratinga jandaya, Cymbidium lowianum. e, Melopsittacus undulatus, Dendrobium bullenianum. f, Psittacula himalayana, Chiloschista parishii.

No. 1489, 38,000d, Like #1487a, with Bangkok 2003 Jamboree emblem added. No. 1490, 38,000d, Like #1488b, with Bangkok 2003 Jamboree emblem added. See illustration A266 for stamps showing Bangkok 2003 Jamboree emblem.

2003

1487	A265	Sheet of 6, #a.-f.	10.00	10.00

1488	A265	10,000d Sheet of 6, #a-f	14.50	14.50

Souvenir Sheets

1489-1490	A265	Set of 2	18.00	18.00

For surcharges, see Nos. 2000-2002, 2007-2009, 2027-2029, 2034-2036, 2054-2056, 2061-2063, 2081-2083, 2088-2090.

Bangkok 2003 Scout Jamboree Emblem and Birds, Orchids, Mushrooms, Insects or Butterflies — A266

No. 1491 — Emblem and various fighting roosters: a, 1000d. b, 2000d. c, 3000d. d, 5000d. e, 6000d. f, 15,000d.

No. 1492 — Emblem and unnamed water birds or orchids: a, 1000d, Bird in flight. b, 2000d, Aerides odorata. c, 3000d, Two birds at nest. d, 5000d, Aerides roaea. e, 6000d, Two birds. f, 15,000d, Aerides quinquevulnera.

No. 1493 — Emblem and mushrooms and orchids: a, 1000d, Xerocomus cubtomentosus, Aerides quinquevulnera. b, 2000d, Suillus placidus, Bulbophyllum wendlandianum. c, 3000d, Boletus edulis, Coelogyne mooreana. d, 5000d, Suillus variegatus, Dendrobium bullenianum. e, 6000d, Tylopilus felleus, Dendrobium crumenatum. f, 15,000d, Aureoboletus gentilis, Ascocentrum garayi.

No. 1494 — Emblem, wasp and mushrooms: a, 1000d, Boletus edulis f. betulicola. b, 2000d, Boletus edulis f. pinicola. c, 3000d, Boletus appendiculatus. d, 5000d, Boletus fechtneri. e, 6000d, Boletus luirdus. f, 15,000d, Boletus impolitus.

No. 1495 — Emblem, mushroom and butterfly: a, 1000d, Russula nigricans, Papilio demoleus. b, 2000d, Lactarius volemus, Libythea geoffroyi. c, 3000d, Russula cyanoxantha, Catonephele numili. d, 5000d, Gomphidius roseus, Doxocopa cherubina. e, 6000d, Russula integra, Dione juno. f, 15,000d, Agaricus bisporus, Philaethria.

No. 1496, 38,000d, Like #1491a. No. 1497, 38,000d, Like #1493c. No. 1498, 38,000d, Like #1494a. No. 1499, 38,000d, Like #1495f.

2003   **Sheets of 6, #a-f**

1491-1495	A266	Set of 5	47.50	47.50

Souvenir Sheets

1496-1499	A266	Set of 4	37.50	37.50

See Nos. 1489-1490 for additional souvenir sheets with Jamboree emblem.

Lord Robert Baden-Powell and Songbirds — A267

Lord Robert Baden-Powell and Cats, Dogs, Butterflies or Owls — A268

No. 1500 — Lord Baden-Powell and unnamed songbirds: a, 1000d. b, 2000d. c, 3000d. d, 5000d. e, 6000d. f, 15,000d.

No. 1501 — Lord Baden-Powell and unnamed cats or dogs: a, 1000d, Cat. b, 2000d, Cat, diff. c, 3000d, Cat, diff. d, 5000d, Dog. e, 6000d, Dog, diff. f, 15,000d, Dog, diff.

No. 1502 — Lord Baden-Powell and butterflies: a, 1000d, Lycaena dispar. b, 2000d, Papilio macheon. c, 3000d, Cethosia biblis. d, 5000d, Netrocoryne repanda. e, 6000d, Eupackardia calleta. f, 15,000d, Gangara thyrsis.

No. 1503 — Lord Baden-Powell and owls: a, 1000d, Bbubo lacteus. b, 2000d, Asio capensis. c, 3000d, Strix woodfordii. d, 5000d, Strix butleri. e, 6000d, Otus insularis. f, 15,000d, Glaucidium perlatum.

No. 1504, 38,000d, Like #1500c. No. 1505, 38,000d, Like #1501e. No. 1506, 38,000d, Like #1502c. No. 1507, 38,000d, Like #1503a.

2003

1500	A267	Sheet of 6, #a-f	9.50	9.50
1501	A268	Sheet of 6, #a-f	9.50	9.50
1502	A268	Sheet of 6, #a-f	9.50	9.50
1503	A268	Sheet of 6, #a-f	9.50	9.50
		Nos. 1500-1503 (4)	38.00	38.00

Souvenir Sheets

1504	A267	38,000d multi	9.00	9.00
1505	A268	38,000d multi	9.00	9.00
1506	A268	38,000d multi	9.00	9.00
1507	A268	38,000d multi	9.00	9.00

A269

Lady Olave Baden-Powell and Pandas — A270

No. 1508 — Lady Baden-Powell and various pandas: a, 1000d. b, 2000d. c, 3000d. d, 5000d. e, 6000d. f, 15,000d.

2003

1508	A269	Sheet of 6, #a-f	9.50	9.50

Souvenir Sheet

1509	A270	38,000d multi	9.00	9.00

Scouting Emblem and Cats or Prehistoric Animals and Minerals — A271

No. 1510 — Scouting emblem and various cats: a, 1000d. b, 2000d. c, 3000d. d, 5000d. e, 6000d. f, 15,000d.

No. 1511 — Scouting emblem, unnamed minerals and prehistoric animals: a, 1000d, Corythosaurus causarius. b, 2000d, Compsognathus. c, 3000d, Edaphosaurus. d, 5000d, Monoclonius. e, 6000d, Rhamphorhynchus. f, 15,000d, Stegosaurus.
38,000d, Like #1511a.

2003

1510	A271	Sheet of 6, #a-f	9.50	9.50

1511 A271   Sheet of 6, #a-f   9.50 9.50
        Souvenir Sheet
1512 A271   38,000d multi   9.00 9.00
                See No. 1522.

Rotary Emblem and Roses — A272

No. 1513 — Rotary emblem and various roses: a, 1000d. b, 2000d. c, 3000d. d, 5000d. e, 6000d. f, 15,000d.
    38,000d, Like #1513e.

2003
1513 A272   Sheet of 6, #a-f   9.50 9.50
        Souvenir Sheet
1514 A272   38,000d multi   9.00 9.00

Rotary or Lions Emblems and Pinnipeds or Birds — A273

No. 1515 — Various pinnipeds and: a, 1000d, Rotary emblem. b, 2000d, Lions emblem. c, 3000d, Rotary emblem. d, 5000d, Lions emblem. e, 6000d, Rotary emblem. f, 15,000d, Lions emblem.
    No. 1516: a, 1000d, Rotary emblem, Polemaetus bellicosus. b, 2000d, Lions emblem, Aquila verreauxi. c, 3000d, Rotary emblem, Circus aeruginosus. d, 5000d, Lions emblem, Aquila nipalensis. e, 6000d, Rotary emblem, Hieraetus fasciatus. f, 15,000d, Lions emblem, Aquila pomarina.
    No. 1517, 38,000d, Like #1515a. No. 1518, 38,000d, Like #1516b.

2003   **Sheets of 6, #a-f**
1515-1516 A273   Set of 2   19.00 19.00
        Souvenir Sheets
1517-1518 A273   Set of 2   18.00 18.00

A274

A275

A276

Dogs and Cats — A277

No. 1519: a, 1000d, Dog. b, 2000d, Cat. c, 3000d, Dogs. d, 5000d, Cat, diff. e, 6000d, Dog, diff. f, 15,000d, Cat, diff.
    No. 1520: a, 1000d, Dog, diff. b, 2000d, Cat, diff. c, 3000d, Dogs, diff. d, 5000d, Cat, diff. e, 6000d, Dog, diff. f, 15,000d, Cat, diff.
    No. 1523, Like #1520e.

2003
1519 A274   Sheet of 6, #a-f   9.50 9.50
1520 A275   Sheet of 6, #a-f   9.50 9.50
        Souvenir Sheets
1521 A276   38,000d multi   9.00 9.00
1522 A277   38,000d multi   9.00 9.00
1523 A275   38,000d multi   9.00 9.00

Sled Dogs — A278

No. 1524 — Various sled dogs: a, 1000d. b, 2000d. c, 3000d. d, 5000d. e, 6000d. f, 15,000d.
    38,000d, Like #1524b.

2003
1524 A278   Sheet of 6, #a-f   9.50 9.50
        Souvenir Sheet
1525 A278   38,000d multi   9.00 9.00

Dolphins — A279

No. 1526 — Various dolphins: a, 1000d. b, 2000d. c, 3000d. d, 5000d. e, 6000d. f, 15,000d.

2003
1526 A279   Sheet of 6, #a-f   8.50 8.50

Rams — A280

Various rams.

2003
1527 A280   7000d Sheet of 6,
                #a-f   8.50 8.50
    For surcharges, see Nos. 1995, 1996, 2004, 2006, 2022, 2023, 2031-2033, 2049, 2050, 2058-2060, 2076, 2077, 2085, 2087.

Hot Air Balloons and Zeppelins — A281

No. 1528: a, 1000d, Balloon. b, 2000d, Zeppelin. c, 3000d, Balloon, diff. d, 5000d, Moored Zeppelin. e, 6000d, Balloons. f, 15,000d, Zeppelin cockpit.
    38,000d, Like #1528e.

2003
1528 A281   Sheet of 6, #a-f   8.00 8.00
        Souvenir Sheet
1529 A281   38,000d multi   7.50 7.50

Aviation, Cent. — A282

No. 1530 — Various military aircraft: a, 1000d, Helicopter. b, 2000d, Airplane. c, 3000d, Helicopter, diff. d, 5000d, Airplanes. e, 6000d, Helicopter, diff. f, 15,000d, Airplane.
    38,000d, Like #1530c.

2003
1530 A282   Sheet of 6, #a-f   9.50 9.50
        Souvenir Sheet
1531 A282   38,000d multi   9.00 9.00

Apollo 11 — A283

Space — A284

Concorde and Spacecraft — A285

Deceased Crew of Space Shuttle Columbia — A286

No. 1532: a, 1000d, Astronaut Edwin Aldrin. b, 2000d, Lift-off. c, 3000d, Crew in capsule. d, 5000d, Retrieval of crew at sea. e, 6000d, Astronauts Neil Armstrong, Michael Collins and Aldrin. f, 15,000d, Astronaut on Moon.
    No. 1533: a, 1000d, Lift-off of Space Shuttle. b, 2000d, Astronaut, vehicle and structures on planet. c, 3000d, Mir Space Station. d, 5000d, Astronauts working in outer space. e, 6000d, Untethered astronaut. f, 15,000d, Lift-off of rocket.
    No. 1534: a, 1000d, Concorde. b, 2000d, Lift-off of Space Shuttle, diff. c, 3000d, Concorde, diff. d, 5000d, Intl. Space Station. e, 6000d, Concorde on runway. f, 15,000d, Space Shuttle in outer space.
    No. 1535, Like #1532e. No. 1536, Like #1533c. No. 1537, Like #1534b.

2003
1532 A283   Sheet of 6, #a-f   9.50 9.50
1533 A284   Sheet of 6, #a-f   9.50 9.50
1534 A285   Sheet of 6, #a-f   9.50 9.50
    Nos. 1532-1534 (3)   28.50 28.50
        Souvenir Sheets
1535 A283   38,000d multi   9.00 9.00
1536 A284   38,000d multi   9.00 9.00
1537 A285   38,000d multi   9.00 9.00
1538 A286   38,000d multi   9.00 9.00

Tandem Bicycles — A287

No. 1539 — Various tandem bicycles and riders: a, 1000d. b, 2000d. c, 3000d. d, 5000d. e, 6000d. f, 15,000d.
    38,000d, Like #1539a.

2003
1539 A287   Sheet of 6, #a-f   9.50 9.50
Souvenir Sheet
1540 A287 38,000d multi   9.00 9.00

Tractor Trailer Trucks — A288

No. 1541 — Trucks with cabs in: a, 1000d,
Red. b, 2000d, Blue. c, 3000d, Red, diff. d,
5000d, White. e, 6000d, Black. f, 15,000d,
Purple.
  38,000d, Like #1542a.

2003
1541 A288   Sheet of 6, #a-f   9.50 9.50
Souvenir Sheet
1542 A288 38,000d multi   9.00 9.00

Volkswagen Beetles — A289

Mercedes-Benz Automobiles — A290

No. 1543: a, 1000d. b, 2000d. c, 3000d. d,
5000d. e, 6000d. f, 15,000d.
No. 1544: a, 1000d. b, 2000d. c, 3000d. d,
5000d. e, 6000d. f, 15,000d.
No. 1545, Like #1543d. No. 1546, Like
#1544d.

2003
1543 A289   Sheet of 6, #a-f   9.50 9.50
1544 A290   Sheet of 6, #a-f   9.50 9.50
Souvenir Sheets
1545 A289 38,000d multi   9.00 9.00
1546 A290 38,000d multi   9.00 9.00

Auto Racing — A291

Formula 1 Racing — A292

Formula 1 Racing — A293

Motorcycle Racing — A294

No. 1547: a, 1000d, Car 4x. b, 2000d, Cars
12 and 21. c, 3000d, Cars 46, 54 and 42. d,
5000d, Cars 11, 37 and 4. e, 6000d, South-
side Fina car. f, 15,000d, Car 16.
No. 1548: a, 1000d, Two cars. b, 2000d,
Two drivers holding trophies. c, 3000d, Car. d,
5000d, Two drivers with champagne bottles. e,
6000d, Car, diff. f, 15,000d, Three drivers.
No. 1549: a, 1000d, Red car with Marlboro
wing. b, 2000d, Yellow car with Benson &
Hedges wing. c, 3000d, Red car, driver with
arms raised. d, 5000d, Black, red and white
car. e, 6000d, Blue and yellow car. f, 15,000d,
Black, red and white car, diff.
No. 1550: a, Yellow motorcycle without number. b, Green motorcycle #1. c, Motorcycle
#26. d, White motorcycle #1. e, Motorcycle #9.
f, Motorcycle #21.
No. 1551, Like #1548a. No. 1552, Like
#1549c.

2003
1547 A291   Sheet of 6, #a-f   9.00 9.00
1548 A292   Sheet of 6, #a-f   9.00 9.00
1549 A293   Sheet of 6, #a-f   9.00 9.00
1550 A294 10,000d Sheet of 6,
              #a-f   13.50 13.50
   Nos. 1547-1550 (4)   40.50 40.50
Souvenir Sheets
1551 A292 38,000d multi   8.50 8.50
1552 A293 38,000d multi   8.50 8.50

For surcharges, see Nos. 2003, 2010, 2030,
2037, 2057, 2064, 2084, 2091.

A295

A296

A297

A298

A299

A300

A301

A302

A303

Trains — A304

Nos. 1553-1562 — Various trains: a, 1000d.
b, 2000d. c, 3000d. d, 5000d. e, 6000d. f,
15,000d.
No. 1563, Like #1553d. No. 1564, Like
#1554c. No. 1565, Like #1555f. No. 1566, Like
#1556d. No. 1567, Like #1557a. No. 1568,
Like #1558e. No. 1569, Like #1559f. No. 1570,
Like #1560b. No. 1571, Like #1561c. No.
1572, Like #1562d.

2003
1553 A295   Sheet of 6, #a-f   9.00 9.00
1554 A296   Sheet of 6, #a-f   9.00 9.00
1555 A297   Sheet of 6, #a-f   9.00 9.00
1556 A298   Sheet of 6, #a-f   9.00 9.00
1557 A299   Sheet of 6, #a-f   9.00 9.00
1558 A300   Sheet of 6, #a-f   9.00 9.00
1559 A301   Sheet of 6, #a-f   9.00 9.00
1560 A302   Sheet of 6, #a-f   9.00 9.00
1561 A303   Sheet of 6, #a-f   9.00 9.00
1562 A304   Sheet of 6, #a-f   9.00 9.00
   Nos. 1553-1562 (10)   90.00 90.00
Souvenir Sheets
1563 A295 38,000d multi   8.50 8.50
1564 A296 38,000d multi   8.50 8.50
1565 A297 38,000d multi   8.50 8.50
1566 A298 38,000d multi   8.50 8.50
1567 A299 38,000d multi   8.50 8.50
1568 A300 38,000d multi   8.50 8.50
1569 A301 38,000d multi   8.50 8.50
1570 A302 38,000d multi   8.50 8.50
1571 A303 38,000d multi   8.50 8.50
1572 A304 38,000d multi   8.50 8.50

Ships — A305

Paintings of various ships by Richard C.
Moore: a, *Constitution* and *Guerriere*; b, Priva-
teer *Rattlesnake*; c, H.M.S. *Victory*; d, H.M.S.
Victory at Trafalgar; e, Clipper Ship *Comet*; f,
U.S.S. *Constitution*.

2003
1573 A305 7000d Sheet of 6,
              #a-f   9.50 9.50

For surcharges, see Nos. 1997-1999, 2024-
2026, 2051-2053, 2078-2080.

2004 Summer Olympics,
Athens — A306

No. 1574 — Various rowing teams: a, 1000d. b, 2000d. c, 3000d. d, 5000d. e, 6000d. f, 15,000d.
38,000d, Like #1574b.

2003

1574 A306   Sheet of 6, #a-f   6.75 6.75

Souvenir Sheet

1575 A306   38,000d multi   7.00 7.00

The editors believe that stamps dated "2004" were not put on sale in St. Thomas and Prince Islands. St. Thomas and Prince postal officials have declared that any stamps dated "2005" are illegal stamps, as well as a sheet of nine 7000d stamps depicting Marilyn Monroe, dated "2006," and a sheet of nine 7000d stamps 2006 World Cup Soccer, dated "2006."

A307

No. 1576 — Sphinx and: a, 7000d, Pyramid stones on ships. b, 9000d, Construction of Pyramid. c, 10,000d, Egyptians and balance scale. d, 14,000d, Egyptians preparing dead man for burial.
No. 1577 — Wolfgang Amadeus Mozart (1756-91), composer: a, 7000d, Wearing black jacket. b, 9000d, Wearing red jacket, at piano. c, 10,000d, Wearing red jacket. d, 14,000d, Wearing gray jacket.
No. 1578 — Gold medalists at 2004 Summer Olympics, Athens: a, 7000d, Keiji Suzuki, judo. b, 9000d, Hicham El Guerrouj, running. c, 10,000d, Seung Min Ryu, table tennis. d, 14,000d, Michael Phelps, swimming.
No. 1579 — Participants at 2006 Winter Olympics, Turin: a, 7000d, Tanith Belbin and Benjamin Agosto, ice dancing. b, 9000d, Carolina Kostner, figure skating. c, 10,000d, Shizuka Arakawa, figure skating. d, 14,000d, Maxim Marinin and Tatiana Totmianina, figure skating.
No. 1580 — European soccer players: a, 7000d, Zinedine Zidane. b, 9000d, Raul Gonzalez. c, 10,000d, David Beckham. d, 14,000d, Pavel Nedved.
No. 1581 — African soccer players: a, 7000d, Nwankwo Kanu. b, 9000d, Patrick Vieira. c, 10,000d, Claude Makelele. d, 14,000d, Aiyegbeni Yakubu.
No. 1582 — Marilyn Monroe (1926-62), actress: a, 7000d, With umbrella. b, 9000d, Wearing red hat and shorts. c, 10,000d, Wearing bikini. d, 14,000d, Wearing dress.
No. 1583 — Spanish painters and their paintings: a, 7000d, El Greco (1541-1614). b, 9000d, Joaquin Sorolla (1863-1923). c, 10,000d, Diego Velazquez (1599-1660). d, 14,000d, Francisco Goya (1746-1828).
No. 1584 — Various views of the Concorde above clouds: a, 7000d. b, 9000d. c, 10,000d. d, 14,000d.
No. 1585, 40,000d, Sphinx. No. 1586, 40,000d, Mozart. No. 1587, 40,000d, Virgilijus Alekna, discus. No. 1588, 40,000d, Seth Wescott, snowboarding. No. 1589, 40,000d, John Terry. No. 1590, 40,000d, Samuel Eto'o. No. 1591, 40,000d, White House and American flag. No. 1592, 40,000d, Pablo Picasso (1881-1973). No. 1593, 40,000d, Concorde.

2006, Apr. 4   Litho.   Perf. 12¾x13¼
Sheets of 4, #a-d

1576-1584 A307   Set of 9   105.00 105.00

Souvenir Sheets
Perf. 13¼ Syncopated

1585-1593 A307   Set of 9   105.00 105.00

Europa Stamps, 50th Anniv. — A308

No. 1594 — Emblems and: a, Charles de Gaulle (1890-1970), French President. b, Wolfgang Amadeus Mozart (1756-91), composer. c, Pope John Paul II (1920-2005). d, Concorde.
40,000d, Emblems and map of Europe.

2006, Apr. 4   Perf. 12¾x13¼

1594 A308   14,000d Sheet of 4,
#a-d   15.00 15.00

Souvenir Sheet
Perf. 13¼ Syncopated

1595 A308   40,000d multi   10.50 10.50

A309

No. 1596 — Turtles: a, 7000d, Testudo graeca. b, 9000d, Pseudemys scripta. c, 10,000d, Clemmys insculpta. d, 14,000d, Trionyx spiniferus.
No. 1597 — Predators: a, 7000d, Crocodylus porosus. b, 9000d, Ursus maritimus. c, 10,000d, Carcharodon carcharias. d, 14,000d, Varanus komodoensis.
No. 1598 — Endangered animals: a, 7000d, Tyto alba. b, 9000d, Phascolarctos cinearus. c, 10,000d, Panthera tigris. d, 14,000d, Balaenoptera musculus.
No. 1599 — Illustrations from book *After Man: A Zoology of the Future* by Dougal Dixon : a, 7000d, Alesimia lapsus. b, 9000d, Aquator adepsicautus. c, 10,000d, Tetraceras africanus. d, 14,000d, Harundopes virgatus.
No. 1600 — Dogs and cats: a, 7000d, Golden retriever, British shorthair cat. b, 9000d, Portuguese Podengo hound, Black smoke Persian cat. c, 10,000d, Greyhound, Norwegian forest cat. d, 14,000d, Black Labrador retriever, Tiffanie cat.
No. 1601 — Owls and mushrooms: a, 7000d, Pseudoscops grammicus, Cortinarius triumphans. b, 9000d, Strix woodfordi, Cortinarius subfulgens. c, 10,000d, Athene noctua, Agaricus augustus. d, 14,000d, Strix nebulosa, Leucocortinarius bulbiger.
No. 1602 — Butterflies and orchids: a, 7000d, Mosaic gynandromorph, Phalaenopsis. b, 9000d, Nymphalidae, Coral Cymbidium. c, 10,000d, Papilio polymnestor, Pleione praecox. d, 14,000d, Charaxes bohemani, Rhyncholaelia glauca.
No. 1603 — Butterflies and bees: a, 7000d, Heliconius nattereri, Apis mellifera scutella. b, 9000d, Nymphalidae, Bombus hypnorum. c, 10,000d, Eterusia, repleta, Bombus terrestris. d, 14,000d, Lasaia mocros, Apis mellifera.
No. 1604 — Dinosaurs and minerals: a, 7000d, Pachycephalosaurus, Spodumene and kunzite. b, 9000d, Psittacosaurus, Opal. c, 10,000d, Troodon, Calcite and limestone. d, 14,000d, Struthiomimus, Barite and calcite.
No. 1605 — Dolphins and Swedish lighthouses: a, 7000d, Lagenorhynchus obliquidens, Berlin Lighthouse. b, 9000d, Delphinus delphis, Brämskär Lighthouse. c, 10,000d, Tursiops truncatus, Hättan Lighthouse. d, 14,000d, Lagenorhynchus acutus, Ursholmen Lighthouse.
No. 1606, 40,000d, Malacochersus tornieri. No. 1607, 40,000d, Carcharodon carcharias,

diff. No. 1608, 40,000d, Felis lynx. No. 1609, 40,000d, Reteostium cortepellium, Cornophilius ophicaudatus. No. 1610, 40,000d, Chow chow, Turkish angora cat. No. 1611, 40,000d, Phodilus badius, mushrooms. No. 1612, 40,000d, Athletes steindachneri moth, Angulocaste orchid. No. 1613, 40,000d, Heliconiinae hermatena, Apidae. No. 1614, 40,000d, Stegosaurus, Topaz. No. 1615, 40,000d, Delphinus delphis, Lista Lighthouse, Norway.

2006, May 25   Perf. 12¾x13¼
Sheets of 4, #a-d, + 4 Labels

1596-1605 A309   Set of 10 110.00 110.00

Souvenir Sheets
Perf. 13¼ Syncopated

1606-1615 A309   Set of 10 110.00 110.00

Paintings — A310

No. 1616 — Paintings by Michelangelo: a, 7000d, Martyrdom of St. Peter. b, 9000d, The Doni Tondo. c, 10,000d, Ezekiel. d, 14,000d, Last Judgment.
No. 1617 — Paintings by Peter Paul Rubens: a, 7000d, The Union of Earth and Water. b, 9000d, Daniel in the Lion's Den. c, 10,000d, The Judgment of Paris. d, 14,000d, Bacchus.
No. 1618 — Paintings by Rembrandt: a, 7000d, Tobit and Anna. b, 9000d, The Apostle Paul in Prison. c, 10,000d, The Militia Company of Captain Frans Banning Cocq. d, 14,000d, The Return of the Prodigal Son.
No. 1619 — Paintings by Gustave Courbet: a, 7000d, The Woman in the Waves. b, 9000d, Still Life: Fruit. c, 10,000d, The Stormy Sea. d, 14,000d, Sleep.
No. 1620 — Paintings by Auguste Renoir: a, 7000d, Bather Arranging Her Hair. b, 9000d, Blonde Nude. c, 10,000d, The Nymphs. d, 14,000d, The Bathers.
No. 1621 — Paintings by Vincent van Gogh: a, 7000d, The Starry Night. b, 9000d, The Church at Auvers-sur-Oise. c, 10,000d, First Steps. d, 14,000d, Midday Siesta.
No. 1622 — Paintings by Henri de Toulouse-Lautrec: a, 7000d, La Goulue Arriving with Two Women. b, 9000d, Yvette Guilbert. c, 10,000d, The Two Girlfriends. d, 14,000d, Rue des Moulins: The Medical Inspection.
No. 1623 — Various unnamed Japanese paintings by: a, 7000d, Utagawa Kuniyoshi. b, 9000d, Toshi Yoshida. c, 10,000d, Tsukioka Yoshitoshi. d, 14,000d, Utagawa Hiroshige II.
No. 1624 — American impressionist paintings: a, 7000d, Mother and Child, by Mary Cassatt. b, 9000d, Rock Garden in Giverny, by Leslie Breck. c, 10,000d, Oyster Gatherers of Cancale, by John Singer Sargent. d, 14,000d, Two Sisters, by William Merritt Chase.
No. 1625 — Paintings by Spanish-speaking artists: a, 7000d, Slave Market with the Disappearing Bust of Voltaire, by Salvador Dali. b, 9000d, The Flower Carrier, by Diego Rivera. c, 10,000d, Self-portrait, by Frida Kahlo. d, 14,000d, Dutch Interior I, by Joan Miró.
No. 1626, 40,000d, The Flood, by Michelangelo. No. 1627, 40,000d, Simon and Pero, by Rubens. No. 1628, 40,000d, Bathsheba at her Bath, by Rembrandt. No. 1629, 40,000d, The Bathers, by Courbet. No. 1630, 40,000d, Nude in the Sunlight, by Renoir. No. 1631, 40,000d, The Night Café, by van Gogh. No. 1632, 40,000d, Ball at the Moulin de la Galette (incorrectly inscribed "The Bathers"), by Toulouse-Lautrec. No. 1633, 40,000d, Painting by Narita Morikane. No. 1634, 40,000d, Sleep, by Frederick Carl Freiseke. No. 1635, 40,000d, A Couple, by Fernando Botero.

2006, Aug. 25   Perf. 12¾x13¼
Sheets of 4, #a-d

1616-1625 A310   Set of 10 110.00 110.00

Souvenir Sheets
Perf. 13¼ Syncopated

1626-1635 A310   Set of 10 110.00 110.00

A311

Nos. 1636 and 1646, 14,000d — Motorcyle and Elvis Presley (1935-77) wearing: a, Lilac shirt (motorcycle rider not visible). b, Red and white shirt. c, White shirt. b, Black and purple shirt.
Nos. 1637 and 1647, 14,000d — Marilyn Monroe (1926-62) and: a, Flash camera. b, Film cans. c, Film reel. b, Director's clapboard.
Nos. 1638 and 1648, 14,000d — Sports and games: a, Garry Kasparov, chess player. b, Won Hee Lee, judo. c, Wang Liqin, table tennis. b, Tiger Woods, golf.
Nos. 1639 and 1649, 14,000d — Lord Robert Baden-Powell (1847-1941), founder of Scouting movement and: a, Mushrooms, opal. b, Flower, owl. c, Mineral, mushrooms. b, Owl, orchid.
Nos. 1640 and 1650, 14,000d — Humanists: a, Pope John Paul II. b, Abraham Lincoln. c, Dr. Albert Schweitzer. b, Mahatma Gandhi.
Nos. 1641 and 1651, 14,000d — The Beatles: a, George Harrison. b, John Lennon. c, Ringo Starr. b, Paul McCartney.
Nos. 1642 and 1652, 14,000d — The Rolling Stones: a, Keith Richards. b, Mick Jagger. c, Charlie Watts. b, Ron Wood.
Nos. 1643 and 1653, 14,000d — Fire vehicles: a, Mercedes-Benz Metz. b, MAN 415 H-LF. c, Mercedes-Benz LF 16. b, Magirus KW 16.
Nos. 1644 and 1654, 14,000d — High-speed trains: a, Shinkansen JR 500. b, Eurostar. c, AGV. b, TGV.
Nos. 1645 and 1655, 14,000d — Scouting emblem, mushrooms and owls: a, Bubo zeylonensis. b, Nyctea ulula. c, Phodilus badius. b, Asio otus.
Nos. 1656 and 1666, 56,000d, Presley with guitar. Nos. 1657 and 1667, 56,000d, Monroe with film reel. Nos. 1658 and 1668, 56,000d, Kim Clijsters, tennis. Nos. 1659 and 1669, 56,000d, Baden-Powell and orchid. Nos. 1660 and 1670, 56,000d, Mother Teresa. Nos. 1661 and 1671, 56,000d, The Beatles. Nos. 1662 and 1672, 56,000d, Jagger. Nos. 1663 and 1673, 56,000d, Fischer fire vehicle. Nos. 1664 and 1674, 56,000d, Swiss Metro. Nos. 1665 and 1675, 56,000d, Strix cinereots.

Litho. & Embossed With Foil Application

2006, Dec. 15   Perf. 12¾x13¼
Without Gum
Sheets of 4 #a-d
Silver Background

1636-1645 A311   Set of 10 165.00 165.00

Gold Background

1646-1655 A311   Set of 10 165.00 165.00

Souvenir Sheets
Silver Background

1656-1665 A311   Set of 10 165.00 165.00

Gold Background

1666-1675 A311   Set of 10 165.00 165.00

Miniature Sheets

A312

No. 1676 — Princess Diana (image at left): a, 7000d, Holding papers. b, 9000d, Walking with Mother Teresa. c, 10,000d, Talking with girl. d, 14,000d, Riding in coach with Prince Charles.

No. 1677 — Steve Irwin (1962-2006), conservationist, with: a, 7000d, Pterois volitans. b, 9000d, Crotalus viridis. c, 10,000d, Crocodylus porosus. d, 14,000d, Myliobatis australis and Phascolarctos cinereus.

No. 1678 — Popes and their arms: a, 7000d, Pope Paul VI. b, 9000d, Pope John Paul I. c, 10,000d, Pope Benedict XVI. d, 14,000d, Pope John Paul II.

No. 1679 — Mushrooms: a, 7000d, Boletus badius and Sir Alexander Fleming (1881-1955), pharmacologist. b, 9000d, Boletus edulis and Leccinum quercinum. c, 10,000d, Amanita pantherina and Russula vesca. d, 14,000d, Amanita muscaria and Fleming.

No. 1680 — Neanderthals and minerals: a, 7000d, Celestine. b, 9000d, Sulfur. c, 10,000d, Pyrargyrite. d, 14,000d, Orthoclase and adularia.

No. 1681 — Minerals: a, 7000d, Barite, calcite and smoky quartz. b, 9000d, Malachite, beryl and emerald. c, 10,000d, Elbaite, rubellite tourmaline, microcline and amazonite. d, 14,000d, Quartz, amethyst and topaz.

No. 1682 — International Polar Year: a, 7000d, Admiral Robert Peary (1856-1920), polar explorer, and expedition members. b, 9000d, Eudyptes chrysolophus. c, 10,000d, Aptenodytes patagonicus. d, 14,000d, Fridtjof Nansen (1861-1930), polar explorer and Ursus maritimus.

No. 1683 — Owls and their prey: a, 7000d, Tyto alba, Ochotona collaris. b, 9000d, Nyctea scandiaca, Lepus arcticus. c, 10,000d, Scotopelia peli, Thunnus albacares. d, 14,000d, Ninox novaeseelandiae, Platacanthomyinae.

No. 1684 — Satellites: a, 7000d, Sputnik 1. b, 9000d, Sputnik 1, diff. c, 10,000d, Sputnik 2. d, 14,000d, Sputnik 2, diff.

No. 1685 — Martian probes: a, 7000d, Mars Odyssey. b, 9000d, Mars Rover. c, 10,000d, Mars Rover, diff. d, 14,000d, Mars Odyssey, diff.

2007, Feb. 2   Litho.   Perf. 12¾x13¼
Sheets of 4, #a-d

1676-1685 A312   Set of 10   110.00 110.00

Souvenir Sheets

U.S. Presidents — A313

No. 1686, 40,000d, George Washington (1732-99). No. 1687, 40,000d, Thomas Jefferson (1743-1826). No. 1688, 40,000d, Abraham Lincoln (1809-65). No. 1689, 40,000d, Franklin D. Roosevelt (1882-1945). No. 1690, 40,000d, Dwight D. Eisenhower (1890-1969). No. 1691, 40,000d, John F. Kennedy (1917-63). No. 1692, 40,000d, Lyndon B. Johnson (1908-73). No. 1693, 40,000d, Ronald Reagan (1911-2004). No. 1694, 40,000d, George H. W. Bush. No. 1695, 40,000d, William J. Clinton.

2007, Feb. 2   Perf. 13¼ Syncopated
1686-1695 A313   Set of 10   110.00 110.00

A314

No. 1696 — Bears: a, 7000d, Three bears. b, 9000d, Three bears in tree. c, 10,000d, Four bears and anthills. d, 14,000d, Three bears, diff.

No. 1697 — Wolves: a, 7000d, Two wolves upright. b, 9000d, Wolf on ground, wolf upright. c, 10,000d, Wolf's head, howling wolf. d, 14,000d, Two woves on ground.

No. 1698 — Birds: a, 7000d, Couroucou oranga. b, 9000d, Couroucou rosalba. c, 10,000d, Ramphocele scarlette. d, 14,000d, Cotinga ouette.

No. 1699 — Birds: a, 7000d, Tangara passe-ver. b, 9000d, Carouge iamacaii. c, 10,000d, Cassique huppe. d, 14,000d, Psittacule caica-barraband.

No. 1700 — Insects and lizards preying on butterflies and moths: a, 7000d, Pseudocreabotra wahlbergi and butterfly. b, 9000d, Spodoptera exigua and lizard. c, 10,000d, Cmenidophorus lemniscatus and moth. d, 14,000d, Asilus crabroniformis and butterfly.

No. 1701 — Animals preying on butterflies: a, 7000d, Frog and Euclidia glyphica. b, 9000d, Aegotheles cristata and butterfies. c, 10,000d, Leiothrix lutea, flowers and butterfly. d, 14,000d, Araneidae, Oxyopidae, and butterflies.

No. 1702 — Fish: a, 7000d, Chaetodon lineolatus, Osphronemidae. b, 9000d, Gymnarchus niloticus, Polyodon spathula. c, 10,000d, Climatius, Dunkleosteus. d, 14,000d, Latimeria chalumnae, Chlorostigma.

No. 1703 — Snakes: a, 7000d, And nest. b, 9000d, And unhatched eggs. c, 10,000d, And hatching eggs. d, 14,000d, With heads raised.

No. 1704 — Dinosaurs: a, 7000d, Velociraptor, Protoceratops. b, 9000d, Deinonychus, Sinosauropteryx. c, 10,000d, Oviraptor, Beipaiosaurus. d, 14,000d, Oviraptors.

No. 1705 — Mushrooms: a, 7000d, Pleurotus salignus, Catathelasma, Suillis luteus. b, 9000d, Lactarius torminosus, Tricholoma portentosum. c, 10,000d, Pleurotus ostreatus, Lactarius necator. d, 14,000d, Pleurotus eryngii, Tricholomopsis rutilans.

No. 1706, 40,000d, Ursus maritimus. No. 1707, 40,000d, Canidae. No. 1708, 40,000d, Fringille daroare. No. 1709, 40,000d, Euphonea diademe. No. 1710, 40,000d, Cyanositta cristata and butterfly. No. 1711, 40,000d, Gerrhonotus multicarinatus and butterflies. No. 1712, 40,000d, Siniperca chuatsi. No. 1713, 40,000d, Snake. No. 1714, 40,000d, Carcharodontosaurus. No. 1715, 40,000d, Entoloma sinuatum, Calocybe gambosa.

2007, Mar. 15   Perf. 12¾x13¼
Sheets of 4, #a-d, + 2 labels

1696-1705 A314   Set of 10   120.00 120.00

Souvenir Sheets

1706-1715 A314   Set of 10   120.00 120.00

Scouting, cent.

Independence of India, 60th Anniv. — A315

No. 1716: a, 9000d, Mahatma Gandhi (1869-1948), Independence leader. b, 10,000d, Indira Gandhi (1917-84), Prime Minister. c, 14,000d, Jawaharlal Nehru (1889-1964), Prime Minister.

40,000d, Vasco da Gama (1469-1524), explorer.

2007, Nov. 5   Perf. 12¾x13¼
1716 A315   Sheet of 3, #a-c, + label   5.00 5.00

Souvenir Sheet
Perf. 13¼ Syncopated
1717 A315 40,000d multi   6.00 6.00

Souvenir sheets of 1 of Nos. 1716a-1716c with colored frames exist.

Cruise Liners — A316

No. 1718: a, 7000d, Queen Mary 2. b, 9000d, Freedom of the Seas. c, 10,000d, Crystal Symphony. d, 14,000d, Star Princess. 40,000d, Titanic.

2007, Nov. 5   Perf. 12¾x13¼
1718 A316   Sheet of 4, #a-d   5.75 5.75

Souvenir Sheet
Perf. 13¼ Syncopated
1719 A316 40,000d multi   5.75 5.75

Souvenir sheets of 1 of Nos. 1718a, 1718b, and 1718d with colored frames exist.

A317

No. 1720 — Chess: a, 7000d, Chess player looking at board, knight. b, 9000d, Queen and pawn, hand moving piece. c, 10,000d, Player, rook and pawns. d, 14,000d, Queen, pieces on board.

No. 1721 — Race cars and Colin McRae (1968-2007), race car driver: a, 7000d, Wearing blue uniform. b, 9000d, Holding bottle of champagne. c, 10,000d, Holding trophy. d, 14,000d, Wearing earphones.

No. 1722 — Luciano Pavarotti (1935-2007), opera singer, and: a, 7000d, Princess Diana. b, 9000d, Spice Girls. c, 10,000d, Placido Domingoa and José Carreras. d, 14,000d, Bono.

No. 1723 — Photographs by Anton Corbijn of: a, 7000d, Miles Davis. b, 9000d, Clint Eastwood. c, 10,000d, Depeche Mode. d, 14,000d, Bono.

No. 1724 — Minerals: a, 7000d, Gypsum. b, 9000d, Rhodonite. c, 10,000d, Cerussite. d, 14,000d, Malachite.

No. 1725 — Lighthouses: a, 7000d, Alexandria Lighthouse. b, 9000d, Tower of Hercules. c, 10,000d, Yokohama Marine Tower. d, 14,000d, Cordouan Lighthouse, France.

No. 1726 — Tangula Express Train, China: a, 7000d, Train, tunnel, bridge. b, 9000d, Train on bridge. c, 10,000d, Train, lake. d, 14,000d, Train, train on bridge.

No. 1727, 40,000d, King, queen, chess players. No. 1728, 40,000d, McRae and race car. No. 1729, 40,000d, Pavarotti. No. 1730, 40,000d, Photograph of Dave Gahan by Corbijn. No. 1731, 40,000d, Fluorite, barite. No. 1732, 40,000d, Statue of Liberty.

2007, Nov. 5   Perf. 12¾x13¼
Sheets of 4, #a-d

1720-1726 A317   Set of 7   42.50 42.50

Souvenir Sheets
Perf. 13¼ Syncopated
1727-1732 A317   Set of 6   37.50 37.50

Souvenir sheets of 1 of Nos. 1725a, 1725c, and 1725d exist.

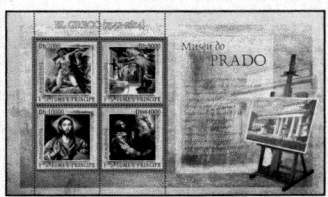

Paintings in Prado Museum by Spanish Artists — A318

No. 1733 — Various paintings by El Greco (1541-1614): a, 7000d. b, 9000d. c, 10,000d. d, 14,000d.

No. 1734 — Various paintings by Diego Velázquez (1541-1614): a, 7000d. b, 9000d. c, 10,000d. d, 14,000d.

No. 1735 — Various paintings by Francisco Goya (1746-1828): a, 7000d. b, 9000d. c, 10,000d. d, 14,000d.

No. 1736 — Various paintings by Joaquín Sorolla (1863-1923): a, 7000d. b, 9000d. c, 10,000d. d, 14,000d.

No. 1737 — Various paintings by Pablo Picasso (1881-1973): a, 7000d. b, 9000d. c, 10,000d. d, 14,000d.

No. 1738, 40,000d, Painting by El Greco, diff. No. 1739, 40,000d, Painting by Velázquez, diff. No. 1740, 40,000d, Painting by Goya, diff. No. 1741, 40,000d, Painting by Sorolla, diff. No. 1742, 40,000d, Painting by Picasso, diff.

2007, Nov. 5   Perf. 12¾x13¼
Sheets of 4, #a-d

1733-1737 A318   Set of 5   32.50 32.50

Souvenir Sheets
Perf. 13¼ Syncopated
1738-1742 A318   Set of 5   32.50 32.50

Souvenir sheets of 1 of Nos. 1733a, 1734b, 1735b, 1736b and 1737d exist.

Marine Science — A319

No. 1743: a, 7000d, Diver and Stenella alymene. b, 9000d, Diver and Natator depressus. c, 10,000d, Jacques Cousteau (1910-97), marine researcher, and submarine. d, 14,000d, Cousteau and research ship. 40,000d, Cousteau, research ship, diff.

2007, Nov. 5   Perf. 12¾x13¼
1743 A319   Sheet of 4, #a-d, + 4 labels   6.00 6.00

Souvenir Sheet
Perf. 13¼ Syncopated
1744 A319 40,000d multi   6.00 6.00

Miniature Sheets

A320

No. 1745, 7000d — Early locomotives: a, Trevithick. b, Marc Seguin. c, Blenkinsop. d, Puffing Billy. e, Rocket. f, Liverpool.

No. 1746, 7000d — Red Cross flag and: a, Airplane. b, Red fire truck with plow attachment. c, Yellow fire truck. d, Ship. e, Helicopter. f, Motorcycle.

No. 1747, 7000d — Divers and marine life: a, Montastrea cavernosa. b, Pisaster ochraceus. c, Gymnothorax javanicus. d, Carassius auratus. e, Octopus vulgaris. f, Lepidochelys olivacea.

No. 1748, 7000d — Extreme sports: a, Skateboarders. b, Motorcyclists. c, Rock climbers. d, Hang gliders. e, Surfer. f, Parachutist.

No. 1749, 7000d — Track and field athletes at 2007 World Championships, Osaka: a, Stefan Holm, high jump. b, Liu Xiang, hurdles. c, Irving Saladino, long jump. d, Steffi Nerius, javelin. e, Agustin Felix, pole vault. f, Liu Xiang running.

No. 1750, 7000d — Rugby players: a, Jonny Wilkinson. b, Felipe Contepomi. c, Chris Paterson. d, Percy Montgomery. e, Jean-Baptiste Elissalde. f, Nick Evans.

No. 1751, 40,000d, Red Cross flag and 1926 Kingsbury motor-driven pumper. No. 1752, 40,000d, Divers and Pomacanthus arcuataus. No. 1753, 40,000d, Monster truck. No. 1754, 40,000d, Alfred Kirwa Yego.

2007, Nov. 5   *Perf. 12¾x13¼*
Sheets of 6, #a-f

1745-1750   A320   Set of 6   36.00   36.00

Souvenir Sheets
Perf. 13¼ Syncopated

1751-1754   A320   Set of 4   23.00   23.00

Souvenir sheets of 1 of Nos. 1745a-1745f, 1746a, 1746c and 1746d with colored frames exist.

A321

No. 1755, 9000d — High-speed trains: a, Transrapid 08. b, TGV. c, Shinkansen. d, TGV Duplex. e, Maglev MLX-01.

No. 1756, 9000d — Paintings by Antoine Wiertz (1806-65): a, The Reader of Novels. b, The Young Witch. c, Beautiful Rosine. d, The Outrage of Belgian Women. e, Esmerelda.

No. 1757, 9000d — Fire engines: a, 1965 Ford Crown. b, 1881 Merryweather. c, 1894 Merryweather 2. d, 1933 Delahaye. e, 1933 Dennis.

No. 1758, 9000d — Automobiles and automotive pioneers: a, Gottlieb Daimler (1834-1900). b, Karl Benz (1844-1929). c, Enzo Ferrari (1898-1988). d, Henry Ford (1863-1947). e, Ferdinand Porsche (1875-1951).

No. 1759, 40,000d, M Set train. No. 1760, 40,000d, Christ in the Tomb, by Wiertz. No. 1761, 40,000d, Fire truck. No. 1762, 40,000d, Juan Manuel Fangio (1911-95), race car driver.

2007, Nov. 5   *Perf. 12¾x13¼*
Sheets of 5, #a-e, + Label

1755-1758   A321   Set of 4   27.50   27.50

Souvenir Sheets
Perf. 13¼ Syncopated

1759-1762   A321   Set of 4   25.00   25.00

Souvenir sheets of 1 of Nos. 1757a-1757e, 1758a-1758e with colored frames exist.

A322

No. 1763 — Various Scouts and dogs: a, 7000d. b, 9000d. c, 10,000d. d, 14,000d.

No. 1764 — Inventors: a, 7000d, Dmitri Mendeleev (1834-1907). b, 9000d, Auguste (1862-1954) and Louis Lumière (1864-1948). c, 10,000d, Joseph Michel (1740-1810) and Jacques Etienne Montgolfier (1745-99). d, Samuel F. B. Morse (1791-1872).

No. 1765 — Orchids and famous Blacks: a, Malcolm X (1925-65). b, Albert Luthuli (1898-1967). c, Dr. Martin Luther King, Jr. (1929-68). d, Steve Biko (1946-77).

No. 1766, 40,000d, Scout and dog, diff. No. 1767, 40,000d, John Logie Baird (1888-1946), inventor. No. 1768, 40,000d, Nelson Mandela.

2007, Dec. 31   *Perf. 12¾x13¼*
Sheets of 4, #a-d

1763-1765   A322   Set of 3   18.00   18.00

Souvenir Sheets

1766-1768   A322   Set of 3   18.00   18.00

Souvenir sheets of 1 of Nos. 1765a-1765d with colored frames exist.

Miniature Sheets

Flora and Fauna — A323

No. 1769 — Rabbits: a, 5000d, Lepus saxatilis. b, 5000d, Pronolagus crassicaudatus. c, 10,000d, Bunolagus monticularis. d, 15,000d, Lepus stracki.

No. 1770 — Hogs: a, 5000d, Phacochoerus africanus. b, 5000d, Potamochoerus porcus. c, 10,000d, Sus scrofa. d, 15,000d, Potamochoerus larvatus.

No. 1771 — Hippopotami: a, 5000d, Hippopotamus amphibius. b, 5000d, Hexaprotodon liberiensis. c, 10,000d, Hexaprotodon liberiensis, diff. d, 15,000d, Hippopotamus amphibius, diff.

No. 1772 — Hyenas: a, 5000d, Lycaon pictus. b, 5000d, Crocuta crocuta. c, 10,000d, Hyaena brunnea. d, 15,000d, Hyaena hyaena.

No. 1773 — Bats: a, 5000d, Mops condylurus. b, 5000d, Cardioderma cor. c, 10,000d, Taphozous mauritianus. d, 15,000d, Hypsignatus monstrosus.

No. 1774 — Cats: a, 5000d, Felis caracal. b, 5000d, Felis serval. c, 10,000d, Felis chaus. d, 15,000d, Felis sylvestris.

No. 1775 — Butterflies: a, 5000d, Charaxes monteiri female. b, 5000d, Papilio leonidas thomasius. c, 10,000d, Hypolimnas salmacis thomensis. d, 10,000d, Charaxes monteiri male. e, 15,000d, Charaxes odysseus.

No. 1776 — Fish: a, 5000d, Ostracion tricornis. b, 5000d, Holocentrus axensionis "Caqui". c, 10,000d, Canthidermis maculatus. d, 10,000d, Rhinecanthus aculeatus. e, 15,000d, Diodon hystrix.

No. 1777 — Medicinal plants: a, 5000d, Buchholzia coriacea. b, 5000d, Piperonia pallucila. c, 5000d, Achyranthes aspera. d, 10,000d, Adenoplus breviflorus. e, 10,000d, Hiliotropium indicum. f, 10,000d, Mimosa pigra. g, 15,000d, Cymbopogon citratus. h, 15,000d, Bryophilllum pinatum.

No. 1778 — Birds: a, 5000d, Alcedo leucogaster nais. b, 5000d, Prinia molleri. c, 5000d, Spermestes cucullatus. d, 5000d, Treron S. thomae. e, 5000d, Euplectes aureus. f, 10,000d, Speirops lugubris. g, 10,000d, Textor grandis. h, 10,000d, Alcedo leucogaster nais, diff. i, 10,000d, Anabathmis hartlaubii. j, 10,000d, Xanthophilus princeps. k, 15,000d, Serinus rufobrunneus. l, 15,000d, Cheatura thomensis. m, 15,000d, Tyto alba thomensis. n, 15,000d, Estrilda astrild.

2007, Dec. 31 Litho.   *Perf. 13x13¼*
Sheets of 4, #a-d

1769-1774   A323   Set of 6   30.00   30.00

Sheets of 5, #a-e

1775-1776   A323   Set of 2   13.00   13.00

Perf. 13¼x13

1777   A323   Sheet of 8, #a-h   11.00   11.00
1778   A323   Sheet of 14, #a-n   19.00   19.00

Dated 2008.

A324

No. 1779 — Napoleon Bonaparte (1769-1821), French emperor, and: a, 5000d, Painting of Napoleon on horseback at right. b, 5000d, Military medal at left. c, 5000d, Military medal at right. d, 70,000d, Painting of Napoleon on horseback at left.

No. 1780 — United States ambulances: a, 5000d, Ambulance and helicopter. b, 5000d, Specialized transport team ambulance. c, 5000d, Ambulance with blue and red stripes. d, 70,000d, Ambulance with blue stripes.

No. 1781 — Japanese ambulances: a, 5000d, Ambulance at hospital ambulance bay, red cross at right. b, 5000d, Ambulance at hospital, red cross at UL c, 5000d, Ambulance at hospital, red cross at UR. d, 70,000d, Ambulance and rear view mirror, red cross at UL.

No. 1782 — European ambulances: a, 5000d, Italian ambulance and Leaning Tower of Pisa. b, 5000d, German ambulance and Cologne Cathedral. c, 5000d, British ambulance and Big Ben. d, 70,000d, French ambulance and Eiffel Tower.

No. 1783 — African ambulances: a, 5000d, Ambulance, people, red cross at LL. b, 5000d, Tractor ambulance, red cross at UL. c, 5000d, Ambulance and Red Cross workers. d, 70,000d, Ambulance with red diagonal stripes.

No. 1784 — Henry Ford (1863-1947), automobile manufacturer, 1908 Model T, and : a, 5000d, Drawing of automobile. b, 5000d, Ford poster, Red Cross flag above Model T ambulance. c, 5000d, Ford advertisement in Spanish. d, 70,000d, Horn.

No. 1785 — Harley-Davidson motorcycles, 105th anniv.: a, 5000d, FLHTCU Ultra Classic Electra Glide. b, 5000d, XL-1200C Sportster 1200 Custom. c, 5000d, FLSTC Heritage Softail Classic. d, 70,000d, FXDC Dyna Super Glide Custom.

No. 1786 — Franz Schubert (1797-1828), composer, and: a, 5000d, Schubert reading book. b, 5000d, Men and women. c, 5000d, Buildings. d, 70,000d, Piano and bench.

No. 1787 — Giacomo Puccini (1858-1924), composer, and: a, 5000d, Puccini and piano. b, 5000d, Costumed man in chair. c, 5000d, Room. d, 70,000d, Man and woman from Puccini opera.

No. 1788 — Nikolai Rimsky-Korsakov (1844-1908), composer, and: a, 5000d, Frog Tsarevna, painting by Viktor Vasnetzov. b, 5000d, Scene from opera "Mlada." c, 5000d, Scene from opera "The Tsar's Bride." d, 70,000d, Scene from opera "Boris Godunov."

No. 1789 — Bee Gees rock band and: a, 5000d, Bee Gees Greatest Hits album cover. b, 5000d, Guitar at left. c, 5000d, Microphone at LR. d, 70,000d, Record of "More Than a Woman" at LL.

No. 1790 — Vivian Ernest Fuchs (1908-99), Polar explorer, and: a, 5000d, Canis lupus familiaris. b, 5000d, Pygoscelis papua. c, 5000d, Stercorarius pomarinus. d, 70,000d, Ursus maritimus.

No. 1791 — Discovery of Halley's comet, 250th anniv.: a, 5000d, Edmond Halley and sextant. b, 5000d, Halley and globe. c, 5000d, Halley and compass, people viewing comet. d, 70,000d, People viewing comet.

No. 1792 — NASA, 50th anniv.: a, 5000d, Pres. John F. Kennedy, space shuttle on launch pad. b, 5000d, Astronaut David R. Scott, Gemini 7. c, 5000d, Astronaut Neil A. Armstrong, Viking lander. d, 70,000d, Crew of Apollo 17 and Lunar Rover.

No. 1793 — Snakes: a, 5000d, Macroprotodon cucullatus. b, 5000d, Python regius. c, 5000d, Bitis arietans and Bitis nasicornis. d, 70,000d, Green mamba.

No. 1794 — Crocodilians: a, 5000d, Caiman crocodilus. b, 5000d, Crocodylus acutus. c, 5000d, Crocodylus niloticus. d, 70,000d, Caiman latirostris.

No. 1795 — Various frogs with background color of: a, 5000d, Blue green. b, 5000d, Yellow orange. c, 5000d, Red orange. d, 70,000d, Blue.

No. 1796 — Butterflies: a, 5000d, Delias aglaia. b, 5000d, Junonia almana. c, 5000d, Junonia coenia. d, 70,000d, Cethosia biblis.

No. 1797 — Naturalists, flora and fauna: a, 5000d, Aristoteles (384 B.C.-322 B.C.), Phalacrocorax. b, 5000d, Theophrastus (372 B.C.-288 B.C.), Arum maculatum. c, 5000d, Pedanius Dioscorides (40-90), illustrations from Dioscorides Neapolitanus. d, 70,000d, Pliny the Elder (23-79), manuscript illustration.

A325

No. 1798 — Frank Sinatra (1915-98), singer, and: a, 5000d, Pres. John F. Kennedy, U.S. flag. b, 5000d, Pres. Ronald Reagan. c, 5000d, Elvis Presley. d, 70,000d, Marilyn Monroe.

No. 1799 — Shells and lighthouses: a, 5000d, Aporrhais pespelecani, Cape Hatteras Lighthouse, U.S., Kéréon Lighthouse, France. b, 5000d, Boroetrophon fraseri, La Laterna Lighthouse, Italy, St. Mary's Lighthouse, United Kingdom. c, 5000d, Conus guanche, Cabo de Palos Lighthouse, Spain, La Martrre Lighthouse, Canada. d, 70,000d, Marginella senegalensis, Kap Arkona Lighthouse, Germany, New Brighton Lighthouse, United Kingdom.

No. 1800 — Billy Karam, race car driver and Porsches: a, 7000d. b, 9000d. c, 10,000d. d, 14,000d.

No. 1801 — Naturalists: a, 15,000d, Andrea Cesalpino (c. 1519-1603), flower illustration, books. b, 15,000d, Conrad Gessner (1516-65), Quadrupedibus illustrations. c, 15,000d, Leonard Fuchs (1501-66), illustration of asparagus. d, 40,000d, Ulisse Aldrovandi (1522-1605), illustrations of mythical beasts.

No. 1802 — Elvis Presley (1935-77) in army uniform: a, 5000d, Wearing cap in foreground and background. b, 10,000d, Wearing cap in background photograph. c, 10,000d, Wearing helmet with goggles in foreground. d, 15,000d, Wearing cap in foreground photograph. e, 15,000d, Guitar in background. f, 30,000d, Reading mail.

No. 1803 — Bridges: a, 5000d, Humber Bridge, United Kingdom, and ship. b, 10,000d, Chain Bridge, Hungary, and police car. c, 10,000d, Erasmus Bridge, Netherlands, and ship. d, 15,000d, Sydney Harbour Bridge, Australia, and rescue boat. e, 15,000d, Brooklyn Bridge, U.S., and airplane. f, 30,000d, Oresund Bridge, Denmark, and hydroplane ambulance.

No. 1804 — Submarines: a, 5000d, Type XXI U-boat, Germany. b, 10,000d, K-21, Soviet Union. c, 10,000d, U-boat 530, Germany, Boat I-52, Japan. d, 15,000d, Royal Navy "S" Class, United Kingdom. e, 15,000d, USS Tang. f, 30,000d, Delta-17, Soviet Union.

No. 1805 — Medicinal plants: a, 5000d, Sophora denudata. b, 10,000d, Mussaenda landia. c, 10,000d, Agarista salicifolia. d, 15,000d, Dodonea viscosa. e, 15,000d, Jumellea fragrans. f, 30,000d, Centella asiatica.

No. 1806, 10,000d, — Mushrooms and orchids: a, Strobilomyces floccopus, Cymbidium. b, Entoloma clypeatum, Calypso bulbosa. c, Gymnopilus spectabilis, Coeloglossum viride. d, Leccinum scabrum, Arachnis annamensis. e, Cortinarius praestans, Galanthus nivalis. f, Cortinarius traganus, Arundina graminifolia. g, Inocybe fastigiata, Aspasia epidendroides. h, Pholiota destruens, Orchis papilionacea. i, Hebeloma radicosum, Dendrophylax lindenii.

No. 1807, 95,000d, Napoleon Bonaparte, diff. No. 1808, 95,000d, Ambulances and airplane. No. 1809, 95,000d, Japanese ambulance and fire station. No. 1810, 95,000d, Ambulance and word "Ambulance" painted on vehicle roof. No. 1811, 95,000d, Animal-drawn ambulance wagon. No. 1812, 95,000d, Ford and Model T. No. 1813, 95,000d, Harley-Davidson FXDWC Dyna Wide Glide motorcycle. No. 1814, 95,000d, Schubert at piano. No. 1815, 95,000d, Puccini, poster for "La Boheme." No. 1816, 95,000d, Rimsky-Korsakov, scene from opera "Sadko." No. 1817, 95,000d, Bee Gees. No. 1818, 95,000d, Vivian Fuchs and Ursus maritimus, diff. No. 1819, 95,000d, Halley and Halley's Comet. No. 1820, 95,000d, Astronauts, Explorer I spacecraft. No. 1821, 95,000d, Osteolaemus. No. 1822, 95,000d, Hyla gratiosa, Pseudis paradoxa. No. 1823, 95,000d, Caligo memnon. No. 1824, 95,000d, Nicolas Steno (1638-86), naturalist, and drawing of shark's head. No. 1825, 95,000d, John Ray (1627-1705), naturalist, drawings of dodo and turkey. No. 1826, 95,000d, Sinatra. No. 1827, 95,000d, Presley. No. 1828, 95,000d, Tower Bridge, United Kingdom, and tugboat. No. 1829, 95,000d, Type XXI U-boat, Germany, diff. No. 1830, 95,000d, Psiloxylon mauritanum. No. 1831, 95,000d, Arundina graminifola, Suillus aeruginascens.

2008, Feb. 4 Litho.   *Perf. 12¾x13¼*
Sheets of 4, #a-d

1779-1795   A324   Set of 17   200.00   200.00
1796-1801   A325   Set of 6   65.00   65.00

Sheets of 6, #a-f

1802-1803   A324   Set of 2   24.00   24.00
1804-1805   A325   Set of 2   24.00   24.00

Miniature Sheet

1806   A325   10,000d   Sheet of 9, #a-i   12.50   12.50

Souvenir Sheets
Perf. 13¼ Syncopated

1807-1831   A324   Set of 25   330.00   330.00

2008 Summer Olympics,
Beijing — A326

Olympic Stamps — A327

No. 1832: a, Tennis. b, Pole vault. c, Weight lifting. d, Rowing.

No. 1833: a, 5000d, Angola #614. b, 5000d, St. Thomas & Prince Islands #838. c, 5000d, Guinea-Bissau #369E. d, 70,000d, Guinea-Bissau #370.

No. 1834: a, 5000d, Cape Verde #826. b, 5000d, Guinea-Bissau #776. c, 5000d, Mozambique #626. d, 70,000d, Mozambique #861.

No. 1835: a, 5000d, Mozambique #945. b, 5000d, St. Thomas & Prince Islands #568. c, 5000d, Guinea-Bissau #936. d, 70,000d, Mozambique #898.

No. 1836: a, 5000d, Guinea-Bissau #612. b, 5000d, St. Thomas & Prince Islands #1170. c, 5000d, St. Thomas & Prince Islands #569. d, 70,000d, Guinea-Bissau #C20.

No. 1837: a, 5000d, St. Thomas & Prince Islands #805c. b, 5000d, Guinea-Bissau #402B. c, 5000d, Guinea-Bissau #369D. d, 70,000d, St. Thomas & Prince Islands #1094.

No. 1838: a, 5000d, Mozambique #1156. b, 5000d, Guinea-Bissau #C18. c, 5000d, Cape Verde #828. d, 70,000d, St. Thomas & Prince Islands #1050C.

No. 1839: a, 5000d, Cape Verde #406. b, 5000d, Angola #843. c, 5000d, Guinea-Bissau #775. d, 70,000d, Angola #1268.

2008, Mar. 10   Perf. 12¾x13¼
1832 A326 5000d Sheet of 4,
          #a-d   2.75   2.75
Sheets of 4, #a-d
1833-1839 A327 Set of 7   72.50 72.50
Nos. 1834a, 1834c, 1838a, 1839b each exist in a souvenir sheet of 1.

A328

A329

No. 1840 — People holding Chinese porcelain, with background color of: a, 5000d, Dull green. b, 5000d, Lilac. c, 5000d, Light blue. d, 70,000d, Light lilac.

No. 1841 — Castles: a, 5000d, Bran Castle, Romania. b, 5000d, Windsor Castle, Great Britain. c, 5000d, Neuschwanstein Castle, Germany. d, 70,000d, Carcassonne, France.

No. 1842 — Herbert von Karajan (1908-89), conductor, with inset photograph of: a, 5000d, Karajan and woman. b, 5000d, Karajan and machine. c, 5000d, Karajan conducting. d, 70,000d, Outer space scene.

No. 1843 — Lord Robert Baden-Powell (1857-1941), founder of Boy Scouts, and: a, 5000d, *The Scout* magazine cover, orchids. b, 5000d, Owl with wings spread, butterfly on flower. c, 5000d, Owl, butterfly, flower. d, 70,000d, *Scouting for Boys* book cover.

No. 1844 — Table tennis players: a, 5000d, Wang Liqin. b, 5000d, Wang Hao. c, 5000d, Werner Schlager. d, 70,000d, Kong Linghui.

No. 1845 — Table tennis players: a, 5000d, Guo Yue. b, 5000d, Zhang Yining. c, 5000d, Wang Nan. d, 70,000d, Deng Yaping.

No. 1846 — Apparition at Lourdes, 150th anniv.: a, 5000d, Lourdes Basilica, photograph and arms of Pope Benedict XVI. b, 5000d, Lourdes Basilica, apparition. c, 5000d, Statue of Virgin Mary, Bernadette Soubirous. d, 70,000d, St. Peter's Basilica, photograph and arms of Pope John Paul II.

No. 1847 — Pandas, Scouting emblem, and: a, 5000d, Tree with foliage. b, 5000d, Snowflakes. c, 5000d, Stars and tree stump. d, 70,000d, Tree, baby panda.

No. 1848 — Loxodonta africana at LR and: a, 5000d, Hippotigris. b, 5000d, Second elephant. c, 5000d, Second elephant and antelope. d, 70,000d, Giraffa camelopardalis.

No. 1849 — Horse racing: a, 5000d, Horse and jockey, denomination over orange red area. b, 5000d, Horse and jockey, denomination over blue area. c, 5000d, Horse and sulky. d, 70,000d, Horse and sulky, diff.

No. 1850 — Waterfalls and wildlife: a, 5000d, Jog Falls, India, Panthera tigris bengalensis. b, 5000d, Gocta Falls, Peru, Vultur gryphus. c, 5000d, Ouzoud Falls, Morocco, Camelus dromedarius. d, 70,000d, Huangguoshu Falls, People's Republic of China, Ailurus fulgens.

No. 1851 — Inventors: a, 5000d, Muhammad al-Khwarizmi, inventor of algebra. b, 10,000d, Alexander Graham Bell, inventor of telephone. c, 10,000d, Christiaan Huygens, inventor of pendulum clock. d, 15,000d, Guglielmo Marconi, inventor of radiotelegraph. e, 15,000d, James Watt, inventor of steam engine. f, 30,000d, Thomas Edison, inventor of long-lasting light bulb.

No. 1852 — Inventors: a, 5000d, Samuel F. B. Morse, inventor of Morse code. b, 10,000d, Blaise Pascal, inventor of mechanical calculator. c, 10,000d, Nicolas Cugnot, inventor of first automobile. d, 15,000d, Emile Berliner, inventor of disc record gramophone. e, 15,000d, Rudolf Diesel, inventor of Diesel engine. f, 30,000d, Ivan Kulibin, inventor of elevator.

No. 1853 — Airbus airplanes: a, 5000d, Airbus 380, Claude Lelaie, test pilot. b, 10,000d, Airbus Beluga. c, 10,000d, Airbus 380, Jacques Rosay, test pilot. d, 15,000d, Airbus 380, cockpit instruments. e, 15,000d, Airbus Beluga, Rosay. f, 30,000d, Airbus 380, passenger cabin.

2008, Mar. 28   Perf. 12¾x13¼
Sheets of 4, #a-d, + 2 labels
Sheets of 4, #a-d
1840-1841 A328 Set of 2   22.50 22.50
Sheets of 4, #a-d
1842-1850 A329 Set of 9 110.00 110.00
Sheets of 6, #a-f
1851-1853 A329 Set of 3   30.00 30.00

A330

No. 1854 — Fire trucks: a, 15,000d, 1906 Shand Mason & Co., Aztec god of fire. b, 25,000d, 1928 Stoughton, Ctesibius, Greek inventor. c, 30,000d, 1939 Scammell, Xiuhtechutli, Aztec lord of volcanoes. d, 30,000d, 1931 Leyland, Mexican god of fire.

No. 1855 — Churches: a, 15,000d, Santa Maria del Fiore Basilica, Florence, Italy, crucifix. b, 25,000d, Basilica of Our Lady of Lichen, Poland, Pope John Paul II. c, 30,000d,

Cologne Cathedral, Germany, Pope Benedict XVI. d, 30,000d, Notre Dame Cathedral, Paris, France, dragon gargoyle.

No. 1856 — Agriculture: a, 20,000d, Grapes and vineyard. b, 20,000d, Bee on flower, beekeeper and hive. c, 20,000d, Wheat stalks and harvested field. d, 40,000d, Tulips and windmill.

No. 1857 — Rotary International emblem and chess champions: a, 20,000d, Bobby Fischer. b, 20,000d, Anatoly Karpov. c, 20,000d, Garry Kasparov. d, 40,000d, Vladimir Kramnik.

No. 1858 — Pre-historic rock art: a, 25,000d, Buffalos, hunters. b, 25,000d, Horned animals, pre-historic man. c, 25,000d, Animal, pre-historic man with spear. d, 25,000d, Animals, stick figures of men.

No. 1859 — Jewelry made with: a, 25,000d, Silver (prata). b, 25,000d, Platinum (platina). c, 25,000d, Pearls (carbonato de cálcio. d, 25,000d, Diamond (diamante).

No. 1860 — European urban transportation: a, 5,000d, Electric train, Budapest. b, 10,000d, Subway train, Barcelona. c, 15,000d, Double-decker bus, London. d, 20,000d, Trolley bus, Milan. e, 20,000d, Taxi, Berlin. f, 30,000d, Subway train, Paris.

No. 1861 — Nobel Peace laureates: a, 5,000d, Henri Dunant, 1901. b, 10,000d, Lech Walesa, 1983. c, 15,000d, Albert Schweitzer, 1953. d, 20,000d, Mikhail Gorbachev, 1990. e, 20,000d, F. W. de Klerk, 1993. f, 30,000d, Dalai Lama Tenzin Gyatso, 1989.

No. 1862 — Albatrosses: a, 5,000d, Phoebastria nigripes. b, 10,000d, Diomedea exulans. c, 15,000d, Phoebetria. d, 20,000d, Thalassarche melanophrys, bird in flight at left. e, 20,000d, Thalassarche melanophrys, bird in water at right. f, 30,000d, Phoebastria immutabilis.

No. 1863 — World War II: a, 5,000d, Sir Winston Churchill, Hawker Tempest airplane. b, 10,000d, Soviet T34/85 tanks. c, 15,000d, Gen. Charles de Gaulle, Bloch MB 210 airplanes. d, 20,000d, Douglas TBD Devastator airplane, HMS Hood. e, 20,000d, Messerscmitt Bf-109E-3 and Bf-109E7/Trop airplanes. f, 30,000d, USS Sawfish.

No. 1864 — Scientists: a, 5,000d, Haroun Tazieff, vulcanologist. b, 10,000d, John Gould, ornithologist. c, 15,000d, Norman L. Bowen, geologist. d, 20,000d, Johann Wolfgang von Goethe, poet and morphologist. e, 20,000d, Ivan Pavlov, physiologist. f, 30,000d, Charles Darwin, naturalist.

No. 1865 — Famous people and dogs: a, 5,000d, Pres. Bill Clinton, Labrador retriever. b, 10,000d, Tony Parker, basketball player, Eva Longoria, actress, Maltese. c, 15,000d, Knud Rasmussen, polar explorer, Husky. d, 20,000d, Madonna, singer, Chihuahua. e, 20,000d, Steve Irwin, conservationist, Staffordshire bull terrier. f, 30,000d, Dorothy Gladys "Dodie" Smith, author, Dalmatian.

No. 1866, 95,000d, St. Peter's Basilica, Vatican City, Pope Benedict XVI. No. 1867, 95,000d, St. Bernard and German shepherd. No. 1868, 100,000d, 1927 Dandy fire engine, fire helmet. No. 1869, 100,000d, Diomedea (albatrosses). No. 1870, 100,000d, Gold nugget and ring.

2008, May 19   Perf. 12¾x13¼
1854 A330 Sheet of 4, #a-d 12.50 12.50
Sheets of 4, #a-d, + 2 labels
1855-1859 A330 Set of 5   62.50 62.50
Sheets of 6, #a-f
1860-1865 A330 Set of 6   75.00 75.00
Souvenir Sheets
Perf. 13¼ Syncopated
1866-1870 A330 Set of 5   60.00 60.00
Nos. 1866-1870 each contain one 50x39mm stamp.

A331

No. 1871 — Animals on bank notes of the world: a, 15,000d, Snake, Aruba 25-florin note. b, 25,000d, Owl, Surinam 25-gulden note. c, 30,000d, Moose, Belarus 25-ruble note. d, 30,000d, Buffalo, Tanzania 500-shilling note.

No. 1872 — Dogs: a, 15,000d, Alaskan malamute. b, 25,000d, Siberian husky. c, 30,000d, Greenland dog. d, 30,000d, Samoyed.

No. 1873 — Various nudes by Pierre-Auguste Renoir (1841-1919) with Renoir at: a, 20,000d, Left, without hat. b, 20,000d, Right, wearing hat. c, 20,000d, Left, wearing hat. d, 30,000d, Right, wearing hat, diff.

No. 1874 — Various nudes by George-Pierre Seurat (1859-91) with Seurat at: a, 20,000d, Left, facing forward. b, 20,000d, Right, facing left. c, 20,000d, Left, facing right. d, 30,000d, Right, facing forward.

No. 1875 — Various paintings by Utagawa Kunisada (1786-1865) with Japanese flag at: a, 20,000d, UL, gray panel at right. b, 20,000d, LL, gray panel at left. c, 20,000d, LL, gray panel at right. d, 30,000d, UL, gray panel at left.

No. 1876 — Orchids and butterflies: a, 25,000d, Cypripedium kentuckiense, Papilio laglaizei. b, 25,000d, Phalaenopsis lindenii toapei, Prepona xenagoras. c, 25,000d, Paphiopedilum, Danaus sita. d, 25,000d, Phragmipedium sedenii, Ornithoptera priamus urvilianus.

No. 1877 — German lighthouses: a, 25,000d, Amrum Lighthouse. b, 25,000d, Neuland Lighthouse. c, 25,000d, Eckernförde Lighthouse. d, 25,000d, List Ost Lighthouse.

No. 1878 — Israel, 60th anniv.: a, 25,000d, Theodor Herzl, arms of Israel. b, 25,000d, David Ben-Gurion, arms of Jerusalem. c, 25,000d, Golda Meir, star of David. d, 25,000d, Dome of the Rock, Jerusalem, menorah.

No. 1879, 100,000d, Paintings by Utagawa Kunisada. No. 1880, 100,000d, Cattleya intermedia, Ornithoptera paradisea.

2008, July 17   Perf. 12¾x13¼
Sheets of 4, #a-d
1871-1878 A331 Set of 8 100.00 100.00
Souvenir Sheets
Perf. 13¼ Syncopated
1879-1880 A331 Set of 2   25.00 25.00
Nos. 1879-1880 each contain one 50x39mm stamp.

A332

No. 1881 — Various trolley cars with background color of: a, 15,000d, Pink. b, 25,000d, Yellow. c, 30,000d, Green. d, 30,000d, Blue.

No. 1882 — Fishermen and fish: a, 15,000d, Sphyraena sphyraena. b, 25,000d, Thunnus alalunga. c, 30,000d, Salmo trutta. d, 30,000d, Lutjanus gibbus.

No. 1883 — Zeppelins: a, 20,000d, LZ-127 Graf Zeppelin over Alps. b, 20,000d, LZ-2 over Friedrichshafen, Germany. c, 20,000d, L-9 over Würzburg, Germany. d, 40,000d, LZ-130 Graf Zeppelin II over Rothenburg, Germany.

No. 1884 — Ancient Egyptian artifacts: a, 20,000d, Bust of Queen Nefertiti, Ankh. b, 20,000d, Sarcophagus, Queen Cleopatra VII. c, 20,000d, Funerary mask of King Tutankhamun, scarab beetle. d, 40,000d, Horus depicted as falcon, King Ramses II.

No. 1885 — Golfers: a, 25,000d, Tiger Woods. b, 25,000d, Todd Hamilton. c, 25,000d, Ernie Els. d, 25,000d, Ben Curtis.

No. 1886 — Circus performers: a, 25,000d, Billy Smart Circus, British flag. b, 25,000d, Moscow State Circus, Russian flag. c, 25,000d, Herman Renz Circus, Netherlands flag. d, 25,000d, Chinese State Circus, flag of People's Republic of China.

No. 1887 — Campaign against AIDS: a, 25,000d, Pres. Bill Clinton, doctor treating child. b, 25,000d, Test tubes in laboratory, woman being treated, AIDS ribbon. c, 25,000d, Doctor getting blood sample from finger, doctor examining infant, AIDS ribbon. d, 25,000d, Hilary Koprowski, immunologist, vials of polio vaccine.

No. 1888, 95,000d, Salmo salar and fisherman. No. 1889, 95,000d, LZ-129 Hindenburg over Lake Constance. No. 1890, 95,000d, Eye of Ra, Anubis attending the mummy of Sennedjem. No. 1891, 95,000d, Woods, diff. No. 1892, 95,000d, Cirque du Soleil performers. No. 1893, 95,000d, Dr. Albert Schweitzer and staff at Lambaréné, Gabon hospital.

2008, July 17   Perf. 12¾x13¼
Sheets of 4, #a-d
1881-1887 A332 Set of 7   90.00 90.00

Souvenir Sheets
Perf. 13¼ Syncopated

1888-1893 A332 Set of 6 75.00 75.00

Nos. 1888-1893 each contain one 50x39mm stamp.

Archaeology — A333

No. 1894 — Archaeologists and items from: a, 20,000d, Paleolithic Era. b, 20,000d, Neolithic Era. c, 20,000d, Bronze Age. d, 40,000d, Iron Age.
100,000d, Archaeologist and items from Persian Period.

2008, Sept. 14   **Perf. 12¾x13¼**
1894 A333 Sheet of 4, #a-d 12.50 12.50
Souvenir Sheet
Perf. 13¼ Syncopated
1895 A333 100,000d multi 12.50 12.50

No. 1895 contains one 38x39mm stamp.

A334

No. 1896 — Various nudes of Paul Gauguin (1848-1903), with Gauguin at: a, 15,000d, Left. b, 25,000d, Right. c, 30,000d, Left, diff. d, 30,000d, Right, diff.
No. 1897 — Various nudes of Pablo Picasso (1881-1973), with Picasso at: a, 15,000d, Left. b, 25,000d, Right. c, 30,000d, Left, diff. d, 30,000d, Right, diff.
No. 1898 — Various nudes of Peter Paul Rubens (1577-1640), with Rubens at: a, 20,000d, Left, in sepia. b, 20,000d, Right. c, 20,000d, Left, in color. d, 40,000d, Right, diff.
No. 1899 — Various nudes of Gustave Moreau (1826-98), with Moreau at: a, 20,000d, Left, in black. b, 20,000d, Right. c, 20,000d, Left, in brown. d, 40,000d, Right, diff.
No. 1900 — Costumes of: a, 20,000d, Ancient Greece. b, 20,000d, France, 18th cent. c, 20,000d, Russia, 17th cent. d, 40,000d, Japan, 19th cent.
No. 1901 — Divers, starfish, and dolphins: a, 20,000d, Delphinus delphis. b, 20,000d, Grampus griseus. c, 20,000d, Platanista gangetica. d, 40,000d, Cephalorhynchus commersonii.
No. 1902 — Dogs: a, 20,000d, Fox terriers. b, 20,000d, Whippets. c, 20,000d, Rhodesian ridgebacks. d, 40,000d, Basset hounds.
No. 1903 — Rescue dogs: a, 20,000d, St. Bernards. b, 20,000d, Labrador retrievers. c, 20,000d, Border collies. d, 40,000d, German shepherds (one with Red Cross identification).
No. 1904 — Domesticated animals: a, 25,000d, Cattle. b, 25,000d, Dogs. c, 25,000d, Cats. d, 25,000d, Horses.
No. 1905 — Horses: a, 25,000d, Cowboy riding chestnut horse (Alazao). b, 25,000d, Friesians. c, 25,000d, Clydesdales. d, 25,000d, Icelandic horses.
No. 1906 — Cat breeds: a, 25,000d, Persian. b, 25,000d, Russian Blue. c, 25,000d, Devon Rex. d, 25,000d, Siamese.
No. 1907 — Sir Peter Markham Scott (1909-89), conservationist and: a, 25,000d, Phascolarctos cinereus. b, 25,000d, Gorilla. c, 25,000d, Ailurus fulgens. d, 25,000d, Ailuropoda melanoleuca.
No. 1908 — Masonic emblem and: a, 25,000d, Alexander Pushkin, writer. b, 25,000d, Louis Armstrong, musician. c, 25,000d, Oscar Wilde, writer. d, 25,000d, Wolfgang Amadeus Mozart, composer.
No. 1909, 100,000d, Tursiops truncatus, starfish and diver, horiz. No. 1910, 100,000d, Two cats, horiz.

2008, Sept. 14   **Perf. 12¾x13¼**
Sheets of 4, #a-d
1896-1908 A334 Set of 13 165.00 165.00

Souvenir Sheets
Perf. 13¼ Syncopated

1909-1910 A334 Set of 2 26.00 26.00

Nos. 1909-1910 each contain one 50x39mm stamp.

A335

No. 1911 — Illustrations of women by Alphonse Mucha (1860-1939) with woman at right with: a, 5000d, Hands in hair. b, 5000d, Hands folded below chin. c, 5000d, Hands on chin. d, 70,000d, Hand at top of chest.
No. 1912 — Charlton Heston (1923-2008), actor, and scenes from: a, 15,000d, The Ten Commandments, 1956. b, 25,000d, Planet of the Apes, 1968. c, 30,000d, The Agony and the Ecstasy, 1965. d, 30,000d, Ben-Hur, 1959.
No. 1913 — Shells: a, 20,000d, Cypraea algoensis, Adamussium colbecki. b, 20,000d, Lunatia grossularia, Trophon geversianus. c, 20,000d, Buccinum undatum, Angaria vicdani. d, 40,000d, Mytilus edulis, Haliotis iris.
No. 1914, 95,000d, The Times of the Day Series, by Mucha. No. 1915, 100,000d, Heston and wife, Lydia Clarke. No. 1916, 100,000d, Cardium edule, Architectonica perspectiva.

2008, Nov. 3   **Perf. 12¾x13¼**
Sheets of 4, #a-d
1911-1913 A335 Set of 3 40.00 40.00
Souvenir Sheets
Perf. 13¼ Syncopated
1914-1916 A335 Set of 3 40.00 40.00

Nos. 1914-1916 each contain one 50x39mm stamp.

A336

No. 1917 — Various nudes of Gustave Courbet (1819-77), with Courbet at: a, 15,000d, Left. b, 25,000d, Right. c, 30,000d, Left, diff. d, 30,000d, Right, diff.
No. 1918 — Various nudes of Edouard Manet (1832-83), with Manet at: a, 15,000d, Left. b, 25,000d, Right. c, 30,000d, Left, diff. d, 30,000d, Right, diff.
No. 1919 — Various nudes of Paul Cézanne (1839-1906), with Cézanne at: a, 15,000d, Left. b, 25,000d, Right. c, 30,000d, Left, diff. d, 30,000d, Right, diff.
No. 1920 — Various nudes of Pierre Bonnard (1867-1947), with Bonnard at: a, 15,000d, Left. b, 25,000d, Right. c, 30,000d, Left, diff. d, 30,000d, Right, diff.
No. 1921 — Jules Verne (1828-1905), and illustrations from his books depicting: a, 15,000d, Spaceship. b, 25,000d, Spaceship, diff. c, 30,000d, Men, hat in air. d, 30,000d, Octopus.
No. 1922 — Dogs: a, 15,000d, Dingos. b, 25,000d, Pharaoh hounds. c, 30,000d, Mexican hairless dogs. d, 30,000d, Basenjis.
No. 1923 — Dogs: a, 20,000d, Groenendael Belgian shepherds. b, 20,000d, Caucasian shepherds. c, 20,000d, Central Asian shepherds. d, 40,000d, German shepherds.
No. 1924 — Red Cross flag and seaplanes: a, 20,000d, Sikorsky S-43. b, 20,000d, Canadair CL-215. c, 20,000d, Shin Meiwa US-1A. d, 40,000d, Grumman HU-16E Albatross.
No. 1925 — Helicopters, cent.: a, 20,000d, Paul Cornu, aircraft engineer. b, 20,000d, Cornu helicopter. c, 20,000d, VS-300A helicopter. d, 40,000d, Igor Sikorsky, helicopter designer, and helicopter.
No. 1926 — Moai of Easter Island and sailing ships: a, 20,000d, Grande Hermine. b, 20,000d, Sparrow. c, 20,000d, Victoria. d, 40,000d, Concorde.
No. 1927 — Animals and dams: a, 25,000d, Lynx lynx, Nurek Dam, Tajikistan. b, 25,000d, Capra ibex nubiana, Aswan High Dam, Egypt.

---

c, 25,000d, Ailurus fulgens, Three Gorges Dam, People's Republic of China. d, 25,000d, Sciurus carolinensis, Fort Peck Dam, U.S.
No. 1928 — Various paintings of Edgar Degas (1834-1917), with Degas at: a, 25,000d, Left, wearing hat. b, 25,000d, Right, without hat. c, 25,000d, Left, without hat. d, 25,000d, Right, holding hat.

2008, Nov. 3   **Perf. 12¾x13¼**
Sheets of 4, #a-d
1917-1928 A336 Set of 12 160.00 160.00

Election of Pres. Barack Obama — A337

No. 1929 — Pres. Obama, U.S. flag, and: a, 13,000d, White House. b, 13,000d, American Indians. c, 39,000d, Slave in chains, group of slaves. d, 39,000d, Statue of Liberty.
100,000d, Pres. Obama, Confederate soldiers.

2008, Dec. 4   **Perf. 12¾x13¼**
1929 A337 Sheet of 4, #a-d 13.00 13.00
Souvenir Sheet
Perf. 13¼ Syncopated
1930 A337 100,000d multi 13.00 13.00

No. 1930 contains one 50x39mm stamp.

Miniature Sheets

Fruits — A338

No. 1931 — Fruit from Republic of China: a, 1000d, Guavas. b, 1500d, Carambolas. c, 2000d, Jujubes. d, 2500d, Wax apples. e, 3000d, Papayas.
No. 1932 — Fruit from St. Thomas & Prince Islands: a, 1000d, Avocados (abacate). b, 1500d, Jackfruit (jaca), horiz. c, 2000d, Soursops (sap-sap). d, 2500d, Cherimoyas (anona). e, 3000d, Mangos (manga).

2008   **Litho.**   **Perf. 12½**
Sheets of 5, #a-e, + 4 labels
1931-1932 A338 Set of 2 6.00 6.00

Cooperation between Republic of China and St. Thomas & Prince Islands, 9th anniv. Dated 2006.

Worldwide Fund for Nature (WWF) A339

Psittacus eritahcus: No. 1933, 25,000d, One bird on branch. No. 1934, 25,000d, Two birds on branch. No. 1935, 25,000d, Chicks in nest. No. 1936, 25,000d, Bird in flight.

2009, Jan. 31   **Perf. 13x13¼**
1933-1936 A339 Set of 4 14.00 14.00
1936a   Souvenir sheet of 8, 2 each #1933-1936 28.00 28.00

A340

No. 1937 — Japanese film and music stars: a, 13,000d, Ken Watanabe. b, 13,000d, Miyavi. c, 39,000d, Chiaki Kuriyama. d, 39,000d, Utada Hikaru.
No. 1938 — Cats: a, 13,000d, Somali cat, Mogadishu, Somalia. b, 13,000d, Singapura cat, Singapore. c, 39,000d, Egyptian Mau cat, Giza Pyramids. d, 39,000d, Russian Blue cat, Red Square, Moscow.
No. 1939 — Polistes fuscatus and flowers: a, 13,000d, Malva sylvestris. b, 13,000d, Helianthus annuus. c, 39,000d, Lantana camara. d, 39,000d, Hebe x franciscana.
No. 1940 — High-speed trains: a, 13,000d, Eurostar. b, 13,000d, JR-Maglev. c, 39,000d, Shinkansen. d, 39,000d, Korea Train Express.
No. 1941 — Chess champions: a, 13,000d, Garry Kasparov. b, 13,000d, Anatoly Karpov. c, 39,000d, Vladimir Kremnik. d, 39,000d, Bobby Fischer.
No. 1942 — Shells: a, 13,000d, Thatcheria mirabilis. b, 13,000d, Amplustrum amplustre. c, 39,000d, Cryptospira elegans. d, 39,000d, Mercenaria mercenaria.
No. 1943 — Liverpool, 2008 European City of Culture: a, 13,000d, SuperLamBanana sculpture, Philharmonic Hall. b, 13,000d, King John, Metropolitan Cathedral. c, 39,000d, The Beatles, Yellow Submarine replica. d, 39,000d, Statue of Emlyn Hughes, Albert Docks.
No. 1944 — Paintings by Lucian Freud (1922-2011): a, 13,000d, Girl with a White Dog. b, 13,000d, Naked Portrait. c, 39,000d, Naked Portrait, diff. d, 39,000d, Naked Girl Asleep II.
No. 1945 — 90th birthday of Nelson Mandela, 1993 Nobel Peace laureate, and butterflies: a, 13,000d, Papilio dardanus. b, 13,000d, Zeuxidia aurelius. c, 39,000d, Speyeria cybele. d, 39,000d, Taenaris horsfieldii birchi.
No. 1946 — Crabs and lighthouses: a, 15,000d, Corystes cassivelaunus, Redonda Island Lighthouse, Sri Lanka. b, 25,000d, Macrocheira kaempferi, Cape Reinga Lighthouse, New Zealand. c, 30,000d, Callinectes sapidus, Hook Head Lighthouse, Ireland. d, 30,000d, Pseudocarcinus gigas, Vieille Lighthouse, France.
No. 1947 — Children, with child at left: a, 25,000d, Touching eye. b, 25,000d, With wound below eye. c, 25,000d, Wearing necklace. d, 25,000d, With flowers in hair.
No. 1948 — Nudes by Paul Delvaux (1897-1994), with inscription: a, 25,000d, O Elogio da Melancolia. b, 25,000d, Pompei. c, 25,000d, O despertar da Floresta. d, 25,000d, As Mulheres diante do Mar.
No. 1949 — Paintings by Tsukioka Yoshitoshi (1839-92), with inscriptions: a, 25,000d, Ichikawa Kodanji IV, Bando Hikosaburo V. b, 25,000d, 28 Assassinatos Famosas, Komagine Hachibyoe. c, 25,000d, Façanhasdo Shogunato Tokugawa, Hideyoshi. d, 25,000d, Apariçao da Princesa Aranha, Marshall Takamori.
No. 1950 — Paul Newman (1925-2008), actor, and: a, 25,000d, Scene from The Life and Times of Judge Roy Bean, 1972. b, 25,000d, Scene from Empire Falls, 2005. c, 25,000d, Wife, Joanne Woodward. d, 25,000d, Scene from The Color of Money, 1986.
No. 1951 — Indian film and music stars: a, 25,000d, Aamir Khan. b, 25,000d, Alka Yagnik. c, 25,000d, Lata Mangeshkar. d, 25,000d, Amitabh Bachchan.
No. 1952, 100,000d, Takeshi Kitano. No. 1953, 100,000d, Angora cats, Sultan Ahmed Mosque, Istanbul, Turkey. No. 1954, 100,000d, Painting of nudes by Delvaux, diff. No. 1955, 100,000d, Paintings by Yoshitoshi, diff. No. 1956, 100,000d, Newman and race car. No. 1957, 100,000d, Asha Bhosle.

2009, Jan. 31   **Perf. 12¾x13¼**
Sheets of 4, #a-d
1937-1951 A340 Set of 15 190.00 190.00

Souvenir Sheets
Perf. 13¼ Syncopated

1952-1957 A340 Set of 6   77.50   77.50

Nos. 1952-1957 each contain one 50x39mm stamp.

A341

No. 1958 — Local dishes: a, 25,000d, Molho no Fogo, map of Prince Island. b, 30,000d, Calúlú, Map of St. Thomas Island.

No. 1959 — Sister Emmanuelle (1908-2008), and: a, 13,000d, Pope John Paul II. b, 13,000d, Child amidst ruins. c, 39,000d, Children. d, 39,000d, Pope Benedict XVI.

No. 1960 — Sharks and jellyfish: a, 15,000d, Isurus oxyrinchus, Carukia barnesi. b, 25,000d, Sphyrna lewini, Aurelia aurita. c, 30,000d, Carcharhinus brevipinna, Phacellophora camtschatica. d, 30,000d, Pristiophorus nudipinnis, Pelagia noctiluca.

No. 1961 — Butterflies and caterpillars: a, 15,000d, Alcides agathyrsus, Papilio machaon caterpillar. b, 25,000d, Danaus sita, Brahmaea wallichi caterpillar. c, 30,000d, Troides aeacus, Danaus chrysippus caterpillar. d, 30,000d, Atrophaneura horishanus, Apatele alni caterpillar.

No. 1962 — Pres. Abraham Lincoln (1809-65), and: a, 25,000d, Son, Tad, head of Lincoln at Mount Rushmore. b, 25,000d, General Winfield Scott. c, 25,000d, Crowd at second inauguration, bust of Lincoln. d, 25,000d, Lincoln in chair, crowd at second inauguration.

No. 1963 — Indian Space Program: a, 25,000d, Abdul Kalam, Endusat satellite. b, 25,000d, Vikram Sarabhai, Aryabhata 1 satellite. c, 25,000d, Mahatma Gandhi, Chandrayaan 1 satellite. d, 25,000d, Astronaut Rakesh Sharma, launch of Chandrayaan 1.

No. 1964 — Joseph Haydn (1732-1809), composer, and: a, 25,000d, Musicians. b, 25,000d, Theater stage and orchestra. c, 25,000d, Hanover Square, London, 1791. d, 25,000d, Harpsichord and chair.

No. 1965 — Felix Mendelssohn (1809-47), composer, and: a, 25,000d, Building. b, 25,000d, Woman on piano bench, musical score. c, 25,000d, Woman and man listening to pianist. d, 25,000d, Mendelssohn's sister, Fanny.

No. 1966 — Louis Braille (1809-52), inventor of Braille writing; and: a, 25,000d, Building, Braille at left. b, 25,000d, Building, Braille at right. c, 25,000d, hand touching Braille text, Braille at left. d, 25,000d, Blind woman writing in Braille, Braille at right.

No. 1967 — Edgar Allan Poe (1809-49), writer, and: a, 25,000d, Poe's home, Bronx, New York. b, 25,000d, Illustration for poem, "The Raven." c, 25,000d, Books and room. d, 25,000d, Poe writing.

No. 1968 — Paintings by Shi Tao (1642-1707): a, 25,000d, Eight Scenic Spots in Huangshan, Shi Tao. b, 25,000d, An Old Man on a Boat. c, 25,000d, Mingxianquan and Hutouyan. d, 25,000d, Spring River.

No. 1969 — Various paintings by Toshusai Sharaku (1770-1825) with white line separating paintings below letters: a, 25,000d, "os" in "Toshusai." b, 25,000d, "us" in "Toshusai." c, 25,000d, "sh" in "Toshusai." d, 25,000d, "To" in "Toshusai."

No. 1970 — Two Strigops habroptilus in trees with animal name at: a, 25,000d, LL. b, 25,000d, UR. c, 25,000d, UL, below date. d, 25,000d, UL, below tree branch.

No. 1971 — New Zealand parrots: a, 25,000d, Strigops habroptilus, orange background. b, 25,000d, Nestor notabilis. c, 25,000d, Heterolocha acutirostris. d, 25,000d, Philesturnus carunculatus.

No. 1972 — Intl. Reconciliation Year: a, 25,000d, Mother Teresa. b, 25,000d, Pope John Paul II. c, 25,000d, Dalai Lama. d, 25,000d, Mohandas Gandhi.

No. 1973 — Primates and fruits: a, 25,000d, Saimiri sciureus, Anacardium occidentale. b, 25,000d, Saguinus oedipus, Passiflora edulis. c, 25,000d, Callithrix jacchus, Mangifera indica. d, 25,000d, Leontopithecus chrysomelas, Feijoa sellowiana.

No. 1974, 100,000d, Isurus paucus, Carukia barnesi. No. 1975, 100,000d, Euplagia quadripunctaria and caterpillar. No. 1976, 100,000d, Lincoln and U.S. flag. No. 1977, 100,000d, Krishnaswamy Kasturirangan, Insat-3c satellite. No. 1978, 100,000d, Periodictus potto, Tarsius spectrum. No. 1979, 100,000d, Panthera leo. No. 1980, 100,000d,

---

Acinonyx jubatus. No. 1981, 100,000d, Felis chaus. No. 1982, 100,000d, Apis mellifica. No. 1983, 100,000d, Jackie Chan, film actor.

2009, Mar. 31   **Perf. 12¾x13¼**
1958 A341   Sheet of 2, #a-
      b, + 2 labels   6.25   6.25

Sheets of 4, #a-d
1959-1973 A341   Set of 15   170.00   170.00

Souvenir Sheets
Perf. 13¼ Syncopated

1974-1983 A341   Set of 10   115.00   115.00

No. 1958 is dated 2008. Nos. 1974-1983 each contain one 50x39mm stamp.

Nos. 608-610, 714, 717-718, 735, 742, 747, 1488c, 1488e, 1527b, 1527e, 1550b & 1573e Srchd. in Black, Silver, Red and Gold

Methods and Perfs As Before
2009, Apr. 15

1984	A93	(8000d) on 50c #714	1.00 1.00
1987	A66	(8000d) on 1.50d #608 (S)	1.00 1.00
1988	A95	(8000d) on 10d #735	1.00 1.00
1990	A66	(8000d) on 11d #609 (S)	1.00 1.00
1991	A93	(8000d) on 15.50d #717	1.00 1.00
1992	A93	(8000d) on 16d #718	1.00 1.00
1993	A66	(8000d) on 17d #610 (S)	1.00 1.00
1994	A95	(8000d) on 18.50d #742 (R)	1.00 1.00
1995	A280	(8000d) on 7000d #1527b (S)	1.00 1.00
1996	A280	(8000d) on 7000d #1527e (S)	1.00 1.00
1997	A305	(8000d) on 7000d #1573e	1.00 1.00
1998	A305	(8000d) on 7000d #1573e (R)	1.00 1.00
1999	A305	(8000d) on 7000d #1573e (G)	1.00 1.00
2000	A265	(8000d) on 10,000d #1488c (S)	1.00 1.00
2001	A265	(8000d) on 10,000d #1488e	1.00 1.00
2002	A265	(8000d) on 10,000d #1488e (S)	1.00 1.00
2003	A294	(8000d) on 10,000d #1550b	1.00 1.00

Dated 2009

2004	A280	(8000d) on 7000d #1527b (R)	1.00 1.00
2006	A280	(8000d) on 7000d #1527e (R)	1.00 1.00
2007	A265	(8000d) on 10,000d #1488c (R)	1.00 1.00
2008	A265	(8000d) on 10,000d #1488e (R)	1.00 1.00
2009	A265	(8000d) on 10,000d #1488e (G)	1.00 1.00
2010	A294	(8000d) on 10,000d #1550b (R)	1.00 1.00

2011	A93	(14,000d) on 50c #714	1.75 1.75
2014	A66	(14,000d) on 1.50d #608 (S)	1.75 1.75
2015	A95	(14,000d) on 10d #735	1.75 1.75
2017	A66	(14,000d) on 11d #609 (S)	1.75 1.75
2018	A93	(14,000d) on 15.50d #717	1.75 1.75
2019	A93	(14,000d) on 16d #718	1.75 1.75
2020	A66	(14,000d) on 17d #610 (S)	1.75 1.75
2022	A280	(14,000d) on 7000d #1527b (S)	1.75 1.75
2023	A280	(14,000d) on 7000d #1527e (S)	1.75 1.75

2024	A305	(14,000d) on 7000d #1573e	1.75 1.75
2025	A305	(14,000d) on 7000d #1573e (R)	1.75 1.75
2026	A305	(14,000d) on 7000d #1573e (G)	1.75 1.75
2027	A265	(14,000d) on 10,000d #1488c (S)	1.75 1.75
2028	A265	(14,000d) on 10,000d #1488e	1.75 1.75
2029	A265	(14,000d) on 10,000d #1488e (S)	1.75 1.75
2030	A294	(14,000d) on 10,000d #1550b	1.75 1.75

Dated 2009

2031	A280	(14,000d) on 7000d #1527b (R)	1.75 1.75
2032	A280	(14,000d) on 7000d #1527b (G)	1.75 1.75
2033	A280	(14,000d) on 7000d #1527e (R)	1.75 1.75
2034	A265	(14,000d) on 10,000d #1488c (R)	1.75 1.75
2035	A265	(14,000d) on 10,000d #1488e (R)	1.75 1.75
2036	A265	(14,000d) on 10,000d #1488e (G)	1.75 1.75
2037	A294	(14,000d) on 10,000d #1550b (R)	1.75 1.75

2038	A93	(14,000d) on 50c #714	1.75 1.75
2041	A66	(14,000d) on 1.50d #608 (S)	1.75 1.75
2042	A95	(14,000d) on 10d #735	1.75 1.75
2044	A66	(14,000d) on 11d #609 (S)	1.75 1.75
2045	A93	(14,000d) on 15.50d #717	1.75 1.75
2046	A93	(14,000d) on 16d #718	1.75 1.75
2047	A66	(14,000d) on 17d #610 (S)	1.75 1.75
2049	A280	(14,000d) on 7000d #1527b (S)	1.75 1.75
2050	A280	(14,000d) on 7000d #1527e (S)	1.75 1.75
2051	A305	(14,000d) on 7000d #1573e	1.75 1.75
2052	A305	(14,000d) on 7000d #1573e (R)	1.75 1.75
2053	A305	(14,000d) on 7000d #1573e (G)	1.75 1.75
2054	A265	(14,000d) on 10,000d #1488c (S)	1.75 1.75
2055	A265	(14,000d) on 10,000d #1488e	1.75 1.75
2056	A265	(14,000d) on 10,000d #1488e (S)	1.75 1.75
2057	A294	(14,000d) on 10,000d #1550b	1.75 1.75

Dated 2009

2058	A280	(14,000d) on 7000d #1527b (R)	1.75 1.75
2059	A280	(14,000d) on 7000d #1527b (G)	1.75 1.75
2060	A280	(14,000d) on 7000d #1527e (R)	1.75 1.75
2061	A265	(14,000d) on 10,000d #1488c (R)	1.75 1.75
2062	A265	(14,000d) on 10,000d #1488e (R)	1.75 1.75
2063	A265	(14,000d) on 10,000d #1488e (G)	1.75 1.75
2064	A294	(14,000d) on 10,000d #1550b (R)	1.75 1.75

2065	A93	(14,000d) on 50c #714	1.75 1.75
2068	A66	(14,000d) on 1.50d #608 (S)	1.75 1.75
2069	A95	(14,000d) on 10d #735	1.75 1.75
2071	A66	(14,000d) on 11d #609 (S)	1.75 1.75
2072	A93	(14,000d) on 15.50d #717	1.75 1.75
2073	A93	(14,000d) on 16d #718	1.75 1.75
2074	A66	(14,000d) on 17d #610 (S)	1.75 1.75
2076	A280	(14,000d) on 7000d #1527b (S)	1.75 1.75
2077	A280	(14,000d) on 7000d #1527e (S)	1.75 1.75
2078	A305	(14,000d) on 7000d #1573e	1.75 1.75
2079	A305	(14,000d) on 7000d #1573e (R)	1.75 1.75
2080	A305	(14,000d) on 7000d #1573e (G)	1.75 1.75
2081	A265	(14,000d) on 10,000d #1488c (S)	1.75 1.75
2082	A265	(14,000d) on 10,000d #1488e (S)	1.75 1.75
2083	A265	(14,000d) on 10,000d #1488e (S)	1.75 1.75
2084	A294	(14,000d) on 10,000d #1550b	1.75 1.75

Dated 2009

2085	A280	(14,000d) on 7000d #1527b (R)	1.75 1.75
2087	A280	(14,000d) on 7000d #1527e (R)	1.75 1.75
2088	A265	(14,000d) on 10,000d #1488c (R)	1.75 1.75
2089	A265	(14,000d) on 10,000d #1488e (R)	1.75 1.75
2090	A265	(14,000d) on 10,000d #1488e (G)	1.75 1.75
2091	A294	(14,000d) on 10,000d #1550b (R)	1.75 1.75

2092	A95	(40,950d) on 46d #747	5.00 5.00

Nos. 1984-2092 (91)   145.25 145.25

Twenty-one additional stamps were issued in this set. The editors would like to examine any examples.

A342

A343

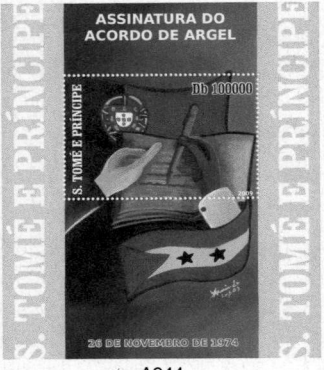

A344

No. 2097 — Rocket launches: a, 13,000d, Delta II. b, 13,000d, Ariane 5. c, 39,000d, CZ-4C. d, 39,000d, Atlas 5.

No. 2098 — Airships: a, 13,000d, U.S. Navy C-7 over Swiss Alps. b, 13,000d, U.S. Navy ZRS-5 Macon over Friedrichshafen, Germany. c, 39,000d, Italian M.1 airship over Rothenburg, Germany. d, 39,000d, LZ-127 Graf Zeppelin, Ferdinand von Zeppelin.

No. 2099 — Native Americans and wildlife: a, 13,000d, Canis lupus. b, 13,000d, Haliaeetus leucocephalus. c, 39,000d, Haliaeetus leucocephalus, diff. d, 39,000d, Aquila chrysaetos.

No. 2100 — Intl. Year of Science: a, 13,000d, Equus grevyi, Serengeti National Park, Tanzania. b, 13,000d, Haroun Tazieff, vulcanologist. c, 39,000d, Dmitri Mendeleev, chemist. d, 39,000d, Dr. Albert Schweitzer and hospital operating room.

No. 2101 — Fishermen and fish: a, 13,000d, Latimeria chalumnae. b, 13,000d, Anabas testudineus. c, 39,000d, Argyropelecus affinis. d, 39,000d, Pantodon buchholzi.

No. 2102 — Movies starring Charlie Chaplin (1889-1977): a, 13,000d, Modern Times, 1936. b, 13,000d, A Dog's Life, 1918. c, 39,000d, City Lights, 1931. d, 39,000d, The Gold Rush, 1925.

No. 2103 — Submarines: a, 15,000d, 1834 Russian submarine made by K. A. Schilder. b, 25,000d, 1866 Russian submarine made by I. F. Alexander. c, 35,000d, 1881 Russian submarine made by S. K. Drzewiecki. d, 35,000d, 1775 Turtle submarine.

No. 2104 — Intl. Year of Science: a, 20,000d, Carl Linnaeus, taxonomist, taxonomic tree. b, 25,000d, Charles Darwin, naturalist, skulls and depiction of evolution of man. c, 25,000d, Albert Einstein, atoms. d, 40,000d, Richard Feynman, energy sources.

No. 2105 — Cyclists: a, 20,000d, Grégory Baugé, French flag. b, 30,000d, Victoria Pendleton, British flag. c, 30,000d, Simona Krupeckaite, Lithuanian flag. d, 30,000d, Cameron Meyer, Australian flag.

No. 2106 — Shells and pre-historic creatures: a, 20,000d, Tylosaurus. b, 30,000d, Hybodus. c, 35,000d, Ichthyosaurus. d, 35,000d, Eurhinosaurus.

No. 2107 — Nude paintings of mythological or religious figures: a, 20,000d, Birth of Venus, by Amaury Duval. b, 30,000d, Susanna and the Elders, by Alessandro Allori. c, 35,000d, Phyllis and Demophon, by Agnolo di Cosimo.

d, 35,000d, Birth of Venus, by William-Adolphe Bouguereau.

No. 2108 — High-speed trains: a, 20,000d, V150. b, 30,000d, Maglev. c, 35,000d, Maglev, diff. d, 35,000d, TGV.

No. 2109 — Intl. Year of Science: a, 25,000d, Wangari Maathai, 2004 Nobel Peace laureate, tropical rain forest. b, 25,000d, Jacques Cousteau, marine conservationist, Tursiops truncatus. c, 25,000d, Nicolaus Copernicus, heliocentric solar system. d, 25,000d, Al Gore, climate change activist, globe.

No. 2110 — North Atlantic Treaty Organization, 60th anniv.: a, 25,000d, B-2 Spirit airplane and dove. b, 30,000d, HMS Bulwark. c, 30,000d, Soldier, child in hospital bed, Red Cross, helicopter and humanitarian supplies. d, 30,000d, Leclerc tanks.

No. 2111 — Pre-historic animals and minerals.: a, 25,000d, Triceratops, Siderite, sphalerite and calcite. b, 30,000d, Batrachognathus, Pyromorphite. c, 30,000d, Caudipteryx, Dioptase. d, 30,000d, Compsognathus, Vanadinite and hollandite.

No. 2112 — Butterflies and moths: a, 25,000d, Attacus atlas. b, 30,000d, Ornithoptera alexandrae. c, 30,000d, Attacus atlas, diff. d, 35,000d, Ornithoptera alexandrae, diff.

No. 2113 — Expedition of Sir Arthur Stanley Eddington to Prince Island, 90th anniv.: a, 13,000d, Forest. b, 13,000d, Mountain. c, 39,000d, Building. d, 39,000d, Beach.

No. 2114 — Dragonflies: a, 15,000d, Libellula depressa. b, 25,000d, Libellula quadrimaculata. c, 30,000d, Enallagma cyathigerum. d, 30,000d, Cordulegaster boltoni.

No. 2115 — Mushrooms, vert.: a, 20,000d, Chanterelle (girolle). b, 20,000d, Hydne. c, 20,000d, Psalliote. d, 40,000d, Xerocomus rubellus.

No. 2116 — Map of Africa, child, handprints, and Postal Union of the Americas, Spain and Portugal (UPAEP) emblem at: a, 25,000d, LR. b, 25,000d, UL. c, 25,000d, Center. d, 25,000d, LL.

No. 2117, 95,000d, Ophiophagus hannah.

No. 2118, 100,000d, Concordes in flight. No. 2119, 100,000d, Eddington, 1919 solar eclipse. No. 2120, 100,000d, Astronaut Rakesh Sharma, GSAT-3 satellite. No. 2121, LZ-129 Hindenburg, Ferdinand von Zeppelin. No. 2122, 100,000d, Native Americans around fire, moccasins and pipe. No. 2123, 100,000d, Caranx hippos and fishermen. No. 2124, Chaplin, Ben Turpin, scene from His New Job, 1915. No. 2125, 100,000d, 1904 Russian submarine Delfin. No. 2126, 100,000d, Anomalocaris and shell. No. 2127, 100,000d, Gen. Hastings Lionel Ismay, NATO conference room. No. 2128, 104,000d, Cyclists Michael Morkov, and Alex Rasmussen, Danish flag. No. 2129, 110,000d, Maglev tain, diff. No. 2130, 110,000d, Platecarpus, Vanadinite. No. 2131, 110,000d, Brephidium exilis.No. 2132, 115,000d, The Bath of Venus, by François Boucher.

No. 2133, 100,000d, Signing of 1974 Argel Accords. No. 2134, 100,000d, Man, woman, AIDS ribbon.

Perf. 12¾x13¼, 13¼x12¾ (#2115)
2009, May 29		Sheets of 4, #a-d		
2097-2112	A342	Set of 16	210.00	210.00
2113-2116	A343	Set of 4	47.50	47.50

Souvenir Sheets
Perf. 13¼ Syncopated
| 2117 | A342 | 95,000d multi | 11.50 | 11.50 |
| 2118-2132 | A343 | Set of 15 | 18.00 | 18.00 |

Perf. 13¼x12¾
| 2133-2134 | A344 | Set of 2 | 24.00 | 24.00 |

Nos. 2118-2132 each contain one 50x39mm stamp. Nos. 2114, 2115, 2117, 2118 are dated 2008.

A345

No. 2135 — Pigeons in military service and : a, 10,000d, Soldier lifting pigeon. b, 20,000d, Soldier with helmet, tanks. c, 40,000d, Soldier with hat with pigeon on finger, tank. d, 50,000d, Pigeon in flight, pilot.

No. 2136 — Table tennis players: a, 13,000d, Werner Schlager, Austrian flag. b, 13,000d, Wang Liqin, flag of People's Republic of China. c, 39,000d, Jörgen Persson, Swedish flag. d, 39,000d, Jan-Ove Waldner, Swedish flag.

No. 2137 — Scouts and mushrooms: a, 13,000d, Clitocybe odora. b, 13,000d, Gomphidius roseus. c, 39,000d, Xerocomus porosporus. d, 39,000d, Russula olivacea.

No. 2138 — Lunar satellites and vehicles: a, 13,000d, LRO. b, 13,000d, LCROSS. c, 39,000d, Lunokhod 1. d, 45,000d, Apollo 15 Lunar Rover.

No. 2139 — Dinosaurs: a, 13,000d, Pterodaustro and Alfred Russel Wallace, naturalist. b, 13,000d, Pelorosaurus and Wallace. c, 39,000d, Xiaosaurus and Wallace. d, 45,000d, Utahraptor.

No. 2140 — Israeli history: a, 13,000d, Golda Meir, prime minister, Báb Shrine, Haifa. b, 23,000d, Pres. Chaim Weizmann, Jerusalem skyline. c, 30,000d, Ron Huldai, mayor of Tel Aviv, arms and skyline of Tel Aviv. d, 49,000d, Theodor Herzl, promulgator of Zionism.

No. 2141 — Malaria prevention: a, 13,000d, Anopheles annulipes, blood test. b, 23,000d, Malaria plasmodium, doctor examining infant. c, 30,000d, Malaria plasmodia, nurse treating child. d, 49,000d, Malaria plasmodium, mother holding child for medical examination.

No. 2142 — 2008 Chess Olympiad champions: a, 13,000d, Gabriel Sargissian, Armenian flag. b, 23,000d, Joanna Majdan, Polish flag. c, 30,000d, Maia Chiburdanidze, Georgian flag. d, 49,000d, Peter Leko, Hungarian flag.

No. 2143 — Jewish Nobel laureates: a, 15,000d, Yitzhak Rabin, Peace, 1994. b, 25,000d, Andrew Fire, Physiology or Medicine, 2006. c, 35,000d, Martin Chalfie, Chemistry, 2008. d, 35,000d, Robert Aumann, Economics, 2005.

No. 2144 — Michael Jackson (1958-2009) singer, wearing: a, 25,000d, Black hat at left, white and red hat at right. b, 25,000d, White shirt with straps at left. c, 25,000d, White shirt and pants at left. d, 25,000d, Black hat and pink shirt at left.

No. 2145 — Natural disasters: a, 25,000d, Tornado. b, 25,000d, Earthquake. c, 25,000d, Flood. d, 25,000d, Tsunami.

No. 2146 — Brigitte Bardot, actress, wearing: a, 26,000d, Red brown dress at right. b, 26,000d, Blue dress at right. c, 26,000d, Striped blouse at right. d, 26,000d, Hat at right.

No. 2147 — Paintings by Amadeo Modigliani (1884-1920): a, 30,000d, Cypress Trees and Houses, 1919. b, 30,000d, Seated Nude, 1918. c, 30,000d, Red-headed Girl in Evening Dress, 1918. d, 30,000d, Self-portrait, 1919.

No. 2148, 100,000d, Table tennis player Wang hao, flag of People's Republic of China. No. 2149, 100,000d, Scouts and Clitocybe gibba. No. 2150, 100,000d, Albert Einstein, 1921 Nobel Physics laureate. No. 2151, 100,000d, Jackson, diff. No. 2152, 100,000d, Forest fire. No. 2153, 100,000d, Bardot, diff. No. 2154, 104,000d, Pigeons in military service, diff. No. 2155, 104,000d, Atlas rocket, LCROSS. No. 2156, 104,000d, Tropeognathus and Charles Darwin. No. 2157, 104,000d, Shimon Peres, Israeli president. No. 2158, 104,000d, Malaria plasmodia, nurse treating infant. No. 2159, 104,000d, Chess player Vladimir Kramnik.No. 2160, 110,000d, Jeanne Hébuterne in Front of a Door, by Modigliani.

2009, July 1		Perf. 12¾x13¼
Sheets of 4, #a-d		
2135-2147	A345	Set of 13　170.00　170.00

Souvenir Sheets
Perf. 13¼ Syncopated
| 2148-2160 | A345 | Set of 13　160.00　160.00 |

A346

A347

No. 2161 — Marilyn Monroe (1926-62), actress, wearing: a, 25,000d, Green plaid blouse at left. b, 25,000d, Pink bathing suit at right. c, 25,000d, Red dress at right. d,

25,000d, Pink dress at left (hands above head).

No. 2162 — Paul Morphy (1837-84), chess player, and chess pieces: a, 25,000d, Black rook and white pawn. b, 25,000d, White knight and black king. c, 25,000d, White pawn and black knight. d, 29,000d, Black queen and white pawn.

No. 2163 — Mushrooms and orchids: a, 25,000d, Russula paludosa, Stanhopea tigrina. b, 25,000d, Tricholomopsis rutilans, Angraecum sesquipedale. c, 25,000d, Boletus reticulatus, Cattleya intermedia. d, 35,000d, Lentinus tigrinus, Scuticaria steelii.

No. 2164 — African animals and steam locomotives: a, 30,000d, Crocodylus niloticus, 4-8-2. b, 30,000d, Equus quagga, 2-8-4. c, 30,000d, Loxodonta africana, Mallett 0-4-4-0. d, 30,000d, Panthera leo, 4-4-0.

No. 2165 — Buddhist temples: a, 10,000d, Puning Temple, People's Republic of China. b, 10,000d, Todai-ji Temple, Japan. c, 30,000d, Jogyesa Temple, South Korea. d, 30,000d, Akshardham Temple, India. e, 30,000d, Horyu-ji Temple, Japan.

No. 2166 — Foods and flags: a, 10,000d, Tacos, Mexican flag. b, 10,000d, Pelmeni, Russian flag. c, 30,000d, Lutefisk, Norwegian flag. d, 30,000d, Kimchi, South Korean flag. e, 30,000d, Pot-au-feu, French flag.

No. 2167 — Asian military aircraft: a, 15,000d, Kawasaki Ki-61-I, Japan. b, 25,000d, T-50 Golden Eagle, South Korea. c, 25,000d, Shijiazhuang Y-5B, People's Republic of China. d, 25,000d, Mitsubishi F-15J Eagle, Japan. e, 25,000d, Chengdu J-10, People's Republic of China.

No. 2168 — Taekwondo gold medalists at 2008 Summer Olympics, Beijing: a, 15,000d, Sujeong Lim, South Korea. b, 25,000d, Kyungseon Hwang, South Korea. c, 25,000d, Jingyu Wu, People's Republic of China. d, 25,000d, Hadi Saei, Japan. e, 25,000d, Guillermo Perez, Mexico.

No. 2169 — Sea birds and lighthouses: a, 15,000d, Rissa tridactyla, Split Point Lighthouse, Australia. b, 25,000d, Neophron percnopterus, Europa Point Lighthouse, Gibraltar. c, 25,000d, Calonectris diomedea, Cabo Espichel Lighthouse, Portugal. d, 25,000d, Larus ridibundus, Pigeon Point Lighthouse, U.S. e, 30,000d, Fulmarus glacialis, Gumundo Lighthouse, South Korea.

No. 2170 — Asian astronauts and spacecraft: a, 15,000d, Yang Liwei, People's Republic of China, Shenzhou 5. b, 25,000d, Koichi Wakata, Japan, Space Shuttle Discovery. c, 25,000d, Fei Junlong, People's Republic of China, Shenzhou 6. d, 25,000d, Soichi Noguchi, Japan, Space Shuttle Discovery. e, 30,000d, Yi So-Yeon, South Korea, Soyuz TMA-9.

No. 2171, 100,000d, Monroe, diff. No. 2172, 100,000d, Morphy, white king, black rook. No. 2173, 100,000d, Omphalotus olearius, Ophrys holoserica. No. 2174, 100,000d, Giraffa camelopardalis, 4-4-0 steam locomotive. No. 2175, 100,000d, Lama Temple, People's Republic of China. No. 2176, 100,000d, Ackee and saltfish, Jamaican flag. No. 2177, 104,000d, KAI KT-1 Woong-Bee airplane, South Korea. No. 2178, 104,000d, Taekwondo gold medalist Maria del Rosario Espinoza, Mexico. No. 2179, 104,000d, Astronaut Chiaki Mukai, Japan, Space Shuttle Discovery. No. 2180, 115,000d, Fratercula arctica, Sunderland Lighthouse, United Kingdom.

2009, July 30		Perf. 12¾x13¼
Sheets of 4, #a-d		
2161-2164	A346	Set of 4　52.50　52.50
Sheets of 5, #a-e		
2165-2170	A347	Set of 6　82.50　82.50

Souvenir Sheets
| 2171-2180 | A346 | Set of 10　125.00　125.00 |

Souvenir sheets of 1 of Nos. 2165c, 2166d, 2167b, 2168b, 2169e, and 2170e with English and Portuguese text exist.

A348

No. 2181 — Medicinal plants: a, 5,000d, Origanum vulgare. b, 10,000d, Angelica archangelica. c, 10,000d, Achillea millefolium. d, 15,000d, Artemissia dracumulus. e, 20,000d, Allium sativum.

No. 2182 — Cetaceans: a, 10,000d, Tursiops truncatus, Balaena mysticetus. b, 10,000d, Unnamed cetaceans. c, 10,000d,

Globicephala melas, Physeter catodon. d, 20,000d, Stenella pernettyi, Lithofaga lithofaga. e, 20,000d, Grampus griseus, Megaptera novaeangliae.

No. 2183 — Famous people and their cats: a, 10,000d, Freddie Mercury, rock star, and cats, Oscar and Tiffany. b, 10,000d, Gustav Klimt, painter, and cat, Katze. c, 15,000d, Pres. Ronald Reagan, wife, Nancy, and cats Cleo and Sara. d, 20,000d, John Lennon and Yoko Ono, rock stars, and cat, Pepper. e, 25,000d, Frank Zappa, rock star, and cat, Marshmoff.

No. 2184 — Automobiles: a, 10,000d, 1930 Walter 6B Sodomka. b, 15,000d, 1923-27 Tatra T11. c, 20,000d, 1935 Walter Junior SS. d, 25,000d, 1931 Aero 662. e, 30,000d, 1932 Wikov 40.

No. 2185 — Dogs in military service: a, 10,000d, Dog and soldier with machine gun. b, 15,000d, Dog and paratrooper in tree. c, 25,000d, Dog with soldier with rifle, airplane in sky. d, 25,000d, Soldier holding dog's leash, boxes at right. e, 25,000d, Soldier with dog, tank at right.

No. 2186 — Birds: a, 10,000d, Falco subbuteo. b, 15,000d, Sarcoramphus papa. c, 25,000d, Bubo virginianus. d, 25,000d, Haliaeetus leucocephalus. e, 35,000d, Ninox strenua.

No. 2187 — Charles Lindbergh (1902-74), pilot, and Spirit of St. Louis: a, 10,000d. b, 15,000d. c, 25,000d, Airplane name below airplane. d, 25,000d, Airplane name above airplane. e, 35,000d.

No. 2188 — Paintings by Paul Cézanne (1839-1906) and Pablo Picasso (1881-1973): a, 10,000d, Still Life, by Cézanne, 1892. b, 15,000d, Jacqueline, by Picasso, 1960. c, 25,000d, Nude Woman, by Cézanne, 1898-99. d, 30,000d, The Bathers, by Cézanne, 1890. e, 35,000d, Gardanne, by Cézanne, 1886.

No. 2189 — Paintings by Pablo Picasso (1881-1973): a, 10,000d, Still Life, 1901. b, 20,000d, Nude on a Divan, 1960. c, 25,000d, Study for "Le Dejeuner sur l'Herbe", 1960. d, 25,000d, Les Demoiselles d'Avignon, 1907. e, 35,000d, The Artist and His Model, 1963.

No. 2190 — Farrah Fawcett (1947-2009), actress: a, 20,000d, Holding drink at left. b, 20,000d, With bicycle at right. c, 20,000d, On skateboard at right. d, 20,000d, In black dress at right, 1890. e, 20,000d, Holding handbag at right.

No. 2191, 60,000d, Artemisia vulgaris. No. 2192, 70,000d, Phocoena phocoena. No. 2193, 80,000d, David Bowie, rock star, and cat, Purrie. No. 2194, 100,000d, Fawcett, diff. No. 2195, 104,000d, 1933 Tatra 52 automobile. No. 2196, 110,000d, Sergeant Stubby, military dog. No. 2197, 110,000d, Five Bathers, by Cézanne, 1877-78. No. 2198, 110,000d, Nude Under a Pine Tree, by Picasso, 1959.

2009, Oct. 20   Perf. 12¾x13¼
Sheets of 5, #a-e
2181-2190 A348   Set of 10   115.00   115.00
Souvenir Sheets
Perf. 13¼ Syncopated
2191-2198 A348   Set of 8   87.50   87.50

Nos. 1400, 1401, 1403 Surcharged in Red

Methods and Perfs As Before
2009, Oct. 25
2199 A220 (8000d) on 3500d
          #1400   1.00   1.00
2200 A220 (8000d) on 5000d
          #1401   1.00   1.00
2201 A220 (8000d) on 7500d
          #1403   1.00   1.00
    Nos. 2199-2201 (3)   3.00   3.00
No. 1402 exists with this surcharge but was not issued.

A349

A350

No. 2202 — Futuristic automobile concepts: a, 20,000d, BMW ZC-6 concept vehicle. b, 25,000d, Magnetic concept vehicle. c, 25,000d, RCA concept vehicle. d, 30,000d, Daedalus concept vehicle.

No. 2203 — Princess Diana (1961-97), with: a, 25,000d, Mother Teresa. b, 25,000d, Sons, William and Harry. c, 25,000d, Prince Charles. d, 25,000d, Child.

No. 2204 — Elvis Presley (1935-77) and Presley: a, 20,000d, In boxing trunks. b, 25,000d, Holding microphone stand. c, 25,000d, Dancing with woman. d, 34,000d, With woman, playing ukulele.

No. 2205 — Various Camargue horses: a, 20,000d. b, 25,000d. c, 30,000d. d, 35,000d.

No. 2206 — Eiffel Tower and Concorde: a, 25,000d, G-BOAC. b, 25,000d, F-BTSD. c, 30,000d, G-BOAC, diff. d, 30,000d, G-BOAF.

No. 2207 — Dinosaurs: a, 25,000d, Quetzalcoatlus, Psittacosaurus. b, 30,000d, Dsungaripterus, Troodon. c, 30,000d, Pteranodon ingens, Stegosaurus. d, 35,000d, Pteranodon, Euoplocephalus.

No. 2208 — Papal visit to Africa: a, 25,000d, Pope Benedict XVI holding crucifix, meeting cardinals. b, 30,000d, Pope Benedict XVI walking with African leader. c, 30,000d, Pope Benedict XVI greeting nuns. d, 35,000d, Pope Benedict XVI on airplane steps.

No. 2209 — Writers and poets: a, 20,000d, Johann Wolfgang von Goethe (1749-1832). b, 20,000d, William Shakespeare (1564-1616). c, 20,000d, George Gordon Byron (Lord Byron) (1788-1824). d, 20,000d, Charles Dickens (1812-70). e, 20,000d, Friedrich von Schiller (1759-1805).

No. 2210 — Humanists: a, 10,000d, Pope John Paul II (1920-2005). b, 15,000d, Tenzin Gyatso, 14th Dalai Lama. c, 25,000d, Mother Teresa (1910-97). d, 30,000d, Mahatma Gandhi (1869-1948). e, 30,000d, Pope Benedict XVI.

No. 2211 — World War II airplanes: a, 10,000d, I-16 Type 18 and I-16 Type 24, Soviet Union. b, 15,000d, Bf 109E-4 and Bf 109F-2, Germany. c, 25,000d, Bf 109E-3 and Me 262, Germany. d, 30,000d, Bf 109F-4Z/Trop, Germany, and Mustang P-51D-15, United States. e, 35,000d, TU-25 and SB-2M-100A, Soviet Union.

No. 2212 — Expensive paintings: a, 15,000d, Rideau, Cruchon et Compotier, by Paul Cézanne. b, 15,000d, Portrait of Dr. Gachet, by Vincent van Gogh. c, 30,000d, Garçon à la Pipe, by Pablo Picasso. d, 30,000d, Massacre of the Innocents, by Peter Paul Rubens. e, 30,000d, Dance at Le Moulin de la Galette, by Pierre-Auguste Renoir.

No. 2213 — Chinese film personalities: a, 5000d, Feng Zhe (1921-69). b, 7000d, Wang Xingang. c, 10,000d, Jiang Wen. d, 13,000d, Shangguan Yunzhu (1920-68). e, 25,000d, Qin Yi. f, 40,000d, Liu Xiaoqing.

No. 2214 — Race car, checkered flag, and Ayrton Senna (1960-94), race car driver, wearing : a, 10,000d, Red racing suit (red and white car). b, 15,000d, White suit, holding helmet (red and white car). c, 15,000d, Red suit (black car). d, 20,000d, Red suit (black car). e, 20,000d, Red suit and black cap (red and white car). f, 20,000d, Black shirt (yellow car).

No. 2215 — Pre-historic crocodilians: a, 10,000d, Guarinisuchus munizi, Metriorhynchus. b, 10,000d, Two Metriorhynchus. c, 15,000d, Steneosaurus. d, 20,000d, Two Metriorhynchus, diff. e, 25,000d, Kaprosuchus saharicus. f, 35,000d, Steneosaurus, Guarinisuchus munizi.

No. 2216 — Cats and dogs: a, 10,000d, Chinese crested dogs. b, 15,000d, Cesky terriers. c, 20,000d, Sphinx cats. d, 20,000d, Oriental shorthair cats. e, 25,000d, Devon Rex cats. f, 25,000d, Italian greyhounds.

No. 2217 — Peter Paul Rubens (1577-1640), painter: a, 10,000d, Cimon and Iphegenia. b, 15,000d, Rubens. c, 20,000d, Pan and Syrinx. c, 20,000d, Jupiter and Calisto. d, 25,000d, Rubens Museum Antwerp, Belgium. e, 30,000d, The Judgement of Paris.

No. 2218, 80,000d, Audi O concept vehicle. No. 2219, 90,000d, Presley and two women. No. 2220, 100,000d, Camargue horses, diff. No. 2221, 100,000d, Senna wearing racing helmet. No. 2222, 104,000d, Princess Diana and Tower Bridge. No. 2223, 104,000d, Shar Peis. No. 2224, 104,000d, Pope Benedict XVI kissing infant. No. 2225, 115,000d, The Four Continents, by Rubens.

No. 2226, 100,000d, Oscar Wilde (1854-1900), writer. No. 2227, 104,000d, Bf 109F-4 and B-71 airplanes, Germany. No. 2228, 110,000d, Nelson Mandela, Tockus erythrorhynchus, Tsavorite. No. 2229, 110,000d, Portrait of Adele Bloch-Bauer I, by Gustav Klimt. No. 2230, 110,000d, Metroryhnchus. No. 2231, 110,000d, Zhang Yimou, film director. No. 2232, 115,000d, Eiffel Tower and Concorde G-BOAC, diff. No. 2233, 115,000d, Euoplocephalus and other dinosaurs.

2010, Jan. 25 Litho. *Perf. 12¾x13¼*
Sheets of 4, #a-d
2202-2208 A349   Set of 7   100.00   100.00
Sheets of 5, #a-e
2209-2212 A350   Set of 4   57.50   57.50
Sheets of 6, #a-f
2213-2217 A350   Set of 5   72.50   72.50
Souvenir Sheets
Perf. 13¼ Syncopated
2218-2225 A349   Set of 8   105.00   105.00
2226-2233 A350   Set of 8   115.00   115.00

Antverpia 2010 National & European Championship of Philately, Antwerp, Belgium (#2217, 2225).

African Mammals — A351

No. 2234 — Primates: a, 10,000d, Cercopithecus neglectus. b, 15,000d, Mandrillus sphinx. c, 20,000d, Pan paniscus. d, 25,000d, Lophocebus albigena. e, 30,000d, Pan troglodytes.

No. 2235 — Elephants (Loxodonta africana): a, 10,000d, Adult and juvenile. b, 15,000d, Adult and juvenile, diff. c, 20,000d, Juvenile and two adults. d, 25,000d, Two adults facing each other. e, 34,000d, Two adults walking.

No. 2236 — Whales: a, 10,000d, Megaptera novaeangliae. b, 15,000d, Physeter catodon. c, 25,000d, Feresa attenuata. d, 30,000d, Orcinus orca. e, 30,000d, Kogia breviceps.

No. 2237 — Lions (Panthera leo): a, 22,000d, Female and cubs. b, 22,000d, Female attacking antelope. c, 22,000d, Male, tail at left. d, 22,000d, Two females attacking buffalo. e, 22,000d, Male, tail at center.

No. 2238 — Bats: a, 10,000d, Chalinolobus gouldii, Tadarida aegyptiaca. b, 15,000d, Taphozous mauritianus, Rousettus aegyptiacus. c, 25,000d, Epomophorus wahlbergi. d, 30,000d, Megaloglossus woermanni. e, 35,000d, Miniopterus schreibersii.

No. 2239, 80,000d, Papio hamadryas, horiz. No. 2240, 80,000d, Loxodonta cyclotis, horiz. No. 2241, 80,000d, Orcinus orca, horiz. No. 2242, 80,000d, Panthera leo, horiz. No. 2243, 80,000d, Plecotus austriacus, Hypsignathus monstrosus, horiz.

2010, Mar. 29   Perf. 12¾x13¼
Sheets of 5, #a-e
2234-2238 A351   Set of 5   60.00   60.00
Souvenir Sheets
Perf. 13¼ Syncopated
2239-2243 A351   Set of 5   45.00   45.00

Nos. 2239-2243 each contain one 50x39mm stamp.

A352

No. 2244 — Albert Camus (1913-60), writer: a, 20,000d, Three book covers. b, 20,000d, Smoking cigarette. c, 20,000d, Standing with arms crossed. d, 20,000d, Book covers and Eiffel Tower. e, 20,000d, Monument to Camus, Villeblevin, France, and gravestone.

No. 2245 — Remembrance of Holocaust victims: a, 20,000d, Cupped hands and spiral. b, 20,000d, Menorah. c, 20,000d, Star of David. d, 20,000d, Symbol with crying eye. e, 20,000d, Heart and barbed wire.

No. 2246 — Paintings by Michelangelo Merisia da Caravaggio (1571-1610): a, 10,000d, Self-portrait as Bacchus, 1593-94. b, 15,000d, Narcissus, 1596. c, 20,000d, The Musicians, 1595. d, 30,000d, Supper at Emmaus, 1601. e, Saint Jerome Writing, 1605.

No. 2247 — Steam locomotives: a, 10,000d, Train facing left. b, 15,000d, Wheels. c, 20,000d, Locomotive on bridge. d, 30,000d, Train facing right, telegraph poles. e, 35,000d, Train and African boys.

No. 2248 — Diego Maradona, soccer player, 50th birthday: a, 10,000d, Maradona and World Cup. b, 15,000d, Maradona and flag of Argentina. c, 20,000d, Maradona cheering. d, 30,000d, Face to Maradona. e, 35,000d, Maradona dribbling ball.

No. 2249 — Moto GP motorcycles and riders: a, 10,000d, Geoff Duke, Gilera motorcycle. b, 15,000d, Valentino Rossi, Yamaha motorcycle. c, 25,000d, Jarno Saarinen, Yamaha motorcycle. d, 30,000d, Daijiro Kato, Honda motorcycle. e, 35,000d, Dani Pedrosa, Honda motorcycle.

No. 2250 — 2010 Winter Olympics gold medalists: a, 10,000d, Simon Ammann, ski jumping, Switzerland. b, 15,000d, Evan Lysacek, figure skating, United States. c, 25,000d, Wang Meng, speed skating, People's Republic of China. d, 30,000d, Jason Lamy-Chappuis, ski jumping, France. e, 35,000d, Andrea Fischbacher, Alpine skiing, Austria.

No. 2251 — Japanese Military Aviation in World War II: a, 10,000d, Japanese airplane. b, 15,000d, Admiral Isoroku Yamamoto (1884-1943). c, 25,000d, Japanese pilots. d, 30,000d, Damaged ships at Pearl Harbor. e, 35,000d, Japanese airplanes.

No. 2252 — Boy Scouts of America, cent.: a, 10,000d, Emblem, Scouts on obstacle course. b, 15,000d, Binoculars, Scouts on rope. c, 25,000d, Emblem, Scouts playing horns. d, 30,000d, Scouts, tents and compass. e, 35,000d, Scout and canteen.

No. 2253 — Firefighting: a, 15,000d, Airplane dropping water on fire. b, 15,000d, Five firefighters. c, 25,000d, Firefighter and truck. d, 30,000d, Helmet and firefighting tools. e, 35,000d, Two firefighters.

No. 2254 — Lighthouses: a, 24,000d, Eddystone Lighthouse, Great Britain. b, 24,000d, Lighthouse and Robert Stevenson (1772-1850), lighthouse builder and civil engineer. c, 24,000d, Ukrainian lighthouse designed by Vladimir G. Shukhov. d, 24,000d, Cockspur Island Lighthouse, United States, Gelochelidon nilotica. e, 24,000d, Kopu Lighthouse, Estonia.

No. 2255, 80,000d, Camus and aerial view of Paris, horiz. No. 2256, 80,000d, The Card Players, by Caravaggio, horiz. No. 2257, 100,000d, Star of David and clouds, horiz. No. 2258, 100,000d, Steam locomotive, horiz. No. 2259, 100,000d, Fire truck, horiz. No. 2260, 100,000d, Casey Stoner, Ducati motorcycle, horiz. No. 2261, 104,000d, Maradona playing soccer and flag of Argentina, horiz. No. 2262, 104,000d, Magdalena Neuner, cross-country skiing, Germany, horiz. No. 2263, 104,000d, Mitsubishi AM-6 Zero, horiz. No. 2264, 110,000d, Boy Scout, tents, emblem, horiz. No. 2265, 110,000d, Pigeon Point Lighthouse, United States, horiz.

2010, Mar. 29   Perf. 12¾x13¼
Sheets of 5, #a-e
2244-2254 A352   Set of 11   140.00   140.00
Souvenir Sheets
Perf. 13¼ Syncopated
2255-2265 A352   Set of 11   125.00   125.00

Nos. 2255-2265 each contain one 50x39mm stamp.

Db 14000

毛泽东同志是当代最伟大的
马克思列宁主义者。毛泽东同志
天才地、创造性地、全面地继承
、捍卫和发展了马克思列宁主
义，把马克思列宁主义提到了一
个崭新的阶段。毛泽东思想是在
帝国主义走向全面崩溃、社会主
义走向全世界胜利的时代的马克
思列宁主义，是全党全军和全国
一切工作的指导方针。

中国人民邮政 4分

S. TOMÉ E PRÍNCIPE 2010

Stamps of
the People's
Republic of
China
A353

Designs: No. 2266, 14,000d, #949 (4f Chinese text). No. 2267, 14,000d, #950 (8f Mao Zedong and text). No. 2268, 14,000d, #951 (8f Mao Zedong waving in crowd). No. 2269, 14,000d, #952, (8f Mao Zedong above crowd). No. 2270, 14,000d, #953 (8f Mao Zedong waving). No. 2271, 14,000d, #954 (8f Mao Zedong leaning on rail, Lin Piao in background). No. 2272, 14,000d, #955 (8f Mao Zedong with arm on rail), horiz. No. 2273, 14,000d, #956 (10f Lin Piao and Mao Zedong reviewing document), horiz. No. 2274, 14,000d, #991 (8f Mao Zedong waving, Chinese text), horiz. No. 2275, 14,000d, #998 (8f Mao Zedong Going to An Yuan).
140,000d, #628 ($3 Mei Lan-fang in opera scene).

Perf. 12¾x13¼, 13¼x12¾

2010, May 5
2266-2275 A353   Set of 10   15.50 15.50
Size: 98x147mm
Imperf
2276 A353   140,000d multi   15.50 15.50

A354

A355

No. 2277 — Clark Gable (1901-60), actor, in scenes from: a, 15,000d, Gone With the Wind, 1939. b, 15,000d, Manhattan Melodrama, 1934. c, 20,000d, Mogambo, 1953. d, 20,000d, Command Decision, 1948. e, 20,000d, It Started in Naples, 1960. f, 25,000d, San Francisco, 1936.
No. 2278 — Year of the Tiger with diagonal lines at: a, 15,000d, UL. b, 15,000d, LL. c, 20,000d, UR. d, 20,000d, LR. e, 20,000d, UL, diff. f, 25,000d, UR, diff.
No. 2279 — Henri Fabre (1882-1984), aviator: a, 15,000d, Beriev A-40 Albatross hydroplane. b, 15,000d, Fabre's 1910 hydroplane. c, 20,000d, Fabre and plane's propeller. d, 20,000d, Fabre and Notre Dame de la Garde, Marseille. e, 25,000d, Fabre's 1910 hydroplane, diff. f, 25,000d, Cessna TU206D hydroplane.
No. 2280 — Buildings at Expo 2010, Shanghai: a, 15,000d, Canadian Pavilion. b, 15,000d, Israeli Pavilion. c, 20,000d, United Africa Pavilion. d, 20,000d, Hong Kong Pavilion. e, 25,000d, Malaysian Pavilion. f, 30,000d, Swedish Pavilion.
No. 2281 — Count Leo Tolstoy (1828-1910), writer and: a, 15,000d, Tales of Sebastopol, 1855. b, 15,000d, The Cossacks, 1863. c, 20,000d, Wife, Sophia. d, 20,000d, Wife, Sophia, and daughter, Alexandra. e, 20,000d,

The Death of Ivan Ilyich, 1886, and stack of books. f, 37,000d, Anna Karenina, 1878.
No. 2282 — Track and field athletes: a, 15,000d, Bryan Clay, decathlete. b, 15,000d, Reese Hoffa, shot putter. c, 20,000d, Meseret Defar, long-distance runner. d, 20,000d, Dwain Chambers, sprinter. e, 25,000d, Dayron Robles, hurdler. f, 32,000d, Veronica Campbell-Brown, sprinter.
No. 2283 — Dinosaurs: a, 15,000d, Alectrosaurus. b, 15,000d, Caudipteryx. c, 20,000d, Gorgosaurus. d, 20,000d, Spinosaurus. e, 25,000d, Plesiosaurus. f, 35,000d, Tapejara.
No. 2284 — Mother Teresa (1910-97): a, 15,000d, Mother Teresa holding child. b, 15,000d, Head of Mother Teresa. c, 20,000d, Mother Teresa holding child, diff. d, 20,000d, Mother Teresa and two angels. e, 25,000d, Mother Teresa and Pope John Paul II. f, 35,000d, Mother Teresa and three putti.
No. 2285 — Brephidium exilis butterfly under magnifying glass with handle at: a, 15,000d, UL. b, 15,000d, Top. c, 20,000d, UR. d, 20,000d, LL. e, 25,000d, Bottom. f, 35,000d, Right.
No. 2286 — Hubble Space Telescope, 20th anniv.: a, 15,000d, Hubble Space Telescope and Lyman Spitzer (1914-97), astronomer. b, 15,000d, Launch of Space Shuttle STS-31. c, 20,000d, Hubble Space Telescope, red violet background. d, 20,000d, Hubble Space Telescope, Eagle Nebula, blue green background. e, 25,000d, Hubble Space Telescope above Earth. f, 35,000d, Hubble Space Telescope and Earth.
No. 2287 — Paintings by Sandro Botticelli (1445-1510): a, 15,000d, The Lamentation Over the Dead Christ. b, 20,000d, The Birth of Venus. c, 20,000d, Madonna and Child and Two Angels. d, 20,000d, Cestello Annunciation. e, 25,000d, Allegory of Spring (Primavera). f, 35,000d, Madonna and Child with Six Saints.
No. 2288 — Lech Kaczynski (1949-2010), President of Poland, and: a, 15,000d, Tupolev TU-154M airplane. b, 15,000d, Flag of Poland. c, 20,000d, Wife, Maria, aerial view and arms of Warsaw. d, 25,000d, Flag of Poland, diff. e, 25,000d, Map and arms of Poland. f, 35,000d, Wife, Maria, and Pope Benedict XVI.
No. 2289, 104,000d, Fabre. No. 2290, 104,000d, Hubble Space Telescope and V838 Monocerotis. No. 2291, 110,000d, Gable and Marilyn Monroe. No. 2292, 110,000d, Tiger, diff. No. 2293, 110,000d, Equatorial Guinea Pavilion. Expo 2010, Shanghai. No. 2294, 110,000d, War and Peace, by Tolstoy. No. 2295, 110,000d, Nodosaur. No. 2296, 115,000d, Ivan Ukhov, high jumper. No. 2297, 120,000d, Mother Teresa holding infant. No. 2298, 120,000d, Self-portrait, by Botticelli. No. 2299, 125,000d, Woman and Ornithoptera goliath. No. 2300, 125,000d, Kaczynski, Pope John Paul II, flag of Poland.

Perf. 13¼x12¾
Sheets of 6, #a-f
2277-2288 A354   Set of 12   170.00 170.00
Souvenir Sheets
Perf. 13¼ Syncopated, 13¼x12¾ (#2300)
2289-2300 A355   Set of 12   155.00 155.00

A356

A357

No. 2301 — World War II military commanders: a, 15,000d, Field Marshal Erwin Rommel (1891-1944), Germany. b, 15,000d, Gen. Dwight D. Eisenhower (1890-1969), United States. c, 20,000d, Marshal Georgy K. Zhukov (1896-1974), Soviet Union. d, 25,000d, Field Marshal Bernard Montgomery (1887-1976), Great Britain. e, 35,000d, Field

Marshal Friedrich Paulus (1890-1957), Germany.
No. 2302 — Cats: a, 24,000d, Two brown and white tabby cats. b, 24,000d, Brown and white tabby cat, Siamese cat. c, 24,000d, Gray and white cat. d, 24,000d, Three Siamese cats. e, 24,000d, Brown and white tabby cat.
No. 2303 — Butterflies and caterpillars: a, 15,000d, Cethosia cyane. b, 20,000d, Danaus plexippus. c, 25,000d, Papilio polyxenes. d, 30,000d, Siproeta epaphus. e, 35,000d, Antheraea polyphemus.
No. 2304 — Pope John Paul II (1920-2005): a, 15,000d, With hand raised. b, 20,000d, With Pope Benedict XVI. c, 25,000d, Holding crucifix. d, 30,000d, With arms of Vatican City. e, 35,000d, Holding young girl.
No. 2305 — Locomotives: a, 20,000d, Canadian Pacific S3 Diesel-electric. b, 20,000d, Class 53 Diesel, Great Britain. c, 25,000d, DB Class V 200. d, 30,000d, Bombardier AGC B 81500, France. e, 35,000d, CN Diesel, Canada.
No. 2306 — Pin-up art of Paul Butvila, with woman: a, 5000d, With life preserver. b, 5000d, With red cross. c, 5000d, With airplane. d, 10,000d, With mirror having image showing hand holding bra. e, 10,000d, In black dress in spotlight. f, 10,000d, With playing cards and poker chips. g, 15,000d, Wearing necklace, as seen from back. h, 15,000d, With binoculars. i, 15,000d, Reclining, with legs above head.
No. 2307, 110,000d, Tabby cat. No. 2308, 115,000d, World War II soldiers. No. 2309, 115,000d, Heliconius charithonia. No. 2310, 115,000d, Rudolf Diesel (1858-1913), inventor, and EMD FT Diesel-electric locomotive.
No. 2311, 90,000d, Tenzin Gyatso, 14th Dalai Lama and Potala Palace, Lhasa, Tibet. No. 2312, 90,000d, Mahatma Gandhi and Sabarnati Ashram. No. 2313, 90,000d, Reclining Nude from the Back, by Amedeo Modigliani.

2010, July 11   **Perf. 12¾x13¼**
Sheets of 5, #a-e
2301-2305 A356   Set of 5   65.00 65.00
2306 A356   Sheet of 9, #a-i   9.75 9.75
Souvenir Sheets
Perf. 13¼ Syncopated
2307-2310 A356   Set of 4   50.00 50.00
Perf. 13¼x12¾
2311-2313 A357   Set of 3   29.00 29.00

A358

No. 2314 — Crustaceans: a, 10,000d, Anonyx nugax, Aristas timidus. b, 15,000d, Leander tenuicornis, Dyastylis glabra. c, 20,000d, Lophozozymus incisus. d, 20,000d, Lybia tessellata, Petrolisthes donadio. e, 25,000d, Leander tenuicornis.
No. 2315 — Intl. Year of Biodiversity: a, 22,000d, Falco punctatus. b, 22,000d, Planting of seedlings. c, 22,000d, Panthera tigris. d, 22,000d, Ursus maritimus. e, 22,000d, Daubentonia madagascariensis.
No. 2316 — Dogs: a, 15,000d, Chinese crested dogs. b, 20,000d, Great Danes (Dogue alemao). c, 20,000d, Samoyeds. d, 25,000d, Australian kelpies. e, 35,000d, Whippets.
No. 2317 — Worldwide Fund for Nature (WWF) stamps of other countries: a, 15,000d, Bulgaria #3401. b, 20,000d, Jamaica #594. c, 20,000d, Maldive Islands #1187. d, 25,000d, Gambia #516. e, 35,000d, South Georgia and South Sandwich Islands #165.
No. 2318 — Robert Schumann (1810-56), composer, and: a, 15,000d, Cover of score for "Papillons." b, 20,000d, Grave monument, Bonn. c, 25,000d, Wife, Clara. d, 25,000d, His house, Germany. e, 35,000d, Wife at piano.
No. 2319 — Oil spills: a, 15,000d, Grounding of the Exxon Valdez, 1989. b, 20,000d, Ixtoc I blowout, 1979. c, 25,000d, Nowruz Field Platform fire, 1983. d, 25,000d, Gulf War well fires, 1991. e, 35,000d, Collision of Atlantic Princess and Aegean Captain, 1979.
No. 2320 — Juliette Gordon Low (1860-1927), founder of Girl Scouts of America, Scouting trefoil, and: a, 20,000d, Dog. b, 20,000d, Three Girl Scout leaders. c, 20,000d, Girl Scouts around campfire. d, 25,000d, Birthplace in Savannah, Georgia. e, 35,000d, Girl Scouts and leaders.
No. 2321 — Korean War, 60th anniv.: a, 20,000d, Zhang Taofang, Chinese sniper. b, 20,000d, Mao Zedong and son, Anying. c,

25,000d, General Douglas MacArthur and officers. d, 25,000d, Chinese Commander Peng Dehuai and North Korean leader Kim Il Sung. e, 35,000d, Negotiators at Panmunjom peace talks.
No. 2322 — Various rabbits and Chinese character (Year of the Rabbit): a, 15,000d, b, 20,000d. c, 25,000d, Rabbit at right. d, 25,000d, Rabbit at left. e, 35,000d.
No. 2323, 80,000d, Cardisoma guanhumi. No. 2324, 100,000d, Ailuropoda melanoleuca. No. 2325, 104,000d, France #2713c and flag of France. No. 2326, 110,000d, Beagles. No. 2327, 110,000d, Zil Elwannyen Sesel #108. No. 2328, 110,000d, Robert Schumann and hands playing piano. No. 2329, 110,000d, Low and Girl Scouts. No. 2330, 115,000d, Deepwater Horizon oil platform explosion, 2010. No. 2331, 120,000d, Wang Hai, Chinese pilot in Korean War. No. 2332, 120,000d, Rabbit and Chinese character, diff.

2010, Sept. 2   **Perf. 12¾x13¼**
Sheets of 5, #a-e
2314-2322 A358   Set of 9   110.00 110.00
Souvenir Sheets
2323-2332 A358   Set of 10   115.00 115.00

Stamp Collectors and Stamps of
Portugal — A359

No. 2333 — Collector and Portugal: a, #1716 (wildcat). b, #2155 (mouse). c, #1503 (dog). d, #1512 (train). e, #2343f (astronaut). f, #1519 (fire truck).
120,000d, Collector and Portugal #1539, 1540.

2010, Sept. 2   **Perf. 12¾x13¼**
2333 A359   20,000d Sheet of 6, #a-f   12.50 12.50
Souvenir Sheet
2334 A359   120,000d multi   12.50 12.50
No. 2334 contains one 50x39mm stamp.

Miniature Sheets

Chinese Zodiac Animals — A360

No. 2335: a, 10,000d, Rat. b, 10,000d, Ox. c, 15,000d, Tiger. d, 20,000d, Rabbit. e, 24,000d, Dragon. f, 25,000, Snake.
No. 2336: a, 10,000d, Horse. b, 10,000d, Goat. c, 15,000d, Monkey. d, 20,000d, Rooster. e, 24,000d, Dog. f, 25,000d, Pig.

2010, Sept. 2   **Perf. 12¾x13¼**
Sheets of 6, #a-f
2335-2336 A360   Set of 2   22.00 22.00

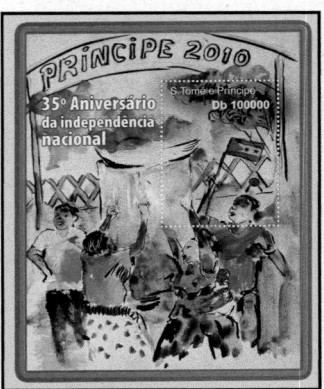

Independence, 35th Anniv. — A361

No. 2337 — Statues of Discoverers and Colonizers of St. Thomas & Prince Islands: a,

10,000d, Joao de Paiva, colonizer. b, 15,000d, Pero Escobar, discoverer. c, 25,000d, Joao de Santarém, discoverer.

No. 2338 — Symbols and maps: a, 10,000d, Map of St. Thomas & Prince Islands. b, 15,000d, Torch, national flag. c, 15,000d, Map of Africa with St. Thomas & Prince Islands circled, building. d, 25,000d, National flag, maps of St. Thomas & Prince Islands, Africa.

No. 2339 — Obverse and reverse of banknotes: a, 10,000d, 5000 dobra note. b, 15,000d, 50,000 dobra note. c, 20,000d, 20,000 dobra note. d, 25,000d, 10,000 dobra note.

No. 2340 — National heroes: a, 10,000d, King of Angolares, orange background. b, 15,000d, King Amador, green background. c, 20,000d, King Amador, yellow background. d, King of Angolares, rose background.

No. 2341, horiz. — Slaves and slave warehouses: a, 10,000d, Slave working on produce drying racks. b, 15,000d, Warehouse. c, 20,000d, Train and buildings. e, 25,000d, Slaves with baskets.

No. 2342, horiz. — Various traditional homes: a, 10,000d, House with painting of dancers. b, 15,000d, Gray house on stilts. c, 20,000d, Curtain in window. d, 25,000d, Blue house on stilts.

No. 2343, horiz. — Beaches: a, 10,000d, Micoló Beach, St. Thomas Island. b, 15,000d, Banana Beach, Prince Island. c, 20,000d, Boats on Café Beach, Ilhéu das Rolas. d, 25,000d, Lagoa Azul Beach, St. Thomas Island.

No. 2344 — Flowers: a, 15,000d, Red flower with stem at bottom. b, 15,000d, Red flower and bud. c, 15,000d, Red and yellow flowers. d, 15,000d, Pink and red five-petaled flowers. e, 15,000d, Red flower, no stem visible. f, 15,000d, Yellow flowers.

No. 2345 — Cuisine of St. Thomas & Prince Islands: a, 10,000d, Plantains. b, 10,000d, Okra. c, 15,000d, Breadfruit. d, 15,000d, Eggplant. e, 25,000d, Calulu de Peixe (fish stew). f, 25,000d, Bananas, diff.

No. 2346, horiz. — Colonial houses: a, 10,000d, House with balcony. b, 10,000d, House with flag. c, 15,000d, House with balcony, sepia-tone photograph. d, 15,000d, House with balcony, colkor photograph. e, 25,000d, House with balcony, diff. f, 25,000d, Road leading to large house.

No. 2347 — Coins: a, 10,000d, 50 centimo coin. b, 15,000d, 1 dobra coin. c, 15,000d, 2 dobra coin. d, 20,000d, 50 dobra coin. e, 20,000d, 100 dobra coin. f, 25,000d, 250 dobra coin.

No. 2348 — Coins: a, 10,000d, 5 dobra coin. b, 15,000d, 10 dobra coin. c, 15,000d, 20 dobra coin. d, 20,000d, 500 dobra coin. e, 20,000d, 1000 dorba coin. f, 25,000d, 2000 dobra coin.

No. 2349 — Agricultural products: a, 10,000d, Yellow cacao pod. b, 15,000d, Green cacao pods on tree. c, 15,000d, Sugar cane. d, 20,000d, Coffee berries. e, 20,000d, Cacao pods approaching ripeness on tree. f, 25,000d, Sugar cane, diff.

No. 2350 — Drawings of people in colonial era dress: a, 10,000d, Woman. b, 15,000d, Man, artist's name at UL. c, 15,000d, Man, diff., artist's name at LL. d, 20,000d, Two women, artist's name at LL. e, 20,000d, Two men, artist's name at UL. f, 25,000d, Man, diff.

No. 2351 — Wood carvings: a, 10,000d, Head and map of St. Thomas & Prince Islands. b, 15,000d, People in rowboats. c, 15,000d, Stylized Africans. d, 20,000d, People and house. e, 20,000d, Statue of woman holding basket. f, 25,000d, Man climbing tree.

No. 2352 — Waterfalls, mountains and rivers: a, 10,000d, Milagrosa Waterfall. b, 10,000d, St. Nicolau Waterfall. c, 15,000d, St. Nicolau Waterfall, diff. d, 15,000d, Vilela Waterfall. e, 20,000d, Foliage near Pico Maria Fernanda. f, 20,000d, Pico Maria Fernanda shrouded in clouds. g, 25,000d, Rio Manuel Jorge. h, 25,000d, Pico Cao Grande.

No. 2353 — Birds and butterflies: a, 10,000d, Speirops lugubris. b, 10,000d, Unidentified bird. c, 15,000d, Ploceus grandis facing right. d, 15,000d, Parrot facing left (incorrectly identified as Ploceus grandis). e, 15,000d, Monarch butterfly. f, 20,000d, Treron sanctithomae. g, 20,000d, Oriolus crassirostris. h, 20,000d, Piombode mato. i, 25,000d, Thomasophantes sanctithomae. j, 25,000d, Prima molleri.

No. 2354, 100,000d, Head of person waving flag of St. Thomas & Prince Islands. No. 2355, 100,000d, Obverse and reverse of 100,000 dobra banknote. No. 2356, 100,000d, First Baron de Agua-Izé Sousa e Almeida, yellow and orange cacao pods. No. 2357, 100,000d, Like #2356, with green cacao pods. No. 2358, 100,000d, Bananas. No. 2359, 100,000d, Okra. No. 2360, 100,000d, Flowers held by gloved hands of woman. No. 2361, 100,000d, Hands of Tchiloli. No. 2362, 100,000d, Wood carving of people and house, basket weaving. No. 2363, 100,000d, Woman in traditional dress. No. 2364, 100,000d, Yellow flower. No. 2365, 100,000d, Bowl of nuts, coconut shells, horiz. No. 2366, 100,000d, National Museum, flag of St. Thomas & Prince Islands, horiz. No. 2367, 100,000d, National Museum, arms of St. Thomas & Prince Islands, horiz.

Perf. 13¼x12¾, 13¼, 12¾x13¼
2010, Dec. 1
2337	A361	Sheet of 3, #a-	
		c	5.50 5.50

Sheets of 4, #a-d
2338-2343	A361	Set of 6	45.00 45.00

Sheets of 6, #a-f
2344-2351	A361	Set of 8	90.00 90.00
2352	A361	Sheet of 8, #a-h	15.50 15.50
2353	A361	Sheet of 10, #a-j	19.00 19.00

Souvenir Sheets
2354-2367	A361	Set of 14	150.00 150.00

Wedding of Prince William and Catherine Middleton — A362

No. 2368: a, Couple skiing. b, Prince William and Princess Diana. c, Princes William, Charles and Harry. d, Middleton with Princes William and Harry.

104,000d, Couple, coat of arms and castle.

Perf. 12¾x13¼
2011, Feb. 14   **Litho.**
2368	A362	27,500d Sheet of 4, #a-d	12.50 12.50

Souvenir Sheet
Perf. 13¼ Syncopated
2369	A362	104,000d multi	12.00 12.00

No. 2369 contains one 50x39mm stamp.

Internazionale Milan, 2010 Winner of FIFA Club World Cup — A363

No. 2370: a, 1964 team. b, 2010 team, Italian Series A champions, player in foreground running. c, Team members, player in foreground holding 2010 European Champions League trophy. d, Players celebrating 2010 Italian Cup championship, player in foreground smiling. e, 2010 team, Italia Supercup champions, player in foreground kicking ball. f, 2010 team celebratin Club World Cup victory.

150,000d, Javier Zanetti holding Club World Cup.

Perf. 12¾x13¼
2011, Feb. 14   **Litho.**
2370	A363	25,000d Sheet of 6, #a-f	17.00 17.00

Souvenir Sheet
Perf. 13¼ Syncopated
2371	A363	150,000d multi	17.00 17.00

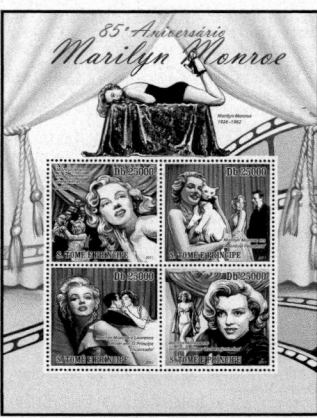

Marilyn Monroe (1926-62), Actress — A364

No. 2372 — Monroe and: a, Men from *Gentlemen Prefer Blondes*. b, Yves Montand and cat from *Let's Make Love*. c, Laurence Olivier from *The Prnce and the Showgirl*. d, Scene from *The Misfits*.

110,000d, Monroe, diff.

Perf. 13¼x12¾
2011, Feb. 25   **Litho.**
2372	A364	25,000d Sheet of 4, #a-d	11.50 11.50

Souvenir Sheet
Perf. 13¼ Syncopated
2373	A364	110,000d multi	12.50 12.50

Miniature Sheets

Nudes — A365

No. 2374, 30,000d — Paintings by Pierre-Auguste Renoir: a, Nude in a Landscape, 1883. b, Seated Bather Drying Her Leg, 1914. c, Woman at the Fountain, 1910. d, After the Bath, 1888.

No. 2375, 31,750d — Paintings by Eugène Delacroix: a, Female Nude Reclining on a Divan, 1825-26. b, Mlle. Rose, 1817-20. c, Reclining Odalisque, 1827. d, The Death of Sardanapalus, 1827.

No. 2376, 32,500d — Paintings by Titian: a, Sacred and Profane Love, 1514. b, Venus with a Mirror, 1555. c, Tarquin and Lucretia, 1568-71. d, Venus Anadyomene, 1520.

No. 2377 — Paintings by Peter Paul Rubens: a, 31,250d, Perseus Liberating Andromeda, 1639-40. b, 31,250d, Diana and Her Nymphs Surprised by the Fauns, 1638-40. c, 31,250d, Venus and Adonis, 1635. d, 312,500d, The Three Graces, 1639.

Perf. 13¼x12¾
2011, Feb. 25   **Litho.**
Sheets of 4, #a-d
2374-2377	A365	Set of 4	87.50 87.50

Miniature Sheets

A366

No. 2378, 31,250d — Protected animals on Christmas Island: a, Sula sula. b, Pipistrellus murrayi. c, Birgus latro. d, Phaethon lepturus.

No. 2379, 31,250d — Dolphins: a, Lagenorhynchus obscurus. b, Stenella attenuata. c, Cephalorhynchus commersonii. d, Tursiops truncatus.

No. 2380, 31,250d — Peonies: a, Paeonia mascula, subspecies russi, Paeonia officinalis. b, Paeonia daurica, Paeonia wittmanniana. c, Paeonia peregrina, Paeonia cambessedesii. d, Paeonia russi var. reverchoni, Paeonia clusii.

No. 2381, 31,250d, vert. — Birds of prey: a, Buteo lagopus lagopus. b, Falco subbuteo subbuteo. c, Aquila chrysaetos chrysaetos. d, Hieraaetus fasciatus fasciatus.

No. 2382, 31,250d, vert. — Pope John Paul II holding crucifix: a, Wearing zucchetto, facing left. b, Wearing miter, facing right. c, Wearing miter, facing forward with hand raised. d, Wearing miter and red stole, hand raised.

No. 2383, 31,750d — Solar-powered items: a, Meguru electric vehicle. b, NanoSail-D2 satellite. c, Solar panels. d, Solar-powered bus.

No. 2384, 31,750d — Cats: a, Acinonyx jubatus raineyii. b, Acinonyx jubatus hecki. c, Panthera leo bleyenberghi. d, Panthera pardus pardus.

No. 2385, 31,750d, vert. — Cats: a, Felis margarita. b, Felis nigripes. c, Prionailurus rubiginosus. d, Felis chaus.

No. 2386, 32,500d — African animals: a, Mellivora capensis. b, Kobus ellipsiprymnus. c, Phacochoerus aethiopicus. d, Orycteropus afer.

No. 2387, 32,500d — Fish: a, Ostracion tricornis. b, Rhinecanthus aculeatus. c, Holocentrus axensionis. d, Diodon hystrix.

No. 2388, 32,500d — Dinosaurs: a, Xiphactinus, Liopleurodon. b, Tyrannosaurus rex, Archaeopteryx. c, Rahonavis ostromi, Ankylosaurus. d, Stegosaurus, Velociraptor.

No. 2389, 32,500d — Service organizations: a, Paul P. Harris, founder of Rotary International, Rotary International emblem and New Orleans skyline. b, Cattleya rex, Rotary Intenational emblem. c, Map of Africa, African child, Lions International emblem. d, Melvin Jones, Lions International founder, Lions International emblem, New Orleans skyline.

No. 2390, 32,500d — Princess Diana (1961-97): a, With sons, William and Harry. b, Dancing with Prince Charles. c, Wearing sailor's hat, holding African child. d, Holding Prince William, holding flowers.

No. 2391, 32,500d, vert. — Owls: a, Tyto soumagnei. b, Bubo lacteus. c, Bubo leucostictus. d, Scotopelia ussheri.

No. 2392, 33,750d — Indian luxury trains: a, Palace on Wheels (Palacio Sobre Carris). b, Deccan Odyssey. c, Golden Chariot (Bigo Dourada). d, Royal Rajasthan.

No. 2393, 33,750d, vert. — Butterflies: a, Urania sloanus. b, Anaea electra. c, Alcides aurora. d, Chrysiridia ripheus.

Perf. 12¾x13¼, 13¼x12¾
2011, Feb. 25   **Litho.**
Sheets of 4, #a-d
2378-2393	A366	Set of 16	230.00 230.00

Souvenir Sheets

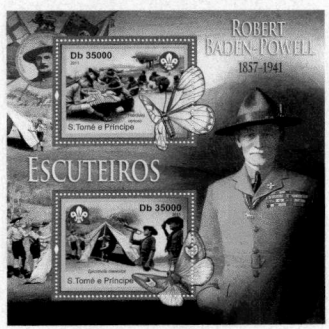

A367

No. 2394, 35,000d — Scouts, scouting emblem and butterflies: a, Hibrildes venosa. b, Epicimelia theresidae.

No. 2395, 35,000d — Ships: a, Adler von Lübeck, 1566. b, Gorch Fock, 1958.

No. 2396, 35,000d — Fire fighters and fire trucks from: a, Wagga Wagga, Australia. b, Sapporo, Japan.

No. 2397, 35,000d — Motorcycles: a, Kiwi Indian Retro 30. b, 2009 Harley-Davidson FLHRC Road King Classic.

No. 2398, 35,000d — Mushrooms: a, Boletus junquilleus. b, Xerocomus badius.

No. 2399, 40,000d — Lighthouses and birds: a, Onychoprion fuscata. b, Diomedea exulans.

No. 2400, 40,000d — Protected species in the Galapagos Islands: a, Conolophus subcristatus. b, Chelonoidis nigra.

No. 2401, 40,000d — Flying dinosaurs: a, Pterodactylus, Anurognathus. b, Pterodactylus, Pterosaur.

No. 2402, 40,000d — Mohandas K. Gandhi (1869-1948), Indian nationalist: a, Waving, with men. b, In bed, young girl sitting on bed.

No. 2403, 40,000d — Maia Chiburdanidze, chess player: a, Playing opponent at right. b, Holding large pawn at left.

No. 2404, 45,000d — Cats: a, Stewie, world's longest cat. b, Scarlett's Magic, world's tallest cat..

No. 2405, 45,000d — Dogs: a, Beagles. b, Airedale terriers.

No. 2406, 45,000d — Minerals: a, Quartz. b, Beryl aquamarine with muscovite.

No. 2407, 45,000d — High-speed trains: a, V150 TGV, France. b, CHR380, China.

No. 2408, 50,000d — World War II aircraft: a, Mitsubishi A5M4 and A5M2, Japan. b, Messerschmitt Me-262A-1a, Focke-Wulf FW-190-A7, Germany.

No. 2409, 50,000d — Yuri Gagarin (1934-68), first man in space, and: a, Vostok 1. b, Floating cosmonaut.

No. 2410, 50,000d — Princess Diana (1961-97): a, Campaigning for land mines elimination in Angola. b, With Zimbabwean Red Cross worker.

No. 2411, 50,000d, vert. — Dogs: a, Alaskan malamute. b, Greenlandic dog.

No. 2412, 50,000d, vert. — Marilyn Monroe (1926-62), actress: a, Leaning backward. b, Leaning forward.

No. 2413, 52,000d — Whales: a, Megaptera novaeangliae. b, Eubalaena glacialis.

No. 2414, 52,000d — Turtles: a, Megalochelis gigantea. b, Chrysemys concinna.

No. 2415, 52,000d, vert. — Butterflies: a, Ornithoptera alexandrae. b, Brephidium exilis.

No. 2416, 52,000d, vert. — Orchids: a, Ansellia africana, Habenaria radiata. b, Calanthe sieboldii, Dracula vampira.

No. 2417, 55,000d — Scouting trefoil and Scouts: a, Hiking. b, Forming human chain.

No. 2418, 55,000d — Ailuropoda melanoleuca: a, Sleeping. b, Eating.

No. 2419, 55,000d — Frogs: a, Gastrotheca cornuta. b, Rhinoderma darwinii.

No. 2420, 55,000d, vert. — Owls: a, Glaucidium californicum. b, Otus asio.

No. 2421, 55,000d, vert. — Mushrooms: a, Amanita muscaria. b, Macrolepiota procera.

No. 2422, 57,500d — Dinosaurs: a, Einiosaurus. b, Medusaceratops.

No. 2423, 57,500d — Red Cross: a, Worker with child, disaster workers, helicopter. b, Worker with child, Worker carrying sack, ambulance.

No. 2424, 57,500d — Wedding of Prince William and Catherine Middleton: a, Prince William at right. b, Middleton at right.

No. 2425, 57,500d, vert. — Fish: a, Regalecus glesne, Lampris guttatus. b, Silurus glanis, Zeus faber.

Perf. 13¼ Syncopated
2011, Mar. 30   **Litho.**
Sheets of 2, #a-b

2394-2425 A367   Set of 32   355.00   355.00

A368

No. 2426, 25,000d — Two images of Babe Ruth (1895-1948), baseball player: a, Ruth

holding brown bat in image at left. b, Ruth holding two bats in image at right. c, Glove and oversized baseball in batter's box at LR. d, Ruth holding brown bat in image at right.

No. 2427, 25,000d — Bobby Fischer (1943-2008), chess champion: a, Wearing red suit. b, Wearing headband and blue suit. c, Wearing no suit. d, Wearing gray suit.

No. 2428, 25,000d — Sebastian Vettel, Formula 1 race car driver, and: a, Race car at LL. b, Race car above Vettel's arm. c, Vettel kissing trophy. d, Vettel wearing racing helmet at left.

No. 2429, 25,000d — 2014 Winter Olympics, Sochi, Russia: a, Ski jumping. b, Ice hockey. c, Speed skating. d, Snowboarding.

No. 2430, 25,000d — Mohandas K. Gandhi (1869-1948), Indian nationalist: a, Gandhi sitting, Indian flag. b, Kanyakumari Temple. c, Dove, head of Gandhi. d, Gandhi facing left.

No. 2431, 25,000d — Pres. John F. Kennedy (1917-63), and: a, Fidel Castro and Minuteman missiles. b, Wife, Jacquline, and Marilyn Monroe. c, Buzz Aldrin on Moon. d, Berlin Wall.

No. 2432, 25,000d — Queen Elizabeth II: a, Wearing crown at left. b, With Australia #259. c, As young child at right. d, With Prince Philip at left.

No. 2433, 25,000d — London Underground, 150th anniv.: a, 1996 train in Notting Hill Gate Station. b, S8 train, Picadilly Station entrance sign, buildings. c, Docklands Light Rail train in tunnel. d, D78 train in Paddington Station.

No. 2434, 25,000d — Ferdinand von Zeppelin (1838-1917), founder of Zeppelin Airship Company: a, With wife, Isabella. b, Graf Zeppelin in air. c, Hindenburg near ground. d, Hindenburg and hangars.

No. 2435, 25,000d — Space flight of Valentina Tereshkova, first woman in space, 50th anniv.: a, Tereshkova wearing helmet. b, Tereshkova feeding infant, emblem of Vostok 5 and 6. c, Tereshkova and Vostok 6. d, Tereshkova and flight technicians.

No. 2436, 25,000d — Rudolf Nureyev (1938-93), ballet dancer: a, Without hat. b, Wearing ski cap at right. c, Wearing ski cap at left. d, Wearing beret at right.

No. 2437, 25,000d — Louis de Funès (1914-83), actor: a, With thumb touching forefinger. b, With finger touching tongue. c, Wearing costume with neck frill. d, Wearing military uniform.

No. 2438, 25,000d — Richard Wagner (1813-83), composer: a, Playing piano at production of Tristan and Isolde. b, And Temple of the Grail from 1882 production of Parsifal. c, And Wagner and Wagner Monument, Berlin. d, And Bayreuth Festival Theater.

No. 2439, 25,000d — Giuseppe Verdi (1813-1901), composer: a, Portrait of Verdi by Francesco Paolo Michetti, musical score. b, Verdi, piano keyboard. c, Caricature of Verdi by Théobald Chartran. d, Verdi in Venice, Verdi's signature.

No. 2440, 25,000d — Jim Morrison (1943-71), rock musician: a, Holding microphone stand, belt visible. b, Two images of Morrison, holding microphone above head at right. c, Two images of Morrison, holding microphone stand at right. d, Holding microphone stand, belt not visible.

No. 2441, 25,000d — Nude paintings by Lucas Cranach the Elder (1472-1553): a, Lucretia, 1538. b, The Three Graces, 1535. c, The Silver Age, 1516. d, The Suicide of Lucretia, 1538.

No. 2442, 25,000d — Paintings by Eugène Delacroix (1798-1863): a, Fanatics of Tangier, 1838. b, The Barque of Dante, 1822. c, The Natchez, 1835. d, Cleopatra and the Peasant, 1838.

No. 2443, 25,000d — Paintings by Pablo Picasso (1881-1973): a, Self-portrait, 1901. b, Les Demoiselles d'Avignon, 1907. c, Three Musicians, 1921. d, Still Life with Bull's Head, 1939.

No. 2444, 25,000d — International Year of Water Cooperation: a, Child carrying water bucket on head. b, Child at faucet. c, Child getting splashed with water. d, Child drinking from bowl.

No. 2445, 25,000d — Year of the Snake: a, Denomination at UL, snake head at LR. b, Denomination at UL, snake head at LL. c, Denomination at UR, snake head at right. d, Denomination and snake head at UL.

No. 2446, 96,000d, Ruth, diff. No. 2447, 96,000d, Fischer, diff. No. 2448, 96,000d, Vettel and race car, diff. No. 2449, 96,000d, Downhill skiing. No. 2450, 96,000d, Gandhi and crowd. No. 2451, 96,000d, Pres. Kennedy and U-2 spy plane. No. 2452, 96,000d, Queen Elizabeth II and scene from her coronation. No. 2453, 96,000d, 1986 train in Canary Wharf London Underground station. No. 2454, 96,000d, Ferdinand von Zeppelin and Zeppelin LZ-11. No. 2455, 96,000d, Tereshkova and Vostok 6, diff. No. 2456, 96,000d, Nurevey and Margot Fonteyn. No. 2457, 96,000d, De Funès and flowers. No. 2458, 96,000d, Wagner, diff. No. 2459, 96,000d, Portrait of Verdi, by Michetti and G clef. No. 2460, 96,000d, Morrison. No. 2461, 96,000d, Nymph of the Spring, by Cranach, the Elder. No. 2462, 96,000d, The Massacre at Chios, by Delacroix. No. 2463, 96,000d,

The Weeping Woman, by Picasso. No. 2464, 96,000d, Child drinking, diff. No. 2465, 96,000d, Snake, diff.

2013, Mar. 29   **Litho.**   *Perf. 13¼*
Sheets of 4, #a-d

2426-2445 A368   Set of 20   210.00   210.00

Souvenir Sheets

2446-2465 A368   Set of 20   200.00   200.00

Animals and Prehistoric
Animals — A369

No. 2466, 25,000d — Rhinoceroses: a, Diceros bicornis facing right. b, Diceros bicornis facing left. c, Adult and juvenile Ceratotherium simum. d, Adult Ceratotherium simum.

No. 2467, 25,000d — Antelopes: a, Gazella cuiveri. b, Gazella spekei. c, Gazella rufifrons. d, Gazella leptoceros.

No. 2468, 25,000d — Cercopithecus mona and fruit: a, Carica papaya. b, Artocarpus rigidus. c, Psidium guajava. d, Annona glabra.

No. 2469, 25,000d — Primates: a, Cercopithecus neglectus, Cercopithecus diana. b, Procolobus badius. c, Two Papio anubis. d, Cercopithecus roloway, Colobus guereza.

No. 2470, 25,000d — Bats: a, Rousettus aegyptiacus. b, Tadarida pumila. c, Taphozous mauritianus. d, Hipposideros ruber.

No. 2471, 25,000d — Cats: a, Leptailurus serval. b, Panthera pardus pardus. c, Acinonyx jubatus and prey. d, Panthera leo and prey.

No. 2472, 25,000d — Loxodonta africana: a, Adult and juvenile. b, Adult and two juveniles. c, Elephants stampeding. d, Two adults.

No. 2473, 25,000d — Dolphins: a, Grampus griseus. b, Steno bredanensis. c, Delphinus delphis. d, Tursiops truncatus.

No. 2474, 25,000d — Whales: a, Feresa attenuata. b, Balaenoptera edeni. c, Kogia breviceps. d, Mesoplodon densirostris.

No. 2475, 25,000d — Birds: a, Sula leucogaster. b, Morus capensis. c, Head of Sula leucogaster and bird in flight. d, Head of Morus capensis, and bird in flight.

No. 2476, 25,000d — Birds: a, Sarkidiornis melanotos. b, Phoenicopterus minor. c, Phoenicopterus roseus. d, Dendrocygne bicolor.

No. 2477, 25,000d — Two Alcedo thomensis: a, Birds sharing prey, denomination at UR. b, Perched bird with fish, bird in flight, denomination at UL. c, Bird on ground at left, bird in flight at right with fish, denomination at UR. d, Two birds on ground, denomination at UL.

No. 2478, 25,000d — Owls: a, Tyto alba. b, Otus senegalensis. c, Otus senegalensis, Tyto alba. d, Tyto alba, Otus hartlaubi.

No. 2479, 25,000d — Apis mellifera: a, Two bees at flowers on branch, denomination in white. b, Two bees on red flower. c, One bee on flower. d, Bee on flower and bee flying near flower.

No. 2480, 25,000d — Butterflies: a, Pseudacraea lucretia. b, Mycalesis sciathis, Myrina marciana. c, Papilio hippocoon, Melantis leda. d, Acraea zetes.

No. 2481, 25,000d — Butterflies: a, Bicyclus dorothea, Hypolimnas salmacis. b, Sevenia boisduvali, Hypolimnas salmacis. c, Graphium angolanus baronis, Leptotes pirithous. d, Precis sinuata, Deudorix lorisona.

No. 2482, 25,000d — Fish: a, Coryphaena hippurus. b, Dactylopterus volitans. c, Histrio histrio. d, Bodianus pulchellus.

No. 2483, 25,000d — Crocodiles: a, Crocodylus cataphractus. b, Crocodylus niloticus. c, Crocodylus suchus. d, Osteolaemus tetraspis.

No. 2484, 25,000d — Turtles: a, Geochelone gigantea. b, Geochelone pardalis. c, Caretta caretta. d, Geochelone sulcata.

No. 2485, 25,000d — Dinosaurs: a, Gorgosaurus. b, Daspletosaurus. c, Dryosaurus. d, Yutyrannus.

No. 2486, 96,000d, Diceros bicornis, diff. No. 2487, 96,000d, Gazella dorcas. No. 2488, 96,000d, Cercopithecus mona and Lycium ferocissimum. No. 2489, 96,000d, Papio anubis. No. 2490, 96,000d, Eidolon helvum. No. 2491, 96,000d, Caracal caracal. No. 2492, 96,000d, Two Loxodonta africana, diff. No. 2493, 96,000d, Stenella frontalis. No. 2494, 96,000d, Megaptera novaeangliae. No. 2495, 96,000d, Morus capensis, diff. No. 2496,

96,000d, Phoenicopterus roseus, diff. No. 2497, 96,000d, Two Alcedo thomensis, diff. No. 2498, 96,000d, Otus senegalensis, Tyto alba, diff. No. 2499, 96,000d, Apis mellifera on honeycomb. No. 2500, 96,000d, Libythea labdaca, Graphium leonidas. No. 2501, 96,000d, Iolaus iulus, Charaxes jasius. No. 2502, 96,000d, Anthias anthias. No. 2503, 96,000d, Crocodylus niloticus and Pluvianus aegyptius. No. 2504, 96,000d, Pelomedusa subrufa. No. 2505, 96,000d, Tyrannosaurus, Edmontosaurus.

2013, May 10   **Litho.**   *Perf. 13¼*
Sheets of 4, #a-d

2466-2485 A369   Set of 20   220.00   220.00

Souvenir Sheets

2486-2505 A369   Set of 20   210.00   210.00

Birth of Prince George of
Cambridge — A370

No. 2506: a, Duke and Duchess of Cambridge with Prince George, blue banner at bottom. b, Princess Diana holding Prince William, Duke of Cambridge holding Prince George. c, Duke and Duchess of Cambridge with Prince George, blue banner at top. d, Duchess of Cambridge holding Prince George.

96,000d, Duke and Duchess of Cambridge with Prince George, diff.

2013, Aug. 2   **Litho.**   *Perf. 13¼*
2506 A370 25,000d Sheet of 4,
     #a-d   11.00   11.00

Souvenir Sheet

2507 A370 96,000d multi   10.50   10.50

A371

No. 2508, 25,000d — Elvis Presley (1935-77): a, With guitar, holding microphone. b, Holding microphone, no guitar. c, With guitar, no microphone. d, Without guitar of microphone.

No. 2509, 25,000d — Marilyn Monroe (1926-62), actress: a, Wearing blue dress. b, Wearing red dress, with Academy Award. c, Wearing potato sack, standing against pillar. d, Wearing blue dress, with Hollywood Walk of Fame star.

No. 2510, 25,000d — Scouts and minerals: a, Scout reading map, Uraninite. b, Scout lifting rock, Orpiment. c, Scouts examining rocks, Emerald. d, Two Scouts, Carbonate.

No. 2511, 25,000d — Scouting trefoil, cats and dogs: a, American Shorthair cat. b, Great Dane. c, Boxer. d, Persian cat.

No. 2512, 25,000d — Rotary International emblem and orchids: a, Cattleya acklandiae. b, Sobralia macrantha. c, Cypripedium lowii. d, Cattleya labiata.

No. 2513, 25,000d — International Red Cross, 150th anniv.: a, Red Cross workers on battlefield. b, Nurse tending to patient with arm in sling. c, Nurse reading newspaper to man in bed. d, Nurse and children.

No. 2514, 25,000d — Pope Benedict XVI and: a, Tiger Woods lily. b, Easter lily with red and white petals. c, Red ginger lily. d, White Easter lily.

No. 2515, 25,000d — Pope Francis and orchids: a, Cattleya walkeriana. b, Vanda tricolor. c, Odontoglossum nevadense. d, Pescatoria lehmanni.

No. 2516, 25,000d — Mushrooms: a, Hygrocybe punicea. b, Amanita phalloides. c, Suillus grevillei. d, Agaricus campester.

No. 2517, 25,000d — High-speed trains: a, Bombardier TWINDEXX Express, Switzerland. b, Talgo 350, Spain. c, Proposed California bullet train. d, West Japan Railways Series 500.

No. 2518, 25,000d — Fire trucks: a, Scania 93. b, Pierce 105-foot truck with rear mount ladder. c, Scania G82M. d, New South Wales Category 11 truck, Australia.

No. 2519, 25,000d — Rescue vehicles: a, Harley-Davidson Ultra Classic fire motorcycle. b, Severn Class lifeboat. c, Christophorus 12 air ambulance. d, Medic 8 ambulance.

No. 2520, 25,000d — Ships and lighthouses: a, Sailing School Vessel Robert C. Seamans. b, Gulden Leeuw, Bremerhaven Lighthouse, Germany. c, Vittoria Lighthouse, Italy. d, Alexander von Humboldt II, Hellevoetsluis Lighthouse, Netherlands.

No. 2521, 25,000d — French people and items: a, Napoleon Bonaparte (1769-1821), emperor. b, Concorde. c, Charles de Gaulle (1890-1970), president. d, TGV Atlantique.

No. 2522, 25,000d — Paintings in Rijksmuseum, Amsterdam: a, The Milkmaid, by Johannes Vermeer, 1658-60. b, Self-portrait with Felt Hat, by Vincent van Gogh, 1887. c, The Square Man, by Karel Appel, 1951. d, The Merry Drinker, by Frans Hals, 1628-30.

No. 2523, 25,000d — Paintings by Paul Cézanne (1839-1906): a, Nude Woman Standing, 1899. b, The Blue Vase, 1887. c, Self-portrait, 1882. d, Bather, 1887.

No. 2524, 25,000d — Paintings of nudes: a, Two Nudes, by Pablo Picasso, 1906. b, Nude Woman on Green Cushions, by Pierre-Auguste Renoir, 1909. c, Seated Female Nude, by Amadeo Modigliani, 1916. d, Adam and Eve, by Tamara de Lempicka, 1932.

No. 2525, 25,000d — 50th birthday of Garry Kasparov, chess player: a, Viewing chessboard with arms folded. b, Wearing red tie. c, Viewing chessboard with hands on head. d, Standing over chessboard.

No. 2526, 25,000d — Guan Tianlang, golfer: a, Crouching, holding putter. b, Swinging golf club. c, Wearing plaid pants. d, Holding golf ball.

No. 2527, 25,000d — Russian postage stamps, 155th anniv.: a, Russia #2. b, Picture post card depicting Yuri Gagarin wearing helmet. c, Russia Nos. 2, 3, 4, 5, 5a, 6, 7 and 11. d, Russia #5266.

No. 2528, 96,000d, Presley with guitar, diff. No. 2529, 96,000d, Monroe and Academy Award, diff. No. 2530, 96,000d, Lord Robert Baden-Powell in Scouting uniform. No. 2531, 96,000d, Scouting trefoil, Italian greyhound, American Shorthair cat. No. 2532, 96,000d, Rotary International emblem and Dendrobium albosanguineum. No. 2533, 96,000d, Red Cross nurse assisting man with crutches. No. 2534, 96,000d, Pope Benedict XVI and lily, diff. No. 2535, 96,000d, Pope Francis and Cymbidium Valley Regent Reggae. No. 2536, 96,000d, Boletus calopus. No. 2537, 96,000d, Italo high-speed train, Italy. No. 2538, 96,000d, Dennis Sabre fire engine, Kent, England. No. 2539, 96,000d, Tanker 910 fire plane. No. 2540, 96,000d, Split Rock Lighthouse, Minnesota. No. 2541, 96,000d, Concorde, diff. No. 2542, 96,000d, The Night Watch, by Rembrandt, 1642. No. 2543, 96,000d, Self-portrait with Palette, by Cézanne. No. 2544, 96,000d, Morning Toilette, by Lotte Laserstein, 1930. No. 2545, 96,000d, Kasparov, diff. No. 2546, 96,000d, Guan Tianlang, diff. No. 2547, 96,000d, Russia #104, 4589, 4779.

2013, Aug. 15   Litho.   Perf. 13¼
Sheets of 4, a-d
2508-2527 A371   Set of 20 220.00 220.00
Souvenir Sheets
2528-2547 A371   Set of 20 210.00 210.00

China International Collection Expo, Beijing (Nos. 2526, 2546); Rossica 2013 International Philatelic Exhibition, Moscow (Nos. 2527, 2547).

Wang Yaping

A372

No. 2548, 25,000d — Wang Yaping, Chinese astronaut: a, Standing in front of capsule wearing space suit. b, At control panel. c, Wearing space suit, waving, parachute in background. d, Waving.

No. 2549, 25,000d — Haroun Tazieff (1914-98), geologist: a, Tazieff and Skutterudite. b, Tungurahua Volcano, Ecuador, andTyrannosaurus rex. c, Karymsky Volcano, Russia, and Pterodactylus. d, Tazieff and Labradorite.

No. 2550, 25,000d — Lions International emblem and: a, Panthera leo, Manis crassicaudata. b, Panthera leo with prey in mouth. c, Panthera leo male, female and cub. d, Male Panthera leo.

No. 2551, 25,000d — Endangered animals: a, Pongo abelii. b, Campephilus principalis. c, Loxodonta africana. d, Lepilemur septentrionalis.

No. 2552, 25,000d — Dolphins: a, Stenella attenuata. b, Lipotes vexillifer. c, Orcaella brevirostris. d, Delphinus delphis.

No. 2553, 25,000d — Birds of prey: a, Pandion haliaetus. b, Strix varia. c, Falco peregrinus. d, Buteo jamaicensis.

No. 2554, 25,000d — Scouting trefoil and parrots: a, Eclectus roratus. b, Ara ararauna. c, Amazona viridigenalis. d, Cacatua alba.

No. 2555, 25,000d — Butterflies and flowers: a, Argynnis paphia, Tulipa gesneriana. b, Danaus plexippus, Hemerocallis. c, Callithea philotima, Alcea setosa. d, Diaethria clymena, Helianthus annuus.

No. 2556, 25,000d — Pope John Paul II: a, Wearing white vestments, St. Peter's Basilica in background. b, Wearing white vestments, doves flying overhead. c, Wearing miter and red robe, doves flying overhead. d, Wearing red robe, St. Peter's Basilica in background.

No. 2557, 25,000d — Nelson Mandela (1918-2013), President of South Africa, and: a, Whitney Houston (1963-2012), singer. b, Princess Diana (1961-97). c, Margaret Thatcher (1925-2013), British Prime Minister. d, Queen Elizabeth II.

No. 2558, 25,000d — Nobel Peace Prize winners: a, Aung San Suu Kyi, 1991. b, Wangari Maathai, 2004. c, Henri Dunant, 1901, and Red Cross flag. d, Dr. Albert Schweitzer, 1952, and Red Cross flag.

No. 2559, 25,000d — James Gandolfini (1961-2013), actor and scenes from: a, The Sopranos (with cigar). b, The Last Castle (wearing Army uniform). c, Lonely Hearts (wearing hat). d, Cinema Verite (with beard).

No. 2560, 25,000d — Magnus Carlsen, chess player: a, With knight. b, At chessboard, with hands clasped. c, With knight and queen. d, With Boris Becker, tennis player.

No. 2561, 25,000d — Brasiliana 2013 Intl. Philatelic Exhibition emblem and soccer players: a, David Luiz, Brazil, and Mario Balotelli, Italy. b, Thiago Silva, Brazil, and Shinji Okazaki, Japan. c, Fred, Brazil, and Walter Gargano, Uruguay. d, Marcelo, Brazil, and Giovani Dos Santos, Mexico.

No. 2562, 25,000d — Paintings by Leonardo da Vinci (1452-1519): a, Lady with an Ermine, 1489-90. b, Madonna Litta, c.1490. c, Virgin and Child with St. Anne, 1508. d, La Belle Ferronière, 1490-96.

No. 2563, 25,000d — Nude paintings by Peter Paul Rubens (1577-1640): a, Andromeda, 1638. b, Venus at Her Toilet, 1608. c, Bathsheba at the Fountain, 1635. d, Hélène Fourment, 1638.

No. 2564, 25,000d — Paintingsby Vincent van Gogh (1853-90): a, La Mousmé, Sitting, 1888. b, Paul Gauguin's Armchair, 1888. c, Still Life: Vase with Fifteen Sunflowers,1889. d, Café Terrace on the Place du Forum, Arles, at Night, 1888.

No. 2565, 25,000d — Steam trains: a, Canadian International Limited, Central 4-4-0. b, London, Midlands and Scotland Railway Jubilee locomotive, Somerset & Dorset Railway 4-4-0. c, Indian Railroad 2-8-2, Royal Scot locomotive. d, Paris-Reims Express, South African Railway 4-8-2.

No. 2566, 25,000d — Year of the Horse: a, Horse with front leg lifted. b, Horse bucking. c, Horse in circle of flowers. d, Horse walking to right.

No. 2567, 96,000d, Wang Yaping, diff. No. 2568, 96,000d, Tazieff, Colima Volcano, Mexico. No. 2569, 96,000d, Lions International emblem, Panthera leo chasing prey. No. 2570, 96,000d, Panthera pardus orientalis. No. 2571, 96,000d, Platanista gangetica. No. 2572, 96,000d, Strix varia, diff. No. 2573, 96,000d, Scouting trefoil and Calyptorhynchus lathami. No. 2574, 96,000d, Agrias hewitsonius, Paeonia officinalis. No. 2575, 96,000d, Pope John Paul II and dove. No. 2576, 96,000d, Mandela and Queen Elizabeth II, diff. No. 2577, 96,000d, Dalai Lama, 1989 winner of Nobel Peace Prize. No. 2578, 96,000d, Gandolfini in The Sopranos, diff. No. 2579, 96,000d, Carlsen and knight, diff. No. 2580, 96,000d, Brasiliana 2013 emblem, Hulk, Brazil, and Sergio Ramos, Spain. No. 2581, 96,000d, Mona Lisa, by Leonardo. No. 2582, 96,000d, Venus, Cupid, Bacchus and Ceres, by Rubens. No. 2583, 96,000d, The Church at Auvers, by van Gogh. No. 2584, 96,000d, Highland Chief 4-4-2, Flying Scotsman locomotives. No. 2585, 96,000d, Three horses in circle.

2013, Sept. 10   Litho.   Perf. 13¼
Sheets of 4, #a-d
2548-2566 A372   Set of 19 210.00 210.00
Souvenir Sheets
2567-2585 A372   Set of 19 200.00 200.00

Sports — A373

No. 2586, 19,000d — Cricket players: a, Hashim Amla. b, Michael John Clarke. c, Alastair Cook. d, Sachin Tendulkar.

No. 2587, 19,000d — Table tennis players: a, Timo Boll. b, Ma Long. c, Xu Xin. d, Liu Shiwen.

No. 2588, 75,000d, Cricket ball. No. 2589, 75,000d, Table tennis ball and paddles.

2013, Dec. 10   Litho.   Perf.
Sheets of 4, #a-d
2586-2587 A373   Set of 2 17.00 17.00
Souvenir Sheets
2588-2589 A373   Set of 2 17.00 17.00

Ursos Polares

A374

No. 2590, 20,000d — Ursus maritimus: a, Adult walking. b, Adult and juvenile. c, Two adults fighting. d, Adult resting.

No. 2591, 20,000d — Gorillas: a, Adult and juvenile Gorilla gorilla gorilla. b, Adult Gorilla gorilla. c, Adult Gorilla gorilla gorilla sitting on rock. d, Adult and juvenile Gorilla beringei beringei.

No. 2592, 20,000d — Marine life: a, Megaptera novaeangliae. b, Makaira nigricans. c, Aluterus scriptus. d, Tursiops truncatus.

No. 2593, 20,000d — Tropical fish: a, Pseudanthias pleurotaenia. b, Ctenochaetus hawaiiensis. c, Ostracion cubicus. d, Symphysodon discus.

No. 2594, 20,000d — Extinct and endangered birds: a, Columba versicolor. b, Rhipidura rufifrons. c, Pyrocephalus rubinus. d, Porphyrio coerulescens.

No. 2595, 20,000d — Mao Zedong (1893-1976), Chinese communist leader: a, With soldiers and peasants, flag at right. b, With young girl. c, Clapping. d, Waving, flag in background.

No. 2596, 20,000d — African trains: a, Blue Train, South Africa. b, Pride of Africa. c, Class 25NC 4-8-4, South Africa. d, Class 19E, South Africa.

No. 2597, 20,000d — Christmas paintings: a, Adoration of the Shepherds, by Charles Le Brun. b, Nativity, by Piero della Francesca. c, Nativity, by Giotto. d, Nativity, by Lorenzo Lotto.

No. 2598, 25,000d — 2013 International Track and Field Championships, Moscow: a, Valerie Adams, shot putter, flag of New Zealand. b, LaShawn Merritt, sprinter, flag of U.S. c, Aleksandr Menkov, long jumper, flag of Russia. d, Pawel Fajdek, hammer thrower, flag of Poland.

No. 2599, 25,000d — Owls: a, Tyto capensis. b, Bubo lacteus. c, Otus ireneae. d, Ninox superciliaris.

No. 2600, 25,000d — Scouting trefoil and turtles: a, Batagur trivittata. b, Pseudemys peninsularis. c, Indotestudo elongata. d, Pseudemys rubriventris.

No. 2601, 25,000d — Paintings by Pierre-Auguste Renoir (1841-1919): a, Gabrielle with Open Blouse, 1907. b, Algiers Landscape, 1895. c, Anemones, 1909. d, After the Bath, 1888.

No. 2602, 25,000d — Impressionist paintings: a, Paris Street, Rainy Day, by Gustave Caillebotte, 1877. b, Woman with Umbrella, by Claude Monet, 1875. c, A Bar at the Folies-Bergère, by Edouard Manet, 1881-82. d, The Dance Class, by Edgar Degas, 1874.

No. 2603, 25,000d — Composers: a, Johann Sebastian Bach (1685-1750). b, Franz Liszt (1811-86). c, Franz Schubert (1797-1828). d, Johannes Brahms (1833-97).

No. 2604, 25,000d — Japanese high-speed trains: a, E5 Series Shinkansen. b, E6 Series Shinkansen. c, 500 Series Shinkansen. d, N700-7000 Series Sakura Shinkansen.

No. 2605, 25,000d — Yuri Gagarin (1934-68), first man in space: a, At left, wearing space helmet. b, Waving. c, Laughing, rocket launch in background. d, At right, wearing space helmet.

No. 2606, 25,000d — Future space flight: a, Space plane with foldable wings. b, Martian lander. c, Asteroid redirection mission. d, Satellite with solar panels at sides.

No. 2607, 79,000d, Ursus maritimus, diff. No. 2608, 79,000d, Gorilla beringei graueri. No. 2609, 79,000d, Sphyrna lewini. No. 2610, 79,000d, Chaetodon capistratus. No. 2611, 79,000d, Vanellus macropterus. No. 2612, 79,000d, Mao Zedong, mountains. No. 2613, 79,000d, Shosholoza Meyl train, South Africa. No. 2614, 79,000d, Holy Family, by El Greco. No. 2615, 96,000d, Svetlana Shkolina, high jumper, flag of Russia. No. 2616, 96,000d, Bubo ascalaphus. No. 2617, 96,000d, Scouting trefoil and Leucocephalon yuwonoi. No. 2618, 96,000d, Self-portrait, by Renoir, 1876. No. 2619, 96,000d, Little Italian Street Singer, by Jean Frédéric Bazille. No. 2620, 96,000d, Joseph Haydn (1732-1809), composer. No. 2621, 96,000d, Series E6 Shinkansen, diff. No. 2622, 96,000d, Gagarin with Valentina Tereshkova, cosmonaut. No. 2623, 96,000d, Mars rocket.

2013, Dec. 10   Litho.   Perf. 13¼
Sheets of 4, #a-d
2590-2606 A374   Set of 17 175.00 175.00
Souvenir Sheets
2607-2623 A374   Set of 17 170.00 170.00

S. Tomé e Príncipe   Db 25000

A375

Personalizable Stamps — A377

2013, Dec. 10　Litho.　Perf. 13¼

2624	A375	25,000d multi	3.00	3.00
		Perf. 12¾		
2625	A376	50,000d multi	5.75	5.75
		Perf. 13¼x13		
2626	A377	150,000d multi	17.00	17.00
		Nos. 2624-2626 (3)	25.75	25.75

Nos. 2624-2626 could be personalized. The stamps exist with a St. Thomas & Prince Islands flag printed in the vignette portion.

Nelson Mandela (1918-2013), President of South Africa — A378

No. 2627 — Mandela wearing: a, Gray suit and tie, b, Yellow and black shirt. c, Dark blue jacket. d, Sports jersey.
96,000d, Black suit jacket with sash.

2014, Jan. 30　Litho.　Perf. 13¼
2627　A378　25,000d Sheet of 4, #a-d　11.00　11.00
Souvenir Sheet
2628　A378　96,000d multi　10.50　10.50

A379

No. 2629, 25,000d — USS Nautilus: a, With crew on top of submarine, flag painted on bow. b, Aerial view. c, Nuclear reactor. d, Submarine leaving wake.
No. 2630, 25,000d — Charles A. Lindbergh (1902-74), aviator: a, Medal of Honor. b, Spirit of St. Louis in flight. c, Bourguet Airport Statue, U.S. #C10. d, Wearing helmet, Spirit of St. Louis in flight.
No. 2631, 25,000d — Adolphe Sax (1814-94), inventor of saxophone, wearing: a, Blue jacket. b, Green jacket. c, Red vest. d, Purple jacket.
No. 2632, 25,000d — Louis Lumière (1864-1948), first filmmaker: a, With brother, Auguste. b, Operating projector at Eden Theater. c, Inspecting film. d, With Walt Disney.
No. 2633, 25,000d — Charlie Chaplin (1889-1977), film actor: a, In City Lights, 1931. b, Behind camera. c, In One A.M., 1916. d, In The Great Dictator, 1940.
No. 2634, 25,000d — Dorothy Lamour (1914-96), actress: a, In Road to Rio, 1947. b, In front of P-51D Mustang. c, With U.S. flag. d, In Typhoon, 1940.
No. 2635, 25,000d — Jawaharlal Nehru (1889-1964), Prime Minister of India, and: a, Queen Elizabeth II. b, Mahatma Gandhi. c, Mother Teresa. d, Albert Einstein.
No. 2636, 25,000d — Ayrton Senna (1960-94), race car driver: a, Wearing cap. b, Wearing racing suit, cars in background. c, Sitting next to helmet. d, Wearing balaclava.
No. 2637, 25,000d — Louis Renault (1877-1944), automobile manufacturer, and: a, Renault Nervastella. b, Renault Type A. c, Renault Type KZ. d, Renault Reinastella.
No. 2638, 25,000d — Eusebio da Silva Ferreira (1942-2014), Brazilian soccer player: a, Preparing to head ball. b, Sitting with ball. c, With Pelé. d, Preparing to kick ball.
No. 2639, 25,000d — 2014 World Cup Soccer Championships, Brazil: a, Purple player. b, Sepia player. c, Green player. d, Blue player.
No. 2640, 25,000d — Opening of Forth Road Bridge, Scotland, 50th anniv: a, Bridge, Sterna paradisaea. b,Queen Elizabeth II, opening of bridge. c, Construction of bridge. d, Bridge under construction, Sterna sandvicensis.
No. 2641, 25,000d — World War I, cent.: a, Bristol F.2b fighter, HMS Caesar, Great Britain. b, Aviatik (Berg) D.I. fighter, SMS Radetzky, Austria-Hungary. c, Sikorsky S-16 fighter, Frunze, Russia. d, Halberstadt CL.IV airplane, SMS Helgoland, Germany.
No. 2642, 25,000d — Paintings by Lavinia Fontana (1552-1614): a, Christ with the Symbols of Passion, 1581. b, Portrait of Constanza Alidosi, 1594. c, Portrait of a Lady with Lap Dog, 1590. d, Holy Family with Saints, 1578.
No. 2643, 25,000d — Paintings by Paul Cézanne (1839-1906): a, Still Life with Apples, 1893-94. b, Self-portrait, 1878-80. c, Pierrot and Harlequin, 1888. d, Fruit and Jug on a Table, 1894.
No. 2644, 25,000d — Paintings by Henri de Toulouse-Lautrec (1864-1901): a, Horsemen Riding in the Bois de Boulogne, 1888. b, Reine de Joie, 1892. c, The Passenger in Cabin 54, 1896. d, Fashionable People at Les Ambassadeurs, 1893.
No. 2645, 25,000d — Paintings by Wassily Kandinsky (1866-1944): a, Cemetery and Vicarage in Kochel, 1909. b, The Singer, 1903. c, Points, 1920. d, Colorful Ensemble, 1938.
No. 2646, 25,000d — Paintings by Henri Matisse (1869-1954): a, Portrait of Madame Matisse, 1905. b, Open Window, Collioure, 1905. c, A Glimpse of Notre Dame in the Late Afternoon, 1902. d, Self-portrait, 1906.
No. 2647, 25,000d — Paintings by Salvador Dalí (1904-89): a, Millet's Architectonic Angelus, 1933. b, Galatea of the Spheres, 1952. c, The Ship, 1943. d, Apparition of Face and Fruit Dish on a Beach, 1938.
No. 2648, 25,000d — Red List of Threatened Species, 50th anniv.: a, Strix uralensis. b, Cyanoramphus unicolor. c, Leontopithecus rosalia. d, Panthera uncia.
No. 2649, 96,000d, USS Nautilus, Adm. Hyman G. Rickover. No. 2650, 96,000d, Lindbergh, route of transatlantic flight. No. 2651, 96,000d, Adolphe Sax and saxophones. No. 2652, 96,000d, Lumiere holding film strip. No. 2653, 96,000d, Chaplin as the Little Tramp. No. 2654, 96,000d, Lamour and Jon Hall in The Hurricane, 1937. No. 2655, 96,000d, Nehru and Gandhi, diff. No. 2656, 96,000d, Senna, diff. No. 2657, 96,000d, Renault Type B. No. 2658, 96,000d, Eusebio holding Golden Boot award. No. 2659, 96,000d, Soccer ball, brown player. No. 2660, 96,000d, Forth Road Bridge, Morus bassanus. No. 2661, 96,000d, Thomas-Morse S-4 airplane, U.S., HIJMS Aki, Japan. No. 2662, 96,000d, Holy Family with St. Catherine of Alexandria, by Fontana, 1581. No. 2663, 96,000d, Madame Cézanne in a Red Armchair, by Cézanne, 1877. No. 2664, 96,000d, Chau U Kao, Chinese Clown, Seated, by Toulouse-Lautrec, 1896. No. 2665, 96,000d, Orange, by Kandinsky, 1923. No. 2666, 96,000d, Woman with a Hat, by Matisse, 1905. No. 2667, 96,000d, The Hallucinogenic Toreador, by Dalí, 1968-70. No. 2668, 96,000d, Tarsius sangirensis.

2014, Mar. 25　Litho.　Perf. 13¼
Sheets of 4, #a-d
2629-2648　A379　Set of 20　225.00　225.00
Souvenir Sheets
2649-2668　A379　Set of 20　215.00　215.00

Worldwide Fund for Nature (WWF) — A380

No. 2669 — Halcyon malimbica: a, Head. b, On horizontal branch, c, On rock. d, In flight. 96,000d, Halcyon malimbica looking over right wing.

2014, Aug. 8　Litho.　Perf. 13x13¼

2669		Horiz. strip of 4	11.00	11.00
a.-d.	A380	25,000d Any single	2.75	2.75
e.		Souvenir sheet of 4, #2669a-2669d	11.00	11.00
f.		Souvenir sheet of 8, 2 each #2669a-2669d, + central label	22.00	22.00

Souvenir Sheet
Perf. 12¾x13¼
2670　A380　96,000d multi　10.50　10.50

No. 2670 contains one 50x39mm stamp.

2014 World Cup Soccer Championships, Brazil — A381

No. 2671: a, Player kicking ball into net, names of four countries in white. b, Soccer ball, names of four countries in white. c, As "b," names of four countries in blue. d, As "a," names of four countries in blue.
96,000d, World Cup trophy, flags of four countries.

Litho. With Foil Application, Litho. (#2671b, 2671c)
2014, Aug. 8　　　　Perf. 13¼
2671　A381　25,000d Sheet of 4, #a-d　11.00　11.00
Souvenir Sheet
2672　A381　96,000d multi　10.50　10.50

A382

No. 2673, 25,000d — Giant Pandas: a, Ailuropoda melanoleuca, bamboo at right. b, Ailuropoda melanoleuca hanging from branch. c, Two Ailuropoda melanoleuca. d, Ailuropoda melanoleuca qinlingensis.
No. 2674, 25,000d — Dolphins: a, Cephalorhynchus hectori. b, Inia geoffrensis. c, Delphinus delphis. d, Platanista gangetica.

No. 2675, 25,000d — Owls: a, Strix nebulosa. b, Bubo scandiacus. c, Bubo bubo. d, Tyto alba.
No. 2676, 25,000d — Eagles: a, Harpia harpyja. b, Haliaeetus leucocephalus. c, Haliaeetus vocifer. d, Pithecophaga jefferyi.
No. 2677, 25,000d — Butterflies: a, Polyommatus icarus. b, Pieris brassicae. c, Delias eucharis. d, Vanessa atalanta, Polyradicion lindenii.
No. 2678, 25,000d — Turtles: a, Clemmys guttata. b, Macroclemys temminckii. c, Trionyx spiniferus. d, Geochelone sulcata.
No. 2679, 25,000d — Dinosaurs: a, Thyreophora. b, Allosaurus. c, Triceratops. d, Pachycephalosaurus.
No. 2680, 25,000d — Orchids: a, Cattleya hardyana. b, Angraecum sesquipedale. c, Burrageara Stefan Isler. d, Dendrobium chrysotoxum.
No. 2681, 25,000d — Mushrooms: a, Pleurotus eryngii. b, Boletus edulis. c, Cantharellus cibarius. d, Flammulina velutipes.
No. 2682, 25,000d — Minerals: a, Stibnite (estibina). b, Rhodochrosite (rodocrosita). c, Hutchinsonite. d, Torbernite.
No. 2683, 25,000d — Deng Xiaoping (1904-97), leader of People's Republic of China: a, Reading, flag in background. b, With Mao Zedong, train and city skyline in background. c, With Mao Zedong and other Chinese officials, flag across table. d, With Pres. Jimmy Carter, map in background.
No. 2684, 25,000d — Canonized popes: a, Pope John Paul II, wearing miter. b, Pope John XXIII, wearing red and white cap. c, Pope John Paul II, wearing zucchetto. d, Pope John XXIII, wearing zucchetto.
No. 2685, 25,000d — Fire engines: a, 1917 Glendale. b, Dennis 4 FJH 324. c, HME 34C. d, Pierce.
No. 2686, 25,000d — Airships: a, NS Airships NS11. b, N-Class ZPG-2. c, Goodyear ZPG-3W (N Class). d, MZ-3A.
No. 2687, 25,000d — Chinese high-speed trains: a, CRH3. b, CRH1, facing left. c, CRH1, facing right. d, CRH2.
No. 2688, 25,000d — Lighthouses: a, Longstone Lighthouse, Great Britain. b, Alexandria Lighthouse, Egypt. c, Portland Head Lighthouse, U.S. d, Bonaire Lighthouse, Caribbean Netherlands.
No. 2689, 25,000d — Worldwide Fund for Nature postage stamps: a, Viet Nam #3392, Cook Islands #1412. b, Hungary #2798, Liechtenstein #1525h. c, Russia #5543, Indonesia #1911. d, Russia #6178, Benin #1086c without denomination.
No. 2690, 25,000d — 2014 Winter Olympics, Sochi, Russia: a, Alpine skiing. b, Snowboarding. c, Ice hockey. d, Figure skating.
No. 2691, 96,000d, Ailuropoda melanoleuca rolling with foot up to mouth. No. 2692, 96,000d, Tursiops truncatus. No. 2693, 96,000d, Strix varia. No. 2694, 96,000d, Haliaeetus pelagicus. No. 2695, 96,000d, Aglais urticae. No. 2696, 96,000d, Eretmochelys imbricata. No. 2697, 96,000d, Tyrannosaurus rex. No. 2698, 96,000d, Cattleya aurea statteriana. No. 2699, 96,000d, Leccinum aurantiacum. No. 2700, 96,000d, Galena. No. 2701, 96,000d, Deng Xiaoping, train. No. 2702, 96,000d, Pope John Paul II, wearing miter, diff. No. 2703, 96,000d, Fire truck, diff. No. 2704, 96,000d, Zeppelin NT. No. 2705, 96,000d, CRH2, diff. No. 2706, 96,000d, Tourlitis Lighthouse, Greece. No. 2707, 96,000d, British Guiana #13. No. 2708, 96,000d, Biathlon.

2014, Aug. 8　Litho.　Perf. 13¼
Sheets of 4, #a-d
2673-2690　A382　Set of 18　195.00　195.00
Souvenir Sheets
2691-2708　A382　Set of 18　185.00　185.00

Nos. 2677, 2680, 2695 and 2698 are impregnated with a floral scent.

Miniature Sheets

Coastal Views — A383

Buildings and Streets — A384

Designs as shown.

2014, Sept. 15	**Litho.**	**Perf. 13¼**
2709 A383 22,000d Sheet of 8, #a-h	18.00	18.00
2710 A384 25,000d Sheet of 8, #a-h	21.00	21.00

See Nos. 2831-2832.

A385

No. 2711, 25,000d — Phascolarctos cinereus (koala): a, Adult carrying juvenile on back. b, Adult sitting in tree. c, Adult holding juvenile. d, Adult climbing tree.

No. 2712, 25,000d — Wolves: a, Canis lupus howling. b, Canis lupus lupus in snow. c,Two canis lupus. d, Canis lupus arctos on rock.

No. 2713, 25,000d — Panthera uncia (snow leopard): a, Walking on ice, mouth closed. b, Sitting near rocks. c, Head. d, Walking on snow, mouth open.

No. 2714, 25,000d — Sled dogs (caes de trenó): a, Three white dogs pulling sled. b, Two dogs with red harnesses. c, Two dogs pulling sled. d, Two dogs with blue and yellow harnesses.

No. 2715, 25,000d — Orcinus orca (killer whales): a, Two whales leaping, heads facing right. b, Whale facing right with open mouth. c, Two whales leaping, heads facing left. d, Whale facing left with open mouth.

No. 2716, 25,000d — Sagittarius serpentarius (secretary bird): a, In tree. b, Head. c, In flight. d, Walking left.

No. 2717, 25,000d — Pheasants: a, Phasianus colchicus, tail at right. b, Phasianus colchicus, with wing feathers spread. c, Phasianus colchicus, no tail visible. d, Lophura nycthemera.

No. 2718, 25,000d — Hornbills: a, Tockus leucomelas. b, Buceros rhinoceros. c, Buceros bicornis. d, Rhyticeros undulatus.

No. 2719, 25,000d — Hummingbirds: a, Chrysuronia oenone. b, Calypte anna. c, Colibri coruscans. d, Selasphorus flammula.

No. 2720, 25,000d — Bee-eaters: a, One Merops leschenaulti. b, Two Merops leschenaulti. c, Merops apiaster. d, Two Merops leschenaulti, one with bee in beak.

No. 2721, 25,000d — Birds and vineyards: a, Agapornis roseicollis and vineyard. b, Cardinalis sinuatus and Chardonnay grapes. c, Ara chloropterus and black grapes. d, Erithacus rubecula and purple grapes.

No. 2722, 25,000d — Shells: a, Lindopecten muscosus. b, Strombidae. c, Naticidae. d, Scaphella junonia.

No. 2723, 25,000d — Snakes: a, Bothriechis schlegelii. b, Crotalus cerastes. c, Python regius. d, Nerodia sipedon insularum.

No. 2724, 25,000d — Lizards: a, Sceloporus occidentalis. b, Trioceros jacksonii. c, Conolophus subcristatus. d, Iguana iguana.

No. 2725, 25,000d — Predators: a, Gyps africanus. b, Panthera pardus. c, Ursus arctos. d, Two Canis lupus lupus.

No. 2726, 25,000d — Fossils: a, Homo erectus skull. b, Shark teeth. c, Tyrannosaurus rex skeleton. d, Trilobite.

No. 2727, 25,000d — Effects of global warming: a, Larus argentatus. b, Polluted water and cracked soil. c, Ursus maritimus and retreating ice. d, Adult and juvenile Aptenodytes forsteri.

No. 2728, 25,000d — Steam locomotives: a, Canadian Pacific Railway 2816. b, Yarra Valley Railway locomotive, Australia. c, Great Western Railway Bradley Manor 7802, Great Britain. d, LV-0283 locomotive, Russia.

No. 2729, 25,000d — Special vehicles: a, HH-65C Dolphin rescue helicopter. b, 1959 Volkswagen Beetle police car. c, 1966 Ford E350 ambulance. d, 1946 American La France 500 Series fire truck.

No. 2730, 25,000d — Electric transportation: a, Segway. b, Golf carts. c, 700 Series Shinkansen train, Japan. d, Electric automobile.

No. 2731, 96,000d, Phascolarctos cinereus on tree branch. No. 2732, 96,000d, Canis lupus, diff. No. 2733, 96,000d, Panthera uncia, diff. No. 2734, 96,000d, Four dogs puling sled. No. 2735, 96,000d, Orcinus orca, diff. No. 2736, 96,000d, Two Sagittarius serpentarius. No. 2737, 96,000d, Phasianus colchicus, diff. No. 2738, 96,000d, Buceros bicornis, diff. No. 2739, 96,000d, Selasphorus sasin. No. 2740, 96,000d, Merops bullockoides. No. 2741, 96,000d, Taeniopygia guttata and red grapes. No. 2742, 96,000d, Nautilus pompilius. No. 2743, 96,000d, Pantherophis spiloides. No. 2744, 96,000d, Varanus salvator. No. 2745, 96,000d, Ursus arctos, diff. No. 2746, 96,000d, Ammonite fossil. No. 2747, 96,000d, Larus dominicanus. No. 2748, 96,000d, Cumbria Mountain Express 60009 locomotive and train, United Kingdom. No. 2749, 96,000d, 1956 Ford police car. No. 2750, 96,000d, Electric scooter.

2014, Sept. 15	**Litho.**	**Perf. 13¼**
Sheets of 4, #a-d		
2711-2730 A385 Set of 20	210.00	210.00
Souvenir Sheets		
2731-2750 A385 Set of 20	200.00	200.00

A386

No. 2751, 25,000d — Robin Williams (1951-2014), actor and comedian: a, With dog. b, Holding Flubber. c, With arms crossed. d, Portraying Theodore Roosevelt.

No. 2752, 25,000d — Spanish royalty: a, King Felipe VI, at left, with Queen Letizia. b, Queen Letizia. c, King Felipe VI, at right, with Queen Letizia. d, King Felipe VI.

No. 2753, 25,000d — Scouting: a, Boy Scouts cooking meal over campfire. b, Boy Scout with model of drawbridge. c, Lord Robert Baden-Powell and Boy Scout. d, Boy Scouts erecting tent and examining butterfly.

No. 2754, 25,000d — Cricket players: a, Sachin Tendulkar. b, Jean-Paul Duminy. c, Alex Hales. d, Virat Kohli.

No. 2755, 25,000d — World War II: a, Sir Winston Churchill (1874-1965), Valentine Mk3 tank, flag of Great Britain. b, Junkers Ju 87

airplane, German Nazi flag. c, Pres. Harry S. Truman, sinking USS Arizona, United States flag. d, Battle of Stalingrad, flag of the Soviet Union.

No. 2756, 25,000d — High-speed trains: a, TGV, France. b, RENFE Class 130, Spain. c, Zefiro 380, People's Republic of China. d, CRH1A, People's Republic of China.

No. 2757, 25,000d — Primates: a, Cercopithecus mona. b, Lagothrix lagotricha. c, Piliocolobus kirkii. d, Theropithecus gelada.

No. 2758, 25,000d — Panthera leo: a, Male with open mouth. b, Female on male. c, Male with closed mouth. d, Female and cub.

No. 2759, 25,000d — Cats: a, Havana. b, Persian. c, Siamese. d, Australian Mist.

No. 2760, 25,000d — Dogs: a, Akita. b, American hairless terrier. c, Afghan hound. d, Black and tan coonhound.

No. 2761, 25,000d — Whales: a, Balaenoptera edeni. b, Eschrichtius robustus. c, Physeter macrocephalus. d, Balaenoptera musculus.

No. 2762, 25,000d — Parrots: a, Trichoglossus rubritorquis. b, Pezoporus flaviventris. c, Eos reticulata. d, Pseudeos fuscata.

No. 2763, 25,000d — Kingfishers: a, Alcedo azurea. b, Tanysiptera galatea. c, Halcyon senegalensis. d, Alcedo atthis.

No. 2764, 25,000d — Flamingos: a, Phoenicopterus andinus. b, Phoenicopterus minor. c, Phoenicoparrus jamesi. d, Phoenicopterus chilensis.

No. 2765, 25,000d — Fish: a, Cheilopogon exsiliens. b, Ostracion cubicus. c, Synchiropus splendidus. d, Scleropages formosus.

No. 2766, 25,000d — Corals: a, Montipora capricornis. b, Wellsophyllia radiata. c, Iciligorgia schrammi. d, Anacropora puertogalerae.

No. 2767, 25,000d — Crocodylus porosus: a, Two crocodiles with mouths open. b, One crocodile with open mouth. c, Two crocodiles with mouths closed. d, One crocodile with closed mouth.

No. 2768, 25,000d — Dinosaurs: a, Styracosaurus. b, Liliensternus. c, Euoplocephalus. d, Caudipteryx hendrickx.

No. 2769, 25,000d — Mushrooms: a, Boletus edulis. b, Macrolepiota procera. c, Cantharellus cibarius. d, Xerocomellus chrysenteron.

No. 2770, 25,000d — Minerals: a, Spessartine. b, Dioptase. c, Boracite. d, Rodocrosita.

No. 2771, 96,000d, Williams holding Academy Award statuette. No. 2772, 96,000d, King Felipe VI. No. 2773, 96,000d, Scouting flag and Boy Scout with bugle. No. 2774, 96,000d, Kohli, diff. No. 2775, 96,000d, Pres. Franklin D. Roosevelt, Allied leaders at Yalta Conference. No. 2776, 96,000d, Zefiro 380, diff. No. 2777, 96,000d, Rhinopithecus roxellana. No. 2778, 96,000d, Male and female Panthera leo. No. 2779, 96,000d, Colorpoint cat. No. 2780, 96,000d, Andalusian dog. No. 2781, 96,000d, Megaptera novaeangliae. No. 2782, 96,000d, Chalcopsitta sintillata. No. 2783, 96,000d, Megaceryle alcyon. No. 2784, 96,000d, Phoenicopterus roseus. No. 2785, 96,000d, Betta splendens. No. 2786, 96,000d, Nemenzophyllia turbida. No. 2787, 96,000d, Two Crocodylus niloticus. No. 2788, 96,000d, Styracosaurus and Triceratops. No. 2789, 96,000d, Morchella esculenta. No. 2790, 96,000d, Amethyst.

2014, Oct. 15	**Litho.**	**Perf. 13¼**
Sheets of 4, #a-d		
2751-2770 A386 Set of 20	200.00	200.00
Souvenir Sheets		
2771-2790 A386 Set of 20	195.00	195.00

Tennis Players — A387

No. 2791: a, Roger Federer. b, Rafael Nadal. c, Novak Djokovic. d, Rod Laver. e, Bjorn Borg. f, Ivan Lendl. g, Jimmy Connors. h, Andre Agassi. i, Pete Sampras. j, John McEnroe.

96,000d, Sampras, diff.

2014, Nov. 17	**Litho.**	**Perf. 13¼**
2791 A387 10,000d Sheet of 10, #a-j	10.50	10.50
Souvenir Sheet		
2792 A387 96,000d multi	9.75	9.75

No. 2792 contains one 30x51mm stamp.

Butterflies — A388

No. 2793: a, Ornithoptera priamus urvillianus. b, Stichophthalma louisa. c, Ornithoptera croesus. d, Teinopalpus imperialis.

96,000d, Thysania agrippina.

2014, Nov. 17	**Litho.**	**Perf. 13¼**
2793 A388 25,000d Sheet of 4, #a-d	10.50	10.50
Souvenir Sheet		
2794 A388 96,000d multi	9.75	9.75

Buceros Rhinoceros — A389

No. 2795: a, Denomination at UL, Latin name at LR. b, Denomination at UL, Latin name at left. c, Denomination at UR, Latin name at LL.

96,000d, Buceros rhinoceros, white background, denomination and country name in green.

2014, Nov. 17	**Litho.**	**Perf. 13¼**
2795 A389 33,000d Sheet of 3, #a-c	10.00	10.00
Souvenir Sheet		
2796 A389 96,000d multi	9.75	9.75

Malaysia 2014 Intl. Stamp Exhibition, Kuala Lumpur.

A390

No. 2797, 25,000d — Marilyn Monroe (1926-62), actress, wearing: a, Blue dress. b, Yellow dress. c, Red dress, with hands touching feet. d, Red dress, hands not visible.

No. 2798, 25,000d — Elvis Presley (1935-77): a, With woman playing ukulele in background. b, With woman on motor scooter. c, With guitar and microphone. d, Playing guitar and surfing.

No. 2799, 25,000d — Pope Francis: a, Seated behind microphone. b, With Queen Elizabeth II. c, Holding child. d, Praying at Western Wall, Jerusalem.

No. 2800, 25,000d — Liberation of Paris, 70th anniv.: a, Tank, French flag, Gen. Charles de Gaulle (1890-1970). b, Arc de Triomphe, French flag, soldier, French women. c, Arc de Triomphe, de Gaulle. d, German General Dietrich von Choltitz (1894-1966), military vehicles.

No. 2801, 25,000d — Paintings depicting chess: a, Chess Players, by Cornelis de Man. b, Chess Match, by Max Oppenheimer. c, Chess Match, by Ludwig Deutsch. d, The Veterans, by Richard Creifelds.

No. 2802, 25,000d — American and Canadian Lighthouses: a, Cape Hatteras Lighthouse, North Carolina. b, Peggys Point Lighthouse, Nova Scotia. c, Brier Island Lighthouse, Nova Scotia. d, Portland Head Lighthouse, Maine.

No. 2803, 25,000d — Japanese high-speed trains: a, Nankai 50000 Series, Yokoham skyline. b, E3 Series Tsubasa, Osaka skyline. c, E6 Series Shinkansen, Sapporo skyline. d, 300 Series Shinkansen, Tokyo skyline.

No. 2804, 25,000d — Fire trucks: a, 1937 Chevrolet American LaFrance. b, 1955 GMC CCKW 353. c, 1937 Leyland Cub. d, 1936 Diamond T.

No. 2805, 25,000d — Concorde: a, Flag of Great Britain, cockpit control panel. b, Flag of France, Concorde with wheels above ground. c, Flag of France, cabin seats. d, Flag of France, Concorde on ground.

No. 2806, 25,000d — Dolphins: a, Stenella frontalis. b, Lagenorhynchus obscurus. c, Steno bredanensis. d, Cephalorhynchus heavisidii.

No. 2807, 25,000d — Owls: a, Strix nebulosa in flight. b, Bubo virginianus in flight. c, Bubo virginianus on tree branch. d, Strix nebulosa on post.

No. 2808, 25,000d — Birds of prey: a, Torgos tracheliotos. b, Sagittarius serpentarius. c, Gypaetus barbatus. d, Harpia harpyja.

No. 2809, 25,000d — Turtles: a, Trachemys scripta elegans. b, Demochelys coriacea. c, Stigmochelys pardalis. d, Astrochelys radiata.

No. 2810, 25,000d — Venomous animals: a, Ophiophagus hannah. b, Phoneutria nigriventer. c, Leiurus quinquestriatus. d, Conus marmoreus.

No. 2811, 25,000d — Orchids: a, Laelia tenebrosa. b, Ophrys apifera. c, Cattleya schilleriana. d, Disa purpurascens.

No. 2812, 25,000d — Christmas paintings: a, Adoration of the Shepherds, by Domenico Ghirlandaio. b, Adoration of the Shepherds, by Ridolfo Ghirlandaio. c, Pierre Bladelin Triptych, by Rogier van der Weyden. d, Adoration of the Magi, by Hendrick Terbrugghen.

No. 2813, 25,000d — New Year 2015 (Year of the Goat): a, Goat with Chinese character at right. b, Chinese character above goat. c, Head of goat with Chinese character at left. d, Goat with Chinese character at left.

No. 2814, 96,000d, Monroe, diff. No. 2815, 96,000d, Presley, diff. No. 2816, 96,000d, Pope Francis and his coat of arms. No. 2817, 96,000d, Arc de Triomphe, soldier and resistance fighter. No. 2818, 96,000d, Almehs Playing Chess in a Café, by Jean-Léon Gérôme. No. 2819, 96,000d, New London Lighthouse, Prince Edward Island. No. 2820, 96,000d, E3-700 Series Shinkansen. No. 2821, 96,000d, 1902 American Steam fire pumper. No. 2822, 96,000d, Flag of Great Britain, Concorde. No. 2823, 96,000d, Tursiops truncatus. No. 2824, 96,000d, Athene brama. No. 2825, 96,000d, Bubo blakistoni. No. 2826, 96,000d, Chelonia mydas. No. 2827, 96,000d, Hapalochlaena lunulata. No. 2828, 96,000d, Laelia xanthina. No. 2829, 96,000d, Adoration of the Magi, by Albrecht Altdorfer. No. 2830, 96,000d, Goat with Chinese character below.

2014, Nov. 17   Litho.   Perf. 13¼
Sheets of 4, #a-d
2797-2813 A390 Set of 17   175.00 175.00
Souvenir Sheets
2814-2830 A390 Set of 17   165.00 165.00

Coastal Views and Buildings and Streets Types of 2014
Miniature Sheets

Designs as before.

2015, Mar. 16   Litho.   Perf. 13¼
2831 A383 30,000d Sheet of 8,
      #a-h   21.50 21.50
2832 A384 38,000d Sheet of 8,
      #a-h   27.00 27.00

Taipei 2015 Intl. Stamp Exhibition — A391

No. 2833: a, Ypthima baldus. b, Choaspes benjaminii. c, Daimio tethys. d, Vanessa cardui.
38,000d, Papilio machaon, horiz.

2015, Mar. 16   Litho.   Perf. 13¼
2833 A391 15,000d Sheet of 4,
      #a-d   5.50 5.50
Souvenir Sheet
2834 A391 38,000d multi   3.50 3.50

2015 Europhilex Stamp Exhibition, London — A392

No. 2835 — Flag of Great Britain and: a, Penny Black. b, Queen Elizabeth II and Buckingham Palace, horiz. c, Eurostar train, horiz. d, Big Ben and telephone booth.
38,000d, Penny Black, horiz.

2015, Mar. 16   Litho.   Perf. 13¼
2835 A392 15,000d Sheet of 4,
      #a-d   5.50 5.50
Souvenir Sheet
2836 A392 38,000d multi   3.50 3.50

A393

No. 2837, 19,000d — Frank Sinatra (1915-98), singer: a, Holding cigarette and Grammy award. b, Holding coat over shoulder, film strip, horiz. c, With Academy award statuette, horiz. d, With G clef and musical staff.

No. 2838, 19,000d — Elvis Presley (1935-77): a, Holding microphone, wearing red scarf. b, Playing guitar to audience, horiz. c, Singing with mouth open, horiz. d, Holding microphone, wearing costume with large silver buttons.

No. 2839, 19,000d — Georg Frideric Handel (1685-1759), and scenes from opera: a, Ottone. b, Almira, horiz. c, Orlando, horiz. d, Teseo.

No. 2840, 19,000d — Ingrid Bergman (1915-82), actress: a, With Humphrey Bogart. b, With Bogart, horiz. c, With Gregory Peck, horiz. d, Alone.

No. 2841, 19,000d — Albert Einstein (1879-1955), physicist: a, With hand on cheek. b, With obverse and reverse of Nobel medal, horiz. c, With diagram of galaxies, horiz. d, Pipe in mouth.

No. 2842, 19,000d — Sir Winston Churchill (1874-1965), Prime Minister of Great Britain: a, Walking with cane. b, With tank, horiz. c, With soldiers, horiz. d, Saluting.

No. 2843, 19,000d — Angela Merkel, Chancellor of Germany: a, With Pope Francis. b, With German coat of arms, horiz. c, At Chancellor's residence, horiz. d, With Pres. Barack Obama.

No. 2844, 19,000d — St. John Paul II (1920-2005): a, Waving, both hands visible. b, With arm extended, horiz. c, With hand on chin, horiz. d, Waving, one hand visible.

No. 2845, 19,000d — Nelson Mandela (1918-2013), President of South Africa: a, Holding World Cup trophy. b, With crowd, horiz. c, With Queen Elizabeth II, horiz. d, With Oprah Winfrey.

No. 2846, 19,000d — Sculpture and paintings by Michelangelo (1475-1564): a, Pieta. b, The Creation of Adam, horiz. c, Adam and Eve, horiz. d, Moses.

No. 2847, 19,000d — Paintings by Vincent van Gogh (1853-90): a, La Mousmé, 1888. b, Noon: Rest from Work (after Millet), 1890, horiz. c, Still Life with Red Cabbages and Onions, 1887, horiz. d, Self-portrait, 1889.

No. 2848, 19,000d — George Stephenson (1781-1848), mechanical engineer: a, Locomotion No. 1. b, Locomotion No. 1, statue of Stephenson holding Locomotion No. 1, horiz. c, Stephenson in blue coat and Locomotion No. 1, horiz. d, Stephenson in purple and Locomotion No. 1 at angle.

No. 2849, 19,000d — Moscow Metro, 80th anniv.: a, Escalator, Komsomolskaya Station. b, Elektrozavodskaya Station and train, horiz. c, Ploshchad Revolyutsii Station and train, horiz. d, Sokol Station and train.

No. 2850, 19,000d — André-Gustave Citroen (1878-1935) automobile manufacturer, and Citroen: a, TPV. b, H Van, horiz. c, Model C61 truck, horiz. d, DS.

No. 2851, 19,000d — Sakigake deep space probe, 30th anniv., and: a, Launch. b, Halley's Comet, horiz. c, Earth, horiz. d, Earth.

No. 2852, 19,000d — Battle of Waterloo, 200th anniv.: a, Arthur Wellesley, Duke of Wellington (1769-1852). b, Napoleon Bonaparte (1769-1821), horiz. c, King William II of the Netherlands (1792-1849), horiz. d, Battle scene.

No. 2853, 19,000d — American Medicare and Medicaid programs, 50th anniv.: a, Hands and pills. b, Doctor and child, horiz. c, Pres. Harry S. Truman and people with signs, horiz. d, Medical personnel and patient.

No. 2854, 19,000d — Independence of St. Thomas and Prince Islands, 40th anniv.: a, Joao de Santarém, co-discoverer or St. Thomas & Prince Islands, and ship. b, Pêro Escobar, co-discover, and ships, horiz. c, Pres. Manuel Pinto da Costa and Presidential residence, horiz. d, Pres. Pinto da Costa and military musicians.

No. 2855, 86,000d, Sinatra and Grammy award, horiz. No. 2856, 86,000d, Presley playing guitar, diff., horiz. No. 2857, 86,000d, Handel, scene from Orlando, horiz. No. 2858, 86,000d, Bergman and Cary Grant, horiz. No. 2859, 86,000d, Einstein and mass-energy equivalence equation, horiz. No. 2860, 86,000d, Churchill, military officers and airplanes, horiz. No. 2861, 86,000d, Merkel and Queen Elizabeth II, horiz. No. 2862, 86,000d, St. John Paul II, diff., horiz. No. 2863, 86,000d, Mandela, broken chain, man with campaign poster, horiz. No. 2864, 86,000d, Delphic Sybil, by Michelangelo, horiz. No. 2865, 86,000d, Field with Poppies, 1890, and Self-portrait, 1889, by van Gogh, horiz. No. 2866, 86,000d, Stephenson, Locomotion No. 1, tunnel, horiz. No. 2867, 86,000d, Moscow Metro Mayakovskaya Station, Alexei Dushkin, Metro station architect, horiz. No. 2868, 86,000d, Citroen and Citroen Model A 10CV, horiz. No. 2869, 86,000d, Sakigake probe, diff., horiz. No. 2870, 86,000d, August Neidhardt von Gneisenau (1760-1831), Prussian field marshal, Waterloo battle scene, horiz. No. 2871, 86,000d, Pres. Lyndon B. Johnson, doctor examining child, caduceus, horiz. No. 2872, 86,000d, Pres. Pinto da Costa, flag of St. Thomas and Prince Islands, horiz.

2015, Mar. 16   Litho.   Perf. 13¼
Sheets of 4, #a-d
2837-2854 A393 Set of 18 125.00 125.00
Souvenir Sheets
2855-2872 A393 Set of 18 140.00 140.00

Singapore 2015 Intl. Stamp Exhibition — A394

No. 2873: a, Caranx ignobilis. b, Centroberyx affinis. c, Epibulus insidiator. d, Plectorhinchus polytaenia.
38,000d, Choerodon schoenleinii.

2015, May 21   Litho.   Perf. 13¼
2873 A394 15,000d Sheet of 4,
      #a-d   5.50 5.50
Souvenir Sheet
2874 A394 38,000d multi   3.50 3.50

Souvenir Sheets

Hindu Statue — A395

Hindu Goddess Durga on Tiger — A396

Litho. With Foil Application and Affixed Stone
Perf. 13¼, 9½ on Diagonal Sides
2015, May 21
2875 A395 86,000d multi   7.75 7.75
Litho. With Stone Affixed, Sheet Margin With Flocking
Perf.
Without Gum
2876 A396 86,000d multi   7.75 7.75

Rainforests — A397

No. 2877, 19,000d — Primates: a, Nasalis larvatus. b, Mandrillus sphinx. c, Cebus capucinus. d, Leontopithecus rosalia.

No. 2878, 19,000d — Wild cats: a, Leopardus pardalis. b, Puma concolor. c, Panthera pardus. d, Panthera tigris tigris.

No. 2879, 19,000d — Dolphins: a, Tursiops truncatus. b, Grampus griseus. c, Stenella longirostris. d, Delphinus capensis.

No. 2880, 19,000d — Manatees: a, Trichechus pygmaeus. b, Two Trichechus manatus. c, Trichechus senegalensis. d, One Trichechus manatus.

No. 2881, 19,000d — Parrots: a, Aratinga jandaya. b, Deroptyus accipitrinus. c, Guaruba guarouba. d, Pyrrhura perlata.

No. 2882, 19,000d — Harpy eagle (Harpia harpyja): a, On branch, facing forward. b, At nest. c, On branch, facing backwards. d, Catching prey.

No. 2883, 19,000d — Toucans: a, Ramphastos ambiguus. b, Ramphastos sulfuratus. c, Selenidera culik. d, Ramphastos toco.

No. 2884, 19,000d — Owls: a, Glaucidium griseiceps. b, Bubo shelleyi. c, Bubo philippensis. d, Bubo poensis.

No. 2885, 19,000d — Butterflies: a, Myscelia cyaniris. b, Hypolimnas misippus. c, Junonia almana. d, Graphium agamemnon.

No. 2886, 19,000d — Piranhas: a, Pristobrycon careospinus. b, Pygopristis denticulata. c, Serrasalmus rhombeus. d, Pygocentrus natterreri.

No. 2887, 19,000d — Frogs: a, Dendrobates tinctorius. b, Agalychnis callidryas. c, Phyllomedusa bicolor. d, Dendrobates leucomelas.

No. 2888, 19,000d — Turtles: a, Podocnemis expansa. b, Trachemys scripta elegans. c, Terrapene carolina carolina, Chelonoidis carbonaria. d, Chelus fimbriata.

No. 2889, 19,000d — Black caimans (Melanosuchus niger): a, With prey in mouth. b, In water. c, Head, with open mouth. d, At nest, with eggs.

No. 2890, 19,000d — Snakes: a, Bothriechis schlegelii. b, Corallus caninus (green snake). c, Corallus caninus (red orange snake). d, Trimeresurus trigonocephalus.

No. 2891, 19,000d — Carnivorous plants and their prey: a, Nepenthes aristolochioides, Danaus plexippus. b, Drosera roraimae, Libellula vibrans. c, Nepenthes rajah, Rattus baluensis. d, Heliamphora ionasi, Chrysopilus thoracicus.

No. 2892, 19,000d — Orchids: a, Cattleya sp. b, Cattleya dowiana. c, Arachnorchis radiata. d, Neomoorea irrorata.

No. 2893, 19,000d — Mushrooms: a, Pleurotus ostreatus. b, Leucocoprinus birnbaumii. c, Cookeina tricholoma. d, Lycoperdon perlatum.

No. 2894, 19,000d — Minerals: a, Fluorite. b, Cobalt and Smithsonite. c, Rhodochrosite. d, Wulfenite.

No. 2895, 86,000d, Saguinus oedipus, horiz. No. 2896, 86,000d, Panthera onca, horiz. No. 2897, 86,000d, Inia geoffrensis, horiz. No. 2898, 86,000d, Trichechus manatus, horiz. No. 2899, 86,000d, Ara macao, Ara ararauna, horiz. No. 2900, 86,000d, Harpia harpyja, horiz. No. 2901, 86,000d, Andigena laminirostris, horiz. No. 2902, 86,000d, Glaucidium brasilianum, horiz. No.. 2903, 86,000d, Heliconius doris, horiz. No. 2904, 86,000d, Pristobrycon striolatus, horiz. No. 2905, 86,000d, Dendrobates tinctorius azureus, horiz. No. 2906, 86,000d, Malaclemys terrapin, horiz. No. 2907, 86,000d, Melanosuchus niger, horiz. No. 2908, 86,000d, Oligodon octolineatus, horiz. No. 2909, 86,000d, Dionaea muscipula, Asterope leprieuri, horiz. No. 2910, 86,000d, Caladenia corynephora, horiz. No. 2911, 86,000d, Hygrocybe miniata, horiz. No. 2912, 86,000d, Emerald, horiz.

2015, May 21   Litho.   Perf. 13¼

Sheets of 4, #a-d

2877-2894   A397   Set of 18   125.00 125.00

Souvenir Sheets

2895-2912   A397   Set of 18   140.00 140.00

Nos. 2895-2912 each contain one 51x43mm stamp.

A398

No. 2913, 31,000d — Mother Teresa (1910-97), humanitarian: a, With hands in prayer and eyes closed. b, Facing froward, hands not visible. c, Holding baby. d, With hands in prayer and eyes open.

No. 2914, 31,000d — Pope Benedict XVI: a, Wearing zucchetto. b, With Queen Elizabeth II. c, Holding crucifix. d, With Pres. Barack Obama.

No. 2915, 31,000d — Queen Elizabeth II, longest-reigning British monarch: a, Wearing tiara. b, Holding Flowers. c, With Prince Philip. d, Waving.

No. 2916, 31,000d — Mahatma Gandhi (1869-1948), Indian nationalist: a, Head of Gandhi. b, With Sita Gandhi (1928-99). c, With Abha Gandhi (1927-95). d, Two images of Gandhi.

No. 2917, 31,000d — Malcolm X (1925-65), human rights activist: a, Holding newspaper. b, Holding child. c, Pointing finger upwards. d, With Dr. Martin Luther King, Jr. (1929-68).

No. 2918, 31,000d — Cricket players: a, Shane Keith Warne. b, Imran Khan. c, Jacques Kallis. d, Brian Lara.

No. 2919, 31,000d — 2014 Nobel Prize Laureates: a, Physics laureates Shuji Nakamura, Isamu Akasaki, and Hiroshi Amano. b, Peace laureate Malala Yousafzai. c, Physiology or Medicine laureates Edvard

Moser, May-Britt Moser, John O'Keefe. d, Economics laureate Jean Tirole.

No. 2920, 31,000d — 23rd International Scout Jamboree, Japan: a, Scouts saluting, butterfly. b, Scouts and tent. c, Scout arranging wood for campfire. d, Scouts with backpacks, mushrooms.

No. 2921, 31,000d — End of World War II, 70th anniv: a, Mistel 2 (Ju 88 G-1 and Fw 190 A-8). b, Messerschmitt Bf 109. c, Supermarine Spitfire. d, Republic P-47 Thunderbolt.

No. 2922, 31,000d — Lighthouses: a, Yaquina Head Lighthouse, Oregon. b, Lange Jaap Lighthouse, Netherlands. c, Whaleback Lighthouse, Maine. d, Roter Sand Lighthouse, Germany.

No. 2923, 31,000d — Fire vehicles: a, U5000 Feuerwehr GW. b, 2003 American LaFrance. c, 2010 MAN GW-L2. d, Citroen 700FPT, Chevy Tahoe ES-11.

No. 2924, 31,000d — Apollo 13 mission: a, Astronaut Jim Lovell, command, service and lunar modules. b, Apollo 13 patch, lunar module. c, Crew members Lovell, Fred Haise, Jack Swigert, capsule re-entry. d, Recovered capsule.

No. 2925, 31,000d — Paintings by Sandro Botticelli (1445-1510): a, Simonetta Vespucci, 1484. b, The Madonna of the Book, 1480. c, Angel from The Annunciation, c. 1485. d, Virgin Mary from The Annunciation, c. 1485.

No. 2926, 31,000d — Paintings by Peter Paul Rubens (1577-1640): a, Wolf and Fox Hunt, c. 1615-21. b, Perseus and Andromeda, c. 1622. c, David Slaying Goliath, c. 1616. d, The Fall of Phaeton, c. 1604.

No. 2927, 31,000d — Paintings by Giovanni Paolo Panini (1691-1765): a, Interior of the Pantheon of Rome, c. 1734. b, Roman Capriccio: The Pantheon and Other Monuments, c. 1735. c, Musical Fête, 1747. d, Interior of St. Peter's in Rome, 1755.

No. 2928, 31,000d — Paintings by Berthe Morisot (1841-95): a, Reading, 1873. b, Harbor in the Port of Fecamp, 1874. c, Hanging the Laundry Out to Dry, 1875. d, Woman Wearing Gloves, 1885.

No. 2929, 31,000d — Paintings by Amedeo Modigliani (1841-95): a, The Cellist, 1909. b, Portrait of Dr. Deveraigne, 1917. c, Lunia Czechowska with Her Left Hand on Her Cheek, 1918. d, Gypsy Woman with Baby, 1919.

No. 2930, 31,000d — Paintings by John James Audubon (1785-1851): a, Self-portrait, 1822-23. b, Bobwhite (Virginia Partridge), 1825. c, Portrait of John James Audubon, by John W. Audubon. d, Canada Geese.

No. 2931, 31,000d — Butterflies: a, Caligo eurilochus. b, Idea leuconoe, Papilio memnon. c, Heliconius cydno. d, Euploea mulciber.

No. 2932, 31,000d — Jurassic age fauna: a, Dilophosaurus wetherilli. b, Sordes pilosus, Coelurus bauri. c, Dsungaripterus weii, Scelidosaurus harrisonii. d, Kentrosaurus aethiopicus.

No. 2933, 96,000d, Mother Teresa and Pope John Paul II (1920-2005), horiz. No. 2934, 96,000d, Popes Benedict XI and Francis, horiz. No. 2935, 96,000d, Queen Elizabeth II, horiz. No. 2936, 96,000d, Mahatma Gandhi, horiz. No. 2937, 96,000d, Malcolm X, horiz. No. 2938, 96,000d, Sir Donald Bradman (1908-2001), cricket player, horiz. No. 2939, 96,000d, Stefan Hell, 2014 Nobel Laureate in Chemistry, horiz. No. 2940, 96,000d, Scouts and mushroom, horiz. No. 2941, 96,000d, Type 156 Beaufighter, horiz. No. 2942, 96,000d, Portland Head Lighthouse, Maine, horiz. No. 2943, 96,000d, 1950 American LaFrance 700 fire truck, horiz. No. 2944, 96,000d, Apollo 13 crew members, Haise, Lovell and Swigert, horiz. No. 2945, 96,000d, The Birth of Venus, by Botticelli, 1482-85, horiz. No. 2946, 96,000d, Self-portrait, by Rubens, 1623, horiz. No. 2947, 96,000d, View of the Colosseum, by Panini, Portrait of Giovanni Paolo Panini, by Louis Gabriel Blanche, horiz. No. 2948, 96,000d, Morisot and The Cradle, by Morisot, 1872, horiz. No. 2949, 96,000d, Modigliani and Landscape, by Modigliani, 1919, horiz. No. 2950, 96,000d, Portrait of Audubon, by John Syme, 1826, Mallards, by Audubon, horiz. No. 2951, 96,000d, Heliconius cydno, horiz. No. 2952, 96,000d, Archaeopteryx siemensii, horiz.

2015, Sept. 23   Litho.   Perf. 13¼

Sheets of 4, #a-d

2913-2932   A398   Set of 20   230.00 230.00

Souvenir Sheets

2933-2952   A398   Set of 20   175.00 175.00

Nos. 2933-2952 each contain one 51x43mm stamp.

Portuguese
Language
800th
Anniv. —
A399

Intl. Association of Portuguese-Speaking Countries, 25th Anniv. — A400

2015, Oct. 9   Litho.   Perf. 13x13¼

2953   A399   22,000d multi   2.00 2.00
2954   A400   30,000d multi   2.75 2.75

See Angola No. , Brazil No. 3300, Cape Verde No. 1004, Guinea-Bissau No. , Macao No. 1440, Moambique No. , Portugal Nos. 3694-3695, Timor No.

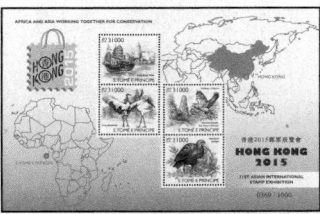

Hong Kong 2015 Intl. Stamp Exhibition — A401

No. 2955: a, Junk and Hong Kong skyline. b, Grus japonensis. c, Psittacus erithacus. d, Bostrychia bocagei.
110,000d, Ailuropoda melanoleuca.

2015, Nov. 18   Litho.   Perf. 13¼

2955   A401   31,000d Sheet of 4, #a-d   11.00 11.00

Souvenir Sheet

2956   A401   110,000d multi   9.50 9.50

A402

No. 2957, 31,000d — Various depictions of Concorde in flight with text, "Concorde" at: a, UR in black. b, Top center in white. c, LR in black. d, LL in black.

No. 2958, 31,000d — High-speed trains: a, ED 250 Pendolino. b, CRH380D. c, Acela Express. d, HEMU-430X.

No. 2959, 31,000d — Soviet space program: a, Yuri Gagarin (1934-68), first man in space. b, Voskhod 2. c, Alexei Leonov taking first spacewalk. d, Valentina Tereshkova, first woman in space.

No. 2960, 31,000d — Table tennis players: a, Jörgen Persson. b, Li Xiaoxia. c, Jan-Ove Waldner. d, Zhang Jike.

No. 2961, 31,000d — Artists and chess pieces: a, Salvador Dalí (1904-89). b, Man Ray (1890-1976). c, Marcel Duchamp (1887-1968). d, Max Ernst (1891-1976).

No. 2962, 31,000d — Paintings by American Impressionists: a, Calm Morning, by Frank Watson Benson, 1904. b, The Cellist, by Joseph DeCamp, 1907. c, Peonies from Spring Flowers, by William Merritt Chase, 1889. d, Woman and peonies from Spring Flowers, by Chase.

No. 2963, 31,000d — Endangered animals: a, Ailurus fulgens. b, Capra falconeri. c, Panthera tigris. d, Pygathrix cinerea.

No. 2964, 31,000d — Dogs: a, Jack Russell terrier, English cocker spaniel. b, Beagle, Portuguese sheepdog. c, Portuguese water dog. d, Chinese crested dog, Pug.

No. 2965, 31,000d — Elephants: a, Elephas maximus maximus. b, Loxodonta africana, latin name at UR, elephant with tusks at left. c, Loxodonta africana, Latin name at UR, elephant with tusks at right. d, Loxodonta cyclotis, juvenile and adult with trunk raised.

No. 2966, 31,000d — Whales: a, Eubalaena glacialis. b, Balaenoptera musculus, Balaenoptera acutorostrata. c, Balaenoptera borealis. d, Physeter macrocephalus, Megaptera novaeangliae.

No. 2967, 31,000d — Owls: a, Surnia ulula. b, Otus sagittatus. c, Glaucidium perlatum, Bubo scandiacus. d, Megascops koepckeae.

No. 2968, 31,000d — Butterflies: a, Zerynthia rumina. b, Polygonia c-album. c, Junonia orithya, Melanargia galathea. d, Colobura dirce.

No. 2969, 31,000d — Shells: a, Nautilus pompilius. b, Strombus alatus gmelin. c, Voluta polypleura. d, Lambis chiragra arthritica.

No. 2970, 31,000d — Turtles: a, Chelonia mydas. b, Graptemys ernsti. c, Caretta caretta. d, Dermochelys coriacea.

No. 2971, 31,000d — Orchids: a, Stelis eublepharis. b, Rhynchostele maculata. c, Cattleya percivaliana. d, Masdevallia veitchiana.

No. 2972, 31,000d — Mushrooms: a, Macrolepiota procera. b, Morchella esculenta. c, Cortinarius triformis. d, Hygrocybe coccinea.

No. 2973, 31,000d — Minerals: a, Proustite. b, Mimetite and wulfenite. c, Carbon. d, Metatorbernite.

No. 2974, 31,000d — Pope Francis: a, Holding censer. b, Greeting Pres. Barack Obama. c, Waving. d, In Popemobile, waving.

No. 2975, 31,000d — Christmas: a, Santa Claus and automobiles. b, Children, Christmas tree, reindeer in flight. c, Sant Claus in sleigh, child on skis, snowman, dog. d, Santa Claus with sack.

No. 2976, 96,000d, Concorde, horiz. No. 2977, 96,000d, Eurostar e320, horiz. No. 2978, 96,000d, Sputnik 1 and Segei Korolev (1907-66), Soviet spacecraft designer, horiz. No. 2979, 96,000d, Zhang Jike holding trophy, horiz. No. 2980, 96,000d, Ernst and chess pieces, horiz. No. 2981, 96,000d, The Fairy Tale, by Chase, 1892, horiz. No. 2982, 96,000d, Lemur catta, horiz. No. 2983, 96,000d, Portuguese podengos, horiz. No. 2984, 96,000d, Elephas maximus indicus, horiz. No. 2985, 96,000d, Balaena mysticetus, horiz. No. 2986, 96,000d, Strix nebulosa, horiz. No. 2987, 96,000d, Polyommatus bellargus, horiz. No. 2988, 96,000d, Bullina lineata, horiz. No. 2989, 96,000d, Emydoidea blandingii, horiz. No. 2990, 96,000d, Stanhopea embreei, horiz. No. 2991, 96,000d, Amanita caesarea. No. 2992, 96,000d, Pyrite, horiz. No. 2993, 96,000d, Pope Francis and his coat of arms, horiz. No. 2994, 96,000d, Child wearing Santa hat, bell, candles.

2015, Nov. 18   Litho.   Perf. 13¼

Sheets of 4, #a-d

2957-2975   A402   Set of 19   205.00 205.00

Souvenir Sheets

2976-2994   A402   Set of 19   160.00 160.00

MonacoPhil 2015 (Nos. 2966, 2970, 2985, 2989). Nos. 2976-2994 each contain one 51x43mm stamp.

A403

No. 2995, 31,000d — Marilyn Monroe (1926-62), actress, and: a, Poster for Niagara, 1953. b, Scene from Something Has to Give, 1962. c, Scene from Some Like it Hot, 1959. d, Scene from River of No Return, 1954.

No. 2996, 31,000d — Princess Diana (1961-97): a, Holding child. b, With child, bush and flowers. c, With flowers and child. d, Wearing tiara.

No. 2997, 31,000d — Paintings of nudes: a, Bathsheba at Her Bath, by Rembrandt, 1654. b, Susannah and the Elders, by Jacob van

Loo, 1658. c, Female Nude Reclining on a Divan, by Eugène Delacroix, 1826. d, Male Nudes, Bathers, by Paul Cézanne, 1900.

No. 2998, 31,000d — Animals and World-wide Fund for Nature (WWF) stamps: a, Cotumix chinensis, Malaysia #821. b, Pelamis platura, Tokelau #389. c, Bos javanicus, Cambodia #747. d, Panthera tigris, Russia #6181.

No. 2999, 31,000d — Lighthouses: a, Fanad Lighthouse, Ireland. b, Pigeon Point Lighhouse, California (Inicie do Ponto). c, Peggy's Point Lighthouse, Canada. d, Portland Head Lighthouse, Maine.

No. 3000, 31,000d — International Year of Light: a, Joshua Bell, violinist. b, Thomas Edison (1847-1931), inventor. c, Light diffraction. d, Andrew, Duke of York, and lighthouse.

No. 3001, 31,000d — Cricket players: a, Players, end of bat near "2015." b, Shahid Afridi. c, Players, end of bat near "Criquete." d, Pakistan player batting.

No. 3002, 31,000d — 2016 Summer Olympics, Rio de Janeiro: a, 100-meter sprint. b, Rugby. c, Basketball. d, Table tennis.

No. 3003, 31,000d — 2018 World Cup Soccer Championships, Russia: a, Roman Shirokov. b, Andrey Arshavin. c, Matryoshka doll, Russian flag. d, Pres. Vladimir Putin and soccer ball.

No. 3004, 31,000d — Ships: a, Christian Radich. b, Concordia. c, Amerigo Vespucci. d, Kruzenshtern.

No. 3005, 31,000d — Steam locomotives: a, Great Western Railway 6000 Class 6024 King Edward I. b, Class DB 10. c, White Pass and Yukon Locomotive No. 69. d, London and North Eastern Railway Peppercorn Class A1 60163 Tornado.

No. 3006, 31,000d — Japanese high-speed trains: a, E5 Series Shinkansen. b, 200 Series Shinkansen. c, N700 Series Shinkansen. d, E2 Series Shinkansen.

No. 3007, 31,000d — Fire vehicles: a, American LaFrance 1000 Series pumper. b, Renault Twizy. c, Old fire truck and automobiles. d, Cadillac sedan.

No. 3008, 31,000d — Cat breeds: a, Norwegian Forest cats (Norueguês da Floresta). b, Devon Rex. c, Kurilian bobtail. d, Tonkinese.

No. 3009, 31,000d — Dolphins: a, Lagenorhynchus obliquidens. b, Two Tursiops truncatus. c, Delphinapterus leucas, Tursiops truncatus. d, Two Tursiops truncatus, red sea vegetation at LL.

No. 3010, 31,000d — Plovers: a, Pluvialis dominica. b, Pluvialis apricaria. c, Pluvialis squatarola. d, Charadrius dubius.

No. 3011, 31,000d — Birds of St. Thomas & Prince Islands: a, Ardeola ralloides. b, Phoenicopterus roseus. c, Sula dactylatra. d, Puffinus gravis.

No. 3012, 31,000d — Birds of prey: a, Athene noctua. b, Buteo buteo. c, Gyps fulvus. d, Pithecophaga jefferyi.

No. 3013, 31,000d — Dinosaurs: a, Dakosaurus maximus. b, Tyrannosaurus rex. c, Brachiosaurus altithorax. d, Spinosaurus aegypticus.

No. 3014, 31,000d — New Year 2016 (Year of the Monkey): a, Macaca mulatta. b, Simia sciureus. c, Cebus capucinus. d, Alouatta puruensis.

No. 3015, 96,000d, Monroe, diff. No. 3016, 96,000d, Princess Diana, tiara, British flag. No. 3017, 96,000d, Seated Bather, by Pierre-Auguste Renoir, 1903. No. 3018, 96,000d, Bubo lacteus, Gambia #381. No. 3019, 96,000d, Cape Agulhas Lighthouse, South Africa. No. 3020, 96,000d, LED lightbulb. No. 3021, 96,000d, Lasith Malinga, cricket player. No. 3022, 96,000d, 100-meter sprint, Christ the Redeemer statue, Rio de Janeiro. No. 3023, 96,000d, Arshavin, diff. No. 3024, 96,000d, Belem. No. 3025, 96,000d, Class GMAM No. 4079 locomotive. No. 3026, 96,000d, Kawasaki efSET train. No. 3027, 96,000d, Flyox I airplane, 2010 Freightliner pumper truck. No. 3028, 96,000d, Prionailurus bengalensis, Prionailurus bengalensis iriomotensis. No. 3029, 96,000d, Delphinus delphis, Grampus griseus. No. 3030, 96,000d, Pluvialis apricaria, diff. No. 3031, 96,000d, Dendrocygna bicolor. No. 3032, 96,000d, Otus hartlaubi. No. 3033, 96,000d, Regaliceratops peterhewsi. No. 3034, 96,000d, Cebus capucinus, diff.

Perf. 13¼, 9½ on Diagonal Sides
2015, Dec. 29 **Litho.**
Sheets of 4, #a-d
2995-3014 A403 Set of 20 220.00 220.00
Souvenir Sheets
3015-3034 A403 Set of 20 170.00 170.00

Miniature Sheets

A404

Biodiversity — A405

No. 3035: a, Turtle. b, Bay. c, Cacao tree. d, Principe Golden Weaver Bird. e, Snakes. f, Parrot. g, Houses near beach. h, Fish.

No. 3036: a, Beach. b, African Green Pigeon. c, Rock outcroppings. d, Cacao pods. e, Butterfly on flower. f, Flower. g, Schlegel's Asity bird. h, Jackfruit.

2016, Jan. 11 **Litho.** **Perf. 13x13¼**
3035 A404 1000d Sheet of 8, #a-h, + central label .75 .75
3036 A405 2000d Sheet of 8, #a-h, + central label 1.50 1.50

Sept. 11, 2001 Terrorist Attacks — A406

No. 3037 — U.S. flag and: a, Fire truck. b, Firemen on World Trade Center rubble. c, Bald eagle and World Trade Center. d, Pres. George W. Bush and fireman.

76,000d, Pres. Barack Obama, U.S. flag and Tribute in Light.

2016, Jan. 26 **Litho.** **Perf. 13¼**
3037 A406 19,000d Sheet of 4, #a-d 6.75 6.75
Souvenir Sheet
3038 A406 76,000d multi 6.75 6.75
2016 World Stamp Show, New York. No. 3038 contains one 51x90mm stamp.

75º aniversário do memorial de
Robert Baden-Powell

A407

No. 3039, 31,000d — Lord Robert Baden-Powell (1857-1941), founder of Scouting movement: a, Baden-Powell and Scouting flag. b, Three Scouts. c, Three Scouts around campfire. d, Baden-Powell and Scouting emblem.

No. 3040, 31,000d — Archbishop Desmond Tutu and: a, Tutu holding Nobel medal. b, United Nations emblem. c, 14th Dalai Lama. d, Nelson Mandela (1918-2013), President of South Africa.

No. 3041, 31,000d — Pope Francis and: a, St. Peter's Square and putto. b, His coat of arms. c, Pres. Barack Obama. d, Patriarch Kirill of Moscow, flag and coat of arms of Cuba.

No. 3042, 31,000d — Queen Elizabeth, 90th birthday: a, Princess Elizabeth of York, by Philip de Laszlo. b, Princess Elizabeth in Auxiliary Territorial Service uniform. c, Queen Elizabeth II wearing crown. d, Queen Elizabeth II with her dogs.

No. 3043, 31,000d — Princess Diana (1961-97): a, With Princes William and Harry. b, With Red Cross worker. c, Wearing hat. d, Receiving flowers from child.

No. 3044, 31,000d — Thomas Edison (1847-1931), inventor, and: a, Nickel- iron battery, IBM computer. b, Film camera. c, Miner's lamp. d, Kinetoscope.

No. 3045, 31,000d — Wolfgang Amadeus Mozart (1756-91), composer: a, Embracing woman. b, With picture of Mozart as child. c, With horse-drawn carriage. d, The Last Hours of Mozart, by Henry Nelson O'Neil.

No. 3046, 31,000d — Louis Armstrong (1901-71), jazz trumpeter, and singers: a, Ella Fitzgerald (1917-96). b, Bing Crosby (1903-77). c, Billie Holiday (1915-59). d, Barbra Streisand.

No. 3047, 31,000d — Elizabeth Taylor (1932-2011), actress: a, In scene from *Cleopatra*. b, In scene from *Ivanhoe*. c, Playing with pearl necklace. d, Holding Academy Award.

No. 3048, 31,000d — BMW motor vehicles, cent.: a, BMW 328 and BMW 501. b, BMW R1200GS LC and R32 motorcycles. c, BMW M1 and BMW i8. d, EMW/BMW 340 and BMW 323i.

No. 3049, 31,000d — First flight of the Hindenburg, 80th anniv: a, Hindenburg over water. b, Hindenburg pilots at controls. c, Hindenburg over Curitba, Brazil. d, Hindenburg and map of Germany-Brazil flight.

No. 3050, 31,000d — Concorde, 40th anniv. of commercial service: a, Air France Concordes in flight and being serviced on ground. b, One British Airways Concorde in flight. c, Air France and British Airways Concordes in flight. d, British Airways Concorde above runway.

No. 3051, 31,000d — First spaceflight of Yuri Gagarin, 55th anniv.: a, Gagarin in ejector seat, Vostok 1 capsule. b, Gagarin and Vostok 1 in orbit. c, Gagarin in space helmet, launch of Vostok 1. d, Parachutes above Gagarin in ejector seat and Vostok 1 capsule.

No. 3052, 31,000d — Edgar Mitchell (1930-2016), astronaut: a, Mitchell and Apollo 14 emblem. b, Mitchell and Lunar Rover. c, Mitchell and Alan Shepard (1923-98) training. d, Apollo 14 crew, Mitchell, Shepard and Stuart Roosa (1933-94).

No. 3053, 31,000d — Battle of Verdun, cent.: a, Two airplanes in dogfight. b, Five airplanes. c, Cannon. d, Soldiers in trench.

No. 3054, 31,000d — Attack on Pearl Harbor, 75th anniv.: a, Airplane attacking ship. b, Lieutenant General Walter Short (1880-1949), ship explosion. c, Osami Nagano (1880-1947), Japanese admiral. d, Japanese airplanes over burning ship.

No. 3055, 31,000d — Paintings by Pierre-Auguste Renoir (1849-1919): a, Self-portrait, 1875. b, Piazza San Marco, Venice, 1881. c, Flowers in a Vase, 1866. d, Self-portrait, 1910.

No. 3056, 31,000d — Paintings by Paul Cézanne (1839-1906): a, Self-portrait, 1895. b, The Bathers, 1898-1905. c, Still Life with Apples, 1893-94. d, Mont Sainte-Victoire, 1895.

No. 3057, 31,000d — Sculptures in Musée d'Orsay, Paris: a, South America, by Aimé Millet. b, Asia, by Alexandre Falguière. c,

---

Oceania, by Mathurin Moreau. d, Europe, by Pierre-Alexandre Schoenewerk.

No. 3058, 124,000d, Baden-Powell, Scouts and Scouting flag. No. 3059, 124,000d, Tutu, 14th Dalai Lama and photographer. No. 3060, 124,000d, Pope Francis, his coat of arms, dove. No. 3061, 124,000d, Queen Elizabeth II waving. No. 3062, 124,000d, Princess Diana, Princes William and Harry, diff. No. 3063, 124,000d, Edison in laboratory. No. 3064, 124,000d, Mozart and his signature. No. 3065, 124,000d, Armstrong playing trumpet. No. 3066, 124,000d, Taylor holding Golden Globe award, Robert Taylor (1911-69), actor. No. 3067, 124,000d, BMW Dixi and 2013 BMW i3. No. 3068, 124,000d, Hindenburg in flight, Ludwig Dürr (1878-1956), designer of Hindenburg. No. 3069, 124,000d, British Airways Concorde in flight, diff. No. 3070, 124,000d, Gagarin in space suit. No. 3071, 124,000d, Mitchell and Presidential Medal of Freedom. No. 3072, 124,000d, Verdun and Pope Benedict XVI. No. 3073, 124,000d, Admiral Husband E. Kimmel (1882-1968) and Japanese airplanes over burning ship. No. 3074, 124,000d, Renoir, diff. No. 3075, 124,000d, Cézanne self-portrait, 1890. No. 3076, 124,000d, Pierre Colboc, architect, and Musée d'Orsay.

2016, Jan. 26 **Litho.** **Perf. 13¼**
Sheets of 4, #a-d
3039-3057 A407 Set of 19 210.00 210.00
Souvenir Sheets
3058-3076 A407 Set of 19 210.00 210.00
Nos. 3058-3076 each contain one 51x90mm stamp.

Philataipei 2016 World Stamp Championship Exhibition, Taipei — A408

No. 3077, 31,000d: a, Prunus mume. b, Urocissa caerulea. c, Onychostoma alticorpus. d, Ursus thibetanus formosanus. 96,000d, Sun Yat-sen Memorial Hall, Taipei.

2016, Mar. 30 **Litho.** **Perf. 17**
3077 A408 31,000d Sheet of 4, #a-d 11.50 11.50
Souvenir Sheet
3078 A408 96,000d multi 9.00 9.00
No. 3078 contains one 71x71mm diamond-shaped stamp.

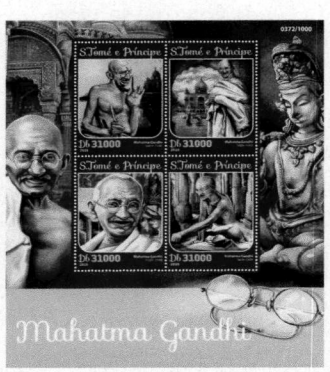

Mahatma Gandhi

A409

No. 3079, 31,000d — Mahatma Gandhi (1869-1948), Indian nationalist: a, Gandhi holding walking stick. b, Gandhi in robe, women in front of temple. c, Head of Gandhi. d, Gandhi seated.

No. 3080, 31,000d — St. John Paul II (1920-2005): a, Kissing head of child. b, Praying at St. Peter's Basilica. c, Head of St. John Paul II. d, Embracing Pope Benedict XVI.

No. 3081, 31,000d — Elvis Presley (1935-77): a, Holding microphone. b, In automobile, wearing Army uniform. c, With Ann-Margret in scene from *Viva Las Vegas*. d, In scene from *Kid Galahad*.

No. 3082, 31,000d — Rugby players: a, Two players, one trying to kick ball. b, Player in green shirt tackling player in black shirt. c,

Player in gray shirt tackling player in yellow shirt. d, Three players.

No. 3083, 31,000d — 2016 Summer Olympics, Rio de Janeiro: a, Cricket. b, Two rugby players and two balls. c, Judo. d, Show jumping.

No. 3084, 31,000d — Fire engines: a, Caterpillar 740. b, EU10FSP of Chelmsford, Essex, United Kingdom. c, Lentner TGM. d, 2011 Ladder truck of North Andover, Massachusetts.

No. 3085, 31,000d — High-speed trains: a, CRH6A, People's Republic of China. b, Series W7 Shinkansen, Japan. c, Frecciarossa 1000, Italy. d, TCDD HT80000, Turkey.

No. 3086, 31,000d — Red Cross campaign against malaria: a, Red Cross worker putting up mosquito netting. b, Red Cross workers in laboratory. c, Red Cross worker with child drinking water. d, Red Cross worker spraying insecticide.

No. 3087, 31,000d — Lighthouses: a, Maiden's Tower (Danzela), Turkey. b, Allainville Lighthouse. c, El Morro Lighthouse, Puerto Rico. d, Point Cabrillo Lighthouse, California.

No. 3088, 31,000d — International Year of Pulses: a, New Holland TR 98 combine, seedlings. b, Woman and child preparing beans. c, Green peas. d, Beans for sale at market.

No. 3089, 31,000d — Dogs: a, Sloughis. b, Pembroke Welsh corgis. c, Tibetan mastiff. d, German shepherds.

No. 3090, 31,000d — Owls: a, Bubo bengalensis. b, Aegolius funereus. c, Glaucidium capense. d, Strix leptogrammica.

No. 3091, 31,000d — Butterflies: a, Zemeros flegyas. b, Cyrestis thyodamas. c, Vanessa virginiensis. d, Papilio ulysses.

No. 3092, 31,000d — Turtles: a, Graptemys pseudogeographica kohni. b, Chrysemys scripta elegans. c, Malaclemys terrapin. d, Caretta caretta.

No. 3093, 31,000d — Endangered animals: a, Pongo pygmaeus. b, Elephas maximus. c, Camelus bactrianus. d, Addax nasomaculatus.

No. 3094, 31,000d — Mushrooms: a, Trametes versicolor. b, Leucocoprinus birnbaumii. c, Amanita phalloides. d, Fomitopsis pinicola.

No. 3095, 31,000d — Minerals: a, Azurite. b, Amazonite. c, Barium. d, Wulfenite.

No. 3096, 31,000d — Marilyn Monroe (1926-62), actress, wearing: a, Black swimsuit, eyes closed. b, White dress. c, Choker. d, Black dress, eyes open.

No. 3097, 31,000d — Whales: a, Balaena mysticetus. b, Balaenoptera musculus. c, Megaptera novaeangliae. d, Physeter macrocephalus.

No. 3098, 96,000d, Gandhi, diff. No. 3099, 96,000d, St. John Paul II, diff. No. 3100, 96,000d, Presley, guitar and Judy Tyler (1932-57), actress. No. 3101, 96,000d, Three rugby players, diff. No. 3102, 96,000d, Table tennis players. No. 3103, 96,000d, Austin 480 and Rosenbauer Panther 6x6 CAS fire trucks. No. 3104, 96,000d, British Railways Class 801, Great Britain. No. 3105, 96,000d, Anopheles gambiae, and mother and child under mosquito netting. No. 3106, 96,000d, Cape Tainaron Lighthouse, Greece. No. 3107, 96,000d, Coracias caudatus, Scarabaeus sacer, people harvesting beans. No. 3108, 96,000d, Rottweilers. No. 3109, 96,000d, Tyto alba, Athene noctua. No. 3110, 96,000d, Rhetus periander. No. 3111, 96,000d, Terrapene carolina carolina. No. 3112, 96,000d, Propithecus coronatus, Propithecus diadema. No. 3113, 96,000d, Lactarius indigo. No. 3114, 96,000d, Amethyst. No. 3115, 124,000d, Monroe, diff. No. 3116, 124,000d, Balaena mysticetus, diff.

2016, Mar. 30 Litho. Perf. 13¼
Sheets of 4, #a-d
3079-3097 A409 Set of 19 220.00 220.00
Souvenir Sheets
3098-3116 A409 Set of 19 175.00 175.00
Nos. 3098-3116 each contain one 51x90mm stamp.

Philataipei 2016 World Stamp Championship Exhibition, Taipei — A410

No. 3117: a, Statue of Genghis Khan (1162-1227) on horseback, Mausoleum of Genghis Khan, Xinjie, People's Republic of China. b, Mausoleum of Genghis Khan and scultpture of Genghis Khan. c, Genghis Khan and Falco rusticolus. d, Warriors on horseback, statue of Genghis Khan on horseback.

76,000d, Statue of Genghis Khan on horseback, diff.

Litho. With Foil Application
2016, July 20 Perf. 13¼
3117 A410 19,000d Sheet of 4,
  #a-d 7.00 7.00
Souvenir Sheet
Perf.
3118 A410 76,000d multi 7.00 7.00
No. 3118 contains one 40mm diameter stamp.

World Youth Day — A411

No. 3119: a, Pope Francis and youths. b, Pope John Paul II (1920-2005) and youths. c, Pope Benedict XVI waving. d, Youths at 2016 World Youth Day celebrations.

96,000d, Youths, flags of Poland and cross.

2016, July 20 Litho. Perf. 13¼
3119 A411 31,000d Sheet of 4,
  #a-d 11.50 11.50
Souvenir Sheet
3120 A411 96,000d multi 8.75 8.75

Animals — A412

No. 3121, 31,000d — Mammals from Africa: a, Acinonyx jubatus. b, Elephantulus myurus. c, Phacochoerus africanus. d, Erythrocebus patas.

No. 3122, 31,000d — Bears (Ursus americanus) from the Americas: a, Bear and squirrel. b, Bear near lake and head of bear. c, Adult bear and cubs climbing tree. d, Three bears, one with fish in mouth.

No. 3123, 31,000d — Mammals from the Arctic: a, Vulpes lagopus. b, Ovibos moschatus. c, Alces alces. d, Lepus arcticus.

No. 3124, 31,000d — Pandas (Ailuropoda melanoleuca) from Asia: a, Four pandas. b, Two pandas. c, One panda. d, Panda in water, farmers in field.

No. 3125, 31,000d — Deer from Europe: a, Dama dama. b, Blastocerus dichotomus. c, Dama dama mesopotamica. d, Axis axis.

No. 3126, 31,000d — Wolves from Europe: a, Canis lupus lupus, tail in foreground. b, Canis lupus albus. c, Canis lupus lupus, head in foreground. d, Two canis lupus lupus fighting.

No. 3127, 31,000d — Jaguars (Panthera onca) from the Americas: a, Head of jaguar and jaguar with black fur. b, Jaguar on log. c, Two jaguars. d, Heads of jaguar and jaguar with black fur.

No. 3128, 31,000d — Tigers from Asia: a, Panthera tigris amoyensis. b, Panthera tigris jacksoni. c, Panthera tigris altaica. d, Panthera tigris corbetti.

No. 3129, 31,000d — Birds from Africa: a, Phalacrocorax carbo. b, Gavia arctica with wings extended. c, Thalassarche melanophris. d, Pelecanus crispus.

No. 3130, 31,000d — Birds from the Americas: a, Falco sparverius. b, Somateria mollissima. c, Meleagris gallopovo. d, Phoenicopterus ruber.

No. 3131, 31,000d — Birds from the Arctic: a, Gavia arctica in water. b, Alca torda. c, Fratercula arctica. d, Somateria spectabilis.

No. 3132, 31,000d — Birds from Asia: a, Plegadis falcinellus. b, Coracias benghalensis. c, Todiramphus chloris. d, Neophron percnopterus.

No. 3133, 31,000d — Owls from Europe: a, Strix uralensis. b, Aegolius funereus. c, Bubo scandiacus. d, Otus scops.

No. 3134, 31,000d — Insects and spiders from the Americas: a, Graphocephala coccinea. b, Acharia stimulea. c, Murgantia histrionica. d, Araneus trifolium.

No. 3135, 31,000d — Butterflies from Asia: a, Melitaea sibina. b, Apatura ilia. c, Sasakia charonda. d, Tatinga thibetanus.

No. 3136, 31,000d — Fish from the Arctic: a, Esox lucius. b, Lota lota. c, Gasterosteus aculeatus. d, Oncorhynchus keta.

No. 3137, 31,000d — Reptiles from Africa: a, Afroablepharus africanus. b, Feylinia polylepis. c, Philothamnus thomensis. d, Hemidactylus principensis.

No. 3138, 31,000d — Predators from Africa: a, Osteolaemus tetraspis. b, Canis mesomelas. c, Caracal caracal. d, Python sebae.

No. 3139, 96,000d, Diceros bicornis. No. 3140, 96,000d, Four Ursus americanus. No. 3141, 96,000d, Canis lupus arctos. No. 3142, 96,000d, Ailurus fulgens. No. 3143, 96,000d, Odocoileus virginianus. No. 3144, 96,000d, Canis lupus lupus, diff. No. 3145, 96,000d, Panthera onca, diff. No. 3146, 96,000d, Panthera tigris tigris. No. 3147, 96,000d, Dromaius novaehollandiae. No. 3148, 96,000d, Fregata magnificens. No. 3149, 96,000d, Anas acuta. No. 3150, 96,000d, Ardeola bacchus. No. 3151, 96,000d, Strix nebulosa. No. 3152, 96,000d, Theatops californiensis. No. 3153, 96,000d, Heliophorus saphir. No. 3154, 96,000d, Salvelinus alpinus. No. 3155, 96,000d, Cordylus tropidosternum. No. 3156, 96,000d, Vulpes zerda.

2016, July 20 Litho. Perf. 13¼
Sheets of 4, #a-d
3121-3138 A412 Set of 18 205.00 205.00
Souvenir Sheets
3139-3156 A412 Set of 18 160.00 160.00

Philataipei 2016 World Stamp Championship Exhibition, Taipei — A413

No. 3157 — 14th Dalai Lama: a, Facing right, holding object with pink strap. b, With Tsai Ing-wen, President of Republic of China. c, With bird, praying. d, With Chen Shui-bian, ex-President of Republic of China.

76,000d, 14th Dalai Lama, Pres. Tsai Ing-wen, flag of Republic of China, birds and flowers.

2016, Sept. 12 Litho. Perf. 13¼
3157 A413 19,000d Sheet of 4,
  #a-d 7.00 7.00
Souvenir Sheet
3158 A413 76,000d multi 7.00 7.00
No. 3158 contains one 47x81mm stamp.

A414

No. 3159, 31,000d — Various stamps, including: a, Cambodia #1631 held in tongs. b, Germany #B206 held in fingers. c, Sharjah bird stamp covered by finger. d, Chad #521 held in tongs.

No. 3160, 31,000d — Nelson Mandela (1918-2013), President of South Africa: a, On 10-rand South African banknote, people with fists raised. b, With military officer. c, Holding finger up at microphone. d, Head facing left.

No. 3161, 31,000d — Fire trucks: a, Mercedes-Benz L6600 DL30. b, Bedford TK. c, ZIL-130. d, Citroen P45.

No. 3162, 31,000d — Steam locomotives: a, Castle class 4-6-0 No. 5013. b, London and North Eastern Railway Gresley K4 61994, The Great Marquess. c, Queensland Railways A10 No. 6. d, Union Pacific Big Boy 4-8-8-4.

No. 3163, 31,000d — High-speed trains of People's Republic of China: a, CRH1E, CRH2C. b, CRH5. c, CRH1. d, Shanghai Transrapid.

No. 3164, 31,000d — Russian soccer players at 2018 World Cup Soccer Championships, Russia, and landmarks: a, Fyodor Smolov, Church of Our Saviour of the Spilled Blood. b, Ramil Sheydayev, Winter Palace. c, Alexandr Kokorin, Bolshoi Theater. d, Aleksandr Golovin, Kizhi Pogost.

No. 3165, 31,000d — Chess players: a, Viswanathan Anand. b, Maxime Vachier-Lagrave. c, Vladimir Kramnik. d, Fabiano Caruana.

No. 3166, 31,000d — Cats: a, Abyssinian. b, Maine Coon cat. c, Cornish Rex. d, Norwegian Forest cat.

No. 3167, 31,000d — Dolphins: a, Stenella clymene. b, Stenella frontalis. c, Steno bredanensis. d, Tursiops truncatus.

No. 3168, 31,000d — Birds of prey: a, Elanus axillaris. b, Aquila fasciata. c, Buteo plagiatus. d, Milvus milvus.

No. 3169, 31,000d — Bee-eaters: a, Merops nubicoides. b, Two Merops apiaster and flower. c, One Merops apiaster. d, Two Merops apiaster, no flower.

No. 3170, 31,000d — Fish and corals: a, Chaetodontoplus conspicillatus, Himerometra robustipinna. b, Paracanthurus hepatus, Gorgonia flabellum. c, Holocentrus rufus, Ocyurus chrysurus, Aplysina fistularis. d, Scarus ferrugineus, Turbinaria reniformis.

No. 3171, 31,000d — Shells and lighthouses: a, Angaria delphinus, Peggys Point Lighthouse, Nova Scotia. b, Tudicla spirillus, Kéréon Lighthouse, France. c, Achatina panthera, Les Eclaireurs Lighthouse, Argentina. d, Drupa morum, Fanad Head Lighthouse, Ireland.

No. 3172, 31,000d — Turtles: a, Aldabrachelys gigantea. b, Eretmochelys imbricata. c, Caretta caretta. d, Gopherus agassizii.

No. 3173, 31,000d — Dinosaurs: a, Edmontosaurus. b, Confuciusornis. c, Velociraptor. d, Sauropelta, Kentrosaurus.

No. 3174, 31,000d — Mushrooms: a, Morchella esculenta. b, Leratiomyces. c, Cyathus striatus. d, Hydnellum peckii.

No. 3175, 31,000d — Orchids: a, Thunia alba. b, Vanilla planifolia. c, Cymbidium sp. d, Caleana major.

No. 3176, 31,000d — Minerals and volcanos: a, Limonite, Galeras Volcano, Colombia. b, Calcite, Taal Volcano, Philippines. c, Biotite, Popocatépetl Volcano, Mexico. d, Malachite and chrysocolla, Mount Merapi, Indonesia.

No. 3177, 31,000d — Christmas Truce of 1914: a, Soldiers shaking hands. b, Soldiers, Christmas tree, barbed wire. c, Soldiers laying down arms. d, Soldier carrying small Christmas tree.

No. 3178, 96,000d, Japan #Z119 held in fingers. No. 3179, 96,000d, Mandela, diff. No. 3180, 96,000d, Ural 43206 fire truck. No. 3181, 96,000d, Great Western Railway 4200 Class 4277. No. 3182, 96,000d, CRH-X Yi train. No. 3183, 96,000d, Igor Shuvalov, head of Russian 2018 World Cup Soccer Championships organizing committee. No. 3184, 96,000d, Magnus Carlsen. No. 3185, 96,000d, Sorrel Somali cat. No. 3186, 96,000d, Sousa teuszii. No. 3187, 96,000d, Pandion halietus. No. 3188, 96,000d, Merops ornatus. No. 3189, 96,000d, Balistoides conspicillum, Stichodactyla haddoni. No. 3190, 96,000d, Cymbiola imperialis, Tillamook Rock Lighthouse, Oregon. No. 3191, 96,000d, Terrapene carolina bauri. No. 3192, 96,000d, Plateosaurus, Coelophysis. No. 3193, 96,000d, Ramaria aurea. No. 3194, 96,000d, Phalaenopsis cornu-cervi. No. 3195, 96,000d, Gormanite, Mauna Loa, Hawaii. No. 3196, 96,000d, Soldiers celebrating Christmas at barrier.

2016, Sept. 12   Litho.   Perf. 13¼
Sheets of 4, #a-d
3159-3177   A414   Set of 19   215.00 215.00
Souvenir Sheets
3178-3196   A414   Set of 19   165.00 165.00

Birds
A415

No. 3197: a, Busarellus nigricollis. b, Spizaetus ornatus. c, Caracara plancus. d, Elanus leucurus. e, Falco deiroleucus. f, Terathopius ecaudatus and snake.

2016, Nov. 10   Litho.   Die Cut
Self-Adhesive
3197   Block of 6   10.50
a.-f.   A415   20,000d Any single   1.75   1.75
Printed in sheets of four blocks, with each block having different background colors.

A416

No. 3198, 31,000d — 2016 World Ice Hockey Championships, Moscow: a, Denomination at UR, puck at LR near stick blades. b, Denomination at UL, player's skate to left of puck. c, Denomination at UR, puck at LR near player's skate. d, Denomination at UL, player's stick blade to left of puck.

No. 3199, 31,000d — Table tennis players: a, Denomination at UR, player's paddle at left. b, Denomination at UL, player's paddle at right, ball at left. c, Denomination at UL, player's paddle at right, ball at right. d, Denomination at UL, player's paddle at left.

No. 3200, 31,000d — Formula 1 race cars: a, Mercedes-Benz W196. b, Haas VF-16. c, Benetton B193B. d, Brabham BT19.

No. 3201, 31,000d — Gold medalists at 2016 Winter Olympics: a, Dominique Gisin. b, Alexander Legkov. c, Martin Fourcade. d, Matthias Mayer.

No. 3202, 31,000d — Rotary International emblem, butterflies and flowers: a, Charaxes thomasius, Brillantaisia owariensis. b, Cyrestis camillus, Heliconia psittacorum. c, Hypolimnas salmacis, Sobralia macrantha. d, Acraea zetes, Cypripedium lowii.

No. 3203, 31,000d — Battle of Moscow, 75th anniv.: a, Portrait of General Ivan Panfilov, by Vasily Yakovlev (1893-1953), and The Exploit of 28 Heroes from Panfilov's Division, by Alexei Komarov (1879-1977). b, Battle of Moscow, by Yevgeny Danilevsky (1928-2010). c, Battle of Moscow, by Pavel Ryzhenko (1970-2014). d, Gunners Fight of December 3, 1941, by Vladimir Korobkov (1951-2014).

No. 3204, 31,000d — Nikola Tesla (1846-1943), inventor: a, Tesla reading book, and electric motor. b, 2011 Tesla Roadster 2.5 S. c, 2018 Tesla Model 3. d, Tesla and Westinghouse alternating current motor.

No. 3205, 31,000d — Space technology: a, Concept of Bigelow Commercial Space Station. b, Orion multi-purpose vehicle. c, Copernicus concept vehicle. d, Commercial space station.

No. 3206, 31,000d — Nobel Laureates: a, 1979 Peace laureate, Mother Teresa (1910-97), and dove. b, 1993 Peace laureate, Nelson Mandela (1918-2013), and flag of South Africa. c, 1913 Literature laureate, Rabindranath Tagore (1861-1941), and Nelumbo nucifera. d, 1989 Peace laureate, 14th Dalai Lama, and Potala Palace.

No. 3207, 31,000d — Red Cross: a, Worker in protective gear feeding infant with bottle. b, Worker with tongue depressor checking patient's mouth. c, Worker with stethoscope checking boy. d, Worker inoculating child.

No. 3208, 31,000d — Sergei Prokofiev (1891-1953), composer, with: a, Dancers from his ballet, Romeo and Juliet. b, Scene from film, Ivan the Terrible. c, Characters from Peter and the Wolf. d, Piano and score.

No. 3209, 31,000d — Paintings by Claude Monet (1840-1926): a, Argenteuil, 1875. b,

Cliffs Near Dieppe, 1882, and 1884 self-portrait. c, Exterior of the Saint-Lazare Station, Sunlight Effect, 1877. d, Poplars on the Epte, 1891.

No. 3210, 31,000d — Paintings by Berthe Morisot (1841-95): a, Boats Under Construction, 1874. b, Two Nymphs Embracing, 1892. c, Girl Playing the Mandolin, 1890, and Young Woman Seated on a Sofa, 1879. d, Girl in Rose Dress, 1888.

No. 3211, 31,000d — Paintings by Odilon Redon (1840-1916): a, Closed Eyes, 1895. b, Reflection, 1900-05. c, Ophelia Among the Flowers, 1905-08. d, Buddha, 1906-07.

No. 3212, 31,000d — Paintings by Pablo Picasso (1881-1973): a, Head, 1926. b, Seated Woman (Jacqueline), 1962. c, Nude Woman with Necklace, 1968. d, Head of a Woman 1922.

No. 3213, 31,000d — American Impressionists and their paintings: a, Day Dreams, 1889, by Theodore Robinson (1852-96). b, End of the Season Sun, 1884, by William Merritt Chase (1849-1916). c, Uplands, Novembere, 1939, by Daniel Garber (1880-1958). d, The End of the Streetcar Line, Oak Park, Illinois, 1893, by Childe Hassam (1859-1935).

No. 3214, 31,000d — Paintings of nudes: a, Red-headed Nude Crouching, 1897, by Henri de Toulouse-Lautrec (1864-1901). b, Rolla, 1878, by Henri Gervex, (1852-1929). c, Reclining Nude with Pink Robe, 1937, by Lev Tchistovsky (1902-69). d, Blonde Girl on a Bed, 1987, by Lucian Freud (1922-2011).

No. 3215, 31,000d — Paintings of roosters (New Year 2017, Year of the Rooster) by: a, Xu Beihong (1895-1953), denomination at UL. b, Chen Dayu (1912-2001). c, Zhang Daqian (1899-1983). d, Xu Beihong, diff., denomination at UR.

No. 3216, 120,000d, Two ice hockey players, diff. No. 3217, 120,000d, Table tennis player, diff. No. 3218, 120,000d, Ferrari SF16-H. No. 3219, 120,000d, Vic Wild. No. 3220, 120,000d, Rotary International emblem, Acraea jodutta, Sobralia macrantha. No. 3221, 120,000d, G. I. Zhukov, Battle of Moscow, 1941, by Nikolay Repin. No. 3222, 120,000d, Tesla and alternating current generator. No. 3223, 120,000d, Concept for Commercial Space Station Hotel. No. 3224, 120,000d, Dr. Martin Luther King, Jr. (1929-68), 1964 Nobel peace laurate, and U.S. Capitol. No. 3225, 120,000d, Red Cross worker holding child, globe. No. 3226, 120,000d, Prokofiev and dancer from his ballet, Cinderella. No. 3227, 120,000d, Argenteuil, Seen from the Small Arm of the Seine, 1872, by Monet. No. 3228, 120,000d, Girl with Dog, 1886, by Morisot. No. 3229, 120,000d, The Birth of Venus, 1910, by Redon. No. 3230, 120,000d, Paloma with Doll, 1952, and Sylvette, 1954, by Picasso. No. 3231, 120,000d, Nurse and Child, 1896-97, and Young Girl Holding a Loose Bouquet, 1880, by Mary Cassatt (1844-1926). No. 3232, 120,000d, Nymphs, 1878, by William-Adolphe Bouguereau (1825-1905). No. 3233, 120,000d, Rooster, by Chen Dayu, diff.

2016, Nov. 10   Litho.   Perf. 13¼
Sheets of 4, #a-d
3198-3215   A416   Set of 18   190.00 190.00
Souvenir Sheets
3216-3233   A416   Set of 18   185.00 185.00

Nos. 3216-3233 each contain one 60x40mm stamp.

Grus Japonensis — A417

No. 3234: a, Bird in flight and wing tip of other bird, Latin name at LL. b, Bird in flight, Latin name at UR. c, Bird landing, Latin name at LL. d, Bird standing.
120,000d, Bird in flight, diff.

2016, Nov. 10   Litho.   Perf. 13¼
3234   A417   31,000d Sheet of 4, #a-d   11.00 11.00
Souvenir Sheet
3235   A417   120,000d multi   10.50 10.50

China 2016 International Stamp Exhibition, Nanning. No. 3235 contains one 48x36mm stamp.

Souvenir Sheet

U.S. President-Elect Donald Trump, and Wife, Melania — A418

2016, Nov. 10   Litho.   Perf. 13¼
3236   A418   120,000d multi   10.50 10.50

2017 Confederations Cup Soccer Tournament, Russia — A419

Venues: No. 3237, 31,000d, Otkrytie Arena, Moscow. No. 3238, 31,000d, Fisht Olympic Stadium, Sochi. No. 3239, 31,000d, Kazan Arena, Kazan. No. 3240, 31,000d, Krestovsky Stadium, St. Petersburg.
120,000d, Soccer player, ball, Russian flag and emblem.

2017, Mar. 13   Litho.   Perf. 13¼
3237-3240   A419   Set of 4   11.00 11.00
Souvenir Sheet
3241   A419   120,000d multi   10.50 10.50

A420

No. 3242, 31,000d — Pandas: a, Two Ailuropoda melanoleuca. b, One Ailuropoda melanoleuca. c, Ailurus fulgens next to tree. d, Ailurus fulgens and fallen tree.

No. 3243, 31,000d — Wild cats: a, Panthera leo. b, Puma concolor. c, Panthera uncia. d, Acinonyx jubatus.

No. 3244, 31,000d — Dolphins: a, Lagenodelphis hosei. b, Tursiops truncatus. c, Feresa attenuata. d, Steno bredanensis.

No. 3245, 31,000d — Aquatic birds: a, Ephippiorhynchus asiaticus. b, Pelecanus occidentalis. c, Podiceps cristatus. d, Phoenicopterus ruber.

No. 3246, 31,000d — Birds of prey: a, Pandion haliaetus. b, Elanus caeruleus. c, Gymnogyps californianus. d, Falco columbarius.

No. 3247, 31,000d — Owls: a, Megascops clarkii. b, Tyto multipunctata. c, Bubo virginianus. d, Otus sunia.

No. 3248, 31,000d — Butterflies: a, Arctia villica. b, Coenonympha pamphilus. c, Zygaena filipendulae. d, Cyclosia papilionaris.

No. 3249, 31,000d — Turtles: a, Terrapene carolina carolina. b, Geochelone elegans. c, Sternothus odoratus. d, Chelydra serpentina.

No. 3250, 31,000d — Dinosaurs: a, Parasaurolophus. b, Stegosaurus. c, Triceratops. d, Tyrannosaurus rex.

No. 3251, 31,000d — Extinct animals: a, Diceros bicornis longipes. b, Panthera tigris sondaica. c, Monachus tropicalis. d, Capra pyrenaica pyrenaica.

No. 3252, 31,000d — Orchids: a, Guarianthe aurantiaca. b, Laeliocattleya Gold Digger. c, Cattleya amethystoglossa. d, Dendrobium victoriae-reginae.

No. 3253, 31,000d — Mushrooms: a, Morchella esculenta. b, Leccinum quercinum and Sciurus vulgaris. c, Gyromitra esculenta and squirrel. d, Cantharellus cibarius.

No. 3254, 31,000d — Minerals: a, Smoky quartz. b, Olivine. c, Galena. d, Quartz.

No. 3255, 31,000d — Lighthouses, light and shells: a, List-West Lighthouse, Germany, Larus delawarensis. b, Stangholmen Lighthouse, Sweden, Chicoreus florifer. c, Touritlis Lighthouse, Greece, Hexaplex regius. d, Sturgeon Bay Ship Canal Pierhead Lighthouse, Wisconsin, and birds.

No. 3256, 31,000d — Scouting movement, 110th anniv.: a, Scout and sculpture The Ideal Scout, by Robert Tait McKenzie (1867-1938). b, Girl Scouts examining flora. c, Scout and leader with bow and arrow. d, Honorary scout, Duchess of Cambridge.

No. 3257, 31,000d — Pres. John F. Kennedy (1917-63): a, With wife, Jacqueline (1929-94). b, With ships and airplanes of the Cuban Missile Crisis. c, Standing in limousine in Tampa, Florida motorcade. d, With Marilyn Monroe (1926-62).

No. 3258, 31,000d — 90th birthday of Pope Benedict XVI: a, On red carpet. b, With arm extended forward, wearing miter. c, Waving. d, Holding aspergillum.

No. 3259, 31,000d — Metropolitan Museum of Art, 145th anniv.: a, Main museum building and The Harvesters, by Pieter Bruegel the Elder. b, Greek and Roman Art gallery and marble sarcophagus with garlands. c, Met Breuer Building and The Charnel House, by Pablo Picasso. d, The Cloisters and Theodosius Entering Ephesus stained-glass window.

No. 3260, 31,000d — New Year 2017 (Year of the Rooster): a, Rooster facing right, bamboo in background. b, Rooster facing left, pagoda in background. c, Rooster with head at left, facing right, torii at LR. d, Rooster facing left, arches at lower left and center.

No. 3261, 124,000d, Two Ailuropoda melanoleuca, diff. No. 3262, 124,000d, Panthera tigris. No. 3263, 124,000d, Gampus griseus. No. 3264, 124,000d, Aix galericulata. No. 3265, 124,000d, Aquila chrysaetos. No. 3266, 124,000d, Pulsatrix perspicillata. No. 3267, 124,000d, Parnassius apollo. No. 3268, 124,000d, Chelonoidis nigra. No. 3269, 124,000d, Hadrosaurus. No. 3270, 124,000d, Thylacinus cynocephalus. No. 3271, 124,000d, Laelia cinnabarina. No. 3272, 124,000d, Pleurotus pulmonarius. No. 3273, 124,000d, Rubies. No. 3274, 124,000d, St. Joseph North Pier Lighthouse, Michigan. No. 3275, 124,000d, Juliette Gordon Low (1860-1927), founder of Girl Scouts of the U.S.A., and Girl Scout. No. 3276, 124,000d, Apollo 15 capsule and space rover, U.S. flag. No. 3277, 124,000d, Pope Benedict XVI, diff. No. 3278, 124,000d, John Taylor Johnston (1820-93), founder of Metropolitan Museum of Art, and human-headed winged lion sculpture. No. 3279, 124,000d, Rooster, diff.

2017, Mar. 13   Litho.   Perf. 13¼
Sheets of 4, #a-d
3242-3260   A420   Set of 19   205.00 205.00
Souvenir Sheets
3261-3279   A420   Set of 19   205.00 205.00

AIR POST STAMPS

Common Design Type
Inscribed "S. Tomé"

1938			Perf. 13½x13

Name and Value in Black

C1	CD39	10c red orange		95.00	67.50
C2	CD39	20c purple		45.00	33.00
C3	CD39	50c orange		3.50	3.00
C4	CD39	1e ultra		9.00	3.50
C5	CD39	2e lilac brown		8.00	5.00
C6	CD39	3e dark green		10.00	6.50
C7	CD39	5e red brown		16.00	14.00
C8	CD39	9e rose carmine		17.00	14.00
C9	CD39	10e magenta		52.50	14.00
		Nos. C1-C9 (9)		256.00	160.50

Common Design Type
Inscribed "S. Tomé e Principe"

1939		Engr.		Unwmk.

Name and Value Typo. in Black

C10	CD39	10c scarlet		.60	.30
C11	CD39	20c purple		.60	.30
C12	CD39	50c orange		.60	.30
C13	CD39	1e deep ultra		.60	.30
C14	CD39	2e lilac brown		1.50	1.00
C15	CD39	3e dark green		2.25	1.60
C16	CD39	5e red brown		5.25	3.00

C17	CD39	9e rose carmine	9.00 5.25
C18	CD39	10e magenta	10.00 5.75
		Nos. C10-C18 (9)	30.40 17.80

No. C16 exists with overprint "Exposicao International de Nova York, 1939-1940" and Trylon and Perisphere.

No. 742 Surcharged in Red

Method and Perf As Before
2009, Apr. 15

C21	A95	(45,000d) on 18.50d	
		#742	*5.50 5.50*

Two additional stamps were issued in this set. The editors would like to examine any examples.

POSTAGE DUE STAMPS

"S. Thomé" — D1

1904 Unwmk. Typo. Perf. 12

J1	D1	5r yellow green	.90 .75
J2	D1	10r slate	.90 .75
J3	D1	20r yellow brown	1.35 .90
J4	D1	30r orange	1.40 .90
J5	D1	50r gray brown	2.75 1.75
J6	D1	60r red brown	3.75 2.10
J7	D1	100r red lilac	5.75 3.25
J8	D1	130r dull blue	5.75 4.00
J9	D1	200r carmine	6.00 4.00
J10	D1	500r gray violet	11.00 8.00
		Nos. J1-J10 (10)	39.55 26.40

Overprinted in Carmine or Green

1911

J11	D1	5r yellow green	.30 .30
J12	D1	10r slate	.30 .30
J13	D1	20r yellow brown	.30 .30
J14	D1	30r orange	.30 .30
J15	D1	50r gray brown	.50 .45
J16	D1	60r red brown	1.40 .80
J17	D1	100r red lilac	1.40 .80
J18	D1	130r dull blue	1.40 .80
J19	D1	200r carmine (G)	1.40 .80
J20	D1	500r gray violet	3.00 2.25
		Nos. J11-J20 (10)	10.30 7.10

Nos. J1-J10 Overprinted in Black

1913 Without Gum

J21	D1	5r yellow green	6.75 4.25
J22	D1	10r slate	9.00 5.50
J23	D1	20r yellow brown	6.75 4.25
J24	D1	30r orange	6.75 4.25
J25	D1	50r gray brown	6.75 5.00
J26	D1	60r red brown	6.75 5.00
J27	D1	100r red lilac	6.75 5.50
J28	D1	130r dull blue	29.00 13.50
a.		Inverted overprint	50.00 42.50
J29	D1	200r carmine	52.50 45.00
J30	D1	500r gray violet	65.00 37.50
		Nos. J21-J30 (10)	196.00 129.75

Nos. J1-J10 Overprinted in Black

1913 Without Gum

J31	D1	5r yellow green	5.25 3.50
a.		Inverted overprint	50.00 40.00
J32	D1	10r slate	5.25 4.00
J33	D1	20r yellow brown	5.25 3.50
J34	D1	30r orange	5.25 3.50
a.		Inverted overprint	55.00
J35	D1	50r gray brown	7.75 5.00
J36	D1	60r red brown	8.00 5.00
J37	D1	100r red lilac	8.00 5.00
J38	D1	130r dull blue	8.00 5.00
J39	D1	200r carmine	11.00 6.75
J40	D1	500r gray violet	23.00 18.00
		Nos. J31-J40 (10)	86.75 59.25

No. J5 Overprinted "Republica" in Italic Capitals like Regular Issue in Green

1920 Without Gum

J41	D1	50r gray brn	40.00 26.00

"S. Tomé" — D2

1921 Typo. Perf. 11½

J42	D2	½c yellow green	.50 .30
J43	D2	1c slate	.50 .30
J44	D2	2c orange brown	.50 .30
J45	D2	3c orange	.50 .30
J46	D2	5c gray brown	.50 .30
J47	D2	6c lt brown	.70 .50
J48	D2	10c red violet	.70 .50
J49	D2	13c dull blue	.70 .50
J50	D2	20c carmine	.70 .50
J51	D2	50c gray	1.60 1.10
		Nos. J42-J51 (10)	6.90 4.60

In each sheet one stamp is inscribed "S. Thomé" instead of "S. Tomé." Value, set of 10, $60.

> Catalogue values for unused stamps in this section, from this point to the end of the section, are for Never Hinged items.

Common Design Type
Photo. & Typo.
1952 Unwmk. Perf. 14
Numeral in Red, Frame Multicolored

J52	CD45	10c chocolate	.30 .30
J53	CD45	30c red brown	.30 .30
J54	CD45	50c dark blue	.30 .30
J55	CD45	1e dark blue	.50 .50
J56	CD45	2e olive green	.70 .70
J57	CD45	5e black brown	1.75 1.75
		Nos. J52-J57 (6)	3.85 3.85

NEWSPAPER STAMPS

N1   N2

Perf. 11½, 12½ and 13½
1892 Without Gum Unwmk.
Black Surcharge

P1	N1	2½r on 10r green	102.50 67.50
P2	N1	2½r on 20r rose	135.00 90.00
P3	N2	2½r on 10r green	140.00 90.00
P4	N2	2½r on 20r rose	150.00 105.00
		Nos. P1-P4 (4)	527.50 352.50

Green Surcharge

P5	N1	2½r on 5r black	72.50 50.00
P6	N1	2½r on 20r rose	140.00 105.00
P8	N1	2½r on 5r black	150.00 90.00
P9	N2	2½r on 10r green	140.00 105.00
P10	N2	2½r on 20r rose	180.00 135.00
		Nos. P5-P10 (5)	682.50 485.00

Both surcharges exist on No. 18 in green.

N3

1893 Typo. Perf. 11½, 13½

P12	N3	2½r brown	1.50 1.20

For surcharges and overprints see Nos. 85, 166, 275, P13.

No. P12 Overprinted Type "d" in Blue

1899 Without Gum

P13	N3	2½r brown	150.00 50.00

POSTAL TAX STAMPS

Pombal Issue
Common Design Types
1925 Unwmk. Perf. 12½

RA1	CD28	15c orange & black	.75 .75
RA2	CD29	15c orange & black	.75 .75
RA3	CD30	15c orange & black	.75 .75
		Nos. RA1-RA3 (3)	2.25 2.25

Certain revenue stamps (5e, 6e, 7e, 8e and other denominations) were surcharged in 1946 "Assistencia," 2 bars and new values (1e or 1.50e) and used as postal tax stamps.

> Catalogue values for unused stamps in this section, from this point to the end of the section, are for Never Hinged items.

PT1

1948-58 Typo. Perf. 12x11½
Denomination in Black

RA4	PT1	50c yellow grn	4.00 1.10
RA5	PT1	1e carmine rose	4.25 1.50
RA6	PT1	1e emerald ('58)	1.75 .75
RA7	PT1	1.50e bister brown	2.50 1.90
		Nos. RA4-RA7 (4)	12.50 5.25

Denominations of 2e and up were used only for revenue purposes. No. RA6 lacks "Colonia de" below coat of arms.

Type of 1958 Surcharged

m   n

1964-65 Typo. Perf. 12x11½

RA8	PT1(m)	1e on 5e org yel	12.00 12.00
RA9	PT1(n)	1e on 5e org yel ('65)	4.75 4.75

The basic 5e orange yellow does not carry the words "Colonia de."

No. RA6 Surcharged: "Um escudo"
1965

RA10	PT1	1e emerald	2.00 2.00

Type of 1948 Surcharged

1965 Typo. Perf. 12x11½

RA11	PT1	1e emerald	.80 .80

POSTAL TAX DUE STAMPS

Pombal Issue
Common Design Types
1925 Unwmk. Perf. 12½

RAJ1	CD28	30c orange & black	.75 .75
RAJ2	CD29	30c orange & black	.75 .75
RAJ3	CD30	30c orange & black	.75 .75
		Nos. RAJ1-RAJ3 (3)	2.25 2.25

ST. VINCENT

sānt 'vin̪t̪-sənt

LOCATION — Island in the West Indies
GOVT. — Independent state in the British Commonwealth
AREA — 150 sq. mi.
POP. — 120,519 (1999 est.)
CAPITAL — Kingstown

The British colony of St. Vincent became an associated state in 1969 and independent in 1979.

12 Pence = 1 Shilling
20 Shillings = 1 Pound
100 Cents = 1 Dollar (1949)

> **Catalogue values for unused stamps in this country are for Never Hinged items, beginning with Scott 152 in the regular postage section, Scott B1 in the semipostal section, and Scott O1 in the officials section.**

Values for unused stamps are for examples with original gum as defined in the catalogue introduction. Early stamps were spaced extremely narrowly on the plates, and the perforations were applied irregularly.

Therefore, very fine examples of Nos. 1-28, 30-39 will have perforations that cut into the design slightly on one or more sides. Also, very fine examples of Nos. 40-53, 55-60 will have perforations touching the design on at least one side. These stamps with perfs clear of the design on all four sides, especially Nos. 1-28, 30-39, are extremely scarce and command substantially higher prices.

Watermarks

Wmk. 5 — Small Star

Wmk. 380 — "POST OFFICE"

Queen Victoria — A1

1861 Engr. Unwmk. Perf. 14 to 16

1	A1	1p rose	62.50	20.00
a.		Imperf., pair	300.00	
c.		Horiz. pair, imperf. vert.	400.00	
1B	A1	6p yellow green	8,250.	250.00

Perfs on Nos. 1-1B are not clean cut. See Nos. 2-3 for rough perfs.

1862-66　　Rough Perf. 14 to 16

2	A1	1p rose	60.00	20.00
a.		Horiz. pair, imperf. vert.	400.00	

3	A1	6p dark green	65.00	21.00
a.		Imperf., pair	1,250.	
b.		Horiz. pair, imperf. between	14,500.	15,500.
4	A1	1sh slate ('66)	425.00	160.00
		Nos. 2-4 (3)	550.00	201.00

1863-69　　Perf. 11 to 13

5	A1	1p rose	45.00	22.50
6	A1	4p blue ('66)	300.00	125.00
a.		Horiz. pair, imperf. vert.		
7	A1	4p orange ('69)	400.00	175.00
8	A1	6p deep green	250.00	82.50
8A	A1	1sh slate ('66)	2,750.	1,000.
9	A1	1sh indigo ('69)	425.00	100.00
10	A1	1sh brown ('69)	550.00	175.00

Perf. 11 to 13x14 to 16

11	A1	1p rose	6,500.	1,250.
12	A1	1sh slate	300.00	140.00

Rough Perf. 14 to 16

1871-78　　Wmk. 5

13	A1	1p black	65.00	15.50
a.		Vert. pair, imperf. btwn.	20,000.	
14	A1	6p dk blue green	350.00	77.50
a.		Watermark sideways		100.00

Clean-Cut Perf. 14 to 16

14A	A1	1p black	65.00	15.50
14B	A1	6p dp bl grn	1,650.	55.00
c.		6p dull blue green	2,250.	55.00
15	A1	6p pale yel green ('78)	800.00	32.50
15A	A1	1sh vermilion ('77)		50,000.

For surcharge see No. 30.

Perf. 11 to 13

16	A1	4p dk bl ('77)	600.00	110.00
17	A1	1sh dp rose ('72)	825.00	160.00
18	A1	1sh claret ('75)	675.00	300.00

Perf. 11 to 13x14 to 16

20	A1	1p black	95.00	16.50
a.		Horiz. pair, imperf. btwn.	25,000.	
21	A1	6p pale yel grn ('77)	725.00	55.00
22	A1	1sh lilac rose ('72)	6,250.	400.00
23	A1	1sh vermilion ('77)	1,100.	100.00
a.		Horiz. pair, imperf. vert.		

See Nos. 25-28A, 36-39, 42-53. For surcharges see Nos. 30, 32-33, 40, 55-60.

Victoria — A2

Seal of Colony — A3

1880-81　　Perf. 11 to 13

24	A2	½p org ('81)	8.00	11.50
25	A1	1p gray green	190.00	5.50
26	A1	1p drab ('81)	800.00	15.50
27	A1	4p ultra	1,350.	130.00
a.		Horiz. pair, imperf. btwn.		
28	A1	6p yel grn	550.00	77.50
28A	A1	1sh vermilion	900.00	65.00
29	A3	5sh rose	1,275.	1,650.

No. 29 is valued well centered with design well clear of the perfs.
See Nos. 35, 41, 54, 598. For surcharges see Nos. 31-33.

No. 14B Bisected and Surcharged in Red

1880, May　　Perf. 14 to 16

30	A1	1p on half of 6p	600.00	425.00
a.		Unsevered pair	2,250.	1,350.

No. 28 Bisected and Surcharged in Red

1881, Sept. 1

31	A1	½p on half of 6p yel grn ('81)	150.	190.
a.		Unsevered pair	525.	550.
b.		"1" with straight top	1,100.	
c.		Without fraction bar, pair, #31, 31c	4,750.	5,500.

Nos. 28 and 28A Surcharged in Black

c

d

1881, Nov.　　Perf. 11 to 13

32	A1(c)	1p on 6p yel grn	500.	400.
33	A1(d)	1p on 1sh ver	1,850.	925.
a.		3 mm spacing between "4d" and bar	3,500.	2,500.

1883-84　　Wmk. 2　　Perf. 12

35	A2	½p green ('84)	110.00	40.00
36	A1	4p ultra	825.00	55.00
37	A1	4p dull blue ('84)	2,500.	275.00
38	A1	6p yellow grn	175.00	350.00
39	A1	1sh orange ver	175.00	65.00
a.		Imperf., pair		

The ½p orange, 1p rose red, 1p milky blue and 5sh carmine lake were never placed in use. Some authorities believe them to be color trials.

Nos. 35-60 may be found watermarked with single straight line. This is from the frame which encloses each group of 60 watermark designs.

Type of A1 Surcharged in Black — e

1883　　Perf. 14

40	A1(e)	2½p on 1p lake	30.00	1.75

1883-97

41	A2	½p green ('85)	1.10	.65
42	A1	1p drab	80.00	3.50
43	A1	1p rose red ('85)	3.00	1.00
44	A1	1p pink ('86)	6.75	1.90
45	A1	2½p brt blue ('97)	10.00	2.25
46	A1	4p ultra	725.00	85.00
47	A1	4p red brn ('85)	1,100.	25.00
48	A1	4p lake brn ('86)	100.00	1.60
49	A1	4p yellow ('93)	2.00	15.00
a.		4p olive yellow	350.00	350.00
50	A1	5p gray brn ('97)	8.75	32.50
51	A1	6p violet ('88)	225.00	225.00
52	A1	6p red violet ('91)	3.00	25.00
53	A1	1sh org ver ('91)	6.00	17.50
54	A3	5sh car lake ('88)	32.50	60.00
a.		5sh brown lake	35.00	60.00

Grading footnote after No. 29 applies equally to Nos. 54-54a.
For other shades, see the *Scott Classic Catalogue.*

No. 40 Resurcharged in Black

1885, Mar.

55	A1	1p on 2½p on 1p lake	37.50	27.50

Examples with 3-bar cancel are proofs.

Stamps of Type A1 Surcharged in Black or Violet

g

h

j

1890-91

56	A1(e)	2½p on 1p brt blue	2.00	.40
a.		2½p on 1p milky blue	27.50	9.50
b.		2½p on 1p gray blue	27.50	.75
57	A1(g)	2½p on 4p vio brn ('90)	90.00	130.00
a.		Without fraction bar	475.00	575.00

1892-93

58	A1(h)	5p on 4p lake brn (V)	40.00	55.00
59	A1(j)	5p on 6p dp lake ('93)	2.00	1.90
a.		5p on 6p carmine lake	22.50	32.50
b.		Double surcharge	7,750.	4,500.

1897

60	A1(j)	3p on 1p lilac	6.00	26.50

Victoria — A13

Numerals of 1sh and 5sh, type A13, and of 2p, 1sh, 5sh and £1, type A14, are in color on plain tablet.

1898　　Typo.　　Perf. 14

62	A13	½p lilac & grn	3.00	3.00
63	A13	1p lil & car rose	5.00	1.70
64	A13	2½p lilac & ultra	6.50	2.25
65	A13	3p lilac & ol grn	4.50	21.00
66	A13	4p lilac & org	7.25	25.00
67	A13	5p lilac & blk	8.25	21.00
68	A13	6p lilac & brn	14.50	55.00
69	A13	1sh grn & car rose	18.50	60.00
70	A13	5sh green & ultra	100.00	175.00
		Nos. 62-70 (9)	167.50	363.95

Edward VII — A14

1902

71	A14	½p redsh lil & grn	4.75	.75
72	A14	1p vio & car rose	4.75	.35
73	A14	2p violet & black	6.50	7.50
74	A14	2½p violet & ultra	5.50	4.00
75	A14	3p violet & ol grn	5.50	7.25
76	A14	6p violet & brn	12.00	50.00
77	A14	1sh grn & car rose	30.00	70.00
78	A14	2sh green & violet	27.50	65.00
79	A14	5sh green & ultra	82.50	140.00
		Nos. 71-79 (9)	179.00	344.85

1904-11　　Wmk. 3　　Chalky Paper

82	A14	½p vio & grn	1.50	1.50
83	A14	1p vio & car rose	26.00	1.75
84	A14	2½p vio & ultra	19.00	52.50
85	A14	6p vio & brn	19.00	55.00
86	A14	1sh grn & car rose	15.50	17.50
87	A14	2sh vio & bl, *bl*	25.00	52.50
88	A14	5sh grn & red, *yel*	19.00	55.00
89	A14	£1 vio & blk, *red*	300.00	400.00
		Nos. 82-88 (7)	125.00	235.75

#82, 83 and 86 also exist on ordinary paper.
Issued: 1p, 1904; ½p, 6p, 1905; 2½p, 1906; 1sh, 1908; 2sh, 5sh, 1909; £1, July 22, 1911.

"Peace and Justice" — A15

1907　　Engr.　　Ordinary Paper

90	A15	½p yellow green	4.00	2.75
91	A15	1p carmine	4.25	.25
92	A15	2p orange	1.75	7.75
93	A15	2½p ultra	45.00	19.00
94	A15	3p dark violet	9.50	18.00
		Nos. 90-94 (5)	64.50	38.75

"Peace and Justice" — A16

1909 — Without Dot under "d"

95	A16	1p carmine	1.50	.35
96	A16	6p red violet	9.25	50.00
97	A16	1sh black, *green*	5.50	11.00
		Nos. 95-97 (3)	16.25	61.35

1909-11 — With Dot under "d"

98	A16	½p yel grn ('10)	2.50	.70
99	A16	1p carmine	4.00	.25
100	A16	2p gray ('11)	6.50	12.00
101	A16	2½p ultra	9.50	4.50
102	A16	3p violet, *yel*	3.00	14.50
103	A16	6p red violet	20.00	11.00
		Nos. 98-103 (6)	45.50	42.95

King George V — A17

1913-17 — Perf. 14

104	A17	½p green	.75	.25
105	A17	1p carmine	1.00	.25
106	A17	2p slate	3.50	42.50
107	A17	2½p ultra	.60	.90
108	A17	3p violet, *yellow*	1.00	7.50
109	A17	4p red, *yellow*	1.00	2.40
110	A17	5p olive green	2.50	17.00
111	A17	6p claret	2.50	5.00
112	A17	1sh black, *green*	1.75	4.25
113	A17	1sh bister ('14)	4.75	35.00
114	A16	2sh vio & ultra	5.75	40.00
115	A16	5sh dk grn & car	15.00	60.00
116	A16	£1 black & vio	125.00	200.00
		Nos. 104-116 (13)	165.10	415.70

Issued: 5p, 11/7; #113, 5/1/14; others, 1/1/13.

For overprints see Nos. MR1-MR2.

No. 112 Surcharged in Carmine

1915

117	A17	1p on 1sh blk, *grn*	11.00	45.00
a.		"PENNY" & bar double	750.00	725.00
b.		Without period	15.00	
c.		"ONE" omitted	1,550.	1,350.
d.		"ONE" double	750.00	
e.		"PENNY" & bar omitted	1,450.	

Space between surcharge lines varies from 8 to 10mm.

1921-32 — Wmk. 4

118	A17	½p green	2.10	.35
119	A17	1p carmine ('21)	1.15	1.00
120	A17	1½p yel brn ('32)	4.00	.25
121	A17	2p gray	3.00	1.00
122	A17	2½p ultra ('26)	1.50	1.75
123	A17	3p ultra	1.15	7.25
124	A17	3p vio, *yel* ('27)	1.15	1.75
125	A17	4p red, *yel* ('30)	2.10	7.25
126	A17	5p olive green	1.15	7.75
127	A17	6p claret ('27)	1.75	4.25
128	A17	1sh ocher ('27)	4.00	20.00
129	A16	2sh brn vio & ultra	9.00	11.00
130	A16	5sh dk grn & car	21.00	37.50
131	A16	£1 blk & vio ('28)	110.00	150.00
		Nos. 118-131 (14)	163.05	255.10

Common Design Types pictured following the introduction.

Silver Jubilee Issue
Common Design Type

1935, May 6 — Perf. 11x12

134	CD301	1p car & dk bl	.55	4.75
135	CD301	1½p gray blk & ultra	1.40	4.50
136	CD301	2½p ultra & brn	2.50	5.00
137	CD301	1sh brn vio & ind	5.00	7.00
		Nos. 134-137 (4)	9.45	21.25
		Set, never hinged	16.00	

Coronation Issue
Common Design Type

1937, May 12 — Perf. 11x11½

138	CD302	1p dark purple	.25	1.25
139	CD302	1½p dark carmine	.25	1.25
140	CD302	2½p deep ultra	.30	2.25
		Nos. 138-140 (3)	.80	4.75
		Set, never hinged	1.50	

Seal of the Colony — A18

Young's Island and Fort Duvernette — A19

Kingstown and Fort Charlotte — A20

Villa Beach — A21

Victoria Park, Kingstown — A22

1938-47 — Wmk. 4 — Perf. 12

141	A18	½p grn & brt bl	.25	.25
142	A19	1p claret & blue	.25	.25
143	A20	1½p scar & lt grn	.25	.25
144	A18	2p black & green	.30	.25
145	A21	2½p pck bl & ind	.25	.25
145A	A22	2½p choc & grn ('47)	.25	.25
146	A18	3p dk vio & org	.25	.25
146A	A21	3½p dp bl grn & ind ('47)	.40	2.25
147	A18	6p claret & blk	.70	.40
148	A22	1sh green & vio	.70	.75
149	A18	2sh dk vio & brt blue	5.25	1.00
149A	A18	2sh6p dp bl & org brn ('47)	.95	4.25
150	A18	5sh dk grn & car	8.75	3.00
150A	A18	10sh choc & dp vio ('47)	7.50	10.00
151	A18	£1 black & vio	22.50	18.00
		Nos. 141-151 (15)	48.55	41.40
		Set, never hinged	55.00	

Issue date: Mar. 11, 1938.
See Nos. 156-169, 180-184.

Catalogue values for unused stamps in this section, from this point to the end of the section, are for Never Hinged items.

Peace Issue
Common Design Type

1946, Oct. 15 — Engr. — Perf. 13½x14

152	CD303	1½p carmine	.25	.25
153	CD303	3½p deep blue	.25	.25

Silver Wedding Issue
Common Design Types

1948, Nov. 30 — Photo. — Perf. 14x14½

154	CD304	1½p scarlet	.25	.25

Engraved; Name Typographed — Perf. 11½x11

155	CD305	£1 red violet	27.50	30.00

Types of 1938

1949, Mar. 26 — Engr. — Perf. 12

156	A18	1c grn & brt bl	.25	1.75
157	A19	2c claret & bl	.25	.50
158	A20	3c scar & lt grn	.55	1.00
159	A18	4c gray blk & grn	.40	.25
160	A22	5c choc & grn	.25	.25
161	A18	6c dk vio & org	.55	1.25
162	A21	7c pck blue & ind	5.50	1.50
163	A18	12c claret & blk	.50	.25
164	A22	24c green & vio	.50	.55
165	A18	48c dk vio & brt bl	4.50	6.00
166	A18	60c dp bl & org brn	2.00	5.50
167	A18	$1.20 dk grn & car	4.75	4.75
168	A18	$2.40 choc & dp vio	6.75	10.00
169	A18	$4.80 gray blk & vio	13.00	19.00
		Nos. 156-169 (14)	39.75	53.55

For overprints see Nos. 176-179.

UPU Issue
Common Design Types
Engr.; Name Typo. on 6c, 12c
Perf. 13½, 11x11½

1949, Oct. 10 — Wmk. 4

170	CD306	5c blue	.25	.25
171	CD307	6c dp rose violet	.55	2.00
172	CD308	12c red lilac	.30	2.00
173	CD309	24c blue green	1.10	.80
		Nos. 170-173 (4)	2.20	5.05

University Issue
Common Design Types

1951, Feb. 16 — Engr. — Perf. 14x14½

174	CD310	3c red & blue green	.50	.50
175	CD311	12c rose lilac & blk	.50	1.50

Nos. 158-160 and 163 Overprinted in Black

1951, Sept. 21 — Perf. 12

176	A20	3c scarlet & lt grn	.30	1.60
177	A18	4c gray blk & grn	.30	.60
178	A22	5c chocolate & grn	.30	.60
179	A18	12c claret & blk	.95	1.25
		Nos. 176-179 (4)	1.85	4.05

Adoption of a new constitution for the Windward Islands, 1951.

Type of 1938-47

1952

180	A18	1c gray black & green	.30	2.25
181	A18	3c dk violet & orange	.30	2.25
182	A18	4c green & brt blue	.30	.25
183	A20	6c scarlet & dp green	.30	2.00
184	A21	10c peacock blue & ind	.45	.35
		Nos. 180-184 (5)	1.65	7.10

Coronation Issue
Common Design Type

1953, June 2 — Perf. 13½x13

185	CD312	4c dk green & blk	.50	.30

Elizabeth II — A23

Seal of Colony — A24

Perf. 13x14
1955, Sept. 16 — Wmk. 4 — Engr.

186	A23	1c orange	.25	.25
187	A23	2c violet blue	.25	.25
188	A23	3c gray	.25	.25
189	A23	4c dk red brown	.25	.25
190	A23	5c scarlet	.25	.25
191	A23	10c purple	.45	.25
192	A23	15c deep blue	.70	1.00
193	A23	20c green	.85	.25
194	A23	25c brown black	1.50	.25

Perf. 14

195	A24	50c chocolate	9.25	3.25
196	A24	$1 dull green	15.00	2.10
197	A24	$2.50 deep blue	15.00	15.00
		Nos. 186-197 (12)	44.00	23.35

See Nos. 205-213.

West Indies Federation
Common Design Type
Perf. 11½x11

1958, Apr. 22 — Wmk. 314

198	CD313	3c green	.30	.25
199	CD313	6c blue	.40	1.00
200	CD313	12c carmine rose	.80	.50
		Nos. 198-200 (3)	1.50	1.75

Freedom from Hunger Issue
Common Design Type

1963, June 4 — Photo. — Perf. 14x14½

201	CD314	8c lilac	.90	.50

Red Cross Centenary Issue
Common Design Type

1963, Sept. 2 — Litho. — Perf. 13

202	CD315	4c black & red	.25	.25
203	CD315	8c ultra & red	.65	.65

Types of 1955
Perf. 13x14

1964-65 — Wmk. 314 — Engr.

205	A23	1c orange	.25	.25
206	A23	2c violet blue	.25	.25
207	A23	3c gray	.55	.60
208	A23	5c scarlet	.30	.30
209	A23	10c purple	.45	.45
a.		Perf. 12½	.25	.25
210	A23	15c deep blue	1.00	.80
a.		Perf. 12½	.45	.30
211	A23	20c green	.70	.75
a.		Perf. 12½	5.00	2.00
212	A23	25c brown black	1.25	1.35
a.		Perf. 12½	.80	1.25

Perf. 14

213	A24	50c chocolate ('65)	5.75	5.50
a.		Perf. 12½	5.00	7.00
		Nos. 205-213 (9)	10.50	10.25

Scout Emblem and Merit Badges — A25

1964, Nov. 23 — Litho. — Perf. 14

216	A25	1c dk brn & brt yel grn	.25	.25
217	A25	4c dk red brn & brt bl	.25	.25
218	A25	20c dk vio & org	.30	.25
219	A25	50c green & red	.45	.60
		Nos. 216-219 (4)	1.25	1.35

Boy Scouts of St. Vincent, 50th anniv.

Breadfruit and Capt. Bligh's Ship "Providence" — A26

Designs: 1c, Tropical fruit. 25c, Doric temple and pond, vert. 40c, Blooming talipot palm and Doric temple, vert.

Perf. 14½x13½, 13½x14½
1965, Mar. 23 — Photo. — Wmk. 314

220	A26	1c dk green & multi	.25	.25
221	A26	4c lt & dk brn grn & yel	.25	.25
222	A26	25c blue, grn & bister	.25	.25
223	A26	40c dk blue & multi	.30	1.10
		Nos. 220-223 (4)	1.05	1.85

Bicentenary of the Botanic Gardens.

ITU Issue
Common Design Type

1965, May 17 — Litho. — Perf. 11x11½

224	CD317	4c blue & yel grn	.25	.25
225	CD317	48c yellow & orange	.55	.65

Boat Building, Bequia A27

Woman Carrying Bananas — A28

Designs: 2c, Friendship Beach, Bequia. 3c, Terminal building. 5c, Crater Lake. 6c, Rock carvings, Carib Stone. 8c, Arrowroot. 10c, Owia saltpond. 12c, Ship at deep water wharf. 20c, Sea Island cotton. 25c, Map of St. Vincent and neighboring islands. 50c, Breadfruit. $1, Baleine Falls. $2.50, St. Vincent parrot. $5, Coat of arms.

Perf. 14x13½, 13½x14

			Wmk. 314	
1965-67		Photo.		
226	A27	1c (BEQUIA)	.25	.75
226A	A27	1c (BEQUIA)	.60	.35
227	A27	2c lt ultra, grn, yel & red	.25	.25
228	A27	3c red, yel & brn	.40	.25
229	A28	4c brn, ultra & yel	.75	.35
a.		Wmkd. sideways	.50	.25
230	A27	5c pur, bl, yel & grn	.25	.25
231	A28	6c sl grn, yel & gray	.25	.30
232	A28	8c pur, yel & grn	.40	.25
233	A27	10c org brn, yel & bluish grn	.40	.25
234	A27	12c grnsh bl, yel & pink	.65	.25
235	A28	20c brt yel, grn, pur & brn	.40	.25
236	A28	25c ultra, grn & vio blue	.45	.25
237	A28	50c grn, yel & bl	.45	.35
238	A28	$1 vio bl, lt grn & dk sl grn	4.00	.45
239	A28	$2.50 pale lilac & multi	19.00	8.50
240	A28	$5 dull vio blue & multi	4.25	10.50
		Nos. 226-240 (16)	32.75	23.55

Issued: No. 226A, 8/8/67; others, 8/16/65.
For overprint see No. 270.

Churchill Memorial Issue
Common Design Type

1966, Jan. 24   **Perf. 14**

Design in Black, Gold and Carmine Rose

241	CD319	1c bright blue	.25	.25
242	CD319	4c green	.25	.25
243	CD319	20c brown	.35	.35
244	CD319	40c violet	.65	.90
		Nos. 241-244 (4)	1.50	1.75

Royal Visit Issue
Common Design Type

1966, Feb. 4   **Litho.**   **Perf. 11x12**

Portrait in Black

245	CD320	4c violet blue	.50	.25
246	CD320	25c dk carmine rose	2.25	1.10

WHO Headquarters Issue
Common Design Type

1966, Sept. 20   **Litho.**   **Perf. 14**

247	CD322	4c multicolored	.25	.25
248	CD322	25c multicolored	.90	.80

UNESCO Anniversary Issue
Common Design Type

1966, Dec. 1   **Litho.**   **Perf. 14**

249	CD323	4c "Education"	.25	.25
250	CD323	8c "Science"	.45	.25
251	CD323	25c "Culture"	1.60	.85
		Nos. 249-251 (3)	2.30	1.35

View of Mt. Coke Area A29

Designs: 8c, Kingstown Methodist Church. 25c, First license to perform marriage, May 15, 1867. 35c, Arms of Conference of the Methodist Church in the Caribbean and the Americas.

Perf. 14x14½

			Wmk. 314	
1967, Dec. 1		Photo.		
252	A29	2c multicolored	.25	.25
253	A29	8c multicolored	.25	.25
254	A29	25c multicolored	.25	.25
255	A29	35c multicolored	.25	.25
		Nos. 252-255 (4)	1.00	1.00

Attainment of autonomy by the Methodist Church in the Caribbean and the Americas, and opening of headquarters near St. John's, Antigua, May 1967.
For overprints see Nos. 268-269, 271.

Caribbean Meteorological Institute, Barbados — A30

Perf. 14x14½

			Wmk. 314	
1968, June 28		Photo.		
256	A30	4c cerise & multi	.25	.25
257	A30	25c vermilion & multi	.25	.25
258	A30	35c violet blue & multi	.25	.25
		Nos. 256-258 (3)	.75	.75

Issued for World Meteorological Day.

Martin Luther King, Jr. and Cotton Pickers A31

Perf. 13½x13

			Wmk. 314	
1968, Aug. 28		Litho.		
259	A31	5c violet & multi	.25	.25
260	A31	25c gray & multi	.25	.25
261	A31	35c brown red & multi	.25	.25
		Nos. 259-261 (3)	.75	.75

Dr. Martin Luther King, Jr. (1929-68), American civil rights leader.

Scales of Justice and Human Rights Flame — A32

3c, Speaker addressing demonstrators, horiz.

Perf. 13x14, 14x13

			Unwmk.	
1968, Nov. 1		Photo.		
262	A32	3c orange & multi	.25	.25
263	A32	35c grnsh blue & vio blue	.25	.25

International Human Rights Year.

Carnival Costume — A33

5c, Sketch of a steel bandsman. 8c, Revelers, horiz. 25c, Queen of Bands & attendants.

1969, Feb. 17   **Litho.**   **Perf. 14½**

264	A33	1c multicolored	.25	.25
265	A33	5c red & dark brown	.25	.25
266	A33	8c multicolored	.25	.25
267	A33	25c multicolored	.25	.25
		Nos. 264-267 (4)	1.00	1.00

St. Vincent Carnival celebration, Feb. 17.

Nos. 252-253, 236 and 255 Overprinted: "METHODIST / CONFERENCE / MAY / 1969"

Perf. 14x14½, 13½x14

			Wmk. 314	
1969, May 14		Photo.		
268	A29	2c multicolored	.25	.25
269	A29	8c multicolored	.25	.25
270	A28	25c multicolored	.25	.25
271	A29	35c multicolored	1.00	2.00
		Nos. 268-271 (4)	1.75	2.75

1st Caribbean Methodist Conf. held outside Antigua.

"Strength in Unity" — A34

5c, 25c, Map of the Caribbean, vert.

Perf. 13½x13, 13x13½

				Litho.
1969, July 1				
272	A34	2c orange, yel & blk	.25	.25
273	A34	5c lilac & multi	.25	.25
274	A34	8c emerald, yel & blk	.25	.25
275	A34	25c blue & multi	.25	.25
		Nos. 272-275 (4)	1.00	1.00

1st anniv. of CARIFTA (Caribbean Free Trade Area.)

Flag and Arms of St. Vincent — A35

Designs: 10c, Uprising of 1795. 50c, Government House.

Perf. 14x14½

			Wmk. 314	
1969, Oct. 27		Photo.		
276	A35	4c deep ultra & multi	.25	.25
277	A35	10c olive & multi	.25	.25
278	A35	50c orange, gray & blk	.75	.50
		Nos. 276-278 (3)	1.25	1.00

Green Heron A36

Birds: ½c, House wren, vert. 2c, Bullfinches. 3c, St. Vincent parrots. 4c, St. Vincent solitaire, vert. 5c, Scalynecked pigeon, vert. 6c, Bananaquits. 8c, Purple-throated Carib. 10c, Mangrove cuckoo, vert. 12c, Black hawk, vert. 20c, Bare-eyed thrush. 25c, Hooded tanager. 50c, Blue-hooded euphonia. $1, Barn owl, vert. $2.50, Yellow-bellied elaenia, vert. $5, Ruddy quail-dove.

Wmk. 314 Upright on ½c, 4c, 5c, 10c, 12c, 50c, $5, Sideways on Others

1970, Jan. 12		Photo.		**Perf. 14**
279	A36	½c multicolored	.25	.25
280	A36	1c multicolored	.25	.25
281	A36	2c multicolored	.25	.25
282	A36	3c multicolored	.25	.25
283	A36	4c multicolored	.25	.25
284	A36	5c multicolored	1.25	.65
285	A36	6c multicolored	.40	.35
286	A36	8c multicolored	.40	.25
287	A36	10c multicolored	.45	.35
288	A36	12c multicolored	.60	.40
289	A36	20c multicolored	.80	.50
290	A36	25c multicolored	.80	.50
291	A36	50c multicolored	1.25	.75
292	A36	$1 multicolored	3.00	1.50
293	A36	$2.50 multicolored	6.00	4.00
294	A36	$5 multicolored	14.00	10.00
		Nos. 279-294 (16)	30.20	20.50

See Nos. 379-381. For surcharges see Nos. 364-366, 3239, 3242, 3265.

Wmk. 314 Upright on 2c, 3c, 6c, 20c, Sideways on Others

1973				
281a	A36	2c multicolored	.35	.45
282a	A36	3c multicolored	.35	.45
283a	A36	4c multicolored	.35	.40
284a	A36	5c multicolored	.35	.30
285a	A36	6c multicolored	.50	.65
287a	A36	10c multicolored	.50	.30
288a	A36	12c multicolored	.75	.65
289a	A36	20c multicolored	.85	.40
		Nos. 281a-289a (8)	4.00	3.60

DHC6 Twin Otter A37

20th anniv. of regular air services: 8c, Grumman Goose amphibian. 10c, Hawker Siddeley 748. 25c, Douglas DC-3.

Perf. 14x13

			Wmk. 314	
1970, Mar. 13		Litho.		
295	A37	5c lt blue & multi	.25	.25
296	A37	8c lt green & multi	.25	.25
297	A37	10c pink & multi	.35	.25
298	A37	25c yellow & multi	.75	.65
		Nos. 295-298 (4)	1.60	1.40

Nurse and Children A38

Red Cross and: 5c, First aid. 12c, Volunteers. 25c, Blood transfusion.

1970, June 1   **Photo.**   **Perf. 14**

299	A38	3c blue & multi	.25	.25
300	A38	5c yellow & multi	.25	.25
301	A38	12c lt green & multi	.35	.25
302	A38	25c pale salmon & multi	.65	.55
		Nos. 299-302 (4)	1.50	1.30

Centenary of British Red Cross Society.

St. George's Cathedral — A39

Designs: ½c, 50c, Angel and Two Marys at the Tomb, stained glass window, vert. 25c, St. George's Cathedral, front view, vert. 35c, Interior with altar.

Perf. 14x14½, 14½x14

			Wmk. 314	
1970, Sept. 7		Litho.		
303	A39	½c multicolored	.25	.25
304	A39	5c multicolored	.25	.25
305	A39	25c multicolored	.25	.25
306	A39	35c multicolored	.25	.25
307	A39	50c multicolored	.25	.30
		Nos. 303-307 (5)	1.25	1.30

St. George's Anglican Cathedral, 150th anniv.

Virgin and Child, by Giovanni Bellini — A40

Christmas: 25c, 50c, Adoration of the Shepherds, by Louis Le Nain, horiz.

1970, Nov. 23   **Photo.**   **Wmk. 314**

308	A40	8c brt violet & multi	.25	.25
309	A40	25c crimson & multi	.25	.25
310	A40	35c yellow grn & multi	.25	.25
311	A40	50c sapphire & multi	.25	.25
		Nos. 308-311 (4)	1.00	1.00

Post Office and St. Vincent No. 1B A41

New Post Office and: 4c, $1, St. Vincent No. 1. 25c, as 2c.

1971, Mar. 29   **Perf. 14½x14**

312	A41	2c violet & multi	.25	.25
313	A41	4c olive & multi	.25	.25
314	A41	25c brown org & multi	.25	.25
315	A41	$1 lt green & multi	.25	.45
		Nos. 312-315 (4)	1.00	1.20

110th anniv. of 1st stamps of St. Vincent.

National Trust Emblem, Fish and
Birds — A42

Designs: 30c, 45c, Cannon at Ft. Charlotte.

Perf. 13½x14

1971, Aug. 4	**Litho.**		**Wmk. 314**	
316	A42	12c emerald & multi	.25	.80
317	A42	30c lt blue & multi	.35	.35
318	A42	40c brt pink & multi	.50	.40
319	A42	45c black & multi	.70	1.00
		Nos. 316-319 (4)	1.80	2.55

Publicity for the National Trust (for conservation of wild life and historic buildings).

Holy Family with Angels (detail), by
Pietro da Cortona
A43

Christmas: 5c, 25c, Madonna Appearing to
St. Anthony, by Domenico Tiepolo, vert.

1971, Oct. 6	**Perf. 14x14½, 14½x14**			
320	A43	5c rose & multi	.25	.25
321	A43	10c lt green & multi	.25	.25
322	A43	25c lt blue & multi	.25	.25
323	A43	$1 yellow & multi	.25	.45
		Nos. 320-323 (4)	1.00	1.20

Careening
A44

Designs: 5c, 20c, Seine fishermen. 6c, 50c,
Map of Grenadines. 15c, as 1c.

1971, Nov. 25	**Perf. 14x13½**			
324	A44	1c dp ver & multi	.25	.25
325	A44	5c blue & multi	.25	.25
326	A44	6c yel grn & multi	.25	.25
327	A44	15c org brn & multi	.25	.25
328	A44	20c yellow & multi	.25	.30
329	A44	50c blue, blk & plum	.50	1.00
a.		Souvenir sheet of 6, #324-329	11.00	11.00
		Nos. 324-329 (6)	1.75	2.30

The Grenadines of St. Vincent tourist issue.

Grenadier
Company
Private,
1764 — A45

Designs: 30c, Battalion Company officer,
1772. 50c, Grenadier Company private, 1772.

1972, Feb. 14	**Perf. 14x13½**			
330	A45	12c gray violet & multi	.30	.30
331	A45	30c gray blue & multi	.80	.50
332	A45	50c dark gray & multi	1.40	1.25
		Nos. 330-332 (3)	2.50	2.05

Breadnut — A46

1972, May 16	**Litho.**	**Perf. 14x13½**		
333	A46	3c shown	.25	.35
334	A46	5c Papaya	.25	.25
335	A46	12c Rose apples	.30	.40
336	A46	25c Mangoes	.80	.75
		Nos. 333-336 (4)	1.60	1.75

Flowers of St.
Vincent — A47

1972, July 31	**Litho.**	**Perf. 13½x13**		
337	A47	1c Candlestick Cassia	.25	.25
338	A47	30c Lobster claw	.30	.30
339	A47	40c White trumpet	.35	.35
340	A47	$1 Flowers, Soufriere tree	.90	1.10
		Nos. 337-340 (4)	1.80	2.00

For surcharge see No. 3266.

Sir Charles Brisbane, Family
Arms — A48

Designs: 30c, Sailing ship "Arethusa." $1,
Sailing ship "Blake."

1972, Sept. 29	**Wmk. 314**	**Perf. 13½**		
341	A48	20c yel, brn & gold	.30	.30
342	A48	30c lilac & multi	.30	.30
343	A48	$1 multicolored	1.15	1.25
a.		Souvenir sheet of 3, #341-343	6.50	6.50
		Nos. 341-343 (3)	1.75	1.85

Bicentenary of the birth of Sir Charles Brisbane, naval hero, governor of St. Vincent.

Silver Wedding Issue, 1972
Common Design Type

Design: Queen Elizabeth II, Prince Philip,
arrowroot plant, breadfruit foliage and fruit.

1972, Nov. 20	**Photo.**	**Perf. 14x14½**		
344	CD324	30c rose brn & multi	.25	.25
345	CD324	$1 multicolored	.30	.30

Columbus Sighting St. Vincent — A49

12c, Caribs watching Columbus' ships. 30c,
Christopher Columbus. 50c, Santa Maria.

1973, Jan. 18	**Litho.**	**Perf. 13**		
346	A49	5c multicolored	.25	.30
347	A49	12c multicolored	.25	.45
348	A49	30c multicolored	.70	.75
349	A49	50c multicolored	1.40	2.25
		Nos. 346-349 (4)	2.60	3.75

475th anniversary of Columbus's Third Voyage to the West Indies.

The Last Supper — A50

Perf. 14x13½				
1973, Apr. 19	**Litho.**		**Wmk. 314**	
350	A50	15c red & multi	.25	.25
351	A50	60c red & multi	.25	.25
352	A50	$1 red & multi	.30	.30
a.		A50 Strip of 3, #350-352	.80	.80

Easter.

William Wilberforce and Slave Auction
Poster — A51

40c, Slaves working on sugar plantation.
50c, Wilberforce & medal commemorating 1st
anniversary of abolition of slavery.

1973, July 11		**Perf. 14x13½**		
353	A51	30c multicolored	.25	.25
354	A51	40c multicolored	.25	.25
355	A51	50c multicolored	.30	.30
		Nos. 353-355 (3)	.80	.80

140th anniv. of the death of William Wilberforce (1759-1833), member of British Parliament who fought for abolition of slavery.

Families — A52

Design: 40c, Families and "IPPF."

1973, Oct. 3		**Perf. 14½**		
356	A52	12c multicolored	.25	.25
357	A52	40c multicolored	.25	.25

Intl. Planned Parenthood Assoc., 21st anniv.

Princess Anne's Wedding Issue
Common Design Type

1973, Nov. 14		**Perf. 14**		
358	CD325	50c slate & multi	.25	.25
359	CD325	70c gray green & multi	.25	.25

Administration Buildings, Mona
University — A53

Designs: 10c, University Center, Kingstown.
30c, Mona University, aerial view. $1, Coat of
arms of University of West Indies.

1973, Dec. 13	**Perf. 14½x14, 14x14½**			
360	A53	5c multicolored	.25	.25
361	A53	10c multicolored	.25	.25
362	A53	30c multicolored	.25	.25
363	A53	$1 multicolored	.25	.50
		Nos. 360-363 (4)	1.00	1.25

University of the West Indies, 25th anniv.

Nos. 291, 286 and 292 Surcharged

1973, Dec. 15	**Photo.**	**Perf. 14**		
364	A36	30c on 50c multi	.25	1.00
365	A36	40c on 8c multi	.35	.35
366	A36	$10 on $1 multi	8.50	8.50
		Nos. 364-366 (3)	9.10	9.85

The position of the surcharge and shape of
obliterating bars differs on each denomination.

Descent from the
Cross — A54

Easter: 30c, Descent from the Cross. 40c,
Pietà. $1, Resurrection. Designs are from
sculptures in Victoria and Albert Museum,
London, and Provincial Museum, Valladolid
(40c).

1974, Apr. 10	**Litho.**	**Perf. 13½x13**		
367	A54	5c multicolored	.25	.25
368	A54	30c multicolored	.25	.25
369	A54	40c multicolored	.25	.25
370	A54	$1 multicolored	.25	.25
		Nos. 367-370 (4)	1.00	1.00

"Istra"
A55

1974, June 28		**Perf. 14½**		
371	A55	15c shown	.25	.25
372	A55	20c "Oceanic"	.25	.25
373	A55	30c "Alexander Pushkin"	.30	.25
374	A55	$1 "Europa"	.80	1.10
a.		Souvenir sheet of 4, #371-374	1.75	1.75
		Nos. 371-374 (4)	1.60	1.85

Cruise ships visiting Kingstown.

Arrows
Circling
UPU
Emblem
A56

UPU, cent.: 12c, Post horn and globe. 60c,
Target over map of islands, hand canceler.
90c, Goode's map projection.

1974, July 25		**Perf. 14½**		
375	A56	5c violet & multi	.25	.25
376	A56	12c ocher, green & blue	.25	.25
377	A56	60c blue green & multi	.25	.25
378	A56	90c red & multi	.25	.30
		Nos. 375-378 (4)	1.00	1.05

Bird Type of 1970

Birds: 30c, Royal tern. 40c, Brown pelican,
vert. $10, Magnificent frigate bird, vert.

Wmk. 314 Sideways on 40c, $10, Upright on 30c

1974, Aug. 29		**Litho.**	***Perf. 14½***
379 A36	30c multicolored	2.00	.75
380 A36	40c multicolored	2.00	.75
381 A36	$10 multicolored	13.00	10.00
Nos. 379-381 (3)		17.00	11.50

Scout Emblem and Badges — A57

		Perf. 13½x14	
1974, Oct. 9			**Wmk. 314**
385 A57	10c lilac & multi	.25	.25
386 A57	25c bister & multi	.25	.25
387 A57	45c gray & multi	.35	.30
388 A57	$1 multicolored	.65	1.10
Nos. 385-388 (4)		1.50	1.90

St. Vincent Boy Scouts, 60th anniversary.

Churchill as Prime Minister — A58

Designs (Churchill as): 35c, Lord Warden of the Cinque Ports. 45c, First Lord of the Admiralty. $1, Royal Air Force officer.

1974, Nov. 28		***Perf. 14½x14***	
389 A58	25c multicolored	.25	.25
390 A58	35c multicolored	.25	.25
391 A58	45c multicolored	.25	.25
392 A58	$1 multicolored	.25	.45
Nos. 389-392 (4)		1.00	1.20

Sir Winston Churchill (1874-1965), birth centenary. Sheets of 30 in 2 panes of 15 with inscribed gutter between.

A59　　　　　A60

1974, Dec. 5		***Perf. 12x12½***	
393 A59	3c like 8c	.25	.25
394 A59	3c like 35c	.25	.25
395 A60	3c like 45c	.25	.25
396 A60	3c like $1	.25	.25
a.	Strip of 4, #393-396	.25	.25
397 A59	8c Shepherds	.25	.25
398 A59	35c Virgin, Child and Star	.25	.25
399 A60	45c St. Joseph, Ass & Ox	.25	.25
400 A60	$1 Three Kings	.25	.40
Nos. 393-400 (8)		2.00	2.15

Christmas. Nos. 396a, 397-400 have continuous picture.

Giant Mask and Dancers — A61

Designs: 15c, Pineapple dancers. 25c, Giant bouquet. 35c, Girl dancers. 45c, Butterfly dancers. $1.25, Sun and moon dancers and float.

Wmk. 314

1975, Feb. 7		**Litho.**	***Perf. 14***
401 A61	1c multicolored	.25	.25
a.	Bklt. pane of 2 + label	.30	
b.	Bklt. pane of 3, #401, 403, 405	.75	
402 A61	15c multicolored	.25	.25
a.	Bklt. pane of 3, #402, 404, 406	1.75	
403 A61	25c multicolored	.25	.25
404 A61	35c multicolored	.25	.25
405 A61	45c multicolored	.25	.25
406 A61	$1.25 multicolored	.25	.45
a.	Souvenir sheet of 6, #401-406	1.75	1.75
Nos. 401-406 (6)		1.50	1.70

Kingstown carnival 1975.

French Angelfish — A62

Type I　　　　　Type II

Two types of $2.50:
I — Line to fish's mouth.
II — Line removed (1976).

Fish and whales — 2c, Spotfin butter-flyfish. 3c, Horse-eyed jack. 4c, Mackerel. 5c, French grunts. 6c, Spotted goatfish. 8c, Ballyhoos. 10c, Sperm whale. 12c, Humpback whale. 15c, Cowfish. 20c, Queen angelfish. 25c, Princess parrotfish. 40c, Red hind. 45c, Atlantic flying fish. 50c, Porkfish. $1, Queen triggerfish. $2.50, Sailfish. $5, Dolphinfish. $10, Blue marlin.

Wmk. 373

1975, Apr. 10		**Litho.**	***Perf. 14***
407 A62	1c shown	.25	.50
408 A62	2c multicolored	.25	.75
409 A62	3c multicolored	.25	.45
410 A62	4c multicolored	.25	.25
411 A62	5c multicolored	.25	.35
412 A62	6c multicolored	.25	.75
413 A62	8c multicolored	.25	2.00
414 A62	10c multicolored	.50	.25
415 A62	12c multicolored	.50	1.75
416 A62	15c multicolored	1.25	1.75
417 A62	20c multicolored	.30	.25
418 A62	25c multicolored	.35	.25
419 A62	35c multicolored	.60	2.00
420 A62	45c multicolored	.60	.90
421 A62	50c multicolored	.70	2.25
422 A62	$1 multicolored	1.50	.90
423 A62	$2.50 Type I	3.25	2.25
a.	Type II	3.00	1.25
424 A62	$5 multicolored	7.00	4.00
425 A62	$10 multicolored	12.00	8.50
Nos. 407-425 (19)		30.30	30.10

The 4c, 10c, 20c, $1, were reissued with "1976" below design; 1c, 2c, 3c, 5c, 6c, 8c, 12c, 50c, $10, with "1977" below design; 10c with "1978" below design.
No. 423a issued 7/12/76.
See Nos. 472-474. For surcharges and overprints see Nos. 463-464, 499-500, 502-503, 572-581, 584-586.

Cutting Bananas — A63

Banana industry: 35c, La Croix packing station. 45c, Women cleaning and packing bananas. 70c, Freighter loading bananas.

1975, June 26		**Wmk. 314**	***Perf. 14***
426 A63	25c blue & multi	.25	.25
427 A63	35c blue & multi	.25	.25
428 A63	45c carmine & multi	.25	.25
429 A63	70c carmine & multi	.30	.30
Nos. 426-429 (4)		1.05	1.05

Snorkel Diving — A64

Designs: 20c, Aquaduct Golf Course. 35c, Steel band at Mariner's Inn. 45c, Sunbathing at Young Island. $1.25, Yachting marina.

Wmk. 373

1975, July 31		**Litho.**	***Perf. 13½***
430 A64	15c multicolored	.30	.25
431 A64	20c multicolored	.65	.40
432 A64	35c multicolored	.95	.40
433 A64	45c multicolored	.95	.40
434 A64	$1.25 multicolored	2.25	2.00
Nos. 430-434 (5)		5.10	3.70

Tourist publicity.
For surcharge see No. 3302.

Presidents Washington, John Adams, Jefferson and Madison — A65

U.S. Presidents: 1c, Monroe, John Quincy Adams, Jackson, Van Buren. 1½c, Wm. Harrison, Tyler, Polk, Taylor. 5c, Fillmore, Pierce, Buchanan, Lincoln. 10c, Johnson, Grant, Hayes, Garfield. 25c, Arthur, Cleveland, Benjamin Harrison, McKinley. 35c, Theodore Roosevelt, Taft, Wilson, Harding. 45c, Coolidge, Hoover, Franklin D. Roosevelt, Truman. $1, Eisenhower, Kennedy, Lyndon B. Johnson, Nixon. $2, Ford and White House.

1975, Sept. 11		**Unwmk.**	***Perf. 14½***
435 A65	½c violet & blk	.25	.25
436 A65	1c green & black	.25	.25
437 A65	1½c rose lilac & blk	.25	.25
438 A65	5c yellow grn & blk	.25	.25
439 A65	10c ultra & blk	.25	.25
440 A65	25c ocher & blk	.25	.25
441 A65	35c brt blue & blk	.25	.25
442 A65	45c carmine & blk	.25	.25
443 A65	$1 orange & blk	.25	.35
444 A65	$2 lt olive & blk	.25	.65
a.	Souvenir sheet of 10, #435-444 + 2 labels	2.75	2.75
Nos. 435-444 (10)		2.50	3.00

Bicentenary of American Independence. Each issued in sheets of 10 stamps and 2 labels picturing the White House, Capitol, Mt. Vernon, etc.

Nativity — A66

No. 445a, 8c, Star of Bethlehem. No. 445b, 45c, Shepherds. No. 445c, $1, Kings. No. 445d, 35c, Nativity.

Se-tenant Pairs, #a.-b.
a. — Top stamp.
b. — Bottom stamp.

Wmk. 314

1975, Dec. 4		**Litho.**	***Perf. 14***
445 A66	3c Triangular block of 4, #a.-d.	.55	.45
446 A66	8c Pair, #a.-b.	.25	.25
447 A66	35c Pair, #a.-b.	.45	.25
448 A66	45c Pair, #a.-b.	.45	.30
449 A66	$1 Pair, #a.-b.	.75	.60
Nos. 445-449 (5)		2.45	1.85

Christmas. No. 445 has continuous design.

Carnival Costumes — A68

Designs: 2c, Humpty-Dumpty people. 5c, Smiling faces (masks). 35c, Dragon worshippers. 45c, Duck costume. $1.25, Bumble bee dance.

		Perf. 13x13½	
1976, Feb. 19		**Litho.**	**Wmk. 373**
457 A68	1c carmine & multi	.25	.25
a.	Bklt pane of 2, #457-458 + label	.25	
458 A68	2c black & multi	.25	.25
a.	Bklt. pane of 3, #458-460	.60	
459 A68	5c lt blue & multi	.25	.25
460 A68	35c lt blue & multi	.25	.25
a.	Bklt. pane of 3, #460-462	2.00	
461 A68	45c black & multi	.25	.25
462 A68	$1.25 carmine & multi	.30	.30
Nos. 457-462 (6)		1.55	1.55

Kingstown carnival 1976.

Nos. 409 and 421 Surcharged with New Value and Bar

1976, Apr. 8		**Wmk. 314**	***Perf. 14***
463 A62	70c on 3c multi	.65	1.00
464 A62	90c on 50c multi	.65	1.25

Yellow Hibiscus and Blue-headed Hummingbird A69

Designs: 10c, Single pink hibiscus and crested hummingbird. 35c, Single white hibiscus and purple-throated carib. 45c, Common red hibiscus and blue-headed hummingbird. $1.25, Single peach hibiscus and green-throated carib.

1976, May 20		**Litho.**	**Wmk. 373**
465 A69	5c multicolored	.25	.25
466 A69	10c multicolored	.35	.30
467 A69	35c multicolored	1.15	1.00
468 A69	45c multicolored	1.75	1.50
469 A69	$1.25 multicolored	5.50	4.00
Nos. 465-469 (5)		9.00	7.05

Map of West Indies, Bats, Wicket and Ball A69a

Prudential Cup — A69b

1976, Sept. 16		**Unwmk.**	***Perf. 14***
470 A69a	15c lt blue & multi	.60	.30
471 A69b	45c lilac rose & blk	1.40	1.00

World Cricket Cup, won by West Indies Team, 1975.

Fish Type of 1975

1976, Oct. 14		**Wmk. 373**	***Perf. 14***
472 A62	15c Skipjack	3.50	2.50
473 A62	70c Albacore	6.50	3.25
474 A62	90c Pompano	6.50	.70
Nos. 472-474 (3)		16.50	6.45

The 15c exists dated "1977."

For overprints see Nos. 501, 582-583.

St. Mary's R.C. Church,
Kingstown — A70

Christmas: 45c, Anglican Church,
Georgetown. 50c, Methodist Church,
Georgetown. $1.25, St. George's Anglican
Cathedral, Kingstown.

1976, Nov. 18		Litho.		Perf. 14	
475	A70	35c multicolored		.25	.25
476	A70	45c multicolored		.25	.25
477	A70	50c multicolored		.25	.25
478	A70	$1.25 multicolored		.30	.55
		Nos. 475-478 (4)		1.05	1.30

For surcharge see No. 3303.

Barrancoid Pot-stand, c. 450
A.D. — A71

Designs (National Trust Emblem and): 45c,
National Museum. 70c, Carib stone head, c.
1510. $1, Ciboney petroglyph, c. 4000 B.C.

1976, Dec. 16				Perf. 13½	
479	A71	5c multicolored		.25	.25
480	A71	45c multicolored		.25	.25
481	A71	70c multicolored		.25	.25
482	A71	$1 multicolored		.25	.45
		Nos. 479-482 (4)		1.00	1.20

Carib Indian art and establishment of
National Museum in Botanical Gardens,
Kingstown.
For surcharges see Nos. 3256, 3290.

Kings William I, William II, Henry I, Stephen A72

Kings and Queens of England: 1c, Henry II,
Richard I, John, Henry III. 1½c, Edward I, II,
III, Richard II. 2c, Henry IV, V, VI, Edward IV.
5c, Edward V, Richard III, Henry VII, VIII. 10c,
Edward VI, Lady Jane Grey, Mary I, Elizabeth
I. 25c, James I, Charles I, II, James II. 35c,
William III, Mary II, Anne, George I. 45c,
George II, III, IV. 75c, William IV, Victoria,
Edward VII. $1, George V, Edward VIII.
George VI. $2, Elizabeth II, coronation.

Wmk. 373
1977, Feb. 7		Litho.		Perf. 13½	
483	A72	½c multicolored		.25	.25
a.		Bkt. pane of 4, #483-486		3.00	
484	A72	1c multicolored		.25	.25
485	A72	1½c multicolored		.25	.25
486	A72	2c multicolored		.25	.25
487	A72	5c multicolored		.25	.25
a.		Bkt. pane of 4, #487-490		3.00	
488	A72	10c multicolored		.25	.25
489	A72	25c multicolored		.25	.25
490	A72	35c multicolored		.25	.25
491	A72	45c multicolored		.25	.25
a.		Bkt. pane of 4, #491-494		3.00	
492	A72	75c multicolored		.25	.25
493	A72	$1 multicolored		.25	.35
494	A72	$2 multicolored		.25	.50
a.		Souv. sheet of 12, #483-494, perf. 14½x14		2.25	3.00
		Nos. 483-494 (12)		3.00	3.35

25th anniv. of the reign of Elizabeth II.
Nos. 483-494 come in a pane of 10 + 2
labels.
Nos. 483a, 487a and 491a are unwmkd.
See No. 508.

Bishop Alfred P. Berkeley, Bishop's
Miters — A73

15c, Grant of Arms to Bishopric, 1951, &
names of former Bishops. 45c, Coat of arms &
map of Diocese. $1.25, Interior of St. George's
Anglican Cathedral & Bishop G. C. M.
Woodroffe.

Wmk. 373
1977, May 12		Litho.		Perf. 13½	
495	A73	15c multicolored		.25	.25
496	A73	35c multicolored		.25	.25
497	A73	45c multicolored		.25	.25
498	A73	$1.25 multicolored		.25	.50
		Nos. 495-498 (4)		1.00	1.25

Diocese of the Windward Islands, centenary.
For surcharge see No. 3304.

Nos. 411, 414, 472, 417, 422 Overprinted in Black or Red: "CARNIVAL 1977/ JUNE 25TH - JULY 5TH"
1977, June 2		Litho.		Perf. 14	
499	A62	5c multi		.25	.25
500	A62	10c multi (R)		.25	.25
501	A62	15c multi (R)		.25	.25
502	A62	20c multi (R)		.25	.25
503	A62	$1 multi		.50	.50
		Nos. 499-503 (5)		1.50	1.50

St. Vincent Carnival, June 25-July 5.
5c, 15c dated "1977", 10c, 20c, $1 "1976."

Girl Guide and
Emblem — A74

Designs: 15c, Early Guide's uniform,
Ranger, Brownie and Guide. 20c, Guide
uniforms, 1917 and 1977. $2, Lady Baden-
Powell, World Chief Guide, 1930-1977.

Wmk. 373
1977, Sept. 1		Litho.		Perf. 13½	
504	A74	5c multicolored		.25	.25
505	A74	15c multicolored		.25	.25
506	A74	20c multicolored		.25	.25
507	A74	$2 multicolored		.30	.75
		Nos. 504-507 (4)		1.05	1.50

St. Vincent Girl Guides, 50th anniversary.

No. 494 with Additional Inscription: "CARIBBEAN / VISIT 1977"
1977, Oct. 27					
508	A72	$2 multicolored		.50	.50

Caribbean visit of Queen Elizabeth II.

"While
Shepherds
Watched"
A75

Christmas: 10c, "Fear not" said He. 15c,
David's Town. 25c, The Heavenly Babe. 50c,
Thus Spake and Seraph. $1.25, All Glory be to
God.

1977, Nov.		Litho.		Perf. 13x11	
509	A75	5c buff & multi		.25	.25
510	A75	10c buff & multi		.25	.25
511	A75	15c buff & multi		.25	.25
512	A75	25c buff & multi		.25	.25
513	A75	50c buff & multi		.25	.25
514	A75	$1.25 buff & multi		.25	.60
a.		Souv. sheet #509-514, perf. 13½		1.50	1.60
		Nos. 509-514 (6)		1.50	1.85

Map of St.
Vincent — A76

		Perf. 14½x14			
1977-78		Litho.		Wmk. 373	
515	A76	20c dk bl & lt bl ('78)		.25	.25
516	A76	40c salmon & black		.30	.30
517	A76	40c car, sal & ocher ('78)		.25	.25
		Nos. 515-517 (3)		.80	.80

Issued: #516, 11/30; #515, 517, 1/31.
For types surcharged see Nos. B1-B4, AR1-AR3.

Painted Lady and Bougainvillea — A77

Butterflies and Bougainvillea: 25c, Silver
spot. 40c, Red anartia. 50c, Mimic. $1.25,
Giant hairstreak.

1978, Apr. 6		Litho.		Perf. 14	
523	A77	5c multicolored		.25	.25
524	A77	25c multicolored		.50	.25
525	A77	40c multicolored		.65	.25
526	A77	50c multicolored		.70	.25
527	A77	$1.25 multicolored		1.40	.85
		Nos. 523-527 (5)		3.50	1.85

For surcharges see Nos. 3259, 3306-3308.

Westminster Abbey — A78

Cathedral: 50c, Gloucester. $1.25, Durham.
$2.50, Exeter.

		Perf. 13x13½			
1978, June 2		Litho.		Wmk. 373	
528	A78	40c multicolored		.25	.25
529	A78	50c multicolored		.25	.25
530	A78	$1.25 multicolored		.25	.25
531	A78	$2.50 multicolored		.25	.25
a.		Souv. sheet, #528-531, perf. 13½x14		.75	1.00
		Nos. 528-531 (4)		1.00	1.00

25th anniv. of coronation of Queen Elizabeth II. Nos. 528-531 issued in sheets of 10.
Nos. 528-531 also exist in booklet panes of
two.

Rotary
Emblem
A79

Emblems: 50c, Lions Intl. $1, Jaycees.

Wmk. 373
1978, July 13		Litho.		Perf. 14½	
532	A79	40c brown & multi		.25	.25
533	A79	50c dark green & multi		.25	.25
534	A79	$1 crimson & multi		.35	.45
		Nos. 532-534 (3)		.85	.95

Service clubs aiding in development of St.
Vincent.
For surcharge see No. 3296.

Flags of
Ontario
and St.
Vincent,
Teacher
A80

Design: 40c, Flags of St. Vincent and Ontario, teacher pointing to board, vert.

1978, Sept. 7		Litho.		Perf. 14	
535	A80	40c multicolored		.25	.25
536	A80	$2 multicolored		.40	.60

School to School Project between children
of Ontario, Canada, and St. Vincent, 10th
anniversary.

Arnos
Vale
Airport
A81

40c, Wilbur Wright landing Flyer I. 50c, Flyer
I airborne. $1.25, Orville Wright and Flyer I.

1978, Oct. 19				Perf. 14½	
537	A81	10c multicolored		.25	.25
538	A81	40c multicolored		.25	.25
539	A81	50c multicolored		.25	.25
540	A81	$1.25 multicolored		.30	.70
		Nos. 537-540 (4)		1.05	1.45

75th anniversary of 1st powered flight.
For overprint see No. 568.

Vincentian Boy,
IYC
Emblem — A82

Children and IYC Emblem: 20c, Girl. 50c,
Boy. $2, Girl and boy.

1979, Feb. 14		Litho.		Perf. 14x13½	
541	A82	8c multicolored		.25	.25
542	A82	20c multicolored		.25	.25
543	A82	50c multicolored		.25	.30
544	A82	$2 multicolored		.25	.50
		Nos. 541-544 (4)		1.00	1.30

International Year of the Child.
For surcharge see No. 3262.

Rowland
Hill
A83

50c, Great Britain #1-2. $3, St. Vincent #1-
1B.

1979, May 31		Litho.		Perf. 14	
545	A83	40c multicolored		.25	.25
546	A83	50c multicolored		.25	.25
547	A83	$3 multicolored		.40	.90
a.		Souvenir sheet of 6		1.50	2.25
		Nos. 545-547 (3)		.90	1.40

Sir Rowland Hill (1795-1879), originator of
penny postage.
No. 547a contains Nos. 545-547 and Nos.
560, 561 and 565.

Buccament Cancellations, Map of St. Vincent — A84

Cancellations and location of village.

1979, Sept. 1　Litho.　Perf. 14

548	A84	1c shown	.25	.25
549	A84	2c Sion Hill	.25	.25
550	A84	3c Cumberland	.25	.40
551	A84	4c Questelles	.25	.30
552	A84	5c Layou	.25	.25
553	A84	6c New Ground	.25	.25
554	A84	8c Mesopotamia	.25	.25
555	A84	10c Troumaca	.25	.30
556	A84	12c Arnos Vale	.25	.30
557	A84	15c Stubbs	.25	.30
558	A84	20c Orange Hill	.25	.30
559	A84	25c Calliaqua	.25	.25
560	A84	40c Edinboro	.25	.25
561	A84	50c Colonarie	.25	.25
562	A84	80c Babou St. Vincent	.40	.35
563	A84	$1 Chateaubelair	.40	.50
564	A84	$2 Kingstown	.50	.80
565	A84	$3 Barrouallie	.55	1.25
566	A84	$5 Georgetown	.75	2.00
567	A84	$10 Kingstown	1.75	4.00
		Nos. 548-567 (20)	7.85	12.75

See No. 547a.
The 5c, 10c, 25c reissued inscribed 1982. Singles of #562-564 from #601a are inscribed 1980.

No. 537 Overprinted in Red: "ST. VINCENT AND THE GRENADINES AIR SERVICE 1979"

1979, Aug. 6　Litho.　Perf. 14½

568	A81	10c multicolored	.40	.40

St. Vincent and Grenadines air service inauguration.

Independent State

St. Vincent Flag, Ixora Coccinea A85

Designs: 50c, House of Assembly, ixora stricta. 80c, Prime Minister R. Milton Cato.

1979, Oct. 27　　Perf. 12½x12

569	A85	20c multi + label	.25	.25
570	A85	50c multi + label	.25	.25
571	A85	80c multi + label	.40	.25
		Nos. 569-571 (3)	.90	.75

Independence of St. Vincent.

Nos. 407, 410-416, 418, 421, 473-474, 422-423, 425 Overprinted in Black: "INDEPENDENCE 1979"

1979, Oct. 27　Litho.　Perf. 14½

572	A62	1c multicolored	.25	.25
573	A62	4c multicolored	.25	.25
574	A62	5c multicolored	.25	.25
575	A62	6c multicolored	.25	.25
576	A62	8c multicolored	.25	.25
577	A62	10c multicolored	.25	.25
578	A62	12c multicolored	.25	.25
579	A62	15c multicolored	.25	.25
580	A62	25c Calliaqua	.25	.25
581	A62	40c multicolored	.40	.30
582	A62	70c multicolored	.70	.35
583	A62	90c multicolored	.70	.40
584	A62	$1 multicolored	.70	.40
585	A62	$2.50 multicolored	.90	1.00
586	A62	$10 multicolored	2.00	4.75
		Nos. 572-586 (15)	7.65	9.45

Silent Night Text, Virgin and Child A86

Silent Night Text and: 20c, Infant Jesus and angels. 25c, Shepherds. 40c, Angel. 50c, Angels holding Jesus. $2, Nativity.

1979, Nov. 1　　Perf. 13½x14

587	A86	10c multicolored	.25	.25
588	A86	20c multicolored	.25	.25
589	A86	25c multicolored	.25	.25
590	A86	40c multicolored	.25	.25
591	A86	50c multicolored	.25	.25
592	A86	$2 multicolored	.25	.40
a.		Souvenir sheet of 6, #587-592	1.10	1.25
		Nos. 587-592 (6)	1.50	1.65

Christmas.

Oleander and Wasp — A87

Oleander and Insects: 10c, Beetle. 25c, Praying mantis. 50c, Green guava beetle. $2, Citrus weevil.

1979, Dec. 13　Litho.　Perf. 14

593	A87	5c multicolored	.25	.25
594	A87	10c multicolored	.25	.25
595	A87	25c multicolored	.25	.25
596	A87	50c multicolored	.50	.50
597	A87	$2 multicolored	.50	.50
		Nos. 593-597 (5)	1.50	1.50

Type of 1880
Souvenir Sheet

1980, Feb. 28　Litho.　Perf. 14x13½

598		Sheet of 3	1.00	1.00
a.		A3 50c brown	.25	.25
b.		A3 $1 dark green	.25	.25
c.		A3 $2 dark blue	.50	.50

Coat of arms stamps centenary; London 1980 Intl. Stamp Exhibition, May 6-14.

London '80 Intl. Stamp Exhibition, May 6-14 — A88

Wmk. 373

1980, Apr. 24　Litho.　Perf. 14

599	A88	80c Queen Elizabeth II	.25	.25
600	A88	$1 GB #297, SV #190	.25	.25
601	A88	$2 Unissued stamp, 1971	.50	.60
a.		Souv. sheet, #562-564, 599-601	1.00	1.75
		Nos. 599-601 (3)	1.00	1.10

Steel Band A89

---

a, shown. b, Drummers, dancers.

1980, June 12　Litho.　Perf. 14

602	A89	20c Pair, #a.-b.	.35	.75

Kingstown Carnival, July 7-8.

Soccer, Olympic Rings — A90

1980, Aug. 7　　Perf. 13½

604	A90	10c shown	.25	.25
605	A90	60c Bicycling	.25	.25
606	A90	80c Women's basket-ball	.30	.40
607	A90	$2.50 Boxing	.30	1.10
		Nos. 604-607 (4)	1.10	2.00

Sport for all.
For surcharges see Nos. 3264, 3278, B5-B8.

Agouti A91

1980, Oct. 2　Litho.　Perf. 14x14½

608	A91	25c shown	.25	.25
609	A91	50c Giant toad	.25	.25
610	A91	$2 Mongoose	.50	.60
		Nos. 608-610 (3)	1.00	1.10

Map of North Atlantic showing St. Vincent — A92

Maps showing St. Vincent: 10c, World. $1, Caribbean. $2, St. Vincent, sail boats, plane.

1980, Dec. 4　Litho.　Perf. 13½x14

611	A92	10c multicolored	.25	.25
612	A92	50c multicolored	.25	.25
613	A92	$1 multicolored	.25	.25
614	A92	$2 multicolored	.50	.30
a.		Souv. sheet of 1, perf. 14	.90	.90
		Nos. 611-614 (4)	1.25	1.05

Ville de Paris in Battle of the Saints, 1782 — A93

60c, Ramillies lost in storm, 1782. $1.50, Providence, 1793. $2, Mail Packet Dee, 1840.

Wmk. 373

1981, Feb. 19　Litho.　Perf. 14

615	A93	50c shown	.35	.25
616	A93	60c multicolored	.45	.40
617	A93	$1.50 multicolored	1.25	1.25
618	A93	$2 multicolored	1.50	1.50
		Nos. 615-618 (4)	3.55	3.40

For surcharges see Nos. 3262A, 3279, 3318.

A94

No. 619a, Arrowroot processing. No. 619b, Arrowroot Cultivation. No. 620a, Banana packing plant. No. 620b, Banana cultivation. No. 621a, Copra drying frames. No. 621b, Coconut plantation. No. 622a, Cocoa beans. No. 622b, Cocoa cultivation.

Wmk. 373

1981, May 21　Litho.　Perf. 14

619	A94	25c Pair, #a.-b.	.25	.40
620	A94	50c Pair, #a.-b.	.35	.60
621	A94	60c Pair, #a.-b.	.35	.60
622	A94	$1 Pair, #a.-b.	.55	1.00
		Nos. 619-622 (4)	1.50	2.60

For surcharge see No. 3297.

Prince Charles, Lady Diana, Royal Yacht Charlotte — A94a

Prince Charles and Lady Diana — A94b

Wmk. 380

1981, July 13　Litho.　Perf. 14

627	A94a	60c Couple, Isabella	.25	.25
a.		Bklt. pane of 4, perf. 12	.60	
628	A94b	60c Couple	.25	.25
629	A94a	$2.50 Alberta	.60	.60
630	A94b	$2.50 like #628	.70	.70
a.		Bklt. pane of 2, perf. 12	1.00	
631	A94a	$4 Britannia	1.25	1.25
632	A94b	$4 like #628	1.50	1.50
		Nos. 627-632 (6)	4.55	4.55

Royal wedding. Each denomination issued in sheets of 7 (6 type A94a, 1 type A94b).
For surcharges and overprints see Nos. 891-892, O1-O6.

Souvenir Sheet

1981　　Litho.　Perf. 12

632A	A95b	$5 Couple	1.25	1.25

Kingstown General Post Office — A95

Wmk. 373

1981, Sept. 1　Litho.　Perf. 14

633	A95	$2 Pair, #a.-b.	1.25	1.90

UPU membership centenary.

First Anniv. of UN Membership A96

Wmk. 373

1981, Sept. 1　Litho.　Perf. 14

634A	A96	$1.50 Flags	.30	.30
634B	A96	$2.50 Prime Minister Cato	.50	.55

"The People that Walked in Darkness . . ." — A97

1981, Nov. 19   Litho.   Perf. 12
635 A97 50c shown .25 .25
636 A97 60c Angel .25 .25
637 A97 $1 "My soul . . ." .25 .25
638 A97 $2 Flight into Egypt .35 .35
  a. Souvenir sheet of 4, #635-638 1.25 1.50
    Nos. 635-638 (4) 1.10 1.10

Christmas. For surcharges see Nos. 674, 3280, 3298, 3320-3321.

Re-introduction of Sugar Industry, First Anniv. — A98

1982, Apr. 5   Litho.   Perf. 14
639 A98 50c Boilers .25 .25
640 A98 60c Drying plant .25 .25
641 A98 $1.50 Gearwheels .45 .65
642 A98 $2 Loading sugar cane .80 1.00
    Nos. 639-642 (4) 1.75 2.15

For surcharges see Nos. 3251, 3260, 3263, 3281, 3322.

50th Anniv. of Airmail Service A99

50c, DH Moth, 1932. 60c, Grumman Goose, 1952. $1.50, Hawker-Siddeley 748, 1968. $2, Britten-Norman Islander, 1982.

1982, July 29   Litho.   Perf. 14
643 A99 50c multicolored .60 .45
644 A99 60c multicolored .75 .50
645 A99 $1.50 multicolored 1.75 1.90
646 A99 $2 multicolored 2.40 2.50
    Nos. 643-646 (4) 5.50 5.35

For surcharges see Nos. 3260A, 3309.

21st Birthday of Princess Diana, July 1 — A99a

Wmk. 380
1982, June   Litho.   Perf. 14
647 A99a 50c Augusta of Saxe, 1736 .30 .30
648 A99a 60c Saxe arms .35 .35
649 A99a $6 Diana 1.60 1.60
    Nos. 647-649 (3) 2.25 2.25

For overprints see Nos. 652-654.

Scouting Year — A100

1982, July 15   Wmk. 373
650 A100 $1.50 Emblem .75 1.00
651 A100 $2.50 "75" 1.10 1.75

For overprints see Nos. 890, 893.

Nos. 647-649 Overprinted: "ROYAL BABY"

1982, July   Wmk. 380
652 A99a 50c multicolored .25 .30
653 A99a 60c multicolored .25 .30
654 A99a $6 multicolored .75 1.40
    Nos. 652-654 (3) 1.25 2.00

Birth of Prince William of Wales, June 21.

Carnival A101

50c, Butterfly float. 60c, Angel dancer, vert. $1.50, Winged dancer, vert. $2, Eagle float.

1982, June 10   Litho.   Perf. 13½
655 A101 50c multicolored .25 .25
656 A101 60c multicolored .35 .35
657 A101 $1.50 multicolored .70 .80
658 A101 $2 multicolored .90 1.25
    Nos. 655-658 (4) 2.20 2.65

Cruise Ships A103

Wmk. 373
1982, Dec. 29   Litho.   Perf. 14
662 A103 45c Geestport .35 .35
663 A103 60c Stella Oceanis .45 .45
664 A103 $1.50 Victoria 1.10 1.40
665 A103 $2 QE 2 1.30 1.90
    Nos. 662-665 (4) 3.20 4.10

For surcharges see Nos. 3310, 3324-3325.

Pseudocorynactis Caribbeorum — A104

Sea Horses and Anemones — 60c, Actinoporus elegans. $1.50, Arachnanthus nocturnus. $2, Hippocampus reidi.
60c, $1.50, $2 vert.

1983, Jan. 12   Wmk. 373   Perf. 12
666 A104 50c shown .90 .90
667 A104 60c multicolored 1.10 1.10
668 A104 $1.50 multicolored 1.90 2.10
669 A104 $2 multicolored 2.10 2.25
    Nos. 666-669 (4) 6.00 6.35

For overprint see No. 886. For surcharges see Nos. 3282, 3311, 3326.

Commonwealth Day — A104a

45c, Map. 60c, Flag. $1.50, Prime Minister Cato. $2, Banana industry.

Wmk. 373
1983, Mar. 14   Litho.   Perf. 14
670 A104a 45c multi .35 .35
671 A104a 60c multi .35 .35
672 A104a $1.50 multi .55 .65
673 A104a $2 multi .80 .90
    Nos. 670-673 (4) 2.05 2.15

For surcharge see No. 3252.

No. 635 Surcharged
Wmk. 373
1983, Apr. 26   Litho.   Perf. 12
674 A97 45c on 50c multi .45 .35

A104b

Wmk. 373
1983, July 6   Litho.   Perf. 12
675 A104b 45c Handshake .25 .30
676 A104b 60c Emblem .25 .35
677 A104b $1.50 Map .50 1.10
678 A104b $2 Flags .90 1.40
    Nos. 675-678 (4) 1.90 3.15

10th anniv. of Chaguaramas (Caribbean Free Trade Assoc.)
For surcharges see Nos. 3233, 3283, 3313, 3327.

A105

45c, Founder William A. Smith. 60c, Boy, officer. $1.50, Emblem. $2, Community service.

Perf. 12x11½
1983, Oct. 6   Litho.   Wmk. 373
679 A105 45c multicolored .25 .25
680 A105 60c multicolored .35 .35
681 A105 $1.50 multicolored .80 1.25
682 A105 $2 multicolored 1.10 1.40
    Nos. 679-682 (4) 2.50 3.25

Boys' Brigade, cent. For overprint see #887. For surcharges see Nos. 3261, 3275, 3284, 3314, 3328.

Christmas — A106

10c, Shepherds at Watch. 50c, The Angel of the Lord. $1.50, A Glorious Light. $2.40, At the Manger.

1983, Nov. 15   Litho.   Perf. 12
683 A106 10c multicolored .25 .25
684 A106 50c multicolored .30 .30
685 A106 $1.50 multicolored .80 1.10
686 A106 $2.40 multicolored 1.50 1.75
  a. Souvenir sheet of 4, #683-686 2.75 2.75
    Nos. 683-686 (4) 2.85 3.40

For surcharge, see No. 3263A.

Classic Cars A107

No. 687, Ford Model T. No. 688, Supercharged Cord. No. 689, Mercedes-Benz. No. 690, Citroen Open Tourer. No. 691, Ferrari Boxer. No. 692, Rolls-Royce Phantom.

Se-tenant Pairs, #a.-b.
a. — Side and front views.
b. — Action scene.

1983, Nov. 9   Litho.   Perf. 12½
687 A107 10c multicolored .25 .25
688 A107 60c multicolored .25 .25
689 A107 $1.50 multicolored .35 .35
690 A107 $1.50 multicolored .35 .35
691 A107 $2 multicolored .35 .35
692 A107 $2 multicolored .35 .35
    Nos. 687-692 (6) 1.90 1.90

See Nos. 773-777, 815-822, 906-911.

Locomotives Type of 1985
No. 699, King Henry VIII. No. 700, Royal Scots Greys. No. 701, Hagley Hall. No. 702, Sir Lancelot. No. 703, B12 Class. No. 704, #1000 Deeley Compound. No. 705, Cheshire. No. 706, Bulleid Austerity.

Se-tenant Pairs, #a.-b.
a. — Side and front views.
b. — Action scene.

1983, Dec. 8   Litho.   Perf. 12½x13
699 A120 10c multicolored .25 .25
700 A120 10c multicolored .25 .25
701 A120 25c multicolored .25 .25
702 A120 50c multicolored .40 .40
703 A120 60c multicolored .40 .40
704 A120 75c multicolored .40 .40
705 A120 $2.50 multicolored .50 .50
706 A120 $3 multicolored .55 .55
    Nos. 699-706 (8) 3.00 3.00

Fort Duvernette A108

Perf. 14x14½
1984, Feb. 13   Litho.   Wmk. 380
715 A108 35c View .25 .25
716 A108 45c Wall, flag .30 .30
717 A108 $1 Canon .60 .60
718 A108 $3 Map 1.75 1.75
    Nos. 715-718 (4) 2.90 2.90

For surcharge see No. 3334.

Flowering Trees — A109

Perf. 13½x14
1984, Apr. 2   Litho.   Wmk. 373
719 A109 5c White frangipani .25 .25
720 A109 10c Genip .25 .25
721 A109 15c Immortelle .25 .25
722 A109 20c Pink poui .25 .25
723 A109 25c Buttercup .25 .25
724 A109 35c Sandbox .30 .30
725 A109 45c Locust .40 .40
726 A109 60c Colville's glory .75 .60
727 A109 75c Lignum vitae .75 .70
728 A109 $1 Golden shower .80 1.40

729	A109	$5 Angelin	3.00 8.00
730	A109	$10 Roucou	6.00 13.00
		Nos. 719-730 (12)	13.25 25.65

For surcharges see Nos. 3247, 3258, 3285-3288.

World War I Battle Scene, King George V — A110

No. 732a, Battle of Bannockburn. No. 732b, Edward II. No. 733a, George V. No. 733b, York Cottage, Sandringham. No. 734a, Edward II. No. 734b, Berkeley Castle. No. 735a, Arms of Edward II. No. 735b, Edward II. No. 736a, Arms of George V. No. 736b, George V.

1984, Apr. 25   Litho.   Perf. 13x12½

731	A110	1c Pair, #a.-b.	.25 .25
732	A110	5c Pair, #a.-b.	.25 .25
733	A110	60c Pair, #a.-b.	.30 .30
734	A110	75c Pair, #a.-b.	.30 .30
735	A110	$1 Pair, #a.-b.	.30 .30
736	A110	$4 Pair, #a.-b.	.60 .60
		Nos. 731-736 (6)	2.00 2.00

Carnival A112

Wmk. 380

1984, June 25   Litho.   Perf. 14

743	A112	35c Musical fantasy	.25 .25
744	A112	45c African woman	.25 .25
745	A112	$1 Market woman	.65 .65
746	A112	$3 Carib hieroglyph	1.75 1.75
		Nos. 743-746 (4)	2.90 2.90

For surcharges see Nos. 3243, 3276.

Locomotives Type of 1985

1c, Liberation Class 141R, 1945. 2c, Dreadnought Class 50, 1967. 3c, No. 242A1, 1946. 50c, Dean Goods, 1883. 75c, Hetton Colliery, 1822. $1, Penydarren, 1804. $2, Novelty, 1829. $3, Class 44, 1925.

Se-tenant Pairs, #a.-b.
a. — Side and front views.
b. — Action scene.

1984, July 27   Litho.   Perf. 12½

747	A120	1c multicolored	.25 .25
748	A120	2c multicolored	.25 .25
749	A120	3c multicolored	.25 .25
750	A120	50c multicolored	.50 .50
751	A120	75c multicolored	.50 .50
752	A120	$1 multicolored	.50 .50
753	A120	$2 multicolored	.70 .70
754	A120	$3 multicolored	.70 .70
		Nos. 747-754 (8)	3.65 3.65

Slavery Abolition Sesquicentennial — A113

35c, Hoeing. 45c, Gathering sugar cane. $1, Cutting sugar cane. $3, Abolitionist William Wilberforce.

1984, Aug. 1   Litho.   Perf. 14

761	A113	35c multicolored	.25 .25
762	A113	45c multicolored	.25 .25
763	A113	$1 multicolored	.65 .65
764	A113	$3 multicolored	1.75 2.40
		Nos. 761-764 (4)	2.90 3.55

For surcharges see Nos. 3273, 3337.

1984 Summer Olympics — A114

No. 765a, Judo. No. 765b, Weight lifting. No. 766a, Bicycling (facing left). No. 766b, Bicycling (facing right). No. 767a, Swimming (back stroke). No. 767b, Breast stroke. No. 768a, Running (start). No. 768b, Running (finish).

1984, Aug. 30   Unwmk.   Perf. 12½

765	A114	1c Pair, #a.-b.	.25 .25
766	A114	3c Pair, #a.-b.	.25 .25
767	A114	60c Pair, #a.-b.	.50 .50
768	A114	$3 Pair, #a.-b.	2.00 2.00
		Nos. 765-768 (4)	3.00 3.00

Car Type of 1983

5c, Austin-Healey Sprite, 1958. 20c, Maserati, 1971. 55c, Pontiac GTO, 1964. $1.50, Jaguar, 1957. $2.50, Ferrari, 1970.

Se-tenant Pairs, #a.-b.
a. — Side and front views.
b. — Action scene.

1984, Oct. 22   Litho.   Perf. 12½

773	A107	5c multicolored	.25 .25
774	A107	20c multicolored	.25 .25
775	A107	55c multicolored	.35 .35
776	A107	$1.50 multicolored	.45 .45
777	A107	$2.50 multicolored	.60 .60
		Nos. 773-777 (5)	1.90 1.90

Military Uniforms — A115

1984, Nov. 12   Wmk. 380   Perf. 14

783	A115	45c Grenadier, 1773	.35 .35
784	A115	60c Grenadier, 1775	.55 .55
785	A115	$1.50 Grenadier, 1768	1.10 1.10
786	A115	$2 Battalion Co. Officer, 1780	1.60 1.60
		Nos. 783-786 (4)	3.60 3.60

For surcharges see Nos. 3289, 3315, 3329.

Locomotives Type of 1985

5c, 1954 R.R. Class 20, Zimbabwe. 40c, 1928 Southern Maid, U.K. 75c, 1911 Prince of Wales, U.K. $2.50, 1935 D.R.G. Class 05, Germany.

Se-tenant Pairs, #a.-b.
a. — Side and front views.
b. — Action scene.

1984, Nov. 21   Litho.   Perf. 12½x13

787	A120	5c multicolored	.25 .25
788	A120	40c multicolored	.30 .30
789	A120	75c multicolored	.30 .30
790	A120	$2.50 multicolored	1.00 1.00
		Nos. 787-790 (4)	1.85 1.85

Cricket Players — A116

5c, N.S. Taylor, portrait. 35c, T.W. Graveney with bat. 50c, R.G.D. Willis at wicket. $3, S.D. Fletcher at wicket.

Se-tenant Pairs, #a.-b.
a. — Side and front views.
b. — Action scene.

1985, Jan. 7   Litho.   Perf. 12½

795	A116	5c multicolored	.25 .25
796	A116	35c multicolored	.40 .40
797	A116	50c multicolored	.60 .60
798	A116	$3 multicolored	2.00 3.00
		Nos. 795-798 (4)	3.25 4.25

Orchids — A117

35c, Epidendrum ciliare. 45c, Ionopsis utricularioides. $1, Epidendrum secundum. $3, Oncidium altissimum.

1985, Jan. 31   Litho.   Perf. 14

803	A117	35c multicolored	.30 .30
804	A117	45c multicolored	.35 .35
805	A117	$1 multicolored	.70 .70
806	A117	$3 multicolored	1.50 1.50
		Nos. 803-806 (4)	2.85 2.85

For surcharge see No. 3338.

Audubon Birth Bicent. — A118

Illustrations of North American bird species by artist/naturalist John J. Audubon: #807a, Brown pelican. #807b, Green heron. #808a, Pileated woodpecker. #808b, Common flicker. #809a, Painted bunting. #809b, White-winged crossbill. #810a, Red-shouldered hawk. #810b, Crested caracara.

1985, Feb. 7   Litho.   Perf. 12½

807	A118	15c Pair, #a.-b.	.25 .25
808	A118	40c Pair, #a.-b.	.45 .45
809	A118	60c Pair, #a.-b.	.45 .45
810	A118	$2.25 Pair, #a.-b.	.90 .90
		Nos. 807-810 (4)	2.05 2.05

Car Type of 1983

1c, 1937 Lancia Aprilia, Italy. 25c, 1922 Essex Coach, US. 55c, 1973 Pontiac Firebird Trans Am, US. 60c, 1950 Nash Rambler, US. $1, 1961 Ferrari Tipo 156, Italy. $1.50, 1967 Eagle-Weslake Type 58, US. $2, 1953 Cunningham C-5R, US.

Se-tenant Pairs, #a.-b.
a. — Side and front views.
b. — Action scene.

1985

815-821	A107	Set of 7 pairs	2.00 2.00

Souvenir Sheet of 4

822	A107	#a.-d.	2.25 2.25

No. 822 contains a pair of $4 stamps like No. 820 (#a.-b.), and a pair of $5 stamps like No. 819 (#c.-d.).
Issued: 1c, 55c, $2, 3/11; others, 6/7.

Herbs and Spices — A119

1985, Apr. 22   Perf. 14

829	A119	25c Pepper	.25 .25
830	A119	35c Sweet marjoram	.25 .25
831	A119	$1 Nutmeg	.50 .50
832	A119	$3 Ginger	1.00 1.00
		Nos. 829-832 (4)	2.00 2.00

For surcharge see No. 3339.

Locomotives of the United Kingdom — A120

1c, 1913 Glen Douglas. 10c, 1872 Fenchurch Terrier. 40c, 1870 No. 1 Stirling Single. 60c, 1866 No. 158A. $1, 1893 No. 103 Class Jones Goods. $2.50, 1908 Great Bear.

Se-tenant Pairs, #a.-b.
a. — Side and front views.
b. — Action scene.

1985, Apr. 26   Perf. 12½

833	A120	1c multicolored	.25 .25
834	A120	10c multicolored	.25 .25
835	A120	40c multicolored	.30 .30
836	A120	60c multicolored	.30 .30
837	A120	$1 multicolored	.50 .50
838	A120	$2.50 multicolored	.80 .80
		Nos. 833-838 (6)	2.40 2.40

See Nos. 699-706, 747-754, 787-790, 849-854, 961-964.

Traditional Instruments — A121

25c, Bamboo flute. 35c, Quatro. $1, Bamboo base, vert. $2, Goat-skin drum, vert.

1985, May 16   Perf. 15

845	A121	25c multicolored	.25 .25
846	A121	35c multicolored	.25 .25
847	A121	$1 multicolored	.50 .50
848	A121	$2 multicolored	1.00 1.00
a.		Sheet of 4, #845-848	2.00 2.00
		Nos. 845-848 (4)	2.00 2.00

For surcharge see No. 3299.

Locomotives Type of 1985

5c, 1874 Loch, U.K. 30c, 1919 Class 47XX, U.K. 60c, 1876 P.L.M. Class 121, France. 75c, 1927 D.R.G. Class 24, Germany. $1, 1889 No. 1008, U.K. $2.50, 1926 S.R. Class PS-4, US.

Se-tenant Pairs, #a.-b.
a. — Side and front views.
b. — Action scene.

1985, June 27   Perf. 12½

849	A120	5c multicolored	.25 .25
850	A120	30c multicolored	.30 .30
851	A120	60c multicolored	.40 .40
852	A120	75c multicolored	.40 .40
853	A120	$1 multicolored	.50 .50
854	A120	$2.50 multicolored	.60 .60
		Nos. 849-854 (6)	2.45 2.45

Queen Mother, 85th Birthday — A122

Nos. 861a, 867a, Facing right. Nos. 861b, 867b, Facing left. Nos. 862a, 866a, Facing right. Nos. 862b, 866b, Facing left. No. 863a, Facing front. No. 863b, Facing right. No. 864a, Facing left. No. 864b, Facing front. No. 865a, Facing right. No. 865b, Facing front.

1985

861	A122	35c Pair, #a.-b.		.25	.25
862	A122	85c Pair, #a.-b.		.25	.25
863	A122	$1.20 Pair, #a.-b.		.35	.35
864	A122	$1.60 Pair, #a.-b.		.35	.35
	Nos. 861-864 (4)			1.20	1.20

Souvenir Sheets of 2

865	A122	$2.10 #a.-b.	.75	.75
866	A122	$3.50 #a.-b.	3.25	3.25
867	A122	$6 #a.-b.	5.50	5.50
	Nos. 865-867 (3)		9.50	9.50

Issued: #861-865, 8/9; #866-867, 12/19.
For overprints see No. 888.

Elvis Presley (1935-77), American
Entertainer — A123

Nos. 874a, 878a, In concert. Nos. 874b, 878b, Facing front. Nos. 875a, 879a, In concert. Nos. 875b, 879b, Facing left. Nos. 876a, 880a, In concert. Nos. 876b, 880b, Facing front. Nos. 877a, 881a, Wearing leather jacket. Nos. 877b, 881b, Facing left.

1985, Aug. 16

874	A123	10c Pair, #a.-b.		.55	.55
875	A123	60c Pair, #a.-b.		.80	.80
876	A123	$1 Pair, #a.-b.		.80	.80
877	A123	$5 Pair, #a.-b.		1.10	1.10
	Nos. 874-877 (4)			3.25	3.25

Souvenir Sheets of 4

878	A123	30c #a.-b.	.90	.90
879	A123	50c #a.-b.	1.50	1.50
880	A123	$1.50 #a.-b.	4.25	4.25
881	A123	$4.50 #a.-b.	12.00	12.00
	Nos. 878-881 (4)		18.65	18.65

Nos. 878-881 contain two of each stamp.
Two $4 "stamps" were not issued.
For other Presley souvenir sheet see No. 1567. For overprints see Nos. 1009-1016.

Flour
Milling
A124

1985, Oct. 17   Wmk. 373   Perf. 15

882	A124	20c Conveyor from elevators		.25	.25
883	A124	30c Roller mills		.25	.25
884	A124	75c Office		.50	.50
885	A124	$3 Bran finishers		2.00	2.00
	Nos. 882-885 (4)			3.00	3.00

Nos. 667, 680, 862, 650, 631-632, 651 Ovptd. "CARIBBEAN / ROYAL VISIT / -1985-" or Srchd. with 3 Black Bars and New Value in Black

1985, Oct. 27   Perfs. as Before

886	A104	60c multi	1.90	1.90
887	A105	60c multi	1.90	1.90
888	A122	85c Pair, #a.-b.	6.00	6.00
890	A100	$1.50 multi	5.25	5.25
891	A94a	$1.60 on $4	5.50	5.50
892	A94b	$1.60 on $4	5.50	5.50
893	A100	$2.50 multi	8.50	8.50
	Nos. 886-893 (7)		34.55	34.55

Michael Jackson (b. 1960), American
Entertainer — A125

No. 894a, Portrait. No. 894b, On stage. No. 895a, Singing. No. 895b, Portrait. No. 896a, Black jacket. No. 896b, Red jacket. No. 897a, Portrait. No. 897b, Wearing white glove.

1985, Dec. 2   Perf. 12½

894	A125	60c Pair, #a.-b.	.45	.45
895	A125	$1 Pair, #a.-b.	.75	.75
896	A125	$2 Pair, #a.-b.	1.50	1.50
897	A125	$5 Pair, #a.-b.	4.00	4.00
	Nos. 894-897 (4)		6.70	6.70

Souvenir Sheets of 4
Perf. 13x12½

898	A125	45c #a.-b.	.70	.70
899	A125	90c #a.-b.	1.40	1.40
900	A125	$1.50 #a.-b.	2.25	2.25
901	A125	$4 #a.-b.	6.25	6.25

#898-901 contain two of each stamp.

Christmas
A126

Children's drawings: 25c, Serenade, 75c, Poinsettia. $2.50, Jesus, Our Master.

1985, Dec. 9   Wmk. 373   Perf. 14

903	A126	25c multicolored	.25	.25
904	A126	75c multicolored	.50	.50
905	A126	$2.50 multicolored	1.75	1.75
	Nos. 903-905 (3)		2.50	2.50

For surcharges see Nos. 3268, 3333.

Car Type of 1983

30c, 1916 Cadillac Type 53, US. 45c, 1939 Triumph Dolomite, UK. 60c, 1972 Panther J-72, UK. 90c, 1967 Ferrari 275 GTB/4, Italy. $1.50, 1953 Packard Caribbean, US. $2.50, 1931 Bugatti Type 41 Royale, France.

Se-tenant Pairs, #a.-b.
a. — Side and front views.
b. — Action scene.

1986, Jan. 27   Perf. 12½

906-911	A107	Set of 6 pairs	7.00	7.00

Halley's
Comet
A127

Wmk. 380

1986, Apr. 14   Litho.   Perf. 15

918	A127	45c shown	.35	.35
919	A127	60c Edmond Halley	.45	.45
920	A127	75c Newton's reflector telescope	.55	.55
921	A127	$3 Local astronomer	2.10	2.10
a.		Souvenir sheet of 4, #918-921	3.50	3.50
	Nos. 918-921 (4)		3.45	3.45

Souvenir Sheets of 2

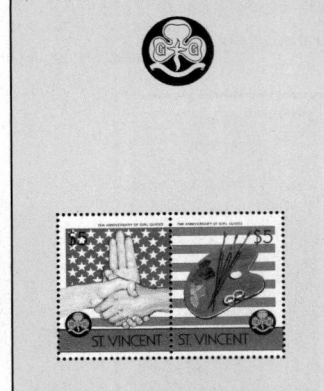

Scouting Movement, 75th
Anniv. — A127a

American flag & Girl Guides or Boy Scouts emblem and: No. 922b, Scout sign, handshake. No. 922c, Paintbrushes, pallet. No. 922Ad, Knots. No. 922Ae, Lord Baden-Powell.

1986, Feb. 25   Litho.   Perf. 13x12½

922	A127a	$5 #b.-c.	4.00	4.00
922A	A127a	$6 #d.-e.	5.00	5.00

"Capex '87" overprints on this issue were not authorized.
Nos. 922-922A exist with decorative selvage. Value, set, $11.50.

Elizabeth II Wearing Crown
Jewels — A128

Various portraits.

1986, Apr. 21   Wmk. 373   Perf. 12½

923	A128	10c multicolored	.25	.25
924	A128	90c multicolored	.50	.50
925	A128	$2.50 multicolored	1.25	1.25
926	A128	$8 multi, vert.	4.50	4.50
	Nos. 923-926 (4)		6.50	6.50

Souvenir Sheet

927	A128	$10 multicolored	5.50	5.50

Elizabeth II at Victoria Park
A129

Designs: No. 929, with Prime Minister Mitchell. No. 930, Arriving at Port Elizabeth. No. 931, at Independence Day Parade.

Perf. 15x14

1986, June 14   Wmk. 373

928	A129	45c multicolored	.40	.40
929	A129	60c multicolored	.55	.55
930	A129	75c multicolored	.70	.70
931	A129	$2.50 multicolored	2.25	2.25
	Nos. 928-931 (4)		3.90	3.90

Souvenir Sheet

932	A129	$3 multicolored	3.75	3.75

Queen Elizabeth II, 60th birthday.

Discovery of America, 500th Anniv.
(1992) — A130

No. 936a, Fleet. No. 936b, Columbus. No. 937a, At Spanish Court. No. 937b, Ferdinand, Isabella. No. 938a, Fruit, Santa Maria. No. 938b, Fruit.

1986, Jan. 23   Litho.   Perf. 12½

936	A130	60c Pair, #a.-b.	.90	.90
937	A130	$1.50 Pair, #a.-b.	2.25	2.25
938	A130	$2.75 Pair, #a.-b.	4.00	4.00
	Nos. 936-938 (3)		7.15	7.15

Souvenir Sheet

939	A130	$6 Columbus, diff.	4.50	4.50

1986 World Cup Soccer
Championships, Mexico — A131

No. 940, Emblem. No. 941, Mexico. No. 942, Mexico, diff. No. 943, Hungary vs. Scotland. No. 944, Spain vs. Scotland. No. 945, England vs. USSR. No. 946, Spain vs. France. No. 947, England vs. Italy.
No. 948, Mexico. No. 949, Scotland. No. 950, Spain. No. 951, England.

1986, May 7   Litho.   Perf. 15

940	A131	1c multicolored	.25	.25
941	A131	2c multicolored	.25	.25
942	A131	5c multicolored	.25	.25
943	A131	5c multicolored	.25	.25
944	A131	10c multicolored	.25	.25
945	A131	30c multicolored	.25	.25
946	A131	45c multicolored	.30	.30
947	A131	$1 multicolored	.60	.60

Perf. 13½
Size: 56x36mm

948	A131	75c multicolored	.40	.40
949	A131	$2 multicolored	1.10	1.10
950	A131	$4 multicolored	2.25	2.25
951	A131	$5 multicolored	2.75	2.75
	Nos. 940-951 (12)		8.90	8.90

1986, July 7   Souvenir Sheets

952	A131	$1.50 like #950	.95	.95
953	A131	$1.50 like #941	.95	.95
954	A131	$2.25 like #949	1.40	1.40
955	A131	$2.50 like #948	1.40	1.40
956	A131	$3 like #946	1.50	1.50
957	A131	$5.50 like #951	3.25	3.25
	Nos. 952-957 (6)		9.45	9.45

Nos. 941-944, 946-947, vert.

Wedding of Prince Andrew and Sarah
Ferguson — A132

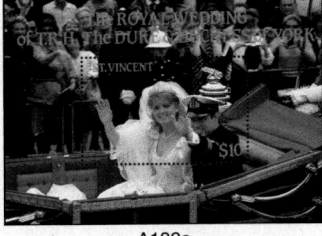

A132a

No. 958a, Andrew. No. 958b, Sarah. No. 959a, Andrew, horiz. No. 959b, Andrew, Nancy Reagan, horiz.

1986   Litho.   Perf. 12½x13, 13x12½

958	A132	60c Pair, #a.-b.	.65	.65
959	A132	$2 Pair, #a.-b.	2.25	2.25
960	A132a	$10 In coach	5.50	5.50
	Nos. 958-960 (3)		8.40	8.40

Issued: $10, Nov.; others, July 23.
For overprints see Nos. 976-977.

A number of unissued items, imperfs., part perfs., missing color varieties, etc., were made available when the Format International inventory was liquidated.

Locomotives Type of 1985

Designs: 30c, 1926 JNR ABT Rack & Adhesion Class ED41 BZZB, Japan. 50c, 1883 Chicago RR Exposition, The Judge, 1A Type, US. $1, 1973 BM & LPRR E60C Co-Co, US. $3, 1972 GM (EMD) SD40-2 Co-Co, US.

a. — Side and front views.
b. — Action scene.

1986, July   Perf. 12½x13
961	A120	30c Pair, #a.-b.	.30	.30
962	A120	50c Pair, #a.-b.	.40	.40
963	A120	$1 Pair, #a.-b.	.55	.55
964	A120	$3 Pair, #a.-b.	.90	.90
		Nos. 961-964 (4)	2.15	2.15

Trees — A133

10c, Acrocomia aculeata. 60c, Pithecellobium saman. 75c, Tabebuia pallida. $3, Andira inermis.

1986, Sept.   Perf. 14
968	A133	10c multicolored	.35	.35
969	A133	60c multicolored	.90	.90
970	A133	75c multicolored	1.10	1.10
971	A133	$3 multicolored	4.25	4.25
		Nos. 968-971 (4)	6.60	6.60

Anniversaries — A134

45c, Cadet Force emblem, vert. 60c, Grimble Building, GHS. $1.50, GHS class. $2, Cadets in formation.

1986, Sept. 30
972	A134	45c multicolored	.40	.40
973	A134	60c multicolored	.50	.50
974	A134	$1.50 multicolored	1.10	1.10
975	A134	$2 multicolored	1.50	1.50
		Nos. 972-975 (4)	3.50	3.50

St. Vincent Cadet Force, 50th anniv., and Girls' High School, 75th anniv.
For surcharges see Nos. 3316, 3330-3331.

Nos. 958-959 Ovptd. "Congratulations to T.R.H. The Duke & Duchess of York" in Silver
Perf. 12½x13, 13x12½

1986, Oct.   Litho.
976	A132	60c Pair, #a.-b.	.75	.75
977	A132	$2 Pair, #a.-b.	2.75	2.75

Stamps of the same denomination also exist printed tete-beche.

The Legend of King Arthur — A134a

30c, King Arthur. 45c, Merlin raises Arthur. 60c, Arthur pulls Excalibur from stone. 75c, Camelot. $1, Lady of the Lake. $1.50, Knights of the Round Table. $2, Holy Grail. $5, Sir Lancelot.

1986, Nov. 3   Perf. 14
979	A134a	30c multi	.30	.30
979A	A134a	45c multi	.45	.45
979B	A134a	60c multi	.50	.50
979C	A134a	75c multi	.65	.65
979D	A134a	$1 multi	.80	.80
979E	A134a	$1.50 multi	1.10	1.10
979F	A134a	$2 multi	1.60	1.60
979G	A134a	$5 multi	4.25	4.25
		Nos. 979-979G (8)	9.65	9.65

St. VINCENT 15c   A134b

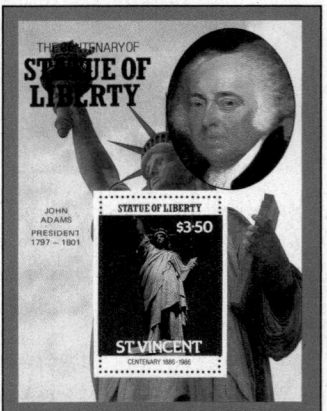

Statue of Liberty, Cent. — A135

Various views of the statue.

1986, Nov. 26   Litho.   Perf. 14
980	A134b	15c multicolored	.25	.25
980A	A134b	25c multicolored	.25	.25
980B	A134b	40c multicolored	.25	.25
980C	A134b	55c multicolored	.35	.35
980D	A134b	75c multicolored	.50	.50
980E	A134b	90c multicolored	.60	.60
980F	A134b	$1.75 multicolored	1.10	1.10
980G	A134b	$2 multicolored	1.25	1.25
980H	A134b	$2.50 multicolored	1.65	1.65
980I	A134b	$3 multicolored	1.90	1.90
		Nos. 980-980I (10)	8.10	8.10

Souvenir Sheets
981	A135	$3.50 multicolored	2.00	2.00
982	A135	$4 multicolored	2.25	2.25
983	A135	$5 multicolored	2.75	2.75

Fresh-water Fishing — A136

No. 984a, Tri tri fishing. No. 984b, Tri tri. No. 985a, Crayfishing. No. 985b, Crayfish.

1986, Dec. 10   Perf. 15
984	A136	75c Pair, #a.-b.	1.10	1.10
985	A136	$1.50 Pair, #a.-b.	2.25	2.25

For surcharges see Nos. 3292-3293, 3317.

Natl. Child Survival Campaign A138

10c, Growth monitoring. 50c, Oral rehydration therapy. 75c, Breast-feeding. $1, Universal immunization.

1987, June 10   Perf. 14x14½
997	A138	10c multicolored	.25	.25
998	A138	50c multicolored	.40	.40
999	A138	75c multicolored	.60	.60
1000	A138	$1 multicolored	.75	.75
		Nos. 997-1000 (4)	2.00	2.00

For overprints see Nos. 1040-1043. For surcharge see No. 3294.

Carnival, 10th Anniv. A139

Designs: 20c, Queen of the Bands, Miss Prima Donna 1986. 45c, Donna Young, Miss Carnival 1985. 55c, M. Haydock, Miss. St. Vincent and the Grenadines 1986. $3.70, Spirit of Hope Year 1986.

1987, June 29   Perf. 12½x13
1001	A139	20c multicolored	.25	.25
1002	A139	45c multicolored	.35	.35
1003	A139	55c multicolored	.40	.40
1004	A139	$3.70 multicolored	2.50	2.50
		Nos. 1001-1004 (4)	3.50	3.50

For surcharges see Nos. 3342-3343.

Nos. 874-881 Overprinted "THE KING OF ROCK AND ROLL LIVES FOREVER . AUGUST 16TH" and "1977-1987" (Nos. 1009-1012) or "TENTH ANNIVERSARY" (Nos. 1013-1016)

1987, Aug. 26   Litho.   Perf. 12½
1009	A123	10c Pair, #a.-b.	.25	.25
1010	A123	60c Pair, #a.-b.	.70	.70
1011	A123	$1 Pair, #a.-b.	1.10	1.10
1012	A123	$5 Pair, #a.-b.	6.00	6.00
		Nos. 1009-1012 (4)	8.05	8.05

Souvenir Sheets
1013	A123	30c Sheet of 4, 2 each #a.-b.	.75	.75
1014	A123	50c Sheet of 4, 2 each #a.-b.	1.25	1.25
1015	A123	$1.50 Sheet of 4, 2 each #a.-b.	3.75	3.75
1016	A123	$4.50 Sheet of 4, 2 each #a.-b.	11.00	11.00

Portrait of Queen Victoria, 1841, by R. Thorburn A140

Portraits and photographs: 75c, Elizabeth and Charles, 1948. $1, Coronation, 1953. $2.50, Duke of Edinburgh, 1948. $5, Elizabeth, c. 1980. $6, Elizabeth and Charles, 1948, diff.

1987, Nov. 20   Litho.   Perf. 12½x13
1017	A140	15c multicolored	.25	.25
1018	A140	75c multicolored	.45	.45
1019	A140	$1 multicolored	.55	.55
1020	A140	$2.50 multicolored	1.25	1.25
1021	A140	$5 multicolored	2.50	2.50
		Nos. 1017-1021 (5)	5.00	5.00

Souvenir Sheet
1022	A140	$6 multicolored	4.00	4.00

Sesquicentennial of Queen Victoria's accession to the throne, wedding of Queen Elizabeth II and Prince Philip, 40th anniv.

Nos. 997-1000 Ovptd. "WORLD POPULATION / 5 BILLION / 11TH JULY 1987"

1987, July 11   Litho.   Perf. 14x14½
1040	A138	10c on No. 997	.40	.40
1041	A138	50c on No. 998	.80	.80
1042	A138	75c on No. 999	1.25	1.25
1043	A138	$1 on No. 1000	1.50	1.50
		Nos. 1040-1043 (4)	3.95	3.95

Automobile Centenary — A143

Automotive pioneers and vehicles: $1, $3, Carl Benz (1844-1929) and the Velocipede, patented 1886. $2, No. 1049, Enzo Ferrari (b. 1898) and 1966 Ferrari Dino 206SP. $4, $6, Charles Rolls (1877-1910), Sir Henry Royce (1863-1933) and 1907 Rolls Royce Silver Ghost. No. 1047, $5, $8, Henry Ford (1863-1947) and Model T Ford.

1987, Dec. 4   Perf. 13x12½
1044	A143	65c multicolored	.65	.65
1045	A143	$2 multicolored	1.00	1.00
1046	A143	$4 multicolored	2.10	2.10
1047	A143	$5 multicolored	2.50	2.50
		Nos. 1044-1047 (4)	6.25	6.25

Souvenir Sheets
1048	A143	$3 like No. 1044	2.00	2.00
1049	A143	$5 like No. 1045	3.25	3.25
1050	A143	$6 like No. 1046	4.00	4.00
1051	A143	$8 like No. 1047	5.50	5.50
		Nos. 1048-1051 (4)	14.75	14.75

Soccer Teams — A144

1987, Dec. 4
1052	A144	$2 Derby County	1.40	1.40
1053	A144	$2 Leeds United	1.40	1.40
1054	A144	$2 Tottenham Hotspur	1.40	1.40
1055	A144	$2 Manchester United	1.40	1.40
1056	A144	$2 Everton	1.40	1.40
1057	A144	$2 Liverpool	1.40	1.40
1058	A144	$2 Portsmouth	1.40	1.40
1059	A144	$2 Arsenal	1.40	1.40
		Nos. 1052-1059 (8)	11.20	11.20

A145

1987 Wimbledon Tennis Championships A137

1987, June 22   Perf. 13x12½
988	A137	40c Hana Mandlikova	.25	.25
989	A137	60c Yannick Noah	.30	.30
990	A137	80c Ivan Lendl	.40	.40
991	A137	$1 Chris Evert Lloyd	.50	.50
992	A137	$1.25 Steffi Graf	.65	.65
993	A137	$1.50 John McEnroe	.85	.85
994	A137	$1.75 Martina Navratilova	.95	.95
995	A137	$2 Boris Becker	1.10	1.10
		Nos. 988-995 (8)	5.00	5.00

Souvenir Sheet
996		Sheet of 2	3.00	3.00
a.	A137	$2.25 like $2	1.50	1.50
b.	A137	$2.25 like $1.75	1.50	1.50

A Christmas Carol,
by Charles Dickens
(1812-1870) — A147

6c, Mr. Fezziwig's Ball. 25c, Ghost of Christmases to Come. 50c, The Cratchits. 75c, Carolers.
$5, Reading book to children.
Portrait of Dickens as left page of book (Nos. 1061a-1064a) and various scenes from novels as right page of book (Nos. 1061b-1064b).

1987, Dec. 17   **Perf. 14x14½**
Horiz. Pairs, #a.-b.

1061	A145	6c multicolored	.35	.35
1062	A145	25c multicolored	.70	.70
1063	A145	50c multicolored	1.25	1.25
1064	A145	75c multicolored	1.90	1.90
		Nos. 1061-1064 (4)	4.20	4.20

Souvenir Sheet

1065	A147	$5 multicolored	3.75	3.75

For surcharge see No. 3267.

Eastern Caribbean Currency — A148

Various Eastern Caribbean coins (Nos. 1069-1081) and banknotes (Nos. 1082-1086) in denominations equaling that of the stamp on which they are pictured.

1987-89   **Litho.**   **Perf. 15**

1069	A148	5c multicolored	.25	.25
1070	A148	6c multicolored	.25	.25
1071	A148	10c multicolored	.25	.25
1072	A148	12c multicolored	.25	.25
1073	A148	15c multicolored	.25	.25
1074	A148	20c multicolored	.25	.25
1075	A148	25c multicolored	.25	.25
1076	A148	30c multicolored	.25	.25
1077	A148	35c multicolored	.30	.30
1078	A148	45c multicolored	.35	.35
1079	A148	50c multicolored	.40	.40
1080	A148	65c multicolored	.50	.50
1081	A148	75c multicolored	.60	.60
1082	A148	$1 multi, horiz.	.75	.75
1083	A148	$2 multi, horiz.	1.50	1.50
1084	A148	$3 multi, horiz.	2.25	2.25
1085	A148	$5 multi, horiz.	3.75	3.75
1086	A148	$10 multi, horiz.	7.50	7.50

Perf. 14

1086A	A148	$20 multi, horiz.	15.00	15.00
		Nos. 1069-1086A (19)	34.90	34.90

Issued: $20, Nov. 7, 1989; others, Dec. 11.
For surcharges see Nos. 3240-3241, 3246, 3249, 3295.

1991   **Perf. 12**

1071a	A148	10c		.25
1073a	A148	15c		.25
1074a	A148	20c		.25
1075a	A148	25c		.25
1078a	A148	45c		.30
1079a	A148	50c		.35
1080a	A148	65c		.45
1081a	A148	75c		.55
1082a	A148	$1		.70
1083a	A148	$2		1.40
1085a	A148	$5		3.50
		Nos. 1071a-1085a (11)		8.25

This perf may not have been issued in St. Vincent.

1991   **Perf. 14**

1071b	A148	10c	.25	.25
1073b	A148	15c	.25	.25
1074b	A148	20c	.25	.25
1075b	A148	25c	.25	.25
1078b	A148	45c	.30	.30
1079b	A148	50c	.35	.35
1080b	A148	65c	.45	.45
1081b	A148	75c	.55	.55
1082b	A148	$1	.70	.70
1083b	A148	$2	1.40	1.40
1085b	A148	$5	3.50	3.50
		Nos. 1071b-1085b (11)	8.25	8.25

For surcharges see Nos. 3242, 3244, 3248, 3249a, 3254-3255, 3257-3257A.

US Constitution Bicentennial A149

Christopher Columbus's fleet: 15c, Santa Maria. 75c, Nina and Pinta. $1, Hour glass, compass. $1.50, Columbus planting flag of Spain on American soil. $3, Arawak natives. $4, Parrot, hummingbird, corn, pineapple, eggs. $5, $6, Columbus, Columbus'l coat of arms and caravel.

1988, Jan. 11   **Perf. 14½x14**

1087	A149	15c multicolored	.25	.25
1088	A149	75c multicolored	.60	.60
1089	A149	$1 multicolored	.75	.75
1090	A149	$1.50 multicolored	1.25	1.25
1091	A149	$3 multicolored	2.25	2.25
1092	A149	$4 multicolored	3.00	3.00
		Nos. 1087-1092 (6)	8.10	8.10

Souvenir Sheets
Perf. 14x14½, 14½x14

1093	A149	$5 multicolored	3.50	3.50
1093A	A149	$6 multicolored	4.25	4.25

US Constitution, bicent.; 500th anniv. of the discovery of America (in 1992).

Brown Pelican — A150

1988, Feb. 15   **Perf. 14**

1094	A150	45c multicolored	.75	.75

See No. 1298.

A151

Tourism — A152

10c, Windsurfing, diff., vert. 45c Scuba diving, vert. $5, Chartered ship.

1988, Feb. 22   **Litho.**   **Perf. 15**

1095	A151	10c multicolored	.25	.25
1096	A151	45c multicolored	.30	.30
1097	A151	65c shown	.45	.45
1098	A151	$5 multicolored	3.25	3.25
		Nos. 1095-1098 (4)	4.25	4.25

Souvenir Sheet
Perf. 13x12½

1099	A152	$10 shown	6.75	6.75

For surcharges see Nos. 3250, 3277.

A153

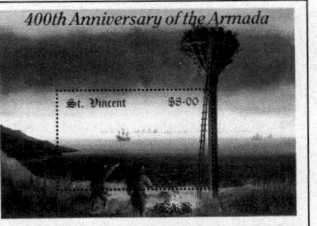

Destruction of the Spanish Armada by the English, 400th Anniv. — A154

16th cent. ships and artifacts: 15c, Nuestra Senora del Rosario, Spanish Chivalric Cross. 75c, Ark Royal, Armada medal. $1.50, English fleet, 16th cent. navigational instrument. $2, Dismasted galleon, cannon balls. $3.50, English fireships among the Armada, firebomb. $5, Revenge, Drake's drum. $8, Shoreline sentries awaiting the outcome of the battle.

1988, July 29   **Litho.**   **Perf. 12½**

1100	A153	15c multicolored	.25	.25
1101	A153	75c multicolored	.40	.40
1102	A153	$1.50 multicolored	.90	.90
1103	A153	$2 multicolored	1.10	1.10
1104	A153	$3.50 multicolored	1.90	1.90
1105	A153	$5 multicolored	2.75	2.75
		Nos. 1100-1105 (6)	7.30	7.30

Souvenir Sheet

1106	A154	$8 multicolored	4.75	4.75

Cricket Players A156

15c, D.K. Lillee. 50c, G.A. Gooch. 75c, R.N. Kapil Dev. $1, S.M. Gavaskar. $1.50, M.W. Gatting. $2.50, Imran Khan. $3, I.T. Botham. $4, I.V.A. Richards.

1988, July 29   **Litho.**   **Perf. 14½x14**

1108	A156	15c multicolored	.25	.25
1109	A156	50c multicolored	.35	.35
1110	A156	75c multicolored	.55	.55
1111	A156	$1 multicolored	.70	.70
1112	A156	$1.50 multicolored	1.00	1.00
1113	A156	$2.50 multicolored	1.75	1.75
1114	A156	$3 multicolored	2.00	2.00
1115	A156	$4 multicolored	2.75	2.75
		Nos. 1108-1115 (8)	9.35	9.35

A souvenir sheet containing a $2 stamp like No. 1115 and a $3.50 stamp like No. 1114 was not issued by the post office.

1988 Summer Olympics, Seoul A158

1988, Dec. 7   **Litho.**   **Perf. 14**

1116	A158	10c Running	.25	.25
1117	A158	50c Long jump, vert.	.35	.35
1118	A158	$1 Triple jump	.65	.65
1119	A158	$5 Boxing, vert.	3.50	3.50
		Nos. 1116-1119 (4)	4.75	4.75

Souvenir Sheet

1120	A158	$10 Torch	6.25	6.25

1st Participation of St. Vincent athletes in the Olympics.
For overprints see Nos. 1346-1351.

Christmas — A159

Walt Disney characters: 1c, Minnie Mouse in freight car. 2c, Morty and Ferdy in open rail car. 3c, Chip 'n Dale in open boxcar. 4c, Huey, Dewey, Louie and reindeer. 5c, Donald and Daisy Duck aboard dining car. 10c, Gramma Duck conducting chorus including Scrooge McDuck, Goofy and Clarabelle Cow. $5, No. 1127, Mickey Mouse in locomotive. $6, Santa Claus in caboose.
No. 1129, $5, Mickey, Minnie Mouse and nephews in train station, vert. No. 1130, $5, Characters riding carousel, vert.

Perf. 14x13½, 13½x14

1121-1128	A159	Set of 8	10.50	10.50

Souvenir Sheets

1129-1130	A159	Set of 2	10.50	10.50

Babe Ruth (1895-1948), American Baseball Star — A160

1988, Dec. 7   **Litho.**   **Perf. 14**

1131	A160	$2 multicolored	2.00	2.00

India '89, Jan. 20-29, New Delhi — A161

Exhibition emblem and Walt Disney characters: 1c, Mickey Mouse as snake charmer, Minnie Mouse as dancer. 2c, Goofy tossing rings at a chowsingha antelope. 3c, Mickey, Minnie, blue peacock. 5c, Goofy and Mickey as miners, Briolette diamond. 10c, Goofy as count presenting Orloff Diamond to Catherine the Great of Russia (Clarabelle Cow). 25c, Regent Diamond and Donald Duck as Napoleon (portrait) in the Louvre. $4, Minnie as Queen Victoria, Mickey as King Albert, crown bearing the Kohinoor Diamond. $5, Mickey and Goofy on safari.
No. 1140, $6, Mickey as Nehru, riding an elephant. No. 1141, $6, Mickey as postman delivering Hope Diamond to the Smithsonian Institute.

1989, Feb. 7   **Litho.**   **Perf. 14**

1132-1139	A161	Set of 8	11.50	11.50

Souvenir Sheets

1140-1141	A161	Set of 2	12.00	12.00

Entertainers of the Jazz and Big Band Eras — A162

Designs: 10c, Harry James (1916-83). 15c, Sidney Bechet (1897-1959). 25c, Benny Goodman (1909-86). 35c, Django Reinhardt (1910-53). 50c, Lester Young (1909-59). 90c, Gene Krupa (1909-73). $3, Louis Armstrong (1900-71). $4, Duke Ellington (1899-1974).
No. 1150, $5, Charlie Parker, Jr. (1920-55). No. 1151, $5, Billie Holiday (1915-59).

1989, Apr. 3   **Litho.**   **Perf. 14**

1142-1149	A162	Set of 8	10.00	10.00

Souvenir Sheets

1150-1151	A162	Set of 2	11.00	11.00

Holiday misspelled "Holliday" on No. 1151.
For surcharge see No. 3274.

Miniature Sheet

Noah's Ark — A163

Designs: a, Clouds, 2 birds at right. b, Rainbow, 4 clouds. c, Ark. d, Rainbow, 3 clouds. e, Clouds, 2 birds at left. f, African elephant facing right. g, Elephant facing forward. h, Leaves on tree branch. i, Kangaroos. j, Hummingbird facing left, flower. k, Lions. l, White-tailed deer. m, Koala at right. n, Koala at left. o, Hummingbird facing right, flower. p, Flower, toucan facing left. q, Toucan facing right. r, Camels. s, Giraffes. t, Sheep. u, Ladybugs. v, Butterfly (UR). w, Butterfly (LL). x, Snakes. y, Dragonflies.

1989, Apr. 10			**Perf. 14**	
1152	A163	Sheet of 25	14.50	14.50
a.-y.		40c any single	.30	.30

Easter
A164

Paintings by Titian: 5c, Baptism of Christ. 30c, Temptation of Christ. 45c, Ecce Homo. 65c, Noli Me Tangere. 75c, Christ Carrying the Cross. $1, Christ Crowned with Thorns. $4, Lamentation Over Christ. $5, The Entombment.
No. 1161, $6, Pieta. No. 1162, $6, The Deposition.

1989, Apr. 17			**Perf. 13½x14**	
1153-1160	A164	Set of 8	12.50	12.50
		Souvenir Sheets		
1161-1162	A164	Set of 2	11.50	11.50

Telstar II and
Cooperation in
Space — A165

Designs: 15c, Recovery of astronaut L. Gordon Cooper, Mercury 9/Faith 7 mission. 35c, Satellite transmission of Martin Luther King's civil rights march address, 1963. 40c, US shuttle STS-7, 1st use of Canadarm, deployment & recovery of a W. German free-flying experiment platform. 50c, Satellite transmission of the 1964 Olympics, Innsbruck (speed skater). 60c, Vladimir Remek of Czechoslovakia, 1st non-Soviet cosmonaut, 1978. $1, CNES Hermes space plane, France, ESA emblem, Columbus space station. $3, Satellite transmission of Pope John XXIII (1881-1963) blessing crowd at the Vatican. $4, Ulf Merbold, W. Germany, 1st non-American astronaut, 1983.
No. 1171, $5, Launch of Telstar II, 5/7/63. No. 1172, $5, 1975 Apollo-Soyuz mission members shaking hands.

1989, Apr. 26		**Litho.**	**Perf. 14**	
1163-1170	A165	Set of 8	10.00	10.00
		Souvenir Sheets		
1171-1172	A165	Set of 2	9.00	9.00

Famous
Ocean
Liners
A166

1989, Apr. 21		**Litho.**	**Perf. 14**	
1173	A166	10c Ile de France	.35	.35
1174	A166	40c Liberte	.50	.50
1175	A166	50c Mauretania	.70	.70
1176	A166	75c France	.95	.95
1177	A166	$1 Aquitania	1.25	1.25
1178	A166	$2 United States	2.50	2.50
1179	A166	$3 Olympic	3.50	3.50
1180	A166	$4 Queen Elizabeth	4.75	4.75
		Nos. 1173-1180 (8)	14.50	14.50
		Souvenir Sheets		
1181	A166	$6 Queen Mary	7.25	7.25
1182	A166	$6 QE 2	7.25	7.25

Nos. 1181-1182 contain 84x28mm stamps.
For overprints see Nos. 1352-1361.

Souvenir Sheet

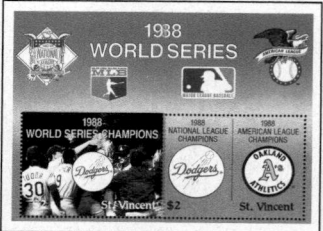

1988 World Series — A167

No. 1183: a, Dodgers emblem and players celebrating victory. b, Emblems of the Dodgers and the Oakland Athletics.

1989, May 3		**Litho.**	**Perf. 14x13½**	
1183	A167	Sheet of 2	6.25	6.25
a.-b.		$2 any single	1.60	1.60

World
Wildlife
Fund, St.
Vincent
Parrots
A168

Indigenous Birds — A169

10c, Parrot's head. 20c, Parrot's wing span. 25c, Mistletoe bird. 40c, Parrot feeding, vert. 70c, Parrot on rock, vert. 75c, Crab hawk. $2, Coucou. $3, Prince bird.
No. 1192, Doctor bird. No. 1193, Soufrieres, vert.

1989, Apr. 5			**Perf. 14**	
1184	A168	10c multicolored	.70	.55
1185	A168	20c multicolored	1.25	.55
1186	A168	25c multicolored	.55	.55
1187	A168	40c multicolored	2.00	2.25
1188	A168	70c multicolored	2.50	1.40
1189	A169	75c multicolored	1.75	1.75
1190	A169	$2 multicolored	2.00	2.00
1191	A169	$3 multicolored	3.00	3.00
		Nos. 1184-1191 (8)	13.75	12.05
		Souvenir Sheets		
1192	A169	$5 multicolored	4.25	4.25
1193	A169	$5 multicolored	4.25	4.25

Fan Paintings — A170

Paintings by Hiroshige unless otherwise stated: 10c, Autumn Flowers in Front of the Full Moon. 40c, Hibiscus. 50c, Iris. 75c, Morning Glories. $1, Dancing Swallows. $2, Sparrow and Bamboo. $3, Yellow Bird and Cotton Rose. $4, Judos Chrysanthemums in a deep ravine in China.
No. 1202, $6, Rural Cottages in Spring, by Sotatsu. No. 1203, $6, The Six Immortal Poets Portrayed as Cats, by Kuniyoshi.

1989, July 6		**Litho.**	**Perf. 14x13½**	
1194-1201	A170	Set of 8	11.00	11.00
		Souvenir Sheets		
1202-1203	A170	Set of 2	10.00	10.00

Hirohito (1901-89) and enthronement of Akihito as emperor of Japan.

First
Moon
Landing,
20th
Anniv.
A171

Apollo 11 Mission: 35c, Columbia command module. 75c, Lunar module Eagle landing. $1, Rocket launch. No. 1207a, Buzz Aldrin conducting solar wind experiments. No. 1207b, Lunar module on plain. No. 1207c, Earthrise. No. 1207d, Neil Armstrong. No. 1208, Separation of lunar and command modules. No. 1209a, Command module. No. 1209b, Lunar module. $6, Armstrong preparing to take man's 1st step onto the Moon.

1989, Sept. 11			**Perf. 14**	
1204	A171	35c multicolored	.40	.30
1205	A171	75c multicolored	1.00	.55
1206	A171	$1 multicolored	1.10	.75
1207		Strip of 4	8.00	8.00
a.-d.	A171	$2 any single	1.40	1.40
1208	A171	$3 multicolored	3.25	3.25
		Nos. 1204-1208 (5)	13.75	12.85
		Souvenir Sheets		
1209		Sheet of 2	6.50	6.50
a.-b.	A171	$3 any single	2.25	2.25
1210	A171	$6 multicolored	6.50	6.50

No. 1207 has continuous design.

Players Elected to
the Baseball Hall
of Fame — A172

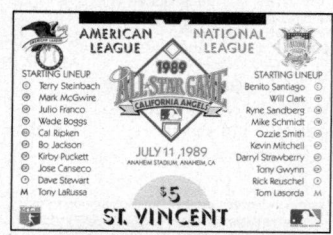

1989 All-Star Game, July 11,
Anaheim, California — A173

1989, July 23		**Litho.**	**Perf. 14**	
1211	A172	$2 Cobb, 1936	1.40	1.40
1212	A172	$2 Mays, 1979	1.40	1.40
1213	A172	$2 Musial, 1969	1.40	1.40
1214	A172	$2 Bench, 1989	1.40	1.40
1215	A172	$2 Banks, 1977	1.40	1.40
1216	A172	$2 Schoendienst, 1989	1.40	1.40
1217	A172	$2 Gehrig, 1939	1.40	1.40
1218	A172	$2 Robinson, 1962	1.40	1.40
1219	A172	$2 Feller, 1962	1.40	1.40
1220	A172	$2 Williams, 1966	1.40	1.40
1221	A172	$2 Yastrzemski, 1989	1.40	1.40
1222	A172	$2 Kaline, 1980	1.40	1.40
		Nos. 1211-1222 (12)	16.80	16.80

"Yastrzemski" is misspelled on No. 1221.

Size: 116x82mm
Imperf

1223	A173	$5 multicolored	5.75	5.75

Baseball Hall of Fame
Members — A173a

No. 1223A, Johnny Bench. No. 1223B, Carl Yastrzemski. No. 1223C, Ernie Banks. No. 1223D, Willie Mays. No. 1223E, Al Kaline. No. 1223F, Ty Cobb. No. 1223G, Ted Williams. No. 1223H, Red Schoendienst. No. 1223I, Jackie Robinson. No. 1223J, Lou Gehrig. No. 1223K, Bob Feller. No. 1223L, Stan Musial.

1989		**Embossed**	**Perf. 13**	
1223A-1223L	A173a	$20 Set of 12		

Miniature Sheets

Rookies and Team Emblems — A174

Rookies of
the Year,
Most
Valuable
Players and
Cy Young
Award
Winners
A175

No. 1224: a, Dante Bichette, 1989. b, Carl Yastrzemski, 1961. c, Randy Johnson, 1989. d, Jerome Walton, 1989. e, Ramon Martinez, 1989. f, Ken Hill, 1989. g, Tom McCarthy, 1989. h, Gaylord Perry, 1963. i, John Smoltz, 1989.
No. 1225: a, Bob Milacki, 1989. b, Babe Ruth, 1915. c, Jim Abbott, 1989. d, Gary Sheffield, 1989. e, Gregg Jeffries, 1989. f, Kevin Brown, 1989. g, Cris Carpenter, 1989. h, Johnny Bench, 1968. i, Ken Griffey Jr., 1989.
No. 1226: a, Chris Sabo, 1988 Natl. League Rookie of the Year. b, Walt Weiss, 1988 American League Rookie of the Year. c, Willie Mays, 1951 Rookie of the Year. d, Kirk Gibson, 1988 Natl. League Most Valuable Player. e, Ted Williams, 1946 Most Valuable Player of 1946 and 1949. f, Jose Canseco, 1988 American League Most Valuable Player. g, Gaylord Perry, Cy Young winner for 1972 and 1978. h, Orel Hershiser, 1988 National League Cy Young winner. i, Frank Viola, 1988 American League Cy Young winner.

Perf. 13½

1224	A174	Sheet of 9	5.00	5.00
a.-i.		60c any single	.50	.50

1225	A174	Sheet of 9	5.00 5.00
		A174 60c any single	.50 .50
1226	A175	Sheet of 9	5.00 5.00
a.-i.		A175 60c any single	.50 .50

For surcharges see Nos. B9-B11.

French Revolution Bicent.,
PHILEXFRANCE '89 — A176

French governors and ships.

1989, July 7		**Litho.**	**Perf. 13½x14**
1227	A176	30c Goelette	.65 .65
1228	A176	55c Corvette	1.00 1.00
1229	A176	75c Fregate 36	1.60 1.60
1230	A176	$1 Vaisseau 74	2.00 2.00
1231	A176	$3 Ville de Paris	6.00 6.00
		Nos. 1227-1231 (5)	11.25 11.25

Souvenir Sheet

1232	A176	$6 Map	6.00 6.00

Miniature Sheet

Discovery of the New World, 500th
Anniv. (in 1992) — A177

No. 1233: a, Map of Florida, queen conch
and West Indian purpura. b, Caribbean reef
fish. c, Sperm whale. d, Columbus's fleet. e,
Cuba, Isle of Pines, remora. f, The Bahamas,
Turks & Caicos Isls., Columbus raising Spanish flag. g, Navigational instruments. h, Sea
monster. i, Kemp's Ridley turtle, Cayman Isls.
j, Jamaica, parts of Cuba and Hispaniola,
magnificent frigatebird. k, Caribbean manatee,
Hispaniola, Puerto Rico, Virgin Isls. l, Caribbean Monk seal, Anguilla and Caribbean isls.
m, Mayan chief, galleon, dugout canoe. n,
Masked boobies. o, Venezuelan village on pil-
ings and the Netherlands Antilles. p, Atlantic
wing oyster, lion's paw scallop, St. Vincent,
Grenada, Trinidad & Tobago, Barbados. q,
Panama, great hammerhead and mako
sharks. r, Brown pelican, Colombia, Hyacin-
thine macaw. s, Venezuela, Indian bow and
spear hunters. t, Capuchin and squirrel
monkeys.

1989, Aug. 31			**Perf. 14**
1233	A177	Sheet of 20	17.00 17.00
a.-t.		50c any single	.70 .70

Major League Baseball: Los Angeles
Dodgers — A178

No. 1234: a, Jay Howell, Alejandro Pena. b,
Mike Davis, Kirk Gibson. c, Fernando
Valenzuela, John Shelby. d, Jeff Hamilton,
Franklin Stubbs. e, Dodger Stadium. f, Ray
Searage, John Tudor. g, Mike Sharperson,
Mickey Hatcher. h, Coaches Amalfitano,
Cresse, Ferguson, Hines, Mota, Perranoski,
Russell. i, John Wetteland, Ramon Martinez.

No. 1235: a, Tim Belcher, Tim Crews. b,
Orel Hershiser, Mike Morgan. c, Mike Scios-
cia, Rick Dempsey. d, Dave Anderson, Alfredo
Griffin. e, Team emblem. f, Kal Daniels, Mike
Marshall. g, Eddie Murray, Willie Randolph. h,
Manager Tom Lasorda, Jose Gonzalez. i,
Lenny Harris, Chris Gwynn, Billy Bean.

1989, Sept. 23			**Perf. 12½**
1234		Sheet of 9	6.50 6.50
a.-i.		A178 60c any single	.55 .55
1235		Sheet of 9	6.50 6.50
a.-i.		A178 60c any single	.55 .55

See Nos. 1344-1345.

1990 World Cup Soccer
Championships, Italy — A179

55c, Youth soccer teams. $1, Natl. team. $5,
Trophy winners.
No. 1240, Youth soccer team. No. 1241,
Natl. team, diff.

1989, Oct. 16		**Litho.**	**Perf. 14**
1236	A179	10c shown	.30 .30
1237	A179	55c multicolored	.60 .60
1238	A179	$1 multicolored	1.10 1.10
1239	A179	$5 multicolored	5.50 5.50
		Nos. 1236-1239 (4)	7.50 7.50

Souvenir Sheets

1240	A179	$6 multicolored	6.50 6.50
1241	A179	$6 multicolored	6.50 6.50

Fauna
and Flora
A180

1989, Nov. 1			
1242	A180	65c St. Vincent parrot	.90 .90
1243	A180	75c Whistling warbler	1.10 1.10
1244	A180	$5 Black snake	7.00 7.00
		Nos. 1242-1244 (3)	9.00 9.00

Souvenir Sheet

1245	A180	$6 Volcano plant, vert.	6.50 6.50

Butterflies
A181

1989, Oct. 16		**Perf. 14x14½, 14½x14**
1246	A181	6c Little yellow	.30 .25
1247	A181	10c Orion	.30 .25
1248	A181	15c American painted lady	.30 .25
1249	A181	75c Cassius blue	.95 .60
1250	A181	$1 Polydamus swallowtail	1.20 1.20
1251	A181	$2 Guaraguao skipper	2.40 2.40
1252	A181	$3 The Queen	3.50 3.50
1253	A181	$5 Royal blue	6.00 6.00
		Nos. 1246-1253 (8)	14.95 14.45

Souvenir Sheets

1254	A181	$6 Monarch	6.50 6.50
1255	A181	$6 Barred sulphur	6.50 6.50

Exhibition
Emblem,
Disney
Characters
and US
Natl.
Monuments
A182

Designs: 1c, Seagull Monument, UT. 2c,
Lincoln Memorial, Washington, DC. 3c, Crazy
Horse Memorial, SD. 4c, Uncle Sam Wilson,
Troy, NY. 5c, Benjamin Franklin Natl. Memo-
rial, Philadelphia, PA. 10c, Statue of George
Washington, Federal Hall, NY. $3, John F.
Kennedy's birthplace, Brookline, MA. $6,

George Washington's home, Mount Vernon,
VA.
No. 1264, $5, Mt. Rushmore, SD. No. 1265,
$5, Stone Mountain, GA.

1989, Nov. 17		**Perf. 13½x14**
1256-1263	A182	Set of 8	12.50 12.50

Souvenir Sheets

1264-1265	A182	Set of 2	13.50 13.50

World Stamp Expo '89.

Souvenir Sheet

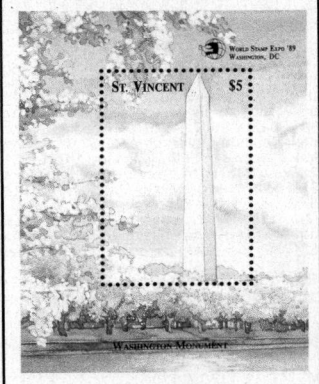

The Washington Monument,
Washington, DC — A183

1989, Nov. 17		**Litho.**	**Perf. 14**
1266	A183	$5 multicolored	4.25 4.25

World Stamp Expo '89.

Major League Baseball — A184

Players, owners and commissioner.
No. 1267, 30c: a, Early Wynn. b, Cecil
Cooper. c, Joe DiMaggio. d, Kevin Mitchell. e,
Tom Browning. f, Bobby Witt. g, Tim Wallach.
h, Bob Gibson. i, Steve Garvey.
No. 1268, 30c: a, Rick Sutcliffe. b, A. Bartlett
Giamatti, commissioner. c, Cory Snyder. d,
Rollie Fingers. e, Willie Hernandez. f, Sandy
Koufax. g, Carl Yastrzemski. h, Ron Darling. i,
Gerald Perry.
No. 1269, 30c: a, Mike Marshall. b, Tom
Seaver. c, Bob Milacki. d, Dave Smith. e,
Robin Roberts. f, Kent Hrbek. g, Bill Veeck,
owner. h, Carmelo Martinez. i, Rogers
Hornsby.
No. 1270, 30c: a, Barry Bonds. b, Jim
Palmer. c, Lou Boudreau. d, Ernie Whitt. e,
Jose Canseco. f, Ken Griffey, Jr. g, Johnny
Vander Meer. h, Kevin Seitzer. i, Dave
Dravecky.
No. 1271, 30c: a, Glenn Davis. b, Nolan
Ryan. c, Hank Greenberg. d, Richie Allen. e,
Dave Righetti. f, Jim Abbott. g, Harold Reyn-
olds. h, Dennis Martinez. i, Rod Carew.
No. 1272, 30c: a, Joe Morgan. b, Tony Fer-
nandez. c, Ozzie Guillen. d, Mike Greenwell.
e, Bobby Valentine. f, Doug DeCinces. g,
Mickey Cochrane. h, Willie McGee. i, Von
Hayes.
No. 1273, 30c: a, Frank White. b, Brook
Jacoby. c, Boog Powell. d, Will Clark. e, Ray
Kroc, owner. f, Fred McGriff. g, Willie Stargell.
h, John Smoltz. i, B. J. Surhoff.
No. 1274, 30c: a, Keith Hernandez. b, Eddie
Matthews. c, Tom Paciorek. d, Alan Trammell.
e, Greg Maddux. f, Ruben Sierra. g, Tony
Oliva. h, Chris Bosio. i, Orel Hershiser.
No. 1275, 30c: a, Casey Stengel. b, Jim
Rice. c, Reggie Jackson. d, Jerome Walton. e,
Bob Knepper. f, Andres Galarraga. g, Christy
Mathewson. h, Willie Wilson. i, Ralph Kiner.

1989, Nov. 30		**Perf. 12½**
		Sheets of 9, #a-i
1267-1275	A184	Set of 9	29.00 29.00

No. 1268d is incorrectly inscribed "Finger."
Cochrane is misspelled "Cochpane" on No.
1272g.
No. 1272d was also issued in sheets of 9.

Achievements of Nolan Ryan,
American Baseball Player — A185

No. 1276 — Portrait and inscriptions: a, 383
League-leading strikeouts, 1973. b, No hitter,
Kansas City Royals, May 15, 1973. c, No hit-
ter, Detroit Tigers, July 15, 1973. d, No hitter,
Minnesota Twins, Sept. 28, 1974. e, No hitter,
Baltimore Orioles, June 1, 1975. f, No hitter,
Los Angeles Dodgers, Sept. 26, 1981. g, Won
100+ games in both leagues. h, Struck out
200+ batters in 13 seasons. i, 5000th Strike-
out, Aug. 22, 1989, Arlington, Texas.

1989, Nov. 30		**Litho.**	**Perf. 12½**
1276		Sheet of 9	12.00 12.00
a.-i.		A185 $2 any single	1.30 1.30

For overprints see Nos. 1336-1337.

Coat of Arms, No.
570 — A186

1989, Dec. 20			**Perf. 14**
1278	A186	65c multicolored	.90 .90

Souvenir Sheet

1279	A186	$10 multicolored	8.75 8.75

Independence, 10th anniv.

Boy Scouts and
Girl
Guides — A187

Lord or Lady Baden-Powell and: No. 1280,
Boy's modern uniform. No. 1281, Guide,
ranger and brownie. No. 1282, Boy's old uniform. No. 1283, Mrs. Jackson. No. 1284, 75th
anniversary emblem. No. 1285, Mrs. Russell
No. 1286, Canoeing, merit badges, No.
1287, Flag-raising, Camp Yourumei, 1985.

1989, Dec. 20			**Perf. 14**
1280	A187	35c multi	.65 .65
1281	A187	35c multi	.65 .65
1282	A187	55c multi	.85 .85
1283	A187	55c multi	.85 .85
1284	A187	$2 multi	3.25 3.25
1285	A187	$2 multi	3.25 3.25
		Nos. 1280-1285 (6)	9.50 9.50

Souvenir Sheets

1286	A187	$5 multi	6.25 6.25
1287	A187	$5 multi	6.25 6.25

Christmas — A188

Paintings by Da Vinci and Botticelli: 10c, The Adoration of the Magi (holy family), by Botticelli. 25c, The Adoration of the Magi (witnesses). 30c, The Madonna of the Magnificat, by Botticelli. 40c, The Virgin and Child with St. Anne and St. John the Baptist, by Da Vinci. 55c, The Annunciation (angel), by Da Vinci. 75c, The Annunciation (Madonna). No. 1294, $5, Madonna of the Carnation, by Da Vinci. $6, The Annunciation, by Botticelli. No. 1296, $5 The Virgin of the Rocks, by Da Vinci. No. 1297, $5, The Adoration of the Magi, by Botticelli.

1989, Dec. 20   **Perf. 14**
1288-1295 A188 Set of 8   12.00 12.00

Souvenir Sheets
1296-1297 A188 Set of 2   8.75 8.75

Bird Type of 1988
1989, July 31 Litho.   Perf. 15x14
1298 A150 55c St. Vincent parrot   .90   .90

Lions Intl. of St. Vincent, 25th Anniv. (in 1989) A189

Services: 10c, Scholarships for the blind, vert. 65c, Free textbooks. 75c, Health education (diabetes). $2, Blood sugar testing machines. $4, Publishing and distribution of pamphlets on drug abuse.

1990, Mar. 5 Litho.   Perf. 14
1303-1307 A189 Set of 5   7.75 7.75
For surcharge see No. 3345.

World War II A190

Historic events: 5c, Defeat of the Graf Spee, 12/13-17/39. 10c, Charles De Gaulle calls the French Resistance to arms, 6/18/40. 15c, The British drive the Italian army out of Egypt, 12/15/40. 25c, US destroyer Reuben James torpedoed off Iceland, 10/31/41. 30c, MacArthur becomes allied supreme commander of the southwest Pacific, 4/18/42. 40c, US forces attack Corregidor, 2/16/45. 55c, HMS King George V engages the Bismarck, 5/27/41. 75c, US fleet enters Tokyo Harbor, 8/27/45. $5, Russian takeover of Berlin completed, 5/2/45. $6, #1317, Battle of the Philippine Sea, 6/18/44. #1318, Battle of the Java Sea, 2/28/42.

1990, Apr. 2   Perf. 14x13½
1308-1317 A190 Set of 10   17.00 17.00

Souvenir Sheet
1318 A190 $6 multi   7.75 7.75

Penny Black, 150th Anniv. — A191

Great Britain No. 1 (various plate positions).

1990, May 3 Litho.   Perf. 14x15
1319 A191 $2 "NK"   2.25 2.25
1320 A191 $4 "AB"   4.50 4.50

Souvenir Sheet
1321 A191 $6 Simulated #1, "SV" 6.75 6.75

Stamp World London '90 — A192

Walt Disney characters in British military uniforms: 5c, Donald Duck as 18th cent. Admiral. 10c, Huey as Bugler, 68th Light Infantry, 1854. 15c, Minnie Mouse as Drummer, 1st Irish Guards, 1900. 25c, Goofy as Lance Corporal, Seaforth Highlanders, 1944. $1, Mickey Mouse as officer, 58th Regiment, 1879, 1881. $2, Donald Duck as officer, Royal Engineers, 1813. $4, Mickey Mouse as Drum Major, 1914. $5 Goofy as Pipe Sergeant, 1918.
No. 1330, $6, Scrooge as Company Clerk and Goofy as King's Lifeguard of Foot. No. 1331, $6, Mickey Mouse as British Grenadier.

1990, May Litho.   Perf. 13½x14
1322-1329 A192 Set of 8   17.00 17.00

Souvenir Sheets
1330-1331 A192 Set of 2   13.50 13.50

A193

1990, July 5   Perf. 14
1332 $2 In robes   1.75 1.75
1333 $2 Queen Mother signing book 1.75 1.75
1334 $2 In fur coat   1.75 1.75
  a. A193 Strip of 3, #1332-1334 5.25 5.25
      Nos. 1332-1334 (3)   5.25 5.25

Souvenir Sheet
1335 A194 $6 Like No. 1334   4.75 4.75

No. 1276 Overprinted

a

b

1990, July 23 Litho.   Perf. 12½
Miniature Sheets
1336 A185(a) $2 Sheet of 9, #a-i   12.50 12.50
1337 A185(b) $2 Sheet of 9, #a-i   12.50 12.50

World Cup Soccer Championships, Italy — A195

Players from participating countries.

1990, Sept. 24 Litho.   Perf. 14
1338 A195 10c Argentina   .35   .25
1339 A195 75c Colombia   .95   .95
1340 A195 $1 Uruguay   1.25 1.25
1341 A195 $5 Belgium   7.00 7.00
      Nos. 1338-1341 (4)   9.55 9.45

Souvenir Sheets
1342 A195 $6 Brazil   5.75 5.75
1343 A195 $6 West Germany   5.75 5.75

Dodger Baseball Type of 1989
No. 1344: a, Hubie Brooks, Orel Hershiser. b, Manager Tom Lasorda, Tim Crews. c, Fernando Valenzuela, Eddie Murray. d, Kal Daniels, Jose Gonzalez. e, Dodger centennial emblem. f, Chris Gwynn, Jeff Hamilton. g, Kirk Gibson, Rick Dempsey. h, Jim Gott, Alfredo Griffin. i, Coaches, Ron Perranoski, Bill Russell, Joe Ferguson, Joe Amalfitano, Mark Cresse, Ben Hines, Manny Mota.
No. 1345: a, Mickey Hatcher, Jay Howell. b, Juan Samuel, Mike Scioscia. c, Lenny Harris, Mike Hartley. d, Ramon Martinez, Mike Morgan. e, Dodger Stadium. f, Stan Javier, Don Aase. g, Ray Searage, Mike Sharperson. h, Tim Belcher, Pat Perry. i, Dave Walsh, Jose Vizcaino, Jim Neidlinger, Jose Offerman, Carlos Hernandez.

Hyphen-hole roulette 7
1990, Sept. 21
1344 Sheet of 9   6.50 6.50
  a.-I. A178 60c any single   .35   .35
1345 Sheet of 9   6.50 6.50
  a.-I. A178 60c any single   .35   .35

Nos. 1116-1120 Overprinted

Overprints: 50c, "CARL / LEWIS / U.S.A.". $1, "HRISTO / MARKOV / BULGARIA". $5, "HENRY / MASKE / E. GERMANY".
No. 1350, USSR, US medals. No. 1351, South Korea, Spain medals.

1990, Oct. 18   Perf. 14
1346 A158 10c shown   .30   .30
1347 A158 50c multicolored   .55   .55
1348 A158 $1 multicolored   .95   .95
1349 A158 $5 multicolored   5.00 5.00
      Nos. 1346-1349 (4)   6.80 6.80

Souvenir Sheets
1350 A158 $10 multicolored   6.75 6.75
1351 A158 $10 multicolored   6.75 6.75

Nos. 1173-1182 Overprinted

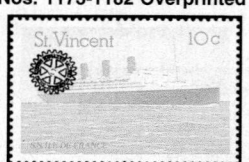

1990, Oct. 18 Litho.   Perf. 14
1352 A166 10c Ile de France   .30   .30
1353 A166 40c Liberte   .35   .35
1354 A166 50c Mauretania   .50   .50
1355 A166 75c France   .70   .70
1356 A166 $1 Aquitania   1.00 1.00
1357 A166 $2 United States   1.90 1.90
1358 A166 $3 Olympic   2.75 2.75
1359 A166 $4 Queen Elizabeth 4.00 4.00
      Nos. 1352-1359 (8)   11.50 11.50

Souvenir Sheets
1360 A166 $6 Queen Mary   5.75 5.75
1361 A166 $6 QE 2   5.75 5.75
Overprint on #1360-1361 is 12mm in diameter.

Orchids — A196

Designs: 10c, Dendrophylax funalis, Dimeranda emarginata. 15c, Epidendrum elongatum. 45c, Comparettia falcata. 60c, Brassia maculata. $1, Encyclia cochleata, Encyclia cordigera. $2, Cyrtopodium punctatum. $4, Cattelya labiata. $5, Bletia purpurea.
No. 1370, $6, Ionopsis utricularioides. No. 1371, $6, Vanilla planifolia.

1990, Nov. 23
1362-1369 A196 Set of 8   20.00 20.00

Souvenir Sheets
1370-1371 A196 Set of 2   17.00 17.00

Christmas A197

Details from paintings by Rubens: 10c, Miraculous Draught of Fishes. 45c, $2, Crowning of Holy Katherine. 50c, St. Ives of Treguier. 65c, Allegory of Eternity. $1, $4, St. Bavo Receives Monastic Habit of Ghent. $5, Communion of St. Francis.
No. 1380, $6, St. Ives of Treguier (entire). No. 1381, $6, Allegory of Eternity. No. 1382, $6, St. Bavo Receives Monastic Habit of Ghent, horiz. No. 1383, $6, The Miraculous Draft of Fishes, horiz.

1990, Dec. 3 Litho.   Perf. 14
1372-1379 A197 Set of 8   13.00 13.00

Souvenir Sheets
1380-1383 A197 Set of 4   16.50 16.50

Intl. Literacy Year A198

Canterbury Tales: a, Geoffrey Chaucer (1342-1400), author. b, "When April with his showers sweet..." c, "When Zephyr also has,..." d. "And many little birds make melody..." e, "And palmers to go seeking out strange strands..." f, Quill pen, open book. g, Bluebird in tree. h, Trees, rider's head with white hair. i, Banner on staff. j, Town. k, Rider's head, diff. l, Blackbird in tree. m, Old monk. n, Horse, rider. o, Nun, monk carrying banner. p, Monks. q, White horse, rider. r, Black horse, rider. s, Squirrel. t, Rooster. u, Chickens. v, Rabbit. w, Butterfly. x, Mouse.

1990, Dec. 12   Perf. 13½
1384 Sheet of 24   17.00 17.00
  a.-x. A198 40c any single   .30   .30

Vincent Van Gogh (1853-1890),
Painter — A198a

Self-portraits.

1990, Dec. 17			Litho.		*Perf. 13*
1385	A198a	1c	1889	.30	.30
1386	A198a	5c	1886	.30	.30
1387	A198a	10c	1888, with hat & pipe	.30	.30
1388	A198a	15c	1888, painting	.30	.30
a.			Strip of 4, #1385-1388	.50	.50
1389	A198a	20c	1887	.30	.30
1390	A198a	45c	1889, diff.	.55	.55
1391	A198a	$5	1889, with bandaged ear	5.75	5.75
1392	A198a	$6	1887, with straw hat	7.00	7.00
a.			Strip of 4, #1389-1392	14.50	14.50
			Nos. 1385-1392 (8)	14.80	14.80

Hummel Figurines — A199

10c, Photographer. 15c, Boy with ladder & rope. 40c, Pharmacist. 60c, Boy answering telephone. $1, Bootmaker. $2, Artist. $4, Waiter. $5, Mailman.

1990, Dec. 30			Litho.		*Perf. 14*
1393	A199	10c	multicolored	.25	.25
1394	A199	15c	multicolored	.25	.25
1395	A199	40c	multicolored	.35	.30
1396	A199	60c	multicolored	.50	.40
1396A	A199	$1	multicolored	.85	.60
1396B	A199	$2	multicolored	1.75	1.75
1397	A199	$4	multicolored	3.75	3.75
a.			Sheet of 4, 15c, 40c, $2, $4	6.00	6.00
1398	A199	$5	multicolored	3.75	3.75
a.			Sheet of 4, 10c, 60c, $1, $5	6.00	6.00
			Nos. 1393-1398 (8)	11.45	11.05

Souvenir Sheets

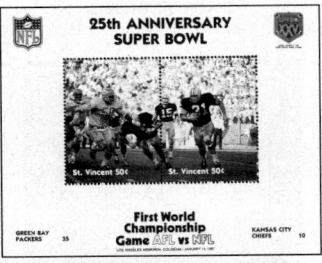

Super Bowl Highlights — A200

Designs: Nos. 1400-1424, Players in action in Super Bowl I (1967) through Super Bowl XXV (1991). Nos. 1400-1423 contain two 50c stamps printed with continuous design showing game highlights. No. 1424 contains three 50c stamps showing AFC and NFC team helmets and the Vince Lombardi Trophy.
Nos. 1425-1449, $2, picture Super Bowl Program Covers. Nos. 1443, 1449 horiz.

1991, Jan. 15		Litho.	*Perf. 13½x14*	
1400-1424	A200	Set of 25	32.00	32.00

Size: 99x125mm

Imperf

| 1425-1449 | A200 | $2 Set of 25 | 60.00 | 60.00 |

Miniature Sheets

Discovery of America, 500th Anniv. (in 1992) — A201

No. 1450: a, 1c, US #230. b, 2c, US #231. c, 3c, US #232. d, 4c, US #233. e, 5c, US #234. g, 6c, US #235. h, 8c, US #236. i, 10c, US #237.
No. 1451: a, 15c, US #238. b, 30c, US #239. c, 50c, US #240. d, $1, US #241. e, $10, Compass rose, sailing ship. f, $2, US #242. g, $3, US #243. h, $4, US #244. i, $5, US #245.
No. 1452, Bow of sailing ship. No. 1453, Ship's figurehead.

1991, Mar. 18		Litho.	*Perf. 14*	
1450	A201	Sheet of 9, #a-i	9.00	9.00
1451	A201	Sheet of 9, #a-i	22.50	22.50

Souvenir Sheets

1452	A201	$6 multicolored	6.75	6.75
1453	A201	$6 multicolored	6.75	6.75

Nos. 1452-1453 each contain one 38x31mm stamp.

Jetsons, The Movie — A202

Hanna-Barbera characters: 5c, Cosmo Spacely, vert. 20c, Elroy, Judy, Astro, Jane & George Jetson, vert. 45c, Judy, Apollo Blue, vert. 50c, Mr. Spacely, George, vert. 60c, George, sprocket factory. $1, Apollo Blue, Judy, Elroy and Grungees. $2, Jane and George in Grungee cavern. $4, George, Elroy, Jane and Little Grungee, vert. $5, Jetsons leaving for Earth, vert.
No. 1463, $6, Jetsons in sprocket factory. No. 1464, $6, Jetsons traveling to Orbiting Ore Asteroid.

1991, Mar. 25		Litho.	*Perf. 13½*	
1454-1462	A202	Set of 9	14.00	14.00

Souvenir Sheets

1463-1464	A202	Set of 2	11.00	11.00

The Flintstones Enjoy Sports — A203

1991, Mar. 25					
1465	A203	10c	Boxing	.35	.25
1466	A203	15c	Soccer	.35	.25
1467	A203	45c	Rowing	.55	.35
1468	A203	55c	Dinosaur riding	.65	.40
1469	A203	$1	Basketball	1.00	.65
1470	A203	$2	Wrestling	2.25	1.75
1471	A203	$4	Tennis	4.50	4.50
1472	A203	$5	Cycling	5.75	5.75
			Nos. 1465-1472 (8)	15.40	13.90

Souvenir Sheets

1473	A203	$6	Baseball, batting	6.75	6.75
1474	A203	$6	Baseball, sliding home	6.75	6.75

Voyages of Discovery A204

Designs: 5c, Sanger 2. 10c, Magellan probe, 1990. 25c, Buran space shuttle. 75c, American space station. $1, Mars mission, 21st century. $2, Hubble space telescope, 1990. $4, Sailship to Mars. $5, Craf satellite, 2000.
No. 1483, $6, Sailing ship, island hopping. No. 1484, $6, Sailing ship returning home.

1991, May 13			
1475-1482	A204	Set of 8	13.00 13.00

Souvenir Sheets

1483-1484	A204	Set of 2	13.00 13.00

Discovery of America, 500th anniv. (in 1992).

Royal Family Birthday, Anniversary Common Design Type

Designs: 20c, 25c, $1, Nos. 1492, 1494, Charles and Diana, 10th wedding anniversary. Others, Queen Elizabeth II, 65th birthday.

1991, July			Litho.		*Perf. 14*
1485	CD347	5c	multicolored	.25	.25
1486	CD347	20c	multicolored	.35	.25
1487	CD347	25c	multicolored	.35	.25
1488	CD347	60c	multicolored	.70	.45
1489	CD347	$1	multicolored	1.10	.70
1490	CD347	$2	multicolored	2.25	2.25
1491	CD347	$4	multicolored	4.25	4.25
1492	CD347	$5	multicolored	5.50	5.50
			Nos. 1485-1492 (8)	14.75	13.90

Souvenir Sheets

1493	CD347	$5	Elizabeth, Philip	6.00	6.00
1494	CD347	$5	Charles, Diana, sons	6.00	6.00

Japanese Trains A205

No. 1495: a, D51 steam locomotive. b, 9600 steam locomotive. c, Chrysanthemum emblem. d, Passenger coach. e, C57 steam locomotive. f, Oil tank car. g, C53 steam locomotive. h, First steam locomotive. i, C11 steam locomotive.
No. 1496: a, Class 181 electric train. b, EH-10 electric locomotive. c, Special Express emblem. d, Sendai City Class 1 trolley. e, Class 485 electric train. f, Sendai City trolley street cleaner. g, Hakari bullet train. h, ED-11 electric locomotive. i, EF-66 electric locomotive.
No. 1497, C55 steam locomotive, vert. No. 1498, Series 400 electric train. No. 1499, C62 steam locomotive, vert. No. 1500, Super Hitachi electric train, vert.

1991, Aug. 12		Litho.	*Perf. 14x13½*	
1495	A205	75c	Sheet of 9, #a.-i.	7.00 7.00
1496	A205	$1	Sheet of 9, #a.-i.	9.75 9.75

Souvenir Sheets

Perf. 13x13½

1497	A205	$6	multicolored	5.75	5.75
1498	A205	$6	multicolored	5.75	5.75
1499	A205	$6	multicolored	5.75	5.75
1500	A205	$6	multicolored	5.75	5.75

Phila Nippon '91. Nos. 1497-1500 each contain 27x44mm or 44x27mm stamps.

Miniature Sheets

Entertainers — A206

No. 1501: a-i, Various portraits of Madonna. No. 1502 — Italian entertainers: a, Marcello Mastroianni. b, Sophia Loren. c, Mario Lanza (1921-59). d, Federico Fellini. e, Arturo Toscanini (1867-1957). f, Anna Magnani (1908-73). g, Giancarlo Giannini. h, Gina Lollobrigida. i, Enrico Caruso (1873-1921). No. 1503: a-i, Various portraits of John Lennon.

1991, Aug. 22			*Perf. 13*	
1501	A206	$1 Sheet of 9, #a.-i.	13.00	13.00
1502	A206	$1 Sheet of 9, #a.-i.	9.25	9.25
1503	A206	$1 +2c, Sheet of 9, #a.-i.	11.00	11.00

Souvenir Sheets

Perf. 12x13

1504	A206	$6 Madonna	11.50	11.50

Perf. 13

1505	A206	$6 Luciano Pavarotti, horiz.	9.00	9.00

No. 1503 is semi-postal with surtax going to the Spirit Foundation.
No. 1504 contains one 28x42mm stamp. Compare with No. 1566. See Nos. 1642-1643, 1729, 2055.

Intl. Literacy Year — A207

Walt Disney characters in "The Prince and the Pauper": 5c, Pauper pals. 10c, Princely boredom. 15c, The valet. 25c, Look alikes. 60c, Trading places. 75c, How to be a prince. 80c, Food for the populace. $1, Captain's plot. $2, Doomed in the dungeon. $3, Looking for a way out. $4, A Goofy jailbreak. $5, Long live the real prince.
No. 1518, $6, Crowning the wrong guy. No. 1519, $6, Mickey meets the captain of the guard. No. 1520, $6, Real prince arrives. No. 1521, $6, Seize the guard.

1991, Nov. 18			*Perf. 14x13½*	
1506-1517	A207	Set of 12	16.00	16.00

Souvenir Sheets

1518-1521	A207	Set of 4	21.00	21.00

1991, Nov. 18

Walt Disney's "The Rescuers Down Under": 5c, Miss Bianca, Heroine. 10c, Bernard, Shy Hero. 15c, Maitre d'Francois. 25c, Wilbur, the Albatross. 60c, Jake, the Aussie kangaroo mouse. 75c, Bernard, Bianca and Jake in the outback. 80c, Bianca and Bernard. $1, Marahute, the magnificent rare eagle. $2, Cody and Marahute. $3, McLeach and his pet Goanna, Joanna. $4, Frank, the frill-necked lizard. $5, Endangered animals: Red Kangaroo, Krebbs Koala, and Polly Platypus.
No. 1534, $6, Cody with the rescuers. No. 1535, $6, Delegates of Intl. Rescue Aid Society. No. 1536, $6, Wilbur's painful touchdown

"down under." No. 1537, $6, Wilbur transports Miss Bianca and Bernard to Australia.

| 1522-1533 | A207 | Set of 12 | 14.00 | 14.00 |

Souvenir Sheets

| 1534-1537 | A207 | Set of 4 | 19.00 | 19.00 |

Brandenburg Gate, Bicent. — A209

Designs: 50c, Demonstrator with sign. 75c, Soldiers at Berlin Wall. 90c, German flag, shadows on wall. $1, Pres. Gorbachev and Pres. Bush shaking hands.
$4, Coat of Arms of Berlin.

1991, Nov. 18   Litho.   Perf. 14

| 1538-1541 | A209 | Set of 4 | 4.00 | 4.00 |

Souvenir Sheet

| 1542 | A209 | $4 multi | 4.00 | 4.00 |

Wolfgang Amadeus Mozart, Death Bicent. A210

Designs: $1, Scene from "Marriage of Figaro." $3, Scene from "The Clemency of Titus."
$4, Portrait of Mozart, vert.

1991, Nov. 18

| 1543 | A210 | $1 multicolored | 1.10 | 1.10 |
| 1544 | A210 | $3 multicolored | 3.25 | 3.25 |

Souvenir Sheet

| 1545 | A210 | $4 multicolored | 4.00 | 4.00 |

17th World Scout Jamboree, Korea — A211

Designs: 65c, Adventure tales around camp fire, vert. $1.50, British defenses at Mafeking, 1900, Cape of Good Hope #179. $3.50, Scouts scuba diving, queen angelfish.

1991, Nov. 18   Litho.   Perf. 14

1546	A211	65c multicolored	.45	.45
1547	A211	$1.50 multicolored	1.00	1.00
1548	A211	$3.50 multicolored	2.50	2.50
		Nos. 1546-1548 (3)	3.95	3.95

Souvenir Sheet

| 1549 | A211 | $5 shown | 3.50 | 3.50 |

Charles de Gaulle, Birth Cent. A212

De Gaulle and: 10c, Free French Forces, 1944. 45c, Churchill, 1944. 75c, Liberation of Paris, 1944.

1991, Nov. 18   Litho.   Perf. 14

1550	A212	10c multicolored	.60	.60
1551	A212	45c multicolored	1.00	1.00
1552	A212	75c multicolored	1.60	1.60
		Nos. 1550-1552 (3)	3.20	3.20

Souvenir Sheet

| 1553 | A212 | $5 Portrait | 3.50 | 3.50 |

Anniversaries and Events — A213

Designs: No. 1554, Woman, flag, map. No. 1555, Steam locomotive. $1.65, Otto Lilienthal, glider in flight. No. 1557, Gottfried Wilhelm Leibniz, mathematician. No. 1558, Street warfare.

1991, Nov. 18

1554	A213	$1.50 multicolored	3.00	3.00
1555	A213	$1.50 multicolored	3.25	3.25
1556	A213	$1.65 multicolored	3.75	3.75
1557	A213	$2 multicolored	4.75	4.75
1558	A213	$2 multicolored	4.25	4.25
		Nos. 1554-1558 (5)	19.00	19.00

Swiss Confedation, 700th anniv. (#1554). Trans-Siberian Railway, 100th anniv. (#1555). First glider flight, cent. (#1556). City of Hanover, 750th anniv. (#1557). Fall of Kiev, Sept. 19, 1941 (#1558).

Heroes of Pearl Harbor — A214

No. 1559 — Congressional Medal of Honor recipients: a, Myrvyn S. Bennion. b, George H. Cannon. c, John W. Finn. d, Francis C. Flaherty. e, Samuel G. Fuqua. f, Edwin J. Hill. g, Herbert C. Jones. h, Isaac C. Kidd. i, Jackson C. Pharris. j, Thomas J. Reeves. k, Donald K. Ross. l, Robert R. Scott. m, Franklin Van Valkenburgh. n, James R. Ward. o, Cassin Young.

1991, Nov. 18   Perf. 14½x15

| 1559 | A214 | $1 Sheet of 15, #a-o | 19.00 | 19.00 |

Famous People — A215

No. 1560 — Golfers: a, Gary Player. b, Nick Faldo. c, Severiano Ballesteros. d, Ben Hogan. e, Jack Nicklaus. f, Greg Norman. g, Jose-Marie Olazabal. h, Bobby Jones.
No. 1561 — Statesmen and historical events: a, Hans-Dietrich Genscher, German Foreign Minister, winged victory symbol. b, Destruction of Berlin Wall. c, Charles de Gaulle delivering radio appeal, Winston Churchill, de Gaulle. d, Dwight D. Eisenhower, de Gaulle, Normandy invasion. e, Brandenburg Gate. f, German Chancellor Helmut Kohl, mayors of East, West Berlin. g, De Gaulle and Konrad Adenauer. h, De Gaulle and John F. Kennedy.
No. 1562 — Chess masters: a, Francois Andre Danican Philidor. b, Adolph Anderssen. c, Wilhelm Steinitz. d, Alexander Alekhine. e, Boris Spassky. f, Bobby Fischer. g, Anatoly Karpov. h, Garri Kasparov.
No. 1563 — Nobel Prize winners: a, Einstein, physics. b, Roentgen, physics. c, William Shockley, physics. d, Charles Townes, physics. e, Lev Landau, physics. f, Marconi, physics. g, Willard Libby, chemistry. h, Ernest Lawrence, physics.
No. 1564 — Entertainers: a, Michael Jackson. b, Madonna. c, Elvis Presley. d, David Bowie. e, Prince. f, Frank Sinatra. g, George Michael. h, Mick Jagger.
No. 1565, Roosevelt, de Gaulle, Churchill at Morocco Conf., 1943. No. 1566, Madonna. No. 1567, Elvis Presley.

1991, Nov. 25   Litho.   Perf. 14½

1560	A215	$1 Sheet of 8, #a-h.	15.50	15.50
1561	A215	$1 Sheet of 8, #a-h.	14.00	14.00
1562	A215	$1 Sheet of 8, #a-h.	11.50	11.50
1563	A215	$1 Sheet of 8, #a-h.	13.00	13.00
1564	A215	$2 Sheet of 8, #a-h.	17.50	17.50

Souvenir Sheets

Perf. 14

1565	A215	$6 multicolored	7.00	7.00
1566	A215	$6 multicolored	5.50	5.50
1567	A215	$6 multicolored	5.50	5.50

Nos. 1565-1567 each contain one 27x43mm stamp.
See Nos. 1642-1643, 1729-1730 for more Elvis Presley stamps.

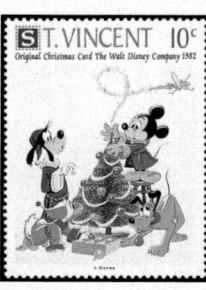

Walt Disney Christmas Cards A216

Designs and year of issue: 10c, Goofy, Mickey and Pluto decorating Christmas tree, 1982. 45c, Mickey, reindeer, 1980. 55c, Christmas tree ornament, 1970. 75c, Baby duck holding 1944 sign, 1943. $1.50, Characters papering globe with greetings, 1941. $2, Lady and the Tramp beside Christmas tree, 1986. $4, Donald, Goofy, Mickey and Pluto reciting "Night Before Christmas," 1977. $5, Mickey in doorway of Snow White's Castle, 1965.
No. 1576, $6, People from around the world, 1966. No. 1577, $6, Mickey in balloon basket with people of different countries, 1966.

1991, Dec. 23   Perf. 13½x14

| 1568-1575 | A216 | Set of 8 | 14.00 | 14.00 |

Souvenir Sheets

| 1576-1577 | A216 | Set of 2 | 14.50 | 14.50 |

Environmental Preservation — A217

1992, Jan.   Litho.   Perf. 14

1578	A217	10c Kings Hill	.30	.30
1579	A217	55c Tree planting	.65	.65
1580	A217	75c Botanical Gardens	.95	.95
1581	A217	$2 Kings Hill Project	2.10	2.10
		Nos. 1578-1581 (4)	4.00	4.00

Queen Elizabeth II's Accession to the Throne, 40th Anniv.

Common Design Type

1992, Feb. 6

1582	CD348	10c multicolored	.25	.25
1583	CD348	20c multicolored	.25	.25
1584	CD348	$1 multicolored	.65	.65
1585	CD348	$5 multicolored	3.25	3.25
		Nos. 1582-1585 (4)	4.40	4.40

Souvenir Sheets

| 1586 | CD348 | $6 Queen, beach | 5.00 | 5.00 |
| 1587 | CD348 | $6 Queen, harbor | 5.00 | 5.00 |

Queen Elizabeth II's Accession to the Throne, 40th Anniv. A217a

Designs: No. 1587A, Queen Elizabeth II. No. 1587B, King George VI.

1993, Mar. 2   Embossed   Perf. 12
Without Gum

| 1587A | A217a | $5 gold |
| 1587B | A217a | $5 gold |

1992 Winter Olympics, Albertville — A218

10c, Women's luge, horiz. 15c, Women's figure skating. 25c, Two-man bobsled, horiz. 30c, Mogul skiing. 45c, Nordic combined, horiz. 55c, Ski jump, horiz. 75c, Giant slalom, horiz. $1.50, Women's slalom. $5, Ice hockey, horiz. $8, Biathlon.
No. 1598, Downhill skiing. No. 1599, Speed skating.

1992, Apr. 21   Litho.   Perf. 14

1588	A218	10c multicolored	.25	.25
1589	A218	15c multicolored	.25	.25
1590	A218	25c multicolored	.25	.25
1591	A218	30c multicolored	.30	.30
1592	A218	45c multicolored	.40	.40
1593	A218	55c multicolored	.45	.45
1594	A218	75c multicolored	.65	.65
1595	A218	$1.50 multicolored	1.10	1.10
1596	A218	$5 multicolored	4.00	4.00
1597	A218	$8 multicolored	6.00	6.00
		Nos. 1588-1597 (10)	13.65	13.65

Souvenir Sheets

| 1598 | A218 | $6 multicolored | 6.75 | 6.75 |
| 1599 | A218 | $6 multicolored | 6.75 | 6.75 |

1992 Summer Olympics, Barcelona — A219

10c, Women's synchronized swimming duet, horiz. 15c, High jump. 25c, Small-bore rifle, horiz. 30c, 200-meter run. 45c, Judo. 55c, 200-meter freestyle swimming, horiz. 75c, Javelin. $1.50, Pursuit cycling. $5, Boxing. $8, Women's basketball. No. 1610, $15, Tennis. No. 1611, $15, Board sailing.

1992, Apr. 21

| 1600-1609 | A219 | Set of 10 | 16.00 | 16.00 |

Souvenir Sheets

| 1610-1611 | A219 | Set of 2 | 25.00 | 25.00 |

World Columbian Stamp Expo '92, Chicago — A220

Walt Disney characters visiting Chicago area landmarks: 10c, Mickey, Pluto at Picasso Sulpture. 50c, Mickey, Donald admiring Frank Lloyd Wright's Robie House. $1, Gus Gander at Calder Sculpture in Sears Tower. $5, Pluto in Buckingham Memorial Fountain.
$6, Mickey painting Minnie at Chicago Art Institute, vert.

1992, Apr.   Litho.   Perf. 14x13½

| 1612-1615 | A220 | Set of 4 | 7.00 | 7.00 |

Souvenir Sheet
Perf. 13½x14

| 1616 | A220 | $6 multi | 6.25 | 6.25 |

Granada
'92 — A221

Walt Disney characters from "The Three Little Pigs" in Spanish military uniforms: 15c, Big Bad Wolf as General of Spanish Moors. 40c, Pig as Captain of Spanish infantry. $2, Pig in Spanish armor, c. 1580. $4, Pig as Spaniard of rank, c. 1550.
$6, Little Pig resisting wolf from castle built of stone.

1992, Apr. 28   **Perf. 13½x14**
1622-1625 A221 Set of 4   7.00 7.00
Souvenir Sheet
1626 A221 $6 multi   6.25 6.25

Discovery
of
America,
500th
Anniv.
A222

5c, Nina. 10c, Pinta. 45c, Santa Maria. 55c, Leaving Palos, vert. $4, Columbus, vert. $5, Columbus' arms, vert.
No. 1638, Map, vert. No. 1639, Sailing ship, vert.

1992, May 22   **Perf. 14**
1632 A222 5c multicolored   .35 .35
1633 A222 10c multicolored   .35 .35
1634 A222 45c multicolored   .60 .60
1635 A222 55c multicolored   .70 .70
1636 A222 $4 multicolored   5.00 5.00
1637 A222 $5 multicolored   6.00 6.00
   Nos. 1632-1637 (6)   13.00 13.00
Souvenir Sheet
1638 A222 $6 multicolored   6.50 6.50
1639 A222 $6 multicolored   6.50 6.50
World Columbian Stamp Expo '92, Chicago. Nos. 1638-1639 contain one 42x57mm stamp.

Bonnie Blair, US
Olympic Speed
Skating
Champion
A223

No. 1641:a, Skating around corner. b, Portrait holding skates. c, On straightaway.

1992, May 25   **Perf. 13½**
1640 A223 $3 shown   4.00 4.00
Souvenir Sheet
1641 A223 $2 Sheet of 3, #a.-c.   6.75 6.75
World Columbian Stamp Expo '92. No. 1641b is 48x60mm.

Entertainers Type of 1991
Miniature Sheet
Various portraits of Elvis Presley.

1992, May 25   **Perf. 13½x14**
1642 A206 $1 Sheet of 9, #a.-i.   12.50 12.50
Souvenir Sheet
Perf. 14
1643 A206 $6 multicolored   9.50 9.50
No. 1643 contains one 28x43mm stamp. See Nos. 1729-1730.

Hummingbirds
A224

Hummingbirds: 5c, Rufous-breasted hermit. 15c, Hispaniolan emerald. 45c, Green-throated carib. 55c, Jamaican mango. 65c, Vervain. 75c, Purple-throated carib. 90c, Green mango. $1, Bee. $2, Cuban emerald. $3, Puerto Rican emerald. $4, Antillean mango. $5, Streamertail.
No. 1656, Antillean crested. No. 1657, Bahama woodstar. No. 1658, Blue-headed.

1992, June 15   **Perf. 14**
1644 A224 5c multi   .25 .25
1645 A224 15c multi   .25 .25
1646 A224 45c multi   .45 .35
1647 A224 55c multi   .55 .40
1648 A224 65c multi   .65 .50
1649 A224 75c multi   .75 .58
1650 A224 90c multi   .90 .70
1651 A224 $1 multi   1.10 .80
1652 A224 $2 multi   2.00 2.00
1653 A224 $3 multi   2.50 2.50
1654 A224 $4 multi   4.00 4.00
1655 A224 $5 multi   5.00 5.00
   Nos. 1644-1655 (12)   18.40 17.33
Souvenir Sheets
1656 A224 $6 multi   6.00 6.00
1657 A224 $6 multi   6.00 6.00
1658 A224 $6 multi   6.00 6.00
Genoa '92 Intl. Philatelic Exhibition.

Butterflies
A225

Designs: 5c, Dull astraptes, vert. 10c, White peacock. 35c, Tropic queen, vert. 45c, Polydamas swallowtail, vert. 55c, West Indian buckeye. 65c, Long-tailed skipper, vert. 75c, Tropical checkered skipper. $1, Crimson-banded black, vert. $2, Barred sulphur, vert. $3, Cassius blue. $4, Florida duskywing. $5, Malachite, vert.
No. 1671, $6, Cloudless giant sulphur, vert. No. 1672, $6, Julia. No. 1673, $6, Zebra longwing.

1992, June 15   **Litho.**   **Perf. 14**
1659-1670 A225 Set of 12   21.00 21.00
Souvenir Sheets
1671-1673 A225 Set of 3   18.00 18.00
Genoa '92.

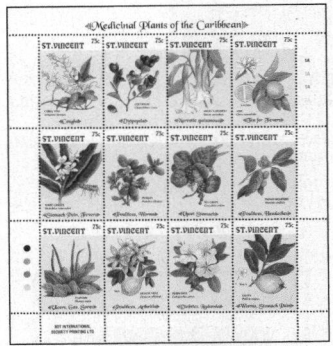

Medicinal plants — A226

No. 1674: a, Coral vine. b, Cocoplum. c, Angel's trumpet. d, Lime. e, White ginger. f, Pussley. g. Sea grape. h, Indian mulberry. i, Plantain. j, Lignum vitae. k, Periwinkle. l, Guava.

1992, July 22   **Litho.**   **Perf. 14**
1674 A226 75c Sheet of 12, #a-l   14.00 14.00

Souvenir Sheets
1675 A226 $6 Aloe   5.50 5.50
1676 A226 $6 Clove tree   5.50 5.50
1677 A226 $6 Wild sage   5.50 5.50

A227

Mushrooms: 10c, Collybia subpruinosa. 15c, Gerronema citrinum. 20c, Amanita antillana. 45c, Dermoloma atrobrunneum. 50c, Inopilus maculosus. 65c, Pulveroboletus brachyspermus. 75c, Mycena violacella. $1, Xerocomus brasiliensis. $2, Amanita ingrata. $3, Leptonia caeruleocaptata. $4, Limacella myochroa. $5, Inopilus magnificus.
No. 1690, Limacella guttata. No. 1691, $6, Amanita agglutinata. No. 1692, $6, Trogia buccinalis.

1992, July 2   **Litho.**   **Perf. 14**
1678-1689 A227 Set of 12   18.00 18.00
Souvenir Sheets
1690-1692 A227 Set of 3   17.00 17.00

Baseball Players — A228

Designs: No. 1693, $4, Ty Cobb. No. 1694, $4, Dizzy Dean. No. 1695, $4, Bob Feller. No. 1696, $4, Whitey Ford. No. 1697, $4, Lou Gehrig. No. 1698, $4, Rogers Hornsby. No. 1699, $4, Mel Ott. No. 1700, $4, Satchel Paige. No. 1701, $4, Babe Ruth. No. 1702, $4, Casey Stengel. No. 1703, $4, Honus Wagner. No. 1704, $4, Cy Young.

Self-Adhesive
Size: 64x89mm
1992, Aug. 5   **Litho.**   **Imperf.**
1693-1704 A228 Set of 12   40.00
Nos. 1693-1704 printed on thin card and distributed in boxed sets. To affix stamps, backing containing player's statistics must be removed.

1992 Albertville Winter Olympics Gold
Medalists — A229

No. 1705: a, Alberto Tomba, Italy, giant slalom. b, Fabrice Guy, France, Nordic combined. c, Patrick Ortlieb, Austria, men's downhill. d, Vegard Ulvang, Norway, cross country. e, Edgar Grospiron, France, freestyle Mogul skiing. f, Kjetil-André Aamodt, Norway, super

giant slalom. g, Viktor Petrenko, Russia, men's figure skating.
No. 1706: a, Kristi Yamaguchi, US, women's figure skating. b, Pernilla Wiberg, Sweden, women's giant slalom. c, Lyubov Yegorova, Unified Team, women's 10-kilometer cross country. d, Josef Polig, Italy, combined Alpine skiing. e, Finn Christian-Jagge, Norway, slalom. f, Kerrin Lee-Gartner, Canada, women's downhill. g, Steffania Belmondo, Italy, women's 30-kilometer cross country.
No. 1707, Alberto Tomba, diff. No. 1708, Kristi Yamaguchi, diff.

1992, Aug. 10   **Litho.**   **Perf. 14**
1705 A229 $1 Sheet of 7, #a.-g.   + label   8.00 8.00
1706 A229 $1 Sheet of 7, #a.-g.   + label   8.00 8.00
Souvenir Sheets
1707 A229 $6 multicolored   6.25 6.25
1708 A229 $6 multicolored   6.25 6.25

Discovery of
America, 500th
Anniv. — A230

1992   **Litho.**   **Perf. 14½**
1709 A230 $1 Coming ashore   1.75 1.75
1710 A230 $2 Natives, ships   3.25 3.25
Organization of East Caribbean States.

Opening of Euro Disney — A231

No. 1711 — Walt Disney movies: a, Pinocchio. b, Alice in Wonderland. c, Bambi. d, Cinderella. e, Snow White and the Seven Dwarfs. f, Peter Pan.

1992   **Litho.**   **Perf. 13**
1711 A231 $1 Sheet of 6, #a.-f.   10.50 10.50
Souvenir Sheet
Perf. 12½
1712 A231 $5 Mickey Mouse   8.75 8.75

Christmas
A232

Details or entire paintings of The Nativity by: 10c, Hospitality Refused to the Virgin Mary and Joseph, by Jan Metsys. 40c, Albrecht Durer. 45c, The Nativity, by Geertgen Tot Sint Jans. 50c, The Nativity, by Tintoretto. 55c, Follower of Jan Joest Calcar. 65c, Workshop of Fra Angelico. 75c, Master of the Louvre Nativity. $1, Filippino Lippi. $2, Petrus Christus. $3, Edward Burne-Jones. $4, Giotto. $5, The Birth of Christ, by Domenico Ghirlandaio.
No. 1725, $6, Nativity, by Jean Fouquet. No. 1726, $6, Sandro Botticelli. No. 1727, $6, Gerard Horenbout.

1992, Nov.   **Litho.**   **Perf. 13½x14**
1713-1724 A232 Set of 12   16.00 16.00
Souvenir Sheets
1725-1727 A232 Set of 3   17.00 17.00

Souvenir Sheet

Jacob Javits Convention Center, NYC — A233

1992, Oct. 28	**Litho.**	**Perf. 14**	
1728	A233	$6 multicolored	10.00 10.00

Postage Stamp Mega Event '92, NYC.

Nos. 1642, 1564, 1567 Overprinted or with Additional Inscriptions

Designs: No. 1729, #1642 inscribed vertically "15th Anniversary."

No. 1729J, #1564 inscribed "15th Anniversary" and "Elvis Presley's Death / August 16, 1977."

No. 1730, #1567 overprinted in margin "15th Anniversary" and "Elvis Presley's Death / August 16, 1977."

1992, Dec. 15		**Perf. 13½x14**	
1729	A206	$1 Sheet of 9, #a-i	14.00 14.00
		Perf. 14½	
1729J	A215	$2 Sheet of 8, #k-r	20.00 20.00

Souvenir Sheet
Perf. 14

1730	A215	$6 multi	13.50 13.50

Baseball Players — A234

1992, Nov. 9	**Litho.**	**Perf. 14**	
1731	A234	$5 Howard Johnson	3.50 3.50
1732	A234	$5 Don Mattingly	3.50 3.50

1992 Summer Olympics, Barcelona.

Members of Baseball Hall of Fame — A235

Player, year inducted: No. 1733, Roberto Clemente, 1973. No. 1734, Hank Aaron, 1982. No. 1735, Tom Seaver, 1992.

1992, Dec. 21			
1733	A235	$2 multicolored	2.50 2.50
1734	A235	$2 multicolored	2.50 2.50
1735	A235	$2 multicolored	2.50 2.50
		Nos. 1733-1735 (3)	7.50 7.50

Fishing Industry A236

1992, Nov.

1736	A236	5c Fishing with rods	.25 .25
1737	A236	10c Inside fishing complex	.25 .25
1738	A236	50c Landing the catch	.50 .50
1739	A236	$5 Fishing with nets	4.00 4.00
		Nos. 1736-1739 (4)	5.00 5.00

Uniting the Windward Islands A237

Children's paintings: 10c, Island coastline. 40c, Four people standing on islands. 45c, Four people standing on beach.

1992, Nov.	**Litho.**	**Perf. 14**	
1740	A237	10c multicolored	.60 .25
1741	A237	40c multicolored	.85 .30
1742	A237	45c multicolored	1.00 .35
		Nos. 1740-1742 (3)	2.45 .90

Miniature Sheets

US Olympic Basketball "Dream Team" — A238

No. 1744: a, Scottie Pippen. b, Earvin "Magic" Johnson. c, Larry Bird. d, Christian Laettner. e, Karl Malone. f, David Robinson.

No. 1745: a, Michael Jordan. b, Charles Barkley. c, John Stockton. d, Chris Mullin. e, Clyde Drexler. f, Patrick Ewing.

1992, Dec. 22	**Litho.**	**Perf. 14**	
1744	A238	$2 Sheet of 6, #a.-f.	8.50 8.50
1745	A238	$2 Sheet of 6, #a.-f.	8.50 8.50

1992 Summer Olympics, Barcelona.

A239

A240

A241

A242

Anniversaries and Events: 10c, Globe and UN emblem. 45c, Zeppelin Viktoria Luise over Kiel Regatta, 1912, vert. 65c, Food products. No. 1749, America's Cup Trophy and Bill Koch, skipper of America 3. No. 1750, Konrad Adenauer, German flag. No. 1751, Adenauer, diff. No. 1752, Snow leopard. $1.50, Caribbean manatee. $2, Humpback whale. No. 1755, Adenauer, John F. Kennedy. No. 1756, Lions Intl. emblem, patient having eye exam. No. 1757, Space shuttle Discovery, vert. No. 1758, Adenauer, Pope John XXIII. $5, Michael Schumacher, race car. No. 1760, Count Zeppelin's first airship over Lake Constance, 1900. No. 1761, Gondola of Graf Zeppelin. No. 1762, Formula I race car. No. 1763, Sailing ship, steam packet. No. 1764, Adenauer at

podium. No. 1765, Woolly spider monkey. No. 1765A, People waving to plane during Berlin airlift.

1992-93		**Litho.**	**Perf. 14**
1746	A239	10c multi	.25 .25
1747	A239	45c multi	5.50 5.50
1748	A242	65c multi	1.50 1.50
1749	A239	75c multi	1.25 1.25
1750	A239	75c multi	8.00 8.00
1751	A239	$1 multi	8.00 8.00
1752	A239	$1 multi	7.50 7.50
1753	A239	$1.50 multi	7.50 7.50
1754	A239	$2 multi	7.50 7.50
1755	A239	$3 multi	2.25 2.25
1756	A239	$3 multi	4.50 4.50
1757	A239	$4 multi	3.00 3.00
1758	A239	$4 multi	3.00 3.00
1759	A240	$5 multi	5.50 5.50
1760	A239	$6 multi	5.50 5.50
		Nos. 1746-1760 (15)	70.75 70.75

Souvenir Sheets

1761	A239	$6 multi	5.50 5.50
1762	A240	$6 multi	5.50 5.50
1763	A241	$6 multi	4.50 4.50
1764	A239	$6 multi	4.50 4.50
1765	A239	$6 multi	4.50 4.50
1765A	A239	$6 multi	4.50 4.50

UN Intl. Space Year (#1746, 1757). Count Zeppelin, 75th anniv. of death (#1747, 1760-1761). Intl. Conference on Nutrition, Rome (#1748). America's Cup yacht race (#1749). Konrad Adenauer, 25th death anniv. (#1750-1751, 1755, 1758, 1764). Earth Summit, Rio de Janeiro (#1752-1754, 1765). Lions Intl., 75th anniv. (#1756). Belgian Grand Prix (#1759, 1762). Discovery of America, 500th anniv. (#1763). Konrad Adenauer, 75th death anniv. (#1765A).

Issued: #1747, 1759-1762, Dec; #1763, 10/28/92; #1746, 1749, 1750-1751, 1755-1758, 1764, Dec; #1752-1754, 1765, Dec. 15; #1765A, 6/30/93.

Care Bears Promote Conservation A243

Designs: 75c, Bear, stork. $2, Bear riding in hot air balloon, horiz.

1992, Dec.	**Litho.**	**Perf. 14**	
1766	A243	75c multicolored	2.00 2.00

Souvenir Sheet

1767	A243	$2 multicolored	3.50 3.50

Elvis Presley (1935-77) — A244

No. 1767A: b, Portrait. c, With guitar. d, With microphone.

1993	**Litho.**	**Perf. 14**	
1767A	A244	$1 Strip of 3, #b.-d.	2.75 2.75

Printed in sheets of 9 stamps.

Walt Disney's Beauty and the Beast — A245

Designs: 2c, Gaston. 3c, Belle and her father, Maurice. 5c, Lumiere, Mrs. Potts and Cogsworth. 10c, Philippe. 15c, Beast and Lumiere. 20c, Lumiere and Feather Duster.

No. 1774: a, Belle and Gaston. b, Maurice. c, The Beast. d, Mrs. Potts. e, Belle and the Enchanted Vase. f, Belle discovers an Enchanted Rose. g, Belle with wounded Beast. h, Belle. i, Household objects alarmed.

No. 1774J: k, Belle and Chip. l, Lumiere. m, Cogsworth. n, Armoire. o, Belle and Beast. p, Feather Duster. q, Footstool. r, Belle. All vert.

No. 1775, Belle reading, vert. No. 1776, Lumiere, diff., vert. No. 1776A, Lumiere, Mrs. Potts. No. 1776B, Belle, lake and castle, vert. No. 1776C, The Beast, vert.

Perf. 14x13½, 13½x14

1992, Dec. 15		**Litho.**	
1768	A245	2c multicolored	.25 .25
1769	A245	3c multicolored	.25 .25
1770	A245	5c multicolored	.25 .25
1771	A245	10c multicolored	.25 .25
1772	A245	15c multicolored	.25 .25
1773	A245	20c multicolored	.25 .25
		Nos. 1768-1773 (6)	1.50 1.50

Souvenir Sheets

1774	A245	60c Sheet of 9, #a.-i.	8.50 8.50
1774J	A245	60c Sheet of 8, #k.-r.	8.50 8.50

Souvenir Sheets

1775	A245	$6 multicolored	6.50 6.50
1776	A245	$6 multicolored	6.50 6.50
1776A	A245	$6 multicolored	6.50 6.50
1776B	A245	$6 multicolored	6.50 6.50
1776C	A245	$6 multicolored	6.50 6.50

Louvre Museum, Bicent. A246

No. 1777, $1 — Details or entire paintings by Jean-Auguste-Dominique Ingres: a, Louis-Francois Bertin. b, The Apotheosis of Homer. c, Joan of Arc. d, The Composer Cherubini with the Muse of Lyric Poetry. e, Mlle Caroline Riviere. f, Oedipus Answers the Sphinx's Riddle. g, Madame Marcotte. h, Mademoiselle Caroline Riviere.

No. 1778, $1 — Details or entire paintings by Jean Louis Andre Theodore Gericault (1791-1824): a, The Woman with Gambling Mania. b, Head of a White Horse. c, Wounded Cuirassier. d, An Officer of the Cavalry. e, The Vendean. f, The Raft of the Medusa. g-h, The Horse Market (left, right).

No. 1779, $1 — Details or entire paintings by Nicolas Poussin (1594-1665): a-b, The Arcadian Shepherds (left, right). c, Ecstasy of Paul. d-e, The Inspiration of the Poet (left, right). f-g, St. John Baptizing (left, right). h, The Miracle of St. Francis Xavier.

No. 1780, $1 — Details or entire paintings by Eustache Le Sueur (1616-1655): a-b, Melpomene, Erato & Polyhymnia (left, right). By Poussin: c, Christ and Woman Taken in Adultery. d, Spring. e, Autumn. f-h, The Plague of Ashdod (left, center, right).

No. 1781, $1: a, The Beggars, by Pieter Brueghel, the Elder (1520-1569). b, The Luncheon, by Francois Boucher (1703-1770). c, Louis Guene, Violin King, by Francois Dumont (1751-1831). d, The Virgin of Chancellor Rolin, by Jan Van Eyck. e, Conversation in the Park, by Thomas Gainsborough. f, Lady Alston, by Gainsborough. g, Mariana Waldstein, by Francisco de Goya. h, Ferdinand Guillemardet, by Goya.

No. 1782, $6, The Grand Odalisque, horiz. No. 1783, $6, The Dressing Room of Esther, by Theodore Chasseriau (1819-1856). No. 1784, $6, Liberty Guiding the People, by Eugene Delecroix (1798-1863), horiz.

1993, Apr. 19		**Perf. 12x12½**	
		Sheets of 8, #a-h, + Label	
1777-1781	A246	Set of 5	34.00 34.00

Souvenir Sheets
Perf. 14½

1782-1784	A246	Set of 3	18.50 18.50

Nos. 1783-1784 each contain a 55x88mm or 88x55mm stamp.

Paintings on Nos. 1777d and 1777h were switched.

A247

A247a

Scenes from
Disney
Animated
Films —
A247b

No. 1787 — Symphony Hour (1942): a, Maestro Mickey. b, Goofy plays a mean horn. c, On first bass with Clara Cluck. d, Stringing along with Clarabelle. e, Donald on drums. f, Clarabelle all fiddled out. g, Donald drumming up trouble. h, Goofy's sour notes. i, Mickey's moment.

No. 1788 — Clock Cleaners (1937): a, Goofy gets in gear. b, Donald on the mainspring. c, Donald in the works. d, Mickey's fine-feathered friend. e, Stork with bundle of joy. f, Father Time. g, Goofy, Mickey leaping upward. h, Donald, Goofy, Mickey out of gear. i, Donald, Goofy, Mickey with headaches.

No. 1789 — The Art of Skiing (1941): a, The ultimate back scratcher. b, Striking a pose. c, And we're off. d, Divided he stands. e, A real twister. f, Hangin' in there. g, Over the hill. h, At the peak of his form. i, Up a tree.

No. 1790 — Orphan's Benefit (1941): a, Mickey introduces Donald. b, Donald recites "Little Boy Blue." c, Orphan mischief. d, Clara Cluck, singing sensation. e, Goofy's debut with Clarabelle. f, Encore for Clara and Mickey. g, A Bronx cheer. h, Donald blows his stack. i, Donald's final bow.

No. 1791 — Thru the Mirror (1936): a, Mickey steps thru the looking glass. b, Mickey finds a tasty treat. c, Mickey's nutty effect. d, Hats off to Mickey. e, What a card, Mickey. f, Mickey dancing with the Queen Hearts. g, A real two-faced opponent. h, Mickey with a pen mightier than a sword. i, Mickey awake at last.

No. 1791J — The Small One: k, Good morning, small one. m, Too old to keep. n, Heatbroken. o, Nazareth markplace. p, Auction mockery. q, Off the auction block. r, Lonely and dejected. s, Happy and useful again.

No. 1792 — The Three Little Pigs (1933): a, Fifer Pig building house of straw. b, Fiddler Pig building house of sticks. c, Practical Pig building house of bricks. d, The Big Bad Wolf. e, Wolf scaring two lazy pigs. f, Wolf blowing down straw house. g, Wolf in sheep's clothing. h, Wolf blowing down twig house. i, Wolf huffs and puffs at brick house.

No. 1792J — How to Play Football (1944): k, Cheerleaders. l, Here comes the team. m, In the huddle. n, Who's got the ball? o, Who, me coach? p, Half-time pep talk. q, Another down, and out. r, Only a little injury. s, Up and at 'em.

No. 1793 — Rescue Rangers: a, Special agents. b, Chip 'n Dale, ready for action. c, Chip 'n Dale on stakeout. d, Gadget in gear. e, Gadget and Monterey Jack rescue Zipper. f, Zipper confers with Monterey Jack. g, Zipper zaps fat cat. h, Team work. i, Innovative Gadget.

No. 1793J — Darkwing Duck: k, Darkwing Duck. l, Launchpad McQuack. m, Gosalyn. n, Honker Muddlefoot. o, Tank Muddlefoot. p, Herb & Binkie Muddlefoot. q, Drake Mallard, aka Darkwing Duck. r, Darkwing Duck logo.

No. 1794, Bird's-eye-view of Goofy. No. 1795, Mickey and Macaroni enjoying applause. No. 1796, On the edge of Goofyness. No. 1797, Gonged-out Goofy.

No. 1798, Film poster for Art of Skiing with Goofy slaloming down mountain. No. 1799, Goofy home in bed at last.

No. 1800, Caveman ballet. No. 1801, Mickey tickles the ivories.

No. 1802, Mickey's true reflection. No. 1803, Mickey hopping home.

No. 1804, Hard Work in Nazareth. No. 1805, Finding a buyer in Nazareth.

No. 1806, Animator's sketch of little pig and brick house. No. 1807, Little pigs playing and singing at piano, vert.

No. 1807A, Goofy demonstrating how to score touchdown. No. 1807B, Goofy shouting "Hooray for the team," vert.

No. 1807C, Gadget at controls of Ranger plane, vert. No. 1807D, Dale, vert.

No. 1807E, Quarterjack. No. 1807F, Darkwing Duck and Launchpad to the rescue in Ratcatcher.

Perf. 14x13½, 13½x14

			1992, Dec. 15		Litho.	
1787	A247	60c	Sheet of 9, #a.-i.		8.50	8.50
1788	A247	60c	Sheet of 9, #a.-i.		8.50	8.50
1789	A247	60c	Sheet of 9, #a.-i.		8.50	8.50
1790	A247	60c	Sheet of 9, #a.-i.		8.50	8.50
1791	A247	60c	Sheet of 9, #a.-i.		8.50	8.50
1791J	A247a	60c	Sheet of 9, #k.-s.		8.50	8.50
1792	A247	60c	Sheet of 9, #a.-i.		8.50	8.50
1792J	A247	60c	Sheet of 9, #k.-s.		8.50	8.50
1793	A247a	60c	Sheet of 9, #a.-i.		8.50	8.50
1793J	A247b	60c	Sheet of 8, #k.-r.		8.50	8.50

Souvenir Sheets

1794	A247	$6 multicolored	5.50	5.50
1795	A247	$6 multicolored	5.50	5.50
1796	A247	$6 multicolored	5.50	5.50
1797	A247	$6 multicolored	5.50	5.50
1798	A247	$6 multicolored	5.50	5.50
1799	A247	$6 multicolored	5.50	5.50
1800	A247	$6 multicolored	5.50	5.50
1801	A247	$6 multicolored	5.50	5.50
1802	A247	$6 multicolored	5.50	5.50
1803	A247	$6 multicolored	5.50	5.50
1804	A247a	$6 multicolored	5.50	5.50
1805	A247a	$6 multicolored	5.50	5.50
1806	A247	$6 multicolored	5.50	5.50
1807	A247	$6 multicolored	5.50	5.50
1807A	A247	$6 multicolored	5.50	5.50
1807B	A247	$6 multicolored	5.50	5.50
1807C	A247a	$6 multicolored	5.50	5.50
1807D	A247a	$6 multicolored	5.50	5.50
1807E	A247b	$6 multicolored	5.50	5.50
1807F	A247b	$6 multicolored	5.50	5.50

See Nos. 2144-2146 for 30c & $3 stamps.

Fish
A248

5c, Sergeant major. 10c, Rainbow parrotfish. 55c, Hogfish. 75c, Porkfish. $1, Spotfin butterflyfish. $2, Trunkfish. $4, Queen triggerfish. $5, Queen angelfish.
No. 1816, Bigeye, vert. No. 1817, Smallmouth grunt, vert.

			1993, Apr. 1	Litho.	Perf. 14	
1808	A248	5c	multicolored		.30	.30
1809	A248	10c	multicolored		.30	.30
1810	A248	55c	multicolored		.55	.40
1811	A248	75c	multicolored		.85	.60
1812	A248	$1	multicolored		1.00	.75
1813	A248	$2	multicolored		2.10	2.10
1814	A248	$4	multicolored		4.25	4.25
1815	A248	$5	multicolored		4.25	4.25
		Nos. 1808-1815 (8)			13.60	12.95

Souvenir Sheets

1816	A248	$6 multicolored	6.25	6.25
1817	A248	$6 multicolored	6.25	6.25

Birds — A249

Designs: 10c, Brown pelican. 25c, Red-necked grebe, horiz. 45c, Belted kingfisher, horiz. 55c, Yellow-bellied sapsucker. $1, Great blue heron. $2, Crab hawk, horiz. $4, Yellow warbler. $5, Northern oriole, horiz. No. 1826, White ibises, map, horiz. No. 1827, Blue-winged teal, map, horiz.

		1993, Apr. 1	Litho.	Perf. 14	
1818-1825	A249	Set of 8		14.50	14.50

Souvenir Sheets

1826-1827	A249	$6 Set of 2	15.00	15.00

Seashells — A250

Designs: 10c, Hexagonal murex. 15c, Caribbean vase. 30c, Measled cowrie. 45c, Dyson's keyhole limpet. 50c, Atlantic hairy triton. 65c, Orange-banded marginella. 75c, Bleeding tooth. $1, Pink conch. $2, Hawk-wing conch. $3, Music volute. $4, Alphabet cone. $5, Antillean cone.
No. 1840, $6, Flame auger, horiz. No. 1841, $6, Netted olive, horiz. No. 1842, $6, Wide-mouthed purpura, horiz.

		1993, May 24	Litho.	Perf. 14	
1828-1839	A250	Set of 12		20.00	20.00

Souvenir Sheets

1840-1842	A250	Set of 3	19.00	19.00

Yujiro Ishihara, Actor — A251

No. 1843 — Name in blue on 2 lines, country name on picture: a, $1, Wearing captain's hat. b, 55c, With tennis racquet. c, $1 Wearing suit. d, 55c, Holding camera. e, 55c, Wearing suit, diff. f, 55c. Wearing striped shirt, smoking. g, $1, Wearing blue shirt and vest. h, 55c, Wearing captain's hat, smoking. i, $1, Wearing pink shirt, smoking.

No. 1844 — Name in gold on one line, countrry name above picture: a, 55c Holding camera. b, $1 Wearing black suit and white tie. c, $2, Wearing white suit. d, $2, Holding guitar.

No. 1845 — Name in gold on one line, country name on picture: a, 55c Wearing captain's hat (like #1843a). b, $2, Wearing striped shirt. c, $1, Smiling. d, $2, Wearing captain's hat (like #1843h).

No. 1846 — Name in white: a, 55c, Wearing yellow suit. b, $2, Wearing yellow shirt. c, $4, Holding drink.

No. 1847 — Name in blue on 2 lines: a, 55c, Smoking, hand near face. b, $4, Smoking, wearing pink shirt. c, $4, Wearing blue shirt and vest (like #1843g).

		1993, May 24	Litho.	Perf. 13½x14	
1843	A251	Sheet of 9, #a.-i.		12.00	12.00

Souvenir Sheets

1844	A251	Sheet of 4, #a.-d.	6.00	6.00

Stamp Size: 32x41mm
Perf. 14½

1845	A251	Sheet of 4, #a.-d.	6.00	6.00

Stamp Size: 60x41mm
Perf. 14x14½

1846	A251	Sheet of 3, #a.-c.	7.00	7.00
1847	A251	Sheet of 3, #a.-c.	9.25	9.25

Automobiles
A252

Designs: $1, 1932 Ford V8, 1915 Ford Model T, Henry Ford's 1st car. $2, Benz 540K, 1928 Benz Stuttgart, 1908 Benz Racer. $3, 1911 Blitzen Benz, 1905 Benz Tourenwagen, 1894 Benz. $4, 1935 Ford, 1903 Ford A Runabout, 1913 Ford Model T Tourer. No. 1852, $6, Karl Benz. No. 1853, $6, Henry Ford.

		1993, May	Litho.	Perf. 14	
1848-1851	A252	Set of 4		10.00	10.00

Souvenir Sheets

1852-1853	A252	Set of 2	11.00	11.00

First Ford motor, cent. (#1848, 1851, 1853). First Benz motor car, cent. (#1849-1850, 1852).

Coronation of Queen Elizabeth II, 40th Anniv. — A253

No. 1854: a, 45c, Official coronation photograph. b, 65c, Opening Parliament, 1980s. c, $2, Coronation ceremony, 1953. d, $4, Queen with her dog, 1970s.
No. 1855, Portrait of Queen as a child.

		1993, June 2	Litho.	Perf. 13½x14	
1854	A253	Sheet, 2 ea #a.-d.		13.00	13.00

Souvenir Sheet
Perf. 14

1855	A253	$6 multicolored	6.25	6.25

No. 1855 contains one 28x42mm stamp.

Moths — A254

10c, Erynnyis ello. 50c, Aellopos tantalus. 65c, Erynnyis alope. 75c, Manduca rustica. $1, Xylophanes pluto. $2, Hyles lineata. $4, Pseudosphinx tetrio. $5, Protambulyx strigilis. No. 1864, Xylophanes tersa. No. 1864A, Utetheisa ornatrix.

		1993, June 14	Litho.	Perf. 14	
1856	A254	10c	multicolored		.25	.25
1857	A254	50c	multicolored		.60	.60
1858	A254	65c	multicolored		.75	.75
1859	A254	75c	multicolored		.85	.85
1860	A254	$1	multicolored		1.10	1.10
1861	A254	$2	multicolored		2.25	2.25
1862	A254	$4	multicolored		4.50	4.50
1863	A254	$5	multicolored		5.75	5.75
		Nos. 1856-1863 (8)			16.05	16.05

Souvenir Sheets

1864	A254	$6 multicolored	5.75	5.75
1864A	A254	$6 multicolored	5.75	5.75

A255

A256

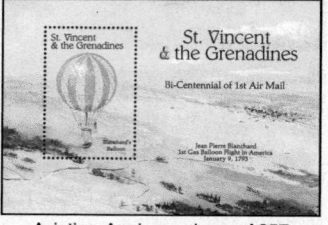

Aviation Anniversaries — A257

Designs: 50c, Supermarine Spitfire. #1866, Graf Zeppelin over Egypt, 1931, Hugo Eckener. #1867, Jean Pierre Blanchard, balloon, George Washington. #1868, De Havilland Mosquito. No. 1869, Eckener, Graf Zeppelin over New York, 1928. $3, Eckener, Graf Zeppelin over Tokyo, 1 929. $4, Philadelphia's Walnut State Prison, balloon lifting off.
No. 1872, Hawker Hurricane. No. 1873, Hugo Eckener, vert. No. 1874, Blanchard's Balloon, vert.

1993, June		Litho.	Perf. 14	
1865	A255	50c multi	.80	.80
1866	A256	$1 multi	1.50	1.50
1867	A257	$1 multi	1.50	1.50
1868	A255	$2 multi	3.00	3.00
1869	A256	$2 multi	3.00	3.00
1870	A256	$3 multi	4.75	4.75
1871	A257	$4 multi	6.00	6.00
	Nos. 1865-1871 (7)		20.55	20.55
Souvenir Sheets				
1872	A255	$6 multi	6.50	6.50
1873	A256	$6 multi	5.00	5.00
1874	A257	$6 multi	5.00	5.00

Royal Air Force, 75th anniv. (#1865, 1868, 1872). Dr. Hugo Eckener, 125th anniv. of birth (#1866, 1869-1870, 1873). First US balloon flight, bicent. (#1867, 1871). Tokyo spelled incorrectly on No. 1870.

Two values and a souvenir sheet commemorating the Wedding of Japan's Crown Prince Naruhito and Masako Owada were printed in 1993 but not accepted by the St. Vincent post office. Set value $5.75, Souvenir Sheet $6.

1994 Winter Olympics, Lillehammer, Norway — A259

Designs: 45c, Marc Girardelli, silver medalist, giant slalom, 1992. $5, Paul Accola, downhill, 1992. $6, Thommy Moe, downhill, 1992.

1993, June 30		Litho.	Perf. 14	
1878	A259	45c multicolored	.45	.45
1879	A259	$5 multicolored	4.25	4.25
Souvenir Sheet				
1880	A259	$6 multicolored	5.75	5.75

Picasso (1881-1973) — A260

Paintings: 45c, Massacre in Korea, 1951. $1, Family of Saltimbanques, 1905. $4, La Joie de Vivre, 1946. $6, Woman Eating a Melon and Boy Writing, 1965, vert.

1993, June 30				
1881	A260	45c multicolored	.50	.50
1882	A260	$1 multicolored	1.00	1.00
1883	A260	$4 multicolored	4.00	4.00
	Nos. 1881-1883 (3)		5.50	5.50
Souvenir Sheet				
1884	A260	$6 multicolored	6.00	6.00

Willy Brandt (1913-1992), German Chancellor — A261

Designs: 45c, Brandt, Richard Nixon, 1971. $5, Brandt, Robert Kennedy, 1967. $6, Brandt at signing of "Common Declaration," 1973.

1993, June 30				
1885	A261	45c multicolored	.50	.50
1886	A261	$5 multicolored	5.00	5.00
Souvenir Sheet				
1887	A261	$6 multicolored	6.00	6.00

A262

Copernicus: 45c, Astronomical instrument. $4, Space shuttle lift-off. $6, Copernicus.

1993, June 30				
1888	A262	45c multicolored	.60	.60
1889	A262	$4 multicolored	5.00	5.00
Souvenir Sheet				
1890	A262	$6 multicolored	6.00	6.00

A263

European Royalty: 45c, Johannes, Gloria Thurn & Taxis. 65c, Thurn & Taxis family, horiz. $1, Princess Stephanie of Monaco. $2, Gloria Thurn & Taxis.

1993, June 30				
1891-1894	A263	Set of 4	3.00	3.00

Inauguration of Pres. William J. Clinton — A264

Designs: $5, Bill Clinton, children. $6, Clinton wearing cowboy hat, vert.

1993, June 30				
1895	A264	$5 multicolored	5.50	5.50
Souvenir Sheet				
1896	A264	$6 multicolored	6.00	6.00

Polska '93 A265

No. 1897, Bogusz Church, Gozlin.
No. 1898: a, $1, Deux Tetes (Man), by S.I. Witkiewicz, 1920, vert. b, $3, Deux Tetes (Woman), vert.
No. 1899, Dancing, by Wladyslaw Roguski, vert.

1993, June 30				
1897	A265	$6 multicolored	5.25	5.25
1898	A265	Pair, #a.-b.	3.50	3.50
Souvenir Sheet				
1899	A265	$6 multicolored	6.00	6.00

1994 World Cup Soccer Qualifying A266

St. Vincent vs: 5c, Mexico. 10c, Honduras. 65c, Costa Rica. $5, St. Vincent goalkeeper.

1993, Sept. 2				
1900-1903	A266	Set of 4	6.75	6.75

Cooperation with Japan — A267

Designs: 10c, Fish delivery van. 50c, Fish aggregation device, vert. 75c, Trawler. $5, Fish complex.

1993, Sept. 2				
1904-1907	A267	Set of 4	7.00	7.00

Pope John Paul II's Visit to Denver, CO A268

Design: $6, Pope, Denver skyline, diff.

1993, Aug. 13				
1908	A268	$1 multicolored	1.50	1.50
Souvenir Sheet				
1909	A268	$6 multicolored	7.00	7.00
No. 1908 issued in sheets of 9.				

Miniature Sheet

Corvette, 40th Anniv. — A269

No. 1910 — Corvettes: a, 1953. b, 1993, c, 1958, d, 1960. e, "40," Corvette emblem (no car). f, 1961. g, 1963. h, 1968, i, 1973. j, 1975. k, 1982. l, 1984.

1993, Aug. 13			Perf. 14x13½	
1910	A269	$1 Sheet of 12,		
		#a.-l.	12.50	12.50

Taipei '93 — A270

Designs: 5c, Yellow Crane Mansion, Wuchang. 10c, Front gate, Chung Cheng Ceremonial Arch, Taiwan. 20c, Marble Peifang, Ming 13 Tombs, Beijing. 45c, Jinxing Den, Beijing. 55c, Forbidden City, Beijing. 75c, Tachih, the Martyrs' Shrine, Taiwan. No. 1917, Praying Hall, Xinjiang, Gaochang. No. 1918, Chih Kan Tower, Taiwan. $2, Taihu Lake, Jiangsu. $4, Chengde, Hebei, Pula Si. No. 1921, Kaohsiung, Cheng Ching Lake, Taiwan. No. 1922, Great Wall.
No. 1923 — Chinese paintings: a, Street in Macao, China, by George Chinnery. b, Pair of Birds on Cherry Branch. c, Yellow Dragon Cave, by Patrick Procktor. d, Great Wall of China, by William Simpson. e, Dutch Folly Fort Off Conton, by Chinnery. f, Forbidden City, by Procktor.
No. 1924 — Chinese silk paintings: a, Rhododendron. b, Irises and bees. c, Easter lily. d, Poinsettia. e, Peach and cherry blossoms. f, Weeping cherry and yellow bird.
No. 1925 — Chinese kites: a, Dragon and tiger fighting. b, Two immortals. c, Five boys playing round a general. d, Zheng Chenggong. e, Nezha stirs up the sea. f, Immortal maiden He.
No. 1926, Giant Buddha, Longmen Caves, Luoyang, Hunan. No. 1927, Guardian and Celestial King, Longmen Caves, Hunan, vert. No. 1928, Giant Buddha, Yungang Caves, Datong, Shanxi, vert.

1993, Aug. 16		Litho.	Perf. 14x13½	
1911-1922	A270	Set of 12	15.00	15.00
1923	A270	$1.50 Sheet of 6,		
		#a.-f.	6.75	6.75
1924	A270	$1.50 Sheet of 6,		
		#a.-f.	6.75	6.75
1925	A270	$1.50 Sheet of 6,		
		#a.-f.	6.75	6.75
Souvenir Sheets				
1926	A270	$6 multicolored	6.00	6.00
		Perf. 13½x14		
1927	A270	$6 multicolored	6.00	6.00
1928	A270	$6 multicolored	6.00	6.00

No. 1925e issued missing "St." in country name. Some sheets of No. 1925 may have been withdrawn from sale after discovery of the error.

With Bangkok '93 Emblem

Designs: 5c, Phra Nakhon Khiri (Rama V's Palace), vert. 10c, Grand Palace, Bangkok. 20c, Rama IX Park, Bangkok. 45c, Phra Prang Sam Yot, Lop Buri. 55c, Dusit Maha Prasad, vert. 75c, Phimai Khmer architecture, Pak Tong Chai. No. 1935, Burmese style Chedi, Mae Hong Son. No. 1936, Antechamber, Central Prang, Prasat Hin Phimai. $2, Brick chedi on laterite base, Si Thep, vert. $4, Isan's Phanom Rung, Korat, vert. No. 1939, Phu Khao

Thong, the Golden Mount, Bangkok. No. 1940, Islands, Ang Thong.

No. 1941 — Thai Buddha sculpture: a, Interior of Wat Hua Kuang Lampang, vert. b, Wat Yai Suwannaram, vert. c, Phra Buddha Sihing, City Hall Chapel, vert. d, Wat Ko Keo Suttharam, vert. e, U Thong B image, Wat Ratburana crypt, vert. f, Sri Sakyamuni Wat Suthat, vert.

No. 1942: a-f: Various details from Mural at Buddhaisawan Chapel.

No. 1943 — Thai painting: a, Untitled, by Arunothai Somsakul. b, Mural at Wat Rajapradit. c, Mural at Wat Phumin (detail). d, Serenity, by Surasit Souakong. e, Scenes of early Bangkok mural (detail). f, Ramayana, vert. No. 1945, Standing Buddha, Hua Hin, vert. No. 1946, Masked dance.

Perf. 13½x14, 14x13½

1993, Aug. 16   **Litho.**

1929-1940	A270	5c Set of 12	14.50	14.50
1941	A270	$1.50 Sheet of 6,		
		#a.-f.	6.50	6.50
1942	A270	$1.50 Sheet of 6,		
		#a.-f.	6.50	6.50
1943	A270	$1.50 Sheet of 6,		
		#a.-f.	6.50	6.50

Souvenir Sheets

1944	A270	$6 multicolored	6.00	6.00
1945	A270	$6 multicolored	6.00	6.00
1946	A270	$6 multicolored	6.00	6.00

With Indopex '93 Emblem

Indopex '93 emblem with designs: 5c, Local landmark, Gedung Sate, 1920. 10c, Masjid Jamik Mosque, Sumenep. 20c, Bromo Caldera, seen from Penanjakan. 45c, Kudus Mosque, Java. 55c, Kampung Naga. 75c, Lower level of Borobudur. No. 1953, Dieng Temple, Dieng Plateau. No. 1954, Temple 1, Gedung Songo group, Semarang. $2, Istana Bogor, 1856. $4, Taman Sari complex, Yogyakarta. No. 1957, $5, Landscape near Mt. Sumbing, Central Java. No. 1958, $5, King Adityawarman's Palace, Batusangar.

No. 1959 — Paintings: a, Female Coolies, by Djoko Pekik. b, Family Outing, by Sudjana Kerton. c, My Family, by Pekik. d, Javanese Dancers, by Arthur Melville. e, Leisure Time, by Kerton. f, In the Garden of Eden, by Agus Djaja.

No. 1960: a, Tayubon, by Pekik. b, Three Dancers, by Nyoman Gunarsa. c, Nursing Neighbor's Baby, by Hendra Gunawan. d, Imagining within a Dialogue, by Sagito. e, Three Balinese Mask Dancers, by Anton H. f, Three Prostitutes, by Gunawan.

No. 1961 — Masks: a, Hanuman. b, Subali/Sugnwa. c, Kumbakarna. d, Sangut. e, Jatayu. f, Rawana.

No. 1962, Relief of Sudamala story, Mt. Lawu. No. 1963, Plaque, 9th Cent., Banyumas, Central Java. No. 1964, Panel from Ramayana reliefs, vert.

1993, Aug. 16   **Litho.**   **Perf. 14x13½**

1947-1958	A270	Set of 12	14.50	14.50
1959	A270	$1.50 Sheet of 6,		
		#a.-f.	6.50	6.50
1960	A270	$1.50 Sheet of 6,		
		#a.-f.	6.50	6.50
1961	A270	$1.50 Sheet of 6,		
		#a.-f.	6.50	6.50

Souvenir Sheets

1962	A270	$6 multicolored	6.00	6.00
1963	A270	$6 multicolored	6.00	6.00

Perf. 13½x14

1964	A270	$6 multicolored	6.00	6.00

Reggie Jackson, Selection to Baseball Hall of Fame — A271

1993, Oct. 4   **Perf. 14**

1965	A271	$2 multicolored	2.00	2.00

Christmas A272

Details or entire woodcut, The Adoration of the Magi, by Durer: 10c, 35c, 40c, $5.

Details or entire paintings by Rubens: 50c, Holy Family with Saint Francis. 55c, 65c, Adoration of the Shepherds. $1, Holy Family.

No. 1974, $6, The Adoration of the Magi, by Durer, horiz. No. 1975, $6, Holy Family with St. Elizabeth & St. John, by Rubens.

Perf. 13½x14, 14x13½

1993, Nov. 18

1966-1973	A272	Set of 8	9.00	9.00

Souvenir Sheets

1974-1975	A272	Set of 2	17.50	17.50

Legends of Country Music — A273

No. 1976 — Various portraits of: a, f, l, Roy Acuff. b, g, j, Patsy Cline. c, h, i, Jim Reeves. d, e, k, Hank Williams, Sr.

1994, Jan. 17   **Litho.**   **Perf. 13½x14**

1976	A273	$1 Sheet of 12,		
		#a.-l.	12.00	12.00

Mickey's Portrait Gallery A274

Mickey Mouse as: 5c, Aviator. 10c, Foreign Legionnaire. 15c, Frontiersman. 20c, Best Pals, Mickey, Goofy, Donald. 35c, Horace, Clarabelle. 50c, Minnie, Frankie, Figuro. 75c, Donald, Pluto today. 80c, Party boy Mickey. 85c, Best Friends, Minnie, Daisy. 95c, Mickey's Girl, Minnie. $1, Cool forties Mickey. $1.50, Mickey, "Howdy!", 1950. $2, Totally Mickey. $3, Minnie, Mickey. $4, Congratulations Mickey, birthday cake. $5, Uncle Sam.

No. 1993, $6, Donald Duck, early photo of Mickey, horiz. No. 1994, $6, Minnie disco dancing, horiz. No. 1995, $6, Mickey photographing nephews, horiz. No. 1996, $6, Pluto, Mickey looking at wall of photos.

1994, May 5   **Litho.**   **Perf. 13½x14**

1977-1992	A274	Set of 16	24.00	24.00

Souvenir Sheets

Perf. 14x13½

1993-1996	A274	Set of 4	28.00	28.00

Breadfruit — A275

10c, Planting. 45c, Captain Bligh, plant. 65c, Fruit sliced. $5, Fruit on branch.

1994, Jan.   **Litho.**   **Perf. 13½x14**

1997	A275	10c multicolored	.25	.25
1998	A275	45c multicolored	.70	.70
1999	A275	65c multicolored	.60	.60
2000	A275	$5 multicolored	5.00	5.00
		Nos. 1997-2000 (4)	6.55	6.55

Intl. Year of the Family — A276

10c, Outing. 50c, Praying in church. 65c, Working in garden. 75c, Jogging. $1, Portrait. $2, Running on beach.

1994, Jan.   **Perf. 14x13½, 13½x14**

2001	A276	10c multicolored	.25	.25
2002	A276	50c multicolored	.50	.50
2003	A276	65c multicolored	.65	.65
2004	A276	75c multicolored	.70	.70
2005	A276	$1 multicolored	1.05	1.05
2006	A276	$2 multicolored	2.10	2.10
		Nos. 2001-2006 (6)	5.25	5.25

Nos. 2001-2004, 2006 are horiz.

Library Service, Cent. A277

1994, Jan.   **Perf. 14x13½**

2007	A277	5c Mobile library	.25	.25
2008	A277	10c Old public library	.25	.25
2009	A277	$1 Family education	.85	.85
2010	A277	$1 Younger, older		
		men	.85	.85
		Nos. 2007-2010 (4)	2.20	2.20

Barbra Streisand, 1993 MGM Grand Garden Concert — A278

1994, Jan.

2011	A278	$2 multicolored	1.60	1.60

A278a

Embossed

Perf. 12

2011A	A278a	$20 gold	25.00	25.00

No. 2011 issued in sheets of 9.

A279

A280

A281

Hong Kong '94 — A282

No. 2012 — Stamps, 19th cent. painting of Hong Kong Harbor: a, Hong Kong #626, ship under sail. b, Ship at anchor, #1548.

No. 2013 — Porcelain ware, Qing Dynasty: a, Bowl with bamboo & sparrows. b, Bowl with flowers of four seasons. c, Bowl with lotus pool & dragon. d, Bowl with landscape. e, Shar-Pei puppies in bowl (not antiquity). f, Covered bowl with dragon & pearls.

No. 2014 — Chinese dragon boat races: a, Dragon boats. b, Tapestry of dragon races. c, Dragon race. d, Dragon boats, diff. e, Chinese crested dog. f, Dragon boats, 4 banners above boats.

No. 2015 — Chinese junks: a, Junk, Hong Kong Island. b, Junk with white sails in harbor. c, Junk with inscription on stern, Hong Kong Island. d, Junk KLN B/G. e, Chow dog, junk. f, Junk with red, white sails, Hong Kong Island.

No. 2016 — Chinese seed stitch purses: a, Vases, fruit on pink purse. b, Peonies, butterflies. c, Vase, fruit on dark blue purse. d, Vases, fruit on light blue purse. e, Fu-dog. f, Flowers.

No. 2017 — Chineses pottery: a, Plate, bird on flowering spray, Qianlong. b, Large dish, Kangxi. c, Egshell plate, cocks on rocky ground, Yongzheng. d, Gladen dish decorated with Qilin curicorn, Yuan. e, Porcelain pug dog. f, Dish with Dutch ship, Uryburg, Qianlong.

No. 2018, vert. — Ceramic figures, Qing Dynasty: a, Waterdropper. b, Two women playing chess. c, Liu-Hai. d, Laughing twins. e, Seated hound. f, Louhan (Ma Ming).

No. 2019, Dr. Sun Yat-sen. No. 2020, Chiang Kai-shek.

No. 2021 — Dinosaurs: a, Triceratops. b, Unidentified, vert. c, Apatosaurus (d). d, Stegosaurus, vert.

1994, Feb. 18   **Perf. 14**

2012	A279	40c Pair, #a.-b.	.85	.85
2013	A280	40c Sheet of 6,		
		#a.-f.	2.25	2.25
2014	A280	40c Sheet of 6,		
		#a.-f.	2.25	2.25
2015	A280	45c Sheet of 6,		
		#a.-f.	2.40	2.40
2016	A280	45c Sheet of 6,		
		#a.-f.	2.40	2.40

2017	A281	50c Sheet of 6,		
		#a.-f.	2.75	2.75

Perf. 13

2018	A280	50c Sheet of 6,		
		#a.-f.	4.00	4.00

Souvenir Sheets

2019	A281	$2 multicolored	1.50	1.50
2020	A281	$2 multicolored	1.50	1.50
2021	A282	$1.50 Sheet of 4,		
		#a.-d.	4.50	4.50

No. 2012 issued in sheets of 10 stamps and has a continuous design.

Portions of the design on No. 2021 have been applied by a thermographic process producing a shiny, raised effect.

New Year 1994 (Year of the Dog) (#2013e, 2014e, 2015e, 2016e, 2017e, 2018e). Hong Kong '94 (#2018, 2021).

Miniature Sheet

Hong Kong '94 — A283

No. 2022 — Butterflies: a, Blue flasher. b, Tiger swallowtail. c, Lustrous copper. d, Tailed copper. e, Blue copper. f, Ruddy copper. g, Viceroy. h, California sister. i, Mourning cloak. j, Red passion flower. k, Small flambeau. l, Blue wave. m, Chiricahua metalmark. n, Monarch. o, Anise swallowtail. p, Buckeye.

1994, Feb. 18   Litho.   Perf. 14½

2022	A283	50c Sheet of 16,		
		#a.-p.	14.50	14.50

Juventus Soccer Team — A284

Players: No. 2023, $1, Causio. No. 2024, $1, Tardelli. No. 2025, $1, Rossi. No. 2026, $1, Bettega. No. 2027, $1, Platini, Baggio. No. 2028, $1, Cabrini. No. 2029, $1, Scirea. No. 2030, $1, Furino. No. 2031, $1, Kohler. No. 2032, $1, Zoff. No. 2033, $1, Gentile. $6, Three European Cups won by team, horiz.

1994, Mar. 22   Litho.   Perf. 14

2023-2033	A284	Set of 11	12.00	12.00

Souvenir Sheet

2034	A284	$6 multicolored	6.00	6.00

Orchids — A285

Designs: 10c, Epidendrum ibaguense. 25c, Ionopsis utricularioides. 50c, Brassavola cucullata. 65c, Encyclia cochleata. $1, Liparis nervosa. $2, Vanilla phaeantha. $4, Elleanthus cephalotus. $5, Isochilus linearis.

No. 2043, $6, Rodriguezia lanceolata. No. 2044, $6, Eulophia alta.

1994, Apr. 6   Litho.   Perf. 14

2035-2042	A285	Set of 8	18.50	18.50

Souvenir Sheets

2043-2044	A285	Set of 2	16.00	16.00

A286

Dinosaurs — A287

No. 2045: a, Protoavis (e). b, Pteranodon. c, Quetzalcoatlus (b). d, Lesothosaurus (a, c, e-h). e, Hetrodontosaurus. f, Archaeopteryx (b, e). g, Cearadactylus (f). h, Anchisaurus.

No. 2046: a, Dimorphodon (e). b, Camarasaurus (e, f). c, Spinosaurus (b). d, Allosaurus (a-c, e-h). e, Rhamphorhynchus (a). f, Pteranodon (b). g, Eudimorphodon (c). h, Ornithomimus.

No. 2047, 75c: a, Dimorphodon (b). b, Pterodactylus (a). c, Rhamphorhynchus (b). d, Pteranodon. e, Gallimimus. f, Stegosaurus. g, Acantholpolis. h, Trachodon (g). i, Thecodonti (j). j, Ankylosaurus (i). k, Compsognathus (j). l, Protoceratops.

No. 2048, 75c: a, Hesperonis. b, Mesosaurus. c, Plesiosaurus. d, Squalicorax (a). e, Tylosaurus (d, g). f, Plesiosoar. g, Stenopterygius ichthyosaurus (j). h, Stenosaurus (f). i, Eurhinosaurus longirostris (e, f, h, l). j, Cryptocleidus oxoniensis. k, Caturus (h, i, j, l). l, Protostega (k).

No. 2049, 75c: a, Quetzalcoatlus. b, Diplodocus (a). c, Spinosaurus (f, g). d, Apatosaurus (c). e, Ornitholestes. f, Lesothosaurus (e). g, Trachodon. h, Protoavis. i, Oviraptor. j, Coelophysis (i). k, Ornitholestes (j). l, Archaeopteryx.

No. 2050, 75c, horiz: a, Albertosaurus. b, Chasmosaurus (c). c, Brachiosaurus. d, Coelophysis (e). e, Deinonychus (d). f, Anatosaurus. g, Iguanodon. h, Baryonx. i, Steneosaurus. j, Nanotyrannus. k, Camptosaurus (j). l, Camarasaurus.

No. 2051, Tyrannosaurus rex.

No. 2052, $6, Triceratops, horiz. No. 2053, $6, Pteranodon, diplodocus carnegii, horiz. No. 2054, $6, Styracosaurus.

1994, Apr. 20   Litho.   Perf. 14

2045	A286	75c Sheet of 8,		
		#a.-h.	7.50	7.50
2046	A286	75c Sheet of 8,		
		#a.-h.	7.50	7.50

Sheets of 12, #a-l

2047-2050	A287	Set of 4	37.50	37.50

Souvenir Sheets

2051	A286	$6 multi	7.00	7.00
2052-2054	A287	Set of 3	21.00	21.00

No. 2048 is horiz.

Entertainers Type of 1991
Miniature Sheet

Various portraits of Marilyn Monroe.

1994, May 16   Perf. 13½

2055	A206	$1 Sheet of 9, #a.-		
		i.	10.00	10.00

1994 World Cup Soccer Championships, US — A288

Team photos: No. 2056, 50c, Colombia. No. 2057, 50c, Romania. No. 2058, 50c, Switzerland. No. 2059, 50c, US. No. 2060, 50c, Brazil. No. 2061, 50c, Cameroon. No. 2062, 50c, Russia. No. 2063, 50c, Sweden. No. 2064, 50c, Bolivia. No. 2065, 50c, Germany. No. 2066, 50c, South Korea. No. 2067, 50c, Spain. No. 2068, 50c, Argentina. No. 2069, 50c, Bulgaria. No. 2070, 50c, Greece. No. 2071, 50c, Nigeria. No. 2072, 50c, Ireland. No. 2073, 50c, Italy. No. 2074, 50c, Mexico. No. 2075, 50c, Norway. No. 2076, 50c, Belgium. No. 2077, 50c, Holland. No. 2078, 50c, Morocco. No. 2079, 50c, Saudi Arabia.

1994   Perf. 13½

2056-2079	A288	Set of 24	14.00	14.00

First Manned Moon Landing, 25th Anniv. — A289

No. 2080, $1 — Famous men, aviation & space scenes: a, Fred L. Whipple, Halley's Comet. b, Robert G. Gilruth, Gemini 12. c, George E. Mueller, Ed White walking in space during Gemini 4. d, Charles A. Berry, Johnsville Centrifuge. e, Christopher C. Kraft, Jr., Apollo 4 re-entry. f, James A. Van Allen, Explorer I, Van Allen Radiation Belts. g, Robert H. Goddard, Goddard Liquid Fuel Rocket, 1926. h, James E. Webb, Spirit of '76 flight. i, Rocco A. Petrone, Apollo 8 coming home.

No. 2081, $1: a, Walter R. Dornberger, missile launch, 1942. b, Alexander Lippisch, Wolfgang Spate's ME-163B. c, Kurt H. Debus, A4b Launch, 1945. d, Hermann Oberth, Oberth's Spaceship, 1923. e, Hanna Reitsch, Reichenberg (type 2) Piloted Bomb. f, Ernst Stuhlinger, Explorer I, 2nd stage ignition. g, Werner von Braun, Rocket Powered He112. h, Arthur Rudolph, Rudolph Rocket Motor, 1934. i, Willy Ley, Rocket Airplane, Greenwood Lake NY.

No. 2082, $6, Holger N. Toftoy. No. 2083, $6, Eberhard Rees.

1994, July 12   Perf. 14
Sheets of 9, #a-i

2080-2081	A289	Set of 2	20.00	20.00

Souvenir Sheets

2082-2083	A289	Set of 2	13.00	13.00

Nos. 2082-2083 each contain one 50x38mm stamp.

D-Day, 50th Anniv. A290

Designs: 40c, Supply armada. $5, Beached cargo ship unloads supplies. $6, Liberty ship.

1994, July 19   Litho.   Perf. 14

2084	A290	40c multicolored	.40	.40
2085	A290	$5 multicolored	4.75	4.75

Souvenir Sheet

2086	A290	$6 multicolored	5.25	5.25

New Year 1994 (Year of the Dog) — A291

Designs: 10c, Yorkshire terrier. 25c, Yorkshire terrier, diff. 50c, Golden retriever. 65c, Bernese mountain dog. $1, Vorstehhund. $2, Tibetan terrier. $4, West highland terrier. $5, Shih tzu.

No. 2095: a, Pomeranian. b, English springer spaniel. c, Bearded collie. d, Irish wolfhound. e, Pekingese. f, Irish setter. g, Old English sheepdog. h, Basset hound. i, Cavalier King Charles spaniel. j, Kleiner munsterlander. k, Shetland sheepdog. l, Dachshund. No. 2096, $6, Afghan hound. No. 2097, $6, German shepherd.

1994, July 21

2087-2094	A291	Set of 8	10.00	10.00
2095	A291	50c Sheet of 12,		
		#a.-l.	4.50	4.50

Souvenir Sheets

2096-2097	A291	Set of 2	9.00	9.00

English Touring Cricket, Cent. A292

Designs: 10c, M. R. Ramprakash, England. 30c, P. V. Simmons, West Indies. $2, Sir. G. St. A. Sobers, West Indies, vert. $3, First English team, 1895.

1994, July 25

2098-2100	A292	Set of 3	3.50	3.50

Souvenir Sheet

2101	A293	$3 multicolored	3.25	3.25

A293

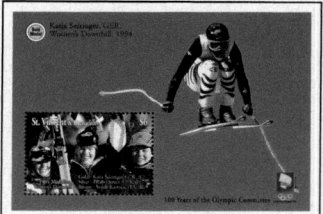

Intl. Olympic Committee, Cent. — A294

Designs: 45c, Peter Frenkel, German Democratic Republic, 20k walk, 1972. 50c, Kijung Son, Japan, marathon, 1936. 75c, Jesse Owens, US, 100-, 200-meters, 1936. $1, Greg Louganis, US, diving, 1984, 1988.

$6, Katja Seizinger, Germany, Picabo Street, US, Isolde Kastner, Italy, women's downhill, 1994.

1994, July 25

2102-2105	A293	Set of 4	3.25	3.25

Souvenir Sheet

2106	A294	$6 multicolored	6.00	6.00

A295

PHILAKOREA '94 — A296

Designs: 10c, Oryon Waterfall. 45c, Outside P'yongyang Indoor Sports Stadium, horiz. 65c, Pombong, Ch'onhwadae. 75c, Uisangdae, Naksansa. $1, Buddha of the Sokkuram Grotto, Kyangju, horiz. $2, Moksogwon, horiz.

No. 2113, 50c: a-h, Various letter pictures, eight panel screen, 18th cent. Choson Dynasty.

No. 2114, 50c — Letter pictures, 19th cent. Choson Dynasty: a, Fish. b, Birds. c-d, h, Various bookshelf pictures. e-g, Various designs from six-panel screen.

No. 2115, $4, Hunting scene, embroidery on silk, Choson Dynasty, horiz. No. 2116, $4, Chongdong Mirukbul.

1994, July 25   **Perf. 14**
2107-2112 A295 Set of 6   8.50 8.50
Sheets of 8, #a-h
Perf. 13½
2113-2114 A296 Set of 2   13.50 13.50
Souvenir Sheets
Perf. 14
2115-2116 A295 Set of 2   7.00 7.00

"All Good Things..."
Star Trek, The Next Generation, 7th Anniv. — A297

A297a

No. 2117: a, Capt. Picard. b, Cmdr. Riker. c, Lt. Cmdr. Data. d, Lt. Worf. e, Cast members. f, Dr. Crusher. g, Lt. Yar, Lt. Worf. h, Q. i, Counselor Troi.
$10, Cast members, horiz.
$20, Starship Enterprise, Capt. Picard.

1994   **Litho.**   **Perf. 14x13½**
2117   A297 $2 Sheet of 9,
         #a.-i.   15.00 15.00
Souvenir Sheet
Perf. 14x14½
2118   A297 $10 multicolored   9.50 9.50
Litho. & Embossed
Perf. 9
2118A A297a $20 gold & multi   25.00 25.00

Issued: Nos. 2117-2118, 6/27; No. 2118, May. No. 2117e exists in sheets of 9. No. 2118 contains one 60x40mm stamp.

Intl. Year of the Family A298

1994   **Perf. 14**
2119 A298 75c multicolored   .95 .95

Order of the Caribbean Community — A299

First award recipients: $1, Sir Shridath Ramphal, statesman, Guyana, vert. $2, Derek Walcott, writer, St. Lucia, vert. $5, William Demas, economist, Trinidad and Tobago.

1994, Sept. 1
2120-2122 A299 Set of 3   8.00 8.00

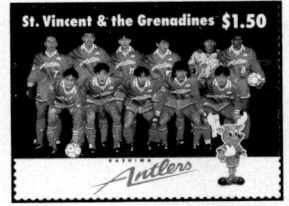

Japanese Soccer — A300

No. 2123: a, Kashima Antlers. b, JEF United. c, Red Diamonds. d, Verdy Yomiuri. e, Nissan FC Yokohama Marinos. f, AS Flugels. g, Bellmare. h, Shimizu S-pulse. i, Jubilo Iwata. j, Nagoya Grampus Eight. k, Panasonic Gamba Osaka. l, Sanfrecce Hiroshima FC.

No. 2124 — Jubilo Iwata, action scenes: a, c-d, 55c. b, e, $1.50. f, $3, Team picture.

No. 2125 — Red Diamonds, action scenes: a, c-d, 55c. b, e, $1.50. f, $3, Team pictue.

No. 2126 — Nissan FC Yokohama Marinos, action scenes: a, c-d, 55c. b, e, $1.50. f, $3, Team picture.

No. 2127 — Verdy Yomiuri, action scenes: a, c-d, 55c. b, e, $1.50. f, $3, Team picture.

No. 2128 — Nagoya Grampus eight, action scenes: a, c-d, 55c. b, e, $1.50. f, $3, Team picture.

No. 2129 — Kashima Antlers, action scenes: a, c-d, 55c. b, e, $1.50. f, $3, Team picture.

No. 2130 — JEF United, action scenes: a, c-d, 55c. b, e, $1.50. f, $3, Team picture.

No. 2131 — AS Flugels, action scenes: a, c-d, 55c. b, e, $1.50. f, $3, Team picture.

No. 2132 — Bellmare, action scenes: a, c-d, 55c. b, e, $1.50. f, $3, Team picture.

No. 2133 — Sanfrecce Hiroshima FC, action scenes: a, c-d, 55c. b, e, $1.50. f, $3, Team picture.

No. 2134 — Shimizu S-pulse, action scenes: a, c-d, 55c. b, e, $1.50. f, $3, Team picture.

No. 2135 — Panasonic Gamba Isajam, action scenes: a, c-d, 55c. b, e, $1.50. f, $3, Team picture.

No. 2136, vert. — League All-Stars: a, $1.50, League emblem. b, 55c, Shigetatsu Matsunaga. c, 55c, Masami Ihara. d, $1.50, Takumi Horiike. e, 55c, Shunzoh Ohno. f, 55c, Luiz Carlos Pereira. g, 55c, Tetsuyo Hashiratani. h, 55c, Carlos Alberto Souza Dos Santos. i, $1.50, Rui Ramos. j, 55c, Yasuto Honda. k, 55c, Kazuyoshi Miura. l, $1.50, Ramon Angel Diaz.

1994, July 1   **Perf. 14x13½**
2123   A300 $1.50 Sheet
               of 12,
           #a.-l.   11.00 11.00
Sheets of 6, #a-f
2124-2135 A300   Set of 12   70.00 70.00
Perf. 13½x14
2136   A300   Sheet of 12, #a.-
            l.   12.00 12.00

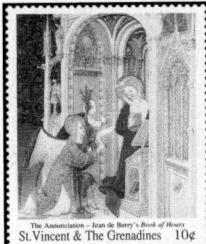

Christmas A301

Illustrations from Book of Hours, by Jean de Berry: 10c, The Annunciation, angel kneeling. 45c, The Visitation. 50c, The Nativity, Madonna seeing infant. 65c, The Purification of the Virgin. 75c, Presentation of Jesus in the Temple. $5, Flight into Egypt. $6, Adoration of the Magi.

1994   **Litho.**   **Perf. 13½x14**
2137-2142 A301 Set of 6   9.50 9.50
Souvenir Sheet
2143 A301 $6 multicolored   7.50 7.50

Disney Type of 1992 Redrawn With New Denominations and Added Inscriptions

Designs: No. 2144, Like #1792. No. 2145, Like #1806. No. 2146, Like #1807.

1995, Jan. 24   **Perf. 14x13½**
2144 A247 30c Sheet of 9, #a.-i.   6.25 6.25
Souvenir Sheets
2145 A247 $3 multi   4.25 4.25
2146 A247 $3 multi   4.25 4.25

Nos. 2144-2146 are inscribed with emblem for "New Year 1995, Year of the Pig."

ICAO, 50th Anniv. A302

Designs: 10c, Bequia Airport. 65c, Union Island. 75c, Liat 8-100, E.T. Joshua Airport. No. 2150, $1, Airplanes, ICAO emblem. No. 2151, $1, J.F. Mitchell Airport, Bequia.

1994, Dec. 1   **Litho.**   **Perf. 14**
2147-2151 A302 Set of 5   4.25 4.25

Cats A303

Parrots — A304

No. 2152 — Cats: a, Snowshoe. b, Abyssinian. c, Ocicat. d, Tiffany (e, h). e, Russian blue. f, Siamese. g, Bi-color. h, Malayan. i, Manx.

No. 2153 — Parrots: a, Mealy Amazon. b, Nanday conure. c, Black-headed caique. d, Scarlet macaw (g). e, Red-masked conure. f, Blue-headed parrot. g, Hyacinth macaw. h, Sun conure. i, Blue & yellow macaw.

No. 2154, White-eared conure. No. 2155, Birman.

1995, Apr. 25   **Litho.**   **Perf. 14**
Sheets of 9, #a-i
2152-2153 A303 $1 Set of 2   18.00 18.00
Souvenir Sheets
2154 A304 $5 multicolored   6.00 6.00
2155 A304 $6 multicolored   7.25 7.25

A305

Birds A306

No. 2156 — World Wildlife Fund, masked booby: a, One standing. b, Two birds. c, One nesting. d, One stretching wings.

No. 2157: a, Greater egret. b, Roseate spoonbill. c, Ring-billed gull. d, Ruddy quail-dove. e, Royal tern. f, Killdeer. g, Osprey. h, Frigatebird. i, Masked booby. j, Green-backed heron. k, Cormorant. l, Brown pelican.

No. 2158, Flamingo, vert. No. 2159, Purple gallinule, vert.

1995, May 2
2156 A305 75c Strip of 4, #a.-
           d.   4.00 4.00
2157 A306 75c Sheet of 12,
           #a.-l.   12.00 12.00
Souvenir Sheets
2158 A306 $5 multicolored   5.00 5.00
2159 A306 $6 multicolored   6.00 6.00

No. 2156 is a continuous design and was issued in sheets of 3.

VE Day, 50th Anniv. A307

No. 2159A: b, Douglas Devastator. c, Doolittle's B25 leads raid on Tokyo. d, Curtis Helldiver. e, USS Yorktown. f, USS Wasp. g, USS Lexington sinks.

No. 2160 — VE Day: a, US First Army nears the Rhine. b, Last V2 rocket fired at London, Mar. 1945. c, 8th Air Force B24 Liberators devastate industrial Germany. d, French Army advances on Strasbourg. e, Gloster Meteor, first jet aircraft to enter squadron service. f, Berlin burns from both air and ground bombardments. g, Soviet tanks on Unter Den Linden near Brandenburg Gate. h, European war is won.

No. 2161, $6, Pilot in cockpit of Allied bomber.

No. 2161A, $6, Ships in Pacific, sunset.

1995, May 8   **Litho.**   **Perf. 14**
2159A A307 $2 Sheet of 6,
         #b-.g + label 11.50 11.50
2160   A307 $2 Sheet of 8,
         #a.-h. + label 15.50 15.50
Souvenir Sheets
2161-2161A A307   Set of 2 15.00 15.00

No. 2161 contains one 57x43mm stamp.

UN, 50th Anniv. — A308

No. 2162: a, Globe, dove. b, Lady Liberty. c, UN Headquarters.
$6, Child.

1995, May 5
2162 A308 $2 Strip of 3, #a.-c. 5.25 5.25

Souvenir Sheet
2163 A308 $6 multicolored 5.25 5.25

No. 2162 is a continuous design and was issued in miniature sheets of 3.

18th World Scout Jamboree, Netherlands A309

Designs: $1, Natl. Scout flag. $4, Lord Baden Powell. $5, Scout handshake.
No. 2167, $6, Scout sign. No. 2168, $6, Scout salute.

1995, May 5
2164-2166 A309 Set of 3 8.75 8.75

Souvenir Sheets
2167-2168 A309 Set of 2 11.50 11.50

Yalta Conference, 50th Anniv. A310

Design: $50, like #2169.

1995, May 8 Litho. Perf. 14
2169 A310 $1 shown 1.75 1.75

Litho. & Embossed
Perf. 9
2169A A310 $50 gold & multi 27.50 27.50

No. 2169 was issued in sheets of 9.

New Year 1995 (Year of the Boar) — A311

No. 2170 — Stylized boars: a, blue green & multi. b, brown & multi. c, red & multi. $2, Two boars, horiz.

1995, May 8
2170 A311 75c Strip of 3, #a.-c. 2.50 2.50

Souvenir Sheet
2171 A311 $2 multicolored 2.50 2.50

No. 2170 was issued in sheets of 3.

FAO, 50th Anniv. — A312

No. 2172: a, Girl holding plate, woman with bowl. b, Stirring pot of food. c, Working in fields of grain.
$6, Infant.

1995, May 8
2172 A312 $2 Strip of 3, #a.-c. 5.25 5.25

Souvenir Sheet
2173 A312 $6 multicolored 5.25 5.25

No. 2172 is a continuous design and was issued in sheets of 3.

Rotary Intl., 90th Anniv. A313

Designs: $5, Paul Harris, Rotary emblem. $6, St. Vincent flag, Rotary emblem.

1995, May 8
2174 A313 $5 multicolored 4.50 4.50

Souvenir Sheet
2175 A313 $6 multicolored 5.25 5.25

Queen Mother, 95th Birthday — A314

No. 2176: a, Drawing. b, Wearing blue hat. c, Formal portrait. d, Wearing lavender outfit. $6, Wearing crown jewels, yellow dress.

1995, May 8 Perf. 13½x14
2176 A314 $1.50 Block or strip of 4, #a.-d. 5.25 5.25

Souvenir Sheet
2177 A314 $6 multicolored 5.25 5.25

No. 2176 was issued in sheet of 2 blocks or strips.
In 2002, sheets of Nos. 2176 and 2177 were overprinted "In Memoriam — 1900-2002" in margin.

Miniature Sheets

Marine Life A315

No. 2178, vert: a, Humpback whale (b, d, e, f, i). b, Green turtle (c). c, Bottlenosed dolphin (f). d, Monk seal (e). e, Krill. f, Blue shark. g, Striped pork fish. h, Chaedolon sedentarius (e, g). i, Ship wreck, bottom of sea.
No. 2179: a, Pomacentrus leucosticus (b). b, Pomacanthus arcuatus (d). c, Microspathodon chrysurus (d). d, Chaedolon capistratus.
No. 2180, $6, Physalia physalis, vert. No. 2181, $6, Sea anemones, vert.

1995, May 23 Perf. 14
2178 A315 90c Sheet of 9, #a.-i. 7.50 7.50
2179 A315 $1 Sheet of 4, #a.-d. 5.00 5.00

Souvenir Sheets
2180-2181 A315 Set of 2 13.00 13.00

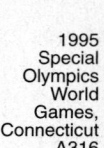

1995 Special Olympics World Games, Connecticut A316

A316a

1995, July 6
2182 A316 $1 blk, yel & bl 1.10 1.10

Embossed
Perf. 9
2182A A316a $20 gold

No. 2182 issued in sheets of 9.

1995 IAAF World Track & Field Championships, Gothenburg & 1996 Summer Olympics, Atlanta — A317

No. 2183: a, Ingrid Kristiansen, Norway. b, Trine Hattestad, Norway. c, Grete Waitz, Norway. d, Vebjorn Rodal, Norway. e, Geir Moen, Norway. f, Steinar Hoen, Norway, horiz.

1995, July 31 Litho. Perf. 14
2183 A317 $1 Sheet of 6, #a.-f. 4.50 4.50

A318

Designs: 15c, Breast, bowl of food, horiz. 20c, Expressing milk, cup, spoon. 90c, Drawing of mother breastfeeding child, by Picasso. $5, Mother, child, olive wreath.

1995, Aug. 4
2184-2187 A318 Set of 4 6.75 6.75
WHO, UNICEF Baby Friendly Program.

A319

Designs: 10c, Leeward Coast, horiz. 15c, Feeder roads project, horiz. 25c, Anthurium andraeanum, horiz. 50c, Coconut palm. 65c, Housing scene, Fairhall, horiz.

1995, Aug. 8
2188-2192 A319 Set of 5 1.90 1.90
Caribbean Development Bank, 25th anniv.

Fudo Myoou (God of Fire), Woodprint, by Shunichi Kadowaki — A320

1995, July 1 Litho. Perf. 14
2193 A320 $1.40 multicolored 1.25 1.25

Nolan Ryan, Baseball Player — A322

Designs: No. 2194, Nolan Ryan Foundation emblem. No. 2195, Emblem of major league All Star Game, Arlington, TX.
No. 2196 — Portraits of Ryan: a, In NY Mets uniform. b, With western hat, dog. c, In Texas Rangers cap. d, Throwing football. e, With son. f, Laughing, without hat. g, With family. h, Wearing Houston Astros cap.
No. 2197 — Ryan in Rangers uniform: a, Blue outfit. b, "34" on front. c, Looking left. d, After pitch looking forward. e, After pitch looking left. f, With bloody lip. g, Ready to pitch ball. h, Holding up cap.
$6, Being carried by team mates.
$30, Ready to pitch (illustration reduced).

1995, Aug. 1 Perf. 13½x14
2194 A321 $1 multicolored .75 .75
2195 A321 $1 multicolored .75 .75
 a. Pair, #2194-2195 1.50 1.50
2196 A321 $1 Sheet of 9, #a.-h. + #2194 12.00 12.00
2197 A321 $1 Sheet of 9, #a.-h. + #2195 12.00 12.00

Souvenir Sheet
2198 A321 $6 multicolored 5.25 5.25

Litho. & Embossed
Perf. 9
2199 A322 $30 gold & multi 35.00 35.00

Nos. 2194-2195 were issued in sheets containing 5 #2194, 4 #2195.

1996 Summer Olympics, Atlanta — A323

No. 2200: a, Jean Shiley, US. b, Ruth Fuchs, Germany. c, Alessandro Andrei, Italy. d, Dorando Pietri, Italy. e, Heide Rosendahl, Germany. f, Mitsuoki Watanabe, Japan. g, Yasuhiro Yamashita, Japan. h, Dick Fosbury, US.
No. 2201: a, Long jump. b, Hurdles. c, Sprint. d, Marathon. e, Gymnastics. f, Rowing.
No. 2202, $5, Magic Johnson. No. 2203, $5, Swimmer's hand, horiz.

1995, Aug. 24 Litho. *Perf. 14*
2200 A323 $1 Sheet of 8, #a.-h. 7.00 7.00
2201 A323 $2 Sheet of 6, #a.-f. 10.50 10.50

Souvenir Sheets
2202-2203 A323 Set of 2 12.00 12.00

Miniature Sheet

Stars of American League Baseball
A324

A324a

No. 2204 — Different portraits of: a, e, i, Frank Thomas, Chicago White Sox. b, f-g, Cal Ripken, Jr., Baltimore Orioles. c-d, h, Ken Griffey, Jr., Seattle Mariners.
No. 2204J, $30, Griffey. No. 2204K, $30, Ripken. No. 2204L, $30, Thomas.

1995, Sept. 6 Litho. *Perf. 14*
2204 A324 $1 Sheet of 9, #a.-i. 8.50 8.50

Litho. & Embossed
Perf. 9
2204J-2204L A324a Set of 3

Entertainers
A325

Nos. 2205-2206, $1: Portraits of Elvis Presley.
No. 2207, $1: Portraits of John Lennon.
Nos. 2208-2210, $1: Portraits of Marilyn Monroe.
No. 2211, $6, Presley, diff. No. 2212, $6, Lennon, diff. No. 2213, $6, Monroe, in black. No. 2214, $6, Monroe, in red.

1995, Sept. 18 *Perf. 13½x14*
2205 A325 $1 Sheet of 6, #a.-f. 7.00 7.00

Sheets of 9, #a-i
2206-2210 A325 Set of 5 40.00 40.00

Souvenir Sheets
2211-2214 A325 Set of 4 26.00 26.00

No. 2208 has serifs in lettering. No. 2209 has pink lettering.

Entertainers — A325a

Designs: $20, Elvis Presley. $30, Marilyn Monroe.

1995 Litho. & Embossed *Perf. 9*
2214A A325a $20 gold & multi 24.00 24.00
2214B A325a $30 gold & multi 36.00 36.00

Passenger Trains — A326

No. 2215: a, German Federal Railway ET4-03, high speed four car electric. b, Tres Grande Vitesse (TGV), France. c, British Railways Class 87 electric. d, Beijing locomotive, Railways of the People's Republic of China. e, American Amtrak turbo. f, Swedish State Railways class RC4 electric.
$6, Eurostar.

1995, Oct. 3 *Perf. 14*
2215 A326 $1.50 Sheet of 6, #a.-f. 7.75 7.75

Souvenir Sheet
2216 A326 $6 multicolored 8.50 8.50

No. 2216 contains one 85x28mm stamp.

Nobel Prize Fund Established, Cent. — A327

No. 2217, $1: a, Heinrich Böll, literature, 1972. b, Walther Bothe, physics, 1954. c, Richard Kuhn, chemistry, 1938. d, Hermann Hesse, literatrue, 1946. e, Knut Hamsun, literature, 1920. f, Konrad Lorenz, medicine, 1973. g, Thomas Mann, literature, 1929. h, Fridtjof Nansen, peace, 1922. i, Fritz Pregl, chemistry, 1923. j, Christian Lange, peace, 1921. k, Otto Loewi, medicine, 1936. l, Erwin Schrodinger, physics, 1933.
No. 2218, $1: a, Giosue Carducci, literature, 1906. b, Wladyslaw Reymont, literature, 1924. c, Ivan Bunin, literature, 1933. d, Pavel Cherenkov, physics, 1958. e, Ivan Pavlov, medicine, 1904. f, Pyotr Kapitsa, physics, 1978. g, Lev Landau, physics, 1962. h, Daniel Bovet, medicine, 1957. i, Henryk Sienkiewicz, literature, 1905. j, Aleksandr Prokhorov, physics, 1964. k, Julius Wagner von Jauregg, medicine, 1927. l, Grazia Deledda, literature, 1926.
No. 2219, $1: a, Bjornstjerne Bjornson, literature, 1903. b, Frank Kellogg, peace, 1929. c, Gustav Hertz, physics, 1925. d, Har Gobind Khorana, medicine, 1968. e, Kenichi Fukui, chemistry, 1981. f, Henry Kissinger, peace, 1973. g, Martin Luther King, Jr., peace, 1964. h, Odd Hassel, chemistry, 1969. i, Polykarp Kusch, physics, 1955. j, Ragnar Frisch, economics, 1969. k, Willis E. Lamb, Jr., physics, 1955. l, Sigrid Undset, literature, 1928.
No. 2220: a, Robert Barany, medicine, 1914. b, Ernest Walton, physics, 1951. c, Alfred Fried, peace, 1911. d, James Franck, physics, 1925. e, Werner Forssmann, medicine, 1956. f, Yasunari Kawabata, literature, 1968. g, Wolfgang Pauli, physics, 1945. h, Jean-Paul Sartre, literature, 1964. i, Aleksandr Solzhenitsyn, literature, 1970. j, Hermann Staudinger, chemistry, 1953. k, Igor Tamm, physics, 1958. l, Samuel Beckett, literature, 1969.
No. 2221: a, Adolf Windaus, chemistry, 1928. No. 2222, $6, Hideki Yukawa, physics, 1949. No. 2223, $6, Bertha von Suttner, peace, 1905. No. 2224, $6, Karl Landsteiner, medicine, 1930.

1995, Oct. 2 Litho. *Perf. 14*
Sheets of 12, #a-l
2217-2220 A327 Set of 4 46.00 46.00

Souvenir Sheets
2221-2224 A327 Set of 4 26.00 26.00

Classic Cars A328

No. 2225: a, 1931 Duesenberg Model J. b, 1913 Sleeve-valve Minerva. c, 1933 Delage D.8. SS. d, 1931-32 Bugatti Royale, Coupe De Ville chassis 41111. e, 1926 Rolls Royce 7668CC Phantom 1 Landauette. f, 1927 Mercedes Benz S26/120/180 PS.
$5, Hispano-Suiza Type H6B tulipwood-bodied roadster by Neuport.

1995, Oct. 3
2225 A328 $1.50 Sheet of 6, #a.-f. 7.75 7.75

Souvenir Sheet
2226 A328 $5 multicolored 7.00 7.00

Singapore '95 (#2225). No. 2226 contains one 85x28mm stamp.

Sierra Club, Cent. — A329

No. 2227: a, Gray wolf in front of trees. b. Gray wolf pup. c, Gray wolf up close. d, Hawaiian goose. e, Two hawaiian geese. f, Jaguar. g, Lion-tailed macaque. h, Sand cat. i, Three sand cats.
No. 2228, horiz.: a, Orangutan swinging from tree. b, Orangutan facing forward. c, Orangutan looking left. d, Jaguar on rock. e, Jaguar up close. f, Sand cats. g, Hawaiian goose. h, Three lion-tailed macaques. i, Lion-tailed macaque.

1995, Dec. 1 Litho. *Perf. 14*
2227 A329 $1 Sheet of 9, #a.-i. 9.00 9.00
2228 A329 $1 Sheet of 9, #a.-i. 9.00 9.00

Natural Wonders of the World A330

No. 2229: a, Nile River. b, Yangtze River. c, Niagara Falls. d, Victoria Falls. e, Grand Canyon, US. f, Sahara Desert, Algeria. g, Kilimanjaro, Tanzania. h, Amazon river.
No. 2230, Haleakala Crater, Hawaii.

1995, Dec. 1
2229 A330 $1.10 Sheet of 8, #a-h 9.50 9.50

Souvenir Sheet
2230 A330 $6 multicolored 6.75 6.75

Disney Christmas — A331

Antique Disney toys: 1c, Lionel Santa car. 2c, Mickey Mouse "Choo Choo." 3c, Minnie Mouse pram. 5c, Mickey Mouse circus pull toy. 10c, Mickey, Pluto wind-up cart. 25c, Mickey Mouse mechanical motorcycle. $3, Lionel's Mickey Mouse handcar. $5, Casey Jr. Disneyland Express.
No. 2239, $6, Silver Link, Mickey the Stoker. No. 2240, $6, Mickey, Streamliner Engine.

1995, Dec. 7 *Perf. 13½x14*
2231-2238 A331 Set of 8 15.50 15.50

Souvenir Sheets
2239-2240 A331 Set of 2 14.00 14.00

Crotons A331a

Codiaeum variegatum: 10c, Mons florin. 15c, Prince of Monaco. 20c, Craigii. 40c, Gloriosum. 50c, Ebureum, vert. 60c, Volutum ramshorn. 70c, Narrenii, vert. 90c, Undutatum, vert. $1, Caribbean. $1.10, Gloriosa. $1.40, Katonii. $2, Appleleaf. $5, Tapestry. $10, Cornutum. $20, Puntatum aureum.

1996, Jan. 1 Litho. *Perf. 14*
2240A A331a 10c multi .25 .25
2240B A331a 15c multi .25 .25
2240C A331a 20c multi .25 .25
2240D A331a 40c multi .30 .30
2240E A331a 50c multi .40 .40
2240F A331a 60c multi .45 .45
2240G A331a 70c multi .55 .55
2240H A331a 90c multi .70 .70
2240I A331a $1 multi .75 .75
2240J A331a $1.10 multi .85 .85
2240K A331a $1.40 multi 1.00 1.00
2240L A331a $2 multi 1.50 1.50
2240M A331a $5 multi 3.75 3.75
2240N A331a $10 multi 7.50 7.50
2240O A331a $20 multi 15.00 15.00
Nos. 2240A-2240O (15) 33.50 33.50

New Year 1996 (Year of the Rat) — A332

Nos. 2241 and 2242 — Stylized rats, Chinese inscriptions within checkered squares: a, lilac & multi. b, orange & multi. c, pink & multi. $2, orange, green & black.

1996, Jan. 2 Litho. *Perf. 14½*
2241 A332 75c Strip of 3, #a.-c. 2.00 2.00
2242 A332 $1 Sheet of 3, #a.-c. 2.40 2.40

Souvenir Sheet
2243 A332 $2 multicolored 1.60 1.60

No. 2241 was issued in sheets of 9 stamps.

A333

Commemorating 30 years of STAR TREK

Star Trek, 30th Anniv. — A333a

No. 2244, $1: a, Spock. b, Kirk. c, Uhura. d, Sulu. e, Starship Enterprise. f, McCoy. g, Scott. h, Kirk, McCoy, Spock. i, Chekov.
No. 2245, $1: a, Spock holding up hand in Vulcan greeting. b, Kirk, Spock in "A Piece of the Action." c. Captain Kirk. d, Kirk, "The Trouble with Tribbles." e, Crew, "City on the Edge of Forever." f, Uhura, Sulu, "Mirror, Mirror." g, Romulans, "Balance of Terror." h, Building exterior. i, Khan, "Space Seed."

$6, Spock, Uhura.
$30, Spock, Kirk, McCoy, Scott, Starship
Enterprise.
Illustration A333a reduced.

1996, Jan. 4   **Perf. 13½x14**
Sheets of 9, #a-i
2244-2245 A333 $1 Set of 2   15.00 15.00
Souvenir Sheet
2246 A333 $6 multicolored   4.50 4.50
Litho. & Embossed
Perf. 9
2246A A333a $30 gold & multi 30.00 30.00

Disney Characters in Various
Occupations — A334

No. 2247 — Merchants: a, Stamp dealer. b,
At supermarket. c, Car salesman. d, Florist. e,
Fast food carhop. f, Street vendor. g, Gift
shop. h, Hobby shop owner. i, Bakery.
No. 2248 — Transport workers: a, Delivery
service. b, Truck driver. c, Airplane crew. d,
Railroad men. e, Bus driver. f, Tour guide. g,
Messenger service. h, Trolley conductor. i, Air
traffic controller.
No. 2249 — Law & order: a, Postal inspec-
tor. b, Traffic cop. c, Private detectives. d,
Highway patrol. e, Justice of the peace. f,
Security guard. g, Judge and lawyer. h, Sher-
iff. i, Court stenographer.
No. 2250 — Sports professionals: a, Bas-
ketball player. b, Referee. c, Track coach. d,
Ice skater. e, Golfer and caddy. f, Sports-
caster. g, Tennis champs. h, Football coach. i,
Race car driver.
No. 2251 — Scientists: a, Paleontologist. b,
Archaeologist. c, Inventor. d, Astronaut. e,
Chemist. f, Engineer. g, Computer graphics. h,
Astronomer. i, Zoologist.
No. 2252, vert. — School of education: a,
Classroom teacher. b, Nursery school
teacher. c, Band teacher. d, Electronic
teacher. e, School psychologist. f, School prin-
cipal. g, Professor. h, Graduate.
No. 2253 — Sea & shore workers: a, Ship
builders. b, Fisherman. c, Pearl diver. d,
Underwater photographer. e, Bait & tackle
shop owner. f, Bathing suit covergirls. g,
Marine life painter. h, Lifeguard. i, Lighthouse
keeper.
No. 2254, $6, Donald in ice cream parlor.
No. 2255, $6, Goofy as an oceanographer.
No. 2256, $6, Grandma, Grandpa, Daisy Duck
as jury, vert. No. 2257, $6, Donald as deep
sea treasure hunter, vert. No. 2258, $6, Minnie
as librarian, vert. No. 2259, $6, Mickey, ducks,
as cheerleaders, vert. No. 2260, $6, Mickey as
seaman, vert.

1996, Jan. 8   **Perf. 14x13½, 13½x14**
2247 A334   10c Sheet of 9,
           #a.-i.   1.10   1.10
2248 A334   50c Sheet of 9,
           #a.-i.   5.75   5.75
2249 A334   75c Sheet of 9,
           #a.-i.   8.25   8.25
2250 A334   90c Sheet of 9,
           #a.-i.   10.00 10.00
2251 A334   95c Sheet of 9,
           #a.-i.   10.50 10.50
2252 A334 $1.10 Sheet of 8,
           #a.-h.   11.00 11.00
2253 A334 $1.20 Sheet of 9,
           #a.-i.   13.50 13.50
Souvenir Sheets
2254-2260 A334 Set of 7   30.00 30.00
#2248-2253 exist in sheets of 7 or 8 10c
stamps + label. The label replaces the following stamps: #2248e, 2249e, 2250e, 2251e,
2252d, 2253e. The sheets had limited release
on Dec. 3, 1996.

Paintings
from
Metropolitan
Museum of
Art — A335

No. 2261: a, Moses Striking Rock, by
Bloemaert. b, The Last Communion, by Botti-
celli. c, The Musicians, by Caravaggio. d,
Francesco Sassetti & Son, by Ghirlandaio. e,
Pepito Costa y Bunells, by Goya. f, Saint
Andrew, by Martini. g, The Nativity, by a fol-
lower of van der Weyden. h, Christ Blessing,
by Solario.
No. 2262 — Art by Cézanne: a, Madame
Cézanne. b, Still Life with Apples and Pears. c,
Man in a Straw Hat. d, Still Life with a Ginger
Jar. e, Madame Cézanne in a Red Dress. f,
Still Life. g, Dominique Aubert. h, Still Life, diff.
i, The Card Players.
No. 2263: a, Bullfight, by Goya. b, Portrait of
a Man, by Frans Hals. c, Mother and Son, by
Sully. d, Portrait of a Young Man, by Memling.
e, Maltilde Stoughton de Jaudenes, by Stuart.
f, Josef de Jaudenes y Nebot, by Stuart. g,
Mont Sainte-Victore, by Cézanne. h,
Gardanne, by Cézanne. i, The Empress Euge-
nie, by Winterhalter.
No. 2264: a, The Dissolute Household, by
Steen. b, Portrait of Gerard de Lairesse, by
Rembrandt. c, Juan de Pareja, by Velázquez.
d, Curiosity, by G. Ter Borch. e, The Compan-
ions of Rinaldo, by Poussin. f, Don Gaspar de
Guzman, by Velázquez. g, Merry Company on
a Terrace, by Steen. h, Pilate Washing Hands,
by Rembrandt. i, Portrait of a Man, by Van
Dyck.
No. 2265, $6, Hagar in Wilderness, by
Corot. No. 2266, $6, Young Ladies from the
Village, by Courbet. No. 2267, $6, Two Young
Peasant Women, by Pissaro. No. 2268, $6,
Allegory of the Planets and Continents, by
Tiepolo.

1996, Feb. 1   **Litho.**   **Perf. 14**
2261 A335   75c Sheet of 8,
           #a.-h.+label   5.00   5.00
2262 A335   90c Sheet of 9,
           #a.-i.   7.00   7.00
2263 A335 $1 Sheet of 9,
           #a.-i.   7.75   7.75
2264 A335 $1.10 Sheet of 9,
           #a.-i.   8.50   8.50
Souvenir Sheets
2265-2268 A335 Set of 4   20.00 20.00
Nos. 2265-2268 each contain one
81x53mm stamp.

A335a

Michael Jordan, Basketball Player,
Baseball Player — A335b

Design: No. 2268E, Jordan as basketball
player.

Perf. 14, Imperf. (#2268Ac)
1996, Apr. 17   **Litho.**
2268A   Sheet of 17, 16 #b, 1
           #c   29.00 29.00
   b. A335a $2 shown   1.50   1.50
   c. A335a $6 Portrait, up close   4.50   4.50

Litho. & Embossed
Perf. 9
2268D A335b $30 shown
2268E A335b $30 gold & multi
No. 2268Ac is 68x100mm and has simulated perforations.

A335c

Joe Montana, Football Player — A335d

No. 2268I: j, In red jersey. k, In white jersey.

Perf. 14, Imperf. (#2268Fh)
1996, Apr. 17   **Litho.**
2268F   Sheet of 17, 16 #g, 1
           #h   29.00 29.00
   g. A335c $2 shown   1.50   1.50
   h. A335c $6 In action   4.50   4.50
Souvenir Sheet
Litho. & Embossed
Perf. 9
2268I   A335d $15 Sheet of 2,
           #j.-k.
No. 2268Fh is 68x100mm and has simulated perforations.

Lou Gehrig and Cal Ripken, Jr.,
Baseball Ironmen — A336

1995   **Litho. & Embossed**   **Perf. 9**
2269 A336 $30 gold & multi

A336a

A337

Star Wars Trilogy — A338

No. 2269: b, In Space Bar. c, Luke,
Emperor. d, X-Wing Fighter. e, Star Destroy-
ers. f, Cloud City. g, Speeders on Forest
Moon.
Nos. 2270, 2273a, Darth Vader, "Star
Wars," 1977. Nos. 2271, 2273c, Yoda, "Return
of the Jedi," 1983. Nos. 2272, 2273b, Storm
troopers, "The Empire Strikes Back," 1980.
No. 2274, $30, Darth Vader, "Star Wars,"
1977. No. 2275, $30, Yoda, "Return of the
Jedi," 1983. No. 2276, $30, Storm Trooper,
"The Empire Strikes Back," 1980.

1996, Mar. 19   **Litho.**   **Perf. 14**
2269A A336a   35c Sheet of 6,
           #b.-g.   9.50 9.50
Self-Adhesive
Serpentine Die Cut 6
2270 A337 $1 sil & multi   3.00 3.00
2271 A337 $1 sil & multi   3.00 3.00
2272 A337 $1 sil & multi   3.00 3.00
Souvenir Sheet
Serpentine Die Cut 9
2273 A338 $2 Sheet of 3, #a.-c. 9.50 9.50
Litho. & Embossed
Perf. 9
2274-2276 A337   Set of 3
Nos. 2270-2272 were issued in sheets of 3
each arranged in alternating order.
Nos. 2274-2276 are gold and multi, and
also exist in silver & multi.
Issued: Nos. 2274-2276, 11/18/95; others
3/19/96.

Butterflies — A339

Designs: 70c, Anteos menippe. $1, Eunica
alcmena. $1.10, Doxocopa lavinia. $2,
Tithorea tarricina.
No. 2281: a, Papilio lycophron. b, Prepona
buckleyana. c, Parides agavus. d, Papilio
cacicus. e, Euryades duponchelli. f, Diaethria
dymena. g, Orimba jansoni. h, Polystichtis
siaka. i, Papilio machaonides.
$5, Adelpha abia. $6, Themone pais.

1996, Apr. 15   **Litho.**   **Perf. 14**
2277-2280 A339 Set of 4   4.50 4.50
2281 A339 90c Sheet of 9, #a.-i. 7.50 7.50
Souvenir Sheets
2282 A339 $5 multicolored   4.75 4.75
2283 A339 $6 multicolored   6.00 6.00

Queen Elizabeth II, 70th
Birthday — A340

No. 2284: a, Portrait. b, In robes of Order of
the Garter. c, Wearing red coat, hat.
$6, Waving from balcony, horiz.

1996, June 12 Litho.   **Perf. 13½x14**
2284 A340 $2 Strip of 3, #a.-c. 5.25 5.25
Souvenir Sheet
Perf. 14x13½
2285 A340 $6 multicolored   5.25 5.25
No. 2284 was issued in sheets of 9 stamps.

Birds
A341

Designs: 60c, Coereba flaveola, vert. $1, Myadestes genibarbis, vert. $1.10, Tangara cucullata, vert. $2, Eulampis jugularis, vert.
No. 2290: a, Progne subis. b, Buteo platypterus. c, Phaethon lepturus. d, Himantopus himantopus. e, Sterna anaethetus. f, Euphonia musica. g, Arenaria interpres. h, Sericotes holosericeus. i, Nyctanassa violacea.
$5, Dendrocygna autumnalis, vert.. $6, Amazona guildingii, vert.

1996, July 11   **Perf. 14**
2286-2289 A341 Set of 4   4.50 4.50
2290 A341 $1 Sheet of 9, #a.-i.   8.00 8.00
Souvenir Sheets
2291 A341 $5 multi   4.25 4.25
2292 A341 $6 multi   5.25 5.25

Radio, Cent.
A342

Entertainers: 90c, Walter Winchell. $1, Fred Allen. $1.10, Hedda Hopper. $2, Eve Arden. $6, Major Bowes.

1996, July 11   **Perf. 13½x14**
2293-2296 A342 Set of 4   4.25 4.25
Souvenir Sheet
2297 A342 $6 multicolored   5.00 5.00

UNICEF, 50th Anniv.
A343

Designs: $1, Boy raising arm. $1.10, Children reading. $2, Girl, microscope. $5, Boy.

1996, July 11   **Perf. 14**
2298-2300 A343 Set of 3   3.25 3.25
Souvenir Sheet
2301 A343 $5 multicolored   3.80 3.80

Chinese Animated Films — A344

Nos. 2302, 15c, 2304, 75c, vert.: Various characters from "Uproar in Heaven."
Nos. 2303, 15c, 2305, 75c, vert.: Various characters from "Nezha Conquers the Dragon King."

1996, May 10   **Litho.**   **Perf. 12**
Strips of 5, #a-e
2302-2303 A344 15c Set of 2   3.50 3.50
Souvenir Sheets
2304-2305 A344 75c Set of 2   4.00 4.00

Nos. 2302-2303 each were issued in a sheet of 10 stamps. CHINA '96, 9th Asian Intl. Philatelic Exhibition.

Jerusalem, 3000th Anniv. — A345

Designs: $1, Knesset. $1.10, Montefiore Windmill. $2, Shrine of the Book. $5, Jerusalem of Gold.

1996, July 11   **Litho.**   **Perf. 14**
2306-2308 A345 Set of 3   4.25 4.25
Souvenir Sheet
2309 A345 $5 multicolored   4.25 4.25
The captions on Nos. 2306 and 2308 are transposed. For overprints see Nos. 2586-2589.

1996 Summer Olympic Games, Atlanta
A346

Designs: 20c, Maurice King, weight lifter, vert. 70c, Eswort Coombs, 400-meter relay, vert. No. 2312, 90c, Runners, Olympia, 530BC. No. 2313, 90c, Pamenos Ballantyne, Benedict Ballantyne, runners, vert. $1, London landmarks, 1908 Olympics, Great Britain. No. 2315, $1.10, Rodney "Chang" Jack, soccer player, vert. No. 2316, $1, Dorando Pietri, marathon runner, London, 1908, vert. $2, Yachting.
No. 2318, $1, vert. — Past winners: event: a, Vitaly Shcherbo, gymnastics. b, Fu Mingxia, diving. c, Wilma Rudolph, track & field. d, Rafer Johnson, decathlon. e, Teofilo Stevenson, boxing. f, Babe Didrikson, track & field. g, Kyoko Iwasaki, swimming. h, Yoo Namkyu, table tennis. i, Michael Gross, swimming.
No. 2319, $1: a, Chuhei Nambu, triple jump. b, Duncan McNaughton, high jump. c, Jack Kelly, single sculls. d, Jackie Joyner-Kersee, heptathlon. e, Tyrell Biggs, boxing. f, Larisa Latynina, gymnastics. g, Bob Garrett, discus. h, Paavo Nurmi, 5000-meters. i, Eric Lemming, javelin.
No. 2320, $1: a, Yasuhiro Yamashita, judo. b, Peter Rono, 1500-meters. c, Aleksandr Kurlovich, weight lifting. d, Juha Tiainen, hammer throw. e, Sergei Bubka, pole vault. f, Q. F. Newall, women's archery. g, Nadia Comaneci, gymnastics. h, Carl Lewis, long jump. i, Bob Mathias, decathlon.
No. 2321, $1, vert. — Sporting events: a, Women's archery. b, Gymnastics. c, Basketball. d, Soccer. e, Water polo. f, Baseball. g, Kayak. h, Fencing. i, Cycling.
No. 2322, $5, Olympic Flag. No. 2323, $5, Carl Lewis, runner, vert. No. 2324, $5, Alexander Dityatin, gymnastics, 1980. No. 2325, $5, Hannes Kolehmainen, marathon runner.

1996, July 19
2310-2317 A346 Set of 8   7.00 7.00
Sheets of 9, #a-i
2318-2321 A346 Set of 4   31.00 31.00
Souvenir Sheets
2322-2325 A346 Set of 4   15.00 15.00
St. Vincent Olympic Committee (#2310-2311, 2313, 2315).

Disney's "The Hunchback of Notre Dame"
A347

No. 2326: a, Quasimodo. b, Phoebus. c, Laverne, Hugo. d, Clopin. e, Frollo. f, Esmeralda. g, Victor. h, Djali.
No. 2327, $6, Esmeralda, Quasimodo, horiz. No. 2328, $6, Esmeralda, Phoebus, horiz.

1996, July 25   **Perf. 13½x14**
2326 A347 $1 Sheet of 8, #a-h   8.00 8.00
Souvenir Sheets
Perf. 14X13½
2327-2328 A347 Set of 2   13.00 13.00

Fish
A348

Designs: 70c, French angelfish. 90c, Red-spotted hawkfish. $1.10, Spiny puffer. $2, Gray triggerfish.
No. 2333, $1: a, Barred hamlet. b, Flamefish. c, Longsnout butterflyfish. d, Fairy basslet. e, Redtail parrotfish. f, Blackbar soldierfish. g, Threespot damselfish. h, Candy basslet. i, Spotfin hogfish.
No. 2334, $1: a, Equetus lanceolatus. b, Acanthurus coeruleus. c, Lutjanus analis. d, Hippocampus hudsonius. e, Serranus annularis. f, Squatina dumerili. g, Muraena miliaris. h, Bolbometopon bicolor. i, Tritonium nodiferum.
$5, Queen triggerfish. $6, Blue marlin.

1996, Aug. 10   **Perf. 14**
2329-2332 A348 Set of 4   4.25 4.25
Sheets of 9, #a-i
2333-2334 A348 Set of 2   14.50 14.50
Souvenir Sheets
2335 A348 $5 multicolored   4.25 4.25
2336 A348 $6 multicolored   5.00 5.00

Flowers
A349

Designs: 70c, Beloperone guttata. $1, Epidendrum elongatum. $1.10, Pettrea volubilis. $2, Oncidium altrissimum.
No. 2341: a, Datura candida. b, Amherstia nobilis. c, Ipomoea acuminata. d, Bougainvillea glabra. e, Cassia alata. f, Cordia sebestena. g, Opuntia dilenii. h, Cryptostegia grandiflora. i, Rodriguezia lanceolata.
No. 2342, Acalypha hispida. No. 2343, Hibiscus rosa-sinensis.

1996, Aug. 15
2337-2340 A349 Set of 4   3.50 3.50
2341 A349 90c Sheet of 9, #a-.i.   6.00 6.00
Souvenir Sheets
2342 A349 $5 multicolored   3.75 3.75
Perf. 14x13½
2343 A349 $5 multicolored   3.75 3.75

John F. Kennedy (1917-63) — A350

No. 2344, $1: a, As young boy. b, Proclamation to send man to the moon. c, With Caroline, Jackie. d, Inauguration. e, Giving speech. f, On PT 109. g, With Jackie. h, Funeral procession, portrait. i, Guard, Eternal Flame.
No. 2345, $1: a, With family on yacht. b, On yacht. c, On yacht holding sail. d, "JFK", portrait. e, Talking to astronauts in space. f, Younger picture in uniform. g, Portrait. h, Riding in motorcade. i, Giving speech, US flag.
No. 2346, $1: a, Up close picture. b, In front of house at Hyannis Port. c, Memorial plaque, picture. d, Photograph among crowd. e, Portrait, flag. f, Rocket, portrait. g, Signing document. h, Martin Luther King, John F. Kennedy, Robert F. Kennedy. i, Painting looking down toward microphones.
No. 2347, $1: a, Photograph with Jacqueline greeting people. b, Formal oval-shaped portrait. c, Photograph. d, With family. e, Space capsule, painting. f, Addressing UN. g, In rocking chair. h, Seated at desk, dignitaries. i, Holding telephone, map.

1996, Aug.   **Perf. 14x13½**
Sheets of 9, #a-i
2344-2347 A350 Set of 4   27.00 27.00

Ships
A351

No. 2348, $1.10: a, SS Doric, 1923, Great Britain. b, SS Nerissa, 1926, Great Britain. c, SS Howick Hall, 1910, Great Britain. d, SS Jervis Bay, 1922, Great Britain. e, SS Vauban, 1912, Great Britain. f, MV Orinoco, 1928, Germany.
No. 2349, $1.10: a, SS Lady Rodney, 1929, Canada. b, SS Empress of Russia, 1913, Canada. c, SS Providence, 1914, France. d, SS Reina Victori-Eugenia, 1913, Spain. e, SS Balmoral Castle, 1910, Great Britain. f, SS Tivives, 1911, US.
No. 2350, $6, SS Imperator, 1913, Germany. No. 2351, $6, SS Aquitania, 1914, Great Britain.

1996, Sept. 5   **Perf. 14**
Sheets of 6, #a-f
2348-2349 A351 Set of 2   11.00 11.00
Souvenir Sheets
2350-2351 A351 Set of 2   9.00 9.00

Elvis Presley's 1st "Hit" Year, 40th Anniv.
A352

Various portraits.

1996, Sept. 8   **Perf. 13½x14**
2352 A352 $2 Sheet of 6, #a.-f.   9.00 9.00

Richard Petty, NASCAR Driving Champion — A353

No. 2353: a, 1990 Pontiac. b, Richard Petty. c, 1972 Plymouth. d, 1974 Dodge. $5, 1970 Plymouth Superbird. $6, 1996 STP 25th Anniversary Pontiac.

1996, Sept. 26   **Perf. 14**
2353 A353 $2 Sheet of 4, #a.-d.   6.50 6.50
Souvenir Sheets
2354 A353 $5 multicolored   3.75 3.75
2355 A353 $6 multicolored   4.75 4.75
No. 2354 contains one 85x28mm stamp.

Sandy Koufax, Baseball Pitcher — A354

A354a

No. 2356: a.-c., Various action shots.

Perf. 14, Imperf. (#2356d)
1996, Sept. 26

2356		Sheet of 17	28.50	28.50
a.-c.		A354 $2 any single	1.50	1.50
d.		A354 $6 Portrait	4.50	4.50

Litho. & Embossed
Perf. 9

2356E A354a $30 gold & multi   25.00 25.00

No. 2356 contains 6 #2356a, 5 each #2356b, 2356c and 1 #2356d. No. 2356d is 70x103mm and has simulated perforations.

Cadet Force, 60th Anniv. — A355

Insignia and: 70c, 2nd Lt. D.S. Cozier, founder. 90c, Cozier, first 12 cadets, 1936.

1996, Oct. 23   Litho.   Perf. 14x13½

2357	A355	70c multicolored	.60	.60
2358	A355	90c multicolored	.80	.80

Christmas
A356

Details or entire paintings: 70c, Virgin and Child, by Memling. 90c, St. Anthony, by Memling. $1, Madonna and Child, by Bouts. $1.10, Virgin and Child, by Lorenzo Lotto. $2, St. Roch, by Lotto. $5, St. Sebastian, by Lotto.
No. 2365, $5, Virgin and Child with St. Roch and St. Sebastian, by Lotto. No. 2366, $5, Virgin and Child with St. Anthony and a Donor, by Memling.

1996, Nov. 14   Perf. 13½x14

2359-2364 A356 Set of 6   9.00 9.00

Souvenir Sheets

2365-2366 A356 Set of 2   8.50 8.50

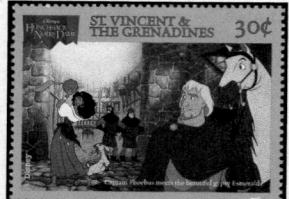

Disney's "The Hunchback of Notre Dame" — A357

Designs: Various scenes from film.
No. 2370, $6, Quasimodo, Phoebus, Esmeralda. No. 2371, $6, Esmeralda, vert. No. 2372, $6, Quasimodo, citizens, vert.

1996, Dec. 12   Litho.   Perf. 13½x14

2367	A357	10c Sheet of 6,		
		#a.-f., vert.	.90	9.00

Perf. 14x13½

2368	A357	30c Sheet of 9,		
		#a.-i.	3.00	3.00
2369	A357	$1 Sheet of 9,		
		#a.-i.	8.00	8.00

Souvenir Sheets

2370-2372 A357 Set of 3   19.50 19.50

Sylvester Stallone in Movie "Rocky IV" — A358

1996   Litho.   Perf. 14
2373 A358 $2 Sheet of 3, #a.-c.   5.00 5.00

A359

New Year 1997 (Year of the Ox) — A359a

Stylized oxen, Chinese inscriptions within checkered squares: Nos. 2374a, 2375a, pale orange, pale lilac & black. Nos. 2374b, 2375b, green, violet & black. Nos. 2374c, 2375c, tan, pink & black.

1997, Jan. 2   Perf. 14½

2374	A359	75c Strip of 3, #a.-		
		c.	1.70	1.70
2375	A359	$1 Sheet of 3,		
		#a.-c.	2.25	2.25

Souvenir Sheet

2376	A359	$2 orange, yellow		
		& blk	1.50	1.50

Litho. & Embossed
Perf. 9

2376A A359a $30 gold & multi   25.00 25.00
No. 2374 was issued in sheets of 9 stamps.

Star Trek Voyager A360

No. 2377: a, Lt. Tuvak. b, Kes. c, Lt. Paris. d, The Doctor. e, Capt. Janeway. f, Lt. Torres. g, Neelix. h, Ens. Kim. i, Cdr. Chakotay.
$6, Cast of characters.

1997, Jan. 23   Litho.   Perf. 14

2377	A360	$2 Sheet of 9, #a.-		
		i.	14.50	14.50

Souvenir Sheet

2378 A360 $6 multicolored   5.00 5.00
No. 2378 contains one 29x47mm stamp.

A361

A361a

Mickey Mantle (1931-95), baseball player.

Perf. 14, Imperf. (#2379b)
1997, Jan. 23

2379		Sheet of 17, 16		
		#2379a, 1 #2379b	28.50	28.50
a.		A361 $2 shown	1.50	1.50
b.		A361 $6 Portrait holding bat	4.50	4.50

Litho. & Embossed
Perf. 9

2379C	A361a	$30 gold &		
		multi	25.00	25.00

No. 2379b is 70x100mm.

Black Baseball Players — A362

No. 2380: a, Frank Robinson. b, Satchel Paige. c, Billy Williams. d, Reggie Jackson. e, Roberto Clemente. f, Ernie Banks. g, Hank Aaron. h, Roy Campanella. i, Willie McCovey. j, Monte Irvin. k, Willie Stargell. l, Rod Carew. m, Ferguson Jenkins. n, Bob Gibson. o, Lou Brock. p, Joe Morgan. q, Jackie Robinson.

Perf. 14x14½, Imperf. (#2380q)
1997, Jan. 23

2380		Sheet of 17	16.50	16.50
a.-p.		A362 $1 any single	.75	.75
q.		A362 $6 Portrait	4.50	4.50

No. 2380q is 66x100mm and has simulated perforations.

Souvenir Sheet

Chongqing Dazu Stone Carving — A363

1996, May 20   Litho.   Perf. 12
2381 A363 $2 multicolored   1.50 1.50
    China '96.
No. 2381 was not available until March 1997.

Hong Kong Changeover — A364

A364a

No. 2382 — Flags of Great Britain, Peoples' Republic of China and panoramic view of Hong Kong: a-e, In daytime. f-j, At night.
No. 2383, $2 — Market scene: a, Vendors, corner of building. b, People strolling. c, Man choosing items to purchase.
No. 2384, $2 — Buddhist religious ceremony: a, Fruit, incense pot, torch. b, Monk at fire. c, Flower.
No. 2385, $2 — Lantern ceremony: a, Boy, girl. b, Couple on bridge. c, Girls with lanterns. Illustration A364a reduced.

1997, Feb. 12   Perf. 14

2382	A364	90c Sheet of 10,		
		#a-j	7.25	7.25

Sheets of 3, #a-c
Perf. 13

2383-2385 A364 Set of 3   14.50 14.50

Litho. & Embossed
Perf. 9

2385D A364a $30 gold & multi   25.00 25.00
    Hong Kong '97.
Nos. 2383-2385 each contain 3 35x26mm stamps.

UNESCO, 50th Anniv. — A365

World Heritage Sites: 70c, Lord Howe Islands, Australia, vert. 90c, Uluru-Kata Tjuta Natl. Park, Australia, vert. $1, Kakadu Natl. Park, Australia, vert. $1.10, Te Wahipounamu, New Zealand, vert. $2, $5, vert., Tongariro Natl. Park, New Zealand.
No. 2392, $1.10, vert. — Various sites in Greece: a, Monastery of Rossanou, Meteora. b, f, h, Painted ceiling, interior, Mount Athos Monastery. c, Monastery Osios Varlaam, Meteora. d, Ruins in Athens. e, Museum of the Acropolis. g, Mount Athos.
No. 2393, $1.10, vert. — Various sites in Japan: a, Himeji-Jo. b, Temple Lake, Gardens, Kyoto. c, Kyoto. d, Buddhist Temple of Ninna-Ji. e, View of city of Himeji-Jo. f, Forest, Shirakami-Sanchi. g, h, Forest, Yakushima.
No. 2394, $1.10, vert: a, City of San Gimignano, Italy. b, Cathedral of Santa Maria Asunta, Pisa, Italy. c, Cathedral of Santa Maria Fiore, Florence, Italy. d, Archaeological site, Valley of the Boyne, Ireland. e, Church of Saint-Savin-Sur-Gartempe, France. f, g, h, City of Bath, England.
No. 2395, $1.50: a, Trinidad, Valley de los Ingenios, Cuba. b, City of Zacatecas, Mexico. c, Lima, Peru. d, Ruins of Monastery, Paraguay. e, Mayan Ruins, Copan, Honduras.
No. 2396, $1.50 — Various sites in China: a, Palace, Wudang Mountains, Hubei Province. b, Cave Sanctuaries, Mogao. c, House, Desert of Taklamakan. d, e, Great Wall.
Nos. 2397, $1.50: a-e, Various sites in Quedlinberg, Germany.
No. 2398, $5, Monastery of Meteora, Greece. No. 2399, $5, Wailing Wall, Jerusalem. No. 2400, $5, Quedlinburg, Germany. No. 2401, $5, Oasis, Dunbuang, China. No. 2402, $5, Himeji-Jo, Japan. No. 2403, $5, Great Wall, China. No. 2404, $5, City of Venice, Italy.

Perf. 13½x14, 14x13½
1997, Mar. 24   **Litho.**
2386-2391 A365 Set of 6   8.00   8.00
Sheets of 8, #a-h, + Label
2392-2394 A365 Set of 3   20.00 20.00
Sheets of 5 + Label
2395-2397 A365 Set of 3   17.50 17.50
Souvenir Sheets
2398-2404 A365 Set of 7   25.00 25.00

Telecommunications in St. Vincent, 125th Anniv. — A366

Designs: 5c, Microwave radio relay tower, Dorsetshire Hill. 10c, Cable & wireless headquarters, Kingstown. 20c, Microwave relay tower, vert. 35c, Cable & wireless complex, Arnos Vale. 50c, Cable & wireless tower, Mt. St. Andrew. 70c, Cable ship. 90c, Eastern telecommunication network, 1872. $1.10, Telegraph map of world, 1876.

Perf. 14x14½, 14½x14
1997, Apr. 3   **Litho.**
2405-2412 A366 Set of 8   4.00   4.00

Birds of the World — A367

Designs: 60c, Smooth-billed ani. 70c, Belted kingfisher. 90c, Blackburnian warbler. $1, Blue tit. $2, Chaffinch. $5, Ruddy turnstone.
No. 2419: a, Blue grosbeak. b, Bananaquit. c, Cedar waxwing. d, Ovenbird. e, Hooded warbler. f, Flicker.
No. 2420: a, Song thrush. b, Robin. c, Blackbird. d, Great spotted woodpecker. e, Wren. f, Kingfisher.
No. 2421, $5, St. Vincent parrot. No. 2422, $5, Tawny owl.

1997, Apr. 7   **Perf. 14**
2413-2418 A367 Set of 6   7.75   7.75
2419 A367 $1 Sheet of 6, #a.-f.   4.50   4.50
2420 A367 $2 Sheet of 6, #a.-f.   9.00   9.00
Souvenir Sheets
2421-2422 A367 Set of 2   7.50   7.50

Water Birds — A368

Designs: 70c, Mandarin duck, horiz. 90c, Green heron, horiz. $1, Drake ringed teal, horiz. $1.10, Blue-footed boobies, horiz. $2, Australian jacana. $5, Reddish egret.
No. 2429: a, Crested auklet. b, Whiskered auklet. c, Pigeon guillemot. d, Adelie penguins. e, Rockhopper penguin. f, Emperor penguin.
No. 2430, $5, Snowy egrets, horiz. No. 2431, $5, Flamingos, horiz.

1997, Apr. 7   **Perf. 15**
2423-2428 A368 Set of 6   8.00   8.00
2429 A368 $1.10 Sheet of 6, #a.-f.   5.00   5.00
Souvenir Sheet
2430-2431 A368 Set of 2   7.50   7.50

Jackie Robinson (1919-72) A369

A369a

Serpentine Die Cut 7
1997, Jan. 23   **Litho.**
Self-Adhesive
2432 A369 $1 multicolored   1.00   1.00
Litho. & Embossed
Perf. 9
2432A A369a $30 gold & multi

No. 2432 was issued in sheets of 3 and was not available until June 1997.

Queen Elizabeth II, Prince Philip, 50th Wedding Anniv. A370

No. 2433: a, Queen. b, Royal arms. c, Portrait of Queen, Prince. d, Queen, Prince, crowd. e, Buckingham Palace. f, Prince.
$5, Queen seated in wedding gown, crown.

1997, June 3   **Litho.**   **Perf. 14**
2433 A370 $1.10 Sheet of 6, #a.-f.   5.50   5.50
Souvenir Sheet
2434 A370 $5 multicolored   4.00   4.00

Paintings by Hiroshige (1797-1858) A371

No. 2435: a, Furukawa River, Hiroo. b, Chiyogaike Pond, Meguro. c, New Fuji, Meguro. d, Moon-Viewing Point. e, Ushimachi, Takanawa. f, Original Fuji, Meguro.
No. 2436, $5, Gotenyama, Shinagawa. No. 2437, $5, Shinagawa Susaki.

1997, June 3   **Perf. 13½x14**
2435 A371 $1.50 Sheet of 6, #a.-f.   7.00   7.00
Souvenir Sheets
2436-2437 A371 Set of 2   9.00   9.00

Paul Harris (1868-1947), Founder of Rotary Intl. — A372

Designs: $2, World Community Service, blankets from Japan donated to Thai children, Harris.
$5, Rotary Intl. Pres. Luis Vincente Giay, US Pres. Jimmy Carter, Rotary award recipient.

1997, June 3   **Perf. 14**
2438 A372 $2 multicolored   1.75   1.75
Souvenir Sheet
2439 A372 $5 multicolored   4.00   4.00

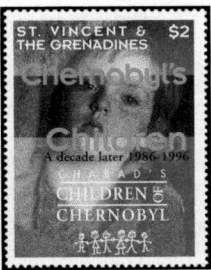

Heinrich von Stephan (1831-97) A373

No. 2440 — Portraits of Von Stephan and: a, Bicycle postman, India, 1800's. b, UPU emblem. c, Zebu-drawn post carriage, Indochina.
$5, Post rider, Indochina.

1997, June 3
2440 A373 $2 Sheet of 3, #a.-c.   4.75   4.75
Souvenir Sheet
2441 A373 $5 gray brown   4.00   4.00
PACIFIC 97.

Chernobyl Disaster, 10th Anniv. A374

Designs: No. 2442, Chabad's Children of Chernobyl. No. 2443, UNESCO.

1997, June 3   **Litho.**   **Perf. 13½x14**
2442 A374 $2 multicolored   1.60   1.60
2443 A374 $2 multicolored   1.60   1.60

Grimm's Fairy Tales A375

No. 2444, $2 — Scenes showing "Old Sultan:" a, With woman, man. b, On hillside. c, With wolf. No. 2446, Man, Old Sultan, girl.
No. 2445, $2 — Scenes from "The Cobbler and the Elves:" a, Cobbler. b, Elves. c, Cobbler holding elf.
No. 2446, $5, Elf. No. 2447, $5, Curly-Locks sewing.

1997, June 3   **Perf. 13½x14**
Sheets of 3, #a-c
2444-2445 A375 Set of 2   9.00   9.00

Souvenir Sheets
2446-2447 A375 Set of 2   8.00   8.00
Perf. 14
2448 A376 $5 multicolored   3.75   3.75

Numbers have been reserved for two additional souvenir sheets with this set.

Inaugural Cricket Test, Arnos Vale — A377

Designs: 90c, Alphonso Theodore Roberts (1937-96), vert. $5, Arnos Vale Playing field.

Perf. 13½x14, 14x13½
1997, June 20   **Litho.**
2451 A377 90c multicolored   .70   .70
2452 A377 $5 multicolored   3.75   3.75

1998 World Cup Soccer Championships, France — A378

Players: 70c, Beckenbauer, W. Germany. 90c, Moore, England. $1, Lato, Poland. $1.10, Pele, Brazil. $2, Maier, W. Germany. $10, Eusebio, Portugal.
No. 2459, $1 — Scenes from England's victory, 1966: a, Stadium. b, c, d, e, f, h, Various action scenes. g, Players coming from field, holding trophy.
No. 2460, $1 — Action scenes from various finals: a, c, Argentina, W. Germany, 1986. b, e, England, W. Germany, 1966. d, Italy, W. Germany, 1982. f, g, Argentina, Holland, 1978. h, W. Germany, Holland, 1974.
No. 2461, $1, vert.: a, Bergkamp, Holland. b, Seaman, England. c, Schmeichel, Denmark. d, Ince, England. e, Futre, Portugal. f, Ravanelli, Italy. g, Keane, Ireland. h, Gascoigne, England.
No. 2462, $1, vert.: a-h, Action scenes from Argentina v. Holland, 1978.
No. 2463, $5, Ally McCoist, Scotland, vert. No. 2464, $5, Salvatori Schillaci, Italy, vert. No. 2465, $5, Mario Kempes, Argentina, vert. No. 2466, $5, Paulao, Angola.

Perf. 14x13½, 13½x14
1997, Aug. 26   **Litho.**
2453-2458 A378 Set of 6   6.00   6.00
Sheets of 8, #a-h, + Label
2459-2462 A378 Set of 4   32.50 32.50
Souvenir Sheets
2463-2466 A378 Set of 4   17.50 17.50

Vincy Mas Carnival, 20th Anniv. A379

Designs: 10c, Mardi Gras Band, "Cinemas." 20c, Queen of the Bands, J. Ballantyne. 50c, Queen of the Bands, vert. 70c, King of the Bands, "Conquistadore." 90c, Starlift Steel Orchestra, Panorama Champs. $2, Frankie McIntosh, musical arranger, vert.

1997, July 24   **Perf. 14½x14, 14x14½**
2467-2472 A379 Set of 6   4.00   4.00

Sierra Club, Cent. A380

No. 2473: a, Snow leopard. b, Polar bear. c, d, Isle Royale Natl. Park. e, f, Denali Natl. Park. g, h, i, Joshua Tree Natl. Park.

No. 2474, vert: a, b, c, Mountain gorilla. d, e, Snow leopard. f, g, Polar bear. h, Denali Natl. Park. i, Isle Royale Natl. Park.

No. 2475, vert: a, b, c, Sifaka. d, e, Peregrine falcon. f, g, h, African Rain Forest. i, China's Yellow Mountains.

No. 2476: a, b, c, Red panda. d, Peregrine falcon. e, f, Galapagos tortoise. g, h, African Rain Forest. i, China's Yellow Mountains.

No. 2477: a, Mountain lion. b, c, Siberian tiger. d, Red wolf. e, Black bear. f, i, Wolong Natl. Reserve. g, h, Belize Rain Forest.

No. 2478, vert: a, Siberian tiger. b, c, Mountain lion. d, e, Black bear. f, g, Red wolf. h, Belize Rain Forest. i, Wolong Natl. Reserve.

No. 2479, vert: a, b, c, Indri. d, e, Gopher tortoise. f, g, Black-footed ferret. h, Haleakala Natl. Park. i, Grand Teton Natl. Park.

No. 2480: a, Black-footed ferret. b, Gopher tortoise. c, d, Grand Teton Natl. Park. e, f, Haleakala Natl. Park. g, h, i, Madagascar Rain Forest.

Scenes in Olympic Natl. Park: No. 2481, $5, Lake, trees. No. 2482, $5, Mountain summit. No. 2483, $5, Snow-topped mountains.

1997, Sept. 18   **Perf. 14**

2473	A380	20c Sheet of 9, #a.-i.		
2474	A380	40c Sheet of 9, #a.-i.	1.40	1.40
2475	A380	50c Sheet of 9, #a.-i.	2.75	2.75
2476	A380	60c Sheet of 9, #a.-i.	3.40	3.40
2477	A380	70c Sheet of 9, #a.-i.	4.00	4.00
2478	A390	90c Sheet of 9, #a.-i.	4.75	4.75
2479	A380	$1 Sheet of 9, #a.-i.	6.00	6.00
2480	A380	$1.10 Sheet of 9, #a.-i.	6.75	6.75
			7.50	7.50

Souvenir Sheets

2481-2483	A380	Set of 3	13.00	13.00

Deng Xiaoping (1904-97), Chinese Leader — A381

No. 2484, $2: a-d, Various portraits in dark brown.
No. 2485, $2: a-d, Various portraits in dark blue.
No. 2486, $2: a-d, Various portraits in black.
No. 2487, Deng Xiaoping, Zhuo Lin, horiz.

1997, June 3   **Litho.**   **Perf. 14**
Sheets of 4, #a-d

2484-2486	A381	Set of 3	18.00	18.00

Souvenir Sheet

2487	A381	$5 multicolored	3.75	3.75

Montreal Protocol on Substances that Deplete Ozone Layer, 10th Anniv. — A382

1997, Sept. 16

2488	A382	90c multicolored	1.10	1.10

Orchids — A383

Designs: 90c, Rhyncholaelia digbyana. $1, Laeliocattleya. $1.10, Doritis pulcherrima. $2, Phalaenopsis.

No. 2493: a, Eulophia speciosa. b, Aerangis rhodosticta. c, Angraecum infundibularea. d, Calanthe sylvatica. e, Phalaenopsis mariae. f, Paphiopedilum insigne. g, Dendrobium nobile. h, Aerangis kotschyana. i, Cyrtorchis chailluana.

No. 2494, $5, Brassavola nodosa. No. 2495, $5, Sanguine broughtonia.

1997, Sept. 18

2489-2492	A383	Set of 4	4.75	4.75
2493	A383	$1 Sheet of 9, #a.-i.	7.75	7.75

Souvenir Sheets

2494-2495	A383	Set of 2	8.75	8.75

Nos. 2494-2495 each contain one 51x38mm stamp.

Diana, Princess of Wales (1961-97) — A384

No. 2496, $2 — Close-up portraits: a, Wearing tiara. b, Black dress. c, Blue dress. d, Denomination in black.

No. 2497, $2: a, White collar. b, Sleeveless. c, Black dress, holding flowers. d, Blue collar, flowers.

No. 2498, $6, Blue dress. No. 2499, $6, White collar.

1997   **Sheets of 4, #a-d**

2496-2497	A384	Set of 2	12.00	12.00

Souvenir Sheets

2498-2499	A384	Set of 2	9.00	9.00

Sinking of RMS Titanic, 85th Anniv. — A385

No. 2500 — Sections of the ship: a, 1st funnel. b, 2nd, 3rd funnels. c, 4th funnel. d, Upper decks. e, Stern.

1997, Nov. 5   **Litho.**   **Perf. 14**

2500	A385	$1 Sheet of 5, #a.-e.	8.00	8.00

1997 Rock & Roll Hall of Fame Inductions, Cleveland A386

Designs: $1, Exterior view of Hall of Fame. $1.50, Stylized guitar, "the house that rock built."

1997, Nov. 5

2501	A386	$1 multicolored	.75	.75
2502	A386	$1.50 multicolored	1.15	1.15

Nos. 2501-2502 were each issued in sheets of 8.

"The Doors" Album Covers — A387

Designs: 90c, Morrison Hotel, 1970. 95c, Waiting for the Sun, 1968. $1, L.A. Woman, 1971. $1.10, The Soft Parade, 1969. $1.20, Strange Days, 1967. $1.50, The Doors, 1967.

1997, Nov. 5

2503-2508	A387	Set of 6	8.25	8.25

Nos. 2503-2508 were each issued in sheets of 8.

20th Cent. Artists — A388

No. 2509, $1.10 — Opera singers: a, Lily Pons (1904-76). b, Donizetti's "Lucia Di Lammermoor," Lily Pons. c, Bellini's "I Puritani," Maria Callas. d, Callas (1923-77). e, Beverly Sills (b. 1929). f, Donizetti's "Daughter of the Regiment," Sills. g, Schoenberg's "Erwartung," Jessye Norman. h, Norman (b.1945).

No. 2510, $1.10: a, Enrico Caruso (1873-1921). b, Verdi's "Rigoletto," Caruso. c, "The Seven Hills of Rome," Mario Lanza. d, Lanza (1921-59). e, Luciano Pavarotti (b. 1935). f, Donizetti's "Elixir of Love," Pavarotti. g, Puccini's "Tosca," Placido Domingo. h, Domingo (b. 1941).

No. 2511, $1.10 — Artists, sculptures: a, Constantin Brancusi (1876-1957). b, "The New Born," Brancusi, 1920. c, "Four Elements," Alexander Calder, 1962. d, Calder (1898-1976). e, Isamu Noguchi (1904-88). f, "Dodge Fountain," Noguchi, 1975. g, "The Shuttlecock," Claes Oldenburg, 1994. h, Oldenburg (b. 1929).

1997, Nov. 5   **Sheets of 8, #a-h**

2509-2511	A388	Set of 3	21.50	21.50

Size: Nos. 2509b-2509c, 2509f-2509g, 2510b-2510c, 2510f-2510g, 2511b-2511c, 2511f-2511g, 53x38mm.

Christmas A389

Paintings (entire or details), or sculptures: 60c, The Sistine Madonna, by Raphael. 70c, Angel, by Edward Burne-Jones. 90c, Cupid, by Etienne-Maurice Falconet. $1, Saint

Michael, by Hubert Gerhard. $1.10, Apollo and the Horae, by Tiepolo. $2, Madonna in a Garland of Flowers, by Rubens and Bruegel the Elder.

No. 2518, $5, The Sacrifice of Isaac, by Tiepolo, horiz. No. 2519, $5, Madonna in a Garland of Flowers, by Rubens and Bruegel the Elder.

1997, Nov. 26

2512-2517	A389	Set of 6	6.25	6.25

Souvenir Sheets

2518-2519	A389	Set of 2	8.00	8.00

New Year 1998 (Year of the Tiger) — A390

No. 2520 — Stylized tigers, Chinese inscriptions within checkered squares: a, light brown & pale olive. b, tan & gray. c, pink & pale violet. $2, yellow orange & pink.

1998, Jan. 5   **Perf. 14½**

2520	A390	$1 Sheet of 3, #a.-c.	2.25	2.25

Souvenir Sheet

2521	A390	$2 multicolored	2.00	2.00

Cooperative Foundation for Natl. Development A391

Designs: 20c, Children going to school. 90c, People working in field, Credit Union office, vert. $1.10, Industry, ship at dock.

1998, Jan. 5   **Litho.**   **Perf. 13½**

2522-2524	A391	Set of 3	2.10	2.10

Jazz Entertainers — A392

No. 2525: a, King Oliver. b, Louis Armstrong. c, Sidney Bechet. d, Nick Larocca. e, Louis Prima. f, Buddy Bolden.

1998, Feb. 2   **Perf. 14x13½**

2525	A392	$1 Sheet of 6, #a.-f.	5.00	5.00

1998 Winter Olympic Games, Nagano
A393   A394

Designs, horiz: 70c, Ice hockey. $1.10, Bobsled. $2, Pairs figure skating. $2, Skier, vert.

No. 2530 — Medalists: a, Bjorn Daehlie. b, Gillis Grafstrom. c, Sonja Henie. d, Ingemar Stenmark. e, Christian Jagge. f, Tomas Gustafson. g, Johann Olav Koss. h, Thomas Wassberg.

No. 2531, $1.50 — Olympic rings in background: a, Downhill skier. b, Woman figure skater. c, Ski jumper. d, Speed skater. e, 4-Man bobsled team. f, Cross country skier.

No. 2532, $1.50 — Olympic flame in background: a, Downhill skier. b, Bobsled. c, Ski jumper. d, Slalom skier. e, Luge. f, Biathlon.

No. 2533, $5, Slalom skiing. No. 2534, $5, Hockey player, horiz.

1998, Feb. 2   **Perf. 14**
2526-2529 A393   Set of 4   5.50   5.50
2530   A394 $1.10 Sheet of 8,
     #a.-h.   7.50   7.50

Sheets of 6, #a-f
2531-2532 A393   Set of 2   15.00 15.00

Souvenir Sheets
2533-2534 A393   Set of 2   8.50   8.50

Butterflies
A395

Designs: 20c, Amarynthis meneria. 50c, Papillo polyxenes. 70c, Emesis fatima, vert. $1, Anartia amathea.
No. 2539, vert.: a, Heliconius erato. b, Danaus plexippus. c, Papillo phorcas. d, Morpho pelaides. e, Pandoriana pandora. f, Basilarchia astyanax. g, Vanessa cardui. h, Colobura dirce. i, Heraclides cresphontes.
No. 2540, $6, Colias eurytheme. No. 2541, $6, Everes comyntas.

1998, Feb. 23   **Perf. 13½**
2535-2538 A395   Set of 4   2.50   2.50
2539   A395 $1 Sheet of 9, #a.-i.   7.50   7.50

Souvenir Sheets
2540-2541 A395   Set of 2   9.50   9.50

Endangered Fauna — A396

Designs: 50c, Anegada rock iguana. 70c, Jamaican swallowtail. 90c, Blossom bat. $1, Solenodon. $1.10, Hawksbill turtle. $2, West Indian whistling duck.
No. 2548, $1.10: a, Roseate spoonbill. b, Golden swallow. c, Short-snouted spinner dolphin. d, Queen conch. e, West Indian manatee. f, Loggerhead turtle.
No. 2549, $1.10: a, Magnificent frigatebird. b, Humpback whale. c, Southern dagger-tail. d, St. Lucia whiptail e, St. Lucia oriole. f, Green turtle.
No. 2550, $5, St. Vincent parrot. No. 2551, $5, Antiguan racer.

1998, Feb. 23   **Perf. 13**
2542-2547 A396   Set of 6   5.25   5.25

Sheets of 6, #a-f
2548-2549 A396   Set of 2   11.50 11.50

Souvenir Sheets
2550-2551 A396   Set of 2   8.50   8.50

Mushrooms
A397

Designs: 10c, Gymnopilus spectabilis. 20c, Entoloma lividium. 70c, Pholiota flammans. 90c, Panaeolus semiovatus. $1, Stropharia rugosoannulata. $1.10, Tricholoma sulphureum.
No. 2558: a, Amanita caesarea. b, Amanita muscaria. c, Aminita ovoidea. d, Amanita phalloides. e, Amanitopsis inaurata. f, Amanitopsis vaginata. g, Psalliota campestris, alfalfa butterfly. h, Psalliota arvensis. i, Coprinus comatus.
No. 2559: a, Coprinus picaceus. b, Stropharia umbonatescens. c, Hebeloma crustuliniforme, figure-of-eight butterfly. d, Cortinarius collinitus. e, Cortinarius violaceus, common dotted butterfly. f, Cortinarius armillatus. g, Tricholoma aurantium. h, Russula virescens. i, Clitocybe infundibuliformis.

No. 2560, $6, Hygrocybe conica. No. 2561, $6, Amanita caesarea.

1998, Feb. 23   **Litho.**   **Perf. 13½**
2552-2557 A397   Set of 6   4.00   4.00
2558   A397 $1 Sheet of 9,
     #a.-i.   8.25   8.25
2559   A397 $1.10 Sheet of 9,
     #a.-i.   9.00   9.00

Souvenir Sheets
2560-2561 A397   Set of 2   9.50   9.50

Mickey Mouse, 70th Birthday — A398

Designs: 2c, Wake up, Mickey. 3c, Morning run. 4c, Getting ready. 5c, Eating breakfast. 10c, School "daze." 65c, Time out for play. $3, Volunteer worker. $4, A date with Minnie. $5, Ready for bed.
Weekly hi-lites from "Mickey Mouse Club," vert: a, The opening march. b, Monday, fun with music day. c, Tuesday, guest star day. d, Wednesday, anything can happen day. e, Thursday, circus day. f, Friday, talent round up day.
Mickey Mouse: No. 2572, $5, Reading, vert. No. 2573, $6, Playing piano, vert. No. 2574, $6, Blowing trumpet. No. 2575, $6, On the Internet, vert.

Perf. 14x13½, 13½x14
1998, Mar. 23   **Litho.**
2562-2570 A398   Set of 9   10.50 10.50
2571   A398 $1.10 Sheet of 6,
     #a.-f.   5.00   5.00

Souvenir Sheets
2572-2575 A398   Set of 4   17.00 17.00

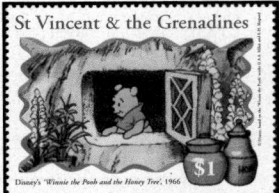

Winnie the Pooh — A399

Scenes from animated films: a, Pooh looking out open window. b, Eeyore, Kanga, Roo. c, Pooh getting honey from tree. d, Rabbit, Pooh stuck in entrance to Rabbit's house. e, Christopher Robin pulling Pooh from Rabbit's house, Owl. f, Piglet sweeping leaves. g, Pooh sleeping. h, Eeyore. i, Tigger on top of Pooh.
No. 2577, Tigger, Pooh, Piglet.

1998, Mar. 23   **Perf. 14x13½**
2576   A399 $1 Sheet of 9, #a.-i.   8.50   8.50

Souvenir Sheet
2577   A399 $6 multicolored   7.00   7.00

Dogs — A400

Designs: 70c, Australian terrier. 90c, Bull mastiff. $1.10, Pomeranian. $2, Dandie dinmont terrier.
No. 2582, $1.10, horiz: a, Tyrolean hunting dog. b, Papillon. c, Fox terriers. d, Bernese mountain dog. e, King Charles spaniel. f, German shepherd.
No. 2583, $1.10, horiz: a, Beagle. b, German shepherd. c, Pointer. d, Vizsla. e, Bulldog. f, Shetland sheepdogs.
No. 2584, $6, Scottish terrier, wooden deck, grass. No. 2585, $6, Scottish terrier, grass, trees.

1998, Apr. 21   **Perf. 14**
2578-2581 A400   Set of 4   4.50   4.50

Sheets of 6, #a-f
2582-2583 A400   Set of 2   12.00 12.00

Souvenir Sheets
2584-2585 A400   Set of 2   10.00 10.50

Nos. 2306-2309 Overprinted

1998, May 19   **Litho.**   **Perf. 14**
2586-2588 A345   Set of 3   3.75   3.75

Souvenir Sheet
2589   A345 $5 multicolored   4.25   4.25

No. 2589 contains overprint "ISRAEL 98 — WORLD STAMP EXHIBITION / TEL-AVIV 13-21 MAY 1998" in sheet margin.

Trains
A401

Designs: 10c, LMS Bahamas No. 5596. 20c, Ex-Mza 1400. 50c, Mallard. 70c, Monarch 0-4-4 OT. 90c, Big Chief. $1.10, Duchess of Rutland LMS No. 6228.
No. 2596, $1.10: a, Hadrian Flyer. b, Highland Jones Goods No. 103. c, Blackmore Vale No. 34023. d, Wainwright SECR No. 27. e, Stepney Brighton Terrier. f, RENFE Freight train No. 040 2184. g, Calbourne No. 24. h, Clun Castle 1950.
No. 2597, $1.10: a, Ancient Holmes J36 060. b, Patentee 2-2-2. c, Kingfisher. d, St. Pierre No. 23. e, SAR Class 19c 4-8-2. f, SAR 6J 4-6-0. g, Evening Star No. 92220. h, Old No. 1.
No. 2598, $5, King George V No. 6000 BR. No. 2599, $5, Caledonia.

1998, June 2   **Litho.**   **Perf. 14**
2590-2595 A401   Set of 6   3.25   3.25

Sheets of 8, #a-h
2596-2597 A401   Set of 2   15.00 15.00

Souvenir Sheets
2598-2599 A401   Set of 2   8.25   8.25

UNESCO
Intl. Year
of the
Ocean
A402

Marine life: 70c, Beluga whale. 90c, Atlantic manta. $1.10, Forceps butterfly fish, copperband butterfly fish, moorish idol. $2, Octopus.
No. 2604, $1, vert.: a, Harlequin wrasse. b, Blue sturgeon fish. c, Spotted trunkfish. d, Regal angelfish. e, Porcupine fish. f, Clownfish, damselfish. g, Lion fish. h, Moray eel. i, French angelfish.
No. 2605, $1, vert.: a, Lemonpeel angelfish. b, Narwhal. c, Panther grouper. d, Fur seal. e, Spiny boxfish. f, Loggerhead turtle. g, Qpah. h, Clown triggerfish. i, Bighead searobin.
No. 2606, $5, Seahorse, vert. No. 2607, $5, Australian sea dragon, vert.

1998, July 1
2600-2603 A402   Set of 4   4.25   4.25

Sheets of 9, #a-i
2604-2605 A402   Set of 2   15.00 15.00

Souvenir Sheets
2606-2607 A402   Set of 2   8.25   8.25

Birds
A403

Designs: 50c, Cock of the rock, vert. 60c, Quetzal, vert. 70c, Wood stork, vert. No. 2611, 90c, St. Vincent parrot, vert. No. 2612, 90c, Toucan. $1, Greater bird of paradise. $1.10, Sunbittern. $2, Green honeycreeper.
No. 2616, vert.: a, Racquet-tailed motmot. b, Red-billed quelea. c, Leadbeater's cockatoo. d, Scarlet macaw. e, Bare-throated bellbird. f, Tucaman Amazon parrot. g, Black-lored red tanager. h, Fig parrot. i, St. Vincent Amazon parrot. j, Peach-faced love birds. k, Blue fronted Amazon parrot. l, Yellow billed Amazon parrot.
No. 2617, $5, Hyacinth macaw, vert. No. 2618, $5, Blue-headed hummingbird, vert.

1998, June 16   **Litho.**   **Perf. 14**
2608-2615 A403   Set of 8   7.00   7.00

Sheet of 12
2616   A403   90c Sheet of 12,
     #a.-l.   10.00 10.00

Souvenir Sheets
2617-2618 A403   Set of 2   9.00   9.00

No. 2611 has different style of lettering.

Diana, Princess of Wales (1961-97) — A404

Designs: No. 2619, Diana in orange jacket. No. 2620, Diana in blue blouse.

Litho. & Embossed
1998, Aug. 1   **Die Cut 7½**
2619   A404 $20 gold & multi   20.00 20.00
2620   A404 $20 gold & multi   20.00 20.00

CARICOM, 25th Anniv. — A405

1998, July 4   **Litho.**   **Perf. 13½**
2621   A405 $1 multicolored   1.25   1.25

Enzo Ferrari (1898-1988), Automobile Manufacturer — A406

No. 2622 — Classic Ferraris: a, 365 GTS. b, Testarossa. c, 365 GT4 BB. $6, Dino 206 GT.

1998, Sept. 15   **Litho.**   **Perf. 14**
2622   A406 $2 Sheet of 3, #a.-c.   5.00 5.00

Souvenir Sheet
2623   A406 $6 multicolored   5.00   5.00

No. 2623 contains one 91x35mm stamp.

Paintings by Pablo Picasso (1881-1973) — A407

Designs: $1.10, Landscape, 1972. No. 2625, $2, The Kiss, 1969. No. 2626, $2, The Death of the Female Torero, 1933. $5, Flute Player, 1962, vert.

1998, Sept. 15		**Perf. 14½**	
2624-2626 A407	Set of 3	4.00	4.00
Souvenir Sheet			
2627 A407	$5 multicolored	4.50	4.50

Organization of American States, 50th Anniv. A408

1998, Sept. 15	**Litho.**	**Perf. 13½**	
2628 A408	$1 multicolored	1.25	1.25

Diana, Princess of Wales (1961-97) — A409

Designs: a, Peach bar with country name on left side. b, Peach bar with country name on right side.

1998, Sept. 15		**Perf. 14½**	
2629 A409	$1.10 Pair, #a.-b.	2.50	2.50
Souvenir Sheet			
Self-Adhesive			
Serpentine Die Cut Perf. 11½			
Size: 53x65mm			
2630 A409	$8 Diana, buildings		

No. 2629 was printed in sheets containing 3 pairs. Soaking in water may affect the image of No. 2630.

Mahatma Gandhi (1869-1948) A411

Design: $5, Seated at table with officials, horiz.

1998, Sept. 15		**Perf. 14**	
2631 A411	$1 shown	1.40	1.40
Souvenir Sheet			
2632 A411	$5 multicolored	6.50	6.50

No. 2631 was issued in sheets of 4.

Royal Air Force, 80th Anniv. A412

No. 2633, $2: a, AEW1 AWACS. b, BAe Eurofighter EF2000. c, Sepcat Jaguar GR1A. d, BAe Hawk T1A.
No. 2634, $2: a, Two Sepcat Jaguar GR1s. b, Panavia Tornado F3. c, Three BAe Harrier GR7s. d, Panavia Tornado F3 IDV.
No. 2635, $6, Mosquito, Eurofighter. No. 2636, $6, Hawk's head, hawk, biplane. No. 2637, $6, Biplane, hawk in flight. No. 2638, $6, Vulcan B2, Eurofighter.

1998, Sept. 15		**Perf. 14**	
Sheets of 4, #a-d			
2633-2634 A412	Set of 2	15.00	15.00
Souvenir Sheets			
2635-2638 A412	Set of 4	22.50	22.50

1998 World Scout Jamboree, Chile — A413

No. 2639: a, Astronaut John Glenn receives Silver Buffalo award, 1965. b, Herb Shriner learns knot tying at 1960 Natl. Jamboree. c, "Ready to go" Boy Scouts break camp, 1940's. $5, Lord Robert Baden-Powell (1857-1941), vert.

1998, Sept. 15			
2639 A413	$2 Sheet of 3, #a.-c.	5.00	5.00
Souvenir Sheet			
2640 A413	$5 multicolored	4.25	4.25

Ancient Order of Foresters Friendly Society, Court Morning Star 2298, Cent. — A414

Designs: 10c, Bro. H.E.A. Daisley, PCR. 20c, R.N. Jack, PCR. 50c, Woman, man shaking hands, emblem. 70c, Symbol of recognition. 90c, Morning Star Court's headquarters.

1998, Oct. 29	**Litho.**	**Perf. 13½**	
2641-2645 A414	Set of 5	2.10	2.10

RMS Titanic — A415

Die Cut 7½

1998, Oct. 29		**Embossed**	
2646 A415	$20 gold	17.50	17.50

Christmas A418

Domestic cats: 20c, Bi-color longhair. 50c, Korat. 60c, Seal-point Siamese. 70c, Red self

longhair. 90c, Black longhair. $1.10, Red tabby exotic shorthair. No. 2653, $5, Seal-point colorpoint. No. 2654, $5, Toirtoiseshell shorthair.

1998, Dec.	**Litho.**	**Perf. 14**	
2647-2652 A418	Set of 6	3.00	3.00
Souvenir Sheets			
2653-2654 A418	Set of 2	8.00	8.00

Hildegard von Bingen (1098?-1179) A419

No. 2655: a, Woman playing flute. b, Hildegard holding tablets. c, Woman playing violin. d, Pope Eugenius. e, Bingen, site of Hildegard's convent. f, Portrait.
$5, Portrait, diff.

1998, Dec. 15	**Litho.**	**Perf. 14**	
2655 A419	$1.10 Sheet of 6, #a.-		
f.		5.75	5.75
Souvenir Sheet			
2656 A419	$5 multicolored	4.25	4.25

New Year 1999 (Year of the Rabbit — A420

No. 2657 — Stylized rabbits: a, Looking right. b, Looking forward. c, Looking left. $2, Like #2657b.

1999, Jan. 4	**Litho.**	**Perf. 14½**	
2657 A420	$1 Sheet of 3, #a.-c.	2.25	2.25
Souvenir Sheet			
2658 A420	$2 multicolored	1.50	1.50

Queen Elizabeth II and Prince Philip, 50th Wedding Anniv. (in 1997) — A421

Litho. & Embossed

1999, Jan. 5		***Die Cut Perf. 6***	
Without Gum			
2659 A421	$20 gold & multi	17.50	17.50

Disney Characters in Winter Sports A422

No. 2660, $1.10 — Wearing checkered outfits: a, Minnie. b, Mickey. c, Goofy. d, Donald. e, Mickey (goggles on head). f, Daisy.
No. 2661, $1.10 — Wearing brightly-colored outfits: a, Daisy. b, Mickey. c, Mickey, Goofy. d, Goofy. e, Minnie. f, Donald.
No. 2662, $1.10 — Wearing red, purple & yellow: a, Mickey. b, Goofy. c, Donald. d, Goofy, Mickey. e, Goofy (arms over head). f, Minnie.

No. 2663, $5, Mickey in checkered outfit. No. 2664, $5, Goofy eating ice cream cone, Mickey, horiz. No. 2665, $5, Mickey in red, purple & yellow.

1999, Jan. 21	**Litho.**	**Perf. 13½x14**	
Sheets of 6, #a-f			
2660-2662 A422	Set of 3	15.00	15.00
Souvenir Sheets			
2663-2665 A422	Set of 3	12.00	12.00

Mickey Mouse, 70th anniv.

World Championship Wrestling A423

No. 2666: a, Hollywood Hogan. b, Sting. c, Bret Hart. d, The Giant. e, Kevin Nash. f, Randy Savage. g, Diamond Dallas Page. h, Bill Goldberg.

1999, Jan. 25	**Litho.**	**Perf. 13**	
2666 A423	70c Sheet of 8, #a.-h.	4.25	4.25

Australia '99, World Stamp Expo A424

Prehistoric animals: 70c, Plateosaurus. 90c, Euoplacephalus. $1.10, Pachycephalosaurus. $1.40, Dilophosaurus.
No. 2671: a, Struthiomimus. b, Indricotherium. c, Giant moa. d, Deinonychus. e, Sabre tooth cat. f, Dawn horse. g, Peittacosaurus. h, Giant ground sloth. i, Wooly rhinoceros. j, Mosasaur. k, Mastodon. l, Syndoyceras.
No. 2672: a, Rhamphorhynchus. b, Pteranodon. c, Archaeopterix. d, Dimetrodon. e, Stegosaurus. f, Parasaurolophus. g, Iguanadon. h, Triceratops. i, Tyrannosaurus. j, Ichthyosaurus. k, Plesiosaurus. l, Hersperonis.
No. 2273, $5, Diplodocus. No. 2674, $5, Wooly mammoth, vert.

1999, Mar. 1	**Litho.**	**Perf. 14**	
2667-2670 A424	Set of 4	4.25	4.25
2671 A424	70c Sheet of 12, #a.-l.	6.50	6.50
m.	As #2671, imperf.	6.50	6.50
2672 A424	90c Sheet of 12, #a.-l.	8.25	8.25
m.	As #2672, imperf.	8.25	8.25
Souvenir Sheets			
2673-2674 A424	$5 Set of 2	7.50	7.50
2673a-2674a	Set of 2, imperf.	7.50	7.50

Flora and Fauna A425

Designs: 10c, Acacia tree, elephant. 20c, Green turtle, coconut palm. 25c, Mangrove tree, white ibis. 50c, Tiger swallowtail, ironweed. 70c, Eastern box turtle, jack-in-the-pulpit, vert. 90c, Praying mantis, milkweed, vert. $1.10, Zebra finch, bottle brush, vert. $1.40, Koala, gum tree, vert.
No. 2683, 70c, vert.: a, Red tailed hawk, ocitillo. b, Morning dove, organ pipe cactus. c, Paloverde tree, burrowing owl. d, Cactus wren, saguaro cactus. e, Ocitillo, puma. f, Organ pipe cactus, gray fox. g, Coyote, prickly pear cactus. h, Saguaro cactus, gila woodpecker. i, Collared lizard, barrel cactus. j, Cowblinder cactus, gila monster. k, Hedgehog cactus, roadrunner. l, Saguaro cactus, jack rabbit.
No. 2684, 70c, vert.: a, Strangler fig, basilisk lizard. b, Macaw, kapok trees. c, Cecropia tree, howler monkey. d, Cecropia tree, toucan. e, Arrrow poison frog, bromiliad. f, Rattlesnake orchid, heliconius phyllis. g, Tree fern, bat eating hawk. h, Jaguar, tillandsia. i, Margay, sierra palm. j, Lesser bird of paradise, aristolchia. k, Parides, erythrina. l, Fer-de-lance, zebra plant.
No. 2685, $5, Alligator, water lilies. No. 2686, $5, Riuolis, hummingbird.

1999, Apr. 12	**Litho.**	**Perf. 14**	
2675-2682 A425	Set of 8	3.75	3.75

Sheets of 12, #a-l

2683-2684	A425	Set of 2	13.00 13.00

Souvenir Sheets

2685-2686	A425	Set of 2	7.50 7.50

Aviation History A426

Designs: 60c, Montgolfier balloon, 1783, vert. 70c, Lilienthal glider, 1894. 90c, Zeppelin. $1, Wright brothers, 1903.

No. 2691, $1.10: a, DH-4 bomber. b, Sopwith Camel. c, Sopwith Dove. d, Jeannin Stahl Taube. e, Fokker DR-1 triplane. f, Albatros Diva. g, Sopwith Pup. h, Spad XIII Smith IV.

No. 2692, $1.10: a, M-130 Clipper. b, DC-3, 1937. c, Beech Staggerwing CVR FT C-17L. d, Hughes H-1 racer. e, Gee Bee Model R-1, 1932. f, Lockheed Sirius Tingmissartoq. g, Fokker T-2, 1923. h, Curtiss CW-16E Floatplane.

No. 2693, $5, Bleriot XI crossing English Channel, 1914. No. 2694, $5, Le Bandy airship, 1903.

1999, Apr. 26

2687-2690	A426	Set of 4	2.50 2.50

Sheets of 8, #a-h

2691-2692	A426	Set of 2	13.50 13.50

Souvenir Sheets

2693-2694	A426	Set of 2	7.50 7.50

'N Sync, Musical Group — A427

1999, May 4   Litho.   Perf. 12½

2695	A427	$1 multicolored	.75 .75

No. 2695 was issued in sheets of 8.

History of Space Exploration, 1609-2000 — A428

Designs: 20c, Galileo, 1609. 50c, Konstantin Tsiolkovsky, 1903. 70c, Robert H. Goddard, 1926. 90c, Sir Isaac Newton, 1668, vert.

No. 2700, $1: a, Luna 9, 1959. b, Soyuz 11, 1971. c, Mir Space Station, 1996. d, Sputnik 1, 1957. e, Apollo 4, 1967. f, Bruce McCandless, 1984. g, Sir William Herschel, telescope, 1781. h, John Glenn, 1962. i, Space Shuttle Columbia, 1981.

No. 2701, $1, vert: a, Yuri Gargarin, 1962. b, Lunar Rover, 1971. c, Mariner 10, 1974-75. d, Laika, 1957. e, Neil A. Armstrong, 1969. f, Skylab Space Station, 1973. g, German V-2 Rocket, 1942. h, Gemini 4, 1965. i, Hubble Telescope, 1990.

No. 2702, $1, vert: a, Explorer, 1958. b, Lunokhod Explorer, 1970. c, Viking Lander, 1975. d, R7 Rocket, 1957. e, Edward H. White, 1965. f, Salyut 1, 1971. g, World's oldest observatory. h, Freedom 7, 1961. i, Ariane Rocket, 1980's.

No. 2703, $5, Atlantis docking with Space Station Mir, 1995. No. 2704, $5, Saturn V, 1969, vert.

1999, May 6   Perf. 14

2696-2699	A428	Set of 4	1.75 1.75

Sheets of 9, #a-i

2700-2702	A428	Set of 3	21.00 21.00

Souvenir Sheets

2703-2704	A428	Set of 2	7.50 7.50

Johann Wolfgang von Goethe (1749-1832), Poet — A430

No. 2709: a, Faust Dying in the Arms of the Lemures. b, Portraits of Goethe, Friederich von Schiller (1759-1805). c, The Immortal Spirit of Faust is Carried Aloft.

No. 2710: a, Faust and Helena with Their Son, Euphonon. b, Mephistopheles Leading the Lemures to Faust.

No. 2711, $5, The Immortal soul of Faust, vert. No. 2712, $5, Portrait of Goethe.

1999, June 25   Litho.   Perf. 14

2709	A430	$3 Sheet of 3, #a.-c.	6.75 6.75
2710	A430	$3 Sheet of 3, #a.-b.	
		+ #2709b	6.75 6.75

Souvenir Sheets

2711-2712	A430	Set of 2	7.50 7.50

Paintings by Hokusai (1760-1849) A431

No. 2713, $1.10: a, Landscape with a Hundred Bridges (large mountain). b, Sea Life (turtle, head LL). c, Landscape with a Hundred Bridges (large bridge in center). d, A View of Aoigaoka Waterfall in Edo. e, Sea Life (crab). f, Women on the Beach at Enoshima.

No. 2714, $1.10: a, Admiring the Irises at Yatsuhashi (large tree). b, Sea Life (turtle, head UL). c, Admiring the Irises at Yatsuhashi (peak of bridge). d, Pilgrims Bathing in Roben Waterfall. e, Sea Life (turtle, head UR). f, Farmers Crossing a Suspension Bridge.

No. 2715, $5, In the Horse Washing Waterfall. No. 2716, $5, A Fisherman at Kajikazawa.

1999, June 25   Perf. 13¾

Sheets of 6, #a-f

2713-2714	A431	Set of 2	10.00 10.00

Souvenir Sheet

2715-2716	A431	Set of 2	7.50 7.50

Wedding of Prince Edward and Sophie Rhys-Jones A432

No. 2717: a, Edward. b, Sophie, Edward. c, Sophie.
$6, Couple, horiz.

1999, June 19   Litho.   Perf. 13½

2717	A432	$3 Sheet of 3, #a-c	6.75 6.75

Souvenir Sheet

2718	A432	$6 multicolored	4.50 4.50

IBRA '99, World Philatelic Exhibition, Nuremberg — A433

Design: $1, Krauss-Maffei V-200 diesel locomotive, Germany, 1852.

1999, June 25   Perf. 14

2720	A433	$1 multicolored	.75 .75

A 90c value was prepared. Its status is unclear.

Souvenir Sheets

PhilexFrance '99, World Philatelic Exhibition — A434

Locomotives: No. 2721, $6, Pacific, 1930's. 2722, $6, Quadrt, electric hight-speed, 1940.

1999, June 25   Perf. 13¾

2721-2722	A434	Set of 2	9.00 9.00

A435

No. 2723 — Children: a, Tyreek Isaacs. b, Fredique Isaacs. c, Jerome Burke III. d, Kellisha Roberts.

No. 2724: a, Girl with braided hair. b, Girl wearing hat. c, Girl holding kitten.
$5, Girl with bow in hair.

1999, June 25   Perf. 14

2723	A435	90c Sheet of 4, #a.-d.	2.75 2.75
2724	A435	$3 Sheet of 3, #a.-c.	6.75 6.75

Souvenir Sheet

2725	A435	$5 multicolored	3.75 3.75

UN Convention on Rights of the Child, 10th anniv.

A436

No. 2726: a, I.M. Pei. b, Billy Graham. c, Barbara Cartland. d, Mike Wallace. e, Jeanne Moreau. f, B.B. King. g, Elie Wiesel. h, Arthur Miller. i, Colin Powell. j, Jack Palance. k, Neil Simon. l, Eartha Kitt.

No. 2727: a, Thomas M. Saunders J.P. b, Mother Sarah Baptiste, M.B.E. c, Sir Sydney Gun-Munro MD, KF, GCMG. d, Dr. Earle Kirby, JP, OBE.

1999, June 25

2726	A436	70c Sheet of 12, #a.-l.	6.25 6.25
2727	A436	$1.10 Sheet of 4, #a.-d.	3.25 3.25

Intl. Year of Older Persons.

World Teachers' Day — A437

No. 2728: a, Henry Alphaeus Robertson. b, Yvonne C. E. Francis-Gibson. c, Edna Peters. d, Christopher Wilberforce Prescod.

1999, Oct. 5   Litho.   Perf. 14¾

2728	A437	$2 Sheet of 4, #a.-d.	6.00 6.00

A438

Queen Mother (b. 1900) — A439

No. 2729: a, In 1909. b, With King George VI, Princess Elizabeth, 1930. c, At Badminton, 1977. d, In 1983.
$6, In 1987. $20, Close-up.

1999   Litho.   Perf. 14

Gold Frames

2729	A438	$2 Sheet of 4, #a.-d., + label	6.00 6.00

Souvenir Sheet

Perf. 13¾

2730	A438	$6 multicolored	4.50 4.50

Litho. & Embossed

Die Cut 9x8¾

Size: 55x93mm

2731	A439	$20 gold & multi	20.00 20.00

Issued: Nos. 2729-2730, 10/18; No. 2731, 8/4. No. 2730 contains one 38x50mm stamp. See Nos. 3010-3011.

Christmas A440

Designs: 20c, The Resurrection, by Albrecht Dürer. 50c, Christ in Limbo, by Dürer. 70c, Christ Falling on the Way to Calvary, by Raphael. 90c, St. Ildefonso with the Madonna and Child, by Peter Paul Rubens. $5, The Crucifixion, by Raphael.
$6, The Sistine Madonna, by Raphael.

1999, Nov. 22   Litho.   Perf. 13¾

2732-2736	A440	Set of 5	5.50 5.50

Souvenir Sheet

2737	A440	$6 multicolored	4.50 4.50

UPU, 125th Anniv. A441

Designs: a, Mail coach. b, Intercontinental sea mail. c, Concorde.

1999, Dec. 7   **Perf. 14**
2738 A441 $3 Sheet of 3, #a.-c.   6.75 6.75

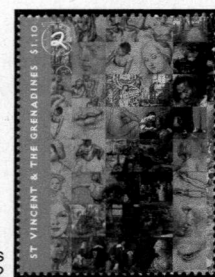

Paintings A442

Various paintings making up a photomosaic of the Mona Lisa.

1999, Dec. 7   **Perf. 13¼**
2739 A442 $1.10 Sheet of 8, #a.-h.   6.50 6.50

See #2744, 2816.

A443

Millennium: No. 2740, Clyde Tombaugh discovers Pluto, 1930.
No. 2741 — Highlights of the 1930s: a, Mahatma Gandhi's Salt March, 1930. b, Like #2740, with colored margin. c, Empire State Building opens, 1931. d, Spain becomes a republic, 1931. e, Franklin D. Roosevelt launches New Deal, 1933. f, Reichstag burns in Germany, 1933. g, Mao Zedong leads China's revolution, 1934. h, Spanish Civil War led by Francisco Franco, 1936. i, Edward VIII abdicates, 1936. j, Diego Rivera, 50th birthday, 1936. k, Golden Gate Bridge opens, 1937. l, First atomic reaction achieved, 1939. m, World War II begins, 1939. n, Television debuts at New York World's Fair, 1939. o, Selection of Dalai Lama, 1939. p, Hindenburg explodes, 1937 (60x40mm). q, Igor Sikorsky builds first practical helicopter, 1939.
No. 2742 — Sculptures by: a, Elizabeth Murray. b, Alexander Calder. c, Charles William Moss. d, Gaston Lachaise. e, Claes Oldenburg. f, Louise Bourgeois. g, Duane Hanson. h, Brancusi. i, David Smith. j, Dan Flavin. k, Boccioni. l, George Segal. m, Lucas Samaras. n, Marcel Duchamp. o, Isamu Noguchi. p, Donald Judd (60x40mm). q, Louise Nevelson.

1999, Dec. 7   **Litho.**   **Perf. 13¼x13**
2740 A443 60c multicolored   .45 .45
        Perf. 12¾x12½
2741 A443 60c Sheet of 17, #a.-
    q. + label   7.50 7.50
2742 A443 60c Sheet of 17, #a.-
    q. + label   7.50 7.50

Inscription on No. 2742e is misspelled. See No. 2764.

Painting Type of 1999

Various flowers making up a photomosaic of Princess Diana.

1999, Dec. 31   **Litho.**   **Perf. 13¾**
2744 A442 $1 Sheet of 8, #a.-h.   6.00 6.00

New Year 2000 (Year of the Dragon) — A444

No. 2745 — Background colors: a, Blue and red lilac. b, Salmon pink and olive. c, Brick red and lilac rose.
$4, Brown and dull green.

2000, Feb. 5   **Litho.**   **Perf. 14¾**
2745 A444 $2 Sheet of 3, #a.-c.   4.50 4.50
      Souvenir Sheet
2746 A444 $4 multi   3.00 3.00

Marine Life — A445

Designs: 50c, High hat. 90c, Spotfin hogfish. $1, Royal gramma. $2, Queen angelfish.
No. 2751: a, Sergeant major. b, Hawksbill turtle, whale's tail. c, Horse-eyed jacks, rear of turtle. d, Two horse-eyed jacks, humpback whale. e, Three horse-eyed jacks, head of humpback whale. f, Black-cap gramma. g, Common dolphins. h, French grunts, with Latin inscription. i, Barracuda. j, Bottlenosed dolphin. k, Sea horse. l, Southern stingray, French grunt. m, French grunts, no Latin inscription. n, Indigo hamlet. o, Basking shark. p, Nassau grouper. q, Nurse shark, ribbonfish. r, Southern stingray. s, Southern stingray, blue shark. t, Spanish hogfish.
No. 2752, $5, Rock beauties. No. 2753, $5, Banded butterflyfish.

2000, Feb. 28   **Litho.**   **Perf. 14**
2747-2750 A445 Set of 4   3.25 3.25
2751 A445 50c Sheet of 20, #a.-
    t.   7.50 7.50
      Souvenir Sheets
2752-2753 A445 Set of 2   7.50 7.50

Fish A446

Designs: 10c, Stoplight parrotfish. 20c, Spotfin hogfish. 70c, Beaugregory. 90c, Porkfish. $1, Barred hamlet. $1.40, Queen triggerfish.
No. 2760, $1.10: a, French angelfish. b, Smooth trunkfish. c, Sargassum triggerfish. d, Indigo hamlet. e, Yellowheaded jawfish. f, Peppermint bass.
No. 2761, $1.10: a, Porcupine fish. b, Blue tang. c, Bluehead wrasse. d, Juvenile queen angelfish. e, Sea horse. f, Small mouth grunt.
No. 2762, $5, Pygmy angelfish. No. 2763, $5, Four-eye butterflyfish.

2000, Feb. 28
2754-2759 A446 Set of 6   3.25 3.25
     Sheets of 6, #a.-f.
2760-2761 A446 Set of 2   10.00 10.00
      Souvenir Sheets
2762-2763 A446 Set of 2   7.50 7.50

Millennium Type of 1999

No. 2764 — Highlights of 1900-1950: a, Sigmund Freud publishes "Interpretation of Dreams." b, First long distance wireless transmission. c, First powered airplane flight. d, Einstein proposes theory of relativity. e, Henry Ford unveils Model T. f, Alfred Wegener develops theory of continental drift. g, World War I begins. h, 1917 Russian revolution. i, James Joyce publishes "Ulysses." j, Alexander Fleming discovers penicillin. k, Edwin Hubble determines universe is expanding. l, Mao Zedong leads "Long March." m, Alan Turing develops theory of digital computing. n, Discovery of fission. o, World War II begins. p, Allied leaders meet at Yalta. q, Mahatma Gandhi and Jawaharlal Nehru celebrate India's independence. r, Invention of the transistor.

2000, Mar. 13   **Perf. 12½**
2764 A443 20c Sheet of 18, a.-r.
    + label   2.75 2.75

Date on No. 2764a is incorrect.

Paintings of Anthony Van Dyck A447

No. 2765, $1: a, Robert Rich, 2nd Earl of Warwick. b, James Stuart, Duke of Lennox and Richmond. c, Sir John Suckling. d, Sir Robert Shirley. e, Teresia, Lady Shirley. f, Thomas Wentworth, 1st Earl of Strafford.
No. 2766, $1: a, Thomas Wentworth, Earl of Strafford, in Armor. b, Lady Anne Carr, Countess of Bedford. c, Portrait of a Member of the Charles Family. d, Thomas Howard, 2nd Earl of Arundel. e, Diana Cecil, Countess of Oxford. f, The Violincellist.
No. 2767, $1: a, The Apostle Peter. b, St. Matthew. c, St. James the Greater. d, St. Bartholomew. e, The Apostle Thomas. f, The Apostle Jude (Thaddeus).
No. 2768, $1: a, The Vision of St. Anthony. b, The Mystic Marriage of St. Catherine. c, The Vision of the Blessed Herman Joseph. d, Madonna and Child Enthroned with Sts. Rosalie, Peter and Paul. e, St. Rosalie Interceding for the Plague-stricken of Palermo. f, Francesco Orero in Adoration of the Crucifixion in the Presence of Sts. Frances and Bernard.
No. 2769, $5, William Feilding, 1st Earl of Denbigh. No. 2770, $5, The Mystic Marriage of St. Catherine, diff. No. 2771, $5, St. Augustine in Ecstasy, horiz.

2000, Apr. 10   **Litho.**   **Perf. 13¾**
     Sheets of 6, #a.-f.
2765-2768 A447 Set of 4   18.00 18.00
      Souvenir Sheets
2769-2771 A447 Set of 3   11.50 11.50

Orchids A448

Designs: 70c, Brassavola nodosa. 90c, Bletia purpurea. $1.40, Blettia cucullata.
No. 2775, $1.50, vert.: a, Oncidium urophyllum. b, Oeceoclades maculata. c, Vanilla planifolia. d, Isolhilus linearis. e, Ionopsis utricularioides. f, Nidema boothii.
No. 2776, $1.50, vert.: a, Cyrtopodium punctatum. b, Dendrophylax funalis. c, Dichaea hystricina. d, Cyrtopodium andersonii. e, Epidendrum secundum. f, Dimerandra emarginata.
No. 2777, $1.50, vert.: a, Brassavola cordata. b, Brassia caudata. c, Broughotnia sanguinea. d, Comparettia falcata. e, Clowesia rosea. f, Caularthron bicornutum.
No. 2778, $5, Neocogniauxia hexaptera, vert. No. 2779, $5, Epidendrum altissimum, vert.

2000, May 25   **Litho.**   **Perf. 14**
2772-2774 A448 Set of 3   2.25 2.25
     Sheets of 6, #a.-f.
2775-2777 A448 Set of 3   21.00 21.00
      Souvenir Sheets
2778-2779 A448 Set of 2   7.50 7.50

The Stamp Show 2000, London.

Prince William, 18th Birthday — A449

No. 2780: a, Wearing checked suit. b, Wearing scarf. c, Wearing solid suit. d, Wearing sweater.
$5, Wearing suit with boutonniere.

2000, June 21   **Litho.**   **Perf. 14**
2780 A449 $1.40 Sheet of 4,
    #a-d   4.25 4.25
      Souvenir Sheet
      Perf. 13¾
2781 A449 $5 multi   3.75 3.75

No. 2780 contains four 28x42mm stamps.

100th Test Match at Lord's Ground — A450

Designs: 10c, Ian Allen. 20c, T. Michael Findlay. $1.10, Winston Davis. $1.40, Nixon McLean.
$5, Lord's Ground, horiz.

2000, June 26   **Perf. 14**
2782-2785 A450 Set of 4   2.10 2.10
      Souvenir Sheet
2786 A450 $5 multi   3.75 3.75

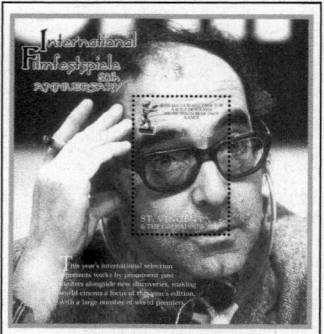

First Zeppelin Flight, Cent. — A451

No. 2787: a, LZ-6. b, LZ-127. c, LZ-129. $5, LZ-9.

2000, June 26
2787 A451 $3 Sheet of 3, #a-c   6.75 6.75
      Souvenir Sheet
2788 A451 $5 multi   3.75 3.75

No. 2787 contains 39x24mm stamps.

Berlin Film Festival, 50th Anniv. — A452

No. 2789: a, Pane, Amore e Fantasia. b, Richard III. c, Smultronstället (Wild Strawberries). d, The Defiant Ones. e, The Living Desert. f, A Bout de Souffle.
$5, Jean-Luc Godard.

2000, June 26
2789 A452 $1.40 Sheet of 6, #a-f 6.25 6.25

Souvenir Sheet
2790 A452 $5 multi 3.75 3.75

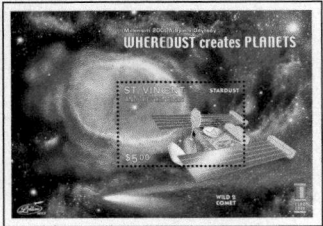

Space — A453

No. 2791, $1.50: a, Comet Hale-Bopp, Calisto. b, Galileo probe. c, Ulysses probe. d, Pioneer 11. e, Voyager 1. f, Pioneer 10.
No. 2792, $1.50: a, Voyager 2, Umbriel. b, Pluto Project. c, Voyager 1, purple background. d, Oort cloud. e, Pluto, Kuiper Express. f, Voayger 2 near Neptune.
No. 2793, $1.50: a, Cassini probe. b, Pioneer 11. c, Voyager 1, green background. d, Huygens. e, Deep Space IV Champollion. f, Voyager 2.
No. 2794, $5, Stardust. No. 2795, $5, Pluto Project, diff.

2000, June 26   **Sheets of 6, #a-f**
2791-2793 A453   Set of 3   21.00 21.00

Souvenir Sheets
2794-2795 A453   Set of 2   7.50 7.50

World Stamp Expo 2000, Anaheim.

Souvenir Sheet

2000 Summer Olympics, Sydney — A454

No. 2796: a, Mildred Didrikson. b, Pommel horse. c, Barcelona Stadium and Spanish flag. d, Ancient Greek horse racing.

2000, June 26
2796 A454 $2 Sheet of 4, #a-d 6.00 6.00

Souvenir Sheet

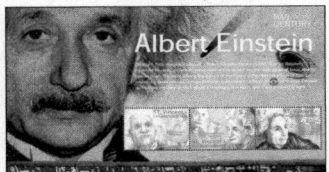

Albert Einstein (1879-1955) — A455

No. 2797: a, Wearing green sweater. b, Wearing blue sweater. c, Wearing black sweater.

2000, June 26
2797 A455 $2 Sheet of 3, #a-c 4.50 4.50

Public Railways, 175th Anniv. — A456

No. 2798: a, Locomotion No. 1, George Stephenson. b, John Bull.

2000, June 26
2798 A456 $3 Sheet of 2, #a-b 4.50 4.50

Mario Andretti, Automobile Racer — A457

No. 2799: a, In car, without helmet. b, In white racing uniform. c, With hands in front of face. d, In car, with helmet. e, In white, standing in front of car. f, With trophy. g, In red racing uniform. h, Close-up.
$5, With trophy, diff.

2000, July 6   **Perf. 12x12¼**
2799 A457 $1.10 Sheet of 8, #a-h 6.50 6.50

Souvenir Sheet
Perf. 13¾
2800 A457 $5 multi 3.75 3.75

Souvenir Sheets

Monty Python's Flying Circus, 30th Anniv. (in 1999) — A458

No. 2801: a, Michael Palin. b, Eric Idle. c, John Cleese. d, Graham Chapman. e, Terry Gilliam. f, Terry Jones.

2000, July 6   **Perf. 12x12¼**
2801 A458 $1.40 Sheet of 6, #a-f 6.25 6.25

Jazz — A459

No. 2802: a, Clarinetist. b, Pianist. c, Trumpeter. d, Guitarist. e, Bassist. f, Saxophonist.

2000, July 6   **Perf. 14**
2802 A459 $1.40 Sheet of 6, #a-f 6.25 6.25

Female Recording Groups of the 1960s — A460

No. 2803, $1.40: a-e, Portraits of the members of The Chantels (green background).
No. 2804, $1.40: a-e, Portraits of the members of The Marvelettes (blue background)

2000, July 6   **Sheets of 5, #a-e**
2803-2804 A460   Set of 2   10.50 10.50

Souvenir Sheet

Barbara Taylor Bradford, Writer — A461

2000, July 6   **Perf. 12x12¼**
2805 A461 $5 multi 3.75 3.75

Betty Boop — A462

No. 2806: a, As Jill, with Jack. b, With three blind mice. c, Jumping over candlestick. d, As fiddler in Hey, Diddle, Diddle. e, On back of Mother Goose. f, As Little Miss Muffet. g, With three cats. h, As candlestick maker, with butcher and baker. i, As Little Jack Horner.
No. 2807, $5, As the Woman Who Lived In a Shoe. No. 2808, $5, As Little Bo Peep.

2000, July 6   **Perf. 13¾**
2806 A462 $1 Sheet of 9, #a-i 6.75 6.75

Souvenir Sheets
2807-2808 A462   Set of 2   7.50 7.50

Artifacts A463

Designs: 20c, Goblet. 50c, Goose. 70c, Boley and calabash. $1, Flat iron.

2000, Aug. 21   **Litho.**   **Perf. 14**
2809-2812 A463   Set of 4   1.75 1.75

Flowers — A464

No. 2813: a, Pink ginger lily. b, Thumbergia grandiflora. c, Red ginger lily. d, Madagascar jasmine. e, Cluster palm. f, Red torch lily. g, Salvia splendens. h, Balsam apple. i, Rostrata.
No. 2814, Red flamingo. No. 2815, Balsam apple, horiz.

2000, Aug. 21
2813 A464 90c Sheet of 9, #a-i 6.00 6.00

Souvenir Sheet
2814-2815 A464 $5 Set of 2 7.50 7.50

Paintings Type of 1999

Various pictures of flowers making up a photomosaic of the Queen Mother.

2000, Sept. 5   **Perf. 13¾**
2816 A442 $1 Sheet of 8, #a-h 6.00 6.00
   i.   As No. 2816, imperf. 6.00 6.00

Magician David Copperfield — A465

No. 2817: a, Head of Copperfield. b, Copperfield's body. c, Copperfield's body vanishing. d, Copperfield's body vanished.

2000, July 6   **Perf. 14**
2817 A465 $1.40 Sheet of 4, #a-d 4.25 4.25

Local Musicians — A466

Designs: No. 2818, $1.40, Horn player with striped shirt. No. 2819, $1.40, Horn player, diff. No. 2820, $1.40, Pianist. No. 2821, $1.40, Fiddler.

2000, Oct. 16   Litho.   Perf. 14
2818-2821 A466 Set of 4   4.25 4.25

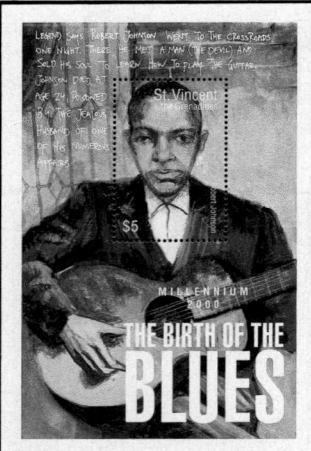

Blues Musicians — A467

No. 2822, $1.40: a, Bessie Smith. b, Willie Dixon. c, Gertrude "Ma" Rainey. d, W. C. Handy. e, Leadbelly. f, Big Bill Broonzy.

No. 2823, $1.40: a, Ida Cox. b, Lonnie Johnson. c, Muddy Waters. d, T-Bone Walker. e, Howlin' Wolf. f, Sister Rosetta Tharpe.

No. 2824, Robert Johnson. No. 2825, Billie Holiday.

2000, Oct. 16   Sheets of 6, #a-f
2822-2823 A467 Set of 2   12.50 12.50
Souvenir Sheets
2824-2825 A467 Set of 2   7.50   7.50

World at War — A468

No. 2826: a, USS Shaw explodes at Pearl Harbor. b, B-24s bomb Ploesti oil fields. c, Soviet T-34 tank moves towards Berlin. d, USS New Jersey off coast of North Korea. e, F-86 Sabre over North Korea. f, USS Enterprise off the Indochina coast. g, B-52 over Viet Nam. h, M-113 tank in Viet Nam.

No. 2827: a, Israeli F-4 Phantoms in action in Six-day War. b, Egyptian T-72 tank destroyed, Six-day War. c, Egyptian SAM-6 missiles, Yom Kippur War. d, Israeli M-48 tanks in desert, Yom Kippur War. e, HMS Hermes, Falkland Islands War. f, British AV-8 harriers in action, Falkland Islands War. g, Iraqi Scud missile launcher in desert, Gulf War. h, M1-A1 Abrams tanks in desert, Gulf War.

No. 2828, Israeli F-4s bomb SAM sites, Yom Kippur War. No. 2829 B-52 bomber, Pershing II missile.

2000, Oct. 16   Sheets of 8, #a-h
2826-2827 A468 Set of 2   12.00 12.00
Souvenir Sheets
2828-2829 A468 $5 Set of 2   7.50   7.50
No. 2829 contains one 56x42mm stamp.

Independence, 21st Anniv. — A469

Designs: 10c, Government House. 15c, First session of Parliament, 1998. 50c, House of Assembly. $2, Financial Complex.

2000, Oct. 27   Litho.   Perf. 14
2830-2833 A469 Set of 4   2.00 2.00

Birds — A470

Designs: 50c, Blue and gold macaw. 90c, English fallow budgerigar. $1, Barraband parakeet. $2, Dominat pied blue.

No. 2838, $2: a, English short-faced tumbler. b, Diamond dove. c, Norwich cropper.

No. 2839, $2: a, Scarlet macaw. b, Blue-fronted Amazon. c, Buffon's macaw.

No. 2840, $2: a, Stafford canary. b, Masked lovebird. c, Parisian full canary.

No. 2841, $2, horiz.: a, Canada goose. b, Mandarin duck. c, Gouldian finch.

No. 2842, $5, Common peafowl, horiz. No. 2843, $5, Budgerigar, horiz.

2000, Nov. 15
2834-2837 A470 Set of 4   4.00 4.00
Sheets of 3, #a-c
2838-2841 A470 Set of 4   18.00 18.00
Souvenir Sheets
2842-2843 A470 Set of 2   7.50 7.50

Shirley Temple in Rebecca of
Sunnybrook Farm — A471

No. 2844, horiz.: a, With man in dark suit. b, With man and woman. c, With woman wearing glasses. d, with blonde woman. e, With man in white hat. f, With three women.

No. 2845: a, At microphone, wearing checked coat and hat. b, Wearing straw hat. c, At microphone, no hat. d, With woman wearing glasses.

No. 2846, With Bill Robinson.

2000, Nov. 29   Perf. 13¾
2844 A471 90c Sheet of 6,
                    #a-f   4.00 4.00
2845 A471 $1.10 Sheet of 4,
                    #a-d   3.25 3.25
Souvenir Sheet
2846 A471 $1.10 multi   .85   .85
See also Nos. 3064-2066.

Queen Mother,
100th
Birthday — A472

2000, Sept. 5   Litho.   Perf. 14
2847 A472 $1.40 multi   1.00 1.00
Printed in sheets of 6.

Christmas — A473

20c, Angel looking right. 70c, Two angels, orange background. 90c, Two angels, blue background. #2851, $5, Angel looking left. No. 2852, Angel, yellow background.

2000, Dec. 7
2848-2851 A473 Set of 4   5.00 5.00
Souvenir Sheet
2852 A473 $5 multi   3.75 3.75

Battle of Britain, 60th Anniv. — A474

No. 2853, 90c: a, Junkers Ju87. b, Two Gloster Gladiators flying left. c, Messerschmitt BF109. d, Heinkel He111 bomber, British fighter. e, Three Hawker Hurricanes. f, Two Bristol Blenheims. g, Two Supermarine Spitfires and ground. h, Messerschmitt BF110.

No. 2854, 90c: a, Two Spitfires, flying left. b, Spitfire. c, Dornier DO217. d, Two Gladiators flying right. e, Four Hurricanes. f, Junkers Ju87 Stuka. g, Two Spitfires flying right. h, Junkers Ju88.

#2855, $5, Spitfire. #2856, $5, Hurricane.

2000, Dec. 18   Perf. 14¼x14½
Sheets of 8, #a-h
2853-2854 A474 Set of 2   10.50 10.50
Souvenir Sheets
Perf. 14¼
2855-2856 A474 Set of 2   7.50 7.50

New Year 2001 (Year of the
Snake) — A475

No. 2857: a, Blue and light blue background. b, Purple and pink background. c, Green and light green background.

2001, Jan. 2   Litho.   Perf. 13x13¼
2857 A475 $1 Sheet of 3, #a-c 2.25 2.25
Souvenir Sheet
2858 A475 $2 shown   1.50 1.50

Paintings of
Peter Paul
Rubens in
the Prado
A476

Designs: 10c, Three women and dog from Diana the Huntress. 90c, Adoration of the Magi. $1, Woman and two dogs from Diana the Huntress.

No. 2862, $2: a, Heraclitus, the Mournful Philosopher. b, Heraclitus, close-up. c, Anne of Austria, Queen of France, close-up. d, Anne of Austria.

No. 2863, $2: a, Prometheus Carrying Fire. b, Vulcan Forging Jupiter's Thunderbolt. c, Saturn Devouring One of His Sons. d, Polyphemus.

No. 2864, $2: a, St. Matthias. b, The Death of Seneca. c, Maria de'Medici, Queen of France. d, Achilles Discovered by Ulysses.

No. 2865, $5, The Judgment of Solomon. No. 2866, $5, The Holy Family with St. Anne.

2001, Jan. 2   Perf. 13¾
2859-2861 A476 Set of 3   1.50 1.50
Sheets of 4, #a-d
2862-2864 A476 Set of 3   18.00 18.00
Souvenir Sheets
2865-2866 A476 Set of 2   7.50 7.50

Rijksmuseum, Amsterdam,
Bicent. — A477

No. 2867, $1.40: a, The Spendthrift, by Cornelis Troost. b, The Art Gallery of Jan Gildermeester Jansz, by Adriaan de Lelie. c, The Rampoortje, by Wouter Johannes van Troostwijk. d, Winter Landscape, by Barend Cornelis Koekkoek. e, Man with white headdress from The Procuress, by Dirck van Baburen. f, Man and woman from The Procuress.

No. 2868, $1.40: a, A Music Party, by Rembrandt. b, Rutger Jan Schimmelpennick and Family, by Pierre Paul Prud'hon. c, Tobit and Anna With a Kid, by Rembrandt. d, The Syndics of the Amsterdam Goldsmiths' Guild, by Thomas de Keyser. e, Portrait of a Lady, by de Keyser. f, Marriage Portrait of Isaac Massa and Beatrix van der Laen, by Frans Hals.

No. 2869, $1.40: a, The Concert, by Hendrick ter Brugghen. b, Vertumnus and Pomona, by Paulus Moreelse. c, Standing couple from Dignified Couples Courting, by Willem Buytewech. d, The Sick Woman, by Jan Steen. e, Seated couple from Dignified Couples Courting. f, Don Ramón Satué, by Francisco de Goya.

No. 2870, $5, Donkey Riding on the Beach, by Isaac Lazarus Israels. No. 2871, $5, The Stone Bridge, by Rembrandt, horiz. No. 2872, $5, Child with Dead Peacocks, by Rembrandt, horiz.

2001, Jan. 15   Perf. 13¾
Sheets of 6, #a-f
2867-2869 A477 Set of 3   19.00 19.00
Souvenir Sheets
2870-2872 A477 Set of 3   11.00 11.00

Birds of
Prey
A478

Designs: 10c, Barred owl. No. 2874, 90c, Lammergeier. $1, California condor. $2, Mississippi kite.

No. 2877, 90c: a, Crested caracara. b, Boreal owl. c, Harpy eagle. d, Oriental bay owl. e, Hawk owl. f, Laughing falcon.
No. 2878, $1.10: a, Bateleur. b, Hobby. c, Osprey. d, Goshawk. e, African fish eagle. f, Egyptian vulture.
No. 2879, $5, Great gray owl. No. 2880, $5, American kestrel.

2001, Feb. 13   **Perf. 14**
2873-2876 A478   Set of 4   3.25 3.25
Sheets of 6, #a-f
2877-2878 A478   Set of 2   9.50 9.50
Souvenir Sheets
2879-2880 A478   Set of 2   8.00 8.00
Hong Kong 2001 Stamp Exhibition (Nos. 2877-2880).

Owls — A479

Designs: 10c, Eagle. 20c, Barn. 50c, Great gray. 70c, Long-eared. 90c, Tawny. $1, Hawk.
No. 2887, horiz.: a, Ural. b, Tengmalm's. c, Marsh. d, Brown fish. e, Little. f, Short-eared.
No. 2888, $5, Hume's. No. 2889, $5, Snowy.

2001, Feb. 13
2881-2886 A479   Set of 6   2.75 2.75
2887 A479 $1.40 Sheet of 6, #a-f   6.75 6.75
Souvenir Sheets
2888-2889 A479   Set of 2   8.00 8.00

Pokémon — A480

No. 2890: a, Kadabra. b, Spearow. c, Kakuna. d, Koffing. e, Tentacruel. f, Cloyster.

2001, Feb. 13   **Perf. 13¾**
2890 A480 90c Sheet of 6, #a-f   4.00 4.00
Souvenir Sheet
2891 A480 $3 Meowth   2.25 2.25

UN Women's Human Rights Campaign — A481

Woman: 90c, With bird and flame. $1, With necklace.

2001, Mar. 8   **Perf. 14**
2892-2893 A481   Set of 2   1.40 1.40

Mushrooms — A482

Designs: 20c, Amanita fulva. 90c, Hygrophorus speciosus. $1.10, Amanita phalloides. $2, Cantharellus cibarius.
No. 2898, $1.40: a, Amanita muscaria. b, Boletus zelleri. c, Coprinus picaceus. d, Stroharia aeruginosa. e, Lepista nuda. f, Hygrophorus conicus.
No. 2899, $1.40: a, Lactarius deliciosus. b, Hygrophorus psittacinus. c, Tricholomopsis rutilans. d, Hygrophorus coccineus. e, Collybia iocephala. f, Gyromitra esculenta.
No. 2900, $1.40: a, Lactarius peckii. b, Lactarius rufus. c, Cortinarius elatior. d, Boletus luridus. e, Russula cyanoxantha. f, Craterellus cornopioioles.
No. 2901, $5, Cyathus olla. No. 2902, $5, Lycoperdon pyriforme, horiz. No. 2903, $5, Pleurotus ostreatus, horiz.

Perf. 13½x13¼, 13¼x13½
2001, Mar. 15
2894-2897 A482   Set of 4   3.25 3.25
Sheets of 6, #a-f
2898-2900 A482   Set of 3   19.00 19.00
Souvenir Sheets
2901-2903 A482   Set of 3   11.00 11.00

A484

A485

Butterflies and Moths A486

Designs: No. 2904, 10c, Tiger. No. 2905, 20c, Figure-of-eight. No. 2906, 50c, Mosaic. No. 2907, 90c, Monarch. No. 2908, $1, Blue-green reflector. No. 2909, $2, Blue tharops.
No. 2910, 10c, Eunica alemena. No. 2911, 70c, Euphaedra medon. No. 2912, 90c, Prepona praeneste. No. 2913, $1, Gold-banded forester.
No. 2914, 20c, Ancycluris formosissima. No. 2915, 50c, Callicore cynosura. No. 2916, 70c, Nessaea obrinus. No. 2917, $2, Eunica alemena.
No. 2918, 90c: a, Orange theope. b, Blue night. c, Small lace-wing. d, Grecian shoemaker. e, Clorinde. f, Orange-barred sulphur.
No. 2919, $1.10: a, Atala. b, Giant swallowtail. c, Banded king shoemaker. d, White peacock. e, Cramer's mesene. f, Polydamas swallowtail.
No. 2920, 90c: a, Cepora aspasia. b, Morpho aega. c, Mazuca amoeva. d, Beautiful tiger. e, Gold-drop helicopsis. f, Esmerelda.
No. 2921, $1.10: a, Lilac nymph. b, Ruddy dagger wing. c, Tiger pierid. d, Orange forester. e, Prepona deiphile. f, Phoebus avellaneda.
No. 2922, $1: a, Calisthenia salvinii flying downward. b, Perisama vaninka. c, Malachite. d, Diaethria aurelia. e, Perisama conplandi. f, Cramer's mesene. g, Calisthenia salvinii flying upward. h, Carpella districata.
No. 2923, $1: a, Euphaedra heophron. b, Milionia grandis. c, Ruddy dagger wiry. d, Bocotus bacotus. e, Cream spot tiger moth. f, Yellow tiger moth. g, Baorisa hiroglyphica. h, Jersey tiger.
No. 2924, $5, Small flambeau. No. 2925, $5, Common morpho, vert. No. 2926, $5, Heliconius sapho. No. 2927 $5 Ornate moth.

No. 2928, $5, Hewitson's blue hair streak. No. 2929, $5, Anaxita drucei.

Perf. 13¼x13½, 13½x13¼
2001, Mar. 22   **Litho.**
2904-2909 A484   Set of 6   3.50 3.50
2910-2913 A485   Set of 4   2.00 2.00
2914-2917 A486   Set of 4   2.50 2.50
Sheets of 6, #a-f
2918-2919 A484   Set of 2   9.00 9.00
2920-2921 A485   Set of 2   9.00 9.00
Sheets of 8, #a-h
2922-2923 A486   Set of 2   12.00 12.00
Souvenir Sheets
2924-2925 A484   Set of 2   7.50 7.50
2926-2927 A485   Set of 2   7.50 7.50
2928-2929 A486   Set of 2   7.50 7.50

Giuseppe Verdi (1813-1901), Opera Composer — A487

No. 2930: a, Mario Del Monaco, Raina Kabaivanska in Othello. b, 1898 Costume design for Iago. c, 1898 costume design for Othello. d, Anna Tomowa-Sintow as Desdemona.
$5, Nicolai Ghiaurov in Othello.

2001, June 12   **Litho.**   **Perf. 14**
2930 A487 $2 Sheet of 4, #a-d   6.00 6.00
Souvenir Sheet
2931 A487 $5 multi   3.75 3.75

Toulouse-Lautrec Paintings — A488

No. 2932: a, Portrait of Comtesse Adèle-Zoé de Toulouse-Lautrec. b, Carmen. c, Madame Lily Grenier.
$5, Jane Avril.

2001, June 12   **Perf. 13¾**
2932 A488 $3 Sheet of 3, #a-c   6.75 6.75
Souvenir Sheet
2933 A488 $5 multi   3.75 3.75

Mao Zedong (1893-1976) — A489

No. 2934: a, In 1924. b, In 1938. c, In 1945. $5, Undated portrait.

2001, June 12
2934 A489 $2 Sheet of 3, #a-c   4.50 4.50
Souvenir Sheet
2935 A489 $5 multi   3.75 3.75

Queen Victoria (1819-1901) — A490

No. 2936: a, As young lady in dark blue dress. b, In white dress. c, With flowers in hair. d, Wearing crown. e, Wearing black dress, facing forward. f, With gray hair.
$5, Sky in background.

2001, June 12   **Perf. 14**
2936 A490 $1.10 Sheet of 6, #a-f 5.00 5.00
Souvenir Sheet
Perf. 13¾
2937 A490 $5 multi   3.75 3.75
No. 2936 contains six 28x42mm stamps.

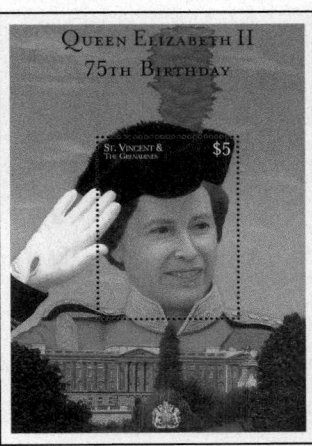

Queen Elizabeth II, 75th Birthday — A491

No. 2938: a, With gray hat. b, In gray jacket, no hat. c, In dark blue dress. d, Wearing tiara. e, With blue hat. f, With green hat.
$5, In uniform.

2001, June 12   **Perf. 14**
2938 A491 $1.10 Sheet of 6, #a-f 5.00 5.00

Souvenir Sheet
Perf. 13¾
2939 A491 $5 multi 3.75 3.75
No. 2938 contains six 28x42mm stamps.

Monet Paintings — A492

Designs: No. 2940, $2, Venice at Dusk (shown). No. 2941, $2, Regatta at Argenteuil. No. 2942, $2, Grain Stacks, End of Summer, Evening Effect. No. 2943, $2, Impression, Sunrise.
$5, Parisians Enjoying the Parc Monceau, vert.

2001, June 12 **Perf. 13¾**
2940-2943 A492 Set of 4 6.00 6.00
Souvenir Sheet
2944 A492 $5 multi 3.75 3.75

Phila Nippon '01, Japan A493

Designs: 10c, The Courtesan Sunimoto of the Okanaya, by Koryusai Isoda. 15c, Oiran at Shinto Shrine-Shotenyama, by Kiyonaga. No. 2947, 20c, Two Girls on a Veranda, by Kiyonaga. No. 2948, 20c, Rooster, from A Variety of Birds, by Hoen Nishiyama, horiz. 50c, On Banks of the Sumida, by Kiyonaga. 70c, Three ducks, from A Variety of Birds, horiz. 90c, Seven ducks, from A Variety of Birds, horiz. $1, Three pigeons and other birds from A Variety of Birds, horiz. $1.10, Two birds, from A Variety of Birds, horiz. $2, Five birds, from A Variety of Birds.
No. 2955, $1.40 — Paintings by Eishi: a, Toriwagi, Geisha of Kanaya, Writing. b, Courtesan Preparing for Doll Festival. c, Two Court Ladies in a Garden. d, Lady With a Lute.
No. 2956, $1.40 — Portraits by Sharaku: a, Oniji Otani II as Edohei, a Yakko. b, Hanshiro Iwai IV. c, Kikunojo Segawa. d, Komazo Ichikawa II.
No. 2957, $1.40 — Paintings by Harunobu Suzuki: a, 6 Tama Rivers, Girls by Lespedeza Bush in Moonlight. b, Warming Sake with Maple Leaves. c, Young Samurai on Horseback. d, 6 Tamu Rivers, Ide No Tamagawa.
No. 2958, $1.40 — Paintings by Harunobu Suzuki: a, Girl on River Bank. b, Horseman Guided by Peasant Girl. c, Komachi Praying for Rain. d, Washing Clothes in the Stream.
No. 2959, $5, Peasants Ferried Across Sumida, by Hokkei. No. 2960, $5, Shadows on the Shoji, by Kikukawa. No. 2961, $5, Boy Spying on Lovers, by Suzuki. No. 2962, $5, Tayu Komurasaki and Hanamurasaki of the Kado Tamaya, by Masanobu Kitao. No. 2963, $5, Gathering Lotus Flowers, by Suzuki.

2001, June 12 **Litho.** **Perf. 13¾**
2945-2954 A493 Set of 10 5.25 5.25
Sheets of 4, #a-d
2955-2958 A493 Set of 4 17.00 17.00
Souvenir Sheets
2959-2963 A493 Set of 5 19.00 19.00

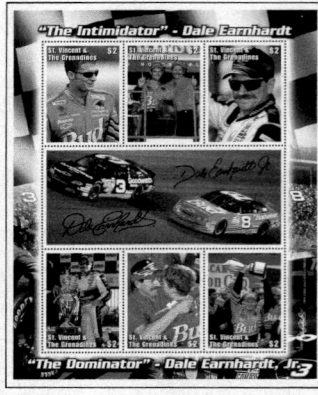

Dale Earnhardt (1951-2001), Stock Car Racer — A494

Designs: a, Dale Earnhardt, Jr. b, Dale and Dale, Jr. with trophy. c, Dale. d, Dale with trophy. e, Dale and Dale, Jr. embracing. f, Dale Jr. with trophy.

2001, July 16
2964 A494 $2 Sheet of 6, #a-f + label 9.00 9.00

Wedding of Norwegian Prince Haakon and Mette-Marie Tjessem Hoiby — A495

2001, Aug. 1 **Perf. 14**
2965 A495 $5 multi 3.75 3.75
Printed in sheets of 4.

Dinosaurs and Prehistoric Animals — A496

Designs: 10c, Mammoth. 20c, Pinacosaurus. No. 2968, 90c, Oviraptor. $1, Centrosaurus. No. 2970, $1.40, Protoceratops. $2, Bactrosaurus.
No. 2972, 90c: a, Saltasaurus. b, Apatosaurus. c, Brachiosaurus. d, Troodon. e, Deinonychus. f, Segnosaurus.
No. 2973, 90c: a, Iguanodon. b, Hypacrosaurus. c, Ceratosaurus. d, Hypsilophodon. e, Herrerasaurus. f, Velociraptor.
No. 2974, $1.40: a, Pteranodon. b, Archaeopteryx. c, Eudimorphodon. d, Shonisaurus. e, Elasmosaurus. f, Kronosaurus.
No. 2975, $1.40: a, Allosaurus. b, Dilophosaurus. c, Lambeosaurus. d, Coelophysis. e, Ornitholestes. f, Eustreptospondylus.
No. 2976, $5, Stegosaurus. No. 2977, $5, Triceratops. No. 2978, $5, Parasaurolophus, vert. No. 2979, $5, Tyrannosaurus, vert.

2001, Oct. 15 **Litho.** **Perf. 14x13¾**
2966-2971 A496 Set of 6 4.25 4.25
Sheets of 6, #a-f
2972-2975 A496 Set of 4 21.00 21.00
Souvenir Sheets
Perf. 13¾
2976-2979 A496 Set of 4 15.00 15.00
Nos. 2976-2977 each contain one 50x38mm stamp; Nos. 2978-2979 each contain one 38x50mm stamp.

Photomosaic of Queen Elizabeth II — A497

2001, Nov. 12 **Perf. 14**
2980 A497 $1 multi 1.10 1.10
Printed in sheets of 8.

2002 World Cup Soccer Championships, Japan and Korea — A498

Players and flags — No. 2981, $1.40: a, Hong Myung-Bo, Korea. b, Hidetoshi Nakata, Japan. c, Ronaldo, Brazil. d, Paolo Maidini, Italy. e, Peter Schmeichel, Denmark. f, Raul Blanco, Spain.
No. 2982, $1.40: a, Kim Bong Soo, Korea. b, Masami Ihara, Japan. c, Marcel Desailly, France. d, David Beckham, England. e, Carlos Valderrama, Colombia. f, George Popescu, Romania.
No. 2983, $5, Seoul World Cup Stadium. No. 2984, $5, International Yokohama Stadium.

2001, Nov. 29 **Sheets of 6, #a-f**
2981-2982 A498 Set of 2 12.50 12.50
Souvenir Sheets
2983-2984 A498 Set of 2 7.50 7.50
Nos. 2983-2984 each contain one 63x31mm stamp.

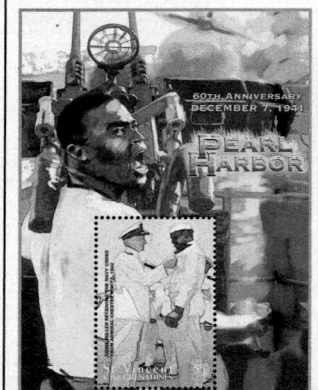

Attack on Pearl Harbor, 60th Anniv. — A499

No. 2985, $1.40, horiz.: a, Japanese bombing Pearl Harbor. b, Japanese pilot ties on a hachimaki. c, Emperor Hirohito. d, Japanese Adm. Isoroku Yamamoto. e, Japanese fighter planes from aircraft carrier Akagi. f, Japanese Zero plane.
No. 2986, $1.40, horiz.: a, Japanese fighter from the Kaga over Ewa Marine Base. b, Hero Dorie Miller downing four Japanese planes. c, Battleship USS Nevada sinking. d, American sailors struggle on the USS Oklahoma. e, Japanese plane takes off from the Akagi. f, Rescue during bombing.
No. 2987, $5, Dorie Miller receiving navy Cross from Adm. Chester Nimitz. No. 2988, $5, Second wave of attack at Wheeler Field, horiz.

2001, Dec. 7 **Sheets of 6, #a-f**
2985-2986 A499 Set of 2 12.50 12.50
Souvenir Sheets
2987-2988 A499 Set of 2 7.50 7.50

Pres. John F. Kennedy — A500

Pres. Kennedy — No. 2989, $1.40: a, With John, Jr. b, With Jacqueline (red dress). c, With Caroline. d, With family, 1963. e, With Jacqueline, at sea. f, With Jacqueline (white dress).
No. 2990, $1.40: a, At 1956 Democratic Convention. b, Campaigning with Jacqueline, 1959. c, At White House, 1960. d, With brother Robert. e, Announcing Cuban blockade, 1962. f, John Jr. saluting father's casket.
No. 2991, $5, Portrait with violet background. No. 2992, $5, Portrait with green background.

2001, Dec. 7 **Sheets of 6, #a-f**
2989-2990 A500 Set of 2 12.50 12.50
Souvenir Sheets
2991-2992 A500 Set of 2 7.50 7.50

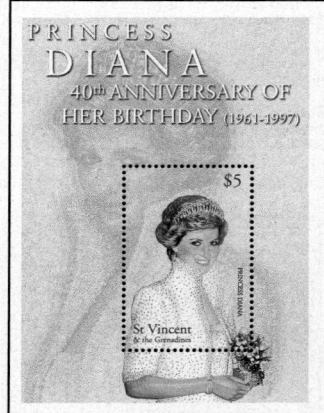

Princess Diana (1961-97) — A501

Flowers and Diana: a, In gray suit. b, In pink dress. c, With tiara.
$5, With tirara and high-necked gown.

2001, Dec. 7
2993 A501 $1.40 Sheet, 2 each #a-c 6.25 6.25
Souvenir Sheet
2994 A501 $5 multi 3.75 3.75

Moths A502

Designs: 70c, Croker's frother. 90c, Virgin tiger moth. $1, Leopard moth. $2, Fiery campylotes.
No. 2999, $1.40: a, Buff-tip. b, Elephant hawkmoth. c, Streaked sphinx. d, Cizara hawkmoth. e, Hakea moth. f, Boisduval's autumnal moth.
No. 3000, $1.40: a, Eyespot anthelid. b, Collenette's variegated browntail. c, Common epicoma moth. d, Staudinger's longtail. e, Green silver lines. f, Salt marsh moth.
No. 3001, $5, Gypsy moth. No. 3002, Orizaba silkmoth caterpillar.

2001, Dec. 10
2995-2998 A502 Set of 4 3.50 3.50
Sheets of 6, #a-f
2999-3000 A502 Set of 2 12.50 12.50
Souvenir Sheets
3001-3002 A502 Set of 2 7.50 7.50

Christmas — A503

Paintings: 10c, Madonna and Child, by Francesco Guardi. 20c, The Immaculate Conception, by Giovanni Battista Tiepolo. 70c, Adoration of the Magi, by Tiepolo. 90c, The Virgin, by Tintoretto. $1.10, The Annunciation, by Veronese. $1.40 Madonna della Quaglia, by Antonio Pisanello.

$5, Madonna and Child Appear to St. Philip Neri, by Tiepolo.

2001, Dec. 12
3003-3008 A503   Set of 6   3.25 3.25
Souvenir Sheet
3009 A503 $5 multi   3.75 3.75

Queen Mother Type of 1999 Redrawn

No. 3010: a, In 1909. b, With King George, Princess Elizabeth, 1930. c, At Badminton, 1977. d, In 1983.
$6, In 1987.

2001, Dec. 13   **Perf. 14**
Yellow Orange Frames
3010 A438 $2 Sheet of 4, #a-d, + label   6.00 6.00
Souvenir Sheet
Perf. 13¾
3011 A438 $6 multi   4.50 4.50

Queen Mother's 101st birthday. No. 3010 contains one 38x50mm stamp with a greener background than that found on No. 2730. Sheet margins of Nos. 3010-3011 lack embossing and gold arms and frames found on Nos. 2729-2730.

New Year 2002 (Year of the Horse) — A504

Scenes from Bo Le and the Horse: a, Man pointing at horse. b, Horse pulling cart. c, Horse snorting. d, Horse drinking. e, Man putting robe on horse. f, Horse rearing.

2001, Dec. 17   **Perf. 13¾**
3012 A504 $1.10 Sheet of 6, #a-f 5.00 5.00

Tourism
A505

Designs: 20c, Vermont Nature Trails. 70c, Tamarind Beach Hotel, horiz. 90c, Tobago Cays, horiz. $1.10, Trinity Falls.

2001, Dec. 31   **Perf. 14**
Stamps + labels
3013-3016 A505   Set of 4   2.25 2.25

Fauna — A506

No. 3017, $1.40, vert.: a, Bumble bee. b, Green darner dragonfly. c, Small lace-wing. d, Black widow spider. e, Praying mantis. f, Firefly.

No. 3018, $1.40: a, Caspian tern. b, White-tailed tropicbird. c, Black-necked stilt. d, Black-billed plover. e, Black-winged stilt. f, Ruddy turnstone.

No. 3019, $5, Blue night butterfly. No. 3020, $5, Brown pelican, vert.

2001, Dec. 10   **Litho.**   **Perf. 14**
Sheets of 6, #a-f
3017-3018 A506   Set of 2   12.50 12.50
Souvenir Sheets
3019-3020 A506   Set of 2   7.50 7.50

Baseball Player Cal Ripken, Jr. — A507

No. 3021: a, Hitting ball. b, Running. c, Without hat. d, Batting (orange shirt). e, Holding trophy. f, Waving hat. g, Greeting fans (68x56mm).
$6, Wearing batting helmet.

2001, Dec. 27   **Perf. 13¼**
3021 A507 $2 Sheet of 7, #a-g 10.50 10.50
Souvenir Sheet
Perf. 13x13¼
3022 A507 $6 multi   4.50 4.50

No. 3022 contains one 36x56mm stamp.

United We
Stand — A508

2001, Dec. 28   **Perf. 14**
3023 A508 $2 multi   1.50 1.50

Reign of Queen Elizabeth II, 50th Anniv. — A509

No. 3024: a, With Prince Philip. b, With Princess Margaret. c, Wearing blue dress. d, In wedding gown.
$5, Wearing orange brown dress.

2002, Apr. 8   **Litho.**   **Perf. 14¼**
3024 A509 $2 Sheet of 4, #a-d   5.50 5.50
Souvenir Sheet
3025 A509 $5 multi   3.25 3.25

Pan-American Health Organization, Cent. — A510

Designs: 20c, Anniversary emblem, vert. 70c, Dr. Gideon Cordice, vert. 90c, Dr. Arthur Cecil Cyrus, vert. $1.10, Headquarters, Christ Church, Barbados.

2002, Apr. 8   **Perf. 14**
3026-3029 A510   Set of 4   2.40 2.40

Vincy Mas, 25th
Anniv. — A511

Designs: 10c, Section of the Bands. 20c, Cocktail, the Blue Dragon, horiz. 70c, Safari, Snake in the Grass. 90c, Bridgette Creese, 2001 Calypso Monarch. $1.10, Heat Wave, horiz. $1.40, Sion Hill Steel Orchestra, horiz.

2002, June 15   **Litho.**   **Perf. 14**
3030-3035 A511   Set of 6   3.50 3.50

Intl. Year of Ecotourism — A512

No. 3036: a, Butterfly. b, Manatee. c, Deer. d, Plant.
$6, Windsurfer, divers and fish.

2002, July 1   **Perf. 13½x13¼**
3036 A512 $2 Sheet of 4, #a-d   6.00 6.00
Souvenir Sheet
3037 A512 $6 multi   4.50 4.50

Intl. Year of Mountains — A513

No. 3038: a, Mt. Ararat, Turkey. b, Mt. Ama Dablam, Nepal. c, Mt. Cook, New Zealand. d, Mt. Kilimanjaro, Tanzania. e, Mt. Kenya, Kenya. f, Giant's Castle, South Africa.
$5, Mt. Aconcagua, Argentina.

2002, July 1
3038 A513 $1.40 Sheet of 6, #a-f 6.25 6.25
Souvenir Sheet
3039 A513 $5 multi   3.75 3.75

20th World Scout Jamboree, Thailand — A514

No. 3040, horiz.: a, Scout with kudu horn. b, Scouts breaking camp. c, Daniel Beard and Lord Robert Baden-Powell.
No. 3041, Scout.

2002, July 1   **Perf. 13¼x13½**
3040 A514 $5 Sheet of 3, #a-c 11.50 11.50
Souvenir Sheet
Perf. 13½x13¼
3041 A514 $5 multi   3.75 3.75

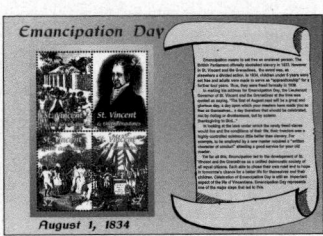

Emancipation Day, 168th
Anniv. — A515

No. 3042: a, Crowd near fence. b, Lieutenant Governor of St. Vincent. c, Black couple dancing, white couple. d, Allegory of freedom.

2002, Aug. 1   *Perf. 14*
3042 A515 $2 Sheet of 4, #a-d   6.00 6.00

2002 Winter Olympics, Salt Lake City A516

Designs: No. 3043, $3, Biathlon. No. 3044, $3, Freestyle skiing.

2002, July 1   **Litho.**   *Perf. 13¼x13½*
3043-3044 A516   Set of 2   4.50 4.50
3044a   Souvenir sheet, #3043-3044   4.50   4.50

Elvis Presley (1935-77) A517

Designs: $1, With red background.
No. 3046: a, Playing guitar. b, In Army uniform. c, In suit, with guitar strap. d, With vertically striped shirt, looking left. e, In horizontally striped shirt. f, In vertically striped shirt, looking forward.

2002, Aug. 19   *Perf. 13¾*
3045 A517 $1 multi   .75 .75
3046 A517 $1.25 Sheet of 6, #a-f   5.75 5.75

No. 3045 printed in sheets of nine.

Souvenir Sheet

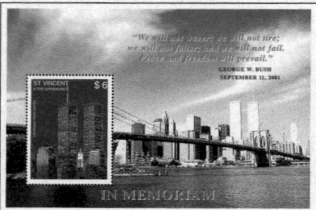

In Remembrance of Sept. 11, 2001 Terrorist Attacks — A518

2002, Sept. 11   *Perf. 13¾*
3047 A518 $6 multi   4.50 4.50

Teddy Bears, Cent. — A519

No. 3048, $2, vert.: a, Cowboy bear. b, Fisherman bear. c, Camper bear. d, Hiker bear.
No. 3049, $2, vert.: a, Bear in kimono. b, Two bears. c, Bear with hair ribbon, baby bear. d, Bear with sunglasses.
No. 3050, vert.: a, Bear with red dress and cap. b, Bear with bonnet. c, Bear with strapless dress. d, Bear with dress with red ruffled collar. e, Bear with blue dress with ribbon.
No. 3051, $5, Four bears by Terumi Yoshikawa. No. 3052, $5, Four bears by Tomoko Suenaga.

2002, Sept. 23   *Perf. 13¾ (#3048), 14*
Sheets of 4, #a-d
3048-3049 A519   Set of 2   12.00 12.00
3050 A519 $2 Sheet of 5, #a-e   7.50 7.50
Souvenir Sheets
3051-3052 A519   Set of 2   7.50   7.50

No. 3048 contains four 38x50mm stamps.

Souvenir Sheets

British Military Medals — A520

Designs: No. 3053, $5, Waterloo Medal. No. 3054, $5, South African War Medal. No. 3055, $5, Queen's South Africa Medal. No. 3056, $5, 1914-15 Star. No. 3057, $5, British War Medal.

2002, Oct. 7   *Perf. 14¼*
3053-3057 A520   Set of 5   19.00 19.00

2002 World Cup Soccer Championship Semifinals, Japan and Korea — A521

No. 3058, $1.40: a, Kleberson and Emre Belozoglu. b, Cafu. c, Roberto Carlos. d, Yildiray Basturk. e, Tugay Kerimoglu and Rivaldo. f, Bulent.
No. 3059, $1.40: a, Ji Sung Park and Dietmar Hamann. b, Miroslav Klose and Tae Young Kim. c, Chong Gug Song and Christoph Metzelder. d, Tae Young Kim and Gerald Asamoah. e, Torsten Frings and Ji Sung Park. f, Oliver Neuville and Tae Young Kim.
No. 3060, $3: a, Ronaldo. b, Cafu, diff.
No. 3061, $3: a, Michael Ballack. b, Oliver Kahn.
No. 3062, $3: a, Bulent, diff. b, Yildiray Basturk, diff.
No. 3063, $3: a, Tae Young Kim. b, Du Ri Cha.

2002, Nov. 4   *Perf. 13¼*
Sheets of 6, #a-f
3058-3059 A521   Set of 2   12.50 12.50
Souvenir Sheets of 2, #a-b
3060-3063 A521   Set of 4   18.00 18.00

Shirley Temple Movie Type of 2000

Temple in "Dimples" — No. 3046, horiz.: a, Embracing man. b, Conducting musicians. c, Seated, in blue dress. d, On stage with actors in black-face. e, Head on pillow. f, With woman, holding plate.
No. 3047: a, Standing on barrel. b, In green dress. c, Adjusting man's ascot. d, With seated woman.
$5, Dancing with man in black face.

2002, Oct. 28   *Perf. 14¼*
3064 A471 $1.40 Sheet of 6,
            #a-f   6.25 6.25
3065 A471 $2 Sheet of 4,
            #a-d   6.00 6.00
Souvenir Sheet
3066 A471 $5 multi   3.75 3.75

Queen Mother Elizabeth (1900-2002) — A522

No. 3067: a, Wearing blue hat and dress. b, Wearing purple hat, dress and corsage. c, Wearing flowered hat.

2002, Nov. 9   **Litho.**   *Perf. 14*
3067 A522 $2 Sheet of 4, #a-b, 2
          #c   6.00 6.00

Christmas — A523

Designs: 20c, Greek Madonna, by Giovanni Bellini. 90c, Kneeling Agostino Barbarigo, by Bellini. $1.10, Presentation of Jesus in the Temple, by Perugino. $1.40, Madonna and Child with the Infant St. John, by Perugino. $1.50, San Giobbe Altarpiece, by Bellini.
$5, Madonna and Child with Saints John the Baptist and Sebastian, by Perugino, horiz.

2002, Nov. 18
3068-3072 A523   Set of 5   4.00 4.00
Souvenir Sheet
3073 A523 $5 multi   3.75 3.75

Souvenir Sheets

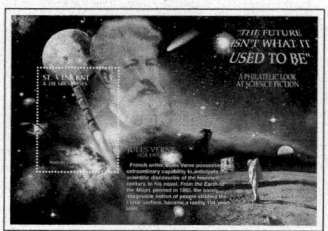

Science Fiction — A524

Designs: No. 3074, $5, From the Earth to the Moon, by Jules Verne. No. 3075, $5, The War of the Worlds, by H. G. Wells. No. 3076, $5, The Time Machine, by Wells.

2002, Dec. 2   *Perf. 13¾*
3074-3076 A524   Set of 3   11.50 11.50

Intl. Federation of Stamp Dealers Associations, 50th Anniv. — A525

2003, Feb. 16   *Perf. 14*
3077 A525 $2 multi   1.50 1.50

British Military Medals Type of 2002
Souvenir Sheets

Designs: No. 3078, $5, Victory Medal. No. 3079, $5, Atlantic Star. No. 3080, $5, 1939-45 Star. No. 3081, $5, Africa Star.

2003, Jan. 27   *Perf. 13¼*
3078-3081 A520   Set of 4   15.00 15.00

New Year 2003 (Year of the Ram) — A526

No. 3082: a, Goat with gray collar. b, Goat facing left. c, Goats and kid. d, Man on goat. e, Goat facing right. f, Goat with piebald coat (flora in background).

2003, Feb. 1   *Perf. 14¼x13¾*
3082 A526 $1 Sheet of 6, #a-f   4.50 4.50

Miniature Sheet

Reign of Queen Elizabeth II, 50th Anniv. (in 2002) — A527

Litho. & Embossed
2003, Feb. 24   *Perf. 13¼x13*
3083 A527 $20 gold & multi   15.00 15.00

Astronauts Killed in Space Shuttle Columbia Accident — A528

No. 3084, $2 — Col. Rick D. Husband: a, Crew photo (green sky). b, Husband, interior of shuttle. c, Shuttle landing. d, Shuttle and space station.
No. 3085, $2 — Commander William C. McCool: a, Crew photo (tan sky). b, McCool in airplane cockpit. c, McCool, interior of shuttle. d, Shuttle in flight, comet.
No. 3086, $2 — Capt. David M. Brown: a, Crew photo (cloudy sky). b, Shuttle being moved to launch pad. c, Shuttle orbiting earth. d, Brown, interior of shuttle.

2003, Apr. 7   **Litho.**   *Perf. 14¼*
Sheets of 4, #a-d
3084-3086 A528   Set of 3   18.00 18.00

Coronation of Queen Elizabeth II, 50th
Anniv. — A529

Designs: No. 3087, $2, Queen arrives at
Westminster Abbey. No. 3088, $2, Queen
seated in Chair of Estate. No. 3089, $2,
Queen's first progress along the nave. No.
3090, $2, Queen leaving Buckingham Palace.
No. 3091, $2, Queen and Duke of Edinburgh
in state coach. No. 3092, $2, Gold state
coach. No. 3093, $2, Westminster Abbey.
$5, Queen's portrait.

2003, Feb. 26	Litho.	Perf. 13¼
3087-3093 A529 Set of 7		10.50 10.50
Souvenir Sheet		
Perf. 14¼		
3094 A529 $5 multi		3.75 3.75

No. 3094 contains one 38x50mm stamp.

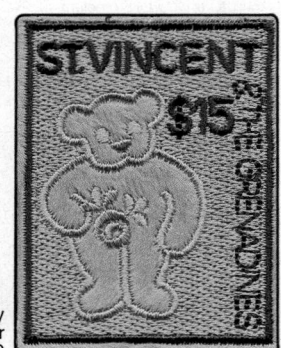

Teddy
Bear
A530

Self-Adhesive

2003, Apr. 30 Embroidered		Imperf.
3095 A530 $15 multi		11.50 11.50

Issued in sheets of 4.

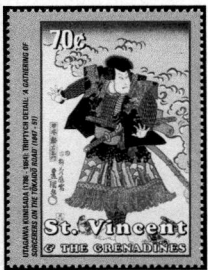

Japanese
Art — A531

Designs: 70c, A Gathering of Sorcerers on
the Tokaido Road (detail), by Kunisada Uta-
gawa. $1.10, Kiyohime and the Moon, by
Chikanobu Yoshu. $1.40, A Gathering of Sor-
cerers on the Tokaido Road (detail), by
Kunisada Utagawa, diff. $3, A Gathering of
Sorcerers on the Tokaido Road (detail), by
Kunisada Utagawa, diff.
No. 3100: a, Snake Mountain, by Kuniyoshi
Utagawa. b, Sadanobu and Oni, by Yoshitoshi
Tsukioka. c, Shoki, by Tsukioka. d, The
Nightly Weeping Rock, by Kuniyoshi Utagawa.
$5, The Ghosts of Matahachi and Kikuno,
by Kunisada Utagawa.

2003, Apr. 30	Litho.	Perf. 14¼
3096-3099 A531 Set of 4		4.75 4.75
3100 A531 $2 Sheet of 4, #a-d		6.00 6.00
Souvenir Sheet		
3101 A531 $5 multi		3.75 3.75

Rembrandt
Paintings
A532

Designs: $1, Portrait of Jacques de Gheyn
III. $1.10, Young Man in a Black Beret. $1.40,
Hendrickje Stoffels. No. 3105, $2, The Polish
Rider, horiz.
No. 3106, $2: a, Belthazzar Sees the Writ-
ing on the Wall. b, Portrait of a Young Man. c,
Jacob Blessing the Sons of Joseph. d, King
Uzziah Stricken with Leprosy.
$5, The Stoning of St. Stephen.

2003, Apr. 30		
3102-3105 A532 Set of 4		4.25 4.25
3106 A532 $2 Sheet of 4, #a-d		6.00 6.00
Souvenir Sheet		
3107 A532 $5 multi		3.75 3.75

Paintings By Pablo Picasso — A533

Designs: 60c, Composition: Woman with
Half-Length Hair. 70c, Sister of the Artist, vert.
90c, Maternity, vert. $1, Bearded Man's Head,
vert. $1.10, Two Seated Children (Claude and
Paloma), vert. $1.40, Woman with a Blue Lace
Collar.
No. 3114: a, Corrida. b, Mandolin, Pitcher
and Bottle. c, The Painter and Model. d,
Reclining Woman Sleeping Under a Lamp.
No. 3115, Reclining Nude. No. 3116, Span-
ish Woman Against an Orange Background,
vert.

2003, Apr. 30		Perf. 14¼
3108-3113 A533 Set of 6		4.25 4.25
3114 A533 $2 Sheet of 4, #a-d		6.00 6.00
Imperf		
Size: 103x82mm		
3115 A533 $5 multi		3.75 3.75
Size: 82x105mm		
3116 A533 $5 multi		3.75 3.75

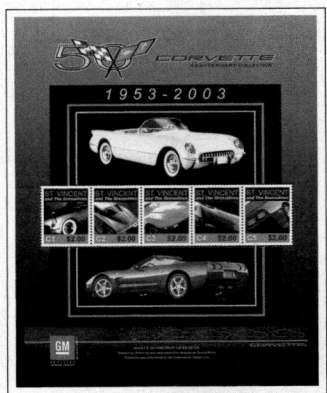

Corvette Automobiles, 50th
Anniv. — A534

No. 3117: a, C1. b, C2. c, C3. d, C4. e, C5.
No. 3118: a, 1953 Corvette. b, 2003
Corvette.

2003, May 5		Perf. 13¼
3117 A534 $2 Sheet of 5, #a-e		7.50 7.50
Perf. 14¼		
3118 A534 $3 Sheet of 2, #a-b		4.50 4.50

No. 3118 contains two 50x38mm stamps.

Prince William, 21st Birthday — A535

No. 3119: a, Wearing suit. b, Wearing polo
jersey. c, Wearing blue shirt.
$5, Wearing suit and tie.

2003, May 13		Perf. 14
3119 A535 $3 Sheet of 3, #a-c		6.75 6.75
Souvenir Sheet		
3120 A535 $5 multi		3.75 3.75

Princess Diana (1961-97) — A536

No. 3121, $2 (vignettes in ovals): a, As child
in baby carriage. b, With Prince Charles on
wedding day. c, With Princes William and
Harry. d, In purple jacket.
No. 3122, $2 (white background): a, Wear-
ing tiara. b, Wearing white gown. c, Wearing
purple sweater. d, Wearing lilac dress.

2003, May 26	Sheets of 4, #a-d	
3121-3122 A536 Set of 2		12.00 12.00

Cadillac Automobiles, Cent. — A537

No. 3123: a, 1953 Eldorado. b, 2002 Eldorado. c, 1967 Eldorado. d, 1962 Series 62.
$5, 1927 LaSalle.

2003, July 1		Perf. 13¼x13¾
3123 A537 $2 Sheet of 4, #a-d		6.00 6.00
Souvenir Sheet		
3124 A537 $5 multi		3.75 3.75

Intl. Year of Fresh Water — A538

No. 3125: a, Owia Salt Pond. b, The Soufriere. c, Falls of Baleine.
$5, Trinity Falls.

2003, July 1		Perf. 13½
3125 A538 $3 Sheet of 3, #a-c		6.75 6.75
Souvenir Sheet		
3126 A538 $5 multi		3.75 3.75

Circus — A539

No. 3127, $2: a, Linny. b, Bruce Feiler. c,
Segey Provirin. d, Weezle.
No. 3128, $2: a, Mermaids. b, Robert Wolf.
c, Elbrus Pilev's Group. d, Stinky.

2003, July 1		Perf. 14
Sheets of 4, #a-d		
3127-3128 A539 Set of 2		12.00 12.00

Tour de France Bicycle Race,
Cent. — A540

No. 3129, $2: a, Antonin Magne, 1931. b,
André Leducq, 1932. c, Georges Speicher,
1933. d, Magne, 1934.
No. 3130, $2: a, Romain Maes, 1935. b,
Sylvére Maes, 1936. c, Roger Lapebie, 1937.
d, Gino Bartali, 1938.
No. 3131, $2: a, Sylvére Maes, 1939. b,
Jean Lazaridés, 1946. c, Jean Robic, 1947. d,
Bartali, 1948.
No. 3132, $5, Magne, 1931, 1934. No.
3133, $5, Fausto Coppi, 1949. No. 3134, $5,
Ferdinand Kubler, 1950.

2003, July 1		Perf. 13¼
Sheets of 4, #a-d		
3129-3131 A540 Set of 3		18.00 18.00
Souvenir Sheets		
3132-3134 A570 Set of 3		11.50 11.50

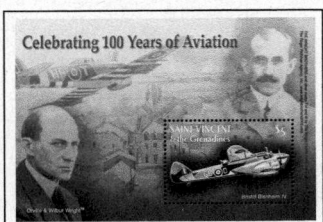

Powered Flight, Cent. — A541

No. 3135, $2: a, Handley Page Heyford. b,
Heinkel He-111B. c, Gloster Gauntlet. d, Cur-
tiss BF2C-1.
No. 3136, $2: a, Mitsubishi A6M Reisen. b,
Dewoitine D520. c, Messerschmitt Bf 109E. d,
Republic Thunderbolt.
No. 3137, $5, Bristol Blenheim IV. No. 3138,
$5, Fairey Flycatcher.

2003, July 15   **Perf. 14**

Sheets of 4, #a-d

3135-3136 A541   Set of 2   12.00 12.00

Souvenir Sheets

3137-3138 A541   Set of 2   7.50 7.50

Salvation Army in
St. Vincent,
Cent. — A542

Designs: 70c, Chief musicians. 90c, District temple. $1, Christmas Kettle Appeal Fund. $1.10, Headquarters, horiz.

2003, Aug. 1

3139-3142 A542   Set of 4   2.75 2.75

Operation Iraqi Freedom — A543

No. 3143: a, Gen. Richard B. Meyers. b, Lt. Gen. David McKiernan. c, Lt. Gen. Michael Moseley. d, Vice Admiral Timothy Keating. e, Lt. Gen. Jay Garner. f, Gen. Tommy R. Franks. g, Lt. Gen. Earl B. Hailston. h, Gen. John Jumper.

No. 3144: a, Private Jessica Lynch. b, Gen. Franks. c, Spectre gunship. d, Stryker vehicle. e, USS Constellation. f, USS Kitty Hawk.

2003, Aug. 25   **Perf. 14¼**

3143 A543 $1 Sheet of 8,   #a-h   6.00   6.00

3144 A543 $1.50 Sheet of 6,   #a-f   6.75   6.75

A544

A545

Marvel Comic Book
Characters — A546

No. 3145 — Spiderman: a, Shooting cable from arm. b, Grasping two cables. c, Grasping one cable. d, Climbing on building.

No. 3146, $2 — The Incredible Hulk: a, Close-up of face, denomination at UR. b, Fire in background, denomination at UL. c, Like "b," denomination at UR. d, Like "a," denomination at UL.

No. 3147, $2 — The Incredible Hulk: a, Punching ground. b, Grasping. c, Showing fists. d, Punching rocks.

No. 3148, $2 — X-Men United: a, Nightcrawler. b, Professor X. c, Iceman. d, Rogue.

No. 3149, $2 — X-Men United: a, Magneto. b, Mystique. c, Stryker. d, Lady Deathstrike.

No. 3150, $2 — X-Men United: a, Jean Grey. b, Storm. c, Wolverine. d, Cyclops.

2003, Sept. 10   **Perf. 13¼**

3145 A544 $2 Sheet of 4, #a-d   6.00 6.00

Sheets of 4, #a-d

3146-3147 A545   Set of 2   12.00 12.00

3148-3150 A546   Set of 3   18.00 18.00

Prehistoric Animals — A547

No. 3151, $2, horiz.: a, Daspletosaurus. b, Utahraptor. c, Scutellosaurus. d, Scelidosaurus.

No. 3152, $2, horiz.: a, Syntarsus. b, Velociraptor. c, Mononikus. d, Massospondylus.

No. 3153, $5, Pterodactylus. No. 3154, $5, Giganotosaurus.

2003, Nov. 5   **Perf. 13¼x13¾**

Sheets of 4, #a-d

3151-3152 A547   Set of 2   12.00 12.00

Souvenir Sheets

Perf. 13¾x13¼

3153-3154 A547   Set of 2   7.50 7.50

Cats — A548

Designs: 50c, British Shorthair. $1, Burmese. $1.40, American Shorthair. $3, Havana Brown.

No. 3159: a, Ocicat. b, Manx. c, Somali. d, Angora.

$5, Abyssinian.

2003, Nov. 5   **Perf. 14**

3155-3158 A548   Set of 4   4.50 4.50

3159 A548 $2 Sheet of 4, #a-d   6.00 6.00

Souvenir Sheet

3160 A548 $5 multi   3.75 3.75

Dogs — A549

Designs: 10c, Chihuahua. 20c, Bulldog. 60c, Weimaraner. No. 3164, $5, Dalmatian.

No. 3165: a, Dachshund. b, Collie. c, Springer spaniel. d, Hamilton hound.

No. 3166, $5, Golden retriever.

2003, Nov. 5

3161-3164 A549   Set of 4   4.50 4.50

3165 A549 $2 Sheet of 4, #a-d   6.00 6.00

Souvenir Sheet

3166 A549 $5 multi   3.75 3.75

Orchids — A550

Designs: 40c, Laelia lobata. 90c, Miltoniopsis phalaenopsis. $1, Phalaenopsis violacea. $3, Trichopilia fragrans.

No. 3171: a, Masdevallia uniflora. b, Laelia flava. c, Barkeria lindleyana. d, Laelia tenebrosa.

$5, Cattleya lawrenceana.

2003, Nov. 5

3167-3170 A550   Set of 4   4.00 4.00

3171 A550 $2 Sheet of 4, #a-d   6.00 6.00

Souvenir Sheet

3172 A550 $5 multi   3.75 3.75

Marine
Life — A551

Designs: 70c, Lutjanus kasmira. 90c, Chaetadon collare. $1.10, Istiophorus platypterus. No. 3176, $2, Pomacanthidae.

No. 3177, $2: a, Equetus lanceolatus. b, Hypoplectrus gutavarius. c, Pomacentridae. d, Cichlidae.

$5, Dolphins.

2003, Nov. 5

3173-3176 A551   Set of 4   3.50 3.50

3177 A551 $2 Sheet of 4, #a-d   6.00 6.00

Souvenir Sheet

3178 A551 $5 multi   3.75 3.75

Christmas — A552

Children's contest-winning art by: 70c, Andrew Gonsalves. 90c, Georgia Gravel. $1.10, Adam Gravel, vert.

2003, Nov. 5   **Perf. 14¼**

3179-3181 A552   Set of 3   2.00 2.00

Playboy Magazine, 50th
Anniv. — A553

Magazine covers depicting: a, Marilyn Monroe. b, Playboy emblem. c, Rabbit and kisses. d, Woman with legs above head. e, Woman licking stamp. f, 50th Anniversary emblem.

2003, Dec. 1   **Litho.**   **Perf. 14**

3182 A553 $1.50 Sheet of 6, #a-f 6.75 6.75

Ma Yuan (1160-1235), Painter — A554

No. 3183: a, Apricot Blossoms. b, Peach Blossoms. c, Unnamed painting, denomination at left. d, Unnamed painting, denomination at right.

$5, On a Mountain Path in Spring.

2004, Jan. 30   **Perf. 13x13½**

3183 A554 $2 Sheet of 4, #a-d   6.00 6.00

Imperf

3184 A554 $5 multi   3.75 3.75

No. 3183 contains four 40x30mm stamps.

Souvenir Sheet

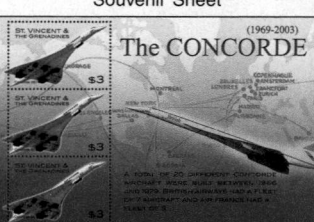

Cessation of Concorde Flights in
2003 — A555

Concorde over map showing: a, Anchorage. b, Los Angeles. c, South Pacific (no cities named).

2004, Feb. 16   **Perf. 13¼x13½**

3185 A555 $3 Sheet of 3, #a-c   6.75 6.75

New Year 2004 (Year of the Monkey) — A556

2004, Jan. 15   Litho.   Perf. 13¼x13
3186   A556 $1.40 buff, lt brn & blk   1.10 1.10
Souvenir Sheet
3187   A556 $3 pink, brn & blk   2.25 2.25
No. 3186 printed in sheets of 4.

A557

MARILYN MONROE

Marilyn Monroe (1926-62), Actress — A558

No. 3188: a, Sepia-toned portrait. b, Wearing blue dress. c, Wearing white dress. d, Wearing black dress.
No. 3189: a, Wearing round white earrings. b, With hand showing. c, Wearing no earrings. d, Wearing different earrings.

2004, May 3   Perf. 14
3188   A557 $2 Sheet of 4, #a-d   6.00 6.00
Perf. 13½x13¼
3189   A558 $2 Sheet of 4, #a-d   6.00 6.00

European Soccer Championships, Portugal — A559

No. 3190, vert.: a, Roger Lemerre. b, Marco Delvecchio. c, David Trezeguet. d, De Kuip Stadium.
$5, 2000 French team.

2004, May 17   Perf. 13½x13¼
3190   A559 $2 Sheet of 4, #a-d   6.00 6.00
Souvenir Sheet
Perf. 13¼
3191   A559 $5 multi   3.75 3.75
No. 3190 contains four 28x42mm stamps.

2004 Summer Olympics, Athens A560

Designs: 70c, Pierre de Coubertin, first Intl. Olympic Committee Secretary General. $1, Pin from 1904 St. Louis Olympics. $1.40, Water Polo, 1936 Berlin Olympics, horiz. $3, Greek amphora.

2004, June 17   Perf. 14¼
3192-3195   A560   Set of 4   4.75 4.75

Babe Ruth (1895-1948), Baseball Player — A561

No. 3196: a, Facing right. b, Facing forward. c, Leaning on bat. d, Swinging bat.

2004, July 1   Perf. 13½x13¼
3196   A561 $2 Sheet of 4, #a-d   6.00 6.00

D-Day, 60th Anniv. A562

Designs: 70c, Air Chief Marshal Sir Trafford Leigh-Mallory. 90c, Lt. Col. Maureen Gara. $1, Gen. Omar Bradley. $1.10, Jean Valentine. $1.40, Jack Culshaw. $1.50, Gen. Dwight D. Eisenhower.
No. 3203, $2: a, British land on Gold Beach. b, British infantry land on Gold Beach. c, Canadians at Juno Beach. d, Canadians land at Juno Beach.
No. 3204, $2: a, Rangers take Pointe du Hoc. b, Rangers hold Pointe du Hoc. c, Invasion announced to press. d, British liberate Hermanville.
No. 3205, $5: Soldiers prepare to board assault landing craft. No. 3206, $5, Code breaking team at work.

2004, July 19   Perf. 14
Stamp + Label (#3197-3202)
3197-3202   A562   Set of 6   5.00 5.00
Sheets of 4, #a-d
3203-3204   A562   Set of 2   12.00 12.00
Souvenir Sheets
3205-3206   A562   Set of 2   7.50 7.50

General Employees' Cooperative Credit Union — A563

Designs: 70c, GECCU children. 90c, GECCU Building. $1.10, Calvin Nicholls, vert. $1.40, Bertrand Neehall, vert.

2004, Sept. 15   Litho.
3207-3210   A563   Set of 4   3.25 3.25

Pres. Ronald Reagan (1911-2004) A564

No. 3211: a, Portrait. b, With flag. c, At microphone.

2004, Oct. 13   Perf. 13½x13¼
3211   Vert. strip of 3   3.25 3.25
a.-c.   A564 $1.40 Any single   1.00 1.00
Printed in sheets containing two strips.

Railroads, 200th Anniv. — A565

No. 3212, $2: a, 1911 0-6-0 Standard, Boston & Maine. b, AG locomotive. c, BA 101 Antigua locomotive. d, Aster 1449.
No. 3213, $2: a, Narrow gauge locomotive W12. b, Gambler. LNV9701 4-4-0 NG. c, No. 4 Snowdon. d, Hiawatha 3-1.
No. 3214, $2: a, CO1604-1. b, CP steam locomotive N135. c, 6042-6. d, E1 narrow gauge 0-4-0T.
No. 3215, $5, NAT2A 01-06-00. No. 3216, $5, Union Pacific 844. No. 3217, $5, Holy War-1, vert.

2004, Oct. 13   Perf. 14
Sheets of 4, #a-d
3212-3214   A565   Set of 3   18.00 18.00
Souvenir Sheets
3215-3217   A565   Set of 3   11.50 11.50

Independence, 25th Anniv. — A566

Designs: 10c, Halimah DeShong. 20c, Winston Davis, cricket player. No. 3220, 70c, Miss Carnival 2003. No. 3221, 70c, Flag, horiz. No. 3222, 70c, Pamenoa Ballantyne, runner, horiz. No. 3223, 90c, Carl "Blazer" Williams. No. 3224, 90c, Breadfruit, horiz. No. 3225, 90c, Rodney "Chang" Jack, soccer player, horiz. $1.10, St. Vincent parrot. No. 3227, $5, Capt. Hugh Mulzac. No. 3228, $5, George McIntosh, political leader. No. 3229, $5, E. T. Joshua, horiz. No. 3230, $10, Joseph Chatoyer, Carib chief, national hero. No. 3231, $10, Robert Milton Cato, politician.

2004, Oct. 25
3218-3231   A566   Set of 14   31.00 31.00

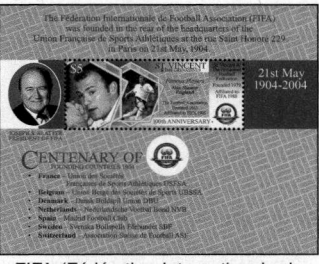

FIFA (Fédération Internationale de Football Association), Cent. — A567

No. 3232: a, David Ginola. b, Paul Scholes. c, Jurgen Kohler. d, Ian Rush. $5, Alan Shearer.

2004, Oct. 27   Perf. 12¾x12½
3232   A567 $2 Sheet of 4, #a-d   6.00 6.00
Souvenir Sheet
3233   A567 $5 multi   3.75 3.75

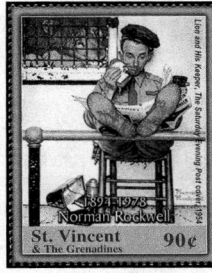

Paintings by Norman Rockwell A568

Designs: 90c, Lion and His Keeper. $1, Weighing In. $1.40, The Young Lawyer. $2, The Bodybuilder. $5, Triple Self-portrait.

2004, Oct. 29   Perf. 14¼
3234-3237   A568   Set of 4   4.00 4.00
Imperf
Size: 66x88mm
3238   A568 $5 multi   3.75 3.75

Various St. Vincent and St. Vincent Grenadines Stamps Surcharged

Surcharge Types on St. Vincent Stamps

10c on 45c No. 1078 — Type 1: "1" without bottom serif, "0" same thickness. Type 2: "1" with bottom serif, "0" thin at top and bottom.
10c on 65c No. 1080b and 10c on 75c No. 1081b — Type 1: "1" with bottom serif, "0" thin at top and bottom. Type 2: "1" without bottom serif, "0" same thickness.
20c on 60c No. 726 — Type 1: New denomination at lower left with small "c." Type 2: New denomination at upper left, with cent sign. Type 3: New denomination below obliterator and approximately 6mm to left of it, with small "c." Type 4: New denomination below obliterator and approximately 16mm to left of it, with small "c."
20c on 75c Nos. 984a-984b horiz. pair — Type 1: Small "c." Type 2: Cent sign.
20c on $1.25 No. 527 — Type 1: New denomination to left of round obliterator, with raised "c" and serifed "2." Type 2: New denomination at lower left, round obliterator with cent sign and serifed "2." Type 3: New denomination below square obliterator, unserifed "2" and "c."
20c on $2 No. 638 — Type 1: New denomination to right and below obliterator, with serifed "2" and small "c" with ball. Type 2: New denomination to right of obliterator, with unserifed "2" and small "c" without ball.
20c on $2 No. 665 — Type 1: New denomination at left, with small "c" with ball and serifed "2." Type 2: New denomination close to obliterator at left, with small "c" without ball and unserifed "2."
20c on $2 No. 975 — Type 1: Cent sign. Type 2: Small "c."
20c on $3.70 No. 1004 — Type 1: New denomination at upper left, with serifed "2," "0"

thin at top and bottom. Type 2: New denomination at upper right with unserifed "2," "0" same thickness.

Surcharge Types on St. Vincent Grenadines Stamps

20c on 75c No. 511 — Type 1: Cent sign. Type 2: Small "c."

20c on 75c No. 593 — Type 1: New denomination at lower left, below obliterator, with cent sign. Type 2: New denomination to right of obliterator, with small "c."

20c on $1.50 No. 277 — Type 1: New denomination at top center, with small "c." Type 2: New denomination at lower left, with cent sign.

20c on $2 No. 186 — Type 1: New denomination to left of obliterator, with small "c." Type 2: New denomination at upper right, with cent sign.

20c on $2.50 No. 265 — Type 1: Unserifed "2," small "c" even with base of numerals. Type 2: Serifed "2," raised small "c."

Methods, Perfs and Watermarks As Before

1994 (?)-2004

On St. Vincent Stamps

3239	A36	10c on 2c #281	125.00	—
3240	A148	10c on 6c #1070	—	—
3241	A148	10c on 12c #1072	—	—
3242	A148	10c on 15c #1073b	—	—
3243	A36	10c on 25c #290	85.00	—
3244	A148	10c on 25c #1075b	—	30.00
3245	A112	10c on 35c #743	50.00	30.00
3246	A148	10c on 35c #1077	—	—
3247	A109	10c on 45c #725	—	—
3248	A148	10c on 45c #1078b, Type 1	—	30.00
3249	A148	10c on 45c #1078, Type 2	—	75.00
a.		On #1078b (perf. 14), Type 2		
3250	A151	10c on 45c #1096	—	25.00
3251	A98	10c on 60c #640	75.00	90.00
3252	A104a	10c on 60c #671	50.00	—
3253	A104b	10c on 60c #676	25.00	10.00
3254	A148	10c on 65c #1080b, Type 1	—	—
3255	A148	10c on 65c #1080b, Type 2	—	—
3256	A71	10c on 70c #481	50.00	—
3257	A148	10c on 75c #1081b, Type 1	—	—
3257A	A148	10c on 75c #1081b, Type 2	—	40.00
3258	A109	10c on $1 #728	—	75.00
3259	A77	10c on $1.25 #527	95.00	—
3260	A98	10c on $1.50 #641	—	—
3260A	A99	10c on $1.50 #645	—	—
3261	A105	10c on $1.50 #681	50.00	—
3262	A82	10c on $2 #544	50.00	—
3262A	A93	10c on $2 #618		
3263	A98	10c on $2 #642		
3263A	A106	10c on $2.40 #686		
3264	A90	10c on $2.50 #607	25.00	25.00
3264A	A108	10c on $3 #718		
3265	A36	20c on ½c #279	15.00	20.00
3266	A47	20c on 1c #337	75.00	50.00
3267	A145	20c on 6c #1061a-1061b horiz. pair	200.00	—
3268	A126	20c on 25c #903	—	85.00
3273	A113	20c on 35c #761	—	200.00
3274	A162	20c on 45c #1145	—	175.00
3275	A105	20c on 45c #679	—	—
3276	A112	20c on 45c #744	—	—

3277	A151	20c on 45c #1096	—	—
3278	A90	20c on 60c #605	150.00	30.00
3279	A93	20c on 60c #616	—	—
3280	A97	20c on 60c #636	200.00	200.00
3281	A98	20c on 60c #640	15.00	20.00
3282	A104	20c on 60c #667	15.00	20.00
3283	A104b	20c on 60c #676	—	50.00
3284	A105	20c on 60c #680	20.00	10.00
3285	A109	20c on 60c #726, Type 1	25.00	10.00
3286	A109	20c on 60c #726, Type 2	10.00	50.00
3287	A109	20c on 60c #726, Type 3	50.00	5.00
3288	A109	20c on 60c #726, Type 4	90.00	35.00
3289	A115	20c on 60c #784	—	30.00
3290	A71	20c on 70c #481	175.00	—
3292	A136	20c on 75c #984a-984b horiz. pair, Type 1	—	150.00
3293	A136	20c on 75c #984a-984b horiz. pair, Type 2		
3294	A138	20c on 75c #999	75.00	50.00
3295	A148	20c on 75c #1081	30.00	—
3296	A79	20c on $1 #534	50.00	15.00
3297	A94	20c on $1 #622a-622b pair	130.00	—
3298	A97	20c on $1 #637	50.00	50.00
3299	A121	20c on $1 #847	—	50.00
3302	A64	20c on $1.25 #434	30.00	40.00
3303	A70	20c on $1.25 #478	30.00	200.00
3304	A73	20c on $1.25 #498	—	—
3306	A77	20c on $1.25 #527, Type 1	—	—
3307	A77	20c on $1.25 #527, Type 2	—	110.00
3308	A77	20c on $1.25 #527, Type 3	85.00	125.00
3309	A99	20c on $1.50 #645	—	—
3310	A103	20c on $1.50 #664	—	100.00
3311	A104	20c on $1.50 #668	15.00	20.00
3313	A104b	20c on $1.50 #677	45.00	50.00
3314	A105	20c on $1.50 #681	—	—
3315	A115	20c on $1.50 #785	35.00	15.00
3316	A134	20c on $1.50 #974	65.00	100.00
3317	A136	20c on $1.50 #985a-985b horiz. pair	140.00	100.00
3318	A93	20c on $2 #618	40.00	100.00
3320	A97	20c on $2 #638, Type 1	40.00	50.00
3321	A97	20c on $2 #638, Type 2	100.00	60.00
3322	A98	20c on $2 #642	—	—
3324	A103	20c on $2 #665, Type 1	—	200.00
3325	A103	20c on $2 #665, Type 2	—	—
3326	A104	20c on $2 #669	40.00	50.00
3327	A104b	20c on $2 #678	15.00	25.00
3328	A105	20c on $2 #682	15.00	15.00
3329	A115	20c on $2 #786	45.00	15.00
3330	A134	20c on $2 #975, Type 1		

3331	A134	20c on $2 #975, Type 2	—	—
a.		Horiz. pair, #3330-3331	—	—
3333	A126	20c on $2.50 #905	20.00	100.00
3334	A108	20c on $3 #718	—	40.00
3337	A113	20c on $3 #764	—	150.00
3338	A117	20c on $3 #806	—	—
3339	A119	20c on $3 #832	—	—
3342	A139	20c on $3.70 #1004, Type 1	80.00	40.00
3343	A139	20c on $3.70 #1004, Type 2	30.00	30.00
3345	A189	20c on $4 #1307	75.00	50.00

On St. Vincent Grenadines Stamps

3346	G3	10c on 1c #33		
3347	G16	10c on 1c #133		
3348	G16	10c on 6c #138		
3349	G35	10c on 35c #433		
3350	G31	10c on 45c #271		
3351	G33	10c on 45c #292		
3351A	G36	10c on 75c #439		
3352	G20	10c on 90c #185		
3353	A90	10c on $1 #192		
3354	G35	10c on $1 #435		
3355	G32	10c on $2 #278		
3356	G36	10c on $3 #440		
3358	A106	20c on 20c #469		
3359	G39	20c on 35c #484		
3360	G31	20c on 45c #271		
3361	A106	20c on 45c #470		
3362	G45	20c on 45c #561		
3363	G7	20c on 50c #71		
3364	G31	20c on 60c #272		
3366	G41	20c on 75c #511, Type 1		
3367	G41	20c on 75c #511, Type 2		
a.		Horiz. pair, #3366-3367		
3368	G50	20c on 75c #588		
3369	G51	20c on 75c #593, Type 1		
3370	G51	20c on 75c #593, Type 2		
a.		Double surcharge		
3371	G20	20c on 90c #185		
3372	G7	20c on $1 #72		
3374	G17	20c on $1.25 #160		
3375	G46	20c on $1.25 #566		
3376	A97	20c on $1.50 #264		
3377	G31	20c on $1.50 #273		
3378	G32	20c on $1.50 #277, Type 1		
3379	G32	20c on $1.50 #277, Type 2		
3381	A76	20c on $2 #128		
3383	G20	20c on $2 #186, Type 1		
3384	G20	20c on $2 #186, Type 2		
3385	G21	20c on $2 #198		
3386	G27	20c on $2 #242		
3387	G32	20c on $2 #278		
3390	A97	20c on $2.50 #265, Type 1		
3391	A97	20c on $2.50 #265, Type 2		
3392	A82	20c on $3 #179		

3394	G35	20c on $3 #436	—	—
3395	G37	20c on $3 #475	—	—
3396	G39	20c on $3 #487	—	—
3397	G43	20c on $3 #536	—	—
3399	G59	20c on $3 #692	—	—
3400	G50	20c on $3.50 #589	—	—
3401	G45	20c on $4 #563	—	—

These surcharges were printed from the mid-1990s to 2004, with the bulk created from 1999 to 2004. Issue dates are not certain as the stamps were available for both revenue and postal use. Numbers are reserved for stamps that printer's records indicate were surcharged. Additional stamps may also have been surcharged.

These stamps were not available through the philatelic agency, but could be bought at post offices, as well as Treasury offices and other locations throughout the country where revenue stamps were used, including retail stores.

The surcharged Grenadines issues were not necessarily sent only to the Grenadines for sale there.

Nos. 3246, 3249a, 3254, 3255, 3257A, 3263, 3347, 3349, 3351, and 3354, which are currently known only with revenue cancels, may also have been used postally.

The shape of the obliterators and the location of new denominations varies.

On No. 3240, the original denomination is obliterated with a marker. No. 3275 is known only with a double surcharge.

Nos. 3260A, 3262A, 3264A, 3351A and 3356, which are known only with revenue cancels, also may have been used postally.

The item illustrated above is a revenue stamp, though it lacks any revenue stamp inscription. 10c on 20c, 20c, 50c, $5 and $60 stamps of this design also exist. Some of these revenue stamps have been used on mail as they were available for sale to the public at the same locations as the surcharged stamps listed above. Non-governmental vendors of these stamps were lax in notifying stamp purchasers that the stamps were intended for revenue use only.

Queen Juliana of the Netherlands (1909-2004) A569

2004, Aug. 25   **Litho.**   *Perf. 13¼*

3405	A569	$2 multi	1.50 1.50

Printed in sheets of 6.

National Soccer Team — A570

2004, Oct. 27   *Perf. 12*

3406	A570	70c multi	.55 .55

Paintings in the Hermitage, St. Petersburg, Russia
A571

Designs: 10c, Head of a Young Girl, by Jean-Baptiste Greuze. 20c, Two Actresses, by Jean-Baptiste Santerre. 40c, An Allegory of History, by José de Ribera. 60c, A Young Woman Trying on Earrings, by Rembrandt. $2, The Girlhood of the Virgin, by Francisco e Zurbarán. No. 3412, $5, Portrait of a Woman, by Frans Pourbus, the Elder.

No. 3413, Landscape with Obelisk, by Hubert Robert. a: b, At the Hermit's, by Robert. c, Landscape with Ruins, by Robert. d, Landscape with Terrace and Cascade, by Robert. e, A Shepherdess, by Jan Siberecht. f, Landscape with Waterfall, by Robert.

No. 3414, $1.40: a, Count N. D. Guriev, by Jean Auguste-Dominque Ingres. b, Portrait of an Actor, by Domenico Fetti. c, Napoleon Bonaparte on the Bridge at Arcole, by Baron Antoine-Jean Gros. d, A Young Man with a Glove, by Frans Hals. e, Portrait of General Alexei Yermolov, by George Dawe. f, A Scholar, by Rembrandt.

No. 3415, The Bean King, by Jacob Jordaens, horiz. No. 3416, Three Men at a Table, by Diego Velázquez. No. 3417, Family Portrait, by Cornelis de Vos, horiz.

2004, Nov. 1 . . . . Perf. 14¼
3407-3412 A571 Set of 6 . . 6.25 6.25
Sheets of 6, #a-f
3413-3414 A571 Set of 2 . 13.00 13.00
Imperf
Size: 98x72mm
3415 A571 $5 multi 3.75 3.75
Size: 78x83mm
3416 A571 $5 multi 3.75 3.75
Size: 88x76mm
3417 A571 $5 multi 3.75 3.75

National Basketball Association Players — A572

Designs: No. 3418, 75c, Gary Payton, Los Angeles Lakers. No. 3419, 75c, Lebron James, Cleveland Cavaliers. No. 3420, 75c, Adonal Foyle, Golden State Warriors. No. 3421, 75c, Peja Stojakovic, Sacramento Kings. No. 3422, 75c, Kirk Hinrich, Chicago Bulls. $3, Steve Francis, Houston Rockets.

2004-05 . . . . Perf. 14
3418-3423 A572 Set of 6 . . 5.25 5.25
Issued: No. 3418, 11/2; Nos. 3419-3420, 11/3; No. 3421, 11/9; Nos. 3422-3423, 2/10/05.

Battle of Trafalgar, Bicent.
A573

Designs: 50c, Captain Thomas Masterman Hardy. $1, Napoleon Bonaparte. $1.50, Admiral Lord Horatio Nelson. $3, Admiral Cuthbert Collingwood.

No. 3428, $5, The Nelson touch. No. 3429, $5, H.M.S. Victory.

2004, Nov. 25 . . . . Perf. 14¼
3424-3427 A573 Set of 4 . . 4.50 4.50
Souvenir Sheets
3428-3429 A573 Set of 2 . . 7.50 7.50

A574

Elvis Presley (1935-77) — A575

No. 3430: a, Country name at UL reading across, denomination at LL. b, Country name at R, denomination at LL. c, Country name at R, denomination at LR. d, Country name at L reading up, denomination at LL.

No. 3431 — Denomination color: a, Green. b, Blue. c, Red. d, Purple.

2004, Nov. 25 . . . . . . Perf. 13¼x13½
3430 A574 $2 Sheet of 4, #a-d . 6.00 6.00
Perf. 13½x13¼
3431 A575 $2 Sheet of 4, #a-d . 6.00 6.00
Souvenir Sheet

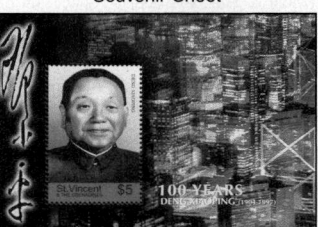

Deng Xiaoping (1904-97), Chinese Leader — A576

2004, Dec. 6 . . . . Perf. 14
3432 A576 $5 multi 3.75 3.75

Subway Systems — A577

No. 3433 — New York City subway: a, 1953 subway token. b, 23rd Street IRT kiosk, c,

1935 Subway car Hi-V 3398. d, 1936 subway car R6 1208 interior. e, Construction of Harlem River Tunnel, 1904. f, Underground construction, early 1900s. g, Hoppers, above ground construction, early 1900s. h, Workers on scaffold, above ground construction early 1900s.

No. 3434, $1.40 — Subway cars from: a, Moscow Metro. b, Tokyo Metro. c, Mexico City Metro. d, Paris Metro. e, Hong Kong MTR. f, Prague Metro.

No. 3435, $1.40 — London Underground: a, Thames Tunnel, 1859. b, City & South London Railway locomotives, 1890. c, East London line. d, Picadilly line. e, Victoria line. f, Jubilee line.

No. 3436, $5, A Train, New York City. No. 3437, $5, Train in station, London Underground. No. 3438, $5, 1992 Tube, Central line, London.

2004, Dec. 13 . . . . . . Perf. 13¼x13½
3433 A577 $1 Sheet of 8, #a-h . 6.00 6.00
Sheets of 6, #a-f
3434-3435 A577 Set of 2 . 13.00 13.00
Souvenir Sheets
3436-3438 A577 Set of 3 . 11.50 11.50

Christmas A578

Paintings by Norman Rockwell: 70c, Santa's Helpers. 90c, Tiny Tim (detail). $1.10, Department Store Santa. $3, The Muggleton Stage Coach.
$5, Extra Good Boys and Girls.

2004, Dec. 13 . . . . Perf. 12
3439-3442 A578 Set of 4 . . 4.25 4.25
Imperf
Size: 64x84mm
3443 A578 $5 multi 3.75 3.75

New Year 2005 (Year of the Rooster) — A579

2005, Jan. 26 . . . . Perf. 12
3444 A579 75c multi . . . . . .55 .55
Issued in sheets of 3.

Miniature Sheet

World Peace — A580

No. 3445: a, Mahatma Gandhi. b, Elie Wiesel. c, Rigoberta Menchu.

2005, Jan. 26 . . . . Perf. 14
3445 A580 $3 Sheet of 3, #a-c . 6.75 6.75

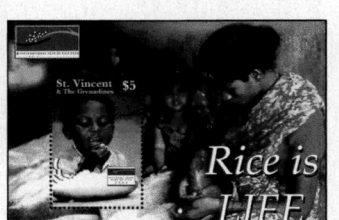

Intl. Year of Rice (in 2004) — A581

No. 3446, horiz.: a, Oxen pulling plow. b, Man and child harvesting rice. c, Man and field.
$5, Child with bowl of rice.

2005, Jan. 26
3446 A581 $3 Sheet of 3, #a-c . 6.75 6.75
Souvenir Sheet
3447 A581 $5 multi 3.75 3.75

Souvenir Sheet

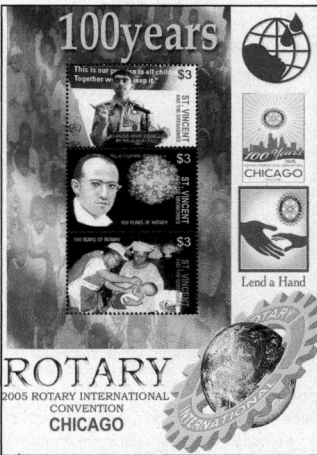

Rotary International, Cent. — A582

No. 3448: a, Jehanzeb Khan, polio victim. b, Dr. Jonas Salk. c, Child receiving polio vaccination.

2005, Apr. 4 . . Litho. . . Perf. 14
3448 A582 $3 Sheet of 3, #a-c . 6.75 6.75

Wedding of Prince Charles and Camilla Parker Bowles — A583

Various photos of couple with oval color of: No. 3449, $2, Blue. No. 3450, $2, Red violet. No. 3451, $2, Purple, horiz.

2005, Apr. 9 . . . . Perf. 13½
3449-3451 A583 Set of 3 . . 4.50 4.50

Vatican City No. 63 — A584

Pope John Paul II (1920-2005) A585

2005, June 1 . . . . Perf. 13x13¼
3452 A584 70c multi . . . . . .55 .55
Perf. 13½
3453 A585 $3 multi 2.25 2.25
No. 3452 issued in sheets of 12; No. 3453, in sheets of 6.

Maimonides (1135-1204), Philosopher A586

No. 3454 — Statue of Maimonides with frame in: a, Yellow. b, Yellow and black.

				Perf. 12
2005, June 7				
3454	A586	$2 Vert. pair, #a-b	3.00	3.00

Printed in sheets containing two pairs.

Souvenir Sheet

Expo 2005, Aichi, Japan — A587

No. 3455 — Woolly mammoth with country name in: a, Red. b, Black. c, White.

				Perf. 12¾
2005, June 7				
3455	A587	$3 Sheet of 3, #a-c	6.75	6.75

Fish A588

Designs: $1, Red Irish lord. $1.10, Deep sea anglerfish. $1.40, Viperfish. $2, Lionfish. $5, Gulper eel.

2005, June 7				
3456-3459	A588	Set of 4	4.25	4.25
Souvenir Sheet				
3460	A588	$5 multi	3.75	3.75

Bats — A589

No. 3461: a, Mexican long-tongued bat. b, Wahlberg's fruit bat. c, Common vampire bat. d, False vampire bat. e, Horseshoe bat. f, Spear-nosed long-tongued bat. $5, Greater long-nosed bat.

2005, June 7				
3461	A589	$1.60 Sheet of 6, #a-f	7.25	7.25
Souvenir Sheet				
3462	A589	$5 multi	3.75	3.75

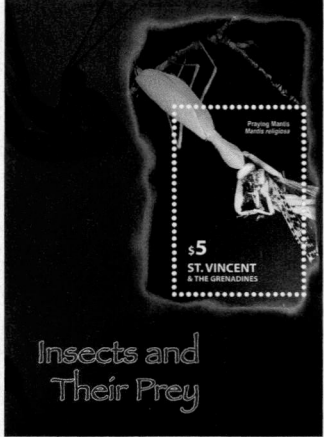

Insects and Spiders — A590

No. 3463: a, Field-digger wasp. b, Water spider. c, Yellow crab spider. d, Mantid. $5, Praying mantis.

2005, June 7				
3463	A590	$2 Sheet of 4, #a-d	6.00	6.00
Souvenir Sheet				
3464	A590	$5 multi	3.75	3.75

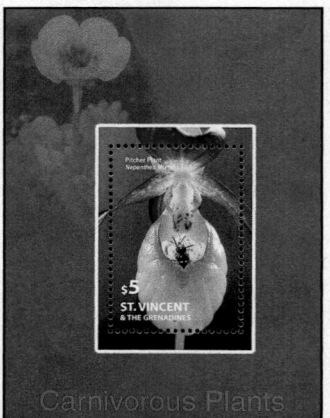

Carnivorous Plants — A591

No. 3465: a, Butterwort, denomination in black. b, Common sundew. c, Venus's flytrap. d, Butterwort, denomination in white. $5, Pitcher plant.

2005, June 7				
3465	A591	$2 Sheet of 4, #a-d	6.00	6.00
Souvenir Sheet				
3466	A591	$5 multi	3.75	3.75

Friedrich von Schiller (1759-1805), Writer — A592

No. 3467 — Schiller: a, At desk. b, Facing right. c, Facing left.

$5, Facing right, diff.

2005, June 7				
3467	A592	$3 Sheet of 3, #a-c	6.75	6.75
Souvenir Sheet				
3468	A592	$5 multi	3.75	3.75

Hans Christian Andersen (1805-75), Author — A593

No. 3469: a, The Brave Tin Soldier. b, The Top and Ball. c, Ole-Luk-Oie, the Dream-God. $5, The Snow Queen.

				Perf. 12¾
2005, June 7				
3469	A593	$3 Sheet of 3, #a-c	6.75	6.75

Souvenir Sheet

Perf. 12x12¼

3470	A593	$5 multi	3.75	3.75

No. 3469 contains three 43x32mm stamps.

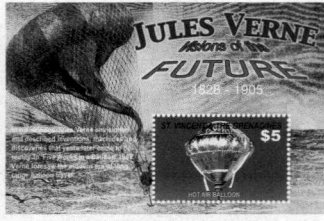

Jules Verne (1828-1905), Writer — A594

No. 3471, $2 — Around the World in 80 Days: a, Princess Aouda. b, Characters in train windows. c, Phileas Fogg. d, Passepartout.

No. 3472, $2 — 20,000 Leagues Under the Sea: a, Mariner using sextant. b, Captain at ship's wheel. c, Sea monster at window. d, Men in diving suits.

No. 3473, $2 — Master of the World: a, Automobile. b, Ship. c, Building. d, Winged vehicle.

No. 3474, $2 — The Castle of the Carpathians: a, Man pointing at beast in sky. b, Women and men looking at woman. c, Two men, woman with arms extended. d, Man pointing.

No. 3475, $2 — From the Earth to the Moon: a, Men and dog. b, Spacecraft and moon. c, Clouds and vapor trail. d, Man on ladder on side of spacecraft.

No. 3476, $5, Hot air balloon. No. 3477, $5, Helicopter.

No. 3478, $5, Atomic bomb. No. 3479, $5, Tank. No. 3480, $5, Blitzkreig of World War II.

				Perf. 12¾
2005, June 7				
Sheets of 4, #a-d				
3471-3472	A594	Set of 2	12.00	12.00
Sheets of 4, #a-d				
3473-3475	A594	Set of 3	18.00	18.00
Souvenir Sheets				
3476-3477	A594	Set of 2	7.50	7.50
3478-3480	A594	Set of 3	11.50	11.50

End of World War II, 60th Anniv. — A595

No. 3481, $2, horiz.: a, USSR T34-85 tank. b, German Tiger tank. c, USA LVT(A)-1. d, Great Britain Cruiser tank Mk VI.

No. 3482, $2, horiz.: a, SBD-3 Dauntless. b, Mitsubishi Zero A6M5. c, USS Yorktown. d, USS Hornet.

No. 3483, $5, Winston Churchill. No. 3484, $5, Gen. Douglas MacArthur signing Japanese surrender instrument, horiz.

2005, June 7		**Sheets of 4, #a-d**		
3481-3482	A595	Set of 2	12.00	12.00
Souvenir Sheets				
3483-3484	A595	Set of 2	7.50	7.50

Souvenir Sheet

Taipei 2005 Stamp Exhibition — A596

No. 3485: a, Panda. b, Formosan rock monkey. c, Formosan black bear. d, Formosan sika deer.

				Perf. 14
2005, Aug. 5				
3485	A596	$2 Sheet of 4, #a-d	6.00	6.00

Souvenir Sheet

Elvis Presley (1935-77) — A597

Litho. & Embossed

				Imperf.
2005, Nov. 21				
Without Gum				
3486	A597	$20 gold & multi	15.00	15.00

Christmas — A598

Designs: 70c, Small Cowper Madonna, by Raphael. 90c, Madonna of the Grand Duke, by Raphael. $1.10, Sistine Madonna, by Raphael. $3, Alba Madonna, by Raphael. $6, Adoration of the Magi, by Rogier van der Weyden.

2005, Dec. 26		**Litho.**		**Perf. 13½**
3487-3490	A598	Set of 4	4.25	4.25
Souvenir Sheet				
3491	A598	$6 multi	4.50	4.50

New Year 2006 (Year of the Dog) A599

2005, Dec. 30
3492 A599 $1 multi   .75 .75
Printed in sheets of 3.

Pope Benedict XVI — A600

2005, Dec. 30
3493 A600 $2 multi   1.50 1.50
Printed in sheets of 4.

Miniature Sheet

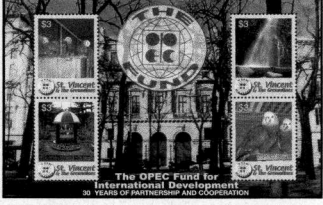

OPEC Intl. Development Fund, 30th Anniv. (in 2006) — A601

No. 3494: a, Three parrots. b, Waterfall. c, Gazebo. d, Two parrots.

2006, Jan. 30   Perf. 12x11½
3494 A601 $3 Sheet of 4, #a-d   9.00 9.00

Miniature Sheets

Children's Drawings — A602

No. 3495, $2 — Flowers: a, Flower Spot, by Tom Brier. b, Flower Vase, by Jessie Abrams. c, Green Flower Vase, by Nick Abrams. d, Red Sunflowers, by Bianca Saad.
No. 3496, $2 — Animals: a, Panda, by Lauren Van Woy. b, Giraffe, by Megal Albe. c, Orange Koala, by Holly Cramer. d, Red Monkey, by Roxanne Hanson.
No. 3497, $2 — Snails and Ladybugs: a, Snail, by Cortland Bobczynski. b, Blue Ladybug, by Jackie Wicks. c, Red Ladybug, by Emily Hawk. d, Snail Boy, by Micah Bobczynski.

2006, Jan. 30   Perf. 13¼
Sheets of 4, #a-d
3495-3497 A602   Set of 3   18.00 18.00

Queen Elizabeth II, 80th Birthday — A603

Inscriptions: No. 3498, $2, The Christening of a Princess. No. 3499, $2, Princess Elizabeth and Margaret. No. 3500, $2, First Radio Broadcast to the Nation. No. 3501, $2, A Decade of War. No. 3502, $2, The Royal Wedding. No. 3503, $2, The Queen's Coronation. No. 3504, $2, The Royal Family. No. 3505, $2, The Queen Awarding the World Cup to England.

2006, Jan. 31   Perf. 13½
3498-3505 A603   Set of 8   12.00 12.00
Each stamp printed in sheets of 8 + label.

Queen Angelfish A604

2006, Feb. 9   Perf. 11½x12
3506 A604 20c multi   .25 .25

Marilyn Monroe (1926-62), Actress — A605

2006, Mar. 31   Perf. 13¼
3507 A605 $3 multi   2.25 2.25
Printed in sheets of 4.

2006 Winter Olympics, Turin A606

Designs: 75c, Poster for 1932 Lake Placid Winter Olympics. 90c, US #716, horiz. $2, Poster for 1924 Chamonix Winter Olympics. $3, Cover with commemorative cancel for 1924 Chamonix Winter Olympics.

2006, May 18   Perf. 14¼
3508-3511 A606   Set of 4   5.00 5.00

Nelson Mandela, 1993 Nobel Peace Prize Winner — A607

2006, May 27   Perf. 11½x12
3512 A607 $3 multi   2.25 2.25
Printed in sheets of 3.

Souvenir Sheet

Airships — A608

No. 3513: a, USS Akron. b, A-170 airship. c, Altair-Z experimental airship.

2006, June 23   Perf. 12¾
3513 A608 $4 Sheet of 3, #a-c   9.00 9.00

Miniature Sheet

Movie Debut of Elvis Presley, 50th Anniv. — A609

No. 3514 — Movie posters: a, King Creole. b, Love Me Tender. c, Loving You. d, Roustabout.

2006, July 12   Perf. 13¼
3514 A609 $3 Sheet of 4, #a-d   9.00 9.00

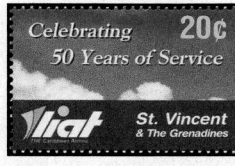

Leeward Islands Air Transport, 50th Anniv. A610

Designs: 20c, Clouds. 50c, Airplane. 70c, Airplane, diff. 90c, Airplane, diff. $5, Frank Delisle, vert.

2006, July 20   Perf. 12¾
3515-3518 A610   Set of 4   1.75 1.75
Souvenir Sheet
3519 A610 $5 multi   3.75 3.75

Christopher Columbus (1451-1506), Explorer — A611

Designs: 50c, Columbus. 70c, Columbus and Queen Isabella, horiz. $2, Santa Maria. $3, Niña, Pinta and Santa Maria, horiz. $5, Pinta.

2006, July 21
3520-3523 A611   Set of 4   4.75 4.75
Souvenir Sheet
3524 A611 $5 multi   3.75 3.75

Souvenir Sheet

Space Achievements — A612

No. 3525 — Viking 1 and Apollo 11: a, Launch of Titan Centaur rocket. b, Viking 1. c, Viking 1 Lander. d, Apollo 11 lunar module. e, Apollo 11 command module. f, Launch of Apollo 11.
No. 3526 — Exploring our Universe: a, Mir Space Station. b, Sputnik 1. c, Soyuz. d, Luna 9.
No. 3527, $6, Conception of crew exploration vehicle for return to Moon. No. 3528, $6, Mir Space Station.

2006, Sept. 27   Perf. 13¼
3525 A612 $1.50 Sheet of 6, #a-f   6.75 6.75
3526 A612 $2.50 Sheet of 4, #a-d   7.50 7.50
Souvenir Sheets
3527-3528 A612   Set of 2   9.00 9.00

Worldwide Fund for Nature (WWF) — A613

No. 3529 — Great white shark: a, Turning right. b, With fish. c, Turning left. d, With mouth open.

2006, Oct. 24   Perf. 14
3529 A613 $1 Block of 4, #a-d   3.00 3.00
   e.   Miniature sheet, 2 #3529   6.00 6.00
No. 3529 printed in sheets of 4 blocks. Value, imperf. sheet of 4 blocks $50. No. 3259e exists imperf. Value $25.

Last Flight of the Concorde — A614

No. 3530, $1.40: a, Concorde coming to Filton. b, Concorde flying past Filton.
No. 3531, $1.40: a, Captains holding British flags. b, Concorde landing at Heathrow Airport.

2006, Dec. 6   Pairs, #a-b
3530-3531 A614   Set of 2   4.25 4.25
Nos. 3530-3531 each printed in sheets containing 3 pairs.

Christmas — A615

Details of Enthroned Madonna with Child Encircled by Saints, by Peter Paul Rubens: 20c, Cherub with flower. 70c, Infant Jesus. 90c, Women. $1.10, Madonna.
No. 3536: a, Like 20c. b, Like 70c. c, Like 90c. d, Like $1.10.

2006, Dec. 6
3532-3535 A615   Set of 4   2.25 2.25
Souvenir Sheet
3536 A615 $2 Sheet of 4, #a-d   6.00 6.00

Diplomatic Relations Between St. Vincent and Republic of China, 25th Anniv. — A616

Designs: 10c, St. Vincent Prime Minister Dr. Ralph Gonsalves and Taiwanese Pres. Chen Shui-bian and other dignitaries. 20c, St. Vincent woman showing dress to Gonsalves and Chen. 50c, Gonsalves and Chen shaking hands. 70c, Chen and St. Vincent honor guard. 90c, Gonsalves and Chen. $1.10, Gonsalves and Chen, diff. $1.40, Children of St. Vincent holding Taiwanese flags.

No. 3544, $5, Chen and Gonsalves seated at table. No. 3545, $5, Chen and another St. Vincent dignitary, flowers. No. 3546, $5, Presentation of gift.

2006, Dec. 12		**Perf. 13½**	
3537-3543	A616	Set of 7	3.75	3.75
		Souvenir Sheets	
3544-3546	A616	Set of 3	11.50	11.50

Rembrandt (1606-69), Painter A617

Designs: 50c, The Jewish Physician Ephraim Bueno. 75c, Portrait of Ariantje Hollaer, Wife of Hendrick Martensz-Sorgh. $1, An Old Man in a Fur Cap. No. 3550, $2, Saskia van Uylenburgh.

No. 3551, $2 — Painting details: a, The Denial of St. Peter (woman with raised hand). b, The Raising of Lazarus (Jesus). c, The Denial of St. Peter (St. Peter). d, The Raising of Lazarus (Lazarus).

No. 3552, $2: a, Portrait of Titia van Uylenburgh. b, The Standing Syndic. c, Polish Officer. d, Seated Girl, in Profile to Left, Half Nude.

No. 3553, $5, Two Young Negroes. No. 3554, $5, Man Standing in Front of a Doorway.

2006, Dec. 22		**Perf. 13¼**	
3547-3550	A617	Set of 4	3.25	3.25
		Sheets of 4, #a-d	
3551-3552	A617	Set of 2	12.00	12.00
		Imperf	
		Size: 70x100mm	
3553-3554	A617	Set of 2	7.50	7.50

Dutch Princesses — A618

No. 3555: a, Princess Amalia (hands showing). b, Head of Princess Amalia. c, Princess Alexia (top of head even with bottom of denomination). d, Princess Alexia (top of head even with top of denomination).

2006			
3555		Vert. strip of 4	4.50	4.50
a.-d.	A618	$1.50 Any single	1.10	1.10

Souvenir Sheet

Wolfgang Amadeus Mozart (1756-91), Composer — A619

2007, Jan. 15			
3556	A619	$5 multi	3.75	3.75

Scouting, Cent. A620

Designs: $4, Dove, Lord Robert Baden-Powell, Earth. $6, Dove, Baden-Powell, horiz.

2007, Jan. 15			
3557	A620	$4 multi	3.00	3.00
		Souvenir Sheet	
3558	A620	$6 multi	4.50	4.50

No. 3557 printed in sheets of 3.

Mushrooms A621

Designs: 75c, Clavulinopsis sp. 90c, Cortinarius sp. $2, Cortinarius cf. $3, Conocybe spp. $6, Galerina paludosa.

2007, Jan. 15		**Perf. 14¼**	
3559-3562	A621	Set of 4	5.00	5.00
		Souvenir Sheet	
3563	A621	$6 multi	4.50	4.50

Pres. John F. Kennedy (1917-63) — A622

No. 3564, $3 — Kennedy as Congressman: a, Wearing pattern tie. b, At microphones. c, Wearing t-shirt. d, Wearing striped tie.

No. 3565, $3, horiz.: a, PT-109. b, PT-109 crew. c, Kennedy in boat. d, Japanese destroyer.

2007, Jan. 15		**Perf. 13¼**	
		Sheets of 4, #a-d	
3564-3565	A622	Set of 2	17.00	17.00

New Year 2007 (Year of the Pig) A623

2007, Feb. 18		**Perf. 14**	
3566	A623	$1.50 multi	1.10	1.10

Printed in sheets of 4.

Map Type of 1977-78
Inscribed "St. Vincent" at Bottom
Map of St. Vincent
Denomination at Upper Left
Perf. 14½x14¼

2007-08		**Litho.**	**Unwmk.**
3566A	A76	30c grn bl, lt bl & blk		100.00

Inscribed "Grenadines of St. Vincent" at Bottom
Map of Bequia

3566B	A76	10c org, lt org & blk	300.00	60.00
3566C	A76	30c org, lt org & blk	50.00	25.00

Map of Mayreau amd Tobago Cays
Denomination at Lower Left

3566D	A76	10c org, lt org & blk	90.00	50.00

Denomination With Thick Numerals at Lower Left

3566E	A76	30c org, lt org & blk	100.00	—

Denomination With Thin Numerals in Center of Stamp

3566F	A76	30c org, lt org & blk		100.00

Earliest known uses: No. 3566A, 11/29; No. 3566B, 3/3; No. 3566C, 2/5/08; No. 3566D, 4/12; No. 3566E, 11/29; No. 3566F, 12/31. No. 3566F exists with denomination shifted to the left.

Birds — A624

No. 3567: a, Bahama yellowthroat. b, Arrow-headed warbler. c, Northern jacana. d, Loggerhead kingbird. $6, Louisiana waterthrush.

2007, Mar. 12	**Litho.**	**Perf. 14**	
3567	A624	$2 Sheet of 4, #a-d	6.50	6.50
		Souvenir Sheet	
3568	A624	$6 multi	4.75	4.75

Butterflies — A625

No. 3569: a, Ancyluris jurgensenii. b, Arcas cypria. c, Stalachtis phlegia. d, Xamia xami. $5, Theritas coronata.

2007, Mar. 12			
3569	A625	$2 Sheet of 4, #a-d	6.50	6.50
		Souvenir Sheet	
3570	A625	$5 multi	4.00	4.00

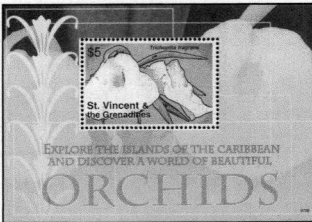

Orchids — A626

No. 3571, vert.: a, Stanhopea grandiflora. b, Psychopsis papilio. c, Vanilla planifolia. d, Tetramicra canaliculata. $5, Trichopilia fragrans.

2007, Mar. 12			
3571	A626	$2 Sheet of 4, #a-d	6.50	6.50
		Souvenir Sheet	
3572	A626	$5 multi	4.00	4.00

Miniature Sheet

Ferrari Automobiles, 60th Anniv. — A627

No. 3573: a, 1968 Dino 166 F2. b, 1958 246 F1. c, 1977 308 GTS. d, 1966 365 P Speciale. e, 2002 Enzo Ferrari. f, 1987 F40. g, 1993 348 Spider. h, 1951 212 Inter.

2007, May 1		**Perf. 13½**	
3573	A627	$1.40 Sheet of 8, #a-h	8.50	8.50

Concorde — A628

Without Gum
Litho. & Embossed

2007, May 1		**Die Cut Perf. 7¾**	
3574	A628	$20 gold & multi	15.00	15.00

Wedding of Queen Elizabeth II and Prince Philip, 60th Anniv. A629

No. 3575: a, Couple in profile. b, Couple, queen wearing tiara. $6, Couple, vert.

2007, May 1   Litho.   Perf. 14
3575 A629 $1.40 Pair, #a-b   2.10 2.10
Souvenir Sheet
3576 A629 $6 multi   4.75 4.75
No. 3575 was printed in sheets containing three of each stamp.

Princess Diana (1961-97) — A630

No. 3577 — Diana wearing: a, Red dress. b, Blue pinstriped jacket. c, Black and white dress. d, White jacket.
No. 3578, $6, Diana wearing black beret. No. 3579, $6, Diana wearing hat in black and white photograph.

2007, May 1
3577 A630 $2 Sheet of 4, #a-d   6.25 6.25
Souvenir Sheets
3578-3579 A630 Set of 2   9.25 9.25

2007 ICC Cricket World Cup, West Indies — A631

Cricket players: No. 3580, 30c, Cameron Cuffy. No. 3581, 30c, Ian Allen. $1.05, Neil Williams. No. 3583, $1.35, Wilfred Slack. No. 3584, $1.35, Michael Findlay. No. 3585, $1.65, Winston Davis. No. 3586, $1.65, Nixon McLean. $2.10, Alphonso (Alfie) Roberts. $6, Arnos Vale Stadium, horiz.

2007, May 1   Perf. 13¼
3580-3587 A631 Set of 8   7.50 7.50
Souvenir Sheet
3588 A631 $6 multi   4.50 4.50

Pope Benedict XVI — A632

2007, July 5
3589 A632 $1.50 multi   1.10 1.10
Printed in sheets of 8.

Miniature Sheet

Elvis Presley (1935-77) — A633

No. 3590 — Presley: a, Wearing dark shirt, sepia photograph. b, Wearing sweater, black and white photograph. c, Wearing sweater, sepia photograph. d, Wearing striped shirt. e, Wearing suit and tie. f, Playing guitar.

2007, July 5   Perf. 14¼
3590 A633 $1.40 Sheet of 6, #a-f   6.00 6.00

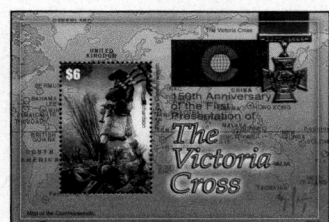

Victoria Cross, 150th Anniv. — A634

No. 3591 — Victoria Cross, recipients and flags of home country: a, Capt. Havildar Lachhiman Gurung, Nepal. b, Ernest Alvia (Smokey) Smith, Canada. c, Nk. Yeshwant Ghadge, India. d, Lt. Col. Eric Charles Twelves Wilson, Great Britain. e, Warrant Officer Class 2 Keith Payne, Australia. f, Lance Corporal Rambahadur Limbu, Nepal.
$6, Piper James Richardson.

2007, Oct. 24   Perf. 13¼
3591 A634 $1.40 Sheet of 6, #a-f 6.00 6.00
Souvenir Sheet
3592 A634 $6 multi   4.75 4.75

Miniature Sheet

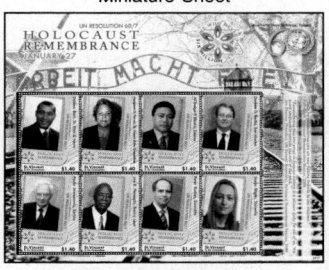

Intl. Holocaust Remembrance Day — A635

No. 3593 — United Nations delegates: a, Delano Bart, St. Kitts & Nevis. b, Margaret H. Ferrari, St. Vincent & the Grenadines. c, Ali'ioaiga F. Elisaia, Samoa. d, Daniele D. Bodini, San Marino. e, Pavle Jevremovic, Serbia. f, Joe R. Pemagbi, Sierra Leone. g, Peter Burian, Slovakia. h, Sanja Stiglic, Slovenia.

2007, Nov. 14
3593 A635 $1.40 Sheet of 8, #a-h   8.00 8.00

Christmas — A636

Paintings: 20c, The Nativity and the Arrival of the Magi, by Giovanni di Pietro. 70c, The Annunciation, by Benozzo Gozzoli. 90c, The Nativity, by Gozzoli. $1.10, The Journey of the Magi, by Sassetta.

2007, Dec. 3   Perf. 12
3594-3597 A636 Set of 4   2.00 2.00

Insects — A637

Designs: 5c, Bumblebee. 10c, Praying mantis. 30c, Firefly, vert. $1.35, Green darner dragonfly, vert.

2007, Dec. 4   Perf. 13¼
3598-3601 A637 Set of 4   1.40 1.40

New Year 2008 (Year of the Rat) A638

2008, Jan. 8   Litho.   Perf. 12
3602 A638 $1.50 multi   1.10 1.10
Printed in sheets of 4.

Miniature Sheet

2008 Summer Olympics, Beijing — A639

No. 3603 — 1952 Summer Olympics: a, Bob Mathias, decathlon gold medalist. b, Poster. c, Josy Barthel, 800-meter gold medalist. d, Lis Hartel, dressage silver medalist.

2008, Jan. 8   Perf. 14
3603 A639 $1.40 Sheet of 4, #a-d   4.00 4.00

America's Cup Yacht Races, Valencia, Spain — A640

No. 3604 — Various yachts with denomination in: a, $1.20, Red. b, $1.80, White. c, $3, Light blue. d, $5, Orange brown.

2008, Jan. 10   Perf. 13¼
3604 A640 Block of 4, #a-d   8.00 8.00

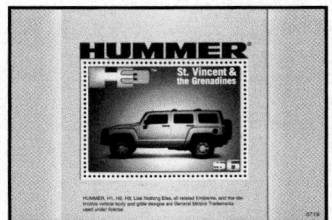

Hummer H3 — A641

Hummer H3 going: a, Uphill, denomination at UL. b, Over rocks. c, In water. d, Uphill, denomination at UR.
$6, Hummer H3 on level ground.

2008, Jan. 10
3605 A641 $1.50 Sheet of 4, #a-d   4.25 4.25
Souvenir Sheet
3606 A641 $6 multi   4.75 4.75

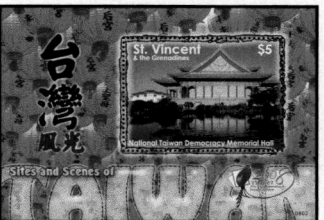

Sites and Scenes of Taiwan — A642

No. 3607, vert.: a, Taipei 101 Building. b, Pagoda. c, High speed railway. d, Lion dance.
$5, National Taiwan Democracy Memorial Hall.

2008, Feb. 8   Perf. 11¼x11½
3607 A642 $1.50 Sheet of 4, #a-d   4.25 4.25
Souvenir Sheet
Perf. 13¼
3608 A642 $5 multi   3.75 3.75
2008 Taipei Intl. Stamp Exhibition. No. 3607 contains four 30x40mm stamps.

Souvenir Sheet

Ocean Liners — A643

No. 3609: a, Queen Victoria. b, Queen Elizabeth 2. c, Queen Mary 2.

2008, May 1   Perf. 13¼
3609 A643 $3 Sheet of 3, #a-c   6.75 6.75

Miniature Sheet

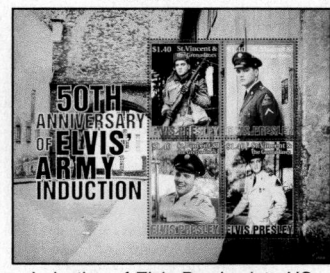

Induction of Elvis Presley into US Army, 50th Anniv. — A644

No. 3610 — Presley: a, Holding rifle. b, Standing against wall. c, In car. d, Standing next to car.

2008, May 1
3610 A644 $1.40 Sheet of 4, #a-d   4.00 4.00

Miniature Sheet

Pope Benedict XVI — A645

No. 3611 — Items in background: a, Cross at LL. b, Blue line near Pope's mouth. c, Tassel at left. d, Shell at left.

2008, May 1
3611 A645 $2 Sheet of 4, #a-d   5.50 5.50

Miniature Sheet

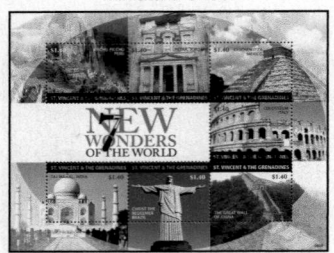

Seven New Wonders of the World — A646

No. 3612: a, Machu Picchu, Peru. b, Petra, Jordan. c, Chichén Itza, Mexico. d, Roman Colosseum, Italy. e, Taj Mahal, India. f, Christ the Redeemer Statue, Brazil. g, Great Wall of China.

2008, May 1   *Perf. 11½*
3612 A646 $1.40 Sheet of 7, #a-g   7.50 7.50

University of the West Indies, 60th Anniv. — A647

Designs: 10c, University crest. 30c, Diploma. 90c, UWDEC Media Center, horiz. $1.05, 60th anniv. emblem.
$6, Crest, diploma, 60th anniv. emblem, horiz.

2008, June 27   *Perf. 12¾*
3613-3616 A647   Set of 4   1.75 1.75
Souvenir Sheet
3617 A647 $6 multi   4.50 4.50

Miniature Sheets

2008 European Soccer Championships — A648

No. 3618 — Teams and flags of: a, Czech Republic. b, Turkey. c, Austria. d, Croatia. e, Switzerland. f, Portugal. g, Poland. h, Germany. i, France. j, Netherlands. k, Greece. l, Sweden. m, Romania. n, Italy. o, Russia. p, Spain.
No. 3619 — Austria team with flag at: a, LR. b, LL. c, UR. d, UL. e, Tivoli Stadium. f, St. Jakob Park Stadium (stadium name at top).
No. 3620 — Croatia team with flag at: a, LR. b, LL. c, UR. d, UL. e, Stade de Geneve.
No. 3621 — Czech Republic team with flag at: a, LR. b, LL. c, UR. d, UL. e, Stade de Suisse Wankdorf.
No. 3622 — France team with flag at: a, LR. b, LL. c, UR. d, UL. e, Stade de Geneve.
No. 3623 — Germany team with flag at: a, LR. b, LL. c, UR. d, UL. e, Worthersee Stadium Hypo Arena.
No. 3624 — Greece team with flag at: a, LR. b, LL. c, UR. d, UL.
No. 3625 — Italy team with flag at: a, LR. b, LL. c, UR. d, UL.
No. 3626 — Netherlands team with flag at: a, LR. b, LL. c, UR. d, UL.
No. 3627 — Poland team with flag at: a, LR. b, LL. c, UR. d, UL. e, Wals-Siezenheim Stadium. f, St. Jakob Park Stadium (stadium name at bottom).
No. 3628 — Portugal team with flag at: a, LR. b, LL. c, UR. d, UL.
No. 3629 — Romania team with flag at: a, LR. b, LL. c, UR. d, UL.

No. 3630 — Russia team with flag at: a, LR. b, LL. c, UR. d, UL.
No. 3631 — Spain team with flag at: a, LR. b, LL. c, UR. d, UL. e, Ernst Happel Stadium.
No. 3632 — Sweden team with flag at: a, LR. b, LL. c, UR. d, UL.
No. 3633 — Switzerland team with flag at: a, LR. b, LL. c, UR. d, UL.
No. 3634 — Turkey team with flag at: a, LR. b, LL. c, UR. d, UL.

2008, Aug. 1   *Perf. 13½*
3618 A648 65c Sheet of 16, #a-p   8.00 8.00
3619 A648 $1.40 Sheet of 6, #3619a-3619f   6.50 6.50
3620 A648 $1.40 Sheet of 6, #3619e, 3620a-3620e   6.50 6.50
3621 A648 $1.40 Sheet of 6, #3619e, 3621a-3621e   6.50 6.50
3622 A648 $1.40 Sheet of 6, #3619e, 3622a-3622e   6.50 6.50
3623 A648 $1.40 Sheet of 6, #3619f, 3623a-3623e   6.50 6.50
3624 A648 $1.40 Sheet of 6, #3621e, 3623e, 3624a-3624d   6.50 6.50
3625 A648 $1.40 Sheet of 6, #3620e, 3623e, 3625a-3625d   6.50 6.50
3626 A648 $1.40 Sheet of 6, #3622e, 3623e, 3626a-3626d   6.50 6.50
3627 A648 $1.40 Sheet of 6, #3627a-3627f   6.50 6.50
3628 A648 $1.40 Sheet of 6, #3621e, 3627e, 3628a-3628d   6.50 6.50
3629 A648 $1.40 Sheet of 6, #3620e, 3627e, 3629a-3629d   6.50 6.50
3630 A648 $1.40 Sheet of 6, #3622e, 3627e, 3630a-3630d   6.50 6.50
3631 A648 $1.40 Sheet of 6, #3619f, 3631e, 3631a-3631e   6.50 6.50
3632 A648 $1.40 Sheet of 6, #3621e, 3631e, 3632a-3632d   6.50 6.50
3633 A648 $1.40 Sheet of 6, #3620e, 3631e, 3633a-3633d   6.50 6.50
3634 A648 $1.40 Sheet of 6, #3622e, 3631e, 3634a-3634d   6.50 6.50
Nos. 3618-3634 (17)   112.00 112.00

Kingstown Cooperative Credit Union, 50th Anniv. A649

Credit Union emblem and: 10c, Children. 30c, Man, vert. 90c, Woman, vert. $1.05, Man wearing sunglasses, vert.
$6, Credit Union Building.

Perf. 12½x12¾, 12¾x12½
2008, Sept. 1
3635-3638 A649   Set of 4   1.75 1.75
Souvenir Sheet
3639 A649 $6 multi   4.50 4.50

Miniature Sheets

Space Exploration, 50th Anniv. (in 2007) — A650

No. 3640, $1.40: a, Space suit of Valentina Tereshkova. b, Tereshkova wearing black suit. c, Vostok 6. d, Tereshkova in space suit and helmet. e, Statue of Tereshkova. f, Tereshkova in space suit without helmet.
No. 3641, $1.40: a, Pioneer 11. b, Pioneer 10 on Atlas Centaur 27 rocket. c, Pioneer plaque. d, Pioneer 10. e, Technical drawing of Pioneer 10 and Pioneer 11. f, Pioneer program.
No. 3642, $1.40: a, Viking 1 on Titan IIIE Centaur rocket. b, Viking 1 orbiter and lander technical drawing. c, Viking 1 lander firing retrorockets. d, Viking 1 above Mars. e, Viking 1 lander technical drawing. f, Picture from Viking 1.
No. 3643, $2: a, Freedom 7 capsule. b, Astronaut Alan Shepard. c, Vostok. d, Cosmonaut Yuri Gagarin.
No. 3644, $2: a, Luna 2. b, Luna 2 ball. c, Lift-off of Luna 2. d, Luna 2 above Moon.
No. 3645, $2: a, Mariner 4 Mars Encounter Imaging Geometry. b, Mariner 4. c, Lift-off of Mariner 4. d, Mariner 4 and Mars.

2008, Oct. 29   *Perf. 14¼*
Sheets of 6, #a-f
3640-3642 A650   Set of 3   19.50 19.50
Sheets of 4, #a-d
3643-3645 A650   Set of 3   18.50 18.50

Christmas — A651

Crèche scenes: 75c, Adoration of the Shepherds. 90c, Angel in manger. $2, Adoration of the Shepherds, diff. $3, Holy Family.

2008, Dec. 8   *Perf. 14*
3646-3649 A651   Set of 4   5.00 5.00

Inauguration of US Pres. Barack Obama — A652

Designs: Nos. 3650, 3652a, Pres. Obama and US flag. $2.75, Pres. Obama, US flag and statue of Abraham Lincoln (26x34mm). No. 3652b, Vice-president Joseph Biden.

Perf. 14x14¾, 12¼x11¾ (#3651)
2009, Jan. 20
3650 A652 $1.75 multi   1.40 1.40
3651 A652 $2.75 multi   2.10 2.10
Souvenir Sheet
3652 A652 $6.50 Sheet of 2, #a-b   10.00 10.00

No. 3650 was printed in sheets of 9; No. 3651, in sheets of 4.

Miniature Sheets

New Year 2009 (Year of the Ox) A653

2009, Jan. 26   *Perf. 12*
3653 A653 $2.50 multi   1.90 1.90
Printed in sheets of 4.

St. Vincent Coat of Arms — A654

2009, Feb. 20   *Perf. 14x14¾*
3654 A654 $1.30 purple + label   1.00 1.00
Printed in sheets of 8 + 8 labels. The labels could be personalized.

Miniature Sheet

Juventus Soccer Team — A655

No. 3655: a, Goalie. b, Three players with gold shirts, one raising fist. c, Three players with gold shirts, one sticking out tongue. d, Four players with gold shirts, one Fans. f, Players in striped shirts, one with fist and open mouth. g, Players in striped shirts, one with arms extended. h, Player in striped shirt kicking ball.

2009, Apr. 23   *Perf. 13½*
3655 A655 $1.50 Sheet of 8, #a-h, + central label   9.00 9.00

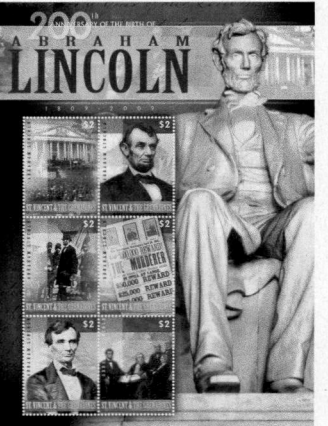

Pres. Abraham Lincoln (1809-65) — A656

No. 3656: a, Inauguration of Lincoln. b, Lincoln with beard. c, Lincoln visiting troops. d, Reward poster for Lincoln's assassin. e, Lincoln without beard. f, Lincoln and four men.
$6, Statue of Lincoln from Lincoln Memorial.

2009, Apr. 23   *Perf. 14¼x14¾*
3656 A656 $2 Sheet of 6, #a-f   9.50 9.50
Souvenir Sheet
                                   Perf. 14¼
3657 A656 $6 multi   4.75 4.75
No. 3657 contains one 38x50mm stamp.

Miniature Sheet

Felix Mendelssohn (1809-47),
Composer — A657

No. 3658: a, A Midsummer's Night Dream, painting by David Scott. b, Portrait of Mendelssohn, by Eduard Magnus. c, Portrait of Cécile Jeanrenaud, wife of Mendelssohn, by Magnus. d, Score of "On Wings of Song." e, Gewandhausorchester. f, Church of the Holy Ghost, drawing by Mendelssohn.

2009, May 18   **Perf. 11¼x11½**
3658 A657 $2.50 Sheet of 6,
          #a-f   11.50 11.50

Miniature Sheet

Pope Benedict XVI — A658

No. 3659 — Pope Benedict XVI: a, $1.50. b, $2. c, $2.50. d, $3.

2009, May 18   **Perf. 11½**
3659 A658 Sheet of 4, #a-d   7.00 7.00

Miniature Sheet

First Man on the Moon, 40th
Anniv. — A659

No. 3660: a, US 2002 Ohio state quarter. b, Apollo 11 Command Module. c, Apollo 11 patch. d, Apollo 11 Lunar Module. e, Drawing of Apollo 11 Command and Lunar Modules. f, Astronaut Neil Armstrong.

2009, May 18   **Perf. 13¼**
3660 A659 $2 Sheet of 6, #a-f   9.50 9.50

Miniature Sheets

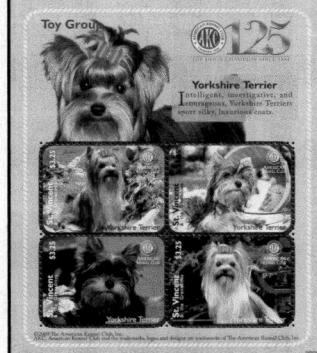

Dogs — A660

No. 3661: a, Yorkshire terrier. b, German shepherd. c, Golden retriever. d, Beagle. e, Dachshund. f, Boxer. g, Poodle. h, Shih tzu. i, Miniature schnauzer.
No. 3662 — Yorkshire terrier: a, With flowers, wearing ribbon. b, With basket at right. c, With flower at left. d, With berries at left, wearing ribbon.

2009, May 18   **Perf. 11½**
3661 A660 $1.60 Sheet of 9,
          #a-i   11.00 11.00
3662 A660 $3.25 Sheet of 4,
          #a-d   9.00   9.00

A661

A662

Michael Jackson (1958-2009),
Singer — A663

No. 3663, 45c: a, Wearing brown striped suit. b, Wearing hat.
No. 3664, 90c: a, Holding microphone. b, Wearing black sweater.
No. 3665, $1.50: a, Wearing jacket and white shirt. b, Wearing red and gold jacket.
No. 3666, $4: a, With goggles on hat. b, Wearing red and gold jacket and white glove.
No. 3667: a, $2.25, Making fist. b, $2.25, Singing. c, $2.75, As "a." d, $2.75, As "b."

No. 3668: a, With microphone in front of chin. b, Holding microphone. c, Pointing. d, With lights in background.

Horiz. Pairs, #a-b

2009   **Perf. 14¼x14¾**
3663-3666 A661 Set of 4   10.50 10.50
Miniature Sheets
Perf. 11½
3667 A662 Sheet of 4, #a-d   7.50 7.50
3668 A663 $2.50 Sheet of 4,
          #a-d   7.50 7.50
Issued: Nos. 3663-3666, 7/7; Nos. 3667-3668, 7/17. Nos. 3663-3666 were each printed in sheets containing two pairs. Compare with Type A125.

Miniature Sheet

Teenage Mutant Ninja Turtles, 25th
Anniv. — A664

No. 3669: a, Michelangelo. b, Donatello. c, Leonardo. d, Raphael.

2009, July 15   **Perf. 11½x12**
3669 A664 $2.50 Sheet of 4, #a-
          d   7.75 7.75

A665

A666

A667

A668

Elvis Presley (1935-77) — A669

No. 3670 — Presley and: a, "L." b, "V." c, "I." d, "S."

2009, July 15   **Perf. 13½**
3670 A665 $2.50 Sheet of 4,
          #a-d   7.75 7.75
Souvenir Sheets
Perf. 14¼
3671 A666 $6 multi   4.75 4.75
3672 A667 $6 multi   4.75 4.75
3673 A668 $6 multi   4.75 4.75
3674 A669 $6 multi   4.75 4.75
    Nos. 3671-3674 (4)   19.00 19.00

Preservation of Polar Regions and
Glaciers — A670

No. 3675: a, Penguin diving, two penguins swimming. b, Nine penguins. c, Three penguins, two with wings extended. d, Adult penguin feeding juvenile.
$6, Five penguins.

2009, Aug. 1   **Perf. 13½**
3675 A670 $3 Sheet of 4, #a-d 9.00 9.00
Souvenir Sheet
3676 A670 $6 multi   4.50 4.50
No. 3676 contains one 38x51mm stamp.

Birds
A671

Designs: $1.20, White-rumped sandpiper. $1.80, Tricolored heron. No. 3679, $3, Masked booby. $5, Red-footed booby, vert. No. 3681, vert: a, Brown pelican. b, Great blue heron. c, Snowy egret. d, Pied-billed grebe. No. 3682, vert.: a, Ring-billed gull. b, Short-billed dowitcher.

2009, Aug. 1	**Litho.**		**Perf. 12**
3677-3680	A671	Set of 4	8.25 8.25
3681	A671	$2.50 Sheet of 4, #a-d	7.50 7.50

Souvenir Sheet

3682	A671	$3 Sheet of 2, #a-b	4.50 4.50

For overprint, see No. 3700.

Miniature Sheet

Stamp Expo 400, Albany, New York — A672

No. 3683: a, Samuel de Champlain (c. 1567-1635), explorer. b, Robert Fulton (1765-1815), steamboat builder. c, Henry Hudson (d. 1611), explorer. d, Ships, US #372.

2009, Sept. 18			**Perf. 11½**
3683	A672	$2.50 Sheet of 4, #a-d	7.50 7.50

Christmas
A673

Designs: 90c, Magi on camels. $1.80, Holy Family. $2.50, Adoration of the Magi. $3, Madonna and Child.

2009, Dec. 10			**Perf. 13x13¼**
3684-3687	A673	Set of 4	6.25 6.25

Miniature Sheets

2010 World Cup Soccer Championships, South Africa — A674

No. 3688, $1.75 — Team from: a, Australia. b, Japan. c, North Korea. d, South Korea. e, Honduras. f, Mexico. g, United States. h, New Zealand.
No. 3689, $1.75 — Team from: a, South Africa. b, Brazil. c, Spain. d, Netherlands. e, Italy. f, Germany. g, Argentina. h, England.
No. 3690, $1.75 — Team from: a, Denmark. b, France. c, Greece. d, Portugal. e, Serbia. f, Slovakia. g, Slovenia. h, Switzerland.
No. 3691, $1.75 — Team from: a, Algeria. b, Cameroon. c, Ivory Coast. d, Ghana. e, Nigeria. f, Chile. g, Paraguay. h, Uruguay.

Sheets of 8, #a-h, + Central Label

2010, Jan. 20			**Perf. 14¼**
3688-3691	A674	Set of 4	45.00 45.00

Ferrari Automobiles and Parts — A675

No. 3692, $1.25: a, Engine of 1970 312 B. b, 1970 312 B.
No. 3693, $1.25: a, Engine of 1973 Dino 308 GT4. b, 1973 Dino 308 GT4.
No. 3694, $1.25: a, Shift console of 1976 400 Automatic. b, 1976 400 Automatic.
No. 3695, $1.25: a, Engine of 1981 126 CX. b, 1981 126 CX.

Vert. Pairs, #a-b

2010, Feb. 18	**Litho.**		**Perf. 12**
3692-3695	A675	Set of 4	8.00 8.00

Miniature Sheets

Inauguration of US Pres. John F. Kennedy, 50th Anniv. — A676

No. 3696: a, White House Oval Office. b, Pres. Kennedy. c, Jacqueline Kennedy. d, Lady Bird Johnson. e, Vice-president Lyndon B. Johnson. f, Capitol Building.
No. 3697: a, Pres. Kennedy. b, John F. Kennedy Presidential Library and Museum, Boston. c, Statue of Pres. Kennedy, Regents Park, London. d, Presidential seal.

2010, Mar. 17			**Perf. 13¼**
3696	A676	$2 Sheet of 6, #a-f	9.00 9.00
3697	A676	$2.75 Sheet of 4, #a-d	8.25 8.25

Miniature Sheets

A677

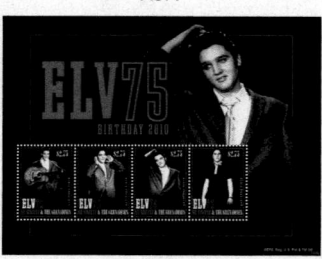

Elvis Presley (1935-77) — A678

No. 3698: a, Without guitar, facing right. b, With guitar, microphone at right. c, With guitar, microphone at left. d, Without guitar, facing left.
No. 3699: a, With guitar. b, With hands near ears. c, Scratching head. d, With arms at side.

2010, Mar. 17			**Perf. 11¼x11½**
3698	A677	$2.75 Sheet of 4, #a-d	8.25 8.25
3699	A678	$2.75 Sheet of 4, #a-d	8.25 8.25

No. 3681 Overprinted With Map of Haiti and "Haiti Earthquake Relief Fund"
Method and Perf. As Before

2010, Jan. 15			
3700	A671	$2.50 Sheet of 4, #a-d	7.75 7.75

A679

Designs: 25c, Huito. 80c, Tiny bladderwort. $1, Purple coral tree. $5, Apple guava. No. 3705, horiz.: a, Soufriere tree. b, Guajacum. c, Nipplefruit. d, Alpine bladderwort. e, Fetid passion flower. f, Shoreline purslane.

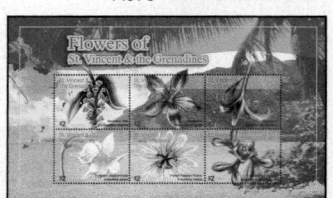

Flowers — A680

2010, Apr. 23	**Litho.**		**Perf. 14x14¾**
3701-3704	A679	Set of 4	5.25 5.25
		Perf. 14¾x14	
3705	A680	$2 Sheet of 6, #a-f	9.00 9.00

Orchids — A681

Designs: 25c, Phragmipedium popowii. 80c, Cattleya dowiana. $1, Brassavola subulifolia. $5, Brassavola acaulis. No. 3710, horiz.: a, Cattleya gaskelliana. b, Cattleya aurea. c, Cattleya mendelii. d, Cattleya schrodera. e, Cypripedium dickinsonianum. f, Phragmipedium longifolium.

2010, Apr. 23	**Litho.**		**Perf. 13¼x13**
3706-3709	A681	Set of 4	5.25 5.25
		Perf. 13x13¼	
3710	A681	$2 Sheet of 6, #a-f	9.00 9.00

Marine Life
A682

Designs: 25c, Leatherback turtle. 80c, Caesar grunt. $1, Atlantic tarpon. $5, Moray eel. No. 3715: a, Caribbean reef shark. b, Loggerhead sea turtle. c, Great barracuda. d, Caribbean lobster. e, Royal gramma. f, Southern stingray.

2010, Apr. 23	**Litho.**		**Perf. 14¾x14**
3711-3714	A682	Set of 4	5.25 5.25
3715	A682	$2 Sheet of 6, #a-f	9.00 9.00

Antverpia 2010 National and European Championship of Philately, Antwerp, Belgium (No. 3715).

Girl Guides, Cent. — A683

No. 3716: a, Two Girl Guides. b, Four Girl Guides. c, Four Girl Guides and trefoil. d, Three Girl Guides.
$6, One Girl Guide, vert.

2010, June 4			**Perf. 13x13¼**
3716	A683	$2.75 Sheet of 4, #a-d	8.25 8.25

Souvenir Sheet
Perf. 13¼x13

3717	A683	$6 multi	4.50 4.50

Miniature Sheet

Accession to Throne of King George V, Cent. — A684

No. 3718: a, King William IV. b, Queen Victoria. c, King Edward VII. d, King George V on coin. e, Portrait of King George V. f, Statue of King George V.

2010, Sept. 1			**Perf. 11½**
3718	A684	$2 Sheet of 6, #a-f	9.00 9.00

Miniature Sheets

A685

Mother Teresa (1910-97), Humanitarian, and Pope John Paul II (1920-2005) — A686

No. 3719 — With dove above Mother Teresa; Pope John Paul II: a, To right of Mother Teresa. b, Touching head of Mother Teresa. c, Wearing miter. d, Holding Mother Teresa's hand.
No. 3720 — Without dove above Mother Teresa; Pope John Paul II: a, Wearing miter. b, Touching head of Mother Teresa. c, At left, holding hand of Mother Teresa. d, At right, holding hand of Mother Teresa.

2010, Sept. 1			**Perf. 13x13¼**
3719	A685	$2.75 Sheet of 4, #a-d	8.25 8.25
3720	A686	$2.75 Sheet of 4, #a-d	8.25 8.25

Miniature Sheet

Kyle Busch, NASCAR Race Car
Driver — A687

No. 3721 — Busch: a, In car wearing helmet. b, With arms raised, wearing helmet. c, Wearing sunglasses. d, Wearing cap.

2010, Oct. 5   **Perf. 12x11½**
3721 A687 $2.75 Sheet of 4, #a-
d   8.25 8.25

Paintings of Sandro Botticelli (1445-
1510) — A688

No. 3722, vert.: a, The Annunciation. b, Portrait of a Young Man. c, Portrait of Simonetta Vespucci. d, Die Verstossene (The Outcast). $6, Mystic Nativity.

2010, Oct. 5   **Perf. 12x11½**
3722 A688 $2.50 Sheet of 4, #a-
d   7.50 7.50
      Souvenir Sheet
          Perf. 13½
3723 A688 $6 multi   4.50 4.50
No. 3722 contains four 30x40mm stamps.

Henri Dunant (1828-1910), Founder of
Red Cross — A689

No. 3724 — Nurse, soldiers and Dunant in: a, Greenish black. b, Brown. c, Violet brown. d, Blue black.
$6, Florence Nightingale, Clara Barton and Dunant.

2010, Oct. 5   **Perf. 12**
3724 A689 $2.50 Sheet of 4, #a-
d   7.50 7.50
      Souvenir Sheet
3725 A689 $6 multi   4.50 4.50

Miniature Sheets

Characters in Star Trek
Movies — A690

No. 3726, $2.75 — Star Trek II, The Wrath of Khan: a, Saavik. b, Spock and Dr. Leonard McCoy. c, Capt. James T. Kirk. d, Khan Noonien Singh.
No. 3727, $2.75 — Star Trek IV, The Voyage Home: a, Montgomery Scott. b, Spock. c, Kirk. d, McCoy.

   Perf. 12x11½, 11½ (#3727)
2010, Oct. 5   **Sheets of 4, #a-d**
3726-3727 A690   Set of 2   16.50 16.50

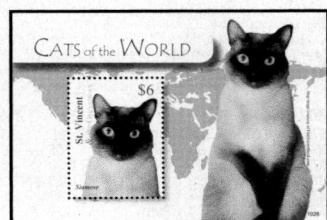

Cats — A691

No. 3728: a, Persian. b, Russian Blue. c, Chartreux. d, Bobtail. e, Selkirk Rex. f, Bengal. $6, Siamese.

2010, Oct. 5   **Perf. 12**
3728 A691 $2 Sheet of 6, #a-f   9.00 9.00
      Souvenir Sheet
3729 A691 $6 multi   4.50 4.50

Miniature Sheets

Pres. Abraham Lincoln (1809-
65) — A692

No. 3730, $2.75: a, Lincoln with hand on chin. b, Statue of Lincoln in Lincoln Memorial. c, Photograph of Lincoln without beard. d, Lincoln Memorial at dusk.
No. 3731, $2.75: a, Photograph of Lincoln with beard. b, Aerial view of Lincoln Memorial. c, First Reading of the Emancipation Proclamation of President Lincoln, painting by Francis Carpenter. d, Lincoln and US No. 1282.

     Sheets of 4, #a-d
2010, Oct. 5   **Perf. 12**
3730-3731 A692   Set of 2   16.50 16.50

Posters of Films Directed by Akira
Kurosawa (1910-98) — A693

No. 3732, $2.50: a, Shubun (Scandal). b, Subarashiki Nichiyobi (One Wonderful Sunday). c, Sugata Sanshiro (Judo Saga). d, Kakushi Toride No San Akunin (The Hidden Fortress).
No. 3733, $2.50: a, Kumonosu-jo (Throne of Blood). b, Waga Seishun Ni Kuinashi (No Regrets for Our Youth). c, Tora No o Wo Fumu Otokotachi (The Men Who Tread on the Tiger's Tail). d, Yoidore Tenshi (Drunken Angel).
No. 3734: a, Rashomon (Samurai with sword). b, Rashomon (woman with knife).

    Sheets of 4, #a-d
2010, Oct. 5   **Perf. 13¼**
3732-3733 A693   Set of 2   15.00 15.00
      Souvenir Sheet
3734 A693 $4 Sheet of 2, #a-b   6.00 6.00

Miniature Sheets

A694

Pres. Barack Obama — A695

No. 3735 — Blue frame, Pres. Obama with: a, Blue tie, microphone at right. b, Red striped tie. c, Black tie, microphone at left. d, Blue tie, flag in background.
No. 3736 — Red frame, Pres. Obama with: a, Black and white striped tie. b, Blue tie, foliage in background. c, Black and white patterned tie, red flag in background. d, Blue tie.

2010, Dec. 6   **Perf. 12x12½**
3735 A694 $2.75 Sheet of 4, #a-
d   8.25 8.25
3736 A695 $2.75 Sheet of 4, #a-
d   8.25 8.25

Christmas
A696

Paintings: 90c, Annunciation, by Domenico di Pace Beccafumi. $1.80, Adoration of the Shepherds, by Gerard van Honthorst. $2.50, Adoration of the Magi, by Guido Reni. $3, Nativity, by Domenico Ghirlandaio.

2010, Dec. 15   **Litho.**   **Perf. 12**
3737-3740 A696   Set of 4   6.25 6.25

British Monarchs
A697

Designs: No. 3741, $2, King Henry I (c. 1068-1135). No. 3742, $2, King John (1166-1216). No. 3743, $2, King Richard II (1367-1400). No. 3744, $2, King Edward V (1470-83 ?). No. 3745, $2, King Edward VI (1537-53). nO. 3746, $2, King Charles II (1630-85). No. 3747, $2, King George III (1738-1820). No. 3748, $2, King George VI (1895-1952).

2011, Jan. 20   **Perf. 13 Syncopated**
3741-3748 A697   Set of 8   12.00 12.00
Nos. 3741-3748 each were printed in sheets of 8 + central label.

A698

Indipex 2011 Intl. Philatelic Exhibition,
New Delhi — A699

No. 3749 — Spices: a, Saffron. b, Chili peppers. c, Curry leaves. d, Turmeric. e, Peppercorns. f, Cinnamon.
No. 3750 — Animals: a, Indian peafowl. b, Indian elephant. c, Red panda. d, Blackbuck. e, King cobra. f, Indian leopard. g, Indian rhinoceros.
No. 3751— Bengal tiger with denominati at: a, LR. b, UL.

2011, Feb. 9

3749	A698	$1.85 Sheet of 6, #a-f	8.25	8.25
3750	A699	$1.85 Sheet of 7, #a-g + 2 labels	9.75	9.75

Souvenir Sheet

3751	A699	$5 Sheet of 2, #a-b	7.50	7.50

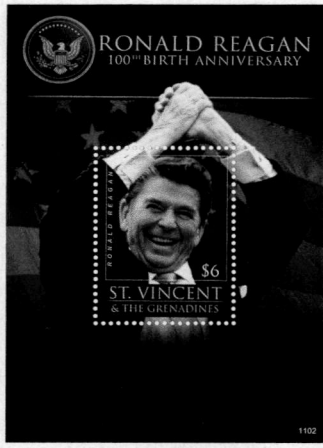

Visit to Japan of President Barack Obama — A700

No. 3752 — Pres. Obama: a, Shaking hands with Japanese Prime Minister Yukio Hatoyama. b, With Hatoyama, flags, Hatoyama waving. c, Walking with Hatoyama. d, At lectern.
$6, Pres. Obama waving.

2011, Feb. 9   *Perf. 12*

3752	A700	$2.75 Sheet of 4, #a-d	8.25	8.25

Souvenir Sheet
Perf. 12¾

3753	A700	$6 multi	4.50	4.50

No. 3753 contains one 51x38mm stamp.

Pres. Ronald Reagan (1911-2004) — A701

No. 3754, horiz. — Pres. Reagan: a, With wife, Nancy, flag and ocean in background. b, At lectern, flag in background. c, At lectern, sign in background. c, With wife on helicopter.
$6, Pres. Reagan with arms raised.

2011, Feb. 9   *Perf. 12*

3754	A701	$2.75 Sheet of 4, #a-d	8.25	8.25

Souvenir Sheet

3755	A701	$6 multi	4.50	4.50

Engagement of Prince William and Catherine Middleton — A702

Designs: No. 3756, Couple, maroon panels. No. 3757, Couple, diff., blue panels. No. 3758, $6, Couple, diff. No. 3759, $6, Prince William, vert.

2011, Feb. 11   *Perf. 12*

3756	A702	$2.50 multi	1.90	1.90

Perf. 13 Syncopated

3757	A702	$2.50 multi	1.90	1.90

Souvenir Sheets

3758-3759	A702	Set of 2	9.00	9.00

Flag of St. Vincent and the Grenadines — A703

2011, Feb. 17   *Perf. 14¾x14¼*

3760	A703	$1 multi	.75	.75

Dolphins — A704

No. 3761: a, Stenella coeruleoalba. b, Langenodelphis hosei. c, Dephinus capensis. d, Delphinus delphis. e, Stenella longirostris. f, Stenella frontalis.
$6, Grampus griseus.

2011, Feb. 17   *Perf. 13 Syncopated*

3761	A704	$2 Sheet of 6, #a-f	9.00	9.00

Souvenir Sheet
Perf. 12

3762	A704	$6 multi	4.50	4.50

Miniature Sheets

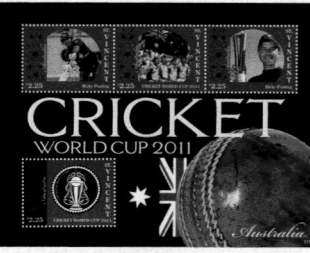

2011 World Cricket Cup, India, Bangladesh, and Sri Lanka — A705

No. 3763, $2.25 — Stamps inscribed "Australia": a, Ricky Ponting wearing helmet. b, Australia team. c, Ponting holding trophy. d, Cricket World Cup emblem.
No. 3764, $2.25 — Stamps inscribed "Bagladesh": a, Shakib Al Hasan wearing helmet. b, Al Hasan without helmet. c, Bangladesh team. d, Cricket World Cup emblem.
No. 3765, $2.25 — Stamps inscribed "England": a, Kevin Pietersen wearing helmet. b, Pietersen without helmet. c, English team. d, Cricket World Cup emblem.
No. 3766, $2.25 — Stamps inscribed "India": a, Sachin Tendulkar wearing helmet. b, Tendulkar without helmet. c, Tendulkar holding trophy. d, Cricket World Cup emblem.
No. 3767, $2.25 — Stamps inscribed "New Zealand": a, Daniel Vettori bowling. b, Vettori

wearing cap. c, New Zealand team holding trophy. d, Cricket World Cup emblem.

Sheets of 4 #a-d

2011, May 2   *Perf. 12*

3763-3767	A705	Set of 5	33.50	33.50

St. Vincent Girls' High School, Cent. A706

School crest and: 30c, 2010 steel drum orchestra. $1.05, Colette Sharlene Charles. No. 3770, $1.35, 1963 West Indian netball team, "BOA" visible on plane. No. 3770A, $1.35, 1963 West Indian netball team, "BOAC" on plane. $1.65, Beryl Baptiste, St. Vincent Director of Audit. No. 3772, $2.10, Grimble Building. No. 3773, $2.10, Betty Boyea-King, diplomat. No. 3774, $2.10, Dame Monica Dacon, deputy to Governor General.
No. 3775, $10, Mrs. Keizer and Mrs. Bowman, headmistresses of school. No. 3776, $10, Laura Smith-Moffett, headmistress. No. 3777, $10, Susan Dougan, cabinet secretary.

2011, May 16   *Perf. 12½*

3768	A706	30c multi	.25	.25
3769	A706	$1.05 multi	.75	.75
3770	A706	$1.35 multi	1.00	1.00
3770A	A706	$1.35 multi	1.00	1.00
3771	A706	$1.65 multi	1.25	1.25
3772	A706	$2.10 multi	1.60	1.60
3773	A706	$2.10 multi	1.60	1.60
3774	A706	$2.10 multi	1.60	1.60
		Nos. 3768-3774 (8)	9.05	9.05

Souvenir Sheets

3775-3777	A706	Set of 3	22.50	22.50

No. 3770A was printed in sheets of 4.

Sumo Wrestler — A707

Fish — A708

No. 3779: a, Pacific bluefin tuna. b, Koi. c, Porcupinefish. d, Cherry salmon.

2011, May 16   *Perf. 12x12½*

3778	A707	$2.75 multi	2.10	2.10

Perf. 12½x12

3779	A708	$2.75 Sheet of 4, #a-d	8.25	8.25

PhilaNippon 2011 Intl. Philatelic Exhibition, Yokohama. No. 3778 was printed in sheets of 4.

Miniature Sheets

A709

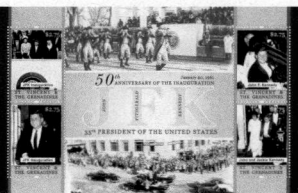

Inauguration of Pres. John F. Kennedy, 50th Anniv. — A710

No. 3780: a, Kennedy taking oath. b, Kennedy on telephone.
No. 3781: a, Kennedy with wife, Jacqueline, and Vice-President Lyndon Johnson on reviewing stand. b, Kennedy at inaugural ball, flowers in background. c, Kennedy near doorway. d, Kennedy walking with wife at inaugural ball.

2011, May 16   *Perf. 13 Syncopated*

3780	A709	$2.75 Sheet of 4, 2 each #a-b	8.25	8.25
3781	A710	$2.75 Sheet of 4, #a-d	8.25	8.25

Paintings by Michelangelo Merisi da Caravaggio (1571-1610) — A711

No. 3782: a, The Denial of Saint Peter. b, The Lute Player. c, The Fortune Teller. d, Supper at Emmaus.
$6, The Cardsharps.

2011, May 16   *Litho.*

3782	A711	$2.50 Sheet of 4, #a-d	7.50	7.50

Souvenir Sheet

3783	A711	$6 multi	4.50	4.50

Beatification of Pope John Paul II — A712

No. 3784 — Pope John Paul II with: a, Charles Eugène de Foucauld de Pontbriand (1858-1916), martyr. b, Sister Marie Simon-Pierre. c, Pope John XXIII. d, Pope Pius IX. e, Mother Teresa. f, Father Jerzy Popieluszko (1947-84), martyr.
$6, Pope John Paul II, dove, St. Peter's Basilica.

2011, May 16

3784	A712	$2 Sheet of 6, #a-f	9.00	9.00

Souvenir Sheet

3785	A712	$6 multi	4.50	4.50

Miniature Sheet

A. C. Milan Soccer Team — A713

No. 3786 — Team emblem and: a, Herbert Kilpin, team founder. b, Franco Baresi. c,

Coach Nereo Rocco and team, 1968. d, Scene from 1969 Intercontinental Cup match. e, Frank Rijkaard, Marco Van Basten, Ruud Gullit. f, Gianni Rivera. g, 1979 team. h, Van Basten. i, Scene from 1994 UEFA Champions League match.

2011, June 15   *Perf. 13¼*
3786 A713 $1.20 Sheet of 9 #a-i   8.00 8.00

A714

Wedding of Prince William and Catherine Middleton
A715

No. 3787: a, Groom. b, Bride. c, Couple.
No. 3788: a, Couple, bride waving. b, Couple, kissing.
$6, Couple in coach.

2011, June 15   *Perf. 12*
3787 A714 $1.20 Block of 4,
    #3787a-
    3787b, 2
    #3787c, + 2
    labels   3.75 3.75
3788 A715 $2.75 Pair, #a-b   4.25 4.25
     Souvenir Sheet
3789 A714 $6 multi   4.50 4.50

No. 3787 was printed in sheets containing 2 blocks. No. 3788 was printed in sheets containing two pairs.

Pres. Abraham Lincoln (1809-65) — A716

No. 3790, $2.75: a, Lincoln, denomination in brown at LL. b, Lincoln, denomination in white at LL. c, Soldiers, flag, at Battle of Fair Oaks, denomination at UR. d, Soldiers, flag and tree at Battle of Fair Oaks, denomination at UL.
No. 3791, $2.75: a, Lincoln, denomination in white at LR. b, Lincoln, denomination in brown at LR. c, Soldiers, horses, flag at Battle of Opequon, denomination at UR. d, Soldiers, horses, flag at Battle of Opequon, denomination at UL.

     Sheets of 4, #a-d

2011, July 13   *Perf. 13¼x13*
3790-3791 A716   Set of 2   16.50 16.50

     Souvenir Sheets

A717

A718

A719

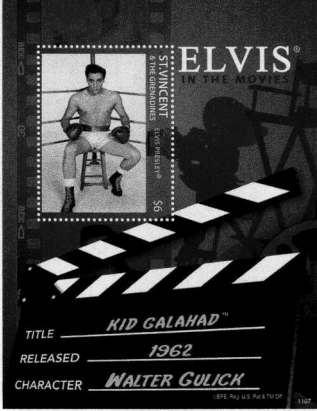

Elvis Presley (1935-77) — A720

2011, July 19   *Perf. 12¾*
3792 A717 $6 multi   4.50 4.50
3793 A718 $6 multi   4.50 4.50
3794 A719 $6 multi   4.50 4.50
3795 A720 $6 multi   4.50 4.50
    Nos. 3792-3795 (4)   18.00 18.00

     Miniature Sheets

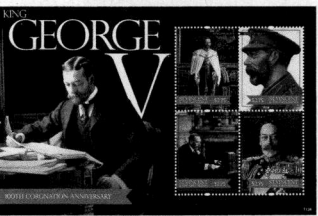

British Royalty — A721

No. 3796, $2.75 — King George V: a, Wearing robes. b, Wearing military uniform and hat. c, Seated at desk. d, Wearing uniform and medals, without hat.
No. 3797, $2.75 — King George VI: a, With Lady Elizabeth Bowes-Lyon. b, Wearing polo shirt. c, Wearing suit and tie. d, Wearing military uniform.
No. 3798, $2.75, horiz. — Queen Elizabeth II: a, Wearing red hat. b, Wearing white blouse. c, As child, in garden. d, In automobile with Prince Philip.
No. 3799, $2.75, horiz. — Prince Philip: a, Wearing uniform, waving. b, With Queen Elizabeth II. c, In palace. d, With family, 1965.

2011, July 26   *Perf. 13 Syncopated*
     Sheets of 4, #a-d
3796-3799 A721   Set of 4   32.50 32.50

     Miniature Sheets

A722

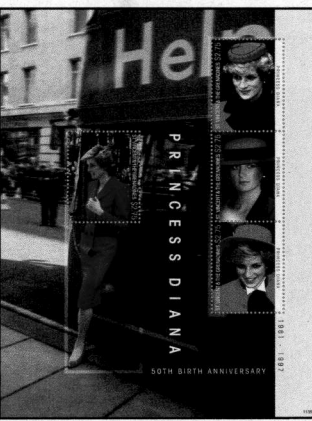

A723

No. 3800 — Princess Diana: a, Wearing striped jacket. b, Wearing dress and choker necklace. c, In vehicle. d, Wearing dark dress, no necklace.
No. 3801 — Princess Diana: a, Wearing red and black hat with veil. b, Leaving bus. c, Wearing red hat with black ribbon. d, Wearing red hat.

2011, July 28   *Perf. 12*
3800 A722 $2.75 Sheet of 4,
     #a-d   8.25 8.25
3801 A723 $2.75 Sheet of 4,
     #a-d   8.25 8.25

Visit to Germany of Pope Benedict XVI — A724

No. 3802 — Various buildings and Pope Benedict XVI: a, Wearing white vestments, with hands together. b, Wearing miter. c, Wearing white vestments, hands not visible. $6, Pope Benedict XVI waving, vert.

2011, Aug. 9   *Perf. 12*
3802 A724 $3 Sheet of 3, #a-c   6.75 6.75
     Souvenir Sheet
3803 A724 $6 multi   4.50 4.50

Sept. 11, 2001 Terrorist Attacks, 10th
Anniv. — A725

No. 3804, horiz.: a, Candles and photograph of World Trade Center at Sept. 13, 2001
New York vigil. b, People at Sept. 13, 2001
New York vigil. c, Sept. 11 Memorial at Pentagon Building. d, Person, flag and flower at
memorial in Stonycreek Township,
Pennsylvania.
$6, Firemen and flags, New York.

2011, Oct. 6   **Perf. 13x13¼**
3804 A725 $2.75 Sheet of 4,
      #a-d   8.25   8.25
Souvenir Sheet
Perf. 13¼x13
3805 A725 $6 multi   4.50   4.50

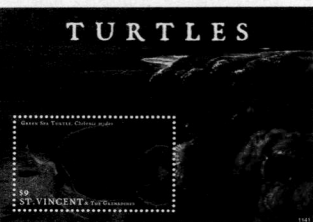

Turtles — A726

No. 3806: a, Chicken turtle. b, Diamondback
terrapin. c, Red-eared slider.
$9, Green sea turtle.

2011, Oct. 26   **Perf. 12**
3806 A726 $3 Sheet of 3, #a-c
          6.75   6.75
Souvenir Sheet
3807 A726 $9 multi   6.75   6.75

Miniature Sheets

A727

Muhammad Ali, 70th Birthday — A728

No. 3808 — Ali: a, Color photograph, wearing red gloves. b, Black-and-white photograph,
during fight. c, Color photograph, wearing
black gloves. d, Black-and-white photograph,
in training ring wearing headgear.
No. 3809 — Ali: a, Color photograph, without shirt, facing forward. b, Black-and-white
photograph, wearing bow tie. c, Color photograph, without shirt, facing right. d, Color photograph, wearing suit and tie.

2011, Nov. 2   **Perf. 13 Syncopated**
3808 A727 $2.75 Sheet of 4,
      #a-d   8.25   8.25
3809 A728 $2.75 Sheet of 4,
      #a-d   8.25   8.25

Christmas
A729

Details from paintings: 30c, Madonna and
Child, by Sandro Botticelli. 90c, Madonna
Enthroned, by Giotto di Bondone. $2,
Madonna and Child, by Carlo Crivelli. $3, Mys-
tic Nativity, by Botticelli.

2011, Nov. 2   **Perf. 12**
3810-3813 A729   Set of 4   4.75   4.75

Miniature Sheet

1908 Olympic Games, London — A730

No. 3814: a, White City Stadium. b,
Dorando Pietri. c, Erik Lemming. d, Poster for
1908 Olympic Games.

2011, Nov. 14   **Perf. 13 Syncopated**
3814 A730 $2.75 Sheet of 4,
      #a-d   8.25   8.25
2012 Summer Olympics, London.

Anoles — A731

No. 3815: a, Barbados anole. b, Martinique's anole. c, Dominican anole. d, Leopard
anole.
$9, Green anole.

2011, Nov. 14   **Perf. 12**
3815 A731 $3.50 Sheet of 4,
      #a-d   10.50 10.50
Souvenir Sheet
3816 A731 $9 multi   6.75   6.75
No. 3816 contains one 30x50mm stamp.

Statue of
Liberty,
125th
Anniv.
A732

2011, Dec. 16
3817 A732 $3 shown   2.25 2.25
Souvenir Sheet
3818 A732 $9 Statue, vert.   6.75 6.75
No. 3817 was printed in sheets of 3. No.
3818 contains one 30x50mm stamp.

Reign of Queen Elizabeth II, 60th
Anniv. — A733

No. 3819 — Queen Elizabeth II: a, With
Prince Philip. b, Wearing flowered hat. c,
Wearing sash and tiara.
$9, Queen Elizabeth II, horiz.

2012, Jan. 1
3819 A733 $3.50 Sheet of 3, #a-
      c   7.75 7.75
Souvenir Sheet
3820 A733 $9 multi   6.75 6.75
No. 3820 contains one 50x30mm stamp.

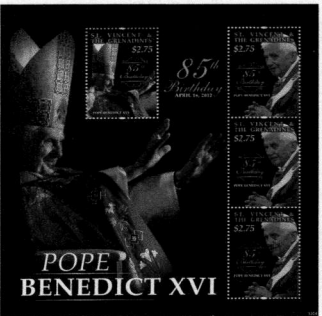

Pope Benedict XVI, 85th
Birthday — A734

No. 3821: a, Facing right, waving. b, Facing
left, wearing green vestments.
$6, Facing left, diff.

2012, Mar. 26   **Perf. 13 Syncopated**
3821 A734 $2.75 Sheet of 4,
      #3821a, 3
      #3821b   8.25 8.25
Souvenir Sheet
3822 A734 $6 multi   4.50 4.50

Miniature Sheets

A735

Elvis Presley (1935-77) — A736

No. 3823 — Presley: a, With guitar. b, Facing right, holding microphone. c, Wearing
striped shirt. d, Facing left, holding
microphone. No. 3824 — "Forever," and Presley: a, Facing right, holding microphone, "Forever" in gray. b, Wearing black jacket. c, Facing right, holding microphone, "Forever" in
white. d, Wearing red jacket.

2012, Mar. 26   **Perf. 13 Syncopated**
3823 A735 $3 Sheet of 4, #a-d   9.00 9.00
3824 A736 $3 Sheet of 4, #a-d   9.00 9.00

Miniature Sheet

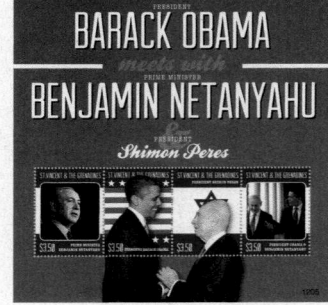

U.S. and Israeli Leaders — A737

No. 3825: a, Israeli Prime Minister Benjamin
Netanyahu. b, Pres. Barack Obama. c, Israeli
Pres. Shimon Peres, Israeli flag. d, Pres.
Obama, Prime Minister Netanyahu.

2012, May 3   **Perf. 13¼x13**
3825 A737 $3.50 Sheet of 4,
      #a-d   10.50 10.50

Miniature Sheets

French National Center for Space Studies, 50th Anniv. — A738

No. 3826, $3.50: a, SPOT satellite (denomination separated from satellite). b, SRET 2. c, Astronaut Jean-Loup Chrétien. d, JASON.
No. 3827, $3.50: a, Astronaut Claudie Haigneré. b, SPOT satellite (denomination covering part of satellite). c, Aureol 1. d, FR 1.

2012, May 3   **Perf. 14**
Sheets of 4, #a-d
3826-3827 A738   Set of 2   21.00 21.00
Nos. 3826-3827 exist imperf. Value, set $25.

Miniature Sheets

Soft Moon Landing — A739

No. 3828, $3.50: a, Lunik 3. b, Luna 10. c, Lunik 2. d, Von Braun vehicle.
No. 3829, #3.50: a, Lunik 9. b, Russian lunar module. c, Lunar orbiter. d, Imaginative spaceship.

2012, June 27   **Perf. 14**
Sheets of 4, #a-d
3828-3829 A739   Set of 2   21.00 21.00
Nos. 3828-3829 exist imperf. Value, set $25.

Miniature Sheet

Duke and Duchess of Cambridge, First Wedding Anniversary — A740

No. 3830: a, Duke of Cambridge. b, Duchess of Cambridge. c, Couple seated in coach. d, Couple standing.

2012, Sept. 5   **Perf. 13¾**
3830 A740 $2.50 Sheet of 4, #a-
            d   7.50 7.50

Butterflies — A741

No. 3831: a, Danaus plexippus. b, Euptoieta hegesia. c, Libytheana carinenta. d, Lycorea halia.
$9, Phocides pigmalion.

2012, Sept. 5   **Perf. 13¾**
3831 A741 $3.50 Sheet of 4,
            #a-d   10.50 10.50
Souvenir Sheet
3832 A741 $9 multi   6.75 6.75

Christmas
A742

Paintings by Raphael: 80c, Madonna and Child with St. Johan and St. Nicholas. $1, The Holy Family with Saints Elizabeth and John. $1.70, Madonna and Child with Saints. $2.20, The Holy Family. $2.65, The Aldobrandini Madonna.
$3.40, The Visitation.

2012, Nov. 28   **Perf. 12¾**
3833-3837 A742   Set of 5   6.25 6.25
Souvenir Sheet
3838 A742 $3.40 multi   2.50 2.50

Beetles — A743

No. 3839: a, Doryphora undata. b, Leptinotarsa lacerata. c, Chrysomela populi. d, Leptinotarsa decemlineata.
$9, Leptinotarsa puncticollis.

2013, Feb. 28   **Perf. 12**
3839 A743 $3.50 Sheet of 4,
            #a-d   10.50 10.50
Souvenir Sheet
            Perf. 12¾
3840 A743 $9 multi   6.75 6.75
No. 3840 contains one 38x51mm stamp.

Dogs — A744

No. 3841: a, Spanish mastiff. b, Poodle. c, Dachshund. d, Basenji.
$9, German shepherd.

2013, Feb. 28   **Perf. 13 Syncopated**
3841 A744 $3.50 Sheet of 4,
            #a-d   10.50 10.50
Souvenir Sheet
3842 A744 $9 multi   6.75 6.75

Coral Reefs — A745

No. 3843: a, Hawksbill turtle. b, Sea sponges and tropical fish. c, Red cushion sea star. d, Ricordea coral.
$9, Turtle, fish, and reef, horiz.

2013, Feb. 28   **Perf. 12**
3843 A745 $3.50 Sheet of 4,
            #a-d   10.50 10.50
Souvenir Sheet
3844 A745 $9 multi   6.75 6.75
No. 3844 contains one 80x30mm stamp.

Miniature Sheet

Crabs — A746

No. 3845: a, Clinging crab. b, Yellowline arrow crab. c, Redeye sponge crab. d, White-spotted hermit crab.
$9, White-spotted hermit crab, vert.

2013, Feb. 28   **Perf. 13 Syncopated**
3845 A746 $3.50 Sheet of 4,
            #a-d   10.50 10.50
Souvenir Sheet
3846 A746 $9 multi   6.75 6.75

Miniature Sheet

Shells — A747

No. 3847: a, Triton's trumpet. b, Flame auger. c, Angular triton. d, Banded tulip. e, Lion's paw scallop.

Perf. 13 Syncopated
2013, Apr. 4   **Litho.**
3847 A747 $2.75 Sheet of 5,
            #a-e   10.50 10.50
Tel Aviv 2013 Multinational Stamp Exhibition.

Images of Celestial Objects Taken by Hubble Space Telescope — A748

No. 3848, $3.25: a, NGC 6302. b, M82. c, Orion Nebula. d, Gas clouds in the Scorpius constellation.
No. 3849, $3.25: a, Eskimo Nebula. b, Carina Nebula. c, Cat's Eye Nebula. d, Cone Nebula.
No. 3850, $9, Eagle Nebula, vert. No. 3851, $9, Saturn, horiz.

2013, Apr. 4   **Litho.**   **Perf. 13¾**
Sheets of 4, #a-d
3848-3849 A748   Set of 2   19.50 19.50
Souvenir Sheets
            Perf. 12¾
3850-3851 A748   Set of 2   13.50 13.50
No. 3850 contains one 38x51mm stamp.
No. 3851 contains one 51x38mm stamp.

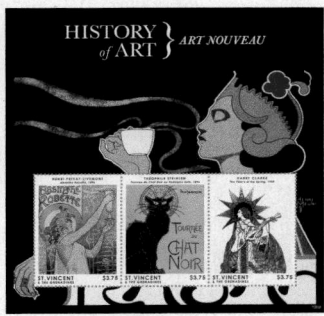

History of Art — A749

No. 3852, $3.75 — Art Nouveau: a, Absinthe Robette, by Henri Privat-Livemont. b, Tournée du Chat Noir de Rodolphe Salis, by Théophile Steinlen. c, The Year's at the Spring, by Harry Clarke.
No. 3853, $3.75 — Paintings by Gustav Klimt (1862-1918): a, The Three Ages of Woman. b, Jurisprudence. c, Judith and the Head of Holofernes.
No. 3854, $9, Ali Baba, by Aubrey Beardsley. No. 3855, $9, Job Cigarette Papers, by Alphonse Mucha, horiz.

2013, Apr. 4   **Litho.**   **Perf. 12¾**
Sheets of 3, #a-c
3852-3853 A749   Set of 2   17.00 17.00
Souvenir Sheets
3854-3855 A749   Set of 2   13.50 13.50

World Environment Day — A750

No. 3856: a, Birds. b, Leaves. c, Fish. d, Sun and clouds.
$9, Owls and leaves, vert.

2013, May 7   Litho.   Perf. 13¾
3856 A750 $3.25 Sheet of 4, #a-
d   9.75 9.75
Souvenir Sheet
Perf. 12¾
3857 A750 $9 multi   6.75 6.75
No. 3857 contains one 38x51mm stamp.

A751

Pres. John F. Kennedy (1917-63) — A752

No. 3858 — Pres. Kennedy: a, Holding paper. b, Seated in rocking chair, hands visible. c, Seated in chair, hands not visible. d, Behind lectern, pointing.
No. 3859 — Pres. Kennedy: a, With man holding medallion in box. b, Signing document. c, With Pres. Dwight D. Eisenhower. d, Standing behind lectern.
No. 3860, $9, Pres. Kennedy behind lectern, diff., denomination in blue. No. 3861, Pres. Kennedy behind lectern, diff., denomination in olive brown.

2013, May 7   Litho.   Perf. 13¾
3858 A751 $3.25 Sheet of 4,
          #a-d   9.75 9.75
3859 A752 $3.25 Sheet of 4,
          #a-d   9.75 9.75
Souvenir Sheets
3860-3861 A752   Set of 2   13.50 13.50

Lady Margaret Thatcher (1925-2013), British Prime Minister — A753

No. 3862 — Thatcher: a, Waving. b, With hand on chin. c, With flowers. d, On telephone.
$9, Thatcher, vert.

2013, June 3   Litho.   Perf. 12
3862 A753 $3.25 Sheet of 4, #a-
d   9.75 9.75
Souvenir Sheet
Perf. 12¾
3863 A753 $9 multi   6.75 6.75
No. 3863 contains one 38x51mm stamp.

Souvenir Sheets

Elvis Presley (1935-77) — A754

Various photographs of Presley in: No. 3864, $9, Black-and-white, frame in black. No. 3865, $9, Color, frame in purple. No. 3866, $9, Black-and-white, frame in red. No. 3867, $9, Color, frame in red. No. 3868, $9, Color, frame in gray.

2013, June 20   Litho.   Perf. 13½
3864-3868 A754   Set of 5   33.50 33.50
Country name is misspelled on No. 3864.

Souvenir Sheet

Elvis Presley (1935-77) — A755

Litho., Margin Embossed With Foil Application
2013, June 25   Imperf.
3869 A755 $25 multi   18.50 18.50

A756

Pride and Prejudice, by Jane Austen — A757

No. 3870: a, Fitzwilliam Darcy, Colonel Fitzwilliam and Elizabeth Bennet at piano. b, Mr. Collins bowing before Elizabeth. c, Lady Catherine de Bourgh and Elizabeth. d, Elizabeth watching her sister and Charles Bingley talking.
No. 3871: a, Men talking about Elizabeth, sitting on bench. b, Man looking at women attending to woman who fainted. c, Elizabeth showing ring to Mrs. Hill and housemaids. d, Woman and tea service.
No. 3872, $9.50, Darcy approaching seated Elizabeth. No. 3873, $9.50, Elizabeth and her father.

2013, July 7   Litho.   Perf. 12¾
3870 A756 $3.25 Sheet of 4,
          #a-d   9.75 9.75
3871 A757 $3.25 Sheet of 4,
          #a-d   9.75 9.75
Souvenir Sheets
3872-3873 A757   Set of 2   14.00 14.00

Mammals — A758

No. 3874: a, Two-toed sloth. b, Nine-banded armadillo. c, Leaf-nosed bat. d, Short-tailed shrew.
$9, West Indian manatee.

2013, Aug. 7   Litho.   Perf. 14
3874 A758 $3.25 Sheet of 4, #a-d
                                 9.75 9.75
Souvenir Sheet
3875 A758 $9 multi   6.75 6.75

Retirement of Concorde G-BOAG to Seattle Museum of Flight, 10th Anniv. — A759

No. 3876: a, Concorde on ground in Seattle. b, Captain Bannister holding microphone. c, Crowd near Concorde. d, Concorde landing at Seattle.
$9, Nose of Concorde, crew holding flags.

2013, Aug. 26   Litho.   Perf. 12¾
3876 A759 $3.25 Sheet of 4, #a-
d   9.75 9.75
Souvenir Sheet
3877 A759 $9 multi   6.75 6.75

St. Joan of Arc (c.1412-31) A760

2013, Sept. 27   Litho.   Perf. 12
3878 A760 $3.50 multi   2.60 2.60
No. 3878 was printed in sheets of 4.

Chess — A761

No. 3879: a, White pawn. b, White queen. c, White rook. d, Black knight. e, Black king. f, Black bishop.
$9, Wilhelm Steinitz (1836-1900), world chess champion.

2013, Sept. 30   Litho.   Perf. 13¾
3879 A761 $2.75 Sheet of 6,
          #a-f   12.50 12.50
Souvenir Sheet
3880 A761 $9 multi   6.75 6.75

Coronation of Queen Elizabeth II, 60th Anniv. — A762

No. 3881 — Queen Elizabeth II: a, As child. b, Wearing crown. c, With Prince Philip. d, Wearing Girl Guide uniform.
$9, Queen Elizabeth II as young girl playing piano.

2013, Oct. 7   Litho.   Perf. 13¾
3881 A762 $3.25 Sheet of 4, #a-d
                                 9.75 9.75
Souvenir Sheet
3882 A762 $9 multi   6.75 6.75

Birth of Prince George of Cambridge — A763

No. 3883: a, Prince George being held by Duchess and Duke of Cambridge. b, Duchess of Cambridge holding Prince George and waving. c, Duchess handing Prince George to Duke.
$9, Prince George, Duke and Duchess of Cambridge, diff.

2013, Oct. 7   Litho.   Perf. 12¾
3883 A763 $3.50 Sheet of 3, #a-
  c   7.75 7.75
Souvenir Sheet
3884 A763 $9 multi   6.75 6.75

Miniature Sheet

Hummingbirds — A764

No. 3885: a, Florisuga mellivora. b, Lampornis violicauda. c, Campylopterus obscurus. d, Thalurania furcata.

2013, Nov. 11   Perf. 12¾
3885 A764 $3.25 Sheet of 4, #a-
  d   9.75 9.75
Brasiliana 2013 Intl. Philatelic Exhibition, Rio de Janeiro.

Reptiles — A765

No. 3886, horiz.: a, Dwarf gecko. b, Hawksbill turtle. c, Brown anole. d, Mona boa.
$9, Iguana.

Perf. 13 Syncopated
2013, Nov. 28   Litho.
3886 A765 $3.50 Sheet of 4,
  #a-d   10.50 10.50
Souvenir Sheet
3887 A765 $9 multi   6.75 6.75

Miniature Sheet

Elvis Presley (1935-77) — A766

No. 3888 — Presley: a, On album cover. b, Touching chin. c, With four women. d, Singing.

2013, Dec. 2   Litho.   Perf. 13¾
3888 A766 $3.25 Sheet of 4, #a-
  d   9.75 9.75

Christmas
A767

Paintings: 80c, Madonna, by Don Lorenzo Monaco. $1.70, The Adoration of the Magi, by Stefano da Verona. $2, Nativity, by Giorigione. $2.20, The Annunciation, by Masolino da Panicale.
$9, Nativity, by Piero della Francesa.

2013, Dec. 2   Litho.   Perf. 12¾
3889-3892 A767   Set of 4   5.00 5.00
Souvenir Sheet
3893 A767 $9 multi   6.75 6.75

Pres. Barack Obama — A768

Designs: $3.25, Pres. Obama.
No. 3895, $9, Pres. Obama sitting. No. 3896, $9, Pres. Obama golfing with Vice President Joseph Biden.

2013, Dec. 9   Litho.   Perf. 14
3894 A768 $3.25 multi   2.40 2.40
Souvenir Sheets
Perf. 12¾
3895-3896 A768   Set of 2   13.50 13.50
No. 3894 was printed in sheets of 4. Nos. 3895-3896 each contain one 38x51mm stamp.

A769

Nelson Mandela (1918-2013), President of South Africa — A770

No. 3898 — Mandela: a, Wearing black and gray shirt. b, Standing in front of building. c, Holding microphone stand. d, With arms extended. e, Pointing. f, With raised fist.
No. 3899, $9, Mandela casting ballot, vert. No. 3900, $9, Mandela standing in front of building, diff., vert.

2013, Dec. 15   Litho.   Perf. 13¾
3897 A769 $2.50 shown   1.90 1.90
3898 A770 $2.50 Sheet of 6,
  #a-f   11.50 11.50
Souvenir Sheets
Perf. 12¾
3899-3900 A770   Set of 2   13.50 13.50
No. 3899-3900 each contain one 38x51mm stamp.

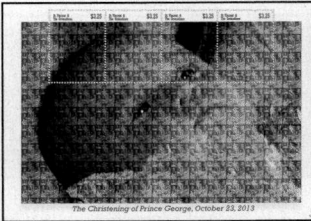

Cat Breeds — A771

No. 3901, $3.25: a, Aegean. b, Mekong Bobtail. c, Australian Mist. d, Brazilian Shorthair.
No. 3902, $3.25: a, American Shorthair. b, British Burmese. c, Ocicat. d, Oriental Shorthair.
No. 3903, $9, Cyprus Shorthair. No. 3904, $9, European Shorthair.

2013, Dec. 18   Litho.   Perf. 13¾
Sheets of 4, #a-d
3901-3902 A771   Set of 2   19.50 19.50
Souvenir Sheets
3903-3904 A771   Set of 2   13.50 13.50

Miniature Sheet

Christening of Prince George of Cambridge — A772

No. 3905: a, Top of head. b, Forehead. c, Eye. d, Upper cheek.

2013, Dec. 31   Litho.   Perf. 14
3905 A772 $3.25 Sheet of 4, #a-
  d   9.75 9.75

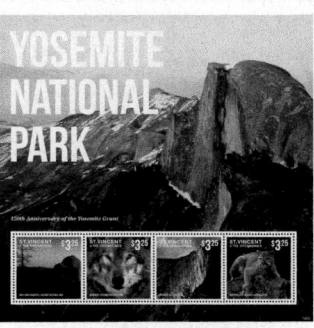

Yoesmite National Park, California — A773

No. 3906, $3.25: a, Half Dome Mountain. b, Gray wolf. c, Firefall at Horsetail Falls. d, Mountain lion.
No. 3907, $3.25: a, Merced River. b, Tenaya Lake. c, Yosemite Waterfalls. d, Yosemite Valley.
No. 3908, $9, Western mule deer, horiz. No. 3909, $9, Rock formation in Yosemite Valley, horiz.

2014, Jan. 2   Litho.   Perf. 13¾
Sheets of 4, #a-d
3906-3907 A773   Set of 2   19.50 19.50
Souvenir Sheets
Perf. 12¾
3908-3909 A773   Set of 2   13.50 13.50
Nos. 3908-3909 each contain one 51x38mm stamp.

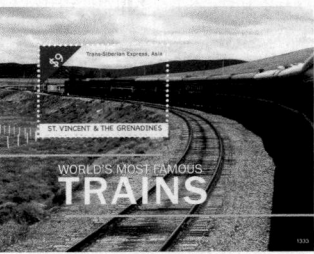

Trains — A774

No. 3910: a, TGV, France. b, Blue Train, South Africa. c, Orient Express, Europe. d, Bullet Train, Japan.
$9, Trans-Siberian Express, Asia.

2014, Jan. 14   Litho.   Perf. 14
3910 A774 $3.25 Sheet of 4, #a-
  d   9.75 9.75
Souvenir Sheet
Perf. 12
3911 A774 $9 multi   6.75 6.75

Garden Flowers — A775

No. 3912: a, Great bougainvillea. b, Hibiscus. c, Iris. No. 3913: a, Lily. b, Bearded iris. c, Bird of paradise.
No. 3914: a, Peony. b, Tulip. No. 3915: a, Iris, diff. b, Hyacinth.

2014, Feb. 6   Litho.   Perf. 12¾
Sheets of 3, #a.-c.
3912-3913 A775 $6.25 Set of
  2   28.00 28.00
Souvenir Sheets of 2, #a.-b.
3914-3915 A775 $9.50 Set of
  2   28.00 28.00

Characters From *Downton Abbey*
Television Series — A776

No. 3916: a, Mr. Bates. b, Thomas Barrow.
c, Mr. Carson. d, Tom Branson.
$9, William Mason and Thomas Barrow,
horiz.

2014, Mar. 5   Litho.   Perf. 14
3916 A776 $3.25 Sheet of 4, #a-
d
9.75 9.75
Souvenir Sheet
3917 A776 $9 multi
6.75 6.75

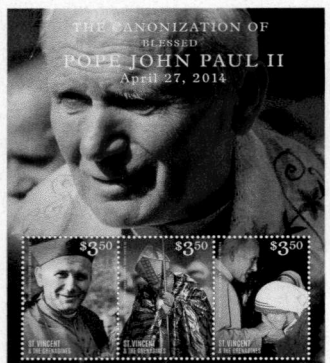

World War I, Cent. — A777

No. 3918, $3.25: a, Austro-Hungarian sol-
dier with rifle. b, Austro-Hungarian soldier
without weapon. c, Russian bugler. d, Russian
artilleryman.
No. 3919, $3.25: a, German cavalryman,
blue gray background. b, Russian cavalryman.
c, German cavalryman, bucking horse, gray
green background. d, British cavalryman.
No. 3920, $5 — German cavalryman with:
a, Blue gray background. b, Dull green
background.
No. 3921, $5, vert.: a, Russian soldier point-
ing pistol. b, Austro-Hungarian soldier pointing
rifle.

2014, Mar. 24   Litho.   Perf. 14
Sheets of 4, #a-d
3918-3919 A777   Set of 2   19.50 19.50
Souvenir Sheets
Perf. 12¾
3920-3921 A777   Set of 2   15.00 15.00
No. 3920 contains two 51x38mm stamps.
No, 3921 contains two 38x51mm stamps.

A778

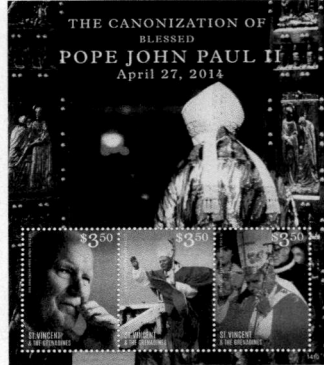

Canonization of Pope John Paul
II — A779

No. 3922 — Pope John Paul II: a, As
younger man, wearing biretta. b, Wearing
miter and striped robe. c, With Mother Teresa.
No. 3923 — Pope John Paul II: a, With hand
near mouth. b, On stairway, holding staff,
wearing miter, waving. c, Wearing miter, holding staff.
No. 3924, $5, horiz. — Pope John Paul II: a,
Facing crowd with arms extended. b, Holding
staff, wearing miter, waving, diff.
No. 3925, $5, horiz. — Pope John Paul II: a,
With Mother Teresa, diff. b, With cardinals.

2014, May 5   Litho.   Perf. 12
3922 A778 $3.50 Sheet of 3,
#a-c
7.75 7.75
3923 A779 $3.50 Sheet of 3,
#a-c
7.75 7.75
Souvenir Sheets of 2, #a-b
3924-3925 A779   Set of 2   15.00 15.00

Panama Canal, Cent. — A780

No. 3926: a, Miraflores Locks, 2014. b,
Miraflores Locks under construction, 1912. c,
Ship in Panama Canal, 2014. d, SS Kroonland
in Panama Canal, 1915.
No. 3927: a, Centennial Bridge. b, Ship in
Panama Canal lock.

2014, May 12   Litho.   Perf. 14
3926 A780 $3.25 Sheet of 4,
#a-d
9.75 9.75
Souvenir Sheet
Perf. 12
3927 A780 $5 Sheet of 2,
#a-b
7.50 7.50

A781

A782

A783

Taekwondo — A784

Various positions, kicks and jumps, as
shown.

2014, May 12   Litho.   Perf. 12¾
3928 A781 $3.25 Sheet of 4, #a-
d
9.75 9.75
3929 A782 $3.25 Sheet of 4, #a-
d
9.75 9.75
Souvenir Sheets
3930 A783 $5 Sheet of 2, #a-
b
7.50 7.50
3931 A784 $5 Sheet of 2, #a-
b
7.50 7.50
Philakorea 2014 World Stamp Exhibition,
Seoul.

Farm Animals — A785

No. 3932, $3.25: a, Anas platyrhynchos
(female ducks). b, Anas platyrhynchos (male
mallard ducks). c, Turkey. d, Chicken.
No. 3933, $3.25: a, Charolais cattle. b,
Zebus. c, Bison. d, Pigs.
No. 3934, $5, vert.: a, Arabian horses. b,
Shetland ponies.
No. 3935, $5, vert.: a, Wild goats. b, Sheep.

2014, May 19   Litho.   Perf. 14
Sheets of 4, #a-d
3932-3933 A785   Set of 2   19.50 19.50
Souvenir Sheets of 2, #a-b
3934-3935 A785   Set of 2   15.00 15.00

A786

A787

Sunflowers — A788

Various sunflowers, as shown.

2014, June 23   Litho.   Perf. 14
3936 A786 $3.25 Sheet of 4, #a-
d
9.75 9.75
3937 A787 $3.25 Sheet of 4, #a-
d
9.75 9.75
Souvenir Sheets
3938 A788 $5 Sheet of 2, #a-
b
7.50 7.50
Perf. 12¾
3939 A787 $10 Sunflower,
horiz.
7.50 7.50
No. 3939 contains one 51x38mm stamp.

A789

A790

A791

Orchids — A792

No. 3940: a, Cattleya mendelii. b, Cattleya trianae. c, Cattleya luddemanniana. d, Cattleya trianae, diff.
No. 3941: a, Cattleya mossiae. b, Cattleya trianae, diff. c, Cattleya mossiae, diff. d, Cattleya trianae, diff.
No. 3942: a, Cattleya trianae, diff. b, Cattleya trianae, diff.
No. 3943: a, Cattleya trianae, diff. b, Cattleya mossiae, diff.

2014, July 1   Litho.   Perf. 14
3940 A789 $3.25 Sheet of 4, #a-d   9.75 9.75
3941 A790 $3.25 Sheet of 4, #a-d   9.75 9.75

Souvenir Sheets
Perf. 12
3942 A791 $5 Sheet of 2, #a-b   7.50 7.50
3943 A792 $5 Sheet of 2, #a-b   7.50 7.50

March 27, 2014 Meeting of Pres. Barack Obama and Pope Francis — A793

Designs: $2, Pres. Obama and Pope Francis.
No. 3945 — Pres. Obama and Pope Francis with: a, Painting behind head of Pope Francis. b, Window behing Pope Francis.
No. 3946, vert.: a, Pope Francis. b, Pres. Obama.
$10, Pres. Obama and Pope Francis, vert.

2014, July 21   Litho.   Perf. 13¾
3944 A793 $2 multi   1.50 1.50
3945 A793 $2.25 Horiz. pair, #a-b   3.50 3.50

Souvenir Sheets
Perf. 12¾
3946 A793 $5 Sheet of 2, #a-b   7.50 7.50
3947 A793 $10 multi   7.50 7.50

No. 3944 was printed in sheets of 6. No. 3945 was printed in sheets of 9, containing six No. 3945a and three No. 3945b. No. 3946 contains two 38x51mm stamps. No. 3947 contains one 38x51mm stamp.

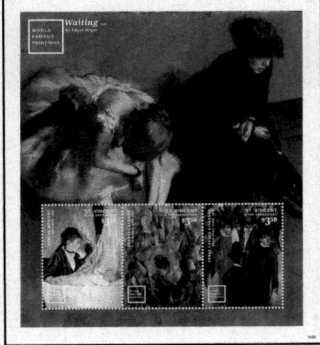

Paintings — A794

No. 3948, $3.50: a, The Cradle, by Berthe Morisot. b, Le Guitare, by Georges Braque. c, Berlin Street Scene, by Ernst Ludwig Kirchner.
No. 3949, $3.50: a, The Football Players, by Henri Rousseau. b, Boy on the Rocks, by Rousseau. c, Still Life with Cherub, by Paul Cézanne.
No. 3950, $10, Open Window, by Henri Matisse. No. 3951, $10, Shore with Red House, by Edvard Munch.

2014, Aug. 14   Litho.   Perf. 12¾
Sheets of 3, #a-c
3948-3949 A794 Set of 2   15.50 15.50
Size: 100x100mm
Imperf
3950-3951 A794 Set of 2   15.00 15.00

Worldwide Fund for Nature (WWF) — A795

Nos. 3952 and 3953: Various depictions of Semipalmated sandpiper, as shown.

2014, Sept. 15   Litho.   Perf. 14
3952 A795 $1.25 Block or vert. strip of 4, #a-d 3.75 3.75
3953 A795 $2.75 Block or vert. strip of 4, #a-d 8.25 8.25

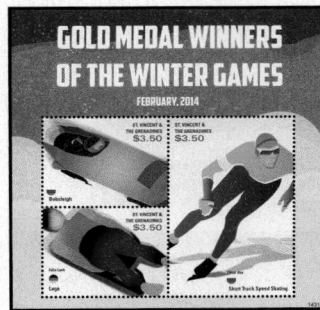

2014 Winter Olympics Gold Medalists — A796

No. 3954: a, Russian Men's two-man bobsled team (40x30mm). b, Felix Lach, luge, Germany (40x30mm). c, Viktor Ahn, short track speed skating, Russia (40x60mm).
No. 3955: a, Michael Mulder, speed skating, Netherlands (40x30mm). b, Alexander Tretiakov, skeleton, Russia (40x30mm).

2014, Sept. 15   Litho.   Perf. 14
3954 A796 $3.50 Sheet of 3, #a-c   7.75 7.75
Souvenir Sheet
3955 A796 $5 Sheet of 2, #a-b   7.50 7.50

2014 World Cup Soccer Championships, Brazil — A797

No. 3956 — Central part of Brazilian flag and: a, Stylized soccer ball and map of Brazil. b, Soccer ball and "Brazil." c, Map of Brazil and "2014."
$10, Christ the Redeemer Statue, Rio de Janeiro.

2014, Sept. 30   Litho.   Perf. 12
3956 A797 $3.50 Sheet of 3, #a-c   7.75 7.75
Souvenir Sheet
3957 A797 $10 multi   7.50 7.50
No. 3957 contains one 30x50mm stamp.

Rare Stamps — A798

No. 3958: a, Great Britain #1. b, Mauritius #1. c, France #3.
$10, United States #1.

2014, Sept. 30   Litho.   Perf. 14
3958 A798 $3.50 Sheet of 3, #a-c   7.75 7.75
Souvenir Sheet
3959 A798 $10 multi   7.50 7.50

Pope Benedict XVI — A799

No. 3960: a, Pope Benedict XVI waving to crowd in St. Peter's Square. b, Pope Benedict XVI praying. c, Pope Benedict XVI waving. d, Hand of Pope Benedict XVI with papal ring.
$10, Back of head of Pope Benedict XVI.

2014, Oct. 20   Litho.   Perf. 12½x12
3960 A799 $3.25 Sheet of 4, #a-d   9.75 9,75
Souvenir Sheet
3961 A799 $10 multi   7.50 7.50

A800

A801

A802

A803

A804

A805

A806

Dome Designs of St. Basil's Cathedral, Moscow — A807

2014, Oct. 27   Litho.   Perf. 14x14¾
3962   Horiz. strip of 4   3.00 3.00
  a. A800 $1 multi   .75 .75
  b. A801 $1 multi   .75 .75
  c. A802 $1 multi   .75 .75
  d. A803 $1 multi   .75 .75
3963   Horiz. strip of 4   3.00 3.00
  a. A804 $1 multi   .75 .75
  b. A805 $1 multi   .75 .75
  c. A806 $1 multi   .75 .75
  d. A807 $1 multi   .75 .75
Nos. 3962-3963 are personalizable stamps. Other vignettes can be found.

A808

A809

A810

Matryoshka Dolls — A811

2014, Oct. 27   Litho.   Perf. 14x14¾

3964		Horiz. strip of 4	3.00 3.00
a.	A808	$1 multi	.75 .75
b.	A809	$1 multi	.75 .75
c.	A810	$1 multi	.75 .75
d.	A811	$1 multi	.75 .75

Nos. 3964a-3964d are personalizable stamps. Other vignettes can be found.

Paintings by El Greco (1541-1614) — A812

No. 3965, $3.50: a, The Disrobing of Christ. b, Portrait of a Cardinal. c, Christ on the Cross with Two Maries and St. John.
No. 3966, $3.50: a, Coronation of the Virgin. b, Female Portrait. c, St. Paul and St. Peter.
No. 3967, $10, An Allegory with a Boy Lighting a Candle in the Company of an Ape and a Fool. No. 3968, $10, The Agony in the Garden of Gethsemane.

Perf. 12, 14 (#3966)
2014, Nov. 3   Litho.
Sheets of 3, #a-c

3965-3966	A812	Set of 2	15.50 15.50

Size: 60x120mm
Imperf

3967-3968	A812	Set of 2	15.00 15.00

Souvenir Sheets

Elvis Presley (1935-77) — A813

Various photographs of Presley: No. 3969, $10, With guitar, hands not visible, blue panel. No. 3970, $10, With guitar, hands visible, blue panel. No. 3971, $10, With arm raised, yellow green panel. No. 3972, $10, As child, with parents, red orange panel.

2014, Nov. 11   Litho.   Perf. 14

3969-3972	A813	Set of 4	30.00 30.00

Christmas A814

Details from paintings by Peter Paul Rubens: $2.20, Assumption of the Virgin Mary, 1626. $2.25, Assumption of the Virgin Mary, 1626, diff. $3.50, Annunciation, 1628. $5, Annunciation, 1615-20.

2014, Nov. 24   Litho.   Perf. 12¾

3973-3976	A814	Set of 4	9.75 9.75

World War I Battle of the Somme — A815

No. 3977, $3.25: a, A ration limber near La Boisselle, 1916. b, David Lloyd George meets with British Minister of Munitions. c, Welsh Guards in a reserve trench near Guillemont. d, London Heavy Battery near Contalmaison, August 1916 (cannon and horse).
No. 3978: a, $3.25: a, British infantry advance at Battle of the Somme, 1916. b, Albert Thomas with French artillery gunners, Fricourt, 1916. c, German prisoners pulling water cart, Contalmaison, 1916. d, London Heavy Battery near Contalmaison, August 1916 (soldiers carrying wounded comrade on litter).
No. 3979, $10, British troops crossing La Boisselle to Contalmaison, July 1916. No. 3980, $10, British infantry waiting to advance at Battle of the Somme, 1916.

2015, Jan. 1   Litho.   Perf. 14
Sheets of 4, #a-d

3977-3978	A815	Set of 2	19.50 19.50

Souvenir Sheets
Perf. 12½

3979-3980	A815	Set of 2	15.00 15.00

Nos. 3979-3980 each contain one 51x38mm stamp.

Fountains — A816

No. 3981: a, Trevi Fountain, Rome. b, Magic Fountain of Montjuïc, Barcelona. c, Fountain of Wealth, Singapore. d, Archibald Fountain, Sydney. e, Founains of Bellagio, Las Vegas. f, Swarovski Fountain, Wattens, Austria.
$10, Friendship of the Peoples Fountain, Moscow, vert.

2015, Jan. 2   Litho.   Perf. 14

3981	A816	$3.15 Sheet of 6, #a-f	14.00 14.00

Souvenir Sheet
Perf. 12

3982	A816	$10 multi	7.50 7.50

Pope John Paul II (1920-2005) — A817

No. 3983 — Pope John Paul II: a, Wearing biretta. b, Wearing miter. c, With Mother Teresa.
No. 3984, horiz. — Pope John Paul II: a, Greeting crowd with arms extended. b, Wearing miter and holding ferula.

2015, Feb. 2   Litho.   Perf. 14

3983	A817	$3.50 Sheet of 3, #a-c	7.75 7.75

Souvenir Sheet

3984	A817	$5 Sheet of 2, #a-b	7.50 7.50

A818

Taipei 2015 Intl. Stamp Exhibition — A819

No. 3985 — Taiwanese buildings and bridges: a, Shorefront buildings, Kaohsiung (30x40mm). b, Dragon and Tiger Pagodas, Kaohsiung (30x40mm). c, Taipei 101 Building, Taipei (30x80mm). d, Wan Yue Bridge, Tainan (30x40mm). e, Waterfront buildings, Taichung (30x40mm). f, Temple, Taipei (30x40mm). g, Skyscrapers, Taichung (30x40mm).
No. 3986 — Taiwanese animals: a, Formosan sambar deer. b, Formosan black bear. c, Common otter. d, Formosan Reeve's muntjac.
No. 3987, $10, Chiang Kai-shek Memorial Hall. No. 3988, $10, Formosan rock macaque, vert.

2015, Mar. 2   Litho.   Perf. 14

3985	A818	$3.15 Sheet of 7, #a-g	16.50 16.50
3986	A819	$3.25 Sheet of 4, #a-d	9.75 9.75

Souvenir Sheets
Perf. 12

3987	A818	$10 multi	7.50 7.50
3988	A819	$10 multi	7.50 7.50

Souvenir Sheet

2015 Cricket World Cup, Australia and New Zealand — A820

2015, Apr. 13   Litho.   Perf. 12

3989	A820	$10 multi	7.50 7.50

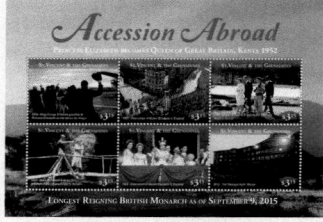

Queen Elizabeth II's Accession to the Throne — A821

No. 3990: a, King George V waving goodbye to Princess Elizabeth as she leaves for Kenya, 1952. b, Coronation parade of Queen Elizabeth II, 1953. c, Queen Elizabeth II's return to Treetops Hotel, Kenya, 1983. d, Princess Elizabeth II and her husband at Sagana Lodge, Kenya, 1952. e, Queen Elizabeth II at coronation, 1953. f, Treetops Hotel, 2012.
$10, Princess Elizabeth at Treetops Hotel, 1952.

2015, May 25   Litho.   Perf. 14

3990	A821	$3.15 Sheet of 6, #a-f	14.00 14.00

Souvenir Sheet
Perf. 12½

3991	A821	$10 multi	7.50 7.50

No. 3991 contains one 51x38mm stamp.

Miniature Sheets

Airships of World War I — A822

No. 3992, $1.15 — British airships: a, His Majesty's Naval Airship No. 2. b, Beta I. c, Beta II. d, Gamma. e, Gamma II. f, Delta. g, ETA. h, Sea Scout (SS). i, Coastal Class (C). j, Sea Scout Zero (SSZ). k, C-Star Class. l, North Sea Class (NS). m, 23r. n, 24r, o, R27. p, R29.
No. 3993, $1.15 — German airships: a, LZ 1. b, LZ 2. c, LZ 4. d, LZ 5 (Z II). e, LZ 7 (Deutschland). f, LZ 8 (Deutschland II). g, LZ 10 (Schwaben). h, LZ 11 (Viktoria Luise). i, LZ 12 (Z III). j, LZ 13 (Hansa). k, LZ 14 (L 1). l, LZ 16 (Z IV). m, LZ 17 (Sachsen). n, LZ 18 (LZ 2). o, LZ 36 (L 9). p, LZ 38.

2015, May 25   Litho.   Perf. 14
Sheets of 16, #a-p, + label

3992-3993	A822	Set of 2	27.50 27.50

Battle of Britain, 75th Anniv. — A823

No. 3994: a, Royal Air Force fighter pilot. b, Hawker Hurricane. c, Old Palace Yard outside the Palace of Westminster. d, Royal Air Force bomber crew.
$10, King George VI and Queen Elizabeth viewing damage to Buckingham Palace.

2015, Aug. 3	Litho.		Perf. 12	
3994	A823	$3.25 Sheet of 4, #a-d	9.75	9.75
Souvenir Sheet				
3995	A823	$10 multi	7.50	7.50

Carnivorous Plants — A824

No. 3996: a, Nepenthes sanguinea. b, Nepenthes burkei. c, Nepenthes mirabilis. d, Nepenthes lowii. e, Nepenthes macfarlanei.
$10, Drosera burmannii.

2015, Aug. 3	Litho.		Perf. 14	
3996	A824	$3.15 Sheet of 5, #a-e	12.00	12.00
Souvenir Sheet				
		Perf. 13¾		
3997	A824	$10 multi	7.50	7.50

Singapore 2015 Intl. Stamp Exhibition. No. 3997 contains one 35x35mm stamp.

Miniature Sheets

85th Birthday of Pope Benedict XVI — A825

Day of Four Popes — A826

Popes Benedict XVI and Francis — A827

No. 3998 — Pope Benedict XVI: a, Wearing miter and white vestments. b, Wearing white zucchetto and cassock, looking to left. c, Wearing white zucchetto and red vestments. d, Wearing miter and red vestments.
No. 3999 — Erroneous inscriptions: a, Pope Francis (Pope John XXIII pictured). b, Pope Benedict XVI (Pope John Paul II pictured). c, Pope John Paul II (Pope Benedict XVI pictured). d, Pope John XXIII (Pope Francis pictured).
No. 4000: a, Pope Benedict XVI (more of zucchetto visible than No. 3998c). b, Pope Francis waving. c, Pope Francis, hand not visible, top of zucchetto not visible. d, Pope Benedict XVI wearing white zucchetto and cassock, looking straight ahead.

2015, Aug. 10	Litho.		Perf. 14	
3998	A825	$3.25 Sheet of 4, #a-d	9.75	9.75
3999	A826	$3.25 Sheet of 4, #a-d	9.75	9.75
4000	A827	$3.25 Sheet of 4, #a-d	9.75	9.75
		Nos. 3998-4000 (3)	29.25	29.25

Reptiles — A828

No. 4001: a, Hawksbill turtle. b, Green iguana. c, Turnip-tailed gecko. d, Leatherback turtle. e, Red-footed tortoise. f, Cuban brown anole.
$10, Tropical house gecko.

2015, Sept. 8	Litho.		Perf. 12½x13¼	
4001	A828	$3.15 Sheet of 6, #a-f	14.00	14.00
Souvenir Sheet				
		Perf. 13¼		
4002	A828	$10 multi	7.50	7.50

No. 4002 contains one 51x38mm stamp.

Paintings by Vincent van Gogh (1853-90) — A829

No. 4003: a, Portrait of a Man, 1888. b, Portrait of Patience Escalier, 1888. c, Portrait of Eugene Boch, 1888. d, Madame Roulin Rocking the Cradle (La Berceuse), 1889. e, Head of a Peasant with a Pipe, 1885. f, Joseph Etienne Roulin, 1889.
$10, Self-portrait with a Gray Felt Hat, 1887.

2015, Sept. 30	Litho.		Perf. 14	
4003	A829	$3.15 Sheet of 6, #a-f	14.00	14.00
Souvenir Sheet				
		Perf. 12½		
4004	A829	$10 multi	7.50	7.50

No. 4004 contains one 38x51mm stamp.

Christmas
A830

Paintings by Fra Angelico (c. 1395-1455): 90c, Madonna of Humility. $2.25, Annunciation of Cortona. $3.50, San Marco Altarpiece. $5, Annunciation.

2015, Nov. 2	Litho.	Perf. 12¾	
4005-4008	A830	Set of 4	8.75 8.75

A831

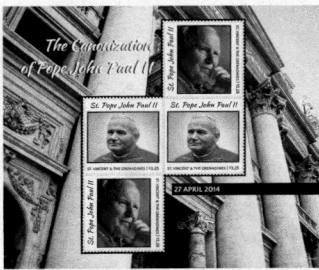

Canonization of Pope John Paul II (1920-2005) — A832

No. 4009, $3.15 — St. John Paul II: a, Facing right, text in white. b, Facing left, text in white. c, Facing left, text in black. d, Facing right, text in black.
No. 4010, $3.25 — St. John Paul II with background color of: a, Green. b, Gray.
No. 4011, $10, St. John Paul II holding crucifix. No. 4012, $10, St. John Paul II with arms raised.

2015, Dec. 1	Litho.		Perf. 13¾	
4009	A831	Sheet of 6, 2 each #4009a-4009b, 1 each #4009c-4009d	14.00	14.00
4010	A832	Sheet of 4, 2 each #4010a-4010b	9.75	9.75
Souvenir Sheets				
		Perf.		
4011-4012	A832	Set of 2	15.00	15.00

Nos. 4011-4012 each have one 38mm diameter stamp.

Battle of Waterloo, 200th Anniv. — A833

No. 4013: a, The Battle of Waterloo, by William Holmes Sullivan. b, The Battle of Waterloo, June 18, 1815, by Clément-Auguste Andrieux. c, The Battle of Waterloo: The British Squares Receiving the Charge of the French Cuirassiers, by Henri Félix Emmanuel Philippoteaux. d, The Storming of Plancenoit, by Ludwig Elsholtz.
$10, The Prussian Attack on Plancenoit, by Adolph Northen.

2015, Dec. 31	Litho.		Perf. 12	
4013	A833	$3.75 Sheet of 4, #a-d	9.75	9.75
Souvenir Sheet				
4014	A833	$10 multi	7.50	7.50

A834

A835

A836

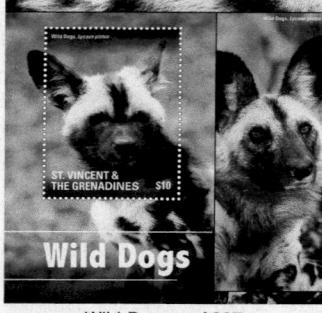

Wild Dogs — A837

Designs as shown. Nos. 4015a-4015b, 4016a-4016b are 35x35mm, Nos. 4015c and 4016c are 35x70mm.

2015, Dec. 31		Litho.		Perf. 13¾
4015	A834	$3.50 Sheet of 3, #a-c		
			7.75	7.75
4016	A835	$3.50 Sheet of 3, #a-c		
			7.75	7.75

Souvenir Sheets
Perf. 12½

4017	A836	$10 multi	7.50	7.50
4018	A837	$10 multi	7.50	7.50

Ducks — A838

No. 4019, $3.25: a, Common merganser. b, Bucephala albeola. c, Common pochard. d, Hooded merganser.
No. 4020, $3.25: a, Smew. b, Freckled duck. c, Surf scoter. d, Canvasback.
No. 4021, $10, Red-crested pochard. No. 4022, $10, Torrent duck, vert.

2015, Dec. 31		Litho.		Perf. 14
Sheets of 4, #a-d				
4019-4020	A838	Set of 2	19.50	19.50

Souvenir Sheets
Perf. 12

| 4021-4022 | A838 | Set of 2 | 15.00 | 15.00 |

A839

Flamingos — A840

Nos. 4023-4024 as shown.
No. 4025 — Head of flamingo facing: a, Right. b, Left.
$10, Flamingo, diff.

2015, Dec. 31		Litho.		Perf. 14
4023	A839	$3.25 Sheet of 4, #a-d		
			9.75	9.75
4024	A840	$3.25 Sheet of 4, #a-d		
			9.75	9.75

Souvenir Sheets
Perf. 12

4025	A840	$5 Sheet of 2, #a-b	7.50	7.50
4026	A840	$10 multi	7.50	7.50

A841

A842

A843

Great Egret — A844

No. 4027: a, Bird standing. b, Bird with extended wings.
No. 4028: a, Bird in flight over water. b, Bird on tree. c, Head of bird. d, Bird in flight.
No. 4029, Adult and chick. No. 4030, Chick.

Perf. 14 (#4027, 4029), 12 (#4028, 4030)

2015, Dec. 31			Litho.	
4027	A841	$3.15 Pair, #a-b	4.75	4.75
4028	A842	$3.25 Sheet of 4, #a-d		
			9.75	9.75

Souvenir Sheets

4029	A843	$10 multi	7.50	7.50
4030	A844	$10 multi	7.50	7.50

Pope Francis in New York City — A845

No. 4031 — Pope Francis: a, Facing forward, denomination at UR. b, Waving, hand below denomination at UL. c, Waving, hand

below denomination at UR. d, Facing forward, denomination at UL. e, Facing right, denomination at UR. f, Waving, hand at level of denomination at UL.
$10, Pope Francis waving, diff.

2015, Dec. 31		Litho.		Perf. 14
4031	A845	$3.15 Sheet of 6, #a-f		
			14.00	14.00

Souvenir Sheet
Perf. 12

4032	A845	$10 multi	7.50	7.50

Paintings — A846

No. 4033, $3.50 — Paintings by Diego Velázquez: a, Las Meninas. b, Portrait of Innocent X. c, The Surrender of Breda.
No. 4034, $3.50: a, The Girl with the Pearl Earring, by Johannes Vermeer. b, Self-portrait, by Albrecht Dürer. c, Laughing Cavalier, by Frans Hals.
No. 4035, $10, Luncheon of the Boating Party, by Auguste Renoir. No. 4036, $10, Judith Beheading Holofernes, by Michelangelo Merisi da Caravaggio.

2015, Dec. 31		Litho.		Perf. 12½
Sheets of 3, #a-c				
4033-4034	A846	Set of 2	15.50	15.50

Size: 100x100mm
Imperf

4035-4036	A846	Set of 2	15.00	15.00

A847

A848

A849

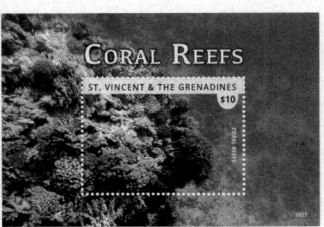

Coral Reefs — A850

Nos. 4037 and 4038 as shown.

2015, Dec. 31   Litho.   *Perf. 14*
4037 A847 $3.15 Sheet of 6,
 #a-f   14.00 14.00
4038 A848 $3.25 Sheet of 4,
 #a-d   9.75 9.75
Souvenir Sheets
Perf. 12½
4039 A849 $10 multi   7.50 7.50
4040 A850 $10 multi   7.50 7.50

Sharks — A851

No. 4041: a, Blacktip reef shark. b, Hammerhead shark. c, Whale shark. d, Caribbean reef shark. e, Lemon shark. f, Nurse shark.
No. 4042: a, Tiger shark. b, Great white shark. c, Bull shark. d, Oceanic whitetip shark.
No. 4043, $10, Zebra shark. No. 4044, $10, Pelagic thresher shark.

2015, Dec. 31   Litho.   *Perf. 14*
4041 A851 $3.15 Sheet of 6,
 #a-f   14.00 14.00
4042 A851 $3.25 Sheet of 4,
 #a-d   9.75 9.75
Souvenir Sheets
Perf. 12½
4043-4044 A851 Set of 2   15.00 15.00
Nos. 4043-4044 each contain one 51x38mm stamp.

Birds — A852

No. 4045: a, Glossy ibis. b, Brown pelican. c, Great blue heron. d, Manx shearwater. e, White-tailed tropicbird. f, Pied-billed grebe.
No. 4046: a, Green heron. b, Magnificent frigatebird. c, Roseate spoonbill. d, Great egret.
$10, Red-billed tropicbird.

2015, Dec. 31   Litho.   *Perf. 14*
4045 A852 $3.15 Sheet of 6,
 #a-f   14.00 14.00
4046 A852 $3.25 Sheet of 4,
 #a-d   9.75 9.75
Souvenir Sheet
4047 A852 $10 multi   7.50 7.50

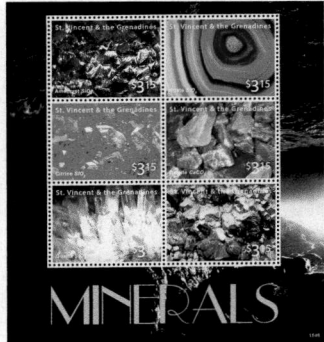

Minerals — A853

No. 4048: a, Amethyst. b, Agate. c, Citrine. d, Calcite. e, Quartz. f, Pyrite.
No. 4049: a, Onyx agate. b, Rose quartz. c, Citrine. d, Emerald.
$10, Amethyst, diff.

2016, Jan. 28 Litho.   *Perf. 12½x13¼*
4048 A853 $3.15 Sheet of 6,
 #a-f   14.00 14.00
Perf. 12½x12
4049 A853 $3.25 Sheet of 4,
 #a-d   9.75 9.75
Souvenir Sheet
4050 A853 $10 multi   7.50 7.50

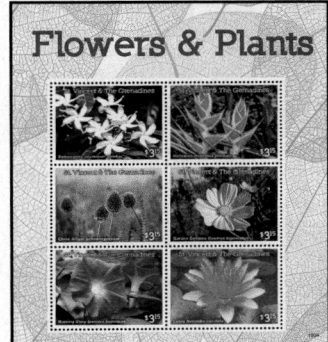

Flora — A854

No. 4051: a, Sampaguita. b, Heliconia. c, Chives. d, Garden cosmos. e, Morning glories. f, Lotus.
No. 4052: a, Hibiscus. b, Frangipani. c, Bird of paradise. d, Maxillaria.
$10, Hibiscus, diff.

2016, Jan. 28   Litho.   *Perf. 14*
4051 A854 $3.15 Sheet of 6,
 #a-f   14.00 14.00
Perf. 12
4052 A854 $3.25 Sheet of 4,
 #a-d   9.75 9.75
Souvenir Sheet
4053 A854 $10 multi   7.50 7.50

Marine Mammals — A855

No. 4054: a, Atlantic spotted dolphins. b, Blue whale. c, Sperm whale. d, Humpback whale. e, Bottlenose dolphins. f, West Indian manatee.

No. 4052: a, Humpback whale, diff. b, Atlantic spotted dolphin. c, Bottlenose dolphin. d, Spinner dolphins.
$10, West Indian manatee, diff.

2016, Jan. 28   Litho.   *Perf. 14*
4054 A855 $3.15 Sheet of 6,
 #a-f   14.00 14.00
4055 A855 $3.25 Sheet of 4,
 #a-d   9.75 9.75
Souvenir Sheet
4056 A855 $10 multi   7.50 7.50

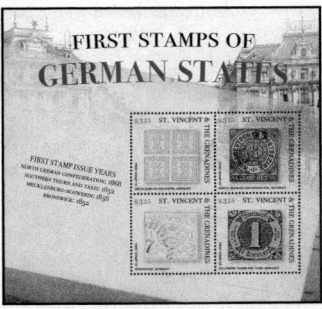

Shells — A856

No. 4057: a, Common American auger. b, Nautilus. c, Scotch bonnet. d, Yellow cockle. e, Rough scallop. f, Longspine star shell.
No. 4058: a, Queen conch. b, Lace murex. c, Abalone. d, Cabrit's murex.
$10, Abalone, diff.

2016, Jan. 28   Litho.   *Perf. 14*
4057 A856 $3.15 Sheet of 6,
 #a-f   14.00 14.00
4058 A856 $3.25 Sheet of 4,
 #a-d   9.75 9.75
Souvenir Sheet
Perf. 12
4059 A856 $10 multi   7.50 7.50

**FIRST STAMPS OF
GERMAN STATES**

German States Stamps — A857

No. 4060: a, Mecklenburg-Schwerin #1. b, North German Confederation #1. c, Brunswick #1. d, Thurn & Taxis Southern District #42.
No. 4061, $3.25: a, Baden #1. b, Bavaria #1. c, Bergedorf #1. d, Bremen #1. e, Brusnwick #3.
No. 4062, $3.25: a, Hamburg #1. b, Hanover #1. c, Lubeck #1. d, Mecklenburg-Schwerin #1a. e, Mecklenburg-Strelitz #1.
No. 4063, $3.25: a, Oldenburg #4. b, Prussia #2. c, Saxony #1. d, Schleswig-Holstein #1. e, Wurttemberg #1.
No. 4064: a, Thurn & Taxis Southern District #42. b, Thurn & Taxis Northern District #1. c, North German Confederation #2.

2016, Jan. 29   Litho.   *Perf. 13¾*
4060 A857 $3.25 Sheet of 4,
 #a-d   9.75 9.75
Sheets of 5, #a-e
4061-4063 A857 Set of 3   36.00 36.00
Souvenir Sheet
4064 A857 $3.50 Sheet of 3,
 #a-c   7.75 7.75

**FIRST STAMPS OF
GERMAN COLONIES**

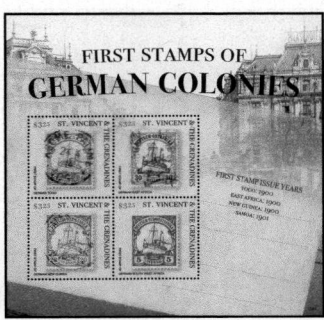

German Colonies Stamps — A858

No. 4065: a, Togo #9. b, German East Africa #27. c, German New Guinea #10. d, German South West Africa #14.
No. 4066: a, Mariana Islands #22. b, Caroline Islands #11. c, Marshall Islands #19. d, Cameroun #19. e, Samoa #68.

2016, Jan. 29   Litho.   *Perf. 13¾*
4065 A858 $3.25 Sheet of 4,
 #a-d   9.75 9.75
4066 A858 $3.25 Sheet of 5,
 #a-e   12.00 12.00

Souvenir Sheet

**FIRST STAMPS OF
GERMAN OFFICES**

German Offices Stamps — A859

No. 4067: a, German Offices in China #1. b, German Offices in Morocco #1. c, German Offices in the Turkish Empire #1.

2016, Jan. 29   Litho.   *Perf. 13¾*
4067 A859 $3.50 Sheet of 3, #a-
 c   7.75 7.75

Jimi Hendrix (1942-70), Rock Musician — A860

No. 4068 — Hendrix: a, With yellow, red orange curves in background. b, Wearing red pants. c, With Jupiter in background. d, With lilac and yellow green curved lines in background.
$10, Hendrix, diff.

2016, Mar. 8   Litho.   *Perf. 12½*
4068 A860 $3.25 Sheet of 4, #a-
 d   9.75 9.75
Souvenir Sheet
4069 A860 $10 multi   7.50 7.50

Queen Elizabeth II, Longest-Reigning British Monarch — A861

No. 4070 — Various photographs of Queen Elizabeth II, as shown.
No. 4071 — Queen Elizabeth II looking: a, Right. b, Left.

2016, Apr. 11   Litho.   Perf. 14
4070 A861 $4 Sheet of 3, #a-c   9.00 9.00
Souvenir Sheet
4071 A861 $6 Sheet of 2, #a-b   9.00 9.00

Magna Carta, 800th Anniv. (in 2015) A862

No. 4072: a, Amerindian petroglyph. b, St. George's Cathedral, Kingstown. c, Argyle International Airport. d, Court House, Kingstown. e, Cadet Force on parade.

2016, May 2   Litho.   Perf. 13¼
4072   Vert. strip of 5   8.25 8.25
  a.   A862 $1 multi   .75   .75
  b.   A862 $1.70 multi   1.25 1.25
  c.   A862 $2.20 multi   1.75 1.75
  d.   A862 $2.65 multi   2.00 2.00
  e.   A862 $3.40 multi   2.50 2.50

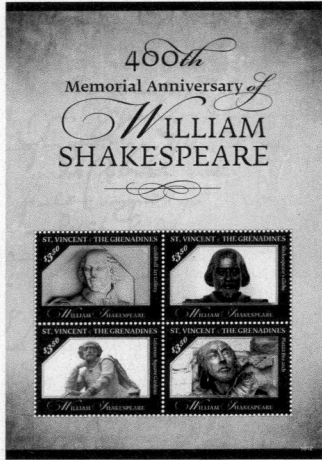

William Shakespeare (1564-1616), Writer — A863

No. 4073 — Statue depicting Shakespeare at: a, Guildhall Art Gallery, London. b, Shakespeare's Globe Theater, London. c, Leicester Square Gardens, London. d, Piazza Bra arch, Verona, Italy.
No. 4074 — Depiction of Shakespeare from: a, The Gallery of Portraits. b, The Leisure Hour Magazine.

2016, May 17   Litho.   Perf. 14
4073 A863 $3.50 Sheet of 4,
              #a-d   10.50 10.50
Souvenir Sheet
4074 A863 $6 Sheet of 2,
              #a-b   9.00 9.00

Souvenir Sheet

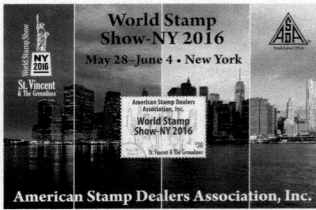

2016 World Stamp Show, New York — A864

2016, May 25   Litho.   Perf. 12½x12
4075 A864 $30 multi   22.50 22.50

New York State Emblematic Items — A865

No. 4076: a, Sweetbriar rose (state flower). b, Nine-spotted ladybug (state insect). c, Bay scallop (state shell). d, Striped bass (state saltwater fish). e, Sycamore maple (state tree). f, Snapping turtle (state reptile).
No. 4077: a, Apple muffin (state muffin). b, Beaver (state animal).

2016, May 26   Litho.   Perf.
4076 A865 $3.15 Sheet of 6,
              #a-f   14.00 14.00
Souvenir Sheet
Perf. 12½x12
4077 A865 $6 Sheet of 2,
              #a-b   9.00 9.00
2016 World Stamp Show, New York. No. 4077 contains two 40x30mm stamps.

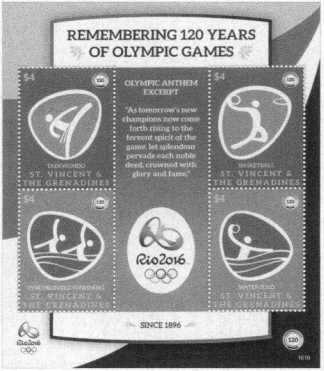

Modern Olympic Games, 120th Anniv. — A866

No. 4078, $4: a, Taekwondo. b, Basketball. c, Synchronized swimming. d, Water polo.
No. 4079, $4: a, Badminton. b, Sailing. c, Road cycling. d, Modern pentathlon.
No. 4080: a, Swimming. b, Shigeo Arai (1916-44), Japanese swimming gold medalist in 1936.

2016, June 7   Litho.   Perf. 14
Sheets of 4, #a-b
4078-4079 A866   Set of 2   24.00 24.00
Souvenir Sheet
Perf. 12½
4080 A866 $7 Sheet of 2, #a-b 10.50 10.50
No. 4080 contains two 38x51mm stamps.

Statue of Liberty 130TH ANNIVERSARY
A867

Statue of Liberty, 130th Anniv. — A868

No. 4081: a, Scaffolding surrounding statue. b, Torch. c, Head, sky in background. d, Head and torch. e, Construction of statue base. f, Head and trees.
No. 4082: a, Torch. b, Head. c, Head and torso. d, Tablet.
$14, Entire statue.

2016, June 7   Litho.   Perf. 13¾
4081 A867 $3.25 Sheet of 6,
              #a-f   14.50 14.50
Perf. 14
4082 A868 $3.50 Sheet of 4,
              #a-d   10.50 10.50
Souvenir Sheet
Perf. 12
4083 A868 $14 multi   10.50 10.50
No. 4083 contains one 30x50mm stamp.

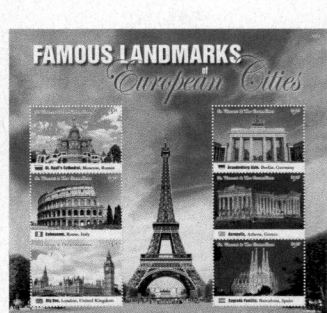

European Landmarks — A869

No. 4084: a, St. Basil's Cathedral, Moscow. b, Brandenburg Gate, Berlin. c, Colosseum, Rome. d, Acropolis, Athens. e, Big Ben, London. f, Sagrada Familia, Barcelona.
$14, Eiffel Tower, Paris, vert.

2016, June 29   Litho.   Perf. 14
4084 A869 $3.25 Sheet of 6,
              #a-f   14.50 14.50
Souvenir Sheet
Perf. 12
4085 A869 $14 multi   10.50 10.50
No. 4085 contains one 30x80mm stamp.

Souvenir Sheets

Elvis Presley (1935-77) — A870

Inscriptions: No. 4086, $14, Memphis charities benefit show. No. 4087, $14, A star is born. No. 4088, $14, Five-star jamboree. No. 4089, $14, Second Grammy "He Touched Me," horiz.

Perf. 13¼x13, 13x13¼
2016, July 7   Litho.
4086-4089 A870   Set of 4   42.00 42.00

Visit of Pres. Barack Obama to Viet Nam — A871

No. 4090: a, Pres. Obama and Vietnamese Prime Minister Nguyen Xuan Phúc shaking hands (120x30mm). b, Pres. Obama (40x30mm). c, Pres. Obama and Prime Minister Nguyen (40x30mm). d, Prime Minister Nguyen.
No. 4091, vert.: a, Pres. Obama. b, Prime Minister Nguyen.

2016, Sept. 21   Litho.   Perf. 14
4090 A871 $4 Sheet of 4, #a-d   12.00 12.00
Souvenir Sheet
4091 A871 $7 Sheet of 2, #a-b   10.50 10.50
No. 4091 contains two 30x80mm stamps.

Paintings by Hieronymus Bosch (c. 1450-1516) — A872

No. 4092 — The Temptation of St. Anthony (details): a, Four men. b, Man in bucket. c, Man and woman on fish. d, Fish and demons.
No. 4093: a, The Ship of Fools. b, Death and the Miser.

2016, Nov. 17   Litho.   Perf. 14
4092 A872 $5.50 Sheet of 4,
              #a-d   16.50 16.50
Souvenir Sheet
Perf. 12
4093 A872 $7.50 Sheet of 2,
              #a-b   11.00 11.00
No. 4093 contains two 30x50mm stamps.

Birds — A873

Designs: $60, Antillean crested humming-bird. $80, St. Vincent Amazon parrot.

2017, Feb. 28 Litho. Perf. 13¼
4094 A873 $60 multi   45.00 45.00
4095 A873 $80 multi   60.00 60.00

A874

Princess Diana (1961-97) — A875

No. 4096: Various photographs of Princess Diana wearing tiara, as shown.
No. 4097 — Princess Diana wearing: a, Hat. b, Gray jacket. c, Red dress. d, Yellow blouse. $10, Princess Diana, diff.

Perf. 12½x13¼
2017, Mar. 30   Litho.
4096 A874 $6 Sheet of 4, #a-
        d   18.00 18.00
Perf. 12x11½
4097 A875 $6 Sheet of 4, #a-
        d   18.00 18.00
Souvenir Sheet
Perf. 12½x12
4098 A874 $10 multi   7.50   7.50

Animals — A876

No. 4099: a, Serval. b, Sunda pangolin. c, Gulf Coast native sheep. d, Red-capped mangabey.
$9, Gee's golden langur.

2017, Apr. 4 Litho. Perf. 12¾x12½
4099 A876 $6 Sheet of 4, #a-d 18.00 18.00
Souvenir Sheet
4100 A876 $9 multi   6.75   6.75

Miniature Sheets

A877

Pres. John F. Kennedy (1917-63) — A878

No. 4101: a, Kennedy with two fingers raised. b, Kennedy pointing. c, Kennedy speaking. d, Kennedy on telephone. e, Neil Armstrong on Moon. f, Color photograph of Kennedy.
No. 4102: a, Kennedy looking upwards. b, Kennedy smiling with teeth visible. c, Kennedy pointing, diff. d, Launch of Apollo 11.

2017, May 15 Litho. Perf. 11½x12
4101 A877 $4 Sheet of 6, #a-f 18.00 18.00
Perf. 13¼
4102 A878 $5 Sheet of 4, #a-d 15.00 15.00

Sharks — A879

No. 4103, $5: a, Tiger shark. b, Whale shark. c, Pacific sleeper shark.
No. 4104, $5: a, Basking shark. b, Great hammerhead shark. c, Great white shark.

2017, June 2 Litho. Perf. 12
Sheets of 3, #a-c
4103-4104 A879 Set of 2   22.50 22.50

September 11, 2001 Terrorist Attacks — A880

No. 4105: a, World Trade Center and U.S. flag. b, Tribute in Light. c, World Trade Center. d, Hillary Clinton. e, Pres. Barack Obama. f, Pres. Donald Trump.
$12, New York City fire fighters at memorial ceremony, vert.

2017, June 29 Litho. Perf. 13¾
4105 A880 $3.15 Sheet of 6,
        #a-f   14.00 14.00
Souvenir Sheet
Perf. 14
4106 A880 $12 multi   9.00   9.00
No. 4106 contains one 30x40mm stamp.

Pres. Donald Trump — A881

No. 4107: a, Pres. Trump and Pres. Barack Obama (40x30mm). b, White House (40x60mm). c, Pres. Trump and wife, Melania (40x30mm). d, Ivanka Trump (40x30mm). e, Barron Trump (40x30mm).
No. 4108, vert.: a, Barron Trump, diff. b, Pres. Trump. c, Pres. Trump with arm raised. d, Melania Trump waving.
$12, Pres. Trump, diff.

2017, July 3 Litho. Perf. 14
4107 A881 $5 Sheet of 5, #a-
        e   18.50 18.50
4108 A881 $7 Sheet of 4, #a-
        d   21.00 21.00
Souvenir Sheet
Perf. 12½
4109 A881 $12 multi   9.00   9.00
No. 4109 contains one 51x38mm stamp.

American Flamingos — A882

No. 4110: Various photographs of flamingos, as shown.
No. 4111, horiz.: a, Two flamingos. b, One flamingo.

2017, Aug. 9 Litho. Perf. 14
4110 A882 $7 Sheet of 4, #a-d 21.00 21.00
Souvenir Sheet
Perf. 12
4111 A882 $7 Sheet of 2, #a-b 10.50 10.50

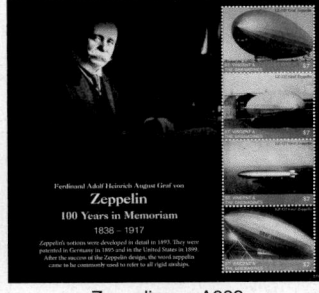

Zeppelins — A883

No. 4112 — LZ-127 Graf Zeppelin: a, With ground crew. b, Outside of hangar. c, In flight. d, In hangar.
$12, Ferdinand von Zeppelin (1883-1917), Zeppelin manufacturer, vert.

Perf. 12½x13¼
2017, Sept. 26   Litho.
4112 A883 $7 Sheet of 4, #a-
        d   21.00 21.00
Souvenir Sheet
Perf. 13¼
4113 A883 £12 multi   9.00   9.00
No. 4113 contains one 38x51mm stamp.

A884

Gold Dust Day Geckos — A885

Various photographs of geckos, as shown.

2017, June 28 Litho. Perf. 12
4114 A884 $7 Sheet of 4, #a-d 21.00 21.00
Souvenir Sheet
Perf. 14
4115 A885 $7 Sheet of 3, #a-c 15.50 15.50

Marine Life — A886

No. 4116 — Actiniaria sea anemones: a, Anemones (30x40mm). b, Anemones, diff. (30x40mm). c, Anemones, diff. (60x40mm). $15, Sea snails, horiz.

2017, Sept. 28 Litho. Perf. 14
4116 A886 $7 Sheet of 3, #a-
        c   15.50 15.50
Souvenir Sheet
4117 A886 $15 multi   11.00 11.00
No. 4117 contains one 80x30mm stamp.

Souvenir Sheets

Elvis Presley (1935-77) — A887

Inscription: No. 4118, $12, Signs first management contract. No. 4119, $12, First paid performance. No. 4120, $12, First professional stage show. No. 4121, $12, First single released, horiz.

2017, Oct. 26 Litho. Perf. 12½
4118-4121 A887 Set of 4   36.00 36.00

70th Wedding Anniversary of Queen Elizabeth II and Prince Philip — A888

No. 4122 — Wedding day photographs: a, Queen Elizabeth II waving. b, Couple in procession with attendants. c, Couple passing soldiers. d, Couple standing in front of curtain. $12, Couple, vert.

2017, Oct. 26   Litho.   Perf. 13¾
4122 A888 $6 Sheet of 4, #a-d   18.00 18.00
Souvenir Sheet
Perf.
4123 A888 $12 multi   9.00 9.00
No. 4123 contains one 34x43mm oval stamp.

World War II, 75th Anniv. — A889

No. 4124: a, Gen. Douglas MacArthur returns to the Philippines, 1944. b, U.S. B-17 bomber over Marienburg, Germany, 1943. c, Gen. Dwight Eisenhower prepares for D-Day, 1944. d, Japan surrenders, 1945. e, USS Arizona sinks at Pearl Harbor, 1941. f, Pres. Franklin Roosevelt, Winston Churchill and Joseph Stalin at Yalta Conference, 1945. $12, Marines raise flag on Iwo Jima, 1945.

2017, Oct. 28   Litho.   Perf. 14
4124 A889 $4 Sheet of 6, #a-f   18.00 18.00
Souvenir Sheet
Perf. 13¾
4125 A889 $12 multi   9.00 9.00
No. 4125 contains one 35x35mm stamp.

Miniature Sheets

Fruits — A890

No. 4126: a, 75c, Starfruits on tree. b, $1.75, Sliced starfruit. c, $2.75, Apple guava on tree. d, $3.75, Sliced apple guavas. e, $4.75, Jackfruits on tree. f, $5.75, Sliced jackfruit.
No. 4127: a, $2, Gooseberry on bush. b, $4, Custard apple on tree. c, $6, Purple star apple on tree. d, $8, Sliced gooseberries. e, $10, Sliced custard apple. f, $12, Sliced purple star apple.

2017, Nov. 18   Litho.   Perf. 11½x12
Sheets of 6, #a-f
4126-4127 A890 Set of 2   46.00 46.00

Miniature Sheets

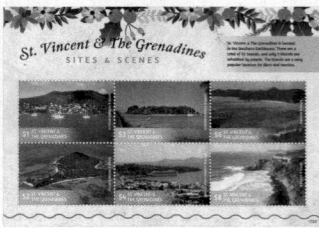

Scenery of St. Vincent — A891

No. 4128: a, $1, Bequia. b, $2, Petit St. Vincent. c, $3, Bequia, diff. d, $4, Kingstown (brown panel). e, $6, Island shoreline. f, $8, Waves reaching shore.
No. 4129: a, $2, Walliabou (42x29mm). b, $4, Kingstown (green panel) (42x29mm). c, $5, Botanical Garden (42x29mm). d, $6, Grenadines (42x29mm). e, $7, Dark View Falls (42x58mm).

2017, Dec. 4   Litho.   Perf. 13¼
4128 A891 Sheet of 6, #a-f   18.00 18.00
4129 A891 Sheet of 5, #a-e   18.00 18.00

Christmas — A892

Inscriptions: 90c, Christmas Celebration! $2.65, Oh, Christmas Tree! $3.40, Merry Christmas! $5, Deck the Halls!
No. 4134: a, Oh, Holy Night. b, Away in a Manger.

2017, Dec. 17   Litho.   Perf. 12½
4130-4133 A892 Set of 4   9.00 9.00
Souvenir Sheet
4134 A892 $2.50 Sheet of 2, #a-b   3.75 3.75

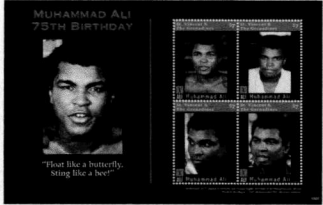

Muhammad Ali (1942-2016), Boxer — A893

No. 4135: Various photographs of Ali, as shown. $12, Ali, diff.

2018, Mar. 7   Litho.   Perf. 14
4135 A893 $7 Sheet of 4, #a-d   21.00 21.00
Souvenir Sheet
Perf. 12½
4136 A893 $12 multi   9.00 9.00
No. 4136 contains one 38x51mm stamp.

Miniature Sheets

Royal Air Force, Cent. — A894

No. 4137: a, $1, Lancaster. b, $2, Hawker Hurricane. c, $3, Douglas Dakota. d, $4, Chipmunk. e, $5, Supermarine Spitfire. f, $6, Supermarine Spitfire, diff.
No. 4138, $4, vert.: a, Distinguished Flying Cross medal. b, General Service medal. c, Long Service and Good Conduct medal. d, Air Force Cross medal. e, Accumulated Campaign Service medal. f, Korea medal.

2018, Mar. 7   Litho.   Perf. 14
4137 A894 Sheet of 6, #a-f   15.50 15.50
Perf. 12
4138 A894 $4 Sheet of 6, #a-f   18.00 18.00

Birds — A895

No. 4139: a, 50c, Lovely cotinga. b, $1, Andean cock-of-the-rock. c, $1.50, Orange-bellied leaf bird. d, $2, Pin-tailed manakin. e, $2.50, Long-tailed broadbill. f, $3, Rufous motmot. g, $3.50, American goldfinch. h, $4, Double-barred finch. i, $4.50, Golden-breated starling. $15, Southern mealy Amazon, Channel-billed toucan, horiz.

2018, Mar. 7   Litho.   Perf. 14
4139 A895 Sheet of 9, #a-i   16.50 16.50
Souvenir Sheet
Perf. 12½
4140 A895 $15 multi   11.00 11.00
No. 4140 contains one 51x38mm stamp.

Parrots — A896

No. 4141: a, $5, Cuban parrot. b, $6, Puerto Rican parrot. c, $7, Yellow-headed parrot. d, $8, St. Vincent parrot. $15, St. Vincent parrot, diff.

2018, Mar. 7   Litho.   Perf. 12
4141 A896 Sheet of 4, #a-d   19.50 19.50
Souvenir Sheet
Perf. 14
4142 A896 $15 multi   11.00 11.00

Marine Life — A897

No. 4143: a, $6, Flying gurnard. b, $6, West Indian manatee. c, $8, Great barracuda. d, $8, Southern stingray.
No. 4144: a, $7, Yellowhead jawfish. b, $8, Longsnout seahorse.

2018, Mar. 7   Litho.   Perf. 14
4143 A897 Sheet of 4, #a-d   21.00 21.00
Souvenir Sheet
Perf. 12
4144 A897 Sheet of 2, #a-b   11.00 11.00

Green Sea Turtles — A898

No. 4145 — Various photographs of turtle: a, $1. b, $2. c, $3. d, $4. e, $5. f, $6.
No. 4146 — Various photographs of turtle: a, $7. b, $8.

2018, Mar. 7   Litho.   Perf. 12
4145 A898 Sheet of 6, #a-f   15.50 15.50
Souvenir Sheet
Perf. 12½
4146 A898 Sheet of 2, #a-b   11.00 11.00
No. 4146 contains two 51x38mm stamps.

Reptiles — A899

No. 4147: a, $6, Thumb-tailed gecko. b, $6, Green iguana. c, $8, Cook's tree boa. d, $8, House gecko. $12, Loggerhead turtle.

2018, Mar. 7   Litho.   Perf. 14
4147 A899 Sheet of 4, #a-d   21.00 21.00
Souvenir Sheet
Perf. 12½
4148 A899 $12 multi   9.00 9.00
No. 4148 contains one 51x38mm stamp.

Miniature Sheet

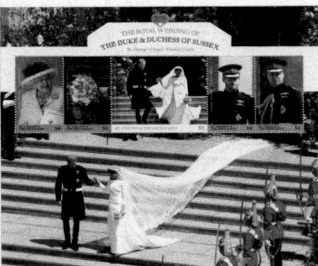

Wedding of Prince Harry and Meghan Markle — A900

No. 4149: a, $4, Queen Elizabeth II (30x50mm). b, $4, Flower bouquet (30x50mm). c, $4, Prince Harry, Duke of Sussex (30x50mm). d, $4, Prince William, Duke of Cambridge (30x50mm). e, $6, Bride and groom (60x50mm).

2018, July 14   Litho.   Perf. 12
4149 A900   Sheet of 5, #a-e   16.50 16.50

Souvenir Sheet

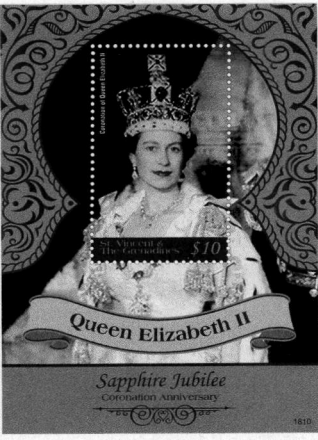

Coronation of Queen Elizabeth II, 65th Anniv. — A901

2018, July 14   Litho.   Perf. 12
4150 A901 $10 multi   7.50 7.50

Miniature Sheets

2018 Winter Olympics and Paralympics, Pyeongchang, South Korea — A902

No. 4151, $6: a, Winter Olympics Alpine skiing. b, Winter Paralympics Alpine skiing. c, Winter Olympics biathlon. d, Winter Paralympics biathlon.
No. 4152, $6: a, Winter Olympics cross-country skiing. b, Winter Paralympics cross-country skiing. c, Winter Olympics ice hockey. d, Winter Paralympics ice hockey.
No. 4153, $6: a, Winter Olympics snowboarding. b, Winter Paralympics snowboarding. c, Winter Olympics curling. d, Winter Paralympics wheelchair curling.

2018, July 14   Litho.   Perf. 12
Sheets of 4, #a-d
4151-4153 A902 Set of 3   53.00 53.00

Miniature Sheet

Visit to Canada of Pres. Donald Trump — A903

No. 4154: a, $4, German Chancellor Angela Merkel, Pres. Trump, Canadian Prime Minister Justin Trudeau. b, $5, Pres. Trump and French President Emmanuel Macron, seated. c, $6, Presidents Trump and Macron standing. d, $7, Pres. Trump and Prime Minister Trudeau.

2018, Oct. 12   Litho.   Perf. 12
4154 A903   Sheet of 4, #a-d   16.50 16.50

Flight of Apollo 11, 50th Anniv. (in 2019) — A904

No. 4155: a, Commander Neil Armstrong. b, Command Module Pilot Michael Collins. c, Lunar Module Pilot Edwin "Buzz" Aldrin. $11, Armstrong in training, horiz.

2018, Oct. 12   Litho.   Perf.
4155 A904 $5 Sheet of 3, #a-c   11.00 11.00
Souvenir Sheet
Perf. 12½
4156 A904 $11 multi   8.25 8.25
No. 4156 contains one 51x38mm stamp.

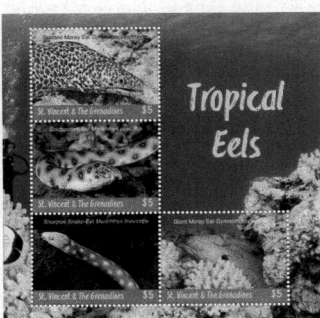

Eels — A905

No. 4157: a, Spotted moray eel. b, Gold-spotted eel. c, Sharptail snake-eel. d, Giant moray eel.
$10, Green moray eel.

2018, Oct. 26   Litho.   Perf. 14
4157 A905 $5 Sheet of 4, #a-d   15.00 15.00
Souvenir Sheet
Perf. 12½
4158 A905 $10 multi   7.50 7.50
No. 4158 contains one 51x38mm stamp.

Miniature Sheet

Western Honey Bees — A906

No. 4159: a, $4, Bee flying near flower. b, $5, Bee. c, $6, Bee on flower. d, $7, Bee moving from flower to flower.

2018, Oct. 26   Litho.   Perf. 14
4159 A906   Sheet of 4, #a-d   16.50 16.50

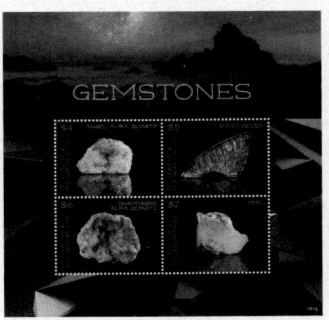

Gemstones — A907

No. 4160: a, $4, Angel aura quartz. b, $5, Super seven crystal. c, $6, Champagne aura quartz. d, $7, Opal.
No. 4161: a, $4, Amazonite. b, $5, Boulder opal. c, $6, Fluorite. d, $7, Benitoite.
No. 4162 — Larimar with background color of: a, Black. b, White.

2018, Oct. 26   Litho.   Perf. 14
Sheets of 4, #a-d
4160-4161 A907 Set of 2   32.50 32.50
Souvenir Sheet
4162 A907 $8 Sheet of 2, #a-b   12.00 12.00

Animals in World War I — A908

No. 4163: a, $4, Dog unspooling wire. b, $5, Russian machine gun mounted on horse. c, $6, Dog carrying pigeons. d, $7, Horse wearing gas mask.
No. 4164: a, Pigeon named Cher Ami. b, Dog named Sergeant Stubby.

2018, Dec. 31   Litho.   Perf. 14
4163 A908   Sheet of 4, #a-d   16.50 16.50
Souvenir Sheet
Perf. 12½
4164 A908 $10 Sheet of 2, #a-b   15.00 15.00
No. 4164 contains two 38x51mm stamps.

Miniature Sheet

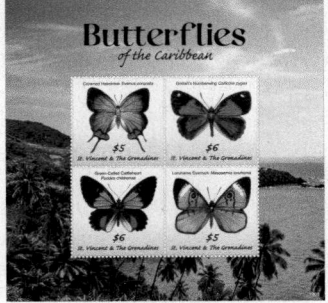

Butterflies — A909

No. 4165: a, $5, Crowned hairstreak. b, $5, Loruhama eyemark. c, $6, Godart's numberwing. d, $6, Green-celled cattleheart.

2019, Jan. 15   Litho.   Perf. 13¾
4165 A909   Sheet of 4, #a-d   16.50 16.50

Miniature Sheet

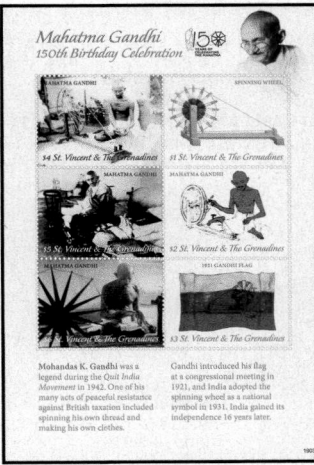

Mohandas K. Gandhi (1869-1948), Indian Nationalist Leader — A910

No. 4166: a, $1, Spinning wheel. b, $2, Drawing of Gandhi at spinning wheel. c, $3, 1921 proposed flag designed by Gandhi. d, $4, Photograph of Gandhi at spinning wheel. e, $5, Photograph of Gandhi turning crank of spinning wheel. f, $6, Photograph of Gandhi reading near spinning wheel.

2019, Jan. 30   Litho.   Perf. 14
4166 A910   Sheet of 6, #a-f   15.50 15.50

Hummingbirds — A911

No. 4167: a, $1, Rufous-breasted hermit. b, $2, Antillean crested hummingbird. c, $3, Puerto Rican emerald. d, $4, Antillean mango. e, $5, Antillean crested hummingbird, diff. f, $6, Blue-headed hummingbird.
$10, Bee hummingbird.

2019, Feb. 7   Litho.   Perf. 14
4167 A911   Sheet of 6, #a-f   15.50 15.50
Souvenir Sheet
Perf. 12½
4168 A911 $10 multi   7.50 7.50
No. 4168 contains one 38x51mm stamp.

Doctorfish Tang — A914

No. 4173 — Doctorfish tang facing: a, $5, Left. b, $6, Right. $14, Doctorfish tang facing left.

2019, July 8   Litho.   Perf. 14
4173 A914   Pair, $a-b   8.25 8.25
Souvenir Sheet
Perf.
4174 A914 $14 multi   10.50 10.50
No. 4173 was printed in sheets containing two pairs. No. 4174 contains one 43x33mm oval stamp.

Souvenir Sheet

Visit to France of Pres. Donald Trump — A915

No. 4175: a, $4, Pres. Trump and wife, Melania, French Pres. Emmanuel Macron and wife, Brigitte. b, $5, Arc de Triomphe and flowers. c, $6, Pres. Trump and wife, Melania.

2019, July 8   Litho.   Perf. 14
4175 A915   Sheet of 3, #a-c   11.00 11.00

Pres. George H. W. Bush (1924-2018) — A916

No. 4176 — Pres. Bush: a, $1, Behind lectern. b, $2, With wife, Barbara, waving. c, $3, Wearing sweater. d, $4, With Queen Elizabeth II. e, $5, With son, Pres. George W. Bush. f, $6, With Pres. Barack Obama.
No. 4177, vert.: a, Official White House portrait of Pres. Bush. b, Sully, service dog of Pres. Bush.

2019, July 14   Litho.   Perf. 14
4176 A916   Sheet of 6, #a-f   15.50 15.50
Souvenir Sheet
Perf. 12½
4177 A916 $8 Sheet of 2, #a-b   12.00 12.00
No. 4177 contains two 38x51mm stamps.

Miniature Sheet

Leonardo da Vinci (1452-1519) — A917

No. 4178: a, Engraving of Leonardo by Raffaello Morghen. b, Portrait of Gian Giacomo Caprotti, by Leonardo. c, Mona Lisa, by Leonardo. d, Monna Vanna, by Leonardo's student, Andrea Salaí.

2019, July 31   Litho.   Perf. 14
4178 A917 $6 Sheet of 4, #a-d   18.00 18.00

Miniature Sheet

Singpex 2019 International Stamp Exhibition, Singapore — A918

No. 4179 — Show emblem and sites in Singapore Botanic Gardens: a, $4, Clock. b, $5, Gazebo. c, $6, Pathway with arches. d, $7, Park bench.

2019, July 31   Litho.   Perf. 12
4179 A918   Sheet of 4, #a-d   16.50 16.50

Miniature Sheet

Birth of Archie Mountbatten-Windsor — A919

No. 4180: a, $4, Duke and Duchess of Sussex. b, $5, Duke and Duchess of Sussex, with son, Archie. c, $6, Duke and Duchess of Sussex, with son, Archie, diff. d, $7, Duke and Duchess of Sussex, with son, Archie, diff.

2019, July 31   Litho. .   Perf. 14
4180 A919   Sheet of 4, #a-d   16.50 16.50

Miniature Sheet

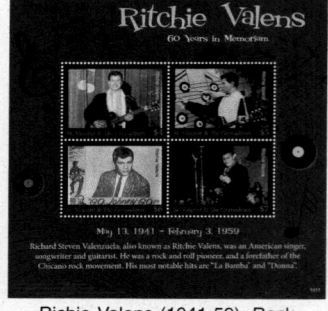

Richie Valens (1941-59), Rock Musician — A920

No. 4181 — Various photographs depicting Valens: a, $4. b, $5. c, $6. d, $7.

2019, Aug. 10   Litho.   Perf. 14
4181 A920   Sheet of 4, #a-d   16.50 16.50

SEMI-POSTAL STAMPS

> Catalogue values for unused stamps in this section are for Never Hinged items.

Map Type of 1977-78 Overprinted: "SOUFRIERE / RELIEF / FUND 1979" and New Values, "10c+5c" etc.
Litho. and Typo.
1979   Wmk. 373   Perf. 14½x14
B1 A76 10c + 5c multi   .25 .25
B2 A76 50c + 25c multi   .25 .25
B3 A76 $1 + 50c multi   .50 .50
B4 A76 $2 + $1 multi   1.00 1.00
    Nos. B1-B4 (4)   2.00 2.00

The surtax was for victims of the eruption of Mt. Soufrière.

Nos. 604-607 Surcharged: "HURRICANE / RELIEF / 50c"
1980, Aug. 7   Litho.   Perf. 13½
B5 A90 10c + 50c multi   .25 .25
B6 A90 60c + 50c multi   .40 .40
B7 A90 80c + 50c multi   .50 .50
B8 A90 $2.50 + 50c multi   1.10 1.10
    Nos. B5-B8 (4)   2.25 2.25

Surtax was for victims of Hurricane Allen.

Nos. 1224-1226 Surcharged "CALIF EARTHQUAKE RELIEF" on 1 or 2 Lines and "+10c"
1989, Nov. 17   Litho.   Perf. 13½x14
B9   Sheet of 9   5.50 5.50
  a.-i. A174 60c +10c #1224a-1224i   .60 .60
B10   Sheet of 9   5.50 5.50
  a.-i. A174 60c +10c #1225a-1225i   .60 .60
B11   Sheet of 9   5.50 5.50
  a.-i. A175 60c +10c #1226a-1226i   .60 .60

WAR TAX STAMPS

No. 105 Overprinted

Type I — Words 2 to 2½mm apart.
Type II — Words 1½mm apart.
Type III — Words 3½mm apart.

1916   Wmk. 3   Perf. 14
MR1   A17 1p car., type III   3.25 25.00
  a.   Double ovpt., type III   275.00 250.00
  b.   1p carmine, type I   12.50 18.50
  c.   Comma after "STAMP", type I   12.50 30.00
  d.   Double ovpt., type I   200.00 200.00
  e.   1p carmine, type II   135.00 87.50
  f.   Double ovpt., type II   1,450.

Overprinted

MR2   A17 1p carmine   1.40 2.25

OFFICIAL STAMPS

> Catalogue values for unused stamps in this section are for Never Hinged items.

Nos. 627-632 Overprinted

1982, Nov.   Litho.   Perf. 14
O1 A94a 60c Couple, Isabella   .25 .25
O2 A94b 60c Couple   .25 .25
O3 A94a $2.50 Couple, Alberta   .45 .45
O4 A94b $2.50 Couple   .65 .65
O5 A94a $4 Couple, Britannia   .80 .80
O6 A94b $4 Couple   .90 .90
    Nos. O1-O6 (6)   3.30 3.30

POSTAL-FISCAL STAMPS

Nos. AR1-AR7 were intended primarily for fiscal use but were also authorized and commonly used for payment of postal charges.

Map of St. Vincent — PF1

1980, Feb.   Litho.   Wmk. 314
AR1 PF1 $5 vio & lavender   2.50 2.50
AR2 PF1 $10 grn & apple grn   4.00 5.00
AR3 PF1 $20 red vio & pale rose lilac   7.00 12.00
    Nos. AR1-AR3 (3)   13.50 19.50

State Seal — PF2

Perf. 14x13¼
1980, May 19   Engr.   Wmk. 373
AR4 PF2 $5 deep blue   2.25 2.75
AR5 PF2 $10 deep green   3.75 4.75
AR6 PF2 $20 carmine rose   6.50 10.50
    Nos. AR4-AR6 (3)   12.50 18.00

Nos. AR4-AR6 are dated "1980" below design.

Perf. 12¼x12
1984, May 22   Engr.   Wmk. 380
AR7 PF2 $20 carmine rose   8.50 13.00

No. AR7 is dated "1984" below design.

ST. VINCENT GRENADINES

sănt ˈvin̪t̪-sənt grə-ˈnā-də

LOCATION — Group of islands south of St. Vincent

CAPITAL — None

St. Vincent's portion of the Grenadines includes Bequia, Canouan, Mustique, Union and a number of smaller islands.

Catalogue values for unused stamps in this area are for Never Hinged items.

Stamps inscribed "Palm Island," "Tobago Cays," and "Young Island" are not listed as they do not meet Scott listing criteria.

The editors would like to examine any commercial covers mailed during 2000-2008 from the islands of Bequia, Canouan, Mayreau, Mustique or Union Island, which are franked only with the island's stamps.

All stamps are designs of St. Vincent unless otherwise noted or illustrated.
See St. Vincent Nos. 324-329a for six stamps and a souvenir sheet issued in 1971 inscribed "The Grenadines of St. Vincent."

Princess Anne's Wedding Issue
Common Design Type

1973, Nov. 14		**Litho.**	**Perf. 14**	
1	CD325	25c green & multi	.25	.25
2	CD325	$1 org brn & multi	.25	.25

Common Design Types pictured following the introduction.

Bird Type of 1970 and St. Vincent Nos. 281a-285a, 287a-289a Overprinted

a

b

1974	**Photo.**	**Wmk. 314**	**Perf. 14**	
3	A36(a)	1c multicolored	.25	.25
4	A36(a)	2c multicolored	.25	.25
5	A36(b)	2c multicolored	.25	.35
6	A36(a)	3c multicolored	.25	.25
7	A36(b)	3c multicolored	.25	.35
8	A36(a)	4c multicolored	.25	.25
9	A36(a)	5c multicolored	.25	.25
10	A36(a)	6c multicolored	.25	.25
11	A36(a)	8c multicolored	.25	.25
12	A36(a)	10c multicolored	.25	.25
13	A36(a)	12c multicolored	.25	.25
14	A36(a)	20c multicolored	.25	.25
15	A36(a)	25c multicolored	.30	.25
16	A36(a)	50c multicolored	.40	.35
17	A36(a)	$1 multicolored	.60	.70
18	A36(a)	$2.50 multicolored	.70	.95
19	A36(a)	$5 multicolored	1.00	1.50
		Nos. 3-19 (17)	6.00	6.95

Nos. 8-9, 12-13, 17-18 vert.
Issue dates: #5, 7, June 7; others, Apr. 24.

Maps of Islands — G1

Perf. 13x12½

1974, May 9		**Litho.**	**Wmk. 314**	
20	G1	5c Bequia	.25	.25
21	G1	15c Prune	.25	.25
22	G1	20c Mayreau	.25	.25
23	G1	30c Mustique	.25	.25
24	G1	40c Union	.25	.25
24A	G1	$1 Canouan	.25	.25
		Nos. 20-24A (6)	1.50	1.50

No. 20 has no inscription at bottom. No. 84 is dated "1976."
See Nos. 84-111.

UPU Type of 1974

2c, Arrows circling UPU emblem. 15c, Post horn, globe. 40c, Target over map of islands, hand canceler. $1, Goode's map projection.

1974, July 25		**Litho.**	**Perf. 14½**	
25-28	A56	Set of 4	.70	.60

Bequia Island G2

Designs: 5c, Boat building. 30c, Careening at Port Elizabeth. 35c, Admiralty Bay. $1, Fishing Boat Race.

1974				
29-32	G2	Set of 4	.75	.70

Shells G3

Designs: 1c, Atlantic thorny oyster. 2c, Zig-zag scallop. 3c, Reticulated helmet. 4c, Music volute. 5c, Amber pen shell. 6c, Angular triton. 8c, Flame helmet. 10c, Caribbean olive. 12c, Common sundial. 15c, Glory of the atlantic cone. 20c, Flame auger. 25c King venus. 35c. Long-spined star-shell. 45c, Speckled tellin. 50c, Rooster tail conch. $1, Green star-shell. $2.50, Incomparable cone. $5, Rough file clam. $10, Measled cowrie.

1974-76			**Wmk. 373**	
33-51	G3	Set of 19	12.50	9.00

Issued: #33-50, 11/27/74; #51, 7/12/76. #36-40, 43, 45, 47-48, exist dated "1976," #40, 42-45, 49-50 dated "1977."
For surcharge see St. Vincent No. 3346.

Churchill Type

Churchill as: 5c, Prime Minister. 40c, Lord Warden of the Cinque Ports. 50c, First Lord of the Admiralty. $1, Royal Air Force officer.

1974, Nov. 28				
52-55	A58	Set of 4	.70	.70

Mustique Island G4

5c, Cotton House. 35c, Blue Waters, Endeavour. 45c, Endeavour Bay. $1, Gelliceaux Bay.

1975, Feb. 27			**Wmk. 373**	
56	G4	5c multicolored	.25	.25
57	G4	35c multicolored	.25	.25
58	G4	45c multicolored	.25	.25
59	G4	$1 multicolored	.25	.25
		Nos. 56-59 (4)	1.00	1.00

Butterflies G5

3c, Soldier martinique. 5c, Silver-spotted flambeau. 35c, Gold rim. 45c, Bright blue, Donkey's eye. $1, Biscuit.

1975, May 15			**Perf. 14**	
60	G5	3c multicolored	.25	.25
61	G5	5c multicolored	.30	.25
62	G5	35c multicolored	.55	.30
63	G5	45c multicolored	.70	.30
64	G5	$1 multicolored	1.40	1.00
		Nos. 60-64 (5)	3.20	2.10

Views of Petit St. Vincent G6

1975, July 24			**Perf. 14½**	
65	G6	5c Resort pavilion	.25	.25
66	G6	35c Harbor	.25	.25
67	G6	45c Jetty	.25	.25
68	G6	$1 Sailing in coral lagoon	.25	.25
		Nos. 65-68 (4)	1.00	1.00

Christmas — G7

Island churches: 5c, Ecumenical Church, Mustique. 25c, Catholic Church, Union. 50c, Catholic Church, Bequia. $1, Anglican Church, Bequia.

1975, Nov. 20			**Wmk. 314**	
69-72	G7	Set of 4	.65	.65

For surcharge see St. Vincent No. 3372.

Union Island G8

5c, Sunset. 35c, Customs and post office. 45c, Anglican Church. $1, Mail boat.

1976, Feb. 26	**Wmk. 373**		**Perf. 13½**	
73	G8	5c Sunset	.25	.25
74	G8	35c multicolored	.25	.25
75	G8	45c multicolored	.25	.25
76	G8	$1 multicolored	.25	.25
		Nos. 73-76 (4)	1.00	1.00

Staghorn Coral — G9

1976, May 13			**Perf. 14½**	
77	G9	5c shown	.25	.25
78	G9	35c Elkhorn coral	.25	.25
79	G9	45c Pillar coral	.25	.25
80	G9	$1 Brain coral	.40	.25
		Nos. 77-80 (4)	1.15	1.00

US Bicentennial Coins — G10

1976, July 15			**Perf. 13½**	
81	G10	25c Washington quarter	.25	.25
82	G10	50c Kennedy half dollar	.25	.25
83	G10	$1 Eisenhower dollar	.25	.25
		Nos. 81-83 (3)	.75	.75

St. Vincent Grenadines Map Type
Bequia Island

1976, Sept. 23		**Litho.**	**Perf. 14**	
84	G1	5c grn, brt grn & blk	.25	.25
85	G1	10c multicolored	.25	.25
a.		Bklt. pane of 3, 2 #84, 85	.35	.35
86	G1	35c multicolored	.25	.25
87	G1	45c multicolored	.25	.25
a.		Bklt. pane of 3, #84, 85, 87	.50	.50
b.		Bklt. pane of 3, 2 #86, 87	.70	.70
		Nos. 84-87 (4)	1.00	1.00

For previous 5c see No. 20.

Canouan Island

1976, Sept. 23				
88	G1	5c multicolored	.25	.25
89	G1	10c multicolored	.25	.25
a.		Bklt. pane of 3, 2 #88, 89	.35	.35
90	G1	35c multicolored	.25	.25
91	G1	45c multicolored	.25	.25
a.		Bklt. pane of 3, #88-89, 91	.50	.50
b.		Bklt. pane of 3, 2 #90, 91	.70	.70
		Nos. 88-91 (4)	1.00	1.00

Mayreau Island

1976, Sept. 23				
92	G1	5c multicolored	.25	.25
93	G1	10c multicolored	.25	.25
a.		Bklt. pane of 3, 2 #92, 93	.35	.35
94	G1	35c multicolored	.25	.25
95	G1	45c multicolored	.25	.25
a.		Bklt. pane of 3, #92-93, 95	.50	.50
b.		Bklt. pane of 3, 2 #94, 95	.70	.70
		Nos. 92-95 (4)	1.00	1.00

Mustique Island

1976, Sept. 23				
96	G1	5c multicolored	.25	.25
97	G1	10c multicolored	.25	.25
a.		Bklt. pane of 3, 2 #96, 97	.35	.35
98	G1	35c multicolored	.25	.25
a.		Bklt. pane of 3, 2 #97, 98	.45	.45
99	G1	45c multicolored	.25	.25
a.		Bklt. pane of 3, #96-97, 99	.50	.50
b.		Bklt. pane of 3, 2 #98, 99	.70	.70
		Nos. 96-99 (4)	1.00	1.00

Petit St. Vincent

1976, Sept. 23				
100	G1	5c multicolored	.25	.25
101	G1	10c multicolored	.25	.25
a.		Bklt. pane of 3, 2 #100, 101	.35	.35
102	G1	35c multicolored	.25	.25
a.		Bklt. pane of 3, 2 #101, 102	.45	.45
103	G1	45c multicolored	.25	.25
a.		Bklt. pane of 3, #100-101, 103	.50	.50
b.		Bklt. pane of 3, 2 #102, 103	.70	.70
		Nos. 100-103 (4)	1.00	1.00

Prune Island

1976, Sept. 23				
104	G1	5c multicolored	.25	.25
105	G1	10c multicolored	.25	.25
a.		Bklt. pane of 3, 2 #104, 105	.35	.35
106	G1	35c multicolored	.25	.25
a.		Bklt. pane of 3, 2 #105, 106	.45	.45
107	G1	45c multicolored	.25	.25
a.		Bklt. pane of 3, #104-105, 107	.50	.50
b.		Bklt. pane of 3, 2 #106, 107	.70	.70
		Nos. 104-107 (4)	1.00	1.00

Union Island

1976, Sept. 23				
108	G1	5c multicolored	.25	.25
109	G1	10c multicolored	.25	.25
a.		Bklt. pane of 3, 2 #108, 109	.35	.35
110	G1	35c multicolored	.25	.25
a.		Bklt. pane of 3, 2 #109, 110	.45	.45
111	G1	45c multicolored	.25	.25
a.		Bklt. pane of 3, #108-109, 111	.50	.50
b.		Bklt. pane of 3, 2 #110, 111	.70	.70
		Nos. 108-111 (4)	1.00	1.00

Mayreau
Island
G11

Designs: 5c, Station Hill school, post office.
35c, Church at Old Wall. 45c, Cruiser at
anchor, La Souciere. $1, Saline Bay.

1976, Dec. 2　　　　　　*Perf. 14½*
112-115　G11　Set of 4　　　　.75　.50

Queen Elizabeth II, Silver
Jubilee — G12

Coins: 25c, Coronation Crown. 50c, Silver
Wedding Crown. $1, Silver Jubilee Crown.

1977, Mar. 3
116-118　G12　Set of 3　　　　.60　.40

Fiddler
Crab
G13

1977, May 19
119　G13　　5c shown　　　　.25　.25
120　G13　35c Ghost crab　　　.25　.25
121　G13　50c Blue crab　　　.25　.25
122　G13　$1.25 Spiny lobster　.50　.90
　　Nos. 119-122 (4)　　　1.25　1.65

Prune
Island
G14

1977, Aug. 25
123　G14　　5c Snorkel diving　　.25　.25
124　G14　35c Palm Island Resort　.25　.25
125　G14　45c Casuarina Beach　.25　.25
126　G14　$1 Palm Island Beach
　　　　　　Club　　　　　　.25　1.00
　　Nos. 123-126 (4)　　　1.00　1.75

Map Type of
1977
Overprinted

　　　　　　　　　Perf. 14½x14
1977, Oct. 31　　　　　Wmk. 314
127　A76　40c multicolored (R)　.25　.25
128　A76　$2 multicolored (B)　.40　.25

For surcharge see St. Vincent No. 3381.

Canouan
Island
G15

5c, Clinic, Charlestown. 35c, Town jetty,
Charlestown. 45c, Mailboat, Charlestown. $1,
Grand Bay.

1977, Dec. 8　Wmk. 373　　*Perf. 14½*
129　G15　　5c multicolored　　.25　.25
130　G15　35c multicolored　　.25　.25
131　G15　45c multicolored　　.25　.25
132　G15　$1 multicolored　　　.25　.90
　　Nos. 129-132 (4)　　　1.00　1.65

Birds
and
Eggs
G16

1c, Tropical Mockingbird. 2c, Mangrove
cuckoo. 3c, Osprey. 4c, Smooth bellied ani.
5c, House wren. 6c, Bananaquit. 8c, Carib
grackle. 10c, Yellow bellied elaenia. 12c, Collared plover. 15c, Cattle egret. 20c, Red footed
booby. 25c, Red-billed tropic bird. 40c, Royal
tern. 50c, Rusty tailed flycatcher. 80c, Purple
gallinule. $1, Broad winged hawk. $2, Common ground dove. $3, Laughing gull. $5,
Brown noddy. $10, Grey kingbird.

1978, May 11　　　　　*Perf. 13x12*
133-152　G16　　Set of 20　　15.00　14.00

　　Nos. 139, 143, 149 exist imprinted "1979,"
Value: $1.60. Nos. 137-138, 140, 142, 144
imprinted "1980." Value: $1.50.
　　Nos. 147-148 imprinted "1979" are from No.
175a. Nos. 145-146, 150 imprinted "1980" are
from No. 189a.
　　For surcharges see No. 266, St. Vincent
Nos. 3347-3348.

Elizabeth II Coronation Anniv. Type

Cathedrals.

1978, June 2　　　　　*Perf. 13½*
153　A78　　5c Worcester　　　.25　.25
154　A78　40c Coventry　　　.25　.25
155　A78　$1 Winchester　　.25　.25
156　A78　$3 Chester　　　　.25　.25
　　　Complete booklet, 2 each #153-
　　　156　　　　　　　2.25
　a.　Souv. sheet, #153-156, perf. 14　.60　.75
　　Nos. 153-156 (4)　　　1.00　1.00

Turtles
G17

1978, July 20　　　　　*Perf. 14*
157　G17　　5c Green turtle　　.25　.25
158　G17　40c Hawksbill turtle　.25　.25
159　G17　50c Leatherback turtle　.30　.30
160　G17　$1.25 Loggerhead turtle　.60　.60
　　Nos. 157-160 (4)　　　1.40　1.40

For surcharge see St. Vincent No. 3374.

Christmas
G18

Christmas scenes and verses from the carol
"We Three Kings of Orient Are".

1978, Nov. 2
161　G18　　5c Three kings follow-
　　　　　　ing star　　　　.25　.25
162　G18　10c Gold　　　　.25　.25
163　G18　25c Frankincense　.25　.25
164　G18　50c Myrrh　　　.25　.25
165　G18　$2 With infant Jesus　.25　.25
　a.　Souvenir sheet of 5 + label,
　　　#161-165　　　　.90　1.25
　　Nos. 161-165 (5)　　1.25　1.25

Sailing
Yachts — G19

1979
166　G19　　5c multicolored　　.25　.25
167　G19　40c multi, diff.　　.25　.25
168　G19　50c multi, diff.　　.25　.25
169　G19　$2 multi, diff.　　.40　.40
　　Nos. 166-169 (4)　　1.15　1.15

Wildlife Type of 1980

1979, Mar. 8　　　　　*Perf. 14½*
170　A91　20c Green iguana　.25　.25
171　A91　40c Manicou　　　.25　.25
172　A91　$2 Red-legged tortoise　.70　.90
　　Nos. 170-172 (3)　　1.20　1.40

Sir Rowland Hill Type of 1979

Designs: 80c, Sir Rowland Hill. $1, Great
Britain Types A1 and A5 with "A10" (Kingstown, St. Vincent) cancel. $2, St. Vincent #41
& 43 with Bequia cancel.

1979, May 31　　　　　*Perf. 13x12*
173　A83　80c multicolored　.25　.25
174　A83　$1 multicolored　.25　.25
175　A83　$2 multicolored　.25　.35
　a.　Souv. sheet, #173-175, 147-149　1.25　2.00
　　Nos. 173-175 (3)　　.75　.85

IYC Type of 1979

Children and IYC emblem: 6c, Boy. 40c,
Girl. $1, Boy, diff. $3, Girl and boy.

1979, Oct. 24　　　　　*Perf. 14x13½*
176　A82　　6c multicolored　.25　.25
177　A82　40c multicolored　.25　.25
178　A82　$1 multicolored　.25　.25
179　A82　$3 multicolored　.25　.25
　　Nos. 176-179 (4)　　1.00　1.00

Independence Type of 1979

Designs: 5c, National flag, Ixora salici-folia.
40c, House of Assembly, Ixora odorata. $1,
Prime Minister R. Milton Cato, Ixora jamaica.

1979, Oct. 27　　　　　*Perf. 12½x12*
180-182　A85　Set of 3　　.45　.45

　Printed se-tenant with label inscribed "Independence of St. Vincent and the Grenadines."

False
Killer
Whale
G20

1979, Jan. 25　　　　　*Perf. 14*
183　G20　10c shown　　　.50　.30
184　G20　50c Spinner dolphin　.50　.35
185　G20　90c Bottle nosed
　　　　　　dolphin　　　　.55　.70
186　G20　$2 Blackfish　　1.40　1.75
　　Nos. 183-186 (4)　　2.95　3.10

For surcharges see St. Vincent Nos. 3352,
3371, 3383-3384.

London '80 Type

1980, Apr. 24　　　　　*Perf. 13x12*
187　A88　40c Queen Elizabeth II　.25　.25
188　A88　50c St. Vincent #227　.25　.25
189　A88　$3 #1-2　　　　.25　1.00
　a.　Souvenir sheet of 6, #187-189,
　　　145-146, 150　　　2.00　2.25
　　Nos. 187-189 (3)　　.75　1.50

Olympics Type of 1980

1980, Aug. 7　　　　　*Perf. 13½*
190　A90　25c Running　　.25　.25
191　A90　50c Sailing　　　.25　.25
192　A90　$1 Long jump　.25　.25
193　A90　$2 Swimming　.25　.25
　　Nos. 190-193 (4)　　1.00　1.00

For surcharge see St. Vincent No. 3353.

Christmas
G21

Scenes and verse from the carol "De Born-
ing Day."

1980, Nov. 13　　　　　*Perf. 14*
194　G21　　5c multicolored　.25　.25
195　G21　35c multicolored　.25　.25
196　G21　60c multicolored　.25　.25
197　G21　$1 multicolored　.25　.25
198　G21　$2 multicolored　.25　.25
　a.　Souvenir sheet of 5 + label,
　　　#194-198　　　　.75　1.25
　　Nos. 194-198 (5)　　1.25　1.25

For surcharge see St. Vincent No. 3385.

Bequia
Island
G22

50c, P.O., Port Elizabeth. 60c, Moonhole.
$1.50, Fishing boats, Admiralty Bay. $2,
Friendship Rose at jetty.

1981, Feb. 19　　　　　*Perf. 14½*
199　G22　50c multicolored　.25　.25
200　G22　60c multicolored　.25　.25
201　G22　$1.50 multicolored　.25　.45
202　G22　$2 multicolored　.25　.50
　　Nos. 199-202 (4)　　1.00　1.45

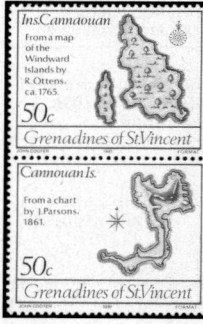

Map by R.
Ottens, c.
1765 — G23

Maps: Nos. 204, 206 by J. Parsons, 1861.
No. 208, by T. Jefferys, 1763.

1981, Apr. 2　　　　　*Perf. 14*
203　50c Ins. Cannaouan　.25　.25
204　50c Cannouan Island　.25　.25
　a.　Pair, #203-204　　.55　.25
205　60c Ins. Moustiques　.25　.25
206　60c Mustique Island　.25　.25
　a.　Pair, #205-206　　.60　.60
207　$2 Ins. Bequia　　.50　.65
208　$2 Bequia Island　.50　.65
　a.　Pair, #207-208　　1.10　1.40
　　Nos. 203-208 (6)　　2.00　2.30

Royal Wedding Types

No. 209, Couple, the Mary. No. 210,
Couple. No. 211, Couple, the Alexandra. No.
213, Couple, the Brittania.

1981, July 17　　　　　Wmk. 380
209　A94a　50c multicolored　.25　.25
　a.　Booklet pane of 4. perf. 12　.60　.60
210　A94b　50c multicolored　.30　.40
211　A94a　$3 multicolored　.25　.25
212　A94b　$3 like #210　　.60　.80
　a.　Booklet pane of 2, perf. 12　2.00　2.00
213　A94a　$3.50 multicolored　.25　.25
214　A94b　$3.50 like #210　.65　.85
　　Nos. 209-214 (6)　　2.30　2.80

Each denomination issued in sheets of 7 (6
type A94a, 1 type A94b).
For surcharges and overprints see Nos.
507-508, O1-O6.

Souvenir Sheet

1981　　　　　　　　*Perf. 12*
215　A94b　$5 like #210　　1.00　1.00

Bar Jack
G25

1981, Oct. 9   Wmk. 373   Perf. 14
218 G25 10c shown .25 .25
219 G25 50c Tarpon .30 .25
220 G25 60c Cobia .40 .25
221 G25 $2 Blue marlin 1.00 .75
    Nos. 218-221 (4) 1.95 1.50

Ships
G26

1982, Jan. 28   Perf. 14x13½
222 G26 1c Experiment .25 .25
223 G26 3c Lady Nelson .25 .25
224 G26 5c Daisy .25 .25
225 G26 6c Carib canoe .25 .25
226 G26 10c Hairoun Star .35 .30
227 G26 15c Jupiter .45 .35
228 G26 20c Christina .45 .35
229 G26 25c Orinoco .60 .40
230 G26 50c Lively .60 .40
231 G26 50c Alabama .85 .45
232 G26 60c Denmark .95 .45
233 G26 75c Santa Maria 1.00 .50
234 G26 $1 Baffin .75 .50
235 G26 $2 QE 2 1.10 1.10
236 G26 $3 Britannia 1.10 1.40
237 G26 $5 Geeststar 1.10 1.60
238 G26 $10 Grenadines Star 1.45 2.50
    Nos. 222-238 (17) 11.75 11.30

For overprint see No. 509.

G27

1982, Apr. 5   Perf. 14
239 G27 10c Prickly pear fruit .25 .25
240 G27 50c Flower buds .30 .30
241 G27 $1 Flower .50 .50
242 G27 $2 Cactus 1.25 1.25
    Nos. 239-242 (4) 2.30 2.30

For surcharge see St. Vincent No. 3386.

Princess Diana Type of Kiribati

50c, Anne Neville. 60c, Arms of Anne Neville. $6, Diana, Princess of Wales.

1982, July 1   Wmk. 380   Perf. 14
243 A99a 50c multicolored .25 .25
244 A99a 60c multicolored .25 .25
245 A99a $6 multicolored .50 .50
    Nos. 243-245 (3) 1.00 1.00

For overprints see Nos. 248-262.

G29

1982, July 1   Wmk. 373   Perf. 14½
246 G29 $1.50 Old, new uniforms .50 .50
247 G29 $2.50 Lord Baden-Powell .80 .80

75th anniversary of Boy Scouts.

Nos. 243-245 Ovptd. "ROYAL BABY / BEQUIA"

1982, July 19   Wmk. 380   Perf. 14
248 A99a 50c multicolored .25 .25
249 A99a 60c multicolored .25 .25
250 A99a $6 multicolored .40 .40
    Nos. 248-250 (3) .90 .90

Nos. 243-245 Ovptd. "ROYAL BABY / CANOUAN"

1982, July 19
251 A99a 50c multicolored .25 .25
252 A99a 60c multicolored .25 .25
253 A99a $6 multicolored .40 .40
    Nos. 251-253 (3) .90 .90

Nos. 243-245 Ovptd. "ROYAL BABY / MAYREAU"

1982, July 19
254 A99a 50c multicolored .25 .25
255 A99a 60c multicolored .25 .25
256 A99a $6 multicolored .40 .40
    Nos. 254-256 (3) .90 .90

Nos. 243-245 Ovptd. "ROYAL BABY / MUSTIQUE"

1982, July 19
257 A99a 50c multicolored .25 .25
258 A99a 60c multicolored .25 .25
259 A99a $6 multicolored .40 .40
    Nos. 257-259 (3) .90 .90

Nos. 243-245 Ovptd. "ROYAL BABY / UNION"

1982, July 19
260 A99a 50c multicolored .25 .25
261 A99a 60c multicolored .25 .25
262 A99a $6 multicolored .40 .40
    Nos. 260-262 (3) .90 .90

Christmas Type of 1981

1982, Nov. 18   Perf. 13½
263 A97 10c Mary and Joseph at inn .25 .25
264 A97 $1.50 Animals of stable .40 .40
265 A97 $2.50 Nativity .50 .50
a.   Souvenir sheet of 3, #263-265 1.10 1.10
    Nos. 263-265 (3) 1.15 1.15

For surcharges see St. Vincent Nos. 3376, 3390-3391.

No. 146 Surcharged

Perf. 13x12
1983, Apr. 26   Wmk. 373
266 G16 45c on 50c multicolored .55 .35

Union Island
G30

50c, Power Station, Clifton. 60c, Sunrise, Clifton Harbor. $1.50, School, Ashton. $2, Frigate Rock, Conch Shell Beach.

1983, May 12   Perf. 13½
267 G30 50c multicolored .25 .25
268 G30 60c multicolored .25 .25
269 G30 $1.50 multicolored .35 .35
270 G30 $2 multicolored .50 .50
    Nos. 267-270 (4) 1.35 1.35

Treaty of Versailles, Bicent. — G31

1983, Sept. 15   Perf. 14½x14
271 G31 45c British warship .25 .25
272 G31 60c American warship .30 .30
273 G31 $1.50 US troops, flag .55 .55
274 G31 $2 British troops in battle .75 .75
    Nos. 271-274 (4) 1.85 1.85

For surcharges see St. Vincent Nos. 3350, 3360, 3364, 3377.

200 Years of Manned Flight
G32

Designs: 45c, Montgolfier balloon 1783, vert. 60c, Ayres Turbo-thrush Commander. $1.50, Lebaudy "1" dirigible. $2, Space shuttle Columbia.

1983, Sept. 15   Perf. 14
275 G32 45c multicolored .25 .25
276 G32 60c multicolored .25 .25
277 G32 $1.50 multicolored .35 .35
278 G32 $2 multicolored .40 .40
a.   Souvenir sheet of 4, #275-278 1.60 1.60
    Nos. 275-278 (4) 1.25 1.25

For surcharges see St. Vincent Nos. 3355, 3378-3379, 3387.

British Monarch Type of 1984

No. 279a, Arms of Henry VIII. No. 279b, Henry VIII. No. 280a, Arms of James I. No. 280b, James I. No. 281a, Henry VIII. No. 281b, Hampton Court. No. 282a, James I. No. 282b, Edinburgh Castle. No. 283a, Mary Rose. No. 283b, Henry VIII, Portsmouth harbor. No. 284a, Gunpowder Plot. No. 284b, James I & Gunpowder Plot.

1983, Oct. 25   Unwmk.   Perf. 12½
279 A110 60c Pair, #a.-b. .30 .30
280 A110 60c Pair, #a.-b. .30 .30
281 A110 75c Pair, #a.-b. .30 .30
282 A110 75c Pair, #a.-b. .30 .30
283 A110 $2.50 Pair, #a.-b. .45 .45
284 A110 $2.50 Pair, #a.-b. .45 .45
    Nos. 279-284 (6) 2.10 2.10

Old Coinage — G33

20c, Quarter and half dollar, 1797. 45c, Nine bits, 1811-14. 75c, Six and twelve bits, 1811-14. $3, Sixty six shillings, 1798.

1983, Dec. 1   Wmk. 373   Perf. 14
291 G33 20c multicolored .25 .25
292 G33 45c multicolored .25 .25
293 G33 75c multicolored .25 .25
294 G33 $3 multicolored .50 .50
    Nos. 291-294 (4) 1.25 1.25

For surcharge see St. Vincent No. 3351.

Locomotives Type of 1985

No. 295, 1948 Class C62, Japan. No. 296, 1898 P.L.M. Grosse C, France. No. 297, 1892 Class D13, US. No. 298, 1903 Class V, UK. No. 299, 1980 Class 253, UK. No. 300, 1968 Class 581, Japan. No. 301, 1874 1001 Class, UK. No. 302, 1977 Class 142, DDR. No. 303, 1899 T-9 Class, UK. No. 304, 1932 Class C12, Japan. No. 305, 1897 Class T15, Germany. No. 306, 1808 Catch-me-who-can, UK. No. 307, 1900 Claud Hamilton Class, UK. No. 308, 1948 Class E10, Japan. No. 309, 1937 Coronation Class, UK. No. 310, 1936 Class 231, Algeria. No. 311, 1927 Class 4P, UK. No. 312, 1979 Class 120, Germany. No. 313, 1941 Class J, US. No. 314, 1900 Class 13, UK. No. 315, 1913 Slieve Gullion Class S, UK. No. 316, 1929 Class A3, UK. No. 317, 1954 Class X, Australia. No. 318, 1895 Class D16, US. No. 319, 1904 J. B. Earle, UK. No. 320, 1879 Halesworth, UK. No. 321, 1900 Class V1, UK. No. 322, 1986 Class 59, UK. No. 323, 1935 Class E18, Germany. No. 324, 1923 Class D50, Japan. No. 325, 1859 Problem Class, UK. No. 326, 1958 Class 40, UK. No. 327, 1875 Class A, US. No. 328, 1907 Star Class, British. No. 329, 1898 Lyn, UK. No. 330, 1961 Western Class, UK. No. 331, 1958 Warship Class 42, UK. No. 332, 1831 Samson Type,

---

US. No. 333, 1854 Hayes, US. No. 334, 1902 Class P-69, US. No. 335, 1865 Talyllyn, UK. No. 336, 1899 Drummond's Bug, UK. No. 337, 1913 Class 60-3 Shay, US. No. 338, 1938 Class H1-d, Canada. No. 339, 1890 Class 2120, Japan. No. 340, 1951 Clan Class, UK. No. 341, 1934 Pioneer Zephyr, US. No. 342, 1948 Blue Peter, UK. No. 343, 1874 Class Beattie Well Tank, UK. No. 344, 1906 Cardean, UK. No. 345, 1840 Fire Fly, UK. No. 346, 1884 Class 1800, Japan.

1984-87 Litho. Unwmk. Perf. 12½
Se-tenant Pairs, #a.-b.
a. — Side and front views.
b. — Action scene.
295 A120 1c multicolored .25 .25
296 A120 1c multicolored .25 .25
297 A120 5c multicolored .25 .25
298 A120 5c multicolored .25 .25
299 A120 10c multicolored .25 .25
300 A120 10c multicolored .25 .25
301 A120 10c multicolored .25 .25
302 A120 10c multicolored .25 .25
303 A120 15c multicolored .25 .25
304 A120 15c multicolored .25 .25
305 A120 15c multicolored .25 .25
306 A120 20c multicolored .25 .25
307 A120 35c multicolored .25 .25
308 A120 35c multicolored .30 .30
309 A120 35c multicolored .35 .35
310 A120 40c multicolored .45 .45
311 A120 40c multicolored .50 .50
312 A120 40c multicolored .25 .25
313 A120 45c multicolored .35 .35
314 A120 45c multicolored .40 .40
315 A120 50c multicolored .55 .55
316 A120 50c multicolored .55 .55
317 A120 60c multicolored .40 .40
318 A120 60c multicolored .40 .40
319 A120 60c multicolored .35 .35
320 A120 60c multicolored .55 .55
321 A120 60c multicolored .55 .55
322 A120 60c multicolored .55 .55
323 A120 70c multicolored .40 .40
324 A120 75c multicolored .40 .40
325 A120 75c multicolored .35 .35
326 A120 75c multicolored .55 .55
327 A120 75c multicolored .60 .60
328 A120 $1 multicolored .40 .40
329 A120 $1 multicolored .40 .40
330 A120 $1 multicolored .40 .40
331 A120 $1 multicolored .60 .60
332 A120 $1 multicolored .60 .60
333 A120 $1.20 multicolored .50 .50
334 A120 $1.25 multicolored .60 .60
335 A120 $1.50 multicolored .50 .50
336 A120 $1.50 multicolored .45 .45
337 A120 $1.50 multicolored .70 .70
338 A120 $1.50 multicolored .80 .80
339 A120 $2 multicolored .50 .50
340 A120 $2 multicolored .80 .80
341 A120 $2 multicolored .80 .80
342 A120 $2.50 multicolored .50 .50
343 A120 $2.50 multicolored 1.20 1.20
344 A120 $3 multicolored .60 .60
345 A120 $3 multicolored 1.00 1.00
a.   Souvenir sheet of 4, #324, 345 3.50 3.50
346 A120 $3 multicolored .60 .60
    Nos. 295-346 (52) 23.70 23.70

Issued: #297, 299, 303, 307, 313, 318, 328, 342, 3/15/84; #295, 298, 306, 308, 319, 329, 335, 344, 10/9/84; #296, 304, 324, 345, 1/31/85; #300, 310, 315, 343, 5/17/85; #309, 323, 333, 339, 9/16/85; #305, 314, 320, 325, 330, 336, 340, 346, 3/14/86; #301, 311, 316, 321, 326, 331, 334, 337, 5/5/87; #302, 312, 317, 322, 327, 332, 338, 341, 8/26/87.

Spotted Eagle Ray
G34

Wmk. 380
1984, Apr. 26   Litho.   Perf. 14
399 G34 45c shown .25 .25
400 G34 60c Queen trigger fish .25 .25
401 G34 $1.50 White spotted file fish .35 .35
402 G34 $2 Schoolmaster .40 .40
    Nos. 399-402 (4) 1.25 1.25

For overprint see No. 504.

Cricket Players Type of 1985

No. 403, R. A. Woolmer, portrait. No. 404, K. S. Ranjitsinhji, portrait. No. 405, W. R. Hammond, in action. No. 406, S. F. Barnes, portrait. No. 407, D. L. Underwood, in action. No. 408, R. Peel, in action. No. 409, M. D. Moxon, in action. No. 410, W. G. Grace, portrait. No. 411, L. Potter, portrait. No. 412, E. A. E. Baptiste, portrait. No. 413, H. Larwood, in action. No. 414, A. P. E. Knott, portrait. No. 415, Yorkshire & Kent county cricket clubs. No.

416, Sir John Berry Hobbs, portrait. No. 417, L. E. G. Ames, in action.

1984-85		Unwmk.	**Perf. 12½**	
		Pairs, #a.-b.		
403	A116	1c multicolored	.25	.25
404	A116	3c multicolored	.25	.25
405	A116	5c multicolored	.25	.25
406	A116	5c multicolored	.25	.25
407	A116	30c multicolored	.55	.55
408	A116	30c multicolored	.45	.45
409	A116	55c multicolored	.45	.45
410	A116	60c multicolored	.70	.70
411	A116	60c multicolored	.45	.45
412	A116	$1 multicolored	.70	.70
413	A116	$1 multicolored	.55	.55
414	A116	$2 multicolored	.80	.80
415	A116	$2 multicolored	.70	.70
416	A116	$2.50 multicolored	.80	.80
417	A116	$3 multicolored	1.10	1.10
		Nos. 403-417 (15)	8.25	8.25

Size of stamps in No. 415: 58x38mm.

Issued: Nos. 403, 407, 410, 412, 414, 417, 8/16/84; Nos. 406, 408, 413, 416, 11/2/84; Nos. 409, 411, 415, 2/22/85.

Canouan Island G35

1984, Sept. 3			**Wmk. 380**	
433	G35	35c Junior secondary school	.25	.25
434	G35	45c Police station	.35	.35
435	G35	$1 Post office	.40	.50
436	G35	$3 Anglican church	1.00	1.60
		Nos. 433-436 (4)	2.00	2.60

For surcharges see St. Vincent Nos. 3349, 3354, 3394.

Night-blooming Flowers — G36

1984, Oct. 15				
437	G36	35c Lady of the night	.30	.30
438	G36	45c Four o'clock	.35	.35
439	G36	75c Mother-in-law's tongue	.45	.45
440	G36	$3 Queen of the night	1.75	1.75
		Nos. 437-440 (4)	2.85	2.85

For surcharges see St. Vincent Nos. 3351A, 3356.

Car Type of 1983

No. 441, 1959 Facel Vega, France. No. 442, 1903 Winton, Britain. No. 443, 1914 Mercedes-Benz, Germany. No. 444, 1936 BMW, Germany. No. 445, 1954 Rolls Royce, Britain. No. 446, 1934 Frazer Nash, Britain. No. 447, 1931 Invicta, Britain. No. 448, 1974 Lamborghini, Italy. No. 449, 1959 Daimler, Britain. No. 450, 1932 Marmon, US. No. 451, 1966 Brabham Repco, Britain. No. 452, 1968 Lotus Ford. No. 453, 1949 Buick, US. No. 454, 1927 Delage, France.

1984-86		Unwmk.	**Perf. 12½**	
		Se-tenant Pairs, #a.-b.		
		a. — Side and front views.		
		b. — Action scene.		
441	A107	5c multicolored	.25	.25
442	A107	5c multicolored	.25	.25
443	A107	15c multicolored	.25	.25
444	A107	25c multicolored	.25	.25
445	A107	45c multicolored	.25	.25
446	A107	50c multicolored	.30	.30
447	A107	55c multicolored	.25	.25
448	A107	60c multicolored	.25	.25
449	A107	$1 multicolored	.30	.30
450	A107	$1 multicolored	.30	.30
451	A107	$1.50 multicolored	.30	.30
452	A107	$1.75 multicolored	.30	.30
453	A107	$3 multicolored	.60	.60
454	A107	$3 multicolored	.50	.50
		Nos. 441-454 (14)	4.40	4.40

Issued: #441, 444, 446, 453, 11/28/84; #442, 447, 449, 451, 4/9/85; #443, 445, 448, 450, 452, 454, 2/20/86.

Stamps issued 2/20/86 not inscribed "Leaders of the World."

Christmas Type of 1983

20c, Three wise men, star. 45c, Journeying to Bethlehem. $3, Presenting gifts.

1984, Dec. 3		**Litho.**		**Perf. 14½**	
469	A106	20c multicolored	.25	.25
470	A106	45c multicolored	.25	.25
471	A106	$3 multicolored	.35	1.00
a.		Souvenir sheet of 3, #469-471	1.00	1.50
		Nos. 469-471 (3)	.85	1.50

For surcharges see St. Vincent Nos. 3358, 3361.

Shellfish G37

1985, Feb. 11			**Perf. 14**	
472	G37	25c Caribbean king crab	.25	.25
473	G37	60c Queen conch	.30	.30
474	G37	$1 White sea urchin	.40	.45
475	G37	$3 West Indian top shell	.80	1.75
		Nos. 472-475 (4)	1.75	2.75

For surcharge see St. Vincent No. 3395.

Flowers — G38

No. 476a, Cypripedium calceolus. No. 476b, Gentiana asclepiadea. No. 477a, Clianthus formosus. No. 477b, Celmisia coriacea. No. 478a, Erythronium americanum. No. 478b, Laelia anceps. No. 479a, Leucadendron discolor. No. 479b, Meconopsis horridula.

1985, Mar. 13		Unwmk.	**Perf. 12½**	
476	G38	5c Pair, #a.-b.	.25	.25
477	G38	55c Pair, #a.-b.	.30	.30
478	G38	60c Pair, #a.-b.	.30	.30
479	G38	$2 Pair, #a.-b.	.55	.55
		Nos. 476-479 (4)	1.40	1.40

Water Sports G39

1985, May 9		**Wmk. 380**	**Perf. 14**	
484	G39	35c Windsurfing	.25	.25
485	G39	45c Water skiing	.25	.25
486	G39	75c Scuba diving	.25	.25
487	G39	$3 Deep sea fishing	.40	.40
		Nos. 484-487 (4)	1.15	1.15

Tourism.

For surcharge see St. Vincent No. 3396.

Fruits and Blossoms G40

1985, June 24			**Perf. 15**	
488	G40	30c Passion fruit	.25	.25
489	G40	75c Guava	.30	.30
490	G40	$1 Sapodilla	.45	.45
491	G40	$2 Mango	.75	.75
a.		Souvenir sheet of 4, #488-491, perf. 14½x15	2.50	2.50
		Nos. 488-491 (4)	1.75	1.75

For overprint see No. 503.

Queen Mother Type of 1985

#496a, Facing right. #496b, Facing forward. #497a, Facing right. #497b, Facing left. #498a, Facing right. #498b, Facing forward. #499a,

Facing right. #499b, Facing left. #500a, As girl facing forward. #500b, Facing left.

1985, July 31		Unwmk.	**Perf. 12½**	
496	A122	40c Pair, #a.-b.	.25	.25
497	A122	75c Pair, #a.-b.	.30	.30
498	A122	$1.10 Pair, #a.-b.	.30	.30
499	A122	$1.75 Pair, #a.-b.	.30	.30
		Nos. 496-499 (4)	1.15	1.15

Souvenir Sheet of 2

500	A122	$2 Pair, #a.-b.	.90	.90

Souvenir sheets containing two $4 or two $5 stamps exist.

Nos. 213-214, 236, 399, 488, and 496-497 Ovptd. or Srchd. "CARIBBEAN ROYAL VISIT 1985" in 1, 2 or 3 Lines

Perfs., Wmks. as Before

1985, Oct. 27				
503	G40	30c On #488	1.00	1.00
504	G37	45c On #399	1.25	1.25
505	A122	$1.10 On #496	2.25	2.25
506	A122	$1.10 On #497	2.25	2.25
507	A94a	$1.50 On $3.50, #213	2.50	2.50
508	A94b	$1.50 On $3.50, #214	22.50	22.50
509	G26	$3 On #236	3.25	3.25
		Nos. 503-509 (7)	35.00	35.00

Traditional Dances G41

1985, Dec. 16		Unwmk.	**Perf. 15**	
510	G41	45c Donkey man	.25	.25
511	G41	75c Cake dance, vert.	.25	.25
512	G41	$1 Bois-bois man, vert.	.35	.35
513	G41	$2 Maypole dance	.55	.55
		Nos. 510-513 (4)	1.40	1.40

For surcharges see St. Vincent Nos. 3366-3367.

Queen Elizabeth II 60th Birthday Type

5c, Elizabeth II. $1, At Princess Anne's christening. $4, As Princess. $6, In Canberra, 1982, vert. $8, Elizabeth II with crown.

1986, Apr. 21			**Perf. 12½**	
514-517	A128	Set of 4	2.00	2.00

Souvenir Sheet

518	A128	$8 multi	2.75	2.75

Handicrafts — G41a

1986, Apr. 22		**Wmk. 380**		**Perf. 15**	
519	G41a	10c Dolls	.25	.25
520	G41a	60c Basketwork	.25	.25
521	G41a	$1 Scrimshaw	.25	.25
522	G41a	$3 Model boat	.55	.55
		Nos. 519-522 (4)	1.30	1.30

World Cup Soccer Championship, Mexico — G42

Perf. 12½, 15 (#525-528)

1986, May 7			Unwmk.	
523	G42	1c Uruguayan team	.25	.25
524	G42	10c Polish team	.25	.25
525	G42	45c Bulgarian player	.30	.30
526	G42	75c Iraqi player	.35	.35
527	G42	$1.50 S. Korean player	.60	.60
528	G42	$2 N. Ireland player	.70	.70

529	G42	$4 Portuguese team	1.00	1.00
530	G42	$5 Canadian team	1.10	1.10
		Nos. 523-530 (8)	4.55	4.55

Souvenir Sheets

531	G42	$1 like #529	.50	.50
532	G42	$3 like #523	1.25	1.25

Size: Nos. 525-528, 25x40mm.

Fungi — G43

45c, Marasmius pallescens. 60c, Leucocoprinus fragilissimus. 75c, Hygrocybe occidentalis. $3, Xerocomus hypoxanthus.

		Wmk. 380		
1986, May 23		**Litho.**	**Perf. 14**	
533	G43	45c multicolored	2.50	2.50
534	G43	60c multicolored	2.75	2.75
535	G43	75c multicolored	3.00	3.00
536	G43	$3 multicolored	8.00	8.00
		Nos. 533-536 (4)	16.25	16.25

For surcharge see St. Vincent No. 3397.

Royal Wedding Type of 1986

No. 539a, Sarah, Diana. No. 539b, Andrew. No. 540a, Anne, Andrew, Charles, Margaret, horiz. No. 540b, Sarah, Andrew, horiz.

1986		Unwmk.	**Perf. 12½**	
539	A132	60c Pair, #a.-b.	.35	.35
540	A132	$2 Pair, #a.-b.	1.10	1.10

Souvenir Sheet

541	A132a	$8 Andrew, Sarah, in coach	3.50	3.50

Issued: #539-540, July 18; #541, Oct. 15.

Nos. 539-540 Ovptd. in Silver "Congratulations to TRH The Duke & Duchess of York" in 3 Lines

1986, Oct. 15				
542	A132	60c Pair, #a.-b.	.60	.60
543	A132	$2 Pair, #a.-b.	2.00	2.00

Dragonflies — G44

45c, Brachymesia furcata. 60c, Lepthemis vesiculosa. 75c, Perithemis domitta. $2.50, Tramea abdominalis, vert.

1986, Nov. 19			**Perf. 15**	
546	G44	45c multicolored	.25	.25
547	G44	60c multicolored	.25	.25
548	G44	75c multicolored	.25	.25
549	G44	$2.50 multicolored	.55	.55
		Nos. 546-549 (4)	1.30	1.30

Statue of Liberty Type
Souvenir Sheets

Each stamp shows different views of Statue of Liberty and a different US president in the margin.

1986, Nov. 26			**Perf. 14**	
550	A135	$1.50 multicolored	.25	.25
551	A135	$1.75 multicolored	.30	.30
552	A135	$2 multicolored	.35	.40
553	A135	$2.50 multicolored	.40	.50
554	A135	$3 multicolored	.50	.50
555	A135	$3.50 multicolored	.60	.60
556	A135	$5 multicolored	.80	.80
557	A135	$6 multicolored	.90	.90
558	A135	$8 multicolored	1.25	1.25
		Nos. 550-558 (9)	5.35	5.50

Birds of
Prey — G45

1986, Nov. 26   **Litho.**

560	G45	10c Sparrow hawk	.75	.75
561	G45	45c Black hawk	1.50	1.50
562	G45	60c Duck hawk	1.75	1.75
563	G45	$4 Fish hawk	8.00	8.00
		Nos. 560-563 (4)	12.00	12.00

For surcharges see St. Vincent Nos. 3362, 3401.

Christmas — G46

45c, Santa playing drums. 60c, Santa wind surfing. $1.25, Santa water skiing. $2, Santa limbo dancing.

1986, Nov. 26

564	G46	45c multicolored	.25	.25
565	G46	60c multicolored	.30	.30
566	G46	$1.25 multicolored	.80	.80
567	G46	$2 multicolored	1.15	1.15
a.		Souvenir sheet of 4, #564-567	8.50	8.50
		Nos. 564-567 (4)	2.50	2.50

For surcharge see St. Vincent No. 3375.

Queen Elizabeth II, 40th Wedding Anniv. Type of 1987

15c, Elizabeth, Charles. 45c, Victoria, Albert. $1.50, Elizabeth, Philip. $3, Elizabeth, Philip, diff. $4, Elizabeth, portrait. $6, Elizabeth as Princess.

1987, Oct. 15   **Perf. 12½**

568	A140	15c multicolored	.25	.25
569	A140	45c multicolored	.25	.25
570	A140	$1.50 multicolored	.30	.30
571	A140	$3 multicolored	.35	.35
572	A140	$4 multicolored	.45	.45
		Nos. 568-572 (5)	1.60	1.60

Souvenir Sheet

573	A140	$6 multicolored	1.90	1.90

Victoria's accession to the throne, 150th anniv.

Marine
Life
G48

45c, Banded coral shrimp. 50c, Arrow crab, flamingo tongue. 65c, Cardinal fish. $5, Moray eel.

No. 578, Puffer fish.

1987, Dec. 17   **Perf. 15**

574	G48	45c multicolored	.55	.55
575	G48	50c multicolored	.60	.60
576	G48	65c multicolored	.70	.70
577	G48	$5 multicolored	2.60	2.60
		Nos. 574-577 (4)	4.45	4.45

Souvenir Sheet

578	G48	$5 multicolored	2.60	2.60

America's Cup
Yachts — G49

1988, Mar. 31   **Perf. 12½**

579	G49	50c Australia IV	.30	.30
580	G49	65c Crusader II	.35	.35
581	G49	75c New Zealand K27	.40	.40
582	G49	$2 Italia	.60	.60
583	G49	$4 White Crusader	.75	.75
584	G49	$5 Stars and Stripes	.75	.75
		Nos. 579-584 (6)	3.15	3.15

Souvenir Sheet

585	G49	$1 Champosa V	.90	.90

Bequia
Regatta
G50

1988, Mar. 31   **Perf. 15**

586	G50	5c Seine boats	.25	.25
587	G50	50c Friendship Rose	.25	.25
588	G50	75c Fishing boats	.25	.25
589	G50	$3.50 Yacht racing	.40	.40
		Nos. 586-589 (4)	1.15	1.15

Souvenir Sheet
Perf. 12½

590	G50	$8 Port Elizabeth	3.50	3.50

For surcharges see St. Vincent Nos. 3368, 3400.

Tourism — G51

Aircraft of Mustique Airways, Genadine Tours.

1988, May 26   **Perf. 14x13½**

591	G51	15c multicolored	.25	.25
592	G51	65c multi, diff.	.25	.25
593	G51	75c multi, diff.	.25	.25
594	G51	$5 multi, diff.	.55	.55
		Nos. 591-594 (4)	1.30	1.30

Souvenir Sheet

595	G51	$10 Waterfall, vert.	3.50	3.50

No. 595 contains one 35x56mm stamp.
For surcharges see St. Vincent Nos. 3369-3370.

Great
Explorers
G52

Designs: 15c, Vitus Bering and the St. Peter. 75c, Bering and pancake ice. $1, David Livingstone and the Ma-Robert. $2, Livingstone meeting Henry M. Stanley. $3, John Speke (1827-1864) and Sir Richard Burton (1821-1890) welcomed at Tabori. $3.50, Speke, Burton at Lake Victoria. $4, Crewman of Christopher Columbus spotting land. $4.50, Columbus, exchange of gifts. $5, Sextant. $6, Columbus' ship landing in Bahamas, 1492.

1988, July 29   **Perf. 14**

596-603	G52	Set of 8	4.50 4.50

Souvenir Sheets

604	G52	$5 multi	1.50	1.50
605	G52	$6 multi	1.75	1.75

Nos. 602-603, 605 picture 500th anniversary discovery of America emblem.

A number of unissued items, imperfs., part perfs., missing color varieties, etc., were made available when the Format International inventory was liquidated.

Cricketers — G53

1988, July 29   **Perf. 15**

606	G53	20c A. I. Razvi	.25	.25
607	G53	45c R. J. Hadlee	.25	.25
608	G53	75c M. D. Crowe	.45	.45
609	G53	$1.25 C. H. Lloyd	.70	.70
610	G53	$1.50 A. R. Border	.85	.85
611	G53	$2 M. D. Marshall	1.10	1.10
612	G53	$2.50 G. A. Hick	1.25	1.25
613	G53	$3.50 C. G. Greenidge, horiz.	1.50	1.50
		Nos. 606-613 (8)	6.35	6.35

A $3 souvenir sheet in the design of the $2 stamp was not a postal issue according to the St. Vincent P.O. Value $6.

Tennis Type of 1987

15c, Pam Shriver, horiz. 50c, Kevin Curran. 75c, Wendy Turnbull. $1, Evonne Cawley. $1.50, Ilie Nastase, horiz. $2, Billie Jean King. $3, Bjorn Borg. $3.50, Virginia Wade.

1988, July 29   **Perf. 12½**

614	A137	15c multicolored	.25	.25
615	A137	50c multicolored	.25	.25
616	A137	75c multicolored	.30	.30
617	A137	$1 multicolored	.40	.40
618	A137	$1.50 multicolored	.45	.45
619	A137	$2 multicolored	.55	.55
620	A137	$3 multicolored	.65	.65
621	A137	$3.50 multicolored	.70	.70
		Nos. 614-621 (8)	3.55	3.55

Souvenir Sheet

622		Sheet of 2	2.00	2.00
a.	A137	$2.25 Stefan Edberg	.80	.80
b.	A137	$2.25 Steffi Graf	.80	.80

No. 616 inscribed "Turnball" in error.

India '89, International Stamp
Exhibition, New Dehli — G54

Disney characters and sites in India — 1c, Fatehpur Sikri. 2c, Palace on Wheels. 3c, Old fort, Delhi. 5c, Pinjore Gardens. 10c, Taj Mahal. 25c, Chandni Chowk. $4, Agra Fort, Jaipur. $5, Gandhi Memorial.
No. 631, Qutab Minar, vert. No. 632, Palace of the Winds.

1989, Feb. 7   **Perf. 14x13½**

623	G54	1c multicolored	.25	.25
624	G54	2c multicolored	.25	.25
625	G54	3c multicolored	.25	.25
626	G54	5c multicolored	.25	.25
627	G54	10c multicolored	.25	.25
628	G54	25c multicolored	.25	.25
629	G54	$4 multicolored	3.50	3.50
630	G54	$5 multicolored	4.75	4.75
		Nos. 623-630 (8)	9.75	9.75

Souvenir Sheets

631	G54	$6 multicolored	6.75	6.75
632	G54	$6 multicolored	6.75	6.75

Japanese Art Type

Paintings: 5c, The View at Yotsuya, by Hokusai. 30c, Landscape at Ochanomizu, by Hokuju. 45c, Itabashi, by Eisen. 65c, Early

Summer Rain, by Kunisada. 75c, High Noon at Kasumigaseki, by Kuniyoshi. $1, The Yoshiwara Embankment by Moonlight, by Kuniyoshi. $4, The Bridge of Boats at Sano, by Hokusai. $5, Lingering Snow on Mount Hira, by Kunitora. No. 641, Colossus of Rhodes, by Kunitora. No. 642, Shinobazu Pond, by Kokan.

1989, July 6   **Perf. 14x13½**

633-640	A170	Set of 8	11.50 11.50

Souvenir Sheets

641	A170	$6 multicolored	5.50	5.50
642	A170	$6 multicolored	5.50	5.50

Miniature Sheet

1990 World Cup Soccer
Championships, Italy — G55

Soccer players and landmarks: a, Mt. Vesuvius. b, The Colosseum. c, Venice. d, Roman Forum. e, Leaning Tower of Pisa. f, Florence. g, The Vatican. h, The Pantheon.

1989, July 10   **Perf. 14**

643	G55	Sheet of 8	13.50	13.50
a.-h.		$1.50 any single	1.60	1.60

Discovery of America 500th Anniv. Type of Antigua & Barbuda

UPAE emblem and American Indians: 25c, Smoking tobacco. 75c, Rolling tobacco. $1, Body painting. No. 647a, Starting campfire. No. 647b, Woman drinking from bowl. No. 647c, Woman frying grain or corn patties. No. 647d, Adult resting in hammock using stone mortar and pestle. $4, Smoothing wood. No. 649, Chief. No. 650, Fishing with bow and arrow.

1989, Oct. 2   **Litho.**   **Perf. 14**

644	A196	25c multicolored	.25	.25
645	A196	75c multicolored	.80	.80
646	A196	$1 multicolored	1.00	1.00
647		Strip of 4	5.00	5.00
a.-d.	A196	$1.50 any single	1.00	1.00
648	A196	$4 multicolored	3.00	3.00
		Nos. 644-648 (5)	10.05	10.05

Souvenir Sheets

649	A196	$6 multicolored	5.00	5.00
650	A196	$6 multicolored	5.00	5.00

No. 647 has continuous design.

1st Moon Landing Type

Designs: 5c, Columbia command module. 40c, Neil Armstrong saluting flag on the Moon. 55c, Command module over Moon. 65c, Eagle liftoff from Moon. 70c, Eagle on the Moon. $1, Command module re-entering Earth's atmosphere. $3, Apollo 11 mission emblem. $5, Armstrong and Buzz Aldrin walking on the Moon. No. 659, Apollo 11 launch, vert. No. 660, Splashdown.

1989, Oct. 2   **Perf. 14**

651-658	A171	Set of 8	12.50 12.50

Souvenir Sheets

659	A171	$6 multi, vert.	5.00	5.00
660	A171	$6 multi	5.00	5.00

Butterflies
G56

5c, Southern dagger tail. 30c, Androgeus swallowtail. 45c, Clench's hairstreak. 65c, Buckeye. 75c, Venezuelan sulphur. $1, Mimic. $4, Common longtail skipper. $5, Carribean buckeye.
No. 669, Flambeau. No. 670, Queen, large orange sulphur. Ramsden's giant white.

1989, Oct. 16   **Litho.**   **Perf. 14x14½**

661	G56	5c multicolored	.45	.45
662	G56	30c multicolored	.75	.75
663	G56	45c multicolored	1.00	1.00
664	G56	65c multicolored	1.10	1.10

665	G56	75c multicolored	1.40	1.40
666	G56	$1 multicolored	1.50	1.50
667	G56	$4 multicolored	6.00	6.00
668	G56	$5 multicolored	7.50	7.50

Nos. 661-668 (8) 19.70 19.70

Souvenir Sheets

| 669 | G56 | $6 multicolored | 9.50 | 9.50 |
| 670 | G56 | $6 multicolored | 9.50 | 9.50 |

Flora — G57

80c, Solanum urens. $1.25, Passiflora andersonii. $1.65, Miconia andersonii. $1.85, Pitcairnia sulphurea.

1989, Nov. 1　　Litho.　　Perf. 14

671	G57	80c multicolored	1.25	1.25
672	G57	$1.25 multicolored	1.75	1.75
673	G57	$1.65 multicolored	2.50	2.50
674	G57	$1.85 multicolored	2.75	2.75

Nos. 671-674 (4) 8.25 8.25

Christmas — G58

Walt Disney characters and classic automobiles — 5c, 1907 Rolls-Royce. 10c, 1897 Stanley Steamer. 15c, 1904 Darracq Genevieve. 45c, 1914 Detroit Electric Coupe. 55c, 1896 Ford. $2, 1904 REO Runabout. $3, 1899 Winton Mail Truck. $5, 1893 Duryea Car. No. 683, 1912 Pope-Hartford. No. 684, 1908 Buick Model 10.

1989, Dec. 20　Perf. 14x13½, 13½x14

675	G58	5c multicolored	.30	.30
676	G58	10c multicolored	.30	.30
677	G58	15c multicolored	.30	.30
678	G58	45c multicolored	.75	.75
679	G58	55c multicolored	1.00	1.00
680	G58	$2 multicolored	2.00	2.00
681	G58	$3 multicolored	2.75	2.75
682	G58	$5 multicolored	4.25	4.25

Nos. 675-682 (8) 11.65 11.65

Souvenir Sheets

| 683 | G58 | $6 multicolored | 7.25 | 7.25 |
| 684 | G58 | $6 multicolored | 7.25 | 7.25 |

Nos. 683-684 vert.

Battles of World War II G59

10c, 1st Battle of Narvik, 4/10/40. 15c, Allies land at Anzio, 1/22/44. 20c, Battle of Midway, 6/4/42. 45c, Allies launch offensive on Gustav Line, 5/11/44. 55c, Allies take over zones in Berlin, 7/3/45. 65c, Battle of the Atlantic, 3/1-20/43. 90c, Allies launch final phase of North African Campaign, 4/22/43. $3, US forces land on Guam, 7/21/44. $5, US 7th Army meets the 3rd Army across the Rhine, 3/26/45. #694, Battle of Leyte Gulf, 10/23/44. #695, The Dambusters Raid, 5/16/43.

1990, Apr. 2　Litho.　　Perf. 14

| 685-694 | G59 | Set of 10 | 20.00 | 20.00 |

Souvenir Sheet

| 695 | G59 | $6 multi | 10.50 | 10.50 |

For surcharge see St. Vincent No. 3399.

Penny Black, 150th Anniv. — G60

$1, Stamp World London '90 emblem. $5, Negative image of the Penny Black. $6, Penny Black with non-existent letters.

1990, May 3　　　Perf. 14x15

| 696 | G60 | $1 pale rose & blk | 1.25 | 1.25 |
| 697 | G60 | $5 pale violet & blk | 6.00 | 6.00 |

Souvenir Sheet

| 698 | G60 | $6 dull blue & blk | 6.75 | 6.75 |

Stamp World London '90.

Disney Characters Portraying Shakespearian Roles — G61

Designs: 20c, Goofy as Marc Antony in "Julius Caesar." 30c, Clarabelle Cow as nurse in "Romeo and Juliet." 45c, Pete as Falstaff in "Henry IV." 50c, Minnie Mouse as Portia in "The Merchant of Venice." $1, Donald Duck holding head of Yorick in "Hamlet." $2, Daisy Duck as Ophelia in "Hamlet." $4, Donald and Daisy Duck as Benedick and Beatrice in "Much Ado About Nothing." $5, Minnie Mouse and Donald Duck portraying Romeo and Juliet. No. 707, Mickey and Minnie Mouse portraying Romeo and Juliet. No. 708, Clarabelle Cow as Titania in "A Midsummer Night's Dream."

1990, May　　　　Perf. 14x13½

| 699-706 | G61 | Set of 8 | 13.00 | 13.00 |

Souvenir Sheets

| 707 | G61 | $6 multi | 6.75 | 6.75 |
| 708 | G61 | $6 multi | 6.75 | 6.75 |

World Cup Soccer Championships, Italy — G62

World Cup Trophy and players from participating countries.

1990, Sept. 24　Litho.　　Perf. 14

709	G62	25c Scotland	.45	.45
710	G62	50c Egypt	.85	.85
711	G62	$2 Austria	2.75	2.75
712	G62	$4 United States	4.75	4.75

Nos. 709-712 (4) 8.80 8.80

Souvenir Sheets

| 713 | G62 | $6 Holland | 7.00 | 7.00 |
| 714 | G62 | $6 England | 7.00 | 7.00 |

Orchids — G63

Designs: 5c, Paphiopedilum. 25c, Dendrobium phalaenopsis, Cymbidium. 35c, Miltonia candida. 50c, Epidendrum ibaguense, Cymbidium Elliot Rogers. $1, Rossioglassum grande. $2, Phalaenopsis Elisa Chang Lou,

---

Masdevallia coccinea. $4, Cypripedium accale, Cypripedium calceolus. $5, Orchis spectabilis. No. 723, Epidendrum ibaguense, Phalaenopsis. No. 724, Dendrobium anosmum.

1990, Nov. 23　　Litho.　　Perf. 14

| 715-722 | G63 | Set of 8 | 18.00 | 18.00 |

Souvenir Sheets

| 723 | G63 | $6 multi | 9.00 | 9.00 |
| 724 | G63 | $6 multi | 9.00 | 9.00 |

Expo '90, Intl. Garden and Greenery Exposition, Osaka, Japan.

Birds G64

5c, Common ground dove. 25c, Purple martin. 45c, Painted bunting. 55c, Blue-hooded euphonia. 75c, Blue-gray tanager. $1, Red-eyed vireo. $2, Palm chat. $3, North American jacana. $4, Green-throated carib. $5, St. Vincent parrot.
$6, Red-legged honeycreeper.

1990, Nov. 26

725	G64	5c multicolored	.40	.40
726	G64	25c multicolored	.40	.40
727	G64	45c multicolored	.70	.70
728	G64	55c multicolored	.80	.80
729	G64	75c multicolored	1.00	1.00
730	G64	$1 multicolored	1.10	1.10
731	G64	$2 multicolored	1.75	1.75
732	G64	$3 multicolored	2.50	2.50
733	G64	$4 multicolored	3.25	3.25
734	G64	$5 multicolored	4.50	4.50

Nos. 725-734 (10) 16.40 16.40

Souvenir Sheets

735		Sheet of 2	5.25	5.25
a.	G64	$3 Bananaquit	2.25	2.25
b.	G64	$3 Magnificent frigatebird	2.25	2.25
736	G64	$6 multicolored	5.25	5.25

Queen Mother 90th Birthday Type

Photographs: Nos. 737a-737i, From 1900-1929. Nos. 738a-738i, From 1930-1959. Nos. 739a-739i, From 1960-1989. Nos. 740-748, Enlarged photographs used for Nos. 737-739.

1991, Feb. 14　　Litho.　　Perf. 14

Miniature Sheets of 9, #a.-i.

737	A193	$2 blue & multi	12.00	12.00
738	A193	$2 pink & multi	12.00	12.00
739	A193	$2 green & multi	12.00	12.00

Souvenir Sheets

740	A193	$5 like #737a	3.25	3.25
741	A193	$5 like #737f	3.25	3.25
742	A193	$5 like #737h	3.25	3.25
743	A193	$5 like #738b	3.25	3.25
744	A193	$5 like #738f	3.25	3.25
745	A193	$5 like #738g	3.25	3.25
746	A193	$5 like #739b	3.25	3.25
747	A193	$5 like #739d	3.25	3.25
748	A193	$5 like #739h	3.25	3.25

Paintings by Vincent Van Gogh — G65

Designs: 5c, View of Arles with Irises in the Foreground. 10c, View of Saintes-Maries, vert. 15c, An Old Woman of Arles, vert. 20c, Orchard in Blossom, Bordered by Cypresses. 25c, Three White Cottages in Saintes-Maries. 35c, Boats at Saintes-Maries-De-La-Mer. 40c, Interior of a Restaurant in Arles. 45c, Peasant Woman, vert. 55c, Self-Portrait, Sept. 1888, vert. 60c, A Pork Butcher's Shop Seen From a Window, vert. 75c, The Night Cafe in Arles. $1, Portrait of Milliet, Second Lieutenant of the Zouaves, vert. $2, The Cafe Terrace on the Place Du Forum Arles, at Night, vert. $3, The Zouave, vert. $4, Two Lovers (Fragment), vert. No. 764, $5, Still Life: Blue Enamel Coffeepot, Earthenware and Fruit.
No. 765, $5, Street in Saintes-Maries. No. 766, $5, A Lane Near Arles. No. 767, $6, Harvest at La Crau, with Montmajour in the Background. No. 768, $6, The Sower.

1991, June 10　Litho.　　Perf. 13½

| 749-764 | G65 | Set of 16 | 27.50 | 27.50 |

Size: 102x76mm

Imperf

| 765-766 | G65 | Set of 2 | 11.00 | 11.00 |
| 767-768 | G65 | Set of 2 | 14.00 | 14.00 |

Royal Family Birthday, Anniversary
Common Design Type

1991, July 5　Litho.　　Perf. 14

769	CD347	10c multicolored	.50	.50
770	CD347	15c multicolored	.50	.50
771	CD347	40c multicolored	.60	.60
772	CD347	50c multicolored	.80	.80
773	CD347	$1 multicolored	1.50	1.50
774	CD347	$2 multicolored	2.25	2.25
775	CD347	$4 multicolored	3.75	3.75
776	CD347	$5 multicolored	5.50	5.50

Nos. 769-776 (8) 15.40 15.40

Souvenir Sheets

| 777 | CD347 | $5 Henry, William, Charles, Diana | 5.75 | 5.75 |
| 778 | CD347 | $5 Elizabeth, Andrew, Philip | 4.25 | 4.25 |

10c, 50c, $1, Nos. 776-777, Charles and Diana, 10th wedding anniversary. Others, Queen Elizabeth II, 65th birthday.

Phila Nippon '91 G66

Japanese locomotives: 10c, First Japanese steam. 25c, First American steam locomotive in Japan. 35c, Class 8620 steam. 50c, C53 steam. $1, DD-51 diesel. $2, RF 22327 electric. $4, EF-55 electric. $5, EF-58 electric. No. 787, $6, Class 9600 steam, vert. No. 788, $6, Class 4100 steam, vert. No. 789, $6, C57 steam, vert. No. 790, $6, C62 steam, vert.

1991, Aug. 12　Litho.　　Perf. 14x13½

| 779-786 | G66 | Set of 8 | 16.50 | 16.50 |

Souvenir Sheets
Perf. 12x13

| 787-790 | G66 | Set of 4 | 19.00 | 19.00 |

Brandenburg Gate Type

Designs: 45c, Brandenburg Gate and Soviet Pres. Mikhail Gorbachev. 65c, Sign. 80c, Statue, soldier escaping through barbed wire. No. 794, Berlin police insignia. No. 795, Berlin coat of arms.

1991, Nov. 18　Litho.　　Perf. 14

791	A209	45c multicolored	.80	.80
792	A209	65c multicolored	1.00	1.00
793	A209	80c multicolored	1.10	1.10

Nos. 791-793 (3) 2.90 2.90

Souvenir Sheets

| 794 | A209 | $5 multicolored | 3.50 | 3.50 |
| 795 | A209 | $5 multicolored | 3.50 | 3.50 |

Wolfgang Amadeus Mozart Type

Portrait of Mozart and: $1, Scene from "Abduction from the Seraglio." $3, Dresden, 1749. No. 799, Portrait, vert. No. 800, Bust, vert.

1991, Nov. 18　Litho.　　Perf. 14

| 797 | A210 | $2 multicolored | 1.00 | 1.00 |
| 798 | A210 | $3 multicolored | 3.50 | 3.50 |

Souvenir Sheets

| 799 | A210 | $5 multicolored | 3.75 | 3.75 |
| 800 | A210 | $5 multicolored | 3.75 | 3.75 |

Boy Scout Type

Designs: $2, Scout delivering mail and Czechoslovakian (local) scout stamp. $4, Cog train, Boy Scouts on Mt. Snowdon, Wales, vert. Nos. 803-804, Emblem of World Scout Jamboree, Korea.

1991, Nov. 18　Litho.　　Perf. 14

| 801 | A211 | $2 multicolored | 2.00 | 2.00 |
| 802 | A211 | $4 multicolored | 4.00 | 4.00 |

Souvenir Sheets

| 803 | A211 | $5 tan & multi | 3.75 | 3.75 |
| 804 | A211 | $5 violet blue & multi | 3.75 | 3.75 |

Lord Robert Baden-Powell, 50th death anniv. and 17th World Scout Jamboree, Korea.

De Gaulle Type

Designs: 60c, De Gaulle in Djibouti, 1959. No. 807, In military uniform, vert. No. 808, Portrait as President.

1991, Nov. 18   **Litho.**   *Perf. 14*

806	A212	60c multicolored	1.45	1.45

Souvenir Sheets

807	A212	$5 multicolored	3.75	3.75
808	A212	$5 multicolored	3.75	3.75

A number has been reserved for additional value in this set.

Anniversaries and Events Type

Designs: $1.50, Otto Lilienthal, aviation pioneer. No. 810, Train in winter, vert. No. 811, Trans-Siberian Express Sign. No. 812, Man and woman celebrating. No. 813, Woman and man wearing hats. No. 814, Georg Ludwig Friedrich Laves, architect of Hoftheater, Hanover. No. 815, Locomotive, Trans-Siberian Railway, vert. No. 816, Cantonal arms of Appenzell and Thurgau. No. 817, Hanover, 750th anniv.

1991, Nov. 18   **Litho.**   *Perf. 14*

809	A213	$1.50 multicolored	1.75	1.75
810	A213	$1.75 multicolored	3.25	3.25
811	A213	$1.75 multicolored	3.25	3.25
812	A213	$2 multicolored	3.00	3.00
813	A213	$2 multicolored	3.00	3.00
814	A213	$2 multicolored	3.00	3.00
		Nos. 809-814 (6)	17.25	17.25

Souvenir Sheets

815	A213	$5 multicolored	6.50	6.50
816	A213	$5 multicolored	5.50	5.50
817	A213	$5 multicolored	5.00	5.00

First glider flight, cent. (#809). Trans-Siberian Railway, cent. (#810-811, 815). Swiss Confederation, 700th anniv. (#812-813, 816). City of Hanover, 750th anniv. (#814, 817). No. 815 contains one 42x58mm stamp.

Pearl Harbor Type of 1991
Miniature Sheet

No. 818: a, Japanese submarines and aircraft leave Truk to attack Pearl Harbor. b, Japanese flagship, Akagi. c, Nakajima B5N2 Kate, attack leader. d, Torpedo bombers attack battleship row. e, Ford Island Naval Air Station. f, Doris Miller earns Navy Cross. g, USS West Virginia and USS Tennessee ablaze. h, USS Arizona destroyed. i, USS New Orleans. j, Pres. Roosevelt declares war.

1991, Nov. 18   *Perf. 14½x15*

818	A214	$1 Sheet of 10, #a.-		
		j.	20.00	20.00

Disney Christmas Card Type

Card design and year of issue: 10c, Mickey in sleigh pulled by Pluto, 1974. 55c, Donald, Pluto, and Mickey watching marching band, 1961. 65c, Greeting with stars, 1942. 75c, Mickey, Donald watch Merlin create a snowman, 1963. $1.50, Mickey placing wreath on door, 1958. $2, Mickey as Santa beside fireplace, 1957. $4, Mickey manipulating "Pinnochio" for friends. $5, Prince Charming and Cinderella dancing beside Christmas tree, 1987.

No. 827, $6, Snow White, 1957, vert. No. 828, $6, Santa riding World War II bomber, 1942, vert.

1991, Nov. 18   *Perf. 14x13½, 13½x14*

819-826	A216	Set of 8	16.50	16.50

Souvenir Sheets

827-828	A216	Set of 2	14.50	14.50

Nos. 819-826 are horiz.

Queen Elizabeth II's Accession to the Throne, 40th Anniv.
Common Design Type

1992, Feb. 6   **Litho.**   *Perf. 14*

829	CD348	15c multicolored	.40	.40
830	CD348	45c multicolored	1.00	1.00
831	CD348	$2 multicolored	2.25	2.25
832	CD348	$4 multicolored	4.00	4.00
		Nos. 829-832 (4)	7.65	7.65

Souvenir Sheets

833	CD348	$6 Queen at left, beach	6.00	6.00
834	CD348	$6 Queen at right, building	6.00	6.00

World Columbian Stamp Expo Type

Walt Disney characters as famous Chicagoans: 10c, Mickey as Walt Disney walking past birthplace. 50c, Donald Duck and nephews sleeping in George Pullman's railway cars. $1, Daisy Duck as Jane Addams in front of Hull House. $5, Mickey as Carl Sandburg. No. 839, Grandma McDuck as Mrs. O'Leary with her cow, vert.

1992, Apr.   **Litho.**   *Perf. 14x13½*

835	A220	10c multicolored	.35	.35
836	A220	50c multicolored	.75	.75
837	A220	$1 multicolored	2.00	2.00
838	A220	$5 multicolored	5.25	5.25
		Nos. 835-838 (4)	8.35	8.35

Souvenir Sheet
Perf. 13½x14

839	A220	$6 multicolored	7.50	7.50

Nos. 840-844 have not been used.

Granada '92 Type

Walt Disney characters as Spanish explorers in New World: 15c, Aztec King Goofy giving treasure to Big Pete as Hernando Cortes. 40c, Mickey as Hernando de Soto discovering Mississippi River. $2, Goofy as Vasco Nunez de Balboa discovering Pacific Ocean. $4, Donald Duck as Francisco Coronado discovering Rio Grande. $6, Mickey as Ponce de Leon discovering Fountain of Youth.

1992, Apr.   *Perf. 14x13½*

845	A221	15c multicolored	.45	.45
846	A221	40c multicolored	1.25	1.25
847	A221	$2 multicolored	1.75	1.75
848	A221	$4 multicolored	4.00	4.00
		Nos. 845-848 (4)	7.45	7.45

Souvenir Sheet
Perf. 13½x14

849	A221	$6 multicolored	6.50	6.50

Nos. 850-854 have not been used.

Discovery of America, 500th Anniv. Type

Designs: 10c, King Ferdinand & Queen Isabella. 45c, Santa Maria & Nina in Acul Bay, Haiti. 55c, Santa Maria, vert. $2, Columbus' fleet departing Canary Islands, vert. $4, Sinking of Santa Maria off Hispanola. $5, Nina and Pinta returning to Spain. No. 861, $6, Columbus' fleet during night storm. No. 862, $6, Columbus landing on San Salvador.

1992, May 22   **Litho.**   *Perf. 14*

855-860	A222	Set of 6	9.25	9.25

Souvenir Sheets

861-862	A222	Set of 2	9.25	9.25

World Columbian Stamp Expo '92, Chicago.

Mushrooms — G67

Designs: 10c, Entoloma bakeri. 15c, Hydropus paraensis. 20c, Leucopaxillus gracillimus. 45c, Hygrotrama dennisianum. 50c, Leucoagaricus hortensis. 65c, Pyrrhoglossum pyrrhum. 75c, Amanita craeoderma. $1, Lentinus bertieri. $2, Dennisiomyces griseus. $3, Xerulina asprata. $4, Hygrocybe acutoconica. $5, Lepiota spiculata.

No. 879, $6, Pluteus crysophlebius. No. 880, $6, Lepiota volvatua. No. 881, $6, Amanita lilloi.

1992, July 2

867-878	G67	Set of 12	21.00 21.00

Souvenir Sheets

879-881		Set of 3	19.00 19.00

Butterfly Type of 1992

Designs: 15c, Nymphalidae paulogramma 20c, Heliconius cydno. 30c, Ithomiidae eutresis hypereia. 45c, Eurytides Columbus koll, vert. 55c, Papilio ascolius. 75c, Anaea pasibula. 80c, Heliconius doris. $1, Nymphalidae persisama pitheas. $2, Nymphalidae batesia hypochlora. $3, Heliconius erato. $4, Elzunia cassandrina. $5, Ithomiidae sais.

No. 894, $6, Pieridae dismorphia orise. No. 895, $6, Nymphalidae podotricha. No. 896, $6, Oleria tigilla.

1992, June 15   **Litho.**   *Perf. 14*

882-893	A225	Set of 12	22.00 22.00

Souvenir Sheets

894-896	A225	Set of 3	18.00 18.00

Genoa '92.

Hummingbirds Type of 1992

5c, Antillean crested, female, horiz. 10c, Blue-tailed emerald, female. 35c, Antillean mango, male, horiz. 45c, Antillean mango, female, horiz. 55c, Green-throated carib, horiz. 65c, Green violet-ear. 75c, Blue-tailed emerald, male, horiz. $1, Purple throated carib. $2, Copper-rumped, horiz. $3, Rufous-breasted hermit. $4, Antillean crested, male. $5, Green breasted mango, male.

No. 909, $6, Blue-tailed emerald. No. 910, $6, Antillean mango, diff. No. 911, $6, Antillean crested, male, diff.

1992, July 7   **Litho.**   *Perf. 14*

897-908	A224	Set of 12	21.00 21.00

Souvenir Sheets

909-911	A224	Set of 3	18.00 18.00

Genoa '92.

Discovery of America Type

1992   **Litho.**   *Perf. 14½*

912	A230	$1 Coming ashore	1.25	1.25
913	A230	$2 Natives, ships	2.75	2.75

Organization of East Caribbean States.

Summer Olympics Type

10c, Volleyball, vert. 15c, Men's floor exercise. 25c, Cross-country skiing, vert. 30c, 110-meter hurdles. 45c, 120-meter ski jump. 55c, Women's 4x100-meter relay, vert. 75c, Triple jump, vert. 80c, Mogul skiing, vert. $1, 100-meter butterfly. $2, Tornado class yachting. $3, Decathlon. $5, Equestrian jumping.

No. 926, Ice hockey. No. 927, Single luge. No. 928, Soccer.

1992, Apr. 21   **Litho.**   *Perf. 14*

914	A219	10c multicolored	.40	.40
915	A219	15c multicolored	.50	.50
916	A218	25c multicolored	.60	.60
917	A219	30c multicolored	.70	.70
918	A218	45c multicolored	.80	.80
919	A219	55c multicolored	1.00	1.00
920	A219	75c multicolored	1.10	1.10
921	A219	80c multicolored	1.25	1.25
922	A219	$1 multicolored	1.40	1.40
923	A219	$2 multicolored	2.00	2.00
924	A219	$3 multicolored	3.25	3.25
925	A219	$5 multicolored	5.50	5.50
		Nos. 914-925 (12)	18.50	18.50

Souvenir Sheets

926	A218	$6 multicolored	5.50	5.50
927	A218	$6 multicolored	5.50	5.50
928	A219	$6 multicolored	5.50	5.50

Christmas Art Type

Details or entire paintings: 10c, Our Lady with St. Roch & St. Anthony of Padua, by Giorgione. 40c, St. Anthony of Padua, by Master of the Embroidered Leaf. 45c, Madonna & Child in a Landscape, by Orazio Gentileschi. 50c, Madonna & Child with St. Anne, by Leonardo da Vinci. 55c, The Holy Family, by Giuseppe Maria Crespi. 65c, Madonna & Child, by Andrea Del Sarto. 75c, Madonna & Child with Sts. Lawrence & Julian, by Gentile da Fabriano. $1, Virgin & Child, by School of Parma. $2, Madonna with the Iris in the style of Durer. $3, Virgin & Child with St. Jerome & St. Dominic, by Filippino Lippi. $4, Rapolano Madonna, by Ambrogio Lorenzetti. $5, The Virgin & Child with Angels in a Garden with a Rose Hedge, by Stefano da Verona.

No. 941, $6, Virgin & Child with St. John the Baptist, by Botticelli. No. 942, $6, Madonna & Child with St. Anne, by Leonardo da Vinci. No. 943, $6, Madonna & Child with Grapes, by Lucas Cranach the Elder.

1992, Nov.   **Litho.**   *Perf. 13½x14*

929-940	A232	Set of 12	20.00 20.00

Souvenir Sheets

941-943	A232	Set of 3	16.50 16.50

Anniversaries and Events — G68

Designs: 10c, Nina in the harbor of Baracoa. No. 948, Columbus' fleet at sea. No. 949, America 3, US and II Moro, Italy. No. 945, Zeppelin LZ3, 1907. No. 946, Blind man with guide dog, vert. No. 947, Guide dog. No. 950, German flag, natl. arms, Konrad Adenauer. No. 951, Hands breaking bread, vert. $2, Mars, Voyager 2. $3, Berlin airlift, Adenauer. No. 954, Wolfgang Amadeus Mozart, Constanze, vert. No. 955, Adenauer, Cologne after World War II. No. 956, Zeppelin LZ 37 shot down over England, World War I. $5, Buildings in Germany, Adenauer.

No. 958, $6, Scene from "Don Giovanni," vert. No. 959, $6, Columbus looking through telescope. No. 960, $6, Count Ferdinand von Zeppelin, facing right. No. 960A, $6, Count Ferdinand von Zeppelin, facing left. No. 961, $6, Mars Observer. No. 962, $6, Adenauer with hand on face, vert. No. 963, $6, Adenauer, diff.

1992, Dec.   *Perf. 14*

944	G68	10c multicolored	1.75	1.75
945	G68	75c multicolored	2.00	2.00
946	G68	75c multicolored	2.75	2.75
947	G68	75c multicolored	2.75	2.75
948	G68	$1 multicolored	3.00	3.00
949	G68	$1 multicolored	2.00	2.00
950	G68	$1 multicolored	1.50	1.50
951	G68	$1 multicolored	3.00	3.00
952	G68	$2 multicolored	3.50	3.50
953	G68	$3 multicolored	2.75	2.25
954	G68	$4 multicolored	7.00	7.00
955	G68	$4 multicolored	3.50	3.50
956	G68	$4 multicolored	4.00	4.50
957	G68	$5 multicolored	3.50	3.00
		Nos. 944-957 (14)	43.00	41.50

Souvenir Sheets

958-963	G68	Set of 7	37.50	37.50

Discovery of America, 500th anniv. (#944, 948, 959). Count Zeppelin, 75th death anniv. (#945, 956, 960-960A). Lions Intl., 75th anniv. (#946-947). Konrad Adenauer, 25th death anniv. (#950, 953, 955, 957, 962-963). America's Cup yacht race (#949). Intl. Conference on Nutrition, Rome (#951). Intl. Space Year (#952, 961). Wolfgang Amadeus Mozart, bicent. of death (in 1991) (#954, 958).

Issued: #945, 956, 960-960A, 12/15; others, Dec.

Walt Disney's Tales of Uncle Scrooge — G69

No. 964, 60c — Goldilocks (Daisy Duck) and the Three Bears: a, Comes upon the house. b, Finds three bowls of soup. c, Finds three chairs. d, Ventures upstairs. e, Tries Papa Bear's bed. f, Falls asleep in Baby Bear's bed. g, The Three Bears return home. h, Baby Bear finds Goldilocks in his bed. i, Goldilocks awakens.

No. 965, 60c — The Princess (Minnie Mouse) and the Pea: a, Prince Mickey in search of a bride. b, Princess Minnie caught in a storm. c, Queen Clarbelle meets the princess. d, Royal family entertains Princess Minnie. e, Queen places a pea on the mattress. f, Mattresses upon mattresses. g, Princess Minnie at her bed-chamber. h, Princess Minnie very tired the next morning. i, A true princess for a real prince.

No. 966, 60c — Little Red Riding Hood (Minnie Mouse): a, Off to Grandmother's. b, Stopping for flowers. c, Followed by the wolf. d, Frightened by the wolf. e, Wolf charges into Grandmother's house. f, Little Red Riding Hood at Grandmother's door. g, "What big teeth you have." h, Calling woodsman for help. i, Woodsman to the rescue.

No. 967, 60c — Hop O'-My-Thumb (Mickey, Minnie, family): a, Poor woodcutter without food for his children. b, Pebbles to find way back. c, Sadly leaving children's forest. d, Surveying from tree top. e, Ogress sends boys to bed. f, Ogre and his magic seven-league boots. g, Ogre chasing boys. h, Taking the magic seven-league boots. i, Running to Royal Palace.

No. 968, 60c — Pied Piper of Hamelin (Donald, Mickey and friends): a, Mayor (Donald) offers reward. b, Piper Mickey accepts the challenge. c, Piper leads rats to the river. d, Piper promises revenge. e, Children follow Piper outside village gates. f, Mayor and townspeople watch from above. g, Children follow Piper through countryside. h, Children pass through the cavern. i, All closed off from Hamelin, except for one.

No. 969, 60c — Puss in Boots (Goofy, Donald and friends): a, Gift for the king. b, Puss brings Marquis of Carabas to bathe in river. c, Puss calls for king's help. d, King introduces his daughter (Daisy Duck) to Puss. e, Puss and reapers. f, Puss received by the Ogre. g, Ogre changed into a lion. h, Ogre changed into a mouse. i, Puss shows off Marquis' castle.

No. 970, $6, The Three Bears in the forest, vert. No. 971, $6, Goldilocks runs home.

No. 972, $6, Prince Mickey's useless search for a true princess. No. 973, $6, Mickey's royal family lived happily ever after.

No. 974, $6, Little Riding Hood on the way to Grandmother's, vert. No. 975, $6, A happy ending.

No. 976, $6, Boy of woodcutter with bag over shoulder. No. 977, $6, Woodcutter's family reunited.

No. 978, $6, Pied Piper leading rats past town square. No. 979, $6, Piper Mickey encouraging children in land of sweets, vert. No. 980, $6, Miller's estate, Donald with cat, Puss, donkey. No. 981, $6, Marriage of Marquis of Carabis to daughter of the king, vert.

Perf. 14x13½, 13½x14

1992, Dec. 15   **Litho.**

Sheets of 9, #a-i

| 964-969 | G69 | Set of 6 | | 37.50 | 37.50 |

Souvenir Sheets

Perf. 13½x14, 14x13½

| 970-981 | G69 | Set of 12 | | 60.00 | 60.00 |

Disney Animated Films Type

No. 982 — Duck Tales (Donald Duck and family): a, Scrooge McDuck, Launchpad. b, Scrooge reads treasure map. c, Collie Baba's treasure revealed. d, Webby finds magic lamp. e, Genie and new masters. f, Webby gets her wish. g, Scrooge McDuck, Genie. h, Retrieving the magic lamp. i, Villain Merlock, Genie.

No. 983 — Darkwing Duck: a, Darkwing Duck. b, Tuskerninni. c, Megavolt. d, Bushroot. e, Steelbeak. f, Eggman. g, Agent Gryzlikoff. h, Director J. Gander Hooter.

No. 984, Webby's tea party, vert. No. 985, Treasure of the lost lamp, vert.

No. 985A, Gosalyn. No. 985B, Honker, horiz.

Perf. 14x13½, 13½x14

1992, Dec. 15   **Litho.**

| 982 | A247a | 60c Sheet of 9, #a.-i. | | 7.75 | 7.75 |
| 983 | A247b | 60c Sheet of 8, #a.-h. | | 7.50 | 7.50 |

Souvenir Sheets

984	A247a	$6 multicolored		5.00	5.00
985	A247a	$6 multicolored		5.00	5.00
985A	A247b	$6 multicolored		5.00	5.00
985B	A247b	$6 multicolored		5.00	5.00

G71

Disney Animated Films — G72

No. 986 — The Great Mouse Detective: a, Olivia and Flaversham. b, Olivia's mechanical mouse. c, Ratigan's evil scheme. d, Ratigan and Mechanical Mouse Queen. e, Fidget pens ransom note. f, Basil studies clues. g, Fidget holds Olivia captive. h, Ratigan in disguise. i, Basil and Dr. Dawson, crime stoppers.

No. 987 — Oliver & Company: a, Dodger. b, Oliver. c, Dodger and Oliver. d, Oliver introduced to the Company. e, Oliver meets Fagin. f, Fagin's bedtime story hour. g, Oliver sleeping with Dodger. h, Fagin's trike. i, Georgette and Tito.

No. 988 — The Legend of Sleepy Hollow: a, Ichabod Crane comes to town. b, Ichabod meets Katrina Van Tassel. c, Schoolmaster Ichabod Crane. d, Ichabod and rival, Brom Bones. e, Ichabod and Katrina at Halloween dance. f, Ichabod is scared of ghosts. g, Ichabod in Sleepy Hollow. h, Ichabod and his horse. i, Meeting the Headless Horseman.

No. 989, $6, Detective Basil holding pipe. No. 990, $6, Detective Basil holding magnifying glass. No. 991, $6, Oliver. No. 992, $6, Oliver and kittens. No. 993, $6, Ichabod Crane, children praying, vert. No. 994, $6, Headless Horseman.

Perf. 14x13½, 13½x14

1992, Dec. 15   **Litho.**

986	G71	60c Sheet of 9, #a.-i.	6.00	6.00
987	G71	60c Sheet of 9, #a.-i.	6.00	6.00
988	G72	60c Sheet of 9, #a.-i.	6.00	6.00

Souvenir Sheets

| 989-994 | G71 | Set of 6 | 30.00 | 30.00 |

Elvis Presley Type of 1993

Designs: a, Portrait. b, With guitar. c, With microphone.

1993   **Litho.**   **Perf. 14**

| 1001 | A244 | $1 Strip of 3, #a.-c. | 3.00 | 3.00 |

Printed in sheets of 9 stamps.

Medicinal Plants — G73

Designs: 5c, Oleander. 10c, Beach morning glory. 30c, Calabash. 45c, Porita tree. 55c, Cashew. 75c, Prickly pear. $1, Shell ginger. $1.50, Avocado. $2, Mango. $3, Blood flower. $4, Sugar apple. $5, Barbados lily.

1994, May 20   **Litho.**   **Perf. 13½x13**

| 1002-1013 | G73 | Set of 12 | 20.00 | 20.00 |

SEMI-POSTAL STAMPS

Nos. 190-193 Surcharged

1980, Aug. 7   **Litho.**   **Perf. 13½**

B1	A90	25c + 50c Running	.25	.30
B2	A90	50c + 50c Sailing	.25	.40
B3	A90	$1 + 50c Long jump	.25	.50
B4	A90	$2 + 50c Swimming	.25	.70
		Nos. B1-B4 (4)	1.00	1.90

OFFICIAL STAMPS

Nos. 209-214 Ovptd. "OFFICIAL"

1982, Oct. 11

O1	A94a	50c on No. 209	.25	.25
O2	A94b	50c on No. 210	.25	.35
O3	A94a	$3 on No. 211	.40	.40
O4	A94b	$3 on No. 212	.40	.70
O5	A94a	$3.50 on No. 213	.45	.45
O6	A94b	$3.50 on No. 214	.45	.70
		Nos. O1-O6 (6)	2.20	2.85

BEQUIA

All stamps are types of St. Vincent ("A" illustration letter), St. Vincent Grenadines ("G" illustration letter) or Bequia ("B" illustration letter).

"Island" issues are listed separately beginning in 1984. See St. Vincent Grenadines Nos. 84-111, 248-262 for earlier issues.

Locomotive Type of 1985

No. 1, 1942 Challenger Class, US. No. 2, 1908 S3/6, Germany. No. 3, 1944 2900 Class, US. No. 4, 1903 Jersey Lily, UK. No. 5, 1882 Gladstone Class, UK. No. 6, 1909 Thundersley, UK. No. 7, 1860 Ser Class 118, UK. No. 8, 1893 No. 999 NY Central & Hudson River, US. No. 9, 1921 Class G2, UK. No. 10, 1902

Jr. Class 6400, Japan. No. 11, 1877 Class G3, Germany. No. 12, 1945 Niagara Class, US. No. 13, 1938 Manor Class, UK. No. 14, 1880 Class D VI, Germany. No. 15, 1914 K4 Class, US. No. 16, 1960 Class U25B, US. No. 17, 1921 Stephenson, UK. No. 18, 1909 Class H4, US. No. 19, 1922 Baltic, UK. No. 20, 1903 J.R. 4500, Japan. No. 21, 1915 Class LS. No. 22, 1841 Borsig, Germany. No. 23, 1943 Royal Scot, UK. No. 24, 1961 Krauss-Maffei, US. No. 25, 1928 River IRT, UK. No. 26, 1890 Electric, UK. No. 27, 1934 A.E.C., UK. No. 28, 1929 No. 10000, UK. No. 29, 1904 City Class, UK. No. 30, 1901 No. 737, UK. No. 31, 1847 Cornwall, UK. No. 32, 1938 Duke Dog Class, UK. No. 33, 1881 Ella, UK. No. 34, 1910 George V Class, UK.

Se-tenant Pairs, #a.-b.
a. — Side and front views.
b. — Action scene.

1984-87		Litho.	Unwmk.		Perf. 12½
1	A120	1c multicolored		.25	.25
2	A120	1c multicolored		.25	.25
3	A120	5c multicolored		.25	.25
4	A120	5c multicolored		.25	.25
5	A120	10c multicolored		.25	.25
6	A120	10c multicolored		.25	.25
7	A120	15c multicolored		.25	.25
8	A120	25c multicolored		.25	.25
9	A120	25c multicolored		.25	.25
10	A120	25c multicolored		.25	.25
11	A120	25c multicolored		.25	.25
12	A120	35c multicolored		.25	.25
13	A120	35c multicolored		.25	.25
14	A120	40c multicolored		.25	.25
15	A120	45c multicolored		.30	.30
16	A120	50c multicolored		.35	.35
17	A120	55c multicolored		.40	.40
18	A120	55c multicolored		.40	.40
19	A120	60c multicolored		.40	.40
20	A120	60c multicolored		.40	.40
21	A120	60c multicolored		.40	.40
22	A120	75c multicolored		.50	.50
23	A120	75c multicolored		.50	.50
24	A120	75c multicolored		.50	.50
25	A120	$1 multicolored		.65	.65
26	A120	$1 multicolored		.65	.65
27	A120	$1 multicolored		.65	.65
28	A120	$1.50 multicolored		.80	.80
29	A120	$2 multicolored		1.00	1.00
30	A120	$2 multicolored		1.00	1.00
31	A120	$2 multicolored		1.00	1.00
32	A120	$2.50 multicolored		1.50	1.50
33	A120	$2.50 multicolored		1.50	1.50
34	A120	$3 multicolored		2.00	2.00
		Nos. 1-34 (34)		18.40	18.40

Issued: #1, 3, 5, 8, 12, 15, 28-29, 2/22/84; #2, 4, 6, 13, 22, 25, 32, 34, 11/26/84; #9, 17, 19, 30, 2/1/85; #10, 18, 20, 23, 26, 33, 8/14/85; #7, 11, 14, 16, 21, 24, 27, 31, 11/16/87.

Stamps issued 11/16/87 are not inscribed "Leaders of the World."

St. Vincent Grenadines Nos. 222-238 Ovptd. "BEQUIA"
Perf. 14x13½

1984, Aug. 23			Wmk. 373
69	G26	1c on No. 222	.25	.25
70	G26	3c on No. 223	.25	.25
71	G26	5c on No. 224	.25	.25
72	G26	6c on No. 225	.25	.25
73	G26	10c on No. 226	.25	.25
74	G26	15c on No. 227	.25	.25
75	G26	20c on No. 228	.25	.25
76	G26	25c on No. 229	.25	.25
77	G26	30c on No. 230	.25	.25
78	G26	50c on No. 231	.35	.35
79	G26	60c on No. 232	.50	.50
80	G26	75c on No. 233	.60	.60
81	G26	$1 on No. 234	.75	.75
82	G26	$2 on No. 235	1.25	1.25
83	G26	$3 on No. 236	2.00	2.00
84	G26	$5 on No. 237	3.50	3.50
85	G26	$10 on No. 238	7.50	7.50
		Nos. 69-85 (17)	18.70	18.70

Car Type of 1983

No. 86, 1953 Cadillac, US. No. 87, 1932 Fiat, Italy. No. 88, 1968 Excalibur, US. No. 89, 1952 Hudson, US. No. 90, 1924 Leyand, UK. No. 91, 1911 Marmon, US. No. 92, 1950 Alfa Romeo, Italy. No. 93, 1968 Ford Escort, UK. No. 94, 1939 Maserati 8 CTF, Italy. No. 95, 1963 Ford, UK. No. 96, 1958 Vanwall, UK. No. 97, 1910 Stanley, US. No. 98, 1948 Ford Wagon, US. No. 99, 1936 Auto Union, Germany. No. 100, 1907 Chadwick, US. No. 101, 1924 Lanchester, UK. No. 102, 1957 Austin-Healy, UK. No. 103, 1935 Brewster-Ford, US. No. 104, 1942 Willys Jeep, UK. No. 105, 1929 Isotta, Italy. No. 106, 1940 Lincoln, US. No. 107, 1964 Bluebird II, UK. No. 108, 1948 Moore-Offenhauser, US. No. 109, 1936 Ford, UK. No. 110, 1936 Mercedes Benz, Germany. No. 111, 1928 Mercedes Benz SSK, Germany. No. 112, 1907 Rolls Royce, UK. No. 113, 1955 Citroen, France. No. 114, 1936 Fiat, Italy. No. 115, 1922 Dusenberg, US. No. 116, 1957 Pontiac Bonneville, US. No. 117, 1916 Hudson Super Six, US. No. 118, 1927 Coyote Ford, US. No. 119, 1960 Porsche, Germany. No. 120, 1970 Plymouth, US. No. 121, 1933

Stutz, US. No. 122, 1910 Benz-Blitzen, Germany. No. 123, 1933 Napier Railton, UK. No. 124, 1978 BMW, Germany. No. 125, 1912 Hispano Suiza, Spain. No. 126, 1954 Mercedes Benz, Germany. No. 127, 1927 Stutz Black Hawk, US.

Se-tenant Pairs, #a.-b.
a. — Side and front views.
b. — Action scene.

1984-87		Unwmk.		Perf. 12½
86	A107	5c multicolored	.25	.25
87	A107	5c multicolored	.25	.25
88	A107	5c multicolored	.25	.25
89	A107	5c multicolored	.25	.25
90	A107	10c multicolored	.25	.25
91	A107	20c multicolored	.25	.25
92	A107	20c multicolored	.25	.25
93	A107	20c multicolored	.25	.25
94	A107	20c multicolored	.25	.25
95	A107	25c multicolored	.25	.25
96	A107	25c multicolored	.25	.25
97	A107	25c multicolored	.25	.25
98	A107	35c multicolored	.25	.25
99	A107	40c multicolored	.30	.30
100	A107	45c multicolored	.35	.35
101	A107	50c multicolored	.40	.40
102	A107	50c multicolored	.40	.40
103	A107	60c multicolored	.45	.45
104	A107	60c multicolored	.45	.45
105	A107	65c multicolored	.50	.50
106	A107	75c multicolored	.50	.50
107	A107	75c multicolored	.50	.50
108	A107	75c multicolored	.50	.50
109	A107	75c multicolored	.50	.50
110	A107	80c multicolored	.55	.55
111	A107	90c multicolored	.65	.65
112	A107	$1 multicolored	.70	.70
113	A107	$1 multicolored	.70	.70
114	A107	$1 multicolored	.70	.70
115	A107	$1 multicolored	.70	.70
116	A107	$1 multicolored	.70	.70
117	A107	$1.25 multicolored	.80	.80
118	A107	$1.25 multicolored	.80	.80
119	A107	$1.50 multicolored	1.00	1.00
120	A107	$1.50 multicolored	1.00	1.00
121	A107	$1.75 multicolored	1.10	1.10
122	A107	$2 multicolored	1.25	1.25
123	A107	$2 multicolored	1.25	1.25
124	A107	$2.50 multicolored	1.50	1.50
125	A107	$3 multicolored	1.75	1.75
126	A107	$3 multicolored	1.75	1.75
127	A107	$3 multicolored	1.75	1.75
		Nos. 86-127 (42)	26.75	26.75

Issued: #86, 99, 112, 119, 9/14; #87, 95, 106, 113, 124-125, 12/19; #88, 96, 101, 114, 117, 122, 6/25/85; #92, 100, 120, 123, 9/26/85; #97, 102, 105, 107, 115, 126, 1/29/86; #93, 103, 108, 111, 116, 127, 12/23/86; #89, 94, 98, 104, 109-110, 118, 121, 7/22/87.

Beginning on Sept. 26, 1985, this issue is not inscribed "Leaders of the World."

1984 Summer Olympics — B1

No. 170a, Men's gymnastics. No. 170b, Women's gymnastics. No. 171a, Men's javelin. No. 171b, Women's javelin. No. 172a, Women's basketball. No. 172b, Men's basketball. No. 173a, Women's long jump. No. 173b, Men's long jump.

1984, Sept. 14   **Perf. 12½**

170	B1	1c Pair, #a.-b.	.25	.25
171	B1	10c Pair, #a.-b.	.25	.25
172	B1	60c Pair, #a.-b.	.40	.40
173	B1	$3 Pair, #a.-b.	1.10	1.10
		Nos. 170-173 (4)	2.00	2.00

Dogs — B2

No. 178a, Hungarian Kuvasz. No. 178b, Afghan. No. 179a, Whippet. No. 179b, Bloodhound. No. 180a, Cavalier King Charles Spaniel. No. 180b, German Shepherd. No. 181a, Pekinese. No. 181b, Golden Retriever.

1985, Mar. 14			Perf. 12½	
178	B2	25c Pair, #a.-b.	.25	.25
179	B2	35c Pair, #a.-b.	.50	.50
180	B2	55c Pair, #a.-b.	.65	.65
181	B2	$2 Pair, #a.-b.	1.90	1.90
		Nos. 178-181 (4)	3.30	3.30

World War II Warships B3

Se-tenant Pairs, #a.-b.
a.— Side and top views.
b. — Action scene.

1985, Apr. 29			Perf. 12½	
186	B3	15c HMS Hood	.60	.60
187	B3	50c HMS Duke of York	1.00	1.00
188	B3	$1 KM Admiral Graf Spee	1.40	1.40
189	B3	$1.50 USS Nevada	2.25	2.25
		Nos. 186-189 (4)	5.25	5.25

St. Vincent Grenadines Flower Type

#194a, Primula veris. #194b, Pulsatilla vulgaris. #195a, Lapageria rosea. #195b, Romneya coulteri. #196a, Anigozanthos manglesii. #196b, Metrosideros collina. #197a, Protea laurifolia. #197b, Thunbergia grandiflora.

1985, May 31			Perf. 12½	
194	G38	10c Pair, #a.-b.	.25	.25
195	G38	20c Pair, #a.-b.	.30	.30
196	G38	70c Pair, #a.-b.	.35	.35
197	G38	$2.50 Pair, #a.-b.	.75	.75
		Nos. 194-197 (4)	1.65	1.65

Queen Mother Type of 1985

Hat: #206a, 212a, Blue. #206b, 212b, Violet. #207a, 211a, Blue. #207b, 211b, Tiara. #208a, Blue. #208b, White. #209a, Blue. #209b, Pink. #210a, Hat. #210b, Tiara.

1985, Aug. 29			Perf. 12½	
206	A122	20c Pair, #a.-b.	.25	.00
207	A122	65c Pair, #a.-b.	.65	.65
208	A122	$1.35 Pair, #a.-b.	.90	.90
209	A122	$1.80 Pair, #a.-b.	1.50	1.50
		Nos. 206-209 (4)	3.30	3.05

Souvenir Sheets of 2

210	A122	$2.05 #a.-b.	1.75	1.75
211	A122	$3.50 #a.-b.	3.00	3.00
212	A122	$6 #a.-b.	5.00	5.00

Queen Elizabeth II Type of 1986

Various portraits.

1986, Apr. 21				
213	A128	5c multicolored	.25	.25
214	A128	75c multicolored	.35	.35
215	A128	$2 multicolored	.50	.50
216	A128	$8 multicolored, vert.	2.10	2.10
		Nos. 213-216 (4)	3.20	3.20

Souvenir Sheet

217	A128	$10 multicolored	3.50	3.50

B4

World Cup Soccer Championships, Mexico, 1986 — B5

No. 218, South Korean team . No. 219, Iraqi team. No. 220, Algerian team. No. 221, Bulgaria vs. France. No. 222, Belgium. No. 223, Danish team. No. 224, Italy vs. W. Germany. No. 225, USSR vs. England. No. 226, Italy, 1982 champions. No. 227, W. Germany. No. 228, N. Ireland. No. 229, England.

1986 July 3			Perf. 12¼, 15 (B5)	
218	B4	1c multicolored	.25	.25
219	B4	2c multicolored	.25	.25
220	B4	5c multicolored	.25	.25
221	B4	10c multicolored	.25	.25
222	B5	45c multicolored	.25	.25
223	B4	60c multicolored	.25	.25
224	B4	75c multicolored	.25	.25
225	B4	$1.50 multicolored	.30	.30
226	B5	$1.50 multicolored	.30	.30
227	B5	$2 multicolored	.50	.50
228	B5	$3.50 multicolored	.70	.70
229	B4	$6 multicolored	1.10	1.10
		Nos. 218-229 (12)	4.65	4.65

Souvenir Sheets

230	B4	$1 like No. 219	.50	.50
231	B4	$1.75 like No. 221	.80	.80

Royal Wedding Type of 1986

No. 232, Andrew. No. 233, Andrew in helicopter. No. 234, Andrew in crowd. No. 235, Andrew, Sarah.
$8, Andrew, Sarah in coach.

1986, July 15			Perf. 12½x13, 13x12½	
232	A132	60c multicolored	.35	.35
233	A132	60c multicolored	.35	.35
234	A132	60c multicolored	.85	.85
235	A132	60c multicolored	.85	.85
		Nos. 232-235 (4)	2.40	2.40

Souvenir Sheet

236	A132a	$8 multicolored	3.75	3.75

Nos. 234-235 horiz.

Railway Engineers and Locomotives — B6

Designs: $1, Sir Daniel Gooch, Fire Fly Class, 1840. $2.50, Sir Nigel Gresley, A4 Class, 1938. $3, Sir William Stanier, Coronation Class, 1937. $4, Oliver V. S. Bulleid, Battle of Britain Class, 1946.

1986, Sept. 30			Perf. 13x12½	
237-240	B6	Set of 4	3.00	3.00

Nos. 232-235 Ovptd.
"Congratulations to TRH The Duke & Duchess of York" in 3 Lines

1986			Perf. 12½x13, 13x12½	
241	A132	60c on No. 232	.75	.75
242	A132	60c on No. 233	.75	.75
243	A132	$2 on No. 234	2.75	2.75
244	A132	$2 on No. 235	2.75	2.75
		Nos. 241-244 (4)	7.00	7.00

Royalty Portrait Type

Portraits and photographs: 15c, Queen Victoria, 1841. 75c, Elizabeth, Charles, 1948. $1, Coronation, 1953. $2.50, Duke of Edinburgh, 1948. $5, Elizabeth c. 1980. $6, Elizabeth, Charles, 1948, diff.

1987, Oct. 15			Perf. 12½x13	
245-249	A140	Set of 5	3.00	3.00

Souvenir Sheet

250	A140	$6 multi	3.00	3.00

Great Explorers Type of St. Vincent Grenadines

Designs: 15c, Gokstad, ship of Leif Eriksson (c. 1000). 50c, Eriksson and bearing dial.

$1.75, The Mathew, ship of John Cabot. $2, Cabot, quadrant. $2.50, The Trinidad, ship of Ferdinand Magellan. $3, Arms, portrait of Christopher Columbus. $3.50, Columbus' ship Santa Maria. $4, Magellan, globe. $5, Anchor, long boat, ship.

1988, July 11			Litho.	Perf. 14	
251-258	G52	Set of 8		3.00	3.00

Souvenir Sheet

259	G52	$5 multi	3.25	3.25

Tennis Type of 1987

1988, July 29			Perf. 13x13½	
260	A137	15c Anders Jarryd	.30	.30
261	A137	45c Anne Hobbs	.30	.30
262	A137	80c Jimmy Connors	.35	.35
263	A137	$1.25 Carling Bassett	.45	.45
264	A137	$1.75 Stefan Edberg, horiz.	.60	.60
265	A137	$2.00 Gabriela Sabatini, horiz.	.70	.70
266	A137	$2.50 Mats Wilander	.90	.90
267	A137	$3.00 Pat Cash	1.10	1.10
		Nos. 260-267 (8)	4.70	4.70

No. 263 inscribed "Carlene Basset" instead of "Carling Bassett."
An unissued souvenir sheet exists.

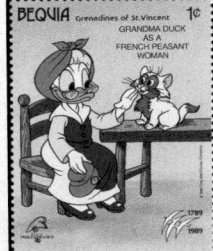

French Revolution Bicentennial B7

Designs: 1c, Grandma Duck as French peasant woman. 2c, Donald & Daisy celebrating liberty. 3c, Minnie as Marie Antoinette. 4c, Clarabelle & patriotic chair. 5c, Goofy in Republican citizen's costume. 10c, Mickey & Donald planting liberty tree. No. 274, $5, Horace taking Tennis Court Oath. $6, Grand Master Mason McDuck.
No. 276, $5, Dancing the Carmagnole. No. 277, $5, Philosophers at Cafe La Procope.

1989, July 7			Perf. 13½x14	
268-275	B7	Set of 8	10.00	10.00

Souvenir Sheets

276-277	B7	Set of 2	6.00	6.00

Anniversaries and Events Type

$5, Otto Lililienthal, aviation pioneer.

1991, Nov. 18			Litho.	Perf. 14	
278	A213	$5 multicolored		5.25	5.25

Japanese Attack on Pearl Harbor, 50th Anniv. B8

Designs: 50c, Kate from second-wave over Hickam Field. $1, B17 sights Zeros in Pearl Harbor attack. $5, Firefighters rescue sailors from blazing USS Tennessee.

1991, Nov. 18				
287	B8	50c multicolored	.70	.70
288	B8	$1 multicolored	1.30	1.30

Souvenir Sheet

289	B8	$5 multicolored	4.25	4.25

Wolfgang Amadeus Mozart, Death Bicentennial — B9

Mozart and: 10c, Piccolo. 75c, Piano. $4, Violotta.
No. 293, $6, Mozart's last composition, Lacrimosa from the Requiem Mass. No. 294, $6, Bronze of Mozart by Adrien-Etienne

Gaudez, vert. No. 295, $6, Score of opening of the "Paris" symphony, K297.

1991			Litho.	Perf. 14	
290-292	B9	Set of 3		5.50	5.50

Souvenir Sheets

293-295	B9	Set of 3	18.00	18.00

Nos. 293-295 each contain one 57x42mm or 42x57mm stamp.

Boy Scout Type

50c, Lord Baden-Powell, killick hitch knot. $1, Baden-Powell, clove hitch knot. $2, Drawing of Boy Scout by Baden-Powell, vert. $3, American 1st Class Scout badge, vert. $6, Baden-Powell, Lark's head knot.

1991				
296-299	A211	Set of 4	8.00	8.00

Souvenir Sheet

300	A211	$6 multicolored	6.75	6.75

Diana, Princess of Wales, (1961-97) — B10

1997, Dec. 10			Litho.	Perf. 14	
301	B10	$1 multicolored		1.75	1.75

No. 301 was issued in sheets of 6.

Paintings Type of 1999

Various pictures of flowers making up a photomosaic of the Queen Mother.

2000, Sept. 5				Perf. 13¾	
302	A442	$1 Sheet of 8, #a-h		6.00	6.00
i.		As No. 302, imperf.		6.00	6.00

Worldwide Fund for Nature (WWF) B11

Leatherback turtle: a, Three on beach. b, One coming ashore. c, One in water. d, One digging nest.

2001, Dec. 10			Litho.	Perf. 14	
303	B11	$1.40 Vert or horiz. strip of 4, #a-d		5.00	5.00

Queen Elizabeth II, 50th Anniv. of Reign Type of 2002

No. 304: a, Without hat. b, Wearing tiara. c, Wearing scarf. d, With Prince Philip and baby. $2, Wearing scarf, diff.

2002, June 17			Litho.	Perf. 14¼	
304	A509	80c Sheet of 4, #a-d		4.50	4.50

Souvenir Sheet

305	A509	$2 multi		4.00	4.00

United We Stand Type of 2001

2002, Nov. 4   ***Perf. 14***
306 A508 $2 multi   2.00   2.00
    Printed in sheets of 4.

Ferrari Race Cars — B12

No. 307: a, 1953 250MM. b, 1962 330LM. c, 1952 340 Mexico. d, 1963 330LM. e, 1952 225S. f, 1956 500TR. g, 1954 750 Monza. h, 1954 375 Plus.

2002, June 10   **Litho.**   ***Perf. 13¾***
307 B12 $1.10 Sheet of 8, #a-h   6.75   6.75

Elvis Presley Type of 2002

2002, Aug. 19
308 A517 $1 multi   1.00   1.00
    Printed in sheets of 9.

Shirley Temple Movie Type of 2000

No. 309, horiz. — Scenes from *Captain January* of Temple with: a, Man at table. b, Woman. c, Two men and bird with bow. d, Boy and teacher. e, Two men at table. f, Three men in boat.
No. 310: a, Man with beard. b, Three men. c, Two men and doll. d, With man, dancing. $5, With sailors.

2002, Aug. 19
309 A471 $1.40 Sheet of 6, #a-f   6.50   6.50
310 A471 $2 Sheet of 4, #a-d   6.50   6.50

Souvenir Sheet
311 A471 $5 multi   5.00   5.00
    Sheet margins are dated "2003."

Queen Mother Elizabeth Type of 2002

No. 312: a, Wearing yellow dress. b, Wearing red dress.

2002, Nov. 4   ***Perf. 14***
312 A522 $2 Pair, #a-b   3.00   3.00
No. 312 printed in sheets containing 2 pairs.

Year of the Horse — B13

No. 313: a, Black horse in foreground, front feet raised. b, White horse in foreground. c, Piebald horse in foreground. d, Black horse in foreground, front feet not raised.

2002, Dec. 17   ***Perf. 13¼x13***
313 B13 $1.40 Sheet of 4, #a-d   5.50   5.50

Teddy Bears Type of 2002

No. 314, $2 — Bears from Germany: a, Balloon pilot bear. b, Bear in lederhosen. c, Bear in pants and ice skates. d, Bear in skirt and ice skates.
No. 315, $2 — Bears from Italy: a, Bear with feathered hat, standing in gondola. b, Bear with cap, seated on gondola. c, Bear with umbrella. d, Gondolier bear.

2003, Jan. 27   ***Perf. 13½x13¼***
    Sheets of 4, #a-d
314-315 A519   Set of 2   13.00   13.00

Year of the Ram Type of 2003

No. 316: a, Ram with white horns and beard, denomination at right. b, Ram with black horns, denomination at left. c, Ram with dark horns, denomination at right. d, Ram with white horns, denomination at left. e, Ram with horns, denomination at left. f, Ram with horns with lines, denomination at left.

2003, Feb. 1   ***Perf. 14¼x13¾***
316 A526 $1 Sheet of 6, #a-f   5.00   5.00

Princess Diana Type of 2003

No. 317, $2: a, Wearing pink hat. b, Wearing gray dress. c, Wearing white blouse. d, Wearing checked pants.
No. 318, $2: a, Wearing black dress. b, Wearing red blouse. c, Wearing black and white hat. d, Wearing white blouse, holding flowers.

2003, May 26   **Litho.**   ***Perf. 14***
    Sheets of 4, #a-d
317-318 A536   Set of 2   13.00   13.00

Corvette Type of 2003

No. 319: a, 1957 convertible. b, 1964 Sting Ray. c, 1954 convertible. d, 1989. $5, 1988.

2003, July 1   ***Perf. 13¼x13½***
319 A534 $2 Sheet of 4, #a-d   7.00   7.00

Souvenir Sheet
320 A534 $5 multi   5.00   5.00

Pres. John F. Kennedy (1917-63) — B14

No. 321: a, Denomination at UL, name at right. b, Denomination at UL, name at left. c, Denomination at UR, name at left. d, Denomination at UR, name at right.

2003, Aug. 25   ***Perf. 14***
321 B14 $2 Sheet of 4, #a-d   7.50   7.50

Elvis Presley (1935-77) — B15

No. 322: a, Silhouette. b, Holding guitar.

2003, Dec. 1   ***Perf. 13½***
322 B15 90c Sheet, #322a, 8   #322b   8.00   8.00

Birds — B16

Designs: 90c, Stripe-headed tanager. $1, Violaceous trogon. $1.40, Barn owl. $2, Green jay.

$5, Montezuma oropendola.

2003, Dec. 1   ***Perf. 13¼***
323-326 B16   Set of 4   4.25   4.25

Souvenir Sheet
327 B16 $5 multi   4.25   4.25

New Year 2004 (Year of the Monkey) B17

Romping Monkeys, by unknown painter: $1.40, Detail. $3, Entire painting.

2004, Jan. 15   **Litho.**   ***Perf. 13¼***
328 B17 $1.40 multi   1.75   1.75

Souvenir Sheet
    Perf. 13½x13¼
329 B17 $3 multi   3.00   3.00

Paintings by Pablo Picasso (1881-1973) — B18

No. 330: a, Bust of a Woman with Self-Portrait. b, Jacqueline in a Turkish Jacket. c, Françoise in an Armchair. d, Still Life on a Pedestal Table. $5, Violin on a Wall.

2004, Apr. 30   ***Perf. 14¼***
330 B18 $2 Sheet of 4, #a-d   6.00   6.00

    Imperf
331 B18 $5 multi   4.00   4.00
No. 330 contains four 38x51mm stamps.

Marilyn Monroe Type of 2004

2004, May 3   ***Perf. 14***
332 A558 70c multi   .55   .55
    Printed in sheets of 12.

Babe Ruth Type of 2004

2004, July 1   ***Perf. 13¼***
333 A561 70c multi   .55   .55
    Printed in sheets of 12.

Ancient Greece B19

Designs: 30c, Palace of Minos, Crete. 70c, Apollo's Temple, Delphi. $1, Statue of Zeus, Olympia. $1.40, Bust of Aphrodite. $2, Bust of Socrates. $3, Parthenon. $5, Panathenaic Stadium, Athens.

2004, Aug. 16   ***Perf. 14***
334-339 B19   Set of 6   7.50   7.50

Souvenir Sheet
340 B19 $5 multi   4.50   4.50

Ronald Reagan Type of 2004

No. 341, horiz.: a, Reagan with wife, Nancy. b, Reagan with George H. W. Bush.

2004, Oct. 13   ***Perf. 13½***
341   Horiz. pair   2.75   2.75
   a.-b.   A564 $1.40 Either single   1.25   1.25
    Printed in sheets containing three each #341a-341b.

Railroads Type of 2004

No. 342, $2: a, GN 2507 Class P 2-4-8-2. b, Great Northern 2507. c, Great Northern. d, GWR King Class 4-6-0.
No. 343, $2: a, LMS 2MT 2-6-2 T. b, Green Arrow. c, LMS Stainer Class 5MT 4-6-0. d, Liner Class A4 Sir Nigel Gresley.
No. 344, $2: a, Barclay 0-4-0 Saddle tank. b, Beyer Peacock. c, BR Class 4MT 2-6-0. d, Dampflok 109.
No. 345, $2: a, British Railways 2-6-4 T. b, Caledonian Railway 0-4-4 T. c, Evening Star. d, Southern Railway Carolina Special.
No. 346, $5, Pakistan Railways SPS 4-4-0. No. 347, $5, Norwegian State Railway. No. 348, $5, Russell Hunslet 2-6-2 T. No. 349, $5, North British Railway 0-6-0.

    Perf. 14½x14, 14 (#344, 348)
2004, Dec. 13   **Sheets of 4, #a-d**
342-345 A565   Set of 4   26.00   26.00

Souvenir Sheets
346-349 A565   Set of 4   16.00   16.00

Christmas B20

Paintings: 55c, Madonna of Port Lligat, by Salvador Dali. 90c, Madonna and Child, by Barolome Esteban Murillo. $1, Madonna and Child, by Jan van Eyck. $4, Madonna of the Meadow, by Giovanni Bellini. $6, Madonna and Child, by Caravaggio.

2004, Dec. 13   ***Perf. 12***
350-353 B20   Set of 4   5.50   5.50

Souvenir Sheet
354 B20 $6 multi   4.75   4.75

End of World War II, 60th Anniv. — B21

No. 355, $2 — Sinking of the Bismarck, 1941: a, Bismarck, Map. b, Aircraft make ready for flight. c, The Bismarck getting pounded by British Navy. d, The Bismarck goes down.
No. 356, $2 — Liberation of Paris: a, Allied troops enter Paris. b, The end of German occupation. c, Allied troops help supply people of Paris. d, Victory at last.
No. 357, $5, Bismarck. No. 358, $5, General De Gaulle returns.

2005, May 9   **Litho.**   ***Perf. 13½***
    Sheets of 4, #a-d
355-356 B21   Set of 2   14.00   14.00

Souvenir Sheets
357-358 B21   Set of 2   8.00   8.00

Vatican Stamp and Pope John Paul II Types of 2005

Designs: 70c, Vatican #64. $4, Pope and crowd, horiz.

2005, June 1   **Perf. 13x13¼**
359 A584 70c multi   .55 .55

         Perf. 13½
360 A585 $4 multi   3.25 3.25

No. 359 printed in sheets of 12; No. 360, in sheets of 4.

Moths — B22

Designs: 90c, Pericallia galactina. $1, Automeris io draudtiana. $1.40, Antherina suraka. $2, Bunaea alcinoe.
$5, Rothschildia erycina nigrescens.

2005, July 26   **Perf. 12¾**
361-364 B22   Set of 4   5.50 5.50
      Souvenir Sheet
365 B22 $5 multi   4.00 4.00

Flowers — B23

No. 366, horiz.: a, Anthurium acropolis. b, Anthurium andraeanum. c, Gloxinia avanti. d, Heliconia psittacorum choconiana.
$5, Dendrobium dearei.

2005, June 26
366 B23 $2 Sheet of 4, #a-d   6.50 6.50
      Souvenir Sheet
367 B23 $5 multi   4.00 4.00

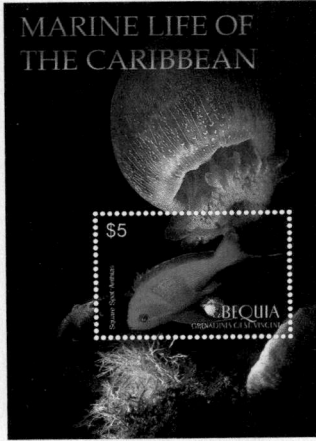

Marine Life — B24

No. 368: a, Hermissenda crassicornis. b, Chromodoris leopardus. c, Chromodoris kuniei. d, Coryphella verrucosa.
$5, Square spot anthias.

2005, June 26
368 B24 $2 Sheet of 4, #a-d   7.00 7.00
      Souvenir Sheet
369 B24 $5 multi   4.00 4.00

Prehistoric Animals — B25

No. 370, $2: a, Tenontosaurus. b, Gorgosaurus. c, Psittacosaurus. d, Parasaurolophus.
No. 371, $2, horiz.: a, Brachiosaurus. b, Seismosaurus. c, Struthiomimus. d, Oviraptor.
No. 372, $2, horiz.: a, Argentinosaurus. b, Triceratops. c, Ankylosaurus. d, Stegosaurus.
No. 373, $5, Quetzalcoatlus. No. 374, $5, Mammoth. No. 375, $5, Pteranodon, horiz.

2005, Sept. 1   **Perf. 14**
     Sheets of 4, #a-d
370-372 B25   Set of 3   19.50 19.50
      Souvenir Sheets
373-375 B25   Set of 3   12.00 12.00

Elvis Presley Type of 2005 and

B26

Elvis Presley (1935-77) — B27

No. 377 — Presley with: a, Tie. b, Hat. c, Lei. d, Guitar.
$20, Like #376.

      Perf. 13½x13¼
2005, Nov. 21   **Litho.**
376 B26 $2 multi   1.50 1.50
377 B27 $2 Sheet of 4, #a-d   5.00 5.00
   Litho. & Embossed
     Without Gum
    Die Cut Perf. 8
378 A597 $20 gold & multi   14.00 14.00

No. 376 was printed in sheets of 4.

Railroads Type of 2004

No. 379, $1: a, British Rail APT. b, Beyer Peacock 4-4-0. c, 1890s steam locomotive, Sao Paolo, Brazil. d, Beijing Limestone 600mm Gauge 0-8-0. e, China Railways QJ 2-10-2 Zhou De. f, Chinese SY 2-8-2 Industrial Baotou. g, Chinese SY Class Mikado 2-8-2. h, Chinese SY Class Overhaul Baotou. i, Derelict colliery, Nanpo, China.
No. 380, $1: a, Class 37 Diesel-electric. b, Indian Railways XB Class. c, Steam locomotive bringing in sugar cane, Java. d, Ji-tong Railway train on bridge, Reshui. e, Ji-tong Railway QJ at Liudigou. f, Ji-tong Railway QJ trains on Simingyi Viaduct. g, Ji-tong Railway train at Nandian. h, Ji-tong Railway QJ trains near Er-di. i, Ji-tong Railway QJ trains and banker.

No. 381, $1, vert.: a, Class 47 Diesel-electric. b, Stanier 8F, Turkey. c, Baldwin 2-8-2, Brazil. d, Sand boy, Borsing 0-8-0, Java. e, Indian Railways meter gauge 2-8-2, girl with pot. f, Locomotive graveyard, Thessaloniki, Greece. g, Greek Z Class meter gauge Peloponnese. h, Burdwan locomotive shed, West Bengal Province, India. i, SY locomotives at shed, Anshan, China.
No. 382, $5, Bridge on Asmara to Masawa line, Eritrea. No. 383, $5, Cornish Riviera Express. No. 384, $5, Zurich to Milan train.

2005, Dec. 30   **Perf. 13½**
     Sheets of 9, #a-i
379-381 A565   Set of 3   22.50 22.50
      Souvenir Sheets
382-384 A565   Set of 3   12.00 12.00

Queen Elizabeth II, 80th Birthday Type

Inscriptions: No. 385, $2, The Investiture of Charles. No. 386, $2, The Queen's 50th Birthday. No. 387, $2, The Queen's Silver Jubilee. No. 388, $2, The Birth of Prince William.

2006, Jan. 31
385-388 A603   Set of 4   7.00 7.00

Each stamp printed in sheets of 8 + label.

     Miniature Sheet

Marilyn Monroe (1926-62), Actress — B28

Various images.

2006, Mar. 31
389 B28 $2 Sheet of 4, #a-d   6.00 6.00

Columbus Type of 2006

Designs: 20c, Columbus and ship. 90c, Columbus, ships and crew, vert. $1.10, Niña, vert. $2, Columbus dicovers New World, 1492. $5, Pinta, vert.

2006, July 21   **Perf. 12¾**
390-393 A611   Set of 4   3.50 3.50
      Souvenir Sheet
394 A611 $5 multi   3.75 3.75

Space Achievements Type of 2006

No. 395, $2 — Luna 9: a, Left half of Luna 9, country name at LL. b, Right half of Luna 9, country name at UR. c, Top half of Luna 9, country name and denomination at UL. d, Luna 9 in space, country name at UL, denomination at UR. e, Bottom half of Luna 9, country name at LR. f, Luna 9 on moon, country name at LR.
No. 396, $3, vert. — Mars Reconnaissance Orbiter: a, Orbiter, country name in white. b, Orbiter, coutnry name in black. c, Mission emblem. d, Exterior of rocket showing Mission and NASA emblems.
No. 397, $6, Viking 1. No. 398, $6, International Space Station.

2006, Sept. 27   **Perf. 14¼**
395 A612 $2 Sheet of 6, #a-f   4.00 4.00
396 A612 $3 Sheet of 4, #a-d   4.00 4.00
      Souvenir Sheets
397-398 A612   Set of 2   4.00 4.00

Mozart Type of 2006

Design: Painting of Mozart, by Johann Georg Edlinger.

2006, Dec. 22   **Litho.   Perf. 13¼**
399 A619 $6 multi   4.75 4.75

     Souvenir Sheet

History of the Zeppelin — B29

No. 400: a, Ludwig Durr (1878-1956), chief engineer. b, Count Ferdinand Adolf August Heinrich von Zeppelin (1838-1917), designer. c, Dr. Hugo Eckener (1868-1954), engineer and pilot.

2006, Dec. 22
400 B29 $3 Sheet of 3, #a-c   7.00 7.00

Scouting, Cent. — B30

Designs: $4, Lord Robert Baden-Powell, Scouting emblem and doves. $6, Baden-Powell, horiz.

2007, Jan. 15
401 B30 $4 purple & blue   2.25 2.25
      Souvenir Sheet
402 B30 $6 brown   4.75 4.75

No. 401 printed in sheets of 3. No. 402 contains one 51x37mm stamp.

Princess Diana Type of 2007
     Miniature Sheet

No. 403 — Various photographs with panel colors of: a, Yellow. b, Red violet. c, Green. d, Blue. e, Purple. f, Black.
$6, Princess Diana and flags.

2007, May 1
403 A630 $1.40 Sheet of 6, #a-f   5.00 5.00
      Souvenir Sheet
404 A630 $6 multi   4.50 4.50

Concorde Type of 2006

No. 405, $1.40 — Concorde landing at Dulles Airport: a, Side view of Concorde. b, Front view of Concorde.
No. 406, $1.40 — Concorde at Boeing Field, Seattle: a, Front view of Concorde. b, Side view of Concorde.

2007, May 1
     Pairs, #a-b
405-406 A614   Set of 2   4.25 4.25

Nos. 405 and 406 were each printed in sheets containing three of each stamp.

John F. Kennedy Type of 2007
     Miniature Sheets

No. 407, $2 — Kennedy: a, As Navy Ensign, 1941. b, With crew at Solomon Islands, 1942. c, Drawing in blue gray. d, At Solomon Islands, 1943.
No. 408, $2: a, Kennedy and R. Sargent Shriver. b, Kennedy giving Peace Corps speech. c, Drawing of Kennedy in claret. d, Peace Corps volunteers.

2007, July 5
     Sheets of 4, #a-d
407-408 A622   Set of 2   13.00 13.00

Wedding of Queen Elizabeth II and Prince Philip, 60th Anniv. Type of 2007

No. 409: a, Couple in coach, denomination in blue. b, Couple crossing street, denomination in blue. c, Couple crossing street, denomination in light green. d, Couple in coach,

denomination in light green. e, Couple in coach, denomination in lilac. f, Couple crossing street, denomination in lilac.
$6, Couple, diff.

2007, July 5
409 A629 $1.40 Sheet of 6, #a-f 7.00 7.00
Souvenir Sheet
410 A629 $6 multi 5.00 5.00

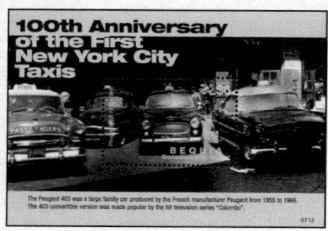

New York City Taxicabs, Cent. — B31

No. 411: a, 1909 Overland Model 31. b, 1910 Rockwell. c, 1916 Yellow Cab Model J. d, 1909 Kayton taxis. e, 1917 Yellow Cab Model K. f, 1919 Yellow Cab.
$6, 1955-66 Peugeot 403.

2007, July 5
411 B31 $1.40 Sheet of 6, #a-f 7.25 7.25
Souvenir Sheet
412 B31 $6 multi 5.00 5.00

1986 Halley's Comet Merchandising Emblem — B32

No. 413 — Emblem and frame color of: a, Light blue. b, Yellow. c, Green. d, Red brown.
$6, Emblem and Halley's Comet orbit diagram.

2007, July 5
413 B32 $2 Sheet of 4, #a-d 6.50 6.50
Souvenir Sheet
414 B32 $6 multi 4.75 4.75

Elvis Presley Type of 2007
Miniature Sheets

No. 415, $2 — Silhouette of Presley and: a, Graceland and gate. b, Piano, television and table in Graceland. c, Graceland and flowers. d, Swimming pool at Graceland.
No. 416, $2.50 — Presley: a, Wearing flowered western shirt, man and woman. b, Playing guitar, with other guitarist. c, Wearing neckerchief. d, Seated.

2007 Sheets of 4, #a-d Perf. 13¼
415-416 A633 Set of 2 13.50 13.50
Issued: No. 415, 7/5; No. 416, 7/12.

Pope Benedict XVI Type of 2007
2007, Oct. 24
417 A632 $1 multi .75 .75
Printed in sheets of 8.

Intl. Holocaust Remembrance Day Type of 2007
No. 418 — United Nations Delegates: a, Marcello Spatafora, Italy. b, Raymond Wolfe, Jamaica. c, Kenzo Oshima, Japan. d, Prince Zeid Ra'ad Zeid Al-Hussein, Jordan. e, Yerzhan Kh. Kazykhanov, Kazakhstan. f, Zachary Muburi-Muita, Kenya. g, Chi Youngjin, Republic of Korea. h, Solveiga Silkalna, Latvia.

2007, Nov. 14
418 A635 $1.40 Sheet of 8, #a-h 11.00 11.00

The editors would like to examine any commercial covers mailed during 2000-2008 from Bequia, which are franked only with the island's stamps.

CANOUAN

Diana, Princess of Wales (1961-97) — C1

1997 Litho. Perf. 14
1 C1 $1 multicolored 1.25 1.25
Issued in sheets of 6.
See Mustique No. 1.

Queen Mother Type of 2000 Inscribed "Canouan"
2000, Sept. 5 Litho. Perf. 14
2 A472 $1.40 multi 1.25 1.25
Issued in sheets of 6.

United We Stand C3

2003, Aug. 25
7 C3 $2 multi 1.75 1.75
Printed in sheets of 4.

Pres. John F. Kennedy (1917-63) — C4

No. 8: a, Peace Corps. b, Space program. c, Nuclear disarmament. d, Civil rights.

2003, Aug. 25
8 C4 $2 Sheet of 4, #a-d 6.50 6.50

Elvis Presley (1935-77) — C5

2003, Dec. 1 Perf. 13½x13¼
9 C5 90c multi 1.00 1.00
Printed in sheets of 9.

Butterflies C6

Designs: 90c, Atala. $1, Calico uranus. $1.40, Ceuptychia. $2, Aphrissa statira.

$5, Phoebis sennae.

2003, Dec. 1 Perf. 13¼
10-13 C6 Set of 4 4.00 4.00
Souvenir Sheet
14 C6 $5 multi 3.75 3.75

Pope John Paul II Type of 2005
2005, June 1 Litho. Perf. 12½x12¾
15 A585 $2 multi 1.75 1.75
Printed in sheets of 4.

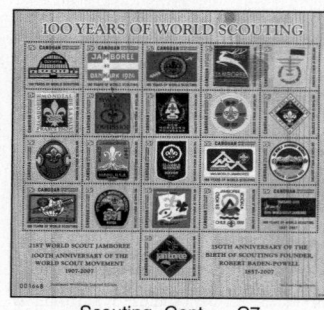

Scouting, Cent. — C7

No. 16 — Patches of International Scout Jamborees: a, Undated patch (1920), Great Britain. b, 1924, Denmark. c, 1929, Great Britain. d, 1933, Hungary. e, 1937, Netherlands. f, 1947, France. g, 1951, Austria. h, 1955, Canada. i, 1957, Great Britain. j, 1959, Philippines. k, 1963, Greece. l, 1967, United States. m, 1971, Japan. n, 1975, Norway. o, 1983, Canada. p, 1987-88, Australia. q, 1991, South Korea. r, 1995, Netherlands. s, 1999, Chile. t, 2003, Thailand. u, 2007, Great Britain.

2007, Jan. 15 Litho. Perf. 13¼
16 C7 75c Sheet of 21, #a-u 12.00 12.00

New York City Taxicabs, Cent. Type of 2007 of Bequia
No. 17 (51x37mm): a, 1913 Model GA. b, 1927 Yellow Cab Model 08. c, 1930 Studebaker Model 53. d, 1948 Checker Model A2. e, 1950's DeSoto. f, 1980's Checker A11.
$6, First gasoline taxi, 1907.

2007, July 5
17 B31 $1.40 Sheet of 6, #a-f 7.00 7.00
Souvenir Sheet
18 B31 $6 multi 5.00 5.00
No. 18 contains one 51x37mm stamp.

Intl. Holocaust Remembrance Day Type of 2007
No. 19 — United Nations diplomats and delegates: a, Jan Eliasson, President of 60th General Assembly. b, Julian Vila Coma, Andorra. c, Ismael A. Gaspar Martins, Angola. d, Victor Camilleri, Malta. e, César Mayoral, Argentina. f, Paulette A. Bethel, Bahamas. g, Christopher Hackett, Barbados. h, Kofi Annan, 7th United Nations Secretary General.

2007, Nov. 14
19 A635 $1.40 Sheet of 8, #a-h 8.50 8.50

Elvis Presley Type of 2007
Miniature Sheet
No. 20 — Presley: a, In olive green suit. b, Silhouette, standing, holding hand-held microphone. c, In purple shirt. d, Silhouette, with guitar. e, In blue shirt. f, Silhouette, crouching, holding hand-held microphone.

2007, Nov. 24
20 A633 $1.50 Sheet of 6, #a-f 8.00 8.00

John F. Kennedy Type of 2006
Miniature Sheet
No. 21 (26x40mm) — Kennedy: a, Facing right. b, In limousine, waving. c, Facing left in crowd. d, With arm extended.

2007, Nov. 24 Perf. 14
21 A622 $2 Sheet of 4, #a-d 6.50 6.50

The editors would like to examine any commercial covers mailed during 2000-2008 from Canouan, which are franked only with the island's stamps.

MAYREAU

All stamps are designs of St. Vincent ("A" illustration letter) unless otherwise illustrated.

Kennedy Type of 2007
Miniature Sheets

No. 1, $2, horiz. — John F. Kennedy and Nikita Khrushchev: a, With others, country name at LL, denomination at UR. b, With others, country name at LR, denomination at UL. c, Without others, country name and denomination at LR. d, With others, country name at LR, denomination at UR.
No. 2, $2, horiz. — Kennedy and: a, Fidel Castro, map of Cuba. b, U.S. Capitol, front page of Washington Post. c, American flag, Nikita Khrushchev, missile. d, Airplane, cameramen.

2006, Nov. 3 Litho. Perf. 12¾
Sheets of 4, #a-d
1-2 A622 Set of 2 13.00 13.00

Wedding of Queen Elizabeth II and Prince Philip, 60th Anniv. Type of 2007
No. 3: a, Parade in the Royal Carriage. b, Official portrait. c, Walking down the aisle (wedding attendees watching). d, Walking down the aisle (bride, groom and attendants). e, Walking down the aisle (attendants assisting bride). f, Saluting the crowd.
$6, Royal couple, vert.

2007, May 1 Litho. Perf. 13¼
3 A629 $1.40 Sheet of 6, #a-f 6.75 6.75
Souvenir Sheet
4 A629 $6 multi 5.00 5.00

Princess Diana Type of 2007
No. 5 — Diana: a, As child in red hooded jacket. b, As young girl in blue sweater. c, As young girl in red, orange and black sweater. d, Wearing pink jacket. e, Wearing lilac jacket. f, Wearing sleeveless dress.
$6, Wearing tiara.

2007, May 1
5 A630 $1.40 Sheet of 6, #a-f 6.75 6.75
Souvenir Sheet
6 A630 $6 multi 4.75 4.75

Pope Benedict XVI Type of 2007
2007, July 5
7 A632 $1.50 multi 1.10 1.10
Printed in sheets of 8.

The editors would like to examine any commercial covers mailed during 2000-2008 from Mayreau, which are franked only with the island's stamps.

MUSTIQUE

All stamps are designs of St. Vincent ("A" illustration letter) or Canouan ("C" illustration letter) unless otherwise illustrated.

Diana, Princess of Wales (1961-97) — M1

1997 Litho. Perf. 14
1 M1 $1 multicolored 1.10 1.10
Issued in sheets of 6.
See Canouan No. 1.

Paintings Type of 1999
Various pictures of flowers making up a photomosaic of the Queen Mother. Stamps inscribed "Mustique".

2000, Sept. 5 — Perf. 13¾
2 A442 $1 Sheet of 8, #a-h   17.50 17.50
i.   As No. 1017, imperf.   27.50 27.50

Coronation of Queen Elizabeth II, 50th Anniv. — M2

No. 3: a, Wearing yellow hat. b, Wearing blue dress. c, Wearing tiara.
$5, Wearing crown.

2003, Feb. 26 Litho. Perf. 14
3 M2 $3 Sheet of 3, #a-c   8.00 8.00
Souvenir Sheet
4 M2 $5 multi   4.50 4.50

Prince William, 21st Birthday Type of 2003

No. 5: a, Looking right. b, Wearing ski cap and goggles. c, Looking down.
$5, Wearing suit.

2003, May 13
5 A535 $3 Sheet of 3, #a-c   7.75 7.75
Souvenir Sheet
6 A535 $5 multi   4.50 4.50

Corvette Type of 2003

No. 7: a, 1960 Shark. b, 1988. c, 1956 convertible. d, 1967.
$5, 1964 Sting Ray convertible.

2003, July 1 Perf. 13¼x13½
7 A534 $2 Sheet of 4, #a-d   7.00 7.00
Souvenir Sheet
8 A534 $5 multi   4.50 4.50

Cadillac Type of 2003

No. 9: a, 1978 Seville. b, 1927 La Salle. c, 1953 Eldorado. d, 2002 Seville.
$5, 1961 Sedan de Ville.

2003, July 1
9 A537 $2 Sheet of 4, #a-d   7.00 7.00
Souvenir Sheet
10 A537 $5 multi   4.50 4.50

Circus Type of 2003

No. 11: a, Josaphine. b, Korolev Group (girl and monkey). c, Korolev Group (monkey). d, Zebra.

2003, July 1 Perf. 14
11 A539 $2 Sheet of 4, #a-d   11.00 11.00

Kennedy Type of Canouan

No. 12: a, On Solomon Islands, 1943. b, On PT 109, 1942. c, Senate campaign, 1952. d, Recieving medal for gallantry, 1944.

2003, Aug. 25
12 C4 $2 Sheet of 4, #a-d   8.00 8.00

United We Stand Type of Canouan

2003, Sept. 8
13 C5 $2 multi   1.60 1.60
Printed in sheets of 4.

Birds
M3

Designs: $1, Red-billed tropicbird. $1.10, Bananaquit. $1.40, Belted kingfisher. $2, Ruby-throated hummingbird. $5, Brown pelican, vert.

2003, Nov. 5 Perf. 13½x13¾
14-17 M3 Set of 4   5.25 5.25
Souvenir Sheet
Perf. 13¾x13½
18 M3 $5 multi   4.25 4.25

Elvis Presley Type of Canouan
2003, Dec. 1 Perf. 13½x13¼
19 C5 90c multi   .90 .90
Printed in sheets of 9.

Pope John Paul II Type of 2005
2005, June 1 Litho. Perf. 12½x12¾
20 A585 $2 multi   1.75 1.75
Printed in sheets of 4.

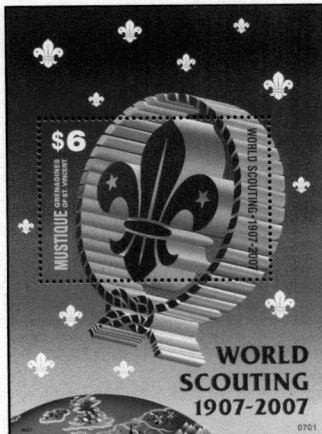

Scouting, Cent. — M4

No. 21, vert.: a, Scouting emblem over globe. b, Emblem of 21st World Scout Jamboree, doves. c, Doves. d, Various national Scouting emblems. e, Doves, map of Mustique, Scouting flag, flag of St. Vincent and the Grenadines. f, Doves, Scout handshake.
$6, Scouting emblem.

2007, July 5 Litho. Perf. 13¼
21 M4 $1.50 Sheet of 6, #a-f   8.50 8.50
Souvenir Sheet
22 M4 $6 multi   4.75 4.75

Intl. Holocaust Remembrance Day Type of 2007

No. 23 — United Nations diplomats and delegates: a, Lebohand Fine Maema, Lesotho. b, Milton Nathaniel Barnes, Liberia. c, Christian Wenaweser, Liechtenstein. d, Dalius Cekuolis, Lithuania. e, Igor Dzundev, Macedonia. f, Zina Andrianarivelo-Razafy, Madagascar. g, Nebojsa Kaludjerovic, Montenegro. h, Asha-Rose Migiro, United Nations Deputy Secretary General.

2007, Nov. 14
23 A635 $1.40 Sheet of 8, #a-h   9.00 9.00

The editors would like to examine any commercial covers mailed during 2000-2008 from Mustique, which are franked only with the island's stamps.

UNION ISLAND

All stamps are types of St. Vincent ("A" illustration letter), St. Vincent Grenadines ("G" illustration letter) or Union ("U" illustration letter).

"Island" issues are listed separately beginning in 1984. See St. Vincent Grenadines Nos. 84-111, 248-262 for earlier issues.

British Monarch Type of 1984

No. 1a, Battle of Hastings. No. 1b, William the Conqueror. No. 2a, William the Conqueror. No. 2b, Abbaye Aux Dames. No. 3a, Skirmish at Dunbar. No. 3b, Charles II. No. 4a, Arms of William the Conqueror. No. 4b, William the Conqueror. No. 5a, Charles II. No. 5b, St. James Palace. No. 6a, Arms of Charles II. No. 6b, Charles II, Great Fire of London.

Perf. 12½
1984, Mar. 29 Litho. Unwmk.
1 A110 1c Pair, #a.-b. .25 .25
2 A110 5c Pair, #a.-b. .25 .25
3 A110 10c Pair, #a.-b. .25 .25
4 A110 20c Pair, #a.-b. .30 .30
5 A111 60c Pair, #a.-b. .50 .50
6 A111 $3 Pair, #a.-b. 3.50 3.50
Nos. 1-6 (6)   5.05 5.05

Locomotives Type of 1985

No. 13, 1813 Puffing Billy, UK. No. 14, 1911 Class 9N, UK. No. 15, 1882 Class Skye Bogie, UK. No. 16, 1912 Class G8, Germany. No. 17, 1954 Class 65.10, Germany. No. 18, 1900 Castle Class, UK. No. 19, 1887 Spinner Class 25, UK. No. 20, 1951 Fell #10100, UK. No. 21, 1942 Class 42, Germany. No. 22, 1951 Class 5MT, UK. No. 23, 1929 P.O. Rebuilt Class 3500, France. No. 24, 1886 Class 123, UK. No. 25, 1976 Class 56, UK. No. 26, 1897 Class G5, US. No. 27, 1947 9400 Class, UK. No. 28, 1888 Sir Theodore, UK. No. 29, 1929 Class Z, UK. No. 30, 1896 Atlantic City RR, US. No. 31, 1906 45xx Class, UK. No. 32, 1912 Class D15, UK. No. 33, 1938 Class U4-b, Canada. No. 34, 1812 Prince Regent, UK. No. 35, 1920 Butler Henderson, UK. No. 36, 1889 Elidir, UK. No. 37, 1934 7200 Class, UK. No. 38, 1911 Class Z, UK. No. 39, 1938 Class C, Australia. No. 40, 1879 Sir Haydn, UK. No. 41, 1850 Aberdeen No. 26, UK. No. 42, 1883 Class Y14, UK. No. 43, 1915 River Class, UK. No. 44, 1936 D51 Class, Japan. No. 45, 1837 L&B Bury, UK. No. 46, 1903 Class 900, US. No. 47, 1904 Class H-20, US. No. 48, 1905 Class L, UK. No. 49, 1952 Class 4, UK. No. 50, 1837 Campbell's 8-Wheeler, US. No. 51, 1934 Class GG1, US. No. 52, 1924 Class 01, Germany. No. 53, 1920 Gordon Highlander, UK. No. 54, 1969 Metroliner Railcar, US. No. 55, 1951 Class GP7, US. No. 56, 1873 Hardwicke Precedent Class, UK. No. 57, 1899 Highflyer Class, UK. No. 58, 1925 Class U1, UK. No. 59, 1880 Class 7100, Japan. No. 60, 1972 Gas Turbine Prototype, France.

Se-tenant Pairs, #a.-b.
a. — Side and front views.
b. — Action scene.

1984-87 Perf. 12½
13 A120 5c multicolored .25 .25
14 A120 5c multicolored .25 .25
15 A120 5c multicolored .25 .25
16 A120 10c multicolored .40 .40
17 A120 15c multicolored .40 .40
18 A120 15c multicolored .40 .40
19 A120 15c multicolored .40 .40
20 A120 15c multicolored .40 .40
21 A120 20c multicolored .40 .40
22 A120 25c multicolored .40 .40
23 A120 25c multicolored .40 .40
24 A120 25c multicolored .40 .40
25 A120 30c multicolored .40 .40
26 A120 30c multicolored .40 .40
27 A120 40c multicolored .50 .50
28 A120 45c multicolored .50 .50
29 A120 45c multicolored .50 .50
30 A120 45c multicolored .50 .50
31 A120 50c multicolored .60 .60
32 A120 50c multicolored .60 .60
33 A120 50c multicolored .60 .60
34 A120 60c multicolored .75 .75
35 A120 60c multicolored .75 .40
36 A120 60c multicolored .75 .75
37 A120 60c multicolored .75 .75
38 A120 60c multicolored .75 .75
39 A120 75c multicolored .90 .90
40 A120 75c multicolored .90 .90
41 A120 75c multicolored .90 .90
42 A120 75c multicolored .90 .90
43 A120 75c multicolored .90 .90
44 A120 $1 multicolored 1.25 1.25
45 A120 $1 multicolored 1.25 1.25
46 A120 $1 multicolored 1.25 1.25
47 A120 $1 multicolored 1.25 1.25
48 A120 $1 multicolored 1.25 1.25
49 A120 $1.50 multicolored 1.75 1.75
50 A120 $1.50 multicolored 1.75 1.75
51 A120 $1.50 multicolored 1.75 1.75
52 A120 $2 multicolored 2.25 2.25
53 A120 $2 multicolored 2.25 2.25
54 A120 $2 multicolored 2.25 2.25
55 A120 $2 multicolored 2.25 2.25
56 A120 $2.50 multicolored 2.75 2.75
57 A120 $2.50 multicolored 2.75 2.75
58 A120 $3 multicolored 3.50 3.50
59 A120 $3 multicolored 3.50 3.50
60 A120 $3 multicolored 3.50 3.50
Nos. 13-60 (48)   53.70 53.35

Issued: Nos. 13, 34, 44, 52, 8/9/84; Nos. 14, 16, 21, 23, 39, 45, 56, 58, 12/18/84; Nos. 15, 31, 35, 53, 3/25/85; Nos. 17, 25, 28, 40, 49, 57, 59, 1/31/86; Nos. 18, 29, 37, 41, 46, 50, 54, 60, 12/23/86; Nos. 19, 24, 27, 32, 38, 42, 47, 55, 9/8/7; Nos. 20, 22, 26, 308, 33, 43, 48, 51, 12/4/87.
Beginning on Jan. 31, 1986, this issue is not inscribed "Leaders of the World."

St. Vincent Grenadines Nos. 222-238 Overprinted "UNION ISLAND"
Perf. 14x13½
1984, Aug. 23 Wmk. 373
109 G26 1c on No. 222 .25 .25
110 G26 3c on No. 223 .25 .25
111 G26 5c on No. 224 .25 .25
112 G26 6c on No. 225 .25 .25
113 G26 10c on No. 226 .25 .25
114 G26 15c on No. 227 .25 .25
115 G26 20c on No. 228 .30 .30
116 G26 25c on No. 229 .30 .30
117 G26 30c on No. 230 .30 .30
118 G26 50c on No. 231 .45 .45
119 G26 60c on No. 232 .50 .50
120 G26 75c on No. 233 .60 .60
121 G26 $1 on No. 234 .90 .90
122 G26 $2 on No. 235 2.00 2.00
123 G26 $3 on No. 236 2.50 2.50
124 G26 $5 on No. 237 4.50 4.50
125 G26 $10 on No. 238 8.00 8.00
Nos. 109-125 (17)   21.85 21.85

Cricket Players Type of 1985

1c, S. N. Hartley. 10c, G. W. Johnson. 15c, R. M. Ellison. 55c, C. S. Cowdrey. 60c, K. Sharp. 75c, M. C. Cowdrey, in action. $1.50, G. R. Dilley, in action. $3, R. Illingworth, in action.

1984, Nov. Unwmk. Perf. 12½
Pairs, #a.-b.
126 A116 1c multicolored .25 .25
127 A116 10c multicolored .30 .30
128 A116 15c multicolored .35 .35
129 A116 55c multicolored .50 .50
130 A116 60c multicolored .55 .55
131 A116 75c multicolored .65 .65
132 A116 $1.50 multicolored .85 .85
133 A116 $3 multicolored 1.75 1.75
Nos. 126-133 (8)   5.20 5.20

Classic Car Type of 1983

No. 142, 1963 Lancia, Italy. No. 143, 1895 Duryea, US. No. 144, 1970 Datsun, Japan. No. 145, 1962 BRM, UK. No. 146, 1927 Amilcar, France. No. 147, 1929 Duesenberg, US. No. 148, 1913 Peugeot, France. No. 149, 1938 Lagonda, UK. No. 150, 1924 Fiat, Italy. No. 151, 1957 Alfa Romeo, Italy. No. 152, 1957 Panhard, France. No. 153, 1954 Porsche, Germany. No. 154, 1904 Darraco, France. No. 155, 1927 Daimler, UK. No. 156, 1949 Oldsmobile, US. No. 157, 1934 Chrysler, US. No. 158, 1965 MG, UK. No. 159, 1922 Fiat, Italy. No. 160, 1934 Bugatti, France. No. 161, 1963 Watson/Meyer-Drake, US. No. 162, 1917 Locomobile, US. No. 163, 1928 Ford, US.

Se-tenant Pairs, #a.-b.
a. — Side and front views.
b. — Action scene.

1985-86 Perf. 12½
142 A107 1c multicolored .25 .25
143 A107 5c multicolored .25 .25
144 A107 10c multicolored .25 .25
145 A107 10c multicolored .25 .25
146 A107 50c multicolored .30 .30
147 A107 55c multicolored .35 .35
148 A107 60c multicolored .40 .40
149 A107 60c multicolored .40 .40
150 A107 60c multicolored .40 .40
151 A107 75c multicolored .50 .50
152 A107 75c multicolored .50 .50
153 A107 75c multicolored .50 .50
154 A107 90c multicolored .55 .55
155 A107 $1 multicolored .60 .60
156 A107 $1 multicolored .60 .60
157 A107 $1 multicolored .60 .60
158 A107 $1.50 multicolored 1.00 1.00
159 A107 $1.50 multicolored 1.00 1.00
160 A107 $1.50 multicolored 1.00 1.00
161 A107 $2 multicolored 1.25 1.25
162 A107 $2.50 multicolored 1.50 1.50
163 A107 $3 multicolored 1.75 1.75
Nos. 142-163 (22)   14.20 14.20

Issued: Nos. 142, 146, 151, 1/4/85; Nos. 143, 148, 155, 158, 5/20/85; Nos. 144, 147, 149, 152, 154, 156, 159, 161, 7/15/85; Nos. 145, 150, 153, 157, 160, 163, 7/30/86.
Beginning on 7/30/86, this issue is not inscribed "Leaders of the World."

Birds — U1

No. 186a, Hooded warbler. No. 186b, Carolina wren. No. 187a, Song sparrow. No. 187b, Black-headed grosbeak. No. 188a, Scarlet tanager. No. 188b, Lazuli bunting. No. 189a, Sharp-shinned hawk. No. 189b, Merlin.

1985, Feb.				Perf. 12½	
186	U1	15c Pair, #a.-b.		.30	.30
187	U1	50c Pair, #a.-b.		.40	.40
188	U1	$1 Pair, #a.-b.		.65	.65
189	U1	$1.50 Pair, #a.-b.		1.50	1.50
		Nos. 186-189 (4)		2.85	2.85

Butterflies — U2

No. 194a, Cynthia cardui. No. 194b, Zerynthia rumina. No. 195a, Byblia ilithyia. No. 195b, Papilio machaon. No. 196a, Carterocephalus palaemon. No. 196b, Acraea anacreon. No. 197a, Anartia amathea. No. 197b, Salamis temora.

1985, Apr. 15					
194	U2	15c Pair, #a.-b.		.25	.25
195	U2	25c Pair, #a.-b.		.35	.35
196	U2	75c Pair, #a.-b.		.55	.55
197	U2	$2 Pair, #a.-b.		1.75	1.75
		Nos. 194-197 (4)		2.90	2.90

Queen Mother Type of 1985

85th birthday — Hats: No. 206a, Mortarboard. No. 206b, Blue. No. 207a, Turquoise. No. 207b, Blue. Nos. 208a, 212a, Without hat. Nos. 208b, 212b, White. Nos. 209a, 211a, White hat, violet feathers. Nos. 209b, 211b, Blue. No. 210a, Crown. No. 210b, Hat.

1985, Aug. 19					
206	A122	55c Pair, #a.-b.		.50	.50
207	A122	70c Pair, #a.-b.		.60	.60
208	A122	$1.05 Pair, #a.-b.		.75	.75
209	A122	$1.70 Pair, #a.-b.		1.40	1.40
		Nos. 206-209 (4)		3.25	3.25

Souvenir Sheets of 2

210	A122	$1.95 #a.-b.		2.25	2.25
211	A122	$2.25 #a.-b.		2.75	2.75
212	A122	$7 #a.-b.		7.00	7.00

Elizabeth II 60th Birthday Type of 1986

Designs: 10c, Wearing scarf. 60c, Riding clothes. $2, Wearing crown and jewels. $8, In Canberra, vert. $10, Holding flowers.

1986, Apr. 21					
213-216	A128	10c Set of 4		3.25	3.25

Souvenir Sheet

217	A128	$10 multi		3.75	3.75

U3

World Cup Soccer Championships, Mexico — U4

1986, May 7		Perf. 12½ (U3), 15 (U4)			
218	U3	1c Moroccan team		.25	.25
219	U3	10c Argentinian team		.25	.25
220	U4	30c Algerian player		.25	.25
221	U4	75c Hungarian team		.30	.30
222	U3	$1 Russian team		.30	.30
223	U4	$2.50 Belgian player		.60	.60
224	U4	$3 French player		.65	.65
225	U4	$6 W. German player		1.25	1.25
		Nos. 218-225 (8)		3.85	3.85

Souvenir Sheets

226	U3	$1.85 like No. 222		2.00	2.00
227	U3	$2 like No. 219		2.25	2.25

Souvenir sheets contain one 60x40mm stamp.

Prince Andrew Royal Wedding Type

No. 228: a, Prince Andrew in cap. b, Prince Andrew in suit.
No. 229:a, Couple. b, Sarah Ferguson.

1986, July 15		Perf. 12½x13, 13x12½			
228	A132	60c Pair. #a.-b.		.75	.75
229	A132	$2 Pair. #a.-b.		1.50	1.50

Nos. 228-229 Overprinted in Silver "CONGRATULATIONS TO T.R.H. THE DUKE & DUCHESS OF YORK" in 3 Lines

1986, Oct.					
230	A132	60c on No. 228a-b		1.75	1.75
231	A132	$2 on No. 229a-b		5.00	5.00

Queen Elizabeth II Wedding Anniv. Type of St. Vincent Grenadines

1987, Oct. 15				Perf. 12½	
236	G47	15c like No. 568		.25	.25
237	G47	45c like No. 569		.35	.35
238	G47	$1.50 like No. 570		.55	.55
239	G47	$3 like No. 571		1.10	1.10
240	G47	$4 like No. 572		1.50	1.50
		Nos. 236-240 (5)		3.75	3.75

U5

Disney characters in various French vehicles: No. 241, 1c, 1893 Peugeot. No. 242, 2c, 1890-91 Panhard-Levassor. No. 243, 3c, 1910 Renault. No. 244, 4c, 1919 Citroen. No. 245, 5c, 1878 La Mancelle. No. 246, 10c, 1891 De Dion Bouton Quadricycle. No. 247, $5, 1896 Leon Bollee Trike. No. 248, $6, 1911 Brasier Coupe.
No. 249, French road race, Mickey, Donald and Goofy racing. No. 250, 1769, Cugnot's artillery tractor, Mickey, Goofy and Donald dressed as soliders.

1989, July 7				Perf. 14x13½	
241-248	U5	Set of 8		16.00	16.00

Souvenir Sheets

249	U5	$6 multicolored		8.50	8.50
250	U5	$6 multicolored		8.50	8.50

PHILEXFRANCE '89.

Diana, Princess of Wales (1961-97) — U6

1997		Litho.		Perf. 14	
251	U6	$1 multicolored		1.50	2.00

No. 251 was issued in sheets of 6.

Paintings Type of 1999

Various pictures of flowers making up a photomosaic of the Queen Mother.

2000, Sept. 5				Perf. 13¾	
252	A442	$1 Sheet of 8, #a-h		7.50	7.50
i.		As No. 252, imperf.		15.00	15.00

New Year 2002 (Year of the Horse) — U7

Horse paintings by Giuseppe Castiglione: a, White horse with head down. b, Brown horse. c, Piebald horse. d, White horse with head up.

2001, Dec. 17		Litho.		Perf. 12¾	
253	U7	$1.40 Sheet of 4, #a-d		5.00	5.00

Worldwide Fund for Nature (WWF) U8

Shortfin mako shark: a, View of underside. b, Side view. c, Pair of sharks. d, Shark at surface.

2002, Nov. 1				Perf. 14	
254		Horiz. or vert. strip		3.25	3.25
a.-d.		U8 $1 Any single		.80	.80
e.		Souvenir sheet of 4, #a-d		27.50	27.50

United We Stand Type of 2001

2002, Nov. 4					
255	A508	$1.40 multi		1.75	1.75

Printed in sheets of 4.

Queen Mother Elizabeth Type of 2002

No. 256: a, Wearing purple hat. b, Wearing green hat. c, Wearing pink hat.

2002, Nov. 4		Litho.		Perf. 14	
256	A522	$2 Sheet of 4, #a-b,			
		2 #c		6.50	6.50

Ferrari Automobiles — U9

Designs: No. 257, $1.10, 1960 Dino 246S. No. 258, $1.10, 1962 248SP. No. 259, $1.10, 1966 330GTC-GTS. No. 260, $1.10, 1967 Dino 206GT. No. 261, $1.10, 1984 Testarossa. No. 262, $1.10, 1989 348TB-TS. No. 263, $1.10, 2002 Enzo Ferrari. No. 264, $1.10, 2002 360 Challenge.

2002, Dec. 9					
257-264		Set of 8		9.00	9.00

Teddy Bears Type of 2002

No. 265, $2 — Bears from Britain: a, Palace Guard bear. b, Bear with crown. c, Bear with bowler hat. d, Beefeater bear.
No. 266, $2 — Bears from Holland: a, Artist bear. b, Bear with black hat. c, Bears in wagon. d, Bear with overalls and checked shirt.

2003, Jan. 27				Perf. 13½x13¼	
		Sheets of 4, #a-d			
265-266	A519	Set of 2		15.00	15.00

Year of the Ram Type of 2003

No. 267 — Color of ram: a, Red violet. b, Red. c, Yellow green. d, Violet. e, Brown. f, Blue green.

2003, Jan. 27				Perf. 14¼x13¾	
267	A526	$1 Sheet of 6, #a-f		4.75	4.75

Princess Diana Type of 2003

No. 268: a, Wearing pink hat, holding roses. b, Wearing lilac dress and necklace. c, Wearing red hat. d, With hand on chin. e, Wearing

pink blouse, holding flowers. d, Wearing blue dress.
No. 269, horiz.: a, Children's Cancer Hospital. b, Meeting with AIDS patients. c, Conference on eating disorders. d, Red Cross child feeding center.

2003, May 26		Litho.		Perf. 14	
268	A536	$1.40 Sheet of 6, #a-f		6.75	6.75
269	A536	$2 Sheet of 4, #a-d		6.50	6.50

Kennedy Type of Bequia

No. 270: a, Denomination at UL, name at right. b, Denomination at UL, name at left. c, Denomination at UR, name at left. d, Denomination at UR, name at right.

2003, Aug. 25					
270	B14	$2 Sheet of 4, #a-d		6.50	6.50

Elvis Presley Type of Bequia

No. 271 — Color of illustration: a, Brown. b, Dark blue. c, Green. d, Purple. e, Yellow brown. f, Red violet. g, Sepia. h, Bright blue. i, Red brown.

2003, Dec. 1				Perf. 13½	
271	B15	90c Sheet of 9, #a-i		6.50	6.50

Fish — U10

Designs: 90c, Great barracuda. $1, French angelfish. $1.40, Reef shark. $2, Tarpon. $5, Queen angelfish.

2003, Dec. 1				Perf. 13¼	
272-275	U10	Set of 4		4.25	4.25

Souvenir Sheet

276	U10	$5 multi		4.25	4.25

Detail from Monkey and Cat, by Yi Yuan-Chi — U11

2004, Jan. 15				Perf. 13½	
277	U11	$1.40 shown		1.60	1.60

Souvenir Sheet
Perf. 13¾

278	U11	$3 Entire painting		5.75	5.75

New Year 2004 (Year of the Monkey). No. 277 printed in sheets of 4. No. 278 contains one 58x35mm stamp.

Marilyn Monroe Type of 2004

Monroe and: No. 279, 75c, Denomination in blue. No. 280, 75c, Denomination in red.

2004, May 3		Litho.		Perf. 13½	
279-280	A558	Set of 2		1.40	1.40

Each stamp printed in sheets of 10.

Ronald Reagan Type of 2004

Reagan and denomination color of: a, Red. b, White. c, Blue.

2004, Oct. 13					
281		Vert. strip of 3		3.75	3.75
a.-c.	A564	$1.40 Any single		1.10	1.10

Printed in sheets containing two strips.

Babe Ruth Type of 2004

2004, Nov. 25				Perf. 14	
282	A561	75c multi		.70	.70

Printed in sheets of 10.

Miniature Sheet

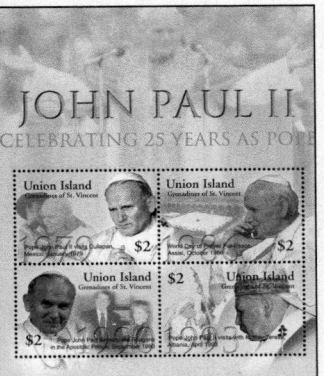

Election of Pope John Paul II, 25th Anniv. (in 2003) — U12

Pope John Paul II: a, With child, Cuilapan, Mexico, 1979. b, At World Day of Prayer for Peace, Assisi, Italy, 1986. c, With Ronald and Nancy Reagan, 1990. d, Visiting Mother Teresa, 1993.

2005, Jan. 26   *Perf. 14*
283 U12 $2 Sheet of 4, #a-d   6.50 6.50

Basketball Players Type of 2004-05

Designs: No. 284, 90c, Mike Bibby, Sacramento Kings. No. 285, 90c, Reggie Miller, Indiana Pacers. No. 286, 90c, Alonzo Mourning, Miami Heat. No. 287, 90c, Paul Pierce, Boston Celtics. No. 288, 90c, Jim Jackson, Phoenix Suns.

No. 289: a, New Jersey Nets emblem. b, Jason Kidd, New Jersey Nets.

2005, Feb. 10   Litho.   *Perf. 14*
284-288 A572 Set of 5   4.00 4.00
Miniature Sheet
289 A572 90c Sheet of 12, 2
      #289a, 10 #289b   8.75 8.75

Nos. 284-288 each printed in sheets of 12.

Vatican Stamp and Pope John Paul II Types of 2005

Designs: 70c, Vatican #64. $3, Pope holding Bible, horiz.

2005, June 1   *Perf. 13x13¼*
290 A584 70c multi   .60   .60
**   *Perf. 13¼x13½***
291 A585 $3 multi   2.50 2.50

No. 290 printed in sheets of 12; No. 291, in sheets of 6.

Railroads Type of 2004

No. 292, $1: a, British Rail intercity high-speed train. b, British-built Edwardian Mogul, Paraguay. c, Fireless locomotive, Ludlow jute mill, Calcutta. d, Welders working on Wisconsin Central. e, Serving breakfast on British intercity train. f, Pacific locomotive, Pulgaon-Avri line, India. g, Locomotive shed laborers, Wankaner, India. h, British Rail train driver with head out of window. i, British Rail train driver at controls.

No. 293, $1: a, Southern Pacific Bullied Pacific "Blackmore Vale." b, Bagnall 0-4-0ST on Assam coalfield. c, Orenstein & Koppel 0-8-0T, Java. d, Baldwin 0-6-6-0 Compound Mallet, Philippines. e, Coal loads on C&I sub, Illinois. f, Class 37 on China Clay, Cornwall. g, BNSF stack train, New Mexico. h, China Railways QJ 2-10-2 near Anshan. i, Kitson 0-6-2 at Suraya Sugar Mill, India.

No. 294, $5, Amtrak Coast Starlight, California. No. 295, $5, Glacier Express.

2005, June 7   *Perf. 12¾*
Sheets of 9, #a-i
292-293 A565 Set of 2   14.50 14.50
Souvenir Sheets
294-295 A565 Set of 2   7.50 7.50

U14

Elvis Presley (1935-77) — U15

No. 297 — Location of spotlights: a, Four spotlights along frame edge at LL, spotlights above and below "S" in "Island." b, Spotlights in top frame near UL corner and above head, spotlights above and below "U" in "Union," spotlight above "S" in "Island." c, Four spotlights in top frame at left, two faint spotlights in left frame at UL. d, Faint spotlight in top frame at UL.

2005, Nov. 21   Litho.   *Perf. 13¼*
296 U14 $2 multi   1.75 1.75
297 U15 $2 Sheet of 4, #a-d   6.50 6.50

No. 296 printed in sheets of 4.

Queen Elizabeth II 80th Birthday Type of 2006

Queen Elizabeth II: No. 298, $2, Riding in coach at Trooping the Color parade, 1987. No. 299, $2, With fireman, 1992. No. 300, $2, At Queen Mother's 100th birthday celebration, 2000. No. 301, $2, Riding in coach in Golden Jubilee parade, 2002.

2006, Jan. 31   *Perf. 13½*
298-301 A603 Set of 4   6.25 6.25

Nos. 298-301 each printed in sheets of 8 + label.

Christopher Columbus Type of 2006

Designs: 10c, Arrival in Hispaniola, 1492. 90c, Columbus and ships. $2, Ships, vert. $3, Ships, diff., vert. $5, Santa Maria, vert.

2006, July 21   *Perf. 12¾*
302-305 A611 Set of 4   4.75 4.75
Souvenir Sheet
306 A611 $5 multi   4.00 4.00

Space Achievements Type of 2006

No. 307, vert. — Venus Express: a, Denomination in white at LL. b, Denomination in white at UL. c, Denomination in black at LL. d, Denomination in black at UL.

No. 308 — First Flight of Space Shuttle Columbia: a, Lift-off. b, Columbia on launch pad. c, Astronaut John W. Young, Columbia. d, Astronaut Robert L. Crippen, Columbia. e, Columbia in space. f, Flight emblem.

$5, Luna 9.

2006, Dec. 22   *Perf. 13¼*
307 A612 $2 Sheet of 4, #a-d   6.50 6.50
308 A612 $3 Sheet of 6, #a-f   14.00 14.00
Souvenir Sheet
309 A612 $5 multi   4.00 4.00

Rembrandt Type of 2006

Self-portraits from: 50c, C. 1632-39. 75c, 1635. $1, 1629. $2, 1634.

No. 314, $2 — Drawings: a, Two Tramps, a Man and a Woman. b, Beggar Leaning on a Stick. c, Ragged Peasant with His Hands Behind Him, Holding a Stick. d, Beggar Man and Beggar Woman Conversing.

No. 315, $2 — Drawings: a, Study for the Drunkenness of Lot. b, A Girl Sleeping. c, Saskia at a Window. d, Old Man with Arms Extended.

No. 316, $5, The Apostle Simon (70x100mm). No. 317, $5, Winter Landscape, horiz. (100x70mm).

2006, Dec. 22   *Perf. 13¼*
310-313 A617 Set of 4   3.50 3.50

Sheets of 4, #a-d
314-315 A617 Set of 2   13.50 13.50
**   *Imperf***
316-317 A617 Set of 2   8.00 8.00

John F. Kennedy Type of 2007
Miniature Sheets

No. 318, $2, horiz. — Inauguration: a, Kennedy shaking hands with Father Richard J. Casey. b, Kennedy and State Department Seal. c, Medal of Kennedy, U.S. flag. d, Portrait of Kennedy, Kennedy with son.

No. 319, $2, horiz. — Cuban Missile Crisis: a, Kennedy, Soviet Premier Nikita Khrushchev, photographer. b, Cuban President Fidel Castro, Soviet trucks at Cuban port. c, Kennedy and map of plan to invade Cuba. d, KA-18A stereo strip camera, map of Cuba.

2006, Dec. 22   *Perf. 13¼*
Sheets of 4, #a-d
318-319 A622 Set of 2   13.00 13.00

Scouting, Cent. Type of Bequia of 2007

Designs: $4, Scouting emblem, doves and figure-eight knots. $6, Scouting emblem.

2007, Jan. 3
320 B30 $4 blue & green   3.75 3.75
Souvenir Sheet
321 B30 $6 multi   5.75 5.75

No. 320 printed in sheets of 3. No. 321 contains one 37x51mm stamp.

Wedding of Queen Elizabeth II and Prince Philip, 60th Anniv. Type of 2007

No. 322 — Couple with Queen wearing: a, Gray hat with black feather. b, Red and lilac hat. c, Black and white hat. d, Light blue jacket, no hat. e, Light blue jacket and hat. f, Light green jacket, red and light green hat.
$6, Couple under umbrella, vert.

2007, July 5   *Perf. 12¾*
322 A629 $1.40 Sheet of 6, #a-f   7.25 7.25
Souvenir Sheet
323 A629 $6 multi   4.75 4.75

Princess Diana Type of 2007

No. 324: a, Reclining. c, Wearing white dress. d, Wearing blue dress. d, Wearing white blouse and jeans. e, Wearing black dress. f, Wearing black sweater, pants and shoes.

No. 325: a, As Red Cross volunteer. b, Touring minefield in Angola. c, With Mother Teresa. d, Holding child at Shri Swaminarayan Mandir, London.
$6, Wearing headphones.

2007, July 5   *Perf. 12¾*
324 A630 $1.40 Sheet of 6, #a-f   7.00 7.00
325 A630 $2 Sheet of 4, #a-d   6.50 6.50
Souvenir Sheet
326 A630 $6 multi   5.00 5.00

Pope Benedict XVI Type of 2007
2007, July 5   *Perf. 13¼*
327 A632 $1.50 multi   1.25 1.25
Printed in sheets of 8.

Elvis Presley Type of 2007

No. 328 — Photographs of Presley from: a, 1946. b, 1956. c, 1962. d, 1970.

2007, Oct. 24
328 A633 $3 Sheet of 4, #a-d   9.50 9.50

First Helicopter Flight, Cent. — U16

Designs: 10c, Benson autogyro. 25c, Agusta-Sikorsky AS-61. 90c, Bell UH-1B/C Iroquois, horiz. $5, Bell UH-1 Iroquois, vert.

No. 333, horiz.: a, Eurocopter/Kawasaki BK 117, denomination at UR. b, Bell UH-1B/C Iroquois, denomination at LL. c, Bell UH-1B/C Iroquois, denomination at UR. d, Eurocopter/Kawasaki BK 117, denomination at UL.

$5, NH 90, horiz.

2007, Oct. 24
329-332 U16 Set of 4   7.00 7.00
333 U16 $2 Sheet of 4, #a-d   8.50 8.50
Souvenir Sheet
334 U16 $5 multi   4.50 4.50

The editors would like to examine any commercial covers mailed during 2000-2008 from Union Island, which are franked only with the island's stamps.

Stamps inscribed "Palm Island," "Tobago Cays," and "Young Island" are not listed as they do not meet Scott listing criteria.

SALVADOR, EL

'el-sal-və-,dor

LOCATION — On the Pacific coast of Central America, between Guatemala, Honduras and the Gulf of Fonseca

GOVT. — Republic
AREA — 8,236 sq. mi.
POP. — 5,839,079 (1999 est.)
CAPITAL — San Salvador

8 Reales = 100 Centavos = 1 Peso
100 Centavos = 1 Colón
100 Cents = 1 Dollar (2003)

Catalogue values for unused stamps in this country are for Never Hinged items, beginning with Scott 589 in the regular postpost section, Scott C85 in the airpost section, and Scott O362 in the official section.

Watermarks

Wmk. 117 — Liberty Cap

Position of wmk. on reprints

Wmk. 172 — Honeycomb

Wmk. 173 — S

Wmk. 240 — REPUBLICA DE EL SALVADOR in Sheet

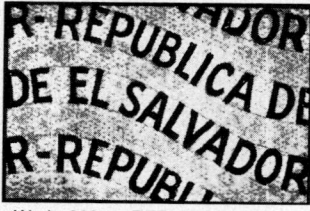
Wmk. 269 — REPUBLICA DE EL SALVADOR

Volcano San Miguel — A1

1867   Unwmk.   Engr.   *Perf. 12*

1	A1	½r dk gray blue	7.00	4.00
2	A1	1r dark red	7.00	4.00
3	A1	2r dark green	8.50	4.50
4	A1	4r dp ol brn	32.50	17.50
		Nos. 1-4 (4)	55.00	30.00

There were at least two printings of Nos. 1-4. Stamps from the second printing are lighter in color. See the *1840-1940 Classic Specialized Catalogue* for detailed listings.

Nos. 1-4 when overprinted "Contra Sello" and shield with 14 stars, are telegraph stamps. For similar overprint see Nos. 5-12.

Counterfeits exist.

Nos. 1-4 Handstamped Either Type I or Type II in Black

Type I

Type II

Type II

1874

5	A1	½r blue	30.00	10.00
6	A1	1r red	20.00	10.00
7	A1	2r green	30.00	10.00
8	A1	4r bister	40.00	20.00
		Nos. 5-8 (4)	120.00	50.00

Nos. 1-4 Handstamped Type III in Black

Type III

9	A1	½r blue	8.00	6.00
10	A1	1r red	8.00	3.00
11	A1	2r green	10.00	3.00
12	A1	4r bister	12.00	10.00
		Nos. 9-12 (4)	38.00	22.00

The overprints on Nos. 5-12 exist double. Counterfeits are plentiful.

Coat of Arms
A2   A3

A4

A5

A6

1879   Litho.   *Perf. 12½*

13	A2	1c green	3.00	1.75
a.		Invtd. "V" for 2nd "A" in "SALVADOR"	6.00	3.00
b.		Invtd. "V" for "A" in "REPUBLICA"	6.00	3.00
c.		Invtd. "V" for "A" in "UNIVERSAL"	6.00	3.00
d.		Thin paper	—	
14	A3	2c rose	4.25	2.25
a.		Invtd. scroll in upper left corner	12.00	7.50
15	A4	5c blue	7.50	1.90
a.		5c ultra	12.00	6.00
16	A5	10c black	15.00	5.25
17	A6	20c violet	24.00	15.00
		Nos. 13-17 (5)	53.75	26.15

There are fifteen varieties of the 1c and 2c, twenty-five of the 5c and five each of the 10 and 20c.

In 1881 the 1c, 2c and 5c were redrawn, the 1c in fifteen varieties and the 2c and 5c in five varieties each.

No. 15 comes in a number of shades from light to dark blue.

These stamps, when overprinted "Contra sello" and arms, are telegraph stamps. Counterfeits of No. 14 exist.

For overprints see Nos. 25D-25E, 28A-28C.

Allegorical Figure of El Salvador — A7

Volcano — A8

1887   Engr.   *Perf. 12*

18	A7	3c brown	2.00	2.00
a.		Imperf., pair	10.00	10.00
19	A8	10c orange	30.00	3.00

For surcharges and overprints see Nos. 25, 26C-28, 30-32.

A9

1888   *Rouletted*

20	A9	5c deep blue	1.50	1.50

For overprints see Nos. 35-36.

A10

1889   *Perf. 12*

21	A10	1c green	.40	
22	A10	2c scarlet	.40	

Nos. 21-22 Overprinted in Black

23	A10	1c green	.40	3.00
24	A10	2c scarlet	.40	

Nos. 21, 22 and 24 were never placed in use.

For overprints see Nos. 26, 29.

No. 18 Surcharged

Type I

Type II

Type I — thick numerals, heavy serifs.
Type II — thin numerals, straight serifs.

25	A7	1c on 3c brn, type II	4.00	*7.00*
a.		Double surcharge	1.50	
b.		Triple surcharge	3.50	
c.		Type I	.65	

The 1c on 2c scarlet is bogus.

Handstamped

1889   Violet Handstamp

25D	A2	1c green	19.00	19.00
25E	A6	20c violet	45.00	45.00
26	A10	1c green, #23	10.50	*15.00*
26C	A7	1c on 3c, #25	50.00	50.00
27	A7	3c brown	7.50	*15.00*
28	A8	10c orange	10.00	*12.50*

Black Handstamp

28A	A2	1c green	22.50	21.00
28B	A3	2c rose	26.00	26.00
28C	A6	20c violet	45.00	45.00
29	A10	1c green, #23	10.50	*15.00*
30	A7	3c brown	10.50	*15.00*
31	A7	1c on 3c, #25	40.00	40.00
32	A8	10c orange	15.00	12.50

Rouletted
Black Handstamp

35	A9	5c deep blue	9.00	*15.00*

Violet Handstamp

36	A9	5c deep blue	9.00	*15.00*

The 1889 handstamps as usual, are found double, inverted, etc. Counterfeits are plentiful.

A13

1890   Engr.   *Perf. 12*

38	A13	1c green	.50	.50
39	A13	2c bister brown	.50	.50
40	A13	3c yellow	.50	.50
41	A13	5c blue	.50	.50
42	A13	10c violet	.50	.50
43	A13	20c orange	.75	*3.00*
44	A13	25c red	1.50	*5.00*
45	A13	50c claret	2.00	*7.50*
46	A13	1p carmine	5.00	*30.00*
		Nos. 38-46 (9)	11.75	48.00

The issues of 1890 to 1899 inclusive were printed by the Hamilton Bank Note Co., New York, to the order of N. F. Seebeck, who held a contract for stamps with the government of El Salvador. This contract gave the right to make reprints of the stamps and such were subsequently made in some instances, as will be found noted in italic type.

Used values of 1890-1899 issues are for stamps with genuine cancellations applied while the stamps were valid. Various counterfeit cancellations exist.

A14

1891

47	A14	1c vermilion	.50	.50
48	A14	2c yellow green	.50	.50
49	A14	3c violet	.50	.50
50	A14	5c carmine lake	2.00	.50
51	A14	10c blue	.50	.50
52	A14	11c violet	.50	.50
53	A14	20c orange	.50	.50
54	A14	25c yellow brown	.50	*2.50*
55	A14	50c dark blue	2.00	*7.50*
56	A14	1p dark brown	.75	*25.00*
		Nos. 47-56 (10)	8.25	38.50

For surcharges see Nos. 57-59.
Nos. 47 and 56 have been reprinted in thick toned paper with dark gum.

Nos. 48, 49 Surcharged in Black or Violet

No. 57   No. 58

No. 59

1891

57	A14	1c on 2c yellow grn	2.25	2.00
a.		Inverted surcharge	8.00	
b.		Surcharge reading up	12.00	
58	A14	1c on 2c yellow grn	1.60	1.40
59	A14	5c on 3c violet	4.00	3.25
		Nos. 57-59 (3)	7.85	6.65

Landing of Columbus — A18

1892   **Engr.**

60	A18	1c blue green	.50	.50
61	A18	2c orange brown	.50	.50
62	A18	3c ultra	.50	.50
63	A18	5c gray	.50	.50
64	A18	10c vermilion	.50	.50
65	A18	11c brown	.50	.50
66	A18	20c orange	.50	.75
67	A18	25c maroon	.50	2.00
68	A18	50c yellow	.50	7.00
69	A18	1p carmine lake	.50	25.00
		Nos. 60-69 (10)	5.00	37.75

400th anniversary of the discovery of America by Columbus.

Nos. 63, 66-67 Surcharged

Nos. 70, 72   Nos. 73-75

Surcharged in Black, Red or Yellow

1892

70	A18	1c on 5c gray (Bk) (down)	3.00	.75
a.		Surcharge reading up	5.00	2.00
72	A18	1c on 5c gray (R) (up)	1.00	3.00
a.		Surcharge reading down	3.00	
73	A18	1c on 20c org (Bk)	1.50	.75
a.		Inverted surcharge	3.50	2.50
b.		"V" of "CENTAVO" inverted	3.50	2.50
		Nos. 70-73 (3)	5.50	4.50

Similar Surcharge in Yellow or Blue, "centavo" in lower case letters

74	A18	1c on 25c mar (Y)	1.50	1.25
a.		Inverted surcharge	2.50	2.50
75	A18	1c on 25c mar (Bl)	250.00	250.00
a.		Double surcharge (Bl + Bk)	275.00	275.00

Counterfeits exist of Nos. 75 and 75a. Nos. 75, 75a have been questioned.

Pres. Carlos Ezeta — A21

1893   **Engr.**

76	A21	1c blue	.50	.50
77	A21	2c brown red	.50	.50
78	A21	3c purple	.50	.50
79	A21	5c deep brown	.50	.50

80	A21	10c orange brown	.50	.50
81	A21	11c vermilion	.50	.50
82	A21	20c green	.50	1.00
83	A21	25c dk olive gray	.50	2.25
84	A21	50c red orange	.50	5.00
85	A21	1p black	.50	20.00
		Nos. 76-85 (10)	5.00	31.25

For surcharge see No. 89.

Founding City of Isabela — A22

Columbus Statue, Genoa — A23

Departure from Palos — A24

1893

86	A22	2p green		.75	—
87	A23	5p violet		.75	
88	A24	10p orange		.75	
		Nos. 86-88 (3)		2.25	

Discoveries by Columbus. No. 86 is known on cover, but experts are not positive that Nos. 87 and 88 were postally used.

No. 77 Surcharged "UN CENTAVO"

1893

89	A21	1c on 2c brown red	1.00	1.25
a.		"CENTNVO"	6.00	5.00

Liberty — A26

Columbus before Council of Salamanca — A27

Columbus Protecting Indian Hostages A28

Columbus Received by Ferdinand and Isabella A29

1894, Jan.

91	A26	1c brown	.75	.50
92	A26	2c blue	.75	.50
93	A26	3c maroon	.75	.50
94	A26	5c orange brn	.75	.50
95	A26	10c violet	.75	.75
96	A26	11c vermilion	.75	.75
97	A26	20c dark blue	.75	1.00
98	A26	25c orange	.75	5.00
99	A26	50c black	.75	10.00
100	A26	1p slate blue	1.10	20.00
101	A27	2p deep blue	1.10	

102	A28	5p carmine lake	1.10	
103	A29	10p deep brown	1.10	
		Nos. 91-103 (13)	11.15	
		Nos. 91-100 (10)		39.50

Nos. 101-103 for the discoveries by Columbus. Experts are not positive that these were postally used.

No. 96 Surcharged

1894, Dec.

104	A26	1c on 11c vermilion	4.50	.65
a.		"Ccntavo"	40.00	40.00
b.		Double surcharge		

Coat of Arms — A31

Arms Overprint in Second Color Various Frames

1895, Jan. 1

105	A31	1c olive & green	.50	.25
106	A31	2c dk green & bl	.25	—
a.		2c dark green & green	.50	.85
107	A31	3c brown & brown	.50	—
108	A31	5c blue & brown	.50	—
109	A31	10c orange & brn	.50	—
110	A31	12c magenta & brn	.50	—
111	A31	15c ver & ver	.50	—
112	A31	20c yellow & brn	.50	—
a.		Inverted overprint	2.00	
113	A31	24c violet & brn	.50	—
114	A31	30c dp blue & blue	.50	—
115	A31	50c carmine & brn	.50	—
116	A31	1p black & brn	.50	—
		Nos. 105-116 (12)	5.75	

As printed, Nos. 105-116 portrayed Gen. Antonio Ezeta, brother of Pres. Carlos Ezeta. Before issuance, Ezeta's overthrow caused the government to obliterate his features with the national arms overprint. The 3c, 10c, 30c exist without overprint. Value $1 each.

All values have been reprinted. Reprints of 2c are in dark yellow green on thick paper. Value, 25c each.

Coat of Arms — A32

Various Frames

1895   **Engr.**   **Perf. 12**

117	A32	1c olive	7.25	.50
118	A32	2c dk blue grn	7.25	.50
119	A32	3c brown	10.00	.75
120	A32	5c blue	2.00	.75
121	A32	10c orange	5.00	.75
122	A32	12c claret	17.50	1.00
123	A32	15c vermilion	22.00	1.00
124	A32	20c deep green	30.00	2.00
125	A32	24c violet	22.50	4.00
126	A32	30c deep blue	30.00	5.00
127	A32	50c carmine lake	3.00	35.00
128	A32	1p gray black	10.00	35.00
		Nos. 117-128 (12)	166.50	86.25

The reprints are on thicker paper than the originals, and many of the shades differ. Value 25c each.

Nos. 122, 124-126 Surcharged in Black or Red

1895

129	A32	1c on 12c claret (Bk)	2.00	1.75
130	A32	1c on 24c violet	2.00	1.75
131	A32	1c on 30c dp blue	2.00	1.75
132	A32	2c on 20c dp grn	2.00	1.75
133	A32	3c on 30c dp blue	3.00	2.75
a.		Double surcharge	9.00	
		Nos. 129-133 (5)	11.00	9.75

"Peace" — A45

1896, Jan. 1   **Engr.**   **Unwmk.**

134	A45	1c blue	2.00	.50
135	A45	2c dark brown	.50	.50
136	A45	3c blue green	.50	.50
137	A45	5c brown olive	2.00	.50
138	A45	10c yellow	.50	.50
139	A45	12c dark blue	4.00	1.00
140	A45	15c brt ultra	.25	—
a.		15c light violet	1.10	2.00
141	A45	20c magenta	4.00	3.00
142	A45	24c vermilion	1.50	5.00
143	A45	30c orange	1.50	5.00
144	A45	50c black brn	3.00	7.50
145	A45	1p rose lake	6.00	20.00
		Nos. 134-145 (12)	25.75	44.00

The frames of Nos. 134-145 differ slightly on each denomination.
For overprints see Nos. O1-O12, O37-O48.

Wmk. 117

145B	A45	2c dark brown	.25	.25

All values have been reprinted. The paper is thicker than that of the originals and the shades are different. The watermark is always upright on original stamps of Salvador, sideways on the reprints. Value 25c each.

Coat of Arms — A46   "White House" — A47

Locomotive A48   Mt. San Miguel A49

Ocean Steamship A50   A51

Post Office A52   Lake Ilopango A53

Atehausillas Waterfall A54   Coat of Arms A55

Coat of Arms A56   Columbus A57

1896

146	A46	1c emerald	.50	1.50
147	A47	2c lake	.50	.90
148	A48	3c yellow brn	.75	.75
149	A49	5c deep blue	.90	.50
150	A50	10c brown	2.00	.90
151	A51	12c slate	2.00	.90
152	A52	15c blue green	1.75	.75
153	A53	20c carmine rose	2.00	1.25
154	A54	24c violet	8.00	1.25
155	A55	30c deep green	5.00	2.00
156	A56	50c orange	10.00	5.00
157	A57	100c dark blue	15.00	12.50

Nos. 146-157 (12)   48.40   28.20

Nos. 146-157 exist imperf.

Unwmk.

157B	A46	1c emerald	3.75	.90
157C	A47	2c lake	3.75	.50
157D	A48	3c yellow brn	6.00	.50
157E	A49	5c deep blue	4.00	.75
157F	A50	10c brown	7.50	.75
157G	A51	12c slate	10.00	1.00
157I	A52	15c blue green	20.00	1.75
157J	A53	20c carmine rose	7.50	1.00
157K	A54	24c violet		1.25
157M	A55	30c deep green	10.00	2.50
157N	A56	50c orange	15.00	7.00
157O	A57	100c dark blue	20.00	15.00

Nos. 157B-157O (12)   117.50   32.90

See Nos. 159-170L. For surcharges and overprints see Nos. 158, 158D, 171-174C, O13-O36, O49-O72, O79-O126.

All values have been reprinted, the 15c, 30c, 50c and 100c on watermarked and the 1c, 2c, 3c, 5c, 12c, 20c, 24c and 100c on unwatermarked paper. The papers of the reprints are thicker than those of the originals and the shades are different. Value, 25c each.

Black Surcharge on
Nos. 154, 157K

1896   **Wmk. 117**

158	A54	15c on 24c violet	4.00	4.00
a.		Double surcharge	20.00	30.00
b.		Inverted surcharge	15.00	

Unwmk.

| 158D | A54 | 15c on 24c violet | 4.00 | 3.00 |

Exist spelled "Qnince."

Types of 1896

1897   **Engr.**   **Wmk. 117**

159	A46	1c scarlet	2.75	.90
160	A47	2c yellow grn	2.75	.50
161	A48	3c bister brn	2.50	.50
162	A49	5c orange	2.50	.75
163	A50	10c blue grn	3.00	.75
164	A51	12c blue	8.00	1.00
165	A52	15c black	20.00	10.00
166	A53	20c slate	8.00	2.00
167	A54	24c yellow	20.00	20.00
168	A55	30c rose	15.00	5.00
169	A56	50c violet	15.00	5.00
170	A57	100c brown lake	30.00	15.00

Nos. 159-170 (12)   129.50   61.40

Unwmk.

170A	A46	1c scarlet	2.00	1.50
170B	A47	2c yellow grn	1.00	.90
170C	A48	3c bister brn	.75	.75
170D	A49	5c orange	.90	.50
170E	A50	10c blue grn	5.00	.90
170F	A51	12c blue	1.00	1.00
170G	A52	15c black	10.00	10.00
170H	A53	20c slate	10.00	10.00
170I	A54	24c yellow	20.00	20.00
170J	A55	30c rose	10.00	10.00
170K	A56	50c violet	9.50	10.00
170L	A57	100c brown lake	50.00	50.00

Nos. 170A-170L (12)   120.15   116.55

The 1c, 2c, 3c, 5c, 12c, 15c, 50c and 100c have been reprinted on watermarked and the entire issue on unwatermarked paper. The papers of the reprints are thicker than those of the originals. Value, set of 20, $5.

Surcharged in Red or
Black

1897   **Wmk. 117**

171	A54	13c on 24c yel (R)	2.50	2.50
172	A55	13c on 30c rose (Bk)	2.50	2.50
173	A56	13c on 50c vio (Bk)	2.50	2.50

174	A57	13c on 100c brn lake (Bk)	2.50	2.50

Unwmk.

174A	A54	13c on 24c yel (R)	2.50	2.50
174B	A55	13c on 30c rose (Bk)	2.50	2.50
174C	A56	13c on 50c vio (Bk)	2.50	2.50

Nos. 171-174C (7)   17.50   17.50

Coat of Arms of
"Republic of Central
America" — A59

ONE CENTAVO:

Originals: The mountains are outlined in red and blue. The sea is represented by short red and dark blue lines on a light blue background.

Reprints: The mountains are outlined in red only. The sea is printed in green and dark blue, much blurred.

FIVE CENTAVOS:

Originals: The sea is represented by horizontal and diagonal lines of dark blue on a light blue background.

Reprints: The sea is printed in green and dark blue, much blurred. The inscription in gold is in thicker letters.

1897   **Litho.**

175	A59	1c bl, gold, rose & grn	1.00	—
176	A59	5c rose, gold, bl & grn	2.00	—

Forming of the "Republic of Central America."

For overprints see Nos. O73-O76.

Stamps of type A59 formerly listed as "Type II" are now known to be reprints.

Allegory of Central
American Union — A60

1898   **Engr.**   **Wmk. 117**

177	A60	1c orange ver	2.25	.50
178	A60	2c rose	2.25	.50
179	A60	3c pale yel grn	2.00	.50
180	A60	5c blue green	2.00	.75
181	A60	10c gray blue	7.50	.75
182	A60	12c violet	8.50	1.00
183	A60	13c brown lake	8.50	1.00
184	A60	20c deep blue	9.50	2.00
185	A60	24c deep ultra	7.50	5.25
186	A60	26c bister brn	10.00	5.00
187	A60	50c orange	10.00	5.00
188	A60	1p yellow	25.00	15.00

Nos. 177-188 (12)   95.00   37.25

For overprints and surcharges see Nos. 189-198A, 224-241, 269A-269B, O129-O142.
The entire set has been reprinted on unwatermarked paper and all but the 12c and 20c on watermarked paper. The shades of the reprints are not the same as those of the originals, and the paper is thicker. Value, set of 22, $5.50.

No. 180 Overprinted
Vertically, up or down
in Black, Violet, Red,
Magenta and Yellow

1899

189	A60	5c blue grn (Bk)	7.50	6.25
a.		Italic 3rd "r" in "Territorial"	12.50	12.50
b.		Double ovpt. (Bk + Y)	37.50	37.50
190	A60	5c blue grn (V)	82.50	82.50
191	A60	5c blue grn (R)	70.00	70.00
191A	A60	5c blue grn (M)	70.00	70.00
191B	A60	5c blue grn (Y)	75.00	75.00

Nos. 189-191B (5)   305.00   303.75

Counterfeits exist.

Nos. 177-184
Overprinted in Black

1899

192	A60	1c orange ver	2.00	.50
193	A60	2c rose	2.50	1.00
194	A60	3c pale yel grn	2.50	.50
195	A60	5c blue green	2.50	.50
196	A60	10c gray blue	4.00	1.25
197	A60	12c violet	6.50	2.50
198	A60	13c brown lake	6.50	2.00
198A	A60	20c deep blue	75.00	75.00

Nos. 192-198 (7)   26.50   8.25

The overprint on No. 198A is only seen on the reprints.

Counterfeits exist of the "wheel" overprint used in 1899-1900.

Ceres
("Estado") — A61

Inscribed: "Estado de El Salvador"

1899   **Unwmk.**   **Litho.**   **Perf. 12**

199	A61	1c brown	.25	
200	A61	2c gray green	.25	
201	A61	3c blue	.25	
202	A61	5c brown org	.25	
203	A61	10c chocolate	.25	
204	A61	12c dark green	.25	
205	A61	13c deep rose	.25	
206	A61	24c light blue	.25	
207	A61	26c carmine rose	.25	
208	A61	50c orange red	.25	
209	A61	100c violet	.25	

Nos. 199-209 (11)   2.75

Nos. 208-209 were probably not placed in use.

For overprints and surcharges see Nos. 210-223, 242-252D, O143-O185.

Same, Overprinted

Red Overprint

210	A61	1c brown	60.00	40.00

Blue Overprint

211	A61	1c brown	2.00	1.50
212	A61	5c brown org	2.00	1.50
212A	A61	10c chocolate	15.00	10.00

Black Overprint

213	A61	1c brown	1.50	.75
214	A61	2c gray grn	2.00	.40
215	A61	3c blue	2.25	1.00
216	A61	5c brown org	1.50	.65
217	A61	10c chocolate	1.50	.80
218	A61	12c dark grn	4.00	4.00
219	A61	13c deep rose	3.50	3.50
220	A61	24c light blue	30.00	27.50
221	A61	26c carmine rose	7.50	7.50
222	A61	50c orange red	9.00	7.50
223	A61	100c violet	10.00	9.00

Nos. 213-223 (11)   72.75   60.10

"Wheel" overprint exists double and triple.

No. 177 Handstamped

1900   **Wmk. 117**

224	A60	1c orange ver	1.00	1.00

No. 177 Overprinted

225	A60	1c orange ver	15.00	15.00

Stamps of 1898
Surcharged in Black

1900

226	A60	1c on 10c gray blue	15.00	15.00
a.		Inverted surcharge	15.00	15.00
227	A60	1c on 13c brn lake	100.00	
228	A60	2c on 12c vio	50.00	50.00
a.		"eentavo"		
b.		Inverted surcharge		
c.		"centavos"	90.00	
d.		As "c," double surcharge		
e.		Vertical surcharge		
229	A60	2c on 13c brn lake	5.00	5.00
a.		"eentavo"	8.00	7.00
b.		Inverted surcharge	12.50	8.00
c.		"1900" omitted	7.50	7.50
230	A60	2c on 20c dp blue	5.00	5.00
a.		Inverted surcharge	8.00	8.00
230B	A60	2c on 26c bis brn		
231	A60	3c on 12c vio	90.00	—
a.		"eentavo"		
b.		Double surcharge		
232	A60	3c on 50c org	35.00	35.00
a.		Inverted surcharge	35.00	35.00
233	A60	5c on 12c vio		—
234	A60	5c on 24c ultra	50.00	50.00
a.		"centavos"	70.00	
235	A60	5c on 26c bis brn	150.00	150.00
a.		Inverted surcharge	35.00	35.00
236	A60	5c on 1p yel	50.00	35.00
a.		Inverted surcharge	60.00	60.00

**With Additional
Overprint in Black**

237	A60	2c on 12c vio	2.50	2.50
a.		Inverted surcharge	2.50	2.50
b.		"eentavo"	8.00	
c.		"centavos" (plural)	75.00	
d.		"1900" omitted		
237H	A60	2c on 13c brn lake	125.00	125.00
a.		"eentavo"	75.00	75.00
238	A60	3c on 12c vio	125.00	125.00
a.		"eentavo"	75.00	75.00
239	A60	5c on 26c bis brn	150.00	150.00
a.		Inverted surcharge		

**Vertical Surcharge
"Centavos" in the Plural**

240	A60	2c on 12c vio	125.00	125.00
b.		Without wheel		
240A	A60	5c on 24c dp ultra	125.00	125.00

With Additional
Overprint in Black

241	A60	5c on 12c vio	50.00	50.00
a.		Surcharge reading downward		

Counterfeits exist of the surcharges on Nos. 226-241 and the "wheel" overprint on Nos. 237-239, 241.

**Same Surcharge on Stamps of 1899
Without Wheel**

1900   **Unwmk.**

242	A61	1c on 13c dp rose	1.50	1.50
a.		Inverted surcharge	4.00	3.00
b.		"eentavo"	4.00	3.00
c.		"ecntavo"	5.00	3.00
d.		"1 centavo 1"	15.00	10.00
e.		Double surcharge		
243	A61	2c on 12c dk grn	8.00	8.00
a.		Inverted surcharge	15.00	15.00
b.		"eentavo"		
244	A61	2c on 13c dp rose	3.00	2.50
a.		"eentavo"	3.00	4.00
b.		"ecntavo"	6.00	2.50
c.		Inverted surcharge	9.00	
245	A61	3c on 12c dk grn	3.00	2.50
a.		Inverted surcharge	9.00	5.00
b.		"eentavo"	12.00	12.00
c.		Double surcharge	9.00	

Nos. 242-245 (4)   15.50   14.50

With Additional Overprint in Black

246	A61	1c on 2c gray grn	1.00	1.00
a.		"eentavo"	4.00	3.00
b.		Inverted surcharge		10.00
247	A61	1c on 13c dp rose	4.00	4.00
a.		"eentavo"	15.00	
b.		"1 centavo 1"		
248	A61	1c on 12c dk grn	5.00	4.00
a.		"eentavo"	15.00	
b.		Inverted surcharge	4.00	4.00
c.		Double surcharge	8.00	
249	A61	2c on 13c dp rose	100.00	100.00
a.		"eentavo"		
b.		Double surcharge	150.00	150.00
250	A61	3c on 12c dk grn	5.00	3.00
a.		Inverted surcharge	5.50	4.00
b.		"eentavo"	8.00	7.00
c.		Date double	15.00	
251	A61	5c on 24c lt bl	12.00	5.00
a.		"eentavo"	20.00	20.00
252	A61	5c on 26c car rose	4.00	4.00
a.		Inverted surcharge	12.00	9.00
b.		"eentavo"	6.00	5.00
252D	A61	5c on 1c on 26c car rose		
		Nos. 246-248,250-252 (6)	31.00	21.00

Counterfeits exist of the surcharges on Nos. 242-252D and the "wheel" overprint on Nos. 246-252D.

Ceres ("Republica") — A63

There are two varieties of the 1c, type A63, one with the word "centavo" in the middle of the label (#253, 263, 270, 299, 305, 326), the other with "centavo" nearer the left end than the right (#270, 299, 305, 326).

The stamps of type A63 are found in a great variety of shades. Stamps of type A63 without handstamp were not regularly issued.

Handstamped in Violet or Black Inscribed: "Republica de El Salvador"

1900

253	A63	1c blue green	.90	.90
a.		1c yellow green	.90	.90
254	A63	2c rose	1.50	1.00
255	A63	3c gray black	1.25	1.00
256	A63	5c pale blue	1.00	.60
a.		5c dark blue	5.00	.60
257	A63	10c deep blue	2.00	.60
258	A63	12c yel green	5.00	3.50
259	A63	13c yel brown	4.00	3.00
260	A63	24c gray	15.00	15.00
261	A63	26c yel brown	7.00	7.00
262	A63	50c rose red	2.00	2.00
		Nos. 253-262 (10)	39.65	34.60

For overprints and surcharges see Nos. 263-269, 270-282, 293A-311B, 317, 326-335, O223-O242, O258-O262, O305-O312.

Handstamped in Violet or Black

263	A63	1c lt green	10.00	4.00
264	A63	2c pale rose	10.00	3.00
265	A63	3c gray black	10.00	3.00
266	A63	5c slate blue	14.00	3.00
267	A63	10c deep blue	—	3.00
268	A63	13c yellow brn	35.00	35.00
269	A63	50c dull rose	15.00	15.00
		Nos. 263-266,268-269 (6)	94.00	63.00

Handstamped on 1898 Stamps Wmk. 117

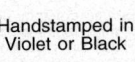

269A	A60	2c rose	30.00	30.00
269B	A60	10c gray blue	30.00	30.00

The overprints on Nos. 253 to 269B are handstamped and, as usual with that style of overprint, are to be found double, inverted, omitted, etc.

Specialists have questioned the existence of No. 267. The editors would like to see authenticated evidence of the existence of a genuine example.

Stamps of Type A63 Overprinted in Black

1900   **Unwmk.**

270	A63	1c light green	1.50	1.00
271	A63	2c rose	7.50	2.00
272	A63	3c gray black	1.50	1.00
273	A63	5c pale blue	7.50	2.00
a.		5c dark blue	6.00	1.00
274	A63	10c deep blue	7.50	2.00
a.		10c pale blue	7.50	2.00
275	A63	12c light green	2.25	1.50
276	A63	13c yellow brown	1.50	1.00
277	A63	24c gray	1.75	1.25
278	A63	26c yellow brown	3.00	2.00
		Nos. 270-278 (9)	34.00	13.75

This overprint is known double, inverted, etc.

Nos. 271-273 Surcharged in Black

1902

280	A63	1c on 2c rose	8.25	6.75
281	A63	1c on 3c black	6.00	4.25
282	A63	1c on 5c blue	3.75	3.00
		Nos. 280-282 (3)	18.00	14.00

Morazán Monument — A64

Perf. 14, 14½

	1903	**Engr.**	**Wmk. 173**	
283	A64	1c green	1.00	.60
284	A64	2c carmine	1.00	.60
285	A64	3c orange	10.00	2.00
286	A64	5c dark blue	1.00	.60
287	A64	10c dull violet	1.00	.60
288	A64	12c slate	1.25	.60
289	A64	13c red brown	1.25	.60
290	A64	24c scarlet	7.50	3.75
291	A64	26c yellow brn	7.50	3.75
292	A64	50c bister	3.75	2.25
293	A64	100c grnsh blue	11.00	7.50
		Nos. 283-293 (11)	46.25	22.85

For surcharges and overprint see Nos. 312-316, 318-325, O253.

Stamps of 1900 with Shield in Black Overprinted

(5¾x13½mm) — a   (5x14¾mm) — b

(4½x16mm) — c   (4½x13½mm) — d

(5x14½mm) — e

1905-06   **Unwmk.**   **Perf. 12**

Blue Overprint

293A	A63 (a)	2c rose	—	—
294	A63 (a)	3c gray blk	8.00	6.00
a.		Without shield		
295	A63 (a)	5c blue	10.00	7.50

Purple Overprint

296	A63 (b)	3c gray blk (Shield in pur)	—	—
296A	A63 (b)	5c bl (Shield in pue)	—	—
297	A63 (b)	3c gray blk	—	—
298	A63 (b)	5c blue	—	—

Black Overprint

298A	A63 (b)	5c blue	—	—

Blue Overprint

299	A63 (c)	1c green	10.00	5.00
299B	A63 (c)	2c rose	.50	.40
c.		"1905" vert.	1.00	
300	A63 (c)	5c blue	6.00	4.00
301	A63 (c)	10c deep blue	2.00	1.00

Black Overprint

302	A63 (c)	2c rose	10.00	5.00
303	A63 (c)	5c blue	25.00	25.00
304	A63 (c)	10c deep blue	12.00	7.00

Blue Overprint

305	A63 (d)	1c green	15.00	10.00
306	A63 (d)	2c rose, ovpt. vert.	9.00	5.00
306B	A63 (d)	3c gray black	8.00	4.00
307	A63 (d)	5c blue	3.00	1.50

Blue Overprint

311	A63 (e)	2c rose	10.00	8.00
a.		Without shield	15.00	12.00

Black Overprint

311B	A63 (e)	5c blue	30.00	20.00
		Nos. 294-295,299-311B (15)	158.50	109.40

These overprints are found double, inverted, omitted, etc. Counterfeits exist.

Regular Issue of 1903 Surcharged

UN CENTAVO   5 CENTAVOS

f   g

1 CENTAVO 1

h

	1905-06	**Wmk. 173**	**Perf. 14, 14½**	

Black Surcharge

312	A64 (f)	1c on 2c car	4.00	2.00
a.		Double surcharge	20.00	20.00

Red Surcharge

312B	A64 (g)	5c on 12c slate	5.00	4.00
c.		Double surcharge		
d.		Black surcharge	15.00	15.00
e.		As "d," double surcharge		

Blue Handstamped Surcharge

313	A64 (h)	1c on 2c car	2.00	2.00
314	A64 (h)	1c on 10c vio	2.00	2.00
315	A64 (h)	1c on 12c sl ('06)		
316	A64 (h)	1c on 13c red brn	22.50	15.00

No. 271 with Handstamped Surcharge in Blue

Unwmk.

317	A63 (h)	1c on 2c rose	—	—
		Nos. 312-316 (6)	37.50	27.00

The "h" is handstamped in strips of four stamps each differing from the others in the size of the upper figures of value and in the letters of the word "CENTAVO," particularly in the size of the "N" and the "O" of that word. The surcharge is known inverted, double, etc.

Regular Issue of 1903 with Handstamped Surcharge

i

j   k

Wmk. 173

Red Handstamped Surcharge

318	A64 (i)	5c on 12c slate	4.00	3.00
319	A64 (j)	5c on 12c slate	6.00	5.00
a.		Blue surcharge		

Blue Handstamped Surcharge

320	A64 (k)	5c on 12c slate	3.50	2.50
		Nos. 318-320 (3)	13.50	10.50

One or more of the numerals in the handstamped surcharges on Nos. 318, 319 and 320 are frequently omitted, inverted, etc.

Regular Issue of 1903 Surcharged

l   m

Blue Handstamped Surcharge

321	A64 (l)	6c on 12c slate	.75	.50
322	A64 (l)	6c on 13c red brn	1.50	.60

Red Handstamped Surcharge

323	A64 (l)	6c on 12c slate	27.50	15.00

Type "l" is handstamped in strips of four varieties, differing in the size of the numerals and letters. The surcharge is known double and inverted.

Black Surcharge

324	A64 (m)	1c on 13c red brn	2.25	1.50
a.		Double surcharge	6.00	4.50
b.		Right "1" & dot omitted		
c.		Both numerals omitted		
325	A64 (m)	3c on 13c red brn	.75	.60

Stamps of 1900, with Shield in Black, Overprinted — n

1905   **Unwmk.**   **Perf. 12**

Blue Overprint

326	A63 (n)	1c green	9.00	6.00
a.		Inverted overprint		
327	A63 (n)	2c rose	5.00	5.00
a.		Vertical overprint	12.50	12.50
b.		Imperforate	9.00	6.00
327B	A63 (n)	3c black	50.00	30.00
327C	A63 (n)	5c blue	25.00	20.00
328	A63 (n)	10c deep blue	15.00	9.00

Black Overprint

328A	A63 (n)	10c deep blue	20.00	15.00
		Nos. 326-328A (6)	124.00	85.00

Counterfeits of Nos. 326-335 abound.

Stamps of 1900, with Shield in Black Surcharged or Overprinted

o   p

q

1906   **Blue and Black Surcharge**

329	A63 (o)	2c on 26c brn org	1.00	.80
a.		"2" & dot double	15.00	15.00
330	A63 (o)	3c on 26c brn org	8.00	6.50
a.		"3" & dot double		

Black Surcharge or Overprint

331	A63 (o)	3c on 26c brn org	9.00	7.00
a.		Disks & numerals omitted		
b.		"3" and disks double		
c.		"1906" omitted		
333	A63 (p)	10c deep blue	6.00	4.00
334	A63 (q)	10c deep blue	6.00	4.00
334A	A63 (q)	26c brown org	50.00	45.00
b.		"1906" in blue		

No. 257 Overprinted in Black

335	A63 (q)	10c dp bl (Shield in violet).	—	—
a.		Overprint type "p"		
		Nos. 329-334A (6)	80.00	67.30

There are numerous varieties of these surcharges and overprints.

Pres. Pedro José
Escalón — A65

1906   **Engr.**   **Perf. 11½**
Glazed Paper
336	A65	1c green & blk	.25	.25
a.		Thin paper	.75	.25
337	A65	2c red & blk	.25	.25
338	A65	3c yellow & blk	.25	.25
339	A65	5c ultra & blk	.25	.25
a.		5c dark blue & black	.25	.25
340	A65	6c carmine & blk	.25	.25
341	A65	10c violet & blk	.25	.25
342	A65	12c violet & blk	.25	.25
343	A65	13c dk brn & blk	.25	.25
345	A65	24c carmine & blk	.35	.35
346	A65	26c choc & blk	.35	.35
347	A65	50c yellow & blk	.35	.45
348	A65	100c blue & blk	3.00	3.00
		Nos. 336-348 (12)	6.05	6.15

All values of this set are known imperforate but are not believed to have been issued in this condition.

See Nos. O263-O272. For overprints and surcharges see Nos. 349-354.

The entire set has been reprinted, perforated 11.8. Value, set of 12, $1.20.

Nos. 336-338
Overprinted in Black

1907
349	A65	1c green & blk	.25	.25
a.		Shield in red	3.50	
350	A65	2c red & blk	.25	.25
a.		Shield in red	3.50	
351	A65	3c yellow & blk	.25	.25
		Nos. 349-351 (3)	.75	.75

Reprints of Nos. 349 to 351 have the same characteristics as the reprints of the preceding issue. Value, set of 3, 15c.

Stamps of 1906
Surcharged with
Shield and

352	A65	1c on 5c ultra & blk	.25	.25
a.		1c on 5c dark blue & black	.25	.25
b.		Inverted surcharge	.35	.35
c.		Double surcharge	.45	.45
352D	A65	1c on 6c rose & blk	.25	.25
e.		Double surcharge	1.25	1.25
353	A65	2c on 6c rose & blk	2.00	1.00
354	A65	10c on 6c rose & blk	.50	.35
		Nos. 352-354 (4)	3.00	1.85

The above surcharges are frequently found with the shield double, inverted, or otherwise misplaced.

National
Palace — A66

Overprinted with Shield in Black
1907   **Engr.**   **Unwmk.**
Paper with or without colored dots
355	A66	1c green & blk	.25	.25
356	A66	2c red & blk	.25	.25
357	A66	3c yellow & blk	.25	.25
358	A66	5c blue & blk	.25	.25
a.		5c ultramarine & black	.25	.25
359	A66	6c ver & blk	.25	.25
a.		Shield in red	3.25	
360	A66	10c violet & blk	.25	.25
361	A66	12c violet & blk	.25	.25

362	A66	13c sepia & blk	.25	.25
363	A66	24c rose & blk	.25	.25
364	A66	26c yel brn & blk	.30	.25
365	A66	50c orange & blk	.50	.35
a.		50c yellow & black	3.50	
366	A66	100c turq bl & blk	1.00	.50
		Nos. 355-366 (12)	4.05	3.35

Most values exist without shield, also with shield inverted, double, and otherwise misprinted. Many of these were never sold to the public.

See 2nd footnote following No. 421.

See Nos. 369-373, 397-401. For surcharges and overprints see Nos. 367-368A, 374-77, 414-421, 443-444, J71-J74, J76-J80, O329-O331.

No. 356 With
Additional Surcharge
in Black

1908
367	A66	1c on 2c red & blk	.25	.25
a.		Double surcharge	1.00	1.00
b.		Inverted surcharge	.50	.50
c.		Double surcharge, one inverted	.50	.50
d.		Red surcharge		

Same Surcharged in
Black or Red

368	A66	1c on 2c	19.00	17.50
368A	A66	1c on 2c (R)	27.50	25.00

Counterfeits exist of the surcharges on Nos. 368-368A.

Type of 1907
1909   **Engr.**   **Wmk. 172**
369	A66	1c green & blk	.25	.25
370	A66	2c rose & blk	.25	.25
371	A66	3c yellow & blk	.25	.25
372	A66	5c blue & blk	.25	.25
373	A66	10c violet & blk	.30	.25
		Nos. 369-373 (5)	1.30	1.25

The note after No. 366 will apply here also.

Nos. 355, 369
Overprinted in Red

1909, Sept.   **Unwmk.**
374	A66	1c green & blk	2.25	1.10
a.		Inverted overprint	10.00	

Wmk. 172
375	A66	1c green & blk	1.75	1.40
a.		Inverted overprint		

88th anniv. of El Salvador's independence.

Nos. 362, 364
Surcharged

1909   **Unwmk.**
376	A66	2c on 13c sep & blk	1.50	1.25
a.		Inverted surcharge		
377	A66	3c on 26c yel brn & blk	1.75	1.40
a.		Inverted surcharge		

A67

Design: Pres. Fernando Figueroa.

1910   **Engr.**   **Wmk. 172**
378	A67	1c sepia & blk	.25	.25
379	A67	2c dk grn & blk	.25	.25
380	A67	3c orange & blk	.25	.25
381	A67	4c carmine & blk	.25	.25
a.		4c scarlet & black	.25	.25
382	A67	5c purple & blk	.25	.25
383	A67	6c scarlet & blk	.25	.25
384	A67	10c purple & blk	.25	.25
385	A67	12c dp bl & blk	.25	.25
386	A67	17c ol grn & blk	.25	.25
387	A67	19c brn red & blk	.25	.25
388	A67	29c choc & blk	.25	.25
389	A67	50c yellow & blk	.25	.25
390	A67	100c turq bl & blk	.25	.25
		Nos. 378-390 (13)	3.25	3.25

See Nos. J81-J87, O293-O304.

A68

5c, José Matías Delgado. 6c, Manuel José Arce. 12c, Centenary Monument.
Paper with colored dots
1911   **Unwmk.**
391	A68	5c dp blue & brn	.25	.25
392	A68	6c orange & brn	.25	.25
393	A68	12c violet & brn	.25	.25

Wmk. 172
394	A68	5c dp blue & brn	.25	.25
395	A68	6c orange & brn	.25	.25
396	A68	12c violet & brn	.25	.25
		Nos. 391-396 (6)	1.50	1.50

Centenary of the insurrection of 1811.

Palace Type of 1907 without Shield
1911   **Paper without colored dots**
397	A66	1c scarlet	.25	.25
398	A66	2c chocolate	.30	.30
a.		Paper with brown dots		
399	A66	13c deep green	.25	.25
400	A66	24c yellow	.25	.25
401	A66	50c dark brown	.25	.25
		Nos. 397-401 (5)	1.30	1.30

José Matías
Delgado — A71

Francisco
Morazán — A73

Trinidad
Cabañas
A75

Manuel José
Arce — A72

Rafael
Campo — A74

Monument of
Gerardo
Barrios
A76

Centenary
Monument
A77

National Palace
A78

Rosales
Hospital — A79

Coat of
Arms — A80

1912   **Unwmk.**   **Perf. 12**
402	A71	1c dp bl & blk	1.00	.25
403	A72	2c bis brn & blk	1.00	.25
404	A73	5c scarlet & blk	1.00	.25
405	A74	6c dk grn & blk	1.00	.25
406	A75	12c ol grn & blk	3.00	.25
407	A76	17c violet & slate	10.00	.25
408	A77	19c scar & slate	3.00	.30
409	A78	29c org & slate	5.00	.30
410	A79	50c blue & slate	5.00	.45
411	A80	1col black & slate	10.00	1.00
		Nos. 402-411 (10)	40.00	3.55

Juan Manuel
Rodríguez
A81

Pres. Manuel E.
Araujo
A82

1914   **Perf. 11½**
412	A81	10c orange & brn	5.00	1.50
413	A82	25c purple & brn	5.00	1.50

Type of 1907 without
Shield Overprinted in
Black

1915
Paper overlaid with colored dots
414	A66	1c gray green	.25	.25
415	A66	2c red	.25	.25
416	A66	5c ultra	.25	.25
417	A66	6c pale blue	.25	.25
418	A66	10c yellow	.60	.30
419	A66	12c brown	.50	.25
420	A66	50c violet	.25	.25
421	A66	100c black brn	1.40	1.40
		Nos. 414-421 (8)	3.75	3.20

Varieties such as center omitted, center double, center inverted, imperforate exist with or without date, date inverted, date double, etc., but are believed to be entirely unofficial.

Preceding the stamps with the "1915" overprint a quantity of stamps of this type was overprinted with the letter "S." Evidence is lacking that they were ever placed in use. The issue was demonetized in 1916.

National
Theater — A83

Various frames.

1916   **Engr.**   **Perf. 12**
431	A83	1c deep green	.25	.25
432	A83	2c vermilion	.25	.25
433	A83	5c deep blue	.25	.25
434	A83	6c gray violet	.25	.25
435	A83	10c black brn	.25	.25
436	A83	12c violet	2.50	.50

437	A83	17c orange	.35	.25
438	A83	25c dk brown	.80	.25
439	A83	29c black	5.00	.75
440	A83	50c slate	20.00	10.00
		Nos. 431-440 (10)	29.90	13.00

Watermarked letters which occasionally appear are from the papermaker's name.

For surcharges and overprints see Nos. 450-455, 457-466, O332-O341.

Nos. O324-O325 with "OFICIAL" Barred out in Black

1917

441	O3	2c red	.90	.90
a.	Double bar		
442	O3	5c ultramarine	1.00	.70
a.	Double bar		

Regular Issue of 1915 Overprinted "OFICIAL" and Re-overprinted In Red

443	A66	6c pale blue	1.25	1.00
a.	Double bar		
444	A66	12c brown	1.75	1.25
a.	Double bar		
b.	"CORRIENTE" inverted		

Same Overprint in Red On Nos. O323-O327

445	O3	1c gray green	3.50	2.50
a.	"CORRIENTE" inverted		
b.	Double bar		
c.	"CORRIENTE" omitted		
446	O3	2c red	3.50	2.50
a.	Double bar		
447	O3	5c ultra	18.00	12.00
a.	Double bar, both in black		
448	O3	10c yellow	2.00	1.00
a.	Double bar		
b.	"OFICIAL" and bar omitted		
449	O3	50c violet	1.00	1.00
a.	Double bar		
		Nos. 443-449 (7)	31.00	21.25

Nos. O334-O335 Overprinted or Surcharged in Red

a   b

450	A83 (a)	5c deep blue	3.00	2.00
a.	"CORRIENTE" double		
451	A83 (b)	1c on 6c gray vio	2.00	1.50
a.	"CORRIENTE"		
b.	"CORRIENRE"		5.00
c.	"CORRIENTE" double		

No. 434 Surcharged in Black

1918

452	A83	1c on 6c gray vio	1.75	1.00
a.	Double surcharge		
b.	Inverted surcharge		

No. 434 Surcharged in Black

1918

453	A83	1c on 6c gray vio	1.50	.75
a.	"Centado"	2.25	1.50
b.	Double surcharge	2.50	1.75
c.	Inverted surcharge		

No. 434 Surcharged in Black or Red

454	A83	1c on 6c gray vio	10.00	6.00
a.	Double surcharge		
b.	Inverted surcharge	5.00	5.00

455	A83	1c on 6c gray vio (R)	10.00	6.00
a.	Double surcharge		
b.	Inverted surcharge	5.00	5.00
		Nos. 454-455 (2)	20.00	12.00

Counterfeits exist of Nos. 454-455.

Pres. Carlos Meléndez — A85

1919   **Engr.**

456	A85	1col dk blue & blk	.50	.50

For surcharge see No. 467.

No. 437 Surcharged in Black

1919

457	A83	1c on 17c orange	.25	.25
a.	Inverted surcharge	1.00	1.00
b.	Double surcharge	1.00	1.00

Nos. 435-436, 438, 440 Surcharged in Black or Blue

1920-21

458	A83	1c on 12c violet	.25	.25
a.	Double surcharge	1.00	1.00
459	A83	2c on 10c dk brn	.25	.25
460	A83	5c on 50c slate ('21)	.40	.25
461	A83	6c on 25c dk brn (Bl)		
		('21)	2.00	1.00

Same Srch. in Black on No. O337

462	A83	1c on 12c violet	1.00	1.00
a.	Double surcharge		
		Nos. 458-462 (5)	3.90	2.75

No. 460 surcharged in yellow and 461 surcharged in red are essays.

No. 462 is due to some sheets of Official Stamps being mixed with the ordinary 12c stamps at the time of surcharging. The error stamps were sold to the public and used for ordinary postage.

Surcharged in Red, Blue or Black

15c Types:

I   II   III   IV

463	A83	15c on 29c blk (III) ('21)	1.00	.40
a.	Double surcharge	2.00	
b.	Type I	1.50	1.00
c.	Type II	1.00	.75
d.	Type IV	2.50	
464	A83	26c on 29c blk (Bl)	1.00	.60
a.	Double surcharge		
466	A83	35c on 50c slate (Bk)	1.00	.60
467	A85	60c on 1col dk bl & blk		
		(R)	.30	.25
		Nos. 463-467 (4)	3.30	1.85

Surcharge on No. 464 differs from 15c illustration in that bar at bottom extends across stamp and denomination includes "cts." One stamp in each row of ten of No. 464 has the "t" of "cts" inverted and one stamp in each row of No. 466 has the letters "c" in "cinco" larger than the normal.

Setting for No. 467 includes three types of numerals and "CENTAVOS" measuring from 16mm to 20mm wide.

No. 464 surcharged in green or yellow and the 35c on 29c black are essays.

A93

1921

468	A93	1c on 1c ol grn	.25	.25
a.	Double surcharge	.75	
469	A93	1c on 5c yellow	.25	.25
a.	Inverted surcharge		
b.	Double surcharge		
470	A93	1c on 10c blue	.25	.25
a.	Double surcharge	.50	
471	A93	1c on 25c green	.25	.25
a.	Double surcharge		
472	A93	1c on 50c olive	.25	.25
a.	Double surcharge		
473	A93	1c on 1p gray blk	.25	.25
a.	Double surcharge		
		Nos. 468-473 (6)	1.50	1.50

The frame of No. 473 differs slightly from the illustration.

Setting includes many wrong font letters and numerals.

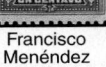

Francisco Menéndez A94   Manuel José Arce A95

Confederation Coin — A96

Delgado Addressing Crowd — A97

Coat of Arms of Confederation A98

Francisco Morazán A99

Independence Monument A100

Columbus A101

1921   **Engr.**   *Perf. 12*

474	A94	1c green	2.50	.25
475	A95	2c black	5.00	.25
476	A96	5c orange	2.00	.25
477	A97	6c carmine rose	2.00	.25
478	A98	10c deep blue	2.00	.25
479	A99	25c olive grn	4.00	.25
480	A100	60c violet	9.00	.50
481	A101	1col black brn	15.00	.75
		Nos. 474-481 (8)	41.50	2.75

For overprints and surcharges see Nos. 481A-485, 487-494, 506, O342-O349.

Nos. 474-477 Overprinted in Red, Black or Blue

a   b

1921

481A	A94 (a)	1c green (R)	5.00	4.00
481B	A95 (a)	2c black (R)	5.00	4.00
481C	A96 (b)	5c orange (Bk)	5.00	4.00
481D	A97 (b)	6c car rose (Bl)	5.00	4.00
		Nos. 481A-481D (4)	20.00	16.00

Centenary of independence.

No. 477 Surcharged

a

b

1923

482	A97 (a)	5c on 6c	4.00	.25
483	A97 (b)	5c on 6c	4.00	.25
484	A97 (b)	20c on 6c	4.00	.25
		Nos. 482-484 (3)	12.00	.75

Nos. 482-484 exist with double surcharge.

No. 475 Surcharged in Red

1923

485	A95	10c on 2c black	4.00	.25

José Simeón Cañas
y Villacorta — A102

1923   **Engr.**   **Perf. 11½**
486   A102   5c blue   .60   .30
    Centenary of abolition of slavery.
For surcharge see No. 571.

**Nos. 479, 481
Surcharged in Red or
Black**

1924   **Perf. 12**
487   A99   1c on 25c ol grn (R)   .30   .25
  a.   Numeral at right inverted
  b.   Double surcharge
488   A99   6c on 25c ol grn (R)   .25   .25
489   A99   20c on 25c ol grn (R)   .60   .25
490   A10120c on 1col blk brn (Bk)   .75   .35
    Nos. 487-490 (4)   1.90   1.10

Nos. 476, 478 Surcharged

1924
491   A96   1c on 5c orange (Bk)   .40   .25
492   A98   6c on 10c dp bl (R)   .40   .25
    Nos. 491-492 exist with double surcharge.
A stamp similar to No. 492 but with
surcharge "6 centavos 6" is an essay.

No. 476
Surcharged

493   A96   2c on 5c orange   .40   .40
  a.   Top ornament omitted   2.00   2.00
    Nos. 491-493 (3)   1.20   .90

No. 480 Surcharged

1924   **Red Surcharge**
494   A100   5c on 60c violet   6.00   5.00
  a.   "1781" for "1874"   13.00   12.00
  b.   "1934" for "1924"   13.00   12.00
    Universal Postal Union, 50th anniversary.
This stamp with black surcharge is an
essay. Examples have been passed through
the post.

Daniel
Hernández
Monument
A106

National
Gymnasium
A107

Atlacatl — A108   Conspiracy of
1811 — A109

Bridge over
Lempa
River — A110

Map of Central
America — A111

Balsam
Tree — A112

Tulla
Serra — A114

Columbus at La
Rábida — A115

Coat of
Arms — A116

Photogravure; Engraved (35c, 1col)
1924-25   **Perf. 12½; 14 (35c, 1col)**
495   A106   1c red violet   .25   .25
496   A107   2c dark red   .40   .25
497   A108   3c chocolate   .30   .25
498   A109   5c olive blk   .30   .25
499   A110   6c grnsh blue   .40   .25
500   A111   10c orange   .85   .25
  a.   "ATLANT CO"   8.00   8.00
501   A112   20c deep green   1.50   .40
502   A114   35c scar & grn   3.50   .50
503   A115   50c orange brown   2.75   .35
504   A116   1col grn & vio ('25)   4.00   .50
    Nos. 495-504 (10)   14.25   3.25
    For overprints and surcharges see Nos.
510-511, 520-534, 585, C1-C10, C19, O350-
O361, RA1-RA4.

No. 480 Surcharged
in Red

1925, Aug.   **Perf. 12**
506   A100   2c on 60c violet   1.50   1.25
    City of San Salvador, 400th anniv.
The variety with dates in black is an essay.

View of San Salvador — A118

1925   **Photo.**   **Perf. 12½**
507   A118   1c blue   1.10   1.00
508   A118   2c deep green   1.10   1.00
509   A118   3c Mahogany red   1.10   1.00
    Nos. 507-509 (3)   3.30   3.00
    #506-509 for the 4th centenary of the found-
ing of the City of San Salvador.

Black Surcharge

1928, July 17
510   A111   3c on 10c orange   1.25   .75
  a.   "ATLANT CO"   20.00   20.00
    Industrial Exhibition, Santa Ana, July 1928.

Red Surcharge

1928
511   A109   1c on 5c olive black   .45   .25
  a.   Bar instead of top left "1"   .60   .25

Pres. Pío Romero Bosque, Salvador,
and Pres. Lázaro Chacón, Guatemala
A121

1929   **Litho.**   **Perf. 11½**
    Portraits in Dark Brown
512   A121   1c dull violet   .60   .45
  a.   Center inverted   11.50   11.50
513   A121   3c bister brn   .60   .45
  a.   Center inverted   35.00   35.00
514   A121   5c gray grn   .60   .45
515   A121   10c orange   .60   .45
    Nos. 512-515 (4)   2.40   1.80
    Opening of the international railroad con-
necting El Salvador and Guatemala.
Nos. 512-515 exist imperforate. No. 512 in
the colors of No. 515.

Tomb of
Menéndez
A122

1930, Dec. 3
516   A122   1c violet   4.50   3.50
517   A122   3c brown   4.50   3.50
518   A122   5c dark green   4.50   3.50
519   A122   10c yellow brn   4.50   3.50
    Nos. 516-519 (4)   18.00   14.00
    Centenary of the birth of General Francisco
Menéndez.

Stamps of 1924-25
Issue Overprinted

1932   **Perf. 12½, 14**
520   A106   1c deep violet   .30   .25
521   A107   2c dark red   .30   .25
522   A108   3c chocolate   .45   .25
523   A109   5c olive blk   .45   .25
524   A110   6c deep blue   .60   .25
525   A111   10c orange   1.50   .25
  a.   "ATLANT CO"   12.00   9.00
526   A112   20c deep green   2.40   .75
527   A114   35c scar & grn   3.25   1.00
528   A115   50c orange brown   4.50   1.50
529   A116   1col green & vio   7.50   3.25
    Nos. 520-529 (10)   21.25   8.00
    Values are for the overprint measuring
7½x3mm. It is found in two other sizes:
7½x3¼mm and 8x3mm.

Types of 1924-25
Surcharged with New Values in Red or
Black

1934   **Perf. 12½**
530   A109   2(c) on 5c grnsh blk   .25   .25
  a.   Double surcharge
531   A111   3(c) on 10c org (Bk)   .45   .25
  a.   "ATLANT CO"   6.00   6.00

**Nos. 503, 504, 502 Surcharged with
New Values in Black**
    Perf. 12½, 14½
532   A115   2(c) on 50c   .45   .25
  a.   Double surcharge   3.00
533   A116   8(c) on 1col   .25   .25
534   A114   15(c) on 35c   .45   .45
    Nos. 530-534 (5)   1.85   1.45

Police Barracks,
Type I — A123

Type II

    Two types of the 2c:
Type I — The clouds have heavy lines of
shading.
Type II — The lines of shading have been
removed from the clouds.

    Wmk. 240
1934-35   **Litho.**   **Perf. 12½**
535   A123   2c gray brn, type I   .25   .25
  a.   2c brown, type II   .25   .25
536   A123   5c car, type II   .25   .25
537   A123   8c lt ultra, type II   .25   .25
    Nos. 535-537,C33-C35 (6)   4.70   2.45

Discus
Thrower
A124

1935, Mar. 16   **Engr.**   **Unwmk.**
538   A124   5c carmine   3.00   2.25
539   A124   8c blue   3.25   2.75
540   A124   10c orange yel   4.50   3.00
541   A124   15c bister   4.50   3.25
542   A124   37c green   6.00   4.50
    Nos. 538-542,C36-C40 (10)   64.75   38.50
    3rd Central American Games.

Same Overprinted in Black

1935, June 27
543   A124   5c carmine   5.00   3.00
544   A124   8c blue   7.00   3.00
545   A124   10c orange yel   7.00   3.50
546   A124   15c bister   7.00   3.50
547   A124   37c green   12.00   5.50
    Nos. 543-547,C41-C45 (10)   71.50   42.70

Flag of El
Salvador — A125

1935, Oct. 26   **Litho.**   **Wmk. 240**
548   A125   1c gray blue   .30   .25
549   A125   2c black brn   .30   .25
550   A125   3c plum   .30   .25
551   A125   5c rose carmine   .45   .25
552   A125   8c ultra   .45   .25
553   A125   15c fawn   .60   .45
    Nos. 548-553,C46 (7)   2.80   2.05

Tree of San
Vicente — A126

Numerals in Black, Tree in Yellow Green

1935, Dec. 26
554	A126	2c black brn	.85	.45
555	A126	3c dk blue grn	.85	.45
556	A126	5c rose red	.85	.45
557	A126	8c dark blue	.85	.55
558	A126	15c brown	.60	.45
	Nos. 554-558,C47-C51 (10)		7.75	5.35

Tercentenary of San Vicente.

Volcano of
Izalco — A127

Wharf at
Cutuco — A128

Doroteo
Vasconcelos
A129

Parade Ground
A130

Dr. Tomás G.
Palomo — A131

Sugar
Mill — A132

Coffee at
Pier — A133

Gathering
Balsam — A134

Pres. Manuel E.
Araujo — A135

1935, Dec.   Engr.   Unwmk.
559	A127	1c deep violet	.25	.25
560	A128	2c chestnut	.25	.25
561	A129	3c green	.25	.25
562	A130	5c carmine	.60	.25
563	A131	8c dull blue	.25	.25
564	A132	10c orange	.60	.25
565	A133	15c dk olive bis	.60	.25
566	A134	50c indigo	3.00	1.75
567	A135	1col black	7.50	4.50
	Nos. 559-567 (9)		13.30	8.00

Paper has faint imprint "El Salvador" on face. For surcharges and overprint see Nos. 568-570, 573, 583-584, C52.

Stamps of 1935 Surcharged with New Value in Black

1938   Perf. 12½
568	A130	1c on 5c carmine	.25	.25
569	A132	3c on 10c orange	.25	.25
570	A133	8c on 15c dk ol bis	.30	.25
	Nos. 568-570 (3)		.80	.75

No. 486 Surcharged with New Value in Red

1938   Perf. 11½
571	A102	3c on 5c blue	.30	.25

Centenary of the death of José Simeón Cañas, liberator of slaves in Latin America.

Map and Flags of US and El
Salvador — A136

Engraved and Lithographed
1938, Apr. 21   Perf. 12
572	A136	8c multicolored	.95	.70

US Constitution, 150th anniv. See #C61.

No. 560 Surcharged with New Value in Black

1938   Perf. 12½
573	A128	1c on 2c chestnut	.25	.25

Indian Sugar
Mill — A137

Designs: 2c, Indian women washing. 3c, Indian girl at spring. 5c, Indian plowing. 8c, Izote flower. 10c, Champion cow. 20c, Extracting balsam. 50c, Maquilishuat in bloom. 1col, Post Office, San Salvador.

1938-39   Engr.   Perf. 12
574	A137	1c dark violet	.25	.25
575	A137	2c dark green	.25	.25
576	A137	3c dark brown	.30	.25
577	A137	5c scarlet	.30	.25
578	A137	8c dark blue	2.00	.25
579	A137	10c yel org ('39)	3.00	.25
580	A137	20c bis brn ('39)	2.75	.25
581	A137	50c dull blk ('39)	3.25	.70
582	A137	1col black ('39)	3.00	1.00
	Nos. 574-582 (9)		15.10	3.45

For surcharges & overprints see Nos. 591-592, C96.

Nos. 566-567, 504
Surcharged in Red

1939, Sept. 25   Perf. 12½, 14
583	A134	8c on 50c indigo	.45	.25
584	A135	10c on 1col blk	.80	.25
585	A116	50c on 1col grn & vio	4.50	3.25
	Nos. 583-585 (3)		5.75	3.75

Battle of San Pedro Perulapán, 100th anniv.

Sir Rowland
Hill — A146

1940, Mar. 1   Perf. 12½
586	A146	8c dk bl, lt bl & blk	6.00	2.00
	Nos. 586,C69-C70 (3)		36.50	22.00

Postage stamp centenary.

Statue of Christ and San Salvador
Cathedral — A147

A148

Wmk. 269
1942, Nov. 23   Engr.   Perf. 14
587	A147	8c deep blue	.80	.25

Souvenir Sheet
Imperf
Without Gum
Lilac Tinted Paper
588	A148	Sheet of 4	25.00	22.00
a.		8c deep blue	10.00	10.00
b.		30c red orange	10.00	10.00

Nos. 587-588 commemorate the first Eucharistic Congress of Salvador. See No. C85.

No. 588 contains two No. 587 and two No. C85, imperf.

> **Catalogue values for unused stamps in this section, from this point to the end of the section, are for Never Hinged items.**

Cuscatlán Bridge, Pan-American
Highway — A149

Arms Overprint at Right in Carmine
Perf. 12½
1944, Nov. 24   Unwmk.   Engr.
589	A149	8c dk blue & blk	.40	.25

See No. C92.

Gen. Juan José
Canas — A150

1945, June 9
590	A150	8c blue	.60	.25

No. 575 Surcharged in Black

a

b

Lake of Ilopango
A151

Ceiba Tree
A152

1944-46
591	A137(a)	1(c) on 2c dk grn	.30	.25
592	A137(b)	1(c) on 2c dk grn ('46)	.30	.25

Water
Carriers — A153

1946-47   Litho.   Wmk. 240
593	A151	1c blue ('47)	.40	.25
594	A152	2c lt bl grn ('47)	.45	.25
595	A153	5c carmine	.40	.25
	Nos. 593-595 (3)		1.25	.75

Isidro Menéndez
A154

2c, Cristano Salazar. 3c, Juan Bertis. 5c, Francisco Duenas. 8c, Ramon Belloso. 10c, Jose Presentacion Trigueros. 20c, Salvador Rodriguez Gonzalez. 50c, Francisco Castaneda. 1col, David Castro.

1947   Unwmk.   Engr.   Perf. 12
596	A154	1c car rose	.25	.25
597	A154	2c dp org	.25	.25
598	A154	3c violet	.25	.25
599	A154	5c slate gray	.25	.25
600	A154	8c dp bl	.25	.25
601	A154	10c bis brn	.45	.25
602	A154	20c green	.45	.25
603	A154	50c black	1.10	.35
604	A154	1col scarlet	2.25	.50
	Nos. 596-604 (9)		5.30	2.60

For surcharges and overprints see Nos. 621-626, 634, C118-C120, O362-O368.

Manuel José
Arce — A163

1948, Feb. 25   Perf. 12½
605	A163	8c deep blue	.45	.25
	Nos. 605,C108-C110 (4)		4.40	2.75

President Roosevelt Presenting
Awards for Distinguished
Service — A164

President
Franklin D.
Roosevelt
A165

A166

Designs: 8c, Pres. and Mrs. Roosevelt. 15c, Mackenzie King, Roosevelt and Winston Churchill. 20c, Roosevelt and Cordell Hull. 50c, Funeral of Pres. Roosevelt.

1948, Apr. 12
Various Frames; Center in Black

606	A164	5c dk bl	.25	.25
607	A164	8c green	.25	.25
608	A165	12c violet	.25	.25
609	A164	15c vermilion	.45	.25
610	A164	20c car lake	.45	.25
611	A164	50c gray	1.10	.70
	Nos. 606-611,C111-C116 (12)		10.65	6.60

Souvenir Sheet
Perf. 13½

612	A166	1col ol grn & brn	4.00	2.25

3rd anniv. of the death of F. D. Roosevelt.

Torch and
Winged
Letter
A167

Perf. 12½
1949, Oct. 9　　Unwmk.　　Engr.

613	A167	8c blue	1.10	.55
	Nos. 613,C122-C124 (4)		26.55	18.55

75th anniv. of the UPU.

Workman and
Soldier Holding
Torch — A168

1949, Dec. 15　Litho.　　Perf. 10½

614	A168	8c blue	.45	.45
	Nos. 614,C125-C129 (6)		9.85	7.25

Revolution of Dec. 14, 1948, 1st anniv.

Wreath and Open
Book — A169

Wreath in Dark Green
Perf. 11½
1952, Feb. 14　Photo.　　Unwmk.

615	A169	1c yel grn	.25	.25
616	A169	2c magenta	.25	.25
617	A169	5c brn red	.25	.25

618	A169	10c yellow	.25	.25
619	A169	20c gray grn	.25	.25
620	A169	1col dp car	1.50	1.00
	Nos. 615-620,C134-C141 (14)		11.75	8.00

Constitution of 1950.

Nos. 598, 600 and
603 Surcharged
with New Values
in Various Colors

1952-53　　　　　　　Perf. 12½

621	A154	2c on 3c vio (C)	.25	.25
622	A154	2c on 8c dp bl (C)	.25	.25
623	A154	3c on 8c dp bl (G)	.25	.25
624	A154	5c on 8c dp bl (O)	.25	.25
625	A154	7c on 8c dp bl (Bk)	.25	.25
626	A154	10c on 50c blk (O)		
		('53)	.25	.25
	Nos. 621-626 (6)		1.50	1.50

Nos. C106 and
C107 Surcharged in
Various Colors

1952-53　　　　　　　Wmk. 240

627	AP31	2c on 12c choc (Bl)	.25	.25
628	AP32	2c on 14c dk bl (R)		
		('53)	.25	.25
629	AP31	3c on 12c choc (Bl)	.25	.25
630	AP32	10c on 14c dk bl (C)	.25	.25
	Nos. 627-630 (4)		1.00	1.00

José
Marti — A170

Perf. 10½
1953, Feb. 27　Litho.　　Unwmk.

631	A170	1c rose red	.25	.25
632	A170	2c bl grn	.25	.25
633	A170	10c dk vio	.30	.25
	Nos. 631-633,C142-C144 (6)		3.05	1.85

José Marti, Cuban patriot, birth cent.

No. 598
Overprinted in
Carmine

1953, June 19　　　　　Perf. 12½

634	A154	3c violet	.25	.25

4th Pan-American Congress of Social Medicine, San Salvador, April 16-19, 1953. See #C146.

Signing of Act
of
Independence
A171

1953, Sept. 15　Litho.　　Perf. 11½

635	A171	1c rose pink	.25	.25
636	A171	2c dp bl grn	.25	.25
637	A171	3c purple	.25	.25
638	A171	5c dp bl	.25	.25
639	A171	7c lt brn	.25	.25
640	A171	10c ocher	.25	.25
641	A171	20c dp org	.70	.25

642	A171	50c green	.95	.30
643	A171	1col gray	1.90	1.25
	Nos. 635-643,C147-C150 (13)		7.10	4.75

Act of Independence, Sept. 15, 1821.

A172

Portrait: 1c, 2c, 5c, 20c: Capt. Gen. Gerardo Barrios. 3c, 7c, 10c, 22c: Francisco Morazan, (facing left).

Overprinted in Black

1953, Dec. 1　　　　　Perf. 11½

644	A172	1c green	.25	.25
645	A172	2c blue	.25	.25
646	A172	3c green	.25	.25
647	A172	5c carmine	.25	.25
648	A172	7c blue	.25	.25
649	A172	10c carmine	.30	.25
650	A172	20c violet	.40	.25
651	A172	22c violet	.60	.25
	Nos. 644-651 (8)		2.55	2.00

The overprint "C de C" is a control indicating "Tribunal of Accounts." A double entry of this overprint occurs twice in each sheet of each denomination.
For overprint see No. 729.

Coastal
Bridge
A173

Motherland
and Liberty
A174

Census
Allegory — A175

Balboa
Park — A176

Designs: Nos. 654, 655, National Palace. Nos. 659, 665, Izalco Volcano. Nos. 660, 661, Guayabo dam. No. 666, Lake Ilopango. No. 669, Housing development. Nos. 670, 673, Coast guard boat. No. 671, Modern highway.

Perf. 11½
1954, June 1　　Unwmk.　　Photo.

652	A173	1c car rose & brn	.25	.25
653	AP43	1c ol & bl gray	.25	.25
654	A173	1c pur & pale lil	.25	.25
655	A173	2c yel grn & lt gray	.25	.25
656	A174	2c car lake	.25	.25
657	A175	2c org red	.25	.25
658	AP44	3c maroon	.25	.25
659	A173	3c bl grn & bl	.25	.25
660	A174	3c dk gray & vio	.25	.25
661	A174	5c red vio & vio	.30	.25
662	AP44	5c emerald	.30	.25
663	A176	7c magenta & buff	.30	.25
664	AP43	7c bl grn & gray bl	.30	.25
665	A173	7c org brn & org	.30	.25
666	A173	10c car lake	.30	.25
667	AP46	10c red, dk brn & bl	.30	.25
668	A174	10c dk bl grn	.30	.25
669	A174	20c org & cr	.40	.25
670	A173	22c gray vio	.40	.25
671	A176	50c org & brn	1.00	.35
672	AP46	1col brn org, dk brn		
		& bl	1.75	.90
673	A173	1col brt bl	1.75	.90
	Nos. 652-673 (22)		9.95	6.90
	Nos. 652-673,C151-C165 (37)		24.90	13.75

For surcharges & overprints see #692-693, 736, C193.

Capt. Gen. Gerardo
Barrios — A177

Wmk. 269
1955, Dec. 20　Engr.　　Perf. 12½

674	A177	1c red	.25	.25
675	A177	2c yel grn	.35	.30
676	A177	3c vio bl	.35	.30
677	A177	20c violet	.50	.30
	Nos. 674-677,C166-C167 (6)		2.15	1.80

Coffee
Picker — A178

Perf. 13½
1956, June 20　Litho.　　Unwmk.

678	A178	3c bis brn	.25	.25
679	A178	5c red org	.25	.25
680	A178	10c dk bl	.25	.25
681	A178	2col dk red	1.90	1.25
	Nos. 678-681,C168-C172 (9)		8.85	5.80

Centenary of Santa Ana Department.
For overprint see No. C187.

Map of Chalatenango — A179

1956, Sept. 14

682	A179	2c blue	.25	.25
683	A179	7c rose red	.45	.30
684	A179	50c yel brn	.70	.45
	Nos. 682-684,C173-C178 (9)		4.30	3.35

Centenary of Chalatenango Department (in 1955).
For surcharge see No. 694.

Coat of Arms of
Nueva San
Salvador — A180

Wmk. 269
1957, Jan. 3　Engr.　　Perf. 12½

685	A180	1c rose red	.25	.25
686	A180	2c green	.25	.25
687	A180	3c violet	.25	.25
688	A180	7c red org	.45	.25
689	A180	10c ultra	.25	.25
690	A180	50c pale brn	.55	.25
691	A180	1col dl red	.80	.75
	Nos. 685-691,C179-C183 (12)		7.10	4.75

Centenary of the founding of the city of Nueva San Salvador (Santa Tecla).
For surcharges and overprints see Nos. 695-696, 706, 713, C194-C195, C197-C199.

Nos. 664-665, 683 and 688
Surcharged with New Value in Black
1957　Unwmk.　Photo.　Perf. 11½

692	A173	6c on 7c bl grn & gray		
		bl	.30	.30
693	A173	6c on 7c org brn & org	.30	.30
1957		**Litho.**	**Perf. 13½**	
694	A179	6c on 7c rose red	.25	.25

Wmk. 269

1957-58			Engr.	Perf. 12½
695	A180	5c on 7c red org ('58)	.25	.25
696	A180	6c on 7c red org	.30	.25
		Nos. 692-696 (5)	1.40	1.35

El Salvador Intercontinental
Hotel — A181

Perf. 11½

1958, June 28   Unwmk.   Photo.
Granite Paper
Vignette in Green, Dark Blue & Red

697	A181	3c brown	.25	.25
698	A181	6c crim rose	.25	.25
699	A181	10c brt bl	.25	.25
700	A181	15c brt grn	.25	.25
701	A181	20c lilac	.30	.25
702	A181	30c brt yel grn	.40	.25
		Nos. 697-702 (6)	1.70	1.50

Presidents Eisenhower and Lemus
and Flags — A182

1959, Dec. 14   Granite Paper
Design in Ultramarine, Dark Brown,
Light Brown and Red

703	A182	3c pink	.25	.25
704	A182	6c green	.25	.25
705	A182	10c crimson	.30	.25
		Nos. 703-705,C184-C186 (6)	1.60	1.50

Visit of Pres. José M. Lemus of El Salvador
to the US, Mar. 9-21.

No. 686 Ovptd.: "5 Enero 1960 XX Aniversario Fundacion Sociedad Filatelica de El Salvador"

1960   Wmk. 269   Engr.   Perf. 12½

706	A180	2c green	.25	.25

Philatelic Association of El Salvador, 20th
anniv.

Apartment
Houses
A183

1960   Unwmk.   Photo.   Perf. 11½
Multicolored Centers; Granite Paper

707	A183	10c scarlet	.25	.25
708	A183	15c brt pur	.25	.25
709	A183	25c brt yel grn	.30	.25
710	A183	30c Prus bl	.35	.25
711	A183	40c olive	.55	.40
712	A183	80c dk bl	.95	.90
		Nos. 707-712 (6)	2.65	2.30

Issued to publicize the erection of multifamily housing projects in 1958.
For surcharges see Nos. 730, 733.

No. 686 Surcharged with New Value

1960   Wmk. 269   Engr.   Perf. 12½

713	A180	1c on 2c grn	.25	.25

Poinsettia — A184

Perf. 11½

1960, Dec.   Unwmk.   Photo.
Granite Paper
Design in Slate Green, Red
and Yellow

714	A184	3c yellow	.25	.25
715	A184	6c salmon	.25	.25
716	A184	10c grnsh bl	.30	.25
717	A184	15c pale vio bl	.30	.25
		Nos. 714-717,C188-C191 (8)	3.40	2.30

Miniature Sheet

718	A184	40c silver	8.00	8.00
a.		Ovptd. in sheet margin ('61)	16.00	16.00
b.		Ovptd. in sheet margin ('61)	16.00	16.00
c.		Ovptd. in sheet margin ('62)	16.00	16.00
d.		Ovptd. in sheet margin ('63)	16.00	16.00
e.		Ovptd. in sheet margin ('63)	16.00	16.00
f.		Ovptd. in sheet margin ('63)	16.00	16.00

Overprints in sheet margin of No. 718:
a, PRIMERA CONVENCION FILATELICA / CENTRO-AMERICANA / SAN SALVADOR, JULIO DE 1961.
b, in purple, Portrait, dates and text commemorating the Death of General Barrios, 96th anniv.
c, in green, Arms of city of Ahuachapan and PRIMER CENTENARIO / Ciudad de Ahuachapan / 1862 22 de Febrero 1962.
d, in blue, Soccer players and text commemorating the 1st North & Central American Soccer Championships 24 March - 2 April, 1963.
e, in blue and green, emblem of Alliance for Progress and text commemorating the 2nd anniversary of the organization.
f, in green, Portrait of Dr. Manuel Araujo and College Arms with text commemorating the 4th Latin American Cong. of Pathological Anatomy and 10th Central American Medical Cong., Dec., 1963.
For surcharge see No. C196.

Fathers
Nicolas,
Vicente
and
Manuel
Aguilar
A185

Parish
Church,
San
Salvador,
1808
A186

Designs: 5c, 6c, Manuel José Arce, José Matias Delgado and Juan Manuel Rodriguez. 10c, 20c, Pedro Pablo Castillo, Domingo Antonio de Lara and Santiago José Celis. 50c, 80c, Monument to the Fathers, Plaza Libertad.

Perf. 11½

1961, Nov. 5   Unwmk.   Photo.

719	A185	1c gray & dk brn	.25	.25
720	A185	2c rose & dk brn	.25	.25
721	A185	5c pale brn & dk ol grn	.25	.25
722	A185	6c brt pink & dk brn	.25	.25
723	A185	10c bl & dk brn	.25	.25
724	A185	20c vio & dk brn	.30	.25
725	A186	30c brt bl & vio	.40	.25
726	A186	40c brn org & sep	.50	.25
727	A186	50c bl grn & sep	.75	.40
728	A186	80c gray & ultra	1.25	.75
		Nos. 719-728 (10)	4.45	3.15

Sesquicentennial of the first cry for Independence in Central America.
For surcharges and overprints see Nos. 731-732, 734-735, 737, 760, 769, 776.

No. 651 Ovptd.: "III Exposición Industrial Centroamericana Diciembre de 1962"

1962, Dec. 21   Litho.   Perf. 11½

729	A172	22c violet	.40	.25
		Nos. 729,C193-C195 (4)	4.15	2.65

3rd Central American Industrial Exposition.

Nos. 708, 726-728 and 673 Surcharged

1962-63   Photo.

730	A183	6c on 15c ('63)	.30	.25
731	A186	6c on 40c ('63)	.30	.25
732	A186	6c on 80c ('63)	.30	.25
733	A183	10c on 15c	.40	.25
734	A186	10c on 50c ('63)	.40	.25
735	A186	10c on 80c ('63)	.40	.25
736	A173	10c on 1col ('63)	.40	.25
		Nos. 730-736 (7)	2.50	1.75

Surcharge includes bars on Nos. 731-734, 736; dot on Nos. 730, 735.

No. 726 Ovptd. in Arc: "CAMPAÑA MUNDIAL CONTRA EL HAMBRE"

1963, Mar. 21

737	A186	40c brn org & sepia	.95	.50

FAO "Freedom from Hunger" campaign.

Coyote
A187

2c, Spider monkey, vert. 3c, Raccoon. 5c, King vulture, vert. 6c, Brown coati. 10c, Kinkajou.

1963   Photo.   Perf. 11½

738	A187	1c lil, blk, ocher & brn	.75	.25
739	A187	2c lt grn & blk	.75	.25
740	A187	3c fawn, dk brn & buff	.75	.25
741	A187	5c gray grn, ind, red & buff	.75	.25
742	A187	6c rose lil, blk, brn & buff	.75	.25
743	A187	10c lt bl, brn & buff	.75	.25
		Nos. 738-743,C200-C207 (14)	35.50	9.45

Christ on
Globe — A188

1964-65   Perf. 12x11½

744	A188	6c bl & brn	.25	.25
745	A188	10c bl & bis	.25	.25
		Nos. 744-745,C208-C209 (4)	1.00	1.00

Miniature Sheets
Imperf

746	A188	60c bl & brt pur	1.60	1.25
a.		Marginal ovpt. La Union	1.25	1.25
b.		Marginal ovpt. Usulutan	1.25	1.25
c.		Marginal ovpt. La Libertad	2.50	2.50

2nd Natl. Eucharistic Cong., San Salvador, Apr. 16-19.
Nos. 746a, 746b and 746c commemorate the centenaries of the Departments of La Union, Usulután and La Libertad.
Issued: #744-746, Apr. 16, 1964; #746a-746b, June 22, 1965; #746c, Jan. 28, 1965.
See #C210. For overprints see #C232, C238.

Pres. John
F. Kennedy
A189

Perf. 11½x12

1964, Nov. 22   Unwmk.

747	A189	6c buff & blk	.25	.25
748	A189	10c tan & blk	.25	.25
749	A189	50c pink & blk	.50	.25
		Nos. 747-749,C211-C213 (6)	1.80	1.50

For overprints & surcharge see #798, 843.

Miniature Sheet
Imperf

750	A189	70c dp grn & blk	1.60	1.25
a.		Overprinted in sheet margin in red brown ('69)	4.50	4.50

President John F. Kennedy (1917-1963).
Overprint on No. 750a reads: "Alunizaje / Apolo-11 / 21 Julio / 1969" and includes pictures of the landing module and astronauts.

Water
Lily — A190

1965, Jan. 6   Photo.   Perf. 12x11½

751	A190	3c shown	.30	.25
752	A190	5c Maquilishuat	.30	.25
753	A190	6c Cinco negritos	.40	.25
754	A190	30c Hortensia	1.25	.25
755	A190	50c Maguey	1.60	.25
756	A190	60c Geranium	1.60	.25
		Nos. 751-756,C215-C220 (12)	12.60	3.05

For overprints and surcharges see Nos. 779, C243, C348-C349.

ICY Emblem
A191

1965, Apr. 27   Photo.   Perf. 11½x12
Design in Brown and Gold

757	A191	5c dp yel	.25	.25
758	A191	6c dp rose	.25	.25
759	A191	10c gray	.25	.25
		Nos. 757-759,C221-C223 (6)	1.55	1.50

International Cooperation Year.
For overprints see #764, 780, C227, C244, C312.

No. 728 Ovptd. in Red: "1er. Centenario Muerte / Cap. Gral. Gerardo Barrios / 1865 1965 / 29 de Agosto"

1965   Unwmk.   Perf. 11½

760	A186	80c gray & ultra	.65	.50
a.		"Garl." instead of "Gral."	1.00	1.00

Capt. Gen. Gerardo Barrios, death cent.

Gavidia
A192

Perf. 11½x12

1965, Sept. 24   Photo.   Unwmk.
Portrait in Natural Colors

761	A192	2c blk & rose vio	.25	.25
762	A192	3c blk & org	.25	.25
763	A192	6c blk & lt ultra	.25	.25
		Nos. 761-763,C224-C226 (6)	2.40	1.65

Francisco Antonio Gavidia, philosopher.
For surcharges see Nos. 852-853.

No. 759 Ovptd. in Carmine: "1865 / 12 de Octubre / 1965 / Dr. Manuel Enrique Araujo"

1965, Oct. 12

764	A191	10c brn, gray & gold	.25	.25

Centenary of the birth of Manuel Enrique Araujo, president of Salvador, 1911-1913. See No. C227.

Fair
Emblem — A193

1965, Nov. 5   Photo.   Perf. 12x11½

765	A193	6c yel & multi	.25	.25
766	A193	10c multi	.25	.25
767	A193	20c pink & multi	.25	.25
		Nos. 765-767,C228-C230 (6)	4.30	3.20

Intl. Fair of El Salvador, Nov. 5-Dec. 4.
For overprints and surcharge see Nos. 784, C246, C311, C323.

WHO Headquarters, Geneva — A194

1966, May 20   Photo.   Unwmk.
768 A194 15c beige & multi   .25 .25
Inauguration of WHO Headquarters, Geneva. See No. C231. For overprints and surcharges see Nos. 778, 783, 864, C242, C245, C322.

No. 728 Ovptd. in Red: "Mes de Conmemoracion / Civica de la Independencia / Centroamericana / 19 Sept. / 1821 1966"

1966, Sept. 19   Photo.   Perf. 11½
769 A186 80c gray & ultra   .40 .40
Month of civic commemoration of Central American independence.

UNESCO Emblem A195

1966, Nov. 4   Unwmk.   Perf. 12
770 A195 20c gray, blk & vio bl   .25 .25
771 A195 1col emer, blk & vio bl   .80 .30
Nos. 770-771,C233-C234 (4)   2.90 1.80
20th anniv. of UNESCO.
For surcharges see Nos. 853A, C352.

Map of Central America, Flags and Cogwheels A196

1966, Nov. 27   Litho.   Perf. 12
772 A196 6c multi   .25 .25
773 A196 10c multi   .25 .25
Nos. 772-773,C235-C237 (5)   1.50 1.35
2nd Intl. Fair of El Salvador, Nov. 5-27.

José Simeon Cañas Pleading for Indian Slaves — A197

1967, Feb. 18   Litho.   Perf. 11½
774 A197 6c yel & multi   .25 .25
775 A197 10c lil rose & multi   .25 .25
Nos. 774-775,C239-C240 (4)   1.10 1.10
Father José Simeon Cañas y Villacorta, D.D. (1767-1838), emancipator of the Central American slaves.
For surcharges see #841A-842, 891, C403-C405.

No. 726 Ovptd. in Red: "XV Convención de Clubes / de Leones, Región de / El Salvador-11 y 12 / de Marzo de 1967"

1967   Photo.
776 A186 40c brn org & sepia   .40 .20
Issued to publicize the 15th Convention of Lions Clubs of El Salvador, March 11-12.

Volcano San Miguel A198

1967, Apr. 14   Photo.   Perf. 13
777 A198 70c lt rose lilac & brn   1.00 .60
Centenary of stamps of El Salvador. See No. C241. For surcharges see Nos. 841, C320, C350.

No. 768 Ovptd. in Red: "VIII CONGRESO / CENTROAMERICANO DE / FARMACIA Y BIOQUIMICA / 5 di 11 Noviembre de 1967"

1967, Oct. 26   Photo.   Perf. 12x11½
778 A194 15c multi   .25 .25
8th Central American Congress for Pharmacy and Biochemistry. See No. C242.

No. 751 Ovptd. in Red: "I Juegos / Centroamericanos y del / Caribe de Basquetbol / 25 Nov. al 3 Dic. 1967"

1967, Nov. 15
779 A190 3c dl grn, brn, yel & org   .25 .25
First Central American and Caribbean Basketball Games, 11/25-12/3. See #C243.

No. 757 Ovptd. in Carmine: "1968 / AÑO INTERNACIONAL DE / LOS DERECHOS HUMANOS"

1968, Jan. 2   Photo.   Perf. 11½x12
780 A191 5c dp yel, brn & gold   .25 .25
Intl. Human Rights Year. See #C244.

Weather Map, Satellite and WMO Emblem A199

1968, Mar. 25   Photo.   Perf. 11½x12
781 A199 1c multi   .25 .25
782 A199 30c multi   .30 .25
World Meteorological Day, Mar. 25.

No. 768 Ovptd. in Red: "1968 / XX ANIVERSARIO DE LA / ORGANIZACION MUNDIAL / DE LA SALUD"

1968, Apr. 7   Perf. 12x11½
783 A194 15c multi   .25 .25
20th anniv. of WHO. See No. C245.

No. 765 Ovptd. in Red: "1968 / Año / del Sistema / del Crédito / Rural"

1968, May 6   Photo.   Perf. 12x11½
784 A193 6c yellow & multi   .25 .25
Rural credit system. See No. C246.

Alberto Masferrer A200

1968, June 22   Litho.   Perf. 12x11½
785 A200 2c multi   .25 .25
786 A200 6c multi   .25 .25
787 A200 25c vio & multi   .30 .25
Nos. 785-787,C247-C248 (5)   1.30 1.25
Centenary of the birth of Alberto Masferrer, philosopher and scholar.
For surcharges and overprints see Nos. 819, 843A, 890, C297.

Scouts Helping to Build — A201

1968, July 26   Litho.   Perf. 12
788 A201 25c multi   .25 .25
Issued to publicize the 7th Inter-American Boy Scout Conference, July-Aug., 1968. See No. C249.

Map of Central America, Flags and Presidents of US, Costa Rica, Salvador, Guatemala, Honduras and Nicaragua — A202

1968, Dec. 5   Litho.   Perf. 14½
789 A202 10c tan & multi   .25 .25
790 A202 15c multi   .25 .25
Nos. 789-790,C250-C251 (4)   1.50 1.25
Meeting of Pres. Lyndon B. Johnson with the presidents of the Central American republics (J. J. Trejos, Costa Rica; Fidel Sanchez Hernandez, Salvador; J. C. Mendez Montenegro, Guatemala; Osvaldo López Arellano, Honduras; Anastasio Somoza Debayle, Nicaragua), San Salvador, July 5-8, 1968.

Heliconius Charithonius — A203

Various Butterflies.

1969   Litho.   Perf. 12
791 A203 5c bluish lil, blk & yel   7.25 .25
792 A203 10c beige & multi   7.25 .25
793 A203 30c lt grn & multi   7.25 .35
794 A203 50c tan & multi   7.25 .55
Nos. 791-794,C252-C255 (8)   78.25 9.65
For surcharge see No. C353.

Red Cross Activities A204

1969   Litho.   Perf. 12
795 A204 10c lt bl & multi   .25 .25
796 A204 20c pink & multi   .25 .25
797 A204 40c lil & multi   .35 .25
Nos. 795-797,C256-C258 (6)   6.60 4.00
50th anniv. of the League of Red Cross Societies.

No. 749 Ovptd. in Green "Alunizaje / Apolo-11 / 21 Julio / 1969"

1969, Sept.   Photo.   Perf. 11½x12
798 A189 50c pink & blk   .55 .30
Man's first landing on the moon, July 20, 1969. See note after US No. C76. See No. C259.

Social Security Hospital A205

1969, Oct. 24   Litho.   Perf. 11½
799 A205 6c multi   .25 .25
800 A205 10c multi, diff.   .25 .25
801 A205 30c multi, diff.   .30 .25
Nos. 799-801,C260-C262 (6)   7.50 4.75
For surcharges see Nos. 857, C355.

ILO Emblem — A206

1969   Litho.   Perf. 13
802 A206 10c yel & multi   .25 .25
50th anniv. of the ILO. See No. C263.

Chorros Spa A207

Views: 40c, Jaltepeque Bay. 80c, Fountains, Amapulapa Spa.

1969, Dec. 19   Photo.   Perf. 12x11½
803 A207 10c blk & multi   .25 .25
804 A207 40c blk & multi   .25 .25
805 A207 80c blk & multi   .55 .40
Nos. 803-805,C264-C266 (6)   1.95 1.70
Tourism.

Euchroma Gigantea — A208

Insects: 25c, Grasshopper. 30c, Digger wasp.

1970, Feb. 24   Litho.   Perf. 11½x11
806 A208 5c lt bl & multi   .40 .25
807 A208 25c dl yel & multi   .75 .25
808 A208 30c dl rose & multi   .75 .25
Nos. 806-808,C267-C269 (6)   14.40 5.50
For surcharges see Nos. C371-C373.

Map and Arms of Salvador, National Unity Emblem A209

1970, Apr. 14   Litho.   Perf. 14
809 A209 10c yel & multi   .25 .25
810 A209 40c pink & multi   .40 .25
Nos. 809-810,C270-C271 (4)   1.70 1.05
Salvador's support of universal human rights. For overprints and surcharge see Nos. 823, C301, C402.

Soldiers with Flag A210

Design: 30c, Anti-aircraft gun.

1970, May 7   Perf. 12
811 A210 10c green & multi ..... .25 .25
812 A210 30c lemon & multi ..... .25 .25
    Nos. 811-812,C272-C274 (5) 1.50 1.25
Issued for Army Day, May 7.
For overprints see Nos. 836, C310.

National Lottery
Headquarters
A211

1970, July 15   Litho.   Perf. 12
813 A211 20c lt vio & multi ..... .25 .25
National Lottery centenary. See No. C291.

UN and
Education
Year
Emblems
A212

1970, Sept. 11   Litho.   Perf. 12
814 A212 50c multi ..... .40 .25
815 A212 1col multi ..... .80 .40
    Nos. 814-815,C292-C293 (4) 3.05 1.70
Issued for International Education Year.

Map of
Salvador,
Globe and
Cogwheels
A213

1970, Oct. 28   Litho.   Perf. 12
816 A213 5c pink & multi ..... .25 .25
817 A213 10c buff & multi ..... .25 .25
    Nos. 816-817,C294-C295 (4) 1.05 1.00
4th International Fair, San Salvador.

Beethoven — A214

1971, Feb. 22   Litho.   Perf. 13½
818 A214 50c ol, brn & yel ..... .85 .25
Second International Music Festival. See
No. C296. For overprint see No. 833.

No. 787 Ovptd. "Año / del Centenario de la / Biblioteca Nacional / 1970"
1970, Nov. 25   Perf. 12x11½
819 A200 25c vio & multi ..... .25 .25
Cent. of the National Library. See No. C297.

Maria Elena
Sol — A215

1971, Apr. 1   Litho.   Perf. 14
820 A215 10c lt grn & multi ..... .25 .25
821 A215 30c multi ..... .30 .25
    Nos. 820-821,C298-C299 (4) 1.35 1.05
Maria Elena Sol, Miss World Tourism, 1970-
71. For overprint see No. 832.

Pietà, by
Michelangelo
A216

1971, May 10
822 A216 10c salmon & vio brn ..... .25 .25
Mother's Day, 1971. See No. C300.

No. 810 Overprinted in Red

1971, July 6   Litho.   Perf. 14
823 A209 40c pink & multi ..... .60 .25
National Police, 104th anniv. See #C301.

Tiger Sharks — A217

1971, July 28
824 A217 10c shown ..... 1.40 .30
825 A217 40c Swordfish ..... 1.75 .35
    Nos. 824-825,C302-C303 (4) 8.75 2.10

Declaration of Independence — A218

Designs: Various sections of Declaration of
Independence of Central America.

1971   Perf. 13½x13
826 A218 5c yel grn & blk ..... .25 .25
827 A218 10c brt rose & blk ..... .25 .25
828 A218 15c dp org & blk ..... .25 .25
829 A218 20c dp red lil & blk ..... .25 .25
    Nos. 826-829,C304-C307 (8) 2.40 2.10
Sesquicentennial of independence of Central America.
For overprints see Nos. C321, C347.

Izalco
Church
A219

Design: 30c, Sonsonate Church.

1971, Aug. 21   Litho.   Perf. 13x13½
830 A219 20c blk & multi ..... .25 .25
831 A219 30c pur & multi ..... .30 .25
    Nos. 830-831,C308-C309 (4) 1.35 1.10

No. 821 Ovptd. in Carmine: "1972 Año de Turismo / de las Américas"
1972, Nov. 15   Litho.   Perf. 14
832 A215 30c multi ..... .35 .25
Tourist Year of the Americas, 1972.

No. 818 Overprinted in Red

1973, Feb. 5   Litho.   Perf. 13½
833 A214 50c ol, brn & yel ..... .35 .25
3rd Intl. Music Festival, Feb. 9-25. See No.
C313.

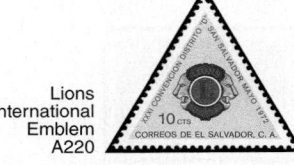

Lions
International
Emblem
A220

1973, Feb. 20   Litho.   Perf. 13
834 A220 10c pink & multi ..... .25 .25
835 A220 25c lt bl & multi ..... .25 .25
    Nos. 834-835,C314-C315 (4) 1.05 1.00
31st Lions International District "D" Convention, San Salvador, May 1972.

No. 812 Ovptd. "1923 1973 / 50 AÑOS FUNDACION / FUERZA AEREA"
1973, Mar. 20   Litho.   Perf. 12
836 A210 30c lem & multi ..... .35 .25
50th anniversary of Salvadorian Air Force.

Hurdling
A221

1973, May 21   Litho.   Perf. 13
837 A221 5c shown ..... .25 .25
838 A221 10c High jump ..... .25 .25
839 A221 25c Running ..... .25 .25
840 A221 60c Pole vault ..... .30 .25
    Nos. 837-840,C316-C319 (8) 6.50 3.05
20th Olympic Games, Munich, Aug. 26-
Sept. 11, 1972.

No. 777
Surcharged

1973, Dec.   Photo.   Perf. 13
841 A198 10c on 70c multi ..... .30 .25
See No. C320.

Nos. 774, C240 Srchd. with New Value and Ovptd. "1823-1973 / 150 Aniversario Liberación / Esclavos en Centroamérica"
1973-74   Litho.   Perf. 11½
841A A197 5c on 6c multi ('74) ..... .25 .25
842 A197 10c on 45c multi ..... .45 .25
Sesquicentennial of the liberation of the
slaves in Central America. On No. 841A two
bars cover old denomination. On No. 842
"Aereo" is obliterated with a bar and old
denomination with two bars.

Nos. 747 and
786
Surcharged

1974   Photo.   Perf. 11½x12
843 A189 5c on 6c buff & blk ..... .30 .25

Litho.   Perf. 12x11½
843A A200 5c on 6c multi ..... .75 .25
No. 843A has one obliterating rectangle and
sans-serif "5."
    Issued: #843, Apr. 22; #843A, June 21.

Rehabilitation
Institute
Emblem
A222

1974, Apr. 30   Litho.   Perf. 13
844 A222 10c multi ..... .25 .25
10th anniversary of the Salvador Rehabilitation Institute. See No. C324.

INTERPOL
Headquarters,
Saint-Cloud,
France — A223

1974, Sept. 2   Litho.   Perf. 12½
845 A223 10c multi ..... .25 .25
50th anniv. of Intl. Criminal Police Organization (INTERPOL). See No. C341.

UN and FAO
Emblems
A224

1974, Sept. 2   Litho.   Perf. 12½
846 A224 10c bl, dk bl & gold ..... .25 .25
World Food Program, 10th anniv. See
#C342.

25c Silver
Coin, 1914
A225

1974, Nov. 19   Litho.   Perf. 12½x13
848 A225 10c shown ..... .25 .25
849 A225 15c 50c silver, 1953 ..... .25 .25
850 A225 25c 25c silver, 1943 ..... .25 .25
851 A225 30c 1c copper, 1892 ..... .25 .25
    Nos. 848-851,C343-C346 (8) 2.55 2.10

No. 763
Surcharged

1974, Oct. 14 Photo. Perf. 11½x12
852 A192 5c on 6c multi .75 .25
12th Central American and Caribbean Chess Tournament, Oct. 1974.

No. 762 and 771
Surcharged

1974-75 Perf. 11½x12, 12
853 A192 10c on 3c multi .35 .25
853A A195 25c on 1col multi ('75) .35 .25
Bar and surcharge on one line on No. 853A. Issued: #853, Dec. 19; #853A, Jan. 13.

UPU Emblem
A226

1975, Jan. 22 Litho. Perf. 13
854 A226 10c bl & multi .25 .25
855 A226 60c bl & multi .35 .30
Nos. 854-855,C356-C357 (4) 1.10 1.05
Cent. of UPU.

Acajutla
Harbor
A227

1975, Feb. 17
856 A227 10c blue & multi .25 .25
See No. C358.

No. 799 Surcharged

1975 Litho. Perf. 11½
857 A205 5c on 6c multi .35 .25

Central Post
Office, San
Salvador
A228

1975, Apr. 25 Litho. Perf. 13
858 A228 10c bl & multi .25 .25
See No. C359.

Map of
Americas
and El
Salvador,
Trophy
A229

1975, June 25 Litho. Perf. 12½
859 A229 10c red org & multi .25 .25
860 A229 40c yel & multi .30 .25
Nos. 859-860,C360-C361 (4) 1.35 1.15
El Salvador, site of 1975 Miss Universe Contest.

Claudia Lars,
Poet, and IWY
Emblem — A230

1975, Sept. 4 Litho. Perf. 12½
861 A230 10c yel & bl blk .25 .25
Nos. 861,C362-C363 (3) .80 .75
Intl. Women's Year 1975.

Nurses
Attending
Patient
A231

1975, Oct. 24 Litho. Perf. 12½
862 A231 10c lt grn & multi .25 .25
Nurses' Day. See No. C364. For overprint see No. 868.

Congress
Emblem — A232

1975, Nov. 19 Litho. Perf. 12½
863 A232 10c yel & multi .25 .25
15th Conference of Inter-American Federation of Securities Enterprises, San Salvador, Nov. 16-20. See No. C365.

**No. 768 Ovptd. in Red "XVI /
CONGRESO MEDICO /
CENTROAMERICANO / SAN
SALVADOR, / EL SALVADOR, / DIC.
10-13, 1975"**

1975, Nov. 26 Photo. Perf. 12x11½
864 A194 15c beige & multi .35 .25
16th Central American Medical Congress, San Salvador, Dec. 10-13.

Flags of
Participants,
Arms of
Salvador
A233

1975, Nov. 28 Litho. Perf. 12½
865 A233 15c blk & multi .25 .25
866 A233 50c brn & multi .30 .25
Nos. 865-866,C366-C367 (4) 1.05 1.00
8th Ibero-Latin-American Dermatological Congress, San Salvador, Nov. 28-Dec. 3.

Jesus and Caritas
Emblem — A234

1975, Dec. 18 Litho. Perf. 13½
867 A234 10c dull red & maroon .25 .25
7th Latin American Charity Congress, San Salvador, Nov. 1971. See No. C368.

**No. 862 Ovptd. "III CONGRESO /
ENFERMERIA / CENCAMEX 76"**

1976, May 10 Litho. Perf. 12½
868 A231 10c lt grn & multi .35 .25
CENCAMEX 76, 3rd Nurses' Congress.

Map of El
Salvador
A235

1976, May 18
869 A235 10c vio bl & multi .25 .25
10th Congress of Revenue Collectors (Centro Interamericano de Administradores Tributarios, CIAT), San Salvador, May 16-22. See No. C382.

Flags of
Salvador
and US,
Torch,
Map of
Americas
A236

The Spirit of
'76, by
Archibald M.
Willard — A237

1976, June 30 Litho. Perf. 12½
870 A236 10c yel & multi .25 .25
871 A237 40c multi .25 .25
Nos. 870-871,C383-C384 (4) 4.50 3.25
American Bicentennial.

American Crocodile — A238

1976, Sept. 23 Litho. Perf. 12½
872 A238 10c shown .30 .25
873 A238 20c Green iguana .65 .25
874 A238 30c Iguana .95 .25
Nos. 872-874,C385-C387 (6) 5.20 1.65

Post-classical
Vase, San
Salvador
A239

Pre-Columbian Art: 15c, Brazier with classical head, Tazumal. 40c, Vase with classical head, Tazumal.

1976, Oct. 11 Litho. Perf. 12½
875 A239 10c multi .25 .25
876 A239 15c multi .25 .25
877 A239 40c multi .30 .25
Nos. 875-877,C388-C390 (6) 2.10 1.65
For overprint see No. C429.

Fair Emblem
A240

1976, Oct. 25 Litho. Perf. 12½
878 A240 10c multi .25 .25
879 A240 30c gray & multi .25 .25
Nos. 878-879,C391-C392 (4) 1.30 1.15
7th Intl. Fair, Nov. 5-22.

Child under
Christmas
Tree — A241

1976, Dec. 16 Litho. Perf. 11
880 A241 10c yel & multi .25 .25
881 A241 15c buff & multi .25 .25
882 A241 30c vio & multi .25 .25
883 A241 40c pink & multi .30 .30
Nos. 880-883,C393-C396 (8) 2.80 2.25
Christmas 1976.

Rotary
Emblem, Map
of Salvador
A242

1977, June 20 Litho. Perf. 11
884 A242 10c multi .25 .25
885 A242 15c multi .25 .25
Nos. 884-885,C397-C398 (4) 1.55 1.25
San Salvador Rotary Club, 50th anniversary.

Cerron Grande Hydroelectric
Station — A243

Designs: No. 887, 15c, Central sugar refinery, Jiboa. 30c, Izalco satellite earth station, vert.

1977, June 29 Perf. 12½
886 A243 10c multi .25 .25
887 A243 10c multi .25 .25
888 A243 15c multi .25 .25
889 A243 30c multi .25 .25
Nos. 886-889,C399-C401 (7) 2.25 1.90
Industrial development. Nos. 886-889 have colorless overprint in multiple rows: GOBIERNO DEL SALVADOR.

**Nos. 785 and 774 Srchd. with New
Value and Bar**

1977, June 30 Perf. 12x11½, 11½
890 A200 15c on 2c multi .25 .25
891 A197 25c on 6c multi .30 .25

Microphone, ASDER Emblem — A244

1977, Sept. 14   Litho.   Perf. 14
892 A244 10c multi   .25   .25
893 A244 15c multi   .25   .25
  Nos. 892-893,C406-C407 (4)   1.00 1.00
Broadcasting in El Salvador, 50th anniversary (Asociacion Salvadoreño de Empresa Radio).

Wooden Drum A245

Design: 10c, Flute and recorder.

1978, Aug. 29   Litho.   Perf. 12½
894 A245 5c multi   .25   .25
895 A245 10c multi   .25   .25
  Nos. 894-895,C433-C435 (5)   1.85 1.40
For surcharge see No. C492.

"Man and Engineering" A246

1978, Sept. 12   Litho.   Perf. 13½
896 A246 10c multi   .25   .25
4th National Engineers' Congress, San Salvador, Sept. 18-23. See No. C436.

Izalco Station A247

1978, Sept. 14   Perf. 12½
897 A247 10c multi   .25   .25
Inauguration of Izalco satellite earth station, Sept. 15, 1978. See No. C437.

Fair Emblem A248

1978, Oct. 30   Litho.   Perf. 12½
898 A248 10c multi   .25   .25
899 A248 20c multi   .25   .25
  Nos. 898-899,C440-C441 (4)   1.00 1.00
8th Intl. Fair, Nov. 3-20.

Henri Dunant, Red Cross Emblem A249

1978, Oct. 30   Perf. 11
900 A249 10c multi   .25   .25
Henri Dunant (1828-1910), founder of the Red Cross. See No. C442.

World Map and Cotton Boll A250

1978, Nov. 22   Perf. 12½
901 A250 15c multi   .25   .25
Intl. Cotton Consulting Committee, 37th Meeting, San Salvador, 11/27-12/2. See #C443.

Nativity, Stained-glass Window A251

1978, Dec. 5   Litho.   Perf. 12½
902 A251 10c multi   .25   .25
903 A251 15c multi   .25   .25
  Nos. 902-903,C444-C445 (4)   1.55 1.25
Christmas 1978.

Athenaeum Coat of Arms — A252

1978, Dec. 20   Litho.   Perf. 14
904 A252 5c multi   .25   .25
Millennium of Castilian language. See No. C446.

Postal Service and UPU Emblems A253

1979, Apr. 2   Litho.   Perf. 14
905 A253 10c multi   .25   .25
Centenary of Salvador's membership in Universal Postal Union. See No. C447.

"75," Health Organization and WHO Emblems — A254

1979, Apr. 7   Perf. 14x14½
906 A254 10c multi   .25   .25
Pan-American Health Organization, 75th anniversary. See No. C448.

Flame and Pillars — A255

1979, May 25   Litho.   Perf. 12½
907 A255 10c multi   .25   .25
908 A255 15c multi   .25   .25
  Nos. 907-908,C449-C450 (4)   1.55 1.25
Social Security 5-year plan, 1978-1982.

Pope John Paul II, Map of Americas A256

1979, July 12   Litho.   Perf. 14½x14
909 A256 10c multi   .25   .25
910 A256 20c multi   .25   .25
  Nos. 909-910,C454-C455 (4)   5.00 3.30

Mastodon A257

1979, Sept. 7   Litho.   Perf. 14
911 A257 10c shown   .30   .25
912 A257 20c Saber-toothed tiger   .30   .25
913 A257 30c Toxodon   .50   .30
  Nos. 911-913,C458-C460 (6)   4.70 2.40

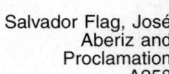

Salvador Flag, José Aberiz and Proclamation A258

1979, Sept. 14   Perf. 14½x14
914 A258 10c multi   .25   .25
National anthem centenary. See No. C461.

Cogwheel around Map of Americas A259

1979, Oct. 19   Litho.   Perf. 14½x14
915 A259 10c multi   .25   .25
8th COPIMERA Congress (Mechanical, Electrical and Allied Trade Engineers), San Salvador, Oct. 22-27. See No. C462.

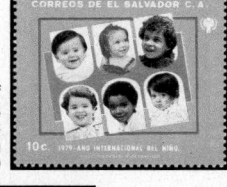

Children of Various Races, IYC Emblem A260

Children and Nurses, IYC Emblem A261

1979, Oct. 29   Perf. 14x14½, 14½x14
916 A260 10c multi   .25   .25
917 A261 15c multi   .25   .25
International Year of the Child.

Map of Central and South America, Congress Emblem — A262

1979, Nov. 1   Litho.   Perf. 14½x14
918 A262 10c multi   .25   .25
5th Latin American Clinical Biochemistry Cong., San Salvador, 11/5-10. See #C465.

Coffee Bushes in Bloom, Coffee Association Emblem A263

Salvador Coffee Assoc., 50th Anniv.: 30c, Planting coffee bushes, vert. 40c, Coffee berries.

1979, Dec. 18   Perf. 14x14½, 14½x14
919 A263 10c multi   .25   .25
920 A263 30c multi   .25   .25
921 A263 40c multi   .30   .30
  Nos. 919-921,C466-C468 (6)   2.60 2.00

Children, Dove and Star — A264

1979, Dec. 18   **Perf. 14½x14**
922 A264 10c multi   .35 .25
Christmas 1979.

Hoof and Mouth Disease Prevention A265

1980, June 3   **Litho.**   **Perf. 14½x14**
923 A265 10c multi   .25 .25
See No. C469.

Anadara Grandis A266

1980, Aug. 12   **Perf. 14x14½**
924 A266 10c shown   .40 .25
925 A266 30c Ostrea iridescens   .80 .25
926 A266 40c Turitello leucos-
     toma   1.25 .25
   Nos. 924-926,C470-C473 (7)   8.40 2.05

Quetzal (Pharomachrus mocino) — A267

1980, Sept. 10   **Litho.**   **Perf. 14x14½**
927 A267 10c shown   1.25 .30
928 A267 20c Penelopina nigra   1.25 .30
   Nos. 927-928,C474-C476 (5)   11.60 1.60

Local Snakes A268

1980, Nov. 12   **Litho.**   **Perf. 14x14½**
929 A268 10c Tree snake   1.60 .30
930 A268 20c Water snake   1.75 .30
   Nos. 929-930,C477-C478 (4)   9.25 1.15

Corporation of Auditors, 50th Anniv. — A269

1980, Nov. 26   **Litho.**   **Perf. 14**
931 A269 15c multi   .25 .25
932 A269 20c multi   .25 .25
   Nos. 931-932,C479-C480 (4)   1.50 1.15

Christmas A270

1980, Dec. 5   **Litho.**   **Perf. 14**
933 A270 5c multi   .25 .25
934 A270 10c multi   .25 .25
   Nos. 933-934,C481-C482 (4)   1.35 1.05

Dental Assoc. Emblems — A271

1981, June 18   **Litho.**   **Perf. 14**
935 A271 15c lt yel grn & blk   .25 .25
Dental Society of Salvador, 50th anniv.;
Odontological Federation of Central America
and Panama, 25th anniv. See No. C494.

Hands Reading Braille Book — A272

1981, Aug. 14   **Litho.**   **Perf. 14x14½**
936 A272 10c multi   .25 .25
   Nos. 936,C495-C498 (5)   2.30 1.70
Intl. Year of the Disabled.

A273

1981, Aug. 28   **Litho.**   **Perf. 14x14½**
937 A273 10c multi   .25 .25
Roberto Quinonez Natl. Agriculture College,
25th anniv. See No. C499.

World Food Day — A274

1981, Sept. 16   **Litho.**   **Perf. 14x14½**
938 A274 10c multi   .25 .25
See No. C500.

1981 World Cup Preliminaries — A275

40c, Cup soccer ball, flags.

1981, Nov. 27   **Litho.**   **Perf. 14x14½**
939 A275 10c shown   .25 .25
940 A275 40c multicolored   .45 .25
   Nos. 939-940,C505-C506 (4)   1.60 1.15

Salvador Lyceum (High School), 100th Anniv. — A276

1981, Dec. 17   **Litho.**   **Perf. 14**
941 A276 10c multi   .25 .25
See No. C507.

Pre-Columbian Stone Sculptures A277

10c, Axe with bird's head. 20c, Sun disc.
40c, Stele Carving with effigy.

1982, Jan. 22   **Litho.**   **Perf. 14**
942 A277 10c multicolored   .25 .25
943 A277 20c multicolored   .25 .25
944 A277 40c multicolored   .30 .30
   Nos. 942-944,C508-C510 (6)   2.00 1.75

Scouting Year — A278

30c, Girl Scout helping woman.

1982, Mar. 17   **Litho.**   **Perf. 14½x14**
945 A278 10c shown   .25 .25
946 A278 30c multicolored   .25 .25
   Nos. 945-946,C511-C512 (4)   1.15 1.00

Armed Forces A279

1982, May 7   **Litho.**   **Perf. 14x13½**
947 A279 10c multi   .25 .25
See No. C514.

1982 World Cup A280

1982, July 14   **Perf. 14x14½**
948 A280 10c Team, emblem   .25 .25
   Nos. 948,C518-C520 (4)   2.60 1.85

10th International Fair — A281

1982, Oct. 14   **Litho.**   **Perf. 14**
949 A281 10c multi   .25 .25
See No. C524.

Christmas 1982 — A282

1982, Dec. 14   **Litho.**   **Perf. 14**
950 A282 5c multi   .25 .25
See No. C528.

Dancers, Pre-Colombian Ceramic Design — A283

1983, Feb. 18   **Litho.**   **Perf. 14**
951 A283 10c shown   .25 .25
952 A283 20c Sower   .25 .25
953 A283 25c Flying Man   .30 .25
954 A283 60c Hunters   .55 .50
955 A283 60c Hunters, diff.   .55 .50
  a.   Pair, #954-955   1.10 1.10
956 A283 1col Procession   .75 .60
957 A283 1col Procession, diff.   .75 .60
  a.   Pair, #956-957   1.75 1.75
   Nos. 951-957 (7)   3.40 2.95
Nos. 953-957 airmail. #955a, 957a have
continuous designs.

Visit of Pope John Paul II — A284

60c, Monument to the Divine Savior, Pope.

1983, Mar. 4   **Litho.**   **Perf. 14**
958 A284 25c shown   .25 .25
959 A284 60c multicolored   .55 .30

Salvadoran Air Force, 60th Anniv. A285

1983, Mar. 24   **Litho.**   **Perf. 14**
960 A285 10c Ricardo Aberle   .25 .25
961 A285 10c Air Force Emblem   .25 .25
962 A285 10c Enrico Massi   .25 .25
  a.   Strip of 3, #960-962   .75 .75

963 A285 10c Juan Ramon Munes .25 .25
964 A285 10c American Air Force
Cooperation Em-
blem .25 .25
965 A285 10c Belisario Salazar .25 .25
a. Strip of 3, #963-965 .75 .75

Arranged se-tenant horizontally with two
Nos. 960 or 963 at left and two Nos. 962 or
965 at right.

Local butterflies — A286

1983, May 31 Litho. **Perf. 14**
966 A286 Pair 1.40 1.40
a. 5c Papilio torquatus .35 .35
b. 5c Metamorpha steneles .35 .35
967 A286 Pair 1.75 1.75
a. 10c Papilio torquatus, diff. .75 .75
b. 10c Anaea marthesia .75 .75
968 A286 Pair 2.25 2.25
a. 15c Prepona brooksiana 1.10 1.10
b. 15c Caligo atreus 1.10 1.10
969 A286 Pair 3.50 3.50
a. 25c Morpho peleides 1.90 1.90
b. 25c Dismorphia praxinoe 1.90 1.90
970 A286 Pair 7.00 7.00
a. 50c Morpho polyphemus 2.25 2.25
b. 50c Metamorphia epaphus 2.25 2.25
Nos. 966-970 (5) 15.90 15.90

Simon Bolivar,
200th Birth
Anniv. — A287

1983, June 23 Litho. **Perf. 14**
971 A287 75c multi .70 .50

Dr. Jose
Mendoza,
College
Emblem.
A288

1983, July 21 Litho. **Perf. 14**
972 A288 10c multicolored .40 .25

Salvador Medical College, 40th anniv.

A289

Perf. 13½x14, 14x13½
1983, Oct. 30 Litho.
973 A289 10c multi .25 .25
974 A289 50c multi, horiz. .40 .40

Centenary of David J. Guzman national
museum. 50c airmail.

World Communications Year — A290

10c, Gen. Juan Jose Canas, Francisco
Duenas (organizers of 1st natl. telegraph service), Morse key, 1870. 25c, Mailman delivering letters. 50c, Post Office sorting center,
San Salvador. 25c, 50c airmail.

Perf. 14x13½, 13½x14
1983, Nov. 23 Litho.
975 A290 10c multi .25 .25
976 A290 25c multi, vert. .25 .25
977 A290 50c multi .40 .30
Nos. 975-977 (3) .90 .80

Dove Over
Globe — A291

25c, Creche figures, horiz.

Perf. 13½x14, 14x13½
1983, Nov. 30
978 A291 10c shown .25 .25
979 A291 25c multicolored .30 .25

Christmas. 25c is airmail.

Environmental
Protection
A292

1983, Dec. 13
980 A292 10c Vehicle exhaust .40 .25
981 A292 15c Fig tree .50 .25
982 A292 25c Rodent .80 .25
Nos. 980-982 (3) 1.70 .75

15c, 25c airmail.

Philatelists'
Day
A293

1984, Jan. 5 **Perf. 14x13½**
983 A293 10c No. 1 .40 .25

Corn — A294

1984, Feb. 21 Litho. **Perf. 14½x14**
984 A294 10c shown .25 .25
985 A294 15c Cotton .25 .25
986 A294 25c Coffee beans .30 .25
987 A294 50c Sugar cane .50 .25
988 A294 75c Beans .80 .25
989 A294 1col Agave .30 .50
990 A294 5col Balsam 1.25 2.40
Nos. 984-990 (7) 3.65 4.15
See Nos. 1047-1051.

Caluco
Church,
Sonsonate
A295

10c, Salcoatitan, Sonsonate. 15c, Huizucar,
La Libertad. 25c, Santo Domingo, Sonsonate.
50c, Pilar, Sonsonate. 75c, Nahuizalco,
Sonsonate.

1984, Mar. 30 **Perf. 14x13½**
991 A295 5c multicolored .25 .25
992 A295 10c multicolored .25 .25
993 A295 15c multicolored .25 .25
994 A295 25c multicolored .25 .25
995 A295 50c multicolored .30 .25
996 A295 75c multicolored .40 .25
Nos. 991-996 (6) 1.70 1.50
Nos. 993-996 airmail.

Central
Reserve
Bank of
Salvador,
50th Anniv.
A296

1984, July 17 Litho. **Perf. 14x14½**
997 A296 10c First reserve note .25 .25
998 A296 25c Bank, 1959 .25 .25
25c airmail.

1984
Summer
Olympics
A297

1984, July 20 **Perf. 14x13½, 13½x14**
999 A297 10c Boxing .30 .25
1000 A297 25c Running, vert. .30 .25
1001 A297 40c Bicycling .40 .25
1002 A297 50c Swimming .50 .25
1003 A297 75c Judo, vert. .75 .30
1004 A297 1col Pierre de
Coubertin 1.00 .30
Nos. 999-1004 (6) 3.25 1.60
Nos. 1000-1004 airmail.
For surcharge see No. C536A.

Govt.
Printing
Office
Building
Opening
A298

1984, July 27 **Perf. 14x13½**
1005 A298 10c multi .40 .25

5th of November Hydroelectric
Plant — A299

Designs: 55c, Cerron Grande Plant. 70c,
Ahuachapan Geothermal Plant. 90c, Mural.
2col, 15th of September Plant. 70c, 90c, 2 col
airmail.

1984, Sept. 13 Litho. **Perf. 14x14½**
1006 A299 20c multi .30 .25
1007 A299 55c multi .50 .25
1008 A299 70c multi .65 .25

1009 A299 90c multi .80 .30
1010 A299 2col multi 1.75 .50
Nos. 1006-1010 (5) 4.00 1.55

Boys Playing
Marbles
A300

1984, Oct. 16 **Perf. 14½x14**
1011 A300 55c shown .25 .25
1012 A300 70c Spinning top .30 .25
1013 A300 90c Flying kite .40 .30
1014 A300 2col Top, diff. .80 .50
Nos. 1011-1014 (4) 1.75 1.30

11th International Fair — A301

1984, Oct. 31 Litho. **Perf. 14½x14**
1015 A301 25c shown .25 .25
1016 A301 70c Fairgrounds .40 .30
70c airmail.

Los
Chorros
Tourist
Center
A302

25c, Plaza las Americas. 70c, El Salvador
International Airport. 90c, El Tunco Beach.
2col, Sihuatehuacan Tourist Center.

1984, Nov. 23 Litho. **Perf. 14½x14**
1017 A302 15c multicolored .25 .25
1018 A302 25c multicolored .40 .25
1019 A302 70c multicolored .55 .25
1020 A302 90c multicolored .65 .25
1021 A302 2col multicolored 1.40 .50
Nos. 1017-1021 (5) 3.25 1.50

The Paper
of Papers,
1979, by
Roberto A.
Galicia (b.
1945)
A302a

Paintings by natl. artists: 20c, The White
Nun, 1939, by Salvador Salazar Arrue (b.
1899), vert. 70c, Supreme Elegy to Masferrer,
1968, by Antonio G. Ponce (b. 1938), vert.
90c, Transmutation, 1979, by Armando Solis
(b. 1940). 2 col, Figures at Theater, 1959, by
Carlos Canas (b. 1924), vert.

1984, Dec. 10 Litho. **Perf. 14**
1021A A302a 20c multi .25 .25
1021B A302a 55c multi .30 .25
1021C A302a 70c multi .50 .30
1021D A302a 90c multi .50 .30
1021E A302a 2col multi 1.25 .50
Nos. 1021A-1021E (5) 2.80 1.60

Nos. 1021B-1021E are airmail. 70c and
2col issued with overprinted silver bar and corrected inscription in black; copies exist without
overprint.

Christmas
1984 — A303

1984, Dec. 19 **Litho.**
1022 A303 25c Glass ornament .25 .25
1023 A303 70c Ornaments, dove .45 .25
No. 1023 airmail.

Birds — A304

15c, Lepidocolaptes affinis. 25c, Spodiornis rusticus barriliensis. 55c, Claravis mondetoura. 70c, Hylomanes momotula. 90c, Xenotriccus calizonus. 1col, Cardellina rubrifrons.

1984, Dec. 21 **Litho.** **Perf. 14½x14**
1024 A304 15c multicolored .55 .30
1025 A304 25c multicolored .90 .30
1026 A304 55c multicolored 2.25 .50
1027 A304 70c multicolored 2.60 .65
1028 A304 90c multicolored 2.25 .70
1029 A304 1col multicolored 3.50 .80
Nos. 1024-1029 (6) 12.05 3.25
Nos. 1026-1029 airmail.

Salvador Bank Centenary A305

1985, Feb. 6 **Litho.** **Perf. 14**
1030 A305 25c Stock certificate .45 .25

Mortgage Bank, 50th Anniv. — A306

1985, Feb. 20 **Litho.** **Perf. 14**
1031 A306 25c Mortgage .45 .25

Intl. Youth Year A307

25c, IYY emblem. 55c, Woodcrafting. 70c, Professions symbolized. 1.50col, Youths marching.

1985, Feb. 28 **Litho.** **Perf. 14**
1032 A307 25c multicolored .30 .25
1033 A307 55c multicolored .50 .30
1034 A307 70c multicolored .60 .30
1035 A307 1.50col multicolored .90 .55
Nos. 1032-1035 (4) 2.30 1.40
Nos. 1033-1035 airmail.

Archaeology A308

15c, Pre-classical figure. 20c, Engraved vase. 25c, Post-classical ceramic. 55c, Post-classical figure. 70c, Late post-classical deity. 1col, Late post-classical figure.
2col, Tazumal ruins, horiz.

1985, Mar. 6 **Litho.** **Perf. 14½x14**
1036 A308 15c multicolored .35 .25
1037 A308 20c multicolored .40 .25
1038 A308 25c multicolored .50 .25
1039 A308 55c multicolored .90 .30
1040 A308 70c multicolored 1.10 .30
1041 A308 1col multicolored 1.25 .40
Nos. 1036-1041 (6) 4.50 1.75

Souvenir Sheet
Rouletted 13½
1042 A308 2col multicolored 2.00 .75
Nos. 1039-1041 airmail. No. 1042 has enlargement of stamp design in margin.

Natl. Red Cross, Cent. A309

25c, Anniv. emblem vert. 55c, Sea rescue. 70c, Blood donation service. 90c, First aid, ambulance, vert.

1985, Mar. 13 **Litho.** **Perf. 14**
1043 A309 25c multicolored .25 .25
1044 A309 55c multicolored .45 .25
1045 A309 70c multicolored .55 .30
1046 A309 90c multicolored .75 .35
Nos. 1043-1046 (4) 2.00 1.15
Nos. 1044-1046 are airmail.

Agriculture Type of 1984
1985 **Perf. 14½x14**
1047 A294 55c Cotton .55 .25
1048 A294 70c Corn .60 .25
1049 A294 90c Sugar cane .80 .30
1050 A294 2col Beans 1.90 .75
1051 A294 10col Agave 6.00 3.50
Nos. 1047-1051 (5) 9.85 5.05
Issued: 55c, 70c, 90c, 4/4; 2col, 10col, 9/4.

Child Survival A310

Children's drawings.

1985, May 3 **Litho.** **Perf. 14x14½**
1052 A310 25c Hand, houses .25 .25
1053 A310 55c House, children .40 .25
1054 A310 70c Boy, girl holding hands .50 .25
1055 A310 90c Oral vaccination .70 .40
Nos. 1052-1055 (4) 1.85 1.15
Nos. 1053-1055 are airmail.

Salvador Army A311

1985, May 17 **Perf. 14**
1056 A311 25c Map .25 .25
1057 A311 70c Recruit, natl. flag .40 .25
No. 1057 is airmail.

Inauguration of Pres. Duarte, 1st Anniv. — A312

1985, June 28 **Perf. 14½x14**
1058 A312 25c Flag, laurel, book .25 .25
1059 A312 70c Article I, Constitution .35 .25

Inter-American Development Bank, 25th Anniv. — A313

25c, Central Hydro-electric Dam, power station. 70c, Map of Salvador. 1col, Natl. arms.

1985, July 5 **Perf. 14x13½**
1060 A313 25c multi .25 .25
1061 A313 70c multi .55 .25
1062 A313 1col multi .70 .40
Nos. 1060-1062 (3) 1.50 .90
Nos. 1061-1062 are airmail.

Fish A314

25c, Cichlasoma trimaculatum. 55c, Rhamdia guatemalensis. 70c, Poecilia sphenops. 90c, Cichlasoma nigrofasciatum. 1col, Astyanax fasciatus. 1.50col, Dormitator latifrons.

1985, Sept. 30 **Perf. 14x14½**
1064 A314 25c multi .45 .25
1065 A314 55c multi .65 .25
1066 A314 70c multi .75 .25
1067 A314 90c multi .85 .30
1068 A314 1col multi 1.00 .30
1069 A314 1.50col multi 1.50 .40
Nos. 1064-1069 (6) 5.20 1.75
Nos. 1065-1069 are airmail.

UNFAO, 40th Anniv. — A315

1985, Oct. 16 **Perf. 14½x14**
1070 A315 20c Cornucopia .30 .25
1071 A315 40c Centeotl, Nahuat god of corn .40 .25

Dragonflies A316

25c, Cordulegaster godmani mclachlan. 55c, Libellula herculea karsch. 70c, Cora marina selys. 90c, Aeshna cornigera braver. 1col, Mecistogaster ornata rambur. 1.50col, Hetaerina smaragdalis de marmels.

1985, Dec. 9 **Perf. 14x14½**
1072 A316 25c multi .40 .25
1073 A316 55c multi .60 .25
1074 A316 70c multi .75 .25
1075 A316 90c multi .85 .30
1076 A316 1col multi 1.00 .30
1077 A316 1.50col multi 1.50 .40
Nos. 1072-1077 (6) 5.10 1.75
Nos. 1073-1077 are airmail.
For surcharge see No. C544.

Summer, 1984, by Roberto Huezo (b.1947) A317

Paintings by natl. artists: 25c, Profiles, 1978, by Rosa Mena Valenzuela (b. 1924), vert. 70c, The Deliverance, 1984, by Fernando Llort (b. 1949). 90c, Making Tamale, 1975, by Pedro A. Garcia (b. 1930). 1col, Warm Presence, 1984, by Miguel A. Orellana (b. 1929), vert. Nos. 1079-1082 are airmail.

1985, Dec. 18 **Perf. 14**
1078 A317 25c multi .25 .25
1079 A317 55c multi .25 .25
1080 A317 70c multi .35 .25
1081 A317 90c multi .45 .30
1082 A317 1col multi .55 .35
Nos. 1078-1082 (5) 1.85 1.40

San Vicente de Austria y Lorenzana City, 350th Anniv. A318

1985, Dec. 20
1083 A318 15c Tower, vert. .25 .25
1084 A318 20c Cathedral .30 .25

Intl. Peace Year 1986 — A319

70c, Dove over people's outstretched arms.

1986, Feb. 21 **Litho.** **Perf. 14**
1085 A319 15c multi .30 .25
1086 A319 70c multi .70 .50
No. 1086 is airmail.

Postal Code Inauguration — A320

1986, Mar. 14 Litho. Perf. 14x14½
1087 A320 20c Domestic mail .25 .25
1088 A320 25c Intl. mail .25 .25

Radio El Salvador, 60th Anniv. A321

1986, Mar. 21
1089 A321 25c Microphone .25 .25
1090 A321 70c Map .50 .40
No. 1090 is airmail.

Mammals A322

15c, Felis wiedii. 20c, Tamandua tetradactyla. 1col, Dasypus novemcinctus. 2col, Pecarii tajacu.

1986, May 30 Litho. Perf. 14x14½
1091 A322 15c multicolored .25 .25
1092 A322 20c multicolored .30 .25
1093 A322 1col multicolored 1.40 .60
1094 A322 2col multicolored 2.75 1.25
Nos. 1091-1094 (4) 4.70 2.35
Nos. 1093-1094 are airmail.

1986 World Cup Soccer Championships, Mexico — A323

Designs: 70c, Flags, mascot. 1col, Players, Soccer Cup, vert. 2col, Natl. flag, player dribbling, vert. 5col, Goal, emblem.

1986, June 6 Perf. 14x14½, 14½x14
1095 A323 70c multi .65 .45
1096 A323 1col multi 1.00 .65
1097 A323 2col multi 1.90 1.40
1098 A323 5col multi 4.50 3.25
Nos. 1095-1098 (4) 8.05 5.75

Teachers — A324

1986, June 30 Litho. Perf. 14½x14
1099 A324 20c Dario Gonzalez .25 .25
1100 A324 20c Valero Lecha .25 .25
a. A324 Pair, #1099-1100 .35 .35
1101 A324 40c Marcelino G. Flamenco .25 .25
1102 A324 40c Camilo Campos .25 .25
a. A324 Pair, #1101-1102 .70 .70
1103 A324 70c Saul Flores .35 .25
1104 A324 70c Jorge Larde .35 .25
a. A324 Pair, #1103-1104 1.10 1.10
1105 A324 1col Francisco Moran .50 .35
1106 A324 1col Mercedes M. De Luarca .50 .35
a. A324 Pair, #1105-1106 1.75 1.75
Nos. 1099-1106 (8) 2.70 2.20
Nos. 1103-1106 are airmail.

Pre-Hispanic Ceramic Seal, Cara Sucia, Ahuachapan, Tlaloc Culture (300 B.C.-A.D. 1200) — A325

1986, July 23 Litho. Perf. 13½
1107 A325 25c org & brn .30 .25
1108 A325 55c grn, org & brn .45 .25
1109 A325 70c pale gray, org & brn .55 .25
1110 A325 90c pale yel, org & brn .80 .30
1111 A325 1col pale grn, org & brn .90 .35
1112 A325 1.50col pale pink, org & brn 1.40 .50
Nos. 1107-1112 (6) 4.40 1.90
Nos. 1108-1112 are airmail.

World Food Day A326

1986, Oct. 30 Litho. Perf. 14x14½
1113 A326 20c multi .40 .25

Flowers A327

20c, Spathiphyllum phryniifolium, vert. 25c, Asclepias curassavica. 70c, Tagetes tenuifolia. 1col, Ipomoea tiliacea, vert.

1986, Sept. 30 Perf. 14
1114 A327 20c multi .65 .25
1115 A327 25c multi .65 .25
1116 A327 70c multi 1.60 .40
1117 A327 1col multi 2.00 .55
Nos. 1114-1117 (4) 4.90 1.45
Nos. 1116-1117 are airmail.

Christmas A328

Perf. 14x14½, 14½x14
1986, Dec. 10 Litho.
1118 A328 25c Candles, vert. .25 .25
1119 A328 70c Doves .60 .25
No. 1119 is airmail.

Crafts A329

1986, Dec. 18
1120 A329 25c Basket-making .35 .25
1121 A329 55c Ceramicware .45 .25
1122 A329 70c Guitars, vert. .55 .30
1123 A329 1col Baskets, diff. .75 .45
Nos. 1120-1123 (4) 2.10 1.25

Christmas A330

Paintings: 25c, Church, by Mario Araujo Rajo, vert. 70c, Landscape, by Francisco Reyes.

1986, Dec. 22
1124 A330 25c multi .25 .25
1125 A330 70c multi .40 .25
No. 1125 is airmail.

Promotion of Philately A331

1987, Mar. 10 Litho. Perf. 14½x14
1126 A331 25c multi .50 .25

Intl. Aid Following Earthquake, Oct. 10, 1986 — A332

1987, Mar. 25
1127 A332 15c multi .30 .25
1128 A332 70c multi .60 .25
1129 A332 1.50col multi 1.00 .50
1130 A332 5col multi 2.75 1.75
Nos. 1127-1130 (4) 4.65 2.75

Orchids — A333

No. 1131, Maxillaria tenuifolia. No. 1132, Ponthieva maculata. No. 1133, Meiracyllium trinasutum. No. 1134, Encyclia vagans. No. 1135, Encyclia cochleata. No. 1136, Maxillaria atrata. No. 1137, Sobrialia xantholeuca. No. 1138, Encyclia microcharis.

1987, June 8 Litho. Perf. 14½x14
1131 20c multi .90 .25
1132 20c multi .90 .25
a. A333 Pair, #1131-1132 1.25 1.25
1133 25c multi 1.10 .25
1134 25c multi 1.10 .25
a. A333 Pair, #1133-1134 1.40 1.40
1135 70c multi 1.50 .55
1136 70c multi 1.50 .55
a. A333 Pair, #1135-1136 3.50 3.50
1137 1.50col multi 3.50 1.10
1138 1.50col multi 3.50 1.10
a. A333 Pair, #1137-1138 3.50 8.50
Nos. 1131-1138 (8) 14.00 4.30
#1133-1138 horiz. #1135-1138 are airmail.

Teachers — A334

Designs: No. 1139, C. de Jesus Alas, music. No. 1140, Luis Edmundo Vasquez, medicine. No. 1141, David Rosales, law. No. 1142, Guillermo Trigueros, medicine. No. 1143, Manuel Farfan Castro, history. No. 1144, Iri Sol, voice. No. 1145, Carlos Arturo Imendia, primary education. No. 1146, Benjamin Orozco, chemistry.

1987, June 30 Litho. Perf. 14½x14
1139 15c greenish blue & blk .25 .25
1140 15c greenish blue & blk .25 .25
a. A334 Pair, #1139-1140 .40 .40
1141 20c beige & blk .25 .25
1142 20c beige & blk .25 .25
a. A334 Pair, #1141-1142 .40 .40
1143 70c yel org & blk .35 .25
1144 70c yel org & blk .35 .25
a. A334 Pair, #1143-1144 1.25 1.25
1145 1.50col lt blue grn & blk .70 .50
1146 1.50col lt blue grn & blk .70 .50
a. A334 Pair, #1145-1146 2.75 2.75
Nos. 1139-1146 (8) 3.10 2.50
Nos. 1143-1146 are airmail.

10th Pan American Games, Indianapolis — A335

1987, July 31 Perf. 14½x14, 14x14½
1147 20c Emblem, vert. .25 .25
1148 20c Table tennis, vert. .25 .25
a. A335 Pair, #1147-1148 .25 .25
1149 25c Wrestling .25 .25
1150 25c Fencing .25 .25
a. A335 Pair, #1149-1150 .30 .30
1151 70c Softball .35 .25
1152 70c Equestrian .35 .25
a. A335 Pair, #1151-1152 .80 .80
1153 5col Weight lifting, vert. 2.40 1.75
1154 5col Hurdling, vert. 2.40 1.75
a. A335 Pair, #1153-1154 6.00 6.00
Nos. 1147-1154 (8) 6.50 5.00
Nos. 1149-1153 are horizontal.
Nos. 1151-1154 are airmail.

Prior Nicolas Aguilar (1742-1818) A336

Famous men: 20c, Domingo Antonio de Lara (1783-1814), aviation pioneer. 70c, Juan Manuel Rodrigues (1771-1837), president who abolished slavery. 1.50col, Pedro Pablo Castillo (1780-1814), patriot.

1987, Sept. 11 Litho. Perf. 14½x14
1155 A336 15c multi .25 .25
1156 A336 20c multi .25 .25
1157 A336 70c multi .30 .25
1158 A336 1.50col multi .70 .50
Nos. 1155-1158 (4) 1.50 1.25
Nos. 1157-1158 are airmail.

World Food Day A337

1987, Oct. 16 Perf. 14x14½
1159 A337 50c multi .45 .25

Paintings by
Salarrue
A338

Perf. 14½x14, 14x14½
1987, Nov. 30
| 1160 | A338 | 25c Self-portrait | .35 | .25 |
| 1161 | A338 | 70c Lake | .55 | .25 |

#1161 is airmail. See #1186-1189.

Christmas
1987
A339

25c, Virgin of Perpetual Sorrow, stained-glass window. 70c, The Three Magi, figurines.

1987, Nov. 18　　　　**Perf. 14x14½**
| 1162 | A339 | 25c multi | .35 | .25 |
| 1163 | A339 | 70c multi | .55 | .25 |

No. 1163 is airmail.

Pre-Columbian Musical
Instruments — A340

Designs: 20c, Pottery drum worn around neck. No. 1165, Frieze picturing pre-Columbian musicians, from a Salua culture ceramic vase, c. 700-800 A.D. (left side), vert. No. 1166, Frieze (right side), vert. 1.50col, Conch shell trumpet.

Perf. 14x14½, 14½x14
1987, Dec. 14　　　　　　　**Litho.**
1164	A340	20c multi	.25	.25
1165	A340	70c multi	.55	.30
1166	A340	70c multi	.55	.30
a.		Pair, #1165-1166	1.25	1.25
1167	A340	1.50col multi	.90	.60
		Nos. 1164-1167 (4)	2.25	1.45

Nos. 1165-1167 are airmail. No. 1166a has a continuous design.

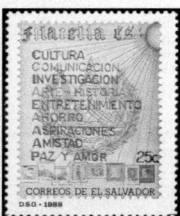

Promotion of
Philately
A341

1988, Jan. 20　Litho.　Perf. 14
| 1168 | A341 | 25c multi | .35 | .25 |

Young Entrepreneurs of El
Salvador — A342

1988　　　　　　　**Perf. 14x14½**
| 1169 | A342 | 25c multi | .40 | .25 |

St. John
Bosco
(1815-88)
A343

1988, Mar. 15　Litho.　Perf. 14x14½
| 1170 | A343 | 20c multi | .40 | .25 |

Environmental Protection — A344

1988, June 3　Litho.　Perf. 14x14½
| 1171 | A344 | 20c Forests | .75 | .25 |
| 1172 | A344 | 70c Forests and rivers | 1.25 | .40 |

No. 1172 is airmail.

1988-1992
Summer
Olympics,
Seoul and
Barcelona
A345

1988, Aug. 31　Litho.　Perf. 13½
1173	A345	1col High jump	.70	.30
1174	A345	1col Javelin	.70	.30
1175	A345	1col Shooting	.70	.30
1176	A345	1col Wrestling	.70	.30
1177	A345	1col Basketball	.70	.30
a.		Strip of 5, Nos. 1173-1177		
b.		Min. sheets of 5 + 5 labels		

Souvenir Sheets
| 1178 | A345 | 2col Torch | 16.00 | — |

Printed in sheets of 10 containing 2 each Nos. 1173-1177.

No. 1177b exists in 2 forms: 1st contains labels picturing 1988 Summer Games emblem or character trademark; 2nd contains labels picturing the 1992 Summer Games emblem or character trademark.

No. 1178 exists in 2 forms: 1st contains 1988 Games emblem; 2nd 1992 Games emblem.

Some, or all, of this issue seem not to have been available to the public.

World Food
Day
A346

1988, Oct. 11　Litho.　Perf. 14x14½
| 1179 | A346 | 20c multi | .60 | .25 |

13th Intl. Fair,
Nov. 23-Dec.
11 — A347

1988, Oct. 25　　　　**Perf. 14½x14**
| 1180 | A347 | 70c multi | .50 | .30 |

Child
Protection
A348

1988, Nov. 10
| 1181 | A348 | 15c Flying kite | .30 | .25 |
| 1182 | A348 | 20c Child hugging adult's leg | .45 | .25 |

Christmas
A349

Paintings by Titian: 25c, *Virgin and Child with the Young St. John and St. Anthony.* 70c, *Virgin and Child in Glory with St. Francis and St. Alvise,* vert.

Perf. 14x14½, 14½x14
1988, Nov. 15
| 1183 | A349 | 25c multi | .40 | .25 |
| 1184 | A349 | 70c multi | .60 | .30 |

70c is airmail.

Return to
Moral Values
A350

1988, Nov. 22　　　　**Perf. 14½x14**
| 1185 | A350 | 25c multi | .60 | .25 |

Art Type of 1987

Paintings by Salvadoran artists: 40c, *Esperanza de los Soles,* by Victor Rodriguez Preza. 1col, *Shepherd's Song,* by Luis Angel Salinas, horiz. 2col, *Children,* by Julio Hernandez Aleman, horiz. 5col, *El Nino de Las Alcancias,* by Camilo Minero. Nos. 1187-1189 are airmail.

Perf. 14½x14, 14x14½
1988, Nov. 30
1186	A338	40c multi	.30	.25
1187	A338	1col multi	.60	.40
1188	A338	2col multi	1.25	.75
1189	A338	5col multi	2.75	1.90
		Nos. 1186-1189 (4)	4.90	3.30

A351

Discovery of America, 500th Anniv. (in
1992) — A352

Ruins and artifacts: a, El Tazumul. b, Multicolored footed bowl. c, San Andres. d, Two-color censer. e, Sihuatan. f, Carved head of the God of Lluvia. g, Cara Sucia. h, Man-shaped vase. i, San Lorenzo. j, Multicolored pear-shaped vase. 2col, Christopher Columbus.

1988, Dec. 21　　　　**Perf. 14x14½**
| 1190 | | Sheet of 10 | 6.50 | 6.50 |
| a.-j. | A351 | 1col any single | .40 | .30 |

Souvenir Sheet
Roulette 13½
| 1191 | A352 | 2col vermilion | 2.00 | 1.25 |

UN
Declaration
of Human
Rights,
40th Anniv.
A353

1988, Dec. 9　Perf. 14½x14, 14x14½
| 1192 | A353 | 25c Family, map, emblem, vert. | .40 | .25 |
| 1193 | A353 | 70c shown | .70 | .30 |

70c is airmail.

World Wildlife
Fund — A354

Felines: a, Felis wiedii laying on tree branch. b, Felis wiedii sitting on branch. c, Felis pardalis laying in brush. d, Felis pardalis standing on tree branch.

1988　　　　　　　**Perf. 14½x14**
1194		Strip of 4	12.00	12.00
a.-b.	A354	25c any single	2.50	.25
c.-d.	A354	55c any single	3.00	.25

World
Meteorological
Organization,
40th
Anniv. — A355

1989, Feb. 3　Litho.　Perf. 14½x14
| 1195 | A355 | 15c shown | .40 | .25 |
| 1196 | A355 | 20c Wind gauge | .40 | .25 |

Meteorology in El Salvador, cent.

Promotion of
Philately
A356

1989, Mar. 15 Litho. Perf. 14½x14
1197 A356 25c Philatelic Soc. emblem .50 .25

See No. 1230.

Natl. Fire Brigade, 106th Anniv. A357

1989, June 19 Litho. Perf. 14x14½
1198 A357 25c Fire truck .75 .25
1199 A357 70c Firemen 1.25 .30

French Revolution, Bicent. A358

1989, July 12
1200 A358 90c Anniv. emblem .50 .35
1201 A358 1col Storming of the Bastille .80 .40

Souvenir Sheets

Stamps on Stamps — A359

Statues of Queen Isabella and Christopher Columbus — A360

Designs: a, No. 88. b, No. 101. c, No. 86. d, No. 102. e, No. 87. f, No. 103.

1989, May 31 Litho. Perf. 14x14½
Miniature Sheet
1202 A359 Sheet of 6 6.75 6.75
a.-f. 50c any single .45 .25

Souvenir Sheet
Rouletted 13½
1203 A360 2col shown 5.00 4.00

Discovery of America, 500th anniv. (in 1992). No. 1203 exists in two forms: margin pictures Natl. Palace with either 500th anniv. emblem or anniv. emblem and "92" at lower right.

Signing Act of Independence — A361

1989, Sept. 1 Perf. 14x14½
1204 A361 25c shown .30 .25
1205 A361 70c Flag, natl. seal, heroes .50 .25

Natl. independence, 168th anniv. No. 1205 is airmail.

Demographic Assoc., 27th Anniv. — A362

1989, July 26
1206 A362 25c multi .55 .25

1990 World Cup Soccer Championships, Italy — A363

Soccer ball, flags of Salvador and: No. 1207, US No. 1208, Guatemala. No. 1209, Costa Rica. No. 1210, Trinidad & Tobago. 55c, Trinidad & Tobago, Guatemala, US, Costa Rica. 1col, Soccer ball, Cuscatlan Stadium.

1989, Sept. 1 Litho. Perf. 14x14½
1207 A363 20c multi .30 .25
1208 A363 20c multicolored .30 .25
a. Pair, #1207-1208 .60 .60
1209 A363 25c shown .30 .25
1210 A363 25c multicolored .30 .25
a. Pair, #1209-1210 .60 .60
1211 A363 55c multicolored .30 .25
1212 A363 1col multicolored .50 .35
Nos. 1207-1212 (6) 2.00 1.60

Beatification of Marcellin Champagnat, Founder of the Marist Brothers Order — A364

1989, Sept. 28
1213 A364 20c multicolored .50 .25

America Issue A365

UPAE emblem and pre-Columbian artifacts: 25c, *The Cultivator*, rock painting. 70c, Ceramic urn.

1989, Oct. 12
1214 A365 25c multicolored .75 .25
1215 A365 70c multicolored 1.50 .30

World Food Day A366

Perf. 14x14½, 14½x14
1989, Oct. 16 Litho.
1216 A366 15c shown .30 .25
1217 A366 55c Aspects of agriculture, vert. .50 .25

Children's Rights A367

1989, Oct. 26 Litho. Perf. 14½x14
1218 A367 25c multicolored .55 .25

Creche Figures A368

1989, Dec. 1
1219 A368 25c shown .30 .25
1220 A368 70c Holy Family, diff. .65 .30

Christmas.

Birds of Prey A369

70c, Sarcoramphus papa. 1col, Polyborus plancus. 2col, Accipiter striatus. 10col, Glaucidium brasilianum.

1989, Dec. 20 Perf. 14½x14, 14x14½
1221 A369 70c multicolored .65 .30
1222 A369 1col multicolored 1.10 .45
1223 A369 2col multicolored 1.75 .80
1224 A369 10col multicolored 7.50 4.00
Nos. 1221-1224 (4) 11.00 5.55

Nos. 1221 and 1223 vert.

Court of Accounts, 50th Anniv. A370

1990, Jan. 12 Litho. Perf. 14x14½
1225 A370 50c multicolored .50 .25

Lord Baden-Powell, 133rd Birth Anniv. — A371

1990, Feb. 23 Perf. 14½x14
1226 A371 25c multicolored 1.00 .25

Intl. Women's Day — A372

1990, Mar. 8 Litho. Perf. 14½x14
1227 A372 25c multicolored .55 .25

Type of 1989 and

Hour Glass — A373

1990 Perf. 14½x14
1228 A373 25c multicolored .25 .25
1229 A373 55c multicolored .35 .25
Souvenir Sheet
Rouletted 13½ with Simulated Perfs.
1230 A356 2col blk & pale blue 2.25 .95

Philatelic Soc., 50th anniv. Nos. 1229-1230 are airmail.

Fight Against Addictions A375

1990, Apr. 26 Litho. Perf. 14x14½
1231 A375 20c Alcohol .30 .25
1232 A375 25c Smoking .40 .25
1233 A375 1.50col Drugs 1.00 .40
Nos. 1231-1233 (3) 1.70 .90

No. 1233 is airmail.

La Prensa, 75th Anniv. — A376

1990, May 14 Litho. Perf. 14½x14
1234 A376 15c multicolored .30 .25
1235 A376 25c "75," newspaper .40 .25

World Cup Soccer Championships,
Italy — A378

Soccer player and flags of: No. 1236, Argentina, USSR, Cameroun, Romania. No. 1237, Italy, US, Austria, Czechoslovakia. No. 1238, Brazil, Costa Rica, Sweden, Scotland. No. 1239, Germany, United Arab Emirates, Yugoslavia, Colombia. No. 1240, Belgium, Spain, Korea, Uruguay. No. 1241, England, Netherlands, Ireland, Egypt.

1990, June 15   **Perf. 14x14½**
1236	A377	55c multicolored	.35	.25
1237	A377	55c multicolored	.35	.25
1238	A377	70c multicolored	.45	.25
1239	A377	70c multicolored	.45	.25
1240	A377	1col multicolored	.55	.35
1241	A377	1col multicolored	.55	.35
1242	A378	1.50col multicolored	.90	.50
		Nos. 1236-1242 (7)	3.60	2.20

For surcharge see No. 1245.

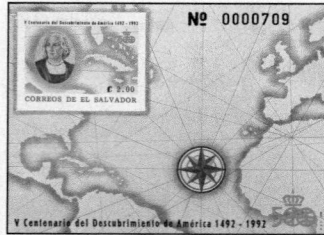

Discovery of America Cent. — A379

Columbus, Map — A380

Stained glass window: a, Christopher Columbus. b, Queen Isabella. c, Columbus' Arms. d, Discovery of America 500th anniv. emblem. e, One boat of Columbus' fleet. f, Two boats.

1990, July 30   **Litho.**   **Perf. 14**
Miniature Sheet
1243	A379	Sheet of 6	6.50	6.50
a.-f.		1col any single	.50	.35

Souvenir Sheet
Rouletted 13 1/2
1244	A380	2col multicolored	5.00	4.00
		See Nos. 1283-1284.		

No. 1239
Surcharged
in Black

1991, Feb.   **Litho.**   **Perf. 14x14½**
1245	A377	90c on 70c multi	1.00	.30

World Summit
for Children
A381

1990, Sept. 25   **Perf. 14½x14**
1246	A381	5col blk, gold & dk bl	2.75	2.00

First
Postage
Stamps,
150th
Anniv.
A382

a, Sir Rowland Hill. b, Penny Black. c, No. 21. d, Central Post Office. e, No. C124.

1990, Oct. 5   **Litho.**   **Perf. 14**
1247		Sheet of 5 + label	9.00	9.00
a.-e.	A382	2col any single	.95	.70

World Food
Day — A383

1990, Oct. 16   **Litho.**   **Perf. 14**
1248	A383	5col multicolored	2.75	1.75

San
Salvador
Electric
Light Co.,
Cent.
A384

1990, Oct. 30
1249	A384	20c shown	.40	.25
1250	A384	90c Lineman, power lines	.70	.35

America
Issue
A385

1990, Oct. 11   **Litho.**   **Perf. 14x14½**
1251	A385	25c Chichontepec Volcano	.50	.25
1252	A385	70c Lake Coatepeque	.90	.25

Chamber
of
Commerce,
75th Anniv.
A386

1990, Nov. 22
1253	A386	1 col blk, gold & bl	.70	.35

Traffic
Safety — A387

Design: 40c, Intersection, horiz.

Perf. 14½x14, 14x14½
1990, Nov. 13
1254	A387	25c multicolored	.35	.25
1255	A387	40c multicolored	.55	.25

Butterflies
A388

15c, Eurytides calliste. 20c, Papilio garamas amerias. 25c, Papilio garamas. 55c, Hypanartia godmani. 70c, Anaea excellens. 1col, Papilio pilumnus. 2col, Anaea proserpina.

Perf. 14x14½, 14½x14
1990, Nov. 28
1256	A388	15c multicolored	.80	.30
1257	A388	20c multicolored	.90	.30
1258	A388	25c multicolored	1.20	.30
1259	A388	55c multicolored	1.40	.40
1260	A388	70c multicolored	1.60	.55
1261	A388	1col multicolored	2.25	.70
		Nos. 1256-1261 (6)	8.15	2.55

Souvenir Sheet
Roulette 13½
1262	A388	2col multicolored	12.00	2.50

Nos. 1259-1261 are vert.

University of
El Salvador,
150th
Anniv. — A389

1991, Feb. 27   **Litho.**   **Perf. 14½x14**
1263	A389	25c shown	.25	.25
1264	A389	70c Sun, footprints, hand	.45	.45
1265	A389	1.50col Dove, globe	1.00	1.00
		Nos. 1263-1265 (3)	1.70	1.70

Christmas
A390

Perf. 14x14½, 14½x14
1990, Dec. 7   **Litho.**
1266	A390	25c shown	.25	.25
1267	A390	70c Nativity, vert.	.50	.50

Month of the
Elderly
A391

1991, Jan. 31   **Perf. 14½x14**
1268	A391	15c purple & blk	.55	.55

Restoration
of Santa
Ana
Theater
A392

1991, Apr. 12   **Perf. 14**
1269	A392	20c Interior	.35	.35
1270	A392	70c Exterior	.65	.65

Amphibians — A393

Designs: 25c, Smilisca baudinii. 70c, Eleutherodactylus rugulosus. 1col, Plectrohyla guatemalensis. 1.50col, Agalychnis moreletii.

1991, May 29   **Litho.**   **Perf. 14x14½**
1271	A393	25c multicolored	.75	.75
1272	A393	70c multicolored	1.20	1.20
1273	A393	1col multicolored	1.90	1.90
1274	A393	1.50col multicolored	2.90	2.90
		Nos. 1271-1274 (4)	6.75	6.75

Aid for
Children's
Village
A394

Designs: 90c, Children playing outdoors.

1991, June 21   **Litho.**   **Perf. 14x14½**
1275	A394	20c multicolored	.30	.30
1276	A394	90c multicolored	.70	.70

United Family
A395

1991, June 28   **Litho.**   **Perf. 14½x14**
1277	A395	50c multicolored	.60	.60

Birds — A396

20c, Melanotis hypoleucus. 25c, Agelaius phoeniceus. 70c, Campylor-hynchus rufinucha. 1col, Cissilopha melanocyanea. 5col, Chiroxiphia linearis.

1991, Aug. 30
1278	A396	20c multicolored	.55	.55
1279	A396	25c multicolored	.65	.65
1280	A396	70c multicolored	1.00	1.00
1281	A396	1col multicolored	1.10	1.10
1282	A396	5col multicolored	4.00	4.00
	Nos. 1278-1282 (5)		7.30	7.30

Discovery of America, 500th Anniv. Type of 1990

No. 1283: a, Hourglass, chart. b, Chart, ship's sails. c, Sailing ship near Florida. d, Corner of chart, ships. e, Compass rose, Cuba, Yucatan Peninsula. f, South America, "500" emblem. No. 1284, Sail, landfall.

1991, Sept. 16   Litho.   Perf. 14
Miniature Sheet
1283	A379	1col Sheet of 6, #a.-f.	6.50	6.50

Souvenir Sheet
Rouletted 6½
1284	A380	2col multicolored	3.00	3.00

America Issue A397

Designs: 25c, Battle of Acaxual. 70c, First missionaries in Cuzcatlan.

1991, Oct. 11   Litho.   Perf. 14x14½
1285	A397	25c multicolored	.75	.75
1286	A397	70c multicolored	1.50	1.50

World Food Day — A398

1991, Oct. 16   Perf. 14½x14
1287	A398	50c multicolored	.60	.60

Wolfgang Amadeus Mozart, Death Bicent. A399

1991, Oct. 23   Perf. 14x14½
1288	A399	1col multicolored	1.00	1.00

Christmas A400

Perf. 14½x14, 14x14½
1991, Nov. 13   Litho.
1289	A400	25c Nativity scene, vert.	.30	.30
1290	A400	70c Children singing	.60	.60

Total Solar Eclipse, July 11 — A401

1991, Dec. 17   Perf. 14x14½
1291		70c shown	.60	.60
1292		70c Eastern El Salvador	.60	.60
a.	A401	Pair, #1291-1292	1.75	1.75

No. 1292a has continous design.

Red Cross Life Guards A402

1992, Feb. 28   Litho.   Perf. 14x14½
1293	A402	3col Rescue	2.00	2.00
1294	A402	4.50col Swimming competition	2.75	2.75

Lions Clubs in El Salvador, 50th Anniv. — A403

1992, Mar. 13   Perf. 14½x14
1295	A403	90c multicolored	.85	.85

Protect the Environment A404

Designs: 60c, Man riding bicycle. 80c, Children walking outdoors. 1.60col, Sower in field. 3col, Clean water. 2.20col, Natural foods. 5col, Recycling center. 10col, Conservation of trees and nature. 25col, Wildlife protection.

1992, Apr. 6   Litho.   Perf. 14x14½
1298	A404	60c multi	.35	.35
1299	A404	80c multi	.45	.45
1300	A404	1.60col multi	1.00	1.00
1302	A404	2.20col multi	1.40	1.40
1303	A404	3col multi	1.75	1.75
1304	A404	5col multi	2.90	2.90
1305	A404	10col multi	5.50	5.50
1307	A404	25col multi	15.00	15.00
	Nos. 1298-1307 (8)		28.35	28.35

Physicians A405

80c, Dr. Roberto Orellana Valdes. 1col, Dr. Carlos Gonzalez Bonilla. 1.60col, Dr. Andres Gonzalo Funes. 2.20col, Dr. Joaquin Coto.

1992, Apr. 30   Perf. 14½x14
1308	A405	80c multicolored	.50	.50
1309	A405	1col multicolored	.60	.60
1310	A405	1.60col multicolored	.90	.90
1311	A405	2.20col multicolored	1.25	1.25
	Nos. 1308-1311 (4)		3.25	3.25

Women's Auxiliary of St. Vincent de Paul Society, Cent. — A406

1992, Mar. 10   Litho.   Perf. 14½x14
1312	A406	80c multicolored	.75	.75

Population and Housing Census A407

80c, Globe showing location of El Salvador.

1992, June 29   Litho.   Perf. 14½x14
1313	A407	60c multicolored	.40	.40
1314	A407	80c multicolored	.60	.60

1992 Summer Olympics, Barcelona A408

1992, July 17   Litho.   Perf. 14½x14
1315	A408	60c Hammer throw	.55	.55
1316	A408	80c Volleyball	.65	.65
1317	A408	90c Shot put	1.00	1.00
1318	A408	2.20col Long jump	1.75	1.75
1319	A408	3col Vault	2.50	2.50
1320	A408	5col Balance beam	4.00	4.00
	Nos. 1315-1320 (6)		10.45	10.45

Simon Bolivar A409

1992, July 24
1321	A409	2.20col multicolored	1.50	1.50

A410

Discovery of America, 500th Anniv. — A411

Designs: No. 1322, European and Amerindian faces. No. 1323, Ship in person's eye. No. 1324, Ship at sea. No. 1325, Ship, satellite over Earth. 3col, Cross, Indian pyramid.

1992, Aug. 28   Litho.   Perf. 14x14½
1322	A410	1col multicolored	1.25	1.25
1323	A410	1col multicolored	1.25	1.25

Perf. 14½x14
1324	A410	1col multicolored	1.25	1.25
1325	A410	1col multicolored	1.25	1.25
a.		Min. sheet, 2 each #1322-1325	10.00	10.00
	Nos. 1322-1325 (4)		5.00	5.00

Souvenir Sheet
Rouletted 13½
1326	A411	3col multicolored	4.50	4.50

Immigrants to El Salvador A412

Designs: No. 1327, Feet walking over map. No. 1328, Footprints leading to map.

1992, Sept. 16   Litho.   Perf. 14x14½
1327	A412	2.20col multicolored	1.50	1.50
1328	A412	2.20col multicolored	1.50	1.50
a.		Pair, #1327-1328	4.00	4.00

General Francisco Morazan (1792-1842) A413

1992, Sept. 28   Perf. 14½x14
1329	A413	1col multicolored	1.00	1.00

Association of Salvadoran Broadcasters A414

1992, Oct. 3
1330	A414	2.20col multicolored	1.50	1.50

Salvadoran Radio Day, Intl. Radio Day.

Discovery of America, 500th Anniv. A415

1992, Oct. 13 Litho. Perf. 14x14½
1331 A415 80c Indian artifacts 2.40 2.40
1332 A415 2.20col Map, ship 6.50 6.50

Exfilna
'92 — A416

1992, Oct. 22 Perf. 14x14½
1333 A416 5col multicolored 5.00 5.00
Discovery of America, 500th Anniv.

Peace in El
Salvador
A417

1992, Oct. 30
1334 A417 50c blk, blue & yel .70 .70

Christmas
A418

Perf. 14x14½, 14½x14
1992, Nov. 23 Litho.
1335 A418 80c shown .80 .80
1336 A418 2.20col Nativity, vert. 1.75 1.75

Wildlife
A419

Designs: 50c, Tapirus bairdii. 70c,
Chironectes minimus. 1col, Eira barbara. 3col,
Felis yagouaroundi. 4.50col, Odocoileus
virginianus.

1993, Jan. 15 Litho. Perf. 14x14½
1337 A419 50c multicolored .40 .40
1338 A419 70c multicolored .60 .60
1339 A419 1col multicolored 1.50 1.50
1340 A419 3col multicolored 2.50 2.50
1341 A419 4.50col multicolored 3.50 3.50
Nos. 1337-1341 (5) 8.50 8.50

Month of
the Elderly
A420

Design: 2.20col, Boy, old man holding tree.

1993, Jan. 27
1342 A420 80c black .60 .60
1343 A420 2.20col multicolored 1.60 1.60

Agape Social Welfare
Organization — A421

Designs: a, Divine Providence Church. b,
People, symbols of love and peace.

1993, Mar. 4 Litho. Perf. 14x14½
1344 A421 1col Pair, #a.-b. 1.40 1.40

Secretary's
Day
A422

1993, Apr. 26 Litho. Perf. 14x14½
1345 A422 1col multicolored .60 .60

Benjamin
Bloom
Children's
Hospital
A423

1993, June 18 Litho. Perf. 14x14½
1346 A423 5col multicolored 3.00 3.00

Visit by
Mexican
President
Carlos
Salinas de
Gortari
A424

1993, July 14
1347 A424 2.20col multicolored 1.50 1.50

Aquatic
Birds
A425

80c, Casmerodius albus. 1col, Mycteria
americana. 2.20col, Ardea herodias. 5col,
Ajaja ajaja.

1993, Sept. 28 Litho. Perf. 14x14½
1348 A425 80c multicolored .65 .65
1349 A425 1col multicolored .90 .90
1350 A425 2.20col multicolored 1.60 1.60
1351 A425 5col multicolored 3.75 3.75
Nos. 1348-1351 (4) 6.90 6.90

Pharmacy Review Commission,
Cent. — A426

1993, Oct. 6
1352 A426 80c multicolored .55 .55

America
Issue
A427

Endangered species: 80c, Dasyprocta
punctata. 2.20col, Procyon lotor.

1993, Oct. 11 Litho. Perf. 14x14½
1353 A427 80c multicolored 1.00 1.00
1354 A427 2.20col multicolored 2.00 2.00

Fifth Central
America
Games
A428

50c, Mascot, torch. 1.60col, Emblem.
2.20col, Mascot, map of Central America.
4.50col, Map of El Salvador, mascot.

Perf. 14½x14, 14x14½
1993, Oct. 29 Litho.
1355 A428 50c multi .50 .50
1356 A428 1.60col multi 1.00 1.00
1357 A428 2.20col multi, horiz. 1.25 1.25
1358 A428 4.50col multi, horiz. 2.50 2.50
Nos. 1355-1358 (4) 5.25 5.25

Miniature Sheet

Medicinal Plants — A429

Designs: a, Solanum mammosum. b,
Hamelia patens. c, Tridex procumbens. d,
Calea urticifolia. e, Ageratum conyzoides. f,
Pluchea odorata.

1993, Dec. 10 Litho. Perf. 14½x14
1359 A429 1col Sheet of 6, #a.-f. 5.00 5.00

Christmas
A430

1993, Nov. 23 Perf. 14x14½
1360 A430 80c Holy Family .50 .50
1361 A430 2.20col Nativity Scene 1.00 1.00

Alberto Masferrer (1868-1932),
Writer — A431

1993, Nov. 30
1362 A431 2.20col multicolored 1.50 1.50

Intl. Year of
the
Family — A432

1994, Feb. 28 Litho. Perf. 14½x14
1363 A432 2.20col multicolored 1.50 1.50

Military
Hospital,
Cent.
A433

1994, Apr. 27 Litho. Perf. 14
1364 A433 1col shown .70 .70
1365 A433 1col Hospital building .70 .70

City of Santa
Ana,
Cent. — A434

Designs: 60c, Arms of Department of Santa
Ana. 80c, Inscription honoring heroic deeds of
44 patriots.

1994, Apr. 29 Litho. Perf. 14
1366 A434 60c multicolored .45 .45
1367 A434 80c multicolored .55 .55

1994 World Cup Soccer
Championships, US — A435

Soccer plays, flags from: 60c, Romania,
Colombia, Switzerland, US. 80c, Sweden,
Cameroun, Russia, Brazil. 1col, South Korea,
Spain, Bolivia, Germany. 2.20col, Bulgaria,
Nigeria, Greece, Argentina. 4.50col, Mexico,
Norway, Ireland, Italy. 5col, Saudi Arabia,
Netherlands, Morocco, Belgium.

1994, June 6 Litho. Perf. 14
1368 A435 60c multicolored .60 .60
1369 A435 80c multicolored .60 .60
1370 A435 1col multicolored .75 .75
1371 A435 2.20col multicolored 1.40 1.40
1372 A435 4.50col multicolored 2.75 2.75
1373 A435 5col multicolored 3.00 3.00
Nos. 1368-1373 (6) 9.10 9.10

Plaza of Sovereign Military Order of Malta
A436

1994, June 24   Litho.   Perf. 14
1374 A436 2.20col multicolored   1.50 1.50

Traditions
A437

Designs: 1col, Tiger and deer dance. 2.20col, Spotted bull dance.

1994, June 30
1375 A437 1col multicolored   .80 .80
1376 A437 2.20col multicolored   1.40 1.40

Nutritional Plants — A438

70c, Capsicum annuum. 80c, Theobroma cacao. 1col, Ipomoea batatas. 5col, Chamaedorea tepejilote.

1994, Aug. 29   Litho.   Perf. 14
1377 A438 70c multicolored   .60 .60
1378 A438 80c multicolored   .60 .60
1379 A438 1col multicolored   .80 .80
1380 A438 5col multicolored   3.00 3.00
      Nos. 1377-1380 (4)   5.00 5.00

Postal Transport Vehicles
A439

1994, Oct. 11   Litho.   Perf. 14
1381 A439 80c Jeep   .75 .75
1382 A439 2.20col Train   2.00 2.00
      America issue.

22nd Bicycle Race of El Salvador
A440

1994, Oct. 26
1383 A440 80c multicolored   .60 .60

16th Intl. Fair of El Salvador
A441

1994, Oct. 31
1384 A441 5col multicolored   3.00 3.00

Christmas
A442

1994, Nov. 16
1385 A442 80c shown   .50 .50
1386 A442 2.20col Magi, Christ child   1.25 1.25

Beetles
A443

80c, Cotinis mutabilis. 1col, Phyllophaga. 2.20col, Galofa. 5col, Callipogon barbatus.

1994, Dec. 16   Litho.   Perf. 14
1387 A443 80c multi   .70 .70
1388 A443 1col multi   .90 .90
1389 A443 2.20col multi   2.25 2.25
1390 A443 5col multi   5.00 5.00
      Nos. 1387-1390 (4)   8.85 8.85

Salvadoran Culture Center, 40th Anniv. — A444

1995, Mar. 24   Litho.   Perf. 14½x14
1391 A444 70c shown   .45 .45
1392 A444 1col "40" emblem   .60 .60

Ceramic Treasures Archeological Site — A445

Designs: 60c, Cup. 70c, Three-footed earthen dish. 80c, Two-handled jar. 2.20col, Long-necked jar. 4.50col, Excavation structure #3. 5col, Excavation structure #4.

1995, Apr. 26   Litho.   Perf. 14½x14
1393 A445 60c multicolored   .40 .40
1394 A445 70c multicolored   .50 .50
1395 A445 80c multicolored   .55 .55
1396 A445 2.20col multicolored   1.40 1.40
1397 A445 4.50col multicolored   2.90 2.90
1398 A445 5col multicolored   3.25 3.25
      Nos. 1393-1398 (6)   9.00 9.00

Fr. Isidro Menendez (1795-1858), Physician
A446

1995, May 19
1399 A446 80c multicolored   .75 .75

La Centro Americana, SA, 80th Anniv. — A447

Designs: 80c, Insuring the future of children. 2.20col, Child wearing costume.

1995, July 7   Litho.   Perf. 14
1400 A447 80c multicolored   .50 .50
1401 A447 2.20col multicolored   1.50 1.50

Sacred Heart College, Cent.
A448

1995, July 26   Perf. 14x14½
1402 A448 80c multicolored   .80 .80

FAO, 50th Anniv. — A449

1995, Aug. 16   Litho.   Perf. 14½x14
1403 A449 2.20col multicolored   1.50 1.50

Tourism
A450

Designs: 50c, Los Almendros Beach, Sonsonate. 60c, Green Lagoon, Apaneca. 2.20col, Guerrero Beach, La Union. 5col, Usulutan Volcano.

1995, Aug. 30   Perf. 14x14½
1404 A450 50c multicolored   .40 .40
1405 A450 60c multicolored   .50 .50
1406 A450 2.20col multicolored   1.50 1.50
1407 A450 5col multicolored   3.25 3.25
      Nos. 1404-1407 (4)   5.65 5.65

Orchids
A451

#1408, Pleurothallis glandulosa. #1409, Pleurothallis grobyi. #1410, Pleurothallis fuegii. #1411, Lemboglossum stellatum. #1412, Lepanthes inaequalis. #1413, Pleurothallis hirsuta. #1414, Hexadesmia micrantha. #1415, Pleurothallis segoviense. #1416, Stelis aprica. #1417, Platystele stenostachya. #1418, Stelis barbata. #1419, Pleurothallis schiedeii.

1995, Sept. 28   Litho.   Perf. 14½x14
1408 A451 60c multicolored   .50 .50
1409 A451 60c multicolored   .50 .50
  a.   Pair, #1408-1409   1.00 1.00
1410 A451 70c multicolored   .70 .70
1411 A451 70c multicolored   .70 .70
1412 A451 1col multicolored   1.00 1.00
1413 A451 1col multicolored   1.00 1.00
1414 A451 3col multicolored   2.75 2.75
1415 A451 3col multicolored   2.75 2.75
1416 A451 4.50col multicolored   4.00 4.00
1417 A451 4.50col multicolored   4.00 4.00
  a.   Pair, #1416-1417   8.00 8.00
1418 A451 5col multicolored   4.75 4.75
1419 A451 5col multicolored   4.75 4.75
      Nos. 1408-1419 (12)   27.40 27.40

America Issue — A452

Martins: 80c, Chloroceryle aenea. 2.20col, Chloroceryle americana.

1995, Oct. 11
1420 A452 80c multicolored   1.25 1.25
1421 A452 2.20col multicolored   3.50 3.50

UN, 50th Anniv. — A453

Design: 2.20col, Hands of different races holding UN emblem, "50."

1995, Oct. 23
1422 A453 80c multicolored   .60 .60
1423 A453 2.20col multicolored   1.75 1.75

Christmas
A454

1995, Nov. 17   Litho.   Perf. 14½x14
1424 A454 80c shown   .60 .60
1425 A454 2.20col Families, clock tower   1.75 1.75

Miniature Sheet

FAUNA DE MONTECRISTO

Fauna — A455

Designs: a, Bubo virginianus. b, Potos flavus. c, Porthidium godmani. d, Felis pardalis (f). e, Dellathis bifurcata. f, Felis concolor (h). g, Mazama americana. h, Leptophobia aripa. i, Bolitoglossa salvinii. j, Eugenes fulgens (h, i).

1995, Nov. 24   **Perf. 14x14½**
1426 A455 80c Sheet of 10,
   #a.-j.   12.00 12.00

Independence, 174th Anniv. — A456

Designs: 80c, Natl. arms, export products, money, textile workers, pharmaceuticals. 25col, Crates of products leaving El Salvador.

1995, Sept. 14   **Perf. 14½x14**
1427 A456   80c shown   .50   .50
1428 A456   25col multicolored   15.00 15.00

2nd Visit of Pope John Paul II — A457

5.40col, Pope John Paul II, Metropolitan Cathedral.

1996, Feb. 8   **Litho.**   **Perf. 14½x14**
1429 A457 1.50col multicolored   1.50 1.50
1430 A457 5.40col multicolored   5.00 5.00

ANTEL, Telecommunications Workers' Day — A458

1.50col, Satellite dish, hand holding cable fibers. 5col, Three globes, telephone receiver.

Perf. 14x14½, 14½x14
1996, Apr. 27   **Litho.**
1431 A458 1.50col multi   1.00 1.00
1432 A458   5col multi, vert.   3.50 3.50

City of San Salvador, 450th Anniv. A459

Designs: 2.50col, Spanish meeting natives. 2.70col, Diego de Holguin, first mayor, mission. 3.30col, Old National Palace. 4col, Heroe's Boulevard, modern view of city.

1996, Mar. 27   **Perf. 14x14½**
1433 A459 2.50col multicolored   1.75 1.75
1434 A459 2.70col multicolored   2.00 2.00
1435 A459 3.30col multicolored   2.25 2.25
1436 A459   4col multicolored   2.75 2.75
    Nos. 1433-1436 (4)   8.75 8.75

Natl. Artists, Entertainers A460

Designs: 1col, Rey Avila (1929-95). 1.50col, María Teresa Moreira (1934-95). 2.70col, Francisco Antonio Lara (1900-89). 4col, Carlos Alverez Pineda (1928-93).

1996, May 17   **Litho.**   **Perf. 14½x14**
1437 A460 1col multicolored   .70   .70
1438 A460 1.50col multicolored   1.00 1.00
1439 A460 2.70col multicolored   1.60 1.60
1440 A460   4col multicolored   2.50 2.50
    Nos. 1437-1440 (4)   5.80 5.80

YSKL Radio, 40th Anniv. A461

1996, May 24   **Perf. 14x14½**
1441 A461 1.40col multicolored   1.20 1.20

1996 Summer Olympic Games, Atlanta A462

Early Greek athletes: 1.50col, Discus thrower. 3col, Jumper. 4col, Wrestlers. 5col, Javelin thrower.

1996, July 3   **Litho.**   **Perf. 14**
1442 A462 1.50col multicolored   1.00 1.00
1443 A462   3col multicolored   2.00 2.00
1444 A462   4col multicolored   2.75 2.75
1445 A462   5col multicolored   3.50 3.50
    Nos. 1442-1445 (4)   9.25 9.25

Birds A463

Designs: a, Pheucticus ludovicianus. b, Tyrannus forficatus. c, Dendroica petechia. d, Falco sparverius. e, Icterus galbula.

1996, Aug. 9   **Litho.**   **Perf. 14x14½**
1446 A463 1.50col Strip of 5,
   #a.-e.   18.00 18.00

Diaro de Hoy Newspaper, 60th Anniv. — A464

1996, Sept. 20
1447 A464 5.20col multicolored   3.50 3.50

Channel 2 Television Station, 30th Anniv. — A465

1996, Sept. 27   **Perf. 14½x14**
1448 A465 10col multicolored   6.00 6.00

UNICEF, 50th Anniv. A466

1996, Oct. 4   **Perf. 14x14½**
1449 A466 1col multicolored   1.00 1.00

Traditional Costumes A467

America issue: 1.50col, Blouse, short flannel skirt, Nahuizalco. 4col, Blouse, long skirt, Panchimalco.

1996, Oct. 11   **Perf. 14½x14**
1450 A467 1.50col multicolored   3.00 3.00
1451 A467   4col multicolored   6.00 6.00

Christmas A468

Designs: 2.50col, Night scene of homes, Christmas tree, church. 4col, Day scene of people celebrating outside homes, church.

1996, Nov. 28   **Litho.**   **Perf. 14½x14**
1452 A468 2.50col multicolored   2.00 2.00
1453 A468   4col multicolored   3.00 3.00

Constitution Day — A469

1996, Dec. 19   **Litho.**   **Perf. 14½x14**
1454 A469 1col multicolored   1.10 1.10

Marine Life — A470

a, Nasolamia velox. b, Scomberomorus sierra. c, Delphinus delphis. d, Eretmochelys imbricata. e, Epinephelus labriformis. f, Pomacanthus zonipectus. g, Scarus perrico. h, Hippocampus ingens.

1996, Dec. 17
1455 A470 1col Sheet of 8,
   #a.-h.   8.00 8.00

Jerusalem, 3000th Anniv. A471

1996, Dec. 5   Litho.   Perf. 14x14½
1456 A471 1col multicolored   .80   .80

El Mundo Newspaper, 30th Anniv. A472

1997, Feb. 6   Litho.   Perf. 14x14½
1457 A472 10col multicolored   7.00 7.00

Exfilna '97 — A473

1997, Feb. 21
1458 A473 4col Baldwin 58441, 1925   4.25 4.25

Carmelite Order of San Jose, 80th Anniv. A474

Design: Mother Clara Maria of Jesus Quiros.

1997, Mar. 19
1459 A474 1col multicolored   1.10 1.10

American School, 50th Anniv. — A475

1997, Apr. 10   Perf. 14½x14
1460 A475 25col multicolored   15.00 15.00

Tropical Fruit — A476

No. 1461: a, Annona diversifolia. b, Anacardium occidentale. c, Cucumis melo. d, Pouteria mammosa.
4col, Carica papaya.

1997, May 28   Litho.   Perf. 14x14½
1461 A476 1.50col Sheet of 4, #a.-d.   6.00 6.00
Souvenir Sheet
Rouletted 13½
1462 A476 4col multicolored   3.50 3.50

Lions Club in El Salvador, 55th Anniv. A476a

1997, Aug. 15   Litho.   Perf. 14
1463 A476a 4col multicolored   3.00 3.00

Montreal Protocol on Substances that Deplete Ozone Layer, 10th Anniv. — A477

1997, Aug. 28   Litho.   Perf. 14
1464 A477 1.50col shown   1.75 1.75
1465 A477 4col Boy drinking water   3.25 3.25
Inter-American Water Day (#1465).

Miguel de Cervantes Saavedra (1547-1616), Writer — A478

1997, Sept. 26   Litho.   Perf. 14
1466 A478 4col multicolored   3.00 3.00

Independence Day — A479

1997, Sept. 10   Litho.   Perf. 14x14½
1467 A479 2.50col shown   1.75 1.75
1468 A479 5.20col Flag, children, dove   3.50 3.50

Scouting in El Salvador, 75th Anniv. — A480

1997, Oct. 3   Perf. 14½x14
1469 A480 1.50col multicolored   1.90 1.90

Life of a Postman A481

America issue: 1col, Postman delivering mail. 4col, Postman on motor scooter, dog.

1997, Oct. 10   Litho.   Perf. 14½x14
1470 A481 1col multicolored   2.00 2.00
1471 A481 4col multicolored   5.00 5.00

ACES (Automobile Club of El Salvador), 26th Anniv. A482

1997, Oct. 28   Perf. 14x14½
1472 A482 10col multicolored   7.00 7.00

Christmas — A483

Children's paintings: No. 1473, Outdoor scene. No. 1474, Indoor scene.

1997, Nov. 20   Litho.   Perf. 14
1473 1.50col multicolored   1.50 1.50
1474 1.50col multicolored   1.50 1.50
  a. A483 Pair, #1473-1474   3.00 3.00

Salesian Order in El Salvador, Cent. — A484

Designs: a, Map, St. John Bosco (1715-88). b, St. Cecilia College. c, San Jose College, priest. d, Ricaldone, students working with machinery. e, Maria Auxiliadora Church. f, City of St. John Bosco, students working with electronic equipment.

1997, Dec. 6
1475 A484 1.50col Sheet of 6, #a.-f.   6.00 6.00

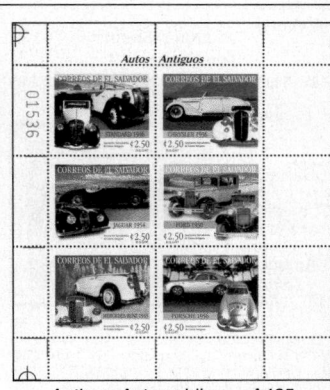

Antique Automobiles — A485

Designs: a, 1946 Standard. b, 1936 Chrysler. c, 1954 Jaguar. d, 1930 Ford. e, 1953 Mercedes Benz. f, 1956 Porsche.

1997, Dec. 17
1476 A485 2.50col Sheet of 6, #a.-f.   10.00 10.00

St. Joseph Missionaries, 125th Anniv. — A486

1col, Image, Church of St. Joseph, Ahuachapan. 4col, Jose M. Vilaseca, Cesarea Esparza.

1998, Jan. 23   Litho.   Perf. 14
1477 A486 1col multicolored   .50   .50
1478 A486 4col multicolored   2.25 2.25

New Intl. Airport A487

1998, Mar. 17   Litho.   Perf. 14
1479 A487 10col multicolored   4.00 4.00

Organization of American States, 50th Anniv. — A488

1998, May 29   Litho.   Perf. 14½x14
1480 A488 4col multicolored   2.00 2.00

1998 World Cup Soccer Championships, France — A489

Soccer player, Paris landmarks: a, Sacre Coeur. b, Eiffel Tower. c, Louvre. d, Notre Dame.
4col, Soccer ball, Arc d'Triumphe, horiz.

1998, May 13
1481 A489 1.50col Strip of 4, #a.-d.   4.00 4.00

Souvenir Sheet
Rouletted 13½
1482 A489   4col multicolored   9.00 9.00

El Salvador, 1997 Champions of the 6th Central American Games — A490

Designs inside medals: No. 1483, Women's gymnastics, weight lifting, judo. No. 1484, Discus, volleyball, women's basketball. No. 1485, Swimming, tennis, water polo. No. 1486, Gymnastics, wrestling, shooting.

1998, July 17   Litho.   Perf. 14
1483 A490   1.50col multicolored   .90 .90
1484 A490   1.50col multicolored   .90 .90
1485 A490   1.50col multicolored   .90 .90
1486 A490   1.50col multicolored   .90 .90
Nos. 1483-1486 (4)   3.60 3.60

Dr. Jose Gustavo Guerrero (1876-1958), President of the World Court — A491

1998, July 22   Litho.   Perf. 14
1487 A491   1col multicolored   .70 .70

18th International Fair — A492

1998, Aug. 28
1488 A492   4col multicolored   2.00 2.00

Painting of the Death of Manuel José Arce, Soldier, Politician — A493

1998, Sept. 1
1489 A493   4col multicolored   2.00 2.00

Hummingbirds and Flowers — A494

a, Archilochus colubris. b, Amazilia rutila. c, Hylocharis eliciae. d, Colibri thalassinus. e, Campylopterus hemileucurus. f, Lampornis amethystinus.

1998, Sept. 7
1490 A494   1.50col Sheet of 6,
    #a.-f.   8.00 8.00

House Social Fund, 25th Anniv. — A495

1998, Sept. 29   Litho.   Perf. 14
1491 A495   10col multicolored   4.25 4.25

Natl. Archives, 50th Anniv. — A496

1998, Oct. 2
1492 A496   1.50col multicolored   1.00 1.00

Famous Women A497

America issue: 1col, Alice Lardé de Venturino. 4col, Maria de Baratta.

1998, Oct. 12
1493 A497   1col multicolored   .70 .70
1494 A497   4col multicolored   2.75 2.75

Christmas A498

Children's drawings: 1col, Clock tower, nativity scene. 4col, Pageant players as angels, Holy Family parading to church, nativity scene.

1998, Nov. 24   Litho.   Perf. 14
1495 A498   1col multicolored   .60 .60
1496 A498   4col multicolored   1.75 1.75

World Stamp Day A499

1998, Nov. 27   Litho.   Perf. 14
1497 A499   1col multicolored   .85 .85

Salvadoran Air Force, 75th Anniv. — A500

Designs: a, C47T transport plane. b, TH-300 helicopter. c, UH-1H helicopter. d, Dragonfly bomber.

1998, Dec. 1   Litho.   Perf. 14¼
1498 A500   1.50col Strip of 4,
    #a.-d.   3.75 3.75

Traditional Foods — A501

Designs: a, Ensalada de papaya y pacaya. b, Sopa de mondongo. c, Camarones en alhuaiste. d, Buñuelos en miel de panela. e, Refresco de ensalada. f, Ensalada de aguacate. g, Sopa de arroz aguado con chipilín. h, Plato típico salvadoreño. i, Empanadas de plátano. j, Horchata.

1998, Dec. 9   Litho.   Perf. 14
1499 A501   1.50col Block of 10,
    #a.-j.   10.00 10.00

Roberto D'Aubuisson Signing New Constitution, 1983 — A502

1998, Dec. 15   Litho.   Perf. 14x14¼
1503 A502   25col multicolored   9.25 9.25

First Natl. Topical Philatelic Exhibition A503

Salvador Railway Company Steamship Service.

1999, Feb. 19   Litho.   Perf. 14
1504 A503   2.50col multicolored   1.25 1.25

Introduction of Television, 40th Anniv. — A504

1999, Feb. 24
1505 A504   4col multicolored   1.50 1.50

European Union Cooperation with El Salvador — A505

1999, May 7   Litho.   Perf. 14x14¼
1506 A505   5.20col shown   2.00 2.00
1507 A505   10col Hands
    clasped   3.50 3.50

Water Birds A506

No. 1508: a, Gallinula chloropus. b, Porphyrula martinica. c, Pardirallus maculatus. d, Anas discors. e, Dendrocygna autumnalis. f, Fulica americana. g, Jacana spinosa. h, Perzana carolina. i, Aramus guarauna. j, Oxyura dominica.
4col, Aythya affinis.

1999, Apr. 22   Perf. 14x14¼
1508 A506   1col Block of 10, #a.-
    j.   8.00 8.00

Souvenir Sheet
Rouletted 8¾
1509 A506   4col multicolored   8.00 8.00

Bats A507

Designs: a, Glossophaga soricina. b, Desmodus rotundus. c, Noctilio leporinus. d, Vampyrum spectrum. e, Ectophilla alba. f, Myotis nigricans.

1999, June 30   Litho.   Perf. 14x14½
1510 A507   1.50col Sheet of 6,
    #a.-f.   7.00 7.00

Visit of US Pres. William J. Clinton — A508

Designs: a, Seals, flags of El Salvador, US. b, Pres. Francisco Flores of El Salvador, Pres. Clinton.

1999, May 19   Perf. 14¼
1511 A508   5col Pair, #a.-b.   5.00 5.00

Quality Control Institute, 20th Anniv. — A509

1999, May 20   Perf. 14¼
1512 A509   5.40col multicolored   2.50 2.50

Geothermic Energy A510

1999, July 16   Litho.   Perf. 14x14½
1513 A510 1col Drilling tower   .50   .50
1514 A510 4col Power station   1.75 1.75

Exports
A511

1999, July 21   Perf. 14½x14
1515 A511 4col multicolored   2.00 2.00

Salvadoran
Journalists'
Association
A512

1999, July 30   Perf. 14x14½
1516 A512 1.50col multicolored   .80   .80

Cattleya Orchids — A513

Designs: a, Skinneri var. alba. b, Skinneri var. coerulea. c, Skinneri. d, Guatemalensis. e, Aurantiaca var. flava. f, Aurantiaca.

1999, Aug. 25
1517 A513 1.50col Sheet of 6, #a.-f. + 4 labels   6.00 6.00

Toño
Salazar,
Caricaturist
A514

Designs: a, Self-portrait. b, Salarrué. c, Claudia Lars. d, Francisco Gavidia. e, Miguel Angel Asturias.

1999, Aug. 31
1518 A514 1.50col Strip of 5, #a.-e.   4.75 4.75

Central
American
Nutrition
Institute
A515

1999, Sept. 14   Litho.   Perf. 14x14½
1519 A515 5.20col Children, food 2.00 2.00
1520 A515 5.40col Food   2.25 2.25

Armed Forces,
175th
Anniv. — A516

1999, Sept. 24   Perf. 14¼x14
1521 A516 1col Gens. Arce & Barrios   .60   .60
1522 A516 1.50col Soldier, flag   .90   .90

Intl. Year of
Older Persons
A517

1999, Oct. 8
1523 A517 10col multicolored   4.25 4.25

America
Issue, A New
Millennium
Without
Arms — A518

1999, Oct. 12
1524 A518 1col Dove, children   .80   .80
1525 A518 4col "No Guns" sign   2.75 2.75

UPU, 125th Anniv. — A519

Designs: a, UPU emblem. b, Mail, jeep, ship, airplane, computer.

1999, Oct. 22
1526 A519 4col Pair, #a.-b.   4.00 4.00

Christmas — A520

Paintings by:
No. 1527: a, Delmy Guandique. b, Margarita Orellana.
No. 1528: a, Lolly Sandoval. b, José Francisco Guadrón.

1999, Nov. 4
1527 A520 1.50col Pair, #a.-b.   1.50 1.50
1528 A520 4col Pair, #a.-b.   3.50 3.50

Inter-American
Development
Bank, 40th
Anniv. — A521

1999, Nov. 24   Litho.   Perf. 14¼x14
1529 A521 25col multi   10.50 10.50

Woodpeckers
A522

Designs: a, Melanerpes aurifrons. b, Piculus rubiginosus. c, Sphyrapicus varius. d, Dryocopus lineatus. e, Melanerpes formicivorus.

1999, Dec. 3
1530 A522 1.50col Vert. strip of 5, #a.-e.   7.00 7.00

Salvadoran
Coffee
Assoc.,
70th Anniv.
A523

1999, Dec. 7   Perf. 14x14¼
1531 A523 10col multi   4.75 4.75

Millennium
A524

2000, Jan. 6   Perf. 14¼x14
1532 A524 1.50col multi   1.35 1.35

Fireman's
Foundation,
25th
Anniv. — A525

Designs: 2.50col, Fireman rescuing child. 25col, Emblem.

2000, Jan. 17   Litho.   Perf. 14¼x14
1533 A525 2.50col multi   1.50 1.50
1534 A525 25col multi   10.00 10.00

Faith and
Happiness
Foundation,
30th
Anniv. — A526

2000, Feb. 10
1535 A526 1col multi   .95   .95

Millennium
A527

No. 1536, Serie I: a, El Tazumal Mayan pyramid. b, Christopher Columbus and ships. c, Spanish soldier, native. d, Independence.
No. 1537, Serie II: a, Salvadoran White House, 1890. b, Shoppers at street market, 1920. c, Trolley and Nuevo Mundo Hotel, 1924. d, Automobiles on South 2nd Avenue, San Salvador, 1924.

2000   Sheets of 4   Perf. 14x14¼
1536 A527 1.50col #a.-d.   4.50 4.50
1537 A527 1.50col #a.-d.   4.50 4.50

Issued: No. 1536, 3/16; No. 1537, 6/16. Nos. 1536 & 1537 includes two labels.

El Imposible
Natl.
Park — A528

No. 1538: a, Gate. b, Ocelot (tigrillo). c, Paca (tepezcuintle). d, Venado River waterfalls. e, Black curassow (pajuil). f, Tree with yellow leaves. g, Orchid (flor de encarnación). h, Honeycreeper (torogoz). i, Bird with purple head (siete colores). j, Vegetation near cliff. k, Interpretation center. l, Bird with black and yellow plumage (payasito). m, Frog. n, Mushrooms (hongos). o, Red flower (guaco de tierra). p, Green toucan (cotuza). s, Ant bear (oso hormiguero). t, Cascaddes of El Imposible.

2000, Apr. 28   Perf. 14¼x14
1538   Sheet of 20   12.00 12.00
  a.-t. A528 1col Any single   .60   .60

La Prensa
Grafica, 85th
Anniv. — A529

2000, May 9
1539 A529 5col multi   2.25 2.25

Canonization
of Marcelino
Champagnat
(1789-1840)
A530

2000, June 2
1540 A530 10col multi   4.25 4.25

2000 Summer Olympics, Sydney A531

No. 1541: a, Runners. b, Gymnast. c, High jumper. d, Weight lifter. e, Fencer. f, Cyclist. g, Swimmer. h, Shooter. i, Archer. j, Judo.

2000, July 20   **Perf. 14x14¼**
1541   Sheet of 10   10.00 10.00
a.-j. A531 1col Any single   .60   .60

Trains A532

No. 1542: a, Baldwin locomotive Philadelphia 58441. b, General Electric locomotive series 65k-15. c, Train car. d, Presidential coach car.

2000, Aug. 3
1542   Vert. strip of 4   7.00 7.00
a.-d. A532 1.50col Any single   1.25 1.25

World Post Day — A533

2000, Oct. 9   **Litho.**   **Perf. 14¼x14**
1543 A533 5col multi   2.25 2.25

Christmas Tree Ornaments A534

No. 1544: a, Snowman. b, Bells. c, Striped pendants. d, Candy cane. e, Candles. f, Sleigh. g, Gifts. h, Santa Claus. i, Santa's hat. j, Santa's boot.

2000, Nov. 9
1544   Block of 10   9.00 9.00
a.-j. A534 1col Any single   .65   .65

Art by Expatriates A535

Art by: a, Roberto Mejía Ruíz. b, Alex Cuchilla. c, Nicolas Fredy Shi Quán. d, José Bernardo Pacheco. e, Oscar Soles.

2000, Dec. 4   **Perf. 14x14¼**
1545   Horiz. strip of 5   17.50 17.50
a.-e. A535 4col Any single   2.50 2.50

Pets A536

No. 1546: a, 1.50col, Dogs. b, 1.50col, Dog and cat.
No. 1547: a, 2.50col, Parakeets. b, 2.50col, Dogs, diff.

2001, Feb. 28   **Litho.**   **Perf. 14x14¼**
Vert. Pairs, #a-b
1546-1547 A536   Set of 2   6.50 6.50
Nos. 1546-1662 show denominations in colons and US dollars.

Saburo Hirao Park, 25th Anniv. A537

Designs: 5col, Playground. 25col, Bridge in gardens.

2001, Mar. 14
1548-1549 A537   Set of 2   23.00 23.00

Claudia Lars (1899-1974), Salvadoran Writer, and Federico Proaño (1848-94), Ecuadoran Writer — A538

2001, Aug. 28   **Litho.**   **Perf. 14x14¼**
1550 A538 10col multi   4.50 4.50

St. Vincent de Paul Children's Home, 125th Anniv. A539

2001, Oct. 26
1551 A539 4col multi   2.00 2.00

Mushrooms A540

No. 1552: a, Lactaius indigo. b, Pleurotus ostreatus. c, Ramaria sp. d, Clavaria vermicularis.
No. 1553: a, Amanita muscaria. b, Phillipsia sp. c, Russula emetica. d, Geastrum triplex.

2001, Dec. 20   **Perf. 14¼x14**
1552   Horiz. strip of 4   5.75 5.75
a.-d. A540 1.50col Any single   1.10 1.10
1553   Horiz. strip of 4   16.50 16.50
a.-d. A540 4col Any single   3.00 3.00

St. Josemaria Escrivá de Balaguer (1902-75), Founder of Opus Dei — A541

Balaguer and: 1col, Plowed field. 5col, People and computers.

2002, Apr. 26   **Litho.**   **Perf. 14¼x14**
1554-1555 A541   Set of 2   5.50 5.50

San Miguel Lions Club, 51st Anniv. — A542

2002, July 31
1556 A542 5col multi   4.00 4.00

Rosales National Hospital, Cent. — A543

2002, June 28
1557 A543 10col multi   8.00 8.00

Peace Accords, 10th Anniv. — A544

Designs: No. 1558, 2.50col, Dove and sun. No. 1559, 2.50col, UN emblem and handshake.
No. 1560: a, 2.50col, Dove with olive branch flying over village. b, 2.50col, Dove, flag.

2002, May 15   **Perf. 14¼x14**
1558-1559 A544   Set of 2   4.00 4.00
Souvenir Sheet
Rouletted Irregularly
1560 A544   Sheet of 2, #a-b   4.00 4.00

19th Central American and Caribbean Games A545

No. 1561: a, Montage of athletes. b, Bicycle race. c, Children's drawing of various athletes. d, Gymnast.
4col, Mascots.

2002, June 13   **Perf. 14¼x14**
1561   Vert. strip of 4   3.75 3.75
a.-d. A545 1col Any single   .70   .70

Souvenir Sheet
Rouletted Irregularly
1562 A545 4col multi   3.50 3.50

A546

2002 World Cup Soccer Championships, Japan and Korea — A547

No. 1563 — Various Korean World Cup stadia and flags of countries in Group: a, A. b, B. c, C. d, D.
No. 1564 — Various Japanese World Cup stadia and flags of countries in Group: a, E. b, F. c, G. d, H.
4col, Flag of winning team, Brazil.

2002, July 11   **Perf. 14x14¼**
1563   Vert. strip of 4   3.25 3.25
a.-d. A546 1col Any single   .75   .75
1564   Vert. strip of 4   6.00 6.00
a.-d. A546 1.50col Any single   1.10 1.10
Souvenir Sheet
Rouletted Irregularly
1565 A547 4col multi   3.75 3.75

Natl. Academy of Public Security, 10th Anniv. — A548

2002, Sep. 6   **Litho.**   **Perf. 14¼x14**
1566 A548 1col multi   1.00 1.00

Central American Parliament, 10th Anniv. (in 2001) A549

2002, Sep. 13   **Perf. 14x14¼**
1567 A549 25col multi   18.50 18.50

Pan-American Health Organization, Cent. — A550

No. 1568: a, Headquarters, Washington, DC. b, Emblem and "100."

2002, Oct. 18   **Litho.**   **Perf. 14¼x14**
1568 A550 2.70col Horiz. pair, #a-b   4.50 4.50

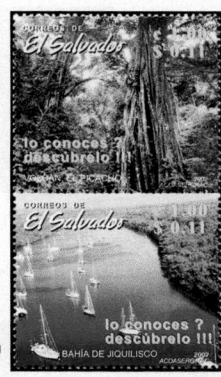

Tourism
A551

No. 1569, 1col: a, Forest, Picacho Volcano. b, Jiquilisco Bay.
No. 1570, 4col: a, Joya de Cerén Archaeological Site. b, Juayua, Sonsonate Department.

2002, Dec. 6   *Perf. 14x14¼*
           Vert. Pairs, #a-b
1569-1570 A551   Set of 2   9.00 9.00

America
Issue —
Youth,
Education,
and Literacy
A552

Designs: 1col, Stylized person, book, block. 1.50col, Teacher and students.

2002, Nov. 26
1571-1572 A552   Set of 2   2.40 2.40

Scouting in El
Salvador, 80th
Anniv. — A553

2002, Dec. 16   *Perf. 14¼x14*
1573 A553 2.70col multi   2.25 2.25

Christmas
A554

Infant Jesus and: 1.50col, Mary. 2.50col, Joseph.

2002, Nov. 29
1574-1575 A554   Set of 2   3.50 3.50

Daughters of
Our Lady Help
of Christians
(Salesian
Sisters) in
Central
America,
Cent. — A555

Designs: 70c, Girls, nun in classroom. 1.50col, Statue of Madonna and Child.

2003, May 26   Litho.   *Perf. 14¼x14*
1576-1577 A555   Set of 2   2.00 2.00

Town of
Sonsonate,
450th
Anniv. — A556

2003, May 28
1578 A556 1.60col multi   1.50 1.50

Grupo
Roble, 40th
Anniv.
A557

No. 1579: a, Tree without leaves. b, Cherries on branch.
4col, Bird and nest.

2003, July 18   *Perf. 14x14¼*
1579 A557 1.50col Vert. pair,
           #a-b   3.00 3.00
        Souvenir Sheet
      Rouletted 12¾x13½
1580 A557   4col multi   3.75 3.75

Regional Sanitary Agricultural
Organization, 50th Anniv. — A558

2003, July 25   *Perf. 14x14¼*
1581 A558 25col multi   21.00 21.00

Agape
Ministries in El
Salvador, 25th
Anniv. — A559

2003, Aug. 25   *Perf. 14¼x14*
1582 A559 1.50col multi   1.25 1.25

A560

Independence, 182nd Anniv. — A561

No. 1583: a, 2.50col, Maria Felipa Aranzamendi y Aguilar. b, 2.70col, Manuela Antonia Arce de Lara.
4col, Cry for Independence, Nov. 5, 1811.

2003, Sept. 30   *Perf. 14¼x14*
1583 A560   Horiz. pair, #a-b   4.25 4.25
        Souvenir Sheet
      Rouletted 13½x13¼
1584 A561 4col multi   3.50 3.50

FAO in El
Salvador, 25th
Anniv. — A562

Designs: 1.50col, Children, farmers. 4col, Child, farmer, food preparation workers.

2003, Oct. 8   *Perf. 14¼x14*
1585 A562 1.50col multi   1.25 1.25
        Souvenir Sheet
      Rouletted 13¼x13¾
1586 A562   4col multi   3.75 3.75

Insects and
Flowers
A563

No. 1587: a, Abejorro sp. b, Chrysina quetzalcoatli. c, Anartia fatima. d, Manduca sp. e, Manduca sexta. f, Tabebuia chrysantha. g, Alpinia purpurata. h, Tecoma stans. i, Tabebuia rosea. j, Passiflora edulis.
4col, Anartia fatima, Tabebuia rosea, vert.

2003, Oct. 23   *Perf. 14x14¼*
1587   Block of 10   13.00 13.00
  a.-j. A563 1.50col Any single   .90 .90
        Souvenir Sheet
      Rouletted 13¼x13¾
1588 A563 4col multi   4.00 4.00

Christmas
A564

Designs: 1.50col, Madonna and Child. 4col, Holy Family.

2003, Nov. 7   *Perf. 14¼x14*
1589-1590 A564   Set of 2   4.50 4.50

Churches
A565

No. 1591: a, Church of the Immaculate Conception, Citalá. b, St. James the Apostle Church, Chalchuapa. c, St. Peter the Apostle Church, Metapán. d, Our Lady of Santa Ana Church, Chapeltique. e, St. James the Apostle Church, Conchagua.
5col, Calvary Church, San Salvador, vert.

2003, Nov. 14   *Perf. 14x14¼*
1591   Horiz. strip of 5   12.00 12.00
  a.-e. A565 4col Any single   2.25 2.25
        Souvenir Sheet
      Rouletted 13¼x13¾
1592 A565 5col multi   3.25 3.25

Tourism
A566

No. 1593: a, Brotherhood of Panchimalco. b, Church cupola, Juayúa. c, Shalpa Beach, La Libertad. d, Tazumal Ruins.

2003, Dec. 10   *Perf. 14x14¼*
1593   Vert. strip of 4   4.75 4.75
  a.-d. A566 1.50col Any single   1.00 1.00

America
Issue -
Flora and
Fauna
A567

Designs: 1.50col, Fernaldia pandurata. 4col, Lepidophyma smithii.

2003, Dec. 19
1594-1595 A567   Set of 2   4.50 4.50

El
Salvador
— Panama
Diplomatic
Relations,
Cent.
A568

Designs: 10col, Flags of El Salvador and Panama. 25col, Flags, ship in lock.

2004, Feb. 17   Litho.   *Perf. 14x14¼*
1596-1597 A568   Set of 2   16.50 16.50

Salvadoran
Cooperation
With
European
Union — A569

Stars and map of: 2.70col, Central America. 5col, Europe.

2004, May 13   *Perf. 14¼x14*
1598-1599 A569   Set of 2   3.75 3.75

Legends
A570

No. 1600, 1col: a, La Carreta Chillona. b, La Siguanaba.
No. 1601, 1.60col: a, Justo Juez de la Noche. b, El Cipitío.

2004, June 30   Perf. 14x14¼
Vert. Tete-beche Pairs, #a-b
1600-1601 A570   Set of 2   2.75 2.75

El Salvador College of Chemistry and Pharmaceuticals, Cent. — A571

2004, Sept. 17
1602 A571 10col multi   3.75 3.75

Santa Tecla (Nueva San Salvador), 150th Anniv. A572

Designs: 1.50col, Adalberto Guirola Children's Home. 4col, Second Avenue.

2004, Oct. 14
1603-1604 A572   Set of 2   2.25 2.25

Powered Flight, Cent. (in 2003) A573

No. 1605: a, Wilbur and Orville Wright, Wright Flyer. b, Alberto Santos-Dumont, 14-Bis. c, Louis Blériot, Blériot XI. d, Glenn Curtiss, Curtiss JN-4D Jenny. e, Hugo Junkers, Junkers J.1.
No. 1606: a, Charles Lindbergh, Spirit of St. Louis. b, Amelia Earhart, Lockheed Vega. c, Chuck Yeager, Bell X-1. d, Robert Withe, X-15. e, Dick Rutan and Jeana Yeager, Voyager.
No. 1607, Wilbur and Orville Wright, Wright Flyer, vert.

2004, Nov. 5   Perf. 14x14¼
1605   Horiz. strip of 5   3.50 3.50
a.-e.   A573 1.50col Any single   .65   .65
1606   Horiz. strip of 5   9.50 9.50
a.-e.   A573 4col Any single   1.75 1.75
Souvenir Sheet
Rouletted Irregularly
1607 A573   4col multi   3.00 3.00

Christmas
A574

Designs: 1.50col, Holy Family. 2.50col, Shepherd and sheep. 4col, Magi. 5col, Flight into Egypt.

2004, Dec. 7   Litho.   Perf. 14x14¼
1608-1611 A574   Set of 4   5.00 5.00

America Issue - Environmental Protection — A575

Marine life: 1.40col, Akko rossi. 2.20col, Chromodoris sphoni.

2004, Dec. 17
1612-1613 A575   Set of 2   2.10 2.10
1613a   Tete-beche pair, #1612-1613 2.25 2.25

La Prensa Newspaper, 90th Anniv. A576

2005, Apr. 7
1614 A576 25col multi   8.00 8.00

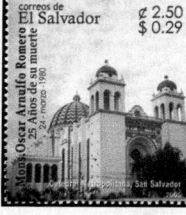

Assassination of Archbishop Oscar Romero, 25th Anniv. — A577

Designs: 2.50col, Metropolitan Cathedral, San Salvador. 5col, Romero (1917-80).

2005, Apr. 23   Perf. 14¼x14
1615-1616 A577   Set of 2   2.75 2.75

Rotary International, Cent. — A578

2005, June 15   Perf. 14¼x14
1617 A578 1.50col shown   1.75 1.75
Souvenir Sheet
Rouletted Irregularly
1618 A578   4col Children   5.00 5.00

Puerto de San Carlos de la Unión, 150th Anniv. A579

2005, July 27   Perf. 14x14¼
1619 A579 10col shown   4.00 4.00
Souvenir Sheet
Rouletted Irregularly
1620 A579   4col Pirigallo Island   2.25 2.25

Tenth Central American Students' Games A580

Designs: 1.60col, Wrestling. 2.20col, High jump. 2.70col, Karate. No. 1624, 4col, Rollerblading.
No. 1625, 4col, Karate, high jump and wrestling.

2005, Sept. 14 Litho. Perf. 14¼x14
1621-1624 A580   Set of 4   5.00 5.00
Souvenir Sheet
Rouletted 11x10¾x10x10½
1625 A580   4col multi   1.75 1.75

Latin American Musicians — A581

No. 1626: a, Agustín Lara (1897-1970), composer, Mexico. b, Pedro Infante (1917-57), singer, Mexico. c, Libertad Lamarque (1906-2000), singer, Argentina. d, Carlos Gardel (1890-1936), singer, Argentina. e, Celia Cruz (1924-2003), singer, Cuba. f, Damaso Pérez Prado (1916-89), composer, Cuba. g, Daniel Santos (1916-92), song writer, Puerto Rico. h, Pedro Vargas (1908-89), singer, Mexico. i, Beny Moré (1919-63), singer, Cuba. j, Jorge Negrete (1911-53), singer, Mexico.
4col, Singer, microphone and guitar.

2005, Oct. 11   Perf. 14¼x14
1626 A581 1.50col Sheet of 10,
            #a-j   7.00 7.00
Souvenir Sheet
Rouletted 11x10¾
1627 A581   4col multi   2.40 2.40

Writers
A582

Designs: No. 1628, 1col, Lilian Serpas (1905-85), poet. No. 1629, 1col, Oswaldo Escobar Velado (1919-61), poet. No. 1630, 4col, Alvaro Menendez Leal (1931-2000), dramatist. No. 1631, 4col, Roque Dalton (1935-75), poet. No. 1632, 5col, Pedro Geoffroy Rivas (1908-79), poet. No. 1633, 5col, Italo Lopez Vallecillos (1932-86), poet.

2005, Oct. 20   Perf. 14¼x14
1628-1633 A582   Set of 6   9.00 9.00

America Issue - Fight Against Poverty A583

Designs: 1.50col, Man holding food. 4col, Children and shack.

2005, Nov. 25   Perf. 14x14¼
1634-1635 A583   Set of 2   2.75 2.75

Christmas — A584

No. 1636 — Creche figures: a, Praying angel. b, Chicken and left half of star. c, Rooster and right half of star. d, Angel with horn. e, Donkey. f, Mary and Jesus. g, Joseph and two sheep. h, Cow. i, Camel with red saddle cloth and Magus. j, Camel without saddle and Magus. k, Camel with blue saddle cloth and Magus. l, Shepherd and three sheep. m, Woman, table and pot. n, Man and oxcart. o, Musicians. p, Bride, groom and church. q, Dog and kneeling woman. r, Sheep and shepherd holding lamb. s, Women with water jugs. t, Birds.

2005, Nov. 30   Perf. 14¼x14
1636 A584 Sheet of 20   8.00 8.00
a.-t.   1col Any single   .40   .40

Diplomatic Relations Between El Salvador and Japan, 70th Anniv. A585

Designs: 2.50col, Flags of El Salvador and Japan, flowers, men shaking hands. 9col, Airport, medical worker and highway.

2005, Dec. 20   Perf. 14x14¼
1637-1638 A585   Set of 2   4.50 4.50

2006 Elections
A586

Ballot box, flag and: 10col, José Mariano Calderón y San Martín. 25col, Miguel José de Castro y Lara.

2006, Feb. 28
1639-1640 A586   Set of 2   12.50 12.50

TACA Airlines, 75th Anniv. A587

No. 1641 — Anniversary emblem, parrot and: a, Stinson airplane, Northern hemisphere. b, Airbus A-319, Southern hemisphere.

2006, Mar. 31   Litho.   Perf. 14x14¼
1641 A587 5col Vert. pair, #a-b   4.00 4.00

Laying of Cornerstone of Santa Ana Cathedral, Cent. — A588

Designs: 1.50col, Religious statues. 2.50col, Santa Ana Cathedral.

2006, Apr. 28   Perf. 14¼x14
1642-1643 A588   Set of 2   2.25 2.25

Flora and Fauna A589

No. 1644: a, Pteroglossus torquatus. b, Smyrna blonfildia. c, Hypanartia dione. d, Sciurus variegatoides. e, Ceiba pentandra. f, Ramphastos sulfuratus. g, Eunica tatila. h, Catonephele numilia. i, Mephitis macroura. j, Enterolobium cyclocarpum.

2006, May 31   Perf. 14x14¼
1644   Block of 10   6.00 6.00
a.-j.   A589 1col Any single   .60 .60

2006 World Cup Soccer Championships, Germany — A590

No. 1645 — Flags, landmarks and people from World Cup host nations: a, Argentina, 1978. b, Spain, 1982. c, Mexico, 1986. d, Italy, 1990.
No. 1646: a, United States, 1994. b, France, 1998. c, Korea and Japan, 2002. d, Germany, 2006.
4col, Soccer ball showing German flags, horiz.

2006, June 29   Perf. 14¼x14
1645   Horiz. strip of 4   3.50 3.50
a.-d.   A590 2.20col Any single   .85 .85
1646   Horiz. strip of 4   4.25 4.25
a.-d.   A590 2.70col Any single 1.00 1.00
Souvenir Sheet
Rouletted 13¼
1647 A590 4col multi   2.50 2.50

Fossils A591

Designs: 1.50col, Mastodon skull. 1.60col, Vertebra of giant sloth. 5col, Mandible of giant sloth. 10col, Paw bones of giant sloth.

2006, July 26   Perf. 14¼x14
1648-1651 A591   Set of 4   7.25 7.25

Disaster Reduction A592

Intl. Year of Deserts and Desertification A593

2006, Aug. 31
1652 A592 1.50col multi   .60 .60
1653 A593   4col multi   1.25 1.25

America Issue, Energy Conservation A594

Designs: 1.50col, Woman in kitchen. 4col, Light bulb and socket.

2006, Sept. 29
1654-1655 A594   Set of 2   2.10 2.10

Republic of China National Day — A595

Designs: 9col, Taipei 101 Building. 10col, President's Mansion, Taipei.

2006, Oct. 9
1656-1657 A595   Set of 2   8.00 8.00

La Constancia Industries, Cent. A596

2006, Oct. 25   Perf. 14x14¼
1658 A596 25col multi   10.50 10.50

Christmas A597

Designs: 1col, Our Lady of Candelaria. 1.50col, Our Lady of Carmen. 5col, Maria Auxiliadora. 10col, Our Lady of Peace.

2006   Perf. 14¼x14
1659-1662 A597   Set of 4   8.00 8.00

2007 Census A598

2007, Mar. 26   Litho.   Perf. 14¼x14
1663 A598 1c multi   .30 .30

Social Peace Year — A599

2007, May 3
1664 A599 $10 multi   30.00 30.00

Scouting, Cent. A600

Designs: No. 1665, 10c, Lord Robert Baden-Powell blowing kudu horn. No. 1666, 10c, Salvadoran Scouts.

2007, June 21   Litho.   Perf. 14x14¼
1665-1666 A600   Set of 2   1.00 1.00

Miniature Sheet

Salvadoran Presidents — A601

No. 1667: a, Juan Lindo, 1841-42. b, Gen. José Escolastico Marin, 1842. c, Dionisio Villacorta, 1842. d, Dr. Juan José Guzmán, 1842-44. e, Gen. Fermin Palacios, 1844, 1845, 1846. f, Gen. Francisco Malespin, 1844. g, Gen. Joaquin Eufrasio Guzmán, 1844-45, 1845-46, 1859. h, Dr. Eugenio Aguilar, 1846-48. i, Tomás Medina, 1848. j, José Felix Quiroz, 1848, 1851.

2007, June 29   Perf. 14¼x14
1667 A601 5c Sheet of 10, #a-j   2.50 2.50

Miniature Sheet

Fauna of Cobanos Reef — A602

No. 1668: a, Apogon dovii. b, Cirrhitus rivulatus. c, Holacanthus passer. d, Acanthurus xanthopterus. e, Thalassoma lucasanum. f, Diodon holocantus. g, Stegastes flavilatus. h, Amphiaster insignis. i, Hypselodoris agassizzi. j, Cypraecassis coarctata.

2007, Aug. 9   Litho.   Perf. 14x14¼
1668 A602 10c Sheet of 10, #a-j   4.00 4.00

El Mundo Newspaper, 40th Anniv. — A603

2007, Sept. 12
1669 A603 $5 multi   17.50 17.50

Archaeology — A604

No. 1670: a, Terracotta figurine. b, Tazumal archaeological site. c, Joya de Cerén. d, San Andres Acropolis.

2007, Oct. 5
1670 A604 25c Block or strip of
4, #a-d　　3.50 3.50

America Issue, Education For All — A605

No. 1671 — Novels: a, El Cristo Negro, by Salarrué. b, Don Quixote de La Mancha, by Miguel de Cervantes.

2007, Oct. 31
1671 A605 $1 Vert. pair, #a-b　7.00 7.00

Christmas — A606

No. 1672: a, Stars on ears of corn. b, Teddy bear and gifts under Christmas tree. c, People touching stars on Christmas tree. d, Candles.

2007, Nov. 14
1672 A606 10c Block or strip of
4, #a-d　　1.50 1.50

Popes A607

Designs: 1c, Pope John Paul II (1920-2005). 10c, Pope Benedict XVI.

2007, Nov. 22　　**Perf. 14x14¼**
1673-1674 A607　Set of 2　1.00 1.00

Birds — A608

No. 1675: a, Bombycilla cedrorum. b, Colaptes auratus. c, Anas clypeata. d, Falco peregrinus.
50c, Passerina ciris, horiz.

2007, Dec. 17　　**Perf. 14¼x14**
1675 A608 10c Block or strip of
4, #a-d　　1.90 1.90

Souvenir Sheet
Rouletted 10½
1676 A608 50c multi　　2.00 2.00

Fire Fighting Corps in El Salvador, 125th Anniv. A609

No. 1677: a, Firemen and truck. b, Fire truck, cab facing right. c, Fire truck, cab facing left. d, Ambulance.

2008, Feb. 15　　**Perf. 14x14¼**
1677　　Vert. strip of 4　2.40 2.40
a.-d.　A609 15c Any single　.60 .60

37th Lions International Latin America and Caribbean Forum — A610

2008, Mar. 7
1678 A610 1c multi　　.55 .55

Miniature Sheets

Salvadoran Presidents — A611

No. 1679: a, Francisco Dueñas, 1851-52, 1852-54, 1856, 1863-71. b, Col. José María San Martín, 1852, 1854-56. c, Rafael Campo, 1856-58. d, Gen. Gerardo Barrios, 1858, 1859-60, 1861-63. e, Dr. Rafael Zaldívar,

1876-84, 1884-85. f, Gen. Fernando Figueroa, 1885, 1907-11. g, Gen. Francisco Menéndez, 1885-90. h, Gen. Carlos Ezeta, 1890-94. i, Gen. Rafael Antonio Gutiérrez, 1894-98. j, Gen. Tomás Regalado, 1898-1903. k, Pedro José Escalón, 1903-07. l, Dr. Manuel Enrique Araujo, 1911-13. m, Carlos Meléndez, 1913-14, 1915-18. n, Dr. Alfonso Quiñones Molina, 1914-15, 1918-19, 1923-27. o, Jorge Meléndez, 1919-23. p, Dr. Pío Romero Bosque, 1927-31. q, Arturo Araujo, 1931. r, Gen. Maximiliano Hernández Martínez, 1931-34, 1935-44. s, Gen. Salvador Castaneda Castro, 1945-48. t, Col. Oscar Osorio, 1950-56.

2008, Apr. 30　　**Perf. 14¼x14**
1679 A611 10c Sheet of 20, #a-t　5.00 5.00

Friendship Between Israel and El Salvador, 60th Anniv. A612

2008, May 29　　**Perf. 14x14¼**
1680 A612 10c multi　　.55 .55

2008 Summer Olympics, Beijing A613

No. 1681 — Salvadoran Olympic Committee emblem and: a, Cycling. b, Tennis. c, Weight lifting. d, Running.
50c, Judo, women's basketball, horiz.

2008, July 3　　**Perf. 14¼x14**
1681　　Horiz. strip of 4　2.00 2.00
a.-d.　A613 20c Any single　.40 .40

Souvenir Sheet
Rouletted 10½
1682 A613 50c multi　　2.00 2.00

Radio El Salvador, 82nd Anniv. A614

Designs: 25c, Engineer and radio control board. 65c, Radio equipment.

2008, July 31　　**Perf. 14¼x14**
1683-1684 A614　Set of 2　2.25 2.25

Central American Integration System A615

2008, Sept. 3　　**Perf. 14x14¼**
1685 A615 $5 multi　　12.50 12.50

Villa Palestina A616

2008, Sept. 4　　**Perf. 14¼x14**
1686 A616 5c multi　　.30 .30

Miniature Sheet

Art of Fernando Llort — A617

No. 1687 — Details: a, Man waving. b, Man and animal. c, House and trees. d, Woman with basket on head holding child. e, Turkey and sun. f, Rooster and path. g, Man on horse on path. h, Short and tall women on path. i, Woman with jug on head, houses. j, Woman at well.

2008, Sept. 19　　**Perf. 14x14¼**
1687 A617 20c Sheet of 10, #a-j　5.00 5.00

Salvadoran Foundation for Economic Development, 25th Anniv. A618

2008, Oct. 22　　**Perf. 14¼x14**
1688 A618 $1 multi　　2.50 2.50

18th Iberoamerican Summit, El Salvador — A619

2008, Oct. 27　　**Perf. 14x14¼**
1689 A619 $1 multi　　2.50 2.50

America Issue, Festivals A620

Designs: 20c, Feria de las Palmas. 75c, Fiestas del Divino Salvador del Mundo.

2008, Nov. 7
1690-1691 A620　Set of 2　3.00 3.00

Ministry of Exterior Relations, 150th Anniv.
A621

2009, Apr. 3   Litho.   Perf. 14x14¼
1692 A621 10c multi   .30   .30

2009 Presidential Elections
A622

2009, May 4   Perf. 14¼x14
1693 A622 10c multi   .30   .30

Intl. Year of Astronomy
A623

No. 1694: a, Galileo Galilei (1564-1642), astronomer. b, Planetary moons discovered by Galileo. c, San Jan Talpa Astronomical Observatory. d, Meade Schmidt-Cassegrain telescope.

2009, May 27
1694   Horiz. strip of 4   2.50   2.50
a.-d. A623 25c Any single   .50   .50

Miniature Sheets

National Symbols and Departmental Arms — A624

No. 1695, 10c: a, Eumomota superciliosa (national bird). b, Arms of Ahuachapan. c, Arms of Santa Ana. d, Arms of Sonsonate. e, Arms of La Libertad. f, Arms of Chalatenango. g, Arms of San Salvador. h, Arms of Cuscatlan.
No. 1696, 10c: a, Yucca elephantipes (national flower). b, Arms of La Paz. c, Arms of Cabañas. d, Arms of San Vicente. e, Arms of Usulutan. f, Arms of San Miguel. g, Arms of Morazan. h, Arms of La Union.

2009, July 22   Perf. 14¼x14
Sheets of 8, #a-h
1695-1696 A624   Set of 2   8.00   8.00

Tourism
A625

No. 1697: a, Butterfly, flower, Sapo River. b, Cranes, Jaltepeque Estuary. c, Butterfly, flowers, San Vicente Volcano. d, Butterfly, flowers, La Unión shoreline.
No. 1698: a, Pottery vendor, building, Guatajiagua. b, Man in costume, street in Izalco. c, Orchids, El Caracol Waterfall,

---

Arambala. d, Native American sculpture, building, Ilobasco.

2009, Sept. 4   Litho.   Perf. 14x14¼
1697   Vert. strip of 4   1.00   1.00
a.-d. A625 5c Any single   .25   .25
1698   Vert. strip of 4   1.00   1.00
a.-d. A625 5c Any single   .25   .25
e.   Block of 8, ##1697a-1697d,
        1698a-1698d   2.00   2.00

America Issue
A626

No. 1699 — Children's games: a, Jump rope. b, Hopscotch.

2009, Oct. 15
1699 A626 $1 Vert. pair, #a-b   5.50   5.50

Christmas
A627

No. 1700: a, Candles, Bible passage, ornament. b, Madonna and child, star of Bethlehem, poinsettia. c, St. Joseph, lamb, dove, poinsettia. d, Magi, poinsettias, ornament.

2009, Nov. 30   Perf. 14¼x14
1700   Horiz. strip of 4   1.25   1.25
a.-d. A627 10c Any single   .25   .25

A628

A629

Oscar A. Romero (1917-80), Assassinated Archbishop of San Salvador — A630

No. 1701: a, Romero with hand raised. b, Romero and silhouette.
No. 1702: a, Romero touching person's head. b, Romero over church.
No. 1703: a, Romero. b, Romero and Salvadoran people.

2010, Mar. 19
1701 A628 $1 Horiz. pair, #a-b   5.00   5.00
1702 A629 $1 Horiz. pair, #a-b   5.00   5.00
1703 A630 $1 Horiz. pair, #a-b   5.00   5.00
     Nos. 1701-1703 (3)   15.00 15.00

City of San Vicente, 375th Anniv. — A631

No. 1704 — Arms and: a, Tempisque tree. b, Our Lady of Pilar Basilica. 50c, Cathedral and Tower of San Vicente.

2010, Dec. 15   Perf. 14¼x14
1704 A631 $1 Horiz. pair, #a-b   6.00   6.00
        Souvenir Sheet
        Rouletted 10x10½
1705 A631 50c multi   1.50   1.50

America Issue
A632

No. 1706 — National symbols: a, Coat of arms. b, Flag.

2010   Perf. 14x14¼
1706 A632 $1 Vert. pair, #a-b   5.75   5.75

Children's Day and Missing Children's Day — A633

Denominations: 10c, $1.

2011, Mar. 25   Perf. 14¼x14
1707-1708 A633   Set of 2   3.50   3.50

First Call for Independence, Bicent. — A634

No. 1709: a, Bell and doves. b, José Matías Delgado (1767-1832), independence leader, with hand on book. c, Gen. Manuel José Arce (1787-1847), holding paper. d, Crowd of people.
No. 1710: a, Monument. b, Delgado and bell. c, Delgado and wreath. d, Arce and wreath.

2011, June 7
1709   Horiz. strip of 4   6.25   6.25
a.-d. A634 50c Any single   1.25   1.25
1710   Horiz. strip of 4   6.25   6.25
a.-d. A634 50c Any single   1.25   1.25

Salvadoran Anniversaries — A635

No. 1711: a, Dr. Sun Yat-sen (1866-1925), President of Republic of China. b, José Matías Delgado (1767-1832), Salvadoran independence leader.

2011, Nov. 14
1711 A635 $1 Horiz. pair, #a-b   6.00   6.00

Diplomatic relations between El Salvador and Republic of China, cent. (#1711a), First call for Salvadoran independence, bicent. (#1711b).

America Issue — A636

No. 1712 — Mailbox with: a, Rounded top. b, Flat top.

2011, Nov. 14
1712 A636 $1 Horiz. pair, #a-b   6.00   6.00

Diplomatic Relations Between El Salvador and Canada, 50th Anniv. — A637

No. 1713: a, Maple leaf, "50," map of El Salvador. b, Canada highlighted on map of North America with Canadian flag, arrows.

2011, Dec. 7
1713 A637 $1 Horiz. pair, #a-b   6.00   6.00

Campaign Against Corruption
A638

No. 1714: a, United Nations emblem in eye. b, Exchange of bribe money, emblem of Organization of American States. c, Magnifying glass over map of El Salvador, arms and flag of El Salvador.

2011, Dec. 9
1714   Horiz. strip of 3   8.25   8.25
a.-c. A638 $1 Any single   2.75   2.75

2012 Elections A639

No. 1715: a, Stylized dove. b, House as ballot box.

2012, Mar. 6 **Perf. 14x14¼**
1715 A639 $1 Vert. pair, #a-b 5.25 5.25

Statues of St. John the Baptist — A640

No. 1716 — Statue in: a, Chalatenango Cathedral. b, Monte San Juan Church, Cuscatlán.

2012, June 18 **Perf. 14¼x14**
1716 A640 $1 Horiz. pair, #a-b 5.25 5.25

Signing of Chapultapec Peace Accords, 20th Anniv. — A641

"XX" and: No. 1717, $1, Dove. No. 1718, $1, Doves, book, pen, hands with olive branch.

2012, Sept. 14
1717-1718 A641 Set of 2 5.75 5.75

Cuscatlán Masonic Lodge, Cent. — A642

2012, Sept. 18
1719 A642 $5 multi 13.00 13.00

America Issue — A643

No. 1720 — Myths and legends of: a, The White Dog. b, The Headless Priest.

2012, Oct. 30
1720 A643 $1 Horiz. pair, #a-b 5.25 5.25

Animals and Their Pre-Columbian Ceramic Depictions — A644

No. 1721, 65c: a, Didelphis marsupialis. b, Pots depicting opossom, c. 900-1524.
No. 1722, $1: a, Panthera onca. b, Figurines depicting jaguars, c. 900-1524.
No. 1723, $5: Sylvilagus floridanus. b, Vessels depicting rabbits, c. 250-900.
No. 1724, $10: a, Ateles geoffroyi. b, Vessels depicting spider monkeys, c. 250-900.

2013, May 14 **Litho.** **Perf. 14¼x14**
Horiz. pairs, #a-b
1721-1724 A644 Set of 4 82.50 82.50

Salvadoran Air Force, 90th Anniv. — A645

Frame color: 65c, Purple. $1, Red brown.

2013, Dec. 9 **Litho.** **Perf. 14¼x14**
1725-1726 A645 Set of 2 3.50 3.50

Ciudad Mujer Women's Services Program A646

2014, June 12 **Litho.** **Perf. 11**
1727 A646 $1 multi 2.00 2.00

Archbishop Oscar Arnulfo Romero (1917-80) A647

2014, June 23 **Litho.** **Perf. 11**
1728 A647 65c multi 1.40 1.40
Renaming of El Salvador International Airport to honor Archbishop Romero.

National Association of the Sovereign Military of Malta, 40th Anniv. — A648

No. 1729: a, Rosales Hospital, San Salvador. b, Embassy of the Sovereign Military Order of Malta, Santa Elena.

2014, June 25 **Litho.** **Perf. 11**
1729 A648 20c Horiz. pair, #a-b .80 .80

University of El Salvador, 173rd Anniv. A649

2014, Dec. 8 **Litho.** **Perf. 11**
1730 A649 20c multi .40 .40

Diplomatic Relations Between El Salvador and Japan, 80th Anniv. — A650

No. 1731: a, 80th anniv. emblem. b, Children with Japanese and Salvadoran flags, 80th anniv. emblem.

2015, Feb. 13 **Litho.** **Perf. 14¼x14**
1731 A650 $2.50 Horiz. pair, #a-b 10.00 10.00

Beatification of Archbishop Oscar Romero (1917-80) A651

Designs: 5c, Romero wearing zucchetto. 10c, Romero wearing stole. 20c, Crypt. $1, Romero with children.

2015, May 23 **Litho.** **Perf. 14¼x14**
1732-1735 A651 Set of 4 2.75 2.75

Decree Declaring Name of Country as Republic of El Salvador, Cent. — A652

Denominations: $1, $5.

2015, June 7 **Litho.** **Perf. 14¼x14**
1736-1737 A652 Set of 2 12.00 12.00

Bonn Challenge to Restore Depleted and Deforested Lands — A653

Designs: 20c, Emblem. $1, Boat on Barra de Santiago.

2015, Aug. 19 **Litho.** **Perf. 14¼x14**
1738-1739 A653 Set of 2 2.40 2.40

Labor Union Day — A654

2015, Oct. 30 **Litho.** **Perf. 11**
1740 A654 3c multi .25 .25

Indigenous People A655

Mi Cultura emblem and: 5c, Group of women. 20c, People drinking.

2015, Nov. 4 **Litho.** **Perf. 11**
1741-1742 A655 Set of 2 .50 .50

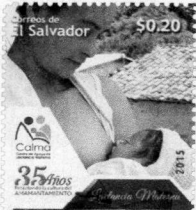

Breastfeeding Help Center, 35th Anniv. A656

2015, Nov. 11 **Litho.** **Perf. 11**
1743 A656 20c multi .40 .40

Court of Accounts, 75th Anniv. A657

Designs: 5c, 75th anniv. emblem. 75c, Building.

2015, Nov. 11 **Litho.** **Perf. 11**
1744-1745 A657 Set of 2 1.60 1.60

Postal Service of El Salvador, 168th Anniv. A658

2015, Nov. 18 **Litho.** **Perf. 11**
1746 A658 $1 multi 2.00 2.00

Campaign to End Violence Against Women A659

2015, Nov. 25 Litho. *Perf. 11*
1747 A659 $2.50 multi 5.00 5.00

See Dominican Republic No. 1583, Ecuador No. 2173, Guatemala No. 717, Venezuela No. 1731.

Department of La Libertad, 150th Anniv. — A660

2015, Nov. 26 Litho. *Perf. 11*
1748 A660 1c multi .25 .25

Salvadoran Philatelic Association, 75th Anniv. — A661

2015, Dec. 7 Litho. *Perf. 11*
1749 A661 20c multi .40 .40

Archbishop Oscar Arnulfo Romero (1917-80) A662

Migrants and Archbishop Romero: $2.50, Wearing miter. $10, Without miter.

2016, May 24 Litho. *Perf. 14¼x14*
1750-1751 A662 Set of 2 25.00 25.00

National Day of Solidarity With People With HIV — A663

2016, May 31 Litho. *Perf. 14¼x14*
1752 A663 5c black & red .25 .25

Ernesto Antonio Claramount Rozeville (1924-2008), Presidential Candidate A664

Rozeville: 10c, Color photograph. 20c, Black-and-white photograph.

2016, July 20 Litho. *Perf. 14¼x14*
1753-1754 A664 Set of 2 .60 .60

National Police Force, 24th Anniv. — A665

Designs: 65c, Police cars. $1, Police officers.

2016, Aug. 15 Litho. *Perf. 14¼x14*
1755-1756 A665 Set of 2 3.50 3.50

Ties Between El Salvador and Republic of China — A666

Flags of El Salvador and Republic of China and: 20c, Tree, bird and volcano. 75c, Trees.

2016, Oct. 14 Litho. *Perf. 14¼x14*
1757-1758 A666 Set of 2 1.90 1.90

Enrique Drews (1844-1916), Orchestra Director A667

2016, Oct. 31 Litho. *Perf. 14¼x14*
1759 A667 $5 multi 10.00 10.00

Chapultepec Peace Accords, 25th Anniv. — A668

2017, Jan. 13 Litho. *Perf. 14¼x14*
1760 A668 25c multi .50 .50

Inter-American Defense Board, 75th Anniv. — A669

Map of North and South America and: 5c, Emblems of Inter-American Defense Board and Armed Forces of El Salvador. 20c, Map of El Salvador, emblems of Salvadoran Army, Air Force and Navy.

2017, Mar. 30 Litho. *Perf. 11¾*
1761-1762 A669 Set of 2 .50 .50

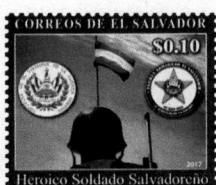

Heroic Soldier, Coat of Arms and Flag of El Salvador, Emblem of Salvadoran Armed Forces A670

2017, May 8 Litho. *Perf. 11*
1763 A670 10c multi .25 .25

First Postage Stamps of El Salvador, 150th Anniv. A671

Vignette color: 5c, Blue. 20c, Red. 75c, Green. $1, Brown.

Perf. 11¾ Rough
2017, May 26 Litho.
1764-1767 A671 Set of 4 4.00 4.00

National Civil Police, 25th Anniv. — A672

2017, Aug. 14 Litho. *Perf. 11¾*
1768 A672 10c multi .25 .25

National Theater A673

National Palace A674

No. 1769 — National Theater: a, Entrance. b, View of ceiling. c, Corner of building. d, View of stage from balcony.
No. 1770 — National Palace: a, Entrance, three windows on top floor on each side of outer pillars. b, Room with tables. c, Entrance, seven windows on top floor on each side of outer pillars. d, Room without tables.

2017, Aug. 23 Litho. *Perf. 11¾*
1769 Vert. strip of 4 8.00 8.00
a.-d. A673 $1 Any single 2.00 2.00
1770 Vert. strip of 4 8.00 8.00
a.-d. A674 $1 Any single 2.00 2.00

Independence, 196th Anniv. — A675

2017, Sept. 12 Litho. *Perf. 11¾*
1771 A675 20c multi .40 .40

Christmas A676

2017, Nov. 13 Litho. *Perf. 11¾*
1772 A676 50c multi 1.00 1.00

Writers A677

No. 1773: a, Hugo Lindo (1917-85). b, Matilde Elena López (1919-2010). c, Salvador Salazar Arrué (1899-1975). d, Lilian Jiménez. e, Francisco Gavidia (1863-1955).

2017, Dec. 6 Litho. *Perf. 11¾*
1773 Horiz. strip of 5 10.00 10.00
a.-e. A677 $1 Any single 2.00 2.00

History of Aeronautics in El Salvador — A678

Designs: 5c, Emblem of International Civil Aviation Organization. 10c, Airplane carrying mail, 1928. 20c, Airplane of Father Domingo Lara. 75c, Enrico Massi (1897-1923), and his airplane.

2017, Dec. 7 Litho. *Perf. 11¾*
1774-1777 A678 Set of 4 2.25 2.25

Japanese International Cooperation Agency, 50th Anniv. in El Salvador — A679

Denominations: 5c, 75c.

2018, Jan. 8 Litho. *Perf. 11¾*
1778-1779 A679 Set of 2 1.60 1.60

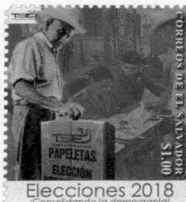

2018 Elections
A680

2018, Mar. 1   Litho.   Perf. 11¾
1780 A680 $1 multi   2.00 2.00

Chancellery of
El Salvador,
160th
Anniv. — A681

2018, June 25   Litho.   Perf. 14¼x14
1781 A681 $10 multi   20.00 20.00

Alberto Masferrer (1868-1932),
Writer — A682

2018, July 24   Litho.   Perf. 14x14¼
1782 A682 50c multi   1.00 1.00

National
Civil Police
Force, 26th
Anniv.
A683

2018, Aug. 13   Litho.   Perf. 14x14¼
1783 A683 $2.50 multi   5.00 5.00

Society of
Mary, 200th
Anniv. (in
2016) — A684

2018, Aug. 17   Litho.   Perf. 14¼x14
1784 A684 $1 multi   2.00 2.00

Literacy
Campaign
A685

2018, Sept. 7   Litho.   Perf. 14¼x14
1785 A685 5c multi   .25   .25

Athenaeum of
El Salvador,
106th
Anniv. — A686

2018, Sept. 20   Litho.   Perf. 14¼x14
1786 A686 75c multi   1.50 1.50

Chirajito (1936-2010), Clown — A687

2018, Sept. 24   Litho.   Perf. 14x14¼
1787 A687 25c multi   .50   .50

Canonization
of St. Oscar
Romero
(1917-80)
A688

Various depictions of St. Oscar Romero,
20c, 25c, 50c, $1.

2018, Oct. 3   Litho.   Perf. 14¼x14
1788-1791 A688   Set of 4   4.00 4.00

A689

2018, Oct. 17   Litho.   Perf. 14x14¼
1792 A689 $1 multi   2.00 2.00
Awarding of Universal Postal Union silver
quality award to El Salvador for Express Mail
Service.

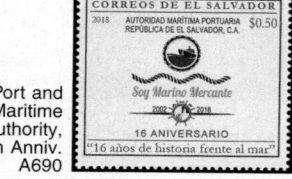

Port and
Maritime
Authority,
16th Anniv.
A690

2018, Oct. 26   Litho.   Perf. 14x14¼
1793 A690 50c multi   1.00 1.00

Military History
Center, 25th
Anniv. — A691

2018, Oct. 30   Litho.   Perf. 14¼x14
1794 A691 $1 multi   2.00 2.00

A692

A693

A694

A695

El Salvador
Travel Sites,
Emblems
and
Slogans
A696

2018, Nov. 16   Litho.   Perf. 14x14¼
1795   Horiz. strip of 5   1.25 1.25
   a. A692 10c multi   .25   .25
   b. A693 10c multi   .25   .25
   c. A694 10c multi   .25   .25
   d. A695 10c multi   .25   .25
   e. A696 10c multi   .25   .25

José Arturo Castellanos (1893-1977),
Diplomat Who Saved Jews in World
War II — A697

2018, Nov. 16   Litho.   Perf. 14x14¼
1796 A697 $5 multi   10.00 10.00

Suchitoto
Tourist
Attractions
A698

No. 1797: a, Los Tercios Waterfall. b, Ale-
jandro Cotto Theater. c, Art Center for Peace
(Centro Arte para la Paz). d, Lake Suchitlán. e,
Santa Lucía Church.

2018, Dec.   Litho.   Perf. 14x14¼
1797   Horiz. strip of 5   7.50 7.50
   a.-e. A698 75c Any single   1.50 1.50

Fe y Alegria
Association in
El Salvador,
50th
Anniv. — A700

2019, Nov. 4   Litho.   Perf. 14¼x14
1799 A700 $1 multi   2.00 2.00

Christmas
A701

2019, Nov. 4   Litho.   Perf. 14¼x14
1800 A701 50c multi   1.00 1.00

Surfing
Beaches
A702

No. 1801: a, Playa El Sunzal. b, Playa Punta
Roca. c, Playa El Zonte. d, Playa Las Flores.
e, Playa El Tunco.

2019, Nov. 8   Litho.   Perf. 14x14¼
1801   Horiz. strip of 5   10.00 10.00
   a.-e. A702 $1 Any single   2.00 2.00

AIR POST STAMPS

Regular Issue of
1924-25 Overprinted
in Black or Red

Back of No. C1

First Printing.
15c on 10c: "15 QUINCE 15" measures
22½mm.
20c: Shows on the back of the stamp an
albino impression of the 50c surcharge.
25c on 35c: Original value canceled by a
long and short bar.
40c on 50c: Only one printing.
50c on 1col: Surcharge in dull orange red.

Perf. 12½, 14
1929, Dec. 28   Unwmk.
C1 A112 20c dp green (Bk)   6.00 5.00
   a.   Red overprint   850.00 850.00
   Counterfeits exist of No. C1a.

**Additional Surcharge of New Values
and Bars in Black or Red**

No. C3   No. C4

No. C5

C3	A111	15c on 10c org	1.10	1.10
a.		"ALTANT CO"	37.50	35.00
C4	A114	25c on 35c scar & grn	2.50	2.25
a.		Bars inverted	10.00	10.00
C5	A115	40c on 50c org brn	.85	.55
C6	A116	50c on 1col grn & bl vio (R)	15.00	10.00
		Nos. C1-C6 (5)	25.45	18.90

No. C7

Back of No. C7

No. C9

No. C10

Second Printing.
15c on 10c: "15 QUINCE 15" measures 20½mm.
20c: Has not the albino impression on the back of the stamp.
25c on 35c: Original value cancelled by two bars of equal length.
50c on 1col: Surcharge in carmine rose.

1930, Jan. 10

C7	A112	20c deep green	1.00	1.00
C8	A111	15c on 10c org	.75	.75
a.		"ALTANT CO"	37.50	35.00
b.		Double surcharge	20.00	
c.		As "a," double surcharge	75.00	
d.		Pair, one without surcharge	175.00	
C9	A114	25c on 35c scar & grn	.90	.90
C10	A116	50c on 1col grn & bl vio (C)	2.00	2.00
a.		Without bars over "UN CO-LON"	4.50	
b.		As "a," without block over "1"	4.50	
		Nos. C7-C10 (4)	4.65	4.65

Numerous wrong font and defective letters exist in both printings of the surcharges.
No. C10 with black surcharge is bogus.

Mail Plane over San Salvador AP1

1930, Sept. 15   Engr.   Perf. 12½

C11	AP1	15c deep red	.40	.25
C12	AP1	20c emerald	.40	.25
C13	AP1	25c brown violet	.40	.25
C14	AP1	40c ultra	.60	.25
		Nos. C11-C14 (4)	1.80	1.00

Simón Bolivar — AP2

1930, Dec. 17   Litho.   Perf. 11½

C15	AP2	15c deep red	6.00	5.00
a.		"15" double	82.50	
C16	AP2	20c emerald	6.00	5.00
C17	AP2	25c brown violet	6.00	5.00
a.		Vert. pair, imperf. btwn.	175.00	
b.		Imperf., pair		
C18	AP2	40c dp ultra	6.00	5.00
		Nos. C15-C18 (4)	24.00	20.00

Centenary of death of Simón Bolivar. Counterfeits of Nos. C15-C18 exist.

No. 504 Overprinted in Red

1931, June 29   Engr.   Perf. 14
C19 A116 1col green & vio   4.50 3.00

Tower of La Merced Church — AP3

1931, Nov. 5   Litho.   Perf. 11½

C20	AP3	15c dark red	4.50	3.25
a.		Imperf., pair	50.00	
C21	AP3	20c blue green	4.50	3.25
C22	AP3	25c dull violet	4.50	3.25
a.		Vert. pair, imperf. btwn.	110.00	
C23	AP3	40c ultra	4.50	3.25
a.		Imperf., pair	60.00	
		Nos. C20-C23 (4)	18.00	13.00

120th anniv. of the 1st movement toward the political independence of El Salvador. In the tower of La Merced Church (AP3) hangs the bell which José Matias Delgado-called the Father of his Country-rang to initiate the movement for liberty.

José Matias Delgado — AP4

1932, Nov. 12   Wmk. 271   Perf. 12½

C24	AP4	15c dull red & vio	1.25	1.10
C25	AP4	20c blue grn & bl	1.60	1.40
C26	AP4	25c dull vio & brn	1.60	1.40
C27	AP4	40c ultra & grn	1.90	1.75
		Nos. C24-C27 (4)	6.35	5.65

1st centenary of the death of Father José Matías Delgado, who is known as the Father of El Salvadoran Political Emancipation. Nos. C24-C27 show cheek without shading in the 72nd stamp of each sheet.

Airplane and Caravels of Columbus — AP5

1933, Oct. 12   Wmk. 240   Perf. 13

C28	AP5	15c red orange	2.00	1.75
C29	AP5	20c blue green	3.00	2.50
C30	AP5	25c lilac	3.00	2.50
C31	AP5	40c ultra	3.00	2.50
C32	AP5	1col black	3.00	2.50
		Nos. C28-C32 (5)	14.00	11.75

Saling of Chistopher Columbus from Palos, Spain, for the New World, 441st anniv.

Police Barracks Type

1934, Dec. 16   Perf. 12½

C33	A123	25c lilac	.60	.25
C34	A123	30c brown	.95	.45
a.		Imperf., pair	80.00	
C35	A123	1col black	2.40	1.00
		Nos. C33-C35 (3)	3.95	1.70

Runner AP7

1935, Mar. 16   Engr.   Unwmk.

C36	AP7	15c carmine	3.75	2.25
C37	AP7	25c violet	3.75	2.25
C38	AP7	30c brown	3.00	1.75
C39	AP7	55c blue	20.00	8.50
C40	AP7	1col black	13.00	8.00
		Nos. C36-C40 (5)	43.50	22.75

Third Central American Games.
For overprints and surcharge see Nos. C41-C45, C53.

Nos. C36-C40 Overprinted in Black

HABILITADO

1935, June 27

C41	AP7	15c carmine	3.00	1.40
C42	AP7	25c violet	3.00	1.40
C43	AP7	30c brown	3.00	1.40
C44	AP7	55c blue	17.00	14.00
C45	AP7	1col black	7.50	6.00
		Nos. C41-C45 (5)	33.50	24.20

Flag of El Salvador Type

1935, Oct. 26   Litho.   Wmk. 240
C46 A125 30c black brown   .40 .35

Tree of San Vicente Type

1935, Dec. 26   Perf. 12½

Numerals in Black, Tree in Yellow Green

C47	A126	10c orange	.75	.60
C48	A126	15c brown	.75	.60
C49	A126	20c dk blue grn	.75	.60
C50	A126	25c dark purple	.75	.60
C51	A126	30c black brown	.75	.60
		Nos. C47-C51 (5)	3.75	3.00

Tercentenary of San Vicente.

No. 565 Overprinted in Red

1937   Engr.   Unwmk.
C52 A133 15c dk olive bis   .35 .25
a.   Double overprint   25.00

No. C44 Surcharged in Red

C53 AP7 30c on 55c blue   1.50 .60

Panchimalco Church — AP10

1937, Dec. 3   Engr.   Perf. 12

C54	AP10	15c orange yel	.30	.25
C55	AP10	20c green	.30	.25
C56	AP10	25c violet	.30	.25
C57	AP10	30c brown	.30	.25
C58	AP10	40c blue	.30	.25

C59	AP10	1col black	1.40	.45
C60	AP10	5col rose carmine	4.50	3.25
		Nos. C54-C60 (7)	7.40	4.95

US Constitution Type of Regular Issue

1938, Apr. 22   Engr. & Litho.
C61 A136 30c multicolored   .95 .70

José Simeón Cañas y Villacorta — AP12

1938, Aug. 18   Engr.

C62	AP12	15c orange	1.40	1.25
C63	AP12	20c brt green	1.75	1.25
C64	AP12	30c redsh brown	1.90	1.25
C65	AP12	1col black	6.00	4.50
		Nos. C62-C65 (4)	11.05	8.25

José Simeón Cañas y Villacorta (1767-1838), liberator of slaves in Central America.

Golden Gate Bridge, San Francisco Bay — AP13

1939, Apr. 14   Perf. 12½

C66	AP13	15c dull yel & blk	.45	.25
C67	AP13	30c dk brown & blk	.45	.25
C68	AP13	40c dk blue & blk	.60	.45
		Nos. C66-C68 (3)	1.50	.95

Golden Gate Intl. Exposition, San Francisco. For surcharges see Nos. C86-C91.

Sir Rowland Hill Type

1940, Mar. 1   Engr.

| C69 | A146 | 30c dk brn, buff & blk | 8.00 | 2.50 |
| C70 | A146 | 80c org red & blk | 22.50 | 17.50 |

Centenary of the postage stamp. Covers postmarked Feb. 29 were predated. Actual first day was Mar. 1.

Map of the Americas, Figure of Peace, Plane — AP15

1940, May 22   Perf. 12

| C71 | AP15 | 30c brown & blue | .45 | .25 |
| C72 | AP15 | 80c dk rose & blk | .85 | .55 |

Pan American Union, 50th anniversary.

Coffee Tree in Bloom — AP16

Coffee Tree with Ripe Berries — AP17

1940, Nov. 27
C73	AP16	15c yellow orange	1.60	.45
C74	AP16	20c deep green	2.25	.45
C75	AP16	25c dark violet	2.50	.55
C76	AP17	30c copper brown	3.00	.25
C77	AP17	1col black	9.00	.70
		Nos. C73-C77 (5)	18.35	2.40

Juan Lindo, Gen. Francisco Malespin and New National University of El Salvador — AP18

Designs (portraits changed): 40c, 80c, Narciso Monterey and Antonio José Canas. 60c, 1col, Isidro Menéndez and Chrisanto Salazar.

1941, Feb. 16 — Perf. 12½
C78	AP18	20c dk grn & rose lake	1.25	.70
C79	AP18	40c ind & brn org	1.25	.70
C80	AP18	60c dl pur & brn	1.40	.70
C81	AP18	80c hn brn & dk bl grn	3.00	2.00
C82	AP18	1col black & org	3.00	2.00
C83	AP18	2col yel org & rose vio	3.00	2.00
a.		Min. sheet of 6, #C78-C83, perf. 11½	15.00	15.00
		Nos. C78-C83 (6)	12.90	8.10

Centenary of University of El Salvador. Stamps from No. C83a, perf. 11½, sell for about the same values as the perf. 12½ stamps.

Catalogue values for unused stamps in this section, from this point to the end of the section, are for Never Hinged items.

Map of El Salvador AP20

Wmk. 269
1942, Nov. 25 Engr. Perf. 14
C85	AP20	30c red orange	.80	.45
a.		Horiz. pair, imperf. between	100.00	

1st Eucharistic Cong. of El Salvador. See #588.

Nos. C66-C68 Surcharged in Dark Carmine

1943 Unwmk. Perf. 12½
C86	AP13	15c on 15c dl yel & blk	.45	.25
C87	AP13	20c on 30c dk brn & blk	.60	.45
C88	AP13	25c on 40c dk bl & blk	1.25	.75
		Nos. C86-C88 (3)	2.30	1.45

Nos. C66-C68 Surcharged in Dark Carmine

1944
C89	AP13	15c on 15c dl yel & blk	.45	.25
C90	AP13	20c on 30c dk brn & blk	.75	.45
C91	AP13	25c on 40c dk bl & blk	1.25	.45
		Nos. C89-C91 (3)	2.45	1.15

Bridge Type of Regular Issue Arms Overprint at Right in Blue Violet
1944, Nov. 24 Engr.
C92	A149	30c crim rose & blk	.45	.25

No. C92 exists without overprint, but was not issued in that form.

Presidential Palace AP22

National Theater AP23

National Palace AP24

1944, Dec. 22 Perf. 12½
C93	AP22	15c red violet	.25	.25
C94	AP23	20c dk blue grn	.25	.25
C95	AP24	25c dull violet	.25	.25
		Nos. C93-C95 (3)	.75	.75

For surcharge and overprint see Nos. C145-C146.

No. 582 Overprinted in Red

1945, Aug. 23 Perf. 12
C96	A137	1col black	1.00	.25

Juan Ramon Uriarte — AP25

Wmk. 240
1946, Jan. 1 Typo. Perf. 12½
C97	AP25	12c dark blue	.45	.25
C98	AP25	14c deep orange	.45	.25

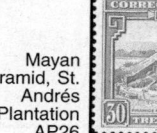

Mayan Pyramid, St. Andrés Plantation AP26

Municipal Children's Garden, San Salvador AP27

Civil Aeronautics School, Ilopango Airport AP28

1946, May 1 Unwmk.
C99	AP26	30c rose carmine	.45	.25
C100	AP27	40c deep ultra	.45	.25
C101	AP28	1col black	1.50	.45
		Nos. C99-C101 (3)	2.40	1.15

For surcharge see No. C121.

Alberto Masferrer — AP29

1946, July 19 Litho. Wmk. 240
C102	AP29	12c carmine	.45	.25
C103	AP29	14c dull green	.45	.25
a.		Imperf., pair	12.50	

Souvenir Sheets

AP30

Designs: 40c, Charles I of Spain. 60c, Juan Manuel Rodriguez. 1col, Arms of San Salvador. 2col, Flag of El Salvador.

Perf. 12, Imperf.
1946, Nov. 8 Engr. Unwmk.
C104	AP30	Sheet of 4	4.50	4.50
a.		40c brown	1.00	1.00
b.		60c carmine	1.00	1.00
c.		1col green	1.00	1.00
d.		2col ultramarine	1.00	1.00

4th cent. of San Salvador's city charter. The imperf. sheets are without gum.

Felipe Soto — AP31

Alfredo Espino — AP32

Wmk. 240
1947, Sept. 11 Litho. Perf. 12½
C106	AP31	12c chocolate	.25	.25
C107	AP32	14c dark blue	.25	.25

For surcharges see Nos. 627-630.

Arce Type of Regular Issue
1948, Feb. 26 Engr. Unwmk.
C108	A163	12c green	.25	.25
C109	A163	14c rose carmine	.45	.25
C110	A163	1col violet	3.25	2.00
		Nos. C108-C110 (3)	3.95	2.50

Cent. of the death of Manuel José Arce (1783-1847). "Father of Independence" and 1st pres. of the Federation of Central America.

Roosevelt Types of Regular Issue

Designs: 12c, Pres. Franklin D. Roosevelt. 14c, Pres. Roosevelt presenting awards for distinguished service. 20c, Roosevelt and Cordell Hull. 25c, Pres. and Mrs. Roosevelt. 1col, Mackenzie King, Roosevelt and Winston Churchill. 2col, Funeral of Pres. Roosevelt. 4col, Pres. and Mrs. Roosevelt.

1948, Apr. 12 Engr. Perf. 12½
Various Frames, Center in Black
C111	A165	12c green	.60	.45
C112	A164	14c olive	.60	.45
C113	A164	20c chocolate	.60	.45
C114	A164	25c carmine	.60	.45
C115	A164	1col violet brn	2.25	1.10
C116	A164	2col blue violet	3.25	1.75
		Nos. C111-C116 (6)	7.90	4.65

Souvenir Sheet
Perf. 13½
C117	A166	4col gray & brn	5.50	3.75

Nos. 599, 601 and 604 Overprinted in Carmine or Black

1948, Sept. 7 Perf. 12½
C118	A154	5c slate gray	.25	.25
C119	A154	10c bister brown	.25	.25
C120	A154	1col scarlet (Bk)	1.90	.60
		Nos. C118-C120 (3)	2.40	1.10

No. C99 Surcharged in Black

1949, July 23
C121	AP26	10(c) on 30c rose car	.25	.25

UPU Type of Regular Issue
1949, Oct. 9 Engr. Perf. 12½
C122	A167	5c brown	.60	.25
C123	A167	10c black	.85	.25
C124	A167	1col purple	24.00	17.50
		Nos. C122-C124 (3)	25.45	18.00

Flag and Arms of El Salvador — AP38

1949, Dec. 15 Perf. 10½
Flag and Arms in Blue, Yellow and Green
C125	AP38	5c ocher	.25	.25
C126	AP38	10c dk green	.25	.25
a.		Yellow omitted	25.00	
C127	AP38	15c violet	.45	.25
C128	AP38	1col rose	.95	.55
C129	AP38	5col red violet	7.50	5.50
		Nos. C125-C129 (5)	9.40	6.80

1st anniv. of the Revolution of 12/14/48.

Isabella I of
Spain — AP39

1951, Apr. 28   Litho.   Unwmk.
Background in Ultramarine, Red
and Yellow

C130	AP39	10c green	.40	.25
C131	AP39	20c purple	.40	.25
a.		Horiz. pair, imperf. between	25.00	
C132	AP39	40c rose carmine	.55	.25
C133	AP39	1col black brown	1.75	.65
		Nos. C130-C133 (4)	3.10	1.40

500th anniv. of the birth of Queen Isabella I
of Spain. Nos. C130-C133 exist imperforate.

Flag, Torch and
Scroll — AP40

1952, Feb. 14   Photo.   Perf. 11½
Flag in Blue

C134	AP40	10c brt blue	.25	.25
C135	AP40	15c chocolate	.25	.25
C136	AP40	20c deep blue	.25	.25
C137	AP40	25c gray	.25	.25
C138	AP40	40c purple	.40	.25
C139	AP40	1col red orange	1.10	.60
C140	AP40	2col orange brn	3.25	2.50
C141	AP40	5col violet blue	3.25	1.40
		Nos. C134-C141 (8)	9.00	5.75

Constitution of 1950.

Marti Type of Regular Issue
Inscribed "Aereo"

1953, Feb. 27   Litho.   Perf. 10½

C142	A170	10c dk purple	.30	.25
C143	A170	20c dull brown	.45	.25
C144	A170	1col dull orange	1.50	.60
		Nos. C142-C144 (3)	2.25	1.10

No. C95 Surcharged "C 0.20" and
Obliterations in Red

1953, Mar. 20   Perf. 12½

C145	AP24	20c on 25c dl vio	.30	.25

No. C95
Overprinted
in Carmine

1953, June 19

C146	AP24	25c dull violet	.55	.25

See note after No. 634.

Bell Tower, La
Merced
Church
AP42

1953, Sept. 15   Perf. 11½

C147	AP42	5c rose pink	.25	.25
C148	AP42	10c dp blue grn	.25	.25
C149	AP42	20c blue	.30	.30
C150	AP42	1col purple	1.25	.65
		Nos. C147-C150 (4)	2.05	1.45

132nd anniv. of the Act of Independence,
Sept. 15, 1821.

Postage Types and

Fishing
Boats — AP43

Gen. Manuel José
Arce — AP44

ODECA
Officials
and Flag
AP46

No. C155, National Palace. No. C157,
Coast guard boat. No. C158, Lake Ilopango.
No. C160, Guayabo dam. No. C161, Housing
development. No. C162, Modern highway. No.
C164, Izalco volcano.

Perf. 11½

1954, June 1   Unwmk.   Photo.

C151	AP43	5c org brn & cr	.30	.25
C152	A175	5c brt carmine	.30	.25
C153	AP44	10c gray blue	.40	.25
C154	A176	10c pur & lt brn	.40	.25
C155	AP43	10c ol & bl blue	.40	.25
C156	AP46	10c bl grn, dk grn & bl	.40	.25
C157	A173	10c rose carmine	.40	.25
C158	A173	15c dk gray	.55	.25
C159	A173	20c pur & gray	.55	.25
C160	A176	25c bl grn & bl	.75	.25
C161	A176	30c mag & sal	.75	.25
C162	A176	40c brt org & brn	1.00	.35
C163	A174	80c red brown	2.00	1.25
C164	AP43	1col magenta & sal	2.25	1.25
C165	A174	2col orange	4.50	1.25
		Nos. C151-C165 (15)	14.95	6.85

Barrios Type of Regular Issue
Wmk. 269

1955, Dec. 20   Engr.   Perf. 12½

C166	A177	20c brown	.35	.30
C167	A177	30c dp red lilac	.35	.35

Santa Ana Type of Regular Issue
Perf. 13½

1956, June 20   Unwmk.   Litho.

C168	A178	5c orange brown	.25	.25
C169	A178	10c green	.25	.25
C170	A178	40c red lilac	.30	.25
C171	A178	80c emerald	.90	.55
C172	A178	5col gray blue	4.50	2.50
		Nos. C168-C172 (5)	6.20	3.80

For overprint see No. C187.

Chalatenango Type of Regular Issue

1956, Sept. 14

C173	A179	10c brt rose	.25	.25
C174	A179	15c orange	.25	.25
C175	A179	20c lt olive grn	.25	.25
C176	A179	25c dull purple	.45	.25
C177	A179	50c orange brn	.70	.45
C178	A179	1col brt vio bl	1.00	.90
		Nos. C173-C178 (6)	2.90	2.35

Nueva San Salvador Type
Wmk. 269

1957, Jan. 3   Engr.   Perf. 12½

C179	A180	10c pink	.25	.25
C180	A180	20c dull red	.25	.25
C181	A180	50c pale org red	.40	.25
C182	A180	1col lt green	.90	.50
C183	A180	2col orange red	2.50	1.25
		Nos. C179-C183 (5)	4.30	2.50

For overprints see Nos. C195, C198.

Lemus' Visit Type of Regular Issue
Perf. 11½

1959, Dec. 14   Unwmk.   Photo.
Granite Paper

Design in Ultramarine, Dark Brown
Light Brown and Red

C184	A182	15c red	.25	.25
C185	A182	20c green	.30	.25
C186	A182	30c carmine	.25	.25
		Nos. C184-C186 (3)	.80	.75

No. C169 Overprinted in Red: "ANO
MUNDIAL DE LOS REFUGIADOS
1959-1960"

1960, Apr. 7   Litho.   Perf. 13½

C187	A178	10c green	.35	.25

World Refugee Year, 7/1/59-6/30/60.

Poinsettia Type of Regular Issue
Perf. 11½

1960, Dec. 17   Unwmk.   Photo.
Granite Paper

Design in Slate Green, Red and
Yellow

C188	A184	20c rose lilac	.35	.25
C189	A184	30c gray	.40	.35
C190	A184	40c light gray	.60	.25
C191	A184	50c salmon pink	.95	.45
		Nos. C188-C191 (4)	2.30	1.30

Miniature Sheet
Imperf

C192	A184	60c gold	8.00	8.00
a.		Ovptd. in sheet margin ('61)	16.00	16.00
b.		Ovptd. in sheet margin ('61)	16.00	16.00
c.		Ovptd. in sheet margin ('62)	16.00	16.00
d.		Ovptd. in sheet margin ('63)	16.00	16.00
e.		Ovptd. in sheet margin ('63)	16.00	16.00
f.		Ovptd. in sheet margin ('63)	16.00	16.00

Overprints in sheet margin of No. C192:
a, PRIMERA CONVENCION FILATELICA /
CENTRO-AMERICANA / SAN SALVADOR,
JULIO DE 1961.
b, in purple, Portrait, dates and text commemorating the Death of General Barrios,
96th anniv.
c, in green, Arms of city of Ahuachapan and
PRIMER CENTENARIO / Ciudad de
Ahuachapan / 1862 22 de Febrero 1962.
d, in blue, Soccer players and text commemorating the 1st North & Central American Soccer Championships 24 March - 2 April, 1963.
e, in blue and green, emblem of Alliance for
Progress and text commemorating the 2nd
anniversary of the organization.
f, in blue, Portrait of Dr. Manuel Araujo and
College Arms with text commemorating the
4th Latin American Cong. of Pathological
Anatomy and 10th Central American Medical
Cong., Dec., 1963.
For surcharge see No. C196.

Nos. 672, 691 and C183 Ovptd. "III
Exposición Industrial
Centroamericana Diciembre de
1962" with "AEREO" Added on Nos.
672, 691

1962, Dec. 21   Perf. 11½, 12½

C193	A174	1col brn org, dk brn & bl	1.50	1.00
C194	A180	1col dull red	.75	.50
C195	A180	2col orange red	1.50	.90
		Nos. C193-C195 (3)	3.75	2.40

3rd Central American Industrial Exposition.
For surcharges see Nos. C197, C199.

Nos. C189, C194, C182 and C195
Surcharged

1963

C196	A184	10c on 30c multi	.35	.25
C197	A180	10c on 1col dl red	.35	.25
C198	A180	10c on 1col lt grn	1.25	.25
C199	A180	10c on 2col org red	1.10	.25
		Nos. C196-C199 (4)	3.05	1.00

Surcharges include: "X" on No. C196; two
dots and bar at bottom on No. C197. Heavy
bar at bottom on No. C198. On No. C199, the
four-line "Exposition" overprint is lower than on
No. C195.

Turquoise-browed Motmot — AP49

Birds: 5c, King vulture (vert., like No. 741).
6c, Yellow-headed parrot, vert. 10c, Spotted-
breasted oriole. 30c, Greattailed grackle.
40c, Great curassow, vert. 50c, Magpie-jay.
80c, Golden-fronted woodpecker, vert.

1963   Unwmk.   Photo.   Perf. 11½
Birds in Natural Colors

C200	AP49	5c gray grn & blk	1.50	.25
C201	AP49	6c tan & blue	1.50	.25
C202	AP49	10c lt bl & blk	1.75	.75
C203	AP49	20c gray & brn	3.00	.90
C204	AP49	30c ol bis & blk	3.75	.90
C205	AP49	40c pale & dk vio	4.50	1.25
C206	AP49	50c lt grn & blk	6.00	1.40
C207	AP49	80c vio bl & blk	9.00	2.45
		Nos. C200-C207 (8)	31.00	7.95

Eucharistic Congress Type
1964-65   Perf. 12x11½

C208	A188	10c slate grn & bl	.25	.25
C209	A188	25c red & blue	.25	.25

Miniature Sheets
Imperf

C210	A188	80c blue & green	1.50	1.00
a.		Marginal ovpt. La Union	1.50	1.00
b.		Marginal ovpt. Usulutan	1.50	1.00
c.		Marginal ovpt. La Libertad	1.00	.85

See note after No. 746.
Issued: #C208-C210, Apr. 16, 1964;
#C210a-C210b, June 22, 1965; #210c, Jan.
28, 1965.
For overprints see Nos. C232, C238.

Kennedy Type of Regular Issue

1964, Nov. 22   Perf. 11½x12

C211	A189	15c gray & blk	.25	.25
C212	A189	20c sage grn & blk	.25	.25
C213	A189	40c yellow & blk	.30	.25
		Nos. C211-C213 (3)	.80	.75

For overprint see No. C259.

Miniature Sheet
Imperf

C214	A189	80c grnsh bl & blk	1.75	1.75
a.		Overprinted in sheet margin in red brown ('69)		

Overprint on No. C214a reads: "Alunizaje /
Apolo-11 / 21 Julio / 1969" and includes pictures of the landing module and astronauts.

Flower Type of Regular Issue

1965, Jan. 6   Photo.   Perf. 12x11½

C215	A190	10c Rose	.65	.25
C216	A190	15c Platanillo	.65	.25
C217	A190	25c San Jose	1.25	.25
C218	A190	40c Hibiscus	1.50	.25
C219	A190	45c Veranera	1.50	.25
C220	A190	70c Fire flower	1.60	.30
		Nos. C215-C220 (6)	7.15	1.55

For overprint and surcharges see Nos.
C243, C348-C349.

ICY Type of Regular Issue
Perf. 11½x12

1965, Apr. 27   Photo.   Unwmk.
Design in Brown and Gold

C221	A191	15c light blue	.25	.25
C222	A191	30c dull lilac	.25	.25
C223	A191	50c ocher	.30	.25
		Nos. C221-C223 (3)	.80	.75

For overprints see Nos. C227, C244, C312.

Gavidia Type of Regular Issue

1965, Sept. 24   Photo.   Unwmk.
Portraits in Natural Colors

C224	A192	10c black & green	.25	.25
C225	A192	20c black & bister	.25	.25
C226	A192	1col black & rose	1.10	.40
		Nos. C224-C226 (3)	1.65	.90

No. C223 Ovptd. in Green "1865 / 12
de Octubre / 1965 / Dr. Manuel
Enrique Araujo"

1965, Oct. 12   Perf. 11½x12

C227	A191	50c brn, ocher & gold	.40	.30

See note after No. 764.

Fair Type of Regular Issue

1965, Nov. 5   Perf. 12x11½

C228	A193	20c blue & multi	.25	.25
C229	A193	80c multi	.55	.30
C230	A193	5col multi	2.75	1.90
		Nos. C228-C230 (3)	3.55	2.45

For overprint see No. C311.

WHO Type of Regular Issue

1966, May 20   Photo.   Unwmk.

C231	A194	50c multicolored	.40	.25

For overprints see Nos. C242, C245.

No. C209 Ovptd. in Dark Green
"1816 1966 / 150 años / Nacimiento
/ San Juan Bosco"

1966, Sept. 3   Photo.   Perf. 12x11½

C232	A188	25c red & blue	.35	.25

150th anniv. of the birth of St. John Bosco
(1815-88), Italian priest, founder of the Salesian Fathers and Daughters of Mary.

UNESCO Type of Regular Issue

1966, Nov. 4   Photo.   Perf. 12

C233	A195	30c tan, blk & vio bl	.25	.25
C234	A195	2col emer, blk & vio bl	1.60	1.00

For surcharge see No. C352.

Fair Type of Regular Issue

1966, Nov. 27　Litho.　*Perf. 12*
C235 A196 15c multicolored　.25　.25
C236 A196 20c multicolored　.25　.25
C237 A196 60c multicolored　.50　.35
　Nos. C235-C237 (3)　1.00　.85

No. C209 Ovptd. "IX-Congreso / Interamericano / de Educacion / Católica / 4 Enero 1967"

1967, Jan. 4　Photo.　*Perf. 12x11½*
C238 A188 25c red & blue　.35　.25
Issued to publicize the 9th Inter-American Congress for Catholic Education.

Cañas Type of Regular Issue

1967, Feb. 18　Litho.　*Perf. 11½*
C239 A197 5c multicolored　.25　.25
C240 A197 45c lt bl & multi　.55　.35
For surcharges see Nos. C403-C405.

Volcano Type of Regular Issue

1967, Apr. 14　Photo.　*Perf. 13*
C241 A198 50c ol gray & brn　.60　.25
For surcharges see Nos. C320, C350

No. C231 Ovptd. in Red "VIII CONGRESO / CENTROAMERICANO DE / FARMACIA & B10QUIMICA / 5 di 11 Noviembre de 1967"

1967, Oct. 26　Photo.　*Perf. 12x11½*
C242 A194 50c multicolored　.45　.40
Issued to publicize the 8th Central American Congress for Pharmacy and Biochemistry.

No. C217 Ovptd. in Red "I Juegos / Centroamericanos y del / Caribe de Basquetbol / 25 Nov. al 3 Dic. 1967"

1967, Nov. 15
C243 A190 25c bl, yel & grn　.30　.25
First Central American and Caribbean Basketball Games, Nov. 25-Dec. 3.

No. C222 Ovptd. in Carmine "1968 / AÑO INTERNACIONAL DE / LOS DERECHOS HUMANOS"

1968, Jan. 2　Photo.　*Perf. 11½x12*
C244 A191 30c dl lil, brn & gold　.40　.30
International Human Rights Year 1968.

No. C231 Ovptd. in Red "1968 / XX ANIVERSARIO DE LA / ORGANIZACION MUNDIAL / DE LA SALUD"

1968, Apr. 7　　　　*Perf. 12x11½*
C245 A194 50c multicolored　.50　.50
20th anniv. of WHO.

No. C229 Ovptd. in Red "1968 / Año / del Sistema / del Crédito / Rural"

1968, May 6　Photo.　*Perf. 12x11½*
C246 A193 80c multicolored　.65　.50
Rural credit system.

Masferrer Type of Regular Issue

1968, June 22　Litho.　*Perf. 12x11½*
C247 A200 5c brown & multi　.25　.25
C248 A200 15c green & multi　.25　.25
For overprint see No. C297.

Scouts Hiking
AP50

1968, July 26　Litho.　*Perf. 12*
C249 AP50 10c multicolored　.30　.25
Issued to publicize the 7th Inter-American Boy Scout Conference, July-Aug., 1968.

Presidents' Meeting Type

1968, Dec. 5　Litho.　*Perf. 14½*
C250 A202 20c salmon & multi　.25　.25
C251 A202 1col lt blue & multi　.75　.50

Butterfly Type of Regular Issue

Designs: Various butterflies.

1969　　　　　Litho.　*Perf. 12*
C252 A203 20c multi　7.25　.30
C253 A203 1col multi　12.00　.70
C254 A203 2col multi　12.00　1.25
C255 A203 10col gray & multi　18.00　6.00
　Nos. C252-C255 (4)　49.25　8.25
For surcharge see No. C353.

Red Cross, Crescent and Lion and Sun Emblems
AP51

1969　　　　　Litho.　*Perf. 11*
C256 AP51 30c yellow & multi　.50　.25
C257 AP51 1col multicolored　1.50　.50
C258 AP51 4col multicolored　3.75　2.50
　Nos. C256-C258 (3)　5.75　3.25
League of Red Cross Societies, 50th anniv. For surcharges see Nos. C351, C354.

No. C213 Ovptd. in Green "Alunizaje / Apolo-11 / 21 Julio / 1969"

1969, Sept.　Photo.　*Perf. 11½x12*
C259 A189 40c yellow & blk　.35　.30
Man's 1st landing on the moon, July 20, 1969. See note after US No. C76.

Hospital Type of Regular Issue

Benjamin Bloom Children's Hospital.

1969, Oct. 24　Litho.　*Perf. 11½*
C260 A205 1col multi　.85　.50
C261 A205 2col multi　1.50　.75
C262 A205 5col multi　4.25　2.50
　Nos. C260-C262 (3)　6.70　4.00
For surcharge see No. C355.

ILO Type of Regular Issue

1969　　　　　Litho.　*Perf. 13*
C263 A206 50c lt bl & multi　.40　.25

Tourist Type of Regular Issue

Views: 20c, Devil's Gate. 35c, Ichanmichen Spa. 60c, Aerial view of Acajutla Harbor.

1969, Dec. 19　Photo.　*Perf. 12x11½*
C264 A207 20c black & multi　.25　.25
C265 A207 35c black & multi　.25　.25
C266 A207 60c black & multi　.40　.30
　Nos. C264-C266 (3)　.90　.80

Insect Type of Regular Issue, 1970

1970, Feb. 24　Litho.　*Perf. 11½x11*
C267 A208 2col Bee　2.50　1.00
C268 A208 3col Elaterida　4.00　1.75
C269 A208 4col Praying
　　　　　　mantis　6.00　2.00
　Nos. C267-C269 (3)　12.50　4.75
For surcharges see Nos. C371-C373.

Human Rights Type of Regular Issue

20c, 80c, Map and arms of Salvador and National Unity emblem similar to A209, but vert.

1970, Apr. 14　Litho.　*Perf. 14*
C270 A209 20c blue & multi　.25　.25
C271 A209 80c blue & multi　.80　.30
For overprint & surcharge see #C301, C402.

Army Type of Regular Issue

Designs: 20c, Fighter plane. 40c, Gun and crew. 50c, Patrol boat.

1970, May 7
C272 A210 20c gray & multi　.25　.25
C273 A210 40c green & multi　.35　.25
C274 A210 50c blue & multi　.40　.25
　Nos. C272-C274 (3)　1.00　.75
For overprint see No. C310.

Brazilian Team, Jules Rimet Cup — AP52

Soccer teams and Jules Rimet Cup.

1970, May 25　Litho.　*Perf. 12*
C275 AP52 1col Belgium　1.10　.65
C276 AP52 1col Brazil　1.10　.65
C277 AP52 1col Bulgaria　1.10　.65
C278 AP52 1col Czechoslova-
　　　　　　kia　1.10　.65
C279 AP52 1col Germany
　　　　　　(Fed. Rep.)　1.10　.65
C280 AP52 1col Britain　1.10　.65
C281 AP52 1col Israel　1.10　.65
C282 AP52 1col Italy　1.10　.65
C283 AP52 1col Mexico　1.10　.65
C284 AP52 1col Morocco　1.10　.65
C285 AP52 1col Peru　1.10　.65
C286 AP52 1col Romania　1.10　.65
C287 AP52 1col Russia　1.10　.65
C288 AP52 1col Salvador　1.10　.65
C289 AP52 1col Sweden　1.10　.65
C290 AP52 1col Uruguay　1.10　.65
　Nos. C275-C290 (16)　17.60　10.40
9th World Soccer Championships for the Jules Rimet Cup, Mexico City, 5/30-6/21/70. For overprints see Nos. C325-C340.

Lottery Type of Regular Issue

1970, July 15　Litho.　*Perf. 12*
C291 A211 80c multi　.65　.25

Education Year Type of Regular Issue

1970, Sept. 11　Litho.　*Perf. 12*
C292 A212 20c pink & multi　.25　.25
C293 A212 2col buff & multi　1.60　.80

Fair Type of Regular Issue

1970, Oct. 28　Litho.　*Perf. 12*
C294 A213 20c multi　.25　.25
C295 A213 30c yel & multi　.30　.25

Music Type of Regular Issue

Johann Sebastian Bach, harp, horn, music.

1971, Feb. 22　Litho.　*Perf. 13½*
C296 A214 40c gray & multi　.75　.25
For overprint see No. C313.

No. C247 Ovptd. "Año / del Centenario de la / Biblioteca Nacional / 1970"

1970, Nov. 25　　　*Perf. 12x11½*
C297 A200 5c brn & multi　.25　.25

Miss Tourism Type of Regular Issue

1971, Apr. 1　Litho.　*Perf. 14*
C298 A215 20c lil & multi　.25　.25
C299 A215 60c gray & multi　.55　.30

Pietà Type of Regular Issue

1971, May 10
C300 A216 40c lt yel grn & vio brn　.35　.25

No. C270 Overprinted in Red Like No. 823

1971, July 6　Litho.　*Perf. 14*
C301 A209 20c bl & multi　.30　.25

Fish Type of Regular Issue

30c, Smalltooth sawfish. 1col, Atlantic sailfish.

1971, July 28
C302 A217 30c lilac & multi　2.10　.35
C303 A217 1col multi　3.50　1.10

Independence Type of Regular Issue

Designs: Various sections of Declaration of Independence of Central America.

1971　　　　　Litho.　*Perf. 13½x13*
C304 A218 30c bl & blk　.25　.25
C305 A218 40c brn & blk　.30　.25
C306 A218 50c yel & blk　.35　.25

C307 A218 60c gray & blk　.50　.25
　a.　Souvenir sheet of 8　2.25　1.60
　Nos. C304-C307 (4)　1.40　1.10
No. C307a contains 8 stamps with simulated perforations similar to Nos. 826-829, C304-C307.
For overprints see Nos. C321, C347.

Church Type of Regular Issue

15c, Metapan Church. 70c, Panchimalco Church.

1971, Aug. 21　Litho.　*Perf. 13x13½*
C308 A219 15c ol & multi　.25　.25
C309 A219 70c multi　.55　.35

No. C274 Overprinted in Red

1971, Oct. 12　Litho.　*Perf. 12*
C310 A210 50c bl & multi　.45　.30
National Navy, 20th anniversary.

No. C229 Ovptd. "V Feria / Internacional / 3-20 Noviembre / de 1972"

1972, Nov. 3　Photo.　*Perf. 12x11½*
C311 A193 80c multi　.90　.50
5th Intl. Fair, El Salvador, Nov. 3-20.

No. C223 Overprinted in Red

1972, Nov. 30　Photo.　*Perf. 11½x12*
C312 A191 50c ocher, brn & gold　.45　.40
30th anniversary of the Inter-American institute for Agricultural Sciences.

No. C296 Overprinted

1973, Feb. 5　Litho.　*Perf. 13½*
C313 A214 40c gray & multi　1.00　.25
3rd International Music Festival, Feb. 9-29.

Lions Type of Regular Issue

Designs: 20c, 40c, Map of El Salvador and Lions International Emblem.

1973, Feb. 20　Litho.　*Perf. 13*
C314 A220 20c gray & multi　.25　.25
C315 A220 40c multi　.30　.25

Olympic Type of Regular Issue

Designs: 20c, Javelin, women's. 80c, Discus, women's. 1col, Hammer throw. 2col, Shot put.

1973, May 21　Litho.　*Perf. 13*
C316 A221 20c lt grn & multi　.45　.25
C317 A221 80c sal & multi　1.00　.35
C318 A221 1col ultra & multi　1.25　.55
C319 A221 2col multi　2.75　.90
　Nos. C316-C319 (4)　5.45　2.05

No. C241 Surcharged Like No. 841

1973, Dec.　　Photo.　*Perf. 13*
C320 A198 25c on 50c multi　.45　.25

No. C307a Ovptd. "Centenario / Cuidad / Santiago de Maria / 1874 1974"

Souvenir Sheet

1974, Mar. 7   Litho.   Imperf.
C321 A218   Sheet of 8   1.90 1.10

Centenary of the City Santiago de Maria. The overprint is so arranged that each line appears on a different pair of stamps.

No. C231 Surcharged in Red

1974, Apr. 22   Photo.   Perf. 12x11½
C322 A194 25c on 50c multi   .35 .25

No. C229 Surcharged

1974, Apr. 24
C323 A193 10c on 80c multi   .45 .25

Rehabilitation Type

1974, Apr. 30   Litho.   Perf. 13
C324 A222 25c multi   .30 .25

Nos. C275-C290 Overprinted

1974, June 4   Litho.   Perf. 12
C325 AP52 1col Belgium   .90 .50
C326 AP52 1col Brazil   .90 .50
C327 AP52 1col Bulgaria   .90 .50
C328 AP52 1col Czech.   .90 .50
C329 AP52 1col Germany   .90 .50
C330 AP52 1col Britain   .90 .50
C331 AP52 1col Israel   .90 .50
C332 AP52 1col Italy   .90 .50
C333 AP52 1col Mexico   .90 .50
C334 AP52 1col Morocco   .90 .50
C335 AP52 1col Peru   .90 .50
C336 AP52 1col Romania   .90 .50
C337 AP52 1col Russia   .90 .50
C338 AP52 1col Salvador   .90 .50
C339 AP52 1col Sweden   .90 .50
C340 AP52 1col Uruguay   .90 .50
   Nos. C325-C340 (16)   14.40 8.00

World Cup Soccer Championship, Munich, June 13-July 7.

INTERPOL Type of 1974

1974, Sept. 2   Litho.   Perf. 12½
C341 A223 25c multi   .25 .25

FAO Type of 1974

1974, Sept. 2   Litho.   Perf. 12½
C342 A224 25c bl, dk bl & gold   .25 .25

Coin Type of 1974

1974, Nov. 19   Litho.   Perf. 12½x13
C343 A225 20c 1p silver, 1892   .25 .25
C344 A225 40c 20c silver, 1828   .30 .25
C345 A225 50c 20p gold, 1892   .50 .25
C346 A225 60c 20col gold, 1925   .50 .35
   Nos. C343-C346 (4)   1.55 1.10

No. C307a Ovptd. "X ASAMBLEA GENERAL DE LA CONFERENCIA / INTERAMERICANA DE SEGURIDAD SOCIAL Y XX / REUNION DEL COMITE PERMANENTE INTERAMERICANO / DE SEGURIDAD SOCIAL, 24 — 30 NOVIEMBRE 1974"

1974, Nov. 18   Litho.   Imperf.
Souvenir Sheet

C347 A218   Sheet of 8   2.50 1.75

Social Security Conference, El Salvador, Nov. 24-30. The overprint is so arranged that each line appears on a different pair of stamps.

Issues of 1965-69 Surcharged

a

b

c

d

1974-75
C348 A190(a) 10c on 45c
   #C219   .60 .25
C349 A190(a) 10c on 70c
   #C220   .60 .25
C350 A198(b) 10c on 50c
   #C241   .75 .25
C351 AP51(d) 25c on 1col
   #C257   .35 .25
C352 A195(c) 25c on 2col
   #C234 ('75)   .75 .25
C353 A203(d) 25c on 2col
   #C234 ('75)   50.00 .25
C354 AP51(d) 25c on 4col
   #C258   .45 .25
C355 A205(d) 25c on 5col
   #C262   .35 .25
   Nos. C348-C355 (8)   53.85 2.00

No. C353 has new value at left and 6 vertical bars. No. C355 has 7 vertical bars.

UPU Type of 1975

1975, Jan. 22   Litho.   Perf. 13
C356 A226 25c bl & multi   .25 .25
C357 A226 30c bl & multi   .25 .25

Acajutla Harbor Type of 1975

1975, Feb. 17
C358 A227 15c bl & multi   .25 .25

Post Office Type of 1975

1975, Apr. 25   Litho.   Perf. 13
C359 A228 25c bl & multi   .35 .25

Miss Universe Type of 1975

1975, June 25   Perf. 12½
C360 A229 25c multi   .25 .25
C361 A229 60c lil & multi   .55 .40

Women's Year Type and

IWY Emblem — AP53

1975, Sept. 4   Litho.   Perf. 12½
C362 A230 15c bl & bl blk   .25 .25
C363 AP53 25c yel grn & blk   .30 .25

International Women's Year 1975.

Nurse Type of 1975

1975, Oct. 24   Litho.   Perf. 12½
C364 A231 25c lt blue & multi   .25 .25

Printers' Congress Type

1975, Nov. 19   Litho.   Perf. 12½
C365 A232 30c green & multi   .25 .25

Dermatologists' Congress Type

1975, Nov. 28
C366 A233 20c blue & multi   .25 .25
C367 A233 30c red & multi   .25 .25

Caritas Type of 1975

1975, Dec. 18   Litho.   Perf. 13½
C368 A234 20c bl & vio bl   .25 .25

UNICEF Emblem — AP54

1975, Dec. 18
C369 AP54 15c lt grn & sil   .25 .25
C370 AP54 20c dl rose & sil   .30 .25

UNICEF, 25th anniv. (in 1971).

Nos. C267-C269 Surcharged

1976, Jan. 14   Perf. 11½x11
C371 A208 25c on 2col multi   2.40 .25
C372 A208 25c on 3col multi   2.40 .25
C373 A208 25c on 4col multi   2.40 .25
   Nos. C371-C373 (3)   7.20 .75

Caularthron Bilamellatum AP55

Designs: Orchids — No. C375, Oncidium oliganthum. No. C376, Epidendrum radicans. No. C377, Epidendrum vitellinum. No. C378, Cyrtopodium punctatum. No. C379, Pleurothallis schiedei. No. C380, Lycaste cruenta. No. C381, Spiranthes speciosa.

1976, Feb. 19   Litho.   Perf. 12½
C374 AP55 25c multi   1.00 .35
C375 AP55 25c multi   1.00 .35
C376 AP55 25c multi   1.00 .35
C377 AP55 25c multi   1.00 .35
C378 AP55 25c multi   1.00 .35
C379 AP55 25c multi   1.00 .35
C380 AP55 25c multi   1.00 .35
C381 AP55 25c multi   1.00 .35
   Nos. C374-C381 (8)   8.00 2.80

CIAT Type of 1976

1976, May 18   Litho.   Perf. 12½
C382 A235 50c org & multi   .55 .25

Bicentennial Types of 1976

1976, June 30   Litho.   Perf. 12½
C383 A236 25c multi   .25 .25
C384 A237 5col multi   3.75 2.50

Reptile Type of 1976

Reptiles: 15c, Green fence lizard. 25c, Basilisk. 60c, Star lizard.

1976, Sept. 23   Litho.   Perf. 12½
C385 A238 15c multi   .50 .25
C386 A238 25c multi   .80 .25
C387 A238 60c multi   2.00 .40
   Nos. C385-C387 (3)   3.30 .90

Archaeology Type of 1976

Pre-Columbian Art: 25c, Brazier with pre-classical head, El Trapiche. 50c, Kettle with pre-classical head, Atiquizaya. 70c, Classical whistling vase, Tazumal.

1976, Oct. 11   Litho.   Perf. 12½
C388 A239 25c multi   .25 .25
C389 A239 50c multi   .45 .25
C390 A239 70c multi   .60 .40
   Nos. C388-C390 (3)   1.30 .90

For overprint see No. C429.

Fair Type of 1976

1976, Oct. 25   Litho.   Perf. 12½
C391 A240 25c multi   .25 .25
C392 A240 70c yel & multi   .55 .40

Christmas Type of 1976

1976, Dec. 16   Litho.   Perf. 11
C393 A241 25c bl & multi   .25 .25
C394 A241 50c multi   .40 .25
C395 A241 60c multi   .50 .30
C396 A241 75c red & multi   .60 .40
   Nos. C393-C396 (4)   1.75 1.20

Rotary Type of 1977

1977, June 20   Litho.   Perf. 11
C397 A242 25c multi   .25 .25
C398 A242 1col multi   .80 .50

Industrial Type of 1977

Designs: 25c, Radar station, Izalco (vert.). 50c, Central sugar refinery, Jiboa. 75c, Cerron Grande hydroelectric station.

1977, June 29   Perf. 12½
C399 A243 25c multi   .25 .25
C400 A243 50c multi   .40 .25
C401 A243 75c multi   .60 .40
   Nos. C399-C401 (3)   1.25 .90

Nos. C399-C401 have colorless overprint in multiple rows: GOBIERNO DEL SALVADOR.

Nos. C271 and C239 Surcharged with New Value and Bar

1977   Perf. 14, 11½
C402 A209 25c on 80c multi   .30 .25
C403 A197 30c on 5c multi   .25 .25
C404 A197 40c on 5c multi   .30 .25
C405 A197 50c on 5c multi   .40 .25
   Nos. C402-C405 (4)   1.25 1.00

Broadcasting Type of 1977

1977, Sept. 14   Litho.   Perf. 14
C406 A244 20c multi   .25 .25
C407 A244 25c multi   .25 .25

Symbolic Chessboard and Emblem — AP56

1977, Oct. 20   Litho.   Perf. 11
C408 AP56 25c multi   .25 .25
C409 AP56 50c multi   .40 .25

El Salvador's victory in International Chess Olympiad, Tripoli, Libya, Oct. 24-Nov. 15, 1976.

Soccer AP57

Boxing
AP58

1977, Nov. 16   Litho.   Perf. 16
C410 AP57 10c shown   .25   .25
C411 AP57 10c Basketball   .25   .25
C412 AP57 15c Javelin   .25   .25
C413 AP57 15c Weight lifting .25   .25
C414 AP57 20c Volleyball   .25   .25
C415 AP58 20c shown   .25   .25
C416 AP57 25c Baseball   .25   .25
C417 AP58 25c Softball   .25   .25
C418 AP58 30c Swimming   .35   .25
C419 AP58 30c Fencing   .35   .25
C420 AP58 40c Bicycling   .45   .25
C421 AP58 50c Rifle shooting .55   .30
C422 AP58 50c Women's tennis .55   .30
C423 AP57 60c Judo   .65   .35
C424 AP57 75c Wrestling   .70   .40
C425 AP58 1col Equestrian hur-
               dles   .90   .50
C426 AP58 1col Woman gymnast .90   .50
C427 AP58 2col Table tennis 1.25   1.00
     Nos. C410-C427 (18)   8.65   6.10

Size: 100x119mm

C428 AP57 5col Games' poster 4.00 4.00

2nd Central American Olympic Games, San Salvador, Nov. 25-Dec. 4.

No. C390 Ovptd. in Red "CENTENARIO / CIUDAD DE / CHALCHUAPA / 1878-1978"

1978, Feb. 13   Litho.   Perf. 12½
C429 A239 70c multi   .60   .55

Centenary of Chalchuapa.

Map of South America, Argentina '78 Emblem AP59

1978, Aug. 15   Litho.   Perf. 11
C430 AP59 25c multi   .30   .25
C431 AP59 60c multi   .50   .40
C432 AP59 5col multi   4.00   3.00
     Nos. C430-C432 (3)   4.80   3.65

11th World Cup Soccer Championship, Argentina, June 1-25.

Musical Instrument Type

Designs: 25c, Drum, vert. 50c, Hollow rattles. 80c, Xylophone.

1978, Aug. 29   Perf. 12½
C433 A245 25c multi   .30   .25
C434 A245 50c multi   .45   .25
C435 A245 80c multi   .60   .40
     Nos. C433-C435 (3)   1.35   .90

For surcharge see No. C492.

Engineering Type of 1978
1978, Sept. 12   Litho.   Perf. 13½
C436 A246 25c multi   .25   .25

Izalco Station Type of 1978
1978, Sept. 14   Perf. 12½
C437 A247 75c multi   .60   .40

Softball, Bat and Globes AP60

1978, Oct. 17   Litho.   Perf. 12½
C438 AP60 25c pink & multi   .25   .25
C439 AP60 1col yel & multi   .80   .50

4th World Softball Championship for Women, San Salvador, Oct. 13-22.

Fair Type, 1978
1978, Oct. 30   Litho.   Perf. 12½
C440 A248 15c multi   .25   .25
C441 A248 25c multi   .25   .25

Red Cross Type, 1978
1978, Oct. 30   Litho.   Perf. 11
C442 A249 25c multi   .25   .25

Cotton Conference Type, 1978
1978, Nov. 22   Perf. 12½
C443 A250 40c multi   .30   .25

Christmas Type, 1978
1978, Dec. 5   Litho.   Perf. 12½
C444 A251 25c multi   .25   .25
C445 A251 1col multi   .80   .50

Athenaeum Type 1978
1978, Dec. 20   Litho.   Perf. 14
C446 A252 25c multi   .25   .25

UPU Type of 1979
1979, Apr. 2   Litho.   Perf. 14
C447 A253 75c multi   .60   .40

Health Organization Type
1979, Apr. 7   Perf. 14x14½
C448 A254 25c multi   .25   .25

Social Security Type of 1979
1979, May 25   Litho.   Perf. 12½
C449 A255 25c multi   .25   .25
C450 A255 1col multi   .80   .50

Games Emblem AP61

1979, July 12   Litho.   Perf. 14½x14
C451 AP61 25c multi   .25   .25
C452 AP61 40c multi   .30   .25
C453 AP61 70c multi   .50   .40
     Nos. C451-C453 (3)   1.05   .90

8th Pan American Games, Puerto Rico, July 1-15.
For surcharge see No. C493.

Pope John Paul II Type of 1979

60c, 5col, Pope John Paul II & pyramid.

1979, July 12
C454 A256 60c multi, horiz.   .50   .30
C455 A256 5col multi, horiz. 4.00   2.50

"25," Family and Map of Salvador — AP62

1979, May 14   Litho.   Perf. 14x14½
C456 AP62 25c blk & bl   .25   .25
C457 AP62 60c blk & lil rose .55   .35

Social Security, 25th anniversary.

Pre-Historic Animal Type
1979, Sept. 7   Litho.   Perf. 14
C458 A257 15c Mammoth   .35   .25
C459 A257 25c Giant anteater,
               vert.   .50   .25
C460 A257 2col Hyenas   2.75   1.10
     Nos. C458-C460 (3)   3.60   1.60

National Anthem Type, 1979
1979, Sept. 14   Perf. 14½x14
C461 A258 40c Jose Aberiz, score .30   .25

COPIMERA Type, 1979
1979, Oct. 19   Litho.   Perf. 14½x14
C462 A259 50c multi   .45   .25

Circle Dance, IYC Emblem AP63

Children's Village and IYC Emblems AP64

1979, Oct. 29   Perf. 14½x14, 14x14½
C463 AP63 25c multi   .25   .25
C464 AP64 30c vio & blk   .30   .25

International Year of the Child.

Biochemistry Type of 1979
1979, Nov. 1   Litho.   Perf. 14½x14
C465 A262 25c multi   .25   .25

Coffee Type of 1979

Designs: 50c, Picking coffee. 75, Drying coffee beans. 1col, Coffee export.

1979, Dec. 18   Perf. 14x14½, 14½x14
C466 A263 50c multi   .40   .25
C467 A263 75c multi   .60   .40
C468 A263 1 col multi   .80   .55
     Nos. C466-C468 (3)   1.80   1.20

Hoof and Mouth Disease Type
1980, June 3   Litho.   Perf. 14½x14
C469 A265 60c multi   .55   .30

Shell Type of 1980

15c, Hexaplex regius. 25c, Polinices helicoides. 75c, Jenneria pustulata. 1col, Pitar lupanaria.

1980, Aug. 12   Perf. 14x14½
C470 A266 15c multi   .40   .25
C471 A266 25c multi   .80   .25
C472 A266 75c multi   2.00   .30
C473 A266 1col multi   2.75   .50
     Nos. C470-C473 (4)   5.95   1.30

Birds Type

25c, Aulacorhynchus prasinus. 50c, Strix varia fulvescens. 75c, Myadestes unicolor.

1980, Sept. 10   Litho.   Perf. 14x14½
C474 A267 25c multi   1.60   .25
C475 A267 50c multi   3.00   .30
C476 A267 75c multi   4.50   .45
     Nos. C474-C476 (3)   9.10   1.00

Snake Type of 1980
1980, Nov. 11   Litho.   Perf. 14½x14
C477 A268 25c Rattlesnake   2.40   .25
C478 A268 50c Coral snake   3.50   .30

Auditors Type
1980, Nov. 26   Litho.   Perf. 14
C479 A269 50c multi   .40   .25
C480 A269 75c multi   .60   .40

Christmas Type
1980, Dec. 5   Litho.   Perf. 14
C481 A270 25c multi   .25   .25
C482 A270 60c multi   .60   .30

Intl. Women's Decade, 1976-85 — AP65

1981, Jan. 30   Perf. 14½x14
C483 AP65 25c ol grn & blk   .25   .25
C484 AP65 1 col orange & black .80   .50

Protected Animals AP66

No. C485, Ateles geoffroyi. No. C486 Lepisosteus tropicus. No. C487, Iguana iguana. No. C488, Eretmochelys imbricata. No. C489, Spizaetus ornatus.

1981, Mar. 20   Litho.   Perf. 14x14½
C485 AP66 25c multicolored   .30   .25
C486 AP66 40c multicolored   .35   .25
C487 AP66 50c multicolored   .45   .25
C488 AP66 60c multicolored   .55   .35
C489 AP66 75c multicolored   .70   .40
     Nos. C485-C489 (5)   2.35   1.50

Heinrich von Stephan, 150th Birth Anniv. — AP67

1981, May 18   Litho.   Perf. 14½x14
C490 AP67 15c multi   .35   .25
C491 AP67 2 col multi   1.60   1.00

Nos. C435, C453 Surcharged
Perf. 12½, 14½x14
1981, May 18   Litho.
C492 A245 50c on 80c, #C435 .40   .25
C493 AP61 1 col on 70c, #C453 .80   .55

Dental Associations Type
1981, June 18   Perf. 14
C494 A271 5 col bl & blk   7.00   3.00

IYD Type of 1981
1981, Aug. 14   Litho.   Perf. 14x14½
C495 A272 25c like #936   .25   .25
C496 A272 50c Emblem   .40   .25
C497 A272 75c like #936   .60   .40
C498 A272 1 col like # C496   .80   .55
     Nos. C495-C498 (4)   2.05   1.45

Quinonez Type
1981, Aug. 28   Litho.   Perf. 14½x14
C499 A273 50c multi   .40   .25

World Food Day Type
1981, Sept. 16   Litho.   Perf. 14x14½
C500 A274 25c multi   .25   .25

Land Registry Office, 100th Anniv. — AP68

1981, Oct. 30   Litho.   Perf. 14x14½
C501 AP68 1 col multi   .80   .55

TACA Airlines, 50th Anniv. AP69

1981, Nov. 10   Litho.   Perf. 14
C502 AP69 15c multi   .25   .25
C503 AP69 25c multi   .25   .25
C504 AP69 75c multi   .60   .40
     Nos. C502-C504 (3)   1.10   .90

World Cup Preliminaries Type
1981, Nov. 27   Litho.   Perf. 14½x14
C505 A275 25c Like No. 939   .30   .25
C506 A275 75c Like No. 940   .60   .40

Lyceum Type
1981, Dec. 17   Litho.   Perf. 14
C507 A276 25c multi   .25   .25

Sculptures Type

1982, Jan. 22   Litho.   Perf. 14
C508 A277 25c Palm leaf with effigy   .25 .25
C509 A277 30c Jaguar mask   .30 .25
C510 A277 80c Mayan flint carving   .65 .45
Nos. C508-C510 (3)   1.20 .95

Scouting Year Type of 1982

1982, Mar. 17   Litho.   Perf. 14½x14
C511 A278 25c Baden-Powell   .25 .25
C512 A278 50c Girl Scout, emblem   .40 .25

TB Bacillus
Cent. — AP70

1982, Mar. 24   Perf. 14
C513 AP70 50c multi   1.50 .25

Armed Forces Type of 1982

1982, May 7   Litho.   Perf. 14x13½
C514 A279 25c multi   .25 .25

Symbolic
Design — AP71

1982, May 14   Perf. 14
C515 AP71 75c multi   .60 .40
25th anniv. of Latin-American Tourist Org.
Confederation (COTAL).

14th World Telecommunications
Day — AP72

1982, May 17   Perf. 14x14½
C516 AP72 15c multi   .25 .25
C517 AP72 2col multi   1.60 1.00

World Cup Type of 1982

1982, July 14
C518 A280 25c Team, emblem   .25 .25
C519 A280 60c Map, cup   .50 .35

Size: 67x47mm

Perf. 11½
C520 A280 2col Team, emblem, diff.   1.60 1.00

1982 World
Cup — AP73

Flags or Arms of Participating Countries;
#C521a, C522a, Italy. #C521b, C522c, Germany. #C521c, C522e, Argentina. #C521d, C522m, England. #C521e, C522o, Spain. #C521f, C522q, Brazil. #C521g, C522b, Poland. #C521h, C522d, Algeria. #C521i, C522f, Belgium. #C521j, C522n, France. #C521k, C522p, Honduras. #C521l, C522l, Russia. #C521m, C522g, Peru. #C521n, #C521o, Chile. #C521o, C522k, Hungary. #C521p, C522s, Czechoslovakia. #C521q, C522u, Yugoslavia. #C521r, C522w, Scotland. #C521s, C522h, Cameroun. #C521t, C522j, Austria. #C521u, C522l, Salvador. #C521v, C522t, Kuwait. #C521w, C522v, Ireland. #C521x, C522x, New Zealand.

1982, Aug. 26
C521   Sheet of 24   7.50
a.-x. AP73 15c Flags   .25 .25
C522   Sheet of 24   7.50
a.-x. AP73 25c Arms   .25 .25

Salvador Team, Cup, Flags — AP74

1982, Aug. 26   Litho.   Perf. 11½
C523 AP74 5col multi   6.00 2.50

International Fair Type

1982, Oct. 14   Litho.   Perf. 14
C524 A281 15c multi   .25 .25

World Food
Day — AP75

1982, Oct. 21   Litho.   Perf. 14
C525 AP75 25c multi   .35 .25

St. Francis of
Assisi, 800th
Birth
Anniv. — AP76

1982, Nov. 10   Litho.   Perf. 14
C526 AP76 1col multi   .80 .60

Natl. Labor
Campaign — AP77

1982, Nov. 30   Litho.   Perf. 14x14½
C527 AP77 50c multi   .40 .25

Christmas Type

1982, Dec. 14   Litho.   Perf. 14
C528 A282 25c multi, horiz.   .25 .25

Salvadoran
Paintings
AP78

#C529, The Pottery of Paleca, by Miguel Ortiz Villacorta. #C530, The Rural School, by Luis Caceres Madrid. #C531, To the Wash, by Julia Diaz. #C532, "La Pancha" by Jose Mejia Vides. #C533, Boats Near The Beach, by Raul Elas Reyes. #C534, The Muleteers, by Canjura.

Perf. 14x13½, 13½x14
1983, Oct. 18   Litho.
C529 AP78 25c multi   .25 .25
C530 AP78 25c multi   .25 .25
a.   Pair, #C529-C530   .65 .65

C531 AP78 75c multi, vert.   .60 .40
C532 AP78 75c multi, vert.   .60 .40
a.   Pair, #C531-C532   1.75 1.75
C533 AP78 1col multi, vert.   .80 .55
C534 AP78 1col multi, vert.   .80 .55
a.   Pair, #C533-C534   2.50 2.50
Nos. C529-C534 (6)   3.30 2.40

Fishing
Industry
AP79

1983, Dec. 20   Litho.   Perf. 14½x14
C535 AP79 25c Fisherman   .40 .25
C536 AP79 75c Feeding fish   1.50 .45

No. 999
Surcharged

1985, Apr. 10   Litho.   Perf. 14
C536A A297 1col on 10c multi   .90 .50

Natl.
Constitution,
Cent. — AP80

1986, Aug. 29   Litho.   Perf. 14
C537 AP80 1col multi   .50 .35

Hugo Lindo
(1917-1985),
Writer — AP81

1986, Nov. 10   Litho.   Perf. 14½x14
C538 AP81 1col multi   .50 .35

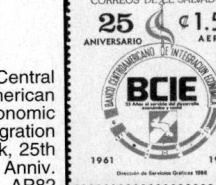

Central
American
Economic
Integration
Bank, 25th
Anniv.
AP82

1986, Nov. 20
C539 AP82 1.50col multi   .70 .50

12th Intl. Fair,
Feb. 14-Mar. 1
AP83

1987, Jan. 20   Litho.   Perf. 14½x14
C540 AP83 70c multi   .35 .25

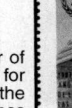

Intl. Year of
Shelter for
the
Homeless
AP84

Perf. 14x14½, 14½x14
1987, July 15   Litho.
C541 AP84 70c shown   .40 .25
C542 AP84 1col Emblem, vert.   .50 .35

Miniature Sheet

06523

Discovery of America, 500th Anniv. (in 1992) — AP85

15th cent. map of the Americas (details) and: a, Ferdinand. b, Isabella. c, Caribbean. d, Ships, coat of arms. e, Base of flagstaff. f, Ships. g, Pre-Columbian statue. h, Compass. i, Anniv. emblem. j, Columbus rose.

1987, Dec. 21   Litho.   Perf. 14
C543 AP85   Sheet of 10   10.00 10.00
a.-j.   1col any single   .65 .35

No. 1075 Surcharged

1988, Oct. 28   Litho.   Perf. 14x14½
C544 A316 5col on 90c multi   3.50 2.00
PRENFIL '88, Nov. 25-Dec. 2, Buenos Aire.

Organization of American States 18th
General Assembly, Nov. 14-19 — AP86

1988, Nov. 19
C545 AP86 70c multi   .40 .30

Handicapped Soccer
Championships — AP87

1990, May 2 Litho. Perf. 14½x14
C546 AP87 70c multicolored .45 .25

REGISTRATION STAMPS

Gen. Rafael Antonio
Gutiérrez — R1

1897 Engr. Wmk. 117 Perf. 12
F1 R1 10c dark blue *125.00*
F2 R1 10c brown lake .25

Unwmk.
F3 R1 10c dark blue .25
F4 R1 10c brown lake .25

Nos. F1 and F3 were probably not placed in use without the overprint "FRANQUEO OFICIAL" (Nos. O127-O128).
The reprints are on thick unwatermarked paper. Value, set of 2, 16c.

ACKNOWLEDGMENT OF RECEIPT STAMPS

AR1

1897 Engr. Wmk. 117 Perf. 12
H1 AR1 5c dark green .25

Unwmk.
H2 AR1 5c dark green .25

No. H2 has been reprinted on thick paper. Value 20c.

POSTAGE DUE STAMPS

D1

1895 Unwmk. Engr. Perf. 12
J1 D1 1c olive green .40 —
J2 D1 2c olive green .40 —
J3 D1 3c olive green .40 —
J4 D1 5c olive green .40 —
J5 D1 10c olive green .40 —
J6 D1 15c olive green .40 —
J7 D1 25c olive green .40 —
J8 D1 50c olive green .90 —
Nos. J1-J8 (8) 3.70

See Nos. J9-J56. For overprints see Nos. J57-J64, O186-O214.

1896 Wmk. 117
J9 D1 1c red .60 —
J10 D1 2c red .60 —
J11 D1 3c red .90 —
J12 D1 5c red 1.10 —
J13 D1 10c red 1.10 —
J14 D1 15c red 1.25 —

J15 D1 25c red 1.25 —
J16 D1 50c red 1.25 —
Nos. J9-J16 (8) 8.05

Unwmk.
J17 D1 1c red .40 —
J18 D1 2c red .40 —
J19 D1 3c red .40 —
J20 D1 5c red .40 —
J21 D1 10c red .40 —
J22 D1 15c red .50 —
J23 D1 25c red .50 —
J24 D1 50c red .50 —
Nos. J17-J24 (8) 3.50

Nos. J17-J24 exist imperforate.

1897
J25 D1 1c deep blue .40 —
J26 D1 2c deep blue .40 —
J27 D1 3c deep blue .40 —
J28 D1 5c deep blue .40 —
J29 D1 10c deep blue .50 —
J30 D1 15c deep blue .50 —
J31 D1 25c deep blue .40 —
J32 D1 50c deep blue .40 —
Nos. J25-J32 (8) 3.40

1898
J33 D1 1c violet 3.00
J34 D1 2c violet 1.00
J35 D1 3c violet 1.00
J36 D1 5c violet 5.00
J37 D1 10c violet 1.00
J38 D1 15c violet 1.00
J39 D1 25c violet 1.00
J40 D1 50c violet 1.00
Nos. J33-J40 (8) 14.00

Reprints of Nos. J1 to J40 are on thick paper, often in the wrong shades and usually with the impression somewhat blurred. Value, set of 40, $2, watermarked or unwatermarked.

1899 Wmk. 117 Sideways
J41 D1 1c orange .40
J42 D1 2c orange .40
J43 D1 3c orange .40
J44 D1 5c orange .40
J45 D1 10c orange .40
J46 D1 15c orange .40
J47 D1 25c orange .40
J48 D1 50c orange .40
Nos. J41-J48 (8) 3.20

Unwmk.
Thick Porous Paper
J49 D1 1c orange .40
J50 D1 2c orange .40
J51 D1 3c orange .40
J52 D1 5c orange .40
J53 D1 10c orange .40
J54 D1 15c orange .40
J55 D1 25c orange .40
J56 D1 50c orange .40
Nos. J49-J56 (8) 3.20

Nos. J41-J56 were probably not put in use without the wheel overprint.

Nos. J49-J56
Overprinted in Black

1900
J57 D1 1c orange 2.00
J58 D1 2c orange 2.00
J59 D1 3c orange 2.00
J60 D1 5c orange 3.00
J61 D1 10c orange 4.00
J62 D1 15c orange 4.00
J63 D1 25c orange 5.00
J64 D1 50c orange 6.00
Nos. J57-J64 (8) 28.00

See note after No. 198A.

Morazán
Monument — D2

Perf. 14, 14½
1903 Engr. Wmk. 173
J65 D2 1c yellow green 1.75 1.25
J66 D2 2c carmine 2.75 1.75
J67 D2 3c orange 2.75 1.75
J68 D2 5c dark blue 2.75 1.75
J69 D2 10c dull violet 2.75 1.75
J70 D2 25c blue green 2.75 1.75
Nos. J65-J70 (6) 15.50 10.00

Nos. 355, 356, 358
and 360 Overprinted

1908 Unwmk. Perf. 11½
J71 A66 1c green & blk .80 .70
J72 A66 2c red & blk .60 .25
J73 A66 5c blue & blk 1.50 1.00
J74 A66 10c violet & blk 2.25 2.00

Same Overprint on No. O275
J75 O3 3c yellow & blk 1.50 1.25
Nos. J71-J75 (5) 6.65 5.20

Nos. 355-358, 360
Overprinted

J76 A66 1c green & blk .50 .50
J77 A66 2c red & blk .60 .60
J78 A66 3c yellow & blk .70 .70
J79 A66 5c blue & blk 1.00 1.00
J80 A66 10c violet & blk 2.00 2.00
Nos. J76-J80 (5) 4.80 4.80

It is now believed that stamps of type A66, on paper with Honeycomb watermark, do not exist with genuine overprints of the types used for Nos. J71-J80.

Pres. Fernando
Figueroa — D3

1910 Engr. Wmk. 172
J81 D3 1c sepia & blk .30 .30
J82 D3 2c dk grn & blk .30 .30
J83 D3 3c orange & blk .30 .30
J84 D3 4c scarlet & blk .30 .30
J85 D3 5c purple & blk .30 .30
J86 D3 12c deep blue & blk .30 .30
J87 D3 24c brown red & blk .30 .30
Nos. J81-J87 (7) 2.10 2.10

OFFICIAL STAMPS

Nos. 134-157O
Overprinted — a

Type a
1896 Unwmk. Perf. 12
O1 A45 1c blue .25
O2 A45 2c dk brown .25
a. Double overprint
O3 A45 3c blue grn 1.00
O4 A45 5c brown ol .25
O5 A45 10c yellow .25
O6 A45 12c dk blue .30
O7 A45 15c blue vio .25
O8 A45 20c magenta 1.00
O9 A45 24c vermilion .25
O10 A45 30c orange 1.00
O11 A45 50c black brn .45
O12 A45 1p rose lake .25
Nos. O1-O12 (12) 5.55

Nos. O1-O12 were not issued.
The 1c has been reprinted on thick unwatermarked paper. Value 25c.

Wmk. 117
O13 A46 1c emerald 4.75 3.00
O14 A47 2c lake 4.75 3.50
O15 A48 3c yellow brn 6.00 4.00
a. Inverted overprint —
O16 A49 5c dp blue 5.00 5.00
O17 A50 10c brown 7.00 3.75
a. Inverted overprint —
O18 A51 12c slate 10.50 9.00
O19 A52 15c blue grn 12.50 8.75

O20 A53 20c car rose 12.50 8.00
a. Inverted overprint
O21 A54 24c violet 12.50 9.00
O22 A55 30c dp green 15.00 12.50
O23 A56 50c orange 25.00 17.00
O24 A57 100c dk blue 40.00 25.00
Nos. O13-O24 (12) 155.50 107.50

Unwmk.
O25 A46 1c emerald 2.50 *3.50*
a. Double overprint
O26 A47 2c lake 2.75 *175.00*
O27 A48 3c yellow brn 3.00 *2.50*
O28 A49 5c dp blue 3.00 .90
O29 A50 10c brown 2.50 2.50
a. Inverted overprint
O30 A51 12c slate 10.00 7.00
O31 A52 15c blue grn 12.00 7.75
O32 A53 15c car rose 20.00 11.00
a. Inverted overprint
O33 A54 24c violet 20.00 11.00
O34 A55 30c dp green — —
O35 A56 50c orange — —
O36 A57 100c dk blue — —
Nos. O25-O36 (12) 75.75 221.15

All values have been reprinted. Value 25c each.

Nos. 134-145
Handstamped in Black
or Violet — b

1896 Type b
O37 A45 1c blue 11.00
O38 A45 2c dk brown 11.00
O39 A45 3c blue green 11.00
O40 A45 5c brown olive 11.00
O41 A45 10c yellow 13.00
O42 A45 12c dk blue 16.00
O43 A45 15c blue violet 16.00
O44 A45 20c magenta 16.00
O45 A45 24c vermilion 16.00
O46 A45 30c orange 16.00
O47 A45 50c black brown 22.50
O48 A45 1p rose lake 22.50
Nos. O37-O48 (12) 182.00

Reprints of the 1c and 2c on thick paper exist with this handstamp. Value, 25c each.
The legitimacy of the "De Officio" handstamp has been questioned. The editors would like to see evidence regarding the authorized use of this handstamp.

Forged overprints exist of Nos. O37-O76, O103-O126 and of the higher valued stamps of O141-O214.

**Nos. 146-157F, 157I-157O, 158D
Handstamped Type b in Black or
Violet**
1896 Wmk. 117
O49 A46 1c emerald 9.00
O50 A47 2c lake 9.00
O51 A48 3c yellow brn 9.00
O52 A49 5c deep blue 9.00
O53 A50 10c brown 9.00
O54 A51 12c slate 16.00
O55 A52 15c blue green 16.00
O56 A53 20c carmine rose 16.00
O57 A54 24c violet 16.00
O58 A55 30c deep green 16.00
O59 A56 50c orange 16.00
O60 A57 100c dark blue 16.00
Nos. O49-O60 (12) 157.00

Unwmk.
O61 A46 1c emerald 9.00
O62 A47 2c lake 9.00
O63 A48 3c yellow brn 9.00
O64 A49 5c deep blue 9.00
O65 A50 10c brown 13.50
O66 A52 15c blue green 16.00
O67 A58 15c on 24c vio 11.50
O68 A53 20c carmine rose 16.00
O69 A54 24c violet 16.00
O70 A55 30c deep green 16.00
O71 A56 50c orange 19.00
O72 A57 100c dark blue 19.00
Nos. O61-O72 (12) 163.00

**Nos. 175-176 Overprinted Type a in
Black**
1897
O73 A59 1c bl, gold, rose & grn .30
O74 A59 5c rose, gold, bl & grn .30
These stamps were probably not officially issued.

**Nos. 175-176 Handstamped Type b
in Black or Violet**
1900
O75 A59 1c bl, gold, rose & grn 22.50
O76 A59 5c rose, gold, bl & grn 22.50

Nos. 159-170L Overprinted Type a in Black

1897   **Wmk. 117**

O79	A46	1c scarlet	8.00	8.00
O80	A47	2c yellow green	8.00	8.00
O81	A48	3c bister brown	7.00	7.00
O82	A49	5c orange	7.00	7.00
O83	A50	10c blue green	9.00	9.00
O84	A51	12c blue	20.00	20.00
O85	A52	15c black	40.00	40.00
O86	A53	20c slate	20.00	20.00
O87	A54	24c yellow	40.00	40.00
a.		Inverted overprint		
O88	A55	30c rose	40.00	40.00
O89	A56	50c violet	40.00	40.00
O90	A57	100c brown lake	100.00	100.00
		Nos. O79-O90 (12)	339.00	

Unwmk.

O91	A46	1c scarlet	5.00	5.00
O92	A47	2c yellow green	3.00	3.00
O93	A48	3c bister brown	2.00	2.00
O94	A49	5c orange	3.00	3.00
O95	A50	10c blue green	10.00	10.00
O96	A51	12c blue	3.00	3.00
O97	A52	15c black	30.00	30.00
O98	A53	20c slate	20.00	20.00
O99	A54	24c yellow	30.00	30.00
O100	A55	30c rose	30.00	30.00
O101	A56	50c violet	20.00	20.00
O102	A57	100c brown lake	50.00	50.00
		Nos. O91-O102 (12)	206.00	

All values have been reprinted. Value 25c each.

Nos. 159-170L Handstamped Type b in Violet or Black

1897   **Wmk. 117**

O103	A46	1c scarlet	7.50	
O104	A47	2c yellow green	7.50	
O105	A48	3c bister brown	7.50	
O106	A49	5c orange	7.50	
O107	A50	10c blue green	8.75	
O108	A51	12c blue		
O109	A52	15c black		
O110	A53	20c slate	15.00	
O111	A54	24c yellow	17.50	
O112	A55	30c rose		
O113	A56	50c violet		
O114	A57	100c brown lake		

Unwmk.

O115	A46	1c scarlet	7.50	
O116	A47	2c yellow grn	7.50	
O117	A48	3c bister brn	7.50	
O118	A49	5c orange	7.50	
O119	A50	10c blue green	7.50	
O120	A51	12c blue		
O121	A52	15c black		
O122	A53	20c slate		
O123	A54	24c yellow		
O124	A55	30c rose	15.00	
O125	A56	50c violet		
O126	A57	100c brown lake	17.50	

Reprints of the 1 and 15c on thick watermarked paper and the 12, 30, 50 and 100c on thick unwatermarked paper are known with this overprint. Value, 25c each.

Nos. F1, F3 Overprinted Type a in Red
Wmk. 117

O127	R1	10c dark blue	.30	

Unwmk.

O128	R1	10c dark blue	.30	

The reprints are on thick paper. Value 15c. Originals of the 10c brown lake Registration Stamp and the 5c Acknowledgment of Receipt stamp are believed not to have been issued with the "FRANQUEO OFICIAL" overprint. They are believed to exist only as reprints.

Nos. 177-188 Overprinted Type a

1898   **Wmk. 117**

O129	A60	1c orange ver	4.50	4.50
O130	A60	2c rose	4.50	4.50
O131	A60	3c pale yel grn	4.00	4.00
O132	A60	5c blue green	4.00	4.00
O133	A60	10c gray blue	15.00	15.00
O134	A60	12c violet	17.00	17.00
O135	A60	13c brown lake	17.00	17.00
O136	A60	20c deep blue	19.00	19.00
O137	A60	24c ultra	15.00	15.00
O138	A60	26c bister brn	20.00	20.00
O139	A60	50c orange	20.00	20.00
O140	A60	100c violet	50.00	50.00
		Nos. O129-O140 (12)	190.00	190.00

Reprints of the above set are on thick paper. Value, 25c each.

No. 177 Handstamped Type b in Violet

O141	A60	1c orange ver	35.00	—

No. O141 with Additional Overprint Type c in Black

c

Type "c" is called the "wheel" overprint.

O142	A60	1c orange ver	—	—

Counterfeits exist of the "wheel" overprint.

Nos. 204-205, 207 and 209 Overprinted

1899   **Unwmk.**

O143	A61	12c dark green	—	50.00
O144	A61	13c deep rose	50.00	—
O145	A61	26c carmine rose	50.00	—
O146	A61	100c violet	100.00	—

Nos. O143-O144 Punched With Twelve Small Holes

O147	A61	12c dark green		
O148	A61	13c deep rose		

Official stamps punched with twelve small holes were issued and used for ordinary postage.

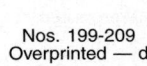

Nos. 199-209 Overprinted — d

1899   **Blue Overprint**

O149	A61	1c brown	.30	
O150	A61	2c gray green	.30	
O151	A61	3c blue	.30	
O152	A61	5c brown orange	.30	
O153	A61	10c chocolate	.30	
O154	A61	13c deep rose	.30	
O155	A61	26c carmine rose	.30	
O156	A61	50c orange red	.30	
O157	A61	100c violet	.30	

Black Overprint

O158	A61	3c blue	.30	
O159	A61	12c dark green	.30	
O160	A61	24c lt blue	.30	
		Nos. O149-O160 (12)	3.60	

Nos. O149-O160 were probably not placed in use.

With Additional Overprint Type c in Black

O161	A61	1c brown	.60	.60
O162	A61	2c gray green	1.10	1.10
O163	A61	3c blue	.60	.60
O164	A61	5c brown org	.60	.60
O165	A61	10c chocolate	.75	.75
O166	A61	12c dark green	—	—
O167	A61	13c deep rose	1.50	1.50
O168	A61	24c lt blue	30.00	30.00
O169	A61	26c carmine rose	.75	.75
O170	A61	50c orange red	1.50	1.50
O171	A61	100c violet	1.50	1.50
		Nos. O161-O165,O167-O171 (10)	38.90	38.90

Nos. O149-O155, O159-O160 Punched With Twelve Small Holes

Blue Overprint

O172	A61	1c brown	5.00	1.00
O173	A61	2c gray green	3.25	5.00
O174	A61	3c blue	8.00	3.75
O175	A61	5c brown org	10.00	3.00
O176	A61	10c chocolate	15.00	5.00
O177	A61	13c deep rose	7.50	7.00
O177A	A61	24c lt blue		
O178	A61	26c car rose	100.00	35.00

Black Overprint

O179	A61	12c dark green	6.00	4.50
		Nos. O172-O177,O178-O179 (8)	154.75	64.25

It is stated that Nos. O172-O214 inclusive were issued for ordinary postage and not for use as Official stamps.

Nos. O161-O167, O169 Punched With Twelve Small Holes

O180	A61	1c brown	1.25	1.10
O180A	A61	2c gray green		
O181	A61	3c blue		
O182	A61	5c brown orange	1.25	
O182A	A61	10c chocolate		
O182B	A61	12c dark green		
O183	A61	13c deep rose	4.00	5.00
O184	A61	26c carmine rose		

No. 209 Ovptd. Types a and e in Black

e

O185	A61	100c violet		

Nos. J49-J56 Overprinted in Black

1900

O186	D1	1c orange	27.50	
O187	D1	2c orange	27.50	
O188	D1	3c orange	27.50	
O189	D1	5c orange	27.50	
O190	D1	10c orange	27.50	
O191	D1	12c orange	62.50	
O192	D1	25c orange	62.50	
O193	D1	50c orange	62.50	
		Nos. O186-O193 (8)	325.00	

Nos. O186-O189, O191-O193 Overprinted Type c in Black

O194	D1	1c orange		25.00
O195	D1	2c orange		25.00
O196	D1	3c orange		25.00
O197	D1	5c orange		25.00
O198	D1	15c orange	16.00	25.00
O199	D1	25c orange	19.00	25.00
O200	D1	50c orange	160.00	

Nos. O186-O189 Punched With Twelve Small Holes

O201	D1	1c orange	45.00	
O202	D1	2c orange	45.00	
O203	D1	3c orange	45.00	
O204	D1	5c orange	45.00	
		Nos. O201-O204 (4)	180.00	

Nos. O201-O204 Overprinted Type c in Black

O205	D1	1c orange	9.00	6.50
O206	D1	2c orange		6.50
O207	D1	3c orange		6.50
O208	D1	5c orange	20.00	6.50

Overprinted Type a in Violet and Type c in Black

O209	D1	2c orange		25.00
a.		Inverted overprint		25.00
O210	D1	3c orange		25.00
O211	D1	10c orange	3.00	

Nos. O186-O188 Handstamped Type e in Violet

O212	D1	1c orange	9.00	7.50
O213	D1	2c orange	9.00	7.50
O214	D1	3c orange	9.00	9.00
		Nos. O212-O214 (3)	27.00	24.00

See note after No. O48.

Type of Regular Issue of 1900 Overprinted Type a in Black

O223	A63	1c lt green	22.50	
a.		Inverted overprint		—
O224	A63	2c rose	27.50	
a.		Inverted overprint		—
O225	A63	3c gray black	17.50	
a.		Overprint vertical		—
O226	A63	5c blue	17.50	
O227	A63	10c black	45.00	
a.		Inverted overprint		—
O228	A63	12c yellow grn	45.00	
O229	A63	13c yellow brn	45.00	
O230	A63	24c gray black	32.50	
O231	A63	26c yellow brn	30.00	—
a.		Inverted overprint		
O232	A63	50c dull rose		
a.		Inverted overprint		
		Nos. O223-O231 (9)	282.50	

Nos. O223-O224, O231-O232 Overprinted in Violet — f

O233	A63	1c lt green	4.75	4.00
O234	A63	2c rose		25.00
a.		"FRANQUEO OFICIAL" invtd.		
O235	A63	26c yellow brown	.50	.50
O236	A63	50c dull rose	.75	.55

Nos. O223, O225-O228, O232 Overprinted in Black — g

O237	A63	1c lt green	5.00	5.00
O238	A63	3c gray black		
O239	A63	5c blue	40.00	
O240	A63	10c blue		
O241	A63	12c yellow green		

Violet Overprint

O242	A63	50c dull rose	10.00	

The shield overprinted on No. O242 is of the type on No. O212.

O1

1903   **Wmk. 173**   **Perf. 14, 14½**

O243	O1	1c yellow green	.45	.25
O244	O1	2c carmine	.45	.25
O245	O1	3c orange	5.00	.85
O246	O1	5c dark blue	5.00	.25
O247	O1	10c dull violet	.70	.35
O248	O1	13c red brown	.70	.35
O249	O1	15c yellow brown	5.00	1.75
O250	O1	24c scarlet	.45	.35
O251	O1	50c bister	.70	.35
O252	O1	100c grnsh blue	.70	.75
		Nos. O243-O252 (10)	19.15	5.50

For surcharges see Nos. O254-O257.

No. 285 Handstamped Type b in Black

1904

O253	A64	3c orange		35.00

Nos. O246-O248 Surcharged in Black

1905

O254	O1	2c on 5c dark blue	6.50	5.50
O255	O1	3c on 5c dark blue		
a.		Double surcharge		
O256	O1	3c on 10c dl vio	18.00	12.00
O257	O1	3c on 13c red brn	1.75	1.40

A 2c surcharge of this type exists on No. O247.

No. O225 Overprinted in Blue

a   b

1905   **Unwmk.**

O258	A63(a)	3c gray black	4.00	3.50
O259	A63(b)	3c gray black	3.50	3.00

Nos. O224-O225 Overprinted in Blue

     c   d

1906

O260	A63(c)	2c rose	22.50	20.00
O261	A63(c)	3c gray black	2.50	2.00
a.		Overprint "1906" in blk		
O262	A63(d)	3c gray black	2.75	2.50
		Nos. O260-O262 (3)	27.75	24.50

Escalón — O2

1906   **Engr.**   **Perf. 11½**

O263	O2	1c green & blk	.40	.25
O264	O2	2c carmine & blk	.40	.25
O265	O2	3c yellow & blk	.40	.25
O266	O2	5c blue & blk	.40	.75
O267	O2	10c violet & blk	.40	.25
O268	O2	13c dk brown & blk	.40	.25
O269	O2	15c red org & blk	.50	.25
O270	O2	24c carmine & blk	.60	.35
O271	O2	50c orange & blk	.60	1.50
O272	O2	100c dk blue & blk	.70	4.50
		Nos. O263-O272 (10)	4.80	8.60

The centers of these stamps are also found in blue black.

Nos. O263 to O272 have been reprinted, perforated 11.8. Value, set of 10, $2.50.

National Palace — O3

1908

O273	O3	1c green & blk	.25	.25
O274	O3	2c red & blk	.25	.25
O275	O3	3c yellow & blk	.25	.25
O276	O3	5c blue & blk	.25	.25
O277	O3	10c violet & blk	.25	.25
O278	O3	13c violet & blk	.25	.25
O279	O3	15c pale brn & blk	.25	.25
O280	O3	24c rose & blk	.25	.25
O281	O3	50c yellow & blk	.25	.25
O282	O3	100c turq blue & blk	.35	.35
		Nos. O273-O282 (10)	2.60	2.60

For overprints see Nos. 441-442, 445-449, J75, O283-O292, O323-O328.

Nos. O273-O282 Overprinted Type g in Black

O283	O3	1c green & blk	3.00	
O284	O3	2c red & blk	4.00	
O285	O3	3c yellow & blk	4.00	
O286	O3	5c blue & blk	5.00	
O287	O3	10c violet & blk	5.00	
O288	O3	13c violet & blk	6.00	
O289	O3	15c pale brn & blk	6.00	
O290	O3	24c rose & blk	8.00	
O291	O3	50c yellow & blk	9.00	
O292	O3	100c turq & blk	10.00	
		Nos. O283-O292 (10)	60.00	

Pres. Figueroa — O4

1910   **Engr.**   **Wmk. 172**

O293	O4	2c dk green & blk	.30	.25
O294	O4	3c orange & blk	.30	.25
O295	O4	4c scarlet & blk	.30	.25
a.		4c carmine & black		
O296	O4	5c purple & blk	.30	.25
O297	O4	6c scarlet & blk	.30	.25
O298	O4	10c purple & blk	.30	.25
O299	O4	12c dp blue & blk	.30	.25
O300	O4	17c olive grn & blk	.30	.25
O301	O4	19c brn red & blk	.30	.25
O302	O4	29c choc & blk	.30	.25
O303	O4	50c yellow & blk	.30	.25
O304	O4	100c turq & blk	.30	.25
		Nos. O293-O304 (12)	3.60	3.00

Regular Issue, Type A63, Overprinted or Surcharged

    a   b

c

1911   **Unwmk.**

O305	A63(a)	1c lt green	.25	.25
O306	A63(b)	3c on 13c yel brn	.25	.25
O307	A63(b)	5c on 10c dp bl	.25	.25
O308	A63(a)	10c deep blue	.25	.25
O309	A63(a)	12c lt green	.25	.25
O310	A63(b)	13c yellow brn	.25	.25
O311	A63(b)	50c on 10c dp bl	.25	.25
O312	A63(c)	1col on 13c yel brn	.25	.25
		Nos. O305-O312 (8)	2.00	2.00

O5

1914   **Typo.**   **Perf. 12**
Background in Green, Shield and "Provisional" in Black

O313	O5	2c yellow brn	.50	.25
O314	O5	3c yellow	.50	.25
O315	O5	5c dark blue	.50	.25
O316	O5	10c red	.50	.25
O317	O5	12c green	.50	.25
O318	O5	17c violet	.50	.25
O319	O5	50c brown	.50	.25
O320	O5	100c dull rose	.50	.25
		Nos. O313-O320 (8)	4.00	2.00

Stamps of this issue are known imperforate or with parts of the design omitted or misplaced. These varieties were not regularly issued.

O6

1914   **Typo.**

O321	O6	2c blue green	.50	.25
O322	O6	3c orange	.50	.25

Type of Official Stamps of 1908 With Two Overprints

1915

O323	O3	1c gray green	1.00	.60
a.		"1915" double		
b.		"OFICIAL" inverted		
O324	O3	2c red	1.00	.60
O325	O3	5c ultra	.35	.70
O326	O3	10c yellow	.35	.60
a.		Date omitted		
O327	O3	50c violet	.90	1.50
O328	O3	100c black brown	1.90	3.25
		Nos. O323-O328 (6)	5.50	7.25

Same Overprint on #414, 417, 429

O329	A66	1c gray green	10.00	1.60
O330	A66	6c pale blue	1.00	.45
a.		6c ultramarine		
O331	A66	12c brown	1.00	.75
		Nos. O329-O331 (3)	12.00	2.80

O323-O327, O329-O331 exist imperf. Nos. O329-O331 exist with "OFICIAL" inverted and double. See note after No. 421.

Nos. 431-440 Overprinted in Blue or Red

1916

O332	A83	1c deep green	.45	.75
O333	A83	2c vermilion	1.60	1.60
O334	A83	5c dp blue (R)	1.25	1.60
O335	A83	6c gray vio (R)	.45	.75
O336	A83	10c black brown	.45	.75
O337	A83	12c violet	2.00	3.25
O338	A83	17c orange	.45	.75
O339	A83	23c dark brown	.45	.75
O340	A83	29c black (R)	.45	.75
O341	A83	50c slate (R)	2.00	.75
		Nos. O332-O341 (10)	9.55	11.70

Nos. 474-481 Overprinted

    a   b

1921

O342	A94(a)	1c green	.25	.25
O343	A95(a)	2c black	.25	.25
a.		Inverted overprint		
O344	A96(b)	5c orange	.25	.25
O345	A97(a)	6c carmine rose	.25	.25
O346	A98(a)	10c deep blue	.30	.25
O347	A99(a)	25c olive green	.75	.35
O348	A100(a)	60c violet	1.00	.60
O349	A101(a)	1col black brown	1.10	.70
		Nos. O342-O349 (8)	4.15	2.90

Nos. 498 and 500 Overprinted in Black or Red

1925

O350	A109	5c olive black	.45	.25
O351	A111	10c orange (R)	.85	.25
a.		"ATLANT CO"	13.00	11.00

Inverted overprints exist.

Regular Issue of 1924-25 Overprinted in Black or Red

1927

O352	A106	1c red violet	.25	.25
O353	A107	2c dark red	.45	.25
O354	A109	5c olive blk (R)	.45	.25
O355	A110	6c dp blue (R)	5.25	4.50
O356	A111	10c orange	.50	.30
a.		"ATLANT CO"	22.50	19.00
O357	A116	1col grn & vio (R)	2.25	1.40
		Nos. O352-O357 (6)	9.15	6.95

Inverted overprints exist on 1c, 2c, 5c, 10c.

Regular Issue of 1924-25 Overprinted in Black

1932   **Perf. 12½**

O358	A106	1c deep violet	.25	.25
O359	A107	2c dark red	.45	.25
O360	A109	5c olive black	.25	.25
O361	A111	10c orange	.85	.35
a.		"ATLANT CO"	22.50	19.00
		Nos. O358-O361 (4)	1.80	1.10

> **Catalogue values for unused stamps in this section, from this point to the end of the section, are for Never Hinged items.**

Regular Issue of 1947 Overprinted in Black or Red

1948   **Unwmk.**   **Engr.**   **Perf. 12**

O362	A154	1c car rose	65.00	32.50
O363	A154	2c deep org	65.00	32.50
O364	A154	5c slate gray (R)	65.00	32.50
O365	A154	10c bis brn (R)	65.00	32.50
O366	A154	20c green (R)	65.00	32.50
O367	A154	50c black (R)	65.00	32.50
		Nos. O362-O367 (6)	390.00	195.00

No. 602 Surcharged in Carmine and Black

1964(?)

O368	A154	1c on 20c green	90.00	—

The X's are black, the rest carmine.

PARCEL POST STAMPS

Mercury PP1

1895   **Unwmk.**   **Engr.**   **Perf. 12**

Q1	PP1	5c brown orange	.45	
Q2	PP1	10c dark blue	.45	
Q3	PP1	15c red	.45	
Q4	PP1	20c orange	.45	
Q5	PP1	50c blue green	.45	
		Nos. Q1-Q5 (5)	2.25	

POSTAL TAX STAMPS

PT1

Overprinted "REVISADO" in Violet, Black or Red

1900-04   Typo.   **Perf. 11½**

RA1	PT1	1c black		
RA2	PT1	1c black, dated "1903"		
RA3	PT1	1c black, dated "1904"		

Use of these stamps was obligatory on all domestic letters. The funds raised were used to maintain the public schools.

Nos. 503, 501 Surcharged

1931   Unwmk.   **Perf. 12½**

RA4	A115	1c on 50c org brn	.50	.40
a.		Double surcharge	5.00	5.00
RA5	A112	2c on 20c dp grn	.50	.40

Nos. 501, 503 Surcharged

RA6	A112	1c on 20c dp grn	.50	.40
RA7	A115	2c on 50c org brn	.50	.40
a.		Without period in "0.02"	3.00	

The use of these stamps was obligatory, in addition to the regular postage, on letters and other postal matter. The money obtained from their sale was to be used to erect a new post office in San Salvador.

SAMOA

sə-'mō-ə

(Western Samoa)

LOCATION — Archipelago in the south Pacific Ocean, east of Fiji
GOVT. — Independent state; former territory mandated by New Zealand
AREA — 1,093 sq. mi.
POP. — 161,298 (1991)
CAPITAL — Apia

In 1861-99, Samoa was an independent kingdom under the influence of the US, to which the harbor of Pago Pago had been ceded, and that of Great Britain and Germany. In 1898 a disturbance arose, resulting in the withdrawal of Great Britain, and the partitioning of the islands between Germany and the US. Early in World War I the islands under German domination were occupied by New Zealand troops and in 1920 the League of Nations declared them a mandate to New Zealand. Western Samoa became independent Jan. 1, 1962.

12 Pence = 1 Shilling
20 Shillings = 1 Pound
100 Pfennig = 1 Mark (1900)
100 Sene (Cents) = 1 Tala (Dollar) (1967)

Catalogue values for unused stamps in this country are for Never Hinged items, beginning with Scott 191 in the regular postage section, Scott B1 in the semipostal section and Scott C1 in the air post section.

Watermarks

 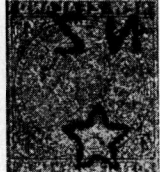

Wmk. 61 — N Z and Star Close Together

Wmk. 62 — N Z and Star Wide Apart

On watermark 61 the margins of the sheets are watermarked "NEW ZEALAND POSTAGE" and parts of the double-lined letters of these words are frequently found on the stamps. It occasionally happens that a stamp shows no watermark whatever.

Wmk. 253 — Multiple N Z and Star

Wmk. 355 — Kava Bowl and WS, Multiple

Issues of the Kingdom

A1

Type I   Type II

Type III   Type IV

Type I — Line above "X" is usually unbroken. Dots over "SAMOA" are uniform and evenly spaced. Upper right serif of "M" is horizontal.
Type II — Line above "X" is usually broken. Small dot near upper right serif of "M."
Type III — Line above "X" roughly retouched. Upper right serif of "M" bends down (joined to dot).
Type IV — Speck of color on curved line below center of "M."

Perf. 11¾, 12½

1877-82   Litho.   **Unwmk.**

1	A1	1p Blue (III), Perf. 11¾ ('79)	37.50	1,000.
1a	A1	1p sky blue (III), Perf. 12½ ('79)	260.00	125.00
2	A1	2p lilac rose (IV), ('82)	25.00	
3c	A1	3p vermilion (I)	450.00	250.00
3d	A1	3p vermilion, rough perfs (III), Perf. 11¾	65.00	—

4	A1	6p lilac (III), Perf. 12½ ('79)	550.00	135.00
4e	A1	6p dl lil (III), Perf. 11¾ ('79)	55.00	100.00
5	A1	9p pale chestnut (IV) ('80)	80.00	425.00
6	A1	1sh orange yellow (II), Perf. 12½ ('78)	325.00	135.00
6c	A1	1sh golden yellow (II), Perf 11¾ ('79)	110.00	260.00
7	A1	2sh Deep brown (III), Perf. 11¾ ('79)	370.00	500.00
7d	A1	2sh dp brn, Perf. 11¾ ('79)	275.00	—
8	A1	5sh emerald green (III), Perf. 12½ ('79)	1,875.	850.00
8a	A1	5sh yellow green (III), Perf. 11¾ ('79)	725.00	

Values are for the least expensive varieties. For detailed listings, see the *Scott Classic Specialized Catalogue*.

The 1p often has a period after "PENNY." The 2p was never placed in use since the Samoa Express service was discontinued late in 1881.

Imperforates of this issue are proofs.

Sheets of the first issue were not perforated around the outer sides. All values except the 2p were printed in sheets of 10 (2x5). The 1p, 3p and 6p type I and the 1p type III were also printed in sheets of 20 (4x5), and six stamps on each of these sheets were perforated all around. These are the only varieties of the original stamps which have not one or two imperforate edges. The 2p was printed in sheets of 21 (3x7) and five stamps in the second row were perforated all around. The 2p was also reprinted in sheets of 40, which are much more common than the sheets of 21.

Reprints are of type IV and nearly always perforated on all sides. They have a spot of color at the edge of the panel below the "M." This spot is not on any originals except the 9p, the original of which may be distinguished by having a rough blind perf. 12. The 2p does show a spot of color.

Forgeries exist.

Palms — A2

Perf. 11, 12x11½ (#14, 17a), 12½ (#16, 18)

1886-1900   Typo.   **Wmk. 62**

9d	A2	½p purple brown	5.75	2.10
10	A2	½p dl bl grn ('99)	4.00	4.50
11f	A2	1p bluish green ('97)	4.00	2.00
12	A2	1p red brown	4.25	20.00
13g	A2	2p bright yellow ('97)	16.00	10.00
14	A3	2½p rose ('92)	80.00	6.00
14b	A3	2½p rose	4.25	10.50
15	A3	2½p black, perf 10x11 ('96)	2.25	3.25
16	A2	4p blue	55.00	13.50
16f	A2	4p deep blue ('00)	1.60	52.50
17a	A2	6p maroon	325.00	12.50
17e	A2	6p maroon ('00)	2.00	62.50
18	A2	1sh rose carmine	67.50	13.50
a.		Perf 12½, diagonal half used on cover ('95)		375.00
18g	A2	1sh carmine ('00)	1.80	
19h	A2	2sh6p deep purple ('98)	5.00	10.00
i.		Vert. pair, imperf. btw.	475.00	

The 2½p has only the 3rd form.
Nos. 9-19 exist in various printings, perf 11, 12½ and 12x11½. Values are for the least expensive varieties. For detailed listings, see the *Scott Classic Specialized Catalogue.*

For surcharges or overprints on stamps or types of design A2 see Nos. 20-22, 24-38.

Nos. 16b and 16c Handstamp Surcharged in Black or Red

a   b

---

c

1893   **Perf. 12x11½**

20	A2(a)	5p on 4p blue (#16c)	65.00	100.00
a.		On 4p deep blue (#16b)	100.00	100.00
21	A2(b)	5p on 4p blue (#16c)	75.00	—
a.		On 4p deep blue (#16b)	100.00	110.00
22	A2(c)	5p on 4p blue (#16c) (R)	42.50	37.50
a.		On 4p deep blue (#16b)	47.50	50.00
		Nos. 20-22 (3)	182.50	137.50

As the surcharges on Nos. 20-21 were handstamped in two steps and on No. 22 in three steps, various varieties exist.

Flag Design — A7

1894-95   Typo.   **Perf. 11½x12**

23	A7	5p vermilion	35.00	7.50
a.		Perf. 11 ('95)	70.00	15.00
b.		As "a," deep red ('00)	5.00	20.00

Types of 1887-1895 Surcharged in Blue, Black, Red or Green

1½p, 2½p   3p

Handstamped Surcharges

1895   **Perf. 11**

24	A2	1½p on 2p org (Bl)	7.50	10.00
a.		1½p on 2p brn org, perf 12x11½ (Bl)	27.50	20.00
b.		1½p on 2p yellow, "2" ends with vertical stroke	5.00	27.50
c.		As No. 24, pair, one without surcharge	650.00	
25	A2	3p on 2p org (Bk)	10.00	15.00
a.		3p on 2p brn org, perf 12x11½ (Bk)	60.00	25.00
b.		3p on 2p org yellow, narrow "R" (Bk)	6.00	50.00
c.		Vert. pair, imperf. btwn.	650.00	
d.		As "b," pair, one without surcharge		

Typographed Surcharges (#26 Handstamped)

1898-1900   **Perf. 11**

26	A2	2½p on 1sh rose (Bk), hstmpd. srch.	50.00	50.00
a.		2½p, typo surcharge	13.00	15.00
b.		As "a," double surcharge	500.00	500.00
27	A2	2½p on 2sh6p vio (Bk)	13.00	20.00
28	A2	2½p on 1p bl grn (R)	1.75	5.00
a.		Inverted surcharge	850.00	425.00
29	A2	2½p on 1sh rose car (R)	8.50	20.00
a.		Double surcharge	400.00	
30	A2	3p on 2p dp red org (G)	5.00	130.00
		Nos. 26-30 (5)	78.25	225.00

No. 30 was a reissue, available for postage. The surcharge is not as tall as the 3p surcharge illustrated, which is the surcharge on No. 25. As Nos. 24-26 are handstamped, various varieties exist.

Stamps of 1886-99 Overprinted in Red or Blue

1899

31	A2	½p dl bl grn (R)	3.50	8.00
32	A2	1p red brown (Bl)	4.25	20.00
33	A2	2p br orange (R)	2.50	20.00
a.		2p deep ocher	4.00	
34	A2	4p rose (R)	1.00	20.00
35	A7	5p dp scarlet (Bl)	3.75	20.00
36	A2	6p maroon (Bl)	2.00	20.00

37	A2	1sh rose car (Bl)	2.00	25.00
38	A2	2sh6p mauve (R)	4.75	40.00
		Nos. 31-38 (8)	23.75	173.00

In 1900 the Samoan islands were partitioned between the US and Germany. The part which became American has since used US stamps.

Issued under German Dominion

Stamps of Germany Overprinted

1900　　Unwmk.　　Perf. 13½x14½

51	A9	3pf dark brown	11.00	16.00
52	A9	5pf green	14.00	21.00
53	A10	10pf carmine	11.00	21.00
54	A10	20pf ultra	22.50	35.00
55	A10	25pf orange	45.00	90.00
56	A10	50pf red brown	45.00	90.00
		Nos. 51-56 (6)	148.50	273.00

Kaiser's Yacht "Hohenzollern"
A12　　　　A13

1900　　Typo.　　Perf. 14

57	A12	3pf brown	1.40	1.50
58	A12	5pf green	1.40	1.50
59	A12	10pf carmine	1.40	1.50
60	A12	20pf ultra	1.40	3.00
61	A12	25pf org & blk, yel	1.50	15.00
62	A12	30pf org & blk, sal	1.60	12.00
63	A12	40pf lake & blk	1.60	15.00
64	A12	50pf pur & blk, sal	1.60	16.00
65	A12	80pf lake & blk, rose	3.50	37.50

Perf. 14½x14
Engr.

66	A13	1m carmine	4.25	75.00
67	A13	2m blue	5.75	130.00
68	A13	3m black vio	10.00	190.00
69	A13	5m slate & car	175.00	650.00
		Nos. 57-69 (13)	210.40	1,148.

1915　Wmk. 125　Typo.　Perf. 14

70	A12	3pf brown	1.40	
71	A12	5pf green	1.60	
72	A12	10pf carmine	1.60	

Perf. 14½x14
Engr.

73	A13	5m slate & car	35.00	

Nos. 70-73 were never put in use.

Issued under British Dominion
Nos. 57-69 Surcharged

On A12

On A13

1914　　Unwmk.　　Perf. 14

101	A12	½p on 3pf brn	60.00	16.00
a.		Double surcharge	800.00	625.00
b.		Fraction bar omitted	90.00	42.50
c.		Comma after "I"	750.00	450.00
102	A12	½p on 5pf grn	65.00	20.00
a.		Double surcharge	800.00	625.00
b.		Fraction bar omitted	140.00	62.50
d.		Comma after "I"	450.00	190.00
103	A12	1p on 10pf car	110.00	42.50
a.		Double surcharge	850.00	675.00
104	A12	2½p on 20pf ultra	62.50	14.00
a.		Fraction bar omitted	95.00	45.00
b.		Inverted surcharge	1,150.	1,050.
c.		Double surcharge	800.00	675.00
d.		Commas after "I"	575.00	375.00
105	A12	3p on 25pf org & blk, yel	80.00	42.50
a.		Double surcharge	1,150.	850.00
b.		Comma after "I"	5,250.	1,150.

106	A12	4p on 30pf org & blk, sal	135.00	62.50
107	A12	5p on 40pf lake & blk	135.00	75.00
108	A12	6p on 50pf pur & blk, sal	67.50	37.50
a.		Inverted "9" for "6"	190.00	110.00
b.		Double surcharge	1,250.	1,150.
109	A12	9p on 80pf lake & blk, rose	210.00	110.00

Perf. 14½x14

110	A13	1sh on 1m car ("1 Shillings")	3,500.	3,750.
a.		"1 Shilling."	11,500.	7,500.
111	A13	2sh on 2m blue	4,000.	3,500.
112	A13	3sh on 3m blk vio	1,600.	1,500.
a.		Double surcharge	10,500.	11,500.
113	A13	5sh on 5m slate & car	1,200.	1,100.
a.		Double surcharge	15,000.	15,000.

G.R.I. stands for Georgius Rex Imperator.
The 3d on 30pf and 4d on 40pf were produced at a later time.
Unauthorized overprints, created as favors, exist on Nos. 101-113.

Stamps of New Zealand Overprinted in Red or Blue

k　　　　　m

Perf. 14, 14x13½, 14x14½
1914, Sept. 29　　Wmk. 61

114	A41(k)	½p yel grn (R)	1.50	.35
115	A42(k)	1p carmine	1.40	.25
116	A41(k)	2p mauve (R)	1.40	1.10
117	A22(m)	2½p blue (R)	2.00	2.00
118	A41(k)	6p car rose, perf. 14x14½	2.25	2.00
a.		Perf. 14x13½	19.00	26.00
119	A41(k)	1sh vermilion	11.00	22.00
		Nos. 114-119 (6)	19.55	27.70

Overprinted Type "m"

1914-25　　Perf. 14, 14½x14

120	PF1	2sh blue (R)	7.00	6.25
121	PF1	2sh6p brown (Bl)	6.25	15.00
122	PF1	3sh vio (R) ('22)	18.00	65.00
123	PF1	5sh green (R)	22.50	11.00
124	PF1	10sh red brn (Bl)	45.00	42.50
125	PF2	£1 rose (Bl)	100.00	85.00
126	PF2	£2 vio (R) ('25)	400.00	
		Nos. 120-126 (7)	598.75	
		Nos. 120-125 (6)		224.75

Postal use of the £2 is questioned.

Overprinted Type "k"
Perf. 14x13½, 14x14½

1916-19　　　　　　Typo.

127	A43	½p yellow grn (R)	1.00	1.40
128	A47	1½p gray blk (R) ('17)	.55	.25
129	A47	1½p brn org (R) ('19)	.35	.50
130	A43	2p yellow (R) ('18)	2.00	.25
131	A43	3p chocolate (Bl)	3.50	22.50

Engr.

132	A44	2½p dull blue (R)	1.25	.60
133	A45	3p violet brn (Bl)	.65	1.25
134	A45	6p carmine rose (Bl)	3.50	3.50
135	A45	1sh vermilion (Bl)	4.75	1.75
		Nos. 127-135 (9)	17.55	32.00

New Zealand Victory Issue of 1919
Overprinted Type "k"

1920, June　　　　Perf. 14

136	A48	½p yellow grn (R)	6.50	16.00
137	A49	1p carmine (Bl)	3.00	21.00
138	A50	1½p brown org (R)	2.00	11.00
139	A51	3p black brn (Bl)	9.25	10.50
140	A52	6p purple (R)	5.25	8.00
141	A53	1sh vermilion (Bl)	15.00	12.50
		Nos. 136-141 (6)	41.00	79.00

British Flag and Samoan House — A22

1921, Dec. 23　Engr.　Perf. 14x13½

142	A22	½p green	5.50	2.00
a.		Perf. 14x14½	5.50	15.00
143	A22	1p lake	6.50	.25
a.		Perf. 14x14½	9.00	1.75

144	A22	1½p org brn, perf. 14x14½	1.50	20.00
a.		Perf. 14x13½	20.00	13.00
145	A22	2p yel, perf. 14x14½	3.00	3.00
a.		Perf. 14x13½	15.00	.90
146	A22	2½p dull blue	2.00	9.50
147	A22	3p dark brown	2.00	6.00
148	A22	4p violet	2.00	4.00
149	A22	5p brt blue	2.00	9.00
150	A22	6p carmine rose	2.00	8.00
151	A22	8p red brown	2.25	16.00
152	A22	9p olive green	2.50	40.00
153	A22	1sh vermilion	2.25	32.50
		Nos. 142-153 (12)	33.50	150.25

For overprints see Nos. 163-165.

New Zealand Nos. 182-183 Overprinted Type "m" in Red

1926-27　　　　Perf. 14½x14

154	A56	2sh dark blue	5.75	21.00
a.		2sh blue ('27)	7.00	50.00
155	A56	3sh deep violet	25.00	50.00
a.		3sh violet ('27)	62.50	110.00

Issued: 2sh, Nov.; 3sh, Oct.; Nos. 154a, 155a, 11/10.

New Zealand Postal-Fiscal Stamps, Overprinted Type "m" in Blue or Red

1932, Aug.　　　　Perf. 14

156	PF5	2sh6p brown	18.00	55.00
157	PF5	5sh green (R)	30.00	57.50
158	PF5	10sh lake	55.00	110.00
159	PF5	£1 pink	80.00	160.00
160	PF5	£2 violet (R)	1,000.	
161	PF5	£5 dk bl (R)	2,600.	
		Nos. 156-159 (4)	183.00	382.50

See Nos. 175-180, 195-202, 216-219.

Silver Jubilee Issue

Stamps of 1921 Overprinted in Black

1935, May 7　　　Perf. 14x13½

163	A22	1p lake	.40	.50
a.		Perf. 14x14½	105.00	190.00
164	A22	2½p dull blue	.75	1.00
165	A22	6p carmine rose	3.25	5.00
		Nos. 163-165 (3)	4.40	6.50
		Set, never hinged	10.00	

25th anniv. of the reign of George V.

Western Samoa

Samoan Girl and Kava Bowl — A23　　　View of Apia — A24

River Scene — A25　　　Samoan Chief and Wife — A26

Samoan Canoe and House — A27　　　"Vailima," Stevenson's Home — A28

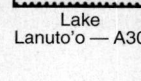

Stevenson's Tomb — A29　　　Lake Lanuto'o — A30

Falefa Falls — A31

Perf. 14x13½, 13½x14
1935, Aug. 7　Engr.　Wmk. 61

166	A23	½p yellow grn	.25	.40
167	A24	1p car lake & blk	.25	.25
168	A25	2p red org & blk, perf. 14	4.00	4.25
			5.00	4.25
169	A26	2½p dp blue & blk	.25	.25
170	A27	4p blk brn & dk gray	.50	.35
171	A28	6p plum	.70	.35
172	A29	1sh brown & violet	.50	.50
173	A30	2sh red brn & yel grn	1.10	.80
174	A31	3sh org brn & brt bl	2.75	3.50
		Nos. 166-174 (9)	10.30	10.65
		Set, never hinged	21.00	

See Nos. 186-188.

Postal-Fiscal Stamps of New Zealand Overprinted in Blue or Carmine

1935　　　　　　Perf. 14

175	PF5	2sh6p brown	10.00	18.00
176	PF5	5sh green	22.50	32.50
177	PF5	10sh dp car	62.50	85.00
178	PF5	£1 pink	55.00	110.00
179	PF5	£2 violet (C)	160.00	400.00
180	PF5	£5 dk bl (C)	235.00	525.00
		Nos. 175-180 (6)	545.00	1,171.

See Nos. 195-202, 216-219.

Samoan Coastal Village — A32　　　Map of Western Samoa — A33

Samoan Dancing Party A34　　　Robert Louis Stevenson A35

Perf. 13½x14
1939, Aug. 29　Engr.　Wmk. 253

181	A32	1p scar & olive	.60	.35
182	A33	1½p copper brn & bl	1.00	.90
183	A34	2½p dk blue & brn	1.10	1.00

Perf. 14x13½

184	A35	7p dp sl grn & vio	3.75	4.25
		Nos. 181-184 (4)	6.45	6.50
		Set, never hinged	12.00	

25th anniv. of New Zealand's control of the mandated territory of Western Samoa.

Samoan Chief — A36

1940, Sept. 2   **Perf. 14x13½**

185 A36 3p on 1½p brown   .50   .35
     Never hinged   .85

Issued only with surcharge. Examples without surcharge are from printer's archives.

Types of 1935 and

Apia Post Office — A37

1944-49   **Wmk. 253**   **Perf. 14**

186 A23 ½p yellow green   .30   21.00
187 A25 2p red orange & blk   2.00   7.50
188 A26 2½p dp blue & blk   5.00   42.50
    ('48)

        Perf. 13½x14

189 A37 5p dp ultra & ol brn   1.40   1.00
    ('49)
    Nos. 186-189 (4)   8.70   72.00
    Set, never hinged   14.50

Issue date: 5p, June 8.

> Catalogue values for unused stamps in this section, from this point to the end of the section, are for Never Hinged items.

Peace Issue
New Zealand Nos. 248, 250, 254, and 255 Overprinted in Black or Blue

p   q

1946, June 1   **Perf. 13x13½, 13½x13**

191 A94(p) 1p emerald   .40   .25
192 A96(q) 2p rose violet (Bl)   .40   .25
193 A100(p) 6p org red & red brn   .80   .25
194 A101(p) 8p brn lake & blk   .45   .25
    (Bl)
    Nos. 191-194 (4)   2.05   1.00

Stamps and Type of New Zealand, 1931-50 Overprinted Like Nos. 175-180 in Blue or Carmine

1945-50   **Wmk. 253**   **Perf. 14**

195 PF5 2sh6p brown   15.00   30.00
196 PF5 3sh green   21.00   18.00
197 PF5 10sh car ('48)   23.00   19.00
198 PF5 £1 pink ('48)   130.00   200.00
199 PF5 30sh choc ('48)   200.00   350.00
200 PF5 £2 violet (C)   210.00   310.00
201 PF5 £3 lt grn ('50)   300.00   425.00
202 PF5 £5 dk bl (C)   425.00   500.00
    ('50)

Making Siapo Cloth — A38

Western Samoa and New Zealand Flags, Village A39

Thatching Hut A40

Samoan Chieftainess A41

Designs: 2p, Western Samoa seal. 3p, Aleisa Falls (actually Malifa Falls). 5p, Manumea (tooth-billed pigeon). 6p, Fishing canoe. 8p, Harvesting cacao. 2sh, Preparing copra.

     Perf. 13, 13½x13

1952, Mar. 10   **Engr.**   **Wmk. 253**

203 A38 ½p org brn & claret   .25   2.00
204 A39 1p green & olive   .25   .40
205 A38 2p deep carmine   .25   .25
206 A39 3p indigo & blue   .50   .25
207 A38 5p dk grn & org brn   9.50   1.25
208 A39 6p dp rose pink & bl   1.00   .25
209 A39 8p rose carmine   .35   .30
210 A40 1sh blue & brown   .25   .25
211 A39 2sh yellow brown   1.10   .50
212 A41 3sh ol gray & vio brn   2.75   2.75
    Nos. 203-212 (10)   16.20   8.20

Coronation Issue
Types of New Zealand 1953

1953, May 25   **Photo.**   **Perf. 14x14½**

214 A113 2p brown   1.25   .30
215 A114 6p slate black   1.25   .50

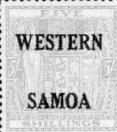

Type of New Zealand 1944-52 Overprinted in Blue or Carmine

       Wmk. 253

1955, Nov. 14   **Typo.**   **Perf. 14**

216 PF5 5sh yellow green   11.00   27.50
217 PF5 10sh carmine rose   11.00   50.00
218 PF5 £1 dull rose   18.00   57.50
219 PF5 £2 violet (C)   100.00   175.00
    Nos. 216-219 (4)   140.00   310.00

Redrawn Types of 1952 and

Map of Western Samoa and Mace A42

Designs: 4p, as 1p. 6p, as 2p.

Inscribed: "Fono Fou 1958" and "Samoa I Sisifo"

     Perf. 13½x13, 13

1958, Mar. 21   **Engr.**   **Wmk. 253**

220 A39 4p rose carmine   .30   .30
221 A38 6p dull purple   .30   .30
222 A42 1sh light violet blue   .85   .50
    Nos. 220-222 (3)   1.45   1.10

Independent State

Samoa College A43

Designs: 1p, Woman holding ceremonial mat, vert. 3p, Public Library. 4p, Fono House (Parliament). 6p, Map of Western Samoa, ship and plane. 8p, Faleolo airport. 1sh, Talking chief with fly whisk, vert. 1sh3p, Government House, Vailima. 2sh6p, Flag of Western Samoa. 5sh, State Seal.

       Wmk. 253

1962, July 2   **Litho.**   **Perf. 13½**

223 A43 1p car & brown   .25   .25
224 A43 2p org, lt grn, red   .25   .25
        & brown
225 A43 3p blue, grn & brn   .25   .25
226 A43 4p dk grn, bl &   .35   .35
        car
227 A43 6p yel, grn & ultra   .80   .50
228 A43 8p blue & emerald   .80   .55
229 A43 1sh brt grn & brn   .35   .85
    Complete booklet, 4 ea. #223-229
    Complete booklet, 4 ea. #223, 225, 227-228
230 A43 1sh3p blue & emerald   1.25   .75
231 A43 2sh6p vio blue & red   2.75   1.75
232 A43 5sh olive gray, red   3.00   2.75
        & dk blue
    Nos. 223-232 (10)   10.05   8.25

Western Samoa's independence.
The booklets described following No. 229 contain marginal blocks of stamps taken from sheets, with glassine interleaving, and stapled into the booklet cover.
See #242-247.

Tupua Tamasese Mea'ole, Malietoa Tanumafili II and Seal — A44

1963, Oct. 1   **Photo.**   **Perf. 14**

233 A44 1p green & blk   .25   .25
234 A44 4p dull blue & blk   .25   .25
235 A44 8p carmine rose & blk   .25   .25
236 A44 2sh orange & blk   .25   .25
    Nos. 233-236 (4)   1.00   1.00

First anniversary of independence.

Signing of Western Samoa-New Zealand Friendship Treaty A45

1964, Sept. 1   **Unwmk.**   **Perf. 13½**

237 A45 1p multicolored   .25   .25
238 A45 8p multicolored   .25   .25
239 A45 2sh multicolored   .25   .25
240 A45 3sh multicolored   .25   .35
    Nos. 237-240 (4)   1.00   1.10

2nd anniv. of the signing of the Treaty of Friendship between Western Samoa and New Zealand. Signers: J. B. Wright, N. Z. High Commissioner for Western Pacific, and Fiame Mata'afa, Prime Minister of Western Samoa.

Type of 1962
      Wmk. 355

1965, Oct. 4   **Litho.**   **Perf. 13½**

242 A43 1p carmine & brn   .40   .75
243 A43 3p blue, grn & brn   37.50   .90
244 A43 4p dk grn, bl & car   .40   .75
245 A43 6p yel, grn & ultra   .50   .45
246 A43 8p blue & emerald   .55   .25
247 A43 1sh brt green & brn   .70   .80
    Nos. 242-247 (6)   40.05   8.00

For surcharge see No. B1.

Aerial View of Deep-Sea Wharf A46

8p, 2sh, View of Apia harbor & deep-sea wharf.

1966, Mar. 2   **Photo.**   **Perf. 13½**

251 A46 1p multicolored   .25   .25
252 A46 8p multicolored   .25   .25
253 A46 2sh multicolored   .30   .25
254 A46 3sh multicolored   .40   .35
    Nos. 251-254 (4)   1.20   1.10

Opening of Western Samoa's first deep-sea wharf at Apia.

Inauguration of WHO Headquarters, Geneva — A47

Design: 4p, 1sh, WHO building and flag.

1966, July 4   **Photo.**   **Wmk. 355**

255 A47 3p gray, ultra & bister   .35   .25
256 A47 4p multicolored   .50   .35
257 A47 6p lt ol grn, pur & grn   .60   .40
258 A47 1sh multicolored   1.50   .60
    Nos. 255-258 (4)   2.95   1.60

Tuatagaloa L.S., Minister of Justice A48

Designs: 8p, F.C.F. Nelson, Minister of Works, Marine and Civil Aviation. 2sh, To'omata T. L., Minister of Lands. 3sh, Fa'alava'au Galu, Minister of Post Office, Radio and Broadcasting.

      Perf. 14½x14

1967, Jan. 16   **Photo.**   **Wmk. 355**

259 A48 3p violet & sepia   .25   .25
260 A48 8p blue & sepia   .25   .25
261 A48 2sh lt olive grn & sepia   .30   .30
262 A48 3sh lilac rose & sepia   .50   .50
    Nos. 259-262 (4)   1.30   1.30

Fifth anniversary of Independence.

Samoan Fales, 1900, and Fly Whisk A49

1sh, Fono House (Parliament) and mace.

1967, May 16   **Perf. 14½**

263 A49 8p multicolored   .35   .35
264 A49 1sh multicolored   .45   .45

Centenary of Mulinu'u as Government Seat.

Wattled Honey-Eater — A50

Birds of Western Samoa: 2s, Pacific pigeon. 3s, Samoan starling. 5s, Samoan broadbill. 7s, Red-headed parrot finch. 10s, Purple swamp hen. 20s, Barn owl. 25s, Tooth-billed pigeon. 50s, Island thrush. $1, Samoan fantail. $2, Mao (gymnomyza samoensis). $4, Samoan white-eye (zosterops samoensis).

      Perf. 14x14½

1967, July 10   **Photo.**   **Wmk. 355**
Birds in Natural Colors
     Size: 37x24mm

265 A50 1s black & lt brown   .25   .25
266 A50 2s lt ultra, blk & brn   .25   .25
         org
267 A50 3s blk, lt brn & emer   .35   .25
268 A50 5s lilac, blk & vio bl   .35   .25
269 A50 7s blk, vio bl & gray   .90   .25
270 A50 10s Prus blue & blk   .90   .25
271 A50 20s dk gray & blue   3.00   .50
272 A50 25s pink, blk & dk grn   1.25   .25
273 A50 50s brn, blk & lt ol grn   2.10   .40
274 A50 $1 yellow & black   5.00   4.50

1969   **Size: 43x28mm**   **Perf. 13½**

274A A50 $2 blk & lt grnsh bl   3.75   7.00
274B A50 $4 dp orange & blk   42.50   17.50
    Nos. 265-274B (12)   60.60   31.65

For surcharge see No. 294.

Child Care A51

Designs: 7s, Leprosarium. 20s, Mobile X-ray unit. 25s, Apia Hospital.

1967, Dec. 1   **Litho.**   **Perf. 14**

275 A51 3s multicolored   .30   .25
276 A51 7s multicolored   .35   .25
277 A51 20s multicolored   .60   .40
278 A51 25s multicolored   .80   .55
    Nos. 275-278 (4)   2.05   1.45

South Pacific Health Service.

Thomas Trood A52

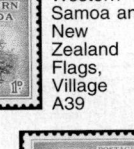

Portraits: 7s, Dr. Wilhelm Solf. 20s, John C. Williams. 25s, Fritz Marquardt.

1968, Jan. 1   Unwmk.   Perf. 13½
279	A52	2s multicolored	.30	.25
280	A52	7s multicolored	.30	.25
281	A52	20s multicolored	.35	.25
282	A52	25s multicolored	.40	.25
	Nos. 279-282 (4)		1.35	1.00

Sixth anniversary of independence.

Samoan Agricultural Development A53

Perf. 13x12½
1968, Feb. 15   Photo.   Wmk. 355
283	A53	3s Cocoa	.30	.30
284	A53	5s Breadfruit	.30	.30
285	A53	10s Copra	.30	.30
286	A53	20s Bananas	.40	.40
	Nos. 283-286 (4)		1.30	1.30

Curio Vendors, Pago Pago A54

20s, Palm trees at the shore. 25s, A'Umi Beach.

Perf. 14½x14
1968, Apr. 22   Photo.   Wmk. 355
287	A54	7s multicolored	.30	.30
288	A54	20s multicolored	.35	.30
289	A54	25s multicolored	.45	.35
	Nos. 287-289 (3)		1.10	.95

South Pacific Commission, 21st anniv.

Bougainville and Compass Rose — A55

Designs: 3s, Map showing Western Samoa Archipelago and Bougainville's route. 20s, Bougainvillea. 25s, Bougainville's ships La Boudeuse and L'Etoile.

1968, June 10   Litho.   Perf. 14
290	A55	3s brt blue & blk	.25	.25
291	A55	7s ocher & blk	.30	.25
292	A55	20s grnsh blk, brt rose & grn	.65	.40
293	A55	25s brt lil, vio, blk & org	.90	.50
	Nos. 290-293 (4)		2.10	1.40

200th anniv. of the visit of Louis Antoine de Bougainville (1729-1811) to Samoa.

No. 270 Surcharged with New Value, Three Bars and "1928-1968 / KINGSFORD-SMITH / TRANSPACIFIC FLIGHT"

1968, June 13   Photo.   Perf. 14x14½
294	A50	20s on 10s multicolored	.90	.90

40th anniv. of the 1st Transpacific flight under Capt. Charles Kingsford-Smith (Oakland, CA to Brisbane, Australia, via Honolulu and Fiji).

Human Rights Flame and Globe A56

Perf. 14½x14
1968, Aug. 26   Photo.   Wmk. 355
295	A56	7s multicolored	.30	.25
296	A56	20s multicolored	.35	.25
297	A56	25s multicolored	.50	.25
	Nos. 295-297 (3)		1.15	.75

International Human Rights Year, 1968.

Martin Luther King, Jr. — A57

1968, Sept. 23   Litho.   Perf. 14
298	A57	7s green & black	.35	.25
299	A57	20s brt rose lil & blk	.45	.25

Rev. Dr. Martin Luther King, Jr. (1929-68), American civil rights leader.

Polynesian Madonna — A58

1968, Oct. 12   Wmk. 355
300	A58	1s olive & multi	.30	.25
301	A58	3s multicolored	.30	.25
302	A58	20s crimson & multi	.30	.25
303	A58	30s dp orange & multi	.40	.25
	Nos. 300-303 (4)		1.30	1.00

Christmas 1968.

Frangipani — A59

Flowers: 7s, Chinese hibiscus, vert. 20s, Red ginger, vert. 30s, Canangium odoratum.

1969, Jan. 20   Unwmk.   Perf. 14
304	A59	2s brt blue & multi	.40	.25
305	A59	7s multicolored	.55	.35
306	A59	20s yellow & multi	.95	.50
307	A59	30s multicolored	1.35	.80
	Nos. 304-307 (4)		3.25	1.90

Seventh anniversary of independence.

R. L. Stevenson and Silver from "Treasure Island" — A60

Robert Louis Stevenson and: 7s, Stewart and Balfour on the moor from "Kidnapped," 20s, "Doctor Jekyll and Mr. Hyde." 22s, Archie Weir and Christiana Elliot from "Weir of Hermiston."

Perf. 14x13½
1969, Apr. 21   Litho.   Wmk. 355
308	A60	3s gray & multi	.35	.30
309	A60	7s gray & multi	.45	.30
310	A60	20s gray & multi	.45	.55
311	A60	22s gray & multi	.45	.55
	Nos. 308-311 (4)		1.70	1.70

75th anniv. of the death of Robert Louis Stevenson, who is buried in Samoa.

Weight Lifting — A61

Perf. 13½x13
1969, July 21   Photo.   Unwmk.
312	A61	3s shown	.25	.25
313	A61	20s Sailing	.25	.25
314	A61	22s Boxing	.35	.30
	Nos. 312-314 (3)		.85	.80

3rd Pacific Games, Port Moresby, Papua and New Guinea, Aug. 13-23.

American Astronaut on Moon, Splashdown and Map of Samoan Islands — A62

1969, July 24   Photo.
315	A62	7s red, blk, silver & grn	.25	.25
316	A62	20s car, blk, sil & ultra	.35	.25

US astronauts. See note after US No. C76.

Holy Family by El Greco A63

Christmas (Paintings): 1s, Virgin and Child, by Murillo. 20s, Nativity, by El Greco. 30s, Virgin and Child (from Adoration of the Kings), by Velazquez.

1969, Oct. 13   Unwmk.   Perf. 14
317	A63	1s gold, red & multi	.25	.25
318	A63	3s gold, red & multi	.25	.25
319	A63	20s gold, red & multi	.25	.25
320	A63	30s gold, red & multi	.35	.25
a.	Souvenir sheet of 4, #317-320		2.00	2.00
	Nos. 317-320 (4)		1.10	1.00

Seventh Day Adventists' Sanatorium, Apia — A64

7s, Father Louis Violette, R. C. Cathedral, Apia. 20s, Church of Latter Day Saints (Mormon), Tuasivi, Safotulafai, vert. 22s, John Williams, London Missionary Soc. Church, Sapapali'i.

1970, Jan. 19   Litho.   Wmk. 355
321	A64	2s brown, blk & gray	.25	.25
322	A64	7s violet, blk & bister	.25	.25
323	A64	20s rose, blk & lt violet	.25	.25
324	A64	22s olive, blk & bister	.25	.25
	Nos. 321-324 (4)		1.00	1.00

Eighth anniversary of independence.

U.S.S. Nipsic A65

Designs: 5s, Wreck of German ship Adler. 10s, British ship Calliope in storm. 20s, Apia after hurricane.

1970, Apr. 27   Perf. 13½x14
325	A65	5s multicolored	.40	.25
326	A65	7s multicolored	.45	.30
327	A65	10s multicolored	.75	.40
328	A65	20s multicolored	1.50	.90
	Nos. 325-328 (4)		3.10	1.85

The great Apia hurricane of 1889.

Cook Statue, Whitby, England — A66

Designs: 1s, Kendal's chronometer and Cook's sextant. 20s, Capt. Cook bust, in profile. 30s, Capt. Cook, island scene and "Endeavour," horiz.

Perf. 14x14½
1970, Sept. 14   Litho.   Wmk. 355
Size: 25x41mm
329	A66	1s silver, dp car & blk	.35	.25
330	A66	2s multicolored	.45	.35
331	A66	20s gold, black & ultra	1.50	.50

Perf. 14½x14
Size: 83x25mm
332	A66	30s multicolored	3.00	1.75
	Nos. 329-332 (4)		5.30	2.85

Bicentenary of Capt. James Cook's exploration of South Pacific.

"Peace for the World" by Frances B. Eccles — A67

Christmas: 3s, Samoan coat of arms and Holy Family, by Werner Erich Jahnke. 20s, Samoan Mother and Child, by F. B. Eccles. 30s, Prince of Peace, by Sister Melane Fe'ao.

Perf. 13½
1970, Oct. 26   Photo.   Unwmk.
333	A67	2s gold & multi	.25	.25
334	A67	3s gold & multi	.25	.25
335	A67	20s gold & multi	.35	.25
336	A67	30s gold & multi	.45	.35
a.	Souvenir sheet of 4, #333-336		2.25	2.25
	Nos. 333-336 (4)		1.30	1.10

Pope Paul VI — A68

Wmk. 355

1970, Nov. 29 Litho. Perf. 14
337	A68	8s Prus blue & black	.25	.25
338	A68	20s deep plum & black	.45	.30

Visit of Pope Paul VI, Nov. 29, 1970.

Lumberjack
A69

8s, Woman and tractor in clearing, horiz. 20s, Log and saw carrier, horiz. 22s, Logging and ship.

Perf. 14x13½, 13½x14
1971, Feb. 1 Litho. Unwmk.
339	A69	3s multicolored	.25	.25
340	A69	8s multicolored	.25	.25
341	A69	20s multicolored	.45	.25
342	A69	22s multicolored	.55	.30
		Nos. 339-342 (4)	1.50	1.05

Development of the timber industry on Savaii Island by the American Timber Company of Potlatch.

Souvenir Sheet

Longboat in Apia Harbor; Samoa #3 and US #3 — A70

1971, Mar. 12 Photo. Perf. 11½
Granite Paper
343	A70	70s blue & multi	2.25	2.25

INTERPEX, 13th Intl. Stamp Exhib., NYC, Mar. 12-14.

Siva Dance
A71

Tourist Publicity: 7s, Samoan cricket game. 8s, Hideaway Resort Hotel. 10s, Aggie Grey and Aggie's Hotel.

Wmk. 355

1971, Aug. 9 Litho. Perf. 14
344	A71	5s orange brn & multi	.40	.25
345	A71	7s orange brn & multi	2.50	.70
346	A71	8s orange brn & multi	.90	.50
347	A71	10s orange brn & multi	.90	.70
		Nos. 344-347 (4)	4.70	2.15

A72

Samoan Legends, carved by Sven Ortquist: 3s, Queen Salamasina. 8s, Lu and his sacred hens (Samoa). 10s, God Tagaloa fishing

Samoan islands of Upolu and Savaii from the sea. 22s, Mt. Vaea and Pool of Tears.

1971, Sept. 20
348	A72	3s dark violet & multi	.25	.25
349	A72	8s multicolored	.25	.25
350	A72	10s dark blue & multi	.30	.30
351	A72	22s dark blue & multi	.45	.45
		Nos. 348-351 (4)	1.25	1.25

See Nos. 399-402.

A73

Christmas: 2s, 3s, Virgin and Child, by Giovanni Bellini. 20c, 30c, Virgin and Child with St. Anne and St. John the Baptist, by Leonardo da Vinci.

1971, Oct. 4 Perf. 14x13½
352	A73	2s blue & multi	.25	.25
353	A73	3s black & multi	.25	.25
354	A73	20s yellow & multi	.35	.25
355	A73	30s dark red & multi	.50	.30
		Nos. 352-355 (4)	1.35	1.05

Samoan Islands, Scales of Justice A74

1972, Jan. 10 Photo. Perf. 11½x12
356	A74	10s light blue & multi	.40	.30

1st So. Pacific Judicial Conf., Samoa, Jan. 1972.

Asau Wharf, Savaii A75

Designs: 8s, Parliament Building. 10s, Mothers' Center. 22s, Portraits of Tupua Tamasese Mea'ole and Malietoa Tanumafili II, and view of Vailima.

Perf. 13x13½
1972, Jan. 10 Litho. Wmk. 355
357	A75	1s bright pink & multi	.25	.25
358	A75	8s lilac & multi	.25	.25
359	A75	10s green & multi	.25	.25
360	A75	22s multicolored	.35	.30
		Nos. 357-360 (4)	1.10	1.05

10th anniversary of independence.

Commission Members' Flags — A76

Designs: 7s, Afoafouvale Misimoa, Secretary-General, 1970-71 and Commission flag. 8s, Headquarters Building, Noumea, New Caledonia, horiz. 10s, Flag of Commission of Samoa, flag and map of South Pacific Commission area, horiz.

1972, Mar. 17 Perf. 14x13½, 13½x14
361	A76	3s ultra & multi	.25	.25
362	A76	7s yellow, black & ultra	.25	.25
363	A76	8s multicolored	.30	.25
364	A76	10s lt green & multi	.30	.25
		Nos. 361-364 (4)	1.10	1.00

South Pacific Commission, 25th anniv.

Sunset and Ships — A77

Designs: 8s, Sailing ships Arend, Thienhoven and Africaansche Galey in storm. 10s, Outrigger canoe and Roggeveen's ships. 30s, Hemispheres with exploration route and map of Samoan Islands. All horiz.

1972, June 14 Perf. 14½
365	A77	2s car rose & multi	.25	.25
366	A77	8s violet blue & multi	.55	.25
367	A77	10s ultra & multi	.65	.25

Size: 85x25mm
368	A77	30s ocher & multi	1.90	1.90
		Nos. 365-368 (4)	3.35	2.65

250th anniv. of Jacob Roggeveen's Pacific voyage and discovery of Samoa in June 1722.

Bull Conch A78

2s, Rhinoceros beetle. 3s, Skipjack (fish). 4s, Painted crab. 5s, Butterflyfish. 7s, Samoan monarch. 10s, Triton shell. 20s, Jewel beetle. 50s, Spiny lobster. $1, Hawk moth. $2, Green turtle. $4, Black marlin. $5, Green tree lizard.

1972-75 Litho. Perf. 14½
Size: 41x24mm
369	A78	1s shown	.30	.30
370	A78	2s multicolored	.30	.30
371	A78	3s multicolored	.30	1.00
372	A78	4s multicolored	.30	.30
373	A78	5s multicolored	.35	.30
374	A78	7s multicolored	2.00	1.50
375	A78	10s multicolored	2.00	1.00
376	A78	20s multicolored	1.25	.30
377	A78	50s multicolored	2.00	2.75

Perf. 14x13½
Size: 29x45mm
378	A78	$1 multicolored	6.50	4.50
378A	A78	$2 multicolored	4.50	2.75
378B	A78	$4 multicolored	6.00	7.00
378C	A78	$5 multicolored	4.00	10.00
		Nos. 369-378C (13)	29.80	32.00

Issued: 1s-$1, Oct. 18, 1972; $2, June 18, 1973; $4, Mar. 27, 1974; $5, June 30, 1975.

Ascension, Stained Glass Window — A79

Stained Glass Windows in Apia Churches: 4s, Virgin and Child. 10s, St. Andrew blessing Samoan canoe. 30s, The Good Shepherd.

Perf. 14x14½
1972, Nov. 1 Wmk. 355
379	A79	1s ocher & multi	.25	.25
380	A79	4s gray & multi	.25	.25
381	A79	10s dull green & multi	.25	.25

382	A79	30s blue & multi	.50	.35
a.		Souvenir sheet of 4, #379-382	2.25	2.25
		Nos. 379-382 (4)	1.25	1.10

Christmas.

Scouts Saluting Flag, Emblems A80

1973, Jan. 29 Perf. 14
383	A80	2s shown	.25	.25
384	A80	3s First aid	.25	.25
385	A80	8s Pitching tent	.30	.25
386	A80	20s Action song	.60	.60
		Nos. 383-386 (4)	1.40	1.35

Boy Scouts of Samoa.

Apia General Hospital — A81

WHO, 25th anniv.: 8s, Baby clinic. 20s, Filariasis research. 22s, Family welfare.

1973, Aug. 20 Wmk. 355
387	A81	2s green & multi	.25	.25
388	A81	8s multicolored	.25	.25
389	A81	20s brown & multi	.35	.35
390	A81	22s vermilion & multi	.45	.40
		Nos. 387-390 (4)	1.30	1.25

"A Prince is Born," by Jahnke — A82

Christmas: 4s, "Star of Hope," by Fiasili Keil. 10s, "Mother and Child," by Ernesto Coter. 30s, "The Light of the World," by Coter.

1973, Oct. 15 Litho. Perf. 14
391	A82	3s blue & multi	.25	.25
392	A82	4s purple & multi	.25	.25
393	A82	10s red & multi	.25	.25
394	A82	30s blue & multi	.55	.50
a.		Souvenir sheet of 4, #391-394	2.10	2.10
		Nos. 391-394 (4)	1.30	1.25

Boxing and Games' Emblem A83

1974, Jan. 24
395	A83	8s shown	.25	.25
396	A83	10s Weight lifting	.25	.25
397	A83	20s Lawn bowling	.25	.25
398	A83	30s Stadium	.75	.75
		Nos. 395-398 (4)	1.50	1.50

10th British Commonwealth Games, Christchurch, New Zealand, Jan. 24-Feb. 2.

Legends Type of 1971

Samoan Legends, Wood Carvings by Sven Ortquist: 2s, Tigilau and dove. 8s, Pili with his sons and famous fish net. 20s, The girl Sina and the eel which became the coconut tree. 30s, Nafanua who returned from the spirit world to free her village.

1974, Aug. 13 Wmk. 355 Perf. 14
399	A72	2s lemon & multi	.25	.25
400	A72	8s rose red & multi	.25	.25

401	A72	20s yellow grn & multi	.40	.30
402	A72	30s lt violet & multi	.70	.70
		Nos. 399-402 (4)	1.60	1.50

Faleolo Airport — A84

Designs: 20s, Apia Wharf. 22s, Early post office, Apia. 50s, William Willis, raft "Age Unlimited" and route from Callao, Peru, to Tully, Western Samoa.

1974, Sept. 4   Unwmk.   Perf. 13½
Size: 47x29mm

403	A84	8s multicolored	.35	.25
404	A84	20s multicolored	.55	.45
405	A84	22s multicolored	.60	.60

Size: 86x29mm

406	A84	50s multicolored	1.50	1.50
a.		Souvenir sheet of 1, perf. 13	1.25	1.25
		Nos. 403-406 (4)	3.00	2.80

Cent. of UPU. The 8s is inscribed "Air Mail"; 20s, "Sea Mail"; 22s, "Raft Mail."

Holy Family, by Sebastiano — A85

Christmas: 4s, Virgin and Child with Saints, by Lotto. 10s, Virgin and Child with St. John, by Titian. 30s, Adoration of the Shepherds, by Rubens.

1974, Nov. 18   Litho.   Perf. 13x13½

407	A85	3s ocher & multi	.25	.25
408	A85	4s fawn & multi	.25	.25
409	A85	10s dull green & multi	.25	.25
410	A85	30s blue & multi	.35	.35
a.		Souvenir sheet of 4, #407-410	2.00	2.00
		Nos. 407-410 (4)	1.10	1.10

Winged Passion Flower A86

20s, Gardenias, vert. 22s, Lecythidaceae, vert. 30s, Malay apple.

Wmk. 355
1975, Jan. 17   Litho.   Perf. 14½

411	A86	8s dull yellow & multi	.30	.30
412	A86	20s pale pink & multi	.40	.40
413	A86	22s pink & multi	.50	.50
414	A86	30s lt green & multi	.80	.80
		Nos. 411-414 (4)	2.00	2.00

Joyita Loading at Apia A87

Designs: 8s, Joyita, Samoa and Tokelau Islands. 20s, Joyita sinking, Oct. 1955. 22s, Rafts in storm. 50s, Plane discovering wreck.

1975, Mar. 14   Photo.   Perf. 13

415	A87	1s multicolored	.25	.25
416	A87	8s multicolored	.30	.25
417	A87	20s multicolored	.50	.45
418	A87	22s multicolored	.60	.55
419	A87	50s multicolored	1.00	1.00
a.		Souvenir sheet of 5, #415-419	3.00	3.00
		Nos. 415-419 (5)	2.65	2.50

17th INTERPEX Phil. Exhib., NYC, 3/14-16.

Pate Drum — A88

1975, Sept. 30   Litho.   Perf. 14½x14

420	A88	8s shown	.25	.25
421	A88	20s Lali drum	.25	.25
422	A88	22s Logo drum	.30	.25
423	A88	30s Pu shell horn	.45	.45
		Nos. 420-423 (4)	1.25	1.20

Mother and Child, by Meleane Fe'ao — A89

Christmas (Paintings): 4s, Christ Child and Samoan flag, by Polataia Tuigamala. 10s, "A Star is Born," by Iosua Toafa. 30s, Mother and Child, by Ernesto Coter.

1975, Nov. 25   Litho.   Wmk. 355

424	A89	3s multicolored	.25	.25
425	A89	4s multicolored	.25	.25
426	A89	10s multicolored	.25	.25
427	A89	30s multicolored	.35	.35
a.		Souvenir sheet of 4, #424-427	1.00	1.00
		Nos. 424-427 (4)	1.10	1.10

Boston Massacre, by Paul Revere — A90

8s, Declaration of Independence, by John Trumbull. 20s, The Ship That Sank in Victory, by J. L. G. Ferris. 22s, Wm. Pitt Addressing House of Commons, by R. A. Hickel. 50s, Battle of Princeton, by William Mercer.

Perf. 13½x14
1976, Jan. 20   Litho.   Wmk. 355

428	A90	7s salmon & multi	.25	.25
429	A90	8s green & multi	.25	.25
430	A90	20s lilac & multi	.60	.40
431	A90	22s blue & multi	.65	.40
432	A90	50s yellow & multi	1.25	1.25
a.		Souvenir sheet of 5, #428-432 + label	6.50	6.50
		Nos. 428-432 (5)	3.00	2.55

Bicentenary of American Independence.

Mullet Fishing A91

1976, Apr. 27   Litho.   Perf. 14½

433	A91	10s shown	.25	.25
434	A91	12s Fish traps	.25	.25
435	A91	22s Fishermen	.40	.40
436	A91	50s Net fishing	1.00	1.00
		Nos. 433-436 (4)	1.90	1.80

Souvenir Sheet

Samoan $100 Gold Coin with Paul Revere and US Map — A92

Unwmk.
1976, May 29   Photo.   Perf. 13

| 437 | A92 | $1 green & gold | 2.75 | 2.75 |

American Bicentennial and Interphil 76 Intl. Phil. Exhib., Philadelphia, PA, May 29-June 6.

Boxing A93

12s, Wrestling. 22s, Javelin. 50s, Weight lifting.

Perf. 14½x14
1976, June 21   Litho.   Wmk. 355

438	A93	10s black & multi	.25	.25
439	A93	12s dark brown & multi	.25	.25
440	A93	22s dark purple & multi	.35	.25
441	A93	50s dark blue & multi	.65	.65
		Nos. 438-441 (4)	1.50	1.40

21st Olympic Games, Montreal, Canada, July 17-Aug. 1.

Mary and Joseph on Road to Bethlehem A94

Christmas: 5s, Adoration of the Shepherds. 22s, Nativity. 50s, Adoration of the Kings.

1976, Oct. 18   Litho.   Perf. 14x13½

442	A94	3s multicolored	.25	.25
443	A94	5s multicolored	.25	.25
444	A94	22s multicolored	.35	.25
445	A94	50s multicolored	.65	.65
a.		Souvenir sheet of 4, #442-445	1.90	1.90
		Nos. 442-445 (4)	1.50	1.40

Presentation of the Spurs of Chivalry — A95

Designs: 12s, Queen and view of Apia. 32s, Royal Yacht Britannia and Queen. 50s, Queen leaving Westminster Abbey.

Perf. 13½x14
1977, Feb. 11   Wmk. 355

446	A95	12s multicolored	.25	.25
447	A95	26s multicolored	.30	.30
448	A95	32s multicolored	.70	.30
449	A95	50s multicolored	.30	.30
		Nos. 446-449 (4)	1.55	1.15

25th anniv. of the reign of Elizabeth II.

Lindbergh and Spirit of St. Louis A96

Designs: 22s, Map of transatlantic route and plane. 24s, Spirit of St. Louis in flight. 26s, Spirit of St. Louis taking off.

1977, May 20   Litho.   Perf. 14

450	A96	22s multicolored	.30	.25
451	A96	24s multicolored	.40	.25
452	A96	26s multicolored	.45	.25
453	A96	50s multicolored	1.00	1.00
a.		Souvenir sheet of 4, #450-453	4.00	4.00
		Nos. 450-453 (4)	2.15	1.75

Charles A. Lindbergh's solo transatlantic flight from New York to Paris, 50th anniv.

Apia Automatic Telephone Exchange — A97

Designs: 13s, Mulinuu radio terminal. 26s, Old wall and new dial telephones. 50s, Global communications (2 telephones and globe).

1977, July 11   Litho.   Perf. 14

454	A97	12s multicolored	.25	.25
455	A97	13s multicolored	.25	.25
456	A97	26s multicolored	.35	.30
457	A97	50s multicolored	.60	.60
		Nos. 454-457 (4)	1.45	1.40

Telecommunications.

Samoa No. 3 and First Mail Notice — A98

13s, Samoa #4 & 1881 cover. 26s, Samoa #1 & Chief Post Office, Apia. 50s, Samoa #4 7 schooner "Energy," which carried 1st mail.

1977, Aug. 29   Wmk. 355   Perf. 13½

458	A98	12s multicolored	.30	.25
459	A98	13s multicolored	.30	.25
460	A98	26s multicolored	.40	.30
461	A98	50s multicolored	.75	.75
		Nos. 458-461 (4)	1.75	1.55

Samoan postage stamp centenary.

Nativity — A99

Christmas: 6s, People bringing gifts to Holy Family in Samoan hut. 26s, Virgin and Child. 50s, Stars over Christ Child.

1977, Oct. 11   Litho.   Perf. 14

462	A99	4s multicolored	.25	.25
463	A99	6s multicolored	.25	.25
464	A99	26s multicolored	.30	.25
465	A99	50s multicolored	.45	.45
a.		Souvenir sheet of 4, #462-465	1.50	1.50
		Nos. 462-465 (4)	1.25	1.20

Polynesian Airlines' Boeing
737 — A100

Aviation Progress: 24s, Kitty Hawk. 26s, Kingsford-Smith Fokker. 50s, Concorde.

Unwmk.

			Perf. 14	
1978, Mar. 21		**Litho.**		
466	A100	12s multicolored	.25	.25
467	A100	24s multicolored	.35	.30
468	A100	26s multicolored	.40	.30
469	A100	50s multicolored	.90	.90
a.		Souvenir sheet of 4, #466-469, perf. 13½	3.00	3.00
		Nos. 466-469 (4)	1.90	1.75

Turtle Hatchery, Aleipata — A101

$1, Hawksbill turtle & Wildlife Fund emblem.

1978, Apr. 14		**Wmk. 355**		**Perf. 14½**	
470	A101	24s multicolored		3.75	1.00
471	A101	$1 multicolored		9.25	3.75

Project to replenish endangered hawksbill turtles.

Common Design Types pictured following the introduction.

Elizabeth II Coronation Anniversary Issue
Souvenir Sheet
Common Design Types

1978, Apr. 21 **Unwmk.** **Perf. 15**		
472	Sheet of 6	2.10 2.10
a.	CD326 26s King's lion	.30 .30
b.	CD327 26s Elizabeth II	.30 .30
c.	CD328 26s Pacific pigeon	.30 .30

No. 472 contains 2 se-tenant strips of Nos. 472a-472c, separated by horizontal gutter with commemorative and descriptive inscriptions and showing central part of coronation procession with coach.

Souvenir Sheet

Canadian and Samoan Flags — A102

		Wmk. 355			
1978, June 9		**Litho.**		**Perf. 14½**	
473	A102	$1 multicolored		1.75	1.75

CAPEX Canadian Intl. Phil. Exhib., Toronto, June 9-18.

Capt. James
Cook — A103

Designs: 24s, Cook's cottage, now in Melbourne, Australia. 26s, Old drawbridge over River Esk, Whitby, 1766-1833. 50s, Resolution and map of Hawaiian Islands.

1978, Aug. 28		**Litho.**		**Perf. 14½x14**	
474	A103	12s multicolored		.30	.25
475	A103	24s multicolored		.40	.35
476	A103	26s multicolored		.50	.45
477	A103	50s multicolored		1.30	1.30
		Nos. 474-477 (4)		2.50	2.35

A104

Cowrie Shells: 1s, Thick-edged Cowrie. 2s, Isabella cowrie. 3s, Money cowrie. 4s, Eroded cowrie. 6s, Honey cowrie. 7s, Banded cowrie. 10s, Globe cowrie. 11s, Mole cowrie. 12s, Children's cowrie. 13s, Flag cone. 14s, Soldier cone. 24s, Cloth-of-gold cone. 26s, Lettered cone. 50s, Tiled cone. $1, Black marble cone. $2, Marlin-spike auger. $3, Scorpion spider conch. $5, Common harp.

1978-80	**Photo.**	**Unwmk.**		**Perf. 12½**	
		Size: 31x24mm			
		Granite Paper			
478	A104	1s multicolored		.25	.25
479	A104	2s multicolored		.25	.25
480	A104	3s multicolored		.25	.25
481	A104	4s multicolored		.25	.25
482	A104	6s multicolored		.25	.25
483	A104	7s multicolored		.25	.25
484	A104	10s multicolored		.25	.25
485	A104	11s multicolored		.25	.25
486	A104	12s multicolored		.25	.25
487	A104	13s multicolored		.25	.25
488	A104	14s multicolored		.25	.25
489	A104	24s multicolored		.25	.25
490	A104	26s multicolored		.30	.25
491	A104	50s multicolored		.40	.30
492	A104	$1 multicolored		1.00	.50

		Perf. 11½			
		Size: 36x26mm			
493	A104	$2 multi ('79)		1.75	.75
494	A104	$3 multi ('79)		2.50	1.50
494A	A104	$5 multi ('80)		4.00	2.25
		Nos. 478-494A (18)		12.95	8.55

Issue dates: 1s-12s, Sept. 15. 13s-$1, Nov. 20. $2, $3, July 18. $5, Aug. 26.

A105

Works by Dürer: 4s, The Virgin in Glory. 6s, Nativity. 26s, Adoration of the Kings. 50s, Annunciation.

		Wmk. 355			
1978, Nov. 6		**Litho.**		**Perf. 14**	
495	A105	4s lt brown & blk		.25	.25
496	A105	6s grnsh blue & blk		.25	.25
497	A105	26s violet blue & blk		.25	.25
498	A105	50s purple & blk		.45	.40
a.		Souvenir sheet of 4, #495-498		1.40	1.40
		Nos. 495-498 (4)		1.20	1.15

Christmas and for 450th death anniv. of Albrecht Dürer.

Boy
Carrying
Coconuts
A106

Designs: 24s, Children leaving church on White Sunday. 26s, Children pumping water. 50s, Girl playing ukulele.

1979, Apr. 10		**Litho.**		**Perf. 14**	
499	A106	12s multicolored		.25	.25
500	A106	24s multicolored		.30	.25
501	A106	26s multicolored		.30	.25
502	A106	50s multicolored		.65	.65
		Nos. 499-502 (4)		1.50	1.40

International Year of the Child.

Charles W.
Morgan
A107

1979, May 29		**Litho.**		**Perf. 13½**	
503	A107	12s multicolored		.30	.25
504	A107	14s Lagoda		.45	.25
505	A107	24s James T. Arnold		.55	.35
506	A107	50s Splendid		1.00	1.00
		Nos. 503-506 (4)		2.30	1.85

See Nos. 521-524, 543-546.

Saturn V
Launch — A108

Designs: 14s, Landing module and astronaut on moon, horiz. 24s, Earth seen from moon. 26s, Astronaut on moon, horiz. 50s, Lunar and command modules. $1, Command module after splashdown, horiz.

Perf. 14½x14, 14x14½				
1979, June 20		**Litho.**	**Wmk. 355**	
507	A108	12s multicolored	.25	.25
508	A108	14s multicolored	.25	.25
509	A108	24s multicolored	.30	.25
510	A108	26s multicolored	.35	.25
511	A108	50s multicolored	.45	.45
512	A108	$1 multicolored	1.00	1.00
a.		Souvenir sheet	2.00	2.00
		Nos. 507-512 (6)	2.60	2.45

1st moon landing, 10th anniv.

Penny Black, Hill
Statue — A109

24s, Great Britain #2 with Maltese Cross postmark. 26s, Penny Black and Rowland Hill. $1, Great Britain #2 and Hill statue.

1979, Aug. 27				**Perf. 14**	
513	A109	12s multicolored		.25	.25
514	A109	24s multicolored		.25	.25
515	A109	26s multicolored		.25	.25
516	A109	$1 multicolored		.60	.60
a.		Souvenir sheet of 4, #513-516		1.75	1.75
		Nos. 513-516 (4)		1.35	1.35

Sir Rowland Hill (1795-1879), originator of penny postage.

Anglican
Church,
Apia
A110

Samoan Churches: 6s, Congregational Christian Church, Leulumoega. 26s, Methodist Church, Piula. 50s, Protestant Church, Apia.

1979, Oct. 22		**Photo.**		**Perf. 12x11½**	
517	A110	4s lt blue & blk		.25	.25
518	A110	6s lt yellow grn & blk		.25	.25
519	A110	26s dull yellow & blk		.25	.25
520	A110	50s lt lilac & blk		.60	.60
a.		Souvenir sheet of 4, #517-520		1.25	1.25
		Nos. 517-520 (4)		1.35	1.35

Christmas.

Ship Type of 1979
Wmk. 355

1980, Jan. 22		**Litho.**		**Perf. 14**	
521	A107	12s William Hamilton		.30	.25
522	A107	14s California		.30	.25
523	A107	24s Liverpool II		.30	.25
524	A107	50s Two Brothers		1.10	1.10
		Nos. 521-524 (4)		2.00	1.85

Map of
Samoan
Islands,
Rotary
Emblem
A111

Missionary Flag, John Williams,
Plaque — A112

Flag-raising Memorial — A113

14s, German flag, Dr. Wilhelm Solf, plaque. 26s, Williams Memorial, Savai'i. 50s, Emblem, Paul P. Harris, founder.

1980, Mar. 26		**Photo.**		**Perf. 14**	
525	A111	12s shown		.60	.25
526	A112	13s shown		.45	1.00
527	A112	14s multicolored		1.00	.25
528	A113	24s shown		1.00	.40
529	A113	26s multicolored		.75	.50
530	A111	50s multicolored		1.25	2.25
		Nos. 525-530 (6)		5.05	4.65

Rotary Intl., 75th anniv. (A111); arrival of Williams, missionary in Samoa, 150th anniv. (13s, 26s); raising of the German flag, 80th anniv. (14s, 24s).

Souvenir Sheet

Village and Long Boat — A114

		Wmk. 355			
1980, May 6		**Litho.**		**Perf. 14**	
531	A114	$1 multicolored		1.25	1.25

London 80 Intl. Phil. Exhib., May 6-14.

Queen Mother Elizabeth Birthday Issue
Common Design Type

1980, Aug. 4		**Litho.**	
532	CD330 50s multicolored	.55	.55

Souvenir Sheet

Samoa No. 239, ZEAPEX
Emblem — A115

Unwmk.

1980, Aug. 23   Litho.   Perf. 14
533 A115 $1 multicolored   1.25 1.25

ZEAPEX '80, New Zealand International Stamp Exhibition, Auckland, Aug. 23-31.

Afiamalu Satellite Earth Station A116

14s, Station, diff. 24s, Station, map of Samoa. 50s, Satellite sending waves to earth. $2, Samoa #536, Sydpex '80 emblem.

1980, Sept. 17   Litho.   Perf. 11½

Granite Paper
534 A116 12s multicolored   .25 .25
535 A116 14s multicolored   .25 .25
536 A116 24s multicolored   .30 .25
537 A116 50s multicolored   .60 .60
     Nos. 534-537 (4)   1.40 1.35

Souvenir Sheet

1980, Sept. 29   Imperf.
538 A116 $2 multicolored   1.75 1.75

Sydpex '80 Natl. Phil. Exhib., Sydney.

The Savior, by John Poynton — A117

Christmas (Paintings by Local Artists): 14s, Madonna and Child, by Lealofi F. Siaopo. 27s, Nativity, by Pasila Feata. 50s, Yuletide, by R.P. Aiono.

Wmk. 355
1980, Oct. 28   Litho.   Perf. 14
539 A117 8s multicolored   .25 .25
540 A117 14s multicolored   .25 .25
541 A117 27s multicolored   .25 .25
542 A117 50s multicolored   .40 .40
a.   Souvenir sheet of 4, #539-542 1.25 1.25
     Nos. 539-542 (4)   1.15 1.15

Ship Type of 1979
1981, Jan. 26   Litho.   Perf. 13½
543 A107 12s Ocean   .30 .30
544 A107 18s Horatio   .45 .45
545 A107 27s Calliope   .70 .70
546 A107 32s Calypso   .80 .80
     Nos. 543-546 (4)   2.25 2.25

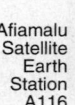

Pres. Franklin Roosevelt and Hyde Park Home A118

IYD: Scenes of Franklin D. Roosevelt — 18s, Inauguration. 27s, Pres. & Mrs. Roosevelt. 32s, Atlantic convoy (Lend Lease Bill). 38s, With stamp collection. $1, Campobello House.

Wmk. 355
1981, Apr. 29   Litho.   Perf. 14
547 A118 12s shown   .25 .25
548 A118 18s multicolored   .25 .25
549 A118 27s multicolored   .25 .25
550 A118 32s multicolored   .30 .30
551 A118 38s multicolored   .30 .30
552 A118 $1 multicolored   .50 .50
     Nos. 547-552 (6)   1.85 1.85

Hotel Tusitala — A119

18s, Apia Harbor. 27s, Aggie Grey's Hotel. 32s, Ceremonial kava preparation. 54s, Piula Pool.

Perf. 14½x14
1981, June 29   Litho.   Wmk. 355
553 A119 12s shown   .25 .25
554 A119 18s multicolored   .25 .25
555 A119 27s multicolored   .30 .25
556 A119 32s multicolored   .30 .25
557 A119 54s multicolored   .50 .50
     Nos. 553-557 (5)   1.60 1.50

Royal Wedding Issue
Common Design Type
Wmk. 355

1981, July 22   Litho.   Perf. 14
558 CD331 18s Bouquet   .25 .25
559 CD331 32s Charles   .25 .25
560 CD331 $1 Couple   .35 .35
     Nos. 558-560 (3)   .85 .85

Tattooing Instruments A120

1981, Sept. 29   Litho.   Perf. 13½x14
561 Strip of 4   2.00 2.00
a. A120 12s shown   .25 .25
b. A120 18s 1st stage   .25 .25
c. A120 27s Later stage   .35 .30
d. A120 $1 Tattooed man   1.00 1.00

Christmas — A121

1981, Nov. 30   Litho.   Perf. 13½
562 A121 11s Milo tree blossom   .25 .25
563 A121 15s Copper leaf   .25 .25
564 A121 23s Yellow allamanda   .25 .25
565 A121 $1 Mango blossom   .85 .85
a.   Souvenir sheet of 4, #562-565 2.25 2.25
     Nos. 562-565 (4)   1.60 1.60

Souvenir Sheet

Philatokyo '81 Intl. Stamp Exhibition — A122

1981, Oct. 9   Litho.   Perf. 14x13½
566 A122 $2 multicolored   2.00 2.00

250th Birth Anniv. of George Washington A123

1982, Feb. 26   Litho.   Perf. 14
567 A123 23s Pistol   .25 .25
568 A123 25s Mt. Vernon   .30 .30
569 A123 34s Portrait   .35 .35
     Nos. 567-569 (3)   .90 .90

Souvenir Sheet
570 A123 $1 Taking oath   1.10 1.10

20th Anniv. of Independence — A124

18s, Freighter Forum Samoa. 23s, Jet, routes. 25s, Natl. Provident Fund building. $1, Intl. subscriber dialing system.

1982, May 24   Litho.   Perf. 13½x14
571 A124 18s multicolored   1.00 .30
572 A124 23s multicolored   1.25 .40
573 A124 25s multicolored   .50 .40
574 A124 $1 multicolored   1.50 1.25
     Nos. 571-574 (4)   4.25 2.35

Scouting Year A125

1982, July 20   Wmk. 355   Perf. 14½
575 A125 5s Map reading   .25 .25
576 A125 38s Salute   .45 .45
577 A125 44s Rope bridge   .55 .55
578 A125 $1 Troop   1.25 1.25
a.   Souvenir sheet   1.75 1.75
     Nos. 575-578 (4)   2.50 2.50

No. 578a contains one stamp similar to No. 578, 48x36mm.

12th Commonwealth Games, Brisbane, Australia, Sept. 30-Oct. 9 — A126

Perf. 14x14½
1982, Sept. 20   Wmk. 373
579 A126 23s Boxing   .25 .25
580 A126 25s Hurdles   .30 .30
581 A126 34s Weightlifting   .40 .40
582 A126 $1 Lawn bowling   .95 .95
     Nos. 579-582 (4)   1.90 1.90

Christmas A127

Children's Drawings: 11s, 15s, Flight into Egypt diff. 38s, $1, Virgin and Child, diff.

1982, Nov. 15   Litho.   Wmk. 355
583 A127 11s multicolored   .25 .25
584 A127 15s multicolored   .25 .25
585 A127 38s multicolored   .45 .45
586 A127 $1 multicolored   .80 .80
a.   Souvenir sheet of 4, #583-586 2.25 2.25
     Nos. 583-586 (4)   1.75 1.75

Commonwealth Day — A128

Perf. 13½x14
1983, Feb. 23   Litho.   Wmk. 373
587 A128 14s Map   .25 .25
588 A128 29s Flag   .35 .35
589 A128 43s Harvesting copra   .35 .35
590 A128 $1 Malietoa Tanumafili
            II   .75 .75
     Nos. 587-590 (4)   1.70 1.70

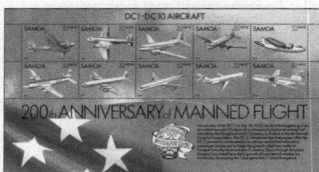

Manned Flight Bicentenary and 50th Anniv. of Douglas Aircraft — A129

a, DC-1. b, DC-2. c, DC-3. d, DC-4. e, DC-5. f, DC-6. g, DC-7. h, DC-8. i, DC-9. j, DC-10.

Wmk. 373
1983, June 7   Litho.   Perf. 14
591 A129 Sheet of 10   8.00 8.00
a.-j.   32s any single   .65 .65

7th South Pacific Games, Apia — A130

1983, Aug. 29   Litho.   Perf. 14x14½
592 A130 8s Pole vault   .45 .45
593 A130 15s Basketball   .55 .55
594 A130 25c Tennis   .70 .60
595 A130 32s Weightlifting   .90 .60
596 A130 35s Boxing   .90 .90
597 A130 46s Soccer   1.10 1.10
598 A130 48s Golf   2.00 1.25
599 A130 56s Rugby   1.50 1.50
     Nos. 592-599 (8)   8.10 6.95

Local Fruit — A131

Perf. 14x13½
1983-84   Litho.   Wmk. 373
600 A131 1s Limes   .35 .35
601 A131 2s Star fruit   .35 .35
602 A131 3s Mangosteen   .35 .35
603 A131 4s Lychee   .35 .35
604 A131 7s Passion fruit   .35 .35
605 A131 8s Mangoes   .35 .35
606 A131 11s Papaya   .35 .35
607 A131 13s Pineapple   .35 .35
608 A131 14s Breadfruit   .35 .35
609 A131 15s Bananas   .35 .35
610 A131 21s Cashew nut   .90 .90
611 A131 25s Guava   1.40 1.40
612 A131 32s Water Melon   1.75 1.75
613 A131 48s Sasalapa   2.00 2.00
614 A131 56s Avocado   2.25 2.25
615 A131 $1 Coconut   2.50 2.50
                Perf. 13½
616 A131 $2 Apples ('84)   3.00 3.00
617 A131 $4 Grapefruit ('84)   6.00 6.00
618 A131 $5 Oranges ('84)   7.00 7.00
     Nos. 600-618 (19)   30.30 30.30

Issued: 1s-15s, 9/28; 21s-$1, 11/30; $2-$5, 4/11.
For overprint see No. 628.

Miniature Sheet

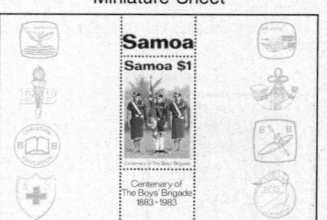

Boys' Brigade Centenary — A132

1983, Oct. 10   Perf. 14½
619 A132 $1 multicolored   3.50 3.50

Togitogiga
Falls, Upolu
A133

32s, Lano Beach, Savai'i. 48s, Mulinu'u
Point, Upolu. 56s, Nu'utele Island.

Wmk. 373

1984, Feb. 15	Litho.	Perf. 14		
620	A133	25s shown	.45	.25
621	A133	32s multicolored	.55	.55
622	A133	48s multicolored	.75	.75
623	A133	56s multicolored	.90	.90
	Nos. 620-623 (4)		2.65	2.45

Lloyd's List Issue
Common Design Type
Perf. 14½x14

1984, May 24	Litho.	Wmk. 373		
624	CD335	32s Apia Harbor	.35	.25
625	CD335	48s Apia hurricane, 1889	.65	.55
626	CD335	60s Forum Samoa	.75	.75
627	CD335	$1 Matua	.80	.80
	Nos. 624-627 (4)		2.55	2.35

**No. 615 Ovptd. "19th U.P.U.
CONGRESS / HAMBURG 1984"**

1984, June 7		Perf. 14x13½		
628	A131	$1 multicolored	1.75	1.75

Los Angeles Coliseum — A134

1984, June 26	Litho.	Perf. 14½		
629	A134	25s shown	.25	.25
630	A134	32s Weightlifting	.35	.35
631	A134	48s Boxing	.45	.45
632	A134	$1 Running	.75	.75
a.	Souvenir sheet of 4, #629-632		2.00	2.00
	Nos. 629-632 (4)		1.80	1.80

1984 Summer Olympics and Samoa's first
Olympic participation.

Souvenir Sheet

Ausipex '84 — A135

1984, Sept. 21	Litho.	Perf. 14		
633	A135	$2.50 Nomad N24	6.00	6.00

Christmas — A136

The Three Virtues, by Raphael.

1984, Nov. 7		Perf. 14½x14		
634	A136	25s Faith	.45	.25
635	A136	35s Hope	.55	.55
636	A136	$1 Charity	1.90	1.90
a.	Souvenir sheet of 3, #634-636		3.75	3.75
	Nos. 634-636 (3)		2.90	2.70

Orchids — A137

48s, Dendrobium biflorum. 56s, Dendrobium vaupelianum kraenzl. 67s, Glomera
montana. $1, Spathoglottis plicata.

Unwmk.

1985, Jan. 23		Perf. 14		
637	A137	48s multicolored	.65	.50
638	A137	56s multicolored	1.10	.90
639	A137	67s multicolored	1.25	1.25
640	A137	$1 multicolored	1.90	1.90
	Nos. 637-640 (4)		4.90	4.55

Vintage Automobiles — A138

48s, Ford Model A, 1903. 56s, Chevrolet
Tourer, 1912. 67s, Morris Oxford, 1913. $1,
Austin Seven, 1923.

Wmk. 373

1985, Mar. 26	Litho.	Perf. 14		
641	A138	48s multicolored	1.25	.75
642	A138	56s multicolored	1.60	1.00
643	A138	67s multicolored	2.00	2.00
644	A138	$1 multicolored	2.50	2.50
	Nos. 641-644 (4)		7.35	6.25

Fungi — A139

48s, Dictyophora indusiata. 56s,
Ganoderma tornatum. 67s, Mycena
chlorophos. $1, Mycobonia flava.

1985, Apr. 17	Litho.	Perf. 14½		
645	A139	48s multicolored	1.50	.75
646	A139	56s multicolored	1.75	1.00
647	A139	67s multicolored	2.00	2.00
648	A139	$1 multicolored	3.00	3.00
	Nos. 645-648 (4)		8.25	6.75

Queen Mother 85th Birthday
Common Design Type

32s, Photo., age 9. 48s, With Prince William
at christening of Prince Henry. 56s, At Liverpool street station. $1, Holding Prince Henry.
$2, Arriving at Tattenham corner station.

Perf. 14½x14

1985, June 7	Litho.	Wmk. 384		
649	CD336	32s multicolored	.50	.35
650	CD336	48s multicolored	.65	.45
651	CD336	56s multicolored	1.75	1.25
652	CD336	$1 multicolored	1.50	1.50
	Nos. 649-652 (4)		4.40	3.55

Souvenir Sheet

| 653 | CD336 | $2 multicolored | 4.00 | 4.00 |

Souvenir Sheet

EXPO '85, Tsukuba, Japan — A140

Unwmk.

1985, Aug. 26	Litho.	Perf. 14		
654	A140	$2 Emblem, elevation map	2.75	2.75

Intl. Youth Year — A141

Portions of world map and: a, Emblem, map
of No. America, Europe and Africa. b, Hands
reaching high. c, Arms reaching, hands limp.
d, Hands clenched. e, Emblem and map of
Africa, Asia and Europe.

1985, Sept. 18		Wmk. 373		
655	A141	Strip of 5	3.25	3.25
a.-e.	60s any single		.55	.55

Christmas
1985 — A142

Illustrations by Millicent Sowerby from A
Child's Garden of Verses, by Robert Louis
Stevenson.

1985, Nov. 5	Unwmk.	Perf. 14x14½		
656	A142	32s System	.30	.30
657	A142	48s Time to Rise	.40	.40
658	A142	56s Auntie's skirts	.45	.45
659	A142	$1 Good Children	.80	.80
a.	Souvenir sheet of 4, #656-659		2.50	2.50
	Nos. 656-659 (4)		1.95	1.95

Butterflies
A143

25s, Hypolimnas bolina inconstans. 32s,
Anapheis java sparrman. 48s, Deudorix
epijarbas doris. 56s, Badamia exclamationis.
60s, Tirumala hamata mellitula. $1,
Catochrysops taitensis.

1986, Feb. 13	Wmk. 384	Perf. 14½		
660	A143	25s multicolored	.55	.35
661	A143	32s multicolored	.65	.45
662	A143	48s multicolored	.90	.75
663	A143	56s multicolored	1.00	1.00
664	A143	60s multicolored	1.10	1.10
665	A143	$1 multicolored	2.00	2.00
	Nos. 660-665 (6)		6.20	5.65

Halley's
Comet
A144

Designs: 32s, Comet over Apia. 48s,
Edmond Halley, astronomer. 60s, Comet orbiting the Earth. $2, Giotto space probe under
construction at British Aerospace.

1986, Mar. 24				
666	A144	32s multicolored	.30	.30
667	A144	48s multicolored	.40	.40
668	A144	60s multicolored	.55	.55
669	A144	$2 multicolored	1.75	1.75
	Nos. 666-669 (4)		3.00	3.00

Queen Elizabeth II 60th Birthday
Common Design Type

Designs: 32s, Engagement to the Duke of
Edinburgh, 1947. 48s, State visit to US, 1976.
56s, Attending outdoor ceremony, Apia, 1977.
67s, At Badminton Horse Trials, 1978. $2, Vis-
iting Crown Agents' offices, 1983.

1986, Apr. 21				
670	CD337	32s scarlet, blk & sil	.30	.30
671	CD337	48s ultra & multi	.35	.35
672	CD337	56s green & multi	.40	.40
673	CD337	67s violet & multi	.50	.50
674	CD337	$2 rose violet & multi	1.00	1.00
	Nos. 670-674 (5)		2.55	2.55

AMERIPEX
'86, Chicago,
May 22-June
1 — A145

1986, May 22		Unwmk.		
675	A145	48s USS Vincennes	.45	.45
676	A145	56s Sikorsky S-42	.55	.55
677	A145	60s USS Swan	.60	.60
678	A145	$2 Apollo 10 splashdown	1.75	1.75
	Nos. 675-678 (4)		3.35	3.35

Souvenir Sheet

Vailima, Estate of Novelist Robert
Louis Stevenson, Upolu Is. — A146

1986, Aug. 4	Litho.	Perf. 13½		
679	A146	$3 multicolored	5.75	5.75

STAMPEX '86, Adelaide, Aug. 4-10.

Fish
A147

1986, Aug. 13	Litho.	Perf. 14		
680	A147	32s Spotted grouper	.50	.50
681	A147	48s Sabel squirrelfish	.70	.50
682	A147	60s Lunartail grouper	.90	.90
683	A147	67s Longtail snapper	1.25	1.25
684	A147	$1 Berndt's soldierfish	2.25	2.25
	Nos. 680-684 (5)		5.60	5.40

US
Peace
Corps in
Samoa,
25th
Anniv.
A148

Statesmen: Vaai Kolone of Samoa, Ronald
Reagan of US and: 45s, Fiame Mata'afa,
John F. Kennedy (1961) and Parliament
House. 60s, Jules Grevy, Grover Cleveland
(1886) and the Statue of Liberty.

1986, Dec. 1		Perf. 14½		
685	A148	45s multicolored	.40	.40
686	A148	60s multicolored	.45	.45
a.	Souvenir sheet of 2, #685-686		4.00	4.00

Christmas, Statue of Liberty, cent.

Natl. Independence, 25th
Anniv. — A149

Perf. 14x14½

			Unwmk.	
1987, Feb. 16		**Litho.**		
687	A149	15s Map, hibiscus	.25	.25
688	A149	45s Parliament	.45	.45
689	A149	60s Rowing race, 1987	.55	.55
690	A149	70s Dove	.65	.65
691	A149	$2 Prime minister, flag	2.00	2.00
		Nos. 687-691 (5)	3.90	3.90

Nos. 687-690 vert.

Marine Life
A150

1987, Mar. 31				
692	A150	45s Gulper	.55	.35
693	A150	60s Hatchet-fish	.65	.65
694	A150	70s Angler	.85	.85
695	A150	$2 Gulper, diff.	2.00	2.00
		Nos. 692-695 (4)	4.05	3.85

Souvenir Sheet

CAPEX '87 — A151

			Perf. 14½	
1987, June 13				
696	A151	$3 Logger, construction workers	3.25	3.25

Landscapes — A152

45s, Lefaga Beach, Upolu. 60s, Vaisala Beach, Savaii. 70s, Solosolo Beach, Upolu. $2, Neiafu Beach, Savaii.

			Perf. 14	
1987, July 29				
697	A152	45s multicolored	.75	.40
698	A152	60s multicolored	1.00	.50
699	A152	70s multicolored	1.10	.90
700	A152	$2 multicolored	2.50	2.50
		Nos. 697-700 (4)	5.35	4.30

Australia Bicentennial A153

Explorers of the Pacific: 40s, Abel Tasman (c. 1603-1659), Dutch navigator, discovered Tasmania, 1642. 45s, James Cook. 80s, Count Louis-Antoine de Bougainville (1729-1811), French navigator, discovered Bougainvelle Is., largest of the Solomon Isls., 1768. $2, Comte de La Perouse (1741-1788), French navigator, discovered La Perouse Strait.

			Perf. 14½	
1987, Sept. 30		**Litho.**		
701	A153	40s multicolored	.60	.35
702	A153	45s multicolored	.75	.55
703	A153	80s multicolored	1.00	1.00
704	A153	$2 multicolored	2.00	2.00
a.		Souvenir sheet of 1	3.00	3.00
		Nos. 701-704 (4)	4.35	3.90

No. 704a Ovptd. with HAFNIA '87 Emblem in Scarlet

1987, Oct. 16				
705	A153	$2 multicolored	3.50	3.50

Christmas 1987 — A154

			Perf. 14	
1987, Nov. 30				
706	A154	40s Christmas tree	.40	.35
707	A154	45s Going to church	.50	.40
708	A154	50s Bamboo fire-gun	.60	.60
709	A154	80s Going home	1.10	1.10
		Nos. 706-709 (4)	2.60	2.45

Australia Bicentennial — A155

a, Samoan natl. crest, Australia Post emblem. b, Two jets, postal van. c, Loading airmail. d, Jet, van, postman. e, Congratulatory aerogramme.

			Perf. 14½	
1988, Jan. 27				
710	A155	Strip of 5	5.75	5.75
a.-e.		45s any single	1.00	1.00

Faleolo Intl. Airport A156

40s, Terminal, Boeing 727. 45s, Boeing 727, Fuatino. 60s, So. Pacific Is. N43SP, terminal. 70s, Air New Zealand Boeing 737. 80s, Tower, jet. $1, Hawaian Air DC-9, VIP house.

Perf. 13x13½

			Unwmk.	
1988, Mar. 24		**Litho.**		
711	A156	40s multicolored	.65	.50
712	A156	45s multicolored	.75	.50
713	A156	60s multicolored	1.00	.90
714	A156	70s multicolored	1.10	1.10
715	A156	80s multicolored	1.25	1.25
716	A156	$1 multicolored	1.60	1.60
		Nos. 711-716 (6)	6.35	5.85

EXPO '88, Brisbane, Australia A157

45s, Island village display. 70s, EXPO complex, monorail and flags. $2, Map.

			Perf. 14½	
1988, Apr. 27				
717	A157	45s multicolored	.65	.65
718	A157	70s multicolored	1.50	1.50
719	A157	$2 multicolored	2.25	2.25
		Nos. 717-719 (3)	4.40	4.40

Souvenir Sheet

Arrival of the Latter Day Saints in Samoa, Cent. — A158

			Perf. 13½	
1988, June 9		**Litho.**		
720	A158	$3 The Temple, Apia	3.00	3.00

1988 Summer Olympics, Seoul — A159

			Perf. 14	
1988, Aug. 10		**Litho.**		
721	A159	15s Running	.25	.25
722	A159	60s Weight lifting	.50	.50
723	A159	80s Boxing	1.00	1.00
724	A159	$2 Olympic Stadium	1.75	1.75
a.		Souvenir sheet of 4, #721-724	3.50	3.50
		Nos. 721-724 (4)	3.50	3.50

Birds — A160

10c, Polynesian triller. 15s, Samoan wood rail. 20s, Flat-billed kingfisher. 25s, Samoan fantail. 35s, Scarlet robin. 40s, Mao. 50s, Cardinal honeyeater. 65s, Samoan whistler. No. 733, Many-colored fruit dove. No. 734, White-throated pigeon. No. 735, Silver gull. No. 736, Great frigatebird. 90s, Eastern reef heron. $3, Short-tailed albatross. $10, Common fairy tern. $20, Shy albatross.

			Perf. 13½	
1988-89		**Unwmk.**		
725	A160	10s multicolored	.30	.45
726	A160	15s multicolored	.30	.45
727	A160	20s multicolored	.30	1.25
728	A160	25s multicolored	.40	.60
729	A160	35s multicolored	.50	1.00
730	A160	40s multicolored	.75	1.50
731	A160	50s multicolored	.90	.90
732	A160	65s multicolored	1.10	1.10
733	A160	75s multicolored	1.25	1.75
734	A160	85s multicolored	1.40	1.40

Perf. 14
Size:45x39mm

735	A160	75s multicolored	1.50	1.75
736	A160	85s multicolored	1.50	1.75
737	A160	90s multicolored	2.40	1.90
738	A160	$3 multicolored	4.50	4.50
739	A160	$10 multicolored	12.00	12.00
740	A160	$20 multicolored	25.00	25.00
		Nos. 725-740 (16)	54.10	57.30

Issue dates: #725-734, 8/17/88; #735-738, 2/28/89; #739-740, 7/31/89.

Conservation — A161

			Perf. 14	
1988, Oct. 25				
741	A161	15s Forests, vert.	.85	.30
742	A161	40s Culture, vert.	1.00	.50
743	A161	45s Wildlife, vert.	2.00	.60
744	A161	50s Water	1.25	.75
745	A161	60s Marine resources	1.25	.90
746	A161	$1 Land and soil	1.50	1.50
		Nos. 741-746 (6)	7.85	4.55

Christmas A162

Designs: 15s, 40s, Congregational Church of Jesus, Apia. 40s, Roman Catholic Church, Leauvaa. 45s, Congregational Christian Church, Moataa. $2, Baha'i Temple, Vailima.

Orchids — A163

Perf. 14x14½

			Unwmk.	
1988, Nov. 14		**Litho.**		
747	A162	15s multicolored	.25	.25
748	A162	40s multicolored	.50	.50
749	A162	45s multicolored	.55	.55
750	A162	$2 multicolored	2.25	2.25
a.		Souvenir sheet of 4, #747-750	3.75	3.75
		Nos. 747-750 (4)	3.55	3.55

			Perf. 14	
1989, Jan. 31		**Litho.**		
751	A163	15s Phaius flavus	.25	.25
752	A163	45s Calanthe triplicata	.75	.75
753	A163	60s Luisia teretifolia	.90	.70
754	A163	$3 Dendrobium mohlianum	2.75	2.75
		Nos. 751-754 (4)	4.65	4.45

Apia Hurricane, 1889 A164

			Unwmk.	
1989, Mar. 16		**Litho.**		
755		Strip of 4	9.50	9.50
a.	A164	50s SMS Eber	1.25	1.25
b.	A164	65s SMS Olga	1.50	1.50
c.	A164	85s SMS Calliope	2.00	2.00
d.	A164	$2 SMS Vandalia	2.50	2.50
e.		Souv. sheet of 2, #c.-d., imperf.	8.00	8.00

World Stamp Expo '89.
#755e, issued Nov. 17, is wmk. 355.

Intl. Red Cross and Red Crescent Organizations, 125th Annivs. — A165

			Perf. 14½x14	
1989, May 15				
756	A165	50s Youths in parade	.40	.40
757	A165	65s Blood donation	.55	.55
758	A165	75s First Aid	.65	.65
759	A165	$3 Volunteers	2.50	2.50
		Nos. 756-759 (4)	4.10	4.10

Moon Landing, 20th Anniv.
Common Design Type

Apollo 14: 18s, Saturn-Apollo vehicle and mobile launcher. 50s, Alan Shepard, Stuart Roosa and Edgar Mitchell. 65s, Mission emblem. $2, Tracks of the modularised equipment transporter. $3, Buzz Aldrin and American flag raised on the Moon, Apollo 11 mission.

1989, July 20		**Wmk. 384**	**Perf. 14**	
Size of Nos. 761-762: 29x29mm				
760	CD342	18s multicolored	.35	.30
761	CD342	50s multicolored	.75	.75
762	CD342	65s multicolored	1.00	.75
763	CD342	$2 multicolored	3.00	3.00
		Nos. 760-763 (4)	5.10	4.55

Souvenir Sheet

764	CD342	$3 multicolored	4.75	4.75

Christmas A166

Perf. 13½x13
1989, Nov. 1   Litho.   Unwmk.

765	A166	18s Joseph and Mary	.40	.30
766	A166	50s Shepherds	.90	.50
767	A166	55s Animals	1.00	.70
768	A166	$2 Three kings	3.50	3.50
		Nos. 765-768 (4)	5.80	5.00

Local Transport — A167

Designs: 18s, Pao pao (outrigger canoe). 55s, Fautasi (longboat). 60s, Polynesian Airlines propeller plane. $3, Lady Samoa ferry.

1990, Jan. 31   Unwmk.   Perf. 14x15

769	A167	18s multicolored	.45	.35
770	A167	55s multicolored	1.10	.75
771	A167	60s multicolored	1.75	1.40
772	A167	$3 multicolored	5.50	5.50
		Nos. 769-772 (4)	8.80	8.00

Otto von Bismarck, Brandenburg Gate — A168

1990, May 3   Perf. 14x13½

773	A168	75s shown	2.00	2.00
774	A168	$3 SMS Adler	6.75	6.75
a.		Pair, #773-774	10.50	10.50

Opening of the Berlin Wall, 1989, and cent. of the Treaty of Berlin (in 1989). No. 774a has a continuous design.

Great Britain No. 1 and Alexandra Palace — A169

1990, May 3

775	A169	$3 multicolored	4.00	4.00

Stamp World London '90 and 150th anniv. of the Penny Black.

Tourism A170

1990, July 30   Litho.   Perf. 14

776	A170	18s Visitors Bureau	.25	.25
777	A170	50s Samoa Village Resorts	.70	.40
778	A170	65s Aggies Hotel	.90	.50
779	A170	$3 Tusitala Hotel	3.50	3.50
		Nos. 776-779 (4)	5.35	4.85

Souvenir Sheet

No. 240, Exhibition Emblem — A171

1990, Aug. 24   Litho.   Perf. 13

780	A171	$3 multicolored	4.75	4.75

World Stamp Exhib., New Zealand 1990.

Christmas — A172

Paintings of Madonna and Child.

1990, Oct. 31   Perf. 12½

781	A172	18s Bellini	.45	.25
782	A172	50s Bouts	.90	.50
783	A172	55s Correggio	1.10	.60
784	A172	$3 Cima	4.75	4.75
		Nos. 781-784 (4)	7.20	6.10

The 55s is "The School of Love," not "Madonna of the Basket."

UN Development Program, 40th Anniv. — A173

1990, Nov. 26   Perf. 13½

785	A173	$3 multicolored	3.75	3.75

Parrots A174

1991, Apr. 8   Litho.   Perf. 13½

786	A174	18s Black-capped lory	.80	.45
787	A174	50s Eclectus parrot	1.50	.70
788	A174	65s Scarlet macaw	1.90	1.00
789	A174	$3 Palm cockatoo	5.00	5.00
		Nos. 786-789 (4)	9.20	7.15

Elizabeth & Philip, Birthdays
Common Design Types
Wmk. 384

1991, June 17   Litho.   Perf. 14½

790	CD346	75s multicolored	1.00	1.00
791	CD345	$2 multicolored	2.25	2.25
a.		Pair, #790-791 + label	3.75	3.75

Souvenir Sheet

1991 Rugby World Cup — A175

1991, Oct. 12   Litho.   Perf. 14½

792	A175	$5 multicolored	11.00	11.00

Christmas A176

Orchids and Christmas carols: 20s, O Come All Ye Faithful. 60s, Joy to the World. 75s, Hark! the Herald Angels Sing. $4, We Wish You a Merry Christmas.

1991, Oct. 31   Litho.   Perf. 14½

793	A176	20s multicolored	.60	.25
794	A176	60s multicolored	1.10	.75
795	A176	75s multicolored	1.40	.90
796	A176	$4 multicolored	5.25	5.25
		Nos. 793-796 (4)	8.35	7.15

See Nos. 815-818, 836-840.

Phila Nippon '91 — A177

Samoan hawkmoths: 60s, Herse convolvuli. 75s, Gnathothlibus erotus. 75s, Hippotion celerio. $3, Cephonodes armatus.

1991, Nov. 16   Perf. 13½x14

797	A177	60s multicolored	1.10	.85
798	A177	75s multicolored	1.30	1.00
799	A177	85s multicolored	1.50	1.40
800	A177	$3 multicolored	5.50	5.50
		Nos. 797-800 (4)	9.40	8.75

Independence, 30th Anniv. — A178

1992, Jan. 8   Litho.   Perf. 14

801	A178	50s Honor guard	.70	.55
802	A178	65s Siva scene	.90	.65
803	A178	$1 Parade float	1.50	1.50
804	A178	$3 Raising flag	4.75	4.75
		Nos. 801-804 (4)	7.85	7.45

Queen Elizabeth II's Accession to the Throne, 40th Anniv.
Common Design Type

1992, Feb. 6   Wmk. 384

805	CD349	20s multicolored	.70	.35
806	CD349	60s multicolored	1.25	.85
807	CD349	75s multicolored	1.40	.80
808	CD349	85s multicolored	1.50	.90

Wmk. 373

809	CD349	$3 multicolored	3.00	3.00
		Nos. 805-809 (5)	7.85	5.90

Souvenir Sheet

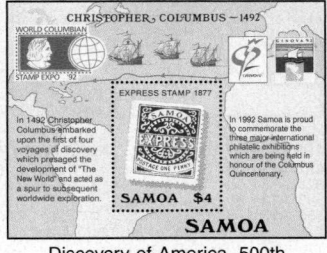

Discovery of America, 500th Anniv. — A179

1992, Apr. 17   Unwmk.   Perf. 14½

810	A179	$4 No. 1	4.75	4.75

World Columbian Stamp Expo '92, Granada '92 and Genoa '92 Philatelic Exhibitions.

1992 Summer Olympics, Barcelona — A180

1992, July 28   Wmk. 373   Perf. 14

811	A180	60s Weight lifting	.90	.75
812	A180	75s Boxing	1.10	.95
813	A180	85s Running	1.40	1.25
814	A180	$3 Stadium, statue	4.25	4.25
		Nos. 811-814 (4)	7.65	7.20

Christmas Type of 1991

Christmas carol, orchid: 50s, "God rest you, merry gentlemen...," liparis layardii. 60s, "While shepherds watched...," corymborkis veratrifolia. 75s, "Away in a manger...," phaius flavus. $4, "O little town...," bulbophyllum longifolium.

1992, Oct. 28   Litho.   Perf. 14½

815	A176	50s multicolored	.65	.40
816	A176	60s multicolored	.75	.65
817	A176	75s multicolored	.90	.80
818	A176	$4 multicolored	4.50	4.50
		Nos. 815-818 (4)	6.80	6.35

Fish A182

60s, Batfish. 75s, Lined surgeonfish. $1, Red-tail snapper. $3, Long-nosed emperor.

1993, Mar. 17   Litho.   Perf. 14

819	A182	60s multicolored	.90	.65
820	A182	75s multicolored	1.10	1.10
821	A182	$1 multicolored	1.60	1.60
822	A182	$3 multicolored	4.50	4.50
		Nos. 819-822 (4)	8.10	7.85

World Cup Seven-a-Side Rugby Championships, Scotland — A183

60s, Team performing traditional dance. 75c, Two players. 85c, Player. $3, Edinburgh Castle.

1993, May 12   Perf. 13½x14

823	A183	60s multi	1.40	.75
824	A183	75s multi, vert.	1.50	.85
825	A183	85s multi, vert.	1.75	1.25
826	A183	$3 multi	5.50	5.50
		Nos. 823-826 (4)	10.15	8.35

Bats
A184

1993, June 10   **Perf. 14x14½**
827	A184	20s Two hanging	1.25	1.25
828	A184	50s Two flying	2.00	2.00
829	A184	60s Three flying	2.50	2.50
830	A184	75s One on flower	3.00	3.00
		Nos. 827-830 (4)	8.75	8.75

World Wildlife Fund.

Souvenir Sheet

Taipei '93, Asian Intl. Invitation Stamp
Exhibition — A185

1993, Aug. 16   **Litho.**   **Perf. 14**
831	A185	$5 multicolored	9.00	9.00

World
Post Day
A186

Designs: 60s, Globe, letter, flowers. 75s,
Customers at Post Office. 85s, Black, white
hands exchanging letter. $4, Globe, national
flags, letter.

1993, Oct. 8   **Litho.**   **Perf. 14**
832	A186	60s multicolored	.70	.45
833	A186	75s multicolored	.95	.55
834	A186	85s multicolored	1.25	1.00
835	A186	$4 multicolored	4.75	4.75
		Nos. 832-835 (4)	7.65	6.75

Christmas Type of 1991

Flowers, Christmas carol: 20s, "Silent Night!
Holy Night!..." 60s, "As with gladness men of
old..." 75s, "Mary had a Baby, Yes Lord..."
$1.50, "Once in Royal David's City..." $3,
"Angels, from the realms of Glory..."

       Perf. 14½
1993, Nov. 1   **Litho.**   **Unwmk.**
836	A176	20s multicolored	.50	.40
837	A176	60s multicolored	1.00	.60
838	A176	75s multicolored	1.25	.75
839	A176	$1.50 multicolored	2.25	2.25
840	A176	$3 multicolored	4.50	4.50
		Nos. 836-840 (5)	9.50	8.50

Corals
A187

1994, Feb. 18   **Litho.**   **Perf. 14**
841	A187	20s Alveropora allingi	.40	.30
842	A187	60s Acropora polys-		
		toma	.80	.60
843	A187	90s Acropora listeri	1.00	1.00
844	A187	$4 Acropora grandis	4.50	4.50
		Nos. 841-844 (4)	6.70	6.40

Ovptd. with Hong Kong '94 Emblem
1994, Feb. 18
845	A187	20s on #841	.30	.30
846	A187	60s on #842	.80	.60
847	A187	90s on #843	1.00	1.00
848	A187	$4 on #844	4.50	4.50
		Nos. 845-848 (4)	6.60	6.40

Manu
Samoa
Rugby
Team
A188

Designs: 70s, Management. 90s, Test
match with Wales. 95s, Test match with New
Zealand. $4, Apia Park Stadium.

1994, Apr. 11   **Litho.**   **Perf. 14**
849	A188	70s multicolored	.80	.75
850	A188	90s multicolored	1.00	1.00
851	A188	95s multicolored	1.10	1.10
852	A188	$4 multicolored	4.75	4.75
		Nos. 849-852 (4)	7.65	7.60

Souvenir Sheet

PHILAKOREA '94 — A189

Butterflies: $5, White caper, glasswing.

1994, Aug. 16   **Litho.**   **Perf. 13**
853	A189	$5 multicolored	6.00	6.00

Teuila
Tourism
Festival
A190

1994, Sept. 22   **Litho.**   **Perf. 13½**
854	A190	70s Singers	1.10	.60
855	A190	90s Fire dancer	1.25	.85
856	A190	95s Parade float	1.40	1.00
857	A190	$4 Police band	6.50	6.50
		Nos. 854-857 (4)	10.25	8.95

For surcharge, see No. 1284.

A191

70s, Schooner Equator. 90s, Portrait. $1.20,
Tomb, Mount Vaea. $4, Vailima House, horiz.

1994, Nov. 21   **Perf. 14**
858	A191	70s multicolored	.85	.65
859	A191	90s multicolored	1.00	1.00
860	A191	$1.20 multicolored	1.40	1.40
861	A191	$4 multicolored	4.75	4.75
		Nos. 858-861 (4)	8.00	7.80

Robert Louis Stevenson (1850-94), writer.

A192

Children's Christmas paintings: 70s, Father
Christmas. 95s, Nativity. $1.20, Picnic. $4,
Greetings.

1994, Nov. 30
862	A192	70s multicolored	.70	.60
863	A192	95s multicolored	1.10	1.10
864	A192	$1.20 multicolored	1.25	1.25
865	A192	$4 multicolored	4.00	4.00
		Nos. 862-865 (4)	7.05	6.95

Scenic
Views
A193

Designs: 5s, Lotofaga Beach, Aleipata. 10s,
Nuutele Island. 30s, Satuiatua, Savaii. 50s,
Sinalele, Aleipata. 60s, Paradise Beach,
Lefaga. 70s, Houses, Piula Cave. 80s, Taga
blowholes. 90s, View from east coast road.
95s, Canoes, Leulumoega. $1, Parliament
Building.

1995   **Litho.**   **Perf. 14½x13**
866	A193	5s multicolored	.25	.50
867	A193	10s multicolored	.25	.50
871	A193	30s multicolored	.25	.35
874	A193	50s multicolored	.30	.35
875	A193	60s multicolored	.35	.35
876	A193	70s multicolored	.40	.40
877	A193	80s multicolored	.45	.45
878	A193	90s multicolored	.50	.50
879	A193	95s multicolored	.50	.50
880	A193	$1 multicolored	.55	.55
		Nos. 866-880 (10)	3.80	4.45

Issued: Nos. 866-867, 871, 874-880, 3/29/95.

1995 World Rugby Cup
Championships, South Africa — A194

Designs: 70s, Players under age 12. 90s,
Secondary Schools' rugby teams. $1, Manu
Samoa test match with New Zealand. $4, Ellis
Park Stadium, Johannesburg.

1995, May 25   **Litho.**   **Perf. 14x13½**
886	A194	70s multicolored	.65	.65
887	A194	90s multicolored	.90	.90
888	A194	$1 multicolored	1.10	1.10
889	A194	$4 multicolored	4.00	4.00
		Nos. 886-889 (4)	6.65	6.65

End of World War II, 50th Anniv.
Common Design Types

Designs: 70s, OS2U Kingfisher over Faleolo
Air Base. 90s, F4U Corsair, Faleolo Air Base.
95s, US troops in landing craft. $3, US
Marines landing on Samoan beach. $4,
Reverse of War Medal 1939-45.

1995, May 31   **Litho.**   **Perf. 13½**
890	CD351	70s multicolored	1.00	.75
891	CD351	90s multicolored	1.25	1.00
892	CD351	95s multicolored	1.50	1.25
893	CD351	$3 multicolored	5.50	5.50
		Nos. 890-893 (4)	9.25	8.50

Souvenir Sheet
Perf. 14
894	CD352	$4 multicolored	6.00	6.00

Year of the Sea
Turtle — A195

1995, Aug. 24   **Litho.**   **Perf. 13x13½**
895	A195	70s Leatherback	.80	.80
896	A195	90s Loggerhead	1.00	1.00
897	A195	$1 Green turtle	1.25	1.25
898	A195	$4 Pacific Ridley	4.50	4.50
		Nos. 895-898 (4)	7.55	7.55

Souvenir Sheet

Singapore '95 — A196

1995, Sept. 1   **Perf. 14**
899	A196	$5 Phaius tankervilleae	6.00	6.00

See No. 935.

UN, 50th Anniv.
Common Design Type

70s, Mobile hospital. 90s, Bell Sioux helicopter. $1, Bell 212 helicopter. $4, RNZAF
Andover.

      Unwmk.
1995, Oct. 24   **Litho.**   **Perf. 14**
900	CD353	70s multicolored	1.00	.70
901	CD353	90s multicolored	1.50	1.00
902	CD353	$1 multicolored	1.60	1.25
903	CD353	$4 multicolored	5.25	5.25
		Nos. 900-903 (4)	9.35	8.20

A197

1995, Nov. 15   **Perf. 14½**
904	A197	25s Madonna &		
		Child	.35	.35
905	A197	70s Wise Man	.75	.55
906	A197	90s Wise Man, diff.	.90	.80
907	A197	$5 Wise Man, diff.	5.00	5.00
		Nos. 904-907 (4)	7.00	6.65

Christmas.

A198

Importance of Water: 70s, Waterfall, bird,
woman, hands. 90s, Girl standing under fountain, "WATER FOR LIFE." $2, Outline of per-
son's head containing tree, birds, waterfall,
girl. $4, Community receiving water from pro-
tected watersheds.

1996, Jan. 26   **Litho.**   **Perf. 14**
908	A198	70s multicolored	.60	.60
909	A198	90s multicolored	.85	.85
910	A198	$2 multicolored	2.00	2.00
911	A198	$4 multicolored	3.75	3.75
		Nos. 908-911 (4)	7.20	7.20

Queen Elizabeth II, 70th Birthday
Common Design Type

Various portraits of Queen, Samoan
scenes: 70s, Apia, Main Street. 90s, Neiafu
beach. $1, Official residence of Head of State.
$3, Parliament Building.
$5, Queen wearing tiara, formal dress.

Perf. 14½

1996, Apr. 22   Litho.   Unwmk.
912	CD354	70s multicolored	.70	.70
913	CD354	90s multicolored	.90	.90
914	CD354	$1 multicolored	.90	.90
915	CD354	$3 multicolored	2.75	2.75
		Nos. 912-915 (4)	5.25	5.25

Souvenir Sheet
916	CD354	$5 multicolored	5.25	5.25

Souvenir Sheet

Moon Festival — A199

1996, May 18   Litho.   Perf. 14
917	A199	$2.50 multicolored	4.25	4.25

CHINA '96.

Souvenir Sheet

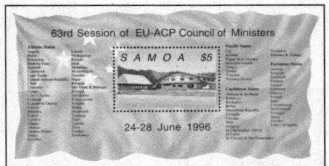

63rd Session of African-Carribean-Pacific-European Union Council of Ministers — A200

1996, June 19   Litho.   Perf. 13½
918	A200	$5 multicolored	5.00	5.00

A201

1996, July 15   Litho.   Perf. 13½
919	A201	70s Boxing	.65	.65
920	A201	90s Running	.95	.95
921	A201	$1 Weight lifting	1.10	1.10
922	A201	$4 Javelin	3.75	3.75
		Nos. 919-922 (4)	6.45	6.45

1996 Summer Olympic Games, Atlanta.

A202

1996, Sept. 13   Litho.   Perf. 14
923	A202	60s Logo	.65	.45
924	A202	70s Pottery	.70	.55
925	A202	80s Stained glass	.80	.80
926	A202	90s Dancing	.90	.90
927	A202	$1 Wood carving	.95	.95
928	A202	$4 Samoan chief	3.00	3.00
		Nos. 923-928 (6)	7.00	6.65

7th Pacific Festival of Arts, Apia.

UNICEF, 50th Anniv. — A203

70s, Children in doctor's waiting room. 90s, Children in hospital undergoing treatment. $1, Child receiving injection. $4, Mothers, children playing.

1996, Oct. 24   Litho.   Perf. 14
929	A203	70s multicolored	.65	.55
930	A203	90s multicolored	.75	.75
931	A203	$1 multicolored	.85	.85
932	A203	$4 multicolored	3.00	3.00
		Nos. 929-932 (4)	5.25	5.15

Souvenir Sheet

Many-Colored Fruit Dove — A204

1997, Feb. 3   Litho.   Perf. 14
933	A204	$3 multicolored	3.25	3.25

Hong Kong '97. See No. 962.

Souvenir Sheet

1st US Postage Stamps, 150th Anniv., 1st Samoan Postage Stamps, 120th Anniv. — A205

1997, May 29   Litho.   Perf. 14½
934	A205	$5 US #2, Samoa #1	4.50	4.50

PACIFIC 97.

Phaius Tankervilleae Type of 1995
Souvenir Sheet
Wmk. 373

1997, June 20   Litho.   Perf. 14½
935	A196	$2.50 multicolored	3.50	3.50

Return of Hong Kong to China, July 1, 1997.

Queen Elizabeth II & Prince Philip, 50th Wedding Anniv. — A206

No. 936, Queen. No. 937, Prince at reins of team, Royal Windsor Horse Show, 1996. No. 938, Queen, horse. No. 939, Prince laughing, horse show, 1995. No. 940, Zara Philips, Balmoral 1993, Prince Philip. No. 941, Queen, Prince William.

$5, Queen, Prince, Royal Ascot 1988.

1997, July 10   Unwmk.   Perf. 13
936	A206	70s multicolored	1.25	1.25
937	A206	70s multicolored	1.25	1.25
a.		Pair, #936-937	2.75	2.75
938	A206	90s multicolored	1.40	1.40
939	A206	90s multicolored	1.40	1.40
a.		Pair, #938-939	3.00	3.00
940	A206	$1 multicolored	1.50	1.50
941	A206	$1 multicolored	1.50	1.50
a.		Pair, #940-941	3.25	3.25
		Nos. 936-941 (6)	8.30	8.30

Souvenir Sheet
942	A206	$5 multicolored	5.75	5.75

Greenpeace, 26th Anniv. — A207

Dolphins: 50s, #947a, Jumping out of water. 60s, #947b, Two swimming right. 70s, #947c, Two facing front. $1, #947d, With mouth open out of water.

1997, Sept. 17   Litho.   Perf. 13½x14
943	A207	50s multicolored	.55	.45
944	A207	60s multicolored	.75	.65
945	A207	70s multicolored	1.00	1.00
946	A207	$1 multicolored	1.25	1.25
		Nos. 943-946 (4)	3.55	3.35

Miniature Sheet
947	A207	$1.25 Sheet of 4, #a.-d.	4.75	4.75

Christmas A208

1997, Nov. 26   Litho.   Perf. 14
948	A208	70s Bells	.65	.55
949	A208	80s Ornament	.75	.65
950	A208	$2 Candle	1.75	1.75
951	A208	$3 Star	2.75	2.75
		Nos. 948-951 (4)	5.90	5.70

Mangroves A209

Bruguiera gymnorrhiza: 70s, Fruit on trees. 80s, Saplings. $2, Roots. $4, Tree at water's edge.

1998, Feb. 26   Litho.   Perf. 13½
952	A209	70s multicolored	.55	.50
953	A209	80s multicolored	.65	.70
954	A209	$2 multicolored	1.50	1.50
955	A209	$4 multicolored	3.00	3.00
		Nos. 952-955 (4)	5.70	5.70

Diana, Princess of Wales (1961-97)
Common Design Type

#956: a, Up close portrait. b, Wearing checkered jacket. c, In red dress. d, Holding flowers.

Perf. 14½x14

1998, Mar. 31   Litho.   Unwmk.
955A	CD355	50s like #956a	1.00	1.00

Sheet of 4
956	CD355	$1.40 #a.-d.	6.00	6.00

No. 956 sold for $5.60 + 75c, with surtax from international sales being donated to the Princess Diana Memorial Fund and surtax from national sales being donated to designated local charity.

Royal Air Force, 80th Anniversary
Common Design Type of 1993
Re-Inscribed

70s, Westland Wallace. 80s, Hawker Fury. $2, Vickers Varsity. $5, BAC Jet Provost.

No. 961: a, Norman-Thompson N.T.2b. b, Nieuport 27 Scout. c, Miles Magister. d, Bristol Bombay.

1998, Apr. 1   Perf. 13½
957	CD350	70s multicolored	.80	.40
958	CD350	80s multicolored	.90	.50
959	CD350	$2 multicolored	1.75	1.75
960	CD350	$5 multicolored	4.50	4.50
		Nos. 957-960 (4)	7.95	7.15

Miniature Sheet
961	CD350	$2 Sheet of 4, #a.-d.	7.75	7.75

Many-Colored Fruit Dove Type of 1997

1998, Sept. 1   Litho.   Perf. 14
962	A204	25s multicolored	.60	.60

Christmas Ornaments — A210

1998, Nov. 16   Litho.   Perf. 14
963	A210	70s Star	.65	.55
964	A210	$1.05 Bell	.95	.85
965	A210	$1.40 Ball	1.25	1.25
966	A210	$5 Cross	4.25	4.25
		Nos. 963-966 (4)	7.10	6.90

Australia '99, World Stamp Expo A211

Boats: 70s, Dugout canoe. 90s, Tasman's ships Heemskerck & Zeehaen, 1642. $1.05, HMS Resolution, HMS Adventure, 1773. $6, New Zealand scow schooner, 1880.

1999, Mar. 19   Litho.   Perf. 14
967	A211	70s multicolored	.60	.40
968	A211	90s multicolored	1.00	.65
969	A211	$1.05 multicolored	1.25	1.00
970	A211	$6 multicolored	4.75	4.75
		Nos. 967-970 (4)	7.60	6.80

Wedding of Prince Edward and Sophie Rhys-Jones
Common Design Type

1999, June 19   Litho.   Perf. 14
971	CD356	$1.50 Separate portraits	1.00	1.00
972	CD356	$6 Couple	4.00	4.00

1st Manned Moon Landing, 30th Anniv.
Common Design Type

70s, Lift-off. 90s, Lunar module separates from Service module. $3, Aldrin deploys solar wind experiment. $5, Parachutes open. $5, Earth as seen from moon.

Perf. 14x13¾

1999, July 20   Litho.   Wmk. 384
973	CD357	50s multicolored	.55	.45
974	CD357	90s multicolored	.65	.60
975	CD357	$3 multicolored	1.90	1.90
976	CD357	$5 multicolored	3.25	3.25
		Nos. 973-976 (4)	6.35	6.20

Souvenir Sheet
Perf. 14
977	CD357	$5 multicolored	6.25	6.25

No. 977 contains one 40mm circular stamp. For surcharge, see No. 1279.

Queen Mother's Century
Common Design Type

Queen Mother: 70s, Talking to tenants of bombed apartments, 1940. 90s, At garden party, South Africa. $2, Reviewing scouts at Windsor. $6, With Princess Eugenie, 98th birthday.

$5, With film showing Charlie Chaplin.

Perf. 13½

1999, Aug. 24   Litho.   Unwmk.
978	CD358	70s multicolored	.70	.50
979	CD358	90s multicolored	.80	.60
980	CD358	$2 multicolored	1.50	1.50
981	CD358	$6 multicolored	4.25	4.25
		Nos. 978-981 (4)	7.25	6.85

Souvenir Sheet
982	CD358	$5 multicolored	5.25	5.25

Christmas and
Millennium — A212

70s, Hibiscus. 90s, Poinsettia. $2, Christmas cactus. $6, Flag, Southern Cross.

Perf. 13½x13¼

			Unwmk.	
1999, Nov. 30	**Litho.**			
983	A212	70s multicolored	.80	.60
984	A212	90s multicolored	.95	.75
985	A212	$2 multicolored	1.50	1.50
986	A212	$6 multicolored	4.50	4.50
	Nos. 983-986 (4)		7.75	7.35

For surcharge, see No. 1277.

Millennium — A213

			Unwmk.	
2000, Jan. 1	**Litho.**		**Perf. 14**	
987	A213	70s shown	1.60	1.60
988	A213	70s Rocks	1.60	1.60
a.		Pair, #987-988	3.25	3.25

For surcharges, see Nos. 1235-1236.

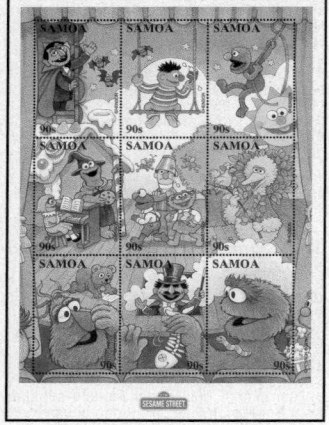

Sesame Street — A214

No. 989: a, The Count. b, Ernie. c, Grover. d, Cookie Monster and Prairie Dawn. e, Elmo, Ernie and Zoe. f, Big Bird. g, Telly. h, Magician. i, Oscar the Grouch.
$3, Cookie Monster.

Perf. 14½x14¾

2000, Mar. 22		**Litho.**		
989	A214	90s Sheet of 9, #a-i	6.25	6.25
		Souvenir Sheet		
990	A214	$3 multi	3.00	3.00

Fire
Dancers — A215

Various dancers. Denominations: 25s, 50s, 90s, $1, $4.

2001, Sept. 3	**Litho.**		**Perf. 13x13¼**	
991-995	A215	Set of 5	6.00	6.00

For surcharges, see Nos. 1234, 1282.

Butterflies — A216

Serpentine Die Cut

2001, Dec. 12			**Litho.**	
		Self-Adhesive		
996		Horiz. strip of 5	7.75	7.75
a.	A216	70s Vagrans egista	.65	.65
b.	A216	$1.20 Jamides bochus	.90	.90
c.	A216	$1.40 Papilio godeffroyi	1.00	1.00
d.	A216	$2 Achraea andromacha	1.10	1.10
e.	A216	$3 Eurema hecabe	1.60	1.60

Intl. Year of
Ecotourism — A217

Designs: 60s, Snorkelers. 95s, Kayakers. $1.90, Village, children, craftsman. $3, Bird watchers.

2002, Feb. 27			**Perf. 13¼**	
997-1000	A217	Set of 4	5.25	5.25
1000a		Horiz strip of 4, #997-1000 + central label	6.25	6.25

For surcharge, see No. 1276.

Independence, 40th Anniv. — A218

Flag and: 25s, Buses, cricket player, huts. 70s, Natives. 95s, Flower, woman, ship, airplane, woman using telephone. $5, Flower, buildings, rugby player, inspection of troops.

Serpentine Die Cut

2002, June 1			**Litho.**	
		Self-Adhesive		
1001-1004	A218	Set of 4	8.00	8.00
1004a		Souvenir sheet of 1, #1004	7.50	7.50

People and Their
Activities — A219

Designs: 5s, Woman holding fish. 10s, Family. 20s, Men carrying baskets. 25s, Two boys smiling. 35s, Woman, girl and flowers. 50s, Toddler and adult. 60s, Male dancer. 70s, Female dancer. 80s, Woman laughing. 90s, Group of women. 95s, Two women with flowers in hair. $1, Boy in stream of water. $1.20, Child smiling. $1.85, Man smiling. $10, People at church.

2002, Aug. 1	**Litho.**		**Perf. 13x13¼**	
1005	A219	5s multi	.25	.25
1006	A219	10s multi	.25	.25
1007	A219	20s multi	.25	.25
1008	A219	25s multi	.25	.25
1009	A219	35s multi	.25	.25
1010	A219	50s multi	.40	.40
1011	A219	60s multi	.45	.45
1012	A219	70s multi	.55	.55
1013	A219	80s multi	.60	.60
1014	A219	90s multi	.65	.65
1015	A219	95s multi	.75	.75
1016	A219	$1 multi	.80	.80
1017	A219	$1.20 multi	.90	.90
1018	A219	$1.85 multi	1.40	1.40
1019	A219	$10 multi	7.50	7.50
	Nos. 1005-1019 (15)		15.25	15.25

For surcharges, see Nos. 1239, 1275, 1278.

Scenic
Views — A220

Designs: 95s, Family on rock. $1.20, Man and woman on beach. $1.40, Waterfall. $2, Woman in ocean.

2002, Sept. 18			**Perf. 14x14¾**	
1020-1023	A220	Set of 4	5.75	5.75
1023a		Souvenir sheet, #1021, 1023	3.25	3.25

For surcharges, see Nos. 1238, 1280.

Ginger
Flowers
A221

Designs: 25s, Alpinia purpurata. $1.05, Alpinia samoensis. $1.20, Etlingeria cevuga. $4, Hedychium flavescens.

2002, Nov. 20			**Perf. 13½**	
1024-1027	A221	Set of 4	6.25	6.25

For surcharge, see No. 1290.

Decorated Buses — A222

Inscriptions on buses: 25s, Return to Paradise. 70s, Misileti Fatu. 90s, Jungle Boys. 95s, Sun Rise Transport. $4, Laifoni.

Serpentine Die Cut

2003, Jan. 22			**Litho.**	
		Self-Adhesive		
1028-1032	A222	Set of 5	7.50	7.50

Marine
Protected
Areas
A223

Designs: 25s, Aleipata. $5, Safata.

Perf. 13½x13¾

2003, Mar. 19			**Litho.**	
1033-1034	A223	Set of 2	5.75	5.75

Artists and Their
Works — A224

Artists: 25s, Vanya Taule'alo. 70s, Michel Tuffery. 90s, Momoe von Reiche. $1, Fatu Feu'u. $4, Lily Laita.

2003, May 7	**Litho.**		**Perf. 13**	
1035-1039	A224	Set of 5	6.25	6.25

Sports
Stars
A225

Designs: 25s, David Tua, boxer. 70s, Beatrice Faumuina, discus. 90s, Michael Jones, rugby. 95s, Rita Fatialofa, netball. $4, Jesse Sapolu, football.

2003, July 16			**Perf. 13½**	
1040-1044	A225	Set of 5	6.50	6.50

For surcharges, see Nos. 1237, 1281.

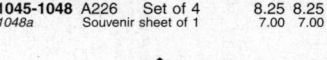

Angelfish — A226

Designs: 25s, Centropyge bicolor. 60s, Centropyge loriculus. 90s, Pygoplites diacanthus. $5, Pomocanthus imperator.

2003, Sept. 10			**Perf. 13x13¼**	
1045-1048	A226	Set of 4	8.25	8.25
1048a		Souvenir sheet of 1	7.00	7.00

Flowers — A227

Designs: 70s, Heliconia caribaea. 80s, Heliconia psittacorum. 90s, Hibiscus rosasinensis. $4, Plumeria rubra.

Perf. 12¾x13¼

2004, Mar. 26			**Litho.**	
1049-1052	A227	Set of 4	7.00	7.00

For surcharges, see Nos. 1288, 1291, 1292.

Birds
A228

Designs: 25s, Black-naped tern. 60s, Crested tern. 70s, Common noddy, vert. 90s, Lesser frigatebird, vert. $4, Reef heron.

2004, June 16   Litho.   Perf. 13¼
1053-1057 A228 Set of 5   8.00 8.00
1057a Souvenir sheet, #1053-
        1057   8.00 8.00

Butterflyfish — A229

Designs: 50s, Chaetodon meyeri. 90s, Chaetodon punctatofasciatus, horiz. $1, Chaetodon ephippium, horiz. $4, Chaetodon flavirostris.

Perf. 14¼x14, 14x14¼
2004, Sept. 29   Litho.
1058-1061 A229 Set of 4   8.00 8.00
1061a Souvenir sheet of 1   7.00 7.00

Women and Flowers A230

Various women and: 25s, Pink flower. 70s, Red flowers, vert. 90s, White flowers. $4, Orange flowers, vert.

2004, Dec. 15   Litho.   Perf. 13¼
1062-1065 A230 Set of 4   6.25 6.25

Scenes From Savaii Island A231

Designs: 25s, Children in small boat. 70s, Women, building. 90s, Women on rope bridge, vert. $4, Coastline, vert.

2005, Feb. 17   Litho.   Perf. 13¼
1066-1069 A231 Set of 4   7.00 7.00

Souvenir Sheet

Dolphins — A232

No. 1070: a, $1, Spinner dolphin. b, $1.75, Rough-toothed dolphin. c, $4, Bottlenose dolphin.

2005, Apr. 21   Litho.   Perf. 13¼
1070 A232 Sheet of 3, #a-c   8.50 8.50

Pacific Explorer 2005 World Stamp Expo, Sydney.

Legends — A233

Designs: 25s, Sau Sau, Dawn of the First Humans. 70s, Tuimanu'a and the Flying Fox. 90s, Fonuea and Salofa Escape Famine. $4, Patea, the Sea Demon.

2005, Sept. 28   Litho.   Perf. 13¼
1071-1074 A233 Set of 4   8.00 8.00

For surcharge, see No. 1289.

European Philatelic Cooperation, 50th Anniv. (in 2006) — A234

Globe, CEPT emblem, stars and various Europa stamps: 60s, $3, $4, $10.

2005, Dec. 7   Perf. 14
1075-1078 A234 Set of 4   17.00 17.00
1078a Souvenir sheet, #1075-
        1078   17.00 17.00

Europa stamps, 50th anniv. (in 2006).

Diplomatic Relations Between Samoa and People's Republic of China, 30th Anniv. A235

Designs: 25s, Chinese and Samoan representatives and flags. 50s, Building. $1, Wooden bowl. $4, Chinese astronauts.

2005, Nov. 6   Litho.   Perf. 13x13¼
1079-1082 A235 Set of 4   8.50 8.50
1082a Souvenir sheet, #1079-1082,
        perf. 12   8.50 8.50

Sunsets A236

Various sunsets: 60s, 90s, $1, $4.

2006, Feb. 15   Perf. 13¼
1083-1086 A236 Set of 4   12.00 12.00

Queen Elizabeth II, 80th Birthday A237

Queen Elizabeth II: $1, As young child. No. 1088, $1.75, Holding young Prince Charles. $4, Without hat. No. 1090, $5, Wearing hat. No. 1091: a, $1.75, Like #1088. b, $5, Like #1089.

2006, Apr. 21   Litho.   Perf. 14
Stamps With White Frames
1087-1090 A237 Set of 4   13.00 13.00
Souvenir Sheet
Stamps Without White Frames
1091 A237 Sheet of 2, #a-b   8.00 8.00

For surcharge, see No. 1283.

Worldwide Fund for Nature (WWF) — A238

Various depictions of Humphead wrasses.

2006, Sept. 20   Perf. 13¼
1092   Horiz. strip of 4   13.00 13.00
a. A238 $1.50 org red & multi 1.50 1.25
b. A238 $2.30 red & multi   2.50 1.90
c. A238 $2.50 yel org & multi   2.75 2.00
d. A238 $3.60 purple & multi   3.50 3.00

Issued in sheets of two strips.

Shells A239

Designs: $1.60, Cypraea cribaria. $2.10, Cypraea aurantium. $2.40, Cypraea mauritiana. $3.10, Ovula ovum.

2006, Nov. 29   Die Cut
1093-1096 A239 Set of 4   12.00 12.00

Houses of Worship — A240

Designs: No. 1097, 50s, Piula College Church, Upolu. No. 1098, 50s, Anglican Church, Apia. No. 1099, 50s, Protestant Church, Apia. No. 1100, 50s, SDA Church, Fusi Saoluafata. No. 1101, $1, Methodist Church, Matafele. No. 1102, $1, Mauga Church, Apia. No. 1103, $1, EFKS Church, Apia. No. 1104, $1, Malua Theological College. No. 1105, $2, Latter Day Saints Temple, Pesega. No. 1106, $2, Mulivai Cathedral, Apia. No. 1107, $2, EFKS Church, Sapapaii. No. 1108, $2, Bahai Temple, Apia.

2007, May 16   Perf. 13¼
1097-1108 A240 Set of 12   16.00 16.00
1108a Miniature sheet, #1097-
        1108   19.00 19.00

South Pacific Games, Apia — A241

Designs: No. 1109, $1, Ele Opeloge, athlete. No. 1110, $1, Apia Park. No. 1111, $1, Aquatic Center. No. 1112, $1, Mana, Games mascot.

2007, Aug. 16
1109-1112 A241 Set of 4   5.00 5.00
1112a Souvenir sheet, 1 #1112 1.75 1.75

Tropical Fruit — A242

Designs: $1.60, Pineapples. $2.10, Coconuts. $2.40, Papayas. $3.10, Mangoes.

2007, Dec. 14   Die Cut
Self-Adhesive
1113-1116 A242 Set of 4   10.00 10.00

2008 Summer Olympics, Beijing — A243

Designs: 50s, Cycling. $1, Boxing. $1.50, Wrestling. $2, Athletics.

2008, June 18   Litho.   Perf. 12
1117-1120 A243 Set of 4   5.50 5.50
1120a Souvenir sheet of 4,
        #1117-1120   5.50 5.50

Peonies, Statue and Temple A244

2009, Apr. 10   Litho.   Perf. 13¼
1121 A244 $1 multi   .85   .85

Printed in sheets of 8.

Intl. Labor Organization, 90th Anniv. — A245

Color of top panel: $2, Green. $2.70, Blue. $3, Yellow brown. $3.90, Lilac.

2009, Apr. 27   Litho.   Perf. 13¼
Granite Paper
1122-1125 A245 Set of 4   90.00 90.00

Worldwide Fund for Nature (WWF) — A246

No. 1126: a, Pacific robin. b, Polynesian triller. c, Polynesian starling. d, Wattled honeyeater.

2009, Sept. 2   Perf. 13¼
1126   Horiz. strip of 4 10.00 10.00
a. A246 50s multi   .50   .50
b. A246 $2 multi   1.50 1.50
c. A246 $2.70 multi   2.00 2.00
d. A246 $5 multi   3.50 3.50

No. 1126 was printed in sheets containing two strips.

Worldwide Fund for Nature (WWF) — A247

No. 1127 — Many-colored fruit dove: a, Two birds. b, Adult and chick in nest. c, Bird eating fruit. d, Two birds, diff.

2011, Apr. 25		**Perf. 14**	
1127	Horiz. strip of 4	10.00	10.00
a.	A247 50s multi	.45	.45
b.	A247 $2 multi	1.75	1.75
c.	A247 $2.70 multi	2.40	2.40
d.	A247 $5 multi	4.50	4.50
e.	Souvenir sheet of 8, 2 each # 1127a-1127d	20.00	20.00

Samoa's Move Across International Date Line — A248

No. 1128: a, Map of Australia and New Zealand, flag and map of Samoa on jigsaw puzzle piece. b, Flag and map of Samoa on jigsaw puzzle piece.

2011, Dec. 15		**Perf. 14¼**	
1128	A248 Horiz. pair + central label	5.00	5.00
a.	$2.50 multi	2.10	2.10
b.	$3 multi	2.50	2.50

Nos. 987-988 Surcharged

Methods and Perfs As Before

2011, Feb. 8				
1129	A213	50s on 70s #987	—	—
a.		Inverted surcharge	—	—
1130	A213	50s on 70s #988	—	—
a.		Pair, #1129-1130	—	—
b.		Inverted surcharge	—	—
c.		Horiz. pair #1129a, 1130b	—	—
1131	A213	$2 on 70s #987	—	—
1132	A213	$2 on 70s #988	—	—
a.		Pair, #1131-1132	—	—
1133	A213	$3 on 70s #987	—	—
1134	A213	$3 on 70s #988	—	—
a.		Pair, #1133-1134	—	—
1135	A213	$10 on 70s #987	—	—
1136	A213	$10 on 70s #988	—	—
a.		Pair, #1135-1136	—	—
		Nos. 1129-1136	125.00	—

Independence, 50th Anniv. — A249

Designs: $1, Longboats. $2, Palm tree and shore. $3, Dancers. $4, Dancer and audience.

2012, May 24	**Litho.**	**Perf. 14¼**	
1137	A249 $1 multi	.90	.90
1137A	A249 $2 multi	1.75	1.75
1137B	A249 $3 multi	2.60	2.60
1137C	A249 $4 multi	3.50	3.50
d.	Souvenir sheet of 4, #1137-1137C	8.75	8.75
	Nos. 1137-1137C (4)	8.75	8.75

Miniature Sheet

Christmas — A250

No. 1138: a, St. Joseph. b, Tree. c, Shepherd with flute. d, Madonna and Child. e, Heads of donkey and cow. f, Shepherd, body of cow. g, Sheep, body of shepherd. h, Sheep, hand of Mary. i, Feed trough and fence. j, Young shepherd holding lamb.

2012, Dec. 21	**Litho.**	**Perf. 13¾**	
1138	A250 50s Sheet of 10, #a-j	4.50	4.50

Miniature Sheet

New Year 2013 (Year of the Snake) — A251

No. 1139 — Background color: a, Yellow. b, Purple. c, Green. d, Orange.

	Perf. 14¼x14¾		
2013, Feb. 19		**Litho.**	
1139	A251 $3 Sheet of 4, #a-d	10.50	10.50

Fuipisia Falls — A252

2013, Feb. 19	**Litho.**	**Perf. 13¾**	
1140	A252 $2.10 shown	1.90	1.90

Souvenir Sheet

	Perf. 14¼x14¾		
1141	A252 $10 multi	8.75	8.75

No. 1141 contains one 24x54mm stamp.

Endangered Bats and Birds — A253

Designs: $1, Emballonura semicaudata. $2.70, Gallinula pacifica. $3, Didunculus strigirostris. $3.90, Lalage sharpei. $4, Zosterops samoensis. $5, Nesofregetta fuliginosa. $6, Numenius tahitiensis. $7.50, Pterodroma brevipes. $8, Pteropus samoensis. $10, Myiagra albiventris. $12.50, Gallicolumba stairi. $15, Gymnomyza samoensis.

2013, May 29	**Litho.**	**Perf. 14**	
1142	A253 $1 multi	.85	.85
1143	A253 $2.70 multi	2.40	2.40
1144	A253 $3 multi	2.60	2.60
1145	A253 $3.90 multi	3.50	3.50
1146	A253 $4 multi	3.50	3.50
1147	A253 $5 multi	4.25	4.25
1148	A253 $6 multi	5.25	5.25
1149	A253 $7.50 multi	6.50	6.50
1150	A253 $8 multi	7.00	7.00
1151	A253 $10 multi	8.75	8.75
1152	A253 $12.50 multi	11.00	11.00
1153	A253 $15 multi	13.00	13.00
	Nos. 1142-1153 (12)	68.60	68.60

Sopoaga Falls and Teuila Flower — A254

2013, Aug. 19	**Litho.**	**Perf. 13¾**	
1154	A254 $2.70 multi	2.25	2.25

Souvenir Sheet

	Perf. 14x14¾		
1155	A254 $20 multi	17.00	17.00

No. 1155 contains one 24x54mm stamp with an image similar to No. 1154 but which is erroneously inscribed "Fuipisia Falls Upolu Island."

Birth of Prince George of Cambridge A255

Designs: Nos. 1156, 1159a, $1, Duchess of Cambridge holding Prince George. Nos. 1157, 1159b, $5, Prince George. Nos. 1158, 1159c, $10, Duke of Cambridge holding Prince George.

2013, Aug. 26	**Litho.**	**Perf. 14**	
Stamps With Photograph 22mm Wide			
1156-1158	A255	Set of 3	13.50	13.50
Souvenir Sheet			
Stamps With Photograph 24mm Wide			
1159	A255	Sheet of 3, #a-c	13.50	13.50

Photographs on Nos. 1159 extend to the tips of the perforations. A white frame is next to the outer sides of the photographs on Nos. 1156-1158.

Miniature Sheet

2013 Pacific Mini Games, Wallis & Futuna Islands — A256

No. 1160 — Inscriptions: a, Athletics. b, Beach volleyball. c, Rugby sevens. d, Sailing. e, Taekwondo. f, Va'a canoeing. g, Bodybuilding. h, Volleyball.

2013, Aug. 28	**Litho.**	**Perf. 13¾**	
1160	A256 $2.50 Sheet of 8, #a-h	17.00	17.00

A257

Teuila Festival — A258

No. 1162: a, Side view of pink teuila flower. b, Side view of red teuila flower. c, View of pink teuila flower from above.

2013, Sept. 17	**Litho.**	**Perf. 13¾**	
1161	A257 50s multi	.45	.45

Souvenir Sheet

1162	A258 $10 Sheet of 3, #a-c	26.00	26.00

Souvenir Sheet

2013 China International Collection Expo, Beijing — A259

No. 1163: a, Painting by Paul Gauguin. b, Beijing Exhibition Center.

2013, Sept. 26	**Litho.**	**Perf. 12**	
1163	A259 $3 Sheet of 2, #a-b	5.25	5.25

Christmas A260

Details of paintings by: $1, Piero della Francesca. $3, Amerighi da Caravaggio.

2013, Nov. 26	**Litho.**	**Perf. 13¼**	
1164-1165	A260	Set of 2	3.50	3.50

Miniature Sheet

New Year 2014 (Year of the Horse) — A261

No. 1166 — Heads of various horses: a, 50s. b, 90s. c, $1.10. d, $2. e, $2.50. f, 3.

2014, Jan. 8   Litho.   Perf. 13¼
1166   A261   Sheet of 6, #a-f   8.50 8.50

Endangered Marine Life and Reptiles — A262

Designs: 50s, Physeter macrocephalus. $1.50, Hippocampus histrix. $2, Bolbometopon muricatum. $2.25, Makaira nigricans. $2.50, Himantura gerrardi. $3.50, Cheilinus undulatus. $5.50, Isurus oxyrinchus. $6.60, Emoia samoensis. $7, Hippopus hippopus. $9, Eretmochelys imbricata. $20, Nebrius ferrugineus. $25, Carcharhinus longimanus.

2014, Jan. 10   Litho.   Perf. 14
1167   A262   50s multi   .45   .45
1168   A262 $1.50 multi   1.25   1.25
1169   A262 $2 multi   1.75   1.75
1170   A262 $2.25 multi   1.90   1.90
1171   A262 $2.50 multi   2.10   2.10
1172   A262 $3.50 multi   3.00   3.00
1173   A262 $5.50 multi   4.75   4.75
1174   A262 $6.60 multi   5.75   5.75
1175   A262 $7 multi   6.00   6.00
1176   A262 $9 multi   7.75   7.75
1177   A262 $20 multi   17.00 17.00
1178   A262 $25 multi   21.50 21.50
        Nos. 1167-1178 (12) 73.20 73.20

Miniature Sheet

Easter — A263

No. 1179 — Various religious paintings by Giovanni Luteri: a, $2, Jesus. b, $2.70, Madonna and Child. c, $3, The Lamentation. d, $3.90, Ascension of Christ.

2014, Apr. 10   Litho.   Perf. 13¼
1179   A263   Sheet of 4, #a-d   10.50 10.50

Souvenir Sheet

Nelson Mandela (1918-2013), President of South Africa — A264

No. 1180 — Various photographs of Mandela: a, $5. b, $10.

2014, May 9   Litho.   Perf. 14¼
1180   A264   Sheet of 2, #a-b   13.00 13.00

Personalizable Stamp A265

2014, Aug. 28   Litho.   Perf. 13¼
1181   A265 $2 multi   1.75   1.75

Small Island Developing States — A266

No. 1182: a, Great barracuda. b, Loggerhead turtle. c, Barbour's seahorse. d, Cutthroat eels. e, Coral reef. f, Samoan coastline. g, Sunset at Fagamalo, Savaii Island. h, Sunset at Savaii. i, Lemafa Peak. j, Stone seawall, Lalomanu. k, Sailboat. l, Cruise ship. m, Tour boat. n, Man in canoe. o, Paddleboarding. p, Flag of Samoa.
No. 1183: a, Like #1182f. b, Like #1182p. c, Like #1182g. d, Like #1182h. e, Like #1182i. f, Like #1182j.
No. 1184: a, Like #1182a. b, Like #1182p. c, Like #1182b. d, Like #1182c. e, Like #1182d. f, Like #1182e.
No. 1185: a, Like #1182l. b, Like #1182c. c, Like #1182k. d, Like #1182m. e, Like #1182n. f, Like #1182o.

2014, Aug. 29   Litho.   Perf. 13¼
1182   A266   Block of 18, #1182a-
              1182o, 3 #1182p   8.25   8.25
 a.-p.   A266   50s Any single   .45   .45

Miniature Sheets

1183   A266   Sheet of 6   16.00 16.00
 a.-f.   A266 $3 Any single   2.60   2.60
1184   A266   Sheet of 6   21.00 21.00
 a.-f.   A266 $3.90 Any single   3.50   3.50
1185   A266   Sheet of 6   21.00 21.00
 a.-f.   A266 $4 Any single   3.50   3.50
        Nos. 1183-1185 (3)   58.00 58.00

No. 1182 was printed in sheets containing 3 blocks of 18. The frame on each stamp in sheet, depicting a map of the Pacific Ocean, differs.

Samoan Participation in the Commonwealth Games, 40th Anniv. — A267

Samoan flag and: $1, Weight lifting. $2, Swimming. $3, Rugby sevens. $4, Boxing.

2014, Sept. 16   Litho.   Perf. 14
1186-1189   A267   Set of 4   8.25   8.25

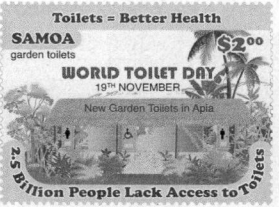

World Toilet Day — A268

No. 1190 — New garden toilets in Apia, with slogan at top: a, "Toilets = Better Health." b, "Toilets = Higher Income." c, "Toilets = Better Education." d, "Toilets = Higher Social Status."

2014, Nov. 19   Litho.   Perf. 13¼
1190   Horiz. strip of 4   7.00   7.00
 a.-d.   A268 $2 Any single   1.75   1.75

World War I, Cent. A269

Designs: $2, New Zealand ships in Samoa. $2.70, New Zealand officers landing to demand German surrender, 1914. $3, New Zealand troops in Western Samoa, 1914. $3.90, New Zealand troops landing in Samoa, 1914.
No. 1195: a, New Zealand troops arriving in three boats to annex Samoa for Britain. b, New Zealand soldiers on board a troop ship en route to Samoa. c, New Zealand troops arriving in one boat to annex Samoa.

2014, Dec. 5   Litho.   Perf. 13¾
1191-1194   A269   Set of 4   9.50   9.50

Souvenir Sheet

1195   A269 $2.50 Sheet of 3, #a-
              c   6.25   6.25

Miniature Sheet

Christmas — A270

No. 1196, a, Head of Santa Claus, Christmas tree, reindeer doll. b, Christmas ornament. c, Christmas stocking. d, Gift.

2014, Dec. 16   Litho.   Perf. 13¼
1196   A270 $2 Sheet of 4, #a-d   6.75   6.75

Souvenir Sheet

New Year 2015 (Year of the Sheep) — A271

No. 1197 — Sheep with background color of: a, $5.50, Blue. b, $6.60, Red orange.

2015, Jan. 5   Litho.   Perf. 13¼
1197   A271   Sheet of 2, #a-b   9.75   9.75

Worldwide Fund for Nature (WWF) — A272

Various photographs of Pacific tree boa: Nos. 1198, 1202, 50s, On tree. Nos. 1199, 1203, $2, On rock. Nos. 1200, 1204, $2.70, On ground. Nos. 1201, 1205, $5, On tree, diff.

2015, Feb. 24   Litho.   Perf. 14
Stamps With White Frames
1198-1201   A272   Set of 4   8.25   8.25
Stamps Without White Frames
1202-1205   A272   Set of 4   8.25   8.25
1205a   Souvenir sheet of 4,
                #1202-1205   8.25   8.25

Nos. 1202-1205 were each printed in sheets of 4.

Endangered Marine Life — A273

No. 1206: a, Brown-marbled grouper. b, Green sea turtle. c, Whale shark.

2015, Mar. 16   Litho.   Perf. 13¼
1206   A273   Horiz. strip of 3 +
              3 labels   50.00 50.00
 a. $6.25 multi + label   5.00   5.00
 b. $12.50 multi + label   10.00 10.00
 c. $45 multi + label   35.00 35.00

Miniature Sheet

Easter — A274

No. 1207 — Pieta paintings by: a, Rogier van der Weyden. b, Enguerrand Quarton. c, Titian. d, Pietro Perugino.

2015, Apr. 2   Litho.   Perf. 14¼x14
1207   A274 $2.70 Sheet of 4, #a-
              d   8.50   8.50

Souvenir Sheet

Birth of Princess Charlotte of
Cambridge — A275

2015, June 24   Litho.   Perf. 13¾
1208 A275 $12.90 multi   10.00 10.00

Magna Carta, 800th Anniv. — A276

Designs: $2, King John on coins. $2.70,
Justice. $3, King John. $3.90, Arms of
England and Samoa.

2015, July 21   Litho.   Perf. 14x14¾
1209-1212 A276   Set of 4   9.00 9.00

Miniature Sheet

2015 Commonwealth Youth Games,
Samoa — A277

No. 1213: a, Aquatics. b, Tennis. c, Track
and field (athletics). d, Lawn bowls. e, Weight
lifting. f, Boxing. g, Archery. h, Rugby 7s. i,
Squash

2015, Sept. 2   Litho.   Perf. 13¼
1213 A277 $2 Sheet of 9, #a-i   14.00 14.00

Miniature Sheet

Diplomatic Relations Between Samoa
and People's Republic of China, 40th
Anniv. — A278

No. 1214 — Flags of Samoa and People's
Republic of China, handshake and: a, $2.50,
Sua Trench. b, $3.70, Samoan government
building. c, $4.70, Samoan Prime Minister Tui-
laepa Lupesoliai Sailele Malielegaoi and Chinese President Xi Jinping. d, $5.40, 2015
Samoan Independence celebrations.

2015, Sept. 4   Litho.   Perf. 13¾
1214 A278   Sheet of 4, #a-d   12.50 12.50

New Year
2016 (Year of
the Monkey)
A279

Designs: $3.90, Monkey holding peach.
$4.70, Monkey scratching head.
No. 1217: a, $5.50, Monkey holding peach.
b, $6.60, Monkey scratching head.

2015, Sept. 25   Litho.   Perf. 13¼
1215-1216 A279   Set of 2   6.50 6.50
Souvenir Sheet
1217 A279   Sheet of 2, #a-b   9.25 9.25

No. 1217 contains two 50x50mm diamond-
shaped stamps.

Oceania 21 Summit, New
Caledonia — A280

No. 1218, $2.50: a, List of participating
countries. b, Wind generator.
No. 1219, $3.70: a, Eiffel Tower. b, List of
participating countries.

2015, Nov. 5   Litho.   Perf. 14
Horiz. Pairs, #a-b
1218-1219 A280   Set of 2   9.50 9.50
1219c   Souvenir sheet of 4, #1218a-
            1218b, 1219a-1219b
                                9.50 9.50

Miniature Sheet

Queen Elizabeth II, Longest-Reigning
British Monarch — A281

No. 1220 — Queen Elizabeth II: a, $1, On
telephone. b, $2, Wearing lime green wide-
brimmed hat. c, $3, Wearing narrow-brimmed
hat. d, $4, In car with Prince Philip.

2015, Nov. 16   Litho.   Perf. 14¼
1220 A281   Sheet of 4, #a-d   7.75 7.75

Souvenir Sheet

Christmas — A282

No. 1221 — Nativity, by Lorenzo Lotto
(details): a, Angels. b, St. Joseph and Virgin
Mary. c, Infant Jesus.

2015, Dec. 4   Litho.   Perf. 13¾
1221 A282 $1 Sheet of 3, #a-c   2.25 2.25

Marine Life and
Birds — A283

Designs: $2, Flower pot coral. $2.50, Spinner dolphins. $2.70, Gray reef shark. $3, Red-
footed booby. $3.70, Bryde's whale. $3.90,
Fairy tern. $4.70, Staghorn coral. $5, Tiger
shark. $5.40, Masked boobies. $6.25,
Galapagos shark. $12.90, Great frigatebird.
$19.25, Bottlenose dolphins.

2016, Mar. 7   Litho.   Perf. 14¼x14¾
1222 A283 $2 multi   1.60 1.60
1223 A283 $2.50 multi   2.00 2.00
1224 A283 $2.70 multi   2.25 2.25
1225 A283 $3 multi   2.40 2.40
1226 A283 $3.70 multi   3.00 3.00
1227 A283 $3.90 multi   3.25 3.25
1228 A283 $4.70 multi   3.75 3.75
1229 A283 $5 multi   4.00 4.00
1230 A283 $5.40 multi   4.25 4.25
1231 A283 $6.25 multi   5.00 5.00
1232 A283 $12.90 multi   10.50 10.50
1233 A283 $19.25 multi   15.00 15.00
        Nos. 1222-1233 (12) 57.00 57.00

Nos. 987, 988,
993, 1018, 1020,
and 1043
Surcharged

Methods and Perfs As Before
2016, Mar. 18
1234 A215 $2 on 90s #993   1.60 1.60
a.   Inverted surcharge   —   —
1235 A213 $2.70 on 70s #987   2.25 2.25
1236 A213 $2.70 on 70s #988   2.25 2.25
a.   Pair, #1235-1236   4.50 4.50
1237 A225 $5 on 95s   4.00 4.00
            #1043
a.   Double surcharge, one in-
        verted   —   —
1238 A220 $15 on 95s
            #1020   12.00 12.00
a.   Inverted surcharge   —   —
1239 A219 $20 on $1.85
            #1018   16.00 16.00
a.   Pair, one without surcharge — —

Souvenir Sheet

Queen Elizabeth II, 90th
Birthday — A284

2016, Apr. 28   Litho.   Perf. 13¼
1240 A284 $10 multi   7.75 7.75

New Year
2017 (Year of
the Rooster)
A285

Designs: $5.50, Brown and gray rooster,
head looking forward. $7, Multicolored rooster,
looking over shoulder.

2016, Aug. 10   Litho.   Perf. 13¼
1241-1242 A285   Set of 2   10.00 10.00
1242a   Souvenir sheet of 2,
            #1241-1242   10.00 10.00

2016 Summer
Olympics, Rio de
Janeiro — A286

Designs: 50s, Swimming. $1.10, Running.
$2.80, Sprint canoeing. $4.20, Weight lifting.
$5.10, Judo.

2016, Sept. 2   Litho.   Perf. 13¾
1243-1247 A286   Set of 5   10.50 10.50

Animals — A287

No. 1248: a, Nine-banded armadillo, b, Dominican red mountain boa. c, Florida panther. d, Mole salamander.

No. 1249: a, Common eland. b, Sumatran tiger. c, Ornate lorikeet. d, Clouded leopard.

No. 1250: a, Koalas. b, Monarch butterflies. c, Lemur leaf frog. d, Australian wood ducks.

No. 1251: a, Lesser Jardine's parrot. b, Porcupine. c, Indian star tortoise. d, Southern three-banded armadillo.

No. 1252: a, Ankole watusi. b, Red-bellied woodpecker. c, Dyeing poison frog. d, Koalas, diff.

2016, Sept. 7   Litho.   Perf. 13¾
1248	A287	60s Block of 4, #a-d	1.90	1.90
1249	A287	70s Block of 4, #a-d	2.25	2.25
1250	A287	80s Block of 4, #a-d	2.50	2.50
1251	A287	$1.20 Block of 4, #a-d	3.75	3.75
1252	A287	$3.60 Block of 4, #a-d	11.50	11.50
		Nos. 1248-1252 (5)	21.90	21.90

Tourism and Culture
A288

Designs: 20s, Trees. 30s, Samoans in canoe. 40s, Samoan men. 50s, Waterfall. 90s, Bat. $1, Dancers. $2, Fire dancer. $2.10, Boats at sea. $2.50, Costume on beach. $2.70, Trees and houses. $3, Tops of palm trees as seen from ground. $3.90, Plants. $4, Palm trees and distant island, vert. $5, Cattle herd and ranchers, vert. $10, Flower, vert. $20, View of Samoa from ocean, horiz.

2016, Dec. 14   Litho.   Perf. 13¼
1253	A288	20s multi	.25	.25
1254	A288	30s multi	.25	.25
1255	A288	40s multi	.30	.30
1256	A288	50s multi	.40	.40
1257	A288	90s multi	.70	.70
1258	A288	$1 multi	.80	.80
1259	A288	$2 multi	1.60	1.60
1260	A288	$2.10 multi	1.60	1.60
1261	A288	$2.50 multi	1.90	1.90
1262	A288	$2.70 multi	2.10	2.10
1263	A288	$3 multi	2.40	2.40
1264	A288	$3.90 multi	3.00	3.00

Size: 36x54mm
1265	A288	$4 multi	3.25	3.25
1266	A288	$5 multi	4.00	4.00
1267	A288	$10 multi	7.75	7.75

Size: 108x54mm
1268	A288	$20 multi	15.50	15.50
		Nos. 1253-1268 (16)	45.80	45.80

Christmas — A289

No. 1269 — Beach scene with: a, Christmas tree and gifts. b, Christmas ornaments and shells. c, Shells in gift box, starfish. d, Stocking caps on beach chairs.

2016, Dec. 21   Litho.   Perf. 13¼
1269	A289	$2.10 Block of 4, #a-d	6.50	6.50

Worldwide Fund for Nature (WWF)
A290

Hawksbill turtle: Nos. 1270, 1274a, 50s, Eating. Nos. 1271, 1274b, $2, Swimming left. Nos. 1272, 1274c, $2.70, On beach. Nos. 1273, 1274d, $5, Swimming right.

2016, Dec. 27   Litho.   Perf. 14¾x14
Stamps With White Frames
1270-1273	A290	Set of 4	8.00	8.00

Stamps Without White Frame
1274	A290	Block of 4, #a-d	8.00	8.00

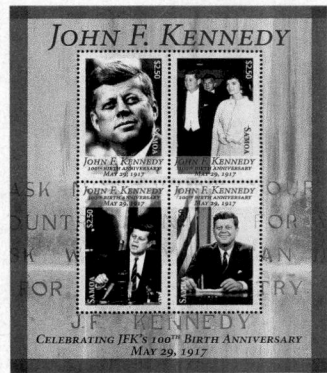

Pres. John F. Kennedy (1917-63) — A291

No. 1275: a, Head of Pres. Kennedy. b, Pres. Kennedy and wife, Jacqueline. c, Pres. Kennedy behind microphones. d, Pres. Kennedy at desk.

2016, Dec. 23   Litho.   Perf. 14
1275	A291	$2.50 Sheet of 4, #a-d	7.75	7.75

Stars — A292

No. 1276: a, Young stars in Carina Nebula. b, Orion Nebula. c, Newborn stars and dwarf galaxy. d, Radiation from a stellar burst ricocheting off dust particles.
$4, Young stars in Carina Nebula, diff.

2016, Dec. 30   Litho.   Perf. 13x13½
1276	A292	$1 Block of 4, #a-d	3.25	3.25

Souvenir Sheet
1277	A292	$4 multi	3.25	3.25

Nos. 855, 973, 985, 994, 998, 1005, 1009, 1022, 1043, 1088 Surcharged

Methods and Perfs. As Before
2017, Mar. 31
1278	A219	$30 on 35s #1009	—	—
1279	A217	$40 on 95s #998	—	—
1280	A212	$50 on $2 #985	—	—
1281	A219	$60 on 5s #1005	—	—
1282	CD357	$70 on 70s #973	—	—
1283	A220	$80 on $1.40 #1022	—	—
1284	A225	$90 on 95s #1043	—	—
1285	A215	$100 on $1 #994	—	—
1286	A237	$150 on $1.75 #1088	—	—
1287	A237	$200 on 90s #855	—	—

Nos. 1026, 1049, 1050, 1052, and 1073 Surcharged

Methods and Perfs. As Before
2018, Apr.
1288	A227	50s on 70s #1049	—	—
1289	A233	50s on 90s #1073	—	—
1290	A221	$2 on $1.20 #1026	—	—
1291	A227	$3 on 80s #1050	—	—
1292	A227	$5 on $4 #1052	—	—

Location of surcharge and obliterator varies.

SEMI-POSTAL STAMP

Catalogue values for unused stamps in this section are for Never Hinged items.

No. 246 Surcharged "HURRICANE RELIEF / 6d"
Wmk. 355
1966, Sept. 1   Litho.   Perf. 13½
B1	A43	8p + 6p blue & emerald	.45	.45

Surtax for aid to plantations destroyed by the hurricane of Jan. 29, 1966.

AIR POST STAMPS

Catalogue values for unused stamps in this section are for Never Hinged items.

Red-tailed Tropic Bird — AP1

Wmk. 355
1965, Dec. 29   Photo.   Perf. 14½
C1	AP1	8p shown	.40	.25
C2	AP1	2sh Flying fish	1.10	.50

Sir Gordon Taylor's Bermuda Flying Boat "Frigate Bird III" — AP2

Designs: 7s, Polynesian Airlines DC-3. 20s, Pan American Airways "Samoan Clipper." 30s, Air Samoa Britten-Norman "Islander."

Perf. 13½x13
1970, July 27   Photo.   Unwmk.
C3	AP2	3s multicolored	.65	.25
C4	AP2	7s multicolored	.85	.25
C5	AP2	20s multicolored	1.25	.90
C6	AP2	30s multicolored	1.25	1.25
a.		Purple omitted	300.00	300.00
		Nos. C3-C6 (4)	4.00	2.65

Used value for No. C6a is for a stamp on a first day cover.

Hawker Siddeley 748 — AP3

Planes at Faleolo Airport: 10s, Hawker Siddeley 748 in the air. 12s, Hawker Siddeley 748 on ground. 22s, BAC 1-11 planes on ground.

1973, Mar. 9   Perf. 11½
Granite Paper
C7	AP3	8s multicolored	.50	.25
C8	AP3	10s multicolored	.70	.25
C9	AP3	12s multicolored	.75	.40
C10	AP3	22s multicolored	1.25	1.25
		Nos. C7-C10 (4)	3.20	2.15

Butterflies — AP4

Designs: $10, Glasswing butterfly. $12.50, Blue tiger butterfly. $56.25, Orange lacewing butterfly. $75, Brown pansy butterfly.

2015, Sept. 15   Litho.   Perf. 14¼
Stamps With White Frames
C11	AP4	$10 multi	7.50	7.50
C12	AP4	$12.50 multi	9.50	9.50
C13	AP4	$56.25 multi	42.50	42.50
C14	AP4	$75 multi	55.00	55.00
a.		Souvenir sheet of 4, #C11-C14	115.00	115.00
		Nos. C11-C14 (4)	114.50	114.50

Stamps Without White Frame
C15		Strip of 4	115.00	115.00
a.		AP4 $10 multi	7.50	7.50
b.		AP4 $12.50 multi	9.50	9.50
c.		AP4 $56.25 multi	42.50	42.50
d.		AP4 $75 multi	55.00	55.00

Stamps on No. C14a have white frames on two adjacent sides.

OFFICIAL STAMPS

Nos. 1142-1153 Overprinted

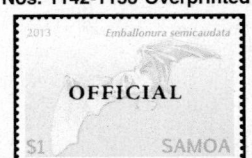

2014, July 23   Litho.   Perf. 14
O1	A253	$1 multi	.80	.80
O2	A253	$2.70 multi	2.25	2.25
O3	A253	$3 multi	2.40	2.40
O4	A253	$3.90 multi	3.25	3.25
O5	A253	$4 multi	3.25	3.25
O6	A253	$5 multi	4.00	4.00
O7	A253	$6 multi	5.00	5.00
O8	A253	$7.50 multi	6.00	6.00
O9	A253	$8 multi	6.50	6.50
O10	A253	$10 multi	8.25	8.25
O11	A253	$12.50 multi	10.00	10.00
O12	A253	$15 multi	12.00	12.00
		Nos. O1-O12 (12)	63.70	63.70

Stamp Show Exhibit Protector Sleeves

Give your treasured exhibit the protection and professional look it deserves with Atlantic Protective Pouches. These expertly crafted, archival quality sleeves are available directly from Amos Advantage in two sizes: 8½ inches by 11 inches, and 11 inches by 17 inches. The standard sleeves come in packs of 16, and the large sleeves are available in packs of eight.

☐ Sleeves made from archival acid-free polyester
☐ 100% transparent and highly polished
☐ Convenient pack sizes to fit exhibit frames

Present Your Exhibit with Max Protection!

tem	Description	Retail	AA
EX100	8 ½ x 11 (Pack of 16)	28.64	22.91
EX120	11 x 17 (Pack of 8)	28.72	22.98

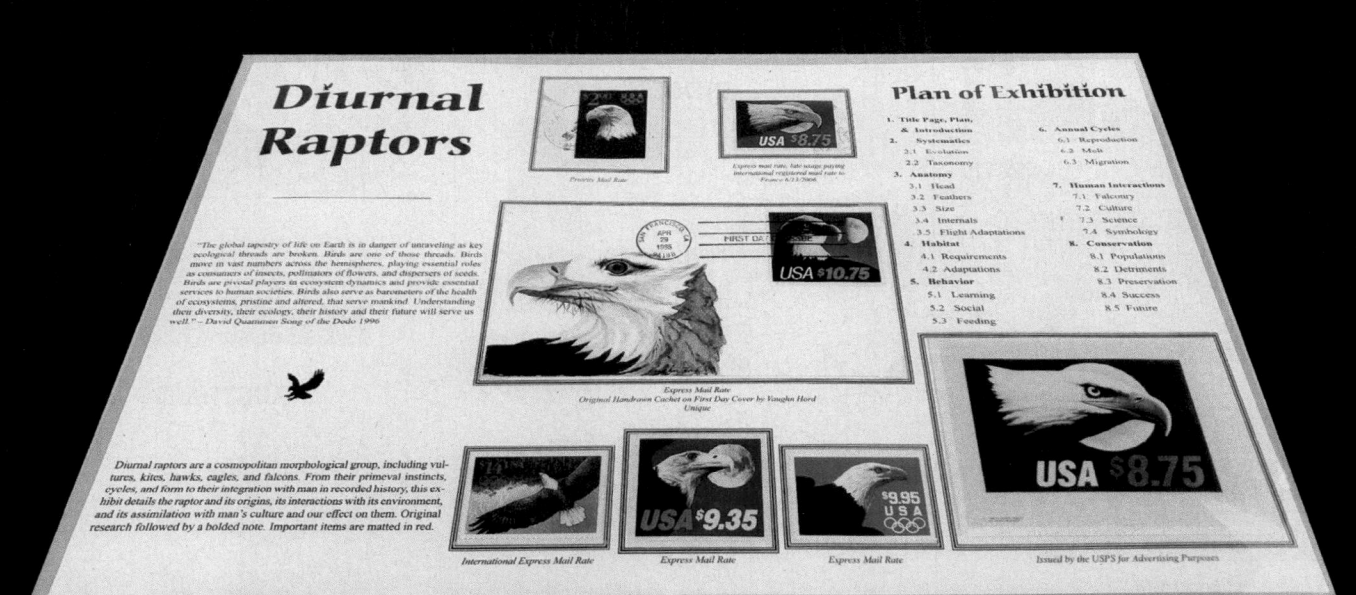

www.AmosAdvantage.com/ExhibitPages

Call **800-572-6885**. Outside U.S. & Canada call: **(937) 498-0800**

Illustrated Identifier

This section pictures stamps or parts of stamp designs that will help identify postage stamps that do not have English words on them.

Many of the symbols that identify stamps of countries are shown here as well as typical examples of their stamps.

See the Index and Identifier for stamps with inscriptions such as "sen," "posta," "Baja Porto," "Helvetia," "K.S.A.", etc.

1. HEADS, PICTURES AND NUMERALS

GREAT BRITAIN

Great Britain stamps never show the country name, but, except for postage dues, show a picture of the reigning monarch.

Victoria

Edward VII   George V   Edward VIII

George VI

Elizabeth II

Some George VI and Elizabeth II stamps are surcharged in annas, new paisa or rupees. These are listed under Oman.

Silhouette (sometimes facing right, generally at the top of stamp)

The silhouette indicates this is a British stamp. It is not a U.S. stamp.

VICTORIA

Queen Victoria

INDIA

Other stamps of India show this portrait of Queen Victoria and the words "Service" (or "Postage") and "Annas."

AUSTRIA

YUGOSLAVIA

(Also BOSNIA & HERZEGOVINA if imperf.)

BOSNIA & HERZEGOVINA

Denominations also appear in top corners instead of bottom corners.

HUNGARY

Another stamp has posthorn facing left

BRAZIL

AUSTRALIA

Kangaroo and Emu

GERMANY

Mecklenburg-Vorpommern

SWITZERLAND

PALAU

2. ORIENTAL INSCRIPTIONS

CHINA

Any stamp with this one character is from China (Imperial, Republic or People's Republic). This character appears in a four-character overprint on stamps of Manchukuo. These stamps are local provisionals, which are unlisted. Other overprinted Manchukuo stamps show this character, but have more than four characters in the overprints. These are listed in People's Republic of China.

Some Chinese stamps show the Sun.

Most stamps of Republic of China show this series of characters.

Stamps with the China character and this character are from People's Republic of China.

Calligraphic form of
People's Republic of China

(一)	(二)	(三)	(四)	(五)	(六)
1	2	3	4	5	6
(七)	(八)	(九)	(十)	(一十)	(二十)
7	8	9	10	11	12

**Chinese stamps
without China character**

REPUBLIC OF CHINA

PEOPLE'S REPUBLIC OF CHINA

Mao Tse-tung

MANCHUKUO

Temple   Emperor Pu-Yi

The first 3 characters are common to
many Manchukuo stamps.

The last 3 characters are common to
other Manchukuo stamps.

Orchid Crest

Manchukuo
stamp
without
these
elements

JAPAN

Chrysanthemum Crest   Country Name

Japanese stamps without these elements

The number of characters in the
center and the design of dragons on
the sides will vary.

RYUKYU ISLANDS

Country Name

PHILIPPINES
(Japanese Occupation)

Country Name

NETHERLANDS INDIES
(Japanese Occupation)

Indicates Japanese Occupation

Java   Sumatra

Country Name   Country Name

Moluccas, Celebes and
South Borneo

Country Name

NORTH BORNEO
(Japanese Occupation)

Indicates Japanese   Country
Occupation   Name

MALAYA
(Japanese Occupation)

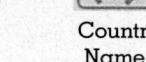

Indicates Japanese   Country
Occupation   Name

BURMA

Union of Myanmar

ပြည်ထောင်စုမြန်မာနိုင်ငံတော်

Union of Myanmar

(Japanese Occupation)

Indicates Japanese Occupation	Country Name

Other Burma Japanese Occupation stamps without these elements

Burmese Script

KOREA

These two characters, in any order, are common to stamps from the Republic of Korea (South Korea) or of the People's Democratic Republic of Korea (North Korea).

This series of four characters can be found on the stamps of both Koreas. Most stamps of the Democratic People's Republic of Korea (North Korea) have just this inscription.

Indicates Republic of Korea (South Korea)

South Korean postage stamps issed after 1952 do not show currency expressed in Latin letters. Stamps wiith " HW," "HWAN," "WON," "WN," "W" or "W" with two lines through it, if not illustrated in listings of stamps before this date, are revenues. North Korean postage stamps do not have currency expressed in Latin letters.

Yin Yang appears on some stamps.

South Korean stamps show Yin Yang and starting in 1966, 'KOREA" in Latin letters

Example of South Korean stamps lacking Latin text, Yin Yang and standard Korean text of country name. North Korean stamps never show Yin Yang and starting in 1976 are inscribed "DPRK" or "DPR KOREA" in Latin letters.

THAILAND

Country Name

King Chulalongkorn

King Prajadhipok and Chao P'ya Chakri

3. CENTRAL AND EASTERN ASIAN INSCRIPTIONS

INDIA - FEUDATORY STATES

Alwar

Bhor

Bundi

Similar stamps come with different designs in corners and differently drawn daggers (at center of circle).

Dhar   Duttia

Faridkot

Hyderabad

Similar stamps exist with different central design which is inscribed "Postage" or "Post & Receipt."

Indore

Jammu & Kashmir

Text varies.

Jasdan

Jhalawar

Kotah

Size and text varies

Nandgaon

Nowanuggur

Poonch

Similar stamps exist
in various sizes with different text

Rajasthan

Rajpeepla

Soruth

Tonk

BANGLADESH

Country Name

NEPAL

Similar stamps are smaller, have squares in
upper corners and have five or nine
characters in central bottom panel.

TANNU TUVA　　**ISRAEL**

GEORGIA

This inscription
is found on other
pictorial stamps.

Country Name

ARMENIA

The four characters are found somewhere
on pictorial stamps. On some stamps only
the middle two are found.

4. AFRICAN INSCRIPTIONS

ETHIOPIA

5. ARABIC INSCRIPTIONS

AFGHANISTAN

Many early Afghanistan stamps show Tiger's head, many of these have ornaments protruding from outer ring, others show inscriptions in black.

Arabic Script

Crest of King Amanullah

Mosque Gate & Crossed Cannons

The four characters are found somewhere on pictorial stamps. On some stamps only the middle two are found.

BAHRAIN

EGYPT

Postage

IRAN

Country Name

Royal Crown

Lion with Sword

Symbol

Emblem

IRAQ

JORDAN

LEBANON

Similar types have
denominations at top
and slightly different
design.

LIBYA

Country Name in various styles

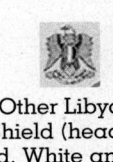

Other Libya stamps show Eagle and
Shield (head facing either direction) or
Red, White and Black Shield (with or with-
out eagle in center).

Without Country Name

SAUDI ARABIA

Tughra (Central design)

 ← Palm Tree and Swords

SYRIA

Arab Government Issues

THRACE   YEMEN

PAKISTAN

PAKISTAN - BAHAWALPUR

→ 924

→

Country Name in top panel, star and crescent

TURKEY

 Star & Crescent is a device found on many Turkish stamps, but is also found on stamps from other Arabic areas (see Pakistan-Bahawalpur)

TURKEY IN ASIA

Tughra (similar tughras can be found on stamps of Turkey in Asia, Afghanistan and Saudi Arabia)

Mohammed V

Mustafa Kemal

Plane, Star and Crescent

Other Turkey in Asia pictorials show star & crescent. Other stamps show tughra shown under Turkey.

6. GREEK INSCRIPTIONS

GREECE

Country Name in various styles (Some Crete stamps overprinted with the Greece country name are listed in Crete.)

Lepta

Drachma   Drachmas   Lepton
Abbreviated Country Name
Other forms of Country Name

No country name

CRETE

Country Name

Crete stamps with a surcharge that have the year "1922" are listed under Greece.

EPIRUS

Similar stamps have text above the eagle.

IONIAN IS.

---

7. CYRILLIC INSCRIPTIONS

RUSSIA

Postage Stamp   Imperial Eagle

Postage in various styles

Abbreviation   Abbreviation   Russia
for Kopeck   for Ruble

Abbreviation for Russian Soviet Federated Socialist Republic RSFSR stamps were overprinted (see below)

Abbreviation for Union of Soviet Socialist Republics

This item is footnoted in Latvia

RUSSIA - Army of the North

"ОКСА"

RUSSIA - Wenden

RUSSIAN OFFICES IN THE TURKISH EMPIRE

These letters appear on other stamps of the Russian offices.

The unoverprinted version of this stamp and a similar stamp were overprinted by various countries (see below).

ARMENIA

BELARUS

FAR EASTERN REPUBLIC

Country Name

FINLAND

Circles and Dots
on stamps similar
to Imperial
Russia issues

SOUTH RUSSIA

Country Name

BATUM

Forms of Country Name

TRANSCAUCASIAN FEDERATED REPUBLICS

Abbreviation for
Country Name

KAZAKHSTAN

KYRGYZSTAN

КЫРГЫЗСТАН

Country
Name

ROMANIA

TAJIKISTAN

Country Name & Abbreviation

UKRAINE

Country Name in various forms

The trident appears
on many stamps,
usually as
an overprint.

Abbreviation for
Ukrainian
Soviet
Socialist
Republic

WESTERN UKRAINE

Abbreviation for
Country Name

AZERBAIJAN

AZƏRBAYCAN

Country Name

A.C.C.P.

Abbreviation for Azerbaijan
Soviet Socialist Republic

MONTENEGRO

ЦРНАГОРА

ЦРНА ГОРА

Country Name in various forms

Abbreviation
for country
name

No country name
(A similar Montenegro
stamp without coun-
try name has same
vignette.)

SERBIA

СРПСКА   **СРБИЈА**

Country Name in various forms

Abbreviation for country name

No country name

MACEDONIA

МАКЕДОНИЈА

Country Name

МАКЕДОНСКИ

Different form of Country Name

SERBIA & MONTENEGRO

YUGOSLAVIA

ЈУГОСЛАВИЈА

Showing country name

No Country Name

BOSNIA & HERZEGOVINA
(Serb Administration)

РЕПУБЛИКА СРПСКА

Country Name

РЕПУБЛИКЕ СРПСКЕ

Different form of Country Name

No Country Name

BULGARIA

Country Name   Postage

Stotinka

Stotinki (plural)   Abbreviation for
Stotinki

Country Name in various forms and styles

No country name

Abbreviation
for Lev, leva

MONGOLIA

ШУУДАН   төгрөг

Country name in   Tugrik in Cyrillic
one word

МОНГОЛ
ШУУДАН   мөнгө

Country name in   Mung in Cyrillic
two words

Mung
in Mongolian

Tugrik
in Mongolian

Arms

No Country Name

STOCK PAGES

You need storage during transition into an album?
You have duplicate stamp issues?
Here are the some solutions for you!

SCOTT ADVANTAGE STOCK PAGES

Scott Advantage Stock sheets provide the protection and durability of crystal acetate pockets. Designed with the collector in mind, the Advantage Stocksheets fit directly in your 3-ring or 2-post binder and match Scott National or Specialty pages in every respect. Perfect or storing new issues, minor varieties and collateral material.
Size: 10" x 11 1/2". Sold in Packs of 10

Item#			Retail	AA
AD11	1 Pocket 242mm	National	$21.99	$19.99
AD21	1 Pocket 242mm	Specialty	$21.99	$19.99
AD12	2 Pocket 119mm	National	$21.99	$19.99
AD22	2 Pocket 119mm	Specialty	$21.99	$19.99
AD13	3 Pocket 79mm	National	$21.99	$19.99
AD23	3 Pocket 79mm	Specialty	$21.99	$19.99
AD14	4 Pocket 58mm	National	$21.99	$19.99
AD24	4 Pocket 58mm	Specialty	$21.99	$19.99
AD15	5 Pocket 45mm	National	$21.99	$19.99
AD25	5 Pocket 45mm	Specialty	$21.99	$19.99
AD16	6 Pocket 37mm	National	$21.99	$19.99
AD26	6 Pocket 37mm	Specialty	$21.99	$19.99
AD17	7 Pocket 34mm	National	$21.99	$19.99
AD27	7 Pocket 34mm	Specialty	$21.99	$19.99
AD18	8 Pocket 31mm	National	$21.99	$19.99
AD28	8 Pocket 31mm	Specialty	$21.99	$19.99

PRINZ STOCK PAGES

Prinz stock pages offer convenience and flexibility. Pages areproduced on thick, archival-quality paper with acetate pockets glued from the bottom of each pocket. Size: 8 1/2" x 11". Sold in Packs of 5

Item#			Retail	AA
S1	1 Pocket 242 mm	Black (Single-Sided)	$11.99	$8.75
S1D	1 Pocket 242 mm	Black (Double-Sided)	$17.99	$12.99
S2	2 Pockets 119mm	Black (Single-Sided)	$11.99	$8.75
S2D	2 Pockets 119mm	Black (Double-Sided)	$17.99	$12.99
S3	3 Pockets 79mm	Black (Single-Sided)	$11.99	$8.75
S3D	3 Pockets 79mm	Black (Double-Sided)	$17.99	$12.99
S4	4 Pockets 58mm	Black (Single-Sided)	$11.99	$8.75
S4D	4 Pockets 58mm	Black (Double-Sided)	$17.99	$12.99
S5	5 Pockets 45mm	Black (Single-Sided)	$11.99	$8.75
S5D	5 Pockets 45mm	Black (Double-Sided)	$17.99	$12.99
S6	6 Pockets 37mm	Black (Single-Sided)	$11.99	$8.75
S6D	6 Pockets 37mm	Black (Double-Sided)	$17.99	$12.99
S7	7 Pockets 31mm	Black (Single-Sided)	$11.99	$8.75
S7D	7 Pockets 31mm	Black (Double-Sided)	$17.99	$12.99
S8	8 Pockets 27mm	Black (Single-Sided)	$11.99	$8.75
S8D	8 Pockets 27mm	Black (Double-Sided)	$17.99	$12.99
S9	3 Pockets 36mm/ 67mm/139mm	Black (Single-Sided)	$11.99	$8.75
S9D	3 Pockets 36mm/ 67mm/139mm	Black (Double-Sided)	$17.99	$12.99

UNIVERSAL BINDERS

We have the binders for you! Take a look at our handsome matching binder and slipcase set. These great binder, slipcase sets are available in blue or black. If you want a heavy duty binder, checkout our metal-hinged, thick panel, 3-ring binder. What are you waiting for?

Item#		Retail	AA
SSBSBL	Blue 3-Ring Binder & Slipcase	$24.99	$19.99
SSBSBK	Black 3-Ring Binder & Slipcase	$24.99	$19.99
SSBMBK	Black Metal-Hinged 3-Ring Binder	$24.99	$19.99

HAGNER STOCK PAGES

The original Hagner Stock sheets are made from archival quality pH board and feature pure polyester film pockets that are glued to each page with special chemically inert glue.
Size: 8 1/2" x 11" . Sold in Packs of 5

Item#			Retail	AA
HGB01	1 Pocket 242 mm	Black (Single-Sided)	$7.25	$6.50
HGB11	1 Pocket 242 mm	Black (Double-Sided)	$11.75	$8.99
HGB02	2 Pockets 119mm	Black (Single-Sided)	$7.25	$6.50
HGB22	2 Pockets 119mm	Black (Double-Sided)	$11.75	$8.99
HGB03	3 Pockets 79mm	Black (Single-Sided)	$7.25	$6.50
HGB33	3 Pockets 79mm	Black (Double-Sided)	$11.75	$8.99
HGB04	4 Pockets 58mm	Black (Single-Sided)	$7.25	$6.50
HGB44	4 Pockets 58mm	Black (Double-Sided)	$11.75	$8.99
HGB05	5 Pockets 45mm	Black (Single-Sided)	$7.25	$6.50
HGB55	5 Pockets 45mm	Black (Double-Sided)	$11.75	$8.99
HGB06	6 Pockets 37mm	Black (Single-Sided)	$7.25	$6.50
HGB66	6 Pockets 37mm	Black (Double-Sided)	$11.75	$8.99
HGB07	7 Pockets 31mm	Black (Single-Sided)	$7.25	$6.50
HGB77	7 Pockets 31mm	Black (Double-Sided)	$11.75	$8.99
HGB08	8 Pockets 27mm	Black (Single-Sided)	$7.25	$6.50
HGB88	8 Pockets 27mm	Black (Double-Sided)	$11.75	$8.99
HGB09	3Pockets 36mm/ 67mm/139mm	Black (Single-Sided)	$7.25	$6.50
HGB99	3 Pockets 36mm/ 67mm/139mm	Black (Double-Sided)	$11.75	$8.99

VARIO STOCK PAGES

Vario stock sheets offer unparalleled quality and versatility. They're a convenient and easy way to store and organize stamps. Vario stock sheets are carefully manufactured to be free of harmful plasticized PVC, and softeners. NOTE: Black sheets have pockets on both sides. Clear sheets have pockets on one side only. "S" in item number denotes black page. "C" in item number denotes clear page.
Size: 8 1/2" x 11". Sold in Packs of 5

Item#			Retail	AA
V1S	1 Pocket 258mm	Black (Double-Sided)	$5.95	$4.98
V1C	1 Pocket 258mm	Clear (Single-Sided)	$5.95	$4.98
V2S	2 Pockets 128mm	Black (Double-Sided)	$5.95	$4.98
V2C	2 Pockets 128mm	Clear (Single-Sided)	$5.95	$4.98
V3S	3 Pockets 84mm	Black (Double-Sided)	$5.95	$4.98
V3C	3 Pockets 84mm	Clear (Single-Sided)	$5.95	$4.98
V4S	4 Pockets 63mm	Black (Double-Sided)	$5.95	$4.98
V4C	4 Pockets 63mm	Clear (Single-Sided)	$5.95	$4.98
V5S	5 Pockets 48mm	Black (Double-Sided)	$5.95	$4.98
V5C	5 Pockets 48mm	Clear (Single-Sided)	$5.95	$4.98
V6S	6 Pockets 39mm	Black (Double-Sided)	$5.95	$4.98
V7S	7 Pockets 33mm	Black (Double-Sided)	$5.95	$4.98
V8S	8 Pockets 29mm	Black (Double-Sided)	$5.95	$4.98
VIB	Interleaving Sheets	Black	$4.50	$3.49

www.AmosAdvantage.com
or Call 800-572-6885 • Outside U.S. & Canada call (937) 498-0800

Glossary of Philatelic Terms

This glossary defines nearly 300 terms frequently encountered by stamp collectors and cover collectors. Precise definitions for many philatelic terms do not exist. One collector, dealer or society may define a term in one way, while others will use the term in a slightly different way.

A

Accessories: Various products and tools commonly used by the stamp collector, including hinges, mounts, stamp tongs, perforation gauges, stock books and magnifiers. Stamp albums, catalogs and philatelic literature can also be regarded as accessories.

Adhesive: 1) The gum on the back of a stamp or label. Some stamps have been issued with no adhesive. Stamp adhesive may be water-activated or pressure-sensitive (self-adhesive). 2) A word generally referring to a stamp that may be affixed to an article to prepay postal fees, in contrast to a design printed directly on an article, as with postal stationery. An adhesive can also refer to a registration label or other label added to a cover.

Admirals: A nickname for three British Commonwealth definitive series, those of Canada, 1912-25 (Scott 104-34); New Zealand, 1926 (182-84); and Rhodesia, 1913-19 (119-38). These stamps depict King George V of Great Britain in naval uniform.

Aerogram: A postage-paid airletter sheet with gummed flaps that is written on and then folded to form an envelope. Aerograms are normally carried at less than the airmail letter rate. No enclosures are permitted.

Aerophilately: A specialized area of collecting concentrating on stamps or covers transported by air.

Agency: 1) An extraterritorial post office maintained at various times by a government within the territory of another government. Examples are the post offices maintained by many European powers in the Turkish Empire until 1923. 2) An organization authorized to publicize or sell new issues of stamps on behalf of a stamp-issuing entity.

Air labels: Air labels, or etiquettes, are used by Universal Postal Union member nations to denote airmail carriage. They are inscribed "Par Avion" (French for "By Airmail"). The text usually includes the same message in the language of the country of origin. Air labels also are adhesives issued by private organizations for specific, unofficial flights.

Airmail: The carriage of mail by air. The first regular airmail service began in 1870, when mail was carried from Paris-then besieged by German forces-over enemy lines by balloon. Many countries have issued postage stamps, stamped envelopes, postal cards and aerograms specially designated for airmail use. The first airmail stamp was issued by Italy in 1917 (Italy Scott C1).

Albino: An uninked impression made by a printing plate. Such errors are scarce on stamps. They are found more frequently on postal stationery.

Album: A binder and pages designed for the mounting and display of stamps or covers. Many early albums were permanently bound books. Albums come in many sizes, styles and themes. See the Album section in this almanac.

Album weed: In general, a forged stamp. It also refers to unusual items that resemble postage stamps but were not intended to pay postage, like publicity labels and bogus issues. *Album Weeds* is the title of a reference book series on forged stamps, written by the Rev. Robert Brisco Ear E.

Aniline: Ink with a coal-tar base. Aniline inks are very sensitive and may dissolve in water or other liquids or chemicals. To prevent the erasure of cancellations and reuse of stamps, aniline inks were used to print some stamps.

Approvals: Priced selections of stamps or covers sent to collectors by mail. The collector purchases the items he chooses, returning the rest to the approval dealer with payment for the purchased items.

Army Post Office: An official United States post office established for use by U.S. military units abroad. An army post office (APO) or military post office is set up to distribute mail to and from military personnel. The APO is indicated by numbers during wartime to prevent revealing personnel locations. The locations become generally known after the conflict ends.

Arrow: On many sheets of stamps, V-shaped arrowlike markings appear in the selvage, generally serving as guides for cutting the sheets into predetermined units. Some collectors save stamps or blocks displaying these marks.

As is: A term written in auction descriptions, or spoken or written during a retail transaction. It indicates that an item or lot is sold without guarantee or return privilege. Stamps are usually sold "as is" when they are damaged or are possibly not genuine.

ATM: 1) In the United States, panes of self-adhesive stamps on a liner the approximate size and shape of U.S. currency, designed for dispensing from automatic teller machines. 2) "Automatenmarken," automatic stamps produced individually by a machine; see also Frama.

Auction: A sale of stamps, covers and other philatelic items where prospective purchasers place bids in an attempt to obtain the desired items. The highest bidder for each lot (described item or items) makes the purchase. Auctions are generally divided into mail sales, where bids are accepted by mail, and public sales, where mail bids are combined with live bidding from individuals present at the auction or participating by telephone.

Authentication mark: A marking, such as initials, placed on the reverse of a stamp examined and certified to be genuine by an expert. Such markings do not detract from the value of the stamps when they represent the endorsement of recognized authorities.

APO: Army Post Office. An official United States post office established for use by U.S. military units abroad. An army post office or military post office is set up to distribute mail to and from military personnel. The APO is indicated by numbers during wartime to prevent revealing personnel locations. The locations become generally known after the conflict ends.

B

Backprint: Printing on the reverse of a stamp. Some stamps have numbers, symbols, advertising or information about the stamp subject printed on the reverse of the stamp.

Backstamp: A postmark applied to mail by the receiving post office or by a post office handling the piece while it is in transit. Backstamps are usually on the back of a cover, but they can be on the front.

Bank mixture: A high-quality mixture of stamps. It generally represents clippings from the mail of banks or other businesses with extensive overseas correspondence, and thus includes a relatively high proportion of foreign stamps of high face value. See also Mission mixture.

Bantams: The nickname of the South African definitive series of 1942-43 (Scott 90-97). Wartime economy measures prompted the manufacture of stamps of small size to conserve paper.

Batonne: A wove or laid paper with watermarklike lines deliberately added in the papermaking process and intended as a guide for handwriting.

Bicolor: Printed in two colors.

Bilingual: Inscribed in two languages. Most Canadian stamps include both English and French text. South African stamps from 1926-49 were printed alternately with English and Afrikaans inscriptions in the same sheet.

Bisect: A stamp cut or perforated into two parts, each half representing half the face value of the original stamp. Officially authorized bisects have often been used during temporary shortages of commonly used denominations. Unauthorized bisects appear on mail from some countries in some periods. Bisects are usually collected on full cover with the stamp tied by a cancel. At times, some countries have permitted trisects or quadrisects.

Bishop mark: The earliest postmark, introduced by Henry Bishop in England circa 1661. A Bishop mark was used to indicate the month and day that a letter was received by a post office. It encouraged prompt delivery by letter carriers.

Black Jack: The nickname of the United States 2¢ black Andrew Jackson stamp issued between 1863 and 1875.

Blind perforation: Intended perforations that are only lightly impressed by the perforating pins, leaving the paper intact, but cut or with a faint impression. Some stamps that appear to be imperforate really are not if they have blind perfs. Stamps with blind perfs are minor varieties carrying little, if any, price premium over normally perforated copies.

Block: A unit of four or more unsevered stamps, including at least two stamps both vertically and horizontally. Most commonly a block refers to a block of four, or a block of stamps two high and two wide, though blocks often contain more stamps and may be irregularly configured (such as, a block of seven consisting of one row of three stamps and one row of four stamps).

Bluenose: The nickname for Canada Scott 158, the 50¢ issue of 1929, picturing the schooner *Bluenose.*

Bogus: A fictitious stamplike label created for sale to collectors. Bogus issues include labels for nonexistent countries, nonexistent values appended to regularly issued sets and issues for nations or similar entities without postal systems.

Booklet: A unit of one or more small panes or blocks (known as booklet panes) glued, stitched or stapled together between thin card covers to form a convenient unit for mailers to purchase and carry. The first officially issued booklet was produced by Luxembourg in 1895. For some modern booklets of self-adhesive stamps the liner (backing paper) serves as the booklet cover.

Bourse: A meeting of stamp collectors and/or dealers, where stamps and covers are sold or exchanged. A bourse usually has no competitive exhibits of stamps or covers. Almost all public stamp exhibitions include a dealer bourse, though many bourses are held without a corresponding exhibition.

Bull's-Eyes: 1) The nickname for the 1843 first issue of Brazil, Scott 1-3. The similar but smaller issues are called goat's eyes. 2) A bull's-eye cancel refers to a "socked-on-the-nose" postmark with the impression centered directly on the stamp so that the location and date of mailing are shown on the stamp.

Burelage: A design of fine, intricate lines printed on the face of security paper, either to discourage counterfeiting or to prevent the cleaning and reuse of a stamp. The burelage on some stamps is part of the stamp design.

Burele: Adjective form for burelage, meaning having a fine network of lines. Some stamps of Queensland have a burele band on the back. Also called moir.

C

Cachet: In French, cachet means a stamp or a seal. On a cover, the cachet is an added design or text, often corresponding to the design of the postage stamp, the mailed journey of the cover, or some type of special event. Cachets appear on modern first-day covers, first-flight covers and special-event covers.

Canceled-to-order: Stamps are "canceled to order," usually in full sheets, by many governments. The cancels may be printed on the stamps at the same time that the stamp design is printed. A stamp with a cancel and with full gum is likely a CTO stamp, as CTOs do not see actual postal use. CTO stamps are sold to stamp dealers at large discounts from face value. Most catalogs say whether they price CTO stamps or genuinely used stamps.

Cancel: A marking intended to show a stamp has been used and is no longer valid as postage. Modern cancels usually include the name of the original mailing location or a nearby sorting facility and the date of mailing. Most cancellations also include a section of lines, bars, text or a design that prints upon the postage stamp to invalidate it. This part of a cancel is called the killer.

Cantonal stamps: Issues of Switzerland's cantons (states) used before the release of national stamps. The cantonal issues of Basel (1845), Geneva (1843-50) and Zurich (1843-50) are among the classics of philately.

Cape Triangles: Common name for the triangular Cape of Good Hope stamps of 1853-64, the first stamps printed in triangular format. The distinctive shape helped illiterate postal clerks distinguish letters originating in the colony from those from other colonies.

Catalog: A comprehensive book or

similar compilation with descriptive information to help identify stamps. Many catalogs include values for the listed items. An auction catalog is published by the auction firm in advance of a planned sale to notify potential customers of the specific items that will be offered.

Catalog value: The value of a stamp as listed in a given catalog for the most common condition in which the stamp is collected. Some catalogs list stamps at a retail value, though actual dealer prices may vary substantially for reasons of condition, demand or other market factors. Most catalogs have a set minimum value for the most common stamps.

Censored mail: A cover bearing a handstamp or label indicating that the envelope has been opened and the contents inspected by a censor.

Centering: The relative position of the design of a stamp in relation to its margins. Assuming that a stamp is undamaged, centering is generally a very important factor in determining grade and value.

Certified mail: A service of most postal administrations that provides proof of mailing and delivery without indemnity for loss or damage.

Chalky paper: A chalk-surfaced paper for printing stamps. Any attempt to remove the cancel on a used chalky-paper stamp will also remove the design. Immersion of such stamps in water will cause the design to lift off. Touching chalky paper with silver will leave a discernible, pencil-like mark and is a means of distinguishing chalky paper.

Changeling: A stamp whose color has been changed-intentionally or unintentionally-by contact with a chemical or exposure to light.

Charity seals: Stamplike labels that are distributed by a charity. They have no postal validity, although they are often affixed to envelopes. United States Christmas seals are one example.

Charity stamp: see Semipostal.

Cinderella: A stamplike label that is not a postage stamp. Cinderellas include seals and bogus issues, as well as revenue stamps, local post issues and other similar items.

Classic: An early issue, often with a connotation of rarity, although classic stamps are not necessarily rare. A particularly scarce recent item may be referred to as a modern classic.

Cleaning (stamps): Soiled or stained stamps are sometimes cleaned with chemicals or by erasing. The cleaning is usually done to improve the appearance of a stamp. A cleaned stamp can also mean one from which a cancellation has been removed, making a used stamp appear unused.

Cliché: The individual unit consisting of the design of a single stamp, combined with others to make up the complete printing plate. Individual designs on modern one-piece printing plates are referred to as subjects.

Coil: Stamps processed in a long single row and prepared for sale in rolls, often for dispensing from stamp-vending and affixing machines. Some coils, including most U.S. coils, have a straight edge on two parallel sides and perforations on the remaining two parallel sides. Some coils are backprinted with sequence or counting numbers.

Collateral material: Any supportive or explanatory material relating to a given stamp or philatelic topic. The material may be either directly postal in nature (post office news releases, rate schedules, souvenir cards, promotional items) or nonpostal (maps, photos of scenes appearing on stamps).

Combination cover: Cover bearing the stamps of more than one country when separate postal charges are paid for the transport of a cover by each country. Also stamps of the same country canceled at two different times on the same cover as a souvenir.

Commatology: Specialized collecting of postmarks. This term was invented before World War II to describe postmark collecting. It is rarely used. Usually, collectors refer to postmark collecting or marcophily.

Commemorative: A stamp printed in a limited quantity and available for purchase for a limited time. The design may note an anniversary associated with an individual, an historic event, or a national landmark. See also Definitive.

Compound perforations: Different gauge perforations on different sides of a single stamp. The sides with the different gauge measurements are usually perpendicular.

Condition: The overall appearance and soundness of a stamp or cover. Positive condition factors include fresh full color, full original gum on unused stamps, and so on. Damage such as creases, tears, thinned paper, short perforation teeth, toning and so on negatively affect condition.

Controlled mail: A system in which the mailer selects philatelically desirable issues for outgoing mail, arranges for a specific manner of cancellation and secures the stamps' return by the addressee. In some cases such controlled mail operations may provide rare examples of specific rate fulfillment, or other similar postal use.

Copyright block: Block of four or more United States stamps with the copyright notice marginal marking of the United States Postal Service. The copyright marking was introduced in 1978 and replaced the Mail Early marking.

Corner card: An imprinted return address, generally in the upper-left corner of an envelope, from a commercial, institutional or private source, similar to business card or letterhead imprints.

Counterfeit: Any stamp, cancellation or cover created for deception or imitation, intended to be accepted by others as genuine. A counterfeit stamp is designed to deceive postal authorities.

Cover: An envelope or piece of postal stationery, usually one that has been mailed. Folded letters that were addressed and mailed without an envelope and the wrappers from mailed parcels are also covers.

Crash cover: A cover that has been salvaged from the crash of an airplane, train, ship or other vehicle. Such covers often carry a postal marking explaining damage or delay in delivery.

Crease: A noticeable weakening of the paper of a stamp or cover, caused by its being folded or bent at some point. Creases substantially lower a stamp's value. Creases particularly affect cover values when they extend through the attached stamp or a postal marking. Stamp creases are visible in watermark fluid.

Cut cancellation: A cancellation that intentionally slices into the stamp paper. Often a wedge-shaped section is cut away. On many issues, such cancellations indicate use of postage stamps as fiscals (revenues) or telegraph stamps rather than as postage. Cut cancellations were used experimentally on early United States postage stamps to prevent reuse.

Cut square: A neatly trimmed rectangular or square section from a stamped envelope that includes the imprinted postage stamp with ample margin. Collectors generally prefer to collect stationery as entire pieces rather than as cut squares. Some older stationery is available only in cut squares.

Cut-to-shape: A nonrectangular stamp or postal stationery imprint cut to the shape of the design, rather than cut square. Cut-to-shape stamps and stationery generally have lower value than those cut square. One of the world's most valuable stamps, the unique 1856 British Guiana "Penny Magenta" (Scott 13), is a cut-to-shape stamp.

Cylinder: A curved printing plate used on a modern rotary press. The plate has no seams. For United States stamps, cylinders are used to print gravure stamps. See also Sleeve.

Cancellation: A marking intended to show a stamp has been used and is no longer valid as postage. Modern cancels usually include the name of the original mailing location or a nearby sorting facility and the date of mailing. Most cancellations also include a section of lines, bars, text or a design that prints upon the postage stamp to invalidate it. This part of a cancel is called the killer.

CTO: Canceled-to-order. Stamps are "canceled to order," usually in full sheets, by many governments. The cancels may be printed on the stamps at the same time that the stamp design is printed. A stamp with a cancel and with full gum is likely a CTO stamp, as CTOs do not see actual postal use. CTO stamps are sold to stamp dealers at large discounts from face value. Most catalogs say whether they price CTO stamps or genuinely used stamps.

Charity stamp: A stamp sold at a price greater than postal value, with the additional charge dedicated for a special purpose. Usually recognized

by the presence of two (often different) values, separated by a "+" sign, on a single stamp.

D

Dead country: A former stamp-issuing entity that has ceased issuing its own stamps. Also, the old name of an active stamp-issuing entity that has changed its name, so that the old name will no longer be used on stamps.

Definitive: Stamp issued in a large indefinite quantity and for an indefinite period, usually several years or more. The United States Presidential issue of 1938 and the 1995 32¢ Flag Over Porch stamps are examples. Definitive stamp designs usually do not honor a specific time-dated event.

Deltiology: Picture postcard collecting.

Denomination: The face value of a stamp, usually indicated by numerals printed as part of the design. Some modern U.S. stamps produced for rate changes are denominated with a letter. A numerical value is assigned when the letter stamps are issued. An example of this is the H-rate Hat stamp of 1998, which represented the first-class rate of 33¢.

Die: The original engraving of a stamp design, usually recess-engraved in reverse on a small flat piece of soft steel. In traditional intaglio printing, a transfer roll is made from a die and printing plates are made from impressions of the transfer roll. When more than one die is used in the production of an issue, distinctive varieties are often identifiable.

Die cut: A form of separation usually employed on self-adhesive stamps. During processing, an edged tool (die) completely penetrates the stamp paper on all sides of the printed stamp, making the removal of the individual stamps from the liner possible. Die cuts may be straight, shaped in wavy lines to simulate perforation teeth, or take other forms.

Directory markings: Postal indication of failed delivery attempt, stating the reason for failure. Examples are "No Such Number," "Address Unknown" and "Moved."

Duck stamp: Popular name for the United States Migratory Bird Hunting and Conservation stamp, issued for use on hunting licenses. Each annual stamp

depicts waterfowl. Also used to describe similar issues from the various states for use by hunters or for sale to collectors.

Dummy stamp: Officially produced imitation stamp used to train employees or to test automatic stamp-dispensing machines. Dummy stamps are usually blank or carry special inscriptions, blocks or other distinguishing ornamentation. They are not valid for postage, nor are they intended to reach the hands of stamp collectors. Some do by favor of postal employees.

Duplex cancel: A two-part postal marking consisting of a canceler and a postmark. The canceler voids the stamp so it cannot be reused. The postmark notes the date and place of mailing.

Duplicate: An additional copy of a stamp that one already has in a collection. Beginners often consider stamps to be duplicates that really are not, because they overlook perforation, watermark or color varieties.

E

Earliest known use: The cover or piece that documents the earliest date on which a stamp or postal stationery item is known to be used. New discoveries can change an established EKU. The EKU for a classic issue may be after the official issue date. Because of accidental early sales, the EKU for modern stamps is often several days before the official first day.

Embossing: The process of giving relief to paper by pressing it with a die. Embossed designs are often found on the printed stamps of postal stationery (usually envelopes and wrappers). Selected stamps of certain countries have been embossed.

Encased postage stamp: A stamp inserted into a small coin-size case with a transparent front or back. Such stamps were circulated as legal coins during periods when coins were scarce.

Entire: An intact piece of postal stationery, in contrast to a cutout of the imprinted stamp. This term is sometimes used in reference to an intact cover or folded letter.

Error: A major mistake in the production of a stamp or postal stationery item. Production errors include imperforate or imperforate-between varieties, missing or incorrect colors, and inversion or doubling of part of the design or overprint. Major errors are usually far scarcer than normal varieties of the same stamp and are highly valued by collectors.

Essay: The artwork of a proposed design for a stamp. Some essays are rendered photographically. Others are drawn in pencil or ink or are painted. Most essays are rejected. One becomes the essay for the accepted design.

Etiquette: A gummed label manufactured for application to an envelope to designate a specific mail service. Airmail etiquettes are most common.

Europa: The "United Europe" theme celebrated annually on stamps of western European nations since 1956. The original Europa stamps were issued by the nations in the European coal and steel association. Today, European nations that are members of the postal and telecommunications association (CEPT) issue Europa stamps.

Expertization: The examination of a stamp or cover by an acknowledged expert to determine if it is genuine. As standard procedure, an expert or expertizing body issues a signed certificate, often with an attached photograph, attesting to the item's status.

Exploded: A stamp booklet that has been separated into its various components, usually for purposes of display. Panes are removed intact: individual stamps are not separated from the pane.

Express mail: Next-day mail delivery service in the United States, inaugurated in 1977.

EKU: The cover or piece that documents the earliest date on which a stamp or postal stationery item is known to be used. New discoveries can change an established EKU. The EKU for a classic issue may be after the official issue date. Because of accidental early sales, the EKU for modern stamps is often several days before the official first day.

F

Face: The front of a stamp; the side bearing the design.

Face value: The value of a stamp as inscribed on its face. For letter-

denominated or nondenominated stamps, the understood postal value of the stamp.

Facsimile: A reproduction of a genuine stamp or cover. Such items are usually made with no intent to deceive collectors or postal officials. Catalog illustrations may also be considered facsimiles.

Fake: A stamp, cover or cancel that has been altered or concocted to appeal to a collector. In a broad sense, fakes include repairs, reperforations and regummed stamps, as well as painted-in cancels, bogus cancels or counterfeit markings. Sometimes entire covers are faked.

Fancy cancel: A general term to describe any pictorial or otherwise unusual obliterating postmark. More specifically, the term is used to describe elaborate handmade pictorial cancels of the 19th century, such as the Waterbury "Running Chicken" of 1869 or the many intricate geometric shapes used during that period in post offices around the country.

Farley's Follies: During 1933-34, U.S. Postmaster General James A. Farley supplied a few imperforate sheets of current commemorative issues to Pres. Franklin D. Roosevelt and other government officials. The resulting uproar from U.S. collectors forced the government to release for public sale 20 issues in generally imperforate and ungummed sheets. They are United States Scott 752-771. Numbers 752-753 are perforated.

Fast colors: Inks resistant to fading.

Field Post Office: A military postal service operating in the field, either on land or at sea. Frequently abbreviated FPO.

Find: A new discovery, usually of something that was not known to exist. It can be a single item or a hoard of stamps or covers.

First-day cover: A cover bearing a stamp tied by a cancellation showing the date of the official first day of issue of that stamp.

Fiscal: A revenue stamp or similar label denoting the payment of tax. Fiscals are ordinarily affixed to documents and canceled by pen, canceler or mutilation. Because of their similarity to postage stamps, fiscals have occasionally been used either legally or illegally to prepay postage. See also Postal fiscal,

Revenues.

Flat plate: A flat metal plate used in a printing press, as opposed to a curved or cylindrical plate.

Flaw: A defect in a plate that reproduces as an identifiable variety in the stamp design.

Fleet Post Office (FPO): An official United States post office for use by U.S. military naval units abroad. Frequently abbreviated FPO.

Forerunner: A stamp or postal stationery item used in a given location prior to the issuing of regular stamps for that location. Turkish stamps before 1918 canceled in Palestine are forerunners of Israeli issues. So are the various European nations' issues for use in Palestine, and the subsequent issues of the Palestine Mandate. The term "forerunner" is also used to describe a stamp issued before another stamp or set, if the earlier issue may have influenced the design or purpose of the later issue.

Forgery: A completely fraudulent reproduction of a postage stamp. There are two general types of forgeries: those intended to defraud the postal authorities (see also Counterfeit), and those intended to defraud the collectors (see also Bogus).

Frama: A general name used for an automatic stamp, derived from the name of the Swiss firm, Frama AG, an early producer of such issues. Automatic stamps are produced individually by a machine on demand in a denomination selected by the customer. There normally is no date on the stamp, as there is on a meter stamp. Also called ATM, from the German word Automatenmarken.

Frame: The outer portion of a stamp design, often consisting of a line or a group of panels.

Frank: An indication on a cover that postage is prepaid, partially prepaid or that the letter is to be carried free of postage. Franks may be written, hand-stamped, imprinted or affixed. Free franking is usually limited to soldiers' mail or selected government correspondence. Postage stamp and postage meter stamps are modern methods of franking a letter.

Freak: An abnormal, usually nonrepetitive occurrence in the production of stamps that results in a variation from the normal stamp, but falls short of producing an error. Most paper folds, overinking and perforation shifts are freaks. Those abnormalities occurring repetitively are called varieties and may result in major errors.

Front: The front of a cover with most or all of the back and side panels torn away or removed. Fronts, while desirable if they bear unusual or uncommon postal markings, are less desirable than an intact cover.

Fugitive inks: Printing inks used in stamp production that easily fade or break up in water or chemicals. To counter attempts at forgery or the removal of cancellations, many governments have used fugitive inks to print stamps.

FPO: Field Post Office. A military postal service operating in the field, either on land or at sea. Also Fleet Post Office. An official United States post office for use by U.S. military naval units abroad.

FDC: First-day cover. A cover bearing a stamp tied by a cancellation showing the date of the official first day of issue of that stamp.

Franking: An indication on a cover that postage is prepaid, partially prepaid or that the letter is to be carried free of postage. Franks may be written, hand-stamped, imprinted or affixed. Free franking is usually limited to soldiers' mail or selected government correspondence. Postage stamp and postage meter stamps are modern methods of franking a letter.

G

Ghost tagging: The appearance of a faint image impression in addition to the normal inked impression. This is caused by misregistration of the phosphor tagging in relation to the ink. Sometimes, a plate number impression will have an entirely different number from the ink plate, giving the impression of an error: one dark (normal) number and one light (ghost) number.

Glassine: A thin, semitransparent paper that is moderately resistant to the passage of air and moisture. Envelopes made of glassine are commonly used for temporary stamp storage. Glassine is also used in the manufacture of stamp

hinges.

Goldbeater's skin: A thin, tough, translucent paper. The 1886 issue of Prussia was printed in reverse on goldbeater's skin, with the gum applied over the printing. These stamps are brittle and virtually impossible to remove from the paper to which they are affixed.

Granite paper: A paper with small colored fibers added when the paper is made. This paper is used as a deterrent against forgery.

Gravure: A printing process utilizing an intaglio printing plate created by photographic and chemical means, rather than by hand engraving. See also Intaglio.

Grill: A pattern of parallel lines (or dots at the points where lines would cross) forming a grid. A grill is usually: 1) the impressed breaks added to stamps as a security measure (United States issues of 1867-71 and Peru issues of 1874-79); or 2) a grill-like canceling device used on various 19th-century issues.

Gum: The mucilage applied to the backs of adhesive postage stamps, revenue stamps or envelope flaps. Gum is an area of concern for stamp collectors. It may crack and harm the paper of the stamp itself. It may stain or adhere to other stamps or album pages under certain climatic conditions. Many collectors are willing to pay extra for 19th- and some 20th-century stamps with intact, undisturbed original gum.

Gutter: The selvage separating panes on a sheet of stamps. The gutter is usually discarded during processing. The gutter may be unprinted, or bear plate numbers, accounting or control numbers, advertising or other words or markings.

Gutter snipe: One or more stamps to which is attached the full gutter from between panes, plus any amount of an adjoining stamp or stamps. This term is typically used in reference to U.S. stamps. Gutter snipes are freaks caused by misregistration of the cutting device or paper foldover.

H

Handstamp: Cancellation or overprint applied by hand to a cover or to a stamp.

Highway Post Office (HPO): Portable mail-handling equipment for sorting mail in transit on highways (normally by

truck). The last official U.S. HPO ran June 30, 1974.

Hinge: Stamp hinges are small, rectangular-shaped pieces of glassine paper, usually gummed on one side. Folded with the gummed side out, the hinge is used to mount stamps. Most modern hinges are peelable. Once dry, they may be easily removed from the stamp, leaving little trace of having been applied.

HPO: Highway Post Office. Portable mail-handling equipment for sorting mail in transit on highways (normally by truck). The last official U.S. HPO ran June 30, 1974.

I

Imperforate: Refers to stamps without perforations or rouletting between the individual stamps in a pane. The earliest stamps were imperforate by design, but after about 1860 most stamps were perforated. Modern imperforates are usually errors or are produced specifically for sale to stamp collectors.

Impression: Any stamped or embossed printing.

Imprimatur: Latin for "let it be printed." The first sheets of stamps from an approved plate, normally checked and retained in a file prior to a final directive to begin stamp production from a plate.

India paper: A thin, tough opaque printing paper of high quality used primarily for striking die proofs.

Indicium: The stamp impression of a postage meter or the imprint on postal stationery (as opposed to an adhesive stamp), indicating prepayment and postal validity. Plural: indicia.

Inscription: The letters, words and numbers that are part of a postage stamp design.

Intaglio: Italian for "in recess." A form of printing in which the inked image is produced by that portion of the plate sunk below the surface. Line engraving and gravure are forms of intaglio printing.

International Reply Coupon: A redeemable certificate issued by member nations of the Universal Postal Union to provide for return postage from recipients in other countries. IRCs are exchangeable for postage at a post office.

Invert: The term generally used to describe any error where one portion of the design is inverted in relation to the other portion(s). An overprint applied upside down is also an invert.

Inverts: The term generally used to describe any error where one portion of the design is inverted in relation to the other portion(s). An overprint applied upside down is also an invert.

IRC: International Reply Coupon. A redeemable certificate issued by member nations of the Universal Postal Union to provide for return postage from recipients in other countries. IRCs are exchangeable for postage at a post office.

J

None

K

Keytype: A basic stamp design utilized for the issues of two or more postal entities, usually differing in the country name and inscription of value. Many of the earlier colonial issues of Britain, France, Spain, Germany and Portugal are keytypes.

Kiloware: A stamp mixture consisting of miscellaneous postally used stamps on envelope corner paper from various sources. Kiloware is sometimes sold by the kilogram (about 2.2 pounds).

L

Label: Any stamplike adhesive that is not a postage stamp or revenue stamp.

Laid paper: One of the two basic types of paper used in stamp printing. Laid paper is distinguished from wove paper by the presence of thin, parallel lines visible when the paper is held to light. The lines are usually a few millimeters apart. See also Batonne.

Letterpress: Printing done directly from the inked, raised surface of the printing plate.

Line engraving: Printing done from an intaglio plate produced from a hand-engraved die and transfer roll rather than by photographic or chemical means. See also Gravure.

Line pair: A pair of coil stamps with a printed line between them. Stamps produced on a flatbed press have a line from the guideline between panes. Stamps produced on a rotary press have a joint line from the space where ink collects between the sections of curved rotary plates.

Liner: Coated paper used as a backing for mint self-adhesive stamps. The liner allows the release of the stamp, which may then be applied with pressure to envelope paper.

Linerless: An experimental form of self-adhesive coil stamp that requires no liner. The mint stamps are rolled upon each other in a manner similar to adhesive tape. See United States Scott 3132, 3133.

Lithography: Printing from a flat surface with a design area that is ink-receptive. The area that is not to print is ink-repellant. The process is based on the principle that an oil-based design surface will attract oily ink.

Locals: Stamps valid within a limited area or within a limited postal system. Local post mail requires the addition of nationally or internationally valid stamps for further service. Locals have been produced both privately and officially.

M

Machin: The name given to a well-known series of British definitive stamps first issued in 1967. The design of the stamp depicts a plaster portrait of Queen Elizabeth II created by artist Arnold Machin.

Mail Early block: U.S. marginal marking block with the selvage bearing the inscription "Mail Early (in the Day)." This first appeared on U.S. marginal selvage in 1968. It was subsequently replaced by the copyright notice. ME blocks typically consist of four or six stamps.

Makeshift booklets: U.S. stamp booklets manufactured using stamps normally issued in individual panes, packaged in generic blue cardboard covers and dispensed by vending machines.

Marcophily: Postmark collecting.

Margin: 1) The selvage surrounding the stamps in a sheet, often carrying inscriptions of various kinds. 2) The unprinted border area around the stamp design. The collectible grades of stamps are determined by the position of the design in relation to the edge of the stamp as perforated or, in the case of imperforate stamps, as cut from the sheet.

Mat: A hard rubber plate used to apply overprints on postage stamps.

Maximaphily: Maximum card collecting.

Maximum card: A picture postcard, a cancel, and a stamp presenting maximum concordance. The stamp is usually affixed to the picture side of the card and is tied by the cancel. Collectors of maximum cards seek to find or create cards with stamp, cancel and picture in maximum agreement, or concordance. The statutes of the International Federation of Philately (FIP) give specific explanatory notes for the postage stamp, the picture postcard, the cancel, concordance of subject, concordance of place and concordance of time. (See Exhibiting chapter.)

Meter: The mechanical or digital device that creates a valid denominated postage imprint known as a meter stamp. Postage is prepaid to the regulating postal authority. Meters were authorized by the UPU in 1920. They are used today by volume mailers to cut the cost of franking mail.

Microprinting: Extremely small letters or numbers added to the designs of selected United States stamps as a security feature. In most cases, 8-power magnification or greater is needed to read microprinting.

Miniature sheet: A smaller-than-normal pane of stamps issued only in that form or in addition to full panes. A miniature sheet is usually without marginal markings or text saying that the sheet was issued in conjunction with or to commemorate some event. See also Souvenir sheet.

Mint: A stamp in the same state as issued by a post office: unused, undamaged and with full original gum (if issued with gum). Over time, handling, light and atmospheric conditions may affect the mint state of stamps.

Mirror image: An offset negative or reverse impression.

Mission mixture: The lowest grade of stamp mixture, containing unsorted but primarily common stamps on paper, as purchased from missions or other institutions. See also Bank mixture.

Missionaries: The first stamps of Hawaii, issued 1851-52, considered among the great classics of philately.

Mixed perforation: See Compound perforation.

Mixed postage: The franking on a cover bearing the stamps of two or more stamp-issuing entities, properly used.

Mixture: A large group of stamps, understood to contain duplication. A mixture is said to be unpicked or picked. A picked mixture may have had stamps removed by a collector or dealer.

Mobile Post Office: Portable mail-handling equipment and personnel, generally in railroad cars, streetcars, trucks or buses.

Mount: Acetate holders, clear on the front and with some sort of adhesive on the back. Collectors use mounts to affix stamps or covers to album or exhibit pages.

Multicolor: More than two colors.

Multiple: An unseparated unit of stamps including at least two stamps, but fewer than the number included in a full pane.

ME block: U.S. marginal marking block with the selvage bearing the inscription "Mail Early (in the Day)." This first appeared on U.S. marginal selvage in 1968. It was subsequently replaced by the copyright notice. ME blocks typically consist of four or six stamps.

MPO: Mobile Post Office. Portable mail-handling equipment and personnel, generally in railroad cars, streetcars, trucks or buses.

N

Native paper: Crude, handmade paper produced locally, as opposed to finer, machine-made paper.

Never hinged: A stamp without hinge marks. A never-hinged (NH) stamp usually has original gum, but this is not always the case.

New issue service: A dealer service that automatically supplies subscribers with new issues of a given country, area or topic. The issues provided are determined by a prearranged standing order that defines the quantity and types of issues.

Newspaper stamps: Stamps issued specifically for the prepayment of mailing rates for newspapers, periodicals and printed matter.

Nondenominated: A stamp with no numerical inscription designating the face value. The value of some nondenominated stamps are marked by a designated letter. Others may have a service inscription that indicates the rate the stamp fulfills.

NH: Never Hinged. A stamp without hinge marks. A never-hinged (NH) stamp usually has original gum, but this is not always the case.

O

Obliteration: 1) A cancellation intended solely to deface a stamp-also called a killer. 2) An overprint intended to deface a portion of the design of a stamp, such as the face of a deposed ruler.

Obsolete: A stamp no longer available from post offices, although possibly still postally valid.

Occupation issue: An issue released for use in territory occupied by a foreign power.

Off-center: A stamp design that is not centered in relation to the edges of the stamp. Generally, off-center stamps are less desirable than stamps more nearly centered in relation to the edges. Stamps that are extremely off-center may be added to collections as production freaks.

Offices abroad: At various times, many nations have maintained post offices in other countries, usually because of the unreliability of the local postal system. In China and the Turkish Empire, especially, many foreign nations maintained their own postal systems as part of their extraterritorial powers. Usually, special stationery and stamps were used by these offices. Most consisted of overprints on the regular issues of the nations maintaining the offices.

Official: Stamp or stationery issued solely for the use of government departments and officials. In many countries such items may be available to collectors in unused condition from the postal authority.

Offset: 1) A printing process that transfers an inked image from a plate to a roller. The roller then applies the ink to paper. 2) The transfer of part of a stamp design or an overprint from one sheet to the back of another, before the ink has dried (also called set off). Such impressions are in reverse (see Mirror image). They are different from stamps printed on both sides.

OHMS: Abbreviation for On His (or Her) Majesty's Service. Used in perfins, overprints or franks to indicate Official use in the British Commonwealth.

Omnibus issue: An issue released by several postal entities to celebrate a common theme. Omnibus issues may or may not share a keytype design.

On paper: Stamps (usually postally used) that are affixed to portions of original envelope or wrapper. Often used to describe stamps prior to soaking.

On piece: A stamp on a portion of the original envelope or wrapper showing all or most of the cancel. Stamps on piece are usually saved that way.

Original gum (OG): The adhesive coating on a mint or unused stamp or envelope flap applied by a postal authority or security printer, usually before the item was issued. Upon request of stamp collectors, postal authorities have at times offered to add gum to items first issued ungummed. See also Regummed.

Overprint: Any printing over the original completed design of a stamp. An overprint that changes the value of a stamp is also called a surcharge.

Oxidation: Darkening of the ink on certain stamps caused by contact with air or light. Some inks used to print stamps, especially oranges, may in time turn brown or black.

P

Packet: 1) A presorted selection of all-different stamps, a common and economical way to begin a general collection; 2) a ship operating on a regular schedule and contracted by a government or post office to carry mail.

Packet letter: A letter carried by a ship operating on a regular schedule and carrying mail by contract with a government or a post office.

Pair: Two unseparated stamps.

Pane: The unit into which a full press

sheet is divided before sale at post offices. What a post office customer may refer to as a "sheet of stamps" is more properly called a pane. Most United States full sheets are divided into four or more regular panes or many more booklet panes before they are shipped to post offices.

Paquebot: Cancellation indicating an item was mailed aboard a ship.

Par Avion: A French phrase meaning "By Air," it appears on airmail etiquettes of most countries, along with a similar phrase in the predominant language of the country of origin.

Parcel post stamps: Special stamps created for payment of parcel post fees.

Part-perforate: A stamp with all perforations missing on one or more sides, but with at least one side perforated.

Paste-up: The ends of rolls of coiled stamps joined together with glue or tape.

Pelure paper: A strong, thin paper occasionally used in stamp printing. Pelure paper is translucent and resembles a slightly dark, thin onion-skin paper.

Pen canceled: Stamps canceled with an ink pen or marker pen rather than a handstamp or machine cancel. Many early stamps were routinely canceled by pen. A pen cancel may also indicate that a stamp was used as a fiscal. Modern stamps may be pen canceled if a sorting clerk or delivery carrier notices a stamp has been missed by a canceling machine.

Penny Black: The black 1-penny British stamp issued May 6, 1840, bearing the portrait of Queen Victoria. It is the world's first adhesive stamp issued for the prepayment of postage.

Perfins: Stamps perforated through the face with identifying initials, designs or holes in coded positions. Perfins are normally used by a business or government office to discourage pilferage or misuse of stamps by employees. Perfins may be either privately or officially produced.

Perforation: The punching out of holes between stamps to make separation easy. 1) Comb perforation-three sides of a stamp are perforated at once, with the process repeated in rows. 2) Harrow perforation-the entire sheet or unit of stamps is perforated in one operation. 3) Line perforation-holes are punched one row at a time. Line perforations are distinguished by the uneven crossing of perforation lines and irregular corners. Comb and harrow perforations usually show alignment of holes at the corners. Some forms of perforation may be difficult to distinguish.

Perforation gauge: A scale printed or designed on metal, transparent or opaque plastic, cardboard or other material to measure the number of perforation holes or teeth within the space of 2 centimeters.

Permit: Franking by the imprint of a number and additional information that identifies a mailer's prepaid postage account, thereby eliminating the need to affix and cancel stamps on large mailings. The mailer must obtain a document (permit) that authorizes his use of this procedure.

Phantom philately: The collection of bogus stamps. The name is derived from Frederick Melville's book *Phantom Philately*, one of the pioneer works on bogus issues.

Philatelic cover: An envelope, postal card or other item franked and mailed by a stamp collector to create a collectible object. It may or may not have carried a personal or business message. A nonphilatelic cover is usually one that has carried business or personal correspondence and has had its stamps applied by a noncollector. Some stamps are known only on collector-created covers. It is impossible to say whether some covers are philatelically inspired or not. See also Used and Postally used.

Philately: The collection and study of postage stamps, postal stationery and postal history.

Phosphor: A chemical substance used in the production of selected stamps to activate machines that automatically cancel mail. The machines react to the phosphor under ultraviolet light. In 1959, Great Britain began to print phosphor lines on some of its stamps. See also Tagging.

Photogravure: A modern stamp-printing process that is a form of intaglio printing. Plates are made photographically and chemically, rather than by hand engraving a die and transferring it to a plate. The ink in this process rests in the design depressions. The surface of the printing plate is wiped clean. The paper is forced into the depressions and picks up the ink, in a manner much like the line-engraved printing process.

Pictorial: Stamp bearing a picture of some sort, other than a portrait or coat of arms.

Plate: The basic printing unit on a press used to produce stamps. Early stamps were printed from flat plates. Curved or cylindrical plates are used for most modern stamps. See also Cylinder and Sleeve.

Plate block: A block of stamps from the corner or side of a pane including the selvage bearing the number(s) of the plate(s) used to print the sheet from which the pane was separated. Some stamp production methods, like booklet production, normally cut off plate numbers. In the United States, plate number blocks are collected normally as blocks of four to 20 stamps, depending on the press used to print the stamps. When each stamp in a pane is a different design, the entire pane is collected as the plate block.

Plate number: Numerals or an alphanumeric combination that identifies the printing plate used to print postage stamp images. In the United States, plate numbers on sheet stamps often appear in corner margin paper or side margin paper. Plate numbers on coil stamps were commonly trimmed off until about 1980; since then the number appears on stamps at specific intervals. Booklet plate numbers are often found on selvage attached to the pane.

Plating: The reconstruction of a stamp pane by collecting blocks and individual stamps representing various positions. This is possible for many older issues, but most modern issues are too uniform to make the identification of individual positions possible.

Plebiscite issue: A stamp issue promoting a popular vote. After World War I, a number of disputed areas were placed under temporary League of Nations administration, pending plebiscites to determine which nation the populace wished to join. Special issues note the upcoming vote in several of these areas; among them, Allenstein, Carinthia, Eastern Silesia, Marienwerder, Schleswig and Upper Silesia.

PNC: 1) A plate number coil stamp; that is, a stamp from a coil that is inscribed with a plate number. The abbreviations PNC3 and PNC5 identify strips of three or five coil stamps with the PNC located in the center position of the strip. 2) A philatelic-numismatic combination: a cover bearing a stamp and containing a coin, medal or token. The coin and stamp are usually related in such cases; often the cover is canceled on the first day of use of the coin.

Pneumatic post: Letter distribution through pressurized air tubes. Pneumatic posts existed in many large cities in Europe, and special stamps and stationery were often produced for the service.

Postage dues: Stamps or markings indicating that insufficient postage has been affixed to the mailing piece. Postage dues are usually affixed at the office of delivery. The additional postage is collected from the addressee.

Postal card: A government-produced postcard bearing a stamp imprint in the upper-right corner representing prepayment of postage.

Postal fiscal: Revenue or fiscal stamps used postally.

Postal history: The study of postal markings, rates and routes, or anything to do with the history of the posts.

Postal stationery: Stationery bearing imprinted stamps, as opposed to adhesive stamps. Postal stationery includes postal cards, lettercards, stamped envelopes, wrappers, aerograms, telegraph cards, postal savings forms and similar government-produced items. The cost to the mailer is often the price of postage plus an additional charge for the stationery item.

Postally used: A stamp or cover that has seen legitimate postal use, as opposed to one that has been canceled-to-order or favor-canceled. The term "postally used" suggests that an item exists because it was used to carry a personal or business communication, without the sender thinking of creating an item to be collected.

Postcard: A small card, usually with a picture on one side and a space for a written message on the other. Postcards have no imprinted stamp, so the mailer must also purchase postage to mail the postcard. See also Postal card.

Postmark: Any official postal marking. The term is usually used specifically in reference to cancellations bearing the name of a post office of origin and a mailing date.

Precancel: Stamp with a special overprint cancellation allowing it to bypass normal canceling. In some cases the precancel also designates a specific mail-handling service, such as "Presorted First-Class." Other precancels may include the city and state of the issuing post office. Precanceled stamps are used by volume mailers who hold a permit to use them. U.S. precancels fall into two categories: 1) Locals have the mark or text applied by a town or city post office; 2) Bureaus have the mark or text applied by the U.S. Bureau of Engraving and Printing. See also Service inscribed.

Prestamp covers: Folded letters or their outer enclosures used before the introduction of adhesive postage stamps or postal stationery.

Prestige booklet: A stamp booklet with oversized panes, descriptive information and stamp issues commemorating a special topic. Prestige booklets often include panes with no stamps that instead bear labels or additional information, along with panes bearing stamps.

Prexies: The nickname for the U.S. 1938-54 Presidential definitive series, Scott 803-34, 839-51.

Printer's waste: Misprinted, misperforated or misgummed stamps often created during the normal process of stamp production. Printer's waste is supposed to be destroyed, but such material enters the philatelic market through carelessness and theft.

Printing: The process of imprinting designs on paper from an inked surface.

Processing: Steps that finish a printed stamp sheet. Processing includes perforation, trimming, dividing the sheet into individual panes, and packaging for distribution.

Pro Juventute: Latin, meaning for the benefit of youth. Switzerland has issued Pro Juventute semipostals nearly every year since 1913.

Proofs: Trial impressions from a die or printing plate before actual stamp production. Proofs are made to examine a die or plate for defects or to compare the results of using different inks.

Provisional: A postage stamp issued for temporary use to meet postal demands until new or regular stocks of stamps can be obtained.

Plate number block: A block of stamps from the corner or side of a pane including the selvage bearing the number(s) of the plate(s) used to print the sheet from which the pane was separated. Some stamp production methods, like booklet production, normally cut off plate numbers. In the United States, plate number blocks are collected normally as blocks of four to 20 stamps, depending on the press used to print the stamps. When each stamp in a pane is a different design, the entire pane is collected as the plate block.

Press sheet: A complete unit of stamps as printed. Stamps are usually printed in large sheets and are separated into two or more panes before shipment to post offices.

Q

Quadripartition: A block or strip of four stamps that together complete a single entire design. See United States Scott 1448-51, the 1972 Cape Hatteras National Seashore issue.

R

Railway Post Office: Portable mail-handling equipment for sorting mail in transit on trains. The last official U.S. RPO ran June 30, 1977. RPOs were used in many countries. See also Mobile Post Office.

Receiving mark: A postmark or other postal marking applied by the receiving, rather than the originating, post office. See also Backstamp.

Redrawn: A stamp design that has been slightly altered yet maintains the basic design as originally issued.

Re-engraved: A stamp with an altered design as the result of a change made to a transfer roll or printing plate prior to a later printing, thereby distinguishing it from the original die.

Regional: Stamp sold or valid in a specific area of a stamp-issuing entity. Great Britain has issued stamps for the regions of Guernsey, Jersey, Isle of

Man, Northern Ireland, Scotland and Wales. Regionals are usually sold only in a given region but are often valid for postage throughout a country.

Registered mail: First-class mail with a numbered receipt, including a valuation of the registered item, for full or limited compensation if the mail is lost. Some countries have issued registered mail stamps. Registered mail is signed for by each postal employee who handles it.

Registration labels: Adhesive labels indicating the registry number and, often, the city of origin for registered articles sent through the mail.

Regummed: A stamp bearing adhesive from an unauthorized source.

Reissue: An official reprinting of a stamp from an obsolete or discontinued issue. Reissues are valid for postage. See also Reprint.

Remainders: Stocks of stamps remaining unsold at the time that an issue is declared obsolete by a post office. Some countries have sold remainders to the stamp trade at substantial discounts from face value. The countries normally mark the stamps with a distinctive cancel. Uncanceled remainders usually cannot be distinguished from stamps sold over the counter before the issue was invalidated.

Repaired stamp: A damaged stamp that has been repaired in some way to reinforce it or to make it resemble an undamaged stamp.

Replica: A reproduction of a stamp or cover. In the 19th century, replica stamps were sold as stamp album space fillers. Replica stamps are often printed in one color in a sheet containing a number of different designs. Replicas can sometimes deceive either a postal clerk or collectors.

Reprint: A stamp printed from the original plate, after the issue has ceased to be postally valid. Official reprints are sometimes made for presentation purposes or official collections. They are often distinguishable in some way from the originals: different colors, perforations, paper or gum. Private reprints, on the other hand, are usually produced strictly for sale to collectors and often closely resemble the original stamps. Private reprints normally sell for less than original copies. Reprints are

not valid for postage. See also Reissue.

Retouch: The repairing of a damaged plate or die, often producing a minor, but detectable, difference in the design of the printed stamps.

Revenues: Stamps representing the prepayment or payment of various taxes. Revenues are affixed to official documents and to merchandise. Some stamps, including many issues of the British Commonwealth, are inscribed "Postage and Revenue" and were available for either use. Such issues are usually worth less fiscally canceled than postally used. In some cases, revenues have been used provisionally as postage stamps. See also Fiscal.

Rocket mail: Mail flown in a rocket, even if only a short distance. Many rocket mail experiments have been conducted since 1931. Special labels, cachets or cancels usually note that mail was carried on a rocket.

Rotary plate: A curved or cylindrical printing plate used on a press that rotates the plate to make continuous impressions. Flat plates make single impressions.

Rouletting: The piercing of the paper between stamps to make their separation more convenient. No paper is actually removed from the sheet, as it is in perforating. Rouletting has been made by dash, sawtooth or wavy line.

Rural Free Delivery: System for free home delivery of mail in rural areas of the United States, begun just prior to the turn of the 20th century.

Rust: A brown mold resembling the rust in iron. Rust affects stamp paper and gum in tropical regions.

RPO: Railway Post Office. Portable mail-handling equipment for sorting mail in transit on trains. The last official U.S. RPO ran June 30, 1977. RPOs were used in many countries. See also Mobile Post Office.

RFD: Rural Free Delivery. System for free home delivery of mail in rural areas of the United States, begun just prior to the turn of the 20th century.

S

SASE: A self-addressed, stamped envelope. An unused envelope bearing the address of the sender and

sufficient return postage. Enclosed with correspondence to make answering easy.

Secret mark: A minute alteration to a stamp design added to distinguish later printings from earlier printings by a different firm. Secret marks may positively distinguish genuine stamps from counterfeits.

Seebeck: The nickname for various Latin American issues produced 1890-99 in contract with Nicholas Frederick Seebeck, the agent for the Hamilton Bank Note Co. of New York. Seebeck agreed to provide new issues of stamps and stationery each year at no charge, in return for the right to sell remainders and reprints to collectors. The resulting furor destroyed Seebeck and blackened the philatelic reputations of the countries involved.

Self-adhesive: Stamp gum that adheres to envelope paper by the application of pressure alone. Most self-adhesive stamps are sold on a coated paper release liner. See also Liner, Linerless, Water-activated.

Selvage: The marginal paper on a sheet or pane of stamps. Selvage may be unprinted or may contain printer's markings or other information.

Semipostal: A stamp sold at a price greater than postal value, with the additional charge dedicated for a special purpose. Usually recognized by the presence of two (often different) values, separated by a "+" sign, on a single stamp.

Series: A group of stamps with a similar design or theme, issued over a period of time. A series may be planned or may evolve.

Service inscribed: A stamp with wording as part of the initial printed design that identifies the mail-handling service for which the stamp is intended, such as "Presorted First-Class." See also Precancel.

Set: Stamps sharing common design elements, often issued at one time and usually collected as a group.

Se-tenant: French for "joined together." Two or more unseparated stamps of different designs, colors, denominations or types.

Shade: The minor variation commonly

found in any basic color. Shades may be accorded catalog status when they are very distinctive.

Sheet: A complete unit of stamps as printed. Stamps are usually printed in large sheets and are separated into two or more panes before shipment to post offices.

Ship letter: Mail carried by private ship.

Short set: An incomplete set of stamps, usually lacking either the high value or one or more key values.

Sleeper: Stamp or other collectible item that seems to be underpriced and may have good investment potential.

Sleeve: 1) A seamless cylindrical printing plate used in rotary intaglio printing. 2) A flat transparent holder, often specifically for protecting and storing a cover.

Soaking: Removal of stamps from envelope paper. Most stamps may be safely soaked in water. Fugitive inks, however, will run in water, and chalky-surfaced papers will lose their designs entirely, so some knowledge of stamps is a necessity. Colored envelope paper should be soaked separately.

Souvenir card: A philatelic card, not valid for postage, issued in conjunction with some special event. The souvenir card often illustrates the design of a postage stamp.

Souvenir page: An announcement of a new United States stamp issue created by the U.S. Postal Service, bearing a copy of the new stamp tied by a first day of issue cancellation.

Souvenir sheet: A small sheet of stamps, including one value or a set of stamps. A souvenir sheet usually has a wide margin and an inscription describing an event being commemorated. Stamps on a souvenir sheet may be perforated or imperforate.

Space filler: A stamp in poor condition used to fill the designated space in a stamp album until a better copy can be found.

Special delivery: A service providing expedited delivery of mail. Called Express by some nations.

Special handling: A U.S. service providing expeditious handling for fourth-class material.

Special printing: Reissue of a stamp of current or recent design, often with distinctive color, paper or perforations.

Specialist: A stamp collector who intensively studies and collects the stamps and postal history of a given country, area, or time period, or who has otherwise limited his collecting field.

Special stamps: Regular postage stamp issues that fall outside the traditional definitions of commemorative and definitive stamps. In the United States, holiday issues such as Contemporary Christmas, Traditional Christmas, Hanukkah and the like are considered special stamps. They are printed in substantially greater quantities than commemorative stamps, and sometimes return to press for additional printings. Love stamps are also considered special stamps.

Specimen: Stamp or stationery item distributed to Universal Postal Union members for identification purposes and to the philatelic press and trade for publicity purposes. Specimens are overprinted or punched with the word "SPECIMEN" or its equivalent, or are overprinted or punched in a way to make them different from the issued stamps. Specimens of scarce stamps tend to be less valuable than the actual stamps. Specimens of relatively common stamps are more valuable.

Speculative issue: A stamp or issue released primarily for sale to collectors, rather than to meet any legitimate postal need.

Splice: The repair of a break in a roll of stamp paper, or the joining of two rolls of paper for continuous printing. Stamps printed over a splice are usually removed and destroyed before the normal stamps are issued.

Stamp: An officially issued postage label, often adhesive, attesting that payment has been rendered for mail delivery. Initially used as a verb, meaning to imprint or impress; as in, to stamp a design.

Stampless cover: A folded sheet or envelope carried as mail without a postage stamp. This term usually refers to covers predating the requirement that stamps be affixed to all letters (in the United States, 1856).

Stock book: A specially manufactured

blank book containing rows of pockets on each page to hold stamps.

Straight edge: Flat-plate or rotary-plate stamps from the margins of panes where the sheets were cut apart. Straight-edge stamps have no perforations on one or two adjacent sides. Sometimes straight-edge stamps show a guideline.

Strip: Three or more unseparated stamps in a row, vertically or horizontally.

Surcharge: An overprint that changes or restates the denomination of a stamp or postal stationery item.

Surface-colored paper: Paper colored on the surface only, with a white or uncolored back.

Surtax: The portion of a semipostal stamp purchase price exceeding the postage value. The surtax is designated for donation to a charity or some other purpose.

Sweatbox: A closed box containing dampened spongelike material, over which stuck-together unused stamps are placed on a grill. Humidity softens the gum, allowing separation of stamps. In some cases, the sweatbox may be used to help remove a postally used stamp from envelope paper.

T

T: Abbreviation for the French "Taxe." Handstamped on a stamp, the T indicates the stamp's use as a postage due. Handstamped on a cover, it indicates that postage due has been charged. Several countries have used regular stamps with a perforated initial T as postage dues.

Tagging: Phosphor material on stamps used to activate automatic mail-handling equipment. This may be lines, bars, letters, part of the design area or the entire stamp surface. The tagging may also permeate the stamp paper. Some stamps are issued both with and without tagging. Catalogs describe them as tagged or untagged.

Teeth: The protruding points along the outer edge of a perforated postage stamp when it has been removed from the pane.

Telegraph stamp: Label used for the prepayment of telegraph fees. Telegraph stamps resemble postage stamps.

Tete-beche: French for "head to tail." Two or more unsevered stamps, one of which is inverted in relation to the other.

Thematic: A collection of stamps or covers relating to a specific topic. The topic is expanded by careful inquiry and is presented as a logical story. See also Topical.

Tied: A stamp is said to be tied to a cover when the cancel extends over both the stamp and the envelope paper. Stamps can also be tied by the aging of the mucilage or glue that holds them to the paper.

Tong: Tweezerlike tool with rounded, polished tips, used to handle stamps. Tongs prevent stamps from being soiled by dirt, oil or perspiration.

Topical: 1) Stamp or cover showing a given subject. Examples are flowers, art, birds, elephants or the Statue of Liberty. 2) The collection of stamps by the topic depicted on them, rather than by country of origin. See also Thematic.

Transit mark: A postal marking applied by a post office between the originating and receiving post offices. It can be on the front or back of a cover, card or wrapper.

Triptych: A se-tenant strip of three related stamps forming one overall design. See United States Scott 1629-31, the 1976 Spirit of 76 issue.

Type: A basic design of a stamp or a set. Catalogs use type numbers or letters to save space. Catalogs show a typical design of one type rather than every stamp with that design or a similar design.

U

Underprint: A fine printing underlying the design of a stamp, most often used to deter counterfeiting.

Ungummed: A stamp without gum. Ungummed stamps are either stamps issued without gum or an uncanceled gummed stamp that has had its gum soaked off. Many countries in tropical climates have issued stamps without gum.

Unhinged: A stamp without hinge marks, but not necessarily with original gum.

Universal Postal Union: An international organization formed in Bern, Switzerland, in 1874, to regulate and standardize postal usage and to facilitate the movement of mail between member nations. Today, most nations belong to the UPU. (See UPU section of this almanac.)

Unused: An uncanceled stamp that has not been used but has a hinge mark or some other characteristic or defect that keeps it from being considered a mint stamp. Uncanceled stamps without gum may have been used and missed being canceled, or they may have lost their gum by accident.

Used: A stamp or stationery item that has been canceled by a postal authority to prevent its reuse on mail. In general, a used stamp is any stamp with a cancel or a precanceled stamp without gum. See also Postally Used and Philatelic Cover.

UPU: Universal Postal Union. An international organization formed in Bern, Switzerland, in 1874, to regulate and standardize postal usage and to facilitate the movement of mail between member nations. Today, most nations belong to the UPU.

V

Variety: A variation from the standard form of a stamp. Varieties include different watermarks, inverts, imperforates, missing colors, wrong colors and major color shifts. See also Freak, Error.

Vignette: The central part of a stamp design, usually surrounded by a border. In some cases the vignette shades off gradually into the surrounding area.

W

Want list: A list of needed stamps or covers, identified by catalog number or some other description, submitted by a collector to a dealer, usually including requirements on condition and price.

Water-activated adhesive: Stamp gum designed to adhere to envelope paper only if the gum is moistened. All gummed stamps before 1963 used water-activated adhesive.

Watermark: A deliberate thinning of paper during its manufacture to produce a semitranslucent pattern. Watermarks appear frequently in paper used in stamp printing or envelope manufacture. See also Batonne.

Web: A continuous roll of paper used in stamp printing.

Wing margin: Early British stamps from the side of a pane with selvage attached. British sheets printed before 1880 were perforated down the center of the gutter, producing oversized margins on one side of stamps adjacent to the gutter. Such copies are distinctive and scarcer than normal copies.

Wove paper: A paper showing few differences in texture and thickness when held to light. In the production of wove paper, the pulp is pressed against a very fine netting, producing a virtually uniform texture. Wove paper is the most commonly used paper in stamp production.

Wrapper: A flat sheet or strip open at both ends that can be folded and sealed around a newspaper or periodical. Wrappers can have an imprinted stamp or have a stamp attached.

X

None

Y

None

Z

Zemstvo: A local stamp issued by Russian municipal governments or zemstvos, in accordance with an imperial edict of 1870.

Zeppelins: The stamps issued for, or in honor of, zeppelin flights. Cacheted covers carried on such flights are Zeppelin covers.

ZIP block: U.S. marginal marking block with the selvage bearing the image of the "Mr. ZIP" cartoon character and/or an inscription urging the use of ZIP code. This first appeared on U.S. marginal selvage in 1964. Typically a ZIP block is a block of four stamps.

ZIP code: The U.S. numerical post code used to speed and mechanize mail handling and delivery. The letters stand for Zoning Improvement Plan.

INDEX AND IDENTIFIER

All page numbers shown are
those in this Volume 5B.
Postage stamps that do not have
English words on them are shown
in the Illustrated Identifier.

A & T ovptd. on French
  Colonies .... Vol. 1A
Aberdeen, Miss. .... Vol. 1A
Abingdon, Va. .... Vol. 1A
Abu Dhabi .... Vol. 1A, Vol. 5A, Vol. 6B
Abyssinia (Ethiopia) .... Vol. 2B
A.C.C.P., A.D.C.P. .... Vol. 1B
A Certo ovptd. on stamps
  of Peru .... Vol. 5A
Acores .... 190, Vol. 1B
Aden .... Vol. 1A
AEF .... Vol. 2B
Aegean Islands (Greek
  Occupation) .... Vol. 3A
Aegean Islands (Italian
  Occupation) .... Vol. 3B
Aeroport International de Kandahar
  (Afghanistan #679) .... Vol. 1A
Afars and Issas .... Vol. 1A
AFF EXCEP .... Vol. 2B
Afghanistan, Afghan, Afghanes ... Vol. 1A
AFR 285
Africa, British Offices .... Vol. 3A
Africa, German East .... Vol. 3A
Africa, German Offices .... Vol. 3A
Africa, German South-West .... Vol. 3A
Africa, Italian Offices .... Vol. 3B
Africa Occidental Espanola .... Vol. 6A
Africa Orientale Italiana .... Vol. 3B
Africa, Portuguese 199
Afrique Equatoriale Francaise ... Vol. 2A,
  Vol. 2B, Vol. 4B, Vol. 6B
Afrique Francaise .... Vol. 2B
Afrique Occidentale Francaise ... Vol. 2B
Agion Oros Athoc (Greece) .... Vol. 3A
Aguera, La .... Vol. 1A
Aguinaldo .... Vol. 5A
AHA (Confed. #44X1) .... Vol. 1A
Aimeliik (Palau #686) .... Vol. 5A
Airai (Palau #686) .... Vol. 5A
Aitutaki .... Vol. 1A
Ajman .... Vol. 1A, Vol. 6B
Aland Islands .... Vol. 1A
Alaouites .... Vol. 1A
Albania .... Vol. 1A
Albania, Greek Occupation .... Vol. 3A
Albania, Italian Offices .... Vol. 3B
Albany, Ga. .... Vol. 1A
Alderney .... Vol. 3A
Aleppo .... Vol. 6A
Alerta ovptd. on stamps of Peru ... Vol. 5A
Alexandretta, Alexandrette .... Vol. 1A
Alexandria, Alexandrie, French
  Offices .... Vol. 2B
Alexandria, Va. .... Vol. 1A
Alexandroupolis .... Vol. 3A
Algeria, Algerie .... Vol. 1A
Allemagne Duitschland .... Vol. 3A
Allenstein .... Vol. 1A
Allied Military Government
  (Austria) .... Vol. 1B
Allied Military Gov. (Germany) ..... Vol. 3A
Allied Military Government
  (Italy) .... Vol. 3B
Allied Military Government
  (Trieste) .... Vol. 3B
Allied Occupation of Azerbaijan .... Vol. 3B
Allied Occupation of Thrace .... Vol. 6B
A L'Ocassion de la Journée
  Internationale de l'Alphabetisation
  (Afghan. #951) .... Vol. 1A
Alsace .... Vol. 2B
Alsace and Lorraine .... Vol. 2B
Alwar .... Vol. 1B
A.M.G. .... Vol. 1B, Vol. 3A, Vol. 3B
A.M.G./F.T.T. .... Vol. 3B
A.M.G./V.G. .... Vol. 3B
AM Post .... Vol. 3A
Anatolia .... Vol. 6B
Ancachs .... Vol. 5A
Andalusian Provinces .... Vol. 6A
Anderson Court House, S.C. ...... Vol. 1A
Andorra, Andorre .... Vol. 1A
Andorre .... Vol. 1A
Angaur (Palau #686) .... Vol. 5A
Angola .... Vol. 1A
Angra .... Vol. 1A
Anguilla .... 624, 661, Vol. 1A
Anhwei .... Vol. 2A
Anjouan .... Vol. 1A
Anna surcharged on France ... Vol. 2B
Anna surcharged on Great

Britain .... Vol. 5A
Anna, Annas .... Vol. 3B
Annam .... Vol. 3B
Annam and Tonkin .... Vol. 1A
Annapolis, Md. .... Vol. 1A
Ano do X Aniversario Comunidade
  dos Paises de Lingua Portuguesa
  (Angola 1298-1300) .... Vol. 1A
Antigua .... Vol. 1A
Antigua & Barbuda .... Vol. 1A
Antioquia .... Vol. 2A
A.O. ovptd. on Congo .... Vol. 3A
AOF on France .... Vol. 2B
A.O.I. ovpt. on Italy .... Vol. 3B
A Payer Te Betalen .... Vol. 1B
A percevoir (see France,
  French colonies, postage due) .... Vol. 2B,
  Vol. 3A
Apurimac .... Vol. 5A
A R .... Vol. 4B
A.R. ovptd. on stamps of
  Colombia .... Vol. 2A
Arabie Saoudite .... Vol. 6A
Arad .... Vol. 3B
A receber (See Portuguese
  Colonies) 187
Arequipa .... Vol. 5A
Argentina .... Vol. 1A
Argyrokastron .... Vol. 2B
Arica .... Vol. 5A
Armenia .... Vol. 1A, Vol. 6B
Armenian stamps ovptd. or
  surcharged .... Vol. 3A, Vol. 6B
Army of the North 596
Army of the Northwest 595
Aruba .... Vol. 1A
Arwad 379
Ascension .... Vol. 1A
Assistencia Nacionalaos
  Tuberculosos 190
Asturias Province .... Vol. 6A
Athens, Ga. .... Vol. 1A
Atlanta, Ga. .... Vol. 1A
Aunus, ovptd. on Finland 595
Austin, Miss. .... Vol. 1A
Austin, Tex. .... Vol. 1A
Australia .... Vol. 1A
Australia, Occupation of Japan ... Vol. 1A
Australian Antarctic Territory ..... Vol. 1A
Australian States .... Vol. 1A
Austria .... Vol. 1B
Austria, Allied Military Govt. ..... Vol. 1B
Austria, Adm. of Liechtenstein ... Vol. 4A
Austria, Lombardy-Venetia .... Vol. 1B
Austria-Hungary .... Vol. 1B
Austrian Occupation of Italy ...... Vol. 3B
Austrian Occupation of
  Montenegro .... Vol. 4B
Austrian Occupation of Romania 378
Austrian Occupation of Serbia ... Vol. 6A
Austrian Offices Abroad .... Vol. 1B
Austrian stamps surcharged or
  overprinted .... 378, Vol. 1B, Vol. 3B, Vol. 6B
Autaugaville, Ala. .... Vol. 1A
Autopaketti, Autorahti .... Vol. 2B
Avisporto .... Vol. 2B
Ayacucho .... Vol. 5A
Aytonomoe .... Vol. 2B
Azerbaijan, Azarbaycan, Azerbaycan,
  Azerbaidjan .... Vol. 1B, Vol. 3B, Vol. 6B
Azirbayedjan .... Vol. 3B
Azores .... 190, Vol. 1B

B .... Vol. 1B, Vol. 5A, Vol. 6A
B ovptd. on Straits Settlements ... Vol. 1B
Baden .... Vol. 3A
Baghdad .... Vol. 4B
Bahamas .... Vol. 1B
Bahawalpur .... Vol. 5A
Bahrain .... Vol. 1B, Vol. 5A
Baja Cal(ifornia) .... Vol. 4B
Bajar Porto .... Vol. 1B
Baku .... Vol. 1B
Balcony Falls, Va. .... Vol. 1A
Baltimore, Md. .... Vol. 1A
Bamra .... Vol. 3B
Banat, Bacska .... Vol. 1B
Bangkok .... Vol. 2B
Bangladesh .... Vol. 1B
Bani ovptd. on Austria 378
Bani ovptd. on Hungary .... Vol. 3B
Baranya .... Vol. 1B
Barbados .... Vol. 1B
Barbuda .... Vol. 1B
Barcelona .... Vol. 6A
Barnwell Court House, S.C. ...... Vol. 1A
Barranquilla .... Vol. 2A
Barwani .... Vol. 3B
Basel .... Vol. 6A

Bashahr .... Vol. 3B
Basque Provinces .... Vol. 6A
Basutoland .... Vol. 1B
Batavia .... Vol. 5A
Baton Rouge, La. .... Vol. 1A
Batum, Batym (British
  Occupation) .... Vol. 1B
Bavaria .... Vol. 3A
Bayar Porto .... Vol. 3B
Bayer., Bayern .... Vol. 3A
B.C.A. ovptd. on Rhodesia .... Vol. 1B
B.C.M. .... Vol. 4B
B.C.O.F. .... Vol. 1A
Beaufort, S.C. .... Vol. 1A
Beaumont, Tex. .... Vol. 1A
Bechuanaland .... Vol. 1B
Bechuanaland Protectorate .... Vol. 1B
Beckmann's City Post .... Vol. 1A
Behie .... Vol. 6B
Belarus .... Vol. 1B
Belgian (Belgisch) Congo .... Vol. 1B
Belgian East Africa 379
Belgian Occ. of German
  East Africa .... Vol. 3A
Belgian Occupation of Germany ... Vol. 3A
Belgien .... Vol. 1B
Belgium, Belgique, Belgie .... Vol. 1B
Belgium (German Occupation) .... Vol. 1B
Belize .... Vol. 1B
Belize, Cayes of .... Vol. 1B
Benadir .... Vol. 6A
Bengasi .... Vol. 3B
Beni .... Vol. 1B
Benin .... Vol. 1B
Benin, People's Republic of .... Vol. 1B
Bequia 840
Bergedorf .... Vol. 3A
Berlin .... Vol. 3A
Berlin-Brandenburg .... Vol. 3A
Bermuda .... Vol. 1B
Besetztes Gebiet Nordfrankreich ... Vol. 2B
Besieged ovptd. on Cape of Good
  Hope .... Vol. 2A, Vol. 6B
Beyrouth, French Offices .... Vol. 2B
Beyrouth, Russian Offices 598
B. Guiana .... Vol. 1B
B. Hneipoe .... Vol. 2B
Bhopal .... Vol. 3B
Bhor .... Vol. 3B
Bhutan .... Vol. 1B
Biafra .... Vol. 1B
Bijawar .... Vol. 3B
B.I.O.T. ovptd. on Seychelles ...... Vol. 1B
Bishop's City Post .... Vol. 1A
Blagoveshchensk .... Vol. 2B
Bluefields .... Vol. 5A
Bluffton, S.C. .... Vol. 1A
B.M.A. Eritrea .... Vol. 3A
B.M.A. Malaya .... Vol. 6A
B.M.A. Somalia .... Vol. 3A
B.M.A. Tripolitania .... Vol. 3B
Bocas del Toro .... Vol. 5A
Boer Occupation .... Vol. 2A
Bogota .... Vol. 2A
Bohemia and Moravia .... Vol. 2B
Bohmen and Mahren .... Vol. 2B
Boletta, Bollettino .... Vol. 3B, Vol. 6A
Bolivar .... Vol. 2A
Bolivia .... Vol. 1B
Bollo .... Vol. 3B
Bollo Postale .... Vol. 6A
Bophuthatswana .... Vol. 6A
Borneo .... Vol. 5A
Boscawen, N.H. .... Vol. 1A
Bosna i Hercegovina .... Vol. 1B, Vol. 6B
Bosnia and Herzegovina ... Vol. 1B, Vol. 6B
Bosnia, Muslim Gov. in Sarajevo ... Vol. 1B
Bosnia, Croat Administration,
  Mostar .... Vol. 1B
Bosnia, Serb Administration,
  Banja Luca .... Vol. 1B
Bosnia stamps overprinted or
  surcharged ...... Vol. 1B, Vol. 3B, Vol. 6B
Bosnien Herzegowina .... Vol. 1B
Boston, Mass. .... Vol. 1A
Botswana .... Vol. 1B
Boyaca .... Vol. 2A
Brattleboro, Vt. .... Vol. 1A
Braunschweig .... Vol. 3A
Brazil, Brasil .... Vol. 1B
Bremen .... Vol. 3A
Bridgeville, Ala. .... Vol. 1A
British Administration of Bahrain ... Vol. 1B
British Antarctic Territory .... Vol. 1B
British Bechuanaland .... Vol. 1B
British Central Africa .... Vol. 1B
British Colonies - Dies I & II .... See
table of contents

British Columbia &
  Vancouver Is. .... Vol. 2A
British Consular Mail .... Vol. 4B
British Dominion of Samoa 896
British East Africa .... Vol. 1B
British Forces in Egypt .... Vol. 2B
British Guiana .... Vol. 1B
British Honduras .... Vol. 1B
British Indian Ocean Territory ... Vol. 1B
British Mandate of Jordan .... Vol. 4A
British Levant .... Vol. 3A
British New Guinea .... Vol. 5A
British North Borneo .... Vol. 5A
British Occupation (of Batum) ...... Vol. 1B
British Occupation of Bushire .... Vol. 1B
British Occupation of Cameroun Vol. 2A
British Occupation of Crete ...... Vol. 2B
British Occupation of Faroe Is. ..... Vol. 2B
British Occ. of German
  East Africa .... Vol. 3A
British Occupation of Iraq .... Vol. 3B,
  Vol. 4B
British Occupation of
  Mesopotamia .... Vol. 4B
British Occ. of Orange River
  Colony .... Vol. 5A
British Occupation overprint .... Vol. 1B
British Occupation of Palestine ..... Vol. 5A
British Occupation of Persia ...... Vol. 1B
British Occupation of Togo .... Vol. 6B
British Occ. of Transvaal .... Vol. 6B
British Offices in Africa .... Vol. 3A
British Offices in China .... Vol. 3A
British Offices in Morocco .... Vol. 3A
British Offices in Tangier .... Vol. 3A
British Off. in the Turkish Empire ... Vol. 3A
British Protectorate of Egypt .... Vol. 2B
British Samoa 896
British Solomon Islands .... Vol. 6A
British Somaliland (Somaliland
  Protectorate) .... Vol. 6A
British South Africa (Rhodesia) 241
British stamps surcharged .... Vol. 6B
British Vice-Consulate .... Vol. 4B
British Virgin Islands .... Vol. 6B
British Zone (Germany) .... Vol. 3A
Brown & McGill's U.S.P.O.
  Despatch .... Vol. 1A
Brunei .... Vol. 1B
Brunei (Japanese Occupation) ... Vol. 1B
Brunswick .... Vol. 3A
Buchanan .... Vol. 1A, Vol. 4A
Buenos Aires .... Vol. 1A
Bulgaria, Bulgarie .... Vol. 1B
Bulgarian Occupation of Romania 378
Bulgarian stamps overprinted
  or surcharged .... 378, Vol. 3A, Vol. 6B
Bundi .... Vol. 3B
Bundi stamps overprinted .... Vol. 3B
Bureau International .... Vol. 6A
Burgenland .... Vol. 1B
Burgos .... Vol. 6A
Burkina Faso .... Vol. 1B
Burma .... Vol. 1B
Burma (Japanese Occupation) ... Vol. 1B
Burundi .... Vol. 1B
Bushire .... Vol. 1B
Bussahir .... Vol. 3B
Buu-Chinh .... Vol. 6B
Buu-Bien .... Vol. 6B
Byelorussia .... Vol. 1B

Cabo, Cabo Gracias a Dios .... Vol. 5A
Cabo Juby, Jubi .... Vol. 2A
Cabo Verde .... Vol. 6A
Cadiz .... Vol. 6A
Caicos .... Vol. 6B
Calchi .... Vol. 3B
Cali .... Vol. 2A
Calino, Calimno .... Vol. 3B
Callao .... Vol. 5A
Camb. Aust. Sigillum Nov. .... Vol. 1A
Cambodia, (Int. Com., India) ..... Vol. 3A
Cambodia, Cambodge .... Vol. 2A, Vol. 3B
Camden, S.C. .... Vol. 1A
Cameroons (U.K.T.T.) .... Vol. 2A
Cameroun (Republique
  Federale) .... Vol. 2A
Campeche .... Vol. 4B
Canada .... Vol. 2A
Canadian Provinces .... Vol. 2A
Canal Zone .... Vol. 2A
Canary Islands, Canarias .... Vol. 6A
Candia .... Vol. 2A
Canouan 844
Canton, French Offices .... Vol. 2B
Canton, Miss. .... Vol. 1A
Cape Juby .... Vol. 2A
Cape of Good Hope .... Vol. 2A

Cape of Good Hope stamps surchd.
(see Griqualand West) .... Vol. 3A
Cape Verde .... Vol. 2A
Carchi .... Vol. 3B
Caribbean Netherlands .... Vol. 2A
Caribisch Nederland .... Vol. 2A
Carinthia .... Vol. 1B, Vol. 6B
Carlist .... Vol. 6A
Carolina City, N.C. .... Vol. 1A
Caroline Islands .... Vol. 2A
Carpatho-Ukraine .... Vol. 2B
Carriacou & Petite Martinique ... Vol. 3A
Carriers Stamps .... Vol. 1A
Cartagena .... Vol. 2A
Cartersville, Ga. .... Vol. 1A
Carupano .... Vol. 6B
Caso .... Vol. 3B
Castellorizo, Castelrosso .... Vol. 2A
Catalonia .... Vol. 6A
Cauca .... Vol. 2A
Cavalla (Greek) .... Vol. 3A
Cavalle, Cavalla (French) .... Vol. 2B
Cayes of Belize .... Vol. 1B
Cayman Islands .... Vol. 2A
CCCP 386
C.CH. on French Colonies .... Vol. 2A
C.E.F. ovptd. on Cameroun .... Vol. 2A
C.E.F. ovptd. on India .... Vol. 3B
Cefalonia ovptd. on Greece ...... Vol. 3B
Celebes .... Vol. 5A
Cent, cents ...... Vol. 1A, Vol. 2B, Vol. 4B,
Vol. 5A
Centenaire Algerie RF
(France No. 255) .... Vol. 2B
Centenary-1st Postage Stamp
(Pakistan #63-64) .... Vol. 5A
Centesimi overprinted on Austria
or Bosnia .... Vol. 3B
Centesimi di corona ...... Vol. 1B, Vol. 2B
Centimes .... Vol. 2B
Centimes ovptd. on Austria .... Vol. 1B
Centimes ovptd. on Germany .... Vol. 3A
Centimos (no country name) ..... Vol. 6A
Centimos ovptd. on France .... Vol. 2B
Central Africa (Centrafricaine) ... Vol. 2A
Central African Republic .... Vol. 2A
Central China .... Vol. 2A
Central Lithuania .... Vol. 2A
Cephalonia .... Vol. 3B
Cerigo .... Vol. 3A, Vol. 6B
Cervantes .... Vol. 6A
Ceska Republica .... Vol. 2B
Ceskoslovenska,
Ceskoslovensko .... Vol. 2B
Ceylon .... Vol. 2B
CF .... Vol. 2B
CFA .... Vol. 2B
C.G.H.S. .... Vol. 6B
Ch .... Vol. 3B, Vol. 4A
Chachapoyas .... Vol. 5A
Chad .... Vol. 2A
Chahar .... Vol. 2A
Chala .... Vol. 5A
Chamba .... Vol. 3B
Channel Islands .... Vol. 3A
Chapel Hill, N.C. .... Vol. 1A
Charkhari .... Vol. 3B
Charleston, S.C. .... Vol. 1A
Charlotte, N.C. .... Vol. 1A
Charlottesville, Va. .... Vol. 1A
Chateau de Beggen (Luxembourg
#1466) .... Vol. 4A
Chateau de Dommeldange
(Luxembourg #1467) .... Vol. 4A
Chattanooga, Tenn. .... Vol. 1A
Chekiang .... Vol. 2A
Chemins des Fer .... Vol. 2B
Cherifien Posts.......................... Vol. 2B
Chiapas .... Vol. 4B
Chiclayo .... Vol. 5A
Chiffre .... See France and French
colonies, postage due
Chihuahua .... Vol. 4B
Chile .... Vol. 2A
Chilean Occupation of Peru ...... Vol. 5A
Chimarra .... Vol. 3A
China, Chinese .... Vol. 2A
China (Japanese Occupation) ... Vol. 2A
China Expeditionary Force
(India) .... Vol. 3B
China, British Offices .... Vol. 3A
China, Formosa .... Vol. 2A, Vol. 4A
China, French Offices .... Vol. 2B
China, German Offices .... Vol. 3A
China, Italian Offices .... Vol. 3B
China, Japanese Offices .... Vol. 3B
China, Northeastern Provinces ... Vol. 2A
China, Offices in Manchuria ..... Vol. 2A
China, Offices in Tibet .... Vol. 2A
China, People's Republic .... Vol. 2A

China, People's Republic Regional
Issues .... Vol. 2A
China, People's Republic
Hong Kong .... Vol. 3B
China, People's Republic Macao ... Vol. 4B
China, Republic of .... Vol. 2A
China, Russian Offices 596
China, United States Offices ..... Vol. 1A
Chine .... Vol. 2B
Chios .... Vol. 3A
Chita .... Vol. 2B
Chosen .... Vol. 4A
Christiansburg, Va. .... Vol. 1A
Christmas Island .... Vol. 2A
Chungking .... Vol. 2B
C.I.H.S. .... Vol. 6B
Cilicia, Cilicie .... Vol. 2A, Vol. 5A, Vol. 6A
Cincinnati, O. .... Vol. 1A
Cinquan Tenaire .... Vol. 5A
Cirenaica .... Vol. 2B
Ciskei .... Vol. 6A
City Despatch Post .... Vol. 1A
City Post .... Vol. 1A
Cleveland, O. .... Vol. 1A
Cluj .... Vol. 3B
c/m .... Vol. 3A
C.M.T. .... Vol. 6B
Coamo .... 212, Vol. 1A
Cochin .... Vol. 3B
Cochin China .... Vol. 3B
Cochin, Travancore .... Vol. 3B
Co. Ci. ovptd. on Yugoslavia ..... Vol. 6B
Cocos Islands .... Vol. 2A
Colaparchee, Ga. .... Vol. 1A
Colis Postaux ... Vol. 1B, Vol. 2B, Vol. 3B
Colombia .... Vol. 2A, Vol. 5A
Colombian Dominion of
Panama .... Vol. 5A
Colombian States .... Vol. 2A
Colon .... Vol. 5A
Colonie (Coloniali) Italiane ...... Vol. 3B
Colonies de l'Empire Francaise ... Vol. 2B
Columbia, S.C. .... Vol. 1A
Columbia, Tenn. .... Vol. 1A
Columbus Archipelago .... Vol. 2B
Columbus, Ga. .... Vol. 1A
Comayagua .... Vol. 3B
Commando Brief .... Vol. 5A
Common Designs .... See table of
contents
Commissioning of Maryan
Babangida (Nigeria #607) .... Vol. 5A
Communicaciones .... Vol. 6A
Communist China .... Vol. 2A
Comores, Archipel des .... Vol. 2A
Comoro Islands (Comores,
Comorien) .... Vol. 2A, Vol. 4B
Compania Colombiana .... Vol. 2A
Confederate States .... Vol. 1A
Congo .... Vol. 1B, Vol. 2A
Congo Democratic Republic ..... Vol. 2A,
Vol. 6B
Congo People's Republic
(ex-French) .... Vol. 2A
Congo, Belgian (Belge) .... Vol. 1B
Congo Francais .... Vol. 2B
Congo, Indian U.N. Force .... Vol. 3B
Congo, Portuguese 200
Congreso .... Vol. 6A
Conseil de l'Europe .... Vol. 2B
Constantinople, Georgian
Offices .... Vol. 3A
Constantinople, Polish Offices 124
Constantinople, Italian Offices ... Vol. 3B
Constantinople, Romanian Offices 379
Constantinople, Russian Offices 597
Constantinople, Turkey .... Vol. 6B
Contribucao Industrial (Macao
A14, P. Guinea WT1) .... 204, Vol. 4B
Convention States (India) .... Vol. 3B
Coo .... Vol. 3B
Cook Islands .... Vol. 2A
Cook Islands, Niue .... Vol. 5A
Cordoba .... Vol. 1A
Corea, Coree .... Vol. 4A
Corfu .... Vol. 2A, Vol. 3B
Corona .... Vol. 1B, Vol. 2B
Correio, Correios e Telegraphos 125
Correo Submarino .... Vol. 6A
Correo, Correos (no name) .... Vol. 1A,
Vol. 2A, Vol. 5A, Vol. 6A
Corrientes .... Vol. 1A
Cos .... Vol. 3B
Costa Atlantica .... Vol. 2B
Costa Rica .... Vol. 2A
Costantinopoli .... Vol. 3B
Cote d'Ivoire .... Vol. 2B
Cote des Somalis .... Vol. 6A
Council of Europe .... Vol. 2B

Cour Permanente de Justice
Internationale .... Vol. 5A
Courtland, Ala. .... Vol. 1A
Cpbnja .... Vol. 6A
Cracow 15, 120
Crete .... Vol. 2A, Vol. 3B
Crete, Austrian Offices .... Vol. 1B
Crete, French Offices .... Vol. 2B
Crete, Italian Offices .... Vol. 3B
Crimea .... 599, Vol. 6A
Croat Administration of Bosnia,
Mostar .... Vol. 1B
Croatia .... Vol. 2A
Croatia-Slavonia .... Vol. 6B
Croissant Rouge Turc. .... Vol. 6B
C.S.A. Postage .... Vol. 1A
CTOT .... Vol. 1B
Cuautla .... Vol. 4B
Cuba stamps overprinted 211
Cuba, U.S. Administration .... Vol. 1A,
Vol. 2A
Cucuta .... Vol. 2A
Cuernavaca .... Vol. 4B
Cundinamarca .... Vol. 2A
Curacao .... Vol. 2A, Vol. 5A
Cuzco .... Vol. 5A
C.X.C. on Bosnia and
Herzegovina .... Vol. 6B
Cyprus .... Vol. 2B
Cyprus, Turkish Republic of
Northern .... Vol. 6B
Cyrenaica .... Vol. 2B, Vol. 3A, Vol. 4A
Czechoslovakia .... Vol. 2B
Czechoslovak Legion Post .... Vol. 2B
Czech Rep. .... Vol. 2B

D .... Vol. 3B
Dahomey .... Vol. 1B, Vol. 2B
Dakar-Abidjan .... Vol. 2B
Dalmatia .... Vol. 2B
Dalton, Ga. .... Vol. 1A
Danish West Indies .... Vol. 1A, Vol. 2B
Danmark .... Vol. 2B
Dansk-Vestindien .... Vol. 1A, Vol. 2B
Dansk-Vestindiske .... Vol. 1A, Vol. 2B
Danville, Va. .... Vol. 1A
Danzig .... Vol. 2B
Danzig, Polish Offices 123
Dardanelles 598
Darlington C.H., S.C. .... Vol. 1A
Datia (Duttia) .... Vol. 3B
D.B.L. ovptd. on Siberia and
Russia .... Vol. 2B
D.B.P. (Dalni Vostochini
Respoublika) .... Vol. 2B
D. de A. .... Vol. 2A
DDR .... Vol. 3A
Debrecen .... Vol. 3B
Deccan (Hyderabad) .... Vol. 3B
Dedeagatch (Greek) .... Vol. 3A
Dedeagh, Dedeagatch (French) ... Vol. 2B
Deficit .... Vol. 6A
Demopolis, Ala. .... Vol. 1A
Denikin .... Vol. 6A
Denmark .... Vol. 2B
Denmark stamps surcharged .... Vol. 2B
Denver Issue, Mexico .... Vol. 4B
Den Waisen ovptd. on Italy .... Vol. 3B
Despatch (US 1LB, 5LB) .... Vol. 1A
Deutsch-Neu-Guinea .... Vol. 3A
Deutsch-Ostafrika .... Vol. 3A
Deutsch-Sudwest Afrika .... Vol. 3A
Deutsche Bundespost .... Vol. 3A
Deutsche Demokratische
Republik .... Vol. 3A
Deutsche Nationalversammlung ... Vol. 3A
Deutsche Post .... Vol. 3A
Deutsche Post Berlin .... Vol. 3A
Deutsche(s) Reich .... Vol. 3A
Deutsche Reich, Nr.21, Nr.16 ...... Vol. 3A
Deutschland .... Vol. 3A
Deutschosterreich .... Vol. 1B
Dhar .... Vol. 3B
Diego-Suarez .... Vol. 2B
Diego-Suarez stamps
surcharged .... Vol. 4B
Dienftmarke (Dienstmarke) ...... Vol. 3A
Dies I & II, British Colonies ... See table
of contents
Diligencia .... Vol. 6B
Dinar .... Vol. 6B
Dire-Dawa .... Vol. 2B
Dispatch (US 1LB) .... Vol. 1A
Distrito ovptd. on Arequipa ...... Vol. 5A
DJ ovptd. on Obock .... Vol. 6A
Djibouti (Somali Coast) ... Vol. 2B, Vol. 6A
Dobruja District 378
Dodecanese Islands ..... Vol. 3A, Vol. 3B

Dollar, ovptd. on Russia 596
Dominica .... Vol. 2B
Dominican Republic,
Dominicana .... Vol. 2B
Don Government .... Vol. 6A
Dorpat .... Vol. 2B
Drzava SHS .... Vol. 6B
Dubai .... Vol. 2B, Vol. 5A, Vol. 6B
Duck Stamps (Hunting Permit) ... Vol. 1A
Duitsch Oost Afrika overprinted
on Congo .... Vol. 3A
Duke de la Torre Regency .... Vol. 6A
Dulce et Decorum est Pro Patria
Mori (Nepal O1) .... Vol. 5A
Dungarpur .... Vol. 3B
Durazzo .... Vol. 3B
Dutch Guiana (Surinam) .... Vol. 6A
Dutch Indies .... Vol. 5A
Dutch New Guinea .... Vol. 5A
Duttia .... Vol. 3B

EA .... Vol. 1A
E.A.F. overprinted on stamps of
Great Britain .... Vol. 3A
East Africa (British) .... Vol. 1B
East Africa (German) .... Vol. 3A
East Africa (Italian) .... Vol. 3B
East Africa and Uganda
Protectorates .... Vol. 2B, Vol. 4A
East Africa Forces .... Vol. 2A
East China .... Vol. 2A
Eastern Rumelia .... Vol. 2B
Eastern Rumelia stamps
overprinted .... Vol. 6B
Eastern Silesia .... Vol. 2B
Eastern Szechwan .... Vol. 2A
Eastern Thrace .... Vol. 6B
East India .... Vol. 3B
East Saxony .... Vol. 3A
East Timor .... Vol. 1A, Vol. 6B
Eatonton, Ga. .... Vol. 1A
Ecuador .... Vol. 2A
E.E.F. .... Vol. 5A
Eesti .... Vol. 2B
Egeo .... Vol. 3B
Egiziane (Egypt types A9-A10) ... Vol. 2B
Egypt, Egypte, Egyptiennes ...... Vol. 2B,
Vol. 5A
Egypt, French Offices .... Vol. 2B
Eire, Eireann (Ireland) .... Vol. 3B
Ekaterinodar .... Vol. 6A
Elobey, Annobon and Corisco ... Vol. 2B
El Salvador 848
Elsas, Elfas .... Vol. 2B
Elua Keneta .... Vol. 1A
Emory, Va. .... Vol. 1A
Empire, Franc, Francais .... Vol. 2B
En .... Vol. 4A
England .... Vol. 2B
Epirus .... Vol. 2B
Equateur (Ecuador #19-21) ...... Vol. 2B
Equatorial Guinea .... Vol. 2B
Eritrea .... Vol. 2B
Eritrea (British Military
Administration) .... Vol. 3A
Escuelas .... Vol. 6B
Espana, Espanola .... Vol. 6A
Estado da India 209
Est Africain Allemand overprinted
on Congo .... Vol. 3A
Estensi .... Vol. 3B
Estero .... Vol. 3B
Estland .... 595, Vol. 2B
Estonia .... 596, Vol. 2B
Etablissments Francais
dans l'Inde .... Vol. 2B
Ethiopia, Etiopia, Ethiopie,
Ethiopiennes .... Vol. 2B, Vol. 3A
Eupen .... Vol. 3A
Europe .... Vol. 3A
Express Letter .... Vol. 2A

15 August 1947 (Pakistan #23) ... Vol. 5A
500 anos, viaje del descubrimiento
de istmo (Panama #897) .... Vol. 5A
F .... Vol. 2B
F. A. F. L. .... Vol. 6A
Falkland Dependencies .... Vol. 2B
Falkland Islands .... Vol. 2B
Far Eastern Republic .... Vol. 2B
Far Eastern Republic surcharged
or ovptd. .... Vol. 6A
Faridkot .... Vol. 3B
Faroe Islands .... Vol. 2B
FCFA ovptd. on France .... Vol. 2B
Federacion .... Vol. 2B
Federal Republic (Germany) ..... Vol. 3A
Federated Malay States .... Vol. 4B
Fen, Fn. (Manchukuo) .... Vol. 4B
Fernando Po, Fdo. Poo .... Vol. 2B

Feudatory States .... Vol. 3B
Fezzan, Fezzan-Ghadames ...... Vol. 4A
Fiera Campionaria Tripoli ...... Vol. 4A
Fiji .... Vol. 2B
Fiji overprinted or surcharged 238
Filipinas, Filipas. .... Vol. 5A
Fincastle, Va. .... Vol. 1A
Finland .... Vol. 2B
Finnish Occupation of Karelia ... Vol. 4A
Finnish Occupation of Russia .... 595, Vol. 4A
Fiume .... Vol. 2B
Fiume-Kupa Zone (Fiumano Kupa) .... Vol. 6B
Five Cents (Confed. #53X) .... Vol. 1A
Florida .... Vol. 6B
F. M. .... Vol. 6B
Foochow, Chinese .... Vol. 2A
Foochow, German .... Vol. 3A
Formosa .... Vol. 2A, Vol. 4A
Foroyar .... Vol. 2B
Forsyth, Ga. .... Vol. 1A
Fort Valley, Ga. .... Vol. 1A
Franc .... Vol. 2B
Franc ovptd. on Austria .... Vol. 1B
Franca ovptd. on stamps of Peru ... Vol. 5A
Francais, Francaise ..... See France and French colonies
France .... Vol. 2B
France (German occupation) ..... Vol. 2B
France D'Outre Mer .... Vol. 2B
Franco Bollo .... Vol. 3B
Franco Marke .... Vol. 3A
Franco Scrisorei 250
Franklin, N.C. .... Vol. 1A
Franqueo .... Vol. 5A
Franquicia .... Vol. 6A
Fraziersville, S.C. .... Vol. 1A
Fredericksburg, Va. .... Vol. 1A
Free .... Vol. 1A
Frei Durch Ablosung .... Vol. 3A
Freimarke (No Country Name) ... Vol. 3A
French Administration of Andorra .... Vol. 1A
French Administration of Saar 618
French Colonies .... Vol. 2B
French Colonies surcharged or overprinted .... Vol. 1A, Vol. 2B, Vol. 3A, Vol. 3B, Vol. 4B, Vol. 5A, Vol. 6A
French Commemoratives Index .... Vol. 2B
French Congo .... Vol. 2B
French Equatorial Africa .... Vol. 2A, Vol. 2B, Vol. 4B, Vol. 6B
French Guiana .... Vol. 2B
French Guinea .... Vol. 2B
French India .... Vol. 2B
French Levant .... Vol. 2B, Vol. 6A
French Mandate of Alaouites ..... Vol. 1A
French Mandate of Lebanon ..... Vol. 4A
French Morocco .... Vol. 2B
French Occupation of Cameroun .... Vol. 2A
French Occupation of Castellorizo .... Vol. 2A
French Occupation of Crete ...... Vol. 2A
French Occupation of Germany ... Vol. 3A
French Occupation of Hungary ... Vol. 3B
French Occupation of Libya ...... Vol. 4A
French Occupation of Syria ...... Vol. 6A
French Occupation of Togo .... Vol. 6B
French Oceania .... Vol. 2B
French Offices Abroad .... Vol. 2B
French Offices in China .... Vol. 2B
French Offices in Crete .... Vol. 2B
French Offices in Egypt .... Vol. 2B
French Offices in Madagascar ... Vol. 4B
French Offices in Morocco .... Vol. 2B
French Offices in Tangier .... Vol. 2B
French Offices in Turkish Empire ... Vol. 6A
French Offices in Turkish Empire surcharged .... Vol. 6A
French Offices in Zanzibar .... Vol. 6B
French Polynesia .... Vol. 2B
French Saar 618
French Southern and Antarctic Territories .... Vol. 2B
French stamps inscribed CFA ... Vol. 2B
French stamps surcharged ... Vol. 2B, Vol. 4B, Vol. 6A
French Sudan .... Vol. 2B
French West Africa .... Vol. 2B
French Zone (Germany) .... Vol. 3A
Frimarke, Frmrk (No Country Name) .... Vol. 2B, Vol. 5A, Vol. 6A
Fujeira .... Vol. 2B, Vol. 6B
Fukien .... Vol. 2A
Funafuti .... Vol. 6B
Funchal .... Vol. 2B

G or GW overprinted on Cape of Good Hope .... Vol. 3A
GAB on French Colonies .... Vol. 3A
Gabon, Gabonaise .... Vol. 3A
Gainesville, Ala. .... Vol. 1A
Galapagos Islands .... Vol. 2B
Galveston, Tex. .... Vol. 1A
Gambia .... Vol. 3A
Gaston, N.C. .... Vol. 1A
Gaza .... Vol. 3B
G & (et) D overprinted on French Colonies .... Vol. 3A
G.E.A. ovptd. .... Vol. 3A, Vol. 6A
General Gouvernement (Poland) 122
Geneva, Geneve .... Vol. 6A
Georgetown, S.C. .... Vol. 1A
Georgia .... Vol. 3A, Vol. 6B
Georgia, Offices in Turkey .... Vol. 3A
Georgienne, Republique .... Vol. 3A
German Administration of Albania .... Vol. 1A
German Administration of Danzig .... Vol. 2B
German Administration of Saar 620
German Democratic Republic ... Vol. 3A
German Dominion of Cameroun ... Vol. 2A
German Dominion of Caroline Islands .... Vol. 2A
German Dominion of Mariana Is. .... Vol. 4B
German Dominion of Marshall Is. .... Vol. 4B
German Dominion of Samoa 896
German Dominion of Togo .... Vol. 6B
German East Africa .... Vol. 3A
German East Africa (Belgian occ.) .... Vol. 3A
German East Africa (British occ.) ... Vol. 3A
German New Guinea .... Vol. 5A
German New Guinea (New Britain) .... Vol. 5A
German Occupation of Belgium ... Vol. 1B
German Occupation of Estonia .... Vol. 2B
German Occupation of France .... Vol. 2B
German Occupation of Guernsey .... Vol. 3A
German Occupation of Ionian Is. .... Vol. 3B
German Occupation of Jersey .... Vol. 3A
German Occupation of Latvia .... Vol. 4A
German Occupation of Lithuania ... 595
German Occupation of Ljubljana .... Vol. 6B
German Occupation of Luxembourg .... Vol. 4A
German Occupation of Macedonia .... Vol. 4B
German Occupation of Montenegro .... Vol. 4B
German Occupation of Poland 122
German Occupation of Romania 378
German Occupation of Russia 595
German Occupation of Serbia ... Vol. 6A
German Occupation of Ukraine 595
German Occupation of Yugoslavia .... Vol. 6B
German Occupation of Zante ... Vol. 3B
German Offices in China .... Vol. 3A
German Offices in China surcharged .... Vol. 4A
German Offices in Morocco .... Vol. 3A
German Offices in Turkish Empire .... Vol. 3A
German Protectorate of Bohemia and Moravia .... Vol. 2B
German South-West Africa .... Vol. 3A
German stamps surchd. or ovptd. .... 378, 595, 617, Vol. 3A, Vol. 6A
German States .... Vol. 3A
Germany .... Vol. 3A
Germany (Allied Military Govt.) ... Vol. 3A
Gerusalemme .... Vol. 3B
Ghadames .... Vol. 4A
Ghana .... Vol. 3A
Gibraltar .... Vol. 3A
Gilbert and Ellice Islands .... Vol. 3A
Gilbert Islands .... Vol. 3A
Giumulzina District .... Vol. 6B
Gniezno 16
Gold Coast .... Vol. 3A
Golfo del Guinea .... Vol. 6A
Goliad, Tex. .... Vol. 1A
Gonzales, Tex. .... Vol. 1A
Gorny Slask .... Vol. 6B
Government (U.S. 1LB) .... Vol. 1A
Governo Militare Alleato .... Vol. 3B
G.P.E. ovptd. on French Colonies .... Vol. 3A
Graham Land .... Vol. 2B
Granada .... Vol. 6A

Granadine Confederation, Granadina .... Vol. 2A
Grand Comoro, Grande Comore .... Vol. 3A
Grand Liban, Gd Liban .... Vol. 4A
Great Britain (see also British) ... Vol. 3A
Great Britain, Gaelic ovpt. ...... Vol. 3B
Great Britain, Offices in Africa ... Vol. 3A
Great Britain, Offices in China ... Vol. 3A
Great Britain, Offices in Morocco ... Vol. 3A
Great Britain, Offices in Turkish Empire .... Vol. 3A
Greater Rajasthan Union .... Vol. 3B
Greece .... Vol. 3A
Greek Occupation of Albania, North Epirus, Dodecanese Islands ... Vol. 3A
Greek Occupation of Epirus ... Vol. 2B, Vol. 3A
Greek Occ. of the Aegean Islands .... Vol. 3A
Greek Occupation of Thrace ..... Vol. 6B
Greek Occupation of Turkey ..... Vol. 3A, Vol. 6B
Greek stamps overprinted ... Vol. 2B, Vol. 6B
Greenland .... Vol. 3A
Greensboro, Ala. .... Vol. 1A
Greensboro, N.C. .... Vol. 1A
Greenville .... Vol. 4A
Greenville, Ala. .... Vol. 1A
Greenville, Tenn. .... Vol. 1A
Greenville Court House, S.C. .... Vol. 1A
Greenwood Depot, Va. .... Vol. 1A
Grenada .... Vol. 3A
Grenadines of Grenada .... Vol. 3A
Grenadines of St. Vincent 833
Grenville .... Vol. 4A
G.R.I. overprinted on German New Guinea .... Vol. 5A
G.R.I. overprinted on German Samoa 896
G.R.I. overprinted on Marshall Is. .... Vol. 5A
Griffin, Ga. .... Vol. 1A
Griqualand West .... Vol. 3A
Grodno District .... Vol. 4A
Gronland .... Vol. 3A
Grossdeutsches Reich (Germany #529) .... Vol. 3A
Groszy 22
Grove Hill, Ala. .... Vol. 1A
Gruzija (Georgia) .... Vol. 3A
Guadalajara .... Vol. 4B
Guadeloupe .... Vol. 3A
Guam .... Vol. 1A
Guanacaste .... Vol. 2A
Guatemala .... Vol. 3A
Guayana .... Vol. 6B
Guernsey .... Vol. 3A
Guernsey, German Occupation ... Vol. 3A
Guiana, British .... Vol. 1B
Guiana, Dutch .... Vol. 6A
Guiana, French .... Vol. 2B
Guine .... 201, Vol. 3A
Guinea .... Vol. 3A, Vol. 6A
Guinea Ecuatorial .... Vol. 2B
Guinea, French .... Vol. 2B
Guinea, Portuguese 202
Guinea, Spanish .... Vol. 6A
Guinea-Bissau, Guine-Bissau ... Vol. 3A
Guinee .... Vol. 2B, Vol. 3A
Guipuzcoa Province .... Vol. 6A
Gultig 9, Armee 378
Guyana .... Vol. 3A
Guyane, Guy. Franc. .... Vol. 2B
G.W. ovptd. on Cape of Good Hope .... Vol. 3A
Gwalior .... Vol. 3B

Habilitado-1/2 (Tlacotalpan #1) .... Vol. 4B
Habilitado on Stamps of Cuba ... Vol. 1A, Vol. 2A, Vol. 5A
Habilitado on Telegrafos or revenues .... Vol. 5A, Vol. 6A
Hadhramaut .... Vol. 1A
Hainan Island .... Vol. 2A
Haiti .... Vol. 3B
Hall, A. D. (Confed. #27XU1) .... Vol. 1A
Hallettsville, Tex. .... Vol. 1A
Hamburg .... Vol. 3A
Hamburgh, S.C. .... Vol. 1A
Hamilton, Bermuda .... Vol. 1B
Hanover, Hannover .... Vol. 3A
Harar .... Vol. 2B
Harper .... Vol. 4A
Harrisburgh, Tex. .... Vol. 1A
Hatay .... Vol. 3B
Hatirasi (Turkey Design PT44) ... Vol. 6B
Hatohobei (Palau #686) .... Vol. 5A
Haute Silesie .... Vol. 6B

Haute Volta .... Vol. 1B
Haut Senegal-Niger .... Vol. 6B
Hawaii, Hawaiian .... Vol. 1A
H B A ovptd. on Russia .... Vol. 6A
Hebrew inscriptions .... Vol. 3B
H.E.H. The Nizam's (Hyderabad) .... Vol. 3B
Heilungkiang .... Vol. 2A
Hejaz .... Vol. 6A
Hejaz-Nejd .... Vol. 6A
Hejaz overprinted .... Vol. 4A, Vol. 6A
Helena, S.C. .... Vol. 1A
Heligoland, Helgoland .... Vol. 3B
Hellas .... Vol. 3A
Helsinki (Helsingfors) .... Vol. 2B
Helvetia, Helvetica (Switzerland) .... Vol. 6A
Heraklion .... Vol. 3A
Herceg Bosna .... Vol. 1B
Herzegovina .... Vol. 1B
Herzogth .... Vol. 3A
H.H. Nawabshah Jahanbegam .... Vol. 3B
H.I. Postage .... Vol. 1A
Hillsboro, N.C. .... Vol. 1A
Hoi Hao, French Offices .... Vol. 2B
Holkar (Indore) .... Vol. 3B
Holland (Netherlands) .... Vol. 5A
Hollandale, Tex. .... Vol. 1A
Holstein .... Vol. 3A
Honan .... Vol. 2A
Honda .... Vol. 2A
Honduras .... Vol. 3B
Honduras, British .... Vol. 1B
Hong Kong .... Vol. 2A, Vol. 3B
Hong Kong (Japanese Occupation) .... Vol. 3B
Hong Kong Special Admin. Region .... Vol. 3B
Hong Kong ovptd. China .... Vol. 3A
Honour's (Hondur's) City .... Vol. 1A
Hopeh .... Vol. 2A
Hopei .... Vol. 2A
Horta .... Vol. 3B
Houston, Tex. .... Vol. 1A
Hrvatska .... Vol. 1B, Vol. 2A, Vol. 6B
Hrzgl. .... Vol. 3A
Huacho .... Vol. 5A
Hunan .... Vol. 2A
Hungary .... Vol. 1B, Vol. 3B
Hungary (French Occupation) ... Vol. 3B
Hungary (Romanian Occupation) .... Vol. 3B
Hungary (Serbian Occupation) ... Vol. 3B
Huntsville, Tex. .... Vol. 1A
Hupeh .... Vol. 2A
Hyderabad (Deccan) .... Vol. 3B

I.B. (West Irian) .... Vol. 3B
Icaria .... Vol. 3A
ICC ovptd. on India .... Vol. 3B
Iceland .... Vol. 3B
Idar .... Vol. 3B
I.E.F. ovptd. on India .... Vol. 3B
I.E.F. 'D' ovptd. on Turkey .... Vol. 4B
Ierusalem 597
Ifni .... Vol. 3B
Ile Rouad 379
Imperio Colonial Portugues 199
Imposto de Selo 210
Impuesto (Impto) de Guerra ... Vol. 6A
Inde. Fcaise .... Vol. 2B
Independence, Tex. .... Vol. 1A
Index of U.S. Issues .... Vol. 1A
India .... 210, Vol. 3B
India, China Expeditionary Force .... Vol. 3B
India, Convention States .... Vol. 3B
India, Feudatory States .... Vol. 3B
India, French .... Vol. 2B
India, Portuguese 205
India stamps overprinted ... Vol. 3B, Vol. 4A, Vol. 5A
India, surcharge and crown ...... Vol. 6A
Indian Custodial Unit, Korea ..... Vol. 3B
Indian Expeditionary Force ...... Vol. 3B
Indian U.N. Force, Congo .... Vol. 3B
Indian U.N. Force, Gaza .... Vol. 3B
Indian Postal Administration of Bahrain .... Vol. 1B
Indo-China, Indo-chine .... Vol. 2B
Indo-China stamps surcharged ... Vol. 6B
Indo-China, Int. Commission ... Vol. 3B
Indonesia .... Vol. 3B, Vol. 5A
Indore .... Vol. 3B
Industrielle Kriegswirschaft .... Vol. 6A
Inhambane .... Vol. 3B
Inini .... Vol. 3B
Inland (Liberia #21) .... Vol. 4A
Inner Mongolia (Meng Chiang) ... Vol. 2A
Insufficiently prepaid .... Vol. 6B

Instrucao .... Vol. 6B
Instruccion .... Vol. 6B
International Bureau of
  Education .... Vol. 6A
International Commission in
  Indo-China .... Vol. 3B
International Court of Justice ..... Vol. 5A
International Labor Bureau .... Vol. 6A
International Olympic
  Committee .... Vol. 6A
International Refugee
  Organization .... Vol. 6A
International Telecommunication
  Union .... Vol. 6A
Ionian Islands, IONIKON
  KPATOE .... Vol. 3B
I.O.V.R. 377
Iran, Iraniennes .... Vol. 3B
Iran (Bushire) .... Vol. 1B
Iran, Turkish Occupation .... Vol. 3B
Iran with Rs. 10 denomination
  (Pakistan #1101) .... Vol. 5A
Iraq .... Vol. 3B
Iraq (British Occupation) ... Vol. 3B, Vol. 4B
Ireland .... Vol. 3A
Ireland, Northern .... Vol. 3A
Irian Barat .... Vol. 3B
Isabella, Ga. .... Vol. 1A
Island .... Vol. 3B
Isle of Man .... Vol. 3A
Isole Italiane dell'Egeo .... Vol. 3B
Isole Jonie .... Vol. 3B
Israel .... Vol. 3A
Istria ovptd. on Greece .... Vol. 6B
Itaca ovptd. on Greece .... Vol. 3B
Ita-Karjala .... Vol. 4A
Italia, Italiano, Italiane .... Vol. 3B
Italian Colonies .... Vol. 3B
Italian Dominion of Albania .... Vol. 1A
Italian Dominion of Castellorizo .... Vol. 2A
Italian East Africa .... Vol. 3B
Italian Jubaland .... Vol. 5A
Italian Occ. of Aegean Islands ... Vol. 3B
Italian Occupation of Austria ... Vol. 1B
Italian Occupation of Corfu ..... Vol. 3B
Italian Occupation of Crete ...... Vol. 2A
Italian Occupation of Dalmatia ... Vol. 2B
Italian Occupation of Ethiopia ... Vol. 2B
Italian Occupation of
  Fiume-Kupa .... Vol. 6B
Italian Occupation of Ionian
  Islands .... Vol. 3B
Italian Occupation of Ljubljana ... Vol. 6B
Italian Occupation of
  Montenegro .... Vol. 4B
Italian Occupation of
  Yugoslavia .... Vol. 6B
Italian Offices Abroad .... Vol. 3B
Italian Offices in Africa .... Vol. 3B
Italian Offices in Albania .... Vol. 3B
Italian Offices in China .... Vol. 3B
Italian Offices in Constantinople ... Vol. 3B
Italian Offices in Crete .... Vol. 3B
Italian Offices in the
  Turkish Empire .... Vol. 3B
Italian Social Republic .... Vol. 3B
Italian Somaliland .... Vol. 6A
Italian Somaliland (E.A.F.) ...... Vol. 3A
Italian stamps surcharged .... Vol. 1B,
  Vol. 2B, Vol. 3B
Italian States .... Vol. 3B
Italy (Allied Military Govt.) .... Vol. 3B
Italy (Austrian Occupation) .... Vol. 3B
Italy .... Vol. 3B
Ithaca .... Vol. 3B
Iuka, Miss. .... Vol. 1A
Ivory Coast .... Vol. 3B

J. ovptd. on stamps of Peru ...... Vol. 5A
Jackson, Miss. .... Vol. 1A
Jacksonville, Ala. .... Vol. 1A
Jacksonville, Fla. .... Vol. 1A
Jaffa 597
Jaipur .... Vol. 3B
Jamaica .... Vol. 4A
Jamhuri .... Vol. 6B
Jammu .... Vol. 3B
Jammu and Kashmir .... Vol. 3B
Janina .... Vol. 3B
Japan, Japanese .... Vol. 4A
Japan (Australian Occ.) .... Vol. 1A
Japan (Taiwan) ...... Vol. 2A, Vol. 4A
Japanese Offices Abroad .... Vol. 4A
Japan Occupation of Brunei ...... Vol. 1B
Japan Occupation of Burma ...... Vol. 1B
Japan Occupation of China ...... Vol. 2A
Japan Occupation of Dutch
  Indies .... Vol. 5A
Japan Occupation of
  Hong Kong .... Vol. 3B

Japan Occupation of Johore ...... Vol. 4B
Japan Occupation of Kedah ...... Vol. 4B
Japan Occupation of Kelantan ... Vol. 4B
Japan Occupation of Malacca .... Vol. 4B
Japan Occupation of Malaya .... Vol. 4B
Japan Occupation of Negri
  Sembilan .... Vol. 4B
Japan Occupation of Netherlands
  Indies .... Vol. 5A
Japan Occupation of North
  Borneo .... Vol. 5A
Japan Occupation of Pahang ...... Vol. 4B
Japan Occupation of Penang ...... Vol. 4B
Japan Occupation of Perak .... Vol. 4B
Japan Occupation of
  Philippines .... Vol. 1A, Vol. 5A
Japan Occupation of Sarawak ... Vol. 6A
Japan Occupation of Selangor ... Vol. 4B
Japan Occupation of
  Sts. Settlements .... Vol. 6A
Japan Occ. of Trengganu .... Vol. 4B
Other Japanese Stamps
  Overprinted .... Vol. 1B, Vol. 2A, Vol. 4A,
  Vol. 5A
Jasdan .... Vol. 3B
Java .... Vol. 3B, Vol. 5A
Jedda .... Vol. 6A
Jeend .... Vol. 3B
Jehol .... Vol. 2A
Jersey .... Vol. 3A
Jersey, German Occupation .... Vol. 3A
Jerusalem, Italian Offices .... Vol. 3B
Jerusalem, Russian Offices 597
Jetersville, Va. .... Vol. 1A
Jhalawar .... Vol. 3B
Jhind, Jind .... Vol. 3B
Johore, Johor .... Vol. 4B
Jonesboro, Tenn. .... Vol. 1A
J. P. Johnson (Confed. #66X1) .... Vol. 1A
Jordan .... Vol. 4A
Jordan (Palestine Occ.) .... Vol. 4A
Journaux .... Vol. 2B
Juan Fernandez Islands (Chile) ... Vol. 2A
Jubile de l'Union Postale Universelle
  (Switzerland #98) .... Vol. 6A
Jugoslavia, Jugoslavija .... Vol. 6B
Junagarh .... Vol. 3B

K .... Vol. 1A
KA3AKCTAH .... Vol. 4A
Kabul .... Vol. 1A
Kalaallit Nunaat, Kalatdlit
  Nunat .... Vol. 3A
Kamerun .... Vol. 2A
Kampuchea .... Vol. 2A
Kansu .... Vol. 2A
Karelia, Karjala .... Vol. 4A
Karema ovptd. on Belgian
  Congo .... Vol. 3A
Karki .... Vol. 3B
Karolinen .... Vol. 3B
Kashmir .... Vol. 3B
Katanga .... Vol. 4A
Kathiri State of Seiyun .... Vol. 1A
Kaunas .... 595; Vol. 4A
Kayangel (Palau #686) .... Vol. 5A
Kazakhstan, Kazakstan,
  Kazakstan .... Vol. 4A
Kedah .... Vol. 4B
Keeling Islands .... Vol. 2B
Kelantan .... Vol. 4B
Kentta Postia .... Vol. 2B
Kenya .... Vol. 4A
Kenya and Uganda .... Vol. 4A
Kenya, Uganda, Tanzania .... Vol. 4A
Kenya, Uganda, Tanganyika ...... Vol. 4A
Kenya, Uganda, Tanganyika,
  Zanzibar .... Vol. 4A
Kerassunde 597
Kermanshah .... Vol. 3B
K.G.C.A. ovptd. on Yugoslavia ... Vol. 6B
K.G.L. .... Vol. 1A, Vol. 2B
Kharkiv .... Vol. 6B
Khmer Republic .... Vol. 2A
Khor Fakkan .... Vol. 6A
Kiangsi .... Vol. 2A
Kiangsu .... Vol. 2A
Kiauchau, Kiautschou .... Vol. 4A
Kibris .... Vol. 6B
Kibris Cumhuriyeti
  (Cyprus #198-200) .... Vol. 2B
Kigoma ovptd. on Belgian
  Congo .... Vol. 3A
Kilis .... Vol. 6A
King Edward VII Land
  (New Zealand #121a) .... Vol. 5A
Kingman's City Post .... Vol. 1A
Kingston, Ga. .... Vol. 1A
Kionga .... Vol. 4A
Kirghizia .... Vol. 4A

Kiribati .... Vol. 4A
Kirin .... Vol. 2A
Kishangarh, Kishengarh .... Vol. 3B
Kithyra .... Vol. 3A, Vol. 3B
K.K. Post Stempel (or Stampel) ..... Vol. 1B
K.K.T.C. (Turk. Rep. N. Cyprus
  #RA1) .... Vol. 6B
Klaipeda .... Vol. 4B
Knoxville, Tenn. .... Vol. 1A
Kolomyia .... Vol. 6B
Kolozsvar .... Vol. 3B
Kon ... 382, 596, Vol. 1B, Vol. 2B, Vol. 4A,
  Vol. 6A
Kongeligt .... Vol. 2B
Kop Koh .... Vol. 2B
Korca, Korce (Albania) .... Vol. 1A
Korea .... Vol. 4A
Korea, Democratic People's
  Republic .... Vol. 4A
Korea (Japanese Offices) .... Vol. 4A
Korea, Indian Custodial Unit ..... Vol. 3B
Korea, North .... Vol. 4A
Korea, Soviet occupation .... Vol. 4A
Korea, U.S. Military Govt. .... Vol. 4A
Koritsa .... Vol. 2B
Koror (Palau #686) .... Vol. 5A
Korytsa (Albania #81) .... Vol. 1A
Kos .... Vol. 3B
Kosova .... Vol. 1A
Kosovo .... Vol. 1A, Vol. 4A
Kotah .... Vol. 3B
Kouang Tcheou-Wan .... Vol. 3B
KPHTH (Crete) .... Vol. 3B
Kr., Kreuzer .... Vol. 1B, Vol. 3B
Kraljevstvo, Kraljevina .... Vol. 6B
K.S.A. .... Vol. 6A
Kuban Government .... Vol. 6A
K.U.K., K. und K. .... 378, Vol. 1B, Vol. 3B
Kunming .... Vol. 2A
Kupa Zone .... Vol. 6B
Kurdistan .... Vol. 4A
Kurland, Kurzeme .... 595, Vol. 4A
Kurus .... Vol. 6B
Kuwait, Koweit .... Vol. 4A, Vol. 5A
Kwangchowan .... Vol. 2B
Kwangsi .... Vol. 2A
Kwangtung .... Vol. 2A
Kweichow .... Vol. 2A
K. Wurtt. Post .... Vol. 3B
Kyiv .... Vol. 6B
Kyrgyz Express Post ....Vol. 4A
Kyrgyzstan .... Vol. 4A

La Aguera .... Vol. 1A
Labuan .... Vol. 4A
La Canea .... Vol. 3B
Lady McLeod .... Vol. 6B
La Georgie .... Vol. 3A
Lagos .... Vol. 4A
La Grange, Tex. .... Vol. 1A
Laibach .... Vol. 6B
Lake City, Fla. .... Vol. 1A
Lanchow .... Vol. 2A
Land Post .... Vol. 4A
Lao, Laos .... Vol. 4A
Laos (Int. Com., India) .... Vol. 3B
L.A.R. .... Vol. 4A
Las Bela .... Vol. 3B
Latakia, Lattaquie .... Vol. 4A
Latvia, Latvija .... 595, Vol. 4A
Laurens Court House, S.C. .... Vol. 1A
Lavaca .... Vol. 1A
League of Nations .... Vol. 6A
Lebanon .... Vol. 4A, Vol. 5A, Vol. 6A
Leeward Islands .... Vol. 4A
Lefkas .... Vol. 3A, Vol. 3B
Lei ovptd. on Austria 378
Lemnos .... Vol. 3A
Lenoir, N.C. .... Vol. 1A
Lero, Leros .... Vol. 3B
Lesbos .... Vol. 3A
Lesotho .... Vol. 4A
Lesser Sundas .... Vol. 5A
Lettland, Lettonia .... Vol. 4A
Levant, British .... Vol. 3A
Levant, French .... Vol. 2B, Vol. 6A
Levant, Italian .... Vol. 3B
Levant, Polish 124
Levant, Romanian 379
Levant, Russian 597
Levant, Syrian (on Lebanon) ..... Vol. 6A
Lexington, Miss. .... Vol. 1A
Lexington, Va. .... Vol. 1A
Liaoning .... Vol. 2A
Liban, Libanaise .... Vol. 4A
Libau ovptd. on German .... Vol. 4A
Liberia .... Vol. 4A
Liberty, Va. .... Vol. 1A
Libya, Libia, Libye .... Vol. 4A
Libyan Arab Republic .... Vol. 4A

Liechtenstein .... Vol. 4A
Lietuva, Lietuvos .... Vol. 4A
Lifland 595
Ligne Aeriennes de la France
  Libre (Syria #MC5) .... Vol. 6A
Lima .... Vol. 5A
Limestone Springs, S.C. .... Vol. 1A
L'Inde .... Vol. 2B
Linja-Autorahti Bussfrakt .... Vol. 2B
Lipso, Lisso .... Vol. 3B
Lithuania .... 595, Vol. 4A
Lithuania, Central .... Vol. 2A
Lithuanian Occupation of
  Memel .... Vol. 4B
Litwa Srodkowa, Litwy
  Srodkowej .... Vol. 2A
Livingston, Ala. .... Vol. 1A
Livonia 595
Ljubljana .... Vol. 6B
Llanes .... Vol. 6A
L McL .... Vol. 6B
Local .... Vol. 6B
Local Post .... Vol. 2A
Lockport, N.Y. .... Vol. 1A
Lombardy-Venetia .... Vol. 1B
Lorraine .... Vol. 2B
Losen .... Vol. 6A
Lothringen .... Vol. 2B
Louisville, Ky. .... Vol. 1A
Lourenco Marques, L. Marques ... Vol. 4A
Lower Austria .... Vol. 1B
L P overprinted on Russian
  stamps .... Vol. 4A
LTSR on Lithuania .... Vol. 4A
Lubeck, Luebeck .... Vol. 3A
Lubiana .... Vol. 6B
Lublin 15
Luminescence .... Vol. 1A
Luxembourg .... Vol. 4A
Lviv .... Vol. 6B
Lydenburg .... Vol. 6B
Lynchburg, Va. .... Vol. 1A

Macao, Macau .... Vol. 4B
Macedonia .... Vol. 4B
Machin Head definitives .... Vol. 3A
Macon, Ga. .... Vol. 1A
Madagascar, Madagasikara ..... Vol. 4B
Madagascar (British) .... Vol. 4B
Madeira .... 194, Vol. 4B
Madero Issue (Mexico) .... Vol. 4B
Madison, Ga. .... Vol. 1A
Madison Court House, Fla. ...... Vol. 1A
Madrid .... Vol. 6A
Madura .... Vol. 5A
Mafeking .... Vol. 2A
Magdalena .... Vol. 2A
Magyar, Magyarorszag .... Vol. 3B
Magy. Kir. .... Vol. 3B
Majunga .... Vol. 4B
Makedonija .... Vol. 4B
Malacca .... Vol. 4B
Malaga .... Vol. 6A
Malagasy Republic .... Vol. 4B
Malawi .... Vol. 4B
Malaya .... Vol. 4B
Malaya (Japanese Occ.) ... Vol. 4B, Vol. 5A
Malaya (Thai Occ.) .... Vol. 4B
Malaya, Federation of .... Vol. 4B
Malaysia .... Vol. 4B
Malay States .... Vol. 4B
Maldive Islands, Maldives .... Vol. 4B
Malgache Republique .... Vol. 4B
Mali .... Vol. 4B
Malmedy .... Vol. 3A
Malta .... Vol. 4B
Maluku Selatan (So. Moluccas) ... Vol. 6A
Man, Isle of .... Vol. 3A
Manchukuo .... Vol. 2A
Manchukuo stamps overprinted ... Vol. 2A
Manchuria .... Vol. 2A
Manizales .... Vol. 2A
Mapka, Mapok .... 383, Vol. 2B
Mariana Islands, Marianen ...... Vol. 4B
Marienwerder .... Vol. 4B
Marietta, Ga. .... Vol. 1A
Marion, Va. .... Vol. 1A
Markka, Markkaa .... Vol. 2B
Maroc, Marocco, Marokko .... Vol. 2B,
  Vol. 3A, Vol. 4B
Marruecos .... Vol. 4B, Vol. 6A
Mars Bluff, S.C. .... Vol. 1A
Marshall Islands, Marschall-Inseln,
  Marshall-Inseln .... Vol. 4B
Marshall Islands (G.R.I. surch.) .... Vol. 5A
Martinique .... Vol. 4B
Martin's City Post .... Vol. 1A
Mauritania, Mauritanie .... Vol. 4B
Mauritania stamps surcharged .... Vol. 2B
Mauritius .... Vol. 4B

Mayotte .... Vol. 4B
Mayreau 844
M.B.D. overprinted .... Vol. 3B
McNeel, A.W. .... Vol. 1A
Mecca .... Vol. 6A
Mecklenburg-Schwerin .... Vol. 3A
Mecklenburg-Strelitz .... Vol. 3A
Mecklenburg-Vorpomm. .... Vol. 3A
Mecklenburg-Vorpommern ...... Vol. 3A
Medellin .... Vol. 2A
Medina .... Vol. 6A
Medio Real .... Vol. 2B
M.E.F. ovptd on Great Britain ..... Vol. 3A
Mejico .... Vol. 4B
Melaka .... Vol. 4B
Melekeor (Palau #686) .... Vol. 5A
Memel, Memelgebiet .... Vol. 4B
Memphis, Tenn. .... Vol. 1A
Meng Chiang .... Vol. 2A
Menge .... Vol. 4B
Mengtsz .... Vol. 2B
Merida .... Vol. 4B
Meshed .... Vol. 3B
Mesopotamia (British
   Occupation) .... Vol. 4B
Metelin 598
Mexico, Mexicano .... Vol. 4B
Micanopy, Fla. .... Vol. 1A
Micronesia .... Vol. 4B
Middle Congo .... Vol. 4B
Middle East Forces .... Vol. 3A
Mihon .... Vol. 4A
Mil .... Vol. 4A
Militarpost (Milit. Post) .... Vol. 1B
Millbury, Mass. .... Vol. 1A
Milledgeville, Ga. .... Vol. 1A
Miller, Gen. 596
Milliemes surch. on French
   Off. in Turkey .... Vol. 2B
Mitau .... Vol. 4A
Milton, N.C. .... Vol. 1A
M. Kir. .... Vol. 3B
Mn. .... Vol. 4A
Mobile, Ala. .... Vol. 1A
Mocambique .... Vol. 4B
Modena, Modones .... Vol. 3B
Moheli .... Vol. 4B
Moldavia .... 250, Vol. 4B
Moldova .... Vol. 4B
Moluccas .... Vol. 5A
Monaco .... Vol. 4B
Monastir .... Vol. 6B
Mongolia .... Vol. 4B
Mongtseu, Mongtze .... Vol. 2B
Monrovia .... Vol. 4A
Mont Athos 598
Montenegro .... Vol. 4B
Monterrey .... Vol. 4B
Montevideo .... Vol. 6B
Montgomery, Ala. .... Vol. 1A
Montserrat .... Vol. 4B
Moquea, Moquegua .... Vol. 5A
Morelia .... Vol. 4B
Morocco .... Vol. 4B
Morocco (British Offices) ...... Vol. 3A
Morocco (German Offices) .... Vol. 3A
Morocco, French .... Vol. 2B
Morocco, Spanish .... Vol. 6A
Morvi .... Vol. 3B
Moschopolis .... Vol. 2B
Mosul .... Vol. 4B
Mount Athos (Greece) .... Vol. 3A
Mount Athos (Turkey) .... Vol. 6B
Mount Athos, Russian Offices ... 598
Mount Lebanon, La. .... Vol. 1A
Mount Pleasant, NC .... Vol. 1A
Moyen-Congo .... Vol. 4B
Mozambique .... Vol. 4B
Mozambique Co. .... Vol. 4B
MQE ovptd. on French Colonies ... Vol. 4B
Muscat and Oman .... Vol. 5A
Mustique 844
M.V.i.R. 378
Myanmar (Burma) .... Vol. 1B
Mytilene .... Vol. 3A

Nabha .... Vol. 3B
Naciones Unidas .... Vol. 1A
Nagyvarad .... Vol. 3B
Namibia .... Vol. 5A, Vol. 6A
Nandgaon .... Vol. 3B
Nanking .... Vol. 2A
Nanumaga .... Vol. 6B
Nanumea .... Vol. 6B
Naples, Napoletana .... Vol. 3B
Nashville, Tenn. .... Vol. 1A
Natal .... Vol. 5A
Nations Unies .... Vol. 1A, Vol. 6A
Native Feudatory States, India ... Vol. 3B
Nauru .... Vol. 5A

Navanagar .... Vol. 3B
Navarra .... Vol. 6A
N.C.E. ovptd. on French
   Colonies .... Vol. 5A
Neapolitan Provinces .... Vol. 3B
Ned. (Nederlandse) Antillen ... Vol. 5A
Ned. (Nederl, Nederlandse)
   Indie .... Vol. 5A
Nederland .... Vol. 5A
Nederlands Nieuw Guinea .... Vol. 5A
Negeri Sembilan .... Vol. 4B
Negri Sembilan .... Vol. 4B
Nejd .... Vol. 6A
Nejdi Administration of Hejaz ... Vol. 6A
Nepal .... Vol. 5A
Netherlands .... Vol. 5A
Netherlands Antilles .... Vol. 5A
Netherlands Indies .... Vol. 5A
Netherlands New Guinea .... Vol. 5A
Nevis .... Vol. 5A
New Britain .... Vol. 5A
New Brunswick .... Vol. 2A
New Caledonia .... Vol. 5A
New Caledonia stamps
   overprinted .... Vol. 5A
Newfoundland .... Vol. 2A
New Granada .... Vol. 2A
New Greece .... Vol. 3A
New Guinea .... Vol. 5A
New Guinea, British .... Vol. 5A
New Guinea, German .... Vol. 3A
New Haven, Conn. .... Vol. 1A
New Hebrides (British) .... Vol. 5A
New Hebrides (French) .... Vol. 5A
New Orleans, La. .... Vol. 1A
New Republic .... Vol. 5A
New Smyrna, Fla. .... Vol. 1A
New South Wales .... Vol. 5A
New York, N.Y. .... Vol. 1A
New Zealand .... Vol. 5A
Nezavisna .... Vol. 2A
N.F. overprinted on
   Nyasaland Pro. .... Vol. 3A
Ngaraard (Palau #686) .... Vol. 5A
Ngardman (Palau #686) .... Vol. 5A
Ngaremlengui (Palau #686) ... Vol. 5A
Ngchesar (Palau #686) .... Vol. 5A
Ngiwal (Palau #686) .... Vol. 5A
Nicaragua .... Vol. 5A
Nicaria .... Vol. 3A
Nieuwe Republiek .... Vol. 5A
Nieuw Guinea .... Vol. 5A
Niger .... Vol. 5A
Niger and Senegambia .... Vol. 6A
Niger and Upper Senegal .... Vol. 6B
Niger Coast Protectorate .... Vol. 5A
Nigeria .... Vol. 5A
Nikolaevsk .... Vol. 6A
Ningsia .... Vol. 2A
Nippon .... Vol. 4A
Nisiro, Nisiros .... Vol. 3B
Niuafo'ou .... Vol. 6B
Niue .... Vol. 5A
Niutao .... Vol. 6B
Nlle. Caledonie .... Vol. 5A
No Hay Estampillas .... Vol. 2A
N. O. P. O. (Confed. #62XU1) ..... Vol. 1A
Norddeutscher Postbezirk ...... Vol. 3A
Noreg (1st stamp #318) .... Vol. 5A
Norfolk, Va. .... Vol. 1A
Norfolk Island .... Vol. 5A
Norge .... Vol. 5A
North Borneo .... Vol. 5A
North China .... Vol. 2A
Northeast China .... Vol. 2A
Northeast Postal Service .... Vol. 2A
Northeastern Provinces (China) ... Vol. 2A
North Epirus (Greek
   Occupation) .... Vol. 3A
Northern Cook Islands .... Vol. 5A
Northern Cyprus, Turkish
   Rep. of .... Vol. 6B
Northern Ireland .... Vol. 3A
Northern Kiangsu .... Vol. 2A
Northern Nigeria .... Vol. 5A
Northern Poland 16
Northern Rhodesia .... Vol. 5A
Northern Zone, Morocco .... Vol. 4B
North German Confederation .... Vol. 3A
North Ingermanland .... Vol. 5A
North Viet Nam .... Vol. 6B
Northwest China .... Vol. 2A
North West (N. W.) Pacific
   Islands .... Vol. 5A
Norway .... Vol. 5A
Nossi-Be .... Vol. 4B
Notopher .... Vol. 3A
Nouvelle Caledonie .... Vol. 5A
Nouvelle Hebrides .... Vol. 5A
Nova Scotia .... Vol. 2A

Novocherkassk .... Vol. 6A
Nowa .... Vol. 1B
Nowa Bb ovptd. on Bulgaria 378
Nowanuggur .... Vol. 3B
Nowta .... Vol. 6A
Nowte .... Vol. 4B
Noyta .... 383, Vol. 1B, Vol. 3A, Vol. 4A,
   Vol. 6B
NP surcharged on Great Britain ... Vol. 5A
Nr. 21, Nr. 16 .... Vol. 3A
N S B ovptd. on French Colonies ... Vol. 5A
N. Sembilan .... Vol. 4B
N. Sembilan .... Vol. 4B
Nueva Granada .... Vol. 2A
Nui .... Vol. 6B
Nukufetau .... Vol. 6B
Nukulaelae .... Vol. 6B
Nyasaland (Protectorate) .... Vol. 5A
Nyasaland and Rhodesia 243
Nyasaland, overprinted .... Vol. 3A
Nyassa .... Vol. 5A
N.Z. .... Vol. 5A

Oakway, S.C. .... Vol. 1A
Oaxaca .... Vol. 4B
Obock .... Vol. 5A
Ob. Ost ovptd. on Germany
   (Lithuania) 595
Occupation Francaise .... Vol. 3B
Oceania, Oceanie .... Vol. 2B
Oesterr. Post, Ofterreich .... Vol. 1B
Offentlig Sak, Off. Sak .... Vol. 5A
Oil Rivers .... Vol. 5A
O K C A (Russia) 596
Oldenburg .... Vol. 3A
Olonets 595
Oltre Giuba .... Vol. 5A
Oman, Sultanate of .... Vol. 5A
ONU (UN Offices in
   Geneva #384) .... Vol. 1A
Oradea .... Vol. 3B
Orange River Colony .... Vol. 5A
Oranje Vrij Staat .... Vol. 5A
Orchha, Orcha .... Vol. 3B
Ore surcharged on Denmark ... Vol. 2B
Orense .... Vol. 6A
Organisation Mondiale de
   la Sante .... Vol. 6A
Oriental .... Vol. 6B
Orts-Post .... Vol. 6B
O.S. .... Vol. 5A
Osten 122
Osterreich .... Vol. 1B
Ostland 595
Ottoman, Ottomanes .... Vol. 2B, Vol. 6B
Oubangi Chari .... Vol. 6B
Outer Mongolia .... Vol. 4B
Oviedo .... Vol. 6A
O.V.S. .... Vol. 5A
Oxford, N.C. .... Vol. 1A
O'zbekiston .... Vol. 6B

P .... Vol. 2A, Vol. 2B, Vol. 4A, Vol. 6A
P on Straits Settlements .... Vol. 4B
Pacchi Postali .... Vol. 3B, Vol. 6B
Pacific Steam Navigation Co. .... Vol. 5A
Packhoi, Pakhoi .... Vol. 2B
Pahang .... Vol. 4B
Paid (Confed. #35X, etc.) .... Vol. 1A
Paid 5 (US #4X1, 7X1,
   many Confed.) .... Vol. 1A
Paid 10 (Confed. #76XU, 101XU,
   80XU) .... Vol. 1A
Paid 2 Cents (Confed. #2XU) .... Vol. 1A
Paid 3 Cents (Confed. #2AXU) .... Vol. 1A
Paita .... Vol. 5A
Pakistan .... Vol. 5A
Pakke-porto .... Vol. 3A
Palau .... Vol. 5A
Palestine .... Vol. 2B, Vol. 5A
Palestine (British Administration) ... Vol. 5A
Palestine (Jordan Occ.) .... Vol. 4A
Palestine overprinted .... Vol. 4A
Palestinian Authority .... Vol. 5A
Panama .... Vol. 5A
Panama (Colombian Dom.) ...... Vol. 2A,
   Vol. 5A
Panama Canal Zone .... Vol. 1A
Papua .... Vol. 5A
Papua New Guinea .... Vol. 5A
Para .... Vol. 2B, Vol. 6B
Para ovptd. on Austria .... Vol. 1B
Para ovptd. on France .... Vol. 2B
Para ovptd. on Germany .... Vol. 3A
Para ovptd. on Italy .... Vol. 3B
Paraguay .... Vol. 5A
Paras .... Vol. 2B, Vol. 6B
Paras ovpt. on Great Britain ... Vol. 3A
Paras ovpt. on Romania 379
Paras ovpt. on Russia 597

Parma, Parm., Parmensi .... Vol. 3B
Pasco .... Vol. 5A
Patiala .... Vol. 3B
Patmo, Patmos .... Vol. 3B
Patterson, N.C. .... Vol. 1A
Patton, N.B. (Confed. #138XU1) ... Vol. 1A
Patzcuaro .... Vol. 4B
Paxos .... Vol. 2A, Vol. 3A, Vol. 3B
PC CP 385
PD 690
P.E. (Egypt #4, etc.) .... Vol. 2B
Pechino, Peking .... Vol. 3B
Peleliu (Palau #686) .... Vol. 5A
Pen, Penna .... Vol. 2B
Penang .... Vol. 4B
Penny Post (US 3LB, 8LB) ...... Vol. 1A
Penrhyn Island .... Vol. 5A
Pensacola, Fla. .... Vol. 1A
Penybnnka Cpncka .... Vol. 1B
People's Republic of China ...... Vol. 2A
Perak .... Vol. 4B
Perlis .... Vol. 4B
Persekutuan Tanah Melayu
   (Malaya #91) .... Vol. 4B
Persia (British Occupation) .... Vol. 1B
Persia, Persanes .... Vol. 3B
Peru, Peruana .... Vol. 5A
Pesa ovpt. on Germany .... Vol. 3A
Petersburg, Va. .... Vol. 1A
Pfennig, Pfg., Pf. .... Vol. 2B, Vol. 3A, Vol. 4A
P.G.S. (Perak) .... Vol. 4B
Philadelphia, Pa. .... Vol. 1A
Philippines .... Vol. 2A, Vol. 5A
Philippines (US Admin.) .... Vol. 1A, Vol. 5A
Philippines (Japanese Occ.) ...... Vol. 1A,
   Vol. 5A
Piast., Piaster ovptd. on Austria .... Vol. 1B
Piaster ovptd. on Germany ...... Vol. 3A
Piaster ovptd. on Romania 379
Piastre, Piastra ovptd. on Italy ... Vol. 3B
Piastre .... Vol. 2B, Vol. 4B, Vol. 6B
Piastre ovptd. on France .... Vol. 3A
Piastres ovpt. on Great Britain ...... Vol. 3A
Piastres ovpt. on Russia 597
Pies .... Vol. 2A, Vol. 3B
Pietersburg .... Vol. 6B
Pilgrim Tercentenary (US #548) ... Vol. 1A
Pilipinas .... Vol. 1A, Vol. 5A
Pisco .... Vol. 5A
Piscopi .... Vol. 3B
Pitcairn Islands 1
Pittsylvania C.H., Va. .... Vol. 1A
Piura .... Vol. 5A
Plains of Dura, Ga. .... Vol. 1A
Pleasant Shade, Va. .... Vol. 1A
Plum Creek, Tex. .... Vol. 1A
P.O. Paid .... Vol. 1A
Pobres (Spain #RA11) .... Vol. 6A
POCCIЯ, POCCIИR 385
Poczta, Polska .... 15, Vol. 2B
Pohjois Inkeri 455
Pokutia .... Vol. 6B
Poland 15
Poland, exile government in
   Great Britain 124
Polish Levant 124
Polish Offices in Danzig 123
Polish Offices in Turkish Empire ... 124
Polska 15
Polynesia, French (Polynesie) .... Vol. 2B
Ponce .... 211, Vol. 1A
Ponta Delgada 124
Р.О.П.иТ. 597
Poonch .... Vol. 3B
Popayan .... Vol. 2A
Port Arthur and Dairen 187
Porteado .... Vol. 5A
Porte de Conduccion .... Vol. 5A
Porte de Mar .... Vol. 4B
Porte Franco .... Vol. 5A
Port Gibson, Miss. .... Vol. 1A
Port Gdansk 123
Port Hood, Nova Scotia .... Vol. 2A
Port Lagos .... Vol. 6A
Port Lavaca, Tex. .... Vol. 1A
Porto .... Vol. 1A, Vol. 1B, Vol. 6B
Porto Gazetei 250
Porto Pflichtige .... Vol. 3A
Porto Rico .... 211, Vol. 1A, Vol. 2A
Port Said, French Offices .... Vol. 2B
Portugal, Portuguesa 125
Portuguese Africa 199
Portuguese Congo 200
Portuguese East Africa
   (Mozambique) .... Vol. 4B
Portuguese Guinea 202
Portuguese India 205
Portuguese India overprinted .... Vol. 6B
Posen (Poznan) 16
Post .... Vol. 3A, Vol. 3B

Post (Postage) & Receipt .... Vol. 3B
Posta .... Vol. 1A, Vol. 6A
Postage(s) .... 211, Vol. 1A, Vol. 3A,
    Vol. 3B, Vol. 4B
Postage Due .... Vol. 1A, Vol. 3A
Postas le hioc .... Vol. 3B
Poste Locale .... Vol. 3B
Postes .... Vol. 1B, Vol. 2B, Vol. 4A
Postes Serbes ovptd. on France ... Vol. 6A
Postgebiet Ob. Ost. 595
Postmarke .... Vol. 1A
Post Office (US #7X, 9X) ...... Vol. 1A
Post Stamp .... Vol. 3B
Postzegel .... Vol. 5A
P.P. ovptd. on French postage
    dues .... Vol. 2B
P.P.C. ovptd. on Poland 124
Pre .... Vol. 6B
Prefecture issues .... Vol. 4A
Preussen .... Vol. 3A
Priamur .... Vol. 4A
Prince Edward Island .... Vol. 2A
Pristina .... Vol. 6B
Province of Canada .... Vol. 2A
Providence (Prov.), R.I. .... Vol. 1A
Prussia .... Vol. 3A
PS .... Vol. 2A, Vol. 3B
P.S.N.C. (Peru) .... Vol. 5A
Puerto Principe .... Vol. 1A, Vol. 2A
Puerto Rico, Pto. Rico .... 211, Vol. 1A,
    Vol. 2A
Puerto Rico (US Admin.) ..... 211, Vol. 1A
Pul .... Vol. 1A
Pulau Pinang .... Vol. 4B
Puno .... Vol. 5A
Puttialla State .... Vol. 3B

Qatar 213
Qu'aiti State in Hadhramaut ..... Vol. 1A
Qu'aiti State of Shihr and
    Mukalla .... Vol. 1A
Queensland .... Vol. 1A
Quelimane 234

R (Armenia) .... Vol. 1A
R (Jind, Iran) .... Vol. 3B
R ovptd. on French Colonies ...... Vol. 2B
Rajasthan .... Vol. 3B
Rajpeepla, Rajpipla .... Vol. 3B
Raleigh, N.C. .... Vol. 1A
Rappen .... Vol. 6A
Rarotonga .... Vol. 2A
Ras al Khaima .... 234, Vol. 6B
R.A.U. .... Vol. 6A
Rayon .... Vol. 6A
Recargo .... Vol. 5A
Redonda (Antigua) .... Vol. 1A
Refugee Relief .... Vol. 3B
Regatul .... Vol. 3B
Reichspost .... Vol. 3A
Reis (Portugal) 125
Repubblica Sociale Italiana ...... Vol. 3A
Republic of China .... Vol. 2A
Republique Arab Unie .... Vol. 6A
Republique Democratique
    du Congo .... Vol. 6B
Reseau d'Etat .... Vol. 3B
Resistance overprinted on Syria .... Vol. 6A
Rethymnon, Retymno .... Vol. 2A
Reunion .... Vol. 2A
R.F. .... See France or French Colonies
RF - Solidarite Francaise .... Vol. 2B
R H .... Vol. 3A
Rheatown, Tenn. .... Vol. 1A
Rheinland-Pfalz .... Vol. 3A
Rhine Palatinate .... Vol. 3A
Rhodes .... Vol. 3B
Rhodesia 241
Rhodesia (formerly So. Rhodesia) ... 244
Rhodesia and Nyasaland 243
Rialtar .... Vol. 3A
Riau, Riouw Archipelago .... Vol. 3B
Ricevuta .... Vol. 3B, Vol. 6A
Richmond, Tex. .... Vol. 1A
Rigsbank Skilling .... Vol. 2B
Ringgold, Ga. .... Vol. 1A
Rio de Oro 247
Rio Muni 248
RIS on Netherlands Indies .... Vol. 3B
Rizeh 598
Rn. .... Vol. 4A
RNS .... Vol. 3B
R. O. ovptd. on Turkey .... Vol. 2B
Robertsport .... Vol. 4A
Rodi .... Vol. 3B
Roepiah .... Vol. 5A
Romagna, Romagne .... Vol. 3B
Romana .... 250, Vol. 3B
Romania, Roumania 250
Romania, Occupation, Offices 379

Romanian Occupation of
    Hungary .... Vol. 3B
Romanian Occupation of
    Western Ukraine .... Vol. 6B
Romania, Offices in the Turkish
    Empire 379
Roman States .... Vol. 3B
Ross Dependency .... Vol. 5A
Rossija 521
Rostov .... Vol. 6A
Rouad, Ile 379
Roumelie Orientale .... Vol. 2B
Rouad, Ile 379
RSA .... Vol. 6A
R S M (San Marino) .... Vol. 6A
Ruanda ovptd. on Congo .... Vol. 3A
Ruanda-Urundi 379
Ruffifch-Polen ovptd. on Germany ... 122
Rumania, Roumania 250
Rumanien on Germany 378
Rupee on Great Britain .... Vol. 5A
Russia 384
Russia (Finnish Occupation) 595,
    Vol. 4A
Russia (German Occupation) 595
Russian Company of Navigation
    & Trade 597
Russian Dominion of Poland 15
Russian Empire, Finland .... Vol. 2B
Russian Occupation of Crete ..... Vol. 2A
Russian Occupation of
    Germany .... Vol. 3A
Russian Occupation of Korea ..... Vol. 4A
Russian Occupation of Latvia ... Vol. 4A
Russian Occupation of
    Lithuania .... Vol. 4A
Russian Offices 596
Russian Offices in China 596
Russian Offices in Turkish Empire ... 597
Russian stamps surch. or
    ovptd. .... 384, 385, 595, 597, Vol. 1A,
    Vol. 2B, Vol. 3A, Vol. 4A, Vol. 6A
Russian Turkestan 384
Rustenburg .... Vol. 6B
Rutherfordton, N.C. .... Vol. 1A
Rwanda, Rwandaise 600
Ryukyu Islands .... Vol. 1A

S on Straits Settlements .... Vol. 4B
S A, S.A.K. (Saudi Arabia) .... Vol. 6A
Saar, Saargebiet, Saar Land 617
Sabah .... Vol. 4B
Sachsen .... Vol. 3A
Sahara Occidental (Espanol) .... Vol. 6A
St. Christopher 624
St. Christopher-Nevis-Anguilla 661
Ste. Marie de Madagascar 684
St. Georges, Bermuda .... Vol. 1B
St. Helena 625
S. Thome (Tome) E Principe 716
St. Kitts 640
St. Kitts-Nevis 661
St. Louis, Mo. .... Vol. 1A
St. Lucia 667
St. Martin 684
St. Pierre and Miquelon 690
St. Thomas and Prince Islands 716
St. Vincent 762
St. Vincent and the Grenadines 762
St. Vincent Grenadines 833
Salamanca Province .... Vol. 6A
Salem, N.C. .... Vol. 1A
Salem, Va. .... Vol. 1A
Salisbury, N.C. .... Vol. 1A
Salonicco, Salonika .... Vol. 3B
Salonika (Turkish) .... Vol. 6B
Salonique .... 598, Vol. 6B
Salvador, El 848
Salzburg .... Vol. 1B
Samoa 895
Samos .... Vol. 2B, Vol. 3A
San Antonio, Tex. .... Vol. 1A
San Marino .... Vol. 6A
San Sebastian .... Vol. 6A
Santa Cruz de Tenerife .... Vol. 6A
Santa Maura .... Vol. 3A, Vol. 3B
Santander .... Vol. 2A
Sao Paulo .... Vol. 1B
Sao Tome and Principe 716
Saorstat .... Vol. 3B
Sarawak .... Vol. 4B, Vol. 6A
Sardinia .... Vol. 3B
Sarre overprinted on Germany
    and Bavaria 617
Saseno .... Vol. 6A
Saudi Arabia .... Vol. 6A
Saudi Arabia overprinted .... Vol. 4A
Saurashtra .... Vol. 3B
Savannah, Ga. .... Vol. 1A
Saxony .... Vol. 3A

SCADTA .... Vol. 2A
Scarpanto .... Vol. 3B
Schleswig .... Vol. 3A, Vol. 6A
Schleswig-Holstein .... Vol. 3A
Schweizer Reneke .... Vol. 6B
Scinde .... Vol. 3B
Scotland .... Vol. 3A
Scutari, Italian Offices .... Vol. 3B
Segel Porto (on Neth. Indies) .... Vol. 3B
Segnatasse, Segna Tassa .... Vol. 3B
Seiyun .... Vol. 1A
Selangor .... Vol. 4B
Selma, Ala. .... Vol. 1A
Semenov .... Vol. 2B
Sen, Sn. ...... Vol. 1A, Vol. 4A, Vol. 5A
Senegal .... Vol. 6A
Senegal stamps surcharged ...... Vol. 2B
Senegambia and Niger .... Vol. 6A
Serb Administration of Bosnia,
    Banja Luca .... Vol. 1B
Serbia, Serbien .... Vol. 6A
Serbia & Montenego ..... Vol. 4B, Vol. 6A
Serbian Occupation of Hungary .... Vol. 3B
Service .... Vol. 3B, Vol. 5A
Sevastopol .... Vol. 6A
Seville, Sevilla .... Vol. 6A
Seychelles .... Vol. 6A
S.H. .... Vol. 3A
Shanghai .... Vol. 2A, Vol. 3A
Shanghai (U.S. Offices) .... Vol. 1A
Shanghai and Nanking .... Vol. 2A
Shansi .... Vol. 2A
Shantung .... Vol. 2A
Sharjah .... Vol. 6A
Shensi .... Vol. 2A
Shihr and Mukalla .... Vol. 1A
Shqipenia, Shqiptare, Shqiperija,
    Shqiperise (Albania) .... Vol. 1A
S.H.S. on Bosnia and
    Herzegovina .... Vol. 6B
S.H.S. on Hungary .... Vol. 6B
Siam (Thailand) .... Vol. 6B
Siberia .... Vol. 6A
Siberian stamps overprinted
    or surcharged .... Vol. 2B
Sicily, Sicilia .... Vol. 3B
Siege de la Ligue Arabe
    (Morocco #44) .... Vol. 4B
Sierra Leone .... Vol. 6A
Sikang .... Vol. 2A
Silesia, Eastern .... Vol. 2B
Silesia, Upper .... Vol. 6B
Simi .... Vol. 3B
Sinaloa .... Vol. 4B
Singapore .... Vol. 6A
Sinkiang .... Vol. 2A
Sint Maarten 684
Sirmoor, Sirmur .... Vol. 3B
Six Cents .... Vol. 1A
Sld. .... Vol. 1B
Slesvig .... Vol. 6A
Slovakia .... Vol. 2B, Vol. 6A
Slovene Coast .... Vol. 6B
Slovenia, Slovenija .... Vol. 6A
Slovenia, Italian .... Vol. 6B
Slovensko, Slovenska,
    Slovensky .... Vol. 2B, Vol. 6A
S. Marino .... Vol. 6A, Vol. 6A
Smirne, Smyrna .... Vol. 3B
Smyrne 598
S O ovptd. on Czechoslovakia,
    Poland .... Vol. 2B
Sobreporte .... Vol. 2A
Sociedad Colombo-Alemana .... Vol. 2a
Sociedade de Geographia
    de Lisboa 190
Societe des Nations .... Vol. 6A
Soldi .... Vol. 1B
Solomon Islands .... Vol. 6A
Somali, Somalia, Somaliya .... Vol. 6A
Somalia, B.M.A. .... Vol. 3A
Somalia, E.A.F. .... Vol. 3A
Somali Coast (Djibouti) .... Vol. 6A
Somaliland Protectorate .... Vol. 6A
Sonora .... Vol. 4B
Sonsorol (Palau #686) .... Vol. 5A
Soomaaliya, Sooomaliyeed .... Vol. 6A
Soruth, Sorath .... Vol. 3B
Soudan .... Vol. 2B, Vol. 6A
South Africa .... Vol. 6A
South African Republic
    (Transvaal) .... Vol. 6B
South Arabia .... Vol. 6A
South Australia .... Vol. 1A
South Bulgaria .... Vol. 2B
South Borneo .... Vol. 5A
South China .... Vol. 2A
Southern Nigeria .... Vol. 6A
Southern Poland 16
Southern Rhodesia .... Vol. 6A

Southern Yemen .... Vol. 6B
South Georgia .... Vol. 2B, Vol. 6A
South Georgia and South
    Sandwich Islands .... Vol. 6A
South Kasai .... Vol. 6A
South Korea .... Vol. 4A
South Lithuania .... Vol. 4A
South Moluccas .... Vol. 6A
South Orkneys .... Vol. 2B
South Russia .... Vol. 6A
South Russian stamps surcharged 599
South Shetlands .... Vol. 2B
South Sudan .... Vol. 6B
South Viet Nam .... Vol. 6B
South West Africa .... Vol. 6A
Southwest China .... Vol. 2A
Soviet Union (Russia) 386
Sowjetische Besatzungs Zone ... Vol. 3A
Spain .... Vol. 6A
Spanish Administration of
    Andorra .... Vol. 1A
Spanish Dominion of Cuba .... Vol. 2A
Spanish Dominion of
    Mariana Islands .... Vol. 4B
Spanish Dominion of
    Philippines .... Vol. 5A
Spanish Dominion of Puerto Rico ... 211
Spanish Guinea .... Vol. 6A
Spanish Morocco .... Vol. 6A
Spanish Sahara .... Vol. 6A
Spanish West Africa .... Vol. 6A
Spanish Western Sahara .... Vol. 6A
Sparta, Ga. .... Vol. 1A
Spartanburg, S.C. .... Vol. 1A
SPM ovptd. on French Cols. 690
Srbija I Crna Gora .... Vol. 6A
Sri Lanka .... Vol. 6A
Srodkowa Litwa .... Vol. 2A
Stamp (Tibet #O1) .... Vol. 6B
Stampalia .... Vol. 3B
Stanyslaviv .... Vol. 6B
Statesville, N.C. .... Vol. 1A
Steinmeyer's City Post .... Vol. 1A
Stellaland .... Vol. 6A
Stempel .... Vol. 1B
Straits Settlements .... Vol. 4B
Straits Settlements overprinted .... Vol. 6A
Strombus gigas Linne
    (Neth. Antilles #1193) .... Vol. 5A
STT Vuja, STT Vujna .... Vol. 6B
Styria .... Vol. 1B
S.U. on Straits Settlements .... Vol. 4B
Submarine mail (Correo
    Submarino) .... Vol. 6A
Sudan .... Vol. 6A
Sudan, French .... Vol. 2B
Suid Afrika .... Vol. 6A
Suidwes-Afrika .... Vol. 6A
Suiyuan .... Vol. 2A
S. Ujong .... Vol. 4B
Sultanate of Oman .... Vol. 6A
Sumatra .... Vol. 3B, Vol. 5A
Sumter, S.C. .... Vol. 1A
Sungei Ujong .... Vol. 4B
Suomi (Finland) .... Vol. 2B
Supeh .... Vol. 2A
Surakarta .... Vol. 3B
Surinam, Suriname,
    Surinaamse .... Vol. 6A
Suvalki 595
Sverige .... Vol. 6A
S.W.A. .... Vol. 6A
Swaziland, Swazieland .... Vol. 6A
Sweden .... Vol. 6A
Switzerland .... Vol. 6A
Switzerland, Administration of
    Liechtenstein .... Vol. 4A
Syria, Syrie, Syrienne ... Vol. 5A, Vol. 6A
Syria (Arabian Government) ..... Vol. 6A
Syrie .... Vol. 6A
Syrie-Grand Liban .... Vol. 6A
Szechwan .... Vol. 2A
Szeged .... Vol. 3B

T .... Vol. 1B, Vol. 2B
T ovptd. on stamps of Peru .... Vol. 5A
Tabora ovptd. on Belgian
    Congo .... Vol. 3A
Tacna .... Vol. 5A
Tadjikistan, Tadzikistan .... Vol. 6A
Tae Han (Korea) .... Vol. 4A
Tahiti .... Vol. 6A
Taiwan (Republic of China) .... Vol. 2A
Taiwan (Formosa) .... Vol. 2A
Taiwan, Japanese ...... Vol. 2A, Vol. 4A
Tajikistan .... Vol. 6A
Takca .... Vol. 1B
Takse .... Vol. 6A
Talbotton, Ga. .... Vol. 1A
Talca .... Vol. 2A

Talladega, Ala. .... Vol. 1A
Tallinn .... Vol. 2B
Tanganyika .... Vol. 6A
Tanganyika and Zanzibar .... Vol. 6A
Tanganyika (Tanzania), Kenya,
  Uganda .... Vol. 4A
Tanger .... Vol. 2B, Vol. 6A
Tangier, British Offices .... Vol. 3A
Tangier, French Offices .... Vol. 2B
Tangier, Spanish Offices .... Vol. 6A
Tannu Tuva .... Vol. 6A
Tanzania .... Vol. 6A
Tanzania-Zanzibar .... Vol. 6B
Tartu .... Vol. 2B
Tasmania .... Vol. 1A
Tassa Gazzette .... Vol. 1B
Taxa de Guerra .... 199, Vol. 4B
Taxyapom .... Vol. 2B
Tchad .... Vol. 6A
Tchongking .... Vol. 2A
T.C. overprinted on Cochin .... Vol. 3B
T.C., Postalari .... Vol. 6A
Te Betalen .... Vol. 1B, Vol. 5A, Vol. 6A
Tegucigalpa .... Vol. 3B
Teheran .... Vol. 6B
Tellico Plains, Tenn. .... Vol. 1A
Temesvar .... Vol. 3B
Ten Cents .... Vol. 1A
T.E.O. ovptd. on Turkey or
  France .... Vol. 2A, Vol. 6A
Terres Australes et Antarctiques
  Francaises .... Vol. 2B
Territorio Insular Chileno
  (Chile #1061) .... Vol. 2A
Teruel Province .... Vol. 6A
Tete .... Vol. 6B
Tetuan .... Vol. 6A
Thailand, Thai .... Vol. 6B
Thailand (Occupation of Kedah) ... Vol. 4B
Thailand (Occupation of
  Kelantan) .... Vol. 4B
Thailand (Occupation of
  Malaya) .... Vol. 4B
Thailand (Occupation of Perlis) ... Vol. 4B
Thailand (Occupation of
  Trengganu) .... Vol. 4B
Thessaly .... Vol. 6B
Thomasville, Ga. .... Vol. 1A
Thrace .... Vol. 6B
Three Cents .... Vol. 1A
Thuringia, Thuringen .... Vol. 3A
Thurn and Taxis .... Vol. 3A
Tibet .... Vol. 6B
Tibet (Chinese province) .... Vol. 2A
Tibet, Chinese Offices .... Vol. 2A
Tical .... Vol. 6B
Tientsin (Chinese) .... Vol. 2A
Tientsin (German) .... Vol. 2A
Tientsin (Italian) .... Vol. 3B
Tiflis .... Vol. 3A
Timbre ovptd. on France .... Vol. 2B
Timor .... Vol. 6B
Timor-Leste .... Vol. 6B
Timor Lorosae .... Vol. 1A, Vol. 6B
Tin Can Island .... Vol. 6B
Tjedan Solidarnosti
  (Yugoslavia #RA82) .... Vol. 6B
Tjenestefrimerke .... Vol. 2B, Vol. 5A
Tlacotalpan .... Vol. 4B
Tobago .... Vol. 6B
Toga .... Vol. 6B
Togo, Togolaise .... Vol. 6B
Tokelau Islands .... Vol. 6B
Tolima .... Vol. 2A
Tonga .... Vol. 6B
Tongareva .... Vol. 5A
Tonk .... Vol. 3A
To Pay .... Vol. 3B
Toscano .... Vol. 3B
Tou .... Vol. 2A
Touva, Tovva .... Vol. 6A
Transcaucasian Federated
  Republics .... Vol. 6B
Trans-Jordan .... Vol. 4A, Vol. 5A
Trans-Jordan (Palestine Occ.) ... Vol. 4A
Transkei .... Vol. 6B
Transvaal .... Vol. 6B
Transylvania .... Vol. 3B
Trasporto Pacchi .... Vol. 3B
Travancore .... Vol. 3B
Travancore-Cochin, State of ...... Vol. 3B
Trebizonde 598
Trengganu .... Vol. 4B
Trentino .... Vol. 1B
Trieste ...... Vol. 1B, Vol. 3B, Vol. 6B
Trinidad .... Vol. 1B, Vol. 6B
Trinidad and Tobago .... Vol. 6B
Trinidad Society (Trinidad &
  Tobago #B1) .... Vol. 6B
Tripoli di Barberia (Tripoli) .... Vol. 3B

Tripoli, Fiera Campionaria .... Vol. 4A
Tripolitania .... Vol. 4A, Vol. 6B
Tripolitania (B.M.A.) .... Vol. 6B
Tristan da Cunha .... Vol. 6B
Trucial States .... Vol. 6B
Tsinghai .... Vol. 6B
Tsingtau .... Vol. 2A, Vol. 4A
T. Ta. C .... Vol. 6B
Tullahoma, Tenn. .... Vol. 1A
Tumbes (Peru #129-133) .... Vol. 5A
Tunisia, Tunisie, Tunis,
  Tunisienne .... Vol. 6B
Turkestan, Russian 384
Turkey, Turkiye, Turk .... Vol. 6B
Turkey (Greek Occupation) ...... Vol. 3A,
  Vol. 6B
Turkey in Asia .... Vol. 6B
Turk Federe Devleti .... Vol. 6B
Turkish Empire, Austrian Offices ... Vol. 1B
Turkish Empire, British Offices ... Vol. 3A
Turkish Empire, French Offices ... Vol. 2B
Turkish Empire, Georgian
  Offices .... Vol. 3A
Turkish Empire, German Offices ... Vol. 3A
Turkish Empire, Italian Offices ... Vol. 3B
Turkish Empire, Polish Offices 124
Turkish Empire, Romanian Offices 379
Turkish Empire, Russian Offices ... 597
Turkish Occupation of Iran .... Vol. 6B
Turkish Republic of Northern
  Cyprus .... Vol. 6B
Turkish stamps surcharged or
  overprinted ...... Vol. 2B, Vol. 3A, Vol. 6A
Turkish Suzerainty of Egypt .... Vol. 2B
Turkmenistan, Turkmenpocta ..... Vol. 6B
Turks and Caicos Islands .... Vol. 6B
Turks Islands .... Vol. 6B
Tuscaloosa, Ala. .... Vol. 1A
Tuscany .... Vol. 3B
Tuscumbia, Ala. .... Vol. 1A
Tuva Autonomous Region .... Vol. 6A
Tuvalu .... Vol. 6B
Two Cents (Confed. #53X5) ...... Vol. 1A
Two Pence .... Vol. 1A
Two Sicilies .... Vol. 3B
Tyosen (Korea) .... Vol. 4A
Tyrol .... Vol. 1B

UAE ovptd. on Abu Dhabi .... Vol. 6B
U.A.R. .... Vol. 2B, Vol. 6A, Vol. 6B
Ubangi, Ubangi-Shari .... Vol. 6B
Uganda, U.G. .... Vol. 6B
Uganda, and Kenya .... Vol. 4A
Uganda, Tanganyika, Kenya ..... Vol. 4A
Ukraine, Ukraina .... Vol. 6B
Ukraine (German Occupation) 595
Ukraine stamps surcharged 599
Ukrainian Soviet Socialist Republic 386
Ukraine, Western .... Vol. 6B
Uku Leta .... Vol. 1A
Ultramar .... Vol. 2A
Umm al Qiwain .... Vol. 6B
UNEF ovptd. on India .... Vol. 3B
UNESCO .... Vol. 2B
U.N. Force in Congo or Gaza
  (India) .... Vol. 3B
Union Island, St. Vincent 845
Union Islands .... Vol. 6B
Union of South Africa .... Vol. 6A
Union of Soviet Socialist
  Republics 386
Uniontown, Ala. .... Vol. 1A
Unionville, S.C. .... Vol. 1A
United Arab Emirates .... Vol. 6B
United Arab Republic (UAR) ..... Vol. 2B,
  Vol. 6A, Vol. 6B
United Arab Republic, Egypt ..... Vol. 2B
United Arab Republic Issues
  for Syria .... Vol. 6A
United Kingdom .... Vol. 3A
United Nations .... Vol. 1A
United Nations European
  Office .... Vol. 1A, Vol. 6A
United Nations Offices in
  Geneva .... Vol. 1A
United Nations Offices in Vienna ... Vol. 1A
United Nations Offices in Vienna .. Vol. 1A, Vol. 4A
United Nations - West New
  Guinea Vol.1A
United State of Saurashtra .... Vol. 3B
United States Adm. of Canal
  Zone .... Vol. 1A
United States Adm. of Cuba ..... Vol. 1A,
  Vol. 2A
United States Adm. of Guam ..... Vol. 1A
U. S. Adm. of Philippines .... Vol. 1A, Vol. 5A
U. S. Adm. of Puerto Rico ... 211, Vol. 1A
U. S. Military Rule of Korea .... Vol. 4A
United States of America .... Vol. 1A
United States of Indonesia .... Vol. 3B

United States of New Granada .... Vol. 2A
United States, Offices in China .... Vol. 1A
Un Real .... Vol. 2B
U.S. Zone (Germany) .... Vol. 3A
Universal Postal Union,
  Intl. Bureau .... Vol. 6A
UNTEA ovptd. on Netherlands
  New Guinea .... Vol. 1A, Vol. 3B
UNTEAT .... Vol. 6B
UPHA ROPA .... Vol. 4B
Upper Austria .... Vol. 1B
Upper Senegal and Niger .... Vol. 6B
Upper Silesia .... Vol. 6B
Upper Volta .... Vol. 1B
Urgente .... Vol. 6A
U.R.I. ovptd. on Yugoslavia ...... Vol. 6B
Uruguay .... Vol. 6B
Urundi ovptd. on Congo .... Vol. 3A
Uskub .... Vol. 6B
U.S. Mail .... Vol. 1A
U.S.PO. .... Vol. 1A
U.S.P.O. Despatch .... Vol. 1A
U.S.S.R. 386
U. S. T.C. overprinted on Cochin .... Vol. 3B
Uzbekistan .... Vol. 6B

Vaitupu .... Vol. 6B
Valdosta, Ga. .... Vol. 1A
Valencia .... Vol. 6A
Valladolid Province .... Vol. 6A
Valona .... Vol. 3B
Valparaiso .... Vol. 2A
Vancouver Island .... Vol. 3A
Van Diemen's Land (Tasmania) ... Vol. 1A
Vanuatu .... Vol. 6B
Varldspost Kongress
  (Sweden #197) .... Vol. 6A
Vasa .... Vol. 2B
Vathy .... Vol. 2B
Vatican City, Vaticane, Vaticano .... Vol. 6B
Venda .... Vol. 6A
Venezia Giulia .... Vol. 1B, Vol. 3B
Venezia Tridentina .... Vol. 1B
Venezuela, Veneza.,
  Venezolana .... Vol. 6B
Venizelist Government .... Vol. 3A
Vereinte Nationen .... Vol. 1A
Vetekeverria .... Vol. 1A
Victoria .... Vol. 1A
Victoria, Tex. .... Vol. 1A
Victoria Land (New Zealand
  #130d-131d) .... Vol. 5A
Vienna .... Vol. 1A, Vol. 1B
Vienna Issues .... Vol. 3B
Viet Minh .... Vol. 6B
Viet Nam .... Vol. 6B
Viet Nam Buu Chinh .... Vol. 6B
Viet Nam Buu Dien .... Vol. 6B
Viet Nam Cong-Hoa .... Vol. 6B
Viet Nam Dan-Chu Cong-Hoa ... Vol. 6B
Viet Nam, Democratic Republic ... Vol. 6B
Viet Nam Doc-Lap .... Vol. 6B
Viet Nam, (Int. Com., India) ...... Vol. 3B
Viet Nam, North .... Vol. 6B
Viet Nam, Republic .... Vol. 6B
Viet Nam, South .... Vol. 6B
Villa Bella (Bolivia #97) .... Vol. 1B
Vilnius .... 596, Vol. 4A
Vineta .... Vol. 3A
Virgin Islands .... Vol. 6B
Vladivostok .... Vol. 2B
Vojna Uprava .... Vol. 6B
Volksrust .... Vol. 6B
Vom Empfanger .... Vol. 2B, Vol. 3A
Vorarlberg .... Vol. 1B
V.R. ovptd. on Transvaal Vol. 2A, Vol. 6B
Vryburg .... Vol. 2A
Vuja-STT, Vujna-STT .... Vol. 6B

Wadhwan .... Vol. 3B
Walachia 250
Wales & Monmouthshire .... Vol. 3A
Wallis and Futuna Islands .... Vol. 6B
Walterborough, S.C. .... Vol. 1A
War Board of Trade .... Vol. 6A
Warrenton, Ga. .... Vol. 1A
Warsaw, Warszawa 15
Washington, Ga. .... Vol. 1A
Watermarks (British Colonies) .... See
  table of contents
Weatherford, Tex. .... Vol. 1A
Weihnachten Joos van Cleve-Geburt
  Christi (Austria 2479) ...... Vol. 1B
Wenden, Wendensche 595
Western Army .... Vol. 4A
Western Australia .... Vol. 1A
Western Samoa 895
Western Szechwan .... Vol. 2A
Western Thrace (Greek
  Occupation) .... Vol. 6B

Western Turkey .... Vol. 3A
Western Ukraine .... Vol. 6B
West Irian .... Vol. 3B
West New Guinea .... Vol. 1A, Vol. 3B
West Saxony .... Vol. 3A
Wet and dry printings .... Vol. 1A
Wharton's U.S. P.O. Despatch Vol.1A
White Russia .... Vol. 1B
Wiederaufbauspende .... Vol. 6B
Wilayah Persekutuan .... Vol. 4B
Wilkesboro, N.C. .... Vol. 1A
Williams City Post .... Vol. 1A
Winnsborough, S.C. .... Vol. 1A
Wir sind frei .... Vol. 2B
Wn. .... Vol. 4A
Wohnungsbau .... Vol. 3A
Wolmaransstad .... Vol. 6B
World Health Organization .... Vol. 6A
World Intellectual Property
  Organization .... Vol. 6A
World Meteorological
  Organization .... Vol. 6A
Worldwide .... Vol. 3A
Wrangel issues 598
Wurttemberg .... Vol. 3A
Wytheville, Va. .... Vol. 1A

Xeimappa .... Vol. 2B

Yambo .... Vol. 6A
Y.A.R. .... Vol. 6B
Yca .... Vol. 5A
Yemen .... Vol. 6B
Yemen Arab Republic .... Vol. 6B
Yemen People's Republic .... Vol. 6B
Yemen, People's Democratic
  Rep. .... Vol. 6B
Yen, Yn. .... Vol. 1A, Vol. 4A
Ykp. H.P. Ykpaiha .... Vol. 6B
Yksi Markka .... Vol. 2B
Yuan .... Vol. 2A
Yucatan .... Vol. 4B
Yudenich, Gen. 596
Yugoslavia .... Vol. 6B
Yugoslavia (German
  Occupation) .... Vol. 6B
Yugoslavia (Italian Occupation) .... Vol. 6B
Yugoslavia (Trieste) .... Vol. 6B
Yugoslavia (Zone B) .... Vol. 6B
Yugoslavia Offices Abroad .... Vol. 6B
Yugoslavia stamps overprinted
  and surcharged .... Vol. 1B
Yunnan (China) .... Vol. 2A
Yunnan Fou, Yunnansen .... Vol. 2B

Za Crveni Krst
  (Yugoslavia #RA2) .... Vol. 6B
Z. Afr. Republiek, Z.A.R. .... Vol. 6B
Zaire .... Vol. 6B
Zambezia .... Vol. 6B
Zambia .... Vol. 6B
Zante .... Vol. 3B
Zanzibar .... Vol. 6B
Zanzibar, French Offices .... Vol. 2B
Zanzibar (Kenya, Uganda,
  Tanganyika) .... Vol. 4A
Zanzibar-Tanzania .... Vol. 6B
Z.A.R. ovptd. on Cape of
  Good Hope .... Vol. 6B
Zelaya .... Vol. 5A
Zentraler Kurierdienst .... Vol. 3A
Zil Eloigne Sesel .... Vol. 6A
Zil Elwagne Sesel .... Vol. 6A
Zil Elwannyen Sesel .... Vol. 6A
Zimbabwe .... Vol. 6B
Zimska Pomoc ovptd. on Italy ... Vol. 6B
Zone A (Trieste) .... Vol. 3B
Zone B (Istria) .... Vol. 6B
Zone B (Trieste) .... Vol. 6B
Zone Francaise .... Vol. 3A
Zuid Afrika .... Vol. 5A, Vol. 6A
Zuidafrikaansche Republiek ...... Vol. 6B
Zuidwest Afrika .... Vol. 6B
Zululand .... Vol. 6B
Zurich .... Vol. 6A

SCOTT-SCHAUBEK UNITED STATES ALBUM SERIES

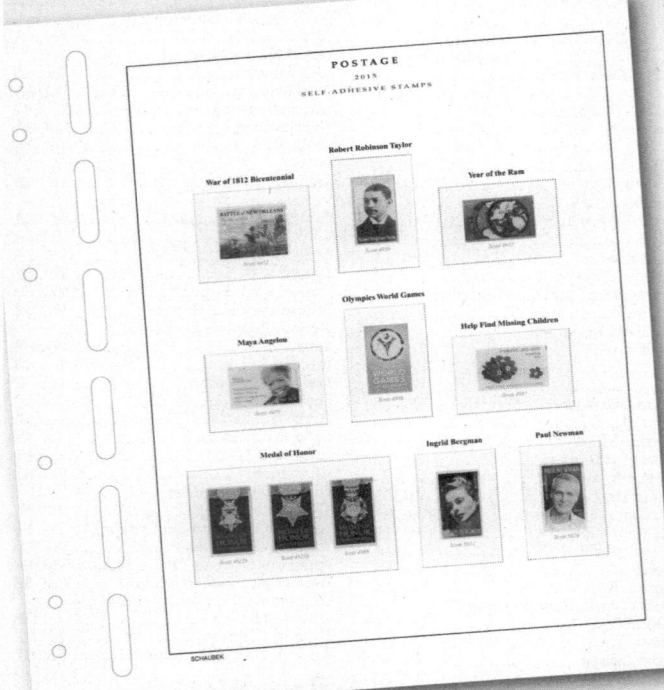

Make life easier with the fully mounted Scott-Schaubek United States album pages. These brilliant pages are equipped with mid-cut clear mounts for maximum protection and display effectiveness. As a bonus, the supplements contain Scott numbers for easy referencing, valuing and tracking. The pages are designed after the Schaubek album series, but with the luxury of the Scott album layout and Scott catalog numbers. The Scott-Schaubek album pages fit in a 6-ring, blue Senator binder and slipcase. If you want to take your collecting enjoyment to the next level, the Scott-Schaubek U.S. album is for you! For complete list of available album pages visit **AmosAdvantage.com.**

Item		Retail	AA*
HUSA01	1845-1934	$299.95	$224.99
HUSA02	1935-1976	$299.95	$224.99
HUSA03	1977-1993	$299.95	$224.99
HUSA04	1994-2000	$299.95	$224.99
HUSA05	2001-2004	$199.95	$148.49
HUSA06	2005-2009	$249.99	$179.99
HUSA07	2010-2015	$249.99	$179.99
HUSA2016	2016	$78.99	$67.99
HUSA2017	2017	$78.99	$67.99
HUSA2018	2018	$78.99	$67.99
HUSA2019	2019	$78.99	$67.99
HRB001	Blue Binder	$39.99	$34.99
HRS001	Blue Slipcase	$19.99	$16.99

United States Album Set

Save BIG when you buy the complete Scott-Schaubek U.S. Hingeless Album Set 1845-2015 from Amos Advantage. This complete Scott-Schaubek album set includes everything you need to collect the United States through the 2015 album supplement. With all the Scott-Schaubek U.S. Hingeless album pages and 8 blue matching, binders, slipcases and labels to house and organize the pages, you can have the complete set you want for your stamp collecting needs.

Item	Retail	AA*
HUSASET	$2,100.00	$1,680.00

Call **800-572-6885** • Outside U.S. & Canada call: **(937) 498-0800**
Visit www.AmosAdvantage.com

Vols. 5A-5B Number Additions, Deletions & Changes

Number in 2020 Catalogue	Number in 2021 Catalogue
Ponta Delgada	
14	deleted
14a	14
Portuguese Congo	
new	127a
new	129a
new	130a
new	131a
new	135a
Portuguese Guinea	
deleted	RA20
Russia	
new	5059a
new	5060a
new	5104a
new	5125a
new	5358a
new	5423a
new	5454a
new	5455a
new	5456a
new	5457a
new	5458a
new	5533a
new	5591a
new	5592a
new	5593a
new	5594a
new	5595a
new	5871a
new	5875a
new	5876a
new	5883a
new	5895a
new	5896a
new	5908a
new	6006a
new	6007a
new	6050a
new	6136a
new	6137a
new	6145a
new	6148a
new	6175a
new	6176a
new	6177a
new	6295a
new	6534a
new	6535a
new	6672a
new	6751a
new	6814a
new	6817a
new	6841a
new	6842a
new	6843a
new	6846a
new	6859a
new	6872a
new	6881a
new	6977a

INDEX TO ADVERTISERS
2021 VOLUME 5B

ADVERTISER	PAGE
– A –	
AG Stamp	385
Almaz Stamps	384
– C –	
Collectors Exchange	242
Colonial Stamp Co.	Yellow Pages
– E –	
Eastern Auctions Ltd.	387
Ercole Gloria	Yellow Pages
– K –	
Kelleher & Rogers LTD.	Inside Front Cover

ADVERTISER	PAGE
– L –	
Loral Stamp Co.	382
– M –	
Gregory Mirsky	383
Mystic Stamp Co.	Back Cover
– P –	
Polish Philately Auth Serv/Andrew Sader	15
– S –	
Liane & Sergio Sismondo	667